Forty-Second Edition

Blue Book of Gun Values™

Edited by Zachary R. Fjestad & Lisa Beuning

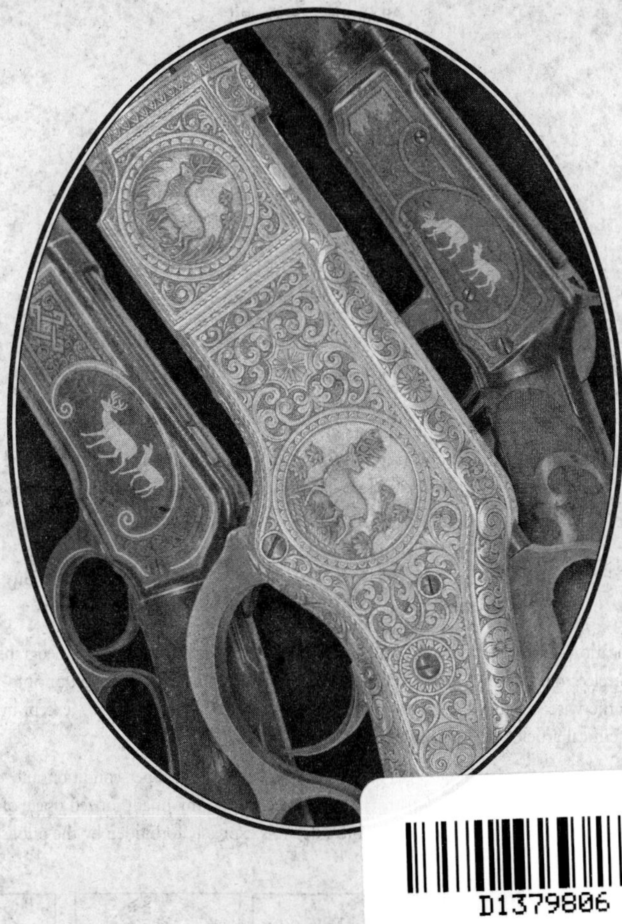

D1379806

MSRP $59.95

PUBLISHER'S NOTE:

This book is the result of nonstop and continuous firearms research obtained by attending and/or participating in trade shows, gun shows, auctions, and also communicating with contributing editors, gun dealers, collectors, company historians, and other knowledgeable industry professionals worldwide each year. This book represents an analysis of prices for which collectible firearms have actually been selling during that period at an average retail level. Although every reasonable effort has been made to compile an accurate and reliable guide, gun prices may vary significantly (especially auction prices) depending on such factors as the locality of the sale, the number of sales we were able to consider, and economic conditions. Accordingly, no representation can be made that the guns listed may be bought or sold at prices indicated, nor shall the author or publisher be responsible for any error made in compiling and recording such prices and related information.

CONTENT DISCLAIMER:

Due to space considerations, this book does not contain information or values on machine guns, NFA classified firearms, secondary/obscure American or European/International antiques, firearms accessories (scopes, bayonets, etc.) airguns, or modern black powder reproductions and replicas. For current information on airguns, modern black powder replicas, and antiques, please refer to the *Blue Book of Airguns,* the *Blue Book of Modern Black Powder Arms,* and the *Blue Book of Antique American Firearms and Values*. Visit BlueBookOfGunValues.com for more information on how to order either online or in print.

Blue Book Publications, Inc.
8009 34th Avenue South, Suite 250
Minneapolis, MN 55425 U.S.A.

Customer Service: 800-877-4867, ext. 3 (domestic only)
Phone: 952-854-5229
Fax: 952-853-1486
General Email: support@bluebookinc.com
Website: BlueBookOfGunValues.com

Published and printed in the United States of America
ISBN 10: 1-947314-26-2
ISBN 13: 978-1-947314-26-9
Library of Congress ISSN number - 1524-6043

Electronic Access ID Code: 40019

Distributed in part to the book trade by Ingram Book Company and Baker & Taylor.
Distributed throughout Europe by:

Visier GmbH
Wipsch 1
D-56130 Bad Ems Germany
www.vsmedien.de

Deutsches Waffen Journal
Rudolf-Diesel-Strasse 46
D-74572 Blaufelden Germany
Website: www.dwj.de

TABLE OF CONTENTS

Title Page 1
Publisher's Note/Copyright 2
Table Of Contents 3
Online Subscriptions/Credits 4
General Information 5
Acknowledgements 6-7
Fallen Comrades 7
About the Cover 8
Introduction by Zachary R. Fjestad 9-10
Foreword by Lisa Beuning 11-12
A Year in Review – What Happened? by Zachary R. Fjestad 13-17
Collecting in the Time of COVID by Mark Rendina 18-23
Blue Book of Gun Values Collectible Firearms Average Index 24-25
How To Use This Book 26-29
Anatomy Of A Handgun 30
Anatomy Of A Rifle 31
Anatomy Of A Shotgun 32
Gun Questions/Appraisals Policy 33
Glossary 34-56
Abbreviations 57-61
Grading Criteria 62
NRA Condition Standards 63
The PPGS - Firearms Grading Made Easy 64
Photo Percentage Grading System™ 65-142
Identifying/Buying Older Editions 143-144
Modern Firearms/Antiques Text & Pricing 145-2,418
NRA Membership Information *766*
NRA National Firearms Museum (NFM) *824*
Buffalo Bill Center of the West Information/Membership *1,152*
NRA National Sporting Arms Museum *1,440*
Firearms/Shooting/Advocacy Organizations 2419
Conservation Organizations 2422
Reference Sources 2423
Store Brand Cross-Over List 2427
Serialization Index 2434
Serialization 2436
Proof Marks 2483
Index 2490
P.S. 2512

ONLINE SUBSCRIPTIONS/CREDITS

Purchasing a *Blue Book of Gun Values* online subscription is another way to ensure you won't miss a thing! Not only is EVERY single manufacturer listed in the online database, but you will also find nearly 15,000 gun images which make identifying your gun even easier! Plus you have the added benefit of creating your own online inventory listing, checking historical pricing, still have access to all your favorite pages like Serialization and the Photo Percentage Grading System™, yet your online subscription is updated MONTHLY so you're always up-to-date on the newest models and latest value trends.

Subscriptions come in different price ranges from month-to-month and up to a 3 year subscription. Prices vary for each subscription, so visit **http://bit.ly/BlueBookSubs** to get started!

SUBSCRIPTION	MONTHLY $3.95	1 YEAR	2 YEAR	3 YEAR
Blue Book of Gun Values	$3.95	$34.95	$54.95	$74.95
Blue Book of Airguns	$3.95	$19.95	$34.95	$44.95
Blue Book of Antique American Firearms	$3.95	$24.95		
Blue Book of AR-15s & Variations	$3.95	$19.95	$34.95	$44.95
Blue Book of Modern Black Powder Arms	$3.95	$19.95	$34.95	$44.95
American Gunsmiths		$29.95		
Ammo Encyclopedia		$24.95		

Our online subscriptions are updated monthly and include:

- Search Capability
- Current Blue Book value
- Thousands of images
- Manufacturer & model information
- Historic price information
- Online Inventory
- Our Photo Percentage Grading System
- Serialization information and more!

42ND *BLUE BOOK OF GUN VALUES* CREDITS

Cover Design, Layout, and Art Direction – Clint H. Schmidt and Zachary R. Fjestad

Inside Layout and Design – Clint H. Schmidt

Editor/Manuscript Supervision – Lisa Beuning

Data Entry Input – Lisa Beuning, Kayla McCarthy, Connor Daine, Alexandra LaDuke, Zachary R. Fjestad

Proofing & Corrections – Sarah Peterson, Zachary R. Fjestad, Lisa Beuning, and Clint H. Schmidt

PPGS Images – courtesy of Rock Island Auctions (RIA), Morphy Auctions, and Dr. Leonardo M. Antaris, MD

Printing – Steve Williamsen, Patrick Willhite, and crew from LSC Communications in Crawfordsville, IN.

GENERAL INFORMATION

While many of you have probably dealt with our company for years, it may be helpful for you to know a little bit more about our operation, including information on how to contact us regarding our various titles and other informational services.

Blue Book Publications, Inc.
8009 34th Avenue South, Suite 250
Minneapolis, MN 55425 USA
GPS Coordinates: N44° 51 28.44, W93° 13.1709

Phone: 952-854-5229 • Customer Service: 800-877-4867, ext. 3 (domestic only)
Fax: 952-853-1486 (available 24 hours a day)
Website: BlueBookOfGunValues.com

Please refer to individual email addresses listed below with phone extension numbers.

To find out the latest information on our products, including availability and pricing, consumer related services, and up-to-date industry information (blogs, trade show recaps with photos/captions, upcoming events, feature articles, etc.), please check our website, as it is updated on a regular basis

BBP STAFF CONTACT INFO:

Ext. 1000 - Beth Schreiber
Operations Manager
(beths@bluebookinc.com)

Ext. 1200 – John Andraschko
Technology Director
(johnand@bluebookinc.com)

Ext. 1300 – Lisa Beuning
Editor/Content Supervisor
(lisab@bluebookinc.com)

Ext. 1400 – Kayla McCarthy
Associate Editor
(kaylam@bluebookinc.com)

Ext. 1500 - Clint H. Schmidt
Art Director
(clints@bluebookinc.com)

Ext. 1600 – Connor Daine
Tactical Marketplace Editor/Research Coordinator
(connord@bluebookinc.com)

Ext. 1800 - Tom Stock
CFO
(toms@bluebookinc.com)

Ext. 2000 – Tom Toupin
Sales Manager
(tomt@bluebookinc.com)

Ext. 2200 – Alexandra LaDuke
Operations/Content
(alexl@bluebookinc.com)

Sarah Peterson
Proofreader
(sarahs@bluebookinc.com)

Zachary R. Fjestad
President/Co-Editor
(zachf@bluebookinc.com)

Office hours are: 8:30am - 5:00pm CST, Monday - Friday.

Additionally, an after-hours message service is available for ordering. All orders are processed within 24 hours of receiving them, assuming payment and order information is correct. Depending on the product, we typically ship UPS, Media Mail, or Priority Mail. Expedited shipping services are also available domestically for an additional charge. Please contact us directly for an expedited shipping quotation.

All correspondence regarding technical information/values on guns or guitars is answered in a FIFO (first in, first out) system. That means that letters, faxes, and email are answered in the order in which they are received, even though some people think that their emails take preference over everything else.

We would like to thank all of you for your business in the past – you are the reason we are successful. Our goal remains the same – to give you the best products, the most accurate and up-to-date information for the money, plus the highest level of customer service available in today's marketplace. If something's right, tell the world over time. If something's wrong, please tell us immediately – we'll make it right.

ACKNOWLEDGEMENTS

Once again we'd like to express our gratitude and appreciation to the following contributing editors and various people throughout the industry that have given their time and support by sharing their extensive knowledge in order to provide us with the necessary updates for this newest 42nd Edition.

*Leonardo M. Antaris, M.D
* Chad Hiddleson
* Josh Loewensteiner
* Lt. Col. Mark Rendina
* Gary Przibilla (the Aussie Perazzi aficionado)
* Jake Streaker - Jaqua's Fine Guns
*Mike Stroud
* Jim Gentile
Bill Allen
Bailey Brower, Jr.
Gurney Brown (Snake Man)
Jerry Bryant
Ken Buch
James A. Buelow
Buffalo Bill Center of the West - Ashley Hlebinsky (Curator), Jessica Bennett, and Rachel Lee
Tim Butler – SIG Sauer
CWO Ric Cameron
Gary Chatham
Kevin Cherry
Richard Churchill
Stefan Cohn
Beverly Haynes (Colt Historian)
Don "Duck" Combs
Aaron Cummins - Browning
Dr. Peter Dallhammer - Umarex Sportwaffen GmbH & Co.
Bob Decker
Richard "Doc" Desira
Leon DeSpain
Matthew DiRisio
John Dougan
Doug Drummond
John Eckert
Dave Eisenried – Anschütz North America
Jim Ellis
Steve Engleson
Jim Fisher
Harvey Frakes
David Gaboury
Joe Gillenwater
Bill Grant
John Groenewold
Bill Hamm
Gordon Hanlan
Mark Hannah
Jay Hansen
Bruce Hart
Jim Hendricks
Holland & Holland - Daryl Greatrex, Guy Davies, Russell Wilkin, and David Winks (ret.)
Peter Horn II
Cindy Jensen - Browning
Rob Johansen - SKB Shotguns
Chris Killoy - Sturm, Ruger & Co.
Bob Knight
John Kopec
David Kosowski (honorary)
H. Krieghoff Gun Co. - Dieter Krieghoff, Alex Diehl, Ralf Muller, & Phil Krieghoff
John Lacy
Charles Layson
Gene Leopold
Richard Littlefield
Jackie Love - Browning
Roy Marcot
Greg Martin
Glen Mattox
Mark May
Bob Maze
Luke Mercaldo
LeRoy Merz
Antonio Miele – Smith & Wesson
Thomas Mintner
Jan Mladek – Smith & Wesson
Bill Mullins
Gene Myszkowski
Richard Nahas
Casey Nanz
Glen Nilson
David Noble
David Noll
Brad Olson
Orvin Olson
Mackenzie "Max" Opdahl
Larry "Iron" Orr
Carlyle H. Pack
William Peets
Scott Pilkington
Joe Pittenger
Linda Powell – Mossberg
Ken Rabeneck
David M. Rachwal
Bob Radaker
Rick Regnier
Jeff Reh – Beretta USA
Rock Island Auctions - Pat & Kevin Hogan, Judy Voss, Alex Janoski, Matt Parise
Stanley J. Ruselowski, Jr. – Glock Collector's Association
Robert Sadowski – Glock Collector's Association
Michael Salisbury

Phil Schreier - NFM & NSAM
Dan Shuck
Randy Shuman
Jeremy Shupe – Browning
Brad Simpson
Ian Skennerton
Danny Spann – Anschutz North America
Eric Suarez – Remington Outdoor Company
Jim Supica - NFM & NSAM
Jim Stubbendieck
Pierangelo Tendas
Dave Trauth
Turnbull Restoration & Mfg. Co. - Doug Turnbull & Stephen Lester
Umarex USA - JB & Adam Blalock
Jon Vander Bloomen – Coach Gun Expert
Anthony Vanderlinden
Fred Vandersnick
Vic Venters
Verney-Carron – Jean Verney Carron
Wolf von Baumbach
Maurice Wadle
Larry Wales
Stephen Wang
Bob Weiss
Doug Wicklund – NFM & NSAM
Tony Wilcox – Morphy Auctions
Carol and the late Don Wilkerson
Joel Ziegler
Browning Collectors Association
Colt Collectors Association (CCA)
German Gun Collectors Association
Jon W. Miller, MD, Ken Rabeneck, Steve Schrott, Jerry Watson, Brad Adams, Bill Bryant, Bob & Mickey Waldinger & the High Standard Collectors Association
L.C. Smith Collectors Association
Mannlicher Collectors Association
Gail Foster, the late Alvin Olson, Dale Peterson, Tony Schwab & the Minnesota Weapons Collectors Association
Remington Society of America – contributing editors include: Randy Davis, David Fagan
Ruger Collectors Association (RCA) – contributing editors include: Steve Adamson, Donnie Findley, Bill Hamm, Jerold Hertel, Robert Livingston, Tyrone Phillips, Lee Sundermeier, Richard Verzal, Gary West, Mike Womble, Terry Workman

FALLEN COMRADES

Unfortunately, 2020 and early 2021 has claimed more gun figures, personalities, and friends of BBP. They'll be greatly missed, and for those of us lucky enough to have known them, they enriched our lives in many ways.

Kenneth Blauch (2019) – contributing editor

Rick Crosier – long-time contributing editor

John Rohner – founder of GRS (engraving)

Dave Wills – contributing editor

ABOUT THE COVER

These are three of the finest engraved and gold inlaid Winchester rifles you will ever see pictured together. Positioned on the cover from left to right is an engraved Model 1886, a Model 1866, and a Model 1894.

The Model 1886 is chambered in .45-70 and features what is likely a number 2 pattern factory engraving. Pictured on the left side of the gun is a two-animal deer scene with a buck and a doe and on the right side of the gun (not pictured on the cover) is a moose. This rifle also features gold outlines on numerous pieces including the frame, the bolt, the front of the takedown ring, and even the for-end cap. Not only does this gun have great engraving scenes and gold outlines, but it is also in remarkable shape for being over 130 years old with 95% of the bluing remaining.

The Model 1866 is the earliest model featured here and most elaborate of the three. The Model 1866 was the first Winchester-branded rifle and is a direct descendent of the former Henry rifle used heavily in the American Civil War. It was chambered in .44 Henry and commonly nicknamed "Yellow Boy" due to the bronze and brass alloy the receiver is made of. The receiver on this one is unique because it is entirely engraved with multiple deer and scrolls.

The Model 1894 is chambered in .25-35 WCF and includes just about every Winchester

feature available including double triggers, a half-octagon extra-light tapered 26 in. barrel, a bird's-eye maple stock carved in Style E, and a nickel-plated Swiss buttplate (not shown). This 94 is also engraved with what appears to be Winchester's pattern number 6. Deer are featured on both sides of this rifle with a buck and a doe on the left side and a single buck on the right side. This is possibly the only factory engraved Model 94 with a bird's-eye maple stock.

The publisher would like to thank LeRoy Merz and his staff in Fergus Falls for allowing us the opportunity to browse their unequaled selection of antique Winchesters and photograph them for the cover. Thanks LeRoy, Rick, Mark and the entire staff!

Blue Book Publications President and co-editor of the Blue Book of Gun Values *Zachary R. Fjestad with his 6-year-old son Joshua pose with this respectable 8-point buck shot 30 minutes after shooting hours began for the Minnesota Deer Opener in November 2020. Taken with one slug from a utilitarian Remington Model 870 Express Deer Gun (not pictured), your gun does not need to be fancy to get the job done.*

Welcome to the 42nd Edition *Blue Book of Gun Values*! It is our sincere hope that we find you in your best health as we begin 2021 and that this book will help you navigate one of the wildest years of firearms sales we have ever seen. This is also the 40th Anniversary of the *Blue Book of Gun Values* – nobody has been compiling firearm information and values for longer, actively, consistently, or more accurately than us. The first book was published in 1981 and since then, we have strived to provide you with the most accurate and up-to-date value guide on firearms.

Yes, most gun values increased in 2020 and the common refrain amongst many is that "all gun values are up." However, the incredulous fact is all guns are not created equal, meaning while there is a good chance your gun increased in value, there are guns that remained stagnant or even depreciated as well. Since day one, the values we publish in this database are compiled from actual sales of firearms – not based on asking prices, suggested prices, speculative thoughts, or any other pie in the sky. Remember, value is defined as "the regard that something is held to deserve; the importance, worth, or usefulness of something." In other words, value is what one party is willing to pay another for an item or good. Our job is to simply report what is currently happening and not justify any spikes or artificial inflation.

PANDEMIC/COVID

As we wrapped up the last edition of the *Blue Book of Gun Values* a year ago, the Coronavirus was still a new word in our vocabulary, but it quickly showed us how vulnerable we are to a disease without a known treatment or vaccine. As this book goes to press, 29 million people were reportedly infected with COVID-19 in the United States since it started and over 525,000 people have reportedly died from the virus or complications related to it. Everyone reacted differently to the "new normal" and "social distancing", but we all know at least one person who was diagnosed/affected by COVID-19 or tragically succumbed to the disease. Whatever your opinions and thoughts are on the Coronavirus, it impacted every one of us and now we must figure out how to move forward.

The pandemic was the first major event of 2020 that started the gun and ammo shortage, but there were several other unfortunate events that exacerbated the situation. I encourage you to read my article in this text called "A Year in Review – What Happened?" starting on page 13 where I explore what caused a record year in gun and ammunition sales and nationwide shortages everywhere. My local gun shop normally sells 600 guns in a year, but in 2020 he sold nearly three times as many. I think most retailers and gun shops share similar stories, but we are all wondering why? Also, longtime contributing editor Mark Rendina makes his editorial debut in this edition with an article called "Collecting in the Time of COVID" starting on page 18.

Gun show promoters had to pull the plug on nearly everything. Preparations for the annual release of the *Blue Book of Gun Values* at the spring Wanenmacher's Tulsa Arms Show were abruptly cancelled, as was every other show in 2020. The 2021 SHOT show was postponed as well, which made gathering gun literature and price lists challenging. However, being that everyone else was in the same boat, the electronic transfer (and the occasional snail mail package) allowed us to update the database like normal. Much of the *Blue Book of Gun Values* is compiled away from the office anyway, so working from home was nothing new to us!

INDUSTRY NEWS

Many major trademarks were in the news over the past 12 months for a variety of reasons. Manufacturers in the AR business come and go, but sales are still very strong. Handguns are very popular right now for self-defense and conceal-carry purposes, and even shotguns are up, because they are an easy choice for home protection. Most manufacturers increased their MSRs in 2021, which is no real surprise as just about everything costs more than it did a year ago. Values in the 100% grading category also went up nearly everywhere, but it depended more on the type of the gun. The shortage of guns is causing them to sell for more when new, and at times even more than MSR. We see this as an anomaly rather than a trend, though.

The biggest news in 2020 was that Remington Outdoor Corporation filed for bankruptcy for the second time in less than 3 years. Upon filing on July 28, 2020, all production halted for Remington's four primary brands: Remington, Marlin, Bushmaster, and DPMS while leaving their fate unknown. They basically

Longtime Luger contributing editor Brad Simpson and Zachary R. Fjestad at the S.P. Fjestad Celebration of Life in October 2019. S.P., the author of this book for nearly 40 editions, passed away in July 2019 and that fall we all came together to celebrate his life and accomplishments.

dismantled the Remington Outdoor Corporation by dividing and selling all their assets. In September 2020, the bankruptcy court held an auction and sold these trademarks to the highest bidder. Remington firearms was sold to the Roundhill Group and are working to restart production at the famed Ilion, NY plant in the first half of 2021. Sturm Ruger bought Marlin and are working to restart that brand as well.

In early February 2021, CZ announced that they were acquiring Colt. While this had been talked about in industry circles for some time, it still came as a surprise to most of us and raised a few eyebrows. Colt, who is predominantly an American company, suddenly has a significant amount of European influence in it. Colt had turned itself around in recent years after filing for bankruptcy in 2015 following their loss of its M4 contract with the military, enough so that CZ closed the deal.

2021 AND AHEAD & PARTING WORDS

The view into my crystal ball is murky on my best days, so to make any bold predictions of where firearms and ammunition will head this year and further down the road is foolish. However, with a new "anti-gun" administration now in control of all 3 branches of the federal government, I do not see any slowing down of "fear acquisition," and we should all be concerned about any new anti-gun legislation. COVID restrictions should let up as the year progresses, and if Remington and Marlin can ramp up production soon, hopefully we can start to solve these gun shortage issues.

If you are buying firearms for their use as a tool, I advise you to do your research and know that you usually "get what you pay for." If you are looking for an investment though, I would proceed with caution as what goes up eventually comes down – it is a matter of how soon that will be. I also encourage you to look at the new *Blue Book of Gun Values* Collector Firearm Value Index (CFVI) starting on page 24. We picked 10 collectible firearms, compiled their values year-by-year starting in 1981 and showed how they have changed in values since we started this book 40 years ago.

I cannot wrap this edition up without acknowledging those who made this edition possible. First, our incredible content team at Blue Book Publications of Alex, Connor, Kayla, Sarah, and especially Lisa for keeping us all on track, deserves a huge thank you for all hanging in there for another frantic two and a half-month race to the finish line. Our production manager and art director Clint Schmidt who assembles this book so effortlessly, we often forget the amount of skill and talent it takes to get this all to fit 2,512 pages. The rest of the Blue Book staff, whether it be operations, IT, or sales, you all step up when needed and we could not do it without you. Thank you all!

Our expansive list of contributing editors deserves to be recognized as well. Without their input and unbiased assessment of the market, we would be scrambling to get this all done by ourselves. I really appreciate what all of you bring to the table, and a great example of "it's not what you know, but who you know." I also encourage anyone who is interested in contributing to the *Blue Book of Gun Values* to reach out to us – we would love to get you involved.

Lastly, I need to thank my incredibly patient wife, Jill and our 3 children, Daniel, Joshua, and Madelyn for allowing my time away these past 2 years to carry on Steve's legacy and keep the *Blue Book of Gun Values* the most relevant firearm publication in the industry. Nobody knows what tomorrow will bring, so please live with the philosophy of putting our best foot forward today and deal with whatever comes tomorrow.

Happy shooting!

Sincerely,

Zachary R. Fjestad
Blue Book Publications President
& *Blue Book of Gun Values* Co-Editor

Zachary R. Fjestad with his family: wife Jill, children Joshua (l), Daniel (m), and Madelyn (r) on Siesta Key beach in Florida. Taken in March 2020, this was the last trip we took in 2020 as COVID-19 restrictions essentially shut everything down a week later.

FOREWORD BY LISA BEUNING

Instead of a Foreword like you read every year,
I thought a "Seuss-style" poem would be fun to see here.
Last year was not pretty, at times kind of rough
from the lockdowns and shutdowns to masks and other stuff.
Stay home for two weeks was what they first said
"Flatten the curve" - "Do your part" - just Please Stop the Spread!
For an unknown virus started sweeping our land
but it became about more than just not shaking hands.
Businesses shut down and nursing homes went quiet
there was looting and protests and even angry riots.
Buildings burned down and traffic was stopped
seemed everyone was screaming and screaming a lot!
Mainstream media was here to just play their part
divide the right from the left – they do not have a heart.
Schools were closed and students sent home
not a prom, not a sporting event, not a graduation was thrown.
A summer without beaches or waterparks or boats
is not a summer at all, for it seemed like a joke!
Stay 6 feet apart, cover your mouth, wash your hands…
there were cases and death counts, or wait, was this planned?

Traveling over New Year's has become an annual tradition for me as I try to sneak in a couple days off before book production begins by visiting my Dad at his winter home in Texas.

Conspiracy theories became a big hit
and we still want to know, is QAnon legit?
Distance learning and Zoom calls are all the new rage
and with masks on our face, they cannot guess your age!
Is it one mask or two masks or three some may say,
do not worry one bit a vaccine is on the way!
The "new normal" had started, strange times had begun
we watched Netflix and news and rerun after rerun.
But some took advantage of time spent at home…
cleaned out closets, did projects, or relaxed while alone.
All work and no play is a hard balancing act
without play you will burn out and that's just a fact!
Fall brought the election and campaign ads that would not end
Cancel Culture and Virtue Signaling seems to be the new trend.
Days became weeks, then months, now a year
how long do they want us to all live in fear?
We still kept on working the entire year through
we had books to get published and to get out to you!

We moved things around at home just a bit
shared office space with our kids, did what was needed to make things fit.

In December we finished a new Airgun book
the 13th edition, have you taken a look?
We have Pocket Guides out that are all up to date
a new Colt book coming soon, will be well worth the wait!
We have plans to update *Modern Black Powder*,
The *Ammo Encyclopedia*, and who knows maybe others.
Things here are busy, that much is true
because gun updates are essential – to me and to you!
This 42nd Edition is jam-packed like the rest
Big thanks to our Contributing Editors – you guys are the BEST!
We made update after update, changing prices galore,
new companies, new models, there's hardly room for much more!

Co-Editor, Zach Fjestad and I showing off some goods we grabbed for others at the estate sale for late author/publisher, S.P. Fjestad.

We made one big change to free up some space -
by moving the Trademark Index to our website, its new home, its new place.
You'll now find what you need on each company there,
their phone number, email, and website address they share.
We try our best each year to bring new things to you,
like Mark's article *Collecting in the Time of Covid* and Zach's *Year in Review.*
Having customers like you brings us great cheer
we cannot wait to see you when the shows open this year!
If this past year has taught us anything at all,
it is that sometimes we're not in control, no, nope, not at all.
Evil is out there it is not going away
so make it a point to bring JOY to each day.
Live life to the fullest even when you do not think you can,
As Steve used to tell me, "You just need a plan."

Shown here with my husband, four sons, nieces, and extended family – we spent a lot of time together this year with everyone being at home. No place I'd rather be!

A YEAR IN REVIEW WHAT HAPPENED?

by Zachary R. Fjestad

A year ago, in my introduction to the 41st Edition *Blue Book of Gun Values*, I made the comment that the Coronavirus (now referred simply and more accurately to as COVID 19) was becoming a global epidemic and that Stephen King's *The Stand* might not be complete fiction. Little did I know that it was just the beginning of a year that most of us could not wait to see in the rearview mirror. What followed included nationwide rioting, a nasty presidential election, and an insurrection of the U.S. Capitol Building to try and stop the certification of said election results capping an already ugly year.

Amidst all that, firearm and ammunition sales have reached all-time highs, surpassing the former "panic" years of 2008 and 2012. S.P. Fjestad, my uncle and the former author of this book, once joked that Bill Clinton and Barack Obama were the best gun-selling presidents of all time. Who knew a rampant virus, a knucklehead police officer, and unpredictable rioters could overshadow the fear mongering of a gun-restrictive Administration? Supply shortages and renewed concerns of self-defense have been catalyzed by domestic and international offenses over the last year, leaving the inauguration of our newest anti-gun President to be the least of our worries.

To illustrate how big of a year 2020 was for firearms, let me share some numbers with you. First, according to the National Instant Criminal Background Check System (NICS), they conducted over 21 million (21,000,000) background checks for the purchase of firearms. The prior year in 2019? A measly 13.2 million. That is a 60% increase in one year! The previous record for background checks in a year was 2016 with 15.7 million. Actual firearm sales are difficult to track, because of different states reporting requirements, but estimates indicate over 20 million guns were sold in 2020. Also, January 2021 set the record for a month of background checks at 4.3 million in just 31 days, so turning the calendar has not slowed things down, at least not yet.

Second, the National Shooting Sports Foundation (NSSF) estimates that 8.4 million Americans bought their first firearm in 2020. That means 2.5% of the entire U.S. population are first-time firearm owners, and these first-time buyers represent roughly 40% of all firearm purchases in 2020.

No, this isn't a store going out of business, but an all too familiar sight in 2020: shelves literally bare of ammunition. This picture, taken at my local sporting goods store in West-Central Minnesota is representative of what we all experienced when trying to buy ammunition. When a supply arrived, it sold immediately.

Third, firearms and ammunition go hand-in-hand; one serves no purpose without the other, aside from collectability. When gun sales go up, naturally ammunition sales follow. There is a lot of confusion, uncertainty, and conspiracy theories going around, but if you simply take those 8.4 million new gun owners and assume they bought a minimum of one box of ammo (say an average of 50 rounds), that's 420 million (420,000,000) rounds that ammo manufacturers didn't count on in 2019. And we're surprised that there's an ammo shortage?

So, what's causing all of this? The perfect storm of a global pandemic, racial injustice, self-defense concerns, and a new Administration; each one played a part. But to what extent? I will explore these one by one.

THE PANDEMIC

Upon the completion of the 41st Edition *Blue Book of Gun Values*, I joined my family for a brief (and much needed) vacation in Florida in early March last year. I questioned the lady sitting next to me on the flight; she was wearing a mask (before they were mandated) and wiping down every surface around her with sanitizer. Upon arriving in Florida (which would become an early COVID hotbed), the news became increasingly grim with reports of new cases, sicknesses, and deaths, which all led me to believe that the lady on the plane was not entirely crazy. We arrived back in Minnesota a week later as the world stopped and changed forever.

Perhaps the slow-burn genesis of Coronavirus will not be remembered as specifically as other tragedies, like the day President Kennedy was shot or 9/11, but I, for one, certainly remember when Utah Jazz basketball player Rudy Gobert famously touched every microphone and recorder in front of him during a press conference to downplay the significance of this new virus…and then came down with COVID-19 a few days later.

When everything shut down in March 2020, we were suddenly forced to stay home and figure out what to do when we could not go anywhere. Many of us cleaned out our houses, basements, and garages, and many of us either took up new hobbies or rediscovered our old hobbies. For example, the musical instrument (MI) industry experienced a great revival in 2020, as many people bought guitars and other instruments to play at home. Recreational shooting experienced a similar revival as many of us opened our gun safes and cycled a few rounds through our favorite iron. Those of us fortunate enough to shoot at home suddenly had ample time to get those guns sighted in.

Meanwhile, the NSSF and other organizations fought hard from the start to keep gun ranges open and manufacturers

This gun case is usually full of pistols and revolvers, but in late 2020, there were only 3 guns available: two Taurus handguns and a Sig Sauer. Increased demand and manufacturing hiccups due to COVID complications helped create the great gun shortage of 2020.

Taken at the Blue Book Publications booth at the Fall Tulsa Gun Show in November 2019 are Blue Book Sales Manager Tom Toupin (l), Tactical Marketplace Researcher and Editor Connor Daine, president Zach Fjestad, and Associate Editor Kayla McCarthy. This would be the last gun show many of us would attend before the pandemic shut large gatherings down and the first Tulsa show without longtime author of the Blue Book of Gun Values, *S.P. Fjestad who passed away from cancer in July 2019.*

working. COVID affected manufacturing in several ways; federal and state regulations forced manufacturers to retool on the go, implementing new safety and testing protocols. When an employee either tested positive or was exposed to COVID, mandatory quarantines forced them to stay at home for up to two weeks – a requirement still in effect for operational businesses today. Transportation was stretched thin as demand increased for everything else as well (remember the toilet paper shortage?), so getting guns and ammunition from the manufacturer to the retailer was not as routine. Also, let us not forget that one of the biggest American gun manufacturers halted production altogether in July 2020, when Remington filed for bankruptcy again. While not directly related to the pandemic, it exacerbated the situation to take thousands of new guns out of production.

Gun shows were put on hold almost immediately, which left retailers (albeit with limited hours) and gun auctions as the two primary sources for buying or selling. Initial results showed that gun sales did not miss a beat, though. With more time to shoot, and more than a few hiccups in manufacturing, the supply/demand ratio started to tip. But as we would learn, this ugly year was just getting started.

GEORGE FLOYD & RACIAL INJUSTICE

On May 25, 2020, George Floyd, an unarmed black man, was killed by a Minneapolis police officer who knelt on his neck for nearly 9 minutes during his arrest for allegedly trying to pass a counterfeit bill shortly before. Floyd's last words of *"I can't breathe"* became the rally cry of freshly opened racial injustice issues across the nation. Protesting and rioting followed immediately, with mobs destroying large parts of Minneapolis including two police precincts. Curfews were enacted while this all played out on local and national television. Minneapolis was considering disbanding the police and moving to a new "community-based system of public safety." I should also mention that all of this happened right in our backyard and we had a front row seat to this tragedy as Blue Book world headquarters is less than five miles fromwhere this all took place.

Since then, murders, assaults, and other violent crimes rose 21% in Minneapolis, while other crimes, such as car-jackings, increased three times in 2020 over 2019. Minneapolis reported 84 homicides in 2020, which is more than twice as many as the 10-year average. Several of these homicides and shootings are between rival gangs, but that doesn't help an innocent bystander. Crime was showing a slight uptick in the first half of 2020, but after the Floyd murder, crime rose exponentially. If they disband the police, how is anyone going to protect or defend themselves? Again, any wonder why 8.4 million Americans bought their first gun in 2020?

Minneapolis is just one city that happened to be the epicenter of all this, but many other cities experienced destruction from looting and rioting, including Atlanta, Chicago, Houston, and Portland, Oregon. Nationally, we saw an overall increase in crime, including a 30% increase in homicides in large cities.

Disbanding the police in a large city seems hard to fathom, but the city of Minneapolis is very serious about it and looking for solutions on how to fix this glaring problem. Even so, law enforcement is still reluctant to enter certain areas, such as the site of George Floyd's killing at the intersection of 38th Street and Chicago Ave. in South Minneapolis. Communities like this started to actualize self-preservation; if you live in a place without recognized, organized protective services and someone steals your car, breaks into your home, assaults you, or worse, what will you do? Thus, people began arming themselves as their only means of safety.

As this edition is going to print, the trial for the first Minneapolis police officer charged in Floyd's death is starting with jury selection and Minneapolis is already preparing for another round of protesting and rioting with 100 activated National Guard soldiers around the courthouse. What is expected to be a heavily covered and scrutinized trial, it will certainly reopen the wounds of racial injustice, regardless of the outcome. The Rodney King beating in Los Angeles was almost exactly 30 years ago (March 3, 1991), and while we have made some progress in racial equality, we still have a long way to go.

SELF-PROTECTION

Many business owners watched their establishments burn to the ground during the riots in Minneapolis, St. Paul, and other cities without protection from the police, the city, or their insurance companies. Mobs ran unobstructed into many neighborhoods, leaving citizens to depend on plywood boards and their own means of defending their property. Unfortunately, the only option for many was to watch the destruction happen without any way to stop it.

The owner of a pawn shop in South Minneapolis, where the pillaging was centered, took matters into his own hands. Two days after Floyd's killing, a group of rioters broke into his shop. Some were armed, some were not. The storeowner shot and fatally injured one of the intruders from approximately seven feet away – a testimony from the only witness. In the chaos, officers and emergency personnel could not attend aid without getting assaulted by the already unruly mob, and ultimately the mob did what they came to do and destroyed the store. The police returned in the morning to find all the security cameras and recording equipment stolen (along with everything else),

Located about 6 miles directly south of the site where George Floyd was killed, this neighborhood in Bloomington was boarded up for nearly a week due to the threat of looting and destruction. Much of the Minneapolis/St. Paul metropolitan area felt threatened as did many areas in the United States.

rendering the witness' statement necessary. The owner was not charged with a crime; there was not enough evidence to prosecute due to the missing security footage.

When faced with protecting your house, your property, and most importantly yourself, a firearm is often the best choice among many. When everyone felt threatened and frightened this past year, many went out and bought their first gun, but plenty "reassessed" their current self-protection and made sure they had the right tool, enough ammo, and proper accessories to feel safe. This is the main reason why pistols and pump shotguns in regular, tactical, or riot configuration became so popular.

THE 2020 PRESIDENTIAL ELECTION

And then we have the 2020 Presidential election, with what many (at least in the gun community) thought of as a surprising win for the Democrats. Again, my point in this article is not to debate the results of the election and whether it was stolen, cheated, or improperly conducted. Even before the new Biden Administration took office in January 2021, the anti-gun rhetoric ramped up once we knew Donald Trump would not get a second term.

Upon the inauguration of President Biden, a handful of bills regarding firearms were introduced at the federal level with many more at the state level. This is fairly routine, and at least two House bills appear to be favorable toward firearms. However, what caught the ire of many is the President's comment in February, where he presented his ideology toward further gun control. It consists of three major planks: universal background checks, a ban on what he calls "assault weapons" and high capacity magazines; and repealing the Protection of Lawful Commerce in America (PLCAA), which protects manufacturers whose products were used in crimes. If you are not familiar with these topics or what is going on in your state, I suggest you read up on it. Often, a bill summary omits many of the "real" intents of the legislation and you can only find the important details by reading everything.

This certainly is not the first time we have feared further restrictive legislation on firearms. We saw this most recently in 2008 when President Obama took office, and again when he won reelection in 2012 with a surge in firearm and ammunition sales. It is ironic that a very anti-gun president could be such a good salesman. I'm not sure if 2020 feels any different or worse yet (time will certainly tell), but it is the first time in 12 years that Democrats hold the Presidency, the majority in the House, and while the Senate is a split 50/50, the presiding officer and ultimate tiebreaker is the Vice President, Kamala Harris – who many view as one of the most anti-gun politicians of all time.

2021 AND AHEAD

We should take all these occurrences, situations, and threats very seriously, but they clearly helped make 2020 a record year for firearm and ammunition sales. So far in 2021, enthusiasm has not slowed down much, as we are all still experiencing empty shelves and gun racks across the county. I think we will see things start to unravel in the order they occurred. Once the pandemic is behind us, we should hopefully all be able to get back to a sense of normalcy. This should put production of manufactured goods and transportation back on the right track.

If we do not have any major incidents involving safety, self-defense, and self-protection, like we experienced in 2020, those impulse purchases will slow down as well. We will be left with an Administration that will look to enact legislation to take away more of our Second Amendment rights. A perfect storm of all these led to an unprecedented year of us all wondering "what's next?" It is my sincere hope that 2021 is calmer and we find a sense of normalcy by the release of the 43rd Edition next spring. Maybe by then we will be able to actually find a box of 9mm on the shelf without waiting in line.

Zachary R. Fjestad

Blue Book of Gun Values

COLLECTING IN THE TIME OF COVID

by Mark Rendina

I am looking back now on 35 years of collecting firearms and I've found that what a person collects tells you a lot about who a person is – or who they want to be. Collectors are a funny lot. American and German firearm collectors cast up images of fighting on the battle lines of 20th century conflagrations. Colt and Winchester collectors envisage the nostalgic narratives of the Old West. We are passionate, informed, curious, and determined – but full of quirks. We feel uneven because we are never satisfied. We want the next acquisition, we are always on the hunt, and that's where the pleasure of collecting originates. That's the high we chase – the next discovery.

A man once talked me out of my collection of P-38s. Before he discovered his affinity for guns, he had spent years and hundreds of thousands of dollars on collecting – wait for it – fountain pens! I was shaken to my core. How can a person who now admires the high and fine art of military arms have also been attracted to fountain pens?

It was humbling. It awakened a curiosity about my own collecting passion, about collecting in general. How similar am I (with a very extensive collection of firearms) to a nice lady who collects figures of owls, angels, or mushrooms? You can't argue aesthetics, since there is no singular answer to what we like to collect – no hierarchy of what we like to look at or what gives us pleasure. Taste cannot be argued.

In early years, I was only interested in German Lugers and P-38s. I felt slightly sorry for anyone who did not own or yearn for them, or those who were drawn to oh, I don't know, cowboy period guns. And my confession (and subsequent penance) is that now I only desire to chase Colts, Winchesters, and Smith & Wessons ranging the antique period to the 1970s. Such fickle things we collectors are! Perhaps I am one step away from collecting fountain pens next?

Now that I collect American-made firearms, have I progressed or merely become jaded with German guns? And did my friend stop collecting fountain pens because he had seen it all (jaded) or had he developed a higher aesthetic? We cannot (and need not) explain our passions; no two people have the same motivation to collect. But ultimately, it seems most collectors are savants of memories-personal, historical, or national nostalgia. For example: men were principally the ones with

COL Mark Rendina stands before his award-winning Buxton WWII P-38 collection. This was also displayed at the Spring 2019 Wanenmacher's Tulsa Arms Show.

These cased Paris retailer 1874 Smith & Wesson New Russians are in mint condition and unfired. The inscription reads, Faure'-Lepage a' Paris, made for famous Peruvian Leader Louis Aretteta Canas. The case is made in Paris as well. These guns were from the famous Dr. Gerald Klaz collection and a historic benchmark set for collectible firearms.

military and hunting experience, and guns were historically a central meeting point for masculine culture, but now we see more and more women who know their way around firearms. Women are in the police force, in the military, and heavily represented in shooting competition. Heck, the Cody Firearm's Museum has a young female curator – and she knows her stuff! That has to be good for the future of collecting and shooting sports – especially now, when so many new female buyers are seeking personal protection after the urban riots of 2020.

So, what is important to a collector? Some level of authenticity, some level of quality, and an ambiguous element of splendor that speaks to the individual. We want to own what we appreciate and value, but that appreciation must be shared with others, otherwise there would be no intrinsic value and the item's worth would be void. And it's paramount that your field of collecting must be deep enough to allow unlimited opportunities, that you may expand and explore new aspects of your interest. We know this to be true, since, when we have obtained all the different variations of a brand, we often move on to other brands – starting from the beginning. (Clearly, it is the hunt that collectors like.)

Firearms have all these qualities; history, workmanship, elegance, cunning design, wide variation, and a mystique that allows the imaginative projection of power.

Which begs the question: how long do we keep our collections? Like beauty, the rich history of firearms is a "gift that keeps on giving". A thing of beauty (or in our case, a valuable firearm) is a joy forever. And how many of us have let a "beauty" go? And why? Time, maturity, space, finances… the list goes on to describe any number of reasons to end – and let go of – a collection. To continue in the hunt for better specimens, we have to trade up and move items that have lost that "special feeling". When I get too many items in my gun safe, I have to face the fact that some firearms have stopped speaking to me as they once did. We have to part as friends.

What I am certain of is that we have lived in a Golden Age of collecting, since WWII Americans have excelled as collectors of industrial art: cars, old toys, and firearms. Most collectors cut their teeth and honed their

Python Madness! COL Mark Rendina stands before his rare and Engraved Colt Pythons along with a copy of Gurney Brown's book *Seven Serpents – The History of Colt's Snake Guns*. He is also holding the never before seen, first-made 1911 from first-year production with nitre blue fire parts – a Colt holy grail – from a world-famous collection.

skills in the phenomenal rise of guns shows in the post-WWII period (from the 1950s to 2019). Some have made collecting their avocation, some have made extra money, many have become dealers, more have spent their lives investigating their collections, displaying them, and even writing books on the subject.

But the industry has evolved; I can't remember buying a single firearm at auction until the 2000s, though I am sure I will going forward. Auction houses have taken over the hub of collecting – growing exponentially since 2000. The time of COVID has only magnified the growth of auction transactions. At Rock Island Auction this February, they had signs looking for "Over the Road Drivers." Post-inauguration (Jan 2021), there are so many collectors letting their guns go that they are short of drivers to go and get them! Yet I observe there are still two buyers for every one! Let's try to see what's going on, see if we can identify some trends.

While online auctions seem to be the primary way of doing business post-COVID, it's challenging to fully inspect the value of a collectable only through photos and ineffective descriptions. Collectors are sticklers for what they want and there are lots of disappointments when the guns arrive. I still make it a point to take my mask and go to auctions personally to inspect a gun face to face. A photo can hide a lot of imperfections and catalogue descriptions fail to present flaws in a clear language. While the world continues to turn via the web, there are still things that are better to do in person.

There were few guns shows in 2020 - before the pandemic shut everything down – but there were many more auctions. Collecting firearms has now become highly centralized at major auction houses since the 1990s. The question has changed from "*what is your next gun show?*" to "*are you attending the next Morphy's or Rock Island Auction event?*" Since 1999 I attended at least 4 auctions each year and it completely changed how I collect firearms.

FIVE EASY TRENDS

I have participated in all national auctions in the past thirty years. I see some important evolutions of the hobby and can anticipate many new trends emerging from the COVID pandemic.

Trend number 1. Third party taxes must now be paid by most residents of the lower 48 states. (I am lucky, since I live in Kansas, which is one of the few states not yet charging third party taxes for items bought at auctions.). However, that has not impacted any significant cooling of the market yet. Collectors pay their taxes and move on.

Trend number 2. Condition and original boxes are king! Minty examples with original boxes get about 30% more than the same guns without their original labeled box. This trend is especially true with 1950-'70 era Colt and Smith & Wesson pistols. Colt Pythons, for example, are still strong but have to be as new in the original box. Pythons with even 2% wear or no box must be sold at discount. Also, I've observed that the top 1% of all antique firearms still get crazy money and have seemed to double in price in the last year. Benchmark condition guns (19th century Winchesters and Colts) sell for multiples of their book value. Here is an example from Amoskeag Auction house: 1885 High Wall Winchester in 50 Express. The estimate was $6-8,000. I bid up to $12,000 (I will admit that was nosebleed for me). The gun sold for $28,200! That's 5 times low estimate! Boom! Hello! No COVID depression here! There are guys who kept their powder dry (not going to gun shows) and were ready to get what they wanted.

Trend number 3. Common, run of the mill guns are flying off internet gun sites! Got a beat up S&W revolver? A common Taurus .357 copy? Small, concealed carry guns are the top sellers now. A standard Ruger Mini 14? Gone! Dealers say that common guns under $1000 are selling instantly – often for a premium. My modern FFL says, "Now I don't have to discount modern guns!"

Why? COVID and a (surprise) Democratic win makes Americans wish they had bought when the "Trump Slump" was in effect before March 2020. Everyone wants to get their gun before the new administration drops the next foot and ramps up gun laws. During these past

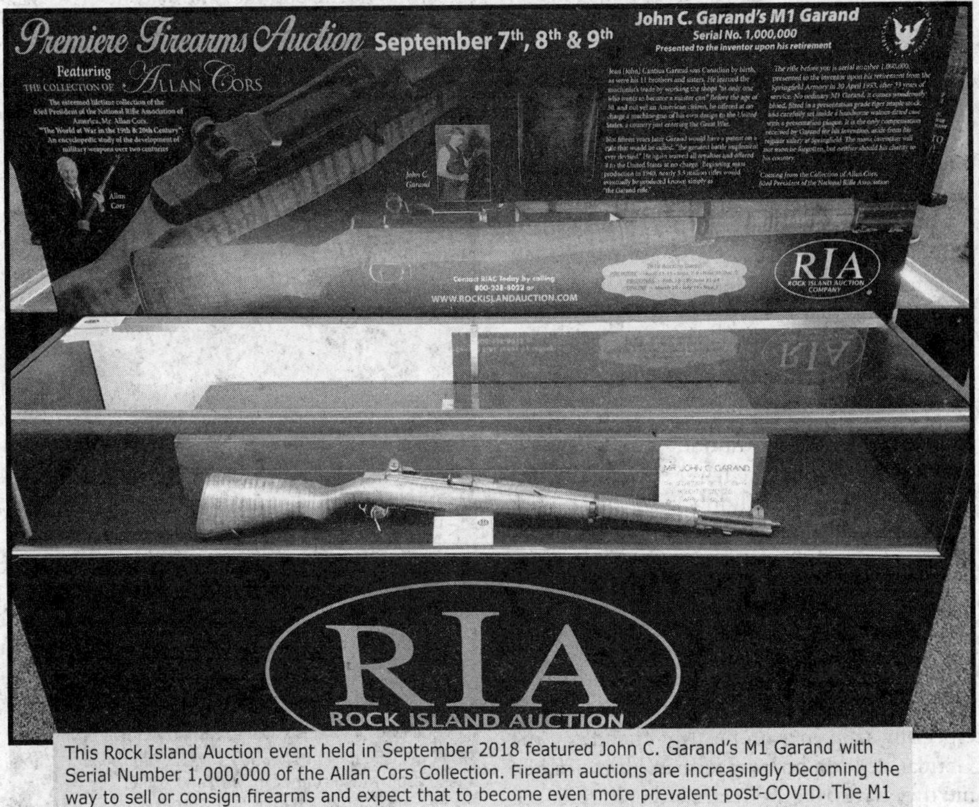

This Rock Island Auction event held in September 2018 featured John C. Garand's M1 Garand with Serial Number 1,000,000 of the Allan Cors Collection. Firearm auctions are increasingly becoming the way to sell or consign firearms and expect that to become even more prevalent post-COVID. The M1 Garand sold for an astounding $287,500, a world record!

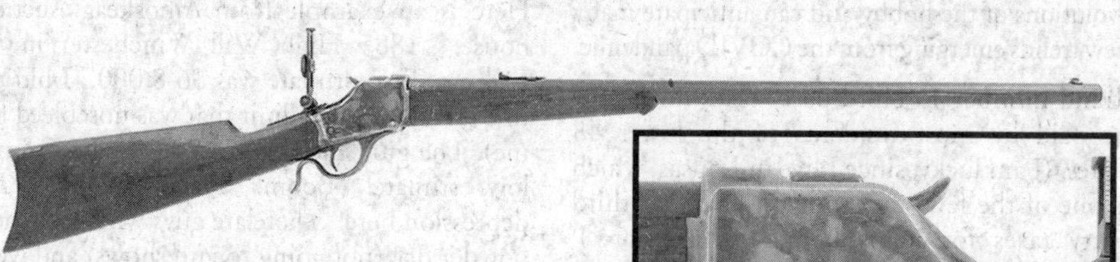

A fine example of Winchester's Model 1885 High Wall Rifle, named for the "high wall" frame used for stronger cartridges and covered most of the firing hammer. Gorgeous case coloring and a desirable .50 Express caliber helped push the selling price of this rifle to unprecedented levels. Images courtesy Amoskeag Auction Company Inc.

12 months of COVID, there have been nearly four million new firearm background checks – nearly doubling the previous year's average totals.

Trend number 4. Ammo is gone. If it is available at all, it is there but at 5-6-7 times the price. I used to buy Russian made Wolf 9mm for my MP40 machine gun for 12 cents a round. Price now? They cost 66 cents a round on a good day. Same for .223 and .45 cal. At a gun show in January 2021 (in Florida), the deal of the show was 500 rounds of 9mm for $400 - that's 80 cents a pop! Reloading components are also 2-3 times as high. Primers are being made only for manufacturers – not the home reloader. Want to buy a 9mm Square B reloading press (to avoid the high cost of factory ammo)? Stand in line. I bought one in December 2020 and was told to wait until March since they were sold out. Now I know why the old guys hoarded ammo from the last Obama scare in 2014 (and it took 4 years to recover from that scarcity). Don't expect prices to go down anytime soon with our new administration waiting in the wings to wave their anti-gun wands.

Trend number 5. Antique guns. Let's be honest - sadly, there are fewer senior collectors to buy civil war and flintlock era firearms. A typical grey $1,800-$1,900 antique with little finish is hard to move unless at bargain prices. U.S. Trapdoor rifles have been at the same price range ($1,200-$1,600) for over 30 years. Many longtime dealers have entire back room warehouses full of these guns and it's hard to see who is going to buy them. The same is especially true in Europe. My friends at the German auction house, Herman Historica, tell me they have 10,000 firearms they cannot sell since European legislatures have frozen an already chilled European market with newly enacted regulations. They are looking for US buyers – with few takers willing to fight the import restrictions.

There are more trends, but we can cover these when the COVID pandemic (hopefully) ends this summer. We know for sure that the new administration will leverage any crisis to place more restrictions and regulations on firearms. In Europe they did it "one crisis at a time," until legislatures totally killed the market in firearms and collecting. Let's hope

COL Mark Rendina holds a rare unfired Colt New Frontier in .357 and nickel finish, of which only 500 were made.

the newly incorporated NRA continues to champion the 2nd amendment right of shooters and collectors.

The world is a different place in many ways. We have lost many lights of the collecting community. Writers such as Warren Buxton and Steven Fjestad have disappeared suddenly from the scene. My close friend, the well-known dealer, Richard Crosier, left us last June. We all feel abandoned and a little lost to face the pandemic without their advice and knowledge. I know I do.

Everyone agrees that collecting firearms will look different on the other side of COVID, just as the world will. A pandemic may lighten your pocketbook, but not your passions. Collecting is a seesawing pursuit, and the old adage "one man's treasure" prevails. If anything, collectors have more time now to look for their treasures while they are working from home. Hobbyists and babies: the two most prominent things that came out of the international shutdown. What I do know is there are more collectors of modern and quality collectable firearms than ever before in American history. Any collector that buys a minty or high-quality firearm will have eager buyers in the future. And that's good news in my book!

Mark Rendina
(Retired military Aviation Officer and past president of the *Missouri Valley Arms Collector Association*.)

Retired military Aviation Officer and past president of the Missouri Valley Arms Collector Association, Mark Rendina stands before some of his recent acquisitions including a pair of Colt Model SAA's, Samurai sword dated 1655, Colt New Service, 1914 Artillery Luger, Walther PP, and period-correct ammo and accessories.

BLUE BOOK OF GUN VALUES
COLLECTIBLE FIREARMS AVERAGE INDEX

2021 marks the 40th Anniversary for the *Blue Book of Gun Values* – the first edition was released 40 years ago in 1981. Since then, we have published a new edition every year (except for 1982 when two editions were released with a mid-year update). This also means we have been compiling firearm information and values for 40 years. We often get asked how a gun's value performed over time. Since we have been doing this for 40 years – the numbers are all there. The challenge (and extremely subjective part) is how we compile them and statistically make them representative of the collectible firearm industry.

Welcome to our inaugural *Blue Book of Gun Values* Collectible Firearms Average Index, where we will show how 10 guns have performed year-by-year in a Dow Jones Industrial Average (DJIA) sort of way. For those of you not familiar with the DJIA, it is a stock market index looking at the performance of 30 large publicly traded companies in the U.S. It gives a current snapshot of the market conditions and generally represents the current health of the economy.

Guns, like this Colt Python, have become very collectible in recent years. In 1981, this gun was listed in the Blue Book of Gun Values *at $375. Today it is worth $3,000+!*

So, after some 11th hour deliberation, I asked contributing editor Mark Rendina to give me ten guns that would fit the following criteria: They must be collectible over the length of our timetable (1981-2021) there needs to be variety (including handguns, rifles, and shotguns), and are common/popular enough that most collectors would seek these out for their collections. We intentionally omitted high value guns (Colt Walkers for example) and left out low end guns as well.

We picked the following guns for consideration:

- Browning Post-WWII Superposed Midas Grade, 12 ga.
- Colt 1st Generation Single Action Army, .45 cal.
- Colt 2nd Generation Single Action Army, .45 cal.
- Colt Model 1911A1 Military in Bright Blue Finish, .45 cal.
- Colt Python from the late 1950s/early 1960s with a 4 in. barrel, .357 cal.
- Smith & Wesson .44 Magnum Pre-Model 29 (5 Screw), .44 Mag. Cal.
- Winchester WWI-era Model 1897 Military Trench Gun, 12 ga.
- U.S. Military M1C Garand Sniper with original paperwork, .30-06 cal.
- Winchester Model 1873 First Model Rifle, .44-40 WCF cal.
- Winchester Model 1886 Carbine .50 Express cal.

COLLECTIBLE FIREARM VALUE INDEX GUIDELINES

All values in the index are based on a gun in original 98% condition and assumes the most common/popular configuration (a certain barrel length, the inclusion of a box, etc.). Each year, I took the 98% condition value for the ten chosen guns, added up all the values for that year, and then divided by ten. This provides a year-by-year average or "mean" to use the proper statistical term. Also, this is meant to look at the long-term value of a firearm in terms of collector value as opposed to new guns and what they sell at for retail.

We have been working with a true database to compile the *Blue Book of Gun Values* since 2005, and one of the features that technology affords us now is year-by-year reporting of each gun's values for that specific year (this is also a shameless plug for our online subscriptions as you can view historical pricing back to 2005). However, prior to the 26th Edition, those books were edited directly in the graphic design program, so I had to go back through all the old copies edition-by-edition and mark these values. This was a tedious task, but it is always fascinating to see how the book changes year-by-year.

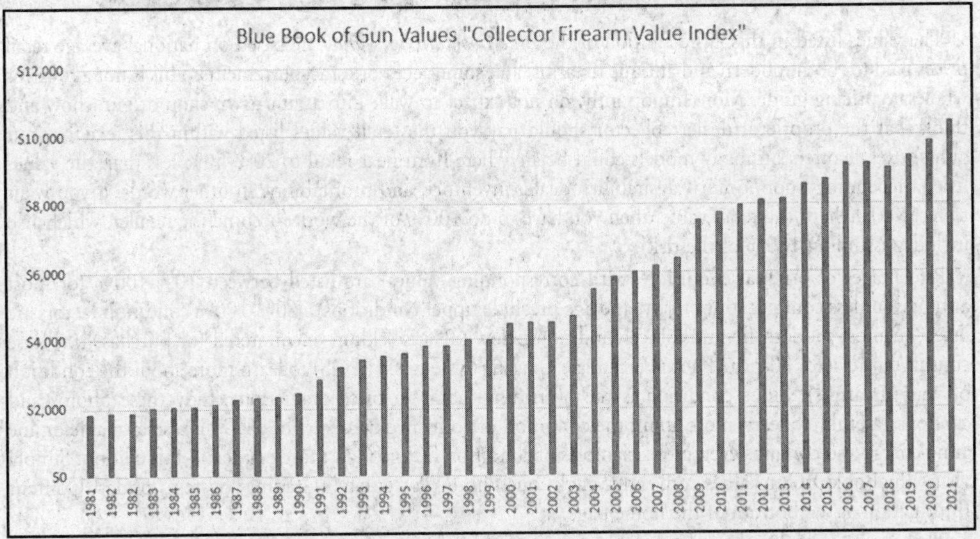

As you can see, the trend is nearly all positive. In 1981, the ten-gun average was $1,869 and 40 years later, the ten-gun average is $10,448. However, I am always amazed at what you learn looking through data after you have taken the time to compile it.

Observation 1. The CFVI has only gone down once in the 40-year history when in 2018 it decreased $137 from 2017 due to a slight correction with the Browning Superposed while the other nine firearms remained the same. Otherwise, every year has shown an increase, even if it is a modest increases such as 1981 to 1982 ($11), 1984 to 1985 ($10), and 2000 to 2001 ($47), but positive, nonetheless.

Observation 2. The CFVI only stayed the same between editions twice: in years 1998 and 1999, and again in 2001 and 2002. I think this is extremely important to note that the values in this book are constantly changing. We picked a diverse group of 10 guns and only twice in the 40-year history have those 10 guns not changed between editions.

Observation 3. 2009 was the best year according to the CFVI with the value increasing 17.5% over the previous year, and that might have something to do with the election of a new president in 2008. Other large increases include 2004 (16.6%), 1991 (16.3%), 1992 (12.8%), and 2000 (11.2%). Interestingly, 2021, which set many records for firearm sales, shows only a respectable 6% increase from 2020. While it seems firearm values are up, these 10 guns do not indicate the anomaly many of us think 2020 represented.

Observation 4. As I stated in my introduction, no two guns are created equal. The increase in value of the CFVI ranges from a modest 312.5% increase on the Browning Superposed while the Colt Model 1911 A1 shows a large 2000% increase and the Winchester Model 97 Military Trench Gun a whopping 2111% increase since we started tracking values in 1981!

I hope to continue the Collector Firearm Value Index into future editions, and I also would like to expand it to include more firearms. Again, our goal is to provide you with a snapshot that is representative of the market. We hope you enjoy this as much as we enjoyed compiling the information and looking back through our history.

Zachary R. Fjestad & Mark Rendina

HOW TO USE THIS BOOK

The values listed in this 42nd Edition of the *Blue Book of Gun Values* are based on national average retail prices paid for both modern and antique firearms, and some accessories/accoutrements. This is not a firearms wholesale pricing guide. More importantly, do not expect to walk into a gun/pawn shop or gun show and think that the proprietor/dealer/collector should pay you the retail values listed within this text for your gun(s). Resale offers on many models could be anywhere from near retail to 20%-50% less than the values listed, depending upon locality, desirability, dealer inventory, and profitability. In other words, if you want to receive 100% of the retail value, then you have to do 100% of the work (become the retailer, which also includes assuming 100% of the risk).

Percentages of original condition (with corresponding values) are listed between 10%-100% for most antiques (unless configuration, rarity, and age preclude upper conditions). 60%-100% condition factors are listed on most modern firearms since condition below 60% is seldom encountered (or purchased). Please consult our revised, 80-page Photo Percentage Grading System™ (PPGS) to learn more about the condition of your firearm(s). Since condition is the overriding factor in price evaluation, study these photos and captions carefully to learn more about the condition of your specimen(s). The PPGS is also available online at no charge and contains even more examples of condition factors than those printed in this edition. Simply visit BlueBookOfGunValues.com and click on Photo Percentage Grading System under Content Information at the bottom of the home page.

Three pages (30-32) are provided (Anatomy of a Handgun, Anatomy of a Rifle, and Anatomy of a Shotgun), to help you identify various parts and firearms nomenclature used within this text. Please refer to the expanded Abbreviations section for a complete listing of abbreviations used within this text. Once again, the Glossary has been updated in this edition, and will explain most of the firearms terminology used in the A-Z sections, especially tactical terminology. You may also want to check out the Store Brand Cross-Over Listings, since hundreds of makes and models can easily be cross-referenced. A Proof Marks section will also help you identify and date many European firearms. Additionally, a Serialization Index has been added to make finding your firearm's serialization easier.

Since the 42nd Edition is 2,512 pages, it may be easier to zero in on a particular manufacturer and category (pistols, rifles, shotguns, etc.) by referring to the updated Index. For trademarks and companies with more than one configuration of firearm, individual category names are listed alphabetically. Alphabetical tabs are located on the tops of the pages next to the page number and heading, making it easier to find all the information you want quickly. Sidebar black markers are also provided, enabling you to zero in on an alphabetical section without opening the book. As in previous editions, the NRA condition standards and grading criteria have been included to make the conversion to percentages easier. This will be especially helpful when evaluating antiques. Additionally, images for NRA condition standards are included in the PPGS.

To find a model in this text, first look under the name of the manufacturer, trademark, brand name, and in some cases, the importer (please consult the Index if necessary). Next, find the correct category name(s) (Commemoratives, Pistols, Rifles, Shotguns, etc.). When applicable, antiques will appear before modern guns, and are typically listed in chronological sequence.

Once you find the correct model or sub-model under its respective subheading, determine the specimen's percentage of original condition (see the Photo Percentage Grading System™) and refer to the corresponding percentage column showing the value. Commemoratives or special/limited editions will generally appear last under a manufacturer's heading.

1. Alphabetical names are located on the top of right-facing, odd-numbered pages and appear as follows:

R SECTION

2. Trademarks, manufacturers, brand names, importers, or organizations are listed alphabetically in uppercase bold typeface, like this:

FOX, A.H.

3. Manufacturer/trademark information is listed directly beneath the trademark heading:

Current manufacturer located in Eckernförde, Germany since 1751 (originally Prussia). Currently imported by Sauer USA, located in San Antonio, TX. Previously manufactured in Suhl pre-WWII. Previously imported and warehoused 1995-2007 by SIG Arms, located in Exeter, NH. Rifles were previously imported until 1995 by the Paul Company Inc. located in Wellsville, KS and until 1994 by G.U., Inc. located in Omaha, NE.

4. Manufacturer notes may appear next under individual heading descriptions and can be differentiated by the following typeface:

In 1972, J.P. Sauer & Sohn entered into a cooperative agreement with SIG. During 2000, SAN Swiss Arms AG purchased SIG Arms AG, including the J.P. Sauer & Sohn trademark. The L&O Group, an international industrial holding company, currently has controlling interest of J.P. Sauer and Sohns. Production remains in Eckernförde, Germany.

5. The next classification is the category name (normally, in alphabetical sequence) in uppercase lettering (inside a screened gray box) which primarily refers to a firearm's configuration. Category names include:

CARBINES: SEMI-AUTO, PISTOLS: SEMI-AUTO, REVOLVERS,

RIFLES: BOLT ACTION, SHOTGUNS: O/U

6. A further sub-classification may appear under a category name, as depicted below. These are sub-categories of a major category name, appear in both upper and lower case type, and typically appear in alphabetical order. Examples include:

Pistols: Semi-Auto, XD Series

7. Following a category or sub-category name, a category note may follow to help explain the category, and/or provide limited information on the models and values listed within the category. This appears as follows:

H&R 1871 began providing the Trigger Guardian trigger locking system beginning Dec. 1, 1999 at no extra charge. During 2008, H&R 1871 reintroduced its Ultragon rifling on its rifled slug barrels, which feature six oval lands and grooves w/o sharp corners. All H&R models are built in the U.S.A.

8. Model names appear flush left, are bold faced, and are in uppercase lettering either in chronological order (normally) or alphabetical order (sometimes, the previous model name and/or close sub-variation will appear at the end in parentheses) and are listed under the individual category and sub-category names. Examples include:

A-BOLT HUNTER II

9. Model descriptions are denoted by the following typeface and usually include the following information:

– calibers, gauges/bore, action type, barrel length(s), finish(es), weight, and other descriptive data are provided adjacent to model names in this typeface. This is where most of the information is listed for each specific model, including identifiable features and possibly some production data, including quantity, date of manufacture, and discontinuance date, if known.

10. Variations (and possible production periods) within a model appear as sub-models - they are differentiated from model names by an artistic icon * prefix, are italicized and indented, and appear in upper and lowercase type, as follows:

*** Mark II Gyro Jet***

This is usually followed by a short description of that sub-model. These sub-model descriptions have the same typeface as the model descriptions:

– additional sub-model information could include finishes, calibers, barrel lengths, special order features, or other production data specific for that sub-model.

11. Also included is yet another layer of model/information nomenclature differentiating sub-models from variations of sub-models or a lower hierarchy of sub-model information. These items are indented from the sub-models, and have the icon graphic », for example:

» **Model 585 Sporting Clays Set**

A description for this level of sub-model information may appear next to the sub-entry, and uses the same typeface as model and sub-model descriptions shown above.

12. Model notes and information appear in smaller type, generally after the price line, and should be read since they contain important, critical, and interesting facts/information. In some cases, factory recalls (some include serialization) are also provided. Examples include:

Many original 1878 barrels have "found their way" on the front end of a SAA frame since the barrels are interchangable. Because of this, many "original" Model 1878 DAs may have an incorrect and/or later SAA Colt barrel attached. Watch yourself here! Also, scarce calibers should be verified with factory.

13. Extra features/special orders which can add or subtract value are placed either under category names, model/sub-model descriptions, or pricing lines. On current models that don't have a price line, the MSR will also appear in this typeface, in addition to other pricing information regarding that model. These individual lines appear bolder than other descriptive typeface, such as the following:

Add 10% for NIB condition.
Subtract 20% for medium action cals.
Current MSR on this model is $1,795.

14. On many discontinued models/variations after 1985, the last MSR (manufacturer's suggested retail price) may appear flush right, in italics at the end of the 100%-60% pricing line. This will fall directly under the Last MSR column that appears at the end of the grading lines. Some MSRs may also appear like this:

Last MSR in 2018 was $1,950.

15. Grading lines normally appear at the top of each page, and in the middle if price lines change. If you are uncertain as to how to properly grade a particular firearm, please refer to the digital color Photo Percentage Grading System™ (PPGS) on pages 65-142 for more assistance. The most commonly encountered grading line (shown with a typical price line underneath) in this text is for 100%-60% condition factors:

GRADING - PPGS™	100%	98%	95%	90%	80%	70%	60%	*LAST MSR*
	$895	$775	$675	$575	$500	$450	$400	

Antique grading lines have additional values listed for 100%-10% and also 95%-10%. Examples (with price lines) are as follows:

100%	98%	95%	90%	80%	70%	60%	50%	40%	30%	20%	10%
$2,250	$1,850	$1,550	$1,350	$1,050	$850	$700	$600	$500	$425	$350	$300
N/A	N/A	$22,000	$18,000	$16,000	$12,000	$10,000	$6,000	$4,000	$2,500	$1,500	$1,000

When "N/A" (Not Applicable) is listed instead of a value, this indicates that this particular model is not encountered enough in those condition factors to warrant a value - especially true on antiques in upper condition factors and with commemoratives and special/limited editions under 95%.

Most commemorative/limited edition grading and price lines will appear as follows:

GRADING - PPGS™	100%	Issued Price	Qty. Made
	$1,250	$575	200

In some cases, an organization's or company's listing (i.e. Turnbull Restoration, etc.) of guns will appear as follows:

Manufacturer/Model	Quantity	Year	Issue Price
ITHACA Model 37 Ultralight 20 ga.	750	1997	N/A

16. Price line formats are as follows - when the price line shown below (with proper grading line) is encountered, it automatically indicates the gun is currently manufactured, and the MSR is shown left of the 100% column.

MSR $1,825	$1,475	$1,150	$1,025	$925	$850	$750	$550
No MSR	$300	$250	$225	$200	$180	$160	$140

Following this are the 100%-60% values. This 100% value is the national average price a consumer will typically expect to pay for that model in NIB unfired condition. 100% specimens without boxes, warranties, etc., which are currently manufactured may be discounted (5%-20%, depending on the desirability of make and model). This 100%

GRADING - PPGS™	100%	98%	95%	90%	80%	70%	60%	LAST MSR

price on currently manufactured guns also assumes not previously sold at retail. Some companies are no longer publishing MSRs, and in this case, No MSR is listed first in the pricing line.

17. When a currently manufactured or discontinued limited/special edition firearm with or without retail pricing is encountered, it typically will not have values listed from 90%-60%, but rather N/As (Not Applicable), as these lower condition factors are seldom encountered. The value lines will appear as follows in this case:

MSR $10,750	**$9,950**	**$8,750**	**$7,500**	**N/A**	**N/A**	**N/A**	**N/A**
	$995	**$850**	**$725**	**N/A**	**N/A**	**N/A**	**N/A**

18. A price line with seven values listed, as represented below, indicates a discontinued, out-of-production model with values shown for 100%-60% conditions. Because stainless steel is almost impervious to visible wear, an 80% - 60% model's value must be determined by the condition of its action and barrel (i.e., how much it has been shot/used), in addition to grip wear. Values are normally not listed for 50%-10% condition factors, since these lower conditions are seldom encountered on recently discontinued models. Examples include:

$1,900	**$1,400**	**$1,200**	**$1,100**	**$995**	**$850**	**$725**
N/A	**$10,000**	**$8,500**	**$7,000**	**$6,000**	**$5,000**	**$3,500**

Values for conditions under 60% will typically be no less than 50% (1/2) of the 60% price, unless the gun has been shot to a point where the action may be loose or questionable. Obviously, no "MSR" will appear in the left margin, but a last manufacturer's suggested retail price may appear flush right in italics within the price line, automatically indicating a discontinued gun, like this:

$300	**$225**	**$185**	**$165**	**$155**	**$145**	**$135**	***$395***

19. Some antiques listed will not have price lines, but rather value ranges for Above Average, Average, and Below Average condition factors. These value range price lines with corresponding grading lines will appear as follows:

Above Average	Average	Below Average
$80,000 - $120,000	**$35,000 - $80,000**	**$20,000 - $35,000**

An explanation of these condition factor ranges appears under the heading "Grading Explanation for Winchester Lever Actions" in the beginning of the Winchester section.

20. Under certain manufacturer/trademark listings you may find the status of the company along with location and mfg. dates only. This is because their category and model listings are no longer available within this printed text but will still appear on our website. Please follow the link to access complete model descriptions and values free of charge.

BINGHAM, LTD.

Previous manufacturer located in Norcross, GA circa 1976-1985.

For individual model listings, please go to BlueBookOfGunValues.com/overflow.

ANATOMY OF A HANDGUN

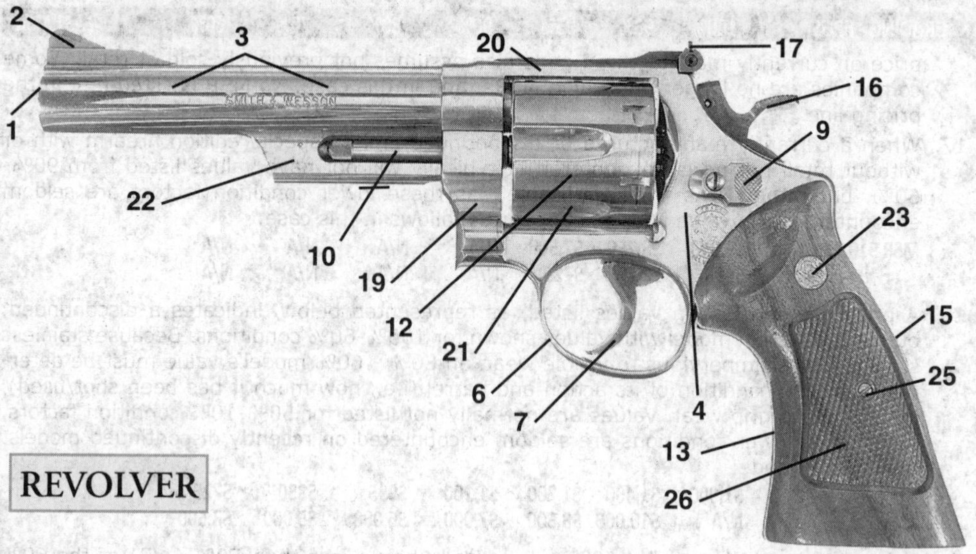

REVOLVER

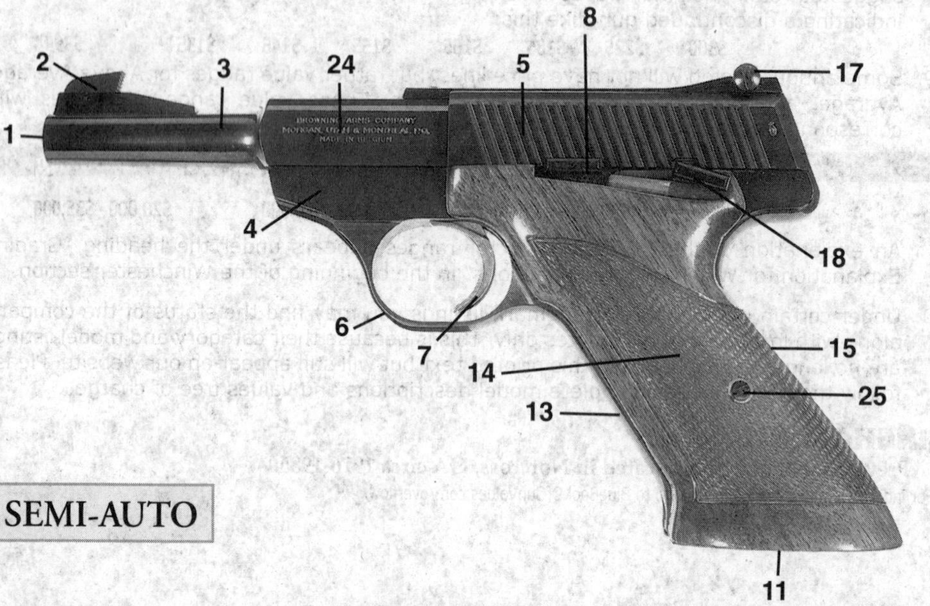

SEMI-AUTO

1. Muzzle
2. Front Sight
3. Barrel
4. Frame
5. Slide (Serrated)
6. Trigger Guard
7. Trigger
8. Slide Release Lever
9. Cylinder Release Latch
10. Cylinder Ejector Rod
11. Magazine (Hidden)
12. Cylinder
13. Front Grip Strap
14. Grip
15. Rear Grip Strap
16. Hammer
17. Rear Sight
18. Safety Lever
19. Crane
20. Top Strap
21. Cylinder Flute
22. Ejector Rod Shroud (Partial Length)
23. Grip Medallion
24. Barrel/Frame Address
25. Grip Screw
26. Grip (Square Butt Type, On Older Mfg.)

ANATOMY OF A RIFLE

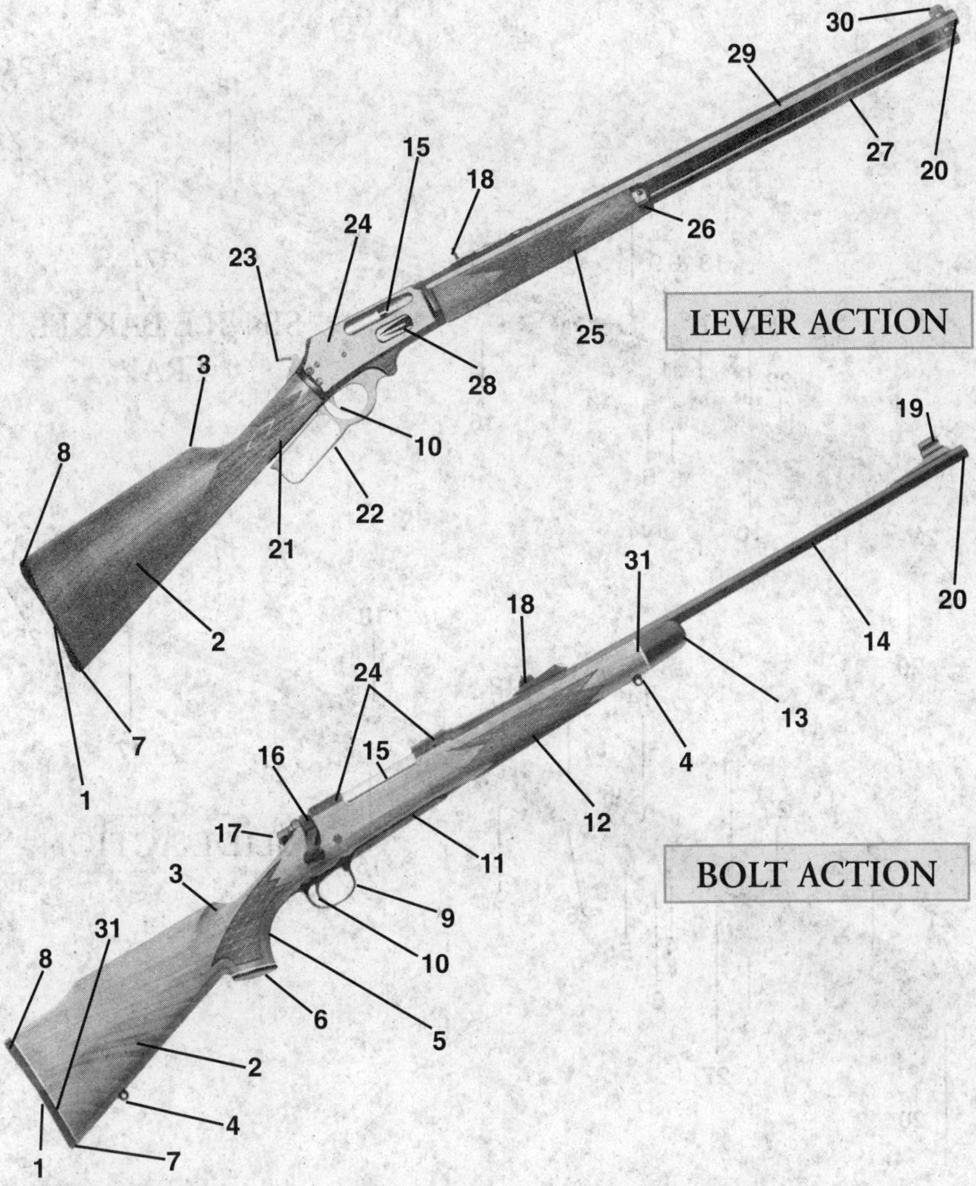

1. Buttplate
2. Buttstock
3. Comb
4. Sling Swivel Stud
5. Semi-Pistol Grip
6. Pistol Grip Cap
7. Toe
8. Heel
9. Trigger Guard
10. Trigger
11. Floor Plate
12. Forend
13. Forend Tip
14. Barrel
15. Bolt
16. Bolt Handle
17. Safety Button
18. Rear Sight
19. Hooded-Ramp Front Sight
20. Muzzle
21. Straight Grip
22. Lever
23. Hammer
24. Receiver
25. Forearm
26. Forearm Cap
27. Magazine Tube
28. Loading Port
29. Octagon Barrel
30. Blade Front Sight
31. Spacer

ANATOMY OF A SHOTGUN

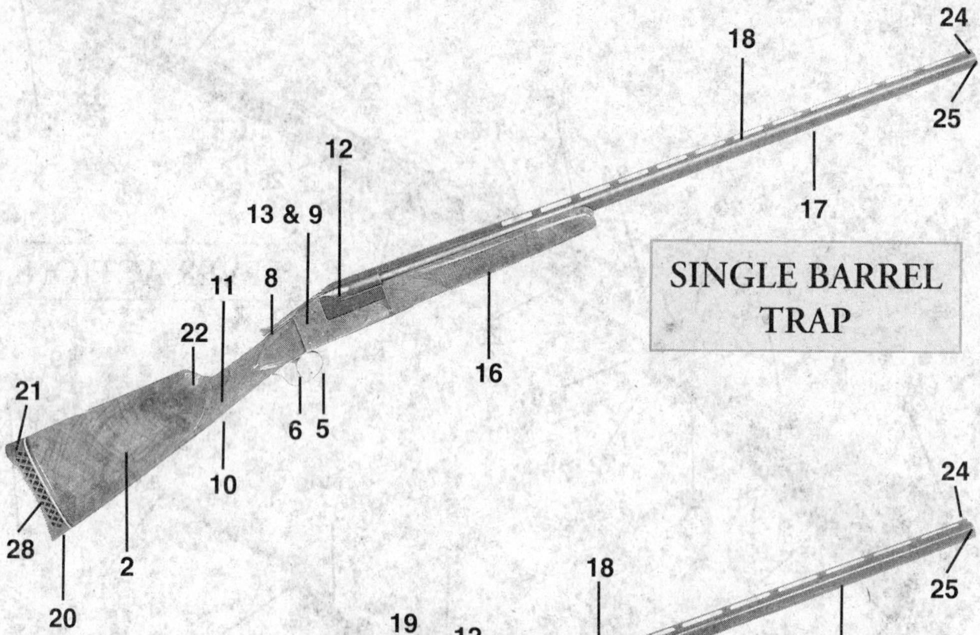

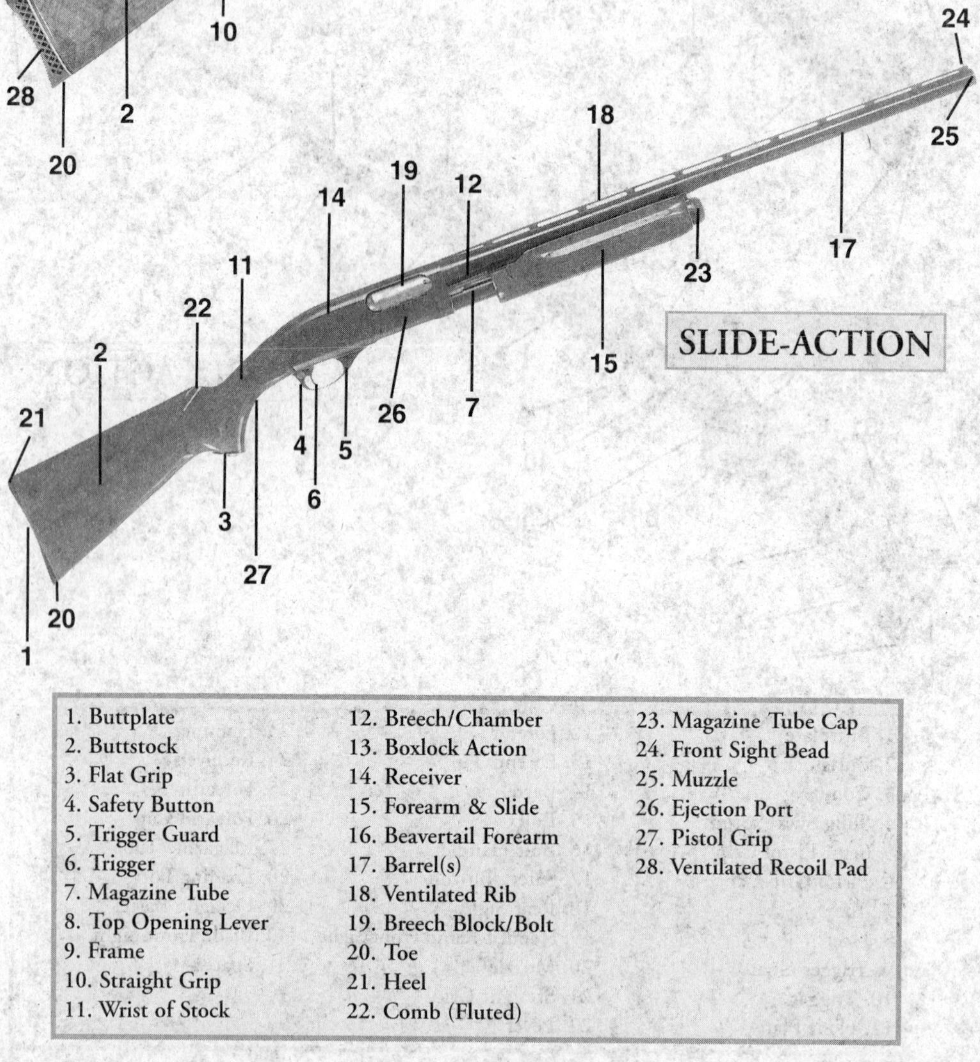

1. Buttplate	12. Breech/Chamber	23. Magazine Tube Cap
2. Buttstock	13. Boxlock Action	24. Front Sight Bead
3. Flat Grip	14. Receiver	25. Muzzle
4. Safety Button	15. Forearm & Slide	26. Ejection Port
5. Trigger Guard	16. Beavertail Forearm	27. Pistol Grip
6. Trigger	17. Barrel(s)	28. Ventilated Recoil Pad
7. Magazine Tube	18. Ventilated Rib	
8. Top Opening Lever	19. Breech Block/Bolt	
9. Frame	20. Toe	
10. Straight Grip	21. Heel	
11. Wrist of Stock	22. Comb (Fluted)	

GUN QUESTIONS/APPRAISALS POLICY

Whether we wanted it or not, Blue Book Publications, Inc. has ended up in the driver's seat as the clearing house for gun information. Because the volume of gun questions now requires almost full-time attention, we have developed a standardized policy that will enable us to provide you with the service you have come to expect from Blue Book Publications, Inc. To that end, we have extended all these services to our website (BlueBookOfGunValues.com).

To ensure that the research department can answer every gun question with an equal degree of thoroughness, an extensive firearms research center has been established. It includes a massive library with well over 1,500 reference books, thousands of both new and old factory catalogs/brochures, price sheets, most major auction catalogs, and dealer inventory listings.

ONLINE SELF SERVICE

Customers can answer most of their gun questions themselves. Simply visit BlueBookOfGunValues.com and visit Appraisals and Evaluations under "Services" at footer of the home page for more information and pricing on these service options. It certainly is a big help to know the manufacturer/trademark and the model to use this service. To further assist you, on our website every firearms manufacturer, category, and model is listed, and a model description is also provided free of charge. This will enable the consumer to ensure he/she selects the right make/model, or manufacturer/trademark before payment is made. There are two different levels of self service. Purchase information and current values on a single model or a one, two, or three-year online subscription for unlimited access to the *Blue Book of Gun Values* (best value). Color images are also available for many models and variations.

PHONE GUN QUESTIONS

The charge is $10 per gun value question, $15 per gun if the firearm's make and/or model needs to be identified first. Phone gun questions are payable with a major credit card. All phone gun questions are answered when time is permitting, on a first-come, first-serve basis. Phone number is 952-854-5229 ext. 2000. All value requests will be given within a range only, based on the accuracy of information the consumer provides – this is the most critical element of phone gun questions. Gun question telephone hours are 10:00 a.m. to 4:00 p.m., M-F, CST, no exceptions please. Phone gun questions are typically answered in 5 business days or less, unless the research staff has a production commitment or is away attending trade/gun shows.

APPRAISAL INFORMATION

Written appraisals will be performed only when time is permitting and if the following criteria are met. Research staff personnel must have good quality photos/images, a complete description(s) including manufacturer's name, model, gauge or caliber, barrel length, and other pertinent information. On some firearms, depending on the manufacturer/trademark and model, a factory letter may be necessary. Remember, since these written appraisals are done without physically inspecting the firearm(s), the appraised value(s) will only be as accurate as the information our research staff receives. High quality images are the single most important element on written appraisals. The charge for a written appraisal is 2% of the appraised value with a minimum of $30 per gun. For email appraisals, please refer to BlueBookOfGunValues.com. Please allow 2-3 weeks response time per appraisal request.

ADDITIONAL SERVICES

Individuals requesting a photocopy of a particular page or section from any edition for insurance or reference purposes will be billed at $5 per page, up to 5 pages, and $3.50 per page thereafter. Please direct all gun questions and appraisals to:

Blue Book Publications, Inc.
Attn: Research Dept.
8009 34th Ave. S., Suite 250
Minneapolis, MN 55425 USA
Phone: 952-854-5229, ext. 2000 • Fax: 952-853-1486 • BlueBookOfGunValues.com
Email: guns@bluebookinc.com
Use "Firearm Inquiry" in the subject line or it may get deleted.

GLOSSARY

1989 BUSH BAN

Refers to the U.S. Federal executive branch study and resulting regulations which banned the importation of firearms which did not meet sporting criteria, i.e. certain paramilitary semi-auto only rifles and shotguns. The study was undertaken in response to the Stockton, CA tragedy in which an AK-47 type rifle was criminally used by a so-called mass murderer. The Federal regulation, U.S.C. Title 18, Section 922r, applies to imported firearms and to firearms assembled in the U.S. using imported components. It is important to note that even though the Assault Weapon Ban (which applied to U.S. manufactured firearms, not imports) has expired, Section 922r remains in effect, and has the force of U.S. Federal law, regardless of its executive branch origin as opposed to U.S. Senate and House of Representatives legislation. Also see Section 922r.

5R

Five groove rifling developed in Russia. Instead of conventional six groove rifling with opposing lands and sharp edged transitions between lands and grooves, 5R lands oppose grooves and the sides of lands are cut at a sixty-five degree angle. Claimed benefits are: decreased bullet deformation, less jacket fouling, increased velocity, and greater accuracy.

A1 STYLE

Refers to an AR style rifle in A1 configuration, or A1 specific components (triangular handguard, short fixed buttstock, receiver with integral carry handle, four slot bird cage flash hider, smooth pistol grip, rear flip sight with short and long range apertures, lighter weight 1:14 twist barrel).

A2 STYLE

Refers to an AR style rifle in A2 configuration, or A2 specific components (circular bi-lateral handguard, longer fixed buttstock, receiver with integral carry handle and spent case deflector, five slot bird cage flash hider, finger rib pistol grip, windage and elevation adjustable rear flip sight with small day and large low light apertures, heavier weight 1:7 twist barrel).

A3 STYLE

Refers to an AR style rifle in A3 configuration, or A3 specific components (circular bi-lateral handguard, collapsible buttstock, receiver with flat top Picatinny rail and detachable carry handle, A2 flash hider/pistol grip/rear sight/barrel).

A4 STYLE

Refers to an AR style rifle in A4 configuration, or A4 specific components (similar to A2 except for flat-top receiver with Picatinny rail, detachable carry handle, and Modular Weapons System handguard).

AK/AKM STYLE ACTION

A gas operated rifle action with a long-stroke gas piston, a tilting breechblock locking design, and a heavy milled (early versions) or lighter sheet metal (later versions) receiver. No regulator is used; the overall design, machining, tolerances, ease of maintenance, and component durability assure reliable function in all circumstances.

AR-15 STYLE ACTION

A gas operated rifle action utilizing a direct gas impingement system (GIO, i.e. no gas piston, no regulator, no moving parts) or a non-gas piston operating mechanism (GPO), a bolt carrier enclosing a multi-lugged rotating bolt locking design, and a two-part light-weight receiver. With the GIO system, propellant gas flows through a gas tube, acts directly upon the bolt carrier to cycle the action, and vents into the receiver. With a GPO, the propellant gas operates a piston which recycles the action. AR-15 style actions have fewer parts, are more adaptable/modifiable, and are significantly lighter than AK, FAL, or HK91 style actions. However, more maintenance, cleaning, and lubrication are required for reliability, especially with the GIO system, in contrast to other gas operated actions.

ACCOUTREMENT

All equipment carried by soldiers on the outside of their uniform, such as buckles, belts, or canteens, but not weapons.

ACCUFIT

Savage's new synthetic stock design on their Model 110 series rifles allows shooters to quickly adjust comb height and length of pull for a customized fit and consistent, more comfortable shooting.

ACTION

An assembly consisting of the receiver or frame and the mechanism by which a firearm is loaded, fired, and unloaded. See ACTION TYPES for the various kinds of actions.

ACTION BAR FLATS

See WATER TABLE.

ACTION TYPES

Actions are broadly classified as either manual or self-loading. Manual actions may be single shot or repeater. Single shot actions include dropping block (tilting, falling, and rolling), break, hinged, and bolt. Repeater actions include revolver, bolt, lever, pump, and dropping block. Self-loading actions may be semiautomatic or automatic. Semi-auto and automatic actions by sub-type are:

a. blowback: simple, lever delayed, roller delayed, gas delayed, toggle delayed, hesitation locked, and chamber-ring delayed.

b. blow-forward.

c. recoil: short, long, and inertia.

d. gas: short stroke piston, long stroke piston, direct impingement, and gas trap.

ADJUSTABLE CHOKE

A device built into the muzzle of a shotgun enabling changes from one choke to another.

ADJUSTABLE FRONT SIGHT

A front sight which can be moved, relative to the barrel's axis, vertically for elevation and/or horizontally for windage adjustments.

ADJUSTABLE REAR SIGHT

A rear sight which can be moved, relative to the barrel's axis, vertically for elevation and/or horizontally for windage adjustments.

ADJUSTABLE SIGHT

A firearm sight which can be adjusted so that the shooter's point of aim and the projectile's point of impact coincide at a desired target distance. On a majority of firearms only the rear sight is adjustable, but front sights may also be adjustable.

AIRGUN

A gun that utilizes compressed air or gas to launch the projectile.

ANY OTHER WEAPON

Any other firearm which is not an NFA defined machine gun, short barrel rifle, short barrel shotgun, modern shoulder stocked pistol, suppressor (BATFE uses the term "silencer"), or destructive device. An AOW is: a device capable of being concealed on a person from which a shot can be discharged through the energy of an explosive; a smooth bore barrel pistol or revolver designed or redesigned to fire a fixed shotgun shell; a weapon with combination shotgun and rifle barrels twelve inches or more but less than eighteen inches in length, from which only a single discharge can be made from either barrel without manual reloading; and any such weapon which may be readily restored to fire. AOW examples: H&R Handyguns, Ithaca Auto-Burglar guns, cane guns, and guns modified/disguised so as to be unrecognizable as firearms.

APERTURE SIGHT

An iron rear sight which has a hole or aperture in a disc or semi-circular blade instead of a rectangular or "vee" notch of an open sight. May also be a front sight, or adjustable for windage/elevation, or have adjustable/interchangeable apertures.

ASSAULT RIFLE

Definition usually depends on if you're pro-gun or anti-gun. If you're pro-gun, it generally refers to a military styled, short to immediate range battle rifle capable of selective fire (semi-auto or full auto). If you're anti-gun, it can include almost anything, including sporter rifles from the turn of the 20th century.

ASSAULT SHOTGUN

Refers to a shotgun manufactured by contract for the military or law enforcement with a barrel shorter than 18 inches, usually a semi-auto or slide action configuration.

ASSAULT WEAPONS BAN

Popular title for the Violent Crime Control and Law Enforcement Act of 1994, Public Law 103-322. See VIOLENT CRIME...LAW 103-322.

AUTO LOADING/LOADER

See SEMI-AUTO ACTION.

AUTOMATIC ACTION

An action design which continuously fires and performs all steps in the operating cycle if the trigger remains fully depressed and ammunition is present in the firearm's magazine or feeding system. Also known as full auto or fully automatic. Machine guns utilize automatic actions, which may be recoil, gas, or externally powered.

AUTOMATIC EJECTOR

See SELECTIVE AUTOMATIC EJECTOR.

BACK BORE/BACK-BORED
A shotgun barrel which has been bored to a diameter greater than normal for its gauge, but not greater than SAAMI specs for that gauge. The advantages of this are: higher shot velocity, more uniform and denser patterns and fewer deformed pellets.

BACK UP IRON SIGHTS
Flip up or fixed iron sights which are not the primary sight system. They are used if the primary optical sight system fails and usually co-witness (optic sight picture and back up sight picture share the same zero).

BACKSTRAP
Those parts of the revolver or pistol frame which are exposed at the rear of the grip.

BARREL
The steel tube (may be wrapped in a sleeve of synthetic material) which a projectile travels through. May or may not be rifled.

BARREL BAND
A metal band, either fixed or adjustable, around the forend of a gun that holds the barrel to the stock.

BARREL FLATS
The lower flat surfaces under the chambers of side-by-side shotgun barrels which contact the corresponding flat areas of the shotgun's receiver. Also see WATER TABLE.

BARREL LUG
A projection which extends from a barrel and performs a locating, supporting, or energy transfer function. Lugs may be separate components, or integral to barrels.

BARREL THROAT
At the breech end of a barrel, the segment of the bore which tapers from a non-rifled projectile diameter to a fully rifled dimension. Also known as a forcing cone, leade, lede, or throat.

BATFE 922r COMPLIANT
A semi-auto paramilitary rifle (assembled with U.S. and foreign manufactured parts) which meets the statutory requirements of Section 922r of the United States code. Also refers to U.S. made parts which bring the rifle into compliance.

BATTUE
A ramped fixed rear sight assembly located on the back of the barrel, allowing quick target acquisition.

BEAVERTAIL FOREND
A wider than normal forend.

BENCH REST STOCK
A rifle stock specifically designed for a "bench rest" competition rifle which is fired from a table or bench, but supported only by sandbags or other devices. Optimized for stability, it often has a very wide flat-bottomed forend.

BESPOKE
A British term for a firearm custom-made to the purchaser's specifications. From the verb "bespeak", which means "to give order for it to be made".

BILLET RECEIVER (LOWER/UPPER)
A billet is a length (usually with square or round profile) of material that has been extruded into shape, either by continuous casting or hot rolling. Manufacturing a final product from a billet usually requires increased machining time.

BIRD'S HEAD
Refers to curved grip configuration on revolvers which resembles the outline of a bird's head, usually with 3 1/2 - 5 1/2 in. barrel lengths. Patterned after the grips on Colt's 1877 Thunderer revolver.

BLIND MAGAZINE
A box magazine which is completely concealed within the action and stock.

BLOWBACK ACTION
A semi-automatic or automatic firearm operating design which uses expanding propellant gasses to push a heavy unlocked breech bolt open, and which relies upon the inertia of its moving parts to keep the action closed until the bullet has exited the muzzle and pressure has decreased to a safe level.

BLUING
The chemical process of artificial oxidation (rusting) applied to gun parts so that the metal attains a dark blue or nearly black appearance.

BOLT
An assembly which reciprocates along the axis of a firearm's bore; it supports the cartridge case head and locks the action. Also see BOLT ACTION.

BOLT (REVOLVER)

The lug or projection which rises from a revolver's frame in order to immobilize the cylinder and align a charge hole with the bore of the barrel. Also called a cylinder stop.

BOLT ACTION

A manual action with a bolt body (usually including locking, firing pin, extractor, and ejector components) enclosed by and moving within the firearm's receiver.

BORE

Internal dimensions of a barrel (smooth or rifled) that can be measured using the Metric system (i.e. millimeters), English system (i.e. inches), or by the Gauge system (see GAUGE). On a rifled barrel, the bore is measured across the lands. Also, it is a traditional English term used when referring to the diameter of a shotgun muzzle (gauge in U.S. measure).

BOX MAGAZINE

A boxlike feed device for a firearm, which allows cartridges to be stacked one on top of the other. Most box magazines are removable for reloading.

BOXLOCK ACTION

Typified by Parker shotguns in U.S. and Westley Richards in England. Generally considered inferior in strength to the sidelock. Developed by Anson & Deeley, the boxlock is hammerless. It has two disadvantages. First, the hammer pin must be placed directly below knee of action, which is its weakest spot. Second, action walls must be thinned out to receive locks. These are inserted from below into large slots in the action body, which is then closed with a plate. If a correctly made Greener crossbolt is used, many of the boxlock's weaknesses can be negated. Also see CROSSBOLT.

BRACE

A device that is designed to aid a shooter in the practice of firing a pistol with a single hand. Designs vary, devices in this category include: Shockwave Technologies "Blade", Gear Head Works "Tailhook", and SB Tactical "SBA3".

BRADY ACT/BILL

See BRADY HANDGUN VIOLENCE PREVENTION ACT.

BRADY HANDGUN VIOLENCE PREVENTION ACT

1998 Federal legislation which established the National Instant Criminal Background Check System (NICS). Also commonly known as the Brady Bill, or the Brady Act. See NATIONAL INSTANT CRIMINAL BACKGROUND CHECK SYSTEM.

BREAK BARREL ACTION

A type of action where the barrels pivot on a hinge pin, allowing access to the chamber(s) in the breech. Configurations include: single shot, SxS, O/U, combination guns, drillings, and Vierlings.

BREAK OPEN ACTION

See BREAK BARREL ACTION

BREECH

The rear end of a barrel where a cartridge is chambered. Also commonly used in reference to the entire chamber, breech, and receiver of long guns.

BREVETTE

French word which, in gun terminology, refers to a European copy (usually English, French, or Belgian) or patterned after a more famous design (i.e., Brevette Remington O/U derringer refers to a copy of the Remington O/U .41 cal. derringer).

BROWNING

An acid oxidation method of applying a rust-resistant finish to steel; so named because of the resultant surface color of the finished metal surface.

BUCKHORN SIGHT

Open metallic rear sight with sides that curl upward and inward.

BULL BARREL

A heavier, thicker than normal barrel with little or no taper.

BULLET BUTTON

A magazine locking device for AR-15 style rifles. It transforms a rifle with a standard manually operable magazine release and detachable magazine functionality into a fixed magazine rifle in order to comply with the State of California's firearm statutes. Depressing the "button" with a tool, e.g. bullet tip, small screwdriver, etc., is the only way to remove the magazine (which cannot hold more than ten rounds).

BULLPUP

A rifle or shotgun configuration with its action and cartridge feed/extract/eject located behind the hand grip and trigger, in an abbreviated buttstock. Advantages are reduced weight and overall length while retaining the barrel length of a conventional long arm configuration. Disadvantages are reduced sight radius, higher sight offset, and degraded trigger pull. Examples: Steyr AUG, French FAMAS, British L85A2, Israeli Tavor, and the Keltec KSG.

BUTTPAD

A rubber or synthetic composition part attached to the buttstock's end; intended to absorb recoil energy, prevent damage to the buttstock, and vary length of pull. May be fixed, solid, ventilated, or adjustable (horizontally, vertically, cant).

BUTTPLATE

A protective plate, usually steel, attached to the back of the buttstock.

BUTT SPIKE

A fixed or adjustable monopod mounted near the rear on the bottom of a rifle's buttstock that, when used with forearm support of the rifle, enables the user to observe the target area for extended periods with minimal fatigue.

BUTTSTOCK

The portion of a stock which is positioned against the user's shoulder; also known as the butt. On AR-15/M16 style or similar long guns, the separate component which is attached to the rear of the receiver. Also see STOCK.

CALIBER

The diameter of the bore (measured from land to land), usually measured in either inches or millimeters/centimeters. It does not designate bullet diameter.

CALIBER INTERCHANGEABILITY

Please refer to Cartridge Interchangeability - Dangerous Combinations (see Table of Contents for location).

CAMO (CAMOUFLAGE) FINISH

Refers to a patterned treatment using a variety of different colors/patterns that enables a gun to blend into a particular outdoors environment. In most cases, this involves a film or additional finish applied on top of a gun's wood and/or metal parts (i.e. Mossy Oak Break-Up, Mossy Oak Brush, Advantage Timber, Realtree Hardwoods, Realtree Max-4, Muddy Girl, etc.). Mossberg introduced camo finishes on its shotguns in the mid-1980s.

CARTOUCHE

Generally refers to a manufacturer's inspector marking impressed into the wood of a military gun, usually in the form of initials inside a circle or oval.

CASE COLORS

See COLOR CASE HARDENING.

CAST OFF

The distance that a buttplate is offset to the right of the line of sight for a right-handed shooter. Especially important in shotgun stocks.

CAST ON

The same as Cast Off, except that the buttplate is offset to the left of the line of sight for a left-handed shooter.

CENTERFIRE

Refers to ammunition with primers centrally positioned in the cartridge case head; or to a firearm which is chambered for centerfire ammunition.

CERAKOTE

A ceramic based firearms coating with improved performance and reliability compared to traditional firearms finishes. Offers abrasion, corrosion, and solvent protection, in many colors and designs.

CHAMBER

Rear part of the barrel which has been reamed out so that it will contain a cartridge. When the breech is closed, the cartridge is supported in the chamber, and the chamber must align the primer with the firing pin, and the bullet with the bore.

CHAMBER THROAT

See BARREL THROAT.

CHARGE HOLE

The hole bored completely through a revolver's cylinder in which cartridges are loaded.

CHARGING HANDLE

A semi-auto firearm component which is manipulated to cycle the action, but which does not fire the cartridge. Also called cocking handle, cocking knob, or operating handle.

CHF

See COLD HAMMER FORGING

CHECKERING

A functional decoration consisting of pointed pyramids cut into the wood or metal surfaces of a firearm. Generally applied to the pistol grip and forend/forearm areas, affording better handling and control.

CHEEKPIECE

An elevated section of the upper buttstock on which the shooter's cheek rests when holding a rifle or shotgun in firing position. It may be integral to the buttstock, or a separate component. Adjustable cheekpieces may be moved in one or more ways: up, down, fore, aft, or side-to-side.

CHOKE

The muzzle constriction on a shotgun which controls the spread of the shot.

CHOKE TUBES

Interchangeable screw-in devices allowing different choke configurations (i.e., cylinder, improved cylinder, improved modified, modified, full). While most choke tubes fit flush with the end of the barrel, some choke tubes now also protrude from the end of the barrel. Most recently made shotguns usually include three to five choke tubes with the shotgun.

CHOPPER LUMP

A method of construction of barrels for double barreled, SxS shotguns in which the "lump" extending beneath the breech of the barrel is forged as an integral part of the barrel. When the barrels are assembled, the two lumps are carefully fitted on their mating surfaces and brazed solidly together into a single unit, into which locking and other functional recesses are cut.

CLIP

A metal or synthetic material formed/shaped to hold cartridges in readiness to be loaded into a magazine or chamber. A clip is NOT a magazine (i.e., stripper clips for most variations of the Mauser Broomhandle). Also known as a stripper or cartridge clip.

COCKING INDICATOR

Any device for which the act of cocking a gun moves it into a position where it may be seen or felt, in order to notify the shooter that the gun is cocked. Typical examples are the pins found on some high-grade hammerless shotguns, which protrude slightly when they are cocked, and also the exposed cocking knobs on bolt-action rifles. Exposed hammers found on some rifles and pistols are also considered cocking indicators.

COIN FINISH

Older definition referring to a metal finish, typically on a rifle or shotgun, which resembles the finish of an old silver coin. Most coin finishes are based on nickel plating (not chrome) and are generally high polish.

COLD HAMMER FORGING

A manufacturing process in which a barrel's rifling and initial outer contour are formed around a mandrel placed inside the bore by a hammer forging machine.

COLLAPSIBLE STOCK

Mostly used in reference to a buttstock which can be shortened or lengthened along its fore to aft axis. Also applies in theory to top-folding, under-folding, and side folding buttstocks; all of which when folded reduce the weapon's length.

COLOR CASE HARDENING

A method of hardening steel and iron while imparting colorful swirls as well as surface figure. Traditional color case hardening using charcoal and bone meal is achieved by putting the desired metal parts in a crucible packed with a mixture of charcoal and finely ground animal bone to temperatures in the 800oC – 900oC range, after which they are slowly cooled. Then they are submerged into cold water, leaving a thin, colorful protective finish. Can also be achieved by treating the necessary metal parts with a cyanide liquid, which helps harden the metal surface, and can be denoted from charcoal color case hardening by a more layered color appearance.

COMB

The portion of the stock on which the shooter's cheek rests.

COMBINATION GUN

Generally, a break-open shotgun-type configuration that is fitted with at least one shotgun barrel and one rifle barrel. Such guns may be encountered with either two or three barrels, and less frequently with as many as four or five, and have been known to chamber as many as four different calibers.

COMPENSATOR

Slots, vents, or ports machined into a firearm's barrel near its muzzle, or a muzzle device, which allow propellant gasses to escape upwards and partially reduce muzzle jump.

CONTROLLED ROUND FEEDING

A bolt action rifle design in which the cartridge is mechanically secured by the extractor and bolt during all parts of the operating cycle.

CRANE

In a modern solid-frame, swing-out cylinder revolver, the U-shaped yoke on which the cylinder rotates, and which holds the cylinder in the frame. The crane/yoke is the weakest part of a revolver's mechanism.

CRIME BILL

Popular title for the Violent Crime Control and Law Enforcement Act of 1994, Public Law 103-322. See VIOLENT CRIME...LAW 103-322.

CRIMP

A turning in of the case mouth to affect a closure or to prevent the projectile(s) from slipping out of the case mouth. Various crimps include: roll, pie, star or folded, rose, stab, and taper.

CROSSBOLT

A transverse locking rod/bar used in many SxS boxlock shotguns and a few rifles, which locks the standing breech and barrels to each other. Originally designed by W.W. Greener, this term is also referred to as the Greener crossbolt. Also a transverse metal bolt which reinforces and prevents damage to the stock from recoil or abusive handling.

CROWNING

The rounding or chamfering normally done to a barrel muzzle to ensure that the mouth of the bore is square with the bore axis and that its edges are countersunk below the surface to protect it from impact damage. Traditionally, crowning was accomplished by spinning an abrasive-coated brass ball against the muzzle while moving it in a figure-eight pattern, until the abrasive had cut away any irregularities and produced a uniform and square mouth.

CRYOGENIC TEMPERING

Computer controlled cooling process that relieves barrel stress by subjecting the barrel to a temperature of -310 degrees Fahrenheit for 22 hours.

CURIO/RELIC

Firearms which are of special interest to collectors by reason of some quality other than that which is normally associated with firearms intended for sporting use or as offensive or defensive weapons. Must be older than 50 years. For more information and a complete up-to-date Curios or Relics List, go to www.atf.gov/publications/firearms/curios-relics/index.html.

CYLINDER

A rotating cartridge holder in a revolver. The cartridges are held in chambers and the cylinder turns, either to the left or the right, depending on the gun maker's design, as the hammer is cocked.

CYLINDER ARM

See CRANE.

DA/SA

A semi-auto pistol fire control design which allows an initial shot to be fired in double action mode, and subsequent shots in single action mode until the magazine is empty or the user decocks the pistol. For most modern semi-auto pistols, the cocking is either manual or automatic; and in both instances the trigger and hammer/striker are returned to their respective double action states. See also DOUBLE ACTION and SINGLE ACTION.

DAMASCENE

The decorating of metal with another metal, either by inlaying or attaching in some fashion.

DAMASCUS BARREL

A barrel made by twisting, forming, and welding thin strips of steel around a mandrel.

DE-HORNING

The removal of all sharp edges from a firearm that would cut or pinch the shooter, the shooter's clothing, and/or holster, but still maintains the nice clean lines of the firearm.

DELAYED IMPINGEMENT GAS SYSTEM

A trademarked gas operating system for AR-15 style carbines, designed by Allan Zitta. Similar to a gas piston action in concept, it has instead an operating rod and recoil spring which run through the receiver, over the barrel, and sleeve the gas tube at the gas block. The gas tube does not enter the receiver, and the recoil spring replaces the buffer and spring in the AR-15 buttstock.

DEMI-BLOC/DEMI-BLOCK

See CHOPPER LUMP.

DERRINGER

Usually refers to a small, concealable pistol with one or two short barrels.

DETACHABLE MAGAZINE

On any gun a detachable magazine permits relatively quick and easy reloading. However, stripper clips, first used on rifles in the late 19th century, may offer as quick a reload as a magazine change (or quicker).

DETACHABLE MILITARY STYLE BIPOD

A bipod designed for severe/heavy use and greater durability, with a Picatinny rail or other type of quick attach/detach mounting system.

DIRECT IMPINGEMENT GAS SYSTEM

A gas operating system in which high pressure and temperature propellant gas is routed into the firearm receiver to make contact with and move action components. There are no "moving parts" (e.g. piston, return spring, operating rod, tappet) in a direct impingement gas system. A typical direct impingement gas system has a gas block surrounding the barrel and covering the gas port, and a gas tube.

DOUBLE ACTION

The principle in a revolver or auto-loading pistol wherein the hammer can be cocked and dropped by a single pull of the trigger. Most of these actions also provide capability for single action fire. In auto loading pistols, double action normally applies only to the first shot of any series, the hammer being cocked by the slide for subsequent shots.

DOUBLE ACTION ONLY

A firearm action which cannot be operated in single action mode. Many newer DAO firearms are either hammerless, or their hammers and triggers cannot be positioned in a single action status.

DOUBLE UNDERLUGS

The two underlugs on the lower barrel of an over/under double barrel shotgun or rifle.

DOUBLE-BARREL(ED)

A gun which has two barrels joined either side-by-side or one over the other.

DOUBLE-SET TRIGGER

A device that consists of two triggers - one to cock the mechanism that spring-assists the other trigger, substantially lightening the other trigger's pull weight.

DOVETAIL

A flaring machined or hand-cut slot that is also slightly tapered toward one end. Cut into the upper surface of barrels and sometimes actions, the dovetail accepts a corresponding part on which a sight is mounted. Dovetail slot blanks are used to cover the dovetail when the original sight has been removed or lost; this gives the barrel a more pleasing appearance and configuration.

DRILLED & TAPPED

Refers to holes drilled into the top of a receiver/frame and threaded, which allow scope bases, blocks, rings, or other sighting devices to be rigidly attached to the gun.

DRILLING

German for triple, which is their designation for a three-barrel gun, usually two shotgun barrels and one rifle barrel.

EJECTOR

A firearm component which propels an extracted cartridge or fired case out of the receiver or chamber. Ejectors may be fixed or movable, spring loaded or manually activated. Also see SELECTIVE AUTOMATIC EJECTOR.

ELASTOMER

A synthetic elastic polymer, soft and compressible like natural rubber, used for seals, grip and stock inlays, and other molded firearm components.

ELECTROCIBLE

Unique reusable target designed like an aircraft propeller that causes it to spin and go in different directions. In competition, electrocibles come out of one of five boxes located 25 meters from the shooter, who must hit it before it crosses over the ring at 21 meters.

ELECTRO-OPTICAL SIGHT

An optical sight (see definition) with the addition of electronic battery powered components which illuminate a reticle (least complex), or which generate a reticle/optional reticles. Electro-optical sights may be: magnifying, non-magnifying, full-tube traditional optical design, or reflex types (see REFLEX SIGHT).

ELEVATION

A firearm sight's vertical distance above the barrel's bore axis; also the adjustment of a sight to compensate for the effect of gravity on a projectile's exterior ballistic path.

ENGINE TURNING

Machined circular polishing on metal, creating a unique overlapping pattern.

ENGLISH STOCK
A straight, slender-gripped stock.

ENGRAVING
The art of engraving metal in decorative patterns. Scroll engraving is the most common type of hand engraving encountered. Much of today's factory engraving is rolled on which is done mechanically. Hand engraving requires artistry and knowledge of metals and related materials.

ERGO SUREGRIP
A Falcon Industries Inc. right hand or ambidextrous replacement pistol grip for AR-15/M-16 style rifles. The grip has finger grooves, upper rear extension to support the web of the shooter's hand, is oil and solvent resistant, and a non-slip textured overmolded rubber surface.

ETCHING
A method of decorating metal gun parts, usually done by acid etching or photo engraving.

EXTRACTOR
A device which partially pulls a cartridge or fired hull/case/casing(s) from the chamber, allowing it to be removed manually.

FALLING BLOCK
A single shot action where the breechblock drops straight down when a lever is actuated.

FALSE SIDELOCK (or Dummy Sidelock)
Ornamental metal panels (complete with dummy pins) attached to a boxlock or other non-sidelock action to give the false representation of a sidelock. See also SIDELOCK and SIDEPLATES.

FARQUHARSON ACTION
A single shot hammerless falling block rifle action patented in 1872 by John Farquharson.

FENCES
The hemispherical formations on a side-by-side shotgun's receiver which are adjacent to the barrel breeches. Originally fences were the curving metal flanges surrounding a percussion ignition firearm's nipple, or a flintlock ignition firearm's priming pan, which protected the shooter from sparks, smoke, and escaping gas.

FIBER OPTIC SIGHT
An iron sight with fiber optic light gathering rods or cylinders; the rod ends are perceived as glowing dots and enhance sight visibility and contrast.

FIT AND FINISH
Terms used to describe over-all firearm workmanship.

FIRE CONTROL GROUP
All components necessary to cause a cartridge to be fired; may be a self-contained assembly, easily disassembled or not user-serviceable, detachable, modular/interchangeable, and may or may not include a safety, bolt release, or other parts.

FIRING PIN
That part of a firearm which strikes the cartridge primer, causing detonation.

FIXED STOCK
A fixed stock is a static position stock that does not have an adjustment feature. They may also contain a space for storage at the end of the stock. Fixed stocks will mount to a rifle length buffer tube, which is smooth and cylindrical in feature. Modern manufacturing has also created fixed stocks that feature adjustable cheek welds. Also see AR-15 TERMINOLOGY section.

FLASH SUPPRESSOR/HIDER
A muzzle attachment which mechanically disrupts and reduces muzzle flash. It does not reduce muzzle blast or recoil.

FLAT-TOP UPPER
An AR-15/M16 style or other tactical semi-auto rifle with a literally flat receiver top. The majority of flat-top uppers have an extended Picatinny rail for mounting iron sights, optical sights, and other accessories, which provides much more versatility than the original "carry handle" receiver design.

FLOATING BARREL
A barrel bedded to avoid contact with any point on the stock.

FLOORPLATE
Usually, a removable/hinged plate at the bottom of the receiver covering the magazine well.

FN FAL STYLE ACTION
A gas operated rifle action with a short-stroke spring-loaded gas piston, a tilting breechblock locking design, and a heavy receiver. A regulator valve allows the user to increase the volume of gas entering the system in order to ensure reliable operation in adverse conditions. Unlike direct gas impingement

or delayed blowback operating systems, propellant gas does not vent into the receiver and fire control components.

FOLDING STOCK

Usually a buttstock hinged at or near the receiver so that it can be "folded" towards the muzzle, reducing the firearm's overall length. Not an adjustable stock as defined above, and usually does not prevent operating/firing when in its folded position.

FORCING CONE

The segment of a shotgun barrel immediately forward of the chamber where its internal diameter is reduced from chamber to bore diameter. The forcing cone aids the passage of shot into the barrel. For revolvers, the tapering portion of the barrel bore from the breech to the rifling.

FOREARM

In this text, a separate piece of wood in front of the receiver and under the barrel used for hand placement when shooting.

FOREARM/FOREND CAP

A separate piece attached to the muzzle end of a forearm; often with a colored spacer, and usually in a contrasting color/material.

FOREND/FORE-END

Usually the forward portion of a one-piece rifle or shotgun stock (in this text), but can also refer to a separate piece of wood.

FORGED RECEIVER (LOWER/UPPER)

Forging is the manufacturing process of applying thermal and mechanical energy to pieces of metal to cause the material to change shape while in a solid state to reduce the amount of machining time needed to produce a final product.

FORWARD BOLT ASSIST

A button, usually found on AR-15 type rifles, which may be pushed or struck to move the bolt carrier fully forward so that the extractor has completely engaged the cartridge rim and the bolt has locked. Mainly used to close/lock the bolt when the rifle's chamber and receiver are excessively fouled or dirty.

FRAME

The part of a firearm to which the action (lock work), barrel, and stock/grip are connected. Most of the time used when referring to a handgun or hinged frame long gun.

FREE FLOATING FOREARM

A forearm which does not contact the barrel at any point, as it attaches and places mechanical stress only on the receiver. An accuracy enhancement for AR-15/M16 style rifles, which by their modular design, are not able to have a conventionally free floated barrel in a one-piece stock.

FREE RIFLE

A rifle designed for international-type target shooting. The only restriction on design is a weight maximum 8 kilograms (17.6 lbs.).

FRONT STRAP

That part of the revolver or pistol grip frame which faces forward and often joins with the trigger guard. In target guns, notably the .45 ACP, the front strap is often stippled to give shooter's hand a slip-proof surface.

FULL AUTO

See AUTOMATIC ACTION

GAS BLOCK (FIXED OR ADJUSTABLE)

On an AR-15 specifically, there is a small "gas port" in the barrel that vents gas when fired. A gas block is mounted over the gas port and directs the gas to the gas tube which then travels through the gas tube into the receiver, where it powers the bolt carrier group and auto-cycles the next round. This is known as a "direct impingement" gas system. A gas block can be fixed or adjustable. A fixed gas block needs to be matched with the correct length gas tube and an adjustable gas block can regulate the amount of gas allowed to the action.

GAS IMPINGEMENT OPERATING SYSTEM

An action in which high pressure propellant gas is diverted from the barrel to supply the energy required to unlock the breech, extract/eject the fired case, load a cartridge, and lock the breech. This type of system generates a large amount of heat and also a considerable amount of fouling directly back into the action.

GAS PISTON OPERATING SYSTEM

A gas operation design in which a piston is used to transfer propellant gas energy to the action components. No gas enters the receiver or makes contact with other action components. Consequently, less heat is absorbed by, and less fouling accumulates in the receiver. This system also has a much different recoil pulse or "feel".

GAS PORT

A small opening in the barrel of a gas operated firearm which allows high pressure gas to flow into the gas system's components. Also an escape vent in a firearm's receiver, a safety feature.

GAS TUBE

On an AR-15 specifically the gas tube is the small tube above the barrel attached to the gas block. When the firearm is fired, it directs the gas into the receiver. Since the amount of gas in the system directly affects felt recoil and function, reliability, and performance of the action, the length of the gas tube needs to be matched proportionately to the length of the barrel. The following are standard recommendations for gas system lengths (distance from receiver to gas port) compared to barrel length.

SYSTEM	BARREL LENGTH	PORT DISTANCE
Pistol Length	UNDER 10"	4"
Carbine Length	10"-18"	7"
Mid-Length	14"-20"	9"
Dissipator Length	16"	12"
Rifle Length	20"+	12"

GAUGE/GA.

A unit of measure used to determine a shotgun's bore. Determined by the amount of pure lead balls equaling the bore diameter needed to equal one pound (i.e., a 12 ga. means that 12 lead balls exactly the diameter of the bore weigh one pound). In this text, .410 is referenced as a bore (if it was a gauge, it would be a 68 ga.).

GAUGE VS. BORE DIAMETER

10-Gauge = Bore Diameter of .775 inches or 19.3mm
12-Gauge = Bore Diameter of .729 inches or 18.2mm
16-Gauge = Bore Diameter of .662 inches or 16.8mm
20-Gauge = Bore Diameter of .615 inches or 15.7mm
28-Gauge = Bore Diameter of .550 inches or 13.8mm
67.5-Gauge = Bore Diameter of .410 inches or 12.6mm

GCA

The Gun Control Act of 1968, 18 USC Chapter 44.

GLACIERGUARDS

AR-15/M-16 carbine length replacement handguard (two-piece) which has fifteen internal heat dispersing fins rather than the standard heat shield. The fins provide greater strength and rigidity; fiber-reinforced polymer shells resist heat and reduce weight. A DPMS product.

GRIP

The handle used to hold a handgun, or the area of a stock directly behind and attached to the frame/ receiver of a long gun.

GRIPS

Can be part of the frame or components attached to the frame used to assist in accuracy, handling, control, and safety of a handgun. Many currently manufactured semi-auto handguns have grips that are molded w/checkering as part of the synthetic frame.

GRIPSTRAP(S)

Typically refers to the front and back metal attached to a handgun frame which supports the grips/ stocks. Also known as the front strap and back strap.

GROOVES

The spiral depressions of the rifling in a barrel bore; created by cutting, swaging, broaching, hammering, cation action, or other methods. Also see LANDS and RIFLING.

HALF COCK

A position of the hammer in a hammer activated firing mechanism that serves as a manual safety.

HAMMER

A part of a gun's mechanism which applies force to the firing pin or other components, which in turn fires the gun.

HAMMERLESS

Some "hammerless" firearms do in fact have hidden hammers, which are located in the action housing. Truly hammerless guns, such as the Savage M99, have a firing mechanism based on a spring-powered striker.

HANDGUARD
A wooden, synthetic, or ventilated metal part attached above the barrel and ahead of the receiver to protect the shooter's hand from the heat generated during semi-auto rapid firing.

HEEL
Back end of the upper edge of the butt stock at the upper edge of the buttplate or recoil pad.

HK91/G3 STYLE ACTION
A roller locked delayed blowback rifle action. There is no gas system per se; gas pressure in the cartridge case pushes the case against the bolt and bolt carrier. Spring-loaded rollers in the bolt resist unlocking and carrier/bolt movement until chamber pressure has dropped to a safe level. Components are heavier, recoil (actual and perceived) is greater, chambers must be fluted to assure extraction, and cocking effort is much greater than direct gas or gas piston weapons.

ILAFLON
Industrielack AG trademarked ceramic reinforced enamel firearms finish coating; highly resistant to abrasion, corrosion, and chemicals/solvent.

INTEGRAL LOCKING SYSTEM
A North American Arms safety system; a key allows the user to internally lock the hammer in place, which prevents discharging the firearm.

INTERCEPTING SEAR
An extra sear which engages the hammer before it falls completely, thus preventing an accidental discharge if a cocked firearm is dropped or jarred – both sears are disengaged when the trigger is pulled.

INTERCHANGEABLE BARRELS
The AR design includes a detachable "upper" – the portion of the gun that includes the barrel. This means that a single AR may be quickly and easily changed for a variety of different uses simply by switching the upper.

INTRAFUSE
A trademarked system of synthetic stocks and accessories designed for tactical firearms.

IN-THE-WHITE
Refers to a gun's finish w/o bluing, nickel, case colors, gold, etc. Since all metal surfaces are normally polished, the steel appears white, hence, "in-the-white" terminology.

IRON SIGHTS
A generic term for metallic front or rear sights which do not use optical lens (magnifying or non-magnifying) components.

JUXTAPOSED
See SIDE-BY-SIDE.

KEYMOD
KeyMod is an accessory mounting system developed through a partnership between Noveske Rifleworks LLC and VLTOR Weapons Systems circa 2012. This mounting system has been integrated with firearms handguards for the attachment of KeyMod compatible accessories. To attach a KeyMod compatible accessory, line up the lugs on the accessory with the round part of the keyhole, push it in, slide it forward, and tighten the set screws.

KRYPTEK
A proprietary camo finish utilizing a multi-directional design to affectively conceal in a multitude of terrains that have either a lateral or vertical flow. The bi-level layering of the patterns incorporate background transitional shading and sharp random geometrical foregrounds to create a three dimensional effect that ensures the utmost in concealment at both close and long ranges. Patterns include Highlander, Typhon, and Raid.

LAMINATED STOCK
A gunstock made of many layers of wood glued together under pressure. The laminations become very strong, preventing damage from moisture or heat, and warping.

LANDS
Portions of the bore left between the grooves of the rifling in the bore of a firearm. In rifling, the grooves are usually twice the width of the land. Land diameter is measured across the bore, from land to land.

LASER SIGHT
An aiming system which projects a beam of laser light onto the target. Usually mounted so the beam is parallel to the barrel bore but not a "traditional" front or rear sight as the shooter does not look through the laser apparatus.

LAST ROUND BOLT HOLD OPEN
A device within the action of a repeating firearm which locks the bolt to the rear upon the last round (shot) being expended from the magazine.

LENS COATINGS

Metallic coatings on optic surfaces which increase light transmission, image brightness, and color rendition. Also used to improve abrasion resistance and filter out unwanted or harmful light.

LEVER ACTION

A manual repeating action operated by an external lever.

LUMP

An English term for an underlug.

M1913 PICATINNY RAIL

Original designation for a Picatinny rail. Also see PICATINNY RAIL.

M4 STYLE

Refers to an AR style rifle in M4 carbine configuration (A2 configuration but with short handguard, short barrel, and relocated gas block).

MACHINE GUN

National Firearms Act and Gun Control Act of 1968 definition:

Any weapon which shoots, is designed to shoot, or can be readily restored to shoot, automatically more than one shot, without manual reloading, by a single function of the trigger. The term shall also include the frame or receiver of any such weapon, any part designed and intended solely and exclusively, or combination of parts designed and intended, for use in converting a weapon into a machine gun, and any combination of parts from which a machine gun can be assembled if such parts are in the possession or control of a person.

MAGAZINE (MAG.)

The container (may be detachable) which holds cartridges under spring pressure to be fed into the gun's chamber. A clip is NOT a magazine. May be a single or double or multiple column, rotary, helical, drum, or other design. The term "high capacity" denotes a magazine capable of holding more than ten rounds.

MAGNUM (MAG.)/MAGNUM AMMUNITION

A term first used by Holland & Holland in 1912 for their .375 H&H Magnum cartridge. The term has now been applied to rimfire, centerfire, or shotshell cartridges having a larger cartridge case, heavier shot charge, or higher muzzle velocity than standard cartridges or shotshells of a given caliber or gauge. Most Magnum rifle cartridges are belted designs.

MAINSPRING

The spring that delivers energy to the hammer or striker.

MANNLICHER STOCK

A full-length slender stock with slender forend extending to the muzzle (full stock) affording better barrel protection.

MELONITE

A trademarked name for a metal case hardening and surface finishing process which provides exceptional wear, abrasion, and corrosion resistance; and very high surface hardness. The generic name for this process is ferritic nitrocarburizing.

MICROMETER SIGHT

A windage and elevation adjustable sight with very precise and small increments of adjustment.

MICRO SLICK

A firearms finish coating which creates a permanently lubricated surface; it impedes galling and seizing of firearm components.

MIL

See MILRADIAN

MIL-DOT

A reticle with dots spaced center-to-center one milradian apart; the distance to an object of known dimension may be calculated based upon the number of milradians which are subtended by the target's known dimension.

MIL-SPEC / MIL-STD

A series of quality control standards used by manufacturers to guarantee machine tolerances ensuring the consistency and interchangeability of parts.

MILRADIAN

The horizontal angle subtended by one unit of measurement at 1,000 units distance. Also called a "mil".

MINUTE OF ANGLE (MOA)

1/60 of a degree of circular angle; at 100 yards it subtends 1.047 inches. Also commonly used to describe a firearm's accuracy and precision capability, i.e. a rifle which shoots under one minute of angle. Abbreviated MOA.

M-LOK
M-LOK is an accessory mounting system developed by Magpul Industries Corp. circa 2014. This mounting system has been integrated with firearms handguards for the attachment of M-LOL compatible accessories. The M-LOK rail utilizes a T-slot nut capable of only 90-degree rotation, reinforced by thread-locking fluid, making it suited for applications on free float handguards. It was designed to work with both metal and polymer parts.

MODERN SPORTING RIFLE
A National Shooting Sports Foundation term for civilian legal semiautomatic AR-15 style rifles. The NSSF promotes its usage to counter the negative anti-gun connotations, confusion, and misunderstandings which have become associated with the term "AR15". A modern sporting rifle is not an automatic or assault rifle, not a regulated NFA weapon, not a military/law enforcement M16 despite its similar cosmetic appearance, and no more powerful than other traditional configuration sporting/hunting/competition rifles of the same caliber. Sometimes called Sport Utility Rifle or SUR. Note: the letters "AR" stand for Armalite Rifle.

MODULAR WEAPONS SYSTEM
A generic term of military origin for quick attach/detach components/systems which allow flexibility and adaptability for using various sighting, illumination, and other accessories, etc. on a weapon. Also see PICATINNY RAIL.

MONOBLOC
A form of construction and assembly for double barreled shotguns wherein the breeching and locking surfaces are cut into a single separate housing or "bloc" into which the breeches of the barrels are brazed or threaded. Compare to CHOPPER LUMP.

MONTE CARLO STOCK
A stock with an elevated comb used primarily for scoped rifles.

MUZZLE
The forward end of the barrel where the projectile exits.

MUZZLE BRAKE
A muzzle device (permanent or removable) or barrel modification which reduces muzzle jump and recoil by diverting propellant gasses sideways or to the rear. Not to be confused with a flash hider or a flash suppressor. Also see COMPENSATOR.

NATIONAL INSTANT CRIMINAL BACKGROUND CHECK SYSTEM (NICS)
A U. S. federal government system which an FFL must, with limited exceptions, contact for information on whether receipt of a firearm by a person who is not licensed under 18 U.S.C. 923 would violate Federal or state law.

NEEDLE GUN
Ignition system invented by Johan Nikolas von Dreyse in 1829. This ignition system used a paper cartridge and became obsolete with the invention of the metallic cartridge.

NFA
The National Firearms Act, 26 USC Chapter 53.

NFA FIREARM
A firearm which must be registered in the National Firearm Registration and Transfer Record, as defined in the NFA and 27 CFR, Part 479. Included are: machine guns, frames or receivers of machine guns, any combination of parts designed and intended for use in converting weapons into machine guns, any combination of parts from which a machine gun can be assembled if the parts are in the possession or under control of a person, silencers and any part designed or intended for fabricating a silencer, short-barreled rifles, short-barreled shotguns, destructive devices, and "any other weapon". NFA semi-auto carbines with less than 16 in. barrels are not listed in this book.

NFA TITLE II OF THE GCA OF 1968
Title II amended the NFA to cure the constitutional flaws pointed out in Haynes. First, the requirement for possessors of unregistered firearms to register was removed Second, a provision was added to the law prohibiting the use of any information from an NFA application or registration as evidence against the person in a criminal proceeding with respect to a violation of law occurring prior to or concurrently with the filing of the application or registration. In 1971, the Supreme Court reexamined the NFA and found that the 1968 amendments cured the constitutional defect in the original NFA. Title II also amended the NFA definitions of "firearm" by adding "destructive devices" and expanding the definition of "machinegun."

NICS CHECK
See NATIONAL INSTANT CRIMINAL BACKGROUND CHECK SYSTEM.

NIGHT SIGHTS

Iron sights with radioactive tritium gas capsules; the capsules are inserted into recesses in the sight body with their ends facing the shooter. The tritium glow provides sight alignment and aiming references in lowlight/no-light conditions.

NP3/NP3 PLUS

An electroless plated nickel-phosphorus alloy firearms finish which offers uniform thickness, lubricity, and hardness equivalent to hard chromium plating.

NON-DETACHABLE BOX MAGAZINE

A rectangular magazine which is never removed during normal use or maintenance of the firearm. It may extend beyond/below the receiver or stock, may be high capacity, and generally is loaded from its top (single cartridges or stripper clips).

NON-DETACHABLE FOLDING BAYONET

An articulated bayonet which cannot be removed from the firearm by the end user. Normally locked into its fully folded or extended position.

NP3/NP3 PLUS

An electroless plated nickel-phosphorus alloy firearms finish which offers uniform thickness, lubricity, and hardness equivalent to hard chromium plating.

OBJECTIVE LENS

A telescopic sight's front, usually larger lens which may be adjustable to reduce parallax error.

OCULAR LENS

The rear lens of a telescopic sight, normally adjustable by rotation to focus the sight image.

OPEN SIGHT

A simple rear iron sight with a notch – the shooter aims by looking through the notch at the front sight and the target.

OPTICAL SIGHT

A generic term for a sight which has one or more optical lenses through which the weapon is aimed. Optical sights usually magnify the target image, but there are many non- magnifying optical sights.

OVER-UNDER (O/U)

A double-barrel gun in which the barrels are stacked one on top of the other. Also called Superposed.

PARALLAX

Occurs in telescopic sights when the primary image of the objective lens does not coincide with the reticle. In practice, parallax is detected in the scope when, as the viewing eye is moved laterally, the image and the reticle appear to move in relation to each other.

PARAMILITARY

Typically refers to a firearm configured or styled to resemble a military weapon with one or more of the military weapon's configurations or features, EXCEPT FOR automatic or selective fire capability. Paramilitary firearms may be slide action (primarily shotguns), bolt action, or semi-automatic (most handguns and rifles).

PARKERIZING

Matte rust-resistant oxide finish, usually dull gray or black in color, found on military guns.

PEEP SIGHT

A rear sight consisting of a disc or blade with a hole or aperture through which the front sight and target are aligned.

PEPPERBOX

An early form of revolving repeating pistol, in which a number of barrels were bored in a circle in a single piece of metal resembling the cylinder of a modern revolver. Functioning was the same as a revolver, the entire cylinder being revolved to bring successive barrels under the hammer for firing. Though occurring as far back as the 16th century, the pepperbox did not become practical until the advent of the percussion cap in the early 1800s. Pepperboxes were made in a wide variety of sizes and styles, and reached their popularity peak during the percussion period. Few were made after the advent of practical metallic cartridges. Both single and double action pepperboxes were made. Single-barreled revolvers after the 1840s were more accurate and easier to handle and soon displaced the rather clumsy and muzzle-heavy pepperbox.

PERCH BELLY

Refers to a rifle's stock configuration where the bottom portion is curved rather than straight between the buttplate and pistol grip.

PICATINNY RAIL

A serrated flat rail typically located on the top of a frame/slide/receiver, but may also be located on the sides and bottom, allowing different optics/sights/accessories to be used on the gun. Developed at the U.S. Army's Picatinny Arsenal.

PINFIRE

An obsolete ignition system; a pinfire cartridge had an internal primer and a small firing pin protruding from the rear sidewall of its metallic case.

PISTOL FOREARM BRACE/PISTOL STABILIZING BRACE

See BRACE

POLYGONAL

Rifling w/o sharp edged lands and grooves. Advantages include a slight increase in muzzle velocity, less bullet deformation, and reduced lead fouling since there are no traditional lands and grooves. See RIFLING.

POPE RIB

A rib integral with the barrel. Designed by Harry M. Pope, famed barrel maker and shooter, the rib made it possible to mount a target scope low over the barrel.

PORTED BARREL

A barrel with multiple holes or slots drilled near the muzzle. See PORTING.

PORTING

Multiple holes or slots drilled into a firearm barrel near the muzzle. Porting reduces felt/perceived recoil, and if located on the upper half of the barrel reduces muzzle jump. Disadvantages are increased muzzle blast and noise.

POST-BAN

See 1989 BUSH BAN, and SECTION 922r.

PRE-BAN

See 1989 BUSH BAN, and SECTION 922r.

PRIMER

A percussion device designed to ignite the propellant charge of a centerfire cartridge or shotshell by generating flame and high temperature expanding gasses.

PRIMER RING

Refers to a visible dark ring around the firing pin hole in a breech or bolt face, created by the impact of centerfire ammunition primer cups when a cartridge is fired.

PRINCE OF WALES GRIP

Refers to a butt stock grip similar to a half pistol grip that is between a straight English grip and a full pistol grip. The radius of the grips curve is more open and longer than a full pistol grip. The name originated with King Edward VII formally the Prince of Wales, his guns had this type of stock.

PROOF MARK

Proof marks are usually applied to all parts actually tested, but normally appear on the barrel (and possibly frame), usually indicating the country of origin and time-frame of proof (especially on European firearms). In the U.S., there is no federalized or government proof house, only the manufacturer's in-house proof mark indicating that a firearm has passed its manufacturer's quality control standards per government specifications.

PUMP ACTION

See SLIDE ACTION.

QUAD RAIL FOREARM

A rifle forearm with upper, lower, and lateral Picatinny rails which allow attachment of multiple accessories.

QUARTER RIB

A short raised portion of a ribbed barrel, which forms a base for a rear metallic or optical sight.

RATE OF TWIST

The distance in which rifling makes one complete revolution; normally expressed as one turn in a specific number of inches or millimeters. Also called rifling pitch, or merely twist.

RECEIVER

That part of a rifle or shotgun (excluding hinged frame guns) which houses the bolt, firing pin, mainspring, trigger group, and magazine or ammunition feed system. The barrel is threaded or pressed into the somewhat enlarged forward part of the receiver, called the receiver ring. At the rear of the receiver, the butt or stock is fastened. In semiautomatic pistols, the frame or housing is sometimes referred to as the receiver.

RECOIL

The rearward motion of a firearm when a shot is fired (i.e. the gun recoiled); the term for the energy or force transferred into the firearm as it discharges a projectile.

RECOIL ACTION/OPERATION

A self-loading or automatic action which uses recoil energy to unlock, extract, eject, cock the firing mechanism, and reload the chamber.

RECOIL SPRING GUIDE ROD

A metal or synthetic rod which positions the recoil spring within the firearm's receiver or slide, and prevents binding/dislocation of the spring during its compression or expansion.

RED DOT SIGHT

See REFLEX SIGHT.

REFLEX SIGHT

An optical sight which generates reticle image upon a partially curved objective lens; the reticle appears superimposed in the field of view and focused at infinity. Most reflex sights are non-magnifying and battery powered. Fiber optic light collectors or tritium may also be used to generate the reticle. Reflex sights are adjustable and virtually parallax free. Popularly known as "red dot" sights; they are NOT laser sights.

RELEASE TRIGGER

A trap shooting trigger which fires the gun when the trigger is released.

RELIC

See CURIO/RELIC.

REPEATER/REPEATING ACTION

A manual action with a magazine or cylinder loaded with more than one cartridge; all cartridges may be fired without reloading.

RETICLE

The shapes, lines, marks, etc. which provide an aiming reference when using an optical sight. Reticles may be illuminated electronically, with tritium, or with fiber optics, and are available in a multitude of designs for many differing requirements.

REVOLVER/REVOLVING ACTION

A manual repeating action so named for its multi-chambered cylinder which rotates on an axis parallel to the barrel bore. Primarily a handgun action, but there have been long gun examples (e.g. Colt Model 1855 Revolving Rifle).

RIB

A raised sighting plane affixed to the top of a barrel.

RIFLING

The spirally cut grooves in the bore of a rifle or handgun barrel. The rifling causes the bullet to spin, stabilizing the bullet in flight. Rifling may rotate to the left or the right, the higher parts of the bore being called lands, the cuts or lower parts being called the grooves. Many types exist, such as oval, polygonal, button, Newton, Newton-Pope gain twist, parabolic, Haddan, Enfield, segmental rifling, etc. Most U.S.-made barrels have a right-hand twist, while British gun makers prefer a left-hand twist. In practice, there seems to be little difference in accuracy or barrel longevity.

RIMFIRE

Self-contained metallic cartridge where the priming compound is evenly distributed within the cartridge head, but only on the outer circumference of the rim. Detonated by the firing pin(s) striking the outer edge of the case head.

RINGS

See SCOPE RINGS.

ROLLING BLOCK ACTION

A single shot action, designed in the U.S. and widely used in early Remington arms. Also known as the Remington-Rider action, the breechblock, actuated by a lever, rotates down and back from the chamber. The firing pin is contained within the block and is activated by hammer fall.

ROUND ACTION

A transitional action design, between the boxlock and sidelock, which has its lock assembly attached to the action's lower rearward projecting trigger bar. Also called a trigger plate action.

SAFETY

A mechanism(s) in/on a gun which prevents it from firing. There are many different types and variations.

SAAMI

The Sporting Arms and Ammunition Manufacturers' Institute; a branch of the National Shooting Sports Foundation.

SAW HANDLE

A distinctive squared off pistol grip design which literally is shaped like a saw handle.

SCHNABEL FOREND/FOREARM

The curved/carved flared end of the forend/forearm that resembles the beak of a bird (Schnabel in German). This type of forend is common on Austrian and German guns. In the U.S., the popularity of the Schnabel forend/forearm comes and goes with the seasons. A Schnabel forend is often seen on custom stocks and rifles.

SCOPE RINGS (BLOCKS/BASES)

Metal mounts used to attach a scope to the top of a gun's frame/receiver.

SEAR

The pivoting part in the firing or lock mechanism of a gun. The sear is linked to the trigger, and may engage the cocking piece, striker, or the firing pin.

SECTION 922r

A 1989 Federal regulation which established sporting criteria for centerfire weapons, either imported, or assembled from imported and domestic components. Firearms which do not meet the criteria are "banned", i.e. non-importable as of the regulation's effective date. Also the source of the popular terms "pre-ban" and post-ban". Due to the complexity of this regulation readers are advised to refer to the actual text of the regulation and contact the BATFE. See 1989 BUSH BAN.

SELECTIVE AUTOMATIC EJECTOR

An ejector which propels only fired cases out of a break open action firearm; and only extracts unfired cartridges. Very often found in double barrel shotguns, and also called an automatic, Southgate, Holland & Holland, or Baker ejector.

SELECTIVE FIRE

Describes a firearm which has more than one firing mode; which is controlled, or "selected", by the user. Most often used in reference to firearms which can fire in semi-auto, burst, or full auto mode.

SEMI-AUTO ACTION/SEMI-AUTOMATIC/SELFLOADING/AUTOLOADING

A pistol, rifle, or shotgun that is loaded manually for the first round. Upon pulling the trigger, the gun fires, ejects the fired round, cocks the firing mechanism, and feeds a fresh round from the magazine. The trigger must be released after each shot and pulled again to fire the next round.

SHELL DEFLECTOR

A protrusion of the receiver near the ejection port which is positioned and shaped to deflect an ejected case away from the shooter's body. Especially appreciated by left-handed shooters when firing a semi-auto with right side ejection.

SHORT ACTION

A rifle action designed for short overall length cartridges.

SHORT BARREL RIFLE

Any rifle having one or more barrels less than sixteen inches in length and any weapon made from a rifle (whether by alteration, modification, or otherwise) if such weapon, as modified, has an overall length of less than twenty-six inches.

SHORT BARREL SHOTGUN

Any shotgun, which was originally equipped with a shoulder stock, with a barrel or barrels less than eighteen inches long and any weapon made from a shotgun (whether by alteration, modification, or otherwise) if such weapon as modified has an overall length of less than twenty-six inches.

SHOTSHELL

An assembly consisting of a rimmed metal head, paper or plastic base wad, 209 battery cup primer, and paper or plastic body. A shotshell cartridge is a shotshell loaded with propellant, wad column, and shot charge or a single large diameter slug.

SIDE-BY-SIDE (SxS)

A two-barrel rifle or shotgun where the barrels are horizontally arranged side-by-side. Also called juxtaposed.

SIDE FOLDING STOCK

A folding stock variation which has its buttstock rotate horizontally, usually to the right side of the firearm's receiver. See FOLDING STOCK.

SIDE LEVER

Refers to opening mechanism lever on either left or right side of receiver/frame.

SIDELOCK

A type of action, usually long gun, where the moving parts are located on the inside of the lock plates, which in turn are inlet in the sides of the stock. Usually found only on better quality shotguns and rifles.

SIDEPLATES

Ornamental metal panels normally attached to a sidelock but also found on some boxlock actions to simulate a sidelock and expand the engravers' "canvas."

SIGHT(S)

Any part or device which allows a firearm to be aimed, versus merely pointed, at a target. There are two main systems: "iron" and optical. Iron sights, also known as "open" sights, are now made of other substances than metal and in many variations. Optical sights have a lens, or lenses, which may or may not magnify the target image.

SILENCER

See SUPPRESSOR.

SINGLE ACTION

A firearms design which requires the hammer to be manually cocked for each shot. Also an auto loading pistol design which requires manual cocking of its mechanism for the first shot only.

SINGLE SHOT ACTION

An action which limits storing or loading only a single cartridge, and is manually operated.

SLIDE ACTION

A manual repeating action with a reciprocating forearm. Sliding the forearm towards the receiver opens the action and extracts/ejects the fired case; forward motion chambers a cartridge and locks the action. Also known as a pump action.

SINGLE TRIGGER

One trigger on a double-barrel gun. It fires each barrel individually by successive pulls, or may be selective, i.e., the barrel to be fired first can be selected via a control button or lever.

SLING SWIVELS

Metal loops affixed to the gun to which a carrying strap is attached.

SOUND SUPPRESSOR

See SUPPRESSOR.

SOUTHGATE EJECTOR(S)

See SELECTIVE AUTOMATIC EJECTOR.

SPECIAL IMPACT MUNITIONS

A class or type of firearm ammunition loaded with one or more projectiles; when fired at a human target the projectiles have a low probability of causing serious injury or death. For example: bean bag, baton, tear gas, and rubber ball rounds. A sub-class of SIMs is known as SPLLAT, or special purpose less lethal anti-terrorist munitions.

SPORT UTILITY RIFLE

See MODERN SPORTING RIFLE.

SPUR TRIGGER

A firearm design which housed the trigger in an extension of the frame in some older guns. The trigger projected only slightly from the front of the extension or spur, and there was no trigger guard.

SQUARE BRIDGE ACTION

A bolt action design which has an enlarged rectangular shaped rear receiver bridge. If the front receiver bridge is also in an enlarged square, the action is termed a double square bridge.

SQUIB LOAD

A cartridge with no propellant, or so little propellant, that when fired in a semi-auto the action does not cycle; and in any type of firearm a squib load most likely results in the projectile remaining in and completely obstructing the barrel's bore.

STAMPED SHEET METAL RECEIVER

A receiver manufactured out of sheet metal which has been cut, stamped into a three-dimensional shape, and welded. An economical alternative to milling a receiver from a solid block of metal.

STANDOFF/BREACHING BARREL

Refers to a barrel that has a jagged muzzle to assist in the physical entry of a door and allows no slipping.

STATE COMPLIANT

Firearms whose features have been changed to comply with state laws/regulations such as CA, MA, MD, NJ, NY, HI, etc. are not listed in this text, as there are almost endless variations. Values of state compliant guns in the secondary marketplace will not be as high as the standard non-compliant models from which they are derived.

STOCK

Usually refers to the buttstock of a long gun, or that portion of a rifle or shotgun that comes in contact with the shooter's shoulder, and is attached to the frame/receiver.

STOCKS

Older terminology used to describe handgun grips. See GRIPS.

STRIKER

An elongated firing pin, or a separate component which imparts energy to a firing pin. Most commonly found in hammerless semi-auto pistols.

STRIKER FIRE ACTION/OPERATION

A striker fire pistol discharges a round when the compressed internal striker spring imparts energy to the striker forcing it to contacting the base of the round in the chamber, which fires the round. The internal striker spring is cocked/compressed when the slide is racked. On some models compressing/pulling the trigger will also increase the pressure on the firing pin spring. When the trigger bar releases the striker lug, the striker moves forward as the striker spring relaxes and causes the striker to impact the primer.

SUICIDE SPECIAL

A mass-produced inexpensive single action revolver or derringer, usually with a spur trigger. Produced under a variety of trade names, these guns earned their nickname by being almost as dangerous to shoot as to be shot at.

SUPERPOSED

Refers to an O/U barrel configuration.

SUPPRESSOR

A mechanical device, usually cylindrical and detachable, which alters and decreases muzzle blast and noise. Commonly referred to, in error, as a silencer, it acts only on the sound of the firearms discharge. It does not have any effect on the sounds generated by: the firearm's moving parts, a supersonic bullet in flight, or the bullet's impact. Legality varies per state.

TACTICAL

An imprecise term referring to certain features on handguns, rifles, and shotguns. Before 2000, a tactical gun generally referred to a rifle or carbine designed for military or law enforcement. In today's marketplace, tactical refers to certain features of both handguns and long arms.

TACTICAL REVOLVERS

Tactical revolvers have at least three of the following factory/manufacturer options or features: non-glare finish (generally but there may be exceptions), Mil Std 1913Picatinny or equivalent rail(s), combat style grips (wood or synthetic), fixed or adjustable low profile primary sights (most often night sights), auxiliary aiming/sighting/illumination equipment, compensators or barrel porting, as well as combat triggers and hammers.

TACTICAL RIFLES

Semi-auto, bolt action, or slide action rifles which have at least two of the following factory/manufacturer options or features: magazine capacity over ten rounds, nonglare finish (generally but there may be exceptions), Mil Std 1913 Picatinny or equivalent rail(s), mostly synthetic stocks which may be fixed, folding, collapsible, adjustable, or with/without pistol grip, most have sling attachments for single, traditional two, or three point slings, tritium night sights, and some Assault Weapon Ban characteristics, such as flash suppressors, detachable magazines, bayonet lugs, etc.

TACTICAL SEMI-AUTO PISTOLS

Tactical semi-auto pistols have at least three of the following factory/manufacturer options or features: magazine capacity over ten rounds, non-glare finish (generally but there may be exceptions), Mil Std 1913 Picatinny or equivalent rail(s), combat style grips (wood or synthetic), fixed or adjustable low profile primary sights (most often night sights), auxiliary aiming/sighting/illumination equipment, and compensators or barrel porting.

TACTICAL SHOTGUNS

Semi-auto or slide action shotguns which have at least two of the following factory/manufacturer options or features: higher capacity (than sporting/hunting shotguns) magazines, or magazine extensions, non-glare finish (generally but there may be exceptions), Mil Std 1913 Picatinny or equivalent rail(s), mostly synthetic stocks which may be fixed, folding, collapsible, adjustable, or with/without pistol grip, most have sling attachments for single, traditional two, or three point slings, some Assault Weapon Ban characteristics, such as bayonet lugs, or detachable high capacity magazines, rifle or night or ghost ring sights (usually adjustable), and short (18-20 inches) barrels with fixed cylinder choke.

TAKEDOWN

A gun which can be easily disassembled into two sections for carrying or shipping.

TANG(S)

Usually refers to the extension straps (upper and lower) of a rifle or shotgun receiver/frame to which the stock or grip is attached.

TARGET STOCK

A stock optimized for accuracy, consistency, ergonomics, and reliability; for firearms used primarily in formal known-distance competition shooting. Rifle versions may have many adjustment options (e.g. length of pull, cast, comb/cheek piece, buttplate, palm rest, hand stop, accessory attachment); handgun versions may have thumb or palm rests, spacers, inserts, etc.

TENIFER

A trademarked name for a metal case hardening and surface finishing process which provides exceptional wear, abrasion, and corrosion resistance; and very high surface hardness. The generic name for this process is ferritic nitrocarburizing.

THUMBHOLE STOCK (CRIME BILL)

An adaptation of the sporter thumbhole stock design which removed a weapon from semi-auto assault weapon legal status. The thumbhole was/is very large and provides the functionality of a true pistol grip stock.

THUMBHOLE STOCK (SPORTER)

A sporter/hunting stock with an ergonomic hole in the grip; the thumb of the shooter's trigger hand fits into the hole which provides for a steadier hold.

TOP BREAK

See BREAK BARREL ACTION.

TOP BREAK ACTION

See BREAK BARREL ACTION.

TOP FOLDING STOCK

A folding stock variation; the buttstock pivots upwards and over the top of the frame/receiver. See FOLDING STOCK.

TOP LEVER

Refers to the opening lever mechanism on top of the upper frame/tang.

TOP STRAP

The upper part of a revolver frame, which often is either slightly grooved - the groove serving as rear sight - or which carries at its rearward end a sight (which may or may not be adjustable).

TORQUE

The force which causes a rifled firearm to counter-rotate when a projectile travels down its bore.

TRACER

A type of military bullet that emits a colored flame from its base when fired allowing the gunner to adjust his fire onto a target.

TRAJECTORY

The curved flight path of a bullet from muzzle to target; resembling but not a true parabolic arc.

TRAJECTORY TABLE

A numerical table of computed data summarizing the down range trajectory of a projectile.

TRAP STOCK

A shotgun stock with greater length and less comb drop (Monte Carlo, in many cases) used for trap shooting, enabling a built-in height lead when shooting.

TRIGGER

Refers to a release device (mechanical or electrical) in the firing system that starts the ignition process. Usually a curved, grooved, or serrated piece of metal which is pulled rearward by the shooter's finger, and which releases the sear or hammer.

TRIGGER GUARD

Usually a circular or oval band of metal, horn, or plastic that goes around the trigger to provide both protection and safety in shooting circumstances.

TRIGGER PLATE ACTION

A shotgun (most typical) or rifle action design in which all components of the lockwork are mounted on the trigger plate (the lower steel bar at the rear of the action). Can be removable or non-removable.

TRIGGER SAFETY

A trigger assembly component which must be depressed or otherwise moved before the trigger can be pulled completely through to fire the weapon. Most often a pivoting blade in the center of a trigger which protrudes from the face of the trigger when it is engaged/"on" and automatically resets itself.

TURRETS

Cylinders on an optical sight's main tube which hold adjustment knobs or screws. A turret is dedicated to one of several functions: windage, elevation, parallax, reticle type, reticle illumination, or ranging.

TWIST BARRELS

A process in which a steel rod (called a mandrel) was wrapped with skelps - ribbons of iron. The skelps were then welded in a charcoal fire to form one piece of metal, after which the rod was driven out to be used again. The interior of the resulting tube then had to be laboriously bored out by hand to remove the roughness. Once polished, the outside was smoothed on big grinding wheels, usually turned by waterpower.

TWIST RATE

Refers to the distance required for one complete turn of rifling, usually expressed as a ratio such as 1:12 in. twist, which refers to one complete twist of rifling within 12 inches of barrel. Typically, the heavier the bullet, the faster the twist rate needs to be.

UNDER FOLDING STOCK

A folding stock variation; the buttstock rotates downwards and underneath the frame/receiver. See FOLDING STOCK.

UNDER-LEVER

Action opening lever that is usually located below or in the trigger guard, can also be side pivoting from forearm.

UNDERLUG

On a break open action firearm, the lug on the chamber end of the barrel which locates the barrel in the receiver, and which locks the barrel into battery when intercepted by the bolt/underbolt. Also called a lump.

UNLOAD

To remove all ammunition/cartridges from a firearm or magazine.

UNSERVICEABLE FIREARM

A firearm that is damaged and cannot be made functional in a minimal amount of time.

UPPER ASSEMBLY

For a semi-auto pistol this includes the barrel and slide assembly, for AR style rifles it includes the barrel, bolt and receiver housing.

VARIABLE POWER OPTICAL SIGHT

An optical sight with a multiple of magnification levels, most common are 3-9 power general purpose scopes.

VENTILATED

Denotes a component with holes, slots, gaps, or other voids which reduce weight, promote cooling, have a structural purpose, or are decorative.

VENTILATED RIB

A sighting plane affixed along the length of a shotgun barrel with gaps or slots milled for cooling and lightweight handling.

VERNIER

Typically used in reference to a rear aperture (peep) sight. Usually upper tang mounted, and is adj. for elevation by means of a highly accurate finely threaded screw.

VIERLING

A German word designating a four-barrel gun.

VIOLENT CRIME CONTROL AND LAW ENFORCEMENT ACT OF 1994, PUBLIC LAW 103-322

On September 13, 1994, Congress passed the Violent Crime Control and Law Enforcement Act of 1994, Public Law 103-322. Title IX, Subtitle A, Section 110105 of this Act generally made it unlawful to manufacture, transfer, and possess semiautomatic assault weapons (SAWs) and to transfer and possess large capacity ammunition feeding devices (LCAFDs). The law also required importers and manufacturers to place certain markings on SAWs and LCAFDs, designating they were for export or law enforcement/government use. Significantly, the law provided that it would expire 10 years from the date of enactment. Accordingly, effective 12:01 am on September 13, 2004, the provisions of the law ceased to apply and the following provisions of the regulations in Part 478 no longer apply:

- Section 478.11- Definitions of the terms "semiautomatic assault weapon" and "large capacity ammunition feeding device"
- Section 478.40- Entire section
- Section 478.40a- Entire section
- Section 478.57- Paragraphs (b) and (c)
- Section 478.92- Paragraph (a)(3) – [NOTE: Renumbered from paragraph (a)(2) to paragraph (a)(3) by TD ATF – 461 (66 FR 40596) on August 3, 2001]
- Section 478.92- Paragraph (c)
- Section 478.119- Entire section- [NOTE: An import permit is still needed pursuant to the Arms Export Control Act- see 27 CFR 447.41(a)]
- Section 478.132- Entire section
- Section 478.153- Entire section

NOTE: The references to "ammunition feeding device" in section 478.116 are not applicable on or after

September 13, 2004.

NOTE: The references to "semiautomatic assault weapons" in section 478.171 are not applicable on or after September 13, 2004.

Information from BATFE Online - Bureau of Alcohol, Tobacco and Firearms, and Explosives an official site of the U.S. Department of Justice.

WAD

A shotshell component in front of the powder charge and has a cup or flat surface that the shot charge rests on. Various types of wads exist with the most common being a column of plastic.

WADCUTTER BULLET

A lead target bullet for revolvers having a flat nose and a sharp outer edge or shoulder which will cut clean holes in paper targets to aid in spotting and scoring.

WATER TABLE

The flat surfaces forward of the standing breech of a side-by-side shotgun. Also called action bar flats or action flats.

WEAVER-STYLE RAIL

A mounting rail system similar in dimensions and use as the Picatinny Rail. Weaver-style grooves are .180 wide and do not always have consistent center-to-center widths. Most Weaver-style accessories will fit the Picatinny system, however Picatinny accessories will not fit the Weaver-style system. Also see PICATINNY RAIL.

WEATHER SHIELD®

Corrosion-resistant coating created for Weatherby rifles to protect them from the elements in any climate.

WILDCAT CARTRIDGE

An experimental or non-standard cartridge, not commercially manufactured, often using a standard cartridge case which has been significantly modified.

WINDAGE

The deflection of a projectile from its trajectory due to wind. Also, adjustment of a firearm's sight(s) to compensate for the deflection.

WING SAFETY

A bolt action rifle safety which has a horizontally rotating lever located on the rear of the bolt assembly. Also known as a Mauser safety, after its designer, Peter Paul Mauser.

WUNDHAMMER GRIP/SWELL

Originally attributed to custom gunsmith Louis Wundhammer, it consists of a bulge on the right side of the pistol grip that ergonomically fills the palm of a right-handed shooter.

YOKE

See CRANE.

YOUTH DIMENSIONS

Usually refers to shorter stock dimensions and/or lighter weight enabling youth/women to shoot and carry a firearm.

ZERO

The procedure of adjusting a firearm's sight(s) so that the point of aim coincides with the bullet's point of impact at a selected range.

ABBREVIATIONS

*	Banned due to 1994-2004 Crime Bill (may be current again)
5R	Five (groove) Rifling
A	Standard Grade Walnut
A.R.M.S.	Atlantic Research Marketing Systems
A2	AR-15 Style/Configuration w/fixed carry handle
A3	AR-15 Style/Configuration w/ detachable carry handle
AA	Extra Grade Walnut
AAA	Best Quality Walnut
ACB	Advanced Combat Bolt (LWRC)
ACP	Automatic Colt Pistol
ACR	Adaptive Combat Rifle
ACS	MAGPUL Adaptable Carbine/ Storage (stock)
ACT	Advanced Combat Trigger (ALG Defense)
adj.	Adjustable
AE	Automatic Ejectors or Action Express
AECA	Arms Export Control Act
AFG	MAGPUL Angled Fore Grip
AK	Avtomat Kalashnikova rifle
ambi.	Ambidextrous
AMU	Army Marksman Unit
AOW	Any Other Weapon (NFA)
appts.	Appointments
AR	Armalite Rifle
ASAP	MAGPUL Ambi Sling Attachment Point
ATACS	Advanced Tactical Concealment System (camo pattern)
ATR	All Terrain Rifle (Mossberg)
ATS	All Terrain Shotgun (Mossberg)
AWB	Assault Weapons Ban
AWR	Alaskan/African Wilderness Rifle
B	Blue
BAC	Browning Arms Company
BAD	MAGPUL Battery Assist Device (bolt catch lever)
BAD-ASS	Battle Arms Development Ambi Safety Selector
BAN/CRIME BILL ERA	Mfg. between Nov. 1989 - Sept. 12, 2004
BAR	Browning Automatic Rifle
BASR	Bolt Action Sniper Rifle (H&K)
BB	Brass Backstrap
BBL	Barrel
BCG	Bolt Carrier Group
BLR	Browning Lever Rifle
BMG	Browning Machine Gun
BOSS	Ballistic Optimizing Shooting System
BOSS-CR	BOSS w/o Muzzle Brake
BP	Buttplate or Black Powder
BPE	Black Power Express
BPS	Browning Pump Shotgun
BR	Bench Rest
BT	Beavertail
BT	Browning Trap shotgun
BUIS	Back-Up Iron Sight(s)
c.	Circa
C/B 1994	Introduced Because of 1994 Crime Bill
CAD	Computer Assisted Design
cal.	Caliber
CAR	Colt Automatic Rifle or Carbine
CAWS	Close Assault Weapons System
CB	Crescent Buttplate
CC	Case Colors
CCA	Colt Collectors Association
CCP	Concealed Carry Pistol (Walther)
CDP	Custom Defense Package (Kimber)
CF	Centerfire
CFR	Code of Federal Regulations
CH	Cross Hair
CHF	Cold Hammer Forged
CLMR	Colt Lightning Magazine Rifle
CMS	Cowboy Mounted Shooter
CMV	Chrome Moly Vanadium Steel
CNC	Computer Numeric Controlled (machining/machinery)
COMM.	Commemorative
COMP	Compensated/Competition
C.O.P.	Continuous Optics Platform (Aero Precision USA)
CQB	Close Quarter Battle
CQC	Close Quarter Combat
C-R	Curio-Relic
CRF	Controlled Round Feed
CRPF	Controlled Round Push Feed
CSAT	Combat Shooting & Tactics (accessories)
CTF	Copper/Tin Frangible (bullet)
CTG/CTGE	Cartridge
CTR	MAGPUL Compact/Type Restricted (stock)
CYL/C	Cylinder
DA	Double Action
DA/SA	Double Action/Single Action
DAGR	Dual aperture Gunsite rifle scope
DAK	Double Action Kellerman Trigger (SIG)
DAO	Double Action Only
DB	Double Barrel

DBM	Detachable Box Magazine
DCM	Director of Civilian Marksmanship
DGR	Dangerous Game Rifle (Weatherby)
DI	Direct Impingement Gas System, see Glossary
DIGS	Delayed Impingement Gas System, see Glossary
DISC or disc.	Discontinued
DLC	Diamond Like Carbon (STI International)
DMR	Designated Marksman Rifle (U.S Army, LWRC)
DPMS	Defense Procurement Manufacturing Services
DSL	Detachable Side Locks
DST	Double Set Triggers
DT	Double Triggers
DWM	DeutscheWaffen and Munitions Fabriken
D.R.I.V.	Dual Regulating Inline Valve gas system (see Savage)
EGLM	Enhanced Grenade Launcher Module (FNH)
EJT	Ejector or Ejectors
EMAG	MAGPUL Export MAGazine
EMP	Enhanced Micro Pistol (Springfield Inc.)
EXC	Excellent
EXT	Extractor or Extractors
F	Full Choke
F&M	Full & Modified
FA	Forearm
FAL	Fusil Automatique Leger
FBT	Full Beavertail Forearm
FC	Full Choke
FDE	Flat Dark Earth (finish color)
FDL	Fleur-de-lis
FE	Forend/Fore End
FFL	Federal Firearms License
FIRSH	Free Floating Integrated Rail System Handguard
FK	Flat Knob
FKLT	Flat Knob Long Tang
FM	Full Mag
FMJ	Full Metal Jacket
FMOS	Full Mass Operating System
FN CAL	FN Carabine Automatique Leger
FN GP	FN Grande Puissance (pistol)
FN LAR	Fabrique Nationale Light Automatic Rifle
FN	Fabrique Nationale
FNAR	FN Automatic Rifle
FNC	Fabrique Nationale Carabine
FNH USA	Fabrique Nationale Herstal (U.S. sales and marketing)
FNH	Fabrique Nationale Herstal
FOL	Foliage (finish)
FPS	Feet Per Second
FQR	First-Gen Quad Rail (Radical Firearms)
g.	Gram
ga.	Gauge
GCA	Gun Control Act
GIO	Gas Impingement Operation
G-LAD	Green Laser Aiming Device
GOVT	Government
GPO	Gas Piston Operation
gr.	Grain
H&H	Holland & Holland
HAMR	High accuracy multi-range rifle scope
HB	Heavy Barrel
H-BAR	H(eavy)-BARrel, AR-15/M16
HC	Hard Case
HK	Heckler und Koch
HMR	Hornady Magnum Rimfire
HP	High Power (FN/Browning pistol)
HP	Hollow Point
HPJ	High Performance Jacket
I	Improved
IAR	Infantry Automatic Rifle (LWRC)
IC	Improved Cylinder
ICORE	International Confederation of Revolver Enthusiasts
ILS	Integral Locking System (North American Arms)
IM	Improved Modified
IMI	Israel Military Industries
in.	Inch
intro.	Introduced
IOM	Individual Officer Model (FNH model suffix)
IPSC	International Practical Shooting Confederation
ISSF	International Shooting Sports Federation
ITAR	International Traffic (in) Arms Regulation
IVT	Italian Value-Added Tax
JCP	Joint Combat Pistol
KAC	Knight's Armament Co.
KCR	Krieger Custom Rifle (Weatherby)
KMC	Knight's Manufacturing Co.
KSG	Kel Tec Shotgun
L	Long
LBA	Lightning Bolt Action (Mossberg)
LBC	Les Baer Custom (Inc.)
lbs.	Pounds
LC	Long Colt
LCW	Lauer Custom Weaponry
LDA	Light Double Action (PARA USA INC.)

LEM	Law Enforcement Model or Modification
LEO	Law Enforcement Only
LM	Lapua Magnum
LMT	Lewis Machine and Tool (Company)
LNIB	Like New in Box
LOP	Length of Pull
LPA	Lightning Pump Action (Mossberg)
LPI	Lines Per Inch
LR	Long Rifle
LHRBO	Last Round Bolt Hold Open
LT	Long Tang or Light
LTR	Light Tactical Rifle (Rem.)
LTRK	Long Tang Round Knob
LWRC	Land Warfare Resources Corporation
LWRC	Leitner-Wise Rifle Company, Inc.
LXX	Trigger by Weatherby (new 2016)
M (MOD.)	Modified Choke
M&P	Military & Police
M-4	Newer AR-15/M16 Carbine Style/ Configuration
Mag.	Magnum Caliber
mag.	Magazine
MARS	Modular Accessory Rail System
MBUS	MAGPUL Back-Up Sight
MC	Monte Carlo
MCS	Modular Combat System (Rem.)
MFG or Mfg.	Manufactured/manufacture
MFT	Mission First Tactical
MIAD	MAGPUL Mission Adaptable (grip, other)
mil	See Glossary
mil-dot	See Glossary
Mil-Spec	Mfg. to Military Specifications
Mil-Std	Mfg. to Military Standards
MK	Mark
mm	Millimeter
MOA	Minute of Angle
MOE	MAGPUL Original Equipment
MOS	Modular Optic System (Glock)
MOUT	Military Operations (on) Urbanized Terrain
MR	Matted Rib
MRP	Monolithic Rail Platform (Lewis Machine & Tool)
MRR	Modular Railed Receiver (Patriot Ordnance Factory)
MS2	MAGPUL Multi Mission Sling System
MSR	Manufacturer's Suggested Retail or Modern Sporting Rifle
MVG	MAGPUL MOE Vertical Grip
MWS	Modular Weapons System
N	Nickel
N/A	Not Applicable or Not Available
NATO	North Atlantic Treaty Org.
NE	Nitro Express
NFA	National Firearms Act (U.S. 1934)
NIB	New in Box
NM	National Match
no.	Number
NP	New Police
NP3/NP3 Plus	Nickel-Phosphorus (firearm coating)
NRS	Not Rifle or Shotgun (Franklin Armory)
NSST	Non Selective Single Trigger
NVD/E	Night Vision Device/Equipment
O/U	Over and Under
OA	Overall
OAL	Overall Length
OB	Octagon Barrel
OBFM	Octagon Barrel w/full mag.
OBO	Or Best Offer
OCT	Octagon
ODG	Olive Drab Green (finish color)
ORB	Oil-Rubbed Bronze finish (Sig Sauer)
ORC	Optics Ready Carbine
OSP	Optical Sight Pistol (Springfield Armory by Springfield Inc.)
oz.	Ounce
P	Police (Rem. rifle/shotgun)
P99AS	Pistol 99 Anti Stress (trigger, Walther)
PAD	Personal Anti-recoil Device (Savage)
Para.	Parabellum
PBR	Patrol Bolt Rifle (FNH)
PDA	Personal Defense Assistant (PARA USA INC.)
PFFR	Percentage of factory finish remaining
PG	Pistol Grip
PGF	Precision Guided Firearm
PK	Pistol Kompact (Walther)
PMAG	MAGPUL Polymer MAGazine
POR/P.O.R.	Price on Request
POST-'89	Paramilitary mfg. after Federal legislation in Nov. 1989
POST-BAN	Refers to production after Sept. 12, 2004
PPC	Pindell Palmisano Cartridge
PPD	Post Paid
PPK	Police Pistol Kriminal (Walther 1931 design)
PPKs	Police Pistol Kriminal (Walther 1968 design)
PPQ	Police Pistol Quick (defense trigger, Walther)
PRE-'89	Paramilitary mfg. before Federal legislation in Nov. 1989

PRE-BAN	Mfg. before September 13, 1994 per C/B or before Nov. 1989.
PRS/PRS2	MAGPUL Precision Rifle/Sniper (stock)
PSD	Personal Security Detail rifle (LWRC)
PSG	PrazisionSchutzenGewehr (H&K rifle)
PSR	Precision Shooting Rifle (FNH)
PXT	Power Extractor Technology (PARA USA INC.)
QD	Quick Detachable
Q.D.S.	Quick Deploy Sight (YHM)
RACS	Remington Arms Chassis System
RAS	Rail Adapter System
RB	Round Barrel/Round Butt
RCM	Ruger Compact Magnum
RCMP	Royal Canadian Mounted Police
RCP	Refined Carry Pistol (Kimber)
RDS	Rapid Deployment Stock
REC	Receiver
REM	Remington
REM. MAG.	Remington Magnum
REPR	Rapid Engagement Precision Rifle (LWRC)
RF	Rimfire
RFB	Rifle Forward (ejection) Bullpup
RFM	Rim Fire Magnum
RIS	Rail Interface system
RK	Round Knob
RKLT	Round Knob Long Tang
RKST	Round Knob Short Tang
RMEF	Rocky Mt. Elk. Foundation
RMR	Rimfire Magnum Rifle (Kel Tec)
RPD	Ruchnoy Pulemyot Degtyaryova (machine gun)
RR	Red Ramp
RSA	MAGPUL Rail Sling Attachment
RSUM	Remington Short-Action Ultra Magnum
RUM	Remington Ultra Magnum
RVG	MAGPUL Rail Vertical Grip
S	Short
S&W	Smith & Wesson
S/N	Serial Number
SA	Single Action
SAA	Single Action Army
SAAMI	Sporting Arms and Ammunition Manufacturers' Institute
SABR	Sniper/Assaulter Battle Rifle (LWRC)
SAE	Selective Automatic Ejectors
SAO	Single Action Only
SAS	SIG Anti Snag (pistol models)
SASS	Single Action Shooting Society or (U.S. Army) Semi Automatic Sniper System
SAUM	Short Action Ultra Magnum
SAW	Semiautomatic Assault Weapon
SAW	Squad Automatic Weapon
SB	Shotgun butt or Steel backstrap
SBR	Short Barrel Rifle
SBS	Short Barrel Shotgun
SCAR	Special (Operations Forces) Combat Assault Rifle (FNH)
SCW	Sub Compact Weapon (Colt)
SDT	Super Dynamic Technology (PARA USA INC.)
ser.	Serial
SFA	Striker Fire Action
SFO	Striker Fire Operation
SG	Straight Grip
SIG	Schweizerische Industriegesellschaft
SIM	Special Impact Munition
SK	Skeet
SLP	Self Loading Police (FNH shotgun)
SMG	Submachine Gun
SMLE	Short Magazine Lee Enfield Rifle
SNT	Single Non-Selective Trigger
SOCOM	Special Operations Command
SOPMOD	Special Operations Peculiar Modification
SP	Special Purpose
SPC	Special Purpose Cartridge
SPEC	Special
SPEC-OPS	Special Operations
SPG	Semi-Pistol Grip
Spl.	Special
SPLLAT	Special Purpose Low Lethality Anti-Terrorist (Munition)
SPR	Special Police Rifle (FNH), Special Purpose Rifle
SPS	Special Purpose Synthetic (Remington)
SPS	Superalloy Piston System (LWRC)
sq.	Square
SR	Solid Rib
SRC	Saddle Ring Carbine
SRS	Smooth Roll Safety
SRT	Short Reset Trigger
SS	Single Shot or Stainless Steel
SSA	Super Short Action
SSR	Sniper Support Rifle (FNH)
SST	Single Selective Trigger or Single Stage Trigger
ST	Single Trigger
SUR	Sport Utility Rifle - see Glossary
SWAT	Special Weapons Assault Team
SWAT	Special Weapons and Tactics
SxS	Side by Side
SX3	Super X3 (Winchester)
SX4	Super X4 (Winchester)

TAS Tactical Adjustable Sight (STI International)
TB Threaded Barrel
TBA To be Announced
TBM Tactical Box Magazine
TD Take Down
TDR Target Deployment Rifle (Rem.)
TFO Tritium Fiber Optic (Sig Sauer)
TFX Tritium Fiber Optic Xtreme (TruGlo)
TGT Target
TH Target Hammer
TiAIN Titanium Aluminum Nitride finish (STI International)
TiN TiN coating (STI International)
TIR Target Interdiction Rifle (Rem.)
TLCI Tactile Loaded Chamber Indicator (S&W)
TLE Tactical Law Enforcement (Kimber)
TPS Tactical Police Shotgun (FNH)
TRP Tactical Response Pistol (Springfield Inc.)
TRPAFD Take Red Pen Away From Dave!
TS Target Stocks
TSOB Scope Mount Rail Weaver Type
TSR XP USA Tactical Sport Rifle - Extreme Performance Ultra Short Action (FNH)
TSR XP Tactical Sport Rifle - Extreme Performance (FNH)
TT Target Trigger
TTR Tactical Target Rifle (PARA USA INC.)
TWS Tactical Weapons System (Rem.)
UBR MAGPUL Utility/Battle Rifle (stock)
UCIW Ultra Compact Individual Weapon (LWRC)
UCP Universal Combat Pistol (H&K)
UIT Union Internationale de Tir
UMC Union Metallic Cartridge Co.
UMP Universal Machine Pistol (H&K)
URX Upper Receiver Extending (free floating barrel system, Knight's Armament)
USA Ultra Safety Assurance (Springfield Inc.)
USAMU U.S. Army Marksmanship Unit
USC Universal Self-Loading Carbine (H&K)
USG United States Government (FNH model suffix)
USP Universal Self-Loading Pistol (H&K)
USPSA United States Practical Shooting Association
USR Urban Sniper Rifle (Rem.)
USSOCOM U.S. Special Operations Command
VAT Value Added Tax
Vent. Ventilated
VG Very Good
VR Ventilated Rib
VTAC Viking Tactics, Inc. (accessories)
VTR Varmint Triangular Profile Barrel (Remington)
w/ With
w/o Without
WBY Weatherby
WC Wad Cutter
WCF Winchester Center Fire
WD Wood
WFF Watch For Fakes
WIN Winchester
WMR Winchester Magnum Rimfire
WO White Outline
WRA Winchester Repeating Arms Co.
WRF Winchester Rim Fire
WRM Winchester Rimfire Magnum
WSL Winchester Self-Loading
WSM Winchester Short Magnum
WSSM Winchester Super Short Magnum
WW World War
X (1X) 1X Wood Upgrade or Extra Full Choke Tube
XD Extreme Duty (Springfield Inc.)
XDM Extreme Duty M Factor (Springfield Inc.)
XX (2X) 2X Wood Upgrade or Extra Extra Full Choke Tube
XXX (3x) 3X Wood Upgrade
YHM Yankee Hill Machine

GRADING CRITERIA

The older NRA modern condition descriptions relied upon adjectives such as "Excellent" or "Fair" – has served the firearms community for many years. However, many of today's dealers/collectors, especially those who deal in modern guns, have turned away from this older, subjective system. There is too much variance within some of the older subjective grades, therefore making accurate grading difficult.

Most dealers and collectors are now utilizing what is essentially an objective method for deciding the condition of a gun: THE PERCENTAGE OF ORIGINAL FACTORY FINISH(ES) REMAINING ON THE GUN. After looking critically at a variety of firearms and carefully studying the Photo Percentage Grading System™ (see Table of Contents), it will soon become evident if a specific gun has 98%, 90%, 70% or less finish remaining. Remember, sometimes an older unfired gun described as NIB can actually be 98% or less condition, simply because of the wear accumulated by taking it in and out of the box and excessive handling. Commemoratives are especially prone to this problem. Of course, factors such as quality of finish(es), engraving (and other embellishments), special orders/features, historical significance and/or provenance, etc. can and do affect prices immensely. Also, it seems that every year bore condition (especially on antiques) becomes more important in the overall grading factor (and price) of both collectible and desirable major trademarks such as Winchester, Remington, Sharps, Schuetzens, older Springfields, etc. Because of this, bore condition must be listed separately for those guns where it makes a difference in value. Never pay a premium for condition that isn't there. Remember, original condition still beats everything else to the bank.

Every gun's unique condition factor – and therefore the price – is best determined by the percentage of original finish(es) remaining, with the key consideration being the overall frame/receiver finish. The key word here is "original", for if anyone other than the factory has refinished the gun, its value as a collector's item has been diminished. The exceptions would be rare and historical guns that have been properly restored. Every year, top quality restorations have become more accepted, and prices have gone up proportionately with the quality of the workmanship. Also popular now are antique finishes, and a new question has come up, "What is 100% antique finish on new reproductions?" Answer – a gun that started out as new, and then has been aged to a lower condition factor to duplicate natural wear and tear.

CAREFULLY STUDY THE HIGH QUALITY DIGITAL IMAGES AND READ THE CAPTIONS IN THE PPGS. The PPGS is also available online at no charge and contains even more examples of condition factors than those printed in this edition. Simply visit BlueBookOfGunValues.com and click on Photo Percentage Grading System under CONTENT INFORMATION. Note where the finishes of a firearm typically wear off first. These are usually places where the gun accumulates wear from holster/case rubbing, and contact with the hands or body over an extended period of time. A variety of firearms have been shown in four-color to guarantee that your "sampling size" for observing finishes with their correct colors is as diversified as possible.

It should be noted that the older a collectible firearm is, the smaller the percentage of original finish one can expect to find. Some very old and/or very rare firearms are sought by collectors in almost any condition!

For your convenience, NRA Condition Standards are listed (see Table of Contents). Converting from this grading system to percentages can now be done accurately. Remember the price is wrong if the condition factor isn't right!

PHOTO PERCENTAGE GRADING SYSTEM CONVERSION GUIDELINES

New/Perfect – 100% condition with or without box. 100% on currently manufactured firearms assumes NIB (New In Box) condition and not sold previously at retail.

Mint – no less than 99% condition with almost no observable wear. Can also include guns sold previously at retail, that may have, only been shot occasionally.

Excellent – 95%+ - 98% condition.

Very Good – 80% - 95% condition (all parts/finish should be original).

Good - 60% – 80% condition (all parts/finish should be original).

Fair – 20% - 60% condition (all parts/finish may or may not be original, but must function properly and shoot).

Poor – under 20% condition (shooting not a factor).

The NRA conditions listed below have been provided as guidelines to assist the reader in converting and comparing condition factors to the Photo Percentage Grading System™ (PPGS, see pages 65-142). NRA antique and modern condition standards are now represented in the PPGS – please refer to pages 65-101 (handguns) and 104-142 (long guns). In order to use this book correctly, the reader is urged to examine these images of NRA condition standards. Once the gun's condition has been accurately assessed, only then can values be accurately ascertained.

NRA MODERN CONDITION DESCRIPTIONS

New – not previously sold at retail, in same condition as current factory production.

Perfect – in new condition in every respect, may have previously been sold at retail.

Excellent – near new condition, used but little, no noticeable marring of wood or metal, bluing near perfect (except at muzzle or sharp edges).

Very Good – in perfect working condition, no appreciable wear on working surfaces, no corrosion or pitting, only minor surface dents or scratches.

Good – in safe working condition, minor wear on working surfaces, no broken parts, no corrosion or pitting that will interfere with proper functioning.

Fair – in safe working condition, but well worn, perhaps requiring replacement of minor parts or adjustments which should be indicated in advertisement, no rust, but may have corrosion pits which do not render article unsafe or inoperable.

NRA ANTIQUE CONDITION DESCRIPTIONS

Factory New – all original parts; 100% original finish; in perfect condition in every respect, inside and out.

Excellent – all original parts; over 80% original finish; sharp lettering, numerals and design on metal and wood; unmarred wood; fine bore.

Fine – all original parts; over 30% original finish; sharp lettering, numerals and design on metal and wood; minor marks in wood; good bore.

Very Good – all original parts; none to 30% original finish; original metal surfaces smooth with all edges sharp; clear lettering, numerals and design on metal; wood slightly scratched or bruised; bore disregarded for collectors firearms.

Good – less than 20% original finish, some minor replacement parts; metal smoothly rusted or lightly pitted in places, cleaned or reblued; principal lettering, numerals and design on metal legible; wood refinished, scratched, bruised or minor cracks repaired; in good working order.

Fair – less than 10% original finish, some major parts replaced; minor replacement parts may be required; metal rusted, may be lightly pitted all over, vigorously cleaned or reblued; rounded edges of metal and wood; principal lettering, numerals and design on metal partly obliterated; wood scratched, bruised, cracked or repaired where broken; in fair working order or can be easily repaired and placed in working order.

Poor – little or no original finish remaining, major and minor parts replaced; major replacement parts required and extensive restoration needed; metal deeply pitted; principal lettering, numerals and design obliterated, wood badly scratched, bruised, cracked or broken; mechanically inoperative, generally undesirable as a collector's firearm.

THE PPGS

FIREARMS GRADING MADE EASY

The next 80 pages of high res color images with captions are easily the most important in this book. If you carefully study all the images, and thoroughly read the accompanying captions, the following color pages will help you accurately determine condition better than anything that's ever been published. This revised Photo Percentage Grading System™ (PPGS) includes images of both NRA new and antique condition factors, in addition to all the 100%-10% percentage conditions for revolvers, pistols, rifles, and shotguns.

Now in its 32nd year, the Photo Percentage Grading System™ has become the industry standard for visibly ascertaining various condition factors based on a percentage system. The 42nd Edition also retains the "PPGS-o-meters" whenever possible, so you can get a quick fix on condition factors. Computer savvy users will be pleased to know that this revised 42nd Edition PPGS™ is also included free of charge on our website at BlueBookOfGunValues.com.

Condition factors pictured (indicated by PPGS-o-meters), unless otherwise noted, refer to the percentage of a gun's remaining finish(es), including blue, case colors, nickel, or another type of original finish remaining on the frame/receiver. On older guns, describing the receiver/frame finish accurately is absolutely critical to ascertain an accurate grade, which will determine the correct value.

Additional percentages of condition may be used to describe other specific parts of a gun (i.e. barrel, wood finish, plating, magazine tube, etc.). Percentages of patina/brown or other finish discoloration factors must also be explained separately when necessary, and likewise be interpolated accurately. **With antiques, the overall percentage within this text is NOT an average of the various condition factors, but again, refers to the overall original condition of the frame/receiver. Being able to spot original condition has never been more important, especially when the prices get into four, five, and six figures. Remember, the price is wrong if the condition factor isn't right!**

Now, more than ever, it takes well-trained senses of sight, hearing, touch, and smell, with a direct connection to the most powerful computer ever built, a trained human brain, to accurately fingerprint a gun's correct condition factor. Regardless of how much knowledge you've accumulated from books, websites, auction catalogs, dealer listings, etc., you're still in potential danger as a buyer if you can't figure out a gun's condition factor(s) accurately. More than anything else, an older gun's overall condition must "add up" (i.e., a Model 12 with visible barrel wear should not have a bright blue magazine tube, and a Model 1911 Colt with 98% frame finish should not have an 80% slide).

While the 42nd Edition's Photo Percentage Grading System™ certainly isn't meant to be the Last Testament on firearms grading, it hopefully goes a lot further than anything else published on the subject. Once you've accumulated the experience necessary to grade guns accurately, a ten-second "CAT scan" is usually all the time that is needed to zero in on each gun's unique condition factor.

In closing, the publisher wishes to express his thanks and gratitude to Rock Island Auctions, Morphy Auctions, and Dr. Leonardo Antaris, M.D. for authorizing the use of their digital images for the Photo Percentage Grading System™ (PPGS).

This PPGS section is also available online free of charge - visit bluebookofgunvalues.com

NIB Condition, Sturm, Ruger & Co. Inc. Mark IV Target Special Edition with color case hardened barrel and upper receiver tube by Turnbull Restoration & Manufacturing Co., .22 LR cal., mfg. late-2016. Firearms special/limited editions like this are getting more popular all the time. Most of these are not listed in factory brochures/price sheets, and due to the way they were originally ordered, manufactured, and initially sold, getting reliable and accurate information on them becomes increasingly difficult every year after their release. Typically, gun distributors (Talo and Davidson's are good examples) order a quantity of a standard production model (500 units or more is common), then add special features. These can be special metal finishes/treatments (like this Mark IV Target), different barrel lengths, unique engraving/embellishments, markings, and other non-standard features. Most special/limited editions do not have unique serialization, unlike factory commemoratives that are made, marketed, and sold by the manufacturers.

The trick to selling these limited/special editions is coming up with the right "mix" of these unique features that add value in the consumer's eyes over the standard models while keeping the price close to the factory offerings. That's much easier said than done. For example: this limited edition Ruger is priced only $66 more than a standard Mark IV Target with blue finish.

The real test on how collectible these editions will be in the future depends on consumer demand after they are discontinued/sold out. With thousands of these makes/models now being bought and sold in the marketplace, each gun has developed its own "desirability mix". Some have gone up in value tremendously, yet most are languishing in relative obscurity and remain close to their original purchase price. Don't forget that many never had an original MSRP when new, so figuring out values will always be more difficult on these special/limited editions than standard production models.

PISTOLS: PPGS CONDITION FACTORS

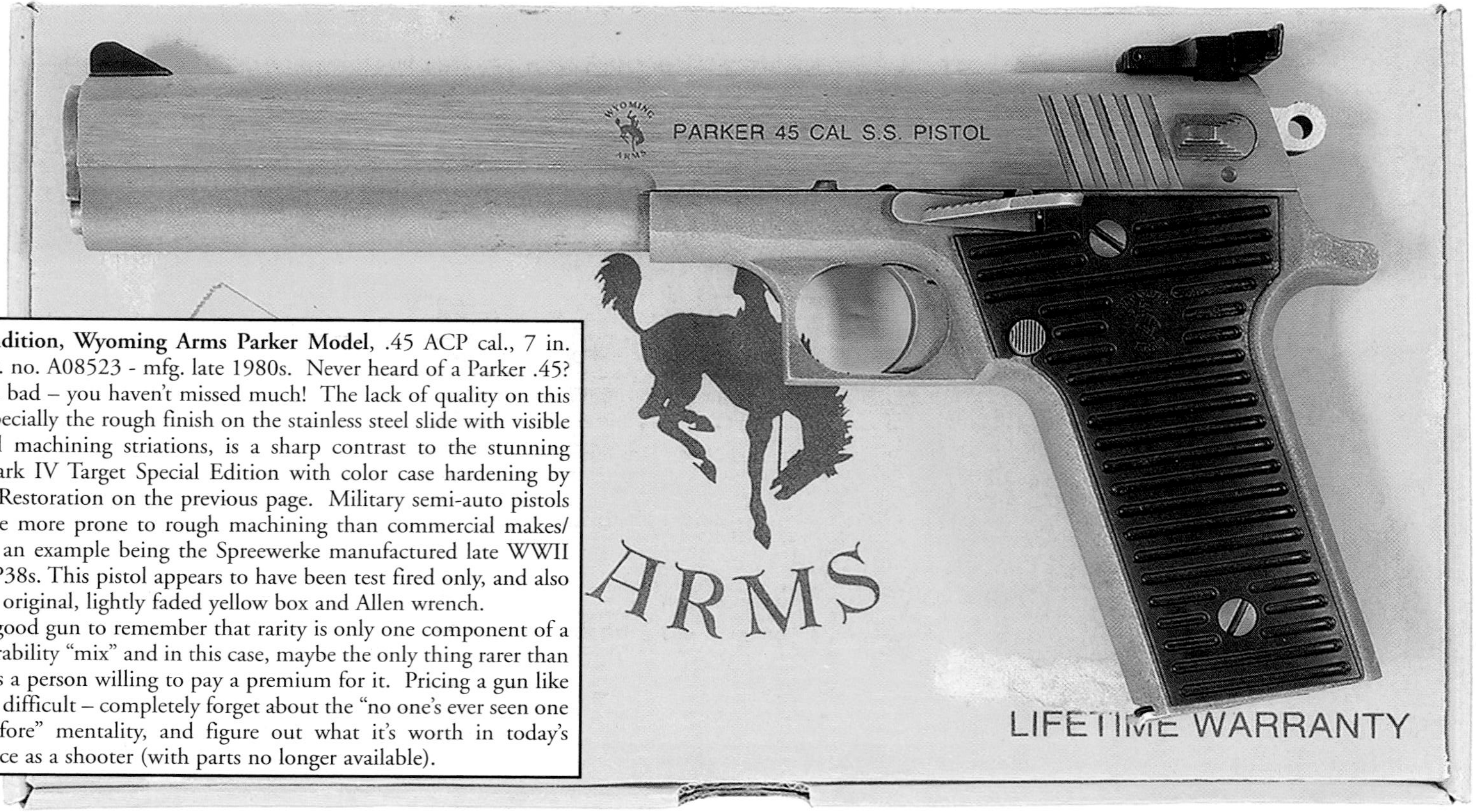

Mint condition, Wyoming Arms Parker Model, .45 ACP cal., 7 in. barrel, ser. no. A08523 - mfg. late 1980s. Never heard of a Parker .45? Don't feel bad – you haven't missed much! The lack of quality on this pistol, especially the rough finish on the stainless steel slide with visible horizontal machining striations, is a sharp contrast to the stunning Ruger Mark IV Target Special Edition with color case hardening by Turnbull Restoration on the previous page. Military semi-auto pistols usually are more prone to rough machining than commercial makes/models – an example being the Spreewerke manufactured late WWII German P38s. This pistol appears to have been test fired only, and also retains its original, lightly faded yellow box and Allen wrench.

This is a good gun to remember that rarity is only one component of a gun's desirability "mix" and in this case, maybe the only thing rarer than this gun is a person willing to pay a premium for it. Pricing a gun like this is not difficult – completely forget about the "no one's ever seen one like it before" mentality, and figure out what it's worth in today's marketplace as a shooter (with parts no longer available).

98% condition, Colt Woodsman Target Second Series Air Force Contract, .22 LR cal., 6 in. barrel, ser. no. 65518-S - mfg. late 1949. Previously, this pistol was described as a Colt Woodsman Second Series, but a contributing editor called in after getting a recent edition, wondering why the caption hadn't included the information that this pistol was a rare Air Force Contract variation, based on its serial number.

This variation has a fixed rear sight, different front sight, no automatic slide stop, and no provision for the usual grip adapter on the backstrap. Only 950 were manufactured circa 1949, 925 for the Air Force (issued for Arctic survival), and 25 for Rock Island. None were marked as U.S. Property or with other U.S. military markings/proofs – all were numbered in the 6XXXX-S range. This is a good example of a savvy buyer purchasing a gun at auction for under the market value. He paid just under $1,000 (w/o buyer's premium) and got a bargain, even though the auction estimate was $450-$600 for a standard Target Second Series. This rare variation is now currently worth over $2,000!

PISTOLS: PPGS CONDITION FACTORS

68

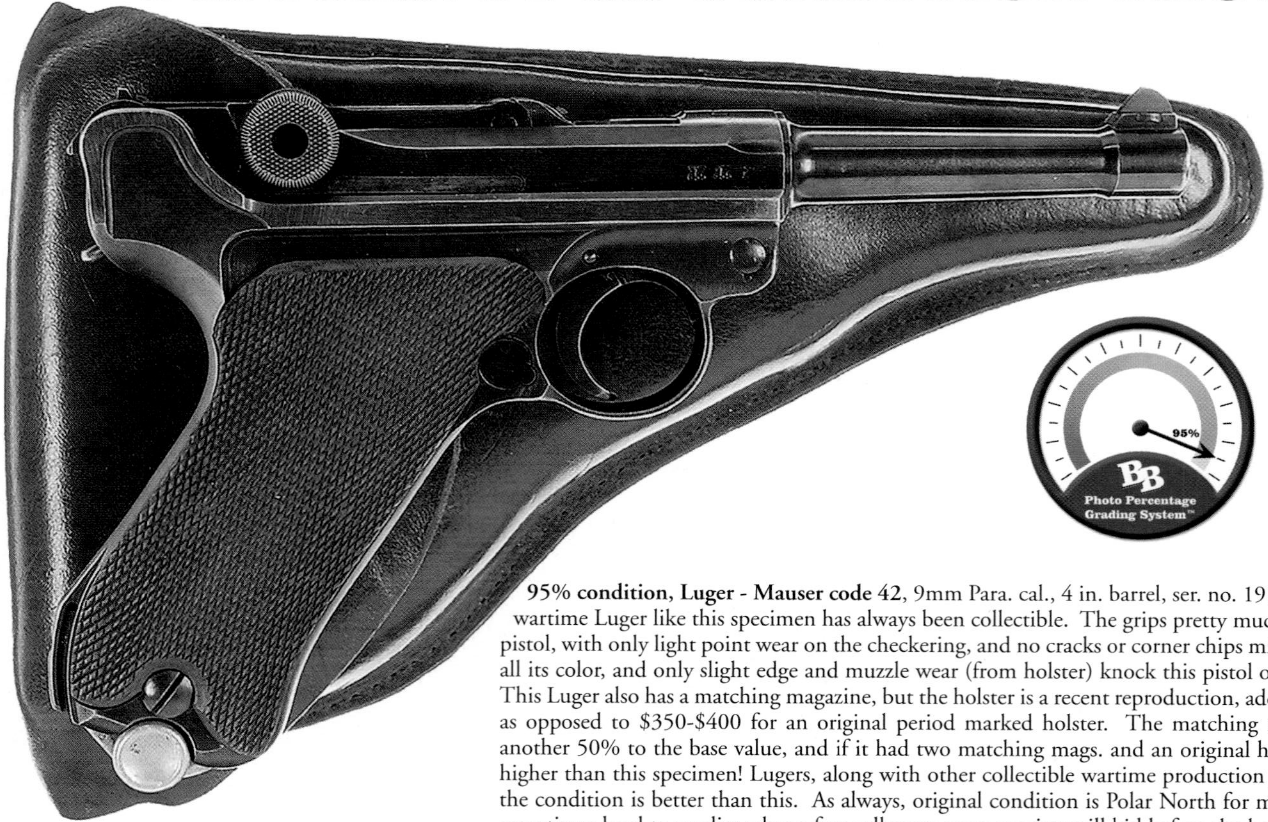

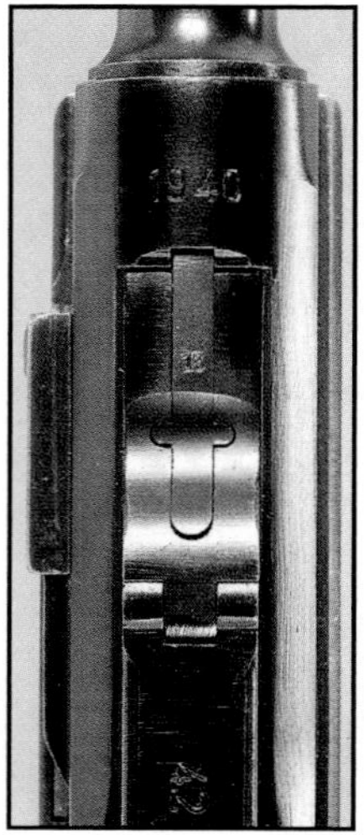

95% condition, Luger - Mauser code 42, 9mm Para. cal., 4 in. barrel, ser. no. 1913b - mfg. 1940. A nice original wartime Luger like this specimen has always been collectible. The grips pretty much tell the story of this Nazi issue pistol, with only light point wear on the checkering, and no cracks or corner chips missing. Blued metal finish retains all its color, and only slight edge and muzzle wear (from holster) knock this pistol out of 98% condition.

This Luger also has a matching magazine, but the holster is a recent reproduction, adding only $75-$100 to the value, as opposed to $350-$400 for an original period marked holster. The matching numbered metal magazine adds another 50% to the base value, and if it had two matching mags. and an original holster, the value might be 400% higher than this specimen! Lugers, along with other collectible wartime production pistols, can get very expensive if the condition is better than this. As always, original condition is Polar North for military pistol collectors, and it is sometimes hard to predict what a few collectors at an auction will bid before the hammer drops!

90% condition, Walther PP w/R.F.V. marking and holster, 7.65mm (.32 ACP) cal., 3¾ in. barrel, ser. no. 986819 – mfg. circa late 1930s. Most of the wear on this pistol has accumulated at the front of the frame and barrel, indicating a lifetime of holster storage. Metal surfaces in back of the trigger guard are an easy 95%. R.F.V. backstrap marking (see inset) indicates this pistol was made for Hitler's Reich Finance Administration. Crown N proof marks indicate pre-April, 1940 mfg. The unmarked holster contains an extra magazine. Original black plastic grips show limited usage and are in excellent condition. Perfect action and crisp bore enhance this gun's value. The original early Walther Models PP and smaller PPK are still benchmarks for quality, reliability, and design. The Walther PP was the world's first commercially successful double action pistol, and pre-war and WWII production have become very collectible. And don't forget, the legendary James Bond carried a PPK for decades.

PISTOLS: PPGS CONDITION FACTORS

PISTOLS: PPGS CONDITION FACTORS

70

80% condition, Walther P.38 Pistol code ac-45 w/holster, 9mm Para. cal., 4 7/8 in. barrel, ser. no. 2622b. This P.38 double action pistol was manufactured toward the end of the war during 1945. The ac-45 code (not shown, left side of slide) designates Walther production (byf was Mauser, and cyq was Spreewerke), and the polishing, bluing, and overall finish were not up to par with earlier manufacture during 1938-1944. During the end of WWII, the Germans were taking quality control shortcuts to get pistols into the hands of the ever decreasing number of desperate German soldiers. Close examination reveals machine cutter lines on both the barrel and side of slide. Also note metal scratching and thinning of the blue in trigger guard area. Not visible in this image is the wear on front grip strap and lower trigger guard, retaining almost no original blue, which decreases this pistol's condition another 10%. Black grips are excellent, and original holster is stamped with the "WaA36" code.

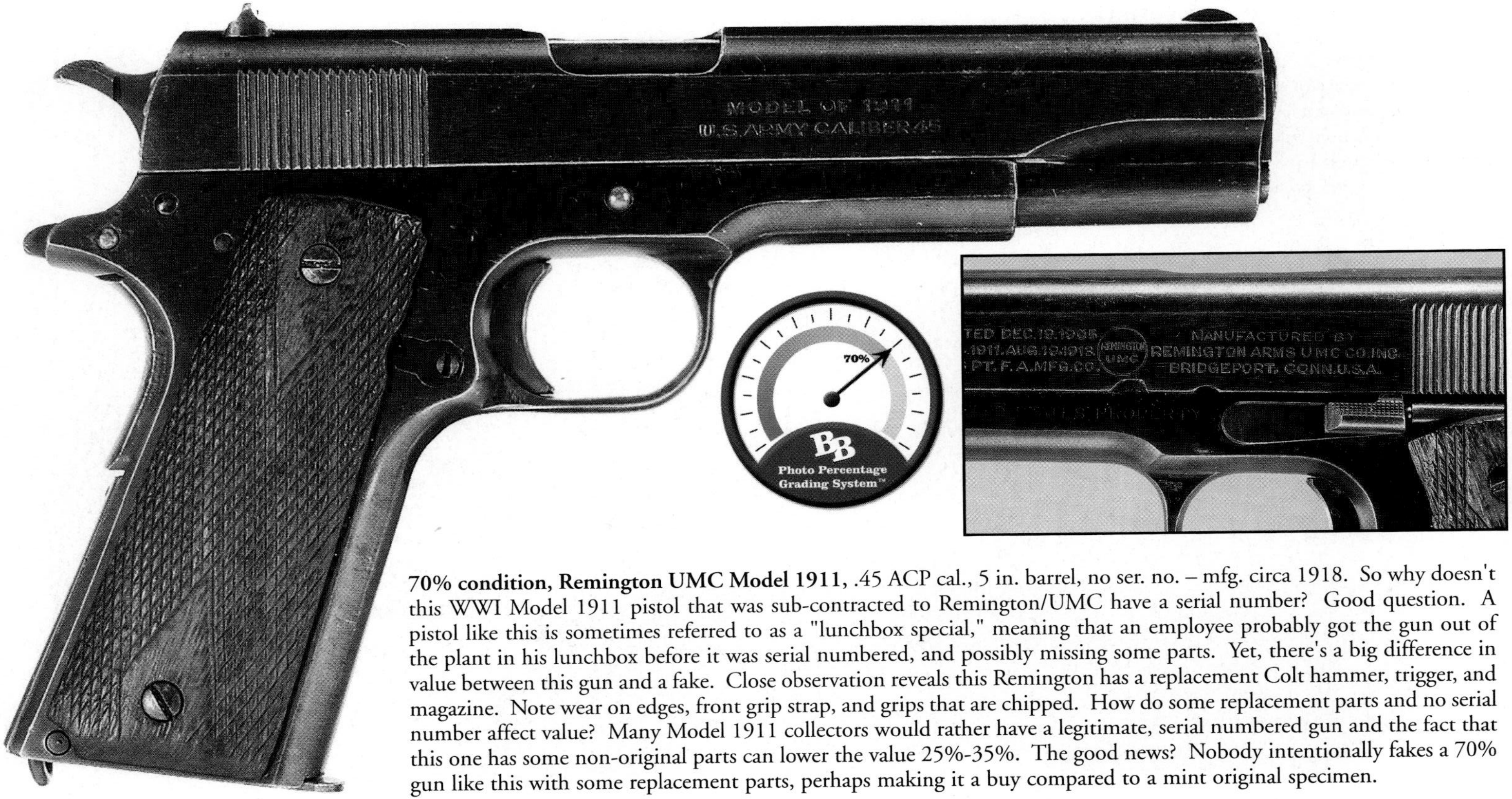

70% condition, Remington UMC Model 1911, .45 ACP cal., 5 in. barrel, no ser. no. – mfg. circa 1918. So why doesn't this WWI Model 1911 pistol that was sub-contracted to Remington/UMC have a serial number? Good question. A pistol like this is sometimes referred to as a "lunchbox special," meaning that an employee probably got the gun out of the plant in his lunchbox before it was serial numbered, and possibly missing some parts. Yet, there's a big difference in value between this gun and a fake. Close observation reveals this Remington has a replacement Colt hammer, trigger, and magazine. Note wear on edges, front grip strap, and grips that are chipped. How do some replacement parts and no serial number affect value? Many Model 1911 collectors would rather have a legitimate, serial numbered gun and the fact that this one has some non-original parts can lower the value 25%-35%. The good news? Nobody intentionally fakes a 70% gun like this with some replacement parts, perhaps making it a buy compared to a mint original specimen.

PISTOLS: PPGS CONDITION FACTORS

71

PISTOLS: PPGS CONDITION FACTORS

72

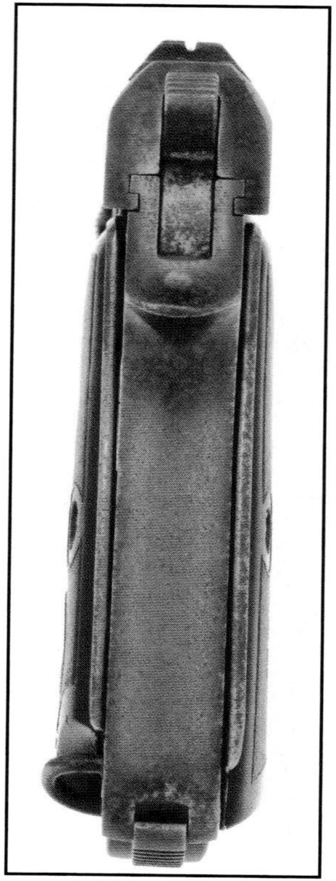

60% condition, Beretta Model 1934, .380 ACP cal., 3 3/8 in. barrel, ser. no. 666496 – mfg. 1937. One of Beretta's most popular pistols, over one million Model 1934s were manufactured from 1934-1980. Some of you may already be concerned about why the slide is a completely different color than the frame (i.e., possibly non-original finish or replaced slide). Not to worry here - this is what happens when the bluing process interacts with metal composition that differs in the carbon makeup from one part to another. In this case, even though the same bluing technique was applied to both the slide and the frame, the slide's metallurgy resulted in a plum-colored finish compared to the normal blued frame. Separate image of back of gun reveals quite a bit of wear, corrosion, and light pitting on both the rear grip strap and metal grip backing. It is especially important on handguns to carefully inspect the grip straps, because if the gun was extensively used, this is where most of the wear should accumulate.

50% condition, Mauser Standard Pre-War Commercial Broomhandle w/Stock, 7.63mm Mauser cal., 5½ in. barrel, ser. no. 95950 – mfg. circa 1909. If only someone would have taken better care of this Broomhandle during its lifetime. The barrel shows a lot of serious pitting, and you can see what happens if you get the steel wool (maybe sandpaper in this case) out and get aggressive! Receiver rail is almost completely shiny, lanyard ring is missing, magazine well housing in front of trigger guard is very scratched, and it has serious pitting on the bottom. Grips are worn, but match this Broomhandle's overall condition factor. Holster and detachable shoulder stock are original, but the stock has been broken and poorly repaired – also, the serial number does not match the pistol. Action is mechanically tight, and bore is very good. This is a classic example of a very collectible pistol losing over 65% of its potential value because the owner(s) didn't give it some TLC when it needed it the most.

PISTOLS: PPGS CONDITION FACTORS

PISTOLS: PPGS CONDITION FACTORS

40% condition, Colt Model 1905, .45 ACP cal., 4 7/8 in. barrel, ser. no. 1656 – mfg. early 1907. As you can see, this gun has problems. Note the original bright bluing on frame, but overall gray finish on slide, indicating that someone acid cleaned this gun thoroughly in the past, probably trying to clean up the heavy pitting on the right side (not shown). Since the frame is one condition factor (thinning blue), and the slide is a totally different condition (gray patina), this pistol's overall condition factor had to be interpolated based on the overall appearance. Note heavy frame scratching next to grips. Grip straps are also worn and gray, and left wood grip has a crack above the top screw. Action is mechanically good, and all parts are original. This gun has lost most of its collector value because of its altered condition and poor eye appeal.

30% condition, Colt Model 1905, .45 ACP cal., 4 7/8 in. barrel, ser. no. 3730 – mfg. 1909. Most of this pistol's lifetime is behind it. Note how the original bluing has turned a dark gray patina, the front of the slide is shiny, and there is pitting throughout the slide. Frame has also turned to a mostly brown patina, and some bluing remains in protected areas. The grip straps are very worn and have turned gray, while the checkered, revarnished grips also show a lot of wear. Action is mechanically okay. This gun is a good example of when value is determined almost completely by collectibility, not shootability. Five hundred of this model were factory slotted for a shoulder stock (this one isn't), making it a rare configuration that automatically adds 50% to the pistol's value, regardless of condition. Most pistols in this condition factor are not very collectible, but this rare Colt is an exception.

PISTOLS: PPGS CONDITION FACTORS

PISTOLS: PPGS CONDITION FACTORS

76

20% condition, Colt Model 1905, .45 ACP cal., 4 7/8 in. barrel, ser. no. 1840 – mfg. 1907. We know what you're thinking – how did the front of this gun become so pitted? Even CSI undergraduates will quickly figure out what happened in this case. At one point (maybe several), the gun and its holster got very wet. Unfortunately, the gun was stored in the wet holster, and witness the results. Serious pitting is an understatement to describe the wear on the front and rear of this unfortunate pistol. The only thing this gun still has going for it is that it can still claim originality and functionality. Grips are well-worn, and the points are long gone on the checkering. Rampant Colt logo is still visible on rear of slide. The only original finish remaining on this gun is in the protected area on the upper frame around the radiused grips.

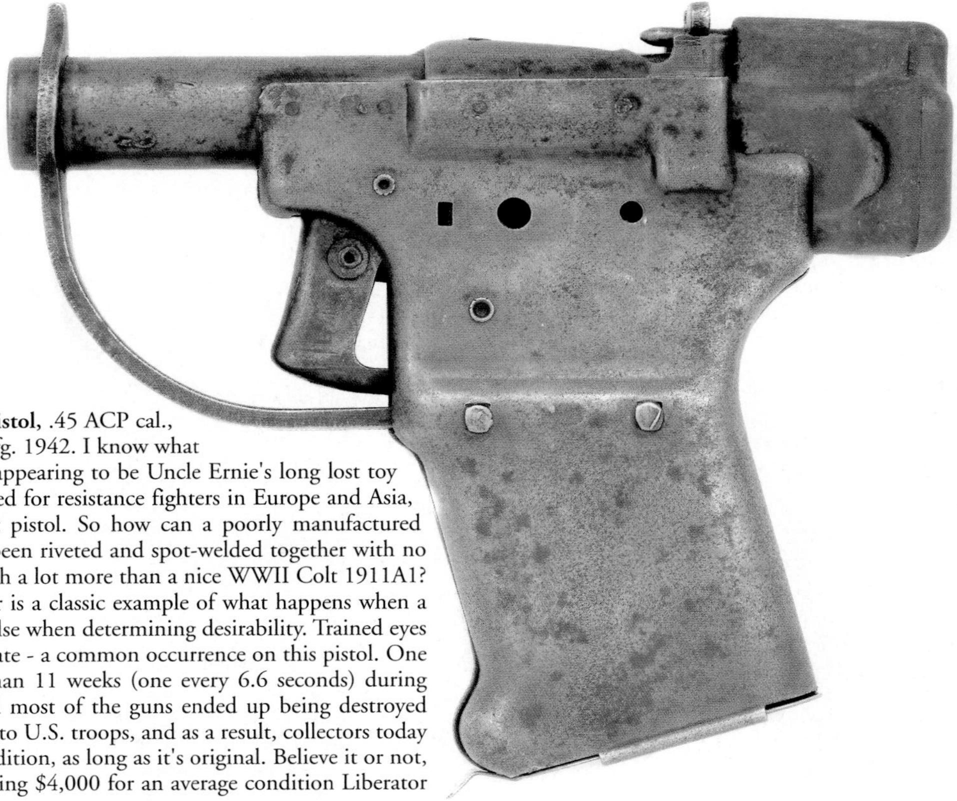

10% condition, Liberator single shot pistol, .45 ACP cal., 4 in. smoothbore barrel, no ser. no. – mfg. 1942. I know what you're thinking, and it's wrong! While appearing to be Uncle Ernie's long lost toy gun, the Liberator was originally designed for resistance fighters in Europe and Asia, and is a very desirable WWII contract pistol. So how can a poorly manufactured handgun made out of pot metal that's been riveted and spot-welded together with no condition or eye appeal possibly be worth a lot more than a nice WWII Colt 1911A1? Even though it's a weirdo, the Liberator is a classic example of what happens when a gun's rarity factor overrules everything else when determining desirability. Trained eyes may spot the shiny replacement floor plate - a common occurrence on this pistol. One million Liberators were made in less than 11 weeks (one every 6.6 seconds) during 1942 at a cost of only $1.73 each, and most of the guns ended up being destroyed overseas after the war. None were issued to U.S. troops, and as a result, collectors today will buy a Liberator in virtually any condition, as long as it's original. Believe it or not, some buyers at major auctions were paying $4,000 for an average condition Liberator like this four or five years ago, but no longer.

77

PISTOLS: NRA MODERN CONDITIONS

NRA Modern New condition (100%), **Browning Hi-Power,** 9mm Para. cal., 4 5/8 in. barrel, ser. no. 245NV56269 – mfg. 1995. The Hi-Power was John M. Browning's last pistol design, and production began in Belgium during 1935. It was immediately accepted, and many military contracts followed shortly. Being a venerable work horse for decades, the HP is still in action around the world today, and its design and functionality are truly ageless. This silver chrome finished HP variation with gold trigger, molded rubber grips with Browning medallions, adj. rear sight, and parkerized small parts was manufactured by F.N. in Herstal, Belgium, and shipped to Portugal for assembly and packaging. Even though NRA Modern New condition generally means not previously sold at retail on currently manufactured guns, this pistol was never fired by its original owner, nor does it show any wear. It is entirely possible for a NIB, unfired gun to accumulate wear if it has been displayed, handled, holstered, improperly stored, or over cleaned. This condition factor means NIB in every respect, with no excuses.

NRA Modern Perfect condition (**Mint - 99%**), **High Standard Model A**, .22 LR cal., 4½ in. barrel, ser. no. 91591 – mfg. late 1941. If you're a .22 cal. pistol collector and like condition, it doesn't get much better than this wartime, boxed High Standard Model A with original receipt from Abercrombie & Fitch. NRA Perfect translates into mint condition in every respect, and this gun certainly qualifies, perhaps test fired only, spending most of its life in the slightly tattered yellow and black two-piece box. Observe the checkered walnut grips with no wear on sharp points, perfect bluing with no wear on edges or end of barrel, and unturned screws still aligned. The older the gun, the harder it is to find one in this condition factor. On many older and desirable collectible firearms, values can double over NRA Excellent. Approximately 7,300 Model As were manufactured circa 1938-1942, but less than a handful may still remain in this condition with original box and bill of sale.

PISTOLS: NRA MODERN CONDITIONS

79

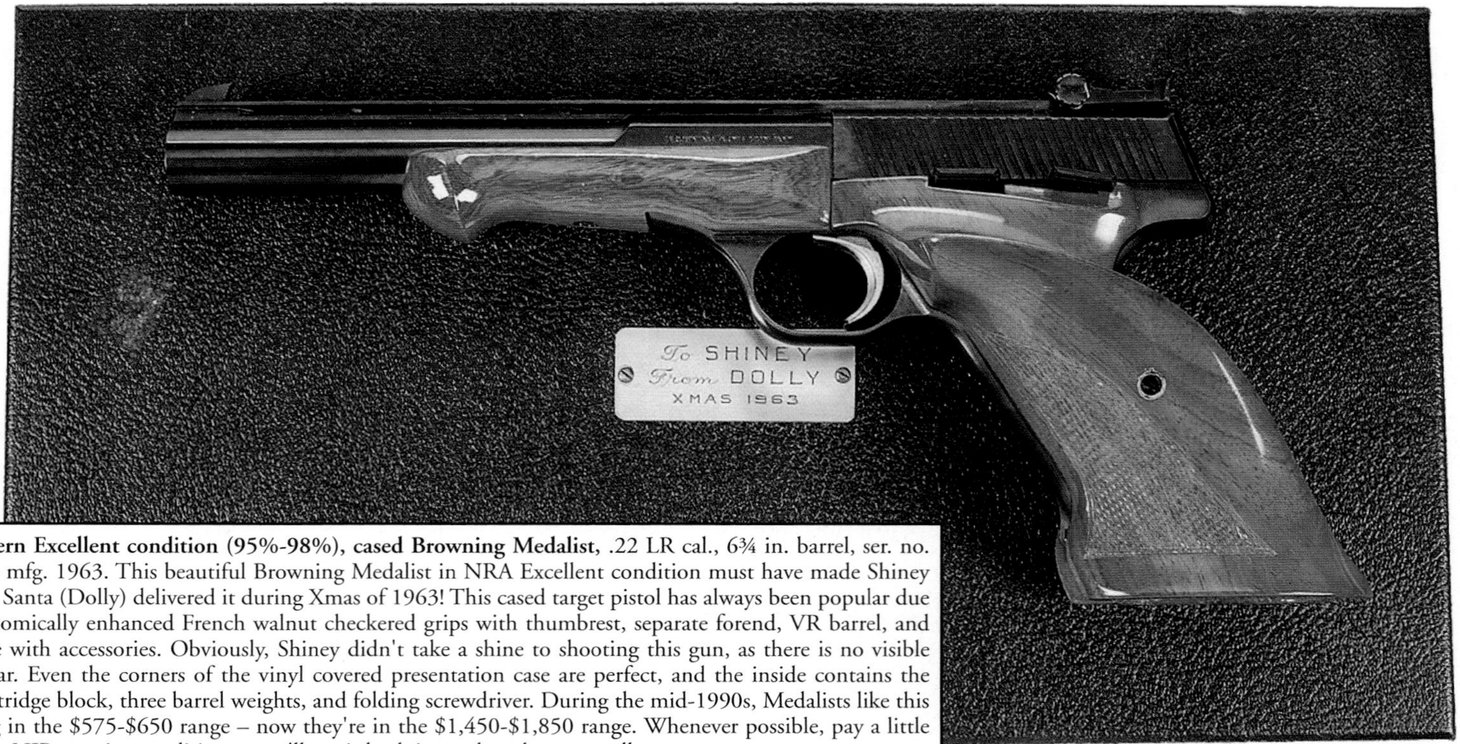

NRA Modern Excellent condition (95%-98%), **cased Browning Medalist**, .22 LR cal., 6¾ in. barrel, ser. no. 30491T3 – mfg. 1963. This beautiful Browning Medalist in NRA Excellent condition must have made Shiney happy after Santa (Dolly) delivered it during Xmas of 1963! This cased target pistol has always been popular due to its ergonomically enhanced French walnut checkered grips with thumbrest, separate forend, VR barrel, and unique case with accessories. Obviously, Shiney didn't take a shine to shooting this gun, as there is no visible exterior wear. Even the corners of the vinyl covered presentation case are perfect, and the inside contains the original cartridge block, three barrel weights, and folding screwdriver. During the mid-1990s, Medalists like this were selling in the $575-$650 range – now they're in the $1,450-$1,850 range. Whenever possible, pay a little bit more for NIB or mint condition – you'll get it back in spades when you sell.

NRA Modern Very Good Refinished condition (80%-95%), Webley & Scott MK I, .455 Webley auto cal., 5 in. barrel, ser. no. 100407 – mfg. 1913. Normally, refinished guns are not pictured in the PPGS, except when they can provide the reader information on condition which can be useful. Notice how the white marker has enhanced a soft, nearly polished off slide legend. This relatively rare, pre-WWI English pistol has been poorly reblued and polished at an earlier date. Note the previous pitting on the frame and barrel, which was poorly polished (observe horizontal slide serrations and rounded corners on slide), then cheaply refinished by hot dipping it into a bluing tank. Rubber grips also show wear, with light cracking, and the action also needs some adjustment. Unfortunately, this pistol's collector value has been virtually ruined, but will provide someone who is not concerned about originality, and is looking for a "buy," with a crude specimen. The problem is, a badly refinished gun like this very rarely goes up in value.

PISTOLS: NRA MODERN CONDITIONS

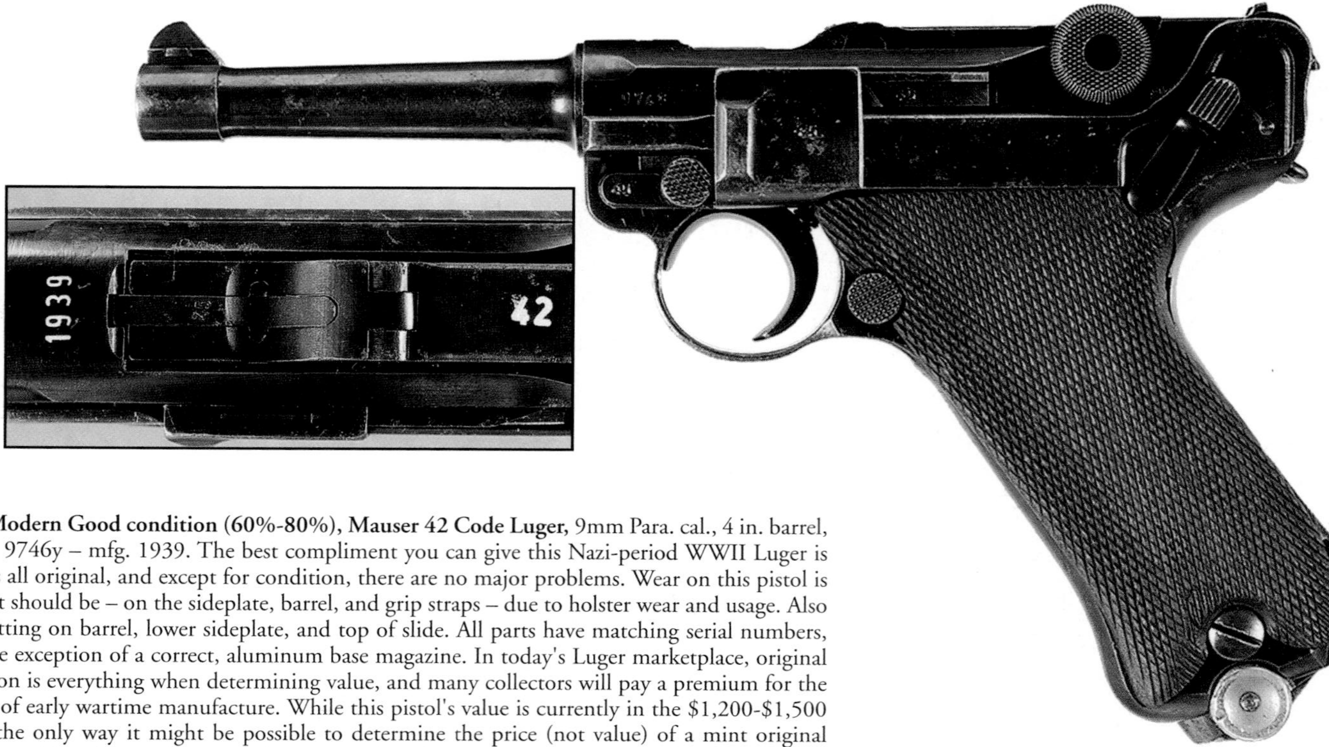

NRA Modern Good condition (60%-80%), Mauser 42 Code Luger, 9mm Para. cal., 4 in. barrel, ser. no. 9746y – mfg. 1939. The best compliment you can give this Nazi-period WWII Luger is that it's all original, and except for condition, there are no major problems. Wear on this pistol is where it should be – on the sideplate, barrel, and grip straps – due to holster wear and usage. Also note pitting on barrel, lower sideplate, and top of slide. All parts have matching serial numbers, with the exception of a correct, aluminum base magazine. In today's Luger marketplace, original condition is everything when determining value, and many collectors will pay a premium for the quality of early wartime manufacture. While this pistol's value is currently in the $1,200-$1,500 range, the only way it might be possible to determine the price (not value) of a mint original specimen with holster and two matching mags. is to buy one in the current auction marketplace.

NRA Modern Fair condition (20%-60%), **CZ Model 27**, 7.65mm cal., 4 ¾ in. barrel, ser. no. 414459 – mfg. circa 1944. Manufactured in late WWII, with not a lot of time left for proper polishing and finishing (note rough horizontal machining marks on slide), this semi-auto pistol originally had a thin phosphate finish, which has turned into a grayish patina overall. Marked with the "WaA76" Waffenampt code on the frame, this Nazi-era pistol could probably tell some interesting stories about its life. Note the plastic grips with the circle CZ logo, indicating manufacture in Czechoslovakia. Observe finish discoloring on trigger and around the trigger guard. In its current condition factor, most collectors would pass on this gun, but this little WWII-era pistol has no major problems, and would still make an inexpensive, decent shooter. When condition lower than this is encountered, it won't make much difference on the price, as it's already bottomed out based on its shooting value.

REVOLVERS: PPGS CONDITION FACTORS

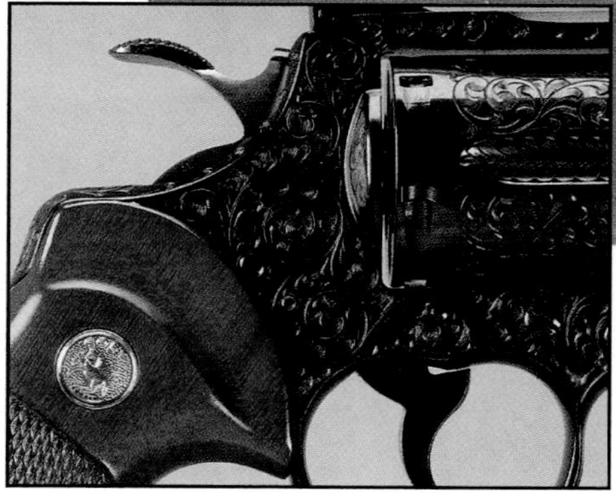

NIB condition, factory engraved Colt Python, .357 Mag. cal., 6 in. vent. rib. barrel, ser. no. 53117E - mfg. 1978. This older, engraved Python letters from Colt's Historical Department, confirming the D standard level factory engraving and blue finish – engraver is not listed. This revolver was shipped to Berns Wholesale Sporting Goods in Denver, CO on Feb. 14, 1978. Most engraved firearms, especially recently manufactured ones, are in 98% or better condition, since their owners seldom, if ever, shoot or use them.

Note scuffed custom shop box, indicating it has seen quite a bit of wear, probably due to either transporting or having been on the bottom of a stack of boxes. One of the best ways to determine a recently manufactured revolver's condition is to look for a vertical drag line between the cylinder lockup notches. Factory engraved major trademarks have always led the pack in terms of investment performance, and this revolver is no exception. When buying or selling upper condition recently manufactured Colt revolvers, it always helps to have a factory letter designating the original configuration when it left the factory.

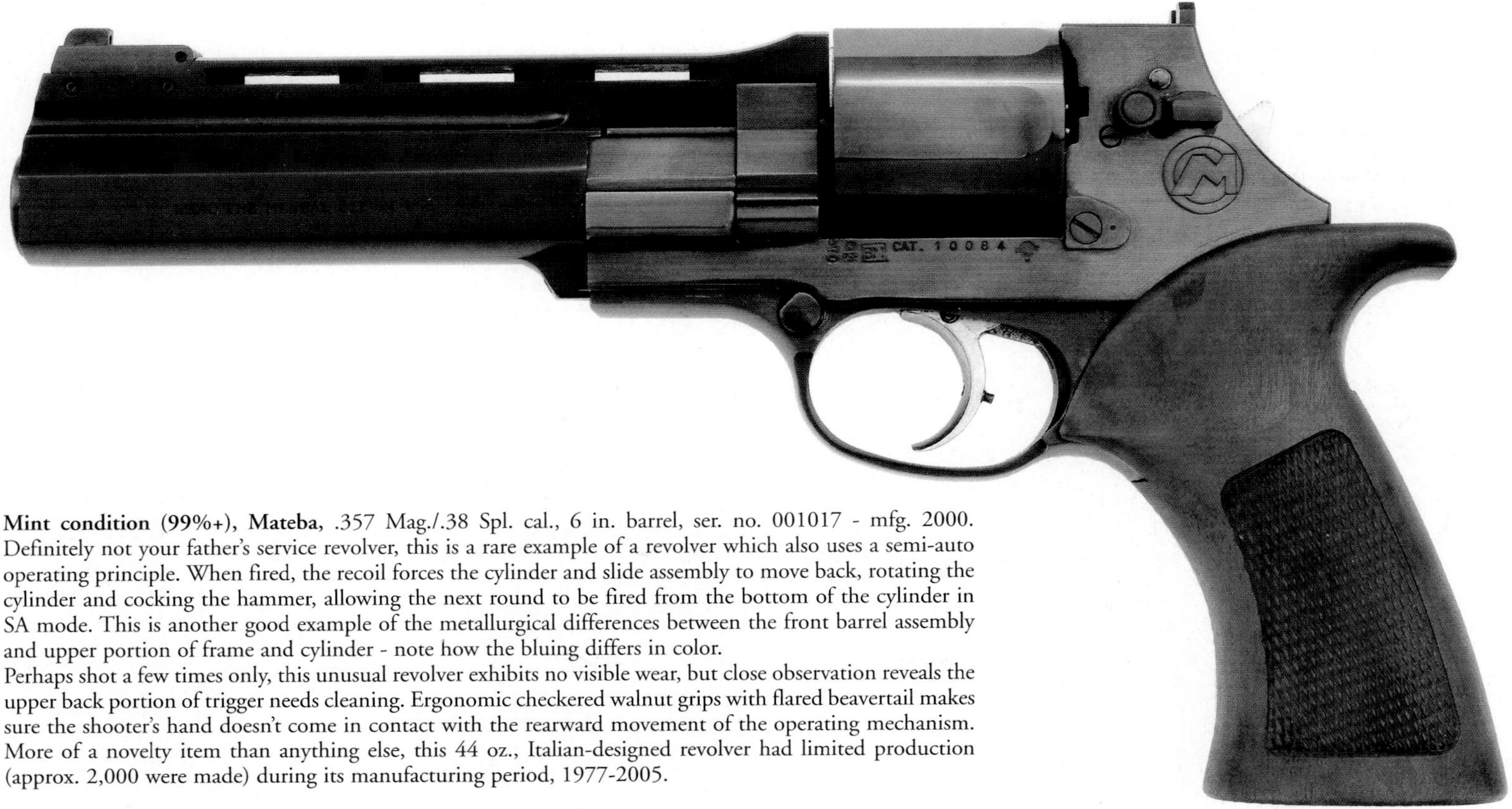

Mint condition (99%+), Mateba, .357 Mag./.38 Spl. cal., 6 in. barrel, ser. no. 001017 - mfg. 2000. Definitely not your father's service revolver, this is a rare example of a revolver which also uses a semi-auto operating principle. When fired, the recoil forces the cylinder and slide assembly to move back, rotating the cylinder and cocking the hammer, allowing the next round to be fired from the bottom of the cylinder in SA mode. This is another good example of the metallurgical differences between the front barrel assembly and upper portion of frame and cylinder - note how the bluing differs in color.

Perhaps shot a few times only, this unusual revolver exhibits no visible wear, but close observation reveals the upper back portion of trigger needs cleaning. Ergonomic checkered walnut grips with flared beavertail makes sure the shooter's hand doesn't come in contact with the rearward movement of the operating mechanism. More of a novelty item than anything else, this 44 oz., Italian-designed revolver had limited production (approx. 2,000 were made) during its manufacturing period, 1977-2005.

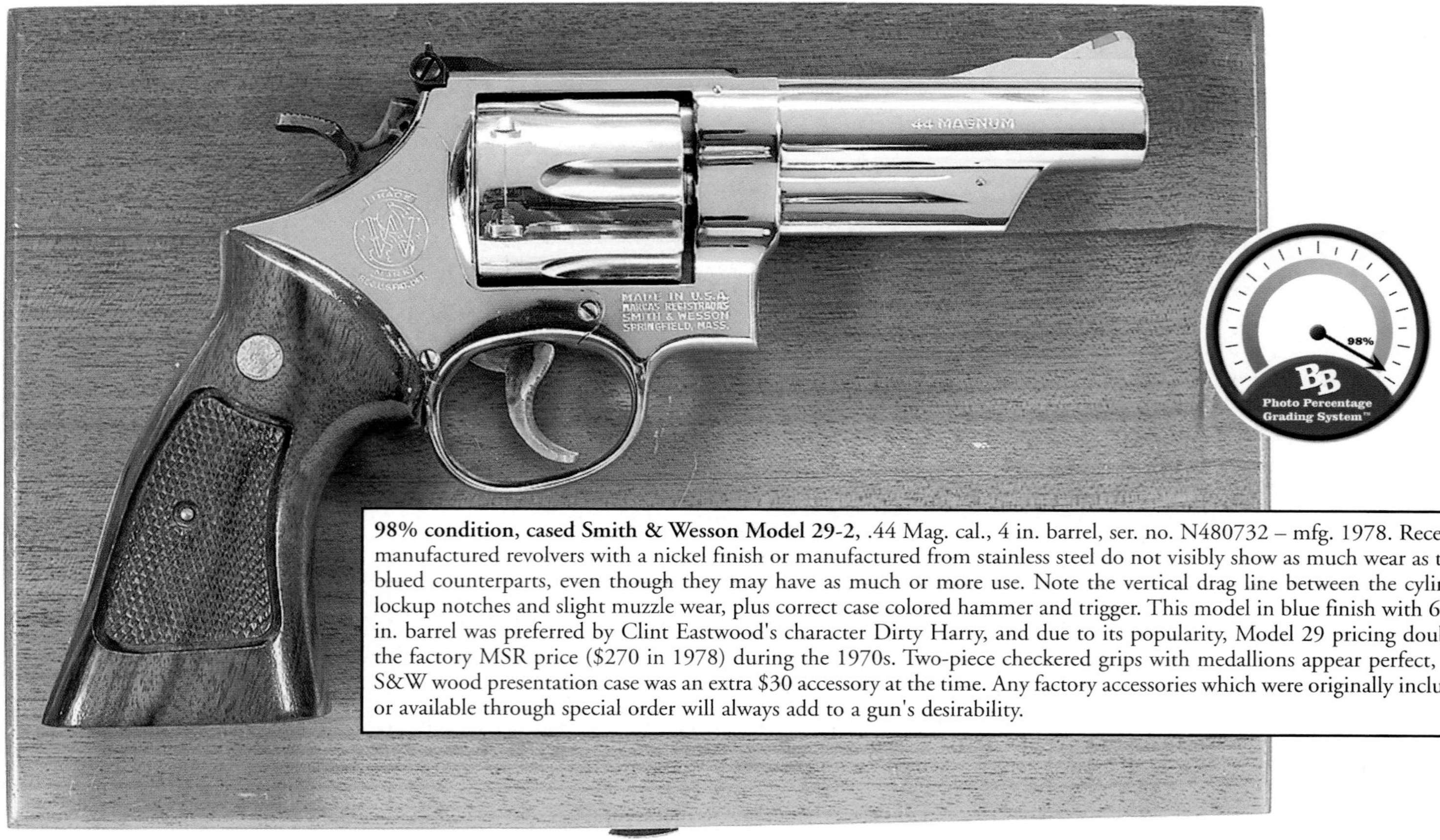

98% condition, cased Smith & Wesson Model 29-2, .44 Mag. cal., 4 in. barrel, ser. no. N480732 – mfg. 1978. Recently manufactured revolvers with a nickel finish or manufactured from stainless steel do not visibly show as much wear as their blued counterparts, even though they may have as much or more use. Note the vertical drag line between the cylinder lockup notches and slight muzzle wear, plus correct case colored hammer and trigger. This model in blue finish with 6 1/2 in. barrel was preferred by Clint Eastwood's character Dirty Harry, and due to its popularity, Model 29 pricing doubled the factory MSR price ($270 in 1978) during the 1970s. Two-piece checkered grips with medallions appear perfect, and S&W wood presentation case was an extra $30 accessory at the time. Any factory accessories which were originally included or available through special order will always add to a gun's desirability.

95% condition, Smith & Wesson Model 34, .22 LR cal., 4 in. barrel, ser. no. 191 – mfg. 1954. 95% on newer mfg. revolvers typically means minor barrel muzzle wear, indicating holster use, and a more noticeable wear line between the cylinder notches. Flat latch cylinder release indicates early mfg., and is worth 25% more than later mfg. Note round butt grip configuration with S&W medallions inset in slightly worn walnut grips with diamond checkering. Careful observation also reveals slight wear on frame and cylinder edges. Bluing is still bright, with several small areas of slight discoloration – case colors on hammer/trigger are near perfect. Whenever a revolver in this condition is encountered, the bore should be near perfect, and the action tight and correctly timed. Overall, a nice example of early S&W quality that can still be used and purchased for a reasonable price.

90% condition, Sturm Ruger Single Six, .22 LR and .22 Mag. cal. cylinders, 6½ in. barrel, ser. no. 260-95611 – mfg. 1985. You might initially think that this gun's condition is actually better than the 95% S&W Model 34. Note that the trigger guard has been chipped and damaged, certainly not indicative of normal wear. Careful observation reveals pitting and metal discoloration on the frame (top and front), hammer, and loading gate (bad), in addition to serious drag marks between the cylinder lock-up notches, which indicates a lot of shooting. Original wood grips also show finish wear and scratching. This revolver is a good example of a 90% condition factor with problems, as opposed to a 90% revolver with normal bluing wear. The areas of pitting, freckling, finish discoloration, etc. need to be measured using the same criteria as regular wear when determining the correct condition, and are actually more detrimental to value than normal wear in the same condition factor. This shooter with problems is worth less than an 80% specimen with ordinary wear, and its only salvation is the original box.

80% condition, Smith & Wesson .455 Hand Ejector 2nd Model with Canadian proof marks, .455 Mark II cal., 6½ in. barrel, ser. no. 54318 - mfg. circa 1916. This gun might have made 90% condition if it wasn't for the barrel wear next to frame. Closer examination reveals an earlier area of small barrel pitting that apparently someone over cleaned to the point where it wore off the bluing around the pitting. Also note some discoloration in the barrel bluing, scratches and nicks on barrel, frame, and cylinder, and four sideplate frame screws. Checkered wooden grips with S&W medallions show some wear, but hammer/trigger case colors are excellent. Note the lanyard ring on the bottom of the grip frame, standard for this model. While unseen in the image, this specimen has both the Commonwealth "BNP" (British Nitro Proof), and Canadian crossed flags, indicating military usage.

REVOLVERS: PPGS CONDITION FACTORS

90

70% condition, Smith & Wesson .38 Military & Police 1st Model (Model 1899 Navy), .38 Military (U.S. Service) cal., 6 in. barrel, ser. no. 5504 – mfg. circa 1900. This specimen is a good example of an older, used revolver in above average condition, even though it has barrel and cylinder discoloration and pitting (brown areas) and worn grips (the diamond pattern around the screw is barely visible). This particular revolver is one of 1,000 that were purchased by the U.S. Navy. Inset photo of bottom of grip frame reveals seven lines of marks, including the U.S. Navy anchor and "CAB" inspector initials. Considering this U.S. Navy Contract model was typically subjected to sea conditions, including salt corrosion, most specimens today are in this condition factor or worse. Even with this much finish wear, however, the action remains very tight, and the bore is still bright with very little corrosion.

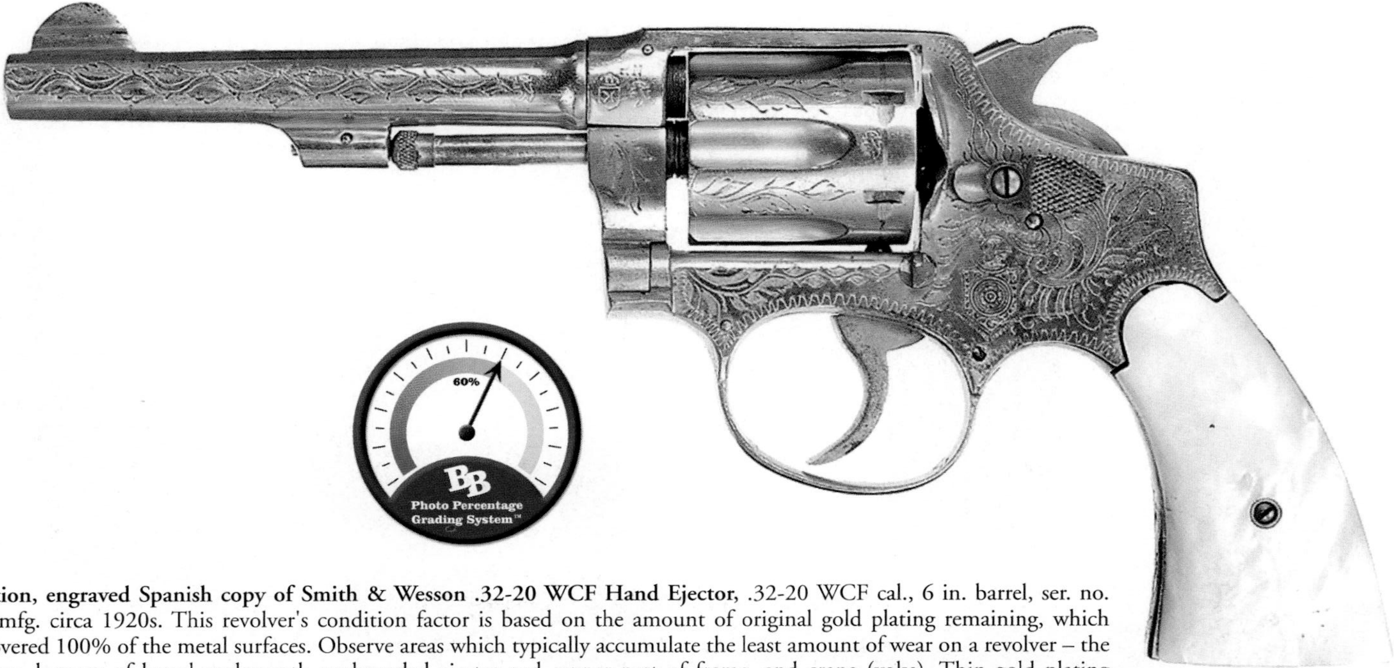

60% condition, engraved Spanish copy of Smith & Wesson .32-20 WCF Hand Ejector, .32-20 WCF cal., 6 in. barrel, ser. no. M12256 – mfg. circa 1920s. This revolver's condition factor is based on the amount of original gold plating remaining, which originally covered 100% of the metal surfaces. Observe areas which typically accumulate the least amount of wear on a revolver – the cylinder flutes, bottom of barrel underneath unshrouded ejector rod, upper part of frame, and crane (yoke). Thin gold plating explains the wear on the barrel and lower frame. Mother-of-pearl grips are probably original, but notice the gap between the arched portion of the grip and the frame. If this was an original factory engraved S&W, someone would care, and pay accordingly, but as a Spanish copy with little or no collectibility, this gun gets priced as a fancy shooter.

50% condition, Smith & Wesson .38 Military & Police 1st Model (Model 1899 Navy), .38 S&W Spl. cal., 6 in. round barrel, ser. no. 5151 - mfg. circa 1900. Compare this slightly more used revolver to the 70% condition Smith & Wesson .38 Military & Police 1st Model. Note that the overall appearance is darker, with the barrel showing more wear, and the rear frame scratching and pitting is very obvious. Even though the barrel, cylinder, and frame metal condition is less than the 60% condition engraved Spanish copy of Smith & Wesson, the case colors on the hammer and trigger are actually better on this revolver. Again, note the inset with USN and anchor markings. The checkered grips are also in worse condition. Nice, straight slots on frame screw heads on this and the 70% condition Smith & Wesson .38 Military & Police 1st Model indicate that these revolvers have probably never been taken apart. Older original revolvers in this condition factor or less typically show more pitting and bluing discoloration.

40% condition, Smith & Wesson .38 Military & Police 1st Model (Model 1899 Navy), .38 S&W Spl. cal., 6 in. barrel, ser. no. 5043 – mfg. circa 1900. This Model 1899 Navy would be at least 70% overall, if it wasn't for the major finish deterioration on the rear of the frame – note the brown patina and pitting in back of the S&W logo. Nicks and gouges on the barrel, frame, and cylinder are also typical of this condition factor. The ejector rod has also turned a brown patina. As you can see, each gun is unique once you get down to these lower condition factors, and each revolver component (barrel, frame, cylinder, grips, case colors, trigger/hammer) has to be taken into consideration before the overall condition factor can be accurately established. In cases where finish wear is excessive on a single part, it is usually prudent to mention/describe that lower condition factor/problem separately.

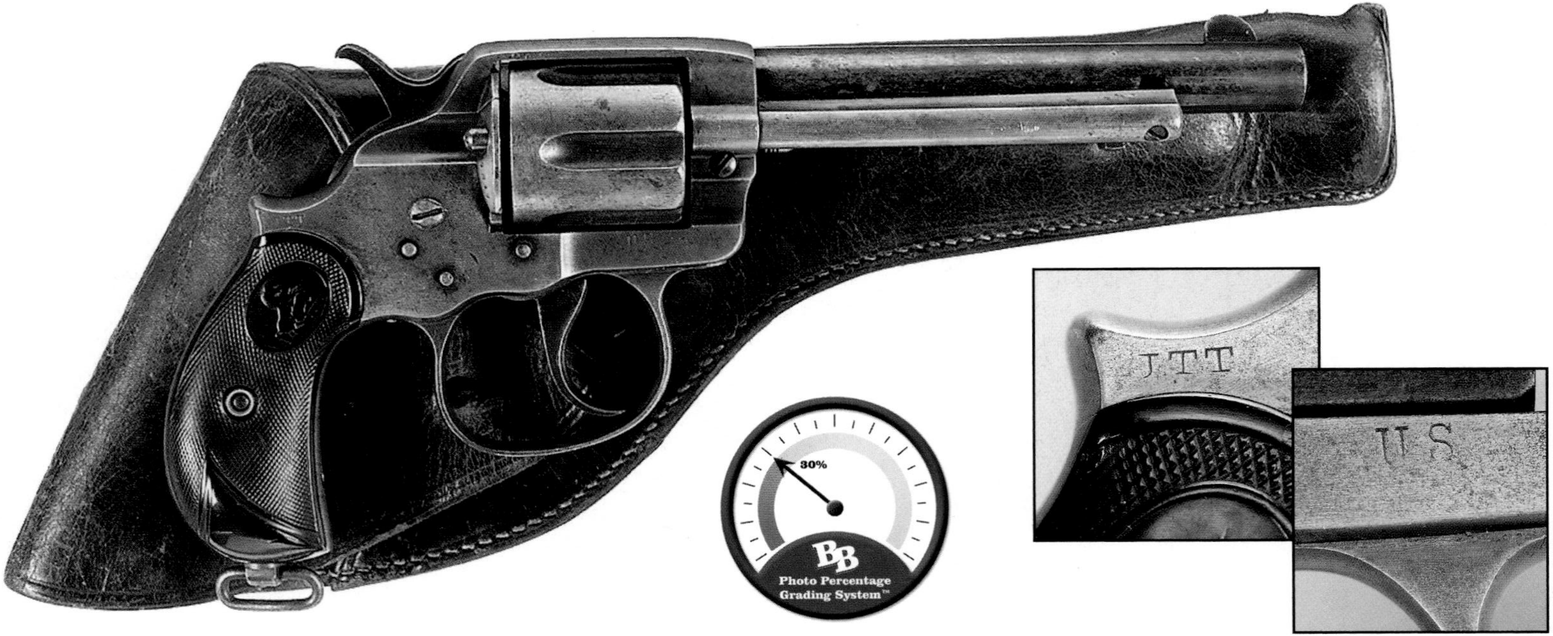

30% condition, U.S. Colt Alaskan Model 1878/1902, .45 LC cal., 6 in. round barrel, ser. no. 45317 – mfg. 1900. Notice how the overall condition of this revolver is approximately in 10% less condition than the 40% condition S&W Military & Police 1st Model. This military marked specimen, which includes "RAC" on left side and "JTT" (John T. Thompson, of Thompson sub-machine gun fame) inspector initials on right side, also has a U.S. property marking. Observe the smooth, overall brownish patina finish, while the barrel exhibits overall pitting, even though the bore is excellent. Note traces of bright barrel blue next to and in front of ejector rod assembly. Screw heads look original, and grips with rampant Colt inserts are worn proportionately with the rest of this gun's finish. Oversize trigger and trigger guard, in addition to the lanyard ring, are distinguishing features of this U.S. military contract model, allowing soldiers to fire it with mittened or gloved hands.

20% condition, Colt Model 1901 New Army & Navy, .38 LC cal., 6 in. barrel, ser. no. 2822 - mfg. 1892. Compare the overall finish on this revolver to the 30% condition U.S. Colt Alaskan Model 1878/1902. This gun's finish has turned mostly brown patina, with the only bright bluing remaining in protected areas (cylinder flutes and front of frame). Note the rust inside of cylinder flutes and upper front portion of frame. Closer examination reveals that frame screws have been amateurishly removed. "RAC" marked grips show moderate wear, but are original and free of major dings and cracks. This revolver's value is enhanced somewhat because it still has a very tight action and bright bore, which is very important to collectors of older revolvers. Many handgun collectors would rather have a no-problem gun in this condition than one in 50% condition, but with major pitting, a dark bore, and other problems. The original holster and belt accompany this well-worn specimen.

REVOLVERS: PPGS CONDITION FACTORS

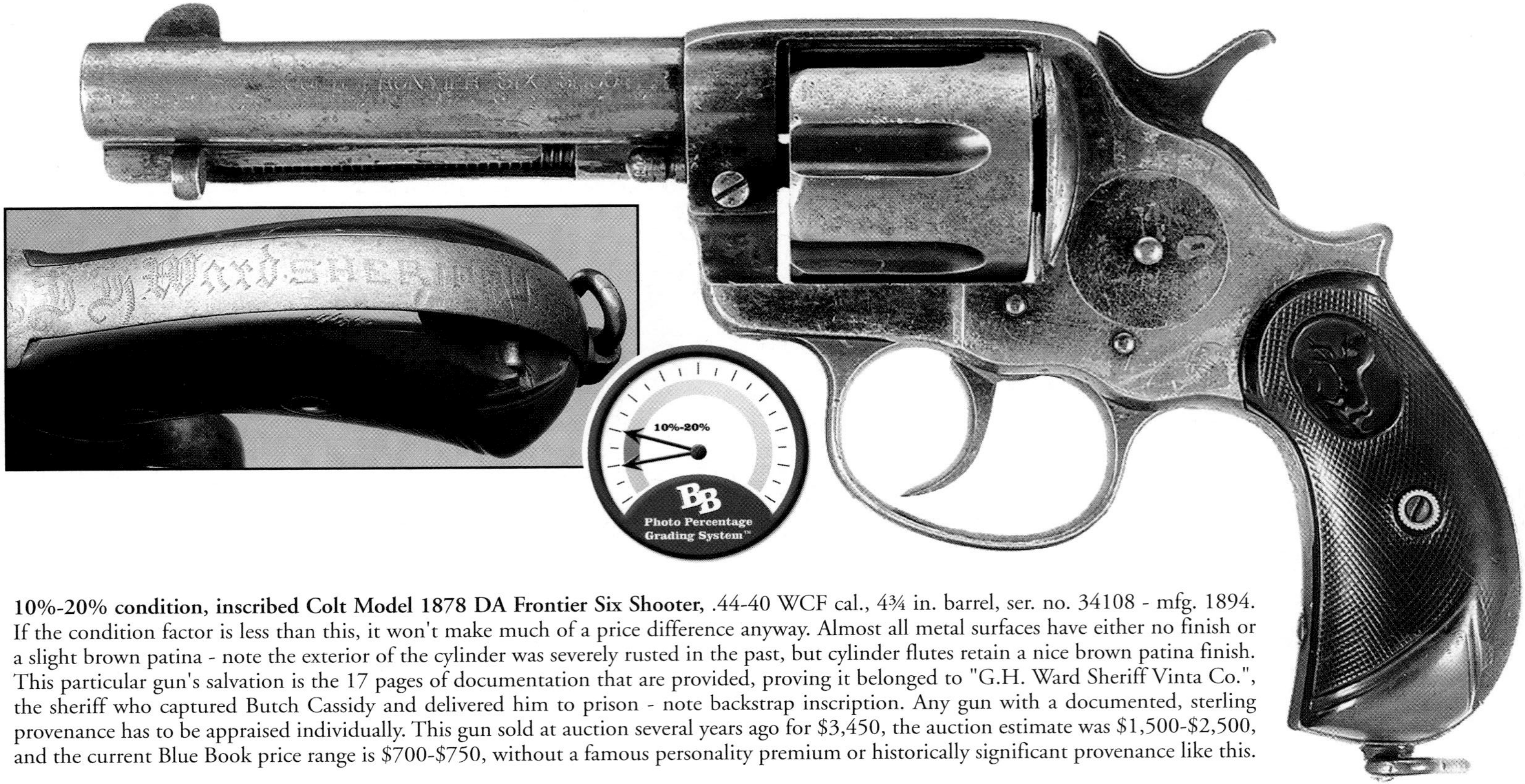

10%-20% condition, inscribed Colt Model 1878 DA Frontier Six Shooter, .44-40 WCF cal., 4¾ in. barrel, ser. no. 34108 - mfg. 1894. If the condition factor is less than this, it won't make much of a price difference anyway. Almost all metal surfaces have either no finish or a slight brown patina - note the exterior of the cylinder was severely rusted in the past, but cylinder flutes retain a nice brown patina finish. This particular gun's salvation is the 17 pages of documentation that are provided, proving it belonged to "G.H. Ward Sheriff Vinta Co.", the sheriff who captured Butch Cassidy and delivered him to prison - note backstrap inscription. Any gun with a documented, sterling provenance has to be appraised individually. This gun sold at auction several years ago for $3,450, the auction estimate was $1,500-$2,500, and the current Blue Book price range is $700-$750, without a famous personality premium or historically significant provenance like this.

NRA Excellent (**over 80% condition**), **inscribed Colt Model 1851 Navy Fourth Model**, .36 cal. percussion, 7½ in. octagon barrel, ser. no. 127080/2 – mfg. 1862. This commercial Colt 1851 Navy was manufactured during the Civil War (1861-1865), and has the late New York barrel address. The frame, barrel, trigger guard, and backstrap all have matching 127080/2 serial numbers, indicating this gun was one of a two-gun presentation set. The backstrap is inscribed "To Major Hill, 45th Reg't OVI" (Ohio Volunteer Infantry). Also verifying this revolver's authenticity is a tintype (older photograph) of Major Hill, his saber and Colt 1851 Navy (not shown). Note the barrel and loading lever retain most of the original finish, strong frame case colors, fire blued untampered frame screws, and excellent original wood grips, all adding up to the NRA Excellent condition factor this revolver deserves. Blue Book value without provenance – approx. $5,000-$7,500.

NRA Fine (30%-80% condition), Remington New Model Army, .44 cal. percussion, 8 in. octagon barrel, ser. no. 19329 – mfg. circa 1866. Overall, a nice, no problem Remington revolver retaining approx. 40%-50% original finish. Octagon barrel retains much of its bright bluing on the flats, while edges are shiny. Most of the frame and unfluted cylinder have turned a nice brown patina, while two-piece grips show normal handling marks with tiny chips. Action remains tight, and this revolver does not have the "New Model" markings used in later manufacture. While some of these guns were converted into .44 rimfire, this specimen retains its original percussion configuration. Also note the brass trigger guard and excellent condition of the screw heads. Since NRA Fine condition covers everything from 30%-80%, this revolver represents the middle of the NRA Fine condition range. Guns in better condition than this generally retain more bright blue, while guns in worse condition will have more patina.

NRA Very Good (0%-30% condition), U.S. Colt SAA Cavalry Model 1873, .45 Colt cal., ser. no. 17579 - mfg. 1875. Except for protected areas, this gun's original blue and case colored finishes have turned a smooth grayish-brown patina. One-piece walnut grips are fine with only minor scratches, and matching serial numbers are on all visible components. Note how serial numbers are marked on the frame and trigger guard in the macro image. On 1st Generation SAAs, it always pays to inspect the numbers very carefully since they were stamped with a rotating roll die. Not only should all the serial numbers match and look the same, but each digit should also retain the same vertical/horizontal positioning in all three areas. The other macro image of "U.S." property stamp marking becomes very important, since revolvers in this serial range were probably issued as replacements to the 7th Cavalry after the Battle of Little Big Horn.

NRA Good (0%-20% condition), Colt Model 1849 Pocket, .31 cal. percussion, 6 in. octagon barrel, ser. no. 181985 - mfg. 1860. Note how the finish on this revolver (10%-20%) has turned an overall plum patina, as opposed to the bright bluing and case colors remaining on the NRA Excellent 1851 Navy. Dark areas on barrel and frame indicate major areas of earlier pitting. Brass trigger guard and frame, originally silver plated, indicate that this revolver is a first type, as the second type has steel grip straps. The cylinder has been filed and renumbered to match the overall serial number, while the grips have been revarnished over the dents and scratches. Screws look good, and this gun's overall condition suggests that it was never abused during its shooting career. This revolver's operating mechanism still functions smoothly, even though the bore is somewhat dark and lightly pitted.

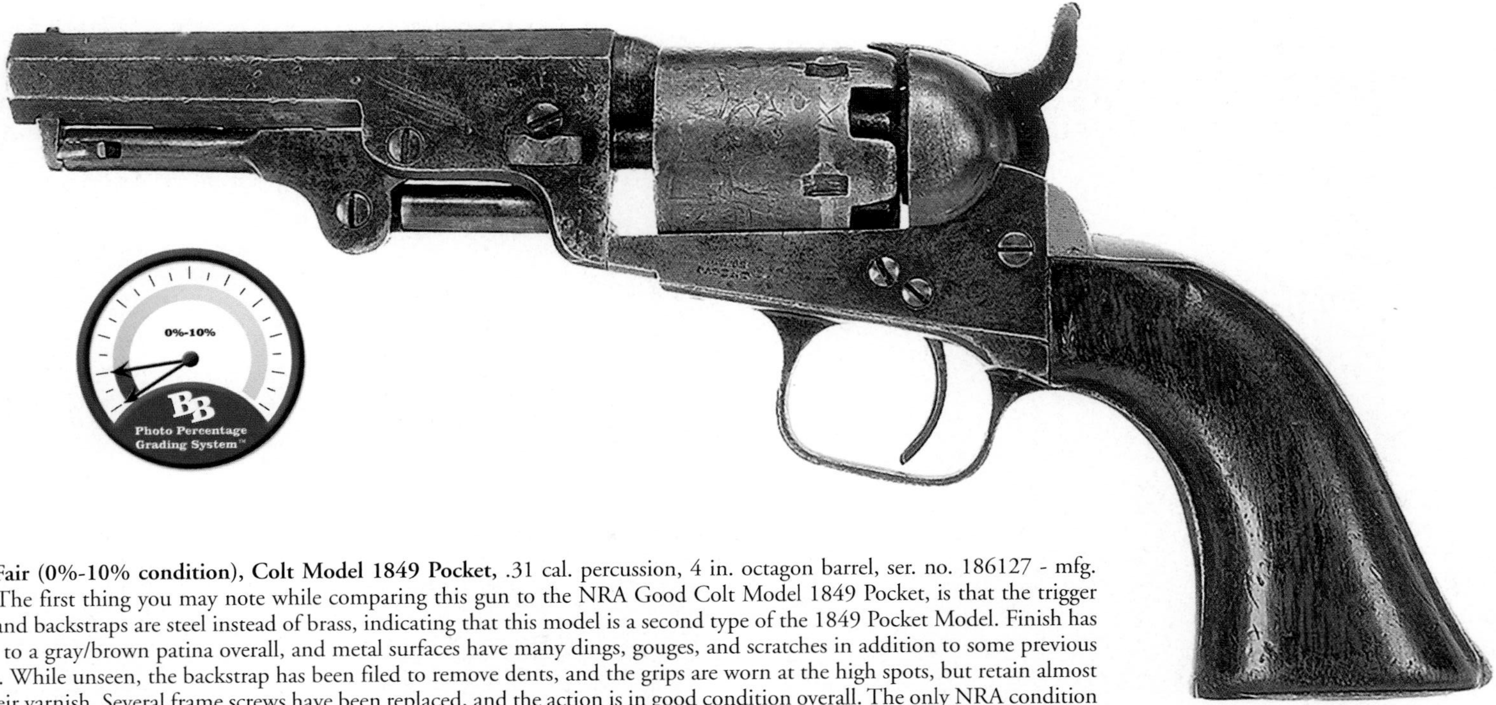

NRA Fair (0%-10% condition), Colt Model 1849 Pocket, .31 cal. percussion, 4 in. octagon barrel, ser. no. 186127 - mfg. 1861. The first thing you may note while comparing this gun to the NRA Good Colt Model 1849 Pocket, is that the trigger guard and backstraps are steel instead of brass, indicating that this model is a second type of the 1849 Pocket Model. Finish has turned to a gray/brown patina overall, and metal surfaces have many dings, gouges, and scratches in addition to some previous pitting. While unseen, the backstrap has been filed to remove dents, and the grips are worn at the high spots, but retain almost half their varnish. Several frame screws have been replaced, and the action is in good condition overall. The only NRA condition factor worse than this is Poor (not pictured), which means that both major and minor parts have been replaced, metal surfaces are deeply pitted, the mechanism is inoperative, and generally the gun is undesirable as a collector's firearm.

APRIL S

			1	2	3
5	6	7	8	9	10
12	13	14	15	16	17
19	20	21	22	23	24
26	27	28	29	30	

MAY

S						S
						1
2	3	4	5	6	7	8
9	10	11	12	13	14	15
16	17	18	19	20	21	22
23	24	25	26	27	28	29
30	31					

JUNE

S						S
		1	2	3	4	5
6	7	8	9	10	11	12
13	14	15	16	17	18	19
20	21	22	23	24	25	26
27	28	29	30			

JULY S

			1	2	3
5	6	7	8	9	10
12	13	14	15	16	17
19	20	21	22	23	24
26	27	28	29	30	31

AUGUST

S						S
1	2	3	4	5	6	7
8	9	10	11	12	13	14
15	16	17	18	19	20	21
22	23	24	25	26	27	28
29	30	31				

SEPTEMBER

S						S
			1	2	3	4
5	6	7	8	9	10	11
12	13	14	15	16	17	18
19	20	21	22	23	24	25
26	27	28	29	30		

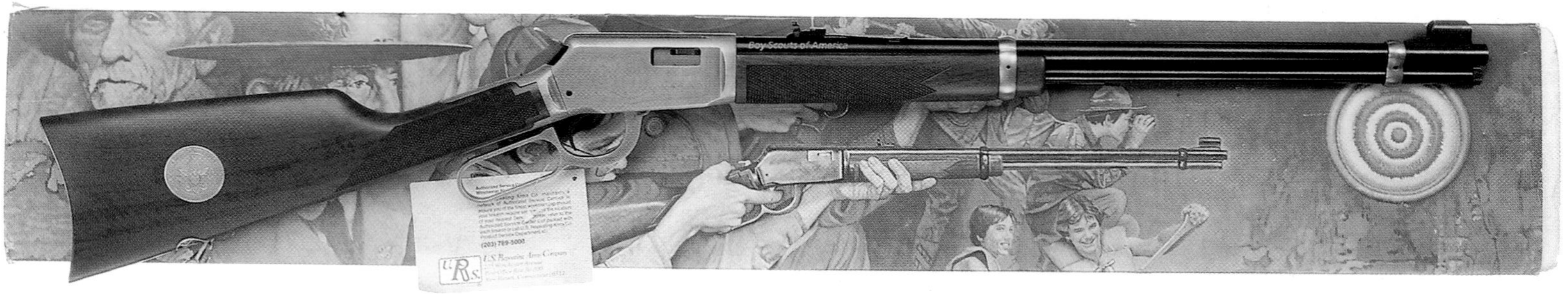

NIB condition, Winchester Model 9422 Boy Scouts of America Commemorative, .22 LR cal., 20 in. round barrel, ser. no. BSA3002 - mfg. 1985. With commemoratives, it is very important to have the box(es), paperwork (including warranty card), and any other accessories/accoutrements that came with the gun when it left the factory. Since most commemoratives are never used or shot, proper storage is the key to keeping them truly NIB - this becomes especially important on silver, gold, or bright nickel finishes, since they have a tendency to naturally tarnish. Commemoratives and limited editions that have been shot and don't have the original box or paperwork are nothing more than fancy shooters most of the time and are priced accordingly with little or no premium.

Because the commemorative consumer is now more in charge (consumers now own most of the guns since distributor/dealer inventories are depleted) than during the 1960s-1980s, commemorative firearms values are possibly as strong as they have ever been. When the supply side of commemorative economics has to be purchased from knowledgeable collectors or savvy dealers and demand stays the same or increases slightly, prices have no choice but to go up. If and when the manufacturers crank up the commemorative production runs again (and it won't be like the good old days), the old marketplace characteristics may reappear. Until then, however, the commemorative marketplace remains steady, with values having become more predictable.

Manufacturers today are focusing their efforts more on special/limited editions rather than factory commemoratives, as these variations are typically subcontracted by other companies and organizations, which means the manufacturers get paid faster without the extra expense of advertising and marketing. Two versions of this model, the Boy Scout (15,000 mfg. - original issue price was $495) and the Eagle Scout (1,000 mfg. - original issue price was $1,710), were manufactured to commemorate the Boy Scouts 75th Anniversary in 1985. Some well-heeled Eagle Scouts at the time paid as much as $5,000 to get an Eagle Scout model! In today's marketplace, a NIB Boy Scout model is valued at $1,350, while the Eagle Scout is $5,500, almost triple its original 1985 MSR!

Mint condition, Russian SKS, 7.62x39mm Russian cal., 20 in. barrel, ser. no. Hh1244 (Cyrillic lettering) – mfg. date unknown. The SKS semi-auto rifle was adopted by the Soviet military in 1949, two years after the select-fire AK-47. Most of the recently imported Russian SKSs came from military stockpiles, and were refurbished at Tula Arms Works. Today, the most collectible SKS models are East German, North Korean, or North Vietnam manufacture. This particular Russian manufactured configuration with brown laminated stock, non-detachable pivoting blade bayonet, and canvas sling became very popular before the Crime Bill was enacted in September of 1994. During this time period, Chinese imports starting flooding the marketplace, reducing the prices of all SKS rifles, despite the fact that the more recent Chinese imports are typically of poor quality with thumbhole stocks. Although millions of SKSs have been imported over the years, NIB examples like this Russian manufactured specimen are actually getting harder to find and prices have gone up. Less than five years ago, it was possible to go to almost any gun show and find an SKS in this condition factor for around $175. Not anymore – currently they are at around $500.

RIFLES: PPGS CONDITION FACTORS

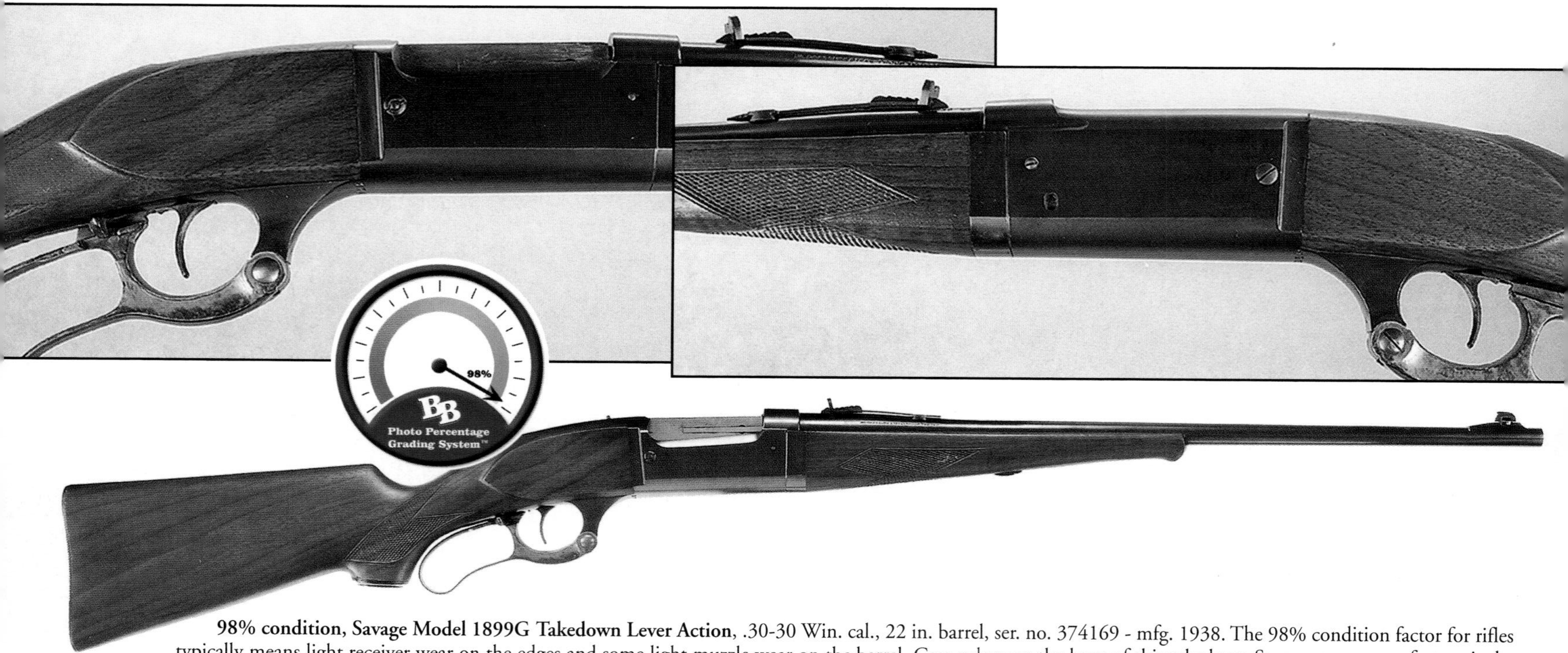

98% condition, Savage Model 1899G Takedown Lever Action, .30-30 Win. cal., 22 in. barrel, ser. no. 374169 - mfg. 1938. The 98% condition factor for rifles typically means light receiver wear on the edges and some light muzzle wear on the barrel. Case colors on the lever of this takedown Savage are near perfect, as is the original stock and forearm finish.

While this gun may have been used only infrequently, it always pays to check the front of the bolt face for noticeable amounts of primer ring impression – always a sign that the gun has been shot more than you think. Corrugated steel buttplate shows no wear, and checkering pattern indicates that it's a Model 1899G, manufactured from 1922-1941. A gun in this original 98% condition factor can still be used for hunting, without deteriorating its condition – with a little caution in the field, and proper maintenance.

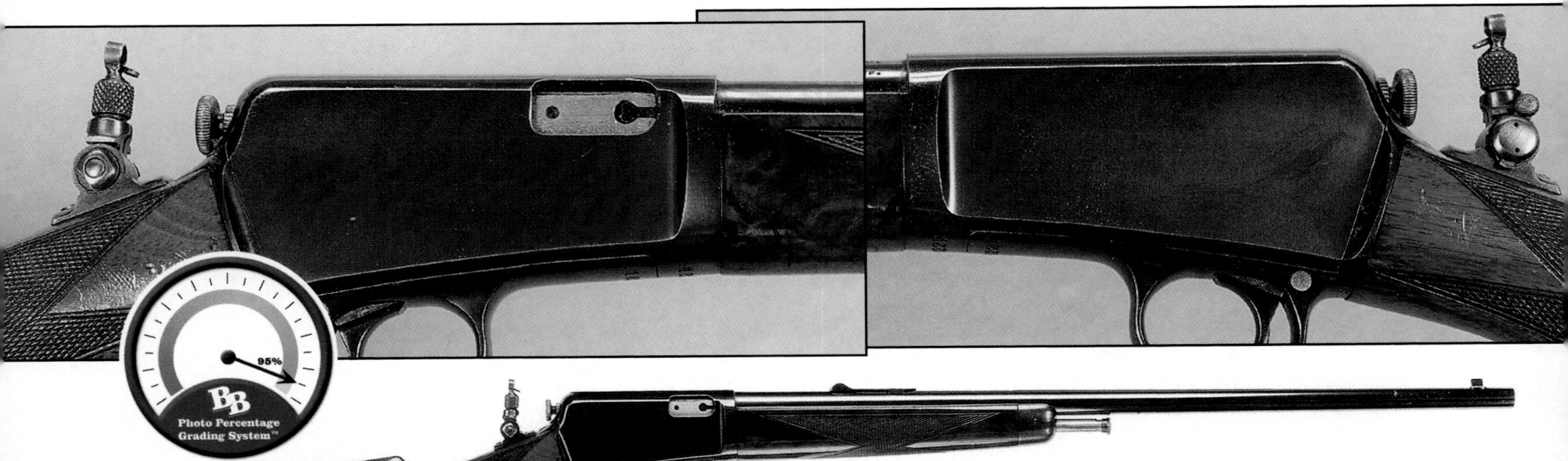

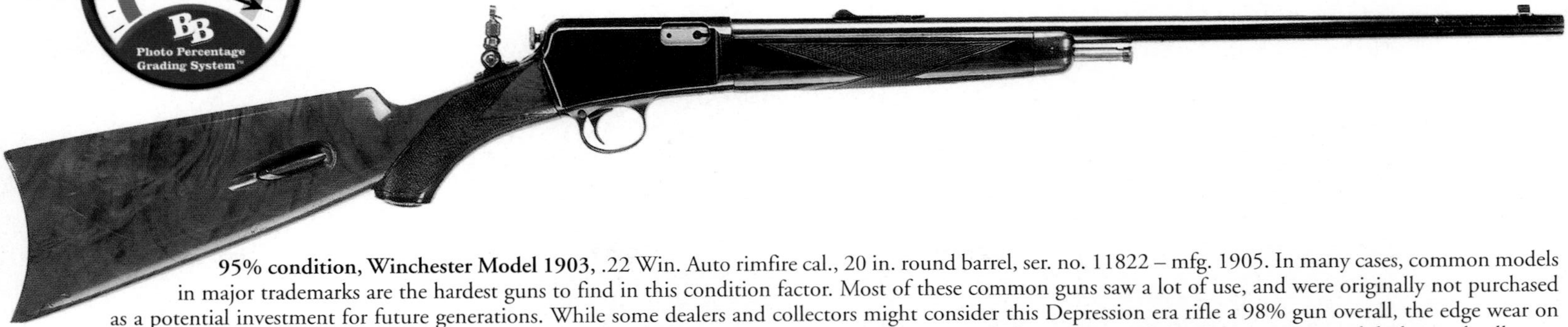

95% condition, Winchester Model 1903, .22 Win. Auto rimfire cal., 20 in. round barrel, ser. no. 11822 – mfg. 1905. In many cases, common models in major trademarks are the hardest guns to find in this condition factor. Most of these common guns saw a lot of use, and were originally not purchased as a potential investment for future generations. While some dealers and collectors might consider this Depression era rifle a 98% gun overall, the edge wear on the sharp corners of both sides of the receiver, in addition to the scratches on right side of stock, lower this rifle to 95% condition. Most experienced dealers and collectors have learned that when buying, selling, or trading, it's better to under evaluate a condition factor rather than overestimate. Deluxe checkered stock and forearm with most of the original varnish is always a big plus for Winchester collectors, especially when the condition is this good.

RIFLES: PPGS CONDITION FACTORS

108

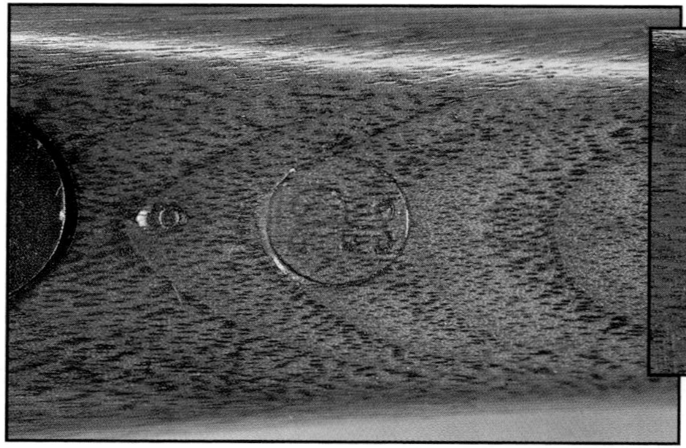

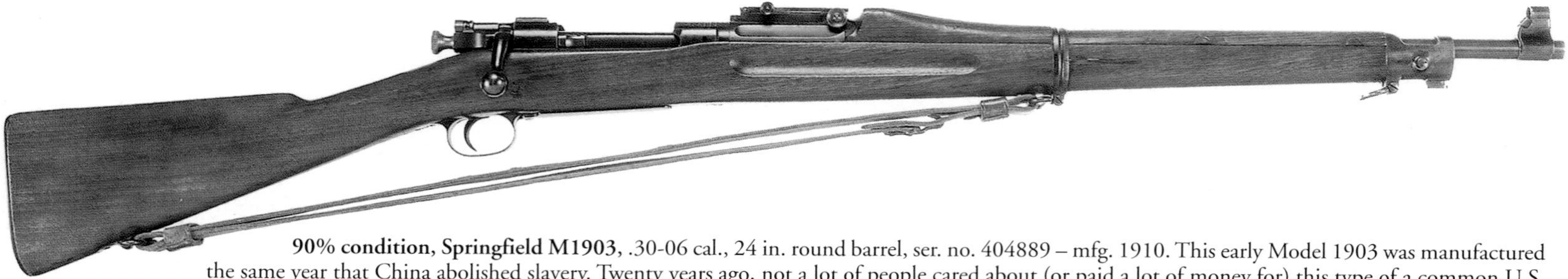

90% condition, Springfield M1903, .30-06 cal., 24 in. round barrel, ser. no. 404889 – mfg. 1910. This early Model 1903 was manufactured the same year that China abolished slavery. Twenty years ago, not a lot of people cared about (or paid a lot of money for) this type of a common U.S. military rifle – that's not the case today. Note the blue and color case hardened metal finishes. It has nice original wood with no problems and "J.F.C." final inspector mark (for J.F. Coyle) in block letters inside rectangle in addition to script "P" in circle proof stamped on underside stock wrist. More than anything else, originality is the key when determining value on this type of 20th century U.S. military rifle – knowing what to look for in proofs/markings, how the original markings appear, and where to find them are absolutely critical when evaluating this rifle's value. Sling is an early RIA (Rock Island Arsenal) 1904 pattern.

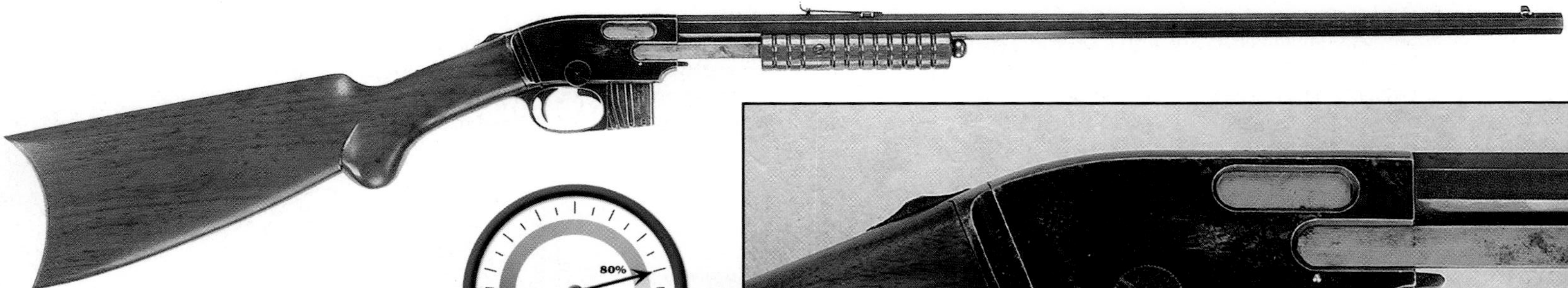

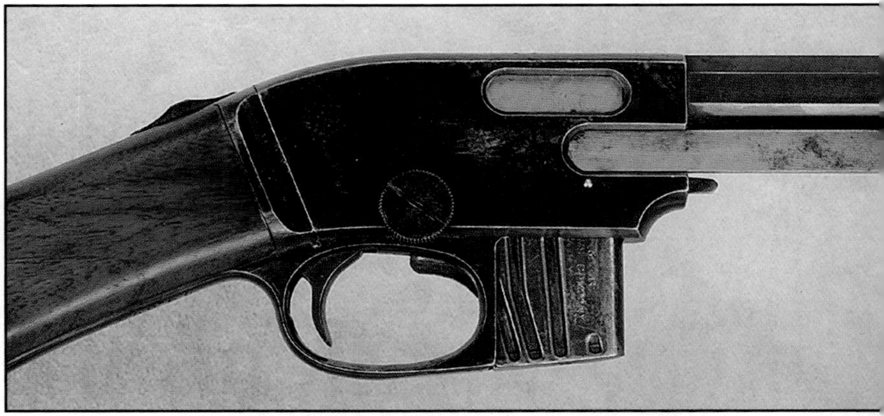

80% condition, Savage Model 1903 slide action, .22 S-L-LR cal., .22 S-L-LR cal., 24 in. octagon barrel, ser. no. 79070 - mfg. circa 1907. On most early 20th century .22 cal. slide action rifles such as this one, which were inexpensively priced when new (typically $10-$15), the hardest thing to find now is superior original condition. Even at 80%, this rifle is probably still in better condition than the vast majority of original slide actions available at the time. Note wear on edges of frame that still retains most of its bright bluing, and small areas of scattered rust on the shiny slide rail and frame. The 7-shot detachable magazine, with vertical indentations located in front of the trigger guard, has also faded and turned a light plum color - consistent with the rest of this gun's overall wear. Barrel bluing also shows light fading and perhaps some over aggressive cleaning. Uncheckered rounded pistol stock with crescent buttplate and eleven groove forearm retain most of the original varnish. If this rifle was in 95% condition, the value would double, and it would be easier to sell.

RIFLES: PPGS CONDITION FACTORS

110

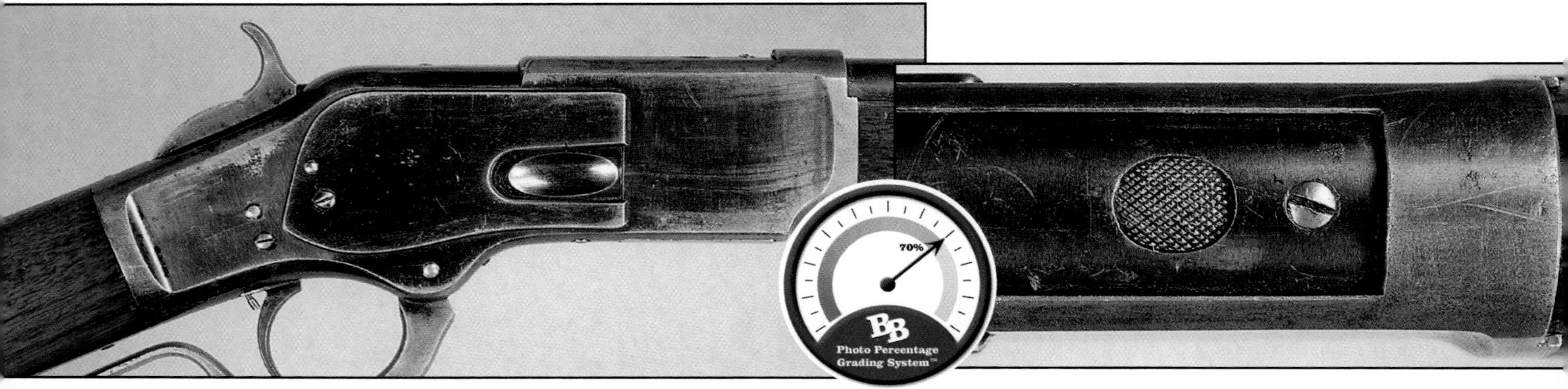

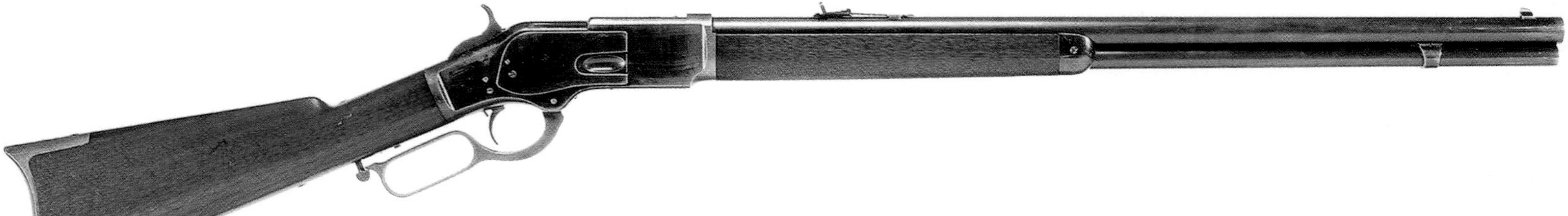

70% condition, Winchester 1873 1st Model Lever Action, .44-40 WCF cal., 24 in. round barrel, ser. no. 6395 - mfg. 1875. Over 140 years old, this 1st Model 1873 (note the thumbprint checkering on upper receiver dust cover) is very rare and desirable in this condition factor. Round barrel and mag. tube show little wear and retain 80%+ original bright blue, while the receiver and sideplate are still bright blue, but show wear next to the front and back edges. Uncheckered walnut straight grip stock and forearm still have most of the original varnish with little wood staining, but with normal dents and scratches. Case colors have mostly faded on the lever, but are still strong on the hammer. A factory letter from the Cody Firearms Museum verifies this rifle's configuration with round barrel and set trigger, and indicates that it was received in the Winchester warehouse on Sept. 1, 1875, and shipped the same day.

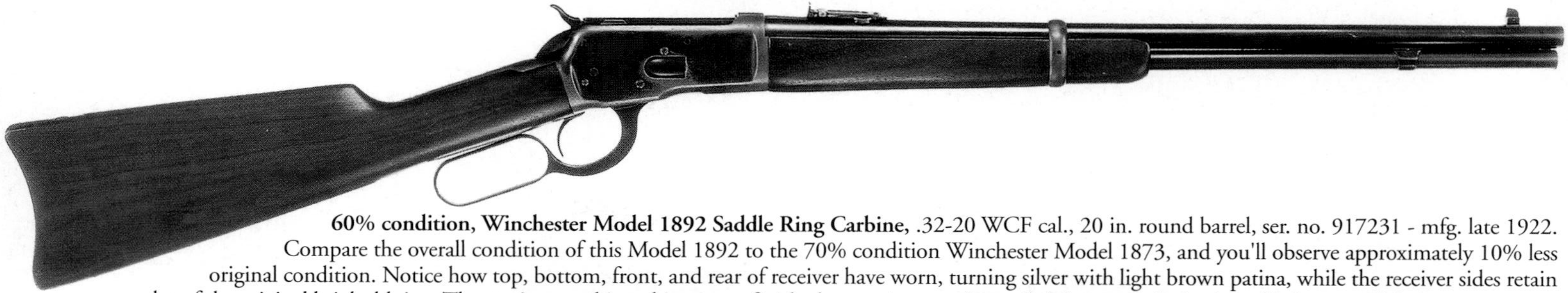

60% condition, Winchester Model 1892 Saddle Ring Carbine, .32-20 WCF cal., 20 in. round barrel, ser. no. 917231 - mfg. late 1922. Compare the overall condition of this Model 1892 to the 70% condition Winchester Model 1873, and you'll observe approximately 10% less original condition. Notice how top, bottom, front, and rear of receiver have worn, turning silver with light brown patina, while the receiver sides retain a lot of the original bright bluing. The receiver on this carbine was refinished some time ago (note slightly rounded edges), and helps to explain its current wear pattern. Saddle ring imprint on rear left side of receiver is normal, and barrel band has turned mostly gray. Uncheckered straight grip walnut stock shows signs of light cleaning, but is still flush with metal. Action remains mechanically perfect, and its overall good eye appeal help elevate its value to above that of a poor reblue.

RIFLES: PPGS CONDITION FACTORS

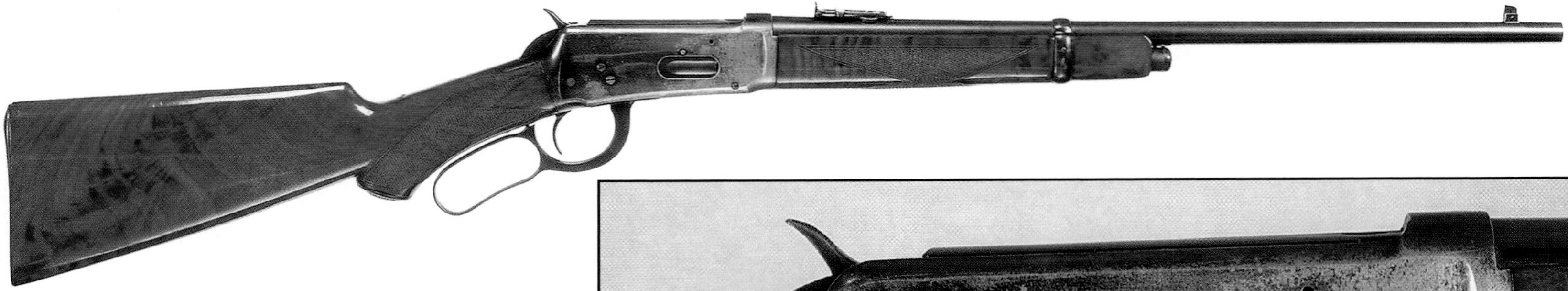

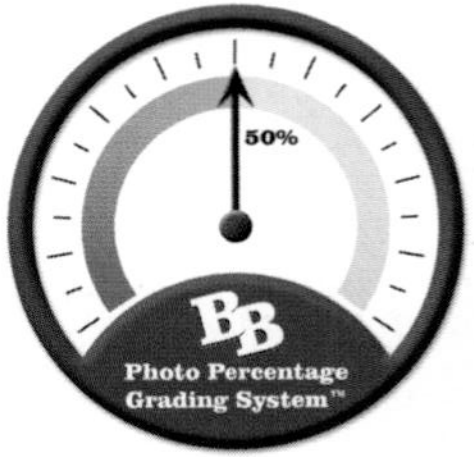

50% condition, Winchester Model 1894 Deluxe Saddle Ring Carbine, .30-30 Win. cal., 20 in. round barrel, ser. no. 582407 – mfg. 1911. Even in this condition factor, this Model 1894 deluxe saddle ring carbine is very desirable, with auction pricing now controlling the final premium paid on most major trademark firearms! Nickel steel barrel with ladder type rear sight and half magazine still has 95%+ original bluing, while the receiver has had much of its bluing flake off. Do not confuse receiver flaking with normal wear and usage – some Winchester lever action rifles can be almost unfired, but show similar frame wear as this specimen. Flaking occurred because the bluing did not adhere properly on guns with a high nickel content in the steel. Deluxe checkered walnut stock with steel shotgun buttplate may have been resprayed at a later date, but the varnish is in excellent condition, and matches the condition of the forearm.

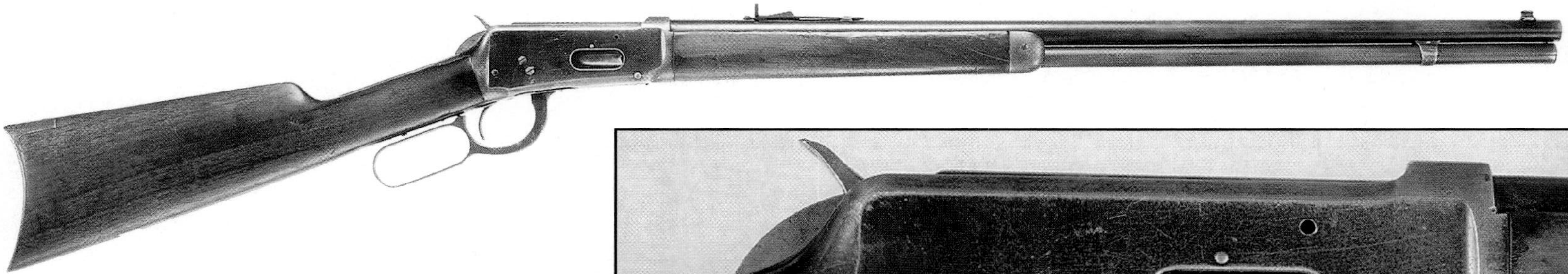

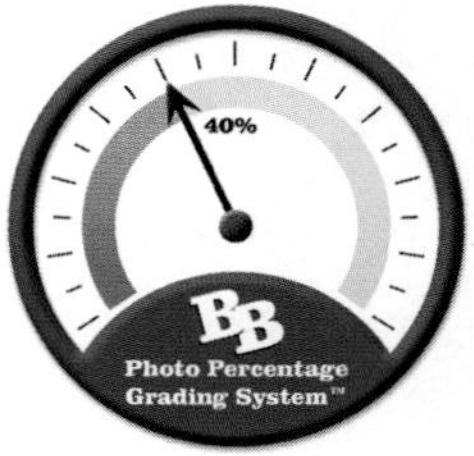

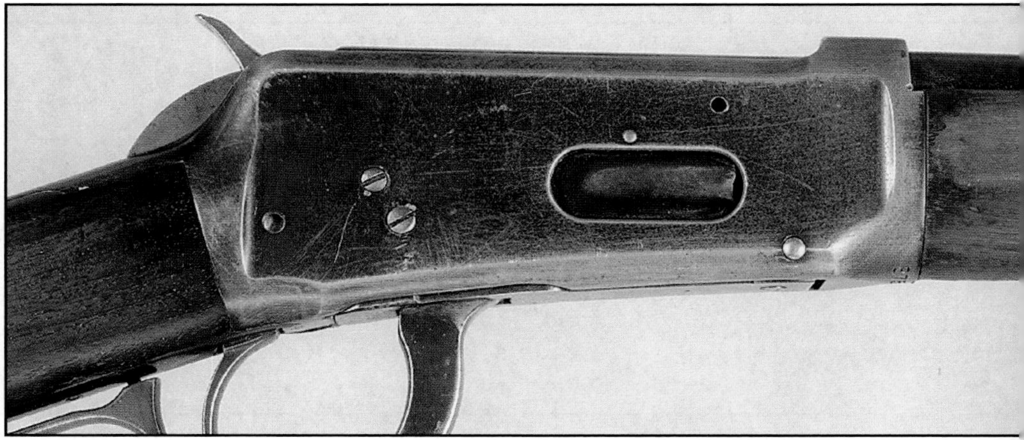

40% condition, Winchester Model 1894 Lever Action, .32 Win. Spl. cal., 26 in. round barrel, ser. no. 875560 – mfg. 1920. In the gun business, this is what you call a gun's condition factors "adding up" correctly. This plain Jane Model 1894 with 26 in. barrel is a study on what to look for when evaluating an older rifle. Note how the nickel steel barrel still has much of its bright blue, while the mag. tube has turned a brown patina overall. Metal forearm cap is mostly shiny, and matches the condition on the receiver and wood. Flat receiver sides still have a lot of bright bluing left, especially at rear – also note how the loading gate finish looks good. The original stock wood and varnish have darkened somewhat, especially next to the receiver (normal) and the forearm shows normal use in the right areas. The receiver screw heads look good, and again, this Winchester still has a lot of eye appeal.

RIFLES: PPGS CONDITION FACTORS

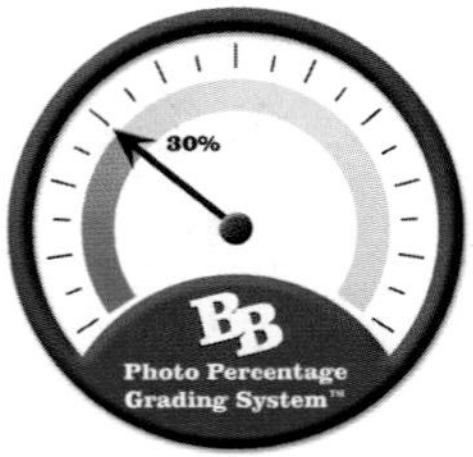

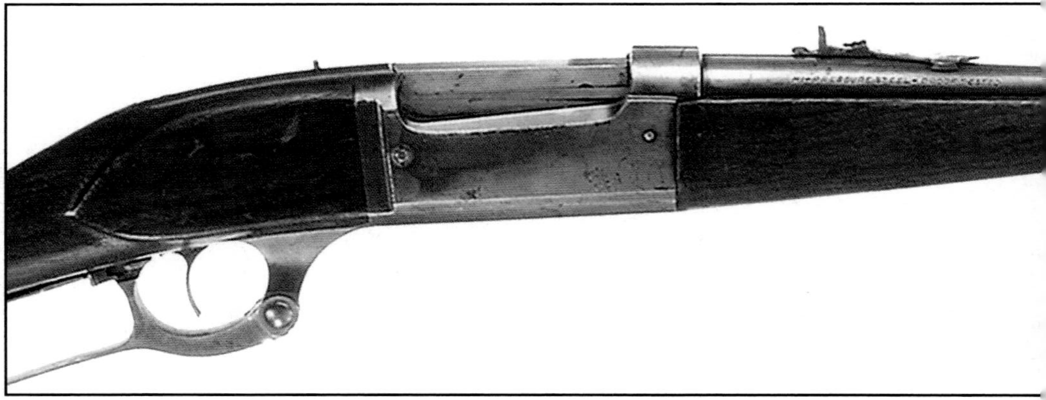

30% condition, Savage Model 1899 Lever Action, .300 Sav. cal., 24 in. round barrel, ser. no. 324301 – mfg. 1929. If this rifle could talk, you'd probably be listening to a lot of interesting older deer hunting tales. Mostly shiny receiver shows previous polishing, while thinning bluing finish on barrel indicates this lever action has been on many previous hunting trips. Uncheckered straight grip walnut stock has turned somewhat dark due to oil staining and handling, and has some dings and scratches. While unseen, serious cracks in the stock have been repaired, and some pitting is present on both the frame and the barrel. Lever is also mostly shiny, attesting to the years of use. This rifle in this condition has now reached shooter status only, since most collectors want better condition in this type of common model. In other words, figure out its price as a shooter, and don't pay a penny more.

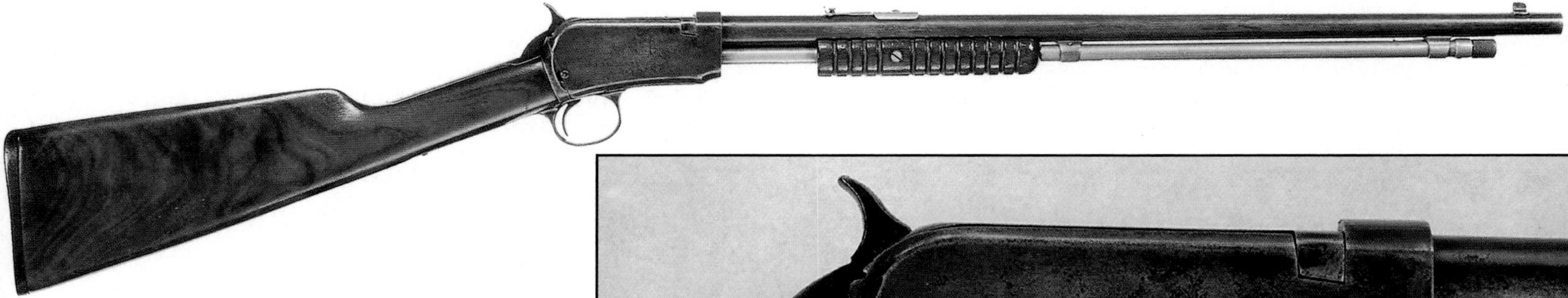

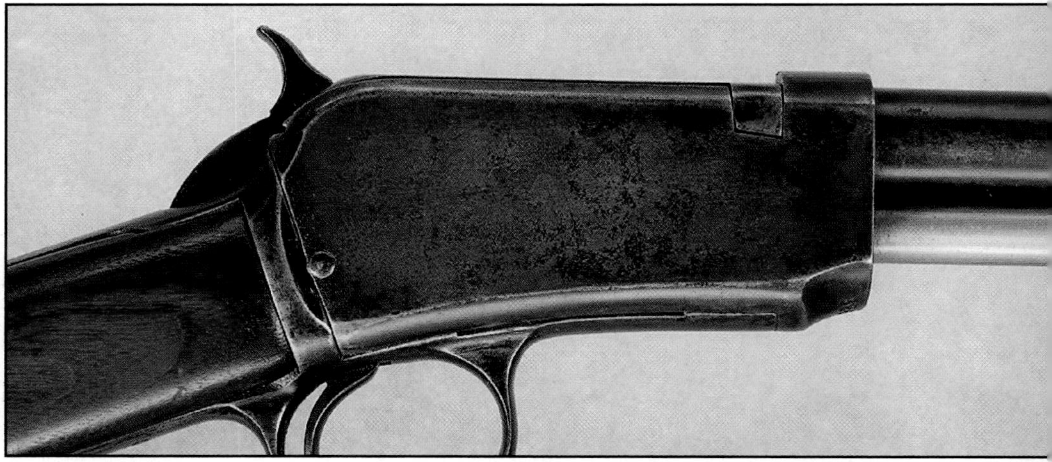

20% condition, Winchester Model 1906 Slide Action, .22 S-L-LR cal., 20 in. round barrel, ser. no. 256876 – mfg. 1911. Two of Winchester's most popular slide action .22 cal. rifles, the Models 1890 and 1906, enjoyed tremendous popularity from 1890-1932, with almost 1.7 million manufactured. Yet, a mint specimen of either model is very rare and only infrequently encountered. This Model 1906 is in below average condition, with the receiver having turned a dark brown patina, and showing major areas of pitting. Barrel has also turned an overall brown patina, while the mag. tube and action bar are nickel plated. Stock and forearm have been revarnished, and do not match the rest of this gun's condition. Action remains tight, while bore is good. This rifle's value has bottomed out in this condition factor, and has limited desirability for Winchester collectors who want better condition.

RIFLES: PPGS CONDITION FACTORS

116

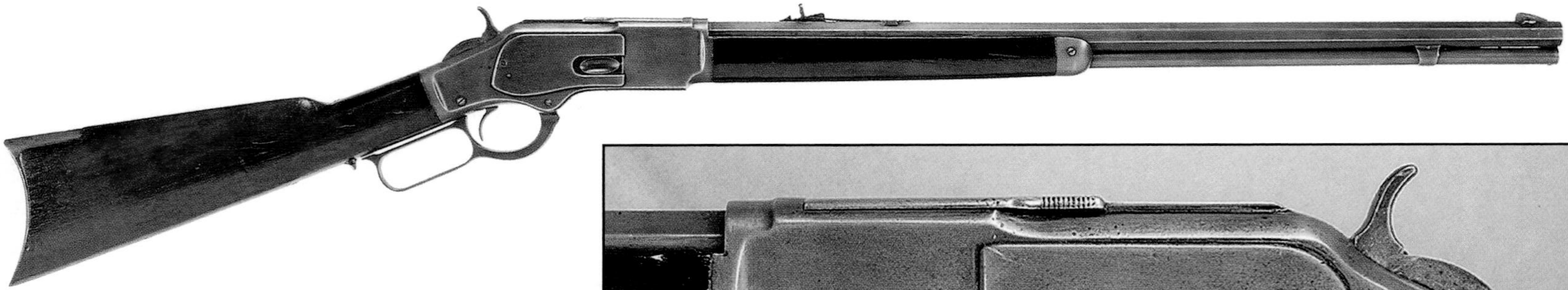

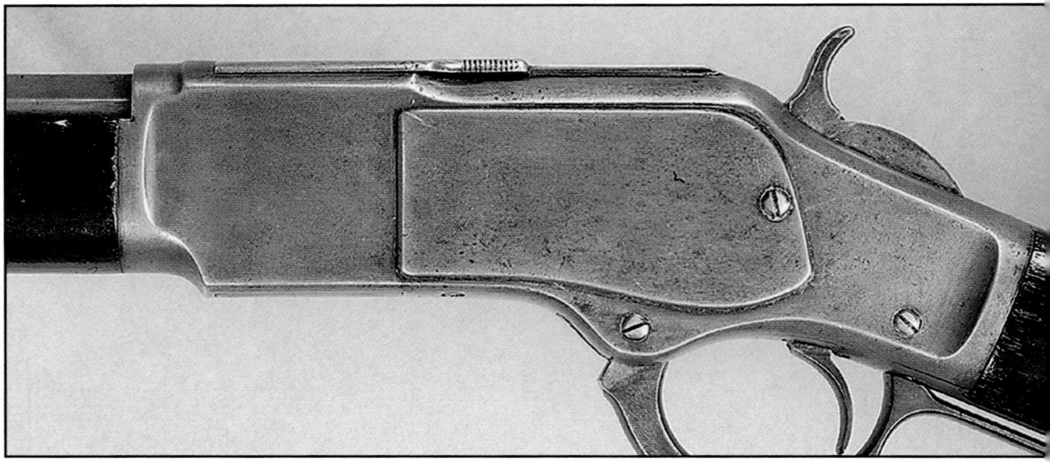

10% condition, Winchester 3rd Model 1873 Lever Action, .32-20 WCF cal., 24 in. octagon barrel, ser. no. 354761B - mfg. 1890. This Model 1873 is a good example of an antique rifle's original finish having turned a smooth gray brown patina overall (compare the finish on this gun to the 70% condition Winchester 1873 1st Model Lever Action). Even though this gun has little original finish left, it does not have major problems like severe pitting, replaced non-original parts, or damaged/cracked wood, even though the stock and forearm have been previously revarnished. All markings remain sharp, the action is mechanically okay, and the bore is fair. Many Winchester collectors would still rather have a no problem, original rifle like this than a 40% overall specimen with major finish problems and alterations. This specimen would be considered an entry-level model for collecting, based on its condition and originality.

0%-10% condition, Remington Rolling Block w/bayonet, .43 Spanish cal., 33 7/8 in. round barrel, no ser. no. – mfg. circa late 19th century. This well-worn Remington Rolling Block rifle made under contract for the Spanish government is a good example of how a gun's value can be reduced to almost nothing if there is very little original condition remaining. The metal finish has turned a grayish patina, with quite a bit of rusting and pitting on the receiver. The stock is also battered, and note that the ramrod and front sling swivel are missing. The bore is as dark as the oil-soaked wood, but at least it has the original bayonet. Remington made hundreds of thousands of rolling block rifles in various configurations and calibers for many countries, and the remaining majority now look like this. While a mint original specimen is both rare and desirable, a contract rolling block in this condition has lost most of its desirability and eye appeal. Typically priced under $250, these contract rifles, in many obsolete calibers, can no longer be considered even as shooters.

RIFLES: NRA ANTIQUE CONDITIONS

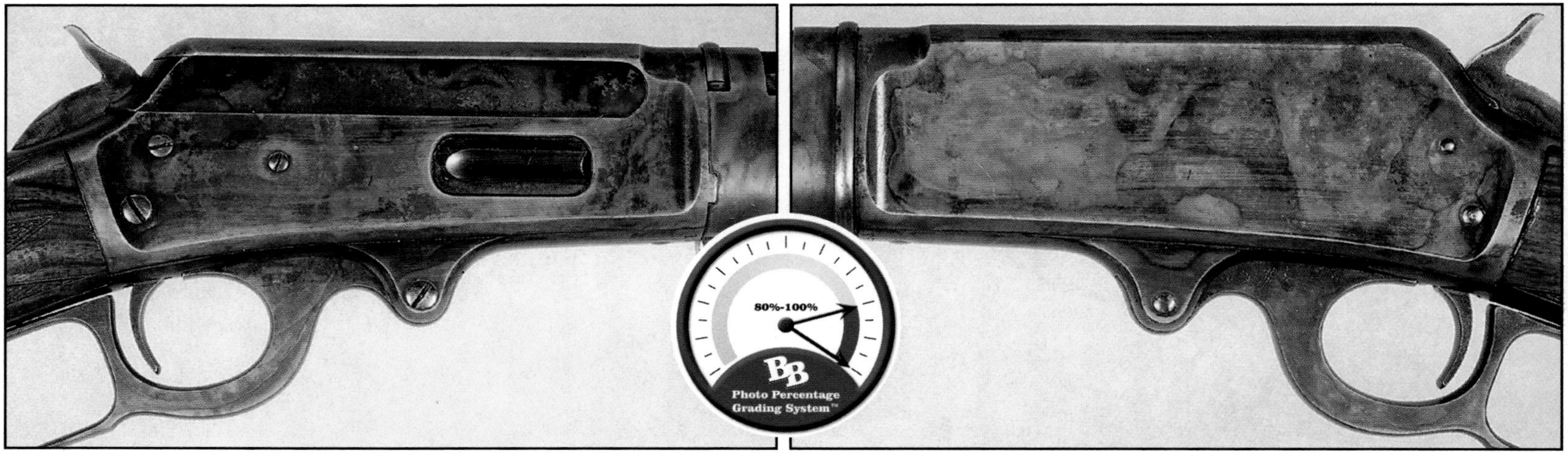

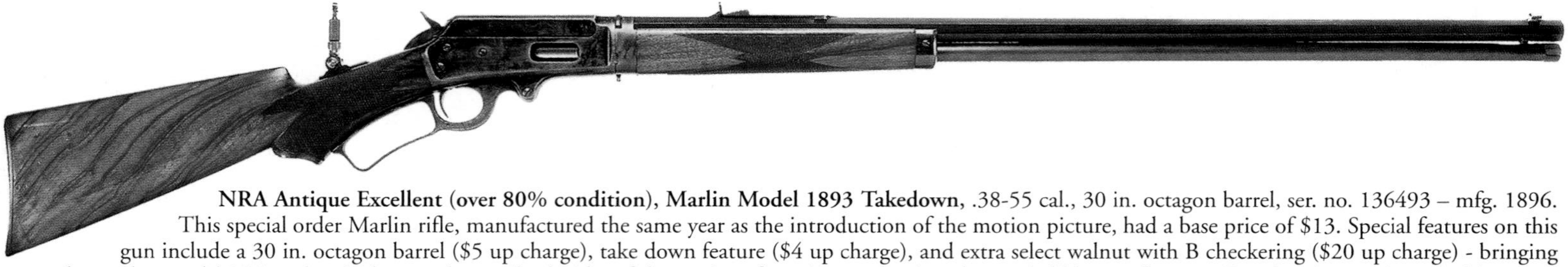

NRA Antique Excellent (over 80% condition), Marlin Model 1893 Takedown, .38-55 cal., 30 in. octagon barrel, ser. no. 136493 – mfg. 1896. This special order Marlin rifle, manufactured the same year as the introduction of the motion picture, had a base price of $13. Special features on this gun include a 30 in. octagon barrel ($5 up charge), take down feature ($4 up charge), and extra select walnut with B checkering ($20 up charge) - bringing the total up to $42! Note the vivid case colors on both sides of the receiver, featuring predominately mottled blues and greens. Barrel and magazine tube bluing are above 95%, and checkered Circassian walnut stock and forearm retain most of the original varnish. Once you start adding up what these special orders/features can do to a major trademark gun in this type of superior original condition in today's marketplace, the price tag gets turbo charged in a hurry!

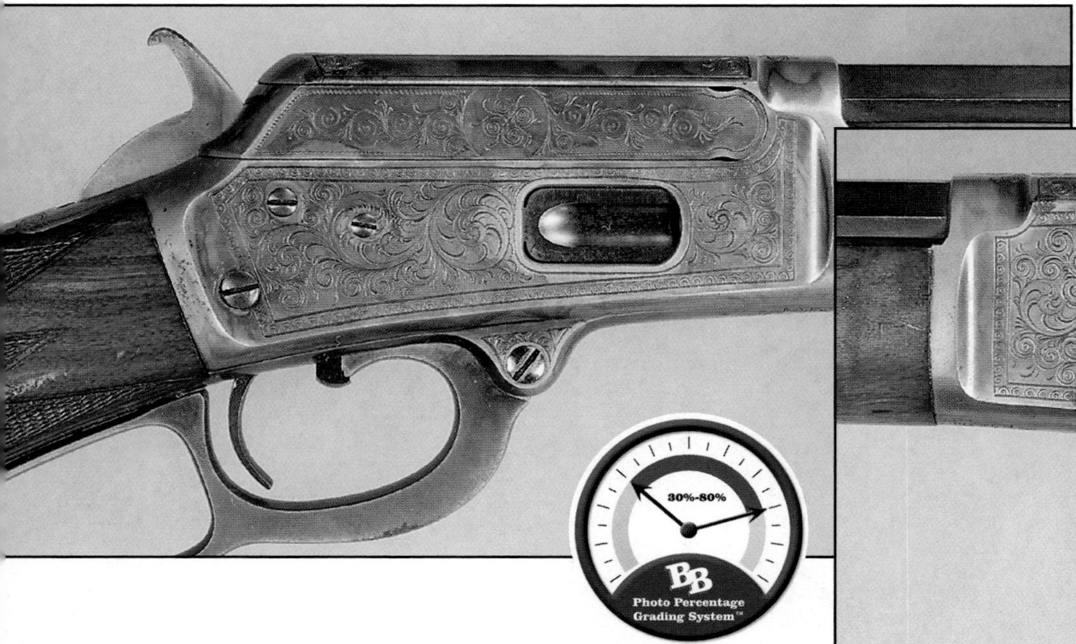

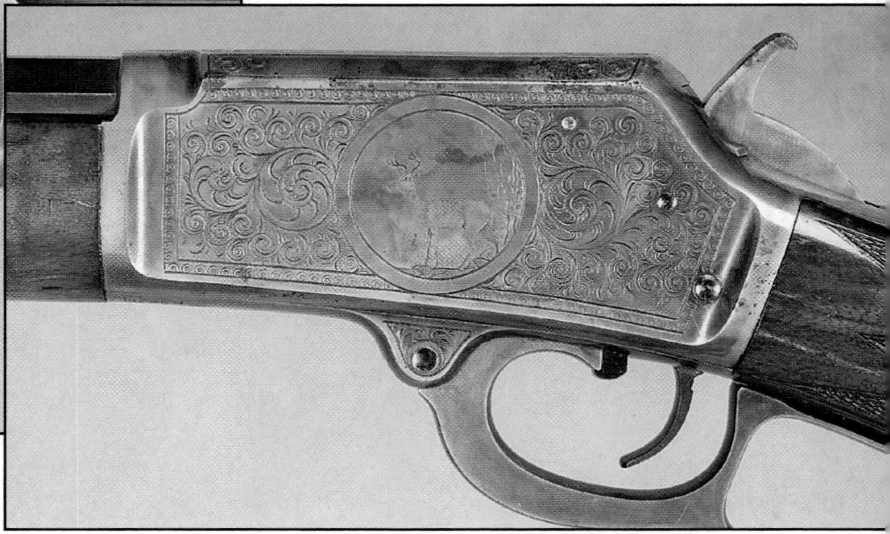

NRA Antique Fine (**30%-80% condition**), **Engraved Marlin Model 1889 Deluxe Lever Action**, .32-20 WCF cal., 24 in. octagon barrel, ser. no. 69896 – mfg. June 18, 1892. As a general rule of thumb, engraved guns appear to have less case colors than non-engraved standard models. Extensive engraving on any case colored rifle actually subdues the case colors somewhat, as the scrollwork tends to break up the overall pattern. Note how front and rear receiver edges have become shiny with light freckling, and how wood to metal fit is perfect. Also note that the case colored lever has coloration left only in the protected area where it pivots. Hammer case colors are nice, and match the overall condition factor of this fine rifle. While some dealers and collectors may refer to this condition as Very Fine, this term is not a proper NRA Antique condition factor.

RIFLES: NRA ANTIQUE CONDITIONS

RIFLES: NRA ANTIQUE CONDITIONS

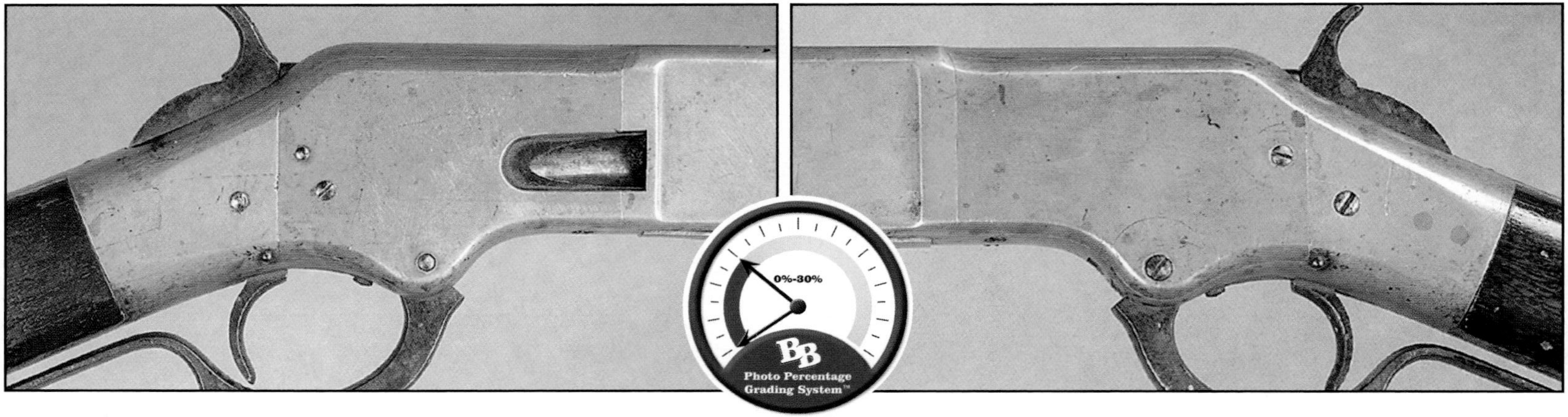

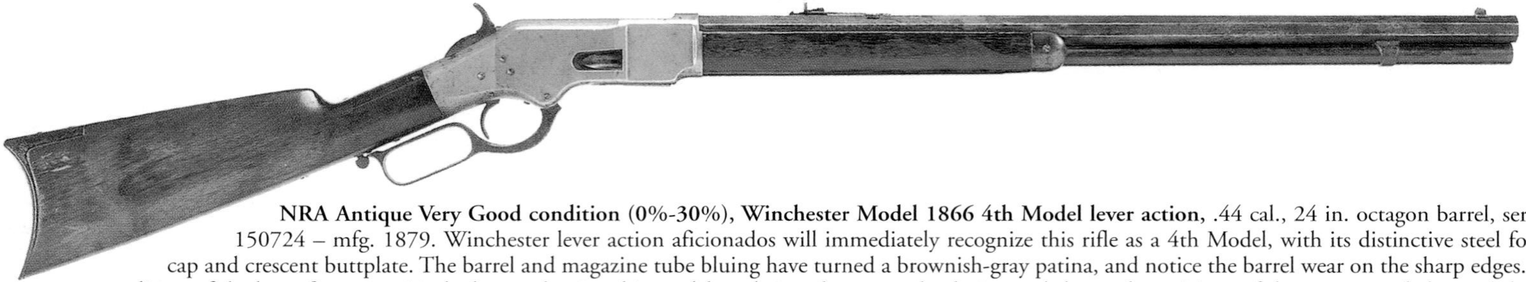

NRA Antique Very Good condition (0%-30%), Winchester Model 1866 4th Model lever action, .44 cal., 24 in. octagon barrel, ser. no. 150724 – mfg. 1879. Winchester lever action aficionados will immediately recognize this rifle as a 4th Model, with its distinctive steel forend cap and crescent buttplate. The barrel and magazine tube bluing have turned a brownish-gray patina, and notice the barrel wear on the sharp edges. The condition of the brass frame is critical when evaluating this model, and note the mustard coloring and sharp edges. Many of these were sanded or polished to make them look newer. The stock may have been lightly sanded at an earlier date, but overall, this is a very nice Model 1866 4th Model. Antique Winchester lever actions like this one used to be commonly seen at most major gun shows, but in recent years, can mainly be found either at auctions or from specialized high end dealers and collectors.

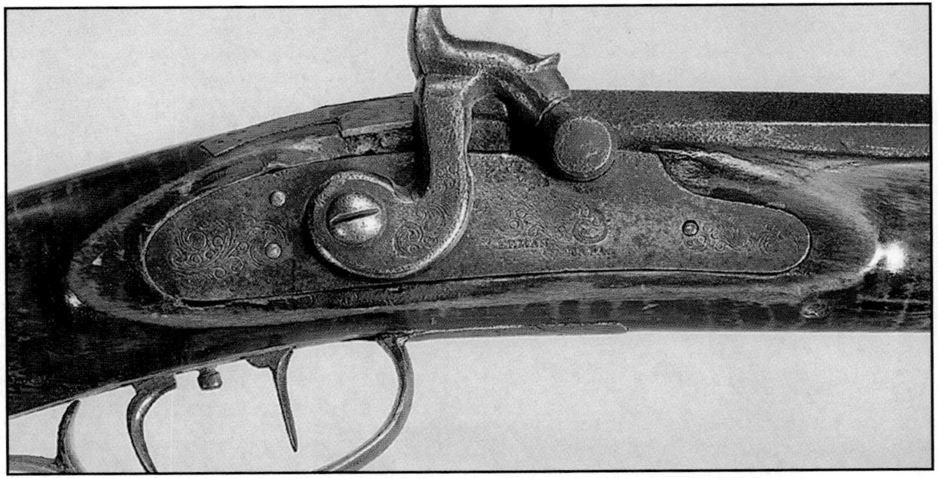

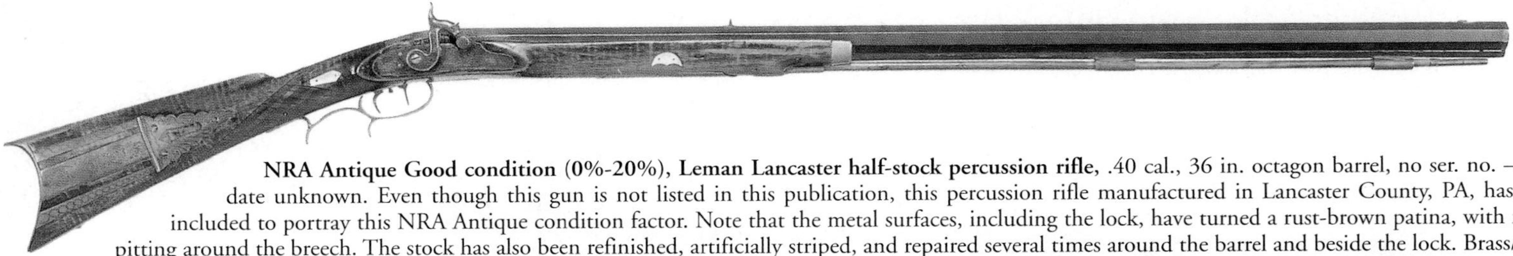

NRA Antique Good condition (0%-20%), **Leman Lancaster half-stock percussion rifle,** .40 cal., 36 in. octagon barrel, no ser. no. – mfg. date unknown. Even though this gun is not listed in this publication, this percussion rifle manufactured in Lancaster County, PA, has been included to portray this NRA Antique condition factor. Note that the metal surfaces, including the lock, have turned a rust-brown patina, with major pitting around the breech. The stock has also been refinished, artificially striped, and repaired several times around the barrel and beside the lock. Brass/silver furniture and mother-of-pearl inlays appear to be original and in good shape. This condition factor takes into consideration pitting, minor replacement parts, and wood refinishing, but in good working order. In general, the older and more common the gun, the less likely it will be found in over NRA Antique Fine condition. Collectors prefer originality over anything else once an older gun like this reaches this condition factor.

RIFLES: NRA ANTIQUE CONDITIONS

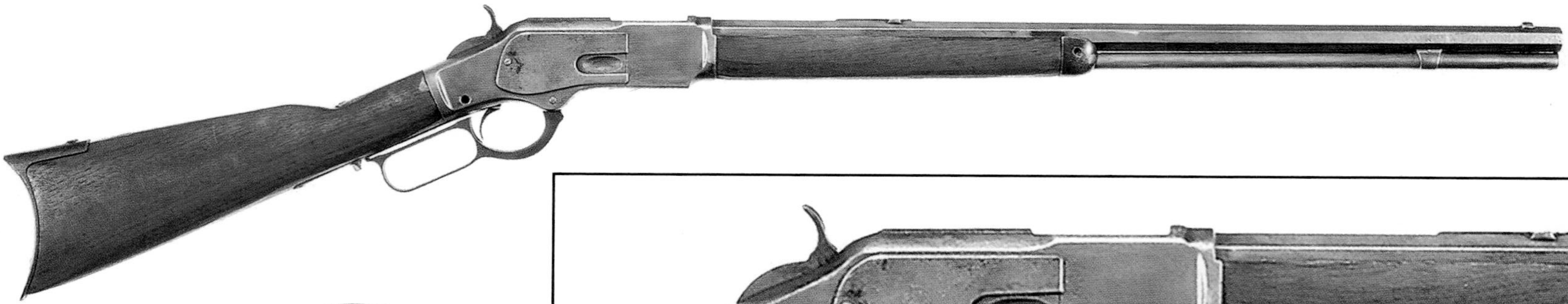

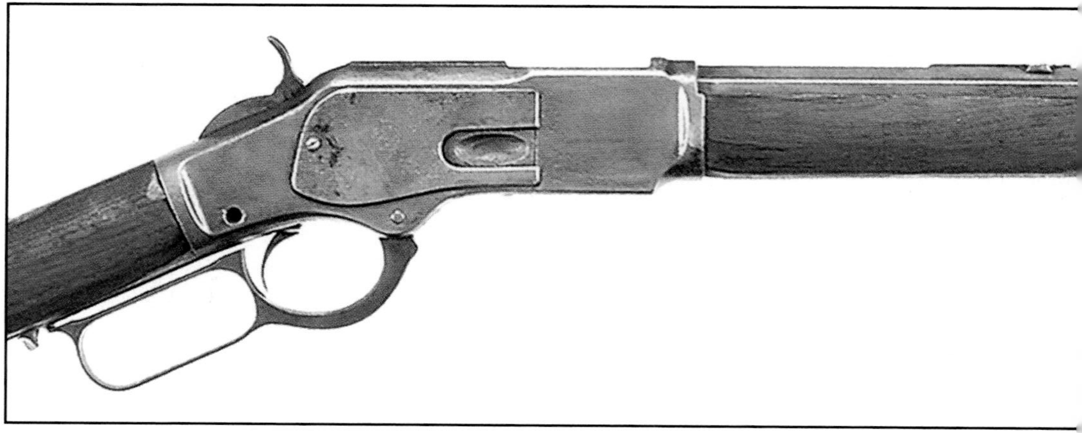

NRA Antique Fair condition (0-10%). **Altered Winchester Model 1873 Lever Action**, .32-20 WCF cal., 24 in. octagon barrel, ser. no. 167428 – mfg. 1884. Except for the forearm cap, there is no original finish remaining on the receiver, barrel, or magazine tube. This gun has had all its metal surfaces polished and is also missing major parts such as the dust cover, receiver screws, and rear sight. Both the stock and the forearm are crude replacements, and fit poorly to the metal. This rifle (or what's left of it) constitutes 0-10% condition (NRA Fair). So what's it worth? The answer is, add up values for the individual parts, and don't include the stock or forearm. In this case, the total is approx. $475-$550, still cheaper than a modern reproduction. Unfortunately, most guns in this condition factor never become more desirable (or expensive) as junk will always be junk, and gets priced accordingly!

NRA Antique Poor condition (no original finish remaining), Modified Sharps New Model 1863 Military parts rifle, .52 cal., 30 in. round barrel, ser. no. C1904 – mfg. circa 1863. This carbine receiver was originally rejected (or perhaps it was on a gun rejected for other reasons) and there are no inspector marks. This rifle has been put together using a rejected carbine receiver and leftover rifle parts. It was probably assembled by Schuyler Hartley & Graham, or Bannerman, using surplus spare parts from other government contracts, and finally sold cheaply in the post-Civil War consumer marketplace. This is a good example of a gun with no eye appeal. Rusted, pitted, and dark splotchy metal surfaces combined with rejected military status, non-original small parts, and an action that needs work lower this rifle's value significantly. The only way this gun can be under priced is if it can be purchased for less than the total value of its parts!

RIFLES: NRA ANTIQUE CONDITIONS

SHOTGUNS: PPGS CONDITION FACTORS

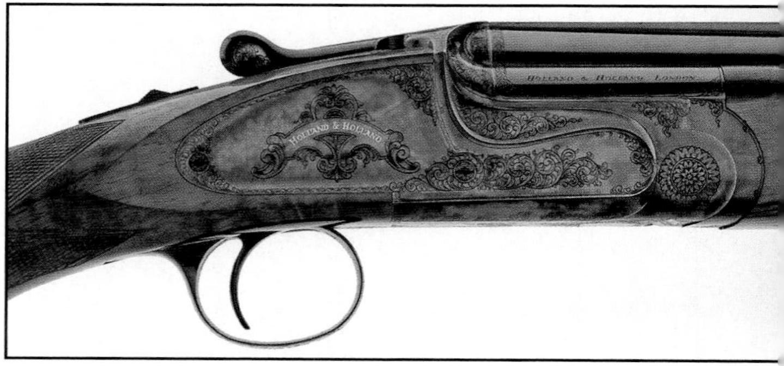

NIB Condition, Holland & Holland Sporting Model O/U, 12 ga., 29 in. barrels - new mfg. One of England's premier gunmakers, Holland & Holland Ltd., has been manufacturing top quality long guns since 1835. This is a new example of their best quality Sporting Model. This shotgun's case colors on the reinforced sidelock frame are spectacular, exhibiting a perfect swirl of blues, greens, and even mottled yellows. Wood-to-metal fit is also flawless, and as you can see, only best quality, oil finished Circassian walnut is used on this special order model - note matching wood buttplate. Also observe the quality of the barrel polishing and bluing, which look like polished black marble.

This Sporting Model features H&H's detachable trigger lock, which can be easily removed for cleaning by a release lever on the trigger guard. If you desire the best, and want to make a statement while shooting game or at the sporting clays range, this is the gun for you. Make sure you have an XXL piggy bank however, because the Sporting Model starts at £55,000.

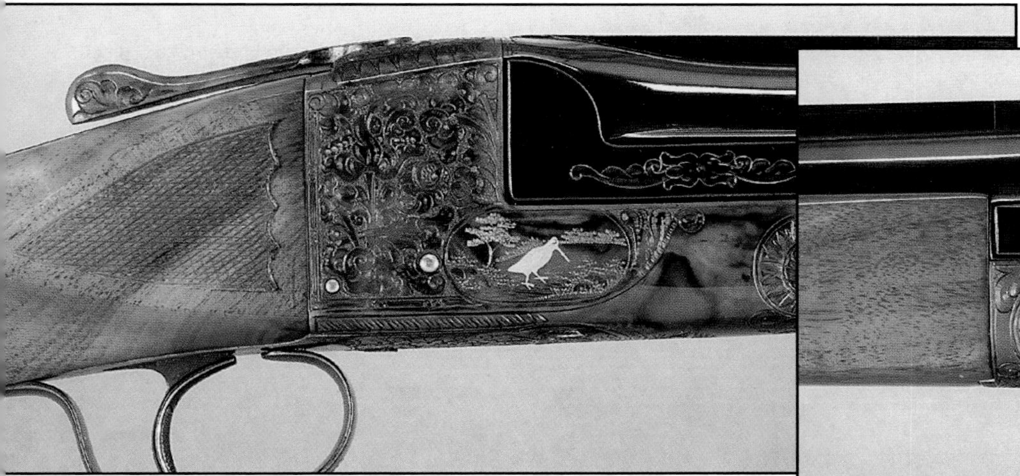

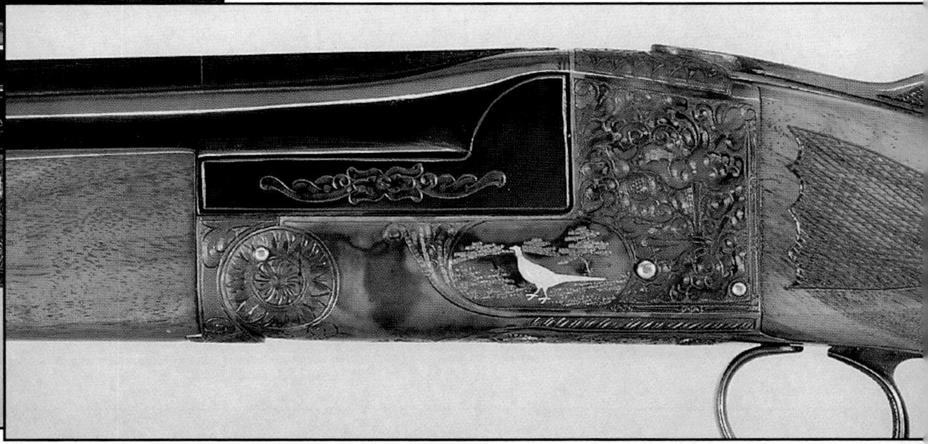

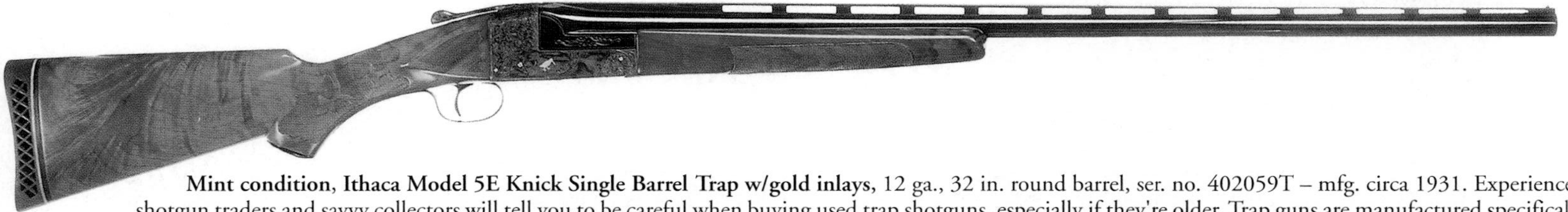

Mint condition, Ithaca Model 5E Knick Single Barrel Trap w/gold inlays, 12 ga., 32 in. round barrel, ser. no. 402059T – mfg. circa 1931. Experienced shotgun traders and savvy collectors will tell you to be careful when buying used trap shotguns, especially if they're older. Trap guns are manufactured specifically to shoot a high volume of shotshells within a relatively brief time frame. Because of this, action wear can accumulate long before wear is visible on the outside of the gun. Always focus on how tight (or loose) the action is, and if the top opening lever is still on the right side of center on upper tang. This nice Ithaca 5E Knick Model has almost no bluing or case color wear, factory engraving and gold bird inlays, definitive of the model. The uncut stock has a replacement Pachmayr recoil pad, typical on trap guns where dimensions are critical and tailored to the individual.

SHOTGUNS: PPGS CONDITION FACTORS

126

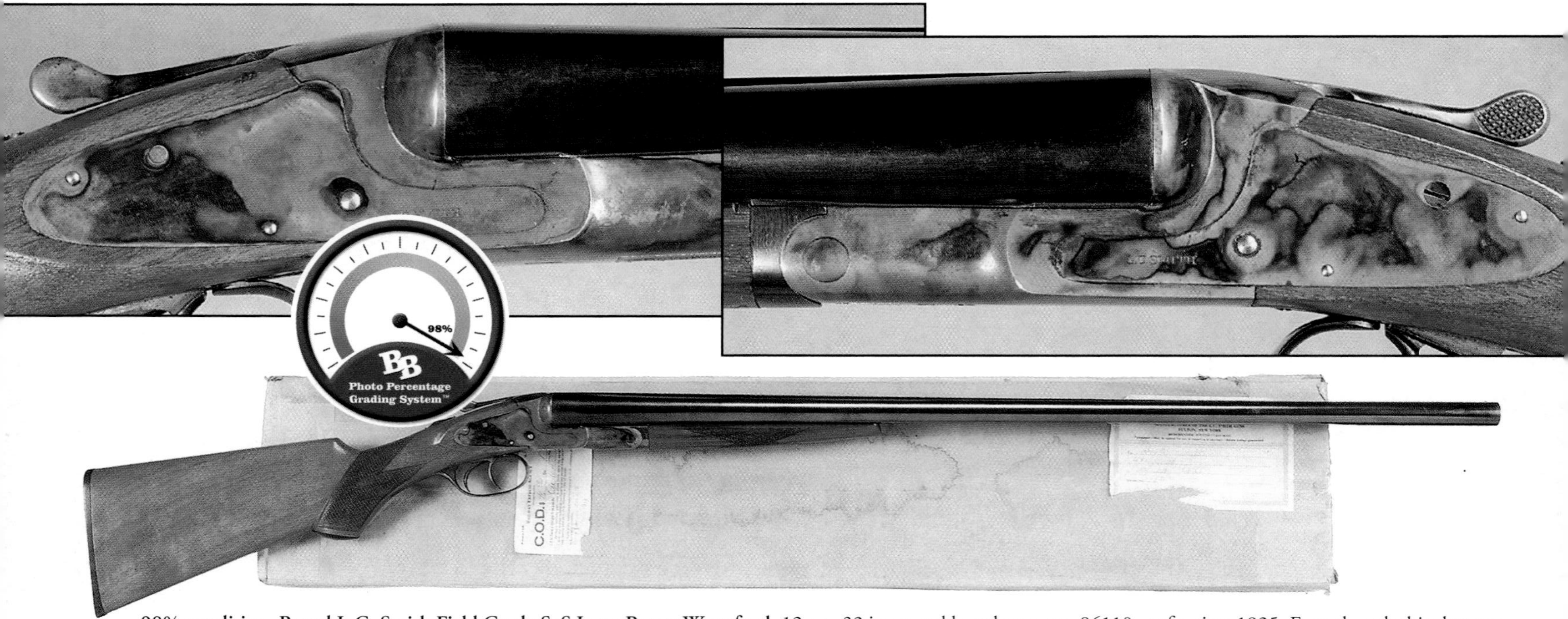

98% condition, Boxed L.C. Smith Field Grade SxS Long Range Waterfowl, 12 ga., 32 in. round barrels, ser. no. 86110 - mfg. circa 1925. Even though this shotgun is both new and unfired, normal storage wear, cleaning, and occasional assembly have all accumulated enough wear to knock this gun's condition factor down to 98%. Original L.C. Smith case colors do not get any better than this - look at the vivid blues and greens surrounded by grayish/brown swirls compared to the 40% condition L.C. Smith 00 Grade SxS (page 133) and the NRA Antique Fine condition L.C. Smith Grade 2 w/ Ejectors SxS (page 138). Also note unstained, light colored, checkered standard grade walnut stock and forearm, and tight wood to metal fit around sideplates. When a desirable gun's condition factor is this good, the value may double or even triple the 90% value. L.C. Smith only had one level of quality - the best, regardless of the grade. Stock and splinter forearm show virtually no wear. In many cases, a 98%+ condition specimen of a factory's most common model is the hardest to find, since most of them were heavily used. Original box is somewhat tattered, and has water staining.

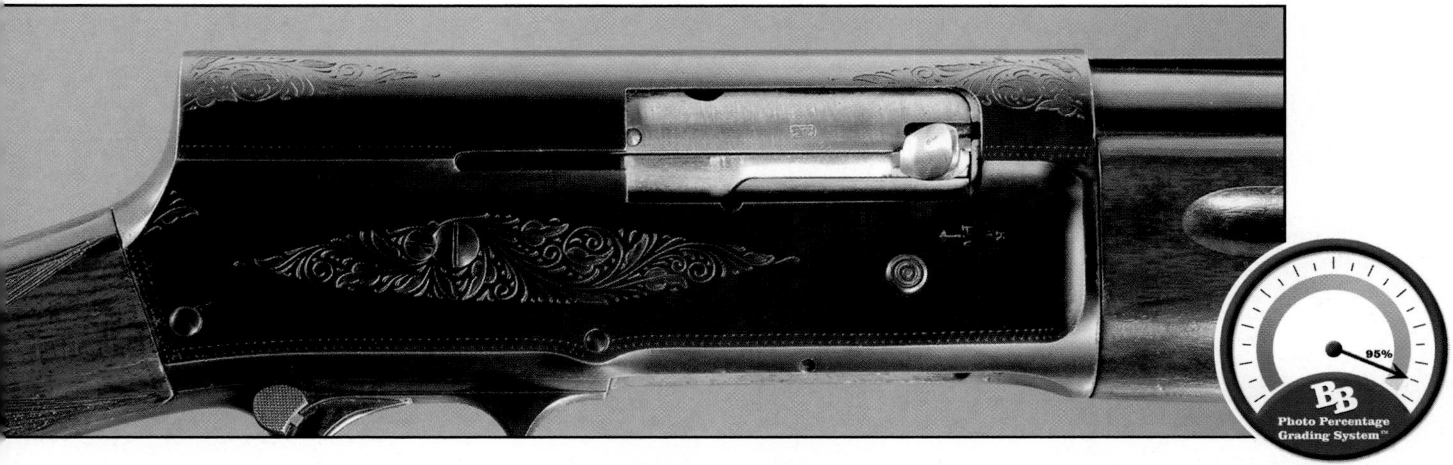

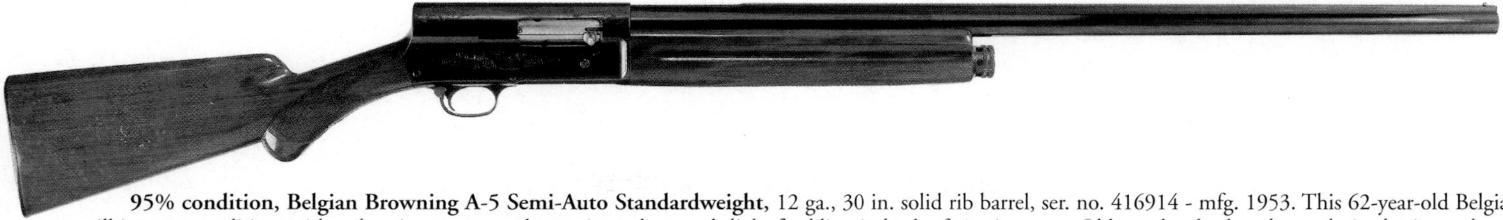

95% condition, Belgian Browning A-5 Semi-Auto Standardweight, 12 ga., 30 in. solid rib barrel, ser. no. 416914 - mfg. 1953. This 62-year-old Belgian A-5 is still in great condition, with only minor wear on the receiver edges, and slight freckling in back of ejection port. Older style, checkered round pistol grip stock and 30 in. solid rib barrel also indicate earlier manufacture. Barrel is marked, "Browning Arms Co, St, Louis, MO." When A-5 condition gets lower than this, prices fall off rapidly, as most Browning collectors prefer 98% or better original condition, whenever possible. After almost 100 years of near continuous production, Browning finally discontinued the venerable Auto-5 shotgun in 1999, but reintroduced it during 2012 as a fixed barrel with the new model designated as the A5. In today's A-5 marketplace, solid rib barrels are more desirable (and expensive) than their vent. rib counterparts, as they are rarer. Also, shorter barrels (26 or 28 in.) with open field chokes are worth more than longer barrels with full chokes.

SHOTGUNS: PPGS CONDITION FACTORS

128

90% condition, Belgian Browning Auto-5 Sweet Sixteen, 16 ga., 28 in. solid rib barrel, ser. no. S14514 – mfg. 1954. Note the additional wear around the lower receiver edges on this Browning compared to the 95% condition Belgian Browning Auto-5 Semi-Auto Standardweight. This Sweet Sixteen Auto-5 is referred to as a round knob, long tang variation, indicating that the pistol grip is rounded (mfg. 1952-1976) instead of flat, and the lower tang is longer than recent manufacture. Note blonde French walnut stock and forearm, typical for this period of production. This is a good example of what a rarer variation of a common model can do to the price tag. While the frequently encountered 12 ga. Auto-5 with 30 in. plain barrel (95% condition Belgian Browning) currently has a retail value of $800, this rarer Sweet 16 with solid matted rib in 90% condition retails in the $1,650-$2,000 range. This same model in 100% condition can top $3,250+, even more if with the original box!

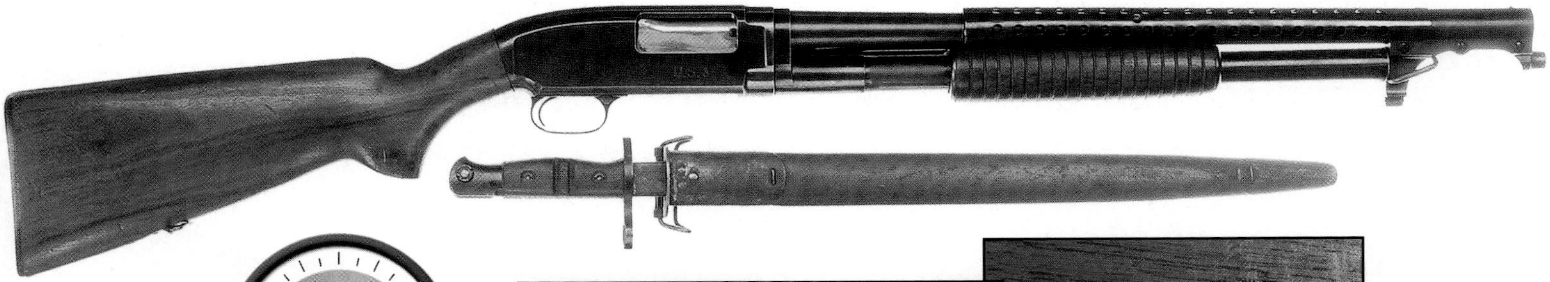

80% condition, Winchester Model 12 Trench Gun w/Bayonet, 12 ga., 20 7/8 in. round barrel, ser. no. 1014064 - mfg. 1943. U.S. military shotguns, like this specimen, were not as collectible (or expensive) as U.S. military handguns up to approximately 20 years ago – then things changed, in a hurry. Originality is Polar North for U.S. military long gun collectors, and knowing exactly what metal proof marks/stock cartouches and where they appear is the only way to determine originality.

Note the "U.S." and ordnance "flaming bomb" proofs on right side of receiver, and crisp stock cartouche, in addition to sling swivels. Compare receiver bluing to the 70%-75% and 60% condition Model 12s on the following pages. While the receiver on this gun is probably closer to 90%, the barrel, barrel shroud, and mag. tube lower this shotgun's condition factor down to 80% overall. Remington 1917 marked bayonet also adds some value to this original WWII U.S. military shotgun.

SHOTGUNS: PPGS CONDITION FACTORS

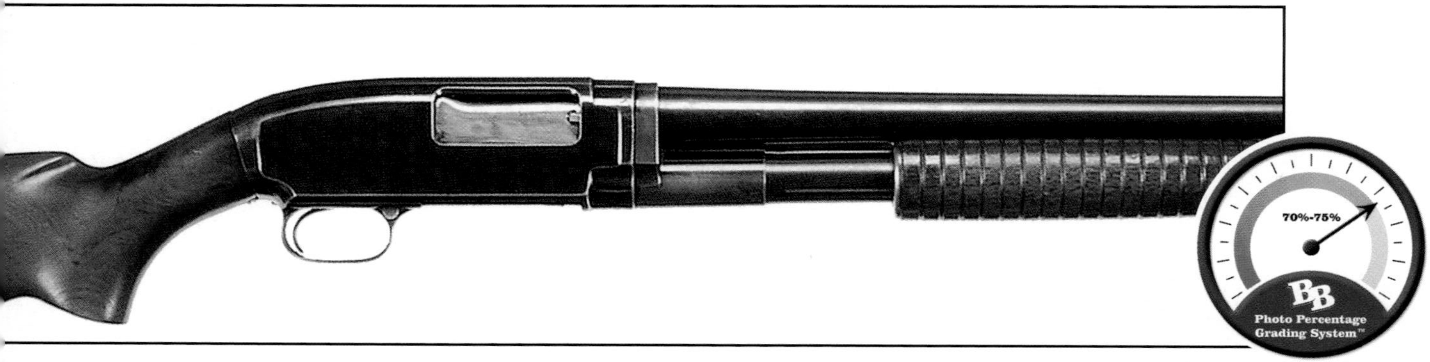

70%-75% condition, Winchester Model 12 Slide Action, 12 ga., 28 in. round barrel, ser. no. 902723 – mfg. 1941. Very few shotgun models are found in such a wide array of condition factors as the Model 12 Winchester. It's pretty hard for any shotgun enthusiast not to have a Model 12 somewhere in his/her gun vault. This particular shotgun shows normal wear, but no abuse. While some dealers and collectors might grade this gun at 80% based on the receiver and barrel bluing, the wear on the mag. tube and ring at end of barrel assembly knock this shotgun's condition down to approx. 70%-75%. Stock has a Pachmayr rubber vent. replacement recoil pad with spacers, but it has not been cut. Horizontal striations and dulling on breech block indicate this shotgun has pumped out more than a few ounces of lead (hopefully, no steel!) in its lifetime.

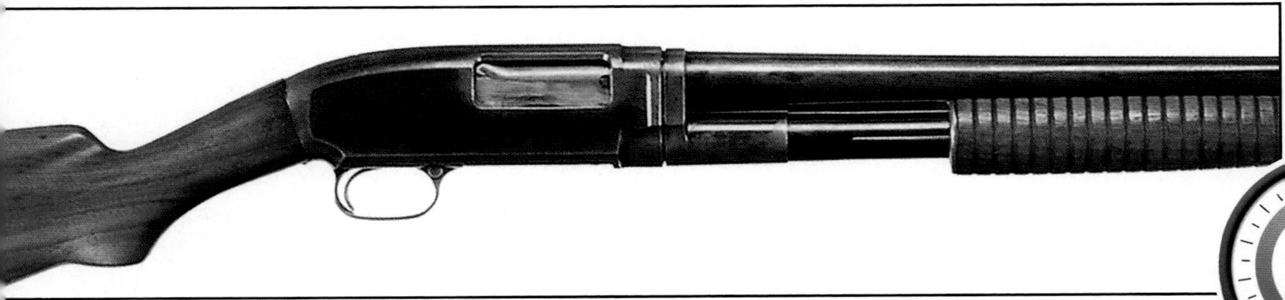

60% condition, Winchester Model 12 Slide Action, 12 ga., 30 in. round barrel, ser. no. 219576 - mfg. early Jan., 1919. When a shotgun gets down to this condition factor, normally the barrel also shows visible wear, as seen on this shotgun. Note how receiver, barrel, and mag. tube have also started to turn a brownish patina. Scuffed breech block and horizontal wear line on mag. tube tell this shotgun's shooting story. The stock has been sanded – note how light it is in the back, but gets dark where it joins the receiver (compare to the 70%-75% condition Winchester Model 12). Most of this gun's value must be determined by its worth as a reliable shooter, since the 12 ga./30 in. full choke barrel is the most common Model 12 configuration. The smaller gauges, especially the 28 ga. and .410 bore, are always more desirable than a 12 ga. in any shotgun model.

SHOTGUNS: PPGS CONDITION FACTORS

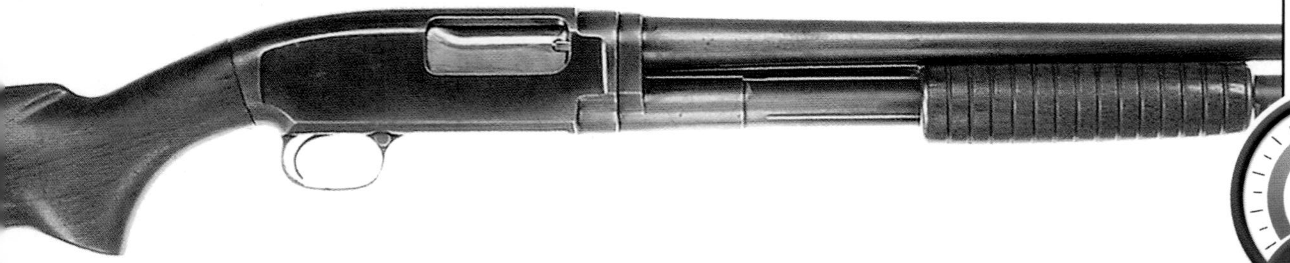

50% condition, Winchester Model 12 Slide Action, 16 ga., 28 in. round barrel, ser. no. 886875 – mfg. 1941. This is a good example of a well used, no problem Model 12. All the major components (wood, receiver, barrel, and mag. tube) are worn in all the right places, as well as not worn in all the right places. When barrel wear reaches this type of brown patina condition, the rest of the gun should look even more worn, as the barrel was normally not handled that much during usage. The mag. tube is equally worn, and the original stock and forearm reveal the right amount of original varnish to match the rest of the gun. Recently, 16 ga. guns have made a comeback in terms of collectibility, and are now priced approximately 20-30% higher than a 12 ga. with similar condition and features.

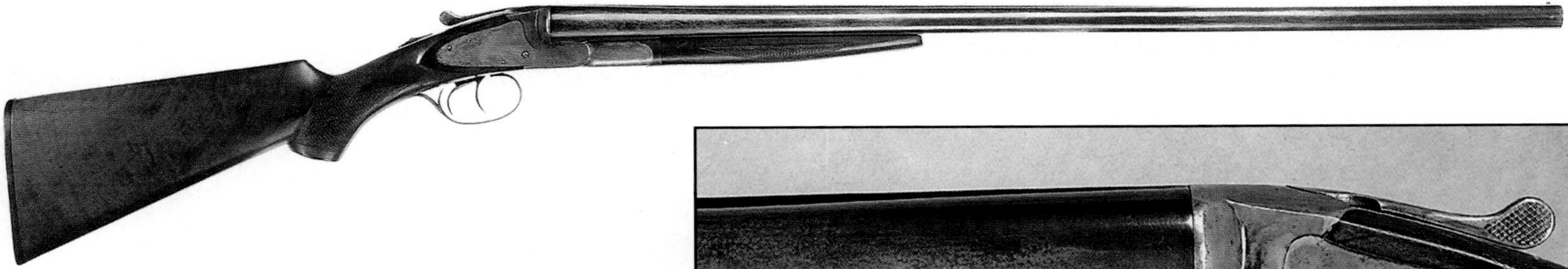

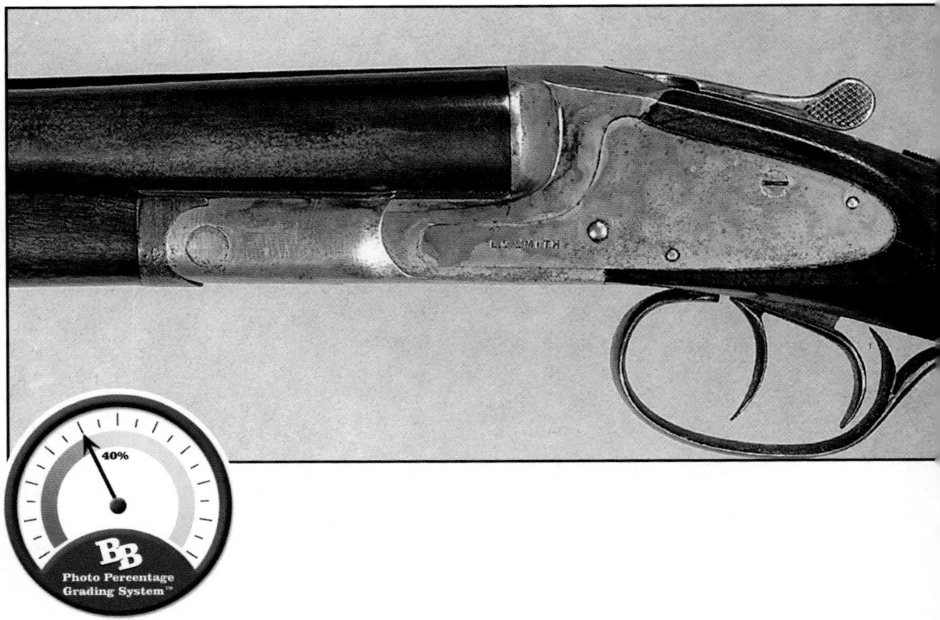

40% condition, L.C. Smith Field Grade SxS, 12 ga., 30 in. barrels, ser. no. 125367 - mfg. circa 1905. The overall condition of this 110-year-old L.C. Smith is a good example of the individual condition factors of the wood finish, frame case colors, and barrel bluing wearing equally. This means no one or two condition factors are a lot better or a lot worse than the others - very important when evaluating older guns for originality. Compare mottled case colors on frame, mostly visible around protected areas, to the vivid patterns depicted on the 98% condition Boxed L.C. Smith Field Grade SxS Long Range Waterfowl (page 126). Checkered Field Grade stock and forearm have darkened somewhat, but do not show major cracks, nicks, or gouges. Bluing on barrels is starting to fade to a patina, but overall, this is a nice original Field Grade L.C. Smith with tight action. Often times, American major trademark Field Grade or Standard Models (including A.H. Fox, Ithaca, Lefever, Parker, Remington, and L.C. Smith) are the hardest models to find in superior original condition, since they were typically used (and possibly abused) the most.

SHOTGUNS: PPGS CONDITION FACTORS

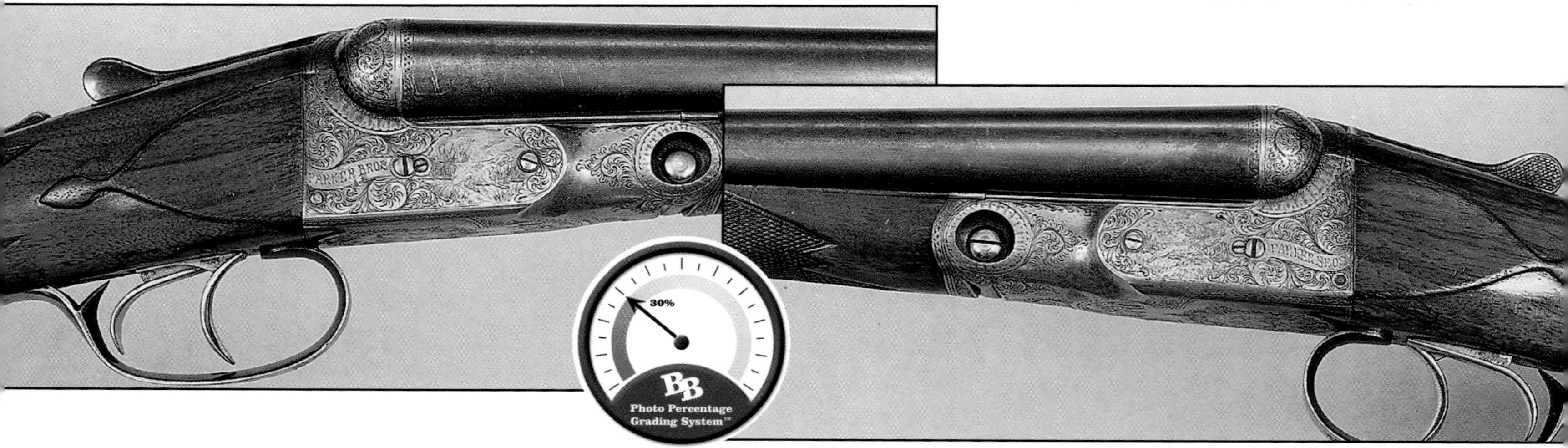

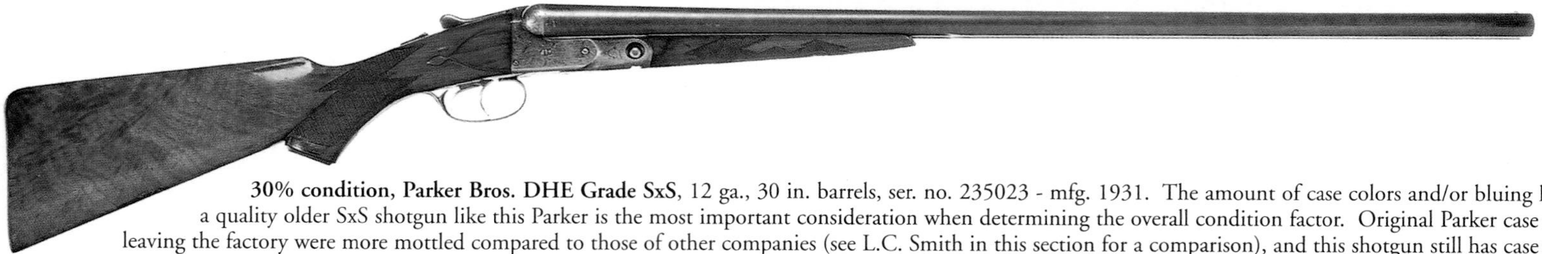

30% condition, Parker Bros. DHE Grade SxS, 12 ga., 30 in. barrels, ser. no. 235023 - mfg. 1931. The amount of case colors and/or bluing left on a quality older SxS shotgun like this Parker is the most important consideration when determining the overall condition factor. Original Parker case colors leaving the factory were more mottled compared to those of other companies (see L.C. Smith in this section for a comparison), and this shotgun still has case colors remaining in protected areas, including where the frame joins the barrels.

Titanic steel barrels with ejectors have turned to a dark grey, but both the stock and splinter forearm have most of the original wood varnish remaining. Stock was special ordered with skeleton steel buttplate (not seen), and DHE pattern engraving is still nice and crisp. Originally selling new for $176, this gun's value has now increased to the $2,000-$3,000 range.

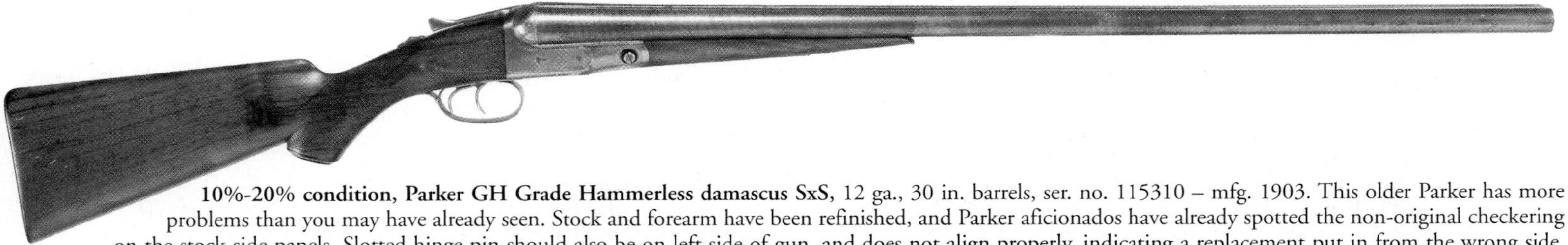

10%-20% condition, Parker GH Grade Hammerless damascus SxS, 12 ga., 30 in. barrels, ser. no. 115310 – mfg. 1903. This older Parker has more problems than you may have already seen. Stock and forearm have been refinished, and Parker aficionados have already spotted the non-original checkering on the stock side panels. Slotted hinge pin should also be on left side of gun, and does not align properly, indicating a replacement put in from the wrong side.

Note that almost all the original frame case colors are gone, and this shotgun's frame may have been previously polished, as some of the engraving has thinned out in areas. The damascus hammerless barrels still show great patterning, and double triggers are to be expected on the Model GH, which retailed for approximately $80 when new, $25 more with ejectors. Parker shotguns have continued to lead the domestic SxS marketplace price appreciation, with pricing for strong, original condition guns in smaller gauges (20 ga. and less) going well above auction reserve levels. But don't forget that originality has always been Polar North for Parker shotgun collectors.

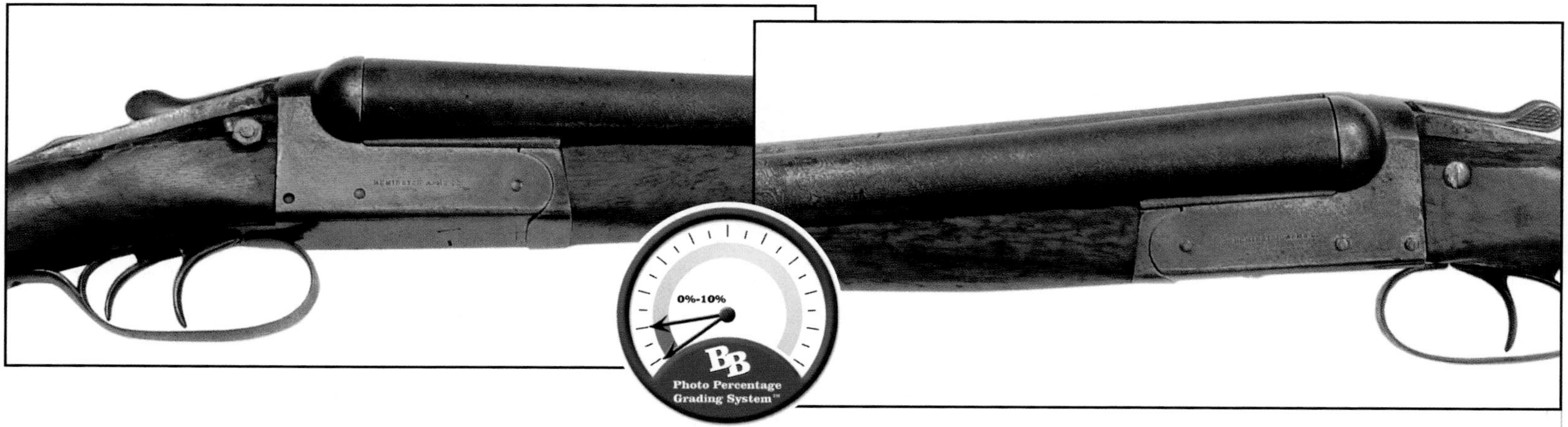

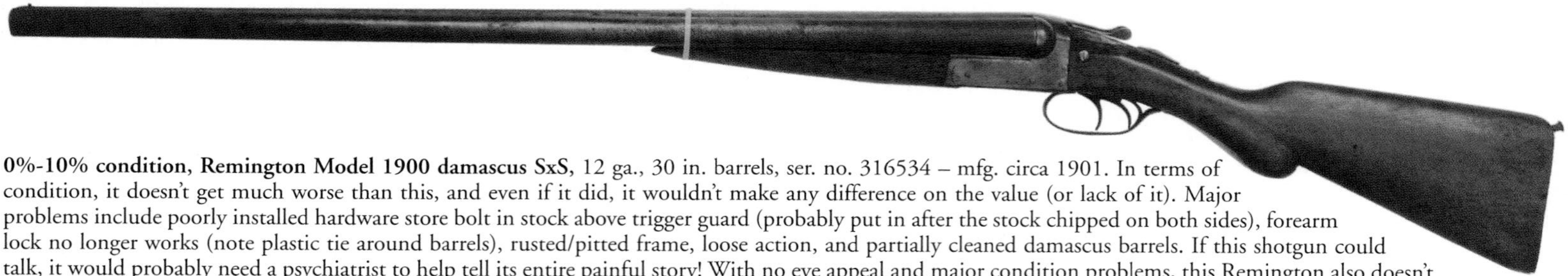

0%-10% condition, Remington Model 1900 damascus SxS, 12 ga., 30 in. barrels, ser. no. 316534 – mfg. circa 1901. In terms of condition, it doesn't get much worse than this, and even if it did, it wouldn't make any difference on the value (or lack of it). Major problems include poorly installed hardware store bolt in stock above trigger guard (probably put in after the stock chipped on both sides), forearm lock no longer works (note plastic tie around barrels), rusted/pitted frame, loose action, and partially cleaned damascus barrels. If this shotgun could talk, it would probably need a psychiatrist to help tell its entire painful story! With no eye appeal and major condition problems, this Remington also doesn't have any shooting value unless a gunsmith extensively went through it, and it wouldn't be worth it. Falling into the rusty iron/kindling category, this gun's value has been under $100 for quite some time, and the problem is, that will never change. Trash will always be trash!

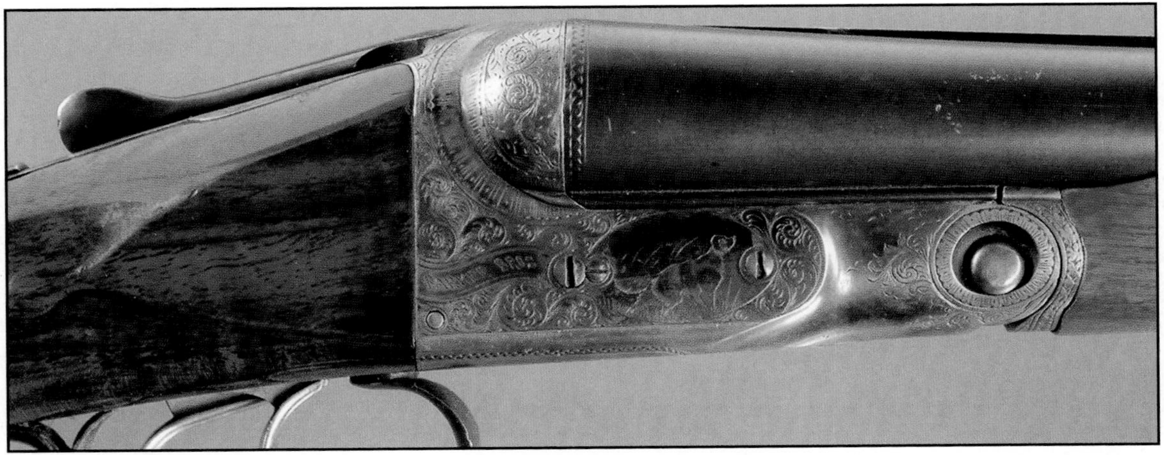

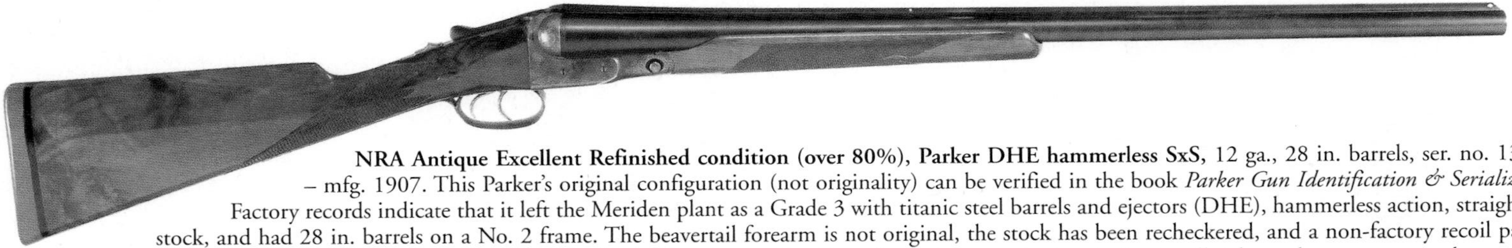

NRA Antique Excellent Refinished condition (over 80%), **Parker DHE hammerless SxS,** 12 ga., 28 in. barrels, ser. no. 139955 – mfg. 1907. This Parker's original configuration (not originality) can be verified in the book *Parker Gun Identification & Serialization.* Factory records indicate that it left the Meriden plant as a Grade 3 with titanic steel barrels and ejectors (DHE), hammerless action, straight grip stock, and had 28 in. barrels on a No. 2 frame. The beavertail forearm is not original, the stock has been recheckered, and a non-factory recoil pad has also been added. The refinished case colors resemble the factory's, and the reblued barrels also have good color. Action is still tight, and as you can see, the engraving is still very sharp. With originality being Polar North for Parker collectors, how do you determine value on a shotgun like this? If this gun was all original, and in 95% condition overall, its value would be in the $11,000-$12,000 range (and easy to sell!). This non-original DHE in this type of refurbished condition would probably be valued in the $3,000-$3,500 range, or less than half of an original.

NRA Antique Fine condition (30%-80%), **L.C. Smith Grade 2 w/Ejectors SxS,** 12 ga., 30 in. barrels, ser. no. 210689 – mfg. early 1909. This older L.C. Smith, manufactured by Hunter Arms Company in Fulton, NY, is a typical example of the condition factor you'll find on older, pre-WWI major trademark American shotguns. The exception is the barrels, which have obviously been reblued and do not match the overall condition of this SxS. Original case colors have mottled/faded over the years, and there appears to be some surface pitting on the front part of the lower frame. Original stock appears to have no cracks around the sidelock mechanism (unusual for an L.C. Smith of this vintage), and the splinter forearm checkering has almost disappeared. This shotgun's single trigger and ejectors will raise its value approximately 65%. Overall, compare the case colors on this L.C. Smith to the 40% and 98% condition L.C. Smiths in the Shotguns: PPGS Condition Factors section (pages 133 and 126). Originality and strong frame case colors are everything when determining value on America's major trademark SxS shotguns.

NRA Antique Very Good condition (0%-30%), **Winchester Repeating Arms Co. Model 1893 Slide Action,** 12 ga., 30 in. barrel, ser. no. WRACO (restamped over original ser. no.) – mfg. circa 1895. During the 1890s, Winchester Repeating Arms Co. attained many achievements with the help of design genius J.M. Browning, which have yet to be duplicated by any other firearms company in such a short time frame. Starting out with the immediately successful 1890 slide action .22 cal rifle, Winchester took the year off in 1891, but a year later, it introduced the lever action Model 1892 rifle/carbine, followed by Browning's first slide action shotgun (pictured above), then the legendary Model 1894 rifle, and finally the Model 1895 with box magazine. At the time, no other company could compete with this onslaught of major new firearms designs and innovations. This Model 1893's condition is typical of the vast majority that has survived. Note how bluing has oxidized to a warm brown patina with little pitting, and for some reason, the mag. tube has been reblued in front of the forearm. Careful observation reveals the slide release button is missing. Plain, uncheckered walnut stock and forearm also have a fresh coat of varnish, and explain the shiny appearance. Designed for black powder ammunition, only 34,050 Model 1893s were manufactured until it was replaced by the Model 1897, which was designed for smokeless powder.

SHOTGUNS: NRA ANTIQUE CONDITIONS

NRA Antique Good condition (0%-20%), Parker VH SxS hammerless, 12 ga., 26 1/8 in. barrels, ser. no. 111718 – mfg. 1902. So what's wrong with this description? If you're a Parker collector, 26 1/8 in. barrels immediately raise a red flag, as they have been shortened from the original factory 30 in. length. Cut barrels on Parkers are a very negative alteration, seriously affecting a Parker's value, regardless of grade. Other problems include stock gouging/chipping, and only a portion of the broken buttplate remains. Original frame and barrel finish are gone and have turned an overall grayish patina. Action still remains tight (no surprise there), and this gun may still be shootable, but must be inspected carefully first. With over 242,000 Parkers manufactured between 1866 and 1938 (Remington took over production 1934-1938), this is a good example of how a lot of them look today – well used, and almost worn out. Most people, including many serious collectors, have never seen an original mint condition Parker – they are that rare!

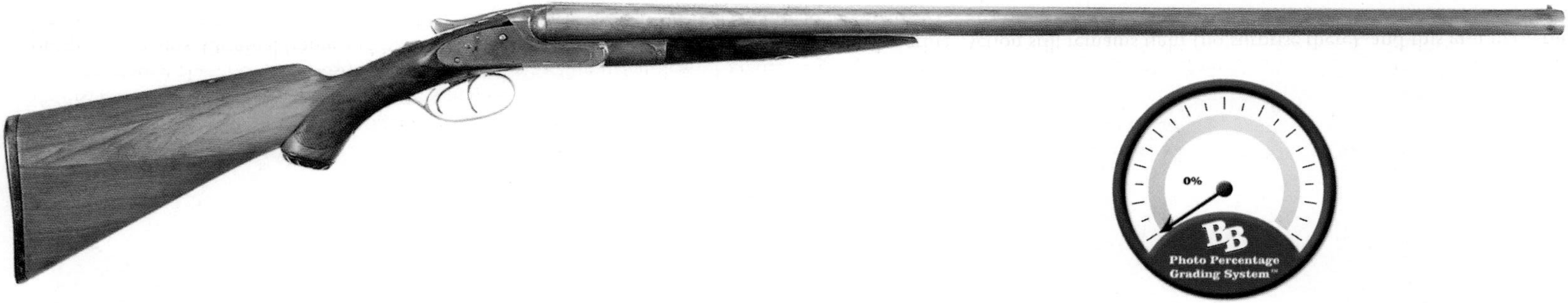

NRA Antique Fair condition (no finish, some major parts replaced), Lefever G Grade SxS, 12 ga., 30 in. barrels, ser. no. 18725 – mfg. 1893. As you can see, with NRA Antique grading factors, once you get down to Good, Fair, or Poor, there isn't a lot of difference when it comes to eye appeal, as guns in this condition are typically not that desirable. The biggest problem with this gun is that the stock was shattered at an earlier date, and a large replacement chunk with non-matching grain has been added. This gun's action is loose, and no metal finish remains on either the barrels or frame. The bores are also dark and pitted (i.e., don't shoot). Close observation will also reveal that the wood surrounding the sidelock is very thin, and appears to have been sanded. Overall, this gun's Fair condition and non-originality have bottomed out its value. Unfortunately, hundreds of similar surviving examples are in this condition factor, which explains why a really good original example is so rare (and expensive) in today's SxS marketplace.

SHOTGUNS: NRA ANTIQUE CONDITIONS

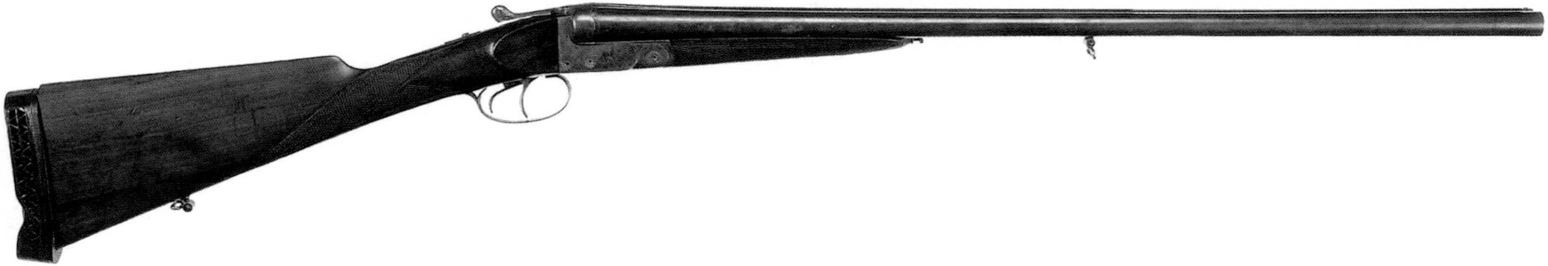

NRA Antique Poor condition (no finish w/replacement parts), French SxS, 16 ga., 28 in. barrels, ser. no. 1513 – mfg. circa 1910-1920. This is truly a no-name shotgun, as no manufacturer's name or marking appears anywhere on this gun — only the proof marks indicate French production. Probably manufactured for a retailer's specifications, this boxlock is only chambered for 2 9/16 in. cartridges, and still has its sling swivels. There is virtually no eye appeal with this shotgun, and the crudely installed recoil pad and major dents on left barrel (not shown) further hurt this gun's overall desirability factor. So how do you determine the value of a gun like this which basically can no longer be shot, and needs to be hidden in the back of your gun cabinet when your friends come over? The answer is thousands of shotguns in this type of condition that are virtually unknown might be rare, but the only thing rarer is the person who might buy it. In other words, don't pay over $125, since in this case even the parts aren't worth anything, as virtually no one is going to have a similar make, model, and gauge.

OLDER EDITIONS

1st Edition (Vol. I, No. I)
1981

2nd Edition (Vol. II, No. I)
1982

3rd Edition (Vol. II, No. II)
1982

4th Edition
1983

5th Edition
1984

6th Edition
1985

7th Edition
1986

8th Edition
1987

9th Edition
1988

10th Edition
1989

11th Edition
1990

12th Edition
1991

13th Edition
1992

14th Edition
1993

15th Edition
1994

16th Edition
1995

17th Edition
1996

18th Edition
1997

19th Edition
1998

20th Edition
1999

21st Edition
2000

22nd Edition
2001

23rd Edition
2002

24th Edition
2003

25th Edition
2004

26th Edition
2005

27th Edition
2006

28th Edition
2007

29th Edition
2008

30th Edition
2009

31st Edition
2010

32nd Edition
2011

33rd Edition
2012

34th Edition
2013

35th Edition
2014

36th Edition
2015

37th Edition
2016

38th Edition
2017

39th Edition
2018

40th Edition
2019

41st Edition
2020

Many of you may want to pick up older editions to start or complete a collection. The rule of thumb is that the older an edition is, the harder it is to find, and the more expensive it will be. We do carry some older editions in stock, but the inventory can change daily. For more information, availability, condition, and pricing, please email: support@bluebookinc.com.

800.877.4867

BlueBookofGunValues.com

2 VETS ARMS CO., LLC

Previous AR-15 style rifle manufacturer located in Eufaula, OK circa 2014-2017.

Please refer to BlueBookOfGunValues.com to order the *Blue Book of AR-15s & Variations*, available as a book or online subscription.

2A ARMAMENT LLC

Current AR-15 style rifle and pistol manufacturer, located in Boise, ID beginning 2009.

Please refer to BlueBookOfGunValues.com to order the *Blue Book of AR-15s & Variations*, available as a book or online subscription.

5TC (5 TOES CUSTOM)

Previous manufacturer of hand-crafted custom pistols and rifles as well as semi-custom AR-15 style rifles, located in Carrollton, TX until 2018.

For individual model listings, please go to BlueBookOfGunValues.com/overflow.

A.A.

Previously manufactured by Azanza & Arrizabalaga, located in Eibar, Spain.

GRADING - PPGS™	100%	98%	95%	90%	80%	70%	60%	LAST MSR

PISTOLS: SEMI-AUTO

A.A. – 7.65mm cal., slide marked "Azanza & Arrizabalaga Model 1916, A.A." in oval on frame.

	100%	98%	95%	90%	80%	70%	60%	LAST MSR
	$250	$200	$165	$135	$115	$85	$75	

REIMS – 6.35mm or 7.65mm cal., copies of M1906 Browning, marked "1914 Model".

	100%	98%	95%	90%	80%	70%	60%	LAST MSR
	$200	$150	$130	$110	$90	$70	$50	

A.A.A.

Previously manufactured by Aldazabal, located in Spain.

PISTOLS: SEMI-AUTO

M1919 – 7.65mm cal.

	100%	98%	95%	90%	80%	70%	60%	LAST MSR
	$110	$100	$85	$70	$65	$60	$55	

A.A. ARMS INC.

Previous manufacturer located in Monroe, NC until 1999.

CARBINES: SEMI-AUTO

AR9 CARBINE – 9mm Para. cal., similar action to AP9, except has carbine length barrel and side folding metal stock. Banned 1994.

	100%	98%	95%	90%	80%	70%	60%	LAST MSR
	$750	$625	$550	$475	$425	$375	$325	

PISTOLS: SEMI-AUTO

AP9 MINI-SERIES PISTOL – 9mm Para. cal., blowback paramilitary design, two barrel lengths, 10 (C/B 1994) or 20* shot mag., phosphate/blue or nickel finish. Disc. 1999, parts cleanup during 2000.

	100%	98%	95%	90%	80%	70%	60%	LAST MSR
	$425	$375	$325	$275	$225	$200	$175	*$245*

Add $20 for nickel finish.
Add $200 for AP9 long barrel Target Model (banned 1994).

A & B HIGH PERFORMANCE FIREARMS

Previous competition pistol manufacturer located in Arvin, CA.

PISTOLS: SEMI-AUTO

LIMITED CLASS – 9mm Para. or .38 Super cal., SA, competition M1911-styled action, STI frame, Ultimatch bull barrel, Caspian slide, Bo-Mar adj. rear sight, blue or chrome finish.

	100%	98%	95%	90%	80%	70%	60%	LAST MSR
	N/A	$1,600	$1,375	$1,150	$925	$700	$550	*$1,875*

OPEN CLASS – 9mm Para. or .38 Super cal., SA, competition M1911-styled action, STI frame, Ultimatch or Hybrid compensated barrel, Caspian slide, C-More scope, blue or chrome finish.

	100%	98%	95%	90%	80%	70%	60%	LAST MSR
	N/A	$2,300	$1,875	$1,600	$1,375	$1,000	$750	*$2,800*

A.R. SALES

Previous manufacturer located in South El Monte, CA, circa 1968-1977.

PISTOLS: SEMI-AUTO

HANDGUN – .45 ACP cal., patterned after Colt Model 1911 Govt., less weight than normal Colt .45.

	100%	98%	95%	90%	80%	70%	60%	LAST MSR
	$295	$250	$225	$205	$175	$155	$145	

GRADING - PPGS™	100%	98%	95%	90%	80%	70%	60%	LAST MSR

RIFLES: SEMI-AUTO

MARK IV SPORTER – .308 Win. cal., M-14 style action, adj. sights. Approx. 200 mfg.

	$725	$650	$575	$500	$450	$400	$350

A06 ARMS

Previous AR-15 style rifle manufacturer located in Fairplay, CO from 2013-2018.

Please refer to BlueBookOfGunValues.com to order the *Blue Book of AR-15s & Variations*, available as a book or online subscription.

ADC (ARMI DALLERA CUSTOM)

Current pistol, rifle, and shotgun manufacturer and customizer located in Concesio, Italy since 1987. Previously located in Gardone, Italy. No current U.S. importer.

ADC manufactures high quality custom pistols, mainly of M1911 design, AR-15 style rifles (including the AR-9 Carabine, AR-308 LR Carabine, Competition Series, Custom Series, M5 Series, and Spartan Series), and the TD Tactical shotgun. Many options and configurations are available. ADC also provides a complete range of customizing and gunsmithing services. Please contact the company directly for more information including pricing, options, and availability.

AFC

Previously manufactured by Auguste Francotte located in Liege, Belgium, 1912-1914. Please refer to the Auguste Francotte listing in the F section.

A. J. ORDNANCE

Previous manufacturer located in Covina, CA.

PISTOLS: SEMI-AUTO

THOMAS – .45 ACP cal., DAO, delayed blowback acton, 3 1/2 in. stainless steel barrel, 6 shot, fixed sights, checkered plastic grips. Disc. mid-1970s.

	$600	$525	$450	$400	$350	$300	$250

Add 50% for chrome or stainless steel.

AK-47 DESIGN CARBINES, RIFLES, & PISTOLS

Select-fire military design rifle originally designed in Russia (initials refer to Avtomat Kalashnikova, 1947). The AK-47 was officially adopted by Russia in 1949. Russian-manufactured select fire AK-47s have not been manufactured since the mid-1950s. Semi-auto AK-47 and AKM clones are currently manufactured by several arsenals in China including Norinco and Poly Technologies, Inc. (currently illegal to import), in addition to being manufactured in other countries including the Czech Republic, Bulgaria, Russia, Egypt, and Hungary. On April 6th, 1998, recent "sporterized" variations (imported 1994-1998) with thumbhole stocks were banned by presidential order. Beginning in 2000, AK-47s were being assembled in the U.S., using both newly manufactured and older original military parts and components.

AK-47s and variations are not rare - approximately 75 million AK-47s and over 100 million AK-74 design carbine/rifles have been manufactured since 1947.

AK-47/AK-74/AKM HISTORY

Since the early 1950s, the AK-47/AK-74/AKM series of select fire rifles has been the standard issue military rifle of the former Soviet Union and its satellites. It continues to fulfill that role reliably today. The AK series of rifles, from the early variants of the AK-47 through the AKM and AK-74, is undoubtedly the most widely used military small arms design in the world. Developed by Mikhail Kalashnikov (the AK stands for Avtomat Kalashnikova) in 1946, the AK went into full production in 1947 in Izhevsk, Russia. In 1953, the milled receiver was put into mass production. Since then, variants of the original AK-47 have been manufactured by almost every former Soviet bloc country and some free world nations, including Egypt. The AK action is the basis for numerous other weapons, including the RPK (Ruchnoy Pulemyot Kalashnikova).

The AK-47 was replaced in 1959 by the AKM, and retained the same basic design. The rifle was simply updated to incorporate easier and more efficient production methods, using a stamped, sheet metal receiver that was pinned and riveted in place, rather than a milled receiver. Other changes included a beavertail forearm, muzzle compensator, and an anti-bounce device intended to improve controllability and increase accuracy.

The AK was designed to be, and always has been, a "peasant-proof" military weapon. It is a robust firearm, both in design and function. Its record on the battlefields around the world is impressive, rivaled only by the great M1 Garand of the U.S. or bolt rifles such as the English Mark III Enfield. The original AK-47 prototypes are on display in the Red Army Museum in Moscow.

All of the current semi-auto AK "clones" are copies of the AKM's basic receiver design and internal components minus the full-auto parts. The Saiga rifle (see separate listing), manufactured by the Izhevsk Machining Plant, in Izhevsk, Russia, is the sole Russian entry into this market. It is available in the standard 7.62x39 mm, 5.45x39 mm (disc.) and 20 gauge or .410 bore. Molot (hammer) JSC also exports semi-automatic AKs to the U.S. under the trade name Vepr. (see separate listing). Saiga is imported by RWC (Russian Weapon Company), and the Vepr. is imported by Robinson Armaments. Molot was the home of the PPSh-41 sub-machine gun during WWII, and also manufactured the RPK and the RPK-74. Other AK European manufacturers include companies in the Czech Republic, Bulgaria, and the former Yugoslavia. The Egyptian-made Maahdi AK clones were also available in the U.S. market.

Interest in the Kalashnikov design is at an all-time high due to the availability of high quality military AK-74, AKS-74, AKS-74U, and RPK-74 parts kits. Some models, such as those produced by Marc Krebs, are of very high quality. Currently, it is hard to go to a gun show or page through a buy/sell firearms magazine and not see a variety of parts, accessories, and high capacity magazines available for many of the AK variants. For shooters, the value represented by these guns is undeniable for the price point.

Values for almost all of the imported AK clones are based solely on their use as sporting or target rifles. Fit and finish varies by country and importer. Most fall on the "low" side. Interest peaked prior to the passage of the 1994 Crime Bill and both AK clones and their "high capacity" magazines were bringing a premium for a short period of time in 1993 and 1994. However, interest waned during 1995-97, and the reduced demand lowered prices. In November of 1997, the Clinton Administration instituted an "administrative suspension" on all import licenses for these types of firearms in order to do a study on their use as "sporting firearms."

On April 6th, 1998, the Clinton Administration, in the political wake of the Jonesboro tragedy, banned the further import of 58 "assault-type" rifles, claiming that these semi-automatics could not be classified as sporting weapons - the AK-47 and most related configurations were included. During 1997, firearms importers obtained permits to import almost 600,000 reconfigured rifles - approximately only 20,000 had entered the country when this ban took effect. When the ban began, applications were pending to import an additional 1,000,000 guns. Previously, thumbhole-stocked AK Sporters were still legal for import, and recent exporters included the Czech Republic, Russia, and Egypt.

AK-47 DESIGN CARBINES, RIFLES, & PISTOLS: RECENT/CURRENT MFG. & IMPORTATION

The following is a listing of both current and recent manufacturers and importers that offer/have offered AK-47 design carbines, rifles, and pistols for sale domestically. Please look under each current company, importer, or brand name/trademark heading for up-to-date information and values on current makes and models that are offered.

These companies include: AKS (AK-47, AK-74, & AKM Copies), American Arms, Inc., American Tactical Imports, Armory USA LLC, Armscor, Arsenal JSCompany(Arsenal Bulgaria), Arsenal Inc., Arsenal USA LLC, B-West, Baikal, Bingham Ltd., Blackheart International LLC, Bushmaster Firearms International LLC, CZ (Ceska Zbrojovka), Century International Arms, Inc., Czechpoint Inc., DDI Arms (Destructive Devices Industries, LLC, new 2017), E.D.M. Arms, E.M.F. Co. Inc., European American Armory Corp., Feather Industries, Inc., Federal Ordnance Inc., FEG, German Sport Guns GmbH, Hakim, Hesse Arms, I.O., Inc., Inter Ordnance of America, LP, Interarms Arsenal, Intrac Arms International Inc., K.B.I., K-VAR Corp., Liberty Arms International, LLC, M+M, Inc., Mitchell Arms, Inc., Molot JSCo, Navy Arms Company, Norinco, Ohio Ordnance Works Inc., Poly Technologies, Inc., Rasheed (Rashid), Robinson Armament Co., Russian American Armory Company, Russian Weapon Company, SAIGA, Samco Global Arms, Inc., Sarco, Inc., Sentinel Arms, TG International, Valmet Inc., Vector Arms Inc., Vepr, Vulcan Armament, and ZDF Import/Export.

PISTOLS: SEMI-AUTO, AK-47 VARIATIONS

Please refer to the individual AK-47 pistol listings and values under the various importers and trademarks.

RIFLES/CARBINES: SEMI-AUTO, AK-47, AK-74, & AKM MODELS

"AK-47" stands for Automatic Kalashnikov Rifle, 1947 Model, first developed in the former Soviet Union by Mikhail Kalashnikov, who passed away in 2013. This gas-operated military rifle was originally designed for select-fire operation, and quickly gained acceptance within the Soviet Union's military forces. While very early military production used stamped receivers, problems in the manufacturing process forced the adoption of milled receivers, which took more time, but solved all of the earlier production problems. The arsenals of Soviet satellite countries, as well as China also began producing AK-47s for military use, but

GRADING - PPGS™	100%	98%	95%	90%	80%	70%	60%	LAST MSR

later also began producing semi-auto variations for commercial sales. In 1959, the AKM (M designates modernized or upgraded) was developed with a stamped receiver and also featured a slanted muzzle brake - it was also approximately 33% lighter than the earlier milled AK-47s. There are far more AKMs available in the American marketplace for sale than semi-auto AK-47s. Chinese importation stopped during late 1990.

AK-47/AKM – 7.62x39mm (most common cal., former Russian M43 military), 5.45x39mm (Romanian mfg. or Saiga/MAK - recent mfg. only), or .223 Rem. cal., semi-auto Kalashnikov action, typically 16 1/2 in. barrel, 5, 10, or 30* (C/B 1994) shot curved mag., stamped (most common) or milled (pre-1959) receiver, wood or synthetic stock and forearm except on folding stock model, 1994-early 1998 importation typically had newer "sporterized" fixed stocks with thumbholes, may be supplied with bayonet, sling, cleaning kit, patterned after former military production rifle of China and Russia.

* ***AK-47/AKM Post-WWII-Pre-1994 Mfg./Importation*** – 7.62x39mm (most common cal., former Russian M43 military), 5.45x39mm (Romanian mfg. or Saiga/MAK - recent mfg. only), or .223 Rem. cal., semi-auto Kalashnikov action, stamped (most common) or milled receiver, typically 16 1/2 in. barrel, 5, 10, or 30* (C/B 1994) shot mag., wood or synthetic stock and forearm except on folding stock model, may be supplied with bayonet, sling, cleaning kit, patterned after former military production rifle of Russia and China. Check markings and/or proofs on gun for country of origin and possible importer.

Romanian mfg.	$1,650	$1,450	$1,250	$1,125	$900	$750	$575	
Yugoslavian mfg.	$1,550	$1,350	$1,165	$1,050	$850	$700	$550	
Hungarian mfg.	$1,750	$1,550	$1,325	$1,175	$950	$775	$625	
Bulgarian mfg.	$1,450	$1,250	$1,075	$950	$800	$650	$500	
Egyptian mfg.	$1,500	$1,300	$1,125	$1,000	$825	$675	$525	

Add 20% for milled receiver.

Add 10% for chrome-lined barrel.

Add 10% for older folding stock variations.

Values are for original guns completely manufactured in the countries listed above and will have various import markings stamped on the receiver or barrel.

* ***AK-47/AKM 1994-2004 Mfg.*** – most feature "sporterized" fixed stocks with thumbholes to comply with the GCA of 1994.

$950	$825	$725	$625	$525	$425	$325	

* ***AK-47/AKM Post 2004 Mfg./Importation*** – most AK-47/AKMs manufactured/imported after 1998 utilize plastic/synthetic furniture, stamped receivers, and folding/telescoping stocks which have different components and construction from those rifles/carbines produced before 1998. Recent U.S. assembly refers to an original stamped European (mostly FEG) or milled receiver with U.S. assembly, using either new parts or matched, older unused original Eastern European-manufactured parts (BATFE 922.R compliant). This newest generation of AK-47/AKMs typically have features as described above, and cannot be sold in several states. Check city and state laws regarding high capacity magazine compliance.

$650	$575	$495	$450	$350	$295	$225	

The most desirable configuration of these recently assembled rifles/carbines has a folding/collapsible stock, high capacity mag., barrel compensator, and a bayonet lug.

These post-2004 AK-47/AKM variations typically do not have import markings, which indicates they have been made up as "parts guns" assembled from various manufacturers, and have usually been put together in the U.S. recently. Additional AK-47 listings can be found under current individual manufacturers and importers listed separately in this text (i.e., Arsenal Inc., Century International, Interarms, etc.).

AK-74/AKM – 5.45x39mm cal., semi-auto action based on the AKM, imported from Bulgaria and other previous Eastern bloc countries, in addition to recent assembly in the U.S., using FEG receivers, Bulgarian parts sets, and additional U.S.-made components.

Bulgarian mfg.	$1,450	$1,275	$1,075	$975	$800	$650	$500	
Recent U.S. assembly	$650	$575	$500	$425	$350	$300	$275	

Add 10%-15% for 5.45x39 mm cal. on Eastern European mfg. (non-recent import).

AMAC

See the "Iver Johnson" section in the I section. AMAC stands for American Military Arms Corporation. Manufactured in Jacksonville, AR. AMAC ceased operations in early 1993.

AMP TECHNICAL SERVICE GmbH

Previous manufacturer located in Puchheim, Germany. Previously imported and distributed 2001-2004 by CQB Products, located in Tustin, CA.

GRADING - PPGS™	100%	98%	95%	90%	80%	70%	60%	LAST MSR

RIFLES: BOLT ACTION

DSR-1 – .300 Win. Mag., .308 Win., or .338 Lapua Mag. cal., 25.6 in. Lothar Walther fluted barrel with muzzle brake and vent. shroud, 4 or 5 shot mag., receiver is made from aluminum, titanium, and polymers, internal parts are stainless steel, two-stage adj. trigger, bullpup design with in-line stock, ambidextrous 3-position safety, includes bipod, 13 lbs. Imported 2002-2004.

	$7,295	$6,300	$5,200	$4,100	$3,000	$2,500	$2,000	*$7,795*

Add $100 for .300 Win. Mag. or $300 for .338 Lapua Mag. cal.

A.M.S.D. (ADVANCED MILITARY SYSTEM DESIGN)

Current manufacturer located in Geneva, Switzerland. No current U.S. importation. Previously distributed 2010-2012 by Loki Weapon Systems, located in Coalgate, OK.

For individual model listings, please go to BlueBookOfGunValues.com/overflow.

AMT (ARCADIA MACHINE & TOOL)

Previous trademark founded circa 1977, manufacturing a variety of firearms, most notably backup pistols, 1911 style pistols, and the "Auto Mag Pistol" large frame magnum automatic pistols. After financial difficulties, the company went bankrupt. The AMT trademark was later acquired by Galena Industries Inc. located in Sturgis, SD, and held from 1999-Jan. 2001, previously located in Irwindale, CA until 1998. From 1998-2001, all AMTs manufactured by Galena Industries Inc. had a lifetime warranty, which is now void. The AMT trademark was then acquired by Crusader Gun Company, Inc., located in Houston, TX. Crusader Gun Company began limited manufacture in late 2004-circa 2015. Also see Irwindale Arms, Inc. and Auto Mag. for older, discontinued models.

Galena Industries phased out the use of the AMT name but continued to use the individual model names until 2001.

During 2005, Crusader Gun Company Inc. acquired the previous tooling of AMT - Auto Mag., and reintroduced the following models with limited production: Auto Mag II, Auto Mag III, AutoMag IV, the Back Up .380, and the Back Up .45.

PISTOLS: SEMI-AUTO

From 1999 to 2001, AMT began using Millett sights exclusively. Between 1993 and 1998, AMT changed from white outline Millett adjustable sights to an adjustable three-dot (white) system manufactured by LPA in Italy. Early production pistols were made in El Monte, CA, and are marked "El Monte".

LIGHTNING – .22 LR cal., SA, stainless steel only, 5 (bull only), 6 1/2, 8 1/2, 10 1/2, or 12 1/2 (disc. 1987) in. bull or tapered barrels, adj. sights and trigger, pistol based on semi-auto Ruger action. 23,903 were mfg. 1984-1987.

	$475	$450	$375	$350	$275	$225	$175	*$289*

This model featured a frame grooved for scope mounts, Clark trigger, Millett sights, and either Pachmayr rubber or Wayland wood grips as standard equipment.

* ***Lightning Bull's Eye Regulation Target*** – similar to 6 1/2 in. Lightning with bull barrel, except has vent. rib, wood grips, extended rear sight. Mfg. 1986 only.

	$675	$575	$500	$450	$375	$300	$240	*$436*

BABY AUTOMAG – .22 LR cal., SA, stainless steel only, 8 1/2 in. vent. rib barrel, Millett adj. rear sight, smooth walnut grips, 1,001 mfg.

	$2,500	$2,200	$1,875	$1,700	$1,375	$1,125	$875	

AUTOMAG II – .22 WMR cal., stainless steel only, 3 3/8 (Compact Model, disc., limited mfg.), 4 1/2 (disc., limited mfg.), or 6 in. barrel, gas-assisted blowback action, adj. white outline Millett adj. rear sight, grooved polymer Lexan grips, 7 (Compact) or 9 shot mag., 24-32 oz. Mfg. 1987-2001, reintroduced late 2004-disc.

	$775	$675	$575	$475	$400	$350	$300	*$850*

Subtract approx. 25% for 3 3/8 or 4 1/2 in. barrel.

AUTOMAG III – .30 Carbine or 9mm Win. Mag. (mfg. 1993 only) cal., stainless steel, 6 3/8 in. barrel, patterned after Colt Govt. Model, white outline Millett adj. rear sight, grooved Lexan grips, 8 shot mag., 43 oz. Mfg. 1992-circa 2014.

	$2,300	$2,000	$1,625	$1,400	$1,275	$1,000	$800	*$549*

GRADING - PPGS™	100%	98%	95%	90%	80%	70%	60%	LAST MSR

AUTOMAG IV – 10mm (disc. 1993) or .45 Win. Mag. cal., 6 1/2 (.45 Win. Mag. only) or 8 5/8 (disc. 1993) in. barrel, 7 or 8 shot mag., Millett adj. rear sight, stainless steel, 46 oz. Mfg. 1992-circa 2014.

	$2,000	$1,750	$1,500	$1,325	$1,100	$900	$700	

AUTOMAG V – .50 AE cal., stainless steel, 6 1/2 in. barrel, gas venting system reduces recoil, 5 shot mag., 46 oz. Mfg. 1993-95.

	$1,900	$1,675	$1,425	$1,275	$1,050	$850	$675	*$900*

AUTOMAG 440 – .440 Cor-Bon cal., special order only. Mfg. 1999-2001.

	$1,600	$1,400	$1,200	$1,100	$875	$725	$550	*$899*

JAVELINA – 10mm cal., 7 in. barrel, 8 shot mag., Millett adj. rear sight, wraparound neoprene grips, wide adj. trigger, long grip safety, 48 oz. Mfg. 1992 only.

	$1,475	$1,300	$1,100	$1,000	$825	$675	$525	*$676*

BACKUP PISTOL SMALL FRAME – .22 LR (limited production, disc. 1987) or .380 ACP cal. (disc. 2000, reintroduced 2004), traditional DA/SA (disc. 1992) or DAO (new 1992), 2 1/2 in. barrel, stainless steel, Lexan grips, 5 (.380 ACP) or 8 (.22 LR) shot mag., 18 (.380 ACP only) or 23 oz. Disc. 2010.

	$380	$330	$275	$250	$220	$175	$140	*$525*

Add approx. 10% for .22 LR cal.
Older disc. walnut grip models are worth a slight premium.

In 1992, AMT reengineered this model and removed all external levers, production resumed late 2004.

BACKUP PISTOL LARGE FRAME – 9mm Para. (mfg. 1995-2006, reintroduced 2011), .357 SIG (mfg. 1996-2010), .38 Super (new 1995), .40 S&W (new 1995), .400 Cor-Bon (mfg. 1997-2010), or .45 ACP (mfg. 1995-2015) cal., traditional DA/SA (disc. 1992) or DAO (new 1992), 3 in. barrel, stainless steel, Lexan grips, 5 (.40 S&W) or 6 shot mag., 23 oz. Disc.

	$400	$350	$300	$275	$225	$180	$140	*$635*

Add $100 for .400 Cor-Bon cal. (disc. 2010).
Older disc. walnut grip models are worth a slight premium.
.38 Super cal. pistols are uncommon and worth a premium.

In 1992, AMT reengineered this model and removed all external levers, production resumed late 2004.

BACKUP PISTOL II – .380 ACP cal., SA, stainless steel, 2 1/2 in. barrel, 5 shot finger extension mag., black carbon fiber grips, 18 oz. Mfg. 1993-98.

	$275	$225	$175	$150	$125	$100	$80	*$369*

.45 ACP STANDARD GOVERNMENT MODEL – .45 ACP cal., similar to Colt semi-auto Govt. Model, stainless steel, 5 in. barrel, fixed rear sight, loaded chamber indicator, adj. trigger, wraparound neoprene grips, 38 oz. Disc. 1999.

	$625	$550	$475	$425	$350	$275	$225	*$399*

HARDBALLER LONGSLIDE – .45 ACP or .400 Cor-Bon (aka .400 Accelerator, new 1998) cal., 7 in. barrel, longer slide assembly, serrated rib, stainless steel slide and frame, adj. trigger, adj. Millet rear sight, wraparound neoprene grips, 46 oz. Disc. circa 2001.

	$1,350	$1,175	$1,000	$925	$750	$600	$475	*$549*

Add $50 for .400 Cor-Bon (.400 Accelerator, new 1998) cal.
Add $300 for 5 in. Longslide conversion kit (disc. 1997).

HARDBALLER II – .45 ACP cal., similar to Colt Gold Cup Model, stainless steel, 5 in. barrel, adj. Millett rear sight, serrated rib, loaded chamber indicator, adj. trigger, wraparound neoprene grips, 38 oz. Disc. 2001.

	$750	$650	$550	$500	$425	$350	$250	*$499*

Add $280 for 7 in. Hardballer conversion kit (disc. 1997).

COMMANDO – .40 S&W cal., 4 in. barrel. Mfg. 1998-2001.

	$800	$700	$600	$550	$450	$375	$275	*$499*

SKIPPER – .45 ACP cal., re-released in 1991 with choice of .40 S&W or .45 ACP cal., similar to Hardballer, except approx. 1 in. shorter slide on pre-1984 mfg. frame, 4 1/4 in. barrel, checkered walnut grips, matte finish stainless steel, Millett adj. rear sight, 7 shot mag., 33 oz. Disc. 1991.

	$600	$450	$375	$300	$250	$210	$175	*$450*

COMBAT SKIPPER – similar to Skipper, but with fixed sights. Disc. 1984.

	$625	$475	$400	$325	$275	$225	$180	

BULL'S EYE TARGET MODEL – .40 S&W cal., similar to Hardballer with 5 in. barrel, 8 shot mag., adj. Millett rear sight, wraparound neoprene grips, 38 oz. Mfg. 1991 only.

	$450	$400	$350	$295	$240	$210	$180	*$500*

GRADING - PPGS™	100%	98%	95%	90%	80%	70%	60%	LAST MSR

"ON DUTY" DOUBLE ACTION – 9mm Para., .40 S&W, or .45 ACP (new late 1994) cal., stainless steel slide and barrel, 4 1/2 in. barrel, 9 (.45 ACP), 10 (C/B 1994), 11* (.40 S&W), or 15* (9mm Para.) shot mag., 3-dot sighting system, anodized aluminum frame, trigger disconnect safety, inertial firing pin, carbon fiber grips, 32 oz. Mfg. 1991-94.

	$650	$500	$425	$350	$300	$250	$200	*$470*

Add $60 for .45 ACP cal.

In 1992, this model became available with either DA/SA with decocking lever or DAO with safety.

RIFLES: BOLT ACTION

AMT manufactured a line of bolt action rifles as well as unbarreled actions that gunsmiths could make custom rifles from. These AMT rifles were discontinued in 1998.

BOLT ACTION STANDARD SINGLE SHOT – 11 various cals., post-1964 push-feed action, pre-1964 3-position side swing safety, cone breech, composite stock, cryogenically treated stainless steel barrel w/o sights, 8 1/2 lbs. Mfg. 1996-97.

	$850	$700	$500	$450	$400	$325	$275	*$1,500*

BOLT ACTION DELUXE SINGLE SHOT – 11 various cals., Mauser-type controlled feeding, short, medium, or long right-hand or left-hand action, pre-1964 3-position side swing safety and claw-type extractor, cryogenically treated stainless steel barrel w/o sights, custom Kevlar stock, approx. 8 1/2 lbs. Mfg. 1996 only.

	$1,025	$825	$675	$550	$475	$425	$350	*$2,400*

BOLT ACTION STANDARD REPEATER – 21 various cals., post-1964 push-feed action, Mauser-type mag., pre-1964 3-position side swing safety, Model 70-type trigger, composite stock, cryogenically treated stainless steel barrel w/o sights. 8 1/2 lbs. Mfg. 1996 only.

	$900	$750	$550	$475	$425	$350	$300	*$1,110*

BOLT ACTION DELUXE REPEATER – similar to Bolt Action Deluxe Single Shot, except has Mauser-type mag. Mfg. 1996 only.

	$1,100	$900	$725	$575	$500	$450	$375	*$1,596*

RIFLES: SEMI-AUTO

LIGHTNING (25/22) – .22 LR cal., based on Ruger 10-22 action, stainless steel, 30 shot mag., 17 1/2 in. bull or tapered barrel, nylon pistol grip handle and forearm, folding stock with recoil pad or youth stock, fixed sights, 6 lbs. Mfg. 1986-93.

	$550	$475	$425	$350	$275	$225	$175	*$296*

SMALL GAME HUNTER (SGH) – .22 LR cal., same mechanical action as Lightning, except has matte black nylon stock with checkered forearm and grip, 22 in. barrel, 10 shot mag., no sights, removable recoil pad allows storage in stock, 6 lbs. Mfg. 1986-93.

	$550	$475	$425	$350	$275	$225	$175	*$300*

SMALL GAME HUNTER II – similar to Small Game Hunter, except has match grade 22 in. heavyweight full-floating barrel, 10 shot rotary mag., black fiberglass nylon stock, no sights, 6 lbs. Mfg. 1993 only.

	$575	$500	$450	$375	$300	$250	$200	*$300*

Add $70 for 17 1/2 in. stainless steel barrel.
Add $150 for 22 1/2 in. stainless steel match grade barrel.

CHALLENGE EDITION (I, II, III) – .22 LR cal., target variation featuring McMillan fiberglass stock, 16 1/4 (choice of 6 in. barrel weight extension or 3 in. muzzle brake, new 1997), 18, 20 (mfg. 1994-96), or 22 (mfg. 1994-96) in. floating stainless steel bull barrel, custom designed or Jewell (new 1997) trigger, custom order through AMT's Custom Shop. Mfg. 1994-98.

	$925	$700	$525	$450	$385	$325	$275	*$1,296*

Subtract $200 if without Jewell trigger.
Add $144 for 16 1/4 barrel with 3 in. muzzle brake (Challenge Edition II, new 1997).
Add $85 for 16 1/4 barrel with 6 in. barrel extension (Challenge Edition III).

* ***Challenge Edition Elite With Bloop Tube*** – 16 1/4 in. barrel with a 6 in. bloop tube extension enabling increased sight radius and muzzle-heavy ergonomics, McMillan fiberglass STC stock. Mfg. 1996-98.

	$1,050	$800	$625	$525	$450	$385	$325	*$1,498*

Subtract $255 if without compensator.

SPORTER EDITION – .22 LR cal., 16 1/2, 18, 20, or 22 in. tapered sporter barrel, McMillan fiberglass sporter stock. Mfg. 1996 only.

	$680	$550	$425	$350	$300	$260	$225	*$900*

GRADING - PPGS™	100%	98%	95%	90%	80%	70%	60%	LAST MSR

HUNTER EDITION I – .22 LR cal., 18, 20, or 22 in. regular barrel with injection-molded sporter stock. Mfg. 1996 only (replaced with Hunter Edition II).

	$550	$475	$425	$350	$275	$225	$175	*$800*

HUNTER EDITION II – .22 LR cal., 22 in. tapered sporter barrel with 2 lb. Jewell trigger, McMillan synthetic sporter stock. Mfg. 1997-98.

	$750	$575	$425	$360	$315	$260	$225	*$1,354*

FLY SWATTER I – .22 LR cal., 16 1/2 in. regular barrel with injection molded (1996 only) or Hogue over-molded (new 1997) sporter stock. Mfg. 1996-97.

	$575	$450	$325	$265	$230	$195	$170	*$822*

FLY SWATTER II – similar to Fly Swatter I, except has 3 in. muzzle brake. Mfg. 1997 only.

	$675	$475	$350	$285	$250	$215	$185	*$936*

BR-50 ACCELERATOR EDITION – .22 LR cal., 16 1/4 (new 1998) or 16 1/2 (disc. 1997) in. bull barrel with 3 in. muzzle brake (new 1998), McMillan bench rest stock, Hoehn barrel tuner (disc. 1997), and Jewell trigger. Mfg. 1997-98.

	$925	$700	$525	$450	$385	$325	$275	*$1,440*

ACCULITE EDITION RIFLE – .22 LR cal., 18 in. Magnum Research graphite barrel with muzzle brake, thumbhole sporter stock, adj. Jewell trigger, 4 3/4 lbs. Mfg. 1998 only.

	$825	$625	$475	$400	$350	$285	$250	*$1,321*

INTIMIDATOR EDITION RIFLE – .22 LR cal., 16 1/4 in. Shilen select match grade barrel with 6 in. bloop tube, adj. Jewell trigger, 6 1/4 lbs. Mfg. 1998 only.

	$1,000	$725	$550	$475	$425	$350	$285	*$1,581*

MAGNUM HUNTER – .22 WMR cal., 20 in. free floating barrel, stainless steel, 10 shot single stack mag., no sights, drilled and tapped for Weaver 87-A scope base, black synthetic stock, 6 lbs. Mfg. 1995-98.

	$450	$375	$295	$225	$175	$140	$125	*$459*

TARGET RIFLE SEMI-AUTO – .22 LR cal., button rifled cryogenically treated barrel with target crown, choice of Fajen laminate or Hogue composite stock, 10 shot mag., one-piece receiver with integral Weaver mount, 7 1/2 lbs. Mfg. 1997-98.

	$500	$425	$350	$275	$225	$195	$165	*$549*

Add $50 for Fajen laminate stock.

APF

Please refer to the Alex Pro Firearms section.

AR 57 LLC

Current AR-15 style rifle manufacturer located in Woodinville, WA. AR 57 LLC's former name was 57 Center LLC and was previously located in Bellevue and Redmond, WA.

Please refer to BlueBookOfGunValues.com to order the *Blue Book of AR-15s & Variations*, available as a book or online subscription.

AR-7 INDUSTRIES, LLC

Previous manufacturer located in Geneseo, IL 1998-2004. Previously located in Meriden, CT, from 1998 to early 2004.

In February 2004, AR-7 Industries, LLC was purchased by ArmaLite, Inc., and recent manufacture was in Geneseo, IL.

RIFLES: BOLT ACTION

AR-7 TAKEDOWN – .22 LR cal., bolt action variation of the AR-7 Explorer rifle, similar takedown/storage configuration, 2 1/2 lbs. Advertised 2002 only.

While advertised during 2002, this model was never manufactured.

RIFLES: SEMI-AUTO

AR-7 EXPLORER RIFLE – .22 LR cal., takedown barrelled action stores in synthetic stock which floats, 16 in. barrel (synthetic sleeve with steel liner), 8 shot mag., aperture rear sight, synthetic stock, stowed length 16 1/2 in., black matte finish on AR-7, silver tone on AR-7S (disc. 2000), camo finish on AR-7C, two-tone (silver receiver with black stock and barrel) on AR-7T (disc. 2000), walnut finish on AR-W (mfg. 2001-2002), 2 1/2 lbs. Mfg. late 1998-2004.

	$175	$150	$125	$110	$100	$90	$80	*$200*

Add $15 for camouflage or walnut finish.

This model was also previously manufactured by Survival Arms, Inc. and Charter Arms - see individual listings for information.

GRADING - PPGS™	100%	98%	95%	90%	80%	70%	60%	LAST MSR

AR-7 SPORTER (AR-20) - .22 LR cal., 16 1/2 in. steel barrel with vent. aluminum shroud, 8 (new 2001) or 16 shot "flip clip" (optional) mag., aluminum shroud, metal skeleton fixed stock with pistol grip, 3.85 lbs. Mfg. late 1998-2004.

$175	$150	$125	$110	$100	$90	$80	*$200*

Add $100 for sporter conversion kit (includes aluminum shrouded barrel, pistol grip stock, and 16 shot flip clip).

This model was also previously manufactured by Survival Arms, Inc. - see individual listing for information.

AR-7 TARGET - .22 LR cal., 16 in. bull barrel with 7/8 in. cantilever scope mount, 8 shot mag., tube stock with pistol grip, 3-9x40mm compact rubber armored scope was optional, 5.65 lbs. Mfg. 2002-2004.

$195	$175	$150	$125	$105	$95	$80	*$210*

Add $60 for compact scope.

AR-15 STYLE CARBINES, RIFLES, PISTOLS, & SHOTGUNS

AR-15 HISTORY

AR-15 refers to the model nomenclature originally given to the select-fire, gas-operated carbine/rifle featuring synthetic furniture and chambered in 5.56 NATO cal., and developed by Eugene Stoner in 1957. At the time, Stoner was under contract by the Armalite division of the Fairchild Aircraft Corp. In 1958, this new AR-15 lost out in military competition to the select-fire M-14 manufactured by Springfield Armory. After losing this competition, Fairchild Aircraft Corp. thought their new carbine/rifle design would never prove to be successful or obtain a military contract. As a result, during 1959 it sold the design and all future manufacturing rights to Colt. In 1962, the U.S. Department of Defense Advanced Research Projects Agency (ARPA) purchased 1,000 AR-15 rifles from Colt which were immediately sent to South Vietnam for field trials. In 1963, Colt was awarded an 85,000 rifle contract for the U.S. Army (designated XM16E1), and another 19,000 for the U.S. Armed Forces (designated M-16). This new select-fire M-16 was a direct variation of Stoner's original AR-15 design, but had U.S. ordnance markings. In 1963, a presidential order given to the U.S. Army made the M-16 its official service rifle.

In 1966, because of the U.S. involvement in the escalating war in Vietnam, the U.S. government submitted an order for 840,000 M-16s to be delivered to the U.S. Armed Forces at a cost of $92 million. Today, the AR-15 is one of the most popular rifles on the market and many companies offer an AR-15 platform.

AR-15 INFORMATION

Because of the consumer popularity and resulting proliferation of the semi-auto AR-15 style carbines/rifles since the early 2000s, there are many companies who now offer the AR-15 style platform for sale with their brand name or trademark stamped on the guns. However, there are only four primary domestic manufacturers which currently produce the majority of lower receivers for the AR marketplace. The following listing includes those manufacturers of AR-15 lower receivers, in addition to those brand names, trademarks, and private labels for other companies.

Lewis Machine & Tool = LMT, Lauer (disc.), DS Arms, PWA, Eagle, Knights Armament, Barrett, Bushmaster (possibly).

Continental Machine & Tool = Stag, RRA, High Standard, Noveske (disc.), Century, Global Tactical, CLE, S&W, MGI (1st variation), Wilson Tactical (not all models), Colt, Ratworx.

LAR = Grizzly, Bushmaster (L Prefix), Ameetech, DPMS (possibly), CMMG, Double Star, Fulton, Spike's Tactical, Noveske.

Mega Machine Shop = Mega, Gunsmoke, Dalphon, POF (forged), Alexander Arms, Singer, Spike's Tactical (disc.).

Additional smaller AR-15 lower receiver manufacturers include JV Precision (Double Star, LRB), Olympic (Olympic, SGW, Tromix, Palmetto, Dalphon, Frankford, Century (disc.), Superior (Superior Arms, Lauer), Grenadier Precision, and Sabre Defense (disc.).

Some companies also manufacture custom cut lower receivers out of solid billets, and they include MGI, Cobb, JP, Socom, Sun Devil, POF, and S&W (Performance Center).

In most cases, the markings on forged lower receivers that appear on the magazine well generally indicate the company or trademark that assembled the lower receiver while the markings that appear above the trigger guard indicate the manufacturer of the lower receiver.

Please look under each current company, importer, or brand name/trademark heading for up-to-date information and values on the AR-15 makes and models that are offered.

ASAI AG (ADVANCED SMALL ARMS INDUSTRIES)

Previous manufacturer located in Solothurn, Switzerland 1994-2004. Previously imported until 2000 by Magnum Research, Inc. located in Minneapolis, MN.

PISTOLS: SEMI-AUTO

ONE PRO .45 – 9mm Para. (limited mfg. in Europe, never imported into the U.S.), .40 S&W (limited mfg. in Europe, never imported into the U.S.), .400 Cor-Bon (conversion only), or .45 ACP cal., SA or DA, steel or alloy (not imported into U.S.) frame, 3 (disc. 1998) or 3 3/4 in. barrel with polygonal rifling, 10 shot mag., steel or alloy (not imported into U.S.) frame, black contoured synthetic grips, includes plastic case, extra 10 shot mag., and cleaning kit, black or two-tone (less than 10 mfg.) finish, 25 or 31 oz. Imported mid-1997 through 2000.

100%	98%	95%	90%	80%	70%	60%	LAST MSR
$595	$485	$410	$360	$330	$300	$275	*$699*

Add $209 for .400 Cor-Bon conversion kit without compensator.

Add $249 for .45 ACP or .400 Cor-Bon conversion kit with extended barrel, compensator, and recoil spring guide.

ASI ARMS (ARAL ARMS)

Current trademark manufactured by Asi Silah San. Tic. Ltd., located in Istanbul, Turkey. In 2018, the company's name changed from Aral Arms to ASI Arms. Aral Arms was a trademark manufactured by Aral Silah San. Tic. Ltd., located in Istanbul, Turkey.

ASI manufactures good quality O/U, semi-auto, slide action, and single barrel shotguns, blank pistols and revolvers, as well as airguns. Currently this trademark has had little or no importation into the U.S. Please contact the company directly for more information, including domestic availability and pricing.

A-SQUARE (CURRENT MFG.)

Current trademark of bolt action rifles and ammunition established in 2013 and owned by the Broadsword Group, located in Glenrock, WY.

RIFLES: BOLT ACTION

A-Square bolt action rifles are built per individual custom order specifications. Please contact the company directly for more information including pricing, options, and availability.

A-SQUARE (PREVIOUS MFG.)

Previous firearms manufacturer located in Glenrock, WY late 2011-2012. Ammunition and administrative offices were located in Chamberlain, SD, from late 2007-late 2011. During 2010, A-Square became a division of Sharps Rifle Company, located in Chamberlain, SD. A-Square was previously located in Jeffersonville, IN, 2003-2007, Bedford, KY until 2002, Louisville, KY until 2000, and in Madison, IN until 1991.

For individual model listings, please go to BlueBookOfGunValues.com/overflow.

ATCSA

Previously manufactured by Armas De Tiro Y Casa located in Spain.

REVOLVERS

COLT POCKET PISTOL COPY – .38 cal., 6 shot.

100%	98%	95%	90%	80%	70%	60%
$155	$140	$110	$100	$90	$75	$65

SINGLE SHOT REVOLVER – target pistol.

100%	98%	95%	90%	80%	70%	60%
$195	$165	$145	$110	$100	$90	$75

ATA ARMS

Current rifle and shotgun manufacturer established circa 1967, and located in Istanbul, Turkey. Select models are currently imported and private labeled beginning 2008 by Weatherby. Previously imported by European American Armory (EAA) Corp located in Cocoa, FL in 2018 only, by Tristar, located in N. Kansas City, MO until 2008 (private label only), and by K.B.I., located in Harrisonburg, PA.

For individual model listings, please go to BlueBookOfGunValues.com/overflow.

AWA USA INC.

Current importer established during late 2004, located in Hialeah, FL.

AWA USA purchased the remaining assets of American Western Arms, Inc. in late 2004, and became the importer of guns manufactured by AWA International, Inc. in Brescia, Italy.

GRADING - PPGS™	100%	98%	95%	90%	80%	70%	60%	LAST MSR

HANDGUNS

1873 CLASSIC SAA – .357 Mag. or .45 LC cal., 4 3/4 or 5 1/2 in. barrel, walnut grips, flat main spring, choice of blue, Turnbull color case hardened, nickel (disc.), or hard chrome (disc.) finish. Importation began 2007.

MSR $440	$395	$360	$330	$295	$250	$225	$195	

Add $125 for color case hardened frame or $195 for nickel (disc.) or hard chrome (disc.) finish.
Subtract $50 for kit gun configuration.

1873 ULTIMATE SAA – .32-20 WCF, .38-40 WCF, .44 Spl., .357 Mag., .44-40 WCF, or .45 LC cal., 4 3/4, 5 1/2, or 7 1/2 in. barrel, walnut grips, coil main spring, blue, Turnbull color case hardened, nickel, or hard chrome finish. Importation began 2007.

MSR $600	$650	$575	$495	$440	$350	$300	$225	

Add $125 for color case hardened frame or $195 for nickel or hard chrome finish.
Add $115 for Jim Martin Ultimate model.
Add $150 for octagon barrel.
Subtract $50 for kit gun configuration.

Custom barrel lengths include 3 1/2, 10, and 12 in.

1884 BISLEY – .357 Mag. or .45 LC cal., 4 3/4 or 5 1/2 in. barrel, walnut grips, choice of blue or Turnbull color case hardened, nickel or hard chrome finish. Imported 2007-2008.

	$395	$360	$330	$295	$250	$225	$195	*$440*

LIGHTNING BOLT SLIDE ACTION – .45 LC cal., 12 in. round barrel, 5 shot, blade front sight, walnut stock and forearm, available in high polish blue, color case hardened, hard chrome, or nickel finish. Importation began 2007.

MSR $1,000	$895	$750	$625	$500	$400	$300	$225	

Add $150 for color case hardened frame or $300 for White Lightningbolt with nickel or hard chrome finish.

RIFLES: SLIDE ACTION

LIGHTNING RIFLE – .32-20 WCF, .38 Spl., .38-40 WCF, .44-40 WCF, or .45 LC cal., patterned after the original Colt Lightning model, 20 or 24 in. round or octagon barrel, standard or limited edition wood stock, choice of blue, color case hardened, white (hard chrome, brushed nickel, or polished nickel) or black frame, standard or limited edition wood stock. Importation began 2007.

MSR $850	$775	$675	$600	$525	$450	$375	$300	

Add $50 for octagon barrel.
Add $100 for upgraded wood with checkering.
Add $150 for 16 in. barrel.
Add $250 for color case hardened frame.
Add $400 for White Lightning with either hard chrome or brushed/polished nickel finish.
Add $525 for Black Lightning w/black chrome finish (disc.)
Add $1,150 for limited edition model (50 each of 20 and 24 in. barrel).
Add $950 for Jerry Harper engraving.

AWC SYSTEMS TECHNOLOGY, LLC

Previous firearms and current suppressor manufacturer currently located in Phoenix, AZ and established circa 1984. AWC also private labels and distributes commercial ammunition manufactured by TTI Armory. In 2010, AWC was acquired by Strategic Armory Corps. Please contact the company directly for more information on its wide range of suppressors.

RIFLES: BOLT ACTION

AWC previously manufactured four bolt action models until 2013. Models included the M91 BDR ($3,995 last MSR), M92 ($3,495 last MSR), M95 ($3,495 last MSR), and the M40A2 ($3,495 last MSR).

AYA (AGUIRRE Y ARANZABAL)

Current manufacturer established in 1915, located in Eibar, Spain. Currently imported by New England Custom Gun Service, Ltd. (NECG), located in Claremont, NH. Previously imported by Fieldsport, located in Traverse City, MI and by AYA USA, located in Old Saybrook, CT, Anglo American Sporting Agency, located in Corona del Mar, CA, H.G. Lomas Gunmakers, located in Elkhart Lake, WI, John F. Rowe, located in Enid, OK, William Larkin Moore 1969-1978 (with Agoura, CA import marking), and 1978-1986 (with West Lake, CA import marking). Diarm also manufactured AYAs circa 1986-1988 in Eibar, Spain.

GRADING - PPGS™	100%	98%	95%	90%	80%	70%	60%	LAST MSR

AYA manufactured shotguns can be identified by serialization. Serial numbers over 600,001 with barrel flats marked "Arms de Chasse" or "Scotia Group" are post-1988 AYA manufactured while specimens numbered under 600,000 may have been manufactured by Diarm circa 1986-1989. Diarm manufacture is not covered by the AYA warranty, nor is the resale the same as values listed below.

Please refer to the AYA and Spanish year of mfg. date codes under Serialization in the back of this text for more information on AYA shotguns.

SHOTGUNS: O/U

AYA also manufactured a Coral boxlock, both in standard and deluxe configurations. The MD Series O/U models completed their European line (2007 MSR was $4,100 - $7,300).

Add 5% for gauges smaller than 12 ga.
Add 5% for 3 in. magnum chambers.

ARRATE – 12 or 20 ga., standard boxlock action or deluxe with sideplates (XBL Model), fixed chokes, ejectors, detachable trigger mechanism, Grade 2 wood stock, light engraving, matte black or classic silver finished receiver. Mfg. 2013-2017.

	100%	98%	95%	90%	80%	70%	60%	LAST MSR
	$5,950	$5,500	$4,500	$3,750	$3,000	$2,500	$2,000	*$6,500*

Add $200 for classic silver finished receiver.
Add $1,300 for BL Model with upgraded wood and more engraving.
Add $2,300 for deluxe boxlock action with sideplates.
Add $1,505-$1,772 for Briley multichokes.
Add $225 for SST.
Add $338 for adj. stock.
Add 40% for extra barrels.
This model is also available in XDL configuration with ornamental scroll and Grade 1 wood stock - please contact the importers directly for pricing.

AUGUSTA – 12 ga. only, deluxe O/U sidelock shotgun, select walnut, Arabesque engraving in deep relief. This model has been imported off and on over the years.

	100%	98%	95%	90%	80%	70%	60%	LAST MSR
MSR $33,323	$28,500	$23,000	$18,500	$14,250	$10,000	$8,750	$7,500	

CORAL "A" – 12 or 16 ga., boxlock action with Kersten crossbolt, VR barrel, ejectors, DT. Disc. 1985.

	100%	98%	95%	90%	80%	70%	60%	LAST MSR
	$1,275	$1,050	$875	$775	$695	$625	$560	*$2,195*

CORAL "B" – similar to Coral "A" model, except for coin-washed engraved receiver. Disc. 1985.

	100%	98%	95%	90%	80%	70%	60%	LAST MSR
	$1,395	$1,100	$925	$820	$720	$650	$595	*$2,450*

EXCELSIOR – 12 or 20 ga., sidelock action, 28 in. VR barrels, fixed chokes, ejectors, DT, elaborately engraved coin finished receiver, available in SNST, SST, or Trap configuration. Disc. 2010.

	100%	98%	95%	90%	80%	70%	60%	LAST MSR
	$6,600	$5,750	$4,875	$4,100	$3,300	$2,600	$1,850	*$7,499*

Add $301 for SNST.
Add $1,101 for SST.
Add $1,701 for Trap configuration.

LEGEND – 12 or 20 ga., 28 in. chrome-lined barrels w/standard choke tubes, non-selective single trigger, straight hand, semi or full pistol grip, Grade 1 oil finished walnut stock, manual safety, maker's name and logo in gold inlay, available in game or clay configuration, Grade 1 grade oil finished walnut. New 2015.

	100%	98%	95%	90%	80%	70%	60%	LAST MSR
MSR $7,539	$6,725	$6,100	$4,950	$4,000	$3,150	$2,625	$2,100	

Add $274 for Legend Sport model (new 2015).

* ***Legend de Luxe*** – 12 or 20 ga., 28 in. chrome-lined barrels w/standard choke tubes, non-selective single trigger, straight, semi, or full pistol grip, manual safety, forged steel monobloc barrels and receiver, English style engraving, maker's name and logo in gold inlay, available in game or clay configuration, double locking system, Grade 1 oil finished walnut stock. New 2015.

	100%	98%	95%	90%	80%	70%	60%	LAST MSR
MSR $8,622	$7,650	$6,800	$5,350	$4,200	$3,350	$2,750	$2,200	

MODEL 37 SUPER (DISC.) – 12, 16, or 20 ga., sidelock, Merkel-style action, various VR barrel lengths and chokes, auto ejector, high grade wood, elaborate engraving. Prices below reflect older models. Disc.

	100%	98%	95%	90%	80%	70%	60%	LAST MSR
12 ga.	$3,200	$2,750	$2,100	$1,900	$1,700	$1,500	$1,250	
16 ga.	$3,200	$2,700	$2,100	$1,700	$1,500	$1,350	$1,150	
20 ga.	$3,750	$2,950	$2,200	$1,900	$1,700	$1,600	$1,475	

NEW MODEL 37 A/B/C (CURRENT MFG.) – detachable sidelock action, nickel steel receiver, game scene engraved. This model has been imported off and on over the years.

GRADING - PPGS™	100%	98%	95%	90%	80%	70%	60%	LAST MSR
* ***Model 37 A***								
MSR $16,601	$12,000	$10,000	$8,500	$6,800	$5,300	$4,250	$3,600	
* ***Model 37 B***								
MSR $16,843	$12,700	$10,750	$8,900	$7,000	$5,500	$4,250	$3,600	
* ***Model 37 C***								
MSR $24,962	$18,700	$16,400	$13,400	$10,650	$8,750	$6,800	$5,750	

MODEL 77 – 12 ga. only, Merkel-style O/U sidelock with Greener crossbolt, deluxe engraving checkering. Disc. 1985.

	$3,100	$2,750	$2,500	$2,255	$2,030	$1,805	$1,600	*$4,100*

MODEL 79 "A" – 12 ga. only, boxlock with double-locking lugs, ejectors, ST. Disc. 1985.

	$1,275	$1,075	$965	$880	$790	$705	$640	*$1,595*

MODEL 79 "B" – similar to Model 79 "A" with more elaborate engraving. Disc. 1985.

	$1,395	$1,200	$1,085	$990	$890	$790	$695	*$1,795*

MODEL 79 "C" – similar to Model 79 "B" with even more elaborate engraving, boxlock, DT on request, Disc. 1985.

	$2,050	$1,825	$1,605	$1,460	$1,315	$1,165	$1,000	*$2,650*

SHOTGUNS: SxS

Current retail values on the AYA shotguns listed below could vary slightly from importer to importer. For the following models, please use these guidelines for special orders and/or features.

On current models listed below, add $1,250 for SNT or approx. $1,250 for SST on recently manufactured guns.

Add $2,300 for self-opening action. Add approx. 40% for extra set of barrels.

BILL HANUS BIRDGUN – 16, 20 (disc. 2005), or 28 ga., similar wood, fit, checkering, and finish as the No. 53 sidelock, except has Anson & Deeley boxlock, patterned after the Westley Richards game gun, frames proportionate to ga., 27 (28 ga.) or 28 (16 ga.) in. barrels with fixed open chokes, ejectors, SST (disc.) or DT, splinter forearm, straight grip, case colored receiver with moderate engraving, includes leather-covered handguard.Imported 1997-2007.

	$2,650	$2,320	$1,990	$1,800	$1,460	$1,195	$930	*$2,995*

This model was available only through Bill Hanus Birdguns LLC. Stocks bent for cast-on and leather-covered decelerator pads were also available at additional cost.

BOLERO – similar to Matador, with non-selective single trigger and extractors. Disc. 1984.

	$450	$395	$340	$305	$250	$205	$160

COUNTRYMAN GAME GUN – 12 or 20 ga. Imported 1998-2002.

	$2,050	$1,795	$1,540	$1,395	$1,130	$925	$720	*$2,295*

IBERIA – 12 or 20 ga., 3 in. chambers, boxlock, DT, plain walnut. Disc. 1984.

	$495	$435	$370	$335	$270	$225	$175

IBERIA II – 12 or 16 ga., 2 3/4 in. chambers, 28 in. barrels, DT, plain walnut stock. Mfg. 1984-1985 only.

	$550	$480	$415	$375	$305	$250	$195	*$570*

MATADOR – 10, 12, 16, 20, 28 ga., or .410 bore, 26, 28, or 30 in. barrels, various chokes, Anson & Deeley boxlock, auto ejectors, beavertail forearm, SST, checkered pistol grip stock. Mfg. 1955-1963.

10, 12, 16, or 20 ga.	$550	$480	$415	$375	$305	$250	$195
28 ga.	$1,100	$965	$825	$750	$605	$495	$385
.410 bore	$1,650	$1,445	$1,240	$1,120	$910	$745	$580

Add 10% for 20 ga.

MATADOR NO. 2 – similar to Matador, vent. rib, 12 or 20 ga. only. Disc.

	$675	$590	$505	$460	$370	$305	$235

Add 10% for 20 ga.

MATADOR NO. 3A – 12 or 20 ga., 3 in. chamber (20 ga.), boxlock, VR barrels, ejectors, SST. Disc. 1985.

	$795	$695	$595	$540	$435	$360	$280	*$1,235*

Add 10% for 20 ga.

SENIOR – 12 ga. only, engraved sidelock action, Beesley or Purdey-type self opener, top-of-the-line quality, select walnut, lighter upland version was available (made-to-order only). Disc. 1987.

	$15,500	$13,565	$11,625	$10,540	$8,525	$6,975	$5,425	*$21,000*

GRADING - PPGS™	100%	98%	95%	90%	80%	70%	60%	*LAST MSR*

SUPREMA – various gauges, sidelock, includes deluxe engraving, made to customer special order per individual specifications.

MSR $23,271	$19,950	$17,250	$15,000	$13,000	$10,750	$8,900	$7,150	

Add $585 for round action.

IMPERIAL – 12, 16, 20, 28 ga. or .410 bore, sidelock action with DTs and hinged front trigger, chopper lump 28 in. barrels, traditional rose and scroll engraved case colored detachable sidelocks, H&H-style self-opening action, exhibition grade walnut with fine checkering, custom order only. Importation began 2008.

MSR $26,345	$23,500	$20,00	$17,000	$14,250	$11,000	$9,000	$8,000	

ADARRA – 12, 16, 20, 28 ga. or .410 bore, boxlock action, double locking mechanism with replaceable hinge pin, 28 in. chopper lump barrels with concave rib (other barrel lengths available by special order), hammerless, double triggers, straight grip Grade 2 hand oil finished walnut stock, automatic safety, engraved receiver, split bottom plate, color case hardened, old silver, or in the white finish, approx. 7 lbs. New 2013.

MSR $6,012	$5,300	$4,600	$3,700	$3,125	$2,650	$2,250	$1,750	

PREMIUM – all gauges, sidelock action. New 2016.

MSR $9,709	$8,750	$7,750	$6,875	$6,000	$5,000	$4,000	$3,000	

Add $285 for round action.

CENTENARY – all gauges, sidelock action. New 2016.

MSR $11,308	$9,950	$8,500	$7,250	$6,250	$5,350	$4,300	$3,300	

Add $554 for round action.

ANNIVERSARY HAMMER – 12 ga. only, forged steel action, exposed hammers with auto ejectors, 30 in. chopper lump barrels with flat hand filed rib, finest scroll engraving with gold inlays, mfg. to celebrate AYA's 50 years in the U.K. marketplace. Limited mfg.

MSR $35,446	$30,000	$25,500	$20,000	$16,000	$12,000	$10,000	$8,000	

NO. 1 – 12, 16, 20, 28 ga. or .410 bore, full sidelock action, straight grip, ejectors, DT, elaborate fine scroll engraving. Importation disc. 1987, resumed in 1991.

MSR $15,002	$12,850	$10,500	$8,750	$7,550	$6,775	$5,475	$4,475	

Add $439 for round action.

* ***No. 1 DeLuxe*** – features bold foliate engraving.

MSR $18,861	$16,500	$14,250	$12,000	$10,750	$8,500	$6,850	$5,325	

Add $931 for rounded action.

* ***No. 1 De Luxe English*** – exhibition quality wood and engraved by Geoff Moore, English metal finish, custom order only.

This shotgun is specifically made for A.S.I., and is sold exclusively in the U.K. marketplace. Current retail is £16,995 (12 ga.) or £17,650 (16, 20, 28 ga. or .410 bore).

NO. 2 – 12, 16, 20, 28 ga., or .410 bore, 3 in. chambers, English-style sidelock, ejector, cocking indicators, DT. Importation disc. 1987, resumed 1991.

MSR $7,008	$5,750	$5,000	$4,375	$3,750	$3,400	$2,750	$2,250	

Add $420 for round action.

* ***No. 2 Bill Hanus Dreamgun Sidelock*** – features Boss rounded action, built per individual custom order, 10 month delivery. Imported 2003-2007.

	$5,500	$4,815	$4,125	$3,740	$3,025	$2,475	$1,925	*$5,950*

This model was only available from Bill Hanus Birdguns LLC.

* ***No. 2 Deluxe*** – 12, 16, 20, 28 ga., or .410 bore, SxS shotgun, sidelock, includes engraving. New 2012.

MSR $8,690	$7,725	$6,800	$5,700	$4,600	$3,800	$3,000	$2,500	

Subtract approx. $250 for round action, depending on ga. and barrel length.

NO. 3-A – 12, 16, 20, 28 ga., or .410 bore, boxlock, extractors, DT. Disc. 1985.

	$675	$590	$505	$460	$370	$305	$235	*$850*

Add 25%-35% for 28 ga. or .410 bore.

NO. 4 – 12, 16, 20, 28 ga., or .410 bore, 3 in. chambers, English-style straight stock, boxlock action, ejectors, DT, straight grip stock, standard wood. Importation disc. 1987, resumed 1991-2008.

	$2,000	$1,750	$1,500	$1,360	$1,100	$900	$700	*$2,300*

GRADING - PPGS™	100%	98%	95%	90%	80%	70%	60%	LAST MSR

* ***No. 4/25 Special Edition*** – 12, 16, 20, 28 ga. or .410 bore, 2 3/4 in. chambers, 29 in. barrels, Westley Richards style boxlock, Anson & Deeley action, auto ejectors, DT, hand rubbed oil finished No. 1 checkered straight grip walnut stock and forearm, coin finished engraved receiver, 6 lbs. 12 oz. Imported mid-2014-2017.

	$3,395	$2,975	$2,550	$2,315	$1,865	$1,525	$1,195	*$3,995*

NO. 4 DELUXE – 12, 20, 28 ga. or .410 bore, English-style boxlock, ejector, stock, forearm, trigger to order. Importation disc. 1985, resumed 1991.

MSR $7,507	$6,400	$5,550	$4,650	$3,825	$3,250	$2,850	$2,300	

Add $472 for rounded action.

NO. 4 RA – 12, 16, 20, or 28 ga., hammerless boxlock ejector, Anson & Deeley action, 28 in. chopper lump barrels with concave rib, double trigger, Grade 1 oil finished walnut stock, split bottom plate, automatic safety, Purdey double underbolt locking system, special floral and scroll engraving with initial oval, disc set firing pins, double locking mechanism with replaceable hinge pin, old silver finish, optional additional barrel lengths and selective or non-selective triggers. Mfg 2015-disc.

Retail pricing was not available for this model.

* ***No. 4L*** – 12, 16, 20, 28 ga., or .410 bore, hammerless boxlock ejector, Anson & Deeley action, 28 in. chopper lump barrels with concave rib, double trigger, Grade 2 oil finished walnut stock, split bottom plate, automatic safety, Purdey double underbolt locking system, laser engraving finished by hand with initial oval, disc set firing pins, double locking mechanism with replaceable hinge pin, color case hardened, old silver, or white finish, optional additional barrel lengths and selective or non-selective triggers, 6 lbs. 10 oz. Mfg. 2015-disc.

While available in Europe, this model was not imported into the U.S.

XXV BOXLOCK (BL) – 12, 20, 28 ga. or .410 bore, similar to No. 4 Deluxe, except 25 in. barrels, Churchill rib. Importation disc. 1986, resumed 1991-2005, reintroduced 2008-2011.

	$3,250	$2,825	$2,400	$2,175	$1,750	$1,425	$1,125	*$3,895*

Add approx. 40% for extra set of barrels (disc.).
Add $196 for gauges other than 12.

NO. 4/53 – similar to No. 4, except has No. 53 wood upgrade. Importation disc. 1987, resumed 1991.

MSR $5,471	$4,800	$4,000	$3,500	$2,950	$2,500	$2,250	$1,825	

Add approx. $500 for .410 bore.
Subtract approx. $250 for 28 ga. Model No. 4/53 Lady Fieldsport importation only.
Add approx. $200 for No. 4/53S (includes wood upgrade, SNT, and round knob pistol grip, disc.).
Add $732 for No. 4 BL with BL engraving (disc.).

XXV SIDELOCK (SL) – 12, 16, 20 (disc. 1997, reintroduced 2008), 28 (disc. 1997, reintroduced 2008) ga., or .410 bore (disc. 1997, reintroduced 2008), sidelock ejector, 25 in. barrels, Churchill rib, stock, forearm, trigger to order. Importation disc. 1986, resumed 1991-2005, reintroduced 2008-2011.

	$6,100	$5,250	$4,450	$4,000	$3,300	$2,725	$2,150	*$6,816*

Add $600 for 28 ga. or .410 bore.

NO. 53 – 12, 16 (disc. 2017), or 20 ga., engraved sidelock, ejector, sideclips, third lock. Stock, forearm, trigger to order. Importation disc. 1986, resumed 1991.

MSR $9,919	$8,650	$7,300	$6,175	$5,200	$4,650	$3,725	$3,050	

NO. 56 – 12, 16 (disc. 2010), or 20 (disc. 2010) ga., engraved sidelock, ejectors, SST. Importation disc. 1985, resumed 1991.

MSR $17,417	$14,650	$11,000	$9,200	$7,750	$6,900	$5,500	$4,600	

NO. 106 – 12, 16, or 20 ga., English-style boxlock, DT, pistol grip, 28 in. barrels. Disc. 1985.

	$550	$480	$415	$375	$305	$250	$195	*$585*

Add 20% for 16 or 20 ga.

107-LI – 12 or 16 ga., English-style boxlock, DT, straight grip, light English scroll engraving. Disc. 1985.

	$775	$680	$580	$525	$425	$350	$270	*$745*

MODEL 116 – 12, 16, or 20 ga., 27-30 in. barrels, any choke, hand detachable H&H sidelocks, DT, engraved, select checkered walnut pistol grip stock. Disc. 1985.

	$1,500	$1,315	$1,125	$1,020	$825	$675	$525	*$1,125*

MODEL 117 – 10, 12, 16, or 20 ga., 3 in. chambers, 26-30 in. barrels, any choke, hand-detachable H&H sidelocks, ejectors, SST, engraved, select checkered walnut pistol grip stock. Disc. 1986.

	$1,750	$1,530	$1,315	$1,190	$965	$790	$615	*$1,075*

GRADING - PPGS™	100%	98%	95%	90%	80%	70%	60%	LAST MSR

MODEL 117 QUAIL UNLIMITED – 12 ga. only, 26 in. barrels choked IC/M with 3 in. chambers, upgraded wood and checkering, high gloss bluing, gold colored ST, engraved by Baron Technologies in PA, only 42 mfg. for Quail Unlimited of North America.

	$1,650	$1,445	$1,240	$1,120	$910	$745	$580	

This model had a retail price of $1,700 but was made available to Quail Unlimited members for approx. $1,200.

MODEL 210 – 12 or 16 ga., boxlock, exposed hammers, DT, plain walnut, light engraving. Disc. 1985.

	$795	$695	$595	$540	$435	$360	$280	*$900*

MODEL 711 SIDELOCK – sidelock action. Mfg. 1985 only.

	$1,450	$1,270	$1,090	$985	$800	$655	$510	*$1,250*

SFERA – 12, 16, 20, 28 ga., or .410 bore, forged steel action, 25 to 32 in. chopper lump forged barrels w/ game rib, double trigger w/front trigger, optional selective or non-selective single trigger, special grade walnut, straight hand stock, automatic safety, intercepting safety sears, double locking underbolt, gas vent screws, Art Nouveau style engraving and other engraving styles available, curved lockplate, available in case color hardened or coin finish, approx. 6 lbs. 14 oz. (12 ga. w/28 in. barrels). New 2017.

MSR $10,395	$8,750	$7,500	$6,500	$5,500	$4,500	$3,500	$2,750	

RIFLES: O/U & SxS

Express rifles are available in both O/U and SxS configurations with a choice of either monoblock or demiblock barrels and boxlock or sidelock action. Please contact the importers directly for a quotation and availability.

ABADIE

Previous trademark of Portuguese military revolvers manufactured by several Belgian makers.

REVOLVERS

MODEL 1878 (OFFICER'S MODEL) – 9.1mm cal., solid frame revolver, 6 shot, ejector rod, officer's issue A.

	$220	$195	$165	$130	$120	$110	$100	

MODEL 1886 (TROOPER'S MODEL) – similar to 1878, but larger, trooper issue A.

	$195	$175	$160	$120	$110	$100	$90	

ABBEY, GEORGE T.

Previous manufacturer of percussion and breech loading firearms located in Utica, NY from 1845-1852, and Chicago, IL from 1852-1874.

For more information on this manufacturer and its models, please refer to the *Blue Book of Antique American Firearms and Values* or visit BlueBookOfGunValues.com.

ABBEY, F.J. & COMPANY

Previous manufacturer of muzzle and breech loading shotguns and rifles located in Chicago, IL, 1858-1878.

For more information on this manufacturer and its models, please refer to the *Blue Book of Antique American Firearms and Values* or visit BlueBookOfGunValues.com.

ABBIATICO & SALVINELLI (FAMARS)

Please refer to the Famars di Abbiatico & Salvinelli srl listing in the F section.

ACCU-MATCH INTERNATIONAL INC.

Previous handgun and pistol parts manufacturer located in Mesa, AZ circa 1996.

PISTOLS: SEMI-AUTO

ACCU-MATCH PISTOL – .45 ACP cal., patterned after the Colt Govt. 1911, SA, competition pistol, stainless steel construction, 5 1/2 in. match grade barrel with 3 ports, recoil reduction system, 8 shot mag., 3-dot sight system. Approx. 160 mfg. 1996 only.

	$795	$700	$625	$550	$450	$375	$325	*$840*

ACCU-TEK

Current trademark manufactured by Excel Industries, Inc., located in Chino, CA. Distributor and dealer direct sales.

GRADING - PPGS™	100%	98%	95%	90%	80%	70%	60%	LAST MSR

PISTOLS: SEMI-AUTO

MODEL AT-9SS – 9mm Para. cal., DAO, 3.2 in. barrel, 8 shot mag., stainless steel, 3-dot sights adj. for windage, no external safety lever, firing pin block, black or brushed stainless finish, 28 oz. Mfg. 1995-96 only.

	$260	$230	$195	$175	$145	$115	$90	*$317*

MODEL AT-25 – .25 ACP cal., similar to AT-32, SA, 2 1/2 in. barrel, 7 shot mag. with finger extension, exposed hammer, stainless steel, aluminum, or alloy construction with choice of stainless, satin aluminum, or black finish, 11 (Model AT-25AL) or 18 (Model AT-25B, disc.) oz. Mfg. 1992-95.

	$150	$130	$115	$100	$85	$70	$55	*$182*

This model was available in satin aluminum (Model AT-25AL) or black (Model AT-25SSB) finish.

MODEL AT-32SS – .32 ACP cal., SA, 2 1/2 in. barrel, 5 shot mag. with finger extension, alloy (disc. 1991) or stainless steel (new 1992) construction, exposed hammer, black synthetic grips, manual safety with firing pin block and trigger disconnect, side mag. release, satin aluminum (disc. 1991), or black (Model AT-32SSB) finish, 1 lb. Mfg. in U.S. 1990-2003.

	$190	$165	$145	$130	$105	$85	$65	*$239*

Add $5 for black finish (Model AT-32SSB).

MODEL AT-40SS – .40 S&W cal., DAO, 3.2 in. barrel, 7 shot mag., firing pin block, no external safety lever, black or brushed stainless finish, 3-dot sights adj. for windage, 28 oz. Mfg. 1995-96 only.

	$260	$230	$195	$175	$145	$115	$90	*$317*

MODEL AT-45SS – .45 ACP cal., similar to Model AT-40SS, except has 6 shot mag., stainless only, 28 oz. Mfg. 1996 only.

	$265	$230	$200	$180	$145	$120	$95	*$327*

MODEL AT-380II (SS/SSB) – .380 ACP cal., 2 3/4 in. barrel, 6 shot mag., alloy (disc. 1991) or stainless steel construction, adj. rear sight, black, purple (new 2013), pink, (new 2013) or grey (new 2013) synthetic grips, current mfg. includes two magazines, one flat buttplate, and one finger extension, black finish (Model AT-380SSB, disc. 1999), 23.5 oz. New 1990.

MSR $289	$250	$225	$195	$175	$150	$125	$100	

Add $5 for black finish (Model AT-380SSB, disc. 1999).

MODEL BL-9 – 9mm Para. cal., DAO, carbon steel, black finish, ultra compact size, includes two 5 shot mags. and lockable case. Mfg. 1997-2002.

	$235	$170	$145	$135	$105	$90	$70	*$232*

MODEL BL-380 – .380 ACP cal., DAO, carbon steel, black finish, compact size, two 5 shot mags., lockable case. Mfg. 1997-99.

	$165	$145	$125	$110	$90	$75	$60	*$199*

MODEL CP-9SS – 9mm Para. cal., DAO, stainless steel, black finish, compact size, 8 shot mag. Mfg. 1997-99.

	$220	$195	$165	$150	$120	$100	$75	*$265*

MODEL CP-40SS – .40 S&W cal., 7 shot mag., otherwise similar to CP-9SS. Mfg. 1997-99.

	$220	$195	$165	$150	$120	$100	$75	*$265*

MODEL CP-45SS – .45 ACP cal., 6 shot mag., otherwise similar to CP-40SS. Mfg. 1997-99.

	$220	$195	$165	$150	$120	$100	$75	*$265*

MODEL HC-380 (SS) – .380 ACP cal., SA, 2.5 (disc.) or 2.8 in. barrel, 10 (C/B 1994) or 13* shot mag., stainless steel, exposed hammer, wrap around grips, manual safety with firing pin block and trigger disconnect, includes two 13 shot mags., lock, and hard case, black finish, 26 oz. Mfg. 1993-2003, reintroduced 2007.

MSR $330	$275	$250	$200	$175	$150	$125	$100	

Add $5 for black finish (Model HC-380B, mfg. 1995-99).

MODEL LT-380 – .380 ACP cal., SA/DA, 2.8 in. barrel, 6 shot mag., aluminum frame and stainless steel slide, choice of black, OD Green, pink, or purple grips, supplied with two mags., features blued or various two-tone finishes, 15 oz. New 2012.

MSR $324	$275	$250	$200	$175	$150	$125	$100	

Add $20 for 6 shot mag. with flat buttplate.
Add $23 for 6 shot mag. with finger extension.

MODEL XL-9SS – 9mm Para. cal., DAO, stainless steel, 3 in. barrel, 5 shot mag., black pebble finished grips, 3-dot adj. sights, 24 oz. Mfg. 1999-2003.

	$235	$190	$160	$145	$120	$95	$75	*$267*

GRADING - PPGS™	100%	98%	95%	90%	80%	70%	60%	LAST MSR

ACCURACY INTERNATIONAL LTD.

Current rifle manufacturer located in Portsmouth, England. Accuracy International North America Inc. located in Fredericksburg, VA offers both law enforcement and military sales. Currently distributed by Euro Optic Limited (civilian sales only) located in Montoursville, PA and by Mile High Shooting Accessories (law enforcement and civilian sales), located in Broomfield, CO. Previously distributed by SRT Supply, located in St. Petersburg, FL, Tac Pro Shooting Center, located in Mingus, TX, and previously imported until 1998 by Gunsite Training Center, located in Paulden, AZ.

RIFLES: BOLT ACTION

In addition to the models listed, Accuracy International also makes military and law enforcement rifles, including the SR98 Australian, G22 German, and the Dutch SLA. On Models AE, AW, AWP, and AWM listed in this section, many options and configurations are available which will add to the base prices listed.

AE MODEL - .243 Win., .260 Rem., .308 Win., or 6.5 Creedmoor cal., 20 or 24 in. stainless barrel, 5 shot mag., Harris bipod attachment point, four sling attachment points, Picatinny rail, black, Green, or Dark Earth finish, approx. 8.5 lbs. Imported 2002-2020.

	100%	98%	95%	90%	80%	70%	60%	LAST MSR
	$3,325	$2,775	$2,400	$2,000	$1,700	$1,425	$1,200	*$3,600*

Add $307 for adj. cheekpiece (disc. 2012) or $422 for folding stock.
Add $213 for standard muzzle brake.
Add $357 for butt spike.
Add $454 for 26 in. barrel.

AT 308 - .308 Win. cal., 20, 24, or 26 in. stainless steel plain barrel, threaded for A1 muzzle brake, Quickloc quick release barrel system bolted and bonded to aluminum chassis, detachable 10 shot double stack mag., extractor, 3-pos. safety, two-stage adj. trigger, fixed stock with adj. cheekpiece and LOP, pistol grip, fixed buttpad with spacers, 1913 action rail, black, green, or Pale Brown stock, black metal finish, 13.9 lbs. New 2014.

	100%	98%	95%	90%	80%	70%	60%
MSR $4,047	$3,995	$3,500	$2,950	$2,500	$2,000	$1,750	$1,500

MSR on this model represents the least expensive base price only.

AW MODEL - .243 Win. (new 2000), .260 Rem., .300 Win. Mag., .308 Win., .338 Lapua Mag. (disc. 2012), or 6.5 Creedmoor cal., precision bolt action, 20, 24, 26, or 27 (disc.) in. 1:12 twist stainless steel standard threaded or fluted barrel with or w/o muzzle brake, 10 shot detachable mag., green synthetic folding (military/LE only) thumbhole adj. stock, 3-lug bolt, AI bipod, 14 lbs. Imported 1995-2018.

	100%	98%	95%	90%	80%	70%	60%	LAST MSR
	$5,500	$4,650	$4,000	$3,400	$2,850	$2,200	$1,800	*$6,050*

Add $203 for fluted barrel.
Add $257 for Picatinny rail or $422 for folding stock.
Add $342 for threaded barrel with muzzle brake.
Add $357 for butt spike.
Add $797 for .300 Win. Mag. cal. with 20 or 26 in. fluted and threaded barrel.
Add $376 for AW-F Model (disc. 2002).

AWP MODEL - .308 Win. cal., similar to AW Model, except has 20 or 24 in. barrel w/o muzzle brake, 15 lbs. Imported 1995-2007.

	100%	98%	95%	90%	80%	70%	60%	LAST MSR
	$4,250	$3,650	$3,150	$2,650	$2,150	$1,800	$1,500	*$4,600*

Add $310 for AWP-F Model (disc. 2002).

AW50 - .50 BMG cal., advanced ergonomic design, built-in anti-recoil system, 5 shot mag., adj. third supporting leg, folding stock, 27 in. fluted barrel with muzzle brake, Picatinny rail, approx. 30 lbs. Mfg. 1998-2012.

	100%	98%	95%	90%	80%	70%	60%	LAST MSR
	$12,500	$10,500	$8,750	$8,000	$7,250	$6,500	$5,750	*$13,096*

AWM MODEL (SUPER MAGNUM) - .300 Win. Mag. or .338 Lapua Mag. cal., 6-lug bolt, 26 or 27 in. 1:9/1:10 twist stainless steel fluted barrel with muzzle brake, 5 shot mag., 15 1/2 lbs. Imported 1995-2009.

	100%	98%	95%	90%	80%	70%	60%	LAST MSR
	$5,600	$4,750	$4,100	$3,500	$2,950	$2,300	$1,900	*$5,900*

Add $100 for .338 Lapua Mag. cal.
Add $324 for AWM-F Model (disc. 2002).

AX MODEL - .243 Win., .260 Rem., .308 Win., .338 Lapua Mag., or 6.5 Creedmoor cal., 10 shot mag., 20, 24, 26, or 27 in. barrel with or w/o muzzle brake, Picatinny rail, pistol grip with adj. cheekpiece, fixed buttpad with additional spacers, choice of green, black, or Dark Earth finished hardware, folding chassis.

	100%	98%	95%	90%	80%	70%	60%
MSR $7,309	$7,250	$6,250	$5,250	$4,250	$3,250	$2,850	$2,650

MSR on this model represents the least expensive base price only.

GRADING - PPGS™	100%	98%	95%	90%	80%	70%	60%	LAST MSR

AXMC (MULTI CALIBER) – .308 Win. (disc., reintroduced 2020), .300 Win. Mag., or .338 Lapua Mag. cal., sniper configuration, solid steel, flat bottomed action bolts to combat tested AI chassis, 20, 24, 26 (disc.), or 27 in. stainless steel plain barrel threaded for muzzle, QuickLoc barrel release system, 10 shot CIP length double stack mag., 6 lug, 60 degree bolt with leaf spring extractor, two-stage trigger with adj. shoe, right side folding stock over bolt, adj. cheekpiece, adj. buttpad with spacers, pistol grip, 3-pos. safety, full length NATO STANAG 4694/Mil-Std. 1913 rail, 16 in. forend tube rail, accessory rails, QD flush cup sling attachments, black, Dark Earth, green, Pale Brown, or Sage Green stock, available in right or left (new 2016) hand configuration, 12.4-15 lbs. New 2014.

MSR $8,426	$6,750	$5,900	$5,000	$4,600	$3,725	$3,000	$2,300	

* ***AX308*** – .308 Win. cal., 20, 24, or 26 in. stainless steel plain barrel, threaded for muzzle brake, detachable 10 shot double stack mag., 3-pos. safety, two-stage trigger, right side folding stock with adj. cheekpiece, adj. buttpad with spacers, pistol grip, Picatinny rail, 13 in. forend tube and accessory rails, 60 degree bolt with leaf spring extractor, available with black or green stock with black metal work or Pale Brown stock and metalwork, 13.9 lbs. New 2014.

Please contact the importers or the factory directly for U.S. retail pricing and availability on this model.

* ***AX50*** – .50 BMG cal., 27 in. stainless match grade barrel with triple chamber muzzle brake, proofed steel action bolted to aluminum chassis, 5 shot detachable mag., Mil-Std 1913 action and forend rail, 6 lug 60 degree bolt with A1 leaf spring extractor, 2-pos. safety, two-stage trigger, integrated quick adjust butt spike, left folding stock, quick adjust butt and cheekpiece, choice of green, black, or Dark Earth finished hardware, 27 1/2 lbs.

MSR $12,132	$12,000	$10,000	$8,750	$8,000	$7,250	$6,500	$5,750	

MSR on this model represents the least expensive base price only.

PALMAMASTER – .308 Win. cal., available with either NRA prone or UIT style stock, 30 in. stainless steel fluted barrel, designed for competition shooting, laminated stock. Disc. 2002.

	$2,600	$2,350	$2,100	$1,900	$1,700	$1,500	$1,250	*$2,850*

CISMMASTER – .22 BR, 6mm BR, .243 Win., .308 Win., 6.5x55mm, or 7.5x55mm cal., designed for slow and rapid fire international and military shooting competition, 10 shot mag., two-stage trigger. Disc. 2002.

	$3,175	$2,850	$2,600	$2,350	$2,100	$1,900	$1,700	*$3,480*

VARMINT RIFLE – .22 Middlestead, .22 BR, .22-250 Rem., .223 Rem., 6mm BR, .243 Win., .308 Win., or 7mm-08 Rem. cal., 26 in. fluted stainless steel barrel. Mfg. 1997-2002.

	$3,200	$2,725	$2,350	$1,950	$1,675	$1,475	$1,300	*$3,650*

ACCURACY X, INC.

Current rifle and semi-auto pistol manufacturer founded by competitive shooter Steve Huff, located in Virginia.

For individual model listings, please go to BlueBookOfGunValues.com/overflow.

ACCURATE ARMS RIFLES LLC

Previous rifle manufacturer established circa 1987-2020, located in Harrisonburg, VA.

For individual model listings, please go to BlueBookOfGunValues.com/overflow.

ACCURATE-MAG PRODUCTS

Current manufacturer of precision bolt action rifles and components located in Monroe, CT. Accurate-Mag Products is currently importing RangeMaster Precision Arms (RPA International LTD.) products.

Accurate-Mag Products is a division of the B.M.L. Tool & Manufacturing Corporation, located in Monroe, CT.

RIFLES: BOLT ACTION

AM 40-A6 RPA – .308 Win. or .300 Win. Mag. cal., RPA Quadlite action, 24 or 26 in. fluted barrel, 6 grooves, standard stock w/fixed buttstock and tactical forend, modular rail system, black or FDE finish, 11 or 13 lbs.

MSR $4,900	$4,500	$3,995	$3,500	$3,000	$2,600	$2,200	$1,850	

Add $130 for FDE finish.
Add $400 for .300 Win. Mag. cal.

This rifle is built on the RangeMaster Precision Arms Quadlite barreled action.

AM 40 A6 308 – .308 Win. or 7.62 NATO cal., Remington 700 Short Action, 24 in. stainless barrel, threaded muzzle, 6 grooves, pull & lock folding buttstock, bi-directional modular rail forend system, adj. cheekpiece and buttpad, black, sand, or FDE Cerakote finish, 13 lbs.

MSR $4,820	$4,450	$3,950	$3,450	$2,950	$2,500	$2,100	$1,750	

Add $130 for sand or FDE Cerakote finish.

GRADING - PPGS™	100%	98%	95%	90%	80%	70%	60%	LAST MSR

AMSR (ADVANCED MULTI-CALIBER SPORTING RIFLE) – .308 Win., 6.5 Creedmoor, .30-06, .300 Win. Mag., .30 Nosler, .33 Nosler, .338 Lapua Mag., .375 H&H Mag., or .416 Rem. Mag. cal., steel or carbon fiber barrel, Jewell trigger, classic walnut stock, features patented Trunnion barrel locking system, advanced military chassis. New 2018.

Please contact the company directly for pricing and availability for this model.

SPECIAL SERVICE RIFLE – .300 or .338 Norma Mag. cal., Savage 110 action, 27 in. Savage Taper barrel, 6 grooves, customized w/butt and forend options, SPORT-TACT straight chassis, black, FDE, or Forest Green finish, 13 lbs.

MSR $3,840	$3,500	$3,000	$2,650	$2,250	$1,850	$1,500	$1,250

Add $130 for FDE or Forest Green finish.

ACCURATE TOOL & MFG. CO.

Previous custom AR-15 style rifle and pistol manufacturer located in Lexington, KY from 1992-late 2018.

Please refer to BlueBookOfGunValues.com to order the *Blue Book of AR-15s & Variations*, available as a book or online subscription.

ACHA

Previous manufacturer located in Eibar, Spain until 1936.

PISTOLS: SEMI-AUTO

MODEL 1916 – 6.35mm cal., SA, 7 shot mag., 1905 Browning copy.

$295	$195	$140	$90	$80	$70	$60

ATLAS – 6.35mm cal., SA, 6 shot mag., slide marked ATLAS, 1905 Browning copy.

$250	$180	$125	$95	$75	$65	$50

LOOKING GLASS – 6.35mm or 7.65mm cal., 6 shot mag., blue or nickel, 1905 Browning copy, slide marked "Looking Glass", many variations.

$295	$190	$140	$90	$80	$70	$60

Add 50% for extended grip.

ACME

Previous trade name of Davenport Arms Company shotguns circa 1880-1884, Maltby Henley & Co. revolvers circa 1888-1893, and Merwin Hulbert & Co. "owl head" revolvers circa 1868-1891.

For more information on this manufacturer and its models, please refer to the *Blue Book of Antique American Firearms and Values* or visit BlueBookOfGunValues.com.

ACME ARMS

Previous trade name for Cornwall Hardware Co., NY.

For more information on this manufacturer and its models, please refer to the *Blue Book of Antique American Firearms and Values* or visit BlueBookOfGunValues.com.

ACME HAMMERLESS

Previously manufactured by Hopkins & Allen, for Hulbert Brothers, 1893.

For more information on this manufacturer and its models, please refer to the *Blue Book of Antique American Firearms and Values* or visit BlueBookOfGunValues.com.

ACTION (M.S.)

Previously manufactured by Modesto Santos, located in Eibar, Spain.

PISTOLS: SEMI-AUTO

MODEL 1915 – 7.65mm cal., semi-auto pistol (French Military).

$245	$175	$140	$105	$90	$75	$65

MODEL 1920 – 6.35mm cal., slide marked "Action".

$195	$150	$110	$85	$65	$45	$40

ACTION ARMS LTD.

Previous firearms importer and distributor until 1994, located in Philadelphia, PA.

Only Action Arms Models AT-84S, AT-88S, and the Model B Sporter will be listed under this heading. Galil, Timberwolf, and Uzi trademarks can be located in their respective sections.

GRADING - PPGS™	100%	98%	95%	90%	80%	70%	60%	LAST MSR

CARBINES: SEMI-AUTO

MODEL B SPORTER – 9mm Para. cal., patterned after the original Uzi Model B Sporter, 16.1 in. barrel, 10 shot mag., adj. rear sight, thumbhole stock with recoil pad, fires from closed bolt, 8.8 lbs. Limited importation from China 1994 only.

$695	$625	$550	$475	$435	$385	$335	*$595*

PISTOLS: SEMI-AUTO

AT-84S – 9mm Para. cal., selective DA/SA design, patterned after the CZ-75, 4.8 in. barrel, 15 shot mag., originally introduced in 1985.

$575	$450	$400	$365	$330	$275	$220

The AT-84S Series was manufactured in Switzerland by Industrial Technology & Machines A.G. and was sold by Action Arms between June of 1987 and 1989. Serial number range is 01201- 06000. No P or H models were ever mfg. in this series (2 or 3 prototypes only).

AT-88S – 9mm or .41 Action Express (available early 1990) cal., selective DA/SA design patterned after CZ-75, 4.8 in. barrel, 15 (9mm) or 10 shot (.41 AE) mag., can be carried "cocked and locked", fixed sights, blue metal, walnut grips, 35.3 oz. Introduced in 1987 with limited production samples imported in 1989.

$550	$450	$395	$360	$330	$275	$220

A very small quantity of AT-88Ss (various configurations) were made by I.T.M. of Switzerland and finishes included all blue, all chrome, or two-tone. These pistols may exhibit both I.T.M. and A.A.L. markings. More recent manufacture was performed by Sphinx-Muller of Switzerland, renamed the AT-2000 Series and previously imported by Sile Distributors.

RIFLES: SLIDE ACTION

TIMBERWOLF – see separate listing in T section, under Timberwolf.

ACTION LEGENDS MFG., INC.

Previous manufacturer, importer, and distributor until circa 2006, located in Houston, TX.

RIFLES

MODEL 888 M1 CARBINE – .22 LR or .30 Carbine cal., 18 in. barrel, mfg. from new original M1 parts and stock and unused GI parts, 10, 15, or 30 shot mag., choice of birch or walnut stock, parkerized finish, metal or wood handguard, 5 1/2 lbs.

$675	$625	$550	$495	$425	$375	$325	*$650*

Add $11 for .22 LR cal.

Add $31 for walnut/metal forearm or $47 for walnut/wood forearm.

MODEL 1903 SPRINGFIELD – .30-06 cal., 24 in. barrel, bolt action, mfg. from new and original GI parts, 5 shot mag., parkerized finish, wood stock, canvas sling.

While previously advertised at a $950 MSR, only a few prototypes were manufactured.

ADAMS

Previously manufactured by Deane, Adams, & Deane, located in London, England.

100%	98%	95%	90%	80%	70%	60%	50%	40%	30%	20%	10%

REVOLVERS: PERCUSSION

Add approx. 25% for case and accessories on the following models.

MODEL 1851 .31 CAL. – .31 cal., double action, 4 1/2 in. barrel.

N/A	N/A	$2,750	$2,500	$2,250	$2,000	$1,850	$1,600	$1,400	$1,200	$1,000	$650

MODEL 1851 .44 CAL. – .44 cal., double action, 6 in. barrel.

N/A	N/A	$2,500	$2,250	$2,000	$1,850	$1,500	$1,200	$900	$675	$475	$325

MODEL 1851 .50 CAL. – .50 cal., double action, 8 in. barrel, Dragoon frame.

N/A	N/A	$3,650	$3,250	$2,600	$2,100	$1,800	$1,400	$1,100	$700	$500	$350

ADAMS ARMS

Current AR-15 style pistol and rifle manufacturer established circa 2007, located in Brooksville, FL. Previously located in Odessa, FL, until late 2019 and Palm Harbor, FL.

Please refer to BlueBookOfGunValues.com to order the *Blue Book of AR-15s & Variations*, available as a book or online subscription.

100%	98%	95%	90%	80%	70%	60%	50%	40%	30%	20%	10%

ADAMS, JOSEPH

Previous manufacturer located in Birmingham, England.

PISTOLS: FLINTLOCK

OFFICER MODEL – .65 cal., flintlock pistol, based on Brown Bess model.

$2,850	$2,500	$2,250	$2,000	$1,800	$1,600	$1,400	$1,100	$900	$825	$725	$600

ADAMY, GEBR. JAGDWAFFEN

Current manufacturer and retailer established circa 1921 and located in Suhl, Germany. Previous limited importation by New England Custom Gun Service, located in Claremont, NH, previously located until 2010 in Plainfield, NH.

The Adamy gunmaking tradition goes back to 1820, and sixth and seventh generation descendants are currently building guns.

Adamy Jagdwaffen currently specializes in custom made, break-open rifles, drillings, and combination guns, SxS and O/U shotguns, and double rifles featuring an Anson & Deeley boxlock action or H&H type sidelocks. Since all guns are made to custom order, please contact the factory directly for information on its current models including pricing, options, and availability.

ADCO ARMS CO., INC. (ADCO SALES INC.)

Current importer located in Woburn, MA. During 2012, the name Adco Sales Inc. was changed to Adco Arms Co., Inc.

Adco Arms Co., Inc. currently imports firearms from the Aselkon, Best Arms, and Redstone brand. Adco previously imported Diamond shotguns circa 2007-2012, 2015-2019. For more information on Best Arms and Diamond models, please refer to the appropriate listings in the B and D sections of this text.

GRADING - PPGS™	100%	98%	95%	90%	80%	70%	60%	LAST MSR

SHOTGUNS: SEMI-AUTO

ASELKON IF1 – 12 ga., 3 in. chamber, 28 in. steel barrel, removable Interpro chokes, 4 shot, aluminum receiver, walnut, polymer, or camo stock, includes ABS case, black or camo finish. Importation began 2021.

MSR $949	$810	$710	$610	$550	$450	$375	$300

Add $10 for walnut stock.
Add $50 for camo stock and camo finish.

ASELKON IT1 – 12 ga., 3 in. chamber, Inter Inertia Technology Locking System, 18 1/2 or 22 in. steel barrel, removable Interpro chokes, 4 shot, aluminum receiver, with or w/o TAC sight, polymer or camo stock, includes ABS case. Importation began 2021.

MSR $559	$475	$415	$355	$325	$260	$215	$175

Add $116 for TAC sight.

AVANTI 3.5 MAGNUM – 12 ga., 3 1/2 in. chamber, Inter Inertia Technology Locking System, 26, 28, or 30 in. steel barrel, removable Interpro chokes (5 Mobile Chokes), two shot mag., aluminum receiver, walnut, polymer, or camo stock, includes ABS case and sling swivels, black or camo finish. Mfg. by Aselkon beginning 2021.

MSR $1,199	$1,025	$895	$775	$700	$575	$475	$375

Add $20 for walnut stock.
Add $50 for camo stock.

REDSTONE RS1 – 12 ga., 3 in. chamber, Inter Inertia Technology Locking System, 18 1/2, 24, 26, or 28 in. steel barrel, removable Interpro chokes, 4 shot mag., aluminum receiver, with or w/o Adco optical sights, walnut or polymer stock, includes ABS case with 5 Mobile chokes and sling swivels, black finish. Importation began 2021.

MSR $559	$475	$415	$355	$325	$260	$215	$175

Add $70 for walnut stock.
Add $90 for dot sights.

ADCOR DEFENSE

Current AR-15 style rifle manufacturer located in Baltimore, MD.

Please refer to BlueBookOfGunValues.com to order the *Blue Book of AR-15s & Variations*, available as a book or online subscription.

ADEQ FIREARMS COMPANY

Current manufacturer of rifles, pistols, and AR-15 style firearms established in 2010 by A.M. de Quesada, located in Tampa, FL.

For individual model listings, please go to BlueBookOfGunValues.com/overflow.

GRADING - PPGS™	100%	98%	95%	90%	80%	70%	60%	LAST MSR

ADIRONDACK ARMS COMPANY

Previous manufacturer located in Plattsburgh, NY, 1870-1874.

For more information on this manufacturer and its models, please refer to the *Blue Book of Antique American Firearms and Values* or visit BlueBookOfGunValues.com.

ADLER

Previously manufactured by Engelbrecht & Wolff located in Blasii, Germany, 1905-1907.

PISTOLS: SEMI-AUTO

SEMI-AUTO PISTOL – 7mm Adler cal., 8 shot mag., cocking lever on top of frame.

100%	98%	95%	90%	80%	70%	60%	LAST MSR
$5,000	$4,000	$3,000	$2,500	$2,000	$1,495	$1,100	

ADLER HUNTING ARMS COMPANY

Current shotgun manufacturer established circa 2007, located in Konya, Turkey. No U.S. importation.

Adler offers a complete line of good quality lever action, bolt action, semi-auto, slide action, O/U, and single barrel shotguns. Please contact the company directly for more information on their current models including pricing and availability.

ADVANCED ARMAMENT CORP.

Previous rifle manufacturer located in Lawrenceville, GA. Advanced Armament Corp. is part of the Remington Outdoor Group. Previously part of the Freedom Group until 2015. AAC currently manufactures silencers and accessories.

RIFLES: BOLT ACTION

MODEL 7 – .300 AAC Blackout cal., Rem. Model 7 bolt action, 16 in. threaded black Nitride barrel, black glass filled polymer stock with adj. cheek riser, X-Mark Pro trigger, includes 20 MOA scope rail, 6 lbs. 8 oz. Disc.

100%	98%	95%	90%	80%	70%	60%	LAST MSR
$775	$685	$615	$550	$485	$415	$370	*$899*

RIFLES: SEMI-AUTO

MPW – 5.56 NATO or .300 AAC Blackout cal., GIO, 16 in. barrel with AAC 51T Blackout flash hider, Geissele two-stage trigger, 6-position Magpul CTR stock, Magpul MOE grip, NiB BCG and cam pin, free floating quad rail sized to match length of barrel. Disc.

100%	98%	95%	90%	80%	70%	60%	LAST MSR
$1,350	$875	$650	$525	$450	$385	$350	*$1,600*

RIFLES: SINGLE SHOT

HANDI-RIFLE – .300 AAC Blackout cal., H&R Handi-Rifle break action, 16.2 in. threaded barrel, black glass filled polymer stock and furniture, H&R transfer bar trigger, 6.9 lbs. Mfg. 2012 only.

100%	98%	95%	90%	80%	70%	60%	LAST MSR
$325	$285	$250	$230	$215	$200	$190	*$360*

ADVANTAGE ARMS USA, INC.

Previous manufacturer located in St. Paul, MN, and distributed by Wildfire Sports, Inc. also located in St. Paul, MN. Advantage Arms USA, Inc. was sold and moved to Tucson, AZ, with the new name of New Advantage Arms, Inc. (see separate listing).

DERRINGERS

MODEL 422 – .22 LR or .22 WMR cal., 4 barrel double action derringer, rotating firing pin, patterned after the Mossberg "Brownie", 2 1/2 in. barrel, high grade alloy frame and barrel, 4 shot, available in blue, nickel, or QPQ (heat treated but appears blue) finish, 15 oz. Mfg. 1986-87 only.

100%	98%	95%	90%	80%	70%	60%	LAST MSR
$150	$135	$115	$105	$95	$85	$75	*$166*

Add 15% for .22 WMR cal. Add $6 for nickel finish. Add $11 for QPQ finish.

AERO PRECISION USA

Current AR-15 style parts and previous rifle manufacturer located in Tacoma, WA.

Please refer to BlueBookOfGunValues.com to order the *Blue Book of AR-15s & Variations*, available as a book or online subscription.

AERON CZ s.r.o.

Current manufacturer established in 1968 and located in Brno, Czech Republic.

Aeron CZ s.r.o. was founded in 1968 by Svazarm, a Czech Army activity club. The company designed, manufactured, and serviced small airplanes. Over the years, the company changed its activities and now manufactures sporting arms, as well as high precision air rifles and pistols. Currently, Aeron firearms are not imported into the U.S. For more information on currently imported Aeron airguns, please refer to the *Blue Book of Airguns* - also available as an online subscription.

GRADING - PPGS™	100%	98%	95%	90%	80%	70%	60%	LAST MSR

AETNA

Previous trademark manufactured by Harrington & Richardson located in Worchester, MA.

For more information on this manufacturer and its models, please refer to the *Blue Book of Antique American Firearms and Values* or visit BlueBookOfGunValues.com.

AETNA ARMS COMPANY

Previous manufacturer located in New York, 1869-1883.

For more information on this manufacturer and its models, please refer to the *Blue Book of Antique American Firearms and Values* or visit BlueBookOfGunValues.com.

AGNER

Previous trademark manufactured by Saxhoj Products Inc. in Denmark. Imported until 1986 by Beeman Arms, Inc. located in Santa Rosa, CA.

PISTOLS: SEMI-AUTO

MODEL M 80 – .22 LR cal. only, stainless steel, semi-auto target pistol, novel design with unique security key safety, adj. French walnut grips, dry fire mechanism, 5.9 in. barrel, 5 shot mag., limited production, 2.4 lbs. Imported 1981-1986.

$1,125	$995	$900	$800	$700	$600	$500	*$1,295*

Add $100 for left-hand action.

AIM SURPLUS, LLC

Current importer and distributor established during 1997 and located in Middletown, OH.

Aim Surplus currently imports a variety of military surplus rifles and pistols. The company also imports surplus European ammunition, in addition to distributing domestic accessories and ammunition. Please contact the company directly for more information including pricing, options, and availability.

AIRBORNE ARMS

Current AR-15 style firearm component manufacturer located in Blaine, MN.

Please refer to BlueBookOfGunValues.com to order the *Blue Book of AR-15s & Variations*, available as a book or online subscription.

AIR MATCH

Previously imported by Kendall International, located in Paris, KY.

PISTOLS: SINGLE SHOT

AIR MATCH 500 – .22 LR cal. match single shot pistol, target grips, adj. front counterweight, 10 1/2 in. barrel. Imported 1984-86.

$550	$495	$450	$425	$395	$360	$330	*$788*

AJAX ARMY

Previously distributed by E.C. Meacham Co., maker unknown, circa 1880s.

For more information on this manufacturer and its models, please refer to the *Blue Book of Antique American Firearms and Values* or visit BlueBookOfGunValues.com.

AKDAL

Previous trademark of pistols and shotguns manufactured by Ücyildiz Silah Sanayi Tic Ltd. Sti. until 2012, and located in Istanbul, Turkey. In late 2014, the company announced plans to open up a subsidiary in the U.S. (Akdal U.S.A.) that will include manufacturing certain models.

Akdal semi-auto pistols were good quality and came in a variety of configurations, including full size polymer frame 9mm cal., as well as chrome and satin finishes, and two different .25 ACP pocket pistols. Akdal also offered slide action and semi-auto shotguns, mostly in 12 ga.

Ücyildiz Silah Sanayi Tic Ltd. Sti. manufactured firearms under a variety of trademarks, including Blow, Akdal, and Voltran.

AKDAS ARMS

Current manufacturer of shotguns established in 1948, and located in Huglu, Konya, Turkey.

Akdas Arms is a family owned company founded by Ömer Akdas, believed to be the first person to ever manufacture a SxS shotgun in Turkey. Sons Sadik and Selim now run the company, which offers a complete line of good quality semi-auto shotguns in hunting and tactical configurations, as well as a line of O/U shotguns in hunting and sporting configurations. The company offers a wide variety of synthetic and wood stock options, receiver finishes, and engraving. Currently, these lines of shotguns have had little or no domestic importation. In addition to hunting and sporting shotguns, Akdas Arms has taken its part in the defense industry. Please

100%	98%	95%	90%	80%	70%	60%	50%	40%	30%	20%	10%

contact the company directly for more information including pricing, options, and availability.

Beginning in 2014, Akdas began manufacture of shotguns imported by SKB. Please refer to the SKB section for current information.

AKKAR

Current shotgun manufacturer established in 1989, located in Istanbul, Turkey. Akkar manufactures Triple barrel, O/U, SxS, single barrel, and slide action shotguns under registered trademarks including Churchill, Mammut, Altay, and Karatay.

Akkar's Churchill brand of shotguns is currently being imported by European American Armory Corp, located in Cocoa, FL. For individual model listings, please go to BlueBookOfGunValues.com/overflow under Akkar to view the Churchill lineup. Akkar shotguns were previously imported on a private label basis by Chiappa Firearms USA and by CZ-USA. Also previously imported by KBI, located in Harrisburg, PA during 2001-2010, and by Samco Global Arms, Inc., located in Miami, FL during 2011-2013..

AKLYS DEFENSE LLC

Current custom specialty firearm and AR-15 style rifle manufacturer founded in 2014, located in Baton Rouge, LA.

For individual model listings, please go to BlueBookOfGunValues.com/overflow.

AKRILL, E.

Previously manufactured in France, circa mid-1800s.

RIFLES: FLINTLOCK

FLINTLOCK RIFLE – .69 cal., breech loaded, octagonal Damascus barrel.

$3,300	$2,750	$2,200	$1,980	$1,460	$1,320	$1,240	$1,075	$935	$800	$745	$660

AKSA ARMS

Current trademark of AR-15 style shotguns, conversions, O/U, SXS, single shot, lever action, semi-auto, and slide action shotguns. Currently manufactured by Silah Insaat Metal SAN. Tic. LTD. STI, located in Konya, Turkey. No current importation.

Please contact the company directly for more information on their current models including pricing, options, and availability.

AKUS

Current trademark of O/U and SxS shotguns manufactured by Akus Silah San Tic A.S., located in Konya, Turkey. Previously imported on a private label basis by GU, located in Omaha, NE.

Akus manufactures a complete line of good quality O/U and SxS boxlock and sidelock shotguns in a variety of configurations, including hunting, trap, and skeet. Currently, the company, in partnership with Akdas Arms, manufactures SKB shotguns on a private label basis beginning in 2013. Please refer to the SKB section for currently imported shotguns.

A wide variety of options are available, including ejectors, receiver finishes, engraving styles, and stock types. Please contact the company directly for more information including pricing, options, and availability.

ALAMO RANGER

Previous manufacturer located in Spain.

REVOLVERS

REVOLVER – .38 Spl. cal., Spanish copy of Colt Model 1929.

GRADING - PPGS™	100%	98%	95%	90%	80%	70%	60%	LAST MSR
	$140	$120	$110	$100	$90	$85	$75	

ALAN & WILLIAM ARMS, INC.

Previous AR-15 style rifle manufacturer located in Cheyenne Wells, CO 2012-2017.

Please refer to BlueBookOfGunValues.com to order the *Blue Book of AR-15s & Variations*, available as a book or online subscription.

ALASKA

Previous trademark manufactured by Hood Firearms Company, Norwich, CT, 1873-1884.

For more information on this manufacturer and its models, please refer to the *Blue Book of Antique American Firearms and Values* or visit BlueBookOfGunValues.com.

GRADING - PPGS™	100%	98%	95%	90%	80%	70%	60%	LAST MSR

ALASKA MAGNUM AR'S

Current manufacturer of AR-15 style rifles, located in Fairbanks, AK.

Please refer to BlueBookOfGunValues.com to order the *Blue Book of AR-15s & Variations*, available as a book or online subscription.

ALASKAN COMMEMORATIVES

For individual model listings, please go to BlueBookOfGunValues.com/overflow.

ALBERTA TACTICAL RIFLE SUPPLY

Current bolt action and AR-15 style rifle manufacturer located in Calgary, Alberta, Canada. No current U.S. importation.

For individual model listings, please go to BlueBookOfGunValues.com/overflow.

ALCHEMY ARMS COMPANY

Previous manufacturer located in Auburn, WA, 1999-circa 2006.

PISTOLS: SEMI-AUTO

SPECTRE STANDARD ISSUE (SI) – 9mm Para., .40 S&W, or .45 ACP cal., SA, SFO, full size design, hammerless firing mechanism, linear action trigger, keyed internal locking device, aluminum receiver with 4 1/2 in. match grade stainless steel barrel and slide, tactical rail, various silver/black finishes, lowered ejection port, 10 shot double column mag, 32 oz. Mfg. 2000-2006.

	100%	98%	95%	90%	80%	70%	60%	LAST MSR
	$675	$585	$525	$465	$415	$350	$300	*$749*

SPECTRE SERVICE GRADE (SG & SGC) – similar to Spectre Standard Issue, except does not have tactical rail and rounded trigger guard, SGC is Commander style with 4 in. barrel and weighs 27 oz. Mfg. 2000-2006, SGC mfg. 2001-2006.

	100%	98%	95%	90%	80%	70%	60%	LAST MSR
	$675	$585	$525	$465	$415	$350	$300	*$749*

SPECTRE TITANIUM EDITION (TI/TIC) – similar to Spectre Series, except features a titanium slide with aluminum receiver, 22 (TIC is Commander style) or 24 oz. Mfg. 2000-2006.

	100%	98%	95%	90%	80%	70%	60%	LAST MSR
	$895	$775	$675	$575	$500	$450	$395	*$999*

ALCHEMY CUSTOM WEAPONRY

Current manufacturer of 1911 style pistols established in 2011, located in Geneseo, IL.

Alchemy Custom Weaponry is a division of Cabot Gun Co, LLC.

PISTOLS: SEMI-AUTO

Alchemy Custom Weaponry offers full custom 1911 builds with a base MSR of $7,000. Please contact the company directly for more information, availability, and pricing.

ANOMALY – .45 ACP, 9mm Para., or .38 Super cal., 1911 style, 4 1/4 in. match grade barrel, 8 shot mag., carbon steel construction, fastback style slide rear w/streamline blended hammer and truncated beavertail, white dot front sight, fixed rear sight w/serrated sight picture, checkered wood or G10 grips, high trigger guard undercut, tuned and polished extractor, lowered ejection port, polished feed ramp, traditional recoil spring and cap, hard pin set, dehorned for carry, polished blued or hard chrome finish. Mfg. 2018-2020.

	100%	98%	95%	90%	80%	70%	60%	LAST MSR
	$2,550	$2,225	$1,915	$1,735	$1,400	$1,150	$900	*$2,995*

BRIMSTONE – .45 ACP or 9mm Para. cal., 1911 style, CCO sized frame and slide, 4 1/4 in. match grade barrel, 7 shot mag., beveled magwell, carbon steel construction, short trigger, serrated front sight with blended dovetail fit, ACW fixed serrated rear sight, checkered wood grips, high trigger guard undercut, tuned and polished extractor, lowered ejection port, 25 LPI checkered front strap, polished feed ramp, traditional recoil spring and cap, hard pin set, dehorned for carry, blued or hard chrome finish. Mfg. 2018-2020.

	100%	98%	95%	90%	80%	70%	60%	LAST MSR
	$2,500	$2,200	$1,900	$1,700	$1,400	$1,150	$900	*$2,795*

PRIME CLASSIC CARRY – .45 ACP, 9mm Para., or .38 Super cal., 1911 style, Commander size frame, 4 1/4 in. Commander length barrel, two 8 shot mags., carbon steel construction, ring hammer, black serrated front sight, fixed serrated rear sight, checkered walnut grips, right-handed safety, polished feed ramp, tuned and polished extractor, lowered ejection port, blued or hard chrome finish. New 2019.

	100%	98%	95%	90%	80%	70%	60%
MSR $2,995	$2,550	$2,225	$1,915	$1,735	$1,400	$1,150	$900

Add $150 for 9mm Para. or .38 Super cal.
Add $250-$495 for hard chrome finish.

PRIME/PRIME COMPACT – .45 ACP, 9mm Para. (new 2020), or .38 Super (new 2020) cal., 1911 style, Govt. size frame, 5 in. Govt. barrel, two 8 shot mags., carbon steel construction, skeletonized hammer,

GRADING - PPGS™	100%	98%	95%	90%	80%	70%	60%	LAST MSR

black serrated front sight, fixed serrated rear sight, checkered wood or G10 grips, right hand or ambi safety, high trigger guard undercut, polished feed ramp, tuned and polished extractor, lowered ejection port, blued or hard chrome finish, also available in compact size (new 2020). New 2018.

MSR $2,795	**$2,500**	**$2,200**	**$1,900**	**$1,700**	**$1,400**	**$1,150**	**$900**

Add $150 for 9mm Para. or .38 Super cal.
Add $250-$495 for hard chrome finish.

PRIME HERITAGE SERIES – .45 ACP or 9mm Para. cal., 1911 style, Govt. size frame, 5 in. match grade throated barrel, two 8 shot mags. w/steel followers, beveled magwell, carbon steel construction, tuned and polished extractor, choice of gold bead (Prime Color Case Hardened model) or serrated black (Prime Charcoal Blue model) front sight w/blended dovetail fit and ACW fixed rear sight, Black Ebony or American Holly grips, cylinder and slide single side thumb safety, traditional guide rod and cap, polished feed ramp, charcoal blued or color case hardened finish. New 2020.

MSR $4,795	**$4,300**	**$3,800**	**$3,250**	**$2,950**	**$2,400**	**$1,950**	**$1,500**

PRIME ELITE/PRIME ELITE HARD CHROME – .45 ACP, 9mm Para., or .38 Super cal., 1911 style, Government sized frame, 5 in. flush cut barrel with reversed muzzle crown, two 8 shot mags., carbon steel construction, tuned and polished extractor, lowered ejection port, skeletonized hammer, gold bead front sight, fixed serrated rear sight, checkered wood grips, right hand or ambi safety, high trigger guard undercut, polished feed ramp, hand-beveled edges, extended magwell, front strap w/ MSH custom bordered checkering, hand polished blued or brushed hard chrome finish, 8.75 in. OAL, 38.4 oz. New 2019.

MSR $3,195	**$2,900**	**$2,500**	**$2,150**	**$1,950**	**$1,600**	**$1,300**	**$1,000**

Add $150 for 9mm Para. or .38 Super cal.
Add $495 for hard chrome finish.

PRODIGY – 9mm Para., .45 ACP, or .38 Super cal., 1911 style, Govt. size frame, 5 in. throated barrel and bushing, two 8 shot mags. w/steel followers, square trigger guard, fiber optic front and full adj. rear sight, walnut grips, ambi thumb safety, checkered front strap, blued finish. New 2021.

MSR $3,095	**$2,800**	**$2,450**	**$2,100**	**$1,900**	**$1,550**	**$1,250**	**$1,000**

QUANTICO – .45 ACP cal., 1911 style, Govt. sized frame, forged steel slide stop, 5 in. polished stainless steel or black coated barrel, two 8 shot mags., beveled magwell, extended billet steel-pinned ejector, ambi safety, traditional guide rod and cap, polished feed ramp, blued finish, available in high capacity. New 2021.

MSR $3,295	**$2,950**	**$2,600**	**$2,200**	**$2,000**	**$1,650**	**$1,350**	**$1,050**

Add $200 for high capacity (Quantico HiCap model).

ALDAZABAL

Previously manufactured by Aldazabal, Leturiondo & Cia., located in Spain.

PISTOLS: SEMI-AUTO

SEMI-AUTOMATIC PISTOL – 7.65mm cal., 7 shot, Eibar style.

	$195	**$165**	**$110**	**$100**	**$90**	**$75**	**$65**

ALERT

Previous trademark manufactured by Hood Firearms Company, Norwich, CT, 1873-1881.

For more information on this manufacturer and its models, please refer to the *Blue Book of Antique American Firearms and Values* or visit BlueBookOfGunValues.com.

ALESSANDRI, LOU, AND SON

Previous custom rifle manufacturer located in Rehoboth, MA 1975-circa 1998.

Lou Alessandri and Son were noted for their top-quality custom rifles (bolt action and side-by-side). Double rifles started at $18,500, while Express bolt actions started at $5,600. All guns were custom built per individual specifications and a wide variety of special order options were available. In addition to building custom rifles, Lou Alessandri and Son also offered a complete line of high-quality cleaning kits and related accessories. To determine the used value of a Lou Alessandri & Son rifle, the configuration has to be evaluated carefully (caliber, grade of wood, embellishments, and overall desirability).

ALEXANDER ARMS LLC

Current manufacturer of AR-15 style rifles and pistols located in Radford, VA. Law enforcement, military, dealer, and consumer sales.

Please refer to BlueBookOfGunValues.com to order the *Blue Book of AR-15s & Variations*, available as a book or online subscription.

100%	98%	95%	90%	80%	70%	60%	50%	40%	30%	20%	10%

ALEXIA

Previous trademark manufactured by Hopkins & Allen, located in Norwich, CT, 1867-1915.

Also known as: Blue Jacket, Captain Jack, Chichester, Defender, Dictator, Monarch, Mountain Eagle, Hopkins & Allen, Towers Police Safety, and Universal.

REVOLVERS

The octagon barreled revolvers listed were single action, solid frame, spur trigger designs. They were an inexpensive vest pocket pistol marketed under numerous names by private companies.

.22 RIMFIRE – 7 shot.

100%	98%	95%	90%	80%	70%	60%	50%	40%	30%	20%	10%
$275	$250	$225	$200	$170	$160	$155	$145	$130	$125	$110	$100

.32 SHORT RIMFIRE – 5 shot.

100%	98%	95%	90%	80%	70%	60%	50%	40%	30%	20%	10%
$170	$165	$160	$155	$150	$140	$125	$105	$95	$85	$75	$70

SINGLE ACTION .38 SHORT RIMFIRE – 5 shot.

100%	98%	95%	90%	80%	70%	60%	50%	40%	30%	20%	10%
$195	$180	$170	$165	$160	$145	$140	$120	$110	$100	$90	$85

.41 SHORT RIMFIRE – 5 shot.

100%	98%	95%	90%	80%	70%	60%	50%	40%	30%	20%	10%
$220	$210	$205	$195	$180	$170	$160	$145	$125	$110	$100	$90

ALEX PRO FIREARMS

Current AR-15 style rifle, pistol, and accessories manufacturer located in Alexandria, MN since 2014.

Please refer to BlueBookOfGunValues.com to order the *Blue Book of AR-15s & Variations*, available as a book or online subscription.

ALFA

Previous trademark manufactured by Armero Especialistas Reunidas, located in Eibar, Spain, circa 1920.

GRADING - PPGS™	100%	98%	95%	90%	80%	70%	60%	LAST MSR

REVOLVERS

All revolvers are marked "Alfa" on grips.

EARLY MODEL – .32, .38, or .44 cal., copies of S&W No. 2 by O. Hermanos.

100%	98%	95%	90%	80%	70%	60%
$145	$130	$120	$110	$105	$95	$75

Add 50% for .44 cal.

LATE MODEL – .22 LR, .32 S&W, or .38 S&W cal., copies of Colt Police Positive and S&W Military and Police.

100%	98%	95%	90%	80%	70%	60%
$160	$150	$130	$120	$110	$100	$90

ALFA PROJ

Current manufacturer established during 1993, located in Brno, Czech Republic. Previously distributed by Czechpoint, Inc. located in Knoxville, TN. Previously imported during 2006 by GunX, LLC, located in Shelton, CT.

For individual model listings, please go to BlueBookOfGunValues.com/overflow.

ALKARTASUNA FABRICA DE ARMAS, S.A.

Previous manufacturer located in Guernica, Spain.

PISTOLS: SEMI-AUTO

ALKARTASUNA CARTRIDGE COUNTER – 6.35mm cal., 7 shot, left grip panel cartridge counter, loaded chamber indicator, grip safety.

100%	98%	95%	90%	80%	70%	60%
$595	$450	$350	$275	$200	$175	$150

ALKARTASUNA RUBY AUTOMATIC – 7.65mm cal., 2 variations - more common is the "Ruby" type, 9 shot, 3 5/8 in. barrel, blue, fixed sights, checkered wood or hard rubber grips, used by French Army in WWI and WWII. Mfg. 1917-22.

100%	98%	95%	90%	80%	70%	60%
$325	$235	$165	$110	$65	$55	$45

Add 25% for extended barrel.

ALLEN & THURBER

Previous manufacturer/trademark originally located in Grafton, Mass. Ethan Allen started many plants to keep up with expanding business after 1832. Listed below is a chronological order of the firms constituting the family dynasty founded by Ethan Allen.

E. Allen - Grafton, Mass. 1832-1837
Allen & Thurber - Grafton, Mass. 1837-1842
Allen & Thurber - Norwich, Conn. 1842-1847
Allen & Thurber - Worcester, Mass. 1847-1854
Allen, Thurber, & Co. - Worcester, Mass. 1854-1856
Allen & Wheelock - Worcester, Mass. 1856-1865
E. Allen & Co. - Worcester, Mass. 1865-1871
Forehand & Wadsworth - Worcester, Mass. 1871-1890
Forehand Arms Co. - Worcester, Mass. 1890-1902

No other 19th-century American firm produced a wider variety of firearms than did Ethan Allen & subsidiaries. In 1902, the Forehand Arms Co. was sold to Hopkins & Allen.

Please refer to the Hopkins & Allen section for approximate values of Forehand Arms Co. revolvers.

ALLEN FIREARMS

Previous importer located in Santa Fe, NM importing A. Uberti firearms until early in 1987. After Allen Firearms closed, Cimarron F.A. Mfg. Co. located in Houston, TX purchased the remaining inventory (in addition to ordering new products under their name).

For individual model listings, please go to BlueBookOfGunValues.com/overflow.

ALMAR

Current trademark of private label shotguns sold by S. Alamanos & Co. O.E., located in Athens, Greece.

Almar is a private label on shotguns available in various configurations. To date, these guns have had little, if any, U.S. importation. Please contact the company directly for more information including pricing, options, and availability.

ALPHA ARMS (ALPHARMS)

Current trademark of shotguns manufactured by Leader Arms Technology. No current U.S. importation.

Please refer to Leader Arms Technology in the L section for more information.

ALPHA ARMS INC.

Previous manufacturer located in Flower Mound, TX from 1983-1987.

For individual model listings, please go to BlueBookOfGunValues.com/overflow.

ALPHA FOXTROT

Current pistol and AR-15 style rifle manufacturer located in Duluth, GA.

For individual model listings, please go to BlueBookOfGunValues.com/overflow.

ALPINE INDUSTRIES

Previous manufacturer located in Los Angeles, CA.

Alpine Industries was a commercial M1 carbine manufacturer which produced approximately 17,000 guns between 1962-1965. Guns were made with newly manufactured cast receivers and military surplus parts, including some from England.

ALTOBELLI ARMS COMPANY

Current shotgun manufacturer established in 1971, located in Konya, Turkey. No current U.S. importation.

Altobelli Arms Company was founded in 1971 by Mustafa Özkiran, who began by producing single barrel shotguns. Currently, the company produces a complete line of O/U, SxS, slide action, and semi-auto shotguns under the Altobelli and Challenger trademarks. Shotguns are available in a variety of configurations, including hunting, sporting, and tactical. A wide variety of finishes, stock options, and engraving are also available. Please contact the company directly for more information including pricing, options, and availability.

GRADING - PPGS™	100%	98%	95%	90%	80%	70%	60%	LAST MSR

ALTOR CORP.

Current single shot pistol manufacturer located in Cave Creek, Arizona.

PISTOLS: SINGLE SHOT

ALTOR PISTOL – 9mm Para. or .380 cal., striker fire, DAO, two parts to connect and load, 6 pieces total, Ergo design, stainless steel barrel, 4 grooves, polymer and metal components, integral extractor, integral sights, fully ambi, traditional button safety, black handle, 10.5 oz.

MSR $119	$110	$100	$85	$75	$65	$50	$45	

Add $10 for 9mm Para. cal.

AMBUSH FIREARMS

Current trademark of AR-15 style hunting rifles manufactured by Daniel Defense located in Black Creek, GA beginning 2011. An additional manufacturing facility is located in Ridgeland, SC.

Please refer to BlueBookOfGunValues.com to order the *Blue Book of AR-15s & Variations*, available as a book or online subscription.

AMERICA REMEMBERS

Current organization located in Ashland, VA, which privately commissions historical, limited/special editions in conjunction with various manufacturers. Previously located in Mechanicsville, VA until 1999.

For individual model listings, please go to BlueBookOfGunValues.com/overflow.

AMERICAN ARMS

Previous manufacturer located in Garden Grove, CA.

PISTOLS: SEMI-AUTO

EAGLE 380 – .380 ACP cal. only, stainless steel semi-auto, copy of Walther PPK/S, 6 shot mag., 3 1/4 in. barrel, limited production, 20 oz.

	$400	$250	$215	N/A	N/A	N/A	N/A	*$289*

Add $25 for case.
Add $50 for case and belt buckle.
Add $25 for black Teflon finish (disc. 1985).

AMERICAN ARMS CO.

Previous manufacturer located in Boston, MA from 1870-1901 and Milwaukee, WI from 1893-1904. American Arms Co. was acquired by Marlin in 1901.

For more information on this manufacturer and its models, please refer to the *Blue Book of Antique American Firearms and Values* or visit BlueBookOfGunValues.com.

AMERICAN ARMS, INC.

Previous importer and manufacturer located in North Kansas City, MO, until 2000. American Arms imported various Spanish shotguns (Indesal, Lanber, Norica, and Zabala Hermanos), Italian shotguns including F. Stefano, several European pistols and rifles, and Sites handguns (1990-2000) mfg. in Torino, Italy. This company also manufactured several pistols in North Kansas City, MO. For more information and pricing on Norica airguns previously imported by American Arms, please refer to the *Blue Book of Airguns* by Dr. Robert Beeman & John Allen (also available online).

In late 2000, TriStar Sporting Arms, Ltd. acquired the parts inventory for some models previously imported by American Arms, Inc. Original warranties from American Arms do not apply to TriStar Sporting Arms, Ltd.

COMBINATION GUNS

RS COMBO – choice of .222 Rem. or .308 Win. rifle barrel under 12 ga. barrel, engraved boxlock frame with antique silver finish, DT, 24 in. VR barrels with shotgun choke tubes, rifle sights, grooved for scope mounting, Monte Carlo stock, 7 lbs. 14 oz. Imported 1989 only.

	$675	$595	$550	$495	$450	$420	$385	*$749*

PISTOLS: SEMI-AUTO

MODEL TT-9MM TOKAREV – 9mm Para. cal., SA, 4 1/2 in. barrel, 9 shot mag., hammer block external safety, 31 oz. Imported 1988-89 only.

	$450	$325	$275	$225	$200	$180	$160	*$289*

This model is patterned after the Tokarev action and was made from machined steel parts in Yugoslavia.

GRADING - PPGS™	100%	98%	95%	90%	80%	70%	60%	LAST MSR

MODEL EP-380 – .380 ACP cal., DA/SA, stainless steel, 3 1/2 in. barrel, 7 shot mag., wood checkered grips, adj. rear sight, 25 oz. Imported 1988-90 only.

$375	$325	$250	$195	$165	$140	$120	*$449*

This model was made in West Germany.

MODEL PK-22 CLASSIC – .22 LR cal., SA, styled after Govt. .45 ACP, 3 1/3 in. barrel, 8 shot finger extension mag., black polymer grips, 22 oz. Mfg. 1988-96.

$165	$140	$115	$100	$90	$80	$70	*$199*

This model was made in North Kansas City, MO. It has patented safety features such as external hammer block and internal blocking of the firing pin until the trigger is pulled.

MODEL CX-22 CLASSIC – .22 LR cal., patterned after Walther PPK, 3 1/3 in. barrel, 8 shot finger extension mag., 22 oz. Mfg. 1990-95.

$175	$145	$125	$110	$100	$90	$80	*$213*

This model was made in North Kansas City, MO. It had patented safety features such as an external hammer block and internal firing pin block.

* ***Model CXC-22*** – similar to CX-22 Classic, except has chrome slide. Mfg. in 1990 only.

$170	$150	$125	$110	$100	$90	$80	*$189*

MODEL PX-22/25 CLASSIC – .22 LR or .25 ACP (mfg. 1991 only) cal., compact variation of the Model CX-22, 2 3/4 in. barrel, 7 shot finger extension mag., 15 oz. New 1989, PX-25 was mfg. 1991 only, PX-22 was disc. 1995.

$175	$145	$125	$110	$100	$90	$80	*$206*

This model was made in North Kansas City, MO. It had patented safety features such as an external hammer block and internal firing pin block.

MODEL P-98 CLASSIC – .22 LR cal., DA/SA patterned after Walther P.38, 5 in. barrel, 8 shot mag., blue/black finish, grooved wraparound grips, 26 oz. Mfg. 1990-96.

$170	$145	$125	$110	$100	$90	$80	*$209*

ESCORT – .380 ACP cal., DAO, 3 3/8 in. barrel, 7 shot mag., unique thin profile, matte stainless steel, soft polymer grips, polygonal rifling, 19 oz. Mfg. 1995-97.

$285	$230	$200	$185	$170	$160	$150	*$349*

SABRE – while this model was advertised, it was never mfg.

SPECTRE – 9mm Para., .40 S&W (mfg. 1991 only), or .45 ACP (new 1993) cal., DA/SA, 6 in. barrel with polygonal rifling, 30 shot mag., ambidextrous safety, decocking lever, adj. sights, 4 1/2 lbs., mfg. in Italy by Sites. Imported 1990-93.

$1,500	$1,325	$1,125	$1,000	$825	$675	$525	*$429*

.45 ACP and .40 S&W cal. variants carry a premium

This model was previously imported by F.I.E. located in Hialeah, FL (1989-1990).

AUSSIE SEMI-AUTO – 9mm Para. or .40 S&W cal., DA/SA, polymer frame with nickeled steel slide and 4 3/4 in. barrel, 10 shot mag., features 5 safeties, last shot slide lock, 23 oz. Limited importation from Spain 1996 only.

$450	$295	$250	$225	$200	$175	$160	*$425*

These guns are marked "FELK TF 919".

REVOLVERS: SAA

REGULATOR MODEL – .357 Mag., .44-40, or .45 LC cal., 4 3/4, 5 1/2 (new 1993), or 7 1/2 in. barrel, reproduction of the Colt Peacemaker, brass trigger guard and backstrap, fixed sights, half-cock and hammer block safeties, blade front and grooved rear sights, color case hardened frame and blue barrel/cylinder or nickel finish (imported 1999 only in .45 LC cal.), walnut grips, 35 oz. Mfg. by Uberti. Imported 1992-2000.

$300	$250	$225	$200	$185	$175	$160	*$320*

Add $55 for nickel finish (disc. 1999).
Add $40 for dual cylinder set (.44-40/.44 Spl. or .45 LC/.45 ACP). Disc. 1998.

* ***Regulator Model Deluxe*** – similar to Regulator Model, except .45 LC cal. only, full charcoal blue finish (mfg. 1996-97) or color case hardened frame (new 1998), case hardened (pre-1993) or blue (post-1993) steel trigger guard and backstrap. Importation disc. 1992, resumed 1994-2000.

$350	$275	$240	$225	$200	$175	$160	*$365*

Add $70 for dual cylinder set (.44-40/.44 Spl. or .45 LC/.45 ACP). Disc. 1992.

GRADING - PPGS™	100%	98%	95%	90%	80%	70%	60%	LAST MSR

* ***Regulator Model Buckhorn*** – .44 Mag. cal., 4 3/4, 6, or 7 1/2 in. barrel, otherwise similar to Regulator Model, 44 oz. Imported 1993-96.

$340	**$275**	**$225**	**$200**	**$185**	**$175**	**$160**	*$379*

Add $10 for Target variation (flat-top and adj. rear sight). Imported 1994 only.

* ***Regulator Model Storekeeper*** – .44-40 WCF or .45 LC cal., 4 in. barrel, smooth walnut curved grips, nickel or B/H nickel finish, 31 oz. Imported 1999 only.

$350	**$300**	**$250**	**$210**	**$185**	**$175**	**$160**	*$375*

Add $44 for B/H nickel finish.

UBERTI BISLEY – .45 LC cal., patterned after the Colt Bisley, case hardened steel frame, 4 3/4, 5 1/2, or 7 1/2 in. barrel with fixed sights, hammer block safety. Imported 1997-98 only.

$475	**$375**	**$300**	**$250**	**$225**	**$200**	**$175**	*$475*

UBERTI .454 SAA – .454 cal., 6 SR or 7 1/2 in. top ported barrel, hammer block safety, satin nickel finish, custom hardwood grips, wide trigger, adj. rear sight. Imported 1996-97 only.

$825	**$700**	**$600**	**$550**	**$500**	**$475**	**$425**	*$869*

SILVERADO – .357 Mag., .44 Mag., or .45 LC cal., 4 3/4, 5 1/2, or 7 1/2 in. barrel, brushed nickel finish, unfluted cylinder, laminated charcoal grips. Mfg. by Uberti, imported 1999-2000.

$375	**$325**	**$250**	**$220**	**$190**	**$175**	**$160**	*$409*

RIFLES: O/U

SILVER EXPRESS – 8x57JRS or 9.3x74R cal., O/U boxlock design, gold SNT, monobloc 28 in. separated barrels, manual safety, silver finished receiver with light engraving, skipline checkered walnut stock and forearm, approx. 7 3/4 lbs. Limited importation 1999-2000.

$1,800	**$1,625**	**$1,500**	**$1,375**	**$1,250**	**$1,125**	**$1,000**	*$1,949*

RIFLES: REPRODUCTIONS

MODEL 1860 HENRY REPLICA – .44-40 WCF or .45 LC cal., 24 1/4 in. blue or in-the-white finish (new 1999) barrel, 9 1/4 lbs. Mfg. by Uberti, importation disc. 2000.

$925	**$700**	**$575**	**$475**	**$400**	**$350**	**$300**	*$940*

Add $50 for white barrel finish.

* ***Model 1860 Henry Trapper Replica*** – similar to the Henry Replica, except has 18 1/2 in. barrel, 8 lbs. Imported 1999-2000.

$925	**$700**	**$575**	**$475**	**$400**	**$350**	**$300**	*$940*

Add $50 for white barrel finish.

MODEL 1866 WINCHESTER REPLICA – .44-40 WCF or .45 LC cal., 19 (Carbine) or 24 1/4 (Rifle) in. barrel, approx. 8 lbs. Mfg. by Uberti, importation disc. 2000.

$725	**$600**	**$500**	**$425**	**$325**	**$275**	**$225**	*$730*

Subtract $20 for Carbine variation (Yellowboy).

MODEL 1873 WINCHESTER REPLICA – .44-40 WCF or .45 LC cal., 24 1/4 or 30 (new 1999) in. octagon barrel, case colored receiver, approx. 8 1/4 lbs. Mfg. by Uberti, importation disc. 2000.

$850	**$675**	**$575**	**$475**	**$400**	**$350**	**$275**	*$860*

Add $80 for 30 in. barrel.

* ***Model 1873 Deluxe Winchester Replica*** – similar to Model 1873 Winchester Replica, except has better quality checkered pistol grip stock and forearm. Disc. 1997.

$1,200	**$850**	**$700**	**$550**	**$475**	**$375**	**$300**	*$1,299*

MODEL 1885 SINGLE SHOT HIGH WALL – .45-70 Govt. cal., 28 in. round barrel, color case hardened frame, 8.82 lbs. Mfg. by Uberti, imported 1998-2000.

$775	**$625**	**$550**	**$450**	**$375**	**$325**	**$275**	*$810*

SHARPS CAVALRY CARBINE – .45-70 Govt. cal., 22 in. heavy round blue barrel, case colored receiver, adj. rear ladder sight, DST, uncheckered walnut stock and forearm, 8 lbs. 3 oz. Imported 1999-2000.

$675	**$575**	**$500**	**$450**	**$400**	**$375**	**$325**	*$660*

SHARPS FRONTIER CARBINE – similar to Cavalry Carbine, except has regular barrel with barrel band and single trigger, 7 lbs. 13 oz. Imported 1999-2000.

$675	**$575**	**$500**	**$450**	**$400**	**$375**	**$325**	*$675*

SHARPS 1874 SPORTING RIFLE – .45-70 Govt. or .45-120 black powder cartridge, 28 in. octagon barrel, checkered walnut stock and forearm, DST, 9 lbs. 3 oz. Imported 1999-2000.

$700	**$600**	**$500**	**$450**	**$400**	**$375**	**$325**	*$685*

GRADING - PPGS™	100%	98%	95%	90%	80%	70%	60%	LAST MSR

* ***Sharps 1874 Deluxe Sporting Rifle*** – similar to Sharps 1874 Sporting Rifle, except has brown barrel finish. Imported 1999-2000.

$725 $600 $500 $450 $400 $375 $325 *$705*

RIFLES: SEMI-AUTO

MODEL ZCY 308 – .308 Win. cal., GPO, AK-47 type action, Yugoslavian mfg. Imported 1988 only.

$775 $650 $550 $450 $400 $375 $350 *$825*

MODEL AKY 39 – 7.62x39mm cal., GPO, AK-47 type action, teakwood fixed stock and grip, flip-up Tritium front and rear night sights, Yugoslavian mfg. Imported 1988-1989 only.

$650 $550 $495 $440 $395 $350 $300 *$559*

This model was supplied with sling and cleaning kit.

* ***Model AKF 39 Folding Stock*** – 7.62x39mm cal., folding stock variation of the Model AKY-39. Imported 1988-89 only.

$725 $625 $550 $475 $425 $375 $325 *$589*

EXP-64 SURVIVAL RIFLE – .22 LR cal., takedown rifle stores in oversize synthetic stock compartment, 21 in. barrel, 10 shot mag., open sights, receiver grooved for scope mounting, crossbolt safety, 40 in. overall length, 7 lbs. Imported 1989-90 only.

$150 $135 $125 $115 $105 $95 $85 *$169*

MINI-MAX – .22 LR cal., 18 3/4 in. barrel, wood or black synthetic stock, 10 shot mag., adj. rear sight, 4 1/3 lbs. Imported in 1990 only.

$85 $75 $65 $55 $45 $40 $35 *$99*

Add $6 for wood stock.

SM 64 TD SPORTER – .22 LR cal., 21 in. takedown barrel, checkered walnut finished hardwood stock and forend, hooded front sight and adj. rear sight, 7 lbs. Imported 1989-90 only.

$130 $115 $105 $95 $85 $75 $65 *$149*

SHOTGUNS: O/U

American Arms imported Spanish shotguns manufactured by Zabala Hermanos, Lanber, and Indesal. Italian shotguns were also imported and mfg. by Stefano Fausti (Models Silver, Waterfowl, and Turkey Special). American Arms also imported Franchi Black Magic semi-auto and O/U shotguns until 1998. These shotguns will appear under the Franchi section in this text. Older Diarm models have been listed below.

LINCE – 12 or 20 ga., 3 in. chambers, boxlock with Greener crossbolt, various barrel lengths and chokings, available in either blue or shiny chrome finish, SST, VR, ejectors. Imported 1986 only.

$510 $400 $380 $360 $340 $320 $300 *$610*

Add $70 for choke tubes.

SILVER MODEL – 12 or 20 ga. only, similar to Lince Model, except has brushed aluminum receiver, no engraving. Imported 1986-1987 only.

$495 $450 $390 $360 $330 $300 $285 *$545*

Add $50 for multi-chokes.

SILVER I – similar to Silver Model, except also available in 24 (Ellett Bros. exclusive), 28 (new 1988), 32 (Ellett Bros. exclusive) ga. or .410 bore (new 1988), single selective trigger became standard in 1988, extractors, engraved frame, fixed chokes, recoil pad. Imported 1986-2000.

$535 $430 $350 $300 $285 $270 $255 *$649*

Add 15% for 28 ga. or .410 bore.
Add 25% for 24 or 32 ga.

Engraved frame became standard in 1987.

SILVER II – similar to Silver I, except was supplied with choke tubes, deluxe walnut, and ejectors, 16 (new 1999) ga. Imported 1987-2000.

$660 $560 $475 $400 $360 $330 $300 *$769*

Add 15% for 28 ga. or .410 bore (fixed chokes only).
Add 25% for 24 or 32 ga.

* ***Silver II Lite (Silver Upland Lite)*** – 12, 20, or 28 (disc. 1995) ga., 3 in. chambers (except for 28 ga.), 26 in. VR barrels, with Franchoke tubes (except for 28 ga.), SST, ejectors, engraved frame with antique silver finish, checkered walnut stock and forearm, 5 3/4-6 1/4 lbs. Imported 1994-98.

$800 $660 $550 $485 $440 $400 $360 *$925*

GRADING - PPGS™	100%	98%	95%	90%	80%	70%	60%	LAST MSR

* ***Silver II Small Gauge Combo*** – included either 20/28 ga. (new 1997) or 28 ga./.410 bore barrels. Imported 1989-2000.

$1,080 $925 $750 $625 $550 $495 $450 *$1,239*

SILVER LITE – 12 or 20 ga., 2 3/4 in. chambers, boxlock action, 26 in. vent. barrels with VR and choke tubes, blue alloy receiver, ejectors, gold SST, checkered walnut stock and forearm, 5 lbs. 14 oz. or 6 (12 ga.) lbs. Mfg. by Lanber. Imported 1990-1992.

$625 $535 $460 $400 $360 $330 $300 *$749*

SILVER HUNTER – 12 or 20 ga., steel boxlock action, SST, extractors, monobloc VR 26 or 28 (12 ga. only) in. barrels with 2 choke tubes, checkered walnut stock and forearm. Imported 1999 only.

$550 $450 $375 $315 $285 $270 $255 *$629*

SILVER SPORTING – 12 ga. or 20 (new 1996) ga., Sporting Clay model, boxlock action, 28, 29 (new 1999), or 30 (new 1993) in. ported vent. barrels with channelled broadway VR, choke tubes, and elongated forcing cones, nickel finished engraved receiver, SST, ejectors, figured walnut stock and forearm with handcut checkering, 7 lbs. 6 oz. Mfg. by Lanber, imported 1990-2000. 1993 manufacture by Pedersoli.

$835 $680 $550 $485 $440 $400 $360 *$965*

SILVER SKEET – 12 ga. only, similar appearance to Silver Sporting, 26 or 28 (new 1993) in. ported vent. barrels with raised VR, 4 choke tubes, recoil pad, 7 lbs. 6 oz. Imported 1992-93 only.

$790 $685 $575 $495 $450 $400 $360 *$899*

SILVER TRAP – similar appearance to Silver Sporting, 30 in. ported barrels with raised VR, 4 choke tubes, recoil pad, trap stock dimensions, 7 3/4 lbs. Imported 1992-1993 only.

$790 $685 $575 $495 $450 $400 $360 *$899*

STERLING/BRISTOL – 12 or 20 ga., 3 in. chambers, boxlock with Greener crossbolt and false sideplates, various barrel lengths and choke tubes, chrome finished receiver with moderate game scene engraving, SST, VR, ejectors. Imported 1986-89.

$695 $550 $495 $450 $400 $375 $350 *$825*

Until 1989, this model was designated the Bristol. In 1988, the engraving pattern was changed from game scene to elaborate scroll type.

SIR – 12 or 20 ga., 3 in. chambers, sidelock with Greener crossbolt, various barrel lengths and chokings, chrome finished receiver with game scene engraving, ST, VR, ejectors, deluxe checkered pistol grip stock and forearm. Imported 1986 only.

$1,100 $900 $750 $675 $610 $565 $520 *$1,090*

Add $75 for choke tubes.

ROYAL – 12 or 20 ga., 3 in. chambers, sidelock with Greener crossbolt, various barrel lengths and chokings, chrome finished receiver with elaborate scroll engraving, ST, VR, ejectors, oil finished deluxe checkered pistol grip and forearm. Imported 1986-87 only.

$1,595 $1,310 $1,080 $960 $850 $750 $675 *$1,730*

Add $65 for choke tubes.

EXCELSIOR – 12 or 20 ga., 3 in. chambers, sidelock with Greener crossbolt, various barrel lengths and chokings, chrome finished receiver with elaborate deep relief engraving and multiple gold inlays, ST, VR, ejectors, oil finished deluxe checkered pistol grip and forearm. Imported 1986-87 only.

$1,775 $1,510 $1,250 $1,100 $975 $885 $780 *$1,925*

Add $70 for choke tubes.

WS/WT - O/U (SILVER) 12 WATERFOWL/TURKEY SPECIAL – 12 ga. only, Mag. chambers (3 1/2 in. was added in 1989), 24 (Turkey - disc. 1996), 26 (Turkey) or 28 (Waterfowl) in. barrels with choke tubes, SST, ejectors, parkerized metal finish, matte finished stock and forearm, Mossy Oak Breakup camo pattern began 1997 for Turkey Special, sling swivels, recoil pad, approx. 7 lbs. Imported 1987-2000.

$650 $550 $460 $395 $360 $330 $300 *$799*

Add $86 for Camo Turkey Model (WT/OU Camo 12, Breakup camo pattern, new 1997).

* ***WS/WT O/U 10 ga. Waterfowl*** – 10 ga. Mag., double triggers, extractors, matte finishes similar to 12 ga. Waterfowl, beavertail forearm. Imported 1988-89 only.

$750 $625 $550 $495 $450 $390 $360 *$829*

WT-O/U10 TURKEY SPECIAL – 10 ga., 3 1/2 in. Mag., 26 in. barrels with choke tubes, SST (became standard in 1990), extractors, recoil pad, non-glare metal finish, 9 lbs. 10 oz. Imported 1988-2000.

$865 $695 $550 $500 $450 $390 $360 *$995*

GRADING - PPGS™	100%	98%	95%	90%	80%	70%	60%	LAST MSR

F.S. 200 – 12 ga., trap or skeet model, 26 or 32 in. separated barrels only, SST, ejectors, boxlock with Greener crossbolt, black or chromed receiver, checkered walnut stock and forearm. Imported 1986-87 only.

$690 $560 $500 $450 $410 $375 $350 *$835*

F.S. 300 – 12 ga., trap or skeet model, 26, 30, or 32 in. separated barrels only, SST, ejectors, boxlock with Greener crossbolt and false sideplates lightly engraved, chromed receiver, checkered walnut stock and forearm. Imported 1986 only.

$825 $675 $610 $555 $510 $470 $440 *$995*

F.S. 400 – 12 ga., trap or skeet model, 26, 30, or 32 in. separated barrels only, ST, ejectors, sidelock with Greener crossbolt, lightly engraved chromed receiver, checkered walnut stock and forearm. Imported 1986 only.

$1,175 $950 $860 $795 $730 $660 $595 *$1,360*

F.S. 500 – same specifications as F.S. 400. Importation disc. 1985.

$1,175 $950 $860 $795 $730 $660 $595 *$1,360*

SHOTGUNS: SxS

American Arms imported Spanish shotguns manufactured by Zabala Hermanos and Grulla. Older discontinued Diarm models will also be shown in this section.

GENTRY/YORK – 12, 16 (disc. 1990), 20, 28 ga., or .410 bore, 3 in. chambers, boxlock, ejectors (extractors after 1986), DT or SST (became standard in 1992), chromed receiver features fine scroll engraving, fixed chokes, pistol grip stock with recoil pad and beavertail forearm. Imported 1986-2000.

$625 $475 $375 $300 $280 $260 $240 *$750*

Add $45 for 28 ga. or .410 bore.

Before 1988 this model was designated York (case coloring began 1988, silver finish began 1993). DT were supplied with 28 ga. or .410 bore 1990-2000.

BRITTANY – 12 or 20 ga., boxlock action, 25 (20 ga. only, disc. 1996), 26, or 27 (12 ga. only, disc. 1996) in. barrels, SST, ejectors, matted solid rib, choke tubes, engraved case colored frame, checkered walnut straight grip stock with recoil pad and semi-beavertail forearm, 6 1/2 or 7 lbs. Imported 1989-2000.

$725 $575 $485 $435 $400 $375 $350 *$885*

The wood finish was changed in this model from oil to semi-gloss in 1991.

SHOGUN – 10 ga., 3 1/2 in. chambers, boxlock, ejectors, DT, chromed receiver features fine scroll engraving. Imported 1986 only.

$440 $350 $325 $300 $280 $260 $240 *$525*

DERBY – 12, 20, 28 (disc. 1991) ga., or .410 bore (disc. 1991) ga., 3 in. chambers, sidelock, ejectors, DT (disc. 1989) or SNT, chromed receiver with fine scroll engraving, fixed chokes, straight grip walnut stock and forearm. Imported 1986-94.

$1,150 $975 $850 $750 $625 $500 $425 *$1,039*

Add 10% for 28 ga. or .410 bore (disc. 1991).
Subtract 10% for DT.
Add approx. 50%-60% for 2-barrel set (20 and 28 ga. - approx. 300 sets mfg.) - disc. 1990.

This model featured a case-colored receiver between 1988-90 and was changed to coin finish in late 1991. At the same time, the wood finish was changed from oil to semi-gloss.

GRULLA NO. 2 – 12, 20, 28 ga., or .410 bore, hand fitted sidelock action, 26 or 28 in. barrels, DT, ejectors, fixed chokes, concave rib, case colored receiver with elaborate engraving, deluxe English-style straight stock and splinter forearm (checkered and hand rubbed), between 5 3/4-6 1/4 lbs. Imported 1989-2000.

Before going to a special order basis, this model retailed for $3,099 (1994).

This model was individually handcrafted with less than 800 mfg. each year.

* ***Grulla No. 2 Small Gauge Set*** – includes choice of 20/28 ga. or 28 ga./.410 bore barrel combination (26 in. fixed choke barrels). Imported 1989-95.

$3,600 $3,000 $2,375 $2,000 $1,650 $1,325 $1,150

Before going to a special order basis, this combination last retailed for $4,219 (1994/5).

WS/SS 10 WATERFOWL SPECIAL – 10 ga. only, 3 1/2 in. chambers, 32 in. barrels, DT, parkerized finish, sling swivels and camouflaged sling, extractors, fixed chokes, recoil pad, 11 lbs. 3 oz. Imported 1987-93.

$560 $500 $440 $400 $375 $350 $325 *$639*

GRADING - PPGS™	100%	98%	95%	90%	80%	70%	60%	LAST MSR

WT/SS 10 – 10 ga. only, 3 1/2 in. chambers, similar to TS/SS 12, except had 28 in. barrels with multi-chokes. Imported 1998-2000.

	$775	$650	$550	$450	$400	$375	$350	*$860*

TS/SS 10/12 TURKEY SPECIAL – 10 (disc. 1995) or 12 ga., 3 or 3 1/2 in. chambers (3 1/2 in. 12 ga. introduced in 1989), 26 in. barrels only, DT, parkerized finish, dull finish stock and forearm, sling swivels, recoil pad, choke tubes, 7 lbs. 6 oz. or 10 lbs. 13 oz. (10 ga.). Imported 1987-2000.

	$665	$550	$450	$400	$375	$350	$325	*$799*

This model in 12 ga. was supplied with a SST.

SHOTGUNS: SEMI-AUTO

PHANTOM FIELD – 12 ga. only, 3 in. chamber, gas operated, 24, 26, or 28 in. VR barrel with 3 choke tubes, black synthetic or checkered walnut stock and forearm, blue finish. Imported 1999-2000.

	$395	$360	$330	$275	$250	$225	$200	*$439*

* ***Phantom HP*** – similar to Phantom Field with synthetic stock and forearm, except had 19 in. threaded barrels for external choke tubes, swivel studs, and extended mag. Imported 1999-2000.

	$400	$365	$330	$275	$250	$225	$200	*$449*

SHOTGUNS: SINGLE SHOT

SINGLE SHOT MODEL – 12, 20 ga., or .410 bore, 3 in. chamber non-exposed hammer, pistol grip stock, non-reflective finish. Imported 1988-89 only.

	$90	$80	$70	$60	$55	$50	$45	*$99*

* ***Single Shot Model Camper Special*** – 12, 20 ga., or .410 bore, 3 in. chamber folding design, 21 in. barrel, pistol grip. Imported 1988-89 only.

	$95	$80	$70	$60	$55	$50	$45	*$107*

* ***Single Shot Model Slugger*** – 12 or 20 ga., 24 in. slug barrel with adj. rear and blade front sights, recoil pad. Imported 1989 only.

	$100	$85	$75	$65	$55	$50	$45	*$115*

* ***Single Shot Model Youth*** – 20 ga. or .410 bore, 26 in. barrel, 12 1/2 in. LOP stock, recoil pad. Imported 1989 only.

	$100	$85	$75	$65	$55	$50	$45	*$115*

* ***Single Shot Model Combo*** – interchangeable rifle and shotgun barrels, choice of .22 Hornet/12 ga. with 28 in. barrel or .22 LR/20 ga. with 26 in. barrel, includes fitted hard case. Imported 1989 only.

	$195	$165	$130	$115	$100	$90	$80	*$235*

* ***Single Shot Model 10 Ga.*** – 10 ga. only, 3 1/2 in. chambers, 26 in. multi-choke or 32 in. full fixed choke barrel, non-exposed hammer, non-reflective finish. Imported 1988-89 only.

	$135	$115	$95	$80	$70	$60	$55	*$149*

Add $30 for multi-chokes (26 in. barrel).

AMERICAN BARLOCK WONDER

Previous trademark manufactured by Crescent Arms for Sears Roebuck & Co.

For more information on this manufacturer and its models, please refer to the *Blue Book of Antique American Firearms and Values* or visit bluebookofgunvalues.com.

AMERICAN BUILT ARMS CO.

Current manufacturer of tactical bolt action rifles using a modular system located in Glen Rock, PA.

RIFLES: BOLT ACTION

.22 CHASSIS RIFLE – .22 LR cal., 16 1/2 in. threaded heavy bull barrel, 7 shot mag., Urban Sniper stock, P*Grip pistol grip, MOD X PT aluminum chassis system, Type III hardcoat anodized finish, 6 lbs. New 2019.

MSR $600	$510	$450	$385	$350	$285	$250	$200	

KEYSTONE PT (PRECISION TRAINER) – .22 LR cal., 16 1/2 in. threaded, heavy bull barrel, 7 shot mag., AB Arms MOD X PT aluminum chassis, Urban Sniper stock (LOP 10 1/2-13 3/4 in.), AB Arms P Grip pistol grip, hardcoat anodized finish, 30 3/4-34 in. OAL, approx. 6 lbs. Mfg. 2017-2019.

	$475	$415	$350	$325	$275	$225	$175	*$550*

This rifle is built on a Keystone Sporting Arms Model 722 barreled action.

GRADING - PPGS™	100%	98%	95%	90%	80%	70%	60%	LAST MSR

MOD X GEN III MODULAR RIFLE SYSTEM – .308 Win. cal., Remington 700 Short Action, 20 in. threaded barrel, aluminum, X-Mark Pro externally adj. trigger, AB Arms Urban Sniper stock, Urban recoil pad and the Ergo 4009-BK pistol grip, 13 1/2 in. free floating modular forearm, hardcoat anodized black or Dark Element finish, approx. 10 lbs. Disc. 2019.

	100%	98%	95%	90%	80%	70%	60%	LAST MSR
	$1,025	$900	$775	$700	$575	$475	$375	*$1,200*

This rifle is built on a Remington Model 700 SPS Tactical AAC-SD barreled action.

AMERICAN CLASSIC

Current trademark of pistols manufactured in the Philippines by MetroArms Corporation (MAC) and imported and distributed by Eagle Imports, Inc., located in Wanamassa, NJ.

PISTOLS: SEMI-AUTO

AMERICAN CLASSIC AMIGO MODEL – .45 ACP cal., SA, Officer's Model configuration, 3 1/2 in. barrel, 7 shot mag., steel frame and slide, dovetail front and Novak-style rear sights, diamond cut checkered mahogany grips, beavertail grip/extended thumb safety, deep blue, hard chrome, or duotone (new 2012) finish, approx. 32 1/2 oz. Mfg. 2011-2020.

	100%	98%	95%	90%	80%	70%	60%	LAST MSR
	$610	$515	$425	$365	$325	$285	$250	*$714*

Add $90 for hard chrome finish.
Add $60 for duotone finish (new 2012).

AMERICAN CLASSIC BOBCUT – .45 ACP cal., SA, steel frame, 4 1/4 in. throated forged steel barrel, 8 shot mag., hammer forged steel slide, skeletal combat trigger, dovetail front and fully adj. Novak style rear sight, custom hardwood grips with MAC logo, stippled front strap serration, blue or chrome finish, approx. 35 oz. New 2021.

	100%	98%	95%	90%	80%	70%	60%
MSR $920	$785	$685	$590	$535	$450	$425	$375

AMERICAN CLASSIC BULLSEYE – .45 ACP or 10mm cal., steel frame, 6 in. throated forged steel barrel, 8 shot mag., hammer forged steel slide with rear slide serrations, skeletal combat hammer and trigger, dovetail front and fully adj. Bomar-type rear sight, custom hardwood grips with MAC logo, stippled front strap serration, blue or chrome finish, 47 oz. New 2021.

	100%	98%	95%	90%	80%	70%	60%
MSR $1,242	$1,055	$925	$790	$715	$580	$475	$400

Add $77 for chrome finish.

AMERICAN CLASSIC COMMANDER MODEL – 9mm Para. (new 2013) or .45 ACP cal., SA, 4 1/4 in. barrel, 8 (.45 ACP) or 9 (9mm) shot mag., blue, hard chrome, or duotone (new 2012, .45 ACP only) finish, steel frame and slide, Novak rear sight, dovetail front sight, flared and lowered ejection port, extended slide stop, beavertail grip safety, combat hammer, combat trigger, rear slide serrations, diamond cut checkered mahogany grips, blue, hard chrome, or duotone (new 2012, .45 ACP only) finish, approx. 36 oz. New 2010.

	100%	98%	95%	90%	80%	70%	60%
MSR $656	$560	$495	$425	$380	$310	$275	$250

Add $79 for duotone finish (new 2012).
Add $102 for hard chrome finish.

* ***American Classic Compact Commander*** – .45 ACP cal., similar to American Classic Commander, except has compact features, 7 shot, blue, duotone, or hard chrome finish. New 2014.

	100%	98%	95%	90%	80%	70%	60%
MSR $750	$635	$555	$475	$430	$350	$285	$250

Add $115 for duotone finish.
Add $101 for hard chrome finish.

AMERICAN CLASSIC CUSTOM – .45 ACP cal., 8 shot mag., blue or hard chrome finish. New 2021.

	100%	98%	95%	90%	80%	70%	60%
MSR $1,066	$910	$795	$685	$620	$500	$425	$350

Add $76 for hard chrome finish.

AMERICAN CLASSIC GOV'T MODEL – .45 ACP, 9mm Para., or .38 Super cal., single action, 1911 Govt. style frame, 5 in. barrel, 8 shot, Mil-Spec sights, checkered wood grips, grip/thumb safety, matte blue or hard chrome (mfg. 2010-2011, reintroduced 2020) finish, 36 oz. Mfg. 2007-2015, reintroduced 2020.

	100%	98%	95%	90%	80%	70%	60%
MSR $601	$510	$430	$365	$325	$295	$275	$250

Add $83 for hard chrome finish.

AMERICAN CLASSIC GOV'T II MODEL – 9mm Para. (new 2013), 10mm (new 2021), or .45 ACP cal., 8 (.45 ACP) or 9 shot mag., 5 in. barrel, dovetail front and Novak rear sights, skeletal combat hammer, beavertail grip safety, lowered ejection port, front and rear slide serrations, deluxe blue, hard chrome (new 2010), or duotone (new 2012, .45 ACP only) finish, 36 oz. New 2007.

	100%	98%	95%	90%	80%	70%	60%
MSR $641	$550	$480	$415	$375	$300	$275	$250

Add $63 for duotone (new 2012).
Add $94 for hard chrome finish.

GRADING - PPGS™	100%	98%	95%	90%	80%	70%	60%	LAST MSR

AMERICAN CLASSIC OFFICER – .45 ACP cal., 7 shot mag., blue, Duo-Tone, or hard chrome finish. New 2021.

MSR $750	$635	$555	$475	$430	$350	$285	$250	

Add $61 for Duo-Tone finish.
Add $94 for hard chrome finish.

AMERICAN CLASSIC RAPIDO SHORT/RAPIDO LONG – 9mm Para. or .38 Super cal., short or long action, 17 shot mag., includes scope mount, blue finish. New 2021.

MSR $2,379	$2,025	$1,775	$1,525	$1,375	$1,115	$925	$785	

AMERICAN CLASSIC TROPHY MODEL – .45 ACP cal., 5 in. barrel, 8 shot mag., steel frame and slide, SA, dovetail fiber optic front sight, adj. Novak rear sight, flared and lowered ejection port, ambidextrous thumb safety, reverse plug recoil system with full-length guide rod, beveled magwell, combat hammer and trigger, front and rear slide serrations, diamond cut checkered mahogany grips, checkered mainspring housing, hard chrome finish, approx. 38 oz. New 2010.

MSR $859	$725	$635	$575	$500	$450	$425	$375	

AMERICAN CLASSIC 22 MODEL – .22 LR cal., patterned after the Colt ACE, 5 in. barrel, checkered walnut diamond grips, Mil-Spec sights, 10 shot mag., matte blue finish, 33 oz. Limited mfg. 2011 only.

	$325	$295	$275	$250	$225	$185	$170	*$365*

AMERICAN CLASSIC 3011 SLD TACTICAL – .45 ACP, .40 S&W, or 9mm Para. cal., 14, 15, or 17 shot mag., includes rail, blue or matte blue finish. New 2021.

MSR $1,897	$1,625	$1,425	$1,225	$1,100	$900	$750	$600	

AMERICAN CLASSIC XB MODEL – 9mm Para., .38 Super (disc.), .40 S&W (disc.), 10mm (new 2021), or .45 ACP cal., SA, 5 in. barrel, 14, 15 (disc.), or 17 shot mag., steel frame, skeletal hammer, combat trigger, Mil-Spec front sight, dovetail rear sight, front and rear slide serrations, standard slide top, blue finish, 39.40 oz. New 2018.

MSR $811	$665	$585	$500	$450	$365	$300	$235	

AMERICAN CUSTOM GUNMAKERS GUILD, INC. (ACGG)

The American Custom Gunmakers Guild is an organization consisting of craftsmen specializing in the artisanship and high quality craftsmanship associated with creating superior sporting firearms. Guild members share a common bond focusing on the betterment of fine custom firearms and the skills needed to come as close to perfection in the field of gunmaking as possible.

There are two membership categories; Professional and Associate. Each Professional Member has passed a rigorous review of his work by his fellow Professional members as part of the application process. Professional members must demonstrate a high degree of creative ability while practicing sound business ethics. The privileges of Professional membership include the right to use the ACGG logo with the word "PROFESSIONAL," use the ACGG Hallmark, voting privileges at the annual Membership meeting, receipt of the quarterly *Gunmaker* magazine, and the option to rent a display table at the annual show in Dallas, TX. Current ACGG Professional members can be found by visiting the Guild's website (www.acgg.org). Associate membership is open to any and all who have an interest in custom guns. The benefits of Associate membership include access to the Guild's website and receipt of the Guild's quarterly publication, *Gunmaker* magazine.

The annual Gunmakers Exhibition at the Dallas Safari Club Show is the most visible activity of the ACGG. This event offers the public a unique opportunity to view the finest in American firearm craftsmanship and meet the individual makers (check acgg.org for more information, including dates). This gathering of ACGG members provides a forum to share technical expertise, honor exemplary work, accept and induct new members, as well as conduct Guild business.

AMERICAN DEFENSE MFG. LLC

Current AR-15 style rifle and pistol manufacturer located in New Berlin, WI.

Please refer to BlueBookOfGunValues.com to order the *Blue Book of AR-15s & Variations*, available as a book or online subscription.

AMERICAN DERRINGER CORPORATION

Current manufacturer located in Waco, TX since 1980.

American Derringer Corp.

DERRINGERS: STAINLESS STEEL

MODEL 1 – available in over 55 cals. including .22 LR through .45-70 Govt. (also available as 2 1/2 in. .410 shot shell.), top break action, O/U stainless steel derringer, top break action, 3 in. barrels, automatic barrel selection, stainless steel, hammer block safety, spur trigger, rosewood, Bacote, walnut, or blackwood grips, hammer block safety, each gun is shipped in its own French fitted leatherette display, satin or high polish finish, 15 oz. New 1980.

GRADING - PPGS™	100%	98%	95%	90%	80%	70%	60%	LAST MSR
* ***Model 1 Rimfire Cals.*** – .22 LR or .22 WMR cal.								
MSR $635	$550	$480	$415	$375	$305	$250	$195	

Add $75 for high polish finish.

* ***Model 1 Centerfire Cals.*** – many cals. between .32 H&R Mag.-.45-70 Govt. cal.								
MSR $715	$635	$550	$475	$425	$350	$285	$225	

Add $75 for high polish finish.
Add approx. $30 for most common Mag. cals.
Subtract approx. $70 for .380 ACP or .38 Spl. cals.
Add $170 for .223 Rem. (disc.) or $140 for .30-30 Win. cal. (disc. 2003).
Add approx. $140 for .22 Hornet (disc. 1989).

This model can be ordered with special ser. nos. and other custom features at additional cost(s).

* ***Model 1 Engraved*** – limited mfg., mostly special ordered.

Please contact the factory regarding a price quotation for this special order model.

* ***Model 1 Millennium 2000 Series*** – .45 LC/.410 shotshell only, 3 in. barrel, 15,000 mfg. beginning 1998 in various configurations including Gambler and Cowboy.

MSR $835	$700	$615	$525	$475	$385	$315	$245	

* ***Model 1 United We Stand Commemorative*** – .45 LC/.410 shotshell only, 3 in. barrel, choice of custom grips, includes red, white and blue presentation case. Limited mfg. 2002-2003.

	$355	$310	$265	$240	$195	$160	$125	*$450*

American Derringer Corporation donated a portion of the proceeds from this commemorative to the post-9/11 recovery effort.

LADY DERRINGER – available in various cals. between .22 LR - .45 LC, and .45 LC/.410 shotshell cal., current cals include .32 H&R Mag., .357 Mag., .38 Spl., .45 LC, and .45 LC/.410 shotshell, O/U top break action, 3 in. barrel, high polish stainless steel, spur trigger, scrimshawed synthetic ivory grips, handfitted action allowing easy cocking, with French styled leatherette display case, 15 1/2 oz. New 1990.

MSR $835	$700	$615	$525	$475	$385	$315	$245	

* ***Lady Derringer Deluxe Engraved*** – similar to Deluxe Grade, except hand engraved with circa 1880 patterns. Disc. 1994.

	$650	$570	$490	$440	$360	$295	$230	*$750*

Mother-of-pearl grips and personalized engraving were available as extra cost options on this model.

* ***Lady Derringer 14Kt. Gold Engraved*** – entire Derringer manufactured out of a 14K gold bar (contains approx. 20 oz. of 14K gold and 3 oz. of stainless steel), custom engraved with diamond sights, special order only until late 1993.

Last MSR was $100,000.

Extreme rarity precludes accurate pricing on this model.

* ***Millenium Lady Derringer*** – similar to Model 1 Millenium 2000 Series. Disc.

	$390	$340	$295	$265	$215	$175	$135	*$470*

LADY DERRINGER II – .22 LR (disc.), .32 ACP (disc.), .38 Spl., or .22 WMR (disc.) cal., O/U pivot design, double action, aluminum frame, trigger guard stops at trigger bottom, 1/2 lb. Mfg. 1999-2003.

	$395	$345	$295	$270	$215	$180	$140	*$480*

GRADING - PPGS™	100%	Issue Price	Qty. Made

MODEL 1 TEXAS COMMEMORATIVE – .38 Spl., .44-40, or .45 LC cal., similar to Model 1 except has brass frame, stainless steel barrel, no stag grips.

.44-40 cal	$575	$440	N/A
.45 cal.	$575	$470	N/A
.32 Mag	$375	$255	500+
.38 Spl.	$375	$385	N/A
.22 LR (mfg. 1991-92)	$350	$238	500
.41 Rimfire (not shootable)	$300	$295	500
Fully engraved model	$795	$750	limited

GRADING - PPGS™	100%	98%	95%	90%	80%	70%	60%	LAST MSR

* ***Model 1 Texas Commemorative (Current Mfg.)*** – . 22 LR (disc.), .32 Mag. (disc.), .38 Spl., .44-40 WCF, .41 Mag. (disc.), or .45 LC cal.

MSR $835	$700	$615	$525	$475	$385	$315	$245	

Add $75 for special serial number on the .45 LC cal. model.

GRADING - PPGS™	100%	Issue Price	Qty. Made

125TH ANNIVERSARY – special edition 125th anniversary variation with pistol case. Disc.

.44-40 or .45 cal.	$395	$320	500
.38 Spl.	$325	$225	500
Deluxe engraved model	$795	$750	limited

GRADING - PPGS™	100%	98%	95%	90%	80%	70%	60%	LAST MSR

MODEL 3 – .32 Mag. (new 1990 - limited availability) or .38 Spl. cal., single shot, 2 1/2 in. barrel, 8 1/2 oz., spur trigger, rosewood grips. Disc. 1994, reintroduced and disc. 2015.

	$635	$550	$475	$425	$350	$285	$225	

Last MSR in 1994 was $120.
Last MSR in 2015 was $709.

MODEL 4 – .357 Mag., .357 Max., .44 Mag. (disc. 2003), .45 ACP, .45-70 Govt. (disc. 2003), .45 LC/.410 shotshell (new 2013), or .45 LC cal. on upper barrel, 3 in. .410 shotshell lower barrel, O/U derringer combination pistol, 4 1/10 in. barrel, rosewood grips, 16 1/2 oz. New 1985.

MSR $760	$665	$580	$500	$450	$365	$300	$235	

Add $110 for oversized grips.
Add $105 for .44 Mag. cal. (oversized grips became standard 1997, disc. 2003).
Add $150 for .45-70 Govt. cal. in both barrels (disc. 2003).
This model was also available on special order in either .50-70 or .50 Saunders cal. (new 1989 - single shot only). MSR was $395.

* ***Model 4 Engraved*** – .45 LC/.410 shotshell cal., allow 12 weeks for delivery. New 1997.

Please contact the factory directly for a price quotation on this special order model.

* ***Model 4 Alaskan Survival Model*** – similar to Model 4, except .45-70 Govt. cal. top barrel, and choice of .44 Mag. (disc.), .45 LC, or .45 LC/.410 shotshell lower barrel.

MSR $870	$725	$635	$525	$475	$385	$315	$245	

Add $90 for high polish finish.

MODEL 6 – .22 WMR (disc.), .357 Mag., .45 LC, .45 ACP, or .45 LC/.410 shotshell cal., O/U, 6 in. barrel, available in high polish, satin (disc. 1994), or grey matte finish (standard), 21 oz. New 1986.

MSR $870	$740	$650	$555	$505	$405	$335	$260	

Add $100 for high polish finish.
Add $13 for satin finish (disc. 1994).
Add $50 for oversized grips (disc. 1994, reinstated 1998-99).

* ***Model 6 Engraved*** – .45 LC/.410 shotshell cal., allow 12 weeks for delivery. New 1997.

Please contact the factory directly for a price quotation on this special order model.

MODEL 7 – .22 LR (disc.), .22 WMR (mfg. 1992-2003), .32 H&R Mag. (disc.), .38 Spl., .38 S&W (disc. 1989), .380 ACP (disc.), or .44 Spl. cal., O/U, same basic specifications as Model 1, except ultra lightweight (7 1/2 oz.). Disc. 2011.

	$575	$505	$430	$390	$315	$260	$200	*$705*

Add $105 for .44 Spl. (reintroduced 2008).

MODEL 8 – .45 LC/.410 shotshell cal., O/U, 8 in. barrel, nickel finish, grooved grips, 24 oz. New 1997.

MSR $915	$725	$625	$520	$475	$380	$315	$245	

Add $150 for high polish finish.

* ***Model 8 Engraved*** – .45 LC/.410 shotshell cal. Limited mfg. 1997-98 only.

	$1,675	$1,465	$1,255	$1,140	$920	$755	$585	*$1,917*

MODEL 10 – .38 Spl. (new 1995), .45 ACP, .45 LC, or .45 LC/.410 shotshell (disc. 1997), O/U, 3 in. barrels, aluminum grip frame and barrels, matte grey finish, 7 1/2 oz. Mfg. 1988-2011.

	$525	$460	$395	$355	$290	$235	$185	*$660*

Add $45 for .45 LC or .45 ACP cal.

GRADING - PPGS™	100%	98%	95%	90%	80%	70%	60%	LAST MSR

MODEL 11 – .22 LR (mfg. 1995-2003), .22 WMR (mfg. 1995-2003), .32 H&R Mag. (mfg. 1995-2003), .380 ACP (mfg. 1995-2003), or .38 Spl. cal., same basic specifications as Model 1, aluminum barrel, matte grey finish, only 11 oz. Disc. 2011.

	$525	$460	$395	$355	$290	$235	$185	*$660*

RIMFIRE DOUBLE ACTION – .22 LR or .22 WMR cal., 3 1/2 in. O/U barrels, double action trigger, dual extractors, hammerless, blue finish with black synthetic grips, 11 oz. Mfg. 1990-1995.

	$145	$125	$110	$100	$80	$65	$50	*$170*

This O/U Derringer was patterned after the original High Standard design.

DS22 – .22 WMR cal., 3 in. barrel, stainless steel with blue finish, 11 oz. Special order beginning 1998.

Please contact the factory directly for a price quotation on this model.

DA 38 DOUBLE ACTION – .22 LR (mfg. 1996-2003), .357 Mag. (new 1991), .38 Spl., 9mm Para., or .40 S&W (mfg. 1993-2012) cal., 3 in. O/U barrels, satin stainless steel with aluminum grip frame, double action trigger design, hammerblock thumb safety, choice of checkered rosewood, walnut, or other hardwood grips, 14 1/2 oz. New 1990.

MSR $690	$575	$505	$430	$390	$315	$260	$200	

Add $50 for .357 Mag. or .40 S&W (disc. 2012) cal.
Add $15 for Lady Derringer Model (scrimshawed synthetic ivory grips, .38 Spl. only. Mfg. 1992-94).

MINI-COP – .22 WMR cal., 4 shot double action design, stainless steel construction, patterned after the original Mini-Cop mfg. in Torrance, CA. Mfg. 1990-94.

	$250	$220	$190	$170	$140	$115	$90	*$313*

4-BARREL DERRINGER – .22 LR, .38 Spl., or .357 Mag. cal., double action, similar design to Mini-Cop, semi-matte finish, 28 oz. While advertised beginning 1991 at $425, only a few prototypes were manufactured during 1997.

CUSTOM TARGET MODELS – .38 Spl. Wadcutter or 9mm Federal (disc.) cal., mfg. for End of Trail Derringer Match, limited production. Mfg. 1990-92.

	$695	$610	$520	$475	$380	$315	$245	*$750*

PISTOLS: PEN DESIGN

MODEL 2 PEN PISTOL – .22 LR, .25 ACP, or .32 ACP cal., unique hinged action allows pen to be converted into a legal pistol within two seconds, folding design, 2 in. barrel, cocks on opening action, firing pin block and grip safeties, brushed stainless finish, 5 oz. Mfg. 1993-1994.

	$500	$450	$425	$375	$350	$325	$300	*$203*

Add $150 for .32 ACP cal.
Add $100 for .25 ACP.

PISTOLS: SEMI-AUTO

STANDARD MODEL

* ***Standard Model .25 Mag. Cal.*** – .25 Mag. cal., SA, less than 100 manufactured in stainless steel only.

	$500	$440	$375	$340	$275	$225	$175

* ***Standard Model .25 ACP Cal.*** – .25 ACP cal., SA, less than 400 manufactured in stainless steel, less than 50 in blue steel.

Stainless	$400	$350	$300	$270	$220	$180	$140
Blue	$550	$480	$415	$375	$305	$250	$195

LM-5 – .25 ACP, .32 H&R Mag. (disc. 1997, reintroduced 2008), or .380 ACP (mfg. 1998-99) cal., compact stainless design, SA, 2 1/4 in. barrel, hammerless, wood grips, 4 (.32 Mag. or .380 ACP) or 5 (.25 ACP) shot mag., 15 oz. Limited mfg. since 1997.

MSR $710	$600	$525	$450	$410	$330	$270	$210

* ***LM-5 .380 ACP*** – limited mfg., disc. 1999.

	$365	$320	$275	$250	$200	$165	$130	*$425*

PISTOLS: SLIDE ACTION

LM-4 (SEMMERLING) – .45 ACP cal., 2 in. barrel, super compact, thumb activated slide mechanism, 4 shot mag., blue (disc.), gray matte, satin, or high polish finish, includes one magazine, 24 oz., very limited manufacture since 1998.

MSR $4,250	$3,825	$3,500	$3,100	$2,625	$2,375	$1,925	$1,575

Add $195 for extra magazine.
Add $200 for high polish finish.

GRADING - PPGS™	100%	98%	95%	90%	80%	70%	60%	LAST MSR

AMERICAN FIREARMS MANUFACTURING CO., INC.

Previous manufacturer located in San Antonio, TX between 1972-1974.

DERRINGERS

AMERICAN .38 SPL. - .38 Spl. cal., O/U configuration, approx. 3,000-4,000 mfg. 1972-74.

	$200	$165	$135	$110	$90	$75	$65	

AMERICAN .380 AUTOMATIC - .380 ACP cal., 8 shot, 3 1/2 in. barrel, stainless steel, smooth walnut grips, approx. 10 mfg. 1972-74.

	$700	$500	$300	$240	$210	$180	$155	

PISTOLS: SEMI-AUTO

AMERICAN .25 AUTOMATIC - .25 ACP cal., 8 shot, 2 1/10 in. barrel, smooth walnut grips. Mfg. 1966-74.

Stainless	$195	$180	$165	$140	$120	$110	$95	
Blue	$165	$150	$140	$120	$100	$90	$85	

AMERICAN FRONTIER FIREARMS MFG., INC.

Previous manufacturer located in Aguanga, CA 1995-2000.

American Frontier Firearms Mfg., Inc. manufactured a line of replica metallic cartridge firing revolvers (black powder or smokeless). These revolvers were manufactured in .22 LR, .32 Spl., .38 Spl., .44 Russian, or .45 LC. During 2000, AFF developed a new cartridge, the .44 A.F.F. It could be used in revolvers firing .44-40 WCF, .44 Russian, .44 Spl., and .44 Mag. It also met S.A.S.S. specifications.

REVOLVERS: CARTRIDGE CONVERSIONS & OPEN TOP

Production on these models was mid-1997 through 2000. Revolvers were supplied with standard finish high polish blue steel parts, color case hardened hammer and/or trigger, silver plated or blue backstrap and trigger guard, and varnished walnut grips. Special orders were also available featuring simulated ivory grips, special finishes, and engraving options. Some models and variations had very limited production, due to problems procuring high quality parts.

1851 NAVY RICHARDS CONVERSION - .38 Spl., .38 LC, .44 Russian, or .44-40 WCF cal., 4 3/4, 5 1/2, or 7 1/2 in. octagon barrel, roll engraved cylinder, blue finish, varnished walnut grips. No ejector rod.

	$695	$550	$375	$325	$295	$265	$235	*$795*

1851 NAVY RICHARDS & MASON CONVERSION - .38 Spl., .38 LC, .44 Russian, or .44-40 WCF cal., 4 3/4, 5 1/2, or 7 1/2 in. octagon barrel with Mason ejector assembly, roll engraved cylinder, blue finish, varnished walnut grips.

	$695	$550	$375	$325	$295	$265	$235	*$795*

1858 REMINGTON NEW ARMY CAVALRY MODEL - .38 Spl., .44-40 WCF, or .45 LC cal., 7 1/2 in. barrel with ejector assembly, blue finish, color case hardened hammer, varnished walnut grips.

	$715	$575	$475	$375	$325	$275	$225	*$795*

1858 REMINGTON NEW ARMY ARTILLERY MODEL - .38 Spl., .44-40 WCF, or .45 LC cal., 5 1/2 in. barrel with ejector assembly, blue finish, color case hardened hammer, varnished walnut grips.

	$715	$575	$475	$375	$325	$275	$225	*$795*

1858 REMINGTON ORIGINAL FACTORY-TYPE CONVERSION - .38 Spl., .44-40 WCF, or .45 LC cal., 5 1/2 or 7 1/2 in. barrels, original loading lever and no gate or ejector assembly, blue finish, color case hardened hammer, varnished walnut grips.

	$715	$575	$475	$375	$325	$275	$225	*$795*

POCKET REMINGTON - .22 LR, .32 S&W Short, or .38 Spl. cal., 3 1/2 in. barrel with or without ejector rod or gate, blue finish, color case hardened hammer, varnished walnut grips.

	$425	$375	$325	$275	$225	$185	$165	*$495*

1860 ARMY RICHARDS CONVERSION - .38 Spl., .38 LC, or .44-40 WCF cal., 4 3/4, 5 1/2, or 7 1/2 in. round barrel, with or without ejector assembly, roll engraved cylinder, blue finish, silver plated trigger guard, varnished walnut grips.

	$695	$550	$375	$325	$295	$265	$235	*$795*

1861 NAVY RICHARDS CONVERSION - .38 Spl., or .38 LC cal., 4 1/2 or 7 1/2 in. round barrel with ejector assembly, blue finish, silver plated backstrap and trigger guard, varnished walnut grips.

	$695	$550	$375	$325	$295	$265	$235	*$795*

POCKET NAVY RICHARDS & MASON CONVERSION – .32 S&W Short cal., 4 1/2 in. octagon barrel with ejector assembly, blue finish, silver plated backstrap and trigger guard, color case hardened trigger and hammer, varnished walnut grips.

$465 $375 $325 $275 $225 $185 $165 *$495*

1871-72 OPEN-TOP FRONTIER MODEL – .38 Spl., .38 LC, or .44-40 WCF cal., 4 3/4, 5 1/2, or 7 1/2 in. round barrel with ejector assembly, blue finish, varnished walnut grips.

$695 $550 $375 $325 $295 $265 $235 *$795*

* ***1871-72 Open-Top Tiffany Model*** – similar to 1871-72 Standard Model, except has engraved gold/silver finished Tiffany grips and also available with 4 3/4 in. barrel. Mfg. 2001.

$995 $895 $700 $525 $450 $395 $350 *$1,200*

AMERICAN GUN CO.

Previous trademark manufactured by Crescent Firearms Co. and distributed by H. & D. Folsom Co.

REVOLVERS

REVOLVER – .32 S&W cal., 5 shot, double action, top-break frame.

N/A $295 $260 $230 $200 $175 $125

SHOTGUNS: SxS

SxS – various gauges, hammer or hammerless, Damascus, or steel barrels.

N/A $495 $400 $395 $300 $250 $200

Add 15% for small gauges or steel barrels.

AMERICAN GUN COMPANY, LLC

Previous rifle and action manufacturer located in Kalispell, MT.

For individual model listings, please go to BlueBookOfGunValues.com/overflow.

AMERICAN HISTORICAL FOUNDATION, THE

Current organization which privately commissions historical commemoratives in conjunction with leading manufacturers and craftsmen around the world. The Foundation is located in Ashland, VA. Previously located in Richmond, VA. During 2005, the assets of the Foundation were acquired by America Remembers, located in Ashland, VA. Direct-to-consumer sales only. Delivery to local FFL holder.

For individual model listings, please go to BlueBookOfGunValues.com/overflow.

AMERICAN HUNTING RIFLES (AHR)

Current manufacturer established in 1998, located in Corvallis, MT since 2007. Previously located in Hamilton, MT 1998-2006.

RIFLES: BOLT ACTION

AHR rifles come in chamberings including but not limited to:

.375 H&H, .375 RUM, .375 Weatherby, .400 H&H, .404 Jeffery, .416 Rem. Mag., .416 Rigby, .458 Win. Mag., .458 Lott, .450 Rigby, .470 Capstick, .500 Jeffery, .500 AHR, .500 A-Square, .505 Gibbs, .550 Magnum, .577 T-Rex, .600 Overkill, .700 AHR, and all Dakota and Weatherby calibers.

600 OVERKILL – .600 Overkill cal., features modified CZ magnum action built by Granite Arms, bull barrel with "X-Brake" muzzle brake, deluxe or fancy English walnut or AHR fiberglass stock.

MSR $6,500 $5,525 $4,825 $4,150 $3,750 $3,050 $2,485 $1,935

Subtract $825 for AHR fiberglass stock.

.700 AHR – .700 AHR cal., Granite Mt. Arms African Magnum action, AHR proprietary X-brake and thread protector, custom made front banded sight, fixed folding sight, hand checkered AAA fancy English walnut stock w/custom LOP, Macassar ebony forend tip and grip cap, custom barrel sling band, custom serial number, custom hand engraving, Satin Gunkote finish on all metal parts. Limited mfg. beginning 2008.

Prices for this model start at $11,500.

AHR BIG GAME – .270 Win., .30-06, 7x57, 9.3x62, and 6 Howell cartridges, built to order on double square bridge CZ-550 standard action, controlled feed claw extractor, custom single stage trigger, fiberglass stock features cheekpiece, grip cap, 1 in. Decelerator recoil pad, and sling swivel studs, 3-pos. wing type safety. Mfg. 2009-Disc.

$2,675 $2,150 $1,850 $1,550 $1,375 $1,050 $925 *$2,995*

Add $75 for stainless steel barrel.

GRADING - PPGS™	100%	98%	95%	90%	80%	70%	60%	LAST MSR

CLASSIC 550 – standard and various Howell proprietary cals., CZ-550 double square bridge standard action, controlled feed claw extractor, 25 in. chrome moly or stainless steel sporter barrel, blue finish, black fiberglass or optional walnut stock with Decelerator recoil pad. Mfg. 1999-2009.

	$1,725	$1,375	$1,075	$900	$775	$650	$550	*$1,895*

Add $75 for stainless steel barrel.
Add $220 for integral and removable muzzle brake, with protective cap.

SAFARI 550 – various Mag. cals., similar to Classic 550, except has Magnum action with integral scope mounts, oil finished fancy walnut stock, trigger guard safety. Mfg. 2001-2011.

	$1,725	$1,375	$1,075	$900	$775	$650	$550	*$1,895*

SAFARI 550 DGR – various cals. from .375 H&H to .700 AHR, based on the double square bridge CZ-550 Magnum blueprinted action, match grade chrome moly barrel using AHR contour, barrel band front sling attachment, controlled feed claw extractor, SST, fixed blade rear and banded ramp front sight with fiber optic bead, AAA fancy English walnut stock, rear sling stud, Macassar ebony forend tip, 1 in. Decelerator recoil pad, 3-position safety, integral scope mounts, Satin Gunkote finish on all metal surfaces. New 2001.

MSR $6,700	$6,200	$5,450	$4,650	$4,225	$3,700	$3,250	$2,700	

Pricing is for base model only, contact the manufacturer directly for several options, delivery time, and availability.

VARMINT 550 PRO – .220 Howell, .220 Swift, .22-250 Rem., .30-06, or .308 Win. cal., CZ-550 double square bridge standard action, 26 in. stainless heavy barrel, SST, black fiberglass stock with Decelerator recoil pad. Mfg. 2001-2007.

	$1,650	$1,325	$1,050	$900	$775	$650	$550	*$1,795*

AMERICAN INDUSTRIES

Please refer to Calico Light Weapons Systems in the C section.

AMERICAN INTERNATIONAL CORP.

Previous manufacturer and importer located in Salt Lake City, UT, circa 1972-1984. American International was a wholly owned subsidiary of ARDCO (American Research & Development). ARDCO's previous name was American Mining & Development. American International imported firearms from Voere, located in Kufstein, Austria. American Arms International (AAI) was another subsidiary of ARDCO.

In 1979, after American International Corp. had dissolved, AAI resumed production using mostly Voere parts. After running out of Voere parts, late production featured U.S. mfg. receivers (can be recognized by not having a pivoting barrel retainer slotted on the bottom of the receiver). American Arms International declared bankruptcy in 1984.

CARBINES: SEMI-AUTO

AMERICAN 180 AUTO CARBINE (M-1) – .22 LR cal., a specialized design for military use, 177 round drum mag., 16 1/2 in. barrel, aperture sight, high impact plastic stock and forearm, aluminum alloy receiver with black finish. Semi-auto variation mfg. 1979-c.1984. Total Voere production (denoted by A prefix serial number) between 1972 and 1979 was 2,300 carbines (includes both full and semi-auto versions). Later mfg. was marked either M-1 (semi-auto) or M-2 (fully auto). "B" serial number prefix was introduced in 1980, and barrel markings were changed to "Amer Arms Intl, SLC, UT."

	$725	$600	$475	$375	$350	$325	$295	

Add $550 for Laser Lok System - first commercially available laser sighting system.
Add approx. $300 for extra drum mag. and winder (fragile and subject to breakage).

AMERICAN LEGACY FIREARMS

Current company located in Ft. Collins, CO since 2004.

American Legacy Firearms specializes in special/limited edition firearms which are based on many popular makes/models. Please contact the company directly for more information on their current models including price, options, and availability.

AMERICAN LEGENDS

Previous trademark of some handguns manufactured by IAI. **Please refer to the IAI, Inc. - American Legends listing in the I section.**

AMERICAN PRECISION ARMS

Current manufacturer established in 2001, located in Jefferson, GA.

For individual model listings, please go to BlueBookOfGunValues.com/overflow.

GRADING - PPGS™ 100% 98% 95% 90% 80% 70% 60% LAST MSR

AMERICAN RIFLE COMPANY

Current bolt action rifle and action manufacturer located in Mukilteo, WA and previously in Kent, WA.

American Rifle Company is known for their "Mausingfield" action, which combines design elements from the Mauser 98 rifle and Springfield 1903 rifle respectively.

RIFLES: BOLT ACTION

ARCHIMEDES RIFLE – 6mm Creedmoor or 6.5mm Creedmoor cal., Archimedes Action based on Remington 700 footprint, 25 in. match grade barrel, ARC 12-point barrel wrench interface, 3 chamber muzzle brake, uses AICS mags., flared magwell, TriggerTech trigger, 20 MOA scope rail, Xylo chassis w/ adj. cheek piece and LOP, adaptable forend featuring mounting compatibility for Arca-Swiss rail, Area 419 ArcaLock rail, Anschutz rail, and M-LOK mounts and accessories, Walnut grip, Remington 700 style safety, integral inclinometer/level system, 11.5 lbs. 44.75 in. OAL. New 2020.

MSR $3,599 $3,100 $2,725 $2,325 $2,100 $1,700 $1,400 $1,000

M2 – 6.5 Creedmoor or .338 Lapua Mag. cal., "Mausingfield" action (includes features from both the Mauser 98 and Spring 1903 Springfield actions), 22 or 27 in. barrel with muzzle brake, detachable 10 shot double stack mag., aerospace grade materials, folding and collapsible stock, AR-15 style grip, ambi bolt handle with rotating knob and 3-pos. safety, green finish with black accessories. Mfg. 2015-2016.

Retail pricing was not available for this model.

NUCLEUS GEN2 RIFLE – 6.5 Creedmoor cal., Nucleus Gen2 Action based on Rem. 700 footprint, 25 in. match grade barrel, barrel profile similar to "Marksman" or "Medium Palma" profile, 3 chamber muzzle brake, uses AICS mags., flared magwell, TriggerTech Special trigger, 20 MOA scope rail, Xylo chassis w/adj. cheekpiece and LOP, adaptable forend featuring mounting compatibility for Arca-Swiss rail, Area 419 ArcaLock rail, Anschutz rail, and M-LOK mounts and accessories, walnut grip, Rem. 700 style safety, integral inclinometer/level system, 11.5 lbs. 44.75 in. OAL. New 2020.

MSR $2,499 $2,125 $1,875 $1,600 $1,450 $1,175 $950 $750

AMERICAN SPIRIT ARMS

Previous AR-15 style rifle and pistol manufacturer established circa 1995, located in Phoenix, AZ until early 2019. Previously located in Scottsdale, AZ until 2018. In April 2015, American Spirit Arms announced its sale to American Spirit Investments, LLC, and confirmed that the American Spirit Arms brand would be retained. They emphasized focus on their patented AR-15 side charger technology.

Please refer to BlueBookOfGunValues.com to order the *Blue Book of AR-15s & Variations*, available as a book or online subscription.

AMERICAN SPIRIT ARMS CORP.

Previous AR-15 style rifle and components manufacturer 1998-2005, located in Tempe, AZ. Previously located in Scottsdale, AZ.

Please refer to BlueBookOfGunValues.com to order the *Blue Book of AR-15s & Variations*, available as a book or online subscription.

AMERICAN TACTICAL (AMERICAN TACTICAL IMPORTS - ATI)

Current manufacturer of AR-15 style rifles and pistols and importer of firearms located in Summerville, SC, beginning late 2013. Previously located in Rochester, NY.

American Tactical imports and assembles a wide variety of firearms and products, including pistols, AR-15 style and AK-47 design semi-auto rifles, and shotguns. Trademarks, imports, and private labels include Alpha shotguns (disc. 2019), American Tactical Imports (ATI), Cavalry O/Us (new 2013), Crusader Shotguns, FMK (disc. 2013), Firepower Xtreme, German Sport Guns (GSG), Head Down Products (mfg. 2012-2013), ISSC (mfg. 2015-2016), Masterpiece Arms (MPA, disc. 2011), Omni, Ottoman Shotguns (disc. 2011), Tisas (imported 2008-2011), and Xtreme Rifles (disc. 2012). Please see individual listings for current or most recent model information and pricing.

PISTOLS: SEMI-AUTO

AT C45 SERIES – .45 ACP cal., 4.6 in. barrel, DA/SA, Picatinny rail, ported slide, 9 shot mag., blue, chrome, or two tone finish. Mfg. in Turkey. Limited importation 2010-2011 only.

$325 $285 $250 $230 $215 $200 $190 *$370*

Add $36 for chrome finish.

AT CS9 SERIES – 9mm Para. cal., 4 in. barrel, DA/SA, Picatinny rail, ported slide, 18 shot mag., blue, chrome, or two tone finish. Mfg. in Turkey. Limited importation 2010-2011 only.

$335 $280 $250 $230 $215 $200 $190 *$380*

Add $60 for chrome finish.

GRADING - PPGS™	100%	98%	95%	90%	80%	70%	60%	LAST MSR

AT CS40 SERIES – .40 S&W cal., 4 in. barrel, DA/SA, Picatinny rail, 12 shot mag., blue, chrome, or two tone finish. Mfg. in Turkey. Limited importation 2010-2011 only.

	$360	$315	$275	$250	$225	$210	$200	*$406*

Add $15 for two tone or $40 for chrome finish.

AT FS9 SERIES – 9mm Para. cal., 5 in. barrel, DA/SA, Picatinny rail, ported slide, 18 shot mag., blue, chrome, or two tone finish, mfg. in Turkey. Limited importation 2010-2011 only.

	$330	$285	$250	$230	$215	$200	$190	*$380*

Add $60 for chrome finish.

AT FS40 SERIES – .40 S&W cal., 5 in. barrel, DA/SA, Picatinny rail, 12 shot mag., blue, chrome, or two tone finish, mfg. in Turkey. Limited importation 2010-2011 only.

	$360	$315	$275	$250	$225	$210	$200	*$406*

Add $14 for two tone or $40 for chrome finish.

AT HP9 SERIES – 9mm Para. cal., 5 in. barrel, DA/SA, 18 shot mag., blue, chrome, or two tone finish, mfg. in Turkey. Limited importation 2010-2011 only.

	$330	$285	$250	$230	$215	$200	$190	*$380*

Add $31 for chrome finish.

AT MS380 SERIES – .380 ACP cal., 3.9 in. barrel, DA/SA, 12 shot mag., black, chrome, or two tone finish, mfg. in Turkey. Disc. 2011.

	$330	$285	$250	$230	$215	$200	$190	*$380*

Add $20 for chrome or black finish.

BB6 – 9mm Para. cal., polymer frame, 5 in. barrel, 15 or 18 shot mag., steel slide, integrated optics mount, quick view "gutter" sight, five different safeties, black finish. Mfg. by BB Techs of Austria. Imported 2016 only.

	$625	$520	$435	$375	$325	$280	$265	*$730*

FIREPOWER XTREME 1911 (FX MILITARY) – .45 ACP cal., 1911 style frame, 5 in. barrel, with (disc. 2020) or w/o compensator, SA, blue finish, 8 shot mag., double diamond checkered wood grips, military style rear slide serrations, slide stop, safety lever and trigger. Mfg. by Shooters Arms Manufacturing in the Philippines beginning mid-2010.

MSR $480	$410	$360	$310	$280	$225	$185	$150	

Add $40 for compensator (disc. 2020).

FX 45K – .45 ACP cal., SA, 5 in. threaded barrel with muzzle cap, 8 shot mag., lower front Picatinny rail, bobbed hammer, beavertail safety, extended ambidextrous safety lever, skeletonized aluminum trigger, checkered mahogany grips, low profile rear sight, blued or FDE (new 2014) finish. Mfg. 2013-2014.

	$625	$520	$435	$375	$325	$280	$265	*$740*

Add $50 for FDE finish (new 2014).

FX 45 TITAN – .45 ACP cal., SA, 1911 style frame, 3 5/8 in. bull barrel, blue (Titan), NiBX (mfg. 2013-2014) finish or stainless steel (Titan SS, disc. 2012), 7 shot mag., double diamond checkered wood grips, low profile rear sights, stainless steel slide, rear slide serrations, military style slide stop, safety lever, skeletonized aluminum trigger. Mfg. by Shooters Arms Manufacturing in the Phillipines mid-2010-2014, reintroduced 2017.

MSR $480	$410	$360	$310	$280	$225	$185	$150	

Add $80 for NiBX finish (mfg. 2013-2014).
Add $100 for Titan SS (stainless steel, mfg. 2010-2012).

* ***FX Titan Lightweight*** – .45 ACP cal., similar to Titan, except has 3 1/8 in. bull barrel, NiBX finish only. Mfg. 2013-2014.

	$525	$465	$400	$340	$300	$265	$250	*$610*

FX FAT BOY – .45 ACP cal., 3.2 in. barrel, SA, blue finish, 10 or 12 shot double stack mag., all steel serrated grips, lightweight configuration became standard 2013. Mfg. by Shooters Arms Manufacturing in the Philippines mid-2010-2014.

	$610	$525	$450	$400	$350	$300	$250	*$720*

FX G.I. – 9mm Para. (mfg. 2017-2020) or .45 ACP cal., SA, 1911 style, Commander size frame, 4 1/4 in. barrel, blue finish, 8 or 9 shot mag., double diamond checkered wood grips, military style rear slide serrations, slide stop, safety lever, matte black trigger, round hammer, beavertail grip safety. Mfg. by Shooters Arms Manufacturing in the Phillipines beginning mid-2010.

MSR $480	$410	$360	$310	$280	$225	$185	$150	

GRADING - PPGS™	100%	98%	95%	90%	80%	70%	60%	LAST MSR

* ***FX G.I. Enhanced*** – .45 ACP cal., similar to G.I. model, except has Novak sights. Mfg. mid-2010-2014.

	$500	$435	$365	$315	$275	$250	$230	*$565*

FX THUNDERBOLT – .45 ACP cal., 1911 style frame, 5 in. non-ported or ported (new 2012) barrel, SA, blue finish or stainless steel (mfg. 2012 only), 8 shot mag., lower Picatinny rail standard, matte chrome round hammer and extended safety, beavertail with safety, dovetail front sight, Champion rear sight, aluminum trigger, double diamond checkered wood grips, wide front and rear slide serrations. Mfg. by Shooters Arms Manufacturing in the Philippines mid-2010-2014.

	$725	$650	$580	$515	$450	$385	$340	*$858*

Add $42 for FX Thunderbolt E with ported slide (new 2012) or $40 for FX Thunderbolt SS with stainless construction (mfg. 2012 only).

FXH-45 – .45 ACP cal., 5 in. steel match grade barrel, 8 shot mag., custom designed stainless steel or Classic Military 70 Series (new 2020) slide, polymer frame with built-in finger grooves, accepts Glock front and rear sights, black or FDE finish. New 2015.

MSR $600	$525	$465	$400	$340	$300	$265	$250	

Subract $50 for Classic Military 70 Series slide (new 2020).

FXH-45C – .45 ACP cal., polymer frame with built-in finger grooves, 4 1/4 in. steel match grade ported (mfg. 2018-2020), threaded (mfg. 2018-2020) or non-threaded barrel, 8 shot mag., custom designed stainless steel slide, accepts Glock front and rear sights, black or FDE (mfg. 2018-2020) finish. New 2017.

MSR $600	$525	$465	$400	$340	$300	$265	$250	

Add $40 for ported barrel (mfg. 2018-2020).
Add $50 for threaded barrel (mfg. 2018-2020).

FXH-45D – .45 ACP cal., polymer frame with built-in finger grooves, 3 1/4 in. steel match grade barrel, 8 shot mag., custom designed stainless steel slide, accepts Glock front and rear sights, black finish. Mfg. 2017-2018.

	$525	$465	$400	$340	$300	$265	$250	*$600*

FXH-45M MOXIE – .45 ACP cal., 1911-style, SA, full-size polymer frame, 8 shot mag., accepts Glock front and rear sights, polymer grips w/built-in finger grooves, removable top plate for optics, black finish, 31.2 oz. New 2020.

MSR $399	$350	$325	$275	$250	$200	$150	$125	

FXH-9 – 9mm Para. cal., polymer frame, stainless steel slide, 5 in. barrel, 8 shot mag., black finish. New 2017.

MSR $670	$585	$500	$435	$365	$325	$280	$265	

FXH-9C – 9mm Para. cal., polymer frame, stainless steel slide, 4 1/4 in. ported (new 2018), threaded (new 2018), or non-threaded barrel, 8 shot mag., black or FDE (new 2018, threaded or ported barrel only) finish. Mfg. 2017-2020.

	$585	$500	$435	$365	$325	$280	$265	*$670*

Add $20 for ported barrel (new 2018).
Add $30 for threaded barrel (new 2018).
Add $30 for FDE finish (new 2018, ported or threaded barrel only).

GALEO PISTOL – 5.56 NATO cal., based on the Galil SAR, long stroke gas piston operated, 13 or 14 in. barrel with birdcage style flash hider, 30 shot Tapco mag., uses Galil style mags., milled steel receiver with stamped steel top cover, hooded front sight post, aperture-type rear sight mounted on top cover, AR-15 style buffer tube receiver adapter plug with blade style pistol stabilizing brace, polymer Galil style handguard and pistol grip, ambi safety, thumb actuated safety lever, shielded mag. catch, Galil style upswept charging handle, phosphate finish. New 2020. .

MSR $1,300	$1,100	$975	$850	$775	$650	$550	$425	

MILSPORT PISTOL – 5.56 NATO or .300 AAC Blackout cal., GIO, 7 1/2 or 8 1/2 (.300 AAC Blackout cal.) in. barrel, low profile gas block, pistol length gas system, A2 flash hider, 30 shot mag., forged receivers, Mil-Spec trigger, pistol buffer tube, 7 in. Keymod or M-LOK handguard, A2 pistol grip, Mil-Spec safety, black anodized finish. New 2017.

MSR $590	$425	$375	$325	$300	$275	$250	$200	

MILSPORT 9MM PISTOL – 9mm Para. cal., blowback operated, 5 1/2 in. barrel, 2 in. flash can, 17 or 31 shot ETS mag., uses Glock 9mm mags., forged upper receiver, billet lower receiver, Mil-Spec trigger, blade brace, 7 in. Keymod or M-LOK handguard, A2 pistol grip, Mil-Spec safety, black anodized finish. Mfg. 2012-2020.

	$650	$525	$475	$400	$375	$350	$325	*$820*

GRADING - PPGS™	100%	98%	95%	90%	80%	70%	60%	LAST MSR

OMNI HYBRID – 5.56 NATO cal., 7 1/2 in. barrel, 30 shot PMAG, Omni Hybrid lower and aluminum upper receiver, 7 in. free float quad rail, black finish, 4 3/4 lbs. Mfg. 2015 only.

	$450	$350	$325	$275	$275	$250	$225	*$600*

OMNI HYBRID 300 – .300 AAC Blackout cal., 8 1/2 in. barrel, 30 shot PMAG, complete Omni Hybrid lower and aluminum upper receiver, 7 in. free float rail, black finish. Mfg. 2015 only.

	$500	$400	$350	$325	$300	$275	$250	*$670*

OMNI HYBRID AR-15 – 5.56 NATO or .300 AAC Blackout cal., 7 1/2 or 8 1/2 in. barrel, two 30 shot PMAGs, complete Omni Hybrid polymer lower receiver, 7 in. buffer tube, 7 in. free float quad rail, flip-up iron or red dot sights, black Nitride finish, 4 3/4-5.2 lbs. Mfg. 2015-2016.

	$475	$375	$325	$300	$275	$250	$225	*$620*

Add $50 for flip-up iron sights or $60 for red dot sights.

OMNI HYBRID MAXX – 5.56 NATO cal., 7 1/2 or 10 1/2 (mfg. 2017 only) in. barrel, A2 flash hider, 30 shot PMAG, low profile gas block, 7 or 10 (mfg. 2017 only) in. free floating KeyMod quad rail, complete Omni Hybrid polymer upper and lower receiver, black finish, 4.8 lbs. New 2015.

MSR $460	$340	$265	$250	$225	$200	$200	$175	

OMNI HYBRID MAXX MXPM – 5.56 NATO or .300 AAC Blackout cal., GIO, 7 1/2 or 8 1/2 (.300 AAC Blackout cal.) in. barrel, low profile gas block, A2 flash hider, 30 shot PMAG, complete Omni Hybrid polymer upper and lower receiver, pistol buffer tube, 7 in. free floating M-LOK handguard, A2 grip, black finish, 4.8 lbs. New 2020.

MSR $470	$350	$275	$250	$225	$200	$200	$175	

OMNI HYBRID MAXX 300 – .300 AAC Blackout cal., low profile gas block, 8 1/2 or 10 1/2 (mfg. 2017 only) in. barrel, 30 shot PMAG, complete Omni Hybrid polymer upper and lower receiver, 7 or 10 (mfg. 2017 only) in. free floating KeyMod rail, optics ready, black finish, 4.95 lbs. New 2015.

MSR $460	$340	$265	$250	$225	$200	$200	$175	

OMNI HYBRID MAXX ADAPTER PISTOL – 9mm Para. cal., 5 1/2 in. barrel w/flashcan muzzle, 31 shot mag., 7 in. KeyMod rail, Mil-Spec control group, OMNI HYBRID MAXX upper and lower receiver, 9mm mag. adapter, black finish. Mfg. late 2018-2019.

	$450	$350	$325	$275	$275	$250	$225	*$600*

OMNI HYBRID MAXX P4/P4B/MP4B – 5.56 NATO or .300 AAC Blackout cal., GIO, 7 1/2 in. barrel, pistol length gas system, low profile gas block, A2 flash hider, 30 shot mag., polymer upper and metal reinforced polymer lower receiver, AR pistol buffer tube, optional blade brace (model P4B), 7 in. KeyMod or M-LOK (model MP4 or MP4B, new 2020) handguard, A2 pistol grip, Picatinny rail, Nano composite parts kit, black, Sniper Grey, FDE, or Battlefield Green finish, 4 3/4 lbs. New 2019.

MSR $400	$300	$250	$2225	$200	$175	$175	$150	

Add $20 for M-LOK handguard (MP4 or MP4B).
Add $50 for blade brace (P4B).
Add $60 for M-LOK handguard and blade brace (MP4B).

RIFLES/CARBINES: SEMI-AUTO

.300 AAC CARBINE – .300 AAC Blackout cal., GIO, 10 or 30 shot mag., 16 in. heavy barrel with muzzle brake, 6-position stock, flat-top receiver with Picatinny rail, 9 in. quad rail handguard, black hardware and finish. Mfg. 2012-2013.

	$850	$550	$465	$395	$350	$325	$295	*$999*

AT-15 – 5.56 NATO cal., AR-15 style, GIO, 16 in. barrel with muzzle brake, flat-top receiver with mid-length quad rail handguard, post front sight, collapsible stock, 30 shot mag. Limited importation 2011 only.

	$615	$495	$415	$360	$325	$300	$275	*$719*

AT-47 – 5.56x45 cal., AK-47 design, GPO, 16 in. M4 barrel, blued finish, A3 flat-top, 30 shot Tapco (disc. 2016) or polymer (new 2017) mag., 6-position original underfolding (disc. 2016) or fixed (new 2017) stock, original wood furniture, includes hard case, unissued M70 Yugo parts kit. Mfg. 2014-2018.

	$840	$735	$630	$570	$500	$425	$380	*$990*

AT-47 MILLED – 7.62x39mm cal., AK-47 design, GPO, 16 1/2 in. match ER Shaw barrel, blue finish, mfg. from unissued Bulgarian parts kit, wood furniture, 30 shot mag., milled receiver, includes hard case. Disc. 2013.

	$685	$615	$550	$475	$420	$365	$335	*$790*

Add $120-$150 for Strikeforce Elite package with adj. polymer stock, pistol grip, recoil system, removable cheekpiece and three Picatinny rails (new 2012).

GRADING - PPGS™	100%	98%	95%	90%	80%	70%	60%	LAST MSR
AT-47 STAMPED – 7.62x39mm cal., AK-47 design, GPO, similar to AT-47 Milled, except has stamped receiver. Mfg. in the U.S. 2011-2013.	$525	$465	$400	$340	$300	$265	$250	*$600*
Add $120-$150 for Strikeforce Elite package with adj. polymer stock, pistol grip, recoil system, removable cheekpiece and three Picatinny rails (new 2012).								
GALEO – 5.56 NATO cal., based on the Galil AR/ARM, long stroke gas piston operated, 18 1/2 in. barrel with birdcage style flash hider, 30 shot Tapco mag., uses Galil style mags., milled steel receiver with stamped steel top cover, hooded front sight post, aperture-type rear sight mounted on top cover, tubular metal right side folding stock, wood or polymer surplus Galil handguards, surplus polymer Galil pistol grip, ambidextrous safety, thumb actuated safety lever, shielded mag. catch, upswept charging handle, phosphate finish. New 2019.								
MSR $1,300	$1,100	$950	$850	$750	$600	$500	$400	
Add $30 for wood handguards.								
HDH16 CARBINE – 5.56 NATO cal., GIO, 10 or 30 shot mag., 16 in. heavy barrel, flat-top receiver with Picatinny rail, 6-position stock, black hardware and finish, includes hard case. Mfg. 2012-2013.	$645	$500	$415	$370	$325	$300	$275	*$750*
MILSPORT AR-15 P3 RIFLE – 5.56 NATO or .300 AAC Blackout cal., 16 in. barrel, 30 shot mag., 6-pos. stock, low profile gas block, 13 in. KeyMod handguard, Picatinny rail, includes Nano Composite Parts Kit. Mfg. 2018 only.	$400	$325	$275	$250	$225	$225	$200	*$530*
MILSPORT M4 CARBINE – 5.56 NATO cal., GIO, 30 shot PMAG, 16 in. barrel, flat-top receiver with Picatinny rail, tubular ribbed handguard, forged aluminum upper and billet aluminum lower, 7 in. drop-in quad rail, 6-position stock, black hardware and finish, includes hard case. Mfg. 2012-2017.	$575	$450	$400	$350	$325	$325	$275	*$770*
MILSPORT .223 WYLDE – .223 Wylde chamber, 18 in. SOCOM profile stainless steel barrel, muzzle covered with thread protector, Extreme Target trigger, optics ready, 6-pos. collapsible Rogers Super-Stoc, 15 in. free float KeyMod rail handguard, forged aluminum upper and lower receiver, carbine buffer. Mfg. 2017-2018.	$525	$425	$375	$325	$300	$275	$250	*$700*
MILSPORT 9MM AR-15 CARBINE – 9mm Para. cal., 16 in. barrel, A2 flash hider, 30 shot mag., 10 in. free float KeyMod rail handguard, forged upper and billet lower receiver, 6-position Rogers Super-Stoc, black finish. New 2012.								
MSR $900	$675	$525	$475	$425	$400	$375	$325	
MILSPORT 5.56 AR-15 CARBINE – 5.56 NATO cal., .223 Wylde chamber, 18 in. match grade barrel, A2 flash hider, 30 shot mag., Rogers Super-Stoc, low profile Nitride steel gas block, 15 in. free floating KeyMod rail handguard, forged upper receiver, Mil-Spec internal parts, black finish. Disc. 2017.	$625	$500	$450	$400	$375	$350	$300	*$840*
MILSPORT AR-15 P3P – 5.56 NATO or .300 AAC Blackout cal., 16 in. phosphate barrel, A2 flash hider, 30 shot mag., pistol grip, Alpha stock, forged aluminum upper and lower receiver, 10 in. KeyMod rail, black finish. New late 2018.								
MSR $600	$450	$350	$325	$300	$275	$250	$225	
MILSPORT AR-15 RIA – 5.56 NATO cal., 16 in. mid-length barrel, A2 flash hider, 13 in. KeyMod rail handguard, anodized black finish. Disc. 2017.	$600	$475	$425	$375	$350	$325	$300	*$800*
MILSPORT AR-15 RIA ALUMINUM – 5.56 NATO, .300 AAC Blackout, or 6.5 Grendel cal., 16 in. barrel, 30 shot mag., 6-pos. M4 stock, aluminum receivers, 10 (6.5 Grendel only) or 13 in. KeyMod rail handguard. New 2018.								
MSR $580	$425	$350	$300	$275	$250	$225	$200	
MILSPORT AR-15 RIA (CURRENT MFG.) – 9mm Para. cal., blowback operation, 16 in. barrel with black Nitride finish, A2 compensator, 6-pos. adj. Rogers Super-Stoc, billet 9mm lower and forged aluminum upper receiver, 10 in. KeyMod rail handguard, Cerakote Burnt Bronze finish. New 2017.								
MSR $959	$725	$575	$500	$450	$425	$400	$350	
MILSPORT AR-15 TRUMP SPECIAL – 5.56 NATO or .300 AAC Blackout cal., 16 in. phosphate barrel, A2 flash hider, 30 shot mag., pistol grip, skeleton stock, forged aluminum upper and lower receiver, 13 in. KeyMod rail, Mil-Spec fire control group. New 2018.								
MSR $640	$475	$375	$350	$300	$275	$250	$225	

GRADING - PPGS™	100%	98%	95%	90%	80%	70%	60%	LAST MSR

MILSPORT AR 450 BUSHMASTER – .450 Bushmaster cal., 16 in. phosphate barrel w/compensator, 5 shot polymer mag., pistol grip, aluminum forged upper and lower receiver, 15 in. KeyMod rail, Mil-Spec fire control group, black finish. New 2019.

MSR $700	$525	$425	$375	$325	$300	$275	$250	

MILSPORT AR-15 CUSTOM SHOP – 5.56 NATO cal.,16 in. phosphate barrel, A2 flash hider, 30 shot mag., 6-position M4 pattern buttstock, pistol grip, forged aluminum upper and lower receiver, 10 in. KeyMod rail, Mil-Spec fire control group, black, Battlefield Green, FDE, Sniper Gray, or Titanium finish. New 2019.

MSR $650	$500	$375	$350	$300	$275	$250	$225	

MILSPORT 3 GUN – 5.56 NATO cal., .223 Wylde chamber, 16 in. barrel, Rifenbark S.O.M. brake, SST, Luth-AR MB4 stock with cheekpiece, Ergo grip, aluminum Milsport receivers, 13 in. free float KeyMod rail handguard, 6.65 lbs. New 2018.

MSR $950	$725	$575	$500	$450	$425	$375	$350	

V916/VX916 CARBINE – 5.56 NATO cal., GIO, 10 or 30 shot mag., 16 in. heavy barrel, flat-top receiver with Picatinny rail, 9 or 13 in. quad rail handguard, 6-position stock, black hardware and finish, includes hard case. Mfg. 2012-2013.

	$765	$515	$440	$375	$335	$315	$295	*$889*

Add $20 for 13 in. quad rail (Model VX916).

OMNI 22 (VK22 STANDARD) – .22 LR cal., AR-15 style, GIO, 16 in. barrel, fixed or telestock, black finish, flat-top receiver with Picatinny rail, 10 or 28 shot mag. Disc. 2013.

	$400	$350	$300	$265	$235	$220	$210	*$470*

OMNI 22 OPS (VK22 TACTICAL) – .22 LR cal., AR-15 style, GIO, 16 in. barrel, fixed or telestock, black finish, flat-top receiver, 10 or 28 shot mag., quad rail, vertical foregrip, tactical rear sight. Disc. 2013.

	$460	$385	$330	$285	$250	$230	$220	*$520*

OMNI 556 – 5.56 NATO cal., GIO, 16 in. M4 style barrel, 10 or 30 shot mag., fixed or telescoping stock, 7 in. quad rail, flat-top receiver with Picatinny rail, Omni polymer lower receiver, black furniture. Mfg. 2013-2015.

	$500	$375	$350	$300	$275	$275	$250	*$650*

OMNI HYBRID M4 – 5.56 NATO cal., GPO, 16 in. barrel, 10 or 30 shot mag., flat-top polymer lower receiver, interlock hammer and trigger pin retainment system, enhanced trigger guard, beveled magwell, 6-position adj. stock, matte black finish, includes AR-15 parts kit, 7 lbs. Mfg. 2014-2015.

	$475	$375	$325	$300	$275	$250	$225	*$620*

OMNI HYBRID 22 COMBO – .22 LR cal. with complete 5.56 aluminum upper and Hybrid lower receiver, 16 in. barrel, 28 (.22 LR) or 30 (5.56) shot PMAG, 10 in. quad rail, 6-position stock, black finish. Mfg. 2015-2016.

	$375	$300	$275	$250	$225	$200	$175	*$495*

OMNI HYBRID 300 AAC BLACKOUT – .300 AAC Blackout cal., 16 in. barrel, 30 shot PMAG, complete Hybrid lower and aluminum upper receiver, 7 in. quad rail, 6-pos. stock, black finish, 6 1/2 lbs. Mfg. 2015-2016.

	$500	$375	$350	$300	$275	$275	$250	*$650*

OMNI HYBRID MAXX – 5.56 NATO cal., 16 in. M4 black Nitride coated barrel, flat-top, optics ready, 10 or 30 shot PMAG, complete Omni Hybrid upper and lower polymer receiver, 6-pos. stock, black or FDE (new 2016) finish, 6 1/4 lbs. Mfg. 2015-2017.

	$500	$400	$350	$325	$300	$275	$250	*$670*

Subtract $60 for no furniture (stripped model ATIGOMX556S).
Add $60 for 13 in. KeyMod rail (ATIGOMX556KM13).

OMNI HYBRID MAXX 5.56 – 5.56 NATO cal., 16 in. barrel, 30 shot PMAG, 7 in. quad rail handguard, complete Omni Hybrid polymer upper and lower receiver, 6-pos. stock, black or FDE (new 2016) finish, 6 1/2 lbs. Mfg. 2015-2017.

	$525	$425	$375	$325	$300	$275	$250	*$695*

OMNI HYBRID MAXX 22 COMBO – .22 LR cal. with complete Omni Hybrid 5.56 upper and lower receiver, 16 in. barrel, 10 in. free float quad rail handguard, 28 (.22 LR) or 30 (5.56) shot PMAG, black or FDE (new 2016) finish. Mfg. 2015-2016.

	$575	$450	$400	$350	$325	$300	$275	*$770*

OMNI HYBRID MAXX 300 – .300 AAC Blackout cal., 16 in. barrel, 30 shot PMAG, 6-pos. stock, 10 in. free float quad rail handguard, complete Omni Hybrid polymer upper and lower receiver, black or FDE (mfg. 2016 only) finish, 6 1/2 lbs. New 2015.

MSR $700	$525	$425	$375	$325	$300	$275	$250	

GRADING - PPGS™	100%	98%	95%	90%	80%	70%	60%	LAST MSR

OMNI HYBRID MAXX TSI – 5.56 NATO or .300 AAC Blackout cal., 16 in. barrel, A2 flash hider, 30 shot mag., iron flip-up sights, 6-pos. Rogers Super-Stoc, pistol grip, OMNI HYBRID MAXX upper and lower receiver, Mil-Spec fire control group, Picatinny rail, black finish. New 2018.

MSR $530 $400 $325 $275 $250 $225 $200 $175

OMNI HYBRID MAXX P3 – 5.56 NATO or .300 AAC Blackout cal., low profile gas block, 16 in. barrel, A2 flash hider, 30 shot mag., 6-pos. M4 stock, 10 in. KeyMod rail, Omni Hybrid polymer upper and metal lower receiver with front and rear metal inserts, features a Saf-T First or Nano composite parts kit, black finish. New 2018.

MSR $450 $350 $275 $250 $225 $200 $175 $175

OMNI HYBRID MAXX P3P – 5.56 NATO or .300 AAC Blackout cal., 16 in. barrel, A2 flash hider, 30 shot mag., polymer upper and lower receiver, 10 in. KeyMod rail, Nano composite parts kit, black, Battlefield Green, FDE, or Sniper Grey finish, 5.5 lbs. New late 2018.

MSR $480 $350 $275 $250 $225 $200 $200 $175

OMNI HYBRID TRANSLUCENT MAXX – 5.56 NATO cal., 16 in. black Nitride coated barrel, two 30 shot PMAGs, 10 in. free float quad rail handguard, low profile gas block, metal reinforced polymer upper and lower receivers, 6-pos. Rogers Super-Stoc, black finish. Mfg. 2015 only.

$700 $425 $375 $325 $300 $275 $250 *$700*

SHOTGUNS: O/U

CAVALRY SPORT – 12, 20, 28 (disc. 2020) ga., or .410 bore, 3 in. chambers, 28 or 30 in. chrome moly barrels, 5 interchangeable chokes, SST, high rib, double bead sights with brass front bead, extractor, Turkish walnut oil finished stock, blued finish on barrels, engraved receiver with matte finish, 6.8 lbs. New 2015.

MSR $670 $575 $500 $425 $390 $315 $260 $220

CAVALRY SVE W/EJECTOR – 12, 20, 28 (disc.) ga., or .410 bore, 3 in. chambers, 18 in. chrome moly steel barrels, aluminum receiver, ejector, SST, brass front bead sight, oil finished Turkish walnut stock, laser engraved design, approx. 6 lbs. New late 2018.

MSR $600 $510 $450 $385 $350 $280 $250 $200

CAVALRY SX – 12, 20, 28 ga., or .410 bore, 3 in. chambers, 26 or 28 (12 ga. only) in. chrome moly steel barrels, blue finish, oil finished checkered Turkish walnut pistol grip stock and forearm, brass bead front sight, alloy receiver with light game scene engraving, five interchangeable chokes, SST, with extractors, black chrome finish. Imported mid-2013-2019.

$550 $450 $350 $295 $260 $230 $200 *$660*

Add $140 for Cavalry SX Combo model with extra 28 ga. barrel.

* ***Cavalry SX Youth*** – 20 ga. or .410 bore, 26 in. barrel, youth configuration, otherwise similar to Cavalry SX. Imported 2014-2019.

$550 $450 $350 $295 $260 $230 $200 *$660*

CAVALRY SXE – 12, 20 ga. or .410 bore, 3 in. chambers, 26 or 28 (12 ga. only) in. chrome moly steel barrels, blue finish, oil finished checkered Turkish walnut pistol grip stock and forearm, brass bead front sight, alloy receiver with light game scene engraving, five interchangeable chokes, SST, with ejectors, black chrome finish. Imported mid-2013-2019.

$565 $450 $350 $295 $260 $230 $200 *$690*

CALVARY TURKEY FOWL – 12 or 20 ga., 3 in. chambers, 21 in. VR barrels with 9 in. choke extensions, extractors, SST, checkered Turkish walnut stock and forearm, perimeter engraving on frame, black chrome finish. Imported 2016-2020.

$510 $450 $385 $350 $280 $250 $200 *$600*

CRUSADER FIELD – 12, 20, 28 ga., or .410 bore, 26 or 28 in. barrels with blued finish, 5 different chokes, SST, fiber optic front sight, oil finished Turkish Walnut stock and forend, laser engraved receiver.

MSR $500 $425 $375 $325 $300 $240 $200 $150

CRUSADER SPORT – 12, 20, 28 ga., or .410 bore, 26, 28, or 30 in. ported barrels with blued finish, extended chokes, SST, fiber optic front sight, oil finished Turkish Walnut stock and forend, laser engraved receiver.

MSR $550 $475 $400 $350 $325 $260 $220 $160

SHOTGUNS: SEMI-AUTO

ALPHA FIELD – 12 ga., 3 in. chamber, inertia recoil system, 28 in. barrel, wide vent. rib, fiber optic front sight, checkered Turkish walnut stock and forearm, black powder coat finish. Mfg. 2015-2019.

$400 $350 $300 $275 $225 $185 $150 *$450*

GRADING - PPGS™	100%	98%	95%	90%	80%	70%	60%	LAST MSR

ALPHA HD – 12 ga., 3 in. chamber, inertia recoil system, 18 1/2 in. barrel, 5 shot, blade sights, synthetic stock and forearm. Mfg. 2015-2016.

	$410	$350	$300	$275	$225	$185	$150	*$470*

ALPHA SPORT – 12 ga., 3 in. chamber, 26 in. barrel, inertia recoil system, 5 shot, synthetic stock and forearm, black finish. Mfg. 2015-2018.

	$360	$315	$275	$250	$225	$200	$150	*$400*

AMTAC-S (TAC-S) – 12 ga., 3 in. chamber, 18 1/2 in. barrel, 5 shot, blue finish, matte black synthetic pistol grip stock and forearm, 6.4 lbs. Imported 2014-2018.

	$225	$195	$170	$150	$125	$100	$80	*$260*

* ***TAC-S Combo*** – 12 ga., similar to TAC-S, except is two barrel set, features 18 1/2 in. cyl. barrel and 28 in. vented ribbed barrel with 3 choke tubes. Imported 2014-2016.

	$370	$315	$275	$250	$225	$200	$150	*$420*

BULL-DOG – 12 ga., 3 in. chamber, bullpup configuration, 18 1/2 in. barrel, 5 or 10 shot mag., in-line stock with adj. cheek riser, Picatinny rail and KeyMod slotted forend, removable adj. open sights, fixed pistol grip, crossbolt safety above trigger guard, shell deflector above ejection port, AR-15 style charging handle, mags. can be inverted and attached to the forend to make a vertical grip, black finish. New 2020.

MSR $500	$425	$375	$325	$300	$240	$200	$150	

MIL-SPORT AR .410 SHOTGUN – .410 ga., 2 1/2 in. chamber, adj. gas system, 18 in. stainless steel barrel, straight choke, 5 shot mag., polymer front and rear flip-up sights, 6-pos. Rogers Super-Stoc, pistol grip, 13 in. custom KeyMod rail, Mil-Spec fire control group, black finish. New 2019.

MSR $720	$615	$495	$415	$360	$325	$300	$275	

OMNI HYBRID MAXX – .410 bore, 2 1/2 in. chamber, GPO, 18 1/2 in. threaded barrel, Remington style chokes, 5 shot mag., 6-pos. adj. Super-Stoc, 10 in. free floating quad rail, ambidextrous sling plate, Omni Hybrid lower receiver, black finish, 6 1/2 lbs. Mfg. 2016 only.

	$700	$550	$500	$425	$400	$375	$350	*$930*

OMNI HYBRID MAXX LIMITED .410 SHOTGUN – .410 bore, straight choke, GPO, 18 or 18 1/2 (disc.) in. barrel, 5 shot mag., 6-pos. adj. Super-Stoc, 13 in. free floating KeyMod rail, Omni Hybrid lower receiver, black finish, 6 1/2 lbs. Mfg. 2017-2020.

	$535	$475	$400	$365	$300	$250	$200	*$630*

SHOTGUNS: SINGLE SHOT

NOMAD – 12, 20 ga., or .410 bore, 2 3/4 and 3 in. chamber, trigger guard release, break open action, folding shotgun, 18 1/2, 26, or 28 in. barrel, single shot, exposed hammer, bead front sight, checkered synthetic stock and forend with sling swivels, high gloss black chrome finish, 12 ga. only for 28 in., approx. 4.8 lbs. New 2018.

MSR $110	$100	$90	$75	$70	$55	$45	$35	

* ***Nomad Grand Slam*** – 12, 20 ga., or .410 bore, 3 in. chamber, trigger guard release, break open action, folding shotgun, 23 in. vent. rib barrel with XXFull and Modified choke tubes, single shot, exposed hammer, fiber optic front sight, checkered synthetic stock and forend with sling swivels, saddle mount with Picatinny rail, camo finished furniture. New 2020.

MSR $170	$150	$130	$120	$100	$85	$70	$50	

SHOTGUNS: SLIDE ACTION

TAC-PX2 (TAC-P) – 12 ga., 3 in. chamber, 18 1/2 in. barrel, 5 shot, forearm with Picatinny rail, matte black finish, fixed synthetic stock with pistol grip, trigger guard mounted safety, ramped front sight, rubber buttpad, 5.95 lbs. Mfg. 2013-2017.

	$215	$190	$160	$145	$120	$95	$75	*$250*

* ***TAC-PX2 Combo (TAC-P Combo)*** – 12 ga., similar to TACPX2, except includes extra barrel and choke tubes. Mfg. 2014-2015.

	$335	$285	$245	$220	$180	$145	$115	*$350*

S-BEAM MB3/MB3-R – 12 ga., 3 in. chamber, 18 1/2 in. barrel, 4 shot mag., bead or blade (MB3-R) sight, synthetic stock, with top Picatinny rail (MB3-R) or without, black finish. New 2017.

MSR $250	$215	$190	$160	$145	$120	$95	$75	

S-BEAM MB3-28/MB3-DW – 12 ga., 18 (MB3-DW, disc. 2020) or 28 (MB3-28) in. barrel, 4 shot mag., bead or blade sight, standard or pistol grip, black finish. New 2019.

MSR $260	$225	$195	$170	$155	$125	$100	$80	

GRADING - PPGS™	100%	98%	95%	90%	80%	70%	60%	LAST MSR

SHOTGUNS: SxS

CAVALRY ROAD AGENT – 12, 20 (mfg. 2018 only) ga. or .410 bore (mfg. 2018 only), 3 in. chambers, 18 1/2 in. carbon steel barrels with black aluminum finish, 5 choke tubes, aluminum receiver with intricate scroll engraving, external hammers with decocker, double triggers, bead front sight, hand-finished Turkish walnut stock and forearm, 5.3 lbs. Mfg. 2017-2019.

	100%	98%	95%	90%	80%	70%	60%	LAST MSR
	$500	$450	$375	$350	$275	$225	$175	*$580*

CAVALRY ROAD AGENT PRIME – 20 ga., 3 in. chambers, 26 in. barrels with 5 choke tubes, silver engraved receiver, external hammers with decocker, Turkish walnut stock, 7.12 lbs. Mfg. 2018 only.

	100%	98%	95%	90%	80%	70%	60%	LAST MSR
	$540	$475	$400	$340	$300	$265	$250	*$626*

AMERICAN WESTERN ARMS, INC.

Previous trademark and importer 1999-2004, and located in Delray Beach, FL. During late 2004, the remaining assets of this company were sold and a new company was established as AWA USA in Hialeah, FL. SAA revolver components were manufactured in the former Armi San Marco factory in Italy (now AWA International, Inc.), and assembled in the U.S.

For individual model listings, please go to BlueBookOfGunValues.com/overflow.

AM-TAC PRECISION

Previous manufacturer of AR-15 style rifles located in Garden City, ID from 2009-2015.

Please refer to BlueBookOfGunValues.com to order the *Blue Book of AR-15s & Variations*, available as a book or online subscription.

AMTEC 2000, INC.

Previous trademark incorporating Erma Werke (German) and H & R 1871 (U.S.) companies located in Gardner, MA until 1999. Amtec 2000, Inc. previously imported the Erma SR 100 rifle (see listing in Erma Suhl section).

REVOLVERS

5 SHOT REVOLVER – .38 S&W cal., 5 shot double action, swing-out cylinder, 2 or 3 in. barrel, transfer bar safety, Pachmayr composition grips, high polish blue, matte electroless nickel, or stainless steel construction, fixed sights, approx. 25 oz., 200 mfg. 1996-99, all were distributed and sold in Europe only (no U.S. pricing).

ANATOLIA MANUFACTURING COMPANY LLC

Current AR-15 style shotgun manufacturer located in Orlando, FL.

Please refer to BlueBookOfGunValues.com to order the *Blue Book of AR-15s & Variations*, available as a book or online subscription.

ANATOLIAN DEFENSE INDUSTRY

Current manufacturer and distributor of various shotgun configurations located in Konya, Turkey. No current U.S. importation.

Please contact the company directly for current information on their impressive model line-up and possible U.S. availability.

ANCIENS ETABLISSEMENTS PIEPER

Please refer to the Bayard listing in the B section for Bayard Models 1908, 1923, and 1930. In addition, Bergmann-Bayard Models 1908 and 1910 mfg. in Liege, Belgium, will appear under the Bergmann heading.

ANDERSON MANUFACTURING

Current AR-15 style rifle, pistol, and components manufacturer established during 2010, located in Hebron, KY.

Please refer to BlueBookOfGunValues.com to order the *Blue Book of AR-15s & Variations*, available as a book or online subscription.

ANDERSON WHEELER

Current long gun and revolver manufacturer established during 2007, located in Dorset, London. Previously located in Mayfair, London. Currently imported by Griffin & Howe, located in Bernardsville, NJ and Greenwich, CT.

REVOLVERS

MARK VII REVOLVER – .357 Mag. cal., DA/SA, top break, 6 in. drop forged barrel, 7 shot, auto ejection, blade front and U-notch rear sights, checkered or non-checkered deluxe Turkish walnut or ebony grips, light rose and scroll custom engraving available upon request, Best London blue or coin finish, 10 1/2 oz. New 2020.

Please contact the manufacturer directly for options, pricing, and delivery time.

RIFLES

Anderson Wheeler rifles are available in the following configurations - Express Double Rifle (.303 British, .375 Flanged, .450-400 Nitro Express, .470 Nitro Express, .500 Nitro Express, .577 Nitro Express, or .600 Nitro Express cal.) and a Bolt Action Magazine rifle (.375 H&H, .404 Jeffery, .416 Rigby, .500 Jeffery, or .505 Gibbs cal.). All models are bespoke and made to individual customer specifications/ requirements. Delivery time is typically 12-18 months. Please contact the company directly for an individual quotation.

SHOTGUNS

Anderson Wheeler makes both a sidelock O/U shotgun in addition to a SxS sidelock shotgun. They are available in 12, 16, 20, 28 ga., or .410 bore. All models are bespoke and made to individual customer specifications/requirements. They are available in either Field or Best Grades. Delivery time is typically 12-18 months - please contact the company directly for an individual quotation.

ANDREAS STRANK BUCHSENMACHERMEISTER

Please refer to the Strank, Andreas Jagdwaffen Buchsenmachermeister listing in the S section.

ANGEL ARMS INC.

Previous manufacturer located in Hayward, CA, 1998-2001.

PISTOLS: SEMI-AUTO

The pistols listed below were designed to shoot a unique integrated case projectile (ICP). These projectiles were hollow, contained the powder charge, and since the case was the projectile, there was no ejection.

MODEL 1000 SE GUN ONE - .45 ICP (Integrated Case Projectile) cal., unique semi-auto design, mag tube is located on top of 6 in. fixed barrel.

While advertised, this model never went into production. $1,900 was the projected MSR.

MODEL QT 427 ZMR - .427 ICP (Integrated Case Projectile) cal., break open action, 5 shot tube or 10 shot staggered mag., 3 1/2 in. barrel located underneath clear mag tube, compact size, 5 oz.

While advertised, this model never went into production. $900 was the projected MSR.

ANGSTADT ARMS

Current AR-15 style rifle and pistol manufacturer specializing in pistol caliber carbines (PCC), located in Charlotte, NC.

Please refer to BlueBookOfGunValues.com to order the *Blue Book of AR-15s & Variations*, available as a book or online subscription.

ANSCHÜTZ

Current manufacturer (J. G. Anschütz, GmbH & Co. KG) established in 1856 and currently located in Ulm, Germany. All Anschutz sporting rifles, target/competition/biathlon/air rifles and accessories are currently imported beginning 2014 by Anschutz North America/GSI, located in Trussville, AL. Anschutz North America (ANA) also has an exclusive on the Meister Grade Series, Custom Shop, and specific limited run production models. During 2015, Anschutz created a relationship with RWS and imports the match grade ammunition and pellets direct from the factory. This allows lot testing for individual rifles with the most accurate ammunition performed in a climate controlled 100 meter underground range. Sporting rifles were previously imported by Steyr Arms, Inc. located in Bessemer, AL 2010-2014, previously located in Trussville, AL until 2013. Merkel USA imported Anschutz from 2005-2010, also located in Trussville, AL.

ANSCHÜTZ ® DIE MEISTER MACHER

Sporting rifles were imported 1996-2003 by Tristar Sporting Arms, Ltd., located in N. Kansas City, MO. Previously distributed until 2000 by Go Sportsmens Supply, located in Billings, MT. Previously imported and distributed through 1995 in the U.S. by Precision Sales International Inc., located in Westfield, MA.

Anschütz was founded by Julius Gottfried Anschütz in 1856, and located in Zella-Mehlis, Germany until 1945. WWII nearly ended the company. Members of the Anschütz family were evacuated to West Germany after the war, while the company's possesions were expropriated and dismantled. Brothers Max & Rudolf Anschütz, grandsons of Julius, re-established the company in Ulm after WWII. In 1968, Max Anschütz turned over general management to his son Dieter (4th generation), who retired on March 31, 2008. The family business is now managed by Dieter's two sons, Jochen (President) and Uwe.

For more information and current pricing on both new and used Anschütz airguns, please refer to the *Blue Book of Airguns* - also available as an online subscription.

GRADING - PPGS™	100%	98%	95%	90%	80%	70%	60%	LAST MSR

ANSCHUTZ HISTORY

Sile Distributors located in NY acted as an import agent during the early 1960s which can be identified by Sile barrel markings. Anschütz rifles imported by Savage were available from 1963-1981 and also have Savage/Anschütz barrel markings. While some of those models might not be listed below, refer to models of similar caliber and quality which are listed to ascertain values.

During the period when Savage was importing Anschütz rifles, certain models in the Anschütz line were designated either "Savage-Anschütz" or "Anschütz-Savage" for sales by Savage in the U.S. Conversely, certain models manufactured by Savage were designated "Anschütz-Savage" for sale by Anschütz in Europe. Some of these models did not have any modifications but others were restocked, supplied with different sights, and had other different features from their original counterparts. In most cases, the original model numbers were used. Some "Anschütz-Savage" rifles have made their way into the U.S. While somewhat rare, these rifles are typically based on the Savage Model 110 action. They are not as desirable as those "Savage-Anschütz" marked rifles utilizing the superior Anschütz actions. Anschütz also manufactured between 1,000-2,000 rifles utilizing SAKO actions in .222 Rem. cal. in the late 1950s-early 1960s. These guns will approximate values shown for the discontinued centerfire models listed in the Rifles: Disc. catergory.

Currently, Anschütz offers 5 different actions. The 1451 action is Anschütz's entry level action, which is lightweight in design, utilizes cam cocking, and has a lateral sliding safety. The 1451 action is currently used in the Models 1451 D KL, 1451 R Sporter Target, and 1451 Target. The Match 64 utilizes a cam cocking system with claw extractor and ejector, grooved receiver, and sliding safety on the right side behind the bolt. The Model 64 match action is used on the Model 1416 and variations, 1418, 64MP R, 1516, 1517 D Classic, 1517 D HB Classic, 1517 D Monte Carlo, 1517 M PR, and the Model 64 Target pistol. The Match 54 is Anschütz's top-of-the-line action, and features dual locking lugs on its bolt eccentrically seated in the receiver, allowing more support for improved stock bedding. It also features a cam cocking system, 2 position pivoting rear safety, and a drilled and tapped receiver. The Match 54 action is currently utilized on the 1710 series, 1712D, 1717, 1720, 1730 series, 1733, and 1740 Models. The other two actions are used on Models 1770 and 1780.

PISTOLS: BOLT ACTION

Anschütz also manufactured an MSP Pistol Series with ergonomic stock for silhouette shooters. This series was designed for target shooting. Anschütz pistols were delivered with a keyed security gun lock.

MODEL 17LP - .17 HMR cal., 4 shot mag., otherwise similar to Model 64LP. Imported 2003-2004.

$650	$575	$495	$400	$335	$300	$250	*$651*

MODEL 64P - .22 LR or .22 WMR (disc. 2001) cal., right-hand Match 64 bolt action pistol, 10 in. drilled and tapped barrel (sights not included), 4 (.22 WMR) or 5 shot mag., two-stage trigger, no sights, weather proof Choate Rynite stock with stippling, 3 1/2 lbs. Imported 1998-2003.

$575	$500	$425	$350	$300	$250	$200	*$509*

Add 10% for .22 WMR cal. (Model 64P Mag., disc. 2001).
Add 15% for accessory sight set.

* ***Model 64LP*** - .22 LR cal., left-hand Match 64 bolt action pistol, 12 in. drilled and tapped barrel (sights not included), 5 shot mag., two-stage trigger, no sights, Choate Rynite stock with stippling, approx. 3 1/2 lbs. Imported 2003-2004.

$625	$550	$475	$395	$335	$300	$250	*$602*

MODEL 1416P/1451P (EXEMPLAR) - .22 LR cal., Match 64 left-hand action (for right-hand shooters), blue finish, 6.92 (original Silhouette Model, mfg. 1994-95) or 10 in. barrel, single shot (Model 1451P, new 1997) or repeater with 5 shot mag. (Model 1416P), two-stage trigger, adj. rear sight, receiver grooved for scope, stippled contoured grip and forestock, 3 1/3 lbs., also available for left-hand shooters. Imported 1987-1997.

$600	$525	$450	$375	$300	$250	$200	*$470*

Add $17 for single shot (Model 1451P).
Add $110 for right-hand action (for left-hand shooters).

This model was previously designated the Exemplar until 1996.

* ***Exemplar Hornet*** - .22 Hornet cal., 5 shot mag., Match 54 left-hand action, 10 in. barrel, grooved receiver, drilled and tapped w/o sights, 4.35 lbs. Imported 1988-1995.

$895	$800	$675	$575	$475	$415	$365	*$995*

This model may also be marked M-1730 MSPE Field.

GRADING - PPGS™	100%	98%	95%	90%	80%	70%	60%	LAST MSR

* ***Exemplar Magnum*** – while advertised in 1987, only one .22 WMR was manufactured.
* ***Exemplar XIV*** – .22 LR cal., similar to Exemplar, except has 14 in. barrel, 4.15 lbs. Imported 1988-1995.

$650	$575	$500	$425	$350	$275	$225	*$562*

MODEL 1416 MSPR/MSPE – .22 LR cal., silhouette variation of the Exemplar pistol, MSPR designates repeater, MSPE designates single shot. Imported 1997 only.

$1,100	$875	$750	$625	$525	$450	$375	*$1,260*

Subract 10% if single shot model (Model MSPE).

MODEL 1416 PISTOL KV – .22 LR cal., Match 64 left-hand bolt action, 14 in. barrel, 5 shot, no. 5098 two-stage trigger, hooded front and adj. rear barrel sight, walnut stock with stippled forend, 4 1/4 lbs. 100 pistols mfg. 2016 only.

$1,100	$975	$850	$775	$650	$525	$400	*$1,099*

MODEL 1730 MSPE FIELD – .22 Hornet cal., 9.3 in. barrel, single shot, target stock with ventilated forend, ergonomic grips, left-handed bolt, 54 Match action, drilled and tapped. Importation disc.

$1,195	$975	$800	$700	$600	$500	$400

RIFLES: BOLT ACTION, DISC.

MARK 10 TARGET RIFLE – .22 LR cal., single shot, 26 in. heavy barrel, globe front sight, adj. rear sight, target stock w/adj. palm stop, full pistol grip. Imported 1963-1981.

$495	$425	$350	$295	$260	$230	$210

MODEL 54 SPORTER – .22 LR cal., Match 54 action, 5 shot mag., 24 in. round tapered barrel, Monte Carlo stock with roll-over cheekpiece, folding leaf rear sight, checkered pistol grip. Imported 1963-1981.

$850	$750	$650	$525	$450	$400	$360

MODEL 54M – similar to Model 54 Sporter, except .22 WMR cal.

$950	$825	$700	$600	$500	$435	$395

MODEL MATCH 64 – .22 LR cal., Match 64 action, single shot, 26 in. barrel, hardwood stock with stippled ergonomic pistol grip, adj. buttpad, grooved receiver, approx. 8 lbs. Disc.

$700	$600	$500	$400	$350	$295	$250

Subtract $150 if w/o correct Anschütz micrometer sights (front and rear).

MODEL 141 – .22 LR cal., 5 shot mag., 23 in. round tapered barrel, Monte Carlo stock, folding leaf rear sight. Disc.

$550	$475	$400	$325	$250	$200	$180

* ***Model 141M (Mag.)*** – similar to Model 141, except .22 WMR cal.

$650	$550	$450	$350	$275	$225	$200

MODEL 153 – .222 Rem. cal., 24 in. barrel, folding leaf rear sight, French walnut stock, rosewood forend tip and pistol grip cap. Imported 1963-1981.

$950	$850	$750	$675	$575	$475	$400

MODEL 153-S – similar to Model 153, 24 in. barrel, DST.

$1,050	$950	$850	$775	$625	$525	$425

MODEL 164 – .22 LR cal., 5 shot mag., 23 in. round tapered barrel, Monte Carlo stock, folding leaf rear sight. Imported 1963-1981.

$575	$450	$375	$300	$250	$200	$180

* ***Model 164M*** – similar to Model 164, except .22 WMR cal.

$650	$550	$450	$350	$275	$225	$200

MODEL 184 – .22 LR cal., 21 1/2 in. barrel, Monte Carlo stock with checkered pistol grip, Schnabel forend, folding leaf rear sight. Imported 1963-1981.

$575	$450	$375	$325	$275	$210	$180

MODEL 1400 – .22 LR cal., standard barrel, with sights. Disc.

$450	$375	$325	$290	$260	$230	$210

The Model 1400D Meistergrade was disc. 1987 - the last advertised retail price was $930.

MODEL 1407 I.S.U. MATCH 54 – .22 LR cal., heavy barrel, match two-stage trigger, stippled walnut stock and forearm with aluminum rail, aperture sights. Disc.

$775	$650	$550	$450	$350	$300	$260	*approx. $530*

GRADING - PPGS™	100%	98%	95%	90%	80%	70%	60%	LAST MSR

MODEL 1408 – .22 LR cal., heavy barrel, no sights. Disc.

	$650	$575	$500	$425	$350	$275	$225	

Add $150 for 1408 ED Model.

MODEL 1411 MATCH 54 – .22 LR cal., prone position target model, heavy barrel, front and rear adj. micrometer sights, pivoting safety, fast lock time, adj. cheekpiece. Disc.

	$650	$550	$475	$400	$350	$300	$260	*approx. $575*

Subtract $150 if w/o correct Anschütz micrometer sights (front and rear).

MODEL 1413 SUPER MATCH 54 – .22 LR cal., top-of-the-line free style international target rifle, adj. cheekpiece and curved buttplate, heavy target barrel, front and rear aperture sights. Disc.

	$950	$850	$700	$575	$450	$375	$325	*approx. $875*

Subtract $150 if w/o correct Anschütz micrometer sights (front and rear).

MODEL 1418 – .22 LR cal., sporter variation, previous importation by Savage Arms.

	$550	$475	$400	$350	$300	$250	$225	

MODEL 1418 MANNLICHER – .22 LR cal., hunting model, fine checkering, 5 shot mag.

	$925	$800	$700	$600	$475	$375	$325	

MODEL 1450 – .22 LR cal., sporter model, 5 shot mag.

	$525	$450	$375	$325	$275	$225	$200	

MODEL 1518 MANNLICHER – deluxe model variation of the Model 1418, full Mannlicher stock.

	$1,075	$950	$850	$725	$625	$525	$450	

MODEL 1574 SPORTER – .22 WMR, .222 Rem., .22-250 Rem., .223 Rem., .243 Win., or .308 Win. cal. Mfg. by Krico (Kriegeskorte, located at Stuttgart) and distributed by Anschütz, approx. 1,000 imported during 1970-1973.

	$825	$725	$595	$540	$485	$430	$375	

Add 15% for centerfire cals.

MODEL 1807 – .22 LR cal., replacement for the Model 1407 Match 54, for I.S.U. and NRA competition, 26 in. barrel, Match 54 action, 10 lbs. Disc.

	$775	$650	$550	$450	$350	$300	$260	

RIFLES: BOLT ACTION, BIATHLON

MODEL 64R BIATHLON SPRINT – .22 LR cal., repeater, 5 shot mag., Match 64 action, 21.2 in. barrel, match trigger, hardwood stock with adj. cheekpiece and buttplate, right or left-hand action, 7.9 lbs. Imported 2004-2020.

	$2,295	$2,010	$1,725	$1,550	$1,275	$1,050	$850	*$2,695*

MODEL 1403B – .22 LR cal., Match 64 action, 21 1/2 in. barrel, blonde finished European hardwood stock with stippled pistol grip, Biathlon design allows 4 mags. to be stored in a housing attached to the forend on right side, entry level Biathlon gun, 8 1/2 lbs. Imported 1990-92.

	$850	$730	$660	$525	$450	$375	$335	*$998*

MODEL 1450B – .22 LR cal., 2000 MK action, 19 1/2 in. barrel, European hardwood with vent. forearm and adj. buttplate, aperture sights, 5 lbs. Imported 1993 only.

	$650	$550	$450	$375	$300	$260	$230	*$765*

MODEL 1827B – .22 LR cal., carries four 5 shot mags. in stock, special Biathlon features, 21 1/2 in. barrel, limited mfg.

	$1,875	$1,550	$1,225	$1,025	$895	$785	$695	*$2,457*

Add $120 for left-hand action (disc. 1989).

In 1990, the stock design was changed permitting 8 mags. to be stored in two housings attached to both the stock and forend on right side.

MODEL 1827 F (BT) FORTNER/MODEL 1827 F JUNIOR – .22 LR cal., 21.7 in. barrel, Fortner straight pull bolt action, right or left-hand action, 5 shot mag., Biathlon style stock, color laminated stock became available 1995, blue, Sprint-Nitride, or stainless barrel, 8.8 lbs. Importation began 1986.

MSR $3,995	$3,395	$2,975	$2,550	$2,310	$1,875	$1,550	$1,300	

Add $200 for Biathlon Comfort stock (new 2018).

Subtract $100 for Model 1827 F Junior (disc. 2020) or Model 1827L F Junior (left-hand variation).

In 1990, the stock design was changed permitting 8 mags. to be stored in two housings attached to the right side of the buttstock and forend.

GRADING - PPGS™	100%	98%	95%	90%	80%	70%	60%	LAST MSR

MODEL 1827 F 160TH ANNIVERSARY - .22 LR cal., Biathlon configuration, features "Anschütz/160" logo carved into stock. Limited mfg. beginning 2016.

MSR $7,995	$7,500	$6,500	$5,750	$5,000	$4,250	$3,500	$2,750	

RIFLES: BOLT ACTION MATCH, CURRENT / RECENT MFG.

These match/target models will vary somewhat in price, depending on the features, options, sights, stock options, and availability. Please contact the importers directly for current model availability and pricing. All currently produced Anschütz match rifles are delivered with a keyed security gun lock.

MODEL 1403D - .22 LR cal., improved Model 64S match rifle, single shot, no sights, adj. trigger, 8 lbs. 6 oz. Importation disc. in 1990.

	$700	$625	$550	$450	$400	$325	$275	*$700*

Add $50 for left-hand action (disc. 1988).

MODEL 1803D - .22 LR cal., Match 64 action, 25 1/2 in. target barrel, single stage adj. trigger, blond finished wood with dark stippling on pistol grip and forearm, adj. cheekpiece and buttplate, 8.6 lbs. Imported 1987-1993.

	$850	$725	$625	$525	$430	$365	$310	*$1,012*

Add $70 for left-hand action (disc. 1989).

MODEL 1808D RT/1808MS R (RUNNING TARGET) - .22 LR cal., single shot running target model, 19 (w/o barrel weights) - 32 1/2 in. barrel, adj. stock, cheekpiece, trigger, heavy beavertail forend, no sights, muzzle barrel weights, 9 1/4 lbs. Importation disc. 1998.

	$1,900	$1,450	$1,100	$950	$800	$695	$595	*$2,220*

Add $50 for left-hand action (disc. 1991).
Subtract 20% for earlier models (Model 1808D RT and Model 1808 ED-Super).

This model was previously designated Model 1808D RT from 1991-96, and also the Model 1808 ED-Super during 1990 and earlier mfg.

MODEL 1813 SUPER MATCH - .22 LR cal., top-of-the-line competition model with sophisticated adj. cheekpiece, buttplate, trigger, pistol grip, and palm rest, Super Match 54 action, stippled walnut stock with thumbhole grip, 15.4 lbs. Mfg. 1979-1988.

	$1,850	$1,600	$1,400	$1,200	$975	$875	$775	

This model previously held all the Olympic and world records. The model nomenclature was changed to Model 1913 Super Match in 1988.

MODEL 1903 - .22 LR cal., 25.4 in. barrel, right or left-hand ation, unstained walnut stock.

MSR $1,495	$1,275	$1,115	$950	$865	$700	$575	$450	

This model is also available in a Junior version with 21.4 in. barrel from Champion Choice at the same price.

MODEL 1903D - .22 LR cal., similar specifications to the Model 1803D, except has new improved target stock and adj. cheekpiece made from walnut finished European hardwood, color laminated stock mfg. 1995-1998, full-length checkering on forend and contoured pistol grip, fully adj. new style buttplate, 9.9 lbs. Imported 1990-circa 2016.

	$1,100	$995	$850	$775	$625	$525	$450	*$1,215*

Add $130 for color laminated stock (disc. 1998).

MODEL 1903 MS R - .22 LR cal., 64 action, 21.4 in. heavy blued barrel, 5 shot mag., two-stage trigger, front dovetail sight, walnut silhouette stock, 7 lbs. 11 oz. Limited mfg. 2019 only.

	$1,275	$1,115	$950	$865	$700	$575	$450	*$1,499*

MODEL 1907 - .22 LR cal., single shot Match 54 action "I.S.U." model, 26 in. button rifled barrel, prone and position shooting design, 5018 two-stage trigger, removable cheekpiece, adj. buttplate, hand stippled stock with ventilated forearm and choice of beechwood (new 1997), walnut, blond laminated (disc.), or color laminated (mfg. 1995-96) wood stock, right or left-hand action, 10 1/2 lbs.

MSR $2,895	$2,475	$2,165	$1,850	$1,685	$1,375	$1,125	$950	

Add $900 for Model 1914 variation with thumbhole walnut stock.
Add $1,400 for 1918 Precise aluminum grip.
Add $125 for quick adj. cheekpiece (disc.).
Add $125 for color laminated stock (disc.).
Add approx. $290 for benchrest model (Model 1907 BR) with walnut stock (disc. 2016).
Subtract $125 for Club Model with non-adj. stock (disc. 2016).

This model is also available with Anschütz stock no. 2213 blue laminate (Alu Color), featuring the most recent innovations in stock technology.

This variation was designated Model 1807 before 1989.

GRADING - PPGS™	100%	98%	95%	90%	80%	70%	60%	LAST MSR

MODEL 1909 – target variation of the Model 1910 Super Match II, limited importation 1997-98 only.

	$1,925	$1,550	$1,225	$1,025	$895	$785	$695	*$2,480*

MODEL 1910 SUPER MATCH II – .22 LR cal., single shot, 27 1/4 in. barrel, diopter sights, fully adj. thumbhole stock, 12 lbs., model down from the 1813 (or 1913), special order only - limited quantities imported until 1998.

	$2,150	$1,750	$1,475	$1,100	$900	$725	$625	*$2,967*

Add $149 for left-hand action.
Subtract 20% for Model 1810.

This variation was designated as Model 1810 before 1988.

MODEL 1911 PRONE MATCH – .22 LR cal., single shot match prone rifle, 27 1/4 in. barrel, beechwood stock with adj. cheekpiece, buttplate, no sights, 11.9 lbs. Disc.

	$1,865	$1,550	$1,200	$995	$925	$825	$700	

Add $99 for stainless steel barrel.
Add $100 for left-hand action (disc. 1993).
Subtract 20% for Model 1811.

This variation was designated Model 1811 before 1988.

MODEL 1912 LADIES SPORT RIFLE – .22 LR cal., designed to meet I.S.S.F. ladies competiton regulations, features 1907 barreled action w/o sights, walnut stock with shorter dimensions, 11.4 lbs. Imported 1999-2013.

	$2,690	$2,175	$1,850	$1,575	$1,350	$1,100	$975	

Add $336 for aluminum stock.
Add $135 for left-hand action.

MODEL 1913 TARGET (SUPER MATCH FREE RIFLE) – .22 LR cal., single shot, top-of-the-line match rifle, every possible refinement, international diopter sights, 27 1/4 in. button rifled barrel, handstop and palm rest, wood (disc. 2007) or blue aluminum Alu Color (new 2000) stock, right or left-hand configuration, 15 1/2 lbs.

MSR $4,395	$3,750	$3,280	$2,815	$2,550	$2,065	$1,695	$1,450	

Add $130 for stainless steel barrel (disc.circa 2016).
Subtract $1,400 for 1913A Benchrest Model with non-adj. walnut stock.

This variation was designated Model 1813 before 1988 (see separate listing).

MODEL 1918 – .22 LR cal., aluminum precision silver/black stock w/choice of grip L or M, with or w/o hook buttplate. New 2016.

MSR $2,395	$2,050	$1,795	$1,550	$1,395	$1,125	$925	$775	

MODEL 1927 – .22 LR cal., Match 54 Fortner straight pull action, 26 in. heavy tapered blued barrel, 5 shot mag., 5020 two-stage trigger, CISM style walnut stock with aluminum buttplate, delivered with hard case, satin blued receiver, 10 lbs. 1 oz. New 2018.

MSR $4,695	$3,995	$3,495	$3,000	$2,715	$2,195	$1,800	$1,400	

MODEL 2000 MK – .22 LR cal., single shot match, 26 in. barrel, aperture sights, 7 1/2 lbs. Disc. 1988.

	$340	$290	$250	$210	$180	$160	$145	*$400*

MODEL 2007 ISSF STANDARD – .22 LR cal., ISSF model, featuring 19 3/4 in. standard or heavy (new 2001) barrel with 8 in. detachable front tube allowing for different sights and counter-weights (total barrel length with tube is 27 1/4 in.), adj. cheekpiece and rubber buttplate, grooved and vented forearm, choice of blond (disc. 2000), walnut, or blue aluminum Alu Color (new 2001) stock, Match 54 action, 12 lbs. Imported 1992-2010.

	$2,525	$2,250	$1,875	$1,550	$1,325	$1,100	$965	

Add $135 for stainless steel barrel.
Add approx. $520 for Alu Color aluminum stock, right-or left-hand.

This model underwent significant engineering changes during 1994, including a heavier receiver.

MODEL 2012 LADIES SPORT RIFLE – .22 LR cal., utilizes 2007 rectangular receiver barreled action designed to meet I.S.S.F. ladies competition regulations, smaller dimensions, walnut stock, 11.4 lbs. Imported 1999-2015.

	$3,295	$2,850	$2,525	$2,100	$1,775	$1,475	$1,200	

MODEL 2013 TARGET (SUPER MATCH "SPECIAL") – .22 LR cal., Match 54 action, top-of-the-line international target rifle, 19 3/4 in. standard (disc.) or 27.1 in. heavy (new 2001) barrel with 8 in. detachable front tube allowing for different sights and counter-weights (total barrel length with tube

GRADING - PPGS™	100%	98%	95%	90%	80%	70%	60%	LAST MSR

is 27 1/4 in.), top grain walnut (disc.), color laminate (disc.), or Alu Color aluminum stock with adj. hand rest, palm rest, cheekpiece, and elaborate metal buttplate, 15.4 lbs. Importation began 1992.

MSR $5,295	$4,500	$3,950	$3,375	$3,060	$2,475	$2,025	$1,750	

This model underwent significant engineering changes during 1994.

* ***Model 2013 BR-50 (Benchrest)*** – .22 LR cal., developed especially for benchrest competition, trigger can be adjusted for either light single or two-stage action, 19.6 (disc.) or 27.1 in. barrel, uncheckered walnut stock with wide forend, 10.3 lbs. Importation began 1999.

MSR $3,895	$3,325	$2,910	$2,495	$2,250	$1,825	$1,500	$1,250	

RIFLES: BOLT ACTION, SILHOUETTE

Currently imported Anschütz silhouette rifles can vary somewhat in price, depending on the importer and inventory. All currently produced Anschütz rifles are delivered with a keyed security gun lock. Certain models may be special order only.

MODEL 54.18MS – .22 LR cal., silhouette target model, 22 in. barrel, Match 54 single shot action, walnut stock with Wundhammer swell, stippled pistol grip and forearm, no sights, 8 lbs. 6 oz. Disc. 1997.

	$1,295	$1,075	$895	$760	$650	$550	$475	*$1,579*

Add $96 for left-hand action.

This model employs the Super Match 54 action.

* ***Model 54.18MS ED*** – same action as Model 54.18MS, except has 19 1/4 in. barrel (7/8 in. diameter) with 14 1/4 in. extension tube, 3 removable muzzle weights. Disc. 1988.

	$1,075	$900	$775	$675	$575	$485	$410	*$1,215*

Add $100 for left-hand action.

MODEL 54.18MS REP – similar to Model 54.18MS, except has repeater action, 5 shot mag., regular beechwood plain stock with or w/o thumbhole, vented forend, or black, grey, or tan-green swirl synthetic stock, 7 3/4 lbs. Importation disc. circa 2016.

	$2,049	$1,750	$1,500	$1,250	$995	$875	$750	

Subtract approx. 10% if w/o thumbhole stock.

This model was introduced in 1989 with a wood stock and a retail price of $1,650.

This model features a Super Match 54 action with detachable box mag. In 1990, the stock was changed to a synthetic McMillan fiberglass finished in grey. Currently, it is available with beechwood or synthetic stock.

* ***Model 54.18MS REP Deluxe*** – deluxe version of the Model 54.18MS REP featuring Fibergrain McMillan stock with advanced thumbhole design and checkering. Imported 1990-1997.

	$2,035	$1,600	$1,275	$1,025	$915	$785	$695	*$2,450*

MODEL 54.30 160TH ANNIVERSARY MODEL – .22 LR cal. top-of-the-line target model w/full-titanium stock and "Anschütz 160" markings on forend. Limited mfg. beginning 2016-2019.

	$10,000	$8,500	$7,000	N/A	N/A	N/A	N/A	*$10,995*

MODEL 54.30 TARGET – .22 LR cal., single shot 54 Match action, 23.6 (disc. 2018) or 25.9 in. barrel, 5018 two-stage trigger, sights not included, various stock configurations, Nitride receiver, top-of-the-line Silhouette model, 10 lbs. 6 oz. New 2015.

MSR $3,895	$3,325	$2,910	$2,495	$2,260	$1,825	$1,500	$1,250	

Add $100 for Model 1907 stock w/aluminum buttplate.
Add $900 for walnut stock.
Add $1,400 for Precise black stock.
Add $1,100 Super Match 1913 walnut stock.

MODEL 64 MP R – .22 LR cal., Match 64 action, 25 1/2 in. heavy barrel, 5 shot mag., 11mm dovetail sight provision, 5098 two-stage trigger, beavertail walnut stock with adj. buttplate, accessory rail on bottom, blued finish, 8 lbs. 7 oz. Disc. 2020.

	$1,400	$1,225	$1,050	$950	$775	$650	$550	*$1,649*

MODEL 64MS/MS R – .22 LR cal., single shot (Model 64MS, disc. 1996) or 5 shot repeater (Model 64MS R), silhouette target model, 21 1/4 in. barrel, no sights, Wundhammer swell stippled pistol grip beechwood stock, adj. trigger, 8 lbs. Disc.

	$925	$800	$650	$550	$450	$350	$275	

Add $50 for left-hand action (disc.).

This variation employs a Match 64 action. R suffix nomenclature started 1997, S suffix began 2003.

GRADING - PPGS™	100%	98%	95%	90%	80%	70%	60%	LAST MSR

* ***Model 64MS - FWT*** – similar to Model 64MS, except SST, 6 1/4 lbs. Disc. 1988.

	$550	$475	$425	$350	$325	$260	$230	*$596*

MODEL 64S RIFLE – .22 LR cal., single shot, 26 in. round barrel, beavertail forearm, adj. SST, aperture sights, target stock with Wundhammer swell grip and adj. buttplate, checkered pistol grip. Imported 1963-1981.

	$475	$425	$375	$325	$285	$240	$220	

Subtract 15% if without sights (Model 64).

This model was available in left-hand or right-hand action.

MODEL 1808MS R – .22 LR cal., 5 shot repeater designed for metallic silhouette shooting, 19.2 in. barrel w/o sights, thumbhole Monte Carlo stock with grooved forearm featuring "ANSCHÜTZ" in panel scene, approx. 8 lbs. Imported 1998-2012.

	$1,695	$1,450	$1,175	$1,025	$900	$800	$700	*$1,916*

This model was distributed by Acusport Corp., Zander's Sporting Goods, Inc., and Ellett Brothers.

MODEL 2013 SUPER-MATCH FREE RIFLE (BR-50) – .22 LR cal., single shot, 20 in. heavy barrel, no sights, black synthetic stock with adj. cheekpiece and widened forend ("ANSCHÜTZ BR-50" is stenciled on sides), 15.4 lbs. Limited importation 1994-1998.

	$2,225	$1,750	$1,375	$1,050	$900	$725	$625	*$2,880*

Add $300 for colored laminated stock (mfg. 1997-98 only).

Model nomenclature changed from the BR-50 to the Model 2013 in 1997.

RIFLES: BOLT ACTION, SPORTER

All currently produced Anschütz rifles are delivered with a keyed security gun lock. Current manufactured Anschütz rifles use the following alphabetical suffixes when describing factory features and options. AV = American Varminter, D = single stage trigger, F = Fortner straight-pull action, G = threaded barrel, HB = heavy barrel, KL = folding leaf sight, KV = heavy tangent sight, L = left-hand action, MP = Multi-Purpose, R = repeater, and ST = double set trigger.

During 2014, a new soft grip stock coating became available on all current rifles in Black, Wood Green, and Wood Orange. Please contact the importer directly for pricing and availability.

MODEL 64 F – .22 LR cal., Model 64 action, 23 in. medium wt. barrel w/o sights, 5 shot mag., No. 5098 two-stage trigger, lower accessory rail on bottom and left side, blue/teal colored laminated stock w/ adj. buttplate and inserts, approx. 8 lbs. Only 25 imported 2016-2018.

	$1,125	$1,025	$875	$775	$675	$575	$450	*$1,299*

MODEL 64 MP R – .22 LR cal., repeater, 5 shot mag., 21.2 regular (disc. 2002) or 25 1/2 (new 2003) in. drilled and tapped, heavy match steel or stainless steel (mfg. 2000-2003) barrel, two-stage trigger, uncheckered walnut stained stock and beavertail forend, adj. rubber buttplate, approx. 9 lbs. Imported 1999-2020.

	$1,275	$1,115	$950	$875	$700	$575	$450	*$1,499*

Add $50 for stainless steel barrel (disc. 2003, reintroduced 2007-2009).
Add $49 for left-hand action (disc. 2006).
Subtract approx. $75 if w/o swivel rail.

* ***Model 64R Sporter Target*** – .22 LR cal., repeater, Match 64 action, two-stage match trigger, 21.4 in. match grade barrel, checkered hardwood stock, 10 shot mag., adj. buttplate and stainless steel rail, 7.7 lbs. Importated 2004-2010.

	$1,100	$950	$800	$700	$600	$500	$450	*$1,149*

This model replaced the Model 1451 Sport Target during 2004.

* ***Model 64 S BR*** – .22 LR cal., features 20 in. heavy target barrel w/o sights, 5 shot mag., two-stage match grade adj. trigger, adj. buttplate, flat beavertail hardwood stock, grooved receiver rail, drilled and tapped, 9 1/2 lbs. Imported 2006-2016.

	$1,350	$1,150	$975	$850	$725	$600	$500	*$1,539*

MODEL 1416 AV MANNERS STOCK – .22 LR cal., Type 64 action, 18 or 23 in. medium weight threaded barrel w/o sights, 5 shot mag., No. 5098 two-stage trigger, Manners T-6 synthetic stock (mixture of carbon fiber and fiberglass) w/adj. buttplate, blue metal finish, GAP camo molded in colors, 6 3/4 lbs. Mfg. 2016-2019.

	$1,525	$1,325	$1,125	$1,000	$825	$685	$550	*$1,749*

Add $100 for 18 in. barrel.

GRADING - PPGS™	100%	98%	95%	90%	80%	70%	60%	LAST MSR

MODEL 1416 AV WALNUT – .22 LR cal., Type 64 action, 18 in. medium weight threaded barrel w/o sights, 5 shot mag., No. 5098 two-stage trigger, walnut stock w/choice of standard forend, beavertail forend, thumbhole, or color laminate thumbhole stock, blue metal finish. Mfg. 2016-2020.

	$1,150	$1,040	$875	$775	$675	$575	$450	*$1,349*

Add $400 for thumbhole or laminate color thumbhole stock.

MODEL 1416D CLASSIC – same specifications as Model 1416D Custom, except straight hardwood stock. Importation Disc. 2011.

	$995	$875	$775	$750	$575	$475	$375	*$1,129*

Add $70 for left-hand action (Model 1416LD).
Add $28 for iron sights (disc. 2006).

* ***1416D Classic Heavy Barrel*** – .22 LR cal., 23 in. heavy barrel, 5 or 10 shot mag., No. 5098 two-stage trigger, no sights, checkered Monte Carlo or thumbhole walnut stock, grooved beavertail forend became standard 2005, right or left (disc. 2019) hand configuration. Mfg. 2000-2001, reintroduced 2003-2020.

	$1,025	$895	$775	$700	$625	$525	$425	*$1,199*

Add $450 for walnut thumbhole stock.

* ***1416D Heavy Barrel Threaded*** – .22 LR cal., 18 in. heavy threaded barrel, 5 or 10 shot mag., No. 5098 two-stage trigger, adj. sights, choice of classic, beavertail, thumbhole or Biathalon (w/o D suffix) stock configuration. Mfg. 2016-2018.

	$1,125	$1,025	$875	$775	$675	$575	$450	*$1,299*

Add $351 for thumbhole and skeletonized stock.

MODEL 1416D CUSTOM (LUXUS) – .22 LR cal., Match 64 action, 22 1/2 in. barrel, 5 or 10 shot mag., cam cocking system on recent mfg., checkered Monte Carlo walnut stock, folding leaf rear sight, 6 lbs. 2 oz. Importation disc. 2007.

	$715	$575	$475	$375	$300	$250	$225	*$819*

Add $40 for left-hand action.

This model utilizes the Match 64 action, and is similar to the Anschütz Model 1413 Target.

* ***Model 1416D Fiberglass*** – similar to Model 1416D Custom, except has McMillan fiberglass stock in hunter brown color with roll-over cheekpiece and checkered Wundhammer palm swell pistol grip, 5 1/4 lbs. Imported 1991 only.

	$755	$650	$575	$525	$475	$415	$365	*$842*

MODEL 1416 HB – .22 LR cal., 23 in. heavy barrrel, 5 shot mag., No. 5098 two-stage trigger, adj. sights, choice of classic walnut stock/forend, beavertail forend, or thumbhole (with or w/o color laminate). Imported 2016-2020.

	$1,075	$950	$800	$725	$595	$485	$400	*$1,249*

Add $400 for thumbhole stock.

* ***Model 1416 D/KL*** – .22 LR cal., similar to Model 1416D HB Classic, except has Monte Carlo stock with pistol grip cap and Schnabel forend, with folding leaf rear sight (KL) or w/o (D) right or left-hand action.

	$975	$850	$775	$700	$625	$525	$425	*$1,099*

MODEL 1418D – .22 LR cal., Match 64 action, Mannlicher full stock, skipline checkering, 19 3/4 in. barrel, same action as Model 1416D, 5 lbs. 5 oz. Importation disc. 1995, resumed 1998-2003.

	$915	$800	$700	$575	$495	$425	$360	*$1,014*

Add $40 for set trigger (mfg. 1985-89).

MODEL 1433D – .22 Hornet cal., special order only, Match 54 target action, Mannlicher full stock, 4 shot mag. Disc. 1986.

	$995	$840	$740	$640	$525	$425	$350	*$826*

Add 5% for set trigger (new 1985).

MODEL 1448D – .22 LR cal., Model 1451 action, 22 1/2 in. smoothbore barrel w/o sights, repeater, 5 shot mag., checkered walnut stained stock and forend. Imported 1999-2001.

	$450	$375	$300	$265	$240	$220	$200	*$349*

MODEL 1449D YOUTH – .22 LR cal., bolt action design, youth dimensions, 16 1/4 in. tapered barrel with adj. rear sight, receiver is grooved for scope mounting, 5 shot mag. with single shot adapter available, European hardwood stock, 12 1/4 in. trigger pull, 3 1/2 lbs. Imported 1990-1991 only.

	$210	$185	$165	$150	$135	$120	$110	*$249*

GRADING - PPGS™	100%	98%	95%	90%	80%	70%	60%	LAST MSR

MODEL 1451 E/R SPORTER/TARGET – .22 LR cal., single shot (Model 1451E) or 5 shot repeater (Model 1451R), Model 1451 action, sporter target model w/o front sight, 22 (new 1998) or 22 3/4 (disc. 1997) in. barrel w/o sights, stippled pistol grip wood stock and vent. forend (with or w/o beavertail), 6 1/2 lbs. Imported 1996-2001.

$435	$395	$360	$330	$300	$280	$260	*$485*

Subtract approx. $100 for Model 1451E (single shot).
Add $110 for Model 1451 Junior Super Target (single shot only).

* ***Model 1451D Classic (Super)*** – .22 LR cal., 5 shot, 22 3/4 in. barrel with front sights, grooved receiver, walnut finished straight hardwood stock, 5 lbs. Imported 1996-2001.

$335	$280	$245	$210	$175	$160	$150	*$398*

This model was designated the 1451 Super during 1996-97.

* ***Model 1451D Custom*** – similar to Model 1451D Classic, except has walnut stock with Monte Carlo cheekpiece, Schnabel forend, and sling swivels, 5 lbs. Imported 1998-2001.

$430	$395	$360	$330	$300	$280	$260	*$480*

* ***Model 1451R Sporter Target Prisma*** – .22 LR cal., entry level, 5 shot repeater, cam cocking, claw extractor, recessed bolt face, sliding safety, fully adj. stippled hardwood stock, 22 in. target barrel, grooved receiver, optional micrometer sights, 6.3 lbs. Imported 2001-2003.

$455	$415	$385	$350	$325	$300	$275	*$515*

This model was replaced by the Model 64R Sporter Target.

* ***Model 1451ST-R*** – .22 LR cal., repeater, 22 in. barrel w/o sights, 5 shot mag., drilled and tapped, cam cocking system, two-stage trigger, uncheckered walnut stained hardwood stock. Imported 1999-2001.

$435	$395	$360	$330	$300	$280	$260	*$485*

MODEL 1466D REPEATER – .22 LR cal., 24 in. tapered barrel with open sights, grooved receiver, checkered Monte Carlo walnut stock and forend. Imported 1996 only.

$660	$525	$435	$375	$315	$260	$235	*$766*

MODEL 1502D HB CLASSIC – .17 Mach 2 cal., features Model 64 bolt action, heavy barrel, 5 shot mag., SST, w/o sights, checkered walnut stock, choice of regular or grooved beavertail forend. Imported 2005-2006.

$695	$595	$550	$495	$450	$415	$385	*$790*

Add $46 for beavertail forend.

MODEL 1516D CUSTOM (LUXUS) – similar to Model 1416D, except .22 WMR cal., 4 shot mag., 6 lbs. 2 oz. Importation disc. 2003.

$630	$530	$465	$385	$335	$275	$250	*$717*

This model utilized the Match 64 action, similar to the Anschütz Model 1403 Target. In 1996, model nomenclature changed from the Model 1516D Custom to Model 1516D Luxus and during 1998, it changed back to Model 1516D Custom.

* ***Model 1516D/DCL KL Classic*** – same specifications as Model 1516D Custom, except regular hardwood stained stock, regular or heavy (new 2000) barrel. Disc. 2016

$950	$775	$650	$575	$500	$450	$400	*$1,169*

* ***Model 1516D HB Classic*** – .22 WMR cal., 23 in. heavy barrel, 4 shot mag., two-stage trigger, adj. iron sights, classic checkered walnut stock/forend or optional beavertail forend. Imported 2016-2020.

$1,075	$925	$815	$700	$600	$500	$400	*$1,249*

Add $50 for beavertail forend.

* ***Model 1516 D HB Thumbhole*** – .22 WMR cal., 23 in. heavy barrel, 4 shot mag., two-stage trigger, adj. iron sights, choice of classic skeletonized and thumbhole walnut stock/forend or colored laminate thumbhole stock. Imported 2016-2020.

$1,400	$1,200	$1,000	$875	$750	$625	$550	*$1,650*

MODEL 1517 AV MANNERS – .17 HMR cal., 18 in. threaded barrel, features Manners T6 stock with adj. buttplate and molded in GAP camo color. Mfg. 2017-2019.

$1,600	$1,365	$1,200	$995	$875	$750	$550	*$1,849*

GRADING - PPGS™	100%	98%	95%	90%	80%	70%	60%	LAST MSR

MODEL 1517D CLASSIC – .17 HMR cal., features Model 64 action with SST, 4 shot mag., checkered walnut stock with or w/o Monte Carlo cheekpiece or colored thumbhole (mfg. 2015-disc.) stock, 18 (threaded, new 2015) or 23 in. regular or heavy (disc. 2011, reintroduced 2016) barrel, 5 1/2 or 6.2 (heavy barrel) lbs. Imported 2003-2019.

$925	$825	$725	$625	$525	$425	$350	*$999*

Add $250 for left-hand action (disc. 2018).
Add $200 for beavertail forend.
Add $250 for heavy 23 in. barrel or $300 for 18 in. barrel (new 2015) - both have No. 5098 trigger group.
Add $600 for colored thumbhole stock (mfg. 2015-disc.) with 23 in. barrel.
Add $21 for Monte Carlo stock (disc. 2006).

* ***Model 1517 D HB*** – .17 HMR cal., 64 action, 23 in. heavy barrel, SST, classic (disc. 2018), beavertail (disc. 2018), walnut thumbhole, or color laminate thumhole stock, blued finish, 6 lbs. 4 oz. Imported 2016-2019.

$1,400	$1,200	$1,000	$875	$750	$625	$550	*$1,650*

Subtract approx. $350 for classic stock (disc. 2018).
Subtract $400 for beavertail forend (disc. 2018).

MODEL 1517 HB AMERICAN VARMINTER – .17 HMR cal., classic stock, 18 in. standard or threaded barrel, 4 shot mag., No. 5098 two-stage trigger, clasic walnut, walnut thumbhole, or color laminate thumbhole stock, blued finish, 5 lbs. 10 oz. Imported 2016-2019.

$1,150	$1,000	$875	$785	$635	$525	$425	*$1,349*

Add $400 for walnut or color laminate thumbhole stock and threaded barrel.

MODEL 1517 HB CLASSIC – .17 HMR cal., 23 in. barrel, No. 5098 two-stage trigger, classic stock. Imported 2016-2018.

$1,050	$925	$795	$725	$585	$475	$375	*$1,249*

MODEL 1517 MP R MULTI-PURPOSE – .17 HMR cal., 25 1/2 in. heavy match barrel, two-stage trigger, no sights, hardwood Monte Carlo stock with beavertail forend, 9 lbs. Imported 2003-2015.

$1,250	$1,100	$940	$825	$725	$625	$500	*$ 1,429*

Subtract $290 for stainless steel barrel (mfg. 2007-2008).

MODEL 1517 S-BR (SPORTER BENCHREST) – .17 HMR cal., 22 in. heavy target barrel w/o sights, repeater action, benchrest stock with wide forend, 4 shot mag., drilled and tapped, 6.6 lbs. Imported 2009-2011.

$1,450	$1,275	$1,050	$925	$800	$700	$600	*$1,639*

MODEL 1518D (LUXUS) – .22 WMR cal., otherwise similar to Model 1418D (Mannlicher stock), 4 shot mag., 5 1/2 lbs. Importation disc. 1995, reintroduced 1997, nomenclature was changed to Model 1518D in 1997, disc. 2001.

$895	$795	$675	$550	$440	$375	$325	*$987*

Add $50 for set trigger (disc. 1995).

MODEL 1532 – .222 Rem. cal., similar to Model 1433, sport model with standard checkered walnut stock and forearm, 24 in. barrel, open sights. Disc.

$895	$800	$725	$660	$600	$550	$475	

MODEL 1533 – .222 Rem. cal., open sights, same action as the Model 1532, except has checkered walnut Mannlicher stock and shorter barrel. Disc. 1994.

$1,100	$975	$875	$750	$625	$500	$400	

MODEL 1700D BAVARIAN – .22 LR, .22 WMR, .22 Hornet, or .222 Rem. cal., 24 in. barrel, 5 shot mag. or clip mag. (.22 WMR cal. only), checkered European style stock with European Monte Carlo cheekpiece and Schnabel forend, 7 1/2 lbs. Mfg. 1988-1995.

$1,165	$935	$775	$650	$550	$450	$375	*$1,364*

Add $199 for Meistergrade variation (select walnut).

MODEL 1700D FEATHERWEIGHT (FWT) – similar to Model 1700D Custom, except has matte black McMillan fiberglass stock configured like the Custom Model, 22 in. barrel, no sights, 6 1/4 lbs. Imported 1989-1995.

$1,075	$895	$775	$650	$550	$450	$375	*$1,230*

* ***Model 1700D Featherweight Deluxe*** – similar specification to the Model 1700D Featherweight, except has skip-line checkered Fibergrain synthetic stock with realistic wood grain. Imported 1990-95.

$1,235	$1,050	$875	$775	$650	$550	$450	*$1,460*

GRADING - PPGS™	100%	98%	95%	90%	80%	70%	60%	LAST MSR

MODEL 1702D HB CLASSIC - .17 Mach 2 cal., Match 54 action, 23 in. heavy barrel w/o sights, 5 shot mag., checkered walnut stock and forend, match grade single stage adj. trigger, 7.3 lbs. Imported 2005-2006.

	$1,300	$1,075	$875	$750	$650	$550	$450	*$1,512*

MODEL 1710 AV GRS SPORTER/VARMINT - .22 LR cal., 1710 HB AV barreled action, 18 in. blued or stainless steel heavy barrel, 5 shot repeating, two-stage 5110/2 trigger, GRS Sporter/Varmint stock, bottom metal and hex-keyed action screws included, 8 lbs. 12 oz. New late 2018.

MSR $2,595	$2,200	$1,925	$1,650	$1,495	$1,210	$995	$775

Add $100 for stainless steel.

MODEL 1710 AV HB CLASSIC - .22 LR cal., Match 54 bolt action repeater, 18 in. heavy threaded blued or stainless steel barrel, 5 shot, blued receiver, 5110 two-stage trigger, no sights, classic walnut stock, 7 lbs. 8 oz.

MSR $2,495	$2,125	$1,860	$1,600	$1,450	$1,175	$950	$750

Add $100 for stainless steel barrel.

MODEL 1710 CLASSIC HIGH GRADE - .22 LR cal., 23 in. stainless steel heavy barrel w/o sights, 150th Anniversary model featuring Anschütz 150 year logo carved in premium walnut stock, wood bolt handle, founder's logo in gold on trigger guard, original Germania 1901 logo on barrel, two different styles of carving/checkering, 8 lbs., limited importation 2007-2010.

	$2,300	$1,995	$1,775	$1,525	$1,350	$1,175	$950	*$2,599*

MODEL 1710D HB CLASSIC - .22 LR cal., Match 54 bolt action rifle, 23 in. regular (disc. 2003), heavy (new 1999), or heavy stainless (mfg. 2000-2003) barrel, single stage trigger, open sights (disc. 1994) or no sights, classic walnut stock, blued finish, 7 lbs. 15 oz. Disc. 1994. Importation resumed 1998.

MSR $2,295	$1,950	$1,700	$1,465	$1,325	$1,075	$885	$750

Add $100 for No. 5109 two-stage trigger (new 2016).
Add $200 for stainless steel barrel (reintroduced 2016).
Add $400 for hand-selected walnut (mfg. 2016-disc.).
Add $340 for Meistergrade (select walnut and gold etched trigger guard, disc. 1994, reintroduced 2000-2011).

This model was also available as a 2000 Signature Series - includes high polish bluing, select American black walnut, "1 of 200" and "Dieter Anschütz 2000" signature in 24Kt. gold on bottom of trigger guard, aluminum case, and dated certificate at no extra charge.

This model was designated 1422DCL Classic until 1989 when it was changed to the Model 1700D Classic with some modifications. The Model 1422DCL Classic Meistergrade was disc. 1987 - the last advertised retail price was $875. In 1998, this model was reintroduced as the Model 1710D Classic.

MODEL 1710D KL CUSTOM (1700D) - .22 LR cal., Match 54 action, 5 shot mag., 23 3/4 (new 1998) or 24 (disc. 1997) in. regular (new 1998) or heavy (disc. 1997) barrel, folding rear sight, single or two-stage trigger (Model 1710 KL, mfg. 2003, reintroduced 2007), Monte Carlo stock with roll-over cheekpiece and skipline checkering, 6 1/2-7 1/4 lbs.

MSR $2,295	$1,950	$1,700	$1,465	$1,325	$1,075	$885	$750

Add $310 for Meistergrade (select walnut and gold etched trigger guard - disc. 1996, resumed 1998-disc. 2011 w/o gold trigger guard).

This model was designated 1422D until 1989 when it was changed to the Model 1700D with some modifications. In 1996, model nomenclature changed from Model 1700D Custom to the Model 1710D Custom.

The Model 1700D Custom employs the Anschütz Match 54 action.

* ***Model 1710D KL Euro Luxus*** - .22 LR cal., 23 in. tapered barrel, single stage gold trigger, adj. iron sights, skip checkered, high-grade Monte Carlo stock with Schnabel forend, 7 lbs. 5 oz. Limited importation 2015-2018.

	$2,250	$1,975	$1,700	$1,475	$1,225	$1,000	$795	*$2,499*

MODEL 1710 HB 150th ANNIVERSARY - .22 LR cal., features laser etched 150th Anniversary emblem in stock, special engraving on top of barrel, and initials ACI intertwined on bottom of trigger guard. Imported late 2006-2011.

	$2,050	$1,825	$1,600	$1,400	$1,200	$1,000	$800	*$2,299*

MODEL 1710 HB GRS HYBRID - .22 LR cal., 1710 HB barreled action, 23 in. heavy blued or stainless (new 2019) barrel, 5 shot repeating, two-stage 5109/2 or 5110/2 (stainless) trigger, GRS Hybrid stock, bottom metal and hex-keyed action screws included, blued finish, 9 lbs. 14 oz. New 2017.

MSR $2,595	$2,200	$1,925	$1,650	$1,495	$1,210	$995	$775

Add $100 for stainless steel (new 2019).

GRADING - PPGS™	100%	98%	95%	90%	80%	70%	60%	LAST MSR

* ***Model 1710D HB GRS Hybrid*** – .22 LR cal., 1710D HB barreled action, 23 in. heavy blued barrel, 5 shot repeating, GRS Hybrid stock, bottom metal and hex-keyed action screws included, blued finish, 9 lbs. 14 oz. New 2017.

MSR $2,495	$2,125	$1,860	$1,600	$1,450	$1,175	$950	$750	

MODEL 1710 HB GRS SPORTER/VARMINT – .22 LR cal., 1710 HB barreled action, 23 in. heavy blued or stainless (new 2019) barrel, 5 shot repeating, two-stage 5109/2 trigger, GRS Sporter/Varmint stock, blued finish, 9 lbs. New 2017.

MSR $2,495	$2,125	$1,860	$1,600	$1,450	$1,175	$950	$750	

Add $100 for stainless steel (new 2019).

* ***Model 1710D HB GRS Sporter/Varmint*** – .22 LR cal., 1710 D HB barreled action, 23 in. heavy blued barrel, 5 shot repeating, 5096 SST, GRS Sporter/Varmint stock, bottom metal and hex-keyed action screws included, 9 lbs. New 2017.

MSR $2,395	$2,050	$1,795	$1,540	$1,395	$1,125	$925	$750	

MODEL 1710 HB KELBLY TRAINER /1710 HB AV KELBLY TRAINER – .22 LR cal., Match 54 bolt action repeater, 18 (threaded) or 23 in. heavy blued or stainless steel barrel, 5 shot mag., 5110 two-stage trigger, no sights, Kelbly's carbon fiber trainer stock w/black and silver flake finish, adj. cheekpiece, blued finish, 7 lbs. 15 oz. Available through the U.S. Custom Shop beginning 2019.

MSR $2,495	$2,125	$1,860	$1,600	$1,450	$1,175	$950	$750	

Add $100 for stainless steel barrel.
Add $100 for AV barreled action with 18 in. threaded barrel.

MODEL 1712 AV GRS SPORTER/VARMINT – .22 LR cal., features 1712 AV barreled action, 18 in. medium-weight blue or stainless steel (new 2019) threaded barrel, 5 shot repeating, no. 5109 two-stage trigger, no sights, GRS Sporter/Varmint stock, includes bottom metal and hex-keyed action screws, blued finish. Importation began 2017.

MSR $2,495	$2,125	$1,860	$1,600	$1,450	$1,175	$950	$750	

Add $100 for stainless steel barrel (new 2019).

MODEL 1712 AV SILHOUETTE SPORTER – .22 LR cal., Match 54 bolt action repeater, 18 in. medium-weight tapered, blued or stainless steel (new 2019) threaded barrel, counter-bored crown, 5 shot, no. 5109 two-stage trigger, no sights, Monte Carlo walnut stock, blued finish, 6 lbs. 4 oz.

MSR $2,395	$2,050	$1,795	$1,540	$1,395	$1,125	$925	$750	

Add $100 for stainless steel (new 2019).

MODEL 1712D – .22 LR cal., top-of-the-line sporter rifle with Match 54 action and deluxe walnut stock/forend. Imported 1997-1998 only.

	$1,300	$1,100	$895	$775	$650	$550	$450	*$1,495*

MODEL 1712 SILHOUETTE SPORTER – .22 LR cal., Match 54 bolt action repeater, 21.5 in. medium-weight tapered barrel, 5 shot, no. 5109 two-stage trigger, no sights, Monte Carlo walnut stock, blued finish, 7 lbs. 3 oz. Importation began 2003.

MSR $2,295	$1,950	$1,700	$1,465	$1,325	$1,075	$885	$750	

Add $310 for Meistergrade (mfg. late 2008-2011).

MODEL 1712 VARMINT 160TH ANNIVERSARY – .22 LR cal., 18 in. threaded barrel w/o sights, No. 5109 two-stage gold trigger, deluxe checkered walnut stock with adj. cheekpiece, "Anschütz/160" logo carved in stock, specially knurled bolt handle, matte blued barrel finish. 160 mfg. (8 separate variations) 2016-2020.

	$3,550	$3,000	$2,600	$2,300	$2,000	$1,750	$1,500	*$3,999*

MODEL 1713 SILHOUETTE – .17 HMR cal., 21.6 in. barrel w/o sights, Monte Carlo stock, Meistergrade features. Limited importation 2008.

	$1,775	$1,475	$1,100	$900	$800	$700	$600	*$2,199*

MODEL 1717D CLASSIC – .17 HMR cal., Match 54 action, 4 shot mag., 23 in. regular or heavy barrel, no sights, 8 lbs. Imported 2002-2011.

	$1,775	$1,575	$1,350	$1,150	$950	$800	$650	*$2,089*

Add $310 for Meistergrade (select walnut and gold etched trigger guard), disc. 2011.

MODEL 1717D KL (CUSTOM) – .17 HMR cal., Match 54 action, 23 in. barrel, no sights, Monte Carlo stock with pistol grip cap and Schnabel forend, 7.3 lbs. Imported late 2002-2011.

	$1,775	$1,575	$1,350	$1,150	$950	$800	$650	*$2,089*

Add $310 for Meistergrade (select walnut and gold etched trigger guard), disc. 2011.

* ***Model 1717 S-BR*** – .17 HMR cal., 22 in. target barrel w/o sights. Limited importation 2008.

	$1,095	$950	$825	$700	$600	$500	$425	*$1,349*

GRADING - PPGS™	100%	98%	95%	90%	80%	70%	60%	LAST MSR

MODEL 1717 SILHOUETTE SPORTER – .17 HMR cal., 21.6 in. barrel w/o sights, Monte Carlo stock with adj. LOP and two-stage trigger. Imported 2008-2011. Reintroduced 2013 only.

	$1,825	$1,550	$1,275	$1,050	$950	$825	$725	*$2,089*

Add $320 for Meistergrade (mfg. late 2008-2011).

MODEL 1700D/1720D CLASSIC – same general specifications as 1700D Custom, straight regular stock, choice of heavy (new 1999), or regular diameter barrel. Importation disc. 1991, resumed 1998, disc. 2001.

	$900	$795	$700	$625	$525	$425	$350	

Last MSR was $1,021 for the Model 1720D Classic.
Last MSR was $1,199 for the Model 1700D Classic.

Add $174 for Meistergrade variation (select walnut).

This model was designated 1522DCL until 1989 and then reintroduced as the Model 1700D with some modifications. In 1998, this model was reintroduced as the 1720D Classic. The Model 1522DCL Classic Meistergrade was disc. 1985 - the last advertised retail price was $660.

MODEL 1720D CUSTOM (1700D) – .22 WMR cal., 5 shot mag., 23 3/4 (new 1998) or 24 (disc. 1991) in. regular (new 1998) or heavy (disc. 1991) barrel, iron sights, Monte Carlo stock with skipline checkering, 6 lbs. 10 oz. to 7 1/4 lbs. Importation disc. 1991, resumed 1998, disc. 2001.

	$995	$875	$750	$650	$550	$450	$375	

Last MSR was $1,104 for the Model 1720D Custom.
Last MSR was $1,229 for the Model 1700D.

Add $174 for Meistergrade variation (select walnut).

This model was designated 1522D until 1989 and then reintroduced as the Model 1700D with some modifications. The Model 1522D Custom Meistergrade was disc. 1985 - last advertised retail price was $678. In 1998, this model was reintroduced as the 1720D Custom.

* ***Model 1700D Graphite*** – similar to Model 1700D Custom, except has McMillan black graphite reinforced stock with Monte Carlo roll-over cheekpiece, includes sling and swivels, 22 in. barrel, 7 1/4 lbs. Imported 1991-95.

	$1,130	$885	$760	$650	$550	$450	$375	*$1,299*

MODEL 1727F – .17 HMR, .22 LR (new 2016), or 17 Mach2 (new 2020) cal., straight pull Fortner repeater action, right or left-hand action, 18 (threaded, new 2016), 22, or 23 (.22 LR cal., mfg. 2016-2018) in. match grade barrel, 4 shot box mag., two-stage match trigger, checkered European walnut stock and Schnabel forend, raised cheekpiece, rubber buttplate, pistol grip. Importation began 2014.

MSR $3,895	$3,300	$2,900	$2,500	$2,250	$1,850	$1,500	$1,150	

Add $100 for 18 in. barrel.
Subtract $400 for 23 in. barrel (mfg. 2016-2018).

MODEL 1727F HB GRS – .22 LR cal., Match 54 Fortner straight pull action, 18 in. heavy tapered threaded barrel, counter-bored crown, 5 shot mag., 5020 two-stage trigger, GRS Sporter/Varmint or GRS Hybrid stock, satin blued receiver and barrel, 9.1 lbs. New 2018.

MSR $3,995	$3,400	$2,975	$2,550	$2,310	$1,875	$1,525	$1,200	

Add $100 for GRS Hybrid stock.

MODEL 1730D CLASSIC (1700D) – .22 Hornet cal., same general specifications as 1700D Custom, except regular stock and 23 1/2 (1432DCL), 5 shot, 23 3/4 regular, heavy (new 1999) - 1730D, or heavy stainless (imported 2001-2002), or 24 (1700D) in. barrel. Disc. 1994, reintroduced 1998. Disc. 2008.

	$1,575	$1,250	$975	$825	$700	$600	$500	

Last MSR was $1,395 on the Model 1700D Classic.
Last MSR was $2,269 on the Model 1730D Classic.

Add $210 for Meistergrade variation (select walnut).
Add $77 for heavy stainless barrel (disc. 2002).

This model was designated 1432D until 1987, and then reintroduced 1989 as the Model 1700D with some modifications. In 1998, this model was reintroduced as the Model 1730D Classic. This model came standard with the Anschütz Match 54 action.

MODEL 1730D KL CUSTOM (1700D) – .22 Hornet cal., 24 in. barrel, folding leaf rear sight, Monte Carlo stock with skipline checkering and rosewood grip cap, 4 shot mag., 7 3/4 lbs. Model 1432D was disc. 1987, and the Model 1700D was introduced 1989. Disc. 2008.

	$1,625	$1,300	$1,100	$900	$800	$700	$600	*$2,399*

Add $220 for Meistergrade variation (select walnut).

This model was designated 1432D until 1987 and then reintroduced 1989 as the Model 1700D with some

GRADING - PPGS™	100%	98%	95%	90%	80%	70%	60%	LAST MSR

modifications. In 1996, model nomenclature changed from the Model 1700D Custom to the Model 1730D Custom. The Model 1432D Custom Meistergrade was disc. 1986 - the last advertised retail price was $770.

The 1700D Custom came standard with the Anschütz Match 54 action.

MODEL 1733D – .22 Hornet cal., 19 3/4 in. barrel with hooded front sight, European walnut Mannlicher full stock featuring skipline checkering with rosewood Schnabel tip, 6 lbs. 6 oz. Imported 1993-95, reintroduced 1998-2002, limited mfg. through 2008.

	$1,595	$1,275	$975	$825	$700	$600	$500	*$2,069*

MODEL 1740D CLASSIC (1700D) – similar to Model 1700D Custom, except regular stock. Disc. 1994, reintroduced 1998-2006.

	$1,375	$1,125	$900	$775	$675	$575	$475	

Last MSR was $1,621.
Last MSR on the Model 1532DCL was $849.
Last MSR on the Model 1700D Classic was $1,395.

Add $274 for Meistergrade variation (select walnut).
Add $77 for heavy stainless barrel (disc. 2002).

This model was designated 1532DCL until 1987 and then reintroduced 1989 as the Model 1700D with some modifications. In 1998, this model was reintroduced as the 1740D Classic.

MODEL 1740D CUSTOM (1700D) – .222 Rem. cal., 3 shot, otherwise similar to Model 1700D Custom, except is also available with 23 3/4 in. barrel. Importation disc. 2006.

	$1,450	$1,175	$1,050	$850	$750	$650	$550	

Last MSR was $1,729.
Last MSR was $909 on the Model 1532D.

Add $270 for Meistergrade variation (select walnut).

This model was designated 1532D until 1987 and then reintroduced 1989 as the Model 1700D with some modifications. In 1996, model nomenclature changed from the Model 1700D Custom to the Model 1740D Custom. The Model 1532D MG Custom Meistergrade was disc. 1986 - the last advertised retail price was $770.

MODEL 1743D – .222 Rem. cal., Mannlicher full stock variation of the Model 1740D, 6.8 lbs. Imported 1997-2001.

	$1,225	$1,000	$850	$750	$625	$500	$400	*$1,373*

MODEL 1761 – .17 HMR, .22 WMR, or .22 LR cal., 1761 bolt action repeater, 18 (threaded, heavy) or 20 in. barrel, 5 shot mag., single stage trigger, polymer trigger guard, classic walnut or thumbhole stock, blued finish, 6.35-6.4 lbs. New 2020.

MSR $1,595	$1,350	$1,180	$1,015	$925	$750	$625	$500	

Add $100 for 18 in. threaded heavy barrel.
Add $400 for thumbhole stock.

MODEL 1761 HB MPR – .22 LR cal., 21.4 in. heavy barrel, MPR hardwood stock. New 2021.

MSR $2,095	$1,785	$1,560	$1,350	$1,225	$980	$825	$700	

MODEL 1761 HB MSR – .22 LR cal., 21.4 in. barrel, 5 shot mag., two-stage light trigger, Classic walnut stock, rubber buttplate, aluminum grooved rail on lower side, blued finish. New 2021.

MSR $2,095	$1,785	$1,560	$1,350	$1,225	$980	$825	$700	

MODEL 1770 D SPORTER – .223 Rem. cal., 22 in. medium target weight barrel with recessed target crown, detachable 3 shot box mag., SST, large bolt handle, 11mm rail is machined to the top of the action, special hardened and polished components, available in either Classic (disc. 2011), Monte Carlo (w/Schnabel forend, disc. 2011), or European style walnut stock. Approx. 7 1/4 lbs. Imported 2009-2016.

	$2,175	$1,800	$1,575	$1,275	$1,050	$900	$800	*$2,495*

MODEL 1771 D SPORTER – .17 Hornet (new 2017), .204 Ruger, .222 Rem., or .223 Rem. cal., 20 (new 2017, special order only) or 22 in. medium target weight barrel with recessed target crown, detachable 3 shot box mag., SST, large bolt handle, 11mm rail is machined to the top of the action, special hardened and polished components, choice of European style walnut or GRS laminated (new 2017) stock. Approx. 7 1/4 lbs. New 2016.

MSR $2,295	$1,950	$1,700	$1,465	$1,325	$1,075	$885	$750	

Add $100 for G-15x1 German stock.
Add $100 for 20 in. barrel (new 2017, special order only).
Add $700 for GRS laminated stock (new 2017).

GRADING - PPGS™ 100% 98% 95% 90% 80% 70% 60% LAST MSR

MODEL 1771 160TH ANNIVERSARY – .222 Rem. cal., 18 in. fluted threaded barrel w/o sights, No. 5097 single stage gold trigger, deluxe checkered walnut stock, "Anschütz/160" logo carved in stock, specially knurled bolt handle, matte blued barrel finish. 160 mfg. (8 separate variations) beginning 2016.

MSR $4,399 $3,850 $3,250 $2,775 $2,450 $2,100 $1,825 $1,650

MODEL 1780 D-FL (SPORTER) – .30-06, .308 Win., 8x57mm (European only), or 9.3x62mm (European only) cal., 21 in. hammer forged barrel with 3-dot target sights, choice of checkered classic or thumbhole deluxe walnut stock with Monte Carlo cheekpiece with or w/o camo, new proprietary action, 4 shot mag., wood bolt handle, SST, aluminum action bedding, Picatinny or Weaver rail can be added to receiver, approx. 7.1 lbs. Imported 2011-2016.

$3,100 $2,750 $2,350 $2,000 $1,750 $1,500 $1,250 *$3,495*

MODEL 1781 D CLASSIC – .30-06 or .308 Win. (new 2017, 18 1/2 in. barrel only) cal., 18 1/2 (new 2017) or 22.1 in. hammer forged barrel with 3-dot target sights, choice of checkered or thumbhole deluxe walnut stock with Monte Carlo cheekpiece, proprietary Anschütz action, 5 shot mag., wood bolt handle, SST, aluminum action bedding, Picatinny or Weaver rail can be added to receiver, approx. 7.1 lbs. Imported 2016-2018.

The last MSR in 2018 was $2,695.
Add $300 for .308 Win. cal. with 18 1/2 in. threaded barrel (new 2017, special order only).
Add $300 for German Walnut stock or $800 for thumbhole stock.

MODEL 1782 – .243 Win., 6.5 Creedmoor, .308 Win., .30-06, 8x57 IS, or 9x3x62 cal., 20.5 in. (threaded with protector) or 22.8 in. Anschutz precision barrel, steel receiver, single stage trigger, Classic or German-style walnut stock, oil finish, rubber buttpad, sling swivel studs, forend checkering, sliding safety catch, 60 degree bolt throw, barreled action milled from soild steel with integrated Picatinny rail. New 2020.

MSR $2,795 $2,375 $2,080 $1,780 $1,615 $1,300 $1,075 $875

Add $100 for German-style stock.
Add $100 for 20.5 in. threaded barrel.

ACHIEVER – .22 LR cal., 19 1/2 in. barrel, single shot, folding leaf rear sight, two-stage trigger, grooved receiver, stippled hardwood stock with vented forearm and adj. length of pull, 5 1/4 lbs. Imported 1987-1995.

$340 $280 $230 $205 $185 $165 $150 *$399*

* ***Achiever ST*** – .22 LR cal., 2000 MK single shot action, slide safety, two-stage trigger, adj. length of pull stock, target sights, approx. 6 1/2 lbs. Imported 1994.

$415 $360 $315 $260 $230 $205 $185 *$485*

DIE MEISTERMACHER – .22 LR cal., Match 54 action, top-of-the-line model, limited edition of 25 guns, select wood, extra polish on metal parts, hand-lapped barrel, with numerous gold inlays including Olympic wreath. Mfg. 1985.

$2,750 $2,000 $1,600 N/A N/A N/A N/A *$2,475*

This variation sold out in late 1988.

KADETT – .22 LR cal., youth dimensions, 22 in. barrel, 5 shot box mag., folding leaf rear sight, SST, grooved receiver, checkered hardwood stock, 5 1/2 lbs. Imported 1987 only.

$235 $200 $180 $165 $150 $135 $120 *$265*

WOODCHUCKER – .22 LR cal., similar to Model 1449D Youth, sold exclusively by R.S.R. Wholesale.

$210 $185 $165 $150 $135 $120 $110

RIFLES: SEMI-AUTO

MODEL 520/61 – .22 LR cal., 24 in. barrel, 10 shot mag., Monte Carlo stock, 6 1/2 lbs. Imported 1983.

$325 $275 $250 $195 $165 $130 $120

MARK 525 SPORTER RIFLE – .22 LR cal., 24 in. barrel, 10 shot mag., adj. rear sight, Monte Carlo stock, 6 1/2 lbs. Limited importation 1984-1995.

$550 $475 $425 $375 $300 $250 $180 *$547*

* ***Mark 525 Carbine*** – similar to Mark 525 Rifle, except has 20 in. barrel. Importation disc. 1986.

$600 $525 $450 $400 $325 $275 $200

MSR RX 22 – .22 LR cal., blowback action, 16 1/2 in. plain barrel, full-length receiver, Picatinny rail with integrated quad rail in forend, folding iron sights, forward cocking lever, folding adj. plastic stock, pistol grip, 2, 5, 10, 20, or 22 shot mag., choice of black (Black Hawk) or Desert Tan finish, ambidextrous safety, adj. trigger, approx. 7 lbs. Mfg. by ISSC in Ried, Austria 2012-2015.

$650 $550 $475 $400 $360 $330 $295 *$895*

GRADING - PPGS™	100%	98%	95%	90%	80%	70%	60%	LAST MSR

MSR RX PRECISION – .22 LR cal., blowback action, 16 1/2 in. plain barrel, full-length receiver, Picatinny rail with folding iron sights, forward cocking lever, 10 shot mag., choice of aluminum anodized or flat black receiver, ambidextrous safety, skeletonized non-folding wood buttstock painted gray, Competition Model has 11 mm prism rail and buttplate carrier with rubber buttplate, pistol grip, adj. trigger, approx. 7 lbs. Mfg. by ISSC in Ried, Austria 2012-2015.

$750	$625	$525	$450	$400	$350	$325	*$995*

SHOTGUNS: O/U

Anschütz marked O/U shotguns were manufactured by Miroku of Japan and distributed in Germany only. Several grades of these shotguns were manufactured and while rarely seen in the U.S., values approximate other Miroku O/Us of similar quality and features ($650-$1,000 assuming 95% or better condition).

ANTREG

Current manufacturer of semi-auto pistols, semi-auto rifles, and accessories located in Vyskov, Czech Republic. No current U.S. importation.

Please contact the company directly for information on models, pricing, and U.S. availability.

ANZIO IRONWORKS CORP.

Current manufacturer established during 2000, located in St. Petersburg, FL. Anzio Ironworks specializes in large bore bolt action rifles and has also been making gun parts and accessories since 1994. Dealer and consumer sales.

For individual model listings, please go to BlueBookOfGunValues.com/overflow.

APACHE

Previous trademark manufactured by Ojanguren Y Vidosa located in Eibar, Spain.

PISTOLS: SEMI-AUTO

SEMI-AUTO – 6.35mm cal., clip fed magazine.

$225	$190	$160	$140	$120	$95	$75

ARCHER MANUFACTURING

Previous AR-15 style rifle and pistol manufacturer located in Hutto, TX from 2015-2018.

Please refer to BlueBookOfGunValues.com to order the *Blue Book of AR-15s & Variations*, available as a book or online subscription.

ARCHON FIREARMS

Currrent semi-auto pistol manufacturer located in Las Vegas, NV.

PISTOLS: SEMI-AUTO

TYPE B – 9mm Para. cal., AF-Speedlock actuated short recoil operation system, striker fired, 4.29 in. match grade barrel, 15 shot double stack mag., integrated flared magwell, flat-faced short reset metal trigger, serrated rear sight with front fiber optic sight, proprietary grip mapping textured frame with beavertail, trigger block, firing pin safety block, lower Picatinny accessory rail, Glock standard sight dovetails, front and rear slide serrations, black Nitride finish (FDE PVD coating available), comes standard with Archon Firearms Malterra range bag and 4 factory magazines, 29.6 oz. New 2017.

MSR $892	$785	$685	$600	$525	$450	$375	$300

Add $52 for FDE slide (new 2019).
Add $101 for night sights (new 2019).

ARCUS CO.

Current trademark of handguns manufactured in Bulgaria. Previously imported by Century International Arms, located in Delray Beach, FL 2005-2015, in Boca Raton, FL 2000-2005, and by Miltex, Inc., located in Waldorf, MD until 2000. No current U.S. importation.

PISTOLS: SEMI-AUTO

MODEL 94/94 COMPACT – 9mm Para. cal., SA or DA (disc. 2000), 4 (compact), 4 3/4 or 5 1/4 (disc. 2000) in. barrel, 10 shot mag., choice of blue (disc.), two-tone, or silver matte (disc.) metal finish, rubber or molded synthetic (disc. 2000) grips, 32-35 oz. Imported 1998-2000, reimported 2003-2008.

$335	$285	$225	$200	$180	$160	$150

MODEL 98DA/98DAC – 9mm Para. cal., DA/SA, blue or duo-tone finish, 10, 13, or 15 shot mag., soft rubber grips with finger grooves, 32 oz. Limited importation 2002-2015.

$390	$340	$295	$265	$215	$190	$175

GRADING - PPGS™	100%	98%	95%	90%	80%	70%	60%	LAST MSR

ARDESA

Current manufacturer located in Vizcaya, Spain. No current U.S. importation.

Ardesa manufactures good quality centerfire external hammer design rifles and single shot shotguns under the Outfitter name. Centerfire rifles utilize Lothar Walther barrels, and come in a variety of configurations. Ardesa has manufactured muzzleloading rifles for over 30 years, and these are imported by Traditions. Ardesa is also a large European distributor for Merkel, Haenel, Fabarm, Caracal, Taurus, and Accuracy International firearms, in addition to optics and ammunition. Please contact the factory directly for more information, including pricing and U.S. availability of Ardesa firearms.

ARES DEFENSE SYSTEMS INC.

Please refer to Fightlite Industries located in the F section.

AREX

Current semi-auto pistol manufacturer located in Slovenia. Currently imported by Global Ordnance, LLC of Sarasota, FL beginning 2020. Previously imported by FIME Group, LLC of Las Vegas, NV from 2016-2019.

PISTOLS: SEMI-AUTO

REX ALPHA – 9mm Para. cal., SA/DA, 5 in. barrel, three 17 shot steel mags., flared magwell, extended mag. release, steel frame and slide, fully adj. black rear sight, fiber optic front sight, black checkered polymer or dimpled aluminum red or blue anodized grips (new 2020), ambi safety levers, undercut trigger guard, ext. beavertail backstrap, compact cleaning kit, black Nitride finish, 8.9 in. OAL, 39 oz. New 2018.

MSR $1,080	$925	$800	$700	$625	$500	$425	$325

REX DELTA – 9mm Para. cal., striker fired operation, 4 in. barrel, one 15 shot and 17 shot mag., polymer frame, Nitrocarburized steel slide, low profile steel sights, textured grip, ambi controls, forward cocking serrations, interchangeable backstraps, takedown w/o trigger pull, black finish, 7 in. OAL, 19.1 oz. New 2019.

MSR $399	$340	$300	$250	$225	$175	$150	$125

Add $50 for AnR Design IWB Holster package.

REX DELTA GEN.2 – 9mm Para. cal., striker fired operation, compact (Gen2.M) or full size (Gen.2 L and X) polymer frame, 4 (Gen.2 M or Gen.2 X) or 4.5 (Gen.2 L) in. barrel, 15 (Gen.2M only), 17, and 19 (Gen2 L and X) shot mag., flared magwell, Nitrocarburized steel slide, low profile steel sights, optional optics ready (OR) slide w/interchangeable sight plates, non-slip stippled textured grip, ambi controls, forward cocking serrations, interchangeable backstraps, takedown w/o trigger pull, black finish, 17.9-21 oz. New 2021.

Please contact the manufacturer/importer directly for price and availability.

* ***REX Delta Gen.2X*** – 9mm Para. cal., striker fired operation, 4 in. barrel, one 17 shot and 19 shot mag., flared magwell, full size polymer frame, Nitrocarburized compact steel slide, low profile steel sights, optional optics ready (OR) slide w/interchangeable sight plates, non-slip stippled textured grip, ambi controls, forward cocking serrations, interchangeable backstraps, takedown w/o trigger pull, black finish, 7.2 in. OAL, 17.9-19.0 oz. New 2021.

Retail pricing was not available for this model.

REX ZERO 1S (STANDARD) – 9mm Para., .40 S&W (disc. 2020), or .32 Auto (disc. 2020) cal., SA/DA, 4 1/4 in. cold hammer forged barrel, two 17 shot mags., ambi mag. release button, aluminum frame, steel slide, external hammer, large trigger guard, white dot iron sight, ambi manual safety, decocking lever, front cocking serrations, loaded chamber indicator, extended Picatinny accessory rail, hardcoat anodized black, FDE (new 2017), or ODG (new 2017) finish or nickel-plated (new 2017) or nickel-plated two-tone finish (new 2017), 1.78 lbs. New 2016.

MSR $670	$575	$500	$425	$400	$325	$275	$200

REX ZERO 1 CP (COMPACT) – 9mm Para. cal., SA/DA, 3.85 in. cold hammer forged barrel, two 15 shot mags., compact aluminum frame, compact steel slide, 3-dot sights, textured black polymer grips, ambi manual safety, decocking lever, full-length dust cover with integral Picatinny accessory rail, hardcoat anodized black or FDE (new 2020) finish, includes hard case, 1.57 lbs. New 2016.

MSR $670	$575	$500	$425	$400	$325	$275	$200

REX ZERO 1T /1TC (TACTICAL/TACTICAL COMPACT) – 9mm Para. cal., SA/DA, 4.5 (1TC, new 2018) or 4.9 in. threaded barrel, two 17 or 20 shot mags., aluminum frame, steel slide, external hammer, large trigger guard, suppressor height white dot steel sights, Arex ROR system (Rex Optics Ready - 4 plates for optics attachment), ambi external safety and mag. release, can be operated either cocked and locked or safely de-cocked for DA/SA operation, forward cocking serrations, loaded chamber indicator, Picatinny railed dust cover, full-length slide rails, includes hard polymer case, cable padlock, operating manual, hardcoat anodized black, FDE, OD Green (1TC, new 2018), or Smoke Grey (ITC, new 20018) finish. New 2017.

MSR $870	$750	$650	$575	$500	$425	$350	$275

GRADING - PPGS™	100%	98%	95%	90%	80%	70%	60%	LAST MSR

ARISAKA

Please refer to Japanese Military in the J section.

ARIZONA ARMORY

Current AR-15 style rifle manufacturer located in Phoenix, AZ since 2007.

Please refer to BlueBookOfGunValues.com to order the *Blue Book of AR-15s & Variations*, available as a book or online subscription.

ARLINGTON ORDNANCE

Previous importer located in Westport, CT until 1996. Formerly located in Weston, CT.

RIFLES/CARBINES: SEMI-AUTO

M1 GARAND RIFLE – .30-06 cal., imported from Korea in used condition, various manufacturers, with import stamp. Imported 1991-96.

	100%	98%	95%	90%	80%	70%	60%	LAST MSR
	$825	$750	$675	$550	$500	$475	$450	

Add $40 for stock upgrade (better wood).

* ***Arsenal Restored M1 Garand Rifle*** – .30-06 or .308 Win. cal., featured new barrel, rebuilt gas system, and reinspected components. Imported 1994-1996.

	100%	98%	95%	90%	80%	70%	60%	LAST MSR
	$850	$700	$650	$600	$575	$550	$500	

Add 5% for .308 Win. cal.

TROPHY GARAND – .308 Win. cal. only, action was original Mil-Spec, included new barrel and checkered walnut stock and forend, recoil pad. Imported 1994-1996.

	100%	98%	95%	90%	80%	70%	60%	LAST MSR
	$925	$825	$725	$675	$575	$525	$475	*$695*

T26 TANKER – .30-06 or .308 Win. cal., included new barrel and other key components, updated stock finish. Imported 1994-1996.

	100%	98%	95%	90%	80%	70%	60%	LAST MSR
	$850	$700	$650	$600	$575	$550	$500	

.30 CAL. CARBINE – .30 Carbine cal., 18 in. barrel, imported from Korea in used condition, various manufacturers, with import stamp. Imported 1991-1996.

	100%	98%	95%	90%	80%	70%	60%	LAST MSR
	$725	$650	$575	$525	$475	$425	$400	

Add approximately $55 for stock upgrade (better wood).

MODEL FIVE CARBINE – while advertised, this model never went into production.

ARMALITE

Previous manufacturer of AR-15 style rifles and other firearms located in Costa Mesa, CA, approx. 1954-circa 1980s.

RIFLES: SEMI-AUTO

AR-7 EXPLORER – .22 LR cal., 16 in. aluminum barrel with steel liner, aperture rear sight, takedown action and barrel store in hollow plastic stock in either brown (rare), black, or multi-color, gun will float, designed by Gene Stoner, mfg. 1959-73 by Armalite, 1973-90 by Charter Arms, 1990-97 by Survival Arms located in Cocoa, FL, and by AR-7 Industries, LLC, located in Meriden, CT, 1998-2004. Current mfg. beginning 1997 by Henry Repeating Arms Co. located in NJ.

	100%	98%	95%	90%	80%	70%	60%	LAST MSR
Black/Multi-color stock	$400	$375	$325	$275	$250	$215	$190	
Brown stock	$550	$500	$450	$375	$325	$260	$220	

Some unusual early Costa Mesa AR-7 variations have been observed with ported barrels, extendable wire stock, hooded front sight, and hollow pistol grip containing a cleaning kit, perhaps indicating a special military contract survival weapon.

AR-7 CUSTOM – similar to AR-7 Explorer, only with custom walnut stock including cheekpiece, pistol grip. Mfg. 1964-70.

	100%	98%	95%	90%	80%	70%	60%	LAST MSR
	$325	$300	$265	$235	$200	$190	$180	

AR-10 – 7.62 NATO cal., GIO, select-fire machine gun, originally designed by Eugene Stoner, 20.8 in. barrel, rotating bolt locks into barrel extension (not receiver), 20 shot detachable mag., hinged aluminum upper and lower receiver, non-detachable carry handle designed to protect top of receiver charge lever, approx. 7 1/2 lbs. Approx. 50 were mfg. circa 1957 by ArmaLite in California (aka Hollywood Model). Approx. 9,900 mfg. for military contracts under ArmaLite licensing agreement to Artillerie Inrichtingen, Holland. Mfg. 1957-1960.

Values for these select-fire rifles depend on originality, condition, and desirability of features and military contract.

AR-15 – .223 Rem. (prototype cals. were also mfg.), GIO, scaled down version of the AR-10, select-fire machine gun, 20 in. barrel, bolt locks into barrel extension, 20 shot detachable mag., hinged aluminum upper and lower receiver, charging handle on top of receiver (early ArmaLite mfg.) or pull handle in

GRADING - PPGS™	100%	98%	95%	90%	80%	70%	60%	LAST MSR

back of receiver (Colt mfg.), with or w/o forward bolt assist on military contracts, approx. 6 1/2 lbs. Less than 20,000 mfg. circa 1958-1963.

Values for these select-fire rifles depend on year of manufacture, originality, and condition.

This model was the final predecessor of the M16 select-fire machine gun introduced during 1964.

AR-180 – .223 Rem. cal., GPO, 18 1/4 in. barrel, folding stock. Manufactured by Armalite in Costa Mesa, CA, 1969-1972, Howa Machinery Ltd., Nagoya, Japan, 1972 and 1973, and by Sterling Armament Co. Ltd., Dagenham, Essex, England.

Sterling Mfg.	**$1,795**	**$1,050**	**$875**	**$625**	**$550**	**$475**	**$425**	
Howa Mfg.	**$2,125**	**$1,325**	**$995**	**$675**	**$595**	**$525**	**$475**	
Costa Mesa Mfg.	**$2,125**	**$1,325**	**$995**	**$675**	**$595**	**$525**	**$475**	

SHOTGUNS: SEMI-AUTO

AR-17 – 12 ga., 24 in. barrel, interchangeable choke tubes, recoil operated, high strength aluminum barrel and receiver, plastic stock and forearm, either gold anodized or black finish. Only 2,000 mfg. 1964-65.

$975 $895 $795 $725 $650 $550 $475

ARMALITE, INC.

Current manufacturer of AR-15 style rifles, pistols, and other firearms and accessories, located in Phoenix, AZ. Previously located in Geneseo, IL until 2018.

New manufacture of firearms under the Armalite, Inc. name began in 1996 after Mark Westrom purchased the ArmaLite trademarks. In July of 2013, Armalite, Inc. was purchased by Strategic Armory Corps. The ArmaLite trademark was originally used by Armalite (no relation to current ArmaLite, Inc.) during manufacture in Costa Mesa, CA, approx. 1959-1973 (see Armalite listing). Dealer and distributor sales.

For Eagle Arms branded/manufactured carbines/rifles, please refer to the Eagle Arms listings in the E section.

PISTOLS: SEMI-AUTO

AR-10 PISTOL – 7.62x51mm/.308 Win. cal., GIO, 13.9 in. black Cerakote finished stainless steel barrel, carbine length gas system, 20 shot Magpul PMAG, two-stage precision trigger, pistol stabilizing arm brace, folding receiver extension, 12 in. aluminum tactical KeyMod handguard, Magpul K2 pistol grip, Raptor ambi charging handle, Mil-Std 1913 Picatinny upper rail, 8.8 lbs. Mfg. 2015-2017.

$2,425 $2,150 $1,875 $1,650 $1,425 $1,150 $925 *$2,699*

AR-19 PISTOL – 9mm Para. cal., blowback operation, 8 1/2 in. barrel, Armalite 9mm Tac Brake, accepts 9mm Glock mags., billet receiver, CMC trigger, Magpul MBUS sights, Shockwave Blade pistol brace, 7 in. free float M-LOK handguard, Magpul MOE grips, black finish, 5.4 lbs. New 2021.

MSR $1,113 $1,000 $875 $775 $675 $600 $475 $375

AR-24 (ULTIMATE) – 9mm Para. cal., full size (AR-24-15 w/4.67 in. barrel) or compact (AR-24K-13 w/3.89 in. barrel) frame, DA/SA, 10, 13 (compact only), or 15 shot mag., 3-dot sights with fixed or adj. rear sight, black parkerized finish, checkered polymer grips, includes case and two magazines, 35 oz. Mfg. by Sarzsilmaz in Turkey. Imported 2007-2013.

$495 $435 $365 $315 $275 $250 $230 *$550*

Add $81 for Model AR-24-10C/15C Combat/Tactical Custom pistol with C-suffix (full or compact size), adj. rear sight and checkered grip straps.

AR-24-15 – 9mm Para. cal., DA/SA, full size frame, 4.67 in. barrel, all steel construction, 15 shot mag., 3-dot sights with fixed or adj. rear sight, black parkerized finish, checkered polymer grips, serrated front and back strap, includes case and two magazines, 35 oz. Mfg. by Sarzsilmaz in Turkey. Imported 2007-2013.

$495 $435 $365 $315 $275 $250 $230 *$550*

* ***AR-24-15C Combat Custom*** – 9mm Para. cal., similar to AR-24-15, except has fully adj. rear sight, checkered front and back strap. Mfg. by Sarzsilmaz in Turkey. Imported 2007-2013.

$500 $450 $400 $350 $310 $270 $255 *$631*

AR-24K-13 COMPACT – 9mm Para. cal., similar to AR-24-15, except has 3.89 in. barrel and 13 shot mag., approx. 31 oz. Mfg. by Sarzsilmaz in Turkey. Imported 2007-2013.

$495 $435 $365 $315 $275 $250 $230 *$550*

Add $81 for Model AR-24-10C/15C Combat/Tactical Custom pistol with C-suffix (full or compact size), adj. rear sight and checkered grip straps.

* ***AR-24K-13C Combat Custom Compact*** – 9mm Para. cal., similar to AR-24K-13, except has fully adj. rear sight, checkered front and back strap, 13 shot mag., 32 oz. Mfg. by Sarzsilmaz in Turkey. Imported 2007-2013.

$550 $480 $415 $350 $310 $270 $255 *$631*

GRADING - PPGS™	100%	98%	95%	90%	80%	70%	60%	LAST MSR

M-15 PISTOL – 5.56 NATO cal., GIO, 6 or 11 1/2 in. double lapped chrome-lined barrel with flash suppressing compensator, 20 shot Magpul PMAG, two-stage precision trigger, pistol stabilizing arm brace, folding receiver extension, light contour aluminum KeyMod handguard (5 in. handguard on 6 in. barrel), Raptor ambi charging handle, Mil-Std 1913 Picatinny upper rail, 6 lbs. Mfg. 2015-2017.

	$1,875	$1,675	$1,450	$1,275	$1,125	$900	$725	*$2,099*

Add $150 for 11 1/2 in. barrel.

RIFLES: BOLT ACTION

AR-30(M) – .300 Win. Mag., .308 Win., or .338 Lapua Mag. cal., scaled down AR-50 action, 26 in. chrome moly barrel, optional muzzle brake, 5 shot detachable mag., Shilen modified SST, 12 lbs. Mfg. 2003-2012.

	$1,850	$1,575	$1,350	$1,125	$1,000	$900	$800	*$2,021*

Add $140 for .338 Lapua Mag. cal.

AR-30A1 STANDARD – .300 Win. Mag. or .338 Lapua Mag. cal., 24 or 26 in. chrome moly barrel with muzzle brake, modified octagonal receiver, metal standard fixed stock, SST, 12.8-13.4 lbs. Mfg. 2013-2017.

	$2,900	$2,550	$2,175	$1,975	$1,600	$1,300	$1,025	*$3,264*

Add $140 for .338 Lapua Mag. cal.

* ***AR-30A1 Target*** – .300 Win. Mag. or .338 Lapua cal., Target configuration, 26 in. chrome moly barrel with muzzle brake, 5 shot mag., fixed buttstock with adj. cheekpiece, steel V-block bedding system, SST, 15.4 lbs. Mfg. 2013-2020.

	$3,125	$2,735	$2,350	$2,125	$1,725	$1,400	$1,095	*$3,460*

Add $139 for .338 Lapua cal.

AR-31 – .308 Win. cal., 18 (disc. 2017) or 24 in. double lapped chrome moly barrel with muzzle brake, 10 shot mag. (accepts AR-10B double stack mags.), SST, detachable sight rail and accessory rails, adj. stock, Hogue pistol grip, matte black finish, 14 lbs. New 2014.

MSR $2,200	$1,875	$1,650	$1,400	$1,275	$1,025	$850	$725	

* ***AR-31 Target*** – 7.62 NATO/.308 Win. cal., short action, 18 in. double lapped chrome moly barrel with muzzle brake, accepts Armalite's AR-10B double-stack mags., SST, adj. buttstock and cheekpiece, 12 1/2 lbs. Mfg. 2017 only.

	$3,125	$2,735	$2,350	$2,125	$1,725	$1,400	$1,095	*$3,460*

AR-50A1 (AR-50) – .50 BMG or .416 Barrett (mfg. 2013-2014, AR-50A1B-416) cal., single shot bolt action, right or left (disc. 2009) hand octagonal action, 30 in. tapered barrel, muzzle brake, bolt w/triple front locking lugs and Sako style extractor, SST, no sights, skeletonized aluminum chassis, removable stock w/adj. cheekpiece and recoil pad, black finish, approx. 34 lbs. New 1999.

MSR $3,359	$3,195	$2,925	$2,600	$2,400	$2,175	$2,000	$1,875	

Add $420 for left-hand action (disc. 2013).

During 2004, this model was produced with a special commemorative stamp notation on the left side of the receiver.

AR-50A1 NATIONAL MATCH – .50 BMG cal., similar to AR-50A1, except features 33 in. chrome moly fluted National Match barrel, right or left-hand action, also includes ArmaLite Skid System, 33.6 lbs. Mfg. 2013-2017.

	$3,800	$3,325	$2,850	$2,575	$2,100	$1,725	$1,325	*$4,230*

RIFLES: SEMI-AUTO

All ArmaLite AR-15 style semi-auto rifles have a limited lifetime warranty. Some previously manufactured models had stainless steel barrels and NM triggers at an additional charge. Descriptions and pricing are for currently manufactured models.

Beginning 2009, a forward bolt assist became standard on all AR-10A4 upper receivers.

Add $99-$228 for A4 carry handle assembly.

Add $150 for 100% Realtree Hardwoods or Advantage Classic camo finish (disc.).

AR-10 SERIES – various configurations, GIO, with or w/o sights and carry handle, choice of standard green, black (new 1999), or camo (disc.) finish, supplied with two 10 shot mags. (until 2004), current mfg. typically ships with one 10 round and one 20 round mag., during 2014, several variations of the AR-10 Series now accept third party polymer mags., two-stage NM trigger became standard during 2008. New late 1995.

* ***AR-10A2 Rifle (Infantry)*** – .243 Win. (disc. 2003) or 7.62 NATO cal., GIO, 20 in. chrome-lined barrel with flash suppressor, forged A2 style upper with forward assist and A2 front sight, forged lower with tactical two-stage trigger, carry handle, Hi-Cap stock, Black or Green finish, includes one 10 shot mag., one 20 shot mag., sling, and hard case, 9.2 lbs. Disc. 2013.

	$1,425	$1,250	$1,100	$950	$825	$675	$550	*$1,583*

GRADING - PPGS™	100%	98%	95%	90%	80%	70%	60%	LAST MSR

* ***AR-10A2 Carbine*** – 7.62 NATO cal., GIO, 16 in. barrel with flash suppressor, forged A2 style upper with forward assist and A2 front sight, forged lower receiver, tactical two-stage trigger, 6-pos. collapsible stock with extended tube, Black or Green finish, includes one 10 shot mag., one 20 shot mag., sling, and hard case, 9 lbs. Disc. 2013.

$1,425	$1,250	$1,100	$950	$825	$675	$550	*$1,583*

Add $74 for 4-way quad rail on front of forearm (mfg. 2004-2008).

* ***AR-10A4 Rifle SPR - Special Purpose Rifle*** – .243 Win. (disc. 2003, reintroduced 2011-2013, black only) or 7.62 NATO cal., GIO, 20 in. chrome-lined barrel with flash suppressor, forged flat-top upper receiver with Picatinny rail and gas block, forward assist, forged lower with tactical two-stage trigger, removable front sight, A2 stock, black (BF) or Green (F, disc. 2013) finish, includes one 10 shot mag., one 20 shot mag. (disc. 2014), sling, and hard case, 8.9 lbs. Disc. 2016.

$1,425	$1,250	$1,100	$950	$825	$675	$550	*$1,571*

Add $35 for permanently affixed muzzle brake (10A4BF-2, new 2013).

* ***AR-10A4 Carbine*** – 7.62 NATO cal., similar to AR-10A4 SPR Rifle, except has 16 in. barrel, mid-length handguard, and 6-pos. collapsible stock with Mil-Spec buffer tube, 7.8 lbs. Disc. 2014.

$1,425	$1,250	$1,100	$950	$825	$675	$550	*$1,571*

Add $414 for SIR System (Selective Integrated Rail System, mfg. 2004-2006).

* ***AR-10A4 Mod 1*** – .308 Win. cal., GIO, 16 in. barrel with flash suppressor, forged one-piece upper receiver/rail system with detachable side and bottom rails, two-stage tactical trigger, collapsible tube stock with pistol grip, black finish and furniture.

While this model was advertised during 2012, it never went into production.

* ***AR-10A2 Carbine (AR-10A4 Tactical Carbine)*** – 7.62 NATO/.308 Win. cal., GIO, 16 in. double lapped chrome-lined chrome moly barrel with flash suppressor, 20 shot Magpul PMAG, two-stage tactical trigger, forged aluminum A4 flat-top upper receiver with Picatinny rail and detachable carry handle, A2 front sight, aluminum handguard tube, 6-pos. collapsible stock, 9 lbs. Mfg. 2014-2017.

$1,425	$1,250	$1,100	$950	$825	$675	$550	*$1,571*

* ***AR-10A4243BF*** – .243 Win. cal., 20 in. match grade chrome moly barrel, two-stage tactical trigger, anodized aluminum lower receiver, forged flat-top upper receiver with Picatinny gas block, forward assist, fixed polymer stock, includes one 5 shot and one 10 shot mag., sling, 9 lbs. Disc. 2013.

$1,425	$1,250	$1,100	$950	$825	$675	$550	*$1,571*

* ***AR-10B Rifle*** – .308 Win. cal., patterned after the early Armalite AR-10 rifle, GIO, featuring tapered M16 handguards, pistol grip, distinctive charging lever on top inside of carry handle (cannot be used to mount sighting devices), original brown color, 20 in. barrel, 9 1/2 lbs. Mfg. 1999-2008.

$2,100	$1,850	$1,600	$1,450	$1,150	$950	$750	*$1,698*

* ***AR-10A Carbine (A10A4CBF/CF)*** – 7.62 NATO/.308 Win. cal., 16 in. double lapped chrome-lined chrome moly threaded barrel with flash suppressor, two-stage tactical trigger, anodized aluminum lower receiver, forged flat-top upper receiver with Picatinny rail and forward assist, 6-pos. collapsible stock, 20 shot Magpul PMAG, standard 8 in. handguard, Picatinny rail gas block, matte black (CBF) or green (CF, disc. 2014) finish, 7 3/4 lbs. Mfg. 2013-2017.

$1,400	$1,250	$1,100	$950	$825	$675	$550	*$1,571*

* ***AR-10 B Series Carbine*** – 7.62 NATO/.308 Win. cal., mid-length gas system, 16 in. double lapped chrome moly threaded barrel, flash suppressor, 20 shot mag., front sight base, tactical two-stage trigger, 8 in. handguard, forged aluminum lower and flat-top upper with Picatinny rail, charging handle, 6-pos. collapsible stock, black anodized finish, 7.6 lbs. Disc. 2017.

$1,400	$1,250	$1,100	$950	$825	$675	$550	*$1,571*

* ***AR-10 National Match*** – 7.62 NATO cal., GIO, 20 in. stainless steel match barrel with stainless A2 flash suppressor, forged flat-top upper receiver with Picatinny rail and forward assist, NM quad rail free float handguard, detachable carry handle, forged lower with two-stage NM trigger, 10 shot mag., Mil-Std 1913 rail handguard, extended elevation NM sights, includes two 20 shot mags., USMC sling, black hard case, 11 1/2 lbs. Mfg. 2009-2013.

$2,125	$1,875	$1,650	$1,450	$1,250	$1,025	$825	*$2,365*

AR-10SOF (SPECIAL OPERATION FORCES) CARBINE – .308 Win. cal., GIO, available in either A2 or A4 configurations, fixed tube stock, 16 in. barrel, black finish only. Mfg. 2003-2004.

$1,350	$1,200	$1,050	$925	$800	$650	$525	*$1,503*

Add $52 for A2 configuration (includes Picatinny rail).

GRADING - PPGS™	100%	98%	95%	90%	80%	70%	60%	LAST MSR

* ***AR-10T Carbine (10TCBNF, Navy Model)*** – 7.62 NATO cal., 16 in. triple lapped stainless barrel with A2 flash suppressor, forged flat-top upper with Picatinny rail and forward assist, Picatinny gas block, round mid-length free floating handguard, forged lower with two-stage NM trigger, Hi-Cap stock, Black finish, includes two 10 shot mags. and hard case, 8 1/2 lbs. Mfg. 2004-2012.

	$1,725	**$1,525**	**$1,325**	**$1,175**	**$1,025**	**$825**	**$675**	***$1,914***

* ***AR-10T Rifle*** – .243 Win. (mfg. 1995-2003, and 2009-2010), .260 Rem. (new 2009-2013), .300 RSAUM (mfg. 2004-2008, Ultra Mag. Model), 7mm-08 Rem. (mfg. 2009-2010), .338 Federal (mfg. 2009-2013), or 7.62 NATO cal., GIO, features 20 (7.62 NATO), 22 (.338 Federal or .260 Rem., disc. 2013), or 24 (disc. 2008) in. stainless steel heavy match barrel, two-stage NM trigger, flat-top receiver with Picatinny rail, w/o sights or carry handle, black fiberglass (disc. 2008) or aluminum handguard tube, fixed A2 buttstock, A2 pistol grip, forward bolt assist became standard in 2009, Green (disc. 2013) or Black finish, includes one (new 2014) or two (disc. 2013) 10 shot mags. and hard case, 9 1/2-10 1/2 lbs. Disc. 2017.

	$1,475	**$1,300**	**$1,150**	**$1,000**	**$875**	**$700**	**$575**	***$1,649***

Add $80 for .338 Federal cal. (disc. 2013).
Add $214 for .300 RSUM cal. (disc. 2008).
Add $250 for Lothar Walther barrel (disc.).

* ***AR-10B Target (10TBNF/NF)*** – .308 Win. cal., 20 in. triple lapped stainless steel match grade barrel, forged flat-top receiver, NM two-stage trigger, Picatinny rail gas block, fixed polymer stock, free float handguard, pistol grip, 10 shot mag., hard anodized matte black (BNF) or green (NF, disc. 2013) finish, 10.3 lbs. Disc. 2015.

	$1,475	**$1,525**	**$1,325**	**$1,175**	**$1,025**	**$825**	**$675**	***$1,914***

AR-10 SASS – .260 Rem. or .308 Win. cal., 20 in. barrel, 25 shot mag., black or brown finish. Mfg. 2017 only.

	$3,150	**$2,775**	**$2,425**	**$2,150**	**$1,850**	**$1,500**	**$1,225**	***$3,499***

AR-10 SASS MKII – 7.62x51mm/.308 Win or .260 Rem. cal, 18 in. stainless steel barrel, AWC PSR thread-over suppressor ready muzzle, 20 shot Magpul PMAG, Timney trigger, Magpul PRS stock, 15 in. enhanced M-LOK handguard, Raptor ambi charging handle, two-pos. selectable gas block, 9.4 lbs. New mid-2018.

Please contact the company directly for pricing and availability for this model.

AR-10 A-SERIES SUPER SASS RIFLE (SUPER SASS RIFLE 10SBF) – .308 Win/7.62 NATO cal., GIO, 20 in. match grade triple lapped Cerakote finished 416R stainless steel barrel, M-4 feed ramps barrel, A2 flash suppressor or mock AAC suppressor (disc.), forged flat-top upper receiver with Picatinny rail, forward assist, SuperSASS quad rail free floating handguard w/rail covers, forged lower receiver, 20 shot mag., Magpul PRS stock, black finish, two-stage NM trigger, available with various accessories, includes one 10 shot mag., one 20 shot mag., USMC quick adjust sling, sling swivel mount, and hard case, 9.4-11.8 lbs. Disc. 2017. Reintroduced 2020.

MSR $3,100	**$2,775**	**$2,475**	**$2,150**	**$1,900**	**$1,650**	**$1,325**	**$1,075**	

* ***AR-10A Super SASS Rifle (A10SBF)*** – 7.62 NATO/.308 Win. cal., 20 in. Cerakote stainless steel match threaded barrel with flash suppressor, 20 shot Mapgul PMAG, National Match two-stage trigger, Armalite floating rail systems handguard, Gas Buster charging handle, quad Mil-Std 1913 rail, Magpul PRS stock, 11.8 lbs. Mfg. 2012-2017.

	$2,775	**$2,475**	**$2,150**	**$1,900**	**$1,650**	**$1,325**	**$1,075**	***$3,099***

This model has magazine interchangeability with the AR-10B.

» **AR-10 CSASS (AR-10A Super SASS Carbine - A10SCBF)** – 7.62 NATO/.308 Win. cal., 16 in. Cerakote stainless steel match barrel with flash suppressor, 20 shot Magpul PMAG, Armalite floating rail systems handguard, Gas Buster charging handle, National Match two-stage trigger, Mil-Std 1913 Picatinny quad rail, B5 buttstock, 9.1 lbs. Mfg. 2014-2017.

	$2,775	**$2,475**	**$2,150**	**$1,900**	**$1,650**	**$1,325**	**$1,075**	***$3,099***

This model has magazine interchangeability with the AR-10B.

AR-10 DEFENSIVE SPORTING RIFLE (DSR10) – 7.62x51mm/.308 Win. cal., GIO, 16 in. double lapped chrome-lined barrel with flash suppressor, 20 shot Magpul PMAG., forged receivers, single stage trigger, 6-pos. collapsible buttstock, 8 in. handguard, Mil-Std 1913 Picatinny rail gas block, 7.9 lbs. New 2015.

MSR $1,099	**$975**	**$875**	**$775**	**$675**	**$575**	**$475**	**$375**	

AR-10 PRC 260 – .260 Rem. cal., GIO, 20 in. stainless steel barrel, Surgeon/AWC PSR thread-over muzzle brake, 20 shot Magpul PMAG, Timney SST, Magpul PRS stock with adj. LOP and comb, 15 in. free floating aluminum handguard w/integrated Mil-Std 1913 Picatinny quad rail sections, Magpul MIAD grip, ambi safety, ambi charging handle, Cerakote finish, 11.4 lbs. Mfg. 2017 only.

	$3,200	**$2,825**	**$2,475**	**$2,175**	**$1,900**	**$1,525**	**$1,225**	***$3,560***

GRADING - PPGS™	100%	98%	95%	90%	80%	70%	60%	LAST MSR

AR-10 QUAD-RAIL (AR-10A4 LOW PROFILE CARBINE) – 7.62x51mm/.308 Win. cal., 16 in. double lapped chrome-lined chrome moly barrel with flash suppressor, anodized aluminum receiver, forged aluminum upper receiver with free float quad rail handguards, low profile gas block, 20 shot Magpul PMAG, two-stage tactical trigger, B5 adjustable stock, 8.8 lbs. Mfg. 2014-2016.

	$1,650	$1,475	$1,275	$1,125	$975	$800	$650	*$1,850*

AR-10 TACTICAL RIFLE – 7.62x51mm/.308 Win. cal., GIO, 13.5, 16, 18, or 20 in. black Cerakote finished stainless steel barrel, flash hiding compensator (permanently attached on 13.5 in. barrel), 25 shot Magpul PMAG, two-stage precision trigger, Magpul MBUS flip-up sights, Magpul STR multi-position collapsible (16 or 18 in.) or Luth-AR MBA-1 (20 in.) buttstock, 12 (13.5 in. barrel only) or 15 in. KeyMod (disc.) or M-LOK handguard, full length Picatinny upper rail, MOE+ pistol grip, ambi safety, Raptor ambi charging handle, 8.8 lbs. New 2015.

MSR $1,999	$1,800	$1,600	$1,375	$1,225	$1,050	$850	$700	

Add $20 for 13.5 in. barrel w/permanently attached flash hiding compensator.
Add $100 for 18 or 20 in. barrel.

AR-10 A SERIES TACTICAL CARBINE – 7.62 NATO/.308 Win. cal., GIO, 16 in. double lapped chrome moly barrel, mid-length gas system, flash suppressor, 20 shot Magpul PMAG, forged receivers, flat-top upper w/Picatinny rail, tactical two-stage trigger, A2 front sight base, 6-pos. collapsible stock, 8 in. handguard, Mil-Spec charging handle and forward assist, black anodized finish, 7.8 lbs. Disc. 2017.

	$1,400	$1,250	$1,100	$950	$825	$675	$550	*$1,571*

AR-10 VSR (VERSATILE SPORTING RIFLE) – 7.62x51mm/.308 Win. cal., 18 in. black Cerakote stainless steel threaded barrel with knurled thread protector, 20 shot Magpul PMAG, top Picatinny rail, 15 in. free floating VSR handguard, Raptor ambi charging handle, two-stage trigger, MBA-1 lightweight precision buttstock adjustable for LOP and comb height, 8.8 lbs. Mfg. 2015-2017.

	$1,700	$1,500	$1,325	$1,175	$1,000	$825	$650	*$1,899*

AR-10 COMPETITION RIFLE (3-GUN COMPETITION RIFLE) – 7.62x51mm/.308 Win. cal., GIO, 18 in. stainless steel barrel, 25 shot Magpul PMAG, Timney 3 or 4 lb. SST, lightweight MBA-1 buttstock w/ adjustable cheekpiece and LOP, 12 or 15 (disc.) in. free floating 3-Gun/Competition handguard, Ergo wide grip, ambi safety and Raptor charging handle, 8.9 lbs. New 2015.

MSR $2,199	$1,975	$1,750	$1,525	$1,350	$1,175	$950	$775	

AR-180B – .223 Rem. cal., GPO, polymer lower receiver with formed sheet metal upper, standard AR-15 trigger group/magazine, incorporates the best features of the M15 (lower group with trigger and magwell) and early AR-180 (gas system, which keeps propellant gas outside of the receiver) rifles, 19.8 in. barrel with integral muzzle brake, 6 lbs. Mfg. 2003-2007.

	$1,250	$825	$575	$475	$425	$375	$350	*$750*

For more information on the original ArmaLite AR-180 and variations, please refer to the previous ArmaLite listing.

M4A1C CARBINE – features GIO, 16 in. chrome-lined 1:9 twist heavy barrel with National Match sights and detachable carrying handle, M4 style handguard, 7 lbs. Disc. 1997.

	$850	$750	$650	$575	$500	$400	$325	*$935*

M4C CARBINE – similar to M4A1C Carbine, except has non-removable carrying handle and fixed sights, 7 lbs. Disc. 1997.

	$775	$700	$600	$525	$450	$375	$300	*$870*

M-15 RIFLE/CARBINE VARIATIONS – .223 Rem. cal. standard unless otherwise noted, GIO, various configurations, barrel lengths, sights, and other features.

* ***M-15 22 LR Carbine*** – .22 LR cal., blowback action, 16 in. barrel with A2 flash suppressor, standard .223 lower with .22 LR upper receiver, forward assist, 6 in. handguard, Picatinny gas block. Mfg. 2011 only.

	$675	$600	$525	$450	$400	$325	$250	*$749*

* ***M-15A4 SPR Mod 1 (15SPR1CB)*** – 5.56 NATO, 6.8 SPC (mfg. 2012-2013, reintroduced 2016), or 7.62x39mm (mfg. 2012-2013) cal., GIO, 16 in. chrome-lined barrel with flash hider, gas block with Picatinny rail, forged flat-top receiver with Picatinny rail and laser engraved t-slots, three extra detachable rails, collapsible stock, tactical two-stage trigger, forged aluminum lower receiver, ARMS polymer (disc. 2013) or flip-up front and rear sights, black furniture, includes one 30 shot mag., sling, and hard case, 6 1/2 lbs. Mfg. mid-2010-2016.

	$1,425	$1,275	$1,100	$975	$850	$675	$550	*$1,589*

Add $35 for mid-length free floating quad rail (disc. 2013).
Add $160 for 7.62x39mm cal. (disc. 2013).
Add $155 for 6.8 SPC cal.

GRADING - PPGS™	100%	98%	95%	90%	80%	70%	60%	LAST MSR

* ***M-15A2/A4 National Match Rifle*** – .223 Rem. cal., GIO, 20 in. stainless steel NM sleeved 1:8 twist barrel with flash suppressor, includes one 30 shot mag., forged receivers, NM two-stage trigger, NM hooded rear sight and A2 NM clamp on front sight, fixed A2 rifle stock, A2 style rifle handguard, black or green furniture, with or w/o detachable carrying handle, includes one 30 shot mag., USMC quick adjust sling and hard case, black or green furniture, 9 lbs. Disc. 2013.

$1,275 $1,125 $975 $875 $750 $600 $500 ***$1,422***

* ***M-15A2 Golden Eagle*** – .223 Rem. cal., GIO, similar to M15A2 National Match Rifle, except has 20 in. heavy barrel, 9.4 lbs. Limited mfg. 1998 only.

$1,200 $1,075 $925 $825 $725 $575 $475 ***$1,350***

* ***M-15A2 Service Rifle*** – 5.56 NATO cal., GIO, includes 20 in. chrome-lined 1:9 twist barrel, green or black furniture, forged A2 receiver, fixed stock, A2 front sight, tactical two-stage trigger, flash suppressor, carrying handle, includes one 30 shot mag., sling, and hard case, 8.2 lbs. Disc. 2013.

$1,050 $925 $825 $725 $625 $500 $400 ***$1,174***

* ***M-15A2 Carbine*** – 5.56 NATO cal., similar to M15A2 Service Rifle, except has 16 in. barrel, 6-position collapsible stock, Mil-Spec carbine buffer tube, includes one 30 shot mag., sling, and hard case, 7 lbs. Disc. 2013.

$1,050 $925 $825 $725 $625 $500 $400 ***$1,174***

* ***M-15A4 National Match SPR*** – .223 Rem. cal., similar to M15A2 National Match, except has forged flat-top receiver with Picatinny rail and NM detachable carry handle, includes one 30 shot mag., USMC quick adjust sling, and hard case, 9.8 lbs. Disc. 2013.

$1,300 $1,150 $1,000 $875 $750 $625 $500 ***$1,435***

* ***M-15A4 SPR (Special Purpose Rifle, 15A4/15A4B)*** – 5.56 NATO cal., GIO, 20 in. chrome-lined HBAR threaded barrel, gas block with rail, forged flat-top upper with Picatinny rail, forged lower with tactical two-stage trigger, Hi-Cap stock, Green (15A4) or Black (15A4B) finish, includes one 30 shot mag., sling, and hard case, 7.8 lbs. Disc. 2013.

$975 $850 $750 $650 $575 $450 $375 ***$1,073***

* ***M-15A4 SPR II National Match (Special Purpose Rifle)*** – 5.56 NATO cal., similar to M-15A4 SPR, except has triple lapped rifled barrel, strengthened free floating barrel sleeve and two-stage match trigger, green or black furniture. Mfg. 2003-2005.

$1,325 $1,175 $1,025 $900 $775 $625 $500 ***$1,472***

* ***M-15A4 Carbine*** – 5.56 NATO, 6.8 SPC (mfg. 2009-2013, reintroduced 2016), or 7.62x39mm (mfg. 2009-2013) cal., 16 in. chrome moly threaded barrel, forged flat-top upper with Picatinny rail, gas block with rail, forged lower with tactical two-stage trigger, 6-pos. collapsible stock, Mil-Spec carbine buffer tube, green (15A4C) or black (15A4CB) furniture, includes one 30 shot mag., sling, and hard case, 6 1/2-7 lbs. Disc. 2015.

$975 $850 $750 $650 $575 $450 $375 ***$1,073***

Add $42 for 6.8 SPC cal.
Add $42 for 7.62x39mm cal. (disc. 2013).
Subtract $60 for fixed front sight w/detachable carry handle (disc.).

* ***M-15A4 CBA2K*** – 5.56 NATO cal., GIO, 16 in. double lapped chrome-lined barrel, flash suppressor, two-stage tactical trigger, forged flat-top receiver with Picatinny rail, A2 front sight, 8 in. mid-length handguard, forged lower receiver, 6-position collapsible stock, Mil-Spec buffer tube, includes one 30 shot mag., sling, and hard case, 6 1/2 lbs. Mfg. 2008-2013.

$925 $825 $725 $625 $550 $450 $350 ***$1,031***

* ***M-15ARTN*** – .223 Rem. cal., GIO, 20 in. stainless steel barrel, National Match trigger, green or black finish. Mfg. 2004-2007.

$1,175 $1,050 $925 $800 $700 $575 $450 ***$1,322***

* ***M-15T Target (15A4TBN Rifle Eagle Eye)*** – 5.56 NATO/.223 Wylde chamber, GIO, 20 or 24 (disc. 2009) in. stainless steel heavy barrel, two-stage NM trigger, smooth green or black fiberglass (disc. 2008) or lightweight aluminum round floating handguard, Picatinny front sight rail but w/o sights and carrying handle, A2 stock, black or green furniture, includes one 10 shot mag. and hard case, 8.6 lbs. Disc. 2005, reintroduced 2007-2016 and 2018-2020.

$1,175 $1,050 $925 $800 $700 $575 $450 ***$1,318***

* ***M-15 Target (15TBN)*** – .223 Wylde chamber, GIO, 18 in. triple lapped stainless steel match barrel, 10 shot mag., forged receivers, flat-top upper receiver, two-stage NM trigger, no sights, B5 Systems collapsible stock, free floating quad rail handguard, A2 pistol grip, matte black finish, 7.9 lbs. Mfg. 2014-2016.

$1,195 $795 $550 $465 $415 $375 $350 ***$1,449***

GRADING - PPGS™	100%	98%	95%	90%	80%	70%	60%	LAST MSR

* ***M-15A4T Carbine (Eagle Eye)*** – GIO, 16 in. stainless steel 1:9 twist heavy barrel, Picatinny rail, smooth fiberglass handguard tube, two-stage trigger, 7.1 lbs. Mfg. 1997-2004.

	$1,250	$1,100	$950	$850	$725	$600	$475	*$1,383*

* ***M-15A4 Predator*** – similar to M-15A4T Eagle Eye, except has 1:12 twist barrel. Disc. 1996.

	$1,200	$1,075	$925	$825	$725	$575	$475	*$1,350*

* ***M-15A4 Action Master*** – GIO, includes 20 in. stainless steel 1:9 twist barrel, two-stage trigger, muzzle brake, Picatinny flat-top design w/o sights or carrying handle, 9 lbs. Disc. 1997.

	$1,050	$925	$825	$725	$625	$500	$400	*$1,175*

* ***M-15SOF (Special Operation Forces) Carbine*** – .223 Rem. cal., GIO, available in either A2 or A4 configurations, fixed tube stock, 16 in. barrel, black finish only. Mfg. 2003-2004.

	$975	$875	$750	$675	$575	$475	$375	*$1,084*

Add $69 for A2 configuration (includes Picatinny rail).

M-15 DEFENSIVE SPORTING RIFLE (DSR15/DSR15F) – .223 Wylde chamber, 16 in. double lapped chrome-lined barrel, A2 flash suppressor, 30 shot Magpul PMAG, 8 in. handguard, Mil-Std 1913 rail gas block or A2 front sight base (DSR15F), single stage trigger, A2 grip, 6-pos. collapsible M4 style buttstock, 6.1 lbs. New 2015.

MSR $799	$725	$625	$550	$500	$425	$350	$275

M-15 BATTALION RIFLE – 5.56 NATO cal., GIO, 16 in. chrome-lined CMV barrel, Picatinny rail gas block, A2 flash hider, forged receivers, enlarged trigger guard, B5 Systems SOPMOD 6-pos. collapsible stock, B5 Systems KeyMod handguard and grip, black hardcoat anodized finish, 6.3 lbs. New 2021.

MSR $899	$800	$725	$625	$550	$475	$375	$300

M-15 LIGHT TACTICAL CARBINE – 5.56 NATO, 6.8 SPC (disc. 2017), or 7.62x39mm (disc. 2017) cal., GIO, 16 in. chrome-lined threaded barrel, flash suppressor, 30 shot mag., forged aluminum receivers, SST, M4 style 6-pos. collapsible stock, 10 in. aluminum tactical KeyMod (disc.) or M-LOK handguard, A2 grip, top Picatinny rail, anodized black finish, 6 lbs. New 2016.

MSR $999	$900	$800	$700	$600	$525	$425	$350

M-15 PISTON – 5.56 NATO cal., GPO, 16 in. chrome moly barrel, adj. long stroke gas piston system, OSS Banner flash hider muzzle brake, 30 shot Magpul PMAG, forged receivers, flat-top Picatinny rail upper receiver, two-stage precision trigger, Magpul MBUS sights, Magpul STR stock, 15 in. KeyMod handguard, Magpul grip, ambi safety, Raptor ambi charging handle, 7.3 lbs. Mfg. 2015-2016.

	$1,800	$1,600	$1,400	$1,225	$1,075	$850	$700	*$2,249*

M-15 TACTICAL – 5.56x45mm/.223 Wylde chamber, GIO, 14.5 or 16 chrome-lined CMV barrel or 18 in. stainless steel barrel, adj. gas block, flash hiding compensator (permanently attached on 14.5 in. barrel), 30 shot Magpul PMAG, forged lower and flat-top upper receiver, two-stage precision trigger, Magpul STR multi-position collapsible stock, 10 or 15 in. aluminum tactical KeyMod or M-LOK handguard, Magpul MOE grip, ambi safety, 7.2 lbs. New 2015.

MSR $1,599	$1,425	$1,275	$1,100	$975	$850	$675	$550

Add $100 for 18 in. barrel.

M-15 VSR (VERSATILE SPORTING RIFLE) – .223 Wylde chamber, GIO, 18 in. black Cerakote stainless steel threaded barrel with knurled thread protector, 20 shot Magpul PMAG, 15 in. free floating VSR handguard, Raptor ambi charging handle, top Picatinny rail, two-stage precision trigger, MBA-1 lightweight buttstock adj. for LOP and comb height, 7 1/2 lbs. Mfg. 2015-2017.

	$1,200	$1,075	$925	$825	$725	$575	$475	*$1,349*

M-15 3-GUN COMPETITION RIFLE – .223 Wylde chamber, GIO, 18 in. free floating stainless steel barrel, adj. gas block, 30 shot Magpul PMAG, 12 in. free floating 3-Gun handguard, two inch Mil-Std rail section, Timney 3 lb. SST, MBA-1 lightweight precision buttstock adjustable for LOP and comb height, 6.6 lbs. New 2015.

MSR $1,699	$1,525	$1,350	$1,175	$1,050	$900	$725	$600

M-15 13 IN. COMPETITION RIFLE – .223 Wylde chamber, GIO, 13.5 in. stainless steel barrel with permanently attached Armalite tunable muzzle brake, 30 shot Magpul PMAG, forged receivers, Timney 4 lb. SST, MBA-1 lightweight precision buttstock adjustable for LOP and comb height, 12 in. free floating Competition handguard, 2 in. Picatinny rail section, Ergo grip, ambi safety, black hardcoat anodized finish, 6.6 lbs. New 2021.

MSR $1,699	$1,525	$1,350	$1,175	$1,050	$900	$725	$600

GRADING - PPGS™	100%	98%	95%	90%	80%	70%	60%	LAST MSR

LEC15A4CBK (LAW ENFORCEMENT CARBINE) – 5.56 NATO cal., GIO, 16 in. double lapped chrome-lined threaded barrel, forged flat-top receiver with Picatinny rail, flash suppressor, A2 front sight, 8 in. handguard, tactical two-stage trigger, 6-pos. collapsible stock, Mil-Spec buffer tube, includes one 30 shot mag., sling, and hard case, 6 1/2 lbs. Mfg. 2009-2016.

$900 $775 $675 $600 $525 $425 $350 ***$989***

ARMAMENT TECHNOLOGY

Previous firearms manufacturer located in Halifax, Nova Scotia, Canada 1988-2003.

Armament Technology discontinued making bolt action rifles in 2003. Currently, the company is distributing optical rifle sights only.

RIFLES: BOLT ACTION

AT1-C24 TACTICAL RIFLE – .308 Win. or .300 Win. Mag. (disc. 2000) cal., similar to AT1-M24, except has detachable mag., adj. cheekpiece, and buttstock adj. for LOP, includes 3.5-10x30mm tactical scope and Mil-Spec shipping case, 1/2 in. MOA guaranteed, available in left-hand action, 14.9 lbs. Mfg. 1998-2003.

$4,095 $3,650 $2,775 $2,250 $1,825 $1,500 $1,275 ***$4,195***

AT1-C24B TACTICAL RIFLE – .308 Win. cal., similar to AT1-C24, except is not available in left-hand, 15.9 lbs. Mfg. 2001-2003.

$4,250 $3,750 $2,850 $2,300 $1,850 $1,525 $1,300 ***$4,695***

AT1-M24 TACTICAL RIFLE – .223 Rem. (new 1998), .308 Win., or .300 Win. Mag. (disc. 2000) cal., tactical rifle with competition tuned right-hand or left-hand Rem. 700 action, stainless steel barrel, Kevlar reinforced fiberglass stock, Harris bipod, matte black finish, competition trigger, 1/2 in. MOA guaranteed, 14.9 lbs. Disc. 2003.

$4,350 $3,850 $2,850 $2,350 $1,900 $1,600 $1,350 ***$4,495***

ARMAMENT TECHNOLOGY CORP.

Previous manufacturer located in Las Vegas, NV between 1972 and 1978.

RIFLES: SEMI-AUTO

In addition to the models listed below, ATC also manufactured the "Firefly II", a select fire pistol.

MODEL 4 POCKET RIFLE – .22 LR cal., semi-auto action (supplied by Mossberg), 5 in. barrel, shortened rifle (18 1/2 in. overall length) with cut stock, 7 shot mag., approx. 450 mfg., approx. 3 lbs.

$350 $295 $260 $230 $195 $175 $150

MODEL 6 – .22 LR cal., full-length variation of the Model 4, Mossberg Model 453-T with ATC trademarks, approx. 12 mfg., approx. 5 1/2 lbs.

$125 $100 $85 $75 $65 $55 $45

M-2 FIREFLY – 9mm Para. cal., unique gas delayed blowback action, collapsible stock, very limited mfg., 4 3/4 lbs.

$695 $625 $550 $475 $395 $350 $295

ARMAS AZOR, S.A.

Previous manufacturer of double rifles located in Eibar, Spain. Previously imported 1994-1997 by Armes De Chasse located in Hertford, NC.

RIFLES: SxS, SIDELOCK

The models listed below are English styled sidelock double rifles. Gold inlay and custom engraving prices were quoted per individual request.

AFRICA MARK I – available in most cals. between 9.3x74R and .375 H&H, nominal engraving and select grade wood.

Previous retail prices ranged between $8,000 and $10,000.

AFRICA MARK II – available in most cals. between 9.3x74R and .375 H&H, African game scene engraving and superior grade wood.

Previous retail prices ranged between $10,000 and $12,000.

AFRICA MARK III – available in most cals. between 9.3x74R and .470 NE Mag., intricate scroll engraving, cartridge trap, top tang, and superior quality grade wood.

Previous retail prices ranged between $13,000 and $18,000.

GRADING - PPGS™	100%	98%	95%	90%	80%	70%	60%	LAST MSR

SHOTGUNS: SxS, SIDELOCK

SIDELOCK MODEL – 12 ga.-.410 bore, English-style sidelock game gun.

	$3,275	$2,700	$2,200	$1,750	$1,500	$1,250	$995	*$3,500*

ARMATIX

Current pistol manufacturer located in Unterfohring, Germany. Limited U.S. importation into California only.

PISTOLS: SEMI-AUTO

iP1 – .22 LR cal., blowback action, 10 shot detachable box mag., integrated color-coded grip safety, pistol is controlled electronically via smartwatch, including the magazine disconnect. Wristwatch must be within 10 in. of the pistol to be operational, interface for additional applications such as a camera, matte black finish, 18.25 oz. Limited importation began 2014.

2014 MSR was $1,800. Please contact the company for current pricing and availability.

ARMED GUNS

Current trademark manufactured by Armed Silah Av Malzemeleri San. Tic. Ltd. Sti. with factory located in Beysehir - Konya, Turkey, and exported by Izmirlioglu Av Malz. San. Tic. Ltd. Sti. located in Izmir, Turkey. Currently, semi-auto, slide action, O/U and single barrel hunting and tactical shotguns private labeled for Iver Johnson Arms, Inc. are being imported into the U.S. (see separate listing).

Izmirlioglu Av Malz. San. Tic. Ltd. Sti. has been manufacturing guns since 2006. A wide variety of firearms are manufactured under the Armed trademarks, including semi-auto (AR-15 style and bullpup), slide action, O/U, and single barrel shotguns. Additionally, the company is making and offering airguns. Please contact the company directly for more information, including pricing and U.S. availability.

ARMERIA DE MADRID, LA

Please refer to the LARM listing in the L section.

ARMES DE CHASSE LLC

Previous importer and distributor located in Norfolk, VA and in Hertford, NC.

SHOTGUNS: SxS

ALBEMARLE GAME GUN SIDELOCK – 12, 16 (special order only), 20, 28 ga., or .410 bore (new 2001), H&H style detachable sidelock action, Purdey style bolt, DT with articulated front trigger, 26, 27, or 28 in. barrels with concave solid rib, ejectors, checkered oil finished walnut English or pistol grip stock and forearm (base price includes custom stock dimensions), extensive lockplate engraving, 5 3/4 (20 ga.) or 6 7/8 (12 ga.) lbs. Spanish importation from 1999-2005.

	$3,100	$2,650	$2,195	$1,800	$1,500	$1,200	$995	*$3,525*

Add 10% for 28 ga. or .410 bore.
Add $1,050 for extra set of barrels.
Add $1,525 for Grade A fine scroll engraving.
Add $1,330 for Grade A black and gold option (mfg. 2000-2003).
Add $1,310 for Grade B ribbon and scroll engraving.
Add $1,100 Grade C game scene engraving.
Add $135 for left-hand.

ALBEMARLE GAME GUN BOXLOCK – 12, 16 (special order only), 20, 28 ga., or .410 bore, H&H style boxlock action, DT, ejectors, old silver or case hardened receiver, beavertail or semi-beavertail forend available. Importation began 2003.

	$2,350	$2,150	$1,875	$1,525	$1,200	$995	$875	*$2,635*

Add $135 for left-hand.
Add 10% for 28 ga. or .410 bore.

ARMES MATHELON

Please refer to Mathelon Armes listing in the M section.

ARMES PIERRE ARTISAN ETS. (P. CHAPUIS)

Current manufacturer located in St. Bonnet Le Chateau, France.

For individual model listings, please go to BlueBookOfGunValues.com/overflow.

ARMI MAGAP

Previous long gun manufacturer located in Marcheno, Italy from 2007-circa 2016.

Armi Magap was founded by Maurizio Piotti during 2007, and the company manufactured custom order, high quality round action boxlock SxS, boxlock O/U with detachable trigger assembly, and hammer sideplate shotguns.

GRADING - PPGS™	100%	98%	95%	90%	80%	70%	60%	LAST MSR

ARMI PERUGINI-VISINI

Please refer to the Perugini-Visini listing in the P section.

ARMI SALVINELLI

Current manufacturer established in 1975, located in Marcheno, Italy. No current U.S. importation.

Armi Salvinelli manufactures high quality O/U competition and hunting shotguns, including a line made specifically for the 2012 Olympics in London. Please contact the company directly for more information, including pricing and availability.

ARMI SAN MARCO

Previous manufacturer located in Gardone, Italy circa early 1960s-2003.

Armi San Marco was one of the first Italian manufacturers to make replica Colt black powder revolvers. Quality varied quite a bit, but typically wasn't as good as other replicas of the day. Some variations had parts that were not heat treated properly. Depending on the model/variation, most black powder derringers/revolvers are currently valued in the $50-$395 range.

ARMI SAN PAOLO

Previous manufacturer located in Concesio, Italy.

During 2002, Armi San Paolo changed its name to Euroarms Italia. Please refer to the Euroarms Italia listing in the E section for recent information.

REVOLVERS

Armi San Paolo manufactured double action .22 and .38 cal. revolvers in both 2 and 6 in. barrel lengths. These revolvers were manufactured in Concesio, Italy under license from J.P. Sauer & Sohn. Assuming 95%+ condition, these handguns are currently priced in the $150-$225 range.

ARMI SPORT di CHIAPPA SILVIA & C. Snc

Please refer to Chiappa Firearms S.r.l. located in the C section.

ARMINEX LTD.

Previous manufacturer located in Scottsdale, AZ.

PISTOLS: SEMI-AUTO

TRI-FIRE - .45 ACP cal., SA, steel frame construction, 5, 6, or 7 (disc. 1984) in. stainless barrel (interchangeable barrels allow caliber conversion), smooth walnut grips, ambidextrous thumb safety (on Target and Presentation only), 38 oz. Approx. 400 mfg. between 1981 and 1985.

	100%	98%	95%	90%	80%	70%	60%	LAST MSR
	$900	$775	$650	$475	$400	$375	$350	*$396*

Add $50 if presentation cased.

Add approx. $130/conversion unit (9mm Para. or .38 Super cal.).

* ***Tri-Fire Target Model*** - same specifications as Tri-Fire, except has 6 or 7 (disc. 1984) in. stainless steel barrel. Very limited mfg.

	100%	98%	95%	90%	80%	70%	60%	LAST MSR
	$950	$725	$550	$450	$400	$360	$330	*$448*

ARMINIUS

Previous trademark of pistols and revolvers manufactured by Weihrauch Sport GmbH, located in Mellrichstadt, Germany. Previously manufactured in Zella-Mehlis, Germany beginning circa 1922 through the mid-1970s.

PISTOLS: SINGLE SHOT

MODEL 1 - .22 LR cal., target model, adj. sights.

	100%	98%	95%	90%	80%	70%	60%
	$1,500	$1,325	$1,125	$1,025	$825	$675	$525

MODEL 2 - similar to Model 1, except has set trigger.

	100%	98%	95%	90%	80%	70%	60%
	$1,650	$1,450	$1,250	$1,125	$925	$750	$575

REVOLVERS

Recently manufactured Arminius revolvers are not individually listed since they were not imported into the U.S. There are however, many models including combat, sport, and target variations. Calibers include .22 LR., .22 WMR, .32 S&W Wadcutter, .357 Mag., and .38 Spl.

HW 3 - .22 LR, .22 Win. Mag, or .32 S&W Long cal., DA/SA, 7 or 8 shot cylinder, brown plastic grips, blued/black finish.

	100%	98%	95%	90%	80%	70%	60%
	$225	$200	$175	$150	$125	$100	$75

GRADING - PPGS™	100%	98%	95%	90%	80%	70%	60%	LAST MSR

HW 4 – .22 LR cal., DA/SA, 2 1/2, 4, or 6 in. barrel, 8 shot cylinder, blued/black finish.

	$200	$175	$150	$135	$110	$90	$70	

HW 5 – .22 LR, .22 Win. Mag, or .32 S&W Long cal., DA/SA, 4 in. barrel, 7 or 8 shot cylinder, brown plastic grips, blued/black finish.

	$225	$200	$175	$150	$125	$100	$75	

HW 7 – .22 LR, .22 Win. Mag., or .32 S&W Long cal., DA/SA, 6 in. vent rib barrel, 7 or 8 shot cylinder, brown plastic grips, blued/black finish.

	$260	$230	$195	$175	$145	$115	$90	

HW 9 – .22 LR cal., DA/SA, 6 in. vent rib barrel, 8 shot cylinder, adj. sights, brown plastic target grips, blued/black finish.

	$275	$240	$210	$185	$160	$125	$100	

HW 22 – .22 LR cal., DA/SA, 2 in. barrel, 8 shot cylinder.

	$225	$200	$175	$150	$125	$100	$75	

HW 38 – .38 Spl. cal., DA/SA, 4 in. vent rib barrel, 6 shot cylinder, adj. sights, brown plastic target grips, blued/black finish.

	$225	$200	$175	$150	$125	$100	$75	

ARMITAGE INTERNATIONAL, LTD.

Previous manufacturer located in Seneca, SC until 1990.

PISTOLS: SEMI-AUTO

SCARAB SKORPION – 9mm Para. cal., blowback operation, paramilitary design patterened after the Czech Model 61, SFO, 4.63 in. barrel, 12 shot (standard) or 32 shot (optional) mag., matte black finish, 3 1/2 lbs. Mfg. in U.S. 1989-90 only.

	$695	$625	$550	$500	$425	$375	$325	*$400*

Add $45 for threaded flash hider or imitation suppressor.

Only 602 Scarab Skorpions were manufactured during 1989-1990.

ARMORY USA LLC

Previous manufacturer/importer until 2008, located in Houston, TX. Previous company name was Arsenal USA LLC.

For individual model listings, please go to BlueBookOfGunValues.com/overflow.

ARMS CORPORATION OF THE PHILIPPINES

Please refer to the Armscor listing in this section.

ARMS LLC

Previous manufacturer of semi-custom AR-15 style rifles and pistols located in Aurora, Oregon 2008-2016.

PISTOLS: SEMI-AUTO

Arms LLC manufactured the ARMS-5 and ARMS-15 AR-15 style pistols. Each model was built to customer specifications.

RIFLES: SEMI-AUTO

Arms LLC manufactured the following AR-15 style models: ARMS-15 Classic, ARMS-15 Elite Custom, ARMS-15 Quadrail, ARMS-15 Long Range, ARMS-5 SBR, and the ARMS-5 rifle. Each model was built to customer specifications.

ARMS MORAVIA, LTD.

Previous European importer/exporter of firearms and accessories located in Ostrava, Czech Republic. Previously imported into the United States by Anderson & Richardson Arms Co., located in Ft. Worth, TX until 2001.

Arms Moravia Ltd. exported a wide variety of European trademarks, including their own line of pistols.

ARMS RESEARCH ASSOCIATES

Previous manufacturer located in Stone Park, IL until 1991.

Arms Research Associates manufactured a KF-System Carbine that was select-fire NFA Class III only. Most NFA firearms are not included in this database.

GRADING - PPGS™	100%	98%	95%	90%	80%	70%	60%	LAST MSR

CARBINES: SEMI-AUTO

KF SYSTEM – 9mm Para. cal., 18 1/2 in. barrel, vent. barrel shroud, 20 or 36 shot mag., matte black finish, 7 1/2 lbs., select-fire NFA class III transferable only.

	$395	$350	$300	$275	$250	$230	$210	*$379*

THE ARMS ROOM (ARMS ROOM LLC)

Previous manufacturer of AR-15 style rifles and pistols located in Orlando, FL until 2017.

For individual model listings, please go to BlueBookOfGunValues.com/overflow.

ARMS TECH LTD.

Previous manufacturer located in Phoenix, AZ 1987-2012.

RIFLES: BOLT ACTION

SBA 2000 – 7.62x51 cal., Sako 75 action, 24 in. fixed barrel, suppressor ready, fully adj. stock, 12 lbs. Disc. 2012.

Retail pricing was not available for this model.

SMIR (SUPER MATCH INTERDICTION RIFLE) – .300WM cal., 26 in. barrel, 13 3/4 lbs. Disc. 2012.

Last MSR in 2012 was $9,000.

TTR-50 (TACTICAL TAKEDOWN RIFLE) – .50 BMG cal., mission configurable heavy sniper rifle, comes standard with a MD50 B suppressor, OAL 59 3/8 in., 26 lbs. Disc. 2012.

Last MSR in 2012 was $9,000.

TTR-700 (TACTICAL TAKEDOWN RIFLE) – 7.62x51 cal., Rem. 700 bolt action, mission configurable sniper rifle, 17 or 24 in. barrel, includes soft "computer case" or optional Pelican hard case, 10.4 lbs. Disc. 2012.

Last MSR in 2012 was $4,500.

VOYAGER – takedown hunting rifle. Disc .2012.

Last MSR in 2012 was $3,000.

RIFLES: SEMI-AUTO, AR-15 STYLE

Previously, the company also offered the Urban Support Rifle for the civilian marketplace.

SUPER MATCH INTERDICTION POLICE MODEL – .243 Win., .300 Win. Mag., or .308 Win. (standard) cal., AR-15 style, GIO, features 22 in. free floating Schnieder or Douglas air gauged stainless steel barrel, McMillan stock, updated trigger group, detachable box mag., 13 1/4 lbs. Limited mfg. 1996-98.

	$3,950	$3,650	$3,300	$3,000	$2,750	$2,350	$2,000	*$4,800*

SHOTGUNS: SLIDE ACTION

ALPHA ENTRY – 12 ga., utilizes Rem. 870 action, 17 in. barrel, folding stock, 8 lbs. Disc. 2012.

Retail pricing was not available for this model.

ARMSAN

Current shotgun manufacturer established in 2006, located in Istanbul, Turkey.

Armsan manufactures good quality O/U (disc.), SxS (disc.), slide action (12 and 20 ga.), and semi-auto (12, 20, and 28 ga.) shotguns in both sporting and tactical configurations. Armsan is currently making private label shotguns in various configurations for Mossberg, TriStar, Verney-Carron, and Weatherby. The Armtac shotgun brand is also a trademark of Armsan - no current U.S. importation.

ARMSCO

Previous North American importer and distributor of Huglu shotguns located in Des Plaines, IL. Please refer to the Huglu listing in the H section for more information.

ARMSCOR

Current trademark of firearms manufactured by Arms Corporation of the Philippines (manufacturing began 1952) established in 1985 (Armscor Precision - API). Rock Island Armory branded firearms are also being manufactured by Armscor USA, located in Pahrump, NV. The Armscor trademark is not being imported into the U.S. currently, but still exists in some foreign marketplaces. Previously imported and distributed 1999-2014 by Armscor Precision International (full line), located in Pahrump, NV. Previously imported 1995-1999 by K.B.I., Inc. located in Harrisburg, PA, by Ruko located in Buffalo, NY until 1995 and by Armscorp Precision Inc. located in San Mateo, CA until 1991.

In 1991, the importation of Arms Corporation of the Philippines firearms was changed to Ruko Products, Inc.,

GRADING - PPGS™	100%	98%	95%	90%	80%	70%	60%	LAST MSR

located in Buffalo, NY. Barrel markings on firearms imported by Ruko Products, Inc. state "Ruko-Armscor" instead of the older "Armscorp Precision" barrel markings. All Armscorp Precision, Inc. models were discontinued in 1991.

The models listed also provide cross-referencing for older Armscorp Precision and Ruko imported models.

PISTOLS: SEMI-AUTO

All semi-auto pistols were discontinued during 2008, and currently Armscor manufactured pistols can be found under the Rock Island Armory trademark.

M-1911-A1 FS (FULL SIZE STANDARD) – .45 ACP cal., patterned after the Colt Govt. Model, SA, 7 shot mag. (2 provided), 5 in. barrel, parkerized (disc. 2001), blue (new 2002), two-tone (new 2002), or stainless steel (new 2002), skeletonized combat hammer and trigger, front and rear slide serrations, hard rubber grips, 38 oz. Imported 1996-97, reintroduced 2001-2008.

$350 $300 $280 $260 $240 $220 $200 *$399*

Add $31 for two-tone finish.
Add $75 for stainless steel.

This model was also available in a high capacity configuration (Model 1911-A2 HC, 13 shot mag., $519 last MSR).

M-1911-A1 MS (COMMANDER) – .45 ACP cal., SA, Commander configuration with 4 in. barrel, otherwise similar to M-1911 A1 Standard, rear slide serrations only. Imported 2001-2008.

$360 $300 $280 $260 $240 $220 $200 *$408*

Add $37 for two-tone finish.
Add $90 for stainless steel.

M-1911-A1 CS (OFFICER) – .45 ACP cal., SA, officer's configuration with 3 1/2 in. barrel, checkered hardwood grips, 2.16 lbs. Imported 2002-2008.

$370 $310 $285 $265 $245 $220 $200 *$423*

Add $52 for two-tone finish.
Add $105 for stainless steel.

M-1911-A1 MEDALLION SERIES – 9mm Para., .40 S&W, or .45 ACP cal., 5 in. barrel, SA, customized model including many shooting enhancements, match barrel, hand fitted slide and frame, choice of checkered wood or Pachmayr grips, available in either Standard or Tactical variation, blue, two-tone or chrome finish. Imported 2002-2008.

$445 $350 $310 $285 $260 $240 $220 *$539*

Add $129 for Tactical Model, add $198 for Tactical Model two-tone, or $203 for Tactical Model chrome.

REVOLVERS

MODEL 200 (DC) – .38 Spl. cal., 6 shot, double action, 2 1/2 (importation disc.), 4 (new 1998) or 6 (new 1998, importation disc.) in. barrel with shroud, transfer bar safety, combat style rubber grips, blue finish only, fixed rear sight, 26 oz. Imported 1996-99, reintroduced 2001-2014.

$230 $195 $165 $140 $125 $115 $100

Add approx. $16 for 6 in. barrel (disc.)

MODEL 202 – similar to Model 200, except does not have barrel shroud. Imported 2001-2008.

$175 $150 $135 $120 $100 $90 $80 *$156*

MODEL 206 – .38 Spl. cal., similar to Model 200, except has 2 in. barrel, checkered wood grips, and parkerized finish, 24 oz. Imported 2001-2014.

$240 $200 $170 $150 $135 $125 $110

MODEL 210 – similar to Model 200, except has 4 in. VR barrel, and adj. rear sight, 28 oz. Imported 2001-2008.

$190 $165 $150 $135 $115 $100 $90 *$196*

RIFLES: BOLT ACTION

M-12Y/12-TY – .22 LR cal., single shot, youth model with 18 3/8 in. barrel. Imported 1997 only, reintroduced during 2001.

$95 $80 $70 $60 $50 $40 $35 *$109*

M-14P – .22 LR cal., 10 shot mag., 23 in. barrel, open sights, hooded bead ramp front sight and leaf type rear sight, 6 lbs. Disc. 1997.

$95 $75 $60 $50 $45 $40 $35 *$129*

A youth model was also available with shorter dimensions at no extra charge (M-14Y).

* ***M-14-D*** – .22 LR cal., similar to M-14P, except has adj. rear sight and checkered mahogany stock. Importation disc. 1995.

$105 $85 $70 $60 $50 $45 $40 *$139*

GRADING - PPGS™	100%	98%	95%	90%	80%	70%	60%	LAST MSR

M-1400LW – .22 LR cal., similar action to M-14P, except has checkered stock and Schnabel forend, 10 shot mag., hard rubber buttpad, 6 lbs. Imported 1990-92.

$185 $165 $150 $135 $120 $105 $95 ***$219***

* ***M-1400S*** – .22 LR cal., similar to M-1500(S), except has 10 shot mag., 6.7 lbs. Imported 1996-97.

$175 $125 $100 $75 $65 $55 $50 ***$224***

* ***M-1400 (SC-Super Classic)*** – .22 LR cal., otherwise similar to M-1500SC, except has 10 shot mag. and 23 in. barrel, 6 lbs. Imported 1990-1997 and 2001-2008.

$200 $150 $110 $85 $70 $60 $55 ***$242***

Add $18 for stainless steel construction (new 2002).

* ***M-1400E*** – .22 LR cal., 6 or 10 shot mag., similar to M-1400, except has checkered stock and Schnabel forend, hard rubber buttpad, fiber optic front sight and adj. rear sight. New 2004.

This model is currently not being imported into the United States.

* ***M-1400 Sportster*** – .22 LR cal., similar to M-1400E, except has competition type stock and scalloped forearm, Monte Carlo style butt with cheekpiece. New 2004.

This model is currently not being imported into the United States.

M-1500S – .22 WMR cal., deluxe bolt action, 5 shot mag., 21 1/2 or 22 5/8 in. barrel, checkered mahogany stock, open sights, 7 lbs. Disc. 1997, reintroduced 2001.

$145 $125 $110 $95 $85 $75 $65 ***$160***

* ***M-1500LW (Lightweight)*** – similar to M-1500, except has lightweight classic European styled stock made of checkered American Walnut, with buttpad. Imported 1990-92.

$190 $170 $150 $135 $120 $105 $95 ***$229***

* ***M-1500 (SC-Super Classic)*** – checkered American Walnut stock with hard rubber pad and Monte Carlo cheekpiece, hardwood forend tip, engine turned bolt, 7 lbs. Imported 1990-1997 and 2001-2008.

$215 $165 $120 $100 $85 $70 $60 ***$260***

Subtract $3 for stainless steel.

M-1800S (CLASSIC) – .22 Hornet cal., 5 shot mag., dual locking lugs, checkered hardwood stock, adj. rear sight, 6.6 lbs. Imported 1996-1997.

$250 $225 $200 $180 $165 $150 $135 ***$358***

* ***M-1800SC (Super Classic)*** – similar to M-1800S, except has checkered walnut stock with forend tip, and high polish bluing, 7 1/4 lbs. Imported 1996-1997, reintroduced during 2001.

$285 $260 $240 $220 $200 $185 $170 ***$323***

RIFLES: SEMI-AUTO

M-1600 – .22 LR cal., blowback action, 10 or 15 (disc.) shot mag., 18 in. barrel, copy of the Armalite M16, ebony stock, 5 1/4 lbs. Importation disc. 2014.

$180 $150 $130 $110 $100 $80 $70

* ***M-1600R*** – .22 LR cal., similar to M-1600, except has stainless steel retractable buttstock and vent. barrel hood, 7 1/4 lbs. Importation disc. 1995, reintroduced 2008-2011.

$155 $135 $115 $105 $85 $70 $55

M-20 – .22 LR cal., 10 shot mag., deluxe checkered hardwood stock and forend, blue or stainless steel. Imported 2002-2008.

$200 $180 $155 $140 $115 $90 $70 ***$245***

Add $15 for stainless steel construction (new 2002).

M-20P – .22 LR cal., 15 shot mag., 20 3/4 in. barrel, open sights, 5 1/2 lbs. Disc. 1997, reintroduced during 2001, again in 2010-2014.

$150 $125 $100 $85 $75 $70 $55

* ***M-20C*** – similar to M-20P, except has carbine style stock, barrel band, and curved steel buttplate, 16 1/2 in. barrel, 5 1/4 lbs. Previously available from K.B.I. only, disc. 2001.

$130 $115 $95 $90 $70 $60 $45 ***$159***

* ***M-20D*** – .22 LR cal., 22 in. barrel, 10 or 15 shot mag., checkered hardwood stock and forend, 6 1/2 lbs. Imported 2002-2008.

$200 $180 $155 $140 $115 $90 $70 ***$245***

Add $15 for stainless steel construction (new 2002).

M-2000(S) – same specifications as M-20P, except has checkered mahogany stock and adj. rear sight. Disc. 1997.

$140 $120 $105 $95 $75 $65 $50 ***$213***

GRADING - PPGS™	100%	98%	95%	90%	80%	70%	60%	LAST MSR

* ***M-2000SC (Super Classic)*** – similar to M-2000, except has checkered American Walnut stock with cheekpiece and hardwood forend tip, engine turned bolt, 6 lbs. Imported 1990-97.

	$270	$235	$200	$185	$150	$120	$95	*$340*

M-50S – .22 LR cal., semi-auto design, 16 1/2 in. shrouded barrel, 25 or 30 shot mag., uncheckered mahogany stock, 6 1/2 lbs. Disc. 1995.

	$155	$135	$115	$105	$85	$70	$55	*$209*

M-AK22(S) – .22 LR cal., copy of the famous Russian Kalashnikov AK-47 rifle, 18 1/2 in. barrel, 10 or 15 (disc.) shot mag., mahogany stock and forearm, 7 lbs. Importation disc. 2014.

	$185	$160	$140	$125	$100	$85	$65	

* ***M-AK22(F)*** – similar to M-AK22, except has metal folding stock, and 30 shot mag. Disc. 1995.

	$275	$240	$205	$185	$150	$125	$95	*$299*

MIG 22 STANDARD – .22 LR cal., 18 in. barrel, blowback action, 15 shot detachable box mag., matte black finish, fixed synthetic stock, top Picatinny rail. Imported mid-2012-2014.

Retail pricing was not available for this model.

MIG 22 TARGET – .22 LR cal., 18 in. heavy barrel, blowback action, 15 shot detachable box mag., matte black finish, skeletonized aluminum stock, top Picatinny rail, 8 lbs. Imported mid-2012-2014.

Retail pricing was not available for this model.

SHOTGUNS: SLIDE ACTION

M-5 – 12 ga., 3 in. chamber, 26 in. shrouded barrel, 4 shot mag., black plastic stock and forearm, parkerized or nickel (new 2011) finish. Importation disc. 2013.

	$240	$195	$170	$150	$125	$110	$100	

Add $40 for matte nickel finish (new 2011).

M-30 F (INTERCHANGEABLE CHOKES) – 12 ga. only, 28 in. plain barrel with 3 choke tubes, 5 shot mag., uncheckered stock and forearm. Disc. 1999.

	$225	$190	$160	$140	$120	$95	$85	*$269*

* ***M-30 D/IC (Deluxe)*** – similar to Model M30 IC, except has checkered walnut stock and forearm with recoil pad. Imported 2001 only.

	$180	$155	$125	$110	$95	$85	$75	*$208*

M-30 DG (DEER GUN) – 12 ga. only, law enforcement version of M-30, 20 in. plain barrel, iron sights, 7 shot mag., approx. 7 lbs. Importation disc. 1999, resumed during 2001.

	$165	$140	$120	$100	$85	$75	$70	*$195*

M-30SAS1 – 12 ga. only, riot configuration with 20 in. barrel and vent. barrel shroud, and Speedfeed 4 shot (disc.) or 6 shot mag., regular synthetic buttstock and forearm, matte finish, 8 lbs. Imported 1996-1999 and 2001-2008.

	$180	$155	$130	$110	$95	$85	$75	*$211*

Add $56 for Speedfeed stock (new 2002).

M-30 R6/R8 (RIOT) – 12 ga. only, similar to M-30DG, except has front bead sight only, 5 or 7 shot mag., cyl. bore. Importation disc. 1999, reintroduced 2001-2008.

	$155	$135	$110	$90	$80	$75	$70	*$181*

Add $7 for 7 shot mag.

M-30BG – 12 ga. only, 18 1/2 in. barrel, 5 shot mag., polymer pistol grip and forearm. New 2004.

This model is currently not being imported into the United States.

M-30F/FS – similar to M-30BG, except has additional folding metal stock unit. Disc. 2008.

	$180	$155	$130	$110	$95	$85	$75	*$211*

M30 C (COMBO) – 12 ga., 20 in. barrel, 5 shot mag., unique detachable black synthetic buttstock which allows pistol grip only operation. Disc. 1995.

	$210	$175	$145	$120	$100	$90	$80	*$289*

M30 RP (COMBO) – 12 ga. only, same action as M-30 DG, interchangeable black pistol grip, 18 1/4 in. plain barrel w/front bead sight, 6 1/4 lbs. Disc. 1995.

	$210	$175	$145	$120	$100	$90	$80	*$289*

ARMSCORP USA, INC.

Previous manufacturer and importer located in Baltimore, MD. Currently Armscorp USA deals in parts only.

GRADING - PPGS™	100%	98%	95%	90%	80%	70%	60%	LAST MSR

PISTOLS: SEMI-AUTO

HI POWER – 9mm Para. cal., patterned after Browning design, 4 2/3 in. barrel, DA/SA, military finish, 13 shot mag., synthetic checkered grips, spur hammer, 2 lbs. mfg. in Argentina, imported 1989-90 only.

$395 $350 $295 $275 $250 $225 $200 *$450*

Add $15 for round hammer.

Add $50 for hard chrome finish w/combat grips (disc. 1989).

* ***Hi Power Compact Detective HP*** – similar to Hi Power, except has 3 1/2 in. barrel, 1.9 lbs. Mfg. 1989 only.

$395 $350 $295 $275 $250 $225 $200 *$475*

SD-9 – 9mm Para. cal., double action only, blowback mechanism, 3.07 in. barrel, 6 shot mag., frame is fabricated mostly of heavy gauge sheet metal stampings, chamber indicator, limited Israeli mfg., 1 1/2 lbs. Imported 1989-90 only.

$350 $250 $230 $210 $195 $180 $170 *$350*

This pistol has also been manufactured by Sirkis Industries - refer to their section.

P22 – .22 LR cal., patterned after the Colt Woodsman, 4 or 6 in. barrel, 10 shot mag., checkered wood grips, mfg. in Argentina. Imported 1989-90 only.

$190 $150 $130 $115 $100 $95 $85 *$225*

RIFLES: SEMI-AUTO

M-14 RIFLE (NORINCO PARTS) – .308 Win. cal., 20 shot mag., mfg. using Norinco parts, wood stock. Mfg. 1991-92 only.

$1,225 $1,150 $1,050 $975 $875 $775 $675 *$688*

M-14R RIFLE (USGI PARTS) – .308 Win. cal., 10 (C/B 1994) or 20* shot mag., newly manufactured M-14 using original excellent condition forged G.I. parts including USGI fiberglass stock with rubber recoil pad. Mfg. 1986-2006.

$1,925 $1,675 $1,400 $1,275 $1,125 $1,000 $850 *$1,895*

Add $80 for medium weight National Match walnut stock (M-14RNS).

Add $25 for G.I. buttplate (disc.).

Add $45 for USGI birch stock (M-14RNSB, disc.).

M-14 BEGINNING NATIONAL MATCH – .308 Win. cal., mfg. from hand selected older USGI parts, except for new receiver and new USGI air gauged premium barrel, guaranteed to shoot 1 1/4 in. group at 100 yards. Mfg. 1993-96.

$2,050 $1,650 $1,350 $1,225 $1,125 $1,025 $925 *$1,950*

M-14 NMR (NATIONAL MATCH) – .308 Win. cal., built in accordance with USAMU Mil-Spec standards, 3 different barrel weights to choose from, NM rear sight system, calibrated mag., leather sling, guaranteed 1 MOA. Mfg. 1987-2006.

$2,675 $2,125 $1,750 $1,400 $1,200 $1,075 $950 *$2,850*

M-21 MATCH RIFLE – .308 Win. cal., NM rear lugged receiver, choice of McMillan fiberglass or laminated wood stock, guaranteed 1 MOA accuracy.

$3,475 $2,900 $2,325 $2,000 $1,650 $1,350 $1,175 *$3,595*

T-48 FAL ISRAELI PATTERN RIFLE – .308 Win. cal., mfg. in the U.S. to precise original metric dimensions (parts are interchangeable with original Belgium FAL), forged receiver, hammer forged chrome-lined Mil-Spec 21 in. barrel (standard or heavy) with flash suppressor, adj. front sight, aperture rear sight, 10 lbs. Imported 1990-92.

$1,650 $1,475 $1,300 $1,150 $1,075 $975 $875 *$1,244*

This model was guaranteed to shoot within 2.5 MOA with match ammunition.

* ***T-48 FAL L1A1 Pattern*** – .308 Win. cal., fully enclosed forend with vents, 10 lbs. Imported 1992 only.

$1,675 $1,500 $1,325 $1,175 $1,100 $1,000 $900 *$1,181*

Add $122 for wood handguard sporter model (limited supply).

* ***T-48 Bush Model*** – similar to T-48 FAL, except has 18 in. barrel, 9 3/4 lbs. Mfg. 1990 only.

$1,625 $1,450 $1,325 $1,175 $1,025 $925 $850 *$1,250*

FRHB – .308 Win. cal., Israeli mfg. with heavy barrel and bipod. Imported 1990 only.

$2,175 $1,900 $1,600 $1,425 $1,325 $1,225 $1,175 *$1,895*

FAL – .308 Win. cal., Armscorp forged receiver, 21 in. Argentinian rebuilt barrel, manufactured to military specs., supplied with one military 20 shot mag., aperture rear sight, 10 lbs. Mfg. 1987-89.

$1,800 $1,575 $1,425 $1,250 $1,125 $1,025 $925 *$875*

Subtract $55 if without flash hider.

GRADING - PPGS™	100%	98%	95%	90%	80%	70%	60%	LAST MSR

Add $75 for heavy barrel with bipod (14 lbs.).
Add $400 (last retail) for .22 LR conversion kit.

This model was guaranteed to shoot within 2.5 MOA with match ammunition.

* ***FAL Bush Model*** – similar to FAL, except has 18 in. barrel with flash suppressor, 9 3/4 lbs. Mfg. 1989 only.

	$2,200	$2,050	$1,925	$1,825	$1,750	$1,500	$1,250	*$900*

* ***FAL Para Model*** – similar to FAL Bush Model, except has metal folding stock, leaf rear sight. Mfg. 1989 only.

	$2,400	$2,150	$1,050	$1,950	$1,750	$1,650	$1,550	*$930*

* ***FAL Factory Rebuilt*** – factory (Argentine) rebuilt FAL without flash suppressor in excellent condition with Armscorp forged receiver, 9 lbs. 10 oz. Disc. 1989.

	$1,675	$1,450	$1,195	$1,025	$950	$775	$695	*$675*

Add 20% for heavy barrel variation manufactured in Argentina under license from F.N.

M36 ISRAELI SNIPER RIFLE – .308 Win. cal., gas operated semi-auto, bullpup configuration, 22 in. free floating barrel, Armscorp M14 receiver, 20 shot mag., includes flash suppressor and bipod, 10 lbs. Civilian offering 1989 only.

	$3,050	$2,650	$2,425	$2,200	$2,050	$1,925	$1,750	*$3,000*

EXPERT MODEL – .22 LR cal., semi-auto, 20.9 in. barrel, 10 shot mag., wood stock with one-screw takedown, iron sights with grooved receiver, 5.1 lbs. Imported 1989-disc.

	$195	$150	$125	$115	$105	$95	$85	*$225*

ARM SPORT LLC

Previous conversion manufacturer and customizer located in Platteville, CO.

Gunsmith R.L. Millington specialized in authentic hand-built conversions of Colt and Remington black powder pistols to metallic cartridges, custom engraving, refinishing, and antique refinishing.

CARTRIDGE CONVERSIONS

Calibers included .32 S&W Short, .38 S&W, .38 LC, .38 Spl., .44-40 WCF, and .45 LC. Antiquing and period-style engraving were options. Arms Sport LLC converted the 1839 Texas Paterson, Colt Pocket Dragoon (Wells-Fargo Model), 1851 Navy, 1861 Navy, and 1862 Pocket Navy/1862 Pocket Police, the 1847 Walker/Dragoon Models and the 1860 Army, the 1858 Remington Army, the Remington Navy, and the Remington Pocket Pistol. All prices were POR.

ARMSPORT, INC.

Previous importer and distributor located in Miami, FL. Armsport imported shotguns (various configurations, manufactured by Sarsilmaz of Turkey) until 2000. Armsport, Inc. imported a revolver and offered a complete line of accessories (snap caps, scope rings, and cleaning kits).

For individual model listings, please go to BlueBookOfGunValues.com/overflow.

ARMY & NAVY

Previous department stores established in the United Kingdom circa 1871, with headquarters in London, England.

The Army & Navy trademark was originally established circa 1871 by a group of Army & Navy officers, and maintained its trademark until 2005, when it was renamed House of Fraser Victoria. In addition to selling domestic goods, the London store also sold guns using the Army & Navy trademark, manufactured by many respected English firms, including Webley & Scott, W.J. Jeffery, and others. These long guns (mostly shotguns, circa 1870s-pre WWII) were offered in a variety of both hammer and hammerless configurations, which included both plain boxlocks and special order sidelocks with elaborate engraving and deluxe wood. A few double rifles were also manufactured in various calibers. Because of the variety of guns that the Army & Navy department stores offered its customers, these guns need to be appraised individually for correct values. A general guideline is that average condition 12 ga. boxlocks sell in the $750-$2,000 range, uncased sidelocks with nice engraving and no problems typically start at $2,500 and can exceed $10,000 for best quality, cased specimens in smaller gauges.

ARMY SERRA

Current trademark of shotguns manufactured by the Hedef Arms Company, located in Konya, Turkey. No current U.S. importation.

A wide variety of semi-auto, slide action, and O/U shotguns are manufactured. Many configurations are available, including wood, synthetic, and carbon fiber stocks, various finishes, engraving, and gold inlays. Please contact the manufacturer for more information, including domestic availability and pricing.

GRADING - PPGS™	100%	98%	95%	90%	80%	70%	60%	LAST MSR

ARNOLD ARMS CO., INC.

Previous rifle manufacturer located in Arlington, WA, 1994-2001.

For individual model listings, please go to BlueBookOfGunValues.com/overflow.

ARRIETA, S.L.

Current manufacturer established circa 1928, located in Elgoibar, Spain. Currently imported by several importers including Wingshooting Adventures, Quality Arms, Griffin & Howe, William Larkin Moore, and Orvis. Previously imported by New England Arms.

RIFLES: SxS

Arrieta rifles have had limited U.S. importation in the past. Please contact the importers directly for pricing, options, and availability.

R-1 – 7x65R, 8x57JRS, or 9.3x74R cal., true sidelock, ejectors, quarter rib barrels with express rear sight.

MSR N/A	$19,000	$16,250	$13,250	$10,750	$9,350	$7,400	$6,200

R-2 – similar to R-1, except has more elaborate H&H style engraving, elongated tangs, and choice of English or reinforced pistol grip with metal cap, ejectors.

This model has a current MSR of $54,300 in .375 H&H, .470 NE, or .500 NE cal.

R-3 – similar to R-1, except includes .375 H&H, .470 NE, .500 NE cal.

This model has a current MSR of $35,000.

R-4 – most dangerous game cals., deluxe engraving and upgraded wood.

This model has a current MSR of $29,500.

This model is available only from Wingshooting Adventures.

R-5 – most dangerous game cals., best quality wood and engraving.

This model has a current MSR of $38,900.

This model is only available from Wingshooting Adventures.

SHOTGUNS: SxS

The models listed below are essentially custom ordered per individual specifications - delivery time is approx. 12 months.

All Arrieta shotguns have frames scaled to individual gauges. Standard gauges are 12 and 16. Most models are available with either color case hardened or coin finished frames. Many factory upgrades and custom options/special orders are available from the individual importers - please contact them directly for availability and current pricing on these special orders.

On the models listed below, there are four different types of sidelock actions. One is used on the Model 550. Another is used on Models 557, 578, and 871. A third is used on Models 590 and 595 (designed for heavy use). Finally, the best quality is used on Models 600-903, except for Model 900 (557 action), and Model 871. All Arrieta actions are assisted opening, except the Models 557, 570, 578, and 871.

MSRs may vary somewhat from importer to importer.

Add 10% for small gauges (20, 24 (disc.), 28, 32 ga., or .410 bore).
Add approx. $1,705 for single trigger depending on action.
Add 10% for matched pair.
Add 10% for rounded action on standard models (except Models 871 and 872).
Extra barrels are priced from $2,465-$3,790/set depending on model.
Add $855 for pistol grip or semi-pistol grip stock or $440 for beavertail forearm.
Add $1,000-$3,000 for wood upgrade, depending on model.
Add $1,515 for fitted leather case.

06 – all gauges, elaborate engraving, assisted opening, ejectors.

MSR N/A	$15,250	$12,000	$10,500	$9,000	$7,250	$6,000	$5,250

557 – 12, 16, or 20 ga., Demi-Bloc steel barrels, detachable engraved sidelocks, double triggers, ejectors.

MSR $6,970	$6,500	$5,500	$3,900	$3,375	$2,350	$1,750	$1,400

570 – 12, 16, or 20 ga., similar to 560 (non-standard model), except has non-detachable sidelocks.

MSR $7,400	$6,950	$5,750	$4,825	$4,275	$3,500	$2,450	$1,975

578 – 12, 16, or 20 ga., similar to 570, except is fine English scrollwork engraved.

MSR $12,165	$11,000	$9,750	$8,500	$7,250	$6,000	$4,750	$3,750

GRADING - PPGS™	100%	98%	95%	90%	80%	70%	60%	LAST MSR
581 – various gauges. Importation began 2016.								
MSR $13,600	$12,500	$10,250	$9,000	$8,000	$6,750	$5,550	$4,250	
600 IMPERIAL – 12, 16, or 20 ga., top-of-the-line self-opening action, very ornate engraving throughout.								
MSR $14,550	$13,250	$11,000	$9,500	$8,450	$7,000	$6,000	$4,850	
601 IMPERIAL TIRO – all gauges, sidelock action with nickel plating, ejectors, SST, self-opening action, border engraving.								
MSR N/A	$9,100	$7,750	$6,350	$5,300	$4,175	$3,300	$2,550	
801 – all gauges, Holland-style detachable sidelocks, self-opening action standard, ejectors, coin-wash finish, finest Churchill style engraving.								
MSR N/A	$12,750	$10,425	$9,100	$8,050	$7,000	$6,000	$4,750	
802 – 12, 16, or 20 ga., similar to 801 only non-detachable sidelocks, finest Holland-style engraving.								
MSR N/A	$12,750	$10,425	$9,100	$8,050	$7,000	$6,000	$4,750	
803 – all gauges, similar to 801, finest Purdey-style engraving.								
MSR $17,375	$15,500	$13,000	$11,000	$9,000	$8,000	$7,000	$5,750	
871 – all gauges, rounded frame sidelock action with Demi-Bloc barrels, scroll engraved, ejectors, DTs.								
MSR $6,450	$6,000	$5,200	$4,500	$3,425	$2,750	$2,100	$1,750	
872 – all gauges, rounded frame sidelock action with Demi-Bloc barrels, elaborate scroll engraving with third lever fastener.								
MSR N/A	$16,000	$12,500	$10,750	$9,000	$7,250	$6,000	$5,250	
873 – all gauges, sidelock action with Demi-Bloc barrels, game scene engraving, ejectors, SST.								
MSR N/A	$16,750	$13,000	$11,000	$9,000	$7,250	$6,000	$5,250	
874 – all gauges, sidelock action with Demi-Bloc barrels, action is gold line engraved.								
MSR N/A	$12,950	$11,500	$9,575	$8,325	$7,300	$6,325	$5,275	
875 – all gauges, top-of-the-line quality, built to individual customer specs. only, elaborate engraving with gold inlays.								
MSR N/A	$18,750	$16,250	$14,550	$11,000	$9,250	$8,100	$7,250	
931 – all gauges, self-opening action, elaborate engraving, H&H selective ejectors.								
MSR $41,050	$36,000	$31,000	$26,000	$21,000	$16,000	$12,500	$9,750	
UPLANDER – small gauges only, engraved sidelock action with upgraded straight grip wood.								
MSR $6,450	$6,000	$5,200	$4,500	$3,425	$2,750	$2,100	$1,750	
This model is available only from Wingshooting Adventures.								
ARRIETA SPECIAL – all gauges, engraved sidelock action, upgraded wood.								
MSR N/A	$5,600	$5,000	$4,475	$3,950	$3,000	$2,100	$1,525	
This model is available only from Wingshooting Adventures.								
"BOSS" ROUND BODY – all gauges, Boss pattern best quality engraving, includes $1,500 wood upgrade.								
MSR N/A	N/A	$8,250	$7,150	$5,950	$5,200	$4,400	$3,600	

ARRIZABALAGA, PEDRO

Current manufacturer located in Eibar, Spain since 1944. Currently imported and distributed by William Larkin Moore, located in Scottsdale, AZ. Previously imported by Harry Marx Hi-Grade Imports located in Los Banos, CA until 2015, and by New England Arms Corp. located in Kittery Point, ME.

Arrizabalaga manufactures best quality guns only, carefully made to individual customer specifications. Shotguns listed below have demi-bloc chopper lump barrels and self-opening hand-detachable locks as standard features. The models listed below are essentially custom ordered per individual specifications - delivery time is approximately 12-18 months.

SHOTGUNS: SxS

Add 10% of MSRs for matched pair. Add 10% for round action shaping. Add $920 for gold oval in stock (includes customers initials). Add $4,750 per extra set of same gauge barrels. Add 10% for 20, 28 ga. or .410 bore. Add $2,100 for single non-selective trigger. Add $625 for beavertail forearm. Add $860 for pistol grip or semi-pistol grip stock. Add $1,000-$3,000 for English or Turkish wood upgrade. Add $1,515 for factory furnished fitted leather case.

HEAVY SCROLL MODEL – all gauges, sidelock action, elaborate engraving, deluxe oil finished stock and forearm.

Current MSR on this model is $24,300.

GRADING - PPGS™	100%	98%	95%	90%	80%	70%	60%	LAST MSR

ENGLISH SCROLL MODEL – all gauges, sidelock action, English scroll engraving, deluxe oil finished walnut stock and forearm.

Current MSR on this model is $24,950.

MODEL DELUXE – all gauges, limited importation.

This model is POR.

BOSS STYLE ROUND ACTION MODEL – all gauges, features English Boss-style scroll engraving.

Current MSR on this model is $26,650.

SPECIAL MODEL – all gauges, sidelock top-of-the-line model, best quality wood and engraving.

This model is POR.

ARSENAL DEMOCRACY

Current semi-auto pistol, AR-15 style rifle, and parts manufacturer established in 2013, located in Freeport, FL.

Please refer to BlueBookOfGunValues.com to order the *Blue Book of AR-15s & Variations*, available as a book or online subscription.

ARSENAL FIREARMS

Current pistol manufacturer located in Gardone, Italy. Currently imported by International Firearms Corp. (IFC) located in Midwest City, OK. Previously distributed by EAA Corp. located in Rockledge, FL and Apex International, located in Middletown, CT.

PISTOLS: SEMI-AUTO

AF2011-DOUBLE BARREL PISTOL – .38 Super or .45 ACP cal., unique design allows side by side 4.92 in. barrels, double hammer with single spur, double independent or single trigger uses two single 8 shot magazines paired together with single floorplate, choice of blue steel with walnut grips and fixed sights, or stainless steel with rubber grips and adj. sights, approx. 51 oz. Importation began 2012.

	100%	98%	95%	90%	80%	70%	60%	LAST MSR
MSR $4,400	**$3,995**	**$3,550**	**$3,100**	**$2,750**	**$2,300**	**$2,100**	**$1,950**	

Add $700 for stainless steel construction with rubber grips and adj. sights.

AF2011 DUELLER PRISMATIC PISTOL – .45 ACP cal., unique design allows side by side 6 1/2 in. barrels w/multiple ports and muzzle brakes, double hammer with single spur, double independent or single trigger uses two single 8 shot magazines paired together with single floorplate, extended beavertail grip safety, black textured synthetic grips, prismatic finish, adj. sights, approx. 60 oz., supplied with plastic case. Limited mfg. beginning 2015.

Please contact the importer directly for pricing and availability on this model.

DBDC TACTICAL – .38 Spl. (left side) and .45 ACP (right side) cals., fires both barrels w/one trigger pull, 5 1/2 inch ported barrel, 16 shot mag., adj. sights, three-hole trigger, solid billet aluminum DBDC grips, black finish, 75.2 oz. Importation began 2015.

Please contact the importer directly for pricing and availability on this model.

STRIKE ONE – 9mm Para. or .40 S&W cal., short recoil, non-tilting barrel locking system, 5 in. barrel, 17 shot mag., short travel trigger, lower accessory rail, fully guided, beveled magwell, reversible mag. release, black Nitride finish, approx. 27 oz. Importation circa 2018 only.

	100%	98%	95%	90%	80%	70%	60%	LAST MSR
	$695	**$625**	**$525**	**$475**	**$400**	**$350**	**$295**	***$800***

Add $2,600 for aluminum frame.

STRYK B – 9mm Para. cal., compact, striker fire, AF-Speedlock mechanism, 4.3 in. barrel, 15 shot mag., ergonomic combat trigger, fiber optic front sights w/blacked out rear, Picatinny rail, front and rear slide serrations, 29.6 oz. Limited importation 2017-2018.

	100%	98%	95%	90%	80%	70%	60%	LAST MSR
	$700	**$615**	**$525**	**$475**	**$385**	**$315**	**$245**	***$780***

ARSENAL INC.

Current importer of JSCo Arsenal AD (Bulgarian Arsenal) firearms, parts, and accessories, primarily AK-type or of Kalashnikov design, established during 2001, located in Las Vegas, NV. Dealer and distributor sales.

For individual model listings, please go to BlueBookOfGunValues.com/overflow.

ARSENAL JSCOMPANY (ARSENAL BULGARIA)

Current manufacturer located in Kazanlak, Bulgaria. Currently imported by Arsenal, Inc., located in Las Vegas, NV. Previously imported exclusively in 1994-1996 by Sentinel Arms located in Detroit, MI. For currently imported models, please refer to the Arsenal, Inc. listing.

For individual model listings, please go to BlueBookOfGunValues.com/overflow.

GRADING - PPGS™	100%	98%	95%	90%	80%	70%	60%	LAST MSR

ARSENAL USA LLC

Previous manufacturer/importer from 1999-2004, located in Houston, TX. During September 2004, Arsenal USA LLC changed its name to Armory USA LLC. Please refer to the Armory USA LLC listing for recently manufactured rifles.

For individual model listings, please go to BlueBookOfGunValues.com/overflow.

ART MANIFATTURA ARMI/ART ARMI

Please refer to Manifaturra Armi Art listing in the M section.

ASELKON

Current shotgun manufacturer located in Konya, Turkey. Imported by Adco Arms, located in Woburn, MA.

For more information on Aselkon models, please refer to the Adco Arms listing within this section.

ASHBURY PRECISION ORDNANCE MANUFACTURING

Current manufacturer established in 1995, located in Ruckersville, VA. Previously located in Charlottesville, VA. APO is a division of the Ashbury International Group, Inc. Consumer direct sales.

RIFLES: BOLT ACTION

Ashbury Precision Ordnance (APO) makes a high quality line of precision tactical rifles called the Asymmetric Warrior Series (ASW) and a Tactical Competition Rifle Series (TCR). During 2014, APO also released a SuperSport precision rifle available in .338 Lapua Mag., .300 Win. Mag., or 6.5 Creedmoor cal. Prices on this model are POR. Specifications, features, and options vary from model to model, so please contact the manufacturer directly for more information and current availability.

.375CT SUPERSPORT XLR – .375 CheyTac cal., 28 in. match grade stainless steel barrel, 7 shot detachable box mag., Arclight muzzle brake, 40-MOA monolithic rail, two-stage trigger, ergonomic adj. folding stock, pistol grip, oversized bolt handle, Desert Tan finish, 22 lbs., 8 oz. Mfg. 2013-2016.

	100%	98%	95%	90%	80%	70%	60%	LAST MSR
	$6,800	$5,850	$5,100	$4,300	$3,550	$2,900	$2,350	*$7,425*

.375CT SUPERSPORT XLR (SSX) – .375 CheyTac, .223 Rem., 6.5 Creedmoor, .308 Win., .300 Win. Mag., or .338 Lapua Mag., SABER VX action, 28 in. Pinnacle series stainless steel barrel, Arclight muzzle brake, A1 7 shot detachable box mag., Huber Tactical two-stage trigger, SABER AVX-A1 w/8 flushcups chassis, Quattro alloy series SuperSport forend w/accessory rails, ergonomic SABER PBA-H2 shoulder stock w/ adj. LOP, cheekpiece, vertical recoil pad drop and grip to trigger distance, Ergo Slimline grip, 40 MOA Mil-Std 1913 Picatinny rail, black, FDE, OD Green, Nordic Gray, or Tungsten Cerakote finish, 18 lbs.

Please contact the manufacturer directly for price and availability.

AMERICAN JAEGER – various cals., SABER stainless steel receiver, match grade barrel w/black Nitride finish, Basix single-stage adj. trigger with aluminum alloy Obendorf style guard, two-piece Talley scope base with 1 in. rings, premium English walnut Grade I or premium Turkish walnut Exhibition Grade II classic sporter stock with high comb, no cheekpiece, 13.5 in. LOP, hand-rubbed old world oil finish.

	100%	98%	95%	90%	80%	70%	60%	LAST MSR
MSR $6,650	$5,650	$4,950	$4,250	$3,850	$3,100	$2,550	$2,000	

Add $2,625 for premium Turkish walnut exhibition grade II stock.

ASW-50 – .50 BMG cal., McMillan repeater, Pinnacle Series 27 (disc.) or 29 in. fluted contour barrel with muzzle brake, target crown, 5 shot detachable box mag. w/ambi paddle release lever, Huber Tactical two-stage trigger, Quattro carbon fiber forend, full-length Mil-Std 1913 rail, PBA-H shoulder stock, Limbsaver recoil pad, Magpul M1AD grip set, Picatinny bottom accessory rail, black, FDE, OD Green, or Nordic Gray finish, 25.75 lbs. Mfg. 2011-2020.

	100%	98%	95%	90%	80%	70%	60%	LAST MSR
	$11,250	$10,000	$9,200	$8,000	$6,750	$5,500	$4,500	*$12,575*

ASW-300 – .300 Win. Mag. cal., Surgeon XL-II action, Pinnacle Series 20 or 24 (disc.) in. fluted stainless steel barrel with AAC Blackout muzzle brake, target crown, 5 shot single stack mag. w/ambi paddle lever release, two-stage trigger, Quattro carbon fiber forend, full-length Mil-Std 1913 rail, fully adj. PBA-H shoulder stock, Limbsaver recoil pad, Magpul M1AD grip, black, FDE, ODG, or Nordic Gray finish, 13 lbs. Disc.

	100%	98%	95%	90%	80%	70%	60%	LAST MSR
	$7,850	$7,100	$6,400	$5,500	$4,600	$3,700	$2,850	*$8,550*

ASW-300NM/ASW-300WM – .300 Norma Mag. (NM) or .300 Win. Mag. (WM) cal., SABER LX octagonal stainless steel receiver w/black Nitride coating, 26 (NM) or 24 (WM) in. Pinnacle Series premium match grade stainless steel fluted barrel, Titan QD suppressor, 5 or 10 shot mag. w/ambi lever, two-stage adj. trigger, AXL-A1A or ALX-A2 MOD-1 carbon fiber series modular chasses, SABER PBA-H tool-less shoulder stock w/optional monopod, Quattro carbon fiber forend, Ergo slimline grips, one-piece monolithic and 4 or 12 in. Picatinny rails, Cerakote finish, 12.5 lbs. New 2019.

	100%	98%	95%	90%	80%	70%	60%	LAST MSR
MSR $7,800	$6,625	$5,800	$4,975	$4,500	$3,650	$2,975	$2,325	

GRADING - PPGS™	100%	98%	95%	90%	80%	70%	60%	LAST MSR

ASW-308WIN/ASW-223/ASW-6.5CM - .223 Wylde, .308 Win., or 6.5 Creedmoor (new mid-2014) cal., SABER SX action, 20 (.223 Wylde, .308 Win.) or 24 (6.5 Creedmoor) in. Pinnacle stainless steel fluted barrel, M4-2000 (.223 Wylde) or 762 SD (6.5 Creedmoor, .308 Win.) sound suppressor, 5 (6.5 Creedmoor, .305 Win.) or 10 shot steel mag. w/ambi release lever, two-stage trigger, SABER ASX-A3 carbon fiber chassis, PBA-H tool-less shoulder stock, fixed, double locking or detachable hinge, Ergo Slimline grips, 20 MOA monolithic and 4 or 12 in. Picatinny rails, Cerakote ceramic finish, 11.25-11.75 lbs. New 2012.

MSR $6,995	$5,950	$5,200	$4,475	$4,050	$3,275	$2,675	$2,325

ASW-338LM/ASW-338NM - .338 Lapua Mag. or .338 Norma Mag. cal., Surgeon XL-II (.338 Lapua Mag. only, disc.) or SABER EX action, 20 (.338 Lapua Mag.) or 27 in. Pinnacle Series stainless steel fluted barrel, target crown, AAC Blacckout muzzle break (.338 Lapua Mag. only, disc.), Titan QD suppressor, 5 or 10 shot steel mag. w/ambi release lever, two-stage trigger, SABER AEX-A1A or AEX-A2 carbon fiber chassis, SABER PBA-H tool-less folding shoulder stock w/fixed, double locking, or detachable hinge, 3-position monopod, Ergo Slimline grip to trigger distance adj., 30 MOA monolithic and 12 or 4 in. Picatinny rails, Cerakote finish, 12.25 (.338 Lapua Mag.) or 14.25 (.338 Norma Mag.) lbs., New 2019 (.338 Norma Mag.).

MSR $8,400	$7,150	$6,255	$5,365	$4,860	$3,935	$3,220	$2,500

ASW-375CT/ASW-408CT - .375 ChetTac or .408 ChetTac cal., SABER VX Magnum action, 28 or 30 in. ULR Conical Pinnacle series premium match grade stainless steel barrel, WindTalker muzzle break and sound suppresor, 7 shot steel mag. w/ambi release lever, two-stage adj. trigger, 40 MOA slant co-linear mounted day and night optics, AVX-A1A MOD-1 (375CT) or AEX-A1 MOD-1 (408CT) carbon fiber SABER modular chassis, PBA-H tool-less fixed or double locking stainless steel hinge, interchangeable buttstock, Ergo Slimline AR15 or M-16 style grips, 12 and 4 in. Picatinny rails, black hardcoat anodized and Cerakote finish, 16-16.3 lbs.

MSR $8,995	$7,650	$6,700	$5,750	$5,200	$4,225	$3,450	$2,675

MODULAR SPORT HUNTER (MSH) - .22-250 Rem., 6.5 Creedmoor, .308 Win., or .300 WSM cal., SABER SX, LX, or EX receiver, 16, 20, or 24 in. fluted stainless steel button rifled barrel, alloy construction, 5 shot mag., single stage trigger, fixed HTA ergonomically adj. shoulder stock, Sporter forend with dual sling studs, Ergo Slimline grip, black Cerakote finish. Mfg. 2015-2016 only.

Retail pricing was not available for this model.

SABER M700 ERT SNIPER'S HIDE SPECIAL EDITION - .308 Win. or 6.5 Creedmoor cal., Remington Model 700 Short Action, 20 or 22 in. medium heavy contour barrel w/threaded muzzle, Arclight SC-3 muzzle brake, 5 or 10 shot Magpul PMAG, TriggerTech adj. single stage trigger, double locking alloy folding stock, octagonal aluminum alloy M-LOK forend, MOE hand grip, monolithic 20 in. MOA Mil-Std 1913 Picatinny rail, black oxide barrel and chassis, Armor Black, FDE, OD Green, or Sniper Grey Cerakote finish, 11.25-11.5 lbs. New 2019.

MSR $1,950	$1,600	$1,000	$775	$575	$495	$425	$395

SABER M700 PRECISION RIFLE - .308 Win. or 6.5 Creedmoor cal., Remington Model 700 SPS Tactical AAC-SD barreled action, Magpul polymer 5 shot AICS type mag., Remington Factory X-Mark Pro externally adj, trigger, Magpul CTR carbine shoulder stock w/6-position telescoping LOP and Magpul cheekpiece, double locking hinge w/adj. tension, Magpul MOE grip, AR-08 octagonal handguard free float w/bipod stud and M-LOK mounting slots.

MSR $1,399	$1,190	$1,040	$900	$810	$650	$525	$425

Add $100 for Sporter Combo.

SABER M700 TACTICAL RIFLE - .223 Rem., .308 Win., or 6.5 Creedmoor cal., APO Accurized Remington Model 700 AAC-SD short action carbon steel receiver w/Armor black Cerakote finish, 20 or 22 in. hammer forged carbon steel armor black finish barrel, AAC Blackout 51T muzzle brake, with or w/o AAC 762SD suppressor, 5 or 10 shot polymer or 10 shot detachable AICS pattern box mag., single-stage adj. enclosed body trigger, RSA-A3 MRCS-AR MOD-1 chassis, PBA-H shoulder stock, interchangeable butt hook, fixed or tension adj. double locking alloy folding hinge or fixed and locking stainless steel stock, Ergo Slimline AR-15 or M-16 style grip, AR-08 octagonal aluminum alloy M-LOK and Picatinny rails, 20 MOA Mil-Std 1913, Co-Linear day & night optics, black hardcoat anodized, Kyptek Camo, Multicam Camo, OD Green, FDE, Armor Black, or Sniper Gray Cerakote finish, 11.3-11.5 lbs.

Please contact the manufacturer directly for price and availability.

SABER PRECISION RIFLE (SPR) - .223 Rem., .308 Win., or .300 AAC Blackout cal., Saber SX receiver, Pinnacle Series 16.5 or 20 in. fluted stainless steel button rifled barrel, 5 shot mag., SABER-FORSST Modular Rifle Chassis System (MRCS), alloy construction, one-piece monolithic top rail, single stage trigger, Quattro Alloy Series V17 Mod-1 forend, 12 in. accessory rail mounts, tactical adj. shoulder stock, Ergo Slimline grip, Cerakote color finish. Mfg. 2015-2016 only.

Retail pricing was not available for this model.

GRADING - PPGS™	100%	98%	95%	90%	80%	70%	60%	LAST MSR

SABER PRECISION RIFLE (SPR)-308 – .308 Win. or 7.62 NATO cal., SX short action receiver, 4140 chrome moly 16.5, 20, or 24 in. Pinnacle stainless steel fluted match grade barrel, AAC Blackout muzzle brake, AAC suppressor, 5 or 10 shot polymer or 5 shot steel box mag., single or two-stage TriggerTech trigger, Quattro alloy tactical forend w/M-LOK attachment system, ASX-A3 alloy tactical chassis, PBA-H shoulder stock, double locking tension adj. hinge, interchangeable butt hook, Ergo Slimline or M16/M4 style grip, Black Nitride or Armor Black Cerakote ceramic finish, left-handed model available, 12.9 lbs.

Please contact the manufacturer directly for price and availability.

SEFR SPORT HUNTER – .30-06 or .300 Win. Mag. cal., Rem. 700 action, 26 in. medium contour free floating barrel, 5 shot detachable box mag. w/ambi paddle lever release, Basix trigger, Sporter composite series forend, HTA ergonomically adj. shoulder stock, LOP spacers, Limbsaver recoil pad, flush cup socket and sling swivel attachment points, Ergo Slimline grips, SABER modular chassis, includes Plano rifle case, Armor Black Cerakote finish.

MSR $1,499	$1,275	$1,125	$950	$875	$700	$575	$475

SEFR SPORT-TAC - .223 Rem., .308 Win., or .300 Blackout cal., Remington 700 barreled action, 20 in. barrel, 5 or 10 shot detachable box mag. w/ambi paddle lever release, Basix trigger, sport composite series forend w/free floating barrel channel, ergonomically hand tool adj. fixed or detachable, foldable locking or double locking hinged shoulder stock, thumbscrew cheekpiece, LOP, and Limbsaver Premium recoil pad drop, Ergo Slimline black rubberized grip w/adj. angle adapter, adj. hand to trigger distance, flush cup socket and sling swivel attachment points, Armor Black, OD Green, or FDE Cerakote ceramic finish.

MSR $1,499	$1,275	$1,125	$950	$860	$700	$575	$450

Add $26 for the .308 Win. cal. model.
Add $36 for 10 shot mag. on .223 Rem. and .300 Blackout cal. models.
Add $60 for 10 shot mag. on .308 Win. cal. model.

SUPRA PRECISION LIGHT RIFLE – various cals. available, SABER SX & LX stainless steel receiver, medium contour Pinnacle series stainless steel or carbon fiber wrapped barrel, recessed target crown w/suppressor adapter muzzle brake, 5 or 10 shot detachable polymer or steel mag., Basix single-stage adj. trigger, ASX or ALX MRCS-AR chassis, LUTH-AR MBA-3 ergonomically adj. shoulder stock w/custom APO cheekpiece, double locking alloy stock joint hinge, adj. Ergo Slimline grip, octagonal AR style slotted handguard w/M-LOK attachment system, 20 or 30 MOA monolithic rail, black Nitride or Cerakote finish, 9.5 lbs.

MSR $3,490	$2,975	$2,600	$2,225	$2,025	$1,630	$1,340	$1,050

Add $985 for Shadow-6 Special Valkyrie Edition (stamped with the Valkyrie and Shadow-6 symbols)
Add $2,000 for base rifle Elite model.

TCR – .223 Rem., .260 Rem., 6.5 Creedmoor, .308 Win. Mag., .300 Win. Mag., or .338 Win. Mag. cal., Surgeon RSR receiver, 20, 22, 24, or 27 in. Pinnacle Series fluted stainless steel barrel with or w/o FTE muzzle brake, target crown, 5 or 10 shot detachable box mag. w/ambi paddle lever release, tactical two-stage trigger, MOD-O Quattro carbon fiber forend, Limbsaver recoil pad, Magpul M1AD modular grip, MOD-O Quattro carbon fiber forend, Mil Std 1913 accessory rail, black, OD Green, FDE, or Nordic Gray finish, 12 lbs., New 2012.

$5,650	$5,100	$4,500	$3,900	$3,300	$2,700	$2,100	*$6,325*

Add $970 for .300 Win. Mag. or .338 Norma Mag. cal.

* ***TCR 300 Short Action/TCR Magnum Series*** – .308 Win., 6.5 Creedmoor, .260 Rem., .223 Rem., .338 Norma Mag., or .300 Win. Mag. cal., Surgeon RSR (300 Short Action) or Surgeon 1086 XL-II Repeater (Magnum Series) action, 20, 22, 24, or 27 in. Rock Creek Pinnacle series fluted barrel with or w/o Badger FTE muzzle brake, A3 (300 Short Action) or A1A (Magnum Series) configuration, 5 or 10 (A3 configuration only) shot detachable box mag., Huber Tactical two-stage trigger, SABER SSA-A3 chassis, Quattro carbon fiber forend, adj. LOP, cheekpiece, and vertical recoil pad placement, Magpul M1AD grips, 20 MOA Mil-Std 1913 scope and 4 in. accessory Picatinny rails, Mil-Std 810G corrosion resistant, dull, non-reflective coating, black w/black carbon fiber forend, FDE, OD Green, or Nordic Gray Cerakote finish, 11-15 lbs.

Please contact the manufacturer directly for price and availability.

ASILSAN

Previous trademark of semi-auto pistols manufactured by Ardesen Silah Sanayi, located in Ankara and Istanbul, Turkey.

PISTOLS: SEMI-AUTO

Ardesen Silah Sanayi manufactured two variations of the Asilsan semi-auto pistol - the Atmaca S3 and the Firtina, both with 15 shot magazines. A wide variety of finishes, engraving, and grip options were available in both variations.

GRADING - PPGS™ 100% 98% 95% 90% 80% 70% 60% LAST MSR

ASP

Previously manufactured customized variation of a S&W Model 39-2 semi-auto pistol (or related variations) manufactured by Armament Systems and Procedures located in Appleton, WI.

PISTOLS: SEMI-AUTO

ASP - 9mm Para. cal., compact, DA/SA, see-through grips with cut-away mag. making cartridges visible, Teflon coated, re-contoured lightened slide, combat trigger guard, spurless hammer, and mostly painted Guttersnipe rear sight (no front sight), supplied with 3 mags., 24 oz. loaded. Approx. 3,000 mfg. until 1981.

$3,500 $1,500 $1,275 $1,050 $875 $775 $695

Add $200 for Tritium filled Guttersnipe sight.

Add 10% for rig holster, mags with pouch.

This pistol is marked "ASP" on the magazine extension.

* ***ASP Quest For Excellence*** - special edition, marked "Quest for Excellence". Included buffalo horn grips, presentation book case and letter opener. Approx. 100 mfg.

$4,000 $3,150 $2,700 $2,400 $2,050 $1,775 $1,525

REVOLVERS

ASP REVOLVER - .44 Spl. cal., conversion of a Ruger Speed or Security Six, 5 shot. Less than 100 mfg., unmarked.

$1,275 $1,075 $950 $875 $775 $700 $650

ASPREY

Previous long gun manufacturer located in London, England. While Asprey was established in 1781, the company manufactured high quality shotguns and rifles only from 1990-1999. During 1998, the name was changed to Asprey & Garrard. Guns are currently manufactured by William & Son, located in London, England.

Please refer to the William & Son listing in the "W" section for currently manufactured models.

ASTRA

Previous manufacturer located in Guernica, Spain. Astra was one of the oldest and most widely recognized trademarks in Spain, with a history dating back to 1908. Though arms were manufactured for many years by Unceta y Compania, S.A., located in Guernica, Spain, corporate reorganization resulted in renaming the same firm Astra-Guernica, S.A. (1995-1997), and Astra Sport Guerniquesa de Mecanizado Tratamiento y Montaje de Armas, S.A. (1997-1998).

Pre-1926 *1926-1965* *1965-1998*

Although Astra had hoped to acquire Star patents and relocate to a smaller facility, the efforts were not successful. Foreclosure sealed the factory doors in July, 1998. Inventory, including the "factory collection", was released for sale in 1999.

PISTOLS: SEMI-AUTO

MODEL 1911 - .25 ACP or .32 ACP cal., may have external or internal hammer.

$425 $375 $325 $250 $200 $165 $150

Add 50% for external hammer.

MODEL 1915/1916 - .32 ACP cal., semi-auto.

$400 $350 $300 $240 $195 $160 $125

Note: Models 1915/1916 were later referred to as Model 100 Special.

CAMPO GIRO 1913 - 9mm Largo cal., mfg. 1913-14. Ser. No. range 1-1,300.

$5,500 $4,500 $3,750 $3,400 $2,750 $2,250 $1,750

Add 20% for magazine with matching ser. number.

CAMPO GIRO 1913-1916 - 9mm Largo cal., mfg. 1915-1919. Serial number range 1-13,625.

$3,500 $3,000 $2,500 $2,000 $1,750 $1,500 $1,250

Engraved w/pearlite grips

$11,000 $9,500 $8,000 $6,500 $5,500 $4,500 $3,500

Add 20% for magazine with matching ser. number.

Add $1,500 for factory presentation case.

GRADING - PPGS™	100%	98%	95%	90%	80%	70%	60%	LAST MSR

MODEL 200 FIRECAT AUTOMATIC PISTOL – .25 ACP cal., 2 1/4 in. barrel, 6 shot, blue, plastic grips. Mfg. 1920-68.

	$295	$260	$220	$200	$160	$135	$105	

100% prices assume N.I.B. condition.
Add 50% for engraved M-200.

Editor's Note: There were no Astras with nickel, they were blued, chromed, silver, or chrome engraved - rarely gold plated and gold damascened. The M200 was blued; M201 chromed (add 20%), M202/3 engraved with silver or chrome plating (add 100% if 95% or better), and M204 was gold damascened (add 400% if NIB, more if with gold damascened grips).

MODEL 300 – .32 ACP or .380 ACP cal., Nazi-proofed .380 ACP pistols, Ser. no. range 350,001-630,475 (blocks of ser. no. were omitted from this range),153,085 were mfg. 1923-1946.

	$900	$750	$500	$400	$300	$200	$150	
lightly engraved	$2,250	$1,750	$1,350	$1,000	$800	$600	$500	
deeply engraved w/salesman sample grips	$3,950	$3,250	$2,500	$2,000	$1,500	$1,250	$1,000	

Add 25% for Nazi-proofed .380 ACP pistols.

Between 1941-1945, a total of 85,390 Model 300s were made for the German Luftwaffe and other German military units (approx. 63,000 in .380 ACP and 22,390 in .32 ACP cal.).

MODEL 400 AUTOMATIC PISTOL – 9mm Largo cal., 9 shot, 6 in. barrel, blue, fixed sights, plastic grips. Mfg. 1921-1945.

	$700	$550	$400	$300	$250	$200	$150	
Nazi variation	$1,750	$1,250	$1,000	$750	$600	$520	$400	
Navy variation	$2,950	$2,500	$2,000	$1,500	$950	$800	$700	

Serial range of Nazi specimens (no special markings) is S/N 92,851-98,850.

This particular model in reworked configuration has recently been imported in large quantities.

* ***Model 400 Copies Marked "F. Ascaso"*** – close copy of the Astra Model 400, produced by the Spanish Republican forces during the later part of the Spanish Civil War, F. Ascaso marked (un-numbered) mags., salt blue, estimated production is approx. 8,000, has identifying logo on slide and grip panels, and base of magazine.

	$1,500	$1,200	$900	$600	$500	$400	$300	

* ***Model 400 Copies Marked R.E. (Republica Espagnola)*** – serial number range to approx. 15,000, has identifying logo on forward slide and grip panels.

	$1,250	$950	$700	$600	$500	$400	$300	

Add $200 for wood serrated grips with brass "RE" medallion.

MODEL 600 MOD. AUTOMATIC – 9mm Para. cal., 8 shot, 5 1/4 in. barrel, blue, fixed sights, wood or plastic grips. Mfg. 1944-1945.

	$550	$475	$400	$300	$250	$225	$200	

Add 100% for Chilean Air Force (450 mfg.), or 50% for Portuguese Navy MRP (800 mfg.).

* ***Nazi Waffenamt proofing***

	$1,500	$1,250	$900	$600	$50	$400	$300	

Serial number range for Nazi Waffenamt proofing is 1-10,500.

MODEL 700 SPECIAL – .32 ACP cal., semi-auto.

	$1,500	$1,315	$1,125	$1,020	$825	$675	$525	

MODEL 800 CONDOR AUTOMATIC – 9mm Para. cal., similar to Model 600, except has exposed hammer. Mfg. 1958-65.

	$1,950	$1,750	$1,500	$1,250	$1,000	$800	$650	

Add 20% if NIB with accessories.

MODEL 900 – 7.63mm cal., Broomhandle copy, parts non-interchangeable with Mauser C96. Mfg. from 1928-1936.

	$4,500	$3,500	$2,500	$1,500	$1,000	$800	$700	

Add $1,250 for non-matching shoulder stock.
Add $1,750 for matching stock.
Add 50% for early Bolo grip variation.
Add 20% for specimens with Chinese characters.

GRADING - PPGS™	100%	98%	95%	90%	80%	70%	60%	LAST MSR

MODEL 902 – 7.63mm Mauser cal., semi-auto, similar to Model 900 except 20 shot mag. Beware of fakes - usually created by welding up selective fire pistols.

	100%	98%	95%	90%	80%	70%	60%	LAST MSR
	$20,000	$17,500	$15,000	$13,600	$11,000	$9,000	$7,000	

Add $2,500 for original "booted" stock, another 50% if matching.
Subtract 60% for selective fire version.

MACHINE PISTOLS – NFA class III, transferrable only, 10 or 20 shot detachable mag., several variations.

	100%	98%	95%	90%	80%	70%	60%	LAST MSR
	$10,000	$8,750	$7,500	$6,800	$5,500	$4,500	$3,500	

MODEL 3000 POCKET AUTOMATIC – .32 ACP or .380 ACP cal., 4 in. barrel, fixed sights, blue, plastic grips. Mfg. 1947-1956.

	100%	98%	95%	90%	80%	70%	60%	LAST MSR
	$950	$750	$700	$550	$400	$200	$150	

Add 100% for lightly engraved M3002.
Add 150% for deeply engraved M3003.
Add $1,000 for metallic cherub grips.

MODEL 1000 OR 1000 SPECIAL – .32 ACP cal., semi-auto, extended frame to hold 12 shot mag.

	100%	98%	95%	90%	80%	70%	60%	LAST MSR
	$1,500	$1,200	$900	$600	$500	$400	$300	

MODEL 2000 CUB – .22 Short or .25 ACP cal., 2 1/4 in. barrel, fixed sights, blue, plastic grips, also chrome finish, mfg. 1954-1998, U.S. importation stopped by GCA 68. Astra also made 2000 Model 2000 Cubs for Colt known as the Jr. Model (see Colt section).

	100%	98%	95%	90%	80%	70%	60%	LAST MSR
	$300	$265	$225	$205	$165	$135	$105	

Add 30% for chrome finish. Add 50% for engraved M-2000.

MODEL 2000 CAMPER – .22 Short cal. only, similar to Model 2000 Cub, with 4 in. barrel. Mfg. 1955-1960.

	100%	98%	95%	90%	80%	70%	60%	LAST MSR
	$450	$350	$300	$250	$200	$150	$125	

Add 10% if in original box.

CONSTABLE – .22 LR (10 shot, disc. 1990), .32 ACP (8 shot, disc. 1984), or .380 ACP (7 shot) cal., double action, exposed hammer, 3 1/2 in. barrel, fixed sights, blue or chrome (disc.) finish, plastic grips. Imported 1965-1991.

	100%	98%	95%	90%	80%	70%	60%	LAST MSR
	$450	$350	$300	$250	$200	$150	$125	*$380*

Add $10 for chrome finish or wood grips (disc. in 1990).
Add 10% for .22 LR cal.

* ***Constable Stainless*** – .380 ACP cal. only, stainless version of the Constable. Mfg. 1986 only.

	100%	98%	95%	90%	80%	70%	60%	LAST MSR
	$650	$570	$490	$440	$360	$295	$230	*$345*

* ***Constable Sport*** – similar to Constable, except has 6 in. barrel, blue finish only, 35 oz. Mfg. 1986-87 only.

	100%	98%	95%	90%	80%	70%	60%	LAST MSR
	$500	$450	$350	$300	$250	$200	$150	*$330*

* ***Constable Blue Engraved*** – blue engraved. Importation disc. 1987.

	100%	98%	95%	90%	80%	70%	60%	LAST MSR
	$600	$500	$425	$375	$305	$250	$195	*$375*

Add $20 for .22 LR or checkered wood grips.

* ***Constable Chrome Engraved*** – chrome engraved. Importation disc. 1987.

	100%	98%	95%	90%	80%	70%	60%	LAST MSR
	$500	$440	$375	$340	$275	$225	$175	*$390*

Add $50 for .22 LR or checkered wood grips.

CONSTABLE A-60 – .380 ACP cal., double action, 3 1/2 in. barrel, 13 shot mag., ambidextrous safety, adj. rear sight, blue finish only. Imported 1986-91.

	100%	98%	95%	90%	80%	70%	60%	LAST MSR
	$425	$355	$295	$270	$215	$180	$140	*$475*

MODEL A-70 – 9mm Para. or .40 S&W cal., single action, 3 1/2 in. barrel, steel frame and slide, 7- (.40 S&W) or 8- (9mm Para.) shot mag., compact design, ambidextrous safety, 3-dot sights, matte blue or chrome (new 1993) finish, 25 3/4 oz. Imported 1991-1996.

	100%	98%	95%	90%	80%	70%	60%	LAST MSR
	$375	$305	$250	$220	$180	$145	$115	*$358*

Add 10% for chrome finish.

* ***Model A-70 Stainless*** – stainless steel variation of the Model A-70. Mfg. 1994 only.

	100%	98%	95%	90%	80%	70%	60%	LAST MSR
	$525	$440	$375	$340	$275	$225	$175	*$435*

MODEL A-75 – 9mm Para., .40 S&W, or .45 ACP (new 1994) cal., action similar to Model A-70, except has selective double action with a decocking lever, steel or aluminum (9mm Para. only) frame. Imported 1993-1998.

* ***Model A-75 9mm Para or .40 S&W*** – choice of blue or chrome, steel frame or lightweight aluminum frame (23 1/2 oz.), 7 (.40 S&W) or 8 (9mm Para.) shot mag. Disc. 1998.

	100%	98%	95%	90%	80%	70%	60%	LAST MSR
	$375	$305	$265	$240	$195	$160	$125	*$303*

Add 10% for chrome finish.
Add $50 for lightweight model (aluminum frame).

GRADING - PPGS™ 100% 98% 95% 90% 80% 70% 60% LAST MSR

* ***Model A-75 .45 ACP*** – blue or chrome finish, 7 shot mag. Disc. 1998.

$400 $350 $300 $250 $195 $160 $125 *$358*

Add 10% for chrome finish.

* ***Model A-75 Stainless*** – stainless steel variation of the Model A-75. Mfg. 1994 only.

$425 $395 $325 $275 $225 $175 $125 *$485*

MODEL A-80 – 9mm Para., .38 Super (disc.), or .45 ACP cal., double action, 15 shot mag. (9 for .45 ACP), 3 3/4 in. barrel. Imported 1982-89.

$450 $400 $350 $300 $250 $215 $175 *$425*

Add 10% for chrome finish (disc.).
Add 20% for .38 Super cal. in chrome finish.

MODEL A-90 – 9mm Para. or .45 ACP cal., 1986 designation for Model A-80 with updated slide mounted safety and pushbutton mag. release, 3 3/4 in. barrel, 14 shot mag. (9mm), or 8 shot (.45 ACP), blue only, approx. 48 oz. Imported 1986-90, replaced by Model A-100.

$500 $425 $350 $300 $250 $215 $195 *$500*

Add 100% if stainless steel (INOX).

MODEL A-100 – 9mm Para., .40 S&W, or .45 ACP cal., replaced the Model A-90 in 1990, with similar specifications, blue or chrome finish, re-engineered 1993 incorporating increased mag. capacity, 10 (C/B 1994), 17*/9mm, 12*/.40 S&W, or 9 shot/.45 ACP, approx. 29 oz. Imported 1990-97.

$450 $400 $350 $300 $250 $215 $195 *$351*

Add 20% for chrome finish.
Add 10% for hi cap mags., new in box.
A small number of pistols with an extended slide were made for the Turkish police - add 100%.

MODEL 4000 FALCON – .22 LR, .32 ACP, or .380 ACP cal., 4 in. barrel, fixed sights, blue, plastic grips, exposed hammer. Mfg. 1956-1986.

$650 $500 $350 $275 $235 $200 $175 *$340*

Add 50% for .22 cal.
Add 10% for .380 ACP.

* ***Model 4000 Tri-cal. Kit*** – includes frame and 3 barrels (.22 LR, .32 ACP, and .380 ACP cals.), may have rust blue, salt blue, or chromed (rare) finish, less than 200 mfg.

$2,250 $1,950 $1,650 $1,225 $990 $810 $630

Subtract 15% if not in factory box.

MODEL 4002 FALCON – similar to Model 4000, except lightly engraved.

$1,500 $1,200 $900 $600 $500 $400 $300

MODEL 4003 FALCON – similar to Model 4002, except deeply engraved.

$2,500 $1,900 $1,500 $1,000 $800 $625 $500

REVOLVERS

CADIX DOUBLE ACTION REVOLVER – .22 LR cal., 9 shot, .38 Spl., 5 shot, 4 or 6 in. barrel, adj. sights, blue, plastic grips. Mfg. 1960-68.

$295 $250 $195 $135 $110 $85 $75

Add 25% for early variation with single piece grip.

.357 D/A REVOLVER – .357 Mag. cal., 6 shot, 3, 4, 6, or 8 1/2 in. barrel, adj. sights, blue, checkered wood grips. Mfg. 1972-88.

$450 $400 $350 $300 $250 $215 $175 *$295*

Add 50% for 8 1/2 in. barrel.

* ***.357 D/A Revolver Stainless Steel*** – 4 in. barrel only. Disc. 1987.

$500 $450 $400 $350 $300 $250 $200 *$330*

LARGE CAL. D/A REVOLVER – .41 Mag. (disc. 1985), .44 Mag., or .45 LC (disc. 1987) cal., 6 shot, 6 or 8 1/2 in. (.44 Mag. only) barrels. Mfg. 1980-87.

$550 $450 $350 $300 $250 $200 $175 *$315*

* ***Large Cal. D/A Revolver Stainless Steel*** – .44 Mag. cal. only, 6 in. barrel only, 2 1/2 lbs. Importation disc. 1993.

$450 $400 $350 $300 $250 $215 $175 *$450*

CONVERTIBLE REVOLVER – 9mm Para. cal. with extra .357 Mag. cal. cylinder, 6 shot, 3 in. barrel, blue only, checkered walnut grips, 2 1/4 lbs. Imported 1986-1993.

$795 $650 $500 $400 $350 $300 $250 *$395*

GRADING - PPGS™	100%	98%	95%	90%	80%	70%	60%	LAST MSR

TERMINATOR – .44 Mag. or .44 Spl. (disc.) cal., 6 shot, adj. rear sight, Pachmayr rubber grips, 2 3/4 in. shrouded barrel only. Inventories were depleted in 1989.

Blue finish	$695	$595	$495	$395	$295	$250	$200	*$250*
Stainless steel	$795	$695	$595	$495	$395	$295	$200	*$275*

These models were distributed by John Jovino, located in Yonkers, NY.

ASTRA ARMS S.A.

Current manufacturer established in 2007 and located in Sion, Switzerland. No current U.S. importation.

Astra manufactures a line of AR-15 style tactical rifles called the Sturmgewher 4 Series. Current models include the Carbine, Commando, and Pistol. Astra also manufactures machine guns MG556 (5.56x5 NATO), MG762 (7.62x51 NATO) and MG127 (12.7x99 NATO-.50 BMB) and launchers GL203 (40x46mm) and SL203 (12/70). These models are not currently imported into the U.S. Please contact the company directly for more information, including availability and pricing.

ATKIN, GRANT & LANG

Current gunmaker established in 1960, and located in Hertfordshire, England. Atkin, Grant & Lang is the parent company which owns the trademarks of Henry Atkin, Stephen Grant, and Joseph Lang. Please refer to these individual trademarks listed separately.

ATKIN, HENRY

Current trademark established in 1877 and currently manufactured by Atkin, Grant & Lang, located in Hertfordshire, England. Henry Atkin joined with Grant & Lang during 1960, forming Atkin, Grant & Lang Ltd. No current U.S. importation.

Henry Atkin was apprenticed to his father at James Purdey & Sons in the mid-19th century. By 1890, he was considered a master craftsman of the gun trade. Atkin is best known for modified Beesley/Purdey action self-openers and modified Southgate type ejectors. Henry Atkin died in 1907, but the firm survived through various family members and later the Hodges family of gunmakers. By 1960, the firm merged with Stephen Grant and Joseph Lang.

Atkin Grant & Lang Ltd. provide a useful historical research service on older Henry Atkin shotguns and rifles. The charge for this service is £25 per gun, and the company will give you all pertinent factory information regarding its history.

Some company information courtesy of David Grant and Vic Venters.

SHOTGUNS: SxS

Prices on Henry Atkin shotguns do not include VAT or importation costs. Please contact the company directly for more information, including availability, delivery time, and a price quotation.

Add 10% for matched pairs.

BOXLOCK MODEL – 28 (2 mfg.) or 20 (3 mfg.) ga., very limited millenium edition.

This model is POR from the factory, based on an individual custom order.

SIDELOCK MODEL – 12, 20 ga., or .410 bore, best quality sidelock ejector model with opening assist.

This model is POR from the factory, based on an individual custom order.

ATLAS FORCES

Current brand name of shotguns manufactured by Guler Arms Silah San. Company, located in Konya, Turkey since 2014. No U.S. importation.

Atlas Forces manufactures O/U, semi-auto, slide action, and single barrel shotguns in sporting and tactical configurations. Please contact the company directly for pricing, options, and availability.

ATLAS GUNWORKS

Current semi-auto pistol manufacturer established in 2014, located in North Ferrisburgh, VT.

Atlas Gunworks manufactures competition 1911-style pistols, built to customer specifications.

PISTOLS: SEMI-AUTO

Atlas Gunworks offers a complete line of high quality custom competition pistols built to customer specifications. Current models reflect base model pricing only. Please contact the company directly for more information on Atlas' custom pistols, including a wide variety of options, gunsmithing services, and availability.

Atlas v2 models are competition (no lock back), or duty (lock back slide stop w/mag. follower) ready and offer short, medium, or large, flat, curved, or convex with black, blue, gold, gray, red or silver finish trigger options, black, blue, gray or red magwell base pads as standard options on most models. All models are shipped with 1 magazine, and a memory foam case.

GRADING - PPGS™	100%	98%	95%	90%	80%	70%	60%	LAST MSR

ARTEMIS v2 – 9mm Para. or .40 S&W cal., tri-topped and lightened rail slide cut, 4.6 in. bull barrel, X-Vario trigger, with or w/o tactical rail, with or w/o optic plates options, Atlas Alpha aluminum (9mm Para. cal.) or stainless steel (.40 S&W) grip w/standard, aggressive standard, palm swell, or aggressive palm swell adj. panels, tactical, regular, or large hand magwell, high grip ambi thumb or slide stop lock-back safety, non-safety beavertail grip, two-tone DLC black/satin silver, all DLC black, or hard chrome matte finish. 39 or 47 oz. New 2020.

MSR $5,900	$5,900	$5,175	$4,425	$4,010	$3,250	$2,650	$2,075	

Add $100 for all DLC black finish.
Add $250 for hard chrome finish.
Add $300 for RDS (red dot system) optic plate.

ATHENA – 9mm Para. cal., full dustcover steel frame, tri-topped and lightened slide cut, 4.6 in. bull barrel, race or duty ready mags., tactical magwell, X-line Vario trigger, removable iron sight plate, various optic plates options, tactical rail, Cheely aluminum E2 grip, DLC black finish. Disc. 2020.

	$5,100	$4,465	$3,825	$3,470	$2,800	$2,300	$1,785	*$5,100*

ATHENA v2 – 9mm Para. cal., tri-topped and lightened rail slide cut, 4.6 in. bull barrel, X-Line Vario trigger, with or w/o tactical rail w/various optic plates, Atlas Alpha aluminum grip w/standard or sweat palm adj. panels, tactical, regular, or large hand magwell, high grip ambi thumb or slide stop lock-back safety, non-safety beavertail grip, two-tone DLC black/satin silver, all DLC black, or hard chrome matte finish. 38 or 39 oz. New 2020.

MSR $5,500	$5,500	$4,825	$4,125	$3,750	$3,025	$2,475	$1,925	

Add $100 for optic plate.
Add $100 for all DLC black matte finish.
Add $250 for hard chrome matte finish.

CHAOS – 9mm Para. or .38 SC cal., tri-top lightened slide, 4.25, 4.6, or 5 in. KKM ported bull barrel, Titanium compensator, Atlas aluminum magwell, flared ejection port, black, blue, gray, or red finished X-Line Vario trigger, AGW reflex mount w/red-dot optic options, PT EVO steel grip, two-tone DLC black/satin silver or all DLC black finish. Disc. 2020.

	$6,500	$5,690	$4,875	$4,425	$3,575	$2,925	$2,275	*$6,500*

Add $100 for all DLC black finish.

EREBUS – 9mm Para. cal., Perfect Zero Engineering, full dust cover steel frame, tri-top lightened slide, 4.6 in. bull barrel, single port compensator, Cheely magwell system, flared ejection port, X-Line Vario trigger, Atlas Gunworks plate for Slide Ride optics w/red dot sight, Cheely aluminum E2 grip, two-tone DLC black/satin silver or all DLC black finish. Disc. 2020.

	$6,250	$5,475	$4,695	$4,250	$3,450	$2,825	$2,195	*$6,250*

Add $100 for tactical rail.
Add $100 for all DLC black finish.

EREBUS v2 – 9mm Para. cal., tri-topped and lightened rail slide cut, 4.6 in. bull barrel, X-Line Vario trigger, with or w/o tactical rail, various optic plate options, Atlas Alpha aluminum grip w/standard or palm swell adj. panels, tactical, regular, or large hand magwell, high grip ambi thumb or slide stop lock-back safety, non-safety beavertail grip, two-tone DLC black/satin silver, all DLC black, or hard chrome matte finish, 39.5 oz. New 2020.

MSR $6,300	$6,300	$5,515	$4,725	$4,285	$3,465	$2,835	$2,200	

Add $100 for all DLC black finish.
Add $250 for hard chrome finish.

HELIOS – 9mm Para. cal., steel frame, square dust cover, tri-topped slide, 4.25 in. barrel, Atlas Gunworks lockback system, Double Alpha Academy mag. base pads, flared ejection port, black, blue, gray, or red finished X-Line Vario trigger, with or w/o tactical rail, Cheely aluminum E2 grip and magwell, thumb and non-working beavertail grip safety, two-tone DLC black/satin silver or all black DLC finish, 40 oz. Disc. 2020.

	$5,000	$4,375	$3,750	$3,400	$2,750	$2,250	$1,750	*$5,000*

Add $100 for tactical rail.
Add $100 for all DLC black finish.

HYPERION – 9mm Para. cal., Perfect Zero engineering, full dust cover steel frame, tri-topped and lightened slide w/polished flats, 4.6 in. KKM bull barrel, single port compensator, black, blue, gray, or red finished X-Line Vario trigger, with or w/o tactical rail, Cheely aluminum E2 grip and magwell, two-tone DLC black/satin silver or all DLC black finish. Disc. 2020.

	$5,200	$4,550	$3,900	$3,535	$2,860	$2,350	$1,825	*$5,200*

Add $100 for tactical rail.
Add $100 for all DLC black finish.

GRADING - PPGS™	100%	98%	95%	90%	80%	70%	60%	LAST MSR

HYPERION v2 – 9mm Para. cal., tri-topped and lightened slide, 4.6 in. KKM bull barrel, X-Line Vario Trigger, fiber front and adj. rear sights with or w/o tactical rail, Atlas Alpha aluminum grip w/standard or palm swell adj. panels, retainer, tactical, regular, or large hand magwell, high grip ambi slide stop lock-back and thumb safety, non-safety beavertail grip, two-tone DLC black/satin silver, all DLC black or hard chrome matte finish, 37.5 oz. New 2020.

MSR $5,200	**$5,200**	**$4,550**	**$3,900**	**$3,535**	**$2,860**	**$2,350**	**$1,825**	

Add $100 for all DLC black finish.
Add $250 for hard chrome finish.

NEMESIS – 9mm Para. or .40 S&W cal., Perfect Zero engineering, steel frame, square dust cover, tri-topped and lightened slide with polished flats, 5 in. KKM bull barrel, flared ejection port, X-Line Vario trigger, custom built sight block, with or w/o tactical rail, PT EVO grip w/magwell options, tool-less guide rod, two-tone DLC black/satin silver, Gradient PVD Smoked gray/DLC black, or all DLC black finish. Disc. 2020.

	$5,500	**$4,815**	**$4,125**	**$3,750**	**$3,025**	**$2,475**	**$1,925**	***$5,500***

Add $100 for tactical rail.
Add $100 for all DLC black finish.

NEMESIS v2 – 9mm Para. or .40 S&W cal., tri-topped and lightened slide, 5 in. bull barrel, X-Line Vario trigger, fiber front and adj. rear sights, with or w/o tactical rail, Atlas Alpha aluminum (9mm Para. cal.) or stainless steel (.40 S&W cal.) grip w/std. delta, std. palm swell, aggressive delta, or aggressive palm swell adj. panels, tactical, regular, or large hand magwell, high grip ambi thumb and slide stop lock-back safety, non-safety beavertail grip, two-tone DLC black/satin silver, all DLC black, or hard chrome matte finish, 54 oz. New 2020.

MSR $5,900	**$5,900**	**$5,175**	**$4,425**	**$4,010**	**$3,250**	**$2,650**	**$2,075**	

Add $100 for all DLC black finish.
Add $250 for hard chrome finish.

NYX – 9mm Para. cal., Regular steel or Ultralite aluminum frame with tri-topped slide with polished flats, 3.5 or 4.25 in. barrel, Atlas Gunworks lockback system, with or w/o tactical rail, full-size Cheely E2 aluminum grip with or w/o Cheely Small IDPA/IPSC magwell, thumb and non-working beavertail grip safety, all DLC black matte finish Disc. 2020.

	$5,500	**$4,815**	**$4,125**	**$3,750**	**$3,025**	**$2,475**	**$1,925**	***$5,500***

Add $100 for tactical rail.

NYX v2/NYX OPTICS v2 – 9mm Para. cal., tri-topped, 4.5 in. flush cut reverse crown bull barrel, X-Line Vario Trigger, fiber front and fixed rear sight, with or w/o tactical rail and various optic plates (NYX Optics v2), Atlas Alpha aluminum carry textured grip w/standard or palm swell adj. panels, high grip ambi thumb, side stop lock-back safety, non-safety beavertail grip, two-tone DLC black/satin silver, all DLC black, or hard chrome matte finish, 36 or 37.5 oz. New 2020.

MSR $5,200	**$5,200**	**$4,550**	**$3,900**	**$3,535**	**$2,860**	**$2,350**	**$1,825**	

Add $100 for all DLC black finish.
Add $250 for hard chrome finish.
Add $300 for NYX Optics v2 model.

TITAN – 9mm Para., .40 S&W, or .45 ACP cal., full dustcover tri-topped lightened cut slide, fixed rear and Fiber or Tritium front sights, Atlas Alpha aluminum or aggressive stainless steel grip, tactical magwell, high grip ambi thumb safety and slide stop lock-back safety, non-safety beavertail grip, two-tone DLC black/satin silver, all DLC black, or hard chrome matte finish, 50-54 oz.

MSR $4,000	**$4,000**	**$3,500**	**$3,000**	**$2,725**	**$2,200**	**$1,800**	**$1,400**	

Add $100 for all DLC black finish.
Add $250 for hard chrome finish.

Limited availability made in small batches released only from mfg. website. This model cannot be ordered or found in dealer networks.

AUSTRIAN SPORTING ARMS

Previous importer located in Ware, MA circa 2010-2011.

Austrian Sporting Arms imported the M22 pistol manufactured by ISSC Handelsgesellschaft, located in Ried, Austria. Litigation brought about by Glock regarding patent and design infringement forced them to cease operations.

AUSTRALIAN AUTOMATIC ARMS PTY. LTD.

Previous AR-15 style rifle and pistol manufacturer located in Tasmania, Australia. Previously imported and distributed by California Armory, Inc. located in San Bruno, CA.

GRADING - PPGS™	100%	98%	95%	90%	80%	70%	60%	LAST MSR

PISTOLS: SEMI-AUTO, AR-15 STYLE

SAP – .223 Rem. cal., GIO, 10 1/2 in. barrel, SA, 20 shot mag., fiberglass stock and forearm, 5.9 lbs. Imported 1986-1993.

$795	$700	$600	$550	$500	$475	$450	*$799*

RIFLES: SEMI-AUTO, AR-15 STYLE

SAR – .223 Rem. cal., GIO, AR-15 style, 16 1/4 or 20 in. (new 1989) barrel, 5 or 20 shot M16 style mag., fiberglass stock and forearm, 7 1/2 lbs. Imported 1986-89.

$1,250	$1,000	$900	$800	$775	$750	$700	*$663*

Add $25 for 20 in. barrel.

This model was also available in a fully automatic version (AR).

SP – .223 Rem. cal., GIO, AR-15 style, sporting configuration, 16 1/4 or 20 in. barrel, wood stock and forearm, 5 or 20 shot M16 style mag., 7 1/4 lbs. Imported late 1991-93.

$850	$750	$650	$600	$550	$500	$475	*$879*

Add $40 for wood stock.

AUSTRALIAN INTERNATIONAL ARMS

Previous manufacturer and exporter located in Brisbane, Australia until circa 2009. Previously, Australian International Arms worked in cooperation with ADI Limited Lithgow, formerly Small Arms Factory, known for its SMLE No. I MKIII and L1A1 rifles. AIA outsourced the manufacture of its designs and specifications. Previously imported in North America by Marstar Canada, located in Ontario, Canada, and imported and distributed until 2004 by Tristar Sporting Arms, Ltd., located in N. Kansas City, MO.

RIFLES: BOLT ACTION, ENFIELD SERIES

M10-A1 – 7.62x39mm cal., redesigned and improved No. 4 MK2 action, parkerized finish, all new components, teak furniture with No. 5 Jungle Carbine style stock with steel or brass buttplate, 20 in. chrome-lined barrel with muzzle brake, adj. front sight, 10 shot mag., Picatinny rail, 8.3 lbs.

While advertised in 2007, this model never went into production.

* ***M10-A2*** – 7.62x39mm cal., similar to M10A2, except has No. 8 style forend, Monte Carlo stock, and 16.1 in. chrome-lined barrel. Limited importation 2003-2004 by Tristar.

$750	$700	$600	$525	$450	$375	$300	*$659*

M10-B1 – .308 Win. cal., redesigned and improved No. 4 MK2 action, matte blue finish, all new components, teak furniture with sporter carbine style stock and steel buttplate, 22 in. barrel, adj. front sight, 10 shot mag., Picatinny rail, 8.3 lbs. Imported 2006-disc.

$575	$500	$425	$350	$300	$275	$250	*$675*

* ***M10-B2*** – .308 Win. cal., similar to M10-B1, except has brass buttplate, gloss blue finish, 25 in. chrome-lined bull barrel, and bipod stud, 10 1/2 lbs. Imported 2006-disc.

$650	$525	$425	$350	$300	$275	$225	*$760*

* ***M10-B3*** – .308 Win. cal., similar to M10-B1, except has chrome steel buttplate, gloss blue finish, and 22 in. lightweight barrel, 7 1/2 lbs. Limited importation 2006-disc.

$900	$800	$700	$600	$500	$425	$350	*$1,000*

NO.4 MK IV – .308 Win. cal., parkerized finish, 25.2 in. chrome-lined medium weight barrel, teak furniture with steel buttplate, 9.1 lbs. Prototype only imported by Tristar. Limited importation beginning 2006.

$575	$500	$425	$350	$300	$275	$250	*$675*

Add $440 for walnut stock, glass bedding, target barrel, elevated Picatinny rail, and accessories (disc.).

M 42 – .308 Win. cal., 27.6 in. barrel with mahogany stock and extra cheekpiece, blue printed action, bright metal/barrel finish, includes Picatinny rail, 8.2 lbs. Imported 2003-2004.

$1,125	$950	$800	$650	$550	$450	$350	*$1,295*

SHOTGUNS: LEVER ACTION

MODEL 1887 – 12 ga., 2 3/4 in. chamber, uncheckered oil finished walnut stock and forearm, blue finish, steel buttplate, 5 shot, exposed hammer with half cock, 22 in. barrel, 8 3/4 lbs. Approx. 100 units mfg. by ADI Lithgow before discontinuance due to ADI technical and quality control problems. Dealer sample importation only 2003-2004.

$995	$850	$750	$650	$600	$550	$500	*$1,195*

GRADING - PPGS™	100%	98%	95%	90%	80%	70%	60%	LAST MSR

AUTAUGA RIFLES, INC.

Previous manufacturer located in Prattville, AL 1996-2002. In 2000, Autauga Arms, Inc. changed their name to Autauga Rifles, Inc.

PISTOLS: SEMI-AUTO

AUTAUGA MKII 32 – .32 ACP cal., double action only, 2 in. barrel, hammerless, blowback action, 6 shot mag., stainless steel, black polymer grips, 3/4 lb. 3,200 mfg. 1996-2000.

	100%	98%	95%	90%	80%	70%	60%	LAST MSR
	$325	$225	$185	$140	$120	$100	$85	*$399*

Early guns did not have the MKII designation.

RIFLES: BOLT ACTION

Autauga Rifles, Inc. manufactured a complete line of precision bolt action rifles which were special ordered per individual customer specifications. Configurations included hunting, long range competition, law enforcement, and military tactical rifles. Complete packages included rifle, optics, hardware, and cleaning equipment. Standard rifle prices varied from $2,500-$3,500, depending on options. Rifles were supplied with a Pelican 1750 case.

AUTO MAG

Previously manufactured (circa 1971-1982) by Auto Mag. Corp. and TDE Corp. Most recent manufacture (Harry Sanford Commemorative) was produced by Galena Industries, located in Sturgis, SD.

Less than 9,000 Auto Mags were produced by all manufacturers. All pistols originally had all stainless steel mags., and a short recoil rotary bolt system made entirely of stainless steel. Most pistols were sold in .44 AMP cal., although .357 AMP was also a popular factory option.

A unique handgun, the Auto Mag was never a commercial success due to high manufacturing costs and initial functioning problems (mostly attributed to hand loading all the ammo - once factory ammo became available, reliability improved significantly). Initial reaction to Dirty Harry's use of this firearm in the movie "Sudden Impact" (1983), as well as Burt Reynolds in "Malone" (1987) made prices escalate considerably, but most values appear to have stabilized since 1989. Be aware of fakes - especially of the XP variety (re-serialized, re-stamped, location of markings, etc.). Also, the ease of barrel swapping should be considered when deciding on a potential purchase. Auto Mags were never Mag-Na-Ported from the factory (only The Custom 100 Series). Non-original Mag-Na-Porting actually detracts from the values listed below, since it is a non-factory alteration.

Serial number ranges for the various models are as follows: Pasadena mfg. - A0000 through A03700. TDE North Hollywood - mostly A02500 through A05015, although some were marked with very low serial numbers. TDE El Monte mfg. - A05016 through A08300. (Note: these numbers should only be used as a guideline - as the company name changed, serial numbers overlapped.)

Although High Standard claimed to be the national sales distributor in 1974 and 1975 and had flyers indicating this, Lee E. Jurras and Associates, Inc. was actually the exclusive world wide distributor. Despite this, High Standard records show sales of 1045 Auto Mags.

High Standard catalog numbers are: 9346 for .44 AMP, and 9347 for .357 AMP. High Standard sold 134 Auto Mags with an "H" prefix. Serial numbers between H1 and H198, with one at H1566 and three between H17,219-H17,222. 108 of these were .44 AMP and 26 were .357 AMP. High Standard also sold 911 Auto Mags between serial numbers A05278-A07637. 777 of these were .44 AMP and 108 were .357 AMP. The "H" prefix guns remain a collectors' item and command a 25% premium over values listed below. It is estimated that an additional 300 barrels were marked High Standard.

DE/OMC marked pistols - B00001 through B00370 are known as the "B" series or solid bolt models (only 370 manufactured). This "B" series also commands collector premiums.

AMT manufactured the last two lots of Auto Mags; the first was the "C" series and was basically the same as the "B" except that only 50 guns were fabricated. The "B" Series was manufactured in 1979. Serial numbered C00001-C00050 "C" Series was manufactured in 1979, and the "Last" Series was manufactured in 1982. The last Auto Mags made by AMT were appropriately serial numbered LAST 1 through LAST 50. These guns had the reputation of being the poorest quality, and do carry collector premiums. One interesting variation is the North Hollywood "two-line" model. Also, the first .357 cal. pistols manufactured did not have the words AUTO MAG appearing on the gun. These are also collectors' items.

In addition to the above calibers, a very few non-factory .22, .25 and .30 LMP (Lomont Magnum Pistols) cal. prototypes were fabricated by Kent Lomont. These specimens will usually demand a premium over the values listed below. Also, some barrels and pistols were made in Covina, CA.

GRADING - PPGS™ 100% 98% 95% 90% 80% 70% 60% LAST MSR

PISTOLS: SEMI-AUTO

ORIGINAL PASADENA - .44 AMP cal. only, 6 1/2 in. VR barrel, ser. no. A0001-A3300.

N/A $3,500 $3,000 $2,750 $2,500 $2,250 $2,000

This model is generally regarded as having the most quality, as all components were milled from Carpenter 455 stainless steel stock.

TDE NORTH HOLLYWOOD - ser. no. range A3400 - A05015.

* ***TDE North Hollywood .44 AMP*** - 6 1/2 in. VR barrel, initial guns were mfg. from existing Pasadena parts, later mfg. required new components made by TDE.

N/A $3,250 $3,000 $2,750 $2,500 $2,250 $1,750

Quality on this model goes down in later mfg. (some small parts are not stainless). Because of this, higher serial numbered guns in this model are less desirable.

* ***TDE North Hollywood .357 AMP*** - two line address, there are no factory records verifying this caliber, and most were assembled with spare barrels.

N/A $2,950 $2,750 $2,500 $2,250 $1,750 $1,550

TDE EL MONTE - ser. no. range A05016-A08300.

* ***TDE El Monte .44 AMP*** - 6 1/2 VR, 8 1/2, or 10 1/2 in. tapered barrel.

N/A $2,750 $2,500 $2,350 $2,050 $1,850 $1,450

* ***TDE El Monte .357 AMP*** - 6 1/2 VR, 8 1/2, or 10 1/2 in. tapered barrel.

N/A $2,250 $2,100 $1,850 $1,625 $1,350 $1,100

HIGH STANDARD - "H" prefixed serial numbers, approx. 132 mfg. by TDE with High Standard markings.

$2,250 $2,100 $1,850 $1,620 $1,335 $1,115 $930

LEE JURRAS STANDARD MODELS - see listings below, custom features would vary from presentation grade polishing of barrel and frame to exotic wood or Micarta grips.

* ***LEJ Standard Automag*** - .357 AMP or .44 AMP cal., 6 1/2 (with vent rib), 8 1/2, or 10 1/2 in. non-rib barrel, TDE markings, lion's head logo. 1,100-1,200 mfg. 1974-76 by Lee Jurras & Associates. - Lee Jurras Custom Models included the 100 (listed below), 200 International (12 mfg.), 300 Alaskan (9 mfg.), 400 Backpacker (5 mfg.), 500 Grizzly (5 mfg.), 600 Condor (2 mfg.), and Metallic Silhouette (2 mfg.). Because of the rarity factor, these models with 12 or less mfg. are difficult to price accurately, and must be evaluated and appraised individually.

N/A $2,225 $2,050 $1,775 $1,560 $1,280 $1,070

Lee Jurras added his Lion's head logo (1974-1976) on TDE manufactured guns. There were also a very limited quantity of original shoulder stocks (less than 12), and were available for the International and Alaskan models only - extreme rarity precludes accurate price evaluation.

Several other calibers and variations were marketed through Lee Jurras including one-of-a-kind exotics like a .30 cal. Cougar with 12 in. barrel and highly polished metal.

LEE JURRAS CUSTOM MODELS

* ***LEJ Custom Model 100*** - .357 AMP, .41 JMP (Jurras Magnum Pistol), or .44 AMP cal., 6 1/2 in. VR or 8 1/2 non-rib (only 10 mfg. in each cal.) polished Mag-Na-Ported barrel, custom laminated wood grips, special carrying case. 100 mfg. in each cal.

N/A $3,150 $2,850 $2,350 $2,065 $1,860 $1,430

TDE/OMC "B" SERIES - 6 1/2 VR or 10 in. barrel, ser. no. range B00001-B00370.

N/A $2,250 $2,100 $1,850 $1,620 $1,335 $1,115

AMT "C" SERIES - 6 1/2 in. VR or 10 in. barrel, ser. no. range C00001 - C00050.

N/A $2,250 $2,100 $1,850 $1,620 $1,335 $1,115

Note: guns were cased (plastic attache style) with accessories. Collector caution - over the years, the foam in these plastic cases can break down, and may cause discoloration and pitting on the gun. Original Auto-Mag ammo (original mfg. only by CDM in Mexico and Norma in Sweden) is currently selling for approx. $75-$95 a box. Starline now has .44 AMP brass, and Corbon loaded .44 AMP ammo also - new 2001.

HARRY SANFORD COMMEMORATIVE AUTO MAG - .44 AMP cal., Automag, Inc. commemorative reissue, "STURGIS, SD" barrel address with Harry Sanford signature on left rear of slide, cased. 1,000 pistols were scheduled to be mfg., but only approx. 300 actually completed by Galena Industries 1999-2000.

N/A $4,000 $3,500 $3,000 N/A N/A N/A *$2,750*

GRADING - PPGS™	100%	98%	95%	90%	80%	70%	60%	LAST MSR

AUTO MAG LTD. CORP

Current manufacture of Auto Mag .44 pistols and parts, established in 2015 and located in Loris, SC.

In 2015, Auto Mag Ltd. Corp. purchased all of the assets and rights to the Auto Mag. The new Auto Mags are produced through an agreement with Excel Industries.

PISTOLS: SEMI-AUTO

AUTO MAG CLASSIC .44 – .44 AMP cal., recoil operated, stainless steel, 6 1/2 or 8 1/2 in. barrel, includes two 7 shot mags., exposed hammer, adj. travel target trigger, fixed front and adj. rear target sights, Hogue G10 or Hogue checkered wooden grips, ambidextrous safety, high polish or brush satin finish, 3.1 to 3.6 lbs. Limited mfg. beginning 2017.

MSR $3,495 $2,975 $2,600 $2,225 $2,025 $1,650 $1,350 $1,050

Add $275 for high polish finish. Add $300 for 8 1/2 in. barrel.

FOUNDER'S EDITION .44 – .44 AMP cal., recoil operated, 8 1/2 in. barrel, 7 shot mag., exposed hammer, fixed front and adj. rear target sights, checkered wood grips, ambidextrous safety, includes wooden presentation case, high polish stainless steel upper, 11.7-13.7 in. OAL, 53-58 oz. Mfg. 2017-2020.

$3,400 $2,950 $2,550 $2,300 $1,850 $1,550 $1,200 *$3,995*

AUTO-ORDNANCE CORP.

Current manufacturer with facilities located in Greeley, PA. Previously located in Worcester, MA. Corporate offices are also located in Greeley, PA. Previously located in Blauvelt, NY. Auto-Ordnance Corp. became a division of Kahr Arms in 1999. Auto-Ordnance Corp. was a division of Gun Parts Corp. until 1999. Previously located in West Hurley, NY.

PISTOLS: SEMI-AUTO

During 1997, Auto Ordnance discontinued all calibers on the pistols listed below, except for .45 ACP or 9mm Para. cal. Slide kits were available for $179. Also, conversion units (converting .45 ACP to .38 Super or 9mm Para.) were available for $195.

All current Auto Ordnance 1911 Models include a spent cartridge case, plastic carrying case, and cable lock.

1911 BOOTLEGGER – .45 ACP cal., 5 in. barrel, 7 shot mag., blade front and rear drift adj. for windage sights, engraved American walnut grips, engraved historical images from 1920s w/"Bootlegger Prohibition Edition", "White Lightning", and " Proof Tennessee Moonshine" on slide, distressed Midnight Blue Cerakote w/clear coating finish, 2.3 lbs. Mfg. 2020 only.

$1,100 $950 $800 $750 $600 $500 $385 *$1,215*

1911 COMPETITION – .38 Super (1996 only) or .45 ACP cal., compensated barrel, commander hammer, white 3-dot sighting system, black textured wraparound grips, beavertail grip safety, flat mainspring housing, includes spent cartridge case, plastic carrying case, and cable lock. Mfg. 1993-1996.

$530 $415 $375 $330 $300 $285 $270 *$636*

Add $10 for .38 Super cal.

1911 A1 100TH ANNIVERSARY – .45 ACP cal., 5 in. barrel, parkerized finish, based on the original military design, diamond checkered wood grips, anniversary laser engraving. Limited mfg. 2011-2013.

$525 $425 $325 $295 $250 $225 $215 *$658*

1911 A1 CUSTOM HIGH POLISH – .45 ACP cal., 8 shot mag., 5 in. barrel, custom combat hammer, beavertail grip safety, rosewood grips with medallions, 3-dot sights, flat mainspring housing, Videcki speed trigger, 39 oz. Mfg. 1997-1999.

$485 $395 $325 $265 $235 $225 $215 *$585*

1911 A1 DELUXE 80 – .38 Super (disc. 1996), 9mm Para. (disc. 1996), or .45 ACP cal., 5 in. barrel, 3-dot sights, wraparound grips, 39 oz. Mfg. 1991-2006.

$480 $385 $315 $260 $240 $225 $215 *$615*

1911 A1 GENERAL – .38 Super (mfg. 1996 only) or .45 ACP cal., 4 1/2 in. barrel with full-length recoil spring guide, 7 shot mag., blue finish, 3-dot fixed Millett sights, black rubber wraparound grips, Commander styling, 37 oz. Mfg. 1992-1998.

$385 $315 $255 $235 $225 $215 $200 *$465*

1911 A1 GI SPECS – .45 ACP or 9mm Para. (new mid-2018) cal., 5 in. barrel, 7 or 9 (9mm Para.) shot mag., carbon steel slide, sear, and disconnector machined from solid bar stock, blade front and rear drift adj. sights, brown checkered plastic grips or checkered wood grips with U.S. logo (.45 ACP cal. only, new 2017), thumb and grip safety, firing pin block, matte black finish, 39 oz. New 2015.

MSR $778 $675 $590 $500 $450 $375 $300 $250

Add $33 for checkered wood grips featuring U.S. logo (.45 ACP cal. only, new 2017).
Add $50 for 9mm Para. cal. (new mid-2018).

GRADING - PPGS™	100%	98%	95%	90%	80%	70%	60%	LAST MSR

1911 A1 GI SPECS COMMANDER MODEL – .45 ACP cal., 4 1/4 in. barrel, 7 shot mag., steel construction, blade front, rear drift adj. for windage sights, brown checkered plastic grips or wood grips with U.S. logo (new 2020), thumb and grip safety, matte black finish, 8 1/2 in. OAL, 39 oz. New 2018.

MSR $828	$675	$590	$500	$460	$375	$300	$250	

Add $33 for wood grips (new 2020).

1911 A1 SPECIAL EDITION – .45 ACP cal., 5 in. barrel, steel frame and slide, iron sights, checkered gray laminate or black rubber grips with Thompson bullet logo, Sniper Green or Black/Hunter Orange Cerakote finish, 39 oz. Limited mfg. 2015-2016.

	$675	$575	$500	$425	$375	$325	$275	*$759*

1911 A1 STANDARD 80 – .45 ACP cal., features firing pin block safety, 5 in. barrel, otherwise similar to 1911 A1 Standard. Mfg. 2004-2007.

	$465	$375	$310	$255	$235	$225	$215	*$609*

1911 A1 STANDARD/COMPACT STANDARD – .38 Super (disc. 1996), 9mm Para. (disc. 1996), .40 S&W (mfg. 1991-93), 10mm (mfg. 1991-96), or .45 ACP cal., 4 1/4 (.45 ACP only, Compact Standard Model), 4 1/2 (.40 S&W cal. only) or 5 (Standard Model) in. barrel, 7 shot mag., single action, parts interchange with the original Colt Govt. Model, blue or nickel finish, checkered plastic grips, 39 oz. Disc. 2005.

	$450	$370	$295	$255	$235	$225	$215	*$592*

Add $28 for satin nickel (mfg. 1990-96) or $37 for duo-tone (mfg. 1992-96) finish (.45 ACP only).

1911 A1 WWII PARKERIZED – .45 ACP cal., 5 in. barrel, no frills variation of the 1911 A1, military parkerizing, G.I. detailing with military style roll stamp, plastic or checkered walnut (disc. 2001, reintroduced 2007) grips, and lanyard loop. Mfg. 1992-2016.

	$585	$510	$440	$400	$325	$275	$225	*$688*

Add $17 for wood grips with U.S. logo (new 2007).

CASE HARDENED 1911 – .45 ACP cal., "GI" pattern 1911 pistol, 5 in. barrel, 7 shot mag., blade front and rear drift adj. for windage sights, checkered wood grips with U.S. logo, thumb and grip safety, case hardened finish, 39 oz. New mid-2018.

MSR $1,390	$1,185	$1,035	$890	$800	$650	$535	$415	

"FLY GIRLS" SPECIAL EDITION 1911 – .45 ACP cal., custom 1911 style pistol honors the Women Airforce Service Pilots (WASPs), 5 in. barrel, 7 shot mag., blade front and rear drift (adj. for windage) sights, checkered wood grips with U.S. logo, custom engraved with the original Fly Girls script, logo, wings, and years of service, also includes the Star Roundel, rivets and panels, two-color black and OD Green Cerakote finish, 35 oz. Limited mfg. Mfg. 2018-2020.

	$1,050	$925	$795	$715	$580	$475	$375	*$1,240*

"I STAND" 1911 – .45 ACP cal., GI pattern, 5 in. barrel, 7 shot mag., blade front and rear drift adj. sights, American flag grips, thumb, grip, and firing pin block safety, engraved with "All Gave Some, Some Gave All" on dust cover, "I Stand" on right slide, and "Freedom Is Not Free" on left side of frame, worn black and gray Cerakote finish, 39 oz. Limited mfg. 2019-2020.

	$1,100	$1,000	$850	$750	$600	$500	$400	*$1,313*

LIBERTY 1911 "DON'T TREAD ON ME" – .45 ACP cal., 5 in. barrel, 7 shot mag., blade front and rear drift adj. sights, custom engraved Goncalo wood grips, "Don't Tread On Me" motto and Gadsen flag marked on frame, brown/black Cerakote finish, 2.3 lbs. New 2020.

MSR $1,278	$1,085	$950	$815	$740	$600	$500	$400	

MODEL ZG-51 "PIT BULL" – .45 ACP cal. only, compact variation of the 1911 A1, 3 5/8 in. standard (disc. 1996) or 4 3/8 in. compensated (new 1997) barrel, 7 shot mag., 36 oz. Mfg. 1988-99.

	$385	$310	$255	$235	$225	$215	$200	*$470*

REVOLUTION SPECIAL EDITION 1911 – .45 ACP cal., 5 in. barrel, 7 shot mag., blade front and rear drift adj. for windage sights, engraved with historical artwork paying tribute to our nation's Founding Fathers, engraved solid copper grips with eagle and Declaration of Independence on the left panel, Liberty Bell on right, thumb safety, grip safety, firing pin block, Distressed Cerakote Midnight Blue finish covered with matte clear finish, 2.3 lbs. New 2020.

MSR $1,338	$1,150	$1,005	$865	$780	$635	$525	$425	

"SQUADRON" SPECIAL EDITION 1911 – .45 ACP cal., custom 1911, 5 in. barrel, 7 shot mag., blade front and rear drift adj. for windage sights, checkered wood grips with U.S. logo, custom engraved to resemble a WWII fighter plane featuring the famous shark mouth artwork, Army Air Corps insignia on both side and a rivet pattern engraved over the gun, worn black and gray Cerakote finish, 39 oz. Limited mfg. beginning mid-2018.

MSR $1,259	$1,070	$935	$800	$725	$595	$485	$400	

GRADING - PPGS™ 100% 98% 95% 90% 80% 70% 60% LAST MSR

"VICTORY GIRLS" SPECIAL EDITION 1911 – .45 ACP cal., WWII themed 1911 designed to honor the women whose strength drove industry at home in support of our boys fighting overseas, 5 in. barrel, 7 shot mag., blade front and rear drift adjustable for windage sights, checkered wood grips with U.S. logo, deep cut laser engraving of a pin-up girl on the right side, updated "Rosie the Riveter" on the left, also features the USAAC Star Roundel on both sides of the frame, two-color worn Cerakote finish of Armor Black and Gunmetal Grey, 39 oz. Mfg. 2018-2020.

$1,050 $925 $795 $715 $580 $475 $375 *$1,240*

"THE GENERAL 1911" 75TH ANNIVERSARY – .45 ACP cal., GI Model 1911, 5 in. barrel, 7 shot mag., GI blade front and rear drift adj. sight, Army eagle badge engraving on both sides of grip, image of General Dwight D. Eisenhower and speech copy on left side of frame and image of General Omar Bradley, Admiral Alan Kirk, battle worn American flag on slide and right-side of frame, Patriot Brown Cerakote finish w/OD Green controls and Armor Black engraving, 2.3 lbs. Mfg. 2019-2020.

$975 $850 $725 $650 $525 $415 $350 *$1,134*

"TRUMP 45" CUSTOM 1911 – .45 ACP cal., 1911-style, 5 in. match grade barrel, 7 shot stainless mag., skeletonized trigger, front and rear dovetail-cut, low profile iron combat sights, checkered inlaid wood laminate grips w/Thompson medallions, high sweep beavertail, full-length guide rod, image of President Trump, White House, and slogan "Make America Great Again" on left side, American flag engraved on both sides of dust cover, stainless steel finish, 39 oz. Mfg. 2019-2020.

This model was a Distributor Exclusive and was available through CSSI. Please contact CSSI directly for information on this model at 1-800-251-4808.

75TH ANNIVERSARY IWO JIMA 1911 – .45 ACP cal., 1911 style, 5 in. barrel, 7 shot mag., blade front and rear drift adj. sight, Raising the Flag wood grips, thumb safety, grip safety, firing pin block, Iwo Jima Operation Detachment battle scenes engraved on steel, custom Cerakote finish, 39 oz. New 2020.

MSR $1,247 $1,060 $930 $800 $725 $585 $475 $400

CARBINES: SEMI-AUTO

For Thompson semi-auto carbine models, please refer to the Thompson listing.

75TH ANNIVERSARY IWO JIMA M1 CARBINE TRIBUTE EDITION – .30 cal., 18 in. barrel, 15 shot stick mag., Cerakoted steel receiver, blade front and flip style rear sight, Iwo Jima Operation Detachment battle scenes and Virtue quote engraved on wooden stock and handguard, Cerakote finish, 5.4 lbs.

MSR $1,391 $1,185 $1,035 $890 $800 $650 $550 $425

M1-CARBINE (.30 CAL.) – .30 Carbine cal., 18 in. barrel, 10 (new 2005) or 15 shot mag., aperture rear sight, birch or walnut (standard beginning 2008) stock, bayonet lug, metal or wood handguard, matte black parkerized receiver, 5.4 lbs. New 2004.

MSR $1,036 $895 $785 $675 $600 $525 $450 $395

* ***M1 Carbine Paratrooper (AOM150)*** – .30 Carbine cal., 18 in. barrel, 15 shot mag., aperture rear sight, birch or walnut forearm and handguard, metal folding stock, bayonet lug, matte black parkerized finish, approx. 5 1/2 lbs. New 2008.

MSR $1,253 $1,075 $940 $800 $725 $600 $500 $400

* ***M1 Carbine Tactical*** – .30 Carbine cal., similar to .30 cal. M1 carbine, except has black polymer folding stock, metal handguard, 15 shot mag. Mfg. 2008-2012.

$650 $575 $475 $375 $325 $300 $275 *$792*

1927 A-1 STANDARD CARBINE – .45 ACP cal., 16 in. plain barrel, solid steel construction, standard military sight, walnut stock and horizontal forearm. Disc. 1986.

$570 $490 $430 $360 $315 $290 $270 *$575*

* ***Special Edition 1927-A1 Deluxe Carbine*** – .45 ACP cal., 16 1/2 in. barrel, 20 shot mag., walnut stock, each gun has engraving of TIG logo, signature, and Beyond the Battlefield logo. Limited mfg. 2018-2019 only.

$1,315 $1,150 $995 $925 $795 $675 $600 *$1,544*

The first 50 guns will be sold as three gun sets (Auto Ordnance, Kahr ST9 Tig, and Magnum Research Desert Eagle TIG models). The set also includes the book *13 Hours: The Inside Account of What Really Happened in Benghazi,* **signed by American Hero, John "TIG" Tiegen.**

"AIRBORNE" WWII CUSTOM M1 CARBINE LIMITED EDITION – .30 cal., 18 in. barrel, 15 shot stick mag., parkerized steel receiver, blade front sight, flip style rear sight, walnut forearm engraved with a battle-worn American flag and the text "St. Michael pray for us", a paratrooper, parachutes, and detailed C-47 transport aircraft are engraved on the opposite side and metal folding stock, matte black parkerized finish, 5.4 lbs. Limited mfg. beginning mid-2018.

MSR $1,518 $1,295 $1,145 $985 $875 $750 $650 $575

GRADING - PPGS™	100%	98%	95%	90%	80%	70%	60%	LAST MSR

"THE RANGER THOMPSON" 75TH ANNIVERSARY – .45 ACP cal., 16 1/2 in. smoothbore barrel, 20 (blued) or 30 shot (OD Green) mag., blade front sight, fixed battle rear sight, fixed walnut stock and horizontal foregrip, pistol grip, custom engraving, Army OD Green w/Patriot Brown Cerakote finish, 11 1/2 lbs. New 2019.

MSR $1,886	$1,600	$1,400	$1,200	$1,100	$900	$700	$550	

"THE SOLDIER M1 CARBINE" – .30 Carbine cal., 18 in. barrel, 15 shot mag., blade front and flip style rear sight, American walnut stock and wood handguard, left side is engraved w/newspaper headlines and General Eisenhower's speech, buttstock has images depicting beach landing, right side is engraved w/patches of United States Army divisions and paratrooper drop gear, additional images of landings and dog-tags for Operation Overlord, super durable Patriot Brown Cerakote finish, 5.4 lbs. New 2019.

Please contact the company directly for pricing and availability on this model.

"VENGEANCE" WWII CUSTOM M1 CARBINE – .30 cal., 18 in. barrel, 15 shot stick mag., parkerized steel receiver, blade front sight, flip style rear sight, walnut stock engraved with images recalling December 7th, 1941, the day Pearl Harbor was attacked, parkerized finish, 5.4 lbs. New mid-2018.

MSR $1,391	$1,195	$1,045	$895	$825	$695	$595	$525	

AUTO-POINTER

Previous trademark manufactured by Yamamoto Co. Formerly imported by Sloans.

SHOTGUNS: SEMI-AUTO

SEMI-AUTO SHOTGUN – 12 or 20 ga., gas operated. Disc.

	$275	$240	$220	$195	$180	$160	$145	

AVIDITY ARMS

Current manufacturer established 2016, located in the USA. Currently distributed exclusively by Eagle Imports, Inc., located in Wanamassa, NJ.

PISTOLS: SEMI-AUTO

PD10 – 9mm Para. cal., striker fire operation, DAO, 4 in. barrel, 10 shot mag., polymer/stainless steel slide, Ameriglo Luma front sight and I.C.E. Claw rear sight, ergonomically sculpted grip, trigger blade/firing pin block, loaded chamber indicator, aggressive rear slide serrations, claw mag. base plate for emergency extraction, black or grey (new 2018) Nitride finish, 6.94 in. OAL, 18.8 oz. New 2017.

MSR $499	$450	$400	$375	$350	$300	$275	$250	

AXELSON TACTICAL

Current AR-15 style rifle and pistol manufacturer and dealer located in Minden, NV.

For individual model listings, please go to BlueBookOfGunValues.com/overflow.

AXIAL PRECISION

Current manufacturer of bolt action rifles established in 2015, located in Boise, ID.

RIFLES: BOLT ACTION

MSR is for standard base models. Please contact the manufacturer directly for custom options, pricing, and availability.

ALLTERRA STEEL/ALLTERRA CARBON – 6mm Creedmoor cal., 24 or 26 (new 2020) in. steel light contour barrel, dual ejectors, Timney trigger, Axial Precision carbon fiber stock, CNC machined stainless steel or carbon (new 2020) receiver, integral or pinned recoil lug, extended mag., ergonomic swept back bolt handle, Graphite Metal finish, 7 lbs.

MSR $5,095	$4,350	$3,800	$3,250	$2,950	$2,400	$1,950	$1,500	

Add $5,750 for Deluxe-Rifle package.

Add $730 for AllTerra Carbon model (new 2020).

ARID – various cals., 20-24 in. match grade stainless steel fluted or non-fluted barrel, detachable mag., dual ejectors, Timney trigger, Manners or McMillan fiberglass/carbon fiber stock, CNC machined stainless steel receiver, integral or pinned recoil lug, Picatinny rail pinned to receiver, extended mag., spiral fluted body, ergonomic swept back bolt handle, Nightforce ATACR scope, 14 lbs. Disc. 2020.

	$4,850	$4,250	$3,650	$3,300	$2,650	$2,200	$1,700	*$5,695*

Add $7,370 for Deluxe-Rifle package.

GRADING - PPGS™	100%	98%	95%	90%	80%	70%	60%	LAST MSR

ARID 1760 – 6mm Creedmoor cal., 24 in. steel heavy contour barrel, Manners MCS-EH1A stock with Elite Tac Gap finish, Graphite metal finish, 11 lbs.

MSR $5,695	$4,850	$4,250	$3,650	$3,300	$2,650	$2,200	$1,700	

HIMALAYAN – available in many popular cals. between .22-250 and .22 Creedmoor, 24 or 26 in. match grade Sendero LC carbon fiber threaded barrel, extended length mag., M16 extractor, lengthened ejection port/dual ejectors, Timney or TriggerTech trigger, AP Carbon Hunter or Manners MCS-SL pillar bedded stock, ATAS and ARD receiver design, integral recoil lug, .25 MOA Swarovski scope, Cerakote metal components or Bead Blast satin finish, approx. 8 lbs. (w/scope). Disc. 2020.

	$4,950	$4,350	$3,700	$3,350	$2,700	$2,250	$1,750	*$5,825*

Add $4,624 for Deluxe-Rifle package.

MOUNTAIN SHADOW – 6.5 Creedmoor cal., 20 in. carbon fiber barrel with threadcap, Axial Precision Carbon Hunter stock with carbon fiber finish, Graphite metal finish, 6 lbs. New 2020.

MSR $5,995	$5,095	$4,460	$3,825	$3,465	$2,800	$2,300	$1,785	

AXTELL RIFLE CO.

Previous rifle manufacturer located in Sheridan, MT. Previously distributed by The Riflesmith Inc., located in Sheridan, MT.

During 2010, the company was sold to Shiloh Mfg. Co., located in Big Timber, MT.

RIFLES: REPRODUCTIONS

New Model 1877 Sharps reproductions were available for both long-range and sporting rifles listed below in the following black powder calibers: .40-50, .40-70, .40-90, .45-70 Govt., .45-90, and .45-100 cal.

NUMBER ONE CREEDMOOR – .40-50, .40-70, .40-90, .45-70 Govt., .45-90, and .45-100 cal., Sharps single shot action rifle, 34 in. Rigby style barrel, long range sights, choice of high-grade black or English checkered walnut stock and forearm with ebony inlays, 10 lbs.

	$5,000	$4,250	$3,600	$3,100	$2,500	$2,000	$1,575	*$5,000*

CUSTOM EXPRESS – .40-50, .40-70, .40-90, .45-70 Govt., .45-90, and .45-100 cal., Sharps single shot action rifle, top-of-the-line model, 32 or 34 in. half round/half octagon barrel, double set triggers, deluxe front and rear sights, select walnut checkered stock, approx. 13 lbs.

	$5,700	$4,550	$3,950	$3,250	$2,650	$2,100	$1,650	*$5,700*

NUMBER TWO LONG RANGE – .40-50, .40-70, .40-90, .45-70 Govt., .45-90, and .45-100 cal., Sharps single shot action rifle, 30-34 in. Rigby style barrel, long range sights, select black or English checkered walnut stock and forearm.

	$4,700	$3,650	$3,150	$2,600	$2,100	$1,650	$1,300	*$4,700*

OVERBAUGH SCHUETZEN – .40-50, .40-70, .40-90, .45-70 Govt., .45-90, and .45-100 cal., Sharps single shot action Schuetzen rifle, 26-30 in. octagon barrel, double-set triggers, short-range sights, Schuetzen buttplate with cheekpiece, palm rest, 11-14 lbs.

	$5,700	$4,550	$3,950	$3,250	$2,650	$2,100	$1,650	*$5,700*

LOWER SPORTER – .40-50, .40-70, .40-90, .45-70 Govt., .45-90, and .45-100 cal., Sharps single shot action rifle, 28 or 30 in. octagon barrel, double-set triggers, steel buttplate with straight grip, standard rifle weight of 9 lbs.

	$3,200	$2,450	$1,875	$1,425	$1,050	$825	$700	*$3,200*

LOWER BUSINESS – .40-50, .40-70, .40-90, .45-70 Govt., .45-90, and .45-100 cal., Sharps single shot action rifle, 28 in. contoured round barrel, double-set triggers, blade front sight, black walnut stock has steel shotgun buttplate with straight grip, hunter tang, approx. 8 1/2 lbs.

	$3,100	$2,400	$1,825	$1,400	$1,050	$825	$700	*$3,100*

AZRA 16

Current trademark of shotguns manufactured by the Hedef Arms Company, located in Konya, Turkey. No current U.S. importation.

A wide variety of semi-auto, slide action, and O/U shotguns are manufactured. Many configurations are available, including wood, synthetic, and carbon fiber stocks, various finishes, engraving, and gold inlays. Please contact the manufacturer for more information, including domestic availability and pricing.

AZTEK ARMS

Previous AR-15 style rifle manufacturer located in Mapleton, UT until 2015.

For individual model listings, please go to BlueBookOfGunValues.com/overflow.

BCI DEFENSE LLC

Previous manufacturer of AR-15 style pistols, rifles, and accessories, located in Bremen, IN from 2012-late 2019.

Please refer to BlueBookOfGunValues.com to order the *Blue Book of AR-15s & Variations*, available as a book or online subscription.

BCM EUROPEARMS

Current manufacturer located in Torino, Italy. No current U.S. importation.

BCM Europearms manufactures high quality bolt action competiton, hunting, and tactical/Law Enforcement pistols and rifles; the Storm semi-auto pistol (in 9x21mm and .40 S&W); and customized Remington 700 rifles. The "Barrel Block" competition rifle features a monolithic stock with integrally machined bedding (no separate bedding components) which allows both action and barrel to free float. The barrel and action are held in the stock by a "cap" which clamps over the barrel's chamber and is attached to the stock, not the action, by eight screws.

Currently these models are not being imported into the U.S. Please contact the company directly for more information, U.S. availability, and pricing.

BJT (BELLMORE JOHNSON TOOL CO.)

Previous manufacturer located in Hamden, CT.

GRADING - PPGS™	100%	98%	95%	90%	80%	70%	60%	LAST MSR

DERRINGERS: O/U

O/U DERRINGER – .38 Spl. or 9mm Para. cal., copy of High Standard derringer. Mfg. 1984-86.

	100%	98%	95%	90%	80%	70%	60%	LAST MSR
	$250	$225	$195	$175	$150	$135	$125	

BNTI ARMS

Current manufacturer of AR-15 style pistols and carbines/rifles, located in Jacksonville, FL.

Please refer to BlueBookOfGunValues.com to order the *Blue Book of AR-15s & Variations*, available as a book or online subscription.

BSA GUNS LIMITED

Current manufacturer (airguns only since circa 1986) and trademark established in 1861 and located in Birmingham, England. BSA (Birmingham Small Arms) currently manufactures airguns only. No current U.S. importation. English made BSA firearms were imported until 1985 by Precision Sports from Ithaca, NY and 1986 by BSA Guns Ltd., located in Grand Prairie, TX. Imported and distributed until 1989 by Samco Global Arms, Inc., located in Miami, FL.

For more information and current pricing on both new and used BSA airguns, please refer to the *Blue Book of Airguns* - also available as an online subscription.

HISTORY OF BIRMINGHAM SMALL ARMS

In a little over a hundred years, BSA has grown from a small union of gunsmiths to become one of Britain's important industrial groups. The story is also part of Britain's history. During 1689, King William III, worried by threats of invasion, sharply criticized the practice of obtaining military weapons from Holland. He was overheard by Sir Richard Newdegate, an MP for Warwickshire, who immediately spoke up on behalf of his Birmingham constituents - many of whom were fine gunsmiths. The result was a trial order for five of the leading Birmingham smiths. It was satisfactorily carried out, and a firm contract was made between the government and the quintet for the supply of 200 snaphance muskets a month "at seventeen shillings per piece, ready money."

This practice of trading with the gunmakers as a group continued for 150 years. At the time of the Crimean War, fourteen of the master smiths formalized their position by joining together as The Birmingham Small Arms Trade Association. On June 7, 1861, a public company was formed as the The Birmingham Small Arms Company Limited.

The company adopted the sign of three crossed rifles, known as the Piled Arms trademark. The company began making small arms by machinery to meet the growing competition from the mechanized government factory at Enfield. A 25 acre site was bought at Small Heath, at that time just outside the Birmingham boundary, and two years later, the factory was in operation. By 1866, the company could record a profit of £7,000 and in a few short years - aided by the turbulent international politics of the time - it became the largest private arms manufacturer in Europe.

One order from the Prussian government, then at war with Austria, was 40 million cartridge cases. Rather

GRADING - PPGS™	100%	98%	95%	90%	80%	70%	60%	LAST MSR

than turn down the order, the directors acquired a munitions factory and changed the company name to the Birmingham Small Arms and Metal Company Limited. The early prosperity was short-lived. As wars ceased, the demand for weapons fell, and the private arms trade was the first to suffer. Towards the end of the 1870s, the Small Heath factory was completely closed for twelve months and the future looked impossibly dark. A small contract enabled the works to be opened again, however, and in 1880 fate took a hand in the shape of an inventor, a Mr. E.C.F. Otto, who had designed a strange type of bicycle with two large wheels on either side of the rider. He demonstrated it by riding on the boardroom table under the noses of the astonished directors - and so impressed them that they put the device into production immediately.

This first venture into the transport field was followed by more conventional bicycles and tricycles, but a sudden increase in the demand for rifles at the end of the 1880s caused the directors to drop cycle work. During the Boer War, the company supplied many thousands of rifles to the British forces. The Birmingham Small Arms and Metal Company Limited name was used until 1897.

In the First World War, the BSA factories were turned over almost entirely to munitions work. Huge quantities of service rifles, machine guns, military motorcycles, and the world's first folding bicycles were supplied to the troops. Right through the 1930s, BSA rifle production had been confined to comparatively small quantities of sporting weapons.

Apart from the company's own factories in Birmingham, Coventry, Redditch, Sheffield and Co. Durham, many dispersal units and shadow factories were used for the purpose of arms production. The Small Heath administration alone (BSA Cycles Ltd and BSA Guns Ltd) controlled 67 factories, employing 28,000 people and containing 25,000 machine tools. This organization produced more than half the small arms supplied to Britain's forces during the war. BSA's war production included nearly half a million of the Browning machine guns with which RAF Spitfires and Hurricanes won the Battle of Britain; one and a quarter million service rifles; 400,000 Sten guns; machine guns, cannon, anti-tank rifles, and gun carriages, ten million shell fuses, over three and a half million magazines, and 750,000 anti-aircraft rockets. Several group factories were heavily bombed and at Small Heath more than 50 employees lost their lives. At this works alone, more machine tools were destroyed or damaged by enemy action than were lost in the whole of the Coventry blitz.

Although the company no longer makes military weapons, BSA Guns Ltd makes and exports air rifles, hunting rifles, and sporting guns to most parts of the world. BSA celebrated its 150th anniversary in 2011.

Company history courtesy of BSA Guns Ltd.

RIFLES: BOLT ACTION

Importation of all BSA rimfire and centerfire rifles was disc. 1987.

MAJESTIC FEATHERWEIGHT DELUXE – .243 Win., .270 Win., .308 Win., .30-06, or .458 Win. Mag. cal., 22 in. barrel, folding sight, checkered European style stock. Mfg. 1959-1965.

	100%	98%	95%	90%	80%	70%	60%	LAST MSR
	$475	$425	$375	$325	$300	$275	$250	
.458 Win. Mag.	$650	$575	$495	$450	$400	$350	$295	

MAJESTIC DELUXE – .222 Rem., .22 Hornet, .243 Win., 7x57mm, .308 Win., or .30-06 cal., heavier barrel.

	100%	98%	95%	90%	80%	70%	60%	LAST MSR
	$475	$425	$375	$325	$300	$275	$250	
.22 Hornet cal.	$950	$850	$750	$650	$600	$550	$500	

MONARCH DELUXE – similar to Majestic Deluxe, but American design stock. Mfg. 1965-74.

100%	98%	95%	90%	80%	70%	60%	LAST MSR
$575	$525	$450	$400	$350	$300	$275	

MONARCH DELUXE VARMINT – similar to Monarch Deluxe, except .222 Rem. or .243 Win. cal., 24 in. heavy barrel. Disc.

100%	98%	95%	90%	80%	70%	60%	LAST MSR
$475	$425	$375	$325	$300	$275	$250	

MARTINI ISU MATCH .22 – .22 LR cal. only, single shot, bolt action, similar to CFT Model. Disc. 1985.

100%	98%	95%	90%	80%	70%	60%	LAST MSR
$825	$720	$620	$560	$455	$370	$290	*$1,000*

Add $100 for Mk. V.H.B. Model.

CF-2 MODELS – .222 Rem., .22-250 Rem., .243 Win., 6.5x55mm, 7x57mm, 7x64mm, 7mm Rem. Mag., .270 Win., .308 Win., .30-06, or .300 Win. Mag. cal., bolt action, barrel length 23-26 in., 7 1/2-8 lbs. CF-2 nomenclature designates an action rather than a model. The following are CF-2 actioned models.

Add $70 for double set trigger option on the following models.

* ***CF-2 Action Sporter/Classic*** – same cals. as CF-2, checkered oil finished walnut stock. Imported 1986-87.

100%	98%	95%	90%	80%	70%	60%	LAST MSR
$475	$425	$375	$325	$300	$275	$250	*$360*

Sporter Model features Monte Carlo stock, rosewood capped forearm and pistol grip stock, and swivels.

GRADING - PPGS™	100%	98%	95%	90%	80%	70%	60%	LAST MSR

* ***CF-2 Action Classic Varminter*** – .222 Rem. - .243 Win. cals. only, heavy barrel, matte finish, with swivels. Imported 1986 only.

$475 $425 $375 $325 $300 $275 $250 *$345*

* ***CF-2 Action Heavy Barrel Model*** – .222 Rem., .22-250 Rem., or .243 Win. cal., approx. 9 lbs., no sights.

$475 $425 $375 $325 $300 $275 $250 *$410*

* ***CF-2 Action Carbine Model*** – 20 in. barrel. Disc. 1985.

$550 $495 $425 $375 $325 $295 $275 *$480*

* ***CF-2 Action Stutzen Rifle*** – Mannlicher style full-length stock, same general specifications as Sporter/Classic, 20 1/2 in. barrel. Not available in 7mm Rem. Mag. or .300 Win. Mag. cal.

$695 $625 $550 $500 $450 $400 $350 *$385*

* ***CF-2 Action Regal Custom*** – similar to Sporter Model, except has slim classic European style stock with Schnabel forend, deluxe walnut with extra checkering, ebony forend cap, engraved action and floorplate. Limited importation 1986 only.

$1,000 $925 $850 $775 $700 $625 $550 *$950*

This model was custom-made by special order only.

CFT TARGET RIFLE – 7.62x51mm NATO cal., single shot, bolt action, globe front and aperture rear sights, 26 1/2 in. barrel, 11 lbs. Disc. 1987.

$675 $590 $500 $460 $370 $300 $235 *$780*

RIFLES: SINGLE SHOT

NO. 12 MARTINI – .22 LR cal., 29 in. barrel, target sights, straight stock, pre-WWII.

$725 $600 $500 $425 $350 $300 $275

MILITARY MARTINI HENRY (MODELS 1871 & 1885) – various cals., pre-WWII mfg. many configurations and barrel lengths. Pricing takes into consideration most commonly encountered types with no engraving or special orders.

Post-1900 mfg. $900 $700 $500 $450 $400 $365 $335

Pre-1899 mfg. $650 $550 $475 $400 $350 $300 $250

MARTINI CADET – various cals., mostly military issue, many thousands previously imported into the U.S. from England, many have been sporterized or modified.

$725 $600 $500 $425 $350 $300 $275

* ***Martini Cadet Australian Junior*** – .310 cal., mfg. by BSA and W.W. Greener, Francotte patent one-piece take out action, various rear sight configurations, some have been converted to modern cartridges.

$550 $475 $375 $325 $275 $235 $200

MODEL 15 – similar to No. 12 Martini, except has pistol grip stock, better grade target sights, pre-WWII.

$725 $600 $500 $425 $350 $300 $275

CENTURION MATCH RIFLE – similar to Model 15, except was guaranteed to shoot a 1 1/2 in. or less group at 100 yards, 24 in. barrel, pre-WWII.

$800 $675 $550 $475 $425 $350 $300

MATCH 12/15 – similar to Model 15, except made after WWII.

$725 $600 $500 $425 $350 $300 $275

MODEL 12/15 – heavy barrel.

$725 $600 $500 $425 $350 $300 $275

MODEL 13 – lighter version of No. 12 Martini.

$725 $600 $500 $425 $350 $300 $275

MODEL 13 SPORTER – similar to Model 13, except has sport sights.

$725 $600 $500 $425 $350 $300 $275

.22 Hornet $950 $825 $725 $625 $525 $425 $325

MARTINI INTERNATIONAL MATCH – .22 LR cal., 29 in. heavy barrel, international sights. Mfg. 1950-53.

$825 $700 $600 $475 $400 $350 $325

INTERNATIONAL LIGHT – 26 in. lightweight barrel.

$775 $675 $550 $450 $400 $350 $325

INTERNATIONAL MKII – improved trigger, ejectors, and stock design. Mfg. 1953-1959.

$950 $825 $700 $600 $550 $500 $450

GRADING - PPGS™	100%	98%	95%	90%	80%	70%	60%	LAST MSR

INTERNATIONAL MKIII – longer action, floating barrel. Mfg. 1959-1967.

	$995	$875	$750	$650	$600	$550	$500	

INTERNATIONAL ISU – modeled to meet ISU standards, 28 in. barrel. Mfg. 1968-disc.

	$1,000	$875	$750	$650	$600	$550	$500	

INTERNATIONAL MARK V – similar to ISU, but heavier barrel, mfg. 1976-disc.

	$1,000	$875	$750	$650	$600	$550	$500	

SHOTGUNS

BSA Imports, located in Ft. Lauderdale, FL, imported O/U, SxS, and semi-auto shotguns from 2004-2006 which were manufactured in Turkey and utilized the BSA logo/trademark.

BSA also manufactured SxS boxlock shotguns in various grades. Normally encountered in 12 ga. with DTs and extractors, these shotguns are of good quality and are typically encountered in the secondary market in the $250-$500 range, assuming standard grade.

SILVER EAGLE O/U – 12 or 20 ga., 3 in. chambers, 26 or 28 in. barrels, multi-chokes, hand-checkered Turkish walnut stock, blue receiver, gold SST, extractors (Silver Eagle) or ejectors (Silver Eagle II). Imported 2004-2006.

	$400	$365	$335	$300	$265	$235	$200	*$489*

Add $100 for ejectors (Silver Eagle II).

FALCON O/U – 12 or 20 ga., 3 in. chambers, boxlock action, 26, 28, or 30 in. barrels, Beretta style multichokes, laser-checkered field grade walnut stock with Schnabel forend, ejectors, case colored engraved receiver, gold SST. Imported 2004-2006.

	$1,000	$900	$800	$700	$600	$500	$400	*$1,199*

SPORTING O/U – 12 ga., 2 3/4 in. chambers, 28 or 30 in. ported barrels, multichokes, checkered walnut target stock, ejectors, silver finished engraved receiver, trigger guard, safety, and opening lever, gold SST. Imported 2004-2006.

	$1,025	$950	$825	$725	$625	$525	$425	*$1,249*

CLASSIC SxS – 12, 16, 20, 28 ga., or .410 bore, 2 3/4 (16 or 28 ga.) or 3 in. chambers, 26 or 28 in. barrels with Beretta style choke tubes, checkered select walnut stock with Prince of Wales pistol grip, ejectors, case colored hardened receiver, gold SST, semi-beavertail forend. Imported 2004-2006.

	$1,065	$975	$850	$750	$650	$550	$450	*$1,299*

ROYAL SxS – 12 or 20 ga., 3 in. chambers, 26 or 28 in. barrels with Beretta style choke tubes, checkered select walnut stock. Imported 2005-2006.

	$1,225	$1,075	$975	$850	$750	$650	$550	*$1,499*

200/300 SERIES SEMI-AUTO – 12, 16, 20, 28 ga., or .410 bore, 2 3/4 (16, 28 ga. or .410 bore), 3 or 3 1/2 (Model 312 only) in. chamber, 24 (Model 312 only), 26 or 28 in. barrels, vent. rib, multichokes, synthetic or checkered Turkish walnut stock, blue receiver, gold trigger, drilled and tapped, firing pin block. Imported 2004-2006.

	$325	$285	$250	$225	$200	$175	$150	*$399*

Add $60 for wood stock.
Add $30 for 16 or 28 ga. or .410 bore.
Add $20 for 3 1/2 in. chamber.

This model was manufactured by Matsan in Turkey, and was also available in 20 ga. at no extra charge.

BWE FIREARMS

Current rifle manufacturer and customizer with gunsmithing services established during 2002, located in Longwood, FL.

BWE Firearms is a full service custom gunsmith shop specializing in NFA firearms, in particular the Uzi and S&W M76/MK Arms 760. It is also a Class II manufacturer. Please contact the company directly for more information on their models and services.

RIFLES: BOLT ACTION

BWE Firearms manufactured a bolt action rifle based on the Remington Model 700 long action. It was chambered for the .300 Blackout/Whisper, .338 Thumper, or .50 Thumper caliber, and features included blue printed actions, fully adjustable Bell and Carlson tactical stock, and Picatinny rail. Finishes included bead blast, polished blue, or parkerizing.

GRADING - PPGS™	100%	98%	95%	90%	80%	70%	60%	LAST MSR

B-WEST

Previous importer/distributor located in Tucson, AZ, until 1997.

B-West previously imported AK-47 design carbines/rifles, Saiga rifles, Dragunov rifles, and others, plus the IJ series .380 ACP Makarov pistol, and the Daewoo DP-51 semi-auto pistol.

BADROCK PRECISION RIFLES

Current manufacturer of bolt action rifles located in Columbia Falls, MT.

For individual model listings, go to BlueBookOfGunValues.com/overflow.

BAER, LES

Please refer to Les Baer Custom, Inc. listing in the L section.

BAFORD ARMS, INC.

Previous manufacturer located in Bristol, TN. Previously distributed by C.L. Reedy & Associates, Inc. located in Melbourne, FL.

DERRINGERS

THUNDER DERRINGER - .44 Spl. cal./.410 shotshell, single shot, side pivoting, 3 in. barrel, blue finish, spur trigger, square butt wood grips. Introduced late 1988 with limited mfg. until 1991, when production permanently ceased.

$130	$110	$95	$90	$85	$80	$75	*$130*

Add $90 for interchangeable barrel kit.

Interchangeable pistol barrels are chambered in various calibers between .22 Short and 9mm Para. There are two types: one fits flush while the other facilitates a scope mounting.

PISTOLS: SEMI-AUTO

MODEL 35 FIRE POWER - 9mm Para. cal., single action, patterned after the Browning Hi-Power, total stainless steel construction, 4 3/4 in. barrel, combat hammer and safety, wood (early mfg.) or Pachmayr grips, removable barrel bushing, Millett Mk. II sights, 14 shot mag., 32 oz. Introduced late 1988 with limited mfg. until 1993.

$950	$650	$525	$425	$325	$275	$225	*$550*

BAIKAL

Current trademark of products manufactured by the Russian Federal State Unitary Plant "Izhevsky Mechanichesky Zavod" (FSUP IMZ), located in Izhevsk, Russia. Currently imported by Kalashnikov USA, a division of the RWC Group located in Tullytown, PA. Previously imported 2011-2015 by U.S. Sporting Goods, Inc. located in Rockledge, FL. Previously imported from late 1998 until 2004 by European American Armory Corp., located in Sharpes, FL, and from 1993-1996 by Big Bear, located in Dallas, TX.

Baikal SxS and O/U hunting guns (including air guns) were imported and distributed exclusively 2005-2009 by U.S. Sporting Goods (USSG), located in Rockledge, FL. Many Baikal shotguns and rifles were marketed domestically by Remington under the Spartan Gunworks trademark until 2008. See listings under Spartan Gunworks for more information.

Please contact the importer directly for more information and availability on Baikal firearms.

Baikal (the name of a lake in Siberia) was one of the key holding companies from the former Soviet Union, specializing in the production of firearms, and science intensive, complex electronic equipment.

The company was founded in 1942 as part of the Russian National Defense Industry. At that time, the plant produced world renowned Tokarev TT pistols. Upon conclusion of WWII, the company expanded its operation to include non-military firearms (O/U, SxS, and single barrel shotguns). FSUP IMZ is one of the world's largest manufacturers of military and non-military firearms. The total amount of guns produced by the FSUP IMZ is 680,000 units per year. The products range from various smoothbore guns, including slide action and self-loading models, rifled and combination guns, to a full array of sporting, civil, and combat pistols, including the internationally famous Makarov pistol. Since 2000, Baikal has produced a new pistol for the Russian Army which was developed by the enterprise designers and named after the group's leader - the Yarygin pistol.

FSUP IMZ features efficient manufacturing capacity and the unique intellectual potential of its qualified engineers-and-technicians staff. The FSUP IMZ is also undertaking the task of reintroducing the world to the "Russian Custom Gunsmith". There is a gunsmith school at the factory area for custom, one-of-a-kind hand engraved shotguns and rifles. The guns produced by the school feature high-quality assembly, attractive appearance, and high functional quality according to the best traditions of Russian gunmakers.

GRADING - PPGS™	100%	98%	95%	90%	80%	70%	60%	LAST MSR

In the past, Baikal shotguns have had limited importation into the U.S. 1993 marked the first year that Baikals were officially (and legally) imported into the U.S. because of Russia's previous export restrictions. In prior years, however, a few O/Us have been seen for sale and have no doubt been imported into this country one at a time. Currently produced Baikals are noted for their good quality at low-level costs.

COMBINATION GUNS

MP94 (IZH-94) O/U – 12 or 20 (new 2001-disc.) ga. over rifle separated rifle barrel, current US cals. include .22 LR, .22 WMR, .223 Rem., .30-06, .308 Win., or 7.62x39mm cal., 3 in. chamber, boxlock action, 19.7 or 23 1/2 (disc.) in. separated barrels with express sights, DT, extractors, fixed or screw-in chokes, checkered walnut stock and forearm, approx. 8 1/2 lbs.

MSR $562	$475	$415	$350	$325	$260	$215	$165	

Add $228 for cals. other than .22 LR or .22 WMR.

This model was also sold in the U.S. under the model name SPR94, and the nomenclature changed to MP94 beginning 2009.

* ***MP94 (IZH-94) .410 Bore/Rimfire*** – .410 bore with 3 in. chamber over choice of .17 HMR (disc. 2010), .22 LR, or .22 WMR cal., 19.7 or 23 1/2 (disc.) in. barrels, extractors, single trigger, open sights, walnut stock and forearm. Imported 2003-2012.

	$425	$350	$295	$265	$240	$220	$200	*$514*

This model was also sold in the U.S. under the model names IZH94 Rimfire and SPR94 Rimfire. The nomenclature changed to MP94 in 2009.

PISTOLS: SEMI-AUTO

IZH-35M – .22 LR cal., semi-auto target pistol featuring fully adj. walnut ergonomic target grip, 6 in. hammer forged barrel, adj. trigger assembly, integral grip safety, 5 shot mag., cocking indicator and detachable scope mount, 2.3 lbs. Imported 2000-disc.

	$425	$385	$335	$300	$275	$250	$225	

U.S. options on this gun include manual lever safety, side-located push-button mag. catch, slide retainer, and removable scope base (not available in standard European version).

IZH-70 (IJ-70) – .380 ACP or 9x18 Makarov cal., double action, all blue steel construction, 4 in. barrel, slide mounted safety with decocking, fully adj. target sights, choice of two 8 shot (IJ- 70), two 10 shot (C/B 1994, Model IJ-70-HC), or two 12*shot mags., holster and cleaning rod, checkered plastic grips, 25 oz. Disc. 1996.

	$175	$150	$135	$120	$105	$95	$85	*$199*

Add $40 for IJ-70-HC (High Capacity).
Add $50 for .380 ACP cal.
Add $10 for nickel finish (disc.).

This model was also imported under the model name Baikal 442.

RIFLES: O/U

IZH-94 EXPRESS – .222 Rem., .223 Rem., .30-06, .308 Win., 6.5x55mm, or 7.62x39mm cal., DT, extractors, monobloc construction, 24 in. barrels with express sights, checkered walnut stock and forearm, 8.3 lbs. Imported 2001-2004.

	$450	$395	$365	$335	$295	$280	$265	*$529*

RIFLES: SxS

MP221 – .223 Rem. (disc.), .270 Win. (disc.), .30-06, .308 Win. (disc.), or .45-70 Govt. cal., 23 1/2 in. barrels, boxlock monobloc action, DT, adj. barrel regulation, 11mm scope rail, checkered walnut stock and forearm with sling swivels, extractors, vent. recoil pad, 7 1/2 lbs. Imported 2003-2009, reintroduced 2011.

MSR $1,155	$985	$860	$750	$675	$550	$450	$350	

This model was also sold in the U.S. under the name SPR22.

RIFLES: SEMI-AUTO

MP161K – .17 HMR (disc. 2010), .22 LR, or .22 WMR (disc. 2010) cal., 19 1/2 in. accurized barrel, grey polymer thumbhole pistol grip stock with adj. LOP and cheekpiece height, 10 shot mag., integral Picatinny rail, adj. open sight, loaded chamber indicator, trigger guard mounted bottom safety, blue recoil pad and inserts in the forend. Importation began 2009.

MSR $437	$375	$325	$275	$250	$200	$175	$140	

Add 20% for .17 HMR or .22 WMR cal. (disc. 2010).

GRADING - PPGS™	100%	98%	95%	90%	80%	70%	60%	LAST MSR

RIFLES: SINGLE BARREL

IZH-18MN – .222 Rem. (disc.), .223 Rem., .243 Win., .270 Win., 7.62x39mm, .308 Win., .30-06, or .45-70 Govt. cal., boxlock action, 23 1/2 in. barrel with extractor and precision spiral cut fluting, underlever action next to trigger guard, blue or nickel frame finish, polymer or checkered walnut (disc.) stock with vent. recoil pad, sling swivels, iron sights or scope rail, 6.8 lbs. Imported 2003-2009.

	$250	$220	$185	$170	$135	$110	$85	*$278*

Add $16 for nickel finish.

This model has also been sold in the U.S. under the names IZH018MN and SPR-18.

MP18MN – .223 Rem., .223 Win., .30-06, or 7.62x39mm cal., boxlock break open action, 23 1/2 in. spiral fluted barrel, adj. open sights, checkered walnut stock and forearm, cocking indicator, opening lever in back of trigger guard, blue finish, 6 3/4 lbs. Limited importation 2012 only.

	$275	$240	$210	$180	$165	$150	$140	*$335*

SHOTGUNS: O/U

IZH-27 – 12, 16, 20, 28 ga., or .410 bore, 3 in. chambers (2 3/4 in. on 16 or 28 ga.) boxlock action, 26 or 28 in. VR barrels with (standard on 12 and 20 ga.) or w/o chokes, monobloc receiver, walnut checkered (with or w/o Monte Carlo) stock and forearm, extractors or ejectors, blue or nickel finish (new 2001), SST. Imported 1999-2004.

	$400	$350	$300	$270	$220	$180	$140	*$475*

Add $10 for 16 or 20 ga.
Add $34 for 28 ga. or .410 bore.
Add $224 for 20 ga. 2 barrel set.
Add $24 for nickel finish.
Add $80 for nickel finish with barrel porting (12 ga. only, disc. 2003).

E nomenclature indicates ejectors. 1C indicates single trigger. This model has also been sold in the U.S. under the model names SPR310 (SST) and SPR320 (DT).

* ***IZH-27 Sporting*** – 12 or 20 ga., 3 in. chambers, SST, ejectors, ported 29 1/2 in. barrels with MC-3 chokes, wide rib, nickel finished frame. Imported 2004.

	$525	$460	$395	$355	$290	$235	$185	*$629*

MP 233 SPORTING – 12 ga., 3 in. chambers, 26, 28, or 29 1/2 in. unported (disc.) or ported barrels with multi-chokes and wide VR, removable trigger group, SST, ejectors, checkered walnut stock and forearm, includes carrying case, 7.2 lbs. Imported 1999-2004.

	$775	$680	$580	$525	$425	$350	$270	*$899*

MP310 – 12, 16 (disc. 2012), 20, 28 (disc. 2010) ga., or .410 bore, 26 or 28 in. vent. rib hammer forged chrome-lined VR barrels with choke tubes, machined steel or nickel receiver, SST, ejectors, checkered walnut stock and forearm, gold trigger, rubber buttpad, approx. 7.4 lbs. Importation began 2009.

MSR $635	$540	$475	$400	$365	$295	$250	$195

Add $20 for nickel finished receiver. Add $47 for 28 ga. (disc.) or $74 for .410 bore.

* ***MP310 Sporting*** – 12 or 20 ga., 28 or 29 1/2 in. vent. rib hammer forged chrome-lined barrels with screw-in chokes, engraved nickel receiver, SST, selective ejectors, checkered walnut stock with right hand palm swell, competition walnut forearm, gold trigger, rubber buttpad, double sight beads, approx. 8 lbs. Limited importation began 2009.

MSR $754	$650	$575	$495	$450	$360	$295	$230

SHOTGUNS: SxS

The IZH Bounty Hunter models were available in either 12 or 20 ga., with 3 in. chambers. These models were designed for cowboy action shooting, with choice of hammers or hammerless action, SST, DT (disc.), or double selective triggers, 20 in. barrels with or w/o choke tubes, hardwood or walnut stock and forearm, engraved receiver, extractors, and weigh approx. 7 lbs.

IZH-43 FIELD MODEL – 12 or 20 ga., DT, extractors, 20, 26 (disc.), or 28 in. barrels. Disc. 1996.

	$235	$200	$175	$160	$130	$100	$80	*$299*

Add $20 for 20 in. barrels bored C/C.

IZH-43 TRADITIONAL HUNTING MODEL – 12, 16, 20, 28 ga., or .410 bore, Anson & Deeley style boxlock action with monobloc, SST, 24, 26, or 28 in. barrels with or w/o (28 ga. and .410 bore) choke tubes, checkered walnut stock and forearm, approx. 7 lbs. Imported 1999-2004.

	$340	$295	$255	$230	$185	$155	$120	*$399*

Add $30 for 16, 20, 28 ga., or .410 bore. Add $20 for nickel finish (new 2004).

This model has been sold in the U.S. under the model names SPR210 (SST), SPR220 (DT), and Stevens Upland Sporter 411.

GRADING - PPGS™	100%	98%	95%	90%	80%	70%	60%	LAST MSR

* ***IZH-43 2 Barrel Set*** – includes both 20 and 28 ga. barrels. Imported 2000-2004.

	$515	$450	$385	$350	$285	$230	$180	*$599*

* ***IZH-43 Traditional Bounty Hunter*** – 12, 20 ga., or .410 bore (mfg. 2001-2002), 2 3/4 in. chambers, hammerless, 20 in. barrels with choice of cyl./cyl. bore or multichokes, nickel receiver (new 2004), DT or SST, hardwood or walnut stock. Imported 2000-2004.

	$275	$240	$200	$185	$150	$125	$95	*$329*

Add $20 for nickel receiver.
Add $40-$50 for walnut stock and forearm.
Add $50-$60 for SST.
Add $159 for .45-70 cal. barrel inserts (only if shotgun is 12 ga., has 2 3/4 in. chambers, and 20 in. barrels with choke tubes).

IZH-43K EXTERNAL HAMMERS – 12 or 20 (disc.) ga., similar to IZH-43 Hunting Model, except has engraved sideplates and external cocking hammers, approx. 6.3 lbs. Imported 2000-2004.

	$330	$290	$245	$225	$180	$150	$115	*$379*

Add $20 for choke tubes.
Add $20 for external firing pins.

* ***IZH-43K External Hammer 2 Barrel Set*** – includes both 20 and 28 ga. barrels. Imported 2000 only.

	$550	$480	$410	$375	$300	$245	$190	*$639*

* ***IZH-43K Bounty Hunter Traditional*** – 12 or 20 (disc. 2002) ga., 20 in. barrels with choice of cyl./cyl. bore or multichokes. Imported 2000-2004.

	$285	$250	$215	$195	$155	$130	$100	*$329*

Add $40 for multichokes or $50 for multichokes and SST.
Add $10 for external firing pins and traditional sideplates.
Add $159 for .45-70 cal. barrel inserts (only if shotgun is 12 ga., has 2 3/4 in. chambers, and 20 in. barrels with choke tubes).

* ***IZH-43KH External Hammers*** – 20 ga., 20 or 28 in. barrels with screw-in chokes, sideplates. Disc.

	$435	$380	$325	$295	$240	$195	$150	

This model has also been sold in the U.S. under the model name SPR220F.

This model has had its nomenclature changed to the MP220F (see new listing).

MP210 – 12, 16 (disc. 2010), 20, 28 (disc. 2010) ga., or .410 bore, boxlock action, 20 (disc. 2011), 26, or 28 in. chrome-lined hammer forged barrels with screw-in chokes, blue steel (disc. 2011), or nickel receiver, checkered walnut stock and forearm, SST, extractors or ejectors, approx. 7.2 lbs. Importation began 2009.

MSR $541	$460	$400	$350	$315	$250	$200	$175	

Add $39 for 28 ga. (disc. 2010) or .410 bore.
Subtract 15% for extractors (disc. 2010).

MP213 – 12 ga. only, 3 in. chambers, hammerless, SST (disc. 2000) or DT, ejectors, removable trigger assembly, 20 (Coach Gun), 24, 26, or 28 in. monobloc barrels with choke tubes, checkered walnut stock and forearm, includes carrying case, approx. 7 lbs. Disc.

	$795	$695	$595	$540	$435	$360	$280	*$939*

Add $159 for .45-70 cal. barrel inserts (only if shotgun is 12 ga., has 2 3/4 in. chambers, and 20 in. barrels with choke tubes).

MP220 – 12 or 20 ga., boxlock action, 20, 26, or 28 in. chrome-lined hammer forged barrels, machined steel or nickel (disc. 2010) receiver, uncheckered walnut stock and forearm, SST, hammerless, steel buttpad, 6.5-7.2 lbs. Importation began 2009.

MSR $382	$325	$285	$250	$225	$180	$150	$125	

Add $48 for choke tubes.
Add $16 for nickel finish (disc. 2010).

* ***MP220F*** – 12 ga., similar to MP220, except has external hammers, toggle firing pin with automatic firing pin block. Importation began 2009.

MSR $580	$495	$435	$375	$335	$275	$225	$175	

SHOTGUNS: SEMI-AUTO

MP151 – 12 ga., 3 in. chamber, 26 or 28 in. plain barrel with 2 choke tubes, black synthetic or checkered walnut Monte Carlo stock, tube or detachable box (available late 1999) mag., approx. 7.8 lbs. Imported 1999 only.

	$275	$240	$200	$185	$150	$125	$95	*$310*

GRADING - PPGS™	100%	98%	95%	90%	80%	70%	60%	LAST MSR

MP153 – 12 ga. only, 3 1/2 in. chamber, 24 (new 2001), 26 or 28 in. VR barrel with choke tubes, blue or camo (new 2011) finish, black synthetic or walnut (disc. 2004) stock and forearm, approx. 8 lbs. Imported 2000-2004, resumed 2011.

MSR $539	$460	$400	$350	$325	$250	$200	$180	

Add $127 for camo finish.
Subtract 15% for black synthetic stock and forearm.

This model has also been sold in the U.S. under the model name SPR453.

SHOTGUNS: SINGLE SHOT

MP18 (IZH-18M-M) – 12, 16 (disc. 2004), 20 ga., or .410 bore, hammerless, 24 (Youth), 26, 28 or 29 1/2 (disc. 2004) in. barrel with fixed or multichokes (12 or 20 ga. only, 2001-2004), ejector (IZH-18EM-M), blue or nickel (new 2001) finish, decocking/cocking lever on rear of trigger guard, cocking indicator, hardwood or walnut (new 2001) stock and forearm, trigger block safety, approx. 5 1/2 lbs. Imported 1998-2004, importation resumed 2011.

MSR $152	$130	$115	$100	$90	$70	$60	$45	

Add $15 for Youth Model (20 ga. or .410 bore only).
Add 15% for nickel finished receiver (IZH-18 Max) with MC-3 multichokes and walnut stock and forearm (disc. 2004).

This model has also been sold in the U.S. under the model name SPR100.

* ***IZH-18 Sporting*** – 12 or 20 (new 2004) ga., 28 (20 ga.) or 29 1/2 in. VR barrel with porting, rubber buttpad, wide rib, ejector, screw-in choke, nickel finish, Monte Carlo stock. Imported 2002-2004.

	$235	$200	$175	$160	$130	$100	$80	*$299*

SHOTGUNS: SLIDE ACTION

IZH-81 – 12 ga. only, 3 in. chamber, 5 shot box mag., 20, 26, or 28 in. plain or VR barrel with (26 or 28 in. barrel only) or w/o choke tubes, hardwood or walnut (disc. 1999) stock and corncob style forearm, blue finish. Imported 1999-2000.

	$235	$200	$175	$160	$130	$100	$80	*$269*

Add $17 for walnut stock (disc. 1999).
Add $68 for VR barrel (walnut stock only).

MP133 – 12 ga., 3 1/2 in. chamber, 20, 24 (new 2001), 26, or 28 in. VR barrel with choke tubes (not available with 20 in. barrel), walnut stock and forearm, approx. 7 lbs. Imported 2000-2004.

	$295	$260	$220	$200	$160	$135	$100	*$359*

BAILONS GUNMAKERS LIMITED

Previous manufacturer located in Birmingham, England until 1993 when operations ceased.

RIFLES: BOLT ACTION

HUNTING RIFLE – various cals., modified Mauser bolt action, barrel length to suit from 18 to 30 in., match or set triggers, Habicht telescopic sight (magnification and reticle to suit), engraving, and types of finishes were available at additional cost, values reflect standard rifle with no options. Imported 1986-1993.

	$2,495	$2,250	$1,995	$1,775	$1,625	$1,450	$1,300	*$2,750*

BAKER, W.H. & CO.

Previously manufactured in Lisle, NY, production was done in Syracuse, NY 1877-1883.

The company was started by William H. and Ellis L. Baker in 1877. Leroy H. and Lyman C. Smith financed the new company, W.H. Baker & Co. In 1880, L.C. Smith bought the interest from the two Baker partners and continued production with "L.C. Smith Maker of the Baker Gun" marked on the rib and "Baker Pat." on the locks. Smith decided to drop the Baker name in 1883 but continued to manufacture this gun and a three-barrel shotgun/rifle combination in Syracuse, NY. The company was sold to the Hunter Brothers in 1889. A new company, Baker Gun & Forging Co., began making both the New Baker shotguns (see separate listing) and the Ithaca gun. The Hunter Arms Company made L.C. Smith shotguns for about 55 years, until the Marlin Firearms Company bought the business in 1945 and formed the L.C. Smith Gun Company in 1946 which produced shotguns until 1950.

Baker guns were originally 10 or 12 ga., and unusual in that the opening mechanism was operated by pressing forward on the front trigger. While relatively uncommon, most original Baker guns (including the three-barrel shotgun/rifle) seldom have much original finish remaining. Most are priced in the $400-$800 range, assuming finish is less than 10%. If condition is better than 40%, guns should be evaluated individually for accurate pricing.

100%	98%	95%	90%	80%	70%	60%	50%	40%	30%	20%	10%

THE BAKER GUN & FORGING CO.

Previous trademark used by W.H. Baker & Co. and L.C. Smith Maker in Syracuse, NY on shotguns manufactured 1877-1888. See L.C. Smith section for listings of the Baker patented three-barrel and two-barrel guns.

This section covers the popular hammer and hammerless guns manufactured 1887-1919 by the Baker Gun & Forging Company, (founded by William H. & Ellis L. Baker) in Syracuse and Batavia, NY and the H&D Folsom Arms Co. 1920-1930 in Norwich, CT. These guns sold in substantial quantities (approx. 190,000) and they attracted a strong and devoted following.

The Baker sidelock shotgun is considered to be one of America's Classic shotguns. Like the L.C. Smith, Parker, Lefever, Fox and Ithaca, collector interest in these high quality shotguns remains high.

The popular Baker Paragon grade hammerless shotguns were made to customer order, and the company went to great lengths to accommodate the customer's requests for configuration, finish and engraving. Therefore, no two guns are exactly alike. Paragon guns with Damascus barrels with 80% or better original finish without pitting, reboring or polishing out are of equal or greater value as shotguns with Krupp steel barrels.

All 'Baker Grade' guns were available with the extra draw lug and firing pin block safeties. However, the 'Batavia Grade' guns did not have these features.

The *Blue Book of Gun Values* strongly recommends an expert examination and appraisal when contemplating the purchase of a high grade Baker in 80% or better original condition.

SHOTGUNS: EXTRA VALUE FEATURES

Add 60% for 16 ga. on all grades.
Add 33% for 10 ga. on all grades.
Add $200-$300 for automatic ejectors.
Add $500 for single selective trigger on all grades valued at $1,500 or more or 33% on guns with values less than $1,500.
Deduct $300 for shortened (cut) barrels.
Deduct $200 for shortened stocks.
Deduct $100 for missing sighting beads.

SHOTGUNS: SXS, BAKER HAMMER-LONDON TWIST OR DAMASCUS, MFG. 1897-1916

MODEL "D" 1897 – sidelock twist bar London action, extra draw lug.

N/A	N/A	N/A	N/A	$1,500	$1,100	$1,000	$900	$800	$750	$700	$650

Add $300 for Damascus barrels.

NEW BAKER 1887-1896 – boxlock twist London action.

N/A	N/A	N/A	N/A	$1,000	$750	$500	$450	$400	$375	$350	$300

SHOTGUNS: SXS, BATAVIA GRADE, SIDELOCK, HAMMERLESS-DAMASCUS OR FLUID STEEL, MFG. 1898-1930

BATAVIA LEADER – London twist, later guns had special steel barrels, plain wood and finish.

N/A	N/A	N/A	N/A	$1,100	$900	$700	$600	$550	$500	$450	$400

Add $300 for Damascus barrels (Batavia Damascus) and $200 for automatic ejectors (Batavia Ejector).

BATAVIA SPECIAL – similar to Leader model, homo-tensile steel.

N/A	N/A	N/A	N/A	$1,200	$900	$700	$600	$550	$500	$450	$400

BLACK BEAUTY – similar to Batavia Special model, cockrill steel, black oxide metal finish.

N/A	N/A	N/A	N/A	$1,100	$800	$600	$450	$400	$350	$300	$275

Add $200 for automatic ejectors.

BLACK BEAUTY SPECIAL – special steel, line engraving, upgraded wood, checkering and finish.

N/A	N/A	N/A	N/A	$1,150	$850	$750	$700	$650	$600	$550	$500

SHOTGUNS: SXS, BAKER GRADE, SIDELOCK, HAMMERLESS-DAMASCUS OR FLUID STEEL, MFG. 1890-1923

Baker Grade hammerless guns were made in 10, 12 and 16 gauges with 26, 28, 30, and 32 inch barrels. Shotguns with Damascus barrels are of equal value if the Damascus barrels are in 80%+ original condition without pitting, reboring or polishing out. The A and B grades were mfg. 1890-1910; R and S grades 1905-1915. The Paragon, Krupp, Pigeon and Deluxe grades were made in the Standard Model 1892-1919. The Paragon, Expert and Deluxe grades were also made in the Model NN style with the L.C. Smith style rotary locking bolt 1909-1915 and the Greener style crossbolt 1915-1919.

100%	98%	95%	90%	80%	70%	60%	50%	40%	30%	20%	10%

S GRADE – fluid tempered steel, plain line and scroll engraving.

N/A	N/A	N/A	N/A	$1,500	$1,100	$950	$850	$750	$650	$600	$550

Add $300 for automatic ejectors.

R GRADE – three rod Damascus or Krupp steel barrels, dog and bird on locks with line and some scroll engraving, better wood and finish.

N/A	N/A	N/A	N/A	$2,300	$1,900	$1,500	$1,200	$1,100	$1,000	$900	$800

Add $500 for Krupp barrels or $300 for automatic ejectors.

B GRADE – London twist, good line and scroll engraving with dog or bird on locks, better wood and finish than Leader model.

N/A	N/A	N/A	N/A	$1,900	$1,500	$1,100	$1,000	$900	$800	$700	$600

Add 33% for early models with elaborate game scene engraving.

A GRADE – three rod Damascus or Krupp steel barrels, same engraving as B Grade, better wood and finish.

N/A	N/A	N/A	N/A	$2,300	$1,900	$1,500	$1,200	$1,100	$1,000	$900	$800

Add 33% for early models with elaborate game scene engraving. Add $500 for Krupp barrels.

PARAGON GRADE – very fine Damascus or Krupp barrels, fine scroll and game scene engraving, best quality wood, checkering and finish. Special order only and made to customer specifications.

N/A	N/A	N/A	N/A	$3,800	$3,200	$2,800	$2,400	$2,000	$1,750	$1,500	$1,400

Add $300 for automatic ejectors.

KRUPP GRADE (N) – Krupp barrels, finer scroll and game scene engraving, better wood, checkering, and finish. Most had straight stocks.

N/A	N/A	N/A	N/A	$4,000	$3,500	$3,000	$2,500	$2,300	$2,100	$1,900	$1,800

Add $300 for automatic ejectors.

PIGEON GRADE (L) – Holland special steel barrels, elaborate scroll and game scene engraving, fancy wood, checkering, and finish.

N/A	N/A	N/A	N/A	$5,500	$4,500	$3,500	$3,000	$2,800	$2,600	$2,400	$2,200

Add $300 for automatic ejectors.

EXPERT GRADE – Holland special steel barrels, ejectors standard, finest scroll and game scene engraving, fancy checkering, wood and finish.

N/A	N/A	N/A	N/A	$6,000	$5,000	$4,000	$3,500	$3,200	$2,900	$2,600	$2,300

DELUXE GRADE – Sir Joseph Whitworth fluid compressed steel barrels, highest quality full coverage scroll and game scene engraving, checkering, wood, and finish. Rare in any condition.

N/A	N/A	N/A	N/A	$12,000	$9,000	$7,500	$6,000	$5,500	$5,200	$4,900	$4,600

Add $600 for automatic ejectors.

SHOTGUNS: SINGLE BARREL TRAP, BOXLOCK, HAMMERLESS, FLUID STEEL, MFG. 1909-1923

The Baker SBT guns were of the highest quality. Made in 12 ga. only with 30, 32, or 34 inch barrels in three grades. They were offered with vent ribs, automatic ejectors, and Monte Carlo stocks with a cheekpiece. The two highest grades had the firing pin block safety. The *Blue Book of Gun Values* recommends an expert appraisal when contemplating the purchase of a high grade SBT Baker in 80% or better original condition.

STERLING GRADE – line border and scroll engraving, semi-fancy wood, neatly checkered.

N/A	N/A	N/A	N/A	$1,600	$1,200	$800	$700	$600	$500	$400	$300

ELITE GRADE – elaborate scroll engraving, fancy wood and checkering.

N/A	N/A	N/A	N/A	$2,400	$2,000	$1,700	$1,500	$1,400	$1,300	$1,200	$1,100

SUPERBA GRADE – ornate scroll and game scene engraving, finest wood and checkering.

N/A	N/A	N/A	N/A	$4,000	$3,300	$2,700	$2,550	$2,400	$2,200	$2,000	$1,800

BALISTIK (SAVUNMA) DEFENSE INDUSTRY AND TRADE INC.

Current manufacturer of Cosmos branded bolt action rifles and accessories, established in 2018, located in Istanbul, Turkey. No current U.S. importation.

Please contact the company directly for more information on their models, pricing, and availability.

BALLARD ARMS, INC.

Previous rifle manufacturer located in Onsted, MI until 2016. Previously located in Cody, WY 1996-2009. Previously named Ballard Rifles LLC until 2006 and Ballard Arms LLC from 2006-2009.

For individual model listings, please go to BlueBookOfGunValues.com/overflow.

GRADING - PPGS™	100%	98%	95%	90%	80%	70%	60%	LAST MSR

BALLESTER MOLINA/RIGAUD (HAFDASA)

Previous trademark of semi-auto pistols manufactured by Hispano Argentino Fabricade Automoviles SA (Hafdasa).

PISTOLS: SEMI-AUTO

The Ballester-Molina was an attempt to market a less expensive alternative to the Colt Model 1927, which was an Argentine-made licensed copy of the Colt Model 1911. During the first three years of production, the pistol was marked "Ballester-Rigaud", and later marked "Ballester-Molina". Although the Ballester-Molina .45 ACP is virtually the same size and shape as the Colt Model 1911, only the barrel is interchangable.

BALLESTER-MOLINA/RIGAUD – .45 ACP or .22 LR (training version) cal., 5 in. barrel, patterned after the Colt M-1911A1 except has pinned trigger, is without grip safety, has different sear mechanism, and distinctive pattern retracting grooves in slide, issued to the Argentine Military and Police (marked on slide), also sold commercially in Latin America, ser. no. stamped on hilt next to magazine floorplate, some also marked with property numbers. Approx. 90,000-110,000 mfg. 1937-1953.

	100%	98%	95%	90%	80%	70%	60%
	$1,250	$950	$800	$700	$600	$500	$400
.22 LR Training Model	$1,800	$1,295	$950	$850	$690	$565	$440

During WWII the British purchased between 10,000 - 15,000 Ballester-Molinas in .45 ACP cal. for both the British military and clandestine activities. These are marked with a B prefix before the serial number. Pistol marked "Ejercito" are Army issue and pistols marked "Armada" are navy issue (this would include the Marines and the Coast Guard). Slides may be marked with various federal and police agency names and issue numbers (not to be confused with the serial number).

Guns marked "Cal. .45" or "11.25mm" will shoot .45 ACP ammo.

Pistols were exported to Columbia, Bolivia, Ecuador, Peru, Uruguay, and Venezuela.

BALTIMORE ARMS COMPANY

Previous manufacturer of SxS shotguns located in Baltimore, MD circa 1895-1902.

SHOTGUNS: SxS

STYLE 1 – this variation does not have the improved Hollenbeck barrel locking mechanism characterized by the eye-shaped hole in the top rib extension. Mfg. 1895-1900.

Prices generally range from $575 to $1,500 depending on condition and grade.

There are 4 grades of Baltimore Arms Company shotguns: Field, Grade A, Grade B, and Grade C.

STYLE 2 – this variation has the improved barrel locking mechanism and is marked with a patent date "FEB. 13, 1900" on the water table. Mfg. 1900-1902.

Prices generally range from $795 to $2,000 depending on condition and grade.

There are 4 grades of Baltimore Arms Company shotguns: Field, Grade A, Grade B, and Grade C.

BANSNER'S ULTIMATE RIFLES, L.L.C.

Previous custom rifle manufacturer located in Adamstown, PA from 1981-late 2013. In 2000, the company name changed from Bansner's Gunsmithing Specialities to Bansner's Ultimate Rifles, L.L.C. In late 2013, Bansner's was bought by firearms retailer Trop Gun Shop, and current firearms are produced under the trademark Legendary Arms Works. Please refer to this listing for current information.

RIFLES: BOLT ACTION

All Bansner's UR rifles up to approx. June 1, 1999 have either Remington 700 or Winchester post-64 claw extractor actions. After this approx. date, Bansner's started using its own proprietary action, and during 2005, released the Sharpshooter model with Nesika Bay action.

ULTIMATE ONE – various cals. and configurations including different metal finishes and special orders, Rem. 700 (disc. 1999), Win. post-64 Model 70 (disc. 1999), Bansner's custom action by Nesika beginning 2004, exclusive action was mfg. by McMillan Bros. Rifle Co., Inc. (steel or stainless steel, mfg. 2001-2003), Douglas premium air gauged (disc.) or Lilja fluted barrel with M-50 muzzle brake, large extractor, plunger ejector, 3 lbs. custom tuned trigger, custom color synthetic stock with Pachmayr Decelerator pad, includes Talley custom scope bases and rings, various weights. Disc. 2013.

100%	98%	95%	90%	80%	70%	60%	LAST MSR
$4,350	$3,875	$3,300	$2,750	$2,300	$1,800	$1,500	*$4,595*

Add $350 for 3 position Model 70 style safety or Lazzeroni calibers (disc. 2007).

GRADING - PPGS™	100%	98%	95%	90%	80%	70%	60%	LAST MSR

ULTIMATE SAFARI HUNTER – various dangerous game cals., Lilja Precision stainless steel 24 in. barrel, scalloped action based on the M-70 Classic (disc.) or Dakota 76 CRF action, M-50 muzzle brake, synthetic stock with Pachmayr Decelerator pad, matte black Teflon metal finish. Mfg. 2003-2008.

	$5,700	$4,985	$4,275	$3,875	$3,135	$2,565	$1,995	*$6,195*

SAFARI HUNTER – various dangerous game cals., Bansner custom stainless steel action, Lilja Precision match grade stainless steel contour barrel, Jewell trigger, High Tech Specialities fiberglass stock, Pachmayr Decelerator pad, custom LOP, drilled and tapped. Disc. 2013.

	$5,300	$4,950	$4,300	$3,650	$3,000	$2,400	$1,950	*$5,595*

BIG FIVE – various dangerous game cals., Dakota 76 action, straddle floorplate, Lilja Precision match grade stainless steel barrel, muzzle brake, polymer K-Kote finish, High Tech Specialties fiberglass pillar bedded and reinforced stock, Pachmayr Decelerator recoil pad, custom LOP, zeroed in at 100 yards. Mfg. 2009-2011.

	$7,150	$6,255	$5,365	$4,860	$3,935	$3,220	$2,500	*$7,465*

CLASSIC HUNTER – various cals., Bansner's stainless steel action with spiral fluted bolt body, Lilja Precision match grade stainless steel barrel, custom "Hunter" trigger with top slide safety, Talley steel bases with fixed rings, all metal coated with polymer black, silver, or Ti K-Kote finish, High Tech Specialties fiberglass pillar bedded stock, Pachmayr Decelerator recoil pad, custom LOP. Mfg. 2009-2011.

	$3,550	$3,105	$2,665	$2,415	$1,955	$1,600	$1,245	*$3,892*

SHARPSHOOTER – various cals., Nesika Bay action, Lilja Precision medium to heavy weight match grade fluted barrel (customer choice of length), with recessed crown, Jewell trigger, brown wood laminate pillar bedded and reinforced fiberglass stock with palm swell, polymer Ti K-Kote metal finish, ebony forend tip, inletted swivel studs. Mfg. 2005-2007.

	$7,900	$6,910	$5,925	$5,370	$4,345	$3,555	$2,765	*$8,495*

SHARPSHOOTER (RECENT MFG.) – various cals., long range light tactical hunting rifle, features accurized and blueprinted stainless Rem. M700 action with Sako extractor, Hart stainless steel match grade barrel with fluting and muzzle brake, Jewell trigger, High-Tech Specialties, Inc. pillar bedded fiberglass stock with Pachmayr Decelerator recoil pad. Mfg. 2012-2013.

	$4,995	$4,400	$3,850	$3,350	$2,800	$2,300	$1,675	*$5,300*

ULTIMATE OVIS SHEEP HUNTER – various cals., Rem. 700 action (disc.) or Banser's custom lightweight stainless steel action (new 2007), accurized, engine turned fluted bolt, skeletonized bolt handle, alloy ADL trigger guard, Jewell trigger, Lilja Precision barrel, fiberglass stock, 5 1/4 lbs. Disc. 2014.

	$4,350	$3,875	$3,300	$2,750	$2,300	$1,800	$1,500	*$4,595*

ULTIMATE VARMINT HUNTER – various cals., Rem. 700 action, accurized and polished, Jewell varmint trigger, Lilja Precision stainless steel barrel, polymer Ti K-Kote metal finish, fully bedded fiberglass stock, Pachmayr Decelerator pad. Disc. 2008.

	$4,550	$3,980	$3,410	$3,095	$2,500	$2,045	$1,590	*$4,995*

ALPINE HUNTER – .300 WSM cal. only, Howa 1500 action, milled receiver, fluted barrel, muzzle brake, tuned trigger, fully bedded fiberglass stock, Pachmayr Decelerator pad, polymer Ti K-Kote metal finish. Disc. 2014.

	$1,995	$1,750	$1,500	$1,350	$1,150	$995	$825	*$2,195*

ALASKAN HUNTER – various cals., Rem. 700 action, accurized, scalloped and polished receiver, fluted bolt, skeletonized handle, alloy ADL trigger guard, Lilja Precision barrel, fiberglass stock, Pachmayr Decelerator pad, approx. 5 lbs. Disc. 2004.

	$3,525	$3,085	$2,645	$2,395	$1,940	$1,585	$1,235	*$3,895*

ULTIMATE RIFLE – various cals., Rem. 700 or Win. 70 action, accurized and polished, 3 lbs. trigger pull, Lilja Precision stainless steel barrel, fully bedded fiberglass stock, Pachmayr Decelerator pad. Disc. 2004.

	$2,995	$2,620	$2,245	$2,035	$1,645	$1,350	$1,050	*$3,300*

HIGH TECH SERIES – various cals., Howa 1500 steel or stainless steel action with factory barrel and Bansner's synthetic stock with Pachmayr Decelerator pad. Mfg. 1997-2004.

	$965	$845	$725	$655	$530	$435	$340	*$1,050*

Add $100 for all stainless steel.

ULTIMATE/TRADITIONAL CLASSIC – various cals., custom Dakota 76 controlled round feed claw extractor action, custom floorplate with release inside trigger bow, Lilja Precision match grade hand lapped barrel, choice of polymer matte blue or Ti K-Kote metal finish, synthetic stock, Pachmayr Decelerator pad. Mfg. 2005-2008.

	$4,450	$3,895	$3,335	$3,025	$2,445	$2,000	$1,555	*$4,895*

GRADING - PPGS™	100%	98%	95%	90%	80%	70%	60%	LAST MSR

LIMITED EDITION SERIES – various cals., customized Bansner's (new 2004) or Rem. 700 action with scalloped receiver, fluted bolt body, Jewell trigger, Gentry 3-position safety, synthetic stock with choice of black or silver Teflon coated metal, 25-50 of each limited edition from 2003-2013.

Retail pricing was not available on this Series. Each rifle should be appraised individually.

25TH ANNIVERSARY MODEL – customer chosen caliber and barrel contour, stainless steel action with custom engraving, sequential serial number, Lilja Precision match grade barrel, Jewell trigger, fiberglass Sheep Hunter stock, Pachmayr Decelerator pad, includes custom aluminum case and black sling. Only 25 mfg. late 2005-2008.

This model had an MSR of $6,195.

BARAK HUNTING ARMS (BARAK SILAH)

Current shotgun manufacturer established in 2004, located in Konya, Turkey. No current U.S. importation.

In the late 2010s, Barak Hunting Arms acquired Bora Hunting Company. Please contact the company directly for more information on their current models, including price, options, and availability.

BARNES PRECISION MACHINE, INC.

Current AR-15 style rifle, pistol, parts, and accessories manufacturer located in Apex, NC. Dealer and consumer direct sales.

Please refer to BlueBookOfGunValues.com to order the *Blue Book of AR-15s & Variations*, available as a book or online subscription.

BARRETT FIREARMS MANUFACTURING, INC.

Current manufacturer and shotgun importer established in 1982, located in Murfreesboro, TN.

Barrett manufactures a line of semi-automatic and bolt action .50 caliber rifles, precision tactical rifles, lightweight hunting rifles, and AR-15 style rifles and pistols. Barrett also imports a line of high quality sporting shotguns.

PISTOLS: SEMI-AUTO

Models come with a Barrett branded soft case and are available through participating Barrett R.E.D. partners and distributors. Please contact Barrett Customer Service at 615-896-2938 for more information and availability.

REC7 DI PISTOL – 5.56 NATO or .300 AAC Blackout cal., GIO, 10.25 in. match grade stainless steel (disc.) or chrome-lined (new 2021) barrel, muzzle brake (disc.) or 3 prong flash hider, 20 shot beveled Magpul mag., ALG Defense ACT (disc. 2020) or QMS (new 2021) trigger, MBUS sights (new 2021), Magpul MOE pistol grip, ambi safety, Barrett KeyMod (disc. 2020) or M-LOK (new 2021) handguard, Bravo Company Gunfighter (disc. 2020) or Radian (new 2021) charging handle, Black, Tungsten Grey, FDE, ODG (disc. 2020), Multi-Role Brown (mfg. 2017-2019), or Burnt Bronze (disc. 2020) Cerakote receiver finish, 5.5 lbs. Limited mfg. beginning mid-2017.

MSR	100%	98%	95%	90%	80%	70%	60%	LAST MSR
MSR $1,899	$1,675	$1,500	$1,375	$1,250	$1,050	$825	$650	

RIFLES: BOLT ACTION

If you currently own a Barrett Model 98B between Serial Number 98B00003 through 98B00775, do not attempt to operate or fire your rifle until it has been examined by the Barrett Firearms Manufacturing, Inc. Service Department. For further information, call Barrett Customer Service at 615-896-2938 between 8am-4pm CST.

MODEL 90 – .50 BMG cal., 29 in. match grade barrel with muzzle brake, 5 shot detachable box mag., includes extendible bipod legs, scope optional, 22 lbs. Mfg. 1990-1995.

MSR	100%	98%	95%	90%	80%	70%	60%	LAST MSR
	$3,450	$2,950	$2,400	$2,150	$1,875	$1,600	$1,500	*$3,650*

Add $1,150 for Swarovski 10X scope and rings.

MODEL 95(M) – .50 BMG cal., 29 in. match grade fluted barrel with high efficiency muzzle brake, 5 shot detachable box mag., includes extendible bipod legs, full-length M1913 receiver optics rail, recoil pad, scope optional, includes carrying case, 23.5 lbs. New 1995.

MSR	100%	98%	95%	90%	80%	70%	60%	LAST MSR
MSR $6,671	$6,250	$5,700	$5,050	$4,250	$3,500	$2,750	$2,200	

Add $1,413 for Leupold scope and Barrett ultra high rings (mfg. 2012-disc.).

Add $2,839 for rifle system including Leupold scope, BORS ultra high rings, 120 rounds of XM33 ammo, Pelican case, and bipod (mfg. 2011-2017).

Add $2,978 for QDL suppressor (mfg. 2013-2019).

MODEL 98B – .338 Lapua Mag. cal., 20 in. heavy unfluted, 26 (new 2013), or 27 (disc. 2012) in. fluted barrel, muzzle brake, includes two 10 shot detachable mags., adj. trigger, adj. stock, Harris bipod, monopod, full-length M1913 optics receiver rail with 3 accessory rails on shroud, two sling loops, ergonomic bolt handle, includes air/watertight case, black finish, 13 1/2 lbs. Mfg. 2009-2016.

MSR	100%	98%	95%	90%	80%	70%	60%	LAST MSR
	$4,400	$3,975	$3,600	$3,100	$2,800	$2,500	$2,150	*$4,827*

GRADING - PPGS™	100%	98%	95%	90%	80%	70%	60%	LAST MSR

Add $153 for 26 in. fluted barrel (new 2013).
Add $1,412 for Leupold scope and Barrett ultra high rings (new 2012).
Add $2,839 for Leupold scope, BORS, and Barrett ultra high rings.
Add $1,300 for Leupold scope and cleaning kit (disc. 2012).

MODEL 98B LIGHTWEIGHT (MODEL 98B FIELDCRAFT) – .260 Rem., .300 Win. Mag., .308 Win. (disc. 2016), .338 Lapua (new 2016), 6.5 Creedmoor (disc. 2016), or 7mm Rem. Mag. cal., 18 (disc. 2016), 22, or 24 in. light barrel, 10 shot detachable box magazine, adj. cheekpiece, adj. match trigger, 8 in. scope rail, black anodized finish or Cerakote finishes in Tungsten Grey, Burnt Bronze, Multi-Role Brown, OD Green, or FDE. Mfg. 2015-2017.

	$3,750	$3,250	$2,775	$2,515	$2,050	$1,675	$1,300	*$4,113*

Add $306 for .300 Win. Mag. or 7mm Rem. Mag. cal.
Add $386 for .338 Lapua cal. (new 2016).

MODEL 98B LEGACY – .338 Lapua cal., 26 in. fluted barrel, 10 shot detachable box magazine, adj. cheekpiece, adj. match grade trigger, quick detach sling loop sockets, 18 in. scope rail, black finish. Mfg. 2015-2016.

	$3,195	$2,795	$2,395	$2,175	$1,750	$1,450	$1,125	*$3,552*

MODEL 98B TACTICAL – .300 Win. Mag., .308 Win., or .338 Lapua (new 2016) cal., 16, 22, or 24 in. heavy barrel with muzzle brake, 10 shot detachable box magazine, adj. cheekpiece, adj. match grade trigger, 17 in. scope rail, black anodized or Tungsten Grey Cerakote receiver finish. Mfg. 2015-2017.

	$3,995	$3,500	$3,000	$2,700	$2,185	$1,795	$1,395	*$4,419*

Add $204 for .300 Win. Mag. or $280 for .338 Lapua (new 2016) cal.

MODEL 99 – .416 Barrett (32 in. barrel only) or .50 BMG cal., single shot, 25 (disc.) or 29 in. lightweight fluted, or 32 in. heavy barrel with muzzle brake, straight through design with pistol grip and bipod, full-length M1913 receiver optics rail, black anodized, brown (disc.), silver (disc.), or tan/FDE Cerakote (new 2012) finish, 23-25 lbs. New 1999.

MSR $4,582	$3,895	$3,410	$2,925	$2,650	$2,150	$1,750	$1,375	

Add $117 for tan/FDE Cerakote finish (new 2012).
Add $177 for 29 in. fluted barrel.

FIELDCRAFT LIGHTWEIGHT HUNTING RIFLE – .243 Win., .22-250 Rem., 6.5 Creedmoor, 6mm Creedmoor, 7mm-08 Rem., .308 Win., .25-06 Rem., .270 Win., .30-06, or 6.5x55 Swedish cal., short or long stainless steel action, 18 (threaded), 21, or 24 in. stainless steel barrel, 4 shot mag., Timney trigger, carbon fiber stock, 44 1/3 in. OAL, 5-6 lbs. Mfg. 2017-2019.

	$1,695	$1,485	$1,275	$1,125	$925	$775	$625	*$1,879*

Add $50 for threaded barrel.

MRAD – .260 Rem. (new 2016), .300 Win. Mag. (new 2014), .308 Win. (new 2014), .338 Lapua Mag. (new 2020), .338 Norma Mag. (new 2020), .300 PRC, 6.5 Creedmoor (new 2016), or 7mm Rem. Mag. (new 2016) cal., 17 (.308 Win. only, new 2014), 20 (mfg. 2012-2020), 22 (.308 Win. only, mfg. 2014-2020), 24 (new 2013), 24 1/2 (disc. 2013), 26 (new 2013) or 27 (mfg. 2012 only) in. fluted or heavy, stainless steel (new 2020) or carbon fiber (disc. 2020) barrel with muzzle brake, user-changeable barrel system, two 10 shot drop free polymer mags., ambi mag. release, aluminum receiver with modular construction, fully adj. two-stage match grade trigger, folding stock with adj. cheekpiece, thumb operated safety, 21 3/4 in. M1913 optics rail plus side rails on vent, forend includes two sling loops, three accessory rails, and Pelican case, Multi-Role Brown, black anodized (new 2013), Grey Cerakote (new 2014), OD Green Cerakote (new 2014), FDE Cerakote (new 2014), or Burnt Bronze (new 2017) finish, 12-14.5 lbs. New mid-2011.

MSR $6,154	$5,225	$4,575	$3,925	$3,550	$2,875	$2,350	$1,850	

Subtract approx. $150 for heavy barrel.
Add $975 for carbon fiber barrel (disc. 2019).
Add $1,565 for heavy (disc.) or fluted barrel or $2,380 for carbon fiber barrel conversion kit (includes complete barrel assembly, bolt, case, and one 10 shot mag. - new 2014).

This model is also available as a military deployment kit in .338 Lapua Mag. cal. with 24 in. fluted FDE barrel - current MSR is $18,792 (new 2018).

* ***MRAD Mark22*** – .338 Norma Mag., 300 Norma Mag., or 7.62 NATO cal., 20 (7.62 NATO), 26 (.300 Norma Mag.), or 27 (.338 Norma Mag.) in. match grade fluted barrel w/suppressor capable muzzle brake, 10 shot drop free polymer ambi release mag., single-stage trigger w/anti-tamper epoxy, oversized trigger guard, lightweight folding stock, ambi adj. polymer cheekpiece, recoil pad w/push button height and LOP adj., M4/M16 grips, ambi thumb safety, user changeable cals., 10 MIL rail, 3-9 slot M-LOK rails, 2 sling mounts, Mil-Spec hard anodized base w/Coyote Cerakote finish, 13.9-15.2 lbs. New 2021.

Please contact the manufacturer directly for price and availability.

GRADING - PPGS™	100%	98%	95%	90%	80%	70%	60%	LAST MSR

* ***MRAD SMR*** – .338 Lapua Mag., .338 Norma Mag., .300 Norma Mag., .300 PRC (new 2020) .300 Win. Mag., .308 Win. (17 or 24 in. bbl. only), or 6.5 Creedmoor (24 in. bbl. only) cal., 17, 24 , or 26 in. fluted barrel, suppressor capable muzzle brake, 10 shot drop-free polymer mag. w/ambi release, two-stage fully adj. trigger oversized trigger guard, fixed stock adj. polymer cheekpiece, M4/M16 grips, ambi thumb safety, 10 MIL rail, M-LOK compatible, Mil-Spec hardcoat anodized black, Tungsten Gray, or FDE Cerakote finish, 10.6-12.3 lbs. New 2020.

MSR $4,995 $4,250 $3,725 $3,195 $2,895 $2,350 $1,925 $1,500

RIFLES/CARBINES: SEMI-AUTO

MODEL 82 RIFLE – .50 BMG cal., semi-auto recoil operation, 33-37 in. barrel, 11 shot mag., 2,850 FPS muzzle velocity, scope sight only, parkerized finish, 35 lbs. Mfg. 1982-1987.

$5,000 $4,350 $3,950 $3,450 $2,700 $2,150 $1,800

Last MSR for consumers was $3,180 in 1985.

This model underwent design changes after initial production. Only 115 were manufactured starting with ser. no. 100.

MODEL 82A1 – .416 Barrett (new 2010) or .50 BMG cal., short recoil operating system, variant of the original Model 82, 20, 29 (new late 1989), or 33 (disc. 1989) in. fluted (current mfg.) or unfluted (disc.) barrel, muzzle brake (current mfg.), 10 shot detachable or fixed (.416 Barrett cal. only) mag., backup iron sights, current mfg. includes elevated M1913 optics rail, watertight case, and cleaning kit, black anodized (disc.), Burnt Bronze (mfg. 2018-2020), OD Green (mfg. 2018-2020, .416 Barrett only), manganese phosphate (new 2020), Tungsten Gray (new 2018), or FDE Cerakote (new 2013) finish, 32 1/2 lbs. for 1989 and older mfg., approx. 30 lbs. for 1990 mfg. and newer.

MSR $8,116 $6,900 $6,050 $5,175 $4,695 $3,800 $3,100 $2,425

Add $181 for tan/FDE (new 2013) or $306 for Burnt Bronze, OD Green, or Tungsten Gray (new 2018, .416 Barrett only) Cerakote finish.
Add $1,413 for Leupold scope, Barrett ultra high rings, and Monopod (mfg. 2012-2018).
Add $2,839 for Leupold scope, BORS, Barrett ultra high rings, and Monopod (mfg. 2012-2018).
Add $384 for pack-mat backpack case (mfg. 1999-2017).
Add $2,800 for rifle system including Leupold scope, ultra high rings, Pelican case, and detachable bipod (mfg. 2011-2014).
Add approx. $4,967 per upper conversion kit (disc. 2014).
Add $1,500 for Leupold Mark IV 4.5-14x50mm scope (disc. 2011).
Add $1,325 for Swarovski 10X scope and rings (disc.).

This model boasts official U.S. military rifle (M107) status following government procurement during Operation Desert Storm. In 1992, a new "arrowhead" shaped muzzle brake was introduced to reduce recoil.

MODEL 82A1 LEGACY – .50 BMG or .416 Barrett cal., recoil operated design, 24 in. non-fluted barrel with 2-port arrow head muzzle brake, 10 shot detachable box mag., 9 in. scope rail with 27 MOA taper, black finish, includes one 10 shot mag. and bipod. Mfg. 2015 only.

$7,775 $7,000 $6,125 $5,250 $4,760 $3,850 $3,150 ***$7,777***

Add approx. $5,000 for upper conversion kit.

MODEL 98 – .338 Lapua Mag. cal., 10 shot box mag., 24 in. match grade barrel with muzzle brake, bipod, 15 1/2 lbs.

While advertised during mid-1999, this model was never produced.

MODEL 107A1 – .50 BMG cal., 20 (new 2012) or 29 in. fluted barrel with four port titanium muzzle brake, 10 shot mag., integrated M1913 full-length receiver optics rail including flip-up iron sights, monopod on buttstock, features new bolt carrier group and aluminum recoil buffer system, detachable adj. lightweight bipod, black (new 2013) or Cerakote finishes in Multi-Role Brown (mfg. 2014-2017), Tungsten Grey (new 2014), OD Green (mfg. 2014-2019), or Tan/FDE, 27.4-28.7 lbs. New mid-2011.

MSR $12,281 $11,650 $10,850 $9,500 $7,500 $6,500 $5,500 $4,500

Add $1,413 for Leupold scope and Barrett ultra high rings (mfg. 2012-2018, black Cerakote finish only).
Add $2,839 for Leupold scope, BORS, and Barrett ultra high rings (mfg. 2012-2018, black Cerakote finish only).
Add $2,978 for QDL suppressor (new 2013).

MODEL M468 – 6.8 SPC cal., 16 in. barrel with muzzle brake, 5, 10, or 30 shot mag., dual spring extractor system, folding front and rear sight, two-stage trigger, aluminum upper and lower receiver, gas block, integrated rail system, choice of full or telescoping 4-position stock, 8 lbs. Mfg. 2005-2008.

$2,375 $2,125 $1,950 $1,775 $1,500 $1,175 $925 ***$2,700***

Add $1,590 for Model M468 upper conversion kit.

GRADING - PPGS™	100%	98%	95%	90%	80%	70%	60%	LAST MSR

MODEL REC7 – 5.56 NATO or 6.8 SPC (disc. 2020) cal., AR-15 style, GPO, 16 in. chrome-lined barrel with A2 flash hider, 30 shot mag., aluminum upper and lower receiver, SST, folding front and ARMS rear sight, 6-pos. MOE stock, ARMS selective integrated rail system (disc.) or Omega X rail (current mfg.), tactical soft case and two mags., 7.62 lbs. Mfg. 2008-2013.

	100%	98%	95%	90%	80%	70%	60%	LAST MSR
	$1,725	$1,550	$1,400	$1,275	$1,075	$850	$675	*$1,950*

Add $1,650 per individual upper conversion kit.
Add $676 for Aimpoint Micro T-1 optics (mfg. 2011-2012).

MODEL REC7 DI – 5.56 NATO, 6.8 SPC (disc. 2020), or .300 AAC Blackout (disc. 2020) cal., GIO, 16 or 18 in. match grade stainless steel barrel, 3-prong flash hider or 2 port muzzle brake, 20 or 30 shot Magpul mag., ALG Defense ACT (disc. 2020) or QMS (new 2021) trigger, Magpul backup iron (disc. 2020) or MBUS (new 2021) sights, 6-pos. Magpul MOE pistol grip stock with adj. LOP, ambi safety, Barrett 15 in. KeyMod handguard, BCM Gunfighter (disc. 2019) or Radian charging handle, black, Tungsten Grey, FDE, ODG (disc. 2020), Multi-Role Brown (disc. 2020), or Burnt Bronze (disc. 2020) receiver finish, 6.2-7.9 lbs. New 2016.

	100%	98%	95%	90%	80%	70%	60%
MSR $1,899	$1,675	$1,500	$1,375	$1,250	$1,050	$825	$650

MODEL REC7 GEN II – 5.56 NATO or 6.8 SPC cal., GPO, 16 in. chrome-lined barrel with PWS Triad (disc. 2020) or 3-prong flash suppressor, 30 shot Magpul mag., beveled magwell, Geissele SSA (disc. 2020) or ALG Defense QMS trigger, PRI flip-up iron (disc. 2020) or Magpul backup sights, Magpul MOE pistol grip stock w/adj. LOP, ambi safety, BCM charging handle, Barrett handguard with KeyMod, includes one KeyMod rail attachment and soft carrying case, Black, Tungsten Grey, FDE, OD Green, Multi-Role Brown (new 2017), or Burnt Bronze (new 2017) finish. New 2014.

	100%	98%	95%	90%	80%	70%	60%
MSR $2,499	$2,200	$1,975	$1,800	$1,650	$1,375	$1,075	$850

MODEL REC7 GEN II DMR – 5.56 NATO or 6.8 SPC cal., GPO, 18 in. stainless steel barrel, Barrett muzzle brake, 20 shot mag., Geissele (disc. 2020) or TriggerTech adaptable trigger, Magpul MBUS Pro (disc. 2020) or Magpul backup (new 2020) sights, Magpul MOE pistol grip stock, ambi safety, Barrett handguard with KeyMod rail attachment, includes soft carrying case, black, Tungsten Grey, FDE, OD Green (disc. 2020), Multi-Role Brown (mfg. 2017-2020), or Burnt Bronze (mfg. 2017-2020) finish, 7.9 lbs. New 2016.

	100%	98%	95%	90%	80%	70%	60%
MSR $2,799	$2,475	$2,200	$2,025	$1,850	$1,550	$1,225	$950

MODEL REC7 GEN II FLYWEIGHT – 5.56 NATO or 6.8 SPC (new 2017) cal., GPO, 16 in. lightweight match grade stainless steel, chrome-lined barrel, thread protector, PWS Triad flash suppressor (disc.) or Barrett 3-prong flash hider, 20 shot beveled Magpul mag., Geissele (disc. 2020) or ALG Defense QMS (new 2021) trigger, Magpul backup sights, Magpul MOE pistol grip stock, Magpul SL-K buttstock w/adj. LOP, ambi safety, Barrett (disc. 2020) or Magpul (new 2021) handguard with KeyMod rail attachment, includes soft carrying case, Black, Tungsten Grey, FDE, OD Green (disc. 2020), Multi-Role Brown (new 2017), or Burnt Bronze (new 2017) finish, 6.1 lbs. New 2016.

	100%	98%	95%	90%	80%	70%	60%
MSR $2,199	$1,950	$1,725	$1,600	$1,450	$1,225	$950	$750

MODEL REC7 (RECENT MFG.) – 5.56 NATO or 6.8 SPC cal., AR-15 style, GPO, 16 in. chrome-lined barrel with A2 flash hider, 30 shot mag., aluminum upper and lower receiver, SST, folding front and ARMS rear sight, 6-position MOE stock, ARMS selective integrated rail system (disc.) or Omega X rail (current mfg.), tactical soft case and two mags., 7.62 lbs. Mfg. 2008-2013.

	100%	98%	95%	90%	80%	70%	60%	LAST MSR
	$1,600	$1,000	$775	$575	$495	$425	$395	*$1,950*

Add $1,650 per individual upper conversion kit.
Add $676 for Aimpoint Micro T-1 optics (mfg. 2011-2012).

MODEL REC10 CARBINE – .308 Win. cal., DI, 16 in. chrome-lined barrel w/Barrett flash hider, 20 shot Magpul mag., ambi bolt release and mag. catch, ALG Defense QMS trigger, Magpul MBUS flip-up iron sights, Magpul MOE-SL pistol grip stock, adj. LOP, ambi safety, BRS M-LOK handguard, Black, FDE, or Tungsten Grey Cerakote finish, 34.5 in. OAL, 8.3 lbs. New 2019.

	100%	98%	95%	90%	80%	70%	60%
MSR $2,995	$2,650	$2,375	$2,175	$1,975	$1,650	$1,300	$1,025

SHOTGUNS: O/U

SOVEREIGN SERIES ALBANY – 12, 20, or 28 ga., 2 3/4 (28 ga.) or 3 in. chambers, 26, 28, or 30 in. polished blue barrels, interchangeable chokes, automatic ejectors, SST, Grade 3A Turkish walnut Prince of Wales stock with classic checkering, rubber recoil pad, splinter or beavertail (28 ga.) forend, steel round body boxlock with ornamental sideplates, includes Barrett branded case and velvet sock, coin finished with custom engraving. Mfg. 2016-2020.

	100%	98%	95%	90%	80%	70%	60%	LAST MSR
	$5,250	$4,600	$4,000	$3,500	$3,000	$2,500	$1,950	*$5,700*

Add $450 for 28 ga.

GRADING - PPGS™	100%	98%	95%	90%	80%	70%	60%	LAST MSR

SOVEREIGN SERIES BxPRO – 12 ga., 3 in. chambers, 30 or 32 in. polished blue VR barrels with rounded forend, interchangeable extended chokes, steel body boxlock design, fiber optic bead sight, automatic ejectors, single selective trigger, A+ walnut pistol grip stock with classic checkering, rubber recoil pad, adj. comb, coin finished receiver with custom engraving. Mfg. 2017-2020.

	$2,795	$2,525	$2,300	$2,050	$1,875	$1,700	$1,495	*$3,075*

SOVEREIGN SERIES RUTHERFORD – 12, 16, 20, or 28 ga., 2 3/4 or 3 in. chambers, 26 or 28 in. polished blue VR barrels, interchangeable chokes, automatic ejectors, single selective trigger, A+ walnut stock with rounded pistol grip and classic checkering, rubber recoil pad, steel body boxlock design, coin finished receiver with custom engraving. Mfg. 2017-2020.

	$2,000	$1,800	$1,600	$1,400	$1,200	$1,000	$850	*$2,200*

Add $320 for 16 or 28 ga.

SHOTGUNS: SxS

SOVEREIGN SERIES BELTRAMI – 12, 20, or 28 ga., 2 3/4 (28 ga.) or 3 in. chambers, 26, 28, or 30 in. polished blue barrels, interchangeable chokes, automatic ejectors, single non-selective trigger, Grade 3A Turkish walnut English stock with classic checkering, rubber recoil pad, steel boxlock design with ornamental sideplates, includes Barrett branded case and velvet sock, coin finished receiver with custom engraving. Mfg. in Italy 2016-2020.

	$5,500	$4,450	$3,850	$3,350	$2,875	$2,425	$1,995	*$6,150*

Add $400 for 28 ga.

BAR-STO

Previous manufacturer located in Palms, CA. Bar-Sto still manufactures barrels and firearms-related accessories.

PISTOLS: SEMI-AUTO

BAR-STO .25 ACP PISTOL – .25 ACP cal., patterned after the Baby Browning, brushed stainless steel finish, walnut grips, approx. 250 manufactured circa 1974.

	$195	$165	$125	$100	$85	$70	$65	

BARTOLOT, WERNER

Please refer to Werner Bartolot listing in the W section.

BASERRI

Previous trademark established mid-2010-2014, and manufactured by Fabarm in Brescia, Italy. Previously imported by Baserri located in Friendswood, TX.

For individual model listings, please go to BlueBookOfGunValues.com/overflow.

BATTAGLIA, MAURO

Current manufacturer established in 1992, located in Ravenna, Italy. No current U.S. importation.

SHOTGUNS: SxS, CUSTOM

Mauro Battaglia manufactures custom order high quality SxS shotguns. He also manufactures a sidelock action with new unique design. Many options are available. Current models include: the Angels, Morena, Mercedes, Manuela, History, Monia Extra, and the Timio. Many engraving options are available and feature engraver Max Gobbi. Please contact the factory directly for more information, including delivery time, options, and a price quotation.

BATTLE ARMS DEVELOPMENT, INC. (B.A.D., INC.)

Current AR-15 style rifle, pistol, and accessories manufacturer located in Henderson, NV since 2009.

Please refer to BlueBookOfGunValues.com to order the *Blue Book of AR-15s & Variations*, available as a book or online subscription.

BATTLE RIFLE COMPANY

Current manufacturer of AR-15 style rifles and pistols established in 2010, located in Houston, TX. Previously located in Seabrook, TX.

Please refer to BlueBookOfGunValues.com to order the *Blue Book of AR-15s & Variations*, available as a book or online subscription.

BAUER FIREARMS CORPORATION

Previous manufacturer located in Fraser, MI circa 1971-1984.

GRADING - PPGS™	100%	98%	95%	90%	80%	70%	60%	LAST MSR

COMBINATION GUNS

THE RABBIT – .22 LR cal. and .410 bore, combination gun with 20 in. barrel, all metal construction, O/U configuration, 4 3/4 lbs. Mfg. 1982-1984.

	100%	98%	95%	90%	80%	70%	60%	LAST MSR
	$250	$225	$175	$150	$125	$100	$85	

PISTOLS: SEMI-AUTO

BAUER .25 ACP – .25 ACP cal., 2 1/2 in. barrel, 6 shot, fixed sights, checkered walnut or pearlite grips. Mfg. 1972-84.

	100%	98%	95%	90%	80%	70%	60%	LAST MSR
	$225	$195	$175	$150	$125	$100	$80	

Note: These guns are identical to the Baby Browning, except stainless steel.

* ***Bauer .25 ACP Bicentennial Model*** – .25 ACP cal., engraved, with buckle and display case.

	100%	98%	95%	90%	80%	70%	60%	LAST MSR
	$300	$200	$150	$120	$100	$90	$80	

BAYARD

Previously manufactured by Anciens Etablissements Pieper located in Herstal, Belgium until 1954 when all operations ceased and the company closed.

Even though Bayard Models 1908, both 1923s, and 1930 were manufactured only by Anciens Etablissements Pieper of Herstal, Belgium, these pistols are listed under this heading as they are most commonly referred to by this trademark designation.

PISTOLS: SEMI-AUTO

MODEL 1908 POCKET AUTOMATIC – .25 ACP, .32 ACP, or .380 ACP cal., 6 shot, 2 1/4 in. barrel, fixed sights, blue, hard rubber grips.

	100%	98%	95%	90%	80%	70%	60%	LAST MSR
	$550	$450	$275	$195	$150	$125	$100	
Factory Engraved	$2,500	$2,200	$1,800	$1,000	$800	$500	$300	

Add 25% if marked with Imperial Eagle, but only if 98% or better.
Add 20% for factory mother-of-pearl or ivory grips if undamaged.
Add 10% for .25 ACP or .380 ACP cal.
Add $300 for original factory box in good condition.

MODEL 1923 & MODEL 1930 .25 POCKET AUTOMATIC – .25 ACP cal., 2 1/2 in. barrel, blue, fixed sights, checkered hard rubber grips.

	100%	98%	95%	90%	80%	70%	60%	LAST MSR
	$675	$495	$350	$300	$275	$200	$175	

Add $300 for original factory box in good condition.

The Model 1930 is a slight improvement over the Model 1923. Both share the same physical characteristics.

BAYARD 1923 & MODEL 1930 POCKET AUTOMATIC – .32 ACP or .380 ACP cal., 6 shot, 3 5/16 in. barrel, fixed sights, blue, checkered hard rubber grips.

	100%	98%	95%	90%	80%	70%	60%	LAST MSR
	$875	$600	$450	$400	$325	$250	$200	

Add 10% for .380 ACP cal.
Add $300 for original factory box in good condition.

The Model 1930 is a slight improvement over the Model 1923. Both share the same physical characteristics.

SHOTGUNS: SxS

Although often recognized in the U.S for their pistols, Anciens Etablissements Pieper, was primarily a fine shotgun manufacturer with roots dating back to 1866. Re-organization and renaming of the company in 1905 brought in modern manufacturing techniques combined with old-world craftsmanship. By 1910 the company was one of Belgium's largest gun manufacturers, employing 1,100 workers. The Bayard trade-name was engraved on all barrels. Often mistaken as antiques, Bayard hammer guns were made through the 1920s and remained available in the 1930s. More than 150 various hammer models and variations were offered at any one time, with most models featuring extensive and luxurious hand engraving. Pricing varies extensively depending on the engraving style and engraving coverage, barrel styles like damascus barrels, wood checkering, etc. Observed pricing for hammer guns have been from $200 to $10,000. Although many model variants exist, hammerless shotguns are outlined below.

BOXLOCK BASIC MODELS – 12 or 16 ga., Anson-Deeley system, standard checkering on walnut stock, minor and simple engraving on select few parts.

	100%	98%	95%	90%	80%	70%	60%	LAST MSR
	$500	$400	$300	$275	$200	$150	$100	

Add 20% for auto ejectors.
Add $40 for semi-pistol grip stock option.

GRADING - PPGS™	100%	98%	95%	90%	80%	70%	60%	LAST MSR

BOXLOCK FINE GRADE MODELS – 12 or 16 ga., Anson-Deeley system, Demi-bloc barrels marked "Tested for Smokeless Powder" in either French, German or English depending on export market, standard checkering on walnut stock, elegant floral and/or game scene engraving styles.

$1,800	$1,600	$1,200	$900	$750	$650	$550	

Add 20% for auto ejectors or semi-pistol grip stock option.
Subtract $400 for Model 560, marked and finished as Fine Grade Models but with almost no engraving.

BOXLOCK LUXURY GRADE MODELS – 12 or 16 ga., Anson-Deeley system, Demi-bloc barrels marked "Tested for Smokeless Powder" in either French, German or English depending on export market, fancy wood checkering, full coverage elegant engraving on all parts.

$4,000	$3,600	$3,000	$2,550	$2,000	$1,300	$800	

Add 20% for auto ejectors or for semi-pistol grip stock option.
Add a minimum of $200 for gold inlay option, depending on coverage but only if 95% condition or better.

SIDELOCK FINE GRADE MODELS – 12 or 16 ga., demi-bloc barrels marked "Tested for Smokeless Powder" in either French, German or English depending on export market, standard checkering on walnut stock, oak leaf engraving or floral and/or game scene engraving styles.

$1,950	$1,750	$1,300	$1,000	$800	$750	$650	

Add 20% for auto ejectors or for semi-pistol grip stock option.

SIDELOCK LUXURY GRADE MODELS – 12 or 16 ga., demi-bloc barrels marked "Tested for Smokeless Powder" in either French, German or English depending on export market, fancy wood checkering, full coverage elegant engraving on all parts.

$4,800	$4,500	$3,900	$3,000	$2,200	$1,500	$900	

Add 20% for auto ejectors or for semi-pistol grip stock option.
Add a minimum of $200 for gold inlay option, depending on coverage but only if 95% condition or better.

BAZOOKA BROTHERS MFG.

Current manufacturer of AR-15 style carbines/rifles, pistols, and components established circa 2002, located in Russiaville, IN.

Please refer to BlueBookOfGunValues.com to order the *Blue Book of AR-15s & Variations*, available as a book or online subscription.

BEAR CREEK ARSENAL

Current AR-15 style pistol, rifle, and parts manufacturer located in Sanford, NC.

Please refer to BlueBookOfGunValues.com to order the *Blue Book of AR-15s & Variations*, available as a book or online subscription.

BECAS

Current trademark of shotguns manufactured by Molot JSC, located in the Kirov Region, Russia.

Becas semi-automatic and slide action rifles and shotguns have had little or no importation into the U.S. Please contact the factory for more information including U.S. model availability.

BEEMAN OUTDOOR SPORTS

Previous importer and distributor located in Santa Rosa, CA.

On April 1, 1993, Beeman Precision Arms, Inc. was split into two independent companies: Beeman Precision Airguns, a division of S/R Industries (Maryland Corp.), located in Huntington Beach, CA retains worldwide distribution of Beeman airguns and accessories. Beeman Outdoor Sports, a Division of Robert's Precision Arms, Inc., located in Santa Rosa, CA distributed Feinwerkbau firearms until 1995.

Beeman Precision Arms, Inc. was a large volume importer, primarily specializing in high quality European air rifles and pistols. Firearms trademarks previously distributed in the U.S. include the following trademarks: Agner (disc. 1986), Erma (disc. 1985), FAS (disc. 1987), Fabarm (disc. 1985), Feinwerkbau, Korth (disc. 1990), Krico (disc. 1988), Unique (disc. 1991), and Weihrauch (disc.). These trademarks appear under their respective alphabetical headings.

For more information and current pricing on both new and used Beeman Precision Airguns, please refer to the *Blue Book of Airguns* - also available as an online subscription.

The following firearms were manufactured to Beeman specifications, and are therefore listed under the Beeman Outdoor Sports heading.

PISTOLS: SEMI-AUTO

BEEMAN MP-08 – .380 ACP cal., Luger type toggle action, 3 1/2 in. barrel, 6 shot mag., blue, 1.4 lbs. Mfg. 1968-90.

$395	$335	$275	$240	$185	$145	$115	*$390*

In 1988, Beeman took over importation of these two models (MP-08 and P-08). These revised models have new Luger style checkered walnut grips and 3 1/2 in. barrel. Previous variations had plastic grips.

GRADING - PPGS™	100%	98%	95%	90%	80%	70%	60%	LAST MSR

BEEMAN P-08 – .22 LR cal., Luger type toggle action, 8 shot mag., 3.8 in. barrel, blue, checkered walnut grips, 1.9 lbs. Mfg. 1969-1990.

$395	$335	$275	$240	$185	$145	$115	*$390*

PISTOLS: SINGLE SHOT

MODEL SP/SPX – .22 LR cal., designed for silhouette shooting, 10 in. heavy bull barrel, blue metal parts, birchwood stocks and forearm, aperture sights, 3.9 lbs. Disc. 1994.

$625	$550	$475	$425	$375	$330	$295	*$700*

Only a few of these models were actually delivered.

* ***Model SPX Deluxe*** – .22 LR cal., similar to Model SPX, except has matte chrome metal finish, hand stippled walnut grips, and Anschütz rear sight. Limited mfg. 1993-94.

$800	$725	$650	$575	$500	$425	$350	*$900*

SP STANDARD – .22 LR cal., sidelever action, 8, 10, 12, or 15 in. barrel, adj. sights and walnut grips, single shot. Made in W. Germany. Imported 1985-86 only.

$250	$220	$180	$170	$160	$150	$140	*$250*

Add $10 or $30 for 12 or 15 in. barrel respectively.

SP DELUXE – .22 LR cal., similar to SP Standard, except has forearm, about 3 1/2 lbs. Made in W. Germany. Imported 1985-86 only.

$275	$240	$200	$185	$170	$155	$145	*$300*

Add $10 for 12 or $30 for 15 in. barrel.

BEHOLLA PISTOL

Previously manufactured by Becker & Hollander located in Suhl, Germany.

PISTOLS: SEMI-AUTO

BEHOLLA POCKET AUTOMATIC – .32 ACP cal., 7 shot, 2.9 in. barrel, blue, serrated wood or rubber grips, mfg. 1915-1920. From 1920-1925 the same gun was mfg. by Stenda-Werke.

$225	$170	$150	$135	$120	$100	$90

BENELLI

Current manufacturer established in 1967, located in Urbino, Italy. Benelli USA was formed during late 1997, and is currently importing all Benelli shotguns and rifles. Benelli pistols (and air pistols) were imported by Larry's Guns, located in Gray, ME from 2003-2019. Company headquarters are located in Accokeek, MD. Shotguns were previously imported 1983-1997 by Heckler & Koch, Inc., located in Sterling, VA. Handguns were previously imported until 1997 by European American Armory, located in Sharpes, FL, in addition to Sile Distributors, Inc., until 1995, located in New York, NY, and Saco, located in Arlington, VA.

For more information on Benelli air pistols, please refer to the *Blue Book of Airguns* - also available as an online subscription.

PISTOLS: SEMI-AUTO

Models B-77, B-80, and MP3S were previously imported by Sile Distributors. Models MP90S and MP95E Atlanta were imported by Benelli USA until 2002 and exclusively imported by Larry's Guns 2003-2019.

MODEL B-76 – 9mm Para. cal., single/double action, all steel, 4 1/4 in. barrel, 8 shot mag., 34 oz. Importation disc. in 1990.

$1,100	$800	$600	$475	$400	$350	$295	*$428*

MODEL B-76S TARGET – 9mm Para. cal., similar to B-76, except has 5 1/2 in. barrel, target grips, and adj. rear sights. Importation disc. 1990.

$1,575	$1,225	$925	$800	$700	$600	$500	*$595*

MODEL B-77 – .32 ACP cal., single/double action, all steel, 4 1/4 in. barrel, 8 shot mag. Importation disc. 1995.

$625	$550	$475	$425	$350	$300	$275	*$385*

MODEL B-80 – .30 Luger cal., single/double action, all steel, 4 1/4 in. barrel, 8 shot mag., 34 oz. Importation disc. 1995.

$500	$425	$350	$300	$275	$225	$175	*$385*

GRADING - PPGS™	100%	98%	95%	90%	80%	70%	60%	LAST MSR

MODEL B-80S TARGET – .30 Luger cal., 5 1/2 in. barrel, 8 shot mag., target grips, and adj. rear sight. Importation disc. 1995.

	$625	$550	$475	$425	$350	$300	$275	*$572*

MODEL B82 – 9x18mm Ultra, .30 Luger, or .32 Auto cal., contract order for Italian police, ser. no. with "D" suffix, limited production.

	$750	$625	$550	$500	$450	$400	$375	

MODEL MP3S – .32 S&W Long Wadcutter or 9mm Para. cal., target variation with 5 1/2 in. barrel, high gloss bluing, target grips, and adj. rear sight. Importation disc. 1995.

.32 S&W Long	$2,250	$1,975	$1,700	$1,525	$1,250	$1,000	$800	
9mm Para.	$4,500	$3,950	$3,375	$3,000	$2,475	$2,025	$1,575	*$785*

Add a premium for factory leather case.

MODEL MP90S (WORLD CUP) – .22 S (disc.), .22 LR, or .32 S&W Wadcutter cal., 4.4 in. barrel, blue finish, black frame finish with chrome bolt on most recent mfg., target pistol featuring forward assisted breech bolt mechanism, anatomic grips, and adj. weight, 5 (disc.), 6, or 9 (optional) shot mag., 2.4 lbs. Imported 1992-2002 by Benelli USA. Imported exclusively by Larry's Guns 2003-2019.

	$1,699	$1,450	$1,225	$1,050	$875	$725	$625	

Add $150 for .32 S&W Wadcutter cal.

Conversion kits were previously available for this model at an extra charge.

MODEL MP95E (ATLANTA) – .22 LR or .32 S&W Wadcutter (disc. 1999, reintroduced 2006) cal., 4.4 in. barrel, inertial recoiling mass system, integral Weaver style base mount, 5 (disc.), 6, or 9 (optional) shot mag., adj. trigger assembly, fully adj. sight, modular firing system, blue or matte chrome finish, smooth laminate (chrome finish only) or choice of checkered adj. (disc.) or non-adj. walnut grips, 2 1/2 lbs. Imported late 1994-2002 by Benelli USA. Imported exclusively by Larry's Guns 2003-2019.

	$1,100	$875	$750	$625	$525	$450	$395	

Add $200 for chrome finish.
Add $150 for .32 S&W Wadcutter cal.

RIFLES: BOLT ACTION

LUPO – .30-06, .300 Win. Mag., .270 Win., 6.5 Creedmoor (new 2021), .308 Win. (new 2021), or .243 Win. (new 2021) cal., 22 or 24 in. free floated threaded Crio barrel, detachable box mag., adj. trigger, drilled and tapped, black synthetic Progressive Comfort stock, Combtech cheek pad, ambi safety, integrated swivel mount, two-piece Picatinny rail, matte blued finish, 7 lbs. New 2020.

MSR $1,699	$1,450	$1,275	$1,095	$985	$800	$650	$525	

RIFLES: SEMI-AUTO

R1 STANDARD CARBINE/RIFLE – .270 WSM (mfg. 2005-2010), .30-06, .308 Win. (mfg. 2002-2010, reintroduced 2019), .300 WSM (mfg. 2005-2010), .300 Win. Mag., or .338 Win. Mag. (new 2011) cal., features AutoRegulating Gas Operated (ARGO) system and rotating 3 lug bolt, 20 (carbine, .30-06 or .300 Win. Mag. only, disc.), 22, or 24 (.300 Win. Mag. and WSM cals.) in. barrel with Crio treatment and interchangeable rear rib, detachable 3 or 4 shot mag., optional sights, forearm is fixed to the alloy receiver, drilled and tapped, Picatinny rail included, available in black or nickel plated (Europe only) receiver finish, optional Realtree APG HD camo treatment (mfg. 2007-2018), black ComforTech synthetic with GripTight inserts (new 2006) or checkered walnut Monte Carlo stock and forearm (current finish is satin), recoil pad is cut into the stock (adj. with shims), ambidextrous safety, approx. 7 lbs. New 2002.

MSR $1,149	$975	$850	$725	$675	$550	$475	$395	

Add $200 for ComforTech GripTight synthetic stock.
Add $230 for Realtree APG camo finish with ComforTech GripTight stock (disc. 2018).

This model is designated the Argo in Europe. An Argo Deluxe is also available for European sales, with better grade wood and hand engraving on both sides of the frame.

* ***R1 Limited Edition Rifle*** – .30-06 cal., 22 in. barrel, 4 shot mag., highly figured AAA satin finished checkered walnut stock and forearm, coin finished receiver with detailed game scenes and gold inlays, fully adj. rear blade and front sight with red fiber optic insert, optional recoil pad, 7.1 lbs., available from World Class dealers only. Imported 2010-circa 2012, still available in Europe.

	$2,475	$2,000	$1,600	$1,250	$1,100	$925	$850	*$2,900*

R1 PRO RIFLE – .30-06 cal., ARGO system action, 22 in. barrel, 4 shot, AA Grade satin walnut stock, Progressive Comfort, 7.2 lbs. New 2017.

MSR $1,499	$1,065	$975	$900	$800	$700	$600	$500	

GRADING - PPGS™	100%	98%	95%	90%	80%	70%	60%	LAST MSR

MR1 CARBINE/RIFLE – 5.56 NATO cal., self-adjusting gas operation (similar to the Benelli M4 shotgun used by Marines) with rotating bolt head featuring three lugs, accepts 5 shot AR-15 style mags., 16 or 20 (Europe only) in. barrel, regular or pistol grip, rifle sights, includes Picatinny rail with ghost ring sights, push-button safety on trigger guard, black finish, approx. 8 lbs. Imported late 2009-2015.

	$1,175	$1,000	$875	$750	$650	$550	$450	*$1,339*

* ***MR1 ComforTech Carbine*** – 5.56 NATO cal., 16 in. barrel features black pistol grip ComforTech stock, otherwise similar to MR1 Carbine/Rifle. Imported 2011-2015.

	$1,275	$1,075	$925	$775	$675	$575	$475	*$1,469*

SHOTGUNS: O/U

828 U – 12 or 20 (new 2020) ga., 3 in. chambers, 26, 28, or 30 (new 2018) in. separated cryogenically treated interchangeable barrels with carbon fiber VR, fiber optic front sight, includes 5 Crio chokes, choice of polished aluminum receiver with combination of scroll and scalloped ornamentation or non-embellished matte black aluminum receiver, pulse ejectors (mechanism is contained in barrels), compact removable trigger assembly, AA grade satin finished walnut stock and forearm with ergonomic recoil pad, gel comb insert, and fish scale pattern carving, top tang safety, patented steel locking system, right or left (new 2018) hand configuration, 6 1/2 lbs. New 2015.

MSR $2,699	$2,295	$1,900	$1,775	$1,575	$1,375	$1,175	$995	

Add $500 for nickel finished aluminum receiver.

Add $500 for left-hand configuration (available on nickel receiver only, new 2018)..

* ***Performance Shop 828U Upland*** – 12 or 20 (new 2021) ga., 3 in. chambers, 24 in. barrels, Crio chokes, AA Grade satin walnut Progressive Comfort stock, anodized bronze/blue receiver finish, 6.4 lbs. New 2019.

MSR $3,499	$2,975	$2,525	$2,300	$2,050	$1,600	$1,350	$1,050	

828 U SPORT – 12 ga., 3 in. chambers, 30 or 32 (new 2020) in. barrels with five extended nickel/red Crio chokes, wide carbon fiber rib with integrated sight channel, movable trigger, AA Grade satin walnut stock, steel receiver and locking plate, Progressive Balancing, blued finish, 8 lbs. New 2019.

MSR $4,399	$3,750	$3,280	$2,825	$2,550	$2,075	$1,700	$1,450	

SHOTGUNS: SEMI-AUTO, 1985-OLDER

Benelli semi-auto 3rd generation (inertia recoil) shotguns were imported starting in the late 1960s. They were marketed as a super fast cycling shotgun. By the time the 5th shell was being ejected, the first shell had not hit the ground! The SL-80 Model 121 had a semi-gloss, black finish, the Model 123 had an ornate photo-engraved receiver, the Model Special 80 had a brushed, white nickel-plated receiver, and the Model 121 M1 had a matte finish receiver, barrel, and stock. All 12 ga. SL-80 Series shotguns will accept 2 3/4 or 3 in. shells, and all SL-80 Series 12 ga. Models have interchangeable barrels (except the 121 M1) with 4 different model receivers (121, 121 M1, 123, and Special 80). All 4 models had fixed choke barrels.

The SL-80 Series shotguns were discontinued in 1985 and later marketed by Beretta as the Vitoria, Pintail, and then the ES-100 Pintail.

Approx. 50,000 SL-80 Series shotguns were mfg. before discontinuance. Choke markings (located on the side or bottom of the barrel) are as follows: *full choke, **imp. mod., ***mod., ****imp. cyl. SL-80 series guns used the same action (different than current mfg.) and all had the desirable split receiver design, similar to the Super Black Eagle. Check forend for cracking in area of the finger grooves.

The marketplace for older Benelli semi-auto shotguns has changed in recent years, with more interest being shown in these older models as they represent a good value compared to Benelli's new offerings. Collector interest on these older SL-80s appears to be occurring also. As a result of this additional interest and demand, values have gone up, after being dormant for many years. The number of guns being offered for sale still remains low. No doubt that people own these SL-80 Series guns are not interested in selling them.

100% values within this section assume NIB condition.

Subtract 5% for "SACO" importation (Saco was located in Arlington, VA).

SL-80 SERIES MODEL SL-121V – 12 ga., field grade, 26 or 28 in. fixed choke VR barrel, anodized and black semi-gloss finish on lower receiver. Disc. 1985.

	$775	$695	$625	$575	$425	$350	$275	*$397*

SL-80 SERIES MODEL SL-121/SL-122 SLUG – 12 ga., features Monte Carlo stock and flat bottom Trap Grade beavertail forearm, 21 1/16 in. cyl. bore barrel, fixed open ring rear iron sights and fixed front ramp, 5 shot mag., recoil pad, 7 lbs. 3 oz. Disc. 1985.

	$875	$795	$700	$600	$495	$350	$250	*$434*

GRADING - PPGS™	100%	98%	95%	90%	80%	70%	60%	LAST MSR

SL-80 SERIES MODEL SL-123V – 12 ga., stylish field grade, Ergal special aluminum alloy receiver with photo engraving, 26 or 28 in. VR barrel with various chokes, approx. 6 lbs. 13 oz. Disc. 1985.

	$875	$775	$695	$575	$450	$300	$250	*$464*

Add $100 for trap stock, $75 for beavertail forearm and $25 for skeet barrel.

The only difference between the SL-123V and SL-121V is the photo engraved receiver and slightly better wood. The SL-123V was at times referred to as the deluxe model when compared to the SL-121V. Both models sold as trap guns by changing stocks and forends.

EX-L – 12 ga., similar in appearance to the Model SL-123V, except has hand-engraved receiver, very limited mfg. with unpredictable premiums over Model SL-123V.

SL-80 SERIES MODEL 121 M1 POLICE/MILITARY – 12 ga. only, similar in appearance to the Super 90 M1, hardwood stock, 7 shot mag., matte metal and wood finish, most stocks had adj. lateral sling attachment inside of buttstock, 18 3/4 in. barrel. Disc. 1985.

	$675	$625	$550	$450	$325	$250	$225	

Since many 121 M1s were sold to the police and military, used specimens should be checked carefully for excessive wear and/or possible damage. Since these guns usually saw extensive use, they are much less desirable than other SL-80s listed in this section. These models are not rare, but few have been traded in recent years.

MODEL 80 SPECIAL SKEET/TRAP – 12 ga. only, 28 in. VR barrel with mod. choke and phosphorescent bead sight, trap/skeet Monte Carlo grade/style wood stock with recoil pad, lower receiver was nickel plated, 7 lbs. 10 oz. Disc. 1985.

	$895	$725	$695	$600	$475	$350	$275	*$531*

Trap guns should have high comb trap stock and trap grade forearm (not field grade/style wood). Trap guns should also be inspected carefully for internal wear before buying/selling. Also inspect the nickel plating carefully before considering a purchase, as it tends to flake.

SL-80 SERIES MODEL SL201 FIELD GRADE – 20 ga., 26 in. VR mod. choke barrel, approx. 5 lbs. 10 oz. Disc. 1985.

	$825	$750	$695	$600	$500	$395	$300	*$399*

Manufactured in smaller numbers compared to the 12 ga. models. Sought after by collectors.

BRI-BENELLI SL-80 123 SLUG GUN – 12 ga. only, custom design, premium slug gun, SL-80 Series action with drilled and tapped rifled barrel by E. R. Shaw Barrel Co., assembled by BRI in the U.S., Monte Carlo stock with beavertail forend, barrels stamped "BRI", ser. nos. 0001-0025, approx. 25 guns total mfg. 1986-1987.

	$1,895	$1,275	$1,025	$875	$750	$625	$525	

Subtract 40% if w/o trap style beavertail forend and Monte Carlo stock.
Subtract 60%-70% if barrel is not stamped "BRI".
Original issue price on this model was $750-$850.

These specimens were marked "BRI-Benelli" on barrel. No warranties exist on this model.

SHOTGUNS: SEMI-AUTO, 1986-NEWER

Unless indicated otherwise, all currently manufactured Benelli shotguns utilize a red fiber optic sight, and are equipped with a patented Benelli keyed chamber lock.

CORDOBA – 12 or 20 ga., 3 in. chamber, 28 or 30 (12 ga. only) in. 10mm ported VR Crio barrel with extended choke tubes, 4 shot mag., matte black finish, black synthetic ComforTech stock with GripTight overcoating on stock and forearm (became standard 2013), or Max 4 HD (12 ga. only, 28 in. barrel, rifle sights, mfg. 2007-2011) camo coverage, 7.2 lbs. Mfg. 2005-2018.

	$1,400	$1,250	$1,100	$1,000	$900	$750	$650	*$2,109*

Add $170 for Max 4 HD camo (not available in 20 ga., mfg. 2007-2011).

* ***Cordoba Performance Shop Edition*** – 12 or 20 ga., 3 in. chamber, 4 shot mag., 28 in. ported barrel with lengthened forcing cone, black synthetic ComforTech stock with GripTight panels, Briley EZ Bolt release and enlarged bolt operating handle, Briley extended chokes, red bar front sight, metal bead mid-sight, 6.7-7.7 lbs. Mfg. 2010-2018.

	$1,900	$1,750	$1,600	$1,450	$1,250	$1,000	$875	*$2,719*

Add $110 for 12 ga.

ETHOS – 12, 20 (new 2016), or 28 (new 2016, 26 in. only) ga., 3 in. chamber, Inertia Driven System, 26 or 28 in. barrel with Crio treatment and 5 chokes, 4 shot mag., black or nickel receiver, easy access cartridge drop lever, enlarged bolt release, improved ergonomics, interchangeable carbon fiber rib, anti-seize mag cap, interchangeable fiber optic sight with red, green, and yellow inserts and metal bead mid-sight, AA Grade satin walnut stock, Progressive Comfort (patented recoil reduction system) recoil and comb pads, includes padded, hard-shell protective gun case, 6 1/2 lbs. Mfg. 2014-2020.

	$1,745	$1,500	$1,400	$1,200	$975	$800	$625	*$1,999*

Add $150 for nickel receiver.

GRADING - PPGS™	100%	98%	95%	90%	80%	70%	60%	LAST MSR

* ***Ethos Sport*** – 12, 20, or 28 ga., 2 3/4 or 3 in. chamber, 28 or 30 (12 ga. only) in. VR ported barrel, extended choke tubes, AA grade satin finished and checkered walnut stock and forearm, engraved nickel receiver, progressive comfort (patented recoil reduction system) with comb pads, 5.4-6.6 lbs. New 2018.

MSR $2,269	$1,995	$1,680	$1,575	$1,275	$1,075	$900	$725	

* ***Performance Shop Ethos Upland*** – 12 or 20 ga., 2 3/4 or 3 in. chamber, 26 in. barrel with gloss blued finish, Crio choke tubes including Triple Threat chokes, 4 shot mag., interchangeable fiber optic front sight, AA Grade satin walnut Progressive Comfort stock, engraved nickel-plated receiver (12 ga.) or engraved nickel-plated alloy receiver (20 ga.), 5.6-6.6 lbs. New 2020.

MSR $2,999	$2,550	$2,225	$1,975	$1,725	$1,400	$1,150	$925	

ETHOS SUPERSPORT – 12, 20, or 28 ga., 2 3/4 or 3 in. chamber, 28 or 30 in. barrel, 5 Crio extended choke tubes, 2 or 4 shot mag., nickel-plated receiver, Comfort Tech 3 stock with carbon fiber finish, gloss blued barrel finish, 5.4-7 lbs. New 2021.

MSR $2,299	$1,960	$1,700	$1,575	$1,400	$1,200	$900	$750	

Add $600 for 20 ga. or $700 for 12 ga. for the Ethos Supersport Performance Center model (new 2021).

B.E.S.T. ETHOS – 12 ga., 2 3/4, 3, or 3 1/2 in. chamber, 28 or 30 in. barrel with B.E.S.T. (Benelli Surface Treatment), Crio chokes, 4 shot, receiver with black anodized finish, interchangeable fiber optic sight, black synthetic ComforTech 3 stock, 6.7 lbs. New 2020.

MSR $2,199	$1,950	$1,650	$1,550	$1,275	$1,075	$800	$675	

* ***B.E.S.T. Ethos Cordoba*** – 12, 20, or 28 ga., 2 3/4 or 3 in. chamber, 28 or 30 in. ported barrel with B.E.S.T. treatment, Crio extended chokes, 2 or 4 shot mags., red fiber optic front sight, black synthetic Comfort Tech 3 stock, anodized black finish, 5.4-7 lbs. New 2021.

MSR $2,349	$1,995	$1,750	$1,500	$1,350	$1,100	$900	$700	

LEGACY MODEL – 12, 20 (new 1999), or 28 (new 2010) ga., 3 in. chamber, 24 (20 or 28 ga. only), 26 or 28 (12 ga. only) in. VR barrel with 5 choke tubes and red bar front sight with bead mid-sight, 4 shot mag., engraved nickel finished alloy lower or all alloy (20 ga. only) receiver, cartridge drop lever, select AA checkered walnut stock with vent. recoil pad and forearm, stock shim kit provided, mfg. to commemorate the 30th Anniversary of Benelli shotgun manufacturing, approx. 5.8 lbs. or 7 1/2 lbs. Imported 1998-2015.

	$1,300	$1,225	$1,150	$1,050	$775	$675	$575	*$1,799*

Add $240 for 28 ga. with WeatherCoat stock and forearm finish.

* ***Legacy Limited Edition*** – 12 or 20 ga., acid etched engraving with gold filled game scenes, only 250 of each ga. mfg. for the new millennium only, deluxe checkered walnut stock and forearm. Limited mfg. 2000 only.

	$1,750	$1,475	$1,250	$1,050	$900	$750	$600	*$1,600*

Add 20% to individual prices for a 2 gun set with matching serial numbers (NIB only).

* ***Legacy Sport*** – 12 ga. only, 3 in. chamber, 28 or 30 in. ported VR barrel with choke tubes, distinctive grey medallion with birds in flight engraved on both sides of receiver, AA grade satin finished walnut stock and forearm, 7 1/2 lbs. Mfg. 2008-2017.

	$1,750	$1,675	$1,600	$1,500	$1,100	$900	$700	*$2,439*

M1 FIELD (SUPER 90) – 12 (disc. 2005) or 20 (new 2001) ga., 3 in. chamber, inertia recoil operating system, alloy receiver, 21 (mfg. 1990-2005, 12 ga. only), 24 (new 1990), 26, or 28 (disc. 2005) in. vent. rib barrel and 3 shot mag., includes 5 screw in choke tubes, satin walnut (mfg. 1994-2005) or black polymer stock, Turkey Models include SteadyGrip buttstock with integral pistol grip (mfg. 2003-2005) or regular pistol grip, red fiber optic front sight, matte finish, 100% Realtree Xtra Brown (mfg. 1997-2001) or Advantage Timber HD (new 2001) camo coverage, approx. 5.8 (20 ga.) or 7.2 (12 ga.) lbs. Disc. 2006.

	$725	$650	$600	$575	$425	$350	$300	*$1,030*

Subtract $30 for 12 ga.
Add $15 for satin walnut stock (12 ga., 26 or 28 in. barrel only, disc. 2005).
Add $120 for Advantage Timber HD camo finish.
Add $195 for Turkey configuration with 24 in. barrel, steady-grip and 100% Timber HD camo coverage (disc. 2005).
Add $100 for Turkey configuration with 24 in. barrel and Timber HD camo finish (disc. 2004).
Add $95 for Realtree Xtra Brown camo finish (disc. 2001).
Add $60 for 11 oz. mercury recoil reducer (synthetic stock only).
Add $20 for left-hand action (mfg. 2000-2003, available in synthetic and camo, 12 ga. only).

During 2000, Benelli improved this model with a stepped VR and oversized safety.

This model was available with an extended magazine tube (26 or 28 in. barrel only).

GRADING - PPGS™	100%	98%	95%	90%	80%	70%	60%	LAST MSR

M1 FIELD SLUG (SUPER 90) – 12 (disc. 2004) or 20 (new 2004) ga., 3 in. chamber, incorporated improvements on the Benelli action, including rotating Montefeltro bolt system, 19 3/4 cyl. bore (disc. 1997) or 24 (new 1998) in. rifled barrel with iron sights (disc. 1997, reintroduced 2001), drilled and tapped beginning 1998, 3 (new 1998) or 7 (disc. 1997) shot mag., Realtree Xtra Brown camo (mfg. 2000-2001), Advantage Timber HD (new 2002) camo, or black fiberglass stock and forearm, 6 1/2-7.6 lbs. Mfg. 1986-2006.

	$775	$700	$600	$475	$375	$335	$300	*$1,105*

Add $110 for Advantage Timber HD camo finish.
Add $105 for Realtree Xtra Brown camo finish (disc. 2001).
Subtract 15% for 19 3/4 in. cyl. bore barrel with iron sights.

M1 DEFENSE (SUPER 90) – similar to Super 90 Slug, except has pistol grip stock, 7.1 lbs. Disc. 1998.

	$850	$775	$700	$625	$550	$475	$400	*$851*

Add $41 for ghost-ring sighting system.

M1 PRACTICAL (SUPER 90) – 12 ga. only, 3 in. chamber, 26 in. plain barrel with muzzle brake, designed for IPSC events, extended 8 shot tube mag., oversized safety, speed loader, larger bolt handle, Mil-Spec adj. ghost ring sight and Picatinny rail, black regular synthetic stock and forearm, matte metal finish, includes 3 choke tubes, 7.6 lbs. Mfg. 1998-2004.

	$925	$785	$675	$575	$450	$350	$300	*$1,285*

M1 TACTICAL (SUPER 90) – 12 ga. only, 3 in. chamber, 18 1/2 in. barrel, fixed rifle or ghost ring sighting system, available with synthetic pistol grip or standard buttstock, includes 3 choke tubes, 5 shot mag., 6.7-7 lbs. Mfg. 1993-2004.

	$900	$825	$750	$675	$600	$500	$400	*$975*

Add $50 for ghost ring sighting system.
Add $50-$65 for pistol grip stock.

* ***M1 Tactical M*** – similar to M1 Tactical, except has military ghost ring sights and standard synthetic stock, 7.1 lbs. Mfg. 1999-2000.

	$900	$825	$750	$675	$600	$500	$400	*$960*

Add $10 for pistol grip stock.

M1 ENTRY (SUPER 90) – 12 ga. only, 14 in. barrel, choice of synthetic pistol grip or standard stock, choice of rifle or ghost ring sights, 5 shot mag. (2 shot extension), approx. 6.7 lbs. Mfg. 1992-2006.

	$810	$675	$585	$450	$395	$340	$310	

Add $15 for synthetic pistol grip stock.
Add $65 for ghost ring sighting system.

This model required special licensing (special tax stamp) for civilians, and was normally available to law enforcement/military only.

M1 SPORTING SPECIAL (SUPER 90) – 12 ga., 18 1/2 in. barrel, matte black finish, ghost ring sighting system, 6 1/2 lbs. Mfg. 1993-1997.

	$750	$650	$550	$450	$395	$340	$310	*$924*

M2 – 12 ga., 2 3/4 or 3 in. chamber, 18 1/2 in. barrel, open or ghost ring sights, matte black finish, pistol grip or straight grip stock, includes three choke tubes, 6.7 lbs. Mfg. 2013-2015.

	$1,300	$1,125	$975	$885	$715	$585	$450	*$1,549*

M2 FIELD – 12 or 20 (new 2007) ga., 3 in. chamber, Inertia Driven system, 21 (12 ga. only), 24, 26, or 28 in. VR barrel with chokes, barrel and chokes have Crio System treatment, redesigned receiver, trigger guard, and safety, left-hand action available on 12 ga. (new 2014) and 20 ga. (new 2013), 3 shot mag., red fiber optic front sight, short forearm with large magazine cap, includes choice of satin walnut (disc. 2012), black synthetic, 100% Realtree Advantage Max-4 HD (disc. 2013), Realtree Max-5 (new 2014), Realtree APG HD (mfg. 2007-2018), Advantage Timber HD (disc. 2007), Gore Optifade Waterfowl Timber (new 2018), or Mossy Oak Shadow Grass Blades (mfg. 2019 only) camo coverage, ComforTech stock system with two recoil reducing gel pads (not available w/walnut stock) became standard 2013, 6.9-7.2 lbs. New 2004.

MSR $1,449	$1,265	$1,075	$1,000	$825	$725	$600	$475	

Add $110 for 100% camo coverage.
Subtract $90 for black synthetic stock without ComforTech and forearm (disc. 2012).

* ***M2 Field Compact*** – 12 or 20 ga., similar to M2 Field, except has shorter LOP, 24 (20 ga., disc. 2017) or 26 (12 ga.) in. barrel, black synthetic ComforTech stock. New 2013.

MSR $1,449	$1,265	$1,075	$1,000	$825	$725	$600	$475	

GRADING - PPGS™	100%	98%	95%	90%	80%	70%	60%	LAST MSR

* ***M2 Field Rifled Slug*** – 12 or 20 ga., 3 in. chamber, 24 in. rifled barrel, adj. rear and ramped front sights, choice of black synthetic or 100% Realtree APG camo coverage (disc. 2016), ComforTech stock and forearm, gel comb insert and recoil pad, 7.3 lbs. New 2004.

MSR $1,559	$1,325	$1,125	$1,025	$875	$700	$575	$475	

Add $100 for camo coverage on 12 ga. (disc. 2016) or $200 for camo on 20 ga. (disc. 2016).
Subtract $30 if without GripTight ComforTech stock.

* ***M2 Field Turkey*** – 12 or 20 ga., 3 in. chamber, inertia driven, 21 (12 ga. only), 24, or 26 (12 ga., left-hand action only) in. barrel with Crio chokes, red-bar front sight, 3 shot mag., drilled and tapped for scope mounting, ComforTech stock system with two recoil reducing gel pads (became standard 2013), black synthetic or 100% Realtree APG camo finish, includes hard case, 5.7-7.1 lbs. Disc. 2015.

	$1,100	$1,025	$950	$850	$600	$525	$450	*$1,469*

Add $50 for 20 ga.
Add $100 for left-hand action (12 ga., 26 in. barrel only).

* ***M2 Performance Shop Turkey*** – 12 (mfg. 2017-2018) or 20 ga., 3 in. chamber, 24 in. VR ported barrel with 3 choke tubes, Burris FastFire II sight, ComforTech stock, 100% Realtree APG (disc. 2018), Mossy Oak Bottomland/Patriot Brown Cerakote (mfg. 2017-2018, 12 ga. only), or Mossy Oak Bottomland/Midnight Bronze Cerakote (new 2019, 20 ga. only) camo finish. New 2016.

MSR $2,999	$2,550	$2,225	$1,975	$1,725	$1,400	$1,150	$925	

Add $800 for 12 ga. with Mossy Oak Bottomland/Patriot Brown Cerakote finish (mfg. 2017-2018).

* ***M2 Performance Shop Waterfowl*** – 12 (mfg. 2017-2018) or 20 ga., 3 in. chamber, 28 in. VR barrel with 3 choke tubes, HiViz comp sight, ComforTech stock, 100% Realtree Max-5 camo (mfg. 2016-2018), Optifade Timber/Texas Tan Cerakote (mfg. 2017-2018, 12 ga. only), Optifade Waterfowl Marsh/Midnight Bronze Cerakote (mfg. 2019 only), or Gore Optifade Marsh (new 2020) finish, 5.9 lbs. New 2016.

MSR $2,699	$2,295	$2,010	$1,725	$1,550	$1,250	$1,050	$850	

Subtract approx. $100 for Optifade Timber/Texas Tan Cerakote finish (mfg. 2017-2018).
Subtract approx. $400 for Realtree Max-5 camo finish (mfg. 2016-2018).

M2 THREE GUN – 12 ga., 3 in. chamber, 21 in. VR barrel with Crio chokes, 3 shot mag., HiViz sights, black synthetic ComforTech stock, designed for 3 gun competition, 7.3 lbs. Mfg. 2012-2015.

	$1,600	$1,525	$1,450	$1,350	$1,200	$1,000	$800	*$2,499*

PERFORMANCE SHOP M2 3-GUN EDITION – 12 ga., 3 in. chamber, 24 in. VR barrel, 3 shot mag., HiViz front and XS express rear sights, black synthetic ComforTech stock, redesigned loading port, includes port caddy for spare shell, 6 3/4 lbs. New 2016.

MSR $2,499	$2,175	$1,850	$1,725	$1,400	$1,250	$1,050	$850	

M2 PRACTICAL – 12 ga. only, 3 in. chamber, 26 in. compensated barrel with ghost ring sights, designed for IPSC competition, 8 shot mag., Picatinny rail. Limited importation 2005.

	$1,135	$965	$825	$650	$550	$475	$425	*$1,335*

M2 TACTICAL – 12 ga. only, 3 in. chamber, Inertia Driven system, 18 1/2 in. barrel with choice of pistol grip, regular stock, or ComforTech stock configuration, matte finish, 5 shot mag., AirTouch checkering pattern on stock and forearm, open rifle or ghost ring sights, 6.7-7 lbs. New 2005.

MSR $1,359	$1,190	$1,000	$925	$775	$650	$500	$400	

Add $110 for ghost ring sights w/ComforTech stock.
Subtract $110 for tactical open rifle sights.

M2 AMERICAN SERIES – 12 ga., 2 3/4 or 3 in. chamber, 26 or 28 in. barrel, synthetic stock with matte black or Realtree Max-4 camo finish, 3 shot mag., red bar front sight, approx. 7 lbs. Mfg. mid-2010-2011.

	$995	$875	$750	$675	$625	$550	$495	*$1,109*

Add $40 for camo.

M3 CONVERTIBLE AUTO/PUMP (SUPER 90) – 12 ga. only, 3 in. chamber, defense configuration incorporating convertible (fingertip activated) pump or semi-auto action, 19 3/4 in. cyl. bore barrel with ghost ring or rifle (disc. 2007) sights, 5 shot mag., choice of standard black polymer stock or integral pistol grip (disc. 1996, reintroduced 1999), approx. 7.3 lbs. Imported 1989-2015.

	$1,150	$1,100	$925	$850	$775	$700	$600	*$1,589*

Add $110 for folding stock (mfg. 1990-disc.) - only available as a complete gun.
Add $340 for Model 200 Laser Sight System with bracket (disc.).
Subtract approx. 10% for rifle sights (disc. 2007).

M3 TACTICAL – 12 ga., 19.8 in. barrel, 5 shot mag., dual-action (semi-auto or slide action operation), ghost ring sights, black synthetic pistol grip stock. New 2017.

MSR $1,599	$1,400	$1,200	$1,050	$850	$775	$700	$575	

GRADING - PPGS™	100%	98%	95%	90%	80%	70%	60%	LAST MSR

M4 TACTICAL – 12 ga. only, 3 in. chamber, consumer version of the U.S. Military M4, includes Auto Regulating Gas Operating (ARGO) system, dual stainless self cleaning pistons, 4 shot mag., matte black phosphated metal standard, H2O coating (mfg. 2012 and 2014), or 100% Desert camo coverage (except for pistol grip, mfg. 2007-2012), 18 1/2 in. barrel with ghost ring sights, pistol grip, tactical (new 2012), telescoping (new 2012), or non-collapsible (disc. 2004) stock and forearm, Picatinny rail, approx. 7.8 lbs. Importation began late 2003.

MSR $1,999	$1,750	$1,500	$1,400	$1,200	$1,050	$850	$750	

Add $300 for ATI Raven stock (mfg. 2013 only).
Add $100 for 100% Desert camo coverage (mfg. 2007-2012).
Add $500 for pistol grip or tactical stock with H20 coating (mfg. 2012, 2014).
Add $370 for tactical stock with H2O coating (mfg. 2012 only) or $500 for telescoping stock with H2O coating (mfg. 2012 only).

* ***M4 Cerakote Tactical*** – 12 ga., 3 in. chamber, 18 1/2 in. barrel, 5 shot mag., ghost ring sights, black synthetic pistol grip or tactical stock, Picatinny rail, Cerakote AIDE finish. Mfg. 2016 only.

	$1,650	$1,575	$1,500	$1,400	$1,200	$900	$750	*$2,299*

* ***M4 H20 Tactical*** – 12 ga., 18 1/2 in. barrel, 5 shot mag., ghost ring sight, black synthetic pistol grip or tactical stock, Picatinny rail, H20 Cerakote finish. New 2016.

MSR $2,269	$1,995	$1,700	$1,575	$1,400	$1,200	$900	$750	

M1014 LIMITED EDITION (CURRENT MFG.) – 12 ga., ARGO system, fixed position skeletonized stock, separate cheekpiece, pistol grip, features United States flag engraved on the receiver in honor of the U.S. Marine Corps., dual stainless self-cleaning gas pistons, patented Benelli rotating bolt, Picatinny rail, anti-reflective Mil-Spec finish. Limited mfg. beginning June 2017.

MSR $2,149	$1,825	$1,595	$1,375	$1,250	$1,000	$825	$700	

M1014 LIMITED EDITION – 12 ga., 3 in. chamber, ARGO system, 18 1/2 in. barrel, synthetic non-collapsible stock, U.S. flag engraved on receiver, Picatinny rail, matte black finish, 8 lbs. Limited edition of 2,500 mfg. 2003-2004.

	$1,375	$1,100	$950	$825	$725	$650	$600	*$1,575*

MONTEFELTRO STANDARD HUNTER (SUPER 90) – 12 or 20 (new 1993) ga., 3 in. chamber, aluminum alloy receiver, right or left-hand (12 ga. only) action, rotary bolt, 21 (disc. 1997), 24, 26, or 28 (12 ga. only) in. VR barrel with 5 choke tubes, matte black metal or 100% Realtree camo (20 ga. only, mfg. 1998-2000) finish, checkered walnut stock and forearm with choice of high gloss (disc. 1997) or satin finish, 4 shot mag., approx. 5 1/2 (20 ga.) or 7.1 lbs. Mfg. 1988-2011.

	$1,050	$900	$800	$700	$600	$525	$425	*$1,269*

Add $100 for 100% Realtree camo finish on 20 ga. only (disc.).

This model is also available in a Youth configuration (12 1/2 in. LOP, 20 ga.) at no extra charge.

* ***Montefeltro Grade II*** – 12 or 20 (disc. 2005) ga., 26 in. VR barrel with 5 chokes, red fiber optic front sight, includes upgraded select walnut and gold accents, 5 1/2 (20 ga.) or 6.9 (12 ga.) lbs. Mfg. 2004-2006.

	$995	$875	$775	$650	$575	$495	$450	*$1,220*

* ***Montefeltro Silver*** – 12 or 20 ga., 3 in. chamber, 26 (20 ga.) or 28 (12 ga.) in. VR barrel with choke tubes, 4 shot mag., nickel/blue receiver with etched game scenes, red-bar front and metal bead mid-sights, AA grade satin finished checkered walnut stock and forearm, 5.6 or 6.9 lbs. New 2007.

MSR $1,769	$1,550	$1,300	$1,225	$1,000	$825	$650	$575	

* ***Montefeltro Silver Featherweight*** – 12 or 20 ga., 2 3/4 or 3 in. chamber, 24 or 26 in. barrel, 2 shot mag., nickel/blue receiver, satin walnut stock with WeatherCoat, etched game scene engraving, 5.3-6.2 lbs. New 2019.

MSR $1,999	$1,700	$1,495	$1,275	$1,150	$950	$775	$650	

* ***Montefeltro Limited Edition (Super 90)*** – 20 ga. only, nickel plated lower receiver with etched gold highlights, 26 in. VR barrel. Limited mfg. 1995-96.

	$1,825	$1,550	$1,325	$1,050	$900	$750	$625	*$2,080*

* ***Montefeltro Turkey Gun*** – 12 ga., similar to Montefeltro Standard Hunter except has 24 in. VR barrel with 3 choke tubes, satin finish wood only, 7 lbs. Imported 1989 only.

	$575	$500	$450	$415	$365	$310	$275	*$675*

* ***Montefeltro Uplander*** – 12 ga., similar to Montefeltro Turkey Gun except has 21 or 24 in. VR barrel with 3 choke tubes, satin finish wood only, 7 lbs. Mfg. 1989-92.

	$650	$575	$500	$450	$415	$365	$310	*$799*

* ***Montefeltro Slug Gun*** – 12 ga., deer gun configuration with 19 3/4 in. slug barrel. Disc. 1992.

	$650	$500	$475	$425	$400	$350	$310	*$799*

GRADING - PPGS™	100%	98%	95%	90%	80%	70%	60%	LAST MSR

MONTEFELTRO – 12 or 20 ga., 3 in. chamber, 24, 26, or 28 (12 ga. only) in. VR barrel, checkered satin finished walnut stock and forearm, also available with left-hand (12 ga. only) ejection. New 2012.

MSR $1,129	$1,000	$850	$775	$625	$525	$450	$395	

Add $170 for combo 20 ga. with 26 in. barrel.

* ***Montefeltro Compact*** – 20 ga., similar to Montefeltro, except has shortened LOP stock, and 24 or 26 in. barrel, satin walnut stock. New 2012.

MSR $1,129	$1,000	$850	$775	$625	$525	$450	$395	

* ***Montefeltro Synthetic Stock*** – 12 ga., similar to Montefeltro, except has 26 or 28 (new 2014) in. barrel and black synthetic stock and forearm, 6.9 lbs. Mfg. 2013-2019.

	$1,000	$850	$775	$625	$525	$450	$395	*$1,129*

* ***Montefeltro Sporting*** – 12 ga., 3 in. chamber, 30 in. ported barrel w/choke tubes, 4 shot mag., checkered satin finish, walnut stock and forearm, 7.2 lbs. New 2017.

MSR $1,329	$1,175	$1,000	$925	$775	$650	$500	$400	

SPORT MODEL – 12 ga., 3 in. chamber, one-piece blued alloy receiver, 26 (disc. 1999, reintroduced during 2001 only) or 28 in. barrel with 5 choke tubes and 2 removable and interchangeable carbon fiber vent. ribs, 4 shot mag., adj. buttpad and buttstock, satin finished select checkered walnut stock and forearm, "Benelli" outlined in red on matte finished receiver side, approx. 7.1 lbs. Mfg. 1997-2002.

	$1,125	$950	$800	$675	$575	$450	$400	*$1,375*

SPORT II – 12 or 20 ga., 3 in. chamber, one-piece satin nickel finished alloy receiver, blued upper receiver and barrel, 26 (disc. 2004), 28, or 30 (new 2005, 12 ga. only) in. Crio treated ported barrel with 5 extra long (not flush with barrel) choke tubes, twin bead sights, 4 shot mag., gel recoil pad with stock spacer kit provided, satin finished select checkered walnut stock and forearm, "Sport II" on receiver side, approx. 7 7/8 lbs. Imported 2003-2020.

	$1,650	$1,400	$1,300	$1,150	$900	$675	$575	*$1,879*

SUPERSPORT – 12 or 20 ga., 3 in. chamber, dimpled black carbon fiber stock and forearm with AirTouch recoil reduction system, 4 shot mag. (shell view feature in 20 ga. only), 28 or 30 in. ported VR Crio treated barrel with extended Crio choke tubes, twin bead sights, satin nickel receiver finish with "Supersport" on right side, 7.9 lbs. Mfg. 2004-2020.

	$1,950	$1,650	$1,550	$1,275	$1,075	$800	$675	*$2,199*

* ***Supersport Performance Shop*** – 12 or 20 ga., 3 in. chamber, 28 (20 ga. only) or 30 (12 ga. only) in. ported barrel with lengthened forcing cones, 4 shot, carbon fiber stock with ComforTech, nickel/blue finish, Briley EZ bolt release and enlarged bolt operating handle, Briley screw-in chokes, red metal accents (including magazine cap and bolt release), front sight and metal bead mid-sight, 6.7-7.7 lbs. New 2010.

	$2,475	$2,100	$1,975	$1,725	$1,275	$1,050	$925	*$2,839*

Add $110 for 12 ga.

ULTRA LIGHT – 12, 20 (new mid-2008), or 28 (new 2012) ga., 3 in. chamber (except for 28 ga.), 24 or 26 (new 2007, 12 or 28 ga.) in. VR blue barrel, satin walnut WeatherCoat stock, 2 shot mag., featherweight alloy receiver, shortened mag. tube and forearm, raised carbon fiber target rib, 6 lbs. Importation began 2006.

MSR $1,669	$1,475	$1,250	$1,175	$975	$850	$600	$550	

Add $130 for 28 ga. (new 2012).

* ***Performance Shop Ultralight Upland*** – 12 or 20 ga., 24 or 26 in. barrel, 3 shot, satin walnut WeatherCoat stock, Burnt Bronze Cerakote finish. Mfg. 2017-2019.

	$2,450	$2,075	$1,950	$1,700	$1,500	$1,200	$895	*$2,799*

VINCI – 12 ga., 3 in. chamber, three-piece modular construction (consists of buttstock module, barrel/receiver module, and trigger group/forearm module), inline inertia operating system with rotating bolt, 3 shot mag., 24 (disc. 2015), 26, or 28 in. VR barrel with 5 choke tubes, push-button safety integrated into trigger guard which is part of lower modular receiver, ComforTech and QuadraFit synthetic stock with vertical grooved forearm integrated into modular lower receiver, choice of black synthetic, Realtree Max-4 HD (disc. 2013), Realtree Max-5 (new 2014), or APG HD 100% Camo coverage (disc. 2015), 6.9 lbs. Mfg. 2009-2020.

	$1,200	$1,025	$950	$850	$725	$600	$475	*$1,349*

Add $100 for 100% Camo coverage.
Add $100 for Slug model with 24 in. barrel and black synthetic stock (mfg. 2014-2015).
Add $180 for Realtree APG HD camo Steadygrip with 24 in. drilled and tapped barrel (disc. 2015).

* ***Vinci Turkey*** – 12 ga., 3 in. chamber, similar to Vinci, except features 24 in. VR barrel with 5 choke tubes, ComforTech or SteadyGrip, Realtree APG HD 100% camo coverage, 6.8 lbs. Imported 2009-2015.

	$1,295	$1,150	$975	$825	$600	$525	$450	*$1,469*

Add $160 for SteadyGrip.

GRADING - PPGS™	100%	98%	95%	90%	80%	70%	60%	LAST MSR

VINCI SPEED BOLT – 12 ga. only, 3 in. chamber, 24 in. barrel, features Speed-Bolt made from tungsten allowing for faster cycling and handling loads down to 1 oz., inline inertia driven system also has less recoil and muzzle climb, black QuadraFit buttstock, 6.7 lbs. Imported 2013-2015.

$1,425 $1,200 $1,075 $950 $775 $650 $575 *$1,599*

VINCI SUPERSPORT – 12 ga., 3 in. chamber, 28 or 30 in. ported barrel with extended choke tubes, Vinci model with Supersport features including carbon fiber finish and ComforTech recoil dampening system, approx. 7 lbs. Imported 2011-2015.

$1,550 $1,475 $1,400 $1,190 $950 $775 $675 *$2,199*

VINCI CORDOBA – 12 ga., 3 in. chamber, In-Line Inertia Driven system, 28 or 30 in. Crio treated ported barrel with choke tubes, 3 shot mag., black synthetic ComforTech stock and forearm with GripTight finish, includes custom fitted hard case, 7 lbs. Imported 2011-2015.

$1,450 $1,375 $1,300 $1,100 $875 $750 $650 *$2,069*

SUPER VINCI – 12 ga., 3 1/2 in. chamber, 26, 28, or 30 (mfg. 2013-2019) in. VR barrel with Crio treated chokes, 3 shot mag., black or camo synthetic ComforTech Plus stock, Max-4 HD (disc. 2013), Realtree Max-5 (new 2014), APG Realtree (disc. 2018), Mossy Oak Shadow Grass Blades (mfg. 2019 only), or Gore Optifade Concealment Marsh (new 2013) camo finish, approx. 7 lbs. New 2011.

MSR $1,599 $1,400 $1,200 $1,125 $975 $775 $600 $525

Add $100 for 100% Realtree Max-5, APG Realtree (disc. 2018), Mossy Oak Shadow Grass Blades (mfg. 2019 only), or Gore Optifade Concealment Marsh camo finish.

* ***Super Vinci Turkey*** – 12 ga. only, 3 or 3 1/2 in. chamber, 26, 28, or 30 in. VR barrel with Crio treated chokes, 3 shot mag., ComforTech stock, 100% Max-4 HD (disc. 2013), Realtree Max-5 (new 2014), Realtree APG, or Gore Optifade Concealment Marsh (new 2013) camo finish approx. 7 lbs. Mfg. 2011-2017.

$1,675 $1,450 $1,225 $1,050 $925 $850 $750 *$1,899*

VINCI TACTICAL – 12 ga., 3 in. chamber, In-Line Inertia Driven operating system, 18 1/2 in. barrel, chokes and barrel with Crio treatment, 3 shot mag., Picatinny rail, ghost ring sight, black synthetic pistol grip or ComforTech Plus stock, ComforTech Plus recoil and comb pads, dual purpose release lever, 6.7 lbs. Mfg. 2014-2020.

$1,300 $1,100 $1,000 $850 $725 $600 $475 *$1,349*

Add $120 for ComforTech Plus stock.

RAFFAELLO SERIES – 12 ga., 3 in. chamber, 26 in. VR barrel with choke tubes, higher grade model with three different levels of embellishments and checkered select walnut stock and forearm, 4 shot mag., available through Benelli World Class dealers only, 7.4 lbs. U.S. Importation began late 2005, and was disc. circa 2012 - still available in Europe.

* ***Raffaello Standard*** – unengraved black receiver with Raffaello marked on right side.

$1,625 $1,350 $1,150 $975 $800 $700 $600 *$1,900*

* ***Raffaello Deluxe*** – features etched fine scroll engraving with game scenes on coin finished lower receiver, fancy walnut.

$1,995 $1,675 $1,425 $1,200 $950 $875 $750 *$2,300*

* ***Raffaello Limited Edition Deluxe Legacy*** – features fine scroll engraved with gold inlaid birds and animals on coin finished lower receiver, deluxe walnut with wood buttplate.

$2,475 $2,000 $1,550 $1,250 $1,100 $925 $850 *$2,900*

RAFFAELLO CRIO 28 – 28 ga., rotating bolt, 2 shot mag., black anodized Ergal receiver with matte and high polish finishes, select checkered walnut stock and forearm, 24 or 26 in. Crio barrel with carbon fiber VR and red fiber optic front sight, 5 1/4 lbs. Released in Europe during 2009, and in the U.S. during 2010. U.S. importation disc. 2012, still available in Europe.

$1,750 $1,575 $1,350 $1,125 $995 $850 $700 *$1,900*

RAFFAELLO EXCLUSIVE LIMITED EDITION – 20 ga., 3 in. chamber, 26 in. VR barrel with choke tubes, satin finished checkered walnut stock and forearm, silver receiver with light scroll and game bird inlays, 4 shot mag., red bar sights, silver "E" inset pistol grip cap, 6 lbs. Importation began 2007, available through World Class dealers only. U.S. importation disc. 2012, still available in Europe.

$2,475 $2,000 $1,550 $1,250 $1,100 $925 $850 *$2,900*

ELITE TWO-GUN SET – 12 and 20 ga., 3 in. chamber, 26 in. VR barrel with choke tubes, oil finished checkered walnut stock and forearm, silver receiver with scroll engraving, gold borders and game bird inlays, 4 shot mag., 5.8 (20 ga.) - 7.4 lbs. U.S. Importation began 2007, available through World Class dealers only. U.S. importation disc. 2012, still available in Europe.

$4,450 $3,900 $3,375 $2,950 $2,600 $2,350 $2,100 *$4,900*

GRADING - PPGS™	100%	98%	95%	90%	80%	70%	60%	LAST MSR

CURATOR LIMITED EDITION TWO-GUN SET – 12 and 20 ga., 26 in. barrel, satin finished AAA Grade checkered walnut stock and forearm, coin finished receiver with deep scrollwork, bevel cut floral engraving and gold inlays, includes sterling silver medallion that can be custom engraved and set into the pistol grip cap, matched walnut buttplate and fitted rubber recoil pad, includes hard case, 6-7.3 lbs., available through World Class dealers only. Limited mfg. of 250 sets beginning 2010-disc.

	100%	98%	95%	90%	80%	70%	60%	LAST MSR
	$5,000	$4,600	$4,250	$3,850	$3,400	$3,000	$2,600	*$5,500*

BIMILLIONAIRE – 12 or 20 ga., 26 in. barrel, 4 shot mag., satin finished checkered walnut stock and forearm, coin finished two-tone receiver with floral scroll and gold game scenes by Giovanelli, walnut buttplate with or w/o recoil pad, includes sterling silver medallion that can be engraved and placed into the pistol grip cap, 6-7.3 lbs., limited mfg. available through World Class dealers only. Imported 2010-2012, still available in Europe.

	100%	98%	95%	90%	80%	70%	60%	LAST MSR
	$2,475	$2,000	$1,550	$1,250	$1,100	$925	$850	*$2,900*

EXECUTIVE SERIES – 12 ga. only, 3 in. chamber, features all-steel greyed.lower receiver engraved by Giovanelli, mid-rib barrel bead, high polish upper receiver and barrel bluing, extra select grade walnut with standard stock dimensions, 5 choke tubes, and other accessories, choice of 21 (disc.), 24 (disc.), 26, or 28 in. VR barrel, approx. 7 3/4 lbs. U.S. importation began 1996, available through World Class dealers only, disc. circa 2012. Still available in Europe.

	100%	98%	95%	90%	80%	70%	60%	LAST MSR
* ***Executive Grade I (Type I)***	$6,500	$5,250	$4,100	$3,650	$3,000	$2,500	$2,100	*$7,600*
* ***Executive Grade II (Type II)***	$7,350	$6,000	$4,750	$3,950	$3,350	$2,800	$2,400	*$8,400*
* ***Executive Grade III (Type III)***	$8,500	$7,000	$5,250	$4,450	$3,650	$3,150	$2,950	*$9,800*

BLACK EAGLE – 12 ga., 3 in. chamber, Montefeltro action, similar to Montefeltro Super 90 Standard Hunter except has black synthetic regular or pistol grip stock and forearm, 21 (disc. 1990), 24 (disc. 1990), 26, or 28 (new 1990) in. VR barrel with 3 choke tubes, right-hand only. Originally imported 1989-90, resumed 1997 only.

	100%	98%	95%	90%	80%	70%	60%	LAST MSR
	$700	$625	$550	$450	$375	$315	$285	*$992*

This configuration changed in 1991 (see Black Eagle Competition Model).

* ***Black Eagle Competition Model*** – 12 ga. only, designed for competition shooting with action adj. for lighter loads, silver finished etched lower receiver, 26 or 28 in. VR barrel with 5 choke tubes and wrench, includes buttstock drop adjustment kit. Mfg. 1991-1997.

	100%	98%	95%	90%	80%	70%	60%	LAST MSR
	$875	$775	$675	$550	$475	$375	$300	*$1,229*

* ***Black Eagle 1994 Limited Edition*** – 12 ga. only, features 26 in. VR barrel with extra fancy grade checkered walnut and gold inlays on receiver sides, 1,000 mfg. 1994-95 only with special serialization.

	100%	98%	95%	90%	80%	70%	60%	LAST MSR
	$1,900	$1,675	$1,425	$1,275	$1,000	$850	$675	*$2,000*

* ***Black Eagle Slug Gun*** – 12 ga., 24 in. rifled barrel with integral scope mounting bases on receiver. Imported 1990-1991 only.

	100%	98%	95%	90%	80%	70%	60%	LAST MSR
	$735	$625	$500	$425	$365	$315	$285	*$859*

SUPER BLACK EAGLE – 12 ga. only, 3 1/2 in. chamber, updated Montefeltro action accepts all 12 ga. loads, right or left-hand (new 1999) action, upper steel/lower alloy receiver, 24, 26, or 28 in. VR barrel with 5 choke tubes and wrench, 3 shot mag., choice of matte finish and satin wood stock, blue finish and high gloss wood finish (26 or 28 in. barrel only, disc. 2004), or 100% coverage Advantage Timber HD (new 2002), or Realtree X-tra Brown camo (mfg. 1997-2001) finish on polymer stock and forearm, Turkey Models include SteadyGrip buttstock with integral pistol grip (new 2003) or regular pistol grip with 24 in. barrel, red fiber optic front sight, black synthetic stock and forearm with matte metal finish was introduced in 1993, vent. recoil pad, includes buttstock drop adjustment kit, approx. 7.4 lbs. Mfg. 1991-2005.

	100%	98%	95%	90%	80%	70%	60%	LAST MSR
	$900	$825	$725	$625	$525	$475	$425	*$1,305*

Add $95 for camo finish (Turkey Models).
Add $95 for 100% coverage Realtree camo wood/metal finish (disc. 2001).
Add $10 for satin walnut stock and forearm (26 or 28 in. barrel only).
Add $45 for 11 oz. mercury recoil reducer (synthetic stock only).
Add $75 for left-hand action for either black synthetic stock/forearm or full coverage camo finish (disc. 2004).
Add $180 for Turkey configuration with 24 in. barrel, steady-grip, and 100% camo coverage.

GRADING - PPGS™	100%	98%	95%	90%	80%	70%	60%	LAST MSR

* ***Super Black Eagle Limited Edition*** – 12 ga. only, features 26 in. VR barrel with extra fancy grade checkered walnut and gold inlays on nickel plated receiver sides, 1,000 mfg. beginning 1997 with special serialization, 7.4 lbs. Disc. 1999.

$2,400	$2,100	$1,800	$1,625	$1,325	$1,075	$850	*$2,095*

* ***Super Black Eagle Limited Edition 10th Anniversary*** – 12 ga., 3 1/2 in. chamber, 26 in. barrel, matte finish, wildlife engraving on both sides of receiver featuring two turkeys and three geese, gold inlays similar to Executive Type III with "Super Black Eagle Tenth Anniversary" on left, "1 of 500", and "SBE10XXX" special serialization on right, 500 mfg. 2002.

$2,250	$1,950	$1,650	$1,325	$1,050	$900	$800	

* ***Super Black Eagle Slug Gun*** – 12 ga., 3 in. chamber, 24 in. rifled barrel with adj. rifle sights, drilled and tapped receiver, choice of matte or camo metal finish, choice of black polymer (new 1993), satin finished wood, or 100% Advantage Timber HD (new 2002) or Realtree X-tra Brown camo (mfg. 2000-2001), 7.6 lbs. Mfg. 1992-2003.

$900	$825	$775	$650	$575	$475	$425	*$1,335*

Add $10 for wood stock.
Add $125 for Advantage Timber HD camo finish.
Add $100 for Realtree X-tra Brown camo finish (disc. 2001).

SUPER BLACK EAGLE I – 12 ga. only, 3 1/2 in. chamber, 24, 26, or 28 in. barrel, choice of satin walnut wood with matte metal finish, synthetic, Advantage Max-4 HD camo (100% coverage), Advantage Timber HD (100% coverage), or SteadyGrip (Turkey, 24 in. barrel only) with Advantage Timber HD, red fiber optic front sight with bead metal sight, 3 shot mag. Mfg. 2005.

$900	$825	$750	$650	$550	$500	$450	*$1,333*

Add $67 for satin walnut stock and forearm.
Add $120 for camo finish.
Add $200 for Turkey configuration with SteadyGrip stock.

* ***Super Black Eagle I Slug*** – 12 ga. only, 24 in. smoothbore barrel, satin walnut stock and forearm, matte metal finish, 3 shot mag., adj. rifle sights. Mfg. 2005.

$1,225	$975	$825	$700	$600	$475	$425	*$1,465*

SUPER BLACK EAGLE II – 12 ga. only, 3 1/2 in. chamber, action similar to Super Black Eagle, with or w/o ComforTech recoil reduction in stock with two gel pads, 3 shot mag., 24, 26, or 28 in. VR barrel with cryogenic treatment, larger trigger guard, AirTouch checkering on stock and shortened forearm, choice of satin finished walnut (disc. 2016), black synthetic, or 100% coverage of Advantage Max-4 HD (disc. 2013), Realtree APG (new 2007), Realtree Max-5 (new 2014), Advantage Timber HD (disc. 2015), Mossy Oak Bottomlands (mfg. 2016 only), Gore Sitka Optifade Timber (mfg. 2016 only), or Gore Sitka Optifade Waterfowl Marsh (mfg. 2016 only) camo, approx. 7.2 lbs. Mfg. 2004-2017.

$1,050	$1,000	$925	$850	$800	$675	$575	*$1,899*

Add $100 for Realtree Max-5 or Realtree APG camo coverage.
Subtract $330 for satin walnut stock (disc. 2016).
Subtract approx. $300-$400 for right-hand configuration (disc. 2016).
Subtract approx. 10% if w/o ComforTech stock (became standard mid-2008).

In 2017, this model became available in left-hand configuration only with ComforTech stock.

* ***Super Black Eagle II Slug*** – 12 ga. only, 3 in. chamber, 24 in. barrel with rifled bore and adj. sights, includes Picatinny rail, choice of satin walnut (disc. 2012) stock and forearm or black synthetic stock, ComforTech became standard 2007, or 100% camo coverage of Timber HD (disc. 2008) or Realtree APG HD, approx. 7.4 lbs. Mfg. 2004-2016.

$1,050	$1,000	$925	$850	$750	$625	$525	*$1,899*

Add $100 for 100% camo treatment.
Subtract approx. $100 if with satin walnut stock and forearm.

* ***Super Black Eagle II SteadyGrip Turkey*** – 12 ga., 3 1/2 in. chamber, similar to Super Black Eagle II, except features 24 in. drilled and tapped barrel, ComforTech (disc. 2015) or SteadyGrip (became standard 2016) pistol grip stock, 100% Realtree APG HD camo coverage, 7.1 lbs. Disc. 2016.

$1,100	$1,000	$925	$850	$750	$675	$525	*$1,999*

Add $100 for SteadyGrip pistol grip stock.
Subtract $100 for left-hand action with ComforTech stock.

* ***Super Black Eagle II Performance Shop Turkey Edition*** – 12 ga., 3 1/2 in. chamber, 3 shot mag., 24 in. ported barrel, 100% APG HD camo with ComforTech synthetic stock with black pistol grip, approx. 7 lbs. Mfg. 2010-2016.

$2,650	$2,250	$2,025	$1,700	$1,450	$1,050	$925	*$2,949*

GRADING - PPGS™	100%	98%	95%	90%	80%	70%	60%	LAST MSR

* ***Super Black Eagle II Performance Shop Waterfowl Edition*** – 12 ga., 3-1/2 in. chamber, 28 in. VR Crio barrel with Bob Roberts custom triple threat choke tubes, features 100% Realtree Max-4 (disc. 2013) or Realtree Max-5 (new 2014) camo coverage, ComforTech stock. Mfg. 2012-2016.

	$2,000	$1,925	$1,800	$1,500	$1,250	$1,000	$875	*$2,669*

* ***Super Black Eagle II Flyway Limited Edition*** – four variations include: the Atlantic, Mississippi, Central, and Pacific Flyways, roll engraved satin grey receiver finish with four gold duck/goose inlays (each Flyway has four different inlays), select checkered walnut stock and forearm, 7.2 lbs. 175 of each Flyway manufactured 2004.

	$2,875	$2,525	$2,150	$1,950	$1,575	$1,275	$1,000	*$2,130*

* ***Super Black Eagle II 25th Anniversary*** – 12 ga., 3 1/2 in. chamber, 28 in. VR barrel with 3 choke tubes, brushed nickel bolt, Realtree Max-5 camo or Black Cerakote finish. Limited mfg. 2016 only.

	$1,350	$1,275	$1,200	$1,000	$800	$700	$625	*$1,999*

* ***Super Black Eagle II 25th Flyway Annivesary*** – 12 ga., 3 1/2 in. chamber, 28 in. gloss blued VR barrel with 3 choke tubes, AAA Grade oil finished American walnut stock and forend, gold inlaid Flyway specific waterfowl scenes and scroll engraving on each side of the nickel plated receivers, configurations include Mississippi Flyway, Atlantic Flyway, Central Flyway, or Pacific Flyway. 400 of each configuration mfg. 2016 only.

	$2,675	$2,300	$2,000	$1,700	$1,500	$1,250	$1,050	*$3,199*

SUPER BLACK EAGLE 3 (III) – 12 or 20 (new 2021) ga., 2 3/4, 3, or 3 1/2 in. chamber, 26 or 28 in. barrel, Crio chokes, 3 shot mag., red bar front and metal bead mid-sight, with or w/o drilled and tapped receiver, Combtech cheek pad, ComforTech 3 stock in A-Grade satin walnut (new 2018), black synthetic, Realtree Max-5, Gore Optifade Marsh (new 2018), Gore Optifade Waterfowl Timber, Mossy Oak Bottomland, or Mossy Oak Shadow Grass Blades (mfg. 2019 only) camo finish, right or left (new 2018) hand action, matte black, camo, Patriot Brown Cerakote (new 2021) or Tungsten Cerakote (new 2021) barrel/receiver finish, approx. 7 lbs. New 2017.

MSR $1,899	$1,650	$1,425	$1,325	$1,100	$950	$800	$600	

Add $20 for satin walnut Progressive Comfort stock (new 2018).
Add $100 for camo finish with or w/o ComforTech stock.
Subtract $100-$200 for 20 ga. depending on chamber, stock, or finish (new 2021).

* ***Super Black Eagle 3 Rifled Slug*** – 12 ga., 2 3/4, 3, or 3 1/2 in. chamber, 24 in. barrel, 3 shot mag., adj. rifle sight, black synthetic ComforTech stock, 7.1 lbs. New 2018.

MSR $1,999	$1,750	$1,525	$1,425	$1,200	$1,050	$900	$700	

* ***Super Black Eagle 3 SteadyGrip*** – 12 ga., 3 1/2 in. chamber, 24 in. barrel, 3 shot mag., SteadyGrip stock, 100% Mossy Oak Bottomland finish, 6.8 lbs. New 2019.

MSR $1,999	$1,450	$1,375	$1,300	$1,200	$975	$800	$625	

* ***Performance Shop SBE 3 Turkey*** – 12 ga., 2 3/4, 3, or 3 1/2 in. chamber, 24 in. ported barrel, 3 shot mag., Burris FastFire II sight, Mossy Oak Bottomland stock, pistol grip, Midnight Bronze Cerakote receiver finish, 6.8 lbs. Mfg. 2019 only.

	$2,650	$2,325	$1,995	$1,800	$1,460	$1,195	$950	*$3,099*

* ***Performance Shop SBE 3 Waterfowl*** – 12 ga., 3 or 3 1/2 in. chamber, 28 in. barrel, three Rob Roberts Triple Threat choke tubes, lengthened and polished forcing cone, 3 shot mag., custom tuned trigger group, HiViz CompSight, ComforTech stock with Optifade Waterfowl Marsh finish, honed and polished action, oversized bolt handle, enlarged bolt release, paracord survival sling, Midnight Bronze Cerakote receiver finish, 7 lbs. New 2019.

MSR $3,199	$2,725	$2,385	$2,050	$1,850	$1,500	$1,225	$950	

B.E.S.T. SUPER BLACK EAGLE 3 – 12 ga., 2 3/4, 3, or 3 1/2 in. chamber, 26 or 28 in. barrel with Crio choke tubes, 3 shot mag., red bar front sight, drilled and tapped, black synthetic Comfort Tech3 stock, featuring B.E.S.T (Benelli Surface Treatment) on barrel, chokes, and sling stud, black anodized receiver finish, 7 lbs. New 2020.

MSR $2,199	$1,950	$1,650	$1,550	$1,275	$1,075	$800	$675	

SHOTGUNS: SLIDE ACTION

All currently manufactured Benelli shotguns are equipped with a patented Benelli keyed chamber lock.

NOVA – 12 or 20 (new 2001) ga., 3 (20 ga. only) or 3 1/2 in. chamber, unique design allows stock and internal metal receiver "shell" to be molded in one unit, utilizing a glass polymer matrix, Montefeltro rotating bolt, dual action bars, 24, 26, or 28 in. VR barrel with 3 choke tubes and red fiber optic front sight, 3 (3 1/2 in. shells) or 4 shot mag., matte metal finish, choice of black synthetic, full

GRADING - PPGS™	100%	98%	95%	90%	80%	70%	60%	LAST MSR

coverage Realtree X-tra brown (disc. 2002), Realtree Max-4 HD (disc. 2013), Realtree Max-5 (new 2014), Realtree APG HD (mfg. 2007-disc.), Realtree APG (disc. 2018), Advantage Timber HD (mfg. 2001-2007, 20 ga. only until 2002), or Mossy Oak Bottomland (new 2019) camo stock and forearm with grooved hand ribs, mag. shell stop button in bottom of forearm, available as Youth Model, approx. 6 1/2 (20 ga.) or 8 lbs. New 1999.

MSR $449	**$400**	**$300**	**$250**	**$200**	**$175**	**$150**	**$125**	

Add $110 for full camo coverage.

Add $60 for 2 (12 ga.) or $45 for 4 (20 ga. only) shot magazine extension. Disc.

Add $90 for recoil reducer - 10 oz. (disc.) or 14 oz. mercury, installed in stock with reduction tube operation (12 ga., disc.).

Add $65 for Realtree X-tra Brown full camo finish (12 ga. only, disc. 2002).

* ***Nova Tactical (Special Purpose Smooth Bore)*** – 12 ga. only, 3 1/2 in. chamber, similar action to Nova, 18 1/2 in. cyl. bore barrel, choice of rifle or ghost ring (new 2000) sights, black synthetic stock and forearm only, 7.2 lbs. New 1999.

MSR $439	**$375**	**$300**	**$250**	**$200**	**$150**	**$100**	**$90**	

Add $10 for ghost ring sights.

* ***Nova H20*** – 12 ga. only, 3 1/2 in. chamber, 18 1/2 in. matte nickel finished barrel, mag. tube, trigger group, and inner metal parts, black synthetic stock and forearm, open rifle sights, 4 shot mag., 7.2 lbs. Importation began 2003.

MSR $669	**$585**	**$500**	**$425**	**$350**	**$300**	**$250**	**$225**	

* ***Nova Slug*** – 12 or 20 ga., 3 in. chamber, features 24 in. rifled bore drilled and tapped barrel with open rifle sights, black synthetic or 100% coverage Advantage Timber HD camo stock and forearm, 8.1 lbs. Mfg. 2000-2006.

	$445	**$390**	**$355**	**$315**	**$285**	**$260**	**$240**	*$535*

Add $90 for Advantage Timber HD camo.

» ***Nova Slug & Field Combo*** – 12 or 20 ga., 3 in. chamber, combo features 24 in. rifled bore drilled and tapped barrel with extra 26 in. field barrel, open rifle sights, black synthetic or 100% coverage Advantage Timber HD camo stock and forearm, 8.1 lbs. Mfg. 2000-2007.

	$460	**$400**	**$365**	**$325**	**$290**	**$260**	**$240**	*$560*

SUPERNOVA – 12 ga. only, 3 1/2 in. chamber, 24, 26, or 28 in. VR barrel with choke tubes, choice of matte black synthetic, Realtree APG HD (mfg. 2007-2018), Realtree Max-5 (new 2014), Advantage Max-4 HD (disc. 2013), or Advantage Timber HD (disc. 2007) 100% camo coverage, includes ComforTech stock system, approx. 8 lbs. New 2006.

MSR $559	**$485**	**$400**	**$350**	**$275**	**$250**	**$225**	**$195**	

Add $110 for 100% camo coverage.

* ***SuperNova SteadyGrip Turkey*** – 12 ga., 24 in. barrel, 4 shot, SteadyGrip buttstock with integral pistol grip, choice of matte finish (disc. 2009), Realtree APG (new 2007), or Advantage Timber HD (disc. 2007) camo, 7.8 lbs. Mfg. 2006-2018.

	$600	**$500**	**$450**	**$400**	**$350**	**$300**	**$250**	*$669*

Subtract 20% if w/matte finish.

* ***SuperNova Tactical*** – 12 ga., 18 (disc.) or 18 1/2 in. barrel, 4 shot, choice of ComforTech or pistol grip synthetic stock, matte finish or Desert camo (mfg. 2007-2012, pistol grip only), choice of rifle or ghost ring sights. New 2006.

MSR $539	**$460**	**$400**	**$350**	**$275**	**$250**	**$225**	**$195**	

Add $10 for pistol grip stock with ghost ring sights or $20 for ComforTech with ghost ring sights.

Add $170 for Desert camo w/pistol grip and ghost ring sights (mfg. 2007-2012).

* ***SuperNova Slug*** – 12 ga., 3 in. chamber, 24 in. rifled bore drilled and tapped barrel with adj. rifle sights, black synthetic ComforTech or 100% coverage Realtree APG HD camo (disc. 2016) stock and forearm, 8.1 lbs. Mfg. 2007-2019.

	$700	**$575**	**$450**	**$375**	**$325**	**$275**	**$250**	*$839*

Add $100 for 100% camo coverage (disc. 2016).

Add 15% for Field & Slug combo with extra 26 in. Field barrel (mfg. 2007 only).

BENSON FIREARMS LTD.

Previous importer for guns manufactured by Aldo Uberti in Italy. Previously imported and distributed from 1987-1989 by Benson Firearms Ltd. located in Seattle, WA. Benson Firearms Ltd. combined with A. Uberti USA Inc. in early 1989 and discontinued importation.

For individual model listings, please go to BlueBookOfGunValues.com/overflow.

GRADING - PPGS™	100%	98%	95%	90%	80%	70%	60%	LAST MSR

BENTON & BROWN FIREARMS, INC.

Previous manufacturer located in Fort Worth, TX and Delhi, LA circa 1993-1996.

RIFLES: BOLT ACTION

MODEL 93 – available in 15 cals. between .243 Win. and .375 H&H Mag., patterned after the Model R-84 Blaser, takedown, free floating 22 or 24 in. barrels, right or left-hand action, checkered walnut stock and forearm, 7-8 1/2 lbs. Mfg. 1993-1996.

	100%	98%	95%	90%	80%	70%	60%	LAST MSR
	$1,875	$1,550	$1,225	$1,100	$995	$875	$750	*$2,075*

Subtract $200 for fiberglass stock.
Add $450 per interchangeable barrel.

BERETTA, DR. FRANCO

Previous manufacturer located in Concesio (Brescia), Italy until 1994.

Please refer to Effebi SRL section for current availability and listings.

SHOTGUNS: O/U, BLACK DIAMOND SERIES

Black Diamond target guns were imported exclusively by Double M Shooting Sports until 1988.

FIELD MODEL – 12, 16, 20, 28 ga., or .410 bore, variety of chokes, coin finish receiver.

	100%	98%	95%	90%	80%	70%	60%	LAST MSR
	$595	$550	$495	$450	$395	$365	$335	*$960*

GRADE ONE – 12, 16, 20, 28 ga., or .410 bore, variety of chokes, coin finish receiver with acid etched engraving, French walnut. Trap or skeet model also available, except in 16 ga.

	100%	98%	95%	90%	80%	70%	60%	LAST MSR
	$1,020	$900	$810	$720	$630	$570	$525	*$1,440*

GRADE TWO – 12, 16, 20, 28 ga., or .410 bore, variety of chokes, coin finish receiver with moderate engraving, French walnut. Trap or skeet model also available, except in 16 ga.

	100%	98%	95%	90%	80%	70%	60%	LAST MSR
	$1,475	$1,320	$1,200	$1,080	$930	$815	$750	*$2,040*

GRADE THREE – 12, 16, 20, 28 ga., or .410 bore, variety of chokes, coin finish receiver with scrollwork engraving, French walnut. Trap or skeet model also available, except in 16 ga.

	100%	98%	95%	90%	80%	70%	60%	LAST MSR
	$2,100	$1,920	$1,775	$1,560	$1,410	$1,200	$1,035	*$3,000*

GRADE FOUR – 12, 16, 20, 28 ga., or .410 bore, variety of chokes, coin finish receiver with elaborate engraving, French walnut. Trap or skeet model also available, except in 16 ga.

	100%	98%	95%	90%	80%	70%	60%	LAST MSR
	$2,500	$2,250	$1,950	$1,650	$1,500	$1,325	$1,100	*$3,960*

SKEET SET – includes 12, 20, 28 ga., and .410 bore barrels, available in Grades One through Four.

Multiply values on Grades One - Four by 275% for 4 ga. skeet sets.

SHOTGUNS: O/U, SxS, & SINGLE BARREL, RECENT MFG.

GAMMA STANDARD O & U – 12, 16, or 20 ga., 26 or 28 in. barrels, coin finish receiver with extensive engraving, Italian walnut. Imported 1984-88.

	100%	98%	95%	90%	80%	70%	60%	LAST MSR
	$400	$360	$330	$300	$275	$260	$240	*$445*

Add $83 with single trigger and ejectors.

* ***Gamma Standard*** – with interchangeable choke tubes. Importation disc. 1993.

	100%	98%	95%	90%	80%	70%	60%	LAST MSR
	$825	$695	$525	$425	$325	$250	$195	*$1,000*

Add 20% for auto ejectors.
Add $100 for single trigger.
Add 36% for Gamma Trap or Skeet variation (ST).

GAMMA DELUXE O & U – 12, 16, or 20 ga., 26 or 28 in. barrels, coin finish receiver with extensive engraving, Italian walnut. Imported 1984-88.

	100%	98%	95%	90%	80%	70%	60%	LAST MSR
	$445	$405	$370	$350	$325	$300	$275	*$480*

Add $84 with single trigger and ejectors.

* ***Gamma Deluxe*** – with interchangeable choke tubes. Importation disc. 1988.

	100%	98%	95%	90%	80%	70%	60%	LAST MSR
	$635	$570	$530	$490	$450	$420	$390	*$685*

GAMMA TARGET O & U – 12 ga., SST, ejectors, Wundhammer swell pistol grip, English walnut stock and beavertail forearm. Imported 1986-1988.

	100%	98%	95%	90%	80%	70%	60%	LAST MSR
	$550	$505	$455	$410	$370	$350	$325	*$595*

ALPHA STANDARD O & U – 12, 16, or 20 ga., 26 or 28 in. barrels, coin finish receiver with extensive engraving, Italian walnut. Imported 1984-88, resumed 1993-1994.

	100%	98%	95%	90%	80%	70%	60%	LAST MSR
	$720	$650	$525	$450	$375	$300	$250	*$780*

Add 18% for auto ejectors. Add $100 for single trigger.

GRADING - PPGS™	100%	98%	95%	90%	80%	70%	60%	LAST MSR

ALPHA DELUXE O & U – 12, 16, or 20 ga., 26 or 28 in. barrels, coin finish receiver with extensive engraving, sling swivels, Italian walnut. Imported 1984-88.

$395 $355 $330 $300 $275 $250 $230 *$435*

Add $75 with single trigger and ejectors.
Add $80 for interchangeable choke tubes (disc. 1985).

AMERICA STANDARD O & U – .410 bore only, 26 or 28 in. barrels, coin finish receiver with extensive engraving, Italian walnut. Imported 1984-88.

$305 $280 $265 $240 $215 $205 $190 *$335*

Add $85 for Deluxe model.

EUROPA O & U – .410 bore only, 26 in. barrels, coin finish receiver with some engraving, Italian walnut. Imported 1984-88.

$275 $250 $235 $220 $210 $200 $185 *$295*

Add $95 for Deluxe model (disc. 1985).

FRANCIA STANDARD SxS – .410 bore only, double triggers, extractors, checkered walnut. Imported 1986-88.

$235 $220 $210 $200 $185 $175 $160 *$255*

Add $19 for Deluxe Model.

OMEGA STANDARD SxS – 12, 16, or 20 ga., 26 or 28 in. barrels, coin finish receiver with extensive engraving, Italian walnut. Imported 1984-93.

$780 $695 $550 $450 $375 $300 $250 *$880*

Add 32% for auto ejectors.
Add 10% for single trigger (disc. 1985).

MILANO O/U – 9mm Flobert, folding design. Imported 1993 only.

$380 $330 $295 $250 $210 $180 $150 *$420*

VERONA/BERGAMO SxS – 9mm Flobert, folding design, Bergamo model has hammers, Verona model is hammerless. Imported 1993 only.

$270 $225 $180 $140 $115 $95 $75 *$300*

BRESCIA SINGLE BARREL – 9mm Flobert, folding design. Imported 1993 only.

$175 $150 $130 $110 $90 $70 $55 *$200*

BETA SINGLE BARREL – 12, 16, 20, 24, 28, 32 ga., or .410 bore, single barrel field gun, VR, chrome finish receiver, folding design. Imported 1985-93.

$215 $185 $160 $145 $135 $125 $115 *$240*

Add 10% for VR.

SHOTGUNS: SEMI-AUTO

ARIETE STANDARD – 12 ga. only, gas operated, 2 3/4 or 3 in. chamber, various barrel lengths, with or without choke tubes, aluminum receiver, checkered stock and forearm, approx. 6.9 lbs. Imported 1993 only.

$995 $795 $525 $425 $325 $250 $195 *$1,180*

Add $20 for 3 in. mag. variation.

SHOTGUNS: SLIDE ACTION

ARIETE – 12 ga. only, 3 in. chamber, various barrel lengths without VR, twin action bars, matte finish, recoil pad. Imported 1993 only.

$780 $695 $550 $450 $375 $300 $250 *$880*

BERETTA

Current manufacturer with headquarters located in Brescia, Italy since 1526. Current manufacturing locations include Brescia, Italy, Accokeek, MD, and Gallatin, TN (new 2014). The company name in Italy is Fabbrica d'Armi Pietro Beretta. Beretta U.S.A. Corp. was formed in 1977 and is located in Accokeek, MD. Beretta U.S.A. Corp. has been importing Beretta Firearms exclusively since 1980. 1970-1977 manufacture was imported exclusively by Garcia. Distributor and dealer direct sales.

Beretta is one of the world's oldest family owned industrial firms, having started business in 1526. In addition to Beretta owning Benelli, Stoeger, and Franchi, the company also purchased Sako and Tikka Companies in late 1999, Aldo Uberti & Co. in 2000, Burris Optics in 2002, Steiner International Optics, and Vitrix Armament (Italy) late 2017. Beretta continues to be a leader in firearms development and safety, and shooters attest to the reliability of their guns worldwide.

GRADING - PPGS™	100%	98%	95%	90%	80%	70%	60%	LAST MSR

On January 29, 2014, Beretta announced that the company will expand its U.S. operations by building a new firearms manufacturing plant in Gallatin, Tennessee.

For more information and current pricing on both new and used Beretta precision airguns, please refer to the *Blue Book of Airguns* - also available as an online subscription.

PISTOLS: SEMI-AUTO, PRE-WWII MFG.

MODEL 1915 - .32 ACP or 9mm Glisenti cal., Beretta's first military pistol, exaggerated slide stop, safety on rear of tang, checkered wood grips, 7 shot mag., serial range 1-16,000.

	100%	98%	95%	90%	80%	70%	60%
	$1,695	$1,350	$1,000	$750	$600	$500	$400

9mm Para. cal. is not interchangeable and potentially dangerous if interchanged with 9mm Glisenti cal.

MODEL 1915-1917 - later 7.65mm cal. variation, 8 shot mag., exaggerated slide stop, wood grips, sold commercially and to the military. A few marked "RM" were issued to the Italian Navy, ser. no. range 16,000-72,000. Mfg. 1917-1921.

	100%	98%	95%	90%	80%	70%	60%
	$750	$600	$450	$350	$275	$225	$175
Navy issue	$1,500	$1,200	$900	$700	$550	$450	$350

MODEL 1922 - successor to the Model 1915-1917, mfg. with more open slide and modern slide stop, wood or pressed metal grips, ser. no. range 200,000-243,000. Mfg. 1922-1932.

	100%	98%	95%	90%	80%	70%	60%
	$700	$550	$450	$350	$275	$225	$175
Navy issue	$1,400	$1,225	$1,050	$950	$770	$625	$495

MODEL 1923 - 9mm Glisenti cal., 8 shot, 4 in. barrel, fixed sights, usually with pressed steel grips, less frequently smooth wood with PB emblem, occasionally slotted for shoulder stock. Most were purchased by the Italian Army and marked "RE," ser. no. range 300,000-310,400. Mfg. 1923-26.

	100%	98%	95%	90%	80%	70%	60%
	$2,000	$1,750	$1,500	$1,250	$1,000	$750	$500

Add 25% if slotted for shoulder stock.

MODEL 1919 - .25 ACP cal., 8 shot mag., offered in several variations, first type in serial range 100,000-156,000, subsequent improvement involved changing the disconnector and left panel in serial range 156,000-185,000.

	100%	98%	95%	90%	80%	70%	60%
	$375	$325	$275	$250	$200	$175	$125

MODEL 1926 - similar to Model 1919, except has wood panels bearing an encircled PB. Approx. 11,000 pistols were mfg. in ser. no. range 187,000-198,000.

	100%	98%	95%	90%	80%	70%	60%
	$350	$315	$275	$220	$190	$160	$130

MODEL 1931 - .32 ACP cal., similar to Model 1926, except has small modifications in the slide, two styles of grips are no longer impressed with the PB monogram, interrupted serial range from 198,000-200,000 and 600,000-601,000.

	100%	98%	95%	90%	80%	70%	60%
	$325	$285	$250	$225	$175	$150	$125

MODEL 318 - .25 ACP cal., 2 1/2 in. barrel, fixed sights, blue, modifications in the slide legend, grip configuration, and magazine floorplate. Limited production during 1936-37, in ser. no. range 609,000-615,000.

	100%	98%	95%	90%	80%	70%	60%
	$275	$250	$200	$185	$160	$140	$120

Add 50%-100% for engraved and plated variations if in 98%+ original condition.

Embellished variations of the Model 318 included the Model 319 (engraved/blue), Model 320 (engraved/nickel plated) and Model 321 (engraved/gold plated).

MODEL 418 - .25 ACP cal., fixed sights, similar to Model 318, but with loaded chamber indicator and grip safety (early type is semi-circular, late type is curved), occasionally was made with an alloy frame, popular pistol mfg. 1937-1961 with minor modifications. Later guns are suffixed with the letters A, B, and C, 178,000 mfg.

	100%	98%	95%	90%	80%	70%	60%
	$250	$225	$200	$175	$150	$135	$120

Add 50%-100% for engraved and plated variations if in 98%+ original condition.

Embellished variations of the Model 418 included the Model 419 (engraved blue), Model 420 (engraved nickel), and Model 421 (engraved gold plated).

MODEL 1932 - 7.65mm (rare) or 9mm Corto (most common) cal., two variations including straight and curved rear grip strap, smooth wood grips bearing PB monogram (commercial) or RM monogram (Italian Navy). 8,000 mfg. in ser. no. range 400,000-408,000.

	100%	98%	95%	90%	80%	70%	60%
	$2,750	$2,000	$1,500	$1,000	$750	$500	$400

Add 20% for RM variation.

GRADING - PPGS™	100%	98%	95%	90%	80%	70%	60%	LAST MSR

MODEL 1934 – 7.65mm or .380 ACP cal., (9mm Corto cal.), 3 3/8 in. barrel, fixed sights, blue, plastic grips, Italy's service weapon in WWII, one of the most common Beretta pistols - over one million manufactured between 1934-1980, many of the military pistols have a parkerized finish, usually with metal-backed grips, later guns have an alphabetical prefix. Post-war production (1946) serial numbers start with C00001.

	100%	98%	95%	90%	80%	70%	60%	LAST MSR
	$650	$500	$375	$300	$250	$225	$200	
Dlx. post-war coml.	$3,500	$2,500	$2,000	$1,750	$1,500	$1,250	$1,000	

Add 20% for high polish, unless post-war production.

Add 20% for Italian Air Force.

The model was sold to the German Army in Italy during 1944. Ser. no. ranges are: 0001AA - 10,000AA and 0001BB - 8903BB - add 100%.

Deluxe post-war commercial pistols were engraved, gold plated, and cased with a spare mag. and cleaning brush.

MODEL 1935 – 7.65mm cal., otherwise similar to the Model 1934, 3 1/2 in. barrel, fixed sights, blue, plastic grips, the wartime model had poor finish, a small number had an experimental slide safety in ser. no. range 500,xxx, military issue was often parkerized. 525,000 mfg. 1935-1967.

	100%	98%	95%	90%	80%	70%	60%	LAST MSR
	$495	$425	$350	$300	$235	$200	$165	
Dlx. post-war coml.	$3,500	$2,500	$2,000	$1,750	$1,500	$1,250	$1,000	
Alloy frame,1937-1939 mfg.	$10,000	$8,500	$7,250	$6,000	$5,000	$4,000	$3,000	

Add 10% for high polish, unless post-war production.

Deluxe post-war commercial pistols were engraved, gold plated, and cased with a spare mag. and cleaning brush.

There are five military groupings on this model. Add 100%. They include: Group I (mfg. for the German Army and Mussolini government in Italy during 1943-44, with ser. no. range 500,000 - 509,000), Group II (ser. no. range 509,000 - 525,000), Group III (sold to the German Army and Imperial Japanese Army, ser. no. range 525,000 - 534,000, control stamp is 4 UT), Group IV (mfg. 1944-45, ser. no. range 534,000 - 599,000, control stamp is 4 UT), and Group V (mfg. Feb. to April of 1945, ser. no. range 599,000 - 616,000).

PISTOLS: SEMI-AUTO, POST WWII MFG.

On Beretta's large frame pistols, alphabetical suffixes refer to the following: F Model - double/single action system with external safety decocking lever, G Model - double/single action system with external decocking only lever, D Model - double action only without safety lever, DS Model - double action only with external safety lever. Pistols have been manufactured in both Italy and America, and country of origin can be determined on the slide legend.

Information and values for state compliant variations are not listed.

The models in this section appear in numerical sequence.

MODEL 20 – .25 ACP cal., double action, alloy frame, 9 shot, 2 1/2 in. barrel, plastic or walnut grips, 10.9 oz. Disc. 1985.

	100%	98%	95%	90%	80%	70%	60%	LAST MSR
	$160	$140	$125	$115	$95	$85	$75	*$214*

MODEL 21(A)-W BOBCAT – .22 LR or .25 ACP cal., double action, alloy frame, 7 (.22 LR) or 8 (.25 ACP) shot mag., 2.4 in. barrel, plastic or walnut (EL Model, disc. 2000) grips, 11 1/2 oz.

* ***Model 21(A)-W Bobcat Blue Finish***

	100%	98%	95%	90%	80%	70%	60%	LAST MSR
	$250	$225	$200	$150	$115	$95	$85	*$300*

Add approx. $75 for engraving and wood grips (EL Model, disc. 2000).

* ***Model 21(A)-W Bobcat Nickel Finish*** – disc. 2000.

	100%	98%	95%	90%	80%	70%	60%	LAST MSR
	$275	$235	$210	$160	$130	$115	$95	*$322*

* ***Model 21(A)-W Bobcat Matte Finish*** – matte finished metal, plastic grips. Mfg. 1992-2013.

	100%	98%	95%	90%	80%	70%	60%	LAST MSR
	$250	$210	$160	$135	$115	$95	$85	*$310*

This model is manufactured by Beretta U.S.A. Corp. in Accokeek, MD.

* ***Model 21(A)-W Bobcat Stainless Steel (Inox)*** – .22 LR cal. only, similar to Model 21 Bobcat, except is stainless steel with plastic grips, approx. 11 1/2 oz. Mfg. 2000-2013, reintroduced 2017.

	100%	98%	95%	90%	80%	70%	60%	LAST MSR
MSR $449	$385	$335	$290	$260	$210	$175	$135	

* ***Model 21(A)-W Bobcat Lady Beretta*** – .22 LR cal. only, similar to Model 21-W, except is specially serial numbered and has gold etching on top of frame and slide sides. Supplied with a blue velvet drawstring bag. 1990 issue.

	100%	98%	95%	90%	80%	70%	60%	LAST MSR
	$245	$185	$160	$140	$130	$115	$100	*$285*

This model was sold exclusively by Lew Horton Distributing Co.

GRADING - PPGS™	100%	98%	95%	90%	80%	70%	60%	LAST MSR

MODEL 21A BOBCAT COVERT – .22 LR cal., blowback operated, DA/SA, aluminum alloy frame, 2.9 in. barrel, 7 shot, two-piece checkered walnut grip panels with Beretta logo, serrated front strap and backstrap, Bruniton finish on slide and barrel, matte black or FDE Cerakote frame finish. New late 2020.

MSR $529	$450	$395	$340	$315	$250	$210	$165	

Add $20 for FDE Cerakote finish.

MODEL U22 NEOS – .22 LR cal., single action, unique design features modular construction and modern styling, 4 1/2 or 6 in. barrel with sights incorporated into integral full-length sight rail, 10 shot mag., interchangeable colored (black, grey, aqua, red) accessory grip frames with aqua, grey, or blue (black standard) rubber inlays, matte black finish, 31 1/2 or 36 oz. Mfg. 2002-2017.

	$260	$200	$170	$145	$120	$100	$90	*$325*

A carbine kit, which includes a 16 in. barrel and skeletonized buttstock was available for $249 (website only, disc. 2013).

* ***Model U22 Neos Inox*** – .22 LR cal., similar to Model U22 Neos, except slide and barrel are stainless steel. Mfg. 2002-2017.

	$285	$225	$200	$165	$130	$110	$100	*$350*

MODEL U22 NEOS DLX – .22 LR cal., similar to Model U22 Neos, except includes adj. trigger and interchangeable front and rear sights (six included), 6 or 7 1/2 in. barrel, laser engraved "U22 NEOS" on slide. Mfg. mid-2003-2007.

	$280	$230	$200	$170	$145	$125	$110	*$350*

* ***Model U22 Neos DLX Inox*** – similar to U22 Neos DLX, except is stainless steel. Mfg. mid-2003-2007.

	$310	$255	$215	$185	$145	$130	$110	*$375*

MODEL 70 (PUMA OR COUGAR) – .32 ACP or .380 ACP cal., 3 1/2 in. barrel, fixed or adj. sights, blue, plastic grips, .32 Puma alloy frame, .380 Cougar steel frame. Disc.

	$225	$195	$175	$150	$125	$115	$100	

Add 10% for .380 ACP cal.

MODEL 70S – .22 LR or .380 ACP cal., single action, 3 1/2 in. barrel, 9 shot, blue finish, plastic grips, steel frame, .22 LR has adj. rear sight on slide, 18 oz. (.22 cal.), or 23 oz.(.380 ACP cal.). Disc. 1985.

	$375	$325	$300	$250	$225	$200	$185	*$295*

MODEL 70T – .32 ACP cal., similar to Model 70, target sights. Disc.

	$325	$275	$250	$220	$195	$165	$150	

MODEL 71 (JAGUAR) – .22 LR cal., single action, 8 shot, 3 1/2 in. barrel, plastic grips with thumb rest, finger extension mag. Jaguar was dropped from the model name in 1983 and used only for marketing purposes in addition to the Jaguar Plinker. Importation disc. 1987.

	$350	$315	$275	$240	$210	$175	$150	*$215*

MODEL 72 JAGUAR – similar to Model 71 Jaguar, except includes extra 6 in. barrel. Disc.

	$350	$275	$230	$200	$180	$160	$150	

MODEL 73 – similar to Model 72, except has 6 in. barrel only, longer grip frame, 10 shot mag., and fixed rear sight moved from slide to barrel.

	$295	$250	$225	$195	$175	$155	$135	

MODEL 74 – similar to Model 73, except has adj. rear sight on barrel.

	$395	$350	$325	$250	$220	$195	$165	

MODEL 75 JAGUAR – similar to Model 71 Jaguar.

	$300	$265	$225	$195	$180	$160	$150	

MODEL 76P-76W TARGET PISTOL – .22 LR cal., single action, 11 shot, steel frame, 6 in. barrel, adj. sights, blue finish, thumb rest plastic grips (76-P). Disc. 1985.

	$795	$725	$650	$575	$500	$450	$395	*$395*

Add $40 for thumb rest wood grips (Model 76-W).

MODEL 80 – .22 Short cal., target pistol, only a couple are known to exist in the U.S.

	$2,000	$1,750	$1,500	$1,250	$995	$750	$500	

MODEL 81P-81W – .32 ACP cal., blowback operation, DA/SA, 3.8 in. barrel, 12 shot double stack mag., round trigger guard, fixed sights, plastic or wood grips (W suffix), ambi frame mounted thumb safety, blue or nickel finish. Imported 1976-1984.

	$450	$400	$350	$300	$250	$200	$160	

Add $90 for nickel finish. Add $20 for wood grips (W suffix).

GRADING - PPGS™	100%	98%	95%	90%	80%	70%	60%	LAST MSR

MODEL 81FS CHEETAH – .32 ACP cal., blowback operation, DA/SA, 3.8 in. barrel, 12 shot double stack mag., squared off trigger guard, fixed 3-dot sights, ambi frame mounted thumb safety, automatic firing pin block safety, Bruniton finish, 24.2 oz. Mfg. 2017 only.

	$675	$535	$475	$400	$350	$300	$250	*$815*

MODEL 82W – .32 ACP cal., blowback operation, DA/SA, 3.8 in. fixed barrel, 9 shot single stack mag., fixed sights, walnut grips (W suffix), slightly thinner grip than Model 81 due to single stack mag., blue or nickel finish, 17 oz. Importation disc. 1984.

	$450	$400	$350	$300	$250	$200	$160	

Add $75 for nickel finish.

MODEL 84B – .380 ACP cal., DA, 3.8 in. barrel, smooth walnut grips, 13 shot mag., blue finish, alloy frame, fixed sights, 22 1/2 oz. Mfg. 1980-approx. 1985.

	$450	$400	$350	$300	$250	$200	$160	

MODEL 84BB – .380 ACP cal., similar to Model 84B, except safety mechanism was modified beginning in 1982, first listed in Beretta catalog during 1985, plastic or walnut grips, 23 oz.

	$450	$400	$350	$300	$250	$200	$160	

MODEL 84W-EL – similar to Model 84 but specially engraved, select walnut grips. Presentation case. Disc. 1984.

	$1,025	$770	$720	$615	$565	$520	$460	

MODEL 84P/84W (CHEETAH) – .380 ACP cal., single/double action semi-auto, 3.82 in. barrel, alloy frame, steel slide, 10 (C/B 1994) or 13* (reintroduced late 2004) shot staggered mag., firing pin block, ambidextrous manual safety (also used as a decocking lever), low profile 3-dot sights, curved trigger guard, plastic or wood (available with nickel finish) grips, blue (disc.), Bruniton, or nickel (disc. 2001, reintroduced 2004) finish, 23.3 oz. Disc. 2013.

	$585	$450	$365	$310	$255	$210	$190	*$770*

Add $30 for wood grips (Model 84W, disc. 2001).
Add $60 for nickel finish (Model 84FS, includes checkered wood grips).

* ***Model 84F*** – similar specifications to the Model 84P-84W, except patterned after the Model 92F Govt. Model, matte black Bruniton finish, squared off trigger guard, plastic or wood grips, 23 oz. Mfg. 1990 only.

	$675	$535	$475	$400	$350	$300	$250	*$479*

MODEL 84 FS CHEETAH – .380 ACP cal., DA, 3.8 in. barrel, 10 or 13 shot staggered mag., 3-dot sights, automatic firing pin block (FS suffix), black Bruniton or nickel finish, 23 oz. Mfg. 2017 only.

	$675	$535	$475	$400	$350	$300	$250	*$815*

Add $100 for nickel finish.

MODEL 85BB – .380 ACP cal., 8 shot mag., similar to Model 84BB, except safety mechanism was modified beginning in 1982, first listed in Beretta catalog during 1985, plastic or checkered walnut grips, blue or nickel plated finish (new 1988), 21.8 oz.

	$450	$400	$350	$300	$250	$200	$160	

MODEL 85F/FS – .380 ACP cal., same general specifications as the Model 84 Cheetah, except slimmer profile because of 8 shot single stack mag., Model 85P has plastic grips, available in nickel or Bruniton finish, 21.9 oz. Disc. 2012, reintroduced 2017 only.

	$675	$535	$475	$400	$350	$300	$250	*$815*

Add $100 for nickel finish.
Add $60 for nickel finish (includes wood grips, disc. 2001, reintroduced 2004).
Add $33 for wood grips with blue finish (Model 85W - disc. 2000).

* ***Model 85F*** – similar specifications to the Models 85P-85W, except has matte black Bruniton finish, squared off trigger guard, plastic or wood grips, 21.8 oz. Mfg. in 1990 only.

	$450	$400	$350	$300	$250	$200	$160	*$440*

Add $25 for wood grips.

MODEL 86P-86W – .380 ACP cal. only, double action, tip-up 4 1/3 in. barrel, 8 shot mag., plastic or walnut grips, 23 oz. While this model was advertised, it was never released.

Advertised MSR was $480 in 1986, walnut grips were $80 extra (86-W).

MODEL 86 – .380 ACP cal., blowback operation, DA/SA, 4.4 in. tip-up barrel, 8 shot mag., checkered walnut grips, matte Bruniton finish, fixed sights, 23.3 oz. Imported 1991-2004.

	$1,000	$875	$750	$680	$550	$450	$350	*$615*

GRADING - PPGS™	100%	98%	95%	90%	80%	70%	60%	LAST MSR

MODEL 87BB – .22 LR cal., similar to Model 85BB, 8 shot single column mag., plastic or checkered walnut grips, blue or nickel plated finish, 20.8 oz.

$795 $725 $650 $575 $475 $375 $275

MODEL 87 CHEETAH – .22 LR cal., single/double action, 7 shot mag., 3.82 or 6 in. target barrel with counterweight (disc. 1994), blue finish, wood grips, 20 oz. (3.82 in. barrel). Imported 1986-2013, reintroduced 2017 only.

$775 $625 $575 $525 $475 $375 $275 *$950*

* ***Model 87 Target*** – .22 LR cal., single action only target variation of the Model 87 with 5.9 in. barrel, 10 shot mag., 23.3 (older mfg.) or 41 (new mfg.) oz., newer mfg. has top Picatinny rail. Disc. 1994, reintroduced 2000-2013, and 2017.

$875 $700 $625 $575 $500 $400 $295 *$1,050*

This model was reintroduced in 2000, and featured adj. rear target sight, integral scope base rail machined on the aluminum barrel sleeve, and Bruniton finish with anodized aluminum frame.

MODEL 89 GOLD STANDARD – .22 LR cal., single action target semi-auto, matte Bruniton black finish on metal parts, 6 in. barrel, 10 shot mag., anatomical wood grips, adj. sights, 41 oz. Imported 1988-2000.

$630 $510 $410 $360 $310 $275 $250 *$802*

MODEL 90 DOUBLE ACTION AUTOMATIC – .32 ACP cal., 3 5/8 in. barrel, fixed sights, blue, plastic grips. Mfg. 1969-83.

$275 $195 $175 $155 $130 $110 $95

Add 25% if without external slide latch.

MODEL 100 – .32 ACP cal., fixed sights. Disc.

$250 $220 $195 $165 $150 $140 $130

MODEL 101 – similar to Model 70T, except in .22 LR cal. Disc.

$250 $220 $195 $165 $150 $140 $130

MODEL 102 – .22 LR cal., target pistol, single action, steel/alloy construction, plastic grips, 10 shot mag. with finger extension, adj. rear sight. Disc.

$575 $500 $450 $400 $375 $350 $325

MODEL 948 – .22 LR cal., 3 1/2 or 6 in. barrel, fixed sights, hammer.

$175 $150 $125 $100 $75 $60 $50

MODEL 949 OLYMPIC TARGET – .22 S or LR cal., 8 3/4 in. barrel, target sights, adj. barrel weights, blue, muzzle brake, checkered wood grips with thumb rest. Limited mfg. 1959-1964.

$660 $550 $495 $385 $305 $250 $195

MODEL 950CC MINX M2 – .22 Short cal., hinged 2 3/8 in. barrel, fixed sights, blue, plastic grips. Mfg. 1955-disc.

$135 $115 $105 $95 $85 $75 $70

MODEL 950CC SPECIAL MINX M4 – similar to M2, with 4 in. barrel.

$135 $115 $105 $95 $85 $75 $70

MODEL 950B JETFIRE – similar to M2, in .25 ACP cal.

$295 $250 $225 $175 $175 $110 $70

MODEL 950 JETFIRE (BS) – .22 Short (disc. 1992) or .25 ACP cal., single action, alloy frame, 8 shot (.25 cal. only) or 6 shot mag., tip-up 2 1/2 and 4 in. (.22 S only) barrel, plastic grips, thumb safety, matte (new 1992, plastic grips only), blue or nickel finish, 9.9 oz. Mfg. in America beginning circa 1978. Disc. 2002.

$295 $250 $225 $175 $150 $110 $70 *$226*

Add $22 for blue finish (disc. 1999).
Add $80 for nickel finish (disc. 1999).

This model was manufactured by Beretta U.S.A. Corp. in Accokeek, MD.

* ***Model 950 Jetfire Stainless (Inox)*** – similar to Model 950 BS, except is stainless steel. Mfg. 2000-2002.

$350 $295 $250 $200 $175 $150 $95 *$267*

* ***Model 950 EL*** – same general specifications as Model 950 BS, only with wood grips and gold plated parts. Disc. 1999.

$275 $230 $200 $180 $165 $125 $80 *$337*

GRADING - PPGS™	100%	98%	95%	90%	80%	70%	60%	LAST MSR

MODEL 1951 (951 BRIGADIER) – 9mm Para. cal., 4 1/2 in. barrel, fixed sights, blue, plastic grips, former Italian service pistol and immediate predecessor to the M92 Series. Mfg. 1952-disc.

$575 $475 $395 $350 $295 $250 $195

Subtract approx. 10% for "Egyptian" (denoted by E prefix) or "Israeli" Model.
Add 20% for NIB.
Add 20% for short slide (about first 1,000 mfg.).
Add 20% if marked for United Arab Republic.
Gold engraved variations sell for $4,000 if NIB.

MODEL 3032 TOMCAT – .32 ACP cal., similar to Model 21 Bobcat, except has 2.45 in. barrel, 7 shot mag., choice of matte or blue (disc. 2007) finish, plastic grips, regular or Tritium AO Big Dot Express (new 2002) sights, approx. 14 1/2 oz., mfg. by Beretta U.S.A. Mfg. 1996-2013.

$300 $240 $200 $175 $150 $135 $120 *$390*

Add $25 for blue finish (disc. 2007).
Add $150 for laser grips (mfg. 2008-2009).
Add $75 for Alley Cat package - includes Tritium AO Big Dot Express sights and in-the-pants Alcantara synthetic holster (disc.).

* ***Model 3032 Tomcat Inox*** – .32 ACP cal., SA/DA, 7 shot, tip-up barrel, adj. rear sight, two-position safety, stainless steel finish. New 2017.

MSR $529 $450 $395 $340 $315 $250 $210 $165

* ***Model 3032 Tomcat Stainless (Inox)*** – .32 ACP cal., similar to Model 3032 Tomcat, except has stainless steel slide and barrel, grey anodized alloy frame, 15.8 oz. Mfg. 2000-2013.

$350 $285 $225 $185 $160 $140 $120 *$430*

* ***Model 3032 Tomcat Titanium*** – similar to Model 3032 Tomcat, except has titanium frame, blue finish only, 16.9 oz. Mfg. 2001-late 2002.

$460 $360 $310 $275 $250 $225 $200 *$589*

MODEL 3032 TOMCAT COVERT – .32 ACP cal., DA/SA, alloy frame, 2.9 in. tip-up barrel, 7 shot, low profile fixed sights, walnut or plastic (FDE model only) grips, matte black Bruniton or FDE Cerakote finish, 14.5 oz. New mid-2020.

MSR $599 $515 $450 $385 $350 $285 $230 $180

Add $20 for FDE Cerakote finish.

MODEL 8000 COUGAR F/D – 9mm Para. cal., single/double (Model 8000 Cougar F) or DA (Model 8000 Cougar D, disc. 2000) only, short recoil system with 3.6 in. rotating barrel, 10 or 13 (became option late 2004) shot mag., fixed sights, anodized aluminum alloy frame, black plastic grips, Bruniton matte black finish, 32.6 oz. Mfg. 1995-2005.

$450 $400 $375 $325 $275 $250 $225 *$800*

* ***Model 8000 Mini Cougar*** – similar to Model 8000 Cougar, except overall height has been reduced to 4 1/2 in. and weight is 27.6 oz. Mfg. 1998-2003.

$400 $350 $325 $275 $250 $225 $200 *$709*

* ***Model 8000L Cougar*** – similar to Model 8000F Cougar, except has shortened grip, 10 or 13 (optional late 2004) shot double stack mag., 28.2 oz. Mfg. 2003-2005.

$450 $400 $375 $325 $275 $250 $225 *$800*

* ***Model 8000 Cougar (Inox)*** – similar to Model 8000F Cougar, except is stainless steel. Limited mfg. 2004 only.

$500 $450 $400 $350 $325 $300 $275 *$875*

MODEL 8040 COUGAR F/D – .40 S&W cal., single/double (Model 8040 Cougar F) or DA (Model 8040 Cougar D, disc. 2000) only, short recoil system with 3.6 in. rotating barrel, 10 or 11 (became optional late 2004) shot mag., fixed sights, anodized aluminum alloy frame, Bruniton matte black finish, 32.4 oz. Mfg. 1995-2005.

$450 $400 $375 $325 $275 $250 $225 *$800*

* ***Model 8040 Cougar (Inox)*** – similar to Model 8040F Cougar, except is stainless steel. Limited mfg. 2004 only.

$500 $450 $400 $350 $325 $300 $275 *$875*

* ***Model 8040 Mini Cougar*** – similar to Model 8040 Cougar, except overall height was reduced to 4 1/2 in. and weight is 27.6 oz., supplied with 8 and extended 10 shot mag. Mfg. 1998-2003.

$450 $400 $350 $300 $275 $250 $225 *$709*

GRADING - PPGS™	100%	98%	95%	90%	80%	70%	60%	LAST MSR

MODEL 8045 COUGAR F/D – .45 ACP cal., 8 shot mag., otherwise similar to Models 8000 and 8040, 32 oz. Mfg. 1998-2004, D Model disc. 2002.

$500 $450 $400 $350 $325 $300 $275 *$860*

Subtract approx. $25 for Model 8045 Cougar D (DA only, disc. 2002).

* ***Model 8045 Mini Cougar D/F*** – similar to Model 8045 Cougar, except overall height was reduced to 4 1/2 in., and weight is 27.6 oz, supplied with 6 shot mag. Importation began 1999, D Model disc. 2002, F disc. in 2003.

$450 $400 $350 $300 $275 $250 $225 *$764*

Subtract approx. $25 for Model 8045 Mini-Cougar D (DA only, disc. 2002).

MODEL 8357 COUGAR F – .357 SIG cal., single/double action, 5 1/2 in. barrel, blue finish with plastic grips, 10 shot mag., 32.4 oz. Mfg. 2001-2004.

$665 $575 $450 $395 $350 $300 $275 *$800*

MODEL 9000S TYPE F/D – 9mm Para. or .40 S&W cal., single/double (Model 9000S Type F) or DA only (Model 9000S Type D, disc. 2003), 3 1/2 in. tilt barrel, 10 or 12 (9mm Para. only, optional late 2004) shot mag., spurless (Type D only) or external (Type F) hammer, ambidextrous safety with hammer decocking, sub-compact pistol utilizing state of the art ergonomic design by Giugiaro Design, matte black techno-polymer frame, overmolded rubber grip, cased, approx. 26 1/2 oz. Mfg. 2000-2005.

$425 $330 $285 $260 $240 $220 $200 *$485*

Add $24 for B-Lok safety system using key lock (mfg. 2003, Type F only).

APX – 9mm Para. or .40 S&W (disc. 2020) cal., striker fire, low profile, black polymer frame, 4 1/4 in. barrel, 10, 15, or 17 (9mm only) shot mag., reversible mag. release, 3-dot sights, ergonomic grip frame, Mil-Spec 1913 Picatinny rail, square trigger guard, striker deactivation button, firing pin block safety, trigger safety, out of the battery disconnection, interchangeable grip frame housing available in FDE (disc. 2020), OD Green (mfg. 2017 only), or Wolf Grey, 28-29 oz. New 2017.

MSR $399 $340 $300 $250 $230 $185 $150 $125

Add $20 for FDE finish (disc. 2020).

APX CARRY – 9mm Para. cal., striker fired, single-stack, sub-compact frame, 3 in. barrel, 6 or 8 (extended) shot mag., DAO style trigger, flat trigger guard, modular chassis design, reversible mag. release, slide serrations, black, FDE, OD Green, or Wolf Grey finish, 19.8 oz. New 2019.

MSR $349 $300 $265 $225 $200 $165 $135 $100

APX CENTURION – 9mm Para. or .40 S&W (disc. 2020) cal., striker fired, 3.7 in. barrel, 10, 13 (.40 S&W, disc.), or 15 (9mm Para.) shot mag., reversible mag. release, SRT, replaceable grips, aggressive slide serrations, ambi slide catch, black or FDE (mfg. 2020 only) finish, 27.7 oz. New mid-2018.

MSR $399 $340 $300 $250 $230 $185 $150 $125

Add $20 for FDE finish (new 2020).

* ***APX Centurion Combat*** – 9mm Para. cal., striker fired, black polymer frame, 4.2 in. threaded barrel, 10 or 15 shot mag., removable front and rear sights, striker deactivation button, firing pin block safety, trigger safety, includes fixed blanking plate, 27 oz. Mfg. 2020 only.

$465 $400 $350 $315 $250 $210 $165 *$549*

* ***APX Centurion RDO*** – 9mm Para. cal., striker fired, 3.7 in. barrel, 10 or 15 shot mag., removable front and rear sights, firing pin block safety, trigger safety, includes fixed blanking plate, pistol plates support mini-red dot optics from Burris, Trijicon, Leupold, and C-More, 27 oz. Mfg. 2020 only.

$465 $400 $350 $315 $250 $210 $175 *$549*

APX COMBAT – 9mm Para. cal., striker fired action, 4.9 in. threaded barrel, 10 or 17 shot, features a factory slide cut to accept one of four different optic plates, ships with fixed banking plate, 33.3 oz. Mfg. 2018-2020.

$495 $435 $375 $335 $275 $225 $175 *$579*

APX COMPACT – 9mm Para. or .40 S&W cal., striker fired, 3.7 in. barrel, 10 or 13 shot mag., reversible mag. release, SRT, removable front and rear sights, replaceable grips, aggressive slide serrations, ambi slide catch, black or FDE (new 2020) finish, 26.4 oz. Mfg. mid-2018-2020.

$340 $300 $250 $230 $185 $150 $125 *$399*

Add $20 for FDE finish (new 2020).

APX RDO – 9mm Para. or .40 S&W cal., striker fired action, SA/DA, 4.9 in. barrel, 10, 15, or 17 shot, features a factory slide cut that allows for optics, 33 oz. Mfg. 2018-2020.

$465 $400 $350 $315 $250 $210 $165 *$549*

GRADING - PPGS™	100%	98%	95%	90%	80%	70%	60%	LAST MSR

APX TARGET – 9mm Para. cal., striker fired, polymer frame, 4.76 in. barrel, 17 shot mag., extended mag. release, target trigger, target adj. sights with fiber optic front, integral red dot ready mount, includes 4 mounting plates compatible with optics, includes three interchangeable back straps, full length slide serrations, ambi extended slide stop, 31.04 oz. Mfg. 2020 only.

	$595	$525	$450	$400	$325	$275	$225	*$699*

ARX 160 – .22 LR cal., 9 in. barrel with flash suppressor, 20 shot STANAG Type mag., matte black finish, Mil-Std 1913 upper and lower rails, polymer flip-up sights, adj. folding stock, pistol grip, ambidextrous mag. release, 5.7 lbs. Mfg. 2013-2014.

	$375	$295	$250	$200	$175	$150	$125	*$545*

BU-9 NANO – 9mm Para. cal., DAO, 3 in. barrel, 6 or 8 (new 2013) shot mag., stainless/alloy steel fiberglass reinforced technopolymer frame, removable dovetailed white dot front sight and rear sight with lockscrews, black or crimson trace (new 2014) grips, black Nitride, Rosa (mfg. 2014-2018), FDE (mfg. 2014-2018), blue (mfg. 2018 only), or Sniper Gray (mfg. 2018 only) finish, 17.1 oz. Mfg. late 2011-2019.

	$375	$300	$275	$225	$200	$175	$150	*$450*

Add $200 for Crimson Trace grips (mfg. 2014-2015).

PICO INOX – .380 ACP (converts to .32 ACP cal. with simple barrel replacement), DAO, 2.7 in. barrel, 6 shot mag., small, ultra-thin polymer frame with matte stainless steel slide, matte black, FDE (disc., reintroduced 2018), white (disc.), pink (disc.), purple (disc.), blue (new 2018), lavender (new 2018), or gray (new 2018) finish, last shot hold open, low profile magazine release, slide lock slide release lever, dovetail white dot front and rear sights, 11 1/2 oz. Mfg. in the U.S. mid-2013-2019.

	$250	$195	$165	$130	$120	$110	$100	*$300*

Add $150 for LaserMax red-laser or light grip frame (mfg. 2016 only).

PX4 STORM – 9mm Para., .40 S&W, or .45 ACP (new 2007) cal., single/double action, 4 in. barrel, polymer frame, locked breech with rotating barrel system, matte black finish with plastic grips, Pronox (disc.) or Super Luminova 3-dot night sights, 9 (.45 ACP only), 10, 14, or 17 shot mag. (varies due to caliber), accessory rail on lower frame, approx. 27 1/2 oz. New mid-2005.

MSR $599	$515	$450	$385	$350	$285	$235	$200	

Add $100 for .45 ACP cal. (new 2007).

The trigger mechanism of this gun can be customized to four different configurations: Type F (single/double action decocker and manual safety), Type D (DAO with spurless hammer, LE only), Type G (single/double action decocker with no manual safety, LE only), or Type C (constant action, spurless hammer). Values are for Type C and Type F variations.

* ***PX4 Storm Compact*** – 9mm Para., .40 S&W (new 2012), or .45 ACP (mfg. 2015 only) cal., similar to Model PX4 Storm, except has compact frame and 3.27 in. barrel, 8 (.45 ACP), 10, 12 (.40 S&W only, new 2012), or 15 (9mm Para. cal. only) shot mag., black, FDE (mfg. 2019 only), or Grey (mfg. 2019 only) finish, 27.3 oz. New late 2010.

MSR $599	$515	$450	$385	$350	$285	$235	$200	

Add $50 for .45 ACP cal. (mfg. 2015 only).

* ***PX4 Storm Compact Carry*** – 9mm Para. cal., DA/SA, compact polymer frame, 3.2 in. cold hammer forged barrel, Grey Cerakote slide, 15 shot double stack mag., reversible mag. release, night sights, Talon grips, Picatinny rail, Stealth Levers Decock only (G-Model), 27.3 oz. New 2018.

MSR $849	$725	$635	$550	$500	$400	$325	$280	

* ***PX4 Storm Sub-Compact*** – 9mm Para. or .40 S&W (mfg. 2007-2019) cal., similar to PX4 Storm, except has 10 (disc. 2019) or 13 (9mm Para. cal. only) shot mag., has sub-compact frame with 3 in. barrel, includes three backstraps, 26 oz. New 2007.

MSR $599	$515	$450	$385	$350	$285	$230	$180	

* ***PX4 Storm Inox*** – 9mm Para. or .40 S&W cal., similar to PX4 Storm, except has stainless steel construction, and 10, 14, or 17 shot only. Mfg. 2012-2019.

	$595	$475	$425	$360	$300	$275	$250	*$700*

* ***PX4 Storm Compact Inox*** – 9mm Para. or .40 S&W cal., DA/SA, 3.2 in. cold hammer forged barrel, stainless steel slide, Commander style hammer, 10, 12, or 15 shot mag., reversible magazine release, interchangeable backstraps, lower Picatinny rail, ambidextrous slide stop, integral and retractable lanyard loop. Mfg. 2015-2019.

	$595	$475	$425	$360	$300	$275	$250	*$700*

GRADING - PPGS™	100%	98%	95%	90%	80%	70%	60%	LAST MSR

* ***PX4 Storm Special Duty*** – .45 ACP cal. only, DA/SA, 4.6 in. extended barrel, Type F action only, dark earth polymer frame and matte black slide, includes one 9 shot flush and two 10 shot extended mags., Commander style hammer, lower Picatinny rail, ambidextrous safety, two additional backstraps and waterproof case, 28.6 oz.

MSR $1,149	$975	$775	$700	$600	$500	$425	$350	

Pistols: Semi-Auto, Model 92 & Variations - 5.9 in. barrel

MODEL 92 COMBAT – 9mm Para. cal., similar to Model 92, except has 5.9 in. target barrel, blue finish, plastic or aluminum grips, only 50 imported into the U.S. for competition.

	$2,500	$1,750	$1,500	$1,250	$1,050	$900	$775	

Pistols: Semi-Auto, Model 92, M9, & Variations - 4.9 or 5.1 in. barrel

MODEL 92 (FIRST SERIES) – 9mm Para. cal., 4.9 in. barrel, early production Model 92s had a step slide, frame mounted safety, and mag. release button at base of pistol grip. Production of the M92 was approx. 5,000 pistols. Originally mfg. 1976. Disc.

	$1,100	$750	$650	$495	$395	$325	$275	

MODEL 92S (SECOND SERIES) – similar to Model 92, except has a slide mounted firing pin blocking safety. Disc.

	$700	$575	$475	$395	$325	$275	$220	

Add 10% for NIB.

Subtract 30% for recent police import.

MODEL 92SB-P (THIRD SERIES) – 9mm Para. cal., double action, 15 shot mag., 4.9 in. barrel, fixed sights, alloy frame, high-polish blue finish, plastic grips (Model 92SB-P), conventionally located push-button magazine release, ambidextrous safety, 34 1/2 oz. Mfg. 1980-1985.

	$675	$495	$450	$375	$300	$275	$270	*$600*

* ***Model 92SB-W*** – similar to above, only with wood grips. Disc. 1985.

	$725	$495	$450	$375	$300	$275	$260	*$620*

MODEL 92D – 9mm Para. cal., double action only, otherwise similar to Model 92F, except does not have a manual safety lever, includes black plastic grips, 3-dot sights, 33.8 oz. Mfg. 1992-1998.

	$550	$450	$395	$350	$275	$250	$190	*$586*

Add $90 for Tritium (new 1994) sight system.

Add 10% for Trijicon (disc.) sights and early guns with Model 92F features.

MODEL 90-TWO TYPE F – 9mm Para. or .40 S&W cal., 4.9 in. barrel, DA/SA, matte metal finish, removable single piece wraparound grip in two sizes, internal recoil buffer and captive recoil spring guide assembly, low profile fixed sights, 10, 12 (.40 S&W cal.), or 17 (9mm Para. cal.) shot mag., lower accessories rail with cover, 32 1/2 oz. Mfg. 2006-2009.

	$600	$475	$425	$400	$350	$300	$275	*$700*

MODEL 92FS & 92F – 9mm Para. cal., official U.S. military variation of 92 Series, 4.9 in. barrel, alloy frame, steel slide, 10 (C/B 1994), or 15* (reintroduced late 2004) shot mag., loaded chamber indicator, matte black Bruniton or olive drab (mfg. 2004 only) finish, squared off trigger guard to facilitate two-hand shooting, extended mag. base, choice of regular or 3-dot sights (new 1991), approx. 34 1/2 oz. Model 92F-P has plastic grips. Model 92F-W has wood grips. Mfg. in Italy or Accokeek, MD. New 1984.

MSR $699	$595	$475	$425	$400	$350	$310	$280	

Add $369 for .22 LR conversion kit (includes slide, barrel, recoil spring, and .22 LR mag., mfg. 2002-disc.).

Add $50 for olive drab finish (mfg. 2004 only).

Add $24 for B-Lok safety system using key lock (mfg. 2003 only).

Add approx. $20 for checkered wood grips (Model 92F-W, disc. 1998).

Add approx. $80 for Tritium sight system (mfg. 1994-98).

Add 10% for Trijicon (disc.) sights.

Add approx. $175 for gold engraving/accenting (Model EL-3, 92F-W only, disc. 1998).

Add $575 for 9mm Competition Conversion Kit (mfg. 1992-98).

The Model 92FS incorporates a slide retaining pin engineering change not included in the Model 92F.

The U.S. military on January 15, 1985 announced that the M9 military variation of the commercial Model 92F would replace the Colt Govt. Model .45 ACP as the standard government issue sidearm. Because of domestic political pressures, Congress requested that a new sidearm competition be conducted again in 1988. The result of this second trial was that the Department of the Army announced on May 22, 1989 that Beretta had won again. This military contract with Beretta U.S.A. Corp. initially involved over 320,000 Model M9s (military designation for the commercial Model 92F) manufactured for U.S. military consumption in the

GRADING - PPGS™	100%	98%	95%	90%	80%	70%	60%	LAST MSR

1990s. Actual delivery of commercial Model 92s began in January of 1986, while M9 delivery to U.S. Armed Forces exceeded 430,000 units, and was completed in 1999.

During 2005, Beretta USA received 13 separate contracts to provide M9 pistols and associated spare parts to the U.S. armed forces. In Jan., 2009, Beretta announced that it had been awarded a U.S. Army contract for 450,000 Model 92FS pistols, for U.S. military customers throughout the world. This contract, if all pistol quantities and associated spare parts are ordered, is worth $220 million.

During 2009, Beretta USA Corp. received another order from the U.S. Army to provide 450,000 Beretta Model 92FS pistols to U.S. military customers worldwide. 50,000 pistols from this contract were scheduled for delivery by the end of 2010.

* ***Model 92FS & 92F Stainless (Inox)*** – 9mm Para. cal., similar to Model 92F/92FS, except is mfg. from stainless steel, 4.9 in. barrel, 10 or 15 shot mag., satin finish with plastic grips, 3-dot sights. Initially released to law enforcement agencies only beginning circa 1990. Disc. 2012. Reintroduced 2014, mfg. in Accokeek, MD or Brescia, Italy.

MSR $799	$675	$550	$465	$415	$350	$315	$285	

Add $180 for laser grips (mfg. 2004-2008).
Add $24 for B-Lok safety system using key lock (mfg. 2003 only).
Add approx. $20 for wood grips (disc. 1998).
Add approx. $90 for Trijicon (1993 only) or Tritium (mfg. 1994-98) sight system.

MODEL 92FSR – .22 LR cal., 4.9 in. barrel, 10 or 15 shot mag., 3-dot sights, lower Picatinny rail, features Sniper Grey frame and black Bruniton slide finish, optional suppressor-ready kit, 26 oz. New 2017.

MSR $399	$340	$300	$255	$230	$185	$155	$125	

Add $50 for suppressor-ready kit.

MODEL 92FS BRIGADIER – similar to the Model 92FS, except has heavier slide to reduce felt recoil, wraparound rubber grips, and 3-dot sights, 35.3 oz. Mfg. 1999-2005.

	$650	$525	$425	$385	$335	$300	$275	*$795*

* ***Model 92FS Brigadier Stainless (Inox)*** – similar to Model 92FS Brigadier, except is stainless steel, 35.3 oz. Mfg. 2000-2005.

	$755	$600	$550	$500	$425	$375	$325	*$845*

MODEL 92FS B.A.T.S. – 9mm Para. cal., 4.9 in. barrel, features black matte Bruniton finish and textured rubber wraparound grips with finger grooves, package includes both 10 and 15 shot mags., Airlight knife, aluminum carrying case, 34.4 oz. Limited mfg. late 2000 only.

	$665	$550	$465	$415	$360	$300	$275	*$785*

MODEL 92FS VERTEC – 9mm Para. cal., DA/SA, straight backstrap grip, special short reach trigger, thin dual textured grip panels, and integral accessory rail on lower frame, removable front sight, beveled magwell, 10 shot mag., Bruniton finish, 32.2 oz. Mfg. 2002-2005.

	$635	$495	$440	$385	$340	$300	$275	*$760*

Add $25 for B-Lok safety system using key lock (mfg. 2003).

* ***Model 92FS Vertec Stainless (Inox)*** – stainless variation of the Model 92FS Vertec. Mfg. 2002-2005.

	$670	$525	$425	$360	$315	$260	$225	*$825*

Add $170 for laser grips (new 2004).
Add $25 for B-Lok safety system using key lock (mfg. 2003).

MODEL 92 BLACK INOX – 9mm Para. cal., single/double action, features black stainless slide and stippled, finger groove plastic grips. Limited mfg. 2002 only.

	$610	$485	$390	$325	$280	$240	$200	*$734*

MODEL 92 BILLENIUM – 9mm Para. cal., single action only, frame mounted safety, contoured steel frame with checkered grip straps and contoured carbon fiber grips, interchangeable sights, oversize mag. release button, unique slide serrations and Billenium engraving, nickel alloy surface treatment finish, included deluxe lockable carrying case, 43.3 oz. Limited mfg. in Italy of 2,000 during 2002-2003.

	$2,000	$1,675	$1,350	$1,000	$750	$650	$575	*$1,429*

MODEL 92 STEEL I – 9mm Para. cal., single action only or DA/SA, plastic grips, features all-steel construction, frame mounted safety, nickel alloy finish, includes two 10 shot mags., 41.1 oz. Mfg. 2004-2005.

	$1,750	$1,350	$975	$825	$750	$675	$595	*$1,600*

MODEL 92FS YEAR 2000 – 9mm Para. cal., 4.9 in. barrel, matte black Bruniton finish, features rosewood laminate grips with Beretta "trident" logo on brass medallions. 2,000 mfg. during 2000 only.

	$615	$500	$450	$400	$350	$300	$275	*$726*

GRADING - PPGS™ 100% 98% 95% 90% 80% 70% 60% LAST MSR

MODEL 92F-ELS – deluxe variation of the Model 92F featuring high polish stainless steel finish with gold highlights, frame etchings, and small parts, plastic grips. Mfg. 1992-1994.

$685 $550 $425 $360 $315 $260 $225 *$790*

MODEL 92F/FS "UNITED WE STAND" LIMITED EDITION – 9mm Para. cal., features laser etched gold American flag and "United We Stand" slide lettering on left side, Bruniton or INOX finish, black plastic grips. Mfg. limited to 2001 (Model 92F) and 3,900 (Model 92FS) pistols in late 2001-early 2002.

$625 $560 $485 $425 $375 $300 $275 *$734*

Beretta USA made a donation from the proceeds of this model to the NYPD Foundation and the Survivor's Fund of the National Capitol Region.

MODEL 92FS 470th ANNIVERSARY LIMITED EDITION – features stainless steel construction with mirror polished finish, smooth select walnut grips with inlaid gold plated medallions, gold filled engraving with Dr. Ugo Gussalli-Beretta's signature, 470th Anniversary logos, only 470 mfg. (with "1 of 470" gold filled on each gun) beginning 1999, lockable walnut case. Disc. 2004.

$1,950 $1,575 $1,100 $985 $795 $675 $565 *$2,217*

MODEL 92F/FS "DESERT STORM" SPECIAL EDITION – 9mm Para. cal., features U.S. Central Command seal, marked "Official Sidearm U.S. Armed Forces" on left side of slide, right side is marked "DESERT STORM", stamped "15 January 1991 - 11 April 1991", special ser. no. Approx. 8,000 mfg. 1991-92.

$625 $560 $485 $425 $375 $300 $275 *$660*

MODEL 92F DELUXE – 9mm Para. cal., deluxe model featuring gold or silver plating and elaborate engraving. Imported 1993-disc.

$5,750 $4,950 $3,750 $2,500 $2,175 $1,950 $1,625 *$6,750*

This model is available at the Beretta Galleries or select Beretta Premium dealers only.

MODEL 92G – 9mm Para. cal., SA/DA, identical to the Model 92F, except features a spring loaded decocking lever which safely lowers the hammer allowing fire-ready when unholstering the pistol. New 1990.

The Model 92G is sold to law enforcement agencies only and prices are slightly higher than the standard Model 92FS. This pistol has been used by French Gendarmes since 1987.

MODEL 92G-SD – 9mm Para. cal., similar to Model 92G, except has an integral accessory rail machined into frame in front of trigger guard, Bruniton finish, 10 shot mag., Tritium sights, 35.3 oz. Mfg. 2003-2005.

$955 $745 $585 $510 $450 $400 $350 *$1,175*

MODEL 92F WITH U.S. M9 MARKED SLIDE/FRAME – 9mm Para. cal., 100 mfg. with special serial no. range, "BER" prefix, government assembly numbers on frame, slide, hammer, mag. etc., includes plastic case and cleaning brush. Mfg. for the Armed Forces Reserve shooters, identical to military M9, except for serial number.

$1,750 $1,525 $1,350 $1,100 $950 $825 $700

MODEL 92FS OPERATION ENDURING FREEDOM – 9mm Para. cal., M9 U.S. Army edition, two 10 shot mags., "BER" prefix, 2,500 mfg. 2003 only.

$625 $500 $425 $360 $315 $260 $225 *$712*

MODEL 92A1 – 9mm Para. cal., DA/SA, 4.9 in. barrel, three 10 or 17 shot mags., removable front sight, frame accessory rail, internal recoil buffer, rounded trigger guard, captive recoil spring assembly, black Bruniton finish, plastic grips, 34.4 oz. Mfg. in Italy beginning 2010.

MSR $749 $640 $560 $480 $435 $350 $300 $250

MODEL 92X PERFORMANCE – 9mm Para. cal., full steel Vertec frame with front and rear checkering, 4.9 in. barrel, Brigadier profile slide, includes two 10 or 15 shot mags., oversized mag. button and oversized rubber magazine pad, skeletonized hammer, Extreme-S trigger mechanism, red fiber optic front sight, full black serrated adj. rear sight, ambi thumb safety, extended beavertail, match takedown lever, saw tooth front and rear serrations, 2.98 lbs. New mid-2019.

MSR $1,499 $1,300 $1,100 $950 $850 $700 $600 $450

M9 – 9mm Para. cal., SA/DA, 4.9 in. barrel, 10 or 15 shot mag., 3-dot sights, checkered grip straps, beveled magwell, black Bruniton finish, 35.3 oz.

MSR $649 $550 $480 $415 $375 $300 $250 $215

M9 LIMITED STANDARD EDITION – commercial limited edition of the U.S. Govt. M9 military pistol, features gold inscribed slide legend "The First Decade 1985-1995", Air Force or Marine Corps emblems on right slide side, 10,000 mfg. during 1995-97.

$600 $475 $425 $360 $315 $260 $225 *$643*

GRADING - PPGS™	100%	98%	95%	90%	80%	70%	60%	LAST MSR

* ***M9 Limited Deluxe Edition*** – features checkered walnut grips, gold-plated hammer, grip screws, and mag. release button. Disc. 1997.

	$695	$525	$475	$415	$360	$300	$255	*$750*

M9 SPECIAL EDITION – patterned after the U.S. Armed Forces M9, special M9- XXXX ser. no. range, one 15 shot mag. (pre-1994 mfg.), dot and post sight system, M9 military packaging including Army operator's manual, Bianchi M12 holster, mag. pouch, and web pistol belt. Mfg. 1998-2000.

	$950	$700	$550	$460	$395	$335	$285	*$861*

M9 20TH ANNIVERSARY – 9mm Para. cal., special edition for 20th anniversary of the U.S. government M9, 10 or 15 shot mag. Mfg. 2006-2009.

	$540	$465	$415	$375	$330	$300	$275	*$625*

M9 (25TH ANNIVERSARY) – 9mm Para. cal., special edition for 25th Anniversary of U.S. Government M9, 4.9 in. barrel, 10 or 15 shot mag., includes military style markings, M9 prefixed serial numbers and dot and post sighting system, limited mfg. circa 2010-2015.

	$575	$495	$440	$385	$350	$310	$280	*$675*

M9 .22 LR – .22 LR cal., DA, 4.9 in. barrel, 10 or 15 shot mag., removable sights, interchangeable grip panels, identical to the M9 with same operation, controls, and takedown, black Bruniton finish, 26 oz. New 2016.

MSR $389	$330	$290	$250	$225	$180	$150	$130	

M9A1 – 9mm Para. cal., DA/SA, features accessory rail on lower frame and checkered grip straps, 10 or 15 shot mag., 3-dot sights, beveled magwell, black Bruniton finish, 35.3 oz. Mfg. 2006-2019.

	$650	$565	$485	$435	$365	$315	$265	*$775*

M9A1 .22 LR – .22 LR cal., DA, 4.9 in. barrel, 10 or 15 shot mag., removable sights, interchangeable grip panels, identical to the M9 with same operation, controls, and takedown, features lower Picatinny rail, black Bruniton finish, 26 oz. New 2017.

MSR $399	$340	$300	$255	$230	$185	$155	$130	

M9A3/M9A3-G – 9mm Para. cal., 10, 15 (disc. 2020), or 17 shot mag., includes 3 mags., removable front sight, removable wrap-around Vertec-style thin grip, convertible from safety - decocker to decocker only, 3-slot Picatinny rail, beveled magazine, G-suffix model nomenclature refers to decocker mode only (M9A3-G model, disc. 2020), two-tone FDE or black (disc. 2020) finish, 33.9 oz. Mfg. in Italy beginning 2016.

MSR $1,099	$925	$850	$775	$725	$650	$525	$500	

* ***M9A3 /M9A3-G Limited Edition Models*** – 9mm Para. cal., DA/SA, 5.1 in. barrel, 10 or 17 shot mag., removable front sight, removable wrap-around Vertec-style thin grip, convertible from safety - decocker to decocker only, 3-slot Picatinny rail, beveled magazine, G-suffix model nomenclature refers to decocker mode only, Black/Gray, Black/Green, FDE/Black, or Green/Black finish, 33.3 oz. Limited mfg. beginning mid-2019.

MSR $1,099	$925	$850	$775	$725	$650	$525	$500	

Pistols: Semi-Auto, Model 92 & Variations - 4.3 and 4.7 in. barrels

MODEL 92D CENTURION – 9mm Para. cal., compact variation with 4.3 in. barrel, plastic grips only, without safety, choice of 3-dot or Tritium sights. Mfg. 1994-98.

	$460	$360	$300	$250	$210	$190	$175	*$586*

Add $90 for Tritium sights.

MODEL 92F & 92FS CENTURION – 9mm Para. cal., similar to Model 92F, except has compact barrel slide unit with full size frame, 4.3 in. barrel, choice of plastic or wood grips, 3-dot sight system, same length as Model 92F Compact, 10 (C/B 1994) or 15* shot mag., 33.2 oz. Mfg. 1992-98.

	$525	$435	$395	$365	$335	$300	$275	*$613*

Add approx. $20 for checkered walnut grips (Model 92F Wood).
Add $90 for Tritium sight system (mfg. 1994-98).
Add 10% for Trijicon sights (disc).

MODEL 92F/92FS COMPACT – similar to Model 92F, except has 4.3 in. barrel, DA/SA, 13 shot mag., plastic or wood grips, 31 1/2 oz. While temporarily suspended in 1986, production was resumed 1989-1993.

	$550	$450	$415	$375	$335	$300	$275	*$625*

Add $20 for checkered walnut grips (Model 92F Wood).
Add $65 for Trijicon sight system.

* ***Model 92F Compact "M"*** – similar to Model 92F Compact, except has 8 shot straight line mag., plastic grips only. Imported 1990-93.

	$550	$450	$415	$375	$335	$300	$275	*$625*

Add $65 for Trijicon sight system.
Add 75% for the approx. 1,200 SBM Models that were imported in the 1980s.

GRADING - PPGS™	100%	98%	95%	90%	80%	70%	60%	LAST MSR

MODEL 92FS BORDER MARSHAL – 9mm Para. cal., commercial equivalent of the I.N.S. (Immigration & Naturalization Service) government contract, 4.7 in. barrel, heavy duty steel slide, Tritium sights, Border Marshal engraving on the slide. Mfg. 1999-2000.

$675	$560	$480	$425	$375	$325	$295	*$802*

MODEL 92FS COMPACT – 9mm Para. cal., similar to Model 92 Compact Type M, except has 10 shot staggered mag., 35.3 oz. Mfg. 1999-2003.

$575	$465	$415	$370	$335	$300	$275	*$691*

* ***Model 92FS Compact Stainless (Inox)*** – similar to Model 92FS Compact, except is stainless steel. Mfg. 2000-2003.

$620	$490	$395	$325	$275	$235	$200	*$748*

* ***Model 92FS Custom Carry*** – 9mm Para. cal., 4.3 in. barrel, shortened grip, low profile control levers, left side only safety lever, blue only, 10 shot staggered mag., plastic grips. Mfg. 1999-2000.

$550	$450	$400	$365	$335	$300	$275	*$655*

* ***Model 92FS Custom Carry II (Type M)*** – 9mm Para. cal., similar dimensions as Custom Carry, except is stainless steel construction with black components and black slide markings, Novak low profile 3-dot sights, 8 shot single stack mag., 30.9 oz. Mfg. 2000.

$560	$455	$410	$345	$295	$245	$215	*$669*

MODEL 92FS COMPACT BRUNITON – 9mm Para. cal., 4 1/4 in. barrel, 10 or 13 shot mag., with (disc. 2016) or without (new 2017) Picatinny rail, Combat trigger guard, 3-dot sights, ambidextrous safety, Bruniton finish on aluminum frame and steel slide, 31.6 oz. Mfg. 2014-2017.

$575	$500	$450	$395	$350	$300	$275	*$699*

Add $75 for Picatinny rail (disc. 2016).

MODEL 92FS COMPACT RAIL STAINLESS (INOX) – 9mm Para. cal., 4 1/4 in. barrel, aluminum alloy frame, stainless steel slide, 10 or 13 shot mag., beveled magwell, 1913 style lower accessory rail, combat trigger guard, ambidextrous safety, stainless steel (Inox) finish, 32 oz. Mfg. 2013-2016, reintroduced 2018-2019.

$725	$600	$500	$450	$375	$325	$285	*$850*

MODEL 92FS COMPACT WITH RAIL (RECENT MFG.) – 9mm Para. cal., DA/SA, 4.3 in. barrel, 10 or 13 shot mag., combat trigger guard, integral Picatinny rail, 5.75 in. OAL, 31.6 oz. Mfg. 2018 only.

$650	$565	$485	$435	$365	$315	$265	*$775*

MODEL 92FS INOX TACTICAL – 9mm Para. cal., 4.7 in. barrel, DA/SA, features satin matte finished stainless steel slide and alloy frame, rubber grips, Tritium sights. Mfg. 1999-2000.

$695	$560	$480	$425	$375	$325	$295	*$822*

MODEL 92G ELITE IA (BRIGADIER) – 9mm Para. cal., similar to Model 92FS Brigadier, DAO, except has 4.7 in. stainless barrel and many standard I.D.P.A. competition features including front and rear serrated slide, skeletonized hammer, and removable 3-dot sighting system, plastic grips, includes Elite engraving on slide, 35.3 oz. Mfg. 1999-2005.

$725	$585	$495	$425	$360	$300	$275	*$875*

* ***Model 92G Elite II (Brigadier)*** – similar to Model 92G Elite, except has stainless steel slide with black "Elite II" markings, target barrel crown, extended mag. release, optimized trigger mechanism, front and back strap checkering, low profile Novak rear sight, 35 oz. Mfg. mid-2000-2005.

$815	$635	$530	$450	$385	$325	$295	*$985*

MODEL 92G ELITE LTT – 9mm Para. cal., M9A1 frame with checkering on front and back strap, 4.7 in. stainless barrel with target crown, beveled magwell with no lanyard loop, oversized mag .release button, includes three 10 or 15 shot mags., D Model hammer spring and skeletonized lightweight hammer, radiused trigger guard and rear slide rail, stainless steel trigger, dovetail fiber optic front sight with square notch rear sight, ultra thin VZ/LTT G10 grips, Vertec/M9A3 slide with front cocking serrations, solid steel guide rod and beveled rear slide, 33.3 oz. New 2018.

MSR $1,099	$925	$850	$775	$725	$650	$525	$500

MODEL 92G ELITE LTT CENTURION – 9mm Para. cal., DA/SA, M9A1 style frame, 4 1/4 in. stainless steel barrel, 10 or 18 shot mag., stainless steel trigger, fiber optic front sight, black out rear sight, Vertec/M9A3 style slide with forward cocking serrations, G style decocker, beveled sharp edges, 31.6 oz. New 2019.

MSR $1,099	$925	$850	$775	$725	$650	$525	$500

This model was made in partnership with Ernest Langdon of Langdon Tactical.

GRADING - PPGS™	100%	98%	95%	90%	80%	70%	60%	LAST MSR

MODEL 92G ELITE LTT COMPACT – 9mm Para. cal., DA/SA, compact M9A1 style frame, 4 1/4 in. stainless steel barrel with target crown, includes three 15 shot mags., spurless hammer, stainless steel trigger, fiber optic front sight, blacked out rear sight, ultra thin VZ/LTT G10 grips, Vertec/M9A3 style slide with forward cocking serrations, G style decocker, beveled sharp edges, solid steel guide rod, 28.5 oz. New 2019.

MSR $1,099	$925	$850	$775	$725	$650	$525	$500	

This model was built in partnership with Ernest Langdon of Langdon Tactical.

MODEL 92SB-P COMPACT – similar to Model 92SB, except has 4.3 in. barrel, 14 shot mag., plastic grips (Model 92SB-P), rarer when front strap has curved lip, 31 oz. Disc. 1985.

	$550	$450	$385	$345	$310	$285	$260	*$620*

Add 15% for nickel finish, if in 95%+ condition.

* ***Model 92SB-W Compact*** – similar to Model 92SB-P Compact, except has wood grips. Disc. 1985.

	$575	$475	$395	$355	$335	$300	$280	*$635*

MODEL 92 TYPE M COMPACT – same features as the Model 92FS, except has 4.3 in. barrel, overall height is 5.3 in., Bruniton matte finish, choice of single/double or double action only (disc. 1998), plastic grips, single column 8 shot mag., 30.9 oz. Mfg. 1998-2003.

	$575	$465	$415	$370	$335	$300	$275	*$691*

Add approx. $90 for Tritium sight system (disc. 1998).
Subtract approx. $25 for double action only (disc. 1998).

* ***Model 92 Type M Compact Stainless (Inox)*** – similar to Model 92 Type M, except is stainless steel. Mfg. 2000-2003.

	$615	$475	$395	$340	$295	$245	$215	*$748*

MODEL 92X CENTURION – 9mm Para. cal., SA/DA, steel Vertec frame with front and rear checkering, 4.3 in. chrome-lined barrel with recessed target crown, includes two 10, 15, or 17 shot mags., extended mag. release, skeletonized hammer, high visibility orange/black combat sights, wraparound textured grips, decocking safety, 3-slot Picatinny rail front of trigger guard, black Bruniton finish on slide, 1.78 lbs. New mid-2019.

MSR $699	$600	$525	$450	$400	$325	$285	$230	

MODEL 92X FULL SIZE – 9mm Para. cal., SA/DA, full size steel Vertec frame with front and rear checkering, 4.7 in. barrel, includes two 10, 15, or 17 shot mags., extended mag. release, skeletonized hammer, high visibility orange/black combat sights, wraparound textured grips, decocking safety, 3-slot Picatinny rail front of trigger guard, black Bruniton finish on slide, 2.08 lbs. New mid-2019.

MSR $699	$600	$525	$450	$400	$325	$285	$230	

* ***Model 92X Compact*** – 9mm Para. cal., SA/DA, compact size, steel Vertec frame with front and rear checkering, 4.3 in. chrome-lied barrel with recessed target crown, includes two 10 or 13 shot mags., extended mag. release, skeletonized hammer, high visibility orange/black combat sights, wraparound textured grips, decocking safety, with or w/o 3-slot Picatinny rail front of trigger guard, black Bruniton finish on slide, 1.7 lbs. New mid-2019.

MSR $699	$600	$525	$450	$400	$325	$285	$230	

Pistols: Semi-Auto, Model 96 & Variations, Recent Mfg.

The models in this section appear in approximate chronological sequence.

MODEL 96D – .40 S&W cal., 4.9 in. barrel, double action only variation of the Model 96F, no safety, 3-dot sight system, 33.8 oz. Mfg. 1992-1998.

	$460	$360	$300	$250	$210	$190	$175	*$586*

Add $90 for Tritium sight system (new 1994).
Add $65 for Trijicon sights (disc.).

* ***Model 96D Centurion*** – similar to Model 96D, except is compact variation with 4.3 in. barrel, 3-dot sights. Mfg. 1994-98.

	$460	$360	$300	$250	$210	$190	$175	*$586*

Add $90 for Tritium sight system.

MODEL 96, 96F, & 96FS – .40 S&W cal., similar to Model 92F, 4.9 in. barrel, plastic grips only, flared grip with grip strap serrations, Bruniton matte black finish, 3-dot sight system, 10 or 11 (optional) shot mag., 34.4 oz. Mfg. 1992-2005.

	$595	$475	$420	$380	$335	$300	$275	*$715*

Add $24 for B-Lok safety system with key lock (mfg. 2003).
Add $91 for Tritium sight system (mfg. 1994-99).
Add 10% for Trijicon sights (disc.).

Current model nomenclature for this pistol is the Model 96.

GRADING - PPGS™	100%	98%	95%	90%	80%	70%	60%	LAST MSR

* ***Model 96, 96FS Stainless (Inox)*** – stainless variation of the Model 96FS, rubber grips, 34.4 oz. Mfg. 1999-2005, reintroduced 2009.

	$600	$515	$435	$395	$350	$315	$285	*$725*

Recent model nomenclature for this pistol is the Model 96 Inox.

* ***Model 96F Compact*** – 4.3 in. barrel, 10 shot mag., 3-dot sights, plastic grips, approx. 32 oz. Mfg. 2000-2003.

	$580	$465	$415	$370	$335	$300	$275	*$691*

While advertised during the 1990s, this gun finally went into production during 2000.

* ***Model 96F Compact Stainless (Inox)*** – similar to Model 96F Compact, except is stainless steel. Mfg. 2000-2003.

	$620	$500	$415	$370	$335	$300	$275	*$748*

* ***Model 96F Centurion*** – similar to Model 96F, except has 4.3 in. barrel, 33.2 oz. Mfg. 1992-99.

	$525	$435	$395	$365	$335	$300	$275	*$613*

Add $91 for Tritium sight system (new 1994).

* ***Model 96 Stainless (Inox) "United We Stand" Limited Edition*** – .40 S&W cal., features laser etched gold American flag and "United We Stand" slide lettering. Mfg. limited to 3,900 pistols in late 2001 - early 2002.

	$625	$560	$485	$425	$365	$305	$260	*$734*

Beretta USA made a donation from the proceeds of this model to the NYPD Foundation and the Survivor's Fund of the National Capitol Region.

* ***Model 96FS B.A.T.S.*** – .40 S&W cal., 4.9 in. barrel, black matte Bruniton finish and textured rubber wraparound grips with finger grooves, included both 10 and 11 shot mags., Airlight knife, aluminum carrying case, 34.4 oz. Limited mfg. mid-2000 only.

	$675	$550	$465	$415	$360	$300	$275	*$785*

Model 96G ELITE IA (BRIGADIER) – .40 S&W cal., similar to Model 96 Brigadier, except has 4.7 in. stainless barrel and many standard I.D.P.A. competition features including front and rear serrated slide, skeletonized hammer, and removable 3-dot sighting system, plastic grips, includes Elite engraving on slide. Mfg. 1999-2005.

	$725	$575	$480	$420	$350	$300	$275	*$875*

* ***Model 96G Elite II (Brigadier)*** – similar to Model 96G Elite, except has stainless steel slide with black "Elite II" markings, target barrel crown, extended mag. release, optimized trigger mechanism, front and back strap checkering, low profile Novak rear sight, 35.3 oz. Mfg. mid-2000-2005.

	$815	$625	$525	$450	$385	$325	$295	*$985*

MODEL 96G-SD – .40 S&W cal., similar to Model 92G, except has an integral accessory rail machined into frame in front of trigger guard, Bruniton finish, 10 shot mag., Tritium sights, 35.3 oz. Mfg. 2003-2005.

	$955	$725	$625	$525	$450	$400	$350	*$1,175*

MODEL 96 STEEL I – .40 S&W cal., single action only or SA/DA, plastic grips, features steel construction, nickel alloy frame, slim vertical grip, frame mounted safety, includes two 10 shot mags. Mfg. 2004-2005.

	$1,295	$1,140	$950	$825	$750	$675	$595	*$1,600*

MODEL 96 COMBAT – .40 S&W cal., single action only, similar to Model 96 Stock, except has factory tuned trigger, 4.9 (new 1998) or 5.9 in. barrel with weight and fully adj. rear target sight, aluminum or plastic grips. Mfg. in Italy 1997-2001.

	$1,350	$1,060	$900	$775	$625	$550	$495	*$1,735*

Add approx. $250 for 5.9 in. barrel (previously available as a Combat Combo).

MODEL 96 VERTEC – .40 S&W cal., single/double action, 4.9 in. barrel, straight backstrap grip, special short reach trigger, thin dual textured grip panels, and integral accessory rail on lower frame, removable front sight, beveled magwell, 10 shot mag., Bruniton finish, 32.2 oz. Mfg. 2002-2005.

	$635	$495	$440	$385	$340	$300	$275	*$760*

Add $25 for B-Lok safety system with key lock (mfg. 2003).

* ***Model 96 Vertec Stainless (Inox)*** – stainless variation of the Model 96 Vertec. Mfg. 2002-2005.

	$670	$530	$430	$365	$320	$260	$225	*$825*

Add $25 for B-Lok safety system with key lock (mfg. 2003).

MODEL 96 BLACK INOX – .40 S&W cal., single/double action, features black stainless slide and stippled finger groove plastic grips. Limited mfg. 2002 only.

	$610	$485	$390	$325	$285	$240	$210	*$734*

GRADING - PPGS™	100%	98%	95%	90%	80%	70%	60%	LAST MSR

MODEL 96 BORDER MARSHAL – .40 S&W cal., commercial equivalent of the I.N.S. (Immigration & Naturalization Service) government contract model, 4.7 in. barrel, heavy duty steel slide, Tritium sights, Border Marshal engraving on the slide. Mfg. 1999-2000.

	$670	$560	$480	$425	$375	$325	$295	*$802*

MODEL 96 BRIGADIER – .40 S&W cal., 4.9 in. barrel, similar to Model 96FS, except has heavier slide to reduce felt recoil, wraparound rubber grips, 3-dot sights, Bruniton matte black finish, 35.3 oz. Mfg. 1999-2005.

	$660	$510	$440	$385	$335	$300	$275	*$795*

* ***Model 96 Brigadier Stainless (Inox)*** – .40 S&W cal., similar to Model 96 Brigadier, except is stainless steel. Mfg. 2000-disc.

	$680	$530	$425	$360	$315	$260	$225	*$845*

MODEL 96 STOCK – .40 S&W cal., designed for practical shooting competition, includes accurized barrel bushing, 4.9 in. barrel, competition frame mounted ambidextrous safety, 3 interchangeable front sights, checkered front and back grip straps, aluminum grips, beveled magwell, cased with two mags. and tool kit, 35 oz. Mfg. 1997-1999, limited quantities remained into 2000.

	$1,200	$995	$865	$725	$600	$550	$495	*$1,407*

MODEL 96 CUSTOM CARRY – .40 S&W cal., 4.3 in. barrel, shortened grip, low profile control levers, left side only safety lever, blue only, 10 shot staggered mag., plastic grips. Mfg. 1999-2000.

	$550	$450	$400	$365	$335	$300	$275	*$655*

MODEL 96A1 – .40 S&W, DA/SA, 4.9 in. barrel, three 10 or 11 shot mags., removable front sight, frame accessory rail, internal recoil buffer, rounded trigger guard, captive recoil spring assembly, ambidextrous safety, black Bruniton finish, plastic grips, 34.4 oz, mfg. in Italy. New 2010.

MSR $729	$725	$635	$545	$495	$400	$325	$255	

REVOLVERS: SINGLE ACTION

Beretta's SAA revolvers were manufactured in Italy between 2005-2012 by Aldo Uberti & Co., S.r.l., which was purchased by Beretta in 2000.

LARAMIE – .38 Spl. or .45 LC cal., patterned after S&W Model 1870 Schofield, 5 or 6 1/2 in. barrel, 6 shot, blued finish with case colored hammer and trigger guard, smooth walnut grips with Beretta medallions, top-break, approx. 37-43 oz. Mfg. 2005-2008.

	$1,025	$795	$750	$650	$550	$475	$375	*$1,200*

Add $175 for nickel finish or 6 1/2 in. barrel.

STAMPEDE SAA – .357 Mag., .44-40 WCF (mfg. 2003), or .45 LC cal., patterned after the Colt SAA, transfer bar and half-cock safeties, 6 shot, 4 3/4, 5 1/2, or 7 1/2 (disc. 2010) in. barrel, various finishes, approx. 37 oz. Mfg. by Uberti beginning mid-2003.

* ***Stampede SAA Blue*** – features blue finish with case colored frame and black polymer grips. Disc. 2012.

	$495	$400	$340	$300	$270	$240	$220	*$600*

* ***Stampede SAA Brushed Nickel*** – .45 LC cal., features brushed nickel finish, smooth walnut grips with Beretta medallions, and fire blued frame screws. Disc. 2010.

	$515	$425	$350	$315	$285	$255	$230	*$625*

* ***Stampede SAA Old West*** – .357 Mag. (new 2008) or .45 LC (disc. 2010) cal., features distressed Old West finish, 4 3/4 (disc. 2010) or 5 1/2 in. barrel. Mfg. 2007-2011.

	$525	$465	$415	$365	$325	$280	$250	*$650*

* ***Stampede SAA Bisley*** – features Bisley styled grips/frame and raked hammer, blue or nickel finish. Mfg. 2005-2008.

	$515	$425	$350	$315	$285	$255	$230	*$650*

Add $50 for nickel finish.

* ***Stampede Buntline Carbine*** – .45 LC cal., 18 in. blue barrel, replica of the Buntline revolver, transfer bar safety, 6 shot, hooked trigger guard, brass crescent buttplate, satin walnut stock with gold Beretta medallions. Mfg. 2007-2008.

	$750	$650	$575	$500	$425	$350	$275	*$850*

* ***Stampede SAA Stainless (Inox)*** – .357 Mag. (new 2011), or .45 LC cal. only, features stainless steel construction, otherwise similar to Stampede. Mfg. 2004-2007, reintroduced 2011-2012.

	$495	$400	$340	$300	$270	$240	$220	*$600*

GRADING - PPGS™	100%	98%	95%	90%	80%	70%	60%	LAST MSR

* ***Stampede SAA Marshal*** – .357 Mag. (disc. 2010) or .45 LC cal., 3 1/2 in. barrel, bird's head grips, blue (disc. 2010) or Old West (.45 LC cal. only) finish. Mfg. 2004-2011.

	$525	$465	$415	$365	$325	$280	$250	*$650*

* ***Stampede SAA Deluxe*** – features charcoal blue metal finish, case colored frame and deluxe smooth walnut grips. Disc. 2010.

	$540	$465	$420	$365	$320	$275	$250	*$695*

* ***Stampede SAA Patton*** – .45 LC cal., features charcoal blue metal finish, engraved case colored frame, light gold accents, simulated ivory grips. Mfg. 2005-2006.

	$925	$800	$700	$600	$525	$450	$375	*$1,095*

This model was also available as a set - MSR was $2,190.

* ***Stamped SAA Matched Pairs*** – .45 LC cal. only, 5 1/2 in. barrel, case colored frame, wood grips with Beretta medallions, Philadelphia Centennial laser engraving (Philadelphia) or German silver trigger guard and backstrap (Gemini), paired serial numbers. Mfg. 2007-2008.

» **Stampede Gemini Matched Pair**

	$1,175	$1,025	$900	$800	$700	$650	$600	*$1,350*

» **Stampede Philadelphia Centennial Matched Pair**

	$1,775	$1,550	$1,325	$1,100	$950	$850	$750	*$2,100*

RIFLES: BOLT ACTION, RECENT MFG.

MODEL 500 CUSTOM – .222 Rem., .223 Rem., .243 Win., .270 Win., .30-06, or .308 Win. cal., 3 action lengths, 24 in. barrel, iron sights, checkered walnut stock with recoil pad. Importation was resumed 1988 only.

	$595	$530	$450	$395	$350	$315	$275	*$725*

Add 10%-15% for .223 Rem. cal.

* ***Model 500 S*** – similar to Model 500, except is equipped with iron sights. Imported 1986 only.

	$615	$560	$460	$400	$350	$315	$275	*$700*

* ***Model 500 DL*** – same specifications as Model 500, only better walnut and light engraving. Disc. 1986.

	$1,395	$1,260	$1,000	$875	$795	$725	$650	*$1,595*

Add 10%-15% for .223 Rem. cal.

* ***Model 500 DLS*** – similar to Model 500 DL, except is equipped with iron sights. Imported 1986 only.

	$1,420	$1,285	$1,020	$875	$795	$725	$650	*$1,625*

* ***Model 500 EELL*** – same specifications as Model 500 DL, only select walnut and more engraving. Disc. 1986.

	$1,550	$1,260	$1,150	$1,000	$875	$800	$725	*$1,745*

Add 10%-15% for .223 Rem. cal.

* ***Model 500 EELLS*** – similar to Model 500 EELL, except is equipped with iron sights. Imported 1986 only.

	$1,575	$1,425	$1,200	$1,120	$875	$800	$725	*$1,785*

MODEL 501 – .243 Win. or .308 Win. cal., Sako medium length receiver, 6 shot, 23 in. barrel, no sights, checkered walnut stock. Disc. 1986.

	$595	$530	$465	$395	$350	$315	$275	*$665*

* ***Model 501 S*** – similar to Model 501, except is equipped with iron sights. Imported 1986 only.

	$615	$560	$460	$400	$350	$315	$275	*$700*

* ***Model 501 DL*** – same specifications as Model 501, only better walnut and light engraving. Disc. 1986.

	$1,395	$1,260	$1,000	$875	$795	$725	$650	*$1,575*

* ***Model 501 DLS*** – similar to Model 501 DL, except is equipped with iron sights. Imported 1986 only.

	$1,420	$1,285	$1,020	$875	$795	$725	$650	*$1,625*

* ***Model 501 EELL*** – same specifications as Model 501 DL, only select walnut and more engraving. Disc. 1986.

	$1,550	$1,260	$1,150	$1,000	$875	$800	$725	*$1,745*

* ***Model 501 EELLS*** – similar to Model 501 EELL, except is equipped with iron sights. Imported 1986 only.

	$1,575	$1,425	$1,200	$1,120	$875	$800	$725	*$1,785*

MODEL 502 – .30-06, .270, or 7mm Rem. Mag. cal., Sako long action receiver, 5 or 6 shot, 24 in. barrel, no sights, checkered walnut stock. Disc. 1986.

	$625	$565	$490	$440	$395	$360	$330	*$710*

* ***Model 502 S*** – similar to Model 502, except is equipped with iron sights. Imported 1986 only.

	$650	$595	$525	$460	$395	$360	$330	*$745*

GRADING - PPGS™	100%	98%	95%	90%	80%	70%	60%	LAST MSR

* ***Model 502 DL*** – same specifications as Model 502, only better walnut and light engraving. Also available in .375 H&H Mag. Disc. 1986.

	$1,495	$1,310	$1,175	$1,025	$900	$775	$695	*$1,640*

* ***Model 502 DLS*** – similar to Model 502, except is equipped with iron sights. Imported 1986 only.

	$1,410	$1,325	$1,175	$1,025	$900	$775	$695	*$1,660*

* ***Model 502 EELL*** – same specifications as Model 502 DL, only select walnut and more engraving. Also available in .375 H&H Mag. Disc. 1986.

	$1,575	$1,425	$1,200	$1,120	$875	$800	$725	*$1,785*

* ***Model 502 EELLS*** – similar to Model 502 EELL, except is equipped with iron sights. Imported 1986 only.

	$1,575	$1,425	$1,200	$1,120	$875	$800	$725	*$1,785*

MATO SYNTHETIC – .270 Win., .280 Rem., .30-06, .300 Win. Mag., .338 Win. Mag., .375 H&H, or 7mm Rem. Mag. cal., 23.6 in. barrel, composite black synthetic stock with integral bedding block, Mauser 98 action with controlled round feeding, 3-position safety, ergonomic bolt handle, 3 or 4 shot detachable box mag., adj. trigger, black satin metal finish, 8 lbs. Mfg. in the U.S. 1997-2002.

	$975	$825	$750	$675	$575	$495	$400	*$1,117*

Add $357 for .375 H&H cal. (includes muzzle brake and iron sights).

Add 20%-40% for Dakota action and Krieger barrel, depending on original condition.

The first 200 rifles manufactured had Dakota actions with Krieger barrels.

* ***Mato Deluxe*** – same cals. as the standard model, features deluxe checkered walnut with ebony forend tip, cased, 7.9 lbs. Mfg. 1997-2002.

	$2,025	$1,575	$1,150	$995	$825	$675	$600	*$2,470*

Add $325 for .375 H&H cal. (includes muzzle brake and iron sights).

* ***Mato Deluxe Safari Grade*** – .375 H&H cal. only, elaborately hand engraved with best quality wood. Available through Beretta Premium dealers only. Disc. 2002.

	$14,750	$12,500	$10,250	$8,000	$6,750	$5,500	$4,350	*$16,500*

RIFLES: LEVER ACTION

1873 RENEGADE SHORT RIFLE – .357 Mag. or .45 LC cal., patterned after the Winchester Model 1873 rifle, case colored frame, 20 in. octagon barrel, 10 shot full mag., uncheckered straight grip walnut stock and forearm. Mfg. 2008-2011.

	$1,150	$925	$750	$650	$525	$425	$375	*$1,350*

MODEL 1876 RIFLE – .45-75 WCF cal., 28 in. octagon barrel with full mag., case colored receiver. Ltd. mfg. 2008.

	$1,350	$1,125	$900	$775	$675	$575	$500	*$1,625*

RIFLES: SEMI-AUTO, RECENT MFG.

BM-59 M-1 GARAND – with original Beretta M1 receiver, M-14 style detachable mag., only 200 imported into the U.S.

	$3,200	$2,900	$2,400	$1,800	$1,500	$1,300	$1,175	*$2,080*

BM-62 – similar to BM-59, except has flash suppressor and is Italian marked.

	$3,200	$2,900	$2,400	$1,800	$1,500	$1,300	$1,175	

AR-70 – .222 Rem. or .223 Rem. cal., 5, 8, or 30 shot mag., diopter sights, epoxy finish, 17.72 in. barrel, 8.3 lbs.

	$1,925	$1,675	$1,375	$1,150	$1,025	$850	$750	*$1,065*

1989 Federal legislation banned the importation of this model into U.S.

ARX 100 – 5.56 NATO cal., lightweight techno-polymer receiver, no pins, matte black or FDE (new 2016) finish, 16 in. quick change cold hammer forged barrel with flash suppressor, can be removed and replaced with various lengths and calibers in a matter of seconds, 30 shot mag., ambidextrous magazine release, accepts AR magazines, case projection can be switched from right to left with a simple push of a button, telescoping folding stock, ambidextrous safety selector, all critical controls are ambidextrous, quad Picatinny rails with full-length upper. Mfg. in the U.S. mid-2013-2017.

	$1,650	$1,000	$795	$595	$495	$425	$395	*$1,950*

ARX 160 – .22 LR cal., 18.1 in. barrel with flash suppressor, 10 (new 2014), 14 (mfg. 2013 only), or 20 (new 2014) shot STANAG-Type mag., matte black finish, quad Picatinny rails with full-length upper, polymer flip-up sights, adj. folding stock, pistol grip, ambidextrous safety lever and mag. release, 6 lbs. 6 oz. Imported 2013-2016.

	$375	$295	$250	$200	$175	$150	$125	*$575*

GRADING - PPGS™	100%	98%	95%	90%	80%	70%	60%	LAST MSR

CX4 STORM CARBINE – 9mm Para. (92 Carbine), .40 S&W (96 Carbine) or .45 ACP (8045 Carbine, disc. 2013.) cal., blowback single action, Giugiaro design featuring tactical styling with one-piece matte black synthetic stock with thumbhole, rubber recoil pad and stock cheekpiece, quad Picatinny rails, ghost ring sights, 16.6 in. hammer forged barrel, reversible crossbolt safety, mag. button, bolt handle, and ejection port, mag. capacities vary depending on caliber, current mfg. has 8 (.45 ACP cal.), 14 (.40 S&W cal., Px4 Storm mag.), 15 (9mm Para. with high cap Model 92 mag.), or 17 (high cap PX4 Storm mag.) shot mag., (this series also accepts Models 96, 8000, 8040, and 8045 pistol mags.), 29.7 in. overall length, 5 3/4 lbs. Mfg. mid-2003-2014, reintroduced 2017-2018.

	$680	$595	$510	$450	$375	$300	$250	*$800*

Add $95 for 92 Carbine package (includes scope, 9mm Para. (disc. 2005) or .40 S&W cal.). Disc.
Add $50 for top rail (only available in 9mm Para. or .40 S&W cal., mfg. 2006-2007).

This model has been available in many variations - 8045 (.45 ACP), 92 Carbine (8000, 9mm Para.), 92 Carbine package (w/scope), and 96 Carbine (8040, .40 S&W).

RX4 STORM CARBINE – .223 Rem. cal., ARGO, gas operating system, available in collapsible five position telescoping stock or sporter style stock with optional pistol grip, black matte finish, ghost ring sights, includes 5 and 10 shot AR-15 style magazines. Limited importation 2007-2008.

	$1,100	$925	$800	$700	$600	$525	$450	*$1,100*

While advertised, only a few samples were brought into the U.S.

RIFLES: O/U, CUSTOM

Current high grade Beretta O/U and SxS rifles are sold only by premium grade franchised Beretta dealers. For a listing of these dealers, contact a Beretta Gallery.

S686/S689 SILVER SABLE – .30-06, 9.3x74R, or .444 Marlin cal. (disc. 1995), boxlock action, single or double (special order only) triggers. Imported 1995-2014.

	$4,000	$3,500	$3,000	$2,700	$2,200	$2,000	$1,800	*$4,200*

Add $500 for 9.3x74R cal.

S689 GOLD SABLE – 9.3x74R or .30-06 cal., boxlock action, nickel (disc. 1985) or case hardened (new 1986) receiver, double triggers, 23 in. barrels, auto ejectors, sling swivels, 7.7 lbs. Disc.

	$7,750	$6,500	$5,250	$4,250	$3,300	$2,750	$2,500	*$9,000*

Add $500 for 9.3x74R cal.
Add approx. $4,500 for scope and quick detachable claw mounts.

S686/S689 EELL DIAMOND SABLE – .30-06, 9.3x74R, or .444 Marlin cal., moderate engraving. New 1995.

This model is POR/special order only. Last published MSR was $12,750.
Add $1,250 for an extra set of 20 ga. barrels with forearm (disc. 2011).
Add approx. $4,500 for scope and quick detachable claw mounts.

SSO EXPRESS – .375 H&H or .458 Win. Mag. cal., sidelock action, case hardened receiver, double triggers, 23 in. barrels, auto ejectors, 11 lbs., cased. Importation disc. 1989.

	$23,500	$15,750	$13,000	$10,500	$8,500	$7,250	$6,500	*$17,533*

SSO5 EXPRESS – similar to SSO Express except has more elaborate engraving and better walnut.

	$23,500	$18,500	$16,250	$14,250	$11,750	$8,750	$7,500	*$19,600*

SSO6 EXPRESS CUSTOM SIDELOCK – 9.3x74R, .375 H&H, or .458 Win. Mag. cal., next to top-of-the-line sidelock double rifle, individually built to the customer's specifications, cased. Mfg. 1990-circa 2014.

Last MSR on this model was $75,000.
Add $12,000 for extra set of barrels.
Add approx. $4,000 for scope mounts for Zeiss 4x32mm scope.

* ***SS06 EELL Gold Custom*** – same cals. as SS06 Express, features multiple gold inlays and best quality wood. Disc.

The last MSR on this model was $125,000.
Add $12,000 for extra set of barrels.
Add approx. $25,000-$45,000 for upgraded master engraving.
Add approx. $4,500 for scope mounts for Zeiss 4x32mm scope.

RIFLES: SxS, CUSTOM

455 SIDE-BY-SIDE – .375 H&H, .416 Rigby, .458 Win. Mag., .470 NE, or .500 3 in. NE cal., top of the line sidelock double rifle, individually built to the customer's specifications, color case hardened (new 2010), cased. Mfg. 1990-disc.

The last MSR range on this model was $100,000 to $125,000, depending on amount of engraving and the engraver.
Add approx. $2,000 for scope mounts for Zeiss 4x32mm scope.

GRADING - PPGS™	100%	98%	95%	90%	80%	70%	60%	LAST MSR

* ***455 EELL*** – similar cals. as Model 455 SxS, top-of-the-line custom sidelock double rifle featuring every refinement of the gunmaker's art, cased.

Last published MSR range on this model was $125,000 to $175,000, depending on amount of engraving and the engraver.
Add approx. $3,500 for scope mounts for Zeiss 4x32mm scope.

RIFLES: SLIDE ACTION

GOLD RUSH CARBINE/RIFLE – .357 Mag. or .45 LC cal., patterned after Colt Lightning model with improved feeding system and hammer block safety, 20 (carbine), 24 1/4, or 26 (mfg. 2005) in. round or octagon barrel, 10-15 shot full mag., case colored receiver, blued barrel/mag. tube, checkered straight grip stock with Beretta medallions and forearm, adj. sights, 6 1/2-7 1/2 lbs. Imported 2005-2008.

$1,325	$1,150	$1,025	$875	$750	$625	$525	*$1,375*

Add 30-40% for deluxe model with oil finished deluxe walnut stock with fish scale checking, charcoal blued barrel and mag. tube, and jeweled hammer.
Add 5% for rifle configuration.

SHOTGUNS: O/U, DISC.

Beretta discontinued O/U Models/Variations 682, 685, 686, 687, Onyx Pro, Whitewing, and Blackwing can be found in the Shotguns: O/U, Field - Recent Mfg. category.

BL-1 – 12 ga., 26, 28, or 30 in. barrels with fixed chokes, blued receiver/barrel finish, boxlock, extractors, double triggers, checkered pistol grip stock, approx. 7 lbs. Mfg. 1968-73.

$395	$350	$300	$250	$200	$150	$125

BL-2 – similar to BL-1, except with single selective trigger, more engraving.

$400	$375	$325	$275	$250	$200	$150

BL-2 STAKE-OUT – riot configuration with 18 in. barrels, DT, blue finish, approx. 6,000 mfg.

$395	$350	$295	$260	$230	$200	$180

BL-2/S – similar to BL-2, with vent. rib and speed trigger. Mfg. 1974-76.

$500	$450	$400	$350	$300	$250	$200

BL-3 – also available in 20 or 28 ga., blued receiver/barrel finish, similar to BL-2, with more engraving and vent. rib., 6-7 1/4 lbs. Mfg. 1968-1976.

$600	$550	$500	$450	$400	$350	$300

Add 100% for 28 ga., if original condition is 90%+.
Add 20% for 20 ga., if original condition is 20%+.

BL-3 SKEET	$600	$550	$500	$450	$400	$350	$275

Subtract 10% for 26 in. barrels.

BL-3 TRAP	$550	$475	$400	$350	$300	$275	$225

BL-4 – 12, 20, or 28 ga., 3 in. chambers (12 and 20 ga. only), blued receiver/barrel finish, deluxe version of BL-3, more engraving, better wood, and ejectors, 6-7 1/4 lbs.

$850	$700	$600	$450	$375	$325	$275

Add 50% for 20 ga. Add 100% for 28 ga.

BL-4 SKEET	$700	$650	$500	$400	$350	$300	$250

Subtract 10% for 26 in. barrels.

BL-4 TRAP	$600	$550	$500	$425	$350	$300	$250

BL-5 – 12, 20, or 28 ga., higher grade version of BL-4 with more engraving, matte grey receiver with blued barrels, full pistol grip stock.

$900	$775	$675	$600	$500	$450	$400

Add 10% for 20 ga. Add 100% for 28 ga.

BL-5 SKEET	$875	$750	$650	$575	$475	$425	$375

Subtract 10% for 26 in. barrels.

BL-5 TRAP	$875	$750	$650	$575	$475	$425	$375

BL-6 – 12, 20, or 28 ga., boxlock with coin finished scroll engraved sideplates, deluxe checkered walnut stock with full pistol grip and slender forearm, ejectors, SST.

$1,395	$1,175	$925	$825	$725	$625	$525

Add 50% for 20 ga. Add 100% for 28 ga.

GRADING - PPGS™	100%	98%	95%	90%	80%	70%	60%	LAST MSR
BL-6 SKEET	$1,200	$1,025	$875	$750	$650	$575	$500	

Subtract 10% for 26 in. barrels.

BL-6 TRAP	$1,200	$1,025	$875	$750	$650	$575	$500	

MODEL S55 B – 12 or 20 ga., 26, 28, or 30 in. barrels, various chokes, boxlock, extractors, selective trigger, checkered pistol grip stock. Disc.

$550 $500 $475 $440 $385 $330 $300

Add 10% for 20 ga.

MODEL S56 E – similar to S55B, with engraved receiver and auto ejectors. Disc.

$750 $700 $675 $650 $600 $550 $500

Add 20% for 20 ga., if original condition is 90%+.

MODEL S58 SKEET – similar to S56E, with 26 in. Bohler steel barrels, skeet bore, wide vent. rib.

$775 $725 $650 $550 $495 $445 $395

Subtract 10% for 26 in. barrels.

MODEL S58 TRAP – similar to S58 Skeet, with 30 in. barrels, imp. mod. and full choke, Monte Carlo stock with pad.

$700 $600 $500 $450 $400 $350 $300

SILVER SNIPE – 12, 20, or 28 ga., 26, 28, or 30 in. barrels, boxlock, extractors, checkered pistol grip stock. Mfg. 1955-1967.

$650 $575 $525 $475 $450 $425 $400

Add 50% for 20 ga.
Add 100% for 28 ga.

* ***Silver Snipe SST*** – with vent. rib and SST.

$850 $750 $675 $595 $550 $495 $425

Add 50% for 20 ga.
Add 25% for ejectors.
Add 25% for 28 ga.

GOLDEN SNIPE – similar to Silver Snipe, with auto ejectors and vent. rib standard.

$900 $800 $700 $600 $550 $500 $425

Add 10% for 20 ga.
Add 100% for 28 ga.

* ***Golden Snipe SST*** – with SST.

$1,075 $900 $800 $700 $600 $550 $500

Add 10% for 20 ga.
Add 100% for 28 ga.

MODEL (S)57 E – higher quality version of Golden Snipe. Mfg. 1955-1967.

$900 $800 $700 $600 $550 $500 $425

Add 10% for 20 ga.
Add 100% for 28 ga.

* ***Model (S)57 E SST*** – with single selective trigger.

$1,075 $900 $800 $700 $600 $550 $500

Add 10% for 20 ga.
Add 100% for 28 ga.

ASE MODEL – 12 or 20 ga., light border scroll engraving, mfg. approx. 1947-1964.

12 ga.	$2,025	$1,700	$1,450	$1,225	$1,000	$825	$650
20 ga.	$2,975	$2,600	$2,200	$1,800	$1,550	$1,275	$975

ASEL MODEL – 12 or 20 ga., 26, 28, or 30 in. barrels, various chokes, single trigger, receiver moderately engraved, checkered pistol grip stock, auto ejectors. Mfg. 1947-1964.

12 ga.	$3,850	$3,250	$2,650	$2,000	$1,700	$1,450	$1,275
20 ga.	$5,750	$4,850	$4,250	$3,750	$2,850	$2,400	$1,925

ASEELL MODEL – 12 or 20 ga., full coverage engraving, rare, very limited mfg.

12 ga.	$5,750	$4,900	$4,275	$3,500	$2,800	$2,350	$1,900
20 ga.	$8,975	$7,750	$6,650	$5,750	$5,000	$4,250	$3,500

GRADE 100 – 12 ga., 26, 28, or 30 in. barrels, any choke, sidelock, double trigger, auto ejectors, checkered pistol grip or straight stock.

$1,550 $1,300 $1,100 $900 $775 $695 $575

GRADING - PPGS™	100%	98%	95%	90%	80%	70%	60%	LAST MSR

MODEL 200 – similar to 100, with chrome-lined bores and action parts, higher quality engraving.

	$2,000	$1,875	$1,650	$1,375	$1,100	$875	$750	

MODEL 680 – 12 ga. only, competition trap and skeet model, boxlock, various chokes, mono-trap model available, silver finish receiver, hand engraved, premium walnut. Disc.

	$900	$850	$800	$700	$600	$550	$500	

Add approx. $300 for 2 barrel combo. package.

SHOTGUNS: O/U, FIELD - CURRENT / RECENT MFG.

All models listed in this category are field grade configuration regardless of model nomenclature.

All currently manufactured Berettas in this category include hardshell cases.

BERETTA CHOKES AND THEIR CODES (ON REAR LEFT-SIDE OF BARREL)

*** designates full choke (F).**

**** designates improved modified choke (IM).**

***** designates modified choke (M).**

****** designates improved cylinder choke (IC).**

******* designates cylinder bore (CYL).**

SK designates skeet (SK).

QUICK REFERENCE GUIDE FOR CURRENT CHOKES

MC3 - includes three Mobilchokes. MC6 - includes six Mobilchokes. MCF - Mobilchoke Field. MCS - Mobilechoke Sport. MCS2 - Mobilechoke Sport 2. OBF - Optima Bore Field. OBF-HP - Optima Bore Field. OBSP - Optima Bore Sporting. OBS - Optima Bore Sport. OBSK - Optima Bore Skeet. OBTR - Optima Bore Trap. OBTS - Optima Bore Trap Single. OCF - Optima Choke Field. OBSP-HP - Optima Bore Sporting HP (5), OBHPe - Optima HP Sporting (3), OBF-HP - Optima HP Field (5), OBF-HP3 - Optima HP FIeld (3), OBF-HP-486 - 18.4mm Optima HP Field (3).

During 2003, Beretta introduced X-Tra Wood on stocks and forearms of select models. X-Tra Wood is a patented and exclusive Beretta wood enhancement finish where average wood is encapsulated with a waterproof film which resembles best quality Circassian walnut. Normal checkering is possible, and all X-Tra Wood stocks are marked clearly on the bottom of the pistol grip cap. It can also be refinished through a special refinishing program available with Beretta USA.

Note: values are for unaltered guns.

Subtract 20% on the following factory multi-choke models if w/o newer Beretta OptimaChokes where applicable (some models only).

MODEL 685 – 12 or 20 ga. 2 3/4 or 3 in. chambers, matte finished chromed receiver, extractors, single trigger. Disc. 1986.

	$600	$550	$485	$440	$360	$320	$295	*$875*

MODEL 686 ONYX – please refer to Ultralight 687. The 686 Onyx model designation was changed to the Ultralight 687 circa 1997.

MODEL 686 WHITE ONYX FIELD (ONYX) – 12, 20, or 28 (new 2003) ga., 2 3/4 (28 ga. only) or 3 in. chambers, boxlock action, 26 or 28 in. barrels with MobilChokes, matte blue metal (disc. 2003) or Dura-Jewel satin nickel alloy (new 2003, became standard 2004) frame, choice of left (disc.) or right-hand standard pistol grip or English straight (disc. 1999) stock with gloss (new 1999), matte (disc. 2003) or X-Tra (standard beginning 2004) wood finish, single trigger, ejectors, approx. 6.2 or 6.8 lbs. Mfg. 1988-2012.

	$1,850	$1,400	$1,250	$1,100	$900	$750	$600	*$2,240*

Add $154 for deluxe wood upgrade (mfg. 2001-2002, included case).
Subtract 10% for matte blue finish.

* ***Model 686 White Onyx Waterfowler Magnum*** – 12 ga. only, similar to Model S686 Onyx, except has 3 1/2 in. chambers, 28 in. barrels only, matte wood and metal finish. Mfg. 1993, reintroduced 1996-2003.

	$1,400	$1,200	$1,000	$800	$650	$525	$450	*$1,648*

* ***Model 686 Onyx Essential*** – 12 ga. only, 3 in. chambers, 26 or 28 in. VR separated barrels with choke tubes, checkered high-gloss walnut stock and forearm, matte finished metal, 6.7 lbs. Mfg. 1994-96.

	$835	$735	$600	$500	$400	$350	$300	*$1,186*

Subtract 10% for 26 in. barrels.

GRADING - PPGS™	100%	98%	95%	90%	80%	70%	60%	LAST MSR

* ***Model S686 Onyx Silver Essential*** – 12 ga. only, 3 in. chambers, 26 or 28 in. VR separated barrels with choke tubes, checkered matte finished walnut stock and forearm, chrome matte finished receiver, 6.7 lbs. Imported 1997-1998 only.

$835	$735	$600	$500	$400	$350	$300	*$1,070*

Subtract 10% for 26 in. barrels.

* ***Model 686 Onyx Quail Unlimited Covey Limited Edition*** – 12 (disc. 2002), 20, or 28 (new 2003) ga., similar to Model 686 Onyx, except includes 6 quail inlays in 24Kt. gold on receiver sides and Quail Unlimited logo on bottom of receiver, marked "1 of 750," deluxe checkered high gloss stock and forearm, cased with 5 choke tubes, 750 of each ga. Mfg. 2002-2004.

$1,600	$1,500	$1,400	$1,200	$1,000	$800	$600	*$2,000*

This model was available through Beretta Showcase Dealers only.

* ***Model 686 Onyx Ringneck Pheasants Forever Limited Edition*** – 12 or 20 ga., similar to Onyx Model 686 Quail Unlimited, except includes multiple ringneck pheasant inlays in 24Kt. gold on receiver sides and Pheasants Forever logo on bottom of receiver, marked "1 of 750," deluxe checkered high gloss stock and forearm, cased with 5 choke tubes, 750 of each ga. Mfg. 2003-2004.

$1,600	$1,500	$1,400	$1,200	$1,000	$800	$600	*$2,027*

MODEL 686 ONYX PRO FIELD – 12 (3 in. chambers), 20, or 28 ga., boxlock action, 30 or 32 in. VR barrels with extended OptimaChoke tubes on 12 ga., flush choke tubes on 20 and 28 ga., gold trigger, oil finished checkered Gr. 3 Turkish walnut stock and Schnabel forearm, "P. Beretta" in gold on receiver sides, high luster bluing on receiver and barrels, 6 1/2-7 1/2 lbs. Mfg. 2017-2018.

$2,800	$2,400	$2,250	$2,000	$1,775	$1,525	$1,175	*$3,100*

* ***Model 686 Onyx Pro Field Small Ga. Combo*** – includes both 20 and 28 ga. barrels, 30 in. VR barrels with flush mounted choke tubes, cased. Mfg. 2017-2018.

$3,950	$3,350	$3,150	$2,900	$1,995	$1,650	$1,275	*$4,300*

ULTRALIGHT 687 (686/ONYX) – 12 ga. only, 2 3/4 in. chambers, Ergal alloy receiver reinforced with titanium plate, electroless nickel finish receiver with game scene engraving (new 1998, restyled 2002 with several gold inlays) or matte black finish on receiver (disc. 1997), 26 (disc. 2001) or 28 in. VR barrels, choice of English (new 2001) straight or pistol grip checkered walnut stock and forearm, matte (new 2001, restyled) or gloss wood finish, choke tubes, gilded lettering and logo (disc. 1997), gold SST, ejectors, very lightweight, 5 lbs. 11 oz. Imported 1992-2011.

$1,850	$1,675	$1,275	$950	$800	$700	$600	*$2,175*

Add approx. $150 for deluxe wood upgrade (includes case, mfg. 2001 only).
Subtract approx. 10%-15% if with matte black finish, depending on condition.

This model is discontinued as a 686 Series.

* ***Ultralight Deluxe (Onyx)*** – 12 ga. only, 2 3/4 in. chambers, similar to 1998 Model 686 Ultralight, except has gold game scene engraving and select walnut stock and forearm, 28 in. barrels. Mfg. 1998-2013.

$2,290	$1,700	$1,550	$1,450	$1,250	$1,000	$800	*$2,550*

ONYX PRO – 12, 20, or 28 ga., 2 3/4 (28 ga. only) or 3 in. chambers, matte blue finish with Dura-Jewel treatment on receiver, X-Tra wood finish on stock and forearm, Gel-Tek recoil pad, gold trigger, TruGlo sights, includes case and 5 choke tubes, 6.8 lbs. (12 ga.). Imported 2003-2006.

$1,100	$900	$800	$700	$650	$575	$500	*$1,875*

* ***Onyx Pro 3.5*** – 12 ga., 3 1/2 in. chambers, otherwise similar to Onyx Pro, 6.9 lbs. Imported 2003-2006.

$1,150	$950	$850	$750	$700	$625	$595	*$1,975*

WHITEWING – 12 or 20 ga., 3 in. chambers, 26 or 28 in. separated VR barrels and MC3 choke tubes, similar to Model 686 Silver Essential, except has checkered gloss finish walnut stock and silver polished receiver with game scene engraving, 6.7 lbs. Mfg. 1999-2003.

$1,200	$1,100	$1,000	$875	$750	$700	$600	*$1,332*

BLACKWING – similar to Whitewing, except has matte black receiver finish, lower stock dimensions, and Schnabel forearm. Mfg. 2002-2003.

$1,200	$1,100	$1,000	$875	$750	$700	$600	*$1,332*

MODEL 686(L) SILVER PERDIZ – 12 (disc. 1990), 20 (disc. 1990), or 28 ga., field model, boxlock action, various barrels/ chokes, ejectors, single trigger, engraved silver finished receiver, special walnut, pistol or straight grip stock, fixed chokes disc. 1987. Importation disc. 1994.

$1,200	$1,100	$1,000	$875	$750	$700	$600	*$1,355*

Subtract 20% with fixed chokes (disc.).
Add 20% for 20 ga., or 30% for 28 ga.

GRADING - PPGS™ 100% 98% 95% 90% 80% 70% 60% LAST MSR

MODEL 686 SILVER PIGEON S & SILVER PIGEON (SILVER PERDIZ) – 12, 20, 28 (mfg. 1995-2001, reintroduced 2004) ga. or .410 bore (new 2005), 3 in. chambers (except for 28 ga.), 26 or 28 in. VR barrels with choke tubes, choice of polished (new 1999) or regular nickel finished receiver with scroll engraving, gold trigger, gloss finish checkered pistol grip or straight grip (disc. 1999) walnut stock and forearm, supplied with carrying case, 5 choke tubes, recoil pad and sling swivels beginning 2004, includes hardshell case, 6.8 lbs. Mfg. 1992-2008.

$1,850 $1,600 $1,500 $1,400 $1,200 $1,100 $1,000 *$2,450*

Add $153 for deluxe wood upgrade (Silver Pigeon only, 12 or 20 ga. only, includes case, mfg. 2001-2002).

During 1996, the model nomenclature was changed from the Silver Perdiz to the Silver Pigeon.

* ***Model 686 Silver Pigeon S King Ranch*** – 20 or 28 ga. only, similar to Model 686 Silver Pigeon, except features special cowboy and western engraving motifs. Mfg. 2006-2010.

$2,500 $2,200 $1,750 $1,500 $1,150 $900 $775 *$2,800*

* ***Model 686 Silver Pigeon S (Silver Perdiz) and 686 Silver Pigeon Combo*** – similar to Model 686 Onyx, except is supplied with 1 set each of 20 ga. (28 in.) and 28 ga. (26 in.) barrels, includes carrying case, 5 choke tubes, recoil pad, and sling swivels, polished receiver became standard 1999. Mfg. 1986-2008.

$2,775 $2,415 $1,900 $1,600 $1,250 $1,000 $875 *$3,175*

Subtract 10% for 26 in. barrels.

MODEL 686 SILVER PIGEON I – 12, 20 (new 2012), 28 (new 2012) ga. or .410 (new 2012) bore 3 in. chambers, 26, 28, or 30 in. VR barrels with 3 MobilChokes, coin finished receiver, checkered oil-finished stock and Schnabel forearm, SST, ejectors. New 2011.

MSR $2,099 $1,800 $1,550 $1,350 $1,200 $1,000 $800 $700

* ***Model S686 Silver Pigeon I Combo*** – choice of 28 in. 20 and 28 ga. barrels or 28 ga/.410 bore barrels. New 2012.

MSR $3,299 $2,800 $2,450 $2,100 $1,900 $1,550 $1,275 $1,100

MODEL S686 EL GOLD PERDIZ – 12 or 20 ga., 3 in. chambers, boxlock action with floral scroll engraved sideplates, silver receiver finish, 26 or 28 (20 ga. only beginning 1997) in. VR barrels with choke tubes, gold SST, checkered walnut stock and forearm, cased, approx. 6.8 lbs. Mfg. 1992-1997.

$1,600 $1,425 $1,200 $1,000 $875 $800 $695 *$1,930*

Add 10% for 20 ga.
Subtract 10% for 26 in. barrels.

MODEL S687(L) SILVER PIGEON – 12 (disc. 1999) or 20 ga., 3 in. chambers, boxlock, various barrels/chokes, ejectors, game scene engraved nickel finished receiver, gloss finished select walnut stock and forearm, approx. 6.8 lbs., fitted case was optional. Disc. 2000.

$1,600 $1,425 $1,200 $1,000 $875 $750 $695 *$2,255*

Subtract 30% without MobilChokes (disc.).
Subtract 10% for 26 in. barrels.

The "L" suffix model nomenclature was disc. 1996.

MODEL S687 SILVER PIGEON II – 12 or 20 ga., similar to Model S687 Silver Pigeon, except has deep relief engraved game scenes on receiver sides and oil finished (matte) walnut stock and forearm, 26 or 28 in. VR barrels with MC3 choke tubes. Mfg. 1999-2011.

$2,130 $1,900 $1,800 $1,650 $1,500 $1,250 $1,000 *$3,050*

* ***Model S687 Silver Pigeon II Combo*** – includes 1 set each of 28 ga. and 20 ga. with 28 in. barrels, cased with 5 choke tubes. Imported 2003-2010.

$3,400 $2,750 $2,275 $1,900 $1,600 $1,400 $1,200 *$4,050*

MODEL 687 SILVER PIGEON III – 12 (disc. 2014), 20, or 28 ga., 26 or 28 in. VR barrels with MobileChokes, engraved boxlock action with game scenes, select checkered walnut stock and forearm, Gel-Tek recoil pad, gold SST, golden Beretta medallion on bottom of receiver, German silver stock oval for owner initials, TruGlo front sight, 6.8 lbs. Mfg. 2004-2017.

$2,675 $2,100 $1,950 $1,750 $1,600 $1,500 $1,250 *$3,425*

A left-hand variation was disc. in 2007.

MODEL 687 SILVER PIGEON III (CURRENT MFG.) – 12, 20, 28 ga., or .410 bore, 2 3/4 or 3 in. chamber, 26, 28, or 30 in. Steelium Optima Bore HP tri-alloy barrels, OBHP or MC chokes, gold SST, finely checkered walnut pistol grip stock and forend with gloss finish, MicroCore buttpad, silver receiver features fine engraving with floral motifs and game scenes highlighted with pheasants and partridges, gloss finish. New 2020.

MSR $2,699 $2,295 $2,010 $1,720 $1,560 $1,275 $1,100 $900

GRADING - PPGS™	100%	98%	95%	90%	80%	70%	60%	LAST MSR

MODEL 687 SILVER PIGEON IV – 12, 20, or 28 ga., 2 3/4 (28 ga. only) or 3 in. chambers, black metal finished receiver with full coverage scroll engraving and 4 gold bird inlays, 26 or 28 in. barrels, checkered oil finished walnut stock with Gel-Tek recoil pad, TruGlo front sight, includes molded case with 5 choke tubes, 6.8 lbs. (12 ga.). Imported 2003-2008. Reintroduced 2014 only.

$3,150 $2,900 $2,750 $2,500 $2,100 $1,700 $1,400 *$3,700*

* ***Model 687 Silver Pigeon IV King Ranch*** – 20 or 28 ga., similar to Model 687 Silver Pigeon IV, except has special cowboy and western engraving motifs. Mfg. 2006-2009.

$3,375 $2,875 $2,175 $1,800 $1,400 $1,050 $875 *$3,375*

MODEL 687 SILVER PIGEON V – 12 (disc. 2017), 20 (disc. 2017), 28 ga., or .410 bore (new 2005), 26 or 28 in. barrels, gold SST, upgraded select oil finished checkered straight grip English or pistol grip walnut stock and forearm, Gel-Tek recoil pad, Schnabel forend, case colored finished receiver with gold bird inlays, case colored finish receiver, 6.8 lbs. Mfg. 2004-2019.

$3,325 $2,950 $2,800 $2,650 $2,500 $2,200 $1,900 *$4,075*

MODEL 687 DU – 12 (1990 release) or 20 ga., mfg. for DU dinner gun auctions and membership, prices may vary significantly from region to region.

$1,200 $1,050 $925 $800 $700 $575 $475

Add 10% for 20 ga.

MODEL 687 BLACK & GOLD TERCENTENNIAL – 12 ga. only, 2 3/4 in. chambers, 28 in. barrels with fixed F/M chokes, bottom of blued receiver features special 1680-1980 Tercentennial logo, inlaid (with gold) and engraved by Giovanelli (signed), ser. no. 001-300.

$2,150 $1,875 $1,625 $1,450 $1,175 $975 $750

MODEL 687 TERCENTENNIAL COMMEMORATIVE – 12 ga. only, 2 3/4 in. chambers, 28 in. barrels, engraved and signed by Giovanelli, with ducks and woodcocks on sides of grey finished frame, oil finished walnut stock and forearm, ser. no. 001-200.

$2,150 $1,875 $1,625 $1,450 $1,175 $975 $750

MODEL 687 L ONYX – 12 or 20 ga., 3 in. chambers, same game scene engraving as standard Model 687 L, except has Onyx blackened receiver, multi-chokes standard. Mfg. 1990 only.

$1,150 $1,000 $900 $750 $650 $575 $525 *$1,590*

Add 15% for 20 ga.

MODEL 687 GOLDEN ONYX – 12 or 20 ga., 3 in. chambers, similar to Model 686 Onyx, except has more engraving, better walnut, and several gold inlays. Imported 1988-89 only.

$1,375 $1,275 $995 $825 $700 $650 $575 *$1,800*

Add 15% for 20 ga.
Subtract 10% for 26 in. barrels.

MODEL S687 EL GOLD PIGEON – same general specifications as Model 687L, except also available in 28 ga. (new 1990) or .410 (new 1990) bore, 20 ga. disc. 2001, 2 3/4 or 3 in. chambers, boxlock with gold inlaid game scene on sideplates, highly figured walnut, and more engraving, oval nameplate, approx. 6.8 lbs, cased. Disc. 2002.

$2,600 $2,200 $1,950 $1,575 $1,350 $1,150 $1,000 *$4,099*

Add $100 for 28 ga.
Subtract 10% for 26 in. barrels.

* ***Model 687 EL DU*** – 28 ga. or .410 bore, small frame, released 1992 for DU auctions and membership.

$2,300 $2,000 $1,800 $1,550 $1,400 $1,200 $1,050

MODEL S687 EL GOLD PIGEON II – 12, 20, 28 ga., or .410 bore, similar to EL Gold Pigeon, except features deep relief engraving on sideplates, 6.8 lbs., cased. Mfg. 2001-2006.

$4,325 $3,525 $3,150 $2,625 $2,050 $1,800 $1,500 *$5,095*

* ***S687 Gold Pigeon II Combo*** – includes either 20 and 28 ga. barrels or 28 ga. and .410 bore barrels, cased with 5 choke tubes. Imported 2003-2007.

$5,475 $4,375 $3,800 $3,200 $2,825 $2,475 $2,050 *$6,400*

MODEL 687 EL ONYX – 12 or 20 ga., 3 in. chambers, simulated sidelock plates with classic scroll engraving. Mfg. 1990 only.

$1,895 $1,700 $1,500 $1,350 $1,075 $950 $800 *$2,660*

Subtract 10% for 26 in. barrels.

GRADING - PPGS™	100%	98%	95%	90%	80%	70%	60%	LAST MSR

MODEL S687 EELL DIAMOND PIGEON – 12, 20, 28 (available in combo only 2012-disc.) ga. or .410 bore (mfg. 2003-disc.), boxlock action, silver receiver with full sideplates and hand engraved game scenes (new motif began 2012, except on .410 bore), 26 (disc.), 28, or 30 in. VR barrels, 3 in. (except 28 ga.) chambers and gold plated trigger, cased, MobilChokes introduced 1988, 6.8 lbs.

MSR $6,999	$5,950	$5,200	$4,450	$4,050	$3,300	$2,700	$2,325	

Add $400 for King Ranch model with special cowboy and western engraving motifs (mfg. 2006-2011).
Add 10%-20% for earlier mfg. with hand chased engraving (non-machine engraved), depending on condition.
Subtract 20% if without MobilChokes.
Subtract 10% for 26 in. barrels.

This model is also available with a straight grip English stock at no extra charge (20 ga. only).

If hand engraved, the engraver's name will be next to the trigger guard.

* ***Model S687 EELL Combo*** – includes either 20 and 28 ga. or 28 ga. and .410 bore (disc. 2014) MobilChoke 26 or 28 in. barrels, cased. Importation disc. 2017.

	$8,350	$6,950	$5,825	$4,750	$3,850	$3,200	$2,700	*$9,850*

Subtract 20% for fixed chokes.

MobileChokes became standard in 1991.

* ***Model S687 EELL Gallery Edition*** – 12, 20, 28 ga., or .410 bore, available as a pair (optional) or 2 barrel sets, featuring special engraving and upgraded wood with oil finish. New 2000.

Prices start at $10,500 for single guns and go up for 2 barrel sets, depending on ga. and options. Pairs start at $23,500. Available at Beretta Galleries only.

MODEL S687 EXTRA – 12, 20, 28 ga., or .410 bore, available in pairs or 2 barrel sets (special order only), features special engraving and upgraded wood with oil finish. New 2001.

Prices start at $8,250 for Field Model, and vary depending on ga. and options. Pairs start at approx. $16,675. Available at Beretta Premium dealers only.

MODEL 690 FIELD I – 12, 20, 28 ga., or .410 bore, 3 in. chambers, boxlock action, 28 in. cold hammer forged barrels with Optima HP field chokes, SST, bead front sight, oiled checkered walnut pistol grip stock, satin nickel receiver finish with etching, 7.4 lbs. Mfg. 2017-2019.

	$2,335	$2,050	$1,750	$1,595	$1,285	$1,050	$825	*$2,750*

MODEL 690 FIELD III – 12 or 20 ga., 3 in. chambers, 26 or 28 in. cold hammer forged barrels with Optima HP Field chokes, right or left-hand action, roll marked game scene engraving on receiver, SST, selective extraction, front bead sight, semi-beavertail forend, oiled walnut pistol grip stock, 7.4 lbs. Mfg. 2015-2019.

	$2,800	$2,450	$2,100	$1,900	$1,540	$1,275	$1,000	*$3,300*

MODEL 690 FIELD I VITTORIA – 20 ga., 28 in. cold hammer forged barrels with Optima bore HP chokes, SST, Grade 2.5 oiled walnut stock with semi-Monte Carlo design and reduced LOP, extra fine checkering on stock and forend, specifically designed for woman, contemporary scroll engraved receiver with Nistan finish. Mfg. 2018-2020.

	$2,335	$2,050	$1,750	$1,595	$1,285	$1,050	$825	*$2,750*

MODEL 695 – 12 or 20 ga., 3 in. chambers, 26 or 28 in. polished Stellium barrels, OptimaBore HP chokes, Grade 3 walnut stock, wood pad, deep Renaissance style premium laser engraving. Mfg. 2018-2020.

	$3,625	$3,175	$2,725	$2,475	$1,995	$1,650	$1,275	*$4,250*

MODEL ASE 90 PIGEON – 12 ga., 28 in. fixed choke (IM/F) barrels with VR, new design features nickel-chromium-molybdenum receiver with special hardening and crossbolt engaging 2 monobloc lugs, detachable trigger grouping, V-shaped main springs, cold hammered barrels, choice of silver or blue receiver with gold etching and no engraving, top quality checkered walnut stock and forearm with vent. recoil pad, choke tubes, 7 lbs. 13 oz., cased. Imported 1992-1994.

	$3,650	$3,225	$2,950	$2,650	$2,300	$2,000	$1,750	*$8,070*

SV10 PERENNIA I – 12 or 20 ga., 26 or 28 in. VR barrels with optima bore field chokes, satin finished receiver with classic floral pattern engraving, checkered walnut stock and forearm, available with standard or Kick-Off recoil pad. Mfg. 2012-2014.

	$2,400	$2,000	$1,850	$1,600	$1,400	$1,200	$975	*$2,895*

Add $400 for Kick-Off recoil pad.

SV10 PERENNIA III – 12 (disc. 2012) or 20 (new 2011) ga., boxlock action, 3 in. chambers, 26, 28, or 30 (disc. 2010) in. barrels, select matte finished checkered pistol grip walnut stock with or w/o Kick-Off recoil mechanism (became standard 2014), titanium SST, semi-beavertail forend, Optima-Choke/s,

GRADING - PPGS™	100%	98%	95%	90%	80%	70%	60%	LAST MSR

patented Q-stock quick takedown system that features shortened stock bolt built into back of trigger system, alloy laser engraved receiver, removable trigger group, approx. 7.3 lbs. Mfg. mid-2008-2014.

$3,200	$2,600	$2,450	$2,250	$1,900	$1,700	$1,400	*$3,945*

Add $325 for Kick-Off recoil system (avail. only in 20 ga. beginning 2011).
Subtract 10% for 12 ga. without Kick-Off recoil system (became standard 2014).

SHOTGUNS: O/U, SKEET - RECENT MFG.

Full descriptions for the following models may be found under the corresponding model numbers in the Field Shotguns category.

QUICK REFERENCE GUIDE FOR CURRENT CHOKES

MC3 - includes three MobilChokes. MC6 - includes six MobilChokes. OBSK - OptimaBore Skeet.

Note: values are for unaltered guns.

Subtract 20% on the following factory MobilChoke models if w/o newer Beretta OptimaChokes (12 ga. only, became standard 2003).

MODEL S682 GOLD SKEET - 12, 20 (disc. 1991), 28 ga. (disc. 1988), or .410 bore (disc. 1988), competition skeet model, 26 (disc.) or 28 in. barrels, boxlock, skeet chokes, silver finish (disc.) or Greystone (titanium nitrate) receiver, hand engraved, premium walnut, cased. Mfg. 1984-99.

$1,595	$1,450	$1,325	$1,075	$950	$850	$750	*$2,850*

Subtract 20% for 26 in. barrels.
Subtract 20% for fixed chokes.
Subtract 20% for silver finish.

* ***Model S682 Gold Skeet With Adj. Stock*** – similar to Model S682 Gold Skeet, except has fully adj. stock, allowing the comb, drop, and cast to be adjusted per shooter. Imported 1999-2000.

$1,750	$1,650	$1,600	$1,400	$1,200	$1,000	$900	*$3,515*

* ***Model S682 Gold E Skeet*** – 12 ga. only, 28 or 30 in. VR barrels with OptimaBore and OptimaChoke, adj. stock with memory system, dual color finished receiver with engraved merging circular lines and gold highlights, including trigger, deluxe wide checkered stock and Schnabel forearm with gloss wood finish, 7.6 lbs. Mfg. 2001-2013.

$3,850	$3,000	$2,750	$2,500	$2,000	$1,650	$1,425	*$4,805*

* ***Model 682 Super Skeet*** – 12 ga. only, 28 in. VR barrels bored SK/SK, factory porting, stock has separate adj. comb cheekpiece. Mfg. 1991-1995.

$1,500	$1,300	$1,200	$1,100	$1,050	$900	$800	*$3,006*

* ***Model 682 Skeet Deluxe*** – similar to Model 682, except deluxe walnut and elaborate engraving. Disc. 1986.

$1,850	$1,700	$1,550	$1,250	$1,050	$900	$800	*$3,000*

* ***Model 682 2-Barrel Skeet Set*** – 12 ga. only, two barrel set bored for skeet and sporting clays competition. Imported 1988 only.

$2,650	$2,350	$2,150	$2,000	$1,700	$1,500	$1,300	*$6,650*

Subtract 25% if w/o choke tubes.

* ***Model 682 4-Ga. Skeet Set*** – four barrel skeet set comes with interchangeable barrels (28 in.) in 12, 20, 28 gauges, and .410 bore. Imported 1985-95.

$3,300	$3,100	$3,000	$2,850	$2,500	$2,175	$1,900	*$6,037*

Subtract 10% for silver frame.

MODEL S686 SKEET SILVER PERDIZ/SILVER PIGEON – 12 ga. only, 28 in. VR barrels bored SK/SK, checkered walnut stock and forearm, Silver Perdiz was disc. 1996 and featured silver finish, while Silver Pigeon nomenclature began 1997 and features nickel finish, 7.6 lbs. Imported 1994-98.

$825	$775	$700	$675	$625	$550	$480	*$1,795*

MODEL S687 EELL SKEET DIAMOND PIGEON – 12 ga. only, fixed chokes, 28 in. barrels, elaborate game scene engraving on sideplates, cased. Disc. 2002.

$3,300	$2,750	$2,325	$2,050	$1,850	$1,500	$1,250	*$4,984*

* ***Model S687 EELL Skeet Diamond Pigeon With Adj. Stock*** – similar to Model S687 EELL Skeet Diamond Pigeon, except has fully adj. stock, allowing the comb, drop, and cast to be adjusted per shooter. Imported 1999-2004.

$4,600	$4,200	$3,950	$3,750	$3,250	$2,600	$2,150	*$6,207*

* ***Model S687 EELL 4-Ga. Skeet Set*** – 4 ga. skeet set, cased. Imported 1988-1998.

$6,000	$5,000	$4,350	$3,750	$3,400	$2,900	$2,450	*$8,405*

GRADING - PPGS™	100%	98%	95%	90%	80%	70%	60%	LAST MSR

MODEL 692 SKEET – 12 ga., 3 in. chambers, satin finished boxlock action, 28 (disc.) or 30 in. Steelium Plus barrels with OBSK-HP chokes, barrel selector on trigger, right or left-hand action, SST, manual extraction or ejection, available with B-Fast adj. comb. (parallel), checkered walnut stock and forearm, soft touch overmolded opening lever, 7.8 lbs. Mfg. 2014-2020.

$3,450	$3,050	$2,800	$2,500	$2,250	$1,950	$1,750	*$5,275*

DT10 TRIDENT SKEET – 12 ga. only, 3 in. chambers, 28 or 30 in. vent. barrels with target VR, specially designed skeet gun featuring removable adj. trigger group, massive crossbolt locking system, OptimaChokes competition choke tubes, OptimaBore internal barrel configuration, specific point of impact, and unique distribution of mass that helps target acquisition and eliminate muzzle rise, adj. walnut stock with memory system, carbon reinforced frame, 7.9 lbs. Mfg. 2000-2009.

$5,000	$4,500	$4,250	$4,000	$3,600	$3,150	$2,550	*$7,900*

DT11 SKEET – 12 ga., 3 in. chambers, 30 in. Steelium Pro VR barrels, OptimaBore HP extended choke tubes, walnut stock, with or w/o adj. drop, MicroCore recoil pad, right or left-hand configuration. Mfg. 2019-2020.

$7,350	$6,425	$5,525	$5,000	$4,050	$3,325	$2,600	*$8,650*

Add $670 for adj. drop.

DT11 BLACK PRO SKEET – 12 ga., 3 in. chambers, 30 in. Steelium Pro barrels with forcing cone, OptimaBore HP extended choke tubes, carbon fiber top rib, B-Fast barrel balancing system, detachable and adj. trigger, carbon fiber trigger plate, Beretta by TSK adj. stock, rounded forend, wide black receiver. New 2019.

MSR $12,400	$10,550	$9,230	$7,915	$7,175	$5,805	$4,750	$3,695

MODEL ASE 90 GOLD SKEET – 12 ga. only, 28 in. fixed choke vent. barrels with VR, similar action and specifications as the Model ASE 90 Pigeon, except has more elaborate hand scroll engraving and extra fine wood, 7.6 lbs., cased. Mfg. 1992-99.

$3,600	$3,400	$3,250	$3,000	$2,750	$2,500	$2,250	*$12,060*

SHOTGUNS: O/U, SPORTING CLAYS - CURRENT / RECENT MFG.

These variations have been specifically designed for sporting clay target shooting. All of the following models have 3 in. chambers, unless specified otherwise. Full descriptions for the following models may be found under the corresponding model numbers in the Field Shotguns category.

QUICK REFERENCE GUIDE FOR CURRENT CHOKES - see all current listings in the Shotguns: O/U, Field - Recent Mfg. section.

Subtract 10% for 28 in. barrels on all used Sporting models in this section.

Subtract 20% on the following factory multi-choke models if w/o newer Beretta OptimaChokes (12 ga. only, became standard 2003).

MODEL S682 CONTINENTAL COURSE – 12 ga. only, 2 3/4 in. chambers, 28 or 30 (disc. 1995) in. VR barrels with MobilChokes, designed for English Sporting Clays courses, previously was Model Super Sport with tapered rib, cased. Mfg. 1993-97.

$1,750	$1,525	$1,300	$1,100	$925	$800	$675	*$2,345*

MODEL S682 GOLD SPORTING – 12 or 20 (mfg. 1992-94) ga., similar specifications to Model 682 Skeet, 2 3/4 in. chambers, 28, 30 (new 1989), or 31 (new 1997) in. unported or ported (new 1995) VR barrels, except over-field stock dimensions and hand engraved silver (disc.) or Greystone (titanium nitrate) finished receiver, cased, 7.6 lbs. MobilChokes were standard. Disc. 2000.

$2,300	$2,000	$1,800	$1,650	$1,450	$1,250	$1,100	*$3,100*

Add $500 for extra set of 12 ga. barrels (combo. package - mfg. 1990-94).

* ***Model S682 Gold E Sporting*** – 12 ga. only, 28 (disc. 2011), 30 or 32 in. VR barrels with OptimaBore and OptimaChokes, dual color finished receiver with engraved merging circular lines and gold highlights, including trigger, select wide checkered stock and Schnabel forearm with gloss wood finish, approx. 7.6 lbs. Mfg. 2001-2014.

$3,100	$2,600	$2,400	$2,200	$1,900	$1,550	$1,225	*$4,050*

MODEL 682 SUPER SPORTING – 12 ga. only, 2 3/4 in. chambers, 28 or 30 in. VR ported (new 1993) barrels with MobilChokes and tapered rib, otherwise similar to Model 682 Sporting, cased, 7.6 lbs. Imported 1989-1995.

$1,650	$1,450	$1,250	$1,100	$950	$875	$800	*$3,017*

Beginning 1993, this model featured a special fully adj. stock and LOP.

MODEL 682 LTD – 12 ga. only, 30 or 32 in. barrels, limited edition mfg. 2006.

$3,750	$3,100	$2,900	$2,650	$2,300	$2,000	$1,650	*$5,075*

GRADING - PPGS™	100%	98%	95%	90%	80%	70%	60%	LAST MSR

MODEL 686 SPORTING/SPECIAL SPORTING – 12 ga. only, 3 in. chambers, deluxe checkered walnut stock and forearm with over-field dimensions, 28 or 30 (new 1991) in. barrels only, MobileChokes standard. Mfg. 1987-1992.

$1,200 $1,100 $925 $825 $675 $625 $550 *$1,940*

The Model 686 Special Sporting is marked "Model S686 Special," and the barrels are marked "Sporting."

* ***Model S686 Silver Pigeon (Silver Perdiz) Sporting*** – 12 or 20 (disc. 2000) ga., 28 or 30 in. VR barrels with MobilChokes, 7.7 lbs. Mfg. 1993-2002.

$1,425 $1,250 $1,050 $950 $800 $650 $500 *$1,931*

Add 10% (Last MSR was $2,070) for deluxe wood upgrade (includes case, mfg. 2001-2002).

Until 1994, this model was named the Model 686 Hunter Sport. Between 1994-95, this model was named the S686 Silver Perdiz, and beginning 1996, this model was again renamed to the 686 Silver Pigeon Sporting.

* ***Model 686 E Sporting*** – 12, 20 or 28 ga., 3 in. chambers, 28 (20 ga. only) or 30 in. VR barrels with 5 chokes, improved styling, oil finished walnut stock and Schnabel forearm, includes accessories, 5 choke tubes, and carrying case, 7.7 lbs. Mfg. 2001-2004.

$1,475 $1,275 $1,075 $975 $850 $750 $650 *$2,008*

* ***Model 686 Silver Perdiz/S686 Silver Pigeon Sporting Combo*** – 12 ga., includes extra set of 30 in. barrels. Model 686 Silver Perdiz was manufactured 1991-95, Model S686 Silver Pigeon was manufactured 1997-99.

$1,925 $1,700 $1,475 $1,250 $1,025 $900 $8000

Last MSR was $2,210.

Last MSR was $2,687 for the 686 Silver Perdiz Combo.

MODEL S686 SILVER PIGEON I SPORTING – 12, 20 (new 2016), 28 (mfg. 2016) ga., or .410 bore (mfg. 2016), 3 in. chambers, 30 or 32 in. cold hammer forged VR barrels with OBSP-HP chokes, extensive floral and scroll engraving, monobloc receiver, dual locking lugs, right or left (new 2016) hand action, Schnabel forend, available with B-Fast adj. comb. (mfg. 2015-2016). Mfg. 2011-disc.

$2,050 $1,600 $1,400 $1,050 $900 $700 $600 *$2,400*

Add $500 for B-Fast adj. comb. (mfg. 2015-2016), not available in 12 ga.

MODEL 686 COLLECTION SPORT – 12 ga. only, features multi-colored checkered wood stock and forearm, 28 in. VR barrels, 7.7 lbs. Mfg. 1996 only.

$995 $850 $725 $625 $525 $425 $375 *$1,499*

MODEL 686 ONYX SPORTING – 12 ga. only, 28 or 30 in. vent. fixed choke barrels with VR, high luster blue finish with gold lettering on receiver sides. Mfg. 1992 only.

$995 $850 $725 $625 $525 $425 $375 *$1,940*

* ***Model 686 Onyx Sporting w/Multi-chokes*** – 12 ga. only, 28 or 30 in. VR barrels with MultiChokes, matte wood finish, choice of semi-matte black (disc. 1998) or polished black receiver with "P. Beretta" engraved in gold, 7.7 lbs. Mfg. 1993-2002.

$1,325 $1,150 $975 $850 $725 $600 $500 *$1,639*

Add approx. 15% for deluxe wood upgrade (includes case, mfg. 2001-2002).

* ***Model 686 English Course*** – 12 ga., 28 in. VR barrels and special reverse tapered VR with special sighting plane designed for English courses. Mfg. 1991-1992.

$995 $895 $775 $675 $600 $500 $400 *$2,015*

MODEL 686 WHITE ONYX SPORTING – 12 ga. only, 30 or 32 in. VR barrels, nickel alloy finish, gold SST, oil finished checkered select walnut stock and forearm, black rubber recoil pad, Schnabel forend, 7-8 1/2 lbs. Mfg. 2004-2012.

$2,050 $1,750 $1,525 $1,300 $1,100 $900 $700 *$2,460*

MODEL 686 ONYX PRO SPORTING – 12 (mfg. 2017 only), 20, or 28 ga., 2 3/4 in. chambers, boxlock action, 30 or 32 in. VR barrels with MCE/MCS choke tubes, gold trigger, oil finished checkered Gr. 3 Turkish walnut stock and Schnabel forearm, "P. Beretta" in gold on receiver sides, high luster bluing on receiver and barrels, 6.5 lbs. Mfg. 2017-2018.

$3,000 $2,550 $2,400 $2,100 $1,900 $1,575 $1,250 *$3,700*

Previously available exclusively from Cabela's, now available to all Beretta dealers.

MODEL S687(L) SILVER PIGEON (SILVER PERDIZ) SPORTING – 12 or 20 ga. only, deluxe checkered walnut stock and forearm with over-field dimensions, game scene engraved, 28 or 30 (12 ga. only) in. barrels, MobilChokes standard. Mfg. 1987-2001.

$1,600 $1,475 $1,300 $1,050 $950 $850 $750 *$2,363*

GRADING - PPGS™	100%	98%	95%	90%	80%	70%	60%	LAST MSR

* ***Model 687 Silver Pigeon Sporting Combo*** – 12 ga., includes set of 28 and 30 in. barrels. Mfg. 2002 only.

	$2,100	$1,875	$1,750	$1,525	$1,325	$1,200	$950	*$3,151*

* ***Model 687 English Course*** – 12 ga. only, features 28 in. VR barrels and special reverse tapered VR with special sighting plane designed for English courses. Mfg. 1991-92.

	$1,650	$1,525	$1,375	$1,150	$1,050	$975	$870	*$2,630*

MODEL S687 SILVER PIGEON II SPORTING – 12, 20 (new 2002), or 28 ga. (new 2002), features deep relief game scene engraving on receiver sides, matte oil finished select walnut stock and forearm, 28, 30, or 32 (12 ga. only, new 2002) in. OptimaBore barrels, OptimaChoke extended tubes became standard on 12 ga. in 2003, 7.7 lbs. Imported 1999-2013.

	$2,100	$1,800	$1,550	$1,400	$1,300	$1,200	$1,075	*$3,700*

Subtract 20% if w/o Optima-Choke/s.

MODEL S687 SILVER PIGEON III SPORTING – 12 ga. only, 30 or 32 in. VR barrels, select checkered walnut stock and forearm, game scene engraving on receiver sides, floral and scroll engraving on bottom of receiver and trigger guard, approx. 8 lbs. Mfg. 2004-2009, reintroduced 2014-2015.

	$2,795	$2,000	$1,800	$1,750	$1,500	$1,225	$975	*$3,375*

MODEL S687 EL GOLD PIGEON SPORTING – 12 ga. only, 28 or 30 in. VR barrels with MobileChokes, 7.7 lbs. Mfg. 1993-2001.

	$2,900	$2,500	$2,100	$1,650	$1,475	$1,200	$950	*$4,182*

MODEL S687 EL GOLD PIGEON II SPORTING – 12, 20 (new 2003), 28 ga., or .410 bore (new 2003), similar to Model S687 Gold Pigeon Sporting, except features deep relief engraving on sideplates, also available in 28 ga. and 32 in. barrels beginning 2002, OptimaBore barrels with OptimaChoke flush tubes became standard on 12 ga. in 2003. Mfg. 2001-2006.

	$4,575	$4,000	$3,500	$3,000	$2,500	$2,125	$1,750	*$5,495*

* ***Model 687 EL Gold Pigeon II Sporting 20 ga./.410 Bore*** – includes set of 20 ga. and .410 bore barrels, cased. Imported 2003 only.

	$4,850	$4,400	$3,650	$3,100	$2,600	$2,200	$1,775	*$6,071*

* ***Model 687 EL Gold Pigeon II Sporting Combo*** – 28 ga. and .410 bore, includes set of 30 in. barrels. Mfg. 2002-2007.

	$5,600	$4,700	$3,995	$3,375	$3,200	$2,975	$2,500	*$6,600*

MODEL S687 EELL DIAMOND PIGEON SPORTING – 12, 20 (disc. 1992, reintroduced 2003), 28 (new 2003) ga. or .410 bore (mfg. 2003-2011), features fine scroll engraving on receiver and sideplates (new motif on 12 ga. only began 2012), deluxe checkered walnut stock and forearm with over-field dimensions, 28 (disc. 2011), 30 (new 1995), or 32 (new 2002) in. barrels only, OptimaBore barrels with OptimaChoke flush tubes became standard on 12 ga. in 2003 or with MobilChokes, cased, 7.6 lbs. Mfg. 1987-2016.

	$7,000	$6,000	$5,850	$4,950	$3,950	$3,100	$2,325	*$8,450*

Add $1,500 for extra set of barrels (combo. package - 1990 mfg. only).
Subtract 10% if w/o OptimaChokes.

MODEL 690 SPORTING – 12 ga. 3 in. chambers, 28 (disc.), 30, or 32 in. VR separated Steelium barrels with extended choke tubes, SST, select checkered walnut stock and forearm, receiver has orange accents, matte polished black finish, 7 3/4 lbs.

MSR $2,999	$2,575	$2,000	$1,900	$1,625	$1,300	$1,100	$995	

MODEL 692 SPORTING – 12 ga., 3 in. chambers, satin finished boxlock action, 30 or 32 in. Steelium Plus barrels with OBSP-HP chokes, barrel selector on trigger, right or left-hand action, SST, manual extraction or ejection, available with B-Fast adj. comb. (parallel), checkered walnut stock and forearm, soft touch overmolded opening lever, 7.8 lbs. Mfg. 2014-2019.

	$3,200	$2,850	$2,600	$2,300	$2,100	$1,850	$1,600	*$4,800*

Add $475 for B-Fast adj. comb.

MODEL 692 SPORTING BLACK EDITION – 12 ga., right or left-hand action, 30 or 32 in. Steelium Plus barrels with OBSP-HP chokes and matte barrel finish, adj. trigger, with or w/o B-Fast adj. comb, wide receiver with black finish. Mfg. 2018-2020.

	$3,500	$3,100	$2,900	$2,650	$2,400	$2,200	$2,100	*$5,250*

Add $500 for B-Fast adj. comb.

GRADING - PPGS™	100%	98%	95%	90%	80%	70%	60%	LAST MSR

MODEL 694 COMPETITION – 12 ga., 3 in. chambers, modern sporting and low profile design, right or left-hand configuration, 30 or 32 in. Steelium Plus Optima HP barrels, fitted ejectors placed behind ejector slide and beneath stop pads, single selective adj. trigger, oil finished checkered wood stock with or w/o B-Fast adj. comb, round or beavertail steel forend w/self-adj. auget button, MicroCore recoil pad, checkered pistol grip, features slide panels w/mirrored profile, blue artwork with "694" logo, matte grey w/anti-glare, Nistan finishing, optional B-Fast adj. heel and Schnabel forend variation. New late 2019.

MSR $4,199	$3,575	$3,130	$2,680	$2,430	$1,965	$1,610	$1,250	

Add $350 for B-Fast adj. comb.

DT10 TRIDENT SPORTING – 12 ga. only, 3 in. chambers, 28, 30, or 32 in. vent. OptimaBore barrels with target VR, specially designed sporting gun featuring removable adj. trigger group, massive crossbolt locking system, OptimaChoke competition choke tubes, specific point of impact, and unique distribution of mass which helps target acquisition and eliminate muzzle rise, deluxe checkered walnut stock and Schnabel forearm, carbon reinforced frame, cased, approx. 8 lbs. Mfg. 2000-2015.

	$5,000	$4,500	$4,250	$4,000	$3,500	$3,100	$2,500	*$7,500*

* ***DT10 Trident L Sporting*** – 12 ga., 30 or 32 in. barrels, floral engraved receiver and trigger guard, palm swell, adj. trigger. Mfg. 2004-2015.

	$6,500	$6,000	$5,250	$4,975	$3,950	$3,300	$2,600	*$9,500*

* ***DT10 Trident EELL Sporting*** – 12 ga., 30 or 32 in. barrels, hand engraved, upgraded wood. Mfg. 2004-2015.

	$14,500	$12,000	$10,250	$9,000	$8,000	$7,000	$6,000	*$15,750*

This model was available by special order through Beretta Galleries only.

DT11 – 12 ga., 3 in. chambers, 30 or 32 in. Steelium Pro barrels with forcing cone, OptimaBore HP chokes, detachable trigger, walnut stock, with or w/o B-Fast adj. comb, MicroCore recoil pad, reinforced locking system, wide receiver, right or left-hand configuration. Mfg. 2019 only.

	$7,650	$6,695	$5,750	$5,200	$4,225	$3,450	$2,700	*$8,999*

Add $321 for B-Fast adj. comb stock.

DT11 BLACK EDITION – 12 ga., 3 in. chambers, 30 or 32 in. Steelium Pro VR barrels with matte black finish, OptimaBore HP extended choke tubes, carbon fiber rib, carbon fiber trigger guard, walnut stock with or w/o B-Fast adj. comb, checkered pistol grip and forend, MicroCore recoil pad, right or left-hand configuration, black receiver. Mfg. 2019 only.

	$9,350	$8,185	$7,025	$6,350	$5,150	$4,225	$3,300	*$10,999*

Add $301 for B-Fast adj. comb.

DT11 BLACK PRO SPORTING – 12 ga., 3 in. chambers, 32 in. Steelium Pro barrels with forcing cone, OptimaBore HP extended choke tubes, carbon fiber top rib, B-Fast barrel balancing system, detachable and adj. trigger, carbon fiber trigger plate, Beretta by TSK adj. stock, rounded forend, wide black receiver. New 2019.

MSR $12,400	$10,550	$9,230	$7,915	$7,175	$5,800	$4,750	$4,000	

DT11 EELL – 12 ga., 3 in. chambers, 30 or 32 in. Steelium Pro barrels, OptimaBore HP extended chokes, hand selected walnut stock, with or w/o B-Fast adj. comb, MicroCore recoil pad, elongated sideplates with exquisite engraving, right or left-hand configuration. New 2019.

MSR $17,500	$14,900	$13,000	$11,150	$10,100	$8,200	$6,700	$5,200	

Add $1,000 for B-Fast adj. comb stock.

DT11 L – 12 ga., 3 in. chambers, top-of-the-line premium firearm, 30 or 32 in. Steelium Pro barrel, OptimaBore HP chokes, detachable trigger, hand finished walnut stock and forend, with or w/o B-Fast adj. comb, engraved receiver, reinforced locking system. New 2019.

MSR $11,712	$9,950	$8,700	$7,475	$6,775	$5,475	$4,485	$3,500	

Add $363 for B-Fast adj. comb stock.

MODEL ASE 90 GOLD SPORTING CLAYS – 12 ga. only, 28, 30, or 31 (new 1997) in. vent. barrels with VR, similar action and specifications to Model ASE 90 Pigeon, 7 1/2 lbs., cased. Mfg. 1992-99.

	$4,500	$3,850	$3,400	$3,250	$3,000	$2,850	$2,500	*$12,145*

SV10 PREVAIL I SPORTING – 12 ga., 30 or 32 in. separated VR barrels with OBSP-HP choke tubes, satin finished boxlock aluminum receiver, choice of extraction or ejection, titanium trigger, quick takedown stock allows disassembly in a few seconds, regular or Kick-Off recoil pad. Mfg. 2012-2013.

	$2,750	$2,200	$1,875	$1,750	$1,500	$1,200	$975	*$2,900*

Add 15% (Last MSR was $400) for Kick-Off recoil pad.

GRADING - PPGS™	100%	98%	95%	90%	80%	70%	60%	LAST MSR

SV10 PREVAIL III SPORTING – 12 ga., 3 in. chambers, 26, 28, 30, or 32 in. OptimaBore barrels with five OptimaChoke High Performance tubes, vent. rib, dual locking lugs, coin finished receiver with or w/o game scene engraving, Alpacca sights, titanium SST, beavertail forend, quick take down stock with pistol grip, optional Kick-Off recoil reduction, rubber recoil pad, sling swivels, and case, approx. 7.7 lbs. Mfg. mid-2009-2013.

	$2,975	$2,450	$2,100	$1,850	$1,600	$1,325	$1,000	*$3,295*

Add 10% (Last MSR was $325) for Kick-Off recoil system.

SHOTGUNS: O/U, TRAP - RECENT MFG.

QUICK REFERENCE GUIDE FOR CURRENT CHOKES

MC3 - includes three Mobilchokes. MC6 - includes six Mobilchokes. OBTR - Optima Bore Trap. OBTS - Optima Bore Trap Single.

Note: values are for unaltered trap guns.

Subtract 20% on the following factory multi-choke models if w/o newer Beretta OptimaChokes (12 ga. only, became standard 2003).

Subtract 10% for 28 in. barrels on used Trap models.

MODEL S682 GOLD TRAP (GOLD X) – 12 ga. only, competition trap model, Greystone (titanium nitrate) or Bruniton finish (matte black, disc.), 30 or 32 in. barrels with or w/o choke tubes (became standard 1996), adj. trigger, supplied with case, 8.8 lbs. Mfg. 1985-2000.

	$1,650	$1,350	$1,200	$1,050	$900	$775	$650	*$3,100*

Subtract 15% for Bruniton finish.

Subtract 20% if w/o choke tubes.

* ***Model S682 Mono/Top Combo Trap (Gold X)*** – 12 ga., supplied with mono under or upper single barrel and O/U barrel sets, MobilChokes became standard 1996, otherwise same specifications as Model S682 Gold Trap, cased. Disc. 2000.

	$2,000	$1,850	$1,700	$1,600	$1,400	$1,200	$1,000	*$4,085*

Subtract 15% for Bruniton finish.

* ***Model S682 Gold Trap Adjustable Stock*** – 12 ga. only, features Monte Carlo style stock with adj. comb, 30 or 32 in. barrels, 8.8 lbs. Mfg. 1998-2000.

	$1,700	$1,600	$1,550	$1,475	$1,250	$1,050	$895	*$3,625*

Add $985 for combo package (includes extra set of 34 in. barrels).

* ***Model 682 Mono*** – single under-barrel trap model, high post vent. rib, 32 or 34 in. barrel. Imported 1985-88.

	$1,250	$1,100	$1,000	$900	$800	$700	$600	*$1,890*

Subtract if w/o choke tubes.

* ***Model S682 Gold Trap Live Bird (Pigeon Trap)*** – 12 ga., includes features for international style pigeon and competition shooters including international style stock, standard or flat (new 1995) VR, and mid-rib sights, Greystone (new 1991) or matte black (disc.) metal finish, semi-gloss American walnut stock, light scroll engraving, sliding trigger, includes MobilChokes, cased, 8.8 lbs. Imported 1990-1998.

	$1,700	$1,625	$1,325	$1,175	$950	$895	$800	*$2,910*

Subtract 15% for matte black.

* ***Model 682 Gold X Trap Mono (Top Single)*** – 12 ga., single over-barrel trap model, 32 or 34 in. barrels. Imported 1986-1995.

	$1,400	$1,275	$1,150	$925	$850	$775	$675	*$2,734*

Subtract 10% if w/o choke tubes.

MobilChokes became standard in 1989.

* ***Model 682 Unsingle Trap*** – 12 ga. only, single under-barrel trap model with 32 in. high post VR, optional choke tubes. Imported 1992-94.

	$1,495	$1,350	$1,150	$925	$850	$775	$675	*$2,650*

Subtract 10% if w/o choke tubes.

MODEL S682 (GOLD X) SUPER TRAP – 12 ga. only, competition trap model, 30 in. barrels, step tapered rib, factory porting, LOP, and separate stock cheekpiece are adjustable, cased. Imported 1991-95.

	$1,800	$1,650	$1,375	$1,050	$900	$800	$700	*$2,907*

* ***Model S682 Top Mono Super Trap (Gold X)*** – 12 ga., single over-barrel trap model, 32 or 34 in. barrel with choice of fixed or MobilChokes. Imported 1991-1995.

	$1,550	$1,375	$1,200	$1,050	$900	$800	$700	*$3,083*

Subtract 10% for 32 in. barrel.

Subtract 10% for fixed choke.

GRADING - PPGS™	100%	98%	95%	90%	80%	70%	60%	LAST MSR

* ***Model S682 Gold Super Trap Top Combo (Gold X)*** – 12 ga., supplied with upper single barrel and O/U barrel sets, otherwise same specifications as Model 682 Super Trap, MobilChokes became standard 1996, cased. Imported 1991-1997.

$2,200	$1,950	$1,825	$1,650	$1,400	$1,125	$895	*$4,040*

MODEL S682 GOLD E TRAP – 12 ga. only, 30 or 32 in. VR OptimaBore barrel, OptimaChokes, adj. stock with memory system, dual color finished receiver with engraved merging circular lines and gold highlights, including trigger, deluxe wide checkered stock with gloss wood finish, bottom single configuration became standard 2009, 7.6 lbs. Mfg. 2001-2010.

$3,400	$2,875	$2,525	$2,150	$1,800	$1,500	$1,300	*$4,350*

* ***Model S682 Gold E Trap Combo Top/Bottom*** – 12 ga. only, includes 30 (scarce, disc. 2001), 32 (disc. 2002) or 34 (new 2002) in. mono top or bottom barrel and choice of 30 or 32 in. O/U barrels, cased. Mfg. 2001-2013.

$4,300	$3,650	$3,150	$2,600	$2,175	$1,725	$1,500	*$5,185*

Add $380 for bottom single combo.

* ***Model S682 Gold E Trap Bottom Single*** – 12 ga., features 34 in. bottom single barrel with OBTR chokes. Disc. 2013.

$3,600	$3,000	$2,650	$2,250	$1,850	$1,550	$1,350	*$4,805*

MODEL S682 LTD. – 12 ga. only, 32 or 34 in. barrel, includes adj. stock. Limited edition mfg. 2006.

$5,400	$4,900	$4,475	$4,200	$3,850	$3,600	$3,300	*$6,775*

MODEL S686 SILVER PIGEON TRAP – 12 ga. only, low profile action, 30 in. VR barrels with 3/8 in. flat rib, matte wood finish, choke tubes, nickel finished receiver with scroll engraving, 7.7 lbs. Mfg. 1997-99.

$1,095	$925	$750	$625	$525	$460	$415	*$1,795*

* ***Model S686 Silver Pigeon Trap Top Mono*** – 12 ga., single over-barrel trap model, 32 or 34 in. barrel with MobilChokes, gloss wood finish, 8.14 lbs. Mfg. 1998-2002.

$1,000	$900	$775	$650	$550	$475	$415	*$1,869*

MODEL 686 INTERNATIONAL TRAP – 12 ga. only, 30 in. VR barrels bored IM/F, checkered walnut stock and forearm. Imported 1994 only.

$900	$800	$725	$650	$550	$500	$460	*$1,300*

MODEL 686 ONYX PRO XTRAP – 12 ga., 3 in. chambers, boxlock action, 30 or 32 in. VR barrels with 3 extended OptimaChoke tubes, gold trigger, oil finished checkered Gr. 3 Turkish walnut stock and Schnabel forearm, "P. Beretta" in gold on receiver sides, high luster bluing on receiver and barrels, 8.8 lbs. Mfg. 2017-2018.

$3,350	$2,850	$2,650	$2,250	$1,825	$1,575	$1,250	*$3,700*

Originally available exclusively from Cabela's, later available to all Beretta dealers.

* ***Model 686 Onyx Pro XTrap Combo*** – 12 ga., 3 in. chambers, includes 30 or 32 in. O/U barrels and a single 34 in. barrel w/high rib. Mfg. 2017-2018.

$4,750	$4,000	$3,750	$3,250	$2,600	$2,425	$1,975	*$5,200*

MODEL S687 EELL DIAMOND PIGEON TRAP (X TRAP) – 12 ga. only, boxlock action with engraved black (new 1992) or silver (disc. 1991) finished sideplates, Monte Carlo stock with recoil pad, 30 in. barrels with choke tubes, cased, 8.8 lbs. Disc. 1999.

$3,600	$3,000	$2,550	$2,200	$1,850	$1,575	$1,300	*$4,815*

* ***Model S687 EELL Diamond Pigeon Trap Top Mono*** – 12 ga. only, single over-barrel trap model, 32 or 34 in. barrel, fixed chokes standard. Imported 1988-92, resumed 1996, disc. 1999.

$3,300	$2,750	$2,350	$2,050	$1,750	$1,500	$1,250	*$5,060*

Subtract 20% if w/o OptimaChokes.

* ***Model S687 EELL Diamond Pigeon X Bottom Mono Trap Combo*** – 12 ga. only, supplied with 30 or 32 in. O/U barrels and a mono trap bottom barrel. Imported 1986-1988, resumed 1994-1995.

$4,600	$3,950	$3,350	$2,850	$2,450	$2,100	$1,650	*$4,984*

Add 5% for MobilChokes.

* ***Model S687 EELL Diamond Pigeon X Top Mono Trap Combo*** – 12 ga. only, supplied with 30 or 32 in. O/U barrels and a mono trap upper barrel, MobilChokes became standard 1995. Mfg. 1988-1997.

$4,975	$4,300	$3,650	$3,100	$2,650	$2,250	$1,750	*$6,070*

GRADING - PPGS™	100%	98%	95%	90%	80%	70%	60%	LAST MSR

MODEL 692 US TRAP – 12 ga., 3 in. chambers, 30, 32, or 34 (new 2018) in. Steelium Plus barrels with OBTR-HP chokes, right or left-hand action, available with B-FAST adj. comb., select Monte Carlo walnut stock with hand rubbed oil finish, Microcore buttplate, locked trigger, rounded forend, mid-bead sights. Mfg. 2015-2019.

	$3,650	$3,000	$2,850	$2,700	$2,500	$2,275	$1,800	*$5,600*

MODEL ASE 90 GOLD TRAP – 12 ga. only, 30 in. vent. barrels with VR, similar action and specifications to Model ASE 90 Pigeon, 8.2 lbs., cased with extra trigger group, MobilChokes became standard 1995. Mfg. 1992-1999.

	$4,675	$4,300	$3,950	$3,425	$2,950	$2,650	$2,450	*$12,145*

Add $1,000 for Trap Combo package.
Subtract 10% if w/o choke tubes.
Subtract $250 if w/o extra trigger assembly.

DT10 TRIDENT TRAP – 12 ga. only, 3 in. chambers, 30 or 32 in. vent. OptimaBore barrels with target VR, specially designed trap gun featuring removable adj. trigger group, massive crossbolt locking system, OptimaChoke competition choke tubes, specific point of impact, and unique distribution of mass that helps target acquisition and eliminate muzzle rise, adj. walnut stock with memory system, carbon reinforced frame, 8.8 lbs., cased. Mfg. 2000-2008.

	$5,000	$4,500	$4,000	$3,700	$3,250	$2,500	$2,000	*$7,400*

* ***DT10 Trident Trap Top Single*** – includes 34 in. top single barrel, cased. Mfg. 2000-2008.

	$5,000	$4,500	$4,000	$3,700	$3,500	$2,700	$2,150	*$7,400*

* ***DT10 Trident Trap Bottom Single*** – includes 34 in. bottom single barrel with adj. rib, cased. Mfg. 2004-disc.

	$5,500	$5,000	$4,500	$4,000	$3,500	$2,700	$2,150	*$8,500*

* ***DT10 Trident Trap Combo*** – includes choice of 30 or 32 in. O/U barrels and a 34 in. top single barrel, cased. Mfg. 2000-2008.

	$6,000	$5,500	$5,000	$4,500	$4,100	$3,750	$3,500	*$10,475*

* ***DT10 Trident Trap Bottom Single Combo*** – includes 34 in. bottom single barrel and choice of 30 or 32 in. O/U barrels, rib on bottom single barrel is adj. for point of impact, cased. Mfg. 2001-2019.

	$6,500	$6,000	$5,500	$5,000	$4,500	$4,000	$3,450	*$11,300*

This model is available by special order through Beretta Galleries only.

DT11 BLACK PRO TRAP – 12 ga., 3 in. chambers, 30 in. Steelium Pro barrels with forcing cone, OptimaBore HP extended choke tubes, carbon fiber top rib, B-Fast barrel balancing system, detachable and adj. trigger, carbon fiber trigger plate, Beretta by TSK adj. stock, rounded forend, wide black receiver. Mfg. 2019 only.

	$10,375	$9,080	$7,780	$7,050	$5,700	$4,675	$3,650	*$12,200*

DT11 INTERNATIONAL TRAP – 12 ga., 3 in. chambers, 30 in. Steelium Pro barrels, OptimaBore HP extended choke tubes, walnut stock, MicroCore recoil pad, right or left-hand configuration, wide receiver. Mfg. 2019 only.

	$7,395	$6,475	$5,550	$5,025	$4,075	$3,350	$2,600	*$8,699*

DT11 X-TRAP – 12 ga., 3 in. chambers, 32 or 34 (unsingle) in. Steelium Pro barrels, OptimaBore HP extended chokes, adj. walnut stock, MicroCore recoil pad, wide receiver. Mfg. 2019 only.

	$8,400	$7,350	$6,300	$5,700	$4,625	$3,785	$2,945	*$9,320*

Add $4,130 for X-Trap Combo - includes 32 and 34 (unsingle) in. barrel.

SV10 PREVAIL I TRAP – 12 ga., 30 or 32 in. VR barrels with OBSP-HP choke tubes, satin finished boxlock aluminum receiver, choice of extraction or ejection, titanium trigger, quick takedown stock allows disassembly in a few seconds, regular or Kick-Off recoil pad. Mfg. 2012-2013.

	$2,500	$2,125	$1,800	$1,650	$1,550	$1,225	$1,000	*$3,000*

Add $450 for Kick-Off recoil pad.

SHOTGUNS: O/U, CUSTOM GRADE - CURRENT / RECENT MFG.

Current high grade Beretta O/U and SxS shotguns are sold only by premium grade franchised Beretta dealers. For a listing of these dealers, contact a Beretta Gallery.

Where applicable, Beretta's new SST, with selector switch built into safety, is more desirable than older manufacture utilizing the disc. single, non-selective trigger.
Subtract 10%-15% for older style non-selective single trigger.

GRADING - PPGS™	100%	98%	95%	90%	80%	70%	60%	LAST MSR

ROYAL PIGEON (GALLERY SPECIAL) – 12 or 20 ga., non-sideplated Model 600 action, hand engraved in the EELL style, upgraded wood, made especially for Beretta Galleries. 40 mfg. in each gauge 2004-disc.

	$5,250	$4,550	$4,100	$3,550	$3,200	$2,800	$2,400	*$5,950*

ASEL – 12 or 20 ga., best SO grade boxlock with vintage 1960s action, SO grade hand finished wood, Boehler Antinit steel barrels, 28 mfg. in 20 ga. (2004-2005), 300 mfg. in 12 ga. Mfg. 2004-2006.

12 ga.	$12,500	$10,500	$9,000	$7,500	$6,000	$5,000	$4,500	*$15,000*
20 ga.	$22,250	$18,500	$14,000	$10,500	$9,500	$8,500	$7,500	*$25,750*

Pairs on this model were available for $59,225 (20 ga. only).

ASE GOLD – see individual models with descriptions under Skeet, Sporting Clays, and Trap category names.

ASE 90 DE LUXE – 12 ga. only, specifications furnished by customer, deep scroll engraving signed by the engraver, upgraded wood, Sporting or Field Model, cased. Mfg. 1996-disc.

	$20,500	$15,000	$10,750	$8,750	$7,250	$6,000	$5,000	*$24,500*

JUBILEE – 12, 20, 28 ga., or .410 bore, choice of Field or Sporting Clays configuration, signed scroll or game scene engraving, upgraded wood, tru-oil finish, and hand polished details throughout, cased. Mfg. 1998-2013.

	$14,995	$12,250	$9,000	$7,250	$6,150	$5,200	$4,750	*$18,000*

Add $3,500 for 2-barrel set (20/28 ga., new 2010).

* ***Jubilee Matched Pair*** – available with consecutive serial numbers, made to special order, cased. Mfg. 2002-2013.

	$35,000	$29,000	$24,000	$18,750	$15,000	$13,250	$11,000	*$42,500*

SL3 – 12 or 20 ga., 3 in. chambers, boxlock w/sideplates, 26 (disc.), 28, or 30 in. OptimaBore HP barrels, extra select checkered walnut stock and forearm, light scroll, deep scroll, game scene engraving, or high polish finish. Mfg. 2018-2019.

	$18,325	$16,050	$13,750	$12,460	$10,080	$8,250	$7,150	*$21,550*

Add $5,000 for high polish finish.

SO-1 – 12 ga. only, entry level SO model, sidelock action with Greener crossbolt, ejectors, DT, checkered walnut stock and forearm, perimeter engraving only, various configurations. Mfg. circa 1935-disc.

	$3,995	$3,500	$3,000	$2,600	$2,250	$1,850	$1,725	

SO-2 – 12 ga., 26-30 in. barrels, sidelock, any chokes, vent. rib, auto ejectors, SST, checkered stock in various configurations (field, skeet, or trap), grades differ in wood, engraving, and finish, cased. SO series mfg. began 1948.

	$3,995	$2,950	$2,350	$1,950	$1,675	$1,475	$1,250	*$4,750*

SO-3 – 2nd grade of the SO series. Disc.

	$4,500	$3,550	$3,200	$2,800	$2,400	$2,100	$1,850	*$6,250*

SO-3 EL – grade-up from SO-3 with better wood and engraving. Disc. 2015.

	$10,000	$6,250	$4,250	$3,600	$3,050	$2,500	$2,200	*$10,000*

SO-3 EELL – best quality SO-3 model, custom specifications, choice of engraving motifs. Disc.

	$14,750	$10,000	$8,500	$7,500	$6,500	$5,500	$4,500	*$14,750*

Add $2,000-$10,000 for master engraving.

SO-4 – 12 ga., sidelock, available in field, skeet, or trap configurations, custom specs., fluorescent sights, wide rib, cased. Disc. 1987, reintroduced 2001-2015.

	$6,500	$5,650	$4,750	$4,225	$3,650	$3,250	$2,800	*$6,500*

SO-5 COMPETITION – best quality O/U, extensively engraved, top quality checkered walnut stock (semi-pistol grip) and forearm, available in either Trap, Skeet, or Sporting configurations, leather cased. Limited importation. Disc.

	$22,000	$14,250	$10,250	$8,250	$6,400	$5,300	$4,500	*$28,000*

Add $10,000 for extra set of barrels.
Add $3,500 for Trap Combo set (disc.).

SO-5 EELL – next to top-of-the-line model, available in either Trap, Skeet, or Sporting Clays configuration, custom built to customer dimensions.

MSR $37,500	$32,000	$22,500	$18,500	$15,000	$12,500	$10,000	$7,500	

GRADING - PPGS™	100%	98%	95%	90%	80%	70%	60%	LAST MSR

SO-6 COMPETITION – 12 ga. only high quality O/U, extensively scroll engraved, top quality checkered walnut stock (semi-pistol grip) and forearm, choice of Field (reintroduced during 1998), Trap, Skeet, or Sporting Clays configuration, built to customer specifications, leather cased, limited importation. Disc. 2002.

	100%	98%	95%	90%	80%	70%	60%	LAST MSR
	$16,650	$13,500	$10,750	$8,500	$7,450	$6,350	$5,100	*$23,900*

Add $6,250 for extra set of barrels.

SO-6 EL FIELD GRADE – 12 ga. only, available with rose and scroll engraving, 28, 30, or 32 in. barrels. Mfg. 2003-disc.

	100%	98%	95%	90%	80%	70%	60%	LAST MSR
	$24,250	$19,750	$15,000	$11,000	$9,750	$8,750	$7,500	*$27,500*

SO-6 EELL – 12 ga., current next to top-of-the-line model, field dimensions, custom built to customer specifications, leather cased. Disc. 2015, reintroduced 2019.

	100%	98%	95%	90%	80%	70%	60%	LAST MSR
MSR $80,000	$68,000	$59,500	$51,000	$46,250	$37,400	$30,600	$26,000	

Special engraving options are available on this model for an additional charge - contact the Beretta Gallery directly for pricing.

SO-6 EESS – 12 ga., features green enamel sideplates with diamond inlays. Mfg. 1998-2011.

The last MSR on this model was $110,000.

SO-9 – 12, 20, 28 ga., or .410 bore, top-of-the-line sidelock model until 2003, 1990 was the first time the SO series was offered in smaller gauges, 28 ga. or .410 bore models have smaller proportionate frames. Mfg. 1990-2013.

	100%	98%	95%	90%	80%	70%	60%	LAST MSR
	$35,000	$27,500	$20,500	$16,000	$12,000	$9,200	$7,000	*$46,725*

Add $10,000 for extra set of barrels.
Add 10%-25% for well-known engravers.
Subtract 10% for 12 ga. on used specimens.

- ***SO-9 EELL Special*** – top-of-the-line O/U model. Disc.

Retail prices ranged from $125,000-$320,000, depending on individual custom-order engraving options. Pairs weae also available from $287,500 to $422,000.

SO-10 – 12, 20, 28 ga., or .410 bore, top-of-the-line O/U sidelock model, 26-32 in. barrels made of nickel, chromium, and molybdenum steel. Limited availability beginning 2003.

	100%	98%	95%	90%	80%	70%	60%	LAST MSR
MSR $120,500	$101,900	$89,200	$76,450	$69,300	$56,050	$45,850	$38,500	

Add $6,000 for .410 ga.

Pairs are available for $215,000. Any level of engraving is available on this model in 20 ga. through 2005. 28 ga. or .410 bore models became available in 2006.

SO-10 EELL – 12, 20, 28 ga., or .410 bore, top-of-the-line premium model, 26-30 in. barrels. Made to customer specifications.

Current base MSR is $145,000.

- ***SO-10 EELL Special*** – top-of-the-line O/U model, extra engraving. Disc.

Prices for single guns, depending on the amount of engraving, ranged from $145,000 - $215,000. Pairs were available from $287,500 to $480,000, depending on the amount of engraving.

GIUBILEO SPORTING – 12 or 20 ga., 28, 30, or 32 in. OptimaBore barrels, OptimaChokes, premium walnut oil finished stock and checkered forearm, coin finished boxlock engraved action with sideplates, scroll engraved receiver with P. Beretta logo, single trigger, available in Sporting configuration and combo, 6.6-7.3 lbs. Mfg. 2007-disc.

	100%	98%	95%	90%	80%	70%	60%	LAST MSR
	$15,500	$12,750	$10,750	$9,000	$8,000	$7,000	$6,000	*$17,500*

Add $1,500 for 12/20 and 20/28 ga. combo.

This model was available by special order through Beretta Galleries only.

DT10 EELL SPORTING – 12 ga. only, scroll or game scene engraved, SST, sporting stock with extra fine wood. Mfg. 2010-2015.

	100%	98%	95%	90%	80%	70%	60%	LAST MSR
	$13,950	$11,500	$9,750	$8,500	$7,250	$6,000	$4,750	*$15,750*

This model was available by special order through Beretta Galleries only.

DT11 GALLERY – 12 ga. only, 30 or 32 in. barrels, engraved action, SST, features upgraded wood and finish. Mfg. 2015-2017.

	100%	98%	95%	90%	80%	70%	60%	LAST MSR
	$12,750	$9,750	$8,500	$7,250	$6,000	$5,000	$4,500	*$14,000*

This model is available by special order through Beretta Galleries only.

GRADING - PPGS™	100%	98%	95%	90%	80%	70%	60%	LAST MSR

SPARVIERE – 12 ga., 3 in. chambers, 28 or 30 in. VR barrels, SST, ejectors, unique "gullwing" sidelock action based on the S0-6 has front hinges allowing sidelocks to be opened for inspection and cleaning by operating the selector button on upper tang, hand engraved action, best quality checkered walnut stock and forearm. Limited importation beginning 2014.

Current base MSR on this model is $85,000, depending on engraving.

SHOTGUNS: SxS, CURRENT / RECENT MFG.

Subtract 20% on the following factory multi-choke models if w/o newer Beretta Optima-chokes (12 ga. only, became standard 2003).

MODEL 409 PB – 12, 16, 20, or 28 ga., 27, 28, and 30 in. barrels, various chokes, double triggers, plain extractors, checkered pistol grip stock. Mfg. 1934-1964.

12 or 16 ga.	$1,650	$1,395	$1,100	$875	$675	$550	$450
20 ga.	$1,995	$1,700	$1,450	$1,075	$925	$775	$695
28 ga.	$2,250	$1,925	$1,625	$1,350	$1,075	$875	$725

MODEL 410 E – higher quality, auto ejector version of 409 PB.

12 ga.	$1,925	$1,650	$1,375	$1,125	$850	$750	$675
20 ga.	$2,500	$2,100	$1,775	$1,475	$1,250	$950	$800
28 ga.	$4,100	$3,550	$3,000	$2,500	$1,975	$1,550	$1,225

MODEL 410 – similar to 410 E, except 10 ga. Mag., 32 in. barrels, full choke, heavier construction. Mfg. 1934-1981.

$1,950	$1,675	$1,375	$1,125	$900	$750	$650

MODEL 411 E – similar to 409 PB, with false sideplates and finer finishing. Mfg. 1934-64.

12 ga.	$2,500	$2,100	$1,750	$1,475	$1,250	$975	$825
20 ga.	$3,100	$2,500	$1,875	$1,425	$1,100	$975	$850
28 ga.	$4,650	$4,000	$3,500	$2,975	$2,500	$1,950	$1,600

MODEL 424-426 – 12 and 20 ga. (Model 426 only), 26 and 28 in. barrels, various chokes, boxlock, extractors, double triggers, light engraving, checkered straight stock.

$1,325	$1,175	$1,025	$900	$775	$675	$550

Add $115 for Model 426.
Add 50% for 20 ga.

MODEL 426 E – similar to 424, with auto ejectors, SST, select wood and more intricate engraving, Silver Pigeon inlay. Disc. 1983.

$1,495	$1,300	$1,200	$1,075	$850	$775	$675

MODEL 470 SILVER HAWK (RECENT MFG.) – 12 or 20 ga., 3 in. chambers, 26 or 28 in. barrels with choice of fixed or multi-chokes (new 1999), satin chrome receiver finish, selector lever on forearm allows either automatic ejection or mechanical extraction, straight grip stock with matte finish, 5.9 or 6 1/2 lbs. Mfg. 1998-2002.

$2,350	$1,975	$1,700	$1,500	$1,225	$1,025	$875	*$2,596*

Add 15% for 20 ga.
Add $130 for MobilChokes (new 1999).

MODEL 470 EL – 12 or 20 ga., 3 in. chambers, 26 (20 ga. only) or 28 in. barrels with MC3 choke tubes, or OptimaBore barrels with OptimaChokes, case colored boxlock receiver with 4 gold inlays (doves and ducks) on sideplates, selector lever on forearm allows either automatic ejection or mechanical extraction, deluxe straight grip stock and splinter forearm with oil finish, 5.9 or 6 1/2 lbs. Mfg. 2002-2006.

$4,500	$4,350	$4,000	$3,750	$3,550	$3,200	$2,800	*$6,495*

This model was available only through select Beretta Showcase dealers.

MODEL 471 SILVER HAWK – 12 or 20 ga., 3 in. chambers, 26 (disc. 2011) or 28 in. barrels with MobilChokes or OptimaChokes, engraved satin chrome or color case hardened (disc. 2010) receiver finish, selector lever on forearm allows either automatic ejection or mechanical extraction, ST, choice of straight grip or pistol grip stock with matte finish, beavertail or splinter forearm (fixed chokes only), 5.9 or 6 1/2 lbs. Mfg. 2003-2013.

$3,660	$3,000	$2,700	$2,200	$1,800	$1,500	$1,200	*$3,850*

Add $625 for color case hardened frame with straight grip stock and splinter forearm (IC/IM fixed chokes only), disc. 2010. Last MSR for this option was $4,475.

MODEL 471 EL – 12 or 20 ga., 3 in. chambers, 26 or 28 in. VR barrels, color case hardened receiver with gold accents, satin finished straight grip English style stock. Mfg. 2005-2010.

$7,500	$6,500	$5,500	$4,500	$3,750	$3,150	$2,750	*$8,450*

GRADING - PPGS™	100%	98%	95%	90%	80%	70%	60%	LAST MSR

MODEL 486 PARALLELO – 12, 20, or 28 ga., 3 in. chambers, scalloped coin finished rounded boxlock action, 28 or 30 in. (disc. 2016) barrels with Triblock system, fixed chokes (30 in. only, disc. 2016) or OBFHP chokes, V-shaped hammer spring, select Turkish walnut pistol grip beavertail stock or straight stock with splinter forearm, SST, single steel bead sight, design allows extraction or ejection of spent cartridges, hand rubbed oil finish, 7.2 lbs. New 2014.

MSR $5,799	$4,935	$4,325	$3,700	$3,350	$2,725	$2,225	$1,725	

MODEL 625 – 12 or 20 ga., 26-30 in. barrels, various chokes, boxlock, extractors, DTs or SST, light engraving, checkered straight stock. Imported 1984-86.

	$1,400	$1,125	$950	$775	$650	$600	$550	*$835*

Add 50% for 20 ga.
Add 15% for SST.

MODEL 626/626E FIELD – 12 or 20 (disc. 1987) ga., 2 3/4 in. chambers, boxlock, 26 and 28 in. barrels, various chokes, blue finish, extractors or ejectors, single trigger or double triggers, moderate engraving, pistol grip or straight checkered stock, 6 3/4 lbs. Imported 1984-1988.

	$1,500	$1,300	$1,150	$995	$850	$775	$675	*$995*

Add 50% for 20 ga.

MODEL 626 ONYX – 12 or 20 ga., 3 in. chambers, 26 or 28 (new 1990) in. VR barrels with MobilChokes, matte finished metal, select checkered walnut stock and forearm. Imported 1988-1993.

	$1,650	$1,350	$1,100	$925	$825	$750	$650	*$1,870*

* ***Model 626 Onyx Magnum*** – 12 ga., 3 1/2 in. chambers. Mfg. 1990-1992.

	$1,650	$1,250	$1,050	$925	$825	$750	$650	*$1,870*

MODEL 627 EL FIELD – 12 and 20 (disc. 1987) ga., 2 3/4 (disc. 1990) or 3 in. (became standard in 1991) chambers, 26 and 28 in. barrels, various chokes, boxlock, ejectors, single trigger, extensive engraving, pistol grip or straight checkered stock, cased. Imported 1985-93.

	$2,250	$2,000	$1,800	$1,500	$1,275	$1,000	$900	*$3,270*

Subtract 10% for fixed chokes and 2 3/4 in. chambers.
Add 25% for 20 ga.

* ***Model 627 EL Sport*** – similar to Model 627 EL Field, except 12 ga. only, knurled rib, sporting clays dimensions. Importation disc. 1988.

	$2,500	$2,200	$1,900	$1,625	$1,350	$1,100	$925	*$1,995*

Add 10% for 20 ga.

MODEL 627 EELL – 12 or 20 (disc. 1987) ga., 2 3/4 (disc.) or 3 (12 ga. only) in. chambers, 26 or 28 in. barrels, various chokes, boxlock, ejectors, single trigger, elaborate engraving, pistol grip or straight English checkered stock, cased. Imported 1985-1993.

	$4,700	$4,000	$3,375	$2,950	$2,525	$2,100	$1,825	*$5,405*

Add 10% for 20 ga.
Add 25% for 28 in. barrels.
Subtract 10% if fixed chokes only.

Multi-chokes became standard in 1991.

MODEL GR-2 – 12 or 20 ga., 26 and 28 in. barrels, various chokes, boxlock, extractors, double triggers, checkered pistol grip stock. Mfg. 1968-1976.

	$900	$800	$700	$600	$400	$330	$275	

Add 50% for 20 ga.

MODEL GR-3 – similar to GR-2, with select wood and more engraving. Mfg. 1968-1976.

	$1,095	$995	$800	$550	$475	$425	$375	

Add 50% for 20 ga.

MODEL GR-4 – similar to GR-3, with auto ejectors. Mfg. 1968-1976.

	$1,300	$1,200	$1,075	$900	$775	$675	$600	

Add 50% for 20 ga.

SILVER HAWK – 12 ga. Mag. (3 in. chambers) or 10 ga. Mag. (3 1/2 in. chambers) with double triggers and extractors. Disc. 1967.

	$795	$700	$600	$400	$300	$275	$250	

Subtract 50% for 10 ga.

GRADING - PPGS™	100%	98%	95%	90%	80%	70%	60%	LAST MSR

SILVER HAWK FEATHERWEIGHT – 12, 16, 20, or 28 ga., 26-32 in. barrels, high solid rib, various chokes, single or double triggers, checkered pistol grip stock, beavertail forearm. Disc. 1967.

Double trigger	$1,250	$1,125	$950	$825	$650	$600	$550	
Single trigger	$1,450	$1,300	$1,050	$850	$700	$625	$575	

Add 50% for 20 ga.
Add 100% for 28 ga.

SHOTGUNS: SxS, CUSTOM GRADE

Current custom grade Beretta O/U and SxS shotguns are sold only by premium grade franchised Beretta dealers. For a listing of these dealers, contact a Beretta Gallery.

Where applicable, Beretta's new SST, with selector switch built into safety, is more desirable than older manufacture utilizing the discontinued single, non-selective trigger. Also, hand chased engraving on earlier mfg. (can be denoted by engraver's signature next to trigger guard) is more desirable, and may add a 10% premium, depending on condition.

MODEL 450 SERIES – 12 ga. only, built to individual customer order, various levels of engraving. Disc.

* ***Model 450 EL*** – incorporates H&H type sidelocks.

$8,750 $7,750 $6,150 $5,350 $4,750 $4,200 $3,600

* ***Model 450 EELL*** – features third fastener with H&H type sidelocks.

$10,750 $8,750 $8,000 $6,250 $5,500 $4,850 $4,300

SO-1 – 12 ga. only, entry level sidelock model with light engraving, ejectors, DT standard, cased with accessories. Mfg. 1934-disc.

$4,750 $3,850 $3,150 $2,650 $2,200 $1,800 $1,600

SO-2 – 12 ga. only, similar to the SO-1 except has monobloc shoulders and forend, an engraved release lever, and English-style engraving. Mfg. 1930s-disc.

$6,000 $5,000 $4,150 $3,400 $2,750 $2,400 $1,900

SO-3 – 12 ga., similar to the SO-2 except does not have swivels and plastic buttplate; instead has select walnut stock/forearm, floral motif engraving, and hand-finished diamond checkering. Mfg. 1930s-disc.

$12,000 $10,250 $8,750 $7,500 $6,250 $5,000 $3,750

* ***SO-3 EL*** – similar to the SO-3 except has superior engraving, specially selected walnut, detachable sidelocks, simple screw takedown, and matted hand-knurled ventilated rib. Mfg. circa 1930s-disc.

$13,500 $11,500 $9,750 $8,250 $6,750 $5,250 $4,000

» **SO-3 EELL** – similar to the SO-3 EL except has gold-plated interior parts, trigger, and locking pin, ivory bead front sight, and best quality engraving signed by artist. Mfg. 1930s-disc.

$15,000 $12,750 $10,250 $8,750 $7,000 $5,500 $4,250

SO-4 – standard engraving motifs and custom stock dimensions, DT standard. Mfg. 1968-mid-1980s.

$7,000 $6,000 $5,000 $4,000 $3,250 $2,500 $2,150

SO-6 – same general specifications and embellishments as the SO series O/U guns, but SxS, removable sidelocks, elaborate scroll engraving, cased with accessories. Mfg. 1988-disc.

$17,500 $14,000 $11,250 $9,000 $7,250 $5,750 $4,750

* ***SO-6 EELL*** – similar to the SO-6 except has master engraved floral and traditional game scene, finest burl walnut. Mfg. 1988-disc.

$39,950 $35,000 $30,000 $25,000 $19,950 $16,000 $12,000

SO-6 SPARVIERE – 12 ga. only, sidelock with auto opening sideplates.

Current MSR is $110,000 with upgraded engraving to $175,000.

SO-7 – top of the line SxS, finest quality wood, more elaborate engraving, only 10 mfg.

$45,000 $40,000 $35,000 $30,000 $24,500 $19,950 $15,000

MODEL 451 SERIES – 12 ga., totally hand-made, sidelock action, ejectors, scroll engraving. Custom made to order with fitted luggage case, various grades have increasing embellishments in EL Models.

* ***Model 451*** – disc. 1987.

$6,850 $6,000 $5,150 $4,600 $4,300 $3,995 $3,600 *$12,375*

* ***Model 451 E*** – 12 ga. only, double triggers, specifications furnished by individual customer. Limited importation 1989-disc.

$7,500 $6,200 $5,500 $4,750 $4,000 $3,500 $2,750 *$7,250*

Add approx. 40% for extra set of barrels.
Add $750 for SST (disc.).

GRADING - PPGS™	100%	98%	95%	90%	80%	70%	60%	LAST MSR

* ***Model 451 EL*** – limited importation, temporarily disc. 1984-disc.

	$16,000	$8,500	$7,400	$6,150	$5,500	$4,950	$4,500	*$15,250*

* ***Model 451 EELL*** – top-of-the-line for Model 451, choice of engraving motifs per customer specifications. Disc. 1987, reintroduced 1989-disc.

	$18,500	$9,250	$8,250	$7,150	$6,350	$5,650	$5,050	*$18,500*

MODEL 452 CUSTOM – 12 ga. only, next to top-of-the-line side-by side shotgun featuring H&H style detachable locks, built to customer's specifications, leather cased. Mfg. 1990-disc.

	$31,500	$17,250	$13,000	$9,650	$7,325	$6,050	$5,500	*$35,000*

Add $6,275 for extra set of barrels.

* ***Model 452 EELL Custom*** – 12 ga. only, top-of-the-line custom sidelock model featuring every refinement, built to customer's specifications, leather cased. Importation began 1992-disc.

	$42,850	$23,000	$17,250	$13,000	$10,000	$7,500	$6,000	*$46,500*

Add $6,275 for extra set of barrels.
Add approx. $8,500-$43,500 for special master engraving options.

MODEL 470 EL CUSTOM – 12 or 20 ga., mfg. by Beretta's custom shop per individual order, custom case hardened frame with 24Kt. bird inlays, upgraded wood with oil finish. Mfg. 1999-2016.

	$8,250	$7,000	$5,750	$3,600	$2,800	$2,300	$1,800	*$9,350*

MODEL JUBILEE II (MODEL 470 EELL) – 12 or 20 ga., scroll or game scene engraving signed by the engraver, select SO quality wood with Tru-oil finish, includes suede case, also available in pairs. Mfg. 1999-2013.

	$15,950	$13,750	$9,250	$7,750	$6,250	$5,250	$4,750	*$18,000*

Pairs were available in this model for $35,075.
This model was designated the Model 470 EELL through 1999.

GIUBILEO II – 12 or 20 ga., 3 in. chambers, 26 or 28 in. barrels with fixed chokes, oil finished premium English straight grip style walnut stock and checkered forearm, coin finished engraved boxlock action with sideplates, scroll and floral engraving, 6 1/2 lbs. Mfg. 2007-2013.

	$15,950	$13,750	$9,250	$7,750	$6,250	$5,250	$4,750	*$18,000*

IMPERIALE MONTE CARLO – 12 or 20 ga., best custom sidelock, top-of-the-line, built to customer's specifications with engraving options. Mfg. 2010-disc.

Last MSR on this model was $131,000.
Add $20,000-$25,000 for master engraving.

DIANA – 12 or 20 ga., external hammer, best quality custom model, completely handmade, available with engraving options. Mfg. 2010-disc.

Last MSR on this model was $150,000.
Add $20,000-$50,000 for master engraving.

SHOTGUNS: SINGLE BARREL, DISC.

MARK II TRAP – 12 ga., 32 or 34 in. wide vent. rib, full choke, boxlock with auto ejector, Monte Carlo stock, recoil pad. Mfg. 1972-76.

	$495	$435	$375	$335	$275	$225	$175	

MODEL FS-1 SINGLE BARREL – 12, 16, 20, 28 ga., or .410 bore, 26 or 28 in. barrels, full choke, checkered semi-pistol grip, under lever break open, folds to length of barrel (also known as Companion).

	$175	$155	$130	$125	$95	$80	$60	

Subtract 20% for 12 ga.

TR-1 TRAP – 12 ga., 32 in. full choke barrel, under lever break open, Monte Carlo pistol grip stock with pad, engraved. Mfg. 1968-1971.

	$275	$250	$225	$195	$140	$110	$100	

TR-2 TRAP – similar to TR-1, with high rib. Mfg. 1969-1973.

	$295	$260	$230	$200	$150	$120	$110	

MODEL 412 – 12, 20, 28 ga., or .410 bore, monobloc construction, folding action, sling swivels, checkered walnut stock and forearm, 5 lbs. Importation disc. 1988.

	$195	$165	$140	$130	$100	$85	$65	*$215*

VANDALIA SPECIAL TRAP – 12 ga., sidelock action with crossbolt, fixed choke, coin finished receiver, light scroll hand engraving with borders, cased with accessories, never offically introduced or released commercially. 6 mfg. circa 1997.

	$9,975	$8,725	$7,475	$6,785	$5,475	$4,495	$3,400	

GRADING - PPGS™	100%	98%	95%	90%	80%	70%	60%	LAST MSR

SHOTGUNS: SLIDE ACTION, MFG. 1960-1996

MODEL SL-2 – 12 ga., 26, 28, or 30 in. barrels, various chokes, vent. rib, checkered pistol grip stock. Mfg. 1968-71.

$300	$275	$250	$220	$195	$165	$140

SILVER PIGEON – 12 ga., various chokes, light engraving.

$250	$200	$175	$160	$150	$140	$130

GOLD PIGEON – 12 ga., various chokes, vent. rib, engraved.

$475	$375	$310	$275	$240	$215	$195

Add $200 for deluxe models.

RUBY PIGEON – 12 ga., various chokes, vent. rib, elaborately engraved, special deluxe walnut.

$600	$475	$395	$350	$295	$260	$230

SHOTGUNS: SEMI-AUTO

It is possible on some of the following models to have production variances occur including different engraving motifs, stock configurations and specifications, finishes, etc. These have occurred when Beretta changed from production of one model to another. Also, some European and English distributors have sold their excess inventory through Beretta U.S.A., creating additional variations/configurations that are not normally imported domestically. While sometimes rare, these specimens typically do not command premiums over Beretta's domestic models.

The following Beretta semi-auto models have been listed in numerical sequence, if possible, disregarding any alphabetical suffix or prefix.

Note: values are for unaltered guns.

Subtract 10% on the following factory multi-choke models if w/o newer Beretta Optima-chokes (12 ga. only, became standard 2003).

MODEL 60 – 12 ga., 2 3/4 in. chamber, gas operated with piston rod, 3 shot mag., 24, 26, or 28 in. plain barrel, approx. 7 lbs. Mfg. 1956-1960.

$295	$260	$240	$220	$200	$185	$170

Add 10% for Model 60 Deluxe with special embellishments.

MODEL 61 – 12 ga., improved version of the Model 60 with recoil spring located in stock, chromium plated action and fine engraving, 24, 26, or 28 in. VR barrel. Mfg. approx. 1961-1965.

$335	$295	$260	$235	$210	$195	$175

SILVER LARK – 12 ga., various chokes.

$295	$260	$240	$220	$200	$185	$170

GOLD LARK – 12 ga., vent. rib, light scroll engraving, select walnut.

$480	$400	$325	$260	$230	$210	$195

RUBY LARK – 12 ga., vent. rib, heavy engraving, deluxe walnut.

$675	$550	$475	$395	$350	$295	$260

MODEL AL-1 – 12 and 20 ga., gas operated, 26, 28, and 30 in. plain barrel, various chokes, checkered pistol grip stock. Mfg. 1971-1973.

$385	$360	$330	$300	$250	$195	$165

MODEL AL-2 – 12 or 20 ga., 26, 28, or 30 in. barrels, vent. rib, various chokes, gas operated, checkered pistol grip stock. Mfg. 1973-75.

$330	$305	$275	$250	$220	$195	$165

MODEL AL-2 SKEET – similar to AL-2, with 26 in. wide rib skeet bored barrel. Mfg. 1973-75.

$395	$360	$320	$275	$220	$200	$185

MODEL AL-2 TRAP – similar to AL-2, with 30 in. full choke barrel, wide rib, Monte Carlo stock, with recoil pad. Mfg. 1973-75.

$375	$345	$315	$285	$250	$195	$165

MODEL AL-2 MAGNUM – 12 or 20 ga., 3 in. chamber, heavier action bar, 28 and 30 in. mod. or full choke. Mfg. 1973-75.

$415	$385	$330	$275	$250	$230	$210

MODEL AL-3 – continuation of the AL-2 series. Mfg. 1975-1976.

Field grade	$395	$360	$330	$260	$240	$220	$190
Magnum grade	$395	$350	$300	$275	$250	$230	$210
Skeet grade	$400	$360	$330	$260	$240	$220	$190
Trap grade	$385	$350	$295	$250	$225	$210	$185

GRADING - PPGS™ 100% 98% 95% 90% 80% 70% 60% LAST MSR

MODEL AL-3 DELUXE TRAP – similar to AL-3, with fully engraved receiver, premium grade wood. Mfg. 1975-76.

$600 $550 $500 $450 $425 $400 $375

MODEL UGB25 XCEL TRAP – 12 ga., 2 3/4 in. chamber, unique two shot (second shell is located outside receiver on cartridge carrier), break open action featuring short recoil operating system, rising lock block system, light alloy black receiver with gold lettering, 30 or 32 (disc.) in. three alloy steel OptimaBore barrel, competition front sight, laser-checkered walnut stock with adj. comb, gold trigger, button safety, Gel-Tek recoil pad, 7.7-9 lbs. Prototypes were introduced late 2004, but regular production started late 2007-2013.

$3,625 $2,500 $2,100 $1,800 $1,450 $1,175 $950 *$4,125*

* ***Model UGB25 Xcel Gold Sporting*** – 12 ga., similar to UGB25 Xcel Trap, except does not have adj. comb, 28 or 30 in. barrel with OptimaChoke High Performance chokes, approx. 8 lbs. Mfg. 2010-2013.

$3,575 $2,500 $2,100 $1,800 $1,450 $1,175 $950 *$3,975*

MODEL PINTAIL/ES100 PINTAIL (VITORIA) – 12 ga., 3 in. chamber, same action as the Benelli SL80 Series shotguns, 24, 26, or 28 (new 1999) in. VR barrel, matte black metal finish, choice of matte finished wood (disc. 1998) or black synthetic stock and forearm (new 1999), includes sling swivels, 7.3 lbs. Frame manufactured in Vitoria, Spain, and barrels were made in Italy. Mfg. 1993-2001, reintroduced 2003 only.

$720 $680 $625 $525 $425 $325 $250 *$682*

Subtract 15-20% for wood stock and forearm.
Subtract 20% for Vitoria market guns.

In 1999, this model was renamed the ES 100 Pintail (with synthetic stock). This Beretta model is the same gun as the Benelli SL80 Series guns, with a few cosmetic changes.

* ***Model ES100 Camouflage*** – 12 ga. only, features 100% Advantage Wetlands, Realtree Hardwoods HD (new 2003), or Mossy Oak Shadowgrass (new 2003) coverage, 28 in. VR barrel only, 7.3 lbs. Mfg. 2000-2003.

$850 $795 $700 $600 $475 $350 $275 *$777*

* ***Model ES100 Rifled Slug (Pintail Rifled Slug)*** – 12 ga., 3 in. chamber, 24 in. rifled barrel with drilled and tapped upper receiver, barrel and upper receiver are permanently joined, anti-glare matte black metal finish, choice of matte finished wood (disc. 1998) or black synthetic (new 1999) stock and forearm, includes sling swivels, 7 lbs. Mfg. 1998-2001, reintroduced 2003 only.

$825 $725 $675 $575 $450 $350 $225 *$749*

Add $148 for combo package (includes extra 28 in. smoothbore barrel with MC3 choke, mfg. 2001).

In 1999, the model nomenclature changed from Pintail Rifled Slug to ES100 Rifled Slug.

* ***Model ES100 Pintail Slug (Vitoria)*** – 12 ga. only, 24 in. slug barrel, includes rifle sights and rifle choke tubes, wood stock, 7 lbs. Imported 1993-95.

$695 $550 $500 $425 $375 $275 $200 *$700*

* ***Model ES100 NWTF Special Camouflage (Pintail)*** – 12 ga. only, 24 in. VR barrel with 3-dot TruGlo fiber optic sight system, includes Briley extended extra-full choke tube and 3 standard MobilChoke tubes, features Mossy Oak Break-Up treatment on synthetic stock and forearm, black matte anti-glare finish on metal components, includes nylon sling. Limited mfg. 1999, reintroduced 2002 only (limited mfg.).

$900 $850 $775 $675 $495 $300 $225 *$966*

MODEL 300/301 – continuation of the AL-3 series, scroll engraved receiver. Mfg. approx. 1968-82.

Field Grade $525 $460 $400 $350 $300 $240 $180
Magnum Grade $575 $500 $425 $400 $325 $260 $200
Skeet Grade $550 $475 $415 $375 $315 $250 $190
Trap Grade $550 $475 $415 $375 $315 $250 $190

Beretta changed model nomenclature rapidly during the Model 300 Series. In approx. 10 months, the evolution of this model had progressed from the 300 to 303 Series. Beginning with the Model 303, all receivers were milled with a 3 in. ejection port window.

MODEL A300 OUTLANDER – 12 ga., 3 in. chamber, gas operation with compensating gas valve and self-cleaning piston, 24 (new 2019) or 28 in. VR barrel with F, M, and IC chokes, black synthetic, oiled wood, or 100% Max-4 (disc. 2013) or Realtree Max-5 (new mid-2014) camo coverage, fitted rubber recoil pad, crossbolt safety, front metal bead sight, 7.1 lbs. New 2012.

MSR $799 $675 $600 $500 $425 $375 $325 $295

Add $100 for oiled wood.
Add $100 for 100% Realtree Max-5 (new 2014) camo coverage.
Add $70 for 100% Max-4 camo coverage (disc. 2013).

GRADING - PPGS™	100%	98%	95%	90%	80%	70%	60%	LAST MSR

* ***Model A300 Outlander Camo True Timber DRT Limited Edition*** – 12 ga., gas operated, 28 in. barrel, MC3 Mobilchokes, 2 shot mag., aluminum alloy receiver, polymer trigger guard, walnut stock, swivel stud, True Timber DRT finish. Limited mfg. beginning 2018.

MSR $900	$795	$725	$650	$575	$525	$450	$395	

This model is only available through Bass Pro Shops.

* ***Model A300 Outlander Sporting*** – 12 ga., 3 in. chamber, 30 in. cold hammer forged barrel with wide sporting rib and three MobilChoke Victory choke tubes, engraved and colored receiver, mid-bead sight, high grade wood sporting stock with enhanced engraving, Micro-Core Sporting pad, gas operated system with locked breech. New 2018.

MSR $1,100	$950	$850	$750	$650	$550	$475	$425	

MODEL A300 OUTLANDER TURKEY CAMO – 12 ga., 3 in. chamber, 24 in. VR barrel w/extended full choke tube, TruGlo sights, 100% Realtree Xtra Green camo finish. Mfg. 2016-2020.

	$795	$725	$650	$575	$525	$450	$395	*$900*

MODEL A300 XTREMA – 12 ga., 3 1/2 in. chamber, 28 in. VR barrel with three Optimabore chokes, 100% coverage Max-4 camo finish. Mfg. 2014 only.

	$1,195	$1,050	$925	$800	$700	$575	$450	*$1,350*

MODEL 301 SLUG GUN – 22 in. barrel, with sights. Disc.

	$395	$365	$340	$310	$280	$255	$225	

MODEL 302 – 12 or 20 ga., self-compensating gas operation semi-auto, designed for both 2 3/4 and 3 in. shells, available with interchangeable chokes, slug barrel, trap and skeet models (disc.), VR, mag. cut-off. Mfg. 1982-87. This model was superceded by the Model 303.

	$395	$365	$340	$310	$280	$255	$225	*$480*

Add $30 for multi-choke set.

* ***Model 302 Super Lusso*** – same specifications as Model A302, but includes hand engraved receiver, many gold plated parts, and stock and forearm made from presentation grade walnut. Disc. 1986.

	$1,700	$1,500	$1,250	$1,025	$900	$800	$700	*$2,500*

MODEL A-303 FIELD – 12 (disc. 1993) or 20 ga., 2 3/4 or 3 in. chambers, same gas operation as the Model 302, 26 or 28 in. VR barrel, high-strength alloy receiver, select wood with choice of pistol grip or straight English stock, beavertail forearm, MobilChokes became standard 1987. Disc. 1996.

	$450	$400	$375	$335	$300	$270	$240	*$799*

Subtract 20% if without multi-chokes.
Subtract $20 for straight grip English stock.

* ***Model A-303 Upland*** – 12 (disc. 1993) or 20 ga., 2 3/4 or 3 in. chamber, 24 in. VR barrel with MobilChokes, English style straight stock, approx. 7 lbs. Imported 1989-1996.

	$450	$400	$380	$335	$300	$270	$240	*$772*

* ***Model A-303 Waterfowl/Turkey*** – 12 ga. only, 3 in. chamber, choice of 24, 26, 28, or 30 in. VR barrel, matte finished wood and metal, MobilChokes are standard. Imported 1991 only.

	$450	$400	$380	$335	$300	$270	$240	*$665*

* ***Model A-303 Sporting*** – 12 (disc. 1994) or 20 (new 1991) ga. only, 2 3/4 in. chambers, sporting clay dimensions, 28 or 30 (12 ga. only) in. VR barrel with MobilChokes. Mfg. 1988-1996.

	$495	$450	$425	$375	$325	$300	$275	*$822*

Subtract 10% for 28 in. barrel.

* ***Model A-303 Skeet*** – 12 (disc. 1994) or 20 ga., 26 in. VR barrel with fixed skeet choking. Importation disc. 1995.

	$400	$375	$350	$315	$275	$250	$225	*$736*

* ***Model A-303 Super Skeet*** – 12 ga. only, 28 in. VR fixed choke barrel, features factory porting, adj. LOP, and adj. separate cheekpiece on stock. Mfg. 1991-92.

	$425	$375	$350	$315	$280	$240	$200	*$1,160*

* ***Model A-303 Trap*** – 12 ga. only, 30 or 32 in. VR barrel with fixed choking or MobilChokes. Importation disc. 1994.

	$450	$400	$380	$350	$325	$300	$275	*$735*

Add $40 for MobilChokes (with Monte Carlo stock).

* ***Model A-303 Super Trap*** – 12 ga. only, 30 or 32 in. VR MobilChoke barrel with step tapered rib, features factory porting, adj. LOP, and adj. separate cheekpiece on stock. Mfg. 1991-1992.

	$550	$525	$500	$450	$425	$365	$300	*$1,210*

GRADING - PPGS™	100%	98%	95%	90%	80%	70%	60%	LAST MSR

* ***Model A-303 Slug*** – 12 or 20 ga., 3 in. chamber (12 ga. only), 22 in. cylinder bore barrel, iron sights. Importation disc. 1991.

	$395	$350	$325	$300	$275	$265	$240	$665

* ***Model A-303 Youth*** – 20 ga. only, 2 3/4 or 3 (disc.) in. chamber, 24 in. VR barrel with MobilChokes, shortened stock, approx. 6 lbs. Mfg. 1988-1996.

	$400	$375	$350	$325	$300	$270	$240	$772

MODEL A304 LARK – 12 ga., 2 3/4 in. chamber, 20 (Silver Slug), 22 (Silver Slug), 24, 26, 28, or 30 in. barrel, vent. rib (except Silver Slug model), MobilChoke or cylinder (Silver Slug) bore, ambidextrous safety, crossbolt, checkered walnut pistol grip stock and semi-beavertail forend, black recoil pad, black matte finished receiver with light scroll work, gold trigger, available in Silver Lark, Silver Slug, or Gold Lark. Mfg. 1994-disc.

	$450	$400	$375	$335	$300	$270	$240	

Add 10% for Silver Lark with scroll engraved black receiver.
Add 20% for White or Black A304 Gold Lark Model with gold filled P. Beretta signature and game scene engraving.

MODEL A350 EXTREMA – 12 ga., 3 1/2 in. chamber, 28 in. VR Steelium barrel w/Optima HP choke tubes, fiber optic front sight, stock features Micro Core recoil pad, adj. LOP, black synthetic or 100% Realtree Max-5 camo (mfg. 2017 only) finish, 7 3/4 lbs. Mfg. in Italy 2017-2018.

	$900	$775	$700	$625	$550	$495	$425	$1,050

Add $100 for Realtree Max-5 camo finish (mfg. 2017 only).

* ***Model A350 Extrema Turkey*** – 12 ga., 3 1/2 in. chamber, gas operating system, 24 in. cold hammer forged Steelium barrel with OBHP chokes, Micro Core recoil pad, 100% Mossy Oak Obsession camo finish. Mfg. mid-2017-2018.

	$1,200	$995	$875	$775	$700	$625	$550	$1,365

MODEL AL390 FIELD SILVER MALLARD – 12 or 20 (new 1997) ga. only, 3 in. chamber, features gas system that accepts all 2 3/4 and 3 in. shotshells, single stainless steel piston with self regulating valve, mag. cut-off on left side of receiver, 22 slug (12 ga. only, new 1994), 24, 26, 28, or 30 (12 ga. only) in. VR barrel with MobilChoke system, choice of gloss or matte (includes sling swivels) wood finish on lightly engraved receiver, adj. checkered walnut stock, gold trigger, 6.4 (20 ga.) or 7.2 (12 ga.) lbs. Mfg. 1992-1999.

	$725	$635	$550	$495	$400	$325	$250	$860

Add $25 for 20 ga.
Subtract $25 for 24 in. barrel.

Beginning 1997, Beretta introduced the "AL" Series of the 390, which is the lightweight variation of the 390. Prior to 1997, this model was designated the A390 Series.

* ***Model AL390 Field Deluxe Gold Mallard*** – similar to Model 390 Field, except has gold accents on receiver, including a gold inlaid snipe, setter, and P. Beretta signature, deluxe walnut, 7.2 lbs. Mfg. 1993-99.

	$850	$750	$650	$575	$475	$385	$300	$1,025

Add $30 for 20 ga.

* ***Model AL390 Lioness Limited Edition*** – 12 ga. only, 28 in. VR barrel with MC3 choke tubes, deluxe checkered walnut stock and forearm. Limited mfg. 2002.

	$2,450	$1,950	$1,600	$1,410	$1,160	$980	$800	$2,969

* ***Model AL390 Silver Mallard Synthetic*** – 12 ga. only, 3 in. chamber, 24, 26, 28, or 30 in. barrel with MobilChoke, black synthetic stock and forearm with sling swivels, matte finish, approx. 7.2 lbs. Mfg. 1996-99.

	$725	$635	$550	$495	$400	$325	$250	$885

* ***Model AL390 Silver Mallard Camouflage*** – 12 ga. only, 3 in. chamber, Advantage camo finish on entire gun, 24 or 28 in. VR barrel with choke tubes, synthetic stock and forearm, 7.2 lbs. Mfg. 1997-99.

	$750	$650	$575	$510	$425	$350	$275	$1,020

* ***Model AL390 Silver Mallard Slug*** – 12 ga. only, 3 in. chamber, 22 in. non-rifled barrel with slug choke, gloss wood finish, adj. rear sight, approx. 6.8 or 7.4 (Model A390) lbs. Mfg. 1995-97.

	$600	$525	$450	$410	$325	$275	$225	$860

* ***Model AL390 Silver Mallard Youth*** – 20 ga. only, 3 in. chamber, gloss wood finish, 24 in. VR barrel only with choke tubes, features youth stock dimensions, 6.4 lbs. Mfg. 1997-99.

	$725	$635	$550	$495	$400	$325	$250	$885

GRADING - PPGS™	100%	98%	95%	90%	80%	70%	60%	LAST MSR

* ***Model AL390 NWTF Special Camouflage*** – 12 ga. only, 3 in. chamber, 24 in. VR barrel with 3-dot TruGlo fiber optic sight system, includes Briley extended extra-full choke tube and 3 standard MobilChoke tubes, full Realtree X-tra Brown camo treatment (including synthetic stock and forearm), includes camo nylon sling. Special Edition released during 1999 only.

	$900	$795	$675	$610	$495	$400	$375	*$1,105*

» **Model AL390 NWTF Special Synthetic** – similar to NWTF Special Camouflage, except has matte black anti-glare finish. Mfg. 1999 only.

	$800	$700	$600	$550	$440	$360	$275	*$970*

* ***Model AL390 NWTF Special Youth*** – 20 ga. only, 3 in. chamber, 24 in. barrel, shorter stock dimensions with 13 1/2 in. LOP, matte finished wood stock and forearm, matte black metal anti-glare finish. Mfg. 1999 only.

	$750	$650	$565	$510	$415	$340	$265	*$910*

MODEL AL390 SPORT SPORTING – 12 or 20 (new 1997) ga., 3 in. chamber, designed for sporting clays competition, similar to Model 390 Sport Skeet, 28 or 30 (12 ga. only) in. VR ported or unported barrel with choke tube, 6.8 (20 ga.) or 7.6 (12 ga.) lbs. Imported 1995-99.

	$775	$675	$575	$525	$425	$350	$275	*$925*

* ***Model AL390 Sport Sporting Collection*** – 12 or 20 (Youth Model) ga., 3 in. chamber, 26 (20 ga. only), 28 in. VR barrel with MobilChoke, features multi-colored, gloss finished stock and forearm, 6.7 (20 ga.) or 7.6 (12 ga.) lbs. Mfg. 1998-99.

	$800	$700	$600	$550	$440	$360	$275	*$965*

The 20 ga. in this model was a youth model with 13 1/2 in. LOP.

* ***Model AL390 Sport Sporting Gold*** – 12 ga. only, 28 or 30 in. VR barrel with MobilChokes, gloss finished wood, gold engraved receiver, 7.6 lbs. Mfg. 1997-99.

	$950	$825	$715	$650	$525	$450	$425	*$1,145*

Subtract 10% for 28 in. barrel.

* ***Model AL390 Sport Sporting Diamond*** – 12 ga. only, 3 in. chamber, silver sided receiver with multiple gold inlays, EELL quality stock and forearm with oil finish, matte 28 or 30 in. barrel with MobilChokes, oval nameplate on stock, 7.6 lbs. Mfg. 1998-99.

	$2,000	$1,650	$1,450	$1,275	$1,200	$995	$825	*$3,075*

Subtract 10% for 26 in. barrel.

* ***Model AL390 Sport Sporting Youth*** – 20 ga. only, 3 in. chamber, matte finished checkered stock and forearm, 26 in. VR barrel only with choke tubes, features youth stock dimensions (13 1/2 in. LOP), 6.7 lbs. Imported 1997-1998 only.

	$750	$650	$565	$510	$415	$340	$265	*$900*

MODEL AL390 SPORT SKEET – 12 ga. only, 3 in. chamber, 26 (disc.) or 28 in. SK bored VR barrel, matte finish on wood and metal, black rubber recoil pad, 7.6 lbs. Imported 1995-99.

	$725	$625	$550	$495	$400	$325	$250	*$890*

* ***Model AL390 Sport Super Skeet*** – 12 ga. only, 28 in. skeet choke VR ported barrels, includes adj. stock comb and LOP (using 3 different recoil pads) approx. 8.1 lbs. Mfg. 1993-99.

	$975	$850	$725	$675	$525	$440	$340	*$1,160*

MODEL AL390 SPORT TRAP – 12 ga. only, 3 in. chamber, 30 or 32 in. VR barrel, matte finish on wood and metal, black rubber recoil pad, 7.8 or 8 1/4 (A390) lbs. Imported 1995-99.

	$725	$625	$550	$495	$400	$325	$250	*$890*

* ***Model AL390 Sport Trap Super*** – 12 ga. only, 30 or 32 in. VR MobilChoke ported barrels, adj. stock comb and LOP, approx. 8 lbs. Mfg. 1993-97.

	$600	$500	$450	$400	$375	$325	$295	*$1,215*

MODEL AL391 URIKA – 12 or 20 ga., 3 in. chamber, features new self-compensating gas valve and receiver recoil absorber for internal shock reduction, satin finished checkered walnut stock and forearm, gas valve is located on the front bottom of the forearm, alloy receiver with thin design, cold hammer forged barrel, black anodized metal surfaces, gold trigger, beginning 2003, all 12 ga. AL391 Urika models include OptimaBore barrels with OptimaChoke Plus tubes, molded synthetic case included, 6.3-7.3 lbs. Mfg. 2000-2006.

* ***Model AL391 Urika Standard*** – 12 or 20 ga., 24 (20 ga. only), 26, 28, or 30 (12 ga. only, disc. 2005) in. VR barrel, available in synthetic stock beginning 2004 at no charge, approx. 5.95 (20 ga.) or 7 1/4 lbs. Mfg. 2000-2006.

	$850	$725	$600	$525	$500	$400	$350	*$1,050*

GRADING - PPGS™	100%	98%	95%	90%	80%	70%	60%	LAST MSR

* ***Model AL391 Urika Synthetic Optima*** – 12 ga. only, 24 (disc. 2003), 26, 28, or 30 (disc. 2003) in. VR barrel with matte finish, features black synthetic stock with oversized grip area for a secure grip and recoil absorption and forearm, OptimaChokes became standard in 2004, approx. 7 1/4 lbs. Mfg. 2000-2006.

	$775	$650	$550	$475	$400	$350	$325	*$998*

Subtract 20% for MobilChokes.

* ***Model AL391 Urika Camouflage*** – 12 ga. only, choice of 100% Hardwoods Green HD (mfg. 2003), RealTree Hardwoods HD (24 in. barrel only, turkey configuration), Max-4 HD (new 2004), or Advantage Wetlands camo (28 in. barrel only, waterfowl configuration, mfg. 2003) finish, with oversized stock grip, approx. 7 1/4 lbs. Mfg. 2000-2006.

	$895	$750	$650	$550	$525	$425	$350	*$1,175*

* ***Model AL391 Urika Youth*** – 20 ga. only, 24 in. VR barrel only, shortened walnut stock and regular forearm, 5.95 lbs. Mfg. 2000-2006.

	$800	$675	$575	$495	$400	$350	$325	*$1,050*

* ***Model AL391 Urika Gold*** – 12 or 20 ga., similar to Model AL391 Urika Standard, except has deluxe checkered walnut stock and forearm, choice of black (standard) or partial silver (lightweight configuration, 12 ga. only) receiver finish, multiple gold receiver inlays, 26 or 28 in. VR barrel, jewelled bolt, 5.9 (20 ga.), 6.6 (12 ga. lightweight), or approx. 7 1/4 lbs. Mfg. 2000-2002.

	$795	$725	$625	$495	$400	$350	$300	*$1,213*

* ***Model AL391 Urika Covey Quail Unlimited*** – 20 ga., matte black receiver with multiple gold quail inlays, deluxe checkered walnut stock and forearm, marked "1 of 1000." 1,000 mfg. 2003-2004.

	$825	$775	$700	$650	$600	$500	$425	*$1,336*

* ***Model AL391 Urika Ringneck Pheasants Forever*** – 12 ga., matte black receiver with multiple gold pheasant inlays, deluxe checkered walnut stock and forearm, includes Gel-Tek recoil pad and OptimaBore barrel with OptimaChokes, marked "1 of 1000." 1,000 mfg. 2003-2004.

	$995	$895	$825	$775	$675	$550	$450	*$1,377*

MODEL AL391 URIKA SPORTING – 12 or 20 ga., 3 in. chamber, gas operating system the same as Model Al391 Urika Standard, 28 or 30 in. wide VR barrel with 2 beads, features special competition checkered walnut sporting stock with rounded solid rubber recoil pad, satin black receiver with silver markings, gold trigger, MobilChoke tubes are standard on 20 ga., OptimaBore barrel with OptimaChoke Flush tubes became standard in 12 ga. during 2003 (AL391 Urika Sporting Optima), molded synthetic case included, 5.95 or 7.3 lbs. Mfg. 2000-2006.

	$1,025	$825	$725	$650	$575	$475	$375	*$1,250*

* ***Model AL391 Urika Gold Sporting*** – similar to Model AL391 Urika Gold, except has deluxe walnut stock and forearm, with choice of black (disc.) or silver receiver and gold accents. Mfg. 2000-2006.

	$1,150	$975	$825	$700	$650	$550	$450	*$1,500*

* ***Model AL391 Urika Diamond Sporting*** – 12 ga. only, 3 in. chamber, silver sided receiver with multiple gold inlays, EELL quality stock and forearm with oil finish, matte 28 in. barrel with MC4 chokes, oval nameplate on stock, 7.6 lbs. Mfg. 2002 only.

	$2,000	$1,850	$1,700	$1,525	$1,200	$995	$775	*$3,139*

MODEL AL391 URIKA TRAP OPTIMA – 12 ga. only, 30 or 32 in. wide VR barrel with 2 beads, Monte Carlo stock with special trap recoil pad, satin black receiver with glossy side panels and silver markings, gold trigger, OptimaBore barrel with OptimaChoke flush tubes became standard in 12 ga. during 2003, molded synthetic case included, 7 1/4 lbs. Mfg. 2000-2006.

	$950	$815	$695	$600	$500	$400	$350	*$1,250*

* ***Model AL391 Urika Trap Gold*** – similar to Model AL391 Urika Trap, except has black receiver with gold filled Beretta logo and P. Beretta signature, jewelled bolt and carrier, 7 1/4 lbs. Mfg. 2000-2002.

	$995	$850	$725	$565	$450	$415	$395	*$1,254*

MODEL AL391 URIKA PARALLEL TARGET RL/SL – 12 ga. only, similar to Model AL391 Urika Trap, except features a Monte Carlo stock with parallel comb and reduced grip radius, RL suffix designates shorter LOP and slimmer grip, molded synthetic case included, 7 1/4 lbs. Mfg. 2000-2006.

	$995	$825	$725	$675	$600	$500	$400	*$1,250*

MODEL AL391 TEKNYS – 12 or 20 ga., 3 in. chamber, multi-colored receiver with unique asymetrical patterns, X-tra Wood stock with Gel-Tek recoil pad, anti-glare receiver top, TruGlo Tru-bead front sight, choice of OptimaBore barrel with OptimaChokes or MobilChokes (20 ga.), includes molded case with 5 choke tubes, 5.9 (20 ga.) or 7.3 (12 ga.) lbs. Imported 2003-2005.

	$1,200	$1,000	$875	$725	$575	$475	$400	*$1,425*

GRADING - PPGS™	100%	98%	95%	90%	80%	70%	60%	LAST MSR

* ***Model AL391 Teknys Gold*** – 12 or 20 ga., 3 in. chamber, 26 or 28 in. VR barrel, receiver has engraved hunting scenes, jewelled breech bolt and carrier, checkered deluxe walnut stock and forearm with green colored enamel inserts in rear receiver and front of stock, includes Gel-Tek recoil pad, and stock recoil reducer. Mfg. 2003-2010.

$2,000	$1,650	$1,425	$1,200	$1,000	$850	$700	*$1,950*

» **Model AL391 Teknys Gold King Ranch** – 12 or 20 ga., similar to AL391 Teknys Gold, except has 26 or 28 in. VR barrel, ranch stable engraving and rope bordered logo. Mfg. 2006-2011.

$2,250	$1,900	$1,675	$1,450	$1,200	$1,000	$800	*$2,075*

* ***Model AL391 Teknys Gold Sporting*** – 12 or 20 ga., similar to Model AL391 Teknys Gold, except has 28 or 30 in. barrel, two-tone dark grey receiver with blue enamel inserts on stock and receiver, interchangeable rib, improved forearm checkering pattern, includes Gel-Tek recoil pad and stock recoil reducer, deluxe checkered walnut stock and forearm, includes hard case, 6.6 (20 ga.) or 7.9 (12 ga.) lbs. Imported 2003-2013.

$2,100	$1,725	$1,475	$1,250	$1,050	$875	$725	*$2,325*

* ***Model AL391 Teknys Gold Trap*** – 12 ga. only, 30 or 32 in. VR barrel, oil finished checkered walnut stock, gold trigger, Gel-Tek recoil pad, includes hardshell case. Imported 2004-2010.

$2,250	$1,900	$1,675	$1,450	$1,200	$1,000	$800	*$2,300*

* ***Model AL391 Teknys Gold Target*** – 12 ga. only, 30 in. VR barrel with interchangeable VRs and Optima-Plus choking, includes 8 1/2 oz. recoil reducer, deluxe checkered walnut stock w/adj. comb, satin nickel finished receiver with blue enamel accents on back of frame and stock. Mfg. 2007-2013.

$2,400	$2,025	$1,775	$1,525	$1,250	$1,050	$850	*$2,540*

MODEL AL391 XTREMA2 3.5 (AL 391 XTREMA 3.5) – 12 ga. only, 3 1/2 in. chamber, features Gel-Tek recoil pad, spring mass and bolt travel recoil reducers lower felt recoil up to 20%, 24 (disc.), 26, or 28 in. VR OptimaBore barrel with OptimaChoke Plus tubes, gas operating system with rotating locking bolt, black synthetic stock and forearm with rubber inserts for firm control instead of traditional checkering, grooved receiver, removable trigger group, includes carrying case, 7.8 lbs. Mfg. 2002-2011.

$1,150	$975	$850	$725	$625	$525	$475	*$1,350*

Add $250 for KO configuration (Kick-Off recoil reduction).

This model's nomenclature changed to Xtrema2 during 2005.

* ***Model AL391 Xtrema2 Camouflage (AL391 Extreme Camouflage)*** – 12 ga. only, similar operating system to Model AL391 Xtrema 3.5, choice of 100% RealTree Hardwoods HD (24 in. barrel only, turkey configuration, disc. 2006), RealTree All-Purpose (new 2007), Max-4 HD (new 2004), Advantage Timber HD camo (26 in. barrel only, disc. 2004) or Advantage Wetlands (26 or 28 in. barrel, disc. 2004) finish, 7.8 lbs. Mfg. 2002-2012.

$1,340	$1,075	$850	$675	$550	$500	$450	*$1,450*

Add $250 for KO configuration (Kick-Off recoil reduction), disc. 2011.

* ***Model AL391 Xtrema2 Slug*** – 12 ga. only, 24 in. rifled OptimaBore barrel. Mfg. 2005-2007.

$1,100	$950	$800	$675	$575	$475	$400	*$1,450*

Add $150 for KO configuration (Kick-Off recoil reduction).

MODEL AL391 URIKA 2 – 12 or 20 ga., 3 in. chamber, features an improved gas system which is both faster and self-cleaning, various configurations. Mfg. 2007-2013.

* ***Model AL391 Urika 2 Standard*** – 12 (disc.) or 20 ga., features Beretta's new proprietary X-Tra grain wood enhancement on stock and forearm, 26 or 28 in. VR barrel w/choice of OptimaChokes or MobilChokes, fine line scroll engraving on receiver. Disc. 2013.

$1,300	$1,050	$925	$800	$675	$550	$495	*$1,565*

* ***Model AL391 Urika 2 Youth*** – 20 ga., 24 in. VR barrel, similar to Standard, except has shorter dimensions. Disc. 2013.

$1,300	$1,050	$925	$800	$675	$550	$495	*$1,565*

* ***Model AL391 Urika 2 Synthetic*** – 12 ga., similar to Standard model, except 28 in. barrel only, features black synthetic stock, available with or w/o Kick-Off recoil reducer (two shock absorbers). Disc. 2013.

$975	$815	$675	$575	$475	$400	$350	*$1,105*

Add $410 for Kick-Off recoil reduction.

Add $425 for Urika 2 Synthetic Sporting Model w/Kick-Off (mfg. 2008-2011).

* ***Model AL391 Urika 2 Camo*** – 12 ga., similar to Standard model, except features Advantage Max-4 or Realtree AP camo treatment, with or w/o Kick-Off recoil reducer. Disc. 2013.

$1,050	$875	$775	$650	$575	$475	$425	*$1,215*

Add $405 for Kick-Off recoil reduction.

GRADING - PPGS™	100%	98%	95%	90%	80%	70%	60%	LAST MSR

* ***Model AL391 Urika 2 Gold*** – 12 or 20 ga., oil finished wood stock and forend, engraved receiver with gold game bird inlays. Disc. 2009.

	$1,375	$1,100	$875	$725	$625	$525	$475	*$1,550*

* ***Model AL391 Urika 2 Sporting*** – 12 or 20 ga., 28 or 30 in. barrel w/either OptimaChoke (12 ga.) or MobilChoke (20 ga.) choke tubes, features Beretta X-Tra Grain wood enhancement on stock and forearm. Disc. 2012.

	$1,300	$1,050	$925	$825	$700	$575	$500	*$1,565*

Add $375 for AL391 Urika 2 Gold Sporting (12 ga. only, includes gold inlays on receiver), disc. 2011.

* ***Model AL391 Urika 2 Parallel*** – 12 ga., 28, 30, or 32 in. VR OptimaBore barrel with OptimaChoke Plus tubes, X-Tra Grain wood enhancement on stock and forearm, available in RL (Youth) or SL configurations. Disc. late 2011.

	$1,300	$1,050	$925	$825	$700	$575	$500	*$1,565*

Add $325 for AL391 Urika 2 Gold Parallel (includes gold inlays on receiver), disc. 2011.

A400 EXTREME PLUS – 12 ga., 3 1/2 in. chamber, 26, 28, or 30 (new 2020) in. Steelium Plus barrel with step rib, 5 OptimaBore HP chokes, black extended choke tube, integral mid-bead and fiber optic front sight, Kick-Off Mega stock with soft comb, adj. LOP, extended charging handle and bolt release, drilled and tapped for Picatinny rail, enlarged loading port, right or left-hand configuration, black synthetic, Mossy Oak Bottomland, Realtree Max-5, True Timber DRT, Optifade Marsh (new 2019), or Optifade Timber finish. New 2018.

MSR $1,749	$1,485	$1,300	$1,115	$1,010	$825	$700	$550	

Add $50 for left-hand configuration (available in black synthetic, Mossy Oak Bottomland, or Realtree Max-5 camo finish only).

Add $100 for Mossy Oak Bottomland, Realtree Max-5, True Timber DRT, Optifade Timber, or Optifade Marsh (new 2019) camo finish.

A400 LITE KO – 12 or 20 ga., 26 or 28 in. barrel, OBHP choke tubes, Kick-Off Technology. Mfg. 2020 only.

	$1,200	$1,050	$900	$815	$650	$550	$425	*$1,420*

* ***A400 Lite MAX-5 KO*** – 20 ga., 26 or 28 in. barrel, OBHP chokes, Kick-Off Technology, Realtree Max-5 camo coverage. Mfg. 2020 only.

	$1,295	$1,135	$975	$875	$710	$585	$500	*$1,520*

A400 LITE SYNTHETIC – 12 or 20 (new 2017) ga., 3 in. chamber, Blink gas operation (allowing 4 shots in less than one second), 26, 28, or 30 (disc. 2017, 12 ga. only) in. VR Steelium barrel w/Optima HP choke tubes, 4 shot mag., S-grip checkered black synthetic stock and forearm w/KO recoil pad, Gunpod 2 electronics in pistol grip allow Bluetooth compliant electronic transmissions to smart phone app, matte black finish or 100% Max-5 camo (mfg. 2017 only, 20 ga. only), features "LITE" logos on receiver sides, 6.6 lbs. Mfg. 2016-2019.

	$1,325	$1,225	$975	$850	$725	$625	$525	*$1,600*

Add $100 for Max-5 camo finish (new 2017, 20 ga. only).

A400 LITE COMPACT SYNTHETIC – 20 ga., 24 or 26 in. barrel with OBF-HP3 chokes, Kick-Off system. Mfg. mid-2017-2020.

	$1,295	$1,135	$975	$875	$710	$585	$500	*$1,520*

A400 UPLAND – 12 or 20 (new 2021) ga., 3 in. chamber, 26 or 28 in. Steelium barrel with OptimaBore HP chokes, fiber optic front bead sight, walnut stock with or w/o Kick-Off Plus technology (became standard with model in 2020), newly designed pistol grip with improved checkering, MicroCore pad, aluminum forend cap, game scene engraved nickel-plated receiver. New 2018.

MSR $1,699	$1,450	$1,275	$1,095	$985	$800	$650	$550	

Subtrace approx. $100 if without Kick-Off Plus technology.

A400 XCEL MULTI-TARGET – 12 ga., 3 in. chamber, 30 or 32 in. VR barrel with a B Fast adj. rib allowing use for skeet, sporting clays, and trap competition, 4 shot mag., checkered walnut stock with 4-pos. adj. cheekpiece, standard MicoCore recoil pad or optional Kick-Off system (KO), receiver with "Xcel/ Multitarget" logo on both sides, right or left-hand, silver anodized finished receiver, 7.7 lbs. New 2017.

MSR $2,749	$2,340	$2,050	$1,750	$1,595	$1,285	$1,075	$850	

Add $150 for Kick-Off system.

A400 XCEL SPORTING – 12 or 20 (new mid-2014) ga., 3 in. chamber, Blink gas operating system, 28, 30, or 32 in. VR OptimaBore barrel with OptimaChoke tubes, features aqua blue aluminum receiver and forearm cap, choice of Micro-core recoil pad or optional Kick-Off recoil system, X-tra grain pistol grip stock and forearm with oil finish, optional Gun Pod system allows digital readout of ambient air temp, cartridge pressure of the last round fired and overall number of rounds fired through the shotgun, balance cap also has 3 interchangeable weights which allow changing the gun's balance, 7.7 lbs. New 2011.

MSR $1,699	$1,450	$1,275	$1,095	$985	$800	$650	$550	

Add $100 for Kick-Off recoil system or $150 for Gun Pod electronics (disc. 2014).

GRADING - PPGS™ 100% 98% 95% 90% 80% 70% 60% LAST MSR

* ***A400 Xcel Sporting Black Edition*** – 12 ga., 28 (new 2018) or 30 in. barrel with OBHPe chokes, with or w/o Kick-Off recoil system, black receiver finish. New mid-2017.

MSR $2,099 $1,785 $1,560 $1,340 $1,215 $980 $825 $650

Add $100 for Kick-Off recoil system.

A400 XCEL PARALLEL TARGET KO – 12 ga. only, 28, 30, or 32 in. VR barrel with external Optima chokes, tapered high rib, Parallel Monte Carlo X-tra Grain stock with oil finish and adj. shim system, features blue anodized receiver and forearm cap, standard length or reduced length stock and forearm, new checkering with Beretta logo, 7.7 lbs. New 2011.

MSR $1,799 $1,530 $1,340 $1,150 $1,050 $850 $700 $550

A400 XPLOR ACTION – 12, 20, or 28 ga., 3 in. chamber (except for 28 ga.), gas operated action, 26, 28, or 30 (disc.) in. VR barrel with OBF-HP3 chokes, bronze colored aluminum alloy receiver, fiber optic sight, new checkering with Beretta logo, checkered walnut stock and forearm with Xtra-Grain oil finish, with or without Kick-Off recoil system (not avail. in 28 ga.), right or left (30 in. only) hand action, approx. 5 1/2-6 1/2 lbs. New 2014.

MSR $1,599 $1,365 $1,195 $1,025 $930 $750 $625 $525

Add $50 for left-hand action (12 ga. only, new 2015).

Add $100 for Kick-Off recoil system (not avail. in 28 ga.).

A400 XPLOR ACTION W/GUNPOD – 12 ga., 3 in. chamber, featuring new Beretta Blink gas system, aluminum alloy brown receiver, 26, 28, or 30 in. VR barrel with OBF-HP chokes, chrome plated trigger, trigger guard with Xplor logo, pistol grip X-tra Grain wood stock with oil finish and checkering with Beretta logo, features Gunpod electronics with digital readout in the pistol grip cap, with or without Kick-Off recoil system, metal bead front sight, 6.8 lbs. Mfg. 2012-2013.

$1,495 $1,250 $1,050 $875 $750 $650 $575 ***$1,620***

Add $205 for Kick-Off recoil system.

A400 XPLOR LIGHT – 12 ga., similar to A400 Xplor Unico, except has 3 in. chamber, 26, 28, or 30 (available with Kick-Off recoil only) in. barrel, approx. 6 1/4 lbs. Mfg. 2011-2012 only.

$1,295 $1,150 $900 $800 $700 $600 $500 ***$1,515***

Add $105 for Kick-Off recoil system.

A400 XPLOR UNICO – 12 ga., Unico chambering with 2 3/4, 3, or 3 1/2 in. chamber, 26, 28, or 30 (KO only, mfg. 2012-2014) in. VR OptimaBore barrel with OptimaChoke, new Beretta Blink gas system, green toned aluminum alloy receiver with light engraving and Beretta logo, chrome plated trigger, Xplor logo on trigger guard, metal bead front sight, X-Tra Grain pistol grip stock with oil finish, 6.6 lbs. Mfg. 2009-2016.

$1,575 $1,350 $1,025 $875 $750 $625 $550 ***$1,750***

Add $100 for Kick-Off recoil system.

A400 XTREME KICK-OFF – 12 ga., 2 3/4, 3, or 3 1/2 in. chamber, gas operated featuring new Beretta "Blink" system, aluminum alloy receiver, 26, 28 or 30 (disc. 2017) in. barrel with OBF-HP chokes, Kick-Off recoil system included, black synthetic pistol grip stock, Micro-Core recoil pad, non-slip rubber grips, fiber optic front sight, right or left (mfg. 2016-2017) hand action, 7.8 lbs. Mfg. 2012-mid-2018.

$1,575 $1,350 $1,025 $875 $750 $625 $550 ***$1,750***

Add $50 for left-hand action (mfg. 2016-2017).

* ***A400 Xtreme Kick-Off Camo*** – 12 ga., similar to A400 Extreme Kick-Off, except has 26, 28, or 30 in. barrel, 100% Max-4 Realtree camo (disc. 2013), Max-5 Realtree camo (new mid-2014), or Gore Optifade Marsh (mfg. 2013-2016, 2018) coverage, right or left (mfg. 2016-2017) hand action, 7.8 lbs. Mfg. 2012-mid-2018.

$1,695 $1,425 $1,100 $975 $850 $750 $650 ***$1,900***

Add $50 for left-hand action (mfg. 2016-2017).

MODEL 1200 FIELD – 12 ga., inertia recoil system, 28 in. VR barrels with MobilChokes, checkered European walnut stock and forearm (pre-1989), matte black polymer stock and forearm (starting 1989), recoil pad, 4 shot mag., approx. 8 lbs. Imported 1984-1989.

$375 $350 $300 $275 $250 $225 $200 ***$580***

* ***Model 1200 Riot*** – 12 ga. only, 2 3/4 or 3 in. chamber, 20 in. cyl. bore barrel with iron sights, extended mag. Imported 1989-90 only.

$400 $375 $350 $295 $250 $225 $200 ***$660***

MODEL 1201 FIELD MAGNUM – 12 ga., 3 in. chamber, short recoil blowback action, 24, 26, or 28 in. VR barrel with two MobilChokes, matte black polymer stock and forearm. Imported 1989-94.

$500 $395 $340 $285 $250 $225 $200 ***$625***

The Model 1201 can be differentiated from the Model 1200 by stock spacers to adjust length.

GRADING - PPGS™	100%	98%	95%	90%	80%	70%	60%	LAST MSR

* ***Model 1201 FP (Riot)*** – 12 ga., riot configuration featuring 18 (new 1997) or 20 (disc. 1996) in. cylinder bore barrel, 5 shot mag, choice of adj. rifle sights (disc.), Tritium sights (disc. 1998) or ghost ring (new 1999, Tritium front sight insert) sights, matte wood (disc.) or black synthetic stock and forearm, matte metal finish (disc.), 6.3 lbs. Mfg. 1991-2004.

	$725	$595	$500	$400	$300	$250	$200	*$890*

Add $80 for Tritium sights (mfg. 1997-98).
Add $45 for pistol grip configuration (Model 1201 FPG3 - mfg. 1994 only).

MODEL 1301 COMPETITION – 12 ga., 3 in. chamber, Blink gas operating system, 21 or 24 in. Steelium barrel with IC Optimabore HP choke and stepped, wide sporting rib, mid bead and front fiber optic sight, oversized cocking handle, bolt release lever, loading and ejection ports, checkered pistol grip synthetic stock and forearm, rubber recoil pad, matte black finish, 6.7 lbs. New 2014.

MSR $1,299	$1,100	$965	$825	$750	$650	$550	$425	

MODEL 1301 COMP PRO – 12 ga., 3 in. chamber, 21 or 24 in. Steelium barrel, OptimaChoke HP Black edition choke tubes, fiber optic sight, blue anodized Ergal stock with Kick-Off Plus system, Soft Comb insert, rubber comfort grip, LOP spacers, MicroCore recoil plate, ergonomic Comfort Grip forend, oversized cocking handle. New 2020.

MSR $1,549	$1,325	$1,160	$995	$900	$750	$625	$500	

MODEL 1301 TACTICAL – 12 ga., 3 in. chamber, Blink gas operating system, 18 1/2 in. fixed choke barrel, oversized charging handle, large textured bolt release, oversized reversible safety button, aggressive checkering on forend and stock, ghost ring with interchangeable front sight, adj. LOP with spacers, top Picatinny rail, synthetic stock, rubber recoil pad, black, FDE (new 2018), OD Green (new 2018), or Tactical Marine (new 2018) finish, 6.7 lbs. New 2014.

MSR $1,259	$1,075	$940	$800	$740	$625	$525	$420	

Add $100 for FDE, OD Green, or Tactical Marine finish (all new 2018).

MODEL AL3901 – 12 or 20 (new 2003) ga., 3 in. chamber, 24 (new 2003), 26 (new 2003), or 28 in. VR barrel with three MobilChokes, choice of regular or shortened (Model AL3901RL) charcoal grey synthetic checkered wood, or Mossy Oak New Break-Up (new 2003), or Mossy Oak New Shadowgrass (new 2003) camo covered stock and forearm, gold trigger, matte metal finish, reversible crossbolt safety, 7 1/2 lbs. Mfg. 2002-2003.

	$450	$425	$375	$335	$280	$250	$230	*$730*

Add $50 for camo finish.

This model was available through Beretta Showcase Dealers only.

MODEL 3901 SERIES – 12 or 20 ga., 3 in. chamber, 26 or 28 in. VR barrel with three MobilChoke tubes, available in five configurations, including Citizen (synthetic stock), Statesman (wood stock, disc. 2010), Ambassador (X-Tra wood, disc. 2006), Target RL (12 ga. only, IC choke, shorter dimensions w/12-13 in. LOP and adj. comb, new 2006), or Rifled Slug (12 ga. only, 24 in. rifled slug barrel, new 2006), gas operating system, 26 or 28 in. steel alloy hammer forged barrel, removable trigger group. Mfg. in America 2005-2011.

	$775	$650	$550	$450	$375	$325	$300	*$895*

Add $100 for Statesman configuration (disc. 2010).
Add $200 for Ambassador configuration (disc. 2006).
Add $105 for Target RL configuration (one IC choke only).
Subtract $25 for Rifled Slug Model (disc. 2010).

MODEL 3901 STANDARD SYNTHETIC – 12 ga., 3 in. chamber, 28 in. VR barrel with three MobilChoke tubes, black synthetic stock and forearm, gas operation, entry level model with full features, mfg. in America. Mfg. 2011 only.

	$575	$500	$450	$400	$365	$335	$295	*$645*

TX4 STORM – 12 ga., 3 in. chamber, gas operated, dual lug action with rotating bolt, 18 in. OptimaBore barrel with OptimaChoke HP cylinder tube, optional TX4 Stand Off Device, 5 shot mag., matte black finish, alloy receiver with integral Picatinny rail, black synthetic stock, ghost ring rear sight, elevated post front sight, includes plastic case, approx. 6.4 lbs. Mfg. 2010-2011.

	$1,200	$995	$850	$725	$625	$525	$450	*$1,450*

COMMEMORATIVES

MODEL A-303 DUCKS UNLIMITED – 12 or 20 ga., D.U. serialization, 5,500 mfg. in 12 ga. 1986-87, 3,500 mfg. in 20 ga. 1987-88.

12 ga.	$525	$450	$350	$285	$250	$215	$185	
20 ga.	$575	$475	$375	$315	$270	$230	$200	

These D.U. Models had no retail pricing from Beretta. Rather, they were auctioned off at D.U. dinners, and as a result, prices could vary substantially from region to region.

GRADING - PPGS™	100%	98%	95%	90%	80%	70%	60%	LAST MSR

MODEL 687 O/U SHOTGUN TERCENTENNIAL – 12 ga., SST and ejectors. Limited production, only 300 manufactured.

	$2,500	$1,950	$1,400	$1,235	$1,000	$870	$700	

MODEL 84 PISTOL TERCENTENNIAL – commemorative, only 300 manufactured. Fully engraved with gold inlays. Presentation case. Only 100 imported to U.S.

	$1,450	$1,100	$850	$740	$620	$515	$440	

BERGARA

Current rifle and barrel manufacturer located in Bergara, Spain. Bolt action rifles are currently imported by Bergara USA, located in Lawrenceville, GA and CVA (select models), located in Lawrenceville, GA. Barrels, muzzleloading firearms, and single shot rifles are imported by Connecticut Valley Arms, located in Duluth, GA. Black Powder Products (BPI) is the North American parent company of both trademarks, located in Lawrenceville, GA.

Bergara manufactures high quality rifle barrels, in addition to bolt action rifles and single shot Apex rifles previously imported by Connecticut Valley Arms. Please refer to the Connecticut Valley Arms section for current single shot rifle information and pricing.

RIFLES: BOLT ACTION

B-14 BMP (MATCH PRECISION) – 6mm Creedmoor (mfg. 2018 only), 6.5 Creedmoor or .308 Win. cal., B-14 action, 20 (.308 Win.), 24 (6.5mm Creedmoor), or 26 (6mm Creedmoor, mfg. 2018 only) in. No. 6 taper barrel, 5 shot detachable AICS mag., 2-lug bolt head with sliding plate extractor, Bergara Performance adj. trigger, BMP chassis, fully adj. buttstock and cheekpiece, AR-15 style grip, integrated QD flush cup mounts, 10.5 lbs. New 2017.

MSR $1,265	$1,075	$950	$800	$725	$600	$475	$375	

B-14 HMR (HUNTING & MATCH RIFLE) – 6mm Creedmoor (disc. 2020), 6.5 Creedmoor, 6.5 PRC (new late 2019), 7mm Rem. Mag. (disc. 2020), .308 Win., .22-250 Rem., .450 Bushmaster (new 2018), .300 PRC (new late 2019), or .300 Win. Mag. cal., B-14 action, 20, 22, 24, or 26 in. No. 6 taper CrMo steel threaded barrel w/muzzle thread protector, 3, 5, or 10 (disc. 2020) shot AICS profile mag., steel receiver, Bergara Performance adj. trigger, brown/black fleck colored molded composite HMR stock with integrated mini-chassis, adj. cheekpiece and LOP spacers, bipod stud, sling swivel studs, and flush QD sling sockets integrated into the stock, matte blued finish, 9-9.9 lbs. New 2017.

MSR $1,150	$975	$850	$725	$675	$550	$450	$375	

Add $29 for left-hand action.

Add $80 for 6.5 PRC or .300 PRC cal. (both new late 2019).

B-14 HUNTER RIFLE – .22-250 Rem. (new 2018), .30-06, .243 Win., .270 Win., .300 Win. Mag., .308 Win., 7mm Rem. Mag., 7mm-08 Rem. (new 2019), or 6.5 Creedmoor cal., B-14 action, 22 or 24 in. No. 4 taper CrMo steel barrel, 3 or 4 shot mag. with hinged floorplate or detachable mag., steel receiver, Bergara Performance adj. trigger, American-style synthetic stock with Soft Touch finish, CrushZone recoil pad, swivel studs, matte blue finish, approx. 7.1-7.3 lbs. New 2015.

MSR $825	$725	$625	$525	$475	$385	$325	$250	

B-14R TRAINER/B-14R TRAINER CARBON – .22 LR, .22 WMR (new 2021), or .17 HMR (new 2021) cal., right or left (new 2021) hand B-14R action, 18 in. free floating barrel, threaded muzzle, 10 shot Bergara rimfire short action, AICS profile mag., HMR stock molded full-length w/mini-chassis, integrated QD flush cup sling and swivel mounts, adj. cheekpiece, floating bolt head design w/non-rotating gas shield, Grey and Black or Black and White (B-14R Trainer Carbon) speckle finish. New late 2019.

MSR $1,150	$975	$850	$725	$675	$550	$450	$375	

Add $95 for B-14R Trainer Carbon model with Black and White speckle finish.

B-14 RIDGE – .300 Win. Mag., .300 PRC (new 2019), .30-06, .270 Win., .308 Win., .243 Win., 6.5 Creedmoor, 6.5 PRC (new 2019), 7mm Rem. Mag., 7mm-08 (new 2019), .22-250 Rem., or .450 Bushmaster (new 2020) cal., B-14 action, 18 (new 2019), 20 (new 2020, .308 Win. only), 22, or 24 in. No. 5 taper CrMo steel threaded barrel with thread protector, 2, 3, or 4 shot mag., hinged floorplate, Bergara Performance adj. trigger, American-style synthetic stock with Soft Touch finish, CrushZone recoil pad, drilled and tapped for Remington 700 style scope bases, dark gray with white and black flecked stock finish, matte blued barrel and action, 7.5 lbs. New 2018.

MSR $865	$750	$650	$575	$500	$425	$350	$275	

Add $80 for 6.5 PRC or .300 PRC cal. (both new 2019).

B-14 SPORTER VARMINT – .308 Win. cal., 24 in. Bergara varmint barrel, adj. trigger, black synthetic Sporter stock, Crush Zone recoil pad, steel receiver, swivel studs, 4+1 floorplate. Mfg. 2017 only.

	$750	$640	$525	$475	$385	$325	$250	*$865*

GRADING - PPGS™	100%	98%	95%	90%	80%	70%	60%	LAST MSR

B-14 TIMBER RIFLE – .30-06, .270 Win., .243 Win., .300 Win. Mag., 7mm-08 (mfg. 2019 only), .308 Win., or 6.5 Creedmoor cal., Bergara B-14 action, 20 (new 2020, .308 Win. only), 22, or 24 in. No. 4 taper CrMo steel barrel, hinged floorplate, steel receiver, adj. trigger, Monte Carlo oil-finished walnut stock with raised comb and cheekpiece, swivel studs, matte blue finish, 7.3-7.6 lbs. New 2015.

MSR $945	$800	$700	$600	$550	$450	$350	$300	

B-14 WOODSMAN – .300 Win. Mag. .308 Win., .243 Win., .30-06, .270 Win., 6.5 Creedmoor, 7mm-08 (new 2019), or 7mm Rem. Mag. cal., 22 or 24 in. steel blued barrel, American Classic style walnut stock, hinged floorplate or detachable magazine (disc. 2018), approx. 7 lbs. Mfg. 2015-2019.

	$800	$700	$600	$550	$450	$350	$300	*$945*

Add $30 for detachable magazine (disc. 2018).

BC15 LONG RANGE HUNTER – .300 Win. Mag. or .300 RUM cal., 24 in. stainless steel contoured Nitride finished barrel, Timney or Shilen trigger, McMillan A3 Sporter stock, custom machined 20 MOA Picatinny rail, pillar bedded with Marine Tex steel filled epoxy, Badger M4 bottom metal, olive finish with tan and black marbling. Mfg. 2013-2015.

	$3,800	$3,400	$2,975	$2,550	$2,310	$1,870	$1,525	*$4,000*

BCR13 SPORT HUNTER – .270 Win., .30-06, or .308 Win. cal., 22 in. stainless steel contoured Nitride finished barrel, Timney or Shilen trigger, Weaver compatible two-piece steel scope base, trigger guard with inside guard floorplate release, pillar bedded with Marine Tex steel filled epoxy, McMillan Hunter stock, olive finish with tan and black marbling, 7.25 lbs. Mfg. 2013-2015.

	$3,250	$2,975	$2,600	$2,225	$2,025	$1,625	$1,350	*$3,500*

BCR17 MEDIUM TACTICAL – .308 Win. cal., 22 in. Nitride finished stainless steel contoured barrel, Timney or Shilen trigger, pillar bedded with Marine Tex steel filled epoxy, custom machined 20 MOA Picatinny rail, Badger M-4 bottom metal, McMillan A1-3 stock, olive finish with tan and black marbling, 9.9 lbs. Mfg. 2013-2015.

	$3,800	$3,400	$2,975	$2,550	$2,310	$1,870	$1,525	*$4,000*

* ***Medium Tactical Chassis Stock*** – .308 Win. cal., 22 in. stainless steel barrel, Bergara custom action, 5 shot detachable mag., Timney trigger, Bergara custom Picatinny rail, APO Sporter Modular chassis stock, adj. comb height, 10.5 lbs. Mfg. 2014-2015.

	$4,200	$3,825	$3,350	$2,875	$2,600	$2,100	$1,725	*$4,500*

BCR19 HEAVY TACTICAL – .308 Win. or .300 Win. Mag. cal., 26 in. Nitride finished stainless steel heavy contour barrel, 5 shot detachable mag., Timney or Shilen trigger, pillar bedded with Marine Tex steel filled epoxy, custom machined 20 MOA Picatinny rail, Badger M-5 bottom metal, six flush-mounted QD sling sockets, bipod mounting stud, McMillan A-4 stock with adj. butt and comb, OD Green finish, 12.5 lbs. Mfg. 2013-2015.

	$4,200	$3,825	$3,350	$2,875	$2,600	$2,100	$1,725	*$4,500*

BCR22 MOUNTAIN HUNTER – .30-06, 6.5x284, .223 Rem., .243 Rem., .270 Win., .308 Win., 6.5 Creedmoor, 6mm Creedmoor, .280 Ackley, or 7mm-08 cal., Bergara Premier action, 18 in. tapered barrel, blind magazine, Timney trigger, fiberglass stock glass bedded with Marine Tex, two sling studs, 3-tone speckle paint pattern finish, 6.5-7 lbs. Disc. 2017.

	$2,750	$2,400	$2,050	$1,850	$1,500	$1,250	$950	*$2,950*

BCR23 SPORT HUNTER – various standard and Mag. cals., Bergara Premier action, 22 or 24 in. tapered barrel, Oberndorf trigger guard, hinged floorplate, Timney trigger, McMillan Hunter stock with Monte Carlo style cheekpiece and slight palm swell, molded in Black Marble or Tan Marble finish, 7.5-7.75 lbs. Disc. 2018.

	$3,500	$2,900	$2,400	$2,100	$1,650	$1,350	$995	*$3,950*

BCR24 VARMINT HUNTER – .308 Win., .243 Rem., 6.5 Creedmoor, 6mm Creedmoor, .22-250, .222 Rem., .223 Rem., or .260 Rem. cal., Bergara Premier action, 24 in. tapered barrel, M4 trigger guard, hinged floorplate, Timney curved or flat trigger, McMillan Remington Varmint stock, McWoody finish, 8.5 lbs. Mfg. 2016-2018.

	$3,600	$3,000	$2,500	$2,200	$1,725	$1,425	$1,050	*$4,100*

BCR25 LONG RANGE HUNTER – various standard and Mag. cals., Bergara Premier action, 24 in. tapered barrel, M4 trigger guard, hinged floorplate, Timney curved or flat trigger, McMillan A3 Sporter stock with high comb, vertical grip, and 3 sling studs, molded in White and Black Marble or Tan Marble finish, 8.5-8.75 lbs. Disc. 2018.

	$3,750	$3,150	$2,650	$2,325	$1,900	$1,500	$1,150	*$4,350*

GRADING - PPGS™	100%	98%	95%	90%	80%	70%	60%	LAST MSR

BCR27 COMPETITION – .308 Win., .243 Win., 6.5 Creedmoor, 6mm Creedmoor, .260 Rem., .300 WSM, or 7mm WSM cal., Bergara Premier action, 26 in. tapered barrel with Dead Air Armament Key Mount muzzle brake/suppressor mount, AICS detachable mag., Timney curved trigger, McMillan A3-5 adj. stock with vertical grip, adj. comp, and adj. LOP spacers, four flush cups, Picatinny rail for Atlas style bipod, black marble finish, 10 lbs. Mfg. 2016-2018.

	$4,450	$3,725	$3,100	$2,750	$2,200	$1,750	$1,350	*$4,950*

BCR28 COMPETITION CHASSIS – .308 Win., .243 Win., 6.5 Creedmoor, 6mm Creedmoor, .260 Rem., .300 WSM, or 7mm WSM cal., Bergara Premier action, 26 in. tapered barrel with Dead Air Armament Key Mount muzzle brake/suppressor mount, AICS detachable mag., Timney curved or flat trigger, KeyMod rail sections, optional night vision, AR-15 style grip, Magpul PRS stock, adj. LOP and comb, black finish, 10 lbs. Mfg. 2016-2017.

	$3,700	$3,250	$2,800	$2,500	$2,050	$1,650	$1,300	*$3,900*

BCR29 HEAVY TACTICAL – 6.5x284 Norma, .300 Win. Mag., .308 Win., .243 Win., 6mm Creedmoor, .260 Rem., .300 WSM, 7mm WSM, or 6.5 Creedmoor cal., short or long action, 24 in. barrel with threaded muzzle, Dead Air Armament Key Mount muzzle brake, AICS detachable mag., Timney flat trigger, McMillan A5 stock with vertical grip, wide width forend, adj. comb and LOP, four flush QD sling sockets, Picatinny rail, green, tan, or black marble colored stock, approx. 12 lbs. Mfg. 2018 only.

	$4,500	$3,925	$3,425	$2,900	$2,650	$2,150	$1,750	*$5,000*

Add $100 for long action.

BCR30 HEAVY TACTICAL CHASSIS – .308 Win., .243 Rem., 6.5 Creedmoor, 6mm Creedmoor, .260 Rem., .300 WSM, 7mm WSM, .300 Win. Mag., or 6.5x284 Norma cal., 24 in. barrel with DeadAir Armament Key Mount muzzle brake/suppressor mount, AICS detachable mag., Timney trigger, Accuracy International AX fully adj. stock, KeyMod forend, flush QD sling sockets, tan, black, or green finish, 11.75-12 lbs. Mfg. 2016-2018.

	$4,300	$3,600	$3,000	$2,650	$2,250	$1,950	$1,600	*$4,800*

Add $50 for long action.

BMR – .22 LR, .17 HMR, or .22 WMR cal., Bergara BMR action, 18 or 20 (.17 HMR and .22 WMR only) in. No. 4 taper threaded steel barrel with match chamber, 5 and 10 shot mag., Bergara Performance Trigger, 30 MOA scope rail, Tactical Grey composite stock with black speckling finish, 5.5-5.8 lbs. New 2021.

MSR $565	$475	$425	$350	$325	$275	$225	$175

* ***BMR Carbon*** – .22 LR, .17 HMR, or .22 WMR cal., Bergara BMR action, 18 or 20 (.17 HMR and .22 WMR only) in. No. 6 taper threaded carbon fiber barrel w/match chamber, 5 and 10 shot mag., Bergara Performance Trigger, 30 MOA scope rail, Tactical Black composite stock with white speckling finish, 5-5.4 lbs. New 2021.

MSR $659	$575	$500	$425	$400	$325	$275	$200

BX-11TAKEDOWN HUNTER – .243 Win., .270 Win., .30-06, .308 Win., or .300 Win. Mag. cal., 22 or 24 (Mag. cals. only) in. chrome moly steel barrel, detachable mag., walnut or black synthetic stock with rubber grip panels and overmolding, 6.6 lbs. Mfg. 2013-2017.

	$1,650	$1,400	$1,200	$1,025	$840	$685	$535	*$1,800*

Add $300 for walnut stock.

HEAVY TACTICAL – .308 Win. cal., Bergara custom action, 24 in. stainless steel barrel, Nitride barrel finish, 10 shot detachable mag., Timney trigger, full length unitized Monolithic rail, tubular aluminum forend with accessory rails and flush QD socket sling mounts, APO Mod-1 Chassis folding stock, adj. comb height, rear monopod, 10.5 lbs. New 2014.

	$4,750	$4,150	$3,550	$3,250	$2,750	$2,150	$1,775

PREMIER SERIES APPROACH – .223 Rem. (mfg. 2018 only), .22-250 Rem., 6mm Creedmoor (disc. 2019), 6.5 Creedmoor, 6.5 PRC, 7mm-08 (new 2019), .308 Win., 7mm Rem. Mag. (new 2019), .300 Win. Mag. (new 2019), .300 PRC (new 2019), .28 Nosler (new 2020), or .450 Bushmaster (disc. 2019) cal., Bergara Premier action, 20, 24, or 26 in. No. 5 taper stainless steel barrel, threaded muzzle with knurled protector (disc. 2019) or Omni muzzle brake (new 2020), 5 shot AICS detachable mag. (disc. 2019) or 2, 3, or 4 shot internal box mag. depending on caliber (new 2020), hinged floorplate, spring-loaded sliding plate extractor, TriggerTech Frictionless Release Technology trigger, hand-laid Greyboe fiberglass stock, removable swivel mount, two-pos. safety, integrated QD flush cup sling mounts and swivel mounts, stainless steel one-piece bolt body, FDE (disc. 2019) or Graphite Black Cerakote (new 2020) finish on barrel and action, 8.2-8.6 lbs. New 2018.

MSR $1,960	$1,665	$1,455	$1,250	$1,125	$910	$750	$625

Add $100 for 6.5 PRC, .28 Nosler, or .300 PRC cal.

GRADING - PPGS™	100%	98%	95%	90%	80%	70%	60%	LAST MSR

MOUNTAIN HUNTER – .243 Win., .270 Win., .30-06, .300 Win. Mag., .308 Win., or 7mm-08 cal., 18 or 20 (disc.) in. stainless steel #2 contour barrel, Bergara custom action, Timney trigger, 2-piece scope base, lightweight fiberglass stock with painted finish, pillar bedded with Marine Tex steel filled epoxy, machined Oberndorf-style trigger guard with internal guard floorplate release, 5.85 lbs. Mfg. 2014-2015.

	$3,500	$3,065	$2,625	$2,375	$1,925	$1,575	$1,225	*$3,750*

PREMIER SERIES CLASSIC – .300 Win. Mag., .30-06, .270 Win., .308 Win., 6.5 Creedmoor, or .280 Ackley cal., 22 or 24 in. barrel, two-pos. safety, hinged floorplate, Timney trigger, Grade 5 American walnut Monte Carlo stock with hand-rubbed oil finish, 7-7.65 lbs. Mfg. 2016-2017.

	$2,050	$1,795	$1,550	$1,400	$1,125	$925	$725	*$2,190*

PREMIER SERIES HIGHLANDER – 6.5 Creedmoor, 6.5 PRC, .270 Win. (mfg. 2019 only), .280 Ackley Improved (mfg. 2019 only), .28 Nosler (new 2020), 7mm-08 (mfg. 2019 only), .308 Win., 7mm Rem. Mag., .30-06 (mfg. 2019 only), .300 PRC, or .300 Win. Mag. cal., Bergara Premier action, 20, 22 (mfg. 2019 only), 24 or 26 (.28 Nosler, new 2020) in. stainless steel No. 5 barrel, pre-threaded muzzle with knurled protector (mfg. 2019 only) or muzzle brake (new 2020), 2, 3, 4, or 5 shot mag. depending on caliber, hinged floorplate, sliding plate extractor, TriggerTech Frictionless Release Technology, composite stock, two-position safety, Sniper Gray Cerakote finish, 7.2-7.7 lbs. New 2019.

MSR $1,885	$1,600	$1,400	$1,200	$1,100	$875	$725	$600	

Add $100 for 6.5 PRC, .28 Nosler, or .300 PRC cal.

PREMIER SERIES HMR PRO – .223 Rem. (mfg. 2018 only), .22-250 Rem., 6mm Creedmoor, 6.5 Creedmoor, 6.5 PRC (new 2019), 7mm-08 (mfg. 2019 only), 7mm Rem. Mag. (new 2019), .28 Nosler (new 2020), .308 Win., .300 Win. Mag. (new 2019), .300 PRC (new 2019), or .450 Bushmaster (mfg. 2019 only) cal., Bergara Premier action, 20, 22 (mfg. 2019 only), 24, or 26 (heavy bbl. new 2019, 6.5 Creedmoor only) in. No. 5.5 or No. 6 taper stainless steel threaded barrel with knurled thread protector, 5 shot AICS style detachable mag., spring-loaded sliding plate extractor, TriggerTech Frictionless Release Technology trigger, speckled black and grey Bergara HMR molded stock with mini-chassis, integrated QD flush cup sling mounts and swivel mounts, adj. cheekpiece and LOP, Tactical Grey Cerakote finish, 9.2-9.7 lbs. New 2018.

MSR $1,715	$1,450	$1,275	$1,095	$985	$800	$650	$550	

Add $100 for 6.5 PRC (new 2019), .28 Nosler (new 2020), or .300 PRC (new 2019) cal.

PREMIER SERIES LONG RANGE – .308 Win., 6.5 Creedmoor, .280 Ackley, .270 Win., 6mm Creedmoor, or .300 Win. Mag. cal., 20 (.308 Win.), 24 (6.5 Creedmoor), or 26 in. tapered barrel, 5 shot detachable mag., Timney trigger w/M4 trigger guard, 100% carbon fiber stock, fully adj. cheekpiece, Picatinny scope rail, full length integrated mini-chassis for repeatable bedding and supports fully free floating barrel, Cerakote finish, 9.6-10 lbs. Mfg. 2017-2018.

	$2,550	$2,225	$1,900	$1,725	$1,395	$1,150	$900	*$2,775*

PREMIER SERIES LRP – .300 Win. Mag. (new 2019), .308 Win., 6.5 Creedmoor, or 6mm Creedmoor cal., Bergara Premier action, aluminum chasis, 20, 24, or 26 in. tapered barrel with Dead Air Armament Key Mount muzzle brake/suppressor mount, 5 shot detachable mag., Timney flat trigger, TriggerTech Frictionless Release Technology, XLR Element chassis stock, AR-15 style grip, adj. LOP and comb, 9.8-10.4 lbs. Mfg. 2016-2019.

	$1,700	$1,490	$1,275	$1,150	$935	$775	$650	*$2,000*

PREMIER SERIES LRP 2.0 – 6.5 Creedmoor, 6.5 PRC, .300 Win. Mag., or .300 PRC cal., Bergara Premier action, 24 or 26 in. No. 6 taper stainless steel threaded barrel with thread protector, 5 shot detachable AICS style mag., TriggerTech Frictionless Release Technology trigger, XLR Element 3.0 stock, ergonomic rubber grip, adj. LOP and comb, Graphite Black Cerakote finish, 9.6-9.8 lbs. New 2020.

MSR $2,000	$1,700	$1,500	$1,275	$1,150	$950	$750	$600	

Add $100 for 6.5 PRC or .300 PRC cal.

PREMIER SERIES LRP ELITE – .308 Win., 6.5 Creedmoor, or 6mm Creedmoor cal., Bergara Premier action, 20 (.308 Win.), 22 (6.5 Creedmoor), or 24 in. tapered barrel with Dead Air Armament Key Mount muzzle brake/suppressor mount, 5 shot detachable mag., Timney flat trigger, self-adjusting recoil lug locking system, KeyMod rail sections, AR-15 style Ergo grip, Magpul PRS buttstock, fully adj. LOP and comb, 10.5-11 lbs. Mfg. 2016-2018.

	$2,600	$2,275	$1,925	$1,750	$1,400	$1,175	$925	*$2,850*

PREMIER SERIES MOUNTAIN – .308 Win., 6.5 Creedmoor, .300 Win. Mag., .280 Ackley Improved, .30-06, or .270 Win. cal., Premier Bergara Action, 22 or 24 in. (.300 Win. Mag. cal. only) barrel, 4 shot mag., curved 510 Timney trigger, carbon fiber stock, hinged floorplate, floating bolt head with non-rotating gas shield, stainless steel, 6.2-6.4 lbs. Disc. 2019.

	$1,865	$1,625	$1,400	$1,275	$1,025	$850	$700	*$2,190*

GRADING - PPGS™	100%	98%	95%	90%	80%	70%	60%	LAST MSR

PREMIER SERIES MOUNTAIN 2.0 – 6.5 Creedmoor, 6.5 PRC, .308 Win., .28 Nosler, .300 Win. Mag., or .300 PRC cal., Bergara Premier action, 22 or 24 in. stainless steel No. 3 taper barrel, 2, 3, or 4 shot internal box mag. depending on caliber, hinged floorplate, spring-loaded sliding plate extractor, TriggerTech Frictionless Release Technology trigger, AG Composite carbon fiber stock w/camo finish, two-position safety, integrated sling swivel mounts, stainless steel one-piece bolt body, Tactical Grey Cerakote finish on barrel and action, 6 1/4-6 1/2 lbs. New 2020.

MSR $2,150	**$1,825**	**$1,600**	**$1,375**	**$1,250**	**$1,000**	**$825**	**$650**	

Add $100 for 6.5 PRC, .28 Nosler, or .300 PRC cal.

PREMIER SERIES RIDGEBACK – 6mm Creedmoor, 6.5 Creedmoor, 6.5 PRC, .28 Nosler (new 2020), .308 Win., .300 Win. Mag., or .300 PRC cal., Bergara Premier action, 20, 24, or 26 in. medium Palma taper stainless steel threaded barrel w/knurled thread protector, 5 shot AICS detachable mag., sliding plate extractor, TriggerTech Frictionless Release Technology, Grayboe fiberglass stock w/M-LOK compatible forearm and adj. cheek rest, LOP spacers, two-position safety, Graphite Black Cerakote finish, 10-10.75 lbs. New 2019.

MSR $2,000	**$1,700**	**$1,500**	**$1,275**	**$1,150**	**$950**	**$750**	**$600**	

Add $100 for 6.5 PRC, .28 Nosler, or .300 PRC cal.

PREMIER SERIES STALKER – .300 Win. Mag., .30-06, .270 Win., .308 Win., 6.5 Creedmoor, or .280 Ackley Improved cal., Bergara Premier action, 22 or 24 in. tapered barrel, fiberglass stock with aluminum bedding block, sling swivels, hinged floorplate, Timney trigger, two-position safety, 3-color textured DuPont paint finish, 6.5-7.15 lbs. Mfg. 2016-2018.

	$1,865	**$1,625**	**$1,400**	**$1,275**	**$1,025**	**$850**	**$700**	***$2,190***

WILDERNESS SERIES B-14 HMR – 6.5 Creedmoor, 6.5 PRC, .308 Win., 7mm Rem. Mag., .28 Nosler, .300 Win. Mag., or .300 PRC cal., B-14 action, 20, 24, or 26 in. No. 6 taper CrMo steel threaded barrel w/Omni muzzle brake, 3 (6.5 PRC only) or 5 shot detachable AICS mag., spring loaded sliding plate extractor, Bergara Performance adj. trigger, molded composite HMR stock with integrated mini-chassis, adj. cheekpiece and LOP spacers, bipod stud, sling swivel studs, flush QD sling sockets, Sniper Gray Cerakote finished barrel and action, stock finished with hand painted camouflage and black webbing, 9.7-9.9 lbs. New 2020.

MSR $1,260	**$1,075**	**$950**	**$800**	**$725**	**$600**	**$475**	**$375**	

Add $80 for 6.5 PRC, .28 Nosler, or .300 PRC cal.

WILDERNESS SERIES B-14 HUNTER – 6.5 Creedmoor, .308 Win., .28 Nosler, 7mm Rem. Mag., or .300 Win. Mag. cal., B-14 action, 22, 24, or 26 in. No. 4 taper CrMo steel barrel with recessed crown, 2, 3, or 4 shot mag., hinged floorplate, spring loaded sliding plate extractor, Bergara Performance adj. trigger, American-style synthetic stock, sling swivel studs, rubber buttpad, Sniper Gray Cerakote finished barrel and action, stock finished with hand painted camouflage, black webbing, and SoftTouch overcoat, 7.1-7.5 lbs. New 2020.

MSR $899	**$765**	**$675**	**$575**	**$525**	**$425**	**$350**	**$275**	

Add $66 for .28 Nosler cal.

WILDERNESS SERIES B-14 RIDGE – 6.5 Creedmoor, 6.5 PRC, .308 Win., 7mm Rem. Mag., .28 Nosler, .300 Win. Mag., or .300 PRC cal., Bergara B-14 action, 18, 20, 22, 24, or 26 in. No. 5 taper CrMo steel barrel with Omni muzzle brake, 2, 3, or 4 shot mag., hinged floorplate, spring loaded sliding plate extractor, Bergara Performance adj. trigger, American-style synthetic stock, sling swivel studs, rubber buttpad, Sniper Gray Cerakote finished barrel and action, stock finished with hand painted camouflage, black webbing, and SoftTouch overcoat, 7.2-7.9 lbs. New 2020.

MSR $975	**$825**	**$725**	**$625**	**$560**	**$450**	**$375**	**$300**	

Add $80 for 6.5 PRC, .28 Nosler, or .300 PRC cal.

WILDERNESS SERIES B-14 TERRAIN – 6.5 Creedmoor, .308 Win., 6.5 PRC, 7mm Rem. Mag., .28 Nosler, .300 Win. Mag., or .300 PRC cal., Bergara B-14 action, 20, 24, or 26 in. No. 5.5 taper CrMo steel barrel w/Omni muzzle brake, 5 shot detachable AICS mag., spring loaded sliding plate extractor, Bergara Performance adj. trigger, molded composite Terrain stock with integrated mini-chassis, adj. cheekpiece and rubber recoil pad, integrated sling swivels and flush mounted QD sling socket cups, bipod swivel, Sniper Gray Cerakote finished barrel and action, stock finished with hand painted camouflage, black webbing, and SoftTouch overcoat, 8.9-10.1 lbs. New 2020.

MSR $1,199	**$1,025**	**$900**	**$775**	**$700**	**$575**	**$450**	**$360**	

Add $80 for 6.5 PRC, .28 Nosler, or .300 PRC cal.

RIFLES: SEMI-AUTO

BXR – .22 LR cal., blowback operated, 16 1/2 in. carbon fiber or fluted steel barrel w/thread protector, 10 shot rotary mag. (10/22 mag. compatible), Bergara BXR trigger, synthetic tactical stock, adj. LOP, Green stock w/Black fleck or Black stock w/White fleck Cerakote finish, integral 30 MOA Picatinny rail, three QD mount studs, four flush cups, 4.75 or 5.2 lbs. New late 2019.

MSR $565	**$475**	**$425**	**$350**	**$325**	**$275**	**$225**	**$175**	

Add $94 for carbon fiber barrel.

100%	98%	95%	90%	80%	70%	60%	50%	40%	30%	20%	10%

BERGMANN

Previous manufacturer located in Gaggenau, Germany circa 1892-1944. Re-established in 1931 under Bergmann Erben.

PISTOLS: SEMI-AUTO

Prices established are for original guns with matching parts.

MODEL 1894 (ANTIQUE) - 8mm "Bergmann Schmeisser" cal. Extremely rare.

100%	98%	95%	90%	80%	70%	60%	50%	40%	30%	20%	10%
N/A	N/A	$29,500	$25,000	$20,000	$15,000	$10,000	$7,500	$6,500	$6,000	$5,500	$5,000

MODEL 1896-NO. 2 - 5mm cal., smaller type frame.

100%	98%	95%	90%	80%	70%	60%	50%	40%	30%	20%	10%
$6,500	$5,500	$4,500	$3,500	$3,000	$2,750	$2,500	$2,250	$2,000	$1,750	$1,200	$1,000

Add 50% for "folding trigger" version.

MODEL 1896-NO. 3 - 6.5mm cal., 80mm barrel.

100%	98%	95%	90%	80%	70%	60%	50%	40%	30%	20%	10%
$5,500	$4,500	$4,000	$3,500	$3,000	$2,750	$2,500	$2,250	$2,000	$1,750	$1,200	$1,000

Add 20% for early pistols without extractors and narrow grips.
Add 30% if hexagonal chamber.

* ***Model 1896-No. 3 Target***

100%	98%	95%	90%	80%	70%	60%	50%	40%	30%	20%	10%
$15,000	$12,500	$10,000	$9,000	$8,000	$7,000	$6,000	$5,000	$4,000	$3,500	$3,000	$2,500

MODEL 1896-NO. 4 - 8mm cal., military contract. Rarely seen.

100%	98%	95%	90%	80%	70%	60%	50%	40%	30%	20%	10%
$8,500	$7,000	$5,500	$4,000	$3,500	$3,000	$2,500	$2,000	$1,750	$1,500	$1,250	$1,000

MODEL 1897-NO. 5 - 7.8mm cal., commercial manufacture. May be fit with shoulder stock.

100%	98%	95%	90%	80%	70%	60%	50%	40%	30%	20%	10%
$12,500	$10,000	$9,000	$8,000	$7,000	$6,000	$5,000	$4,000	$3,500	$3,000	$2,500	$2,000

* ***Model 1897-No. 5 w/Shoulder Stock***

100%	98%	95%	90%	80%	70%	60%	50%	40%	30%	20%	10%
$25,000	$20,000	$15,000	$12,500	$10,000	$9,000	$8,000	$7,000	$6,000	$5,000	$4,000	$3,000

Add 20% if stock and pistol serial numbers match.

* ***Model 1897-No. 5 Long Barrel Carbine***

100%	98%	95%	90%	80%	70%	60%	50%	40%	30%	20%	10%
$30,000	$25,000	$20,000	$15,000	$12,500	$10,000	$7,500	$6,000	$5,000	$4,000	$3,500	$3,000

BERGMANN SIMPLEX - 8mm cal., 2.7 in. barrel, 10 shot mag., scaled down design, first and most common variation has mag. release button in front of mag. housing, later and much scarcer version has push-button mag. release mounted on side of frame. Mfg. circa 1901-1914.

* ***Bergmann Simplex First Variation***

100%	98%	95%	90%	80%	70%	60%	50%	40%	30%	20%	10%
$4,500	$4,000	$3,500	$3,000	$2,500	$2,250	$2,000	$1,850	$1,650	$1,475	$1,350	$1,225

* ***Bergmann Simplex Second Variation***

100%	98%	95%	90%	80%	70%	60%	50%	40%	30%	20%	10%
$5,500	$5,000	$4,500	$4,000	$3,500	$3,000	$2,750	$2,350	$2,100	$1,800	$1,600	$1,475

BERGMANN MARS MODEL 1903 - .30 or 9mm Bergmann cal.

100%	98%	95%	90%	80%	70%	60%	50%	40%	30%	20%	10%
$9,500	$7,500	$6,000	$5,500	$5,000	$4,500	$4,000	$3,500	$3,000	$2,500	$2,000	$1,500

Add 25% if .30 caliber (first 100 pistols).
Add $3,500-$7,000 for original shoulder stock, depending on condition.

MODEL 2 - .25 cal., small frame.

100%	98%	95%	90%	80%	70%	60%	50%	40%	30%	20%	10%
$400	$350	$300	$275	$250	$225	$200	$175	$150	$125	$100	$75

Add $100 for Model 2A.

MODEL 3 - .25 cal., small frame.

100%	98%	95%	90%	80%	70%	60%	50%	40%	30%	20%	10%
$450	$375	$300	$275	$250	$225	$200	$175	$150	$125	$100	$75

Add $100 for Model 3A.

ERBEN - .25 cal., Models I, II, and Special (.32 cal.).

100%	98%	95%	90%	80%	70%	60%	50%	40%	30%	20%	10%
$500	$400	$350	$300	$250	$215	$180	$160	$135	$115	$95	$80

PISTOLS: SEMI-AUTO - BERGMANN-BAYARD

Even though the Bergmann-Bayard models listed were manufactured only by Anciens Etablissements Pieper of Herstal, Belgium, these pistols are listed under this heading as they are most commonly referred to by this trademark designation.

MODEL 1908 STANDARD COMMERCIAL - 9mm Bergmann/Bayard cal., identified by a mounted knight on the left magazine housing and is without finger cuts at base of magazine housing.

100%	98%	95%	90%	80%	70%	60%	50%	40%	30%	20%	10%
$4,200	$3,800	$3,400	$2,750	$1,900	$1,600	$1,100	$900	$700	$600	$500	$400

Add 25% if backstrap is slotted for shoulder stock.
Add $3,500 for excellent original leather/wood shoulder stock.

MODEL 1908 SPANISH CONTRACT – 9mm Bergmann/Bayard cal., total contract was for 3,000 pistols, can be identified from standard commercial pistols by the Spanish military acceptance stamp struck on the receiver.

100%	98%	95%	90%	80%	70%	60%	50%	40%	30%	20%	10%
$4,000	$3,500	$3,000	$2,500	$1,600	$1,100	$900	$800	$700	$600	$500	$400

Add 10% for matched numbered magazine.

Prices are for guns with original finish and grips - many Spanish contract guns were arsenal refinished.

MODEL 1910 STANDARD COMMERCIAL – 9mm Bergmann/Bayard cal., mechanically similar to Model 1908 Standard Commercial except has finger cuts in bottom of magazine housing, circular grooves are present on each side of magazine base.

100%	98%	95%	90%	80%	70%	60%	50%	40%	30%	20%	10%
$3,500	$3,000	$2,750	$2,200	$1,700	$1,200	$900	$800	$700	$600	$500	$400

Add 10% for matching numbered magazine.

MODEL 1910 DANISH GOVERNMENT CONTRACT – 9mm Bergmann/Bayard cal., total contract was for 4,840 pistols with mfg. and delivery 1911-1914. This variation can be identified by the Danish proof mark on the left receiver side and Danish inventory number on right side of receiver. Most pistols were converted in Denmark, Trolite grips were part of the original conversion, followed later by wood replacements, Converted pistols are marked "1910/21". Few pistols escaped conversion and have just Trolite replacement grips, those pistols lack the "1910/21" marking.

100%	98%	95%	90%	80%	70%	60%	50%	40%	30%	20%	10%
$2,950	$2,500	$2,000	$1,800	$1,300	$1,000	$900	$800	$700	$600	$500	$400

Add 15% for matching numbered magazine.

Add 25% for pistols that were not converted and lack the 1910/21 marking.

Subtract 25% for late wood replacement grips.

MODEL 1910/21 TOJHUS – 9mm Bergmann/Bayard cal., these pistols are marked "Haerens Tojhus" and are numbered from 1-900, original grips were black Trolit, replacement grips are either all smooth or with checkered circles above and below grip screw.

100%	98%	95%	90%	80%	70%	60%	50%	40%	30%	20%	10%
$2,950	$2,600	$2,200	$1,950	$1,450	$1,100	$900	$800	$700	$600	$500	$400

This contract was manufactured by the Danish Royal Arsenal located in Copenhagen.

MODEL 1910/21 RUSTKAMMER – 9mm Bergmann/Bayard cal., pistols are marked "Haerens Rustkammer", and numbered 901-2204, grip replacements are the same as noted for Haerens Tojhus.

100%	98%	95%	90%	80%	70%	60%	50%	40%	30%	20%	10%
$2,750	$2,350	$2,000	$1,800	$1,300	$1,000	$900	$800	$700	$600	$500	$400

This contract was manufactured by the Danish Royal Arsenal located in Copenhagen.

WAYNE BERGQUIST CUSTOM PISTOLS

Previous custom pistolsmith and gun dealer established during 1980 and located in Naples, FL until April 2021.

BERNARDELLI, GIULIO

Current shotgun manufacturer established in 2010, located in Gardone, Italy. No current U.S. importation.

Giulio Bernardelli Manifattura Armi manufactures both high quality O/U and SxS (hammer or hammerless) boxlock shotguns in all gauges, in addition to O/U rifles. Every gun is a special order manufactured per individual customer specifications. Please contact the company directly for a price quotation and length of delivery.

BERNARDELLI, VINCENZO

Current trademark of pistols and long arms mostly produced under private label by various manufacturers in Turkey, with headquarters located in Brescia, Italy beginning mid-2002. No current U.S. importation. Previously manufactured from 1721 to August, 1997 in Gardone, VT, Italy. Previously imported and distributed until 1997 by Armsport, Inc. located in Miami, FL. Previously imported and distributed by Magnum Research, Inc. located in Minneapolis, MN (1989-1992), Quality Arms, Inc. located in Houston, TX, Armes De Chasse located in Chadds Ford, PA, Stoeger located in New York, NY, and Action Arms, Ltd. located in Philadelphia, PA.

For individual model listings, please go to BlueBookOfGunValues.com/overflow.

BERSA

Current manufacturer established circa 1958, located in Ramos Mejia, Argentina. Currently distributed exclusively by Eagle Imports, Inc. located in Wanamassa, NJ. Previously imported and distributed before 1988 by Rock Island Armory located in Geneseo, IL, Outdoor Sports Headquarters, Inc. located in Dayton, OH, and R.S.A. Enterprises, Inc. located in Ocean, NJ. Distributor sales only.

GRADING - PPGS™	100%	98%	95%	90%	80%	70%	60%	LAST MSR

PISTOLS: SEMI-AUTO

THUNDER 9 – 9mm Para. cal., DA, 3 1/2 in. barrel, 10 (C/B 1994) or 14* shot mag., ambidextrous manual safety and decocking lever, automatic firing pin safety, 3-dot sights, aluminum frame, wraparound matte black polymer grips, link-free locked breech design, non-glare matte blue, satin nickel (new 1995), or duo-tone (new 1995) finish. Imported 1993-95.

	$400	$350	$300	$270	$220	$180	$140	*$475*

Add $17 for duo-tone finish. Add $50 for satin nickel finish.

THUNDER 22 (DISC. MODEL 23) – .22 LR cal., DA, 9 shot mag., 3 1/2 in. barrel, black polymer (new 1997) or walnut (disc. 1996) grips, 24 1/2 oz. Imported 1988-1998.

	$230	$200	$170	$155	$125	$100	$80	*$265*

Add $17 for satin nickel finish.

THUNDER 22 (CURRENT MFG.) – .22 LR cal., DA/SA (disc., reintroduced 2019), 3 1/2 in. standard or threaded (new 2019, matte only) barrel, 10 shot mag. with finger extension, alloy frame/steel slide, combat style trigger guard, 3-dot sights, integral locking system, manual, firing pin, or mag. disconnect safety, black checkered polymer grips, matte, satin nickel, or duo-tone (new 2012) finish, 18.9 oz.

MSR $306	$255	$225	$190	$175	$140	$115	$100	

Add $4 for duo-tone finish (new 2012).
Add $15 for nickel finish.
Add $24 for threaded barrel (new 2019).

THUNDER 32 – .32 ACP cal., matte, duo-tone, or nickel finish, 10 shot mag. Mfg. 2012 only.

	$275	$240	$200	$185	$150	$125	$95	*$323*

Add $6 for duo-tone finish. Add $19 for nickel finish.

THUNDER 380 – .380 ACP cal., DA, 3 1/2 in. barrel, fixed sights, 7 shot mag., deep blue, satin nickel, duo-tone (disc. 1995) finish, rubber grips, 25 3/4 oz. Imported 1995-98.

	$325	$285	$245	$220	$180	$145	$115	*$275*

Add $16 for satin nickel.
Add $16 for duo-tone finish (disc. 1995).

* ***Thunder 380 Deluxe*** – .380 ACP cal., 9 shot mag., black polymer grips, extended slide release and mag. bottom, polished blue, 3-dot sights, 23 oz. Mfg. 1997-2010.

	$295	$260	$220	$200	$160	$135	$100	*$360*

* ***Thunder 380 Plus*** – similar to Thunder 380, except has 15 shot mag. Mfg. 1995-1997.

	$265	$230	$200	$180	$145	$120	$95	*$316*

Add $32 for satin nickel finish. Add $17 for duo-tone finish.

THUNDER 380 (95) – .380 ACP cal., DA/SA, 3 1/2 in. barrel, 8 shot mag., alloy frame/steel slide, combat trigger guard, 3-dot fixed sights, black polymer or pink rubber wrap-around (mfg. 2015-2019) grips, features integral locking system, manual, firing pin, or mag. disconnect safety, matte blue, satin nickel, matte plus (mfg. 2007-disc.), Duotone (3,000 mfg. 2001, reintroduced 2008), Cerakote Robin Egg Blue (new 2018), Cerakote Purple (new 2018), Cerakote White (mfg. 2019 only), or Reverse Duotone (mfg. 2019 only) finish, 20 oz. New 1995.

MSR $306	$255	$225	$190	$175	$140	$115	$100	

Add $15 for satin nickel finish.
Add $24 for threaded barrel (new 2019).
Add $6 for pink rubber wrap-around grips (mfg. 2015-2019).
Add $165 for Crimson Trace grips (matte - mfg. 2010-2015, Duotone - mfg. 2010-2019, or matte with pink grips - mfg. 2016-disc.).

* ***Thunder 380 CC*** – .380 ACP cal., DA/SA, 3.2 in. barrel, 8 shot mag., alloy frame/steel slide, low profile sights with notched rear and integral front sight, ergonomic finger groove black polymer grips, loaded chamber indicator, matte black or Duotone (disc. 2019) finish, 16.4 oz.

MSR $319	$275	$240	$200	$185	$150	$125	$100	

Add $10 for Duotone finish (disc. 2019).
Add $163 for Crimson Trace grips (matte black finish only), mfg. 2015-2018.

* ***Thunder 380 Combat*** – .380 ACP cal., DA/SA, 3 1/2 in. barrel, 8 or 15 (Combat Plus, new late 2015) shot mag., alloy frame/steel slide, rounded trigger guard, combat sight system, olive wrap-around rubber grips, features integral locking system, manual, firing pin, or mag. disconnect safety, combat trigger guard, matte black finish, 20 oz. New 2012.

MSR $314	$265	$230	$195	$180	$145	$120	$100	

Add $88 for 15 shot mag. (Combat Plus, new late 2015).

GRADING - PPGS™	100%	98%	95%	90%	80%	70%	60%	LAST MSR

* ***Thunder 380 Plus (Current Mfg.)*** – .380 ACP cal., DA/SA, 3 1/2 in. standard or threaded (new 2021) barrel, 15 shot double stack mag., alloy frame/steel slide, combat trigger guard, 3-dot fixed sights, rubber grips, matte black or satin nickel finish, 20.5 oz.

MSR $373	$315	$275	$235	$215	$175	$140	$115	

Add $20 for threaded barrel (new 2021).
Add $36 for nickel finish.

TPRC 9 (THUNDER PRO 9MM ULTRA-COMPACT) – 9mm Para. cal., DA/SA, 3 1/4 in. standard or threaded (new 2019) barrel, 10 (disc. 2018) or 13 (new 2006) shot mag., skeletonized hammer, Sig Sauer type interchangeable sights, checkered black polymer grips, loaded chamber indicator, current mfg. includes lower accessory rail, choice of matte black, nickel (disc. 2009), Duotone (new 2008), or stainless steel (disc. 2008), 23 oz. New 2004.

MSR $482	$410	$360	$325	$290	$235	$195	$150	

Add $15 for Duotone finish.
Add $36 for threaded barrel (new 2019).
Add $58 for stainless steel (disc. 2008).

TPRC 40 (THUNDER PRO 40 ULTRA-COMPACT) – .40 S&W cal., similar to Thunder Pro 9mm Ultra-Compact, except has 10 shot mag., matte black or Duotone (disc.) finish, 23 oz. Mfg. late 2004-2018.

	$415	$375	$330	$290	$235	$195	$150	*$480*

Add $9 for Duotone (disc.).
Add $42 for stainless steel (disc.).
Add $20 for nickel finish (mfg. 2006-2009).

TPRC 45 (THUNDER PRO 45 ULTRA-COMPACT) – .45 ACP cal., DA/SA, alloy frame/steel slide, 3.6 in. barrel, 7 shot mag., interchangeable Sig Sauer type sights, checkered black polymer grips, choice of matte, Duotone (mfg. 2003, reintroduced 2008), stainless steel (mfg. 2004-2007), or satin nickel (disc. 2009) finish, 27 oz. Imported 2003-2018.

	$415	$375	$330	$290	$235	$195	$150	*$480*

Add $14 for Duotone finish.
Add $36 for satin nickel finish (disc. 2009).
Add $58 for stainless steel (disc. 2007).

TPR (THUNDER PRO HC 9/40) – 9mm Para. or .40 S&W (disc. 2017) cal., DA/SA, 4 1/4 in. threaded (new 2019) or standard barrel with interchangeable SIG Sauer type 3-dot sights, alloy frame/steel slide, 17 (9mm Para. cal.), or 13 (.40 S&W cal., disc. 2017) shot mag., checkered black polymer grips, integral locking system, Picatinny lower rail, polygonal rifling, loaded chamber indicator, ambidextrous releases, matte black or Duotone (9mm Para. only) finish, 30.7 oz.

MSR $482	$410	$360	$325	$290	$235	$195	$150	

Add $15 for Duotone finish.
Add $36 for threaded barrel (new 2019).

THUNDER PRO XT – 9mm Para. cal., DA/SA, 5 in. barrel, 17 shot mag., aluminum construction, dovetailed front and adj. rear sights, checkered black polymer grips, firing pin or manual safety, ambidextrous, matte (new 2017) or Duotone finish, 33.9 oz. New 2015.

MSR $865	$735	$650	$550	$500	$400	$330	$250	

FIRESTORM 380 – .380 ACP cal., DA/SA, PPK type design, 3 1/2 in. barrel, 7 shot mag., alloy frame, steel slide, combat style trigger guard, fixed sights, anatomic finger grooved rubber grips, matte black finish, 20 oz. New 2011.

MSR $321	$275	$240	$200	$185	$150	$125	$100	

* ***Firestorm 22*** – .22 LR cal., similar to Firestorm 380, except has 10 shot mag., 18.9 oz. While advertised during 2011, this model never went into production.

BPCC – 9mm Para., .380 ACP, or .40 S&W (disc. 2018) cal., short reset DAO, SFO, high impact polymer frame, 3.3 in. standard or threaded (new 2019) barrel, 7 (.40 S&W, disc. 2018) or 8 shot mag., interchangeable Sig Sauer type front and Glock type rear sights, loaded chamber indicator, ambidextrous mag. release, integral grips and front Picatinny rail, steel slide, black, OD (new 2014), FDE (new 2016), Urban Grey (new 2016), or full FDE Cerakote frame (new 2021), 21.5 oz. New 2010.

MSR $318	$275	$240	$200	$185	$150	$125	$100	

Add $19 for Full FDE Cerakote frame (new 2021.)
Add $19 for threaded barrel (new 2019).

MODEL 38BA – .380 ACP cal., DA, 3 1/2 in. barrel, blue finish, walnut grips, 6 shot mag., 24 1/2 oz.

	$325	$285	$245	$220	$180	$145	$115	

GRADING - PPGS™	100%	98%	95%	90%	80%	70%	60%	LAST MSR

MODEL 83 – .380 ACP cal., DA, 3 1/2 in. barrel, blue or satin nickel finish, custom walnut grips, 6 shot mag., 24 1/2 oz. Imported 1988-1994.

$295 $260 $220 $200 $160 $135 $100 *$288*

Add $34 for satin nickel finish.

MODEL 85 – .380 ACP cal., similar specifications to Model 83 except has 12 or 13 shot mag., 30 1/2 oz. Imported 1988-94.

$350 $315 $265 $240 $195 $165 $125 *$340*

Add $47 for satin nickel finish.

MODEL 86 – .380 ACP cal., blue matte or nickel finish, undercover model, wraparound rubber grips, 12 shot mag. Imported 1991-94.

$350 $315 $265 $240 $195 $165 $125 *$375*

Add $29 for nickel finish.

MODEL 90 – 9mm Para. cal., single action, steel frame, checkered walnut grips, 13 shot mag., deep blue finish. Imported 1990-91 only.

$325 $285 $245 $220 $180 $145 $115 *$384*

MODEL 97 – .380 ACP or 9mm Para. cal., single blowback action, 3 1/2 in. barrel, 6 shot mag. Disc. 1984.

$350 $315 $265 $240 $195 $165 $125

MODEL 223 – .22 LR cal., single action, 10 shot mag., 3 1/2 in. barrel, blue finish, squared-off trigger guard, nylon grips. Importation disc. 1987.

$250 $225 $195 $175 $135 $115 $95 *$239*

MODEL 224 – similar to Model 223, except has 4 in. barrel. Imported 1987 only.

$250 $225 $195 $175 $135 $115 $95 *$239*

MODEL 225 – similar to Model 223, except has 5 in. barrel and 10 shot mag. Disc. 1987.

$250 $225 $195 $175 $135 $115 $95 *$170*

MODEL 226 – similar to Model 225, except has 6 in. barrel. Importation disc. 1987.

$250 $225 $195 $175 $135 $115 $95 *$239*

MODEL 323 – .32 ACP cal., single action, 8 shot mag., thumb rest plastic grips, 25 oz. Disc. 1987.

$230 $200 $170 $155 $125 $100 $80 *$125*

MODEL 383 – .380 ACP cal., DA/SA, 3 1/2 in. barrel, blue finish, nylon grips, 7 shot mag. Imported 1984-1988.

$250 $225 $195 $175 $135 $115 $95

Last MSR was $188 for single action. Last MSR was $239 for double action.

Add $15 for double action.

REVOLVERS

FIRESTORM 38 – .38 Spl. +P cal., DAO, w/bobbed hammer, 2 in. barrel, 6 shot, fixed sights, black wood boot grips, choice of satin nickel, polished nickel, or parkerized finish, 24 oz. Mfg. by Armscor Precision. Limited importation 2011 only.

$295 $250 $225 $200 $185 $170 $160 *$364*

BERTUZZI, F.LLI

Previous manufacturer located in Gardone, VT, Italy 1886-2009. Previously distributed during 2009 by Sporting Products, LLC, located in Palm Beach, FL, also by Dewing's Fly & Gun Shop, located in W. Palm Beach, FL, and by New England Arms Corp. located in Kittery Point, ME.

For individual model listings, please go to BlueBookOfGunValues.com/overflow.

BESCHI, MARIO

Previous manufacturer until circa 1983 located in Italy.

SHOTGUNS: O/U

BOXLOCK MODEL – 12 or 20 ga., standard model with light engraving.

$3,000 $2,600 $2,300 $1,950 $1,600 $1,300 $995

SHOTGUNS: SxS

EXTRA LUSSO SIDELOCK – 12 or 20 ga., elaborate game scene engraving.

12 ga.	$12,000	$10,750	$9,250	$8,000	$6,750	$5,500	$4,250
20 ga.	$12,000	$10,750	$9,250	$8,000	$6,750	$5,500	$4,250

BOXLOCK MODEL – prices assume moderate engraving.

$1,650 $1,475 $1,300 $1,050 $850 $650 $500

GRADING - PPGS™	100%	98%	95%	90%	80%	70%	60%	LAST MSR

BEST ARMS (BEST HUGLU)

Current manufacturer of semi-auto (sporting and tactical configurations), slide action, and single shot shotguns established circa 2000, located in Konya, Turkey. No current U.S. importation.

THE BEST OF THE WEST

Current trademark of bolt action rifles manufactured in Cody, WY. Sold exclusively through Best of the West's Long Range Store.

RIFLES: BOLT ACTION

Prices listed below reflect base MSRs only. Many options are available for these models. Please contact the manufacturer directly for special orders, options, and pricing.

HUNTER ELITE/HUNTER ELITE LITE SERIES – 7mm Rem. Mag., .28 Nosler, .300 Win. Mag., 6.5 Creedmoor, or 6.5x284 cal., 26 in. fluted stainless steel barrel, Timney trigger, fiberglass, carbon fiber reinforced stock, Cerakote finish, 9.25 lbs.

MSR	100%	98%	95%	90%	80%	70%	60%	LAST MSR
MSR $5,499	$5,225	$4,575	$3,925	$3,555	$2,875	$2,350	$1,825	

MOUNTAIN HUNTER SERIES - .28 Nosler, 7mm Rem. Mag., .300 Win. Mag., .300 PRC (disc. 2020), 6.5 PRC (disc. 2020), 6.5 Creedmoor, or 6.5x284 cal., right or left-hand action, 26 in. fluted stainless steel barrel, 3 shot mag., Timney or Jewell trigger, sporter style, carbon fiber stock, includes 4-16x42 Huskemaw scope, scope rings, 1 box of ammo, and hard case, Cerakote finish, 9.5 lbs.

MSR	100%	98%	95%	90%	80%	70%	60%	LAST MSR
MSR $6,399	$6,080	$5,325	$4,550	$4,125	$3,350	$2,740	$2,125	

* ***Mountain Scout*** – 6.5 Creedmoor, 6.5 PRC, 6.5x284, or 7mm Rem. Mag. cal., Titanium action, 22 or 24 in. carbon fiber barrel w/side-port muzzle brake, Jewell trigger, sporter style carbon fiber stock, Huskemaw BD scope, includes Atlas bipod, 7.5 lbs. New 2019.

MSR	100%	98%	95%	90%	80%	70%	60%	LAST MSR
MSR $9,050	$8,750	$8,000	$7,250	$6,500	$5,750	$5,000	$4,500	

SIGNATURE SERIES - .300 PRC (disc. 2020), 6.5 PRC (disc. 2020), 6.5 Creedmoor, 6.5x284, 7mm Rem. Mag., 28 Nosler, .300 Win. Mag., .300 RUM, .375 H&H (new 2021), or .338 Lapua Mag. (new 2020) cal., right or left-hand action, 26 in. stainless steel or carbon fiber wrapped barrel w/side port muzzle brake, 3 shot mag., Jewell trigger, carbon fiber stock, Cerakote finish, 8.3 lbs.

MSR	100%	98%	95%	90%	80%	70%	60%	LAST MSR
MSR $8,199	$7,790	$6,825	$5,850	$5,300	$4,280	$3,500	$2,725	

Add $1,000 for carbon fiber wrapped barrel.

* ***Signature Tactical*** - .300 PRC, .300 Win. Mag., 7mm Rem. Mag., .28 Nosler, 6.5 PRC, or 6.5x284 cal., right or left-hand action, 26 in. carbon fiber or stainless steel barrel, 3 shot mag., Jewell trigger, carbon stock w/adj. cheekpiece, 7.85 lbs.

MSR	100%	98%	95%	90%	80%	70%	60%	LAST MSR
	$4,750	$4,350	$3,750	$3,250	$2,750	$2,500	$2,000	*$4,999*

SHOTGUNS: BOLT ACTION

SLUG GUN SERIES – 20 ga., Savage Arms Model 110 action and Huskemaw Optics, fully rifled stainless steel barrel w/Cerakote finish, detachable box mag., AccuTrigger, gray laminate stock w/aluminum pillar bedding, 1 MOA at 100 yards, matte metal finish, 11.5 lbs. New 2017.

MSR	100%	98%	95%	90%	80%	70%	60%	LAST MSR
MSR $3,199	$3,050	$2,660	$2,275	$2,060	$1,675	$1,375	$1,060	

BETTINSOLI, TARCISIO, Srl

Current manufacturer located in Brescia, Italy. Currently imported by Bettinsoli USA, established in 2019 and located in Eberfeld, IN. Previously imported on a private label basis by Franchi. Distributed in Europe by Bignami, located in Bolzano, Italy.

Bettinsoli manufactures fine quality O/U shotguns, express O/U rifles, and combination guns. Certain models were private labeled under the Franchi trademark in the U.S. and distributed under the Bettinsoli name in Europe. Select models are being imported by Bettinsoli USA. Please contact the importer directly for more information.

SHOTGUNS

Select Bettinsoli guns are being imported by Bettinsoli USA. Select models include: Grand Prix Deluxe w/adj. stock (MSR $4,999), Grand Prix w/adj. stock (MSR $4,299), Overland EELL-12 and 20 ga. (MSR $3,799), Overland ELS-12 and 20 ga. (MSR $3,799), Overland ELS-28 ga. (MSR $3,999), Overland EELL-.410 bore (MSR $3,999), Overland ELS-.410 bore (MSR $3,999), Diamond Deluxe Lite-12 and 20 ga. (MSR $2,849), Diamond Deluxe-12 and 20 ga. (MSR $2,649), Omega Sport w/adj. stock (MSR $2,799), Omega Lite-12 and 20 ga. (MSR $2,199), Omega Steel-12 and 20 (MSR $1,999), Omega Steel-28 ga. (MSR $2,149), and X-Trail Camo (MSR $1,999). Please contact the importer directly for more information and availability on these models.

GRADING - PPGS™	100%	98%	95%	90%	80%	70%	60%	LAST MSR

BIG BEAR ARMS & SPORTING GOODS INC.

Previous firearms importer located in Carrollton, TX 1992-1999, specializing in the importation of both Russian military surplus and new firearms.

PISTOLS: SEMI-AUTO

IZH-70 MAKAROV – .380 ACP or 9mm Makarov cal., 8 shot mag., mfg. in Russia. Imported 1994-1999.

	100%	98%	95%	90%	80%	70%	60%	LAST MSR
	$265	$185	$155	$135	$115	$100	$90	*$325*

RIFLES: SEMI-AUTO

SAIGA SPORTER RIFLE – 7.62x39mm cal., semi-auto with improved Kalashnikov design, checkered hardwood (disc.) or synthetic stock and forearm, 5 or 10 (disc.) shot mag. Imported 1996-99.

	100%	98%	95%	90%	80%	70%	60%	LAST MSR
	$575	$400	$325	$250	$225	$200	$175	*$750*

Add $169 for 3.5X scope and mount.

SHOTGUNS

SAIGA SEMI-AUTO – .410 bore, 3 in. chamber, tactical configuration. Imported 1996-1999.

	100%	98%	95%	90%	80%	70%	60%	LAST MSR
	$425	$350	$295	$250	$200	$180	$165	*$499*

IJ-27 O/U – 12 ga., 2 3/4 in. chambers. Imported 1995-99.

	100%	98%	95%	90%	80%	70%	60%	LAST MSR
	$425	$350	$295	$250	$200	$180	$165	*$499*

IJ-39E O/U – 12 ga., 2 3/4 in. chambers. Imported 1995-99.

	100%	98%	95%	90%	80%	70%	60%	LAST MSR
	$760	$600	$495	$400	$360	$330	$295	*$895*

IJ-43 SxS – 12 ga., 2 3/4 in. chambers. Imported 1995-99.

	100%	98%	95%	90%	80%	70%	60%	LAST MSR
	$325	$250	$200	$175	$155	$145	$135	*$399*

BIG HORN ARMORY INC.

Current manufacturer located in Cody, WY.

PISTOLS: SEMI-AUTO

AR500 PISTOL – .500 Auto Max cal., 10 in. barrel with flash suppressor, 5 shot mag., no sights, forearm brace, M-LOK forend, adj. gas block, full Picatinny rail. New 2018.

	100%	98%	95%	90%	80%	70%	60%	LAST MSR
MSR $2,199	$1,875	$1,650	$1,400	$1,275	$1,025	$850	$700	

RIFLES: LEVER ACTION

In addition to custom alterations, special checkering, engraving, upgraded wood, and metal finishes are also available. Options and pricing on request.

Exhibition Grade wood mated to color cased receivers and octagon barrels are available for all models. MSR begins at $6,500.

MODEL 89 CARBINE – .500 S&W Mag., patterned after the Winchester Model 1886 lever action, 16 (new 2017) or 18 in. barrel, recessed crown, stainless steel action, 7 shot mag., sling swivels, aperture rear sight on bolt, blade front sight, integral front and stud rear sling swivel mounts, standard or fancy checkered American black walnut, Hot Wood maple (disc.), or laminate pistol grip buttstock, 1 in. recoil pad, Blue (disc.), Hunter Black stainless steel, Matte stainless steel, or case color hardened metal finish, approx. 7 1/2 lbs.

	100%	98%	95%	90%	80%	70%	60%	LAST MSR
MSR $2,499	$2,125	$1,875	$1,600	$1,450	$1,185	$975	$775	

Add $50 for Hot Wood maple (disc.) or laminate stock.
Add $150 for Scout scope mount.
Add $600 for upgraded walnut stock or Matte stainless steel metal finish.
Add $750 for octagon barrel.
Add $1,200 for case color hardened metal finish.
Add $1,200 for .500 Linebaugh or .475 Linebaugh cal.
Add $650 for Blued steel metal finish (disc. 2015).

MODEL 89 RIFLE – .500 S&W Mag. cal., patterned after the Winchester Model 1886 lever action, 22 in. barrel, recessed crown, stainless steel action, 5 shot mag., sling swivels, aperture rear sight on bolt, blade front sight, integral front and stud rear sling swivel mounts, standard or fancy checkered American black walnut, Hot Wood maple (disc. 2016), or laminate pistol grip buttstock, 1 in. recoil pad, Blue (disc.), Hunter Black stainless steel, Matte stainless steel, or case color hardened metal finish, approx. 7 1/2 lbs.

	100%	98%	95%	90%	80%	70%	60%	LAST MSR
MSR $2,699	$2,285	$1,990	$1,700	$1,550	$1,250	$1,025	$800	

Add $50 for Hot Wood maple (disc. 2016) or laminate stock.
Add $600 for upgraded walnut stock or Matte stainless steel finish.
Add $1,200 for case color hardened metal finish.
Add $650 for blued metal finish (disc. 2015).

GRADING - PPGS™	100%	98%	95%	90%	80%	70%	60%	LAST MSR

MODEL 89 TRAPPER – .500 S&W Magnum cal., 16 (carbine) or 22 (rifle) in. stainless steel barrel, recessed crown, 6 shot mag., aperture rear and post front sights, American black walnut pistol grip stock and forend with synthetic satin finish, integral front and stud rear sling swivel mounts, 1 in. recoil pad, Matte stainless steel, Hunter Black stainless steel, or color case hardened finish, 7 lbs. 10 oz. New 2017.

MSR $2,799	$2,375	$2,075	$1,785	$1,625	$1,300	$1,075	$900	

Add $150 for Scout scope mount.
Add $600 for Matte stainless steel finish.
Add $750 for octagon barrel.
Add $1,200 for color case hardened finish.

MODEL 90 CARBINE – .460 S&W or .454 Casull cal., 18 in. barrel, recessed crown, stainless steel action, 7 shot mag., integral front and stud rear sling swivel mounts, aperture rear and post front sights, standard or fancy American black walnut, Hot Wood maple (disc. 2016), or laminate stock with 1 in. recoil pad and synthetic satin stock finish, available in Hunter satin stainless (mfg. 2015 only), Hunter Black stainless steel, Matte stainless steel, Blued (mfg. 2015 only), or case color hardened metal finish, 8 lbs. 2 oz. New 2015.

MSR $2,849	$2,425	$2,125	$1,825	$1,650	$1,350	$1,100	$875	

Add $200 for .454 Casull or .45 LC cal.
Add $50 for Hot Wood (disc. 2016) maple or laminate stock.
Add $150 for Scout scope mount.
Add $600 for upgraded walnut stock or Matte stainless steel.
Add $750 for octagon barrel.
Add $650 for Blued Steel (disc.).
Add $1,200 for case color hardened metal finish.

MODEL 90 RIFLE – .460 S&W, .454 Casull, or .45 LC cal., 22 in. barrel, recessed crown, stainless steel action, 5 shot mag., integral front and stud rear sling swivel mounts, aperture rear and post front sights, standard or fancy American black walnut, Hot Wood maple (disc. 2016), or laminate stock with 1 in. recoil pad and synthetic satin stock finish, available in Hunter satin stainless (mfg. 2015 only), Hunter Black stainless steel, Blued (mfg. 2015 only), Matte stainless steel, or case color hardened metal finish, 8 lbs. 2 oz. New 2015.

MSR $3,149	$2,675	$2,350	$2,000	$1,825	$1,475	$1,200	$950	

Add $200 for .454 Casull or .45 LC cal.
Add $50 for Hot Wood maple (disc. 2016) or laminate stock.
Add $150 for Scout scope mount.
Add $600 for upgraded walnut stock or Matte stainless steel.
Add $750 for octagon barrel.
Add $1,200 for case color hardened metal finish.
Add $650 for Blued Steel (disc.).

RIFLES: SEMI-AUTO

AR500 – .500 Auto Max cal., 18 in. barrel, flash suppressor, 5 shot mag., no sights, adj. buttstock, M-LOK forend, adj. gas block, full Picatinny rail, includes hard plastic case. New 2018.

MSR $1,999	$1,700	$1,495	$1,275	$1,150	$950	$775	$650	

SHOTGUNS: O/U

STERLING FIELD – 12 ga., 3 in. chambers, 26, 28, or 30 in. vent. rib alloy steel barrels, checkered Grade 3 Turkish walnut stock, includes ten choke tubes, SST, detachable trigger lock, engraved Nitride receiver, ejectors, elongated forcing cones, 6 lbs. 14 oz.-7 lbs. 6 oz. Mfg. 2010-2016.

	$2,750	$2,300	$1,950	$1,725	$1,500	$1,350	$1,100	*$2,999*

STERLING TARGET – 12 ga., 2 3/4 in. chambers, 28, 30 or 32 in. vent. rib barrels, engraved Nitride receiver, checkered Turkish two-way adj. oil finished walnut stock, includes ten choke tubes, 7 lbs. 12 oz - 8 lbs. 4 oz. Mfg. 2010-2016.

	$3,150	$2,755	$2,365	$2,150	$1,750	$1,425	$1,125	*$3,499*

STERLING REGAL – similar to Sterling Target and Field models, except has gold trigger and locks, exhibition grade walnut, special engraving, rust blued barrels, and bone charcoal case coloring.

While advertised, this model was not manufactured.

GRADING - PPGS™	100%	98%	95%	90%	80%	70%	60%	LAST MSR

BIG HORN ARMS CORP.

Previous manufacturer located in Watertown, SD.

PISTOLS: SINGLE SHOT

TARGET PISTOL – .22 Short cal. only, unique action permitting auto. ejection, ambidextrous stock made of molded Tufflex with carvings, 26 oz. Approx. 1,200 mfg. Disc. in the late 1960s.

$175	$150	$135	$125	$115	$105	$95	

SHOTGUNS: SINGLE SHOT

LIL' MAGNUM SHOTGUN – .410 diameter reloadable shot cartridge, single shot open bolt operation, included reloading equipment, approx. 2,000 mfg. in the late 1960s.

$125	$100	$75	$65	$55	$50	$45	

BIGHORN RIFLE CO.

Previous manufacturer located in Orem, UT.

PISTOLS: BOLT ACTION

BIGHORN PISTOL – .22 LR cal., bolt action design.

Lack of information on this pistol precludes accurate pricing.

RIFLES: BOLT ACTION

BIGHORN RIFLE – Mauser action, choice of calibers, custom made bolt action of high quality, interchangeable barrels (gun was supplied with 2 barrels), adj. trigger, deluxe walnut stock, many custom options. Mfg. 1984 only.

$2,100	$1,800	$1,600	$1,400	$1,200	$1,000	$850	

BILL HANUS BIRDGUNS LLC

Previous dealer and importer located in Newport, OR. Bill Hanus imported select private label models from various manufacturers, including AyA, Fausti, Sabatti, Remington, Grulla, Merkel, Browning, and Fabarm. Previously, he had his own private label model manufactured by Armas Ugartechea (see separate listing) located in Eibar, Spain until 1997. A champion of small shotgun gauges, Bill passed away on Sept. 12, 2012.

BINGHAM, LTD.

Previous manufacturer located in Norcross, GA circa 1976-1985.

For individual model listings, please go to BlueBookOfGunValues.com/overflow.

BISHOP AMMUNITION & FIREARMS

Current ammunition and rifle manufacturer located in Antelope, CA.

For individual model listings, please go to BlueBookOfGunValues.com/overflow.

BITTNER

Previously manufactured by Gustav Bittner located in Vieprty, Bohemia (Austria, Hungary), circa 1893.

PISTOLS

BITTNER MODEL 1893 – 7.7mm Bittner cal., pistol with hand activated repeater mechanism, box magazine, checkered grips, limited manufacture circa 1893.

$15,000	$12,500	$10,000	$7,500	$6,000	$5,000	$4,000	

BLACK ACES TACTICAL

Current trademark of shotguns and parts established in 2011, located in Longwood, FL.

For individual model listings, please go to BlueBookOfGunValues.com/overflow.

BLACK COLLAR ARMS

Current bolt action pistol manufacturer, located in Austin, TX.

PISTOLS: BOLT ACTION

PORK SWORD PISTOL – .223 Wylde, .300 AAC Blackout, 6mm Creedmoor, 6mm ARC (new 2021), 6.5 Grendel, 6.5 Creedmoor, .308 Win., .375 Raptor, .224 Valkyrie, .243 Win., 6x47 Lapua, 6.5x47 Lapua, 6mm BR, .260 Rem., 6.8 SPC, 7mm-08 Rem., .270 WSM, .300 WSM, .338 Federal, .350 Legend, .358 Win., 45 Raptor (new 2021), or .450 Bushmaster cal., Bighorn Origin action with salt bath Nitride finish, 6, 6 1/2, 8, 9, 10, 12, or 14 in. X-Caliber match grade or KAK Industries barrel, AICS profile mag. compatibility, choice of factory, black or red ELF 700 trigger, or TriggerTech Primary or Diamond flat shoe trigger, right or left-handed Pork Sword Chassis system, 8 or 12 in. Tri-LOK FARend forearm w/M-LOK slots or optional ARCA rail compatibility (new 2020), KAK Shockwave kit or SB SF1913, A2, Ergo, or Magpul K grips, black finish, 4.1-5.2 lbs. New late 2019.

GRADING - PPGS™	100%	98%	95%	90%	80%	70%	60%	LAST MSR
MSR $1,795	**$1,525**	**$1,350**	**$1,150**	**$1,000**	**$850**	**$700**	**$550**	

The first 100 models are engraved "First Run x/100" on the action, these models carry a slight premium.

MSR reflects base price. Please contact the manufacturer directly for more information on the various options available for this model.

BLACK CREEK PRECISION

Current manufacturer of AR-15 style pistols, rifles, and shotguns located in Jacksonville, FL.

Please refer to BlueBookOfGunValues.com to order the *Blue Book of AR-15s & Variations*, available as a book or online subscription.

BLACK DAWN ARMORY (BLACK DAWN INDUSTRIES)

Previous manufacturer of semi-auto pistols and rifles located in Sedalia, MO, 2010-2018.

Please refer to BlueBookOfGunValues.com to order the *Blue Book of AR-15s & Variations*, available as a book or online subscription.

BLACK FORGE LLC

The assets of Black Forge were acquired by Invincible Arms, LLC located in Willoughby, OH, beginning 2015. Invincible Arms operates that brand exclusively as the parts and components arm of the company. Black Forge previously manufactured semi-auto pistols and rifles until 2014, and was located in Orlando, FL.

For individual model listings, please go to BlueBookOfGunValues.com/overflow.

BLACKHEART FIREARMS (BLACKHEART INTERNATIONAL LLC)

Previous pistol and rifle manufacturer located in Clarksburg, WV until 2019. Previously located in Fairmont and Philippi, WV.

For individual model listings, please go to BlueBookOfGunValues.com/overflow.

BLACKOPS TECHNOLOGIES

Previous manufacturer located in Columbia Falls, MT until 2014.

For individual model listings, please go to BlueBookOfGunValues.com/overflow.

BLACK RAIN ORDNANCE, INC.

Current AR-15 style rifle and pistol manufacturer established in 2009, located in Neosho, MO. Dealer and distributor sales.

Please refer to BlueBookOfGunValues.com to order the *Blue Book of AR-15s & Variations*, available as a book or online subscription.

BLACK RIFLE COMPANY LLC

Previous AR-15 style rifle and accessories manufacturer located in Clackamas, OR until 2014.

Please refer to BlueBookOfGunValues.com to order the *Blue Book of AR-15s & Variations*, available as a book or online subscription.

BLACK WEAPONS ARMORY

Previous AR-15 style custom manufacturer located in Tucson, AZ until 2014.

Please refer to BlueBookOfGunValues.com to order the *Blue Book of AR-15s & Variations*, available as a book or online subscription.

BLAND, THOMAS & SONS GUNMAKERS LTD.

Current manufacturer located in England since 1840. This firm was purchased in 1990 by Woodcock Hill located in Benton, PA.

For individual model listings, please go to BlueBookOfGunValues.com/overflow.

BLASER

Currently manufactured by Blaser Jagdwaffen GmbH in Isny im Allgäu, Germany. Currently imported and distributed beginning late 2006 by Blaser Group (formerly known as Blaser USA), located in San Antonio, TX. Previously located in Stevensville, MD. Previously imported and distributed 2002-2006 by SIG Arms located in Exeter, NH, and circa 1988-2002 by Autumn Sales Inc. located in Fort Worth, TX. In January 2020, Blaser USA became Blaser Group. This name change transition was done to establish consistent branding around the world.

The Blaser Company was founded in 1963 by Horst Blaser. In 1986, the company was taken over by Gerhard Blenk. During 1997, the company was sold to SIG. In late 2000, SIG Arms AG, the firearms portion of SIG, was

GRADING - PPGS™	100%	98%	95%	90%	80%	70%	60%	LAST MSR

purchased by two Germans, Michael Lüke and Thomas Ortmeier, who have a background in textiles. Today the Lüke & Ortmeier group (L&O Group) includes independently operational companies such as Blaser Jadgwaffen GmbH, Mauser Jagdwaffen GmbH, J.P. Sauer & Sohn GmbH, SIG-Sauer Inc., SIG-Sauer GmbH and SAN Swiss Arms AG.

Blaser currently makes approximately 20,000 rifles and shotguns annually, with most being sold in Europe.

DRILLINGS

Blaser makes a D99 Drilling in a variety of combinations, including a rifle over two shotgun barrels, a single shotgun barrel with a rifle barrel on the top and on the side (Duo), and three rifle barrels (Trio). Many centerfire calibers are available, and the shotgun barrel is chambered for 3 in. 20 ga. This model is not currently imported into America, and is available by special order only. Please contact the importer directly for availability and pricing.

PISTOLS: BOLT ACTION

R-93 HHS (HUNTING HANDGUN SYSTEM) – various cals. between .222 Rem.-.375 H&H, features R93 right or left-hand straight pull bolt action, 14 in. hammer forged free floating barrel (interchangeable), matte black receiver with choice of wood, case colored, or game scene sideplates, Turkish walnut stock and pistol grip, 3-4 shot mag., 5 lbs. Limited importation 2004-2006.

	100%	98%	95%	90%	80%	70%	60%	LAST MSR
	$2,475	$2,050	$1,775	$1,500	$1,350	$1,200	$1,025	*$2,900*

Add $200 for left-hand bolt assembly.
Add $900 per interchangeable barrel.

RIFLES: BOLT ACTION

The R-93 rifle system's biggest advantage is its component interchangeability. Both barrels and bolt heads/assemblies can be quickly changed making the R-93 a very versatile rifle platform. Many special orders and features were available.

Add $487 for saddle scope mount on all current Blaser rifles.
Add $445 for left-hand stock available on currently manufactured R-8 models.
Add $317 for Kickstop recoil pad on currently manufactured Blaser rifles.
Beginning late 2006, Blaser began offering graded wood between Grades 3 and Grade 10 (Grade 11 was discontinued in 2020) on most models. Please refer to these listings under each current model.

R-8 PROFESSIONAL – available in many standard and metric cals. between .222 Rem.-10.3x60R cal., improved R-93 action featuring detachable mag. (includes double release buttons and locking device), Desmodromic mechanical trigger (available in both removable or fixed trigger assemblies), optimized barrel bedding, and new stock design that decreases felt recoil, 20 1/2, 23, or 25 3/4 in. interchangeable barrel with white outline contrast sights on barrel, right or left-hand action, Dark Green, Dark Brown, or Savannah (new 2013) synthetic one-piece stock is standard with black thermo elastic inlays, recoil pad, palm swell, and black forearm tip, approx. 6 3/8-8 3/4 lbs. New 2011.

	100%	98%	95%	90%	80%	70%	60%
MSR $4,292	$3,650	$3,195	$2,750	$2,480	$2,010	$1,650	$1,425

Add 903 for camo.
Add $532 for adj. comb. (disc. 2020).
Add $445 for steel receiver (mfg. 2012 only).
Add $1,377-$3,232 per interchangeable barrel, depending on caliber and configuration.

This model is also available in additional higher grades, including the Jaeger (Grade 3 wood, MSR $5,445, new late 2010), Intuition (MSR $5,998), Compact (MSR $5,998), Classic Sporter (Grade 4 wood, last MSR in 2017 was $4,699, Grade 7 wood last MSR in 2015 was $6,657), Luxus (Grade 4 wood, MSR $6,409, new late 2010), Attache (Grade 7 wood, MSR $9,672), Custom (Grade 7 wood, disc. 2012 - last MSR was $12,425), Baronesse (Grade 8 wood, MSR $17,277), Ruthenium (Grade 8 wood, $13,040 MSR), Stradivari (Grade 10 wood, $19,880 MSR), Success (Grade 4 wood, MSR $5,434), Success Individual (MSR $6,969), Custom I (Grade 6 wood, $19,206 MSR), Custom II (Grade 7 wood, POR), Custom III (Grade 8 wood, POR), Custom IV (Grade 9 wood, POR), Super Luxus (Grade 7 wood, last MSR in 2014 was $18,370), Exclusive (Grade 8 wood, last published MSR was $22,232 in 2011), Super Exclusive (Grade 8 wood, last published MSR was $29,615 in 2011), and Imperial (Grade 8 wood, last published MSR was $43,511 in 2011).

Wood upgrade MSR's are as follows: Grade 3 - $1,780, Grade 4 - $2,013, Grade 5 - $2,649, Grade 6 - $2,596, Grade 7 - $4,663, Grade 8 - $5,960, Grade 9 - $7,150, Grade 10 - $10,200, Grade 11 - (last MSR in 2020 was $10,559).

* ***R-8 Professional Hunter*** – dangerous game cals., 20 1/2, 23, or 25 3/4 in. Selous barrel, steel receiver, detachable mag., synthetic stock in Dark Green, Savannah, or Black/Brown, elastomer inlays on forend and pistol grip, ring sling swivel, Professional recoil pad, includes Kickstop. New 2014.

	100%	98%	95%	90%	80%	70%	60%
MSR $9,009	$7,650	$6,695	$5,750	$5,200	$4,225	$3,500	$3,000

GRADING - PPGS™	100%	98%	95%	90%	80%	70%	60%	LAST MSR

* ***R-8 Kilombero (Big Bore Edition)*** – dangerous game cals., Selous barrel, steel receiver, Safari sights, Grade 4 (disc. 2020) or Grade 7 (new 2021) wood, Safari buttstock and forearm with ebony forearm tip, silver recoil red pad, includes kickstop. New 2014.

MSR $12,589	$10,700	$9,365	$8,025	$7,275	$5,885	$5,000	$4,000	

Last MSR in 2020 with Grade 4 wood was $8,995.

* ***R-8 Selous (Big Bore Edition)*** – dangerous game cals., Selous barrel, integrated custom case hardened steel receiver, gold plated trigger, Grade 7 wood, Safari buttstock, silver recoil pad in red, ring sling swivel, Safari forearm with forearm ebony tip, Selous lettering inlayed in gold, includes Kickstop. New 2014.

MSR $17,807	$15,150	$13,250	$11,365	$10,300	$8,335	$6,825	$5,925	

R-8 PROFESSIONAL SUCCESS – similar to R-8 Professional, except has Dark Green or Dark Brown synthetic thumbhole stock, black thermo elastic inlays standard, or optional leather inlays (in Dark Brown only). New 2013.

MSR $4,875	$4,150	$3,650	$3,100	$2,800	$2,300	$1,850	$1,450	

Add $1,272 for leather inlays.

Add $916 for R8 Long Range Professional Success model (.338 Lapua Mag., includes muzzle brake, disc. 2018).

Add $2,120 for Black Edition model (new 2015) or $2,754 for Ruthenium Model (new 2015).

Add $5,914 for Success Carbon model with carbon fiber stock/forearm and brown leather inlays.

* ***R-8 Professional Success Monza*** – DLC coated trigger, bolt head, and knob, black anthracite stock with leather inlays and recoil pad in black with red contrast stitchings. New 2013.

MSR $6,873	$5,850	$5,125	$4,390	$3,980	$3,225	$2,650	$2,275	

* ***R-8 Professional Success Stutzen*** – Desmodromic trigger mechanism, dark green or black brown stock with elastomere inlays or leather inlays. New 2013.

MSR $5,405	$4,595	$4,025	$3,450	$3,125	$2,525	$2,075	$1,700	

Add $1,093 for leather inlays.

R-8 SUCCESS/SUCCESS MONO – black receiver, gold plated trigger, Grade 4 walnut stock with brown leather inlays, black ebony forend tip, rubber recoil pad.

MSR $7,578	$6,450	$5,650	$4,850	$4,400	$3,550	$3,000	$2,500	

Subtract $1,333 for R-8 Success Mono model with Grade 4 wooden thumbhole stock (disc. 2020).

R-8 SUCCESS BLACK EDITION – matte black receiver, Grade 7 hand selected Caucasian walnut thumbhole stock with premium black leather inlays, black ebony forearm tip, rubber recoil pad, gold colored accents, wooden bolt head.

MSR $11,984	$10,185	$8,915	$7,650	$6,925	$5,600	$4,700	$3,975	

R-8 ULTIMATE – black/brown ergonomic synthetic thumbhole stock with black elastomer inlays. New mid-2019.

MSR $4,875	$4,150	$3,630	$3,115	$2,825	$2,285	$1,875	$1,625	

Add $349 for Recoil Absorption System.

Add $542 for adj. comb.

Add $604 for adj. recoil pad.

R-8 ULTIMATE LEATHER – ergonomic synthetic brown/black thumbhole stock with cocoa leather inlay. New late 2019.

MSR $6,147	$5,225	$4,575	$3,925	$3,550	$2,875	$2,400	$2,000	

Add $349 for Recoil Absorption System.

Add $604 for adj. recoil pad.

Add $636for adj. comb.

R-84 – .22-250 Rem. (disc. 1993), .243 Win., 6mm Rem., .25-06 Rem., .270 Win., .280 Rem., or .30-06 standard cals., .257 Wby. Mag., .264 Win. Mag., 7mm Rem. Mag., .300 Win. Mag., .300 Wby. Mag., .338 Win. Mag., or .375 H&H cal., 23 or 24 (Mag. cals. only) in. interchangeable barrel, scroll engraving on receiver, short bolt action with 60 degree rotation, checkered Turkish walnut stock and forearm, approx. 7 lbs. Mfg. 1988-94.

	$2,100	$1,575	$1,275	$1,050	$950	$850	$775	*$2,300*

Add $50 for left-hand action.

Add $600 per interchangeable barrel (w/scope mounts).

This model has the scope mounted directly to the barrel (and not the receiver). Since the scope mounts are on the barrel extension, this takedown rifle is unique in that it does not require re-zeroing when the rifle is reassembled.

GRADING - PPGS™	100%	98%	95%	90%	80%	70%	60%	LAST MSR

* ***R-84 Deluxe*** – features a better grade of Turkish walnut with a North American game scene engraved on receiver, silver pistol grip cap with animal scene engraving.

	$2,375	$2,025	$1,650	$1,200	$1,000	$925	$825	*$2,600*

Add $50 for left-hand action.

* ***R-84 Super Deluxe*** – best grade Turkish walnut with receiver featuring African game scene engraving (animals are in gold and silver), and silver pistol grip cap with gold animal engraving.

	$2,675	$2,225	$1,775	$1,300	$1,100	$975	$895	*$2,950*

Add $50 for left-hand action.

R-93 CLASSIC – available in various domestic (.22-250 Rem.-.416 Rem. Mag.) and European (6.5x55mm and 7x57mm) cals., 22, 24 (Mag. cals.), or 27 1/2 (disc.) in. barrel, unique patented rifle features straight pull bolt action (0 degree bolt lift), 360 degree radial locking system eliminates bolt rotation, unique safety offering cartridge in chamber capability, 3 shot mag., features interchangeable barrel system and newly designed bolt, searfree trigger mechanism, matte finished nickel receiver with engraving, non-glare "black velvet" barrel finish, integrated low scope mounts standard (1994-1997 only), custom gun case with combination lock became standard 1998, 6 1/2-7 lbs. Importation began 1994, R-93 Classic introduced 1998, disc. May 2002.

	$2,600	$2,200	$1,850	$1,675	$1,500	$1,375	$1,250	*$2,950*

Add $595 per interchangeable barrel (w/o mounts).

During 1998, this model's nomenclature changed to the R-93 Classic. Scope mounts were no longer included. Between 1994-1997, this model retailed for approx. $2,800 and a Deluxe Grade was available for $3,100, while the Super Deluxe Grade retailed for $3,500.

* ***R-93 Classic Safari*** – .416 Rem. Mag. cal., features 24 in. heavy barrel, open sights, large forearm, 9 1/2 lbs., this model was renamed the R-93 Classic in 1998. Imported 1994-2002.

	$3,575	$3,100	$2,650	$2,275	$1,825	$1,350	$1,150	*$4,140*

R-93 LUXUS – available in 20 calibers from .222 Rem. - .375 H&H., similar to the R-93 Classic, except has Grade 4 wood and ebony forend tip, choice of sideplates with game portraits or wood, available in right or left-hand action, case not included. Mfg. 2002-2010.

	$4,150	$3,625	$2,850	$2,300	$1,850	$1,525	$1,350	*$4,594*

Add $700 for Luxus Plus Model with upgraded wood, black receiver and choice of color case hardened steel, wood, or animal sideplates (mfg. 2005-2007).

* ***R-93 Luxus Safari*** – .375 H&H or .416 Rem. Mag. cal., similar to R-93 Classic Safari, except has higher quality walnut and ebony forend tip, available in right or left-hand action, case not included. Mfg. 2002-2008.

	$4,875	$4,450	$3,700	$3,150	$2,400	$2,100	$1,800	*$5,470*

R-93 SUPER LUXUS – various cals., oil finished Grade 6 stock, engraved sideplates with animals and different styles of engraving were optional. Mfg. 2007-2010.

The last base price on this special order model was $10,643.

R-93 ATTACHE – various cals., features premium walnut stock and forearm with receiver wood panel inserts, wood bolt knob, ebony forearm tip, fluted barrel, current mfg. includes Grade 7 walnut, includes case, approx. 6 1/2 lbs. Mfg. 1998-2010.

	$5,895	$5,200	$4,550	$3,750	$3,250	$2,600	$2,025	*$6,360*

R-93 OCTAGON – various cals., Grade 6 wood, black receiver with wooden sideplates, full octagon barrel. Disc. 2008.

	$7,100	$6,000	$5,000	$4,000	$3,250	$2,650	$2,475	*$7,883*

R-93 GRAND LUXE – various cals., deluxe model with high grade checkered Grade 5 stock and forearm, fully hand engraved receiver with sideplates (various styles available), 3 shot mag., 6 1/2-7 lbs. Mfg. 1999-2003, reintroduced 2007-2010.

	$7,950	$6,800	$5,750	$4,600	$3,600	$2,750	$2,600	

Last MSR during 2003 was $5,160, and last MSR during 2010 was $8,409.

R-93 SELOUS – .375 H&H, .300 Win. Mag., or .416 Rem. cal., color case hardened steel receiver, compact design, Safari barrel, gold trigger, gold lined bolt handle, sling straps, named after big game hunter Frederick Courteney Selous, with Selous name in gold on receiver. Mfg. 2009-2010.

	$15,750	$12,750	$10,500	$9,000	$8,000	$7,000	$6,000	*$17,058*

Add $2,417 per interchangable barrel.

GRADING - PPGS™	100%	98%	95%	90%	80%	70%	60%	LAST MSR

R-93 PROFESSIONAL – various cals., one-piece dark green synthetic stock with black thermo-elastic inlays, ergonomic pistol grip and rubber recoil pad, also available in Mossy Oak (disc. 2010) or Orange camo (disc.), approx. 6 3/4 lbs. Currently available exclusively through Mad Dog Guns. Imported 2007-late 2017.

$2,950	$2,525	$2,100	$1,625	$1,450	$1,225	$1,050	*$3,288*

Add $723 for semi-weight, $600 for match grade (disc. 2011), or $1,356 for Safari barrel configuration.
Add $1,214 per extra R-93 barrel with standard taper (includes mag.).
Add $1,746 for R-93 rimfire conversion kit (.17 HMR, .22 LR, or .22 WMR cal., includes barrel, magazine, bolt assembly, and bolt catch insert, mfg. 2008-2012).
Add $1,134 for Professional Tracking Model with open sights and detachable sling swivels (disc. 2008).
Add $470 for left handed, EU style stock (disc. 2015).
Add $502 for camo coverage (disc. 2010).

The basic Professional Model was also available as a receiver, stock, and bolt assembly - last MSR (2011) was $2,001, or as a receiver and stock only - last MSR was $1,369 (2011).

Last MSRs in 2015 for wood upgrades were as follows: Grade 3 - $1,399, Grade 4 - $2,203, Grade 5 - $2,156, Grade 6 - $3,009, Grade 7 - $4,437, Grade 8 - $4,429, Grade 9 - $5,421, Grade 10 - $7,834, Grade 11 - $9,985.

R-93 LRS 2 (LONG RANGE SPORTER 2) – various standard and metric cals., competition styled long range sporter with adj. trigger and stock, 5 or 10 (disc. 1999) shot removable box mag., free floating fluted barrel, many competition features, 10.4 lbs. Mfg. 1999-2017.

$3,950	$3,325	$2,800	$2,150	$1,725	$1,400	$1,200	*$4,405*

Add $184 for left-hand action.
Add 10% for .338 Lapua cal. (disc. 2006).
Add $1,804 per interchangeable barrel (w/o mounts).
Add $358 for right-hand bolt head, bolt assembly, and mag.
Add $1,600 for Package II or $2,600 for Package II in .338 Lapua cal. or $1,600 for Package III (includes Leupold scope, mounts, muzzle brake, bi-pod, and hard carry case). Disc. 2006.

R-93 SYNTHETIC – available in 21 cals. between .22-250 Rem. - .416 Rem. Mag., also available by special order in the same European cals. as the Model R-93 Repeater, features one-piece conventional black, wood grain (new 2004), or Mossy Oak camo (new 2004) synthetic stock, 22 or 26 in. barrel, without scope mounts and rings, 6 1/2 - 7 lbs. Mfg. 1998-2006.

$1,800	$1,450	$1,150	$1,000	$875	$775	$675	*$2,100*

Add $400 for black synthetic Safari Model in .375 H&H or .416 Rem. Mag.
Add $600 for wood grain or camo stock.
Add $700 per interchangeable barrel (w/o mounts) in standard cals.

R-93 TACTICAL 2 – please refer to listing in the Sig Sauer section under the Rifles: Bolt Action category.

This model is distributed by Sig Sauer Inc., located in Exeter, NH.

R-93 VARMINT – various cals., fluted match barrel, adj. comb, integrated rail, beavertail forend, removable sling swivels, Grade 3 wood. Imported 2007-2010.

$4,675	$4,100	$3,650	$3,100	$2,650	$2,150	$1,725	*$5,145*

Add $306 for bipod.

* ***R-93 Varmint Success*** – similar to Varmint model, except has Grade 5 one-piece wood thumbhole stock. Mfg. 2008-2010.

$6,375	$5,725	$5,150	$4,500	$3,650	$3,225	$2,500	*$6,802*

R-93 LX – similar cals. as Model R-93 Synthetic, features checkered walnut stock and forearm, coin finished stippled receiver sides, without scope mounts and rings, 6.5-7 lbs. Mfg. 1998-2002.

$2,000	$1,750	$1,500	$1,350	$1,100	$900	$700	*$1,990*

Add $275 for Safari LX Model in .416 Rem. Mag. cal.
Add $595 per interchangeable barrel (w/o mounts).

R-93 PRESTIGE – similar to R-93 LX, except receiver has fine scroll engraving, and Grade 3 wood, case not included. Mfg. 2002-2010.

$2,975	$2,600	$2,125	$1,750	$1,500	$1,300	$1,100	*$3,373*

Add $977 for Prestige Safari Model in .375 H&H or .416 Rem. Mag. cal. (disc. 2007).

R-93 EXCLUSIVE – various cals., high quality oil finished Grade 7 walnut stock, engraved sideplates, trigger guard, and bolt assembly, various levels of engraving available. Imported 2007-2010.

The last base price on this special order model was $15,448.

GRADING - PPGS™	100%	98%	95%	90%	80%	70%	60%	LAST MSR

R-93 SUPER EXCLUSIVE – various cals., similar to Exclusive, except has gold line engraving with deeper relief and Grade 8 stock and forearm.

The last base price on this special order model was $23,264.

R-93 IMPERIAL – various cals., top-of-the-line R-93 model, Grade 9 wood, highest quality engraving with gold line and animal scenes, engraved bolt assembly and trigger guard, wood ball on bolt handle, titanium trigger and bolt head. Imported 2007-2010.

The last base price on this special order model was $32,615.

R-93 STUTZEN – various cals., octagon barrel, full two-piece Grade 4 stock, sling swivels, various configurations available. Imported 2007-2010.

$6,575	**$5,925**	**$5,250**	**$4,500**	**$3,950**	**$3,500**	**$2,750**	***$7,028***

This model was also available in the following special order configurations: Stutzen Attache ($10,432 Last MSR), Stutzen Grand Luxe ($10,208 Last MSR), Stutzen Super Luxus ($12,441 Last MSR), Stutzen Exclusive ($17,247 Last MSR), Stutzen Super Exclusive ($25,063 Last MSR), and the Stutzen Imperial ($34,413 Last MSR).

ULTIMATE BOLT ACTION – .22-250 Rem., .243 Win., .25-06 Rem., .270 Win., .308 Win., .30-06, 7x57mm, 7x64mm, .264 Win. Mag., 7mm Rem. Mag., .300 Win. Mag., .338 Win. Mag., or .375 H&H cal., unique bolt action design with 60 degree bolt throw, interchangeable barrel capability, 3 locking lugs, safety lever cocks and uncocks the firing pin spring, exposed hammer, 22 or 24 in. barrel, single set trigger, silver finished aluminum receiver has light engraving, select checkered walnut stock and forearm, 6 3/4 lbs. Extra interchangeable barrels were $545 each, extra bolt heads were $175 each. Mfg. 1985-89.

$1,350	**$1,100**	**$975**	**$925**	**$825**	**$750**	**$675**	***$1,495***

All models were available in left-hand version at no extra charge.

ULTIMATE BOLT ACTION - SPECIAL ORDER – all of the following models may have been ordered with a buttstock cartridge trap - add $250-$500 depending on model. Mfg. was disc. 1989 on all models.

* ***Ultimate Deluxe*** – similar to Ultimate, except better wood and game scene engraving.

$1,425	**$1,175**	**$1,000**	**$950**	**$850**	**$775**	**$700**	***$1,595***

* ***Ultimate Deluxe Carbine*** – .243 Win. or .308 Win. cal. only, 19 1/2 in. barrel with full length forearm. Mfg. 1986-1989.

$1,600	**$1,375**	**$1,150**	**$1,000**	**$900**	**$825**	**$750**	***$1,800***

* ***Ultimate Super Deluxe*** – similar to Ultimate Deluxe, except features better wood and game scene engraving. Mfg. 1986-1989.

$3,750	**$3,250**	**$2,900**	**$2,600**	**$2,300**	**$2,100**	**$1,850**	***$4,030***

* ***Ultimate Exclusive*** – similar to Ultimate Super Deluxe, except features better wood and game scene engraving. Mfg. 1986-1989.

$4,850	**$4,300**	**$3,500**	**$2,975**	**$2,600**	**$2,275**	**$1,975**	***$5,655***

Add $700 per interchangeable barrel.

* ***Ultimate Super Exclusive*** – similar to Ultimate Exclusive, except features better wood and game scene engraving. Mfg. 1986-1989.

$7,700	**$6,800**	**$5,750**	**$4,700**	**$3,950**	**$3,450**	**$2,950**	***$8,905***

Add $950 per interchangeable barrel.

* ***Ultimate Royal*** – best quality Ultimate, featuring Bavarian cheekpiece and checkering/carving on stock and forearm, elaborate game scene engraving, gold plated hammer. Mfg. 1986-1989.

$9,000	**$7,500**	**$6,750**	**$6,000**	**$5,375**	**$4,600**	**$4,000**	***$11,500***

Add $1,200 per interchangeable barrel.

RIFLES: SxS

S2 – various cals. between .22 Hornet-.308 Win., including various metric cals., scalloped boxlock action false sideplates (higher grades only), 22.6 or 24 in. free floating barrels with quarter rib and iron sights, interchangeable easily regulated barrels, tilting lock block, manual cocking safety, checkered Turkish walnut stock and forearm (Grade 1 standard), approx. 7.7 lbs. for standard cals. Limited importation 2004-2005, reintroduced 2007-2014.

$7,350	**$6,650**	**$5,850**	**$5,100**	**$4,550**	**$3,995**	**$3,500**	***$7,954***

Add $5,140 for extra set of standard cal. barrels.

This model is also available in higher grades by special order, including the S2 Luxus - $9,025 MSR, S2 Super Luxus - $15,087 w/sideplates, S2 Exclusive - POR, last published MSR was $17,765 in 2011, S2 Super Exclusive - POR, last published MSR was $23,305 in 2011, and the S2 Imperial - POR, last published MSR was $33,033 in 2011. Previously available in S2 Royal - last MSR was $29,000.

GRADING - PPGS™	100%	98%	95%	90%	80%	70%	60%	LAST MSR

* ***S2 Safari*** – .375 H&H, .470 NE, .416 Rem. Mag. (disc.), .416 NE, or .500 NE cal., 24.4 in. barresl, Grade 1 wood standard, similar to S2 model, except has Monte Carlo stock with cheekpiece, Kickstop in buttstock, rubber recoil pad, and semi-beavertail forend. Disc. 2014.

	$10,150	$8,900	$8,000	$7,150	$6,300	$5,550	$4,995	*$11,060*

Add $6,694 for extra set of standard cal. barrels (not interchangeable on the standard S2 model).

This model is also available in higher grades by special order, including the S2 Safari Luxus -$12,133 MSR, S2 Safari Super Luxus -$18,202 w/sideplates, S2 Safari Exclusive - POR, last published MSR was $20,583 in 2011, S2 Safari Super Exclusive - POR, last published MSR was $26,133 in 2011, and the S2 Safari Imperial - POR, last published MSR was $35,868.

RIFLES: SINGLE SHOT

MODEL BL 820 – various American and European cals., falling block action, adj. trigger, 26 1/2 in. barrel, available in Standard to Royal configurations. Mfg. 1982-89.

Standard Model	$1,550	$1,300	$1,075	$925	$800	$700	$600	*$2,900*

Add 30% for Royal configuration.

MODEL K77 A – .22-250 Rem., .243 Win., 6.5x55mm, .270 Win., 7x57R, 7x65R, or .30-06 standard cals., 7mm Rem. Mag., .300 Win. Mag. or .300 Wby. Mag. cal., break open action, 23 or 24 in. barrel, 3 piece take down, upper tang safety, checkered walnut stock and forearm, engraved silver finished receiver, sling swivels, 5 1/2 lbs. Imported 1988-90.

	$2,250	$2,200	$1,875	$1,700	$1,375	$1,125	$875	*$2,280*

Add $50 for Mag. calibers.
Add $730-$778 per interchangeable barrel.

K95 JAEGER (PRESTIGE) – .222 Rem., .22 Hornet (new 2006), .243 Win., .25-06 Rem. (new 2006), .270 Win., .308 Win., .30-06, 7mm Rem. Mag., .300 Win. Mag., or .300 Wby. Mag. cal., break open action, 22 (standard cals.) or 25 (Mag. cals.) in. barrel, upper tang safety/cocking lever, 3 piece takedown, checkered Grade 3 stock and forearm, scroll engraved sideplates, sling swivels. Importation began 2000.

MSR $6,820	$5,795	$5,075	$4,350	$3,950	$3,185	$2,650	$2,200	

Add $2,115 for interchangable barrel.
Add $3,650 for octagonal barrel.

The following special order models are available in K95 configuration: K95 Attache (Grade 7 wood, MSR $12,032), K95 Custom I (Grade 6 wood, $16,287 MSR), K95 Stradivari (Grade 10 wood, $23,582 MSR), K95 Super Luxus (Grade 6 wood, last MSR in 2014 was $12,595), K95 Baronesse (Grade 7 wood, MSR $23,686), K95 Exclusive (Grade 7 wood, POR, last published MSR was $16,156 in 2011), K95 Super Exclusive (Grade 8 wood, POR, last published MSR was $22,255 in 2011), and the K95 Imperial (Grade 9 wood, POR, last published MSR was $32,296 in 2011).

K95 LUXUS – similar to K95 Prestige, except has Grade 4 checkered stock and forearm, engraved sideplates and receiver. Importation began 2000.

MSR $7,470	$6,350	$5,550	$4,765	$4,325	$3,500	$2,900	$2,485	

Add $2,115 for interchangable barrel.
Add $3,650 for octagonal barrel.

K95 STUTZEN LUXUS – various cals., features engraved aluminum frame, 20 in. octagon barrel and full-length forearm, deluxe checkered Turkish Grade 4 wood, iron sights, 6 lbs. Importation began 2004.

MSR $10,444	$8,900	$7,750	$6,650	$6,050	$4,900	$4,000	$3,475	

Add $3,725 for interchangable barrel.

The following special order models are available in K95 Stutzen configuration: K95 Attache (Grade 7 wood, MSR $14,521), K95 Super Luxus (Grade 6 wood, last MSR wwas $16,764), K95 Stutzen Baronesse (Grade 7 wood, MSR $24,496), K95 Exclusive (Grade 7 wood, POR, last published MSR was $18,751in 2011), K95 Super Exclusive (Grade 8 wood, POR, last published MSR was $24,850 in 2011), and the K95 Imperial (Grade 9 wood, POR, last published MSR was $35,130 in 2011).

K95 ULTIMATE CARBON – standard round carbon fiber barrel, black receiver, two-piece ergonomically designed thumbhole stock with cocoa leather inserts, gold colored K95 logo. New 2019.

MSR $14,477	$12,300	$10,775	$9,225	$8,375	$6,800	$5,600	$4,825	

SHOTGUNS: O/U

Add $582 for adj. comb stock.
Add $210 for stock balancer or $250 for barrel balancer on all currently manufactured Blaser O/U shotguns (allows weight distribution, on both stock and forearm).
Add $900 for custom LOP.

GRADING - PPGS™	100%	98%	95%	90%	80%	70%	60%	LAST MSR

F3 GAME STANDARD – 12 or 20 (new 2008) ga., 3 in. chambers, boxlock action with satin oxide finish, SST, ejectors, 27, 28, or 29 in. VR barrels with 2 Briley choke tubes, similar to Competition model, except has Schnabel forearm, Grade 4 wood, 7.3 lbs. Mfg. 2007-2009, reintroduced 2014 only.

	$6,250	$5,325	$4,525	$4,095	$3,325	$2,725	$2,175	*$6,695*

Add $2,550 per extra O/U barrel assembly.

This model is also available in the following special order configurations: Luxus (Grade 5 wood, $8,422 MSR), Baron (Grade 7 wood, MSR $10,077), Baron DeLuxe (Grade 7 wood, $11,907 MSR), Grand Luxe (Grade 6 wood, MSR $11,315), Super Luxus (Grade 6 wood, $12,995 MSR), Baronesse (Grade 7 wood, $14,902 MSR), Exclusive (Grade 7 wood, MSR POR), Super Exclusive (Grade 8 wood, MSR POR), and the Imperial (Grade 9 wood, MSR POR). Previously available in Attache configuration (Grade 7 wood, last MSR was $8,875).

F3 COMPETITION SPORTING STANDARD – 12, 20, 28 ga. or .410 bore, 3 in. chambers, boxlock action with monobloc barrels, 28 (12 ga. only), 30, 32, or 34 (12 ga. only) in. VR barrels with 5 Briley extended spectrum choke tubes, SST, ejectors, Grade 4 wood, greyed receiver finish, 8-8.4 lbs. New 2005.

MSR $8,650	$7,350	$6,425	$5,500	$5,000	$4,000	$3,300	$2,575	

Add $3,306 per O/U barrel assembly.

This model is also available in additional higher grades, including the Luxus (Grade 5 wood, $10,248 MSR), Baron (Grade 7 wood, MSR $12,066), Baron DeLuxe (Grade 7 wood, $14,076 MSR), Grand Luxe (Grade 6 wood, MSR $13,249), Attache (Grade 7 wood, $12,339), Bonsi - Scroll (Grade 6 wood, $14,749 MSR), Custom I (Grade 6 wood, $15,273 MSR), Baronesse (Grade 7 wood, $16,473 MSR), Heritage (Grade 8 wood, $21,950 MSR), Custom II (Grade 7 wood, POR), Custom III (Grade 8 wood, POR), Custom IV (Grade 9 wood, POR), Exclusive (Grade 7 wood, last published MSR was $15,575 in 2011), Super Exclusive (Grade 8 wood, last published MSR was $23,750 in 2011), and the Imperial (Grade 9 wood, last published MSR was $29,950 in 2011). Previously available in F3 Competition Royal ($25,895 last MSR) and the Super Luxus (Grade 6 wood, last MSR was $13,913).

Wood upgrade MSR's are as follows: Grade 4 - $2,364, Grade 5 - $2,966, Grade 6 - $4,120, Grade 7 - $5,129, Grade 8 - $5,825, Grade 9 - $6,910, Grade 10 - $9,216, Grade 11 - $11,532.

* ***F3 Sporting Ladies*** – Grade 4 wood, black action, gold colored F3 logo.

MSR $8,563	$7,800	$6,500	$5,750	$5,000	$4,250	$3,500	$2,750	

* ***F3 Sporting Youth*** – Grade 2 wood, black action with F3 youth logo. Disc. 2017.

	$5,250	$4,800	$4,400	$3,750	$3,250	$2,500	$1,850	*$5,707*

F3 SKEET – similar to F3 Competition Sporting Standard, original mfg. had choice of heavyweight (approx. 4 1/2 lbs.) or lightweight (LST, 3 1/2 lbs.) and 2 Briley choke tubes, current mfg. offers 28 (12 ga. only), 30, 32, or 34 (12 ga. only) in. VR barrels with 5 Briley extended spectrum choke tubes, Monte Carlo stock and semi-beavertail forearm, approx. 8.2 lbs. Mfg. 2007-2013.

	$6,875	$5,750	$5,000	$4,000	$3,350	$2,650	$2,250	*$7,613*

Add $3,012 per O/U barrel assembly.

Please refer to the F3 Competition Sporting Standard model for recent MSRs on the higher grades and wood upgrades.

F3 SUPERSKEET STANDARD – 12 ga. only, 3 in. chambers, 28, 30, or 32 in. VR barrels with 2 Briley titanium (disc.) or 5 Briley extended Spectrum choke tubes, Grade 4 (disc. 2020) or Grade 5 (new 2021) wood. New 2014.

MSR $9,645	$8,200	$7,175	$6,150	$5,575	$4,510	$3,700	$3,200	

Add $3,709 per O/U barrel assembly.

This model is also available in additional higher grades, including the Luxus (Grade 5 wood, MSR $11,447), Baron (Grade 7 wood, MSR $13,461), Baron DeLuxe (Grade 7 wood, MSR $16,790), Grand Luxe (new 2012 - Grade 6 wood, MSR $15,348), Attache (Grade 7 wood, MSR $13,779), Baronesse (Grade 7 wood, $11,735 MSR), Bonsi - Scroll (Grade 6 wood, $16,417 MSR), Heritage (Grade 8 wood, $24,915 MSR), Custom I (Grade 6 wood, $21,811 MSR), Custom II (Grade 7 wood, POR), Custom III (Grade 8 wood, POR), and Custom IV (Grade 9 wood, POR).

F3 SUPERSPORT STANDARD – 12 ga. only, action similar to F3 Competion Sporting Standard, 3 in. chambers, 30 or 32 in. VR barrels with 5 Briley extended spectrum choke tubes and adj. rib, free floating barrels with adj. barrel hanger system, checkered walnut stock with adj. comb and Schnabel forearm, Grade 3 wood, black action, gold colored F3 logo, 3 1/2 lb. trigger pull, approx. 9 lbs. New 2011.

MSR $11,082	$9,425	$8,250	$7,075	$6,410	$5,185	$4,250	$3,695	

Add $4,192 per O/U barrel assembly (12 ga. only).

This model is also available in additional higher grades, including the Luxus (Grade 5 wood, MSR $12,778), Baron

GRADING - PPGS™	100%	98%	95%	90%	80%	70%	60%	LAST MSR

(Grade 7 wood, MSR $14,805), Baron DeLuxe (Grade 7 wood, MSR $18,164), Attache (Grade 7 wood, $15,110 MSR), Bonsi-Scroll (Grade 6 wood, MSR $17,790), Grand Luxe (Grade 6 wood, $16,720), Baronesse (Grade 7 wood, $19,710 MSR), Heritage (Grade 8 wood, MSR $25,990), Custom I (Grade 6 wood, MSR $23,248), Custom II (Grade 7 wood, POR), Custom III (Grade 8 wood, POR), or Custom IV (Grade 9 wood, POR).

Wood upgrade MSRs are as follows: Grade 4 - Last MSR was $3,170, Grade 5 - $4,239, Grade 6 - $5,511, Grade 7 - $6,571, Grade 8 - $7,419, Grade 9 - $8,585 Grade 10 - $11,129, Grade 11 - Last MSR was $12,337.

F3 AMERICAN SUPER TRAP STANDARD – similar to F3 Competition Sporting Standard, except has 30 (disc. 2011), 32 in. barrels, also available as Unsingle with 34 in. barrel, approx. 8.1 lbs. New 2007.

MSR $11,082 $9,425 $8,250 $7,075 $6,410 $5,185 $4,250 $3,695

Add $4,192 for extra single barrel or O/U barrels.

MSRs $15,274-$30,182 for combo package (includes either Unsingle or extra O/U barrel assembly) with adj. comb stock, depending on wood and engraving options.

This model is also available in additional higher grades, including the Luxus (Grade 5 wood, MSR $12,778), Grand Luxe (new 2012, Grade 6 wood, MSR $16,720), Baron (Grade 7 wood, $14,805 MSR), Baron DeLuxe (Grade 7 wood, $18,1645 MSR), Baroness (Grade 7 wood, $18,999), Attache (Grade 7 wood, $15,110 MSR), Bonsi - Scroll (Grade 6 wood, $17,760 MSR), Heritage (Grade 8 wood, $25,990 MSR), Custom I (Grade 6 wood, $23,248 MSR), Custom II (Grade 7 wood, POR), Custom III (Grade 8 wood, POR), Custom IV (Grade 9 wood, POR), Exclusive (Grade 7 wood, last published MSR was $16,561 in 2011), Super Exclusive (Grade 8 wood, last published MSR was $24,736 in 2011), and the Imperial (Grade 9 wood, last published MSR was $30,936 in 2011).

Wood upgrade MSRs are as follows: Grade 5 - $4,239, Grade 6 - $5,511, Grade 7 - $6,571, Grade 8 - $7,419, Grade 9 - $8,585, Grade 10 - $11,129, Grade 11 - Last MSR was $12,337.

F3 VANTAGE – 12 (disc. 2017), 20, 28 ga. or .410 bore, 3 in. chambers, boxlock action with monobloc barrels, 28 (12 ga. only, disc. 2017), 30, 32, or 34 (12 ga. only, disc. 2017) in. raised VR barrels with 5 Briley extended spectrum choke tubes, SST, ejectors, Kick-Eez recoil pad, matte black action, available in sporting and trap variations, right or left-hand models, 8-8.4 lbs. New 2015.

MSR $9,963 $8,475 $7,415 $6,350 $5,765 $4,660 $3,900 $3,300

Add $4,027 per O/U barrel assembly.

This model is also available in additional higher grades, including the Luxus (Grade 5 wood, MSR $11,765), Baron (Grade 7 wood, MSR $13779), Baron DeLuxe (Grade 7 wood, MSR $17,151), Attache (Grade 6 wood, $14,094 MSR), Bonsi-Scroll (Grade 6 wood, MSR $16,779), Grand Luxe (Grade 6 wood, $15,709), Baronesse (Grade 7 wood, $18,698 MSR), Heritage (Grade 8 wood, MSR $25,274), Custom I (Grade 6 wood, MSR $22,129), Custom II (Grade 7 wood, POR), Custom III (Grade 8 wood, POR), or Custom IV (Grade 9 wood, POR).

Wood upgrade MSR's are as follows: Grade 5 - $3,285, Grade 6 - $4,557, Grade 7 - $5,723, Grade 8 - $6,959, Grade 9 - $8,207, Grade 10 - $9,216, Grade 11 - $11,434.

F16 GAME – 12 ga., 3 in. chambers, 28 or 30 in. barrels with 3 chokes, nickel silver front bead sight, Grade 2 (disc. 2020) or Grade 4 (new 2021) laser enhanced wood, English style forearm, rubber recoil pad, basic design with gun metal gray receiver and silver colored F16 logo. New 2018.

MSR $4,769 $4,050 $3,550 $3,050 $2,750 $2,250 $1,825 $1,585

This model is also available in additional higher grades, including the Grand Luxe (Grade 6 wood, $8,479), and Heritage (Grade 8 wood, $11,659).

F16 GAME INTUITION – 12 ga., 3 in. chambers, built specifically for women, 28 or 30 in. barrels with three chokes, nickel silver front bead sight, Grade 2 laser enhanced specially shaped compact Monte Carlo stock (reduced stock length), English style forearm, extra soft rubber recoil pad, reduced pitch angle, ergonomically designed pistol grip, basic design with gun metal gray receiver and silver colored F16 logo. New 2018.

MSR $4,769 $4,050 $3,550 $3,050 $2,750 $2,250 $1,825 $1,585

This model is also available in additional higher grades, including the Grand Luxe (Grade 6 wood, $8,479), and Heritage (Grade 8 wood, $11,659).

F16 SPORTING – 12 ga., 3 in. chambers, 30 or 32 in. barrels with 5 Briley extended Spectrum choke tubes, adj. trigger, luminescent red bead sight, Grade 2 (disc. 2019) or Grade 4 (new 2020) laser enhanced wood stock, English style forearm, rubber recoil pad, gun metal gray receiver with red colored F16 logo, features the Balancer System (barrel and stock balancer). New 2018.

MSR $5,299 $4,500 $3,940 $3,375 $3,060 $2,475 $2,100 $1,750

This model is also available in additional higher grades, including the Grand Luxe (Grade 6 wood, $8,903), and Heritage (Grade 8 wood, $11,997).

GRADING - PPGS™	100%	98%	95%	90%	80%	70%	60%	LAST MSR

F16 SPORTING INTUITION – 12 ga., 3 in. chambers, built specifically for women, 30 or 32 (disc. 2020) in. barrel with 5 Briley extended Spectrum choke tubes, adj. trigger, luminescent red bead sight, Grade 2 (disc. 2020) or Grade 4 (new 2021) laser enhanced specially shaped compact Monte Carlo wood stock (reduced stock length), English style forearm, extra soft rubber recoil pad, ergonomically designed pistol grip, reduced pitch angle, gun metal gray receiver with red colored F16 logo, features the Balancer System (barrel and stock balancer). New 2018.

MSR $5,299	$4,500	$3,940	$3,375	$3,060	$2,475	$2,100	$1,750	

This model is also available in additional higher grades, including the Grand Luxe (Grade 6 wood, $8,903), and Heritage (Grade 8 wood, $11,977).

BLEIKER, HEINRICH

Current match rifle and accessories manufacturer located in Bütschwil, Switzerland. Currently imported by Pardini USA, LLC, located in Tampa, FL.

RIFLES: BOLT ACTION

CHALLENGER SERIES – .22 LR cal., Bleiker action featuring minimum firing pin resonance and precise head space, super match trigger, match barrel, choice of walnut, all aluminum or wood/aluminum laminated stock, many options/configurations available, including left-hand action. New 2002.

MSRs on this model and variations range from $9,500-$9,900.

MATCH 300 M FREE RIFLE SERIES – 6mm BR, 6xC Norma, 6.5x47 Lapua, .308 Win., or 7.5x55mm Swiss cal., alloy Bleiker action featuring titanium hardening/coating, integrated magazine, super match trigger, match barrel, many options/configurations available, including different colors. New 2002.

MSRs on this model and variations can range from $9,200-$10,200.

BLUEGRASS ARMORY

Current rifle manufacturer located in Ocala, FL. Previously located in Richmond, KY. Consumer direct sales. During 2010, Bluegrass Armory was purchased by Good Times Outdoors.

For individual model listings, please go to BlueBookOfGunValues.com/overflow.

BOBCAT WEAPONS INC.

Previous manufacturer from April 2003-circa 2006, located in Mesa, AZ. During late 2006, the company name was changed to Red Rock Arms.

For individual model listings, please go to BlueBookOfGunValues.com/overflow.

BOBERG ARMS CORPORATION

Previous pistol manufacturer located in White Bear Lake, MN circa 2013-2016.

In late 2016, Bond Arms Inc. purchased the assets and product lines of Boberg Arms Corp. Bond Arms Inc. is planning to build the next generation of Bullpup pistols under the Bond Arms Inc. name on a limited basis at its Texas facility (see the Bond Arms Inc. listing for more information).

PISTOLS: SEMI-AUTO

XR9 SERIES – 9mm Para. cal., DAO, 3.35 standard (S) or 4.2 (L) in. rotating barrel, locked breech, black polymer frame with stainless steel slide and barrel, choice of standard (satin finish two-tone), onyx (all black), or Platinum (nickel/chrome two-tone) finish, 7 shot mag., low profile 3-dot sights, reverse feed technology features no feed ramp into chamber, two safeties, includes two mags., carrying case and lock, 17.4 or 18.4 oz. Mfg. 2013-2016.

	$975	$850	$750	$650	$550	$450	$350	*$1,049*

Add $50 for 4.2 in. barrel (XR9-L) with standard two-tone finish.
Add $149 for Tritium night sights.
Add $300 for Onyx all black or Platinum two-tone finish.

XR45-S – .45 ACP cal., DAO with long pull trigger (6 lbs.), aluminum frame with DuPont Zytel polymer grip panels, stainless steel slide, 3 3/4 in. rotating stainless steel barrel, 3-dot sights, 6 shot, two-tone (black frame, Silver Satin slide) finish, black grip, features rear feeding magazine system with no feed ramp, no manual safety, 21 oz. Mfg. 2014-2016.

	$1,050	$950	$800	$725	$500	$485	$375	*$1,199*

Add $114 for Tritium night sights.

BOHICA

Previous manufacturer and customizer located in Sedalia, CO circa 1993-1994.

GRADING - PPGS™	100%	98%	95%	90%	80%	70%	60%	LAST MSR

RIFLES: SEMI-AUTO

M16-SA – .223 Rem. or various custom cals. GIO, 16 or 20 in. barrel, A2 sights, standard handguard, approx. 950 were mfg. through September 1994.

	$1,385	$895	$675	$525	$450	$385	$350	

Add $100 for flat-top receiver with scope rail.
Add $65 for two-piece, free floating handguard.

In addition to the rifles listed, Bohica also manufactured a M16-SA Match variation (retail was $2,295, approx. 10 mfg.), a pistol version of the M16-SA in both 7 and 10 in. barrel (retail was $1,995, approx. 50 mfg.), and a limited run of M16-SA and uppers in .50 BMG cal. (retail was $1,695, approx. 25 mfg.).

BOITO

Previous manufacturer located in Brazil. Previously imported by F.I.E. Corp. located in Hialeah, FL.

Boito shotguns were inexpensive, utilitarian shotguns that are shootable, but not collectible. Because of this, prices typically range between $75 - $175, depending on the gauge and condition.

BOLLIGER, JOHN

Please refer to Mountain Riflery, LLC listing in the M section.

BOND ARMS, INC.

Current manufacturer located in Granbury, Texas beginning 1995.

In late 2016, Bond Arms Inc. purchased the assets and product lines of Boberg Arms Corp. Please contact the company directly for availability and pricing.

DERRINGERS: O/U

A key entry internal safety locking device was introduced for all Defender models beginning in 2000. This device locks the preexisting crossbolt safety in the on-safe position.

All Bond models can be made available with optional barrels in the following calibers, unless otherwise noted: .357 Mag/.38 Spl., .45 ACP, .45 LC, .45 GAP, .44 Special, .44-40 WCF, .40 S&W, 10mm, 9mm Para., .32 H&R Mag., .22 LR, .22 WMR, .327 Fed. Mag., .45 LC/.410, .30 Carbine, or .380.

Add $10 for bead blasted finish.
Add $30 for left-handed configuration.
Add $130 per extra set of 2 1/2 in. barrels, $160 for 3 in. barrels, $180 for 3 1/2 in. barrels, $225 for 4 1/4 in. barrels, $375 for 4 1/4 in. Mag-Na-Port (disc. 2019, reintroduced 2021), or $310 for 6 in. barrels (limited mfg. beginning 2020) barrels.

BACKUP – .45 ACP or 9mm Para. cal., O/U derringer, compact stainless steel frame, 2 1/2 in. barrel, patented rebounding hammer, rubber grips, crossbolt safety, retracting firing pins, spring-loaded cammed locking lever, black finish frame, bead-blast matte finished barrel, 18-20 oz. New 2014.

MSR $540	$460	$400	$350	$315	$250	$200	$175

BLACKJACK SPECIAL EDITION – .45 LC/.410 cal., 3 1/2 in. stainless steel double barrel and frame w/ engraved spade logo, auto extractor, trigger guard, front blade and fixed rear sight, ext. black ash grips w/spade on sides, crossbolt safety, retracting firing pins, spring-loaded cammed locking lever, all black finish, 22 oz. New 2019.

MSR $689	$600	$500	$450	$400	$325	$275	$200

BOND MINI – .45 LC cal., 2 1/2 in. barrel, compact stainless steel frame, accepts all optional barrels, patented rebounding hammer, crossbolt safety, retracting firing pins, spring-loaded cammed locking lever, no trigger guard, satin finish, rosewood grips, 19 oz. New 2012.

MSR $534	$460	$400	$350	$315	$250	$200	$175

* ***Bond Girl Mini*** – .357/.38 Spl. cal., similar to Bond Mini, except has pink wood grips, 19 oz. New 2012.

MSR $534	$460	$400	$350	$315	$250	$200	$175

CENTURY 2000 DEFENDER (C2K)/COWBOY CENTURY 200 – .357/.38 Spl. (new 2012) or .410 bore/.45 LC cal., compact stainless steel frame, 2 1/2 in. chambers and 3 in. barrels or 3 in. chambers and 3 1/2 in. barrels (.410 bore), patented rebounding hammer, crossbolt safety, retracting firing pins, spring-loaded cammed locking lever, trigger guard, satin finish, custom laminated black ash (disc.) or rosewood grips. New 1999.

MSR $567	$485	$425	$365	$325	$265	$225	$175

GRADING - PPGS™	100%	98%	95%	90%	80%	70%	60%	LAST MSR

COWBOY DEFENDER – .22 LR, .22 WMR, 9mm Para., 10mm, .327 Fed. Mag., .357/.38 Spl., .40 S&W, .44-40 WCF, .45 GAP, .45 ACP, .45 LC, or .45/.410 cal., compact stainless steel frame, 3 in. barrel, patented rebounding hammer, crossbolt safety, retracting firing pins, spring-loaded cammed locking lever, no trigger guard, satin finish, rosewood grips, 20 oz. New 1995.

MSR $543 $460 $400 $350 $315 $250 $200 $175

CUB – .357 Mag./38 Spl. cal., spring-loaded cammed locking lever, 2 1/2 in. stainless steel double barrel and frame, auto extractor, trigger guard, front blade and fixed rear sight, rubber grip, crossbolt safety, 4 1/2 in. OAL, 19 oz. New 2019.

MSR $541 $460 $400 $350 $315 $250 $200 $175

GRIZZLY – .45 LC/.410 bore, 3 in. stainless steel barrel, stainless steel frame, trigger guard, extended rosewood grips w/Grizzly logo, "Rough and Tumble" bead blasted finish, 20 oz. New 2020.

MSR $377 $325 $275 $250 $225 $175 $150 $100

MAMA BEAR – .357/.38 Spl. cal., compact stainless steel frame, 2 1/2 in. barrel, patented rebounding hammer, crossbolt safety, retracting firing pins, spring-loaded cammed locking lever, trigger guard, satin finish, pink "Mama Bear" wood grips, 19 oz. New 2015.

MSR $541 $460 $400 $350 $315 $250 $200 $175

NICKEL BORON GUN – .45 LC/.410 cal., 3 1/2 in. stainless steel double barrel and frame, rebounding hammer, auto extractor, trigger guard, front blade and fixed rear sight, extended black ash grips with spade on sides, crossbolt safety, black accents w/star design, retracting firing pins, spring-loaded cammed locking lever, NiB coating, 22 oz. Mfg. 2019-2020.

$600 $500 $450 $400 $325 $275 $200 *$689*

OLD GLORY – .45 LC/.410 cal., 3 1/2 in. stainless steel double barrel and frame, auto extractor, trigger guard, front blade and fixed rear sight, extended black ash grips, crossbolt safety, retracting firing pins, spring-loaded cammed locking lever, American flag Cerakote finish, 22 oz. New 2019.

MSR $697 $600 $500 $450 $400 $325 $275 $200

PAPA BEAR – .45 LC/.410 cal., 3 in. barrel, compact stainless steel frame, patented rebounding hammer, crossbolt safety, retracting firing pins, spring-loaded cammed locking lever, trigger guard, satin finish, extended "Papa Bear" rubber grips, 20 oz. New 2015.

MSR $560 $485 $425 $365 $325 $265 $225 $175

PATRIOT – .45/.410 or .357/.38 Spl. cal., compact stainless steel frame, 3 in. barrel, patented rebounding hammer, crossbolt safety, retracting firing pins, spring-loaded cammed locking lever, trigger guard, satin finish, extended "Patriot" rosewood grips, includes tan BAD holster, 22 oz. New 2015.

MSR $648 $550 $480 $415 $375 $300 $250 $200

PROTECT THE 2ND AMENDMENT (PT2A45/410 PT2A357/38) – .45 Colt cal./.410 bore (2.5 or 3 in. chamber) or .357 Magnum/.38 Special cal., break open action, 4 1/4 in. barrel, fixed sights, custom ext. rosewood American flag grips, crossbolt safety, custom PT2A laser engraving w/Gold tint, leather holster included, stainless steel finish, 23.5 oz. New 2016.

MSR $887 $775 $675 $575 $525 $450 $385 $325

RANGER – .410 bore/.45 LC or .357/.38 Spl. cal., 4 1/4 in. barrel, compact stainless steel frame, patented rebounding hammer, crossbolt safety, retracting firing pins, spring-loaded cammed locking lever, no trigger guard, black ash extended grips w/inlayed silver star, hard shell carry case replaced black nylon bag in 2011, includes black custom driving/concealed leather holster, satin finish, 22 oz. Mfg. 2008-2015.

$625 $550 $475 $425 $350 $285 $225 *$726*

RANGER II – .45/.410 or .357/.38 Spl. cal., similar to Ranger, except has trigger guard, includes black BAD holster. New 2011.

MSR $761 $650 $575 $495 $450 $360 $300 $250

RUSTIC RANGER SPECIAL EDITION – .45 LC/.410 cal., 4 1/4 in. stainless steel double barrel and frame, auto extractor, trigger guard, front blade and fixed rear sight, extended rosewood grips w/inlayed silver star, crossbolt safety, spring-loaded, cammed locking lever, retracted firing pins, leather premium holster, 23.5 oz. Limited mfg. beginning 2019.

MSR $761 $650 $550 $475 $450 $350 $300 $225

Available only through Cabelas.

ROUGHNECK – 9mm Para., .357Mag./.38 Spl., or .45 ACP cal., 2 1/2 in. barrel w/polished flats, trigger guard, front blade and fixed rear sights, standard rubber grips, "Rough and Tumble" bead blasted finish, 19 oz. New 2019.

MSR $269 $225 $200 $175 $150 $125 $100 $75

GRADING - PPGS™	100%	98%	95%	90%	80%	70%	60%	LAST MSR

ROWDY – .45LC/.410 cal., 3 in. barrel w/polished flats, trigger guard, front blade and fixed rear sights, standard rubber grips, "Rough and Tumble" bead blasted finish, 20 oz. New 2019.

MSR $299	$250	$225	$200	$175	$150	$125	$100	

SNAKE SLAYER – .357/.38 Spl. (new 2012) or .410 bore/.45 LC cal. with 3 in. chambers and 3 1/2 in. barrels, compact stainless steel frame, patented rebounding hammer, crossbolt safety, retracting firing pins, spring-loaded cammed locking lever, trigger guard, satin finish, extended rosewood "Snake Slayer" grips, 22 oz. New 2005.

MSR $603	$515	$450	$385	$350	$285	$225	$185	

SNAKE SLAYER IV – .45/410 or .357/.38 Spl. cal., similar to the Snake Slayer, except has 4 1/4 in. barrels, 23 oz. New 2005.

MSR $648	$550	$480	$415	$375	$300	$250	$200	

SUPER DEFENDER – .450 AutoBond cal., 3 in. barrels, rosewood grips, stainless steel construction, 20 oz. Limited mfg. 2003-2004.

	$325	$280	$250	$225	$180	$150	$125	*$369*

TEXAN – .410/.45 Colt, 6 in. stainless steel double barrel and frame, patented rebounding hammer, front blade sights, fixed rear sights, extended rosewood grips w/custom "Texan" engraving, crossbolt safety, automatic spent casing extractor, retracting firing pins. spring-loaded cammed locking lever, 27 oz. New 2016.

MSR $700	$600	$525	$450	$410	$330	$270	$210	

TEXAS DEFENDER – .22 LR, .22 WMR, 9mm Para., 10mm, .32 H&R Mag. (disc. 2015), .327 Fed. (new 2012), .357 Mag./.38 Spl., .357 Max (disc.), .40 S&W, .44 Spl. (disc. 2015), .44 Mag. (disc.), .44-40 WCF, .45 GAP, .45 ACP, .45 LC, or .45 LC/.410 shot shell cals., O/U design, compact stainless steel frame, 3 in. barrel, accepts all optional barrels, patented rebounding hammer, crossbolt safety, retracting firing pins, spring-loaded cammed locking lever, trigger guard, satin finish, rosewood grips, 20 oz. New 1995.

MSR $543	$460	$400	$350	$315	$250	$200	$175	

TEXAS RANGER SPECIAL EDITION – .45/.410 cal., compact stainless steel frame, 3 1/2 in. barrel, patented rebounding hammer, crossbolt safety, retracting firing pins, spring-loaded cammed locking lever, trigger guard, extended Texas mesquite wood grips w/Ranger badge inlay, features Texas Rangers and 200th Anniversary gold engraved on the barrel, includes custom glass top display case and Buck knife with matching grips (disc.). Limited mfg. beginning 2012.

MSR $1,355	$1,150	$1,000	$865	$780	N/A	N/A	N/A	

USA DEFENDER – .45/.410 or .357/.38 Spl. cal., compact stainless steel frame, 3 in. interchangeable barrels, design similar to Remington O/U Derringer, crossbolt safety, trigger guard, satin finish, extended rosewood grips, includes BAD Driving holster, 22 oz. 5,000 mfg. beginning 2012. Disc. 2015.

	$510	$450	$385	$350	$285	$240	$195	*$598*

WICKED – 9mm Para. cal., 4 1/4 in. stainless steel double barrel and frame, automatic extractor, rebounding hammer, front blade and fixed rear sights, standard rubber grips, crossbolt safety, retracting firing pins, spring-loaded cammed locking lever, 30 oz., includes extra 4 1/4 in. barrel in .45LC/.410 cal. as part of a package. Limited mfg. 2019 only.

	$600	$550	$450	$400	$325	$275	$200	*$711*

This model was a Special Edition Serialized Gun Package honoring the appearance of a Bond Arms gun in the 2019 film "John Wick 3".

Z-SLAYER – .45 LC/.410 cal., 3 1/2 in. stainless steel double barrel and frame, auto extractor, trigger guard, rebounding hammer, front blade and fixed rear sight, extended black ash grips, crossbolt safety, retracting firing pins, spring-loaded cammed locking lever, Zombie Green finish w/light "blood" splatter pattern, 22 oz. New 2019.

MSR $697	$600	$500	$450	$400	$325	$275	$200	

PISTOLS: SEMI-AUTO

.450 AUTOBOND – .450 AutoBond/.45 ACP cal., based on Colt 1911 design, full size frame, 5 in. barrel.

While advertised during 2003, this model never went into production.

BOND BULLPUP – 9mm Para. cal., DAO, ultra compact size, 3.35 in. barrel, two 7 shot mags., dovetail 3-dot sights, signature Bond Arms engraved rosewood grips, two internal safeties, patterned after the Boberg Arms XR9 w/reverse feed technology featuring no feed ramp into the chamber, 17.5 oz. New 2017.

MSR $1,099	$950	$825	$725	$650	$525	$425	$375	

GRADING - PPGS™	100%	98%	95%	90%	80%	70%	60%	LAST MSR

BORA HUNTING ARMS COMPANY

Previous manufacturer located in Konya, Turkey until 2019.

Bora Hunting Arms Company manufactured a complete line of semi-auto shotguns and rifles in sporting and tactical configurations. The company also manufactured tactical slide action shotguns and sporting semi-auto shotguns. A variety of finishes and options were available. In the late 2010s, Bora Hunting Arms Company was acquired by Barak Hunting Arms (Barak Silah). Please refer to their listing in the B section for additional information.

BORCHARDT

Previous pistol design originating in Germany circa 1894-1897.

PISTOLS: SEMI-AUTO

Prices below assume matching parts and original condition.

MODEL 1893 – 7.65mm Borchardt cal., original Luger design, 6 1/2 in. barrel, blue finish with fire-blue small parts, checkered walnut grips, 8 shot mag., distinguished by elongated spring mechanism housing located behind the toggle assembly, may include accessories (mags., holster, stock) and/or case.

* ***Model 1893 Ludwig Loewe Mfg.*** – serial numbered 1-1104.

$26,500	$21,945	$18,740	$15,280	$13,250	$11,000	$9,240	

Original stocks (with attached leather holster) are priced starting at $5,000.

» **Model 1893 Ludwig Loewe Mfg. Cased With Accessories** – original cased gun was supplied with matching shoulder stock, detachable cheekpiece, leather holster, 3 regular mags. and a hold-open mag., plus tools.

$52,500	$40,425	$35,000	$28,665	$21,945	$18,745	$15,275	

* ***Model 1893 DWM Mfg.*** – starting approx. 1895, serial numbered 1105-3000.

$26,000	$21,265	$18,375	$14,965	$12,335	$10,445	$8,555	

Original stocks (with attached leather holster) are priced starting at $4,750.

» **Model 1893 DWM Mfg. Cased With Accessories** – original cased gun was supplied with shoulder stock, detachable cheekpiece, leather holster, 3 regular mags. and a hold-open mag., plus tools.

$52,000	$40,950	$34,965	$28,085	$22,420	$18,585	$15,380	

At a recent nationally publicized auction a cased Borchardt with all major accessories in 90-95% condition sold for $36,350. A Prototype #6 with accessories in 98% condition sold for $161,000.

BORDEN RIFLES

Current bolt action rifle manufacturer located in Springville, PA. Consumer sales through FFL.

For individual model listings, please go to BlueBookOfGunValues.com/overflow.

BOROVNIK, LUDWIG KG

Current long gun manufacturer located in Ferlach, Austria. No current U.S. importation.

Ludwig Borovnik is a third generation gunmaker who manufactures long guns by custom order only. Please contact him directly for more information.

BOSIS, LUCIANO

Current manufacturer established in 1977 and located in Travagliato, Brescia, Italy. Currently imported (beginning 2011) by Alamo Sporting Arms, located in Boerne, TX, Cole Fine Guns & Gunsmithing, located in Naples, FL and Harpswell, ME, and British Sporting Arms Ltd., located in Millsbrook, NY. Previously imported by Covey & Nye, located in Manchester Village, VT, JTH Agency, located in Pittsford, NY, Dewing's Fly & Gun Shop, located in W. Palm Beach, FL, Old Friends Hunting & Shooting Co., located in Livingston, MT, New England Arms, located in Kittery Point, ME, Sporting Products, LLC, located in Palm Beach, FL. and by William Larkin Moore & Co., located in Scottsdale, AZ, and Larry's Trading Post located in Gaithersburg, MD.

All Luciano Bosis guns are truly Bespoke, and all are manufactured on a custom order only basis. Bosis works with only Italy's finest master engravers and customers work directly with the engravers without a markup from Bosis. Annual production is approximately 12 best quality guns. Delivery time varies by the type of gun and engraving, as well as the engraver. Please contact the manufacturer or the importer directly for more information, including a custom order quotation, and delivery time. Used Bosis shotguns need to be appraised individually to accurately determine current value.

SHOTGUNS

Add 20% for matched pair on most models listed.
Add 20% for small gauges as 28 and .410.
Add €2,000 for leather case, depending on configuration.

MICHAELANGELO SIDELOCK O/U – 12, 16, 20, 28 ga., or .410 bore, pinned Boss style sidelock action, 26-32 in. chopper lump barrels, scaled frame, supplied in-the-white, exhibition quality walnut, w/o engraving, optional case and chokes.

This model has a MSR of €60,000 without engraving.
Add 20% for 28 ga. or 20% for .410 bore.
Add €1,500 for single trigger. Add €1,500 for automatic safety.
Add €18,000 for extra set of barrels without forearm.

* ***Michaelangelo O/U Extra*** – 12, 16, 20, 28 ga., or .410 bore, pinless Boss style sidelock action, 28 in. chopper lump barrels, scaled frame, best quality Turkish walnut and engraving. Importation disc. 2010.

Last MSR on this model was €71,000 without engraving.

CHALLENGER TITANIUM SIDELOCK O/U – 12 or 20 ga., 26-30 in. chopper lump barrels, scaled frame, supplied in-the-white, exhibition quality walnut, w/o engraving, optional case and chokes.

The current MSR on this gun is €85,000 without engraving.

WILD COMPETITION O/U – 12 ga., boxlock action with optional sideplates, 26-34 in. monobloc barrels, 100% handmade stock and forearm with no CNC operations, best handmade bluing, regular or round action, engraving per customer specifications, supplied in-the-white.

This model has a current MSR of €28,500 without engraving on sideplate model.
Add €21,500 for boxlock model.
Add €9,500 for extra set of barrels.

WILD ROUND BODY GAME GUN O/U – 20 or 28 ga., hand forged, 26-34 in. monobloc barrels, 100% handmade stock and forearm with no CNC operations, best handmade bluing, regular or round action, engraving per customer specifications, supplied in-the-white.

The current MSR on this model is €30,500 without engraving.
Add €9,500 for extra set of barrels.

HAMMER GUN SxS – 12 ga., sidelock back action, regular or round action, stock and forearm are handmade, engraving depends on customer specifications, supplied in-the-white. Limited importation.

The current MSR on this gun is €30,000 without engraving.

QUEEN SIDELOCK SxS – 12, 16, 20, 28 ga., or .410 bore, H&H type sidelock action, hand forged 26-32 in. chopper lump barrels.

This model has a MSR of €30,000 without engraving.
Add 10% for 28 ga. or 20% for .410 bore.
Add €10,000 for extra set of barrels.

COUNTRY SxS – 12, 20, or 28 ga., Anson & Deeley type scalloped boxlock action, hand forged 26-32 in. chopper lump barrels, DT, checkered deluxe English straight grip stock and forearm.

This current MSR on this model is €28,000 without engraving.
Add €8,000 for extra set of barrels.

LAURA O/U – 12, 20, 28 ga. or .410 bore, 27-30 in. barrels, fixed or Briley screw-in chokes, solid or vent. rib, square back trigger plate action, checkered walnut stock, built on B. Rizzini frame, custom order engraving, with or w/o sideplates. New 2011.

This current MSR on this model is €9,000 without engraving.

BOSS & CO., LTD.

Current manufacturer located in London, England 1812 to date. Direct sales from the manufacturer only.

For individual model listings, please go to BlueBookOfGunValues.com/overflow.

BOSWELL, CHARLES

Current manufacturer established in 1869, located in London, England. Currently imported by Chris Batha beginning 2004, and located in Okatie, SC. Previously imported by Saxon Arms, Ltd., located in Clearwater, FL. Consumer direct sales.

All new prices do not include English VAT. Delivery time for new guns is 12 to 18 months.

CHARLES BOSWELL COMPANY HISTORY

Charles Boswell was not only a fine gunmaker but an expert shot in the sport of live pigeon shooting and accordingly specialized in the building of high quality competition shotguns and rifles. He founded his business in 1869 at Edmunton, but by 1884 had moved to 126 The Strand in central London. In 1914,

GRADING - PPGS™	100%	98%	95%	90%	80%	70%	60%	LAST MSR

Boswell's son, Osbourne George, assumed management and in 1922 the firm moved to South Moulton Street. Charles Boswell died in 1924, and in 1932, the firm moved again to 15 Mill Street, where the company was bombed by the Luftwaffe in April of 1941. Osbourne George passed away a few months later, and his widow ran the business until 1944 - after which point the family connection apparently ends.

In 1988, Charles Boswell was purchased by U.S. interests and Cape Horn International (previously Cape Horn Outfitters) located in Charlotte, NC, was retained to sell and manufacture the Boswell Guns in the U.S. In addition to acquiring their entire inventory of English manufactured firearms, Charles Boswell fabricated new shotguns and double rifles in the U.S. using the best materials, including English lock mechanisms and retained the Charles Boswell Co. trademark. Every gun was custom ordered to an individual client's requirements/specifications.

After several post WWII overseas ownerships, the brand was revived by British shooting instructor Chris Batha, with American owner Garfield R. Beckstead. Batha acquired the company name, records, and goodwill in January of 2004 and continues the heritage of building best guns of superior craftsmanship and outstanding quality of shotguns and rifles in all gauges and calibers.

Some information appears courtesy of David Grant and Vic Venters.

The most collectible Boswell guns are pre-WWII, including the hammer guns that were lightweight with great shooting dynamics.

RIFLES: BOLT ACTION

BOLT ACTION RIFLE – all standard calibers, built on Mauser or Mannlicher action, 3/4 rib with standard and two folding leaf rear sight, finest well figured hand checkered Turkish walnut, with pistol grip and cheekpiece. Delivered in leather motor case with accessories.

Last MSR for a base model was $35,000.

Pinless, scopes, Kurz or Magnum actions were available by individual quotation.

RIFLES: SxS

SIDELOCK DOUBLE RIFLE – all standard calibers, best quality reinforced sidelock ejector with pinless lock plates, folding leaf rear sight on 3/4 rib, finest well figured hand checkered Turkish walnut, with pistol grip and cheekpiece. Delivered in leather motor case with accessories.

The current MSR for base model is $125,000.

Deluxe and game scene engraving is POR.

BOXLOCK RIFLE – .300 Express, .375 H&H, .458 Win. Mag., or .500 NE cal., made to individual order, choice of game scene engraving, Anson & Deeley boxlock actions, select European hybrid walnut, double triggers, leather cased. Disc. 1996.

	100%	98%	95%	90%	80%	70%	60%	LAST MSR
	$18,950	$16,750	$14,750	$12,500	$10,500	$9,000	$8,000	*$35,000*

Add 40% for .458 Win. Mag. cal. or 50% for .500 NE cal.

* ***Boxlock Rifle .600 Nitro Express***

The 1991 MSR on this model was $123,000, and it was discontinued in 1996.

SIDELOCK RIFLE – .300 Express, .375 H&H, or .458 Win. Mag. cal., made to individual order, choice of game scene engraving, H&H sidelock action, select European hybrid walnut, double triggers, leather cased. Disc. 1996.

	100%	98%	95%	90%	80%	70%	60%	LAST MSR
	$35,000	$29,500	$25,000	$20,000	$18,000	$17,000	$16,000	*$65,000*

Add 40% for .375 H&H cal. or 50% for .458 Win. Mag. cal.

* ***Sidelock Rifle .600 Nitro Express***

	100%	98%	95%	90%	80%	70%	60%	LAST MSR
	$65,000	$55,000	$45,000	$37,500	$33,500	$29,500	$25,000	*$125,000*

SHOTGUNS: O/U, SIDELOCK

MERLIN – 12, 16, 20, 28 ga., or .410 bore, best quality sidelock ejector, pinless lock plates, single or double triggers, finest well figured hand checkered Turkish walnut. Delivered in leather motor case with accessories.

Current MSR for base model is $85,500.

PENDRAGON – 20 ga. only, best quality sideplate ejector pinless lock plates, trigger plate model with Boss style forend iron, finest well figured hand checkered Turkish walnut. Delivered in leather motor case with accessories.

Current MSR for base model is $85,500.

SHOTGUNS: SxS

Charles Boswell hammer guns in all gauges have a base price of $85,500. Live Pigeon guns with side clips, third bite and Magnum frame have a base price of $105,000. Please contact Mr. Batha directly for more information.

GRADING - PPGS™	100%	98%	95%	90%	80%	70%	60%	LAST MSR

MERLIN SIDELOCK MODEL – 12, 16, 20, 28 ga., or .410 bore, best quality sidelock ejector, pinless lock plates, single or double triggers, finest well figured hand checkered Turkish walnut. Delivered in leather motor case with accessories.

Current MSR for base model is $70,000.

BOXLOCK MODEL – previously made to individual order, choice of engraving - including game scenes with gold, Anson & Deeley boxlock actions, select European hybrid walnut, double triggers, leather cased. While each shotgun was priced per individual special order, the listed prices represented standard features and embellishments. Disc. 1996.

* ***Boxlock Model Best Quality***

	$5,950	$5,250	$4,500	$3,950	$3,425	$2,900	$2,250	*$9,500*

* ***Boxlock Model Deluxe Grade*** – game scene engraved.

	$7,450	$5,600	$4,800	$4,300	$3,850	$3,200	$2,650	*$10,500*

Add $900 for single trigger.
Add $2,800 for extra set of barrels.
Add $2,200 for 28 ga. or .410 bore.

FEATHERWEIGHT MONARCH GRADE – lavishly engraved with gold game scenes, lightweight model, specifications per individual customer special order. Mfg. 1989-96.

* ***Featherweight Monarch Grade Boxlock Model***

	$10,500	$8,150	$6,750	$5,500	$4,800	$4,150	$3,450	*$12,500*

* ***Featherweight Monarch Grade Sidelock Model***

	$18,000	$15,500	$13,250	$10,750	$9,100	$7,750	$6,750	*$25,000*

SIDELOCK MODEL – previously made to individual order, choice of game scene engraving, H&H sidelock action, select European hybrid walnut, double triggers, leather cased, while each shotgun was priced per individual special order, the listed values represented standard features and embellishments.

	$12,950	$10,500	$9,000	$7,600	$6,500	$5,500	$4,400	*$17,500*

Add $4,000 for smaller gauges except .410 bore - add $5,000.
Add $2,800 for extra set of barrels.
Add $2,800 for extra set of .410 bore barrels.
Subtract 50% for post-1988 mfg.

BOWEN, BRUCE & COMPANY

Current shotgun manufacturer established 1996 and located in Sturgis, SD. Consumer direct sales only. Bruce Bowen & Company is a division of NIP Manufacturing, Inc.

SHOTGUNS: SINGLE SHOT

BOWEN TRAP GUN – 12 ga. only, unique break open action similar to Seitz trap gun, 32, 33, 34, or 35 in. fixed full choke barrel with four different rib configurations, allowing for four different points of impact, both release and pull triggers included, deluxe checkered walnut with either regular or Monte Carlo stock, adj. comb (available upon request), individually made per customer's specifications, 9 lbs.

The base price for the Bowen Trap Gun is $16,900 for fixed rib and $13,500 for adj. rib. Please contact the factory directly for a firm price quotation on various options and a delivery date.

BOXALL & EDMISTON LTD.

Current shotgun manufacturer established during 2010, located in Shropshire, U.K.

Boxall & Edmiston Ltd. was founded during 2010 by Peter Boxall, former manufacturing director of Holland & Holland, and James Edmiston, former managing director of the Sterling Armament Co.

SHOTGUNS: O/U

Current O/U models include: 12 ga. in either round (case colored action with choice of border or full scroll engraving) or square action (with sideplates and minimal engraving). MSRs are £24,600 for round action or £25,200 for sideplated square action, 16 ga. in either round (case colored action with choice of border or full scroll engraving) or square action (with sideplates and minimal engraving). MSRs are £28,800 for round action or £29,400 for sideplated square action, and a 20 ga. in either round (case colored action with choice of border or full scroll engraving) or square action (with sideplates and minimal engraving). MSRs are £27,000 for round action or £27,600 for sideplated square action. 28 ga. round action MSRs are £29,400 or £30,000 for square sideplated action. All pricing includes 20% VAT. Delivery is currently 10-14 months.

GRADING - PPGS™	100%	98%	95%	90%	80%	70%	60%	LAST MSR

SHOTGUNS: SxS

Boxall & Edmiston currently offers fine quality SxS Anson & Deeley boxlock shotguns in either 12 or 20 (mfg. 2012-disc.) ga. with and w/o sideplates. Prices start at £30,000 w/o sideplates, and £25,200 with sideplates. The company also offers a 12 or 20 (mfg. 2012-disc.) ga. sidelock SxS shotgun and prices start at £36,000 for 12 ga. or £38,000 for 20 ga. (disc.). 30 in. barrels are standard. Engraving is available, and can be personalized. All guns are made to order and a variety of options are available, including small gauges, upgraded wood, and color case hardening. Prices include 20% VAT. Please contact the company for more information, including a custom quotation, delivery time, and availability.

BOY'S RIFLES

Rifle configuration generally denoting small caliber single shot rifles designed for youth circa 1890-early 1940s.

U.S. manufactured Boy's rifles are generally single shot, small caliber, rimfire rifles. The era of Boy's rifles is considered to be from the mid-1880s to the beginning of the U.S. involvement in World War II in the early 1940s.

Many Boy's rifles are not marked with the maker's name, model, caliber, or serial number. Therefore, identification and evaluation should be left to an expert in the field for those unmarked guns. Many are clearly marked and are familiar to many gun enthusiasts. Many marked Boy's rifles are included in this book, e.g., Remington No. 4, Quackenbush Safety Rifles, Winchester Thumb Trigger, Stevens Favorite, et cetera. Unfortunately, due to various circumstances, many brands of Boy's rifles are not listed in this book, such as the various Hamilton guns, Davenport, Page Lewis, Meriden, Heal, Nicholson, Clive, et cetera.

In the beginning, Boy's rifles were all single shot and mostly falling block actions. Later when the bolt action became common, Boy's rifles started to appear with bolt actions. Then even later, repeaters started to emerge as Boy's rifles.

The most common caliber was .22 rimfire in all cartridge lengths. Some were available in .25 or .32 rimfire.

Most Boy's rifles were cheaply made and, therefore, barely safe. Those that have seen excessive wear or have a loose action are definitely not safe to be used with modern ammunition. They were designed to be inexpensive so children could afford them. Most were of diminutive size to suit young boys and girls. Most were made in the northeast and midwestern parts of the U.S.

It is not uncommon to find these in rough condition with poor bores. This is primarily due to the low quality steel used, lack of proper care by youngsters, and lack of proper cleaning (many Boy's rifles were used with black powder and/or corrosive ammunition) and are only worth a few dollars. However, one in excellent or close to like new condition with box and literature can command many thousands of dollars.

The publisher would like to thank Mr. John Groenewold for providing this information.

BRAVO COMPANY MFG., INC. (BCM)

Current pistol and AR-15 style rifle and parts manufacturer located in Hartland, WI.

Please refer to BlueBookOfGunValues.com to order the *Blue Book of AR-15s & Variations*, available as a book or online subscription.

BRAZIER, JOSEPH, LTD.

Previous manufacturer established circa 1700, located in West Sussex, England. Previously represented in the U.S. by Joseph Brazier, Ltd - Karl Lippard, gunmaker, located in Colorado Springs, CO.

For individual model listings, please go to BlueBookOfGunValues.com/overflow.

BREDA FUCILI (BREDA MECCANICA BRESCIANA)

Current semi-auto shotgun manufacturer located in Brescia, Italy. Currently imported beginning 2015 by Breda USA/Esquire Estate Firearms & Collectibles, LLC located in Mullica Hill, NJ. Previous company names were Breda Meccanica Bresciana, and Ernesto Breda. Previously imported 2007-2008 by Legacy Sports International located in Reno, NV, during 2002-2005 by Tristar, located in No. Kansas City, MO, during 2000-2001 by Gryphon International, located in Kansas City, MO, and by Diana Imports Co., located in San Francisco, CA. Dealer direct sales.

SHOTGUNS: O/U

VEGA SPECIAL – 12 or 20 ga., boxlock action, 26 or 28 in. barrels, single trigger, ejectors, blue only.

	100%	98%	95%	90%	80%	70%	60%	LAST MSR
	$625	$550	$500	$475	$440	$400	$375	*$650*

VEGA SPECIAL TRAP – 12 ga. only, boxlock action, triggers and locks designed for competition shooting, 30 or 32 in. barrels, single trigger, ejectors, blue only.

	100%	98%	95%	90%	80%	70%	60%	LAST MSR
	$975	$900	$825	$800	$750	$700	$625	*$1,114*

GRADING - PPGS™	100%	98%	95%	90%	80%	70%	60%	LAST MSR

VEGA LUSSO – 12 ga. only, scalloped boxlock action, 3 in. chambers, SST, ejectors, 26 or 28 in. VR barrels, coin finished receiver with light perimeter engraving, deluxe checkered Circassian walnut stock and forearm. Imported 2001-2002.

$1,875	$1,500	$1,225	$1,075	$925	$800	$650	*$1,858*

SIRIO STANDARD – 12 or 20 ga., boxlock action, 26 or 28 in. barrels, single trigger, ejectors, blue only, action extensively engraved. Also available in skeet model (28 in. barrels).

$2,200	$2,000	$1,775	$1,575	$1,450	$1,325	$1,150	*$2,225*

PEGASO HUNTER – 12 or 20 ga., boxlock action, 3 in. chambers, 26, 28 (12 ga. only), or 30 (Sporting Clays only) in. VR barrels with 7mm (Hunter) or 11mm (Sporting Clays) rib, 5 interchangeable chokes, removable trigger group, engraved silver steel (Hunter Model) or blue finished (Sporting Clays), inertia SST, oil finished deluxe walnut stock and forearm, approx. 7-7.5 lbs. Imported 2004 only.

$2,650	$2,250	$2,000	$1,825	$1,575	$1,325	$1,050	*$2,739*

* ***Pegaso Sporting Clays*** – features upgraded wood, Breda logos in 24Kt. gold, removable trigger group, supplied with ABS fitted case. Imported 2004 only.

$3,600	$3,150	$2,650	$2,250	$1,875	$1,600	$1,325	*$3,644*

PEGASO HUNTING – 12 or 20 ga., 3 in. chambers, 28 in. blued VR barrels with three flush choke tubes, boxlock stainless steel receiver, SST, ejectors, checkered pistol grip stock and forearm, 6.2 - 6.8 lbs. Limited importation 2007.

$2,650	$2,200	$2,000	$1,825	$1,575	$1,325	$1,000	*$2,729*

PEGASO SPORTING – 12 or 20 ga., 3 in. chambers, 28 in. blued VR barrels with three flush choke tubes, blue boxlock receiver, SST, ejectors, checkered pistol grip stock and forearm, 7.9 lbs. Limited importation 2007.

$3,400	$2,875	$2,525	$2,200	$1,875	$1,550	$1,250	*$3,509*

PEGASO TRAP – 12 or 20 ga., 3 in. chambers, 28 in. blued VR barrels with three flush choke tubes, chrome plated boxlock receiver, checkered pistol grip stock and forearm, SST, ejectors, 7.8 lbs. Limited importation 2007.

$3,400	$2,875	$2,525	$2,200	$1,875	$1,550	$1,250	*$3,509*

ZENITH (ZENITH BLACK/ZENITH NICKEL) – 12 ga., 3 in. chambers, dual locking lugs, 28, 30, or 32 in. VR barrel w/fixed chokes or removeable Mobile chokes, forged steel action w/inlaid titanium "Breda" logo plate on both sides, adj. 7 pos. trigger blade, fiber optic front sight, hand oiled walnut stock and forearm w/fine checkering, 5 chokes (if applicable), choke key, black or "Nickel Extreme" nickel plated finish, ABS hard case, 8 lbs. New 2019.

These models are not currently imported into the U.S.

* ***Zenith L*** – 12 ga., 3 in. chambers, 28, 30, or 32 in. VR barrel, similar to the Zenith, but features greater receiver engraving embellishment including "Zenith L" engraving on the bottom of the action, also features higher grade walnut w/refined stock and forearm checkering, "Nickel Extreme" nickel plated finish, ABS hard case, 8 lbs. New 2019.

These models are not currently imported into the U.S.

SHOTGUNS: SxS

ANDROMEDA SPECIAL – 12 ga., ejectors, single trigger, select checkered walnut, elaborate engraving, satin finish receiver. Disc.

$700	$600	$525	$475	$400	$325	$275	*$685*

SHOTGUNS: SEMI-AUTO

Add approx. 5% for vent. rib on those discontinued models below where applicable.
Add approx. 10% for choke tubes on discontinued models.

930I SPORTING – 12 ga., inertia operating system, 28 or 30 in. VR barrel w/three extended competition chokes, hand tuned trigger w/aluminum alloy trigger assembly, high visibility-low profile fiber optic front sight, hand-oiled walnut stock w/adj. comb, weight system (4 weights) in front of forearm cap, extended bolt handle and ergonomic bolt release, blue or red select small parts. Imported 2015-2020.

$2,200	$1,850	$1,550	$1,275	$1,100	$950	$800	*$2,599*

ALTAIR – 12 or 20 ga., 3 in. chamber, gas operated, two-tone (disc.) or blue alloy receiver finish with 28 in. VR barrel and three choke tubes, checkered walnut stock and forearm, 5.7 - 6.1 lbs. Imported 2007-2008.

$1,275	$1,050	$925	$800	$675	$600	$525	*$1,320*

ALTAIR SPECIAL – 12 ga., 2 3/4 in. chamber, gas operated, 25 or 27 in. barrel, alloy construction, interchangeable choke tubes on recent mfg., vent. rib is standard, choice of blue or chromed receiver.

$475	$425	$375	$350	$325	$300	$275	*$495*

GRADING - PPGS™	100%	98%	95%	90%	80%	70%	60%	LAST MSR

ARIES 2 – 12 ga. only, 2 3/4 in. chamber, gas operated, engraved two-tone receiver, 28 or 30 in. VR barrel, deluxe checkered Circassian walnut stock and forearm. Limited importation 2001 only.

	$900	$800	$650	$600	$550	$500	$425	*$925*

ASTRO – 12 (disc. 2002) or 20 ga., 3 in. chamber, inertia movement action, 22 (slug), 24, 26, 28, or 30 in. VR barrel with choke tube, choice of black synthetic, Advantage camo, or Circassian walnut stock (recoil pad on 20 ga. only) and forearm. Imported 2001-2004.

	$1,150	$900	$750	$650	$575	$500	$450	*$1,215*

Add $100 for Advantage camo coverage (disc. 2002).

ASTROLUX – similar to Astro, except has two-tone receiver with engraving and deluxe checkered Circassian walnut stock and forearm. Imported 2001-2002.

	$1,625	$1,325	$1,100	$975	$825	$700	$600	*$1,665*

B12I COMPETITION/TACTICAL – 12 ga., 3 in. chamber, inertia operating system, 18 1/2, 21, 24, 28, or 30 in. step-rib barrel or 24 or 26 in. barrel w/front rifle sight, 4 shot tubular mag., extended tube available, high luminosity fiber optic front sight, ghost ring rear sight optional, recoil reducing Tri-Polymer synthetic stock, includes 5 flush mount chokes, drilled receiver for optics, oversized charging handle, ergonomic/large bolt release, oversized loading port, black or Kryptek Highlander or Kryptek Mandrake camo finish. Importation began circa 2018.

MSR $1,299	$1,100	$950	$825	$725	$625	$525	$425	

Add $200 for Kyptek Highlander or Mandrake Camo finish.

B12IS "SPORT" – 12 ga., 3 in. chamber, inertia operating system, 18 1/2-30 in. VR barrel, 5 flush mount chokes, rounded action/receiver, high luminosity fiber optic front sight, walnut stock w/Shim System, oversized charging/bolt handle, ergonomic/large bolt release, black receiver, other options include: flat rib field barrel, 4-way adj. comb walnut stock, Tri-Polymer synthetic stock, fancy or semi-fancy wood upgrades. Importation began circa 2015.

MSR $1,349	$1,150	$975	$850	$750	$625	$525	$450	

B3.5 SM – 12 ga., 3 1/2 in. chamber, inertia operating system, 18 1/2, 24, 26, 28, or 30 in. VR barrel, high luminosity fiber optic front sight, Tri-Polymer stock w/adj. Shim System and recoil reducing pad, extended bolt release and Ergo bolt handle, black, tan, or green finish, Marsh Grass, Kryptek Highlander, or Kryptek Mandrake Camo finishes also available, other options include: 24 in. smoothbore barrel w/ iron sight or high capacity extension tube, 7.1 lbs. Importation began circa 2018.

MSR $1,399	$1,200	$1,050	$900	$800	$650	$550	$450	

Add $100 for tan, green, Marsh Grass, or Kyptek camo finishes.

CHIRON – 12 ga., 3 in. chamber, Breda Technology Inertia operation w/vertical lug locking system, 24, 26, 28, or 30 in. VR barrel, 2 (w/plug) or 3 shot mag., steel receiver, fiber optic sight, black synthetic stock and forend w/Soft-Touch inserts and covering, transverse button safety behind the trigger, gold fill "Breda" and "Chiron" engraving, blued finish, 4.8-5.5 lbs. New circa 2016.

MSR $1,449	$1,225	$1,075	$925	$825	$675	$550	$425	

ECHO – 12 or 20 ga., 3 in. chamber, inertia mechanism, blue, bronze, or nickel finished receiver with accents, 28 in. VR barrel and three choke tubes, grooved/checkered walnut stock and forearm, 6-6.5 lbs. Imported 2007-2008.

	$1,550	$1,275	$1,050	$900	$800	$700	$600	*$1,897*

Add $317 for nickel finished receiver.
Add $72 for bronze finished receiver.

ECHO T9 – 12 ga., 3 in. chamber, Breda Technology Inertia System, 26, 28, or 30 in. steel barrel, Technopolymer matte finished trigger, high luminosity fiber optic sight, synthetic stock and forend with Soft Touch covering treatment, comb insert, high density recoil pad, transverse button safety, sandblasted and anodized receiver, 11 lbs. Disc. 2020.

	$1,150	$1,000	$865	$780	$635	$525	$425	*$1,349*

ERMES SERIES (2000/2000 L) – 12 ga., 3 in. chamber, inertia recoil operating system, aluminum alloy receiver, nickel plated or blue (lower receiver only) finish, 24, 26, or 28 in. barrel with choke tube, deluxe checkered Circassian walnut stock and forearm. Imported 2001-2005.

	$1,150	$1,000	$875	$775	$650	$550	$450	*$1,339*

Add $417 for Ermes 2000 L with nickel finished receiver.

* ***Ermes Silver*** – similar to Ermes 2000, except has engraved nickel plated finish on lower receiver. Imported 2002-2005.

	$1,550	$1,325	$1,075	$900	$775	$625	$550	*$1,834*

GRADING - PPGS™	100%	98%	95%	90%	80%	70%	60%	LAST MSR

* ***Ermes Gold*** – similar to Ermes 2000, except has nickel plated finish with engraving and 24Kt. animal gold inlays on lower receiver. Imported 2002-2005.

	$1,700	$1,475	$1,175	$1,000	$850	$725	$600	*$2,060*

GOLD SERIES – 12 or 20 (lightweight) ga., 2 3/4 in. chamber, recoil operated, 25 or 27 in. VR barrels, interchangeable choke tubes on recent mfg.

* ***Antares Standard*** – all steel construction. Importation disc. 1988.

	$475	$425	$375	$350	$325	$275	$260	*$495*

* ***Argus*** – lightweight standard, weighs only 6.6 lbs. Importation disc. 1988.

	$450	$380	$340	$310	$285	$260	$240	*$510*

* ***Aries*** – Magnum, 3 in. chamber, 7.9 lbs. Importation disc. 1988.

	$500	$450	$385	$350	$325	$300	$275	*$525*

GLD (SALIENT GLD) – 12 ga, 3 in. chamber, inertia operating system, 18 1/2, 24, 26, 28, or 30 in. barrel, 7 shot mag., extractor, hand tuned trigger, Hi-Viz optic front sight, SAI straight stock and forearm stippling, SAI upgraded safety, gold anodized breechblock, custom lightened and TiN coated bolt carrier, machined and polished loading port, SAI custom charging handle and oversized bolt release, modified recoil pad. This model is available through Salient Arms International only.

MSR $3,040	$2,600	$2,275	$1,950	$1,775	$1,425	$1,175	$925	

GRADE 1 – 12 ga., similar to standard, except with fancier wood and engraving.

	$625	$575	$525	$475	$450	$425	$375	

GRADE 2 – 12 ga., exceeds Grade 1 embellishments.

	$750	$675	$625	$550	$500	$475	$425	

GRADE 3 – 12 ga., top-of-the-line semi-auto.

	$925	$875	$775	$700	$650	$600	$525	

GRIZZLY – 12 ga., 3 1/2 in. chamber, inertia operation with rotary bolt, 28 in. VR barrel with choke tubes, choice of matte black, 100% Advantage Timber HD camo, Desert Tan, or green camo finish, sling swivels, includes fitted case, 7 1/2 lbs. Imported 2004, 2007-2008, and beginning circa 2015-Disc.

	$1,350	$1,150	$1,000	$875	$750	$625	$525	*$1,549*

Add $100 for camo finish.

ICARO – 20 ga., 3 in. chamber, Breda Technology inertia operation, rotating locking system, 23 (Youth Model), 24, 26, 28, or 30 in. barrel, 2 (plug fitted) or 4 (w/o plug) shot mag., two-piece aluminum alloy receiver, Technopolymer matte finish trigger guard, high luminosity fiber optic sight, standard walnut, oil-finished stock w/checkered forend, tranverse bottom behind trigger with red "ready to shoot" signal, hand polished and black anodized finish, approx. 5 lbs. Importation began circa 2015.

MSR $1,299	$1,100	$950	$825	$725	$625	$525	$425	

MAGNUM MODEL – 12 ga. only, chambered for 3 in. shells.

	$525	$450	$425	$375	$350	$325	$300	

MIRA – 12 ga. only, 3 in. chamber, gas operated, Ergal aluminum alloy receiver, choice of anodized black metal or Advantage camo finish, 22 (slug), 24, 26, 28, or 30 in. VR barrel with choke tube, Circassian walnut or black synthetic (disc. 2002) stock and forearm. Imported 2001-2005.

	$875	$775	$700	$600	$500	$425	$350	*$938*

Subtract 10% for black synthetic stock and forearm.
Add $12 for Sporting Clays configuration.

STANDARD – 12 ga., 2 3/4 in. chamber, recoil operated, 25 or 27 in. barrel, lightly engraved, interchangeable choke tubes on recent mfg. Disc.

	$350	$325	$300	$275	$260	$240	$215	

TITANO – 12 or 20 ga., 3 in. chamber, inertia operation, rotating bolt locking system, 24, 26, 28, or 30 in. VR barrel, 4 shot capacity w/o plug, 2 shot capacity w/plug, aluminum alloy receiver, LPA high visibility fiber optic front sight, oil-finished semi-fancy grade walnut forend and stock w/high density recoil pad, stippled checkering, 5 chokes, choke key, detachable sling swivels, ABS hard case, high polish upper w/black finish, hand brushed lower receiver w/engravings, 6.8 lbs. Imported beginning circa 2020.

Please contact the manufacturer/importer directly for price and availability.

* ***Titano L*** – 12 or 20 ga., 3 in. chamber, inertia operation, rotating bolt locking system, similar to the Titano, but features greater receiver engraving embellishment including gold and blue colorations, and refined stock and forearm checkering, 6.8 lbs. Imported beginning circa 2020.

Please contact the manufacturer/importer directly for price and availability.

GRADING - PPGS™	100%	98%	95%	90%	80%	70%	60%	LAST MSR

XANTHOS – 12 ga., 3 in. chamber, inertia operation, 28 in. VR blue barrel with three choke tubes, receiver colors include blue, grey, or chrome with accents, deluxe checkered walnut stock and forearm, 6 1/2 lbs. Imported 2007-2008.

MSR N/A	$1,995	$1,750	$1,500	$1,250	$995	$850	$750	*$2,309*

Add $142 for grey receiver with colored accents.
Add $1,097 for chrome receiver with colored accents.

XANTHOS DAMASCO/XANTHOS GOLD – 12 ga., 3 in. chamber, Breda Technology Inertia operation w/ vertical lug locking system, 24, 26, 28 or 30 in. barrel, 2 (w/plug fitted) or 3 (w/o plug) shot mag., steel receiver, Technopolymer matte finished trigger guard, high luminosity fiber optic sight, select walnut/oil-finished forend and stock w/high density recoil pad, tranverse safety button behind trigger w/"ready to shoot" indicator, Damask engraving on both sides of receiver w/gold embellishment and manual polishing, nickel plating bath and ruthenium finish (Damasco model) or manually polished steel receiver w/engraving and gold and silver wire inlays w/black surface finish (Gold model), 6.6 lbs. Imported beginning circa 2018.

MSR $2,999	$2,600	$2,200	$1,850	$1,500	$1,300	$1,150	$995	

BREEDING, RYAN

Current custom rifle manufacturer located in Nampa, ID. Previously located in Palmdale, CA.

RIFLES: BOLT ACTION

Ryan Breeding specializes in making high quality, custom built rifles in .22-.585 cal. Many configurations and upgrades are available on his custom safari guns. Ryan works alongside rifle maker and African Hunter, Gil Van Horn. Please contact Ryan Breeding directly for more information, including pricing, availability, and a customized quote.

BRE-MAC Srl

Current manufacturer of Renato Gamba shotguns located in Gardone, Italy. Please refer to Gamba, Renato listing in the G section.

BREN 10 (PREVIOUS MFG.)

Previous trademark manufactured 1983-1986 by Dornaus & Dixon Ent., Inc., located in Huntington Beach, CA.

Bren 10 magazines played an important part in the failure of these pistols to be accepted by consumers. Originally, Bren magazines were not shipped in some cases until a year after the customer received his gun. The complications arising around manufacturing a reliable dual caliber magazine domestically led to the downfall of this company. For this reason, original Bren 10 magazines are currently selling for $150-$175 if new (watch for fakes). Standard Black Hogue grips selling for $75-$100.

PISTOLS: SEMI-AUTO

Note: the Bren 10 shoots a Norma factory loaded 10mm auto cartridge. Ballistically, it is very close to a .41 Mag. Bren pistols also have unique power seal rifling, with five lands and grooves. While in production, Bren pistols underwent four engineering changes, the most important probably being re-designing the floorplate of the magazine to prevent the magazine from dislocating as the pistol recoiled. Beware of cobbled together parts - some have appeared at recent gun shows.

100% values in this section assume NIB condition. Add 5% for extra original factory mag. Subtract 10% without box/manual.
Add $30 for a 10 round box of factory ammunition, add $100 for a 50 round box.

BREN 10 STANDARD MODEL – 10mm cal. only, semi-auto selective double action design, blue slide/ silver frame finish, 5 in. barrel, 11 shot, stainless steel frame, usually supplied with two mags. although early mfg. did not include a mag. because of design problems, "83SM" ser. no. prefix. Mfg. 1984-86.

	$3,250	$2,500	$1,950	$1,500	$1,000	$750	$550	*$500*

Add $900 for .45 conversion unit.

BREN 10 MILITARY/POLICE MODEL – 10mm cal. only, DA/SA, identical to standard model, except has all black finish, 5 in. barrel, "83MP" ser. no. prefix. Mfg. 1984-1986.

	$4,000	$3,000	$2,500	$2,000	$1,500	$1,000	$950	*$550*

BREN 10 SPECIAL FORCES MODEL – 10mm cal. only, DA/SA, 4 in. barrel, commercial version of the military pistol submitted to the U.S. gov't. Model D has dark finish. Model L has light finish, "SFD" ser. no. prefix on Model D, "SFL" ser. no. prefix on Model L. Disc. 1986.

Dark finish - Model D	$3,800	$3,000	$2,400	$2,000	$1,500	$1,000	$750	
Light finish - Model L	$4,000	$3,100	$2,500	$2,100	$1,600	$1,100	$775	*$600*

GRADING - PPGS™	100%	98%	95%	90%	80%	70%	60%	LAST MSR

BREN 10 DUAL-MASTER PRESENTATION MODEL – 10mm and .45 ACP cal., supplied with extra slide and barrel (numbered to gun) to accommodate the .45 ACP, same mags. (two) for both cals., extra fine finish, light scroll engraving, with wood presentation case, "83DM" ser. no. prefix, less than 50 mfg. Disc. 1986.

$5,200 $4,150 $3,350 $2,500 $2,000 $1,400 $995 *$800*

Be wary of Standard Models with wooden cases and conversion kits - they are fakes!

BREN 10 JEFF COOPER COMMEMORATIVE – 10mm cal. only, while 2,000 were annnounced for mfg., sources now believe that approx. 5 were actually made, 22Kt. gold plated detailing, laser engraved stocks, special presentation chest. Disc. 1986.

Last MSR was $2,000

Extreme rarity factor precludes accurate pricing on this model. An individual appraisal is recommended. Current pricing guidelines, depending on condition, are approx. $7,500-$15,000.

MARKSMAN MODEL – .45 ACP cal., approx. less than 250 mfg. (in its own ser. range) for "The Marksman" retail shop in Chicago, action similar to Bren 10 Standard Model, "MSM" ser. no. prefix.

$1,950 $1,600 $1,500 $950 $850 $750 $525

Add $900 for 10mm conversion unit.

Add $400 for original nylon carrying case marked "Marksman."

Initial models were faulty and returned to D&D for repairs. Due to the closure of D&D, it is doubtful that all 250 guns were actually sent to Chicago.

BREN 10 (RECENT MFG.)

Previous trademark manufactured in limited quantities from 2010-2011 by Vltor Mfg., located in Tucson, AZ. Vltor Mfg. was acquired by Abrams Airborne Manufacturing, Inc. in 2004. Previously distributed exclusively until early 2011 by Sporting Products, LLC, located in W. Palm Beach, FL.

BREN-TEN.COM

PISTOLS: SEMI-AUTO

Very few of the following pistols were actually mass produced.

SM SERIES – 10mm or .45 ACP cal., 5 in. barrel, DA/SA, stainless steel frame with blue slide, 10 (SM45) or 15 (SM10) shot mag., two-tone finish, synthetic grips, approx. 500 (SM10) or 300 (SM45) were scheduled to be mfg., but very few were produced mid-2010-2011.

$1,095 $995 $875 $750 $650 $550 $450 *$1,200*

SMV SERIES – 10mm or .45 ACP cal., 5 in. barrel, DA/SA, stainless steel frame, hard chrome slide, 10 (SMV10) or 15 (SMV15) shot mag., black synthetic grips, approx. 500 (SMV10) or 300 (SMV45) were scheduled to be produced, but very few were mfg. mid-2010-2011.

$1,175 $1,050 $925 $800 $700 $600 $495 *$1,299*

SFD45 – .45 ACP cal., 4 in. barrel, DA/SA, matte black finished frame and slide, synthetic grips, 10 shot mag., approx. 500 were scheduled to be produced, but very few were mfg. mid-2010-2011.

$995 $895 $800 $700 $600 $500 $425 *$1,100*

SFL45 – .45 ACP cal., 4 in. barrel, DA/SA, matte finished stainless steel frame, hard chrome slide, 10 shot mag., synthetic grips, two-tone finish, approx. 200 were scheduled to be produced, but very few were mfg. mid-2010-2011.

$1,095 $995 $875 $750 $650 $550 $450 *$1,200*

BRETTON-GAUCHER

Current manufacturer established in 2000, and located in Saint-Etienne, France. No current U.S. importation. Previously imported and distributed by Mandall Shooting Supplies, Inc. located in Scottsdale, AZ.

The Bretton trademark was established in 1934, and specialized in Baby lightweight shotguns. Gaucher dates back to 1834, and specialized in Express double rifles. The two companies merged in 2000.

RIFLES

Bretton-Gaucher manufactures a variety of single shot and small caliber rifles, in addition to Express double rifles. To date, these guns have had little or no importation into the U.S. Please contact the factory directly for more information, including pricing and availability.

SHOTGUNS: O/U

All Bretton shotguns are extremely lightweight and well balanced because of their unique design (permitting total disassembly including barrels) and use of various composition alloys. Current MSR's reflect European pricing without shipping, export, and duty costs to the U.S.

GRADING - PPGS™	100%	98%	95%	90%	80%	70%	60%	LAST MSR

BABY STANDARD (SPRINT MODEL) – 12 or 20 ga. only, sliding breech action allows barrels to move straight forward, 27 1/2 in. separated barrels, double triggers, side opening lever, blue action and barrels, recoil pad, checkered walnut stock and forearm, 4.8 lbs. Limited importation.

MSR €1,140	$995	$885	$700	$625	$575	$475	$430	

Add €240 for Baby Luxe.

SPRINT DELUXE – 12, 16 (disc.), or 20 ga., action similar to Baby Standard, engraved coin finished receiver, 27 1/2 in. separated barrels, deluxe checkered walnut stock and forearm, extremely lightweight, 4.8 lbs. Limited importation.

	$895	$725	$625	$575	$475	$430	$395	*$975*

Prices reflect most recent importation information.

FAIR-PLAY – 12 or 20 ga., differs from Sprint Models in that action pivots like a normal O/U, 27 1/2 in. separated barrels, lightweight construction, 4.8 lbs. Limited importation.

MSR €1,395	$1,325	$1,125	$975	$850	$675	$625	$575	

Add €235 for Fair-Play Luxe model with engraved coin finished receiver.
Add €5 for Fair-Play MXT model with open sights (12 ga. only).
Add 10% for Fair-Play Limited Model.

TINY – 20 ga., double triggers, extremely lightweight, approx. 4.2 lbs.

Current French MSR on this model is €1,185.
Add €245 for Tiny Luxe model with coin finished receiver and engraving.

BRIGADE FIREARMS

Current AR-15 style pistol, rifle, and parts manufacturer located in Miami, FL.

Please refer to BlueBookOfGunValues.com to order the *Blue Book of AR-15s & Variations*, available as a book or online subscription.

BRIGNOLI, SILVIO

Current firearms manufacturer, importer, and distributor established in 1965, located in Brescia, Italy.

Silvio Brignoli manufactured a Brescia Model boxlock SxS shotgun in most gauges and various configurations.

BRILEY

Current trademark of pistols and rimfire semi-auto rifles with choke tubes currently manufactured in Houston, TX. Current pistol and rifle manufacture is sub-contracted to other manufacturers using the Briley trademark. Briley has previously produced both pistols and rifles, including those listed, in addition to manufacturing a complete line of top quality shotgun barrel tubes and chokes since 1976. Additionally, beginning late March, 2006-2007 Briley Manufacturing imported and distributed Mauser Models 98 and 03 bolt action rifles from Germany.

For individual model listings, please go to BlueBookOfGunValues.com/overflow.

BRITARMS

Previous trademark manufactured by Berdan Gunmakers Ltd. located in England. Previously imported and distributed until 1994 by Mandall Shooting Supplies, Inc. located in Scottsdale, AZ, and by Action Arms Ltd. (1982-1983) located in Philadelphia, PA.

Britarms Target Pistols had very limited importation into the U.S. While Britarms manufactured other models, only the Model 2000 is listed since it was formally imported through U.S. firms.

PISTOLS: SEMI-AUTO

MODEL 2000 (MK II) – .22 LR cal., standard fire target semi-auto pistol, adj. trigger and rear sight, anatomical adj. grips, 5.82 in. barrel, 5 shot mag., 3 lbs., limited importation, including approx. 2000 through Action Arms Ltd.

	$995	$825	$700	$625	$550	$495	$450	*$1,295*

This model features a bolt hold-open mechanism which serves as a manual safety to allow importation.

BRITISH ORDNANCE COMPANY

Current manufacturer located in the U.K., established during 2013 and imported by Chris Batha, located in Okatie, SC.

SHOTGUNS: O/U

O/U BOXLOCK – all gauges, boxlock action, removable V spring trigger plate. New 2013.

Base price on this model ranges from $30,000-$35,000.

BRIXIA SHOTGUNS Srl

Current pistol and shotgun manufacturer established during 2012 and located in Gardone, Italy. Previously imported (select models only) by International Firearms Corp. (IFC) from 2017-2019, located in Midwest City, OK. No current U.S. importation.

Brixia Shotguns manufactures good quality semi-auto, slide action, sporting, O/U, and tactical shotguns in various configurations, in addition to a line of M1911 style semi-auto pistols. Please contact the company directly for more information, pricing, and U.S. availability.

SHOTGUNS: O/U

Previously, only select models were being imported by the International Firearms Corp. (IFC) Please contact the manufacturer directly for more information on models not listed here, including U.S. availability and pricing.

RAVEN – 12 or 20 ga., 2 3/4 or 3 in. chambers, steel or aluminum receiver, 26 or 30 in. barrels, raised top rib and bead, compatible with JEBS Precision choke tubes, auto ejectors, barrel select on trigger, fiber optic sight, walnut coated stock with "soft touch" technology, auto safety, available in trap configuration, 7 lbs. (steel receiver). Imported 2019 only.

Please contact the manufacturer directly for pricing and availability on this model.

BRNO ARMS (ZBROJOVKA BRNO)

Previously manufactured by Zbrojovka Brno located in Brno, Czech Republic (formerly Czechoslovakia) from 1918-2006. Brno 98 bolt action rifles and actions were imported by EAA Corp, located in Sharpes, FL until 2002. Also previously imported and distributed by Euro-Imports, located in El Cajon, CA until 2001 and by Bohemia Arms located in Fountain Valley, CA until 1997. Brno rifles, shotguns, and combination guns produced at the Brno factory were previously imported and distributed by Magnum Research Inc. located in Minneapolis, MN (c. 1994-1996). In the early '50s, Brno rifles were imported by Continental Arms Corp. located in New York City. Pragotrade located in Ontario, Canada also imported this trademark for Canada exclusively. Previously imported by T.D. Arms located in New Baltimore, MD.

As more history is becoming available on this important European trademark, the following biographical sketch will provide some information. Circa 1918, some military personnel took over the controlling interest of the Austro-Hungarian armament shop in Brno, Czechoslovakia, renaming it The State Armament and Engineering Works. Approximately a year later, the name was changed to Czechoslovak State Armament Works. The former provinces of Bohemia and Moravia had long been firearms manufacturing centers within their regions. Prior to 1924, this firm was involved mainly with Mauser Model 98 type rifles (both assembly and mfg.).

Pistol manufacture was tranferred from Brno to Ceská Zbrojovka, located in Strakonice, Czechoslovakia, circa 1923. During 1964-1966, the Czech government transferred the production of long guns from Zbrojovka Brno to Ceská Zbrojovka Uhersky Brod. During the 1970s & 1980s, the arms production of Zbrojovka Brno accounted for less than 3% of its total capacity. The activities of this company were deverted into the production of typewriters, diesel motors, and automatic machine tools. While many firearm designs originated in Brno, Zbrojovka Brno was not the manufacturer. Because of this, the long guns manufactured in the mid-1960s, including the ZKK 600 - 602 series and ZKM rimfires, were manufactured in CZ Uhersky Brod. Because of the Czech government's decision to merge manufacture within both companies, the Brno trademark was also used by Ceská Zbrojovka Uhersky Brod.

This relationship was terminated in 1983, when both companies became part of the Agrozet conglomerate. While confusing, the arms utlizing the Brno trademark were not produced in Brno during this time. All firearms exported from Czechoslovakia at the time carried the Brno logo, and most of them were manufactured by Ceská Zbrojovka Uhersky Brod.

Brno was declared bankrupt in March 2003. Shortly after, Brno emerged from bankruptcy, but fell back in during Oct. 2003. The company continued to trade under administration until Zbrojovka Brno finally closed in 2006. The facilities were bought by a Slovak firm, and the owners wanted to support various business activities in the future. The majority of the firm's employees transferred to Brno Rifles a subsidiary of Ceska Zbrojovka (CZ), which was established in Brno to continue production of Brno firearms. Please refer to Brno Rifles for current manufacture.

Brno's famous Z banner trademark was sold to an undisclosed buyer on November 6, 2007.

CZ PISTOLS & RIFLES

See separate listing under CZ.

PISTOLS: SEMI-AUTO

MODEL ZBP-99 – 9mm Para. or .40 S&W cal., double action.

While advertised in 1998, this gun never went into production.

GRADING - PPGS™	100%	98%	95%	90%	80%	70%	60%	LAST MSR

REVOLVERS

ZKR 551 – .32 S&W Long or .38 Spl. cal., double action, solid frame with Colt SAA style shrouded ejector rod, 6 shot cylinder, adj. sights, checkered wood grips with thumb rest, 6 in. barrel, approx. 2 lbs. Imported 1999-2002.

$1,375	$1,100	$978	$875	$775	$675	$600	

RIFLES: BOLT ACTION

The Brno Lightweight Sporter was introduced in the late 1930s. A small quantity was manufactured during pre-war and WWII. Most production occured between 1946-1955. Total production of this model was approx. 40,000+ units. A design change was implemented at approximately serial number 23,000, at which time the receiver was changed to a double square bridge dovetailed to accept scope mounts.

Earlier mfg. had a rounded receiver and some had claw type scope mounts installed. These guns were referenced as Models 21 and 22 domestically, but no model designation appears on the gun. Available cals. were 6.5x57mm, 7x57mm, 7x64mm, 8x57mm, or 8x60mm. Configuration was small ring Mauser 98 receiver with double set trigger(s), butterknife bolt, checkered walnut pistol grip stock (half or full length), with cheekpiece and sling swivels, late production incorporated four variations and two barrel lengths (20.5 or 23.6 in.).

Brno rifles may be dated by the two digit date beside the proofmarks. Brno's rifle designations typically indicated the Brno Z brand and the designer. Hence, a ZG47 was manufactured by the factory in Zbrojovka Brno, G refers to Otakar Galas, the designer, and 47 is most likely the year of design.

HORNET SPORTER (MODEL ZKW 465) – various cals., miniature Mauser action, 22 3/4 in. barrel, 5 shot box mag., 3-leaf express sight, double set trigger(s), checkered pistol grip stock, also called Z-B Mauser, serial range noted is 00111-38262, approx. 40,000 mfg. between 1946-1974.

$1,200	$1,050	$900	$815	$660	$540	$425	

There are few examples in .218 Bee and .222 Rem. cal. - premiums can be added.

This model was redesigned with a subsequent designation of ZKB 680 Fox in approx. 1971. Please refer to the CZ section for this model.

MODEL ZG-47 – .270 Win., .30-06, 7x57mm, 7x64mm, 8x64S, 8x57mm, 9.3x62mm, or 10.75x68mm cal., large ring Mauser 98 action with 20mm dovetails on receiver ring and bridge, single trigger, hinged floorplate, rollover type safety and bolt handle designed for low scope mounting, 23 1/2 in. barrel, checkered pistol grip walnut stock with sling swivels and Schnabel forend, approx. serial range is 0-20,000, mfg. and exported world-wide between 1956-62 (approx.).

$1,125	$985	$845	$765	$620	$505	$395	

Early specimens of this model are marked "BRNO MADE IN CZECHOSLOVAKIA". This model is generally regarded as being one of the finest rifles that Brno has manufactured. Circa 1961-1966, Parker-Hale Limited, of Birmingham, England, built some Hussar and International model rifles on Brno Model ZG-47 actions. Calibers were .243, .270, .308, .30-06 and .308 Norma Mag. As no Brno/Czech markings appear on these guns, collectors should look for the integral scope mount dovetails on the receiver. Internationals were advertised in the 1963 *Gun Digest* for $149.95. The Magnum was an additional $10.

MODEL G 33-40 – 8mm cal., mfg. between 1940-42, prices below assume sporterized condition.

$350	$305	$260	$240	$190	$155	$120	

MODEL 21 – 6.5x57mm, 7x57mm, 7x64mm (scarce), 8x57mm, or 8x60mm cal., featherweight style design of the small ring Mauser type action, with (post-1949) or without 20mm dovetails on receiver ring and bridge, 20 1/2 or 23 in. barrel, butterknife style bolt handle, double set triggers, 2-leaf rear sight, checkered pistol grip walnut stock with cheekpiece and plastic buttplate/grip cap, small Schnabel forend, sling swivels included, noted serialization is 2,303-41,787, mfg. approx. 1942-1956.

$1,495	$1,325	$1,175	$1,050	$900	$825	$675	

The Brno Models 21 and 22 were available in 4 different variations: short barrel/short stock, short barrel/full length stock, long barrel/short stock, long barrel/full length stock. The left receiver rail on these models is marked "ZBROJOVKA BRNO, NARODNI PODNIK". Examples with dovetailed (post-1949) receivers and later ZG 47-type bolts have been observed. Collectors sometimes classify these (unofficially) as "transition models."

MODEL 22 – similar to 21, with full length stock. Disc.

$1,400	$1,225	$1,050	$950	$770	$630	$490	

The Brno Models 21 and 22 were available in 4 different variations: short barrel/short stock, short barrel/full length stock, long barrel/short stock, long barrel/full length stock. The left receiver rail on these models is marked "ZBROJOVKA BRNO, NARODNI PODNIK".

GRADING - PPGS™	100%	98%	95%	90%	80%	70%	60%	LAST MSR

MODEL 1 – .22 LR cal., 22 3/4 in. barrel, 3-leaf sight, 5 shot box mag., 6 lbs. Mfg. 1945-1957.

$675 $595 $525 $450 $400 $325 $275

Add a premium for the deluxe model with checkered pistol grip and walnut stock.

This model is also known as the Model ZKM 451.

In 1957, some Model 1s were built on the then-new Model 2 (ZKM 452) action. Observed serial numbers are 48532, 48545, and 48690 (which conform with the Model 2 serialization). In the same year, Brno renamed this configuration Model 5 (ZKM 573) with serialization commencing with No. 00001.

ZKM 468 – .22 LR cal., single shot. Mfg. 1948.

$200 $175 $150 $135 $110 $90 $70

MODEL 2 – similar to Model 1, except has 24.8 in. barrel and Mauser type tangent rear sight, walnut stock. Mfg. 1954-disc.

$635 $555 $475 $430 $350 $285 $220

Add a premium for deluxe model with checkered walnut stock.

This model is also known as the Model ZKM 452.

MODEL 3 – .22 LR cal., target rifle model with 27 1/2 in. heavy barrel, adj. click target sights, 5 shot box mag., plain target style stock with large swivels, 9 1/2 lbs. Mfg. 1949-1956.

$635 $555 $475 $430 $350 $285 $220

This model is also known as the Model ZKM 455.

MODEL 4 – similar to Model 3, except has improved trigger design and safety. Mfg. 1956-1962.

$700 $610 $525 $475 $385 $315 $245

This model is also known as the Model ZKM 456.

MODEL 5 (ZKM 573) – similar to Model 1, except has improved trigger design and safety. Noted mfg. 1957-1978.

$750 $675 $595 $525 $450 $400 $325

BRNO 98 STANDARD – .243 Win., .270 Win., .30-06, .308 Win., .300 Win. Mag., 6.5x55mm SE, 7mm Rem. Mag. (new 2000), 7x57mm, 7x64mm, 8x57 JS, or 9.3x62mm cal., Mauser 98 style action, 23.6 in. barrel with or without iron sights, checkered walnut stock with Bavarian cheekpiece, or synthetic stock (disc.) and forearms (new 2002) single or set trigger, 7 1/4 lbs. Disc.

$625 $525 $450 $400 $365 $335 $295

Subtract approx. 10% for synthetic stock (disc.).
Add 10% for Mag. cals.
Add 5% for single set trigger.
Add $25 for Battue ramp sights.

This model is historically significant as it was the last centerfire bolt action rifle assembled in the famous Brno factory. Guns were built on refurbished military M98 actions from various makers, sourced primarily from the former Yugoslavia.

* ***Brno 98 Mannlicher*** – similar to Brno 98 Standard, except has full length stock and set trigger. Disc.

$825 $725 $625 $525 $450 $375 $325

Add 10% for Mag. cals.

* ***Brno 98 Damask*** – similar cals. to Brno 98 Standard, features unique individually welded Damascus steel barrel (no two are identical). Seldomly encountered.

N/A $1,950 $1,750 $1,500 $1,250 $1,000 $800

MODEL ZOM-451 – .22 LR cal., straight pull bolt action, limited importation by Century International Arms during 1998.

$215 $190 $160 $145 $120 $95 $75

MODEL ZKM-451 – .22 LR cal. Imported 1995-2002.

$595 $520 $445 $405 $325 $270 $210

Add approx. 10% for Lux Model (deluxe checkered wood).

It is possible that these guns are refurbished Model 1s, and have been seen with older proof date stamps.

MODEL ZKM-456 LUX SPORTER – .22 LR cal., bolt action, 5 or 10 shot mag., 24.4 in. barrel, folding rear sight, blue finish, beechwood stock with pistol grip, 6.8 lbs., mfg. by Aeron. Imported 1992-1998.

$315 $275 $235 $215 $175 $140 $110 *$370*

Add $18 for micrometer rear sight (ZKM-456 MI).

GRADING - PPGS™	100%	98%	95%	90%	80%	70%	60%	LAST MSR

* ***Model 456 L/LK Target*** – .22 LR cal., Target variation of the ZKM-456 Lux featuring 25 or 28 in. barrel with adj. front and rear sights, 10.1 lbs., mfg. by Aeron. Imported 1992-1998.

$305	$265	$230	$205	$170	$135	$105	*$358*

Add $7 for 25 in. barrel.

* ***Model 456 Match Single Shot*** – .22 LR cal., designed for UIT competition at 50 M, features 27 1/2 in. barrel, adj. cheekpiece and buttplate, aperture sights, 9.9 lbs., mfg. by Aeron. Imported 1992-1998.

$375	$330	$280	$255	$205	$170	$130	*$459*

ZKK 600 – please refer to the CZ section for this model.

ZKK 601 – please refer to the CZ section for this model.

ZKK 602 – please refer to the CZ section for this model.

ZKB 680 (FOX/FOX II) – please refer to the CZ section for this model.

RIFLES: O/U

ZH-344, 348, & 349 – 7x57R (Model ZH-344), 7x65R (Model ZH-348), or 8x57JRS (Model ZH-349) cal., 23.6 in. VR barrels, double triggers, skip line checkering, sling swivels, approx. 7 1/2 lbs. Imported 1998-disc.

$1,100	$978	$875	$775	$675	$600	$550

Add $324-$357 per additional set of shotgun barrels, $418 per additional rifle barrel, and $829 for additional Mag. cal. rifle barrels.

SUPER EXPRESS – 7x65R, 9.3x74R, .375 H&H, or .458 Win. Mag. (disc.) cal., sidelock action with Kersten breech crossbolt, hand engraved, skipline checkering, approx. 9 lbs. Importation disc. 1992.

$3,450	$2,875	$2,300	$1,875	$1,600	$1,375	$1,200	*$3,900*

This model previously could be ordered with 6 different types of engraving options. They were: Grade I - add $2,060, Grade II - add $1,030, Grade III - add $1,545, Grade IV - add $1,030, Grade V - add $620, Grade VI - add $660.

SUPER SAFARI – 7x64R, .375 H&H Mag., or 9.3x74R cal., action derived from the Super Express, sidelock, DT with set trigger built in, adj. point of impact, 23.6 in. barrels with open sights, deluxe skipline checkered walnut stock and forearm with vent. recoil pad, approx. 9 lbs. Imported 1992-disc.

$2,375	$1,975	$1,675	$1,450	$1,225	$1,000	$900

MODEL 803 – various cals., includes set trigger.

$1,350	$1,175	$1,000	$875	$750	$650	$550

RIFLES: SEMI-AUTO

ZKM-611 – .17 HMR (new 2006), .22 WMR cal., 20 1/2 in. barrel, 6, 10 (C/B 1994), or 12* shot mag., black metal finish, beechwood (new 1996) or checkered walnut stock and forend, grooved receiver, 6.2 lbs.

$800	$725	$650	$575	$500	$425	$350

Add 20% for walnut stock (disc. 1999).

The prototype of this model was designed by Mr. Kautsky in 1962. Development was completed in early 1990, and production began in 1992.

MODEL 581 – .22 LR cal., select walnut stock, adj. sights, 5 shot mag. Mfg. 1959-disc.

$600	$540	$495	$440	$395	$350	$295

RIFLES: SINGLE SHOT

ZK-05 – various cals., upgraded variation of the ZK-99, set trigger, many other design improvements.

$575	$500	$430	$390	$315	$260	$200

ZK 99 – various cals., break open action with top lever, quarter rib on barrel, checkered walnut stock with cheekpiece and Schnabel forearm, includes swivels and slings, 5 3/4 lbs. Imported 2000-2003.

$875	$765	$655	$595	$480	$395	$305

MODEL ZKB-110 – .22 Hornet, .222 Rem., 5.6x52R, 5.6x50R Mag., 6.5x57R (disc. 1999), 7x57R (disc. 1999), or 8x57JRS (disc. 1999) cal., single shot break open rifle/shotgun, top lever opening, 23.6 in. barrel, uncheckered (Standard Model) or checkered walnut stock with Bavarian cheekpiece and forearm (Lux Model), includes sling swivels, 6 lbs. Imported 1998-2003.

$225	$195	$170	$155	$125	$100	$80

Add $77 for ZKB-110 Lux Model.
Add $205 for ZKB-110 Super Lux Model (new 2000).
Add $48 for 7x57R or 8x57JRS cal. (disc. 1999).
Add $132 (standard) or $142 (Lux) for an interchangeable 12 ga. shotgun barrel.

GRADING - PPGS™	100%	98%	95%	90%	80%	70%	60%	LAST MSR

EFFECT – .30-06 cal., 23.6 in. barrel, single set trigger, light engraved blue receiver, iron sights, sling swivels, checkered walnut stock, 6 lbs.

	$1,295	$1,135	$970	$880	$710	$585	$455	

Please refer to Brno Rifles section for current mfg.

SHOTGUNS/COMBINATION GUNS: O/U

Many of the following models were imported and distributed by Euro-Imports, located in El Cajon, CA.

ZH-300 SHOTGUN – 12 ga. only, double triggers with rear trigger doubling as single trigger, 27 1/2 in. barrels, 7 lbs. Imported 1986-92.

	$530	$465	$395	$360	$290	$240	$185	*$599*

This model was available in skeet, trap, or field configuration.

ZH-301 FIELD SHOTGUN – 12 or 16 ga. field, 27 1/2 in. barrels, optional Monte Carlo stock (disc.).

	$600	$525	$450	$410	$330	$270	$210	

Add $20 for Monte Carlo stock.

ZH-302 SKEET SHOTGUN – 12 ga., skeet model, 26 in. barrels, optional Monte Carlo stock (disc.).

	$650	$570	$485	$440	$355	$290	$225	

Add $20 for Monte Carlo stock.

ZH-303 TRAP SHOTGUN – 12 ga., trap model, 30 in. barrels, optional Monte Carlo stock (disc.).

	$650	$570	$485	$440	$355	$290	$225	

Add $20 for Monte Carlo stock.

ZH-300 SERIES COMBINATION GUNS – 7x57R x 12 ga. (ZH-304), 6x52R x 12 ga. (ZH-305), 6x50R Mag. x 12 ga. (ZH-306), .22 Hornet x 12 ga. (ZH-307), 7x65R x 12 ga. (ZH-308), 8x57JRS x 12 ga. (ZH-309), 7x57R x 16 ga. (ZH-324), 7x65R x 16 ga. (ZH-328), combination rifle/shotgun, optional adj. trigger and Monte Carlo stock. Importation disc. 1994 - reintroduced 1999-2003.

	$695	$610	$520	$470	$380	$315	$245	

Add $73 for cheekpiece and set trigger.
Add $35 for adj. trigger (disc.).
Add $20 for Monte Carlo stock (disc.).

ZH 300 Series over and unders are unique in that they permit 8 different interchangeable barrels including rifle and shotgun sets, interrupter on double trigger, blued action, engraving, diamond checkered walnut.

M6 SCOUT COMBINATION GUN – See separate listing under Springfield Armory.

MODEL ZH-300 COMBO SET – Model ZH-300 style engraving and features, equipped with 8 interchangeable O/U shotgun/shotgun and rifle/shotgun barrels in various gauges and calibers. Imported 1986-1991.

	$2,950	$2,580	$2,210	$2,005	$1,620	$1,325	$1,030	*$3,500*

MODEL 500/501 SHOTGUN – 12 ga. only, 28 in. VR barrels, double or single (disc. 1999) trigger.

	$845	$740	$635	$575	$465	$380	$295	

Add $50 for single trigger (disc. 1999).

* ***Model 500 Combo Set*** – shotgun/rifle set comprised of 4 barrels including 12 ga. over barrels with choice of 5.6x52R (disc.), 7x57R, 7x65R, or 12 ga. under barrels (in either field, skeet, or trap chokings), sling swivels, set trigger on rifle/shotgun combo, chemically engraved, about 7 1/2 lbs. Imported 1987-91.

	$1,925	$1,685	$1,445	$1,310	$1,060	$865	$675	*$2,169*

This model was available in limited quantity.

MODEL 502 SERIES COMBINATION GUN – 12 ga. only, ejectors, combination shotgun/rifle available in .222 Rem., .243 Win., .30-06, .308 Win., and 4 metric cals., fixed choke, acid etched engraving, skipline checkering and cheekpiece. Imported 1986-2003.

	$1,050	$920	$785	$715	$575	$470	$365	

Add $699 for interchangeable 12 ga. shotgun barrels (new 1998).

BS-571/572 SHOTGUN/COMBINATION GUN – 12 ga. only, boxlock action with ejectors, 6x65R (disc.) or 7x65R rifle cal. only. Limited importation 1992-95.

	$825	$720	$620	$560	$455	$370	$290	*$995*

Add approx. $115 for rifle/shotgun (12 ga. only) combination (Model 572).

GRADING - PPGS™	100%	98%	95%	90%	80%	70%	60%	LAST MSR

MODEL 571 SUPER SERIES – 12 ga. field, skeet, and trap configuration as well as combination shotgun/rifle in 12 ga. x 7x57R or 7x65R cal. Importation disc. 1991.

	$800	$700	$600	$545	$440	$360	$280	*$899*

Add $70 for single trigger or trap/skeet configuration (disc.).
Add $700 for extra set of 12 ga. field barrels.
Add $1,101 for hand engraving.

* ***Model 571 Super Combo*** – 3 barrel set including 12 ga., 7x57R, and 7x65R barrels. Imported 1987-90.

	$1,925	$1,685	$1,445	$1,310	$1,060	$865	$675	*$2,169*

MODEL 801 SERIES SHOTGUN – 12 ga. only, 2 3/4 or 3 in. chambers, ejectors, SST, machine engraved receiver, checkered walnut stock and forearm, VR barrels with or without choke tubes, left-hand version in various configurations that include field, sporting, trap, and skeet available at no additional charge.

	$875	$765	$655	$595	$480	$395	$305	

Add $276 for Sporting Model with 4 interchangeable choke tubes.

Please refer to Brno Rifles section for current manufacture (Models 801.1 and 801.2).

MODEL 802 COMBINATION GUN – 12 ga., 3 in. chambers, various American and metric cals., includes set trigger, extractors, machined engraved receiver, checkered walnut stock and forearm, interchangeable barrels.

	$1,000	$875	$750	$680	$550	$450	$350	

COMBO RIFLE/SHOTGUN – .243 Win., .30-06, or .308 Win. cal. over 12 ga., 23 1/2 in. barrels, black receiver, checkered pistol grip walnut stock, extractors, sling mount on barrel, shotgun barrel fired by rear trigger, front trigger has set function for precision rifle shooting, 7 1/2 lbs.

	$1,800	$1,575	$1,350	$1,225	$990	$810	$630	

SHOTGUNS: SxS

ZP-49 – 12 ga. only, ejectors, double triggers, true sidelock, Purdey-type top bolt, cocking indicators, walnut stock, swivels. Imported 1986-91.

	$535	$460	$420	$385	$350	$320	$290	*$589*

Add $20 for engraving.

ZP-149 – 12 ga., similar to ZP-49, except has game scene engraving on sideplates, choice of English or pistol grip stock. Imported 1986-1998.

	$575	$495	$425	$350	$300	$250	$225	*$676*

Add $23 for pistol grip stock.

ZP-349 – 12 ga. only, extractors, double triggers, true sidelock, Purdey-type top bolt, cocking indicators, walnut stock with cheekpiece, beavertail forearm, swivels, 7.3 lbs. Imported 1986 only.

	$450	$390	$360	$325	$300	$270	$250	*$520*

Add $20 for engraving.

SHOTGUNS: SINGLE SHOT

ZBK 100 – 12 or 20 ga., 3 in. chamber, walnut stock and forearm. Imported 1999-2003.

	$180	$160	$140	$120	$105	$95	$85	

BRNO RIFLES

Current trade/brand name of fixed breech Brno O/U and single shot rifles, O/U shotguns, and O/U combination guns, manufactured by Zbrojovka Brno, established circa 2007, and located in Brno, Czech Republic. During 2010, the company changed its name to Zbrojovka Brno, and it remains as part of the CZUB Uhersky Brod group. Previously imported by CZ USA, located in Kansas City, KS. Please refer to Zbrojovka Brno in the Z section for model listings and MSRs/Values.

BROADSWORD GROUP

Previous parent company of A-Square rifles and ammunition, Sharps Rifle Company, and H.H. Heizer Holsters and Saddlery, located in Glenrock, WY 2013-circa 2018. Please refer to A-Square and Sharps Rifle Company sections for current information.

BROCKMAN'S RIFLES

Current custom rifle manufacturer and gunsmith established in 1986, located in Gooding, Idaho. Consumer direct sales only.

For individual model listings, please go to BlueBookOfGunValues.com/overflow.

GRADING - PPGS™	100%	98%	95%	90%	80%	70%	60%	LAST MSR

BROLIN ARMS, INC.

Previous importer of handguns (FEG mfg.), rifles (older Mauser military, see Mauser listing), shotguns (Chinese mfg.), and airguns from 1995 to 1999. Previously located in Pomona, CA, until 1999, and in La Verne, CA until 1997.

PISTOLS: SEMI-AUTO, SINGLE ACTION

LEGEND SERIES MODEL L45 - .45 ACP cal., patterned after the Colt 1911 Government Model, features include throated match 5 in. barrel, polished feed ramp, flared ejection port, beveled magwell, flat-top slide, flat mainspring housing, front strap high relief cut, aluminum lightweight extended trigger, high visibility sights, 7 shot mag., commander style hammer and checkered walnut grips, 38 oz. Mfg. 1995-1998.

$425	$365	$325	$295	$275	$250	$225	*$500*

* ***Legend Series Model L45C (Compact)*** - similar to Model L45, except has 4 in. barrel, 35 oz. Mfg. 1995-98.

$440	$380	$330	$295	$275	$250	$225	*$520*

* ***Legend Series Model L45T*** - features standard frame with compact slide, 4 in. barrel, 36 oz. Mfg. 1997-98.

$440	$380	$330	$295	$275	$250	$225	*$520*

PATRIOT SERIES MODEL P45 COMP - .45 ACP cal., patterned after the Colt 1911 Government model, one-piece match 4 in. barrel with integral dual port compensator, 7 shot mag., Millett or Novak combat sights (new 1997), polished feed ramp, flared ejection port, beveled magwell, flat-top slide, flat mainspring housing, front strap high relief cut, aluminum lightweight extended trigger, Commander style hammer, checkered walnut grips, test target provided, choice of blue or satin (frame only) finish, 38 oz. Mfg. 1996-97 only.

$585	$475	$415	$365	$325	$285	$250	*$649*

Add $70 for Novak combat sights (new 1997).
Add $20 for T-tone finish (frame only).

* ***Patriot Series Model P45C (Compact)*** - .45 ACP cal., similar to Model P45 Comp, except has 3 1/4 in. barrel with integral conical lock-up system, 34 1/2 oz. Mfg. 1996-97.

$610	$495	$425	$375	$325	$285	$250	*$689*

Add $70 for Novak combat sights.
Add $20 for T-tone finish (frame only).

* ***Patriot Series Model P45T*** - features standard frame with compact slide, 3 1/4 in. barrel, 35 1/2 oz. Mfg. 1997 only.

$620	$500	$425	$375	$325	$285	$250	*$699*

Add $60 for Novak combat sights (new 1997).
Add $10 for T-tone finish (frame only).

PRO STOCK MODEL COMPETITION PISTOL - .45 ACP cal., competition pistol featuring most state-of-the-art competitive improvements, 5 in. barrel, 8 shot mag., blue or satin (frame only) finish, signature wood grips, 40 oz. Mfg. 1996-97.

$685	$550	$475	$415	$360	$295	$260	*$779*

Add $20 for T-tone finish (frame only).

* ***Pro Comp Model Competition Pistol*** - similar to Pro Stock Model, except has 4 in. dual port compensated heavy match barrel, blue or satin (frame only) finish, 40 oz. Mfg. 1996-97.

$800	$650	$525	$435	$375	$325	$295	*$919*

Add $10 for T-tone finish (frame only).

TAC 11 - .45 ACP cal., 5 in. conical barrel w/o bushing, beavertail grip safety, 8 shot mag., T-tone or blue finish, Novak low profile combat or Tritium sights, black rubber contour grips, 37 oz. Mfg. 1997-98.

$595	$485	$425	$365	$325	$285	$250	*$670*

Add $90 for Tritium sights (disc. 1997).

* ***Tac 11 Compact*** - similar to Tac 11, except has shorter barrel. Mfg. 1998 only.

$610	$495	$435	$365	$325	$285	$250	*$690*

Add $60 for hard chrome finish.

GOLD SERIES - .45 ACP cal., 5 in. barrel w/o barrel bushing and supported chamber, IPSC configuration with many features, adj. aluminum trigger, front and rear slide serrations, stainless steel construction with choice of natural stainless or blue stainless finish. Limited mfg. 1998 only.

$715	$625	$525	$440	$385	$325	$280	*$800*

GRADING - PPGS™	100%	98%	95%	90%	80%	70%	60%	LAST MSR

PISTOLS: SEMI-AUTO, DOUBLE ACTION

The following models had limited manufacture 1998 only.

TAC SERIES SERVICE MODEL – .45 ACP cal., full sized service pistol, DA/SA, 8 shot single column mag., front and rear slide serrations, combat style trigger guard, royal or satin blue finish, low profile 3-dot sights. Mfg. 1998 only.

	$360	$315	$285	$260	$240	$220	$200	$400

Add $20 for royal blue finish.

TAC SERIES FULL SIZE MODEL – 9mm Para., .40 S&W, or .45 ACP cal., DA/SA, similar to Tac Series Service Model, except longer barrel, checkered walnut or plastic grips, 8 (.45 ACP only) or 10 shot mag. Mfg. 1998 only.

	$360	$315	$285	$260	$240	$220	$200	$400

Add $20 for royal blue finish.

TAC SERIES COMPACT MODEL – 9mm Para. or .40 S&W cal., DA/SA, shortened barrel/slide with full size frame, 10 shot mag. Mfg. 1998 only.

	$360	$315	$285	$260	$240	$220	$200	$400

Add $20 for royal blue finish.

TAC SERIES BANTAM MODEL – 9mm Para. or .40 S&W cal., super compact size, DA/SA, with concealed hammer, all steel construction, 3-dot sights. Mfg. 1998 only.

	$360	$315	$285	$260	$240	$220	$200	$399

BANTAM MODEL – 9mm Para. or .40 S&W cal., DA/SA, super compact size, concealed hammer, all steel construction, 3-dot sights, royal blue or matte finish. Limited mfg. by FEG 1999 only.

	$360	$315	$285	$260	$240	$220	$200	$399

PISTOLS: CUSTOM

Brolin Arms manufactured a small quantity of high performance M1911 based custom combat and competition pistols during 1998 only. The Formula Z Model Custom Combat Model retail price range was $1,300-$1,600, the Formula One RS Limited Class Competition Model was priced at $2,000-$2,300, and the Formula One RZ Competition Race Gun Model topped the line at $2,450- $2,750.

SHOTGUNS: SEMI-AUTO

MODEL BL-12 – 12 ga. only, 3 in. chamber, 18 1/2 (security) or 28 (field) in. VR barrel with 3 choke tubes (Beretta compatible), satin blue finish, choice of wood or synthetic stock and forearm. Mfg. 1998 only.

	$375	$325	$300	$280	$260	$240	$220	$430

MODEL SAS-12 – 12 ga. only, 2 3/4 in. chamber, 24 in. barrel with IC choke tube, 3 (standard) or 5 shot (disc. late 1998) detachable box mag., synthetic stock and forearm, gas operated. Mfg. 1998-99.

	$445	$385	$335	$300	$280	$260	$240	$499

Add $39 for extra 3 or 5 (disc.) shot mag.

SHOTGUNS: SLIDE ACTION

Brolin shotguns were manufactured in China by Hawk Industries, and were unauthorized copies of the Remington Model 870. Most of these slide action models were distributed by Interstate Arms, and it is thought that Norinco or China North Industries were connected to the manufacturer during the importation of these shotguns.

FIELD SERIES – 12 ga. only, 3 in. chamber, 24, 26, 28, or 30 in. VR barrel with mod. choke tube, steel receiver and aluminum trigger guard, choice of black synthetic or wood stock, bead sights, 5 shot mag., matte finish, 7.3 lbs. Mfg. 1997-98.

	$195	$170	$155	$140	$130	$120	$110	$240

* ***Field Combo*** – includes choice of extra 12 ga. 18 1/2 or 22 in. barrel, choice of regular or pistol grip stock. Mfg. 1997-98.

	$230	$195	$175	$155	$140	$130	$120	$270

Add approx. $25 for rifled deer barrel.

LAWMAN MODEL – 12 ga. only, 3 in. chamber, action patterned after the Rem. Model 870 (disc. 1998) or the Ithaca Model 37 (new 1999) 18 1/2 in. barrel, choice of bead, rifle (disc. 1998), or ghost ring (disc. 1998) sights, matte (disc. 1998), nickel (disc. 1997), royal blue (new 1998), satin blue (new 1998) or hard chrome finish, black synthetic or hardwood stock and forearm, 7 lbs. Mfg. in China 1997-99.

	$165	$155	$145	$135	$125	$115	$105	$189

Add $20 for nickel finish (disc. 1997).
Add $20 for hard chrome finish.
Add $20 for ghost ring sights.

GRADING - PPGS™	100%	98%	95%	90%	80%	70%	60%	LAST MSR

SLUG SPECIAL – 12 ga. only, 3 in. chamber, choice of 18 1/2 or 22 in. barrel with either rifle sights, ghost ring, or cantilevered scope mount, wood or synthetic stock, choice of fixed IC choke, 4 in. extended rifled choke, or fully rifled barrel, 5 shot mag. Mfg. 1998 only.

$230	$180	$165	$150	$140	$130	$120	*$270*

Add $10 for rifled barrel.

Add $20 for cantilevered scope mount.

SLUGMASTER – 12 ga. only, 3 in. chamber, action patterned after the Model 37 Ithaca, bottom ejection, choice of royal blue metal finish with wood stock or satin blue metal with synthetic stock, rifle sights, mfg. in China. Limited importation 1999 only.

$165	$155	$145	$135	$125	$115	$105	*$189*

TURKEY SPECIAL – 12 ga. only, 3 in. chamber, 22 in. VR barrel with extra-full extended turkey choke, choice of wood or synthetic stock. Mfg. 1998 only.

$215	$165	$155	$145	$135	$125	$115	*$250*

BRONCO

Current trademark of shotguns manufactured by Ottomanguns located in Istanbul, Turkey. No current U.S. importation.

BRONCO (PISTOLS)

Previous trademark manufactured by Echave Y Arizmendi, located in Eibar, Spain.

PISTOLS: SEMI-AUTO

MODEL 1918 POCKET AUTOMATIC – 7.65mm cal., 6 shot, 2 1/2 in. barrel, fixed sights, blue, hard rubber grips. Mfg. 1918-25.

$175	$150	$100	$80	$70	$60	$50

VEST POCKET AUTOMATIC – 6.35mm cal., small frame. Disc.

$160	$125	$110	$95	$80	$60	$40

BRONCO (LONG ARMS)

Previous trademark of rifles and shotguns imported by Firearms International Sporting Arms circa 1969-1970.

The Bronco was available in both a single shot rifle (.22 LR cal.) and .410 bore (3 in. chamber) shotgun. It featured a skeletonized aluminum stock and receiver with no forend. A forward trigger lever allowed a swing out action to pivot for loading, and the regular trigger operated a hammerless action. The Bronco also featured compact youth dimensions, crossbolt safety and adj. rear sight, and was approx. 3-3 1/2 lbs.

Average-above average condition specimens sell in the $150-$275 range - add approx. 10% more for .410 bore.

A.A. BROWN & SONS

Current long gun manufacturer established in 1938, located in Birmingham, England.

A.A. BROWN COMPANY HISTORY

Albert Arthur Brown was an action maker who founded his business in 1929 in Birmingham's gun quarter. In 1938, he was joined by sons Albert Henry and Sidney Charles, and from that time on the firm was known as A.A. Brown & Sons. Much of the work done during the Depression era was for other British makers such as E.J. Churchill. During WWII, the company was involved in defense related contract work and the Sand Street premises were bombed.

By the late 1950s, A.A. Brown & Sons were building a wide variety of guns for Cogswell & Harrison, E.J. Churchill, and Holland & Holland. During 1960, the firm moved to Westley Richards' factory complex and built Westley's sidelocks. Robin Brown, grandson of the founder and son of Sidney Charles, joined as an apprentice in 1961. He left the Westley Richards location in 1974 to establish a factory in Alvechurch, south of Birmingham, and began building best quality sidelocks.

After the deaths of his father and uncle in 2001 and 2006, Robin Brown became the sole proprietor. Much of the work remains in-house, although Robin uses London trained barrel makers and stockers for his guns.

Information appears courtesy of David Grant and Vic Venters.

SHOTGUNS: O/U, SxS, CUSTOM

A.A. Brown & Sons manufactures high quality SxS English sidelock ejector shotguns in all gauges with many options available, as well as a Beretta EELL over and under modified for the English game shooter.

For more information, including a price quotation, customer options, availability and delivery time, please contact the company directly.

GRADING - PPGS™	100%	98%	95%	90%	80%	70%	60%	LAST MSR

B.B. GAME de LUXE (THE BROWN BERETTA) – O/U, modified 687 EELL Beretta, oil-finished stock is converted to a straight hand or Prince of Wales grip, English shaped comb with leather covered recoil pad, hand checkered buttplate, or wooden buttplate, inserted tear drop points, Schnabel type forend is slimmed to a rounded splinter shape, forend and stock are recheckered by hand, trigger guard tang is added, many other options and embellishments can be added per customer specification.

Prices for this model start at £9,600. Converted customer gun begins at £3,600.
Standard wood upgrade is £2,500.

SUPREME DE LUXE – 12, 16, 20, 28 ga. or .410 bore, best gun with chopper lump barrels, lengths 25 to 30 in., sidelock ejector with standard or rounded action shape.

Prices for this model start at £55,000 including standard engraving.
28 ga. and .410 bore are built to special order, and start at £60,000. Pairing or matching sets start at £3,000 per gun.
There are many engraving choices - both in terms of the engravers and engraving styles. Individual quotations are provided per order. As a guide, standard patterns range from £6,000 to £12,000. Cases, cleaning kits, and other accessories are also available.

DAVID MCKAY BROWN (GUNMAKERS) LTD.

Current long gun manufacturer established in 1974 and located in Bothwell, Glasgow, Scotland. Available through the manufacturer directly or U.S. agents, Griffin & Howe, New York City and Bernardsville, NJ, and Wingshooting Adventures, located in Coopersville, MI.

For individual model listings, please go to BlueBookOfGunValues.com/overflow.

ED BROWN CUSTOM, INC.

Please refer to Ed Brown Custom, Inc. located in the E section.

ED BROWN PRODUCTS, INC.

Please refer to Ed Brown Products, Inc. located in the E section.

BROWN PRECISION, INC.

Current manufacturer established in 1968, located in Cameron, TX since 2020. Previously located in Los Molinos, CA until 2019. Previously manufactured in San Jose, CA. Consumer direct sales.

Brown Precision Inc. manufactures rifles primarily using Remington or Winchester actions and restocks them using a combination of Kevlar, fiberglass, and graphite (wrinkle finish) to save weight. Stock colors are green, brown, grey, black, camo brown, camo green, or camo grey. Chet Brown pioneered the concept of the fiberglass rifle stock in 1965. He started blueprinting actions and using stainless steel match grade barrels on hunting rifles in 1968, and became the first custom gunmaker to use high tech weather-proof metal finishes on hunting rifles during 1977.

PISTOLS: BOLT ACTION

CUSTOM XP-100 HIGH COUNTRY – various cals., includes highly tuned XP-100 single shot action with Shilen stainless match grade barrel, electroless nickel or Teflon finish, fiberglass stock. Limited mfg. 1993-96.

$1,550	$1,375	$1,150	$950	$775	$650	$525	*$1,690*

RIFLES: BOLT ACTION

Brown Precision will also stock a rifle from a customer supplied action. This process includes a Brown Precision stock, custom glass bedding with totally free floated barrel, recoil pad, custom length of pull, stock finish, sling swivel studs, etc. All other hardware to be supplied by the customer. Prices begin at $995.

BLASER BOLT ACTION RIFLE – standard Camex Blaser cals. and action, fiberglass stock and nickel plated barrel. Disc. 1989.

$1,395	$1,220	$1,045	$950	$765	$630	$490	*$1,395*

BROWN PRECISION WINCHESTER 70 – .270 Win. or .30-06 cal., 22 in. featherweight barrel, camo stock in four colors with black recoil pad, 6 1/4 lbs. Mfg. 1989-1992.

$650	$570	$485	$440	$355	$290	$225	*$750*

Add $20 for 7mm Rem. Mag. (24 in. sporter barrel).

CUSTOM HIGH COUNTRY – includes fully blueprinted Remington 700, Remington Model 7, Ruger 77 (disc.), Win. Model 70 push feed (disc.), or Winchester Model 70 action, Match Grade stainless steel barrel, custom chamber, recessed target crown, custom glass bedded Brown Precison fiberglass/Kevlar

GRADING - PPGS™	100%	98%	95%	90%	80%	70%	60%	LAST MSR

(disc.) stock, with choice of recoil pad, length of pull, and color, electroless nickel (disc.) or Teflon metal finish (choice of color), finely tuned trigger. New 1975.

MSR $5,995	$5,625	$4,950	$4,300	$3,650	$3,125	$2,600	$1,950	

Add $159 for cryogenic barrel treatment.
Add $800 for take down action (new 2006, includes torque wrench Talley scope mounts, and custom travel case).
Subtract $1,300 if action is supplied by customer.
Subtract approx. $800 for Ruger M77 action and steel barrel (disc. 2012).

Beginning 2006, this model's standard features include a choice of a fully blueprinted Winchester Model 70 (controlled round feeding), Rem. Model 700, or Rem. Model 7 action, and a match grade stainless steel barrel.

* ***Custom High Country ES II*** – similar to Custom High Country, except includes cryogenic barrel treatment and speed lock firing pin spring, includes 60 rounds of custom ammo. Disc. 2003.

	$3,400	$2,975	$2,550	$2,310	$1,870	$1,530	$1,190	*$3,995*

Add $100 for Rem. 700 BDL or Model 7 action.
Add $300 for stainless steel Rem. 700 BDL action.
Add $500 for Win. Model 70 Classic action with controlled round feeding.
Add $300 for left-hand action.
Subtract $700 if action is supplied by customer.

HIGH COUNTRY YOUTH RIFLE – various cals., choice of Rem. Model 7 or 700 factory barreled action, fiberglass stock. Mfg. 1993-2000.

	$1,250	$1,095	$935	$850	$685	$560	$435	*$1,435*

Add $145 for lengthening stock.

LAW ENFORCEMENT SELECTIVE TARGET – .308 Win. cal., Model 700 Varmint action with 20, 22, or 24 in. factory barrel, OD Green camouflage treatment. Disc. 1992.

	$995	$870	$745	$675	$545	$450	$350	*$1,086*

This model could have been special ordered with similar options from the Custom High Country Model, with the exception of left-hand action.

MODEL 7 SUPER LIGHT – .223 Rem., .243 Win., 6mm Rem., 7mm-08 Rem., or .308 Win. cal., Model 7 action, 18 in. factory barrel, no sights, 5 lbs. 4 oz. Disc. 1992.

	$995	$870	$745	$675	$545	$450	$350	*$1,059*

This model could have been special ordered with similar options from the Custom High Country Model, with the exception of left-hand action.

PRO HUNTER – available in over 25 cals., Model 700 ADL action is standard, match grade stainless steel barrel, custom chamber, recessed target crown, glass bedded Brown Precision Alaskan style fiberglass stock, Teflon metal finish (choice of color), 8x40 Magnum base screws, standard express sights. New 1988.

MSR $6,495	$5,675	$4,775	$3,900	$3,375	$2,700	$2,250	$2,000	

Subtract $1,300 if action is supplied by customer.

In late 1991, improvements were made including decelerator recoil pad, barrel band swivel, and speed lock firing pin spring.

* ***Pro Hunter Elite*** – various cals., custom tuned Winchester Model 70 Super Grade action with controlled feed claw extractor, match grade stainless steel barrel, custom chamber, recessed target crown, glass bedded Brown Precision Alaskan style fiberglass stock, Teflon metal finish (choice of color), 8x40 Magnum base screws, Talley custom scope mounts, banded express sights, barrel band swivel, Speedlock firing pin spring, finely tuned trigger. New 1993.

MSR $7,795	$7,050	$6,000	$4,950	$3,950	$3,375	$2,900	$2,450	

Add $899 for drop box trigger guard (allows additional round in mag.).
Subtract $1,300 if action is supplied by customer.
Add $600 for take down action (includes torque wrench and custom travel case).

PRO/LIGHT VARMINTER – various cals., includes fully blueprinted Rem. 700 action or custom tuned Rem. Model 700 ADL action (disc.), Shilen (disc.) or select match grade stainless steel barrel, custom chamber, recessed target crown, glass bedded Brown Precision fiberglass stock. New 1993, Light Varminter new 2006.

MSR $5,195	$4,675	$4,200	$3,550	$2,925	$2,550	$2,050	$1,700	

Subtract $1,300 if action is supplied by customer.
Add $600 for optional Rem. Model 40-XB action with target trigger (disc. 2012).

GRADING - PPGS™	100%	98%	95%	90%	80%	70%	60%	LAST MSR

SUPER BOLT RIMFIRE – .22 LR or .22 WMR cal., modified Ruger 77/22 action, 20 in. heavy Shilen match grade steel or stainless steel barrel, extended mag. release, choice of lightweight fiberglass or Kevlar stock, blue or silver metal finish, 6 1/2 lbs. Disc. 2005.

	$1,600	$1,400	$1,200	$1,090	$880	$720	$560	*$1,895*

Add $100 for stainless steel barrel.
Add $200 for stainless steel action & barrel.

TACTICAL ELITE – various cals. and custom features, includes fully blueprinted Rem. 700 action, Shilen (disc.) select match grade stainless steel barrel, custom chamber, recessed target crown, glass bedded Brown Precision Tactical Elite style stock, Teflon metal finish (choice of color), customized per individual order. New 1997.

MSR $6,595	$5,975	$5,400	$4,475	$3,750	$3,200	$2,700	$2,050	

Subtract $1,300 if action is supplied by customer.
Add $675 for 3 way adj. buttplate (disc.).

THE UNIT – .270 Win., .300 Win. Mag., .300 Wby. Mag., .338 Win. Mag., 7mm-08 Rem., 7mm Rem. Mag., or 7mm STW cal., Rem. 700 BDL or Win. Mod. 70 controlled feed action, various lengths match grade stainless steel barrel with cryogenic treatment, Teflon or electroless nickel finish, Brown Precision Kevlar or graphite reinforced fiberglass stock, includes 60 rounds of custom ammo. Limited mfg. 2001 only.

	$3,225	$2,820	$2,420	$2,195	$1,775	$1,450	$1,130	*$3,795*

Add $500 for Win. Model 70 Super Grade action with controlled round feeding.
Add $200 for left-hand action.
Subtract $600 if action was supplied by customer.

RIFLES: SEMI-AUTO

CUSTOM TEAM CHALLENGER – .22 LR cal., modified Ruger 10/22 action, 20 in. heavy Shilen match grade steel or stainless steel barrel, extended mag. release, choice of lightweight fiberglass or Kevlar stock, blue or silver metal finish, disc. 2005.

	$1,350	$1,075	$825	$675	$550	$450	$400	*$1,595*

Add $100 for stainless steel barrel.
Add $200 for stainless steel barrel & action.

BROWNELLS, INC.

Current firearms trademark (including a private label line of Retro AR-15 style rifles), accessories, and gunsmithing distributor established circa 1939 in Montezuma, IA. In mid-2016, Brownells expanded operations, including a retail store in Grinnell, IA.

For individual model listings, please go to BlueBookOfGunValues.com/overflow.

BROWNING

Current manufacturer with U.S. headquarters located in Morgan, UT. Browning guns originally were manufactured in Ogden, UT, circa 1880. Browning firearms are manufactured by Fabrique Nationale in Herstal and Liège, Belgium. Beginning 1976, Browning also contracted with Miroku of Japan and A.T.I. in Salt Lake City, UT to manufacture both long arms and handguns. In 1992, Browning (including F.N.) was acquired by GIAT of France. During late 1997, the French government received $82 million for the sale of F.N. Herstal from the Walloon business region surrounding Fabrique Nationale in Belgium.

The category names within the Browning section have been arranged in an alphabetical format: - PISTOLS (& variations), RIFLES (& variations), SHOTGUNS (& variations), SPECIAL EDITIONS, COMMEMORATIVES & LIMITED MFG., and SHOT SHOW SPECIALS.

The author would like to express his sincere thanks to the Browning Collectors Association for continuing to make their important contributions to the Browning section.

Beginning in 2004, Browning also offered various models/variations that were available only at the annual SHOT SHOW. For complete model descriptions of all SHOT Show Specials, please go to BlueBookOfGunValues.com/overflow.

BROWNING HISTORY

The Browning firm, first known as J.M. Browning & Bro., was established in Ogden, Utah about 1880. Later known as Browning Brothers and Browning Arms Company (BAC), the firm actually manufactured only one gun - the Model 1878 Single Shot which was John M.'s first patent. Winchester bought the production and distribution rights to this gun in 1883, bringing it out as the Winchester M1885. From that time until 1900, Mr. Browning sold Winchester the exclusive rights to 31 rifles and 13 shotguns, of

which Winchester produced only 7 rifles (M1885SS: the lever actions M1886, 1892, 1894 and 1895: and the slide action .22s M1890 and 1906) and 3 shotguns (M1887, M1893 and M1897). The other models were bought from Browning simply to keep them out of the hands of other arms makers.

John M. Browning, perhaps the greatest firearms inventor the world has ever known, was directly responsible for an estimated 80 separate firearms that evolved from his 128 patents. During his most prolific period from 1894 to 1910, Browning sold the rights to his rifles, semi-auto pistols, shotguns and machine guns to Winchester, Remington, Colt and Stevens in this country and to Fabrique Nationale (Belgium) for sale outside the U.S. Every Colt and F.N. semi-auto pistol is based on a Browning patent. In 1902, Browning broke off relations with Winchester when the company refused to negotiate a royalty arrangement for his new semi-auto shotgun (A-5). Browning took the prototype to F.N. Since 1902, F.N. has produced numerous automatic pistols, 3 rifles and 2 shotguns designed by John M. Browning and is still a major producer of arms sold by Browning in the U.S. and by F.N. distributors worldwide.

Our American military was armed for many years with Browning designed weaponry, not the least of which is the venerable "Old Slabside" 1911 Govt. Model .45 ACP. Today, the firm that bears the Browning name still stands at the forefront with the other makers of fine sporting firearms.

BROWNING FACTS

Note: Between 1966-1971 Browning used a salt-curing process on some of its raw wood to speed the drying time needed to produce its walnut stock blanks. Unfortunately, the salt would be released from the wood and oxidize (rust) the metal surface(s) after a period of time. Although not all Browning guns were salty, those affected guns, especially bolt action rifles in all grades, some BARs, Superposed shotguns, and T-bolt models should be examined carefully around where the metal contacts with the wood for signs of freckling and rust. Discount values on guns which show tell-tale characteristics of salt corrosion range from 25%-40%, depending on how severe the rust damage is. Check all screws which have direct contact with wood and the wood under the buttplate as well. Original Superposed owners of salt wood guns who still have their original owner's warranty card are still eligible for Browning factory refurbishing of affected parts only without charge. Otherwise, Browning has a standardized repair charge for each model.

Since the inception and standardization of steel shot for hunting purposes, the desirability factor of shotguns has changed considerably. On newer manufacture, most shooters/buyers now expect choke tubes, and shotguns without choke tubes must be discounted somewhat. Browning does not recommend using steel shot in any Superposed (B-25) or older Belgian Auto-5 barrels.

Browning's Miroku plant in Japan, in addition to making models specifically for the Browning Arms Company (BAC) in the U.S., also makes a wide variety of makes and models specifically for European sale. These models are normally not imported into the U.S., and because of this, they are not included in this section. You may be able to find more information on the current European models by visiting Browning's international website: browningint.com.

BROWNING VALUES INFORMATION

Editor's Note: It is important to note the differences in values of Browning firearms manufactured in Belgium by F.N. and those made recently in Japan by Miroku. We feel that these values are somewhat higher because of collector interest in Belgian guns, and not as the result of any inferiority of the quality of Browning guns made anywhere else.

AS A FINAL NOTE: Most post-war Brownings are collectible only if in 95% or better condition as most models have relatively high mfg. and are not that old. Condition under 95% is normally very shootable, but not as collectible and values for 95% or less condition could be lower than shown in some areas.

All add-ons or deductions on Browning's currently manufactured models reflect retail pricing without any discounting. On higher grade Browning firearms that are engraved, signed specimens by FN's master engravers Funken, J. Baerten, Vrancken, and Watrin will command premiums over the values listed.

BROWNING SERIALIZATION

In addition to the Belgian Browning serialization listed in the back of this text, the following codes will determine the year and origin of those guns made from 1975 to date. The 2 letters in the middle of the serial number are the code designations for year of manufacture. They represent the following: RV - 1975, RT - 1976, RR - 1977, RP - 1978, RN - 1979, PM - 1980, PZ - 1981, PY - 1982, PX - 1983, PW - 1984, PV - 1985, PT -1986, PR - 1987, PP - 1988, PN - 1989, NM - 1990, NZ - 1991, NY - 1992, NX - 1993, NW - 1994, NV - 1995, NT - 1996, NR - 1997, NP - 1998, NN - 1999, MM - 2000, MZ - 2001, MY - 2002, MX - 2003, MW - 2004, MV - 2005, MU - 2006, MT - 2007, MS - 2008, MN - 2009, ZM - 2010, ZZ - 2011, ZY-2012, ZX-2013, ZW-2014, ZV-2015, ZT-2016, ZR-2017, ZP-2018, ZN-2019, ZM-2020, YZ-2021, YY-2022.

GRADING - PPGS™	100%	98%	95%	90%	80%	70%	60%	LAST MSR

Since most recently manufactured Browning's use a 3-digit model identification code with the two-letter year code in the serial number (appearing before the year code on European and U.S. mfg. guns, and after the year code on Japanese mfg.) the configuration of a model can also be determined. For example, S/N 611RP2785 would be a Model B-2000 made in 1978 with 2785 being the shotgun's number. S/N 01001NY873 would be the first production example of a Citori Grade III 28 gauge Lightning Model shotgun manufactured in 1992. Refer to Browning Serialization in the back of this text of additional information on Browning model codes.

BROWNING CUSTOM SHOP

Browning's Custom Shop in Herstal, Belgium, continues to make a wide variety of firearms, a number of which have limited importation into the U.S. Current Custom Shop Superposed prices and model information have been provided in the Superposed section. For more information on the Browning Custom Shop's additional offerings, please look under the various category names for availability and current pricing. Please refer to Browning's website at browning.com for more information on the wide variety of firearms available from the Browning Custom Shop in Belgium, or contact Browning directly.

PISTOLS: SEMI-AUTO, CENTERFIRE, F.N. PRODUCTION UNLESS OTHERWISE NOTED

In addition to the models listed below, Browning has also released SHOT Show specials on some models that were available by dealers ordering them at the SHOT Show only. Complete descriptions for these models can be found under SHOT SHOW SPECIALS - PISTOLS at BlueBookOfGunValues.com/overflow.

MODEL 1899-FN STANDARD (PRODUCTION MODEL) – 7.65mm cal., first Belgian Browning, 4 in. barrel, similar to later M-1900 but w/o safety markings or lanyard ring, almost 15,000 mfg. 1899-1901.

$3,900 $3,250 $2,000 $1,750 $1,000 $600 $550

Add 15% for guns manufactured in 1899 (ser. nos. 1-3900, without "A" prefix).
Add 30% for factory nickel finish (nickel finish with blue trigger and blue safety lever) - if 95% condition or better.
Add $2,200 for factory Model 1899 presentation case with accessories including wooden screwdriver.
Add $1,200 for factory Model 1899 presentation case without wood-handled screwdriver.

MODEL 1899-FN LARGE (MILITARY TRIALS MODEL) – 7.65mm cal., 4 3/4 in. barrel, similar to Standard M1899, except has oversized slide, frame, and magazine. Frame lacks reinforced sides. Only 7 made for military trials and evaluations in Belgium, U.K., Imperial Russia, Denmark, and others. Pistols are internally numbered (1-7), wooden or hard rubber grips. Made as FN tool room prototpyes, these pistols exhibit exceedingly fine workmanship and tolerances. This is the rarest FN Browning model. Mfg. 1899-1900.

$25,000 $20,000 $15,000 $10,000 $7,500 $6,500 $5,500

Values assume correct magazine and intact original grips.

This model was extensively copied in Asia resulting in thousands being dispersed worldwide. These copies display various levels of workmanship, usually valued in the $300-$650 range.

MODEL 1900-FN - 7.65mm cal., 4 in. barrel, standard safety markings are in French: Feu and Sur. 724,500 mfg. 1900-1914.

$1,800 $1,500 $1,000 $750 $600 $500 $350

Add 75% for factory nickel finish (nickel finish with blue trigger and safety lever) - if 95% condition or better.
Add $1,250 for factory Model 1900 presentation case with accessories.
Add $3,000 for Imperial Russian contract (crossed rifles marking on blue or nickel guns).
Add $200 for Imperial German contracts with German safety markings (Feuer & Sicher).
Add $250 minimum for special contract or retailer markings.

MODEL 1903-FN – 9mm Browning Long cal., 5 in. barrel. 58,400 mfg. 1903-1927.

$3,500 $2,950 $2,500 $2,000 $1,500 $1,000 $750

Add 50% if slotted to accept shoulder stock - beware of fakes.
Add $200 minimum for special contract or retailers markings, except Swedish acceptance markings.
Add $2,000 for Paraguayan, Salvadorian, or Imperial Russian contracts with factory contract markings.
Subtract 50% for .380 conversions.

This variation was also manufactured with a detachable shoulder stock. This accessory is rare and can add $2,500 (shoulder stock w/o extended magazine) or $2,500-$3,500 (shoulder stock with extended magazine and cleaning rod) to the values listed.

GRADING - PPGS™	100%	98%	95%	90%	80%	70%	60%	LAST MSR

MODEL 1905-FN (VEST POCKET) – 6.35mm cal. (.25 ACP), 6 shot mag. dubbed "Vest Pocket" model, 2 in. barrel, manufactured by Fabrique Nationale, Herstal, Belgium. 1,086,133, mfg. 1906 to circa 1949.

* ***Model 1905-FN First Variation*** – no slide lock/safety lever.

	$650	$525	$375	$325	$275	$225	$175	

Add 50% for factory nickel finish (nickel finish with blue trigger and blue safety lever) - if 95% condition or better.
Add $900 for factory presentation case.
Add $300 for original factory box with instructions.
Add $3,000 for Imperial Russian contract (crossed rifles marking on blue or nickel guns).
Add $250 minumum for special contract or retailer markings.

* ***Model 1905-FN Second Variation*** – post 1908, with slide lock/safety lever.

	$600	$475	$325	$275	$225	$175	$125	

Add 50% for factory nickel finish (nickel finish with blue trigger and blue safety lever) - if 95% condition or better.
Add $900 for factory presentation case.
Add $300 for original factory box with instructions.
Add $3,000 for Imperial Russian contract (crossed rifles marking on blue or nickel guns).
Add $250 minimum for special contract or retailers markings.

MODEL 1907 HUSQVARNA MFG. – 9mm Browning Long cal., identical to FN Browning 1903, mfg. by Husqvarna in Sweden to supply the Swedish military. Mfg. started in 1917 because the FN Browning 1903 was not available from Belgium during WWI, produced 1917-1942. Most were arsenal refinished in Sweden featuring a dull blue finish over sandblasted metal. Many were imported into the U.S. and converted to .380 ACP cal. in the U.S.

	$1,000	$900	$800	$750	$650	$550	$450	

Add 50% for original early factory high polish blue finish.
Add 20% for early "Browning's Patent" slide legend.
Add 10% for "System Browning" slide legend.
Subtract 20% for .380 ACP conversion.

MODEL 1910-FN (MODEL 1955) – 7.65mm (.32 ACP) or Browning 9mm short (.380 ACP) cal., 3 7/16 in. barrel. FN manufacture. 701,266 mfg. 1912-1983.

	$800	$650	$500	$300	$250	$195	$150	

Subtract 20% for FN marked.
Add 20% if BAC marked and 7.65mm cal., or if FN marked and .380 ACP cal.
Add $200 for original factory box with instructions.
Add $100 for original pouch and instructions (1964-1968).
Add $100 minimum for special contract or retailer markings.

This model is also referred to as the Model 1910/55. BAC marked pistols were imported 1954-1968. Importation ceased after the 1968 GCA.

* ***Model 1955 Renaissance*** – Renaissance engraved model. Most often encountered with BAC slide legend, rarely encountered in the U.S. with "Fabrique Nationale" slide legend.

	$2,500	$1,995	$1,800	N/A	N/A	N/A	N/A	

Add $400 for original Browning clamshell case or $100 for original pouch and instructions (1964-1968).

MODEL 1922 OR 10/22 FN – 7.65mm (.32 ACP) or .380 ACP cal., 4 1/2 in. barrel, Model 10/22 and 1922 are the same. The Model 1910 was modified by FN technicians for sale to the Yugoslav military in 1922, includes a longer barrel, larger frame and magazine. Made primarily for police and military contracts, it was also sold in France, Holland, Greece, Germany, Turkey, and many other nations. Several hundred thousand were mfg. during the Nazi occupation of FN during 1940-44. Most common variations are wartime "WaA140" marked pistols.

	$600	$425	$375	$325	$275	$225	$200	
WaA613 marked in .32 cal.								
	$1,050	$850	$750	$650	$550	$450	$400	
WaA613 trigger guard marked in .380 ACP								
	$1,300	$1,050	$925	$800	$675	$550	$500	

Add 30% if WaA103 marked.
Add 30% if Wartime commercial Eagle N marked.
Add 25% for post liberation "A" prefix ser. no.
Add at least $100 for special prewar contract markings.
Subtract 10% for common WaA140 wartime marked pistols.

GRADING - PPGS™	100%	98%	95%	90%	80%	70%	60%	LAST MSR

FN "BABY" MODEL – 6.35mm (.25 ACP) cal., 6 shot mag., 2 in. barrel, w/o grip safety or slide lock lever, under BAC trademark from 1954-1968+ in standard blue finish, lightweight (1955-1968) solid chrome and alumnium frame, and engraved Renaissance models. Over 510,000 mfg. 1931-1983. Reintroduced during the 1990s for the European market.

* ***FN "Baby" Model: FN Marked*** – slide marked "Fabrique Nationale", blue finish standard.

	$775	$600	$475	$425	$350	$300	$225	

Add 75% for pre-war production (ser. no. 1-50140) if 95% or better.
Add $100 for original cardboard or plastic box with extras.
Add $700 for pre-war factory presentation case.
Add $150 minimum for special contract or retailers markings.

* ***FN "Baby" Model: BAC Marked*** – slide marked "Browning Arms Co.", blue finish standard.

	$700	$650	$500	$350	$250	$200	$150	

Add $50-$150 for original box and manual, or $50-$100 for original BAC pouch and manual.

* ***FN "Baby" Model: Lightweight Model*** – BAC marked, nickel or aluminum (introduced 1955) frame, with pearl grips.

	$825	$650	$525	$375	$275	$225	$200	

Add $50-$150 for original box and manual, or $50-$100 for original BAC pouch and manual.

* ***FN "Baby" Model: Renaissance Model*** – engraved, satin grey finish.

	$1,995	$1,750	$1,500	$1,200	$900	$800	$600	

Add $300 for original Clamshell case.

FN/BROWNING MODEL 10/71 – .380 ACP cal., 4 1/2 in. barrel, modified version of Model 1922 (10/22), grip safety, includes target sights and grips in addition to incorporating a magazine finger tip extension designed to comply with GCA of 1968. Sold in U.S. by BAC 1970-1974 as the "Standard .380," still mfg. by FN as Model 125.

	$725	$625	$500	$400	$375	$350	$300	

Add $50-100 for original pouch and instructions.

* ***FN/Browning Model 10/71 Renaissance Model***

	$3,250	$2,400	$1,600	$1,300	$1,150	$925	$700	

Add $50-100 for original pouch and instructions (estimated only 483 sold).

MODEL 1935 HI-POWER (HP) – 9mm Para. cal., 13 shot mag., 4 21/32 in. barrel, John M. Browning's last pistol design, mfg. 1935 to date in variations for commercial, military, and police use in over 68 countries, first introduced under BAC trademark in 1954.

Please refer to the Fabrique Nationale section of this book for pre-1954 variations (including pre-WWII, WWII, and earlier commercial models), as well as contemporary production of those variations not imported by BAC.

HI-POWER: POST-1954-2017 MFG. – 9mm Para. or .40 S&W (mfg. 1995-2010) cal., SA, similar to FN Model 1935, has BAC slide marking, 10 (C/B 1994) or 13* shot mag., 4 5/8 in. barrel, polished blue finish, checkered walnut grips, fixed sights, molded grips were introduced in 1985 (disc. in 2000), ambidextrous safety was added to all models in 1989, approx. 32 (9mm Para.) or 35 (.40 S&W) oz., mfg. by FN in Belgium, 1954-2017.

Even though Hi Power commercial production from Portugal ceased during 2017, Browning's Custom Shop continued to manufacture them in very limited quantities through 2019.

* ***Hi-Power Standard - Polished Blue Finish (1954-1988)*** – 9mm Para., includes fixed front and lateral adj. rear sight, 32 oz.

	$1,325	$1,100	$800	$500	$425	$350	$325	

Add 50% for ring hammer and internal extractor.
Add 20% for ring hammer and external extractor (post 1964-1970 mfg.).
Add 30% for thumb print feature.
Add 15% for T-prefix serial number.
Older specimens in original dark green, maroon, or red/black cardboard or plastic boxes were introduced 1954-1964 and are scarce - add $100+ in value. Black pouches (circa 1964-1984, especially with gold metal zipper) will also command a $50-$100 premium, depending on condition.

Major identifying factors of the Hi-Power are as follows: the "Thumb-Print" feature was mfg. from the beginning through 1958. Old style internal extractor was mfg. from the beginning through mid-1964, the "T" SN prefix (T-Series start visible extractor) was mfg. 1964-mid-1970s for all U.S. imports by BAC, 69C through 77C S/N prefixes were mfg. 1969-1977. Rounded type Ring Hammers with new external extractor were mfg. from 1962-1970. Spur Hammers have been mfg. 1971-present, and the "245" S/N prefix has been mfg. since mid-1977.

GRADING - PPGS™	100%	98%	95%	90%	80%	70%	60%	LAST MSR

* ***Hi-Power Standard Fixed Sights - Polished Blue Finish (1989-2017 Mfg., Assembled in Portugal)*** – 9mm Para. or .40 S&W (mfg. 1995-2010) cal., 4 5/8 in. barrel, 10 or 13 shot mag., fixed front sights, single action trigger, ambidextrous thumb safety, select walnut panel grips, polished blued finish, 32 or 35 oz. "245" prefix with 511 prefix showing up circa 2000. Disc. 2017, but final shipments were made during 2018.

$1,150 $975 $700 $495 $425 $375 $350 *$1,120*

During September of 2016,"Hi Power" was roll-marked in front of the ejection port. The last commercial Hi Powers had special ser. nos. LASTHP1701 - LASTHP1725 (17 designated the year and the last two digits 01-25 referred to the final 25 pistol mfg.)

In September of 2016, Browning changed the right side slide markings to "HI POWER/MADE IN BELGIUM/ASSEMBLED IN PORTUGAL" (three lines) with the right side "BROWNING ARMS COMPANY MORGAN, UTAH & MONTREAL P.Q.". This is the first time this pistol has been marked "HI-POWER".

* ***Hi-Power Standard with Adj. Rear Sight (1989-2017 Mfg.)*** – 9mm Para. or .40 S&W cal. (disc. 2010), similar to Hi-Power Standard blue, except has adj. rear sight. Disc. late 2017, final shipments were made during 2018.

$1,175 $1,000 $725 $550 $450 $400 $375 *$1,200*

During September of 2016,"Hi Power" was roll-marked in front of the ejection port. The last commercial Hi Powers had special ser. nos. LASTHP1701 - LASTHP1725 (17 designated the year and the last two digits 01-25 referred to the final 25 pistol mfg.)

* ***Hi-Power Standard - Polished Blue Finish 75th Anniversary Edition*** – 9mm Para. cal. only, similar to Hi-Power Standard Polished Blue Finish, except has "75 years 1935-2010" etched on the top of slide. Limited production 2011 only.

$1,150 $975 $700 $450 $400 $350 $325 *$1,030*

Add $45 for adj. rear sight.

* ***Hi-Power Mark III (1989-2017 Mfg.)*** – 9mm Para. or .40 S&W (mfg. 1994-2000, reintroduced 2003-2010) cal., 4 5/8 in. barrel, non-glare matte blue (disc. 2005) or black epoxy (new 2006) finish, 10 or 13 shot mag., ambidextrous safety, tapered dovetail rear fixed sight, single action trigger, two-piece molded grips, Mark III designation became standard in 1994, approx. 35 oz. Disc. 2017, final shipments were made during 2018.

$1,000 $850 $625 $495 $425 $375 $350 *$1,110*

During September of 2016,"Hi Power" was roll-marked in front of the ejection port.

Add 50% for black epoxy military FN model marked "Made in Belgium." (without Assembled in Portugal) with box and accessories (98%+ condition).

» ***Hi-Power Mark III 75th Anniversary Edition*** – 9mm Para. cal. only, features "75th year" logo etched on top of slide. Limited production 2011 only.

$1,000 $850 $525 $450 $400 $350 $325 *$1,030*

* ***Hi-Power Silver Chrome Finish*** – 9mm Para. or .40 S&W (new 1995) cal., entire gun finished in silver chrome. Not to be confused with stainless steel (never offered in the Hi-Power). Gold trigger w/ blued adj. sights, hammer, safety, slide stop, magazine release and with Pachmayr rubber grips. 36 (9mm Para.) or 39 (.40 S&W) oz. Assembled in Portugal and imported 1991-2000.

$1,150 $975 $700 $500 $425 $400 $375 *$718*

Add 50% for circa 1981-1985 Belgian model marked "Made in Belgium".

* ***Hi-Power Practical Model*** – 9mm Para. or .40 S&W (new 1995) cal., features blue (disc. 2005) or black epoxy slide, silver-chromed frame finish, wraparound Pachmayr rubber grips, round style serrated hammer, and choice of adj. sights (mfg. 1993-2000), 36 (9mm Para.) or 39 (.40 S&W) oz. Imported 1990-2000, reintroduced 2002-2006.

$1,150 $975 $700 $450 $425 $400 $375 *$863*

Add $45 for adj. sights (disc. 2000).

* ***Hi-Power Nickel*** – 9mm Para. cal., gold trigger with "B" medallion walnut grips (early manufactured fixed sights were found without medallions), fixed or adj. sights, bright nickel finish. Mfg. 1980-1985.

$1,850 $1,450 $900 $650 $425 $400 $375 *$525*

* ***1974 Hi-Power Nickel*** – 9mm Para. cal., comes with Nacrolac grips (fake pearl), finish not as above described nickel, appears Renaissance without engraving (satin chrome) BAC refers to it as "Nickel" finish. 100 received by BAC in 1974.

$2,250 $1,750 $1,450 N/A N/A N/A N/A

GRADING - PPGS™	100%	98%	95%	90%	80%	70%	60%	LAST MSR

* ***Hi-Power .30 Luger cal.*** – .30 Luger cal., mfg. for European sales (most are marked BAC on slide), approx. 1,500 imported late 1986-89, similar specifications as 9mm Para. model.

	$1,500	$1,250	$1,000	$550	$450	$425	$375	

This model was never cataloged for sale by BAC in the U.S. A few earlier specimens have been noted with F.N. markings and ring hammer.

* ***Hi-Power GP Competition*** – 9mm Para. cal., competition model with 6 in. barrel, detent adj. rear sight, rubber wraparound grips, front counterweight, improved barrel bushing, decreased trigger pull, either BAC or FN marked, this model was not cataloged, approx. 36 1/2 oz.

	$1,650	$1,375	$1,100	$875	$700	$600	$500	

Add 10% for black case NIB.
Subtract 30% if FN marked model.

The original GP Competition came in a black plastic case w/accessories, is BAC marked, and more desirable than later FN marked importation that came in a styrofoam box. FN model was never offered for sale by BAC in the U.S., and is not serviced by Browning.

* ***Hi-Power Tangent Rear Sight*** – 9mm Para. cal., manufactured from 1965-1978. 50-500 meter tangent sight. A total of approx. 7,000 were imported by Browning Arms Co. Early pistols are designated by "T" prefix and were mfg. 1964-69, later pistols mfg. 1972-76, had spur hammers and followed the 69C-76C ser. no. prefixes.

	$2,150	$1,850	$1,200	$950	$825	$725	$625	

Add $400 for "T" prefix.
Add $100 for original pouch and instruction manual.

* ***Hi-Power Tangent Capitan Polished Blue Finish*** – 9mm Para. cal., features 50-500 meter tangent rear sight, blue finish with walnut grips, slide is marked "Made in Belgium, Assembled in Portugal", 32 oz. Imported 1993-2000.

	$1,200	$1,075	$900	$500	$400	$350	$300	*$764*

Capitan refers to a Mark III variant featuring an adj. tangent rear sight, ring hammer, checkered walnut grips, and a blue finish.

* ***Hi-Power Tangent Rear Sight & Slotted*** – 9mm Para. cal., variation with grip strap slotted to accommodate shoulder stock. Early pistols had "T" prefixes. Later pistols had spur hammers and are in the serial range 73CXXXX-74CXXXX.

	$2,700	$2,400	$2,100	$1,500	$1,150	$875	$650	

Add $350 if with "T" prefix.
Add $100 for original pouch and instruction booklet.

This variation will command a premium; beware of fakes, however (carefully examine slot milling and look for ser. no. in 3 places).

Vektor Arms in N. Salt Lake, UT, imported this model again in limited quantities circa 2004 with both the "245" and seldom seen "511" (includes wide trigger, loaded chamber indicator and external extractor) ser. no. prefixes. These guns are not arsenal refinished or refurbished, and were sold in NIB condition, with two 13 shot mags. Original pricing was $895 for the "245" prefix, and $995 for the "511" prefix (milled slot will not accept original shoulder stock). Current price range is around $1,250-$1,350.

BCA EDITION HI-POWER – 9mm Para. cal., limited edition made specifically for the Browning Collectors Association in 1980, approx. 100 were delivered, in wood case.

	$1,750	$1,500	$1,000	N/A	N/A	N/A	N/A	

GOLD LINE HI-POWER – 9mm Para. cal., blue finish with gold line perimeter engraving.

	$7,500	$6,500	$5,000	N/A	N/A	N/A	N/A	

Check this model carefully for factory originality.

RENAISSANCE HI-POWER – 9mm Para. cal., extensive scroll engraving on grey silver slide and frame, synthetic pearl grips, gold plated trigger. Disc. approx. 1978.

Round Hammer	$4,250	$3,850	$3,200	N/A	N/A	N/A	N/A	
Spur Hammer	$3,850	$3,250	$2,800	N/A	N/A	N/A	N/A	

Add $100 for internal extractor (pre-1964 mfg.)
Add $100 for "Thumb Print."
Add $100 for original pouch and booklet.
Add $600 for older individual blue leatherette European case.
Add $300-$500 for hi-polished nickel finish, depending on condition.
Subtract $350 for Models 1975 and later as these are not all hand engraved.

Target sights do not affect the value of this model significantly.

GRADING - PPGS™	100%	98%	95%	90%	80%	70%	60%	LAST MSR

HI-POWER: CUSTOM SHOP MODELS

The Browning Custom Shop in Belgium is no longer making any custom shop Hi-Power models. Previous models included: 75th Anniversary Model (last MSR was $7,131), Renaissance "Dore" or Gold (last MSR was $7,083), Renaissance Silver/Nickel (last MSR was $6,975), L1 (last MSR was $4,858), I1 (last MSR was $7,850), and B2 (last MSR was $5,475). Beginning 2017, this Custom Shop series is now part of the John M. Browning Collection of special order guns. Last MSRs were from 2006-2007.

CASED RENAISSANCE SET – one pistol each in .25 ACP, .380 ACP (rarest cal. of the three), and 9mm Para. cal., Hi-Power Renaissance models in walnut or black vinyl case, ser. no. not related to other calibers but shipped as a set. Offered 1954-1968.

$9,600	$8,400	$6,600	N/A	N/A	N/A	N/A	

Add 30% for coin finish/high polish in early walnut case.
Add $100 for "St. Louis" slide address.
Add $150 for old style Hi-Power extractor.

All original Renaissance cased sets had 9mm Para. Hi-Powers with Ring Hammers.

CASED GRADE I (BLUE) SET – one pistol each in .25 ACP, .380 ACP, and 9mm Para. cal., Hi-Power Grade I Models in walnut or black vinyl case, ser. no. not related to other calibers, but shipped as a set.

$3,650	$3,150	$2,250	N/A	N/A	N/A	N/A	

Add $100 for walnut presentation case.
Add $100 for thumbprint.
Add $100 for "St. Louis" slide address.
Add $100 for old style Hi-Power extractor.

All original Grade I blue cased sets had 9mm Para. Hi-Powers with Ring Hammers sold through 1968.

CENTENNIAL MODEL HI-POWER – similar to fixed sight Hi-Power, chrome plated with inscription "Browning Centennial/1878-1978", engraved on side, checkered walnut grips with "B" in circle, cased, 3,500 mfg. in 1978. Original issue price was $495.

$2,350	$1,600	$1,100	N/A	N/A	N/A	N/A	

CENTENAIRRE MODEL HI-POWER 1 OF 100 – 9mm Para. cal., unique pattern chemically etched, signed by the engraver, checkered walnut grips with border. 100 mfg. during 1989, 61 were sold in U.S., the others in Europe.

$7,500	$6,250	$5,000	N/A	N/A	N/A	N/A	

LOUIS XVI MODEL – 9mm Para., chemically etched throughout in leaf scroll patterns, satin finish, checkered grips, walnut case. Disc. 1984.

$2,500	$1,950	$1,400	N/A	N/A	N/A	N/A	

CLASSIC HI-POWER – 9mm Para. cal., less than 2,500 manufactured. Features multiple engraved scenes, and a special silver grey finish, presentation grips, cased. Mfg. 1984-86.

$2,600	$2,100	$1,500	N/A	N/A	N/A	N/A	*$1,000*

* ***Gold Classic Hi-Power*** – engraved, 5 gold inlays, select walnut grips are both checkered and carved. Approx. 500 mfg. 1984-1986.

$4,800	$4,025	$3,100	N/A	N/A	N/A	N/A	*$2,000*

125th ANNIVERSARY HI-POWER – 9mm Para. cal., silver nitride finish with scroll engraving, gold enhanced 125th Browning Anniversary logo with image of John M. Browning in gold on slide, 10 shot mag., fixed sights, smooth oil finished walnut grips. 125 mfg. 2003-2004 only.

$2,600	$2,125	$1,600	N/A	N/A	N/A	N/A	*$1,516*

D-DAY COMMEMORATIVE (1 of 150) – 9mm Para. cal., uncheckered walnut grips, blued receiver with gold plated adornment, packaged in hard plastic case with accompanying leather pouch and D-Day patch, engraved with gold to commemorate D-Day landing at Normandy June 6, 1944, ser. no. range 245DD00001 - 245DD00150. Mfg. in Belgium in 1994.

W/Box and Accessories	$2,600	N/A	N/A	N/A	N/A	N/A	N/A	

BROWNING DOUBLE ACTION – this model was first listed in the Browning catalog in 1985 but was never imported commercially. The advertised 1985 retail price was $494.

Please refer to BDA Model listing.

BDM/BPM/BRM SINGLE/DOUBLE ACTION – 9mm Para. cal., double mode design featuring slide selector allowing choice between pistol (true double action operation) or revolver mode (full hammer decocking after each shot), available in double mode, single mode (BPM-D decocker, mfg. 1997), or double action only (BRM-DAO, mfg. 1997), dual purpose decocking lever/safety, 4.73 in. barrel, 10 (C/B 1994) or 15* shot mag., matte blue finish, black molded wraparound grips, unique breechblock allows visible cartridge inspection, adj. rear sight, 31 oz. Mfg. in U.S. 1991-1997.

$600	$450	$400	$350	$300	$280	$260	*$551*

This model features hammer block and firing pin block safeties.

GRADING - PPGS™	100%	98%	95%	90%	80%	70%	60%	LAST MSR

* ***BDM Practical*** – similar to Standard BDM, except has matte blue slide and silver chrome frame. Mfg. 1997-98.

	$600	$450	$400	$350	$300	$280	$260	*$571*

* ***BDM Silver Chrome*** – similar to Standard BDM, except has silver chrome finish. Only 119 mfg. in 1997 only.

	$650	$500	$400	$350	$300	$280	$260	*$571*

FN DA/DAO – 9mm Para. cal., choice of double action or double action only, 4 5/8 in. barrel, molded rubber grips, 10 shot mag., 31 oz., small quantities of both versions were imported and sold by FN Manufacturing in SC and PW Arms in Redmond, WA. during the 1990s.

	$650	$600	$495	$400	$350	$325	$295	*$613*

* ***FN DAc/DAOc Compact*** – 9mm Para. cal., compact variation of the FN DA/DAO, 4 in. barrel, molded rubber grips, 10 shot mag., 28 oz. Mfg. by FN.

	$795	$700	$600	$500	$400	$350	$325	

PRO-9/PRO-40 – 9mm Para. or .40 S&W cal., DA/SA, 4 in. barrel, 10, 14 (.40 S&W cal. only), or 16 (9mm Para. cal. only) shot mag., ambidextrous decocking and safety, black polymer frame with satin stainless steel slide, under barrel accessory rail, interchangeable backstrap inserts, fixed sights only, 30 (9mm Para.) or 33 oz. Mfg. in the U.S. by FNH USA 2003-2006.

	$550	$450	$375	$340	$315	$295	$260	*$641*

Please refer to FNH USA handgun listing for current manufacture.

BDA MODEL – 9mm Para. (9 shot, 2,740 mfg.), .38 Super (752 mfg.), or .45 ACP (7 shot) cal., mfg. from 1977-80 by Sig-Sauer of W. Germany (same as Sig-Sauer 220).

9mm Para.	$910	$675	$560	$450	$375	$300	$250	
.38 Super	$1,175	$950	$700	$600	$525	$450	$375	
.45 ACP	$950	$700	$600	$500	$375	$300	$250	

Add $50 for box.

BDA-380 – .380 ACP cal., blowback operation, DA/SA, 3.8 in. barrel, 10 (C/B 1994) or 13 shot mag., fixed sights, smooth walnut grips, ambi slide mounted safety, 23 oz. Introduced 1977 - all production was by Beretta. Disc. 1997.

Blue finish	$750	$575	$475	$395	$325	$275	$225	*$564*
Nickel finish	$900	$650	$525	$450	$350	$295	$250	*$607*

BLACK LABEL 1911-380 – .380 ACP cal., 4 1/4 in. barrel, 8 shot mag., composite frame with blackened stainless steel slide, bobbed hammer, skeletonized trigger, fixed combat sights, checkered composite grips, extended ambidextrous thumb safety, extended slide release, beavertail grip safety, ABS carry case included, matte black finish, 17 1/2 oz. Mfg. in USA, new 2015.

MSR $710	$600	$525	$450	$410	$335	$300	$275	

* ***Black Label 1911-380 Compact*** – .380 ACP cal., locked breech action, composite frame with blackened stainless steel slide, 3 5/8 in. barrel, target crown, 8 shot mag., skeletonized hammer, skeletonized trigger, fixed combat sights, checkered composite grips, beavertail grip safety, extended ambidextrous thumb safety, extended slide release, includes ABS carry case, matte black finish, 16 oz. New 2017.

MSR $710	$600	$525	$450	$410	$335	$300	$275	

BLACK LABEL 1911-380 PRO – .380 ACP cal., locked-breech action, composite frame, 4 1/4 in. barrel, target crown, 8 shot mag., blackened stainless steel slide, skeletonized hammer, steel 3-dot combat sights or night sights dovetailed into slide, G10 composite grips, extended ambidextrous manual thumb safety, beavertail grip safety, extended slide release, includes ABS case, matte black finish, 17 1/2 oz. Mfg. 2016-2020.

	$675	$575	$500	$415	$375	$325	$295	*$800*

Add $30 for Picatinny rail.
Add $80 for night sights.

* ***Black Label 1911-380 Pro Stainless*** – .380 ACP cal., locked-breech action, composite frame, 4 1/4 in. barrel, target crown, 8 shot mag., stainless steel slide, skeletonized hammer, SAT, steel 3-dot combat sights or night sights dovetailed into slide, black/white G10 composite grips, extended ambidextrous manual thumb safety, beavertail grip safety, extended slide release, with or without accessory rail on dust cover, includes ABS case, satin silver finish, 17 1/2 oz. Mfg. 2018-2020.

	$675	$575	$500	$415	$375	$325	$295	*$800*

Add $30 for accessory rail.
Add $80-$100 for night sights.

GRADING - PPGS™	100%	98%	95%	90%	80%	70%	60%	LAST MSR

BLACK LABEL 1911-380 PRO COMPACT – .380 ACP cal., locked-breech action, composite frame, 3 5/8 in. barrel, target crown, 8 shot mag., blackened stainless steel slide, skeletonized hammer, steel 3-dot combat sights or night sights dovetailed into slide, G10 composite grips, with or w/o lower Picatinny rail, extended ambidextrous manual thumb safety, beavertail grip safety, extended slide release, includes ABS case, matte black finish, 16 oz. Mfg. 2017-2020.

	100%	98%	95%	90%	80%	70%	60%	LAST MSR
	$650	$550	$475	$415	$375	$325	$295	*$800*

Add $30 for lower Picatinny rail.
Add $80-$110 for night sights.

* ***Black Label 1911-380 Pro Stainless Compact*** – .380 ACP cal., locked-breech action, composite frame, 3 5/8 in. barrel, target crown, 8 shot mag., stainless steel slide, skeletonized hammer, SAT, steel 3-dot combat sights or night sights dovetailed into slide, black/white G10 composite grips, extended ambidextrous manual thumb safety, beavertail grip safety, extended slide release, with or w/o accessory rail on dust cover, includes ABS case, satin silver finish, 16 oz. Mfg. 2018-2020.

	100%	98%	95%	90%	80%	70%	60%	LAST MSR
	$650	$550	$475	$415	$375	$325	$295	*$800*

Add $30 for lower Picatinny rail.
Add $80-$100 for night sights.

BLACK LABEL 1911-380 MEDALLION PRO – .380 ACP cal., composite frame, 4 1/4 in. barrel, target crown, 8 shot mag., blackened stainless steel finish with silver brush polished flats on slide, skeletonized hammer, single action trigger, steel 3-dot combat sights or night sights dovetailed into slide, intricately checkered rosewood grips with gold Buckmark, extended ambidextrous manual thumb safety, beavertail grip safety, extended slide release, includes two mags. and ABS carry case, matte black finish, 17 1/2 oz. New 2017.

	100%	98%	95%	90%	80%	70%	60%
MSR $840	$720	$630	$540	$490	$395	$325	$295

Add $80 for night sights.

* ***Black Label 1911-380 Medallion Pro Compact*** – .380 ACP cal., composite frame, 3 5/8 in. barrel, target crown, 8 shot mag., blackened stainless steel finish with silver brush polished flats on slide, skeletonized hammer, single action trigger, steel 3-dot combat sights or night sights dovetailed into slide, intricately checkered rosewood grips with gold Buckmark, extended ambidextrous manual thumb safety, beavertail grip safety, extended slide release, includes two mags. and ABS carry case, matte black finish, 16 oz. New 2017.

	100%	98%	95%	90%	80%	70%	60%
MSR $840	$720	$630	$540	$490	$395	$325	$295

Add $80 for night sights.

1911-380 HIGH GRADE/HIGH GRADE COMPACT – .380 ACP cal., full size or compact composite frame with 7075 aluminum sub-frame and slide rails, 3 5/8 (compact) or 4 1/4 (full size) in. barrel, two 8 shot mags., stainless steel slide with extensive engraving on the slide flats, steel 3-dot sights, black imitation pearl grips with gold-colored metal Buckmark, includes pistol rug, 18 oz. New 2021.

	100%	98%	95%	90%	80%	70%	60%
MSR $1,020	$880	$750	$650	$590	$475	$395	$325

1911-380 MEDALLION STAINLESS ENGRAVED/COMPACT – .380 ACP cal., full size or compact composite frame with 7075 aluminum sub-frame and slide rails, 3 5/8 (compact) or 4 1/4 (full size) in. barrel, two 8 shot single stack mags., stainless steel slide with neo-classical engraving, polished flats, and matte curves, steel 3-dot sights dovetailed into slide, imitation white pearl grips with gold-colored Buckmark, includes pistol rug, 16-17.5 oz. New 2021.

	100%	98%	95%	90%	80%	70%	60%
MSR $920	$820	$685	$590	$535	$430	$375	$300

1911-380 SPEED/SPEED COMPACT – .380 ACP cal., full size or compact composite frame with A-TACS AU Camo finish and 7075 aluminum sub-frame, 3 5/8 (compact) or 4 1/4 (full size) in. barrel, two 8 shot mags., stainless steel slide with Cerakote Burnt Bronze finish, steel 3-dot sights, A-TACS AU Camo composite grips, includes pistol rug, matte barrel finish, 17.5 oz. New 2021.

	100%	98%	95%	90%	80%	70%	60%
MSR $820	$720	$615	$525	$475	$385	$325	$295

PISTOLS: SEMI-AUTO, .22 CAL. RIMFIRE

In addition to the models listed below, Browning has also released SHOT Show specials on some models that were available by dealers ordering them at the SHOT Show only. Complete descriptions for these models can be found under SHOT SHOW SPECIALS - PISTOLS at BlueBookOfGunValues.com/overflow.

NOMAD MODEL – .22 LR cal., 10 shot, 4 1/2 and 6 3/4 in. barrel, steel or alloy frame, adj. sights, blue finish, black plastic grips. Mfg. 1961-1974 by FN.

	100%	98%	95%	90%	80%	70%	60%
	$700	$600	$400	$300	$225	$200	$175

Add 10% for alloy frame.
Add $100 for red/black plastic box and manual or $75 for original pouch and manual.

GRADING - PPGS™	100%	98%	95%	90%	80%	70%	60%	LAST MSR

CHALLENGER MODEL – .22 LR cal., 10 shot, 4 1/2 and 6 3/4 in. barrels, steel frame, adj. sights, checkered walnut or plastic (mfg. 1974 only) wraparound grips, gold plated trigger. Mfg. 1962-1975 by FN.

$850 $700 $550 $400 $350 $300 $250

Add $100 for red/black plastic box and manual or $75 for original pouch and manual.

* ***Challenger Renaissance*** – engraved satin nickel finish, 437 mfg. total (121 with 4 1/2 in. barrel, and 316 with 6 3/4 in. barrel).

$3,400 $2,550 $1,900 N/A N/A N/A N/A

Add 15% for 4 1/2 in. barrel.

* ***Challenger Gold Line*** – blue finish, gold line border on perimeter of frame surfaces, 293 mfg. total (147 with 4 1/2 in. barrel, and 146 with 6 3/4 in. barrel).

$3,500 $2,600 $1,950 N/A N/A N/A N/A

CHALLENGER II – .22 LR cal., Salt Lake City mfg., 6 3/4 in. barrel, steel frame, plastic impregnated hardwood grips, 38 oz. Mfg. 1975-82.

$550 $475 $400 $250 $200 $175 $150

Add $75 for original box and manual.

CHALLENGER III – .22 LR cal., Salt Lake City mfg., 5 1/2 in. bull barrel, 11 shot, alloy frame, adj. sights, 35 oz. Mfg. 1982-1985.

$525 $400 $325 $200 $175 $150 $135 *$240*

Add $75 for original box and manual.

* ***Challenger III BCA Commemorative*** – .22 LR cal., mfg. to commemorate BCA's fourth anniversary.

$625 $475 $400 N/A N/A N/A N/A

CHALLENGER III SPORTER – .22 LR cal., similar to Challenger III, except has 6 3/4 in. round barrel, wide trigger, 29 oz. Mfg. 1983-1985.

$525 $400 $325 $200 $175 $150 $135 *$240*

Add $75 for original pouch and manual.

MEDALIST MODEL – .22 LR cal., 6 3/4 in. barrel, vent. rib, adj. target sights and counter weight support with 3 counter weights, screwdriver tool, (2) keys, blue finish, target walnut grips with thumbrest, dry-fire mechanism, 46 oz., black case with red cloth interior. 24,001 mfg. 1962-1976 by FN.

$1,850 $1,400 $1,150 $950 $825 $725 $625

Subtract 20%-30% if without case and accessories, depending on condition.

The following is a breakdown on how many USA Medalists were manufactured per year: 1962 - 1,068, 1963 - 4,661, 1964 - 1,666, 1965 - 1,170, 1966 - 1,400, 1967 - 2,631, 1968 - 3,039, 1969 - 2,897, 1970 - 1,131, 1971 - 425, 1972 - 1507, 1973 - 708, 1974 - 906, 1975 - 792, 1976-10 (no case or accessories).

* ***Medalist Gold Line*** – 407 mfg. 1962-1975.

$4,600 $3,500 $2,750 N/A N/A N/A N/A

* ***Medalist Renaissance Model*** – one mfg. 1962, exhibition engraved with full coverage, satin chrome finished (displayed at 1962 World's Fair in Seattle, WA). 10 mfg. 1963-1967, full coverage engraving, coin finished. 382 mfg. 1970-1975, w/o full coverage engraving, baked enamel finish. Mfg. by FN 1962-1975.

$5,650 $5,000 $3,250 N/A N/A N/A N/A

Add 140% for full coverage engraving.

* ***Medalist BCA Engraved Edition*** – this BAC edition was a special order (not regular production), featured full coverage engraving. 60 mfg. 1986 only.

$8,000 $7,200 $5,000 N/A N/A N/A N/A

The BCA Medalist features full coverage engraving (similar to 1962-1967 Renaissance mfg.), and has a satin chrome finish, maroon case.

INTERNATIONAL MEDALIST – target variation model manufactured (early model) 1970, 1971, 1974, 5 7/8 in. round barrel, polished blue (681 mfg. for 1971, 1974 only), T serial, or slab side, matte finish, 5 15/16 in. barrel (late model) 1977-1988, I75-I76 serial all BAC marked (no productions figures for 1970, 1977-1988).

Early Model $1,300 $1,100 $850 $725 $600 $525 $400

Late Model $1,100 $950 $750 $625 $525 $475 $425

Subtract 10% for International II, same as Late Model except made in France with two letter date code.

Add $75 for original pouch and manual for Early Model or $100 for original box, tools, and manual for late model.

GRADING - PPGS™	100%	98%	95%	90%	80%	70%	60%	LAST MSR

BUCK MARK STANDARD URX – .22 LR cal., blowback action, 5 1/2 in. slabside barrel, 10 shot mag., aluminum frame, gold trigger, Pro-Target adj. rear and front blade sights, composite grips with skipline checkering (disc. 1990), molded rubber grips (mfg. 1991-2006), or URX grips (ambidextrous with finger grooves, new 2006, became standard during 2007), matte blue or nickel (mfg. 1991-2005) finish, 34-36 oz. New 1985.

MSR $500	$425	$375	$325	$290	$235	$190	$150	

Add $58 for nickel finish (mfg. 1991-2005).
Subtract approx. 10% for composite or molded rubber grips.

Buck Mark models are manufactured in Salt Lake City, UT.

* ***Buck Mark Standard Stainless URX*** – .22 LR cal., blowback action, 5 1/2 in. tapered bull stainless steel barrel with polished flats, 10 shot mag., alloy frame, SAT with gold plated finish, Pro-Target adj. rear and blade front sights, Ultragrip RX ambidextrous grips, includes ABS case, matte black finish, 34 oz. New 2005.

MSR $550	$465	$400	$350	$315	$250	$210	$165	

Subtract 10% for molded rubber grips (mfg. 2005-2006).

BUCK MARK MICRO STANDARD URX – similar to Buck Mark Standard, except has 4 in. barrel, choice of standard or nickel finish, URX grips became standard 2007, 32 oz. Mfg. 1992-2013.

	$375	$295	$250	$200	$175	$150	$135	*$460*

Add $58 for nickel finish (disc. 2005).
Subtract approx. 10% for composite or molded grips.

* ***Buck Mark Micro Standard Stainless URX*** – similar to Buck Mark Micro Standard, except stainless steel, URX grips became standard 2007, 34 oz. Mfg. 2005-2010.

	$375	$295	$250	$200	$175	$150	$135	*$469*

* ***Buck Mark Micro Plus*** – similar to Buck Mark Micro, except has ambidextrous contoured laminated wood grips, nickel (new 1996) or blue finish. Disc. 2001.

	$325	$275	$225	$200	$170	$145	$130	*$350*

Add $33 for nickel finish.

BUCK MARK STANDARD MICRO URX – .22 LR cal., blowback action, 4 in. slabside barrel, 10 shot mag., alloy frame, single action gold trigger, Pro-Target adj. sights, Ultragrip RX ambidextrous grips, blued finish, includes pistol rug, 32 oz. Mfg. 2016-2020.

	$400	$350	$300	$275	$225	$175	$150	*$470*

* ***Buck Mark Micro Challenge*** – similar to Buck Mark Challenge, except has 4 in. barrel. 23 oz. Mfg. 1999-2000.

	$295	$250	$200	$175	$150	$135	$125	*$311*

BUCK MARK BULLSEYE TARGET – .22 LR cal., Bullseye model featuring 16 click per turn Pro-Target rear sight, 7 1/4 in. fluted barrel, matte blue finish, adj. trigger pull, contoured rosewood target or wraparound finger groove (disc.) grips, 10 shot mag., 36 oz. Mfg. 1996-2005.

	$495	$395	$295	$225	$190	$165	$150	*$604*

* ***Buck Mark Bullseye Target Stainless*** – similar to Buck Mark Bullseye Target, except is stainless steel and has laminated rosewood grips, 39 oz. Mfg. 2006-2011.

	$595	$475	$350	$285	$250	$195	$175	*$759*

* ***Buck Mark Bullseye Standard*** – similar to Buck Mark Bullseye Target, except has molded composite ambidextrous grips, 36 oz. Mfg. 1996-2006.

	$375	$295	$250	$200	$160	$145	$125	*$468*

BUCK MARK BULLSEYE URX – .22 LR cal., 7 1/4 in. fluted barrel, matte blue finish, URX ambidextrous grips with finger grooves, 39 oz. Mfg. 2006-2010.

	$460	$375	$300	$250	$210	$185	$165	*$579*

BUCK MARK CAMPER – .22 LR cal., features 5 1/2 in. heavy barrel, ambidextrous molded black composite grips, matte blue or satin nickel finish, Pro-Target sights, 34 oz. Mfg. 1999-2012.

	$295	$250	$200	$175	$150	$135	$125	*$380*

Add $33 for satin nickel finish (disc. 2005).

* ***Buck Mark Camper Stainless*** – similar to Buck Mark Camper, except stainless steel, 34 oz. Mfg. 2005-2012.

	$315	$260	$210	$175	$150	$135	$125	*$420*

GRADING - PPGS™	100%	98%	95%	90%	80%	70%	60%	LAST MSR

* ***Buck Mark Camper Stainless URX Field*** – .22 LR cal., alloy frame, 5 1/2 in. stainless tapered bull barrel, ambidextrous Ultragrip RX grips, matte blued finish, Pro-Target adj. rear sight, TruGlo/Marbles fiber optic front sight, 34 oz. Available from Full Line Browning dealers only. Mfg. 2008-2015.

	$325	$275	$225	$200	$170	$145	$130	*$430*

This model was originally featured as a SHOT Show Special during 2007.

BUCK MARK CAMPER UFX – .22 LR cal., blowback action, alloy frame, 5 1/2 in. tapered bull barrel with matte blue finish, 10 shot mag., Pro-Target adj. rear sight, ramp front sight, ambidextrous overmolded black/grey UFX grips, matte black finish, 34 oz. New 2013.

MSR $420	$360	$315	$275	$250	$200	$160	$125

* ***Buck Mark Camper Stainless UFX*** – .22 LR cal., similar to Buck Mark Camper UFX, except has satin finished stainless steel barrel and slide assembly, 34 oz. New 2013.

MSR $460	$400	$350	$300	$275	$225	$185	$140

BUCK MARK CAMPER STAINLESS URX – .22 LR cal., blowback action, 5 1/2 in. slabside stainless steel barrel, 10 shot mag., alloy frame, SAT with gold plated finish, Pro-Target adj. rear and TruGlo/Marble Arms fiber optic front sights, Ultragrip RX ambidextrous grips, matte black finish, 34 oz. New 2016.

MSR $500	$425	$375	$325	$290	$235	$190	$150

BUCK MARK CHALLENGE – .22 LR cal., features smaller grip circumference for smaller hands, smooth (disc.) or checkered walnut grips with medallions, matte blue finish, 5 1/2 in. lightweight barrel, Pro-Target sights, 25 oz. Mfg. 1999-2010.

	$350	$285	$225	$190	$160	$140	$130	*$429*

BUCK MARK CHALLENGE ROSEWOOD – .22 LR cal., blowback action, compact alloy frame, 5 1/2 in. light tapered round barrel with matte blued finish, 10 shot mag., single action gold trigger, Pro-Target adj. rear and TruGlo/Marble Arms fiber optic front sights, rosewood laminated checkered grips with scroll engraving, includes pistol rug, matte black finish, 25 oz. New 2016.

MSR $580	$495	$435	$375	$335	$275	$225	$175

BUCK MARK COMMEMORATIVE – features 6 3/4 in. Challenger style tapered barrel, white bonded ivory grips with scrimshaw style patterning including "1 of 1,000 Commemorative Model" on sides, matte blue finish, gold trigger, 30 1/2 oz. 1,000 mfg. 2001 only.

	$395	$315	$250	N/A	N/A	N/A	N/A	*$437*

BUCK MARK CONTOUR URX – .22 LR cal., 5 1/2 (new 2021) or 7 1/4 in. specially contoured steel or alloy (Lite) sleeved barrel with full length scope base, 10 shot mag., SAT with gold plated finish, Patridge front and Pro-Target adj. rear sights, URX grips, Picatinny cross slots, includes pistol rug, matte blue finish, 36-39 oz. (Contour Lite variation is 8 oz. less than standard). New 2006.

MSR $590	$500	$440	$375	$340	$275	$225	$175

Add $10 for 7 1/4 in. barrel.

Add $50 for Contour Lite variation (alloy sleeved barrel, 8 oz. less than steel, disc. 2010).

* ***Buck Mark Contour Stainless URX*** – .22 LR cal., blowback action, 5 1/2 or 7 1/4 in. special contour stainless steel barrel with polished flats, 10 shot mag., SAT with gold plated finish, Patridge front and Pro-Target adj. rear sights, Ultragrip RX ambidextrous grips, Picatinny optics rail, includes pistol rug, matte stainless, 36-39 oz. New 2016.

MSR $620	$525	$460	$400	$350	$300	$250	$200

Add $10 for 7 1/4 in. barrel.

BUCK MARK CONTOUR GRAY URX – .22 LR cal., Gray anodized frame, 5 1/2 in. special contour matte blued steel barrel, polished flats, 10 shot mag., gold-plated trigger, Pro-Target adj. rear sight, Patridge front sight, URX grips with textured grip panels, Picatinny optics rail, includes pistol rug, 36 oz. New 2021.

MSR $580	$500	$440	$375	$340	$275	$225	$175

BUCK MARK 5.5 FIELD – same action and barrel as the Target 5.5, except sights are designed for field use, anodized blue finish, choice of contoured walnut, cocobolo (became standard 2005), or walnut wraparound finger groove grips (new 1992-disc.), 35 1/2 oz. Mfg. 1991-2011.

	$450	$375	$300	$225	$190	$165	$150	*$619*

BUCK MARK FIELD TARGET/FIELD TARGET SUPPRESSOR READY – .22 LR cal., blowback action, 5 1/2 or 5 7/8 (Suppressor Ready model) in. heavy round bull barrel, 10 shot mag., gold plated trigger, Patridge front and Pro-Target adj. sights, laminated cocobolo target grips, full length Picatinny scope base, shipped in 13 in. pistol rug, matte black finish, 38 oz. New 2017.

MSR $620	$525	$460	$395	$355	$290	$240	$200

Add $20 for Field Target Suppressor Ready model 5 7/8 in. barrel and thread protector.

GRADING - PPGS™	100%	98%	95%	90%	80%	70%	60%	LAST MSR

BUCK MARK HUNTER – .22 LR cal., blowback action, 7 1/4 in. round heavy bull barrel with integral scope base and matte blued finish, 10 shot mag., alloy frame, single action trigger, Pro-Target adj. rear and TruGlo/Marble Arms fiber optic front sight, Picatinny optics base, laminated cocobolo target grips, includes pistol rug, matte black finish, 38 oz. New 2005.

MSR $540	$460	$400	$350	$315	$250	$200	$175	

BUCK MARK LITE UFX – .22 LR cal., blowback action, 5 1/2 in. matte black alloy barrel sleeve with steel insert, Buckmark logo machined into barrel sleeve, 10 shot mag., SAT with gold plated finish, TruGlo/Marble Arms fiber optic front and Pro-Target adj. rear sights, Ultragrip FX ambidextrous grips with rubber overmolding, Picatinny accessory rail under barrel, matte black finish, 28 oz. Mfg. 2017, reintroduced 2020.

MSR $590	$515	$465	$415	$365	$315	$265	$215	

BUCK MARK LITE FLUTE UFX – .22 LR cal., blowback action, 5 1/2 in. barrel, aluminum alloy outer sleeve with deep flutes, 10 shot mag., gold plated trigger, Pro-Target adj. rear and Marble Arms violet fiber optic front sights, black rubber overmolded Ultragrip FX ambidextrous grips, matte black finish, 28 oz. Mfg. 2017 only.

	$485	$435	$365	$315	$265	$215	$165	*$560*

BUCK MARK LITE GREEN URX – .22 LR cal., blowback action, matte green anodized alloy frame, fluted alloy sleeved 5 1/2 in. barrel, 10 shot mag., Ultragrip RX ambidextrous grips, Pro-Target adj. rear sight and TruGlo/Marble Arms fiber optic front sight, 28-30 oz. Mfg. 2010-2013, reintroduced 2016.

MSR $620	$525	$460	$400	$350	$300	$250	$200	

BUCK MARK LITE SPLASH URX – .22 LR cal., 5 1/2 or 7 1/4 in. round barrel, aluminum barrel and receiver feature gold splash annodizing, URX grips standard, adj. sights with TruGlo fiber optic front sight, 28 or 30 oz. Mfg. 2006-2009.

	$370	$290	$230	$180	$150	$135	$120	*$489*

Add $20 for 7 1/4 in. barrel.

BUCK MARK MEDALLION ROSEWOOD – .22 LR cal., 5 1/2 in. blackened stainless steel slabside barrel with polished flats, 10 shot, gold plated trigger, Pro-Target adj. rear sight, TruGlo/Marble Arms fiber optic front sight, laminated rosewood colored grips with gold Buckmark, 34 oz. New 2019.

MSR $550	$470	$410	$350	$325	$260	$215	$185	

BUCK MARK PLUS CAMPER UFX SUPPRESSOR READY – .22 LR cal., blowback action, alloy frame, 6 in. tapered bull barrel with matte blue finish, threaded for suppressor, 10 shot mag., gold single action trigger, Pro-Target white outline adj. rear and TruGlo/Marble Arms fiber optic front sights, Picatinny rail for optics, Ultragrip FX ambidextrous grips with overmolding, matte black finish, includes pistol rug, 36 oz. New 2018.

MSR $550	$470	$410	$350	$325	$260	$215	$185	

BUCK MARK PLUS LITE FLUTE UFX SUPPRESSOR READY – .22 LR cal., blowback action, alloy frame, 6 in. matte black alloy barrel sleeve with steel insert, available with or w/o fluting, suppressor ready with thread protector, 10 shot mag., SAT with gold plated finish, Pro-Target adj. rear and TruGlo/Marble Arms fiber optic green front sights, Ultragrip FX ambidextrous grips with rubber overmolding, Picatinny optics rail, matte black finish, includes pistol rug, 28 oz. New 2018.

MSR $660	$560	$490	$420	$380	$310	$250	$200	

BUCK MARK PLUS LITE GRAY URX – .22 LR cal., blowback action, matte gray anodized alloy frame, 5 1/2 or 7 1/4 (disc. 2010, reintroduced 2016) in. fluted matte gray alloy barrel sleeve with steel insert, 10 shot mag., Pro-Target adj. rear sight and TruGlo/Marble Arms fiber optic front sight, Ultragrip RX ambidextrous grips, 28-30 oz. Mfg. 2010-2020.

	$500	$450	$400	$350	$300	$250	$200	*$580*

Add $10 for 7 1/4 in. barrel with pistol rug (disc. 2010, reintroduced 2016).

BUCK MARK PLUS PRACTICAL URX – .22 LR cal., blowback action, alloy frame, 5 1/2 in. tapered bull barrel with matte black finish, 10 shot mag., SAT with gold plated finish, Pro-Target white outline adj. rear sight and TruGlo/Marble Arms fiber optic front sight, Picatinny rail for optics, Ultragrip RX ambidextrous grips, matte gray finish, includes pistol rug, 35 oz. New 2017.

MSR $500	$425	$375	$325	$295	$235	$195	$165	

BUCK MARK PLUS UDX – .22 LR cal., 5 1/2 in. barrel, 10 shot mag., gold single action trigger, Pro-Target adj. rear and TruGlo/Marble Arms fiber optic front (new 2002) sights, uncheckered laminated wood (disc. 2006) or walnut ambidextrous DX Ultragrips (new 2007), choice of high polish blue or nickel (mfg. 1996-2006) finish, includes pistol rug, 34 oz. Mfg. 1987-2007, reintroduced 2010-2020.

	$475	$425	$375	$325	$275	$225	$175	*$550*

Add approx. 10% for nickel finish (disc. 2006).

This model with a Challenge size frame, 5 1/2 in. bull barrel and slide, finger grooved laminated walnut Ultra DX grips, Pro-Target rear and TruGlo/Marble's fiber optic front sight was featured as a SHOT Show Special in 2006.

GRADING - PPGS™	100%	98%	95%	90%	80%	70%	60%	LAST MSR

* ***Buck Mark Field Plus UDX (Classic Plus)*** – .22 LR cal., similar to Buck Mark Plus, except has rosewood grips (disc. 2006, reintroduced 2010) or DX Ultragrips (mfg. 2007), and TruGlo Marble front sight. Mfg. 2002-2007, reintroduced 2010-2013.

	100%	98%	95%	90%	80%	70%	60%	LAST MSR
	$395	$325	$275	$235	$210	$190	$170	*$520*

This model is available from Full-Line dealers only.

This model with laminated rosewood grips and Challenge size frame was featured as a 2006 SHOT Show Special.

* ***Buck Mark Plus Rosewood UDX*** – .22 LR cal., blowback action, 5 1/2 in. matte blued slabside barrel with polished flats, 10 shot mag., alloy receiver, SAT with gold plated finish, TruGlo/Marble Arms fiber optic front and Pro-Target adj. rear sights, rosewood laminated UDX grips, Picatinny optics rail, includes pistol rug, 34 oz. New 2016.

	100%	98%	95%	90%	80%	70%	60%	LAST MSR
MSR $600	$510	$450	$385	$350	$275	$225	$175	

* ***Buck Mark Plus Stainless UDX*** – .22 LR cal., aluminum alloy frame, 5 1/2 in. stainless steel barrel/slide with polished flats, 10 shot mag., SAT with gold plated finish, Pro Target white outline adj. rear sight, TruGlo/Marble Arms fiber optic front sight, choice of black or brown (disc. 2010) laminated UDX grips, Picatinny top rail, includes pistol rug, choice of high polish blue or nickel finish (mfg. 1996-2006), 35 oz. Mfg. 2007, reintroduced 2010.

	100%	98%	95%	90%	80%	70%	60%	LAST MSR
MSR $640	$540	$475	$400	$365	$300	$250	$200	

Subtract $35 for brown laminate grips (disc. 2010).

This model with black laminated Ultra DX grips was originally featured as a 2006 SHOT Show Special.

BUCK MARK PLUS VISION UFX – .22 LR cal., 5.9 in. suppressor-ready threaded alloy sleeved steel Vision barrel, removable muzzle brake, gold-plated trigger, white outline Pro-Target adj. rear sight, TruGlo/Marble Arms fiber optic front sight, Picatinny optics rail, UFX overmolded grips, includes pistol rug, matte black, anodized red, or anodized blue frame, slide, and barrel, 27 oz. New 2021.

	100%	98%	95%	90%	80%	70%	60%	LAST MSR
MSR $740	$625	$545	$475	$425	$345	$275	$225	

BUCK MARK PRACTICAL URX – .22 LR cal., alloy matte gray finished frame, tapered 5 1/2 in. bull barrel, matte blue finish, 10 shot mag., Ultragrip RX ambidextrous grips, single action gold trigger, Pro-Target adj. rear sight, TruGlo/Marble Arms fiber optic front sight, 34 oz. Mfg. 2010-2016.

	100%	98%	95%	90%	80%	70%	60%	LAST MSR
	$325	$275	$235	$210	$185	$165	$140	*$440*

This model was originally featured as a 2008 and 2009 SHOT Show Special.

BUCK MARK SILHOUETTE – .22 LR cal., silhouette variation of the Buck Mark, 9 7/8 in. bull barrel with serrated top rib allowing adj. sight positioning, hooded target sights, laminated wood stocks and forearm, choice of contoured walnut or walnut wraparound finger groove grips (new 1992), matte blue, 53 oz. Mfg. 1987-99.

	100%	98%	95%	90%	80%	70%	60%	LAST MSR
	$395	$325	$265	$240	$210	$185	$160	*$448*

* ***Buck Mark Unlimited Silhouette (Match)*** – similar to Silhouette Model featuring 14 in. barrel with set back front sight, choice of contoured walnut or walnut wraparound finger groove grips (new 1992), 64 oz. Mfg. 1991-99.

	100%	98%	95%	90%	80%	70%	60%	LAST MSR
	$495	$400	$350	$275	$240	$210	$175	*$536*

BUCK MARK 5.5 TARGET – .22 LR cal., same action as Buck Mark, 5 1/2 in. barrel with serrated top rib allowing adj. sight positioning, target sights, matte blue or nickel (mfg. 1994-2000) finish, choice of contoured walnut (disc. 2004), cocobolo (became standard 2005), or walnut wraparound finger groove grips (new 1992-disc.), 35 oz. Mfg. 1990-2009.

	100%	98%	95%	90%	80%	70%	60%	LAST MSR
	$440	$365	$285	$235	$190	$170	$150	*$579*

Add $54 for nickel finish (mfg. 1994-2000).

* ***Buck Mark 5.5 Gold Target*** – similar to 5.5 Target, except has gold anodized frame and top rib. Mfg. 1991-1999.

	100%	98%	95%	90%	80%	70%	60%	LAST MSR
	$375	$295	$250	$200	$160	$145	$125	*$477*

BUCK MARK VARMINT – .22 LR cal., same action as Buck Mark, 9 7/8 in. barrel with serrated top rib allowing adj. sight positioning, laminated wood grips, choice of contoured walnut or walnut wraparound finger groove grips (new 1992), optional detachable forearm, matte blue, 48 oz. Mfg. 1987-1999.

	100%	98%	95%	90%	80%	70%	60%	LAST MSR
	$375	$300	$250	$225	$195	$175	$150	*$403*

1911-22 A1 FULL SIZE ALLOY – .22 LR cal., blowback action semi-auto pistol patterned after the Colt Model 1911-A1, matte black or gray (new 2021) anodized alloy frame, 4 1/4 in. stainless steel barrel, target crown, 10 shot mag., alloy frame and slide, single action trigger, fixed sights, diamond patterned checkered walnut grips, manual thumb and grip safeties, 15-15 1/2 oz. Mfg. in the USA beginning 2011.

	100%	98%	95%	90%	80%	70%	60%	LAST MSR
MSR $640	$550	$475	$425	$375	$325	$275	$225	

Pistols made during 2011 include a limited edition canvas and leather zippered commemorative case, plus a collector's certificate.

GRADING - PPGS™	100%	98%	95%	90%	80%	70%	60%	LAST MSR

1911-22 A1 COMPACT ALLOY – .22 LR cal., blowback action, alloy frame and slide, 3 5/8 in. stainless steel barrel w/target crown, detachable 10 shot mag., single action trigger, fixed sights, walnut grips with double diamond pattern cut checkering, manual thumb and grip safeties, includes ABS carry case, matte black or matte gray (new 2021) anodized finish, 14 oz. New 2011.

MSR $660	$560	$495	$425	$380	$325	$275	$225	

Add $10 for matte black anodized finish.

1911-22 A1 FULL SIZE COMPOSITE – .22 LR cal., blowback action, semi-auto pistol patterned after the Colt Model 1911-A1, Desert tan composite frame w/aluminum subframe, 4 1/4 in. stainless steel barrel w/target crown, 10 shot mag., matte black alloy slide, fixed sights, checkered black composite grips, manual thumb and grip safeties, approx. 14 oz. Mfg. in the USA 2014-2016.

	$500	$450	$400	$350	$300	$250	$200	*$580*

Pistols made during 2011 include a limited edition canvas and leather zippered commemorative case, plus a collector's certificate.

1911-22 A1 COMPACT COMPOSITE – .22 LR cal., blowback action, matte black (disc.) or Desert Tan (new 2014) composite frame, 3 5/8 in. barrel, detachable 10 shot mag., matte black finished aluminum slide, fixed sights, checkered black composite (new 2014) or walnut grips with double diamond pattern and cut checkering (disc.), includes ABS carry case, 15 oz. Mfg. 2011-2019.

	$500	$450	$400	$350	$300	$250	$200	*$580*

1911-22 BCA EDITION – .22 LR cal., special 1911 Anniversary Edition, "BCA" is incorporated into the serial number, only 100 mfg. during 2011-2012.

	$925	$825	$725	N/A	N/A	N/A	N/A	*$850*

1911-22 BLACK LABEL FULL SIZE COMPOSITE – .22 LR cal., blowback action, composite frame w/ aluminum subframe and slide rails, 4 1/4 in. stainless steel barrel w/target crown, 10 shot detachable mag., skeletonized hammer, skeletonized single action trigger, fixed combat or fiber optic (mfg. 2017-2020, Gray model only) sights, black laminated wood grips, extended ambidextrous thumb safety, beavertail grip safety, with or w/o Picatinny accessory rail, extended slide release, includes ABS case, matte black or gray (mfg. 2017-2020) anodized aluminum slide finish, 14 oz. New 2015.

MSR $680	$600	$510	$450	$400	$350	$300	$250	

Add $30 for lower Picatinny rail.
Add $60 for gray anodized finish and fiber optic sights (mfg. 2017-2020).
Add $80 for gray finish, fiber optic sights and lower Picatinny rail (mfg. 2017-2020).

1911-22 BLACK LABEL COMPACT COMPOSITE – .22 LR cal., blowback action, composite frame w/ aluminum subframe and slide rails, 3 5/8 in. barrel, 10 shot detachable mag., bobbed Commander hammer, skeletonized trigger, fixed combat or fiber optic (mfg. 2017-2020, gray model only) sights, black laminated wood grips, extended ambidextrous thumb safety, beavertail grip safety, with or w/o lower Picatinny accessory rail, extended slide release, matte black or gray (mfg. 2017-2020) anodized finish, 13 oz. New late 2014.

MSR $680	$600	$510	$450	$400	$350	$300	$250	

Add $30 for lower Picatinny rail.
Add $60 for gray anodized finish and fiber optic sights (mfg. 2017-2020).
Add $80 for gray finish, fiber optic sights and lower Picatinny rail (mfg. 2017-2020).

1911-22 BLACK LABEL FULL SIZE SUPPRESSOR READY COMPOSITE – .22 LR cal., blowback action, composite frame w/aluminum subframe and slide rails, 4 7/8 in. stainless steel barrel, target crown, threaded muzzle protector, detachable 10-shot mag., skeletonized hammer, skeletonized SAT, steel 3-dot sights dovetailed into slide, black/white textured G10 composite grips, extended ambidextrous manual thumb safety, beavertail grip safety, extended slide release, lower Picatinny rail, includes ABS case, matte black finish, 14 oz. New 2016.

MSR $780	$665	$580	$500	$450	$400	$350	$300	

1911-22 BLACK LABEL COMPACT SUPPRESSOR READY COMPOSITE – .22 LR cal., blowback action, composite frame w/aluminum subframe and slide rails, 4 1/4 in. barrel, target crown, threaded muzzle protector, detachable 10 shot mag., skeletonized hammer, single action skeletonized trigger, steel 3-dot sights dovetailed into slide, textured G10 composite grips, extended ambidextrous manual thumb safety, beavertail grip safety, extended slide release, lower Picatinny rail, includes ABS case, matte black finish, 14 oz. New 2016.

MSR $780	$665	$580	$500	$450	$400	$350	$300	

GRADING - PPGS™	100%	98%	95%	90%	80%	70%	60%	LAST MSR

1911-22 BLACK LABEL MEDALLION FULL SIZE ALLOY – .22 LR cal., blowback action, patterned after the Colt Model 1911-A1, 4 1/4 in. stainless steel barrel, target crown, 10 shot detachable mag., alloy frame and slide, skeletonized hammer, skeletonized SAT, steel 3-dot sights dovetailed into slide, checkered rosewood grips w/gold Buckmark, extended ambidextrous manual thumb safety, beavertail grip safety, extended slide release, includes ABS carry case, matte black finish w/brushed polished flats, approx. 15 oz. Mfg. in the USA beginning 2017.

MSR $710	$600	$525	$465	$415	$365	$315	$265	

1911-22 BLACK LABEL MEDALLION COMPACT ALLOY – .22 LR cal., blowback action semi-auto pistol patterned after the Colt Model 1911-A1, 3 5/8 in. stainless steel barrel, target crown, 10 shot mag., alloy frame and slide, skeletonized hammer, skeletonized single action trigger, steel 3-dot sights dovetailed into slide, checkered rosewood grips w/gold Buckmark, extended ambidextrous manual thumb safety, beavertail grip safety, extended slide release, matte black finish w/brushed polished flats, 13 oz. Mfg. in the USA beginning 2017.

MSR $710	$600	$525	$465	$415	$365	$315	$265	

1911-22 SPEED – .22 LR cal., full size or compact composite frame with A-TACS AU Camo finish and 7075 aluminum sub-frame and slide rails, 3 5/8 (compact) or 4 1/4 (full size) in. stainless steel barrel, two 10 shot mags., alloy slide with Burnt Bronze Cerakote finish, steel 3-dot sights dovetailed into slide, A-TACS AU Camo composite grips, includes pistol rug, 13 or 15 oz. New 2021.

MSR $620	$540	$460	$400	$350	$300	$250	$200	

RIFLES: BOLT ACTION

In addition to the models listed below, Browning has also released SHOT Show specials on some models that were available by dealers ordering them at the SHOT Show only. Complete descriptions for these models can be found under SHOT SHOW SPECIALS - RIFLES BOLT ACTION at BlueBookOfGunValues.com/overflow.

MODEL 52 LIMITED EDITION – .22 LR cal., virtually identical to the original Winchester Model 52C Sporter, except for minor safety enhancements, bolt action, 24 in. drilled and tapped barrel, 5 shot detachable mag., pistol grip walnut stock with oil style finish, deep blue finish, adj. trigger, two-position safety, 7 lbs. 5,000 mfg. 1991-92.

	$950	$850	$700	N/A	N/A	N/A	N/A	*$500*

AB3 COMPOSITE STALKER – .243 Win. (new 2015), .270 Win., .30-06, .308 Win. (new 2015), .270 WSM (new 2015), .300 WSM (new 2015), .300 Win. Mag., 7mm-08 Rem. (new 2015), 6.5 Creedmoor (new 2017), or 7mm Rem. Mag. cal., short (new 2015) or long action, 22, 23 (new 2015, WSM cal. only), or 26 in. free floating barrel, target crown, 4, 5, or 6 shot detachable box mag., steel receiver, no sights, matte black composite stock with textured gripping surfaces, Inflex Technology recoil pad, top tang safety, bolt lock override button, sling swivel studs, matte blued finish, approx. 7 lbs. New 2014.

MSR $630	$535	$475	$400	$365	$335	$300	$275	

AB3 MICRO STALKER – .243 Win., 6.5 Creedmoor, 7mm-08 Rem., or .308 Win. cal., 20 in. free floating Sporter barrel with matte blued finish, 6 shot detachable box mag., drilled and tapped, matte black composite stock with textured gripping surfaces, 13 in. LOP, Pachmayr Decelerator recoil pad, sling swivel studs, top tang safety, 6 lbs. 7 oz. New 2017.

MSR $630	$535	$475	$400	$365	$335	$300	$275	

AB3 HUNTER – .243 Win., 7mm-08 Rem., .308 Win., .270 WSM, .300 WSM, .270 Win., .30-06, 7mm Rem. Mag., 6.5 Creedmoor (new 2017), or .300 Win. Mag. cal., 22, 23, or 26 in. free floating Sporter barrel with matte blue finish, target crown, 4, 5, or 6 shot detachable box mag., steel receiver drilled and tapped for scope mounts, satin finished checkered walnut stock, Inflex recoil pad, top tang safety, sling swivel studs, approx. 7 lbs. New 2016.

MSR $720	$615	$540	$460	$425	$350	$325	$295	

ACERA MODEL – .30-06 or .300 Win. Mag. cal., features straight pull action, Teflon coated breechblock face, 7 lug bolt, 22 or 24 (.300 Win. Mag.) in. barrel, available w/o sights, with sights (disc. 1999), or with BOSS, detachable box mag., checkered walnut stock, gloss metal finish, 7 lbs. 3 oz -7 lbs. 9 oz. Mfg. 1999-2000, reintroduced during 2002 only.

	$895	$800	$650	$575	$475	$375	$285	*$896*

Add $34 for .300 Win. Mag. cal.
Add $24 for iron sights (disc. 1999).
Add $80 for barrel BOSS (.30-06 cal. mfg. 2002 only).

GRADING - PPGS™	100%	98%	95%	90%	80%	70%	60%	LAST MSR

BBR – .25-06 Rem., .270 Win., .30-06, 7mm Mag., .300 Win. Mag. or .338 Win. Mag. cal., short action available in .22-250 Rem., 243 Win., 257 Roberts, 7mm-08 Rem., or .308 Win. cal., 24 in. standard or heavy barrel, 60 degree bolt throw, fluted bolt, adj. trigger, hidden detachable mag., no sights, checkered pistol grip, Monte Carlo stock. Mfg. 1978-84 by Miroku.

	$695	$600	$475	$400	$325	$250	$200	

Some rare production calibers will add premiums to the values listed (i.e., add 50% for .243 Win. cal.).

BBR RIFLE ELK ISSUE – 7mm Rem. Mag. cal., deeply blued receiver which has multiple animals gold inlaid, high grade walnut stock and forearm feature skipline checkering. 1,000 mfg. Disc. 1986.

	$1,800	$1,500	$1,100	N/A	N/A	N/A	N/A	*$1,395*

T-BOLT SPORTER (NEW MFG.) – .17 HMR (new 2008), .22 LR, or .22 WMR (new 2008) cal., original straight pull action with enlarged bolt handle, right or left (mfg. 2009-2019) hand action, 22 in. free floating medium sporter barrel, recessed crown, 10 shot double helix rotary mag., blued steel receiver, adj. gold trigger, no sights, matte black composite stock with textured gripping surfaces and spare magazine storage compartment (mfg. 2008-2019) or satin finished walnut stock with cut checkering, sling swivel studs installed, top tang safety, drilled and tapped for scope mounts, 4 lbs. 14 oz. New 2006.

MSR $780	$665	$580	$500	$450	$365	$300	$235	

Add $40 for .17 HMR or .22 WMR cal.

Add $50 for left-hand action in .17 HMR or .22 WMR cal. (mfg. 2009-2019).

T-BOLT TARGET/VARMINT (NEW MFG.) – .17 HMR (new 2008), .22 LR, or .22 WMR (new 2008) cal., original straight pull action with enlarged bolt handle, right or left (mfg. 2009-2019) hand action, 22 in. free floating heavy target barrel, recessed crown, 10 shot double helix rotary mag., blued steel receiver, adj. gold trigger, no sights, matte black composite stock with textured gripping surfaces and spare magazine storage compartment (mfg. 2008-2019) or satin finished walnut stock with raised cheekpiece and cut checkering, sling swivel studs installed, top tang safety, drilled and tapped for scope mounts, 5 1/2 lbs. New 2007.

MSR $800	$680	$600	$500	$450	$375	$300	$250	

Add $30 for .17 HMR or .22 WMR cal.

Add $50 for left-hand action in .17 HMR or .22 WMR cal. (mfg. 2009-2019).

T-BOLT GRAY LAMINATED TARGET/VARMINT STAINLESS – .22 LR, .22 WMR, or .17 HMR cal., straight pull bolt action, 22 in. medium target free floating stainless steel barrel, threaded for suppressor with thread protector, recessed crown, blued steel receiver drilled and tapped for scope mounts, 10 shot double Helix mag., gold adj. trigger, gray laminated wood stock with Monte Carlo cheekpiece and checkered gripping surfaces, sling swivel studs, top tang safety. New 2018.

MSR $960	$810	$750	$650	$550	$450	$375	$300	

Add $60 for .22 WMR or .17 HMR cal.

T-BOLT T-1 – .22 LR cal., straight pull bolt action, 5 shot mag., 22 in. barrel, adj. rear sight, 5 1/2 lbs., plain pistol grip stock. Mfg. 1965-1974 by FN.

	$600	$525	$450	$410	$330	$270	$210	

Add 10%-15% for left-hand model (mfg. 1967-1974 only).

An aperture rear sight was standard for the first nine years of production.

Watch for salt wood.

T-BOLT T-2 – similar to T-1, only with select checkered walnut stock (lacquer finished), pinned front sight blade, 24 in. barrel, 6 lbs.

	$875	$765	$655	$595	$480	$395	$325	

Add 10%-15% for left-hand model (mfg. 1967-1974 only).

Watch for salt wood.

* ***T-Bolt T-2 Late Production*** – features oil finished stock, press fit plastic front sight, and Browning computerized serialization.

	$600	$525	$435	$375	$305	$250	$200	

T-BOLT TARGET WITH MUZZLE BRAKE – .22 LR, .22 WMR, or .17 HMR cal., straight pull bolt action, 16 1/2 in. free floating heavy bull target barrel, muzzle brake, target crown, 10 shot Double Helix mag., steel receiver, drilled and tapped for scope mounts, adj. trigger, satin finish walnut stock with Monte Carlo comb, wide forend and cut checkering, top tang safety, matte blue finish, 6.2 lbs. New 2021.

MSR $700	$600	$525	$450	$410	$325	$275	$225	

Add $40 for .22 WMR or .17 HMR cal.

GRADING - PPGS™	100%	98%	95%	90%	80%	70%	60%	LAST MSR

FN HIGH-POWER MODEL - .222 Rem. (Sako action), .222 Rem. Mag. (Sako action), .22-250 Rem. (Sako action), .243 Win., .257 Roberts, .264 Win. Mag., .270 Win., .284 Win. (Sako action), .30-06, .308 Win., 7mm Mag., .300 Win. Mag., .308 Norma Mag., .300 H&H, .338 Win. Mag., .375 H&H, or .458 Win. Mag. cal., standard Mauser type action with either short or long (more desirable) extractor, 22 or 24 in. (heavy available) barrel, folding leaf sight, checkered pistol grip stock. Mfg. 1960-1974 by FN.

The .243 Win. and .308 Win. cals. were built on the small ring Mauser action prior to using the Sako medium action.

Note: Grades differ in engraving, finish, checkering, and grade of wood. It should be noted that the salt wood problem is more common in these high powered models. Guns should be checked carefully for rust below wood surfaces.

* ***FN High-Power Safari Grade Basic Model*** - basic model with blue finish.

Standard cals.	$1,675	$1,475	$1,275	$1,175	$995	$850	$550	
Mag. cals.	$1,850	$1,650	$1,425	$1,275	$1,075	$900	$650	
.257 Roberts	$2,825	$2,500	$2,150	$1,875	$1,500	$1,250	$1,150	
.308 Norma Mag.	$2,250	$1,950	$1,550	$1,375	$1,250	$1,050	$975	
.338 Win. Mag.	$1,995	$1,750	$1,400	$1,250	$1,050	$900	$800	
.375 H&H	$2,195	$1,850	$1,500	$1,350	$1,150	$1,000	$900	

Add 15% for Magnum long extractor models.

Between 1963 and 1974, Browning also offered short and medium barrelled actions in the Safari, Medallion and Olympian Grades. These models have Sako barrelled actions and were stocked by FN. Medium weight barrels could also be ordered.

* ***FN High-Power Safari Grade Short Sako Action*** - .222 Rem. or .222 Rem. Mag. cal., short action.

	$1,675	$1,475	$1,275	$1,175	$995	$850	$695	

* ***FN High-Power Safari Grade Medium Sako Action*** - .22-250 Rem., .243 Win., .284 Win. or .308 Win. cal., medium action.

	$1,595	$1,375	$1,175	$1,050	$900	$750	$550	

Add 75% for .284 Win. cal. (mfg. 1965-76).

In .284 Win. cal., only 162 rifles were mfg. in Safari Grade, 29 in Medallion Grade, and 10 in Olympian Grade.

* ***FN High-Power Medallion Grade*** - features select figured walnut with skipline checkering, rosewood grip and forearm caps, blue/black lustre bluing, receiver and barrel portion scroll engraved, ram's head engraved on floorplate.

	$3,250	$2,950	$2,500	$2,200	$1,850	$1,500	$1,200	

Add 20%-60% for rare calibers, depending on rarity.
Add 15% for Mag. cals. with long extractor.

Caliber rarity is as follows: .30-06 (least rare), .300 H&H, .375 H&H long extractor, .264 Win. Mag., .222 Rem./.222 Rem. Mag., .284 Win. (rarest).

This model was also available with a Sako short or medium action - cals. are the same as listed for the Sako Safari.

* ***FN High-Power Olympian Grade*** - top-of-the-line model featuring highly figured walnut stock that is both checkered and carved. Receiver, floorplate, and trigger guard are chrome plated in a satin finish that has deep relief animal scenes engraved, as well as deep scroll work on other metal parts.

	$9,250	$8,000	$6,850	$6,200	$5,200	$4,400	$3,850	

Add 20%-60% for rare calibers, depending on the rarity.
Add 15% for Mag. cals. with long extractor.

Caliber rarity is as follows: .30-06 (least rare), .308 Norm. Mag., .300 H&H, .375 H&H long extractor, .264 Win. Mag., .222 Rem./.222 Rem. Mag., .284 Win. (rarest).

This model was also available with a Sako short or medium action - cals. are the same as listed for the Sako Safari.

RIFLES: BOLT ACTION, CENTERFIRE A-BOLT I SERIES

In addition to the models listed below, Browning has also released SHOT Show specials on some models that were available by dealers ordering them at the SHOT Show only. Complete descriptions for these models can be found under SHOT SHOW SPECIALS - RIFLES BOLT ACTION at BlueBookOfGunValues.com/overflow.

GRADING - PPGS™	100%	98%	95%	90%	80%	70%	60%	LAST MSR

A-BOLT HUNTER MODEL I – available in .25-06 Rem., .270 Win., .280 Rem. (new 1988), .30-06, 7mm Rem. Mag., .300 Win. Mag., or .338 Win. Mag. cal. in long action, short action available in .223 Rem. (new 1988), .22-250 Rem., .243 Win., .257 Roberts, .284 Win. (new 1989), 7mm-08 Rem., or .308 Win. cal., 3 or 4 shot mag., matte blue finish, 3 lug rotary bolt locking, 22 (short action only), 24 in. (disc. 1987), or 26 in. barrel (new 1988 - long action Mag. cals. only), 60 degree bolt throw, adj. trigger, hidden detachable mag., with or without sights, top tang thumb safety, checkered pistol grip stock, 6 lbs. 3 oz. - 7 lbs. 11oz. Mfg. 1985-93 by Miroku. Replaced by A-Bolt Model II in 1994.

$495 $425 $325 $295 $240 $195 $150 *$510*

Add $65 for open sights.

* ***A-Bolt Hunter Medallion Model*** – same A-Bolt specifications, except also available in .375 H&H cal., features better grade walnut stock with rosewood pistol grip and forend cap, synthetic floorplate, high lustre bluing, no sights. Disc. 1993. Replaced by A-Bolt Medallion Model II in 1994.

$625 $525 $425 $355 $290 $235 $185 *$597*

Add $25 for left-hand action (avail. in long action cals. only).
Add $100 for .375 H&H cal. (open sights only).

Left-hand action available in .25-06 Rem., .270 Win., .280 Rem., .30-06, 7mm Rem. Mag., .300 Win. Mag., .338 Win. Mag., or .375 H&H cal.

* ***A-Bolt Hunter Micro Medallion Model*** – .223 Rem. (new 1988), .22-250 Rem., .243 Win., .257 Roberts, .284 Win., .308 Win., or 7mm-08 Rem. cal., scaled down variation of the A-Bolt Hunter Model, 20 in. barrel, short action only, 13 5/16 in. LOP, 3 shot mag., no sights, 6 lbs. 3 oz. for short action. Mfg. 1988-93. Replaced by A-Bolt Micro Medallion Model II in 1994.

$625 $525 $425 $355 $290 $235 $185 *$597*

* ***A-Bolt Hunter Gold Medallion Model*** – .270 Win., .30-06, .300 Win. Mag. (new 1993), or 7mm Rem. Mag. cal., similar to Medallion Model, except has extra select walnut stock with continental style cheekpiece, gold lettering and light engraving, no sights. Mfg. 1988-93. Replaced by A- Bolt Gold Medallion Model II in 1994.

$750 $650 $550 $500 $405 $330 $255 *$810*

* ***A-Bolt Hunter Euro-Bolt*** – .22-250 Rem., .243 Win., .270 Win., .30-06, .308 Win., or 7mm Rem. Mag. cal., features European styling including Schnabel style forearm, rounded rear receiver, Mannlicher style bolt, European cheekpiece on satin finished checkered stock, low-lustre bluing, hinged floorplate with removable mag., cocking indicator, upper tang thumb activated safety, 6 lbs. 14 oz.-7 lbs. 6 oz. (Mag.). Mfg. 1993-96.

$675 $550 $475 $425 $345 $280 $220 *$700*

* ***A-Bolt Hunter Stainless Stalker*** – .22-250 Rem. (left-hand only, new 1993), .25-06 Rem., .270 Win., .280 Rem., .30-06, 7mm Rem. Mag., .300 Win. Mag., .338 Win. Mag. or .375 H&H (new 1990) cal., action and barrel are stainless steel, matte black graphite fiberglass composite stock, dull stainless finish, no sights, 6 lbs. 11 oz.-7 lbs. 3 oz. Mfg. 1987-93. Replaced by Stainless Stalker II in 1994.

$625 $525 $450 $410 $330 $270 $210 *$665*

Add $100 for .375 H&H cal.
Add $20 for left-hand action.

Originally, this model was offered in .270 Win., .30-06, or 7mm Rem. Mag. cal. only.

* ***A-Bolt Hunter Camo Stalker*** – .270 Win., .30-06, or 7mm Rem. Mag. cal., laminated black and green wood stock, matte finish on metal parts, no sights. Mfg. 1987-89.

$475 $425 $350 $300 $250 $190 $150 *$483*

* ***A-Bolt Hunter Composite Stalker*** – .25-06 Rem., .270 Win., .280 Rem., .30-06, 7mm Rem. Mag., .300 Win. Mag., or .338 Win. Mag. cal., black graphite fiberglass composite stock, matte non-glare metal finish, 6 lbs. 11 oz.-7 lbs. 3 oz. Mfg. 1988-93. Replaced by Composite Stalker II in 1994.

$525 $425 $350 $300 $250 $190 $150 *$525*

A-BOLT BIGHORN SHEEP ISSUE – .270 Win. cal. only, 22 in. barrel, high grade walnut stock with gloss finish and skipline checkering, deep relief engraving on receiver barrel, floorplate, and trigger guard, two 24Kt. inlays depicting bighorn sheep. 600 mfg. 1986-87 only.

$1,450 $1,100 $950 $850 $725 $550 $500 *$1,365*

A-BOLT PRONGHORN ISSUE – .243 Win. cal., presentation grade walnut with skipline checkering and pearl borders, receiver and barrel engraving, multiple gold inlays on receiver top and floorplate. 500 mfg. 1987 only.

$1,450 $1,100 $950 N/A N/A N/A N/A *$1,302*

GRADING - PPGS™	100%	98%	95%	90%	80%	70%	60%	LAST MSR

RIFLES: BOLT ACTION, CENTERFIRE A-BOLT II SERIES

The A-Bolt II Series was introduced in 1994, and differs from the original A-Bolt variations (disc. 1993) in that a new anti-bind bolt featuring a non-rotating bolt sleeve has been incorporated in addition to an improved trigger system. Action feeding is similar to A-Bolt I Series, with a hinged floorplate featuring a detachable box magazine. Consumers also may have their name/inscription engraved on the flat bolt-face on any A-Bolt II Series variation for an additional $25. Browning introduced the BOSS (Ballistic Optimizing Shooting System) in 1994 as an option on A-Bolt rifles, except Micro-Medallion models. It is a user-adjustable barrel tuning attachment which greatly improves accuracy. The BOSS version has porting, which functions as a muzzle brake and reduces recoil by approx. 30%. The BOSS-CR (Conventional Recoil) is not ported, and does not have the substantially increased noise/muzzle blast of the BOSS.

During 2010, the A-Bolt celebrated its 25th Anniversary, and in commemoration, select A-Bolt rifles have a "25th Anniversary A-Bolt" etched on the floorplate.

In addition to the models listed below, Browning has also released SHOT Show specials on some models that were available by dealers ordering them at the SHOT Show only. Complete descriptions for these models can be found under SHOT SHOW SPECIALS - RIFLES: BOLT ACTION at BlueBookOfGunValues.com/overflow.

A-BOLT HUNTER MODEL II – available in various cals. between .22-250 Rem. - .338 Win. Mag. (disc.), currently available in .270 WSM, 7mm WSM cals. (new 2002), .300 WSM (new 2001), or .325 WSM (new 2005) cal., 22 (disc.), 23 (.300 WSM cal. only), 24, or 26 in. barrel with (disc. 1998) or w/o open sights, walnut stock with gloss finish, top tang safety, low lustre bluing, 60 degree bolt throw, right-hand action was disc. during 2007, except for Full Line dealer model, left-hand action disc. 2010. 6 lbs. 7 oz. - 7 lbs. 3 oz. Disc. 2012.

$825	$630	$575	$475	$375	$335	$300	*$1,030*

Subtract approx. $70 for left-hand action (disc. 2010).
Subtract approx. $65 for Mag. cals. on left-hand action.
Add approx. $60 for open sights (available in 8 cals., disc. 1998).

Beginning 2007, right hand action in this model was only available through Full Line Browning dealers.

* ***A-Bolt Hunter Model II WSSM*** – .223 WSSM, .25 WSSM (new 2004), or .243 WSSM cal., 3 shot mag., super short action, 21 or 22 (new 2004) in. barrel, walnut stock with satin finish and smaller dimensions, 6 1/4 lbs. Mfg. 2003-2007.

$650	$575	$450	$375	$325	$280	$240	*$770*

* ***A-Bolt Hunter Model II with BOSS*** – same cals. as Hunter Model II until 1999, available only in .22-250 Rem., .243 Win., .270 Win., .280 Rem., .30-06, or .308 Win. cal. during 1999, features 22 or 26 (Mag. cals. only, disc. 1998) in. barrel with BOSS. Mfg. 1994-99.

$595	$500	$425	$350	$300	$275	$250	*$617*

A-BOLT HUNTER FIELD II (CLASSIC HUNTER) – .270 Win. (disc. 2001), .270 WSM (new 2002), .30-06 (disc. 2001), .300 Win. Mag. (disc. 2001), .300 WSM (new 2002), .325 WSM (new 2005) 7mm Rem. Mag. (disc. 2001), or 7mm WSM (new 2002) cal., 22 (disc. 2001), 23 (new 2002, WSM cals. only), or 26 (disc. 2001) in. barrel, 3-5 shot mag., features low-lustre bluing and select checkered satin finished Monte Carlo walnut stock and forend, approx. 6 1/2 - 7 1/4 lbs. Mfg. 1999-2006.

$695	$595	$475	$395	$325	$275	$250	*$808*

This model was available to Full-line and Medallion dealers only.

* ***A-Bolt Hunter Field II WSSM (Classic Hunter)*** – .223 WSSM, .25 WSSM (new 2004), or .243 WSSM cal., 3 shot mag., super short action, 22 in. barrel, satin finished Monte Carlo walnut stock with palm swell and double bordered checkering, low lustre bluing, 6 1/4 lbs. Mfg. 2003-2006.

$725	$600	$500	$400	$350	$300	$275	*$829*

This model was available to Full-line and Medallion dealers only.

A-BOLT RMEF SPECIAL HUNTER – .325 WSM cal., similar to Medallion Model II, except has satin finished Monte Carlo stock and special RMEF logo insert on floorplate. Mfg. 2007-2008.

$725	$625	$495	$395	$350	$300	$275	*$864*

A-BOLT NRA WILDLIFE CONSERVATION COLLECTION – .243 Win. cal., 22 in. barrel, blue finish, features NRA Heritage logo laser engraved in satin finished walnut stock, approx. 6 1/2 lbs. Limited mfg. 2006-2007.

$725	$625	$495	$395	$350	$300	$275	*$813*

GRADING - PPGS™	100%	98%	95%	90%	80%	70%	60%	LAST MSR

A-BOLT MICRO HUNTER II – .22 Hornet (only available cal. in right hand action beginning 2009), .22-250 Rem. (disc. 2010), .223 Rem. (mfg. 2000-2005), .243 Win. (disc. 2010), .260 Rem. (disc. 2001), .270 WSM (mfg. 2003-2010), 7mm WSM (mfg. 2003-2010), .300 WSM (mfg. 2003-2010), .325 WSM (mfg. 2005-2010), .308 Win. (disc. 2010), or 7mm-08 Rem. (disc. 2010) cal., 3 shot mag., features shorter LOP and 20 or 22 in. barrel w/o sights, checkered walnut stock and forend, approx. 6 1/4 lbs. Mfg. 1999-2012.

$675 $500 $385 $335 $285 $250 $225 *$870*

Add $60 for Mag. cals. (disc. 2009)
Add $30 for left-hand action (new 2003).

A-BOLT MEDALLION MODEL II – .375 H&H cal., previously available in various cals. between .22-250 Rem. (disc.) - .338 Win. Mag., similar to Medallion Model with A-Bolt II improvements, without sights, except for .375 H&H cal. (open sights standard), gloss finished walnut stock with rosewood grip and forend caps, right hand action w/o BOSS was disc. 2007, 6 lbs. 7 oz. - 7 lbs. 1 oz. Mfg. 1994-2011.

$775 $625 $525 $400 $350 $295 $275 *$990*

Subtract approx. $30 for standard, non-Mag. cals., including WSM.
Subtract approx. $20 for right hand action w/o BOSS (only available in .375 H&H cal. beginning 2007).

* ***A-Bolt Medallion Model II WSSM*** – .223 WSSM, .25 WSSM (new 2004), or .243 WSSM cal., 3 shot mag., super short action, 22 in. barrel, engraved receiver, Monte Carlo gloss finished walnut stock with rosewood pistol grip and forend caps, palm swell and double bordered checkering, no sights, low lustre bluing, 6 1/4 lbs. Mfg. 2003-2007.

$695 $575 $475 $425 $385 $365 $335 *$872*

* ***A-Bolt Medallion Model II with BOSS*** – various cals. between .223 WSSM - .375 H&H, similar to Medallion Model II, except has 22, 23 (new 2002, WSM cals. only), or 26 in. BOSS barrel. Mfg. 1994-2013.

$885 $700 $565 $450 $400 $375 $335 *$1,120*

Add $30 for normal Mag. and WSM cals. or $51 for WSSM (disc. 2007) cals.
Add $32 for left-hand action (disc. 2005).

* ***A-Bolt Micro Medallion Model II*** – .22 Hornet, .22-250 Rem., .223 Rem., .243 Win., 7mm-08 Rem., .284 Win. (disc. 1997), or .308 Win. cal., similar to Micro Medallion Model with A-Bolt II improvements, 20 or 22 (.22 Hornet only) in. barrel without sights, 6 lbs. Mfg. 1994-98.

$525 $465 $400 $350 $300 $275 $250 *$636*

A-BOLT CUSTOM TROPHY II – .270 Win., .30-06, .300 Win. Mag., or 7mm Rem. Mag. cal., features 24 or 26 (Mag. cals. only) in. octagon barrel with gold band at muzzle, no sights, gold outlines on barrel and receiver, checkered select American walnut stock with shadowline cheekpiece and skeleton pistol grip, approx. 7 1/2 lbs. Mfg. 1998-2000.

$1,150 $925 $800 $660 $525 $450 $375 *$1,428*

A-BOLT GOLD MEDALLION MODEL II – .270 Win., .30-06, .300 Win. Mag., or 7mm Rem. Mag. cal., similar to Gold Medallion Model, except has A-Bolt II improvements, 22 or 26 in. barrel, approx. 7 1/2 lbs. Mfg. 1994-98.

$695 $595 $450 $375 $335 $300 $265 *$855*

* ***A-Bolt Gold Medallion Model II with BOSS*** – mfg. 1994-97.

$750 $625 $525 $450 $375 $325 $285 *$916*

A-BOLT WHITE GOLD MEDALLION MODEL II – .270 WSM (new 2004), .270 Win., .30-06, .300 Win. Mag., .300 WSM (new 2004), .325 WSM (new 2005), 7mm WSM (new 2004), or 7mm Rem. Mag. cal., stainless steel receiver and 22, 23 (new 2004), or 26 in. barrel, gold engraving, checkered high gloss Monte Carlo walnut stock with rosewood cap on forend and pistol grip, 6 lbs. 6 oz. - 7 lbs. 11 oz. Mfg. 1999-2009.

$1,025 $775 $625 $525 $425 $360 $300 *$1,279*

Add $30 for Mag. cals.

* ***A-Bolt White Gold Medallion II RMEF*** – 7mm Rem. Mag. (disc. 2006) or .325 WSM (new 2007) cal., similar to White Gold Medallion, includes RMEF logo on pistol grip cap, gold engraved, stainless steel receiver and 26 in. barrel, select walnut stock, contrasting spacers and rosewood caps on forend and pistol grip, continental style cheekpiece and sling swivels, 7 lbs., 11 oz. Limited edition 2003-2008.

$1,045 $785 $630 $515 $450 $375 $325 *$1,312*

* ***A-Bolt White Gold Medallion II with BOSS*** – similar to White Gold Medallion, except has barrel with BOSS, and not available in WSM cals. Disc. 2006.

$985 $765 $610 $500 $435 $375 $320 *$1,235*

Add $28 for non-WSSM Mag. cals.

GRADING - PPGS™	100%	98%	95%	90%	80%	70%	60%	LAST MSR

A-BOLT ECLIPSE HUNTER II WITH BOSS – .22-250 Rem. (disc. 1999), .243 Win. (disc. 1997), .270 Win., .30-06, .308 Win. (disc. 2000), or 7mm Rem. Mag. cal., features laminated thumbhole wood stock with cheekpiece, long action, 22 or 26 (7mm Rem. Mag. only) in. barrel with BOSS, approx. 7 1/2 lbs. Mfg. 1996-2013.

	$1,100	$850	$650	$550	$425	$350	$325	*$1,430*

Add $30 for 7mm Rem. Mag. cal.

* ***A-Bolt Eclipse Varmint II with BOSS*** – .22-250 Rem., .223 Rem., or .308 Win. cal., 24 in. heavy barrel with BOSS, 4 shot mag., otherwise similar to Eclipse Model, approx. 9 lbs. Mfg. 1996-99.

	$810	$655	$535	$455	$375	$325	$285	*$969*

A-BOLT ECLIPSE M-1000 II – .22-250 Rem. (new 2006), .270 WSM, 7mm WSM, .300 WSM, or .308 Win. (new 2006) cal., features 26 in. heavy blue barrel, 3 shot mag., adj. trigger, laminated Gray satin finished thumbhole grip stock, Monte Carlo cheekpiece, recoil pad, 9 lbs. 14 oz. Mfg. 2004-2013.

	$1,050	$800	$665	$535	$400	$350	$300	*$1,340*

Add $20 for WSM cals.

* ***A-Bolt Eclipse M-1000 II with BOSS*** – .22-250 Rem. (new 2006), .300 Win. Mag., .308 Win. (new 2006), .270 WSM (new 2006), 7mm WSM (new 2006), or .300 WSM (new 2006) cal., features special 26 in. heavy target barrel, refined trigger system, 10 lbs. Disc. 2013.

	$1,150	$925	$750	$635	$525	$425	$350	*$1,440*

Add $30 for Mag. cals.

* ***A-Bolt Eclipse M-1000 II Stainless*** – similar to Eclipse M-1000 II, except features 26 in. stainless bull barrel, 9 lbs., 14 oz. Mfg. 2004-2013.

	$1,325	$1,150	$975	$875	$700	$575	$475	*$1,600*

Add $100 for BOSS. Add $40 for WSM cals.

A-BOLT VARMINT II WITH BOSS – .22-250 Rem., .223 Rem., or .308 Win. (new 1995) cal., features A-Bolt II improvements, 22 in. heavy barrel with BOSS, blue/gloss or satin/matte (new 1995, .223 Rem. disc. 1999) finish, black laminated wood stock with checkering, palm swell, and solid recoil pad, without sights, 9 lbs. Mfg. 1994-2000.

	$715	$600	$465	$380	$335	$300	$265	*$879*

A-BOLT EURO-BOLT II – .243 Win., .270 Win., .30-06, .308 Win., or 7mm Rem. Mag. cal., similar to Euro-Bolt with A-Bolt II improvements, 22 or 26 (7mm Rem. Mag. only) in. barrel w/o sights, 6 lbs. 7 oz. - 7 lbs. 3 oz. (Mag.). Mfg. 1994-96.

	$625	$510	$410	$355	$300	$265	$250	*$824*

* ***A-Bolt Euro-Bolt II with BOSS*** – .243 Win., .270 Win., or .308 Win. cal., 22 in. barrel with BOSS, 6 lbs. 7 oz.

	$725	$600	$500	$425	$350	$325	$295	*$922*

A-BOLT STAINLESS STALKER II – similar to Stainless Stalker with A-Bolt improvements, available in various cals, between .22-250 Rem. - .375 H&H, .223 Rem. reintroduced during 2004 in super short action only, no sights, right-hand action w/o Boss was disc. 2007, 6 lbs. 1 oz. - 7 lbs. 3 oz. Mfg. 1994-2010.

	$885	$625	$450	$375	$325	$275	$250	*$1,099*

Add $40 for normal Mag. or WSM cals.

Subtract approx. $20 for right-hand action (available in .375 H&H cal. only beginning 2007).

* ***A-Bolt Stainless Stalker II WSSM*** – .223 WSSM, .25 WSSM (new 2004), or .243 WSSM cal., 3 shot mag., super short action, 21 (disc.) or 22 in. barrel, walnut stock with satin finish and smaller dimensions, 6 lbs., 1 oz. Mfg. 2003-2007.

	$790	$585	$425	$350	$300	$250	$215	*$966*

* ***A-Bolt Stainless Stalker II with BOSS*** – various cals. between .22-250 Rem. and .375 H&H, 22, 23 (new 2002, .300 WSM cal. only), 24 (.375 H&H cal. only) or 26 (Mag. cals. only) in. barrel with BOSS. Approx. 6 1/4 - 7 lbs. Disc. 2013.

	$995	$750	$525	$400	$350	$300	$285	*$1,240*

Add $30 for normal Mag. or WSM cals., or $51 for WSSM cals. (mfg. 2004-2007).

Add $30 for left-hand action.

A-BOLT CARBON FIBER STAINLESS STALKER II – .22-250 Rem. or .300 Win. Mag. cal., features Christensen lightweight 22 or 26 in. carbon fiber barrel with steel liner, stainless steel action, black synthetic stock, 4 or 5 shot mag., approx. 6 1/4 or 7 1/4 lbs. Mfg. 2000-2001.

	$1,475	$1,225	$975	$860	$700	$600	$500	*$1,750*

A-BOLT COMPOSITE STALKER II – various cals. between .22-250 Rem. - .338 Win. Mag., similar to Composite Stalker with A-Bolt II improvements, 22, 23 (WSM cals. only), 24, or 26 (Mag. cals. only) in. barrel without sights, 6 lbs. 1 oz. - 7 lbs. 3 oz. Mfg. 1994-2007.

	$595	$525	$400	$350	$300	$250	$225	*$719*

Add $30 for all Mag. cals.

GRADING - PPGS™	100%	98%	95%	90%	80%	70%	60%	LAST MSR

* ***A-Bolt Composite Stalker II WSSM*** – .223 WSSM, .25 WSSM (new 2004), or .243 WSSM cal., 3 shot mag., super short action, 21 (disc.) or 22 in. barrel, black composite stock with matte blued metal and smaller dimensions, 6.1 lbs. Mfg. 2003-2007.

$650	$535	$435	$380	$335	$295	$260	*$770*

* ***A-Bolt Composite Stalker II with BOSS*** – various cals., 22, 23 (WSM cals. only), or 26 (Mag. cals. only) in. barrel with BOSS, 6 lbs. 6 oz.-7 lbs. 3 oz. Disc. 2013.

$815	$625	$525	$425	$350	$300	$275	*$1,000*

Add $30 for standard Mag. and WSM cals., or $51 for WSSM cals. (mfg. 2004-2007).

A-BOLT VARMINT STALKER II – .22-250 Rem. or .223 Rem. (SSA only beginning 2004) cal., 24 or 26 (.22-250 Rem. cal. only) in. heavy barrel, features Dura-Touch armor coated composite stock with slight palm swell, matte blue metal, 4 or 6 shot mag., approx. 7 3/4 lbs. Mfg. 2002-2008.

$715	$575	$450	$360	$300	$255	$230	*$895*

* ***A-Bolt Varmint Stalker II WSSM*** – .223 WSSM, .25 WSSM (new 2004), or .243 WSSM cal., 3 shot mag., super short action, 21 (mfg. 2003 only) or 24 (new 2004) in. barrel, features Dura-Touch armor coated composite stock with slight palm swell, matte blue metal, 7 lbs. 13 oz. Mfg. 2003-2007.

$745	$580	$475	$395	$335	$295	$275	*$928*

A-BOLT II MOUNTAIN TI – .243 Win. (new 2006), .308 Win. (new 2006), 7mm-08 Rem. (new 2006), .270 WSM, .300 WSM, 7mm WSM, .223 WSSM (mfg. 2005-2010), .243 WSSM (mfg. 2005-2010), .25 WSSM (mfg. 2005-2010), or .325 WSM (new 2006) cal., features titanium short action receiver with composite bolt sleeve and stainless steel 23 in. barrel, fiberglass Bell & Carlson stock with Mossy Oak New Break-Up or Break-Up Infinity (new 2010) camo and Dura-Touch armor coating, Pachmayr Decelerator recoil pad, approx. 5 1/2 lbs. Mfg. 2004-2011.

$1,565	$1,225	$985	$850	$725	$625	$525	*$1,960*

Add $30 for WSM cals.

A-BOLT II GREYWOLF – .25-06 Rem., .270 Win., .280 Rem., .30-06, .300 Win. Mag., .338 Win. Mag., or 7mm Rem. Mag. cal., stainless steel, classic sporter with select walnut stock. Limited mfg. during 1994 only.

$850	$675	$595	$525	$450	$400	$350	*$935*

A-BOLT TARGET II – .223 Rem., .308 Win., .300 WSM cal., 28 in. heavy contour bull barrel, 4 or 6 shot mag., matte blue finish, satin grey checkered laminated wood stock with adj. comb, right-hand palm swell, drilled and tapped, 13 lbs. Mfg. 2009-2013.

$1,200	$925	$750	$650	$550	$450	$395	*$1,480*

Add $20 for .300 WSM cal.

* ***A-Bolt Target Stainless II*** – .223 Rem., .308 Win., .300 WSM cal., similar to A-Bolt Target, except has 28 in. stainless steel barrel. Mfg. 2009-2013.

$1,425	$1,225	$1,050	$900	$775	$675	$575	*$1,730*

Add $50 for .300 WSM cal.

RIFLES: BOLT ACTION, CENTERFIRE X-BOLT SERIES

The X-Bolt Series was introduced during 2008, and features a new three-lever Feather trigger system, which is adjustable from 3-5 lbs. It also has a 3-4 shot detachable rotary mag., 60-degree bolt lift, top safety with bolt unlock button feature, free floating barrel, X-lock scope mounting system (four screws per base, instead of two), and a soft recoil pad using Inflex technology. The various models listed all have these features.

In addition to the models listed below, Browning has also released SHOT Show specials on some models that were available by dealers ordering them at the SHOT Show only. Complete descriptions for these models can be found under SHOT SHOW SPECIALS - RIFLES BOLT ACTION at BlueBookOfGunValues.com/overflow.

X-BOLT COMPOSITE STALKER – .223 Rem. (mfg. 2020 only), .22-250 (new 2020), .243 Win. (new 2020), 6.5 Creedmoor (new 2020), 7mm-08 Rem., .308 Win., .270 WSM, .300 WSM, .25-06 Rem., .270 Win., .280 Rem. (disc. 2020), .30-06, 7mm Rem. Mag., .300 Win. Mag., or .338 Win. Mag. (disc. 2020) cal., 22, 23, 24, or 26 in. free floating Sporterr barrel, 3, 4, or 5 shot detachable rotary mag., steel receiver, drilled and tapped, three lever Feather trigger system, no sights, adj. trigger, Buck Mark engraved in gold on trigger guard, matte black (disc. 2019) or dark gray (new 2020) composite stock with palm swell and textured gripping surfaces, DuraTouch Armor coating (disc. 2019) or non-glare composite finish (new 2020), Inflex recoil pad, sling swivel studs, top tang safety with bolt unlock button, X-Lock scope mounting system, matte blue finish, 6 lbs. 6 oz.-7 lbs. New 2008.

MSR $940	$800	$700	$600	$550	$450	$350	$300

Add $50 for standard Mag. or WSM cals.

GRADING - PPGS™	100%	98%	95%	90%	80%	70%	60%	LAST MSR

X-BOLT ECLIPSE HUNTER – .243 Win., 6.5 Creedmoor (new 2017), 7mm-08 Rem., .308 Win., .270 WSM, .300 WSM, .25-06 Rem., .270 Win., .30-06, 7mm Rem. Mag., or .300 Win. Mag. cal., 22, 23, 24, or 26 in. free floating barrel, target crown, 4 or 5 shot detachable rotary mag., steel receiver, glass bedded and drilled and tapped for scope mounts, adj. feather trigger, no sights, laminated gray satin varnish finished checkered stock with thumbhole grip and Monte Carlo cheekpiece, Inflex recoil pad, sling swivel studs, top tang safety, bolt unlock button, matte blued metal finish, 6.5-7.5 lbs. Mfg. 2014-2017.

	$865	$750	$650	$575	$475	$385	$300	*$1,020*

Add $40 for standard Mag. or WSM cals.

X-BOLT ECLIPSE HUNTER STAINLESS – .243 Win., 6mm Creedmoor (mfg. 2018-2019), 6.5 Creedmoor, 7mm-08 Rem., .308 Win., .270 WSM, .300 WSM, .25-06 Rem., .270 Win., .30-06, 7mm Rem. Mag., or .300 Win. Mag. cal., 24 or 26 in. free floating matte gray stainless steel sporter barrel, threaded muzzle brake, target crown, 4 or 5 shot detachable rotary mag., steel receiver, drilled and tapped for scope mounts, adj. feather trigger, no sights, laminated gray satin varnish finished checkered stock with thumbhole grip and Monte Carlo cheekpiece, Inflex recoil pad, top tang safety, bolt unlock button, sling swivel studs, matte blue metal finish, approx. 6.5-7.5 lbs. New 2018.

MSR $1,310	$1,100	$965	$825	$750	$600	$500	$425	

Add $30 for standard Mag. or WSM cals.

X-BOLT ECLIPSE TARGET – 6.5 Creedmoor or .308 Win. cal., short action, 28 in. heavy free floating bull barrel, target crown, 5 shot detachable rotary mag., steel receiver, glass bedded, drilled and tapped, adj. feather trigger, laminated gray satin varnish finished stock with thumbhole grip and raised cheekpiece, Inflex recoil pad, top tang safety, swivel stud for bipod, two QD swivel cups, bolt unlock button, matte blue metal finish, 10 lbs. Mfg. 2015-2017.

	$900	$785	$675	$600	$500	$400	$325	*$1,070*

X-BOLT ECLIPSE TARGET STAINLESS – 6mm Creedmoor, 6.5 Creedmoor, or .308 Win. cal., 28 in. fluted heavy free floating matte gray stainless steel bull barrel, target crown, 5 shot detachable rotary mag., steel receiver, glass bedded, drilled and tapped, adj. feather trigger, laminated gray satin varnish finished stock with thumbhole grip and raised cheekpiece, Inflex recoil pad, top tang safety, swivel stud for bipod, two QD swivel cups, bolt unlock button, matte blue metal finish, 10 lbs. Mfg. 2018-2019.

	$1,215	$1,065	$910	$825	$675	$550	$425	*$1,430*

X-BOLT ECLIPSE VARMINT – .204 Ruger, .22-250 Rem., or .223 Rem. cal., 26 in. free floating heavy bull barrel, target crown, 5 or 6 shot detachable rotary mag., adj. feather trigger, no sights, laminated gray satin varnish finished stock with thumbhole grip, raised cheekpiece, and Inflex recoil pad, swivel stud for bipod, two QD swivel cups, matte blue metal finish, 10 lbs. Mfg. 2015-2017.

	$900	$785	$675	$600	$500	$400	$325	*$1,070*

X-BOLT ECLIPSE VARMINT STAINLESS – .204 Ruger, .223 Rem., or .22-250 Rem. cal., 26 in. free floating fluted heavy matte gray stainless steel bull barrel, target crown, 5 or 6 shot detachable rotary mag., steel receiver, glass bedded, drilled and tapped, adj. feather trigger, laminated gray satin varnish finished stock with thumbhole grip and raised cheekpiece, Inflex recoil pad, swivel stud for bipod, two QD swivel cups, top tang safety, bolt unlock button, matte blued finish, 9 1/2 lbs. Mfg. 2018-2019.

	$1,215	$1,065	$910	$825	$675	$550	$425	*$1,430*

X-BOLT HELL'S CANYON LONG RANGE – 6.5 Creedmoor, 6mm Creedmoor (mfg. 2018-2020), 6.5 PRC (new 2020), .270 WSM, .300 WSM, .26 Nosler (mfg. 2017-2019), 7mm Rem. Mag., .28 Nosler, .300 Win. Mag., .30 Nosler (new 2020), .300 PRC (new 2021), or .300 RUM (new 2020) cal., 22 (mfg. 2017 only), 23 (mfg. 2017 only), or 26 in. heavy sporter fluted barrel with threaded muzzle brake, target crown, 3 (mfg. 2017), 4, or 5 shot detachable rotary mag., steel receiver, adj. feather trigger, composite stock with textured gripping surfaces, palm swell, A-TACS AU Camo finish, Dura-Touch Armor coating, sling swivel studs, Inflex recoil pad, top tang safety, Cerakote Burnt Bronze finish on receiver and barrel, 7.3-7.8 lbs. New 2017.

MSR $1,320	$1,125	$985	$850	$765	$625	$500	$425	

Add $40 for 6.5 PRC (new 2020), .300 RUM (new 2020), .300 PRC (new 2021), all WSM, or Mag. cals.
Add $70 for Nosler cals.

X-BOLT HELL'S CANYON LONG RANGE MCMILLAN – 6mm Creedmoor (disc. 2020), 6.5 Creedmoor, 6.5 PRC (new 2020), 7mm Rem. Mag., .300 WSM (mfg. 2018-2019), .26 Nosler (mfg. 2018-2019), .28 Nosler, .300 Win. Mag., .30 Nosler (new 2020), .300 PRC (new 2021), or .300 RUM (new 2020) cal., 26 in. free floating fluted heavy sporter barrel, threaded muzzle brake with thread protector, target crown, 3 or 4 shot detachable rotary mag., steel receiver, glass bedded, drilled and tapped, adj. feather trigger, ATACS AU camo finished McMillan Game Scout composite stock with textured gripping surfaces, palm swell, Dura-Touch Armor coating, QD sling swivel studs, bipod stud, Pachmayr Decelerator recoil

GRADING - PPGS™	100%	98%	95%	90%	80%	70%	60%	LAST MSR

pad, top tang safety, bolt unlock button, Picatinny rail, Cerakote Burnt Bronze finish on receiver and barrel, right or left (mfg. 2018 only) hand action. New 2018.

MSR $2,310	$1,950	$1,700	$1,465	$1,325	$1,075	$885	$750	

Add $50 for 6.5 PRC (new 2020) .300 RUM (new 2020), .300 PRC (new 2021), or Mag. cals.
Add $80 for Nosler cals.

X-BOLT HELL'S CANYON MAX LONG RANGE – 6.5 Creedmoor, 6.5 PRC, 7mm Rem. Mag., .28 Nosler, .300 Win. Mag., .30 Nosler, .300 PRC, or .300 RUM cal., 26 in. fluted heavy sporter barrel, Recoil Hawg muzzle brake, thread protector, 3 or 4 shot mag., A-TACS AU Camo composite Max stock with adj. comb, includes 1/4 in. and 2/3 in. LOP spacers and three swivel studs, extended bolt handle, Cerakote Burnt Bronze finish, 8.3-8.7 lbs. New 2021.

MSR $1,430	$1,225	$1,075	$925	$835	$675	$550	$450	

Add $60 for 6.5 PRC, 7mm Rem. Mag., .300 Win. Mag., .300 PRC, or .300 RUM cal.
Add $70 for .28 Nosler or .30 Nosler cal.

X-BOLT HELL'S CANYON SPEED A-TACS AU CAMO – .243 Win., 6mm Creedmoor (mfg. 2018-2020), 6.5 Creedmoor, 6.5 PRC (new 2020), 7mm-08 Rem., .308 Win., .270 WSM, .300 WSM, .26 Nosler (mfg. 2016-2019), .28 Nosler (new 2017), .270 Win., .30-06, 7mm Rem. Mag., .300 Win. Mag., .30 Nosler (new 2020), .300 PRC (new 2021), or .300 RUM (new 2020) cal., 22, 23, 24 (new 2020, 6.5 PRC cal. only), or 26 in. fluted free floating lightweight sporter contour barrel with muzzle brake and thread protector, target crown, 3, 4, or 5 (disc. 2020) shot detachable rotary magazine, steel receiver, glass bedded, drilled and tapped for scope mounts, adj. feather trigger, A-TACS AU camo composite stock with palm swell and textured gripping surfaces, Inflex recoil pad, top tang safety, bolt unlock button, sling swivel studs, Cerakote Burnt Bronze finish on barrel and receiver, approx. 6 1/2 lbs. New 2016.

MSR $1,300	$1,100	$965	$825	$750	$600	$500	$400	

Add $40 for 6.5 PRC (new 2020), .300 RUM (new 2020), .300 PRC (new 2021), WSM, or Mag. cals.
Add $60 for Nosler cals.

X-BOLT HELL'S CANYON SPEED A-TACS TD-X CAMO – 6.5 Creedmoor, .308 Win., .300 WSM, .270 Win., .30-06, 7mm Rem. Mag., .28 Nosler, or .300 Win. Mag. cal., 22, 23, or 26 in. fluted Sporter contour barrel with threaded muzzle brake, 3 or 4 shot detachable mag., steel receiver, gold plated trigger, Buck Mark engraved in gold on trigger guard, composite stock with A-TACS TD-X camo, Inflex recoil pad, textured grip panels, drilled and tapped, Burnt Bronze Cerakote finish, 6 lbs. 5 oz. New 2020.

MSR $1,300	$1,100	$965	$825	$750	$600	$500	$400	

Add $40 for WSM or Mag. cals.
Add $60 for .28 Nosler cal.

X-BOLT HUNTER – .223 Rem., .22-250 Rem., .243 Win., 6mm Creedmoor (mfg. 2018-2019), 6.5 Creedmoor, 7mm-08 Rem., .308 Win., .270 WSM, .300 WSM, .25-06 Rem., .270 Win., .280 Rem., .30-06, 7mm Rem. Mag., .300 Win. Mag., .338 Win. Mag., or .375 H&H Mag. cal., right or left (new 2011) hand action, 22, 23, 24, or 26 in. free floating barrel w/o sights (.375 H&H Mag. includes open sights), target crown, 4, 5, or 6 shot detachable rotary mag., steel receiver, glass bedded, drilled and tapped, adj. Feather trigger, satin finished walnut stock with checkering, Inflex technology recoil pad, top safety with bolt unlock button, 60 degree bolt lift, X-lock scope mounting system, low luster blue finish, approx. 6 1/2-7 lbs. New 2008.

MSR $1,000	$850	$750	$650	$575	$475	$385	$325	

Add $40 for standard Mag. or WSM cals.
Add $30 for left-hand action (new 2011, certain cals. only).

* ***X-Bolt Hunter Full Line Dealer*** – .243 Win., 7mm-08 Rem., .308 Win., .270 WSM, .300 WSM, .270 Win., .30-06, 7mm Rem. Mag., or .300 Win. Mag. cal., 22, 23, or 26 in. free floating round barrel, target crown, 4 or 5 shot detachable rotary mag., steel receiver, glass bedded, drilled and tapped for scope mounts, gold adj. Feather Trigger, no sights, satin finished checkered walnut pistol grip stock with raised hunter cheekpiece, Inflex recoil pad, top safety with bolt unlock button, sling swivel studs, matte blue metal finish, approx. 6 3/4 lbs. Mfg. 2008-2016.

	$875	$750	$650	$585	$475	$400	$325	*$1,040*

Add $40 for Mag. or WSM cals.

* ***X-Bolt High Grade Hunter Full Line Dealer*** – .243 Win., 6.5 Creedmoor (new 2017), 7mm-08 Rem. (disc. 2016), .308 Win., .270 WSM, .300 WSM, .270 Win., .30-06, 7mm Rem. Mag., or .300 Win. Mag cal., 22, 23, or 26 in. free floating full octagon barrel, 3-4 shot detachable rotary mag., steel receiver, drilled and tapped, gold adj. Feather trigger, no sights, oil finished Grade III/IV checkered full pistol grip walnut stock with rosewood forend grip and pistol caps, Inflex recoil pad, top tang safety with bolt unlock button, sling swivel studs, matte blue metal finish, approx. 6 3/4 lbs. Mfg. 2015-2018.

	$1,250	$1,100	$950	$850	$700	$575	$475	*$1,470*

Add $40 for Mag. or WSM cals.

GRADING - PPGS™	100%	98%	95%	90%	80%	70%	60%	LAST MSR

X-BOLT HUNTER LONG RANGE – 6.5 Creedmoor, 6.5 PRC, .308 Win., .270 Win., .30-06, 7mm Rem. Mag., or .300 Win. Mag. cal., 22, 24, or 26 in. heavy sporter barrel, muzzle brake, 3 or 4 shot detachable rotary mag., adj. trigger, Buck Mark engraved in gold on trigger guard, satin finish checkered walnut stock with ambidextrous adj. comb, Inflex recoil pad, extended bolt handle, short throw bolt, drilled and tapped, matte blued finish, 7 lbs. 11 oz.-8 lbs. New 2020.

MSR $1,350	$1,150	$1,000	$865	$780	$635	$525	$450	

Add $30 for 6.5 PRC, 7mm Rem. Mag., or .300 Win. Mag. cal.

X-BOLT LONG RANGE HUNTER – 6.5 Creedmoor, .270 WSM, .300 WSM, .26 Nosler, 7mm Rem. Mag., or .300 Win. Mag. cal., 26 in. stainless steel fluted free floating barrel with threaded muzzle brake, target crown, 4 or 5 shot detachable rotary mag., stainless steel receiver, drilled and tapped, adj. Feather trigger, carbon fiber finished composite stock with palm swell and textured gripping surfaces, Dura-Touch Armor coating, Inflex recoil pad, sling swivel studs, top tang safety with bolt unlock button, approx. 7-8 lbs. Mfg. 2016 only.

	$1,215	$1,050	$900	$815	$650	$550	$450	*$1,430*

Add $40 for Mag. or WSM cals.

X-BOLT MAX LONG RANGE – 6mm Creedmoor (disc. 2020), 6.5 Creedmoor, 6.5 PRC (new 2020), .308 Win., .300 WSM, .26 Nosler (mfg. 2019 only), 7mm Rem. Mag., .28 Nosler, .30 Nosler (new 2020), .300 Win. Mag., .300 PRC (new 2021), or .300 RUM cal., 26 in. free floating stainless steel fluted heavy sporter barrel with satin gray finish, removable or Recoil Hawg (new 2021) muzzle brake, 3 or 4 shot rotary mag., gold engraved Buck Mark on trigger guard, black and gray textured composite Max stock with adj. comb, Inflex Technology recoil pad, slim pistol grip, top tang safety, X-Lock Scope Mounting System, sling and bipod studs, extended bolt handle, 8.3-8.7 oz. New 2019.

MSR $1,340	$1,140	$1,000	$855	$775	$625	$515	$445	

Add $40 for 6.5 PRC (new 2020), .300 WSM, 7mm Rem. Mag., .300 Win. Mag., .300 PRC (new 2021), or .300 RUM cal.

Add $60 for .28 Nosler or .30 Nosler (new 2020) cal.

X-BOLT MAX VARMINT/TARGET – .204 Ruger, .223 Rem., .22-250 Rem., 6.5 Creedmoor, .308 Win., .28 Nosler, or .300 Win. Mag. cal., 26 in. match grade stainless steel bull barrel with fluting and satin gray barrel finish, Recoil Hawg (new 2021) muzzle brake, 5 shot mag., gold plated trigger, trigger guard engraved with Buck Mark in gold, drilled and tapped, matte black Max stock with adj. comb, LOP spacers, and vertical pistol grip, Inflex recoil pad, textured grip panels, extended bolt handle, Picatinny rail for bipod mounting, matte black finish, 9 lbs.-9 lbs. 6 oz. New late 2019.

MSR $1,380	$1,175	$1,025	$875	$800	$650	$550	$450	

Add $40 for .300 Win. Mag. cal.

Add $80 for .28 Nosler cal.

This model was originally featured as a 2019 SHOT Show Special.

X-BOLT MEDALLION – .223 Rem., .22-250 Rem., .243 Win., 6mm Creedmoor (mfg. 2018-2019), 6.5 Creedmoor, .308 Win., .270 WSM, .300 WSM, .25-06 Rem., .270 Win., .280 Rem., .30-06, 7mm Rem. Mag., .300 Win. Mag., .338 Win. Mag. (mfg. 2008-2019), or .375 H&H Mag. cal., right or left (new 2011) hand action, 22, 23, 24, or 26 in. free floating barrel with blued finish, target crown, 3-5 shot detachable rotary mag., steel engraved receiver with polished blued finish, drilled and tapped, adj. Feather trigger, gloss finished checkered walnut stock with rosewood pistol grip and forend caps, Inflex technology recoil pad, top tang safety with bolt unlock button, 60 degree bolt lift, X-lock scope mounting system, sling swivel studs, 6.6-7 lbs. New 2008.

MSR $1,140	$975	$850	$725	$675	$550	$450	$375	

Add $40 for standard Mag., WSM, or .375 H&H (new 2012) cals.

Add $20-$60 for left-hand action, depending on caliber (new 2011, certain cals. only).

This model was also featured as a 2011 SHOT Show Special (in .375 H&H cal.).

X-BOLT MEDALLION SAFARI GRADE – .243 Win., 6.5 Creedmoor, .308 Win., .300 WSM, .270 Win., .30-06, 7mm Rem. Mag., .300 Win. Mag., .338 Win. Mag., .300 H&H Mag., or .375 H&H Mag. cal., 24 in. fluted heavy sporter barrel with gold accented engraving, 4 or 5 shot detachable rotary mag., adj. Feather trigger, gloss finish checkered Grade IV/V walnut stock, rosewood forend grip and pistol grip cap, sling swivel studs, Inflex recoil pad, top tang safety. Mfg. 2017 only.

	$1,625	$1,400	$1,075	$950	$825	$725	$625	*$1,870*

Add $30 for WSM and Mag. cals.

X-BOLT MICRO COMPOSITE – .243 Win., 6mm Creedmoor (disc. 2020), 6.5 Creedmoor, 7mm-08 Rem., or .308 Win. cal., 20 in. free floating light sporter barrel, threaded muzzle brake with thread protector, target crown, 4 shot detachable rotary mag., steel receiver, glass bedded, drilled and tapped, adj.

GRADING - PPGS™	100%	98%	95%	90%	80%	70%	60%	LAST MSR

feather trigger, composite stock with palm swell and textured gripping surfaces, Dura-Touch Armor coating, 13 in. LOP, Pachmayr Decelerator recoil pad, sling swivel studs, top tang safety, bolt unlock button, matte blued finish, 6 lbs. New 2018.

MSR $1,030	$875	$765	$650	$595	$475	$400	$325	

X-BOLT MICRO HUNTER – various cals., 20 or 22 in. blue barrel, right or left (new 2011) hand action, 3 or 4 shot mag., low luster blue finish, satin finished walnut stock, smaller dimensions, drilled and tapped, approx. 6 lbs. Mfg. 2009-2014.

	$750	$650	$550	$500	$400	$350	$300	*$900*

Add $50 for WSM cals.
Add $40 for left-hand action (new 2011, certain cals. only).

X-BOLT MICRO MIDAS – .22-.250 Rem., .243 Win., 6mm Creedmoor (mfg. 2018-2019), 6.5 Creedmoor (new 2017), .308 Win., 7mm-08 Rem., .270 WSM (mfg. 2015-2016), or .300 WSM (mfg. 2015-2016) cal., short or super short action, 20 or 22 (disc.) in. free floating barrel, target crown, 4 or 5 shot detachable rotary mag., steel receiver, adj. Feather trigger, no sights, satin finished checkered walnut stock with three 1/4 in. stock spacers, Inflex Technology recoil pad, top tang safety with bolt unlock button, 60 degree bolt lift, X-lock scope mounting system, matte blue metal finish, approx. 6 lbs. New 2011.

MSR $940	$800	$700	$600	$550	$450	$350	$300	

Add $50 for left-hand action (certain cals. only).
Add $40 for .270 WSM or .300 WSM cals. (mfg. 2015-2016).

The Micro Midas Left-Hand version was available as a 2012 SHOT Show Special and also featured an Inflex Technology recoil pad and sling swivel studs. MSR was $900.

X-BOLT PRO BURNT BRONZE – 6mm Creedmoor (disc. 2019), 6.5 Creedmoor, 6.5 PRC (new 2020), .308 Win., .300 WSM, .26 Nosler (disc. 2019), .270 Win., .30-06, 7mm Rem. Mag., .28 Nosler, .300 Win. Mag., .30 Nosler (new 2020), .300 PRC (new 2021), or .300 RUM (new 2020) cal., 22, 23, 24 (new 2020, 6.5 PRC cal. only), or 26 in. free floating fluted stainless steel lightweight sporter contour barrel, threaded muzzle brake, target crown, 3, 4, or 5 shot detachable rotary mag., stainless steel receiver, glass bedded, drilled and tapped for X-Lock scope mounts, adj. feather trigger, Second generation carbon fiber stock with palm swell and textured gripping surfaces, Inflex recoil pad, top tang safety, bolt unlock button, spiral fluted bolt body, ergonomic spiral fluted bolt handle, sling swivel studs, Cerakote Burnt Bronze finish, approx. 6 1/2 lbs. New 2018.

MSR $2,280	$1,940	$1,700	$1,450	$1,325	$1,065	$900	$750	

Add $60 for 6.5 PRC (new 2020), .300 RUM (new 2020), .300 PRC (new 2021), all WSM, or Mag. cals.
Add $110 for Nosler cals.

This model was featured as a 2017 SHOT Show Special.

X-BOLT PRO LONG RANGE BURNT BRONZE – 6mm Creedmoor (disc. 2019), 6.5 PRC (new 2020), 6.5 Creedmoor, .270 WSM (disc. 2019), .300 WSM, .26 Nosler (disc. 2019), 7mm Rem. Mag., .28 Nosler, .300 Win. Mag., .30 Nosler (new 2020), .300 RUM (new 2020), or .300 PRC (new 2021) cal., 26 in. free floating fluted stainless steel heavy sporter barrel, threaded muzzle brake, target crown, 4 or 5 shot detachable rotary mag., stainless steel receiver, glass bedded, drilled and tapped for X-Lock scope mounts, adj. feather trigger, Second generation carbon fiber stock with textured gripping surfaces and palm swell, Inflex recoil pad, spiral fluted bolt body, ergonomic spiral fluted bolt handle, sling swivel studs, top tang safety, bolt unlock button, Cerakote Burnt Bronze finsh, approx. 7 1/2 lbs. New 2018.

MSR $2,340	$2,000	$1,750	$1,500	$1,350	$1,100	$900	$775	

Add $50 for 6.5 PRC (new 2020), .300 RUM (new 2020), .300 PRC (new 2021), all WSM, or Mag. cals.
Add $90 for Nosler cals.

X-BOLT PRO TUNGSTEN – 6.5 Creedmoor, 6.5 PRC (new 2020), .308 Win., .300 WSM, .26 Nosler (mfg. 2019 only), .270 Win., .30-06, 7mm Rem. Mag., .28 Nosler, .300 Win. Mag., .30 Nosler (new 2020), or .300 RUM (new 2020) cal., 22, 23, 24 (new 2020, 6.5 PRC only), or 26 in. stainless steel lightweight sporter fluted barrel, threaded muzzle brake, 3, 4, or 5 shot detachable mag., gold plated trigger, Generation 2 carbon fiber stock, textured grip panels, spiral fluted bolt handle and body, Cerakote Tungsten finish, 6.1-6.10 oz. New 2019.

MSR $2,280	$1,940	$1,700	$1,450	$1,325	$1,065	$900	$750	

Add $60 for 6.5 PRC (new 2020), .300 RUM (new 2020), all WSM, or Mag. cals.
Add $110 for Nosler cals.

X-BOLT RMEF SPECIAL HUNTER – .300 WSM or .325 WSM (disc.) cal., 23 in. free floating barrel, target crown, 3 shot detachable rotary mag., steel receiver, drilled and tapped, three lever Feather trigger system, checkered satin finished walnut stock with raised cheekpiece, rosewood grip cap with RMEF logo inset, Inflex recoil pad, top tang safety with bolt unlock button, 60 degree bolt lift, X-lock scope mounting system, sling swivel studs, low-luster blue finish, 6 lbs. 14 oz. Mfg. 2009-2016.

	$925	$800	$685	$625	$500	$425	$325	*$1,110*

GRADING - PPGS™	100%	98%	95%	90%	80%	70%	60%	LAST MSR

X-BOLT RMEF WHITE GOLD MEDALLION – .300 Win. Mag. or .325 WSM (disc.) cal., 26 in. stainless steel free floating barrel, target crown, 4 shot detachable rotary mag., stainless steel receiver with scroll engraving on front and rear, drilled and tapped for scope mounts, adj. Feather trigger, gloss finished Grade IV/V checkered walnut stock with raised cheekpiece, rosewood forend grip and pistol grip caps with RMEF logo inset, Inflex recoil pad, top tang safety with bolt unlock button, sling swivel studs, polished stainless finish, 7 lbs. New 2009.

MSR $1,670	**$1,425**	**$1,250**	**$1,075**	**$975**	**$785**	**$650**	**$550**	

X-BOLT STAINLESS STALKER – .223 Rem. (disc. 2020), .22-250 Rem. (disc. 2020), .243 Win., 6mm Creedmoor (mfg. 2018-2019), 6.5 Creedmoor, 7mm-08 Rem., .308 Win., .270 WSM, .300 WSM, .25-06 Rem., .270 Win., .280 Rem. (disc. 2020), .30-06, 7mm Rem. Mag., .300 Win. Mag., .338 Win. Mag., or .375 H&H Mag. cal., 22, 23, 24, or 26 in. free floating stainless steel sporter barrel, target crown, 3, 4, or 5 (disc. 2020) shot detachable rotary mag., stainless steel receiver, drilled and tapped for scope mounts, adj. Feather trigger, matte black composite stock with palm swell and textured gripping surfaces, Dura-Touch Armor coating, Inflex recoil pad, sling swivel studs, top tang safety, 6.6-7 lbs. New 2008.

MSR $1,230	**$1,050**	**$920**	**$790**	**$715**	**$580**	**$475**	**$400**	

Add $40 for regular Mag. or WSM cals. or .375 H&H with open sights (new 2011).

This model in .375 H&H cal. was featured as a 2010 SHOT Show Special.

X-BOLT TARGET MCMILLAN A3-5 AMBUSH – 6.5 Creedmoor, 6.5 PRC (new 2020), .308 Win. (mfg. 2019 only), .26 Nosler (mfg. 2019 only), 7mm Rem. Mag. (mfg. 2019 only), .28 Nosler, or .300 Win. Mag. cal., 26 in. stainless steel fluted bull barrel, Recoil Hawg (new 2021) muzzle brake with suppressor threads and thread protector, 3 or 4 shot detachable mag., composite McMillan A3-5 stock with adj. comb, Pachmayr Decelerator recoil pad, QD sling swivel studs, textured grip panels, extended bolt handle, upper and lower Picatinny rail, Urban Carbon Ambush camo finish, 10 lbs. New 2019.

MSR $3,240	**$2,750**	**$2,400**	**$2,065**	**$1,875**	**$1,515**	**$1,275**	**$1,075**	

Add $40 for 6.5 PRC (new 2020) or .300 Win. Mag. cal.
Add $70 for Nosler cals.

This model was originally a 2018 SHOT Show Special.

X-BOLT VARMINT STALKER – .22-250 Rem., .223 Rem., .243 Win., or .308 Win. cal., 24 or 26 in. heavy blue barrel, low luster blue finish, 4 or 5 shot mag., matte black checkered composite stock with Dura-Touch Armor coating and palm swell, approx. 8 lbs. Mfg. 2009-2014.

	$925	**$725**	**$625**	**$525**	**$425**	**$375**	**$350**	***$1,070***

X-BOLT VARMINT STALKER CAMO – .204 Ruger, .22-250 Rem., .223 Rem., .243 Win., 6.5 Creedmoor (new 2017), or .308 Win. cal., 22 (new 2017, 6.5 Creedmoor only), 24, or 26 in. heavy free floating sporter contour barrel, target crown, 5 shot detachable rotary mag., steel receiver, drilled and tapped for scope mounts, adj. feather trigger, Mossy Oak Brush camo composite stock with palm swell and textured gripping surfaces, DuraTouch Armor coating, Inflex recoil pad, sling swivel studs, top tang safety with bolt unlock button, 60 degree bolt lift, matte blue metal finish, approx. 6 1/2 lbs. Mfg. 2015-2017.

	$800	**$700**	**$600**	**$550**	**$450**	**$350**	**$300**	***$940***

X-BOLT WESTERN HUNTER – 6.5 Creedmoor, 6.5 PRC, .270 Win., 7mm Rem. Mag., .28 Nosler, .300 Win. Mag., or .300 PRC cal., 24 or 26 in. heavy sporter contour barrel, threaded muzzle brake and thread protector, 3 or 4 shot removable mag., A-TACS AU Camo composite stock with new adj. comb system, top tang thumb safety, extended bolt handle, matte blued finish, 6.5-7 lbs. New 2021.

MSR $1,070	**$900**	**$790**	**$675**	**$610**	**$495**	**$400**	**$325**	

Add $30 for 6.5 PRC, 7mm Rem. Mag., .300 Win. Mag., or .300 PRC cal.
Add $110 for .28 Nosler cal.

X-BOLT WESTERN HUNTER LONG RANGE – 6.5 Creedmoor, 6.5 PRC, .270 Win., 7mm Rem. Mag., .28 Nosler, .300 Win. Mag., .30 Nosler, .300 PRC, or .300 RUM cal., 26 in. heavy sporter contour barrel, threaded muzzle brake, A-TACS AU Camo composite stock with new adj. comb system, extended bolt handle, matte blued finish, 7.7-7 lbs. 12 oz. New 2021.

MSR $1,100	**$940**	**$825**	**$700**	**$640**	**$515**	**$425**	**$350**	

Add $40 for 6.5 PRC, 7mm Rem. Mag., .300 Win. Mag., .300 PRC, or .300 RUM cal.
Add $80 for Nosler cals.

X-BOLT WESTERN HUNTER LONG RANGE FIBER FUSION – 6.5 Creedmoor, 6.5 PRC, .270 Win., .30-06, 7mm Rem. Mag., .28 Nosler, .300 Win. Mag., .30 Nosler, .300 RUM, or .300 PRC cal., short or long action, stainless steel heavy sporter contour fluted barrel with threaded muzzle brake, rotary mag., gold plated three-lever Feather trigger, Hard Core Fiber Fusion stock with Cerakote FDE finish with

GRADING - PPGS™	100%	98%	95%	90%	80%	70%	60%	LAST MSR

black spider web graphic, new adj. comb system, Inflex Technology recoil pad, textured grip panels, top tang thumb safety, ergonomic extended bolt handle, Buck Mark in gold engraved on trigger guard, matte gray barrel finish.

MSR $2,040	$1,735	$1,525	$1,300	$1,180	$950	$780	$680	

Add $30 for .300 PRC, .300 RUM, or Mag. cals.
Add $80 for Nosler cals.

X-BOLT WHITE GOLD MEDALLION – .223 Rem. (mfg. 2010-2019), .22-250 Rem., .243 Win., 6mm Creedmoor (mfg. 2018-2020), 6.5 Creedmoor, 7mm-08 Rem., .308 Win., .270 WSM, .300 WSM, .25-06 Rem., .270 Win., .280 Rem. (disc. 2020), .30-06, 7mm Rem. Mag., .300 Win. Mag., or .338 Win. Mag. (disc. 2020) cal., 22, 23, 24, or 26 in. stainless steel free floating barrel, target crown, 3, 4, or 6 (disc. 2020) shot detachable rotary mag., stainless steel receiver with scroll engraving on front and rear, drilled and tapped for scope mounts, three lever Feather trigger system, gloss finished Grade IV/V checkered walnut stock with raised cheekpiece, rosewood forend grip and pistol grip cap, Inflex recoil pad, top tang safety with bolt unlock button, 60 degree bolt lift, X-lock scope mounting system, sling swivel studs, polished stainless finish, 6 lbs. New 2010.

MSR $1,550	$1,320	$1,155	$990	$900	$725	$600	$515	

Add $40 for Mag. or WSM cals.

During 2014, this model's nomenclature was changed from X-Bolt White Gold to X-Bolt White Gold Medallion.

RIFLES: BOLT ACTION, RIMFIRE A-BOLT SERIES

In addition to the models listed below, Browning has also released SHOT Show specials on some models that were available by dealers ordering them at the SHOT Show only. These models are listed in the separate category SHOT SHOW SPECIALS LISTINGS: RIFLES BOLT ACTION.

A-BOLT GRADE I RIMFIRE – .22 LR or .22 WMR (new 1989) cal., 60 degree bolt throw, 22 in. barrel, checkered walnut stock and forearm or laminated stock (scarce - approx. 1,500 mfg., 390 had no sights), 5 or 15 (optional) shot mag., adj. trigger, available with or without open sights, 5 lbs. 9 oz. Mfg. 1986-96.

* ***A-Bolt Grade I .22 LR cal.***

	$575	$495	$425	$350	$295	$250	$210	*$425*

Add $14 for open sights.

A 15 shot mag. was also available for this model at $45 retail.

* ***A-Bolt Grade I .22 WMR cal.***

	$650	$550	$450	$375	$325	$295	$250	*$493*

Add $21 for open sights.

A-BOLT GOLD MEDALLION RIMFIRE – .22 LR cal. only, similar to A-Bolt, except has high grade select walnut stock checkered 22 lines per inch, rosewood pistol and forend cap, high gloss finish, gold filled lettering and moderate engraving, solid recoil pad. Mfg. 1988-96.

	$625	$550	$450	$385	$325	$295	$250	*$567*

RIFLES: LEVER ACTION

In addition to the models listed below, Browning has also released SHOT Show specials on some models that were available by dealers ordering them at the SHOT Show only. Complete descriptions for these models can be found under SHOT SHOW SPECIALS - RIFLES: LEVER ACTION at BlueBookOfGunValues.com/overflow.

BL-17 – .17 Mach 2 cal., otherwise similar to the BL-22, 5 lbs., 2 oz. New 2005.

* ***BL-17 Grade I*** – uncheckered stock with choice of blued or nickel (BL-17 Field) receiver, blued trigger. Mfg. 2005.

	$420	$370	$325	$285	$240	$200	$160	*$484*

Add $32 for nickel.

* ***BL-17 Grade II*** – features choice of engraved blued or nickel (Field) receiver, gold trigger, checkered stock and forearm. Mfg. 2005.

	$465	$400	$350	$315	$255	$210	$165	*$524*

Add $53 for nickel.

* ***BL-17 Grade II Field Octagon*** – similar to BL-22 Classic/Field octagon, 5 lbs., 6 oz., mfg. 2005 by Miroku.

	$750	$675	$600	$550	$450	$375	$295	*$744*

GRADING - PPGS™	100%	98%	95%	90%	80%	70%	60%	LAST MSR

BL-22 GRADE I – .22 S, L, and LR cal., 20 in. barrel, short throw (33 degree) lever, folding leaf sight, 15 shot (LR) mag., blue finish, exposed hammer, Western style gloss finished uncheckered stock and forearm, 5 lbs. Mfg. 1970-2003 by Miroku.

	$450	$395	$335	$290	$250	$210	$165	*$436*

* ***BL-22 Grade I (Classic)*** – .22 S, L, and LR cal., 20 in. barrel, recessed crown, 15 shot tubular mag., exposed hammer, adj. sights with front bead, gloss finished American walnut straight grip stock and forearm, blue finish, 5 lbs. New 1999, mfg. by Miroku.

MSR $670	$565	$490	$420	$380	$310	$250	$200	

* ***BL-22 Grade I Field Full Line Dealer*** – .22 S, L, and LR cal., 20 in. barrel with blued finish, recessed crown, 15 shot tubular mag., satin nickel finished steel receiver grooved for scope mounts, adj. sights with front bead, satin finished American walnut straight grip stock, 5 lbs. New 2005.

MSR $700	$600	$525	$450	$410	$325	$275	$225	

This model is available through Full Line and Medallion dealers only.

* ***BL-22 Grade I Micro Midas*** – .22 LR cal., 16 1/4 in. barrel, recessed crown, 12 shot tubular mag., steel receiver grooved for scope mounts, adj. sights with front bead, gloss finished walnut straight grip stock, 12 in. LOP, blued finish, 4 3/4 lbs. New 2011.

MSR $620	$525	$460	$395	$355	$290	$240	$200	

* ***BL-22 Grade I NRA*** – similar to BL-22 Grade I, except has NRA logo laser engraved in stock. Mfg. 2006-2007.

	$485	$415	$365	$325	$265	$220	$175	*$514*

BL-22 GRADE II – same general specifications as BL-22, except scroll engraved blue receiver and deluxe high gloss checkered walnut stock and forearm. Disc. 2003.

	$550	$475	$415	$350	$300	$250	$195	*$494*

* ***BL-22 Grade II (Classic)*** – .22 S, L, or LR cal., 20 in. barrel, 15 shot tubular mag., scroll engraved steel receiver, grooved for scope mounts, gold colored trigger, adj. sights with front bead, gloss finished American walnut straight grip stock with cut checkering, blue finish, 5 lbs. New 1999, mfg. by Miroku.

MSR $760	$640	$550	$475	$425	$350	$285	$250	

* ***BL-22 Grade II Classic/Field Octagon Full Line Dealer*** – .22 S, L, or LR cal., 24 in. octagon barrel with blued finish, recessed crown, 15 shot 3/4 length tubular mag., scroll engraved satin nickel finished steel receiver, grooved for scope mounts, gold-colored trigger, adj. sights with front gold bead, satin finished American walnut straight grip stock with cut checkering, 5 1/4 lbs. New 2004, mfg. by Miroku.

MSR $1,060	$900	$790	$675	$610	$500	$410	$350	

This model is available through Full-Line and Medallion dealers only.

* ***BL-22 Grade II Field Full Line Dealer*** – .22 S, L, or LR cal., 20 in. barrel with blued finish, recessed crown, 15 shot tubular mag., scroll engraved satin nickel finished steel receiver, grooved for scope mounts, gold colored trigger, adj. sights with front bead, satin finished American walnut straight grip stock with cut checkering, 5 lbs. New 2005.

MSR $820	$700	$615	$525	$475	$385	$315	$250	

This model is available through Full Line and Medallion dealers only.

MODEL 53 DELUXE LIMITED EDITION – .32-20 WCF cal. (round nose or hollow point bullets only), patterned after the original Winchester Model 53 (redesigned Model 1892), 7 shot tube mag., high polished blue metal, open sights, 22 in. tapered barrel, high grade checkered walnut stock featuring full pistol grip cap and shotgun style metal buttplate, 6 1/2 lbs. Only 5,000 mfg. in 1990.

	$925	$795	$675	N/A	N/A	N/A	N/A	*$675*

MODEL 65 GRADE I LIMITED EDITION – .218 Bee cal., patterned after the Winchester Model 65, round tapered 24 in. barrel, open sights (hooded front), blue metal finish, 7 shot tube mag., uncheckered pistol grip stock and semi-beavertail forearm, metal buttplate, 6 3/4 lbs. 3,500 total mfg. for Grade I in 1989 only, inventory depleted in 1990.

	$725	$625	$525	N/A	N/A	N/A	N/A	*$550*

* ***Model 65 High Grade*** – greyed receiver (and lever) with scroll engraving and gold plated animals, gold plated trigger, deluxe checkered walnut stock and semi-beavertail forearm. 1,500 total mfg. in 1989, inventory depleted in 1990.

	$1,050	$925	$800	N/A	N/A	N/A	N/A	*$850*

GRADING - PPGS™	100%	98%	95%	90%	80%	70%	60%	LAST MSR

MODEL 71 LIMITED EDITION CARBINE – .348 Win. cal., reproduction of the Winchester Model 71 Carbine, 20 in. barrel, open sights, 4 shot mag., 8 lbs. New 1987 with inventory depleted in 1990.

* ***Model 71 Limited Edition Carbine Grade I*** – uncheckered satin finished walnut stock and forearm. 4,000 mfg. 1986-87 only.

$950	$795	$650	N/A	N/A	N/A	N/A	*$600*

* ***Model 71 Limited Edition Carbine High Grade*** – deluxe checkered walnut stock and forearm with high gloss finish, scroll engraved grey receiver with gold inlays and trigger. 3,000 mfg. 1986-1987 only.

$1,425	$1,150	$925	N/A	N/A	N/A	N/A	*$980*

MODEL 71 LIMITED EDITION RIFLE – .348 Win. cal., reproduction of the Winchester Model 71 Rifle, 24 in. barrel, open sights, 4 shot mag., 8 lbs. 2 oz. Mfg. 1986-87 only with inventory depleted in 1990.

* ***Model 71 Grade I Rifle*** – uncheckered satin finished walnut stock and forearm. 3,000 mfg. 1986-1987 only.

$950	$825	$675	N/A	N/A	N/A	N/A	*$600*

* ***Model 71 High Grade Rifle*** – deluxe checkered walnut stock and forearm with high gloss finish, scroll engraved grey receiver with gold inlays and trigger. 3,000 mfg. 1986-1987 only.

$1,595	$1,250	$900	N/A	N/A	N/A	N/A	*$980*

BLR USA – .243 Win. or .308 Win. cal., this model was originally scheduled to be manufactured by TRW in Cleveland, OH for Browning. Originally assembled in 1966, these rifles are considered prototypes as they were never sold through regular channels and at one time were scheduled to be destroyed. Approx. 50-250 of these rifles exist, some still NIB.

$995	$875	$750	$675	$550	$450	$350	

This variation has a 2-line legend on the right side marked "MADE IN USA" and "PATENT PENDING". This model is dangerous to operate and should not be fired.

BLR BELGIAN – .243 Win. or .308 Win. cal., mfg. was moved to FN in Belgium with original assembly beginning 1969 and concluding in 1973. This FN model included a number of small dimensioning and engraving changes.

$925	$825	$700	$625	$525	$425	$325	

BLR JAPAN – .243 Win. or .308 Win. cal., mfg. was moved to Miroku in Japan 1974-1980. Early guns during 1974 had stocks with impressed checkering. By 1975, cut checkering and gloss wood finish was used on stocks and forearms. Last ser. no. for Belgian production was 27,XXX. Japanese mfg. started with ser. no. 30,000.

$775	$675	$575	$525	$425	$350	$275	*$550*

Add $40 without sights (scarce).

BLR SHORT ACTION – .22-250 Rem., .222 Rem. (disc. 1989), .223 Rem., .243 Win., .257 Roberts (disc. 1992), 7mm-08 Rem., .284 Win. (disc. 1994), .308 Win., or .358 Win. (disc. 1992) cal., steel receiver, rotary bolt locking lugs, 20 in. barrel with band, 3 (.284 Win. only) or 4 shot detachable mag., adj. rear sight, checkered straight grip stock, recoil pad, no sights optional 1988-89, approx. 7 lbs. Mfg. 1970-1981.

.243 Win. and .308 Win. cals. are the most popular in this model.

BLR '81 SHORT ACTION (MIROKU) – similar cals. and features as Model BLR short action, mfg. 1981-1995 by Miroku in Japan.

Standard cals.	$700	$625	$550	$450	$375	$300	$250	
.284 Winchester	$1,100	$800	$675	$600	$500	$425	$350	
.257 Roberts	$900	$795	$675	$600	$500	$425	$350	
.222 Rem.	$1,650	$1,450	$1,200	$1,050	$875	$725	$575	*$550*

BLR '81 LONG ACTION – .270 Win., .30-06, or 7mm Rem Mag. cal., incorporates distinct design changes, 22 or 24 in. barrel, approx. 8 1/2 lbs. Mfg. 1991-95 by Miroku.

$750	$675	$595	$525	$450	$375	$295	*$580*

LIGHTNING BLR (SHORT ACTION) – .22-250 Rem., .223 Rem. (disc. 1998), .243 Win., 7mm-08 Rem., or .308 Win. cal., rotary bolt locking lugs, 20 in. barrel w/o barrel band, similar action as the BLR 81, but features aluminum alloy receiver, checkered pistol grip stock and forearm, rack and pinion geared slide, fold down hammer, trigger travels with lever, 3-5 shot detachable mag., adj. rear sight, approx. 6 1/2 lbs. Mfg. by Miroku late 1995-2002.

$625	$550	$495	$425	$350	$275	$225	*$681*

GRADING - PPGS™	100%	98%	95%	90%	80%	70%	60%	LAST MSR

LIGHTNING BLR (LONG ACTION) – .270 Win., .30-06, .300 Win. Mag. (new 1997), or 7mm Rem. Mag. cal., 22 or 24 (Mag. cals.) in. barrel, approx. 7 1/4-7 3/4 lbs. Mfg. by Miroku 1995-2002.

	$650	$575	$515	$440	$365	$295	$240	*$721*

BLR LIGHTWEIGHT '81 (LONG ACTION) – .270 Win., .30-06, .300 Win. Mag. (disc.), or 7mm Rem. Mag. (disc.) cal., 22 or 24 in. barrel, crowned muzzle, 4 shot detachable box mag., alloy receiver, drilled and tapped for scope mounts, adj. sights, gloss finished checkered walnut straight grip stock or checkered pistol grip and Schnabel forend (disc.), recoil pad, blue finish, 7 1/4 or 7 3/4 lbs. Mfg. by Miroku beginning 2003.

MSR $1,080	$915	$800	$685	$620	$500	$410	$350

Add $260 for takedown action (mfg. 2007-disc.).
Add $60 for checkered pistol grip and Schnabel forend (disc.).

* ***BLR Lightweight Pistol Grip Long Action*** – .270 Win., .30-06, .300 Win. Mag., or 7mm Rem. Mag. cal., 22 or 24 in. barrel w/o band, crowned muzzle, 4 or 5 shot detachable box mag., alloy receiver, drilled and tapped, adj. sights, gloss finished walnut checkered pistol grip stock with Schnabel forearm, recoil pad, sling swivel studs, polished blue finish, approx. 7 lbs.

MSR $1,140	$975	$850	$725	$675	$550	$450	$375

* ***BLR Lightweight Stainless Long Action*** – .270 Win., .30-06, 7mm Rem. Mag., or .300 Win. Mag. cal., 20 (disc.), 22, or 24 in. matte stainless steel barrel, crowned muzzle, 4 or 5 shot detachable box mag., satin nickel finished receiver, drilled and tapped, adj. sights, gloss finished walnut checkered pistol grip stock with Schnabel forearm, recoil pad, sling swivel studs, 7 1/4 or 7 3/4 lbs. New 2010.

MSR $1,220	$1,040	$910	$780	$700	$575	$475	$400

This model was also featured as a 2009 SHOT Show Special.

BLR LIGHTWEIGHT '81 (SHORT ACTION) – .22-.250 Rem., .223 Rem. (new 2010), .243 Win., 6.5 Creedmoor (new 2021), .270 WSM (mfg. 2004-disc.), 7mm-08 Rem., .325 WSM (pistol grip only, mfg. 2005-disc.), .300 WSM (mfg. 2004-disc.), 7mm WSM (mfg. 2004-disc.), .308 Win., .358 Win., or .450 Marlin (disc.) cal., 20 or 22 (WSM cals. only) in. barrel with barrel band, solid or takedown (mfg. 2007-disc.) action, aluminum alloy receiver, choice of checkered Model 81 styled straight grip and forearm with gloss finish or checkered, gloss finished pistol grip with Schnabel forearm w/o barrel band (mfg. 2005-disc.) stock, sling swivels (pistol grip only), rack and pinion geared slide with rotating breech head, fold down hammer, trigger travels with lever, 3-4 shot detachable mag., adj. rear sight, approx. 6 1/2-7 lbs. Mfg. by Miroku beginning 2003.

MSR $1,030	$875	$765	$650	$595	$475	$400	$325

Add $80 for WSM cals. (mfg. 2004-disc.).
Add $60 for checkered pistol grip stock and Schnabel forearm (new 2005-disc.).
Add $270 for takedown action (mfg. 2007-disc).
Add $70 for one-piece scope mount (mfg. 2007-disc.).

* ***BLR Lightweight Stainless Short Action*** – .223 Rem., .22-250 Rem., .243 Win., 6,5 Creedmoor (new 2021), 7mm-08 Rem., .308 Win., .358 Win., .450 Marlin, .270 WSM (mfg. 2010-2019), or .300 WSM cal., 20 or 22 in. matte stainless steel barrel, crowned muzzle, 3-4 shot detachable box mag., satin nickel finished receiver, adj. rear sight, gloss finished checkered pistol grip walnut stock with Schnabel forearm, recoil pad, sling swivel studs, 6 1/2-7 lbs. New 2010.

MSR $1,160	$985	$850	$725	$675	$550	$450	$375

Add $80 for WSM cals.

This model was also featured as a SHOT Show Special in 2009.

* ***BLR Lightweight With Pistol Grip Short Action*** – .223 Rem., .22-250 Rem., .243 Win., 7mm-08 Rem., .308 Win., .358 Win., .450 Marlin, .270 WSM, or .300 WSM cal., 20 or 22 in. barrel without band, crowned muzzle, 4 or 5 shot detachable box mag., alloy receiver, drilled and tapped, gloss finished walnut checkered pistol grip stock and Schnabel forearm, recoil pad, sling swivel studs, high gloss blue finish, approx. 6 1/2 lbs.

MSR $1,080	$915	$800	$685	$620	$500	$410	$350

Add $80 for WSM cals.

BLR LIGHTWEIGHT '81 STAINLESS TAKEDOWN – .223 Rem. (mfg. 2010-2019), .22-250 Rem. (disc. 2018), .243 Win., 6.5 Creedmoor (new 2021), 7mm-08 Rem., .308 Win., .358 Win. (disc. 2020), .450 Marlin (disc. 2020), .300 WSM, .270 Win. (mfg. 2010-2019), .30-06, 7mm Rem. Mag. (disc. 2018), or .300 Win. Mag. cal., 20, 22, or 24 in. matte stainless steel barrel, crowned muzzle, 4 shot detachable box mag., satin nickel finished alloy receiver, drilled and tapped for scope mounts, gold-plated trigger, adj. sights, satin finished gray laminate checkered wood straight grip stock, recoil pad, 6 lbs. 8 oz.-7 lbs. 12 oz. New 2010.

MSR $1,300	$1,100	$965	$825	$750	$600	$500	$425

Add $50 for long action cals. or $80 for WSM cals.

GRADING - PPGS™	100%	98%	95%	90%	80%	70%	60%	LAST MSR

MODEL 1886 LIMITED EDITION GRADE I RIFLE – .45-70 Govt. cal. only, patterned after the Winchester Model 1886, blue receiver, 26 in. octagon barrel, 8 shot full mag., crescent buttplate, open sights, w/o top tang safety. 7,000 mfg. 1986 only.

	$2,150	$1,750	$1,500	N/A	N/A	N/A	N/A	*$578*

* ***Model 1886 Limited Edition High Grade Rifle*** – same general specifications as Model 1886, except has checkered high grade walnut stock and forearm, greyed steel receiver, with game scene engraving including elk and American Bison, gold accenting with "1 of 3,000" engraved on top of barrel. 3,000 mfg. 1986 only.

	$2,400	$2,150	$1,675	N/A	N/A	N/A	N/A	*$935*

* ***Model 1886 Montana Centennial Rifle*** – similar to Model 1886 High Grade. 2,000 mfg. 1989 only to commemorate Montana Centennial.

	$2,250	$1,850	$1,575	N/A	N/A	N/A	N/A	*$935*

MODEL 1886 LIMITED EDITION GRADE I CARBINE – .45-70 Govt. cal. only, saddle ring carbine, patterned after the Winchester Model 1886 Carbine, blue receiver, 22 in. round barrel, 7 shot full mag., crescent buttplate, open sights. 7,000 total mfg. 1992-93.

	$2,200	$1,775	$1,500	N/A	N/A	N/A	N/A	*$750*

* ***Model 1886 Limited Edition High Grade Carbine*** – same general specifications as Model 1886, except has checkered high grade walnut stock and forearm, greyed steel receiver, with game scene engraving including bear and elk, gold accenting, 3,000 total mfg. 1992-93.

	$2,400	$2,150	$1,675	N/A	N/A	N/A	N/A	*$1,175*

B-92 CARBINE – .357 Mag. or .44 Rem. Mag. cal., 20 in. barrel, patterned after the Winchester Model 92, 11 shot mag. (tubular), blue finish. Disc. 1986.

	$600	$525	$450	$400	$340	$285	$235	*$342*

Add 25% for .357 Mag. cal.

* ***B-92 Centennial*** – .44 Mag. cal., 6,000 mfg. in 1978.

	$685	$600	$515	N/A	N/A	N/A	N/A	*$220*

* ***B-92 BCA Commemorative*** – mfg. to commemorate BCA's third anniversary.

	$750	$650	$550	N/A	N/A	N/A	N/A	

MODEL 1895 LIMITED EDITION GRADE I – .30/40 Krag or .30-06 cal. only, patterned after the Winchester Model 1895, blue receiver, 24 in. barrel, 4 shot mag. (box type), select walnut, rear buckhorn sight, 8 lbs. Mfg. 1984 only.

.30/40 Krag	$925	$800	$700	N/A	N/A	N/A	N/A	
.30-06	$875	$750	$650	N/A	N/A	N/A	N/A	

Production totaled 6,000 in the .30-06 cal. and 2,000 in .30/40 Krag for this model.

* ***Model 1895 Limited Edition High Grade*** – same general specifications as Model 1895, except gold plated game scenes on satin finish receiver, gold trigger, and finely checkered select French walnut.

	$1,625	$1,420	$1,220	N/A	N/A	N/A	N/A	

Production totaled 1,000 in the .30-06 cal. and 1,000 in .30/40 Krag for this model.

RIFLES: O/U

Currently, the Browning Custom Shop in Belgium is producing the CCS25 double rifle in the following grades: B5 ($15,404), D5G ($33,177 MSR), M1 ($44,335 MSR), Bavarian ($17,675 MSR).

Previous custom shop models included: CCS Africa ($15,266 last MSR, disc. 2005), CCS25 B2E (last MSR $15,059, disc. 2013), CCS Herstal (last MSR was $11,150, disc. 2013), and the .375 H&H African Classic (last MSR was $27,256, disc. 2013).

In addition to the models listed below, Browning has also released SHOT Show specials on some models that were available by dealers ordering them at the SHOT Show only. Complete descriptions for these models can be found under SHOT SHOW SPECIALS - RIFLES: O/U at BlueBookOfGunValues.com/overflow.

EXPRESS RIFLE – .270 Win., .30-06 cal., or 9.3x74R cal., Superposed Superlight style action. 24 in. barrels, checkered straight grip stock and forearm, auto ejectors, Fleur-de-lis engraving, single trigger, folding leaf rear sight, 6 lbs. 14 oz., cased. Disc. 1986.

	$6,000	$5,500	$4,775	$4,250	$3,500	$2,750	$2,250	*$3,125*

GRADING - PPGS™	100%	98%	95%	90%	80%	70%	60%	LAST MSR

GRADE I CONTINENTAL SET – includes .30-06 O/U rifle barrels with extra set of 20 ga. O/U shotgun barrels (26 1/2 in.), rifle barrels are 24 in., 20 ga. frame, SST, ejectors, blue receiver with scroll engraving, straight grip checkered stock and forearm, supplied with 2 barrel takedown case. Mfg. 1978-86.

	$7,500	$6,500	$5,500	$4,850	$3,925	$3,225	$2,500	

RIFLES: SEMI-AUTO, .22 LR

Miroku manufactured .22s can be determined by year of manufacture in the following manner: RV suffix - 1975, RT - 1976, RR - 1977, RP - 1978, RN - 1979, PM - 1980, PZ - 1981, PY - 1982, PX - 1983, PW - 1984, PV - 1985, PT -1986, PR - 1987, PP - 1988, PN - 1989, NM - 1990, NZ - 1991, NY - 1992, NX - 1993, NW - 1994, NV - 1995, NT - 1996, NR - 1997, NP - 1998, NN - 1999, MM - 2000, MZ - 2001, MY - 2002, MX - 2003, MW - 2004, MV - 2005, MU - 2006, MT - 2007, MS - 2008, MN - 2009, ZM - 2010, ZZ - 2011, ZY - 2012, ZX - 2013, ZW - 2014, ZV - 2015, ZT - 2016, ZR - 2017, ZP - 2018, ZN - 2019, ZM - 2020.

Currently, the Browning Custom Shop in Belgium is making the following .22 LR cal. semi-auto models: Grade II ($2,440 MSR), and the Grade III ($3,485 MSR).

On the following FN (Belgian mfg.) models, add approx. 10% if in NIB condition.

In addition to the models listed below, Browning has also released SHOT Show specials on some models that were available by dealers ordering them at the SHOT Show only. These models are listed in the separate category SHOT SHOW SPECIALS LISTINGS: RIFLES SEMI-AUTO/SINGLE SHOT.

AUTO RIFLE GRADES I - VI – .22 LR or .22 Short (FN only, disc. - rare) cal., takedown design, 10 shot (16 for .22 Short) tube mag. in buttstock, 19 1/4 in. barrel for all .22 LR, .22 Shorts had various barrel lengths according to mfg. year: 19 1/4 in. for 1956, 22 3/8 in. for 1957, and 22 in. from 1958 until general production was disc. in 1983, checkered pistol grip stock, semi-beavertail forearm, stock has hole machined halfway to allow partial filling of tube mag., adj. folding rear or earlier wheel sight, grades differ in finish, amount of engraving, and quality of wood, 4 3/4-5 3/4 lbs. Early top loaders were mfg. from 1914 until approx. 1955. Modern tube loader mfg. 1956 to 1974 by FN Belgium. Mfg. beginning 1976 by Miroku in Japan.

* ***Auto Rifle Grade I - FN (Belgian Mfg.)***

	$875	$750	$650	$550	$450	$400	$350	

Add 50% for guns in .22 Short cal., if in 98% or better condition.
Add 25% for wheel sight guns if in 98% or better condition.
Add $150 for 100% condition with box.
Subtract 30% if w/o BAC barrel marking - "Fabrique Nationale D'armes de Guerre, Herstal Belgique" barrel marking only.

FN Postwar Grade Is have a lightly engraved blue steel receiver, checkered walnut, blue trigger, and a variety of rear sights.

» **Auto Rifle Grade I - FN Custom Shop**

	$1,100	$900	$750	$650	$525	$450	$375	

Add 10% for .22 Short cal.

* ***SA-22 Grade I (Auto Rifle Grade I - Miroku (Japan Mfg.)*** – .22 LR cal., 19 3/8 in. barrel, drilled and tapped for scope mounts, 10 shot tubular mag., steel receiver with scroll engraving, takedown design, bottom ejection, blued trigger, adj. sights with gold bead front and folding leaf rear, gloss finished and checkered select American walnut stock and forearm, Crossbolt safety, polished blue finish, approx. 5 1/4 lbs. Mfg. by Miroku in Japan.

MSR $740	$625	$545	$475	$425	$345	$275	$225	

* ***Auto Rifle Grade II - FN (Belgian Mfg.)***

	$1,850	$1,350	$1,100	$975	$825	$675	$525	

Add $100 for guns initialed by the engraver.
Add $200 for guns fully signed by the engraver.
Add $150 for original box.
Add 20% for Grade II with wheel sight.
Add 50% for guns in .22 Short cal., if in 95% or better condition.
Subtract 30% if w/o BAC barrel marking - "Fabrique Nationale D'armes de Guerre, Herstal Belgique" barrel marking only.

FN Grade IIs have grey receiver, deluxe wood with finer checkering, gold plated trigger, and engraving depicting two squirrels and two prairie dogs. Unsigned, signed, or initialed by engraver.

» **Auto Rifle Grade II - FN Custom Shop**

	$1,895	$1,500	$1,250	$1,050	$825	$675	$525	

Add 10% for .22 Short cal.

GRADING - PPGS™	100%	98%	95%	90%	80%	70%	60%	LAST MSR

* ***Auto Rifle Grade II - Miroku (Japan Mfg.)*** – disc. 1984.

	$895	$700	$575	$525	$425	$350	$275	

Add $50 for original box.

* ***Auto Rifle Grade III - FN (Belgian Mfg.)***

	$3,350	$2,925	$2,500	$2,275	$1,950	$1,575	$1,225	

Add 15% for guns signed by the engraver.
Add $200 for original box.
Add 50% for guns in .22 Short cal., if in 98% or better condition.
Subtract 25% if w/o BAC barrel marking - "Fabrique Nationale D'armes de Guerre, Herstal Belgique" barrel marking only.

FN Grade IIIs have coin finish or grey chromed receiver, extra deluxe walnut with skipline checkering, gold plated trigger, and more elaborate game scene engraving usually featuring a dog flushing ducks or upland game. Signed or unsigned by engraver (Funken, J. Baerten, Vrancken, and Watrin will command premiums over values listed). A few were also special ordered with blue finish and special engraving - these command an extra premium.

» **Auto Rifle Grade III - FN Custom Shop**

	$3,400	$2,900	$2,500	$2,275	$1,950	$1,575	$1,225	

Add 15% for guns signed by the engraver.

* ***Auto Rifle Grade III "Transition" (Japan Mfg.)*** – only available in Grade III, Japan mfg., Belgium engraved.

	$2,400	$2,000	$1,750	$1,600	$1,295	$1,050	$825	

Add $100 for box.

* ***Auto Rifle Grade III - Miroku (Japan Mfg.)*** – disc. 1983.

	$1,650	$1,375	$1,275	$995	$800	$675	$525	

Add $100 if signed by engraver.
Add $100 for original box.

SA-22 GRADE II OCTAGON – .22 LR cal., 19 3/8 in. octagon barrel, 10 shot, gold colored trigger, satin finished Grade II/III walnut stock with gloss finish and cut checkering, scroll engraving, satin nickel receiver finish, 5.3 lbs. New 2019.

MSR $1,040	$885	$775	$665	$600	$485	$415	$325	

* ***SA-22 Grade VI (Auto Rifle Grade VI - Miroku (Japan Mfg.)*** – .22 LR or .22 Short (disc.) cal., 19 3/8 in. barrel, drilled and tapped, 10 or 16 (.22 Short cal.) shot tube mag., choice of blue or greyed steel receiver, game scene engraving with 24Kt. gold accents (typically fox and squirrel on receiver sides), bottom ejection, gold trigger, adj. sights, gloss finished and checkered select American walnut stock, Crossbolt safety, 5 lbs. 3 oz. Mfg. by Miroku in Japan. New 1987.

MSR $1,700	$1,450	$1,275	$1,095	$985	$800	$650	$550	

Add at least 50% for small run of .22 Short cal. Grade VI mfg. during 2003.

* ***Auto Rifle Grade VI 125th Anniversary Miroku*** – features silver nitride receiver with gold enhanced 125th Anniversary logo and delicate scroll engraving. 500 mfg. 2003-2004.

	$1,195	$975	$795	N/A	N/A	N/A	N/A	*$1,271*

BUCK MARK RIFLE – .22 LR cal., Buck Mark pistol blowback action, 18 in. tapered barrel with Hi-Viz fiber optic sights (Sporter Rifle), heavy barrel w/o sights (Target or Field Target Rifle), or carbon composite barrel (disc. 2006), includes integral scope rail, uncheckered walnut or grey laminate (new 2002, no sights) Monte Carlo stock that attaches to non-detachable, one-piece skeletonized and enclosed rear grip assembly, separate forearm, 10 shot mag., 3 lbs. 10 oz. (Classic Carbon -disc. 2006), 4 lbs. 6 oz. (Sporter) or approx. 5 1/2 lbs. (Target & Classic Target). New 2001.

MSR $700	$600	$525	$450	$410	$325	$275	$225	

Add $40 for grey laminate stock (Classic/Field Target Rifle, new 2002).
Add $95 for carbon composite barrel (disc. 2006).

The Buck Mark Classic/Field Target with grey laminate stock & Classic/Field Carbon Rifles are available through Full-Line and Medallion dealers only.

* ***Buck Mark Target Fluted Gray Laminate*** – .22 LR cal., straight blowback action, 18 3/8 in. fluted heavy bull barrel with muzzle brake and thread protector, 10 shot mag., gold plated trigger, gray laminated stock and grips, Picatinny style optics rail, serrated slide, anodized finish, 6.8 lbs. New 2019.

MSR $740	$625	$545	$475	$425	$345	$275	$225	

GRADING - PPGS™	100%	98%	95%	90%	80%	70%	60%	LAST MSR

RIFLES: SEMI-AUTO, BAR SERIES

Currently, the Browning Custom Shop in Belgium is making the following BAR custom shop rifles: Grade 4 VB ($9,294 MSR), Grade 4 PH ($9,294 MSR). Until 2006, the Custom Shop produced the Grade D ($6,543 last MSR).

In addition to the models listed below, Browning has also released SHOT Show specials on some models that were available by dealers ordering them at the SHOT Show only. Complete descriptions for these models can be found under SHOT SHOW SPECIALS - RIFLES: SEMI-AUTO/SINGLE SHOT at BlueBookOfGunValues.com/overflow.

BROWNING PATENT 1900 – please refer to model listing under F.N.

BAR SEMI-AUTO – .243 Win., .270 Win., .280 Rem. (new 1990), .308 Win., or .30-06 cal. available in standard model, Mag. cals. include 7mm Rem., .300 Win., and .338 Win. Mag. (reintroduced 1990), gas operated, blued steel receiver, 22 or 24 (Mag. only) in. barrel, rotary bolt with seven lugs, folding leaf sight, walnut stock, grades differ in engraving, finish, and quality of wood, in 1993, to celebrate the 25th Anniversary of the BAR, Browning introduced the BAR MK II Safari (see model listing), approx. 7 lbs. 6 oz. New 1967 (includes BAR MK II).

Add 20% for FN mfg. and assembled BARs (marked "Made in Belgium").
Add 10% for .338 Win. Mag. cal. (FN mfg. only).

Note: Original .338s were limited production, mostly seen in the deluxe Grade II only. During the last year of FN .338 production, several were delivered in a Grade I by FN. Although being rarer than the Grade II, it is not as desirable. The following prices are for Portuguese assembled guns, manufactured by FN, and so stamped on the barrel.

* ***BAR Grade I*** – standard grade without engraving, blue finish. Ordering this model without sights became an option in 1988. Disc. 1992.

$775	$650	$595	$525	$450	$400	$350	*$633*

Add 15% for .280 Rem. cal. if in 98%+ condition.

FN mfg. and assembled Grade Is can be denoted by light scroll engraving on the receiver.

* ***BAR Grade I Magnum*** – standard grade without engraving, with recoil pad, 8 lbs. 6 oz. Disc. 1992.

$875	$750	$650	$575	$500	$450	$395	*$680*

Subtract $16 without sights.

Ordering this gun without sights became an option in 1988.

* ***BAR Grade II*** – blue receiver, engraved with big game heads. Mfg. 1967-74.

$1,250	$1,100	$950	$800	$700	$550	$475

This model was previously designated Deluxe.

* ***BAR Grade II Magnum*** – magnum version of Grade II. Mfg. 1967-74.

$1,350	$1,175	$1,000	$875	$775	$675	$550

* ***BAR Grade III*** – features antelope and deer game scenes etched on greyed steel receiver, select checkered stock and forearm. Disc. 1984.

$1,750	$1,500	$1,275	$1,100	$950	$825	$725

* ***BAR Grade III Magnum*** – magnum version of Grade III, features elk and moose game scenes. Disc. 1984.

$1,850	$1,600	$1,375	$1,200	$1,050	$925	$825

* ***BAR Grade IV*** – engraved satin finish greyed receiver depicts big game animal scenes and trigger guard, carved borders on checkering. Disc. 1989.

$2,800	$2,500	$2,200	$1,825	$1,525	$1,275	$1,050	*$1,670*

* ***BAR Grade IV Magnum*** – magnum version of Grade IV. Disc. 1984.

$2,950	$2,650	$2,350	$2,000	$1,650	$1,375	$1,150	*$1,720*

* ***BAR Grade V*** – more elaborate engraving than Grade IV, with gold inlays. Mfg. 1971-74.

$6,500	$5,700	$4,900	$4,500	$3,515	$2,875	$2,250

* ***BAR Grade V Magnum*** – magnum version of Grade V.

$6,850	$5,995	$5,150	$4,650	$3,775	$3,075	$2,400

BAR NORTH AMERICAN DEER RIFLE ISSUE – .30-06 cal. only, BAR style action with silver grey finish and engraved action, 600 total production, walnut cased with accessories. Disc. 1983 but were sold through 1989.

$4,500	$3,950	$3,400	$3,100	N/A	N/A	N/A	*$3,550*

GRADING - PPGS™	100%	98%	95%	90%	80%	70%	60%	LAST MSR

BAR SAFARI 100TH ANNIVERSARY – .30-06 cal., 22 in. hammer forged barrel, 5 shot detachable box mag., steel receiver with scroll engraving, oil finished Grade V Turkish walnut checkered stock with rounded forearm, recoil pad, sling swivel studs, crossbolt safety, includes limited edition commemorative box sleeve, polished blue finish, 8 lbs. 100 rifles mfg. 2017-2018.

	$2,400	$2,100	$1,875	$1,675	$1,500	$1,375	$1,225	*$2,700*

BAR MK II ONE MILLIONTH COMMEMORATIVE – .30-06 cal., satin finish frame features scrolled on left-side "Limited Edition One Of 500", 22 in. barrel.

	$2,250	$1,850	$1,650	$1,450	N/A	N/A	N/A	

BAR MK II SAFARI – .22-250 Rem. (mfg. as prototype only during 1997), .25-06 Rem. (new 1997), .243 Win. (disc. 2013), .270 Win., .30-06, .308 Win., .270 Wby. Mag. (mfg. 1996-2000), 7mm Rem. Mag. (disc. 2013), .300 Win. Mag., or .338 Win. Mag. (disc.) cal., improved BAR action featuring redesigned bolt release, new gas operating system, and reduced recoil, removable trigger assembly, 22, 23 (WSM cals. only, disc.), or 24 in. barrel with (adj. for windage and elevation) or without sights, blue finish with scroll engraved receiver, checkered walnut stock and forearm, gold trigger, detachable 3 (.300 WSM cal. only), 4 (Mag. cals. only) or 5 shot box mag., approx. 7 lbs. 6 oz. except for Mag. cals. (8 lbs. 6 oz.). Mfg. by FN in Belgium. New 1993.

MSR $1,320	$1,125	$985	$850	$765	$625	$500	$425	

Add $120 for .300 Win. Mag. cal.

Add $19 for open sights (not available in .270 Wby. Mag., disc.).

This model was also featured as a 2012 SHOT Show Special but included sights. MSR range was $1,340-$1,470, depending on caliber.

The new BAR MK II Safari does not have interchangeable magazine capability with the older pre-1993 BARs.

* ***BAR Classic Mk II Safari*** – .270 Win. (disc. 2001), .270 WSM (new 2003), .30-06 (disc. 2001), 7mm Rem. Mag., (disc. 2001), 7mm WSM (new 2003), .300 Win. Mag. (disc. 2001), or .300 WSM (new 2002) cal., similar to BAR Mark II Safari, except has satin finished checkered stock and forearm, 7 lbs. 6 oz. or 8 lbs. 6 oz. Mfg. 1999-2003.

	$775	$650	$595	$525	$450	$400	$350	*$908*

Subtract approx. 10% for non-Mag. cals.

Add $17 for open sights (disc. 2000).

This model was available through Full-line and Medallion dealers only.

* ***BAR MK II Safari with BOSS*** – .243 Win. (disc. 1999), .308 Win. (disc. 1999), .270 Win., .270 WSM (mfg. 2003-2013), .30-06, 7mm Rem. Mag. (disc. 2013), 7mm WSM (mfg. 2003-2013), .300 Win. Mag., .300 WSM (mfg. 2003-2013), or .338 Win. Mag. (disc. 2018) cal., similar to BAR MK II Safari, with BOSS (ballistic optimizing shooting system), avalable with ported (approx. 30% less recoil) or unported BOSS-CR (Conventional Recoil) muzzle brake, no sights, approx. 7 1/2 or 8 1/2 lbs. New 1994.

MSR $1,500	$1,275	$1,115	$950	$865	$700	$600	$500	

Add $140 for Mag. and WSM (disc.) cals.

BAR MK II LIGHTWEIGHT – .243 Win., .270 Win., .30-06, .308 Win., 7mm Rem. Mag. (new 1999), .300 Win. Mag. (new 1999), or .338 Win. Mag. (new 1999) cal., features alloy receiver and 20 or 24 (Mag. cals. only) in. barrel, matte wood and barrel finish, open sights, 7 lbs. 2 oz. or 7 lbs. 12 oz. Mfg. 1997-2003.

	$825	$700	$650	$575	$500	$450	$400	*$850*

Add $77 for Mag. cals. (new 1999).

* ***BAR MK II Lightweight with BOSS*** – 7mm Rem. Mag., .300 Win. Mag., or .338 Win. Mag. (disc. 1999) cal., similar to BAR Mark II Lightweight, except has 24 in. barrel with BOSS, 8 lbs., 6 oz. Mfg. 1999-2000.

	$875	$750	$675	$600	$525	$475	$425	*$939*

* ***BAR MK II Lightweight Stalker*** – .243 Win., .270 Win., .270 WSM (new 2003), .30-06, .308 Win., 7mm Rem. Mag. (disc. 2004), 7mm WSM (new 2003), .300 Win. Mag., .300 WSM (new 2002), or .338 Win. Mag. cal., similar to BAR Mark II Safari, except has aluminum alloy receiver and checkered black synthetic stock and forearm, matte metal finish, 20, 22, 23 (new 2002, WSM cals. only), or 24 (Mag. cals. only) in. barrel with open sights, 7 lbs. 2 oz. - 7 lbs. 12 oz. Mfg. 2001-2012.

	$995	$850	$750	$650	$575	$525	$475	*$1,230*

Add $110 for Mag. or WSM cals.

GRADING - PPGS™	100%	98%	95%	90%	80%	70%	60%	LAST MSR

» **BAR MK II Lightweight Stalker with BOSS** – .270 WSM (new 2003), 7mm Rem. Mag., 7mm WSM (new 2003), .300 Win. Mag., .300 WSM (new 2002), or .338 Win. Mag. cal., similar to BAR Mark II Stalker, except has 23 (new 2002, WSM cals. only) or 24 in. barrel with BOSS, approx. 7 3/4 lbs. Mfg. 2001-2003.

	$875	$750	$675	$600	$525	$475	$425	*$981*

* ***BAR MK II High Grade*** – .270 Win., .30-06, .300 Win. Mag., or 7mm Rem. Mag. cal., satin finished receiver with either whitetail/mule deer or moose/elk etched game scenes and gold border, checkered high grade gloss finished walnut stock and forearm, no sights, 7 lbs. 6 oz. or 8 lbs. 6 oz. Mfg. 2001-2003.

	$1,475	$1,295	$1,150	$1,000	$875	$725	$600	*$1,856*

Add $58 for Mag. cals.

* ***BAR MK II Grade III*** – features Grade III engraving pattern. Mfg. by the FN custom shop 1996-99.

	$3,400	$2,975	$2,550	$2,300	$1,875	$1,525	$1,195	*$3,754*

* ***BAR MK II Grade IV*** – features Grade IV engraving pattern. Mfg. by the FN custom shop beginning 1996.

	$3,500	$3,075	$2,625	$2,375	$1,925	$1,575	$1,225	*$3,859*

BAR MK III – .243 Win., 7mm-08 Rem., .308 Win., .270 WSM, .300 WSM, .270 Win., .30-06, 7mm Rem. Mag., or .300 Win. Mag. cal., 22, 23, or 24 in. hammer forged barrel, 4 or 5 shot detachable box mag., satin nickel finished alloy receiver with high relief engraving, drilled and tapped for scope mounts, composite trigger guard and floorplate, oil finished Grade II checkered walnut stock with stylized forearm, shim adjustable, sling swivel studs, crossbolt safety, blue finish, right or left (new 2021) hand configuration, approx. 7 1/2 lbs. New 2016.

MSR $1,340	$1,140	$1,000	$855	$775	$625	$515	$445	

Add $100 for WSM and Mag. cals.
Add $40 for left-hand in .308 Win. or .30-06 cal. or $130 for lef-hand in .300 Win. Mag. cal. (all new 2021).

BAR MK 3 HELL'S CANYON SPEED – .243 Win., 7mm-08 Rem., .308 Win., .270 WSM, .300 WSM, .270 Win., .30-06, 7mm Rem. Mag., or .300 Win. Mag. cal., 22, 23, or 24 in. barrel, 4 or 5 shot mag., gold plated trigger, composite stock with overmolded gripping panels and A-TACS AU camo finish, shim adjustable, Inflex recoil pad, drilled and tapped for scope, Cerakote Burnt Bronze finish, 7.5-7.8 lbs. New 2019.

MSR $1,660	$1,410	$1,235	$1,060	$960	$775	$650	$550	

Add $90 for WSM or Mag. cals.

BAR MK 3 CAMO – .243 Win., 7mm-08 Rem., .308 Win., .270 WSM, .300 WSM, .270 Win., .30-06, 7mm Rem. Mag., or .300 Win. Mag. cal., 22, 23, or 24 in. barrel, 4 or 5 shot detachable box mag., alloy receiver, composite trigger guard and floorplate, composite stock with overmolded gripping panels, shim adjustable, front sling swivel stud and two QD sling swivel cups, crossbolt safety, high relief engraving, 100% Mossy Oak Break-Up Country finish. New 2017.

MSR $1,460	$1,240	$1,085	$930	$850	$685	$575	$475	

Add $130 for WSM and Mag. cals.

BAR MK 3 DBM – .308 Win. cal., 18 in. fluted barrel, 10 shot detachable box mag., alloy receiver, composite trigger guard and floorplate, black composite stock with overmolded gripping panels, Inflex recoil pad, shim adjustable, front sling swivel stud and two QD sling swivel cups, crossbolt safety, matte black finish, includes ABS case. New 2017.

MSR $1,560	$1,330	$1,155	$990	$900	$725	$600	$515	

BAR MK 3 DBM WOOD – .308 Win. cal., 18 in. fluted barrel, 10 shot detachable box mag., alloy magwell, alloy receiver with integrated Picatinny rails for mounting optics, oil finished Grade II Turkish walnut stock, shim adjustable for cast on/off and drop at comb, Inflex recoil pad, non-reflective matte blued finish, includes ABS case, 7.6 lbs. New 2019.

MSR $1,590	$1,350	$1,180	$1,000	$910	$735	$600	$500	

BAR SHORTTRAC – .243 Win., .270 WSM, .300 WSM, .308 Win., 7mm-08 Rem. (new 2010), 7mm WSM, or .325 WSM (new 2009) cal., features new styling with black (disc. 2008) or satin nickel finished (new 2009) aluminum alloy gas operated short action receiver with light etching and gold Browning logo at rear, composite trigger guard and mag. floorplate, 22 or 23 in. hammer forged barrel w/o sights, drilled and tapped, checkered satin (disc. 2008) or oil (new 2009) finished walnut stock supplied with 6 adj. shims and squared off forearm, 3 or 4 shot detachable mag., 6 lbs. 10 oz (regular cals.) or 7 1/4 lbs. (WSM cals.). Mfg. in Belgium 2004-2015.

	$1,050	$925	$795	$715	$580	$500	$400	*$1,230*

Add $110 for WSM cals.
Add $40 for left-hand model with left-side ejection port.

The left-hand model was featured as a 2006 SHOT Show Special.

GRADING - PPGS™	100%	98%	95%	90%	80%	70%	60%	LAST MSR

BAR MK 3 STALKER – .243 Win., 7mm-08 Rem., .308 Win., .270 WSM (disc. 2020), .300 WSM (disc. 2020), .270 Win., .30-06, 7mm Rem. Mag., or .300 Win. Mag. cal., 22, 23, or 24 in. barrel, 4 or 5 shot detachable box mag., alloy receiver, composite trigger guard and floorplate, composite stock with overmolded gripping panels, shim adjustable, front sling swivel stud and two QD sling swivel cups, crossbolt safety, high relief engraving, matte black finish. New 2017.

MSR $1,340	$1,140	$1,000	$855	$775	$625	$515	$445	

Add $100 for WSM (disc. 2020) or Mag. cals.

* ***BAR Shorttrac Stalker*** – similar to BAR Shorttrac, except has matte black metal finish and black composite stock and forearm. Mfg. 2006-2015.

	$1,050	$875	$750	$650	$525	$425	$325	*$1,260*

Add $90 for WSM cals.

* ***BAR Shorttrac Camo*** – similar to BAR Shorttrac, except has 100% Mossy Oak New Break Up (disc. 2009), Break-Up Infinity (2010-2014), or Mossy Oak Break-Up Country (new 2015) camo coverage. Mfg. 2007-2015.

	$1,175	$995	$850	$750	$650	$495	$375	*$1,360*

Add $120 for WSM cals.

This model was originally featured as a 2006 SHOT Show Special.

BAR LONGTRAC – .270 Win., .30-06, .300 Win. Mag., or 7mm Rem. Mag. cal., similar to BAR Shorttrac, except has long action, 3 or 4 shot mag., 7 or 7 1/2 lbs. Mfg. 2004-2015.

	$995	$850	$725	$625	$525	$450	$375	*$1,230*

Add $110 for Mag. cals. Add $40 for left-hand model with left-side ejection port.

The left-hand model was originally featured as a 2006 SHOT Show Special.

* ***BAR Longtrac Stalker*** – similar to BAR Longtrac, except has matte black metal finish and black composite stock and forearm. Mfg. 2006-2015.

	$1,050	$875	$750	$650	$525	$425	$325	*$1,260*

Add $90 for Mag. cals.

* ***BAR Longtrac Camo*** – similar to BAR Longtrac, except has 100% Mossy Oak New Break Up (disc. 2009), Mossy Oak Break Up Infinity (2010-2014), or Mossy Oak Break-Up Country (new 2015) camo coverage. Mfg. 2007-2015.

	$1,175	$995	$850	$750	$650	$495	$375	*$1,360*

Add $120 for Mag. cals.

This model was originally featured as a 2006 SHOT Show Special.

BAR ZENITH – various cals., features a manual cocking system on the upper tang and wood inserts in the receiver, 20 in. barrel with Battue/fixed rear sight and fiber optic front sight. European distribution only. New 2012.

This model is not available for U.S. importation, and is sold in Europe exclusively.

BAR-22 – .22 LR cal., 20 1/4 in. barrel, 15 shot tube mag., folding leaf sight, high polish steel receiver, checkered pistol grip stock, 5 lbs. 13 oz. Mfg. 1977-85 by Miroku.

	$795	$625	$550	$450	$350	$300	$250	*$245*

Add $100 for NIB.

BAR-22 GRADE II – engraved model of BAR-22 featuring game scenes on silver greyed steel receiver, select French walnut. Disc. 1985.

	$1,300	$975	$800	$725	$575	$450	$350	*$350*

Add $150 for NIB.

RIFLES: SEMI-AUTO, FAL & CAL SERIES

FN manufactured FALs and CALs imported by BAC can be found under the Fabrique Nationale heading.

	Above Average	Average	Below Average

RIFLES: SINGLE SHOT

MODEL 1878 STANDARD – various cals., J.M. Browning's first patent, falling block action, fewer than 600 made (highest known ser. no. is 542) by Browning Brothers in Ogden, Utah between 1878-1883, octagon barrel marked "Browning Bros. Ogden, Utah USA", plain wood stock and forearm with and without pistol grips, crescent steel buttplate, with or without ramrod, several receiver configurations, a very few were made in the deluxe model, seldom found in better than average used condition, with or w/o serial number. Approx. only 100 have survived - Browning Arms Co. and the Winchester Museum have no factory records on this model.

	$50,000 - $40,000	$35,000 - $30,000	$25,000 - $20,000

Add 50% for Deluxe Rifle (checkered stock and forearm), 10% for Early Rifle with Sharps Borchardt type

GRADING - PPGS™	100%	98%	95%	90%	80%	70%	60%	LAST MSR

lever, 40% for Early Rifle stamped "Ogden, U.T.", 20% for any caliber other than .40-70 SS or .45-70 Govt., 25% for Late Model with ramrod under barrel held by two thimbles (known as "Montana Model"). Subtract 20% if the original sights have been removed or replaced incorrectly.

Please refer to the grading explanation for Winchester lever actions regarding descriptions for the above condition factors.

Calibers in this model are listed from rarest to most commonly encountered: .50-70 Govt., .45 Sharps, .44 Rem., .40-90 Sharps, .44-77 Sharps, .45-70 Govt., and .40-70 Sharps Straight.

This model is rare since approx. only 550 were mfg. (approx. ser. range 1-550). This patent was sold to Winchester, which became their Model 1885 single shot. To date, less than 100 original Model 1878s have been encountered indicating a high mortality rate (most remaining specimens are in poor original condition). An inherent weakness of the original design was the way the stock attached to the action - Winchester later corrected this design flaw. A few remaining examples are not serial numbered. Barter guns are rifles which have Browning stamped actions but with another gunsmith's barrel.

B-78 - .22-250 Rem., 6mm Rem., .243 Win. (only 671 mfg.), .25-06 Rem., 7mm Mag., .30-06, or .45-70 Govt. (octagon barrel only) cal., 24 or 26 in. round or octagon barrel, lever activated falling block, no sights except .45- 70 Govt., checkered walnut stock, approx. 24,000 mfg. 1973-1982.

$1,495	$1,275	$1,125	$1,000	$825	$675	$525	

Add 35% for .243 Win. cal.
Add 25% for octagon barrel.
Add 10% for 7mm Rem. Mag or .25-06 Rem. cal.

Production statistics on the various calibers are as follows: .22-250 - 2,431 mfg. in round barrel, 3,482 mfg. in octagon, .243 Win. - 280 mfg. in round barrel, 391 mfg. in octagon, 6mm Rem - 1,280 mfg. in round barrel, 1,911 mfg. in octagon, .25-06 - 1,475 mfg. in round barrel, 3,293 mfg. in octagon, .30-06 - 1,588 mfg. in round barrel, 2,330 mfg. in octagon, .45-70 - 0 mfg. in round barrel, 3,839 mfg. in octagon, 7mm Rem. Mag. - 635 mfg. in round barrel, 961 mfg. in octagon.

The Model B-78 was superceded by the Model 1885 in 1985.

* ***B-78 Sporter*** - various cals., utilizes a Model 1885 barrelled action with B-78 wood (pistol grip and cheekpiece).

$1,325	$1,200	$1,075	$950	$795	$650	$500	

Add 10% for highly figured wood.

MODEL 1885 HIGH WALL - .22-250 Rem., .223 Rem. (disc. 1994), .270 Win., .30-06, 7mm Rem. Mag., .45-70 Govt., or .454 Casull (new 1998) cal., falling block action, sear safety, 28 in. octagonal barrel, adj. gold trigger, no sights, checkered straight grip English walnut stock without cheekpiece and Schnabel forearm, exposed hammer, approx. 8 3/4 lbs. Mfg. 1985-2001.

$1,600	$1,375	$1,150	$1,000	$800	$675	$525	*$1,027*

This model was equipped with open sights in .45-70 Govt. and .454 Casull cals.

MODEL 1885 LOW WALL - .22 Hornet, .223 Rem. (disc. 2000), .243 Win. (disc. 2000), or .260 Rem. (new 1999) cal., action patterned after the Winchester Low Wall receiver, features thinner 24 in. barrel, adj. trigger, 6 1/4 lbs. Mfg. 1995-2001.

$1,225	$1,070	$920	$835	$675	$550	$430	*$997*

Add $300 for .260 Rem. cal. (rare caliber).

MODEL 1885 HIGH WALL TRADITIONAL HUNTER - .30-30 Win., .38-55 WCF or .45-70 Govt. cal., High-Wall action, 30 in. octagon barrel with ejector, blue receiver, rear tang aperture sight, crescent buttplate, checkered stock and forearm, approx. 9 lbs. Mfg. 1997-2000.

$1,325	$1,160	$995	$900	$730	$595	$465	*$1,220*

* ***Model 1885 High Wall Traditional Hunter 125th Anniversary*** - .45-70 Govt. cal., features delicate scroll receiver engraving and gold enhanced 125th anniversary logo with gold border. 500 mfg. 2003-2004 only.

$1,750	$1,575	$1,355	N/A	N/A	N/A	N/A	*$1,516*

MODEL 1885 LOW WALL TRADITIONAL HUNTER - .357 Mag., .44 Mag., or .45 LC cal., 24 in. half-round, half-octagon barrel, case colored receiver and buttplate, gold bead front, semi-buckhorn rear, and rear tang aperture sights, 6 1/2 lbs. Mfg. 1998-2001.

$1,375	$1,205	$1,030	$935	$755	$620	$480	*$1,289*

MODEL 1885 BPCR (BLACK POWDER CARTRIDGE RIFLE) - .40-65 Win. (black powder only) or .45-70 Govt. (black powder or smokeless) cal., case colored high wall action, 30 in. half-round, half-octagon

GRADING - PPGS™	100%	98%	95%	90%	80%	70%	60%	LAST MSR

barrel, checkered pistol grip stock with shotgun butt, w/o ejector system and shell deflector, vernier tang rear sight and globe front sight with spirit level, approx. 11 lbs. Mfg. 1996-2001.

$1,900	$1,665	$1,425	$1,290	$1,045	$855	$665	*$1,766*

* ***Model 1885 BPCR Creedmoor*** – .45-90 cal., blue receiver, 34 in. half-round, half-octagon barrel with globe front and aperture rear tang sights, 11 3/4 lbs. Mfg. 1998-1999.

$1,900	$1,665	$1,425	$1,290	$1,045	$855	$665	*$1,764*

RIFLES: SLIDE ACTION

BPR – .243 Win., .270 Win., .30-06, .308 Win., .300 Win. Mag., or 7mm Rem. Mag. cal., 7 lug rotary bolt, blue alloy receiver, 22 or 24 (Mag. cals. only) in. barrel with open sights, features downward camming slide action assembly, checkered walnut stock and forend, crossbolt safety, 3 or 4 shot mag., approx. 7 lbs. 3 oz. Mfg. 1997-2001.

$750	$650	$525	$475	$375	$315	$250	*$725*

Add $55 for Mag. cals.

BPR-22 – .22 LR or .22 WMR cal., short-stroke action, 20 1/4 in. barrel, 11 shot tube mag., mfg. 1977-1982.

$900	$650	$525	$425	$350	$295	$250

Add 30% for .22 WMR cal.
Add $100 for NIB.

* ***BPR-22 Grade II*** – similar to BPR-22, only engraved action, select walnut.

$1,200	$900	$775	$650	$525	$450	$350

Add 30% for .22 WMR cal.
Add $100 for NIB.

TROMBONE MODEL – .22 LR cal. only, slide action with tube mag., fixed sights, takedown, 24 in. barrel, hammerless, with either FN or U.S. (rare) barrel address, approx. 150,000 Grade I's were mfg.

Add $150 for original box.

* ***Trombone Model w/FN Barrel Address*** – most common variation.

$1,650	$1,275	$1,050	$950	$750	$625	$475

Add $200 for 100% condition with box.

* ***Trombone Model w/BAC Barrel Markings*** – approx. 3,200 Grade Is were imported by BAC during the late 1960s.

$2,250	$1,800	$1,525	$1,375	$1,100	$875	$700

Add $250 for original box.

* ***Trombone Model Grade I*** – limited mfg. for the BCA circa 1985, 30 mfg., with only 10 sold individually, engraved by Custom Shop at FN for wholesaler.

$1,895	$1,550	$1,250	$1,000	$800	$650	$500

Add $100 for NIB.

* ***Trombone Grades I & II 2 Gun Set*** – limited mfg. for the BCA circa 1985, 10 sets mfg., available in 2 gun set.

$4,200	$3,500	$3,000	$2,500	$2,150	$1,750	$1,500

* ***Trombone Grades I, II, & III 3 Gun Set*** – 10 sets mfg. for BCA circa 1985.

$8,500	$6,575	$5,625	N/A	N/A	N/A	N/A

* ***Trombone Custom Shop Models*** – limited mfg. from the FN Custom Shop.

Values for 100% rifles are as follows: Grade I - $1,500, Grade II - $2,500, Grade III - $4,000, Grade III C or Grade III w/gold inlays (sometimes referred to as Grade IV) - $4,500, Grade V (wood and water or Squirrel gun) - $3,000.

SHOTGUNS: BOLT ACTION, A-BOLT SERIES

A-BOLT SHOTGUN MODEL (DISC.) – 12 ga. only, 3 in. chamber, 2 shot mag., same bolt system as A-Bolt II Rifle, 22 or 23 in. barrel (rifled or Invector with rifled tube), available in Stalker Model with graphite fiberglass composite stock or Hunter Model with select satin finished walnut stock, dull matte finished barrel and receiver, top tang safety, choice of no sights (new 1996) or adj. rear sight, drilled and tapped receiver, approx. 7 lbs. Mfg. by Miroku 1995-98.

* ***A-Bolt Stalker Model Shotgun***

$625	$540	$500	$425	$400	$360	$340	*$720*

Add $45 for open sights.
Add $150 for rifled barrel.

GRADING - PPGS™	100%	98%	95%	90%	80%	70%	60%	LAST MSR

* ***A-Bolt Hunter Model Shotgun***

	$625	$540	$500	$425	$400	$360	$340	*$805*

Add $40 for open sights.
Add $150 for rifled barrel.

A-BOLT SHOTGUN HUNTER – 12 ga. only, 3 in. chamber, 22 in. rifled barrel with adj. rear and TruGlo fiber optic front sights, matte blued finish, 60 degree bolt lift, 2 shot detachable mag., satin finished checkered walnut stock, vent. recoil pad, sling swivels, approx. 7 lbs. Mfg. 2011-2015.

	$985	$800	$765	$725	$585	$475	$360	*$1,280*

* ***A-Bolt Shotgun Camo*** – 12 ga. only, similar to A-Bolt Shotgun Hunter, except available with Mossy Oak Break-Up Infinity (2010-2014) or Mossy Break-Up Country (new 2015) camo finish with armor coating. Mfg. 2011-2015.

	$985	$800	$765	$725	$585	$475	$360	*$1,300*

* ***A-Bolt Shotgun Stalker*** – 12 ga. only, similar to A-Bolt Shotgun Hunter, except as black composite stock with Dura-Touch Armor coating and textured gripping surfaces. Mfg. 2011-2015.

	$900	$720	$675	$625	$585	$475	$360	*$1,150*

SHOTGUNS: O/U, CYNERGY SERIES

In addition to the models listed below, Browning has also released SHOT Show specials on some models that were available by dealers ordering them at the SHOT Show only. Complete descriptions for these models can be found under SHOT SHOW SPECIALS - SHOTGUNS: O/U at BlueBookOfGunValues.com/overflow.

CYNERGY SERIES – 12, 20 (new 2005), 28 (new 2005) ga., or .410 bore (new 2007), silver nitride finished receiver, features new MonoLock hinge system allowing low receiver profile, mechanical striker based SST, Reverse Striker ignition system (triple trigger system included on Sporting models), 26 or 28 in. backbored and ported vent. barrels with VR, Vector Pro lengthened forcing cones became standard on all 12 and 20 ga. models beginning 2010, Invector Plus chokes, choice of wood or composite (12 ga. only) stock and forearm, solid, vent., or Inflex recoil pad, impact ejectors. New 2004.

* ***Cynergy Field (Current Mfg.)*** – 12, 20, 28 (disc. 2017) ga., or .410 bore (disc. 2017), 3 in. chambers, Reverse Striker ignition system, 26 or 28 in. lightweight profile barrel with ventilated top and side ribs, matte blue finish, Vector Pro lengthened forcing cones (12 and 20 ga.), three Invector-Plus choke tubes (12 and 20 ga.), three standard Invector choke tubes (28 and .410), silver Nitride finished engraved receiver, impact ejectors, gold trigger, ivory front bead sight, satin varnish finished Grade I/II walnut stock, Inflex recoil pad, 1/4 in. stock spacer, top tang barrel selector/ safety, approx. 6-7 3/4 lbs. New 2015.

MSR $2,040	$1,735	$1,520	$1,300	$1,180	$955	$780	$680	

Add $70 for 20 ga.
Add $70 for 28 (disc. 2017) ga. or .410 bore (disc. 2017).

* ***Cynergy Field (Mfg. 2010-2014)*** – 12, 20, 28 ga. or .410 bore, similar to discontinued Cynergy Field, except has Vector Pro lengthened forcing cones on 12 and 20 ga., engraving features pheasants and ducks on 12 ga., or quail and grouse on small gauge, gloss oil finished Grade II/III walnut stock, approx. 6-7 3/4 lbs. Mfg. 2010-2014.

	$2,375	$1,850	$1,700	$1,450	$1,150	$925	$775	*$2,800*

Add $50 for 20, 28 ga. or .410 bore.

* ***Cynergy Field (Mfg. 2004-2007)*** – 12 (disc. 2006), 20, or 28 ga., 2 3/4 (28 ga. only) or 3 in. chambers, 26 or 28 in. non-ported barrels with 5/16 in. slanted VR, flush choke tubes, silver nitride finished receiver with clay pigeon motif, checkered Grade I walnut or non-glare black composite (disc. 2006) stock and forearm, stock has adj. comb with built in Inflex recoil pad system allowing LOP adjustment, approx. 6 1/4-7 1/2 lbs. Mfg. 2004-2007.

	$1,575	$1,200	$950	$875	$775	$700	$625	*$2,062*

Subtract approx. 10% for composite stock and forearm.

* ***Cynergy Classic Field*** – 12, 20 (new 2007), 28 ga. (new 2007), or .410 bore (new 2007), 3 in. chambers, features traditional satin finished walnut stock with standard vent. recoil pad and Schnabel forearm, etched mallard and pheasant on receiver sides, approx. 6 1/4 - 7 3/4 lbs. Mfg. 2006-2013.

	$2,150	$1,825	$1,550	$1,325	$1,100	$900	$700	*$2,530*

Add $60 for 20, 28 ga. or .410 bore.

GRADING - PPGS™ 100% 98% 95% 90% 80% 70% 60% LAST MSR

* ***Cynergy Classic Field Grade III*** – 12 or 20 ga., 3 in. chambers, similar to Classic Field, except has gloss finished upgraded wood (Grade III/Grade IV) and fully engraved receiver, approx. 6-8 lbs. Mfg. 2007-2013.

$3,400 $2,850 $2,450 $2,100 $1,775 $1,500 $1,200 *$4,000*

Add $50 for 20 ga.

* ***Cynergy Classic Field Grade VI*** – 12 or 20 ga., similar to Classic Field Grade III, except has upgraded wood (Grade V/VI), fully engraved receiver with multiple gold inlays. Mfg. 2007-2013.

$5,185 $4,400 $3,800 $3,250 $2,750 $2,300 $1,800 *$6,100*

Add $30 for 20 ga.

* ***Cynergy Composite Ultimate Turkey Mossy Oak Break-Up Country*** – 12 ga., 3 1/2 in. chambers, Reverse Striker ignition system, 24 or 26 in. lightweight profile barrels with ventilated top and side ribs, Vector Pro lengthened forcing cones, extended ultimate full turkey and spreader choke tubes, impact ejectors, Marbles Arms Bullseye rear sight with fiber optic front sight, composite stock, comb is adj. for drop, Inflex recoil pad with one 1/4 in. spacer, textured grip panels, ultra low profile steel receiver with MonoLock hinge, short Picatinny rail, 100% Mossy Oak Break-Up Country camo finish, 7 lbs. 6 oz.

MSR $2,470 $2,100 $1,840 $1,575 $1,430 $1,155 $950 $820

* ***Cynergy Euro Field*** – 12, 20, 28 ga. or .410 bore, 26 or 28 in. barrel, jewelled monobloc, full coverage high relief engraving (pheasants and ducks on 12 ga., quail and grouse on 20 ga.) on receiver, forearm iron and top lever, gloss oil finished Grade II/III walnut stock and forearm, choke tubes, 5 lbs., 15 oz. - 7 lbs., 11 oz. Mfg. 2009.

$2,125 $1,800 $1,550 $1,300 $1,100 $900 $700 *$2,509*

Add $20 for 20, 28 ga. or .410 bore.

This model's nomenclature was changed to the Cynergy Field during 2010.

* ***Cynergy Feather (Current Mfg.)*** – 12 or 20 ga., 3 in. chambers, 26 or 28 in. non-ported VR barrels and Vector Pro choke tubes, matte blue finish, lightweight alloy engraved receiver with steel breech face, MonoLock hinge, impact ejectors, gold trigger, ivory front bead sight, checkered satin finished Grade I/II walnut stock/forearm with Inflex recoil pad, 1/4 in. stock spacer, top tang barrel selector/safety, approx. 5 1/2-6 3/4 lbs. Mfg. 2015-2017.

$1,795 $1,550 $1,325 $1,100 $925 $825 $725 *$2,140*

Add $60 for 20 ga.

* ***Cynergy Feather Composite*** – 12 ga., 3 in. chambers, 26 or 28 in. non-ported VR barrels and three Invector Plus choke tubes, matte blue finish, lightweight alloy engraved receiver with steel breech face and gold enhanced grayed finish, impact ejectors, gold trigger, ivory front bead sight, charcoal gray composite stock with black rubber overmolding in grip areas, adj. comb, Inflex recoil pad, 1/4 in. stock spacer, top tang barrel selector/safety, approx. 5 1/2-6 3/4 lbs. Mfg. 2015-2017.

$1,750 $1,525 $1,300 $1,075 $900 $800 $700 *$2,070*

* ***Cynergy Feather (Mfg. 2007-2014)*** – 12, 20 (new 2008), 28 (new 2008) ga. or .410 bore (new 2008), 3 in. chambers, choice of checkered black composite stock with adj. comb or checkered satin-finished walnut stock and Schnabel forearm, Inflex recoil pad, 26 or 28 in. barrels with flush Invector Plus choke tubes, jewelled monobloc (new 2009), approx. 5 1/2 - 6 3/4 lbs. New 2007.

$2,525 $2,025 $1,650 $1,325 $1,100 $950 $800 *$2,900*

Add $30 for 20, 28 ga. or .410 bore.

Subtract $100 for black adj. composite stock and forearm (12 ga. only).

* ***Cynergy Micro Midas*** – 12 (disc. 2016), 20, 28 (disc. 2016) ga. or .410 bore (disc. 2016), 3 in. chambers, Reverse Striker ignition system, 24 or 26 in. lightweight profile barrel with ventilated top and side ribs, matte blued finish, Vector Pro lengthened forcing cones, three Invector Plus choke tubes, silver nitride finished steel engraved receiver with MonoLock hinge, impact ejectors, gold trigger, ivory front bead sight, satin varnish finished Grade I/II walnut stock, Inflex recoil pad, compact 13 in. LOP, three 1/4 in. stock spacers, top tang barrel selector/safety, approx. 6-7 3/4 lbs. New 2015.

MSR $2,040 $1,735 $1,520 $1,300 $1,180 $955 $780 $680

* ***Cynergy Sporting (Recent Mfg.)*** – 12 ga., 3 in. chambers, 30 or 32 in. ported VR barrels with floating top rib, matte blued finish, three Invector Plus Midas Grade choke tubes, Vector Pro lengthened cones, silver Nitride finished engraved steel receiver, impact ejectors, gold trigger, HiViz Pro-Comp fiber optic sight, ivory mid-bead sight, satin varnish finished Grade I/II walnut stock with or without adj. cheekpiece, Inflex recoil pad, adj. LOP, 1/4 in. stock spacer, top tang barrel selector/safety, approx. 8 lbs. Mfg. 2015-2017.

$1,995 $1,600 $1,500 $1,250 $1,000 $900 $800 *$2,400*

Add $270 for adj. comb

GRADING - PPGS™	100%	98%	95%	90%	80%	70%	60%	LAST MSR

* ***Cynergy Sporting (Mfg. 2004-2007)*** – 12 (disc. 2006), 20, or 28 ga., 2 3/4 in. chambers, 28, 30, or 32 in. ported barrels with tapered VR (non-tapered 5/16 in. rib on 28 ga.), Hi-Viz fiber optic front sight, silver Nitride receiver with clay pigeon motif, oil finished checkered walnut (with or w/o adj. comb) or black composite (12 ga. only, disc. 2006) stock and forearm, stock has adj. comb with built in Inflex recoil pad system allowing LOP adjustment (disc. 2006), extended choke tubes, approx. 6 1/2-8 lbs. Mfg. 2004-2007.

$1,875 $1,600 $1,500 $1,250 $1,000 $845 $655 ***$3,080***

Add 25% for adj. comb (mfg. 2006 only).

Subtract approx. 20% for composite stock and forearm.

* ***Cynergy Classic Sporting*** – 12, 20 (new 2007), 28 ga. (new 2007) or .410 bore (new 2007), 2 3/4 or 3 in. chambers, 28, 30, or 32 in. ported barrels with extended choke tubes, features traditional oil finished walnut stock with solid recoil pad and Schnabel forearm, etched Browning logo on receiver sides, approx. 6 1/4 - 8 lbs. Mfg. 2006-2013.

$3,100 $2,000 $1,850 $1,750 $1,550 $1,400 $1,100 ***$3,600***

Add $30 for 20, 28 ga. or .410 bore.

Add $400 for adj. comb (new 2007, not available in 28 ga. or .410 bore).

* ***Cynergy Sporting (Euro Sporting)*** – 12 or 20 (new 2008) ga., 2 3/4 in. chambers, 28, 30, or 32 in. VR barrels with porting and extended choke tubes, features traditional checkered oil finished walnut stock and Schnabel forearm, or black composite (adj. comb only) stock with Inflex recoil pad, jewelled monobloc (new 2009), high relief scroll engraving on receiver forearm and top lever (new 2009), approx. 6 1/4 - 8 lbs. Mfg. 2007-2014.

$3,525 $1,800 $1,650 $1,500 $1,250 $1,100 $1,000 ***$4,000***

Add $500 for adj. comb (12 ga. only) with oil finished walnut stock and Schnabel forearm.

Add $30 for 20 ga.

Subtract $120 for adj. comb black composite stock and forearm (not available in 20 ga.).

Subtract 10% if w/o scroll engraving.

This model's nomenclature changed from Euro Sporting to Sporting during 2010.

* ***Cynergy Classic Trap*** – 12 ga. only, 2 3/4 in. chambers, 30 or 32 in. VR barrels with porting, extended Invector-Plus chokes and Hi-Viz fiber optic front sight, checkered walnut stock with or w/o adj. comb and competition forearm, vent. recoil pad, approx. 8 3/4 lbs. Mfg. 2007-2014.

$3,340 $2,000 $1,850 $1,700 $1,600 $1,500 $1,300 ***$3,880***

Add $400 for adj. comb.

* ***Cynergy Classic Trap Unsingle Combo (Current Mfg.)*** – 12 ga. only, 2 3/4 in. chambers, includes choice of ported single barrel and choice of O/U ported barrels with adj. top rib in 32/34, 32/32 (disc. 2019), or 30/34 (disc. 2019), Vector Pro forcing cones, four Invector Plus Midas Grade choke tubes, silver Nitride finished engraved receiver, impact ejectors, HiViz Pro-Comp fiber optic sight, ivory mid-bead sight, Gray laminated Monte Carlo stock with palm swell, adj. comb, and semi-beavertail forearm with finger grooves, adj. LOP, includes green canvas/leather fitted case with Cynergy logo, approx. 8 3/4 lbs. New 2015.

MSR $4,360 $3,700 $3,240 $2,775 $2,515 $2,035 $1,665 $1,450

* ***Cynergy Classic Trap Unsingle Combo (Disc.)*** – 12 ga. only, includes choice of 32 or 34 in. ported single barrel and choice of 30 or 32 in. O/U ported barrels with adj. top rib, gloss finished Grade III/VI walnut stock with adj. comb and semi-beavertail forearm with finger grooves, includes aluminum (disc.) or green canvas case, approx. 8 3/4 lbs. Mfg. 2008-2014.

$5,180 $3,200 $2,900 $2,700 $2,500 $2,265 $1,800 ***$6,000***

* ***Cynergy CX*** – 12 ga., 3 in. chambers, Reverse Striker ignition system, 28 (new 2018), 30, or 32 in. VR barrels, Vector Pro lengthened forcing cones, three Invector Plus Midas Grade choke tubes, steel engraved receiver, impact ejectors, ivory front and mid-bead sights, satin finish Grade I walnut stock, Inflex recoil pad, 1/4 in. stock spacer, with (new 2018) or w/o adj. comb, top tang barrel selector/safety, silver Nitride finish, approx. 8 lbs. New 2017.

MSR $1,900 $1,615 $1,415 $1,225 $1,100 $900 $725 $625

Add $420 for adj. comb (new 2018).

* ***Cynergy CX Composite*** – 12 ga., 3 in. chambers, Reverse Striker ignition system, 28 (new 2018), 30, or 32 in. VR barrels, Vector Pro lengthened forcing cones, three Invector Plus Midas Grade choke tubes, steel engraved receiver, MonoLock hinge, impact ejectors, ivory front and mid-bead sights, charcoal gray composite stock with black rubber overmolding in grip areas, adj. comb, adj. LOP, 1/4 in. stock spacer, top tang barrel selector/safety, silver Nitride finish, 7 lbs. 11 oz. New 2017.

MSR $1,820 $1,550 $1,355 $1,165 $1,055 $855 $700 $600

GRADING - PPGS™	100%	98%	95%	90%	80%	70%	60%	LAST MSR

* ***Cynergy Wicked Wing Mossy Oak Shadow Grass Habitat*** – 12 ga., 3 1/2 in. chambers, 26, 28, or 30 in. barrels, three extended Goose Band choke tubes, white bead front sight, adj. comb, Inflex recoil pad, 1/4 in. stock spacer, Cerakote Burnt Bronze camo on receiver and Burnt Bronze finish on barrel, 7.6-7.10 lbs. New 2021.

MSR $2,340	$1,990	$1,740	$1,500	$1,350	$1,100	$900	$750

SHOTGUNS: O/U, CITORI HUNTING SERIES

All Citori shotguns which incorporate the Invector choke tube system may be used with steel shot. Invector Plus choke tubes are designed for backbored barrels. DO NOT USE Standard Invector choke tubes in barrels marked for the Invector Plus choking system.

Hand engraving was replaced by machine engraving in late 1982 on all higher grade models.

In addition to the models listed below, Browning has also released SHOT Show specials on some models that were available by dealers ordering them at the SHOT Show only. These models are listed separately under: SHOT SHOW SPECIALS LISTINGS: SHOTGUNS O/U.

Subtract $100 for 26 in. barrels on used guns.

CITORI CX – 12 ga., 3 in. chambers, crossover design for trap, skeet, or sporting clays, 28, 30, or 32 in. lightweight profile VR barrels, 3 extended Midas Grade choke tubes, Vector Pro forcing cones, high post rib, interchangeable choke tubes, steel high polished blue receiver with Citori CX logo on sides in gold, Triple Trigger System, ivory bead sight and mid-bead, gloss finished Grade II American walnut stock with or w/o Graco adj. comb, Inflex recoil pad, locking bolt and hinge pin, 60/40 POI, 8.1-8.9 lbs. New 2019.

MSR $2,270	$1,930	$1,685	$1,450	$1,310	$1,060	$875	$750

Add $430 for Graco adj. comb.

CITORI CX MICRO WITH ADJUSTABLE LOP – 12 ga., 3 in. chambers, 28 or 30 in. barrel, three Midas Grade extended choke tubes, 3-pos. trigger with one trigger shoe, ivory bead sight and mid-bead, gloss finished Grade II American walnut stock with Graco buttpad plate, gold enhancement, Inflex recoil pad, 13 1/4 in. LOP, 8 lbs. 1 oz. New 2020.

MSR $2,550	$2,170	$1,900	$1,630	$1,475	$1,195	$1,000	$850

This model was originally featured as a 2019 SHOT Show Special.

CITORI CXS – 12 ga., 3 in. chambers, 28, 30, or 32 in. ported VR barrel with floating top rib, Vector Pro lengthened forcing cones, three Invector Plus Midas Grade choke tubes, steel receiver with gold accented engraving, hammer ejectors, Triple Trigger System with one trigger piece, ivory front and mid-bead sights, gloss finished Grade II American walnut stock with or w/o adj. comb, Inflex recoil pad, top tang safety, blued finish, approx. 7-8 lbs. New 2018.

MSR $2,320	$1,975	$1,730	$1,480	$1,350	$1,085	$900	$775

Add $430 for adj. comb.

CITORI CXS MICRO – 12 or 20 ga., 3 in. chambers, 24 or 26 in. lightweight barrels, 3 Midas grade extended Invector-Plus choke tubes, Vector Pro lengthend forcing cones, vent. top and side ribs, steel high polished blue receiver with Citori CXS logo on sides in gold, Triple Trigger System, ivory bead sight and mid-bead, gloss finished Grade II American walnut stock, Inflex recoil pad, compact 13 in. LOP, 8.6 lbs. New 2019.

MSR $2,270	$1,930	$1,685	$1,450	$1,310	$1,060	$875	$750

CITORI FIELD SPORTING GRADE VII – 12 (mfg. 2020 only), 20 (new 2021), 28 (new 2021) ga., or .410 bore (new 2021), 2 3/4 (28 ga. only, new 2021) or 3 in. chambers, 30 or 32 in. barrels with polished blued finish, five extended black Midas Grade choke tubes, Triple Trigger System with three shoes, HiViZ Pro Comp sight and ivory mid-bead, gloss oil finished Grade VI/VII walnut stock with nameplate inlay for owner's initials, Inflex recoil pad, extensive engraving with silver bird and dog accents, 7.5-8 lbs. New 2020.

MSR $6,460	$5,500	$4,815	$4,125	$3,740	$3,025	$2,475	$2,150

Add $80 for 28 ga. or .410 bore (both new 2021).

CITORI HUNTER MODELS – 12, 16 (mfg. 1986-89), 20, 28 ga. (disc. 1994) or .410 bore (disc. 1994), 26, 28, or 30 in. barrels, various chokes, boxlock, auto ejectors, SST, vent. rib, checkered semi-pistol grip stock with grooved semi-beavertail forearm, grades differ in amount of engraving, finish, and wood. Invector chokes became standard in 1988, Invector Plus chokes became standard 1995 on 12 or 20 ga., 6 lbs. 9 oz.-8 lbs. 5 oz. Mfg. 1973-2001 by Miroku.

* ***Citori Hunter Grade I 12 or 20 ga.*** – blue finish with light scroll engraving beginning 1978.

GRADING - PPGS™	100%	98%	95%	90%	80%	70%	60%	LAST MSR
» **Citori Hunter Grade I Earlier Mfg. without Invector Choking**								
	$950	$800	$700	$600	$575	$500	$450	

Add 15% for 16 ga. if in 90%+ original condition.
Add approx. 40% for extra 20 ga. barrels originally ordered with gun.

» ***Citori Grade I Hunter Model w/Invector Choking*** – recent mfg. with Invector Choking, 12 or 20 ga., 3 in. chambers, 20 ga. available with Standard Invector or Invector Plus (new 1994) choking system, Invector Plus choking standard on recently mfg. 12 and 20 ga., 6 lbs. 9 oz. - 8 lbs. 5 oz. Disc. 2001.

	100%	98%	95%	90%	80%	70%	60%	LAST MSR
	$1,150	$950	$825	$700	$650	$575	$525	*$1,486*

Add $100 for Invector Plus choke tubes.

* ***Citori Hunter Grade I Smaller Gauges***

» ***Citori Hunter Grade I 28 ga. or .410 bore*** – without Invector choking. Disc. 1994.

	100%	98%	95%	90%	80%	70%	60%	LAST MSR
	$1,000	$850	$700	$600	$550	$500	$450	*$1,097*

* ***Citori Hunter Grade II*** – 12, 20, 28 ga., or .410 bore. Mfg. 1978-1983.

	100%	98%	95%	90%	80%	70%	60%	LAST MSR
	$1,400	$1,250	$1,100	$900	$600	$550	$500	

* ***Citori Hunter Grade III*** – 12, 16 (mfg. 1986-89), 20, 28 ga. (disc. 1994), or .410 bore (disc. 1994), greyed steel receiver with engraved game scenes featuring grouse (20 ga.) and ducks (12 ga.), Invector chokes standard, Invector Plus became standard in 12 ga. in 1994. Mfg. 1985-95.

	100%	98%	95%	90%	80%	70%	60%	LAST MSR
	$1,500	$1,400	$1,325	$1,000	$800	$700	$600	*$1,875*

Add 15% for 16 ga. if in 90%+ original condition.
Add 15%-25% for 28 ga. or .410 bore (both disc. 1989).
Subtract $200 for standard Invector chokes.

* ***Citori Hunter Grade V*** – 12, 20, 28 ga., or .410 bore, extensive deep relief hand engraving with game scenes on satin grey receiver. Disc. 1984.

	100%	98%	95%	90%	80%	70%	60%	LAST MSR
	$4,950	$4,500	$4,000	$3,500	$3,000	$2,600	$2,200	

Add 15-25% for 28 ga., .410 bore, depending on condition.

* ***Citori Hunter Grade VI*** – 12, 16 (mfg. 1986-89), 20, 28 ga. (disc. 1992), or .410 bore (disc. 1989), hand engraved (1983-1984 only, signed by the engraver) or machine engraving on blue (1983-1984 mfg. only) or grey (new late 1984) receiver with extensive engraving including multiple gold inlays, Standard Invector (12 ga. disc. 1993) or Invector Plus chokes. Mfg. 1983-1995.

	100%	98%	95%	90%	80%	70%	60%	LAST MSR
1983-1984 mfg. (hand engraved)	$5,150	$4,600	$4,000	$3,500	$3,000	$2,600	$2,200	
1985-1995 mfg.	$3,000	$2,750	$2,200	$1,900	$1,600	$1,350	$1,225	*$2,715*

Add 15% for 16 ga. if in 90%+ original condition.
Add 15%-25% for 28 ga. or .410 bore, depending on condition.
Subtract $200 for standard Invector chokes.

* ***Citori Hunter 3 1/2 in. Magnum Model*** – 12 ga., 3 1/2 in. chambers, 28 or 30 in. VR barrels with back-bored Invector plus choke tubes, with recoil pad, approx. 8 lbs. 9 oz. Mfg. 1989-2000.

	100%	98%	95%	90%	80%	70%	60%	LAST MSR
	$1,000	$900	$825	$695	$600	$550	$495	*$1,563*

* ***Citori Sporting Hunter*** – 12 or 20 ga., 3 or 3 1/2 (12 ga. only) in. chambers, 26, 28, or 30 (12 ga. only) in. barrels with Invector Plus choking, configured for both hunting and sporting clays shooting, Superposed style forearm, contoured recoil pad, front and middle bead sights, gloss or satin (3 1/2 in. only) wood finish, 6 lbs. 9 oz. - 8 lbs. 9 oz. Mfg. 1998-2001.

	100%	98%	95%	90%	80%	70%	60%	LAST MSR
	$1,000	$900	$825	$695	$600	$550	$495	*$1,607*

* ***Citori Satin Hunter*** – 12 ga. only, 3 or 3 1/2 (disc. 2000) in. chambers, 26, 28, or 30 (3 1/2 in. Mag. only, disc. 1998) in. VR backbored barrels with Invector Plus choking, features satin wood finish, approx. 8 1/4 lbs. Mfg. 1998-2001.

	100%	98%	95%	90%	80%	70%	60%	LAST MSR
	$1,000	$895	$700	$600	$500	$450	$375	*$1,535*

* ***Citori Upland Special*** – 12, 16 (mfg. 1989 only), or 20 ga. (2 3/4 in. chambers), shortened checkered straight grip walnut stock (14 in. LOP) and Schnabel forearm, 24 in. barrels, blue finish, Invector (12 ga. disc. 1993) or Invector Plus choking, 6-6 3/4 lbs. Mfg. 1984-2000.

	100%	98%	95%	90%	80%	70%	60%	LAST MSR
	$1,195	$975	$725	$625	$500	$450	$375	*$1,514*

Add 15% for 16 ga. if in 90%+ original condition.
Subtract $200 for Invector choking.

* ***Citori White Upland Special*** – 12 or 20 ga., 2 3/4 in. chambers, similar to Upland Special, except features silver nitride finished receiver, 6 1/8 or 6 1/2 lbs. Mfg. 2000-2001.

	100%	98%	95%	90%	80%	70%	60%	LAST MSR
	$1,250	$1,000	$875	$750	$650	$600	$550	*$1,583*

GRADING - PPGS™	100%	98%	95%	90%	80%	70%	60%	LAST MSR

CITORI SATIN HUNTER MICRO MIDAS – 12 or 20 ga., 3 in. chambers, 24 or 26 in. VR barrels with Vector Pro lengthened forcing cones, includes 3 Invector Plus choke tubes, blued receiver, SST, checkered satin finished walnut stock and forearm, 13 in. LOP, vent. recoil pad on 12 ga., 6-7 3/4 lbs. Mfg. 2011-2017.

$1,425 $1,175 $1,055 $900 $750 $650 $500 *$1,650*

CITORI SUPERLIGHT MODELS – 12, 16, 20, 28 ga., or .410 bore, 2 3/4 in. chambers except for .410 bore, English stock, oil finish, Invector chokes became standard in 1988, Invector Plus became standard 1995 for 12 or 20 ga., approx. 5 lbs. 11 oz.-6 3/4 lbs. New 1983.

* ***Citori Superlight Grade I 12, 16, or 20 ga.***

» **Citori Superlight Grade I Earlier Mfg. without Invector Choking**

$1,150 $1,000 $850 $725 $600 $550 $500

» **Citori Superlight Grade I w/Invector Choking** – recent mfg. with Invector Choking 12 or 20 ga., 20 ga. available with Standard Invector or Invector Plus (new 1994, became standard 1995) choking system, Invector Plus choking standard on recently mfg. 12 ga. Disc. 2002.

$1,450 $1,250 $1,050 $900 $750 $600 $525 *$1,590*

Subtract $200 for Standard Invector choking in 12 or 20 ga.

* ***Citori Superlight Grade I 28 ga. or .410 bore*** – without Invector choking until 1993, Invector choking became an option in 1994 and standard in 1995. Disc. 2002.

$1,500 $1,300 $1,100 $950 $750 $625 $550 *$1,666*

Subtract $200 if without Invector choke tubes.

* ***Citori Superlight Feather*** – 12 or 20 (new 2002) ga., 2 3/4 in. chambers, 26 in. VR barrels with three Invector Plus choke tubes, alloy receiver with high relief engraving, hammer ejectors, single selective trigger, silver front bead sight, gloss finished walnut English-style straight grip stock and scaled down Schnabel forearm, top tang barrel selector/safety, 5 3/4 or 6 1/4 lbs. Mfg. 1999-2017.

$1,500 $1,300 $1,100 $950 $750 $625 $550 *$2,390*

* ***Citori Superlight Grade III*** – same gauges as Grade I, Standard Invector on 12 or 20 (disc.) ga. or Invector Plus (standard in 12 ga. beginning 1994) chokes. Mfg. 1986-2002.

$2,100 $1,800 $1,500 $1,300 $1,000 $700 $600 *$2,300*

Add $270 for 28 ga. or .410 bore (disc. 1997).

Subtract $300 if without Invector choke tubes or $200 for standard Invector choke tubes.

* ***Citori Superlight Grade V*** – sideplate available. Disc. 1984.

$2,950 $2,300 $1,900 $1,500 $1,250 $1,075 $900

* ***Citori Superlight Grade VI*** – older mfg. has Invector chokes standard (option on 28 ga. or .410 bore beginning 1994) or Invector Plus (standard and available in 12 or 20 ga. only) chokes, choice of blue or grey (new 1996) receiver finish. Mfg. 1983-2002.

$2,950 $2,350 $2,000 $1,700 $1,450 $1,325 $1,200 *$3,510*

Subtract 10% for 28 ga. or .410 bore without choke tubes.

Subtract $200 for standard Invector choke tubes.

Add $270 for 28 ga. or .410 bore with Standard Invector choking.

* ***Citori Superlight Grade VI Sideplate*** – 20 ga. only. Disc.

$3,500 $2,950 $2,250 $1,950 $1,825 $1,650 $1,475

CITORI SPORTER MODELS – similar to Citori Superlight, except with 3 in. chambers, 26 in. barrels, various chokes, straight grip stock, Schnabel forearm. Disc. 1983.

$1,250 $1,100 $1,050 $900 $750 $600 $500

Add 10% for 28 ga. or .410 bore.

* ***Citori Sporter Grade II*** – 12, 20, 28 ga., or .410 bore.

$1,600 $1,400 $1,200 $1,000 $850 $750 $600

Add 10% for 28 ga.

* ***Citori Sporter Grade V*** – 12, 20, 28 ga., or .410 bore.

$4,750 $4,150 $3,565 $3,225 $2,615 $2,150 $1,675

Add 10% for 28 ga. or .410 bore.

CITORI LIGHTNING MODELS – 12, 16 (disc. 1989), 20, 28 ga., or .410 bore, 2 3/4 (28 ga. only), or 3 in. (standard on 12 ga., 20 ga., and .410 bore) chambers, 26, 28, or 30 (disc.) in. barrels, Invector chokes standard on newer mfg. smaller ga.'s, Invector Plus became standard 1995 for 12 or 20 ga., boxlock, auto ejectors, SST, vent. rib, features checkered round knob pistol grip stock and slimmer forearm, grades differ in amount of engraving, finish, and quality of wood, approx. 6.5-8 lbs. Introduced 1988.

GRADING - PPGS™	100%	98%	95%	90%	80%	70%	60%	LAST MSR

* ***Citori Lightning Grade I 12, 16, or 20 ga.***

» **Citori Lightning Grade I Earlier Mfg. w/o Invector Choking** – without Invector Choking.

	$1,100	$1,000	$900	$750	$600	$550	$500	

Add 15% for 16 ga.

» **Citori Lightning Grade I w/Invector Choking** – 12 or 20 ga., current mfg. with Invector Choking, 12 or 20 ga., Invector (disc. 1994) or Invector Plus choking (became standard on 12 ga. in 1994, 20 ga. in 1995), gloss finished walnut stock and forearm, buttplate replaced vent. recoil pad in 2010, 6 1/2-8 lbs. Disc. 2016.

	$1,200	$1,050	$975	$925	$875	$750	$625	*$1,990*

Subtract 10% for Standard Invector choking.

This model was supplied with scroll engraving with rosette design until 2004. Beginning 2004, standard engraving is high relief, intricate, and sculpted.

* ***Citori Lightning Grade I Smaller Gauges*** – 28 ga. or .410 bore, without Invector choking until 1993, Invector choking became an option in 1994, Mfg. 1995-2017.

	$1,425	$1,200	$1,050	$975	$925	$900	$750	*$2,070*

Subtract $200 if without Standard Invector choking.

* ***Citori Lightning Grade III*** – 12, 16 (disc. 1989), or 20 ga., greyed steel receiver with engraved game scenes (mallards/pheasants on 12 ga., quail/grouse on 20 ga.), older mfg. may or may not have Invector choking, Invector Plus choking is now standard on 12 or 20 ga. Mfg. 1988-2004.

	$2,000	$1,700	$1,450	$1,200	$1,000	$850	$600	*$2,464*

Subtract 10% if without Invector choking.
Add 15% for 16 ga. (disc. 1989).

» **Citori Lightning Grade III 28 ga. or .410 bore** – features quail and grouse scene engraving. Disc. 2004.

	$2,150	$1,825	$1,550	$1,375	$1,250	$1,175	$995	*$2,754*

* ***Citori Lightning Grade IV*** – 12 or 20 ga., high relief engraving on grey receiver (pheasants on left, mallards on right on 12 ga., quail and grouse on 20 ga.) trigger guard and tang screws, high gloss finished walnut stock and forearm. Mfg. 2005-2012.

	$3,030	$2,380	$1,950	$1,575	$1,250	$1,030	$800	*$3,500*

» **Citori Lightning Grade IV 28 ga. or .410 bore** – features quail and grouse inlays. Disc. 2012.

	$3,095	$2,475	$2,100	$1,900	$1,700	$1,500	$1,100	*$3,590*

* ***Citori Lightning Grade VI*** – 12, 16 (disc. 1989), or 20 ga., blue or greyed receiver with extensive deep relief engraving with 7 gold inlays, including mallards/pheasants on receiver sides. Disc. 2004.

	$2,825	$2,400	$2,000	$1,650	$1,450	$1,225	$1,050	*$3,797*

Add 15% for 16 ga. (disc. 1989).

» **Citori Lightning Grade VI 28 ga. or .410 bore** – disc. 2004.

	$3,075	$2,550	$2,100	$1,750	$1,550	$1,325	$1,100	*$4,090*

* ***Citori Lightning Grade VII*** – 12 or 20 ga., deep relief engraving on grey or blue receiver, trigger guard, top tang, takedown lever and bracket, 24Kt. gold bird inlays (two flushing ringnecks and pointer on right side with three mallards on left side on 12 ga., quail and grouse on 20 ga.), high gloss finished walnut stock and forearm. Mfg. 2005-2012.

	$4,800	$3,840	$3,275	$2,625	$2,225	$1,895	$1,600	*$5,560*

» **Citori Lightning Grade VII 28 ga. or .410 bore** – features quail and grouse inlays. Disc. 2012.

	$4,875	$3,900	$3,300	$2,800	$2,400	$1,925	$1,650	*$5,660*

CITORI GRADE III – 12 ga., 3 in. chambers, 28 in. VR barrels with 3 Invector Plus choke tubes, raised teardrops behind sideplates, case colored receiver with sideplates and laser engraving, ejectors, gloss oil finished checkered stock with round knob and Schnabel forearm, recoil pad, includes ABS elite case, 8 1/4 lbs. A combined total of 500 Grade III and Grade VI were mfg. during 2014.

	$4,150	$3,700	$3,300	$2,950	$2,500	$2,250	$1,950	*$4,670*

CITORI GRADE VI – 12 ga., similar to Citori Grade III, except features better walnut and eight gold inlays on sideplates and bottom of frame, also includes a Crazy Horse leather case. A combined total of 500 Grade III and Grade VI were mfg. during 2014.

	$6,500	$5,750	$5,000	$4,500	$4,000	$3,500	$2,950	*$7,340*

GRADING - PPGS™	100%	98%	95%	90%	80%	70%	60%	LAST MSR

CITORI LIGHTNING FEATHER – 12 or 20 (new 2000) ga., 3 in. chambers, greyed alloy receiver with dovetailed steel breech face and steel hinge pin, 26 or 28 in. Invector Plus choked VR barrels, select checkered round knob walnut stock and forearm with gloss finish, vent. recoil pad, approx. 6 1/4-7 lbs. Mfg. 1999-2007.

	$1,650	$1,400	$1,200	$1,000	$800	$650	$500	*$1,944*

* ***Citori Lightning Feather Combo*** – includes set of 27 in. 20 ga. (3 in. chambers) and 28 ga. barrels with Invector Plus (20 ga.) and Standard Invector (28 ga.) chokes, checkered high gloss round knob stock and forearm, includes luggage case, approx. 6 1/4 lbs. Mfg. 2000-2017.

	$3,150	$2,525	$2,100	$1,800	$1,500	$1,350	$1,125	*$3,580*

CITORI FEATHER LIGHTNING – 12 or 20 ga., 3 in. chambers, greyed alloy receiver with dovetailed steel breech face and steel hinge pin, 26 or 28 in. Invector Plus choked VR barrels, satin nickel finished receiver with laser engraving, select checkered round knob walnut stock and forearm with gloss finish, solid recoil plate, approx. 6-6 1/2 lbs. Mfg. 2012-2017.

	$1,875	$1,500	$1,225	$1,000	$850	$725	$625	*$2,180*

CITORI FEATHER LIGHTNING (CURRENT MFG.) – 12 or 20 (new 2020) ga., 3 in. chambers, 26 or 28 in. barrels, 3 extended black Midas Grade choke tubes, lightweight alloy receiver with steel breech face and hinge pin, ivory bead sight and mid-bead, oil finished Grade III/IV walnut lightning-style stock, Inflex recoil pad, rounded pistol grip and forearm, intricate broad coverage engraving, polished blued barrels, 7 lbs. New 2019.

MSR $2,960	$2,515	$2,200	$1,885	$1,710	$1,385	$1,150	$985	

CITORI GRAN LIGHTNING (GL) MODEL – 12, 20, 28 ga. (new 1994), or .410 bore (new 1994) only, 2 3/4 (28 ga. only) or 3 in. chambers, similar to Lightning Model, except has Grade III walnut stock and forearm with satin/oil finish, includes recoil pad, 26 or 28 in. barrels, Invector chokes standard on newer mfg. smaller ga.'s, Invector Plus became standard 1995 for 12 or 20 ga., 6 1/4 - 8 lbs. Mfg. 1990-2005.

	$2,000	$1,700	$1,450	$1,200	$1,000	$850	$725	*$2,429*

Add $128 for 28 ga. or .410 bore.

Subtract $200 for standard Invector chokes on 12 or 20 ga.

Beginning 2004, high relief intricate sculpted engraving replaced rosette, scroll type engraving.

CITORI GRAN LIGHTNING (CURRENT MFG.) – 12, 20 (new 2020), 28 (new 2020) ga. or .410 bore (new 2020), 2 3/4 or 3 in. chambers, 26 or 28 in. barrels, 3 extended black Midas Grade choke tubes, high relief engraved receiver, ivory bead sight and mid-bead, oil finished Grade V/VI walnut lightning-style stock, Inflex recoil pad, rounded pistol grip and forearm, intricate broad coverage engraving with detailed gold accents, polished blued barrels, 6 lbs. 12 oz.-8 lbs. New 2019.

MSR $3,440	$2,925	$2,560	$2,195	$1,990	$1,610	$1,325	$1,125	

Add $70 for 20, 28 ga., or .410 bore (all new 2020).

CITORI WHITE LIGHTNING – 12, 20, 28 (new 2000) ga., or .410 bore (new 2000), 3 in. chambers, 26 or 28 in. VR barrels with Invector Plus choking, silver nitride finished receiver with high relief engraving, hammer ejectors, single selective trigger, silver front bead sight, Gloss oil finished Grade II/III walnut round pistol grip stock and vent. recoil pad, top tang barrel selector/safety, 6 lbs. 7 oz. 8 lbs. 2 oz. Mfg. 1998-2017.

	$1,785	$1,475	$1,250	$1,075	$925	$795	$695	*$2,070*

Add $70 for .28 ga. or .410 bore (new 2000).

Beginning 2004, high relief intricate sculpted engraving replaced rosette, scroll type engraving.

CITORI WHITE LIGHTNING (CURRENT MFG.) – 12, 20 (new 2020), 28 (new 2020) ga., or .410 bore (new 2020), 2 3/4 or 3 in. chambers, 26 or 28 in. barrels, 3 extended black Midas Grade choke tubes, steel receiver "in the white", ivory bead sight and mid-bead, oil finished Grade III/IV walnut lightning-style stock with 18 LPI cut checkering, Inflex recoil pad, rounded pistol grip and forearm, intricate broad coverage engraving, polished blued barrels, 6 lbs. 12 oz.-8.2 lbs. New 2019.

MSR $2,750	$2,335	$2,050	$1,750	$1,590	$1,285	$1,050	$915	

Add $80 for 20, 28 ga., or .410 bore (all new 2020).

CITORI MICRO LIGHTNING – 20 ga. only, 2 3/4 in. chambers, 24 in. VR barrels, Invector (disc. 1993) or Invector Plus (new 1994) choking, 13 3/4 in. LOP (1/2 in. shorter), 6 lbs. 3 oz. Mfg. 1991-2001.

* ***Citori Micro Lightning Grade I***

	$1,250	$1,000	$850	$750	$650	$575	$525	*$1,591*

Subtract 10% for standard Invector choking.

GRADING - PPGS™	100%	98%	95%	90%	80%	70%	60%	LAST MSR

* ***Citori Micro Lightning Grade III*** – Invector (disc. 1993) or Invector Plus choking. Mfg. 1993-94.

$1,600 $1,300 $1,175 $950 $825 $700 $550 *$1,850*

Subtract $200 for Standard Invector choking.

* ***Citori Micro Lightning Grade VI*** – Mfg. 1993-94.

$2,025 $1,725 $1,500 $1,250 $1,025 $900 $825 *$2,680*

Subtract $200 for standard Invector choking.

CITORI CLASSIC LIGHTNING GRADE I – 12 or 20 ga., 3 in. chambers, 26 or 28 in. vent. rib barrels, Invector Plus chokes, silver nitride receiver with Grade I Superposed engraving, Grade II/III oil finished slender lightning style walnut stock and forearm with vent. recoil pad, 6 lbs. 10 oz.- 8 lbs. 2 oz. Mfg. 2005-2007.

$1,600 $1,300 $1,100 $850 $725 $650 $500 *$1,968*

CITORI CLASSIC LIGHTNING FEATHER GRADE I – 12 or 20 ga., 3 in. chambers, 26 or 28 in. vent. rib barrels, Invector Plus chokes, lightweight alloy receiver with high relief sculpted engraving, Grade II/III satin finished lightning style stock and Schnabel forearm, vent. recoil pad, 6 lbs. 3 oz. - 7 lbs. Mfg. 2005-2006.

$1,650 $1,350 $1,100 $850 $725 $650 $550 *$1,991*

CITORI SUPER LIGHTNING GRADE I – 12 or 20 ga., 3 in. chambers, 26 or 28 in. vent. rib barrels, Invector Plus chokes, deep blue receiver with gold border accents, Grade II/III gloss finished lightning style stock with buttplate and Schnabel forearm, 6 lbs. 7 oz. - 8 lbs. 2 oz. Mfg. 2005-2007.

$1,600 $1,300 $1,000 $825 $700 $600 $500 *$1,941*

CITORI 525 FIELD – 12 (disc. 2007), 20, 28 (new 2003) ga. or .410 bore (new 2003), 3 in. chambers (except 28 ga.), engraved silver nitride receiver, 26 or 28 in. unported barrels featuring VR with forward angled posts, oil finished checkered walnut stock with pronounced pistol grip and European comb, flush fit Invector Plus choke tubes, vent. recoil pad, Schnabel forearm, 6 lbs. 6 oz. - 8 lbs. Mfg. 2002-2008.

$1,650 $1,395 $1,175 $1,000 $750 $650 $550 *$2,144*

Add $31 for 28 ga. or .410 bore.
Subtract $50 for 12 ga.

CITORI 525 FIELD GRADE III – 12 ga. only, 3 in. chambers, similar to 525 Field, except has Grade III/VI wood and more engraving, includes case, approx. 8 lbs. Mfg. 2007.

$1,950 $1,650 $1,400 $1,200 $800 $700 $600 *$2,532*

CITORI 525 FEATHER – 12, 20 (new 2008), 28 (new 2008) ga. or .410 bore (new 2008), 3 in. chambers, silver nitride alloy receiver featuring high relief engraving, traditional oil finished checkered stock and Schnabel forearm, approx. 6 1/4 lbs. Limited mfg. 2007-2008.

$1,750 $1,400 $1,200 $1,000 $800 $675 $550 *$2,278*

Add $17 for 28 ga. or .410 bore.

CITORI ESPRIT – 12 ga. only, 3 in. chambers, 28 in. barrels with VR and 3 choke tubes, features removable and interchangeable sideplates, satin finished receiver, choice of scroll or pointer engraving scenes, gold enhancements were optional, 8 1/4 lbs. Mfg. 2002-2003.

$1,950 $1,350 $1,025 $875 $725 $625 $550 *$2,502*

CITORI PRIVILEGE – 12 or 20 (new 2001) ga., 3 in. chambers, boxlock with extensively hand engraved sideplates, silver finished receiver, 26 or 28 in. barrels with 5/16 in. VR and Invector Plus choking, approx. 8 lbs. Mfg. 2000-2003.

$4,235 $3,600 $3,050 $2,600 $2,475 $2,025 $1,750 *$5,537*

CITORI 625 FIELD – 12 (disc. 2011), 20 (new 2009), 28 (new 2009) ga. or .410 (new 2009) bore, 3 in. chambers, 26 or 28 in. VR barrels with Vector Pro choking system with extended forcing cones, gloss finished Grade II/III special cut checkered walnut stock and Schnabel forearm, vent. recoil pad, silver nitride finished receiver with laser engraving, approx. 6 1/2-7 3/4 lbs. Mfg. 2008-2013.

$2,275 $1,825 $1,525 $1,300 $1,100 $950 $795 *$2,630*

Add $30 for 28 ga. or .410 bore.

CITORI 625 FEATHER – 12 (disc. 2011), 20, 28 ga., or .410 bore, 2 3/4 (20 or 28 ga.) or 3 in. chambers, 26 or 28 in. lightweight VR barrels with three Invector Plus choke tubes (12 or 20 ga.) or Standard Invector (28 ga. or .410 bore), lightweight alloy receiver with steel breech face and hinge pin, laser engraving, SST, ejectors, gloss finished Grade II/III pistol grip walnut stock with Schnabel forearm, approx. 5 lbs. 9 oz.-7 lbs. Mfg. 2009-2013.

$2,425 $1,975 $1,575 $1,350 $1,100 $1,000 $800 *$2,800*

Add $60 for 28 ga. or .410 bore.

GRADING - PPGS™	100%	98%	95%	90%	80%	70%	60%	LAST MSR

CITORI 725 FIELD – 12, 20 (new 2014), 28 (new 2016) ga., or .410 bore (new 2016), 2 3/4 or 3 in. chambers, boxlock action, 26 or 28 in. VR barrels with three Invector-DS choke tubes, Fire Lite mechanical gold single trigger, gloss oil finished Grade II/III checkered walnut pistol grip stock, Inflex recoil pad, low profile silver nitride finished steel receiver with high relief engraving, 6 1/4 or 7 1/4 lbs. New 2012.

MSR $2,680	$2,285	$1,990	$1,700	$1,550	$1,250	$1,025	$875	

Add $70 for 28 ga. or .410 bore (new 2016).

Beginning in 2020, new accented high relief engraving was added to this model.

CITORI 725 FIELD GRADE VI – 12 or 20 ga., 3 in. chambers, 26 or 28 in. VR barrels, Vector Pro lengthened forcing cones, three Invector DS extended choke tubes, low profile steel receiver with silver Nitride finish and gold accented engraving, hammer ejectors, Fire Lite mechanical trigger system, ivory front and mid-bead sights, gloss oil finished Grade V/VI walnut stock with close radius pistol grip and palm swell, Inflex recoil pad, top tang barrel selector/safety. Mfg. 2018-2019.

	$5,100	$4,475	$3,825	$3,475	$2,800	$2,300	$1,800	*$6,000*

CITORI 725 FEATHER – 12 or 20 (new 2015) ga., 3 in. chambers, 26 or 28 in. VR barrels with three invector-DS choke tubes, hammer ejectors, Fire Lite mechanical gold single trigger, ivory front and mid-bead sights, gloss oil finished Grade II/III walnut pistol grip stock, Inflex recoil pad, top tang barrel selector/safety, lightweight alloy frame, low profile silver Nitride finished receiver with accented high relief engraving, approx. 6 1/2 lbs. New 2013.

MSR $2,830	$2,400	$2,100	$1,800	$1,630	$1,320	$1,100	$940	

Beginning in 2020, new accented high relief engraving was added to this model.

CITORI 725 FEATHER SUPERLIGHT – 12 or 20 ga., 2 3/4 in. chambers, 26 in. barrels, 3 choke tubes, lightweight alloy receiver with steel breech face and hinge pin, ivory bead sight, gloss oil finished Grade II/III walnut stock with straight grip and Schnabel forearm, Inflex recoil pad, accented engraving, engraved silver Nitride finish, 5.7-6.2 lbs. New 2019.

MSR $2,750	$2,335	$2,050	$1,750	$1,590	$1,285	$1,100	$915	

CITORI 725 GRADE III – 12 ga. only, 26 or 28 in. VR barrels with three invector-DS choke tubes, features engraved pheasants on left side of frame, mallards on the right side, and a dog on the bottom, Grade III/IV checkered walnut with high gloss finish, Inflex II recoil pad, Fire Lite mechanical SST trigger, includes ABS case, approx. 7 3/8 lbs. 300 mfg. 2013 only.

	$3,250	$2,725	$1,425	$1,950	$1,650	$1,450	$1,125	*$3,730*

CITORI 725 GRADE V – 12 ga. only, 26 or 28 in. VR barrels with three invector-DS choke tubes, features gold enhanced pheasants on left and mallards on the right side, Grade V/VI checkered walnut with high gloss finish, Inflex II recoil pad, Fire Lite mechanical SST trigger, includes canvas/Crazy Horse leather case, approx. 7 3/8 lbs. 200 mfg. 2013 only.

	$4,950	$4,450	$3,700	$3,200	$2,700	$2,300	$1,950	*$5,600*

CITORI 725 GRADE VII SMALL GAUGE – 20, 28 ga., or .410 bore, 2 3/4 or 3 in. chambers, 28, 30, or 32 in. separated VR barrels with floating rib, Vector Pro forcing cones and five black extended choke tubes, low profile steel receiver with gold accented Grade VII deep relief engraving, blued finish, hammer ejectors, ivory front and mid-bead sights, oil finished Grade VI/VII walnut stock with pistol grip and palm swell, 1/2 in. recoil pad, top tang barrel selector/safety, includes John M. Browning Signature fitted case, 7-7 lbs. 8 oz. Limited mfg. 2016 only.

	$5,500	$4,750	$4,000	$3,500	$3,000	$2,650	$2,300	*$6,270*

CITORI 725 HIGH GRADE SIDE PLATE FOUR GAUGE COMBO – 12, 20, 28 ga. and .410 bore (four barrel set), 3 in. chambers, 30 or 32 in. barrels with chokes, gold plated trigger, ivory bead sight with mid-bead, gloss oil finished Grade VI/VII walnut stock, Inflex recoil pad, sideplates feature full coverage engraving with gold bird and dog accents, Nitride receiver finish, approx. 8 lbs. Mfg. 2019 only.

	$9,625	$8,425	$7,225	$6,550	$5,300	$4,325	$3,700	*$11,330*

SHOTGUNS: O/U, CITORI SKEET

Hand engraving was replaced by machine engraving in late 1982 on all higher grade models.

In addition to the models listed below, Browning has also released SHOT Show specials on some models that were available by dealers ordering them at the SHOT Show only. These models are listed in the separate category SHOT SHOW SPECIALS LISTINGS: SHOTGUNS O/U.

Subtract 10%-15% for all Skeet models with 26 in. barrels.

CITORI SKEET/SPECIAL SKEET MODELS – 12, 20, 28 ga., or .410 bore, same action as Citori Field, only with high post target rib (standard 1985), 26 and 28 in. skeet barrels, recoil pad, Invector chokes became standard in 1990 in 12 and 20 ga., Invector Plus chokes with ported barrels were an option during 1992 and became standard on the 12 ga. in 1994, new Special Skeet models were introduced during 1995 with decreased weight (1/4 lb. lighter) and better swing/balance characteristics.

GRADING - PPGS™	100%	98%	95%	90%	80%	70%	60%	LAST MSR

* ***Citori Skeet Grade I***

» **Citori Skeet Grade I 12 or 20 Ga.** – Invector Plus choking, high-post target rib, and ported barrels became standard in 1994, 7 1/4 - 8 lbs. Disc. 2000.

	$1,295	$1,095	$995	$800	$625	$575	$500	*$1,742*

Add $100 for factory adj. comb (mfg. 1995-98).
Subtract 10% if without Invector Plus chokes.
Subtract 30% for fixed chokes.
Add approx. 40% for extra 20 ga. skeet barrels originally ordered with gun.
Add $50 for 20 ga.

Earlier mfg. skeet guns had a low profile, wide VR.

» **Citori Skeet Grade I Smaller Gauges** – 28 ga. or .410 bore, 6 lbs. 15 oz. Disc. 1999.

	$1,400	$1,000	$850	$650	$550	$500	$450	*$1,627*

Subtract 20% if without Invector chokes.

* ***Citori Skeet Grade II*** – 12, 20, 28 ga., or .410 bore, high rib. Disc. 1983.

	$1,600	$1,235	$925	$740	$690	$650	$600	

* ***Citori Skeet Grade III*** – 12 or 20 ga., Invector chokes originally in 12 and 20 ga. and invector plus choking, high-post target rib, and ported barrels became standard in 1994. Mfg. 1986-1999.

	$1,700	$1,300	$1,000	$800	$700	$650	$600	*$2,310*

Add $100 for factory adj. comb (mfg. 1995-98).
Subtract 10% if w/o Invector Plus choke system.

» **Citori Skeet Grade III Smaller Gauges** – 28 ga. or .410 bore, invector chokes became an option in 1994. Mfg. 1986-1999.

	$1,800	$1,500	$1,300	$1,000	$700	$650	$600	*$2,316*

Subtract 20% if without standard Invector choking (new 1994).

* ***Citori Skeet Grade V*** – 12, 20, 28 ga., or .410 bore, high rib. Disc. 1984.

	$2,200	$2,000	$1,800	$1,500	$1,250	$1,050	$850	

Add 20% for 20 ga. or 30% for 28 ga.or .410 bore.

* ***Citori Skeet Grade VI*** – 12 or 16 ga., choice of blue or grey finished receiver with multiple gold inlays, deluxe walnut, Invector Plus choking high post target rib and ported barrels became standard in 1994. Disc. 1995.

	$2,300	$2,100	$1,800	$1,300	$1,100	$900	$800	*$2,555*

Add approx. 35% for hand engraving (mfg. 1983-1984 only).
Subtract 10% if w/o Invector Plus choke system.

» **Citori Skeet Grade VI Smaller Gauges** – 28 ga. or .410 bore, barrels are choked SK/SK.

	$3,000	$1,700	$2,250	$2,000	$1,750	$1,400	$1,100	*$2,518*

Add approx. 35% for hand engraving (mfg. 1983-1984 only).

* ***Citori Skeet Golden Clays (GC)*** – 12 or 20 ga., 26 or 28 in. ported VR barrels with Invector (disc. 1995) or Invector Plus choking, high post target rib and ported barrels (12 ga. only), Skeet features, satin grey receiver with Grade VI level of engraving and gold inlays depicting a transitional hunting to clay pigeon scene. Mfg. 1993-1999.

	$2,725	$2,400	$2,250	$2,000	$1,650	$1,300	$1,000	*$3,434*

Add $100 for factory adj. comb (mfg. 1995-98).
Subtract approx. 20% if without Invector Plus choking.

» **Citori Skeet Golden Clays Smaller Gauges** – 28 ga. or .410 bore, Standard Invector or fixed SK/SK choking.

	$3,000	$2,650	$2,400	$2,250	$1,800	$1,500	$1,250	*$3,356*

Subtract approx. 20% with fixed choking.

CITORI XS SKEET (ULTRA XS SKEET) – 12 or 20 (new 2001) ga., 2 3/4 in. chambers, ported 28 or 30 in. barrels with raised 5/16 in. VR and Invector Plus choking, silver nitride receiver with gold accents, checkered walnut stock available with or without adj. comb, Hi-Viz fiber optic front sight, includes Triple Trigger System, approx. 7 - 8 1/4 lbs. Mfg. 2000-2013.

	$2,750	$2,200	$2,000	$1,700	$1,450	$1,200	$1,000	*$3,180*

Add $420 for adj. comb.

This model's nomenclature was changed from Ultra XS Skeet to Citori XS Skeet in 2002.

This model was featured as a SHOT Show Special in 2013 (Citori XS Skeet Small Gauge), and was available in 28 ga. and .410 bore with 30 in. barrels.

GRADING - PPGS™	100%	98%	95%	90%	80%	70%	60%	LAST MSR

CITORI 725 SKEET – 12 ga., 3 in. chambers, 28 or 30 in. VR barrels with porting and HiViz Pro-comp sights, Vector Pro lengthened forcing cones, three Invector-DS choke tubes, Triple Trigger System, ejectors, steel receiver with silver nitride finish and small geometric etching, gold Browning logos next to forearm, gloss oil finished Grade III/IV walnut stock with pistol grip and palm swell, semi-beavertail forearm with finger grooves, Inflex II recoil pad, with or w/o adj. comb, 7 lbs. 11 oz. Mfg. 2014-2017.

$2,725	$2,150	$2,000	$1,700	$1,500	$1,250	$1,000	*$3,140*

Add $390 for adj. comb.

CITORI 3-GAUGE SKEET SETS – supplied with one 20 ga. frame and one forearm, and 3 barrels consisting of 20, 28 ga., and .410 bore, cased. Mfg. 1987-1996.

* ***Citori 3-Gauge Skeet Set Grade I*** – with high post target rib, Standard Invector choking became standard 1994.

$2,650	$2,000	$1,800	$1,450	$1,275	$1,050	$975	*$3,100*

* ***Citori 3-Gauge Skeet Set Grade III*** – with high post target rib, available with Standard Invector choking (new 1994) or fixed SK/SK chokes.

$3,400	$2,450	$2,000	$1,600	$1,395	$1,250	$1,125	*$3,900*

Subtract 20% for fixed SK/SK chokes.

* ***Citori 3-Gauge Skeet Set Grade VI*** – with high post target rib, fixed SK/SK chokes only. Disc. 1994.

$3,600	$2,800	$2,300	$1,775	$1,600	$1,400	$1,275	*$3,990*

* ***Citori 3-Gauge Skeet Set Golden Clays*** – features Golden Clays accents and engraving, standard Invector choking. Mfg. 1994-95 only.

$5,800	$5,000	$4,600	$4,000	$3,500	$3,000	$2,600	*$5,100*

CITORI 4-GAUGE SKEET SETS – supplied with one 12 ga. frame and forearm, and 4 barrels consisting of 12, 20, 28 ga., and .410 bore, cased. Imported 1985 only.

* ***Citori 4-Gauge Skeet Set Grade I*** – with high post target rib, choice of standard Invector (new 1994) or fixed SK/SK choking.

$3,500	$2,750	$2,400	$1,975	$1,800	$1,775	$1,600	*$4,450*

Subtract 10% for fixed SK/SK choking.

* ***Citori 4-Gauge Skeet Set Grade III*** – with high post target rib, choice of Standard Invector (new 1994) or fixed SK/SK choking.

$4,250	$3,000	$2,700	$2,250	$1,950	$1,800	$1,700	*$5,450*

Subtract 20% for fixed SK/SK choking.

* ***Citori 4-Gauge Skeet Set Grade VI*** – with high post target rib, fixed SK/SK choking only. Disc. 1994.

$5,000	$4,250	$4,000	$3,600	$3,100	$2,600	$1,900	*$5,225*

* ***Citori 4-Gauge Skeet Set Golden Clays*** – features Golden Clays accents and engraving, Standard Invector choking. Mfg. 1994 only.

$5,650	$4,100	$3,300	$2,600	$2,350	$2,100	$1,975	*$6,750*

SHOTGUNS: O/U, CITORI SPORTING CLAYS

All sporting clays models mfg. after 1994 have the Triple Trigger System which includes 3 interchangeable trigger shoes.

In addition to the models listed below, Browning has also released SHOT Show specials on some models that were available by dealers ordering them at the SHOT Show only. Complete descriptions for these models can be found under SHOT SHOW SPECIALS - SHOTGUNS: O/U at BlueBookOfGunValues.com/overflow.

Subtract 10% for 28 in. barrels on used guns.

CITORI 325 GRADE II – 12 or 20 ga., 28, 30, or 32 (12 ga. only) in. 10mm VR barrels with Invector Plus choking, ported barrels, European styling featuring checkered walnut stock and Schnabel forearm, greyed nitrous finished receiver, top tang safety, SST, ejectors, 6 lbs. 12 oz. - 7 lbs. 15 oz. Mfg. 1993-94.

$1,300	$1,100	$950	$800	$700	$600	$450	*$1,625*

CITORI 325 GOLDEN CLAYS – 12 or 20 ga., 28, 30, or 32 in. ported (12 ga. only) or unported (20 ga. only) VR barrels, Invector Plus choking, Model 325 Grade II features, satin grey receiver with engraving and gold inlays depicting a transitional hunting to clay pigeon scene. Mfg. 1994 only.

$2,100	$1,900	$1,700	$1,400	$1,200	$1,000	$825	*$3,030*

CITORI 425 SPORTING CLAYS GRADE I – 12 or 20 ga., 28, 30, or 32 (disc. 2000 - 12 ga. only, adj. comb) in. 10mm VR barrels with Invector Plus choking, 12 ga. has ported barrels, with or without adj. comb (disc. 2000), European styling featuring checkered walnut stock and Schnabel forearm, monobloc action with greyed nitrous finished receiver, top tang safety, SST, ejectors, solid pad, approx. 6 3/4 - 8 lbs. Mfg. 1995-2001.

$1,500	$1,300	$1,150	$1,000	$800	$625	$525	*$2,006*

Add $231 for adj. comb.

GRADING - PPGS™	100%	98%	95%	90%	80%	70%	60%	LAST MSR

CITORI 425 GOLDEN CLAYS – 12 or 20 ga., 28, 30, or 32 (disc. 1999) in. ported (12 ga. only) or unported (20 ga. only) VR barrels, with (disc. 1998) or without adj. comb, Invector Plus choking, Model 425 Grade I features, satin grey receiver with engraving and gold inlays depicting a transitional hunting to clay pigeon scene, 6 lbs., 13 oz. - 7 lbs., 14 oz. Mfg. 1995-2001.

	$2,100	$1,900	$1,700	$1,400	$1,200	$1,000	$825	*$3,977*

Add $100 for factory adj. comb (disc. 1998).

CITORI 425 WSSF – 12 ga. only, special dimensions for Women's Shooting Sports Foundation, features painted turquoise finish with WSSF logo on stock or natural walnut finish (new 1997), 7 1/4 lbs. Mfg. 1995-99.

	$1,400	$1,200	$1,050	$925	$800	$675	$550	*$1,855*

CITORI 525 SPORTING – 12, 20, 28 (new 2003) ga., or .410 bore (new 2003), 2 3/4 or 3 (.410 bore) in. chambers, 28, 30, or 32 (new 2003) in. vent. barrels with 8-11 mm (12 ga. only) or 10 mm (20 ga. only) width canted VR and porting (12 or 20 ga. only), silver nitride receiver finish with high relief engraving, Hi-Viz Pro-Comp sights, redesigned stock, includes full set of Midas Grade Invector Plus choke tubes (non-flush), oil finished European style checkered Grade III/IV walnut stock with palm swell and forearm, approx. 7-8 1/2 lbs. Mfg. 2002-2008.

	$2,000	$1,750	$1,600	$1,450	$1,100	$800	$695	*$3,035*

Add $11 for 28 ga. or .410 bore.
Add $298 for adj. comb stock (mfg. 2004-2007, 12 or 20 ga.).

* ***Citori 525 Sporting Grade I*** – 12 ga. only, 3 in. chambers, 28, 30, or 32 in. ported barrels, silver nitride receiver with light 525 style field engraving, oil finished Grade I American walnut stock and Schnabel forearm, right hand palm swell, tapered floating rib, triple trigger system, three flush Invector-Plus choke tubes, Hi-Viz Pro-Comp sight, approx. 8 lbs. Mfg. 2005-2007.

	$1,700	$1,450	$1,300	$1,050	$800	$675	$575	*$2,461*

CITORI 525 GOLDEN CLAYS – 12, 20, 28 (new 2003) ga. or .410 bore (new 2003), similar features to the Model 525 Sporting, except has oil finished Grade V/VI walnut stock with solid pad and Schnabel forearm, engraving pattern that depicts the transition of a game bird into a clay bird in 24Kt. gold, includes 5 Midas Grade Invector Plus choke tubes (non-flush), 7-8 1/2 lbs. Mfg. 2002-2007.

	$2,500	$2,250	$2,000	$1,850	$1,500	$1,250	$995	*$4,722*

Add $215 for 28 ga. or .410 bore.

CITORI 625 SPORTING – 12 (disc.), 20 (new 2009), 28 (new 2009) ga., or .410 bore (new 2009), 2 3/4 or 3 (.410 bore only) in. chambers, 28, 30, or 32 in. ported VR barrels with Vector Pro choking system with extended forcing cones, checkered gloss finished Grade III/IV walnut stock with or w/o adj. comb and Schnabel forearm, Triple Trigger System, Hi-Viz fiber optic front sight, silver nitride finished receiver with gold accents, approx. 7-8 lbs. Mfg. 2008-2013.

	$2,150	$1,950	$1,750	$1,600	$1,450	$1,200	$1,000	*$3,550*

Add $50 for adj. comb. (12 ga. only), disc.
Add $30 for 28 ga. or .410 bore.

CITORI 725 SPORTING – 12, 20 (new 2014), 28 (new 2016) ga., or .410 bore (new 2016), 3 in. chambers, lower profile silver Nitride boxlock action receiver, 28, 30, or 32 in. vent ported barrels with VR and five Invector-DS choke tubes, hammer ejectors, gold triple trigger system, oil finished Grade III/IV checkered forearm and walnut stock with palm swell, Inflex II recoil pad, with or without adj. comb, top tang barrel selector/safety, approx. 7 1/2 lbs. New 2012.

MSR $3,310	$2,815	$2,465	$2,110	$1,915	$1,550	$1,275	$1,100	

Add $70 for 28 ga. or .410 bore (new 2016).
Add $400 for adj. comb.
Add $490 for high rib and adj. comb (new 2015).
Add $70 for high rib only (mfg. 2015-2019 in 12 ga. only).

This model with adj. comb was originally featured as a 2012 SHOT Show Special.

CITORI 725 SPORTING GOLDEN CLAYS – 12 ga., 2 3/4 in. chambers, 30 or 32 in. ported VR barrels, floating rib, Vector Pro lengthened forcing cones, five Invector-DS extended choke tubes, steel receiver with gold accented engraving, hammer ejectors, Triple Trigger System, HiViz Pro-Comp sight and ivory mid-bead, gloss oil finished Grade V/VI walnut stock with pistol grip and palm swell, Pro Fit adj. comb, Inflex recoil pad, top tang barrel selector/safety, silver Nitride finish, 7 lbs. 13 oz. New 2017.

MSR $5,620	$4,775	$4,180	$3,580	$3,245	$2,625	$2,175	$1,875	

CITORI 725 SPORTING GRADE V – 12 ga., 3 in. chambers, 30 or 32 in. ported VR barrels, Vector Pro lengthened forcing cones, five Invector-DS extended choke tubes, low profile silver nitride finished steel

GRADING - PPGS™	100%	98%	95%	90%	80%	70%	60%	LAST MSR

receiver with Grade V deep relief engraving, hammer ejectors, HiViz Pro-Comp sight and ivory mid-bead, oil finished Grade IV/V walnut pistol grip stock with palm swell, Inflex recoil pad, top tang barrel selector/safety, includes fitted canvas/distressed leather case, 7 lbs. 10 oz. Limited mfg. 2015 only.

	$4,500	$3,550	$3,300	$3,000	$2,500	$2,000	$1,750	*$5,340*

CITORI 725 SPORTING GRADE VII – 12 ga., 3 in. chambers, 30 or 32 in. ported VR barrels, Vector Pro lengthened forcing cones, five Invector-DS extended choke tubes, low profile steel receiver with gold accented Grade VII deep relief engraving, blued finish, hammer ejectors, HiViz Pro-Comp sight and ivory mid-bead, oil finished Grade VI/VII walnut pistol grip stock with palm swell, Inflex recoil pad, top tang barrel selector/safety, includes John M. Browning Signature fitted case, 7 lbs. 10 oz. Limited mfg. 2015 only.

	$5,500	$4,000	$3,700	$3,500	$3,000	$2,650	$2,300	*$6,270*

CITORI 725 PRO SPORTING WITH ADJ. COMB – 12 or 20 ga., 2 3/4 in. chambers, 30 or 32 in. ported VR barrels with floating rib, Vector Pro lengthened forcing cones, five Invector-DS extended choke tubes, Pro Balance System, silver nitride finished steel receiver with gold accented engraving, Triple Trigger System, HiViz Pro-Comp sight and ivory mid-bead, gloss oil finished Grade III/IV walnut pistol grip stock with palm swell, Pro Fit adj. comb, Inflex recoil pad, top tang barrel selector/safety, includes Elite ABS case, 7 lbs. 5 oz. New 2015.

MSR $4,220	$3,585	$3,135	$2,690	$2,440	$1,975	$1,625	$1,400	

CITORI 802 EXTENDED SWING (ES) SPORTING – 12 ga. only, 2 3/4 in. chambers, features 28 in. ventilated ported VR barrels (low post, 6.2mm wide) which accept either Invector Plus stainless steel 2 or 4 in. extension tubes (extends barrels to 30 or 32 in.), adj. pull trigger, slimmer checkered and Schnabel forearm, 7 lbs. 5 oz. Mfg. 1996-2001.

	$1,395	$1,100	$975	$800	$700	$600	$550	*$2,063*

CITORI GTI GRADE I – 12 ga. only, 28 or 30 in. barrel with 13mm vent. rib and barrels, red lettering on receiver during 1989 only - changed to gold lettering and borders with Browning logo in 1990, checkered stock and semi-beavertail forearm, ported barrels were introduced 1990 and became standard 1992, Invector chokes standard, back-bored Invector Plus chokes became standard in 1990, approx. 8 lbs. Mfg. 1989-1994.

	$1,400	$1,200	$1,100	$950	$700	$550	$475	*$1,450*

Subtract $100 for standard chokes.
Add $35 for Signature Painted Model.

The Signature Painted Model includes special paint treatment on stock and forearm featuring Browning logos and trademark - new 1993.

CITORI GTI GOLDEN CLAYS – 12 ga. only, 28, 30, or 32 in. ported VR barrels, Invector Plus choking, GTI features, satin grey receiver with Grade VI level of engraving and gold inlays depicting a transitional hunting to clay pigeon scene. Mfg. 1993-94.

	$2,350	$1,950	$1,600	$1,300	$1,050	$925	$825	*$2,930*

CITORI GRADE I SPECIAL SPORTING – 12 ga. only, 2 3/4 in. chambers, target dimensions, high-post tapered rib, 28, 30, or 32 in. barrels, full pistol grip with palm swell, adj. comb became optional in 1994, approx. 8 lbs. 3 oz. Mfg. 1989-99.

	$1,295	$1,150	$1,000	$850	$750	$600	$450	*$1,636*

Add $100 for factory adj. comb.
Add $35 for Signature Painted Model (disc. 1994).
Add $800 for 2 barrel set (28 and 30 in. barrels), disc. 1990.

The Signature Painted Model includes special paint treatment on stock and forearm featuring Browning logos and trademark - mfg. 1993-94.

Ported barrels were new in 1990 and became standard in 1992.

In 1990, the Grade I designation was added to this model. Changes include back-bored barrels with Invector plus choke tubes.

CITORI SPECIAL SPORTING GOLDEN CLAYS (GC) – 12 ga. only, 28, 30, or 32 in. ported barrels with high-post VR, Invector Plus choking, Special Sporting features, satin grey receiver with Grade VI level of engraving and gold inlays depicting a transitional hunting to clay pigeon scene. Mfg. 1993-98.

	$2,250	$1,900	$1,600	$1,250	$995	$875	$825	*$3,203*

Add $100 for factory adj. comb.

CITORI GRADE I SPECIAL SPORTING PIGEON GRADE – 12 ga. only, Invector Plus choking and ported barrels, higher grade of Special Sporting model featuring higher grade walnut and gold line receiver accents. Mfg. 1993-94.

	$1,395	$1,150	$950	$800	$700	$625	$550	*$1,630*

GRADING - PPGS™	100%	98%	95%	90%	80%	70%	60%	LAST MSR

CITORI ULTRA SPORTER – 12 ga. only, 28, 30, or 32 in. barrels with vent. rib separating barrels, low tapered 13-10mm VR, blue or grey (new 1996) receiver with gold accents, satin finished checkered pistol grip stock and forearm, Invector Plus choking, 7 lbs. 10 oz. - 8 lbs. 4 oz. Mfg. 1995-99.

$1,400	$1,050	$875	$750	$575	$495	$450	*$1,800*

Add $210 for adj. comb (disc. 1998).

This model was designated GTI until 1995.

* ***Citori Ultra Sporter Golden Clays (GC)*** – 12 ga. only, features better wood and satin finished engraved receiver with gold inlays clay target scene. Mfg. 1995-99.

$2,250	$1,900	$1,700	$1,500	$1,275	$1,075	$925	*$3,396*

Add $210 for adj. comb (disc. 1997).

CITORI FEATHER XS SPORTING – 12, 20, 28 ga., or .410 bore, 2 3/4 in. chambers (3 in. standard on .410 bore), 28 or 30 in. vent. barrels with tapered VR (12 ga. only) and Invector Plus choking on 12 and 20 ga. (Standard Invector on 28 ga. and .410 bore, 28 in. barrels), alloy receiver with dovetailed steel breech face and hinge pin, satin finished checkered walnut pistol grip stock with Schnabel forearm, Hi-Viz comp. sighting system (includes 8 interchangeable colored light pipes), Nitex receiver finish, includes Triple Trigger System (3 interchangeable trigger shoes), 6 lbs. (28 ga. or .410 bore) - approx. 7 lbs. (12 ga., 30 in. barrels). Mfg. 2000-2002.

$1,700	$1,375	$1,150	$995	$875	$775	$675	*$2,311*

CITORI XS GOLDEN CLAYS – 12 or 20 ga. only, similar to 525 Golden Clays, except has traditional checkering pattern and 1/2 - 3/8 in. width VR, includes 3 choke tubes. Mfg. 2002-2003.

$3,150	$2,600	$2,050	$1,650	$1,400	$1,150	$925	*$3,914*

CITORI XS SPORTING (ULTRA) – 12, 20, 28 ga. (disc. 2003), or .410 bore (disc. 2003), greyed steel receiver with silver nitride finish, 24Kt. gold accents and light engraving, 28, 30, or 32 (new 2003) in. barrels, with or w/o (30 in. barrels only) barrel porting, 12 ga. features flush Invector Plus choking and right-hand palm swell, Hi-Viz Pro-Comp sight, Triple Trigger System, select checkered walnut stock with satin finish and Schnabel forearm, 6 lbs. 5 oz.-8 lbs. Mfg. 1999-2007.

$1,900	$1,600	$1,300	$995	$875	$750	$650	*$2,597*

Add 10% for 28 ga. or .410 bore.

CITORI GRAND PRIX SPORTER – 12 ga. only, 2 3/4 in. chambers, steel receiver with silver nitride finish and gold enhanced engraving, 28, 30, or 32 in. VR ported barrels with extended Invector-Plus Midas Grade choke tubes and Hi-Viz fiber optic front sight, oil finished checkered pistol grip walnut stock and Schnabel forearm, select ejector system allows for either ejection or manual extraction, cased, approx. 8 1/4 lbs. Mfg. 2007-2009.

$1,600	$1,400	$1,250	$1,100	$1,000	$900	$800	*$3,439*

CITORI LIGHTNING SPORTING (GRADE I) – 12 ga. only, features 3 in. chambers, rounded pistol grip, Lightning style forearm, choice of high or low post VR, standard or adj. (new 1995) comb stock, "Lightning Sporting Clays Edition" inscribed and gold-filled on receiver, triple trigger system, 28 in. ported or 30 in. ported or unported (disc.) barrels, approx. 8 1/2 lbs. Mfg. 1989-2004.

$1,300	$1,045	$885	$765	$650	$550	$495	*$1,794*

Add $100 for adj. comb (disc. 1998).
Subtract $100 for low rib.

The Signature Painted Model includes special paint treatment on stock and forearm featuring Browning logos and trademark - mfg. 1993-94. Ported barrels were new in 1990 and became standard in 1992. Between 1990-2000, the Grade I designation was added to this model. Changes include back-bored barrels with Invector plus choke tubes.

* ***Citori Lightning Sporting Golden Clays (GC)*** – 12 ga. only, 28, 30, or 32 (disc.) in. ported barrels with choice of low or high-post VR, standard or adj. (new 1995) comb stock, Invector Plus choking, Lightning Sporting features, satin grey receiver with Grade VI level of engraving and gold inlays depicting a transitional hunting to clay birds scene, approx. 8 1/2 lbs. Mfg. 1993-98.

$2,600	$2,200	$1,750	$1,400	$1,175	$1,000	$875	*$3,092*

Add $100 for factory adj. comb.
Subtract $100 for low post rib.

CITORI GRADE I LIGHTNING SPORTING PIGEON GRADE – 12 ga. only, higher grade model featuring higher grade walnut and gold line receiver accents. Mfg. 1993-94.

$1,500	$1,200	$950	$700	$575	$495	$450	*$1,566*

Subtract $100 for low post rib.

GRADING - PPGS™	100%	98%	95%	90%	80%	70%	60%	LAST MSR

CITORI SPORTING HUNTER – please refer to description and pricing under Shotguns: O/U Citori Hunting Series category.

SHOTGUNS: O/U, CITORI TARGET

During 2010, Vector Pro chokes became standard on 12 and 20 ga. models.

In addition to the models listed below, Browning has also released SHOT Show specials on some models that were available by dealers ordering them at the SHOT Show only. Complete descriptions for these models can be found under SHOT SHOW SPECIALS - SHOTGUNS: O/U at BlueBookOfGunValues.com/overflow.

CITORI XS SPECIAL – 12 ga. only, 2 3/4 in. chambers, 30 or 32 in. vent. barrels, silver nitride receiver with XS Special engraving, satin finished stock with adj. comb and semi-beavertail forearm, low/regular or high-post (new 2007) floating 8-11mm tapered rib, includes Triple Trigger System and 5 Midas Grade Invector Plus chokes (non-flush), approx. 8 3/4 lbs. Mfg. 2004-2013.

	100%	98%	95%	90%	80%	70%	60%	LAST MSR
	$2,250	$1,800	$1,650	$1,500	$1,400	$1,325	$1,150	*$3,600*

CITORI GTS GRADE I – 12 ga. only, 3 in. chambers, 28 or 30 in. 10mm VR barrels with flush Invector-Plus choke tubes, steel silver nitride finished receiver with game bird transforming into clay target engraving, oil finished checkered Grade II/III walnut pistol grip stock and Schnabel forearm, Hi-Viz front sight, includes case, approx. 8 1/4 lbs. Mfg. 2007-2009.

	100%	98%	95%	90%	80%	70%	60%	LAST MSR
	$1,950	$1,400	$1,250	$1,150	$950	$800	$700	*$2,349*

CITORI GTS HIGH GRADE – 12 ga. only, similar to Grade I, except has gold game bird/clay target engraving. Mfg. 2007-2009.

	100%	98%	95%	90%	80%	70%	60%	LAST MSR
	$3,475	$2,500	$2,350	$1,925	$1,600	$1,300	$1,175	*$4,309*

CITORI ULTRA XS PRESTIGE – 12 ga., similar to Citori GTS High Grade, except has gloss oil finished adj. stock and gold accented Ultra XS special engraving, ported barrels, Hi-Viz fiber optic sight, includes case, approx. 8 lbs. Mfg. 2008-2009.

	100%	98%	95%	90%	80%	70%	60%	LAST MSR
	$4,000	$2,350	$2,000	$1,600	$1,350	$1,125	$1,000	*$4,759*

SHOTGUNS: O/U, CITORI TRAP

Hand engraving was replaced by machine engraving in late 1982 on all higher grade models.

In addition to the models listed below, Browning has also released SHOT Show specials on some models that were available by dealers ordering them at the SHOT Show only. Complete descriptions for these models can be found under SHOT SHOW SPECIALS - SHOTGUNS O/U at BlueBookOfGunValues.com/overflow

CITORI TRAP MODELS – 12 ga., similar to Standard Citori, 30 or 32 in. barrels, trap chokes, Monte Carlo stock, recoil pad. Invector chokes became standard in 1988, Invector Plus chokes with ported barrels became an option in 1992, and were made standard in 1993, new Special Trap models were introduced during 1995 with decreased weight (1/4 lb. lighter) and better swing/balance characteristics. Mfg. 1974-2017.

* ***Citori Trap Grade I*** – w/o choke tube, mfg. 1974-1978, with choke tube 1979-1994.

	100%	98%	95%	90%	80%	70%	60%	LAST MSR
w/o Choke Tube	$1,000	$900	$800	$650	$525	$495	$450	
w/ Choke Tube	$1,150	$1,025	$900	$800	$750	$650	$525	

* ***Citori Grade I Special Trap*** – approx. 8 1/2 lbs. Mfg. 1995-1999.

	100%	98%	95%	90%	80%	70%	60%	LAST MSR
	$1,395	$1,200	$1,000	$900	$850	$600	$450	*$1,658*

Add $100 for factory adj. comb.
Subtract 20% without Invector chokes or high rib.

* ***Citori Trap Combination Set*** – Grade I only, 32 in. O/U and 34 in. single barrel, or extra set of barrels in same ga., cased. Disc.

	100%	98%	95%	90%	80%	70%	60%	LAST MSR
	$1,500	$1,275	$1,100	$900	$825	$775	$725	

Add approx. 40% for extra 20 ga. barrels originally ordered with gun.

* ***Citori Grade I Plus Trap*** – features adj. rib and stock, back-bored barrels, Invector Plus choke system. Mfg. 1990-94.

	100%	98%	95%	90%	80%	70%	60%	LAST MSR
	$1,900	$1,525	$1,225	$995	$700	$600	$500	*$2,005*

Add 5% for ported barrels.

In 1991 this model included a travel vault gun case at no extra charge. Subtract $50 for older mfg. without travel case.

* ***Citori Grade I Plus Trap Combo*** – includes ported barrels with Invector Plus choking and extra standard single ported barrel, luggage case. Mfg. 1992-94.

	100%	98%	95%	90%	80%	70%	60%	LAST MSR
	$2,775	$2,475	$2,100	$1,900	$1,700	$1,500	$1,250	*$3,435*

GRADING - PPGS™	100%	98%	95%	90%	80%	70%	60%	LAST MSR

* ***Citori Plus Trap Golden Clays*** – 12 ga. only, 30 or 32 in. ported VR barrels, Invector Plus choking, Trap features, satin grey receiver with Grade VI level of engraving and gold inlays depicting a transitional hunting to clay birds scene. Mfg. 1993-94.

$3,000	$2,600	$2,000	$1,600	$1,400	$1,200	$995	*$3,435*

* ***Citori Plus Trap Golden Clays Combo*** – includes O/U ported barrels with Invector Plus choking and extra standard single ported barrel, luggage case. Mfg. 1993-94.

$4,425	$3,300	$2,775	$2,250	$1,925	$1,800	$1,700	*$5,200*

* ***Citori XT Trap (Older Mfg.)*** – 12 ga. only, features greyed receiver with 24Kt. gold accents and light engraving, Triple Trigger System (includes 3 interchangeable triggers for 1/8 in. adj. on LOP), 30 or 32 in. vent. backbored barrels with high-post VR, checkered high gloss Monte Carlo walnut stock and forearm, right-hand palm swell, Hi-Viz front sight, waffle-style recoil pad, approx. 8 1/2 lbs. Mfg. 1999-2013.

$2,300	$1,900	$1,750	$1,400	$1,100	$850	$650	*$2,950*

Add $440 for adj. comb.

* ***Citori XT Trap, Grade I (Recent Mfg.)*** – 12 ga. only, 30 or 32 in. vent. backbored ported barrels with high-post VR, Triple Trigger system, HiViz Pro-Comp sights, checkered high gloss Monte Carlo Grade II/III walnut stock and forearm with right-hand palm swell, vent. recoil pad, blued receiver with 24Kt. gold accents and high relief engraving, approx. 8 1/2 lbs. Mfg. 2014-2017.

$2,275	$1,825	$1,525	$1,325	$1,125	$950	$800	*$2,650*

Add $350 for adj. comb.

* ***Citori XT Trap Gold*** – 12 ga. only, 2 3/4 in. chambers, features intricate "Golden Clays" engraving with game bird/clay bird, Grade V/VI American walnut stock and semi-beavertail forearm, vented 30 or 32 in. ported barrels with high post VR and Invector Plus choke system with five flush Midas Grade chokes, adj. comb, adj. GraCoil recoil reduction system, Triple Trigger System, Hi-Viz Pro-Comp, and mid-bead sights, approx. 9 lbs. Mfg. 2005-2013.

$4,950	$3,850	$3,050	$2,375	$1,875	$1,475	$1,175	*$5,700*

* ***Citori Trap Pigeon Grade*** – 12 ga. only, features extra deluxe walnut, Invector Plus ported barrels, and receiver gold accents. Mfg. 1993-94.

$1,715	$1,250	$950	$800	$700	$600	$500	*$2,225*

* ***Citori Trap Signature Painted*** – 12 ga. only, features painted red/black stock with Browning logos on stock and forearm, Invector Plus ported barrels. Mfg. 1993-94.

$1,595	$1,200	$940	$800	$700	$600	$500	*$2,065*

* ***Citori Trap Grade II*** – high post rib. Mfg. 1978-1983.

$1,200	$900	$800	$700	$650	$600	$500	

* ***Citori Trap Grade III*** – 12 ga. only, high post rib, Invector Plus choking and ported barrels became standard in 1994. Mfg. 1986-99.

$1,500	$1,200	$900	$800	$725	$650	$550	*$2,310*

Add $100 for factory adj. comb.
Subtract 10% if without Invector Plus chokes or ported barrels.

* ***Citori Trap Grade V*** – high post rib. Mfg. 1978-1984.

$1,750	$1,400	$1,100	$880	$795	$710	$620	

* ***Citori Trap Grade VI*** – 12 ga. only, Invector chokes became standard in 1985, Invector Plus chokes became standard in 1994. Disc. 1994.

$1,995	$1,600	$1,300	$1,100	$960	$875	$825	*$2,555*

Add approx. 20% for hand engraving (mfg. 1983-1984 only).
Subtract $150 if without Invector Plus chokes or ported barrels.
Subtract $250 for fixed chokes.

* ***Citori Trap Golden Clays (GC)*** – 12 ga. only, 30 or 32 in. ported VR barrels, Invector Plus choking, Trap features, Monte Carlo or regular stock, satin grey receiver with Grade VI level of engraving and gold inlays depicting a transitional hunting to clay pigeon scene. Mfg. 1993-99.

$2,750	$2,400	$2,100	$1,750	$1,500	$1,250	$1,025	*$3,434*

Add $220 for adj. comb (new 1995).

CITORI CXT – 12 ga., 3 in. chambers, 30 or 32 in. ported VR barrels with high-post floating top rib, Vector Pro lengthened forcing cones, three Invector Plus Midas Grade choke tubes, steel receiver with gold accented engraving, hammer ejectors, Triple Trigger System with one trigger piece, ivory front and mid-bead sights, gloss finished Grade II American walnut stock with raised cheekpiece or adj. comb, semi-beavertail forearm with finger grooves, Inflex recoil pad, top tang safety. New 2018.

MSR $2,390	$2,025	$1,775	$1,525	$1,375	$1,115	$925	$750

GRADING - PPGS™	100%	98%	95%	90%	80%	70%	60%	LAST MSR

Add $440 for adj. comb.

CITORI CXT MICRO WITH ADJUSTABLE LOP – 12 ga., 3 in. chambers, 28 or 30 in. barrels, 3 extended Midas Grade choke tubes, steel receiver, gold plated 3-pos. trigger, ivory bead sight and mid-bead, gloss finished Grade II American walnut Monte Carlo stock, Inflex recoil pad, Graco buttpad plate allows for LOP adjustment, high shooting 70/30 POI, gold enhancement, polished blue finish, 8.9-8.11 lbs. New 2020.

MSR $2,550	$2,170	$1,900	$1,630	$1,475	$1,195	$1,000	$850	

CITORI XS PRO-COMP – 12 ga. only, 2 3/4 in. chambers, 28 or 30 in. vent. and ported VR barrels with spreader chokes, adj. comb, beavertail forearm, GraCoil recoil reduction system, right-hand palm swell, Triple Trigger System, features removable tungsten alloy forearm weight which approximates the same weight as barrel tubes, also has removable front barrel weight to adj. the swing through, approx. 9 lbs. Mfg. 2002-2004.

	$2,750	$2,300	$1,900	$1,425	$1,100	$975	$850	*$4,027*

CITORI 725 PRO TRAP WITH ADJ. COMB – 12 ga., 2 3/4 in. chambers, 30 or 32 in. ported VR barrel with floating rib, Vector Pro lengthened forcing cones, five Invector-DS extended choke tubes, Pro Balance System, silver nitride finished steel receiver with gold accented engraving, hammer ejectors, Triple Trigger System, HiViz Pro-Comp sight and ivory mid-bead, gloss finished Grade III/IV walnut pistol grip stock with palm swell, Pro Fit adj. comb, semi-beavertail forearm with finger grooves, top tang barrel selector/safety, includes Elite ABS case, 8 lbs. 8 oz. New 2015.

MSR $4,220	$3,585	$3,135	$2,690	$2,440	$1,975	$1,625	$1,400	

CITORI 725 TRAP – 12 ga., 2 3/4 in. chambers, 30 or 32 in. separated ported barrels with high post rib and HiViz Pro-Comp sights, Vector Pro lengthened forcing cones, three Invector-DS choke tubes, silver nitride finished steel receiver, ejectors, top tang safety, gloss finished Grade III/IV walnut stock with pistol grip and palm swell, Monte Carlo cheekpiece, semi-beavertail forearm with finger grooves, vent recoil pad, Triple Trigger System, with or w/o adj. comb, 8 1/2 lbs. New 2014.

MSR $3,510	$2,985	$2,610	$2,240	$2,030	$1,650	$1,400	$1,175	

Add $430 for adj. comb.

CITORI 725 TRAP GOLDEN CLAYS – 12 ga., 2 3/4 in. chambers, 30 or 32 in. ported VR barrels with floating rib, Vector Pro lengthened forcing cones, five Invector DS extended choke tubes, low profile steel receiver with silver Nitride finish and gold accented engraving, hammer ejectors, Fire Lite mechanical trigger system, Triple Trigger System, HiViz ProComp sight and ivory mid-bead, gloss oil finished Grade V/VI walnut stock with close radious pistol grip and right-hand palm swell, Pro Fit adj. Monte Carlo comb, Graco buttpad plate, Pachmayr Decelerator XLT recoil pad, top tang barrel selector/safety, adj. GraCoil recoil reduction system. New 2018.

MSR $6,040	$5,135	$4,500	$3,850	$3,490	$2,825	$2,325	$2,000	

CITORI 725 TRAP GRADE V (RECENT MFG.) – 12 ga., 2 3/4 in. chambers, 30 or 32 in. ported VR barrels with high post floating top rib, Vector Pro lengthened forcing cones, five extended Invector-DS choke tubes, steel receiver with Grade V deep relief engraving, hammer ejectors, Fire Lite mechanical trigger system, HiViz Pro-Comp sight and ivory mid-bead, oil finished Grade V/VI walnut stock with pistol grip and palm swell, Monte Carlo cheekpiece, ventilated trap recoil pad, semi-beavertail forearm with finger grooves, top tang barrel selector/safety, includes canvas/distressed leather fitted case, silver Nitride finish, 8 lbs. 10 oz. Mfg. 2017-2018.

	$4,650	$3,700	$3,550	$3,000	$2,500	$2,000	$1,725	*$5,340*

CITORI 725 TRAP GRADE VII – 12 ga., 2 3/4 in. chambers, 30 or 32 in. ported VR barrels, high post floating top rib, Vector Pro lengthened forcing cones, five extended Invector-DS choke tubes, steel receiver with gold accented Grade VII deep relief engraving, hammer ejectors, Fire Lite Mechanical trigger system, HiViz Pro-Comp sight and ivory mid-bead, oil finished Grade VI/VII walnut stock with pistol grip and palm swell, Monte Carlo cheekpiece, ventilated trap recoil pad, semi-beavertail forearm with finger grooves, top tang barrel selector/safety, includes canvas/distressed leather fitted case, blued finish, 8 lbs. 7 oz. Mfg. 2017-2018.

	$5,450	$4,400	$4,150	$3,750	$3,100	$2,650	$2,150	*$6,400*

CITORI 725 TRAP MAX – 12 ga., 2 3/4 in. chambers, 30 or 32 in. barrels, five extended choke tubes, adj. rib, Triple Trigger System with three trigger shoes, Buck Mark engraved in gold on trigger guard, gold plated trigger, HIVIZ Pro Comp sight and ivory mid-bead, gloss finished Grade V/VI walnut stock with close radius pistol grip and palm swell, Pachmayr Decelerator XLT recoil pad, Graco adj. Monte Carlo comb, adj. GraCoil Recoil Reduction System, Graco buttpad plate, 9 lbs. New 2020.

MSR $6,040	$5,135	$4,500	$3,850	$3,490	$2,825	$2,325	$2,000	

GRADING - PPGS™	100%	98%	95%	90%	80%	70%	60%	LAST MSR

SHOTGUNS: O/U, SUPERPOSED GENERAL INFO & CHOKE CODES

SUPERPOSED MODEL – 12, 20 (introduced circa 1948-49), 28 ga. (introduced 1959) or .410 bore (introduced 1958), 26 1/2, 28, 30, or 32 in. barrels, various chokes, boxlock, auto ejectors, various trigger combinations (single & double), checkered pistol grip stock, mfg. 1931-40 and 1948-76 by FN, grades differ in amount of engraving, inlays, general quality of workmanship and wood.

NOTE: The use of steel shot is NOT recommended in any Superposed Series manufactured in Belgium (B-25 variations).

BROWNING CHOKES AND THEIR CODES (MARKED NEXT TO EJECTORS)

*** designates full choke (F).**

***- designates improved modified choke (IM).**

**** designates modified choke (M).**

****- designates improved cylinder choke (IC).**

****$ designates skeet (SK).**

***** designates cylinder bore (CYL).**

SKEET MODELS were available in every ga. and grade.

TRAP MODELS were available in every grade in 12 ga. only.

BROADWAY TRAP MODELS (mfg. 1961-75) featured a 5/8 in. wide vent. rib and were also available in every grade.

Please refer to the Browning Superposed serialization section for determining year of manufacture.

SHOTGUNS: O/U, JOHN M. BROWNING COLLECTION

B15 BEAUCHAMP – premium model, part of the John M. Browning collection, available in four grades with choice of engraving and wood quality, buttstocks and forends are also included. Introduced 2015.

* ***B15 Beauchamp Grade B*** – 12 ga., 3 in. chambers, 26 or 28 in. polished blued barrels with solid top rib, 5 Invector Plus choke tubes, steel trigger guard, no sights, checkered Grade V stock with satin oil finish, low profile receiver with full sideplates, extensive engraving of pheasant and quail scenes plus additional chasing, silver Nitride receiver finish, 7.6 lbs. New 2015.

MSR $13,000	$11,700	$10,250	$8,775	$7,800	$6,450	$5,275	$4,300

* ***B15 Beauchamp Grade C*** – 12 ga., 3 in. chambers, 26 or 28 in. polished blued barrels with solid top rib, 5 Invector Plus choke tubes, steel trigger guard with laser engraving, no sights, checkered Grade V wood stock with satin oil finish, highly embellished Grade C engraving includes acanthus scroll pattern on bottom and sides of receiver, engraving features hand chasing to increase the contrast and depth within the pattern, silver Nitride receiver finish, 7.4-7.6 lbs.

MSR $15,500	$13,950	$12,200	$10,475	$9,500	$7,675	$6,300	$5,000

* ***B15 Beauchamp Grade D*** – 12 ga., 3 in. chambers, 26 or 28 in. polished blued barrels, 5 Invector Plus choke tubes, steel receiver, laser engraved trigger guard, no sights, highly configured Grade V wood stock with smooth satin oil finish, engraved grip cap and skeletonized buttplate, mock 3-piece style forearm, Grade D precision engraving on full sideplate receiver, additional chasing, pheasant, and quail scenes, 7.4-7.6 oz.

MSR $18,000	$16,200	$14,175	$12,150	$11,000	$8,925	$7,300	$6,000

* ***B15 Beauchamp Grade E*** – 12 ga., 3 in. chambers, 26 or 28 in. back bored polished blued barrels, 5 stainless steel chokes, solid top rib, highly configured Grade 5 wood stock with smooth satin oil finish, engraved pistol grip and skeletonized buttplate, mock 3-piece style forearm, extensive chasing to the acanthus scroll engraving on entire receiver and every steel surface, includes B15 leather case, 7.6 lbs.

MSR $20,500	$17,425	$15,250	$13,075	$11,850	$9,585	$7,850	$6,750

CLASSIC B25 – built per customer specifications.

Please contact the company directly for pricing, options, and availability.

* ***B25 Sporter New Generation*** – built per customer specifications including vented top and side ribs, Olympic trigger, deeply figured walnut stock with choice of fixed of adj. comb.

Please contact the company directly for pricing, options, and availability.

SUPERPOSED: 1931-1940 MFG. (PRE-WWII)

The Superposed was introduced in 1931 during the Great Depression, which seriously affected prewar sales figures. Pre-1938 guns had long slender forearms with a metal plate at the front called a "horseshoe

GRADING - PPGS™	100%	98%	95%	90%	80%	70%	60%	LAST MSR

plate". A new forearm was introduced during 1937 for the Lightning model eliminating the horseshoe plate - this forearm was smaller with a transverse bolt to hold it on. The early forearm with horseshoe plate had a long bolt that ran from front to back through the metal plate. The earlier transverse bolts were recessed into the sides of the forearms. Later the head and opposing fastener of the forearm were flush with the wood. Only the smaller forearm was carried over to postwar production.

Prewar Superposed furniture was finished with lacquer, this lacquer finish cracked over time like craquelure. Fine cracking of the lacquer is a sign of original finish and should not affect values.

Original buttplates are important to collectors, these buttplates featured intertwined twin circles and were made of horn.

Pre-war cases were made in genuine leather or leatherette, machine grained, both materials were available in brown or black. Insides were lined with grey or blue cloth, and the Browning brass label was on the inside of the case, not the outside. Depending on original condition, these cases sell in the $600-$900 range - single barrel cases are more common than multi-barrel ones. Cases are easily confused with similar prewar Auto-5 cases.

Extra barrels could be ordered with the original gun. Original extra barrel sets can demand up to a 40% premium depending on the overall condition of the gun and barrels.

SUPERPOSED STANDARD GRADE/GRADE I/LIGHTNING – 12 ga. only, boxlock action, blue receiver w/ decorative border engraving, standard from 1931-1937 for the U.S. Browning market. (This engraving pattern remained available for FN's world market well into the 1950s). During 1937 a simple small center rosette engraving pattern with simpler border engraving was introduced in the U.S. The lighter Lightning model with new forearm was first cataloged with the Standard Model Grade 1 in 1937.

	100%	98%	95%	90%	80%	70%	60%
	N/A	$2,900	$2,200	$1,800	$1,200	$1,000	$800

Subtract 15%-25% for recoil pad (depending on originality, deterioration, and condition).
Add at least $100 for ventilated rib barrel if 90% or better.
Add $100 for "horseshoe plate" forearm if 90% or better.
Add $100 for early guns with hand engraved "Browning Superposed" on top of barrel if 90% or better.
Add 10% for original double trigger, many were retrofitted by Browning to selective single trigger.

There were multiple pre '38 trigger options (depending on year): double normal, selective single with the selector on the bottom next to the trigger, twin single, and non-selective single. In 1938, the trigger system was changed to single-selective trigger with the selector on the top tang.

SUPERPOSED PIGEON GRADE – polished in-the-white engraved receiver with two pigeons on either side, pre-war guns have larger engraved pigeons than postwar production. Mfg. 1931-1940.

	100%	98%	95%	90%	80%	70%	60%
12 ga.	N/A	$5,050	$4,100	$3,350	$2,500	$2,000	$1,700

Subtract 25%-35% for recoil pad (depending on originality, deterioration, and condition).

The Pigeon Grade style of engraving is the only pre-war style that was continued after WWII. Pre-war Pigeon, Diana, and Midas Grades were usually not signed by the engraver.

SUPERPOSED DIANA GRADE – polished in-the-white receiver with fine, delicate engraving. Boars and stags were pictured in the 1931 catalog, but dogs and birds could also be special ordered at no additional cost until 1936, after which it became extra cost, dogs and birds engraving are more common than boars and stag. Mfg. 1931-1940.

	100%	98%	95%	90%	80%	70%	60%
12 ga.	N/A	$7,650	$5,750	$4,450	$3,525	$3,150	$2,475

Subtract 25%-35% for recoil pad (depending on originality, deterioration, and condition).

The Diana Grade was changed dramatically in post-WWII production.

SUPERPOSED MIDAS GRADE – features gold inlaid pigeons with stretched out wings on blue receiver. Gold inlays are prominent. This fine engraving exhibited the best of FN's engraving department.

	100%	98%	95%	90%	80%	70%	60%
12 ga.	N/A	$10,625	$7,225	$5,750	$4,250	$3,600	$2,700

Carefully inspect the rust blue on the receiver as restorations circulate, values above reflect original finish only. Refinished/restored guns are only worth a fraction of original values.
Subtract 25%-35% for recoil pad (depending on originality, deterioration, and condition).
Add 15% for original high-grade wood with teardrop and fine checkering, only if 95% or better and with original horn buttplate.

The Midas Grade was changed dramatically in post-WWII production.

SUPERPOSED: 1948-1960 MFG. (POST-WWII)

Model nomenclature was changed from pre-war designations to Grades I-VI. During this period, extra barrels could only be ordered in the same gauge as the original gun. Hardshell cases from this era are

GRADING - PPGS™	100%	98%	95%	90%	80%	70%	60%	LAST MSR

referred to as Tolex cases - they have blue velvet lining, and a brass Browning label on the outside top.

Engraved guns signed by Browning's top engravers (Funken, Vrancken, Watrin, Doyen, Müller, and Magis) will command a premium over unsigned guns. Felix Funken retired in 1960, and died in 1966.

On most Superposed with added recoil pads, the stock has usually been cut to keep the LOP the same. The correct LOP on a Superposed is 14 1/4 inches, with or w/o a recoil pad.

The twin circle buttplate was always horn, and was used on very early post war guns until 1949-1950.

Barrel addresses appeared as follows: circa 1947-1958 "St. Louis, M.O." (earliest BAC markings) or "St. Louis, Missouri", 1959-1968 "St. Louis, Missouri and Montreal P.Q.", and 1969-1975 "Morgan, Utah and Montreal, P.Q." Make sure barrel address date matches year of mfg. (see listings in the back of this text).

The original factory configuration of almost all Superposed shotguns can be verified by grade, gauge/bore, and barrel length. To obtain information on a specific Belgian Superposed serial number, please contact the Browning historian directly through their website at www.browning.com.

Add approx. 35%-50% per extra set of barrels (same ga. only), depending on condition.
Add $300-$500 for correct Tolex hardshell case with paperwork.
Subtract 25% for non-original recoil pads on Grade I models, depending on condition.
Subtract 25% for non-original recoil pads on the higher grades, depending on condition.
Special order Superposed with non-standard factory engraving, checkered buttstocks, 3 piece forearms, and other special orders will command premiums over standard configurations.

SUPERPOSED GRADE I STANDARD WEIGHT – 12 or 20 ga. (3 in. chambers were introduced in the 12 ga. during 1955, and in 20 ga. during 1957), otherwise similar to pre-war mfg., blue finish and triggers until 1955, gold trigger(s) became standard in 1955, raised (standard until 1959) or vent. rib only beginning in 1959, round knob long tang (RKLT) stock configuration, this earlier period of mfg. also featured smaller, narrower forearms and thinner pistol grip stock with horn buttplate (can be determined by the rounded "g" in Browning, not square), early post-war production had similar pre-WWII minimal engraving until circa 1952-53, more standard engraving continued through 1955, when Grade I models featured considerably more engraving, post-war 12 ga. serialization began at approx. 17,100, and with 200 on 20 ga. Mfg. 1948-1960.

12 ga.	N/A	$1,450	$1,250	$1,100	$900	$800	$700	
20 ga.	N/A	$2,525	$2,375	$1,900	$1,500	$1,200	$1,000	

Grade I models had 3 levels of standard engraving coverage.

* ***Superposed Grade I Lightning Hunting Model*** – 12 or 20 ga., 6 oz. lighter than Standard Weight. Introduced in all Grades beginning 1956.

12 ga.	N/A	$1,450	$1,250	$1,100	$900	$800	$700	
20 ga.	N/A	$2,525	$2,375	$1,900	$1,500	$1,250	$1,100	

* ***Superposed Grade I Magnum*** – 12 ga. only, 3 in. chambers, 28, 30, or 32 (rare) in. barrels with raised or vent. rib, recoil pad standard, introduced in all Grades in 1955.

	N/A	$1,550	$1,350	$1,150	$1,050	$950	$750	

This model with 30 or 32 (rare) in. barrels is now popular again, as Sporting Clays shooters like this desirable configuration.

* ***Superposed Grade I Trap Standard Weight Model*** – 12 ga. only, various configurations. Introduced 1952.

	N/A	$1,550	$1,350	$1,150	$1,050	$950	$725	

Pre-war trap guns and those manufactured post-war until approx. 1955 were virtually indistinguishable from field guns as they had field style forearms, round knob (semi-pistol grip) and long tangs. The only way to tell the difference is they had a longer LOP (14 1/2 in.) and a shorter drop at the heel - 1 3/4 in. vs. 2 1/2 in. for field stocks. These early trap guns did not come with recoil pads. Between 1956-1960, trap guns had the forearm changed to semi-beavertail. These late guns with semi-beavertail forearms are very desirable today due to their rarity and overall desirability.

SUPERPOSED GRADE II – 12 or 20 ga., featured pre-war Pigeon Grade engraving with large pigeons, some early post- war mfg. were signed by Funken.

12 ga.	N/A	$3,575	$3,150	$2,800	$2,250	$2,000	$1,550	
20 ga.	N/A	$6,200	$5,450	$4,900	$4,150	$3,420	$2,700	

GRADING - PPGS™	100%	98%	95%	90%	80%	70%	60%	LAST MSR

SUPERPOSED GRADE III – 12 or 20 ga., European style engraving, commonly referred to as "fighting cocks," pheasants on right side, fighting cocks on left, most were signed by the engraver.

12 ga.	N/A	$4,100	$3,575	$3,225	$2,550	$2,250	$1,700
20 ga.	N/A	$9,000	$7,875	$7,100	$5,675	$4,675	$3,600

SUPERPOSED GRADE IV – 12 or 20 ga., features deeper European style engraving with dogs and foxes, most were signed by the engraver.

12 ga.	N/A	$6,800	$5,950	$5,350	$4,250	$3,750	$2,875
20 ga.	N/A	$11,875	$10,400	$9,400	$7,500	$6,175	$4,750

SUPERPOSED GRADE V – 12 or 20 ga., features deeper engraving than pre-war Diana Grade, pheasants and ducks on receiver, most were signed by the engraver - Doyen was prevalent on this model.

12 ga.	N/A	$5,950	$5,200	$4,675	$3,750	$3,275	$2,525
20 ga.	N/A	$10,800	$9,450	$8,500	$6,500	$5,150	$4,000

SUPERPOSED GRADE VI – 12 or 20 ga., engraving pattern similar to later production Midas Grade, almost all of these were signed by Müeller. Introduced in July, 1957, changed in 1960, limited production, and rarest of the 6 grades.

12 ga.	N/A	$10,200	$8,300	$7,450	$6,715	$5,675	$4,675
20 ga.	N/A	$17,500	$15,000	$12,900	$11,500	$9,750	$7,750

SUPERPOSED: 1960-1976 MFG.

In early 1960, a major change was made in the manner in which the various grades of Superposed were designated. The Roman numerals used in the 1950s were dropped, and Browning once again returned to names. The Pigeon, Diana, and Midas names used for pre-war designations were brought back and replaced the Grade II, Grade V, and Grade VI respectively. Grades III & IV were dropped and replaced by the Pointer. The Grade I remained unchanged.

The Broadway Trap Model was introduced in 1961. Browning's lifetime Superposed warranty began in 1963. During 1965, the Hydro Coil stock (1 year only) and barrel Super Tubes were introduced. During 1966, a major change was implemented to save money when Browning switched from a long tang to short tang. During 1970-71, the stock configuration was once again changed to a full pistol grip (referred to as flat knob), and the long tang was brought back. Also at this time, mechanical triggers were implemented vs. the older inertial design, and silver solder vent. ribs vs. tin solder. As a result, this period of Superposed manufacture was mechanically better and more reliable. The Superlight Model was introduced in 12 ga. during 1967, 20 ga. during 1969, and became available in all Grades beginning in 1971. All gauge Skeet sets became available in all Grades during 1972.

During late 1966, Browning's salt wood problems began to emerge, and continued until 1970. The majority of salt wood Superposed models from this era are in the round knob short tang configuration (RKST), but some flat knob short tang (FKST) guns with salt problems have also been observed. Depending on the damage (it can vary a lot), values for salt damaged guns can be reduced by as much as 50% (heavy pitting and original salt wood). Those salt guns that have been restocked by Browning are accepted by the shooting fraternity, and can command as much as 90% of the value of non-salt original guns. To determine if a Superposed has salt damage, examine carefully any gun where the serial number is within the 1966-1971 production range (please refer to the Browning Superposed serialization section), and carefully inspect the wood around the buttplate, forearm, and where the wood joins the receiver metal for any telltale rusting or pitting.

Engraved guns signed by Browning's top engravers (Funken, Vrancken, Watrin, Magis, Müeller, and J. Baerten) will command a premium over unsigned guns. Also, more and more Superposed models are appearing with Angelo Bee's signature (while non-factory, Mr. Bee's work is universally recognized. He engraved in Belgium at FN from 1951-1974.) Louis Vrancken and Andre Watrin took over as heads of the engraving department in 1960.

The following values are for 1960-1976 Superposed production non-salt damaged guns. Most desirable period of mfg. is 1960-1966 (round knob, long tang, limited salt, rarely encountered with salt damage). Guns made during 1972-1976 (FKLT) are worth more than RKST. Lowest values are for 1966-1971 mfg. (round/flat knob, short tang - should be inspected carefully for potential salt wood problems). Many Browning collectors/dealers feel that round/flat knob, short tang Superposed are getting harder to sell every year.

Barrel addresses appeared as follows: circa 1947-1958 "St. Louis, M.O." (earliest BAC markings) or "St. Louis, Missouri", 1959-1968 "St. Louis, Missouri and Montreal P.Q.", 1969-1975 "Morgan, Utah and Montreal, P.Q." Make sure barrel address date matches year of mfg. (see listings in the back of this text).

The original factory configuration of almost all Superposed shotguns can be verified by grade, gauge/bore,

GRADING - PPGS™	100%	98%	95%	90%	80%	70%	60%	LAST MSR

and barrel length. To obtain information on a specific Belgian Superposed serial number, please contact the Browning historian directly through their website at www.browning.com.

SUPERPOSED WITH EXTRA BARREL(S) OR SUPER-TUBES – The Superposed could be special ordered from the factory in the following combinations: 12 or 20 ga. with one extra set of barrels in same ga., 12 ga. with one extra set in 20 ga., 12 or 20 ga. with two extra barrel sets of same ga., 20 ga. with one extra set in either 28 ga. or .410 bore, 20 ga. with both 28 ga. and .410 bore barrel sets, and 28 ga. with extra set of .410 bore barrels. Super-Tubes were adaptable on 12 ga. guns only; came from the factory cased with accessories, 16 1/2 in. long, factory installation.

Add 40%-50% of the gun's value for each Grade I extra barrel set(s). For higher grades, add approx. $1,000-$2,500 per barrel set, depending on grade.
Add $250 for Super-Tubes - available for 12 ga. only, introduced in 1965.
Add $400 for Super-Tube Set - 3 ga. set (20, 28 ga., and .410 bore).
Subtract $150-$500 for non-original recoil pads on Grade I models, depending on condition.
Subtract $250-$750 for non-original recoil pads on the higher grades, depending on condition.

SUPERPOSED VARIATIONS – On most Superposed with added recoil pads, the stock has usually been cut to keep the LOP the same. The correct LOP on a Superposed is 14 1/4 inches (14 1/2 in. on Trap & New Style Skeet), with or w/o a factory recoil pad, unless special ordered from the factory. Except for the Superlight Model, individual configurations have not been broken out on the Pigeon, Pointer, Diana, and Midas grades, but values will be similar to each other in most cases.

Subtract approx. 25%-40% for salt wood (depending on extent of damage).
Subtract 10% for new style Skeet configuration on models.
Subtract 15%-20% for Broadway Trap Model.
Special order Superposed with non-standard factory engraving, checkered buttstocks, 3 piece forearms, and other special orders will command premiums over standard configurations.

SUPERPOSED GRADE I STANDARD WEIGHT & LIGHTNING – 12, 20, 28 ga., or .410 bore (the 28 ga. & .410 bore were not cataloged until 1960), 28 ga. and .410 bore were built on a 20 ga. frame, the buttplate was changed from horn to plastic during 1961, 12 and 20 ga. Lightning Models were approx. 6 oz. lighter than Standard Weight.

12 ga.	$1,700	$1,375	$1,100	$850	$750	$675	$625	
20 ga.	$3,250	$2,525	$2,375	$1,900	$1,550	$1,275	$1,100	
28 ga.	$5,950	$5,525	$4,675	$3,825	$2,925	$2,500	$2,050	
.410 bore	$5,500	$4,750	$4,000	$3,000	$2,200	$1,475	$1,225	

Subtract 10%-15% for Grade I Standardweight (12 ga. only).
Add 20%-25% for round knob, long tang stock variations (pre-1966), unless Skeet choked.

* ***Superposed Grade I Magnum*** – 12 ga. only, 3 in. chambers, 28, 30, or 32 (rare) in. barrels with vent. rib, recoil pad standard.

12 ga.	$1,700	$1,375	$1,100	$850	$750	$675	$625	

This model with 30 or 32 (very rare) in. barrels is now popular again, as Sporting Clays shooters like this desirable configuration.

* ***Superposed Grade I Superlight*** – 12 (mfg. 1967-1976), 20 (1969-1976), 28 (very rare, approx. 12-14 mfg.) ga. or .410 bore (mfg. 1970-76) features lightweight construction and straight grip stock. During 1971, the Superlight was offered in all Grades.

12 ga.	$2,750	$2,250	$2,000	$1,700	$1,200	$1,000	$875	
20 ga.	$4,500	$4,000	$3,650	$2,850	$2,000	$1,650	$1,425	
28 ga.	$17,500	$16,250	$13,750	$10,500	$8,125	$6,625	$5,750	
.410 bore	$8,250	$6,750	$5,250	$4,500	$3,300	$2,200	$1,850	

A Quail Unlimited limited edition was also available in the Superlight Series, add 10%-15% if in 98%+ original condition.
20 ga. with solid rib barrels are very rare and will command a premium over vent. rib variations.

* ***Superposed Grade I Skeet/New Model Skeet*** – 12, 20, 28 ga. or .410 bore, 26 1/2 or 28 in. VR barrels with fixed SK/SK chokes, New Model Skeet was introduced during 1968, and was available in both Standard and Lightning weights in 12 and 20 ga., this New Model featured a flat bottom pistol grip stock with factory vent. recoil pad and beavertail forearm, pre-'68 mfg. was basically a hunting model with skeet chokes. Mfg. circa 1950s-1976.

12 ga.	$1,675	$1,400	$1,100	$950	$825	$750	$700	
20 ga.	$2,450	$2,100	$1,700	$1,250	$975	$850	$775	
28 ga.	$4,950	$4,500	$3,500	$2,750	$2,250	$1,550	$1,275	
.410 bore	$2,800	$2,400	$1,950	$1,450	$1,100	$925	$850	

GRADING - PPGS™	100%	98%	95%	90%	80%	70%	60%	LAST MSR

Add approx. 10%-15% for pre 1968 mfg. (w/o beavertail forearm and recoil pad.)
Subtract 20% for 26 in. (New Skeet style) barrels.

* ***Superposed Grade I Four Gauge Skeet Set*** – includes 12, 20, 28 ga. and .410 bore barrels, 26 1/2 or 28 in. VR barrels, 12 ga. frame, beavertail forearm, includes fitted luggage case. Mfg. 1972-1976.

	$5,250	$4,950	$4,500	$4,150	$3,850	$3,350	$2,650

Subtract 20% for 26 in. (New Skeet style) barrels.

* ***Superposed Grade I Trap Model (Lightning and Broadway)*** – 12 ga. only, FKLT, Trap dimension stock with recoil pad, 14 3/8 in. LOP, semi-beavertail forearm, 30 or 32 (rare in Lightning model) in. barrels with either standard 5/16 in. VR (Lightning) or 5/8 in. Broadway VR, first cataloged in 1961, this new Lightning Model Trap was approx. 6 oz. lighter than previous mfg., front and middle ivory bead sights standard, Broadway is approx. 1 lbs. heavier than Lightning with same length barrels.

	$1,950	$1,600	$1,200	$1,000	$825	$750	$700

SUPERPOSED PIGEON GRADE – 12, 20, 28 ga. or .410 bore, features a silver grey receiver with 2 smaller flying pigeons surrounded by fine scroll engraving on each side of the frame, receiver bottom and tangs also exhibit fine scroll work. Disc. 1974.

12 ga.	$4,675	$3,275	$2,475	$1,700	$1,525	$1,350	$1,275
20 ga.	$9,000	$7,500	$6,000	$4,000	$2,750	$2,100	$1,850
28 ga.	$12,500	$9,000	$7,800	$6,000	$4,500	$3,500	$2,500
.410 bore	$9,000	$7,500	$6,000	$4,500	$3,300	$2,800	$2,200

Add 20%-25% for round knob, long tang stock variations (pre-1966), unless Skeet choked.
Subtract 20% for newer Skeet style model with beavertail forearm and recoil pad.

Between 1948-1960, this model was designated the Grade II.

* ***Superposed Pigeon Grade Superlight*** – 12 (mfg. 1967-1976), 20 (1969-1976), 28 (very rare, approx. 6 mfg.) ga., or .410 bore (mfg. 1970-76) features lightweight construction and straight grip stock. During 1971, the Superlight was offered in all Grades.

12 ga.	$7,225	$5,825	$4,675	$3,525	$2,650	$1,975	$1,750
20 ga.	$11,500	$10,000	$8,750	$7,500	$6,250	$5,000	$4,000
28 ga.	$15,000	$12,500	$9,250	$7,750	$6,150	$5,000	$3,750
.410 bore	$12,000	$10,500	$9,250	$8,000	$6,750	$5,500	$4,500

SUPERPOSED POINTER GRADE – features engraved silver grey receiver with a pointer on one side, and a setter on the other, select checkered walnut, early production was engraved by Funken, while the final design was executed by Vrancken. Mfg. 1959-disc. 1966, except for special orders.

12 ga.	$7,450	$5,825	$4,950	$4,150	$3,100	$2,200	$1,800
20 ga.	$15,000	$12,500	$9,250	$7,600	$6,000	$5,000	$3,750
28 ga. (rare)	$21,500	$18,000	$15,500	$12,500	$8,000	$5,000	$3,800
.410 bore (rare)	$17,500	$14,000	$12,250	$9,250	$6,000	$4,600	$3,500

Add 40% for round knob, long tang stock variations (pre-1966), unless Skeet choked (add 40% if 28 ga.).
Subtract 20% for newer Skeet style model with beavertail forearm and recoil pad.

* ***Superposed Pointer Grade Superlight*** – this model was available by special order only, and was never cataloged by BAC (approx. 10 mfg. in 28 ga.).

12 ga.	$10,400	$8,650	$6,925	$5,800	$4,350	$3,075	$2,525
20 ga.	$21,000	$17,500	$12,950	$10,500	$8,400	$7,000	$5,250
28 ga. (very rare)	$30,000	$25,750	$19,750	$15,000	$11,000	$8,500	$7,000
.410 bore (very rare)	$25,000	$21,000	$15,500	$12,000	$9,000	$7,750	$6,000

SUPERPOSED DIANA GRADE – deeper engraving with duck and pheasant game scenes - similar to 1948-60 mfg. Grade V. Disc. 1976.

12 ga.	$6,975	$5,525	$4,300	$2,750	$2,450	$2,200	$1,975
20 ga.	$13,000	$10,000	$8,500	$5,950	$4,850	$3,650	$3,150
28 ga.	$22,500	$18,000	$15,000	$10,000	$7,350	$5,750	$4,750
.410 bore	$14,500	$12,000	$9,000	$6,550	$5,000	$4,200	$3,650

Add 20% for round knob, long tang stock variations (pre-1966, add 40% if 28 ga.).
Subtract 20% for newer Skeet style model with beavertail forearm and recoil pad.

Between 1948-1960, this model was designated the Grade V.

GRADING - PPGS™	100%	98%	95%	90%	80%	70%	60%	LAST MSR

* ***Superposed Diana Grade Superlight*** – 12 (mfg. 1967-76), 20 (1969-76), 28 (very rare, approx. 7-9 mfg.) ga. or .410 bore (mfg. 1970-76) features lightweight construction and straight grip stock. During 1971, the Superlight was offered in all Grades.

12 ga.	$9,900	$8,300	$6,450	$3,850	$3,425	$3,075	$2,775	
20 ga.	$18,000	$15,000	$11,500	$8,000	$6,500	$4,950	$4,000	
28 ga. (very rare)	$35,000	$30,000	$25,000	$21,000	$17,500	$14,000	$10,000	
.410 bore (very rare)	$27,500	$23,000	$17,000	$13,500	$10,000	$8,500	$7,250	

SUPERPOSED MIDAS GRADE – features new design by Vrancken with deep relief scroll engraving with gold inlaid ducks and pheasants on frame sides and a quail on the bottom, ejector trip rods, ejector hammers, and firing pins are also 18Kt. gold plated, best quality walnut with fine checkering. Disc. 1976.

12 ga.	$10,625	$8,925	$7,450	$5,325	$4,500	$3,600	$3,250	
20 ga.	$19,500	$16,500	$14,000	$11,750	$8,750	$7,250	$5,000	
28 ga.	$27,500	$23,000	$20,000	$16,500	$12,500	$9,000	$7,350	
.410 bore	$19,500	$16,500	$14,000	$11,750	$8,750	$7,250	$5,000	

Add 20% for round knob, long tang stock variations (pre-1966), unless Skeet choked (add 40% if 28 ga.).
Subtract 20% for newer Skeet style model with beavertail forearm and recoil pad.

Between 1948-1960, this model was designated the Grade VI.

* ***Superposed Midas Grade Superlight*** – 12 (mfg. 1967-76), 20 (1969-76), 28 (very rare, approx. 9 mfg.) ga., or .410 bore (mfg. 1970-76) features lightweight construction and straight grip stock. During 1971, the Superlight was offered in all Grades.

12 ga.	$15,625	$13,125	$11,000	$7,800	$6,250	$5,000	$4,375	
20 ga.	$24,375	$20,500	$17,500	$14,500	$11,000	$9,000	$6,250	
28 ga. (very rare)	$39,500	$33,500	$26,000	$21,000	$17,500	$14,750	$11,500	
.410 bore (very rare)	$27,250	$23,000	$19,500	$16,450	$12,250	$10,150	$7,000	

SUPERPOSED BICENTENNIAL SUPERLIGHT – specially engraved limited edition Model, 51 mfg. - one for each state and Washington, D.C. Left side has U.S. Flag, bald eagle and state emblem inlaid in gold. Right side has gold inlaid hunter and turkey. Blue receiver, fancy checkered English stock, Schnabel forend, velvet lined wood case. Made 1976 by FN.

	$12,000	$10,000	$8,000	N/A	N/A	N/A	N/A	

SUPERPOSED EXPOSITION/EXHIBITION MODEL – this specially manufactured Superposed saw limited production from pre-WWII through 1976. There are true exhibition models and a "C" series. Most "C" series did not have carved stocks, and were a special BAC sale of FN guns which did not sell well in Europe. True exhibition guns had gold lettering on the barrels in most cases, and many also had carved stocks. These guns were made for a very special reason, purpose, or person. Prices usually start in the 5 digit level - the C Series is typically priced between $20,000-$50,000, with the Exhibition guns comparably priced as long as they are not Trap or Skeet guns. Field choked RKLT and Superlite small bore guns bring the most, with small bore, all option side plated Exhibitions at the top of the heap, whether C Series or not.

SUPERPOSED PRESENTATION MODELS (P1-P4) – custom made versions of the Lightning Field, Super Light, Trap, and Skeet guns, specifications the same as Standard models, with differences in finish, engraving and inlay(s), and grade of wood and checkering. These guns were introduced by FN in 1977 and were disc. after 1984. Gauge premiums below refer to Models P1-P3.

Add 50% for 20 ga.
Add 75% for 28 ga.
Add 40% for .410 bore.
Add $1,500 for each P1 extra barrel set(s). For higher grades, add approx. $1,500-$2,500 per barrel set, depending on grade.
Subtract 25% for P Series Trap Models.
Subtract 25% for P Series Broadway Trap Models.
Subtract 20% for P Series Skeet 12 and 20 ga. guns.

Since P Series Superposed were disc. in 1985, collector interest has increased substantially. Interestingly, the P series models are rarer than most of the pre-1976 high grade Superposed models.

* ***Superposed Presentation 1*** – silver grey or blue receiver, oak leaf and fine scroll engraved, choice of 6 different animal scenes.

	$3,500	$2,750	$2,150	$1,850	$1,500	$1,250	$1,000	

GRADING - PPGS™	100%	98%	95%	90%	80%	70%	60%	LAST MSR

* ***Superposed Presentation 1 w/Gold Inlays*** – similar to Presentation 1, only with gold inlays.

	$5,000	$3,750	$3,150	$2,100	$1,825	$1,700	$1,500	

* ***Superposed Presentation 2*** – silver grey or blue receiver, high relief engraving, choice of 3 different sets of game scenes.

	$5,000	$4,250	$3,000	$2,150	$1,825	$1,700	$1,500	

* ***Superposed Presentation 2 w/Gold Inlays*** – similar to Presentation 2, only with gold inlays.

	$7,250	$6,150	$4,200	$2,150	$1,925	$1,750	$1,550	

* ***Superposed Presentation 3*** – silver grey or blue receiver, more elaborate high relief engraving with choice of partridges, mallards, or geese depicted on frame sides in 18Kt. gold.

	$9,250	$7,750	$5,750	$3,750	$3,200	$2,875	$2,300	

* ***Superposed Presentation 4*** – features engraved sideplates in either silver grey or blue finish, hand engraved game scenes include waterfowl on right frame side, 5 pheasants on left frame side, 2 quail on receiver bottom, and a retriever's head on trigger guard. Extra figure walnut stock and forearm.

	$8,250	$7,000	$5,250	$4,000	$3,350	$2,950	$2,375	

Add 30% for 20 ga., 70% for 28 ga., or 50% for .410 bore.

* ***Superposed Presentation 4 w/Gold Inlays*** – similar to Presentation 4, only with game scenes inlaid in 18Kt. gold.

	$12,500	$10,750	$8,700	$6,000	$4,250	$3,650	$2,950	

Add 50% for 20 ga., 75% for 28 ga., or 50% for .410 bore.

SUPERPOSED PRESENTATION SERIES SUPERLITE (PI - PIV) – available in various configurations including multi-barrel sets.

* ***Superposed Presentation I Superlite w/Gold*** – G, H, I, J, K, or L style engraving.

12 ga. (25 mfg.)	$6,750	$6,000	$5,200	$3,600	$3,000	$2,250	$1,800	
20 ga. (80 mfg.)	$9,500	$8,000	$7,000	$5,500	$4,000	$3,200	$2,500	
28 ga. (38 mfg.)	$13,000	$11,000	$9,800	$7,700	$6,200	$4,000	$3,400	
.410 bore (47 mfg.)	$9,500	$8,500	$6,800	$5,500	$4,000	$3,200	$2,600	

Add $1,500 per extra barrel.
Add 40% for an all option gun (checkered buttstock, oil finish, three piece forend, rare).
Add 15% for J. Baerten signed gun (rare).
Subtract 35% for Trap or Skeet Models.
Subtract 30% for A, B, C, D, E, or F models w/o gold.

* ***Superposed Presentation II Superlite*** – P, Q, or R style engraving.

12 ga. (23 mfg.)	$9,500	$9,000	$8,000	$7,000	$6,000	$4,500	$2,200	
20 ga. (93 mfg.)	$14,000	$12,500	$9,500	$7,500	$6,000	$5,000	$3,000	
28 ga. (57 mfg.)	$16,000	$14,500	$11,000	$9,000	$7,500	$6,000	$4,000	
.410 bore (44 mfg.)	$14,000	$12,500	$9,500	$7,500	$6,000	$5,000	$3,000	

Add $2,000 per extra barrel.
Add 40% for an all option gun (checkered buttstock, oil finish, three piece forend, rare, 50% if 28 ga.).
Add 15% for J. Baerten signed gun (rare).
Subtract 40% for Trap or Skeet Models.
Subtract 30% for M, N, or O models w/o gold.

* ***Superposed Presentation III Superlite*** – S, T, or U style engraving.

12 ga. (16 mfg.)	$13,000	$12,000	$10,000	$8,500	$7,000	$5,000	$3,500	
20 ga. (85 mfg.)	$18,500	$17,000	$14,000	$10,000	$7,500	$5,500	$4,500	
28 ga. (36 mfg.)	$22,500	$20,500	$17,000	$14,000	$10,000	$8,000	$6,500	
.410 bore (37 mfg.)	$18,000	$16,500	$13,500	$9,500	$7,000	$5,000	$4,000	

Add $2,000 per extra barrel.
Add 30% for an all option gun (checkered buttstock, oil finish, three piece forend, 40% if 28 ga.).
Add 25% for an all option FKLT gun (very rare).
Add 15% for J. Baerten signed gun (rare).
Subtract 40% for Trap or Skeet Models.

GRADING - PPGS™	100%	98%	95%	90%	80%	70%	60%	LAST MSR

* ***Superposed Presentation IV Superlite w/Gold*** – W style engraving.

12 ga. (14 mfg.)	$21,000	$20,000	$17,500	$14,000	$11,000	$8,500	$6,000	
20 ga. (44 mfg.)	$25,000	$23,000	$19,500	$15,000	$10,000	$8,000	$6,500	
28 ga. (20 mfg.)	$32,000	$30,000	$24,000	$18,000	$15,000	$12,000	$10,000	
.410 bore (35 mfg.)	$25,000	$23,000	$19,500	$15,000	$10,000	$8,000	$6,500	

Add $3,000 per extra barrel.
Add 40% for an all option gun (checkered buttstock, oil finish, three piece forend, 50% if 28 ga.).
Add 40% for an all option FKLT gun (very rare).
Add 15% for J. Baerten signed gun (rare).
Subtract 35% for Trap or Skeet Models.
Subtract 35% for plain models w/o gold.

LIEGE (FN B-26) – 12 ga., 26 1/2, 28 or 30 in. barrels, various chokes, boxlock, auto ejectors, non-selective single trigger, vent. rib, checkered pistol grip stock. Approx. 10,000 mfg. 1973-1975 by FN.

	$1,325	$1,050	$850	$685	$610	$570	$540	

This model is also known as the B-26.

GRAND LIEGE – similar to Liege, except has deluxe checkered walnut stock and forearm, and engraved receiver. Disc.

	$1,750	$1,275	$1,000	$850	$750	$700	$650	

B-26 – with BAC markings. Mfg. 1973-75.

	$1,325	$1,050	$825	$685	$610	$570	$540	

B-27 – F.N. manufactured modified B-26, imported into the U.S. in 1984, same action as Liege (B 26), blue or satin finished receiver with light engraving, no BAC markings and never cataloged.

* ***B-27 Standard Game*** – 28 in. barrels, 9/32 in. vent. rib, pistol grip stock, Schnabel forearm, SST, blue receiver, choking M/F only.

	$1,395	$1,000	$850	$685	$610	$570	$540	

Also available in Skeet model with gold "Browning" logo on blue receiver. Prices are the same.

* ***B-27 Deluxe Game (Grade II)*** – similar to Standard Grade, except has 30 in. barrels, better wood and English scroll engraved satin finished receiver, choking M/F only.

	$1,500	$1,150	$1,000	$850	$750	$650	$550	

* ***B-27 Grand Deluxe Game*** – 28 in. IC/IM & M/F choked barrels, game scene engraved, signed by the engraver, 90% receiver coverage.

	$1,650	$1,250	$1,075	$900	$775	$660	$595	

This model was also available in a Trap configuration - values are about the same as above.

* ***B-27 Deluxe Skeet*** – similar to Deluxe Game (Grade II), except is designed for skeet shooting.

	$1,325	$1,050	$850	$685	$610	$570	$540	

International Skeet was also available at same price; hand fit pistol grip with stippling and International Type recoil pad.

* ***B-27 Deluxe Trap*** – similar to Deluxe Game (Grade II), except is configured for trap shooting.

	$1,395	$1,100	$850	$685	$610	$570	$540	

* ***B-27 City of Liege Commemorative*** – limited edition of 250 units manufactured to commemorate the 1,000th anniversary of the city of Liege, cased. Only 29 imported into the U.S.

	$1,875	$1,550	$1,225	N/A	N/A	N/A	N/A	

ST-100 – 12 ga., Belgian mfg., O/U trap configuration with separated barrels and adj. point of impact, manufactured 1979-81 for European sale mostly, floating VR, ST, deluxe checkered walnut stock and forearm, non-BAC model.

	$3,500	$2,750	$2,000	$1,850	$1,200	$975	$825	

SUPERPOSED WATERFOWL SERIES – 12 ga., 500 made of each issue, 7 gold inlays with extensive engraving on French Grey receiver, lightning action, 28 in. barrels, checkered buttstock, full-length walnut case, factory inventories were depleted on Mallard, Pintail, and Black Duck Issues in 1989.

Add 20% for 3 gun set with same serial number.

* ***Superposed Waterfowl 1981 Mallard Issue***

	$9,995	$7,750	$6,000	N/A	N/A	N/A	N/A	*$7,000*

This issue was sold out in 1988.

GRADING - PPGS™	100%	98%	95%	90%	80%	70%	60%	LAST MSR
* ***Superposed Waterfowl 1982 Pintail Issue***								
	$9,995	$7,750	$6,000	N/A	N/A	N/A	N/A	*$7,000*
* ***Superposed Waterfowl 1983 Black Duck Issue***								
	$9,995	$7,750	$6,000	N/A	N/A	N/A	N/A	*$8,800*

SUPERPOSED SHOTGUN: 1983-86 MFG. – 12 or 20 ga. In 1983, Browning announced renewed production of the famous Belgian "Superposed" O/U in Grade I only. Available in Lightning or Superlight models, 3 in. chambers in Lightning 20 ga., 26 1/2 or 28 in. barrels. Belgian manufactured from 1983-86.

* ***Superposed Shotgun Grade I (1983-86 Mfg.)*** – limited mfg., not compatible with steel shot, featured select walnut stock/forearm and extra engraving.

	100%	98%	95%	90%	80%	70%	60%	LAST MSR
Lightning	$2,800	$2,150	$1,550	$950	$800	$675	$550	
Superlight	$3,750	$3,300	$2,750	$1,850	$1,400	$1,000	$850	*$1,995*

Add 25% for 20 ga.

SUPERPOSED CLASSIC SERIES – 20 ga. only, 26 in. barrels, less than 2,500 manufactured in Classic model and under 350 manufactured in Gold Classic. Both editions feature multiple engraved scenes and a special silver grey finish. Select American walnut featuring oil finish. Available 1986 only.

	100%	98%	95%	90%	80%	70%	60%	LAST MSR
	$4,250	$3,500	$2,750	N/A	N/A	N/A	N/A	*$2,000*

* ***Superposed Gold Classic*** – 8 gold inlays, select walnut forearm and stock are both checkered and carved, many were shipped back to Belgium due to poor sales domestically. Available 1986 only.

	100%	98%	95%	90%	80%	70%	60%	LAST MSR
	$7,750	$6,250	$4,350	N/A	N/A	N/A	N/A	*$6,000*

SHOTGUNS: O/U, SUPERPOSED HIGH GRADES: 1985-PRESENT

Browning, in 1985, resumed production of the Superposed in Pigeon, Pointer, Diana, and Midas grades. They were available in 12 and 20 ga. only, in either a Lightning or Superlight configuration. These higher grades were custom ordered from the factory with delivery ranging from 8 to more than 12 months. Custom options could be special ordered on each grade with corresponding prices being higher than shown below. B-25 engraving patterns on these various grades will nearly duplicate those styles manufactured before 1976. Skeet models were not available.

Be wary of non-factory upgraded Superposed higher grade models. These upgraded guns have very nice workmanship, but are valued at approx. 50% less than a factory gun in similar grade/gauge, and barrel length. Non-factory engraving has been done by: R. Capece, Dubois, Diet, and Bee. It is strongly advised to get a factory letter from the Browning Historical Department to guarantee the original configuration of a Superposed.

Superposed: Custom Shop Current Pricing & Models

In 2000, Browning changed the nomenclature of their B-25 shotgun Series. All current models are POR. These new boxlock grades include: Special Woodcock $16,558 (importation disc. 2013), Special Duck POR/last MSR in 2015 was $17,355, Special Pigeon POR/last MSR in 2015 was $18,506, Trap Evolution 2 POR/last MSR in 2015 was $19,655, Traditionnel POR/last MSR in 2015 was $17,355, Sporting 207 Gold last MSR in 2013 was $17,273, Diana UK POR/last MSR in 2015 was $22,415, and Grades B11 - POR/last MSR in 2015 was $18,296 (disc. 2003, reintroduced 2006), B12 - POR/last MSR in 2015 was $18,506 (disc. 2003, reintroduced 2006), B2G - POR/last MSR in 2015 was $18,715 (disc. 2003, reintroduced 2004), C11 - last MSR in 2013 was $21,668, C12 - $22,896 (importation disc. 2013), C1G - $19,421 (importation disc. 2013), C2G - POR/last MSR in 2015 was $23,420, C3 - $25,553 (importation disc. 2013), D11 - $30,970 (importation disc. 2013), D12 - $29,845 (importation disc. 2013), D2L $37,309 (importation disc. 2013), D4G POR/last MSR in 2015 was $36,592, D5G - POR/last MSR in 2015 was $36,592, Special Automn - POR/last MSR in 2015 was $37,638, Cheverny - $41,907 (importation disc. 2013).

Additionally, the Browning Custom Shop also offers the following shotguns in various grades with engraved sideplates: Grade II - $23,234 (disc. 2003), C2S - POR/last MSR in 2015 was $32,724, Grade E1 - POR/last MSR in 2015 was $41,867, Grade F1 - POR/last MSR in 2015 was $40,931, Grade I1 - POR/last MSR in 2015 was $40,931, Grade M1 - POR/last MSR in 2015 was $44,335, Grade M2 - POR/last MSR was in 2015 was $44,335, Special Perdrix - POR/last MSR in 2015 was $55,296, Windsor Or - POR/last MSR in 2015 was $55,296, Chenonceau - POR/last MSR in 2015 was $57,664, Cheverny - POR/last MSR in 2015 was $56,376, D5G Sideplate - POR/last MSR in 2015 was $57,664, and the Special Automn POR/last MSR in 2015 was $57,664. These new grades are special order only through the Browning Custom Shop.

Grade I Traditional, Pigeon Grade, Pointer Grade, Diana Grade, and Midas Grade Superposed are listed separately under the B-25 model listing.

GRADING - PPGS™	100%	98%	95%	90%	80%	70%	60%	LAST MSR

Add 20% for 20 ga. on previously owned models.
Add approx. $1,250 for a previously owned extra set of barrels.
Add $6,479 - $11,954 per extra set of barrels on currently manufactured Superposed models, depending on the grade.

B-25 – 12 or 20 ga. only, original Superposed Model manufactured entirely from parts fabricated in Herstal, Belgium. Also available in Superlight configuration. This older nomenclature series was discontinued domestically in 1999, but the Custom Shop is still producing these grades.

* ***B-25 Grade I Traditional***

	100%	98%	95%	90%	80%	70%	60%	LAST MSR
	$10,500	$8,750	$6,500	N/A	N/A	N/A	N/A	*$19,433*

* ***B-25 Pigeon Grade*** – Disc.

	100%	98%	95%	90%	80%	70%	60%	LAST MSR
	$12,850	$9,700	$7,350	N/A	N/A	N/A	N/A	*$17,675*

* ***B-25 Pointer C Grade*** – Disc.

	100%	98%	95%	90%	80%	70%	60%	LAST MSR
	$14,750	$10,925	$8,650	N/A	N/A	N/A	N/A	*$19,353*

* ***B-25 Diana C Grade***

	100%	98%	95%	90%	80%	70%	60%	LAST MSR
MSR $20,341	$16,000	$11,950	$9,650	N/A	N/A	N/A	N/A	

* ***B-25 Midas D Grade*** – Disc.

	100%	98%	95%	90%	80%	70%	60%	LAST MSR
	$18,150	$12,750	$10,250	N/A	N/A	N/A	N/A	*$26,265*

B-25 125th ANNIVERSARY – 12 ga. only, 2 3/4 in. chamber, 28 in. VR barrels with fixed M/F chokes and 8mm rib, Lightning style stock and forearm with oil finish and black buttplate, case colored receiver with gold border and gold enhanced 125th Anniversary logo. 10 mfg. 2003 only.

	100%	98%	95%	90%	80%	70%	60%	LAST MSR
	$13,750	$5,250	$3,750	N/A	N/A	N/A	N/A	*$15,219*

B-125 – 12 or 20 ga. only, retains all the features of the original Superposed, except parts were subcontracted worldwide to decrease production costs and were assembled "in the white" at Herstal's Custom Gun Shop in Belgium, choice of three different engraving styles and two receiver finishes. Mfg. 1988-2003.

* ***B-125 Hunting Model*** – available in either Hunting Lightning or Superlight configuration.

» **B-125 Hunting Model w/"A" Style Engraving** – blue frame with border engraving featuring Browning logo engraved on each side.

	100%	98%	95%	90%	80%	70%	60%	LAST MSR
	$3,400	$2,750	$2,150	$1,700	$1,450	$1,275	$1,050	*$3,925*

» **B-125 Hunting Model w/"B" Style Engraving** – coin finished frame with smaller game scene engravings.

	100%	98%	95%	90%	80%	70%	60%	LAST MSR
	$3,700	$3,100	$2,250	$1,800	$1,500	$1,300	$1,100	*$4,360*

» **B-125 Hunting Model w/"C" Style Engraving** – coin finished frame with elaborate scroll work and game scene engraving.

	100%	98%	95%	90%	80%	70%	60%	LAST MSR
	$4,100	$3,475	$2,450	$1,900	$1,600	$1,400	$1,200	*$4,903*

* ***B-125 Sporting Clays Model*** – 12 ga. only, designed for sporting clays competition and included Invector-Plus choke tube system.

» **B-125 Sporting Clays Model w/"A" Style Engraving** – blue frame with border engraving featuring Browning logo engraved on each side.

	100%	98%	95%	90%	80%	70%	60%	LAST MSR
	$3,400	$2,750	$2,150	$1,700	$1,450	$1,275	$1,050	*$3,925*

» **B-125 Sporting Clays Model w/"B" Style Engraving** – coin finished frame with smaller game scene engravings.

	100%	98%	95%	90%	80%	70%	60%	LAST MSR
	$3,700	$3,100	$2,250	$1,800	$1,500	$1,300	$1,100	*$4,360*

» **B-125 Sporting Clays Model w/"C" Style Engraving** – coin finished frame with elaborate scroll work and game scene engraving.

	100%	98%	95%	90%	80%	70%	60%	LAST MSR
	$4,100	$3,475	$2,450	$1,900	$1,600	$1,400	$1,200	*$4,903*

* ***B-125 Trap Model*** – standard F-1 style engraving.

	100%	98%	95%	90%	80%	70%	60%	LAST MSR
	$4,950	$3,550	$2,325	$1,750	$1,450	$1,275	$1,050	*$5,452*

SHOTGUNS: SxS

The Browning Custom Shop in Herstal, Belgium offered several SxS sidelock models manufactured by Lebeau-Courally until circa 2006. Models include the LC1 (blued receiver, $17,516 last MSR), and LC2 (coin finished receiver, $22,799 last MSR).

GRADING - PPGS™	100%	98%	95%	90%	80%	70%	60%	LAST MSR

B-SS – 12 or 20 ga., 26, 28, or 30 in. barrels, various chokes, engraved boxlock action, auto ejectors, checkered pistol grip walnut stock, beavertail forearm, SST. Mfg. 1971-1988 by Miroku.

12 ga.	$1,325	$1,150	$1,000	$875	$800	$700	$600	
20 ga.	$2,000	$1,800	$1,650	$1,525	$1,300	$1,100	$950	*$775*

Early guns had a single non-selective trigger (silver plated) - subtract 10%.

* ***B-SS Grade II*** – 12 or 20 ga., satin greyed steel receiver featuring an engraved pheasant, duck, quail, and dogs. Disc. 1983.

	$3,250	$2,850	$2,250	$1,775	$1,350	$1,100	$925	

B-SS SPORTER – 12 or 20 ga., straight grip stock, longer lower tang, slimmed down beavertail forearm, oil finish, 26 or 28 in. barrels. Disc. 1988.

	$2,250	$1,950	$1,650	$1,300	$1,000	$800	$650	*$775*

Add 50% for 20 ga., if in 95%+ condition.

* ***B-SS Sporter Grade II*** – 12 or 20 ga., satin greyed steel receiver featuring an engraved pheasant, duck, quail and dogs. Disc. 1983.

	$3,150	$2,700	$2,225	$1,800	$1,350	$1,100	$925	

Add 50% for 20 ga., if in 95%+ condition.

* ***B-SS "Bottle" Sporter Set*** – 12 and 20 ga., wild turkey and wood duck inlays on 12 ga., wood ducks only on 20 ga., straight grip sporter stock, shoulders are sculpted and engraved, Exhibition grade walnut, engraving was done in Belgium by custom shop, cased in Browning Airways case. Less than 100 mfg. circa 1976.

Set	$9,500	$8,750	$7,500	$6,250	$5,000	$4,500	$4,000	
12 ga.	$2,995	$2,750	$2,400	$2,100	$1,850	$1,600	$1,400	
20 ga.	$3,750	$3,300	$2,950	$2,650	$2,300	$2,000	$1,800	

This model got its nickname from a Mr. Bottles Sporting Goods store in Wichita, KS, who special ordered 100 sets of these guns circa 1976.

B-SS SIDELOCK – 12 or 20 ga., engraved sidelock action in satin grey finish, ST, 26 or 28 in. barrels, English select walnut stock, splinter forend. Mfg. 1983-88 by Miroku in Japan.

12 ga.	$3,750	$3,300	$2,725	$2,275	$1,875	$1,500	$1,250	
20 ga.	$6,000	$5,000	$4,250	$3,500	$3,000	$2,500	$1,500	*$2,000*

SHOTGUNS: SEMI-AUTO, AUTO-5 1903-1998, 2012-CURRENT MFG.

BROWNING CHOKES AND THEIR CODES (ON REAR LEFT-SIDE OF BARREL)

*** designates full choke (F).**

***- designates improved modified choke (IM).**

**** designates modified choke (M).**

****- designates improved cylinder choke (IC).**

****$ designates skeet (SK).**

***** designates cylinder bore (CYL).**

INV. designates barrel is threaded for Browning Invector choke tube system.

INV. PLUS designates back-bored barrels.

Miroku manufactured A-5s can be determined by year of manufacture in the following manner: RV suffix - 1975, RT - 1976, RR - 1977, RP - 1978, RN - 1979, PM - 1980, PZ - 1981, PY - 1982, PX - 1983, PW - 1984, PV - 1985, PT - 1986, PR - 1987, PP - 1988, PN - 1989, NM - 1990, NZ - 1991, NY - 1992, NX - 1993, NW - 1994, NV - 1995, NT - 1996, NR - 1997, NP - 1998, ZY - 2012, ZX - 2013, ZW - 2014, ZV - 2015, ZT - 2016, ZR - 2017, ZP - 2018, ZN-2019, ZM-2020, YZ-2021, YY-2022.

Browning resumed importation from F.N. in 1946. On November 26, 1997, Browning announced that the venerable Auto-5 would finally be discontinued. Final shipments were made in February, 1998. Over 3 million A-5s were manufactured by Fabrique Nationale in all configurations between 1903-1976. 1976-1998 manufacture was by Miroku in Japan. The A-5 was reintroduced in 2012 with a Kinematic Drive System, aluminum receiver, and a fixed barrel.

NOTE: Barrels are interchangeable between older Belgian A-5 models and recent Japanese A-5s manufactured by Miroku, if the gauge and chamber length are the same. A different barrel ring design and thicker barrel wall design might necessitate some minor sanding of the inner forearm on the older model, but otherwise, these barrels are fully interchangeable.

NOTE: The use of steel shot is recommended ONLY in those recent models manufactured in Japan -

GRADING - PPGS™	100%	98%	95%	90%	80%	70%	60%	LAST MSR

NOT in the older Belgian variations.

The "humpback" design on the Auto-5 (both Belgian and Japanese mfg.) features recoil operation with a scroll engraved steel receiver. During 1909, Browning introduced the magazine cutoff, and moved the safety from inside to the front of the triggerguard. 1946-1951 mfg. has a safety in front of triggerguard. 1951-1976 mfg. has crossbolt safety behind the trigger. Post-war 16 ga. imports by Browning are chambered for 2 3/4 in., and have either a horn (disc. 1964) or plastic (1962-1976) buttplate, high luster wood finish (disc. 1962) or glossy lacquer (1962-1976) finish. Walnut buttstock has either round knob pistol grip (disc. 1967) or flat knob (new 1967). In today's Auto-5 marketplace, all gauges of the A-5 have become extremely collectible. Obviously, the Belgian A-5s are the most desirable. However, the pre-1998 Miroku guns are gaining in collectible popularity. It also has become very apparent that the demand for the FN lightweight 20 ga. has superceded the Sweet 16 due to availablilty. Both the lightweight 20 ga. and the Sweet 16 are the most desirable and have seen a dramatic increase in collectibility. Rarity of configurations such as choke designations, and barrel lengths are very important factors in determinging value. Older rare barrels such as the solid rib and the 16 and 20 ga. guns with shorter barrels and open chokes are more desirable than a 30 in. 12 ga. gun with full choke barrel.

In addition to the models listed below, Browning has also released SHOT Show specials on some models that were available by dealers ordering them at the SHOT Show only. Complete descriptions for these models can be found under SHOT SHOW SPECIALS - SHOTGUNS SEMI-AUTO at BlueBookOfGunValues.com/overflow.

Add 15% for NIB condition on Belgian mfg. Auto-5 models only, depending on desirability. Beware of reproduced boxes and labels, especially on the more desirable configurations.

Add 15% for the round knob (rounded pistol grip knob on stock, pre-1967 mfg.) variation on FN models only, depending on desirability.

Add $250-$500 per additional barrel, depending on the gauge, barrel length, choke, condition, and rarity (smaller gauge open chokes are the most desirable).

Add 20% for reddish stock and forearm configurations (Belgian mfg. - pre 1962).

Add 15% on FN models with blonde stock and forearm - mfg. mid-1960s.

AUTO-5 STANDARD - 1903-1940 MFG. – 12 ga. (introduced in Sept., 1903, Browning discontinued imports Dec., 1903), 16 ga. (introduced in 1909, but not in the U.S.), in 1923, Browning resumed importing both 12 and 16 ga. in four grades that differ in engraving, inlays, and grade of wood, both gauges were available with 26-32 in. barrel, recoil operated, 4 shot mag. with cutoff, various chokes, checkered pistol grip stock, horn buttplate, also available in a 3 shot version with shorter magazine tube to limit capacity to 3 rounds from 1932-1940. Importation temporarily ceased in 1940 with the German occupation of Belgium, ser. no. range 1-224,596 (12 ga.) and 1-126,175 (16 ga.). Mfg. in Herstal, Belgium 1903-1940.

Grade 1	$925	$825	$700	$575	$525	$475	$450
Solid matte rib	$1,175	$1,075	$975	$875	$775	$675	$625
With vent. rib	$1,075	$975	$875	$775	$665	$575	$525
Grade 2 (disc.1937)	$1,625	$1,375	$1,150	$1,025	$925	$850	$775
Solid matte rib	$2,150	$1,925	$1,625	$1,350	$1,125	$1,075	$725
With vent. rib	$2,050	$1,825	$1,525	$1,250	$1,025	$975	$875
Grade 3 (disc. 1940)	$3,050	$2,725	$2,425	$2,175	$1,825	$1,600	$1,325
Solid matte rib	$3,700	$3,250	$2,900	$2,625	$2,325	$2,025	$1,675
With vent. rib	$3,600	$3,150	$2,800	$2,525	$2,225	$1,925	$1,575
Grade 4 (disc. 1940)	$4,500	$4,050	$3,650	$3,300	$2,800	$2,300	$1,900
Solid matte rib	$5,250	$4,650	$4,450	$3,550	$3,150	$2,650	$2,450
Grade 4 w/vent. rib	$5,150	$4,550	$4,350	$3,450	$3,050	$2,550	$2,350

Add 100% for first year production (No. 1-10,000) with "Browning Automatic Arms Co." marking on barrel.

Subtract 25% for pre-WWII 16 ga. A-5s chambered for 2 9/16 in. shells.

Early models with safety mounted in front of trigger guard are not as desirable as there are potential safety problems inherent in the design.

Pre-WWII 16 ga. A-5s could be chambered for 2 9/16 in. shells. These shotguns are considerably less desirable than 16 ga. A-5s chambered for 2 3/4 in. modern shotshells. Since some guns have been modified to 2 3/4 in., careful inspection is advised before purchasing or shooting. The 2 9/16 chambered guns can be modified by the Browning Service Dept. to accept 2 3/4 in. shells if so desired.

GRADING - PPGS™	100%	98%	95%	90%	80%	70%	60%	LAST MSR

"AMERICAN BROWNING" AUTO-5 – 12, 16, or 20 ga., Remington-produced variation of the Browning Auto-5, very similar to the Remington Model 11, except with Browning logo, mag. cut-off, and different engraving, over 38,000 mfg. in 12 ga. (ser. no. range B5000- B43129), over 14,000 in 16 ga. (ser. no. range A5000-A19450), and 11,000 in 20 ga. (ser. no. range C5000- C16152), stocks have Remington style round knob pistol grip. Mfg. 1940-1947.

	$695	$575	$500	$450	$400	$375	$350	

Add 15% for 20 ga.

An easy way to identify this configuration is to look for the "A", "B", or "C" serial number prefix on the left side of receiver.

AUTO-5 STANDARDWEIGHT – 12 (disc. 1970) or 16 (disc. 1964) ga., 26-32 in. barrel, various chokes, checkered walnut stock and forearm, between 7 1/3-8 lbs. Browning resumed importation from F.N. in 1946.

Plain barrel	$1,150	$975	$800	$675	$600	$550	$500	
Matted rib (solid)	$1,450	$1,275	$1,100	$1,000	$900	$800	$700	
Vent. rib	$1,350	$1,175	$1,000	$900	$800	$700	$600	

Add 20% for 16 ga.
Subtract 20% for front safety.

Note: Watch for cracked forearms on all A-5 models (due to barrel recoil.)

Barrel addresses appeared as follows: circa 1930-1958 "St. Louis, M.O.", 1959-1968 "St. Louis, Missouri and Montreal P.Q.", 1969-1976 "Morgan, Utah and Montreal, P.Q." Barrels are serial numbered to the gun until 1953. Make sure barrel address date matches year of mfg. (see Serialization section).

AUTO-5 LIGHTWEIGHT (LIGHT 12 & LIGHT 20) – 12 (new 1947) or 20 (new 1958) ga., recoil operated, 26, 28, or 30 in. barrel, various chokes, gold plated trigger, checkered pistol grip round knob (disc. 1967) or flat knob (mfg. 1967-1976) stock, approx. 10 oz. lighter than Standard weight.

FN model	$1,300	$1,125	$925	$850	$750	$650	$550	
FN-vent. rib	$1,525	$1,350	$1,125	$1,050	$950	$850	$750	

Add 60% for 20 ga.
Add 15% for round knob NIB condition.
Add 15% for blonde stock and forearm (mfg. mid-1960s).
Add 20% for reddish stock and forearm configurations, Belgian mfg. pre-1962.
Subtract 30% for Cutts or Polychoke.

* ***Auto-5 Light 12 Miroku*** – 12 ga. only, 22, 26, 28, or 30 in. VR (became standard 1986) barrel with Invector choke system, approx. 8-8 1/2 lbs. Mfg. 1976-Feb. 1998.

	$1,050	$925	$775	$700	$625	$550	$500	*$840*

Subtract 10% without Invector chokes.

* ***Auto-5 Light 20 Miroku*** – 20 ga. only, 2 3/4 in. chamber, similar to original Belgian Light 20, VR, 22 (new 1995), 26, or 28 in. barrel, Invector chokes standard until 1993, Invector Plus choking became standard 1994, 6 lbs. 12 oz - 7 lbs. 2 oz. Mfg. 1987-1997.

	$1,350	$1,225	$975	$900	$825	$750	$650	*$840*

SUPER LIGHTWEIGHT AUTO-5 – 12, 16, and 20 ga . In 1958, FN introduced the 12 and 16 ga. Super lightweight Auto-5 . Mfg. of the 20 ga. began in 1969. Pre-1969 Super Lightweight models were mfg. with a light alloy trigger guard and mechanism parts designed for weight reduction (approx.10 oz. lighter than the Lightweight A-5). In 1969, to further reduce weight, FN mfg. these models with alloy receivers. The alloy receiver Auto-5 were of a gray or black matte textured finish. Prior to 1972, the Super Lightweight A-5 were prone to flaking of these textured finishes. Stock and forearm cracking issues were also prevalant. FN modified its mfg. process and resolved these issues in 1972.

Black matte	$2,175	$2,000	$1,725	$1,500	$1,300	$1,175	$1,050	
Gray matte	$2,200	$2,025	$1,750	$1,525	$1,325	$1,200	$1,075	
Pattern 1	$2,400	$2,225	$1,950	$1,725	$1,525	$1,400	$1,275	
Pattern 2	$2,625	$2,450	$2,175	$1,950	$1,750	$1,625	$1,500	
Pattern 3	$2,800	$2,625	$2,350	$2,125	$1,925	$1,800	$1,675	

Add 30% for 16 or 20 ga.
Add 15% for NIB condition.
Add $200 for vent rib models.
Add $300 for solid rib models.
Subtract 20% for 2 9/16 in.chamber.
Subtract 20% for pre 1969 mfg.
Beware of mismatched configurations.

GRADING - PPGS™	100%	98%	95%	90%	80%	70%	60%	LAST MSR

Three patterns of engraving exist. All engraved Super Lightweight A-5 have frosted receiver finishes and varnished wood. Engraving patterns are as follows: Pattern (Type) 1 -Leaf , Pattern 2 -Bouquet and leaf, Pattern 3-Ribbon and foliage. These patterned Super Lighweight Auto 5's command a premium.

AUTO-5 MAGNUM – 12 (new 1958) or 20 (new 1967) ga., 3 in. chamber, 26, 28, 30, or 32 in. barrels, various chokes, VR or etched, 8 1/2 - 9 lbs. Mfg. 1958-1976 by FN, 1976-Feb. 1998 by Miroku.

FN model	$1,150	$975	$800	$675	$600	$550	$500	
FN-vent. rib.	$1,350	$1,175	$1,000	$900	$800	$700	$600	

Add 50% for 20 ga.
Add 15% for round knob, NIB condition.
Add 15% for blonde stock and forearm (mfg. mid-1960s).
Add 20% for reddish stock and forearm configurations, Belgian mfg. pre-1962.

Between 1976-1985 approx. 2,000 Belgian 12 ga. A-5 Mags. were imported into the U.S. These late models can be differentiated by serialization - also, slight premiums may be asked.

* ***Auto-5 Mag. Miroku*** – 12 or 20 ga., VR barrel with Invector choke system until 1993, Invector Plus choking became standard 1994, 8 1/2 - 9 lbs. Disc. 1997.

$1,025	$900	$750	$675	$595	$525	$475	*$866*

Add 30% for 20 ga.
Subtract 10% without Invector chokes.

AUTO-5 STALKER – 12 ga. only, 2 3/4 (Light-12) or 3 (Mag. Stalker) in. chamber, 22 (Light-12 only), 26, 28, 30, or 32 (Mag. only) in. VR barrel with Invector chokes, black matte finish graphite-fiberglass stock and forearm, matte finished metal, recoil pad, 8 lbs. 1 oz. - 8 lbs. 13 oz. Mfg. by Miroku 1992-1997.

$975	$825	$675	$625	$550	$525	$450	*$840*

Add approx. $100 for Mag. Stalker.

AUTO-5 BUCK SPECIAL – 12, 16, or 20 ga., included Lightweight, Standardweight, and Magnum Models, 24 in. barrel, slug bore, adj. sight, optional sling studs and sling, between 1985-88, Buck Special barrels were available at additional cost. Introduced in 1962, mfg. by F.N. until 1976, and by Miroku from 1976-1984, and again in 1989.

* ***Auto-5 Buck Special FN Mfg. 12 Ga.***

$1,375	$1,200	$1,000	$925	$825	$725	$625

Add 75% for Sweet 16 model.
Add 60% for 20 ga.
Add 50% for Standard Weight 16 ga.

This model was made in Light 12, Standard 12, 3 in. Mag. 12, Sweet 16, Standard 16, Lightweight 20 and Lightweight 20 Mag. (new 1967) configurations.

* ***Auto-5 Buck Special Miroku Model*** – mfg. 1989-97.

$1,050	$925	$775	$700	$625	$575	$525	*$829*

AUTO-5 SKEET – 12, 16, or 20 ga., Lightweight models with 26 or 28 in. skeet bored, vent. rib barrel. Pre 1976 mfg. by F.N., 1976-1983 mfg. by Miroku.

* ***Auto-5 Skeet FN Mfg.***

$1,325	$1,150	$950	$875	$775	$675	$575

Add 20% for vent. rib.
Add 60% for 20 ga.

* ***Auto-5 Skeet Miroku Model***

$1,000	$895	$750	$675	$600	$550	$500

Add 30% for 20 ga.

AUTO-5 TRAP MODEL – 12 ga. only, similar to Standard, 30 in. full vent. rib barrel, 8 1/2 lbs., mfg. by FN until 1970.

$1,300	$1,125	$925	$850	$750	$650	$550

AUTO-5 SWEET 16 – 16 ga., 2 9/16 in. chamber from 1937-1940, and 2 3/4 in. chamber from 1947-1975, similar configuration to Lightweight, 12 and 20 ga., gold plated trigger, 10 oz. lighter than Standardweight Model 16 ga., 1937-1940 mfg. Sweet Sixteens were available in pre-war Grades I, III, and IV. Mfg. 1937-1975 by F.N.

Plain Barrel	$1,700	$1,400	$1,200	$1,100	$1,000	$875	$800
Solid Matte Rib	$2,500	$2,100	$1,625	$1,425	$1,275	$1,175	$1,075
Vent. Rib	$2,400	$2,000	$1,525	$1,325	$1,175	$1,075	$975

GRADING - PPGS™	100%	98%	95%	90%	80%	70%	60%	LAST MSR

Add 15% for round knob, NIB condition.
Add 15% for blonde stock and forearm (mfg. mid-1960s).
Add 20% for reddish stock and forearm configurations, Belgian mfg. pre-1962.
Subtract 20% for front safety.
Subtract 20% for 2 9/16 in. chamber.

* ***Auto-5 Sweet 16 Miroku*** – 16 ga. only, similar to original Belgian Sweet 16, VR, Invector choke standard. Mfg. 1987-92.

	100%	98%	95%	90%	80%	70%	60%	LAST MSR
	$1,625	$1,325	$1,175	$1,075	$975	$825	$750	*$720*

AUTO-5 TWO MILLIONTH COMMEMORATIVE – 12 ga., 2,500 mfg., 1971-74 mfg., special walnut, engraving, high-lustre bluing, cased with Browning book. Issue price was $550-$700, serial range 2,000,000-1 to 2,000,000-2,500.

	100%	98%	95%	90%	80%	70%	60%	LAST MSR
	$2,950	$2,250	$1,750	N/A	N/A	N/A	N/A	

Subtract 25%-40% for guns damaged from salt wood problems, depending on salt wood damage.

AUTO-5 POLICE CONTRACT – 12 ga. only, 5 or 8 (factory extended) shot mag., black enamel finish on receiver and barrel, can be recognized by the European "POL" police markings below serial number, 24 in. barrel. Imported in limited quantities during 1999.

	100%	98%	95%	90%	80%	70%	60%	LAST MSR
5 shot mag.	N/A	$700	$650	$625	$575	$525	$500	
8 shot mag.	N/A	$1,300	$1,095	$995	$895	$850	$750	

AUTO-5 CLASSIC SERIES – 12 ga., 5,000 mfg. in Classic model, 500 mfg. in Gold Classic. Both editions feature game scenes, John M. Browning's profile, and other inscriptions, special silver grey finished receiver. Introduced 1984.

* ***Auto-5 Gold Classic Model*** – features 4 gold inlays depicting duck hunting scenes, plus head silhouette of John Browning. 500 mfg. beginning 1986 with inventory depleted during 1989.

	100%	98%	95%	90%	80%	70%	60%	LAST MSR
	$9,950	$7,450	$5,200	N/A	N/A	N/A	N/A	*$6,500*

* ***Auto-5 Classic Model*** – no inlays. Factory inventories were depleted in 1987.

	100%	98%	95%	90%	80%	70%	60%	LAST MSR
	$2,950	$2,100	$1,850	N/A	N/A	N/A	N/A	*$1,260*

FN CENTENARY EDITION – 12 or 16 ga., limited production mfg. 1989 to commemorate the 100th anniversary of FN, available for worldwide FN sales and not limited to Browning.

* ***FN Centenary Edition 12 ga.*** – 2 3/4 in. chamber, 28 in. VR barrel, Mod. choke, more engraving than a standard A-5, gold relief FN logo on left side of receiver, high grade French walnut flat knob pistol grip stock, 20 LPI checkering, ser. no. CENT 211 001 - 100, 100 mfg.

	100%	98%	95%	90%	80%	70%	60%	LAST MSR
	$2,900	$2,200	$1,500	N/A	N/A	N/A	N/A	*$2,100*

* ***FN Centenary Edition 16 ga.*** – 2 3/4 in. chamber, 26 in. VR barrel, Mod. choke, ornate engraving with gold relief inlay (24Kt.), commemorative FN medallion on left side of receiver, high grade French walnut flat knob pistol grip stock, 25 LPI checkering, ser. no. CENT 221 001 - 010, 10 mfg.

	100%	98%	95%	90%	80%	70%	60%	LAST MSR
	$8,000	$6,250	$4,750	N/A	N/A	N/A	N/A	*$6,855*

AUTO-5 BCA COMMEMORATIVE – 12 ga., 3 in. Mag., round knob, Belgian mfg., 1984 issue price was $595.

	100%	98%	95%	90%	80%	70%	60%	LAST MSR
	$1,550	$1,275	$1,000	N/A	N/A	N/A	N/A	

AUTO-5 DU 50TH ANNIVERSARY

* ***Auto-5 DU Light 12*** – 12 ga. only, 5,500 mfg. in 1987 only for Ducks Unlimited chapters throughout North America.

	100%	98%	95%	90%	80%	70%	60%	LAST MSR
	$2,100	$1,700	$1,200	N/A	N/A	N/A	N/A	

* ***Auto-5 DU Sweet 16*** – 16 ga. only, companion 1988-89 DU auction gun, 4,500 mfg. 1988 only.

	100%	98%	95%	90%	80%	70%	60%	LAST MSR
	$2,450	$2,050	$1,350	N/A	N/A	N/A	N/A	

* ***Auto-5 DU Light 20*** – 20 ga. only, companion 1990 DU auction gun, 4,500 mfg. 1990 only.

	100%	98%	95%	90%	80%	70%	60%	LAST MSR
	$2,200	$1,800	$1,350	N/A	N/A	N/A	N/A	

AUTO-5 FINAL TRIBUTE – 12 ga. only, limited edition of 1,000 guns, features elaborate engraving on white receiver, the last of the A-5 semi-autos. Mfg. 1999 only, sellout occurred during 2000.

	100%	98%	95%	90%	80%	70%	60%	LAST MSR
	$3,200	$2,700	$2,300	N/A	N/A	N/A	N/A	*$1,330*

A5 CAMO – 12 ga., 3 or 3 1/2 in. chamber, 26, 28, or 30 (mfg. 2012-2019) in. VR barrel with 3 invector-DS choke tubes, fiber optic front and ivory mid-bead sights, composite pistol grip stock with textured gripping surfaces, shim adjustable for LOP, Dura-Touch Armor Coating, 1/4 and 1/2 in. stock spacers, Inflex recoil pad, lightweight aluminum alloy receiver with black anodized bi-tone finish, includes ABS

GRADING - PPGS™	100%	98%	95%	90%	80%	70%	60%	LAST MSR

case, 100% Mossy Oak Duck Blind (disc. 2012), Mossy Oak Break-Up Infinity (disc. 2014), Mossy Oak Shadow Grass Blades (mfg. 2013-2020), Mossy Oak Break-Up Country (new 2015), or Mossy Oak Shadow Grass Habitat (new 2021) camo coverage, approx. 7 1/4 lbs. New 2012.

MSR $1,720	$1,525	$1,315	$1,100	$995	$825	$700	$575	

Add $140 for 3 1/2 in. chamber (new 2014).

This model with 3 1/2 in. chamber was featured as a SHOT Show Special for 2013.

A5 HUNTER – 12 ga. only, 3 or 3 1/2 (new 2014) in. chamber, recoil operated humpback design with fixed barrel featuring Kinematic Drive System, aluminum receiver, bi-tone black anodized finish, 26, 28, or 30 (mfg. 2012-2019) in. VR barrel with 3 Invector-DS choke tubes, checkered gloss finish walnut stock with Inflex II recoil pad and forearm, speed loading/unloading, ergonomic bolt latch, includes extra stock spacers and ABS case, approx. 6 3/4 lbs. New 2012.

MSR $1,720	$1,525	$1,315	$1,100	$995	$825	$700	$575	

Add $140 for 3 1/2 in. chamber (new 2014).

This model with 3 1/2 in. chamber was featured as a SHOT Show Special for 2013.

A5 HUNTER HIGH GRADE – 12 ga., 3 in. chamber, recoil operated Kinematic Drive, 26 or 28 in. flat VR barrel with gloss blued finish, Vector Pro lengthened forcing cone, three Invector-DS choke tubes, gloss black aluminum alloy receiver has engraving pattern of pheasants on left side and mallards on the right surrounded by intricate scrollwork, fiber optic front and ivory mid-bead sight, Grade 2.5 varnish finished and checkered walnut stock with pistol grip, shim adj. for LOP, 1/4 and 1/2 in. stock spacers, Inflex recoil pad, includes ABS case, 6 lbs. 11 oz. New 2017.

MSR $1,960	$1,665	$1,455	$1,250	$1,125	$910	$750	$625	

A5 SWEET SIXTEEN – 16 ga., 2 3/4 in. chamber, 26 or 28 in. lightweight profile flat VR barrel, Vector Pro forcing cone, three Invector-DS choke tubes, fiber optic front and ivory mid-bead sights, gloss finished walnut checkered pistol grip stock, shim adjustable for LOP, 1/4 and 1/2 in. stock spacers, Inflex recoil pad, lightweight aluminum alloy black anodized bi-tone finished receiver, includes ABS case, 5 lbs. 12 oz. New 2016.

MSR $1,790	$1,525	$1,335	$1,145	$1,035	$840	$695	$595	

A5 STALKER – 12 ga., 3 or 3 1/2 in. chamber, 26, 28, or 30 (mfg. 2012-2019) in. VR barrel with three Invector-DS choke tubes, aluminum alloy receiver, fiber optic front and ivory mid-bead sight, Dura-Touch armor coated black composite stock and forearm with textured gripping surfaces, Inflex recoil pad, includes ABS case, matte black metal finish, approx. 7 1/4 lbs. New 2012.

MSR $1,590	$1,350	$1,180	$1,000	$910	$735	$600	$500	

Add $130 for 3 1/2 in. chamber (new 2014).

This model with 3 1/2 in. chamber was featured as a SHOT Show Special for 2013.

A5 ULTIMATE – 12 ga., 3 in. chamber, 26 or 28 in. vent. rib barrel, satin finished lightweight aluminum alloy receiver with etched pheasants on left and mallards on right surrounded by light scroll, blue finish, Grade III gloss oil finished checkered pistol grip walnut stock and forearm, Vector Pro lengthened forcing cone, three Invector-DS choke tubes, fiber optic front sight, Inflex II recoil pad, includes ABS case, 6 lbs. 12 oz. New mid-2013.

MSR $2,100	$1,785	$1,550	$1,324	$1,200	$950	$800	$650	

This model was featured as a 2013 SHOT Show Special.

A5 WICKED WING – 12 ga., 3 or 3 1/2 in. chamber, Kinematic Drive, 26, 28, or 30 (mfg. 2017-2019) in. flat VR barrel with chromed bore, Vector Pro lengthened forcing cone, three extended Invector-DS banded choke tubes, aluminum alloy receiver, fiber optic front and ivory mid-bead sight, composite stock with pistol grip and textured gripping surfaces, shim adjustable for LOP, DuraTouch Armor coating, 1/4 and 1/2 in. stock spacers, Inflex recoil pad, Briley extended bolt handle and oversize bolt release, includes ABS case, Cerakote Burnt Bronze finish on barrel and receiver, Mossy Oak Shadow Grass Blades camo finish on stock and forearm, approx. 7 1/2 lbs. Mfg. 2017-2020.

	$1,590	$1,390	$1,195	$1,080	$875	$715	$600	*$1,870*

Add $130 for 3 1/2 in. chamber.

* ***A5 Wicked Wing Mossy Oak Shadow Grass Habitat*** – 12 ga., 3 or 3 1/2 in. chamber, Kinematic Drive recoil operation, 26, 28, or 30 in. barrel with Cerakote Burnt Bronze finish, three extended Invector-DS Goose band choke tubes, gold plated trigger, fiber optic front and ivory mid-bead sight, pistol grip composite stock with textured gripping surfaces and Mossy Oak Shadow Grass Habitat camo finish, Inflex Technology recoil pad, oversized bolt release, includes ABS case, Cerakote Burnt Bronze camo finish on receiver, 7 lbs. 3 oz. New 2021.

MSR $2,000	$1,700	$1,490	$1,275	$1,150	$935	$775	$650	

Add $70 for 3 1/2 in. chamber.

GRADING - PPGS™	100%	98%	95%	90%	80%	70%	60%	LAST MSR

BROWNING SPECIAL AUTO-5 – 12 or 16 ga., 3 or 5 shot magazine tubes, solid rib or ventilated rib barrels, hand engraved full foliage Grade 2 patterned Auto 5, hand checkered and hand selected stock and forearm. Mfg. between 1934-1940 and post war between 1946-1947.

Solid Matte Rib	$2,250	$2,125	$1,825	$1,525	$1,225	$1,175	$875	
Vent Rib	$2,150	$2,025	$1,725	$1,425	$1,125	$1,075	$775	

Add 15% for NIB condition.

Add 40% for Sweet 16 models.

AUTO-5 THREE SHOT – 12 or 16 ga., and Sweet 16, features shorter magazine tube (holding only two shots), and 3 shot stamped on the forearm. Produced for federal regulations on migratory fowl. Mfg. between 1932-1940 (in all grades) and post war between 1946-1947 (by special order only in the Browning Special).

Grade I	$1,025	$925	$800	$675	$625	$575	$550	
Solid Matte Rib	$1,275	$1,175	$1,075	$875	$825	$775	$750	
Vent Rib	$1,175	$1,075	$975	$775	$725	$675	$650	

Add 15% for NIB condition.

Add 40% for Sweet 16 models.

Grade 2 values refer to the Browning Special Auto 5 section.

Grades 3 and 4 are extremely rare, scarcity precludes accurate pricing. Factory letters should be obtained before purchase.

SHOTGUNS: SEMI-AUTO, DOUBLE AUTO MODELS

Add 15% for NIB condition on the following models.

Double auto raised rib barrels are currently selling for $375-$450 if in excellent condition, VR barrels are selling for $325-$400 if in excellent condition.

STANDARD DOUBLE AUTO – 12 ga. only, 2 shot, 26, 28, or 30 in. barrel, various chokes, checkered pistol grip stock and forearm, blued steel receiver, approx. 7 1/2 lbs. Mfg. 1952-1960.

	$1,050	$900	$700	$600	$450	$400	$375	
w/Vent. or Raised Rib	$1,350	$1,150	$900	$800	$700	$650	$500	

LIGHTWEIGHT DOUBLE AUTO – similar to Standard Model, except has hiduminum (aircraft alloy) frame, anodized in velvet grey, dragon black, autumn brown, or forest green, approx. 6 3/4 lbs. Approx. 67,000 (all variations) mfg. 1952-1956.

	$1,225	$1,100	$850	$700	$600	$550	$500	
w/Vent. or Raised Rib	$1,550	$1,425	$1,150	$1,000	$900	$850	$750	

Add 50% for autumn brown or forest green receiver.

Add 150%+ for all other colors (rare, only a few mfg.).

TWELVETTE DOUBLE AUTO – similar to Lightweight model, except has "Twelvette" stamped above loading port. Mfg. 1957-1971.

	$1,225	$1,100	$850	$700	$600	$550	$500	
w/Vent. or Raised Rib	$1,600	$1,425	$1,150	$1,000	$900	$850	$750	

Add 50% for autumn brown or forest green receiver.

Add 150%+ for all other colors (rare, only a few mfg.).

TWENTYWEIGHT DOUBLE AUTO – similar to Twelvette, but 3/4 pound lighter, jet black finish with engraving accented with gold foil, "Twentyweight" stamped above loading port, 26 1/2 in. barrel only. Mfg. 1957-1971.

	$1,325	$1,100	$850	$700	$600	$550	$500	
w/Vent. Rib	$1,650	$1,475	$1,200	$1,000	$900	$850	$750	

SHOTGUNS: SEMI-AUTO, MISC. - CURRENT / RECENT MFG.

BROWNING CHOKES AND THEIR CODES (ON REAR LEFT-SIDE OF BARREL)

* designates full choke (F).

*- designates improved modified choke (IM).

** designates modified choke (M).

**- designates improved cylinder choke (IC).

**$ designates skeet (SK).

*** designates cylinder bore (CYL).

In addition to the models listed below, Browning has also released SHOT Show specials on some models that were available by dealers ordering them at the SHOT Show only. Complete descriptions for these models can be found under SHOT SHOW SPECIALS - SHOTGUNS: SEMI-AUTO at BlueBookOfGunValues.com/overflow.

Add $195-$375 per additional barrel, depending on the condition and configuration.

GRADING - PPGS™	100%	98%	95%	90%	80%	70%	60%	LAST MSR

B/2000 STANDARD – 12 or 20 ga. (new 1975), 2 3/4 in. chamber, 26, 28, or 30 in. VR barrel, various chokes, gas operated, checkered pistol grip stock, Belgian manufactured but assembled in Portugal, approx. 115,000 imported (approx. 95,000 in 12 ga., and 20,000 in 20 ga.) into the U.S. between 1974-1983.

	$495	$425	$375	$350	$325	$300	$275	*$475*

Add 20% for 20 ga.

This model could be converted to accept 3 in. Mag. shotshells by simply installing a barrel chambered for 3 in. shells. Even though production on this model ceased in 1979, assembly and sales were not discontinued until 1983.

B/2000 MAGNUM – similar to B/2000 Auto Shotgun, except with 3 in. chambered barrel (all receivers were the same), recoil pad, vent. rib.

	$495	$425	$375	$350	$325	$300	$275	

B/2000 SKEET – similar to Standard, with 26 in. skeet bored barrel, floating vent. rib, skeet stock, pad.

	$450	$395	$350	$325	$300	$275	$250	

B/2000 TRAP – similar to Standard, with 30 or 32 in. barrel bored F or IM, floating rib, Monte Carlo trap stock.

	$450	$395	$350	$325	$300	$275	$250	

B/2000 BUCK SPECIAL – 12 or 20 ga., rifle sights on 24 in. barrel.

	$450	$395	$350	$325	$300	$275	$250	

1976 CANADIAN OLYMPICS B2000 – 12 ga., 100 manufactured in 1976 for Canadian sales only, high polish blue with multiple gold inlays including Olympic crest, 30 in. barrel, cased. Issue price was $1,295.

	$1,495	$1,095	$850	N/A	N/A	N/A	N/A	

MODEL B-80 – 12 or 20 ga., offers 2 3/4 or 3 in. capability by changing barrel, gas operation, 4 shot, hunting models use choice of steel or aluminum receiver, anodized aluminum was used in the Superlight (12 ga. mfg. 1984 only), 6 to 8 lbs. 1 oz. Buck special disc. 1984. Components manufactured by Beretta of Italy and finished and assembled at FN's plant in Portugal. Mfg. 1981-late 1988, final inventory was sold in 1991. Invector chokes became standard in 1985.

	$450	$375	$325	$295	$275	$250	$230	*$562*

Add 10% for Invector chokes.

Steel frames were reintroduced into production again in 1988.

* ***Model B-80 Upland Special*** – 12 or 20 ga., 2 3/4 in. chamber, 22 in. vent. rib barrel, straight grip stock, Invector chokes. Mfg. 1986-88.

	$525	$450	$395	$350	$325	$300	$275	*$562*

MODEL B 80 DU COMMEMORATIVE – mfg. for American DU Chapters (The Plains and others), price fluctuates greatly as collector support is sometimes limited. Unless new, this model's values approximate those of the regular Model B-80. If NIB, values recently have been in the $795-$995 range.

A-500 (R) HUNTING – 12 ga. only, 3 in. chamber, new design utilizing short recoil system with a four-lug rotary bolt design, capable of shooting all 12 gauge loads interchangeably, magazine cut-off, 26, 28, or 30 in. VR barrel with Invector chokes standard, 24 in. barrel on Buck Special (fixed choke), high polished blue finish with red accents on receiver sides, gold trigger, checkered semi-pistol grip walnut stock with vent. recoil pad, 7 lbs. 11 oz. - 8 lbs. 1 oz. Mfg. 1987-1993.

	$525	$450	$395	$350	$325	$300	$275	*$560*

Add $33 for Buck Special variation (Invector chokes).

This model features fewer moving parts than many other semi-auto shotguns due to the short recoil operating system. From 1987-90, this model was the Model A-500 - R suffix was added in 1991.

A-500G HUNTING – similar to A-500, except is gas operated, distinguishable by "A-500G" in gold accents on receiver, capable of shooting all 2 3/4 or 3 in. shells interchangeably, approx. 8 lbs. Mfg. 1990-93.

	$575	$495	$425	$375	$340	$325	$295	*$653*

A Buck Special variation was mfg. until 1992. No premiums currently exist.

* ***A-500G Sporting Clays*** – 12 ga. only, Sporting Clays variation with 30 in. VR barrel, 8 lbs. 2 oz. Mfg. 1992-93.

	$575	$495	$425	$375	$340	$325	$295	*$653*

GRADING - PPGS™	100%	98%	95%	90%	80%	70%	60%	LAST MSR

GOLD 3 IN. HUNTER – 12 or 20 ga., 3 in. chamber, self-cleaning piston rod gas action with self-regulation, alloy receiver with non-glare black finish and "Gold Hunter" on receiver side, 26, 28, or 30 (12 ga. only, disc. 2001) in. VR Invector Plus (12 ga. only) or Invector (20 ga. only) choked barrel with high polish bluing, crossbolt safety, gloss finish checkered walnut stock and forearm with recoil pad (vent on 12 ga.), includes 3 choke tubes, 6 lbs. 12 oz.-7 lbs. 10 oz. Parts mfg. in Belgium and final assembly in Portugal. Mfg. 1994-2005.

$825 $575 $450 $375 $300 $275 $250 *$1,025*

Do not use 12 ga. 3 1/2 in. chambered barrels on either a 2 3/4 or 3 in. receiver, or vice versa.

* ***Gold Superlite Hunter*** – 12 or 20 ga., similar to Gold 3 in. Hunter, except has new alloy magazine, "Gold SL" on receiver sides, 6 lbs. 7 oz.-7 lbs., 15 oz. Mfg. 2006-2008.

$975 $750 $535 $425 $325 $275 $250 *$1,161*

GOLD 3 1/2 IN. HUNTER – 12 ga., 3 1/2 in. chamber, 24 (mfg. 2002-2003), 26, 28, or 30 (disc. 2003) in. VR barrel with Invector Plus choking, otherwise similar to Gold Hunter, 3-4 shot mag., approx. 7 3/4 lbs. Mfg. 1998-2005.

$985 $725 $600 $550 $450 $375 $335 *$1,190*

* ***Gold 3 1/2 In. Superlite Hunter*** – 12 ga., similar to Gold 3 1/2 in. Hunter, except has new alloy magazine, "Gold SL" engraved on receiver sides, approx. 7 1/4 lbs. Mfg. 2006-2007.

$1,075 $900 $700 $525 $425 $350 $300 *$1,279*

* ***Gold 3 1/2 In. Turkey/Waterfowl Hunter*** – similar to Gold 3 1/2 in. Hunter, full coverage (including barrel) Mossy Oak Break-Up camo finish, 24 in. VR barrel with extra full choke tube, 7 1/4 lbs. Mfg. 1999-2000.

$875 $695 $600 $500 $425 $375 $335 *$1,038*

* ***Gold 3 1/2 In. NWTF Mossy Oak Break-Up*** – 12 ga. only, 3 1/2 in. chamber, 24 in. VR barrel with 4 choke tubes and Hi-Viz sight, full coverage Mossy Oak Break-Up camo pattern, Dura-Touch armor coating became standard 2003, 7 1/4 lbs. Mfg. 2001-2002.

$875 $695 $600 $525 $450 $385 $335 *$1,221*

* ***Gold 3 1/2 In. Mossy Oak New Break-Up/New Shadow Grass*** – similar to Gold 3 1/2 in. Hunter, choice of full coverage (including barrel) Mossy Oak Break-Up, New Break-Up (standard beginning 2004) or Shadow Grass camo finish, 24 (Mossy Oak Break-Up only, disc. 2001), 26 (Mossy Oak Shadow Grass only), or 28 (Mossy Oak Shadow Grass only) in. VR back-bored barrel with Invector Plus choke tubes, Dura-Touch armor coating became standard 2003, approx. 7 1/2 lbs. Mfg. 1999-2007.

$900 $750 $650 $600 $500 $400 $350 *$1,359*

* ***Gold 3 1/2 In. Mossy Oak Duck Blind*** – 12 ga. only, similar to Gold Mossy Oak New Break-Up, except has Mossy Oak Duck Blind camo coverage. Mfg. 2007.

$900 $750 $650 $600 $500 $400 $350 *$1,359*

* ***Gold 3 1/2 In. NWTF Ultimate Turkey Gun*** – 12 ga. only, similar to Gold NWTF Mossy Oak New Break-Up, except has extended full strut turkey choke tube and neoprene sling, 7 1/4 lbs. Mfg. 2003-2007.

$1,100 $900 $725 $675 $600 $500 $450 *$1,469*

GOLD FIELD HUNTER (CLASSIC) – similar to Gold Hunter, except has semi-hump back receiver design, magazine cutoff, adj. comb, and satin finished wood, 26 or 28 in. VR barrel. Mfg. 1999-2005.

$800 $575 $450 $375 $300 $275 $250 *$1,025*

This model was available through Full-line and Medallion dealers only.

* ***Gold Superlite Field Hunter*** – 12 or 20 ga., similar to Gold 3 in. Superlite Hunter, except is semi-humpback design, approx. 6 1/2 - 7 lbs. Mfg. 2006-2007.

$1,025 $725 $525 $400 $300 $275 $250 *$1,105*

* ***Gold Turkey/Waterfowl Hunter Camo*** – similar to Gold Hunter, full coverage (including barrel) Mossy Oak Break-Up camo finish, 24 in. VR barrel with Hi-Viz sights and extra full choke tube, 7 lbs. Mfg. 1999-2000.

$750 $500 $400 $350 $295 $275 $250 *$867*

* ***Gold Mossy Oak New Break-Up/Shadow Grass*** – 12 ga., similar to Gold 3 in. Hunter, choice of full coverage (including barrel) Mossy Oak New Break-Up or New Shadow Grass camo finish (New became standard in 2004), 24 (Mossy Oak Break-Up only, disc. 2004), 26, or 28 in. VR back-bored barrel with Invector Plus choke tubes, Dura-Touch armor coating became standard 2003, approx. 7 1/2 - 7 3/4 lbs. Mfg. 1999-2007.

$850 $700 $525 $450 $325 $285 $250 *$1,150*

* ***Gold Mossy Oak Duck Blind*** – 12 ga. only, similar to Gold Mossy Oak New Break-Up, except has Mossy Oak Duck Blind camo coverage. Mfg. 2007.

$850 $700 $525 $450 $325 $285 $250 *$1,150*

GRADING - PPGS™	100%	98%	95%	90%	80%	70%	60%	LAST MSR

* ***Gold NWTF Mossy Oak New Break-Up*** – 12 ga. only, 3 in. chamber, drilled and tapped receiver, 24 in. VR barrel with 4 choke tubes and Hi-Viz sight, full coverage Mossy Oak New Break-up camo pattern, Dura-Touch armor coating became standard 2003, 7 lbs. Mfg. 2001-2007.

	$850	$700	$575	$450	$375	$300	$250	*$1,226*

* ***Gold Classic High Grade Hunter*** – 12 (disc. 2001) or 20 ga. (new 2002), similar to Gold Classic Hunter, except has satin nickel finished receiver featuring multiple gold inlays with ducks, pheasants, and dogs (12 ga.) or doves and quail (20 ga.) and light scroll engraving, deluxe checkered gloss finished walnut stock and forearm, 28 in. barrel only, 6 lbs. 14 oz. Mfg. 1999-2004.

	$1,575	$1,250	$1,050	$875	$725	$625	$550	*$1,838*

This model was available through Full-line and Medallion dealers only.

GOLD MICRO – 20 ga. only, 3 in. chamber, 24 (new 2002) or 26 in. VR barrel, features shorter stock (13 7/8 LOP) and lighter weight, 6 lbs., 10 oz. Mfg. 2001-2005.

	$775	$575	$450	$375	$300	$275	$250	*$1,025*

* ***Gold Superlite Micro*** – 20 ga. only, 3 in. chamber, 26 in. VR barrel, features shorter stock (13 7/8 LOP) and lighter weight, 6 lbs., 3 oz. Mfg. 2006-2007.

	$850	$650	$525	$400	$300	$275	$250	*$1,105*

GOLD UPLAND SPECIAL – 12 or 20 ga., 3 in. chamber, 24 or 26 (20 ga. only) in. VR barrel, checkered satin finished straight grip stock, 6 3/4 (20 ga.) or 7 lbs. Mfg. 2001-2005.

	$775	$575	$450	$375	$300	$275	$250	*$1,025*

GOLD FUSION – 12 or 20 (new 2002) ga., 3 in. chamber, 26, 28, or 30 (12 ga. only, new 2002) in. wide profile lightweight VR barrel with 5 Invector Plus chokes and Hi-Viz Pro-Comp sight system, checkered oil finished Turkish walnut stock and forearm, shim adj. stock system, alloy mag. tube, includes hardshell case, 6.25 - 7 lbs. Mfg. 2001-2007.

	$900	$650	$550	$400	$350	$295	$260	*$1,152*

* ***Gold Fusion High Grade*** – 12 or 20 ga., 3 in. chamber, silver nitride receiver with engraving and gold inlays (mallards and lab on 12 ga., quail and pointer on 20 ga.), 26, 28, or 30 in. barrel with five interchangeable Invector Plus chokes, high grade Turkish walnut stock and forearm, shim adj. stock system with 1/4 in. adj. range, Hi-Viz TriComp sight system, includes hard case, 6 lbs., 6 oz. - 7 lbs. Mfg. 2005-2007.

	$1,825	$1,300	$1,125	$950	$850	$725	$625	*$2,137*

GOLD EVOLVE – 12 ga. only, 3 in. chamber, features updated engraved receiver, magazine cap, and canted VR design, 26, 28, or 30 in. barrel, includes shim adj. stock system, newly designed checkered satin finished walnut stock and forearm, alloy mag. tube, Hi-Viz Pro-Comp sight system, approx. 7 lbs. Mfg. 2004-2007.

	$900	$650	$525	$425	$335	$285	$250	*$1,220*

* ***Gold Evolve Sporting*** – 12 ga. only, similar to Gold Evolve, except has 2 3/4 in. chamber, 28 or 30 in. ported barrel, gold receiver accents, includes case, approx. 7 lbs. Mfg. 2006-2007.

	$950	$700	$550	$450	$350	$300	$250	*$1,287*

Subtract 10% for 28 in. barrel on used guns.

GOLD DEER HUNTER – 12 or 20 (new 2001) ga., 3 in. chamber, 22 in. barrel with choice of 5 in. rifled Invector choke (disc. 1998) or rifled plain barrel, checkered satin finished stock and forearm, cantilevered scope mount, sling swivels, 6 3/4 (20 ga.) or 7 3/4 lbs. Mfg. 1997-2007.

	$900	$650	$525	$400	$325	$285	$250	*$1,154*

Subtract approx. 10% for rifled choke tube (disc. 1998).

* ***Gold Deer Hunter with Mossy Oak Break-Up Camo*** – 12 ga., similar to Gold Deer Hunter, except has full Mossy Oak Break-Up or New Break-Up (standard 2004) camo coverage, rifled barrel standard. Mfg. 1999-2007.

	$950	$750	$625	$550	$450	$365	$335	*$1,242*

GOLD 3 IN. STALKER – 12 ga., similar to Gold Hunter (3 in. chamber), except has checkered black composite stock and forearm with sling swivels, approx. 7 3/8 lbs. Mfg. 1998-2007.

	$800	$625	$475	$375	$300	$275	$250	*$1,001*

* ***Gold 3 In. Stalker Field (Classic)*** – similar to Gold Stalker, except has semi-hump back receiver design, magazine cutoff and adj. comb, 26 or 28 in. VR barrel. Mfg. 1999-2007.

	$800	$625	$475	$375	$300	$275	$250	*$1,001*

This model was available through Full-line and Medallion dealers only.

GRADING - PPGS™	100%	98%	95%	90%	80%	70%	60%	LAST MSR

* ***Gold 3 In. Turkey/Waterfowl Stalker*** – similar to Gold Stalker, except has 24 in. VR barrel with extra full choke tube, Hi-Viz sights, matte non-glare wood and finish, 7 lbs. Mfg. 1999-2000.

	$650	$500	$400	$350	$300	$275	$250	*$850*

* ***Gold 3 In. NWTF Stalker*** – 12 ga. only, 3 in. chamber, 24 in. VR barrel with 3 choke tubes and Hi-Viz sight, 7 lbs. Mfg. 2001-2002.

	$635	$475	$415	$350	$300	$275	$250	*$744*

* ***Gold 3 In. Rifled Deer Stalker*** – 12 ga. only, 22 in. rifled barrel, cantilevered scope mount, sling swivels, 7 3/4 lbs. Mfg. 1997-2007.

	$850	$625	$475	$400	$340	$300	$265	*$1,108*

GOLD 3 1/2 IN. STALKER – 12 ga., 3 1/2 in. chamber, 26, 28, or 30 (disc. 2002) in. VR barrel with Invector Plus choking, otherwise similar to Gold Stalker, 3-4 shot mag., approx. 7 lbs. 10 oz. Mfg. 1998-2007.

	$985	$725	$625	$525	$425	$375	$335	*$1,171*

* ***Gold 3 1/2 In. Turkey/Waterfowl Stalker*** – similar to Gold 3 1/2 Stalker, except has 24 in. VR barrel with extra full choke tube, matte non-glare wood and finish, 7 1/4 lbs. Mfg. 1999-2000.

	$800	$650	$595	$500	$420	$375	$335	*$1,022*

GOLD SPORTING CLAYS – 12 ga. only, similar specs as the Gold Hunter, except has 2 3/4 in. chamber, 28 or 30 in. ported barrel with Invector Plus choking, gloss finished walnut stock and forearm, adj. stock shims, Hi-Viz front sight, approx. 7 3/4 lbs. Mfg. 1996-2008.

	$1,000	$850	$700	$600	$500	$400	$350	*$1,184*

This model was supplied standard with 2 interchangeable gas pistons for light or heavy loads.

* ***Gold Golden Clays*** – 12 ga. only, 2 3/4 in. chamber, engraved coin finished alloy receiver with gold accents and game birds, new scroll motif was introduced during 2005, deluxe satin finished checkered walnut stock and forearm, 28 or 30 in. VR ported barrel with Hi-Viz Tri-Comp front sight and mid-bead, approx. 7 3/4 lbs. Mfg. 1999-2008.

	$1,650	$1,225	$950	$850	$750	$650	$550	*$1,941*

Subtract approx. 10% if with older engraving motif (non-scroll, disc. 2004).

* ***Gold Sporting Ladies/Youth*** – similar to Gold Sporting Clays, except has shorter 13 1/2 in. LOP stock, 28 in. barrel only, approx. 7 1/2 lbs. Mfg. 1999-2008.

	$1,000	$850	$700	$600	$500	$400	$350	*$1,184*

» **Gold Golden Clays Ladies/Youth** – similar to Gold Sporting Ladies/Youth, except features coin finished receiver with "golden clays" rose motif and gold enhancements, satin finished select walnut stock and forearm. Mfg. 2005-2007.

	$1,575	$1,175	$925	$850	$750	$650	$550	*$1,848*

GOLD NRA SPORTING – 12 ga. only, 2 3/4 in. chamber, similar to Gold Sporting Clays, except has NRA logo/banner on left side of receiver, approx. 7 3/4 lbs. Mfg. 2006-2007.

	$950	$800	$650	$550	$450	$400	$350	*$1,160*

This model was supplied standard with 2 interchangeable gas pistons for light or heavy loads.

BSA 10 – while advertised, this gun had its model nomenclature changed to the Gold 10 Ga. before mfg. started.

GOLD LIGHT 10 GA. 3 1/2 IN. (HUNTER/STALKER) – 10 ga. Mag., 3 1/2 in. chamber, short stroke self-cleaning gas action, 4 shot mag., steel (disc. 2000) or aluminum (new 2001) receiver, choice of high polish (Hunter Model, disc. 2000), dull finish (Stalker Model, disc. 1999, reintroduced 2000) bluing, 24 (NWTF Model only with Break-Up, new 2001), 26, 28, or 30 (disc. 2001) in. VR Standard Invector choke barrel, available with either high-gloss checkered walnut (Hunter, disc. 2002) stock/forearm, matte black fiberglass (Stalker, disc. 1998, reintroduced 2000-2003) stock/forearm, or choice of 100% camo treatment in Shadow Grass (disc. 2003), Break-Up (mfg. 2001-2003), New Shadow Grass (mfg. 2005-2008), Mossy Oak Duck Blind (mfg. 2007-disc.), New Break-Up (mfg. 2004-2009), Break-Up Infinity (mfg. 2010-disc.), Mossy Oak Shadow Grass Blades, or Mossy Oak Break-Up Country (mfg. 2015-2019), vent. recoil pad, Dura-Touch armor coating became standard for camo finishes during 2003, approx. 9 1/2 lbs. (aluminum receiver) or 10 lbs. 10 oz. (steel receiver, disc. 2000), mfg. by Miroku, Japan 1994-2020.

	$1,585	$1,380	$1,180	$1,075	$875	$725	$600	*$1,860*

Add $120 for NWTF model with camo finish (disc. 2019).
Add 10% for extra 24 in. turkey barrel.
Subtract approx. 10% for matte black fiberglass stock and forearm.
Subtract 15% for steel receiver.

During 1999-2001, this model was packaged to include an extra 24 in. turkey barrel.

GRADING - PPGS™	100%	98%	95%	90%	80%	70%	60%	LAST MSR

GOLD LIGHT 10 CAMO – 10 ga., 3 1/2 in. chamber, 26 or 28 in. barrel, standard Invector interchangeable choke tube system, silver bead front sight, composite stock with textured gripping surfaces, 100% Mossy Oak Shadow Grass Habitat or Mossy Oak Break-Up Country camo finish, 9.9-9.10 lbs. New 2021.

MSR $1,860	$1,585	$1,380	$1,180	$1,075	$875	$725	$600	

MAXUS ALL PURPOSE – 12 ga., 3 1/2 in. chamber, Power Drive gas system, Vector Pro forcing cone, aluminum alloy receiver, 26 in. barrel with 4 Invector Plus chokes, 4 shot mag., gold Lightning trigger, synthetic pistol grip stock and speed lock forearm, recoil pad, Dura-touch Mossy Oak Break-up Infinity camo finish, 7.9 lbs. Mfg. 2014 only.

	$1,425	$1,250	$1,075	$975	$785	$650	$500	*$1,679*

MAXUS ALL PURPOSE HUNTER – 12 ga., 3 1/2 in. chamber, Power Drive gas system, aluminum alloy receiver, 26 in. VR barrel with 4 Invector Plus flush chokes, 4 shot tubular mag., gold-plated trigger, Hi-Viz magnetic combo front sights, integral sling swivel studs, composite stock, textured grip panels, Inflex 1 recoil pad with hard heel insert, 100% Dura-touch Mossy Oak Break-up Country camo finish, 7 lbs. Mfg. mid-2015-2020.

	$1,550	$1,325	$1,135	$1,025	$835	$685	$575	*$1,780*

MAXUS CAMO – 12 ga., 3 (mfg. 2009-2019) or 3 1/2 in. chamber, gas operated, 26 or 28 in. VR barrel with three Invector Plus choke tubes, Vector Pro lengthened forcing cone, turnkey magazine plug, aluminum alloy receiver, fiber optic front and ivory mid-bead sight, composite pistol grip stock with textured gripping surfaces, Speek Lock forearm, shim adj., 1/4 in. stock spacer, Dura-Touch Armor coating, Inflex recoil pad, 100% Mossy Oak Duck Blind (disc. 2012) or Mossy Oak Shadow Grass Blades (new 2013) camo finish, 7 lbs. Mfg. 2009-2020.

	$1,450	$1,275	$1,095	$985	$800	$650	$550	*$1,700*

Subtract approx. $140 for 3 in. chamber (mfg. 2009-2019).

MAXUS HUNTER – 12 ga., 3 or 3 1/2 in. chamber, 26, 28, or 30 in. VR barrel with Vector Pro lengthened forcing cone, three Invector Plus choke tubes, satin nickel finished aluminum alloy receiver with laser engraved duck and pheasant, brass front bead sight, ivory mid-bead sight, gloss finished Grade I checkered walnut stock with close radius pistol grip, Speed Lock forearm, Inflex Technology recoil pad, includes shims and spacers, approx. 7 lbs. Mfg. mid-2010-2020.

	$1,350	$1,180	$1,000	$910	$735	$600	$500	*$1,590*

Add $150 for 3 1/2 in. chamber.

This model was also featured as a 2013 SHOT Show Special with Grade II/III Maple stock. MSR was $1,600.

MAXUS RIFLED DEER CAMO – 12 ga., 3 in. chamber, 22 in. fully rifled barrel with cantilever sight base and w/o sights, 100% Mossy Oak Break-Up Infinity (disc. 2014) or Mossy Oak Break-Up Country (new 2015) camo coverage, includes extra shims and spacer, approx. 7 1/4 lbs. Mfg. 2011-2017.

	$1,395	$1,225	$1,050	$950	$775	$625	$525	*$1,640*

MAXUS RIFLED DEER STALKER – 12 ga., 3 in. chamber, 22 in. fully rifled barrel with cantilever sight base and no sights, black composite pistol grip stock and speed lock forearm, textured gripping surfaces, 1/4 in. stock spacer for LOP adjustment, black metal finish, approx. 7 1/4 lbs. Mfg. 2011-2017.

	$1,300	$1,150	$975	$885	$715	$600	$500	*$1,520*

MAXUS SPORTING – 12 ga., 3 in. chamber, 28 or 30 in. VR barrel with Vector Pro lengthened forcing cone, includes 5 Invector Plus choke tubes, aluminum alloy receiver with satin nickel finish and full coverage engraving featuring game birds transforming into a clay target, HiViz TriComp fiber optic front and ivory mid-bead sight, gloss varnish finished high grade checkered walnut stock with close radius pistol grip, Speed Lock forearm, Inflex Technology recoil pad, shim adjustable for LOP, two 1/4 in. stock spacers, includes ABS case, approx. 7 lbs. Mfg. 2011-2020.

	$1,595	$1,335	$1,145	$1,035	$835	$685	$575	*$1,800*

MAXUS SPORTING CARBON FIBER – 12 ga., 3 in. chamber, Power Drive Gas System, 28 or 30 in. flat VR carbon fiber barrel, Vector Pro lengthened forcing cone, five Invector Plus choke tubes, lightweight aluminum alloy receiver with carbon fiber finish, HiViz TriComp fiber optic front and ivory mid-bead sights, matte black composite pistol grip stock with Speed Lock forearm, textured gripping surfaces, Dura-Touch Armor coating, Inflex recoil pad, two 1/4 in. stock spacers, includes ABS case, approx. 7 lbs. Mfg. mid-2010-2020.

	$1,350	$1,180	$1,000	$910	$735	$600	$500	*$1,590*

This model was originally featured as a 2010 SHOT Show Special.

GRADING - PPGS™	100%	98%	95%	90%	80%	70%	60%	LAST MSR

MAXUS SPORTING GOLDEN CLAYS – 12 ga., 3 in. chamber, Power Drive gas system, 26 (disc. 2014), 28, or 30 in. VR barrel with Vector Pro lengthened forcing cone, five Invector Plus choke tubes, satin nickel finished aluminum alloy receiver with gold enhanced game birds transforming into a clay target on receiver sides, HiViz TriComp fiber optic front sight and ivory mid-bead, gloss varnish finished Grade III checkered walnut stock with pistol grip, Speed Lock forearm, Mfg. 2013-2020.

	$1,785	$1,550	$1,324	$1,200	$950	$800	$650	*$2,100*

This model was also featured as a 2012 SHOT Show Special.

MAXUS STALKER – 12 ga., 3 or 3 1/2 in. chamber, gas operated with new Power Drive gas system, 26 or 28 in. VR barrel with Vector Pro lengthened forcing cone (became standard 2010), three Invector Plus choke tubes, turnkey magazine plug, aluminum alloy receiver, fiber optic front sight and ivory mid-bead, matte black composite pistol grip stock with Speed Lock forearm, textured gripping surfaces, shim adj., includes one 1/4 in. stock spacer, Dura-Touch Armor coating, Inflex recoil pad, approx. 6 lbs. 15 oz. Mfg. 2009-2020.

	$1,190	$1,050	$900	$815	$675	$550	$450	*$1,400*

Add $190 for 3 1/2 in. chamber.

MAXUS ULTIMATE – 12 ga., 3 in. chamber, gas operated, 26, 28, or 30 in. flat VR barrel with three Invector Plus choke tubes, Vector Pro lengthened forcing cone, magazine cutoff, satin nickel finished aluminum alloy receiver featuring laser engraved pheasant on right side, and mallard on left, brass front bead sight, checkered gloss oil finish Grade III walnut stock, Speed Lock forearm, Inflex Technology recoil pad, shim adj., two 1/4 in. stock spacers, engine turned bolt, includes hardshell ABS case, approx. 7 1/4 lbs. Mfg. 2013-2020.

	$1,725	$1,475	$1,265	$1,150	$925	$750	$650	*$1,980*

This model was also featured as a 2012 SHOT Show Special.

MAXUS WICKED WING – 12 ga., 3 or 3 1/2 in. chamber, Power Drive Gas System, 26 or 28 in. flat, fully chromed VR barrel, Vector Pro lengthened forcing cone, three extended Invector-Plus choke tubes, aluminum alloy receiver, fiber optic front and ivory mid-bead sight, composite stock with pistol grip and textured gripping surfaces, Speed Lock forearm, shim adjustable for LOP, 1/4 in. stock spacer, DuraTouch Armor coating, Inflex recoil pad, Briley extended bolt handle and oversize bolt release, Cerakote Burnt Bronze finish on receiver and barrel, Mossy Oak Shadow Grass Blades camo finish on stock and forearm, 7 lbs. 2 oz. Mfg. 2017-2020.

	$1,495	$1,200	$1,100	$1,000	$800	$675	$525	*$1,780*

Add $120 for 3 1/2 in. chamber.

MAXUS II CAMO – 12 ga., 3 or 3 1/2 in. chamber, Power Drive Gas System, 26 or 28 in. barrel, three knurled/extended Invector Plus choke tubes, screw-on magazine cap, Nickel Teflon coating on hardware, ramped trigger guard, Lightning trigger, fiber optic front and ivory mid-bead sight, trimmable composite stock with rubber overmolding on stock and forearm, SoftFlex cheek pad, Inflex recoil pad, speed load plus, new oversize bolt release and bolt handle, includes ABS case, 100% Mossy Oak Shadow Grass Habitat, Mossy Oak Break-Up Country, or Retro Vintage Tan camo finish, 7 lbs. New 2021.

MSR $1,790	$1,525	$1,335	$1,145	$1,035	$840	$695	$595	

Add $110 for 3 1/2 in. chamber.

MAXUS II SPORTING CARBON FIBER – 12 ga., 3 in. chamber, 28 or 30 in. barrel, five extended Midas Grade choke tubes, chrome chamber and bore, screw-on mag. cap, HiViz TriComp fiber optic front with mid-bead sight, carbon fiber dip composite stock with rubber overmolding on gripping surfaces, SoftFlex cheek pad, Inflex recoil pad, oversized controls, includes ABS hard case, 7 lbs. 2 oz. New 2021.

MSR $1,860	$1,585	$1,385	$1,180	$1,075	$875	$725	$600	

MAXUS II STALKER – 12 ga., 3 or 3 1/2 in. chamber, 26 or 28 in. barrel, chrome chamber and bore, three Invector Plus choke tubes, screw-on mag. cap, new receiver styling, HiViz Tri-Comp fiber optic front sight and ivory mid-bead, trimmable pistol grip composite stock, rubber overmolded gripping surfaces, SoftFlex cheek pad, Inflex recoil pad, oversized controls, includes ABS hard case, no glare matte black finish, 6 lbs. 14 oz. New 2021.

MSR $1,590	$1,350	$1,180	$1,000	$910	$735	$600	$500	

Add $190 for 3 1/2 in. chamber.

MAXUS II WICKED WING CAMO – 12 ga., 3 or 3 1/2 in. chamber, Power Drive gas system, 26 or 28 in. barrel with Cerakote Burnt Bronze finish, three extended Invector-Plus Goose Band choke tubes, chrome bore and chamber, turnkey mag. plug, screw-on magazine cap, new trigger guard design, lightning trigger, fiber optic front and ivory mid-bead sight, Mossy Oak Shadow Grass Habitat camo trimmable composite stock with close radius pistol grip, overmolded gripping surfaces, shim adj. for LOP, Inflex recoil pad, SoftFlex cheekpad, oversized bolt handle and enlarged bolt release, Speed Load Plus feeding system, includes ABS case, 7-7.2 lbs. New 2021.

MSR $1,940	$1,650	$1,450	$1,240	$1,125	$910	$750	$625	

Add $130 for 3 1/2 in. chamber.

GRADING - PPGS™	100%	98%	95%	90%	80%	70%	60%	LAST MSR

SILVER 3 1/2 IN. CAMO – 12 ga. only, 3 1/2 in. chamber, 26 or 28 in. VR barrel with 3 Invector Plus choke tubes, brass bead front sight, composite stock, Dura-Touch Armor coating, aluminum alloy receiver, semi-humpback design, 100% Mossy Oak New Break-Up (disc. 2009), Mossy Oak Break-Up Infinity (mfg. 2010-disc.), Mossy Oak Duck Blind (mfg. 2007-disc.), New Shadowgrass (mfg. 2006 only), Mossy Oak Shadow Grass Blades (new 2013), or Mossy Oak Break-Up Country (mfg. 2015-2016) camo finish, 7 1/2 lbs. Mfg. 2006-2017.

	100%	98%	95%	90%	80%	70%	60%	LAST MSR
	$1,165	$950	$825	$725	$625	$495	$425	*$1,360*

SILVER BLACK LIGHTNING – 12 ga., 3 in. chamber, active valve system, 26 or 28 in. VR barrel with gloss blued finish, three Invector-Plus choke tubes, semi-humpback aluminum alloy receiver, brass front bead sight, Lightning style gloss finished Grade 2.5 Turkish walnut stock, 7 lbs. 6 oz. New 2017.

	100%	98%	95%	90%	80%	70%	60%	LAST MSR
MSR $1,180	$1,000	$875	$750	$680	$550	$450	$385	

SILVER FIELD – 12 or 20 ga., 3 in. chamber, 26 or 28 in. barrel, three Invector Plus choke tubes, brass bead front sight, satin finished walnut stock with cut checkering, silver/matte black bi-tone receiver finish, 6.5-7.5 lbs. New 2018.

	100%	98%	95%	90%	80%	70%	60%	LAST MSR
MSR $1,140	$975	$850	$725	$675	$550	$450	$375	

Add $60 for 20 ga.

SILVER FIELD CAMO – 12 ga., 3 1/2 in. chamber, 26 or 28 in. lightweight VR barrel, three Invector Plus choke tubes, aluminum alloy receiver with semi-humpback design and black/charcoal bi-tone finish, brass front bead sight, composite stock, Mossy Oak Shadow Grass Blades (disc. 2020) or Mossy Oak Shadow Grass Habitat (new 2021) camo finish, 7 lbs. 9 oz. New 2018.

	100%	98%	95%	90%	80%	70%	60%	LAST MSR
MSR $1,220	$1,040	$910	$780	$700	$575	$475	$400	

SILVER FIELD COMPOSITE – 12 ga., 3 or 3 1/2 in. chamber, 26 or 28 in. lightweight VR barrel, three Invector Plus choke tubes, aluminum alloy receiver with semi-humpback design and black/charcoal bi-tone finish, brass front bead sight, matte black composite stock, 7 lbs. 9 oz. New 2018.

	100%	98%	95%	90%	80%	70%	60%	LAST MSR
MSR $1,070	$910	$795	$685	$620	$500	$410	$350	

Add $70 for 3 1/2 in. chamber.

SILVER FIELD MICRO MIDAS – 12 (mfg. 2018-2019) or 20 ga., 3 in. chamber, 24 or 26 in. barrel with three Invector Plus choke tubes, brass bead front sight, satin finished walnut stock with cut checkering, silver/matte black bi-tone receiver finish, 6-7 1/2 lbs. New 2018.

	100%	98%	95%	90%	80%	70%	60%	LAST MSR
MSR $1,200	$1,025	$900	$775	$700	$575	$475	$400	

Subtract approx. $70 for 12 ga. (mfg. 2018-2019).

SILVER HUNTER – 12 or 20 ga., 3 or 3 1/2 in. chamber, gas operating system, 26, 28, or 30 in. VR barrel, includes three Invector-Plus choke tubes, silver finished aluminum alloy receiver, semi-humpback design, brass bead front sight, checkered satin finished stock and forearm with Inflex recoil pad, approx. 6 1/4-7 1/2 lbs. Mfg. 2006-2016.

	100%	98%	95%	90%	80%	70%	60%	LAST MSR
	$1,040	$835	$650	$575	$495	$425	$375	*$1,200*

Add $160 for 3 1/2 in. chamber.

SILVER HUNTER MICRO MIDAS – 12 or 20 ga., 3 in. chamber, 24 or 26 in. VR barrel, includes three choke tubes, aluminum alloy receiver with semi-humpback design and silver finish, brass bead front sight, checkered satin finished walnut stock and forearm, Inflex recoil pad, 1/4 in. stock spacer, approx. 6-7 3/8 lbs. Mfg. 2011-2016.

	100%	98%	95%	90%	80%	70%	60%	LAST MSR
	$1,025	$900	$775	$700	$575	$475	$400	*$1,200*

SILVER MATTE HUNTER – 12 or 20 ga., 3 in. chamber, gas operated, active valve system, 26 or 28 in. VR barrel with matte black finish, three Invector Plus choke tubes, semi-humpback aluminum alloy receiver, brass front bead sights, satin finished walnut stock, Inflex recoil pad, silver/matte black bi-tone receiver finish, 6 1/2-7 1/2 lbs. Mfg. 2017 only.

	100%	98%	95%	90%	80%	70%	60%	LAST MSR
	$995	$800	$625	$550	$475	$425	$375	*$1,150*

SILVER MATTE HUNTER MICRO MIDAS – 12 or 20 ga., 3 in. chamber, gas operated, active valve system, 24 or 26 in. VR barrel with matte black finish, three Invector Plus choke tubes, semi-humpback aluminum alloy receiver, brass front bead sights, satin finished walnut stock, Inflex recoil pad, 1/4 in. stock spacer, silver/matte black bi-tone receiver finish, 6-7 1/2 lbs. Mfg. 2017 only.

	100%	98%	95%	90%	80%	70%	60%	LAST MSR
	$995	$800	$625	$550	$475	$425	$375	*$1,150*

SILVER LIGHTNING – 12 ga., 3 in. chamber, 26 or 28 in. VR barrel, silver finished aluminum alloy receiver, semi-humpback design, gloss finished Lightning style walnut stock, three Invector Plus choke tubes, approx. 7 1/2 lbs. Mfg. 2008-2016.

	100%	98%	95%	90%	80%	70%	60%	LAST MSR
	$1,040	$835	$650	$575	$495	$425	$375	*$1,200*

This model is available only through Browning Full Line and Medallion dealers.

This model was also available in 20 ga. with ivory bead front sight as a SHOT Show Special in 2008, MSR was $997.

GRADING - PPGS™	100%	98%	95%	90%	80%	70%	60%	LAST MSR

SILVER 3 1/2 IN. LIGHTNING – 12 ga., similar to Silver Lightning 3 In., except has 3 1/2 in. chamber., 26 or 28 in. VR barrel with 3 Invector Plus choke tubes. Mfg. 2008-2013.

	$1,125	$850	$750	$625	$550	$500	$450	*$1,360*

This model is available only through Browning Full Line and Medallion dealers.

SILVER MICRO – 20 ga., 3 in. chamber, 26 in. VR barrel, lightweight aluminum alloy receiver, semi-humpback design, satin finished walnut stock and forearm, compact dimensions for smaller shooters, three Invector Plus choke tubes, 6 lbs., 3 oz. Mfg. 2008-2014.

	$1,025	$825	$650	$575	$495	$425	$375	*$1,180*

SILVER NWTF CAMO – 12 ga., 3 in. chamber, 24 in. VR barrel, aluminum alloy receiver, composite stock and forearm with Dura-Touch Armor coating and 100% Mossy Oak New Break-Up (disc. 2009) or Mossy Oak Break Up Infinity (new 2010) camo treatment, NWTF logo, Hi-Viz 4 in 1 fiber optic sight, three Invector Plus choke tubes, 7 lbs. Mfg. 2008-2014.

	$1,175	$1,000	$850	$675	$550	$500	$450	*$1,360*

SILVER 3 1/2 IN. NWTF CAMO – 12 ga., 3 1/2 in. chamber, 24 in. barrel, three Invector Plus choke tubes, aluminum alloy receiver, Hi-Viz 4 in 1 fiber optic sight, composite stock and forearm with Dura-Touch Armor coating and 100% Mossy Oak New Break-Up (disc. 2014), Break-Up Infinity (2009-2014), or Mossy Oak Break-Up Country (new 2015) camo treatment, NWTF logo, 7 1/4 lbs. Mfg. 2008-2017.

	$1,350	$1,125	$950	$800	$675	$500	$425	*$1,580*

SILVER RIFLED DEER CAMO – 12 or 20 (new 2009) ga., 3 in. chamber, 22 in. rifled deer barrel, aluminum alloy receiver, composite stock and forearm with Dura-Touch Armor coating and 100% Mossy Oak New Break-Up (disc. 2009), Break-Up Infinity (2009-2014), or Mossy Oak Break-Up Country (new 2015) camo treatment, cantilever scope mount, 7 lbs. 12 oz. New 2008.

MSR $1,340	$1,140	$1,000	$855	$775	$625	$515	$445	

Add $60 for 20 ga. (new 2009).

SILVER RIFLED DEER MATTE – 20 ga., 3 in. chamber, gas operated, 22 in. thick-walled fully rifled barrel, semi-humpback aluminum alloy receiver, satin finished walnut stock, features cantilever scope mount, 6 lbs. 12 oz. New 2017.

MSR $1,240	$1,060	$925	$790	$715	$580	$475	$400	

SILVER RIFLED DEER SATIN – 12 or 20 ga., 3 in. chamber, 22 in. rifled deer barrel, satin finished walnut stock with Dura-Touch Armor coating, cantilever scope mount, 7 lbs. 12 oz. Mfg. 2008-2016.

	$1,165	$950	$825	$725	$625	$495	$425	*$1,360*

SILVER RIFLED DEER STALKER – 12 ga., 3 in. chamber, semi-humpback design, 22 in. fully rifled deer barrel, aluminum alloy receiver, non-glare matte black composite stock and forearm, Dura-Touch Armor coating, cantilever scope mount, 7 lbs. 12 oz. Mfg. 2008-2016.

	$1,125	$875	$750	$650	$525	$475	$425	*$1,310*

SILVER SPORTING – 12 ga. only, 2 3/4 in. chamber, 28 or 30 in. ported barrel with flush choke tubes, semi-humpback silver fnished alloy receiver, HiViz TriComp fiber optic and mid-bead sights, adj. satin finished walnut stock with Pachmayr Decelerator recoil pad, 7 1/2 lbs. Mfg. 2009-2016.

	$1,115	$925	$775	$675	$575	$475	$425	*$1,320*

SILVER SPORTING MICRO – 12 ga., 2 3/4 in. chamber, 28 in. VR ported barrel, lightweight aluminum alloy receiver, brass bead and mid-bead sights, semi-humpback design, satin finished walnut stock and forearm, features 13 3/4 in. LOP adj. in 1/4 in. increments using three included adj. spacers, premium Pachmayr Decelerator pad, three Invector Plus chokes, 7 lbs. Mfg. 2008-2016.

	$1,115	$925	$775	$675	$575	$475	$425	*$1,320*

SILVER STALKER – 12 ga. only, 3 1/2 in. chamber, 26 or 28 in. VR barrel, three Invector Plus choke tubes, brass front bead sight, matte black composite stock and forearm, Dura-Touch armor coating, semi-humpback alloy receiver, matte black metal finish, approx. 7 1/2 lbs. Mfg. 2006-2017.

	$1,075	$865	$725	$625	$525	$475	$425	*$1,230*

SHOTGUNS: SINGLE BARREL, BT-99 & BT-100

During 2010, the Vector Pro lengthened 2 1/2 inch forcing cone became standard on the following current models.

In addition to the models listed below, Browning has also released SHOT Show specials on some models that were available by dealers ordering them at the SHOT Show only. Complete descriptions for these models can be found under SHOT SHOW SPECIALS - SHOTGUNS SINGLE SHOT at BlueBookOfGunValues.com/overflow.

GRADING - PPGS™	100%	98%	95%	90%	80%	70%	60%	LAST MSR

BT-99 STANDARD TRAP GUN – 12 ga., 32 or 34 in. vent. rib barrel, mod., imp. mod., or full choke, boxlock, auto ejector, checkered pistol grip with Monte Carlo or conventional style stock, beavertail forearm. Invector chokes became standard in 1986 and ported barrel with Invector Plus chokes and back boring became standard in 1992. Values below assume Invector Plus choking with ported barrel. Mfg. 1968-94 by Miroku.

	$900	$800	$700	$600	$550	$500	$450	*$1,288*

Subtract $125 without Invector chokes or ported barrels.

* ***BT-99 2 Barrel Set*** – 12 ga., without Invector choking or barrel porting. Disc. 1983.

	$1,150	$995	$850	$750	$700	$650	$600	

* ***BT-99 Pigeon Grade*** – 12 ga., features higher grade walnut and gold receiver accents, Invector chokes and ported barrels. Mfg. 1993-1994.

1978-1985 Mfg.	$1,700	$1,500	$1,200	$1,100	$650	$575	$525	
1986-1994 Mfg.	$1,395	$1,150	$875	$600	$525	$495	$450	*$1,505*

Older Pigeon Grade guns featured a satin grey receiver with deep relief, engraved pigeons in a fleur-de-lis background.

* ***BT-99 Signature Painted*** – 12 ga., features painted red/black stock with Browning logos on stock and forearm, Invector Plus ported barrels. Mfg. 1993-1994.

	$1,250	$1,050	$900	$700	$600	$500	$330	*$1,323*

* ***BT-99 Stainless*** – 12 ga., features all stainless construction with Invector Plus ported 32 or 34 in. black VR barrel. Mfg. 1993-1994.

	$1,500	$1,200	$1,000	$700	$575	$495	$450	*$1,738*

BT-99 (CURRENT MFG.) – 12 ga., choice of 32 or 34 in. back bored unported barrel with 11/32 in. high post rib and one full Invector Plus choke tube, satin finished walnut stock, beavertail forearm, ventilated trap recoil pad, ejector only, 8 lbs. 5 oz. New 2001.

MSR $1,560	$1,325	$1,160	$995	$900	$730	$600	$520	

Add $390 for adjustable buttplate and comb (new 2017).

BT-99 GOLDEN CLAYS – 12 ga., 2 3/4 in. chamber, features gloss finished Grade V/Grade VI wood and gold outline receiver and inlays depicting a transitional hunting to clay pigeon scene, current mfg. includes 32 or 34 in. ported barrel, adj. comb and LOP, and GraCoil recoil reduction, approx. 9 lbs. Mfg. 1994, reintroduced 2003-2018.

	$3,740	$3,180	$2,700	$2,300	$1,850	$1,475	$1,185	*$4,340*

Subtract 15% for older mfg. w/o current features.

BT-99 GRADE III – 12 ga., similar to BT-99, except has silver Nitride receiver finished with gold accents, gloss finished Grade III/IV Monte Carlo stock with beavertail forearm, 32 or 34 in. ported barrel, approx. 8 1/2 lbs. Mfg. 2008-2014.

	$2,440	$2,075	$1,750	$1,485	$1,175	$950	$750	*$2,540*

Add $290 for adj. comb.

BT-99 MICRO – 12 ga., 2 3/4 in. chamber, 30 or 32 in. high post VR barrel, one Invector-Plus choke tube, steel receiver, extractors only, ivory front and mid-bead sights, satin finished walnut checkered pistol grip with Monte Carlo or conventional style stock, beavertail forearm, shortened 13 3/4 in. LOP, blue finish, approx. 7 3/4 lbs. New 2004.

MSR $1,560	$1,325	$1,155	$990	$900	$725	$600	$515	

Add $390 for adjustable buttplate and comb (new 2017).

* ***BT-99 Micro with Adjustable LOP*** – 12 ga., 2 3/4 in. chamber, 30 or 32 in. barrel with full chokes, gold plated trigger, Buck Mark engraved in gold on trigger guard, ivory front sight with mid-bead, satin finished walnut stock, trap-style recoil pad, Graco buttpad plate allows for adjustment of LOP, satin blued finish, 7 lbs. 12 oz. New 2020.

MSR $1,720	$1,460	$1,275	$1,095	$985	$800	$650	$550	

BT-99 MICRO MIDAS – 12 ga., 2 3/4 in. chambers, 28 or 30 in. VR barrel with one Invector-Plus choke tube, compact variation with 13 in. LOP, blued finish, extractor, satin finished walnut stock, beavertail forearm, recoil pad, approx. 7 3/4 lbs. Mfg. 2013-2019.

	$1,295	$1,050	$900	$750	$600	$525	$450	*$1,470*

BT-99 PLUS GRADE I – similar to BT-99, except has adj. rib to control point of impact and new recoil reduction system that reduces felt recoil by 50%, stock has adj. comb and buttplate (recoil pad), back-bored barrel, Invector chokes, 8 3/4 lbs. Mfg. 1989-94.

Older Mfg.	$1,775	$1,525	$1,275	$1,100	$1,000	$800	$700	*$1,835*

Add 5% for ported barrel.

GRADING - PPGS™	100%	98%	95%	90%	80%	70%	60%	LAST MSR

In 1990, the Grade I designation was added to this model. In 1991, this model was supplied with a travel vault gun case as standard equipment. Older mfg. will not have these cases as an original accessory.

Beginning 1991, a Micro Plus Model was introduced that incorporates smaller dimensions (shorter stock and choice of shorter barrel). Values are the same as listed.

* ***BT-99 Plus Stainless Grade I*** – features all stainless construction with Invector Plus ported 32 or 34 in. black VR barrel. Mfg. 1993-94.

$1,950	$1,725	$1,425	$1,255	$1,020	$885	$715	*$2,240*

Beginning 1991, a Micro Plus Model was introduced that incorporates smaller dimensions (shorter stock and choice of shorter barrel). Values are the same as listed.

* ***BT-99 Plus Pigeon Grade Grade I*** – 12 ga., features higher grade walnut and gold receiver accents, Invector chokes and ported barrels. Mfg. 1993-disc.

$1,875	$1,600	$1,250	$1,100	$895	$785	$630	*$2,065*

Beginning 1991, a Micro Plus Model was introduced that incorporates smaller dimensions (shorter stock and choice of shorter barrel). Values are the same.

* ***BT-99 Plus Signature Painted Grade I*** – features painted red/black stock with Browning logos on stock and forearm, Invector Plus ported barrels. Mfg. 1993-94.

$1,750	$1,525	$1,250	$1,100	$895	$785	$630	*$1,890*

Beginning 1991, a Micro Plus Model was introduced that incorporates smaller dimensions (shorter stock and choice of shorter barrel). Values are the same.

* ***BT-99 Plus Golden Clays Grade I*** – features high-grade wood and gold outline receiver and inlays depicting a transitional hunting to clay pigeon scene. Mfg. 1994 only.

$2,700	$2,350	$2,050	$1,850	$1,700	$1,550	$1,395	*$3,205*

Beginning 1991, a Micro Plus Model was introduced that incorporates smaller dimensions (shorter stock and choice of shorter barrel). Values are the same.

BT-99 PLUS (NEW MFG.) – 12 ga., 32 or 34 in. ported high post VR barrel with Vector Pro lengthened forcing cone, gloss oil finished Grade III/IV checkered walnut stock/forearm with Pachmayr Decelerator XLT recoil pad, adj. comb, blue finish with high relief engraving, approx. 8 1/2 lbs. New 2015.

MSR $3,160	$2,685	$2,350	$2,015	$1,825	$1,475	$1,225	$1,050

BT-99 MAX – 12 ga. only, choice of blue steel with engraving or stainless steel barrel, receiver, and trigger guard, 32 or 34 in. high post VR ported barrel, thin forearm with finger grooves, select walnut pistol grip stock (regular or Monte Carlo) with high gloss finish, ejector/extractor selector, no safety, approx. 8 lbs. 10 oz. Mfg. 1995-96.

$1,300	$1,000	$800	$600	$525	$495	$450	*$1,496*

Add $400 for stainless steel.

BT-99 MAX HIGH GRADE – 12 ga., 2 3/4 in. chamber, adj. Graco Recoil Reduction System, 32 or 34 in. barrel, three extended Midas Grade choke tubes, adj. rib, Hull ejector, gold plated trigger, HiViz Pro Comp fiber optic front sight with mid-bead, gloss oil finished Grade V/VI black walnut stock, adj. Graco comb and buttpad plate, Pachmayr Decelerator XLT recoil pad, beavertail forearm, includes brown BT trap fitted case, blued finish, 9 lbs. 5 oz. New 2019.

MSR $5,620	$4,775	$4,180	$3,580	$3,250	$2,625	$2,200	$1,875

BT-100 STANDARD TRAP GUN – 12 ga. only, 32 or 34 in. steel high-post ported Invector Plus or fixed choked (F) barrel, without safety, choice of blue or stainless steel receiver, removable trigger assembly, ejector selector (either ejects or extracts) adj. comb and thumbhole stock (disc. 1999) are optional, approx. 8 lbs. 10 oz. Mfg. 1995-2002.

$1,900	$1,600	$1,300	$795	$575	$495	$450	*$2,266*

Subtract approx. 10% for fixed choke.
Add $100 for adj. comb.
Add $558 for replacement trigger assembly (blue or stainless).

* ***BT-100 Stainless*** – features stainless steel barrel, receiver, trigger guard and top lever. Disc. 2002.

$2,210	$1,800	$1,600	$1,000	$815	$695	$580	*$2,742*

Subtract approx. 10% for fixed choke.
Add $100 for adj. comb.
Add $558 for replacement trigger assembly (blue or stainless).

GRADING - PPGS™	100%	98%	95%	90%	80%	70%	60%	LAST MSR

BT-100 SATIN (LOW LUSTER) – features 32 or 34 in. Invector Plus barrel, satin/low luster metal/wood finish, conventional type stock without Monte Carlo, quick removable trigger with adj. trigger pull, 8 lbs. 10 oz. Mfg. 1998-2000.

	$1,400	$1,200	$1,000	$775	$650	$575	$495	$1,684

SHOTGUNS: SINGLE BARREL, RECOILLESS TRAP

RECOILLESS SINGLE BARREL TRAP – 12 ga., special bolt action design that eliminates 72% of felt recoil, 27 (also available in Micro Model) or 30 in. high-post vent. rib Invector Plus choked back-bored barrel, rib adjusts for 3 points of impact (3, 6, or 9 in.), stock has adj. pull (2 sizes) and comb height, anodized receiver, no safety, approx. 8 1/2 lbs. Mfg. 1994-96.

	$995	$750	$675	$600	$525	$500	$450	$1,995

The Micro Model featured a 27 in. barrel and shorter length of pull.

* ***Recoilless Single Barrel Trap Signature Painted*** – features painted red/black stock with Browning logos on stock and forearm, Invector Plus ported barrels. Mfg. 1994 only.

	$995	$750	$675	$600	$525	$500	$450	$1,900

SHOTGUNS: SLIDE ACTION

Do not use BPS barrels chambered for 3 1/2 in. shotshells on a BPS 3 in. receiver or vice versa. In addition to the models listed below, Browning has also released SHOT Show specials on some models that were available by dealers ordering them at the SHOT Show only. Complete descriptions for these models can be found under SHOT SHOW SPECIALS - SHOTGUNS: SLIDE ACTION at BlueBookOfGunValues.com/overflow.

BPS FIELD – 12, 16 (mfg. 2018 only), 20, 28 (mfg. 2018 only) ga., or .410 bore (disc. 2019), 2 3/4 or 3 in. chamber, 26 or 28 in. VR barrel, three standard or Invector Plus (with 12 and 20 ga.) choke tubes, forged steel receiver, bottom ejection, gold plated trigger, satin finished walnut stock with checkered gripping surfaces (new 2020), Inflex recoil pad, top tang safety, dual steel action bars, matte blue finish, approx. 7 lbs. New 2018.

MSR $700	$600	$525	$450	$410	$325	$275	$225	

Add $20 for 20 ga.
Add $40 for .410 bore (disc. 2019).
Add $40 for 16 or 28 ga. (mfg. 2018 only).

In 2020, this model went through design changes, including a newly designed stock with textured gripping surfaces and a larger trigger guard.

BPS FIELD COMPOSITE – 12 or 20 ga., 3 or 3 1/2 in. chamber, 26 or 28 in. barrel, three Invector Plus choke tubes, forged steel receiver, bottom ejection and loading, oversized trigger guard with Buck Mark engraved in gold, silver bead front sight, black composite stock with textured gripping surfaces, Inflex recoil pad, top tang safety, matte blued finish, 7 lbs. 1 oz - 8 lbs. 1 oz. New 2020.

MSR $660	$550	$485	$415	$375	$300	$250	$200	

Add $20 for 20 ga.
Add $20 for 3 1/2 in. chamber.

BPS FIELD COMPOSITE CAMO – 12 or 20 ga., 3 or 3 1/2 in. chamber, 26 or 28 in. barrel, three Invector Plus choke tubes, floating rib, larger trigger guard, brass bead front sight, composite stock with textured gripping surfaces, Inflex recoil pad, 100% Mossy Oak Shadow Grass Blades camo coverage, 7-8 lbs. New 2020.

MSR $780	$665	$580	$500	$450	$365	$300	$235	

BPS HUNTER/FIELD MODEL – 12, 16 (new 2008), 20, 28 (new 1994) ga., or .410 bore (new 2000), 2 3/4 (28 ga. only) or 3 in. chamber, bottom ejection, double action bars, top tang safety, 5 shot capacity, vent. rib, all steel receiver with variety of finishes, receiver engraving became standard 1991 and was disc. during 1998, 20 and 28 ga. are approx. 1/2 lb. lighter than 12 ga. Field Models, Invector or Invector Plus (new 1994 in 20 ga.) choking, various barrel lengths, Invector Plus choking became standard 1995 (except 28 ga.), back bored barrels on 12 and 20 ga. BPS Models (except Game guns) became standard during 2003, 7-7 3/4 lbs. Mfg. by Miroku. Mfg. 1977-2019.

	$595	$465	$375	$275	$230	$195	$175	$700

Add $30 for 16, 28 ga., or .410 bore.
Subtract 10% if without Invector Plus choke tubes.

The 16 ga. model was featured as a 2007 SHOT Show Special before it was added to the line in 2008.

* ***BPS Stalker Model*** – 12 ga. 3 or 3 1/2 in. chamber, all metal parts have a dull matte finish, non-glare black synthetic composite stock and forearm, 24 (disc. 1997, reintroduced 1999-2000), 26,

GRADING - PPGS™	100%	98%	95%	90%	80%	70%	60%	LAST MSR

28, or 30 (disc. 1997) in. VR barrel, three Invector Plus choke tubes, silver colored front bead sight, approx. 8 lbs. Mfg. 1987-2019.

$595 $475 $365 $275 $230 $195 $175 ***$700***

Add $100 for 3 1/2 in. chamber.

* ***BPS Camo 3 In.*** – 12 or 20 (disc. 2006) ga., 3 in. chamber, features Mossy Oak Shadow Grass (disc. 2006), Mossy Oak Duck Blind (mfg. 2007-2013), Mossy Oak Break-Up (mfg. 2000-2003), Break-Up Infinity (mfg. 2010-disc.), New Break-Up (mfg. 2004-2009), Mossy Oak Shadow Grass Blades (new 2013), or Mossy Oak Break-Up Country (new 2015) full camo treatment, 24 (disc.), 26, or 28 in. barrel, Dura-Touch armor coating became standard during 2003, approx. 8 lbs. Mfg. 1999-2019.

$700 $615 $525 $475 $385 $315 $250 ***$820***

* ***BPS NWTF Camo*** – 12 ga., 3 or 3 1/2 in. chamber, 24 in. VR barrel, three Invector Plus coke tubes, steel receiver, drilled and tapped for scope mounts, bottom ejection, HiViz fiber optic sight, composite stock with Dura-Touch Armor coating, top tang safety, NWTF buttstock decal, 100% Mossy Oak Break-Up (mfg. 2000-2009, 3 1/2 in. chamber), Mossy Oak Break-Up Infinity (disc. 2014) or Mossy Oak Break-Up Country (new 2015) camo finish, 7 lbs. 15 oz. Mfg. 2001-2019.

$800 $700 $600 $550 $450 $350 $300 ***$950***

Add $80 for 3 1/2 in. chamber.

* ***BPS Pigeon Grade*** – 12 ga., 3 in. chamber, 26 or 28 in. VR barrel with Invector chokes, gold trimmed receiver, high grade walnut stock, 7 lbs. 10 oz. Mfg. 1992-1998.

$550 $465 $395 $350 $310 $290 $275 ***$603***

* ***BPS Upland Special*** – 12, 16 (new 2008), or 20 ga., 2 3/4 (16 ga.) or 3 in. chamber, 22 (12 and 20 ga.), 24, or 26 in. VR barrel, Invector (pre-1994) or Invector Plus (new 1994, standard 1995) choking, bottom ejection, silver-colored front bead sight, English-style straight grip satin finished walnut stock and forearm, top tang safety, forged and machined steel high polished blued receiver, 6 3/4 or 7 1/2 lbs. Mfg. 1985-2017.

$595 $475 $365 $275 $230 $195 $175 ***$700***

Add $30 for 16 ga.

Subtract 10% if without Invector Plus choke tubes.

The 16 ga. model was featured as a 2007 SHOT Show Special before it was added to the line in 2008.

* ***BPS Turkey Special*** – 12 ga. only, 3 in. chamber, 20 1/2 in. lightened barrel, non-glare walnut stock, matte finished barrel and receiver, receiver is drilled and tapped for scope base, rifle-style stock dimensions, sling swivels, new extra-full Invector choke tube, 7 lbs. 8 oz. Mfg. 1992-2001.

$400 $340 $275 $240 $215 $190 $175 ***$500***

* ***BPS Micro*** – 20 ga. only, 22 in. vent. rib barrel, pistol grip stock (13 1/4 in. LOP), Invector Plus choking (includes 3 chokes), 6 3/4 lbs. Mfg. 2001-2013.

$565 $480 $385 $300 $230 $195 $175 ***$650***

* ***BPS Micro Midas*** – 12 (disc. 2017), 20, 28 (disc.) ga., or .410 bore, 3 in. chamber, 22 (new 2014), 24 or 26 in. VR barrel with three Invector Plus choke tubes, bottom ejection, silver colored front bead sight, checkered satin finished walnut stock and forearm includes two stock spacers, Inflex recoil pad, top tang safety, 13 in. LOP, forged steel receiver with high polish blue finish, 7-7 1/2 lbs. Mfg. 2013-2019.

$600 $525 $450 $425 $345 $275 $225 ***$700***

Add $30 for 28 ga. (disc.) or .410 bore.

* ***BPS Micro - Youth and Ladies Model*** – 20 ga. only, 22 in. vent. rib barrel, straight grip shortened stock (13 1/4 in. LOP), Invector (pre-1994) or Invector Plus (new 1994, standard 1995) choking, 6 3/4 lbs. Mfg. 1986-2002.

$385 $300 $260 $225 $200 $185 $170 ***$473***

Subtract 10% if without Invector Plus choke tubes.

* ***BPS Rifled Deer Hunter/Special (DG, DS or DH)*** – 12 or 20 (new 2007) ga., 3 in. chamber, 20 1/2 (disc. 2000) or 22 in. barrel with 5 in. rifled choke tube (disc. 2013) or rifled barrel (DH, cantilever scope mount with satin finish only, new 1997), iron sights (disc.) or w/o sights, scope mount base, choice of gloss (DG, disc. 1997), satin (DS, disc. 2000), or non-glare wood finish checkered stock with recoil pad and forearm, sling swivels, polished or matte finished metal, approx. 7 1/2 lbs. Mfg. 1992-2019.

$700 $615 $525 $475 $385 $315 $250 ***$830***

Subtract approx. 10% for rifled choke tube.

Add $10 for 20 ga. (new 2007).

GRADING - PPGS™	100%	98%	95%	90%	80%	70%	60%	LAST MSR

* ***BPS Rifled Deer Camo*** – 12 or 20 ga., 3 in. chamber, 22 in. rifled barrel with cantilever scope mount, steel receiver, bottom ejection, composite (12 ga.) or walnut (20 ga.) stock, Dura-Touch Armor coating, top tang safety, 100% Mossy Oak New Break-Up (disc. 2009), Mossy Oak Break-Up Infinity (mfg. 2010-2014), or Mossy Oak Break-Up Country (new 2015) camo coverage, approx. 7 1/2 lbs. Mfg. 2007-2019.

	$740	$650	$550	$500	$400	$350	$285	*$870*

Add $110 for 20 ga.

* ***BPS Buck Special*** – 12 or 20 (disc. 1984) ga., 3 in. chamber, 24 in. cyl. bore barrel, iron sights, 7 lbs. 10 oz. Reintroduced 1988-disc. 1998.

	$335	$275	$230	$200	$185	$175	$160	*$409*

* ***BPS All Purpose*** – 12 or 20 ga., 26 (20 ga.) or 28 (12 ga.) in. barrel, 4 shot mag., three Invector Plus choke, 100% Realtree AP camo coverage stock and forearm, HiViz fiber optic sights, drilled and tapped, approx. 8 lbs. Mfg. 2013-2014.

	$795	$695	$595	$540	$435	$360	$280	*$930*

BPS MAGNUM HUNTER 12 GA. 3 1/2 IN. – 12 ga., 3 1/2 in. chamber, 24 (disc. 1997), 26, 28, or 30 (disc. 1997) in. barrel with Invector chokes and vent. rib, 4 shot mag., 7 3/4 lbs. Disc. 2002.

	$675	$525	$450	$375	$325	$275	$250	*$800*

In 1990, the back-bored Invector Plus choke tube system became standard in 12 ga. 3 1/2 in. chamber only.

* ***BPS Camo 3 1/2 In. (Magnum Hunter)*** – 12 ga., 3 in. chamber, 26 or 28 in. VR barrel, three Invector-Plus choke tubes, steel receiver, bottom ejection, silver colored front bead sight, composite stock, top tang safety, 100% Mossy Oak Shadow Grass (disc. 2006), Mossy Oak Duck Blind (mfg. 2007-2012), Mossy Oak Break-Up Infinity (mfg. 2010-disc.), Mossy Oak Break-Up (mfg. 2000-2009), Mossy Oak Shadow Grass Blades (new 2013), or Mossy Oak Break-Up Country (new 2015) camo finish, approx. 8 lbs. Mfg. 1999-2019.

	$800	$700	$600	$550	$450	$350	$300	*$950*

* ***BPS Magnum Hunter Waterfowl*** – 10 ga., 3 1/2 in. Mag. with choice of 28 or 30 in. matte finished VR barrel with Standard Invector choking, features higher grade walnut and gold trimmed receiver with Waterfowl outlined, approx. 9 lbs. 6 oz. Mfg. 1993-1998.

	$615	$500	$400	$375	$350	$315	$285	*$750*

* ***BPS Magnum 3 1/2 In. Buck Special*** – 10 or 12 (disc. 1994) ga., 3 1/2 in. chambers, 24 in. cyl. bore barrel, 7 lbs. 10 oz. Mfg. 1990-1997.

	$500	$450	$400	$370	$335	$310	$290	*$677*

BPS MAGNUM STALKER 10 GA. (HUNTER MODEL) – 10 ga., 3 1/2 in. chamber, 26 or 28 in. barrel with three Standard Invector choke tubes, currently available in Stalker (matte black synthetic stock and forearm), with Dura-Touch coating configuration, no longer available in Hunter Model, 10 1/2 lbs. Disc. 2001, reintroduced 2004-2019.

	$680	$600	$500	$450	$375	$300	$250	*$800*

BPS 10 GA. CAMO – 10 ga., 3 1/2 in. chamber, 26 or 28 in. barrel with three Standard Invector choke tubes, brass bead front sight, composite stock with Dura-Touch Armor coating, Mossy Oak New Break-Up (disc. 2009), Mossy Oak Break-Up Infinity (mfg. 2010-2013), Mossy Oak Duck Blind (mfg. 2007-2012), New Shadowgrass (disc. 2006), Mossy Oak Shadow Grass Blades (new 2013), Mossy Oak Break-Up Country (new 2015) camo finish, 10 1/2 lbs. Disc. 2019.

	$795	$675	$600	$525	$450	$375	$295	*$950*

BPS 10 GA. NWTF – 10 ga., 3 1/2 in. chamber, 24 in. VR barrel and extra full XF extended turkey choke tube, 4 shot mag., forged steel receiver, drilled and tapped for scope mounts, bottom ejection, HiViz TriViz fiber optic sights, composite stock with Dura-Touch Armor coating, NWTF logo on buttstock, top tang safety, 100% Mossy Oak New Break-Up (disc. 2009), Break-Up Infinity (mfg. 2010-2014), or Mossy Oak Break-Up Country (new 2015) camo coverage, 10 lbs. 3 oz. Disc. 2019.

	$875	$765	$650	$595	$475	$400	$325	*$1,030*

BPS TRAP MODEL – 12 ga., 30 in. barrel. Disc. 1984 but trap barrels were available separately for several years.

	$360	$300	$270	$230	$210	$190	$170	

BPS TRAP (CURRENT MFG.) – 12 ga., 2 3/4 in. chamber, 30 in. VR barrel, magazine cutoff, HiViz front sight, checkered satin finished Monte Carlo walnut stock and forearm, dark grey receiver with full coverage engraving, approx. 8 1/2 lbs. Mfg. 2007-2019.

	$750	$600	$475	$375	$300	$275	$225	*$840*

GRADING - PPGS™	100%	98%	95%	90%	80%	70%	60%	LAST MSR

* ***BPS Micro Trap*** – 12 ga. only, similar to BPS Trap, except has 28 in. VR barrel and 13 3/4 in. LOP, approx. 8 lbs. Mfg. 2007-2019.

$750	$600	$475	$375	$300	$275	$225	*$840*

BPS WILD TURKEY FEDERATION COMMEMORATIVE – only 500 manufactured. Disc. 1991.

$550	$425	$325	N/A	N/A	N/A	N/A

BPS PACIFIC EDITION DU – limited mfg., DU serialization, cased.

$595	$475	$350	$285	$250	$215	$185

BPS COASTAL DU – limited mfg., DU serialization, cased.

$595	$475	$350	$285	$250	$215	$185

BPS WATERFOWL DELUXE – 12 ga. Mag., gold trigger and etching, Invector chokes, limited mfg.

$625	$525	$450	$385	$335	$280	$235

MODEL 12 LIMITED EDITION SERIES

* ***Model 12 Limited Edition Grade I 20 Ga.*** – 20 ga. only, 2 3/4 in. chamber only, reproduction of the famous Winchester Model 12 with slight design improvements, 26 in. VR barrel bored modified, 5 shot mag., high post floating rib, walnut stock and forearm with semi-gloss finish, take down, serialization format similar to 28 ga., 7 lbs. 1 oz. 8,000 mfg. in 1988 with inventory depleted 1990.

$800	$675	$525	N/A	N/A	N/A	N/A	*$735*

* ***Model 12 Limited Edition Grade V 20 Ga.*** – similar specifications to Grade I, except has select walnut checkered 22 lines per inch with high gloss finish, extensive game scene engraving including multiple gold inlays serialization format similar to 28 ga. 4,000 mfg. 1988 only.

$1,400	$1,175	$900	N/A	N/A	N/A	N/A	*$1,187*

* ***Model 12 Limited Edition Grade I 28 Ga.*** – 28 ga. only, similar to Grade I 20 Ga., except in 28 ga., 26 in. VR modified choke barrel, 5 digit ser. no. with NM872 suffix. 7,000 mfg. 1991-92.

$1,150	$950	$750	N/A	N/A	N/A	N/A	*$772*

* ***Model 12 Limited Edition Grade V 28 ga.*** – 28 ga. only, similar to Grade V 20 ga., except in 28 ga., 26 in. VR modified choke barrel, 5 digit ser. no. with NM972 suffix. 5,000 mfg. 1991-92.

$1,850	$1,450	$1,100	N/A	N/A	N/A	N/A	*$1,246*

MODEL 42 LIMITED EDITION

* ***Model 42 Limited Edition Grade I*** – .410 bore, 3 in. chamber, reproduction of the Winchester Model 42 with slight design improvements, 26 in. VR full choke barrel, select walnut stock, 5 digit ser. no. with NZ882 suffix, 6 lbs. 12 oz. 6,000 mfg. late 1991-1993.

$950	$825	$650	N/A	N/A	N/A	N/A	*$800*

* ***Model 42 Limited Edition Grade V*** – .410 bore, engraving and embellishments similar to the Model 12 Grade V, 5 digit ser. no. with NZ982 suffix, 6,000 mfg. late 1991-1993.

$1,600	$1,300	$995	N/A	N/A	N/A	N/A	*$1,360*

SPECIAL EDITIONS, COMMEMORATIVES, & LIMITED MFG.

Please refer to the *Blue Book of Modern Black Powder Arms* (online also) for more information and prices on Browning black powder rifles.

BICENTENNIAL 1876-1976 SET – .45-70 Govt. cal., Model 78 rifle with specially engraved receiver, silver finish, fancy wood, cased, with engraved knife and medallion, 1,000 sets mfg. in 1976. Issue price - $1,500.

$1,975	$1,550	$1,200	N/A	N/A	N/A	N/A

CENTENNIAL O/U RIFLE/SHOTGUN – 20 ga. O/U shotgun w/extra set of .30-06 O/U rifle barrels. Shotgun barrels are 26 1/2 in., rifle barrels are 24 in., SST, ejectors, elaborate scroll engraved receiver with 2 gold inlays, straight grip special oil finished walnut stock and forearm, deluxe walnut full-length case. 500 mfg. 1978 only.

$6,750	$6,250	$5,250	N/A	N/A	N/A	N/A	*$7,000*

CENTENNIAL SET – complete Browning set mfg. in 1978, includes the Centennial O/U rifle/shotgun, 9mm Hi-Power, B92 .44 Mag., Mountain Rifle, and a set of three knives.

$8,750	$7,750	$6,250	N/A	N/A	N/A	N/A

1 OF 50 BICENTENNIAL RIFLE – .30-06 cal., Model 78 single shot with 26 in. octagon barrel, includes special engraving by Neil Hartliep (non-factory), extra fine walnut, 4X wide angle scope, special luggage case. 50 mfg. (one for each state) during 1976 only and sold by silent mail order bidding (minimum bid was $3,100 in 1976).

As very few specimens are bought or sold each year, pricing is rather unpredictable. A few specimens have been sold in the $6,000 range recently. Remember, this is not a "factory edition" as the work on this gun was subcontracted by Centennial Guns (division of Frigon Guns located in Clay Center, KS).

GRADING - PPGS™	100%	98%	95%	90%	80%	70%	60%	LAST MSR

BUCK MARK COMMEMORATIVE PISTOL - features 6 3/4 in. Challenger style tapered barrel, white bonded ivory grips with scrimshaw style patterning including "1 of 1,000 Commemorative Model" on sides, matte blue finish, gold trigger, 30 1/2 oz. 1,000 mfg. 2001-2002.

	$335	$275	$225	N/A	N/A	N/A	N/A	*$437*

SHOT SHOW SPECIALS

Since 2004 Browning has introduced SHOT (Shooting, Hunting, Outdoor Trade) Show Specials annually for its dealers who attend the SHOT Show. These are typically variations of existing models, but with different features, finishes, calibers/gauges, etc. These guns can only be ordered during the SHOT Show, and the quantity depends on the amount of dealer orders received during the show. Unfortunately, the total quantity of each SHOT Show Special variation is not available. If a SHOT Show Special is well received by the dealers, it may go into production as a standard model. If this happens, these variations can be found in the regular categories. These SHOT Show Specials are not Limited or Special Editions. Models listed in this section have only the MSRs at the time of their releases, and secondary values must be based off the variation from which they are derived. SHOT Show Specials manufactured during 2006-current will appear alphabetically according to category. For complete model descriptions and information, please go to BlueBookOfGunValues.com/overflow. Unfortunately, Browning does not have records on the quantities produced on these SHOT Show Special models.

BROZ ARMS CZ

Current pistol and rifle manufacturer established circa 2004, located in Roudne, Czech Republic. No current U.S. importation.

Broz Arms manufactures single shot falling block pistols and rifles, historic firearm replicas, and Damascus steel weaponry. Please contact the manufacturer directly for more information on these models.

BRUCHET

Previous trademark manufactured by Darne until circa 2011 and previous manufacturer located in Saint Etienne, France. Distributed exclusively from 1982-1989 by Wes Gilpin located in Dallas, TX. In 1989, Bruchet was able to get permission to use the older Darne trademark and all new manufacture can be found under the Darne listing.

Paul Bruchet manufactured his shotguns patterned after the Darne action circa 1981-2011, following his tenure at Darne as line foreman until 1979 (at which time the Darne plant closed). These new Bruchet Models were designated "A" or "B". All shotguns were totally hand made with approx. 50 guns being mfg. each year.

Since Paul Bruchet was able to retain the Darne trademark in 1989, please refer to the Darne section for current manufacture.

SHOTGUNS: SxS

MODEL A - 12, 16, 20, 28 ga., or .410 bore, small key opening, ejectors, double triggers only, basically 4 variations (1, 1A, 2, and 2A), wide assortment of customer specified special orders.

Retail values were as follows: Model 1A started at under $2,000, the Model 2 started at $3,000, and the Model 2A started at $3,500.

Each additional grade represented more embellishments and better grade of walnut. Magnum chambers could be ordered at a small surcharge. Importation began 1982, values represent the last published retail prices from 1989.

MODEL B - 12, 16, 20, 28 ga., or .410 bore, large key opening, self-opening (assisted) action, ejectors, double triggers only, basically special ordered to individual customer specifications.

Retail values were as follows: Model B started at $5,800 and included deluxe carrying case.

Each additional upgrade represented more embellishments and a better grade of walnut. Magnum chambers could be ordered at a small surcharge. Importation began 1982, values represent the last published retail prices from 1989.

BRUGGER & THOMET

Current manufacturer established in 1991 and located in Thun, Switzerland. Currently imported by B&T USA located in Tampa, FL beginning 2016. Previously imported by D.S.A., located in Barrington, IL until 2016.

For individual model listings, please go to BlueBookOfGunValues.com/overflow.

BRYCO ARMS

Previous manufacturer located in Irvine, CA until 2003. Previously distributed by Jennings Firearms, Inc. located in Carson City, NV.

GRADING - PPGS™	100%	98%	95%	90%	80%	70%	60%	LAST MSR

PISTOLS: SEMI-AUTO, SINGLE ACTION

MODEL T-22 – while advertised during 1997 at a retail price of $179, this model was never produced.

MODEL J-25 – .25 ACP cal., aluminum alloy frame, 2 1/2 in. barrel, single action, synthetic ivory, walnut, or black combat grips, positive safety, 11 oz. Mfg. 1988-95, reintroduced 1999.

$110	$95	$85	$75	$60	$50	$40	*$79*

This model was available in either satin nickel, bright chrome, or black Teflon finish.

MODEL M-32/M-38 – .22 LR (disc.), .32 ACP, or .380 ACP cal., semi-auto single action, 2.8 in. barrel, pressure cast fabrication using non-ferrous alloy, chrome or blue finish, black combat grips, 16 oz. Mfg. 1991-disc.

$110	$95	$85	$75	$60	$50	$40	*$79*

Add $20 for .380 ACP cal.

MODEL M-48 – .22 LR, .32 ACP, or .380 ACP cal., semi-auto single action, 4 in. barrel, larger frame variation of the M-38, chrome or blue finish, black combat grips, 24 oz. Mfg. 1991-95.

$125	$110	$95	$85	$70	$55	$45	*$96*

MODEL M-5 – .380 ACP or 9mm Para. cal., 3 1/4 in. barrel, 10 or 12 shot mag., blue or nickel finish, black synthetic grips, 36 oz. Disc. 1995.

$130	$115	$100	$90	$70	$60	$50	

Add $15 for 9mm Para. cal.
Last MSR was $100 for the .380 ACP, $119 for 9mm Para.

MODEL M-59 – .380 ACP or 9mm Para. cal., 4 in. barrel, 10 shot mag., blue or nickel finish, black synthetic grips, 36 oz. Disc. 1995.

$140	$125	$110	$95	$75	$65	$50	*$119*

Add $15 for 9mm Para. cal.

JENNINGS NINE – 9mm Para. cal., single action, redesigned model 59, frame mounted ejector, contour grips, loaded chamber indicator, 30 oz. Mfg. 1997-2003.

$150	$130	$115	$100	$85	$70	$60	*$145*

BUDISCHOWSKY

Previous trade name of firearms designed by Edgar Budischowsky, initially manufactured in Ulm, Germany by Korriphila GmbH, and subsequently by Norton Armament Corporation (NORARMCO) in Mt. Clemens, MI.

PISTOLS: SEMI-AUTO

TP-70 – .22 LR or .25 ACP cal., double action, 2.6 in. barrel, stainless steel, fixed sights, 6 shot mag., plastic grips, 12 oz. Mfg. 1973-1977.

$440	$385	$330	$265	$230	$195	$175	

Note: In 1977, Norton Arms marketed this pistol. Quality of workmanship is not on par with early Budischowsky, and values are approx. 35% less.

SEMI-AUTO PISTOL – .223 Rem. cal., 11 5/8 in. barrel, 20 or 30 shot mag., fixed sights, a novel tactical designed type pistol.

$470	$415	$385	$360	$305	$250	$220	

RIFLES: SEMI-AUTO

TACTICAL DESIGN RIFLE – .223 Rem. cal., 18 in. barrel, wood tactical stock.

$500	$440	$415	$385	$330	$275	$250	

TACTICAL DESIGN RIFLE W/FOLDING STOCK – .223 Rem. cal., 18 in. barrel, folding stock.

$575	$500	$450	$425	$395	$360	$330	

BUEHLER CUSTOM SPORTING ARMS

Current custom gun manufacturer established during 2005, located in Medford, OR.

Reto Buehler manufactures high quality custom order bolt action and single shot rifles. He also specializes in the repair and restocking of double rifles, shotguns, and combination guns. Since all guns are built or repaired per customer's specifications, please contact him directly for available options, pricing, and delivery time.

BUFFALO ARMS

Previous manufacturer located in Tonowanda, NY.

DERRINGERS: O/U

MODEL 1 – .357 Mag. or .38 Spl. cal., nickel finish. Disc.

$250	$225	$195	$175	$150	$135	$125	

GRADING - PPGS™	100%	98%	95%	90%	80%	70%	60%	LAST MSR

BULA DEFENSE SYSTEMS

Current manufacturer and custom builder of commercial and military spec rifles and accessories, located in Cleveland, OH.

RIFLES: SEMI-AUTO

M14 (BATTLE RIFLE) – .308 Win., .450 Bushmaster (disc. 2020), or 6.5 Creedmoor (disc. 2020) cal., GPO, M14 platform, 19 1/4 (Paratrooper), 20 (disc. 2020), or 22 in. medium weight Bull (disc. 2020), National Match, Paratrooper, or modified USGI barrel, USGI flash hider w/bayonet lug, 4 grooves, 20 shot mag., fully adj. aperture rear sight, American walnut stock, forged Mil-Spec receiver, integrated optics scope rail, removable solid mount, two sling swivels, manganese phosphate finish, right or left-hand action, 41-44 in. OAL, 9-10 lbs.

MSR $2,250	$1,925	$1,685	$1,450	$1,310	$1,075	$875	$700	

Add $50 for National Match barrel.
Add $150 for left-hand.
Add $200 for tactical stock.
Add $200 for 6.5 Creedmoor cal. with National Match barrel (disc. 2020).

M21 DMR (DESIGNATED MARKSMAN RIFLE) – 7.62 NATO or .308 Win. cal., GPO, M14 platform, 19 1/4 or 22 in. modified USGI or National Match barrel, USGI flash hider w/bayonet lug, 4 grooves, 20 shot mag., iron sights, carbon fiber (disc.), tactical, or American walnut stock, forged Mil-Spec receiver, solid Picatinny rail, integrated optics scope rail, removable solid mount, manganese phosphate finish, 41-44 in. OAL, 9-10 lbs.

MSR $2,395	$2,050	$1,800	$1,550	$1,400	$1,125	$925	$725	

Add $50 for National Match barrel.
Add $150 for left-hand action.
Add $200 for tactical stock.

XM21 CBR (CARBON FIBER BATTLE RIFLE) – .308 Win. cal., GIO, Garand style action, 16 1/4 or 18 1/2 in. National Match barrel, AG composite CBR stock with Mil-Spec buffer tube, 6-pos. telescoping M4 style buttstock, pistol grip, Mil-Spec 1913 Picatinny rails at 3, 6, and 9 o'clock positions, forged XM21 flat-top receiver, forward top rail on plane with milled rail on the receiver for BUIS alignment, black Nitride finish, multiple color options available, 7.8 lbs. Mfg. 2017-2020.

	$2,550	$2,250	$1,775	$1,525	$1,250	$1,050	$925	*$2,895*

BULLARD REPEATING ARMS COMPANY

Previous manufacturer located in Springfield, MA, circa 1882-1891.

Designed by prolific inventor James Bullard, the design, quality, and workmanship of Bullard rifles rivaled those of any competitor during the 1880s. Bullard made two basic rifles: a lever action repeater and a single shot. The repeater was made in two frame styles: large and small. The single shot was also made in two basic styles; solid frame and detachable-interchangeable barrel model. Total production is estimated at 2,800 rifles.

The author would like to thank Mr. Gene Weicht for providing information and values for this section.

100%	98%	95%	90%	80%	70%	60%	50%	40%	30%	20%	10%

RIFLES: LEVER ACTION

LEVER ACTION REPEATER – rack and pinion style lever activated mechanism, mag. mounted under barrel, loaded through underside of action while lever was opened, blue finish with various parts (including receiver) sometimes case hardened, approx. 1,700 mfg.

* ***Lever Action Large Frame*** – .45-70 Govt., .45-75, .50-95, .40-70 Bullard, .40-75 Bullard, .40-90 Bullard, .45-85 Bullard, or .50-115 Bullard cal., 26 or 28 in. round, octagon, or part round barrel, crescent steel or hard rubber buttplates with elk motif, ser. no. range 1-1,500 and 2,000-3,000.

N/A	N/A	$4,150	$3,500	$3,000	$2,700	$2,400	$2,100	$1,700	$1,550	$1,200	$1,125

Add 25% for .40-90 Bullard, .50-95, or .50-115 Bullard cal.
Add 25% for deluxe checkered wood with pistol grip.

Various military and experimental models are found in this frame size and will command significant premiums.

Large frame repeating rifles up to ser. no. 113 will be marked "Bullard Repeating Arms Association". Ser. no. 114-4067 will be marked Bullard Repeating Arms Company.

* ***Lever Action Small Frame*** – .32-40 Bullard or .38-45 Bullard cal., (other calibers cataloged, but essentially unknown), 24, 26, or 28 in. round, octagon, or part round barrel, crescent steel or hard rubber buttplates with turkey motif, ser. no. range 1,500-2,000. Approx. 500 mfg.

N/A	N/A	$3,500	$3,000	$2,750	$2,350	$2,000	$1,750	$1,500	$1,250	$1,000	$950

100%	98%	95%	90%	80%	70%	60%	50%	40%	30%	20%	10%

Add 25% for deluxe checkered wood with pistol grip.
Add 40% for any caliber other than .32-40 and .38-45.

Although the small frame saw less production and is scarcer than the large frame repeater, it is not as desirable among collectors, and is typically priced less than a large frame model.

RIFLES: SINGLE SHOT

SINGLE SHOT MODEL – thin receiver with full lever, similar in appearance to small frame repeater action, except shorter (several parts will interchange), 26, 28, or 30 in. round, octagon, or part round barrel, blue finish with various parts sometimes case hardened (including receiver), crescent steel or hard rubber (turkey motifs) buttplates, ser. no. range 3,500-4,100. Approx. 600 mfg.

* ***Single Shot Solid Frame*** – wide variety of cals. from .22 rimfire to .50 cal., (.22 and .32-40 are most common), made in both frame sizes, narrow width or wide width action.

100%	98%	95%	90%	80%	70%	60%	50%	40%	30%	20%	10%
N/A	N/A	$3,900	$3,350	$2,950	$2,500	$2,275	$2,000	$1,775	$1,500	$1,250	$1,150

* ***Single Shot Detachable-interchangeable Barrel Model*** – same cals. as small frame model with two frame sizes - small (.38 cal. and smaller) and large (usually .40 cal. and larger, but some small calibers were mfg.), interchangeable barrels could not be switched between the two frame sizes, barrel and breech detach from action, narrow or wide width action.

100%	98%	95%	90%	80%	70%	60%	50%	40%	30%	20%	10%
N/A	N/A	$3,800	$3,175	$2,800	$2,450	$2,100	$1,950	$1,775	$1,550	$1,175	$1,125

Add 15% for large frame models in less than .40 cal.
Add 30% for .50 cals.
Add 30% for extra barrel with forend (numbers matching).
Add 30% for Schuetzen model.
Add 25% for deluxe checkered wood with pistol grip.
Values are for models with original sights and no stock alterations - subtract 15% if not original.

BULLSEYE GUN WORKS

Previous manufacturer located in Miami, FL circa 1954-1959.

CARBINES: SEMI-AUTO

Bullseye Gun Works initially started as a gun shop circa 1954, and several years later, they started manufacturing M1 carbines using their own receivers and barrels. Approx. 2,000 - 2,500 were manufactured with their name on the receiver side until the company was reorganized as Universal Firearms Corporation circa late 1950s. Values are typically in the $200 - $350 range, depending on originality and condition.

BUL ARMORY / BUL LTD. (TRANSMARK)

Current pistol manufacturer located in Tel Aviv, Israel since 1990. Currently imported by GP Arms located in Dandridge, TN beginning 2019. Bul M1911 parts were previously imported by All America Sales, Inc. located in Piggot, AR. Previously imported by International Firearms Corp. until late 2019. Previously imported 2003-early 2010 by K.B.I., located in Harrisburg, PA. Previously imported and distributed in North America during 2009 by Legacy Sports International, located in Reno, NV, and during 2002 by EAA Corp., located in Sharpes, FL. Previously imported and distributed 1997-2001 by International Security Academy (ISA) located in Los Angeles, CA, and from 1996-1997 by All America Sales, Inc. located in Memphis, TN. Dealer sales only.

BUL ARMORY

PISTOLS: SEMI-AUTO

Please refer to the Charles Daly: 1976-2010 section in this text for the most recent information and prices on Charles Daly imported Bul Transmark pistols (domestic imports were marked Charles Daly 2004-early 2010). Non-domestic Bul Pistols are typically marked Bul M-5 on left side of slide except for the Cherokee and Storm models. M-5 frame kits were previously available at $399 retail.

Many options, accessories, and finishes are available. Please contact the manufacturer directly.

1911 GOVERNMENT (BUL 1911 CLASSIC GOVERNMENT) – 9mm Para., .45 ACP, or 9x21 cal., short recoil operated, Govt. size steel frame and slide, 5 in. conventional barrel or bushingless bull barrel, 8 or 10 shot, internal extractor, skeletonized hammer and trigger, fixed 3-dot sights or adj. rear sight and fiber optic front sight (9mm Para. only.), textured G10 grips, extended safety lever, front and rear slide serrations, black oxide, stainless steel, or two-tone finish, approx. 2 1/2 lbs.

GRADING - PPGS™	100%	98%	95%	90%	80%	70%	60%	LAST MSR
MSR $830	$750	$650	$560	$525	$400	$350	$260	

Add $20 for stainless steel finish. Add $120 for adj. rear sight and fiber optic front sight.

GRADING - PPGS™	100%	98%	95%	90%	80%	70%	60%	LAST MSR

1911 COMMANDER (BUL 1911 CLASSIC COMMANDER) – 9mm Para., .45 ACP, or 9x21 cal., short recoil operated, 8, 9, or 10 shot, Commander steel frame and slide, 4 1/4 in. bushingless bull barrel, internal extractor, skeletonized hammer and trigger, fixed 3-dot sights, textured G10 grips, extended safety lever, front and rear slide serrations, black oxide, stainless steel, or two-tone finish, approx. 2 1/4 lbs.

MSR $830	$750	$650	$560	$525	$400	$350	$260	

Add $20 for stainless steel finish.

1911 ULTRA (BUL 1911 CLASSIC ULTRA) – 9mm Para., .45 ACP, or 9x21 cal., short recoil operated, "Ultra" Officer size aluminum frame and steel slide, 3 1/4 in. bushingless bull barrel, two 7 or 8 shot 1911 Ultra mags., internal extractor, skeletonized hammer and trigger, fixed front sight, adj. rear sight, textured G10 grips, extended safety lever, rear slide serrations, black oxide, stainless steel, or two-tone finish, approx. 1 1/2 lbs.

MSR $990	$880	$775	$660	$600	$480	$400	$300	

» **1911 Ultra Light (UL, Ultralight)** – 9mm Para. or .45 ACP cal., short recoil operated, "Ultra" Officer size aluminum frame and Ultralight steel slide, 3 1/4 in. fluted bushingless bull barrel, two 7 or 8 shot 1911 Ultra mags., internal extractor, skeletonized hammer, skeletonized trigger, fixed fiber optic front sight, adj. rear sight, textured G10 grips, extended safety lever, forward and rear slide serrations, black oxide, stainless steel, or two-tone finish, approx. 1 1/2 lbs.

MSR $990	$880	$775	$660	$600	$480	$400	$300	

1911 TROPHY (BUL 1911 CLASSIC TROPHY)/1911 TROPHY SAW – 9mm Para., 9x21, .45 ACP (Classic), or .40 S&W (SAW) cal., short recoil operated, Govt. size steel frame and slide, 5 in. stainless steel conventional or bushingless bull barrel, Gold Titanium Nitride barrel finish available, flared magwell, enlarged mag. release, three 1911 mags. w/polymer base plates, internal extractor, skeletonized hammer and trigger, fixed front fiber optic sight, adj. rear sight, textured G10 grips, extended safety lever, front and rear (Classic) or deep front, rear, and top (SAW) slide serrations, full length stainless steel guide rod, black oxide, stainless steel, or two-tone finish, approx. 2 1/2 lbs.

MSR $1,750	$1,575	$1,375	$1,175	$1,075	$860	$725	$550	

Add $100 for 1911 Trophy SAW.

Add $60 for two-tone polish. Add $150 for two-tone high polish finish (SAW model only).

* ***1911 Trophy CESAR*** – 9mm Para., .40 S&W, or 9x21 cal., short recoil operated, Govt. size steel frame and slide, 5 in. bushing or bushingless Bul barrel w/gold PVD finish, extended and flared oversized magwell, three 1911 mags., spring loaded competition internal extractor, CNC race hammer, match grade modular trigger kit, fixed front fiber optic sight, adj. rear sight, fully machined cross-checkered steel grips, extended ambi shielded safety levers, front and rear slide "Cesar" bullet shaped slide cuts, full length stainless steel guide rod, black oxide or stainless steel finish, approx. 2 1/2 lbs.

MSR $2,250	$2,000	$1,750	$1,500	$1,360	$1,100	$900	$700	

The Trophy CESAR model is an homage to Robert "Cesar" Cernigoj for winning the 2019 European Handgun Championship.

1911 TAC GOVERNMENT/COMMANDER (BUL 1911 TACTICAL CARRY GOVT/COMMANDER) – 9mm Para., .45 ACP, or 9x21 cal., short recoil operated, Govt. or Commander size slide and frame w/ Picatinny rail, 4 1/4 (Commander) or 5 (Govt.) in. conventional or bushingless barrel, two 1911 mags., internal extractor, skeletonized hammer and trigger, fixed 3-dot sights or adj. rear sight and fiber optic front sight (9mm Para. Govt. model only.), textured G10 grips, ambi ext. safety lever, front and rear slide serrations, black oxide finish, approx. 2 1/2 lbs.

MSR $950	$850	$750	$650	$575	$475	$375	$300	

Add $120 for adj. rear sight and fiber optic front sight.

1911 TACTICAL CARRY COMP (1911 TACTICAL STREET COMP) – 9mm Para., .45 ACP, or 9x21 cal., short recoil operated, Commander size steel slide and frame w/Picatinny rail, 4 1/4 in. bull barrel with single port compensator, three 1911 mags. w/polymer base plates, internal extractor, skeletonized hammer and trigger, fixed 3-dot sights, optional fiber optic sights, textured G10 grips, ambi ext. safety lever, front and rear slide serrations, black oxide finish, approx. 2 1/2 lbs. Disc. 2020.

	$1,150	$1,000	$860	$775	$640	$525	$400	*$1,280*

* ***1911 Ultra Tac Street Comp/Ultra Tac Shield*** – 9mm Para. or .45 ACP cal., short recoil operated, "Ultra" Officer frame w/Picatinny rail and steel slide, 3 1/4 in. bull barrel with single port compensator, internal extractor, skeletonized hammer and trigger, adj. rear (Street) or RMS-C red dot (Shield) sight, fixed fiber optic front sight, textured G10 grips, ext. safety lever, front and rear slide serrations, black oxide finish. Disc. 2020.

	$1,250	$1,100	$950	$850	$700	$560	$440	*$1,390*

Add $390 for Ultra Tac Shield model with RMS-C red dot sight.

GRADING - PPGS™	100%	98%	95%	90%	80%	70%	60%	LAST MSR

» **1911 Ultra Tactical Shield** – 9mm Para., or .45 ACP cal., short recoil operated, "Ultra" Officer frame w/Picatinny rail and steel slide, 3 1/4 in. bull barrel with single port compensator, internal extractor, skeletonized hammer, skeletonized trigger, Shield RMS-C red dot sight, fixed fiber optic front sight, textured G10 grips, ext. safety lever, front and rear slide serrations, black oxide finish. Disc. 2020.

$1,600 $1,400 $1,200 $1,100 $880 $725 $560 *$1,780*

1911 TARGET 6 IN. – 9mm Para., .45 ACP, or 9x21 cal., short recoil operated, Govt. size steel frame and ext. 6 in. steel slide, 6 in. conventional bushing barrel, two 8 (.45 ACP) or 10 (9mm Para.) shot mags., internal extractor, skeletonized hammer and trigger, adj. rear and fixed front sight, textured G10 grips, extended safety lever, full length guide rod, front and rear slide serrations, black oxide, stainless steel, two-tone, or PVD coated finish, approx. 2 1/2 lbs.

Please contact the importer directly for pricing and availability on this model.

BUL 1911 GOVERNMENT (M-5 STANDARD) – .38 Super, 9mm Para., .40 S&W, or .45 ACP cal., SA, 5 in. barrel, polymer double column frame, steel slide, aluminum speed trigger, checkered front and rear grip straps, blue or chrome (new 2000) finished slide, 10 shot staggered mag., 31-33 oz. Imported 1995-2000, reintroduced 2002-2003.

$525 $460 $395 $355 $290 $235 $185 *$559*

Add 10% for .38 Super or .40 S&W cal.

* ***Bul Commander (M5 Standard)*** – similar to M-5 Government, except has 3.8, 4 1/3, or 4 1/4 in. barrel, 29-30 oz. Imported 1998-2000, reintroduced 2002-2003. Disc.

$525 $460 $395 $355 $290 $235 $185 *$559*

Add 10% for .38 Super or .40 S&W cal.
Add 25% for early mfg. in 9mm Para. cal. with 18 shot mag. and Bul frame.
Add $40 for matte chrome finished slide.

* ***Bul M-5 Stinger*** – similar to Bul 1911 Government, except has 10 shot mag., 3 in. barrel, 24 oz. Imported 2002-2003.

$525 $460 $395 $355 $290 $235 $185 *$559*

* ***Bul M-5 Standard Street Comp.*** – similar to M-5 Standard Commander, except has single port compensated 4 1/4 in. barrel, 32 oz. Imported 1998-99.

$960 $840 $720 $650 $530 $430 $335 *$1,060*

Add $28 for .38 Super or .40 S&W cal.

* ***Bul M-5 Multi Caliber*** – similar cals. as the M-5 Standard Government, includes 3 upper-ends including Commander length, another with adj. sights, and a third with a single port compensator, cased. Imported 1999-2000.

$1,575 $1,380 $1,180 $1,070 $865 $710 $550 *$1,768*

BUL M-5 STANDARD IPSC – .38 Super, 9mm Para., .40 S&W, or .45 ACP cal., configured for IPSC competition, with custom slide to frame fit and match grade barrel bushing. Imported 1998-2001, reintroduced 2003. Disc.

$925 $810 $695 $630 $510 $415 $325 *$990*

Add $111 for .38 Super or .40 S&W cal. (disc. 2001).
Add $70 for chrome finish (mfg. 2000-2001).

BUL M-5 STANDARD MATCH – IPSC custom race gun, includes multi-port compensator system. Imported 1998-99.

$1,200 $1,050 $900 $815 $660 $540 $420 *$1,655*

Add $24 for .38 Super or .40 S&W cal.

BUL M-5 JET – same cals. as the M-5 Standard IPSC, features Commander length with 4 1/4 in. barrel and 4 port compensator, 31 oz. Imported 1999-2000.

$875 $765 $655 $595 $480 $395 $305 *$1,158*

Add $51 for .38 Super or .40 S&W cal.

BUL M-5 MODIFIED – 9mm Para., .38 Super, .40 S&W, or .45 ACP cal., designed for open division competition, features new Optima 2000 optical sight fitted to slide, 5 port compensator, includes carrying case, 38 oz. Imported 1998-2001.

$1,075 $940 $805 $730 $590 $485 $375 *$1,430*

BUL M-5 TARGET – same cals. as the M-5 Modified, features long slide and 6 in. barrel, choice of sights, and match grade oversize barrel bushing, includes 3 mags and carrying case, 38 oz. Imported 1999-2001.

$895 $785 $670 $610 $490 $405 $315 *$1,196*

Add $315 for Aristocrat Tri-state sights.

GRADING - PPGS™	100%	98%	95%	90%	80%	70%	60%	LAST MSR

BUL M-5 ULTIMATE RACER – top-level open division IPSC competition gun, includes 3 mags. and carrying case, 38 oz. Imported 1998-2001.

	$1,050	$920	$785	$715	$575	$470	$365	*$1,573*

Add $306 for fitted C-More optical sight.

BUL 1911 LIGHTWEIGHT CARRY – 9mm Para. or .45 ACP cal., Series 70 design, aluminum frame, 3 1/4 in. match grade bull barrel, 6 or 8 shot mag., lightweight match hammer, 3-hole trigger, low-mount adj. combat sights, G-10 grips, high-rise beavertail grip safety, extended thumb safety, full-length stainless steel guide rod, rear cocking serrations, flared ejection port, black oxide finish. Importation began 2019.

	$650	$550	$475	$425	$350	$275	$225	*$699*

BUL CHEROKEE FS (CHEROKEE) – 9mm Para. cal., DA/SA, full size polymer frame, steel forged slide, 4.45 in. barrel, two 17 shot mags., exposed hammer, squared off trigger guard, 3-dot sights, black polymer finger groove grips, manual thumb safety, integral Picatinny rail, includes hard case and cleaning kit. Imported 2009, reintroduced 2019.

MSR $490	$425	$375	$325	$300	$225	$180	$150

* ***Bul Cherokee Compact*** – similar to Cherokee except has compact polymer frame and 3.66 in. barrel. Imported 2009, reintroduced 2019.

MSR $490	$425	$375	$325	$300	$225	$180	$150

BUL STORM & COMPACT – while advertised during 1999, this model was never produced.

BUL IMPACT – while advertised during 1999, this model was never produced.

SAS II SL AIR (SAS II AIR) – 9mm Para., .40 S&W, 9x21, or 9x23 Win. cal. (2019 only), short recoil operated, 5 in. match grade ramped bull barrel with TiN gold finish, three 17 (.40 S&W cal.) or 19 shot double-stack mag., oversized adj. mag. release button, competition magwell, full length steel dust cover frame with or w/o Picatinny rail, lightweight ported steel slide, lightweight skeletonized hammer and trigger, adj. rear sight, fixed fiber optic front sight, polymer grip, high-rise beavertail safety, ambi ext. safety levers, black stainless or stainless steel finish, approx. 2 1/3 lbs. Importation began 2019.

MSR $2,550	$2,250	$1,975	$1,700	$1,525	$1,240	$1,025	$800

SAS II BULLESTEROS – 9mm Para., 9x21, 9x23 Win. (2019 only), or .38 Super cal., short recoil operated, match grade one-piece 5.7 in. hybrid compensated ramped bull barrel, TiN gold barrel finish optional, three 19 shot mags. w/aluminum baseplates, oversized adj. mag. release, enlarged brass or aluminum magwell, full length steel dust cover frame, Govt. length lightened and ported stainless steel slide, lightweight skeletonized hammer, modular aluminum match trigger w/replaceable trigger shoes, Nikko Stirling 6 MOA red dot sight, Cmore RTS and Vortex Razor optics supported, optics mount w/ thumb rest, stainless steel grip, ambi wide shielded safety levers, full-length stainless steel guide rod, oversized slide racker, stainless or black stainless finish, approx. 3 1/2 lbs. Importation began 2019.

MSR $4,759	$4,275	$3,750	$3,200	$2,900	$2,350	$1,925	$1,500

SAS II EDC – 9mm Para., .38 Super, 9x21, 9x23 Win., or .45 ACP cal., short recoil operated, Govt. or Commander length slide, double stack frame with short dust cover, 4 1/4 or 5 in. stainless conventional (Govt. slide only), fluted, or bushingless bull barrel, 13 or 19 shot double-stack mag., oversized mag. release, competition magwell, aluminum skeletonized trigger, fixed 3 dot sights, high-rise beavertail ambi safety, front and rear slide serrations, black oxide or stainless finish, approx. 2 1/8 lbs. Imported 2019 only.

Retail pricing was not available for this model.

SAS II RADICAL – 9mm Para., .40 S&W, 9x21, or 9x23 Win. cal. (2019 only), short recoil operated, RADICAL match grade 5.4 or 5.7 in. ramped bull barrel, three 17 (.40 S&W cal.) or 19 shot mags. w/aluminum or brass floorplates, oversized adj. mag. release button, shortened competition brass magwell, steel full length dust cover frame, steel slide, lightweight skeletonized or flattened hammer, aluminum skeletonized trigger, adj. rear sight, barrel mounted fixed fiber optic front sight, polymer grip, high-rise shortened beavertail safety, ambi ext. safety levers, front and rear slide serrations, full length guide rod, stainless steel finish, approx. 2 1/2 lbs.

MSR $3,090	$2,775	$2,425	$2,075	$1,875	$1,525	$1,250	$975

Add $100 for 5.7 in. barrel.

These pistols were designed to fit specifically into IPSC Standard Division boxes without sacrificing barrel length or other performance features.

SAS II SL SAW (SAS II SAW) – 9mm Para., .40 S&W, 9x21, or 9x23 Win. cal. (2019 only), short recoil operated, 5 in. match grade ramped stainless bull barrel, TiN gold barrel finish optional, three 17 (.40 S&W cal.) or 19 shot mags., oversized adj. mag. release button, competition magwell, steel full length dust cover frame, steel slide, lightweight skeletonized hammer, aluminum skeletonized trigger, adj. rear sight, fixed fiber optic front sight, polymer grip, high-rise beavertail safety, ambi ext. safety levers, deep front, rear, and top SAW slide serrations, black stainless or stainless steel finish, approx. 2 1/3 lbs.

MSR $2,350	$2,125	$1,875	$1,600	$1,450	$1,175	$950	$750

GRADING - PPGS™	100%	98%	95%	90%	80%	70%	60%	LAST MSR

SAS II SL (SAS II STANDARD LIMITED) – 9mm Para., .40 S&W, 9x21, or 9x23 Win. cal. (2019 only), short recoil operated, 5 in. match grade ramped stainless bull barrel, three 17 (.40 S&W cal.) or 19 shot mags., oversized adj. mag. release button, competition magwell, steel full length dust cover frame with or without Picatinny rail, steel slide, lightweight skeletonized hammer, aluminum skeletonized trigger, adj. rear sight, fixed fiber optic front sight, polymer grip, high-rise beavertail safety, ambi ext. safety levers, front and rear slide serrations, black stainless or stainless steel finish, approx. 2 1/4 lbs.

MSR $2,190	$1,975	$1,725	$1,475	$1,350	$1,075	$880	$700

SAS II TAC GOVERNMENT/COMMANDER (SAS II TACTICAL CARRY) – 9mm Para., .38 Super (disc. 2020), 9x21, 9x23 Win. (2019 only), or .45 ACP cal., short recoil operated, Govt. or Commander length slide and tactical mid-length (Govt.) or 3/4 length (Commander) frame w/Picatinny rail, 4 1/4 (Commander) or 5 (Govt.) in. stainless conventional bushing (Govt. only), fluted, or bushingless bull barrel, 14 (.45 ACP cal.) or 19 shot mags., oversized mag. release, competition magwell, aluminum skeletonized trigger, fixed 3-dot sights or adj. rear sight and fiber optic front sight (9mm Para. only.), high-rise beavertail ambi safety, front and rear slide serrations, black oxide or two-tone finish, approx. 2 1/8 lbs. Importation began 2019.

MSR $1,350	$1,225	$1,075	$925	$825	$675	$550	$425

Add $120 for adj. rear sight and fiber optic front sight (9mm Para. only).

* ***SAS II Tac Commander SC (SAS II StreetComp)*** – 9mm Para., 9x21 (new 2020) or .45 ACP cal., short recoil operated, Commander size slide, 4 1/2 in. bull barrel with single port compensator, two 14 (.45 ACP cal.) or 19 shot mags., double stack 3/4 length tactical frame with dust cover Picatinny rail and steel slide, internal extractor, skeletonized hammer and trigger, fixed 3-dot sights, optional fiber optic sights, ambi ext. safety lever, front and rear slide serrations, black oxide finish, approx. 2 lbs.

MSR $1,590	$1,425	$1,250	$1,075	$975	$775	$650	$500

SAS II ULTIMATE RACER (UR) – 9mm Para., 9x21 (new 2019), 9x23 Win. (2019 only), or .38 Super (new 2019) cal., short recoil operated, 5 in. match grade compensated bull barrel, TiN gold barrel finish optional, three 19 shot mags. w/aluminum baseplate, oversized adj. mag. release, enlarged magwell, steel short dust cover frame, Govt. length lightened and ported stainless steel slide, lightweight skeletonized hammer and trigger, with or w/o Nikko Stirling 4 or 6 (new 2019) MOA red dot sight, polymer grip, wide ambi ext. safety levers, full-length stainless steel guide rod, oversized slide racker, black T or stainless finish, optional 27 shot mag. available. Importation began 2019.

MSR $3,490	$3,125	$2,740	$2,350	$2,125	$1,720	$1,400	$1,100

* ***SAS II Ultimate Racer Shorty*** – 9mm Para., 9x21, 9x23 Win. (disc. 2020), or .38 Super cal., short recoil operated, 4 1/4 in. match grade compensated bull barrel, TiN gold barrel finish optional, three 120mm length mags. w/aluminum baseplate, oversized adj. mag. release, enlarged magwell, stainless steel short dust cover frame, commander length lightened and ported stainless steel slide, internal extractor, skeletonized hammer, skeletonized trigger, Nikko Stirling 6 MOA red dot sight, polymer grip, ambi ext. safety levers, oversized slide racker, approx. 2 1/2 lbs.

MSR $3,450	$3,100	$2,725	$2,325	$2,100	$1,700	$1,400	$1,075

* ***SAS II UR F*** – 9mm Para., 9x21, or .38 Super cal., short recoil operated, 5 in. match grade compensated bull barrel, TiN gold barrel finish optional, three 19 shot mags. w/aluminum baseplate, oversized adj. mag. release, enlarged magwell, full length dust cover frame, Govt. length lightened stainless steel slide, lightweight skeletonized hammer, aluminum skeletonized trigger, Nikko Stirling 6 MOA red dot sight, polymer grip, wide ambi ext. safety levers, full-length stainless steel guide rod, oversized slide racker, stainless steel or black stainless finish, optional 27 shot mag. available, 2.7 lbs. New 2020.

MSR $3,550	$3,200	$2,800	$2,400	$2,175	$1,760	$1,440	$1,125

* ***SAS II UR Heavy Metal (SAS II Heavy Metal)*** – 9mm Para., 9x21 (disc. 2020), 9x23 Win. (disc. 2020), or .38 Super cal., short recoil operated, 5 in. match grade compensated bull barrel, TiN gold barrel finish optional, three 19 shot mags. w/aluminum baseplate, oversized adj. mag. release, enlarged magwell, full length steel dust cover frame, Govt. length lightened and ported stainless steel slide, lightweight skeletonized hammer and trigger, with or w/o Nikko Stirling 4 or 6 (new 2020) MOA red dot sight, polymer grip, wide ambi ext. safety levers, full-length stainless steel guide rod, oversized slide racker, integrated thumb rest on optics mount, black or stainless finish.

MSR $3,550	$3,200	$2,800	$2,400	$2,175	$1,775	$1,450	$1,125

SAS II FS (SAS II ULTRA FS) – 9mm Para., or .45 ACP cal., short recoil operated, full size double stack aluminum frame with Picatinny rail dust cover, steel Officer size slide, 3 1/4 in. ramped bull barrel, two 14 (.45 ACP cal.) or 19 shot mags. with aluminum baseplate, internal extractor, skeletonized hammer and trigger, adj. rear and fixed front sight, polymer grip panels, ext. safety lever, rear slide serrations, black oxide or two-tone finish, approx. 1 1/2 lbs.

MSR $1,090	$975	$850	$725	$660	$540	$450	$350

GRADING - PPGS™	100%	98%	95%	90%	80%	70%	60%	LAST MSR

* ***SAS II UL/UL Shield (SAS II Ultralight/Shield)*** – 9mm Para. or .45 ACP cal., short recoil operated, short (Ultralight) or full (Shield) size double stack aluminum frame with Picatinny rail dust cover, Ultralight machined Officer size slide, 3 1/4 in. ramped fluted bull barrel, two 14 (.45 ACP cal. Ultralight model only), 15, or 19 (9mm Para. Shield model) shot mags. with aluminum baseplates, internal extractor, skeletonized hammer and trigger, adj. rear or RMS-C red dot (Shield) sight, fixed fiber optic front sight, polymer grip panels, ext. safety lever, front, rear, and top slide serrations, black oxide or two-tone (Ultralight only) finish, approx. 1 1/3-1 1/2 lbs.

MSR $1,270 $1,150 $1,000 $880 $775 $640 $525 $400

* ***SAS II UL Viper (SAS II Viper)*** – 9mm Para. or .45 ACP (2019 conly) cal., short recoil operated, full size double stack aluminum frame with Picatinny rail dust cover, steel Officer size slide, 3 1/4 in. fluted and ramped bull barrel with single port compensator, two 14 (.45 ACP cal.) or 19 shot mags. with aluminum baseplate, internal extractor, skeletonized hammer and trigger, RMS-C red dot optic, fixed blade or fiber optic front sight, polymer grip panels, ext. safety lever, front and rear slide serrations, black oxide finish, approx. 1 1/2 lbs.

MSR $1,880 $1,680 $1,475 $1,260 $1,150 $925 $750 $600

RIFLES: SEMI-AUTO

BL9 PCC – 9mm Para. cal., direct blowback operation, 14 1/2 or 16 in. stainless barrel, aluminum muzzle brake (permanently attached on 14 1/2 in. barrel), uses Glock pattern mags., curved or flat single stage competition trigger, ext. aluminum trigger guard, FAB Defense GL-Core S buttstock, lightweight aluminum M-LOK handguard, FAB Defense AGR-43 grip, ambi safety, ambi charging handle, forward handstop, offset 45 deg. optics mount, functional LRBHO, red, blue, purple, or black anodized finish. New 2019.

Please contact the importer directly for pricing and availability on this model.

BUMAR

Current military supplier and exporter of armament, as well as manufacturing some makes/models available to the civilian marketplace. Distributed exclusively by Beryl ASG. The Bumar Group consists of 27 manufacturing and trading defense sector companies specializing in small arms, munitions, and large scale military weapons and accessories. Please contact the company directly for current civilian offerings, U.S. availability, and pricing.

THE BURGESS GUN CO.

Previous manufacturer located in Buffalo, NY circa 1892-1899.

Andrew Burgess was a prolific firearms designer who held many firearms patents and designed guns for Colt, Marlin, and Whitney before forming The Burgess Gun Co. Burgess manufactured slide action rifles and shotguns of a unique design that incorporated an iron sleeve fitted over the wrist portion of the stock which operated the action.

RIFLES: SLIDE ACTION

Burgess rifles are very rare and need to be appraised individually. Also refer to the Colt section for the Colt-Burgess lever action model.

SHOTGUNS: SLIDE ACTION

Burgess shotguns have either a takedown or folding frame that was hinged on the bottom and manufactured in both plain/standard and fancy/deluxe grades. It is believed production may have reached a few thousand, with the vast majority being 12 gauge shotguns and only very few rifles. These long guns should be treated as a collectible and not fired. Solid frame shotguns are valued $300-$1,500 range, depending on condition. Folding frame shotguns are currently in the $600-$3,500 range, depending on original condition. Deluxe examples will bring premiums.

BUSHMASTER FIREARMS

Current trademark of AR-15 style carbines, rifles, and pistols established in the 1970s, currently manufactured in Huntsville, AL, with company headquarters located in Madison, NC. Previously located in Windham, ME until 2011.

Bushmaster was initially manufactured by Gwinn Arms Co. located in Winston-Salem, NC between 1972 and 1974. The Quality Parts Co. gained control in 1986. During 2003, Bushmaster purchased Professional Ordnance, previous maker of the Carbon 15 Series of semi-auto pistols and rifles/carbines (for pre-2003 Carbon 15 manufacture, please refer to the Professional Ordnance section). In April, 2006, Bushmaster was sold to Cerberus Capital Management and became part of the Freedom Group. On March 31, 2011, Freedom Group Inc. announced that Bushmaster's manufacturing facility in Windham, ME would be closing, and new Bushmaster

GRADING - PPGS™	100%	98%	95%	90%	80%	70%	60%	LAST MSR

products would be produced in other Freedom Group facilities. In 2015, the Freedom Group was renamed as Remington Outdoor Company. In January 2020, Remington announced that they would no longer be producing Bushmaster firearms. As part of Remington's bankruptcy proceedings, Bushmaster was sold off at auction in September, 2020 to Crotalus Holdings, Inc. and the current status of production is unknown.

PISTOLS: SEMI-AUTO

ACR PISTOL – 5.56 NATO cal., 10 1/2 in. chrome moly steel barrel, Advanced Armament Blackout flash hider, quick-detach sling mount receiver endplate, accepts QD sling attachments, AAC SquareDrop modular handguard (KeyMod compatible), fully ambidextrous controls with full time ambi charging handle, black finish, 6 1/2 lbs. New 2019.

MSR $2,149	$1,600	$1,275	$1,150	$1,000	$950	$875	$800	

BUSHMASTER ARM PISTOL – .223 Rem. cal., bullpup configuration, AK-47 design, top (older models with aluminum receivers) or side mounted charging handle (most recent mfg.), steel frame on later mfg., 11 1/2 in. barrel, parkerized finish, adj. sights, 5 1/4 lbs., original mfg. by Gwinn Arms Co. beginning circa 1972-1974. Disc. circa 1988.

N/A	$3,500	$3,000	$2,650	$2,385	$1,925	$1,575	*$375*

Add 10% for electroless nickel finish (disc. 1988).
Add 20% for matte nickel finish (mfg. circa 1986-1988).

This model uses a 30 shot M-16 mag. and the AK-47 gas piston operating system.

During 1985-1986, a procurement officer for the U.S. Air Force ordered 2,100 of this model for pilot use with a matte nickel finish. Eventually, this officer was retired or transferred, and the replacement officer turned down the first batch, saying they were "too reflective". Bushmaster then sold these models commercially circa 1986-1988.

CARBON-15 TYPE P21S/TYPE 21 – 5.56 NATO cal., GIO, ultra lightweight carbon fiber upper and lower receivers, 7 1/4 in. "Profile" stainless steel barrel, quick detachable muzzle compensator, ghost ring sights, 10 or 30 (new late 2004) shot mag., A2 pistol grip, also accepts AR-15 type mags., Stoner type operating system, tool steel bolt, extractor and carrier, 40 oz. Mfg. 2003-2012 (Bushmaster mfg.).

$725	$625	$550	$475	$400	$325	$295	*$871*

Subtract approx. $200 if without full-length barrel shroud and Picatinny rail (Type 21, disc. 2005).

CARBON-15 TYPE 97/TYPE P97S – GIO, similar to Professional Ordnance Carbon 15 Type 20, except has fluted barrel, Hogue overmolded pistol grip and chrome plated bolt carrier, Type 97S has full-length barrel shroud, upper and lower Picatinny rail, 46 oz. Mfg. 2003-2012 (Bushmaster mfg.).

$695	$600	$525	$450	$375	$300	$285	*$825*

Add $78 for Model P97S with full-length barrel shroud and lower Picatinny rail.
Subtract approx. $100 if w/o full-length barrel shroud and lower Picatinny rail (disc.)

CARBON-15 9MM – 9mm Para. cal., blowback operation, carbon fiber composite receivers, 7 1/2 in. steel barrel with A1 birdcage flash hider, A2 front sight, full-length Picatinny optics rail, Neoprene foam sleeve over buffer tube, 10 or 30 shot mag, 4.6 lbs. Mfg. 2006-2012.

$785	$710	$625	$550	$475	$400	$325	*$871*

PIT VIPER AP-21 – 5.56 NATO cal., 7 1/4 in. barrel with A2 flash hider, 30 shot mag., forged upper and lower receivers, padded buffer tube, visible barrel nut, no forward handguard, Hogue rubberized grip, Mil-Spec safety, upper receiver Picatinny rail, visible gas tube, black anodized finish, approx. 3 1/2 lbs. Limited mfg. 2011 only.

$725	$625	$550	$475	$400	$325	$295	*$873*

SQUAREDROP PISTOL – 5.56 NATO or .300 AAC Blackout cal., 7, 9, or 10 in. chrome moly steel barrel, AAC SquareDrop and Blackout flash hider, 30 shot mag., Mil-Std upper and lower receiver, SquareDrop rail, SB tactical arm brace, ALG defense fire control group. New 2018.

MSR $1,399	$1,050	$825	$750	$650	$625	$575	$525	

XM-15 PATROLMAN'S AR PISTOL – 5.56 NATO cal., GIO, 7 or 10 1/2 in. stainless steel barrel with A2 flash hider, knurled free float tubular handguard, flat-top receiver with Picatinny rail, Phase 5 ambi single point sling attachment, A2 pistol grip and standard trigger guard, aluminum pistol buffer tube with foam featuring laser engraved Bushmaster logo, 30 shot mag., approx. 5 1/2 lbs. Mfg. 2013-2015.

$725	$575	$525	$450	$425	$400	$350	*$973*

XM-15 ENHANCED PATROLMAN'S AR PISTOL – 5.56 NATO cal., GIO, 7 or 10 1/2 in. stainless steel barrel with AAC 3-prong flash hider, 30 shot mag., free float lightweight quad rail handguard, Phase 5 ambi single point sling attachment, Magpul MOE pistol grip and trigger guard, aluminum pistol buffer tube with foam featuring laser engraved Bushmaster logo. Mfg. 2013-2015.

$925	$725	$650	$575	$550	$500	$450	*$1,229*

GRADING - PPGS™	100%	98%	95%	90%	80%	70%	60%	LAST MSR

RIFLES: BOLT ACTION

BA50 CARBINE/RIFLE – .50 BMG cal., 22 (carbine, disc. 2011) or 30 (rifle) in. Lothar Walther free floating barrel with vent. forend, AAC Cyclops muzzle brake/silencer adapter (new 2014), 10 shot mag., left side bolt handle, full-length receiver Picatinny rail, Magpul PRS adj. buttstock with LimbSavr recoil pad, high efficiency recoil reducing muzzle brake, steel bipod with folding legs, ErgoGrip deluxe tactical pistol grip, aluminum lower receiver, Manganese Phosphate finish on steel parts, hard anodized black finish on aluminum parts, includes Storm hardcase and two mags., 20 or 27 lbs. New 2009.

MSR $5,657	$4,995	$4,500	$4,000	$3,500	$3,000	$2,650	$2,300	

Last MSR on the carbine was $5,261.

VARMINTER – 5.56 NATO cal., Model 700 action, 24 in. barrel w/o sights, Hogue overmolded green pillar bedded stock, 4 shot internal box magazine, features a TrackingPoint 3x-21x zoom scope with laser range finder, gyroscopes, and camera, programmable optics software adjusts for different ammunition, 10.3 lbs. Mfg. 2014-2015.

	$4,250	$3,720	$3,195	$2,895	$2,350	$1,925	$1,500	*$5,000*

RIFLES: SEMI-AUTO

All current AR-15 style Bushmaster rifles are shipped with a hard plastic lockable case. Most Bushmaster barrels are marked "5.56 NATO", and can be used safely with either 5.56 NATO (higher velocity/pressure) or .223 Rem. cal. ammo.

Information and values for state compliant variations are not listed.

During 2006, Bushmaster began offering a complete gas piston upper receiver/barrel assembly. Last MSRs ranged from $580-$990, depending on caliber and configuration.

The XM-10 typically refers to 7.62 NATO cal., and XM-15 refers to 5.56 NATO cal. on the current models listed.

.300 AAC BLACKOUT – .300 AAC Blackout cal., GIO, 16 in. M4 contour barrel with AAC Blackout muzzle brake, Magpul ACS stock and MOE grip, free floating quad rail, 30 shot mag. (AR compatible), flat-top receiver with Picatinny rail, 6 1/2 lbs. Mfg. 2012-2015.

	$1,125	$900	$800	$700	$650	$625	$550	*$1,508*

.450 CARBINE/RIFLE – .450 Bushmaster cal., GIO, 16 (carbine) or 20 in. chrome moly steel barrel, 5 shot mag., solid A2 buttstock with trapdoor, A2 pistol grip, forged aluminum A3 flat-top upper receiver with Picatinny rail, free floating vented aluminum forend, 8 1/2 lbs. New 2008.

MSR $1,199	$900	$725	$650	$575	$525	$500	$450	

450 BM SD CARBINE – .450 Bushmaster cal., 16 or 20 in. chrome moly steel barrel with muzzle brake, 5 shot mag., ALG advanced combat trigger, B5 SOPMOD stock (16 in. barrel) or Remington R25 stock with recoil pad (20 in. barrel), Hogue grip, Mil-Std upper and lower receiver, rifle length AAC Squaredrop handguard, 6 lbs. New 2018.

MSR $1,299	$975	$775	$700	$600	$575	$525	$475	

6.8mm SPC/7.62x39mm CARBINE – 6.8mm SPC or 7.62x39mm (new 2010) cal., GIO, 16 in. M4 profile barrel with Izzy muzzle brake, 6-position telescoping stock, available in A2 (disc. 2012) or A3 configuration, 26 shot mag., includes black web sling, extra mag. and lockable carrying case, approx. 7 lbs. Mfg. late 2006-late 2013.

	$1,175	$775	$550	$465	$415	$375	$350	*$1,402*

Add $100 for A3 configuration (disc. 2010).

ORIGINAL BUSHMASTER TACTICAL RIFLE - EARLY GWINN MFG. – 5.56 NATO cal., GPO, 18 1/2 in. barrel, 30 shot M-16 mag., steel receiver (recent mfg.), adj. sights, wood or left-side folding stock, A1 style grip, top charging handle (older models with aluminum receivers) or side charging handle (recent mfg.), parkerized or electroless nickel (disc. 1988) finish, base values are for folding stock model. Early mfg. by Gwinn Arms Co. Disc.

	N/A	$2,500	$2,150	$1,850	$1,650	$1,450	$1,300	*$350*

* ***Bushmaster Rifle Combination System*** – GPO, includes rifle with both metal folding stock and wood stock with pistol grip.

	$745	$500	$435	$375	$335	$315	$295	*$450*

TARGET/COMPETITION A-2/A-3 RIFLE (XM15-E2S) – 5.56 NATO cal., GIO, patterned after the Colt AR-15, 20, 24 (disc. 2012), or 26 (disc. 2002) in. Govt. spec. match grade chrome-lined or stainless steel (new 2002) barrel with A2 flash hider, 10 or 30 shot mag., manganese phosphate or Realtree Camo (20 in. barrel only, mfg. 2004-late 2006) finish, rear sight adj. for windage and elevation, cage flash suppressor (disc. 1994), approx. 8.3 lbs. Mfg. began 1989 in U.S.

MSR $969	$725	$575	$525	$450	$425	$400	$350	

GRADING - PPGS™	100%	98%	95%	90%	80%	70%	60%	LAST MSR

Add $30 for A3 configuration with removable carry handle.
Add $88 for stainless steel barrel with A3 removable carry handle (disc. 2015).
Add $194 for heavy 1 in. diameter competition barrel (disc. 2011).
Add $50 for fluted barrel or $40 for stainless steel barrel (mfg. 2002-2009).
Add $10 for 24 in. (disc. 2012) or $25 for 26 in. (disc. 2002) barrel.
Add $60 for Realtree Camo finish (disc.).

HEAVY BARREL CARBINE A-2/A-3 (XM15-E2S, SHORTY CARBINE) – 5.56 NATO cal., GIO, 11 1/2 (LE only, disc. 1995), 14 (LE only, disc. 1994), or 16 in. heavy barrel with birdcage flash suppressor, 30 shot mag., choice of A2 or A3 configuration, fixed (disc.) or telescoping buttstock, approx. 7.4 lbs. Mfg. began 1989.

MSR $895	$675	$525	$475	$425	$400	$375	$325	

Add $52 for A3 configuration with removable carry handle.

This model does not have the target rear sight system of the XM15-E2S rifle.

* ***M4 Post-Ban Carbine (XM15-E2S)*** – 5.56 NATO cal., GIO, 16 in. barrel, fixed or telestock (new late 2004) tubular stock, pistol grip, black, FDE, OD Green, phosphate (disc.), A-TACS camo, or Desert Camo (stock, pistol grip, and forearm only, disc. 2005) finish, M4 carbine configuration with permanently attached Izzy muzzle brake, 30 shot mag. became standard in late 2004. Mfg. 2003-2015.

	$1,000	$800	$700	$625	$575	$550	$500	*$1,331*

Add $107 for A-TACS camo.
Add $35 for desert camo finish (disc. 2005).
Add $85 for A3 removable carrying handle (disc. 2012).

* ***XM-15 Limited Edition 20th Anniversary Rifle*** – GIO, 20 in. barrel, features 20th Anniversary engraving on upper and lower receiver, special medallion in buttstock, includes hardwood presentation case. Limited mfg. 1998-99.

	$1,385	$895	$675	$525	$450	$385	$350	

* ***XM-15 Limited Edition 25th Anniversary Carbine*** – GIO, skeletonized tubular stock, pistol grip, A3 type flat-top with flip-up sights, laser engraved 25th Anniversary crest on lower magwell, nickel plated ejection port cover. Limited mfg. of 1,500 during 2003.

	$1,385	$895	$675	$525	$450	$385	$350	*$1,695*

* ***E2 Carbine*** – 5.56 NATO cal., GIO, 16 in. match chrome-lined barrel with new M16A2 handguard and short suppressor, choice of A1 or E2 sights. Mfg. 1994-1995.

	$765	$515	$440	$375	$335	$315	$295	

Add approx. $50 for E2 sighting system.

AK CARBINE – 5.56 NATO cal., 17 in. barrel featuring AK-47 style muzzle brake, telestock standard, choice of A2 or A3 configuration, ribbed oval forearm, approx. 7 1/2 lbs. Mfg. 2008-2010.

	$1,025	$625	$495	$450	$395	$350	$325	*$1,215*

Add $85 for A3 removable carry handle.

DISSIPATOR CARBINE – 5.56 NATO cal., GIO, 16 in. heavy barrel with full-length forearm and special gas block placement (gas block system is located behind the front sight base and under the rifle length handguard), 30 shot mag., A2 or A3 style with choice of solid buttstock or 6-position telestock, lockable carrying case. Mfg. 2004-2010.

	$1,050	$650	$495	$450	$395	$350	$325	*$1,246*

Add $25 for telestock.
Add $50 for fluted barrel (disc. 2005).
Add $115 for A3 removable carrying handle.

MOE DISSIPATOR CARBINE – 5.56 NATO cal., GIO, 16 in. barrel with chrome-lined bore and chamber, mid-length gas system, flat-top Picatinny rail, features Magpul Original Equipment (MOE) accessories such as 30 shot PMAG, rifle length handguard, MBUS rear flip sight, Magpul MOE adj. stock with rubber buttpad, MOE grip, black finish, 6.42 lbs. New 2011.

MSR $1,099	$825	$650	$575	$525	$475	$450	$400	

MOE .223 MID-LENGTH – 5.56 NATO cal., GIO, 16 in. barrel with chrome-lined bore and chamber, 30 shot Magpul PMAG, MBUS rear flip sight, Magpul MOE stock, Magpul MOE pistol grip, mid-length handguard, black or FDE (disc. 2014) finish, 6 1/2 lbs. New 2011.

MSR $1,099	$825	$650	$575	$525	$475	$450	$400	

MOE .308 MID-LENGTH – .308 Win. cal., GIO, otherwise similar to MOE .223 Mid-length, except has 20 shot mag., Black, OD Green, or FDE finish, 6.1 lbs. Mfg. 2011-2015.

	$1,150	$925	$825	$725	$675	$625	$575	*$1,546*

GRADING - PPGS™	100%	98%	95%	90%	80%	70%	60%	LAST MSR

MOE M4-TYPE CARBINE/A-TACS CARBINE – 5.56 NATO cal., GIO, 16 in. heavy profile M4 barrel, 30 shot PMAG, Magpul adj. A-frame buttstock, Magpul MOE handguard, grip, enhanced trigger guard, and Magpul MBUS rear flip sight, Black, OD Green (disc. 2014), FDE (disc. 2014), or A-TACS camo (disc. 2014) finish, 6.42 lbs. Mfg. 2011-2016.

	$825	$650	$575	$525	$475	$450	$400	*$1,099*

Add $106 for A-TACS camo (disc. 2014).

M4 A.R.M.S. CARBINE – 5.56 NATO cal., GIO, 16 in. chrome moly vanadium steel barrel with chrome-lined bore and chamber, 30 shot mag., A3 removable carry handle, black, Foliage Green (new 2010), or FDE (new 2010) anodized finish, Magpul adj. buttstock with optional MOE (new 2010), Hogue pistol grip, optional Troy four rail handguard and front sights or A.R.M.S. 41-B front and rear flip-up sights (new 2010, became standard 2011), 6.2 lbs. Mfg. 2009-2011.

	$1,050	$650	$495	$450	$395	$350	$325	*$1,247*

Subtract approx. 10% if without A.R.M.S. front and rear flip-up sights.

PATROLMAN'S CARBINE – 5.56 NATO, 6.8 SPC, or 7.62x39mm NATO cal., GIO, 16 in. standard barrel, choice of A2 (bullet button) or A3 configuration, two-piece tubular handguard, 6-position adj. stock, black finish only, approx. 6 1/2 lbs. Disc. 2013.

	$1,065	$650	$500	$450	$395	$350	$325	*$1,275*

M4 PATROLMAN'S CARBINE – 5.56 NATO cal., GIO, choice of A2 or A3 configuration, 16 in. chrome-lined M4 barrel with A2 flash hider, 30 shot mag., 6-position telestock, detachable carry handle (A3 only), black anodized finish, approx. 6 1/2 lbs. New 2009.

MSR $895	$675	$525	$475	$425	$400	$375	$325

Add $52 for A3 detachable carry handle.

M4 A3 PATROLMAN'S CARBINE CERAKOTE – 5.56 NATO cal., GIO, 16 in. M4 barrel with A2 flash hider, A3 upper with removable carry handle, A2 carbine two-piece handguard, 6-position M4 stock, 30 shot mag., choice of OD Green or FDE Cerakote finished receiver, 6.7 lbs. Mfg. 2013-2014.

	$1,100	$675	$525	$450	$400	$350	$325	*$1,321*

M4 A3 PATROLMAN'S CARBINE W/QUAD RAIL – 5.56 NATO cal., 16 in. M4 chrome-lined barrel with A2 flash hider, 30 shot mag., aluminum free float quad rail handguard, forged A3 flat-top upper with detachable carry handle, forged lower with 6-position lightweight M4 stock. New 2011.

MSR $1,099	$825	$650	$575	$525	$475	$450	$400

M17S BULLPUP – 5.56 NATO cal., GIO, semi-auto bullpup configuration featuring gas operated rotating bolt, 10 (C/B 1994) or 30* shot mag., 21 1/2 plain or 22 (disc.) in. barrel with flash suppressor (disc.), glass composites and aluminum construction, phosphate coating, 8 1/4 lbs. Mfg. 1992-2005.

	$750	$650	$525	$475	$425	$400	$385	*$765*

MINIMALIST-SD – 5.56 NATO/.223 Rem. or .300 AAC Blackout cal., 16 in. lightweight or heavy (.300 AAC Blackout) barrel, AAC 51T flash hider, ACT trigger, Mission First Tactical Minimalist stock and grip, QD cup, rounded rubber buttpad, rifle length AAC SquareDrop handguard, A3 flat-top upper receiver, 6-6.3 lbs. New late 2016.

MSR $1,169	$875	$700	$625	$550	$500	$475	$425

MINIMALIST-SD M-LOK – 5.56 NATO or .300 AAC Blackout cal., 16 in. chrome moly barrel, AAC 51T Blackout fast attach silencer mount, Mission First Tactical Minimalist stock, QD cup, rounded rubber buttpad, Mission First Tactical grip, Samson M-LOK handguard, black finish, 6 lbs. New 2019.

MSR $1,169	$875	$700	$625	$550	$500	$475	$425

MODULAR CARBINE – 5.56 NATO cal., GIO, 16 in. barrel with flash suppressor, includes many Bushmaster modular accessories, such as skeleton telestock and four-rail free floating tubular forearm, detachable folding front and rear sights, 10 or 30 (new late 2004) shot mag., 6.3 lbs. Mfg. 2004-2014.

	$1,475	$950	$725	$550	$475	$395	$350	*$1,793*

SUPERLIGHT CARBINE – 5.56 NATO cal., GIO, 16 in. lightweight barrel, choice of fixed (disc.), 6-position telestock, or stub (disc.) stock with finger groove pistol grip, A2 or A3 type configuration, 30 shot mag., black finish, 5.8-6 1/4 lbs. Mfg. 2004-2013.

	$1,075	$675	$500	$450	$400	$350	$325	*$1,291*

Subtract 5% if without telestock.
Subtract approx. $75 if without A3 removable carry handle.

ACR – .450 BM or 6.8mm Rem. SPC cal., 16 or 18 1/2 (.450 BM cal. only) in. chrome moly barrel, Advanced Armament Blackout flash hider, 7-position collapsing and folding stock, adj. for LOP and cheek rise, AAC SquareDrop modular handguard (KeyMod compatible), fully ambidextrous controls with full time ambi charging handle, black finish, 8-8.2 lbs. New 2019.

MSR $2,249	$1,795	$1,050	$875	$625	$550	$475	$425

GRADING - PPGS™	100%	98%	95%	90%	80%	70%	60%	LAST MSR

ACR BASIC A-TACS CARBINE – 5.56 NATO cal., GPO, 16 1/2 in. barrel with A2 flash hider, 30 shot PMAG, fixed A-frame composite stock with rubber buttpad and sling mounts, black (disc. 2013), Coyote Brown (disc. 2010), or A-TACS camo finish, 8.2 lbs. Disc. 2014.

	$2,125	$1,325	$995	$675	$595	$525	$475	*$2,604*

ACR BASIC FOLDER – .223 Rem. or 6.8 SPC (mfg. 2013-2015) cal., GPO, 16 1/2 in. barrel with A2 flash hider, 30 shot PMAG, Magpul MBUS front/rear flip-up sights, composite handguard with heat shield, folding and 6-position polymer stock with rubber buttpad and sling mount, black or Coyote Brown finish, 8.2 lbs. New mid-2011.

MSR $2,149	$1,725	$1,050	$850	$625	$550	$475	$425	

ACR BASIC ORC CARBINE – 5.56 NATO cal., GPO, 16 1/2 in. barrel with muzzle brake, full-length top Picatinny rail w/o sights and fixed stock, 30 shot mag., Black or Coyote Brown finish, 8.2 lbs. Mfg. 2011-2013.

	$1,875	$1,100	$895	$650	$575	$495	$425	*$2,343*

ACR BASIC FOLDER ORC – 5.56 NATO cal., GPO, 16 1/2 in. barrel with muzzle brake, similar to ACR Enhanced Carbine, except does not have 3-sided aluminum handguard with Picatinny rails, Black or Coyote Brown finish, 8.2 lbs. Mfg. 2011 only.

	$1,975	$1,150	$925	$650	$575	$495	$425	*$2,490*

ACR DMR – 5.56 NATO cal., 18 1/2 in. stainless steel Melonite-treated barrel, AAC 51T Blackout flash hider, Geissele trigger, ACR railed handguard, Magpul PRS style stock, 8 3/4 lbs. Mfg. 2014-2015.

	$2,225	$1,395	$1,050	$675	$595	$525	$475	*$2,799*

ACR DMR (RECENT MFG.) – 5.56 NATO/.223 Rem. cal., GPO, 18 1/2 in. hammer forged stainless, Melonite-treated barrel with 51T AAC flash hider, Geissele trigger, modular system for changing barrels and calibers instantly, Magpul PRS2 stock with LOP and cheek weld adjustments, three-rail aluminum handguard, 10.4 lbs. Mfg. 2017-2019.

	$2,050	$1,250	$950	$650	$575	$495	$475	*$2,569*

ACR ENHANCED – 5.56 NATO or 6.8 SPC (while advertised in 2010, this caliber hasn't been mfg. to date) cal., Bushmaster proprietary GPO, modular design allows caliber interchangeability by changing the barrel, magazine, and bolt head, 16 1/2 in. chrome moly steel barrel with Melonite coating, AAC Blackout NSM flash hider, ambidextrous controls, adj. two-position gas piston, 30 shot mag., folding or 6-position telestock, black or Coyote Brown finish, three sided aluminum handguard, Magpul MBUS front/rear flip-up sights, upper and lower accessory rails, includes sling, hard case, and extra mag., 8.2 lbs. New 2010.

MSR $2,249	$1,795	$1,050	$875	$625	$550	$475	$425	

ACR ORC BULLET BUTTON – .223 Rem. cal., 16 in. M4 contour barrel with A2 flash hider, 10 shot mag., Bullet Button lower receiver. Mfg. 2015-2016.

	$1,795	$1,050	$875	$625	$550	$475	$425	*$2,249*

ACR PATROL CARBINE – 5.56 NATO or 6.8 SPC cal., GPO, 16 1/2 in. chrome moly steel barrel with Melonite coating, AAC Blackout flash hider, ratchet-style suppressor mounting, 30 shot mag., fixed stock, adj. cheekpiece, Picatinny rail, includes sling and three mags, 8.2 lbs. Mfg. 2010-2014.

	$2,050	$1,250	$950	$650	$575	$495	$475	*$2,552*

ACR SPECIAL PURPOSE CARBINE – 5.56 NATO cal., GPO, 16 1/2 in. cold hammer forged barrel, folding and 6-position telescoping polymer stock with rubber buttpad and sling mounts, quad Picatinny rails, and includes three 30 shot PMAG magazines and soft nylon case, black finish only, 8.3 lbs. Mfg. 2011-2014.

	$2,225	$1,395	$1,050	$675	$595	$525	$475	*$2,799*

ORC (OPTICS READY CARBINE) – 5.56 NATO or .308 Win. (mfg. 2010-2012) cal., GIO, 16 in. barrel with A2 birdcage flash suppressor, receiver length Picatinny rail with risers ready for optical sights, 6-position telestock, 30 shot mag., oval M4 type forearm, 6 lbs. Mfg. 2008-2013.

	$935	$575	$475	$415	$350	$325	$300	*$1,112*

Add $239 for .308 Win. cal. (mfg. 2010-2012).

ORC 5.56 – 5.56 NATO cal., GPO, 16 or 18 (disc.) in. heavy profile barrel with flash suppressor, full-length receiver Picatinny rail, heavy oval handguard, 6-position telescoping stock, 10 or 30 shot mag., black finish, 7 3/4 lbs. Mfg. 2011-2014.

	$915	$575	$475	$415	$350	$325	$300	*$1,083*

GRADING - PPGS™	100%	98%	95%	90%	80%	70%	60%	LAST MSR

MOE/ORC GAS PISTON CARBINE – 5.56 NATO cal., GPO, 16 in. barrel, MOE carbine features many Magpul accessories, is available in black, OD Green, or FDE finish, ORC model does not have MOE features, but 6-position tactical stock and receiver length Picatinny rail with risers for optics, approx. 6.3 lbs. Mfg. 2011-2012.

$1,050 $650 $495 $450 $395 $350 $325 *$1,247*

Add $89 for ORC model. Add $100-$149 for extra Magpul features on MOE model.

GAS PISTON CARBINE – 5.56 NATO cal., GPO, 16 in. M4 profile barrel with flash suppressor, telestock, ribbed oval forearm with flip-up sight. Mfg. 2008-2010.

$1,525 $975 $750 $575 $495 $425 $375 *$1,850*

HUNTER – .308 Win. cal., GIO, 20 in. fluted barrel, vented free floating aluminum forearm tube, 10 shot mag., Hogue rubberized pistol grip (Hunter) or A2 grip (Vista, disc. late 2011), Grey/Green or camo finish, 8.2 lbs. Mfg. 2011-2013.

$1,385 $895 $675 $525 $450 $385 $350 *$1,685*

Add $100 for Vista Hunter model (disc. late 2011).

PREDATOR – 5.56 NATO/.223 Rem. cal., GIO, includes DCM (disc.) 20 in. extra fluted, or stainless steel (disc. 2006) predator barrel, two-stage competition trigger, rubberized pistol grip, flat-top receiver with mini-risers (adds 1/2 in. height for scope mounting), free floating vented tube forearm, 5 or 10 (disc.) shot mag., controlled ejection path, choice of black or A-TACS Digital Camo (mfg. 2011-2013, compliant configuration only) finish, 8 lbs. Mfg. 2006-2013, reintroduced 2017.

MSR $1,159 $875 $700 $625 $550 $500 $475 $425

Last MSR in 2013 was $1,415.

Add $104 for A-TACS Digital Camo finish (compliant configuration only, disc. 2013).

The stainless variation included an adj. ergonomic pistol grip.

DCM COMPETITION RIFLE – 5.56 NATO cal., GIO, includes DCM competition features such as modified A2 rear sight, 20 in. extra heavy 1 in. diameter competition barrel, custom trigger job, and free floating handguard. Mfg. 1998-2005.

$1,250 $825 $575 $475 $425 $375 $350 *$1,495*

DCM-XR COMPETITION RIFLE – 5.56 NATO cal., GIO, 20 in. extra heavy competition barrel, dual aperture rear sight and competition ground for clarity front sight, free floating ribbed forearm, competition trigger, choice of A2 solid or A3 removable carry handle, 13 1/2 lbs. Mfg. 2008-2010.

$950 $595 $495 $425 $365 $335 $300 *$1,150*

Add $100 for A3 removable carry handle.

CARBINE-15 COMPETITION – 5.56 NATO cal., GIO, various configurations, choice of extra heavy or heavy barrel in 20 or 24 in. with or w/o muzzle brake, A2 or A3 configuration, various type of sights, 8.5-13.85 lbs. Mfg. 2011 only.

$935 $575 $475 $415 $350 $325 $300 *$1,112*

Add approx. $75 for A3 removable carry handle. Add $194 for heavy 1 in. diameter competition barrel.

CARBON-15 R21 – 5.56 NATO cal., GIO, Stoner type operating system, 16 in. "Profile" stainless steel barrel, quick detachable muzzle compensator, ultra lightweight carbon fiber upper and lower receivers, tool steel bolt, extractor and carrier, optics mounting base, fixed tube stock, 10 or 30 (new late 2004) shot mag., also accepts AR-15 type mags., 3.9 lbs. Mfg. 2003-2009 (Bushmaster mfg.).

$850 $550 $465 $395 $350 $325 $295 *$990*

* ***Carbon-15 Lady*** – 5.56 NATO cal., GIO, 16 in. barrel, includes overall tan finish (except for barrel) and webbed tube stock with recoil pad, chrome/nickel plating on small parts, supplied with soft case, 4 lbs. Mfg. 2004-2006.

$850 $550 $465 $395 $350 $325 $295 *$989*

CARBON-15 (R97/97S) – 5.56 NATO cal., AR-15 style, GIO, 16 in. fluted stainless steel barrel, quick detachable muzzle compensator, ultra lightweight carbon fiber upper and lower receivers, hard chromed tool steel bolt, extractor and carrier, optics mounting base, 10 or 30 (new late 2004) shot mag., quick detachable stock, also accepts AR-15 type mags., 3.9 or 4.3 (Model 97S) lbs. Mfg. 2003-2010.

$1,075 $675 $500 $450 $400 $350 $325 *$1,300*

Subtract approx. $175 without Picatinny rail and "Scout" extension, double walled heat shield foregrip, ambidextrous safety, and multi-carry silent sling (Model Type 97, disc. 2005).

CARBON-15 .22 LR – .22 LR cal., GIO, similar to Carbon-15 R21, 16 in. barrel, Picatinny rail, 10 shot mag., fixed stock, approx. 4.4 lbs. Disc. 2009.

$675 $500 $425 $375 $335 $315 $295 *$790*

Bushmaster also made a Carbon-15 .22 rimfire upper receiver/barrel assembly, which is exclusively designed for Bushmaster lower receivers - last MSR was $387 (new 2005).

GRADING - PPGS™	100%	98%	95%	90%	80%	70%	60%	LAST MSR

CARBON-15 9MM – 9mm Para. cal., blowback operation, carbon fiber composite receiver, 16 in. steel barrel with A1 birdcage flash suppressor, A2 front sight and dual aperture rear sight, Picatinny optics rail, collapsible stock, 10 or 30 shot mag., 5.7 lbs. Mfg. 2006-2012.

	$800	$525	$450	$385	$340	$325	$295	*$933*

CARBON-15 TOP LOADING RIFLE – 5.56 NATO cal., GIO, carbon fiber composite receiver, 16 in. M4 profile barrel with Izzy suppressor, A2 front sight and dual aperture rear sight, Picatinny optics rail, collapsible stock, 10 shot top-loading internal mag., 5.8 lbs. Mfg. 2006-2010.

	$915	$575	$475	$415	$350	$325	$300	*$1,100*

CARBON-15 MODEL 4 CARBINE – 5.56 NATO cal., GIO, carbon composite receiver, collapsible tube stock, 14 1/2 (LE only) or 16 (disc. 2012) in. barrel with compensator, 30 shot mag., semi-auto design styled after the military M4, 5 1/2 lbs. Mfg. 2005-2013.

	$825	$535	$450	$385	$340	$325	$295	*$956*

CARBON-15 FLAT-TOP CARBINE – 5.56 NATO cal., GIO, 16 in. M4 barrel, muzzle fitted with Izzy flash hider, 30 shot mag., receiver length Picatinny rail with dual aperture flip-up rear sight, 6-position stock, black finish, 5 1/2 lbs. Mfg. 2006-2015.

	$725	$575	$500	$450	$425	$400	$350	*$956*

CARBON-15 SUPERLIGHT ORC W/RED DOT – 5.56 NATO cal., GIO, 16 in. super light contour barrel with A2 flash hider, 10 (disc. 2013) or 30 shot mag., red dot optical sight with rings and riser blocks, 6-position stock, black finish. Mfg. 2012-2015.

	$650	$525	$450	$400	$375	$350	$325	*$866*

CARBON-15 M4 QUAD RAIL – 5.56 NATO cal., GIO, 16 in. M4 barrel with A2 flash hider, 30 shot mag., fixed front sight base and bayonet lug, Mission First Tactical polymer quad rail with rail covers, 6-position stock, black finish, 6 1/4 lbs. Mfg. 2014-2015.

	$650	$525	$450	$400	$375	$350	$325	*$866*

CARBON-15 C22 COMBO – .22 LR and 5.56 NATO cals., GIO, includes two barrels chambered for .22 LR and 5.56 NATO cals., flat-top receiver with Picatinny rail, 16 in. M4 style barrels with A2 flash hiders, fixed front sight base, Mission First Tactical polymer quad rail with rail covers, 6-position stock, supplied with 25 shot (.22 LR cal.) and 30 shot (5.56 NATO) magazines. Mfg. 2013-2015.

	$925	$725	$650	$575	$525	$500	$450	*$1,222*

CARBON 22 – .22 LR cal., 16 in. M4 contour barrel with A2 flash hider, 25 shot mag., 6-position stock assembly, Mission First Tactical polymer quad rail with rail covers. Mfg. 2014-2015.

	$375	$300	$275	$250	$235	$200	$175	*$499*

V-MATCH COMPETITION RIFLE – 5.56 NATO cal., GIO, top-of-the line match/competition rifle, flat-top receiver with extended aluminum barrel shroud, choice of 20, 24, or 26 (disc. 2002) in. barrel, 8.3 lbs. Mfg. 1994-2010.

	$935	$575	$475	$415	$350	$325	$300	*$1,115*

Add $50 for fluted barrel.
Add $10 for 24 in. or $25 for 26 in. (disc. 2002) barrel.
Add $117 for A3 removable carry handle.

* ***V-Match Commando Carbine*** – 5.56 NATO cal., GIO, 16 in. barrel, flat-top receiver with extended aluminum barrel shroud. Mfg. 1997-2010.

	$935	$575	$475	$415	$350	$325	$300	*$1,105*

Add $50 for fluted barrel.
Add $117 for A3 removable carry handle.

VARMINTER – 5.56 NATO/.223 Rem. cal., GIO, includes DCM (disc.) 24 in. extra heavy fluted or stainless steel (disc. 2013) varmint barrel, competition trigger, rubberized pistol grip, flat-top receiver with mini-risers (adds 1/2 in. height for scope mounting), free floating vented tube forearm, 5 shot mag., controlled ejection path, choice of Black or A-TACS Digital camo (mfg. 2011-2013, compliant configuration only) finish. Mfg. 2002-2013, reintroduced 2017.

MSR $1,159	$875	$700	$625	$550	$500	$475	$425	

Add $71 for stainless steel barrel (compliant variation only, disc. 2013).
Add $105 for A-TACS Digital camo coverage (compliant configuration only, disc. 2013).

The stainless variation included an adj. ergonomic pistol grip.

VARMINTER W/2020 OPTICS – 5.56 NATO cal., GIO, 24 in. fluted barrel, features Remington's new 2020 Digital Optic System, Magpul stock, includes wheeled hard case with custom fitted foam insert. Mfg. 2014 only.

	$4,000	$2,850	$1,775	$1,200	$875	$775	$700	*$5,000*

GRADING - PPGS™	100%	98%	95%	90%	80%	70%	60%	LAST MSR

BUSHMASTER .308 SERIES – .308 Win. cal., GIO, 16 or 20 in. phosphate coated heavy alloy steel barrel with Izzy compensator, 20 shot mag., solid buttstock or skeletonized stock, available in A2 or A3 style with a variety of configurations, including muzzle brakes, flash suppressors, and sighting options. Mfg. late 2004-2005.

	$1,425	$925	$700	$550	$475	$395	$350	*$1,750*

Add $10 for 20 in. barrel.
Add $25 for A3 removable carry handle.
Add $50 (16 in. barrel) or $60 (20 in. barrel) for skeletonized stock.
Add approx. $100 for free floating foream.

XM-10 .308 ENHANCED ORC – .308 Win. cal., GIO, 16 in. chrome-lined barrel, Troy modular free floating handguard, Magpul PRS stock and MIAD grip, two-stage trigger, 9 lbs. Mfg. 2014-2016.

	$1,200	$950	$850	$750	$700	$650	$600	*$1,599*

XM-10 DMR – 7.62 NATO cal., 18 1/2 in. stainless Cerakote bull barrel, Troy free floating handguard, Magpul PRS stock, MIAD grip and trigger guard, AAC 51T Blackout muzzle brake, Geissele trigger, 10 1/2 lbs. Mfg. 2014 only.

	$1,650	$1,000	$795	$595	$495	$425	$395	*$1,999*

XM-10 ORC GEN 1 (ORC .308) – 7.62 NATO cal., GPO, 16 or 18 (disc.) in. heavy profile barrel with A2 birdcage flash suppressor, full-length receiver Picatinny rail, heavy oval handguard, 6-position telescoping stock, 20 shot mag., black finish, 7 3/4 lbs. Mfg. 2011-2015, reintroduced 2017.

MSR $1,249	$925	$750	$675	$575	$550	$500	$450

XM-15 ORC – .300 AAC Blackout cal., AR-15 style, FNC barrel, A2 flash hider, 30 shot PMAG, collapsible stock, vented and knurled free float tube, forged Teflon coated upper and lower receiver. New 2018.

MSR $929	$700	$550	$500	$425	$400	$375	$350

XM-15 TACTICAL ORC (BASIC TACTICAL CARBINE) – 5.56 NATO cal., GIO, 16 in. mid-length stainless steel barrel with AAC 51T Blackout flash hider, 15 in. Barnes Precision modular free float handguard, Magpul MOE grip, Magpul MOE stock, two-stage match trigger, enhanced trigger guard, 7 3/4 lbs. Mfg. 2014-2015.

	$1,025	$800	$725	$625	$600	$550	$500	*$1,350*

XM-15 QRC (QUICK RESPONSE CARBINE) – 5.56 NATO cal., GIO, 16 in. superlight contour chrome moly barrel with A2 birdcage flash hider, 10 shot mag., quick detach mini red dot sight, forged lower and A3 flat-top upper receiver, 6-position collapsible M4 stock, Melonite coated barrel. New 2016.

MSR $769	$575	$450	$400	$350	$325	$325	$275

Subtract $30 if without mini red dot sight (Optics Ready model).

XM-15 3-GUN ENHANCED CARBINE – 5.56 NATO cal., GIO, 16 in. mid-length stainless steel barrel, Rolling Thunder compensator, 15 in. AP Custom carbon fiber handguard, Timney trigger, Magpul MIAD grip, Magpul MOE stock, PVD bolt carrier group, crimson anodized receiver, Bravo Company charging handle, ambi selector switch, Arrendondo mag. release, black finish, 7 3/4 lbs. Mfg. 2014-2015.

	$1,325	$1,050	$925	$825	$775	$700	$650	*$1,750*

BUTLER ARMS USA

Previous shotgun manufacturer located in Salt Lake City, UT. Previously located in Whitefish, MT.

SHOTGUNS: SEMI-AUTO

BUTLER XX12 – 12 ga. only, 2 3/4 in. chamber, utilizes a proprietary HE (high efficiency) gas system and bottom barrel technology to reduce recoil, bottom ejection, side loading, quick detachable trigger, 30 in. barrel features adj. carbon fiber vent. rib, includes Briley chokes and luggage travel case, checkered Claro walnut stock with adj. comb. Mfg. 2012-2013.

	$6,875	$6,000	$5,150	$4,675	$3,775	$3,095	$2,400	*$8,100*

BUTLER ASSOC., INC.

Previous manufacturer located in New Haven, CT.

DERRINGERS

SINGLE SHOT – .22 Short cal. only, side pivoting Thuer action, various metal finishes and grips, including wood and mother-of-pearl, spur trigger, uses same parts as Colt's Lord & Lady derringers, cased and uncased, B prefix serialization.

Derringer only	$150	$130	$95	$85	$75	$65	$60
Cased set	$375	$325	$275	$240	$200	$175	$150

BÜYÜK HUGLU

Current shotgun manufacturer located in Konya, Turkey. Currently imported on a limited basis by Bud's Gun Shop beginning 2014, located in Lexington, KY.

Büyük Huglu manufactures good quality O/U, slide action, and semi-auto shotguns in various configurations. Importation is limited so please contact the importer or manufacturer directly for more information on their model line-up, including pricing, options, and U.S. availability.

C3 DEFENSE, INC.

Previous manufacturer of AR-15 style rifles, upper/lower receivers, and related components located in Hiram, GA until 2013.

Please refer to BlueBookOfGunValues.com to order the *Blue Book of AR-15s & Variations*, available as a book or online subscription.

C&H PRECISION WEAPONS

Current rifle manufacturer located in Richmond Hill, GA since 2013.

In addition to building precision rifles, C&H Precision Weapons also customizes handguns. Please contact them directly for more information.

RIFLES: BOLT ACTION

C&H Precision Weapons specializes in high quality bolt action rifles for recreational shooting, long range hunts, and competitive long range/ELR matches. Current lineup includes the Competitor Series - base packages start at $3,250, and the Heritage Series - base packages start at $3,995. Since each rifle is built to customer specifications, it is important that you contact the company directly for options, pricing, and availability.

CEO GUNS

Current manufacturer of semi-auto, O/U, and single shot shotguns located in Konya, Turkey. No current U.S. importation.

Please contact the company directly for more information including pricing, options, and availability.

CETME

Previous manufacturer located in Madrid, Spain. CETME is an abbreviation for Centro Estudios Technicos de Materiales Especiales.

GRADING - PPGS™	100%	98%	95%	90%	80%	70%	60%	LAST MSR

RIFLES: SEMI-AUTO

AUTOLOADING RIFLE – 7.62x51mm NATO cal., 17 3/4 in. barrel, roller lock delayed blowback action, similar to HK-91 in appearance, wood military style stock, aperture rear sight.

	100%	98%	95%	90%	80%	70%	60%	LAST MSR
	$3,950	$3,500	$2,950	$2,650	$2,350	$2,000	$1,725	

The H&K G3 is the next generation of this rifle, and many parts are interchangeable between the CETME and the G3.

CFS GUNS

Previous firearms and airgun manufacturer circa 1997-2006, located in Istanbul, Turkey.

CFS Guns manufactured a wide variety of O/U, SxS, slide action, and semi-auto shotguns. Some models were imported under the BSA trademark.

CK ARMS

Current firearms and parts manufacturer located in Camilla, GA.

For individual model listings, please go to BlueBookOfGunValues.com/overflow.

CMMG INC.

Current manufacturer of AR-15 style carbines/rifles, pistols, and related components and accessories established in 2002, located in Fayette, MO.

Please refer to BlueBookOfGunValues.com to order the *Blue Book of AR-15s & Variations*, available as a book or online subscription.

C-MORE COMPETITION

Current manufacturer of shotguns, including the M26 MASS system for the U.S. military. Located in Warrenton, VA since 1999.

SHOTGUNS: BOLT ACTION

M26-CMC-M1 – 12 ga., 2 3/4 in. or 3 in. shells, straight-pull bolt action, 18 in. barrel, 3 or 5 shot detachable mag., adj. 4 pos. energy absorbing buttstock, ventilated aluminum handguard with detachable Picatinny rail sections, A2 grip, reversible safety, reversible bolt handle, black anodized finish, M26 marked specialized cleaning kit available separately, 6.2 lbs.

MSR	100%	98%	95%	90%	80%	70%	60%
MSR $1,399	$1,250	$1,100	$950	$850	$700	$575	$450

The M26 Shotgun system offered by C-More Competition also comes in a variety of NFA configurations, please contact the manufacturer for more information on availability and pricing of these models.

GRADING - PPGS™	100%	98%	95%	90%	80%	70%	60%	LAST MSR

C.O. ARMS

Previous manufacturer located in Millington, TN until 2011.

PISTOLS: SEMI-AUTO

SCORPION – .45 ACP cal., 4 1/4 in. stainless steel barrel, stainless steel slide with rear cocking serrations, diamond checkered wood grips, Novak sights, lightweight adj. trigger, beavertail grip safety, lowered and flared ejection port, full length guide rod, extended rear slide stop.

$1,050 $925 $800 $700 $600 $500 $400 *$1,199*

AWP (ALL WEATHER PISTOL) – .45 ACP cal., 3 1/2 in. stainless steel bull barrel, carbon steel slide, aluminum frame, checkered front strap, XS Express big dot sights, Commander style hammer, solid adj. trigger, beavertail grip safety, lowered and flared ejection port, stippled synthetic grips, full length guide rod.

$1,425 $1,200 $1,025 $925 $825 $750 $675 *$1,599*

CVA

Please refer to the Connecticut Valley Arms listing in this section.

CZ (CESKÁ ZBROJOVKA)

Current manufacturer located in Uhersky Brod, Czech Republic since 1936. Previous manufacture was in Strakonice, Czechoslovakia circa 1923-late 1950s. Newly manufactured CZ firearms are currently imported exclusively by CZ USA located in Kansas City, KS. Previously imported by Magnum Research, Inc. located in Minneapolis, MN until mid-1994. Previously imported before 1994 by Action Arms Ltd. located in Philadelphia, PA. Dealer and distributor sales.

For CZ manufactured airguns, please refer to the *Blue Book of Airguns* - also available as an online subscription.

CZ USA currently has four product lines, which include CZ (pistols, rifles, and shotguns), Safari Classics (best quality bolt action rifles), Dan Wesson (semi-auto pistols), and Brno (combination guns and rifles). Please refer to the individual listings for more information and current values.

CZ HISTORY

Ceská Zbrojovka simply means Czech weapons factory. CZ's full name is Ceská Zbrojovka a.s. Uhersky Brod, often abbreviated to CZUB a.s., meaning joint stock company. Uhersky Brod is the town the factory is located in. Zbrojovka Brno means weapons or arms factory located in Brno.

Zbrojovka Brno was built in 1916-1918, as a subsidiary of the Vienna Arsenal. In 1919 the Jihoceska Zbrojovka (South Bohemian Arms Factory) merged with the Hubertus Engineering firm to form the Ceska Zbrojovka (Bohemian Arms Factory), better known as CZ. After WWI, this factory was given the responsibility of providing the newly formed Czechoslovakian military with infantry weapons, specifically rifles and light machine guns. Circa 1923, pistol manufacture was transferred from Brno to Ceská Zbrojovka, located in the town of Strakonice, southwest of Bohemia. Since the location change, Zbrojovka Brno has never produced pistols on any great scale (please refer to the Brno section in this text for more information).

Ceská Zbrojovka Strakonice began developing many innovative and revolutionary pistol designs. These models, including the CZ-24, CZ-27, and CZ-52 are certainly well-known throughout the world. During the mid-1950s, CZ's facilities were converted to making motorcycles and precision engineering products.

Ceská Zbrojovka, located in the town of Uhersky Brod, was founded in 1936, as a subsidiary of Ceská Zbrojovka Strakonice, in a government decision designed to move firearms production further away from the German border, and out of the reach of German bombers. Uhersky Brod is located approx. 60 miles east of Brno. Before WWII, the factory produced aircraft machine guns (LK-30), the military pistol (CZ-38 in 9mm Para.), and rifle Models Z242-Z247. During WWII, the factory was taken over by the Germans, and the facilities were used for the production of aircraft machine guns (German designed MG 17s) and related components for other models of military weapons.

Shortly after WWII, Ceská Zbrojovka Uhersky Brod resumed production of firearms for the civilian marketplace, including the CZ 241 semi-auto shotgun, and some O/U shotguns. The production of pistols commenced during the mid-1950s, with the introduction of the Model CZ-50 and other small pistol models named DUO in 6.35mm cal. Up to this point, the main pistol producer in Czechoslovakia was CZ Strakonice as stated above. The CZ-52 pistol was the last model they produced. Since the end of the 1950s, Ceská Zbrojovka Uhersky Brod has become the sole producer of pistols.

After WWII, the Ceská Zbrojovka Uhersky Brod became massively involved in other types of production

GRADING - PPGS™	100%	98%	95%	90%	80%	70%	60%	LAST MSR

besides sporting and hunting firearms. Production reached a high during the 1980s, when hunting/sporting firearms manufacture resulted in approx. 30% of total production. The balance of manufacture was devoted to the production of power hydraulics for tractors, while gears and accessory drive boxes for speed reduction in turbo prop airplane engines made up the rest.

During 1964-1966, the Czech government transferred the production of long guns from Zbrojovka Brno to Ceská Zbrojovka Uhersky Brod. During the 1970s & 1980s, the arms production of Zbrojovka Brno accounted for less than 3% of its total capacity. The activities of this company were diverted into the production of typewriters, diesel motors, and automatic machine tools. While many firearm designs originated in Brno, Zbrojovka Brno was not the manufacturer. Because of this, the long guns manufactured in the mid-1960s, including the ZKK 600-602 series and ZKM rimfires, were manufactured in CZ Uhersky Brod. Because of the Czech government's decision to merge manufacture within both companies, the Brno trademark was also used by Ceská Zbrojovka Uhersky Brod.

This relationship was terminated in 1983, when both companies became part of the Agrozet conglomerate. While confusing, the arms utlizing the Brno trademark were not produced in Brno during this time. All firearms exported from Czechoslovakia at the time carried the Brno logo, and most of them were manufactured by Ceská Zbrojovka Uhersky Brod.

During 1975, Ceská Zbrojovka Uhersky Brod designed and began manufacture of the famous CZ-75 pistol. Production in quantity began in 1977. To date, over one million CZ-75s have been produced. This semi-auto has been made in many variations and/or modifications to suit many military and commercial contracts. During the mid-1980s, the CZ factory released the CZ-85, basically a CZ-75 with ambidextrous safety and slide stop. In the mid-1990s, production of the CZ-100 began - this new model featured a polymer frame. The CZ 550 line of rifles was also introduced at this same time.

During 2009, after the Brno factory closure, many of Brno's employees transferred to Brno Rifles, Ltd., a subsidiary of CZ, which was established in Brno to continue production of Brno firearms using the original Brno trademark. Please refer to the Brno section for current listings.

COMBINATION GUNS

CZ 584 SOLO - 12 ga. over choice of 7x57mm Mauser (importation disc. 1999), 7x57Rmm, 7x65Rmm, .222 Rem. (importation disc. 1999), .223 Rem. (imported 1994-99), .243 Win. (imported 1994-99), .30-06 (new 1994), 7mm Mauser (imported 1994-99), and .308 Win. (importation disc. 1999) cals., 24 1/2 in. barrels, similar action to CZ 581 O/U shotgun, extractors or ejectors, rifle sights, approx. 7.4 lbs. Importation disc. 1986, resumed 1994. Disc. 1995, importation resumed 1999. Disc. 2003.

	100%	98%	95%	90%	80%	70%	60%	LAST MSR
	$775	$655	$595	$515	$450	$385	$350	*$917*

Add 20% for ejectors.

PISTOLS: SEMI-AUTO, DISC.

The models listed below were made in Ceská Zbrojovka Strakonice, with the exception of some models manufactured in Ceská Zbrojovka Prague during the Nazi occupation of Czechoslovakia. The VZ38 was also produced in Uhersky Brod.

"DUO" POCKET AUTOMATIC - .25 ACP cal., 6 shot, 2 1/8 in. barrel, fixed sights, blue or nickel, plastic grips. Mfg. beginning 1926 (current Z pistol by Brno).

	100%	98%	95%	90%	80%	70%	60%
	$300	$275	$225	$200	$175	$150	$125

Add 40% for WWII years.

This model was manufactured by Dushek and is similar to the Z pistol equivalent by Brno.

CZ 22 - .380 ACP cal., derived from Mauser variation and manufactured under license from Mauser. Mfg. 1923 only.

	100%	98%	95%	90%	80%	70%	60%
	$1,250	$1,000	$750	$600	$500	$400	$300

CZ 24 - .380 ACP cal.

* ***CZ 24 Standard Frame*** - 8 shot mag., over 175,000 mfg. 1924-1938, over half issued to Czech Army, same general design as CZ 22 except no gap between trigger and frame. Production continued to 1941.

	100%	98%	95%	90%	80%	70%	60%
Standard Mfg.	$850	$650	$450	$350	$300	$275	$250
Kriegsmarine Proofed	$1,275	$1,125	$975	$875	$800	$700	$600

Add $50 for Nazi proof.

Beware of counterfeit markings on Kriegsmarine proofed models.

GRADING - PPGS™	100%	98%	95%	90%	80%	70%	60%	LAST MSR

* ***CZ 24 Long Frame*** – 9 shot mag.

	$2,500	$2,000	$1,750	$1,500	$1,250	$1,000	$750	

Add 50% if fit with stock slot (either standard frame or long frame).

CZ 27 – .32 ACP cal.

* ***CZ 27 "CESKA" Slide Legend Variation*** – slanted slide grooves, high polish, available as Prewar Commercial, DR proofed, or Nazi proofed. Ser. no. range 1 - 21,500.

	$1,300	$1,150	$975	$885	$725	$600	$450	

Add 50% for DR proofed.

* ***CZ 27 "BÖHMISCHE" Slide Legend Variation*** – vertical slide grooves, high or medium polish, standard or Nazi Police pistols dated 1941, 1942, or 1943 marked with Eagle/K on left trigger guard web, ser. no. range 21,500-261,000.

Standard mfg.	$350	$300	$250	$200	$150	$135	$100	
1941 dated	$775	$675	$550	$450	$325	$275	$225	
1942-1943 dated	$700	$600	$500	$400	$300	$275	$200	
Kriegsmarine proofed	$1,050	$900	$750	$600	$475	$400	$350	

Beware of counterfeit markings on Kriegsmarine proofed models.

* ***CZ 27 "fnh" Slide Legend Variation*** – medium polish or phosphate finish. Ser. no. range 261,000-476,000.

	$325	$275	$225	$175	$150	$125	$100	

Add 50% for late phosphate war finish.

* ***CZ 27 Sound Suppressor Barrel Variation*** – a small number of phosphate pistols were fitted with an extended barrel for suppressor attachment. Usually in 450,000-460,000 ser. no. range.

	$3,500	$3,000	$2,500	$2,250	$2,000	$1,750	$1,500	

* ***CZ 27 Post-WWII mfg.*** – dated 1945, 1946, 1947, 1948, 1949, 1950, 1951. These models will have the "NARODNI PODNIK" inscription on slide.

Currently, these variations average $250 in 95%+ condition while reworks (very common) average under $200.

CZ 28 – .32 ACP cal., blue finish, smooth hardwood grips, four slanted slide serrations on rear of slide, marked "C.S. STRAZ KARLOVY VARY" on right side, "CESKA ZBROJOVKA AS v PRAZE" on top of frame, and "CZ 28" on left side below serrations.

	$600	$525	$450	$400	$325	$275	$200	

VZ 36 – .25 ACP cal., 8 shot, 2 1/2 in. barrel, fixed sights, blue finish, plastic grips, DA, similar to VZ 45, but scarce, some examples mfg. with safety lever on the left frame, some made w/o the lever. Mfg. 1936-1942.

	$600	$550	$500	$450	$400	$350	$300	

VZ 38 (MODEL 39T) DOUBLE ACTION AUTOMATIC – .380 ACP cal., 9 shot, double action only, 4 5/8 in. barrel, fixed sights, blue, brown, plastic grips. Mfg. 1938-1939.

	$700	$600	$500	$400	$300	$250	$200	
Waffenamt proofed	$3,250	$2,750	$2,250	$1,750	$1,500	$1,250	$850	

Model nomenclature was changed to Model 39T after 1939.

Waffenamt proofed variations (E/WaA76 markings on barrel and left frame), are usually phosphate finished, either unnumbered or in B291,000-B293,000 ser. no. range, and with black grips.

VZ 38 "BULGARIAN CONTRACT" – .380 ACP cal., 9 shot, single or double action, prominent safety on left frame. Usually in 420,000-423,000 ser. no. range.

	$3,250	$2,750	$2,250	$1,500	$1,000	$750	$500	

VZ 45 – .25 ACP cal., 8 shot, 2 1/2 in. barrel, fixed sights, blue finish, plastic grips, DA, similar to VZ 36, but slightly modified and with no safety lever. Mfg. 1945-1952.

	$300	$275	$250	$225	$200	$175	$150	

PISTOLS: SEMI-AUTO, CURRENT/RECENT MFG.

CZ-75 P-01 – 9mm Para. cal., based on CZ-75 design but with metallurgical improvements, DA/SA, aluminum alloy frame, hammer forged 3.7 in. barrel, 10 or 14 (new 2005) shot mag., fixed sights, swappable safety (new 2016)/decocker, includes M3 rail on bottom of frame, checkered rubber grips, matte black polycoat finish, 27.2 oz. Importation began 2003.

MSR $725	$615	$540	$460	$425	$345	$275	$225	

Add $99 for tactical block with bayonet (mfg. 2006-2012).
Add $67 for Crimson Trace Lasergrips (mfg. 2007-2010).

GRADING - PPGS™	100%	98%	95%	90%	80%	70%	60%	LAST MSR

* ***CZ-75 P-01 Omega Convertible*** – 9mm Para. cal., forged alloy frame, 3.7 in. barrel, 10 or 15 shot mag., swappable trigger system, black rubber grips, can be converted from decocker to safety operation with minimal tools, black polycoat finish. New 2016.

MSR $725	$615	$540	$460	$425	$345	$275	$225	

CZ-75 P-01 URBAN GREY SUPPRESSOR-READY – 9mm Para. cal., DA/SA, aluminum frame, 4 1/2 in. barrel with threaded muzzle, two 10 or 15 shot extended mags., high suppressor sights, black rubber grips, swappable safety/decocker, Urban Grey polycoat slide finish, 1.88 lbs. New 2016.

MSR $769	$655	$575	$490	$450	$360	$300	$250	

CZ-75 P-06 – .40 S&W cal., 3.7 in. hammer forged barrel, 10 shot mag., light aluminum alloy frame, M3 rail, dual slide serrations, squared trigger guard, checkered black rubber grips, fixed night sights, decocker, black polycoat finish, 1.82 lbs. Mfg. 2008-2009, reintroduced 2011-2016.

	$575	$500	$450	$395	$335	$295	$265	*$680*

Add $99 for tactical block with bayonet (disc. 2012).

CZ P-07 DUTY – 9mm Para. or .40 S&W cal., DA/SA, 3.8 in. standard or threaded (new 2012) barrel, black polycoat or OD Green (new 2012) polymer frame with black slide, squared off trigger guard, 10 (9mm only), 12 (.40 S&W only) or 16 shot mag., fixed sights, decocking lever, Omega trigger system, 27 oz. Mfg. 2009-2013.

	$450	$370	$325	$280	$260	$240	$220	*$483*

Add $13 for .40 S&W cal.
Add $6 for OD Green frame in 9mm Para. cal. with 16 shot mag. (new 2012).
Add $45 for threaded barrel (9mm Para. cal. only) with black finish (new 2012).

CZ P-07 – 9mm Para. or .40 S&W (disc. 2018) cal., SA/DA, updated version of the CZ P-07 Duty including interchangeable backstraps, integrated Picatinny rail, nitrated slide finish, and updated trigger shape, 3.8 in. barrel, 10 (9mm), 12 (.40 S&W, disc. 2018) or 15 (9mm) shot mag., metal 3-dot sights, interchangeable ambi safety or decocking lever, firing pin block, black or OD Green (new 2018) polymer frame, 1.7 lbs. New 2014.

MSR $540	$460	$400	$335	$315	$250	$200	$175	

Add $24 for OD Green finish (new 2018).
Add $14 for .40 S&W cal. (disc. 2018).
Add $249 for CZ P-07 Kadet Kit (enables users to train using .22 LR ammo, includes 10 shot mag. and fully reciprocating slide), mfg. 2016-2020.

* ***CZ P-07 Suppressor Ready*** – 9mm Para. cal., DA/SA, polymer frame, 4.36 in. cold hammer forged barrel, 17 shot double stack mag., high Tritium 3-dot sights, stippled grips, interchangeable ambidextrous decocker/manual safety. New 2017.

MSR $559	$475	$415	$350	$325	$260	$215	$185	

CZ-75 P-07 URBAN GREY SUPPRESSOR-READY – 9mm Para. cal., DA/SA, Urban Grey polymer frame, black slide, 4 1/2 in. barrel with threaded muzzle, suppressor ready, two 10 or 17 shot extended mags., interchangeable backstraps, high suppressor sights, rubber grips, ambi safety or decocker, firing pin block, 1 3/4 lbs. New 2016.

MSR $585	$500	$440	$375	$340	$275	$225	$195	

CZ P-09 (P-09 DUTY) – 9mm Para. or .40 S&W (disc. 2018) cal., full size variation of the P-07 Duty, 4 1/2 in. barrel, 10, 15 (.40 S&W, disc. 2018) or 19 (9mm Para.) shot staggered mag., includes lower Picatinny rail and low profile sights, Omega SA/DA trigger, black or OD Green (new 2018) polymer frame and black steel slide, polymer grips, approx. 30 oz. New 2013.

MSR $555	$475	$415	$350	$325	$260	$215	$185	

Add $74 for OD Green finish (new 2018).
Add $100 for suppressor ready (9mm Para. only), 19 shot mag. (new 2014).
Add $14 for .40 S&W cal. (disc. 2018).
Add $249 for .22 LR Kadet Adapter (mfg. 2017-2020).

* ***CZ P-09 FDE*** – 9mm Para. cal., 4.53 in. barrel, 19 shot mag., Tritium night sights, interchangeable backstraps, FDE finish, 1.84 lbs. Mfg. 2014-2015.

	$525	$475	$415	$365	$315	$235	$185	*$596*

CZ P-09 URBAN GREY SUPPRESSOR-READY – 9mm Para. cal., DA/SA, Urban Grey polymer frame, black slide, 4 1/2 in. barrel with threaded muzzle, two 17 shot extended mags., interchangeable backstraps, high suppressor sights, rubber grips, ambi safety or decocker, firing pin block, 1 3/4 lbs. New 2016.

MSR $655	$560	$485	$420	$375	$300	$250	$200	

GRADING - PPGS™	100%	98%	95%	90%	80%	70%	60%	LAST MSR

CZ P-10 C – 9mm Para. or .40 S&W (mfg. 2017 only) cal., striker fire action, black or FDE compact polymer frame, 4 in. cold hammer forged barrel, 15 or 12 shot mag., black or white (mfg. 2018 only) Nitride slide, ambidextrous mag. release, 3-dot or Tritium (FDE model only) sights, mild palm swell, deep beavertail, three interchangeable backstraps, 26 oz. New 2017.

MSR $525	$450	$395	$340	$300	$250	$200	$175	

Add $24 for FDE finish.
Add $17 for .40 S&W cal. (mfg. 2017 only).
Add $40 for FDE frame and white Nitride slide (mfg. 2018 only).

* ***CZ P-10 C Optics Ready*** – 9mm Para. cal., compact carbon fiber reinforced polymer frame, 4 in. barrel, 15 shot mag., front Tritium night sight and rear serrated combat sight, firing pin block safety, reversible mag. release, blank fill plate, Nitride finish, 26.3 oz. New 2019.

MSR $600	$510	$450	$385	$350	$275	$225	$200	

* ***CZ P-10 C Suppressor Ready*** – 9mm Para. cal., striker fire, polymer frame, 4.61 in. extended threaded barrel, 17 shot mag., high metal night sights, black polymer grips, Nitride finish, 26 oz. New 2017.

MSR $585	$500	$440	$375	$340	$275	$225	$195	

CZ P-10 C URBAN GRAY SUPPRESSOR-READY – 9mm Para. cal., striker fired, Urban Grey polymer frame, 4 1/2 in. barrel with threaded muzzle, suppressor ready, two 10 (mfg. 2018 only) or 17 shot extended mags., black Nitride slide finish, high suppressor sights, polymer grips, ambi safety or decocker, interchangeable backstraps, firing pin block, 1 3/4 lbs. New 2018.

MSR $585	$500	$440	$375	$340	$275	$225	$195	

CZ P-10 F – 9mm Para. cal., striker fired, full size fiber reinforced polymer frame in black, FDE, or OD Green finish, 4 1/2 in. cold hammer forged barrel, 10 or 19 shot mag., swappable mag. release, fixed 3-dot sights, polymer grip, firing pin block safety, mild palm swell, deep beavertail, three interchangeable backstraps, Nitride slide finish, 28.2 oz. New 2019.

MSR $579	$495	$435	$375	$335	$275	$225	$195	

Add $40 for FDE or OD Green frame finish.

* ***CZ P-10 F Optics Ready*** – 9mm Para. cal., full size fiber reinforced polymer frame, 4 1/2 in. cold hammer forged barrel, 19 shot mag., swappable mag. release, single Tritium lamp in front with a large orange surround and serrated black rear, optics ready configuration (shipped with a blank fill plate for the Trijicon RMR or Leupold DeltaPoint Pro), polymer grip, firing pin block and trigger safety, Nitride finish, 28.2 oz. New 2019.

MSR $649	$550	$480	$415	$375	$310	$260	$215	

* ***CZ P-10 F Suppressor Ready*** – 9mm Para. cal., striker fired, full size fiber reinforced polymer frame in black or Urban Grey finish, 5.11 in. cold hammer forged threaded barrel, 21 shot mag., swappable mag. release, high Tritium 3-dot sights, polymer grip, firing pin block safety, mild palm swell, deep beavertail, three interchangeable backstraps, Nitride finish, 30 oz. New 2019.

MSR $635	$540	$475	$400	$365	$300	$250	$200	

CZ P-10 S – 9mm Para. cal., striker fired, sub-compact fiber reinforced polymer frame, 3 1/2 in. cold hammer forged barrel, 10 or 12 shot mag., polymer grip, front Tritium night sight and rear serrated combat sight, firing pin block and trigger safety, black, FDE (new 2020), or OD Green (new 2020) finish, 24.4 oz. New 2019.

MSR $605	$515	$450	$385	$350	$285	$230	$200	

Add $14 for FDE or OD Green finish (new 2020).

* ***CZ P-10 S Optics Ready*** – 9mm Para. cal., striker fired, sub-compact fiber reinforced polymer frame, 3 1/2 in. cold hammer forged barrel, 10 or 12 shot mag., swappable mag. release, single Tritium lamp in front with a large orange surround and serrated black rear, optics ready configuration (shipped with a blank fill plate for the Trijicon RMR or Leupold DeltaPoint Pro), polymer grip, firing pin block and trigger safety, Nitride finish, 28.2 oz. New 2019.

MSR $635	$540	$475	$400	$365	$300	$250	$210	

CZ-40B/CZ-40P – .40 S&W cal. only, CZ-75B operating mechanism in alloy (CZ-40B) or polymer (CZ-40P) M1911 style frame, DA/SA, black polycoat finish, 10 shot double column mag., fixed sights, firing pin block safety. Limited importation 2002 only, reintroduced 2007 only.

	$425	$365	$325	$290	$275	$250	$225	*$499*

* ***CZ-40 P Compact*** – .40 S&W cal., 1,500 imported 2004, reimported 2006.

	$325	$285	$265	$245	$225	$200	$175	*$370*

CZ-50 – .32 ACP cal., DA/SA, blowback action, 3 3/4 in. barrel, loaded chamber indicator, 8 shot mag.

	$450	$370	$325	$280	$260	$240	$220	

GRADING - PPGS™	100%	98%	95%	90%	80%	70%	60%	LAST MSR

CZ-52 – 7.62 Tokarev or 9mm Para. cal., roller locked short recoil operation, single action only, 4.9 in. barrel, 8 shot mag., heel magazine release, external hammer, bakelite grip panels with metal retaining band, frame mounted thumb safety/decocker, military models feature parkerized or grey oxide finish, some import packages may include extra 9mm Para. barrel. Mfg. in Strakonice.

$450	$400	$375	$325	$275	$200	$125	

Add $40 for extra 9mm Para. barrel.

Currently imported used CZ-52 pistols are priced in the $250-$300 range, depending on condition, and will have the current importer's mark visible on the gun.

CZ-70 – 7.65mm/.32 ACP cal., DA/SA, similar to Walther PP, 8 shot mag., 1 lb. 9 oz. Disc.

$250	$225	$195	$175	$150	$125	$100	

A very limited quantity of this model was imported.

CZ-75 SERIES – 9mm Para. or .40 S&W (disc. 1997, reintroduced 1999) cal., Poldi steel, selective double action, double action only, or single action only, frame safety, 4 3/4 in. barrel, 10 (C/B 1994, standard for .40 S&W cal.), 15* (disc.), or 16 (9mm Para. cal. only) shot mag., currently available in black polycoat/polymer (standard, DA and SA only), matte blue (disc. 1994), high polish (disc. 1994), glossy blue (mfg. 1999-2010), dual tone (mfg. 1998-2012), satin nickel (mfg. 1994-2012), high polished stainless steel, or matte stainless steel (new 2006) finish, black plastic grips, non-suffix early guns did not have a firing pin block safety, reversible mag. release, or ambidextrous safety, and were usually shipped with two mags., B suffix model nomenclature was added 1998, and designated some internal mechanism changes, BD suffix indicates decocker mechanism, 34.3 oz. New 1975.

"First Model" variations, mostly imported by Pragotrade of Canada, are identifiable by short slide rails, no half-cock feature, and were mostly available in high polish blue only. Current values may reach $3,000 if NIB. Chrome engraved $3,200 (NIB), factory competition $3,500 (NIB).

* ***CZ-75 25th Anniversary*** – 9mm Para. cal., features include 25th Anniversary markings. Limited mfg. of 500 during 2000 only.

$625	$450	$375	$315	$270	$230	$200	*$699*

* ***CZ-75 30th Anniversary*** – 9mm Para. cal., features special 30th anniversary engraving with 24Kt. gold plated controls and accents, 10 or 15 shot mag., high gloss blue finish, birch grips with carved "30". 1,000 mfg. (ser. no. 1-1,000) 2005-2006.

$875	$750	$625	$500	$450	$395	$350	*$999*

* ***CZ-75 Semi-Compact*** – 9mm Para. cal. only, 13 shot mag., choice of black polymer, matte, or high polish blue finish. Imported 1994 only.

$350	$300	$275	$250	$230	$250	$200	*$519*

Add $20 for matte blue finish.

Add $40 for high polish blue finish.

* ***CZ-75 Champion*** – 9mm Para. (mfg. 2000-2008) or .40 S&W cal., dual tone finish, IPSC competition features including 3 port compensator, finger grooved synthetic grips, target trigger and sights, 4 1/2 in. barrel, approx. 2.2 lbs. Imported 1999-2004, reintroduced 2006-2009.

$1,425	$1,200	$1,050	$875	$725	$600	$500	*$1,739*

* ***CZ-75 Modified*** – similar to Standard, except has dual port compensator and red dot reflex sight, approx. 2.8 lbs. Imported 2001-2002.

$1,250	$1,075	$975	$875	$735	$600	$500	*$1,567*

* ***CZ-75 Special Editions*** – 9mm Para. cal., similar to CZ-75, except has optional special edition finishes including all matte nickel, bright nickel frame, matte chrome, all brushed chrome, bright chrome, or gold frame, choice of matching finish slide, master blue slide, gold small parts, or master blue slide with gold small parts, price line refers to all matte nickel finish. Imported 1993-94 by Action Arms only.

$525	$465	$415	$375	$335	$310	$285	*$699*

Add approx. $120 for matte nickel frame with master blue small parts.

Add approx. $180 for matte nickel with gold small parts, matte nickel frame with master blue slide and gold small parts, master blue with gold small parts, or gold frame with master blue slide.

CZ-75 B – 9mm Para. or .40 S&W (disc. 2018) cal., DA/SA, steel frame, 4.6 in. hammer forged barrel, 10 (.40 S&W) or 16 (9mm Para.) shot mag., plastic grips, black polycoat, glossy blue (disc. 2008), dual tone (disc. 2012) or satin nickel (disc. 2012) finish, 3-dot sights (Tritium night sights available), firing pin block safety, ergonomic grip and controls, slide-in-frame design for better recoil control, manual (9mm) or ambidextrous manual safety, 2.2 lbs. New 1998.

MSR $699	$600	$525	$450	$410	$325	$275	$225

Add $13 for .40 S&W cal. (disc. 2018).

GRADING - PPGS™	100%	98%	95%	90%	80%	70%	60%	LAST MSR

Add $431 for CZ-75 Kadet .22 LR Adapter I (mfg. 1998-2010), or $435 for Adapter II (includes .22 LR upper slide assembly and mag., fits Omega System, new 2012).
Add $81 for Crimson Trace Lasergrips (black polycoat finish only, mfg. 2007 only).

* ***CZ-75 BD*** – 9mm Para. cal., similar to CZ-75 B, except features a decocking lever, 10 or 16 shot mag., black polycoat finish only.

MSR $699	$600	$525	$450	$410	$325	$275	$225	

* ***CZ-75 B Limited Edition*** – similar to CZ-75 B, except is stainless steel, tritium night sights. Limited mfg. 2010 only.

	$695	$625	$550	$475	$400	$350	$300	*$806*

* ***CZ 75 B 40th Anniversary Limited Edition*** – 9mm Para. cal., DA/SA, 4.6 in barrel, steel frame, fixed sights, each pistol is hand engraved in the Czech Republic, deep glossy blue finish, controls, extractor, grip screws and magazine base plate are finished in rainbow titanium nitride, high-grade birds eye maple grips, ships in leather-bound presentation case with two 16 shot magazines. Only 1,000 manufactured with individual number and certificate of authenticity 2015 only.

	$1,350	$1,175	$995	$875	$750	$625	$500	*$1,499*

* ***CZ-75 B 45th Anniversary*** – 9mm Para. cal., SA/DA, steel frame, 4.5 in. cold hammer forged barrel, 16 shot, fixed Tritium night sights, engraved wooden grips, manual safety, safety stop on hammer, firing pin block safety, deep engraving on slide and frame, high gloss blued finish, 35.2 oz. Limited mfg. of 1,000, 2020 only.

	$1,450	$1,300	$1,100	$1,000	$800	$650	$500	*$1,720*

* ***CZ 75 B Omega Convertible*** – 9mm Para. cal., DA/SA, steel frame, 4.6 in. cold hammer forged barrel, 16 shot double stack mag., black plastic grips, fixed three-dot sights, swappable ambi safety and decocker, safety stop on hammer, firing pin block safety, 2.2 lbs. New 2016.

MSR $699	$600	$525	$450	$410	$325	$275	$225	

* ***CZ-75 B Military*** – 9mm Para. cal. Imported 2000-2002.

	$365	$315	$270	$250	$225	$210	$195	*$429*

* ***CZ-75 B SA*** – 9mm Para. or .40 S&W (disc. 2013, reintroduced 2015-2016) cal., similar to CZ-75 B, except features SAO trigger mechanism and drop-free magazine, 10 or 16 (9mm only) shot mag., full length slide rails, extended beavertail, ambidextrous safety, black polycoat finish only. Disc. 2018.

	$525	$460	$400	$350	$300	$250	$200	*$612*

Add $49 for .40 S&W cal. (reintroduced 2015-2016).

* ***CZ-75 B Stainless*** – 9mm Para. cal., similar to CZ-75 B, except features matte or high polish stainless steel finish, 10 or 16 shot mag., ambidextrous manual safety, and rubber grips. Disc. 2019.

	$685	$600	$515	$465	$400	$350	$300	*$806*

* ***CZ-75 B Tactical*** – 9mm Para. cal., similar to CZ-75 B, except has ODG frame and matte black slide, includes CZ knife. Limited importation during 2003.

	$425	$355	$305	$270	$225	$210	$195	*$499*

* ***CZ-75 B Target*** – similar to CZ-75, except SAO with custom shop target features. Limited importation 2010 only.

	$1,050	$900	$750	$625	$525	$525	$350	*$1,182*

* ***CZ-75 B Urban Grey Suppressor-Ready*** – 9mm Para. cal., DA/SA, steel frame, Urban Grey polycoat slide, 5.2 in. barrel with threaded muzzle, two 10 or 18 shot extended mags., high suppressor sights, black rubber grips, swappable safety/decocker, 2.63 lbs. New 2016.

MSR $739	$625	$545	$475	$425	$345	$275	$225	

CZ-75 COMPACT – 9mm Para. or .40 S&W (mfg. 2005-2010) cal., 3.7 in. barrel, steel frame, 10 (C/B 1994), 13* (disc.), or 14 shot mag., fixed sights, checkered walnut (disc.) or plastic grips, manual safety, black, glossy blue (disc. 2006), dual tone (disc. 2012), or satin nickel (disc. 2012) finish, 33 oz. New 1993.

MSR $725	$615	$540	$460	$425	$345	$275	$225	

Add $41 for glossy blue (disc. 2006), dual tone (disc. 2012), or satin nickel (disc. 2012) finish.
Add $41 for .40 S&W cal. (disc. 2010).
Add $99 for tactical block with bayonet (.40 S&W cal. only) mfg. 2006-2012.
Add $431 for CZ Kadet .22 LR adapter I or II (includes .22 LR upper slide assembly and mag., mfg. 1998-disc.).

GRADING - PPGS™	100%	98%	95%	90%	80%	70%	60%	LAST MSR

* ***CZ-75 Compact SDP*** – 9mm Para. cal., DA/SA, 3.7 in. barrel, black alloy frame with black aluminum grips, lower Picatinny rail, low profile Tritium two-dot night sights, 14 shot mag., front and rear slide serrations, bobbed hammer, 28 1/2 oz. Mfg. 2013-2018.

	$1,265	$1,075	$925	$800	$700	$600	$500	*$1,453*

CZ-75 D PCR COMPACT – 9mm Para. cal., 3.7 in. barrel, black polymer alloy frame, decocker, PCR stands for Police of Czech Republic, 10 or 14 shot mag., black rubber grip, fixed snag free sights, loaded chamber indicator, 1.7 lbs. Importation began 2000.

MSR $695	$600	$525	$450	$410	$325	$275	$225	

CZ-75 KADET – .22 LR cal., black polymer finish, 10 shot mag, 4.7 in. barrel, 37.9 oz. Mfg. 1999-2004, reintroduced 2006-2012.

	$560	$500	$450	$400	$350	$300	$275	*$690*

CZ-75 SHADOW – 9mm Para. cal., DA/SA or SAO (new 2013), black or dual-tone finish, competition hammer/trigger with beavertail frame, stainless steel guide rod, ambidextrous extended manual safety, new style 85 combat trigger, includes two 16 (SAO, new 2013), or 18 shot mags. and test target, fiber optic front sight and shadow rear sight, checkered black plastic grips, 39 oz. Mfg. in Czech Republic, assembled in USA. Mfg. 2011-2013.

	$915	$800	$725	$650	$575	$500	$425	*$1,053*

Subtract $74 for SAO (new 2013, includes two 16 shot mags.).

* ***CZ-75 Shadow T*** – 9mm Para. cal., similar to CZ-75 Shadow, except is DA/SA, and has black rubber grips and full adj. rear sight. Mfg. 2011-2013.

	$1,075	$940	$815	$725	$650	$575	$500	*$1,180*

CZ-75 SHADOW CTS LS-P – 9mm Para. cal., DA/SA, black polycoat frame/grips, satin nickel long slide, adj. sights. Mfg. 2012-2013.

	$1,300	$1,150	$1,025	$875	$775	$675	$550	*$1,521*

CZ-75 SHADOW TAC II – 9mm Para. cal., DA/SA, 4.61 in. barrel, 16 shot mag., steel frame, Pre-B style slide, plain black serrated Combat II rear sight, Trijicon Tritium front sight, factory 85 Combat trigger, extended magazine release, stainless steel guide rod, short dust cover, high-rise beavertail, checkered aluminum grips, black polycoat finish, 2.4 lbs. Mfg. 2015-2017.

	$1,150	$1,000	$875	$750	$650	$525	$450	*$1,349*

CZ SHADOW 2 BLACK & BLUE/CZ SHADOW 2 SA – 9mm Para. cal., SA/DA or SAO (new 2020), steel frame, 4.89 in. cold hammer forged barrel, 17 shot mag., undercut trigger guard, fiber optic front and HAJO rear sights, optics ready (new 2020), checkered blue aluminum grips, ambidextrous manual safety, black polycoat finish, 46.5 oz. New 2018.

MSR $1,359	$1,160	$1,000	$865	$775	$625	$525	$475	

Add $246 for optics ready (new 2020).
Add $435 for Kadet adapter kit.

CZ SHADOW 2 ORANGE – 9mm Para. cal., SA/DA, steel frame with black polycoat, 4.89 in. cold hammer forged barrel, barrel bushing, 17 shot, adj. extended mag. release button, fiber optic front and serrated black HAJO rear sight, thin aluminum orange grips, ambidextrous manual safety, front and backstrap checkering, Nitride finish, 46.5 oz. New 2020.

MSR $2,245	$1,915	$1,675	$1,435	$1,300	$1,055	$875	$750	

CZ SHADOW 2 URBAN GREY – 9mm Para. cal., SA/DA, steel frame, 4.89 in. cold hammer forged barrel, 17 shot mag., undercut trigger guard, fiber optic front and HAJO rear sights, checkered black aluminum grips, ambidextrous manual safety, Urban Grey polycoat finish, 46.5 oz. New 2017.

MSR $1,359	$1,160	$1,000	$865	$775	$625	$525	$475	

CZ-75 STANDARD IPSC – .40 S&W cal., IPSC features, 5.4 in. barrel, dual tone finish, checkered wood grips, 10 or 16 (new 2005) shot mag., 45 oz. Mfg. 1999-2005.

	$1,000	$900	$750	$625	$550	$450	$350	*$1,152*

CZ-75 TACTICAL SPORT – 9mm Para. or .40 S&W cal., 5.3 in. barrel, steel frame, 10, 16 (.40 S&W cal.), or 20 (9mm Para. cal.) shot mag., ambidextrous safety, checkered wood grips, fixed sights, dual tone finish, 45 oz. Mfg. 2006-2018.

	$1,125	$975	$850	$725	$600	$500	$450	*$1,310*

* ***CZ-75 Tactical Sport Orange*** – 9mm Para. or .40 S&W cal., steel frame, 5.4 in. barrel, 10 (disc.), 17, or 20 shot mag., SAO trigger, fully adj. target sights, orange grips/mag. bases, thumb stop, black polycoat finish. New 2016.

MSR $1,949	$1,650	$1,450	$1,240	$1,125	$910	$750	$625	

GRADING - PPGS™	100%	98%	95%	90%	80%	70%	60%	LAST MSR

CZ-75 TS CZECHMATE – 9mm Para. cal., includes two 5.4 in. barrels and all accessories necessary to shoot in IPSC open or limited division, aluminum grips, competition hammer, undercut trigger guard, three 20 shot mags. and one 26 shot mag., black polycoat finish. Mfg. by Custom Shop beginning 2011.

MSR $3,659	$3,110	$2,725	$2,335	$2,115	$1,710	$1,400	$1,215	

CZ-75 SP-01 – 9mm Para. cal., 4 3/4 in. barrel, two 10 or 18 shot mags., adj. Tritium sights, checkered black rubber grips, ambidextrous thumb safety, lower Picatinny rail, ambidextrous decocking lever (SP-01 Tactical model only), matte black polycoat finish, 38 oz. New 2006.

MSR $829	$700	$615	$525	$475	$385	$315	$275	

Add $435 for Kadet adapter kit.

* ***CZ-75 SP-01 Phantom*** – 9mm Para. cal., SA/DA, polymer frame, 4.6 in. cold hammer forged barrel, 18 shot mag. (also fits standard CZ-75 models), steel slide, squared off trigger guard, fixed (disc. 2013) or 3-dot (new 2017) sights, two interchangeable grip inserts, decocking lever, black polycoat finish, 29.4 oz. Mfg. 2009-2013, reintroduced 2017-2019.

	$540	$475	$400	$365	$300	$250	$200	*$636*

CZ-75 SP-01 ACCU-SHADOW (AccuShadow) – 9mm Para. cal., 4.6 in. barrel, features Accu-Bushing system enabling precise barrel placement and better accuracy, competition hammer, lighter springs, short reset disconnector, fiber optic front and Hajo serrated target rear sight, lower Picatinny rail, black finish, 38 1/2 oz. Mfg. 2013-2014.

	$1,475	$1,295	$1,075	$925	$800	$700	$600	*$1,715*

CZ ACCUSHADOW 2 – 9mm Para. cal., SA/DA, steel frame, 4.89 in. cold hammer forged barrel, 17 shot mag., undercut trigger guard, fiber optic front and HAJO rear sights, checkered black aluminum grips, ambidextrous manual safety, black polycoat finish. Mfg. by Custom Shop beginning 2018.

MSR $2,269	$1,930	$1,685	$1,450	$1,310	$1,060	$875	$750	

CZ-75 SP-01 SHADOW – 9mm Para. cal. Limited mfg. by the Custom Shop.

	$625	$550	$475	$425	$365	$335	$295	*$724*

* ***CZ-75 SP-01 Shadow Custom*** – 9mm Para. cal., adj. competition rear and fiber optic front sight, 19 shot mag., custom tuned action and trigger, competition hammer, reduced power springs, stainless guide rod, thin black aluminum grips, dual tone finish. Custom Shop mfg. 2011 only.

	$1,050	$900	$750	$600	$500	$400	$325	*$1,199*

CZ-75 SP-01 SHADOW TARGET – 9mm Para. cal., similar to SP-01 Series, except has Custom Shop target features, including Champion style hammer, fiber optic front sight and competition rear sight, extended mag. release, fully beveled magwell, 19 shot mag., rubber grips, 2.6 lbs. Custom Shop mfg. 2010-2014.

	$1,175	$995	$825	$700	$600	$500	$425	*$1,361*

CZ 75 SP-01 SHADOW TARGET II – 9mm Para. cal., DA/SA, steel frame, 4.61 in. barrel, short reset single action trigger, fully adj. rear sight, fiber optic front sight, stainless steel guide rod, extended magazine release, checkered aluminum grips, black polycoat finish, 2.4 lbs. Mfg. by Custom Shop 2015-2020.

	$1,465	$1,280	$1,100	$995	$800	$650	$525	*$1,721*

CZ-75 SP-01 TACTICAL – 9mm Para. or .40 S&W (disc. 2016) cal., 4.6 in. barrel, 12 or 18 shot mag., lower Picatinny rail, decocker, Tritium sights, black rubber grips, black polycoat finish.

MSR $829	$700	$615	$525	$475	$385	$315	$275	

Add $79 for .40 S&W cal. (disc. 2016).

Add $99 for tactical block with bayonet (disc. 2012).

CZ 75 SP-01 TACTICAL URBAN GREY SUPPRESSOR-READY – 9mm Para. cal., DA/SA, steel frame, Urban Grey polycoat slide, 5.2 in. barrel with threaded muzzle, two 10 or 18 shot extended mags., high suppressor sights, black rubber grips, ambi decocking lever, firing pin block, 2.63 lbs. New 2016.

MSR $855	$725	$635	$550	$500	$400	$325	$280	

CZ-82 – 9x18mm Makarov cal., current Czech military sidearm, most recent exportation was to W. Germany in Makarov chambering.

This model is similar to the CZ-83 except for cal. Prices are similar to the model CZ-83.

CZ-83 – .32 ACP (disc. 1994, reintroduced 1999-2002 and 2006), .380 ACP (new 1986), or 9mm Makarov (mfg. 1999-2001) cal., modern design, 3-dot sights, 3.8 in. barrel, DA/SA, choice of carry models, blue (disc. 1994), glossy blue (new 1998), satin nickel (new 1999, not available in .32 ACP), or black polymer (disc. 1997) finish, black synthetic grips, 10 (C/B 1994), 12* (.380 ACP) or 15* (.32 ACP) shot mag., 26.2 oz. Mfg. began 1985, but was imported into the U.S. 1992-2012.

	$375	$315	$265	$235	$200	$175	$160	*$452*

Add $36 for satin nickel.

GRADING - PPGS™	100%	98%	95%	90%	80%	70%	60%	LAST MSR

* ***CZ-83 Special Editions*** – .380 ACP cal. only, similar to CZ-83, has optional special edition finishes including all matte nickel, master high polish blue, bright nickel, matte chrome, all brushed chrome, bright chrome, or gold frame, choice of matching finish or master blue slide with gold small parts, price line refers to all matte nickel or high polish blue finish. Importation disc. 1994.

	$425	$375	$335	$295	$250	$225	$200	*$569*

Add approx. $90 for matte nickel frame with master blue small parts.
Add approx. $175 for matte nickel with gold small parts, matte nickel frame with master blue slide and gold small parts, master blue with gold small parts, or gold frame with master blue slide.

CZ-85, CZ-85 B – 9mm Para. or 9x21mm (imported 1993-94 only) cal., DA/SA, variation of the CZ-75 with ambidextrous controls, 4.6 in. barrel, new plastic grip design, sight rib, available in black polycoat, matte blue (disc. 1994), glossy blue (mfg. 2001 only), or high-gloss blue (9mm Para. only, disc. 1994) finish, includes firing pin block and finger rest trigger, plastic grips, 10, 15 (disc.), or 16 shot mag. New 2005, B suffix model nomenclature was added during 1998, approx. 2.2 lbs. Disc. 2016.

	$550	$465	$410	$375	$330	$295	$275	*$628*

Add 50% for early guns w/high-gloss blue.
Add $431 for CZ Kadet .22 LR adapter (includes .22 LR upper slide assembly and mag., mfg. 1998 only).

* ***CZ-85 Combat*** – 9mm Para. cal., similar to CZ-85B, except has fully adj. rear sight, available in black polymer, matte blue (disc. 1994), glossy blue (mfg. 2001-2010), dual-tone (disc. 2012), satin nickel (disc. 2012), or high-gloss blue (disc. 2010) finish, walnut (disc. 1994) or black plastic (new 1994) grips, extended mag. release, drop free 15 (mfg. 1995-2011) or 16 shot mag. Imported 1992-2016.

	$550	$465	$425	$375	$350	$325	$295	*$664*

Add $50 for glossy blue (disc. 2010), satin nickel (disc. 2012), or dual-tone (disc. 2012) finish.
Add $291 for CZ Kadet .22 LR adapter (includes .22 LR upper slide assembly and mag., mfg. 1998 only).

* ***CZ-85 Champion*** – .40 S&W or 9x21mm cal., similar to CZ-75 Champion. Imported 1999 only.

	$1,325	$1,100	$975	$850	$725	$600	$500	*$1,484*

* ***CZ-85 Special Editions*** – 9mm Para. cal., similar to CZ-85, has optional special edition finishes including all matte nickel, bright nickel, matte chrome, all brushed chrome, bright chrome, or gold frame, choice of matching finish slide, master blue slide, gold small parts, or master blue slide with gold small parts, price line refers to all matte nickel finish. Imported 1993-94 only.

	$575	$495	$450	$395	$350	$325	$285	*$749*

Subtract $60 for matte nickel frame with master blue slide.
Add $130 for matte nickel frame with master blue small parts, matte nickel with gold small parts, matte nickel frame with master blue slide and gold small parts, master blue with gold small parts or gold frame with master blue slide.

* ***CZ-85 Combat Special Editions*** – 9mm Para. cal., finishes similar to Model CZ-85 Special Editions, price line refers to all matte nickel finish. Limited importation 1994-95.

	$775	$725	$650	$595	$525	$450	$375	*$1,049*

Subtract $125 for matte nickel frame with master blue small parts.
Add $245 for matte nickel with gold small parts, matte nickel frame with master blue slide and gold small parts, master blue with gold small parts, or gold frame with master blue slide.

CZ-97 B – .45 ACP cal., DA/SA, 4.84 in. barrel, all steel construction, front and rear slide serrations, extended beavertail, manual safety and firing pin block safeties, short recoil system, loaded chamber indicator, black polycoat or glossy blue (disc. 2014) finish, checkered wood (disc. 2012) or aluminum (new 2013) grips, fixed (disc. 2012) or fiber optic (new 2013) front sight, double column 10 shot mag., last shot hold open slide, 40 oz. New 1998.

MSR $819	$700	$615	$525	$475	$385	$315	$275	

Add $27 for glossy blue finish (disc. 2014).

* ***CZ-97 BD*** – .45 ACP cal., similar to CZ-97 B, except has decocker, Tritium night sights, black polycoat finish, 41 oz. New 2009.

MSR $945	$800	$700	$600	$550	$450	$350	$300	

CZ-100 – 9mm Para. or .40 S&W (disc.) cal., DAO, firing pin blocking safety, w/o external manual safety, black polymer finish, adj. 3-dot sights, high impact plastic frame, 10 or 12 (new 2005, 9mm Para. cal. only) shot mag., 3.9 in. barrel, approx. 24 oz. Mfg. 1996-2007, reintroduced 2009 only.

	$450	$395	$340	$285	$240	$220	$195	*$517*

CZ-122 B SPORT – .22 LR cal., SAO, 6 in. solid ribbed barrel with adj. rear sight, 10 shot mag., manual and firing pin block safety, last shot hold open slide, steel frame and slide with two-tone finish, ribbed black polymer grips, 30 oz. Limited mfg. 1998 only.

	$225	$190	$175	$160	$150	$140	$135	*$259*

GRADING - PPGS™	100%	98%	95%	90%	80%	70%	60%	LAST MSR

CZ 805 BREN S1 (PS1) PISTOL – 5.56 NATO or .300 AAC Blackout (mfg. 2017 only) cal., 11 in. barrel, one-piece aluminum upper receiver with monolithic Picatinny rail, 30 shot STANAG mag., single point sling attachment, adj. aperture rear and post front sights, black composite/bronze anodized or FDE (new 2016) finish, includes accessory arm brace adapter. Mfg. 2015-2018.

	100%	98%	95%	90%	80%	70%	60%	LAST MSR
	$1,525	$1,335	$1,150	$1,050	$850	$700	$550	*$1,799*

Add $100 for FDE finish (new 2016).

CZ BREN 2 Ms PISTOL – 5.56 NATO or 7.62x39 cal., carbon fiber reinforced polymer frame, 8, 9, 11, or 14 in. cold hammer forged barrel, 30 shot detachable mag., folding adj. sights, modular forend, stippled grips, ambi safety, flushed rear plate for AR-style buffer tube attachment, black finish, approx. 5 1/2 lbs. New 2019.

	100%	98%	95%	90%	80%	70%	60%	LAST MSR
MSR $2,075	$1,750	$1,525	$1,325	$1,185	$975	$800	$675	

CZ-2075 RAMI – 9mm Para. or .40 S&W (disc. 2016) cal., DA/SA, 3 in. barrel, double stack 7 (.40 S&W cal. new 2012), 8 (.40 S&W cal.), 10 (9mm Para. cal., flush fit) or 14 (9mm Para. cal., disc. 2013) shot mag. with finger extension, snag free (disc.) or fixed sights, black polycoat finish with black rubber checkered grips, alloy or polymer (mfg. 2006-2011) frame, 25 oz. Mfg. 2005-2020.

	100%	98%	95%	90%	80%	70%	60%	LAST MSR
	$545	$475	$410	$375	$300	$250	$200	*$645*

Add $12 for 10 shot mag.
Add $19 for .40 S&W cal. with 7 shot mag. (mfg. 2012-2016).
Subtract approx. $100 for polymer frame with black polycoat finish (disc. 2011).

* ***CZ-2075 RAMI BD*** – 9mm Para. cal., DA/SA, 3 in. barrel, 10 or 14 shot mag., similar to CZ-2075 RAMI, except has decocking lever, weight reduction scallop on slide, Tritium 3-dot night sights, 23 1/2 oz. Mfg. 2009-2020.

	100%	98%	95%	90%	80%	70%	60%	LAST MSR
	$595	$520	$450	$400	$325	$275	$225	*$699*

CZ VZ 61 SKORPION – imported by CZ 2009-2010. Please refer to this model listing in the Skorpion section.

CZ SCORPION EVO 3 S1 PISTOL – 9mm Para. cal., blowback operation, black polymer frame, 7 3/4 in. barrel, 10 (new 2016) or 20 shot double stack polymer mag., low profile sights, quad rails with 11 in. top Picatinny rail, ambidextrous controls, non-reciprocating charging handle, includes an arm brace adapter which allows for adding an AR-style pistol buffer tube, black, FDE (new 2016), OD Green (new 2018), or Battleship Grey (new 2018) finish, 5 lbs. New 2015.

	100%	98%	95%	90%	80%	70%	60%	LAST MSR
MSR $995	$850	$750	$640	$580	$470	$400	$350	

Add $30 for FDE (new 2016), OD Green (new 2018), or Battleship Grey (new 2018) finish.

CZ SCORPION EVO 3 S1 PISTOL W/FLASH CAN – 9mm Para. cal., SA, polymer frame, 7.7 in. barrel, muzzle threaded, includes 5 in. KAK flash can, 10 or 20 shot double stack mag., extended forend, factory folding stock, polymer grips, ambidextrous thumb safety, M-LOK attachment points, with (new 2018) or without SB Tactical arm brace, includes accessory adaptor kit, black finish, 5.7 lbs. New 2017.

	100%	98%	95%	90%	80%	70%	60%	LAST MSR
MSR $1,099	$935	$825	$700	$635	$515	$425	$365	

Add $76 for SB Tactical arm brace (new 2018).

The CZ Scorpion EVO 3 S1 Pistol is legally classified by the ATF as a pistol, and is intended by CZ-USA to be used as a pistol. Under current federal law and ATF policy, attaching a stock to this pistol - or attaching a device which is then used as a stock or intended to be used as a stock - constitutes the making of a short-barreled rifle which requires registration with ATF and the payment of the applicable tax.

CZ SCORPION EVO 3 S2 MICRO W/BRACE – 9mm Para. cal., SA, polymer frame, 4 in. barrel, muzzle threaded, includes faux suppressor from SilencerCo., 20 shot double stack mag., HB Industries forend, telescoping SB Tactical arm brace, ambidextrous thumb safety, black finish, 5 1/2 lbs. Mfg. 2018-2019.

	100%	98%	95%	90%	80%	70%	60%	LAST MSR
	$1,025	$895	$750	$675	$550	$450	$350	*$1,211*

CZ SCORPION EVO 3 S2 PISTOL MICRO W/FOLDING BRACE – 9mm Para. cal., SA, fiber-reinforced polymer frame, 4.12 in. cold hammer forged threaded barrel, 20 shot double stack polymer mag., Magpul MBUS back-up iron sights, folding SB Tactical brace, ambi thumb safety, HB Industries short handguard, black finish, 5.3 lbs. New 2020.

	100%	98%	95%	90%	80%	70%	60%	LAST MSR
MSR $1,349	$1,150	$1,000	$865	$780	$635	$525	$450	

CZ TS 2 – 9mm Para. cal., steel frame, 5.28 in. cold hammer forged barrel, 20 shot double stack mag., SAO trigger, serrated fiber optic front and serrated fixed rear sights, thin aluminum grips with checkering and magwell cap, safety stop on hammer and ambi manual safety, front and rear cocking slide serrations, 48.5 oz. New 2021.

	100%	98%	95%	90%	80%	70%	60%	LAST MSR
MSR $1,699	$1,450	$1,275	$1,095	$985	$800	$650	$550	

GRADING - PPGS™	100%	98%	95%	90%	80%	70%	60%	LAST MSR

CZ 1911 A1 – .45 ACP cal., 5 in. stainless steel barrel, carbon steel slide and frame, two 7 shot mags., serrated slide stop, aluminum trigger, manual safety, fixed sights, fully checkered walnut grips, black oxide finish, 2.42 lbs. Mfg. 2015 only.

$725 $650 $575 $500 $450 $400 $350 *$849*

CZC A01-LD – please refer to listing under CZ Custom within this section.

RIFLES: BOLT ACTION, RIMFIRE, COMMERCIAL MFG.

Ceská Zbrojovka began manufacturing rifles circa 1936. Long gun production was discontinued between 1948-1964, with the exception of the massive military contracts during that time period.

CZ 452 STYLE (ZKM-452) – .22 LR or .22 WMR (disc. 1998) cal., bolt action, 5, 6 (.22 WMR only), or 10 shot mag., 24.8 in. barrel, choice of black synthetic stock and matte nickel metal finish (new 1999) or uncheckered hardwood stock with Schnabel forend and blue metal finish (disc. 1998), adj. rear sight, 6.6 lbs. Importation began 1995 from CZ, earlier mfg. was by Brno. Reintroduced 2007-2011.

$360 $300 $260 $230 $200 $175 $150 *$443*

Add $50 for .22 WMR cal. (disc. 1998).

Satin nickel finish became the only finish on this model beginning 2011.

* ***CZ 452 Lux/Deluxe (ZKM-452D)*** – similar to CZ 452 Style (ZKM-452) only with checkered walnut stock, .22 WMR cal. in right hand action (disc. 2010). Imported 1995-2013.

$365 $310 $265 $230 $200 $175 $150 *$451*

Add $34 for .22 WMR cal. (disc. 2010).

Left-hand action became standard on this model beginning 2011.

* ***CZ 452 Ultra Lux*** – .22 LR cal., 28 in. barrel, beechwood stock, 10 shot mag., features gold accents, 6.8 lbs. Mfg. 2006-2015.

$365 $310 $265 $230 $200 $175 $150 *$450*

* ***CZ 452 American Classic (ZKM-452)*** – .17 HMR (new 2003), .17 Mach 2 (mfg. 2005-2009), .22 LR, or .22 WMR (disc. 2010) cal., 5 shot mag., 16 (mfg. 2007-disc.) or 22 1/2 in. barrel w/no sights, American style walnut stock, right (disc. 2010) or left (new 2011) hand action, approx. 6 lbs. Imported 1999-2018.

$375 $315 $265 $230 $200 $175 $150 *$464*

Add $28 for .17 HMR cal.
Add $34 for .22 WMR cal. (disc. 2010).

This model became standard with left-hand action only beginning 2011, except for 16 in. barrel.

* ***CZ 452 FS Mannlicher*** – .17 HMR (new 2005), .22 LR, or .22 WMR cal., 5 shot detachable mag., 21 in. barrel, features full length walnut Mannlicher stock, tangent rear adj. sight, 6.4 lbs. Mfg. 2004-2011.

$425 $365 $325 $275 $250 $225 $200 *$504*

Add $10 for .22 WMR or .17 HMR cal.

* ***CZ 452 Grand Finale Limited Edition*** – .22 LR cal., 452 action, 5 shot detachable mag., adj. trigger, upgraded American walnut stock with oil finish, ebony forend and grip cap, two-position safety, embellished with hand engraved scrollwork on the action, barrel, andbottom metal, includes 1 in. scope rings, jewelled bolt, deep glossy blue metal finish. Limited mfg. Disc.

$1,075 $950 $800 $750 $600 $500 $400 *$1,189*

* ***CZ 452 Silhouette*** – .22 LR cal., similar to CZ-452 American Classic, except has black synthetic stock and blue metal, 5.3 lbs. Mfg. 2003-2011.

$335 $275 $230 $210 $180 $160 $145 *$414*

* ***CZ 452 Scout (ZKM-452)*** – .22 LR cal. only, youth configuration, 16.2 in. sporter barrel, adj. trigger, adj. sights, uncheckered beechwood or pink synthetic (mfg. 2009-2010) stock, 5 shot mag., includes single shot adapter, 5 lbs. Imported 2000-2016.

$250 $215 $185 $165 $140 $120 $100 *$312*

Add $15 for pink finish (disc. 2010).

* ***CZ 452 Special Military Training Rifle*** – .17 HMR (Special only) or .22 LR (disc. 2010, reintroduced 2013) cal., similar to CZ-452 Lux, except has beechwood stock and 5 shot mag., 6.4 lbs. Mfg. 2002-2013.

$335 $285 $240 $210 $180 $150 $125 *$395*

Subtract $21 for .22 LR cal.

GRADING - PPGS™	100%	98%	95%	90%	80%	70%	60%	LAST MSR

* ***CZ 452 Varmint (ZKM-452)*** – .17 HMR (new 2005), .17 Mach 2 (mfg. 2005-2009), .22 LR, or .22 WMR (new 2004) cal. only, similar to Model 452 Lux/Deluxe, except has 21 in. heavy barrel and no sights, 6.8 lbs. Imported 1998-2011.

$385 $330 $290 $260 $225 $185 $165 ***$448***

Add $16 for .22 WMR cal.
Add $26 for .17 HMR cal.
Add $65 for brown laminated thumbhole stock (new 2010).

CZ 453 AMERICAN/VARMINT – .17 Mach 2 (disc. 2006), .17 HMR (new 2007), or .22 LR cal., 5 shot detachable shot mag., 20.9 (Varmint) or 22 1/2 (American) in. fluted or non-fluted barrel, two-position safety, regular (disc. 2009) or single set trigger (became standard 2010), no sights, 6.1 (American) or 7 (Varmint) lbs. Mfg. 2006-2012.

$455 $400 $350 $300 $265 $225 $200 ***$534***

Add $27 for .17 HMR cal.
Add $13 for Varmint Model.
Add $74 for fluted barrel (.17 HMR cal. only).

CZ 455 AMERICAN – .17 HMR, .22 LR, or .22 WMR cal., 5 shot detachable mag., 20 1/2 in. sporter barrel, w/o sights, black polymer (.22 LR only, new 2013) or checkered Turkish walnut stock with sling swivels, adj. trigger, approx. 6.2 lbs. Mfg. 2010-2018.

$345 $275 $240 $225 $200 $175 $150 ***$421***

Add $17 for .17 HMR or .22 WMR cal.
Add $27 for left hand action (mfg. 2012 only).
Subtract $36 for black polymer stock (new 2013).
Add $136 for American Combo (includes both .22 LR and .17 HMR cal. barrels), new 2011.

* ***CZ 455 American Stainless Synthetic*** – .17 HMR, .22 LR, or .22 WMR cal., 20 1/2 in. stainless steel sporter barrel, 5 shot detachable mag., adj. trigger, no sights, black synthetic American style stock, two-position safety, 5.94 lbs. Mfg. 2017-2018.

$350 $275 $240 $225 $200 $175 $150 ***$434***

Add $17 for .17 HMR or .22 WMR cal.

* ***CZ 455 American Suppressor Ready*** – .22 LR cal., 16 1/2 in. threaded sporter barrel, 5 shot detachable mag., no sights, black synthetic American-style stock, adj. trigger, 5 1/2 lbs. Mfg. 2014-2018.

$345 $275 $240 $225 $200 $175 $150 ***$421***

CZ 455 FS MANNLICHER – .17 HMR, .22 LR, or .22 WMR cal., 20 1/2 in. sporter barrel, 5 shot detachable mag., adj. trigger, full length forearm, Mannlicher style Turkish walnut stock, hooded front sight, 6.38 lbs. Mfg. 2012-2018.

$425 $385 $350 $325 $295 $265 $225 ***$514***

Add $26 for .17 HMR or .22 WMR cal.

CZ 455 LUX – .22 LR or .22 WMR cal., 20 1/2 in. barrel, 5 shot detachable mag., adj. rear sight and hooded front sight, adj. trigger, deluxe checkered Turkish walnut stock, blue finish, 6.1 lbs. Mfg. 2011-2018.

$375 $330 $280 $250 $200 $175 $150 ***$440***

Add $29 for .22 WMR cal.

CZ 455 SCOUT – .22 LR cal., 16 1/2 in. cold hammer forged barrel, detachable mag., adj. trigger, adj. iron sights, integrated 11mm dovetail, beechwood American style stock, 12 in. LOP, two-position safety, includes single shot adapter, blue finish, 5 lbs. Mfg. 2017-2018.

$290 $260 $225 $200 $185 $175 $150 ***$339***

CZ 455 SUPER MATCH – .22 LR cal., 10 shot detachable box mag., 20 in. barrel, uncheckered beech wood pistol grip stock, adj. rear sight, approx. 6.2 lbs. New 2010.

While advertised in 2010, this model never went into production.

CZ 455 TRAINING RIFLE – .17 HMR (new 2015) or .22 LR cal., 24.8 in. sporter barrel, 5 shot detachable mag., tangent rear sight, beechwood Lux stock, Schnabel forend, adj. trigger, 6.3 lbs. Mfg. 2014-2018.

$325 $285 $245 $225 $200 $185 $170 ***$374***

Add $25 for .17 HMR cal. (new 2015).

CZ 455 TRAINING RIFLE RUSTIC – .22 LR cal., 24.8 in. barrel, 5 shot detachable mag., tangent adj. sights, aged beechwood stock with Schnabel forend, two-position safety, feature integral dovetail for scope mounting, 6.81 lbs. Mfg. 2017 only.

$335 $285 $245 $225 $200 $185 $170 ***$399***

GRADING - PPGS™	100%	98%	95%	90%	80%	70%	60%	LAST MSR

CZ 455 ULTRA LUX – .22 LR cal., 28.6 in. cold hammer forged barrel, 10 shot detachable mag., tangent rear sight, interchangeable barrels and stocks, Lux Beechwood stock with cheekpiece, blue finish, 6.8 lbs. Mfg. 2015-2018.

$385 $335 $295 $260 $210 $175 $150 *$449*

CZ 455 VARMINT – .17 HMR, .22 LR, or .22 WMR cal., 20 1/2 in. heavy barrel without sights, 5 shot detachable mag., adj. trigger, Turkish walnut stock with American style comb, blue finish, 7 lbs. Mfg. 2012-2018.

$400 $360 $325 $295 $270 $250 $225 *$469*

Add $28 for .17 HMR or .22 WMR cal.

* ***CZ 455 Varmint Evolution*** – .17 HMR (new 2013) or .22 LR cal., 20 1/2 in. free floating heavy barrel, 5 shot detachable mag., adj. trigger, no sights, blue (mfg. 2012-2015), Coyote (new 2016), or Gloss Pink (mfg. 2016) laminated Boyds skeletonized stock, 7.2 lbs. Mfg. 2012-2018.

$460 $415 $375 $335 $300 $275 $250 *$538*

Add $27 for .17 HMR cal. (new 2013).

* ***CZ 455 Varmint Precision Trainer*** – .22 LR cal., 20 1/2 in. heavy barrel w/o sights, 5 shot detachable mag., adj. trigger, tan (disc. 2013) or camo paint (new 2014) Manners composite target stock, 7.8 lbs. Mfg. 2012-2018.

$795 $675 $600 $525 $450 $400 $350 *$940*

* ***CZ 455 Varmint Precision Trainer Suppressor Ready*** – .22 LR cal., 16 1/2 or 24 in. heavy barrel, 5 shot detachable mag., adj. trigger, no sights, Manners camo composite stock, 6.4-8 lbs. Mfg. 2016-2018.

$795 $675 $600 $525 $450 $400 $350 *$940*

Add $27 for 24 in. barrel.

* ***CZ 455 Varmint SST*** – .17 HMR or .22 LR cal., 20 1/2 in. heavy barrel w/o sights, features single set trigger, checkered walnut stock, 5 shot mag., 7 lbs. Mfg. 2013-2015.

$440 $415 $375 $335 $300 $275 $250 *$509*

Add $27 for .17 HMR cal.

* ***CZ 455 Varmint Thumbhole*** – .17 HMR or .22 LR cal., 20 1/2 in. heavy fluted barrel w/o sights, single set trigger, 5 shot mag., forest camo laminate thumbhole stock, 7 lbs. Mfg. 2013 only.

$495 $425 $375 $335 $300 $275 $250 *$588*

Add $27 for .17 HMR cal.

* ***CZ 455 Varmint Thumbhole Fluted*** – .22 LR cal., 20 1/2 in. heavily fluted barrel, 5 shot detachable mag., adj. trigger, no sights, nutmeg-colored laminate thumbhole stock, 7.2 lbs. Mfg. 2015-2016.

$465 $420 $375 $335 $300 $275 $250 *$549*

* ***CZ 455 Varmint Tacticool*** – .22 LR cal., 16 1/2 in. threaded (new 2014) or 20 1/2 (mfg. 2013 only) in. heavy barrel w/o sights, 5 shot detachable mag., adj. trigger, black painted laminate composite stock featuring Monte Carlo cheekpiece and ambidextrous palm swells, beavertail forend, suppressor ready became available 2014, 6.6 or 7.4 (20 1/2 in. bbl.) lbs. Mfg. 2013-2018.

$465 $420 $375 $335 $300 $275 $250 *$549*

CZ 457 AMERICAN – .22 LR, .17 HMR, or .22 WMR cal., 24.8 in. cold hammer forged Sporter barrel, 5 shot detachable mag., adj. trigger, no sights, Turkish walnut stock with high flat comb and classic checkering pattern, two-position push-to-fire safety, Nitride finish, 6.17 lbs. New 2019.

MSR $515 $440 $385 $330 $300 $240 $195 $170

* ***CZ American Synthetic Suppressor-Ready*** – .22 LR, .22 WMR, or .17 HMR cal., 20 in. cold hammer forged barrel, 5 shot detachable mag., no sights, integrated 11mm dovetail, black synthetic American-style stock, Nitride finish, 5.4 lbs. New 2021.

MSR $475 $400 $350 $300 $275 $225 $185 $155

CZ 457 AMERICAN COMBO – .22 LR and .17 HMR cal., 24.8 in. barrel, 5 shot detachable mag., fully adj. trigger, no sights, 11mm dovetail, American-style Turkish walnut stock with high, flat comb and classic checkering pattern, two-pos. push-to-fire safety, 6.17 lbs. New 2020.

MSR $655 $550 $480 $415 $375 $310 $260 $215

CZ 457 JAGUAR – .22 LR cal., 28.6 in. cold hammer forged barrel, threaded muzzle, 10 shot detachable mag., fully adj. trigger, rear tangent sight, European beechwood stock with cheekpiece, 13.75 in. LOP, grip stippling with Jaguar motif, two-position push-to-fire safty, 6.39 lbs. New 2020.

MSR $585 $500 $440 $375 $340 $275 $225 $195

CZ 457 LONG RANGE PRECISION – .22 LR cal., 20 in. fluted barrel, 5 shot, no sights, integrated 11mm dovetail, painted laminate stock, Nitride finish. New 2021.

MSR $1,195 $1,025 $900 $775 $700 $575 $475 $400

GRADING - PPGS™	100%	98%	95%	90%	80%	70%	60%	LAST MSR

CZ 457 LRP – .22 LR cal., 20 in. fluted varmint barrel with threaded muzzle and muzzle brake, 5 shot mag., adj. pistol grip stock with Picatinny rail underneath for bag rider or monopod, extended forend, textured grip surfaces, includes 3 LOP spacers, user-configurable comb and buttpad, 25 MOA Weaver-style rail, oversized bolt knob, includes premium 4M rifle case. New 2020.

Please contact the manufacturer directly for pricing and availability on this model.

CZ 457 LUX – .22 LR, .17 HMR, or .22 WMR cal., 24.8 in. cold hammer forged Sporter barrel, 5 shot detachable mag., adj. trigger, adj. iron sights, Turkish walnut Lux stock with cheekpiece, two-position push-to-fire safety, Nitride finish, 6.17 lbs. New 2019.

MSR $549	$470	$410	$350	$325	$260	$215	$185

CZ 457 SCOUT – .22 LR cal., 16 1/2 in. cold hammer forged Sporter barrel, single shot adapter, 5 shot detachable mag., adj. trigger, adj. iron sights, Beechwood youth stock, 12 in. LOP, two-position push-to-fire safety, 4.92 lbs. New 2019.

MSR $475	$400	$350	$300	$275	$225	$185	$155

CZ 457 TRAINING RIFLE – .22 LR cal., 24.8 in. cold hammer forged Sporter barrel, 5 shot detachable mag., adj. trigger, tangent rear sight, Beechwood stock with Schnabel forend, two-position push-to-fire safety, Nitride finish, 6.17 lbs. New 2019.

MSR $475	$400	$350	$300	$275	$225	$185	$155

CZ 457 PREMIUM – .22 LR cal., 24.8 in. barrel, threaded muzzle, 5 shot detachable mag., adj. trigger, fiber optic front and tangent rear sight, European-style Turkish walnut Monte Carlo stock with decorative Schnabel forend tip, cheekpiece, two-pos. push-to-fire safety, 6.39 lbs. New 2020.

MSR $799	$680	$600	$500	$450	$375	$300	$265

CZ 457 PRO VARMINT SUPPRESSOR-READY – .22 LR cal., 16 1/2 in. heavy threaded Varmint barrel, 5 shot detachable mag., fully adj. trigger, no sights, black painted laminate stock, two-position push-to-fire safety, Nitride finish, 7.3 lbs. New 2019.

MSR $615	$525	$460	$395	$355	$290	$240	$200

CZ 457 ROYAL – .22 LR cal., 16 1/2 or 20 1/2 in. cold hammer forged barrel, 5 shot detachable mag., adj. trigger, no sights, integrated 11mm dovetail, Turkish walnut stock with decorative tip, two-pos. safety, 5.95-6.17 lbs. New 2020.

MSR $769	$655	$575	$490	$450	$360	$300	$250

CZ 457 VARMINT – .22 LR, .17 HMR, or .22 WMR cal., 20 1/2 in. heavy Varmint barrel, 5 shot detachable mag., fully adj. trigger, no sights, Turkish walnut stock with American style comb, laser cut stippling on grips and forend, two-position push-to-fire safety, Nitride finish, 7 lbs. New 2019.

MSR $565	$475	$415	$350	$325	$260	$215	$185

CZ 457 VARMINT AT-ONE – .22 LR cal., 16 1/2 or 24 in. threaded heavy Varmint barrel, 5 shot detachable mag., fully adj. trigger, no sights, Boyds AT-ONE nutmeg laminate stock, adj. comb and LOP, Nitride finish, 7.23-7.73 lbs. New 2019.

MSR $689	$585	$510	$440	$400	$325	$275	$230

CZ 457 VARMINT MTR – .22 LR cal., 20 1/2 in. cold hammer forged Varmint profile barrel, 5 shot detachable mag., adj. trigger, no sights, Target style Turkish walnut stock, large flat forend with dual QD studs, vertical grip with palm swell and laser stippling, two-position push-to-fire safety, Nitride finish, 7 1/2 lbs. New 2019.

MSR $785	$665	$580	$500	$450	$365	$300	$260

CZ 457 VARMINT PRECISION CHASSIS SUPPRESSOR READY – .22 LR cal., 16 1/2 or 24 in. heavy cold hammer forged barrel, 5 shot detachable mag., fully adj. trigger, no sights, integral 11mm dovetail, adj. Luth-AR stock, aluminum chassis, AR-style grip, QD sling sockets, two-position push-to-fire safety, 7-7.65 lbs. New 2020.

MSR $1,039	$885	$775	$665	$600	$485	$415	$325

CZ 457 VARMINT PRECISION TRAINER – .22 LR cal., 20 1/2 in. Varmint barrel, 5 shot detachable mag., fully adj. trigger, no sights, black carbon fiber composite stock, 7.88 lbs. Mfg. 2019-2020.

	$975	$850	$725	$665	$535	$450	$375	*$1,144*

* ***CZ 457 Varmint Precision Trainer MTR*** – .22 LR cal., 16 1/2 in. heavy threaded barrel, MTR match chamber, 5 shot detachable mag., adj. trigger, carbon fiber Manners composite stock finished in a two-color camo pattern with orange highlights, 7.1 lbs. New 2021.

MSR $1,449	$1,230	$1,075	$925	$835	$675	$550	$450

GRADING - PPGS™	100%	98%	95%	90%	80%	70%	60%	LAST MSR

* ***CZ 457 Varmint Precision Trainer Suppressor-Ready*** – .22 LR cal., 16.5, 20 (disc. 2020), or 24 (disc. 2020) in. tapered Varmint threaded barrel, 5 shot detachable mag., fully adj. trigger, no sights, Target style Manners carbon fiber composite stock with three-color camo pattern, two-position push-to-fire safety, Nitride finish, 7.48-7.95 lbs. New 2019.

MSR $1,189	$1,010	$875	$750	$680	$550	$450	$385	

CZ 513 BASIC – .22 LR cal., 5 shot detachable mag., 20.9 in. barrel, non-adj. trigger, uncheckered beechwood stock, iron sights, includes single shot adaptor, 5 3/4 lbs. Mfg. 2004-2005, reintroduced 2007-2012.

	$245	$210	$180	$160	$140	$120	$100	*$307*

CZ 513 HUNTER – .22 LR cal., entry level bolt action, 5 shot detachable mag., beechwood stock. Imported 1994 only.

	$195	$175	$150	$125	$95	$80	$65	*$225*

Add $30 for Farmer Model.

This model was imported exclusively by Action Arms.

RIFLES: BOLT ACTION, CENTERFIRE, COMMERCIAL MFG.

Ceská Zbrojovka began manufacturing rifles circa 1936. Long gun production was discontinued between 1948-1964, with the exception of the massive military contracts during that time period.

CZ USA MODEL 3 – .270 WSM, 7mm WSM, or .300 WSM cal., Mauser style claw extractor, adj. M-70 type trigger, bottom floorplate with 3 shot fixed mag., three position safety, blue or stainless matte finished action and 24 in. barrel, right or left-hand action, drilled and tapped, American black walnut stock with fleur-de-lis, no sights, 7.9 lbs. Limited mfg. in the U.S. 2005 only.

	$725	$600	$550	$495	$450	$400	$350	*$872*

Add $10 for left-hand action.
Add $21 for stainless steel action and barrel.

CZ 527 AMERICAN (CLASSIC) – .17 Hornet (new 2013), .22 Hornet, .204 Ruger, .221 Fireball (mfg. 2004-2013, reintroduced 2016), 6.5 Grendel (new 2017), 7.62x39mm (new 2017), .222 Rem. (disc. 2018), or .223 Rem. cal., 21.9 in. sporter weight hammer forged barrel w/o sights, SST, recessed target crown, maple (disc.), brown laminate (disc.), spring camo laminate (disc.), sunset camo laminate (disc.), English walnut (disc.), fancy American walnut (disc.) or American pattern stock, scope rings included, approx. 6 1/2 lbs. New 1999.

MSR $752	$635	$555	$475	$430	$350	$285	$250	

Add $14 for left-hand action - available in .223 Rem. or .204 Ruger (disc. 2017) cal. only.
Add $122 for English walnut (disc.) stock or $178 for fancy American walnut stock (disc.)
Subtract $13 for laminated stock (disc.).

* ***CZ 527 American Rustic*** – 6.5 Grendel or 7.62x39mm cal., 21.9 or 24 in. sporter barrel, 5 shot detachable mag., SST, no sights, aged beechwood American style stock, blue finish, 6.41 lbs. Mfg. 2017 only.

	$625	$550	$475	$425	$350	$285	$250	*$733*

* ***CZ 527 American Synthetic Suppressor Ready*** – .300 AAC Blackout (mfg. 2017-2019), .223 Rem. (new 2019), 6.5 Grendel (new 2019), or 7.62x39mm cal., 16 1/2 or 21.9 in. threaded sporter barrel, 5 shot detachable mag., no sights, black synthetic American style stock, blue finish, 5.87 lbs. New 2017.

MSR $779	$665	$580	$500	$450	$365	$300	$260	

Add $20 for 7.62x39mm cal.

CZ 527 CARBINE – .223 Rem. (new 2001) or 7.62x39mm cal., carbine configuration with 18 1/2 in. barrel with open rear and bead front sights, 5 shot detachable mag., SST, straight comb walnut or aged beechwood (new 2017, 7.62x39mm only) stock, approx. 6 lbs. New 1999.

MSR $785	$665	$580	$500	$450	$365	$300	$260	

* ***CZ 527 Youth Carbine*** – .223 Rem. or 7.62x39mm cal., micro-Mauser action, 18 1/2 in. barrel, 5 shot detachable mag., SST, fixed sights, 12.75 in. LOP, Turkish walnut stock, 5.61 lbs. Mfg. 2015-2018.

	$625	$550	$475	$425	$350	$285	$250	*$733*

CZ 527 FS MANNLICHER – .22 Hornet (disc. 2013), .222 Rem. (disc. 2013), or .223 Rem. cal., 20 1/2 in. barrel, SST, fixed sights, 5 shot detachable mag., checkered full length Mannlicher walnut stock with steel muzzle cap, vent. recoil pad, 6 1/4 lbs. Imported 1995-2018.

	$675	$595	$535	$450	$400	$325	$275	*$784*

GRADING - PPGS™	100%	98%	95%	90%	80%	70%	60%	LAST MSR

CZ 527 LUX – .22 Hornet, .222 Rem. (disc. 2017), or .223 Rem. cal., Mauser style bolt action with silent safety, 21.9 (disc.) or 23.6 in. sporter barrel with open sights, 5 shot detachable mag., hardwood (disc.) or checkered Turkish walnut stock and forend, 6.2 lbs. Importation began 1995.

MSR $780	$665	$580	$500	$450	$365	$300	$260	

Add $26 for left-hand action (.223 Rem. cal. only, disc. 2019).

CZ 527 M1 AMERICAN – .223 Rem. cal., styling similar to U.S. military M1 carbine featuring 3 shot flush detachable mag., no sights, redesigned trigger guard (new 2015), walnut (disc. 2013) or black synthetic stock, approx. 6 lbs. Mfg. 2008-2019.

	$565	$475	$420	$365	$335	$295	$250	*$686*

Add $66 for walnut stock (disc. 2013).

* ***CZ 527 M1 Ultralight Predator*** – .223 Rem. cal., synthetic stock with 100% Badland West camo coverage, 22 in. sporter weight barrel, single set trigger, 3 shot detachable mag., no sights, 5 3/4 lbs. Mfg. 2009-2011.

	$695	$595	$500	$450	$400	$350	$295	*$830*

CZ 527 PRESTIGE – .22 Hornet (disc. 2008) or .223 Rem. (disc. 2006, reintroduced 2009) cal., Mauser style bolt action with silent safety, 23.6 in. sporter barrel, 5 shot detachable mag., deluxe checkered walnut stock and forend, no sights, jewelled bolt, SST, scope rings included, 6.3 lbs. Limited mfg. 2001-2009.

	$895	$750	$625	$500	$400	$350	$300	*$1,022*

CZ 527 VARMINT – .17 Hornet (new 2013), .17 Rem. (mfg. 2005-2006, reintroduced 2007-2013 and 2016), .204 Ruger (new 2005), .222 Rem. (disc. 2013), or .223 Rem. cal., varmint configuration with 24 in. heavy barrel and no sights, SST, choice of walnut, maple (.223 Rem. cal., disc. 2006), laminated (mfg. 2002-2014), or H-S Precision Kevlar (mfg. 2002-2011) black stock, approx. 8 lbs. Importation began 2001.

MSR $779	$665	$580	$500	$450	$365	$300	$260	

Add $6 for .204 Ruger cal.

Add $50 for grey laminate stock (.223 Rem. cal. only, disc. 2014) or $178 for H-S Precision Kevlar stock (not available in .17 Rem.), disc. 2011.

* ***CZ 527 Varmint Suppressor-Ready*** – 6.5 Grendel cal., 25.6 in. cold hammer forged threaded Varmint barrel, 5 shot detachable box mag., SST, no sights, controlled round feed, claw extractor, Turkish walnut stock, matte blue finish, 7.8 lbs. New 2019.

MSR $815	$700	$615	$525	$475	$385	$315	$275	

* ***CZ 527 Varmint Target*** – .204 Ruger or .223 Rem. cal., 24 in. barrel, 5 shot detachable mag., vertical grip Kevlar stock with wide forearm and aluminum bedding. Mfg. 2012-2013.

	$775	$725	$625	$550	$500	$450	$400	*$885*

* ***CZ 527 Varmint Thumbhole*** – .223 Rem. cal., 24 in. hammer forged heavy barrel, 5 shot detachable box mag., Shady Camo laminate thumbhole stock with palm swell and wide forend, claw extractor, SST, integrated scope mount, matte blue finish, 7.8 lbs. Mfg. 2015-2016.

	$650	$575	$495	$440	$360	$300	$250	*$775*

CZ 527 VARMINT MTR – .223 Rem. or 6.5 Grendel cal., 25.6 in. heavy Varmint barrel, 5 shot detachable box mag., adj. trigger, no sights, Turkish walnut Target stock with vertical pistol grip and wide forend, two-position safety, 8.7 lbs. New 2019.

MSR $925	$785	$685	$625	$560	$475	$425	$375	

CZ 531 – .243 Win., .270 Win., .308 Win., .30-06, 7x64mm, 8x57mm, 8x60mm, 8x64mm, or 8x68mm, 4 shot detachable (.243 and .308 only) or internal 5 shot (4 shot, 8x68) mag., receiver drilled and tapped for scope bases, short extractor and plunger type ejector, double set trigger, tang safety with locking button, 23.6 in. (25.6 in., 8x68) barrel, adj. open sights, checkered walnut stock with Bavarian style cheekpiece, recoil crossbolts and vent. recoil pad, approx. 7-7 3/4 lbs. 766 rifles mfg. 1985-1988.

	$1,750	$1,500	$1,300	$1,150	$950	$800	$725	

CZ 531 was the firm's initial departure from the Brno-type (improved Mauser) centerfire rifle designs. Only .30-06 cal. rifles have been observed. Not until the introduction of CZ 555 in 2006 did CZ return to the push-feed style (short extractor, plunger ejector) action.

CZ 537 – .243 Win., .270 Win., .30-06, .308 Win., or 7x57mm cal., detachable 4 shot (.243 Win. and .308 Win. cals. only) or 5 shot fixed mag., choice of regular or Mannlicher (.30-06 or .308 Win. cal. only) stock, hooded ramp front sight, 7 1/4 lbs. Importation 1995 only.

	$495	$425	$370	$330	$300	$275	$250	*$649*

Add $100 for Mannlicher style stock.

GRADING - PPGS™ 100% 98% 95% 90% 80% 70% 60% LAST MSR

* ***CZ 537 Mountain Carbine*** – .243 Win. cal. only, 19 in. barrel, 5 shot detachable mag., includes ring mounts, 7.1 lbs. Imported 1994 only.

$525 $450 $375 $330 $300 $275 $250 *$669*

CZ 550 STANDARD – various cals. have been imported to date, 4 shot detachable (.243 Win. or .308 Win. only) or internal 5 shot mag., 23.6 in. barrel, receiver drilled and tapped for Remington 700 style scope base, no sights, checkered walnut stock and forearm, 7 1/4 lbs. Imported 1995-2000.

$475 $395 $340 $310 $285 $260 $240 *$561*

Add $21 for .243 Win. or .308 Win. cal. with detachable mag.

* ***CZ 550 Lux*** – various cals., similar to CZ 550 Standard, except has deluxe checkered walnut stock with Bavarian style cheekpiece and vent. recoil pad. Mfg. 1998-2004.

$495 $415 $350 $315 $285 $260 $240 *$588*

Add $20 for detachable mag. (.22-250 Rem., .243 Win., or .308 Win. cal., disc.).

» ***CZ 550 Battue Lux*** – similar to CZ 550 Lux, except has 20 1/2 in. barrel with integral barrel fixed rear sight. Limited mfg. 1998 only.

$450 $375 $330 $300 $280 $260 $240 *$519*

Add $30 for .243 Win. or .308 Win. cal. with removable mag.

* ***CZ 550 Prestige*** – .270 Win. or .30-06 cal., similar to CZ 550 Lux, except has deluxe checkered walnut stock and forend, no sights, scope rings included. Imported 2001, reintroduced 2003-2005.

$740 $510 $405 $380 $325 $285 $260 *$854*

* ***CZ 550 American (Classic)*** – .22-250 Rem., .243 Win., .270 Win., .30-06, .308 Win., 6.5x55mm (new 2001), 7x57mm (disc. 2004), or 9.3x62mm cal., American style walnut or Kevlar (.270 Win., .30-06, 6.5x55mm, or 9.3x62mm cals.) stock, fixed or detachable mag., scope rings included, no sights, approx. 8 lbs. Mfg. mid-1999-2013.

$695 $575 $475 $425 $375 $325 $275 *$815*

Add $38 for 9.3x62mm cal.

Add $145 for Kevlar stock (new 2009).

* ***CZ 550 Varmint/Varmint Tacticool*** – .22-250 Rem. (mfg. 2002-2013) or .308 Win. cal., 25.6 in. barrel w/o sights, 4 shot detachable mag., SST, no sights, checkered walnut (.308 Win. cal. only), H-S Precision Kevlar (mfg. 2005-2103), grey laminated (mfg. 2002-2013), or Boyds laminate Foliage Green (new 2014, Varmint Tacticool model) stock with vent. recoil pad, approx. 9 - 10 3/4 lbs. Imported 2000-2015.

$750 $625 $525 $450 $400 $350 $295 *$865*

Add $59 for Boyds laminate stock (new 2014).

Add $66 for laminated stock (mfg. 2002-2013).

Add $139 for H-S Precision Kevlar stock (mfg. 2005-2013).

* ***CZ 550 Carbine*** – .30-06 or 9.3x62mm cal., 20.6 in. sporter barrel with adj. rear iron sight and hooded front sight, fixed 4 shot mag., 3-position safety, SST, black Kevlar (disc.) or American-pattern Aramid composite stock, 7 lbs. Mfg. 2011-2016.

$950 $815 $700 $600 $500 $400 $350 *$1,080*

Add $49 for 9.3x62mm cal.

* ***CZ 550 FS Mannlicher*** – .243 Win., .270 Win., .30-06, .308 Win., 6.5x55mm, or 9.3x62mm cal., 20 1/2 in. barrel, fixed 5 shot or 4 shot detachable mag. (.243 Win. or .308 Win. cal. only), adj. sights, Turkish walnut Bavarian-style Mannlicher stock with steel muzzle cap, 7.4 lbs. Imported 1996-98, reintroduced 2001-2017.

$780 $660 $550 $450 $400 $350 $295 *$890*

Add $49 for 9.3x62mm cal.

* ***CZ 550 Battue FS Mannlicher*** – similar to CZ 550 FS Mannlicher, except has integral barrel fixed rear sight. Limited mfg. 1998 only.

$525 $465 $425 $395 $360 $330 $300 *$609*

Add $30 for .243 Win. or .308 Win. cal. with removable mag.

* ***CZ 550 Minnesota*** – similar to CZ 550 Lux, except has select walnut stock w/o cheekpiece, and barrel has no sights. Limited mfg. 1998 only.

$445 $375 $330 $300 $280 $260 $240 *$505*

Add $30 for .243 Win. or .308 Win. cal. with removable mag.

GRADING - PPGS™	100%	98%	95%	90%	80%	70%	60%	LAST MSR

* ***CZ 550 Medium Magnum*** – .300 Win. Mag. (disc. 2012) or 7mm Rem. Mag. cal., checkered walnut stock and forearm, open sights, (.300 Win. Mag. has Battue quarter rib, detachable mag. and fiber optic front sight), 23.6 in. barrel, 7 3/4 lbs. Mfg. 2007-2014.

$825 $740 $625 $550 $495 $450 $395 ***$947***

Add $182 for Kevlar stock (7mm Rem. Mag. only, new 2011).

CZ 550 MAGNUM STANDARD – .300 Win. Mag., .375 H&H, .416 Rem. Mag. (disc. 1998), .416 Rigby, .458 Win. Mag., or 7mm Rem. Mag. (importation disc. 1997) cal., 3-5 shot fixed mag., 25 in. barrel with express rear sight, checkered hardwood stock, 9 1/4 lbs. Limited mfg. 1998 only.

$525 $475 $440 $400 $375 $350 $335 ***$595***

Add $40 for .416 Rem. Mag., .416 Rigby, or .458 Win. Mag. cal.

* ***CZ 550 Magnum Standard Lux*** – similar to CZ 550 Magnum, except has select checkered walnut, last cals. were .300 Win. Mag. and 7mm Rem. Mag., 7.7-9.4 lbs. Mfg. 1998-2005.

$600 $500 $445 $395 $350 $335 $300 ***$690***

Add $185 for .375 H&H., .416 Rigby, or .458 Win. Mag. (disc.) cal.

* ***CZ 550 Safari Magnum*** – .300 Win. Mag. (mfg. 2008-2009), .375 H&H, .416 Rigby, or .458 Win. Mag. cal., 25 in. heavy sporter barrel, 4 or 5 shot fixed mag., express sights, single set trigger, checkered walnut stock with curved cheekpiece, 9.4 lbs. Mfg. 2004-2020.

$1,065 $925 $800 $725 $585 $475 $400 ***$1,252***

Add $106 for .416 Rigby or .458 Win. Mag. (new 2012).

CZ 550 AMERICAN SAFARI MAGNUM FIELD GRADE – .375 H&H, .416 Rigby, .458 Win. Mag., .458 Lott, or .505 Gibbs cal., 24 or 25 in. barrel, 3 or 5 shot fixed mag., SST, express sights, field grade walnut stock, right or left (.375 H&H only, disc. 2018) hand action, blue finish, 9.1-10.94 lbs. Mfg. 2004-2020.

$1,065 $925 $800 $725 $585 $475 $400 ***$1,252***

Add $106 for .416 Rigby or .458 Win. Mag. cal. Add $137 for .458 Lott in Field grade.
Add $1,968 for .505 Gibbs cal.
Add $784 for left-hand action (.375 H&H cal. only) with premium walnut stock (disc. 2012, reintroduced 2016-2018).

* ***CZ 550 American Safari Magnum Field Fancy*** – .375 H&H, .416 Rigby, .458 Win. Mag., or .458 Lott cal., 25 in. heavy sporter barrel, 4 (.416 Rigby only) or 5 shot fixed mag., SST, express sights, fancy grade walnut stock, blue finish, 9.9 lbs. Mfg. 2004-2020.

$1,750 $1,575 $1,375 $1,200 $1,050 $900 $775 ***$1,999***

* ***CZ 550 American Safari Magnum Field Kevlar/Aramid Composite*** – .375 H&H, .416 Rigby, .458 Win. Mag., or .458 Lott cal., 25 in. barrel, 4 or 5 shot fixed mag., Kevlar (disc.) or Aramid composite stock, 9.9 lbs. Mfg. 2009-2020.

$1,500 $1,325 $1,100 $900 $750 $600 $550 ***$1,757***

Add $56 for .458 Lott cal.

* ***CZ 550 American Safari Magnum Field Laminate*** – .375 H&H, .416 Rigby, .458 Win. Mag., or .458 Lott cal., 25 in. barrel, 4 or 5 shot fixed mag., choice of brown, spring camo, or sunset camo laminate stock, 9.9 lbs. Mfg. 2004-2013.

$1,150 $950 $850 4750 $650 $550 $450 ***$1,387***

Add $37 for .458 Lott cal.

* ***CZ 550 American Safari Magnum Deluxe*** – .375 H&H, .416 Rigby, .458 Win. Mag., or .458 Lott cal., similar to Field Grade, except has deluxe walnut stock. Mfg. 2004-2011.

$1,700 $1,475 $1,225 $1,025 $925 $825 $725 ***$1,911***

Add $57 for .458 Lott cal.

CZ 550 SAFARI CLASSICS EXPRESS/MAGNUM EXPRESS RIFLE (CUSTOM GRADE SAFARI MAGNUM) – .270 Win., .30-06, .300 H&H (new 2007), .338 Lapua Mag. (new 2008), .338 Win. Mag. (new 2008), .375 H&H (disc. 2014), .375 Ruger, .404 Jeffery, .416 Rem. (new 2008), .416 Taylor, .425 Westley Richards, .450 Rigby, .500 Jeffrey (new 2007), or .505 Gibbs cal., custom Magnum action, 24 in. heavy Sporter barrel, 5 shot mag., single set trigger adjustable per individual requirements, express sights, checkered fancy grade American walnut stock and forend, dual crossbolts and straight comb, two-position safety, glossy or matte blue metal finish, built per individual custom order. Mfg. by the Custom Shop beginning 2005.

Last MSR in 2015 was $3,268.

This model is currently P.O.R.
In 2015, these were the final advertised MSRs for the following calibers: Add $408 for .338 LM, .500 Jeffery cal., or .505 Gibbs cal. (includes built-in recoil reducer and glass bedded action).
Subtract $547 for .375 H&H cal. with 20 in. barrel (disc. 2014).

GRADING - PPGS™	100%	98%	95%	90%	80%	70%	60%	LAST MSR

SAFARI CLASSICS CRAIG BODDINGTON SIGNATURE SERIES – .375 H&H cal., 550 Magnum action, 24 in. barrel, front sight, barrel band forward sling swivel stud, 13 1/2 in. LOP, red 1 in. Decelerator recoil pad fitted to the XX Claro walnut stock, jeweled bolt, Craig's signature is engraved on the floorplate and "Craig Boddington Series" designation is engraved just forward of the action on top of the barrel, includes canvas sling, cartridge slide from Trader Keith, and a leather-bound hunting journal. Limited Edition of 50 pieces including 45 right-hand models and 5 left-hand models. Mfg. 2015-2018.

Last MSR on this model was $3,099.

CZ 550 MAGNUM H.E.T. (HIGH ENERGY TACTICAL) – .300 Win. Mag., .300 Rem. Ultra Mag., or .338 Lapua cal., 28 in. barrel, flat black finish, Kevlar tactical stock, 4 to 6 shot fixed mag., SST, muzzle brake, oversized bolt handle, 13 lbs. Mfg. 2009-2013.

$3,500 $3,125 $2,625 $2,250 $1,950 $1,575 $1,325 *$3,929*

CZ 550 H.E.T. II (HIGH ENERGY TACTICAL) – .338 Lapua cal., 550 Magnum action, 25 in. barrel with muzzle brake, 5 shot detachable mag., adj. trigger, Manners carbon fiber composite stock with adj. cheekpiece and molded-in Midnight Camo finish, low-mount Picatinny rail, includes QD sling flush cups, 14 lbs. Mfg. 2014-2018.

$3,500 $3,125 $2,625 $2,250 $1,950 $1,575 $1,325 *$3,929*

CZ 550 BADLANDS WESTERN SERIES – .338 Lapua cal., 25 in. threaded heavy Sporter barrel with custom muzzle brake, 4 shot mag., SST, integral scope bases, Kevlar (disc.) or Aramid composite stock, two-position safety, full length aluminum bedding block, blue finish, 9.2 lbs. Mfg. 2014-2019.

$2,325 $2,050 $1,750 $1,575 $1,275 $1,050 $825 *$2,599*

CZ 550 SONORAN WESTERN SERIES – .270 Win., .30-06, .300 Win. Mag., 7mm Rem. Mag., or .26 Nosler (new 2015) cal., 24 or 26 in. fluted barrel, 3 or 5 shot internal mag., SST, Manners 100% Olive Drab carbon fiber stock with Wundhammer swell pistol grip, flat black Nitride finish, approx. 7 1/2 lbs. Mfg. 2014-2017.

$2,875 $2,525 $2,150 $1,950 $1,575 $1,300 $1,000 *$3,199*

CZ 550 ULTIMATE HUNTING RIFLE (UHR) – .300 Win. Mag. cal. only, 23.6 in. heavy sporter barrel, 4 shot fixed mag., SST, no sights, extra craftsmanship guarantees one MOA accuracy to 600 yards, Kevlar (mfg. 2011-2014), Aramid composite (mfg. 2015-2016) or deluxe checkered walnut stock and forend, includes scope rings, 8 lbs. Mfg. 2007-2018.

$1,200 $1,025 $875 $750 $625 $500 $425 *$1,361*

Add $2,097 for Nightforce 5.5-22x50 mm scope (disc).

Add $136 for Kevlar (mfg. 2011-2014) or Aramid composite (mfg. 2015-2016) stock.

CZ 550 URBAN COUNTER SNIPER – .308 Win. cal., 16 in. barrel with SureFire muzzle brake, OD Green Kevlar stock, 10 shot mag. Mfg. 2010-2013.

$2,275 $2,000 $1,750 $1,500 $1,250 $1,000 $825 *$2,530*

CZ 555 SPORTER – .30-06 or .308 Win. cal., push-feed style action, short extractor, side release 3 shot detachable mag., 24 in. hammer forged barrel with sights, single set trigger, two position safety, deluxe walnut stock with sling swivels, 7 1/4 lbs. Mfg. 2006-disc.

$795 $725 $650 $575 $500 $450 $400

CZ 557 AMERICAN – 6.5x55, .270 Win., .30-06, .243 Win. (disc. 2020), 6.5 Creedmoor, 7mm-08 (mfg. 2019 only), or .308 Win. (disc. 2020) cal., long or short action, 24 in. cold hammer forged Sporter barrel, 4 (detachable) or 5 shot mag., adj. trigger, no sights, integral scope bases, Turkish walnut stock with oil finish, palm swell, high comb, two-position push-to-fire safety, square bridge receiver, blue finish, 7.05 lbs. New 2019.

MSR $909 $775 $680 $580 $525 $425 $350 $300

* ***CZ 557 American Synthetic*** – 6.5x55, .270 Win., .30-06, .243 Win., 6.5 Creedmoor, 7mm-08 (mfg. 2019 only), or .308 Win. cal., short or long action, 24 in. cold hammer forged barrel, 4 (detachable) or 5 shot mag., adj. trigger, no sights, black synthetic stock with high flat comb, two-position push-to-fire safety, blue finish, 6.83 lbs. Mfg. 2019-2020.

  $675 $585 $500 $450 $350 $285 $250 *$792*

CZ 557 CARBINE – .243 Win. (mfg. 2014 only), .270 Win., .30-06, .308 Win. (mfg. 2014 only), or 6.5x55 cal., 20 1/2 in. barrel, adj. trigger, 4 shot mag., iron sights, satin finished walnut stock, 7 1/4 lbs. Mfg. 2014-2016.

$725 $625 $575 $525 $450 $395 $350 *$812*

CZ 557 ECLIPSE – 6.5 Creedmoor, .308 Win., or 30-06 cal., 20 1/2 in. cold hammer forged barrel, 5 shot hinged floorplate, fully adj. trigger mech, no sights, integrated 19mm dovetails, black synthetic American style stock, two-position push to fire safety, 6.83 lbs. New 2020.

MSR $659 $560 $490 $420 $380 $310 $260 $215

GRADING - PPGS™	100%	98%	95%	90%	80%	70%	60%	LAST MSR

CZ 557 LEFT HAND – .30-06 or .308 Win. (new 2019) cal., 24 in. cold hammer forged Sporter barrel, 4 (detachable) or 5 shot mag., adj. trigger, no sights, integral scope bases, Turkish walnut American style with oil finish, two-position push-to-fire safety, blue finish, 7.05 lbs. New 2018.

MSR $899	$765	$670	$575	$525	$425	$350	$300	

CZ 557 SPORTER – .243 Win. (mfg. 2014, reintroduced 2016), .270 Win., .30-06, .308 Win. (mfg. 2014, reintroduced 2016), or 6.5x55 cal., short action, 20 1/2 in. forged barrel w/o sights, matte blue metal finish, fixed 4 shot mag., adj. trigger, forged steel receiver with integral scope dovetails, short extractor and plunger style ejector, receiver mounted two-position safety, American style walnut with cheekpiece or Manners 100% carbon fiber (not available in .243 Win. or .308 Win.) stock, 7 1/4 lbs. Mfg. 2014-2018.

	$725	$650	$595	$540	$465	$415	$365	*$832*

Add $33 for left-hand action (.308 Win. cal. only).
Add $436 for Manners 100% carbon fiber stock.

* ***CZ 557 Sporter Synthetic*** – .270 Win., .30-06, or 6.5x55 cal., 20 1/2 in. barrel, fixed 4 shot mag., adj. trigger, no sights, black synthetic stock with parallel comb, full grip, wider forend, and a soft-touch rubberized finish, 6.7-8 lbs. Mfg. 2015-2018.

	$660	$600	$540	$495	$425	$385	$340	*$779*

CZ 557 VARMINT – .308 Win. or .243 Win. (mfg. 2017-2018) cal., 25.6 in. heavy Varmint barrel, 10 shot detachable box mag., fully adj. trigger, no sights, integral dovetails, Turkish walnut stock with palm swell, laser-cut checkering, and flat forend, two-position safety, blue finish, 11 lbs. New 2016.

MSR $925	$790	$690	$625	$560	$475	$425	$375	

CZ 700 SNIPER – .308 Win. cal., sniper design features forged billet receiver with permanently attached Weaver rail, 25.6 in. heavy barrel w/o sights, 10 shot detachable mag., black synthetic thumbhole stock with adj. cheekpiece and buttplate, large bolt handle, fully adj. trigger, 11.9 lbs. Limited importation 2001 only.

	$1,875	$1,575	$1,250	$1,025	$895	$775	$650	*$2,097*

CZ 700M1 SNIPER – .308 Win. cal., similar to CZ 700 Sniper, except has laminated stock. Limited importation 2001 only.

	$1,875	$1,575	$1,250	$1,025	$895	$775	$650	

CZ 750 SNIPER – .308 Win. cal., sniper design, 26 in. barrel w/muzzle brake, includes two 10 shot mags., thread protector, and mirage shield, black synthetic thumbhole stock with adj. comb, scope mounting via detachable Weaver rail or integral CZ 19mm dovetail, 11.9 lbs. Limited mfg. 2006-2015.

	$1,775	$1,550	$1,250	$1,050	$925	$775	$675	*$1,999*

ZKK 600 – .270 Win., .30-06, or 7x57mm cal., improved Mauser type action, 23 1/2 in. barrel, checkered walnut stock, 5 shot internal mag., thumb safety, 7.2 lbs. Importation disc. 1995.

	$500	$425	$370	$330	$300	$275	$250	*$589*

ZKK 601 – .222 Rem., .223 Rem., .243 Win. or .308 Win. cal., otherwise similar to ZKK 600. Importation disc. 1995.

	$500	$425	$370	$330	$300	$275	$250	*$589*

ZKK 602 – .300 Win. Mag. (disc.), .375 H&H, .416 Rigby (new 1996), .416 Rem. (new 1996), 8x68mm (disc.), or .458 Win. Mag. cal., similar to ZKK 600, except has 25.2 in. barrel and 3 leaf express rear sight, 9.3 lbs. Disc. 1997.

	$675	$575	$495	$450	$395	$350	$310	*$799*

ZKB 680 (FOX/FOX II) – .22 Hornet or .222 Rem. cal., 23 1/2 in. barrel, 5 shot mag., set triggers, 5 lbs. 12 oz. Importation disc. 1991.

	$445	$380	$340	$295	$255	$230	$200	*$499*

The Fox model in .222 Rem. cal. began production circa 1971. During the mid to late 1970s, this model was revamped into the Fox II, and was available in .222 Rem. and .22 Hornet.

RIFLES: O/U

CZ-589 STOPPER – .458 Win. Mag. cal. only, Kersten style boxlock action with Blitz type trigger, checkered Turkish walnut stock and forearm, fixed iron sights, includes sling swivels, 9.3 lbs. Approx. 5 mfg. and imported 2001 only.

	$2,695	$2,300	$2,000	$1,750	$1,500	$1,250	$1,050	*$2,999*

Add $1,000 for sideplates and special engraving/checkering.

GRADING - PPGS™	100%	98%	95%	90%	80%	70%	60%	LAST MSR

RIFLES: SEMI-AUTO

CZ-M52 (1952) – 7.62x45mm Czech cal., 20 2/3 in. barrel, 10 shot detachable mag., tangent rear sight, this model was also imported briefly by Samco Global Arms, Inc. located in Miami, FL.

	100%	98%	95%	90%	80%	70%	60%	LAST MSR
	$550	$450	$350	$300	$250	$200	$150	

CZ-M52/57 (1957) – 7.62x39mm cal., later variation of the CZ-M52.

	100%	98%	95%	90%	80%	70%	60%	LAST MSR
	$425	$375	$325	$300	$250	$200	$150	

CZ-511 – .22 LR cal., blowback action, 22.2 in. barrel, uncheckered beechwood (disc. 2001) or checkered walnut (new 2006) stock, flip-up rear sight, receiver top slotted for scope mounts, 8 shot mag., approx. 5 1/2 lbs. Previously disc. 1986, importation resumed 1998-2001. Imported 2005-2006.

	100%	98%	95%	90%	80%	70%	60%	LAST MSR
	$320	$275	$235	$200	$180	$160	$150	*$389*

CZ 512 STANDARD – .22 LR (mfg. 2011-2019) or .22 WMR cal., hammer forged 20.6 in. barrel with adj. rear and hooded front sight, dual guide rods, modular design with aluminum alloy upper receiver and fiberglass reinforced polymer lower receiver, 5 shot mag., uncheckered beechwood stock and forearm with sling swivels, integral 11mm dovetail on receiver, 5.9 lbs. New 2011.

	100%	98%	95%	90%	80%	70%	60%	LAST MSR
MSR $550	$470	$410	$350	$325	$260	$215	$185	

Subtract approx. $31 for .22 LR cal. (mfg. 2011-2019).

CZ 512 AMERICAN – .22 LR (mfg. 2016-2019) or .22 WMR cal., 20 1/2 in. cold hammer forged barrel, 5 shot detachable mag., aluminum alloy upper receiver and fiberglass-reinforced polymer lower receiver, no sights, Crossbolt safety, blue finish, Turkish walnut stock with laser-cut checkering, 5 lbs. New 2016.

	100%	98%	95%	90%	80%	70%	60%	LAST MSR
MSR $585	$500	$440	$375	$340	$275	$225	$195	

Subtract approx. $32 for .22 LR cal. (mfg. 2016-2019).

CZ 512 CARBINE – .22 LR or .22 WMR (mfg. 2016 only) cal., 16 1/2 in. cold hammer forged threaded barrel, extended 10 shot mag., tangent adj. rear and fiber optic front sights, dual guide rods, integral 11mm dovetail, crossbolt safety, blue finish, beechwood stock, 5.12 lbs. Mfg. 2016-2018.

	100%	98%	95%	90%	80%	70%	60%	LAST MSR
	$420	$350	$300	$275	$250	$225	$195	*$493*

Add $31 for .22 WMR cal. (mfg. 2016 only).

CZ 512 TACTICAL – .22 LR or .22 WMR cal., 16 1/2 in. threaded sporter barrel, 10 or 25 shot detachable single stack mag., top Picatinny rail, crossbolt safety, 6-position stock with adj. comb, black finish, 6.1 lbs. Mfg. 2016-2019.

	100%	98%	95%	90%	80%	70%	60%	LAST MSR
	$425	$385	$350	$325	$295	$265	$225	*$509*

Add $31 for .22 WMR cal.

CZ 805 BREN S1 CARBINE – 5.56 NATO or .300 AAC Blackout (mfg. 2017 only) cal., aluminum frame, 16.2 in. cold hammer forged threaded barrel with two port muzzle brake, 30 shot STANAG mag., flip-up adj. iron sights, folding adj. stock, polymer grips, ambi thumb safety, top and bottom Picatinny rails, black or FDE finish, 8.02 lbs. Mfg. 2016-2018.

	100%	98%	95%	90%	80%	70%	60%	LAST MSR
	$1,685	$1,465	$1,225	$1,085	$935	$800	$660	*$1,999*

Add $100 for FDE finish.

CZ BREN 2 MS CARBINE – .223/5.56x45mm cal., 6.5 in. cold hammer forged barrel, 10 or 30 shot detachable or AR-15/M16 style (low capacity) mag., no sights, carbon fiber reinforced polymer stock, stippled grips, ambi manual safety, full Picatinny rail, 7.3 lbs. New 2020.

	100%	98%	95%	90%	80%	70%	60%	LAST MSR
MSR $2,255	$1,915	$1,675	$1,435	$1,300	$1,055	$875	$750	

CZ SCORPION EVO 3 S1 CARBINE – 9mm Para. cal., fiber reinforced polymer frame, 16 1/2 in. barrel with either a two-port compensator or faux suppressor, 10 or 20 shot double stack polymer mag., low profile aluminum adj. sights, folding adj. stock, black polymer grips, ambi thumb safety, non-reciprocating charging handle, forend with M-LOK attachment points, top Picatinny rail, black or FDE (new 2018) finish, 6.1 lbs. New 2016.

	100%	98%	95%	90%	80%	70%	60%	LAST MSR
MSR $1,209	$1,025	$900	$775	$700	$575	$475	$400	

Add $30 for FDE finish (new 2018).
Add $46 for faux suppressor.

VZ 58 MILITARY/TACTICAL SPORTER – 7.62x39mm cal., short stroke GPO, milled receiver, 16.14 in. barrel, tilting breechblock, choice of Zytel skeletonized (Tactical) or plastic impregnated wood (Military) stock, alloy 30 shot mag., 7.32 lbs. Mfg. 2008-2011.

	100%	98%	95%	90%	80%	70%	60%	LAST MSR
	$925	$850	$750	$650	$550	$450	$350	*$999*

Add $30 for Tactical Sporter model (available with synthetic or folding (new 2010) stock).

GRADING - PPGS™	100%	98%	95%	90%	80%	70%	60%	LAST MSR

SHOTGUNS: O/U

ALL-AMERICAN – 12 ga., 2 3/4 in. chambers, fires bottom barrel first, 30 or 32 in. barrels, extended black chokes, ejectors, Turkish walnut stock with adj. comb and buttplate, target forend, manual tang safety, raised steel rib, gloss blue finish, 8 1/2 lbs. New 2017.

MSR $2,649	$2,250	$1,975	$1,690	$1,530	$1,250	$1,025	$880	

ALL-AMERICAN TRAP COMBO (TWO-BARREL SET) – 12 ga., 3 in. chambers, 32 in. barrels with gloss blue finish, ejectors, Turkish walnut stock with adj. comb and target style forend, ships as a two barrel set (one as a single shot "un-single" with a dual adj. aluminum rib, the other with O/U barrels and stepped rib), hardened in the white receiver finish, 8 1/2 lbs. New 2016.

MSR $3,575	$3,040	$2,660	$2,280	$2,065	$1,675	$1,375	$1,185	

CZ 581 SOLO – 12 ga., 2 3/4 in. chambers, boxlock action with Kersten upper locking mechanism, ejectors, checkered walnut stock and forearm, approx. 7.4 lbs. Importation disc. 1995, resumed 1999-2005.

	$740	$625	$570	$490	$425	$385	$350	*$872*

Add 10% for single trigger (disc.).

CANVASBACK (103D) – 12 or 20 ga., 3 in. chambers, 26 or 28 in. VR barrels with 5 choke tubes, black chrome finished receiver and barrels, extractors, blued frame with light perimeter engraving, SST, stock/forearm similar to Redhead, 6.3 - 7 1/2 lbs. Mfg. 2005-2013.

	$675	$550	$450	$400	$350	$300	$275	*$786*

CANVASBACK GOLD – 12, 20, 28 ga., or .410 bore (26 in. bbl. only), updated version of the Canvasback, 26 or 28 in solid mid-rib barrels, SST, extractors, with 5 choke tubes or fixed IC/M chokes (.410 bore only), checkered pistol grip walnut stock and forearm, black chrome receiver with two gold birds inlaid on each side, 6-7 1/2 lbs. Mfg. 2014-2015.

	$700	$575	$475	$400	$350	$300	$275	*$827*

Add $132 for 28 ga. or .410 bore.

DRAKE – 12, 20, 28 (new 2018) ga., or .410 bore (new 2018), 3 in. chambers, 28 in. barrels with 5 choke tubes, extractors, single selectable trigger, Turkish walnut pistol grip stock with laser-cut checkering, gloss black chrome finish, 7.4 lbs. New 2016.

MSR $675	$565	$495	$425	$385	$320	$270	$220	

Add $50 for 28 ga. or .410 bore (new 2018).

* ***Drake Southpaw*** – 12 or 20 ga., 3 in. chambers, 28 in. barrels with 5 choke tubes, extractors, SST, Turkish walnut pistol grip stock with laser-cut checkering, gloss black chrome finish, 7.4 lbs. New 2018.

MSR $675	$565	$495	$425	$385	$320	$270	$220	

DRAKE ALL-TERRAIN – 12 or 20 ga., 3 in. chambers, 28 in. barrels with 5 extended black chokes, extractor, SST, Turkish walnut pistol grip stock, manual tang safety, OD Green Cerakote barrel and receiver finish, 7 lbs. New 2020.

MSR $815	$700	$615	$525	$475	$385	$315	$275	

MALLARD (104A) – 12 or 20 ga., 3 in. chambers, 28 in. VR barrels with multichokes, DT, extractors, coin finished alloy receiver, checkered Turkish walnut stock and forearm, 6 1/2 (20 ga.) or 7 1/2 (12 ga.) lbs. Mfg. 2005-2015.

	$485	$415	$350	$300	$275	$250	$225	*$583*

QUAIL – 20 ga., 3 in. chambers, 28 in. VR barrels, 5 chokes, walnut stock with checkered grip and forend, 13 3/4 in. LOP, blue finish, 6.3 lbs. New 2019.

MSR $655	$550	$480	$415	$375	$310	$260	$215	

REAPER MAGNUM – 12 ga., 3 1/2 in. chambers, 26 in. barrels with 5 extended black choke tubes, top Picatinny rail, polymer stock, front and back QD swivels, Realtree Xtra Green camo finish, 7.1 lbs. New 2018.

MSR $1,025	$865	$750	$650	$590	$475	$400	$325	

REDHEAD DELUXE (103DE) – 12 or 20 ga., boxlock action, SST, ejectors, checkered round knob Turkish walnut pistol grip stock and Schnabel forearm, coin finished frame and trigger guard, 26 or 28 in. VR barrels with 5 screw-in chokes, 6.7 - 7.9 lbs. Mfg. 2005-2014.

	$815	$715	$625	$550	$500	$450	$395	*$953*

Subtract $80 for shortened LOP (20 ga. only, 24 in. barrels, and 13 in. LOP - new 2008).
Add $35 for retractable sling system (12 ga. only, disc.).

* ***Redhead 103 D (Mini)*** – 28 ga. or .410 bore, scaled down frame, otherwise similar to Redhead Deluxe, but w/o ejectors, 5.7 (.410 bore) or 6.2 lbs. Mfg. 2005-2013.

	$795	$725	$625	$550	$500	$450	$395	*$960*

GRADING - PPGS™	100%	98%	95%	90%	80%	70%	60%	LAST MSR

* ***Redhead Custom Shop Enhanced*** – 12 ga., 28 in. barrels, similar to Redhead, except has hand rubbed oil finished stock, tuned action and trigger job from custom shop. Mfg. 2010 only.

	$1,675	$1,450	$1,250	$1,050	$900	$800	$700	*$1,899*

* ***Redhead Target*** – 12 ga. only, 30 in. barrels with stepped VR and standard choke tubes (disc. 2012), or 6 Kicks extended stainless steel choke tubes (new 2013), Monte Carlo checkered walnut stock and grooved forearm, silver finished receiver. Mfg. 2012-2014.

	$1,125	$975	$825	$725	$625	$525	$450	*$1,389*

Subtract 5% for standard choke tubes (disc. 2012).

REDHEAD PREMIER – 12, 16 (new 2020), 20, 28 (mfg. 2016-2017) ga., or .410 bore (mfg. 2016-2017), 2 3/4 or 3 in. chambers, 24, 26, or 28 in. barrels with five flush-mount choke tubes, one-piece receiver, laser-cut checkering, solid mid-ribs, ejectors (12 and 20 ga.) or extractors (28 and .410, new 2016), single trigger, 13 or 14 1/2 in. LOP, pistol grip, Turkish walnut stock, includes hard plastic case, 6-7.7 lbs. New 2015.

MSR $1,019	$865	$750	$650	$590	$475	$400	$325

Add $98 for 28 ga. or .410 bore (mfg. 2016-2017).
Subtract $64 for 13 in. LOP, 20 ga. only (Redhead Reduced Length model).

* ***Redhead Premier Target*** – 12 or 20 (new 2020) ga., 3 in. chambers, 30 in. barrels with 6 Kicks stainless steel extended choke tubes, ST, ejectors, laser cut checkering, one-piece CNC'd receiver, Monte Carlo stock with right-hand palm swell, 8 lbs. New 2015.

MSR $1,475	$1,250	$1,095	$940	$850	$685	$575	$475

REDHEAD PREMIER ALL-TERRAIN – 12 or 20 ga., 2 3/4 or 3 in. chambers, 28 or 30 in. flat rib barrels with 5 extended black chokes, ejectors, SST, Turkish walnut stock with pistol grip, manual tang safety, OD Green Cerakote barrel and receiver finish, 7-8 lbs. New 2020.

MSR $1,159	$985	$850	$725	$675	$550	$450	$375

SHARP TAIL TARGET – 12 ga., 3 in. chambers, 30 in. barrel with 6 Kicks stainless steel choke tubes, 14 3/4 in. LOP, single selectable trigger, Turkish walnut stock with semi-beavertail forend, color case hardened receiver, black hard chrome barrel finish, 7 1/2 lbs. New 2015.

MSR $1,329	$1,125	$985	$850	$765	$625	$500	$425

CZ SPORTER G2 (CZ SPORTER) – 12 ga., boxlock action, ejectors, SST, 30 or 32 in. VR backbored barrels with standard choke tubes (disc. 2012), or 6 Kicks extended stainless steel choke tubes (new 2013), No. 3 Circassian walnut stock and forearm with adj. comb and palm swell, added for 2015 is the full forend, laser-cut checkering, and one-piece CNC'd receiver, approx. 8 1/2 lbs. Mfg. 2008-2016.

	$2,100	$1,825	$1,625	$1,325	$1,100	$900	$775	*$2,497*

Subtract 5% if with standard choke tubes (disc. 2012).

In 2015 this model was updated and model nomenclature was changed to CZ Sporter G2.

CZ SPORTER STANDARD GRADE G2 – 12 ga. only, 30 or 32 in. vent. barrels with VR or adj. rib (new 2014), includes 6 Kicks extended stainless steel choke tubes, checkered adj. Monte Carlo stock and Schnabel forearm, ejectors and SST, added in 2015 is the full forend, laser-cut checkering, and one-piece CNC'd receiver, 8 1/2 lbs. Mfg. 2013-2016.

	$1,675	$1,425	$1,200	$1,025	$875	$750	$625	*$1,899*

Add $1,223 for adj. rib (mfg. 2014-2015).

In 2015 this model was updated and nomenclature changed to CZ Sporter Standard Grade G2.

CZ SUPER SCROLL COMBO SET – includes 20 and 28 ga. 30 in. barrels with VR, coin finished receiver with hand engraved sideplates, ejectors, SST, includes 5 choke tubes, deluxe checkered walnut stock and forearm, supplied with aluminum Americase, 6.7 lbs. Mfg. 2013-2017.

	$3,475	$3,100	$2,750	$2,400	$2,100	$1,825	$1,600	*$3,899*

CZ SUPER SCROLL LIMITED EDITION – 12 ga., 3 in. chambers, 28 in. barrels, boxlock, mechanical selective triggers, checkered Turkish walnut stock with Schnabel forend, ejectors, interchangeable choke tubes. Limited mfg. of 50 beginning 2011.

	$2,250	$1,975	$1,750	$1,525	$1,325	$1,125	$850	*$2,499*

CZ SUPREME FIELD – 12, 20, or 28 ga., 2 3/4 or 3 in. chambers, 28 in. barrels with gloss black chrome finish, 5 extended black choke tubes, one-piece CNC polished nickel chrome receiver, auto ejectors, Grade III Turkish walnut stock, sharply checkered forend, deep relief engraving, shipped in protective hard case, 6-8 lbs. New 2018.

MSR $1,839	$1,565	$1,370	$1,175	$1,065	$860	$715	$610

GRADING - PPGS™	100%	98%	95%	90%	80%	70%	60%	LAST MSR

SWAMP MAGNUM – 12 ga., 3 1/2 in. chambers, 30 in. barrels with 5 extended black choke tubes, polymer stock in black (mfg. 2017-2019) or Realtree Max-5 camo, auto safety, all black metalwork, 7.1 lbs. New 2017.

MSR $1,109	$935	$825	$700	$635	$515	$425	$350	

WINGSHOOTER – 12, 20, 28 (limited mfg. 2011 only) ga. or .410 bore (limited mfg. 2011 only), 3 in. chambers, silver engraved boxlock action featuring black sideplates with gold inlaid birds, 28 in. VR barrels with 5 multi-chokes, SST, ejectors (12 and 20 ga.), or extractors (28 ga. and .410 bore), checkered Turkish walnut stock and forearm, 6-7.9 lbs. Mfg. 2011-2014.

	$875	$750	$625	$550	$495	$450	$395	*$999*

Add $41 for 28 ga. or .410 bore. (disc. 2011).

WINGSHOOTER ELITE – 12 or 20 ga., 3 in. chambers, 28 in. barrel with 5 flush-mount choke tubes, one-piece receiver, fully hand engraved sideplates, single selectable trigger, solid mid-ribs, ejectors, laser cut checkering, two-tone chrome finish, Turkish walnut stock, includes hard plastic case, approx. 7 lbs. New 2015.

MSR $1,139	$975	$850	$725	$675	$550	$450	$375	

WOODCOCK DELUXE 103FE – 12 or 20 ga., ejectors, SST, 26 or 28 in. barrels with screw-in chokes, color case hardened boxlock frame with sideplates and trigger guard, hand engraving, checkered round knob Turkish walnut stock and Schnabel forearm, 6.8 (20 ga.) or 7.8 (12 ga.) lbs. Mfg. 2005-2010.

	$1,075	$875	$725	$600	$500	$450	$395	*$1,246*

* ***Woodcock 103F Mini*** – 28 ga. or .410 bore, scaled down frame, otherwise similar to Woodcock Deluxe, but w/o ejectors, 6-6 1/4 lbs. Mfg. 2005-2010.

	$1,100	$900	$800	$700	$600	$500	$450	*$1,332*

WOODCOCK DELUXE CUSTOM GRADE – 20 ga. only, 28 in. barrels, features color case hardened frame, No. 4 deluxe checkered Circassian walnut stock and forearm. Mfg. 2006-2010.

	$1,895	$1,550	$1,325	$1,100	$950	$800	$700	*$2,309*

LADY STERLING – 12 ga., 3 in. chambers, 28 in. VR barrels with 5 choke tubes, ejectors, single trigger, Turkish walnut stock with (new 2016) or without adj. comb, laser stippling, and female dimensions, 14 in. LOP, two-tone satin and gloss chrome receiver finish, gloss black barrel finish, 7 1/2 lbs. Mfg. 2014-2017.

	$1,150	$1,015	$900	$800	$700	$625	$550	*$1,321*

Subtract approx. $40 for stock without adj. comb.

SCTP STERLING – 12 ga., 3 in. chambers, 28 (disc. 2019) or 30 (new 2020) in. barrels with 5 choke tubes, optics rail, Turkish walnut stock with adj. comb, 7 1/2 lbs. New 2018.

MSR $1,445	$1,225	$1,070	$920	$835	$675	$550	$450	

Subtract approx. $40 for 28 in. barrels (disc. 2019).

This model is also available for left-handed shooters (SCTP Sterling Southpaw) at no extra charge.

SOUTHPAW STERLING – 12 ga., 3 in. chambers, boxlock, 29 (disc. 2015) or 30 (new 2016) in. barrels with five flush-mount choke tubes, ejectors, coil-operated hammers, single trigger, Turkish walnut stock, hand checkering, built for left-handed shooters, gloss black chrome barrel finish, two-tone satin gloss chrome receiver finish, 7 1/2 lbs. Mfg. 2015-2018.

	$885	$775	$700	$600	$500	$400	$325	*$999*

UPLAND STERLING – 12 ga. only, 3 in. chambers, 28 in. barrels with 5 screw-in choke tubes, two-toned CNC milled receiver and trigger guard, checkered Turkish walnut stock with stippled grip area on the wrist and forend, 7 1/2 lbs. Mfg. 2013-2019.

	$885	$775	$700	$600	$500	$400	$325	*$1,038*

* ***Upland Sterling Southpaw*** – 12 ga., 3 in. chamber, 30 in. VR barrels with gloss black chrome finish, 5 choke tubes, Turkish walnut stock with laser stippling, 14 1/2 in. LOP, two-tone satin and gloss chrome receiver finish, 7 1/2 lbs. Mfg. 2019 only.

	$885	$775	$700	$600	$500	$400	$325	*$1,038*

UPLAND ULTRALIGHT – 12 or 20 (new 2016) ga., 3 in. chambers, 26 or 28 (disc. 2019) in. VR matte black barrels with 5 choke tubes, matte black or green (mfg. 2016-2019) alloy receiver, checkered Turkish walnut pistol grip stock and forearm, 6 lbs. New 2010.

MSR $809	$680	$600	$500	$450	$375	$300	$265	

UPLAND ULTRALIGHT ALL-TERRAIN – 12 or 20 ga., 2 3/4 or 3 in. chambers, 28 in. flat rib barrels, 5 extended black chokes, extractor, SST, Turkish walnut pistol grip stock, manual tang safety, OD Green Cerakote finish on barrel and receiver, 5.9-6.3 lbs. New 2020.

MSR $919	$780	$685	$585	$530	$430	$350	$300	

GRADING - PPGS™	100%	98%	95%	90%	80%	70%	60%	LAST MSR

LIMITED EDITION (DISC.) – 12 ga., 28 in. barrels, Circassian walnut stock and forearm, engraved boxlock action, gold trigger, 50 mfg. 2008-2009.

	$1,975	$1,725	$1,500	$1,300	$1,100	$900	$775	*$2,466*

SHOTGUNS: SxS

AMARILLO – 12 or 20 ga., boxlock action, 20 in. barrels with multichokes, double triggers, checkered Turkish walnut round knob stock and splinter forearm, 5.9 (20 ga.) or 6 1/2 lbs. Imported 2005-2006.

	$625	$550	$475	$375	$300	$250	$200	*$695*

BOBWHITE (202B) – 12, 16 (new 2006), 20, 28 ga., or .410 bore, 3 in. chambers, 26 or 28 (disc.) in. barrels with multichokes (N/A in .410 bore), color case hardened boxlock action, DT, extractors, checkered Turkish walnut straight grip English style stock and semi-beavertail forearm, 5.2-7 lbs. Mfg. 2005-2015.

	$665	$585	$500	$425	$350	$300	$250	*$778*

Add $196 for 16 or 28 ga., or .410 bore.

BOBWHITE G2 – 12, 20, or 28 ga., 2 3/4-3 in. chambers, boxlock, 28 in. barrels, 5 chokes, CNC receiver, single extractor, double triggers, Turkish walnut straight grip stock, black chrome finish on barrels and receiver, 5 1/2-7.3 lbs. New 2019.

MSR $675	$565	$495	$425	$385	$320	$270	$220	

Add $50 for 28 ga.

BOBBHITE G2 ALL-TERRAIN – 12 or 20 ga., 2 3/4 or 3 in. chambers, 28 in. flat rib barrels with 5 chokes, extractor, double triggers, English-style straight grip stock, splinter forend, manual tang safety, OD Green Cerakote finish on barrel and receiver, 6-7.3 lbs. New 2020.

MSR $855	$725	$635	$550	$500	$400	$325	$280	

DURANGO – 12 or 20 ga., hammerless contoured boxlock action with color case hardened frame, 20 in. barrels, single trigger, multichokes, checkered Turkish walnut round knob stock and splinter forearm, 6 (20 ga.) or 6.7 (12 ga.) lbs. Imported 2005-2006.

	$725	$625	$525	$425	$350	$300	$250	*$795*

GROUSE – 12, 20, 28 ga., or .410 bore, 26 (28 ga. or .410 bore) or 28 (12 or 20 ga.) in. barrels, silver receiver, ST, choke tubes. Limited importation 2008.

	$875	$750	$650	$575	$500	$425	$350	*$995*

Add $211 for 28 ga. or .410 bore.

HAMMER CLASSIC MODEL – 12 ga., 3 in. chambers, 30 in. barrels with five multi chokes, DT, extractors, Turkish walnut stock, detailed hand engraving, color case hardened receiver, 7 1/2 lbs. New 2010.

MSR $1,049	$895	$785	$675	$605	$495	$425	$350	

HAMMER COACH MODEL – 12 ga., 3 in. chambers, case colored action, 20 in. barrels with fixed chokes bored C/C, DT, exposed hammers, walnut stock, 6.7 lbs. New 2006.

MSR $999	$850	$750	$650	$575	$475	$385	$325	

RINGNECK (201A) – 12, 16, or 20 ga., 3 in. chambers, features engraved boxlock action with sideplates, 26 or 28 in. barrels with multi chokes, ST, extractors, checkered straight (new 2012, 20 ga. only) or pistol grip walnut stock and splinter forearm, 6.3-7.1 lbs. Mfg. 2005-2014.

	$895	$785	$675	$575	$500	$425	$350	*$1,022*

Add $207 for 16 ga.

PARTRIDGE – 12, 20, 28 ga., or .410 bore, 26 (28 ga. or .410 bore) or 28 (12 or 20 ga.) in. barrels, silver receiver, DT, straight grip English stock, choke tubes. Limited importation 2008.

	$675	$600	$525	$450	$375	$300	$250	*$765*

Add $193 for 28 ga. or .410 bore.

* ***Ringneck Mini (201A)*** – 28 ga. or .410 bore, frame proportioned to gauge, otherwise similar to Ringneck 201A, 28 ga. is supplied with 5 choke tubes, 5 1/4 (.410 bore) or 6 (28 ga.) lbs. Mfg. 2005-2014.

	$1,050	$885	$775	$675	$575	$475	$400	*$1,229*

RINGNECK TARGET – 12 ga., 30 in. barrels with 5 choke tubes (disc. 2012) or 6 Kicks extended stainless steel choke tubes (new 2013), checkered walnut pistol grip stock and splinter forearm, case colored receiver with blued barrels. Mfg. 2012-2014.

	$1,100	$925	$800	$700	$600	$495	$425	*$1,298*

Subtract 5% if with standard choke tubes (disc. 2012).

GRADING - PPGS™	100%	98%	95%	90%	80%	70%	60%	LAST MSR

RINGNECK DELUXE CUSTOM GRADE – 20 ga., 3 in. chambers, 28 in. barrels, features color case hardened engraved frame with sideplates, deluxe checkered pistol grip walnut stock and forearm, 6.3 lbs. Mfg. 2006-2012.

	$1,695	$1,450	$1,250	$975	$850	$725	$625	*$1,983*

RINGNECK COMPETITION – 12 ga., 28 in. ported barrels, adj. comb, lengthened forcing cones, hand honed action from custom shop. Mfg. 2010-2011.

	$2,725	$2,200	$1,825	$1,525	$1,375	$1,150	$995	*$3,189*

RINGNECK STRAIGHT GRIP – 20 ga. only, 3 in. chambers, 26 in. barrels with 5 choke tubes, straight grip English stock and semi-beavertail forearm, SST, case colored receiver with sideplates, 6.3 lbs. Limited importation 2013 only.

	$875	$775	$675	$575	$500	$425	$350	*$993*

SHARP-TAIL – 12, 16 (new 2018), 20, 28 ga., or .410 bore, 3 in. chambers, 28 in. barrels, 5 flush choke tubes, coil spring operated hammers, single selective trigger, one-piece receiver, single extractor, Turkish walnut stock, color case hardened receiver finish, includes plastic case, 5.9-7.3 lbs. New 2015.

MSR $1,105	$935	$825	$700	$635	$515	$425	$350	

Add $224 for 28 ga. or .410 bore.

SHARP-TAIL COACH – 12 or 20 ga., 2 3/4 or 3 in. chambers, boxlock action, 20 in. barrels with 3 choke tubes, color case hardened receiver, extractor, SST, Turkish walnut stock, 6.7 lbs. New 2018.

MSR $1,039	$885	$775	$665	$600	$485	$415	$325	

SHOTGUNS: SEMI-AUTO

CZ 712/720 G2 (CZ-712/720) – 12 (Model 712) or 20 (Model 720) ga., 3 in. chamber, gas operated, 26 or 28 in. VR barrel, multichokes, matte black chrome, aluminum receiver, 13 (Reduced Length Model, 20 ga., 24 in. barrel, mfg. 2008-2013, reintroduced 2016) or 14 1/2 in. LOP, checkered Turkish walnut stock, Mossy Oak Shadow Grass (disc. 2005) or Mossy Oak Obsession camo treatment (disc. 2005), jeweled bolt, single trigger, laser engraved checkering (new 2015 with G2 version), right-hand palm swell (new 2015), 6.3-7.3 lbs. Limited mfg. 2005, reintroduced 2008.

MSR $535	$460	$400	$350	$315	$250	$200	$175	

Add $10 for 20 ga. (Model 720).

Add approx. 10% for 100% camo coverage (disc. 2005).

In 2015, the 712/720 models were udpated and the nomenclature changed to 712/720 G2.

* ***CZ 712/720 ALS G2 (CZ 712/720 ALS)*** – 12 or 20 (new 2014) ga., 24 (20 ga. only, new 2014), 26, or 28 in. barrel with 3 choke tubes, features fully adj. LOP, black adj. ATI polymer stock, fiber optic front sight. Mfg. 2012-2018.

	$485	$430	$365	$335	$300	$275	$250	*$579*

Add $20 for 20 ga. (new 2014).

In 2015, the 712/720 ALS models were updated and the model nomenclature was changed to 712 ALS G2/720 ALS G2.

* ***CZ 712 G2 Green*** – 12 ga., 3 in. chamber, 26 in. barrel with 5 chokes, 4 shot mag., Turkish walnut stock with palm swell, green anodized receiver, matte black chrome barrel finish, 7.4 lbs. Mfg. 2016-2019.

	$445	$390	$335	$300	$250	$200	$175	*$518*

* ***CZ 712 Target G2 (CZ 712 Target)*** – 12 ga. only, 3 in. chamber, gas operated, 30 in. barrel with stepped VR and screw in chokes, fiber optic front sight, ejector, walnut stock, 7.6 lbs. New 2012.

MSR $725	$615	$540	$460	$425	$345	$275	$225	

In 2015, the 712 Target received some updates and the model nomenclature changed to 712 Target G2.

* ***CZ 712 Utility G2 (CZ 712 Utility)*** – 12 ga., 3 in. chamber, gas operated, 20 in. VR barrel with 3 choke tubes, single trigger, black polymer stock, matte black chrome finish, 6.6 lbs. New 2009.

MSR $535	$460	$400	$350	$315	$250	$200	$175	

In 2015, this model was updated and nomenclature changed to CZ 712 Utility G2.

CZ-712 MAGNUM – 12 ga. only, 3 1/2 in. chamber, 24 or 28 in. barrel, single trigger, vent. rib, matte black chrome receiver, checkered walnut, Mossy Oak Shadowgrass (28 in. barrel) or Mossy Oak Obsession (24 in. barrel) camo finish, 7 1/2 lbs. Limited mfg. 2005.

	$425	$375	$325	$295	$265	$235	$200	*$499*

Add $100 for 100% camo coverage.

GRADING - PPGS™	100%	98%	95%	90%	80%	70%	60%	LAST MSR

CZ 712 PRACTICAL G2 (CZ 712 PRACTICAL) – 12 ga., 3 in. chamber, 22 in. barrel with 5 choke tubes, 9 shot extended mag., 6-position M4 style adj. stock, matte black finish, 8.1 lbs. Mfg. 2014-2015.

	$595	$550	$495	$450	$415	$385	$335	*$699*

In 2015, this model was updated and nomenclature changed to CZ 712 Practical G2.

CZ 712 SYNTHETIC G2 12 GAUGE – 12 ga., 3 in. chamber, 28 in. barrel with 5 flush-mount choke tubes, black matte hard chrome finish on all metal surfaces, ejector, black synthetic buttstock and forend, ships in plastic case, 6.7 lbs. Mfg. 2015-2018.

	$425	$370	$320	$290	$235	$190	$150	*$499*

* ***CZ 712 Synthetic G2 Camo*** – 12 ga., 3 in. chamber, 28 in. barrel with three extended choke tubes, polymer stock, 100% Mossy Oak Shadow Grass Blades camo finish, 6.7 lbs. Mfg. 2016-2018.

	$590	$510	$425	$385	$350	$325	$295	*$679*

CZ 712 3-GUN G2 – 12 ga., 3 in. chamber, 22 in. vent. rib barrel with three black extended choke tubes, 9 shot ATI fluted mag. extension, black synthetic stock, extended bolt handle and oversized bolt release, matte black chrome finish, 6.9 lbs. Mfg. 2016 only.

	$540	$475	$400	$365	$300	$250	$200	*$629*

CZ 812 WATERFOWL 12 GAUGE – 12 ga., 3 in. chamber, gas operated, 28 in. barrel with five extended black choke tubes, 4 shot, oversized trigger guard, single trigger, ejector, 100% Realtree Max-4 camo finish, rubber recoil pad, includes plastic hard case, 6.7 lbs. Mfg. 2015 only.

	$595	$520	$450	$400	$325	$275	$225	*$699*

CZ 912 G2/CZ 920 G2 (CZ 912/920) – 12 or 20 (new 2013) ga., 3 in. chamber, gas operated, black alloy receiver, 28 in. VR barrel with 3 choke tubes, high gloss Turkish checkered walnut stock and forearm, advanced design recoil pad, 6.4 or 7.3 lbs. Mfg. 2011-2020.

	$475	$415	$360	$315	$275	$250	$225	*$561*

Add $12 for 20 ga. (new 2013).

CZ 1012 – 12 ga., 2 3/4-3 in. chamber, inertia operating system, 26 (new 2021) or 28 in. barrel, 5 extended choke tubes, 4 shot mag., Turkish walnut stock, gloss black chrome barrel finish, blued, grey, or bronze receiver, 6 1/2 lbs. New 2019.

MSR $645	$540	$475	$400	$365	$300	$250	$210

* ***CZ 1012 Synthetic*** – 12 ga., 2 3/4-3 in. chamber, inertia operating system, 26 (new 2021) or 28 in. barrel, 5 extended black choke tubes, 4 shot mag., synthetic stock, black or 100% Waterfowl, Mossy Oak Bottomlands (new 2020), or Mossy Oak Shadow Grass Blades (new 2021) camo coverage, 6 1/2 lbs. New 2019.

MSR $645	$540	$475	$400	$365	$300	$250	$210

Add $70 for 100% Mossy Oak Bottomlands (new 2020) or Waterfowl camo coverage.

CZ 1012 ALL-TERRAIN – 12 ga., 3 in. chamber, inertia driven, 28 in. barrel with 5 extended black chokes, Turkish walnut pistol grip stock, sling swivels, Crossbolt safety, OD Green Cerakote finish, 6.5 lbs. New 2020.

MSR $715	$615	$540	$460	$425	$345	$275	$225

SHOTGUNS: SINGLE SHOT

CZ ALL-AMERICAN SINGLE TRAP – 12 ga., 3 in. chamber, 30, 32, or 34 in. ported barrel with lengthened forcing cone, 5 extended black chokes, high vented rib, ejectors, white front bead and small white mid-bead sights, Turkish walnut stock with 4-way adj. comb/buttplate, wide beavertail forend, 14.5-15.5 in. LOP, manual safety, gloss blue finish, 8 1/2 lbs. New 2019.

MSR $1,349	$1,150	$1,000	$865	$780	$635	$525	$450

COTTONTAIL – 20 ga. or .410 bore, 24 (Youth) or 28 in. barrel with Mod. choke, designed for beginning shooters, silver receiver with black hard chrome barrel finish, checkered pistol grip walnut stock, exposed hammer, transfer bar safety. Limited mfg. 2009.

	$195	$160	$130	$120	$115	$100	$90	*$255*

SHOTGUNS: SLIDE ACTION

CZ 612 FIELD – 12 ga., 3 in. chamber, 28 in. barrel with 3 chokes, single trigger, walnut stock, satin chrome finish, 6.2 lbs. New 2014.

MSR $395	$340	$315	$275	$245	$215	$200	$185

CZ 612 HC-P – 12 ga., 20 in. barrel with cyl. choke tube, tactical configuration features black polymer pistol grip stock and grooved forearm, ghost ring sights with fiber optic dots, matte black metal finish, 6 1/2 lbs. Mfg. 2013-2015.

	$310	$285	$250	$225	$200	$185	$170	*$369*

GRADING - PPGS™	100%	98%	95%	90%	80%	70%	60%	LAST MSR

CZ 612 HOME DEFENSE – 12 ga., 18 1/2 in. barrel with fixed cyl. choke and front bead sight, black synthetic stock and forearm, matte black metal finish, 6 lbs. Mfg. 2013-2015.

	$265	$235	$210	$190	$170	$150	$135	*$304*

Add $105 for Home Defense Combo two barrel set with extra 26 in. barrel (new 2014).

CZ 612 MAGNUM TURKEY – 12 ga., 3 1/2 in. chamber, 26 in. barrel with two chokes, ST, hydrodipped in Realtree Xtra Green camo finish, 6.8 lbs. New 2015.

MSR $445	$380	$335	$285	$260	$210	$175	$145	

CZ 612 MAGNUM WATERFOWL – 12 ga., 3 1/2 in. chamber, 28 in. barrel with five extended black choke tubes, hydrodipped in Realtree Max-4 camo finish, 6.8 lbs. New 2015.

MSR $445	$380	$335	$285	$260	$210	$175	$145	

CZ 612 TARGET – 12 ga., 3 in. chamber, 32 in. barrel, 3 extended choke tubes, raised rib, 4 shot, select grade Turkish walnut Monte Carlo stock with glossy oil finish, crossbolt safety, polished blue metal finish, 7.3 lbs. New 2017.

MSR $585	$500	$440	$375	$340	$275	$225	$195	

CZ 612 TRAP – 12 ga., 3 in. chamber, 32 in. ported barrel with 3 or 5 (disc. 2015) extended choke tubes, high ventilated target rib, spring loaded ejector, gold trigger, parallel comb on walnut Monte Carlo stock, crossbolt safety, matte blue finish, 7.3 lbs. Mfg. 2015, reintroduced 2017 only.

	$425	$370	$320	$290	$235	$190	$150	*$499*

CZ 612 WILDFOWL MAGNUM – 12 ga., 3 1/2 in. chamber, 26 in. VR barrel with M and XF choke tubes, 100% camo coverage, 6.8 lbs. Mfg. 2013-2014.

	$375	$335	$300	$260	$230	$210	$185	*$428*

CZ 620 BIG GAME – 20 ga., 3 in. chamber, 22 in. smoothbore barrel with Weaver-style rail, extended rifled choke, single trigger, matte black synthetic stock, 5.2 lbs. Mfg. 2014-2017.

	$345	$315	$275	$245	$215	$200	$185	*$399*

CZ 620 YOUTH – 20 ga., 3 in. chamber, 24 in. barrel with three choke tubes, matte black synthetic stock and forearm, reduced length buttstock, single trigger, 5.2 lbs. Mfg. 2014-2017.

	$285	$250	$225	$200	$185	$175	$65	*$349*

CZ 620/628 FIELD SELECT – 20 or 28 ga., 2 3/4 or 3 in. chamber, 28 in. barrel with three chokes tubes, select grade Turkish walnut stock with pistol grip, crossbolt safety, glossy blue finish, 5.4 lbs. New 2017.

MSR $445	$380	$335	$285	$260	$210	$175	$145	

CZ (STRAKONICE)

Current manufacturer established in 1919, located in Strakonice, Czech Republic. No current U.S. importation. Previously imported by Adco Sales, Inc., located in Woburn, MA.

HISTORY OF THE CZ TRADEMARK

In September 1919, the first factories were built under the name The South Bohemian Armory in Strakonice in the south of the Czech Republic. They took over the production of the firearms. This merger resulted in the new trademark CZ (in a circle).

Pre-World War II: The majority of products were for military and professional forces. Realizing the growing danger of war in 1936, and considering that Strakonice was about an hour drive from the Austrian and German borders, the company relocated to Uherský Brod in the eastern part of the country.

World War II: During World War II, firearms manufacturing continued but the production range consisted of firearms designed and made in German armouries.

Post-World War II: In 1954, the entire firearms production was, (for safety), moved to the branch plant in Uherský Brod. Because of political and economic changes in 1989 in the Czech Republic, the plant in Uherský Brod became independent. They continued to use the original trademark until 1992 when they registered their own - CZ UB.

Modern CZ Strakonice History: When CZ Strakonice production resumed in the first half of 1990, the company was divided into several divisions and firearms were allocated to CZ Strojirna Ltd. CZ Strojirna Ltd. produced 50,000 M6 for the U.S. Army between 1993 to 2001.

LUVO Prague Ltd.: (LUVO Firearms) took over firearms production from CZ Strojirna Ltd. in 2006. The company continues to use the trademark CZ (in a circle) and produces pistols, assault rifles, semi-

GRADING - PPGS™	100%	98%	95%	90%	80%	70%	60%	LAST MSR

automatic snipers, semi-automatic rifles, and grenade launchers in 40x46 caliber. Luvo Prague Ltd. has had little or no importation into the United States. For more information on Luvo Prague Ltd., please refer to Luvo Prague in the L section.

PISTOLS: SEMI-AUTO

Older Strakonice manufacture can be found in the CZ (Ceska Zbrojovka) section.

CZ-75 – 9mm Para. cal., DA/SA, 4 3/4 in. barrel, steel frame, 10 shot mag., blue finish only. Limited importation 2004 only.

	100%	98%	95%	90%	80%	70%	60%	LAST MSR
	$475	$425	$375	$325	$295	$275	$225	*$569*

CZ-TT – 9mm Para., .40 S&W, or .45 ACP cal., DA/SA, polymer frame, 3.77 in. ported or unported barrel, matte finish, 10 shot mag., 26.1 oz. Imported 2004-2006.

	100%	98%	95%	90%	80%	70%	60%	LAST MSR
	$450	$415	$375	$325	$295	$275	$250	*$479*

Add $30 for ported barrel (disc.).
Add $40 for ported barrel and slide serrations (disc.).
Add $399 for conversion kit with one mag.

CZ-T POLYMER COMPACT – similar to CZ-TT, except has shorter barrel. Limited importation 2004 only.

	100%	98%	95%	90%	80%	70%	60%	LAST MSR
	$475	$425	$375	$325	$295	$275	$225	*$559*

ADCO/CZ 1911-A1 – .38 Super or .45 ACP cal., standard size government model with 5 in. barrel, black matte finish. Limited importation 2004.

	100%	98%	95%	90%	80%	70%	60%	LAST MSR
	$475	$425	$375	$325	$295	$275	$225	*$559*

Add $10 for .38 Super cal.

CZ ST9 – 9mm Para. cal., 5 in. barrel, 16 shot mag., DA/SA, manual safety lever, matte blue finish, checkered wood grips.

This model has not been imported into the U.S.

RIFLES: SEMI-AUTO

CZ Strakonice also manufactures a .22 LR cal. AR-15 style training rifle, as well as .22 LR and .17 Mach 2 adapters for the AR-15. These guns are not imported into the U.S.

CZ CUSTOM

Current custom shop and manufacturer located in Mesa, AZ. CZ Custom specializes in CZ (Ceská zbrojovka) pistols and their derivatives. CZ Custom also manufactures a line of in-house pistols based off of the CZ-75 design.

CZ Custom manufactures an in-house line of pistols, but also maintains a strong relationship to CZ-USA/CZUB and regularly collaborates on the production of custom models with those companies. CZ-USA does not themselves operate a custom shop, but will advertise and sell models that CZ Custom makes. For CZ factory manufactured firearms, please refer to the CZ (CESKÁ ZBROJOVKA) section.

PISTOLS: SEMI-AUTO

CZC A01-LD – 9mm Para. cal., DA/SA, short recoil, tilting barrel action, 4.9 in. match grade stainless steel bull barrel, two 19 shot CZ P-09 mags., hammer forged steel frame, steel slide, ring hammer, stainless steel short reset trigger, CZ Custom low-mount rear sight, fiber optic front sight, CZ Custom grip panels with 25 LPI checkering on the front and backstrap of the pistol grip, ambi enlarged manual safety, enlarged and full length dustcover, rounded trigger guard with deep undercut, internal magwell, CZC slide markings, blued or Tungsten (disc. 2020) frame finish, 51.2 oz. Mfg. by Custom Shop beginning 2019.

	100%	98%	95%	90%	80%	70%	60%	LAST MSR
MSR $2,385	$2,025	$1,775	$1,525	$1,375	$1,115	$925	$750	

Add $35 for Picatinny railed variant (A01-LD-R), disc. 2020.
Add $125 for Tungsten finished lower frame (disc. 2020).
Add $380 for optics ready variant with removeable rear sight plate (disc. 2020).

CZC A01-SD – 9mm Para. cal., DA/SA, short recoil, tilting barrel action, 4.925 in. match grade stainless steel bull barrel, two 19 shot CZ P-09 mag., hammer forged steel frame, steel slide, CZC Ghost Competition hammer, CZC 85 Gunsmith stainless trigger, tuned 8.5 lb DA trigger pull and 3.5 lb SA trigger pull with short reset, CZC low-mount rear sight, fiber optic front sight, CZC grip panels with 25 LPI checkering on the front and backstrap of the pistol grip, ambi enlarged manual safety, short dustcover, rounded trigger guard with deep undercut, internal magwell, CZC slide markings, blued finish, 47 oz. New 2019.

	100%	98%	95%	90%	80%	70%	60%	LAST MSR
MSR $2,325	$1,975	$1,725	$1,475	$1,350	$1,100	$900	$700	

Add $230 for optics ready variant with removeable rear sight plate.

GRADING - PPGS™	100%	98%	95%	90%	80%	70%	60%	LAST MSR

CABANAS

Previous trademark manufactured by Industrias Cabanas, S.A. in Aguilas, Mexico 1949-1999. Previously imported and retailed by Mandall Shooting Supplies, Inc. located in Scottsdale, AZ.

Cabanas manufactured a unique single shot bolt action rifle which shot oversized .177 pellets/BBs powered by .22 blanks at 1,150 feet per second. There were at least 8 variations, and secondary market prices today for 95%+ original condition ranges from approx. $65-$120. Transfer requires FFL. This trademark had limited U.S. importation.

CABELA'S INC.

Current sporting goods dealer and catalog company headquartered in Sidney, NE. Consumer direct (store or mail order catalog) sales only.

For individual model listings, please go to BlueBookOfGunValues.com/overflow.

CABOT GUN COMPANY LLC

Current pistol manufacturer located in Cabot, PA. Consumer and dealer sales.

PISTOLS: SEMI-AUTO, 1911 STYLE

Cabot Guns also manufactures one-of-a-kind pistols with unique features and finishes. Values are not shown for 90% and less condition factors as they are almost never encountered in these lower conditions. Please contact the factory directly on these special order pistols. From 2016-2018, Cabot introduced the Cabot of the Month Club (a 1911 delivered each month). Models included: Jan. - S100, Feb. - S103, March - Vintage Classic, April - The Ultimate Bedside 1911, May - Two-Tone DLC Custom Commander, June - Drako Garra (new), July - American Joe Commander, August - S103 9mm, Sept. - Cabot Elite Special Edition (ONLY for CE2017 members), Oct. - S100 9mm, Nov/Dec. - Custom built pistol set for the owner ($15K value). In 2020, the Gun of the Month Specials returned with 12 Limited Edition 1911 models. Only 20 of each model will be produced and each gun will have a custom serial number to ensure provenance. Total price for the set is $74,000. Models include: Jan. - The Demon GT, Feb. - The Son of Drako, March - Golden Joe, April - Case Color 1911, May - Prospector Icon, June - Belligerent Gentleman, July - Damascus Tornado, August - Rhone, Sept. - Rebellion VC, Oct. - Valley of Darkness, Nov. - Cabot Safari, and Dec. - NERO Damascus.

Trump 45 Pistols are also available. Prices range between $15,000-$80,000, depending on the serial number.

Cabot pistols commonly come with a bushing wrench and gun lock.

Add $75 for fixed Tritium front sight.
Add $100 for Ambi safety.
Add $75-$125 for fiber optic front sight.
Add $125 for Low Mount adj. or fixed Tritium rear sight.
Add $175 for Low Mount adj. Tritium rear sight.
Add $195 for gold bead front sight.
Add $200 for front and rear fixed tritium sights.
Add $250 for threaded barrel.
Add $295 for factory equipped Surefire X300 weaponlight.

AMERICAN JOE – .45 ACP cal., modern full size 1911 style, enhanced frame to slide fit, included exclusive custom design aluminum American flag grips, engraving design by Joe Faris. Mfg. 2013-2017.

	100%	98%	95%	90%	80%	70%	60%	LAST MSR
	$6,700	$5,875	$5,000	N/A	N/A	N/A	N/A	*$7,450*

AMERICAN JOE COMMANDER – 9mm Para. or .45 ACP cal., 4 1/4 in. stainless steel match grade barrel w/flush cut crown, hand fit stainless commander size steel frame and slide, lowered and flared ejection port, Tristar trigger, reverse dovetail front white dot, gold bead, or Tritium sights, low mount fixed or adj. rear sights, aluminum American flag grips, beavertail grip safety, top and rear slide serrations, 24 LPI rhombus cut front strap and mainspring housing checkering, USA motif engraving on slide, 33.5 oz. New 2017.

	100%	98%	95%	90%	80%	70%	60%	LAST MSR
MSR $4,595	$4,150	$3,600	$3,100	N/A	N/A	N/A	N/A	

APOCALYPSE – 9mm Para. or .45 ACP cal., Commander or Govt. frame, 4 1/4 or 5 in. stainless steel hand-fit match grade barrel w/flush fit crown cut or optional threading, two 8 (.45 ACP) or 9 (9mm Para.) shot mags., stainless steel slide and frame w/integrated rail, lowered and flared ejection port, flat serrated trigger, reverse dovetail front and ledge rear sight w/optional MRDS mount, G-10 tactical grips, bushing wrench and gun lock, one-piece guide rod, VC Heritage finish. New 2021.

	100%	98%	95%	90%	80%	70%	60%	LAST MSR
MSR $7,495	$6,750	$5,900	$5,100	N/A	N/A	N/A	N/A	

Add $395 for MRDS mount.
Add $1,045 for factory installed MRDS mount w/2.5 MOA Trijicon SRO.

GRADING - PPGS™	100%	98%	95%	90%	80%	70%	60%	LAST MSR

BLACK DIAMOND – .45 ACP cal., full size frame, all black finish, similar to Jones 1911, carry model. Mfg. 2014-2016.

	$5,625	$4,925	$4,225	N/A	N/A	N/A	N/A	$6,250

BLACK DIAMOND DELUXE, LIMITED EDITION – .45 ACP cal., full size frame, billet steel construction, front and rear strap checkering, Blind Sight front sight, Tristar trigger, Mammoth tooth grips, black blued finish. Limited mfg. of approx. 10 per year beginning 2017. A total of of 50 units were sold. Disc. 2019.

	$10,800	$9,450	$8,100	N/A	N/A	N/A	N/A	$11,995

BULLSEYE – .45 ACP cal., full size frame and slide, includes Aimpoint Micro H-1 optic, similar to Jones 1911, integrated optic mouting rail lowered into rear of slide. Mfg. 2014 only.

	$6,075	$5,325	$4,550	N/A	N/A	N/A	N/A	$6,750

CGI CLASSIC (CONTEMPORARY GOVERNMENT ISSUE CLASSIC) – .45 ACP cal., vintage M1911A1 style, 5 in. National Match grade barrel w/polished feed ramp, 8 shot Chip McCormick Power Mag., full size CNC machined frame and slide w/rear slide serrations, aluminum skeletonized trigger, GI style fixed sights, American Box Elder grips, GI style right hand thumb safety, custom fitted case or customized aluminum Technoframe display case, bright blue hand polished finish, jeweled barrel and magazine optional, 40 oz. Mfg. 2011-2013.

	$4,450	$3,900	$3,350	N/A	N/A	N/A	N/A	$4,950

CHARLEY – 9mm Para. or .45 ACP cal., 5 in. hand fit match grade barrel w/flush cut crown, two 8 shot mags., billet mag. release, beveled magwell, full size hand polished stainless steel bobtail frame and slide, lowered and flared ejection port, Cabot aluminum Tristar trigger, Cabot reverse dovetail front sight, ACW fixed rear sight, satin Ironwood or High Tactile G10 grip panels, billet beavertail grip safety, billet thumb safety, top and side slide serrations, 24 LPI rhombus cut front strap checkering, one-piece full length guide rod with engraved star. Mfg. 2019-2020.

	$4,050	$3,550	$3,050	N/A	N/A	N/A	N/A	$4,495

THE CLONE COMMANDER (CLONE TECHNOLOGY CARRY PISTOL) – .45 ACP cal., 1911 style, bobtailed frame, precision grade Tristar trigger, black G10 grips, grip-assuring checkering at the front and rear straps. Mfg. mid-2015-2018.

	$5,625	$4,925	$4,225	N/A	N/A	N/A	N/A	$6,250

DAMASCUS LADDER DELUXE – 9mm Para. or .45 ACP cal., 5 in. stainless steel hand fit match grade barrel w/flush cut crown, hand fit frame and slide, two 8 shot mags., beveled and chamfered magwell, lowered and flared ejection port, standard or aluminum Tristar trigger, reverse dovetail front sight, ext. rear sight, Sonoran Desert Ironwood, Mammoth Ivory or Molar (new 2020), or Morrissey Damascus (disc.) grips, beavertail grip safety, "Racing Stripes" rear slide serrations, 24 LPI rhombus cut front strap and mainspring housing checkering, engraved star on one-piece full length guide rod, Super-Etch Damascus finish, 2.35 lbs. New 2018.

MSR $7,995	$7,200	$6,300	$5,400	N/A	N/A	N/A	N/A	

Add $125 for Tristar trigger.

Add $800 for Mammoth Ivory or $850 Mammoth Molar grips (new 2020).

Add $2,000 for 10 Unit Limited Edition Morrissey Damascus grips (disc.).

DRAGON FIRE – .45 ACP cal., stainless steel construction, hand engraved dragon motif and stippling by FEGA Master Engraver Lee Griffiths. One-of-a-kind pistol features slide with polished fangs fore of the dust cover, rearward on each side of the slide a pair of "eyes" is featured containing jet black Marquis Cut diamond pupils surrounded by 24 rubies, genuine ruby front sight, custom hand made rear sight, Serial No. "Dragon1911". New 2021.

Original price at sale: $129,000.

THE DRAKO GARRA (DRAKO GARRA) – 9mm Para. or .45 ACP cal., stainless steel construction, 5 in. stainless steel match grade barrel, two 8 shot mags., Cabot Dragon Claw front and rear slide serrations, beveled magwell, lowered and flared ejection port, Dragon Claw trigger, diagonal cut front strap checkering, billet thumb safety and beavertail grip safety, engraved star at front of guide rod, reverse dovetail front sight, low mount fixed rear sight, Piano Black Ebony wood grips. Mfg. 2017-2018.

	$4,775	$4,200	$3,575	N/A	N/A	N/A	N/A	$5,295

* ***Drako Garra 2.0*** – 9mm Para. or .45 ACP cal., 5 in. stainless steel match grade barrel, polished feed ramp, 416 stainless steel billet frame and slide, two 8 shot mags., beveled magwell, lowered and flared ejection port, Cabot Claw trigger, reverse dovetail front sight (stainless steel blank, optional gold-dot or Tritium) and Cabot Dante rear sight, optional Novak low mount adj. rear sight (black or Tritium bar), Chatoyant carbon fiber grips with inlaid Cabot medallion, billet thumb safety and beavertail grip safety, Trinity Stripes rear slide serrations, matte finish, 38.4 oz. Mfg. 2019-2020.

	$5,000	$4,375	$3,750	N/A	N/A	N/A	N/A	$5,595

GRADING - PPGS™	100%	98%	95%	90%	80%	70%	60%	LAST MSR

THE GENTLEMANS CARRY – 9mm Para. or .45 ACP cal., 4 1/4 in. barrel w/flush cut recessed crown, two 8 (.45 ACP) or 9 (9mm Para.) shot mags., stainless steel carry cut slide w/13 degree slide serrations and bobtail cut frame, black aluminum Tristar trigger, front sight reverse dovetail with Tritium, rear sight warren style U-notch with Tritium, double diamond checkered Walnut grips w/Cabot medallions, right-hand thumb safety, beavertail grip safety, 24 LPI rhombus cut front strap and mainspring housing checkering, all black or stainless steel (new 2020) finish. New 2018.

MSR $4,795	$4,325	$3,775	$3,250	N/A	N/A	N/A	N/A	

GI CLASSIC (GOVERNMENT ISSUE CLASSIC) – .45 ACP cal., vintage M1911A1 style, full size CNC machined frame, 5 in. National Match grade barrel, polished feed ramp, blued solid trigger with front stippling, rear slide serrations, right hand thumb safety, extended slide stop, arched main spring housing, retro fixed style sights, 8 shot original ordnance style mag., Isonited glare resistant finish, ordinance style GI grips. Limited mfg. 2012-2013.

	$4,275	$3,750	$3,200	N/A	N/A	N/A	N/A	*$4,750*

GRAN TORINO SS (STAINLESS STEEL) – .45 ACP or 9mm Para. cal., 5 in. National Match grade barrel, reverse crown, two 8 shot mags., beveled magwell, high polish stainless steel frame and slide, lowered and flared ejection port, "Perfect Fit" ejector, aluminum Tristar trigger, reverse dovetail front sight, black low mount fixed rear sight, Chatoyant carbon fiber grips with inlaid Cabot medallion, ext. beavertail grip safety, billet thumb safety, full length guide rod w/inlaid star, Racing Vector slide serrations, top slide serrations, 24 LPI rhombus cut front strap and mainspring housing checkering. New 2019.

MSR $4,495	$4,050	$3,550	$3,050	N/A	N/A	N/A	N/A	

THE ICON – 9mm Para. or .45 ACP cal., 4 1/4 (Commander size) or 5 (Government size) in. National Match Grade barrel with recessed crown, two 8 shot mags., Cabot Icon racking buttons, flat-top slide, Cabot Idiot-Scratch-Proof slide stop with countersunk and recessed notch, full length guide rod w/inlaid star, lowered and flared ejection port, no-dot reverse dovetail front sight and ACW fixed rear sight, aluminum Icon trigger, right-hand thumb safety, beveled magwell, 24 LPI rhombus cut front strap and mainspring housing checkering, beavertail grip safety, stainless steel monochrome grips, all stainless finish. New 2018.

MSR $4,995	$4,500	$3,950	$3,375	N/A	N/A	N/A	N/A	

JONES 1911 – .45 ACP cal., 5 in. National Match grade barrel w/polished feed ramp, full size CNC machined and ground frame and slide, lowered and flared ejection port, aluminum (mfg. 2012 only) or Tristar (new 2013) trigger, rear and front checkered serrations, right hand or ambidextrous thumb safety, ext. slide stop, 20 LPI front strap checkering, titanium firing pin, low mount adj. 2-dot rear sight, front dot sight, engraved star on guide rod, chamfered magwell, 8 shot mag., bright blue hand polished finish, Desert Ironwood grips, includes customized case, 40 oz. Mfg. 2012-2016.

	$5,800	$5,075	$4,350	N/A	N/A	N/A	N/A	*$6,450*

JONES DELUXE – .45 ACP cal., similar to Jones 1911 with added refinements, including hand polishing and finishing resulting in a mirror-like finish, TriStar trigger, Ironwood grips, front and rear checkered slide serrations, beveled and chamfered magwell, CNC engraved star on guide rod. Mfg. 2012-2019.

	$9,000	$7,875	$6,750	N/A	N/A	N/A	N/A	*$9,995*

MONARCH LIMITED EDITION 1911 – .45 ACP cal., 5 in. National Match grade barrel w/polished feed ramp, 8 shot flush fit mag., beveled magwell, full size CNC machined frame and slide, lowered and flare ejection port, stainless Tristar trigger with rounded and knurled front pad, gold bead front sight, adj. rear sight, Ancient Mammoth Ivory grip scales, RH thumb safety, beavertail grip safety, 13 degree rear slide serrations, 20 LPI front strap and mainspring housing checkering, acrylic and aluminum display case, mirror polish blued slide finish, satin finish blued frame finish. Mfg. 2016-2019.

	$9,000	$7,875	$6,750	N/A	N/A	N/A	N/A	*$9,995*

NAKED 1911 – .45 ACP cal., stainless steel frame and slide, 5 in. National Match barrel, 8 shot mag., lowered and flared ejection port, beveled and chamfered magwell, low mount fixed rear sight, polished feed ramp, aluminum Tristar trigger, smooth front strap, Cabot engraved CG logo on rear slide, G10 or walnut grips, beavertail grip safety, matte stainless or black Nitride finish. Mfg. 2017 only.

	$2,975	$2,600	$2,225	N/A	N/A	N/A	N/A	*$3,295*

Add $100 for walnut checkered grips.

NATIONAL STANDARD (RECENT MFG.) – .45 ACP cal., 5 in. NM barrel w/polished feed ramp, 8 shot mag., full size stainless steel frame and slide, lowered and flared ejection port, Tristar trigger, adj. 2-dot rear sight, blind front sight, Desert Ironwood grips, RH thumb safety, rear slide serrations, top slide serrations, ext. slide stop, 20 LPI front strap checkering. Mfg. 2012-2016.

	$6,100	$5,325	$4,550	N/A	N/A	N/A	N/A	*$6,750*

GRADING - PPGS™	100%	98%	95%	90%	80%	70%	60%	LAST MSR

NATIONAL STANDARD (CURRENT MFG.) – 9mm Para. or .45 ACP cal., 4 1/4 or 5 in. hand fit match grade barrel w/polished feed ramp and flush cut crown, two 8 (.45 ACP) or 9 (9mm Para.) shot mags., stainless steel frame and slide, lowered and flared ejection port, Tristar trigger, reverse dovetail white-dot front sight and fixed rear sight, smooth figured Walnut grips, optional Fibonacci or checkered Walnut grips or Desert Ironwood grips, billet thumb safety, beavertail grip safety, one-piece guide rod, 24 LPI rhombus cut front strap and mainspring housing checkering. New 2021.

MSR $3,995	$3,600	$3,150	$2,700	N/A	N/A	N/A	N/A	

NATIONAL STANDARD DELUXE – .45 ACP cal., similar to National Standard, except has closer tolerances, hand polished to a two micron mirror finish, mammoth ivory grips. Mfg. 2012, limited reintroduction 2015-2016.

	$10,350	$9,000	$7,775	N/A	N/A	N/A	N/A	$11,500

NERO – 9mm Para. or .45 ACP cal., 4 1/4 or 5 in. stainless steel match grade barrel w/polished feed ramp and flush cut crown, two 8 (.45 ACP) or 9 (9mm Para.) shot mag., one-piece ext. magwell, Cabot machined fit ejector, lowered and flared ejection port, flat serrated trigger, reverse dovetail red fiber optic front sight, Cabot/ACW ledge rear sight, G10 tactile grips, billet beavertail grip and thumb safety, top, front, and rear slide serrations, integrated frame rail, 24 LPI rhombus cut front strap and mainspring housing checkering, black finish w/hardening. Limited mfg. beginning mid-2019.

MSR $4,695	$4,225	$3,700	$3,175	N/A	N/A	N/A	N/A	

RANGEMASTER – .45 ACP cal., 5 in. National Match grade barrel w/polished feed ramp, 8 shot Chip McCormick Power Mag., CNC machined full size frame and slide, lowered and flared ejection port, aluminum Tristar trigger, Novak adj. 3-dot sights, Pachmayr American Legend (disc. 2013) or G10 (new 2013) grips, RH thumb safety, polished feed ramp, rear checkered slide serrations, ext. slide stop, includes customized case, semi-bright blue hand polished finish, 40 oz. Mfg. 2012-2014.

	$4,725	$4,125	$3,550	N/A	N/A	N/A	N/A	$5,250

REBELLION – 9mm Para. cal., 4 1/2 in. stainless steel match grade bull barrel w/polished feed ramp and flush cut crown, two 9 shot mags., stainless steel slide w/front, top, and rear serrations and carry cut, aircraft aluminum frame w/speed cut rails, lowered ejection port, flat serrated trigger, reverse dovetail white dot front sight and ledge rear sight, G-10 tactile grips, beavertail grip safety and thumb safety, one-piece full-length guide rod, 24 LPI rhombus cut front strap and mainspring housing checkering, black or two-tone finish, 28.3 oz. New 2020.

MSR $4,295	$3,875	$3,375	$2,900	N/A	N/A	N/A	N/A	

S100 1911 – 9mm Para. or .45 ACP cal., Government Model, stainless steel construction, 5 in. match grade hand fit barrel w/polished feed ramp and flush cut crown, right or left-hand action, 8 shot mag., beveled magwell, Fibonacci patterned or Tactile G10 grips, Cabot "Trinity Stripes" top and rear checkered slide serrations, lowered and flared ejection port, aluminum Tristar trigger, low mount fixed rear sight and reverse dovetail front sight, beavertail grip safety, matte finish, 2.35 lbs. Mfg. 2015-2020.

	$3,325	$2,900	$2,500	N/A	N/A	N/A	N/A	$3,695

Add $100 for checkered walnut grips.

* ***S100 Southpaw Edition*** – 9mm Para. or .45 ACP cal., full size 1911 designed for left-handed shooters, stainless steel construction, 5 in. match grade barrel, beveled magwell, top and rear slide serrations, lowered and flared ejection port, aluminum Tristar trigger, reverse dovetail white dot front sight, low mount fixed rear sight, one-piece full length guide rod, billet left-hand thumb safety, slide stop, and mag. release, Fibonacci G10 or optional Fibonacci Walnut grips, beavertail grip safety, matte finish, 2.35 lbs. New late 2016.

MSR $4,995	$4,500	$3,950	$3,375	N/A	N/A	N/A	N/A	

Add $100 for walnut checkered grips.
Add $750 for DLC finish.

S103 COMMANDER CARRY – 9mm Para. or .45 ACP cal., stainless steel Commander frame and slide, 4 1/4 in. National Match barrel w/flush cut crown, 8 shot mag., Tristar trigger, lowered and flared ejection port, front strap checkering, "Trinity Stipe" checkered serrations, blind sight white dot front and low mount fixed rear sight, beavertail grip safety, High Tactile G10,scalloped Fibonacci G10, or checkered walnut grips, matte stainless or black Nitride finish, 33.5 oz. Mfg. 2015-2020.

	$3,325	$2,900	$2,500	N/A	N/A	N/A	N/A	$3,695

Add $100 for checkered walnut grips.

GRADING - PPGS™	100%	98%	95%	90%	80%	70%	60%	LAST MSR

* ***S103 Commander Southpaw (Southpaw Commander)*** – 9mm Para. or .45 ACP cal., true left-handed Commander size 1911, stainless steel frame and slide, 4 1/4 in. match grade hand fit barrel w/ flush cut crown, 8 shot mag., reverse dovetail front white dot, gold bead, or Tritium sight, "Trinity Stripe" top and rear slide checkered serrations, lowered and flared ejection port, Tristar trigger, front strap checkering, beavertail grip safety, Fibonacci G10, Fibonacci Walnut, or checkered Walnut grips, matte stainless or black Nitride finish. New late 2016.

MSR $4,995 $4,500 $3,950 $3,375 N/A N/A N/A N/A

Add $100 for checkered walnut grips.

* ***S103 LTD*** – 9mm Para. or .45 ACP cal., 1911 style, hand fit frame and slide, stainless steel construction, 4 1/4 in. NM barrel, crowned flush barrel, two 8 shot mags., beveled and chamfered magwell, black Nitride finished small parts, front blind white dot sight, low mount fixed rear or adj. sights, front strap checkering, lowered and flared ejection port, rear slide Trinity Stripe serrations, Tristar trigger, beavertail grip safety, G10 black Fibonacci grips, matte stainless or black Nitride finish. Mfg. 2016-2020.

$3,600 $3,150 $2,700 N/A N/A N/A N/A *$3,995*

Add $155 for smooth Ebony w/inlay medallion or $195 for Ebony Fibonacci grips.

SOB - SON OF RELIC – .45 ACP cal., stainless steel construction, billet hammer, deep curve Tristar trigger, reverse dovetail front sight, Mammoth Ivory grips, hand-engraved Germanic scroll by FEGA Master Engraver Otto Carter, sepia-toned acid etched finish, 10 models mfg. 2019 only.

$7,200 $6,300 $5,400 N/A N/A N/A N/A *$7,995*

SOB - SON OF RELIC 2.0 – .45 ACP cal., stainless steel frame and slide, 5 in. stainless steel match grade barrel w/polished feed ramp, two 8 shot mags., billet mag. release, Tristar trigger, reverse dovetail front and ledge rear sight, select Hawaiian Heart of Mango wood grips w/inlaid Cabot medallion, billet thumb and beavertail grip safety, 24 LPI rhombus cut checkered front strap and mainspring housing, top slide serrations, hand engraved by FEGA Master Engraver Otto Carter, acid etched Relic finish, optional Mammoth Ivory grips. Limited mfg. of 20 in 2020.

$7,200 $6,300 $5,400 N/A N/A N/A N/A *$7,995*

SOUTH PAW – .45 ACP cal., designed for left-handed shooters, National Match grade barrel w/polished feed ramp, lowered and flared ejection port, aluminum Tristar trigger, rear slide serrations, left hand thumb safety, ext. slide stop, arched main spring housing, 20 LPI front strap checkering, Harrison design fixed rear sight, Rozic blind front sight, 8 shot mag., hand polished blue or Nitride Penn Gray finish, Box Elder or CA Olive wood grips, 40 oz. Mfg. 2012-2016.

$5,350 $4,675 $4,000 N/A N/A N/A N/A *$5,950*

ULTIMATE BEDSIDE 1911 – 9mm Para. or .45 ACP cal., 5 in. stainless steel hand fit match grade barrel w/polished feed ramp and flush cut crown, two 8 (.45 ACP) or 9 (9mm Para.) shot mags., beveled and chamfered magwell, Damasteel Damascus stainless steel slide, black DLC finished frame, lowered and flared ejection port, Tristar trigger, low mount fixed or adj. rear sight, front blind white dot sight, Fibonacci G10 grip, beavertail grip safety, 24 LPI rhombus cut front strap and mainspring housing checkering, full length guide rod w/engraved star, with or w/o rail and/or Surefire light. New 2016.

MSR $6,595 $5,925 $5,200 $4,450 N/A N/A N/A N/A

Add $150 for smooth Ebony w/inlaid medallion or $195 for Ebony Fibonacci grips.

UTOPIA LIMITED EDITION – .45 ACP cal., full size 120 layer Damascus steel frame and slide, Widmanstätten patterned Meteorite Tristar trigger, basepads, and sights, polished Meteorite Bark grips. Limited mfg. of 3 beginning 2020.

Current MSR is $59,000.

THE VINTAGE CLASSIC 1911 (VINTAGE CLASSIC 1911) – 9mm Para. or .45 ACP cal., right-hand or left-hand (disc.) configuration, 5 in. hand fit match grade barrel w/polished feed ramp and flush cut crown, two 8 (.45 ACP) or 9 (9mm Para.) shot mags., beveled magwell, Government or Commander size stainless steel frame and slide, lowered and flared ejection port, perfect fit ejector, aluminum Tristar trigger, reverse dovetail gold dot front sight, low mount fixed black or Tritium rear sight, highly figured Turkish Walnut checkered grips with inlaid Cabot medallion or White American Holly grips, billet beavertail grip safety, Cabot "Trinity Stripes" rear slide checkered serrations, top slide serrations, 24 LPI rhombus cut front strap and mainspring housing checkering, billet one-piece full length guide rod, proprietary Vintage Classic finish. New late 2016.

MSR $4,295 $3,875 $3,400 $2,900 N/A N/A N/A N/A

Add $800 for Mammoth Ivory grips.

Add $1,000 for left-hand configuration (disc.).

GRADING - PPGS™	100%	98%	95%	90%	80%	70%	60%	LAST MSR

CADEX DEFENCE

Current bolt action rifle and accessories manufacturer with U.S.A. office located in Swanton, VA. Previously located in Valdosta, GA.

RIFLES: BOLT ACTION

Several finish options include: Black, Tan, OD Green, Stealth Shadow Vortex, Sniper Grey, Hunter Orange, Stormtrooper White, Robin's Egg Blue, Hybrid Tan/Black, Hybrid Green/Black, Hybrid Stealth Shadow, Hybrid Grey/Black, Hybrid Orange/Black, Hybrid White/Black, or Hybrid Robin's Egg Blue.

CDX-30 LITE RIFLE SERIES (GUARDIAN LITE RIFLE) - .308 Win., .260 Rem., 6 Creedmoor, 6.5 Creedmoor, or 6.5x57 Lapua cal., 20, 24, or 26 in. fluted match grade barrel with threaded muzzle, M16-style extractor, oversized trigger guard and mag. release, reverse folding buttstock, rubberized Ergo grip with finger grooves, detachable base, full length lite top rail, tool-free adj. buttpad, adj. LOP and cheek rest, black, tan, Hybrid Tan/Black, OD Green, Grey, Stealth Shadow Vortex, Hybrid Stealth Black, Hybrid Grey/Black, or Hybrid Green/Black finish, 14.2 lbs. New 2015.

MSR $5,719	$4,850	$4,250	$3,650	$3,300	$2,700	$2,200	$1,700

CDX-30 TAC RIFLE SERIES (GUARDIAN TAC RIFLE) - 6mm Creedmoor, 6.5 PRC (new 2020), .260 Rem., 6.5 Creedmoor, 6.5x47 LM, or .308 Win. cal., 20, 24, or 26 in. fluted match grade barrel with threaded muzzle, multiple magazine sleeves, oversized trigger guard and mag. release, fully adj. stock with integrated monopod attachment, rubberized Ergo grip with finger grooves, detachable base, full length lite top rail, black, tan, OD Green, Stealth Shadow Vortex, Sniper Grey, Hybrid Green/Black, Hybrid Grey/Black, or Hybrid Tan/Black finish, 12.2-13.2 lbs. New 2015.

MSR $5,719	$4,850	$4,250	$3,650	$3,300	$2,700	$2,200	$1,700

CDX-33 LITE RIFLE SERIES (PATRIOT LITE) - .338 Lapua, .300 Norma, or .338 Norma cal., 27 in. fluted match grade barrel with threaded muzzle, M16-style extractor, oversized trigger guard and mag. release, reverse folding buttstock, rubberized Ergo grip with finger grooves, detachable base, full length lite top rail, tool-free adj. buttpad, adj. LOP and cheek rest, Black, Tan, Hybrid Tan/Black, OD Green, Hybrid Grey/Black, or Hybrid Green/Black finish, 14.2 lbs. New 2015.

MSR $5,719	$4,850	$4,250	$3,650	$3,300	$2,700	$2,200	$1,700

CDX-33 TAC RIFLE SERIES (PATRIOT TAC) - .300 Norma Mag., .338 Norma Mag., or .338 Lapua Mag. cal., 26 or 27 in. fluted match grade barrel with 5R Mil-Spec point-cut rifling, multiple magazine sleeves, oversized trigger guard and mag. release, fully adj. stock with integrated monopod attachment, rubberized Ergo grip with finger grooves, detachable base, full length lite top rail, Black, Tan, OD Green, Sniper Grey, Stealth Shadow Vortex, Hybrid Green/Black, Hybrid Stealth Shadow, or Hybrid Tan/Black finish, 12.2-13.3 lbs. New 2015.

MSR $5,139	$4,350	$3,800	$3,300	$2,950	$2,400	$1,950	$1,550

CDX-40 SHADOW - .375 CheyTac, .408 CheyTac, or .375 EnABLER (new 2020) cal., 29 or 32 in. fluted Bartlein stainless steel barrel, single or double stage trigger, oversized trigger guard and mag. release, folding buttstock, adj. buttpad, LOP, and cheek rest, Ergo finger grooved grips, detachable base, full length light top rail, black, tan, OD Green, Sniper Grey, Stealth Shadow Vortex, Hybrid Green/Black, Hybrid Grey/Black, Hybrid Stealth Shadow, Hybrid Tan/Black, and additional Cerakote finish options, 18 1/2 lbs. New 2016.

MSR $7,369	$6,250	$5,500	$4,700	$4,250	$3,450	$2,800	$2,200

CDX-50 TREMOR - .50 BMG cal., 29 or 32 in. fluted match grade heavy stainless steel barrel, barrel band and threaded muzzle, 5 shot mag., stainless action and bolt, single or double stage trigger, oversized trigger guard and mag. release, folding buttstock, tool-free adj. cheek rest, rubberized Ergo grip, detachable base, full length dual top rail, black, tan, OD Green, Stealth Shadow Vortex, Sniper Grey, Hybrid Black/Tan, Hybrid Black/Green, Hybrid Grey/Black, Hybrid Stealth Shadow, 23.8 lbs. New 2016.

MSR $8,109	$6,900	$6,050	$5,150	$4,700	$3,800	$3,100	$2,400

CDX-300 LITE RIFLE (FREEDOM LITE) - .300 Win. Mag. cal., 24 or 26 in. fluted match grade barrel with threaded muzzle, M16-style extractor, oversized trigger guard and mag. release, reverse folding buttstock, rubberized Ergo grip with finger grooves, detachable base, full length lite top rail, tool-free adj. buttpad, adj. LOP and cheek rest, Black, Tan, Hybrid Tan/Black, OD Green, Hybrid Grey/Black, or Hybrid Green/Black finish, 14.2 lbs. New 2015.

MSR $5,719	$4,850	$4,250	$3,650	$3,300	$2,700	$2,200	$1,700

CDX-300 TAC RIFLE SERIES (FREEDOM TAC) - .300 Win. Mag. or .300 PRC (new 2020) cal., 24 or 26 in. fluted match grade barrel with threaded muzzle, multiple magazine sleeves, oversized trigger guard and mag. release, fully adj. stock with integrated monopod attachment, rubberized Ergo grip with finger grooves, detachable base, full length lite top rail, Black, Tan, OD Green, Sniper Grey, Stealth Shadow Vortex, Hybrid Green/Black, Hybrid Stealth Shadow, or Hybrid Tan/Black finish, 13-13.2 lbs. New 2015.

MSR $5,486	$4,650	$4,100	$3,500	$3,150	$2,550	$2,100	$1,650

GRADING - PPGS™	100%	98%	95%	90%	80%	70%	60%	LAST MSR

CDX-MC KRAKEN – .260 Rem., 6 Creedmoor, 6.5 Creedmoor, 6.5 PRC (new 2020), 6.5x47 Lapua, .300 PRC (new 2020), .308 Win., .300 Win. Mag., .300 Norma Mag., .338 Lapua Mag., or .338 Norma cal., 20, 24, 26, or 27 in. barrel, muzzle brake ready, folding buttstock, tool-free adj. buttpad, LOP, and cheek rest, full length top rail, detachable base, black, tan, ODG, Stealth Shadow Vortex, Hybrid tan/black, Hybrid green/black, or Hybrid Stealth Shadow finish, 15.8 lbs. New 2017.

MSR $7,195	$6,100	$5,350	$4,600	$4,150	$3,350	$2,750	$2,150	

CDX-R7 C.O.P.S. (CARBINE OPTIMISEE POUR SNIPER) – .308 Win. cal., repeater, 16 1/2 in. Bartlein straight taper fluted match grade barrel, AICS mag. compatible (5 or 10 shot), DV2 Evo two-stage trigger, Magpul MOE stock, field QD chassis, 20 MOA full-length top rail, 3, 6, and 9 o'clock accessory rail, optional MX2 tactical muzzle brake, 10.49 lbs. black, tan, OD Green, Sniper Grey, Stealth Shadow Vortex, Hybrid tan/black, Hybrid green/black, Hybrid grey/black.

MSR $4,799	$3,925	$2,800	$1,750	$1,150	$875	$775	$700	

Add $75 for MX2 tactical muzzle brake.

CDX-R7 CPS SERIES – .308 Win. or 6.5 Creedmoor cal., 16.5 in. straight taper fluted, match grade Bartlein barrel, optional muzzle brake, AICS mag. compatible, stainless steel construction, DX2 EVO single/two stage trigger, Field QD chassis w/ultra-fast buttstock takedown system, accessory rails, interchangeable pinned full-length top rail, several Cerakote finish options available, optional vision rail, approx. 10.5 lbs. New 2020.

MSR $4,480	$3,800	$3,325	$2,850	$2,585	$2,090	$1,710	$1,500	

Add $190 for 6.5 Creedmoor cal.

CDX-R7 CRBN – 6.5 Creedmoor, 6.5 PRC, .308 Win., .300 WSM, 7mm Rem Mag., .28 Nosler, .300 Win. Mag., .300 PRC, or .338 Lapua Mag. cal., 20, 24, 26, or 27 in. Proof Research carbon fiber barrel, hunting style muzzle brake, AICS mag. compatible, stainless steel construction, Tundra Strike synthetic Monte Carlo rifle stock w/aluminum bedding, rubberized grip, interchangeable pinned top rail, several finish options available, approx. 8.3 lbs. New 2020.

Please contact the manufacturer directly for pricing and availability on this model.

CDX-R7 LCP/CDX-R7 FCP – 260 Rem., 6mm Creedmoor, 6.5 Creedmoor, 6.5x47 Lapua, 6.5 PRC (new 2020), .308 Win., .300 Win. Mag., .300 PRC (new 2020), .300 Norma, or .338 Lapua Mag. cal., 20, 24, 26, or 27 in. fluted match grade Bartlein barrel, optional MX1 muzzle brake, 5 or 10 shot AICS mag., stainless steel construction, DX2 trigger, oversized trigger guard, fixed skeleton stock (Field Model) or reverse folding buttstock with adj. cheek rest and buttpad rubberized Ergo grip, black, tan, OD Green, or several Cerakote finish options available, approx. 13 lbs. New 2018.

MSR $4,900	$4,175	$3,650	$3,125	$2,840	$2,300	$1,880	$1,625	

Add $440 for CDX-R7 LCP.

CDX-R7 LITE COMP/CDX-R7 FIELD COMP – 6mm Creedmoor, .260 Rem., 6.5 Creedmoor, 6.5x47 Lapua Mag., .308 Win., .300 Win. Mag., .300 Norma Mag., or .338 Lapua Mag. cal., R7 action, 20, 24, 26, or 27 in. Bartlein fluted match grade barrel with barrel band and threaded muzzle, 5 or 10 shot AICS mag., stainless steel construction, oversized trigger guard, DX2 trigger, fixed skeleton stock (Field model) or reverse folding buttstock with adj. cheek rest, LOP, and buttpad, rubberized Ergo grip, black, tan, OD Green, or several other Cerakote finish options available, approx. 13 lbs. Mfg. 2018-2019.

	$4,285	$3,750	$3,200	$2,900	$2,350	$1,950	$1,525	*$5,043*

Subtract $471 for CDX-R7 Field Comp.

CDX-R7 SHP SERIES SHORT ACTION (SHEEPDOG) – .260 Rem., 6.5 Creedmoor, 6.5 PRC (new 2021), 6.5x47 Lapua, or .308 Win. cal., 20, 24, 26, or 27 in. barrel, MX2 muzzle brake ready, fully adj. synthetic stock, adj. buttpad, adj. LOP, tool-free adj. cheek rest, built-in micro chassis system, action rail, black, tan, OD Green, Hybrid Stealth Shadow, Stealth Shadow Vortex, Hybrid tan/black, or Hybrid green/black finish, 13 lbs. New. 2017.

MSR $3,270	$2,800	$2,450	$2,100	$1,900	$1,550	$1,250	$1,000	

CDX-R7SHP SERIES LONG ACTION (SHEPHERD) – .300 Win. Mag., .300 Norma Mag., .300 PRC (new 2021), or .338 Lapua Mag. cal., 24, 26, or 27 in. barrel, muzzle brake ready, fully adj. synthetic stock, adj. buttpad, adj. LOP, tool-free adj. cheek rest, built-in micro chassis system, action rail, Black, Tan, OD Green, Hybrid Stealth Shadow, Stealth Shadow Vortex, Hybrid Tan/Black, or Hybrid Green/Black finish, 13 1/2 lbs. New 2017.

MSR $3,370	$2,850	$2,500	$2,150	$1,950	$1,600	$1,300	$1,000	

Add $612 for .300 Norma Mag. cal.

CDX-R7 SPTR – 6.5 Creedmoor, 6.5 PRC, .308 Win., .300 WSM, 7mm Rem. Mag., .28 Nosler, .300 Win. Mag., .300 PRC, or .338 Lapua Mag. cal., 20, 24, 26, or 27 in. Cadex Sporter stainless steel fluted barrel, hunting style muzzle brake, AICS mag. compatible, stainless steel construction, Tundra Strike synthetic Monte Carlo rifle stock w/aluminum bedding, rubberized grip, interchangeable pinned top rail, several finish options available, approx. 8.5 lbs. New 2020.

Please contact the manufacturer directly for pricing and availability on this model.

GRADING - PPGS™	100%	98%	95%	90%	80%	70%	60%	LAST MSR

CAEM, RENATO

Previous manufacturer of small gauge SxS shotguns located in Marcheno Val Trompia, Italy until 2008.

Renato Caem manufactured approx. 5 best quality scalloped boxlock SxS shotguns annually, only in 20 ga., 28 ga., or .410 bore. This trademark has had very little importation into the U.S, and guns should be appraised individually.

CAESAR GUERINI, Srl

Current manufacturer located in Marcheno, Italy. Currently imported beginning 2003 by Caesar Guerini USA LLC.

SHOTGUNS: O/U, FIELD/HUNTING

All Caesar Guerini 12, 20, and 28 ga. Field Grade shotguns include 5 nickel plated flush choke tubes. On some of the following models, 28 ga. and .410 bore are available as special order only. Please contact the company directly for a current quotation on these small bore offerings.

Add $260 for left-hand or English stock on models, where applicable.

Add $307 for double triggers on 12 ga.

APEX – 12, 20, 28 ga. or .410 bore (combination set only), 26, 28, or 30 in. chrome-lined barrels with 5 choke tubes, SST, full length trigger guard with skeletal grip cap, brass (disc.) or silver bead front sight, hand rubbed oil finish stock with Prince of Wales grip, coin finished w/Invisalloy full coverage scroll engraved receiver, available as combination package, double triggers on 12. ga., left-hand with sideplates, 6 lbs. 5oz.-7 lbs.

MSR $9,295	$7,900	$6,915	$5,925	$5,375	$4,350	$3,555	$3,100	

Add $400 for left-hand stock (available by special order only).

Combination sets were also available on this gun - prices ranged from $9,840-$12,100 (disc.).

This model is available through Caesar Guerini Elite dealers only.

ELLIPSE – 20 ga., 3 in. chambers, round action, 28 in. solid rib barrels, non-selective trigger, checkered round knob stock and forearm with wood buttplate, light perimeter receiver etching, coin finish with Invisalloy, approx. 6 1/2 lbs. Mfg. 2017-2018.

	$4,100	$3,250	$2,950	$2,600	$2,100	$1,675	$1,300	*$4,650*

ELLIPSE CURVE – 12 (disc.), 20, 28 ga., or .410 bore (disc.), 2 3/4 or 3 in. chambers, round body frame, 26 (disc.), 28, or 30 (disc.) in. barrels with 5 nickel plated flush fitting choke tubes, tapered solid rib, non-selective trigger, silver front bead sights, hand rubbed oil finished checkered walnut stock and Ellipse rounded forearm, wooden buttplate recoil pad, pistol grip, manual safety, left-hand stock available, hand polished coin finished receiver with Invisalloy protective finish and fantasy style rose and scroll engraving, approx. 6 1/2 lbs. New mid-2014.

MSR $7,895	$6,725	$5,885	$5,050	$4,575	$3,700	$3,050	$2,625	

Combination package is available on this model with a current MSR of $10,270 (20/28 ga. combo).

This model is available through Caesar Guerini Elite dealers only.

ELLIPSE EVO – 12 (new 2012), 20, or 28 ga., 2 3/4 or 3 in. chambers, rounded action, 28 in. barrels, hand polished coin finish alloy receiver with Invisalloy protective finish, silver front bead sight, checkered walnut stock with hand rubbed oil finish, Ellipse rounded forend and buttplate, checkered pistol grip, manual or automatic safety, scroll and floral engraving, 20 and 28 ga. combo, left-hand stock, English style stock, includes plastic hard case, 6 lbs. 5 oz.-7 lbs. New mid-2010.

MSR $7,225	$6,150	$5,380	$4,615	$4,180	$3,385	$2,800	$2,400	

A 20/28 ga. combination package was available until 2020 (last MSR was $9,370).

* ***Ellipse Evo Light*** – 12, 20, 28 ga. or .410 bore, 2 3/4 or 3 in. chambers, 28 in. barrels, similar to Ellipse Evo, except is lightweight, 5 1/2 lbs. New mid-2012.

MSR $7,225	$6,150	$5,380	$4,615	$4,180	$3,385	$2,800	$2,400	

ELLIPSE LIMITED – 20 or 28 ga., 28 in. barrels, 2 3/4 (28 ga.) or 3 (20 ga.) in. chambers, color case hardened receiver with light border line engraving, semi-deluxe checkered Turkish walnut stock with hand rubbed oil finish, gold trigger, approx. 6 1/2 lbs. Limited mfg. 2012.

	$3,825	$3,250	$2,750	$2,350	$1,800	$1,500	$1,200	*$4,395*

A combination set was available in this model for $6,175.

ESSEX – 12, 20, 28 ga. or .410 bore, 26 (disc.), 28, or 30 (20 ga. only) in. barrels, tapered solid rib, round knob pistol grip stock, coin finished sideplates with English rose and scroll engraving, combination package. Less than 100 mfg. for importation during 2006.

	$4,200	$3,575	$3,150	$2,675	$2,275	$1,950	$1,650	*$4,895*

Add $155 for .410 bore.

Combination packages were available on this model and had MSRs in the $6,620-$8,500 range.

GRADING - PPGS™	100%	98%	95%	90%	80%	70%	60%	LAST MSR

* ***Essex Limited*** – 20 or 28 ga., similar to Essex, except has case colored finish, full coverage English scroll engraving, 28 in. barrels. Mfg. 2009-2011.

	$4,300	$3,650	$3,175	$2,700	$2,300	$2,000	$1,500	*$5,095*

FLYWAY – 12 ga., 3 in. chambers, 28 or 30 in. barrels, beavertail forend, multichokes, blued boxlock receiver with satin finish and gold mallard on bottom, parallel 10mm top rib, shipped with hard case, 7 lbs.14 oz.-8 lbs.

	$1,795	$1,495	$1,295	$1,095	$895	$800	$725	*$2,295*

FORUM – 12, 20, 28 ga., or .410 bore (new 2006), 2 3/4 or 3 in. chambers, 26, 28, or 30 in. barrels, multichokes, Schnabel forend, checkered stock with oil finish, Prince of Wales grip, coin finished boxlock receiver, blind sideplates with no visible screws, Bulino style engraving with game scenes and floral scroll, combination packages, factory hard case, left-hand available by special order only, 6 lbs. 5 oz.-7 lbs.

MSR $12,225	$10,400	$9,100	$7,800	$7,075	$5,725	$4,700	$4,100	

Combination packages were available on this model, and had MSRs in the $11,700-$13,915 range (disc.).

This model is available through Caesar Guerini Elite dealers only.

MAGNUS – 12, 20, 28 ga., or .410 bore (mfg. 2006-disc.), 2 3/4 or 3 in. chambers, 26 (disc.), 28, or 30 in. chrome-lined barrels, 5 nickel plated flush fitting chokes, coin finish (mfg. 2013-disc.) or case colored steel receiver with Invisalloy protective finish, SST, silver front bead sight, checkered wood stock with hand rubbed oil finish, Schnabel forend, wood buttplate, Prince of Wales grip, gold grouse, pheasant, and quail game scenes, includes plastic hard case, left-hand or English stock, available in combination packages, 6 lbs. 4 oz.-7 lbs.

MSR $5,385	$4,575	$4,000	$3,430	$3,110	$2,515	$2,075	$1,800	

Add $165 for .410 bore (mfg. 2006-disc.).

Combination packages are available on this model, and have current MSRs of $7,715 (20/28 ga. combo) or $10,250 (20/28/.410 ga. combo).

* ***Magnus Light*** – 12, 20, 28 ga., or .410 bore (mfg. 2006-2018), 2 3/4 or 3 in. chambers, similar to the Magnus, left-hand or English stock, combination package, 5 lbs. 4 oz.-6 lbs.

MSR $5,385	$4,575	$4,000	$3,430	$3,110	$2,515	$2,075	$1,800	

Add $165 for .410 bore (mfg. 2006-2018).

Combination packages are available on this model, and have current MSRs of $7,715 (20/28 ga. combo) or $10,250 (20/28/.410 ga. combo).

MAXUM – 12, 20, 28 ga., or .410 bore (disc.), 26 (disc.), 28, or 30 (disc.) in. chrome-lined barrels, SST, silver front bead sight, deluxe checkered oil finished Turkish walnut stock, Schnabel forend and wood buttplate, manual or automatic safety, deep relief floral scroll engraving, coin finished sideplates w/Invisalloy protective finish receiver, left-hand or English stock, combination packages, 6 lbs. 5 oz.-7 lbs. Importation began 2006.

MSR $7,175	$6,100	$5,350	$4,575	$4,150	$3,350	$2,750	$2,395	

Combination packages was available on this model, and had MSRs in the $7,875-$9,925 range (disc.).

* ***Maxum Light*** – 12, 20, 28 ga. or .410 bore, similar to Maxum, except is lighter weight and available with 28 in. barrels only. Mfg. mid-2010-2012.

	$5,050	$4,300	$3,650	$3,100	$2,500	$2,100	$1,625	*$5,775*

Add $215 for left-hand or English stock.

Combination packages were available with MSRs in the $7,595-$9,650 range.

REVENANT – 20 ga., 3 in. chambers, round body action, 26 (special order only), 28 or 30 in. chrome-lined barrels w/tapered solid top and mid-rib, multi-chokes, non-selective trigger, long trigger guard, silver front bead sight, hand-rubbed oil finished checkered stock, wood buttplate, ellipse rounded forend, manual safety, winged forend iron and inlaid escutcheon, optional automatic safety, includes choke wrench and special Revenant hard case, right or left-hand stock, 6 lbs. 11 oz. New 2019.

MSR $13,895	$11,800	$10,325	$8,850	$8,025	$6,500	$5,325	$4,630	

Add $400 for left-hand stock (available by special order only).

This model is available through Caesar Guerini Elite dealers only.

TEMPIO – 12, 20, 28 ga., or .410 bore (new 2006), 2 3/4 or 3 in. chambers, 26, 28, or 30 in. chrome-lined barrels, multi-chokes, SST, silver front bead sight, checkered wood stock and buttplate with hand rubbed oil finish, Schnabel forend, Prince of Wales grip, manual safety, grey "Tinaloy" boxlock receiver featuring gold grouse, quail, and pheasant game scenes surrounded by scroll, includes plastic hard case, hand polished coin finished receiver with Invisalloy, left-hand or English stock, available in combination packages, 6 lbs. 4 oz.-7 lbs.

MSR $4,525	$3,850	$3,370	$2,890	$2,620	$2,120	$1,735	$1,500	

Add $200 for .410 bore (new 2006, MSR $4,725).

Combination packages are available on this model, and have current MSRs of $6,810(20/28 ga. combo) or $9,290 (20/28/.410 ga. combo).

GRADING - PPGS™	100%	98%	95%	90%	80%	70%	60%	LAST MSR

* ***Tempio Light*** – 12, 20 or 28 ga., 2 3/4 or 3 in. chambers, similar to Tempio, except has lighter barrels and stock, 26 or 28 in. chrome-lined barrels, nickel alloy receiver with Invisalloy and bulino style engraving with gold inlays, available as 20/28 ga. combination package, 6 lbs. 4 oz.-7 lbs. New mid-2008.

MSR $4,525	$3,850	$3,370	$2,890	$2,620	$2,120	$1,735	$1,500	

Combination package is available on this model, and has a current MSR of $6,810 (20/28 ga. combo).

TEMPIO SE "SOUTHEAST EDITION" – 20, 28 ga., or .410 bore, 2 3/4 or 3 in. chambers, 28 in. barrels, 5 nickel plated flush fitting chokes, receiver has choice of case colored or hand polished coin finish, both with Invisalloy protective finish, single selective gold trigger, silver front bead sight, checkered wood stock with hand rubbed oil finish, wood buttplate, Schnabel forend, doves and game scene engraving on left receiver, pair of Bobwhite quail and game scene on the right, includes plastic hard case, case colored finish, 6 lbs. 5 oz.-6 lbs. 10 oz. Limited mfg. 2019-2020.

	$3,675	$3,225	$2,750	$2,500	$2,025	$1,650	$1,285	*$4,325*

Current MSR for the 20/28 ga. combo is $6,475.
Current MSR for the 20/28/.410 combo is $8,815.

WOODLANDER – 12, 20, 28 ga., or .410 bore (mfg. 2006-2018), 2 3/4 or 3 in. chambers, right or left-hand acton, 26, 28 (12 ga. only), or 30 in. barrels, 5 nickel plated flush fitting chokes, 6mm top rib, SST, silver front bead sight, checkered wood stock with hand rubbed oil finish, wood buttplate, Schnabel forend, Prince of Wales grip, manual safety, case hardened boxlock receiver with Bulino style engraving (ruffed grouse in gold on bottom of receiver), Invisalloy finish, includes plastic hard case, 6 lbs. 5 oz.-6 lbs. 14 oz.

MSR $3,995	$3,400	$2,975	$2,550	$2,310	$1,877	$1,550	$1,325	

Add $260 for left-hand stock.
Combination packages are available on this model, and have current MSRs of $6,725 (20/28 ga. combo) or $8,760 (20/28/.410 ga. combo).

SHOTGUNS: O/U SKEET

Add $260 for left-hand stock.

CHALLENGER IMPACT SKEET – 12 ga., 28 or 30 in. barrels w/adj. Impact VR barrels and 6 chokes, hand polished coin finished receiver, gold trigger, deluxe checkered wood stock, Acanthus leaf and scroll engraving, four gauge Skeet set optional, approx. 8 1/2 lbs. Mfg. 2012-2018.

	$6,300	$5,000	$4,500	$4,075	$3,275	$2,675	$2,075	*$7,350*

A four gauge Skeet set was available in this model for $10,225.

SUMMIT IMPACT SKEET – 12 ga., 28 (disc.) or 30 in. VR barrels, Impact rib is 40% lower than usual, Briley Ultra-Lite skeet tubes, satin blue receiver light floral scroll engraving, DTS trigger system, oil finished checkered walnut stock with adj. comb and semi-beavertail forearm, four gauge Skeet is optional, available in left-hand stock, approx. 8 lbs. Disc. 2020.

	$5,185	$4,535	$3,895	$3,525	$3,000	$2,600	$2,000	*$6,100*

A four gauge Skeet set is available for $8,625.

SHOTGUNS: O/U, SPORTING CLAYS

On some of the following models, 28 ga. and .410 bore are available as special order only. Please contact the company directly for a current quotation on these small bore offerings.
Add $260 for left-hand stock where applicable.
Add $410 for adj. comb where applicable.
Add $285 for double triggers on 12 ga.
Add $200 for left-hand with sideplates (disc. 2012).

APEX SPORTING – 12, 20, 28 ga., or .410 bore, 30, 32, or 34 in. barrels, similar to Apex Field, except has high grade English walnut stock, approx. 8 lbs. New 2009.

MSR $9,750	$9,600	$8,400	$7,200	$6,530	$5,280	$4,325	$3,250	

Combination sets and left-handed stocks are available on this model by special order only (disc.).

This model is available through Caesar Guerini Elite dealers only.

CHALLENGER ASCENT SPORTING – 12 ga. only, 2 3/4 in. chambers, 30 or 32 in. VR barrels with 6 MAXIS choke tubes, engraved coin finished receiver, DTS trigger system with two trigger pull weight options, deluxe checkered walnut stock and forearm, includes plastic hard case, left-hand stock available. New 2014.

MSR $6,995	$5,950	$5,200	$4,465	$4,050	$3,275	$2,680	$2,325	

GRADING - PPGS™	100%	98%	95%	90%	80%	70%	60%	LAST MSR

CHALLENGER IMPACT – 12 ga., 28, 30, 32, or 34 in. barrels w/adj. Impact VR barrels and 6 MAXIS chokes, hand polished coin finished receiver with Invisalloy, gold trigger, deluxe checkered wood stock w/4-position adj. comb, Acanthus leaf and scroll engraving, approx. 8 1/2 lbs. Mfg. 2012-2018.

$6,300 $5,000 $4,500 $4,075 $3,275 $2,675 $2,075 *$7,350*

CHALLENGER IMPACT SPORTING – 12 ga., 2 3/4 in. chambers, 32 or 34 in. w/adj. Impact VR barrels and 6 chokes, gold trigger, hand polished coin finished receiver with Acanthus leaf and scroll engraving, deluxe checkered wood stock, approx. 8 1/2 lbs. Mfg. 2012-2016.

$6,450 $4,225 $4,500 $4,075 $3,275 $2,675 $2,075 *$7,350*

CHALLENGER SPORTING – 12 ga., 30, 32, or 34 in. barrels, coin finished receiver with Invisalloy finish, DTS trigger system, hand rubbed oil finished checkered walnut stock and forearm, vent. rib, six competition chokes, 7 lbs., 14 oz.-8 lbs. 2 oz. Mfg. 2013-2018.

$4,600 $3,650 $3,250 $2,950 $2,350 $1,925 $1,495 *$5,275*

ELLIPSE CURVE GOLD SPORTING (LIMITED EDITION) – 20 or 28 ga., 2 3/4 or 3 in. chambers, boxlock, round body frame, 28 in. barrel with 5 nickel plated flush fitting choke tubes, tapered solid rib, non-selective trigger, silver front bead sights, hand rubbed oil finished deluxe grade Turkish walnut stock and forearm with wooden buttplate recoil pad, Ellipse rounded forend, pistol grip, manual safety, hand polished coin finish with Invisalloy protective finish and fantasy style rose and scroll engraving with gold accents, approx. 6 1/2 lbs. Limited edition mfg. late 2016-2020.

$7,025 $6,150 $5,275 $4,775 $3,875 $3,200 $2,750 *$8,275*

This model is available through Caesar Guerini Elite dealers only.

ELLIPSE EVO SPORTING – 12 ga., 30 or 32 in. VR barrels, alloy receiver, DTS trigger system, White Bradley style front silver center bead sight, hand rubbed oil stock finish, Ellipse rounded forend, checkered pistol grip, manual safety (automatic optional), bold leaf and scroll engraving, black rubber recoil pad, left-hand stock, 7 lbs.14 oz - 8 lbs. Mfg. 2012-2018.

$6,000 $4,800 $4,200 $3,575 $2,875 $2,300 $1,850 *$6,950*

ELLIPSE EVOLUTION SPORTING – 12 ga., 32 in. barrels, bold leaf and scroll engraving, deluxe checkered Turkish walnut stock. Mfg. mid-2012-2018.

$7,500 $6,050 $5,400 $4,775 $3,850 $3,125 $2,425 *$8,775*

Left-hand stock is only available with a custom stock purchase.

ESSEX LIMITED GOLD SPORTING (LIMITED EDITION) – 12 ga., 2 3/4 in. chambers, 30 or 32 in. VR barrels, 6 MAXIS competition chokes, case colored receiver with Invisalloy protective finish, white, rose, and yellow gold subjects framed by English scroll engraving, DTS trigger system, white Bradley style front sight with silver center bead, extra deluxe Turkish walnut checkered stock and rounded forend, hand rubbed oil finish, black rubber recoil pad, includes hard plastic case, 8 lbs. Limited importation beginning 2017.

MSR $8,350 $7,100 $6,215 $5,325 $4,830 $3,900 $3,225 $2,775

FORUM SPORTING – 12, 20, 28 ga., or .410 bore (new 2006), 30, 32, or 34 (12 ga. only) in. barrels, DTS trigger system, Premium English walnut stock with hand-rubbed oil finish, rounded forend, manual safety (automatic optional), Bulino style game scene engraving, blind sideplates with no visible screws, coin finished sideplate boxlock receiver, left-hand stock available, approx. 8 lbs.

MSR $12,995 $11,050 $9,670 $8,290 $7,515 $6,080 $4,975 $4,325

This model is available through Caesar Guerini Elite dealers only.

INVICTUS I ASCENT – 12 ga., 2 3/4 in. chambers, 30 or 32 in. VR barrels with 6 Maxis extended choke tubes, adj. DPS trigger, oil finished deluxe Turkish Monte Carlo walnut stock and round forearm, coin finish with Invisalloy, left-hand stock and adj. comb options available, approx. 8 1/4 lbs. New 2017.

MSR $8,795 $7,475 $6,540 $5,600 $5,085 $4,110 $3,375 $2,925

INVICTUS III ASCENT – 12 ga., 2 3/4 in. chambers, 30 or 32 in. VR barrels w/6-Maxis extended choke tubes, adj. DPS trigger (available as ST or DT), White Bradley style front silver center bead sight, oil finished deluxe walnut stock and round forearm, manual safety, black rubber recoil pad, includes plastic hard case, coin finish with Invisalloy, left-hand stock and adj. comb options available, approx. 8 1/4 lbs. New late 2018.

MSR $9,975 $8,485 $7,425 $6,365 $5,775 $4,665 $3,825 $3,325

INVICTUS V ASCENT – 12 ga., 2 3/4 in. chambers, modular locking system, sideplate action, 30 or 32 in. chrome-lined VR barrels w/6-Maxis competition choke tubes, adj. DPS trigger (available as ST or DT), White Bradley style front silver center bead sight, oil finished deluxe walnut stock and round forearm, manual safety, full-coverage engraving, black rubber recoil pad, includes plastic hard case, coin finish with Invisalloy, left-hand stock option available, approx. 8 1/4 lbs. New late 2018.

MSR $10,795 $9,175 $8,030 $6,880 $6,240 $5,050 $4,130 $3,600

This model is available through Caesar Guerini Elite dealers only.

GRADING - PPGS™	100%	98%	95%	90%	80%	70%	60%	LAST MSR

INVICTUS I SPORTING/INVICTUS I SPORTING M-SPEC – 12 ga., 2 3/4 in. chamber, wider target frame, hinge trunions extend out from monobloc, 28, 30, or 32 in. vent. rib barrels with 6 Maxis competition chokes or fixed chokes (Invictus I Sporting M-Spec, new 2017), white Bradley style front silver center bead sight, hand rubbed oil finished 26 LPI checkered pistol grip walnut stock and forearm, rubber recoil pad, light scroll engraving, five DuoCon forcing cones, hand polished coin finished receiver with Invisalloy protective finish, left-hand stock and adj. comb options available, approx. 8 lbs. New 2014.

MSR $7,775	$6,600	$5,775	$4,950	$4,490	$3,630	$2,975	$2,600	

INVICTUS II SPORTING – 12 ga., 2 3/4 in. chambers, 32 in. VR barrels, 6 MAXIS competition chokes, case colored receiver with Invisalloy protective finish, DPS trigger system, white Bradley style front sight with silver center bead, checkered wood stock with hand rubbed oil finish, rounded forend, black rubber recoil pad, includes plastic hard case, 8 lbs. 3 oz. New 2020.

MSR $7,925	$6,750	$5,900	$5,065	$4,590	$3,715	$3,050	$2,625	

INVICTUS III SPORTING – 12 ga., 2 3/4 in. chambers, 30 or 32 in. barrels, 6 MAXIS competition chokes, 5 in. DuoCon forcing cones, DPS ultra-crisp trigger system, white Bradley style front sights with silver center bead, hand rubbed oil finished wood stock, rounded forend, black rubber recoil pad, 26 LPI checkering, includes plastic hard case, hand polished coin finish receiver with Invisalloy, left-hand stock and adj. comb options available, 8 lbs. New 2019.

MSR $8,915	$7,585	$6,635	$5,690	$5,160	$4,175	$3,425	$2,975	

* ***Invictus III Sporting Limited (Limited Edition)*** – 12 ga., 2 3/4 in. chamber, 30 or 32 in. VR chrome-lined barrel, 6 MAXIS competition chokes, 5 DuoCon forcing cones, case colored receiver with Invisalloy protective finish, White Bradley style front sight with silver center bead, wood stock with hand rubbed oil finish, rounded forend, black rubber recoil pad, 26 LPI checkering, includes plastic hard case, 8-8.3 lbs. Limited mfg. beginning 2021.

MSR $8,695	$7,400	$6,475	$5,550	$5,030	$4,070	$3,330	$2,900	

INVICTUS V SPORTING – 12 ga., 2 3/4 in. chambers, wider target frame, hinge trunions extend out from monobloc, 30 or 32 in. VR barrels with 6 Maxis competition chokes, coin-finished engraved sideplates with gold inlays, white Bradley-style front sight with silver center bead, oil rubbed 26 LPI checkered pistol grip, walnut stock and forearm, rubber recoil pad, light scroll engraving, hand polished coin finished receiver with Invisalloy, left-hand stock and adj. comb options available, approx. 8 lbs. New 2017.

MSR $9,895	$8,400	$7,350	$6,300	$5,710	$4,620	$3,780	$3,300	

This model is available through Caesar Guerini Elite dealers only.

INVICTUS VII SPORTING – 12 ga., 2 3/4 in. chambers, 30 or 32 in. VR barrels, 6 MAXIS competition chokes, 5 in. DuoCon forcing cones, DPS trigger system, white Bradley-style front sights with silver center bead, oil rubbed wooden stock, black rubber recoil pad, rounded forend, 26 LPI checkering, includes plastic hard case, receiver has hand polished coin finish with Invisalloy, left-hand stock and adj. comb options available, 8 lbs. 1 oz. New 2019.

MSR $9,920	$8,450	$7,400	$6,300	$5,750	$4,650	$3,800	$2,950	

This model is available through Caesar Guerini Elite dealers only.

MAGNUS SPORTING – 12, 20, 28 ga., or .410 bore (mfg. 2006-2012), 30, 32, or 34 (12 ga. only, disc. 2018) in. barrels, sideplate grey "Tinaloy" boxlock receiver featuring gold grouse, quail, and pheasant game scenes, 10mm parallel vent. top rib, vent. barrels, pistol grip stock and Schnabel forend, adj. trigger, extended choke tubes, factory hard case, 7 lbs. 4 oz.-8 lbs. 2 oz.

MSR $6,095	$5,185	$4,535	$3,890	$3,525	$2,850	$2,335	$2,025	

Add $165 for .410 bore (disc. 2012).

Add $405 for case hardened receiver.

Combination packages are available on this model, and have current MSRs of $8,870 (20/28 ga. combo) or $11,800 (20/28/.410 ga. combo).

* ***Magnus Sporting Limited Edition*** – 12 ga., 30, 32, or 34 in. barrels, case hardened receiver with engraved sideplates and gold inlays, deluxe grade oil finished Turkish walnut stock and forearm. Mfg. mid-2008-2012.

	$4,400	$3,750	$3,175	$2,700	$2,150	$1,750	$1,375	*$5,055*

* ***Magnus Sporting Limited (Current Mfg.)*** – 12, 20, or 28 ga., 2 3/4 in. chamber, 30 or 32 in. chrome-lined VR barrel, 6 MAXIS or CCP competition chokes, White Bradley style front sight with silver center bead, case colored receiver with Invisalloy protective finish, DTS trigger, wood stock with hand rubbed oil finish, Schnabel forend, black rubber recoil pad, includes plastic hard case, 7.6-8 lbs.

MSR $6,500	$5,525	$4,835	$4,145	$3,755	$3,040	$2,485	$2,150	

Combination packages are available on this model and have current MSRs of $9,275 (20/28 ga. combo) or $12,205 (20/28/.410 ga. combo).

GRADING - PPGS™	100%	98%	95%	90%	80%	70%	60%	LAST MSR

MAXUM SPORTING – 12, 20 (disc.), 28 (disc.) ga., or .410 (disc.) bore, 28 (disc.), 30, 32, or 34 (disc.) in. barrels, extended sporting chokes, DTS trigger system, White Bradley style front silver center bead sights, deluxe checkered oil finished Turkish walnut stock and forearm, Schnabel forend, manual safety (automatic optional), coin finished sideplates with deep relief floral scroll engraving, hand polished coin finish receiver, extended sporting chokes, combination packages available, approx. 7 1/2-8 lbs. Importation began 2006.

MSR $7,725	$6,575	$5,755	$4,930	$4,475	$3,615	$2,960	$2,575	

Combination packages had MSRs in the $8,495-$10,675 range.

MAXUM GOLD SPORTING (LIMITED EDITION) – 12 ga., 2 3/4 in. chamber, 30 or 32 in. barrels, 6 MAXIS competition chokes, DTS trigger system with two trigger pull weight options, take up, over travel, and LOP adjustments, White Bradley style front silver center bead sights, Turkish walnut stock with 26 LPI checkering and natural oil finish, black rubber recoil pad, Schnabel forend, deep relief gothic scroll engraving on receiver, sideplates, and forend assembly, hand polished coin finish receiver with Invisalloy, includes plastic hard case with fit interior and velvet stock and barrel sleeve, approx. 8 lbs. Limited mfg. late 2018-2020.

	$6,975	$6,100	$5,250	$4,750	$3,850	$3,150	$2,450	*$7,750*

Add $240 for left-hand stock.
Add $385 for adj. comb.

MAXUM IMPACT – 12 ga., 30 or 32 in. barrels w/adj. Impact rib and 6 Maxis choke tubes, coin finished sideplates with deep relief floral scroll engraving, deluxe checkered oil finished Turkish walnut stock w/4-position comb with grooved forearm, left-hand stock available. Importation began 2006.

MSR $9,815	$8,350	$7,305	$6,265	$5,680	$4,595	$3,775	$3,275	

MAXUM IMPACT SPORTING – 12 or 20 ga., 30, 32, or 34 in. barrels, also available in Unsingle Combo in 12 ga., 7 lbs. 11 oz. - 8 lbs., 7 oz. Mfg. mid-2010-2013.

	$7,700	$6,150	$5,350	$4,750	$3,825	$3,125	$2,425	*$8,450*

Add $2,350 for Unsingle Combo in 12 ga.
Add $220 for left-hand (not available in 20 ga.).

SUMMIT ASCENT SPORTING – 12 ga., 30 or 32 in. barrels, 10mm high tapered top rib, checkered walnut stock with adj. comb, case colored hardened receiver with light engraving, gold trigger, left-hand stock available. New 2012.

MSR $5,395	$4,585	$4,000	$3,430	$3,110	$2,515	$2,075	$1,800	

SUMMIT IMPACT – 12 or 20 (disc. 2018) ga., 3 in. chambers, 30, 32, or 34 in. barrels w/adj. Impact rib and 6 MAXIS choke tubes, gold trigger, deluxe Turkish walnut stock w/4-position comb and choice of round or grooved semi-beavertail forearm, blued finish, left-hand stock available, 7 3/4-8 3/4 lbs. New 2017.

MSR $6,425	$5,475	$4,790	$4,100	$3,725	$3,010	$2,465	$2,140	

SUMMIT IMPACT SPORTING – 12 or 20 ga., 30, 32, or 34 in. VR barrels, oil finished checkered walnut stock with adj. comb, satin blue receiver with light floral scroll engraving, DTS trigger system, Impact rib is 40% lower than usual, six choke tubes, approx. 8 lbs. Mfg. 2009-2018.

	$5,000	$4,000	$3,750	$3,400	$3,000	$2,600	$2,000	*$5,750*

An Unsingle combo is available for $5,795. A four gauge Skeet set is available for $7,850.

SUMMIT SPORTING – 12, 20, 28 ga., or .410 bore (new 2006), 30, 32, or 34 (12 ga. only) in. vent. barrels, grey "Tinaloy" boxlock receiver with neo-modern engraving, 10mm parallel vent. top rib, adj. trigger, pistol grip stock, Schnabel forend, right hand palm swell, extended choke tubes, factory case, 7 lbs. 4 oz.-8 lbs. 2 oz.

MSR $4,250	$3,625	$3,175	$2,725	$2,465	$1,995	$1,630	$1,425	

Add $200 for .410 bore.
Combination packages are available on this model, and have current MSRs of $6,975 (20/28 ga. combo) or $9,855 (20/28/.410 ga. combo).

* ***Summit Sporting Compact*** – 12 ga., 2 3/4 in. chamber, 28, 30, or 32 (disc. 2018) in. VR barrels, features 13 3/4 in. LOP fixed Monte Carlo stock, grey "Tinaloy" boxlock receiver with neo-modern engraving, 8-10mm parallel vent. top rib, adj. trigger, pistol grip stock, Schnabel forend, right hand palm swell, extended choke tubes, factory case, approx. 7 3/4 lbs.

MSR $4,250	$3,625	$3,175	$2,725	$2,465	$1,995	$1,630	$1,425	

* ***Summit Limited Sporting*** – 12, 20, 28 ga., or .410 bore, 30 or 32 in. barrels, similar to Summit Sporting, except has case hardened receiver.

MSR $4,995	$4,250	$3,700	$3,200	$2,900	$2,350	$1,900	$1,500	

Add $200 for .410 bore.
Combination packages are available on this model, and have current MSRs of $7,845 (20/28 ga. combo) or $10,725 (20/28/.410 ga. combo).

GRADING - PPGS™	100%	98%	95%	90%	80%	70%	60%	LAST MSR

SUMMIT SPORTING BLACK LIMITED EDITION – 12 ga., 2 3/4 in. chambers, 30 or 32 in. barrels, 6 MAXIS competition chokes, 5 in. DuoCon forcing cones, DTS trigger system, white Bradley front sight with silver center bead, hand rubbed oil finished walnut stock, Schnabel forend, black rubber recoil pad, 26 LPI checkering, includes hard plastic case, receiver has satin blued finish with Invisalloy clear protection, 7 lbs. 14 oz. Mfg. 2019-2020.

	$3,595	$2,700	$2,450	$2,100	$1,675	$1,375	$1,075	*$3,975*

SHOTGUNS: O/U, TRAP

APEX TRAP – 12 ga., 32 or 34 in. barrels, available in Unsingle, Top Single Barrel, and combo set configuration, special production run, approx. 9 lbs. Mfg. 2010-2013.

	$8,675	$7,395	$6,325	$5,725	$4,650	$3,800	$2,950	*$9,950*

Combination sets were available starting at $12,295.

CHALLENGER TRAP – 12 ga., 2 3/4 in. chambers, 32 or 34 in. barrels, gold trigger, hand polished coin finished receiver with Acanthus leaf and scroll engraving, deluxe checkered wood stock, approx. 9 lbs. Mfg. 2012-2018.

	$6,400	$5,050	$4,625	$4,100	$3,275	$2,675	$2,075	*$7,350*

An Unsingle combination set is also available in this model for $9,895.

FORUM TRAP – 12 ga., 32 or 34 in. barrels, available in Unsingle, Top Single Barrel, and combo set configuration, special production run, approx. 9 lbs. Mfg. 2010-2012.

	$10,100	$8,600	$7,300	$6,050	$5,200	$4,500	$4,000	*$11,595*

Combination sets were available in this model starting at $13,845.

INVICTUS I TRAP – 12 ga., 32 or 34 in. barrel(s), choice of O/U or Unsingle configuration, manual (automatic is optional), DPS trigger system, white Bradley-style silver centered bead front sight, Monte Carlo stock with DTS 4-way adj. comb and semi-beavertail forend with finger grooves, hand polished coin finish with Invisalloy protective finish, left-hand stock option available, 8-9 lbs. New 2016.

MSR $9,755	$8,300	$7,250	$6,200	$5,650	$4,550	$3,750	$2,900	

A combination set of this model was available for MSR $13,175.

INVICTUS III TRAP – 12 ga., 32 or 34 (unsingle) in barrels., DPS trigger, white Bradley silver center bead front sights, Monte Carlo stock w/adj. comb and semi-beavertail forend w/finger grooves, soft black rubber recoil pad, includes hard case and tools, coin finish, 8-9 lbs. Importation began 2019.

MSR $14,375	$12,220	$10,690	$9,165	$8,310	$6,720	$5,500	$4,275	

INVICTUS V TRAP COMBO SET – 12 ga., 2 3/4 in. chamber, 30, 32 (O/U), or 34 (Unsingle) barrel, standard Invictus features, left-hand stock option available. New 2017.

MSR $15,295	$13,000	$11,400	$9,750	$8,850	$7,150	$5,850	$4,550	

MAGNUS TRAP – 12 ga., 30, 32, or 34 (unsingle only) barrels, case colored action and sideplates, scroll engraved with gold game scenes, deluxe Turkish walnut, 8 - 9 lbs. Mfg. 2007-2012.

	$5,925	$5,025	$4,300	$3,825	$3,225	$2,750	$2,150	*$6,795*

A combination set of this model was available for $9,045.

MAXUM TRAP – 12 ga., 30 (either available as O/U - disc. or Unsingle), 32 (either available as O/U - disc. or Unsingle), or 34 (Unsingle only) in. barrels, hand polished coin finish action, deep engraved receiver, extra deluxe Turkish walnut stock, left-hand stock available, approx. 9 lbs. New 2007.

MSR $9,815	$8,350	$7,300	$6,265	$5,680	$4,595	$3,760	$3,275	

A combination set of this model has an MSR of $12,720.

SUMMIT TRAP – 12 ga., 30 (disc.), 32, or 34 (Unsingle only) in. barrels, adj. comb, grey alloy receiver, choice of O/U, Unsingle, or Top Single configuration, light scroll engraving, adj. comb, approx. 8-8 1/2 lbs. New 2007.

MSR $6,425	$5,475	$4,800	$4,115	$3,725	$3,025	$2,475	$2,150	

A combination set of this model is available for MSR $9,330.

* ***Summit Trap Compact*** – 12 ga., 30, 32, or 34 (Unsingle only) in. barrels, adj. comb, grey alloy receiver, features 13 3/4 in. LOP stock, choice of O/U or Unsingle configuration, light scroll engraving, adj. comb, approx. 8-8 1/2 lbs. New 2017.

MSR $6,425	$5,475	$4,800	$4,115	$3,725	$3,025	$2,475	$2,150	

A combination set of this model is available for MSR $9,330.

SUMMIT IMPACT TRAP – 12 ga., 34 in. VR barrels w/adj. Impact rib, satin blue receiver light floral scroll engraving, DTS trigger system, oil finished checkered walnut stock with adj. comb and semi-beavertail forearm, approx. 8 1/2 lbs. Disc. 2020.

	$5,185	$4,535	$3,895	$3,525	$3,000	$2,600	$2,000	*$6,100*

An Unsingle combination variation is also available on this model with a current MSR of $8,825.

GRADING - PPGS™	100%	98%	95%	90%	80%	70%	60%	LAST MSR

CALICO LIGHT WEAPON SYSTEMS

Current pistol and rifle manufacturer established during 1986, located in Elgin, OR. Previously located in Cornelius, OR from 2010-circa 2018, Hillsboro, OR from 2002-2010, Sparks, NV from 1998-2001, and in Bakersfield, CA.

PISTOLS: SEMI-AUTO

LIBERTY III – 9mm Para. cal., roller delayed blowback action, 6 in. chrome moly ported barrel, 6 lands and grooves, choice of 50 or 100 shot helical feed mag., glass-filled polymer construction, adj. front sight and flip-up (both ghost-ring and notched) rear sight, ribbed forend, rotating sear block safety, 2 1/4 lbs. w/o mag., black or tan/black finish. New 2010.

MSR $862	$725	$650	$580	$515	$450	$385	$340	

* ***Liberty IIIT*** – 9mm Para. cal., roller delayed blowback action, 6 in. chrome moly ported barrel, 6 lands and grooves, choice of 50 or 100 helical feed shot mag., adj. front sight and flip-up (both ghost-ring and notched) rear sight, ribbed forend, rotating sear block safety, aluminum quad rail, black finish, 2 1/4 lbs. w/o mag. New 2011.

MSR $939	$800	$700	$600	$550	$450	$350	$275	

M-110 – .22 LR cal., blowback action, 6 in. chrome moly barrel with muzzle brake, 100 shot helical feed mag., glass-filled polymer construction, includes notched rear sight and adj. windage front sight, 10 1/2 in. sight radius, pistol grip storage compartment, ambidextrous trigger and hammer lock safety, black, tan/black, or Urban Camo/black finish, 2.21 lbs. Mfg. 1989-2001, reintroduced 2007.

MSR $650	$575	$500	$435	$365	$325	$280	$265	

M-950 – 9mm Para. cal., same operating mechanism as the M-900 Carbine, 6 in. barrel, 50 (standard) or 100 shot helical feed mag., 2 1/4 lbs. Mfg. 1989-1994, reintroduced late 2007-2010.

	$775	$700	$650	$600	$500	$450	$400	*$872*

RIFLES/CARBINES: SEMI-AUTO

LIBERTY I CARBINE/LIBERTY I TACTICAL – 9mm Para. cal., roller delayed blowback, 16 in. chrome moly barrel, 50 or 100 shot Helical feed mag., flip-up rear (ghost ring and notched) and adj. front sight, skeletal adj. stock with pistol grip, (some early post-ban specimens had full wood stocks with thumbhole cutouts), rotating sear block safety, aluminum receiver, with (Liberty I, new 2010) or w/o quad rails, glass-filled polymer furniture, black or black/tan (Liberty I Tactical model only) finish, 5 lbs. Mfg. 1995-2001, reintroduced 2007.

MSR $912	$775	$680	$580	$525	$425	$350	$300	

Add $77 for quad rails (Liberty I Tactical, new 2010).

LIBERTY II CARBINE/LIBERTY II TACTICAL – 9mm Para. cal., roller delayed blowback, 16 in. chrome moly, 50 or 100 shot Helical feed mag., flip sight rear (both ghost ring and notched) and adj. front sight, fixed stock with pistol grip, rotating sear block safety, aluminum receiver, with (Liberty II, new 2010) or w/o quad rails, glass-filled polymer construction, black finish, 5.25 lbs. Mfg. 1995-2001, reintroduced 2007.

MSR $932	$795	$695	$595	$540	$435	$375	$310	

Add $77 for quad rails (Liberty II Tactical, new 2010).

LIBERTY 50/LIBERTY 100 CARBINE – 9mm Para. cal., roller delayed blowback, 16 in. chrome moly barrel, 50 or 100 shot Helical feed mag., flip-up rear (ghost ring and notched) and adj. front sight, fixed stock with pistol grip, (some early post-ban specimens had full wood stocks with thumbhole cutouts), rotating sear block safety, aluminum receiver, glass-filled polymer furniture, black finish, 5 lbs. Mfg. 1995-2001, reintroduced 2007.

MSR $781	$665	$575	$500	$450	$375	$300	$250	

Add $51 for 100 shot Helical feed mag. (Liberty 100).

* ***Liberty 50 Tactical/Liberty 100 Tactical*** – 9mm Para. cal., roller delayed blowback action, 16 in. chrome moly barrel, 50 or 100 shot helical feed mag., aluminum alloy receiver, adj. front sight and flip-up (both ghost-ring and notched) rear sight, synthetic fixed stock with pistol grip, ambi rotating sear block safety, quad rails, black finish, 6 1/2 lbs. New 2010.

MSR $859	$725	$635	$550	$500	$400	$325	$285	

Add $50 for Liberty 100 Tactical (100 shots).

M-100 – .22 LR cal., blowback action, 16.1 in. chrome moly, shrouded barrel with flash suppressor/muzzle brake, 100 shot helical feed mag., aluminum alloy receiver, glass-filled polymer construction, adj. front sight for windage, notched rear sight, pistol grip, folding buttstock, ambidextrous (trigger and hammer lock) safety, black, Plumb Crazy Purple/black, or tan/black finish, 4.2 lbs. Mfg. 1986-1994, reintroduced late 2007.

MSR $602	$525	$465	$400	$340	$300	$265	$250	

GRADING - PPGS™	100%	98%	95%	90%	80%	70%	60%	LAST MSR

* ***M-100 Tactical*** – .22 LR cal., similar to M-100, except has quad rails and black, pink/black, or tan/black finish. New 2010.

MSR $675	$585	$500	$435	$365	$325	$280	$265	

* ***M-100 FS*** – .22 LR cal., blowback action, 16.1 in. shrouded barrel, 100 shot helical mag., aluminum receiver, adj. sights, solid stock, ambidextrous (trigger and hammer) safety, black, OD Green/black, or Urban Camo/black finish. Mfg. 1996-2001, reintroduced late 2007.

MSR $602	$525	$465	$400	$340	$300	$265	$250	

* ***M-100 FS Tactical*** – .22 LR cal., similar to M-100 FS, except has quad Picatinny rail, black or OD Green/black finish, 4 1/2 lbs. New 2010.

MSR $675	$585	$500	$435	$365	$325	$280	$265	

M-101 – while advertised, this model never went into production.

M-105 SPORTER – similar to M-100, except has walnut distinctively styled buttstock and forend, 4 3/4 lbs. empty. Mfg. 1989-1994.

	$650	$550	$495	$450	$350	$295	$250	*$335*

M-106 – while advertised, this model never went into production.

M-900 – 9mm Para. cal., roller delayed blowback action, wood (disc.) or collapsible buttstock, cast aluminum receiver with stainless steel bolt, static cocking handle, 16 in. barrel, fixed rear sight with adj. post front, 50 (standard) or 100 shot helical feed mag., ambidextrous safety, black polymer pistol grip and forend, approx. 3.7 lbs. Mfg. 1989-1990, reintroduced 1992-1993, again during 2007-2010.

	$775	$700	$650	$600	$500	$450	$400	*$875*

Add $157 for 100 shot mag.

* ***M-900S*** – similar to M-900, except has non-collapsible shoulder stock. Disc. 1993.

	$700	$625	$525	$475	$400	$350	$300	*$632*

* ***M-901 Canada Carbine*** – 9mm Para. cal., similar to M-900, except has 18 1/2 in. barrel and sliding stock. Disc. 1992.

	$675	$595	$550	$475	$350	$300	$285	*$643*

This model was intended for the Canadian export market and was also available with solid fixed stock (Model 901S).

M-951 TACTICAL CARBINE – 9mm Para. cal., 16.1 in. barrel, similar appearance to M-900 Carbine, except has muzzle brake and extra pistol grip on front of forearm, 4 3/4 lbs. Mfg. 1990-94.

	$775	$700	$650	$600	$500	$450	$400	*$556*

* ***M-951S*** – similar to M-951, except has synthetic buttstock. Mfg. 1991-94.

	$700	$625	$525	$475	$400	$350	$300	*$567*

CAMDON DEFENSE

Current AR-15 manufacturer established in 2017, located in Yuma, AZ.

Please refer to BlueBookOfGunValues.com to order the *Blue Book of AR-15s & Variations*, available as a book or online subscription.

CAMEX-BLASER USA, INC.

Previous importer/distributor of Blaser Jagdwaffen Gmbh rifles.

Previously imported Camex-Blaser rifles can be located in the Blaser section.

CANIK (55)

Current trademark of pistols manufactured by Samsun Domestic Defence and Industry Corporation (a subsidiary of Aral Industry Corporation), established in 1997 and located in Samsun, Turkey. Currently imported beginning 2014 by Century Arms, located in Delray Beach, FL. Previously imported by Tristar circa 2013-2018, located in N. Kansas City, MO. Previously imported circa mid-2010-2011 by Canik-USA, located in Pueblo West, CO.

PISTOLS: SEMI-AUTO

The Canik brand currently includes the striker-fired TP9 Series with variations (see Century Arms for current listings). Canik also produced a line of 1911-style and CZ75 design pistols that included the Shark Series, Stingray Series, Piranha Series, LSC Series, S-FC 100 Series, MKEK Series, and Dolphin Series.

GRADING - PPGS™	100%	98%	95%	90%	80%	70%	60%	LAST MSR

CAPRINUS

Previous shotgun manufacturer located in Varberg, Sweden.

SHOTGUNS: O/U

CAPRINUS SWEDEN – 12 ga., boxlock action, ejectors, ST, stainless steel receiver, unique design breaks down without forearm disassembly, 29 1/2 in. barrels with choke tubes, limited mfg. during early 1980s.

$3,750 $3,250 $2,850 $2,400 $2,000 $1,600 $1,200 *approx. $5,955*

CARACAL

Current manufacturer of semi-auto pistols and rifles (including AR-15 style rifles and pistols) established in 2006, located in Abu Dhabi, United Arab Emirates. Currently imported beginning 2012 by Caracal USA, located in Boise, ID. Previously located in Newinton, NH, Trussville, AL, and Knoxville, TN. Currently distributed in Italy exclusively by Fratelli Tanfoglio Snc, located in Brescia, Italy.

For individual model listings, please go to BlueBookOfGunValues.com/overflow.

CARBON 15

Please refer to the Professional Ordnance (discontinued mfg.) and Bushmaster (current mfg.) listings for more information on this trademark.

CARL GUSTAF

Previous manufacturer located in Eskilstuna, Sweden. Previously imported by Hansen & Co. located in Southport, CT during 1994-1995, and by Precision Sales International located in Westfield, MA during 1991-1993.

RIFLES: BOLT ACTION

MODEL CG 2000 STANDARD GRADE – 6.5x55mm, 7x64mm, 9.3x62mm, .243 Win., .270 Win., .30-06, .308 Win., 7mm Rem. Mag., or .300 Win. Mag. cal., bolt action, Monte Carlo walnut stock with checkering and Wundhammer grip, 24 in. barrel, detachable 3 or 4 shot mag., with or without sights, cold-swaged barrel, 60 degree bolt, 3-way slide safety, 7 1/2 lbs. Imported 1991-95.

$1,325 $1,050 $875 $725 $575 $475 $375 *$1,535*

Add $540 for Mag. cals.

This model was supplied with individual 80 meter signed test targets. This model was also imported as the Fairfax 2000 series.

* ***Model 2000 Luxe Grade*** – .270 Win., .30-06, .308 Win., or 6.5x55mm cal., features choice of regular or Mannlicher deluxe walnut stock. Imported 1995 only.

$1,695 $1,400 $1,200 $975 $825 $650 $475 *$1,935*

A Model 2000 Super-Luxe was also available in 6.5x55mm or .30-06 cal. - retail was $4,250.

MODEL 3000 – various cals., features Sauer action with non-rotating bolt. Previously imported by Aimpoint.

$675 $575 $475 $400 $375 $350 $325

STANDARD BOLT ACTION RIFLE – 6.5x55mm, 7x64mm, .270 Win., 7mm Rem. Mag., .308 Win., .30-06, or 9.3x62mm cal., 24 in. barrel, folding rear sight, checkered classic style stock. Mfg. 1970-77.

$475 $425 $350 $315 $285 $250 $225

* ***Standard Bolt Action Rifle w/Monte Carlo stock***

$525 $450 $395 $350 $300 $275 $250

GRADE II – similar to Monte Carlo Standard, in .22-250 Rem., .25-06 Rem., 6.5x55mm, .270 Win., 7mm Rem. Mag., .308 Win., .30-06, or .300 Win. Mag. cal., select stock and rosewood pistol grip cap, and forearm tip.

$500 $425 $375 $325 $295 $275 $250

GRADE III – similar to Grade II, except fancy wood, deluxe high gloss finish.

$575 $475 $425 $350 $325 $300 $275

DELUXE – similar to Grade III, except engraved floorplate and trigger guard, Deluxe French walnut, and jeweled bolt.

$675 $575 $475 $400 $375 $350 $325

VARMINT TARGET MODEL – .222 Rem., .22-250 Rem., .243 Win., or 6.5x55mm cal., bolt action, fast lock time, 27 in. barrel, no sights, large bakelite bolt knob, target type stock. Mfg. 1970. Disc.

$550 $495 $440 $385 $360 $320 $290

GRADING - PPGS™	100%	98%	95%	90%	80%	70%	60%	LAST MSR

GRAND PRIX SINGLE SHOT TARGET – .22 LR cal., fastest lock time bolt action, 27 in. heavy barrel with adj. weight, no sights, target stock, adj. buttplate. Mfg. 1970. Disc.

	$550	$495	$440	$385	$360	$320	$290	

CAROLINA ARMS GROUP

Previous pistol manufacturer located in Mooresville, NC until circa 2018.

For individual model listings, please go to BlueBookOfGunValues.com/overflow.

CASARTELLI, CARLO

Previous manufacturer located in Brescia, Italy until 2000. Previously imported and distributed until 1999 by New England Arms Corp. located in Kittery Point, ME.

Casartelli rifles and shotguns were available through special order only. Virtually any custom gun configuration could be manufactured to the customer's exact specifications and requirements.

RIFLES

AFRICA MODEL - BOLT ACTION – various heavy and Mag. cals., square bridge Mauser action, full coverage game scene engraving appropriate to caliber, takedown, limited production.

	$10,200	$7,500	$5,900	$5,300	$4,700	$4,100	$3,600	*$12,000*

SAFARI MODEL - BOLT ACTION – standard cals., regular Mauser action, full coverage game scene engraving, limited production.

	$6,250	$5,900	$5,250	$4,950	$4,150	$3,650	$3,150	*$8,250*

KENYA - DOUBLE RIFLE – most standard and Mag. cals., sidelock action, elaborate game scene and/or scroll engraving, limited production.

	$24,250	$21,500	$17,750	$14,750	$12,000	$9,950	$8,250	*$35,000*

SHOTGUNS: SxS

SIDELOCK MODEL – various gauges, elaborate game scene and/or scroll engraving, limited production.

	$13,000	$9,750	$7,900	$6,500	$5,200	$4,250	$3,750	*$17,000*

CASPIAN ARMS, LTD

Current parts manufacturer established during 1976, located in Wolcott, VT. Dealer direct sales only. Caspian Arms, LTD. is a subsidiary of Foster Industries, Inc.

Caspian Arms currently fabricates high quality aluminum (new 2012), steel, stainless steel, titanium (new 2002), and alloy (disc. 2006) frames for the Colt Government Model 1911/A1, both in standard and high capacity frames. Frame sizes include the Government, Commander, and Officer's. Caspian Arms Ltd. also manufactures slides, including a damascus variation, and related small parts, in addition to having many special order machine operations available. Please contact them directly for current information on their extensive line of pistol-related components.

PISTOLS: SEMI-AUTO

VIETNAM COMMEMORATIVE – .45 ACP, total production was 1,000, hand engraved by J.J. Adams, nickel plated, service branch medallion installed in grips. Limited mfg. 1986-93.

	$1,450	$995	$795	N/A	N/A	N/A	N/A	*$1,500*

Add $350 for gold plating.
Add $200 for serial numbers below RVN100.

This Vietnam Commemorative was also available in 24Kt. gold hand inlay edition for $14,000 - very limited production.

CASULL ARMS CORPORATION

Previous manufacturer and distributor located in Afton, WY 1996-2005.

For individual model listings, please go to BlueBookOfGunValues.com/overflow.

CATMA ARMS

Current manufacturer of shotguns established in 2015, located in Konya, Turkey. No current U.S. importation.

Catma Arms currently manufactures O/U, SxS, and semi-auto (including AR-15 style) shotguns in a variety of configurations. Please contact the company directly for more information and availability.

GRADING - PPGS™	100%	98%	95%	90%	80%	70%	60%	LAST MSR

CAVALRY

Current trademark of O/U shotguns imported by American Tactical Imports. Please refer to their listing in the "A" section.

CAVALRY ARMS CORPORATION

Previous AR-15 style manufacturer located in Gilbert, AZ until 2010. Previously located in Mesa, AZ.

Please refer to BlueBookOfGunValues.com to order the *Blue Book of AR-15s & Variations*, available as a book or online subscription.

CENTURION ARMS

Current manufacturer of AR-15 style pistols, rifles, parts, and accessories located in Morgantown, IN.

Please refer to BlueBookOfGunValues.com to order the *Blue Book of AR-15s & Variations*, available as a book or online subscription.

CENTURION ORDNANCE, INC.

Previous importer located in Helotes, TX. Centurion Ordnance also imported Aguila ammunition.

SHOTGUNS: SLIDE ACTION

POSEIDON – 12 ga., 1 3/4 in. chamber (shoots "mini-shells" and slugs), 18 1/4 in. smoothbore barrel, 13 in. LOP, black synthetic stock and forearm, 6 shot mag., adj. rear sight, 5 lbs., 5 oz. Limited importation 2001.

	100%	98%	95%	90%	80%	70%	60%	LAST MSR
	$285	$250	$225	$200	$185	$170	$155	

While prototypes of this model were imported briefly during 2001, this gun never made it into the consumer marketplace.

Mini-shells retailed for $12.60 for a box of 20 (shot sizes include 7, #4 & #1 buckshot).

CENTURY ARMS

Previous manufacturer circa 1996-1998 located in Balwyn, Victoria, Australia.

RIFLES: SINGLE SHOT

REWA RIFLE – 4 bore ball, break open action, massive single shot with case colored and engraved action, deluxe checkered stock and forearm with ebony tip, iron sights, production limited to a few prototypes only (a convertible shotgun barrel was also planned).

Extreme rarity precludes accurate pricing on this model.

CENTURY ARMS (CENTURY INTERNATIONAL ARMS, INC.)

Current importer and distributor founded in 1961 with current corporate offices located in Delray Beach, FL. Century International Arms, Inc. was previously headquartered in St. Albans, VT until 1997, and Boca Raton, FL from 1997-2004. The company rebranded in late 2014 and is now known as Century Arms.

Century Arms imports a variety of currently manufactured pistols, carbines, rifles, and shotguns, in addition to surplus military rifles, shotguns, and pistols. Because inventory changes often, especially on tactical style rifles, carbines and pistols, please contact the company directly for the most recent offerings and pricing.

Additionally, Century Arms imports a wide range of accessories, including bayonets, holsters, stocks, magazines, grips, mounts, scopes, misc. parts, new and surplus ammunition, etc., and should be contacted directly.

PISTOLS: SEMI-AUTO

Century International Arms Inc. also imported the Arcus pistols from Bulgaria and Daewoo pistols from South Korea. Please refer to the individual sections for more information.

C39V2 – 7.62x39mm cal., 10.6 in. chrome moly barrel, birdcage flash hider, 30 shot mag., larger T-shaped mag. catch, RAK-1 enhanced trigger group, standard AKM sights, front sight gas block, MOE AK pistol grip, milled ordnance quality steel Nitride treated receiver, compatible with AKM furniture, QD attachments on rear of receiver, MOE AK handguard, 6.9 lbs. Mfg. in the U.S. 2016-2020.

	100%	98%	95%	90%	80%	70%	60%	LAST MSR
	$750	$650	$565	$510	$415	$350	$285	*$880*

Add $70 for Shockwave blade (pistol brace).

C93 PISTOL – 5.56 NATO cal., patterned after the HK53, roller delayed blowback action, 8 1/2 in. barrel with flash suppressor, fluted chamber, includes two 40 shot mags., adj. rear sight, 6.4 lbs. Mfg. 2012-2014.

	100%	98%	95%	90%	80%	70%	60%	LAST MSR
	$900	$795	$675	$625	$495	$400	$315	

GRADING - PPGS™	100%	98%	95%	90%	80%	70%	60%	LAST MSR

CENTURION 39 AK PISTOL – 7.62x39mm cal., AK-47 design, features 11 3/8 in. barrel with M16 style birdcage muzzle brake, machined receiver, quad Picatinny rails, Tapco G2 trigger, ergonomic pistol grip, black polymer furniture, optional Shark Fin front sight, 5.4 lbs. Mfg. in the U.S. 2011-2016.

	$630	$550	$475	$425	$350	$285	$240	*$735*

* ***Centurion 39 Micro Pistol*** – 7.62x39mm cal., AK-47 design, similar to C39 pistol, except has 6 1/4 in. barrel, includes one 10 shot mag. and one 30 shot mag. Mfg. 2014-2016.

	$800	$700	$625	$550	$485	$415	$375	*$940*

COLEFIRE MAGNUM – 7.62 Tokarev cal., styled after the Sterling Mk7 pistol, Manganese Phosphate finish coated with black wrinkle paint, enlarged and knurled charging handle, 4 1/2 in. barrel, SA, optional accessory rail. Disc.

	$575	$500	$425	$400	$325	$275	$200	

This model did not include a magazine (sold separately).

CZ 40/CZ 40 COMPACT – .40 S&W cal., 3 1/2 (Compact) or 4 1/4 in. barrel, 10 shot double column mag., ambidextrous controls, white dot sights, inertial firing pin, loaded chamber indicator, decocking lever, mfg. by Zastava. Imported 2013-2014.

	$375	$325	$275	$250	$200	$175	$125	

CZ 999/CZ 999 COMPACT – 9mm Para. cal., 3 1/2 (Compact) or 4 1/4 in. barrel, DA/SA, 15 shot double column mag., ambidextrous controls, white dot sights, inertial firing pin, loaded chamber indicator, decocking lever, mfg. by Zastava. Imported 2013-2014.

	$375	$325	$275	$250	$200	$175	$125	

DRACO AK47 PISTOL – 7.62x39mm cal., 10 1/2 in. barrel, 30 shot mag., accepts AK-47 mag. or drum, standard AKM sights, maple wood handguard, stamped receiver, 6.3 lbs. Imported 2010-2012, importation from Romania and U.S. mfg. resumed mid-2017.

MSR $725	$625	$550	$475	$425	$350	$275	$225	

DRACO MINI/MICRO – 7.62x39mm cal., 6 1/4 or 7 3/4 in. barrel, 30 shot mag., accepts AK-47 mags. or drums, standard AKM tangent rear sight or top cover mounted notch rear sight (Micro Draco Only), maple wood handguard, stamped receiver, approx. 4 1/2-5 1/2 lbs. Imported from Romania, also manufactured in the USA beginning mid-2017.

MSR $899	$750	$650	$600	$500	$425	$350	$275	

DRACO NAK9 – 9mm Para. cal., blowback operation, 11 1/8 in. barrel, 33 shot mag., accepts Glock 17 and 19 mags., standard AKM sights, hardwood forearm, stamped receiver w/Picatinny rail, rear sling mount, 6.4 lbs. New 2018.

MSR $699	$600	$500	$450	$400	$325	$275	$200	

DRACO NAK9X – 9mm Para. cal., blowback operation, 11 1/8 in. threaded barrel, 33 shot mag., accepts Glock 17 and 19 mags., standard AKM sights, Shockwave blade stock forearm, Magpul MOE handguard and grip stamped receiver with Picatinny rail, rear sling mount, 19 in. OAL, 6.38 lbs. Mfg. 2018-disc.

	$650	$575	$500	$450	$375	$300	$250	*$760*

K100 Mk7 – 9mm Para. cal., similar to P1 Mk7, except has 4 1/4 in. barrel, 25 oz. Mfg. by Grand Power. Imported mid-2013-2020.

	$500	$440	$375	$340	$275	$225	$175	

M57 – 7.62x25mm Tokarev cal., 4 1/2 in. barrel, Browning-style short recoil, tilting barrel action, based on Soviet TT design, 9 shot mag., solid steel, blue finish, factory installed safety, includes extra mag., 23 oz. Mfg. by Zastava, imported 2013-2020.

	$250	$225	$210	$200	$190	$180	$150	*$265*

M70A – 9mm Para. cal., 4 1/2 in. barrel, Browning-style short recoil, tilting barrel action, based on Soviet TT design, 9 shot mag., solid steel, blue finish, factory installed safety, includes extra mag., 23 oz. Mfg. by Zastava, imported 2013-2014.

	$300	$275	$225	$200	$165	$135	$100	

M88A – 9mm Para. cal., Browning-style short recoil, tilting barrel action, based on Soviet TT design, 3.78 in. hammer forged barrel and slide, includes two 8 shot mags., checkered polymer grips, external safety, blue finish. Imported 2014-2020.

	$300	$265	$225	$200	$165	$135	$100	

GRADING - PPGS™	100%	98%	95%	90%	80%	70%	60%	LAST MSR

M-1911 STYLE PISTOLS – .45 ACP cal., SA, patterned after the Colt Govt. Model 1911, choice of 4 1/4 (Blue Thunder Commodore, Commodore 1911, or GI-Officer's Model) or 5 (SAM Elite/SAM Standard, Military, or SAM Chief/Falcon or Scout) ported (disc. 2002) or unported barrel, 7 or 8 shot mag., various configurations and finishes, target features are available on select models, approx. 41 oz. Imported from the Philippines beginning 2001, previously mfg. by Shooter's Arms. Disc. 2020.

	100%	98%	95%	90%	80%	70%	60%	LAST MSR
	$500	$450	$375	$350	$275	$225	$175	

Add $35 for Commodore Blue Thunder Model with squared off trigger guard (disc. 2013).

PAP M85 PV – .223 Rem. cal., GPO, AK-47 design, 10 in. cold hammer forged barrel, 30 shot mag., dual aperture Krinkov style rear sight, bolt hold-open notch on selector, steel alloy bolt and barrel, stamped receiver, hinged top cover, 6.4 lbs. Mfg. by Zastava, imported 2013-2020.

	100%	98%	95%	90%	80%	70%	60%	LAST MSR
	$455	$400	$340	$310	$250	$230	$220	*$535*

Add $30 for Krinkov muzzle brake.

PAP M92 PV – 7.62x39mm cal., GPO, AK-47 design, 10 in. cold hammer forged barrel, 30 shot mag., dual aperture Krinkov style rear sight, bolt hold-open notch on selector, steel alloy bolt and barrel, stamped receiver, hinged top cover, 6.6 lbs. Mfg. by Zastava, imported 2013-2020.

	100%	98%	95%	90%	80%	70%	60%	LAST MSR
	$625	$550	$475	$425	$350	$285	$240	*$725*

Add $30 for Krinkov muzzle brake.

P1 Mk 7 – 9mm Para. cal., 3.7 in. stainless steel barrel, polymer frame, integral Picatinny rail, fully ambidextrous, four interchangeable grip backstraps, matte black finish, includes two 15 shot mags., 24 oz. Mfg. by Grand Power, imported mid-2013-2020.

	100%	98%	95%	90%	80%	70%	60%	LAST MSR
	$500	$440	$375	$340	$275	$225	$175	

RAS47 – 7.62x39mm cal., 10.6 in. chrome moly barrel, birdcage flash hider, 30 shot mag., larger T-shaped mag. catch, RAK-1 enhanced trigger group, standard AKM sights, front sight gas block, MOE AK pistol grip, stamped steel Nitride treated receiver, compatible with AKM furniture, QD attachments on rear of receiver, MOE AK handguard, 6.55 lbs. Mfg. 2015-2020.

	100%	98%	95%	90%	80%	70%	60%	LAST MSR
	$615	$540	$470	$400	$350	$285	$240	*$700*

STINGRAY-C – 9mm Para. cal., 3 1/2 in. chrome-lined cold forged barrel, includes two 15 shot mags., adj. rear sight, ambidextrous safety lever and slide release, loaded chamber indicator, Picatinny rail, black, chrome, desert, OD green, or titanium finish. Imported 2014-2020.

	100%	98%	95%	90%	80%	70%	60%	LAST MSR
	$390	$340	$295	$265	$215	$175	$135	

TP9DA – 9mm Para. cal., DA, 4.07 in. match grade barrel, top slide mounted disassembly button, 10 or 18 shot mag., reversible mag. catch, Warren Tactical sights with dot front sight, dovetail sight cuts, striker status indicator, Mil-Std 1913 Picatinny rail, includes two mags., poly holster, paddle and belt attachment, interchangeable backstraps, cleaning rod, and brush, black or Burnt Bronze Cerakote finish, 1.73 lbs, mfg. by Canik in Turkey. New 2021.

	100%	98%	95%	90%	80%	70%	60%	LAST MSR
MSR $380	$325	$300	$250	$225	$175	$150	$125	

TP9 ELITE COMBAT – 9mm Para. cal., 4.73 in. fluted and Nitride-coated match grade barrel, proprietary convex thread protector, 10 or 18 shot mag., aluminum speed funnel magwell, aluminum Plus 3 magazine extension, enhanced trigger, optics ready slide with adapter plates and charging hndle, fiber optic sight set, advanced coatings on all steel and internal parts, new retention holster with slide lock release, FDE Cerakote finish, 25.8 oz. Designed in collaboration with Salient Arms. Mfg. by Canik in Turkey beginning 2018.

	100%	98%	95%	90%	80%	70%	60%	LAST MSR
MSR $850	$725	$635	$550	$500	$400	$325	$275	

* ***TP9 Elite Combat Vortex Viper Red Dot*** – 9mm Para. cal., similar to TP9 Elite Combat, except has two 15 or 18 shot mags., Vortex Viper red dot. Designed in collaboration with Salient Arms. Mfg. by Canik in Turkey 2018-2020.

	100%	98%	95%	90%	80%	70%	60%	LAST MSR
	$850	$750	$650	$600	$475	$375	$300	

Last MSR $940.

TP9 ELITE COMBAT EXECUTIVE – 9mm Para. cal., black polymer frame topped with Nitride coated jeb black slide, 4.73 in. gold fluted match grade barrel with PVD over Nitride coating, thread protector, 15 shot mag., aluminum Speed Funnel magwell, aluminum Plus 3 mag. extension, extended mag. release, slide, barrel, and small steel parts are Nitride coated, flat-face aluminum trigger, fiber optic sight set, optics ready slide with one adapter plate and charging handle, retention holster with slide lock release, black Cerakote finish, 25.8 oz. Designed in collaboration with Salient Arms. Mfg. by Canik in Turkey beginning 2019.

	100%	98%	95%	90%	80%	70%	60%	LAST MSR
MSR $779	$650	$600	$500	$450	$375	$300	$225	

GRADING - PPGS™	100%	98%	95%	90%	80%	70%	60%	LAST MSR

TP9 ELITE SC – 9mm Para. cal., 3.6 in. match grade barrel, 12 (optional finger rest base plate) or 15 (extended base plate) shot mag. w/reversible mag. release, phosphorous front white dot or blackout rear sights, integral Mil-Std 1913 Picatinny rail, micro red-dot interface w/co-witness feature, interchangeable backstrap (small and large), includes toolbox, manual, concealed carry holster w/reversible clips, Tungsten Cerakote finish over black Nitride slide finish, 24.78 oz. Mfg. by Canik in Turkey beginning 2019.

MSR $440	$375	$325	$275	$250	$200	$175	$125	

Add $259 for Shield Optic.

TP9SA – 9mm Para. cal., SA, SFO, new trigger and frame assembly, 4.47 in. match grade barrel, ambi top-slide mounted decocker, 10 (new 2016) or 18 shot mag., reversible mag. catch, Cerakoted slide with 3-dot steel sights, front and rear grip panels, loaded chamber indicator, striker status indicator, also includes poly holster, paddle attachment, belt attachment, two interchangeable backstraps, cleaning rod, brush, and limited lifetime manufacturer's warranty, black or Desert Tan Cerakote finish, 1.8 lbs. Mfg. by Canik in Turkey. Imported 2015-2019.

	$340	$300	$250	$230	$185	$150	$125	*$400*

TP9SA MOD.2 – 9mm Para. cal., 4.46 in. match grade barrel, top slide mounted disassembly button, 10 or 18 shot mag., reversible mag. release, improved SAT, dovetail sight cuts, Warren Tactical sights with rear U-notch and white dot front, loaded chamber indicator, striker status indicator, Mil-Std 1913 Picatinny rail, AFC magazine coating, includes two mags., poly holster, paddle and belt attachment, interchangeable backstraps, and cleaning rod, black or Desert Tan Cerakote finish, 1.78 lbs. Mfg. by Canik in Turkey. Importation began 2018.

MSR $360	$300	$275	$225	$200	$175	$150	$125	

TP9SF – 9mm Para. cal., 4.46 in. match grade barrel, two 10 or 18 shot mags., reversible mag. catch, single action trigger, dovetail sights, loaded chamber indicator, striker status indicator, reversible magazine catch, Mil-Std 1913 Picatinny rail, AFC magazine coating, includes interchangeable backstraps, poly holster, paddle and belt attachment, cleaning rod, and brush, black, Desert Tan, or FDE Cerakote finish, 1.78 lbs. Mfg. by Canik in Turkey 2014-2020.

	$325	$300	$250	$225	$175	$150	$125	*$380*

TP9SF ELITE – 9mm Para. cal., 4.19 in. match grade barrel, 10 or 15 shot mag., reversible mag. catch, improved SAT, Warren Tactical sights with red and green fiber optic front sight, front and rear slide serrations, loaded chamber indicator, striker status indicator, ambi slide release, Mil-Std 1913 Picatinny rail, includes two mags., poly holster, paddle/belt attachment, interchangeable backstraps and cleaning rod, black, FDE (new 2020), or Tungsten Grey Cerakote finish, 1.77 lbs. Mfg. by Canik in Turkey.

MSR $430	$375	$325	$275	$250	$200	$175	$125	

Add $10 for FDE finish (new 2020). Add $10 for Robin's Egg Blue frame finish (disc.).

* ***TP9SF Elite-S*** – 9mm Para. cal., 4.19 in. match grade barrel, 10 or 15 shot mag., reversible mag. catch, improved SAT, Warren Tactical sights with red and green fiber optic front sight, front and rear slide serrations, loaded chamber indicator, striker status indicator, ambi slide release, Mil-Std 1913 Picatinny rail, black, Tungsten Grey, or OD Green Cerakote finish, 1.77 lbs. Mfg. by Canik in Turkey. Disc 2020.

	$425	$375	$325	$295	$235	$195	$165	*$500*

TP9SFL – 9mm Para. cal., 5.2 in. match grade barrel, two 10 or 18 shot mags., improved SAT, Warren Tactical sights with dot front sight, standard dovetail sight cuts, forward slide serrations, loaded chamber indicator, striker status indicator, reversible mag. catch, Mil-Std 1913 Picatinny rail, poly holster, paddle and belt attachment, interchangeable backstraps, cleaning rod, black Cerakote finish, 1.87 lbs. Mfg. by Canik in Turkey late 2017-2020.

	$445	$390	$335	$300	$250	$200	$175	*$520*

TP9SFT – 9mm Para. cal., 5 in. 13.5x1mm LH threaded match grade barrel, one 18 shot and one 20 shot mag., reversible mag. catch, single action trigger, dovetail sights, loaded chamber indicator, striker status indicator, reversible magazine catch, Mil-Std 1913 Picatinny rail, AFC magazine coating, includes interchangeable backstraps, poly holster, paddle and belt attachment, cleaning rod, and brush, black or Desert Tan Cerakote finish, 1.78 lbs. Mfg. by Canik in Turkey. Imported 2018-2020.

	$445	$390	$335	$300	$250	$200	$175	*$520*

TP9SFX – 9mm Para. cal., 5.2 in. match grade barrel, two 10 shot mags., lightning cuts on slide, improved SAT, Warren Tactical sights with red and green fiber optic front sight, standard dovetail sight cuts, removable red dot cover, four red dot interface plates, forward slide serrations, reversible ambi cocking lever, extended ergonomic slide release, adj. length reversible magazine catch, striker status indicator, Mil-Std 1913 Picatinny rail, AFC magazine coating, poly holster, paddle attachment, interchangeable backstraps, Tungsten Grey or FDE (new 2018) Cerakote over phosphate finish, 1.83 lbs. Mfg. by Canik in Turkey beginning 2016.

MSR $550	$475	$400	$350	$325	$250	$200	$175	

GRADING - PPGS™	100%	98%	95%	90%	80%	70%	60%	LAST MSR

* ***TP9SFX Vortex Viper Red Dot*** – 9mm Para. cal., similar to TP9SFX, except has two 20 shot mags., Vortex Viper red dot, Tungsten Grey or FDE Cerakote over phosphate finish, 1.9 lbs. Mfg. by Canik in Turkey beginning 2017.

MSR $759	$650	$550	$475	$450	$350	$300	$225	

TP9SF ONE SERIES – 9mm Para. cal., striker fired, 4.46 in. barrel, 18 shot mag., short reset SA trigger design, Warren Tactical sights, loaded chamber indicator, side reversible mag. catch and alternate backstraps, Mil-Std 1913 under-barrel rail, includes hard plastic case, Nitride finish (black models) or Cerakote over Nitride (color models) finish, 1.78 lbs. Mfg. by Canik in Turkey 2019 only.

	$250	$225	$200	$175	$150	$125	$100	*$300*

* ***TP9SF One Series Elite*** – 9mm Para. cal., striker fired, 4.19 in. match grade barrel, 15 shot mag., improved SA trigger, Warren Tactical sights with red and green fiber optic front sight, standard dovetail sight cuts, loaded chamber and striker status indicator, front and rear slide serrations, ambi slide release, side reversible mag. catch and alternate backstraps, Mil-Std 1913 Picatinny rail, includes hard plastic case, black Nitride finish, 28.32 oz. Limited mfg. by Canik in Turkey 2019-2020.

	$275	$250	$200	$185	$150	$125	$100	*$325*

TP9V2 – 9mm Para. cal., polymer frame, 4.07 in. match grade barrel, two 13 or 18 shot mags., improved DA/SA trigger, ambi top slide mounted decocker, loaded chamber indicator, reversible magazine catch, Mil-Std 1913 Picatinny rail, AFC magazine coating, interchangeable backstraps, cleaning rod, black Cerakote finish, 1.81 lbs. Mfg. by Canik in Turkey 2014-2020.

	$340	$300	$250	$230	$185	$150	$125	*$400*

REVOLVERS: SAA

MODEL 1873 SAA MILLENNIUM – .22 LR (new 2014), .357 Mag., .44-40 WCF (new 2014), or .45 LC cal., 4 3/4, 5 1/2, or 7 1/2 (new 2014) in. barrel, black matte or case colored steel frame, 6 shot, smooth walnut-stained hardwood grips, grooved top strap and fixed blade front sight, 35 oz. Mfg. by Pietta, importation began mid-2013. Disc. 2020

	$325	$285	$250	$225	$175	$150	$115	*$380*

Add $70 for case colored frame.

RIFLES: BOLT ACTION

Century International also imports a complete line of .22 LR and .22 WMR cal. rimfires. MSRs range from $140-$250. Please contact the company directly for current availability and pricing.

M70 – .243 Win., .270 Win., .30-06, .308 Win., 7mm Rem. Mag., or .300 Win. Mag. cal., right or left-hand action, 20 or 23.6 in. barrel, 3, 4, or 5 shot integral mag., walnut Monte Carlo or Mannlicher style stock, 7.72 lbs. Mfg. by Zastava, importation began 2013. Disc. 2020.

	$520	$450	$395	$350	$285	$235	$180	

Add $30 for Mannlicher stock.
Add $30 for Mag. cals.

M85 "MINI MAUSER" – .223 Rem., 7.62x39mm, or .22 Hornet cal., right or left-hand action, 18, 20, or 22 in. barrel, 5 shot integral or detachable (.22 Hornet cal. only) mag., walnut Monte Carlo or Mannlicher style stock, approx. 6.2 lbs. Mfg. by Zastava, imported 2013-2020.

	$550	$475	$425	$375	$300	$250	$195	

Add $20 for Mannlicher stock (disc.).

TYPE 53 (TYPE 53 REPEATER) – 7.62X54R cal., Mosin-Nagant type rifle, 20.4 in. barrel, 5 shot, tangent rear sight, hooded post front sight, straight grip wood stock, blue finish, includes folding bayonet, Chinese mfg., 8 lbs. 14 oz. Disc. 2020.

	$160	$140	$120	$110	$90	$70	$55	

Add $340 for modern Archangel tactical stock (new 2014).

CZ99 – .17 HMR, .22 LR, or .22 WMR cal., 22 in. cold forged barrel, includes two 5 shot mags., adj. trigger, adj. sights, checkered pistol grip walnut stock and forearm, receiver dovetailed for scope mounts. Imported 2014-2020.

	$300	$265	$225	$200	$165	$135	$100	

RIFLES/CARBINES: SEMI-AUTO

AES10-B RPK STYLE – 7.62x39mm cal., 23 1/8 in. heavy barrel with folding bipod, laminated stock and forend, includes two AK style 40 shot mags., 10.9 lbs. Imported 2012, reimported 2019.

MSR $1,599	$1,350	$1,200	$1,000	$900	$750	$600	$475	

GRADING - PPGS™	100%	98%	95%	90%	80%	70%	60%	LAST MSR

AK-63 DS – 7.62x39mm cal., 16 1/2 in. barrel w/slant cut muzzle brake, 30 shot mag., metal underfolding stock, mfg. from Hungarian surplus military parts, stamped receiver, blonde wood furniture, black phosphate finish, 7 1/2 lbs. Assembled in the U.S. Disc.

	$625	$550	$500	$450	$395	$315	$295	*$710*

M74 BULLPUP (AK-74 BULLPUP) – 5.45x39mm cal., AK-47 design, 16 1/4 in. barrel with muzzle brake, vent. handguard, top Picatinny rail, two 30 shot mags., 7.35 lbs. Limited importation 2010-2011.

	$575	$500	$425	$365	$335	$295	$275	*$650*

AK-74 SPORTER – 5.45x39mm cal., AK-47 design, 16 1/4 in. barrel with muzzle brake, side mount rail, bayonet lug, fixed wood stock, includes two 30 shot mags., sling, mag. pouch, cleaning rod and oil bottle, 7.6 lbs. Imported 2014-2020.

	$790	$695	$595	$535	$435	$350	$275	

AKMS – 7.62x39mm cal., AK-47 design, 16 1/4 in. barrel with muzzle brake, features laminate wood handguards, pistol grip, and steel folding buttstock with skeleton buttplate, includes two 30 shot mags., 7.8 lbs. Imported 2011-2013.

	$625	$550	$500	$425	$350	$275	$225	*$700*

C15A1 SPORTER – 5.56 NATO cal., AR-15 style, based on M16A1, GIO, triangular "Vietnam era" style handguard, 16 in. barrel with muzzle brake, fixed stock, includes two original Colt 30 shot mags. (disc. 2011) or fixed 10 shot mag. (current mfg.), choice of green polymer or walnut wood furniture, A3 carry handle and sights. Mfg. mid-2010-2020.

This model was POR.

Add 15% for High Cap Mag. model.

C15 M4 – 5.56 NATO cal., GIO, 16 in. Govt. profile barrel, carbine length gas system, front sight gas block, birdcage flash hider, 30 shot mag., forged upper and lower receivers, adj. Tapco T6 stock, flat-top receiver with detachable carry handle, black anodized finish. Mfg. 2014-disc.

	$425	$375	$325	$300	$275	$250	$200	*$599*

C39v2 & VARIATIONS – 7.62x39mm cal., AK-47 design, 16 1/2 in. barrel, 10 or 30 shot mag., standard AKM sights, choice of fixed wood or MOE Magpul black synthetic folding stock and forearm, bolt holed open safety selector, milled receiver, approx. 7 1/2 lbs. Mfg. in USA, disc. 2020.

	$775	$675	$575	$525	$425	$350	$300	*$900*

Add $46 for Magpul MOE furniture.

Add $50 for high grade walnut stock, forearm, and pistol grip.

Add $185 for Magpul Zhukov forearm and folding stock.

C308 – .308 Win. cal., roller lock delayed blowback system, 18 in. chrome moly 4140 barrel, one 5 shot mag. and two 20 shot G3 or CETME mags., Mil-Spec 1913 Picatinny scope rail integrally mounted to receiver, Chevron brake, polymer (disc. 2020) or original wood furniture, choice of 100% matte black or Patriot Brown finish. New 2014.

MSR $849	$700	$650	$550	$500	$400	$325	$250	

CENTURION 39 – 7.62x39mm cal., 16 1/2 in. barrel, V-shape Chevron compensator, available in Tactical (fixed black synthetic stock) or Sporter (black synthetic stock) configurations, black finish, fixed buttstock with pistol grip, four Picatinny rails, includes two 30 shot mags., 8.2 lbs. All parts mfg. in U.S. mid-2010-2020.

	$800	$700	$600	$550	$450	$360	$295	

* ***Centurion 39 Classic*** – 7.62x39mm cal., similar to Centurion 39, except has laminated wood stock in Black (new 2014), Brown (new 2014), and Blonde (new 2014), adj. rear sight. All parts mfg. in U.S. mid-2010-2020.

	$800	$700	$600	$550	$450	$360	$295	

CENTURION UC-9 CARBINE – 9mm Para. cal., patterned after the Israeli UZI submachine gun, straight blowback closed bolt action, 16 in. barrel, parkerized finish, folding steel stock, includes two 32 shot all steel double column mags., approx. 9 lbs. Imported mid-2012-2020.

	$725	$650	$575	$475	$400	$350	$295	*$805*

CETME SPORTER – .308 Win. cal., new mfg. Cetme action, 19 1/2 in. barrel, 20 shot mag., choice of blue or Mossy Oak Break-Up camo (disc.) metal finish, wood (disc.) or synthetic stock, pistol grip, and vent. forearm, refinished condition only, 9.7 lbs. Imported 2002-2011.

	$550	$475	$400	$350	$300	$275	$250	*$635*

GRADING - PPGS™	100%	98%	95%	90%	80%	70%	60%	LAST MSR

DEGTYAREV MODEL – 7.62x54R cal., semi-auto closed bolt copies of the WWII Soviet machine gun, available in three variations, 23.8 in. barrel, 47 or 63 (DTX /DTM variant only) shot pan magazine mounted on top of receiver, adj. sights, wood furniture, blued metal, includes bipod, approximately 18 1/2 lbs. w/out mag. Imported 2011-2012.

* ***DP 28*** – 7.62x54R cal., 23.8 in. barrel, gas operated, 47 shot drum mag., full shoulder stock. Disc.

$3,500 $3,060 $2,625 $2,380 $1,925 $1,575 $1,225

* ***DPM 28*** – 7.62x54R cal., 23.8 in. barrel, gas operated, 47 shot drum mag., pistol grip stock. Disc.

$3,500 $3,060 $2,625 $2,380 $1,925 $1,575 $1,225 ***$2,000***

* ***DTX Tank Model*** – 7.62x54R cal., 23.8 in. barrel, 63 shot drum mag., collapsible stock, approx. 10 lbs. Disc.

$3,500 $3,060 $2,625 $2,380 $1,925 $1,575 $1,225

DRAGUNOV (TIGER) – 7.62x54R cal., milled receiver, based on the Russian Dragunov designated marksman rifle, thumbhole stock, 20 3/4 or 24 in. barrel, supplied with scope and cleaning kit. Mfg. in Russia. Disc.

$8,000 $7,000 $6,000 $5,450 $4,400 $3,600 $2,800

FAL SPORTER – .308 Win. cal., short stroke GPO, various configurations, new US made barrel, 20 shot mag., new US made receiver, wood or synthetic furniture, bipod optional, parkerized finish, Mfg. 2004-2006, limited manufacture afterwards. Disc.

$950 $825 $725 $650 $525 $425 $350

G-3 SPORTER – .308 Win. cal., mfg. from genuine G3 parts, and American made receiver with integrated scope rail, includes 20 shot mag., 19 in. barrel, pistol grip stock, matte black finish, refinished condition only, 9.3 lbs. Imported 1999-2006.

$785 $685 $590 $535 $430 $355 $275

GOLANI SPORTER – .223 Rem. cal., 21 in. barrel, 35 shot mag., folding stock, optional bayonet lug, approx. 8 lbs., mfg. using original Israeli parts. Disc.

$900 $800 $675 $600 $500 $400 $325 ***$700***

Add $30 for bayonet lug (disc.).

GORYUNOV SG43 – 7.62x54R cal., copy of Soviet model, gas operated, 28.3 in. barrel, 250 shot belt fed, charging handle, spade grips, includes wooden crate, folding carriage, 3 ammo belts, 96 lbs. Disc. 2011.

$6,500 $5,700 $4,875 $4,425 $3,575 $2,925 $2,275 ***$5,325***

GP 1975 – 7.62x39mm cal., AK-47 design, 16 1/4 in. barrel, black synthetic furniture, new U.S. receiver and barrel, includes two 30 shot mags., approx. 7.4 lbs. Importation disc. 2011.

$595 $425 $375 $325 $275 $250 $225 ***$675***

Add approx. $140 for collapsible stock and Picatinny rail forearm.

GP WASR-10 HIGH-CAP SERIES – 7.62x39mm cal., AK-47 design, 16 1/4 in. barrel, various configurations, includes two 30 shot double stack mags., 7 1/2 lbs. Mfg. by Cugir Arms Factory (ROMARM) of Romania. Disc.

$585 $510 $435 $365 $325 $280 $265 ***$670***

Add $10 for bayonet.
Add $133 for 100 shot drum mag.
Add $250 for factory installed slide fire stock (new 2014).
Add $67 for recoilless buttstock (new 2012).
Add $60 for 50th Anniversary model with Century Arms logo on back right of receiver (only 50 mfg. during 2012).

GP WASR-10 LO-CAP – 7.62x39mm cal., AK-47 design, 16 1/4 in. barrel, wood stock and forearm, includes one 5 and one 10 shot single stack mags., 7 1/2 lbs. Mfg. by Romarm of Romania. Importation disc. 2011.

$400 $350 $315 $275 $250 $225 $200 ***$450***

L1A1/R1A1 SPORTER – .308 Win. cal., current mfg. receiver patterned after the British L1A1, includes carrying handle, synthetic furniture, 20 shot mag., 22 1/2 in. barrel, fold over aperture rear sight, 9 1/2 lbs. Mfg. in U.S., disc. 2010.

$975 $850 $750 $650 $575 $500 $450

Subtract approx. $200 for L1A1 Sporter.

M70 SERIES – 7.62x39mm cal., based on Yugoslavian Paratrooper variant, 16 1/4 in. barrel, includes two 30 shot double stack mags., classic wood furniture (disc.) or black polymer upper and lower handguards, black under folding stock (AB2) or fixed synthetic stock (B1), slant muzzle brake, bayonet lug, approx. 7 1/2 lbs. Limited importation 2013-2020.

$700 $625 $525 $475 $400 $325 $250

Add $40 for AB2 Model.

GRADING - PPGS™	100%	98%	95%	90%	80%	70%	60%	LAST MSR

M-76 SNIPER/SPORTER MODEL – 8mm Mauser cal., semi-auto version of the Yugoslavian M76 rifle, new U.S. receiver and 21 1/2 in. barrel, includes original scope, mount, and 10 shot mag., 11.3 lbs. Importation disc. 2011.

	$1,495	$1,200	$1,000	$875	$750	$650	$550	*$1,725*

MEXSAR – .22 LR cal., 21 1/4 in. barrel, 16 shot mag., fiber optic front sight, uncheckered pistol grip hardwood stock, dovetailed for scope mounts, blue finish, 6.2 lbs. Imported 2014-2020.

	$230	$200	$175	$150	$125	$100	$80	

PAP M77 PS – .308 Win. cal., 16 1/4 in. cold hammer forged barrel, 30 shot mag., black polymer thumbhole stock with upper and lower handguard, Picatinny rail, dust cover. Mfg. by Zastava. Importation began 2013.

No MSR	$650	$575	$495	$440	$360	$295	$250	

MISR-10 HIGH-CAP – 7.62x39mm cal., long stroke GPO, AK-47 design, 16 in. chrome-lined barrel, non-threaded, no bayonet lug tabs, accepts standard double stack AK mags., double stack magwell, "XY" stamped and dimpled steel receiver, non-hooded front sight block, fixed wooden buttstock, laminate wooden handguards, black polymer pistol grip, AK style right side lever safety, marked "MISR-10 SEMI-AUTO CAL. 7.62x39mm" on the left side of the rear sight block and "MADE BY MAADI CO IN EGYPT IMPORTER CAI ST ALBANS VT" on the right side of the receiver, black painted finish. Importation disc.

	$800	$700	$600	$550	$425	$350	$275	

PAP SERIES – 7.62x39mm or 7.62x51mm cal., 16 1/4 in. cold hammer forged barrel, choice of classic wood stock with pistol grip, black thumbhole stock with polymer handguard, or T6 collapsible stock with plastic handguard, 10 or 30 shot mag., accessory rail, 7.7-8 lbs. Mfg. by Zastava. Importation began 2013.

No MSR	$580	$510	$435	$395	$325	$260	$200	

Add $80 for Hi-Cap Model with fixed wood buttstock, handguard, and two 30 shot mags. (new 2014).
Add $120 for DF Model with T6 collapsible stock.

PSL 54 – 7.62x54R cal., DMR rifle, 24 1/2 in. chrome-lined barrel, muzzle brake, 10 shot mag., Russian PO 4x24 optic, laminate thumbhole skeletonized stock, reinforced front trunnion, mfg. in Romania. Importation began 2019.

MSR $2,545	$2,300	$2,000	$1,700	$1,550	$1,250	$1,050	$800	

RAS47 – 7.62x39mm cal., AK-47 design, 16 1/2 in. barrel, slant muzzle brake, stamped receiver, two 30 shot Magpul mags., T-shaped magazine catch, side scope rail, bolt hold open safety, AK sights, compatibility with AKM furniture, AK stock, pistol grip, and handguard, includes enhanced dust cover, 7.8 lbs. Mfg. 2015-disc.

	$685	$615	$550	$475	$420	$365	$335	*$799*

* ***RAS47 Black*** – 7.62x39mm cal., similar to RAS47, except has RAK-1 enhanced trigger group, Magpul MOE AK furniture, black Nitride finish, 7.37 lbs. Mfg. 2015-disc.

	$685	$615	$550	$475	$420	$365	$335	*$799*

S.A.R. 1 – 7.62x39mm cal., AK-47 design, 16 1/2 in. barrel, wood stock and forearm, scope rail mounted on receiver, includes one 10 and two 30 shot double stack mags., 7.08 lbs. Mfg. by Romarm of Romania. Importation disc. 2003.

	$750	$655	$560	$510	$410	$335	$260	

S.A.R. 2 – 5.45x39mm cal., AK-47 design, 16 in. barrel, wood stock and forearm, includes one 10 and one 30 shot double stack mags., 8 lbs. Mfg. by Romarm of Romania. Importation disc. 2003.

	$750	$655	$560	$510	$410	$335	$260	

S.A.R. 3 – .223 Rem. cal., AK-47 design, 16 in. barrel, wood stock and forearm, includes one 10 and one 30 shot double stack mag., 8 lbs. Mfg. by Romarm of Romania. Importation disc. 2003.

	$750	$655	$560	$510	$410	$335	$260	

SAIGA SERIES – 5.45x39mm or 7.62x39mm cal., 16 1/4 (Hi-Cap) or 16 1/2 in. chrome-lined barrel, 10 or 30 (Hi-Cap) shot mag., iron sights, fixed plastic straight grip stock with pistol grip or checkered synthetic pistol grip stock, side mount rail, matte black finish, approx. 8 lbs. Imported 2014-2020.

	$650	$575	$495	$450	$375	$295	$250	

Add $310 for Hi-Cap Model.

STERLING SA – 9mm Para. cal., blowback action, semi-auto version of the Sterling submachine gun, 16 1/4 in. barrel, American made receiver and barrel, original style crinkle painted finish, folding stock, includes two 34 shot mags., available in Type I (disc.) or Type II, L sight with 100 and 200 yard apertures, front post sight, full length heat shield, unique port feed angle, 9.2 lbs. Disc. 2020.

	$800	$700	$600	$550	$450	$350	$275	

GRADING - PPGS™	100%	98%	95%	90%	80%	70%	60%	LAST MSR

TANTAL SPORTER – 5.45x39mm cal., 18 in. barrel, parkerized finish, side folding wire stock, flash hider, includes extra mag., 8 lbs.

$850 $750 $650 $575 $475 $375 $300 *$550*

VZ2008 SPORTER – 7.62x39mm cal., copy of the Czech VZ58, 16 1/4 in. barrel, steel receiver, dull matte finish, bead blasted metal parts, wood, plastic (disc. 2011), or folding steel buttstock, 7 lbs. Importation disc. 2011, reimported 2014-2020.

$600 $525 $450 $410 $325 $275 $210

WASR RIFLE – 7.62x39mm cal., 16 1/4 in. barrel, 30 shot mag., stamped receiver, with or w/o bayonet lug or compensator, 7 1/2 lb, available as underfolding stock. Mfg. in Romania, assembled in the United States with U.S. parts.

MSR $989 $850 $750 $650 $550 $450 $375 $300

Add $10 for muzzle nut and bayonet lug.
Add $110 for underfolding stock.

* ***Wasr-M*** – 9mm Luger cal., semi-auto rifle, 17 1/2 in. barrel, muzzle thread, 33 shot Glock mag., fully adj. front sight and fixed rear sight, approx. 7 1/2 lbs. Mfg. in Romania, assembled in the United States with U.S. parts.

MSR $819 $700 $600 $500 $475 $375 $325 $250

VSKA - 7.62x39mm cal., AK-47 design, chrome moly 4150 barrel, 30 shot mag., RAK-1 enhanced rigger group, synthetic shoulder stock and handguards or American maple wood buttstock and forend, 1/16 in. stamped steel receiver, 4140 steel bolt, heat treated S7 steel carrier, feed ramp, front trunnion, magnesium phosphate finish. Mfg. in U.S. beginning 2019.

MSR $749 $650 $550 $475 $425 $350 $275 $225

Add $50 for American maple wood buttstock and forend.

RIFLES: SLIDE ACTION

PAR 1 OR 3 - 7.62x39mm (PAR 1) or .223 Rem. (PAR 3) cal., AK-47 receiver design, 10 shot mag., accepts double stack AK magazines, wood stock, pistol grip, and forearm, 20.9 in. barrel, 7.6 lbs. Mfg. by PAR, and imported 2002-2009.

$360 $300 $275 $250 $225 $200 $175

SHOTGUNS

ARTHEMIS (SUPER ARTHEMIS) O/U - 12, 20, 28 (new 2004) ga., or .410 bore, 3 in. chambers, 28 in. VR barrels, SST, extractors, checkered walnut stock and forearm, 5.3-7.4 lbs. Mfg. by Khan in Turkey, importation disc.

$450 $395 $335 $305 $245 $200 $155

Add $25 for 20 or 28 ga.
Add $50 for .410 bore.

PHANTOM SEMI-AUTO – 12 ga. only, 3 in. chamber, 24, 26, or 28 in. VR barrels with 3 choke tubes, black synthetic stock and forearm. Mfg. in Turkey, importation disc.

$265 $230 $200 $180 $145 $120 $95

SAS-12 SEMI-AUTO – 12 ga. only, 2 3/4 in. chamber, detachable 3 (Type II) or 5 shot mag., black synthetic stock and forearm, 22 or 23 1/2 in. barrel. Previously mfg. by PRC in China, disc. 2020.

$200 $175 $150 $130 $110 $100 $75

Add approx. $25 for ghost ring rear with blade front or bead sight.

CATAMOUNT FURY I SEMI-AUTO – 12 ga., 2 3/4 or 3 in. chamber, adj. gas system, 20.1 in. barrel, includes 3 choke tubes, full, modified, and cylinder bore, Picatinny rail mounted to hinged dust cover, fixed combat sights, AK-style safety lever, 5 shot AK style detachable box mag., fixed black synthetic stock with pistol grip, matte black finish, 8.7 lbs. Mfg. 2013-2020.

$585 $515 $435 $365 $325 $280 $265 *$670*

* ***Catamount Fury II Semi-Auto*** – 12 ga., 3 in. chamber, adj. gas system, 20.1 in. barrel, extended magwell, straight drop 5 shot mag, Dragunov-style skeletonized stock, AK-style safety lever, top optics rail, matte black finish, Mfg. 2013-2020.

$585 $515 $435 $365 $325 $280 $265 *$670*

JW-2000 COACH SxS – 12, 20 ga., or .410 bore (disc. 2012), exposed hammers, 20 in. barrels, DT, steel contruction, checkered walnut stock and forearm, includes sling swivels, approx. 7.9 lbs. Mfg. in China, importation disc. 2020.

$285 $250 $225 $210 $200 $190 $180 *$330*

GRADING - PPGS™	100%	98%	95%	90%	80%	70%	60%	LAST MSR

MODEL YL12-1J2 SLIDE ACTION (IJ2) – 12 ga. only, 2 3/4 or 3 in. chamber, 19 in. barrel with ghost ring sights or fiber optic front sights, fixed choke only, 7.2 lbs. Mfg. in China. Disc.

$200	$175	$150	$135	$110	$90	$70	

ULTRA 87 SLIDE ACTION – 12 ga., 3 in. chamber, 19 in. barrel with iron sights, optional pistol grip, metal heat shield (disc.), fixed black synthetic (current mfg.) or side folding (disc.) stock, 8.2 lbs.

$185	$160	$145	$130	$115	$100	$90	*$200*

Add $65 for extra 28 in. barrel.

MKA 1919 – 12 ga., AR-15 styled, GIO, aluminum alloy upper, one-piece polymer lower receiver, pistol grip fixed stock, matte black or 100% camo finish, right side magwell mag. release, bolt stop, 5 shot detachable mag., A2 removable carry handle and front sight, three internal chokes, integral Picatinny rail, approx. 6 1/2 lbs. Imported from Turkey circa 2012-disc.

$850	$750	$640	$575	$475	$385	$300	

PW87 LEVER ACTION – 12 ga., 2 3/4 in. chamber, 20 in. barrel, cylinder choke, blue finish, uncheckered hardwood pistol grip stock and forearm, patterned after the Winchester Model 1887. Mfg. in China, imported 2013-2020.

$295	$265	$225	$210	$200	$190	$180	*$335*

PIETTA SEMI-AUTO – 20 ga., 3 in. chamber, lightweight aluminum alloy receiver is cut to allow Weaver style scope rings or clamp on base, 28 in. chrome-lined vent. rib steel barrel with chokes, 4 shot mag., fiber optic sight, black fiberglass reinforced polymer stock, matte black, dark nickel, or bright nickel finish, 6.2 lbs. Imported 2014-2020.

$750	$650	$565	$510	$415	$340	$265	

SPM – 12 ga. or .410 bore, PW87 lever action style, 20 in. barrel, steel construction, fully fuctional rabbit ear hammer, double triggers, brass bead front sight, oil rubbed walnut stained hardwood stock, checkered forearm, rubber buttpad, checkered grips, sling swivels, 7.9 lbs. Mfg. 2016-2020.

Please contact the company directly for pricing and availability for this model.

CENTURY MFG., INC.

Previous manufacturer located in Knightstown, IN, Feb. 2002-late 2004. Previously manufactured in Evansville and Greenfield, IN 1973-circa 1999. Consumer direct and dealer sales.

This revolver design was originally manufactured in 1972 by Russell Wilson, who sandcasted the bronze frame (cloned from the Colt SAA configuration) in Evansville, IN. Gene Phelps purchased the manufacturing rights for this gun and formed a partnership with Earl Keller to produce a redesigned frame, also using sandcast bronze.

The original Century revolver was made in Evansville, IN beginning in 1973 (1973 was the 100th anniversary of the .45-70 Govt. cartridge - hence the term Century) and production was halted in 1976 at ser. no. 524. In late 1976, Phelps and Keller (the two original partners on the venture) dissolved their partnership and each began manufacturing their own version of the .45-70 revolver. Gene Phelps completely redesigned the gun's interior and began manufacturing the Heritage I, with an investment-cast steel frame, and without the Century's novel cross-bolt safety. Keller's Century Manufacturing, Inc. continued to produce the original Century, with some design refinements, and in 1985 the company was purchased by Dr. Paul Majors, who died in Dec. of 2001.

The most recent Century revolver featured a manganese bronze frame and other components in addition to having a cross-bolt safety. They were produced in .45-70 and various other cals., in Greenfield, IN. Earl Keller died in 1986. The second series was made in Greenfield, IN with limited production resuming in 1986. Earlier handmade "Evansville" Model 100s (disc.) are currently selling for between $2,500-$3,500, depending on the region.

In Feb. 2002, Century Mfg. was purchased by Dave Lukens and Jeff Yelton and moved to Knightstown, IN. New production guns also included a revolving rifle built on the Model 100 frame. These new production guns carried a limited lifetime guarantee.

REVOLVERS

Less than 3,000 Model 100s were manufactured 1976-2001. The values below are for .45-70 Govt. cal. Other calibers were priced from $2,000 on up.

MODEL 100 – .30-30 Win. (new 1987), .375 Win. (new 1986), .444 Marlin (new 1986), .45-70 Govt., .50-70 Govt. (new 1987), or .50-110 cal., single action 6 shot, manganese bronze frame, steel cylinder, 6 1/2, 8, 10, or 12 (disc.) in. round or octagon barrel, unique crossbolt safety that locks the hammer, adj. sights, walnut grips, 5 lbs. 14 oz. Disc. 2000, reintroduced 2002-2004.

GRADING - PPGS™	100%	98%	95%	90%	80%	70%	60%	LAST MSR

* ***Model 100 .45-70 Govt. and other cals.*** – includes all cals. except .50-110.

	$1,295	$1,100	$995	$900	$850	$800	$750	

Last MSR (2002-2004) was $1,295.
Previous mfg. Last MSR was $2,000.

Add $200 for calibers other than .45-70 Govt.
Add $110 for normal octagon barrel.
Add $200 for stainless steel fabrication.

* ***Model 100 .50-110 cal.***

	$2,895	$2,350	$1,950	$1,700	$1,500	$1,250	$1,025	*$2,895*

CHAMPLIN FIREARMS, INC.

Current custom manufacturer, gunsmith, and importer located in Enid, OK. Champlin Firearms was established in 1966. Direct sales only.

Champlin Firearms, Inc. manufactures handcrafted rifles built around a patented bolt action of their own design. Most guns are built per individual customer order and specifications. Values will vary greatly depending on the configuration, desirability, and special order specifications. All Champlin rifles are built along classic lines with best quality wood and exemplary workmanship. They have been used successfully on safaris and have shot dangerous game throughout the world.

Champlin Firearms, Inc. also inventories a wide selection of high grade, top-quality shotguns and rifles (especially top trademark doubles and bolt actions). Contact George Caswell (owner) directly for a current listing. Additional services include a complete gunsmithing service for all grades of English double rifles and shotguns. Custom stocks are also built to individual customer specifications. All double rifles are test fired and checked thoroughly upon completion of manufacture or repair. Champlin Firearms should be contacted for consultation and quotation regarding this additional work.

RIFLES: BOLT ACTION

BOLT ACTION RIFLE – various cals., round or octagon barrel, adj. trigger, each rifle is built to customer specifications. Values below represent base gun with standard wood, no options, and no engraving.

	$8,500	$8,000	$7,000	$6,750	$6,000	$5,250	$4,500	*$8,500*

CHAPARRAL ARMS

Previous trademark of firearms manufactured in Brescia, Italy until 2013. Previously imported circa 2010-2011 by Chapparal Firearms Inc., located in Melbourne, FL. Previously imported by Tristar, located in Kansas City, MO, by Charter 2000, located in Shelton, CT, and K.B.I., located in Harrisburg, PA

Chaparral Arms manufactured reproductions of the Winchester Model 1866, 1873, 1876, Colt 1878, and Sharps 1874 rifles, and Colt 1873 SAA revolvers.

RIFLES: LEVER ACTION, REPRODUCTIONS

MODEL 1866 – .357 Mag./.38 Spl., or .45 LC cal., 19 (round barrel carbine), 20 or 24 (octagon rifle) in. barrel. Imported late 2007-2008.

	$695	$625	$550	$475	$425	$375	$325	*$800*

MODEL 1873 – .357 Mag., .38-40 WCF, .44-40 WCF, or .45 LC cal., patterned after the Model 1873 Winchester, uncheckered straight grip stock, case colored frame, choice of 19 in. round (carbine), 20 or 24 in. octagon barrel. Imported late 2006-2008.

	$895	$775	$675	$600	$525	$450	$375	*$1,050*

MODEL 1876 – .40-60, .45-60, .45-75, or .50-95 (new 2008) cal., patterned after the Model 1876 Winchester, uncheckered straight grip stock and forearm, case colored frame, 22, 26, or 28 in. octagon barrel. Imported late 2006-2008.

	$1,095	$950	$850	$750	$650	$550	$450	*$1,250*

Add $100 for NWMP (Northwest Mounted Police) carbine with 22 in. barrel, and full length forearms, .45-75 cal. only.

CHAPUIS ARMES

Current manufacturer located in St. Bonnet Le Chateau, France. Currently imported by William Larkin Moore, located in Scottsdale, AZ and JJ Perodeau Gunmaker, located in Sand Springs, OK. Select double rifles are also imported by Evolution USA, located in White Bird, ID. Previously imported by Heirloom Armes, located in Howard Lake, MN, Chadick's, Ltd. (limited importation) located in Terrell, TX, by GSI, Inc. located in Trussville, AL until 1995, and by Armes De Chasse located in Chadds Ford, PA until 1993.

For individual model listings, please go to BlueBookOfGunValues.com/overflow.

GRADING - PPGS™	100%	98%	95%	90%	80%	70%	60%	LAST MSR

CHAPUIS, P. ETS

Previous manufacturer located in Saint-Bonnet le Chateau, France.

P. Chapuis specialized in custom order rifles and shotguns. This company developed a process to color the receiver sideplates while using traditional engraving techniques - resulting in a unique 3-D scene. This is a different company than Chapuis Armes.

CHARLES DALY: PRUSSIAN MFG.

Previous trademark manufactured in Prussia, England, Belgium, and the U.S. circa 1875-pre-WWII.

Charles Daly was a gentleman (not a company) whose goal was to give the U.S. shotgun consumer a European-manufactured gun of similar quality to the premier American shotguns of the same era. Accordingly, he had various European firms fabricate shotguns with American shooting features and preferences. Many "Prussian" Dalys were built by various firms in Suhl, Germany. Importation ceased prior to WWII. These Prussian Charles Dalys utilized the finest materials and best workmanship of their time.

In 1865, Charles Daly was one of two partners who founded the sporting goods business named Schoverling & Daly. They were importers and dealers located in New York City. In 1873, the company reorganized to include a third partner, and the corporate name was changed to Schoverling, Daly & Gales.

Marking the Charles Daly name on firearms began some time around 1875. Daly's name was chosen because it had an appealing sound and would likely influence potential buyers to choose their firearms. Schoverling, Daly & Gales established their lofty reputation by dealing in top-quality merchandise. Because they were known for their high standard of excellence, the Charles Daly brand garnered much esteem.

Schoverling, Daly & Gales made every effort to select only the finest quality firearms for sale in the United States. Initially, manufacturers in Prussia, such as Schiller and Lindner, and later Heym and Sauer of Germany, were selected for their superbly constructed shotguns. Early manufacturers also included J&W Tolley of England, Newmann of Belgium, and even Lefever Arms of New York.

Schoverling, Daly & Gales changed ownership several times throughout the years. Eventually, the company's primary asset was the Charles Daly trademark. In 1919, Henry Modell bought the company, and controlled it for several years. In the 1920s, he sold out to the Walzer family, owners of Sloan's Sporting Goods of Ridgefield, CT. The Walzers established a branch of Sloan's in New York known as Charles Daly & Company. Sloan's imported quality shotguns from many companies, including Italian gun makers Beretta and Vincenzo Bernardelli, Miroku of Japan, and Garbi of Spain.

DRILLINGS

DRILLING MODEL – 12, 16, or 20 gauges and .25-20 WCF, .25-35 WCF, or .30-30 WCF cal., 3 barrel combination gun, extractors, double triggers, engraved action, select walnut, mfg. by both Lindner and Sauer. Lindner mfg. guns are extremely rare - very few specimens are to be found domestically. Sauer guns were not marked for grade, but rather had three levels of engraving which determined the grade. Most Sauer guns had a tang mounted aperture rear sight and a separate rifle cock and were sidelocks. Disc. 1933.

* ***Drilling Model Superior Quality*** – borderline engraving only.

Sauer mfg.	**$4,500**	**$3,750**	**$3,000**	**$2,600**	**$2,300**	**$2,000**	**$1,700**

* ***Drilling Model Diamond Quality*** – full scroll engraving.

Sauer mfg.	**$7,500**	**$6,500**	**$5,500**	**$4,800**	**$4,400**	**$4,000**	**$3,500**

* ***Drilling Model Regent Diamond Quality*** – top-of-the-line model featuring full game scene coverage.

Lindner mfg.	**$20,000**	**$15,000**	**$12,000**	**$11,000**	**$10,000**	**$9,000**	**$7,000**
Sauer mfg.	**$10,000**	**$8,000**	**$7,000**	**$6,700**	**$6,000**	**$5,000**	**$4,000**

Add approx. 25% for gold inlays.

RIFLES

BOLT ACTION GRADE I – .22 Hornet cal., mfg. by F. Jaeger & Co. of Suhl, Germany, 5 shot mag., 24 in. barrel, miniature Mauser bolt action, deluxe walnut. Very limited mfg.

$2,000	**$1,750**	**$1,500**	**$1,250**	**$1,025**	**$825**	**$650**

SHOTGUNS

In the higher grade Prussian Daly variations, there is quite a bit of difference in their manufacture, including engraving options, levels of wood embellishment, and other extra cost features at the time. H.A. Lindner produced approx. 2,500 guns (ser. numbered accordingly), and many of the higher grades show a noticeable difference in the amount of engraving (from minimal to considerable game scene engraving). These guns can be either case colored only or have gold inlaid birds and animals (the number

GRADING - PPGS™	100%	98%	95%	90%	80%	70%	60%	LAST MSR

of which can also vary) and barrels can have various levels of engraving on both the breech and muzzle ends. All of these factors have considerable impact on the overall value of a particular specimen. It is estimated that it took three craftsmen one year to produce a single Diamond Regent gun.

Add 25% - 50% for 20 ga., depending on condition.
Add 200% for 28 ga. on higher grade models (very rare).
Add 100% for .410 bore on higher grade models.
Add approx. 20% for 10 ga. on the following models that apply.

COMMANDER O/U – 12, 16, 20, 28 ga., or .410 bore, Anson & Deeley boxlock action, single or double triggers, ejectors. Mfg. in Belgium circa 1947-1964.

Add 30% for 28 ga. or .410 bore.
Add 10% for single trigger.

* ***Commander O/U Model 100***

	100%	98%	95%	90%	80%	70%	60%	LAST MSR
	$1,200	$975	$800	$700	$625	$550	$475	

Add $100 for single trigger.

* ***Commander O/U Model 200*** – similar to Model 100, except has deluxe walnut.

	100%	98%	95%	90%	80%	70%	60%	LAST MSR
	$1,500	$1,275	$1,075	$900	$800	$700	$600	

EMPIRE O/U – 12, 16, or 20 ga., various barrel lengths, Anson & Deeley boxlock, ejectors and double triggers, fine engraving, deluxe walnut. Disc. 1933.

	100%	98%	95%	90%	80%	70%	60%	LAST MSR
	$4,000	$3,400	$2,750	$2,375	$2,000	$1,825	$1,625	

DIAMOND O/U – similar to Empire model, only finer workmanship and materials.

	100%	98%	95%	90%	80%	70%	60%	LAST MSR
	$6,000	$5,150	$4,300	$3,475	$3,000	$2,600	$2,300	

SUPERIOR SxS – 10, 12, 20, 28 ga., or .410 bore, Anson & Deeley boxlock, various barrel lengths, extractors. Disc. 1933.

	100%	98%	95%	90%	80%	70%	60%	LAST MSR
10 ga.	$2,750	$2,300	$1,850	$1,600	$1,350	$1,125	$995	
12 ga.	$1,650	$1,425	$1,200	$975	$825	$675	$550	
20 ga.	$2,200	$1,875	$1,675	$1,400	$1,175	$995	$825	

28 ga. and .410 bore specimens are too rare to accurately evaluate, and should be appraised individually.

EMPIRE SxS – similar to Superior, only more engraving and better wood.

	100%	98%	95%	90%	80%	70%	60%	LAST MSR
Lindner mfg.	$5,500	$4,650	$4,150	$3,700	$2,950	$2,300	$1,500	
Sauer mfg.	$4,750	$3,850	$3,300	$3,000	$2,300	$1,800	$1,400	

DIAMOND SxS – similar to Empire model, only more elaborate engraving.

	100%	98%	95%	90%	80%	70%	60%	LAST MSR
Lindner mfg.	$11,000	$9,995	$9,000	$8,650	$7,450	$6,250	$4,500	
Sauer mfg.	$7,750	$6,500	$5,750	$5,100	$4,100	$3,000	$2,000	

DIAMOND REGENT SxS – top-of-the-line Prussian side-by-side with or w/o engraving and gold inlays.

	100%	98%	95%	90%	80%	70%	60%	LAST MSR
Lindner mfg.	$18,500	$15,000	$12,000	$11,000	$8,500	$7,000	$5,000	
Sauer mfg.	$15,000	$12,000	$9,200	$8,000	$7,000	$6,000	$5,000	

Subtract 20% - 25% if w/o gold inlays.

EMPIRE SINGLE BARREL TRAP – 12 ga., 30-34 in. barrel, Anson & Deeley boxlock, ejector, vent. rib, finely engraved with select walnut, chopper lump extension, top quality. Disc. 1933.

	100%	98%	95%	90%	80%	70%	60%	LAST MSR
Lindner mfg.	$5,000	$4,500	$4,000	$3,500	$3,100	$2,800	$2,200	
Sauer mfg.	$4,000	$3,500	$3,100	$2,750	$2,350	$2,000	$1,700	

DIAMOND REGENT SINGLE BARREL TRAP – 12 ga., 30-34 in. barrel, six locking bolts, ejector, vent. rib, elaborately engraved and checkered.

	100%	98%	95%	90%	80%	70%	60%	LAST MSR
Lindner mfg.	$15,000	$12,750	$10,500	$8,500	$6,500	$5,000	$4,000	
Sauer mfg.	$10,500	$9,150	$8,000	$7,000	$6,000	$4,750	$3,750	

SEXTUPLE SINGLE BARREL TRAP EMPIRE QUALITY

	100%	98%	95%	90%	80%	70%	60%	LAST MSR
Lindner mfg.	$6,000	$5,400	$4,600	$4,150	$3,650	$3,100	$2,800	

SEXTUPLE SINGLE BARREL TRAP DIAMOND REGENT QUALITY

	100%	98%	95%	90%	80%	70%	60%	LAST MSR
Lindner mfg.	N/A	$18,000	$15,000	$12,000	$9,250	$7,500	$6,000	

CHARLES DALY: JAPANESE MFG.

Private label of shotguns previously manufactured circa 1963-1972 by B.C. Miroku, located in Kochi, Japan.

In 1971, a typhoon almost destroyed the factory. Because of this, all factory records were lost, and these earlier models cannot be researched.

GRADING - PPGS™	100%	98%	95%	90%	80%	70%	60%	LAST MSR

SHOTGUNS: O/U

In the early sixties, C. Daly guns were manufactured by the firm of B.C. Miroku in Kochi, Japan. This Japanese gun manufacturing company has produced guns for many companies, Browning being the biggest current customer. Miroku guns are high quality with excellent fit and finish. Many of them are highly engraved and are fine examples of the gunmaker's art. Charles Daly Miroku Guns are becoming quite collectible in some areas (smaller gauges with open chokes). Their production ceased in 1976.

O/U MODELS - 12, 20, 28 ga., or .410 bore, 26, 28, or 30 in. vent. rib barrels, various chokes, boxlock, auto ejectors, SST, select walnut checkered pistol grip stock, Superior and Diamond Grade Trap have Monte Carlo stocks, the grades differ in amount of engraving and wood. Mfg. 1963-1976 by Miroku.

Add 20% for 20 ga. on models listed below.
Add 50% for 28 ga. on models listed below.
Add 60% for .410 bore on models listed below.
Add 300% for original 28 ga. Lightweight models in 98%+ condition (rare).

Approx. 1,000 28 ga. Lightweight guns were manufactured. All 28 ga. Lightweights (approx. observed ser. range 230011-230998) have barrel spacing 3/4 in. center to center, while the normal 28 ga. has a measurement of 7/8 in. After the Charles Daly line of O/Us were mechanically redesigned, both the 28 ga. and .410 bore were only made on the new 20 ga. frame. To date, no one has observed a .410 bore Lightweight Charles Daly.

FIELD GRADE - 12 or 20 ga., light engraving.

	100%	98%	95%	90%	80%	70%	60%	LAST MSR
	$1,000	$900	$825	$725	$625	$525	$375	

VENTURE GRADE - all gauges, moderate engraving.

	100%	98%	95%	90%	80%	70%	60%	LAST MSR
	$1,175	$1,050	$925	$875	$625	$500	$450	

VENTURE SKEET - 26 in. barrels choked skeet and skeet.

	100%	98%	95%	90%	80%	70%	60%	LAST MSR
	$1,200	$1,100	$900	$800	$700	$600	$450	

VENTURE TRAP - 30 in. imp. mod. and full.

	100%	98%	95%	90%	80%	70%	60%	LAST MSR
	$950	$850	$700	$600	$475	$425	$375	

SUPERIOR GRADE - all gauges, select checkered walnut stock with round knob, scroll engraving similar to Grade I Browning Superposed.

	100%	98%	95%	90%	80%	70%	60%	LAST MSR
	$1,500	$1,300	$1,000	$850	$800	$700	$650	
SUPERIOR TRAP	$1,250	$1,000	$750	$675	$600	$500	$400	

This model has an optional selective ejection system enabling the shooter to deactivate the ejectors.

DIAMOND GRADE - all gauges, extensive engraving with better quality wood.

	100%	98%	95%	90%	80%	70%	60%	LAST MSR
	$2,800	$2,300	$1,500	$1,200	$1,000	$925	$800	

DIAMOND GRADE SKEET

	100%	98%	95%	90%	80%	70%	60%	LAST MSR
	$2,700	$2,400	$1,550	$1,200	$1,100	$925	$800	

DIAMOND GRADE TRAP

	100%	98%	95%	90%	80%	70%	60%	LAST MSR
	$2,200	$1,700	$1,300	$1,000	$900	$800	$650	

DIAMOND GRADE FLATTOP TRAP W/WIDE RIB

	100%	98%	95%	90%	80%	70%	60%	LAST MSR
	$2,300	$1,900	$1,300	$1,000	$900	$725	$650	

DIAMOND REGENT GRADE - mostly 12 ga., extensive frame engraving with gold inlays, rare.

	100%	98%	95%	90%	80%	70%	60%	LAST MSR
	$4,500	$4,000	$3,500	$3,000	$2,400	$2,000	$1,700	

SHOTGUNS: SXS

EMPIRE SHOTGUN - 12, 16, or 20 ga., 26, 28, or 30 in. barrels, various chokes, boxlock, extractors, single trigger, checkered pistol grip stock, early production guns were made by Beretta in Italy. Mfg. 1968-1971.

	100%	98%	95%	90%	80%	70%	60%	LAST MSR
	$1,000	$900	$825	$725	$600	$450	$375	
Vent. rib	$1,200	$1,000	$900	$750	$650	$500	$425	

Add 25% for 20 ga.

MODEL 500 - 12 or 20 ga., 26 or 28 in. barrels with raised or vent. rib, DT, extractors.

	100%	98%	95%	90%	80%	70%	60%	LAST MSR
	$1,100	$875	$650	$500	$450	$300	$275	

Add 20% for vent. rib.

1974 WILDLIFE COMMEMORATIVE - duck scene engraved, Diamond Grade, Trap, or Skeet, limited to 500 guns. Mfg. 1974 only.

	100%	98%	95%	90%	80%	70%	60%	LAST MSR
	$2,500	$1,200	$1,700	N/A	N/A	N/A	N/A	

GRADING - PPGS™	100%	98%	95%	90%	80%	70%	60%	LAST MSR

SHOTGUNS: SINGLE BARREL, TRAP

SUPERIOR GRADE SINGLE BARREL TRAP – 12 ga., 32 or 34 in. vent. rib, full choke barrel, auto ejector, Monte Carlo stock with recoil pad. Mfg. 1968-1976.

	$625	$575	$525	$495	$440	$385	$330	

CHARLES DALY: 1976-2010

Previous manufactured trademark imported late 1996-early 2010 by KBI, Inc. located in Harrisburg, PA. Previously imported by Outdoor Sports Headquarters, Inc. located in Dayton, OH until 1995.

In 1976, Sloan's Sporting Goods sold the Daly division to Outdoor Sports Headquarters, Inc., a sporting goods wholesaler located in Dayton, OH. OSHI continued the importation of high-grade Daly shotguns, primarily from Italy and Spain. By the mid-1980s, the Charles Daly brand was transformed into a broad consumer line of excellent firearms and hunting accessories.

In 1996, OSHI was sold to Jerry's Sports Center, Inc. of Forest City, PA, a major wholesaler of firearms and hunting supplies. Within a few months of Jerry's acquisition of OSHI, K.B.I., Inc. of Harrisburg, PA, purchased the Charles Daly trademark from JSC. As it turned out, Michael Kassnar, president of K.B.I., Inc., had produced almost all of the Charles Daly products for OSHI from 1976-1985 in his capacity of president of Kassnar Imports, Inc. K.B.I., Inc. resurrected the complete line of O/U and SxS shotguns in early 1997.

In 1998, the line expanded to include rimfire rifles and the first pistol produced under the Daly name, a Model 1911-A1 in .45 ACP cal. In 1999, semi-auto and slide action shotguns were also reintroduced. In 2000, the additions included 3 1/2 in. slide actions and semi-autos, Country Squire .410 bore shotguns, bolt action centerfire rifles, and the DDA 10-45, the first double action pistol produced under the Charles Daly name.

During 2004, Charles Daly began importing Bul Transmark pistols from Israel. In 2007, the Little Sharps single shot rifles were introduced.

In 2008, a Charles Daly Defense line was established, which included AR-15 style semi-auto rifles.

On Jan. 29, 2010, K.B.I. announced it was shutting its doors and discontinued importation of all models.

COMBINATION GUNS

SUPERIOR COMBINATION MODEL – 12 ga. (multi-chokes became standard in 2001) over choice of .22 Hornet, .22-250 Rem. (disc. 1998), .223 Rem., .243 Win. (disc. 1998), .270 Win. (disc. 1998), .30-06, or .308 Win. (disc. 1998) cal., boxlock action with dovetailed receiver (accepts scope mounts and iron sights), 23 1/2 in. barrels with iron sights, approx. 7 5/8 lbs. Mfg. by Sabatti in Italy. Imported 1997-2005.

	$1,260	$1,105	$945	$855	$695	$565	$440	*$1,479*

EMPIRE COMBINATION MODEL – 12 ga. (multi-chokes became standard in 2001) over choice of .22 Hornet, .22-250 Rem. (disc. 1998), .223 Rem., .243 Win. (disc. 1998), .270 Win. (disc. 1998), .30-06, or .308 Win. (disc. 1998) cal., boxlock action, 23 1/2 in. barrels, engraved with choice checkered walnut stock and forearm. Mfg. by Sabatti in Italy. Imported 1997-2005.

	$1,800	$1,575	$1,350	$1,225	$990	$810	$630	*$2,189*

HANDGUNS: LEVER ACTION

MODEL 1892 – .357 Mag. or .45 LC cal., similar to Model 1892 rifle, except has 12 in. blue barrel, color case hardened finish, walnut stock. Mfg. 2009.

	$1,195	$1,050	$900	$775	$675	$575	$475	*$1,309*

PISTOLS: SEMI-AUTO

During 2001, the nomenclature on these 1911 models was changed to include a new "E" prefix. The "E" stands for enhanced, and features included extended high-rise beavertail grip safety, combat trigger, combat hammer, beveled magwell, flared and lowered ejection port, dovetailed front and low profile rear sights, and hand checkered double diamond grips. The Enhanced pistols were manufactured by Armscor of the Philipines. M-5 pistols are manufactured by Bul Transmark in Israel.

GOVERNMENT 1911-A1 FIELD EFS/FS – .38 Super (mfg. 2005-2007), .40 S&W (mfg. 2005-2007), .45 ACP cal., steel frame, single action, skeletonized combat hammer and trigger, ambidextrous safety, 8 or 10 shot mag., extended slide release and beavertail grip safety, oversized and lowered ejection port, 5 in. barrel with solid barrel bushing, matte blue (Field FS), stainless slide/blue frame (Superior FS, mfg. 1999-2002), or all stainless (Empire EFS, new 1999) finish, includes two 8 or 10 shot mags. and lockable carrying case, 39 1/2 oz. Mfg. 1998-2008.

	$475	$415	$355	$325	$260	$215	$165	*$589*

Add $50 for Superior EFS Model (disc. 2002).
Add $199 for .22 LR conversion kit with adj. sight (disc. 1999).

GRADING - PPGS™	100%	98%	95%	90%	80%	70%	60%	LAST MSR

* ***Government 1911A1 Field EFS Stainless Empire*** – .45 ACP cal. only, similar to Field FS, except is stainless steel. Disc. 2007.

	$575	$505	$430	$390	$315	$260	$200	*$709*

GOVERNMENT 1911-A1 TARGET EFST/FST – similar to Government 1911-A1 Field FS, except has target sights. Imported 2000-2007.

	$550	$480	$415	$375	$305	$250	$195	*$679*

Add $40 for Superior FST Model (disc. 2000). Add $65 for Empire FST Model (disc. 2000).

* ***Government 1911-A1 Target EFST Stainless Empire*** – .45 ACP cal. only, similar to Target EFST, except is stainless steel. Mfg. 2001-2007.

	$650	$570	$490	$440	$360	$295	$230	*$789*

* ***Government 1911-A1 Target Field EFST*** – .45 ACP cal., 5 3/4 in. compensated barrel with 3 ports, blue or stainless steel, 44.5 oz. Limited importation 2001 only.

	$550	$480	$415	$375	$305	$250	$195	*$679*

Add $100 for stainless steel (Empire EFSTC).

EMPIRE ECMT CUSTOM MATCH – .45 ACP cal., 5 in. barrel, match features, high polish stainless steel, 38 1/2 oz. Imported 2001-2007.

	$750	$650	$575	$500	$425	$350	$275	*$895*

COMMANDER 1911-A1 FIELD EMS/MS – similar to Government 1911-A1, except has 4 in. Commander barrel and features, 37 oz. Imported 1999-2008.

	$475	$415	$355	$325	$260	$215	$165	*$589*

Add $40 for Superior MS Model (includes stainless steel slide and blue frame, disc. 2000).

* ***Commander 1911-A1 Field EMS Stainless Empire*** – .45 ACP cal. only, similar to Field EMS/MS, except is stainless steel. Imported 1999-2007.

	$575	$505	$430	$390	$315	$260	$200	*$709*

* ***Commander 1911-A1 Field EMSCC*** – carry comp., similar to Commander Field EMS, except has single port compensator, blue or stainless. Imported 2001 only.

	$540	$475	$405	$365	$295	$245	$190	*$619*

OFFICER'S 1911-A1 FIELD ECS/CS – similar to Commander, except has 3 1/2 in. barrel and Officer's Model features, 34 1/2 oz. Imported 1999-2008.

	$475	$415	$355	$325	$260	$215	$165	*$589*

Add $40 for Superior CS Model (includes stainless steel slide and blue frame, disc. 2000).

* ***Officer's 1911-A1 Field ECS Stainless Empire*** – .45 ACP cal. only, similar to Field ECS/CS, except is stainless steel. Imported 1999-2008.

	$575	$505	$430	$390	$315	$260	$200	*$709*

* ***Officer's 1911-A1 Field ECSCC*** – carry comp., similar to Officer's Field ECS, except has single port compensator, blue or stainless. Importation began 2001.

	$540	$475	$405	$365	$295	$245	$190	*$619*

Add $100 for Empire ECS Model (full stainless steel construction).

COMMANDER 1911-A1 POLYMER FRAME PC – .45 ACP only, features polymer frame, 4 in. barrel, available in matte blue (Field PC) or stainless slide/blue frame (Superior PC). Imported 1999-2000.

	$460	$405	$345	$315	$255	$205	$160	*$530*

Add $25 for Superior PC Model (includes stainless steel slide and blue frame).

GOVERNMENT 1911-A2 FIELD EFS HC – .40 S&W or .45 ACP cal., 5 in. barrel, SA, similar to Government 1911 A-1 Field EFS, 13 (.45 ACP cal.), or 15 (.40 S&W cal.) shot mag., blue finish only. Imported 2005-2007.

	$595	$520	$445	$405	$325	$270	$210	*$725*

Add $124 for Target Model (.45 ACP cal. only, new 2005).

MODEL DDA 10-45 FS (DOUBLE ACTION) – .40 S&W (disc. 2001) or .45 ACP cal., DA/SA, 4 3/8 in. barrel, polymer frame with checkering, double stack 10 shot mag. with interchangeable base plate (allowing for extra grip length), matte black or two-tone (new 2001) finish, 28 1/2 oz. Imported 2000-2002.

	$450	$395	$340	$305	$250	$205	$160	*$519*

Add $40 for two-tone finish.

* ***Model DDA 10-45 CS*** – similar to Model DDA 10-45 FS, except has 3 5/8 in. barrel, 26 oz. Imported 2000-2002.

	$450	$395	$340	$305	$250	$205	$160	*$519*

Add approx. $10 for colored frame (yellow, OD green, or fuschia, new 2001) and compensated barrel.

GRADING - PPGS™	100%	98%	95%	90%	80%	70%	60%	LAST MSR

FIELD HP HI-POWER – 9mm Para. cal., SA, 4 3/4 in. barrel, patterned after the Browning Hi-Power, blue or hard chrome (mfg. 2005) finish, 10 or 13 shot mag., XS Express sight system, mfg. in U.S. Mfg. late 2003-2006.

	$385	$335	$290	$260	$210	$175	$135	*$458*

Add $120 for hard chrome finish (mfg. 2005).

This model has been produced both by Dan Wesson (2003-2004) and Magnum Research (2005-2006).

CD9 – 9mm Para. cal., 4.46 in. barrel, SA, SFO, black polymer frame and finish, adj. sights, trigger safety, forward/lower accessory rail, 10 or 15 shot mag., three grip inserts. Imported 2009 only.

	$400	$330	$280	$255	$205	$170	$130	*$437*

G4 1911 SERIES – .45 ACP cal., SA, 5 in. barrel, 7 shot, black finish carbon or stainless steel construction, beveled magwell, flared and lowered ejection port, beavertail grip safety, internal extractor, Novak sights, three slot aluminum trigger, available in Standard, Target, and Tactical configurations, mfg. in Israel. Imported 2009 only.

	$750	$655	$565	$510	$415	$340	$265	*$867*

Add $96 for either Tactical or Target model.
Add $96 for stainless steel.
Add $354 for .22 LR conversion kit.

M-5 FS STANDARD (BUL 1911 GOVERNMENT) – 9mm Para. (new 2010), .40 S&W or .45 ACP cal., 5 in. barrel, polymer double column frame, SA, steel slide, aluminum speed trigger, checkered front and rear grip straps, blue or chrome finished slide, 10, 14, or 17 (9mm Para. cal.) shot staggered mag., 31-33 oz. Mfg. by Bul Transmark in Israel. Imported 2004-2009.

	$665	$580	$500	$450	$365	$300	$235	*$803*

* ***M-5 MS Standard Commander*** – .40 S&W or .45 ACP cal., similar to M-5 FS Standard, except has 4 1/3 in. barrel, 29-30 oz. Imported 2004-2009.

	$665	$580	$500	$450	$365	$300	$235	*$803*

* ***M-5 Ultra-X*** – 9mm Para. or .45 ACP cal., 10 or 12 (9mm Para. cal. only) shot mag., compact variation with 3.15 in. barrel. Imported 2005-2009.

	$665	$580	$500	$450	$365	$300	$235	*$803*

M-5 IPSC – .40 S&W, or .45 ACP cal., configured for IPSC competition, 5 in. barrel, with custom slide to frame fit and match grade barrel bushing. Mfg. by Bul Transmark in Israel. Imported 2004-2007.

	$1,250	$1,095	$940	$850	$690	$565	$440	*$1,439*

JERICHO SERIES – 9mm Para., .40 S&W, or .45 ACP cal., 3 1/2 (Compact), 3.82 (Mid-Size), or 4.41 (Full Size) in. barrel, DA/SA, 10, 12, 13, or 15 shot mag., polymer or steel frame with black or chrome (Mid-size .45 ACP cal. only) finish, combat style trigger guard, slide mounted thumb decocker, two slot accessory rail (except Compact), ergonomic grips, mfg. by IWI, Ltd. (formerly IMI) in Israel. Limited importation 2009.

	$595	$520	$445	$405	$325	$270	$210	*$699*

Add $198 for steel frame and chrome finish (Full or Mid-size only).

ZDA MODEL – 9mm Para. or .40 S&W cal., DA/SA, 4 1/8 in. barrel, 12 (.40 S&W cal.) or 15 (9mm Para. cal.) shot mag., mfg. by Zastava. Limited importation 2005 only.

	$490	$430	$370	$335	$270	$220	$170	*$589*

REVOLVERS: DOUBLE ACTION

S222/S224/S226 SERIES – .22 LR cal., 2 (S222), 4 (S224) or 6 (S226) in. barrel, blue finish, 9 shot, rubber grips, fixed (S222) or adj. (S224 or S226) sights, steel construction. While advertised during 2006, this Series was never imported.

	$265	$230	$200	$180	$160	$140	$120	*$321*

S352/S354/S356 SERIES – .357 Mag. cal., 2 (S352), 4 (S354), or 6 (S356) in. barrel, blue finish, 6 shot, fixed (S382) or adj. (S384 or S386) sights, rubber grips, steel construction. While advertised during 2006, this Series was never imported.

	$300	$265	$240	$215	$185	$165	$145	*$350*

S382/S384/S386 SERIES – .38 Spl. cal., 2 (S382), 4 (S384), or 6 (S386) in. barrel, blue finish, 6 shot, fixed (S382) or adj. (S384 or S386) sights, rubber grips, steel construction. While advertised during 2006, this Series was never imported.

	$265	$230	$200	$180	$160	$140	$120	*$321*

GRADING - PPGS™	100%	98%	95%	90%	80%	70%	60%	LAST MSR

Z222/Z224/Z226 SERIES – .22 LR cal., 2 (Z222), 4 (Z224) or 6 (Z226) in. barrel, blue finish, 9 shot, rubber grips, fixed (Z222) or adj. (Z224 or Z226) sights. While advertised during 2006, this Series was never imported.

$200	$180	$160	$140	$120	$100	$80	*$244*

Z382 – .38 Spl. cal., 2 in. barrel, blue finish, 6 shot, fixed sights, rubber grips. While advertised during 2006, this Series was never imported.

$210	$185	$160	$140	$125	$110	$95	*$249*

REVOLVERS: SINGLE ACTION

Models were manufactured by Flli. Pietta in Italy.

MODEL 1873 CLASSIC – .357 Mag. or .45 LC cal., 4 3/4, 5 1/2, or 7 1/2 in. barrel, case hardened frame, blue finish, choice of brass (.45 LC only) or steel backstrap and trigger guard. Imported 2004-2007.

$415	$365	$310	$280	$230	$185	$145	*$485*

Add $20 for steel backstrap and trigger guard.

* ***Model 1873 Classic Stainless*** – similar to Model 1873, except has matte finish, stainless construction with steel backstrap and trigger guard. Imported 2004-2006.

$515	$450	$385	$350	$285	$230	$180	*$587*

MODEL 1873 SONORA – similar to Model 1873 Classic, except has matte blue finish, and not available with steel backstrap and trigger guard. Imported 2006-2007.

$325	$285	$245	$220	$180	$145	$115	*$399*

MODEL 1873 BIRDSHEAD – .45 LC cal. only, 4 3/4 in. barrel, color case hardened finish, steel backstrap and trigger guard. Imported 2006-2007.

$445	$390	$335	$305	$245	$200	$155	*$549*

* ***Model 1873 Birdshead Sheriff*** – .45 LC cal. only, 3 in. barrel, color case hardened finish, steel backstrap and trigger guard. Imported 2006-2007.

$445	$390	$335	$305	$245	$200	$155	*$549*

MODEL 1873 LIGHTNING – .45 LC cal. only, 4 3/4 in. barrel, color case hardened finish, steel backstrap and trigger guard. Imported 2006-2007.

$445	$390	$335	$305	$245	$200	$155	*$549*

* ***Model 1873 Lightning Sheriff*** – .45 LC cal. only, 3 in. barrel, color case hardened finish, steel backstrap and trigger guard. Imported 2006-2007.

$445	$390	$335	$305	$245	$200	$155	*$549*

MODEL 1874 RUSSIAN – .44 Russian or .45 LC cal., 6 1/2 in. barrel, blue finish. Limited importation 2006.

$800	$700	$600	$545	$440	$360	$280	*$931*

RIFLES: BOLT ACTION

K.B.I. also imported a wide variety of Mauser and Mini-Mauser actions until 2006. MSRs ranged between $319-$659.

MAUSER 98 – various cals., Mauser 98 action, 22 (new 2001) or 23 (disc.) in. barrel, 3-5 shot mag., hinged floorplate, fiberglass/graphite composite (Field Grade) or checkered European walnut (Superior Grade) stock, open sights, drilled and tapped receiver, side safety. Mfg. by Zastava. Importation began 1998, and resumed 2001-2005.

* ***Mauser 98 Field Grade*** – features fiberglass/graphite composite stock, matte blue finish or matte stainless steel.

$395	$345	$295	$270	$215	$180	$140	*$459*

Add $90 for stainless steel.
Add $30 for Mag. cals. (.300 Win. Mag. or 7mm Rem. Mag.).
Add 50% for .375 H&H or .458 Win. Mag. cal. (disc.).

* ***Mauser 98 Superior Grade*** – features checkered European walnut stock and high polish blue finish.

$525	$460	$395	$355	$290	$235	$185	*$599*

Add $190 for .375 H&H or .458 Win. Mag. cal.
Add $30 for Mag. cals. (.300 Win. Mag. or 7mm Rem. Mag.).
Add $30 for left-hand action (.30-06 cal. only).

MINI-MAUSER 98 – .22 Hornet, .22-250 Rem. (disc.), .223 Rem., or 7.62x39mm cal., similar to Mauser 98, except has 18.1 (new 2001) or 19 1/4 (disc.) in. barrel, 5 shot mag.

* ***Mini-Mauser 98 Field Grade*** – features fiberglass/graphite composite stock.

$345	$300	$260	$235	$190	$155	$120	*$399*

GRADING - PPGS™	100%	98%	95%	90%	80%	70%	60%	LAST MSR

* ***Mini-Mauser 98 Superior Grade*** – features checkered European walnut stock.

$525 $460 $395 $355 $290 $235 $185 *$599*

Add $30 for left-hand action (.223 Rem. cal. only).

FIELD HUNTER – .22 Hornet, .223 Rem., .243 Win., .270 Win., .30-06, .308 Win., .300 Rem. Ultra Mag., .300 Win. Mag., .338 Win. Mag., or 7mm Rem. Mag. cal., 22 or 24 (Mag. cals. only) in. barrel w/o sights, detachable mag. on short action cals. (.22 Hornet, .223 Rem., or .243 Win.), high polish bluing, checkered walnut stock and forend, right or left-hand action, gold trigger, approx. 7 1/3 lbs. Imported 2000 only.

$475 $415 $355 $325 $260 $215 $165 *$565*

Add approx. $31 for left-hand action (.223 Rem., .243 Win., .270 Win., .30-06, .300 Rem. Ultra Mag., or 7mm Rem. Mag.).

* ***Field Hunter Stainless/Polymer*** – similar to Field Hunter, except has stainless steel barrel and action, black polymer stock with checkering. Imported 2000 only.

$495 $435 $370 $335 $270 $225 $175 *$580*

FIELD GRADE .22 LR CAL. – .22 LR cal., 16 1/4 (True Youth Standard), 17 1/2 (Youth), or 22 5/8 (Standard) in. barrel, single shot (True Youth Standard) or 6 shot mag., all steel shrouded action, grooved receiver, walnut finished hardwood stock. Imported 1998-2002.

$110 $95 $85 $75 $60 $50 $40 *$135*

Add $14 for repeater Youth Model (6 shot, new 2000).
Add $20 for single shot True Youth Standard with shortened dimensions.

* ***Field Grade .22 LR Cal. Polymer/Hardwood*** – similar to Field Grade, except has stainless steel action and barrel with black polymer (disc.) or hardwood (new 2001) checkered stock, 6 1/3 lbs. Imported 2000-2002.

$120 $105 $90 $80 $65 $55 $40 *$149*

* ***Field Grade .22 LR Cal. Superior Grade*** – .22 LR (disc. 2001), .22 WMR, or .22 Hornet cal., 22 5/8 in. barrel, 5 or 6 shot mag., features checkered walnut finished stock with adj. rear sight. Imported 1998-2002.

$175 $155 $130 $120 $95 $80 $60 *$209*

Add $160 for .22 Hornet cal.
Subtract $20 for .22 LR cal. (disc. 2001).

* ***Field Grade .22 LR Cal. Empire Grade*** – similar to Superior Grade, except has checkered California walnut stock with rosewood grip and forend caps, high polish bluing and damascened bolt. Imported 1998-2001.

$290 $255 $220 $195 $160 $130 $100 *$349*

Add $20 for .22 WMR cal.
Add $130 for .22 Hornet cal.

SUPERIOR II RIMFIRE – .17 HMR, .22 LR, or .22 WMR cal., 22 in. barrel, walnut stock. Limited importation 2005 only.

$215 $190 $160 $145 $120 $95 $75 *$259*

Add $40 for .22 WMR or $75 for .17 HMR cal.

RIFLES: LEVER ACTION, REPRODUCTIONS

MODEL 1866 – .38 Spl., .357 Mag., or .45 LC cal., brass or case colored blue (rifle, .357 Mag. cal. only) frame, choice of 19 (carbine), 20 (short rifle), or 24 1/4 (rifle) in. barrel, patterned after the Winchester Model 1866, mfg. by Chapparal. Limited importation 2008.

$725 $635 $545 $495 $400 $325 $255 *$849*

MODEL 1873 – .357 Mag. or .45 LC cal., case colored frame, choice of 18 (Trapper), 19 (carbine), 20 (short rifle), or 24 1/4 (rifle) in. barrel, patterned after the Winchester Model 1873, mfg. by Chapparal. Limited importation 2008.

$740 $660 $550 $475 $400 $350 $295 *$875*

Add $40 for half-round, half-octagon rifle or for Triwood stock.

MODEL 1876 – .45-60 WCF or .45-75 WCF cal., case colored or blue (NWMP short rifle) frame, choice of 22 (short rifle or musket), 26, or 28 in. barrel, patterned after the Winchester Model 1876, mfg. by Chapparal. Limited importation 2008.

$875 $765 $655 $595 $480 $395 $305 *$1,019*

Add $250 for NWMP short rifle or musket.
Add $90 for short rifle or $46 for Triwood stock.

GRADING - PPGS™	100%	98%	95%	90%	80%	70%	60%	LAST MSR

1892 RIFLE/CARBINE – .357 Mag. or .45 LC cal., color case hardened frame, 20 (Carbine) or 24 1/4 (Rifle) in. barrel, patterned after the Winchester Model 1892, mfg. by Armi Sport. Disc. 2009.

$925	$810	$695	$630	$510	$415	$325	*$1,094*

* ***1892 Rifle/Carbine Takedown*** – .357 Mag. or .45 LC cal., color case hardened receiver, 20 (Carbine) or 24 1/4 (Rifle) in. barrel, takedown action. Disc. 2009.

$1,075	$940	$805	$730	$590	$485	$375	*$1,249*

RIFLES: O/U

SUPERIOR EXPRESS – .30-06 cal., 23 1/2 in. barrels with quarter rib and leaf sights, dovetailed receiver for scope mounting, silver finished boxlock receiver, gold SST, checkered walnut stock and forearm, 7 3/4 lbs. Imported 2000-2005.

$1,900	$1,665	$1,425	$1,290	$1,045	$855	$665	*$2,259*

EMPIRE EXPRESS – .30-06, .375 H&H (new 2005), or .416 Rigby (new 2005) cal., 23 1/2 in. barrels with quarter rib and leaf sights, dovetailed receiver for scope mounting, silver finished boxlock receiver with shoulders, gold SST, checkered European style walnut stock with Bavarian cheekpiece and forearm, 7 3/4 lbs. Imported 2000-2005.

$2,525	$2,210	$1,895	$1,715	$1,390	$1,135	$885	*$2,949*

Add $710 for .375 H&H or .416 Rigby cal.

RIFLES/CARBINES: SEMI-AUTO

All recently manufactured semi-auto rifles have forged aluminum alloy receivers that are hardcoat Mil-Spec anodized and Teflon coated, manganese phosphate barrel (except stainless), radiused aluminum magazine release button, aluminum trigger guard, safety selector position on right side of receiver, dust cover, brass deflector, forward assist, and include one magazine and hard plastic carrying case. All recently manufactured rifles were covered by a lifetime repair policy.

SEMI-AUTO RIFLE – .22 LR cal., steel receiver, 20 3/4 in. barrel with adj. rear sight, 10 shot mag. Mfg. 1998-2002.

* ***Semi-Auto Rifle Field Grade*** – features uncheckered walnut finished hardwood stock.

$110	$95	$85	$75	$60	$50	$40	*$135*

* ***Semi-Auto Rifle Field Grade Polymer/Hardwood*** – similar to Field Grade, except has stainless steel action and barrel with black polymer (disc.) or hardwood checkered stock, 6 1/8 lbs. Mfg. 2000-2002.

$120	$105	$90	$80	$65	$55	$40	*$149*

* ***Semi-Auto Rifle Superior Grade*** – features checkered walnut finished stock. Disc. 2001.

$175	$155	$130	$120	$95	$80	$60	*$209*

* ***Semi-Auto Rifle Empire Grade*** – features checkered California walnut stock. Disc. 2001.

$275	$240	$205	$185	$150	$125	$95	*$334*

D-M4/D-M4P CARBINE – 5.56 NATO cal., GIO, 16 in. chrome moly match barrel with M-203 mounting groove, A2 birdcage flash hider, 10, 20, or 30 shot mag., forged "F" front sight base with bayonet lug and rubber coated sling swivel, A3 detachable carry handle, T-marked flat-top upper, 6-position telestock, oval double heat shield M4 forend. Mfg. 2008-2009.

$950	$595	$495	$425	$365	$335	$300	*$1,143*

Add $90 for M4 feed ramps (Model DM-4).

D-M4LE CARBINE – 5.56 NATO cal., GIO, similar to D-M4 carbine, except has Mil-Spec diameter receiver extension with "H" buffer. Mfg. 2008-2009.

$1,135	$725	$525	$465	$415	$375	$350	*$1,373*

D-M4S CARBINE – 5.56 NATO cal., GIO, similar to D-M4 carbine, except has two Picatinny riser blocks, oval double heat shield M4 forend with QD sling swivel and swivel/bipod stud installed, Magpul enhanced trigger guard. Mfg. 2008-2009.

$995	$625	$495	$450	$395	$350	$325	*$1,189*

D-M4LT CARBINE – 5.56 NATO cal., GIO, chrome-lined lightweight A1 barrel, permanently attached Phantom suppressor, 30 shot Magpul PMAG, Mil-Spec diameter receiver extension with "H" buffer, slim carbine type forend. Limited mfg. 2009.

$1,135	$725	$525	$465	$415	$375	$350	*$1,373*

Add $890 for permanently attached Smith Vortex flash suppressor, Magpul CTR stock with buttpad, and Daniel Defense light rail (Model D-M4LTD, mfg. 2009 only).

Add $1,050 for VLTOR Modstock, mid-length gas system, Smith Vortex suppressor, Daniel Defense light rail, and Magpul grip (Model D-M4MG, mfg. 2009 only).

Add $150 for A2 birdcage flash hider, full-length handguard, Troy flip-up BUIS (Model D-M4MLL, mfg. 2009 only).

GRADING - PPGS™	100%	98%	95%	90%	80%	70%	60%	LAST MSR

D-M4LX CARBINE – 5.56 NATO cal., GIO, 16 in. chrome moly HBAR fluted match barrel, Phantom flash suppressor, M4 feed ramps, T-marked flat-top upper, flip-up rear sight, folding front gas block with bayonet lug, aluminum free floating quad rail forend with swiveling sling stud, nine 5-slot low profile ladder style quad rail covers, Ace M4 SOCOM standard length telestock with half buttpad, Ergo Ambi AR grip. Mfg. 2008-2009.

$1,475	$950	$725	$550	$475	$395	$350	*$1,783*

D-MCA4 RIFLE – .223 Rem. cal., 20 in. chrome-lined Govt. profile barrel with A2 birdcage flash hider, 30 shot Mil-Spec mag., A3 detachable carry handle, forged front sight base, A2 handguard, A2 buttstock. Limited mfg. 2009.

$1,100	$675	$525	$450	$400	$350	$325	*$1,317*

Add $622 for KAC M5 quad rail with KAC panels (Model D-MCA4-M5).

D-M4LED CARBINE – 5.56 NATO cal., GIO, 16 in. chrome-lined Govt. profile barrel, A2 birdcage flash hider, Magpul CTR Mil-Spec buttstock, M4 feed ramps, Daniel Defense light rail, Magpul MIAD grip, Troy rear BUIS, FDE finish. Limited mfg. 2009.

$1,795	$1,050	$875	$625	$550	$475	$425	*$2,209*

D-MR20 RIFLE – 5.56 NATO cal., GIO, 20 in. Wilson Arms stainless steel fluted bull barrel, Magpul PRS II stock, three slot riser blocks, Daniel Defense light rail forearm with Picatinny rail gas block, two-stage match trigger, Phantom suppressor, 20 shot mag. Mfg. 2009.

$1,650	$1,000	$795	$595	$495	$425	$395	*$1,979*

DR-15 TARGET – 5.56 NATO cal., GIO, 20 in. chrome moly match HBAR barrel, A2 upper with carry handle, fixed A2 buttstock, A2 birdcage flash hider, forged front sight tower with bayonet lug and rubber coated sling swivel. Limited mfg. 2008.

$915	$575	$475	$415	$350	$325	$295	*$1,089*

DV-24 MATCH TARGET/VARMINT – 5.56 NATO cal., GIO, 24 in. free float match stainless steel bull barrel, T-marked flat-top upper, two Picatinny riser blocks, ported aluminum tube forend with swivel/bipod stud installed, Ace skeletonized buttstock, Picatinny rail milled gas block, two-stage match trigger. Mfg. 2008-2009.

$1,150	$750	$550	$465	$415	$375	$350	*$1,389*

JR CARBINE – 9mm Para. (JR9), .40 S&W (JR40), or .45 ACP (JR45) cal., GIO, 16 1/4 in. triangular contoured barrel, 13 (.45 ACP), 15 (.40 S&W), or 17 (9mm) shot mag., features unique magwell interchangability, allowing the owner to use handgun magazine of choice, matte black synthetic 6-position telescoping AR stock, anodized aluminum receiver, Picatinny rail, free float quad rail forearm, ergonomic AR grip, includes two mags., approx. 6 1/2 lbs. Disc. 2009.

$850	$550	$465	$395	$350	$325	$295	*$987*

RIFLES: SINGLE SHOT

FIELD GRADE – .22 Hornet, .223 Rem., .243 Win., or .270 Win. cal., single shot break open action, 22 in. barrel with mount base, drilled and tapped, adj. or no sights, checkered hardwood stock and forearm. Limited importation 2001 only.

$165	$145	$125	$110	$90	$75	$60	*$189*

Add $10 for adj. sights.

This model was also available in a Youth configuration at no extra charge.

MODEL 1874 LITTLE SHARPS – .17 HMR, .218 Bee, .22 LR (new 2008), .22 Hornet, .22 WMR (new 2009), .357 Mag., .30-30 Win., .38-55 WCF (new 2008), .44-40 WCF (new 2008), or .45 LC cal., 24 (rimfire only) or 26 in. tapered octagon barrel, case colored frame, straight grip uncheckered walnut stock and forearm, mfg. by Armi Sport. Mfg. 2007-2009.

$1,075	$940	$805	$730	$590	$485	$375	*$1,249*

SHOTGUNS: O/U

Recent O/U production was from Italy and Turkey.

PRESENTATION MODEL – 12 or 20 ga., with choke tubes, Purdey double underlug locking action with decorative engraved sideplates, French walnut, single trigger, ejectors. Disc. 1986.

$995	$870	$745	$675	$545	$450	$350	*$1,165*

COUNTRY SQUIRE MODEL – .410 bore only, 3 in. chambers, case colored boxlock action, gold DT, 25 1/2 in. vent. barrels with VR and F/F chokes, checkered straight grip stock and Schnabel forearm, approx. 6 lbs. Disc. 2002.

$640	$560	$480	$435	$350	$290	$225	*$715*

GRADING - PPGS™	100%	98%	95%	90%	80%	70%	60%	LAST MSR

FIELD II HUNTER – 12, 16 (new 2001), 20, 28 ga., or .410 bore, similar to DeLuxe Model except has fixed chokes, extractors, machine-cut stock checkering, and blue receiver, 5 1/2 - 7 lbs., depending on ga./barrel lengths. Imported 1989-2005.

$850 $745 $640 $580 $470 $385 $300 *$1,029*

Add $100 for 28 ga. or .410 bore.

* ***Field II Hunter with Ejectors*** – similar to Field II Hunter, except has ejectors and multi-chokes (not available on 28 ga. or .410 bore), Monte Carlo stock. Imported 1997-2005.

$1,065 $900 $800 $675 $575 $475 $375 *$1,279*

* ***Field II Hunter Ultra-Light*** – 12 or 20 ga., alloy frame, 26 in. VR barrels only with fixed IC/M (disc. 2000) or multi-chokes (new 2001), thin forearm, approx. 5 1/2 lbs. Imported 1999-2005.

$965 $840 $725 $625 $525 $425 $325 *$1,199*

DELUXE MODEL – 12, 20, 28 ga. (disc. 1995), or .410 bore (disc. 1995), boxlock with self adj. crossbolt, 26 or 28 in. chrome-lined VR barrels with internal choke tubes, SST, ejectors, antique silver finish on receiver, deluxe hand checkered walnut stock and forearm. Imported 1989-96.

$650 $570 $490 $440 $360 $295 $230 *$770*

SPORTING CLAYS MODEL – 12 ga. only, SST, ejectors, silver engraved receiver, checkered walnut stock and forearm, screw-in chokes, 28 (disc.) or 30 (new 1996) in. VR ported barrels. Imported 1995-96.

$775 $680 $580 $525 $425 $350 $270 *$895*

SUPERIOR II – 12 or 20 ga., various chokes, boxlock action, single trigger, ejectors, engraved. Disc. 1988.

$675 $590 $505 $460 $370 $305 $235 *$875*

Add $35 for 12 ga. Mag. (disc. 1987).

FIELD III – 12 or 20 ga., various chokes, boxlock action, single trigger. Disc. 1989.

$395 $345 $295 $270 $215 $180 $140 *$450*

SUPERIOR II HUNTER – 12, 20, 28 ga. (new 1998), or .410 bore, 3 in. chambers (except 28 ga.), boxlock action, ejectors, 26, 28, or 30 in. VR barrels with multi-chokes (except 28 ga. and .410 bore), barrel porting became standard during 2000, select checkered walnut stock and forearm, 6 1/8-7 lbs. Imported 1997-2005.

$1,325 $1,160 $995 $900 $730 $595 $465 *$1,519*

Subtract $70 for 28 ga. or .410 bore.

* ***Superior II Hunter Sporting*** – 12 or 20 ga. (disc. 1998), 26 (disc. 1998), 28, or 30 (12 ga. only) in. 10mm VR barrels with multi-chokes and ported barrels. Imported 1997-2005.

$1,400 $1,225 $1,050 $950 $770 $630 $490 *$1,659*

* ***Superior II Hunter Trap*** – 12 ga. only, 30 or 32 (disc. 2001) in. VR barrels with choice of fixed chokes or multi-chokes, regular or Monte Carlo stock. Imported 1997-2005.

$1,450 $1,270 $1,090 $985 $800 $655 $510 *$1,699*

Subtract 10% if w/o multi-chokes with Monte Carlo stock.

* ***Superior II Hunter Skeet*** – 12 or 20 ga., 26 in. VR barrels with choice of Skeet fixed chokes or multi-chokes, regular or Monte Carlo stock. Imported 1997-98.

$935 $820 $700 $635 $515 $420 $325 *$1,039*

Add $120 for multi-chokes with Monte Carlo stock.

EMPIRE DL HUNTER – 12, 20, 28 ga., or .410 bore, boxlock action, silver receiver with game scene engraving, ejectors, SST, 26 or 28 (12 or 20 ga. only) in. VR barrels with multi-chokes (except 28 ga. and .410 bore). Imported 1997-98.

$1,025 $875 $750 $650 $550 $475 $395 *$1,159*

Add $65 for 28 ga. or $110 for .410 bore.

EMPIRE II EDL HUNTER – similar to Empire DL Hunter, except has engraved sideplates featuring game scenes. Imported 1998-2005.

$1,675 $1,465 $1,255 $1,140 $920 $755 $585 *$2,029*

Subtract $10 for 28 ga. or .410 bore.

* ***Empire II EDL Hunter Sporting*** – 12 or 20 ga. (disc. 1999), 26 (disc. 1999), 28, or 30 (12 ga. only) in. VR barrels with multi-chokes. Imported 1997-2005.

$1,675 $1,465 $1,255 $1,140 $920 $755 $585 *$2,049*

* ***Empire II EDL Hunter Trap*** – 12 ga. only, 30 or 32 (disc. 2000) in. VR barrels with choice of fixed chokes (32 in. barrel only) or multi-chokes, regular (disc. 1998) or Monte Carlo stock. Imported 1997-2005.

$1,700 $1,490 $1,275 $1,155 $935 $765 $595 *$2,099*

Subtract 10% if w/o multi-chokes.

GRADING - PPGS™	100%	98%	95%	90%	80%	70%	60%	LAST MSR

* ***Empire II EDL Hunter Mono Trap*** – features 30 or 32 in. single top barrel, standard or adj. Monte Carlo stock. Imported 1999-2005.

	$2,825	$2,400	$2,150	$1,800	$1,425	$1,150	$925	*$3,249*

Subtract approx. 20% if w/o adj. Monte Carlo stock.

* ***Empire II EDL Hunter Trap Combo*** – includes mono 32 in. barrel and extra set of 30 in. O/U barrels, standard or adj. Monte Carlo stock. Imported 1999-2005.

	$3,500	$3,150	$2,700	$2,250	$1,925	$1,625	$1,375	*$3,919*

Subtract approx. 20% if w/o adj. Monte Carlo stock.

* ***Empire II EDL Hunter Skeet*** – 12 or 20 ga., 26 in. VR barrels with choice of Skeet fixed chokes or multi-chokes, regular or Monte Carlo stock. Imported 1997-98.

	$1,050	$920	$790	$715	$580	$475	$370	*$1,189*

Add $125 for multi-chokes with Monte Carlo stock.

DIAMOND FIELD – 12 or 20 ga. (disc. 1986) Mag., with choke tubes. Same action as Presentation Model without sideplates, engraved, select walnut, single trigger, ejectors. Disc. 1986.

	$695	$610	$520	$475	$380	$315	$245	*$895*

* ***Diamond Field Trap or Skeet*** – 12 ga. only, 26 or 30 in. barrels only. Disc. 1986.

	$850	$745	$640	$580	$470	$385	$300	*$1,050*

Subtract $50 for Skeet Model.

DIAMOND GTX DL HUNTER – 12, 20, 28 ga., or .410 bore, sidelock action, ejectors, SST, elaborate engraving with select checkered walnut stock and forearm, 26, 28 (12 or 20 ga. only), or 30 (12 ga. only) in. VR barrels with multi-chokes (except 28 ga. and .410 bore). Imported 1997 only.

	$11,250	$9,845	$8,440	$7,650	$6,190	$5,065	$3,940	*$12,399*

* ***Diamond GTX EDL Hunter*** – more elaborate variation of the Diamond GTX DL Hunter. Imported 1997 only.

	$13,750	$12,030	$10,315	$9,350	$7,565	$6,190	$4,815	*$15,999*

DIAMOND GTX SPORTING – 12 or 20 (disc. 1998) ga., boxlock Boss action with light perimeter engraving, 28 or 30 (12 ga. only) in. VR barrels with multi-chokes and porting. Imported 1997-2001.

	$5,260	$4,605	$3,945	$3,575	$2,895	$2,365	$1,840	*$5,849*

DIAMOND GTX TRAP – 12 ga. only, boxlock Boss action with light perimeter engraving, 30 in. VR barrels with choice of fixed (disc. 1999) or multi-chokes with barrel porting, regular or adj. (new 1999) Monte Carlo stock. Imported 1997-2001.

	$5,865	$4,900	$4,400	$3,825	$3,175	$2,750	$2,175	*$6,699*

Subtract 10% w/o fixed chokes.

DIAMOND GTX MONO TRAP – features single top barrel, adj. Monte Carlo stock. Imported 1999-2001.

	$5,795	$4,850	$4,400	$3,825	$3,150	$2,750	$2,175	*$6,619*

* ***Diamond GTX Mono Trap Combo*** – includes 32 in. mono barrel and extra set of 30 in. O/U barrels, adj. Monte Carlo stock. Imported 1999-2001.

	$6,775	$5,930	$5,080	$4,605	$3,725	$3,050	$2,370	*$7,419*

DIAMOND GTX SKEET – 12 or 20 ga., 26 or 28 (20 ga. only with Monte Carlo stock) in. VR barrels with choice of Skeet fixed chokes or multi-chokes, regular or Monte Carlo stock. Imported 1997-98.

	$4,700	$4,115	$3,525	$3,195	$2,585	$2,115	$1,645	*$5,149*

Add $140 for multi-chokes with Monte Carlo stock.

DIAMOND REGENT GTX DL HUNTER – 12, 20, 28 ga., or .410 bore, sidelock action, ejectors, SST, best quality engraving with premium checkered walnut stock and forearm, 26, 28 (12 or 20 ga. only), or 30 (12 ga. only) in. VR barrels with multi-chokes (except 28 ga. and .410 bore). Imported 1997 only.

	$19,750	$17,280	$14,815	$13,430	$10,865	$8,890	$6,915	*$22,299*

* ***Diamond Regent GTX EDL Hunter*** – top-of-the-line model incorporating best quality engraving and premium walnut. Imported 1997 only.

	$23,000	$20,125	$17,250	$15,640	$12,650	$10,350	$8,050	*$26,429*

MODEL 105 – 12 ga., 26 or 28 in. barrels, fixed chokes, extractors, DT, silver engraved receiver, Turkish walnut stock, mfg. in Turkey. Imported 2006-2007.

	$355	$310	$265	$240	$195	$160	$125	*$409*

MODEL 106 – 12, 20, 28 ga. or .410 bore, 26 or 28 in. barrels, SST, extractors, fixed (.410 bore) or multi-chokes, inlaid blue receiver, mfg. in Turkey. Imported 2006-2007.

	$525	$460	$395	$355	$290	$235	$185	*$599*

GRADING - PPGS™	100%	98%	95%	90%	80%	70%	60%	LAST MSR

MODEL 206 – 12 ga., 3 in. chambers, extractors or ejectors, 26 or 28 in. VR barrels with three multichokes, SST, silver receiver, select Turkish Monte Carlo walnut stock, mfg. in Turkey. Imported 2007-2009.

$685	$600	$515	$465	$375	$310	$240	*$793*

Add $126 for auto ejectors.

* ***Model 206 Sporting*** – 12 ga., 28 or 30 in. VR barrels with 5 multichokes, ejectors, SST. Imported 2007-2009.

$925	$800	$700	$600	$500	$400	$350	*$1,059*

Add $240 for adj. comb.

* ***Model 206 Trap*** – 12 ga., 30 in. VR barrels with 5 multichokes, ejectors. Imported 2007-2009.

$975	$850	$750	$650	$550	$450	$375	*$1,123*

Add $240 for adj. comb.

DALY UL – 12 ga., aluminum receiver, SST, ejectors, 26 in. barrels with five multi-chokes. Imported 2007 only.

$525	$460	$395	$355	$290	$235	$185	*$599*

MAXI-MAG – 12 ga., 3 1/2 in. chambers, boxlock action, 26 or 28 in. VR barrels with three choke tubes, SST, extractors, checkered walnut stock and forearm. Imported 2007 only.

$485	$425	$365	$330	$265	$220	$170	*$559*

Add $60 for Advantage Max-4 or Realtree HD camo finish.

SHOTGUNS: SXS

FIELD III – 12 or 20 ga., various chokes, boxlock action, single trigger. Disc.

$350	$305	$265	$240	$195	$160	$125	

COUNTRY SQUIRE MODEL – .28 ga. or .410 bore, 3 in. chambers, case colored boxlock action, gold DT, 26 in. barrels with fixed chokes, checkered stock and splinter forearm, approx. 6 lbs. Disc. 2000.

$600	$525	$450	$410	$330	$270	$210	*$680*

FIELD II HUNTER MODEL – 10 (disc. 2002), 12, 16 (new 2005), 20, 28 ga., or .410 bore, boxlock action, 26, 28, 30 (12 ga. only), or 32 (10 ga. only) in. barrels, fixed (disc. 2000) or multi-chokes (12 or 20 ga. only), 6-7 3/ 8 lbs., or 11 1/4 (10 ga.) lbs. Imported 1997-2005.

$975	$875	$750	$650	$550	$450	$375	*$1,189*

Subtract $90 for 16 ga., 28 ga. or .410 bore (extractors only).
Subtract approx. 15% if w/o ejectors and multi-chokes (not available in 28 ga. or .410 bore).

SUPERIOR – 12 or 20 ga., boxlock action, various chokes, single trigger. Disc. 1985.

$550	$480	$415	$375	$305	$250	$195	*$624*

SUPERIOR HUNTER – 12, 20, or 28 (new 1999) ga., or .410 bore (new 2000), 26 or 28 in. barrels with fixed (disc. 2000) or multi-chokes (new 2001, 12 or 20 ga. only), 5 7/8-6 3/4 lbs. Imported 1997-2005.

$1,395	$1,220	$1,045	$950	$765	$630	$490	*$1,659*

Subtract $30 for 28 ga. or .410 bore.

LUXE MODEL – 12 (disc. 1991) or 20 ga., boxlock action, SST, ejectors, 26 in. barrels with choke tubes, checkered pistol grip walnut stock with semi-beavertail forearm, recoil pad. Imported 1990-94.

$575	$505	$430	$390	$315	$260	$200	*$650*

This model was manufactured by Hermanos located in Spain.

EMPIRE HUNTER – 12, 20, or 28 (disc. 1998) ga., 26 or 28 in. barrels with fixed or multi-chokes (new 2001), 6-6 7/8 lbs. Imported 1997-2005.

$1,700	$1,490	$1,275	$1,155	$935	$765	$595	*$2,119*

DIAMOND DL – 12, 20, 28 ga., or .410 bore, case colored sidelock action with 3rd lever fastener, scroll engraving, select checkered walnut stock and splinter forearm, 26 or 28 in. barrels with fixed chokes. Importation began 1997.

$6,060	$5,305	$4,545	$4,120	$3,335	$2,725	$2,120	*$6,999*

DIAMOND REGENT DL – 12, 20, 28 ga., or .410 bore, sidelock action with best quality engraving and premium checkered walnut stock and forearm, 26 or 28 in. barrels with fixed chokes. Imported 1997 only.

$18,950	$16,580	$14,215	$12,885	$10,425	$8,530	$6,635	*$21,659*

MODEL 306 – 12 or 20 (new 2007) ga., 3 in. chambers, engraved boxlock action, 26 or 28 in. barrels with three multichokes, gold SST, extractors, checkered Turkish walnut stock and forearm, 6 1/2-7 lbs. Importation from Turkey 2006-2007.

$580	$510	$435	$395	$320	$260	$205	*$649*

GRADING - PPGS™	100%	98%	95%	90%	80%	70%	60%	LAST MSR

CLASSIC COACH GUN – 12 ga., 3 in. chambers, engraved boxlock action, 20 in. barrels with three multichokes, gold SST, extractors, checkered Turkish walnut stock and forearm, 6.3 lbs. Imported 2007.

	$550	$480	$415	$375	$305	$250	$195	*$635*

SHOTGUNS: LEVER ACTION

MODEL 1887 – 12 ga., patterned after the Winchester Model 1887, case-colored frame, 22 or 28 in. barrel. Imported 2007-2009.

	$1,100	$950	$800	$700	$600	$500	$450	*$1,279*

Add $60 for 28 in. barrel.

SHOTGUNS: SEMI-AUTO

The Charles Daly "Novamatic" shotguns were produced in 1968 by Breda in Italy. The Novamatic series was not imported by Outdoor Sport Headquarters, Inc.

NOVAMATIC LIGHTWEIGHT MODEL – 12 ga., 26 or 28 in. barrel, various chokes, available with quick choke interchangeable tubes, checkered pistol grip stock, similar to the Breda shotgun. Mfg. 1968 only.

	$305	$265	$230	$205	$170	$135	$105	

Add $25 for vent. rib.
Add $15 for quick choke.

NOVAMATIC SUPER LIGHTWEIGHT – 12 or 20 ga., similar to Lightweight, except approx. 1/2 lb. lighter.

	$330	$290	$250	$225	$180	$150	$115	

Add $25 for vent. rib.
Add $15 for quick choke.

NOVAMATIC MAGNUM – 12 or 20 ga. with 3 in. chambers, similar to Lightweight, 28 or 30 in. vent. rib barrel, full choke.

	$330	$290	$250	$225	$180	$150	$115	

NOVAMATIC TRAP – similar to Lightweight, with 30 in. full vent. rib barrel, Monte Carlo stock.

	$360	$315	$270	$245	$200	$160	$125	

MULTI-XII – 12 ga. only, 3 in. chamber, 27 in. VR multichoke barrel, self-adjusting gas operation, deluxe checkered walnut stock with recoil pad and forearm. Imported 1987-88 only.

	$425	$370	$320	$290	$235	$190	$150	*$498*

CHARLES DALY AUTOMATIC – 12 ga., 2 3/4 or 3 in. chambers, gas operation, alloy frame, pistol grip (high gloss) or English stock, vent. rib, 5 shot mag. Also available as slug gun with iron sights. Invector chokes became standard in 1986. Disc. 1988.

	$320	$280	$240	$220	$175	$145	$110	*$365*

Add $15 for oil finished English stock.

FIELD GRADE ERCT – 12 or 20 ga., 22 in. barrel, adj. sight or cantilever scope mount, blue finish or RealTree Hardwoods camo coverage, extended rifle choke tube, deer variation, mfg. in Turkey. Imported 2006-2007.

	$340	$300	$255	$230	$185	$155	$120	*$399*

Add $70 for Youth Model.
Add $10 for cantilever scope mount.
Add $60 for 100% camo coverage.

FIELD GRADE FRB – 12 ga., 22 in. fully rifled barrel with choice of fiber optic sights or cantilever scope mount, blue or camo finish, mfg. in Turkey. Imported 2007-2008.

	$385	$335	$290	$260	$210	$175	$135	*$449*

Add $70 for 100% camo coverage.
Add $180 for combo variation with cantilever mount barrel and extra 28 in. multi-choke barrel.
Add $16 for cantilever scope mount.

FIELD IV (FIELD HUNTER) – 12, 20 (new 2002), or 28 (new 2002) ga., 3 in. chamber (12 or 20 ga.), gas operated, aluminum receiver, 22 (Youth or smoothbore slug), 24-30 in. VR barrel with multi-chokes, choice of standard wood/black metal or 100% Next (new 2009), Advantage (disc. 2001), Advantage Timber HD (mfg. 2002-2008), Realtree (disc. 2001), RealTree Hardwoods HD (disc. 2009), Advantage Max-4 HD (12 ga. only, mfg. 2004-2009), Realtree APG (mfg. 2008-2009), Advantage Wetlands (mfg. 2001-2003), or Advantage Classic (disc. 2001) camo coverage, synthetic stock and forearm, 6 7/8-7 1/8 lbs. Imported 1999-2009.

	$440	$385	$330	$300	$240	$200	$155	*$509*

GRADING - PPGS™	100%	98%	95%	90%	80%	70%	60%	LAST MSR

Add $74 for 100% camo coverage.
Add $20 for 28 ga.
Add $124 for Turkey Model with 24 in. barrel, pistol grip stock, and camo coverage (new 2009).
Add $28 for left-hand action (12 ga. only).
Add $20 for Advantage Timber HD camo (20 ga. only, disc. 2008).

* ***Field Hunter Slug*** – 12 ga. only, 22 in. cyl. bore barrel with adj. sights, black synthetic stock and forearm, nickel (disc. 2002) or black chrome finish, adj. open sights. Imported 1999-2003.

$355	$310	$265	$240	$195	$160	$125	*$409*

Add $20 for satin nickel finish (disc. 2002).
Add $40 for fully rifled barrel with adj. sights (new 2002).

FIELD HUNTER MAXI-MAG – 12 ga. only, 3 1/2 in. chamber, 24, 26 (new 2001), or 28 in. 7mm VR barrel with multi-choke, choice of wood/metal or 100% camo coverage similar to Field Hunter, 6 7/8-7 1/8 lbs. Importation began 2000.

$440	$385	$330	$300	$240	$200	$155	*$499*

Add $75 for 100% camo coverage.

* ***Field Hunter Maxi-Mag Turkey*** – 12 ga. only, includes 24 in. barrel, Hi/TriViz fiber optic sights and XX full ported turkey choke tube, Advantage Timber or Realtree Hardwoods HD camo treatment, Uncle Mike's camo sling and sling swivels. Mfg. 2002-2009.

$550	$480	$415	$375	$305	$250	$195	*$639*

SUPERIOR II/IV HUNTER – similar to Field Hunter, except has 20 LPI checkered Turkish walnut stock and forearm, gold highlights and trigger. Imported 1999-2009.

$565	$495	$425	$385	$310	$255	$200	*$675*

Add $32 for 28 ga.
Add $100 for left-hand action (12 ga. only, disc. 2006).

Model nomenclature was changed from Superior II Hunter to Superior IV Hunter during 2009.

* ***Superior II/IV Hunter Sporting*** – 12, 20, or 28 ga., similar to Superior Hunter, except has 28 or 30 in. ported 10mm VR barrels. Imported 1999-2009.

$625	$525	$450	$410	$330	$270	$210	*$739*

Add $236 for adj. comb.
Add $30 for 28 ga.

* ***Superior II/IV Hunter Trap*** – 12 ga. only, 30 or 32 (disc. 2007) in. ported barrel with front and mid bead sights. Imported 1999-2009.

$640	$540	$460	$420	$340	$275	$215	*$769*

Add $230 for adj. comb.

TACTICAL – 12 ga., 18 1/2 in. barrel, matte black synthetic pistol grip stock, Picatinny rail, ghost ring sights, extended tactical choke tube. Limited mfg. 2009.

$495	$435	$370	$335	$270	$225	$175	*$587*

Add $80 for 100% A-Tacs camo finish (new 2010).

SHOTGUNS: SLIDE ACTION

FIELD ERCT – 12 or 20 ga., 22 in. barrel with rifled choke tubes, blue or RealTree Hardwoods HD camo finish, available with either adj. sights or cantilever scope mount, also available in Youth Model (20 ga. only), deer variation. Imported 2006-2007.

$220	$195	$165	$150	$120	$100	$75	*$259*

Add $10 for cantilevered scope mount.
Add $60 for 100% camo coverage.
Add $6 for Youth Model (20 ga. only).

FIELD HUNTER – 12 or 20 (new 2001) ga., 3 in. chamber, 22 (Youth, 20 ga. only), 24, 26, 28, or 30 in. VR barrel with multi-choke, black or pink (Youth only) synthetic stock and forearm, choice of standard wood/metal, chrome (Youth only) or 100% Next (new 2009), Advantage Timber HD (mfg. 2002-2008), Realtree APG (mfg. 2008-2009), Realtree AP HD (mfg. 2008-2009), Realtree Hardwoods HD 12 ga. only, (mfg. 2002-2008) or Advantage Classic (disc. 2001) camo coverage, 5 5/8-6 7/8 lbs. Imported 1999-2009.

$240	$210	$180	$165	$130	$110	$85	*$299*

Add $14 for Youth model with pink synthetic stock (new 2009).
Add $80 for camo.
Add $124 for Turkey Model with pistol grip stock and camo (new 2009).

GRADING - PPGS™	100%	98%	95%	90%	80%	70%	60%	LAST MSR

* ***Field Hunter Slug*** – 12 ga. only, 18 1/2 in. cyl. bore or 22 in. fully rifled (new 2002) barrel with adj. sights, black synthetic stock and forearm, black chrome or dull nickel finish. Imported 1999-2003.

	$210	$185	$160	$145	$115	$95	$75	*$229*

Subtract 15% for 18 1/2 in. barrel.

FIELD HUNTER MAXI-MAG – 12 ga. only, 3 1/2 in. chamber, 24, 26 (new 2001), or 28 in. 7mm VR barrel with multi-choke, choice of wood/metal or 100% camo coverage similar to Field Hunter, approx. 6 3/4 lbs. Imported 2000-2009.

	$270	$235	$205	$185	$150	$120	$95	*$339*

Add $80 for camo.
Add $114 for Turkey Model with camo, Hi/TriViz fiber optic sights and XX full ported turkey choke tube - also includes sling and sling swivels (new 2002).

TACTICAL – 12 or 20 (new 2009) ga., 3 in. chamber, 18 1/2 in. cyl. bore barrel with front sight, black synthetic stock and forearm or 100% camo coverage (new 2009), matte blue metal or chrome finish, 6 lbs. Imported 2000-2009.

	$250	$220	$190	$170	$140	$115	$90	*$289*

Add $24 for Field Tactical AW with chrome finish and adj. sights.
Add $74 for pistol grip stock, ghost ring sights, and MC1 multichoke.
Add $134 for pistol grip stock, ghost ring sights, Picatinny rail, and extended choke tube.
Add $124 for camo with ghost ring and fiber optic sights (new 2009).

CHARLES DALY: 2011-PRESENT

Current trademark of shotguns and pistols owned and imported by Chiappa Firearms USA Ltd. located in Dayton, OH beginning late 2016. Currently manufactured by Chiappa Firearms S.r.L. located in Brescia, Italy. Previously imported by Samco Global Arms located in Miami, FL.

In September 2012, Samco Global Arms, Inc. purchased the Charles Daly trademark from the Kassnar family and imported Charles Daly guns from 2012-2015. In late 2016, Chiappa Firearms USA Ltd. took over the Charles Daly trademark and introduced a new line of Charles Daly shotguns, including O/U, SxS, semi-auto, slide action, and a unique triple barrel.

Service can be provided directly by Samco on Akkar and Charles Daly shotguns imported by Samco during 2011-2012, as well as service parts and accessories for 1999-2010 Charles Daly semi-auto, pump, and O/U shotguns (which can be identified by the serial number) imported by K.B.I. Inc. made by the Akkar factory in Turkey.

Contact Armscor for parts pertaining to other Charles Daly firearms imported by K.B.I. Inc. (such as 1911 pistols). Contact Sabatti or Fausti for shotguns made in Italy. Contact Browning for Miroku shotguns made in Japan.

PISTOLS: SEMI-AUTO

1911 EMPIRE GRADE – 9mm Para. or .45 ACP cal., 5 in. barrel, two 8 shot mags., combat hammer, combat trigger, target sights, VZ grips, beavertail grip safety, checkered front strap, black finish, 2.57 lbs. New 2018.

MSR $899	$765	$670	$575	$520	$420	$350	$300

1911 SUPERIOR GRADE – 9mm Para. or .45 ACP cal., 5 in. barrel, two 8 shot mags., combat hammer, combat trigger, fiber optic sights, diamond checkered walnut grips, beavertail grip safety, black finish, 2.57 lbs. New 2018.

MSR $699	$600	$525	$450	$410	$325	$275	$225

PAK-9 – 9mm Para. cal., blowback action, 6.3 in. blued barrel, two 10 shot Beretta 92 style mags., interchangeable magazine adapter, steel blued receiver, integrated trigger guard (new 2021), standard AK-style sights (disc. 2020) or tactical flip-up adj. sights (new 2021), black synthetic grips (updated in 2021 for a slimmer feel), matte black finish, 6 lbs. New 2017.

MSR $649	$550	$480	$415	$375	$310	$260	$215

Add $30 for Glock mag. adapter and arm brace adapter (new 2019).

In 2021, the PAK-9 had a slight makeover that included a few changes and upgrades to the previous design.

SHOTGUNS: O/U

202 SERIES – 12 or 20 ga., 3 in. chambers, 26 or 28 in. chrome-lined VR barrels, MC-3 Mobil choke tubes, ejector, single selective trigger, fiber optic front sight, checkered walnut (with laser engraved checkering) or synthetic stock, white or black receiver finish, 7.1-7.3 lbs. Mfg. 2018-2019.

	$475	$425	$350	$325	$250	$225	$175	*$554*

Add $22 for walnut stock.

GRADING - PPGS™	100%	98%	95%	90%	80%	70%	60%	*LAST MSR*

202 O/U SHOTGUN – 12, 20 ga., or .410 bore, 3 in. chambers, break open action, 26 or 28 in. chrome-lined barrels with ventilated side ribs, MC-5 choke tubes with Beretta/Benelli mobile threads, extractor, single selective mechanical trigger or double triggers (12 ga. only, mfg. 2020 only), fixed fiber optic front sight, walnut stock with laser engraved checkering on stock and forend, white (steel) finish, 6.2-7.3 lbs. New 2020.

MSR $569 $475 $415 $350 $325 $260 $215 $185

Add $124 for single selective mechanical reset trigger (mfg. 2020 only).

202A O/U SHOTGUN – 12, 20 ga., or .410 bore, 3 in. chambers, break open action, 26 or 28 in. chrome-lined barrels with ventilated side ribs, MC-5 choke tubes with Beretta/Benelli mobile threads, extractor, single selective mechanical reset trigger, fixed fiber optic front sight, walnut stock with laser engraved checkering on stock and forend, aluminum receiver engraved with dog scene, white (aluminum) finish, 7.3 lbs. New 2020.

MSR $499 $425 $375 $325 $295 $235 $195 $165

204X FIELD – 12 or 20 ga., 3 in. chambers, 26 or 28 in. barrels, MC-5 choke tubes with Rem Choke thread pattern, extractor, single selective trigger, fiber optic front sight, walnut stock with checkered grip and forend, matte black finish, 43-45 in. OAL, 6.1-6.8 lbs. Mfg. 2017-2019.

$680 $600 $500 $450 $375 $300 $250 *$799*

* ***204X Field Camo*** – 12 ga., 3 1/2 in. chambers, 24 in. barrels, MC-5X choke tubes with Rem choke thread pattern, Maxi-Mag extractor, fiber optic front sight, single selective trigger, synthetic stock with checkered grip and forend, 100% Realtree Xtra Green camo finish, 41 in. OAL, 7.1 lbs. Mfg. 2017-2019.

$750 $650 $565 $510 $425 $350 $275 *$880*

204XT TACTICAL – 12 or 20 ga., 3 in. chambers, 20 in. barrel, MC-5B choke tubes with Rem choke thread pattern, extractor, SST, synthetic stock with checkered grip and forend, 6-6.8 lbs. New 2017.

MSR $815 $700 $600 $500 $475 $375 $325 $250

Add $84 for 12 ga.

204X MAXI-MAG – 12 ga., 3 1/2 in. chambers, break open action, 24 in. barrels, MC-5X choke tubes with Rem choke thread pattern, Maxi-Mag extractor, single selective mechanical reset trigger, fixed fiber optic front sight, checkered synthetic stock and forend, Mossy Oak Obsession or Realtree APG camo coverage, 8.6 lbs. New 2020.

MSR $899 $765 $675 $575 $525 $425 $350 $275

214E FIELD – 12 or 20 ga., 3 in. chambers, 26 or 28 in. barrels, MC-5 choke tubes with Rem choke thread pattern, ejector, fiber optic front sight, single selective trigger, walnut stock with checkered grip and forend, black finish, 43-45 in. OAL, 6.4-7.3 lbs. New 2017.

MSR $869 $740 $650 $550 $500 $400 $335 $260

Add $90 for 20 ga.

* ***214E Field Compact*** – 12 or 20 ga., 3 in. chambers, 26 or 28 in. barrels, MC-5 choke tubes with Rem choke thread pattern, ejector, single selective trigger, fiber optic front sight, walnut stock with checkered grip and forend, black finish, 41-43 in. OAL, 6.4-7.3 lbs. New 2018.

MSR $914 $775 $680 $580 $525 $425 $350 $275

Add $85 for 20 ga.

* ***214E Field Maxi-Mag Camo*** – 12 ga., 3 1/2 in. chambers, 28 in. barrels, MC-5 choke tubes with Rem choke thread pattern, Maxi-Mag ejector, fiber optic front sight, single selective trigger, synthetic stock with checkered grip and forend, 100% Realtree Max-5 camo finish, 45 in. OAL, 7.1 lbs. New 2017.

MSR $899 $765 $675 $575 $525 $425 $350 $275

214E SPORTING CLAYS – 12 ga., 3 in. chambers, 30 in. ported barrels, MC-5 choke tubes with Rem choke thread pattern, fiber optic front sight, single selective trigger, walnut stock with checkered grip and forend, silver finish, 47.6 in. OAL, 7.6 lbs. New 2018.

MSR $1,449 $1,230 $1,075 $925 $835 $675 $550 $450

SHOTGUNS: SxS

500 SERIES (512 FIELD/520 FIELD/528 FIELD) – 12, 20, 28 ga., or .410 bore (new 2019), 3 in. chambers, break action, 26 or 28 in. barrels, MC-5 choke tubes with Rem choke thread pattern, extractor, single trigger, checkered walnut stock, gloss blued finish, 43-45 in. OAL, 5.4-6 lbs. New 2017.

MSR $945 $800 $700 $600 $550 $450 $375 $300

GRADING - PPGS™	100%	98%	95%	90%	80%	70%	60%	LAST MSR

* ***500 Black/Gold Engraved*** – .410 bore, break open action, 28 in. barrel, Beretta/Benelli Mobil chokes, two shot, extractor, double triggers, brass bead sights, checkered walnut stock and forend, black or black/gold finish, 4.4 lbs. New 2020.

MSR $725	$625	$550	$475	$425	$350	$280	$225	

Add $150 for gold.

512T/520T COACH – 12 or 20 ga., 3 in. chambers, 20 in. barrels, MC-5 flush mount choke tubes with Rem choke thread pattern, walnut stock with checkered grip and forend, 5.3-5.5 lbs. New 2017.

MSR $945	$800	$700	$600	$550	$450	$375	$300	

536 FIELD – .410 bore, 3 in. chambers, break action, 26 in. barrels, MC-5 choke tubes with Rem choke thread pattern, extractor, single selective trigger, bead front sight, checkered walnut stock, white frame and gloss blued finish barrels, 43 in. OAL, 5.4 lbs. New 2019.

MSR $945	$800	$700	$600	$550	$450	$375	$300	

SHOTGUNS: SEMI-AUTO

600 FIELD – 12 or 20 ga., 3 in. chamber, gas operated, right or left (new 2018) hand configuration, 26 or 28 in. barrel, MC-3 choke tubes with Rem choke thread pattern, aluminum receiver, fixed fiber optic front sight, synthetic stock with checkered grip and forend, black finish, 7 lbs. Mfg. 2017-2019.

	$400	$350	$300	$275	$225	$175	$150	*$480*

Add $109 for left-hand configuration with camo finish (new 2018).

* ***600 Field 28 Ga.*** – 28 ga., 3 in. chamber, gas operated, 26 in. barrel, MC-3 choke tubes with Rem choke thread pattern, aluminum receiver, fixed fiber optic sights, wood stock with checkered grip and forend, black finish, 6.4 lbs., 49 in. OAL. New 2019.

MSR $549	$465	$400	$350	$315	$250	$210	$175	

* ***600 Field Camo*** – 12 or 20 ga., 3 in. chamber, gas operated, 22 (20 ga., new 2019), 26, or 28 in. barrel, MC-3 choke tubes with Rem choke thread pattern, fixed fiber optic sights, synthetic stock with checkered grip and forend, drilled and tapped for scope mount, 100% Realtree Xtra Green camo finish, 6.8-7.1 lbs. Mfg. 2017-2019.

	$480	$425	$360	$325	$275	$225	$175	*$565*

* ***600 Field Compact*** – 20 ga., 3 in. chamber, gas operated, right or left (new 2018) hand configuration, 22 in. barrel, MC-3 choke tubes with Rem choke thread pattern, aluminum receiver, fixed fiber optic sights, synthetic stock with checkered grip and forend, drilled and tapped for scope mount, 100% Realtree Xtra Green camo finish, 5.1 lbs. Mfg. 2017-2018.

	$480	$425	$360	$325	$275	$225	$175	*$565*

Add $24 for left-hand configuration (new 2018).

600 LEFT HAND – 20 ga., 3 in. chamber, left-hand configuration, 22 (compact) or 26 in. barrel, MC-3 choke tubes with Rem choke thread pattern, 5 shot, aluminum receiver, auto ejection, fixed fiber optic front sights, checkered synthetic stock and forend, Mossy Oak Obsession camo coverage, 5.1 lbs. (compact) or 6.8 lbs. New 2020.

MSR $609	$525	$460	$395	$350	$290	$235	$185	

600 SPORTING CLAYS – 12 ga., 3 in. chamber, gas operated, 30 in. gloss ported barrel, MC-5 extended choke tubes with Rem choke thread pattern, 5 shot mag., fixed fiber optic front sight, walnut stock with adj. comb and checkered grip and forend, 7.26 lbs. New 2018.

MSR $885	$750	$650	$565	$510	$415	$350	$275	

600T TACTICAL – 12 ga., 3 in. chamber, gas operated, 18 1/2 in. barrel, MC-3B choke tubes with Rem choke thread, 5 shot, hooded fixed fiber optic front sight, ghost ring with Picatinny rail rear sight, black synthetic stock with checkered grip and forend, black finish, 6.8 lbs. Mfg. 2017-2019.

	$425	$375	$325	$300	$225	$200	$150	*$499*

601 CAMO – 12 or 20 ga., 3 in. chamber, 22 (compact), 26 or 28 in. barrel, MC-3 chokes with Beretta/Benelli Mobil choke thread pattern, 5 shot, aluminum receiver, auto ejection, fixed fiber optic front sight, checkered synthetic stock, 100% Realtree Max-5, Realtree Edge, or Mossy Oak Obsession (compact only) camo coverage, 5.5-7.2 lbs. New 2020.

MSR $379	$325	$285	$250	$225	$180	$150	$125	

Add $30 for 20 ga.

601 DPS – 12 ga., 3 in. chamber, gas operated, 18 1/2 in. steel barrel with Beretta/Benelli Mobil choke thread MC-3B (IC/M/B), 5 shot mag., aluminum receiver, auto ejection, fixed hooded front sight and ghost ring rear with Picatinny rail, black synthetic stock, black synthetic pistol grip, 8.05 lbs. New 2021.

MSR $649	$550	$485	$425	$375	$300	$250	$195	

GRADING - PPGS™	100%	98%	95%	90%	80%	70%	60%	LAST MSR

601 FIELD – 12 ga., 3 in. chamber, gas operated, 28 in. barrel, 5 shot mag., brass bead front sight, wood stock with detailed laser engraved checkering on stock and forend or black synthetic stock, aluminum alloy receiver grooved for scope mount, 7.2 lbs. Mfg. 2018-2019.

	$265	$225	$200	$180	$150	$125	$100	*$309*

Add $16 for wood stock.

601 SYNTHETIC – 12 or 20 ga., 3 in. chamber, 26 or 28 in. barrel, MC-3 chokes with Beretta/Benelli Mobil choke thread pattern, 4 shot, aluminum alloy receiver with black anodized finish, auto ejection, fixed fiber optic front sight, checkered synthetic stock and forend, blued barrel finish, 6.2-7.2 lbs. New 2020.

MSR $319	$275	$240	$200	$185	$150	$125	$100	

Add $79 for 20 ga.

601 SEMI-AUTO/601 COMPACT SEMI-AUTO – 12 or 20 (compact model only) ga., 3 in. chamber, gas operated, 22 (compact) or 28 in. steel barrel with Beretta/Benelli Mobil Choke Thread MC-3 (IC/M/F), 4 shot mag., aluminum receiver, auto ejection, single trigger, fixed fiber optic front sight, checkered synthetic stock and forend, Mossy Oak Bottomland camo finish with FDE finish on receiver and barrel, 7-7.2 lbs. New 2021.

MSR $354	$300	$265	$225	$200	$165	$135	$115	

Add $44 for 20 ga.

601 TACTICAL – 12 ga., 3 in. chamber, 18 1/2 in. barrel, MC-3B choke tubes with Rem choke thread pattern, 5 shot, auto extraction, hooded fiber optic front and ghost ring rear sights, black synthetic stock with pistol grip, black finish, 6.8 lbs. New 2020.

MSR $289	$250	$225	$195	$175	$140	$120	$95	

601 WOOD – 12 ga., 3 in. chamber, 28 in. barrel, MC-3 chokes with Beretta/Benelli Mobil choke thread pattern, 4 shot, aluminum receiver with black anodized finish, auto ejection, fiber optic front sight, checkered wood stock, blued barrel finish, 7.3 lbs. New 2020.

MSR $339	$285	$250	$210	$195	$150	$125	$100	

CA612 FIELD – 12 or 20 ga., 3 in. chamber, inertia driven rotary bolt system, 28 in. barrel, MC-5 choke tubes with Beretta/Benelli mobile threads, 5 shot, synthetic stock, black or 100% Realtree Max-5 camo finish, 49.6 OAL, 6 lbs. Mfg. 2017-2019.

	$550	$475	$400	$375	$300	$250	$175	*$629*

Add $60 for 100% Realtree Max-5 camo finish.

CA612 – 12 ga., 3 in. chamber, inertia driven rotary bolt system, 28 in. barrel, MC-5 choke tubes with Beretta/Benelli mobile threads, 4 shot, auto ejection, fixed fiber optic front sight, synthetic checkered stock and forend, 100% Realtree Max-5 camo coverage, 7 lbs. New 2020.

MSR $529	$450	$395	$340	$300	$250	$200	$160	

CA612 SUPERIOR GRADE – 12 ga., 3 in. chamber, inertia driven rotary bolt system, 28 in. barrel, MC-5 chokes with Beretta Optima Plus/Benelli Crio Plus choke threads, 4 shot, aluminum receiver with black anodized finish, auto ejection, fixed fiber optic sights, checkered walnut stock and forend, blued barrel finish, 6.9 lbs. New 2020.

MSR $499	$425	$375	$325	$295	$235	$195	$165	

CA612 TACTICAL (RECENT MFG.) – 12 ga., 3 in. chamber, inertia driven rotary bolt system, 22 in. barrel, MC-5B choke tubes, Beretta/Benelli mobile thread pattern, aluminum receiver, synthetic stock, black finish, 6.6 lbs. Mfg. 2017-2020.

	$395	$350	$300	$275	$215	$180	$140	*$459*

CA612 TACTICAL (CURRENT MFG.) – 12 ga., 3 in. chamber, inertia driven rotary bolt, 22 in. steel barrel, Beretta/Benelli Mobil Choke Thread MC-5B (M/IM/F/+2 Breacher), 4 shot mag., aluminum receiver, auto ejection, fixed hooded front sight, ghost ring rear with Picatinny rail, synthetic pistol grip stock and forend, matte black finish, 6.7 lbs. New 2021.

MSR $473	$400	$350	$300	$275	$225	$185	$155	

CA612 TURKEY – 12 ga., 3 in. chamber, inertia driven rotary bolt system, 24 in. barrel, MC-5X choke tubes with Beretta/Benelli mobile threads, 5 shot, synthetic stock, 100% Realtree Xtra Green camo finish, 6.7 lbs. Mfg. 2017-2020.

	$450	$395	$340	$300	$250	$200	$160	*$529*

635 FIELD – 12 ga., 3 1/2 in. chamber, gas operated, right or left (mfg. 2018-2019) hand configuration, 28 in. ported barrel, MC-5 choke tubes with Rem choke thread pattern, aluminum receiver, Maxi-Mag, fixed fiber optic front sight, synthetic stock with checkered grip and forend, drilled and tapped for scope mount, 100% Realtree Max-5 camo finish, 7.1 lbs. New 2017.

MSR $685	$585	$510	$440	$400	$325	$265	$225	

Add $30 for left-hand configuration (mfg. 2018-2019).

GRADING - PPGS™	100%	98%	95%	90%	80%	70%	60%	LAST MSR

635 TURKEY – 12 ga., 3 1/2 in. chamber, gas operated, 24 in. ported barrel, MC-5X choke tubes with Rem choke thread pattern, 5 shot mag., Maxi-Mag, fixed fiber optic front sights, synthetic stock with black Soft Touch pistol grip and checkered forend, drilled and tapped for scope mount, 100% Realtree Xtra Green (mfg. 2017-2018), Realtree APG (new 2019), or Mossy Oak Obsession (new 2020) camo finish, 7.1 lbs. New 2017.

MSR $685	$585	$510	$440	$400	$325	$275	$225	

AR-12A – 12 ga., 3 in. chamber, gas operated, 18 1/2 in. steel barrel, modified Beretta/Benelli Mobil Choke tube, 5 shot mag., aluminum receiver, auto ejection, adj. front and rear flip-up sights, synthetic pistol grip stock with adj. comb, black finish, 8.2 lbs. New 2021.

MSR $458	$395	$350	$300	$275	$215	$180	$150	

AR-12S – 12 ga., gas operated, 18 1/2 (new 2021) or 20 (disc. 2020) in. barrel, Beretta/Benelli Mobil Choke tube, 5 shot mag., fixed (disc. 2020) or adj. (new 2021) front sight and carry handle rear sight, synthetic pistol grip stock, adj. comb, black finish, approx. 7.5 lbs. New 2019.

MSR $413	$350	$300	$265	$240	$195	$160	$135	

AR-12T – 12 ga., 3 in. chamber, gas operated, 18 1/2 in. steel barrel, Beretta/Benelli Mobil Choke Thread MC-1 (M), barrel shroud, 5 shot mag., aluminum receiver, auto ejection, adj. front and rear flip-up sights, synthetic pistol grip stock and forend, adj. comb, top charging handle, black finish, 9 lbs. New 2021.

MSR $529	$450	$395	$340	$300	$250	$200	$175	

HONCHO TACTICAL SEMI-AUTO – 12 ga. with 3 in. chamber, 14 in. barrel, 5 shot tube mag., auto ejection, fixed brass bead front sight, black synthetic forend, synthetic bird's head grip, black anodized finish with blued barrel, includes ambidextrous sling attachment, 27 in. OAL, 5.3 lbs. New 2019.

MSR $499	$435	$385	$325	$300	$245	$200	$150	

N4S BULLPUP – 12 ga., 3 in. chamber, 20 in. barrel, 5 shot removable mag., adj. flip-up front and rear sights, synthetic stock, forend, and grip, black finish, 29 1/4 in. OAL, 9.3 lbs. Mfg. 2019-2020.

	$550	$485	$425	$375	$300	$250	$195	*$649*

N4S BULLPUP G2

MSR $529	$450	$395	$340	$300	$250	$200	$175	

SHOTGUNS: SINGLE BARREL

101 SINGLE BARREL – 12, 20 ga., or .410 bore, 3 in. chamber, 26 or 28 in. barrel, MC-1 mobile choke or fixed mod choke (.410 bore only), bead front sight, walnut or adj. synthetic stock, black finish, 4 3/4-5 lbs. Mfg. 2018-2019.

	$150	$130	$115	$100	$85	$70	$55	*$176*

Add $9 for walnut stock.

101 SINGLE BARREL (CURRENT MFG.) – 12, 20 ga., or .410 bore, 3 in. chamber, break open action, 20 (new 2021), 26, or 28 in. barrel, Beretta/Benelli Mobil Chokes, extractor, brass bead front sights, black or checkered walnut stock and forend, black finish, 5 lbs. New 2020.

MSR $119	$100	$90	$75	$70	$55	$45	$40	

Add $10 for 20 ga. or .410 bore.
Add $10 for 12 ga. with 28 in. barrel and checkered walnut stock and forend.

101 SINGLE BARREL CAMO – .410 bore, break open action, 20 in. barrel, Beretta/Benelli Mobil Choke Thread MC-1 (XXF), fixed fiber optic sight, Picatinny rail, Mossy Oak Bottomland checkered synthetic stock and forend, FDE finish on receiver and barrel, 4.55 lbs. New 2021.

MSR $219	$190	$165	$145	$130	$105	$85	$70	

SHOTGUNS: SLIDE ACTION

C6 TACTICAL – 12 ga., 3 in. chamber, 18 1/2 in. barrel, MC-1 choke tube with Rem choke thread pattern, 5 shot mag., synthetic field stock with pistol grip, matte black or nickel (new 2018) finish, 5.8 lbs. Mfg. 2017-2019.

	$285	$250	$215	$195	$150	$125	$100	*$329*

Add $30 for nickel finish (new 2018).

300 FIELD – 12 or 20 ga., 3 in. chamber, 26 or 28 in. barrel, MC-3 choke tubes with Rem choke thread pattern, 5 shot mag., fixed fiber optic front sight, synthetic stock with checkered grip and forend, matte black finish, 5.4-6.4 lbs. Mfg. 2017-2019.

	$300	$275	$225	$200	$175	$125	$100	*$349*

* ***300 Field Camo*** – 12 or 20 ga., 3 in. chamber, 26 or 28 in. barrel, MC-3 choke tubes with Rem choke thread pattern, 5 shot mag., synthetic stock with checkered grip and forend, drilled and tapped for scope mount, 100% Realtree Xtra Green camo finish, 5.4-6.4 lbs. Mfg. 2017-2019.

	$375	$325	$275	$250	$200	$175	$125	*$445*

GRADING - PPGS™ 100% 98% 95% 90% 80% 70% 60% LAST MSR

* ***300 Field Compact*** – 20 ga., 3 in. chamber, 22 in. barrel, MC-3 choke tubes with Rem choke thread pattern, 5 shot mag., synthetic stock with checkered grip and forend, Realtree Xtra Green camo finish, 5 lbs. Mfg. 2017-2019.

$325 $275 $250 $225 $175 $150 $125 *$385*

300 RIFLED SLUG – 12 ga., 3 in. chamber, 24 in. barrel, interchangeable Rem choke tube, 5 shot mag., 4-pos. adj. folding stock, cantilever, matte black finish, 7.38 lbs. New 2018.

MSR $434 $375 $325 $275 $250 $200 $175 $125

300T TACTICAL – 12 ga., 3 in. chamber, 18 1/2 in. barrel, MC-1 choke tube with Rem choke thread pattern, 5 shot mag., fixed blade front sight, folding black synthetic pistol grip 4-pos. stock with adj. cheekpiece, black finish, 6 lbs. Mfg. 2017-2019.

$300 $265 $225 $200 $165 $135 $100 *$350*

301 – 12 or 20 ga., 3 in. chamber, 26 (20 ga.) or 28 (12 ga.) in. blued steel barrel, MC-3 chokes with Beretta/Benelli Mobil choke thread pattern, 5 shot, aluminum receiver with black anodized finish, automatic extraction, matte black finish, 6.4-7.4 lbs. New 2020.

MSR $265 $225 $195 $175 $150 $125 $100 $85

Add $14 for 20 ga.

* ***301 Camo*** – 12 or 20 ga., 3 in. chamber, 22 (compact), 26, or 28 in. steel barrel, MC-3 chokes with Beretta/Benelli Mobil choke thread pattern, 5 shot, aluminum receiver, auto extraction, fixed fiber optic sights, checkered synthetic stock, 100% Realtree Max-5 or Mossy Oak Obsession camo coverage, 6-7.4 lbs. New 2020.

MSR $319 $275 $240 $200 $185 $150 $125 $100

Add $50 for 26 or 28 in. barrel.

* ***301 FDE Synthetic*** – 12 ga., 3 in. chamber, 18 1/2 in. steel barrel with heat shield, Beretta/Benelli Mobil Choke Thread MC-3, 5 shot tube magazine, aluminum receiver, auto ejection, fixed fiber optic front and ghost ring rear sight with Picatinny rail, FDE synthetic stock and forend, black synthetic pistol grip, 6.8 lbs. New 2021.

MSR $279 $240 $210 $180 $165 $130 $110 $90

* ***301 Tactical*** – 12 ga., 3 in. chamber, 18 1/2 in. steel barrel, MC-3B/MC-3 chokes with Beretta/Benelli Mobil Choke thread pattern, 5 shot, aluminum receiver, fixed fiber optic front, fixed synthetic stock or folding 4-pos. stock with adj. comb, pistol grip, Picatinny rail, black finish, 6 lbs. New 2020.

MSR $249 $215 $190 $160 $150 $125 $95 $75

* ***301 Wood*** – 12 or 20 ga., 3 in. chamber, 26 (20 ga.) or 28 (12 ga.) in. blued steel barrel, MC-3 choke tubes with Beretta/Benelli Mobil choke thread pattern, 5 shot, aluminum receiver, brass bead front sight, gloss wood checkered stock and forend, black finish, 6-7.1 lbs. New 2020.

MSR $289 $250 $225 $195 $175 $140 $120 $95

Add $6 for 20 ga.

301 FIELD – 12 ga., 3 in. chamber, 28 in. barrel with MC-1 choke tube, 5 shot mag., synthetic or gloss wood stock, ventilated recoil pad, black finish, 6.7-7 lbs. Mfg. 2018-2019.

$215 $190 $160 $145 $120 $95 $75 *$249*

Add $40 for gloss wood stock.

335 FIELD – 12 ga., 3 or 3 1/2 in. chamber, 24 (new 2019), 26 (disc.), or 28 in. barrel, MC-3 or MC-3T (new 2018) choke tubes with Rem choke thread pattern, 5 shot mag., Maxi-Mag, synthetic stock with checkered grip and forend or 4-pos. folding synthetic stock (new 2018), 100% Max-5, Realtree Xtra Green (new 2018), Realtree APG (new 2018), or Mossy Oak Obsession (new 2020) camo finish, 6.7-6.9 lbs. New 2017.

MSR $489 $415 $365 $310 $280 $230 $185 $150

Add $10 for 4-pos. folding stock with Realtree Xtra Green or Realtree APG camo finish (new 2018).
Add $28 for 4-pos. folding stock with Mossy Oak Obsession camo finish (new 2020).

HONCHO PUMP – 12 (new 2020) or 20 ga., 3 in. chamber, 14 in. barrel, 5 shot tube mag., fixed blade front sight, ribbed synthetic forend, synthetic bird's head grip, ambi sling attachment, matte black finish, 27 in. OAL, 4.7 lbs. New 2019.

MSR $309 $265 $235 $200 $175 $145 $125 $95

HONCHO SPRING ASSISTED PUMP – .410 bore, 14 in. barrel, 5 shot tube mag., fixed blade front sight, ribbed synthetic forend, synthetic bird's head grip, matte black finish, 27 in. OAL, 4.1 lbs. New 2019.

MSR $369 $325 $285 $245 $225 $185 $150 $125

GRADING - PPGS™	100%	98%	95%	90%	80%	70%	60%	LAST MSR

HONCHO TACTICAL MAG-FED PUMP – 12 ga., 3 in. chamber, 14 in. barrel, 5 shot detachable mag., ribbed synthetic forend, synthetic bird's head grip, matte black finish, 27 1/4 in. OAL, 5.7 lbs. New 2019.

MSR $339	$285	$250	$215	$185	$150	$125	$100	

SHOTGUNS: TRIPLE BARREL

HONCHO TACTICAL TRIPLE – 12 ga. or .410 bore, 3 in. chamber, triple barrel shotgun, break open action, 18 1/2 in. barrel, 3 shot, extractors, single non-selective trigger w/mechanical reset, fixed brass bead front sight, synthetic forend, black synthetic grip, right, left, top firing sequence, black finish, 27 in. OAL, 6 lbs. New 2019.

MSR $1,329	$1,125	$985	$850	$765	$625	$500	$450	

TRIPLE CROWN – 12, 20, 28 ga. or .410 bore, 3 in. chamber, 26 or 28 in. barrels, MC-5 choke tubes with Rem choke thread pattern, fixed fiber optic front sight, walnut stock with checkered grip and forend, right, left, top firing sequence, includes Break Down case, white finish, 43-45 in. OAL, 6.8-8.7 lbs. New 2017.

MSR $1,979	$1,685	$1,475	$1,265	$1,150	$925	$775	$600	

* ***Triple Crown Compact*** – 12 or 20 ga., 3 in. chamber, 26 or 28 in. barrels, MC-5 choke tubes with Rem choke thread pattern, fixed fiber optic front sight, walnut stock with checkered grip and forend, right, left, top firing sequence, includes Break Down case, white finish, 41-43 in. OAL, 7-8 lbs. New 2017.

MSR $1,979	$1,685	$1,475	$1,265	$1,150	$925	$775	$600	

* ***Triple Crown Two Barrel Set*** – .410/28 ga., 26 in. barrels, MC-5 (extended on .410 bore) choke tubes with Rem choke thread pattern, fixed fiber optic front sight, walnut stock with checkered grip and forend, right, left, top firing sequence, includes Break Down case, white finish, 41 in. OAL, 7 lbs. New 2018.

MSR $2,825	$2,400	$2,100	$1,800	$1,630	$1,325	$1,085	$900	

TRIPLE MAGNUM SHOTGUN – 12 ga., 3 1/2 in. chamber, 28 in. barrel, MC-5 choke tubes with Rem choke thread pattern, Maxi-Mag, fiber optic front sight, synthetic stock with checkered grip and forend, includes Break Down case, 100% Realtree Max-5 camo finish, 43 in. OAL, 8.6 lbs. New 2017.

MSR $2,069	$1,750	$1,530	$1,315	$1,190	$965	$795	$625	

TRIPLE THREAT – 12, 20 ga., or .410 bore, 3 in. chamber, 18 1/2 in. barrel, MC-5 choke tubes with Rem choke thread pattern, fixed fiber optic sights, two-piece walnut stock with checkered grip and forend (buttstock is removable), right, left, top firing sequence, includes Break Down case, black receiver, 7.1-8.2 lbs. New 2017.

MSR $2,015	$1,715	$1,500	$1,285	$1,175	$950	$775	$600	

* ***Triple Threat Synthetic Stock*** – 12 ga., 3 in. chamber, 18 1/2 in. barrel, MC-5 choke tubes with Rem choke thread pattern, fixed fiber optic front sight, black synthetic stock with checkered grip and forend, right, left, top firing sequence, includes Break Down case, blued finish, 8.2 lbs. New 2017.

MSR $1,969	$1,675	$1,465	$1,250	$1,150	$925	$750	$650	

CHARLIN ARMS

Previous manufacturer located in St. Etienne, France.

Charlin Arms previously made shotguns which were patterned after Darne firearms. Typically, they are very high quality and values seem to approximate the Darne guns. Once you have determined the comparable model in Darne, please refer to the Darne section.

CHARTER ARMS (1964-1996 MFG.)

Previously manufactured by Charco, Inc. located in Ansonia, CT 1992-1996.
Previously manufactured by Charter Arms located in Stratford, CT 1964-1991.

The company's first model was the Undercover.

PISTOLS: SEMI-AUTO

MODEL 40 – .22 LR cal. only, DA/SA, 3.3 in. barrel, 8 shot mag., 21 1/2 oz., fixed sights, stainless steel. Mfg. 1984-86.

	$265	$240	$220	$170	$135	$125	$105	*$319*

MODEL 79K – .32 or .380 ACP cal., DA/SA, 3.6 in. barrel, 7 shot mag., 24 1/2 oz., fixed sights, stainless steel. Mfg. 1984-86.

	$325	$300	$280	$230	$200	$170	$145	*$390*

GRADING - PPGS™	100%	98%	95%	90%	80%	70%	60%	LAST MSR

EXPLORER II & S II PISTOL – .22 LR cal., SA survival pistol, barrel unscrews, 8 shot mag., black, gold (disc.), silvertone, or camouflage finish, 6, 8, or 10 in. barrels, simulated walnut grips. Disc. 1986.

$90 $80 $70 $60 $55 $50 $45 *$109*

This model uses a modified AR-7 action.

Manufacture of this model was by Survival Arms located in Cocoa, FL.

MODEL 42T (COMPETITION II TARGET) – .22 LR cal. only, SA, 5.9 in. barrel, target model with checkered walnut grips, adj. sights, blue finish only. Mfg. 1984-85 only.

$490 $450 $395 $350 $300 $260 $220 *$599*

REVOLVERS: DOUBLE ACTION

All Charter Arms revolvers had a hammer block safety system, 8 groove rifling, unbreakable beryllium copper firing pin, triple safety features, no sideplate, steel frames, and lifetime warranty to the original owner.

BONNIE & CLYDE SET – .32 H&R Mag. (Bonnie) and .38 Spl. (Clyde) cal., matched pair, 6 shot, 2 1/2 in. fully shrouded barrel, wood laminate grips (color coordinated), blue finish, pistols individually marked "Bonnie" or "Clyde" on barrels, supplied with gun rugs. Mfg. 1989-91.

$425 $365 $335 $295 $260 $240 $220

LADY ON DUTY – .32 S&W or .38 Spl. cal., 5 (.38 Spl.) or 6 shot, 2 in. shrouded barrel, fixed sights, rose neoprene grips, cased. Mfg. 1995-96.

$195 $165 $145 $130 $115 $100 $85 *$219*

PATHFINDER – .22 LR or .22 WMR (disc. 1989) cal., 6 shot, 2, 3, or 6 (disc. 1985) in. barrels, round butt, adj. sights, walnut grips, wide trigger and spur hammer. Disc. 1990.

$185 $150 $125 $110 $90 $70 $50

* ***Pathfinder - Square Butt*** – .22 LR or .22 WMR (disc. 1989) cal., 6 in. barrel, square butt, otherwise similar to Pathfinder. Disc. 1990.

$190 $155 $125 $110 $90 $70 $50

* ***Pathfinder Stainless*** – .22 LR or .22 WMR (disc. 1989) cal., stainless variation, 3 1/2 in. shrouded barrel. Disc. 1990.

$185 $150 $130 $105 $90 $75 $70

UNDERCOVER – .32 S&W (disc. 1989) or .38 Spl. cal., 5 shot in .38 Spl., 6 shot in .32 S&W, 2 (.38 Spl.) or 3 in. barrel, wide trigger and spur hammer, fixed sights, .38 Spl. was also available with pocket hammer. Disc. 1991.

$175 $145 $115 $100 $90 $85 $80

* ***Undercover Stainless*** – 2 in. shrouded barrel only. Disc. 1994.

$260 $195 $140 $110 $95 $80 $70 *$304*

UNDERCOVERETTE – .32 S&W Long cal., similar to Undercover, 6 shot, 2 in. barrel, blue. Disc.

$155 $140 $110 $100 $90 $70 $55

BULLDOG – .44 Spl. cal., 2 1/2 or 3 (disc. 1988) in. barrels, 5 shot, spur or pocket hammer, wide trigger, checkered bulldog grips (walnut or neoprene), blue or electroless nickel finish, Disc. 1991, reinstated 1994-1996.

$225 $195 $155 $125 $110 $90 $70 *$268*

Add $22 for electroless nickel finish.

* ***Bulldog Stainless*** – 2 1/2 in. bull or 3 (disc. 1989) in. regular barrel. Disc. 1991.

$195 $155 $125 $100 $85 $70 $65

* ***Bulldog Target*** – .357 Mag. or .44 Spl. cal., 5 shot, 4 in. shrouded barrel, adj. sights, square butt only, blue finish. Mfg. 1976-1988.

$225 $150 $125 $100 $85 $70 $65 *$255*

Subtract $10 for .357 Mag. cal.

* ***Bulldog Stainless Target*** – 9mm Federal, .357 Mag., or .44 Spl. cal., 5 shot, 5 1/2 in. shrouded VR barrel, adj. sights, square butt target grips only, matte finished, 28 oz. Mfg. 1989-91.

$250 $175 $125 $100 $85 $70 $65

BULLDOG PUG – .44 Spl. cal., 5 shot, 2 1/2 in. shrouded barrel, fixed sights, walnut or neoprene grips. Mfg. 1986-93.

$240 $195 $160 $130 $110 $100 $90 *$279*

GRADING - PPGS™ 100% 98% 95% 90% 80% 70% 60% *LAST MSR*

* ***Bulldog Pug Stainless*** – 2 1/2 in. shrouded barrel. Mfg. 1987-93.

$300 $235 $175 $135 $115 $100 $85 *$334*

BULLDOG TRACKER – .357 Mag. (.38 Spl.) cal., 5 shot, 2 1/2, 4 (disc. 1989), and 6 (disc. 1989) in. bull barrels, adj. sights, blue only, checkered bulldog grips, square butt on 4 or 6 in. barrel only. Disc. 1986, reintroduced 1989-91.

$185 $150 $125 $110 $100 $90 $80

MAGNUM PUG – .357 Mag. cal., 5 shot, fixed sights, 2.2 in. shrouded barrel, blue finish. Mfg. 1995-96.

$225 $195 $155 $125 $110 $90 $70 *$268*

POLICE BULLDOG – .32 H&R Mag., .38 Spl., or .44 Spl. cal., 5 (.44 Spl. only) or 6 shot, fixed sights, blue only, 3 1/2 or 4 in. barrel, Neoprene grips or square butt (.44 Spl. only). Disc. 1991.

$175 $140 $120 $105 $95 $85 $75

Add $20 for either .44 Spl. cal or 3 1/2 in. shrouded barrel.

* ***Bulldog Stainless Police*** – .32 Mag., .357 Mag. (new 1989), .38 Spl. (disc. 1988 - reintroduced 1990), or .44 Spl. (new 1989) cal., 5 (.357 Mag. or .44 Spl.) or 6 (.32 Mag. or .38 Spl.) shot, square butt, 3 1/2 or 4 in. shrouded barrel. Mfg. 1987-91.

$195 $160 $150 $140 $115 $95 $80

Add $20 for .357 Mag. or .44 Special cal.

Neoprene grips are standard on these models except for the .357 Mag. (square butt).

POLICE UNDERCOVER – .32 H&R Mag. or .38 Spl. cal., 6 shot, spur or pocket hammer, 2.2 in. shrouded barrel, checkered walnut grips, fixed sights, blue or electroless nickel (new 1994) finish. Disc. 1996.

$205 $175 $145 $120 $100 $85 $75 *$238*

Add $14 for electroless nickel finish.

* ***Police Undercover Stainless*** – similar to Police Undercover. Disc. 1993.

$240 $185 $150 $120 $105 $90 $80 *$276*

OFF DUTY – .22 LR (new 1993), .22 WMR (new 1994), or .38 Spl. cal., DA or DAO, 5 (.38 Spl.) or 6 (.22 LR) shot, 2 in. barrel, fixed sights, blue, matte black (disc.), or electroless nickel (new 1994) finish. Disc. 1996.

$170 $145 $120 $105 $90 $85 $80 *$200*

Add $39 for electroless nickel finish.
Add $7 for double action only.

* ***Off Duty Stainless*** – similar to Off Duty. Disc. 1993.

$235 $180 $145 $115 $100 $85 $75 *$268*

PIT BULL – 9mm Federal (rare), .357 Mag. (disc. 1989), or .38 Spl. (disc. 1989) cal., 5 shot, 2 1/2, 3 1/2, or 4 (disc. 1989) in. full shrouded barrel, Neoprene grips, approx. 26 oz. Mfg. 1989-91.

$230 $180 $150 $125 $115 $100 $90

* ***Pit Bull Stainless*** – 2 1/2 or 3 1/2 in. shrouded barrel. Disc. 1991.

$240 $190 $155 $125 $115 $100 $90

RIFLES: SEMI-AUTO

AR-7 EXPLORER RIFLE – .22 LR cal., SA, takedown, barreled action stores in Cycolac synthetic stock, 8 shot mag., adj. sights, 16 in. barrel, black finish on AR-7, silvertone on AR-7S. Camouflage finish new 1986 (AR-7C). Mfg. until 1990.

$125 $100 $85 $75 $65 $55 $50 *$146*

In 1990, the manufacturing of this model was taken over by Survival Arms located in Cocoa, FL. Current mfg. AR-7 rifles will be found under the Henry Repeating Arms Company.

CHARTER ARMS (CURRENT MFG.)

Current manufacturer located in Shelton, CT established during 1998. Previously marketed and distributed mid-2005-late 2010 by MKS Supply, Inc., located in Dayton, OH. Previous company name was Charter 2000, Inc. Dealer sales only.

Charter 2000, Inc. acquired the rights to reproduce the original Charter Arms Undercover Model. Otherwise, it is not affiliated with Charter Arms in any way, nor is it responsible for repair or service on older Charter Arms handguns.

GRADING - PPGS™	100%	98%	95%	90%	80%	70%	60%	LAST MSR

DERRINGERS

DIXIE DERRINGER – .22 LR or .22 WMR cal., 1 1/8 in. barrel, 5 shot, spur trigger, hardwood grips, hammer block safety, choice of black frame with stainless cylinder (new 2011), combo cylinder (new 2009), 6 oz. Mfg. 2002-2012.

	100%	98%	95%	90%	80%	70%	60%	LAST MSR
	$180	$155	$130	$110	$90	$75	$65	*$211*

Add $10 for .22 WMR or black frame with stainless cylinder.
Add $53 for combo cylinder (new 2009).

REVOLVERS

Charter Arms revolvers offer a multitude of various colored finishes the company refers to as "Guns of Color". A select few Charter Arms models have a Blacknitride+ proprietary process, to add hardness to the finish to create a scratch resistant surface and reduce friction and wear to your revolver.

BOOMER – .44 Spl. cal., DAO, large frame, 2 in. ported barrel, 5 shot, full rubber combat grips, matte stainless steel or Nitride (mfg. 2017-2019) finish, 20 oz. New 2016.

	100%	98%	95%	90%	80%	70%	60%	LAST MSR
MSR $439	$375	$325	$275	$250	$200	$175	$145	

Add $21 for Nitride finish (mfg. 2017-2019).

BULLDOG – .44 Spl. or .45 LC (new 2018) cal., DA or DAO, 2 1/2 in. barrel, 5 shot, steel or stainless steel construction, choice of standard or pocket hammer, fixed sights, round butt w/finger groove or Crimson Trace Lasergrips, hammer block safety, black, Nitride (Blacknitride+, new 2017), or matte stainless steel finish, 19-22 oz. New late 1999.

	100%	98%	95%	90%	80%	70%	60%	LAST MSR
MSR $426	$365	$325	$275	$250	$200	$175	$140	

Add $12 for matte stainless steel.
Add $13 for DAO (new 2008)
Add $15 for .45 LC cal. (new 2018).
Add $34 for Nitride finish (Blacknitride+, new 2017).
Add $206 for Crimson Trace Lasergrips (stainless steel only, new 2009).

* ***Bulldog 50th Anniversary*** – .44 Spl. cal., carbon steel frame, 3 in. barrel, 5 shot, wood grips, engraved, features gold inlay in frame, Black finish, 20 oz. Mfg. 2014-2017.

	100%	98%	95%	90%	80%	70%	60%	LAST MSR
	$775	$685	$585	$525	$425	$375	$285	*$894*

* ***Bulldog On Duty*** – .44 Spl. cal., DA, large frame, 2 1/2 in. barrel, 5 shot, matte stainless steel construction, bobbed hammer, fixed sights, round butt with finger groove grips, hammer block safety, 21 oz. Mfg. 2013-2014, reintroduced 2016.

	100%	98%	95%	90%	80%	70%	60%	LAST MSR
MSR $448	$380	$335	$285	$260	$210	$180	$150	

* ***Classic Bulldog*** – .44 Spl. cal., carbon steel frame, 3 in. barrel, 5 shot, fixed sights, standard hammer, wood grip, blue finish, 20 oz.

	100%	98%	95%	90%	80%	70%	60%	LAST MSR
MSR $453	$385	$335	$285	$260	$210	$180	$150	

* ***Target Bulldog*** – .357 Mag. (disc.) or .44 Spl. cal., DA, large frame, 4 (disc.), 4.2 (new 2016), 5 (disc.), or 6 (mfg. 2018-2020) in. barrel, 5 shot, standard hammer, adj. sights, full grip, matte stainless steel finish 22 oz. New 2009.

	100%	98%	95%	90%	80%	70%	60%	LAST MSR
MSR $493	$420	$375	$315	$285	$230	$200	$160	

Add $8 for 6 in. barrel (new 2018).
Add $10 for 5 in. barrel (disc.).
Add $12 for .357 Mag. cal. (disc.).

* ***Tiger Bulldog*** – .44 Spl. cal., 2 1/2 in. barrel, 5 shot, steel or stainless steel construction, standard hammer, fixed sights, round butt with finger groove grips, hammer block safety, black with green stripe finish, 19 oz. New 2011.

	100%	98%	95%	90%	80%	70%	60%	LAST MSR
MSR $481	$410	$360	$310	$280	$225	$185	$160	

* ***Heller Commemorative Bulldog*** – .44 Spl. cal., 5 shot unfluted cylinder, matte stainless steel, checkered finger groove rubber grips, fully engraved, commemorates Heller vs. DC court case, wood presentation case with glass etched top and certificate of authenticity, 22 oz. Limited to 250 models. Mfg. 2019-2020.

	100%	98%	95%	90%	80%	70%	60%	LAST MSR
	$1,475	$1,350	$995	N/A	N/A	N/A	N/A	*$1,595*

The proceeds from this limited edition gun will be donated to the U.S. Bill of Rights Foundation which assists Mr. Heller in our fight for liberty.

GRADING - PPGS™	100%	98%	95%	90%	80%	70%	60%	LAST MSR

CHIC LADY – .38 Spl. cal., small aluminum frame, 2 in. barrel, 5 shot, spur hammer, fixed sights, Crimson Trace Laser (new 2016) or three finger groove grips, includes pink faux alligator case, high polished and pink, lavender (new 2013), leopard skin (mfg. 2016-2020), or gold (mfg. 2017-2020) finish, 14-15 oz. New 2012.

MSR $492	$420	$375	$315	$285	$230	$190	$165	

Add $193 for Crimson Trace Lasergrips (new 2016).

* ***Chic Lady Off Duty*** – .38 Spl. cal., DAO, small aluminum frame, 2 in. barrel, 5 shot, concealed hammer, fixed sights, compact grips, includes pink faux alligator case, pink & high polish stainless finish, 12 oz. New 2012.

MSR $502	$425	$375	$315	$285	$230	$200	$160	

FIRST RESPONDER – .38 Spl. cal., aluminum frame, 2 in. barrel, 5 shot, standard hammer, fixed sights, full grip, black finish with red or blue line, 14 oz. Mfg. 2019-2020.

	$385	$335	$285	$260	$210	$180	$150	*$454*

MAG PUG – .357 Mag. or .41 Magnum (new 2018) cal., stainless steel frame, 2.2 or 2 1/2 (.41 Magnum only, new 2018) in. ported barrel, 5 shot, standard or DAO hammer, fixed sights, full rubber finger grooved or Crimson Trace laser (new 2009) grips, black, stainless steel, or Blacknitride+ (new 2017) finish, 21-23 oz. New 2001.

MSR $403	$345	$300	$260	$235	$190	$150	$125	

Add $6 for stainless steel finish.
Add $7 for DAO with stainless steel finish only.
Add $38 for .41 Magnum cal. with 2 1/2 in. barrel (new 2018).
Add $198 for Crimson Trace Lasergrips (new 2009).

* ***Mag Pug Hi-Polish*** – .357 Mag. cal., stainless steel frame, 3 in. barrel, 5 shot, standard hammer, adj. sights, black finger grooved rubber grips, Hi-Polish finish, 21 oz. New 2019.

MSR $476	$410	$360	$310	$280	$225	$185	$160	

* ***Mag Pug On Duty*** – refer to ON DUTY.

* ***Target Magnum (Mag Pug Target)*** – .357 Mag. cal., stainless steel frame, 4.2 or 6 (new 2018) in. barrel, 5 shot, standard hammer, adj. rear sight, full size black finger grooved rubber grips, 25-27 oz.

MSR $489	$420	$375	$315	$285	$230	$200	$160	

Add $7 for 6 in. barrel (new 2018).

* ***Tiger III (Mag Pug Tiger)*** – .357 Mag. cal., stainless steel frame, 2.2 in. barrel, 5 shot, standard hammer, fixed sights, black finger grooved rubber grips, black with green tiger stripes, 21 oz. New 2001.

MSR $475	$410	$360	$310	$280	$225	$185	$160	

OFF DUTY – .38 Spl. cal., DAO, aluminum frame, 2 in. barrel, 5 shot, enclosed hammer, fixed sights, black compact synthetic or Crimson Trace laser (mfg. 2009-disc.) grips, black, brushed aluminum, black/aluminum matte stainless, lavender/stainless steel (disc.), or black/high polished finish, 12 oz. New 2002.

MSR $420	$360	$325	$275	$250	$200	$175	$140	

Add $15 for black or black/stainless finish.
Add $32 for black/high polish finish.
Add $195 for Crimson Trace Lasergrips (mfg. 2009-disc.).

* ***Pink Lady Off Duty*** – .38 Spl. cal., DAO, aluminum frame, 2 in. barrel, 5 shot, concealed hammer, fixed sights, black compact grips, pink/stainless steel finish, 14 oz.

MSR $441	$375	$325	$275	$250	$200	$175	$140	

ON DUTY – .357 Mag. (Mag Pug On Duty) or .38 Spl. (Undercover Lite On Duty) cal., DA or DAO, aluminum (Undercover Lite) or stainless steel (Mag Pug) frame, 2 (Undercover Lite) or 2.2 (Mag Pug) in. barrel, 5 shot, semi-concealed hammer, fixed sights, black finger grooved rubber or Crimson Trace laser (disc. 2015) grips, 12 oz. New 2009.

MSR $419	$360	$325	$275	$250	$200	$175	$140	

Add $247 for Crimson Trace Lasergrips (disc. 2015).

PATHFINDER – .22 LR or .22 WMR cal., stainless steel frame, 2 or 4 (disc.) in. barrel, 6 shot, stainless construction, fixed or adj. (disc.) sights, checkered walnut (disc.) or black rubber grips with finger grooves, 20 oz. New 2002.

MSR $378	$325	$285	$250	$225	$185	$150	$125	

Add $3 for .22 Mag. cal.
Add $179 for combo with .22 LR/.22 WMR cylinder and adj. sights (disc. 2009, reintroduced 2011-2016).

GRADING - PPGS™	100%	98%	95%	90%	80%	70%	60%	LAST MSR

* ***Pathfinder Concealed Compact*** – .22 WMR cal., DA revolver, 2 in. barrel, concealed hammer, compact grip, lavender/stainless steel or pink/stainless steel, 12 oz. Mfg. 2017 only.

	$360	$325	$275	$250	$200	$175	$125	*$425*

* ***Pathfinder Lavender Lady*** – .22 LR or .22 Mag. cal., aluminum frame, 2 in. barrel, 6 shot, standard hammer, fixed sights, full black rubber grips with finger grooves, lavender/stainless steel finish, 16 oz.

MSR $395	$340	$300	$250	$225	$185	$150	$125	

* ***Pathfinder Lite*** – .22 LR (new 2018) or .22 Mag. cal., aluminum frame, 2 in. barrel, 6 shot, standard hammer, fixed or adj. sights, black rubber grip with finger grooves, brushed aluminum, pink/stainless steel, lavender/stainless steel, or black/anodized finish, 16-21 oz.

MSR $395	$340	$300	$250	$225	$185	$150	$125	

Add $31 for pink/stainless steel or lavender/stainless steel.

* ***Pathfinder Pink Lady*** – .22 LR or .22 Mag. cal., aluminum frame, 2 in. barrel, 6 shot, standard hammer, fixed sights, full black rubber grips with finger grooves, pink/stainless steel finish, 16 oz.

MSR $395	$340	$300	$250	$225	$185	$150	$125	

* ***Pathfinder Target*** – .22 LR or .22 WMR cal., stainless steel frame, 4.2 in. barrel, 6 shot, adj. sights, rubber grips with finger grooves, 24 oz. New 2007.

MSR $426	$365	$325	$275	$250	$200	$175	$140	

PATRIOT – .327 Federal cal., 2.2 or 4 in. barrel, 6 shot, stainless steel Bulldog frame, fixed or adj. sights, rubber finger groove grips, 23 oz. Mfg. 2009-2012.

	$345	$300	$260	$235	$190	$155	$120	*$390*

Add $180 for Crimson Trace Lasergrips and Kershaw knife. Add $50 for Target model.

PITBULL – .40 S&W, 9mm Para., .380 ACP (new 2019), or .45 ACP (new 2017) cal., DA revolver, small or large stainless steel frame, 2.2 (9mm), 2.3 (.40 S&W), 2 1/2 (.45 ACP), 3 (.380 ACP, new 2019), 4.2 (9mm, new 2019), or 6 (9mm, new 2018) in. barrel, 5 or 6 (.380 ACP, new 2019) shot fluted cylinder, exposed hammer, fixed or adj. (new 2019) sights, checkered black rubber finger groove or Neoprene grips, dual coil spring assembly, matte stainless steel or Nitride (Blacknitride+, new 2017) finish, 20-22 oz. New 2013.

MSR $465	$395	$350	$300	$275	$215	$185	$150	

Add $14 for 9mm Para. cal.
Add $42 for .40 S&W or .45 ACP cal.
Add $49 for adj. sights (new 2019, .40 S&W cal.).
Add $56 for 9mm Para. cal.
Add $63 for Nitride finish (Blacknitride+, new 2017).
Add $70 for 4.2 in. or $88 for 6 in. barrel (9mm Para. cal. w/adj. sights, new 2019).

* ***Tiger IV Pitbull*** – .45 ACP cal., stainless steel frame, 2.2 in. barrel, 5 shot, standard hammer, fixed sights, full grips, green/black stripe finish, 22 oz. New 2019.

MSR $414	$355	$325	$275	$250	$200	$175	$140	

POLICE BULLDOG – .38 Spl. cal., 5 shot, large frame, 4 in. tapered or bull barrel, exposed ejector rod, full rubber grips, approx. 23 oz. Mfg. 2002-2007.

	$255	$225	$190	$175	$140	$115	$90	*$299*

* ***Police Bulldog (Recent Mfg.)*** – .38 Spl. cal., large frame, 6 shot, 4 in. barrel, black finish (disc. 2014), standard hammer, steel (disc. 2014) or stainless steel frame, fixed sights. Mfg. 2013-2016.

	$335	$285	$260	$240	$195	$160	$125	*$408*

Add $20 for steel construction w/black finish (disc. 2014).

* ***Heller Commemorative Police Bulldog*** – .44 Spl. cal., stainless steel, fully engraved, commemorates Heller vs. DC court case, smooth finger groove wood grips, includes engraved knife, wood presentation case with glass etched top, and certificate of authenticity. 250 mfg. beginning 2011. Disc.

	$1,475	$1,350	$995	N/A	N/A	N/A	N/A	*$1,595*

The proceeds from this gun were donated to the U.S. Bill of Rights Foundation.

POLICE UNDERCOVER – .38 Spl. cal., stainless steel frame, 2, 4 (disc. 2007), or 4.2 (mfg. 2017 only) in. barrel, 6 shot, stainless steel, standard hammer, fixed sights, full black rubber grips, stainless steel finish, 20 oz. New late 2006.

MSR $409	$350	$300	$260	$235	$190	$150	$125	

PROFESSIONAL – .32 H&R Mag. cal., 3 in. barrel, 7 shot cylinder, LitePipe front and fixed back sights, walnut grips, Blacknitride+ finish. New 2021.

MSR $438	$375	$330	$280	$250	$200	$175	$145	

GRADING - PPGS™	100%	98%	95%	90%	80%	70%	60%	LAST MSR

SOUTHPAW – .38 Spl. cal., true left-hand design with cylinder release and opening from the right side, all aluminum one-piece frame, 2 in. barrel, 5 shot, fixed sights, black finger groove rubber grips, anodized or two-tone pink/stainless steel (new 2009) finish, 14 oz. New 2008.

MSR $435	$375	$325	$275	$250	$200	$175	$140	

Add $35 for two-tone pink/stainless steel (two-tone) finish (new 2009).

UNDERCOVER – .38 Spl. cal., DA or DAO, standard or compact stainless steel frame, 2 in. barrel, 5 shot, fixed sights, full rubber or boot compact grips with finger grooves, or Crimson Trace Laser grips (new 2009), black, BlackNitride+ (new 2017), or stainless steel finish, 16-17 oz. New late 1998.

MSR $358	$300	$265	$225	$200	$165	$135	$100	

Add $6 for compact frame with DAO. Add $14 for stainless steel with standard frame, or $20 for stainless steel with compact frame (DAO).
Add $175 for BlackNitride+ finish (new 2017).
Add $208 for Crimson Trace Lasergrips (new 2009).
Add $42 for blue titanium (mfg. mid-2012-2013, reintroduced 2016 only).

* ***Undercover Gator*** – .38 Spl. cal., DA, stainless steel frame, 2 in. barrel, 5 shot, checkered compact round butt (standard hammer), fixed sights, full black rubber grips with finger grooves, OD Green (mfg. 2011 only) or Gator Skin finish, 14 oz.

MSR $440	$375	$325	$275	$250	$200	$175	$140	

* ***Undercover Hi-Polish*** – .38 Spl. cal., stainless steel frame, 2 in. barrel, 5 shot, standard hammer, fixed sights, wood grips, Hi-Polish finish, 17 oz. New 2018.

MSR $403	$345	$300	$260	$235	$190	$150	$125	

* ***Undercover Panther*** – .38 Spl. cal., small frame, 5 shot, 2 in. barrel, full grips, standard hammer, fixed sights, camo finish. Mfg. 2013-2014.

	$350	$300	$275	$250	$200	$160	$125	*$421*

* ***Undercover Tiger II (Tiger)*** – .38 Spl. cal., DA, stainless steel frame, 2 in. barrel, 5 shot, checkered compact round butt (standard hammer), fixed sights, full black rubber grips with finger grooves, black with green stripes, 14 oz. New 2011.

MSR $420	$360	$325	$275	$250	$200	$175	$140	

UNDERCOVERETTE – .32 H&R Mag. cal., small aluminum or stainless steel frame, 2 in. barrel, 5 shot, standard hammer, fixed sights, Crimson Trace (mfg. 2009-2012) or black rubber grips, available in matte black (disc.), stainless, pink/stainless (Pink Lady), lavender/stainless (Lavender Lady), or gold/black (Goldfinger, disc.) finish, 15-18 oz. New late 2006.

MSR $389	$335	$295	$250	$225	$185	$150	$115	

Add $13 for matte black finish (disc.).
Add $41 for Pink Lady (pink/stainless steel finish) or Lavender Lady (lavender/stainless steel finish).
Add $44 for Goldfinger (gold/black finish, disc.).
Add $123 for Crimson Trace Lasergrips (mfg. 2009-2012) or $173 for Crimson Trace Lasergrips with pink/stainless finish (disc.).

UNDERCOVER LITE – .32 H&R Mag. (disc. 2012) or .38 Spl. cal., ultralight compact aluminum frame, 2 in. barrel, 5 shot, traditional spurred hammer, fixed sights, full black rubber grips with finger grooves, black anodized, red/stainless, red/black, green/black, green/stainless, OD Green/black (disc.), turquoise/stainless, turquoise/black, earth tone/black, black/stainless, gold/black, light bronze/black (disc.), dark grey/stainless (disc.), brown camo/black (disc.), or tiger/black (disc.) finish, 12 oz. New 2009.

MSR $397	$340	$300	$250	$225	$185	$150	$125	

Add $18 for red, green (Shamrock), turquoise (Santa Fe Sky), earth tone (Earthborn), or gold (Goldfinger) finish with black or stainless steel.

* ***Undercover Lite Chameleon*** – .38 Spl. cal., aluminum frame, 2 in. barrel, 5 shot, standard hammer, fixed sights, full rubber finger grooved black grips, black components, iridescent finish, 14 oz. Mfg. 2018-2020.

	$385	$335	$285	$260	$210	$180	$150	*$454*

* ***Undercover Lite Hi-Polish*** – .38 Spl. cal., aluminum frame, 2 in. barrel, 5 shot, standard hammer, fixed sights, rose gold, magenta (new 2018), black, or blue diamond /hi-polish finish, 14 oz.

MSR $454	$385	$335	$285	$260	$210	$180	$150	

* ***Undercover Lite Lavender Lady*** – .38 Spl. cal., aluminum frame, 2 in. barrel, 5 shot, standard or DAO hammer, fixed sights, standard or full black rubber grips with finger grooves or Crimson Trace lasergrips (lavender/stainless steel, .32 H&R Mag. cal. only, disc.), lavender/stainless steel or lavender/black finish, 12 oz. New 2009.

MSR $430	$365	$325	$275	$250	$200	$175	$140	

Add $6 for DAO with compact grips (lavender/stainless steel only).
Add $263 for Crimson Trace Lasergrips (disc.).

GRADING - PPGS™	100%	98%	95%	90%	80%	70%	60%	LAST MSR

* ***Undercover Lite Old Glory*** – .38 Spl. cal., aluminum frame, 2 in. barrel, 5 shot, standard hammer, fixed sights, full black rubber finger groove grips, red/white/blue finish, 14 oz.

MSR $480	$410	$360	$310	$280	$225	$200	$160	

* ***Undercover Lite Pink Lady*** – .32 H&R Mag. (mfg. 2009-2012) or .38 Spl. cal., aluminum frame, 2 in. barrel, 5 shot, standard or DAO hammer, fixed sights, full or compact black rubber grips or Crimson Trace laser grips (Pink/stainless steel finish, .32 H&R Mag. cal. only), pink/stainless steel, pink camo/stainless steel (disc. 2018), or pink/black finish, 13-14 oz. New 2009.

MSR $430	$365	$325	$275	$250	$200	$175	$140	

Add $5 for DAO with compact grips (pink/stainless steel only).
Add $263 for Crimson Trace Lasergrips, disc.

RIFLES: BOLT ACTION

FIELD KING – .243 Win. (disc. 2000), .25-06 Rem., .270 Win., or .30-06 cal., blue or stainless Mauser long action, 4 shot mag., blue or stainless 22 in. E.R. Shaw barrel, checkered black fiberglass reinforced stock with recoil pad, 6 3/4 lbs. Mfg. 2000-2002.

	$300	$260	$225	$205	$165	$135	$105	*$345*

Subtract $46 for non-stainless standard blue rifle.

* ***Field King Carbine*** – .308 Win. only, similar to Field King, except is available in 18 in. barrel with compensator only, blue finish or stainless steel. Mfg. 2000-2002.

	$300	$260	$225	$205	$165	$135	$105	*$345*

CHATTAHOOCHEE GUN WORKS, LLC

Current custom firearms manufacturer and manufacturer of AR-15 style firearms located in Phenix City, AL.

Please refer to BlueBookOfGunValues.com to order the *Blue Book of AR-15s & Variations*, available as a book or online subscription.

CHEROKEE FIREARMS

Current AR-15 style pistol and rifle manufacturer located in Springfield, MO.

Please refer to BlueBookOfGunValues.com to order the *Blue Book of AR-15s & Variations*, available as a book or online subscription.

CHEYTAC USA, LLC

Current manufacturer located in Summerville, SC. Previously located in Charleston, SC, Nashville, GA, and Arco, ID. Previously distributed by SPA Defense, located in Ft. Lauderdale, FL, and by Knesek Guns, Inc. located in Van Buren, AR.

RIFLES: BOLT ACTION

Cheytac previously manufactured the following models: M300 A5 McMillan, M300 Precision Engagement Rifle, Perses Tactical Engagement Rifle, Vidar, and Safeside.

CHEYTAC USA CT 10 – .308 Match or 6.5 Creedmoor cal., rifle length gas system, adj. gas block, 18 in. barrel, Magpul mag., Timney trigger, fully adj. folding stock, ambi selector and bolt release, 15 in. M-LOK Atlas bipod, match billet receiver set, captured buffer, includes hard case and cleaning kit, black finish, 9 lbs. New 2021.

Please contact the company directly for pricing, options, and availability.

CHEYTAC USA CT 15 – 5.56 NATO cal., low profile gas system, 16 in. vanadium steel SOCOM barrel, A2 muzzle brake, custom CT "D" stock, B5 polymer pistol grip, ambi safety, aluminum upper and lower receiver, 13 in. M-LOK handguard, Mil-Std charging handle, M16 BCG, Type III hardcoat black anodized finish, 8 lbs. New 2021.

Please contact the company directly for pricing, options, and availability.

M200 INTERVENTION – .375 CheyTac or .408 CheyTac cal., long action, 29 in. takedown/interchangeable barrel, removable muzzle brake, 7 shot detachable box mag., adj. Timney Elite trigger, CNC machined receiver, integral bipod and monopod, 5-position fully adj. stock, Cerakote Armor Black (standard), FDE, OD Green, Nordic Gray, Tungsten, or Kryptek camo finish, includes custom case, 6 1/2 lbs.

Current MSR is $11,850-$12,870, depending on finish.

PRAETORIAN (M300 INTERVENTION) CARBON FIBER – .375 CheyTac or .408 CheyTac cal., 29 in. fluted barrel, detachable muzzle brake, 7 shot detachable box mag, adj. match or Timney trigger, Push-Button Adjustable Hybrid (PBA-H) shoulder stock, adj. cheekpiece, premium Limbsaver custom recoil pad, Ergo tactical handle grip, integral trigger guard and magwell, ambi paddle lever mag. release, carbon fiber ergonomic enclosed forend with free floating barrel channel, full length Picatinny rails, flush cup swing swivel attachment points, fully adj. folding buttstock, includes CheyTac USA logo and laser engraving and custom case, optional Atlas bipod, Cerakote Armor Black (standard), FDE, OD Green, Nordic Gray, Tungsten, or Kryptek camo finish, 21 lbs.

Current MSR is $10,650-$10,970, depending on finish.

GRADING - PPGS™	100%	98%	95%	90%	80%	70%	60%	LAST MSR

PRAETORIAN (M300 INTERVENTION) COMPOSITE – .375 CheyTac or .408 CheyTac cal., 29 in. fluted barrel, removable muzzle brake, 7 shot detachable box mag., Picatinny rail mount, adj. match or Timney trigger, V-Block stock with adj. cheekpiece, flush cups for sling mounts, OD Green or Kryptek camo finish, includes custom case, 19 lbs.

Current MSR is $6,850-7,170, depending on finish.

M300 LIGHTWEIGHT ALUMIINUM – .300 Win. Mag., .308 Win., .375 Cheytac, .338 Lapua, .or .408 CheyTac cal., 29 in. fluted barrel, muzzle brake, 7 shot box mag., lightweight aluminum chassis with built in V block design, 40 MOA optic rail, adj. target trigger, fully adj. stock, ergonomic pistol grip, sling mounting flush cups, Cerakote Armor Black (standard), FDE, OD Green, Nordic Gray, Tungsten, or Kryptek camo finish, includes custom case, 19 lbs. Disc. 2016.

Last MSR was $8,700-$9,160, depending on finish.

PALADIN – .300 Win. Mag., 7mm Mag., or 6.5x284 Norma cal., 26 1/2 in. barrel, 5 shot detachable box mag., Timney adj. trigger, KRG Whiskey 3 stock, black, FDE, or OD Green finish, 15 lbs.

Current MSR on this model is $4,925.

PERSES – .338 Lapua Mag., .338 Norma, or .300 Norma cal., CheyTac long action w/20 MOA base, 26 1/2 in. MTU contour Bartlein barrel, 5 shot detachable box mag., Timney 510 or Calvin Elite trigger, MDT ESS chassis, custom case included, Atlas bipod (optional), black, FDE, or OD Green finish, 18 lbs.

Current MSR on this model is $5,900.

SAPP – .300 Win. Mag., 7mm Mag., or 6.5x284 Norma cal., CheyTac short action w/20 MOA base, 20 or 24 in. barrel, 5 shot detachable box mag., Timney adj. trigger, KRG Whiskey 3 or Bravo stock, black, FDE, or OD Green finish, Atlas bipod (optional), 15 lbs.

Current MSR on this model is $4,100.

CHIAPPA FIREARMS USA LTD.

Current manufacturer established during 2008 and located in Dayton, OH. Previously marketed until 2014 by MKS Supply, located in Dayton, OH with sales through various domestic distributors. Chiappa Firearms USA Ltd. is one division of the Chiappa Group, which includes Chiappa Firearms Srl (firearms and replica firearms manufacturer established in 1958), Chiappa Firearms USA (firearms manufacturer), Kimar Srl (firearms manufacturer), Costa Srl (metal surface finish treatment), ACP (laser training system), FAS (airguns and target pistols), and Charles Daly brand.

Chiappa Firearms Ltd. manufactures a wide variety of firearms including reproductions and replicas. The models listed in this section were marketed exclusively by MKS Supply, Inc. until 2014, and are marked Chiappa Firearms on the guns. Chiappa also manufactures private label guns for Cimarron Firearms, Legacy Sports, and Taylor's and Company. Please refer to these sections for more information on those Chiappa mfg. models.

COMBINATION GUNS

DOUBLE BADGER – .22 LR, .22 WMR, or .243 Win. (new 2019) cal. over .410 bore (3 in. chamber) or 20 ga./.22 LR (new 2016), 19 in. barrels, Rem. Choke thread pattern (new 2016, 20 ga./.22 LR only), adj. fiber optic rear sight, folding design (19 in. total length), checkered walnut or semi-gloss beechwood (new 2016) stock and forearm, sling swivels, blue or color case (new 2019) finish, double triggers, 5.8 lbs. New 2013.

MSR $441	$375	$325	$275	$250	$200	$175	$165

Add $64 (MSR $505) for 20 ga./.22 LR with Rem. Choke thread pattern (new 2016).
Add $206 (MSR $647) for .410/.243 Win. with color case receiver finish (new 2019).

CHIAPPA M6 SHOTGUN/RIFLE – 12 ga./.22 LR (new 2016), 12 ga./.22 WMR (new 2016), 20 ga/.22 LR (disc.), or 20 ga./.22 WMR (disc.) cal., 18 1/2 in. blue barrel, cylinder bore (disc.) or Rem Choke thread pattern (new 2016), steel blue receiver, foam and steel stock, adj. rear sight, cleaning kit included in stock. New 2014.

MSR $729	$620	$540	$450	$390	$315	$260	$200

X-CALIBER SURVIVAL SHOTGUN/RIFLE – 12 ga. over .22 LR cal. with 8 caliber adapters included, 12 ga. over .22 WMR (new 2016, with 8 inserts), 20 ga. over .22 LR with 4 adapters included, or 20 ga. over .22 WMR cal (new 2016 with 4 inserts), 2-3/4-3 in. chamber, folding break open action, 18 1/2 in. blue steel barrel, blue steel receiver, double triggers, fixed fiber optic front and adj. rear sights, top tang manual safety, matte black finish, three Picatinny quad rails, steel and foam stock, cleaning kit included in stock, 5.8 lbs. New 2014.

MSR $799	$675	$595	$500	$460	$375	$300	$235

Add $200 (MSR $999) for 12 ga./.22 LR or 12 ga./.22 WMR adapter set.

GRADING - PPGS™	100%	98%	95%	90%	80%	70%	60%	LAST MSR

DRILLINGS

Chiappa Drillings were manufactured by Akkar, located in Istanbul, Turkey.

TRIPLE CROWN – 12, 20 (new 2014), or 28 (new 2016) ga., 3 in. chambers, 26 (20 or 28 ga.) or 28 (12 ga.) in. barrels with VR on top barrel, Rem. Chokes, fiber optic sights, checkered walnut stock and splinter forearm, nickel finished receiver, single gold trigger, 7-8.7 lbs. Imported from Turkey 2013-19.

	$1,650	$1,450	$1,250	$1,150	$925	$750	$625	*$1,929*

TRIPLE THREAT – 12 or 20 (new 2016) ga., 3 in. chambers, 18 1/2 in. barrels without VR and fixed front sight, rear of stock detaches for portability, Mare's Leg configuration, black or nickel (disc.) finished receiver, gold trigger, two-piece walnut stock. Imported from Turkey 2013-19.

	$1,675	$1,475	$1,250	$1,150	$925	$750	$625	*$1,955*

TRIPLE MAGNUM – 12 ga., 3 1/2 in. chambers, 28 in. barrels, MC-5 chokes, fiber optic sights, synthetic stock and forearm, black receiver, black (disc. 2015) or Realtree Max-5 camo finish, 8.6 lbs. Imported 2014-2017.

	$1,925	$1,685	$1,450	$1,310	$1,075	$875	$685	*$2,139*

Last MSR for black synthetic stock in 2015 was $1,733.

TRIPLE TOM – 12 ga., 3 1/2 in. chambers, 24 in. barrels, black receiver, fiber optic sights, MC-5T synthetic stock and forearm, Realtree Xtra Green camo, 8.3 lbs. Imported 2014-2017.

	$1,925	$1,685	$1,450	$1,310	$1,075	$875	$685	*$2,139*

PISTOLS: LEVER ACTION

1892 MARE'S LEG PISTOL – .45 LC, .44 Mag., .357 Mag. cal., 4 shot mag., 9 or 12 in. round barrel, walnut stock and forend, fixed rear sight, color case hardening, oversized finger lever, blue finish, 4.8-5.5 lbs. New 2013.

MSR $1,288	$1,095	$960	$825	$750	$600	$500	$400	

1892 MARE'S LEG THIRD VERSION – .44-40 or .45 Colt cal., 9 in. octagonal barrel, 4 shot, steel receiver, barrel band, and large lever loop, walnut pistol grip stock and forend, receiver mounted saddle ring, antique finished metal parts, 4.8 lbs. Mfg. 2016-2017.

	$1,325	$1,160	$995	$900	$730	$600	$475	*$1,479*

PISTOLS: SEMI-AUTO

1911-22 STANDARD – .22 LR cal., SA blowback, 5 in. barrel, blue steel or two tone (disc.) finish, 10 shot mag., checkered wood grips, fixed front sight, adj. rear sight, Black, OD/Black (olive drab, mfg. 2011-2017), or Tan/Black (mfg. 2011-2017) finish, includes two mags., approx. 33 oz. New mid-2010.

MSR $269	$230	$195	$170	$145	$120	$95	$75	

Add $20 for OD Green/Black or Tan/Black finish (disc. 2017).

* ***1911-22 Pistol*** – .22 LR cal., full size, 5 in. barrel, two 10 shot mags., Hogue grips, matte black frame and OD Green or Tan slide.

MSR $317	$270	$235	$200	$175	$150	$125	$95	

* ***1911-22 Target*** – .22 LR cal., black frame, 5 in. threaded barrel with muzzle brake, two 10 shot mags., dovetail front sight, Williams rear sight, checkered wood grips, matte black finish. New mid-2010.

MSR $336	$285	$250	$215	$195	$150	$125	$100	

* ***1911-22 Tactical*** – .22 LR cal., similar to 1911-22, except has 5 in. threaded barrel with fake suppressor, fiber optic front sights, black finish only. Mfg. mid-2010-2016.

	$365	$320	$280	$250	$200	$175	$150	*$408*

1911-22 COMPACT – .22 LR cal., SA blowback, 10 shot mag., 4 in. fixed barrel, Novak style rear sight and fiber optic front sight, diamond checkered walnut grips, combat hammer, serrated grip frame, black finish.

MSR $295	$250	$225	$200	$175	$150	$125	$95	

1911-22 CUSTOM – .22 LR cal., SA blowback, 5 in. fixed barrel, two 10 shot mags., Novak style rear and fiber optic front sights, diamond checkered walnut grips, combat hammer, serrated grip frame, adj. target trigger, checkered slide back, optional lower Picatinny tactical rail, extended flared magwell, extended magazine bumpers, black finish.

MSR $324	$275	$240	$200	$185	$150	$125	$100	

1911-22 CRUISER – .22 LR cal., SA blowback, 10 shot mag., 5 in. barrel, Novak fiber optic sights, diamond checkered walnut grips, satin nickel slide/black receiver finish. Disc. 2013.

	$275	$250	$200	$175	$150	$125	$100	*$309*

GRADING - PPGS™	100%	98%	95%	90%	80%	70%	60%	LAST MSR

1911 CUSTOM PISTOL – .45 ACP cal., SA, short recoil operating system, 8 shot mag., 5 in. barrel, Novak style fiber optic sights, checkered olive wood grips, skeletonized trigger, lower Picatinny rail, extended beavertail safety, Tactical Black finish. Mfg. 2013-2016.

	$525	$435	$370	$300	$275	$250	$225	*$659*

CBR-9 BLACK RHINO – 9mm Para. cal., blowback system, polymer frame, 9 in. barrel, flash hider, two 18 shot mags., fixed fiber optic sights, polymer sliding stock or fixed stock with synthetic pistol grip, arm brace, reversible fire-safety selector and cocking lever, Mil-Std 1913 full length rail, ambi bolt release, sling swivel front point, includes hard plastic case with sling, sights, speed loader, cleaning kit, thread adapter, and quick release QD mount, matte black finish, 4.8 lbs. New 2020.

MSR $2,269	$1,925	$1,675	$1,450	$1,275	$1,000	$800	$675	

M FOUR-22 GEN II – .22 LR cal., blowback action, replica of the M4 carbine, 6 in. steel barrel, blue finish, fire control group, finger groove pistol grip, dust cover, adj. sights, 10 or 28 shot mag., faux flash hider, machined quad rail forearm, includes two mags. Mfg. 2011-2017.

	$400	$350	$300	$265	$235	$220	$210	*$489*

M9-22 – .22 LR cal., replica of the Beretta M9, 5 in. barrel, fixed or Novak style fiber optic sights, choice of wood or checkered black plastic grips, includes two 10 shot mags., 37 oz. New 2011.

MSR $244	$215	$190	$160	$145	$120	$95	$75	

Add $15 (MSR $259) for wood grips and threaded barrel.

M9 – 9mm Para. or .40 S&W cal., DA/SA, 10 or 15 shot, 4.9 in. barrel, drift adj. sights, plastic grips with walnut option, finger groove front strap, Tactical Black finish. Mfg. 2013-2016.

	$485	$400	$350	$285	$260	$240	$220	*$599*

Add $60 for .40 S&W cal.

* ***M9 Compact*** – 9mm Para. or .40 S&W cal., similar to M9, except features 4.3 in. barrel. Mfg. 2013-2016.

	$485	$400	$350	$285	$260	$240	$220	*$599*

Add $60 for .40 S&W cal.

MC14 – .380 ACP cal., short recoil, DA/SA, 3.82 in. cold forged barrel, 13 shot mag. Mfg. 2014-2017.

	$425	$375	$300	$250	$200	$170	$130	*$519*

MC27 – 9mm Para. or .40 S&W (disc.) cal., DA/SA or DAO, short recoil operating system, 15 shot mag., 3.9 in. barrel, drift adj. sights, plastic grips with walnut option, lower Picatinny rail, Tactical Black finish. Mfg. 2013-2016.

	$485	$400	$350	$285	$260	$240	$220	*$599*

MC28 – 9mm Para. cal., SA, 3.82 or 4 1/4 in. barrel, two 15 shot mags., black finish. Mfg. 2015 only.

	$325	$365	$300	$265	$235	$220	$210	*$469*

Add $30 for 4 1/4 in. barrel.

PAK-9 PISTOL – 9mm Para. cal., blowback action, 6.3 in. barrel, includes two 10 shot Beretta 92 style mags., interchangeable magazine adapter allows user to convert from Beretta style to Glock style mags., matte black finish, 6 lbs. Mfg. 2016-19.

	$510	$435	$365	$315	$275	$250	$230	*$569*

Add $50 for Glock magazine adapter.

REVOLVERS

RHINO REVOLVER SERIES – 9mm Para. (disc.), .357 Mag. or .40 S&W (new 2013) cal., barrel is in line with the lowest cylinder chamber, matte black or brushed nickel (White Rhino) finish, hexagonal cylinder, checkered wood or neoprene grips, fixed or adj. sights, available in 2 (Model 20DS or Model 200D), 4 (Model 40DS), 5 (Model 50DS), or 6 (Model 60DS) in. barrel, with or w/o lower tactical rail, approx. 24-33 oz. New mid-2010.

Add $75 for checkered walnut, or $86 for checkered olive wood or checkered laminate grips.

* ***Rhino 30DS*** – .357 Mag. cal., 3 in. barrel, 6 shot, fiber optic front sights, black rubber or walnut (on "Hunter" model only) grip, 3 moon clips, black, nickel, or "Hunter" OD Green frame finish, 1.7 lbs. New 2018.

MSR $1,136	$975	$850	$725	$625	$510	$425	$325	

Add $95 (MSR $1,231) for nickel finish.

Add $145 (MSR $1,287) for OD Green frame finish.

* ***Rhino 30DS Special Edition "White Rhino"*** – 9mm Para. or .357 Mag. cal., 3 in. barrel, 6 shot, gray and black G10 laminate grips, includes three moon clips, matte black cylinder, Cerakote and laser etched frame makes it look like a rhino hide, 1.7 lbs. Mfg. 2017 only.

	$1,295	$1,150	$995	$850	$700	$600	$500	*$1,465*

GRADING - PPGS™	100%	98%	95%	90%	80%	70%	60%	LAST MSR

* ***Rhino 30DS X "Special Edition"*** – .357 Mag. cal., SA/DA, 3 in. stainless steel barrel, 6 shot, fiber optic sights, G10 grips, internal safety, 7.5 in. OAL, 2.8 lbs. New 2020.

MSR $1,539	$1,325	$1,150	$1,000	$850	$695	$575	$475	

* ***Rhino 30 SAR*** – .357 Mag. cal., SAO, 3 in. barrel, 6 shot, fiber optic front sights, black rubber or walnut ("Hunter" model only) grips, 3 moon clips, black, nickel, or "Hunter" OD Green frame finish. New 2018.

MSR $1,136	$975	$850	$725	$625	$510	$425	$325	

Add $95 (MSR $1,231) for nickel finish.
Add $145 (MSR $1,287) for OD Green frame finish.

* ***Rhino 40DS*** – 9mm Para. (new 2018), .357 Mag. or .40 S&W cal., aluminum frame, 4 in. barrel, 6 shot, fiber optic front and adj. rear sight, medium walnut grips, 3 moon clips, chrome (mfg. 2013-disc.), nickel, or matte black finish, 29.6 oz.

MSR $1,181	$1,000	$850	$725	$650	$550	$450	$350	

Subtract $34 (MSR $1,147) for .40 S&W cal. (new 2013).
Add $112 (MSR $1,293) for nickel finish.
Add $120 for White Rhino with brushed nickel finish (disc. 2014).
Add $226 for extra 9mm Para. cylinder and five moon clips (mfg. 2013-disc.).

* ***Rhino 40 SAR*** – 9mm Para., .357 Mag., or .40 S&W cal., SAO, 4 in. barrel, 6 shot, fiber optic sights, medium walnut grip, 3 moon clips, black or nickel finish, 1.87 lbs. New 2017.

MSR $1,181	$1,000	$850	$725	$650	$550	$450	$350	

Subtract $34 (MSR $1,147) for .40 S&W cal.
Add $112 (MSR $1,293) for nickel finish.

* ***Rhino 50DS*** – 9mm Para., .357 Mag., or .40 S&W (new 2013) cal., aluminum frame, 5 in. barrel, 6 shot, fiber optic adj. rear sight, walnut medium grips, includes three moon clips, brushed nickel or matte black finish, 31.4 oz.

MSR $1,228	$1,050	$900	$750	$675	$550	$450	$350	

Subtract $40 (MSR $1,188) for .40 S&W cal.
Add $117 (MSR $1,345) for brushed nickel finish.

* ***Rhino 50 SAR*** – 9mm Para., .357 Mag., or .40 S&W cal., SAO, aluminum frame, 5 in. barrel, 6 shot, fiber optic sights, medium walnut grips, includes three moon clips, nickel or matte black finish, 1.97 lbs. New 2017.

MSR $1,228	$1,050	$900	$750	$675	$550	$450	$350	

Subtract $40 (MSR $1,188) for .40 S&W cal.
Add $117 (MSR $1,345) for brushed nickel finish.

* ***Rhino 60DS*** – 9mm Para., .357 Mag., or .40 S&W (new 2013) cal., aluminum frame, 6 in. barrel, 6 shot, fiber optic adj. rear sight, medium walnut grips, includes three moon clips, brushed nickel, matte black, "Hunter" OD Green Cerakote (new 2018), or gold (new 2013) finish, 33.2 oz.

MSR $1,243	$1,050	$900	$760	$695	$560	$450	$350	

Subtract $28 (MSR $1,215) for .40 S&W cal.
Add $118 (MSR $1,361) for brushed nickel finish.
Add $136 (MSR $1,379) for "Hunter" OD Green Cerakote finish (new 2018).
Add $281 (MSR $1,524) for gold finish (new 2013).

* ***Rhino 60DS Charging Rhino*** – 9mm Para. cal., DAO, black anodized alloy frame, 6 in. barrel, 6 shot chrome cylinder, no external hammer/cocking lever, tuned internal hammer, light trigger pull, improved trigger, fixed red fiber optic front and adj. green fiber optic rear sight, gray laminate grips, includes 10 moon clips, 2 lbs. New 2017.

MSR $1,509	$1,325	$1,175	$1,000	$850	$700	$600	$500	

* ***Rhino 60DS Charging Rhino Gen II*** – 9mm Para. cal., DAO, Ergal frame, 6 in. barrel, 6 shot chrome cylinder, no external hammer/cocking lever, tuned internal hammer, light trigger pull, improved trigger, fixed red fiber optic front and adj. green fiber optic rear sight, gray laminate grips, Cerakote slate finish, includes 10 moon clips, 2 lbs. New 2021.

MSR $1,624	$1,375	$1,200	$1,025	$850	$700	$600	$500	

* ***Rhino 60DS Match Master*** – .38 Spl. cal., DA/SA, Ergal frame, 6 shot, Aristocrat sights, Hogue Micarta grip, licensed by Richard Wilson Custom Guns, Grey PVD finish, 2.9 lbs. New 2020.

MSR $2,990	$2,550	$2,225	$1,915	$1,735	$1,400	$1,150	$950	

GRADING - PPGS™	100%	98%	95%	90%	80%	70%	60%	LAST MSR

* ***Rhino 60DS Nebula Special Edition*** – .357 Mag. cal., 6 in. barrel, 6 shot, fiber optic sights, blue laminate medium grip with 3 moon clips, "Nebula" mixed color PVD finish, 2.1 lbs. New 2019.

MSR $1,725	$1,475	$1,295	$1,105	$1,000	$810	$675	$575	

* ***Rhino 60 SAR*** – 9mm Para., .357 Mag., or .40 S&W cal., SAO, 6 in. barrel, 6 shot, fiber optic front and adj. rear sights, medium walnut grip, 3 moon clips, black, gold, "Hunter" OD Green, or nickel finish.

MSR $1,243	$1,050	$900	$760	$695	$560	$450	$350	

Subtract $28 (MSR $1,215) for .40 S&W cal.
Add $118 (MSR $1,361) for brushed nickel finish.
Add $136 (MSR $1,379) for "Hunter" OD Green Cerakote finish (disc. 2020).
Add $281 (MSR $1,524) for gold finish (new 2013).

* ***Rhino 60 SAR Charging Rhino*** – 9mm Para. cal., SA, black frame with nickel cylinder, 6 in. barrel, 6 shot, adj. rear sight, gray laminate grips, includes 10 moon clips, 2.06 lbs. New 2017.

MSR $1,509	$1,325	$1,175	$1,000	$850	$700	$600	$500	

* ***Rhino 60 SAR Nebula Special Edition*** – .357 Mag. cal., SAO, 6 in. barrel, 6 shot, fiber optic sights, blue laminate medium grip with 3 moon clips, "Nebula" mixed color PVD finish, 2.1 lbs. New 2019.

MSR $1,509	$1,325	$1,175	$1,000	$850	$700	$600	$500	

* ***Rhino 200D*** – 9mm Para. (2017-2020), .357 Mag. or .40 S&W (new 2013) cal., DAO, 2 in. barrel, matte black or nickel (.40 S&W only) finish, 6 shot, black aluminum frame, fiber optic front sight, black rubber small grips, includes brown leather holster and three moon clips, 1 1/2 lbs.

MSR $1,082	$925	$800	$700	$600	$485	$400	$310	

Subtract $17 (MSR $1,065) for .40 S&W cal.
Add $131 (MSR $1,213) for chrome or nickel finish.
Add $135 for extra 9mm Para. cylinder and five moon clips (mfg. 2013-disc.).

* ***Rhino 200DS*** – 9mm Para. (2017-2020), .357 Mag. or .40 S&W (new 2013) cal., aluminum frame, 2 in. barrel, 6 shot, fiber optic front sight, small black rubber grips, includes brown leather holster and three moon clips, brushed nickel or matte black finish, 24 oz.

MSR $1,082	$925	$800	$700	$600	$485	$400	$310	

Subtract $17 (MSR $1,065) for .40 S&W cal (new 2013).
Add $131 (MSR $1,213) for brushed nickel finish (new 2013).
Add $135 for extra 9mm Para. cylinder and five moon clips (mfg. 2013-disc.).

» **Rhino 200DS Polymer** – similar to Rhino 200DS, except has black polymer frame, 18 oz. Imported 2014-2015.

	$650	$575	$500	$450	$400	$375	$350	*$749*

SAA 1873 – .22 LR cal., SA, 4 3/4, 5 1/2, or 7 1/2 in. barrel, 6 shot, black plastic grips with "CF" medallions, approx. 2.2 lbs. Mfg. late 2011-2012.

	$170	$155	$140	$130	$120	$110	$100	*$189*

Add $40 for dual cylinder (includes .22 LR and .22 WMR cal. cylinders) or Target model with adj. rear sight.

SAA 1873 SCOUT REVOLVER – .22 LR cal., 4 3/4, 5 1/2, 7 1/2 in. barrel, 6 shot, choice of black or antique finish, rotary safety on left recoil shield, black plastic checkered grips, Target variation has adj. rear sight, approx. 35 oz. Mfg. late 2011-2012.

	$165	$145	$130	$120	$110	$100	$90	*$189*

Add $10 for 7-1/2 in. barrel.
Add $40 for either dual cylinder (.22 LR/.22 WMR) or Target Model with adj. rear sight.

1873 SAA BUNTLINE – .22 LR or .22 LR/.22 WMR (extra cylinder) cal., SA, aloy frame, 12 in. barrel, fixed sights, 6 shot, checkered black plastic grips with gold medallions, blue or black (disc.) frame, 2.8 lbs. New 2013.

MSR $287	$250	$225	$195	$175	$150	$125	$100	

Add $27 (MSR $314) for dual cylinder.

1873 SAA 22-6 SHOT – .22 LR cal., 4 3/4 in. barrel, 6 shot, choice of Antique, Blue, Black/Ivory (disc.), Black/Silver (disc.), or Black/Gold (disc.) finish, New Frontier style frame with adj. rear sight, includes red fire indicator, black plastic grips. New mid-2014.

MSR $189	$175	$160	$140	$130	$120	$110	$95	

Add $10 (MSR $199) for wood grips.
Add $20 (MSR $209) for .22 LR/.22 WMR cal. combo.
Add $10 for Black/Silver (disc.) or $11 for Black/Gold finish (disc.).

GRADING - PPGS™	100%	98%	95%	90%	80%	70%	60%	LAST MSR

1873 SAA 22-10 SHOT/1873 SAA 22-10 TARGET – .22 LR or .22 LR/.22 WMR (extra cylinder) cal., SA, 4 3/4, 5 1/2, or 7 1/2 (Target model) in. barrel, fixed sights, 10 shot, checkered black plastic grips with gold medallions, black frame. New 2013.

MSR $224	$195	$170	$145	$135	$100	$90	$70	

Add $12 (MSR $236) for 5 1/2 in. barrel.
Add $25 (MSR $249) for Target model with 7 1/2 in. barrel.
Add $40 (MSR $264) for extra .22 WMR cylinder.
Add $20 for case colors (mfg. 2015 only).

1873 SAA 17 REVOLVER – .17 HMR cal., SA, alloy frame, 4.75 in. barrel, 6 shot, fixed front sight, black plastic grips, blued finish, 2.2 lbs.

MSR $205	$175	$150	$130	$110	$90	$75	$60	

1873 SAA 17-10 SHOT – .17 HMR cal., SA, 7 1/2 in. Target barrel, adj. sights, otherwise similar to SAA 22-10. New 2014.

MSR $265	$225	$195	$170	$150	$120	$95	$75	

1873 SAA 38-6 REGULATOR – .38 Spl. or .45 LC cal., aircraft aluminum frame, 4 3/4 in. barrel, 6 shot, fixed front sight, black polymer grips, transfer bar, 3 lbs. Mfg. 2016-2017.

	$300	$265	$235	$215	$200	$185	$175	*$359*

RIFLES/CARBINES: LEVER ACTION

1886 CARBINE HUNTER – .45-70 Govt. cal., 22 in. round barrel, 7 shot, Skinner rear sight, red fiber optic front sight, black rubber coated walnut stock, "D" lever, 7.4 lbs. Mfg. 2015-2017.

	$1,475	$1,275	$1,050	$900	$775	$650	$525	*$1,669*

1886 CLASSIC CARBINE – .45-70 cal., 22 in. round blued barrel with two barrel bands, interchangeable blade front and semi-buckhorn rear sight, standard uncheckered walnut stock and forearm, case colored receiver finish, 7.4 lbs. New 2013.

MSR $1,629	$1,385	$1,210	$1,040	$950	$760	$625	$525	

1886 KODIAK – .45-70 Govt. cal., 18 1/2 in. half octagon barrel, 4 shot mag., ejector, fiber optic front and Skinner peep rear sights, straight grip black synthetic overmolded (disc.) or rubber coated walnut stock, drilled and tapped, sling swivels, "D" lever, brushed nickel (disc.) or matte chrome finish, 7.8 lbs. New 2011.

MSR $2,099	$1,785	$1,550	$1,324	$1,200	$950	$800	$650	

1886 KODIAK TRADITIONAL (TRAPPER) – .45-70 Govt. cal., 18 1/2 in. full octagon barrel, straight grip walnut stock, traditional sights, 5 shot mag., color case hardened finish. Limited importation 2011-2014.

	$1,350	$1,175	$975	$850	$725	$600	$500	*$1,540*

1886 RIFLE – .45-70 cal., 26 in. octagon barrel, 8 shot, buckhorn rear sight, color case hardened receiver and forearm tip, crescent buttplate, uncheckered walnut stock and forend, or fancy checkered select walnut stock and forend (Deluxe model), 9 lbs. New 2013.

MSR $1,709	$1,450	$1,275	$1,090	$985	$800	$650	$550	

Add $171 for Deluxe model with fancy checkered walnut stock.

1886 RIDGE RUNNER TAKEDOWN RIFLE – .45-70 Govt. cal., 18 1/2 in. barrel, flash hider, mag. tube, steel construction, ejectors, fixed fiber optic front and Skinner Peep rear sight, rubber coated walnut stock, matte blue or matte chrome w/Soft-Touch finish, 7.8 lbs. New 2020.

MSR $1,728	$1,465	$1,275	$1,100	$995	$800	$675	$525	

Add $102 for matte chrome finish.

1886 SKINNER CARBINE – .45-70 Govt. cal., 16 in. round barrel, 4 shot, ejector, Skinner peep rear sight, fiber optic front sight, hand oiled walnut stock, matte blue finish, 7 lbs. Disc. 2017.

	$1,425	$1,250	$1,025	$875	$750	$650	$525	*$1,629*

1886 TRAPPER CARBINE – .45-70 cal., 16 in. barrel pre-drilled for Weaver mounts, Skinner rear sight and fiber optic front sight, 4 shot mag., rubber buttplate, walnut stock and forearm, matte blue finish. Disc.

	$1,200	$1,050	$925	$800	$700	$600	$475	*$1,399*

1886 TRAPPER RIFLE – .45-70 Govt. cal., 18 1/2 in. octagon barrel, 4 shot, Buckhorn rear and dovetail front sights, walnut stock and forend. Disc. 2017.

	$1,550	$1,325	$1,100	$950	$825	$725	$600	*$1,759*

1886 WILDLANDS TAKEDOWN RIFLE – .45-70 cal., takedown, 18 1/2 in. threaded barrel, 4 shot, ejector, fixed fiber optic front and Skinner peep rear sight, Gray laminate stock, Dark Gray Cerakote or matte black (new 2021) finish, 9.5 lbs. New 2020.

MSR $2,069	$1,750	$1,525	$1,325	$1,185	$975	$800	$675	

Add $136 for Dark Gray Cerakote finish.

GRADING - PPGS™	100%	98%	95%	90%	80%	70%	60%	LAST MSR

1892 60TH ANNIVERSARY ENGRAVED BLACK COMMEMORATIVE – .45 LC cal., 24 in. octagonal barrel, 12 shot, black engraved receiver, adj. windage blade front and long buckhorn rear sight, hand-finished high gloss select walnut stock and forend, 7 lbs. Limited mfg. 1 of 60, 2018-2019.

	$2,275	$1,995	$1,700	$1,545	$1,250	$1,025	$795	*$2,665*

1892 60TH ANNIVERSARY ENGRAVED GOLD COMMEMORATIVE – .45 LC cal., 24 in. octagonal barrel, 12 shot, gold engraved receiver, long buckhorn rear sight, hand-finished high gloss select walnut stock and forend, 7 lbs. Limited mfg. 1 of 6, mfg. 2018-2019.

	$2,275	$1,995	$1,700	$1,545	$1,250	$1,025	$795	*$2,665*

1892 CARBINE – .357 Mag., .45 LC, .44-40 Win. (disc.), .44 Mag., .38 Spl. (disc.), or .38-40 Win. (disc.) cal., 16 (new 2020) or 20 in. round barrel, 10 shot, fixed blade front and short Buckhorn rear sight, hand oiled walnut stock and forend, color case receiver/blued barrel finish, 6.6 lbs.

MSR $1,329	$1,125	$985	$850	$775	$625	$500	$425	

Add $70 for 16 in. barrel (new 2020).
Add $81 for .38 Spl., .38-40 Win., or .44-40 Win. cal. (disc.)

1892 RIFLE – .357 Mag., .38 Spl. (disc.), .38-40 WCF (disc.), .44-40 WCF (disc.), .44 Mag. (mfg. 2013, reintroduced 2020), or .45 LC cal., 16 (new 2020), 20, or 24 in. octagon barrel, 10 shot mag., long Buckhorn rear sight, walnut stock and forearm, case colored receiver, blue (disc.) or case color receiver finish, 6.6-7.3 lbs. New 2013.

MSR $1,329	$1,125	$985	$850	$775	$625	$500	$425	

Add $81 for .38 Spl., .38-40 WCF, or .44-40 WCF cal. (mfg. 2013 only).

1892 TAKEDOWN RIFLE CLASSIC – .45 LC, .357 Mag. (new 2020), or .44 Mag. (new 2020) cal., 20 (new 2020) or 24 in. octagon barrel with buckhorn rear sight, takedown action, 10 or 12 shot mag., case colored receiver, checkered walnut stock and forearm, 6.6-7.3 lbs. New 2013.

MSR $1,435	$1,225	$1,075	$925	$835	$675	$550	$475	

1892 TRAPPER CLASSIC CARBINE – .45 LC, .44 Mag., or .357 Mag. cal., 16 in. round barrel, 9 shot mag., walnut stock and forearm, two barrel bands, front sight with interchangeable blades, buckhorn rear sight, case colored receiver, blue finish. New 2013.

MSR $1,399	$1,190	$1,050	$900	$815	$675	$550	$450	

1892 TRAPPER SKINNER CARBINE – .44 LC, .44 Mag., or .357 Mag. cal., 16 in. round barrel with 9 shot mag., receiver drilled for Weaver scope mount, Skinner rear sight and fiber optic front sight with interchangeable blades, oversized finger lever, matte blue finish, walnut stock and forend with rubber buttplate. Mfg. 2013-2017.

	$1,275	$1,115	$950	$865	$700	$575	$475	*$1,489*

1892 WILDLANDS – .44 Mag. cal., takedown or solid frame configuration, 16 1/2 in. threaded barrel, 5 shot, ejector, fixed fiber optic front and Skinner peep rear sights, Gray laminate stock and forend or walnut stock, matte black (new 2021), color case, or Dark Gray Cerakote finish, 6.2-6.9 lbs. New 2020.

MSR $1,579	$1,340	$1,175	$1,000	$910	$735	$600	$515	

Add $120 for Dark Gray Cerakote finish.
Add $167 for takedown model (laminate stock only).

CHIAPPA 39 LEVER ACTION RIFLE – .22 S, L, or LR cal., 18 1/2 in. blue barrel, take down action, synthetic pistol grip or wood stock, 15 shot, drilled and tapped, black or case colored finished receiver, 5-5 1/2 lbs. Mfg. 2014-2017.

	$360	$315	$275	$240	$195	$170	$150	*$419*

Add $40 for wood stock.

CHIAPPA LA322 TAKEDOWN RIFLE – .22 LR cal., takedown, 18 1/2 in. steel blued barrel, 15 shot, fixed tunnel front sight, adj. rear sights, straight or pistol grip (new 2020) English style wood stock with plastic buttplate, matte black or color case (disc.) finish, 5.5 lbs. New 2015.

MSR $389	$335	$295	$250	$230	$185	$150	$125	

Add $10 for pistol grip stock.
Add $80 for case colored finish (disc.).

CHIAPPA LA322 DELUXE TAKEDOWN RIFLE – .22 LR cal., takedown, 18 1/2 in. blued barrel, case colored (disc.), polished black nickel (mfg. 2015 only) or black chrome (new 2016) frame, hand oiled walnut finish stock with rubber buttplate, checkered pistol grip, 5 1/2 lbs. New 2015.

MSR $576	$495	$435	$375	$335	$275	$225	$175	

Add $10 for case colored (disc.) or polished nickel (mfg. 2015 only) frame finish.

GRADING - PPGS™	100%	98%	95%	90%	80%	70%	60%	LAST MSR

CHIAPPA LA322 KODIAK CUB TAKEDOWN RIFLE – .22 LR cal., takedown, 18 1/2 in. chrome barrel, 15 shot, English style black soft touch stock with rubber buttplate, 3/8 in. dovetail rail for scope mounts, matte hard chrome finish, 5 1/2 lbs. New 2016.

MSR $754	$650	$575	$495	$440	$360	$300	$250	

SPENCER RIFLE/CARBINE – .44-40 WCF, .45 Schofield (disc. 2013), .45 LC or .56-50 Spencer cal., 20 (carbine), 22 (carbine, disc.), 30 (rifle), or 33 (rifle, disc.) in. round blue barrel, rifle has 3 barrel bands, oil finished walnut stock and forearm, color case hardened finish.

MSR $1,925	$1,650	$1,450	$1,250	$1,125	$910	$750	$625	

Add $100-$106 for .45 LC cal.
Add $118 for Spencer Rifle.

RIFLES: REPRODUCTIONS, SINGLE SHOT

LITTLE SHARPS CLASSIC – .17 HMR (disc.), .22 LR, .22 WMR, .22 Hornet, .30-30 Win., .38-55 Win., .218 Bee (disc. 2015), .44-40 (disc. 2015, reintroduced 2020), or .45 LC cal., single shot, 24 or 26 in. octagon barrel, blade front and diopter rear tang sight, DT, case colored receiver, uncheckered straight grip walnut stock and forearm, drilled and tapped for Weaver style scope.

MSR $1,389	$1,185	$1,035	$895	$800	$650	$535	$450	

LITTLE SHARPS HUNTER – .17 Hornet cal., single shot, 24 in. drilled and tapped half octagon, half round barrel w/o sights, case colored receiver, DST, rubber buttplate, uncheckered walnut stock and forearm, matte blue finish. Disc. 2015.

	$975	$840	$750	$675	$575	$475	4375	*$1,109*

LITTLE SHARPS TARGET – .17 Hornet cal., single shot, 26 in. octagonal heavy barrel with spirit level front sight and middle range diopter tang rear sight, white satin finished receiver, DST, blue barrel finish, checkered walnut stock and forearm, drilled and tapped. Disc. 2015.

	$1,125	$975	$850	$725	$625	$525	$425	*$1,319*

SHARPS CREEDMORE – .45-70 Govt. cal., 34 in. round blued barrel, tang sight and tunnel front sight, walnut stock, DT, color case hardened finish. Disc. 2014.

	$1,495	$1,310	$1,125	$1,025	$825	$675	$525	*$1,759*

1863 NEW MODEL SHARPS CARBINE – .45-70 Govt. or .50-70 cal., 22 in. round blue barrel, ST, oil finished walnut stock and forearm, color case hardened finish.

MSR $1,456	$1,250	$1,075	$925	$815	$675	$550	$450	

Add $29 (MSR $1,485) for .45-70 Govt. cal.

1874 SHARPS BERDAN – .45-70 Govt. cal., falling block action, 30 in. round blued barrel, double trigger, extractor, fixed blade front and ladder adj. rear sights, hand oiled walnut stock with patchbox, color case receiver finish, 10.6 lbs.

MSR $1,559	$1,325	$1,150	$975	$885	$710	$585	$500	

1874 SHARPS BUSINESS – .45-70 Govt. cal., falling block action, 28 in. octagon blue barrel, DT, oil finished walnut stock and forearm, color case hardened finish, 8.5 lbs.

MSR $1,418	$1,200	$1,050	$900	$815	$660	$550	$450	

1874 SHARPS DOWN UNDER – .38-55 WCF (disc.), .45-70 Govt., .45-90 (disc.), .45-110 (disc.), .45-120 (disc.), or .50-90 (disc.) cal., 34 in. octagon blued barrel, double triggers, walnut stock with patchbox, pewter tip forend, color case hardened finish.

MSR $1,893	$1,600	$1,350	$1,150	$1,035	$850	$685	$575	

1874 SHARPS SPORTING – .45-70 Govt. cal., 32 in. octagonal blued barrel, extractor, double trigger, adj. sight, walnut stock or checkered walnut stock with patchbox and pewter tip forend (new 2016), color case receiver finish, 10.2 lbs.

MSR $1,489	$1,275	$1,100	$950	$825	$675	$550	$450	

Add $269 (MSR $1,758) for checkered walnut stock with patchbox and pewter tip forend (new 2016).

1874 SHARPS TEXAS CAVALRY – .45-70 Govt. or .50-70 cal., 22 in. octagon blue barrel, ST, oil finished walnut stock and forearm, color case hardened finish, 9.7 lbs. Disc.

Retail pricing was not available for this model.

RIFLES: SEMI-AUTO

CBR-9 RIFLE – 9mm Para. or 9x21 cal., 18.6 in. barrel, 18 shot mag., adj. front and rear flip-up sights, fixed stock, black synthetic grip, matte black finish, 5.5-6.6 lbs. New 2020.

Please contact the manufacturer directly for pricing and availability.

GRADING - PPGS™	100%	98%	95%	90%	80%	70%	60%	LAST MSR

M-22 SERIES – While a Carbine, National Match, and Precision Match were advertised during 2011, this series never went into production and was not imported.

M FOUR-22 – .22 LR cal., blowback action, 5, 10 or 28 shot, 16 in. barrel with flash hider, forward assist and bolt release, black or tan finish, fixed tube stock, ribbed tube-type forearm, A-4 adj. sights, Picatinny flat-top, detachable carry handle, accepts Mil-Spec handguards, 5 1/2 lbs. Disc. 2012.

	$360	$325	$300	$265	$230	$200	$180	*$419*

Add $30 for red dot scope.

M1 CARBINE – please refer to listing under Citadel.

M1-22 CARBINE – .22 LR cal., 18 in. barrel, two 10 shot mags., fully adj. rear sight, wood or polymer stock, matte blue metal finish, 5 1/2 lbs.

MSR $333	$285	$240	$200	$170	$140	$120	$100	

Add $127 (MSR $460) for wood stock.
Add $70 for Muddy Girl stock finish (disc. 2016).

M1-9 CARBINE – 9mm Para. cal., 19 in. matte blue barrel and receiver, two 10 shot mags., polymer or wood stock, dovetail rail for scope mounts.

MSR $597	$500	$425	$350	$325	$260	$215	$165	

Add $79 (MSR $676) for wood stock.

M FOUR-22 GEN II PRO CARBINE – .22 LR cal., blowback action, 16 in. heavy match threaded barrel, 10 or 28 shot mag., 7.8 in. free floating aluminum quad rail with 8-position Picatinny rail, pistol grip, 6-position collapsible stock, parkerized or Muddy Girl (disc. 2017) finish, 5.7 lbs. New 2013.

MSR $494	$420	$360	$315	$285	$240	$190	$160	

Add $60 for Muddy Girl finish (disc. 2017).

Chiappa also offers an M Four-22 conversion unit (upper only) - current MSR is $339-$354, depending on forend length (new 2012).

M FOUR-22 GEN II PRO RIFLE – .22 LR cal., blowback action, 16 in. heavy match threaded barrel, 10 or 28 shot mag., 11.8 in. free floating aluminum quad rail with 8-position Picatinny rail, pistol grip, 6-position collapsible stock, parkerized or Muddy Girl (disc. 2017) finish. New 2013.

MSR $569	$485	$425	$365	$330	$265	$225	$185	

Add $60 for Muddy Girl finish (disc. 2017).

Chiappa also offers an M Four-22 conversion unit (upper only) - current MSR is $339-$354, depending on forend length (new 2012).

M FOUR-22 GEN II RIFLE – .22 LR cal., blowback action, black or tan (mfg. 2015-2019) polymer frame, 16 in. heavy match threaded barrel, 10 or 28 shot mag., fixed stock, matte black barrel and receiver. New 2014.

MSR $473	$400	$350	$300	$275	$225	$180	$150	

M FOUR-22 GEN III PRO RIFLE – .22 LR cal., 16 in. heavy barrel, 10 or 28 shot mag., adj. flip-up front and rear sights, 6-pos. stock, 11.8 in. forend, 8-pos. Picatinny rail, black finish, 5.7 lbs. New 2019.

This model is not available in the U.S. Please contact the company directly for more information.

AK-22 RIFLE – .22 LR cal., blued steel receiver, 17 1/4 in. blue barrel, synthetic or wood stock, includes two 10 shot mags., 6-6.7 lbs. Mfg. 2014-disc.

	$365	$325	$275	$250	$200	$165	$130	*$429*

Add $35 for wood stock.

RAK-22 RIFLE – .22 LR cal., blowback action, 17 1/4 in. blued barrel, two 10 shot mags., wood stock with synthetic pistol grip, 6.6 lbs. New 2016.

MSR $665	$565	$495	$425	$385	$315	$250	$200	

RAK-9 RIFLE – 9mm Para. cal., blowback action, 17 1/4 in. blued barrel, two 10 shot mags., AK-style adj. sights, matte black stock with synthetic pistol grip, raised comb, AK-style selector switch, black finish, 6.6 lbs. New 2019.

MSR $719	$625	$545	$475	$425	$345	$285	$225	

RIFLES: SINGLE SHOT

LITTLE BADGER – .17 HMR (new 2015), .22 LR, or .22 WMR cal., 16 1/2 in. threaded barrel, extractor, fixed front and adj. rear sight, folding design with wire stock and 12 shot ammunition holder, small quad rail on barrel, includes backpack, matte black finish, 3 1/2 lbs. New 2013.

MSR $228	$195	$165	$140	$125	$100	$85	$65	

Add $15 (MSR $243) for .17 HMR cal. (new 2015).

GRADING - PPGS™	100%	98%	95%	90%	80%	70%	60%	LAST MSR

* ***Little Badger With Scope*** – .22 LR cal., break-open action, alloy frame, 16 1/2 in. threaded steel barrel, M1 style sights, steel wire stock, quad Picatinny forend, includes scope and hammer extension, Black or OD Green finish, 31 in. OAL, 3.6 lbs. New 2020.

MSR $233	$200	$170	$145	$130	$105	$90	$70	

* ***Little Badger Deluxe*** – .22 LR or .22 WMR cal., break-open action, alloy frame, 16 1/2 in. threaded steel barrel with protective plastic cap, half cock hammer, fixed M1 style front and adj. M1 style rear sight, wood stock and forend, includes backpack, black finish, 31 in. OAL, 3.6 lbs.

MSR $273	$235	$200	$175	$160	$130	$100	$80	

Add $3 (MSR $276) for .22 WMR cal.

SHOTGUNS: LEVER ACTION

MODEL 1887 – 12 ga., 2 3/4 in. chamber, 22 or 28 in. round blued barrel with three chokes (IC/Mod/F), 2 (fast load, new 2015) or 5 shot mag., oil finished walnut stock and forearm, chrome (mfg. 2015 only) or color case hardened finish, 9 lbs.

MSR $1,480	$1,250	$1,095	$950	$850	$700	$575	$475	

Add $150 for chrome receiver (mfg. 2015 only).

1887 MARE'S LEG – 12 ga., 2 3/4 in. chamber, 18 1/2 in. round blued barrel, 5 shot mag., bead sight, oil finished walnut stock and forearm, color case receiver finish, 7.8 lbs.

MSR $1,409	$1,200	$1,025	$875	$775	$650	$525	$425	

1887 ROSEBOX LIMITED EDITION – 12 ga., 2 3/4 in. chamber, 18.5 in. barrel 5 shot mag., hand oil finished walnut stock and forearm, black finish, 7.8 lbs. 1 of 300 numbered pieces celebrating the 30th anniversary of the movie *Terminator 2: Judgement Day*. New 2021.

MSR $1,449	$1,225	$1,075	$925	$800	$675	$550	$450	

1887 T-MODEL – 12 ga., 2 3/4 in. chamber, 18 1/2 in. round barrel, 5 shot mag., extractor, black soft touch walnut stock and forend, matte blue finish, 7.9 lbs. New 2015.

MSR $1,370	$1,165	$1,025	$875	$800	$650	$525	$425	

1887 TROPHY HUNTER – 12 ga., 2 3/4 in. chamber, 22 in. rifled barrel, 5 shot mag., extractor, Skinner peep rear and fiber optic front sights, walnut stock and forend, rubber buttplate, matte blue finish, 9 lbs. Disc. 2017.

	$1,500	$1,300	$1,100	$925	$800	$675	$575	*$1,709*

SHOTGUNS: SINGLE SHOT

LITTLE BADGER DELUXE SHOTGUN – 9mm Flobert cal., break-open action, 24 in. barrel, half cock hammer, M1 style sights, wood stock and forend, black finish, 38.5 in. OAL, 3.6 lbs.

MSR $258	$225	$195	$175	$150	$125	$100	$80	

SHOTGUNS: O/U

204X – 12 or 20 ga., 3 in. chambers, 26 (20 ga.) or 28 (12 ga.) in. barrels, extractors, walnut stock and forearm, black receiver. Mfg. 2014-2016.

	$850	$750	$650	$585	$475	$400	$325	*$999*

* ***204X Camo*** – 20 ga., 3 1/2 in. chambers, 24 or 28 in. barrels, 5 chokes, with or without Rem Choke thread pattern, synthetic stock, Realtree Max-5 or Realtree Extra Green camo finish, 7.1 lbs. Disc. 2016.

	$925	$810	$695	$630	$525	$425	$350	*$1,089*

Add $40 for 28 in. barrels with 5 chokes and Rem Choke thread pattern.

214E – 12 or 20 ga., 3 in. chambers, 26 (20 ga.) or 28 (12 ga.) in. barrels, ejectors, walnut stock and forearm, black receiver. Mfg. 2014-2016.

	$950	$830	$715	$650	$525	$450	$350	*$1,109*

SHOTGUNS: SLIDE ACTION

C6 SERIES – 12 ga., 3 in. chamber, 18 1/2 in. barrel with fixed front sight and one Rem Choke, 5 shot mag., choice of black synthetic stock with pistol grip or pistol grip only, or four-position adj. stock (black finish only), matte black or satin nickel finish. Mfg. 2013-2017.

	$325	$275	$250	$225	$200	$175	$150	*$389*

Add $10 for field stock with pistol grip.
Add $40 for satin nickel finish.

* ***C6 Compact*** – 20 ga., 3 in. chamber, 22 in. barrel, MC-1, Next G1 camo stock and forend, matte black metal finish, 5 lbs. Disc. 2017.

	$365	$300	$275	$250	$200	$165	$135	*$409*

GRADING - PPGS™	100%	98%	95%	90%	80%	70%	60%	LAST MSR

C6 FIELD PUMP SHOTGUN – 12 or 20 ga., 3 in. chamber, 26 in. barrel, interchangeable choke tubes, 5 shot, synthetic stock, black or RealTree Xtra Green camo (20 ga. only) finish, 5.4-6.4 lbs. Mfg. 2016-2017.

$350	$300	$275	$250	$200	$165	$135	*$409*

Add $90 for Realtree Xtra Green camo finish.

C6 MAG PUMP SHOTGUN – 12 ga., 3 1/2 in. chamber, 24 or 28 in. barrel, interchangeable choke tubes, 5 shot, fiber optic front sight, Realtree Max-5 or Realtree Xtra Green camo finish, 6.7 lbs. Mfg. 2016 only.

$450	$395	$340	$300	$250	$200	$175	*$519*

Add $30 for Realtree Xtra Green camo finish.

C9 SERIES – 12 ga. only, 3 in. chamber, 22 in. barrel, black synthetic stock with pistol grip, 8 shot mag., fixed or fiber optic front, ghost ring Picatinny rear sight, matte black or satin nickel finish. Mfg. 2013-2016.

$300	$265	$225	$200	$175	$150	$125	*$349*

Add $28 for satin nickel finish.

Add $35 for full length pistol grip stock, ghost ring sights and rail, and breecher tube.

SHOTGUNS: SEMI-AUTO

CA612 FIELD – 12 ga., 3 in. chamber, rotary bolt/ inertia action, 28 in. barrel, black or Realtree Max-5 camo finish, synthetic stock and forearm, 7.1 lbs. Mfg. 2014-2017.

$560	$495	$425	$385	$310	$250	$200	*$629*

Add $60 for camo.

CA612 TURKEY – 12 ga., 3 in. chamber, 24 in. barrel, 4 shot, black finish, synthetic stock, Realtree Xtra Green camo, 6.7 lbs. Mfg. 2014-2016.

$625	$550	$475	$425	$350	$285	$225	*$689*

CA612M FIELD – 12 ga., 3 1/2 in. chamber, 28 in. barrel, Beretta/Benelli mobile thread pattern, MC-5, synthetic stock, 100% Mossy Oak Shadow Grass Blades camo finish. Mfg. 2016-2017.

$635	$550	$475	$425	$350	$285	$225	*$709*

CA612M TURKEY – 12 ga., 3 1/2 in. chamber, 24 in. barrel, MC-5X, pistol grip synthetic stock, Mossy Oak Breakup Infinity camo finish, 7.1 lbs. Mfg. 2016-2017.

$635	$550	$475	$425	$350	$285	$225	*$709*

CA612 TACTICAL – 12 ga., 3 in. chamber, rotary bolt/inertia, 22 in. barrel, ghost ring sights, breecher tube, 4 shot, synthetic pistol grip stock, black finish, 6.6 lbs. Mfg. 2014-2016.

$625	$550	$475	$425	$350	$285	$225	*$699*

SHOTGUNS: SxS

MODEL 512 – 12, 20, or 28 ga., 2 3/4 in. chambers, 28 in. barrels with interchangeable choke tubes, walnut stock, white receiver. Mfg. 2016-disc.

$1,050	$925	$795	$715	$580	$475	$385	*$1,169*

MODEL 520 – 20 ga., 3 in. chambers, 26 in. barrels, Rem Choke thread pattern, MC-5, extractor, select trigger, checkered walnut stock, gloss blued finish. Mfg. 2016-disc.

$1,050	$925	$795	$715	$580	$475	$385	*$1,169*

MODEL 528 – 28 ga., 2 3/4 in. chambers, 26 in. barrels, Rem Choke thread pattern, MC-5, extractor, select trigger, checkered walnut stock. Mfg. 2016-disc.

$1,050	$925	$795	$715	$580	$475	$385	*$1,169*

CHIAPPA FIREARMS Srl (ARMI SPORT di CHIAPPA SILVIA & C. Snc)

Current manufacturer established in 1958, and located in Brescia, Italy. Chiappa Firearms Srl (recently changed its name from Armi Sport di Chiappa Silvia & C. Snc) is one division of the Chiappa group, which includes Chiappa Firearms Srl (firearms and replica firearms manufacturer established in 1958), Chiappa Firearms USA Ltd. (firearms manufacturer), Kimar Srl (firearms manufacturer), Costa srl (metal surface finsh treatment), ACP (laser training system), FAS (airguns and target pistols), and Charles Daly brand. Currently distributed by various U.S. companies.

See Chiappa Firearms USA Ltd. for current firearms listings. Chiappa Firearms Srl also manufactures firearms that are currently imported by Cimarron, Dixie Gun Works, and Taylor's & Co. Please refer to the individual headings for listings on various models.

Chiappa Firearms Srl also manufactures a complete line of percussion and flintlock blackpowder reproductions and replicas, including both pistols and rifles. For more information on these replicas, please refer to the *Blue Book of Modern Black Powder Arms* (also available online).

GRADING - PPGS™	100%	98%	95%	90%	80%	70%	60%	LAST MSR

RIFLES: REPRODUCTIONS

Please refer to the distributor's listings for current information on these models, including U.S. pricing and availability.

CHINA SOUTH INDUSTRIES

Current manufacturer of firearms and unrelated industrial products located in Beijing, China. Current trademarks include EMEI and Jianshe. No current U.S. importation.

Please contact the company directly for more information including price and availability.

CHIPMUNK RIFLES

Current trademark established in 1982 and currently manufactured by Keystone Sporting Arms, located in Milton, PA. Previously manufactured by Rogue Rifle Co., Inc., located in Lewiston, ID, 2001-2007. Previously located in Prospect, OR from 1997-2001. Previously manufactured by Oregon Arms, Inc. located in Prospect, OR 1988-1996, and by Chipmunk Manufacturing located in Medford, OR until 1988.

Rogue Rifle Co. Inc. was purchased by Keystone Sporting Arms, LLC in Jan. 2007. Keystone is also the manufacturer of Crickett rifles (see separate listing).

PISTOLS: SINGLE SHOT

SILHOUETTE PISTOL – .22 LR cal., bolt action design with 14 7/8 in. barrel, iron sights, rear grip walnut stock. Mfg. 1984-88.

	100%	98%	95%	90%	80%	70%	60%	LAST MSR
	$135	$115	$95	$80	$70	$60	$50	*$150*

HUNTER/SILHOUETTE – .17 HMR (disc.), .17 Mach 2 (disc.), .22 LR, or .22 WMR cal., left-handed bolt action, 10 in. blued steel or stainless steel barrel, current mfg. now comes standard with threaded barrel and cap, open or Truglo (disc.) sights, walnut stock or blue (disc.), black, brown (disc. 2020), pink (disc.), purple (disc.), or camo laminate target style stock, current mfg. has Barracuda style forend, ergonomic grip, drilled and tapped. New 2005.

	100%	98%	95%	90%	80%	70%	60%
MSR $219	$190	$165	$145	$130	$100	$85	$70

Add $10 for .22 WMR cal. (MSR $229).
Add $10 for black or camo laminate stock (MSR $229).
Add $20 for stainless steel (new 2006, MSR $239).
Add $10 for blue, brown (disc. 2020), pink, or purple laminate stock (all disc).
Add $25 for .17 HMR or.17 Mach 2 cal. (disc.).

RIFLES: BOLT ACTION, SINGLE SHOT

BARRACUDA CHIPMUNK – .17 HMR (disc.), .17 Mach 2 (disc.), .22 WMR (disc.), or .22 LR cal., free floating (standard, disc.) or bull blued steel or stainless steel barrel, no sights, ergonomic pistol grip, receiver Picatinny rail, skeletonized thumbhole (disc.), walnut (disc. 2020), or laminated stock in black (disc. 2019), brown (disc.), or camo.

	100%	98%	95%	90%	80%	70%	60%
MSR $269	$230	$200	$175	$155	$125	$110	$90

Add $20 for stainless (available on walnut - disc. 2019, or camo laminated stock only, MSR $289).
Add $25 for .17 HMR, .17 Mach 2, or .22 WMR cal. (disc.).

CHIPMUNK STANDARD RIFLE – .17 HMR (mfg. 2002-disc), .17 Mach 2 (mfg. 2005-disc.), .22 WMR (disc. 1987, reintroduced 1999-disc.), .22 Short, Long, or LR cal., youth model, 16 1/8 in. blued steel or stainless steel barrel and 12 in. LOP, iron sights (adj. aperture rear) or Truglo sights (mfg. 2005-disc.), choice of black coated wood stock (disc.), walnut, black or brown laminate (mfg.1999-disc.), camo (new 2002, various colored woods), synthetic (mfg. 2004-disc.), birch (mfg. 2006-disc.), or uncheckered Monte Carlo walnut stock, 2 1/2 (standard barrel) or 4 (bull barrel, disc.) lbs. New circa 1982.

	100%	98%	95%	90%	80%	70%	60%
MSR $219	$185	$150	$150	$125	$100	$75	$75

Add $10 for left-hand (walnut stock only, MSR $229).
Add $20 for black, brown (disc.), or camo laminated stock (MSR $239).
Add $30 for Deluxe rifle with hand checkered deluxe Monte Carlo walnut stock (MSR $249).
Add $30 for stainless steel (available with black or camo laminated stock only, MSR $249).
Add $20 for .17 HMR or .17 Mach 2 (disc.).
Add approx. 15% for bull barrel (disc.).
Add 75% for target rifle with 18 in. heavy barrel (disc.).
Subtract approx. 10% for black coated wood stock (disc.).

GRADING - PPGS™	100%	98%	95%	90%	80%	70%	60%	LAST MSR

* ***Chipmunk Special Alaska Edition*** – .22 LR cal., walnut stock, Alaska "907", includes blue case. Mfg. 2020 only.

	$215	$190	$160	$145	$120	$95	$80	*$249*

* ***Chipmunk Special Edition Deluxe*** – .22 LR cal., blued barrel, walnut stock with gloss finish (black details on stock at pistol grip end and forend), includes low profile compact gloss black scope and Chipmunk logo case. New 2020.

MSR $349	$300	$265	$225	$200	$165	$135	$115	

SHOTGUNS: SINGLE SHOT

CHIPMUNK .410 SHOTGUN – .410 bore, single shot, manual cocking shotgun, 18 1/4 in. smoothbore barrel, walnut stock, 11 1/2 in. LOP, blue finish only, approx. 3 1/4 lbs. Mfg. mid-2002-2005.

	$175	$150	$130	$100	$90	$80	$70	*$190*

CHRISTENSEN ARMS

Christensen Arms

Current manufacturer of AR-15 style rifles and pistols, bolt action rifles, and 1911 style handguns. Established in 1995, currently located in Gunnison, UT. Previously located in Fayette, UT from 2000-2010, and in St. George, UT from 1995-1999. Direct sales only.

PISTOLS: SEMI-AUTO

1911 A4 – 9mm Para. or .45 ACP cal., aluminum frame, 4 in. stainless steel match grade barrel, 7 (.45 ACP) or 9 (9mm) shot mag., stainless steel slide with two tone (polished steel/black) finish, skeletonized hammer and trigger, raised night sights, G10 grips, beavertail grip safety, checkered mainspring housing, adj. overtravel, full-length guide rod, checkered front strap, black anodized finish, 2 lbs. Mfg. 2017-2020.

	$1,795	$1,600	$1,400	$1,225	$1,050	$900	$775	*$1,995*

1911 A5 – 9mm Para. or .45 ACP cal., aluminum frame, 5 in. stainless steel match grade barrel, 7 (.45) or 9 (9mm) shot mag., stainless steel slide with two tone (polished steel/black) finish, skeletonized hammer and trigger, raised night sights, G10 grips, beavertail grip safety, checkered mainspring housing, adj. overtravel, full length guide rod, checkered front strap, black anodized finish, 2.2 lbs. Mfg. 2017-2020.

	$1,795	$1,600	$1,400	$1,225	$1,050	$900	$775	*$1,995*

1911 A5-TR – 9mm Para. or .45 ACP cal., aluminum frame, 5 in. stainless steel match grade threaded barrel, threaded muzzle, 7 (.45 ACP) or 9 (9mm) shot mag., extended flared magwell, stainless steel slide with two tone (polished steel/black) finish, skeletonized hammer and trigger, suppressor sights, G10 grips, beavertail grip safety, tactical rail, adj. overtravel, full length guide rod, checkered front strap, checkered mainspring housing, black anodized finish, 2.4 lbs. Mfg. 2017-2020.

	$1,795	$1,600	$1,400	$1,225	$1,050	$900	$775	*$1,995*

1911 C4 – 9mm Para. or .45 ACP cal., full size, single stack 1911 stainless steel frame, bobtail, 4 in. stainless steel match grade barrel, 7 shot, stainless steel or damascus slide, skeletonized hammer and trigger, Novak night sights, VZ G10 or carbon fiber (disc.) grips, beavertail grip safety, checkered front strap, full length guide rod, extended slide stop, adj. overtravel, Natural or Cerakote in Black, FDE (disc.), Burnt Bronze, OD Green (disc.), or Tungsten frame and slide finish, 2.4 lbs. Mfg. 2016-2020.

	$2,625	$2,295	$1,975	$1,785	$1,450	$1,185	$925	*$2,895*

Add $1,300 for damascus slide.

* ***1911 C4 Ti*** – 9mm Para. or .45 ACP cal., similar to the 1911 C4, except features 4.5 in. barrel, 7 (.45 ACP) or 9 (9mm Para.) shot mag. bobtail cut or standard titanium frame, raised night sights, carbon fiber grips, natural titanium finish, 2.1 lbs.

MSR $5,095	$4,590	$4,050	$3,450	$3,120	$2,525	$2,070	$1,700	

1911 CA – .45 ACP cal., stainless steel frame, 4 or 5 in. stainless steel barrel, 8 shot mag., skeletonized hammer and trigger, optics ready slide, removable rear sight, composite grips, beavertail grip safety, checkered front strap, full length guide rod, with or w/o accessory rail, checkered mainspring housing, black Nitride finish, 2.6 lbs. Mfg. 2020 only.

	$1,525	$1,350	$1,150	$1,050	$850	$685	$550	*$1,395*

1911 OFFICER – .45 ACP cal., stainless steel or titanium frame with natural finish, 3.65 in. barrel without bushing, stainless slide with black cerakote finish, Novak 3-dot Trijicon sights, skeletonized trigger, bobbed hammer, bi-directional textured black G10 grips, 6 shot mag., full length guide rod, 30 oz. Mfg. 2013-2015.

	$2,050	$1,800	$1,550	$1,400	$1,150	$925	$725	*$2,395*

Add $800 for titanium frame.

GRADING - PPGS™	100%	98%	95%	90%	80%	70%	60%	LAST MSR

1911 GOVERNMENT DAMASCUS – .45 ACP cal., 5 in. barrel without bushing, titanium frame with natural finish, patterned damascus slide with front and rear serrations, stippled grip straps, skeletonized trigger and hammer, Novak 3-dot Trijicon sights, smooth carbon fiber grips, 7 shot mag., full length guide rod, 36 oz. Mfg. 2013-2015.

	$4,100	$3,650	$3,175	$2,750	$2,375	$2,000	$1,700	*$4,595*

1911 G5 – 9mm Para. (new 2017) or .45 ACP cal., stainless steel frame, 5 in. stainless steel match grade barrel, 7 (.45 ACP) or 9 (9mm) shot mag., stainless steel or damascus slide, skeletonized hammer and trigger, raised night sights, VZ G10 grips, beavertail grip safety, checkered mainspring housing, front strap checkering, extended slide stop, full length guide rod, Cerakote in Black (disc.), FDE (disc. 2016), Burnt Bronze, OD Green (disc. 2016), Tungsten, FDE/Black (disc. 2016), OD Green/Black (disc. 2016), or Natural/Black frame and slide finish, 2 1/2 lbs. Mfg. 2016-2020.

	$2,600	$2,275	$1,850	$1,725	$1,400	$1,150	$900	*$2,895*

Add $1,300 for damascus slide.
Add $100 for Cerakote finishes (disc. 2016).

* ***1911 G5-Ti*** – 9mm Para. or .45 ACP cal., similar to to the 1911 G5, excepts features titanium frame, Damascus slide, carbon fiber grips, natural titanium finish, and is 2.2 lbs. New 2016.

MSR $4,795	$4,315	$3,775	$3,230	$2,930	$2,375	$1,950	$1,600	

1911 G5-TARGET – .45 ACP cal., full size, single stack 1911 stainless steel frame, 5 in. stainless steel match grade barrel, 7 shot, extended magwell, stainless steel slide, adj. target sights, VZ G10 or carbon fiber grips, ambidextrous safety, beavertail grip safety, front strap checkering, extended slide stop, full length guide rod, black slide and satin frame finish. Mfg. 2016 only.

	$2,700	$2,365	$2,025	$1,835	$1,485	$1,225	$950	*$2,999*

1911 G5-TR – 9mm Para. or .45 ACP cal., full size, single stack 1911 stainless steel frame, 5 in. stainless steel match grade threaded barrel, threaded muzzle, 8 (.45 ACP) or 10 (9mm) shot mag., extended flared magwell, stainless steel or damascus slide, skeletonized hammer and trigger, Heinie night sights, VZ G10 grips, ambi and beavertail grip safety, checkered front strap and mainspring housing, extended slide stop, full length guide rod, tactical rail, Natural, Black, or Cerakote FDE (disc. 2016), Burnt Bronze, OD Green (disc. 2016), Tungsten, FDE/Black (disc. 2016), or ODG/Black (disc. 2016) frame and slide finish, 2.7 lbs. Mfg. 2016-2019.

	$2,600	$2,275	$1,850	$1,725	$1,400	$1,150	$900	*$2,895*

Add $1,400 for damascus slide.
Add $100 for Cerakote frame and slide finish (disc. 2016).

CA 9MM PISTOL – 9mm Para. cal., direct blowback, 7.5 or 10.5 in. Aerograde carbon fiber wrapped, buttoned barrel w/Nitride finish, threaded muzzle, 3-prong stainless steel flash hider, flared magwell, SBA3 pistol brace, forged aluminum upper and lower receiver, 9.25 (10.5 in. bbl.) or 6.25 (7.5 in. bbl) in. aluminum M-LOK handguard, full rail, 2 QD mounts, anodized black finish, 5.5 lbs. New 2021.

MSR $1,495	$1,350	$1,180	$1,015	$920	$745	$610	$475	

CARBON ONE PISTOL SINGLE SHOT – various cals., graphite barrel lengths up to 14 in., uses Thompson Center Encore or Contender pistol frame, less than 1 in. grouping for 3 shots at 100 yards, satin nickel receiver, approx. 2.5-3 lbs. Limited mfg. beginning 1999.

This model is a special order, please contact the company directly.

COMMANDER (COMMANDER LITE) – .45 ACP cal., stainless steel slide with tungsten carbide runners, steel or titanium frame, 4.29 in. match barrel (threaded barrel is optional), VZ G10 grips, adj. trigger, Tritium night sights, aerospace aluminum mainspring housing, 34.3 oz. Mfg. 2011-2015.

	$2,750	$2,350	$1,995	$1,775	$1,500	$1,250	$995	*$3,095*

Add $1,000 for titanium frame.
Add $250 for Ed Brown Bobtail Commander model.

* ***Tactical Commander*** – .45 ACP cal., similar to the Commander model, except has flared magwell and Picatinny rail. 38.1 oz. Mfg. 2013-2015.

	$2,775	$2,425	$2,075	$1,885	$1,525	$1,250	$975	*$3,250*

Add $1,000 for titanium frame.

GOVERNMENT (CLASSIC GOVERNMENT LITE) – 9mm Para., .40 S&W, or .45 ACP cal., patterned after Colt M1911, SA, 5.05 in. match barrel, stainless steel or titanium frame with a hand fit slide, front and rear slide serrations, extended ambidextrous thumb safety, SPRINCO recoil reducing system, carbon fiber grips, Trijicon/Novak Tritium sights, 8 (.45 ACP), 9 (.40 S&W), or 10 (9mm, disc. 2011) shot mag., 3 1/4-3 3/4 lb. trigger pull. Mfg. 2011-2015.

	$2,750	$2,350	$1,995	$1,775	$1,500	$1,250	$995	*$3,095*

Add $1,000 for titanium frame.

GRADING - PPGS™	100%	98%	95%	90%	80%	70%	60%	LAST MSR

* ***Tactical Government (Tactical Lite)*** – .45 ACP cal., similar to Government model, except has Picatinny rail, and flared magwell. Mfg. 2011-2015.

	$2,825	$2,350	$2,050	$1,775	$1,500	$1,250	$1,050	*$3,250*

Add $1,000 for titanium frame.

OFFICER LITE – similar to the Classic Government Lite, except has 3.65 in. barrel, low profile ambidextrous thumb safety, 7 (.40 S&W or .45 ACP cal.), or 8 (9mm) shot mag., two-piece reverse plug recoil system, titanium pin and hammer strut, aluminum mainspring housing. Mfg. 2011-2013.

	$2,750	$2,350	$1,995	$1,775	$1,500	$1,250	$995	*$3,095*

RIFLES: BOLT ACTION

In addition to the models listed below, Christensen Arms also offers the Carbon One Custom barrel installed on a customer action (any caliber) for $1,100 ($695) if short chambered by competent gunsmith), as well as providing a Carbon Wrap conversion to an existing steel barrel ($795). Additionally, a Custom Long Range Package is available for $6,695, as well as an Extreme Long Range Package for $4,650.

Add $150 for Realtree (disc. 2013), Mossy Oak (disc. 2013), King's Desert (mfg. 2011-2013), King's Snow (mfg. 2011-2013) or Natural Gear (disc. 2010) camo stock.

BA TACTICAL – .223 Rem., 6mm Creedmoor (new 2020), 6.5 Creedmoor, 6.5 PRC, .308 Win. (disc 2020), .300 Win. Mag., .300 PRC, .300 Norma Mag. (disc. 2020), .338 Lapua Mag., or .338 Norma Mag. (disc. 2020) cal., 16, 20, 22, 24, 26, or 27 in. carbon fiber wrapped 416R stainless steel barrel with target contour, SS thread protector, SS side-port muzzle brake, 5 shot detachable mag., tactical mag. release, 3-way adj. single stage trigger, carbon fiber composite long range tactical stock with Black/Gray webbing finish, adj. cheekpiece via inserts, adj. LOP via 1/4 in. spacers, front stud with five flush cups, dual sling studs, modified beavertail forearm, Limbsaver recoil pad, full integral Picatinny rail, oversized fluted bolt knob, tactical grip, tactical hook, black Nitride finish, approx. 7.7-8.1 lbs. New 2016.

MSR $2,795	$2,525	$2,210	$1,895	$1,715	$1,395	$1,150	$885	

Add $200 for .338 Lapua Mag. cal.

* ***BA Tactical VTAC*** – .223 Rem., 6.5 Creedmoor, .308 Win., or .300 AAC Blackout cal., similar to BA Tactical, except has 16 in. barrel, 7.1-7 1/2 lbs. Mfg. 2016 only.

	$2,525	$2,210	$1,895	$1,715	$1,395	$1,150	$885	*$2,799*

CARBON CLASSIC TACTICAL – .22-250 Rem., .223 Rem., .270 WSM, 7mm Rem. Mag., .308 Win., .300 WSM, .300 Win. Mag., .300 RUM, or .338 Lapua cal., 18 to 26 in. carbon wrapped select match grade barrel, spiral fluted, lightened, and teflon coated bolt, tuned trigger, graphite, black with grey webbing, tan with black webbing, green with black webbing, or green with tan and black webbing carbon fiber sporter or thumbhole stock, recoil pad, 7.6 lbs. Disc. 2013.

	$3,350	$2,925	$2,515	$2,275	$1,850	$1,510	$1,175	*$3,950*

CARBON CUSTOM TACTICAL – .22-250 Rem., .223 Rem., .270 WSM, 7mm Rem. Mag., .308 Win., .300 WSM, .300 Win. Mag., .300 RUM, .30-378 Wby., .338 RUM, or .338 Lapua cal., 18 to 28 in. carbon wrapped select match grade barrel, diamond fluted, lightened, and teflon coated bolt, graphite, black with grey webbing, tan with black webbing, green with black webbing, or green with tan and black webbing carbon fiber sporter or thumbhole stock, 7.2 lbs. Disc. 2013.

	$4,475	$3,915	$3,350	$3,050	$2,460	$2,015	$1,565	*$5,275*

CARBON ONE 10TH ANNIVERSARY MODEL – .270 WSM, .300 WSM, or .325 WSM cal., Rem. titanium action, graphite stock, titanium muzzle brake, stainless floorplate, SST, laser engraving, individually numbered 1-50. Limited mfg. beginning mid-2005.

Retail pricing was not available for this model.

CARBON ONE CUSTOM – most popular cals., features Remington 700 BDL short action or Winchester Model 70 action, barrel (up to 32 in. long) features a match grade Shilen/Christensen precision 416R stainless steel barrel liner inside a larger diameter graphite/epoxy barrel casing with crown, black synthetic stock, Shilen trigger, 5 1/2 - 7 lbs. Mfg. 1996-2013.

	$4,225	$3,695	$3,175	$2,875	$2,325	$1,900	$1,475	*$4,975*

Add $1,955 for long range rifle package including Swarovski Z5 3-18x44mm BRH scope, Talley rings, 100 rounds of ammo, accessories, and custom rifle case (new 2011).

Variations have included the Carbon Lite (5 lbs.), Carbon King (6-7 lbs., .25-.308 cal.), Carbon Cannon (includes muzzle brake, 6 1/2-7 1/2 lbs., Magnum series), or Carbon Tactical (includes muzzle brake, 6 1/2 lbs., new 1997), or Carbon Conquest (new 1998).

GRADING - PPGS™	100%	98%	95%	90%	80%	70%	60%	LAST MSR

CARBON ONE EXTREME – various cals., 18-26 in. carbon wrap free floating barrel, choice of carbon classic or thumbhole Christensen Arms stock, Teflon coated and lightened action, 3 lb. trigger pull, 5 1/2-7 lbs. Mfg. 2007-2012.

	$2,875	$2,400	$1,900	$1,500	$1,200	$975	$800	*$3,295*

CARBON ONE HUNTER – various popular cals., features Remington M700 (regular or stainless) or Winchester Model 70 stainless action, available with HS Precision (disc.), or synthetic (disc.), or Bell & Carlson stock with Dura-Touch (new 2011) finish, 18-26 in. large diameter graphite barrel with stainless steel barrel liner, 5 1/2-7 lbs. Mfg. 1999-2012.

	$1,825	$1,525	$1,250	$1,050	$900	$775	$650	*$2,150*

Subtract approx. 15% if without 2011 updates (drilled bolt handle, Bell & Carlson stock).

CARBON ONE R93 – various cals., features Blaser R93 action, 24 or 26 in. carbon fiber barrel with carbon classic stock, 5.5-7 lbs. Mfg. 2011-2012.

	$3,775	$3,300	$2,825	$2,575	$2,075	$1,700	$1,350	*$4,195*

CARBON ONE RANGER (CONQUEST) – .50 BMG cal., single shot (disc. 2010) or repeater (5 shot), McMillan stainless steel bolt action, max barrel length is 32 in. with muzzle brake, Christensen composite stock with bipod, approx. 16 (single shot) - 24 lbs. Mfg. 2001-2014.

	$8,200	$6,700	$5,450	$4,500	$3,750	$2,850	$2,500	*$8,995*

Add $300 for Tac-50 stock.
Add $240 for Atlas Bipod BT10.
Add $200 for camo stock dip.
Subtract 20% for single shot action (disc. 2010).

CARBON ONE TACTICAL – various cals., grey synthetic stock, various barrel lengths, stainless steel free floating Shilen barrel with muzzle brake, glass bedded barrel assembly, precision trigger, many options available per customer request, 5.5-7 lbs. Mfg. 2010-2012.

	$4,150	$3,650	$3,125	$2,825	$2,285	$1,875	$1,500	*$4,595*

CARBON RANGER – .50 BMG cal., large diameter graphite barrel casing (up to 36 in. long), no stock or forearm, twin rails extending from frame sides are attached to recoil pad, Omni Wind Runner action, bipod and choice of scope are included, 25-32 lbs. Limited mfg. 1998-2000.

	$9,950	$8,900	$8,000	$7,100	$6,200	$5,300	$4,400	*$10,625*

CLASSIC CARBON (CARBON CLASSIC CUSTOM) – .22-250 Rem., .223 Rem., .270 WSM, 7mm Rem. Mag., .308 Win., .300 WSM, .300 Win. Mag., .300 RUM or .338 Lapua cal., 18 to 26 in. carbon wrapped select match grade barrel, Cerakoted spiral fluted bolt, black with grey webbing, tan with black webbing, green with black webbing, or green with tan and black webbing Bell & Carlson stock, tuned trigger, 6.4 lbs. Disc. 2016.

	$2,525	$2,210	$1,895	$1,715	$1,395	$1,150	$885	*$2,795*

Add $850 for Tier 1 stock.

* ***Classic Steel*** – similar to Classic Carbon model, except features steel barrel. Disc. 2016.

	$1,725	$1,510	$1,295	$1,175	$950	$775	$600	*$1,900*

Add $850 for Tier 1 stock.

CLASSIC (CLASSIC II) – .243 Win.-.375 H&H cal., 24, 26, or 27 in. stainless steel carbon fiber wrapped barrel with light target contour, titanium muzzle brake, SS thread protector, aluminum hinged floorplate, 3-way adj. single stage trigger, carbon fiber composite Sporter or Monte Carlo (new 2017) stock, modified beavertail forearm, raised comb, full palm swell, Limbsaver recoil pad, spiral fluted bolt, scalloped bolt knob, dual front studs, integrated split Picatinny rail, painted Black w/Gray webbing or Green w/Black webbing, 6.8-7.1 lbs. Mfg. 2016-2018.

	$2,700	$2,375	$2,025	$1,850	$1,485	$1,225	$975	*$2,995*

Add $200 for .338 Lapua Mag. cal.

ELR – 6.5 Creedmoor, 6.5 PRC (new mid-2018), 6.5-284 Norma (disc. 2020), .26 Nosler (disc. 2020), .28 Nosler, 7mm Rem. Mag., .308 Win. (disc. 2020), .30-06 (disc. 2020), .30 Nosler (disc. 2020), .300 WSM (disc. 2020), .300 Win. Mag., .300 PRC (new 2019), .300 RUM (disc. 2020), or .338 Lapua Mag. (disc. 2020) cal., 24 (disc. 2018), 26, or 27 in. 416R stainless steel carbon fiber wrapped barrel with target contour and titanium side-port muzzle brake, black Nitride finish spiral fluted bolt and scalloped bolt knob, SS thread protector, aluminum hinged floorplate, 3-way adj. single stage trigger, carbon fiber composite extreme long range hunting stock, adj. cheekpiece via inserts, adj. LOP with 1/4 in. spacers, dual sling studs, modified beavertail forearm, dual front studs with flush cups, Limbsaver recoil pad, tactical grip, full integral Picatinny rail, painted black/gray webbing, 7 1/2 lbs. New 2016.

MSR $2,795	$2,525	$2,210	$1,895	$1,715	$1,395	$1,150	$885	

Add $200 for .338 Lapua Mag. cal. (only available with dropbox mag.).

GRADING - PPGS™	100%	98%	95%	90%	80%	70%	60%	LAST MSR

* ***Ultra ELR*** – 6.5 Creedmoor-.338 Lapua Mag. cal., similar to ELR, except has Aerograde carbon fiber extended long range stock and natural carbon fiber finish, 6.4-6.8 bs. Mfg. 2016 only.

	$4,050	$3,550	$3,050	$2,750	$2,250	$1,825	$1,425	*$4,499*

Add $200 for .338 Lapua Mag. cal.

MESA – .308 Win., 6.5 Creedmoor, .300 Win. Mag., 7mm-08 Rem., 7mm Rem. Mag., .28 Nosler (2017 only), .300 PRC (new 2019), .450 Bushmaster (new mid-2017), or 6.5 PRC (new 2019) cal., Rem. 700 action, right or left (new mid-2018) hand configuration, 20, 22, 24, or 26 in. 416R stainless steel free floating barrel, threaded muzzle, thread protector, removable seamless radial brake, 3 or 4 shot mag., enlarged ejection port, M16 style extractor, adj. match grade trigger, carbon fiber composite Sporter stock with black/gray webbing finish, Limbsaver recoil pad, skeletonized bolt handle, fluted bolt knob, Tungsten or Burnt Bronze (new late 2017) Cerakote finish, 6.5-7.3 lbs. New 2017.

MSR $1,295	$1,165	$1,020	$875	$790	$640	$525	$410	

Add $250 for left-hand configuration (new mid-2018).

MESA LONG RANGE – 6.5 Creedmoor, .308 Win., .28 Nosler, .300 Win. Mag., 7mm Rem. Mag., .300 PRC (new 2019), .338 Lapua Mag. (new 2019), or 6.5 PRC (new mid-2018) cal., 24, 26, or 27 (new 2019) in. Christensen Arms 416R stainless steel free floating barrel with threaded muzzle and Tungsten or Burnt Bronze (new mid-2018) Cerakote finish, 3 or 4 shot mag., enlarged ejection port, match grade trigger, carbon fiber composite long range stock, adj. comb, modified beavertail forearm, forward mount rail with sling stud, tactical grip, skeletonized bolt handle, oversized fluted bolt knob, black w/ gray or green with black/tan (new mid-2018) webbing on stock, 8.9-9.9 lbs. New 2018.

MSR $1,595	$1,435	$1,250	$1,075	$975	$795	$650	$525	

MESA TITANIUM EDITION – .308 Win., 6.5 Creedmoor, 6.5 PRC, .28 Nosler (new 2021), .300 PRC (new 2021), 7mm Rem. Mag. (new 2021), or .300 Win. Mag. cal., titanium action, 22 or 24 in. featherlight contour 416R stainless steel barrel with bead blasted finish, removable seamless radial brake, titanium receiver, M16 style extractor, enlarged ejection port, match grade trigger, carbon fiber composite Sporter stock in Metallic Grey with black webbing, Limbsaver recoil pad, skeletonized bolt handle, custom Titanium Edition floorplate, 6.1 lbs. New 2020.

MSR $1,795	$1,600	$1,400	$1,200	$1,090	$880	$725	$600	

MODERN PRECISION RIFLE – .223 Rem. (new 2019), 6mm Creedmoor (new 2020), 6.5 Creedmoor, 6.5 PRC (new 2018), .300 PRC (new 2019), .300 Win. Mag. (new 2018), .300 Norma Mag. (new 2018), .308 Win., or .338 Lapua Mag. (new 2018) cal., short or long action, 16, 20, 22, 24, or 26 in. 416R stainless steel carbon fiber wrapped barrel, AICS compatible detachable mag., tactical mag. release, enlarged ejection port, M16 style extractor, match grade flat trigger, Remington 700 optics base compatible, adj. carbon fiber cheek riser, adj. LOP, folding stock with locking hinge and Magnelock Technology, QD flush cup mounts, standard AR grip, stainless steel receiver, oversized fluted bolt knob, skeletonized bolt handle, billet aluminum chassis, 14 or 17 in. carbon fiber handguard with M-LOK, 20 MOA rail, Monopod Picatinny mount ready, hardcoat anodized black or Desert Brown (new 2019) finish, 6.9-7.9 lbs. New late 2017.

MSR $2,295	$2,075	$1,825	$1,550	$1,425	$1,150	$950	$750	

Add $100 for long action.

Christensen Amrs 416R stainless steel barrel (#4 contour) with black Cerakote finish is available in current calibers and 20, 22, 24, 26, or 27 in. lengths. Current MSR is $1,795 for short action or $1,895 for long action.

RANGER 22 – .22 LR cal., Christensen arms carbon fiber tension rimfire barrel, threaded muzzle, Ruger 10/22 compatible mag., black anodized aluminum receiver with steel recoil lug, dual ejectors, TriggerTech Rem. 700 trigger, black/gray webbing or tan/black webbing carbon fiber composite rimfire stock, palm swell, recoil pad, flat forend, sling studs, palm hook, ambidextrous grip, Picatinny rail, threaded bolt handle, 5.1 lbs. New 2020.

MSR $795	$715	$625	$535	$485	$400	$325	$250	

REBEL – .223 Rem.-.300 RUM cal., 22-26 in. stainless steel fluted barrel, MagSporter contour, threaded muzzle with protector, 3-way adj. single stage trigger, hand-laid fiberglass stock, dual front studs, aluminum hinged floorplate, Painted Black finish, 7-7 1/2 lbs. Mfg. 2016 only.

	$1,800	$1,575	$1,350	$1,225	$995	$825	$650	*$1,999*

RIDGELINE – .450 Bushmaster, .22-250 Rem., .243 Win., 6.5 Creedmoor, 6.5 PRC (new mid-2018), 6.5-284 Norma, .26 Nosler, .270 Win., .270 WSM, 7mm-08 Rem., .280 Ackley, .28 Nosler, 7mm Rem. Mag., .308 Win., .30-06, .30 Nosler, .300 PRC (new 2020), .300 WSM, .300 Win. Mag., .300 PRC (new 2019), or .300 RUM cal., right or left (new mid-2018) hand configuration, 20, 22 (disc.), 24, or 26 in. 416R stainless steel aerograde carbon fiber wrapped barrel, light target contour, stainless steel

GRADING - PPGS™	100%	98%	95%	90%	80%	70%	60%	LAST MSR

muzzle brake, spiral fluted bolt, enlarged ejection port, M16 style extractor, 3-way adj. single stage trigger, black or green carbon fiber composite Sporter style stock with black/gray webbing or black/tan webbing, stainless steel or Burnt Bronze Cerakote (new 2019) action finish, Limbsaver recoil pad, one-piece 1913 Mil-Std base, scalloped bolt knob, dual front studs, aluminum hinged floorplate, 6.3-6.7 lbs. New 2015.

MSR $1,995	$1,795	$1,550	$1,325	$1,100	$925	$775	$650	

Add $100 for Burnt Bronze Cerakote finish (new 2019).
Add $250 for left-hand configuration (new mid-2018).

RIDGELINE TITANIUM EDITION – .308 Win., 6.5 Creedmoor, 6.5 PRC, .28 Nosler (new 2021), .300 PRC (new 2021), 7mm Rem. Mag. (new 2021), or .300 Win. Mag. cal., titanium action, 22 or 24 in. 416R stainless steel carbon fiber wrapped barrel, removable titanium radial brake, spiral fluted bolt, titanium receiver, enlarged ejection port, M16 style extractor, match grade trigger, carbon fiber composite Sporter stock in Metallic Grey with black webbing, Limbsaver recoil pad, fluted bolt knob, hinged floorplate, 5.8 lbs. New 2020.

MSR $2,495	$2,250	$1,975	$1,695	$1,525	$1,250	$1,025	$800	

ROGUE – .243 Win.-.375 H&H cal., 24-27 in. carbon fiber wrapped barrel, light target contour, titanium muzzle brake, detachable carbon fiber in-line feed magazine, 3-way adj. single stage trigger, Monte Carlo hand-laid carbon fiber stock, spiral fluted bolt, scalloped bolt knob, dual front studs, painted black with gray webbing, 6.8-7.1 lbs. Mfg. 2016 only.

	$2,700	$2,375	$2,025	$1,850	$1,485	$1,225	$975	*$2,999*

Add $200 for .338 LM cal.

SUMMIT CARBON – multiple calibers available, carbon fiber barrel, fluted bolt, adj. Timney trigger, Tier 1 carbon stock in Sporter or Thumbhole configuration, graphite bed block, glass bedded, 6 lbs. Mfg. 2014-2015.

	$5,075	$4,450	$3,800	$3,450	$2,795	$2,285	$1,775	*$5,645*

Subtract $850 for Bell & Carlson stock.

* ***Summit Steel*** – similar to Summit Carbon model, except features steel barrel. Mfg. 2014-2015.

	$4,125	$3,625	$3,095	$2,800	$2,275	$1,850	$1,450	*$4,595*

Subtract $850 for Bell & Carlson stock.

SUMMIT Ti/SUMMIT Ti-TH – .25-06 Rem., 6.5 Creedmoor, 6.5-284 Norma, .26 Nosler, .270 Win., .270 WSM, .280 Ackley, .28 Nosler, 7mm Rem. Mag., 6.5 PRC (new mid-2018), .30-06, .308 Win., .30 Nosler, .300 WSM, .300 Win. Mag., .300 RUM, .300 PRC (new 2019), .338 Lapua Mag. (mfg. 2016-2019), or .375 H&H cal., titanium bolt action, 24, 26, or 27 in. 416R stainless steel carbon fiber wrapped barrel with light target contour and titanium muzzle brake, fully adj. match trigger, carbon fiber Sporter or thumbhole (Summit TH, disc. 2020) stock, modified beavertail forearm, enhanced comb (thumbhole), Limbsaver recoil pad, dual front studs, aluminum hinged floorplate, integrated split Picatinny rail, natural carbon fiber finish or painted black/gray webbing, green/black webbing, green/black and tan webbing, 5.5-6 lbs. New 2016.

MSR $5,495	$4,950	$4,325	$3,725	$3,375	$2,725	$2,250	$1,750	

Add $200 for .338 Lapua Mag. cal. (mfg. 2016-2019).

TACTICAL FORCE MULTIPLIER (TFM) CARBON – .223 Rem. (mfg. 2014-2019), 6mm Creedmoor (new 2020), .300 Win. Mag., .308 Win., 6.5 Creedmoor (new 2019), 6.5 PRC (new 2019), .300 PRC (new 2019), .300 Norma Mag. (new 2019), .338 Norma Mag. (new 2019), or .338 Lapua Mag. cal., 16 (new 2019), 20, 24, 26, or 27 in. 416R stainless steel carbon fiber wrapped barrel with target profile, titanium muzzle brake, SS thread protector, drop-box magazine, adj. Timney trigger, carbon fiber long range tactical stock, adj. comb, adj. LOP, modified beavertail forearm, palm swell, tactical hook, Limbsaver recoil pad, tactical grip, oversized fluted bolt knob, integral Picatinny rail, black Nitride finish, 7.3-7.6 lbs. New 2014.

MSR $4,895	$4,400	$3,850	$3,300	$2,995	$2,425	$1,985	$1,550	

Add $200 for .338 Lapua Mag. cal.

* ***Tactical Force Multiplier (TFM) Steel*** – .223 Rem., .300 Win. Mag., .308 Win., or .338 Lapua Mag. cal., similar to TFM Carbon model, except features steel barrel. Disc. 2015.

	$4,350	$3,800	$3,275	$2,950	$2,395	$1,950	$1,525	*$4,845*

* ***Tactical Force Multiplier (TFM) VTAC*** – 6.5 Creedmoor, .300 AAC Blackout, or .308 Win. Mag. cal., 16 in. carbon fiber wrapped barrel with target contour and muzzle brake, 5 shot detachable mag., 3-way adj. single stage trigger, Aerograde carbon fiber TFM stock, front stud with five flush cups, Natural carbon fiber finish, 7.1-7 1/2 lbs. Mfg. 2016 only.

	$4,400	$3,850	$3,300	$2,995	$2,425	$1,985	$1,550	*$4,899*

GRADING - PPGS™	100%	98%	95%	90%	80%	70%	60%	LAST MSR

TRAVERSE – .22-250 Rem., .243 Win., 6.5 Creedmoor, 6.5 PRC, 6.5-284 Norma, .26 Nosler, .270 Win., .270 WSM, 7mm-08 Rem., .280 Ackley, .28 Nosler, 7mm Rem. Mag., .308 Win., .30-06, .30 Nosler, .300 WSM, .300 Win. Mag., .300 PRC, .300 RUM, or .338 Lapua (new 2020) cal., 20, 24, or 26 in. LC carbon fiber threaded 416R stainless steel barrel, M16 style extractor, dual ejector, match grade trigger, Monte Carlo carbon fiber composite stock, modified beavertail forearm, raised comb, stainless steel side-baffle brake, 0-MOA optic rail, 4 in. bottom Picatinny rail, Limbsaver recoil pad, enlarged bolt handle, black w/gray or green w/black webbing finish, 7.3 (short action) or 7.7 (long action) lbs. New 2019.

MSR	100%	98%	95%	90%	80%	70%	60%	LAST MSR
MSR $2,395	$2,150	$1,875	$1,595	$1,450	$1,150	$950	$795	

RIFLES: SEMI-AUTO

Christensen Arms also offered a Carbon One Challenge drop-in barrel (16 oz.) for the Ruger Model 10/22. Last MSR was $499 (disc. 2010).

CARBON ONE CHALLENGE (CUSTOM) – .17 HMR, .22 LR, or .22 WMR cal., features Ruger 10/22 Model 1103 action with modified bolt release, synthetic bull barrel with precision stainless steel liner, 2 lb. Volquartsen trigger, Fajen brown laminated wood (disc.) or black synthetic stock with thumbhole, approx. 3.5-4 lbs. Mfg. 1996-2010.

MSR	100%	98%	95%	90%	80%	70%	60%	LAST MSR
	$1,500	$1,250	$1,050	$875	$750	$600	$500	*$1,750*

Add $350 for .17 HMR or .22 WMR cal.

The 100% price represents the base model, with no options.

* ***Carbon One Challenge*** – .22 LR cal., non-custom shop variation, 4 lbs. New 1999.

MSR	100%	98%	95%	90%	80%	70%	60%	LAST MSR
	$550	$495	$440	$400	$365	$330	$295	*$599*

CARBON CHALLENGE II – similar to Carbon Challenge I, except has AMT stainless receiver and trigger, black synthetic stock, approx. 4 1/2 lbs. Limited mfg. 1997-1998 only.

MSR	100%	98%	95%	90%	80%	70%	60%	LAST MSR
	$1,150	$975	$875	$800	$725	$650	$525	*$1,299*

CA5five6 – 5.56 NATO cal., DI, 16 in. Christensen Arms 416R stainless steel carbon fiber wrapped barrel, button rifled, threaded muzzle, 3 prong stainless steel flash hider, black Nitride finish on barrel and BCG, forged aluminum receiver, TriggerTech trigger, MFT battlelink Minimalist stock, 14 3/4 (disc. 2020) or 15 in. carbon aluminum hybrid handguard with full rail, carbon fiber panels, 2 QD mounts, M-LOK, hardcoat anodized black or Cerakote finish in Tungsten or Burnt Bronze, 6.3 lbs. New 2020.

MSR	100%	98%	95%	90%	80%	70%	60%	LAST MSR
MSR $1,495	$1,350	$1,200	$1,100	$975	$825	$700	$600	

CA9MM – 9mm Para. cal., direct blowback, 16 in. Christensen Arms 416R stainless steel carbon fiber wrapped barrel, button rifled, threaded muzzle, 3 prong stainless steel flash hider, black Nitride finish on barrel and BCG, TriggerTech trigger, MFT Battlelink Minimalist stock, forged aluminum receiver, 2 QD mounts, 14 3/4 in. carbon aluminum hybrid handguard with full rail, carbon fiber panels, M-LOK, hardcoat anodized black or Cerakote finish in Tungsten or Burnt Bronze, 6.6 lbs. Mfg. 2020 only.

MSR	100%	98%	95%	90%	80%	70%	60%	LAST MSR
	$1,350	$1,200	$1,100	$975	$825	$700	$600	*$1,495*

CA-10 DMR – .243 Win. (mfg. 2016-2020), .260 Rem. (mfg. 2016-2020), 6.5 Creedmoor (new 2016), or .308 Win. cal., GIO, 18, 20, 22, or 24 in. match grade carbon fiber wrapped 416R stainless steel barrel, threaded with titanium side baffle brake, Christensen LTM (disc.) or TriggerTech trigger, Magpul adj. STR buttstock, Hogue overmolded grip, carbon fiber handguard with integrated carbon Picatinny rails in KeyMod or M-LOK, ambidextrous mag. release, extended charging handle, oversized bolt release, Type III hardcoat anodized black or Cerakote finish in Burnt Bronze or Tungsten, 7.1 lbs. New 2014.

MSR	100%	98%	95%	90%	80%	70%	60%	LAST MSR
MSR $3,245	$2,924	$2,625	$2,375	$2,125	$1,825	$1,550	$1,300	

CA-10 G2 – 6.5 Creedmoor or .308 Win. cal., DI, 18 or 20 in. 1:8/1:10 twist 416R stainless steel or carbon fiber wrapped barrel, threaded muzzle, stainless steel or titanium flash hider, flared magwell, integrated undercut trigger guard, match grade trigger, BCM Gunfighter stock, 15 in. KeyMod or M-LOK handguard, Christensen Arms G2 Edition aluminum lower receiver, hardcoat anodized black finish, 7.2-7.7 lbs. New 2016.

MSR	100%	98%	95%	90%	80%	70%	60%	LAST MSR
MSR $2,595	$2,325	$2,100	$1,900	$1,700	$1,450	$1,225	$1,050	

Add $400 for carbon fiber wrapped barrel.

CA-10 RECON – .243 Win., 6.8 Creedmoor, .308 Win., or .338 Federal cal., GIO, 16-24 in. carbon fiber match grade barrel, various stock configurations, flat-top receiver with Picatinny rail, adj. Timney trigger, carbon fiber handguard, 20 shot mag., black carbon fiber or camo forearm finish, 6-8 lbs. Mfg. 2011-2013.

MSR	100%	98%	95%	90%	80%	70%	60%	LAST MSR
	$3,025	$2,650	$2,275	$2,050	$1,675	$1,375	$1,100	*$3,575*

Subtract $200 for steel barrel.

GRADING - PPGS™	100%	98%	95%	90%	80%	70%	60%	LAST MSR

CARBON ONE CA-15 SERIES (AR-15) – .223 Rem. cal., GIO, forged aluminum upper and lower receiver, choice of round shroud with quad rails or integrated forearm with full Picatinny rail on top, adj. stock, carbon fiber wrapped stainless steel barrel, ambidextrous charging handle, Timney adj. drop-in trigger, 30 shot detachable AR-15 style mag., 5.5-7 lbs. Mfg. 2009-2010.

	$2,500	$2,190	$1,875	$1,700	$1,375	$1,125	$875	*$2,950*

CA-15 C2 – .204 Ruger, .223 Wylde chamber, or .300 AAC Blackout cal., GIO, fixed gas block, 16-24 in. threaded barrel with stainless steel flash suppressor, match grade trigger, Magpul adj. CTR stock, Magpul MOE grip, carbine, rifle, or mid-length gas tube, CA carbon fiber Slim-Line profile KeyMod or M-LOK 15 in. handguard, billet upper and lower receivers, Type III hardcoat anodized black finish, 5.65 lbs. Mfg. 2016 only.

	$1,800	$1,625	$1,450	$1,300	$1,125	$950	$800	*$1,999*

CA-15 G2 – .223 Wylde chamber, DI, 16 in. stainless steel or carbon fiber wrapped barrel, threaded muzzle, stainless steel or titanium flash hider, flared magwell, match grade trigger, BCM Gunfighter stock, Christensen Arms G2 Edition upper and lower aluminum receivers, 14 3/4 in. slim-line carbon fiber KeyMod or M-LOK handguard, hard anodized black or Cerakote finish in Tungsten or Burnt Bronze, 5.8-5.9 lbs. New 2016.

MSR $1,749	$1,575	$1,425	$1,275	$1,150	$975	$825	$700	

Add $546 for carbon fiber wrapped barrel and titanium flash hider.

CA-15 3G – .223 Wylde chamber, GIO, 16 or 18 in. stainless steel carbon fiber wrapped barrel, titanium side baffle brake, flared magwell, Hiperfire trigger, integrated undercut trigger guard, BCM Gunfighter stock, Christensen Arms G2 Edition upper and lower receivers, 14 3/4 in. slim-line carbon fiber M-LOK handguard, hard anodized black finish, 5.9 lbs. Mfg. 2016-2017.

	$2,750	$2,475	$2,225	$2,000	$1,700	$1,450	$1,225	*$3,045*

CA-15 PREDATOR – .223 Rem., .204 Ruger, 6.8 SPC, or 6.5 Grendel cal., GIO, 20 or 24 in. carbon fiber match grade barrel, collapsible stock, flat-top receiver with Picatinny rail, ambidextrous controls, adj. Timney trigger, 20 shot mag., Hogue pistol grip, black, King's Desert Shadow, or King's Snow Shadow finish, 5.5-7 lbs. Mfg. 2011-2012.

	$2,550	$2,250	$1,900	$1,750	$1,400	$1,150	$900	*$2,995*

CA-15 RECON – .204 Ruger, .223 Wylde chamber, 6.5 Grendel, 6.8 SPC, or .300 AAC Blackout cal., GPO, 16 or 20 in. match grade carbon fiber barrel, titanium birdcage flash suppressor, 30 shot mag., carbon fiber handguard with built-in Picatinny rails, adj. stock, adj. Timney trigger, Hogue pistol grip, factory black synthetic, Digital Desert Brown, King's Desert Shadow, or King's Snow Shadow finish, 5.5-7 lbs. Mfg. 2011-2015.

	$3,050	$2,750	$2,475	$2,225	$1,900	$1,625	$1,350	*$3,395*

CA-15 VTAC – .223 Wylde chamber or .300 AAC Blackout (disc. 2016) cal., GIO, 16 in. straight fluted stainless steel black Nitride finished barrel or carbon fiber wrapped barrel, titanium (became standard 2017) flash hider, flared magwell, VTAC self-contained trigger, BCM Gunfighter stock, Magpul MOE pistol grip, 15 in. free float KeyMod or M-LOK handguard with integral rails, machined billet upper and lower receivers, Picatinny rail, Type III hardcoat anodized black finish, 5 1/2 lbs. Mfg. mid-2015-2017.

	$2,550	$2,300	$2,075	$1,875	$1,600	$1,350	$1,150	*$2,845*

Subtract approx. $150 if with Nitride finished barrel and standard flash hider.

* ***CA-15 VTAC 3G*** – .243 Win., .260 Rem., 6.5 Creedmoor, or .308 Win. cal., 16 in. threaded stainless steel or carbon fiber wrapped barrel with titanium flash suppressor, BCM Gunfighter buttstock, Magpul MOE grip, low mass bolt carrier, adj. gas block, billet receivers with top Picatinny rail, mid-length gas tube, 15 in. KeyMod or M-LOK handguard, Type III hardcoat anodized black finish, 5 1/2 lbs. Mfg. 2016 only.

	$2,375	$1,525	$1,150	$700	$625	$550	$475	*$2,999*

Add $200 for carbon fiber wrapped barrel.

CD-15 RECON – .223 Wylde or 5.56 NATO cal., GIO, 16-24 in. match grade carbon fiber wrapped barrel, OSS suppressor, Christensen LTM trigger, aluminum receiver, carbon fiber handguard with integrated carbon Picatinny rails, nickel boron coated bolt carrier, ambidextrous magazine release, oversized bolt release, extended charging handle, Hogue overmolded grip, Type III hardcoat anodized black or Cerakote receiver colors, numerous finish options available, 7.3 lbs. Mfg. 2014-2015.

	$3,925	$2,800	$1,750	$1,150	$875	$775	$700	*$4,890*

CHRISTIAN ARMORY WORKS

Current custom AR-15 style rifle manufacturer located in Rock Spring, GA.

GRADING - PPGS™	100%	98%	95%	90%	80%	70%	60%	LAST MSR

CHRISTOPH FUNK GEWEHRFABRIK SUL

Previous gunmaker located in Suhl, Germany from 1835-1965.

Christoph Funk manufactured a variety fine shotguns, rifles, and drillings. These firearms were mainly produced for the European market, and are seldom seen imported into the United States. For more information, please visit the website currently operated by Peter Ravn Lund.

CHURCHILL

Previous trademark imported and distributed by Ellett Brothers located in Chapin, SC until 1993. Previously imported (until 1988) by Kassnar Imports, Inc. located in Harrisburg, PA. Not affiliated with E.J. Churchill Gunmakers, Ltd.

For individual model listings, please go to BlueBookOfGunValues.com/overflow.

E.J. CHURCHILL GUNMAKERS

Current manufacturer established in 1891, and located in High Wycombe, England since 1996. Previously imported until 2001 by Aspen Outfitters, located in Aspen, CO. Previously manufactured in London, England. This company underwent various trading forms until Churchill, Atkin, Grant & Lang Ltd. closed in 1981. Currently, Churchill Gunmakers' rifles and shotguns are manufactured in High Wycombe, England.

For individual model listings, please go to BlueBookOfGunValues.com/overflow.

CIMARRON F.A. CO.

Current importer, distributor, and retailer located in Fredricksburg, TX. Cimarron is currently importing A. Uberti, D. Pedersoli, Chiappa Firearms, Pietta, and Armi-Sport firearms and black powder reproductions and replicas. Previous company name was Old-West Co. of Texas. Dealer sales only.

Please refer to the *Blue Book of Modern Black Powder Arms* (also available online) for more information and prices on Cimarron's lineup of modern black powder models.

DERRINGERS: O/U

DIABLO – .22 LR/.22 WMR, or .32 H&R Mag./.38 Spl. cal. 2 barrel set, 2.4 (.22 LR/.22 WMR cal.) or 2 3/4 (centerfire) in. VR barrels, chrome or black finish, tip-up action, spur trigger, walnut Cimarron grips with horse and rider logo, mfg. by Cobra Enterprises of Utah. Mfg. 2010-2014.

	100%	98%	95%	90%	80%	70%	60%	LAST MSR
	$185	$160	$150	$130	$115	$100	$90	*$227*

Add $13 for .32 H&R Mag. or .38 Spl.

TITAN – 9mm Para. or .45 LC/.410 shotshell cal., 3 1/2 in. VR rifled barrels with fixed front sight, 2 shot, SA, polished, brushed, or black stainless steel frame, rebounding hammer, rosewood grips with Cimarron logo, removable trigger guard, 16.4 oz. Mfg. 2011-2014.

	100%	98%	95%	90%	80%	70%	60%	LAST MSR
	$375	$335	$295	$250	$200	$160	$145	*$425*

Add $42 for snug case (9mm only, disc. 2011).

The Titan was made exclusively for Cimarron by Cobra Firearms. For parts and repairs, please contact either Cimarron or Cobra Firearms.

PISTOLS: SEMI-AUTO

M4-22 – .22 LR cal., AR-15 style, blowback action, 6 in. barrel with muzzle brake, quad rail, includes A2 carry handle, black finish, 5, 10, or 28 shot Atchison style conversion mag., cased with cleaning kit, 3.9 lbs. Mfg. by Armi Chiappa in Italy. Imported 2011-2012.

	100%	98%	95%	90%	80%	70%	60%	LAST MSR
	$450	$375	$325	$275	$250	$225	$195	*$587*

MODEL 1911 (MODEL 1911A1) – .45 ACP cal., 5 in. barrel, 8 shot, diamond checkered walnut grips, blue (disc. 2013), parkerized (new 2014), polished, or nickel finish, 2.47 lbs. Mfg. by Armi Chiappa in Italy. Importation began 2011.

	100%	98%	95%	90%	80%	70%	60%	LAST MSR
MSR $571	$485	$425	$360	$330	$260	$225	$190	

Add $229 for polished or nickel finish

MODEL 1911 22 TACTICAL – .22 LR cal., 5 in. barrel, 10 shot mag., fixed sights, diamond checkered walnut grips with CF logo, mfg. by Armi Chiappa in Italy. Imported 2011-2012.

	100%	98%	95%	90%	80%	70%	60%	LAST MSR
	$290	$260	$230	$200	$185	$170	$160	*$335*

GRADING - PPGS™	100%	98%	95%	90%	80%	70%	60%	LAST MSR

WILD BUNCH 1911 WWI G.I. COMBO – .45 ACP cal., original 1911 frame, 5 in. barrel, 8 shot mag., replica of WWI model, Type 1 smooth mainspring housing, correct historical markings, polished/high luster blue finish, diamond checkered walnut grips, includes tanker shoulder holster, 2.47 lbs. New mid-2013.

MSR $956	$815	$715	$610	$550	$450	$365	$320	

REVOLVERS: REPRODUCTIONS, COLT

The Cimarron reproductions of the 1873 Colt Peacemaker, mostly mfg. by Uberti, with the exception of previous limited production by Armi San Marco, are available in two configurations listed below. Beginning in 1984, Cimarron arms reproductions began incorporating many of the features of the 1st Generation Colt SAAs. These SAA revolvers are extremely accurate reproductions of the original Colt pre-war Peacemaker and are marked (and machined) the same as the originals, including serial numbers on frames, backstrap, trigger guard, and cylinder. Barrels are radiused and cylinders are beveled. Frames are color case hardened, stocks are walnut - choice of 4 3/4, 5 1/2, or 7 1/2 in. barrel. All Cimarron SAAs are currently barrel marked "- CIMARRON F.A. MFG. Co. FREDERICKSBURG, TX. U.S.A. -". The "Old Model" configuration has the older style black powder frame, screw-in cylinder pin retainer, and circular "bullseye" ejector head. The Standard Model includes the post-1890 style frame with spring loaded cross-pin cylinder retainer and "half-moon" ejector head. Only the Old Model is available in the authentic old style "charcoal blue" finish (sometimes referred to as fire-bluing).

During 1998, Cimarron introduced an Original Finish (antiqued) that resembles the older, worn finish seen on many of the well-used, original Colt revolvers. This distressed finish is a greyish-brown patina color, and certain areas of these guns (end of barrel, grip straps, frame/cylinder edges, and grips) have been artifically aged to give them an authentic "been carried and used for 100 years" appearance.

Add $70 for Antique Original Finish (aged and antique looking) on SAAs listed below.
Add approx. $70 for charcoal blue finish.
Add $260 for antique custom nickel or custom nickel finish.
Add $358 for silver plating.
Add $250 for U.S. Armory finish utilizing bonemeal case coloring.
Add $488 for old style color case hardening and Carbona blue finish (disc. 2003).
Add $45 for hand checkered walnut grips (disc. 2003).
Add $64 for various styles of grips. Add $140 for oversize grips (new 2011).
Add $305 ($455 fitted) for Sumbar custom stag grips.
Add $225 Izit ivory grips (disc. 2006).
Add $325 for Izit ivory steer head grips (mfg. 2004-2006).
Add $325 for Micarta grips.
Add $845 for geniune ivory grips. Add $326 for mother-of-pearl grips (disc. 2006).
Add $195 for Tru Ivory (stark white, slightly aged, antique or ultra antique ivory) grips (new 2007).
Add $850 for "A" style engraving (30% coverage) on SAAs listed below (disc 2004).
Add $1,069 for "B" style engraving (50% coverage) on SAAs listed below.
Add $1,800 for "C" style engraving (70% coverage), on SAAs listed below (disc. 2004).
Add $2,400 for "Texas Cattle Brands" or full (100% coverage) engraving pattern (disc. 2004).
Add $789 for Patton engraving.
Add $842 for Teddy Roosevelt laser engraving or $1,707 for Teddy Roosevelt hand engraving (disc. 2013).
Add $1,557 for Open Top Standard laser engraving (disc.).
Add $2,600 for Judge Roy Bean engraving (disc.).
Add $2,470 for Wild Bill conversion engraving (disc.).

1872 OPEN TOP ARMY – .45 LC, .44 Colt/Russian, .44 Spl. (new 2011), or .38 Colt/Spl. cal., Open Top Army style, patterned after the Colt 1871-1872 Open Top, 7 1/2 in. barrel, one-piece walnut Army grips, case hardened frame, standard blue or nickel (new 2019) finish, 2 1/2 lbs. Mfg. by A. Uberti beginning 1999.

MSR $591	$500	$440	$380	$345	$280	$225	$200	

Add $128 for nickel finish in .45 LC cal. only (new 2019).
Add $1,557 for standard engraving (disc. 2016).
Add $2,334 for standard engraving and nickel finish (disc. 2010).

GRADING - PPGS™	100%	98%	95%	90%	80%	70%	60%	LAST MSR

1872 OPEN TOP NAVY – .38 Long Colt (disc.), .38 S&W Spl. (disc.), .38 Colt/Spl., .44-40 WCF (disc.), .44 Colt/S&W Spl./Russian (new 2011), .44 Colt/Russian (disc. 2016), .45 Colt (new 2006), or .45 Schofield cal., 4 3/4 (new 2004), 5 1/2, or 7 1/2 in. barrel, patterned after the Colt 1871-1872 Open Top, brass or silver plated (disc. 2010), 1.91 lbs. Mfg. by A. Uberti beginning 1999.

MSR $560	$475	$415	$350	$325	$260	$215	$185	

Add $40 for silver plated backstrap and trigger guard (disc. 2010).
Add $1,557 for standard engraving (disc. 2016).
Add $2,334 for standard engraving and nickel finish (disc. 2010).

BAD BOY – .44 Mag., 10mm (new 2020), or 10mm/.38-40 (new 2021) cal., Pre-War frame, 6 or 8 in. octagon barrel, flat-top with target sights, brown wood Army grips, with or w/o Picatinny rail, standard blue finish. New 2017.

MSR $743	$625	$545	$475	$425	$345	$275	$225	

Add $35 for Picatinny rail.
Add $88 for 10mm/.38-40 cal. combo.

BADLANDS SAA MODEL – .357 Mag. or .45 LC cal., 4 3/4 in. barrel, brass backstrap and trigger guard, flat black frame and barrel finish, steel frame, smooth wood grips, case colored hammer. Mfg. 2005-2007.

	$275	$240	$205	$185	$150	$125	$95	*$325*

BISLEY SAA – .357 Mag./.38 Spl., .44 Spl., .44-40 WCF, or .45 LC cal., 4 3/4, 5 1/2, or 7 1/2 in. barrel, Pre-War configuration, Bisley configured grips, case colored receiver, standard blue finish, smooth walnut grips, flat-top target model available with 7 1/2 in. barrel in .44-40 WCF or .45 LC cal. only (disc. 2010), mfg. by Uberti. Importation began 2002.

MSR $687	$580	$510	$440	$400	$320	$260	$230	

BLACK EL DIABLO – .45 LC cal., Frontier style, 4 3/4 in. barrel, black frame and finish, one-piece walnut grips. Mfg. 2012-2016.

	$685	$600	$515	$465	$375	$325	$250	*$801*

BUCKHORN – .44 Spl. or .44 Mag. cal., reinforced variation of the Cimarron SAA designed for more powerful cartridges, 4 3/4, 6, or 7 1/2 in. barrel, brass or steel backstrap, mfg. by Uberti. Disc. 1993.

	$355	$310	$265	$240	$195	$160	$125	*$400*

* ***Buckhorn Buntline*** – .44-40 WCF, .44 Spl., or .44 Mag. cal., 18 in. barrel, fixed or target sights. Disc. 1989.

	$370	$325	$275	$250	$205	$165	$130	*$419*

Add $30 for target sights.

* ***Buckhorn Carbine*** – .44-40 WCF, .44 Spl., or .44 Mag. cal., 18 in. barrel, includes non-detachable shoulder stock with brass hardware and lanyard ring. Disc. 1990.

	$375	$330	$280	$255	$205	$170	$130	*$429*

Add $30 for target sights.

* ***Buckhorn Convertible Model*** – .44 Mag. and .44-40 WCF cylinders, 4 3/4, 6, or 7 1/2 in. barrel. Disc. 1989.

	$375	$330	$280	$255	$200	$170	$130	*$427*

Add $12 for target sights.

* ***Buckhorn Target Model*** – .44 Spl. or .44 Mag. cal., 4 3/4, 6, or 7 1/2 in. barrel, adj. rear sight. Importation disc. 1991.

	$370	$325	$275	$250	$200	$165	$130	*$420*

BUNTLINE MODEL – .357 Mag., .44-40 WCF, or .45 LC cal., 18 in. barrel, brass or steel gripstraps cut for shoulder stock. Disc. 1989.

	$355	$310	$265	$240	$195	$160	$125	*$400*

Add $10 for target sights.

EVIL ROY SAA – .357 Mag./.38 Spl., .44-40 WCF (disc. 2020), or .45 LC cal., 4 3/4 or 5 1/2 in. barrel, features wide square notch rear sight and constant width front sight, smooth or checkered slim grips, lightened trigger and hammer springs, color case hardened finish on frame, blue or stainless steel, Evil Roy signature on bottom of grip strap, 2.33 lbs. Mfg. by Uberti. New 2005.

MSR $841	$715	$625	$535	$485	$400	$320	$280	

Add $197 for stainless steel (new 2010).

This model is also available in Old Model or low wide hammer, both with standard blue finish at no additional charge.

GRADING - PPGS™	100%	98%	95%	90%	80%	70%	60%	LAST MSR

"HAND OF GOD" HOLY SMOKER – .45 LC cal., 4 3/4 in. barrel, case hardened pre-war frame, standard blue finish, one-piece walnut grip with gold cross inlay on both sides, 2 1/4 lbs. Mfg. by Uberti. Disc. 2014.

	$650	$575	$495	$425	$375	$325	$295	*$761*

JUDGE ROY BEAN COMMEMORATIVE – mfg. to commemorate Judge Roy Bean's Texas cattlebrand. Disc. 1996.

	$1,500	$1,310	$1,125	$1,020	$825	$675	$525	*$1,695*

LIGHTNING – .22 LR (new 2007), .38 Colt (disc.), .38 S&W Spl., .41 LC (new 2007), or .32 WCF/.32 H&R (dual cylinder) cal., patterned after the original Colt Lightning, 3 1/2, 4 3/4, 5 1/2, or 6 1/2 (new 2012) in. barrel, 10 shot mag. (3 1/2 in. barrel, .22 LR cal. only, new 2020), one-piece smooth walnut, bird's head, or checkered grips, standard blue finish. Mfg. by A. Uberti 1999-2001, reintroduced in 2003.

MSR $557	$475	$415	$350	$325	$260	$215	$185	

Add $25 for 10 shot (new 2020).
Add $39 for .38 Spl. cal.
Add $68 for .41 LC cal.
Add $147 for dual cylinder (.32-20 WCF/.32 H&R Mag. cal., new 2004).

MAN WITH NO NAME SAA – .45 LC cal., 4 3/4 or 5 1/2 in. barrel, case hardened pre-war frame, one-piece walnut grip with silver rattlesnake inlay on both sides, standard blue finish, approx. 2 3/4 lbs. Mfg. by Uberti. Disc. 2014.

	$660	$580	$495	$450	$360	$295	$260	*$774*

MODEL P SAA – .32-20 WCF, .38-40 WCF, .357 Mag./.38 Spl. (dual cylinder), .44-40 WCF, .44 Spl., or .45 LC cal., 4 3/4, 5 1/2, or 7 1/2 in. barrel, features pinched frame (.45 LC cal. with 7 1/2 in. barrel only, disc. 2006), Old Model (OM) or Pre-War (PW) configuration, blue (standard), charcoal blue, or original finish, importation began 1996.

MSR $597	$510	$450	$385	$350	$275	$225	$200	

Add $3 for .44 Spl. or .44-40 WCF cal.
Add $6-$28 for Pre-War configuration depending on caliber.
Add $50 for target model with adj. sights and flat-top frame (.45 LC cal. with 7 1/2 in. barrel or .44-40 WCF cal., disc. 2006).
Add $60 for hard rubber grips (disc. 2010).
Add $91 for charcoal blue finish.
Add $130 for original finish.
Add $133 for convertible .45 ACP cylinder.
Add $1,169 for Deluxe Buffalo Bill engraving - charcoal blue, case hardened Old Model frame with William F. Cody signature on backstrap (mfg. 2019-2020).

* ***Model P Jr. SAA*** – .22 LR (new 2007), .38 Spl., .32 WFC/.32 H&R (new 2004), .38 Colt/S&W Spl. (disc.), or .41 LC (mfg. 2007-2010) cal., features 20% smaller frame size than full size SAA, but with standard single action grip frame, 3 1/2, 4 3/4, or 5 1/2 in. barrel, blue finish, smooth walnut or checkered (disc. 2012) grips, brass (.22 LR cal. only) or steel backstrap, 1.79 lbs. Mfg. by A. Uberti 2000-2001, reintroduced 2004-2016, 2019.

MSR $518	$440	$385	$330	$300	$240	$200	$175	

Add $45 for checkered walnut grips (disc. 2012).
Add $48 for 10 shot in .22 LR cal. with 3 1/2 in. barrel (new 2019).
Add $166 for dual cylinder (.32-20 WCF/.32 H&R Mag. cal., new 2004).
Subtract $41 for .41 LC cal. (disc. 2010).

* ***Model P Jr. Black Stallion*** – .22 LR/.22 WMR cal., dual cylinder, 4 3/4 in. barrel, black steel finish, brass backstrap and trigger guard, wood grips with gold medallions. New 2010.

MSR $588	$500	$440	$375	$340	$275	$225	$195	

* ***Model P Stainless*** – .357 Mag./.38 Spl. or .45 LC cal., 4 3/4, 5 1/2, or 7 1/2 in. barrel, pre-war frame, smooth walnut grips. New 2004.

MSR $803	$680	$600	$500	$450	$375	$300	$265	

NEW SHERIFF – .357 Mag./.38 Spl., .44-40 WCF, or .45 LC cal., 3 1/2 in. barrel, case hardened frame, blue finish only, smooth walnut grips. Mfg. by Uberti. New 2011.

MSR $597	$510	$450	$385	$350	$275	$225	$200	

Add $20 for .44 WCF cal.

GRADING - PPGS™	100%	98%	95%	90%	80%	70%	60%	LAST MSR

PISTOLERO – .357 Mag./.38 Spl., .22 LR (new 2018), or .45 LC cal., similar to the Model P, except has brass gripstraps and trigger guard, 4 3/4, 5 1/2 (disc. 2010), or 7 1/2 (disc.) in. barrel, case hardened frame with blue barrel and cylinder, nickel, or Millenium (disc.) finish, one-piece smooth walnut grips. Mfg. by Uberti 1997 only, reintroduced 2007-2013. Reintroduced again in 2017, mfg. by Pietta.

MSR $454	$385	$335	$230	$260	$210	$175	$135	

Add $65 for Pre War.
Add $90-$147 for nickel finish, depending on caliber (Pietta mfg. only, new 2017).

PLINKERTON – .22 LR cal., 4 3/4 in. barrel, matte black metal finish, checkered black plastic or wood (mfg. 2011-2012) grips, 34 oz. Mfg. by Chiappa 2007-2015, reintroduced in 2020.

MSR $193	$165	$145	$125	$110	$90	$75	$65	

Add $37 for dual cylinders (.22 LR and .22 WMR, disc.).
Add $22 for wood grips (mfg. 2011-2012).

ROOSTER SHOOTER – .357 Mag. (disc. 2015), .44-40 WCF (disc. 2015), or .45 LC cal., 4 3/4 in. barrel, replica of John Wayne's gun from many of his westerns, including *True Grit*, antique original finish, one-piece orange finger grooved grips. Mfg. by Uberti. Importation began 2010.

MSR $958	$815	$715	$610	$555	$450	$365	$320	

THUNDERER – .357 Mag./.38 Spl., .45 LC/.45 ACP (dual cylinder), .44 Spl., .44-40 WCF or .45 LC cal., patterned after Colt's Thunderer Model, 3 1/2, 4 3/4, or 5 1/2 (new 2000) in. barrel with full ejector rod housing, smooth or checkered walnut grips, choice of case colored (disc.), nickel (disc.), original (disc.), charcoal blue (disc.), standard blue, or stainless steel (disc.) finish, mfg. by Uberti. Importation began 1994.

MSR $621	$525	$460	$395	$355	$290	$240	$200	

Add $14 for .44 Spl. or .44 WCF cal.
Add $60 for hard rubber grips (disc. 2010).
Add $116 for 3 1/2 or 4 3/4 in. convertible .45 ACP cylinder.

* ***Thunderer Stainless*** – .357/.38 Spl. or .45 LC cal., Pre-War frame, 3 1/2 or 4 3/4 in. barrel, stainless steel. Mfg. by Uberti.

MSR $811	$690	$600	$525	$475	$380	$310	$270	

* ***Thunderer Long Tom*** – .357 Mag., .44-40 WCF or .45 LC cal., 7 1/2 in. barrel, mfg. by Uberti. Mfg. 1997-2009.

	$445	$390	$335	$300	$245	$200	$155	*$534*

Add $45 for checkered walnut grips.

THUNDERER DOC HOLLIDAY – .357 Mag./.38 Spl. (disc. 2016), or .45 LC cal., 3 1/2 in. barrel, custom nickel finish, Tru (disc.) or poly Ivory grips, with Huckleberry shoulder rig and numbered dagger, mfg. by Uberti. New late 2008.

MSR $1,606	$1,365	$1,200	$1,025	$930	$750	$615	$535	

* ***Thunderer Doc Holliday Stainless*** – .45 LC cal., 3 1/2 in. barrel, poly ivory grips, engraved, with or w/out Huckleberry shoulder rig with dagger, stainless steel. New 2019.

MSR $1,094	$930	$815	$700	$630	$510	$420	$365	

Add $224 for Huckleberry shoulder rig with dagger.

THUNDERSTORM – .357 Mag./.38 Spl. or .45 LC cal., 3 1/2, 4 3/4, or 5 1/2 in. barrel, pre-war configuration, standard blue finish or stainless steel. Disc. 2015.

	$630	$525	$465	$410	$350	$300	$250	*$748*

Add $226 for stainless steel.

THUNDERSTORM COMPETITION – .45 LC cal., 3 1/2 or 4 3/4 in. barrel, checkered Model P or Thunderer grips, stainless steel or blue finish, wide front sights, deep rear notch sights, knurled hammer, designed for competition shooting. New 2011.

MSR $870	$740	$650	$550	$500	$400	$340	$290	

Add $156 for stainless steel.

* ***Thunderstorm Competition Short Stroke*** – .45 LC or .357 Mag. cal., short stroke, 3 1/2 or 4 3/4 in. standard or octagon (disc. 2019) barrel, low wide groovy hammer, checkered Model P or Thunderer grips, stainless steel or blue finish. New 2019.

MSR $870	$740	$650	$550	$500	$400	$340	$290	

Add $13 for octagon barrel (disc. 2019).
Add $156 for stainless steel.

U.S. ARTILLERY MODEL – .45 LC cal., 5 1/2 in. barrel, Rinaldo A. Carr 1895 U.S. Artillery Model Commemorative. Limited mfg.

	$495	$425	$365	$335	$295	$250	$210	*$499*

GRADING - PPGS™	100%	98%	95%	90%	80%	70%	60%	LAST MSR

U.S.V. ARTILLERY (ROUGH RIDER) – .45 LC cal. only, 5 1/2 in. barrel, case colored Old Model frame, smooth walnut grips, standard blue, charcoal blue, or antique original finish. Mfg. by Uberti or Pietta. New 1996.

MSR $647	$550	$480	$415	$375	$305	$250	$215	

Add $20 for Uberti mfg.
Add $117 for charcoal blue, Uberti mfg. only.
Add $165 for original finish, Uberti mfg. only.

U.S. CAVALRY MODEL P (A.P. CASEY) – .45 LC cal. only, 7 1/2 in. barrel, Old Model frame. Mfg. 1996-97.

	$495	$425	$365	$335	$295	$250	$210	*$499*

7TH CAVALRY CASED SET – .45 LC cal., revolver, U.S. Cavalry Model, in case with accessories. Disc. 1990.

	$600	$495	$425	$365	$335	$295	$250	*$780*

U.S. 7TH CAVALRY CUSTER MODEL – .45 LC cal., authentic reproduction of original Colt military cavalry contract SAA, 7 1/2 in. barrel, marked "U.S." on lower left frame, one-piece walnut grips with military cartouche, standard blue, charcoal blue, or original finish. Mfg. by Uberti or Pietta.

MSR $647	$550	$480	$415	$375	$305	$250	$215	

Add $20 for Uberti mfg.
Add $117 for charcoal blue.
Add $165 for original finish.

* ***U.S. 7th Cavalry Custer Scout Model*** – .45 LC cal., authentic reproduction of original Colt military cavalry contract SAA, 7 1/2 in. barrel, marked "U.S." on lower left frame, one-piece walnut grips with military cartouche, nickel plated finish, 2.56 lbs. Mfg. by Uberti.

MSR $799	$680	$600	$500	$450	$375	$300	$265	

WILD BILL ELLIOT TEXAS CATTLEBRAND – .45 LC cal. Mfg. 1994-96.

	$1,225	$1,070	$920	$835	$675	$550	$430	*$1,395*

WYATT EARP LIMITED EDITION BUNTLINE – .45 LC cal. only, Old Model case hardened frame, 10 in. barrel, one-piece walnut grip with inlaid sterling silver medallion, shield, case colored receiver, standard blue finish, 2.69 lbs. Mfg. by Uberti or Pietta (new 2021). Importation began 2002.

MSR $918	$780	$685	$585	$530	$430	$350	$300	

Add $35 for Uberti model.

ELIMINATOR 8 – .45 LC, .357/.38 Spl. cal., Cowboy Comp U.S. action job, 4 3/4 in. octagon barrel, 25% shorter hammer stroke, modified Army grip, standard blue finish. Mfg. by Pietta 2016-2018.

	$650	$575	$490	$440	$350	$300	$250	*$761*

ELIMINATORC (COMPETITION) – .45 LC, .357/.38 Spl. cal., Cowboy Comp U.S. action job, 4 3/4 in. barrel, standard hammer or low wide hammer, standard blue finish or stainless steel. Mfg. by Pietta 2016-2017.

	$600	$525	$450	$400	$340	$295	$235	*$715*

Add $26 for low wide hammer.
Add $196 for stainless steel.

ELIMINATOR CM – .45 LC cal., 3 1/2 or 4 3/4 in. barrel, CM Groovy hammer, standard or Thunderer grips, stainless steel or standard blue finish. Mfg. 2017-2018.

	$650	$575	$490	$440	$360	$300	$250	*$753*

Add $209 for stainless steel.

ELIMINATOR TS (THUNDERSTORM) – .45 LC cal., 3 1/2 or 4 3/4 in. barrel, stainless steel, standard hammer, standard or Thunder grip. Mfg. by Pietta. Imported 2016 only.

	$825	$720	$600	$550	$450	$375	$295	*$974*

PISTOLEER – .45 LC or .375 Mag. cal., color case hardened frame, 4.75 in. barrel, steel or nickel backstrap and trigger guard, walnut grips w/Cimarron Firearms embedded coin, fully auto safety hammer, blued finish. New 2021.

MSR $519	$440	$380	$330	$300	$240	$200	$175	

REVOLVERS: REPRODUCTIONS, COLT, FRONTIER MODELS

The following current models are all manufactured by F. LLI Pietta.

BIG IRON – .357 Mag. or .45 LC cal., brass gripstraps and trigger guard, 4 3/4 in. barrel, case hardened frame with blue barrel and cylinder or Millenium (matte black) finish, one-piece smooth walnut grips, approx. 2 1/2 lbs. Mfg. by Pietta 2011-2015.

	$425	$350	$300	$275	$245	$225	$195	*$480*

GRADING - PPGS™	100%	98%	95%	90%	80%	70%	60%	LAST MSR

EL MALO – .357/.38 Spl. (new 2017) or .45 LC cal., color case hardened pre-war frame, 4 3/4, 5 1/2 (new 2017), or 7 1/2 in. octagon barrel with standard blue finish, smooth walnut grips, 2.5 lbs. New late 2016.

MSR $607	$515	$450	$385	$350	$285	$230	$200	

EL MALO 2 – .45 LC or .357/.38 Spl. cal., pre-war frame, 3 1/2, 4 3/4, 5 1/2, or 7 1/2 in. octagon barrel, low wide hammer, Army or Thunderer (3 1/2 in. barrel only) grips, blue finish. New 2019.

MSR $649	$550	$480	$415	$375	$310	$260	$215	

FRONTIER SIX SHOOTER (DISC.) – .22 LR (disc. 1995), .22 WMR (disc.), .357 Mag., .38 Spl. (disc.), .38-40 WCF, .44 Spl. (new 1998), .44-40 WCF, or .45 LC cal., 4 3/4, 5 1/2, or 7 1/2 in. barrel lengths, steel backstraps and trigger guard.

* ***Frontier Six-Shooter (USA Finish)*** – .32 WCF, .357 Mag., .38 WCF, .44 Spl., .44 WCF, or .45 LC cal., this variation is disassembled and then refinished in the U.S. in the same type of finish as the original Colt SAA from the late 19th century. Mfg. 2008-2010.

	$725	$650	$575	$485	$440	$355	$300	*$860*

* ***Frontier Six-Shooter Standard or Old Model***

	$395	$345	$295	$270	$235	$215	$190	*$469*

Add $30 for convertible .45 ACP cylinder.

* ***Frontier Six-Shooter Sheriff's Model*** – .44-40 WCF or .45 LC cal., w/o ejector, 3 or 4 (disc. 1992) in. barrel, steel backstraps and trigger guard. Disc. 1998, reintroduced 2000-2001.

	$395	$345	$295	$270	$235	$215	$190	*$469*

* ***Frontier Six-Shooter New Sheriff Model*** – .357 Mag., .44-40 WCF, .44 Spl., or .45 LC cal., 3 1/2 in. barrel with ejector, Old Model frame only. Imported 1995-2010.

	$450	$385	$335	$295	$260	$230	$210	*$548*

Add $40 for charcoal blue finish (disc.).
Add $45 for checkered walnut grips.

* ***Frontier Six-Shooter Target Model*** – similar to Standard Model, except has fully adj. target rear sight, brass or steel backstrap. Importation disc. 1991.

	$395	$345	$295	$270	$235	$215	$190	*$400*

Add $40 for .357 Mag. cal.

This variation was available in the Standard Model configuration only and with standard finish.

FRONTIER (CURRENT MFG.) – .357 Mag./.38 Spl., .44-40 WCF (new 2012), or .45 LC cal., 3 1/2 (PW only), 4 3/4, 5 1/2, or 7 1/2 in. barrel, pinched frame, Old Model or pre-war configuration, standard blue or charcoal blue (disc. 2012) finish. Mfg. by Pietta. New 2011.

MSR $580	$495	$435	$375	$335	$275	$225	$195	

Add $293 for Armory old-style bone meal color case hardening (disc. 2019).

* ***Frontier Bird's Head*** – .45 LC cal., 3 1/2 or 4 3/4 in. barrel, features pre-war configuration, standard blue finish. Mfg. by Pietta, limited importation 2011 only.

	$465	$400	$350	$300	$270	$240	$220	*$535*

* ***Frontier Buntline*** – .45 LC cal., 10 in. barrel, Old Model configuration, standard blue finish. Mfg. by Pietta beginning 2014.

MSR $647	$550	$480	$415	$375	$310	$260	$215	

* ***Frontier Cody Wild West*** – .45 LC cal., 5 1/2 in. barrel, nickel plated, checkered walnut grip, deluxe "Cody Wild West" tribute engraving with "Buffalo Bill" signature on backstrap. New 2019.

MSR $842	$715	$625	$535	$485	$340	$320	$280	

* ***Frontier Stainless*** – .357 Mag./.38 Spl., or .45 LC cal., pre-war configuration, stainless steel, 3 1/2, 4 3/4, 5 1/2, or 7 1/2 (new 2011) in. barrel, standard walnut grips. Mfg. by Pietta. New 2011.

MSR $794	$675	$590	$500	$460	$375	$300	$265	

* ***Frontier Sheriff*** – .45 LC cal., pre-war configuration, standard blue finish, 3 1/2 in. barrel. Mfg. by Pietta. Limited importation 2011 only.

	$475	$410	$360	$310	$280	$250	$225	*$546*

FRONTIER SHORT STROKE MODEL – .357/.38 Spl. or .45 LC cal., 4 3/4 or 5 1/2 in. barrel, pre-war configuration, checkered walnut grips, standard blue or stainless finish. Mfg. by Pietta 2014-2016.

	$500	$425	$350	$315	$275	$240	$220	*$597*

Add $196 for stainless steel.

GRADING - PPGS™	100%	98%	95%	90%	80%	70%	60%	LAST MSR

* ***Frontier Short Stroke Model With U.S. Action Job*** – .357/.38 Spl. or .45 LC cal., 4 3/4 or 5 1/2 in. barrel, pre-war configuration, includes U.S. action job, checkered walnut grips, standard blue or stainless finish. Mfg. by Pietta 2014-2016.

	$615	$550	$475	$425	$350	$300	$250	*$714*

Add $195 for stainless steel.

GEORGE S. PATTON FRONTIER – .45 LC cal., pre-war frame, 4 3/4 or 5 1/2 (disc. 2018) in. barrel, laser engraved, nickel finish.

MSR $845	$720	$630	$540	$490	$395	$325	$280

HOLY SMOKER – .45 LC cal., 4 3/4 in. barrel, case hardened pre-war frame, standard blue finish, gold-plated sterling silver Jesus on the cross inlay on one or both sides of one-piece walnut grips, accurate replica of Russell Crowe's gun from *3:10 to Yuma*, 2 1/4 lbs. Mfg. by Pietta, new 2010.

MSR $785	$670	$585	$500	$450	$370	$300	$260

Add $168 for sterling silver cross inlay on both sides of the grips (disc. 2012).

MAN WITH NO NAME SAA – .45 LC cal., 4 3/4 or 5 1/2 in. barrel, case hardened pre-war frame, standard blue finish, walnut grips with sterling silver rattlesnake inlay on one or both sides, accurate replica of Clint Eastwood's spaghetti western gun. Mfg. by Pietta. New 2010.

MSR $799	$680	$600	$500	$450	$375	$300	$265

Add $168 for sterling silver rattlesnake inlay on both sides (disc. 2012).

NEW SHERIFF – .45 LC cal., 3 1/2 in. barrel, pre-war configuration, standard blue finish. Mfg. by Pietta, disc. 2012.

	$465	$400	$350	$300	$270	$240	$220	*$546*

ROOSTER SHOOTER – .45 LC cal., SA, 4 3/4 in. barrel, pre-war configuration, one-piece orange finger grooved grip, antique original finish, 2 1/2 lbs. Mfg. by Pietta. Disc. 2014.

	$725	$650	$575	$485	$440	$355	$300	*$883*

TEDDY ROOSEVELT FRONTIER – .45 LC cal., 7 1/2 in. barrel, pre-war frame, laser engraved, nickel finish.

MSR $903	$765	$670	$575	$520	$420	$350	$300

TEXAS RANGER FRONTIER – .45 LC cal., 4 3/4 in. barrel, pre-war frame, poly ivory grip, "Texas Ranger" engraving, nickel plated. New 2017.

MSR $897	$765	$670	$575	$520	$420	$350	$300

THUNDERBALL – .357 Mag./.38 Spl. or .45 LC cal., patterned after Colt's Thunderer Model, 3 1/2 or 4 3/4 in. barrel with full ejector rod housing, bird's head grips, blue or stainless steel finish. Mfg. by Pietta. New 2011.

MSR $581	$495	$435	$375	$335	$275	$225	$195

Add $233 for stainless steel.

TOMBSTONE (WYATT EARP) FRONTIER BUNTLINE – .45 LC cal. only, Old Model case hardened frame, 10 in. barrel, one-piece walnut grip with inlaid sterling silver medallion, case colored receiver, standard blue finish, 2.69 lbs. Mfg. by Pietta. Importation began 2002.

MSR $918	$780	$685	$585	$530	$430	$350	$300

Add $35 for Tombstone mfg. by Uberti.
Subtract $265 if without inlay (disc.).

REVOLVERS: REPRODUCTIONS, COLT CONVERSIONS

All guns are manufactured (current and previous) by Uberti.

Add approx. $60 for charcoal blue (disc. 2011) or $74 for Original finish (2011).

1851 NAVY RICHARDS-MASON – .38 Spl. cal., 4 3/4, 5 1/2, or 7 1/2 in. barrel, patterned after the original Richards-Mason 1851 Navy Conversion, available in standard blue, charcoal blue (disc. 2011), original (disc. 2011), or nickel (new 2019) finish. Mfg. by Uberti. Importation began 2003.

MSR $600	$510	$450	$385	$350	$275	$225	$200

Add $47 for nickel finish (new 2019).
Add $25 for silver plated gripstraps and trigger guard (disc. 2006).

1851 MAN WITH NO NAME CONVERSION – .38 Colt/S&W Spl. cal., 7 1/2 in. barrel, blue finish, patterned after the original 1851 model used in the 1960s spaghetti westerns, one-piece walnut grip. New 2007.

MSR $631	$535	$475	$400	$365	$300	$250	$210

Add $252 for right side sterling silver rattlesnake grip inlay.
Add $448 for sterling silver rattlesnake grip inlay on both sides (disc. 2012).

GRADING - PPGS™	100%	98%	95%	90%	80%	70%	60%	LAST MSR

1860 ARMY RICHARDS-MASON – .38 Spl. (new 2007), .44 WCF and Russian, .45 LC (new 2007), or .45 Schofield (disc.) cal., 4 3/4 (disc. 2010), 5 1/2 or 8 in. barrel, patterned after the original Richards-Mason 1860 Conversion, available in standard blue, charcoal blue (disc. 2011), or original (disc. 2011) finish. Mfg. by Uberti. Importation began 2003.

MSR $631	$535	$475	$400	$365	$300	$250	$210	

1862 POCKET CONVERSION – .380 ACP cal., 3 1/2 or 6 (new 2019) in. barrel, blue or nickel (new 2020) finish. New 2018.

MSR $602	$510	$450	$385	$350	$275	$225	$200	

Add $61 for nickel finish (new 2020).

1868 THUER CONVERSION OF 1860 ARMY – .44-40 WCF cal., Thuer conversion ring and cylinder, cartridge loading tool, all other specifications same as 1860 Army, prototype only.

This model required a special hand-loaded round in .44 cal for the Thuer Conversion. While it was advertised with an MSR $418, this model was only available as a prototype before being shelved by Uberti in 2002.

TYPE II RICHARDS TRANSITION MODEL – .38 Spl., .44 Colt, .44 Spl., or .45 LC cal., 5 1/2 or 8 in. barrel, blue or nickel (new 2019) finish, case hardened frame, one-piece walnut grips. New 2007.

MSR $680	$580	$510	$435	$395	$320	$260	$225	

Add $117 for nickel finish (new 2019).

REVOLVERS: REPRODUCTIONS, SMITH & WESSON

These guns are S&W reproductions, and are manufactured by Uberti.

MODEL NO. 3 AMERICAN – .45 LC, .44-40 WFC (new 2021), .44 Russian/Colt/S&W Spl. (new 2021) cal., early 1st Model frame and grip, 5 or 8 in. barrel, 6 shot cylinder, period, two-piece walnut grips, case colored top latch, trigger, and hammer, blued or nickel finish, civilian or military model, military revolvers martially marked with U.S. markings, inspector stamp and a grip cartouche. New 2019.

MSR $1,199	$1,020	$895	$765	$695	$560	$460	$400	

Add $27 for .45 LC cal.

MODEL NO. 3 RUSSIAN – .44 Russian or .45 LC cal., 6 1/2 in. barrel, blue finish, two-piece walnut grips, blue frame, mfg. by Uberti. New 2007.

MSR $1,220	$1,040	$910	$780	$700	$575	$475	$400	

SCHOFIELD MODEL NO. 3 – .38 Spl. (disc. 1997), .38-40 WCF (disc. 1997), .44 Russian/Spl., .44-40 WCF, .45 Schofield, .45 ACP (disc.), or .45 LC cal., available in 7 (Civilian or Military) or 5 (Wells Fargo only) in. barrel. Mfg. by Armi San Marco 1996-99.

	$730	$640	$545	$495	$400	$330	$255	*$849*

Add $100 for nickel finish.
Add $150 for custom nickel finish.

This model was also available as a "Little Big Horn" variation with sub-inspector markings and "SBL" cartouche.

SCHOFIELD MODEL NO. 3 (CURRENT MFG.) – .38 Spl., .44-40 WCF, or .45 Schofield/LC cal., 3 1/2, 5, or 7 in. barrel, blue or nickel (new 2021) finish. Mfg. by Uberti beginning 2007.

MSR $1,214	$1,030	$900	$775	$700	$565	$465	$400	

Add $117 for nickel finish.

REVOLVERS/PISTOLS: REPRODUCTIONS, REMINGTON

These guns are reproductions of the Models 1858, 1871, 1875, and 1890, and are manufactured by Uberti.

1858 ARMY NEW MODEL CONVERSION – .38 Spl., .44-40 WCF, or .45 LC cal., 5 1/2, 7 3/8, or 8 in. barrel, forged steel frame, blue or nickel (new 2019) finish, walnut grips, brass trigger guard. New 2007.

MSR $612	$520	$455	$390	$355	$285	$235	$200	

Add $6 for .44 WCF or .45 LC.
Add $117 for nickel finish (new 2019).
Add $72 for dual cylinder (.45 LC/.44 cal. Percussion, disc. 2010).

1871 ROLLING BLOCK TARGET PISTOL – .22 LR, .22 Hornet (new 1990), .22 WMR, or .357 Mag. cal., 9 1/2 in. barrel. Importation disc. 1990.

	$350	$275	$225	$200	$185	$170	$160	*$280*

Add 10% for centerfire or .22 WMR cals.

GRADING - PPGS™	100%	98%	95%	90%	80%	70%	60%	LAST MSR

MODEL 1875 OUTLAW – .357 Mag./.38 Spl., .44-40 WCF, or .45 LC cal., 5 1/2 (new 2010) or 7 1/2 in. barrel, case colored frame, standard blue, charcoal blue (disc. 2012), nickel (new 2019), or original (disc. 2012) finish, plain wood grips. Disc. 1993, reintroduced 2010.

MSR $624	$530	$465	$400	$360	$290	$240	$210	

Last MSR in 1993 was $390.

Add $110 for dual cylinder (.45 LC/.45 ACP cal., 7 1/2 in. only).
Add $117 for nickel finish (new 2019).

MODEL 1890 – .357 Mag./.38 Spl., .44-40 WCF, or .45 LC cal., 5 1/2 or 7 1/2 (disc.) in. barrel, case colored frame, standard blue finish, plain wood grips, lanyard loop. Disc. 1993, reintroduced 2010.

MSR $639	$540	$475	$400	$365	$300	$250	$210	

Last MSR in 1993 was $390.

Add $104 for dual cylinder (.45 LC/.45 ACP cal.).

RIFLES: CUSTOM SHOP OPTIONS

The following wood upgrades and special options apply to all rifles imported by Cimarron.

Add $200 for AA select wood (disc.), $552 for AAA premium select wood, or $1,040 for super premium (fine European walnut, disc. 2013). Add $150 for fine hand oil finish (disc.) or $201 for super fine stock finish. Add $80 for antique finish. Add $293 for Armory Old Style Bone Meal color case hardening, or $488 for Armory Old Style color case hardening.

RIFLES: REPRODUCTIONS, BURGESS

1883 BURGESS CARBINE/RIFLE – .44-40 WCF (new 2011) or .45 LC cal., 20 or 25 1/2 in. barrel, 10 (20 in. barrel) or 15 (25 1/2 in. barrel) shot mag., sliding dust cover over loading port, side plate, lever action design. Mfg. by Uberti, imported 2010-2016.

	$1,300	$1,125	$975	$850	$675	$550	$430	*$1,528*

Add $31 for rifle configuration.

RIFLES: REPRODUCTIONS, COLT

LIGHTNING MAGAZINE RIFLE – .357 Mag., .44-40 WCF, or .45 LC cal., 20, 24, or 26 in. round (not available with 24 or 26 in. barrel) or octagon barrel, walnut stock, blue or case colored frame, patterned after Colt Lightning rifle. Mfg. by Pedersoli. Imported 2006-2012.

	$1,375	$1,175	$975	$875	$700	$600	$500	*$1,581*

Add $98 for octagon barrel.
Add $243 for case colored frame.

RIFLES/CARBINES: REPRODUCTIONS, REMINGTON ROLLING BLOCK

MODEL 1871 ROLLING BLOCK BABY CARBINE – .22 LR, .22 Hornet (new 1990), .22 WMR, or .357 Mag. cal., 22 in. barrel and walnut stock and forearm, brass trigger guard and buttplate. Importation disc. 1990.

	$495	$450	$375	$325	$275	$250	$225	*$340*

Add 10% for centerfire and .22 WMR cals.

MODEL 1875 CARBINE – .45-70 Govt. cal., 18 in. barrel, includes non-detachable shoulder stock with brass hardware and lanyard ring. Importation disc. 1990.

	$495	$450	$375	$325	$275	$250	$225	*$460*

ROLLING BLOCK SPORTING RIFLE – .45-70 Govt. cal., 30 in. barrel, walnut stock and forearm. Imported 1989-90 only.

	$825	$725	$625	$550	$475	$400	$350	*$620*

* ***Deluxe Rolling Block Sporting Rifle*** – similar to standard model, except has select wood. Importation disc. 1990.

	$925	$825	$700	$600	$525	$450	$375	*$720*

REMINGTON ROLLING BLOCK LONG RANGE CREEDMOOR – .45-70 Govt. cal., 30 in. tapered octagon barrel, deluxe checkered walnut stock. Importation began 1997.

	$1,375	$1,175	$975	$850	$725	$625	$525	*$1,295*

"ADOBE WALLS" ROLLING BLOCK – .45-70 Govt. cal., 30 in. octagon barrel, hand checkered walnut stock, case hardened receiver, German silver nose cap, optional Creedmoor sight, blue finish, 10.35 lbs. Mfg. by Pedersoli, importation began 2004.

MSR $1,774	$1,510	$1,325	$1,130	$1,025	$830	$680	$590	

GRADING - PPGS™	100%	98%	95%	90%	80%	70%	60%	LAST MSR

RIFLES/CARBINES: REVOLVING

BUNTLINE CARBINE – .22 LR/.22 WMR (convertible cylinders, disc.), .357 Mag., .44-40 WCF, or .45 LC cal., 18 in. barrel, includes non-detachable shoulder stock with brass hardware and finger extension trigger guard. Mfg. by Uberti, importation disc. 1991, reintroduced 2006-2011.

	$695	$575	$495	$450	$395	$350	$285	*$811*

Add 5% for target sights or .22 LR/.22 WMR combo (disc.).

REVOLVING CARBINE – .357 Mag./.38 Spl., .44-40 WCF, or .45 LC cal., single action, color case hardened pre-war frame, 18 in. barrel, uncheckered straight walnut stock with brass buttplate, standard blue finish.

MSR $869	$740	$650	$550	$500	$400	$340	$290	

THUNDERSTORM CARBINE – .45 LC cal., 6 shot, 18 in. barrel, color case hardened frame, standard blue finish, one-piece walnut brass buttplate, 3.9 lbs. Mfg. by Uberti 2012-2014.

	$825	$675	$575	$495	$425	$375	$325	*$984*

RIFLES: REPRODUCTIONS, SHARPS

ARMI-SPORT BILLY DIXON MODEL 1874 SPORTING RIFLE – .38-55 WCF (disc. 2013), .45-70 Govt., .45-90 Win. (disc. 2013), .45-110 (mfg. 2003-2013), or .50-90 (mfg. 2003-2013) cal., 32 in. barrel, nickel silver front blade and forearm cap, checkered deluxe walnut stock, double set triggers. Mfg. by Armi-Sport, importation began 1997.

MSR $1,640	$1,395	$1,220	$1,045	$950	$765	$630	$545	

ARMI-SPORT RIFLE FROM DOWN UNDER (QUIGLEY) II MODEL 1874 SPORTING RIFLE – .38-55 WCF (mfg. 2011-2012), .45-70 Govt., .45-90 Win. (disc. 2012), .45-110 (mfg. 2004-2012), .45-120 Sharps (disc. 2012), or .50-90 (mfg. 2002-2012) cal., 34 in. octagon barrel with storage compartment in stock. Mfg. by Armi-Sport, importation began 2000.

MSR $1,833	$1,555	$1,360	$1,165	$1,055	$855	$700	$610	

Add $28 for cals. other than .45-70 Govt. (disc. 2012).

ARMI-SPORT SHARPS 1874 SPORTING RIFLE – .45-70 Govt. cal., 32 in. barrel, A or AAA Grade wood stock and forend. New 2019.

MSR $1,488	$1,265	$1,100	$950	$860	$700	$575	$500	

Add $136 for AAA Grade wood stock and forend.

ARMI-SPORT SHARPS "PRIDE OF THE PLAINS" II MODEL 1874 – .45-70 Govt. cal., similar to original "Pride of the Plains", except comes with or w/o telescopic sight, silver forearm cap. Mfg. by Armi-Sport mid-2008-2009.

	$1,250	$1,075	$925	$825	$695	$575	$450	*$1,429*

Add $450 for extended tube telescopic sight.

LITTLE RASCAL MINI-SHARPS – .22 LR, .22 Hornet (new 2012), .30-30 Win. (new 2012), .38-55 WCF, or .45 LC cal., 3/4 scale Sharps rifle with original patent markings, 26 in. octagon barrel with blade front and aperture rear sight on upper tang, polished steel (white finish) or standard blue color case hardened frame. Mfg. by ArmiSport. Imported 2011-2015.

	$1,150	$950	$800	$700	$600	$500	$450	*$1,325*

Subtract $91 for white finish.

MCNELLY CARBINE – .45-70 cal., single shot, 22 in. round barrel, case colored receiver, American black walnut stock, blued steel barrel and parts. Mfg. 2017-2018.

	$1,340	$1,175	$1,000	$885	$710	$585	$475	*$1,572*

PEDERSOLI BILLY DIXON MODEL 1874 SPORTING RIFLE – .45-70 Govt., .45-90 Win. (disc.2020), or .50-70 (mfg. 2004-2006, reintroduced 2010 only) cal., 32 in. barrel, nickel silver front sight blade and forearm cap, checkered deluxe walnut stock, double set triggers. Mfg. by Pedersoli, importation began 1997.

MSR $2,262	$1,925	$1,685	$1,450	$1,310	$1,060	$875	$755	

Add $40 for .45-90 Win. cal.

PEDERSOLI BILLY DIXON OFFICER'S RIFLE – .45-70 Govt. cal., 26 in. barrel. Mfg. 2015-2017.

	$2,050	$1,795	$1,540	$1,395	$1,125	$925	$800	*$2,404*

PEDERSOLI BILLY DIXON TRAPDOOR CARBINE – .45-70 Govt. cal., 26 in. barrel. New 2019.

MSR $2,824	$2,400	$2,100	$1,800	$1,630	$1,320	$1,080	$940	

GRADING - PPGS™	100%	98%	95%	90%	80%	70%	60%	LAST MSR

PEDERSOLI RIFLE FROM DOWN UNDER II (QUIGLEY) MODEL 1874 SPORTING RIFLE - .45-70 Govt., .45-90 Win. (disc.), .45-110 (disc. 2012), .45-120 Sharps, .50-70 (mfg. 2004-2006), or .50-90 (mfg. 2002-disc.) cal., 34 in. octagon barrel with storage compartment in stock. Mfg. by Pedersoli, importation began 2000.

MSR $2,387	$2,030	$1,775	$1,525	$1,380	$1,110	$920	$795	

Add $47 for .45-90 Win. cal. (disc.)
Add $187 for .45-120 Sharps cal.
Add $314 for .50-70 (disc.) or .50-90 (mfg. 2012-disc.) cal.

PEDERSOLI SHARPS BUSINESS RIFLE - .45-70 Govt., 32 in. octagon barrel w/case color hardening, double-set triggers, blade front sight and buckhorn rear sight, straight walnut stock/post-1875 Schnabel-tipped forearm and shotgun style buttplate, 11.89 lbs. New 2017.

MSR $1,574	$1,340	$1,175	$1,000	$910	$735	$600	$525	

PEDERSOLI SHARPS "PRIDE OF THE PLAINS" MODEL 1874 - .45-70 Govt. cal., 32 in. matte black octagon barrel, hand checkered walnut stock, nickel receiver, Creedmoor rear sight. Mfg. by Pedersoli, importation began 2004.

MSR $2,249	$1,910	$1,675	$1,435	$1,300	$1,050	$860	$750	

SHARPS BIG 50 LONG RANGE MODEL 1874 SPORTING RIFLE - .50-90 cal., 34 in. barrel, double set triggers, aperture rear sight, checkered stock and forearm. Mfg. by Pedersoli, imported 2004-2020.

	$2,585	$2,250	$1,950	$1,750	$1,425	$1,175	$1,000	*$3,038*

SHARPS MCNELLY CARBINE MODEL 1874 (TEXAS RANGER) - .45-70 Govt. or .50-70 (disc. 2012) cal., 22 in. round blue barrel, American black walnut stock, case colored receiver, marked with Lone Star between TS initials on barrel. Mfg. by Armi Sport, importation began 2004.

MSR $1,585	$1,350	$1,180	$1,015	$925	$745	$610	$530	

Add $42 for .50-70 cal. (disc. 2012).

SHARPS PROFESSIONAL HUNTER MODEL 1874 - .45-70 Govt. cal., 32 in. barrel. Mfg. by Pedersoli, imported 2005-2014.

	$1,350	$1,150	$975	$875	$725	$575	$445	*$1,525*

SHARPS ROCKY MOUNTAIN II MODEL 74 - .45-70 Govt. cal., 30 in. octagon barrel, silver receiver, checkered walnut stock, available with optional 6X Malcolm rifle scope, mfg. by Armi Sport. Imported 2010-2014.

	$1,495	$1,275	$1,000	$875	$775	$675	$575	*$1,689*

Add $619 for Malcolm scope.

SLOTTER & CO. SHARPS RIFLE - .45-70 Govt. cal., 34 in. barrel, choice of maple or walnut (disc.) stock. Mfg. by Pedersoli, importation began 2011.

MSR $2,512	$2,135	$1,875	$1,600	$1,450	$1,175	$960	$840	

SPORTING #1 RIFLE - .40-65 Win. or .45-70 Govt. cal., 32 in. octagon barrel, pistol grip stock. Mfg. by Pedersoli, imported 2000-2002.

	$1,100	$975	$850	$725	$625	$525	$425	*$1,095*

SPORTING #1 SILHOUETTE RIFLE - .45-70 Govt. (disc. 2012) or .50-70 cal., 32 in. octagon barrel with silhouette sights, pistol grip stock. Mfg. by Pedersoli. Imported 2003-2018.

	$1,495	$1,310	$1,125	$1,015	$825	$675	$585	*$1,766*

U.S.A. SHOOTING TEAM CREEDMOOR SHARPS - .45-70 Govt. cal., color case hardened frame, blue finish, 34 in. round barrel, walnut stock, mfg. by Armi-Sport. Disc. 2014.

	$1,375	$1,175	$1,000	$900	$725	$575	$445	*$1,559*

Add $246 for carrying case.

Cimarron donated a portion of the sales from this rifle to the U.S.A. shooting team.

RIFLES: REPRODUCTIONS, SPENCER

1860 SPENCER RIFLE - .56-50 cal., 30 in. barrel, uncheckered walnut stock and forearm, three barrel bands, case colored receiver, trigger guard, and hammer. Mfg. by Armi-Sport mid-2008-2012.

	$1,550	$1,325	$1,100	$975	$775	$625	$550	*$1,791*

1865 SPENCER REPEATING RIFLE - .44-40 WCF (disc. 2012) .45 Schofield (disc. 2012), .45 LC, or .56-50 (disc. 2016) cal., 20 or 30 (.56-50 cal. only, disc. 2009) in. barrel, blue finish, case colored receiver and frame, straight grip walnut stock, includes slings. Mfg. by Armi-Sport, importation began 2005.

MSR $1,968	$1,675	$1,465	$1,255	$1,140	$920	$755	$655	

Add $182 for 30 in. barrel (disc. 2009).

GRADING - PPGS™	100%	98%	95%	90%	80%	70%	60%	LAST MSR

RIFLES: REPRODUCTIONS, SPRINGFIELD

SPRINGFIELD TRAPDOOR CAVALRY CARBINE – .45-70 Govt. cal., single shot, case hardened steel frame, 22 in. barrel, ladder rear sight, uncheckered straight grip walnut stock with one barrel band, standard blue finish. Importation began late 2013.

MSR $1,687	$1,435	$1,250	$1,075	$975	$790	$645	$560

RIFLES: REPRODUCTIONS, WINCHESTER

The rifles listed below are manufactured by A. Uberti, unless otherwise indicated.

1860 CIVILIAN HENRY RIFLE/CARBINE – .44-40 WCF, .44 Spl. (mfg. 1993-95), or .45 LC (new 1993) cal., 24 in. barrel (rifle), 22 in. barrel (carbine, disc. 1995, .44-40 WCF cal. only), brass or case colored steel (.44-40 WCF and .45 LC cal., new 2002) frame, standard blue, charcoal blue, or original finish. Mfg. by Uberti.

MSR $1,576	$1,340	$1,175	$1,000	$910	$735	$600	$525

Add $50 for in-the-white finish (disc.).
Add $130 for charcoal blue finish.
Add $195 for original finish.
Add $3,014 for Lincoln Presentation hand engraving (disc. 2009, reintroduced 2011-2019).
Prior to 1997, this model could also be special ordered with Grade A engraving ($450 extra), Grade B engraving ($550 extra), and Grade C engraving ($725 extra).

1860 CIVIL WAR HENRY RIFLE – .44-40 WCF or .45 LC (new 1998) cal., 24 in. barrel, patterned after the U.S. issue original inspected by Chas. G. Chapman (C.G.C.) with military inspector's marks and cartouche, military sling swivels became standard in 1996, choice of standard blue, charcoal blue, or original finish. Importation began 1993.

MSR $1,734	$1,475	$1,290	$1,100	$1,000	$810	$660	$580

Add $65 for in-the-white finish (disc.).
Add $130 for charcoal blue.
Add $195 for original finish.
Add $2,509 for standard hand engraving (disc. 2009).
Add $3,055 for standard hand engraving and deluxe wood (disc. 2009).
Add $4,225 for Lincoln hand engraving (disc. 2009).
Add $4,810 for Lincoln hand engraving and deluxe wood (disc. 2009).

1860 STEEL FRAMED HENRY RIFLE – .44-40 WCF or .45 LC cal., 24 in. barrel, 12 shot, Henry steel frame, walnut stock and forearm, 9 lbs.

MSR $1,662	$1,410	$1,235	$1,060	$960	$775	$650	$550

1866 YELLOWBOY SHORT RIFLE – .32-20 WCF, .38-40 WCF, .38 Spl., .44 Spl., .44-40 WCF, or .45 LC cal., lever action, 20 in. short octagon barrel, brass receiver and endplate, standard blue finish. New 2000.

MSR $1,339	$1,140	$1,000	$855	$775	$625	$515	$445

Add $26 for .32-20 WCF, or .38-40 WCF cal.

1866 YELLOWBOY SPORTING RIFLE – .22 LR (disc. 1993, reintroduced 2012), .22 WMR (disc. 1993), .32-20 WCF (new 2002), .38 Spl. (new 1995), .38-40 WCF (new 2002), .44 Spl. (new 2006), .44-40 WCF, or .45 LC (new 1993) cal., brass receiver, 24 in. octagon barrel, standard blue, charcoal blue, or original finish.

MSR $1,339	$1,140	$1,000	$855	$775	$625	$515	$445

Add $26 for .32-20 WCF or .38-40 WCF cal.
Add $130 for charcoal blue (.45 LC cal. only) or $195 for original finish (.45 LC cal. only).
Add $100 for charcoal blue or $150 for original finish in .44-40 WCF cal. (disc. 2018).
Add $1,116 for standard engraving (new 1997-disc.).
Add $3,379 for Mexican Eagle engraving (new 1997-disc.) or $2,535 for Red Cloud engraving (mfg. 2005-2008).
Add $500 (retail) for A engraving, $650 for B engraving, $1,175 for C engraving (disc.).

1866 YELLOWBOY CARBINE – .22 LR (new 2013), .32-20 WCF, .38 Spl., .38-40 WCF, .38-55 WCF (disc. 2011), .44 Spl., .44-40 WCF, or .45 LC cal., similar to Model 1866 Yellowboy Sporting Rifle, except has 19 in. round barrel with 2 bands, with or w/o (.22LR only) saddle ring, uncheckered walnut stock and forearm. Mfg. by Uberti.

MSR $1,321	$1,125	$985	$850	$765	$625	$500	$440

Add $61 for .38 Spl., .44 Spl., .44-40 WCF, or .45 LC cal.
Add $81 for .32-20 WCF, or .38-40 WCF cal.
Add $100 for charcoal blue or $150 for original finish (.44-40 WCF cal. only, disc. 2020).
Add $191 for charcoal blue or $256 for original finish (.45 LC cal. only).

GRADING - PPGS™	100%	98%	95%	90%	80%	70%	60%	LAST MSR

Add $2,067 for standard engraving (disc. 2009).
Add $2,567 for standard engraving and deluxe wood (disc. 2009).
Add $2,957 for deluxe engraving and deluxe wood (disc. 2009).
Add $4,875 for Mexican Eagle engraving with deluxe wood and silver accents (disc. 2009).
Add $4,095 for Red Cloud engraving, studded wood and blue finish (disc. 2009).

* ***1866 Trapper Carbine*** – .38 Spl. (new 2002), .44-40 WCF, or .45 LC (new 2005) cal., 16 in. round barrel, standard blue finish. Importation disc. 1990, reintroduced 2002.

MSR $1,301	$1,100	$965	$825	$750	$600	$500	$435	

Add $35 for saddle ring (disc.).

* ***1866 Pawnee (Yellowboy Indian) Carbine*** – .22 LR (disc.), .22 WMR (disc.), .38 Spl. (disc.), .44-40 WCF (disc.), or .45 LC (new 2012) cal., 19 in. round barrel, photo engraved (disc. 1989), plain brass, or nickel (new 2019-2020) frame includes tacks in forearm and rear of stock. Disc. 1989, reintroduced 2012.

MSR $1,473	$1,250	$1,095	$940	$850	$685	$575	$490	

Last MSR in 1989 was $649.

Add $266 for nickel finish (new 2019-2020).

* ***1886 Red Cloud Commemorative Carbine*** – same cals. as Yellowboy Indian Carbine, includes special engraving representing Oglalla Indian tribe symbols, brass tacks in forearm and stock. Disc. 1989.

	$950	$825	$725	$625	$500	$425	$350	*$649*

1873 EVIL ROY SADDLE RING RIFLE – .357 Mag., .44-40 WCF (new 2012), or .45 LC cal., 20 in. barrel, features Evil Roy shooting improvements, standard finish. Imported 2005-2007, reintroduced 2012 only.

	$1,750	$1,500	$1,300	$1,125	$1,020	$825	$675	*$2,027*

1873 LARRY CROW SIGNATURE SERIES RIFLE – .357 Mag. or .45 LC cal., 20 in. barrel, features Larry Crow shooting improvements and signature. Imported 2005-2007.

	$1,850	$1,575	$1,350	$1,150	$1,025	$825	$675	*$2,275*

1873 LONG RANGE SPORTING RIFLE – .44-40 WCF or .45 LC cal., 30 in. octagon barrel with full mag., case hardened receiver, iron sights, with or w/o pistol grip, standard blue finish. New 1990.

MSR $1,468	$1,250	$1,095	$940	$850	$685	$575	$490	

Add $105 for Deluxe Model with checkered pistol grip.

1873 SADDLE RIFLE – .44-40 WCF, .357/.38 Spl., or .45 LC cal., lever action, 18 in. octagon barrel. New 2017.

MSR $1,480	$1,260	$1,100	$950	$850	$700	$560	$490	

1873 SADDLE RING CARBINE – .22 LR (disc. 1993), .22 WMR (disc. 1993), .32-20 WCF (new 2002), .357 Mag./.38 Spl., .38-40 WCF (new 2002), .44 Mag. (mfg. 2012-2018), .44 Spl. (mfg. 2002-2014), .44-40 WCF, or .45 LC cal., blue steel receiver, saddle ring, 19 in. round barrel, standard blue, charcoal blue (disc. 2017), or original (disc. 2017) finish.

MSR $1,437	$1,220	$1,075	$910	$830	$675	$550	$425	

Add $21 for .32-20 WCF, .38-40 WCF, or .44 Spl. (disc. 2014) cal.
Add $65 for .44 Mag. (mfg. 2012-2018).
Add $100 for charcoal blue (disc. 2017) or $150 for original finish (.44-40 WCF or .45 LC cal., disc. 2017).
Add $90 for nickel plating (disc.).

* ***1873 Saddle Ring Shorty*** – .357 Mag./.38 Spl., .44-40 WCF, or .45 LC cal., 18 in. barrel with iron sights, standard action or with short stroke kit. Disc. 2014.

	$1,150	$995	$850	$750	$625	$525	$425	*$1,351*

Add $80 for short stroke kit.

1873 SHORT RIFLE – .32-20 WCF (new 2002), .357 Mag./.38 Spl. (new 2000), .38-40 WCF (new 2002), .44 Spl. (pistol grip only, new 2002), .44-40 WCF, or .45 LC cal., 20 in. octagon barrel, case hardened receiver, iron sights, standard blue finish. Importation began 1990.

MSR $1,408	$1,195	$1,050	$900	$815	$660	$540	$470	

Add $32 for .44 Spl. cal.
Add $22 for .32-20 WCF or .38-40 WCF cal. (1873 Short Rifle)
Add $32 for .32-20 WCF or .38-40 WCF cal. (Deluxe pistol grip)
Add $103 for Deluxe Border Model with checkered pistol grip.

GRADING - PPGS™	100%	98%	95%	90%	80%	70%	60%	LAST MSR

1873 SPORTING RIFLE – .22 LR (disc. 1993), .22 WMR (disc. 1993), .32-20 WCF (new 2002), .357 Mag./.38 Spl., .38-40 WCF (new 2002), .44 Spl. (new 2002), .44-40 WCF, or .45 LC cal., 24 in. octagon barrel, case hardened receiver, full mag., iron sights, standard blue, charcoal (disc. 2017), or original finish. Mfg. by Uberti.

MSR $1,408	$1,195	$1,050	$900	$815	$660	$540	$470	

Add $22 for .32-20 WCF, .38-40 WCF, or .44 Spl. cal.
Add $103 or $135 (.44-40 WCF) for Deluxe Sporting Model with checkered pistol grip.
Add $100 for charcoal blue (.44-40 WCF or .45 LC cal. only) disc. 2017.
Add $195 (.45 LC) or $228 (.44-40 WCF) for original finish.
Add $425 for old style color case hardening (disc.).
Add $500 (retail) for A engraving, $650 for B engraving, $1,075 for C engraving (disc. 2002).
Add $1,207 for standard engraving or $3,103 for 1 of 1,000 engraving.

1873 TEXAS BRUSH POPPER – .357 Mag./.38 Spl., .44-40 WCF, or .45 LC cal., 18 in. half-round, half-octagon barrel w/o barrel bands, case colored receiver, choice of straight (disc. 2017) or checkered pistol grip stock.

MSR $1,539	$1,310	$1,150	$985	$890	$725	$590	$510	

Subtract $98 for straight stock (disc. 2017).

* ***1873 "Evil Roy" Texas Brush Popper*** – .357 Mag./.38 Spl., .44-40 WCF, or .45 LC cal., features 18 in. half-round, half-octagon barrel w/o barrel bands, choice of straight or checkered pistol grip stock, custom Marble sights, leather butt tamer, short stroke kit, tuned action, designed for competition cowboy action shooting. Imported 2010-2013.

	$1,700	$1,450	$1,250	$1,050	$950	$800	$650	*$1,875*

Add $84 for Deluxe Model with pistol grip.

1873 TRAPPER CARBINE – .357 Mag./.38 Spl. (new 1990, reintroduced 2004), .44-40 WCF (disc. 1990, reintroduced 2005), or .45 LC (mfg. 1990, reintroduced 2005) cal., 16 in. barrel, blue finish. Mfg. by Uberti, importation disc. 1990, reintroduced 2004.

MSR $1,382	$1,175	$1,025	$875	$800	$650	$550	$460	

Add $55 for color case hardened frame.

1873 U.S. MARSHALL CARBINE – .44 Mag. cal., 18 in. barrel, saddle ring. Mfg. 2018-2020.

	$1,250	$1,095	$945	$850	$695	$565	$475	*$1,471*

1873 U.S. MARSHALL INDIAN TERRITORY CARBINE – .357 Mag., .44 Spl.+P, or .45 LC cal., 18 1/2 in. barrel, with saddle ring. New 2019.

MSR $1,513	$1,285	$1,125	$965	$875	$700	$580	$500	

1876 CENTENNIAL SPORTING RIFLE – .40-60 WCF (disc. 2014, reintroduced 2021), .45-60 WFC, .45-75 WCF (disc. 2020), or .50-95 WCF cal., 22 (short rifle, disc. 2013) or 28 in. octagon barrel, blue finish and case hardened frame, full mag., iron sights, walnut stock and forearm. Mfg. by Uberti, importation began 2006.

MSR $1,795	$1,525	$1,335	$1,145	$1,035	$840	$695	$600	

Add $42 for .50-95 WCF or .45-75 WCF (disc. 2020) cal.
Add $104 for short rifle (disc. 2013).
Add $3,315 for standard engraving (disc. 2009).
Add $3,900 for standard engraving and deluxe wood (disc. 2009).

1876 CARBINE N.W.M.P. ROYAL CANADIAN MOUNTED POLICE MODEL – .45-60 WCF or .45-75 cal., 22 in. round barrel with full length forend and barrel band, blued frame, saddle ring. Mfg. by Uberti, importation began 2010.

MSR $1,964	$1,670	$1,460	$1,255	$1,135	$920	$750	$655	

1876 CROSSFIRE CARBINE – .45-75 or .45-60 cal., 22 in. round barrel with full length forend and barrel band, color case hardened frame, exact replica of carbine used in *Crossfire Trail*. Mfg. by Uberti. Importation began 2010.

MSR $2,014	$1,710	$1,500	$1,280	$1,160	$940	$775	$675	

1876 PRESIDIO RIFLE (SHORT RIFLE PARA MUERTE DE DIABLOS) – .50-95 cal., 20 in. barrel, button mag. New 2017.

MSR $1,949	$1,650	$1,450	$1,240	$1,125	$910	$750	$650	

1876 TOM HORN RIFLE – .45-60 cal., 28 in. octagon barrel, Centennial rifle, Tom Horn sight, walnut stock, engraved name, standard blue frame and finish, 10.05 lbs. New 2017.

MSR $1,847	$1,570	$1,375	$1,180	$1,075	$865	$700	$620	

GRADING - PPGS™	100%	98%	95%	90%	80%	70%	60%	LAST MSR

1885 HIGH WALL RIFLE – .30-40 Krag (mfg. 2004-2018), .348 Win. (mfg. 2004-2017), .38-55 WCF (new 2000), .405 Win. (mfg. 2006-2017), .40-65 WCF (disc. 2018), .45-70 Govt., .45-90 WCF (mfg. 2000-2018), or .45-120 WCF (mfg. 2002-2004) cal., 28 (disc.) or 30 in. octagon barrel, case hardened finish on frame, iron sights (standard) or optional aperture rear and globe front sight (new 2002). Mfg. by Uberti. New 1998.

MSR $1,161	$985	$850	$725	$675	$550	$450	$390	

Add $26 for cals. other than .45-70 Govt.
Add $159 for Deluxe Model with adj. sights, pistol grip (new 2002), and double set trigger.

1885 HI-WALL RIFLE (PEDERSOLI) – .38-55 WCF, .45-70 Govt., or .45-90 WCF cal., 32 in. heavy barrel, single set trigger, straight grip walnut stock, case colored receiver. Mfg. by Pedersoli, limited importation 2010-2011 only.

	$1,975	$1,725	$1,525	$1,300	$1,100	$900	$725	*$2,278*

1885 LOW WALL RIFLE – .22 LR, .22 Hornet, .22 WMR, .30-30 Win. (disc. 2007), .32-20 WCF, .357 Mag. (disc. 2007), .38-40 WCF, .44 Mag. (disc. 2007), .38-55 (disc. 2007), .44-40 WCF, .45-70 Govt. (custom shop only), or .45 LC cal., 30 in. octagon barrel, hand checkered walnut stock, single or double set trigger, case colored frame. Mfg. by Uberti, imported 2005-2018.

	$895	$775	$650	$550	$475	$400	$350	*$1,039*

Subtract $26 for .22 LR or .22 WMR cal.
Add $104 for checkered pistol grip and double set triggers on Deluxe model.
Add $1,004 for standard engraving (.45-70 Govt. cal., custom shop only, mfg. 2010).
Add $1,285 for standard engraving with pistol grip (45-70 Govt. cal., custom shop only, mfg. 2010).

1886 CARBINE/RIFLE – .45-70 Govt. cal., 22 (carbine, disc. 2015) or 26 (rifle) in. octagon barrel, walnut stock and forearm, case colored frame, with or w/o pistol grip, standard blue finish. Mfg. by ArmiSport. Importation began 2011.

MSR $1,709	$1,450	$1,275	$1,095	$985	$800	$650	$570	

Add $125 for Deluxe Rifle (mfg. 2019-2020).
Add $292 for Deluxe pistol grip (new 2020).
Add $375 for pistol grip rifle (mfg. 2017-disc.).
Subtract $91 for 22 in. carbine model (disc. 2015).

* ***1886 Premium Sporting Classic*** – .45-70 cal., 26 in. round barrel, pistol grip stock. New 2019.

MSR $1,969	$1,675	$1,465	$1,250	$1,140	$925	$750	$655	

Add $93 for Premium pistol grip model.

1892 RIFLE – .357 Mag. (disc. 2016), .44 Mag. (disc. 2016), .44-40 WCF (disc. 2016), or .45 LC cal., 20 (disc. 2013, reintroduced 2021) or 24 in. barrel, available in either solid or takedown (disc. 2010) frame, uncheckered walnut stock and forearm, case colored receiver. Mfg. by ArmiSport, imported 2005-2013, reintroduced 2015.

MSR $1,446	$1,230	$1,075	$925	$835	$675	$550	$480	

Add $155 for takedown frame (disc. 2010).

1892 CARBINE – .357 Mag. (disc. 2020), .44 Mag. (mfg. 2010-2013, reintroduced 2021), .44-40 WCF (disc. 2013), or .45 LC cal., 16 (Trapper, disc. 2010) or 20 in. (saddle ring) barrel, solid frame, standard lever. Mfg. by ArmiSport, importation began 2006.

MSR $1,446	$1,230	$1,075	$925	$835	$675	$550	$480	

Subtract $187 for Trapper model with 16 in. barrel (disc. 2010).

1892 COGBURN CARBINE – .45 LC cal., 20 in. blued round barrel, American black walnut stock, big loop lever, saddle ring, case color hardened. New 2017.

MSR $1,476	$1,250	$1,100	$940	$850	$690	$560	$490	

1892 EL DORADO – .357/.38 Spl. or .45 LC cal., 20 in. barrel, big loop, saddle ring. Disc. 2017.

	$1,000	$875	$775	$675	$575	$475	$395	*$1,208*

1894 CARBINE – .30-30 or .38-55 cal., 20 in. round barrel, blue or case color hardened frame (new 2020). New 2019.

MSR $1,275	$1,080	$945	$810	$735	$600	$485	$425	

Add $50 for case color hardened frame (new 2020).

1894 RIFLE – .30-30 or .38-55 cal., 20 (short rifle, new 2021), 24 1/4 (.38-55 cal. only, mfg. 2020 only), or 26 in. octagon barrel. New 2019.

MSR $1,272	$1,080	$950	$810	$725	$595	$485	$425	

Add $53 for 26 in. octagon barrel.
Add $183 for Deluxe model.

GRADING - PPGS™	100%	98%	95%	90%	80%	70%	60%	LAST MSR

MODEL 71 CLASSIC – .45-70 or .348 (new 2017) cal., lever action, 24 in. round barrel. Mfg. 2015-2018.

$1,725 $1,510 $1,300 $1,175 $950 $775 $650 *$2,014*

Add $34 for .45-70 cal.

MODEL 71 HOGZILLA KILLA – .45-70 cal., lever action, 19 in. round barrel, scope sight optional. Mfg. 2015-2017.

$1,575 $1,325 $1,050 $950 $825 $675 $575 *$1,846*

MODEL 71 PREMIUM RIFLE – .45-70 or .348 (new 2017) cal., lever action, 24 in. round barrel, color case hardened frame. New 2015.

MSR $1,974 $1,675 $1,465 $1,250 $1,140 $925 $750 $660

Add $38 for 45-70 cal.

RIFLES: SEMI-AUTO

M4 22 TACTICAL – .22 LR cal., 19 in. solid steel barrel, fire control group, 28 shot, dust cover, adj. sights, pseudo flash hider, bayonet lug, forward assist, and bolt release, quad rail capable forearm, includes two mags, black polymer grips, matte black finish, 5 1/2 lbs. Mfg. by Chiappa 2011-2012.

$475 $400 $350 $315 $285 $260 $240 *$579*

PPS/50 CARBINE – .22 LR cal., patterned after the Russian WWII PPS military rifle, full-length barrel shroud, 50 shot drum mag., walnut stock. Imported by Pietta. Imported 2012 only.

$675 $525 $450 $395 $350 $300 $250 *$805*

SHOTGUNS: REPRODUCTIONS

1878 SxS COACH GUN – 12 ga., 3 in. chambers, 20 or 26 (new 2010) in. barrels, standard blue, original (disc. 2014), or USA (mfg. 2010-2017) finish, hammers, DT, uncheckered American walnut stock with pistol grip, mfg. in China by Polytech. Importation began 2007.

MSR $636 $540 $475 $400 $365 $300 $250 $210

Add $13 for 26 in. barrels.

Add $100 for Original finish (disc. 2014) or $257 for USA finish (mfg. 2010-2017).

Add $112 for 20 in. barrel Deluxe model.

Add $99 for 26 in. barrel Deluxe model.

1881 SxS HAMMERLESS COACH GUN – 12 ga., 2 3/4 in. chambers, 20 (mfg. 2010, reintroduced 2013-2014), 22 (disc. 2014), 26, 28, or 30 in. barrels with choke tubes, hammerless, straight grip walnut stock, DT, standard blue finish. Mfg. in China by Polytech, imported 2010-2015.

$600 $525 $450 $400 $350 $300 $250 *$722*

Add $39 for Deluxe model with deluxe wood.

1883 DOUBLE BARREL SHOTGUN – 12 ga. or .410 bore, SxS, 18 (disc. 2018), 22, 26, or 28 in. barrels, splinter or beavertail forend. Mfg. 2015-2019.

$750 $650 $565 $510 $415 $350 $295 *$883*

1887 LEVER ACTION – 12 ga., 2 3/4 in. chamber, 20 (disc.), 22 (disc.), 24 (mfg. 2010-disc.), or 28 in. barrel, standard blue or original (disc.) finish, uncheckered pistol grip stock. Mfg. by ArmiSport Chiappa, imported 2010-2018.

$1,215 $1,065 $910 $825 $675 $550 $475 *$1,429*

1887 LEVER ACTION SHOTGUN – 12 ga., 2 3/4 in. chamber, 20 or 30 in. barrel with chokes. New 2019.

MSR $501 $425 $375 $325 $295 $235 $195 $165

Add $31 for 30 in. barrel.

1887 TERMINATOR LEVER ACTION – 12 ga., 2 3/4 in. chamber, 20 (mfg. 2010-disc.) or 22 in. barrel, standard blue or original (disc.) finish, uncheckered pistol grip stock. Mfg. by ArmiSport Chiappa, imported 2010-2018.

$1,215 $1,065 $910 $825 $675 $550 $475 *$1,429*

1889 DOUBLE BARREL SHOTGUN – 12 ga. or .410 bore, SxS, 18, 20, or 22 in. barrels, beavertail or splinter forend. Mfg. 2015-2020.

$675 $595 $500 $460 $375 $300 $250 *$792*

Add $26 for .410 bore.

1897 SLIDE ACTION – 12 ga., 2 3/4 in. chamber, patterned after the Model 1897 Winchester, 20 in. barrel with choke tubes, uncheckered American walnut stock with pistol grip, blue or original (disc. 2010) finish. Mfg. in China by Polytech. Imported 2007-2014, reintroduced 2017.

MSR $467 $395 $345 $295 $275 $215 $180 $150

Add $86 for original finish (disc. 2010).

GRADING - PPGS™	100%	98%	95%	90%	80%	70%	60%	LAST MSR

1897 SLIDE ACTION TRENCH SHOTGUN - 12 ga., 2 3/4 in. chamber, 20 in. barrel with choke tubes. New 2019.

MSR $511	$435	$380	$325	$300	$250	$200	$165	

DOC HOLLIDAY SHOTGUN - 12 ga., 20 in. barrel. New 2015.

MSR $1,624	$1,380	$1,210	$1,035	$940	$760	$625	$540	

WYATT EARP SxS SHOTGUN - 12 ga., 20 in. barrel, standard blue finish. Mfg. 2013-2014.

	$1,325	$1,125	$925	$825	$725	$625	$525	*$1,554*

CITADEL

Current trademark imported beginning 2009 by Legacy Sports International, located in Reno, NV.

PISTOLS: SEMI-AUTO

M-1911 FLAG PISTOL + AMMO CAN PACKAGE - 9mm Para. or .45 ACP cal., Series 70 firing system, extended slide stop, 5 in. barrel w/full-length guide rod, two 8 shot mags., beveled magwell, skeletonized hammer and trigger, extended ambi thumb safety and beavertail grip safety, choice of matching American Flag theme ammo cans in red, white, and blue (CITC45FUSAAC), Grayscale (CITC45FUSGAC) or Bazooka Green (CITC45FUSBAC) Reno Cerakote finish, 2.38 lbs. Importation began late 2019.

MSR $959	$800	$700	$600	$550	$450	$375	$275	

This package is available through Bill Hicks & Co Ltd., Davidson's, Sport's South LLC, Williams Shooters Supply, Grice Wholesale, or Chattanooga Shooter Supply.

M-1911 GOVERNMENT - 9mm Para. (disc. 2019), .38 Super (disc. 2014), or .45 ACP cal., full size 1911 style frame, 5 in. barrel, SA, matte black, brushed nickel (mfg. 2010-2014), or polished nickel (mfg. 2010-2014), steel slide, 8 or 10 shot (disc. 2019), skeletonized hammer and trigger, Novak sights, lowered and flared ejection port, extended ambidextrous safety, checkered wood or Hogue wraparound (available in black, green, or sand, mfg. 2010-2016) grips, includes two magazines and lockable plastic case, 2.3 lbs. Imported 2009-2014, reintroduced 2016.

MSR $599	$515	$445	$395	$365	$325	$275	$250	

Add $26 for Hogue wraparound grips in black, green, or sand (disc.).
Add $89 for brushed nickel (disc. 2014) or $108 for polished nickel (disc. 2014).
Add $250 for Wounded Warrior Project configuration with matte black finish (disc.).
Add $360 for laser etched Damascus design "Madagascar" (new 2019).
Add $501 for laser etched Warbird design with Battleworn grips (new 2019).

M-1911 OFFICER - 9mm Para. or .45 ACP cal., 3 1/2 in. barrel, 6 (disc.), 7, or 8 shot, similar to Citadel M-1911 FS, except has compact frame, not available in polished nickel, 2.1 lbs. Imported 2009-2014, re-imported 2016-2019.

	$515	$445	$395	$365	$325	$275	$250	*$599*

Add $26 for Hogue grips in black, OD Green, or sand (disc.).
Add $89 for brushed nickel (disc. 2014).

M-1911 BABY CITADEL - .380 ACP cal., aluminum frame, 3 3/4 in. steel barrel, 7 shot, skeletonized hammer and trigger, beveled magwell, Champagne and Crushed Orchard finish, 1.47 lbs. Importation began 2020.

MSR $669	$575	$495	$425	$385	$345	$285	$265	

M-1911 CERAKOTE - 9mm Para. or .45 ACP cal., full size 1911 style frame, 5 in. barrel with full length guide rod, 7 or 8 shot, beveled magwell, extended slide stop, extended ambi thumb and beavertail grip safety, lowered and flared ejection port, skeletonized hammer and trigger, Cerakote OD Green frame and black slide, black frame and Pewter slide (disc. 2015), FDE frame and Black slide (new 2016), or black frame and Brushed Nickel slide (disc. 2015), Hogue Piranha G10 (new 2016), Hogue Dymondwood Rosewood, or Hogue Black and OD Green wraparound grips (brushed nickel only, disc. 2015), 2.3 lbs. Imported 2014-2017.

	$675	$595	$500	$450	$350	$300	$240	*$785*

* ***M-1911 Cerakote Compact*** - 9mm Para. or .45 ACP cal., similar to M-1911 Cerakote, except has compact frame, 3 1/2 in. barrel, 2.1 lbs. Imported 2014-2017.

	$675	$595	$500	$450	$350	$300	$240	*$785*

M-1911 COMMANDER - 9mm Para. (disc. 2019) or .45 ACP cal., Series 70 firing system, compact frame, 4 1/4 in. bushingless barrel, 6 (disc.), 7 (disc. 2019), or 8 shot, beveled magwell, lowered and flared ejection port, skeletonized hammer and trigger, extended beavertail grip safety, matte black finish, 2.3 lbs. Importation began 2019.

MSR $599	$515	$445	$395	$365	$325	$275	$250	

GRADING - PPGS™	100%	98%	95%	90%	80%	70%	60%	LAST MSR

M-1911-22 TARGET MODEL – .22 LR cal., patterned after the M1911, 5 in. barrel, matte black finish, features wood (new 2012) or Hogue grips, standard (new 2012) or fiber optic sights and key operated safety, supplied with two 10 shot mags., lanyard loop, 2.1 lbs. Mfg. by Chiappa Firearms. Imported 2011-2014.

	$265	$235	$210	$195	$180	$170	$160	*$310*

Add $39 for Hogue grips and fiber optic sights.

M-1911 TAC ULTRA – 9mm Para. or .45 ACP cal., SA, full size 1911 style frame, 5 in. barrel, 8 or 10 shot, matte black steel slide, lowered and flared ejection port, skeletonized hammer, skeletonized trigger, adj. fiber optic sights, gray checkered G10 grips, extended ambidextrous safety, full tactical rail, includes two magazines and lockable plastic case, black parkerized finish, 2.8 lbs. Imported 2019 only.

	$750	$650	$565	$500	$425	$345	$275	*$859*

CARBINES: SEMI-AUTO

M1 CARBINE – .22 LR cal., M1 design, 18 in. threaded (new 2013) barrel with fixed front sight and adj. rear sight, black synthetic, Harvest Moon camo (mfg. 2013-2015), Muddy Girl camo (new 2013), Outshine camo (mfg. 201302915), or wood (new 2012) stock, 10 shot mag., blued finish, 4.8 lbs. Mfg. by Chiappa in Italy, imported 2011-2016.

	$265	$235	$200	$185	$170	$160	$150	*$309*

Add $70 for Muddy Girl, Harvest Moon (disc. 2015), or Outshine camo (mfg. 2013-2015) stock.
Add $100 for wood stock (new 2012).

M1 9MM CARBINE – 9mm Para. cal., blowback action, 18 in. barrel, two Beretta style 10 shot mags., fixed front and adj. rear sights, synthetic bayonet lug, wood or black synthetic stock with oiler and nylon sling cutout, 5.8 lbs. Imported 2014 only.

	$475	$415	$350	$325	$225	$225	$175	*$539*

RIFLES: BOLT ACTION

TRAKR 22 LR – .22 LR cal., 18 in. barrel, vented forend, 10 shot mag., hooded fiber optic front sight, black synthetic stock, pistol grip, Nikko Stirling 3-9x40 scoped packages available. Importation began 2020.

MSR $199	$175	$150	$125	$115	$100	$95	$75	

RIFLES: LEVER ACTION

LEVTAC-92 – .357 Mag., .44 Mag., or .454 Casull cal., 18 in. blued barrel, 8 shot, front blade and rear peep sight, Picatinny rail, modular M-LOK forend, black synthetic stock. Importation began 2020.

MSR $799	$700	$600	$500	$450	$375	$300	$250	

SHOTGUNS: SEMI-AUTO

BOSS-25 – 12 ga., 3 in. chamber, 18 3/4 in. barrel with muzzle brake, 4 shot mag., adj. folding raised tactical sights, black synthetic stock with adj. cheekpiece, pistol grip, Picatinny rail on top receiver and lower forend, matte black, FDE, Tactical Gray, or USA Flag finish. Importation began 2020.

MSR $579	$500	$425	$375	$325	$275	$225	$175	

BOSSHOG – 12 or 20 ga., 3 in. chamber, 20 in. chrome-lined barrel with 3 chokes, 4 shot mag., black synthetic stock, 13.6 in. LOP, 7 lbs. New 2021.

Please contact the manufacturer directly for price and availability.

CDA-12 – 12 ga., 3 in. chamber, 20 in. barrel, MC-1 chokes, blade front sight, black synthetic stock and forearm with recoil pad, 14 1/2 in. LOP, matte black finish, 40 in. OAL, 7.3 lbs. Imported 2019-2020.

	$350	$300	$250	$225	$200	$150	$125	*$399*

CDA-12 FORCE – 12 ga., 3 in. chamber, 20 in. barrel, adj. rear and high post front sights, black synthetic stock and forearm, 14 1/2 in. LOP, pistol grip, oversize bolt handle, Picatinny rail, matte black finish, 41 in. OAL, 6.8 lbs. Imported 2019-2020.

	$350	$300	$250	$225	$200	$150	$125	*$399*

RSS1 – 12 ga., 3 in. chamber, 28 in. barrel, mod. choke, adj. rear and high post front sights, black synthetic stock and forearm with Picatinny rail, recoil pad, pistol grip, 14 in. LOP, matte black metal finish, 40 in. OAL, 8 lbs. Imported 2019-2020.

	$675	$595	$500	$465	$375	$300	$235	*$799*

SHOTGUNS: SLIDE ACTION

CITADEL LE TACTICAL – 12 ga., 20 (disc. 2011) or 22 (new 2012) in. barrel, 7 shot mag., matte black finish, available in Standard, Spec-Ops (features Blackhawk Spec-Ops stock with recoil reduction), Talon (features thumbhole stock with Blackhawk recoil reduction), or Pistol grip w/heat shield (features interchangeable stock and removable pistol grip) configuration, approx. 5.8-7 lbs. Mfg. in the U.S. 2010-2012.

$385 $335 $285 $240 $210 $180 $150 ***$466***

Add $41 for Pistol grip w/heat shield or $166 for either Spec-Ops or Talon configuration.

CDP-12 – 12 ga., 3 in. chamber, 20 in. barrel, blade front sight, black synthetic stock and forearm with recoil reduction, 14 1/2 in. LOP, matte black or nickel (Marine) Cerakote finish, 40 1/2 in. OAL, 6.1 lbs. Imported 2019-2020.

$215 $195 $165 $145 $125 $95 $75 ***$249***

CDP-12 FORCE – 12 ga., 3 in. chamber, 20 in. barrel with muzzle brake, adj. rear on Picatinny rail and high post front sight, black synthetic stock and forearm with Picatinny rail, recoil reduction and pistol grip, 14 1/2 in. LOP, matte black finish, 42 in. OAL, 6.4 lbs. Imported 2019-2020.

$215 $195 $165 $145 $125 $95 $75 ***$249***

CIVILIAN FORCE ARMS

Previous 1911 style pistol and AR-15 style pistol, rifle, and parts and accessories manufacturer located in Yorkville, IL late 2014-2018.

For individual model listings, please go to BlueBookOfGunValues.com/overflow.

CLARIDGE HI-TEC INC.

Previous manufacturer located in Northridge, CA 1990-1993. In 1990, Claridge Hi-Tec, Inc. was created and took over Goncz Armament, Inc.

All Claridge Hi-Tec firearms utilized match barrels mfg. in-house, which were button-rifled. The Claridge action is an original design and does not copy other actions. Claridge Hi-Tec models can be altered (Law Enforcement Companion Series) to accept Beretta 92F or Sig Model 226 magazines.

PISTOLS: SEMI-AUTO

Add $40 for polished stainless steel frame construction.

L-9 PISTOL – 9mm Para., .40 S&W, or .45 ACP cal., blowback telescoping bolt operation, SA, 7 1/2 (new 1992) or 9 1/2 (disc. 1991) in. shrouded barrel, aluminum receiver, choice of black matte, matte silver, or polished silver finish, one-piece grip, safety locks firing pin in place, 10 (disc.), 17 or 30 shot double row mag., adj. sights, 3 3/4 lbs. Mfg. 1991-1993.

$595 $525 $375 $300 $265 $225 $200 ***$598***

Add $395 for a trigger activated laser sight available in Models M, L, C, and T new mfg.

S-9 PISTOL – similar to L-9, except has 5 in. non-shrouded threaded barrel, 3 lbs. 9 oz. Disc. 1993.

$695 $625 $550 $475 $350 $280 $250 ***$535***

T-9 PISTOL – similar to L-9, except has 9 1/2 in. barrel. Mfg. 1992-93.

$550 $495 $375 $300 $265 $225 $200 ***$598***

M PISTOL – similar to L Model, except has 7 1/2 in. barrel, 3 lbs. Disc. 1991.

$575 $515 $375 $300 $265 $225 $200 ***$720***

CARBINES: SEMI-AUTO

C-9 CARBINE – same cals. as L and S Model pistols, 16.1 in. shrouded barrel, choice of black graphite composite or uncheckered walnut stock and forearm, 5 lbs. 12 oz. Mfg. 1991-1993.

$650 $595 $525 $450 $395 $350 $300 ***$675***

Add $74 for black graphite composite stock.
Add $474 for integral laser model (with graphite stock).

This model was available with either gloss walnut, dull walnut, or black graphite composite stock.

LAW ENFORCEMENT COMPANION (LEC) – 9mm Para., .40 S&W, or .45 ACP cal., 16 1/4 in. button rifled barrel, black graphite composition buttstock and foregrip, buttstock also provides space for an extra mag., available in either aluminum or stainless steel frame, matte black finish, available with full integral laser sighting system. Limited mfg. 1992-93.

$750 $650 $575 $495 $425 $375 $325 ***$749***

Add $400 for integral laser sighting system.

CLARK CUSTOM GUNS, INC.

Current custom gun maker and gunsmithing shop located in Princeton, LA. Clark Custom Guns, Inc. has been customizing various configurations of handguns, rifles, and shotguns since 1950. It would be impossible to list within the confines of this text the many conversions this company has

GRADING - PPGS™	100%	98%	95%	90%	80%	70%	60%	LAST MSR

performed. Please contact the company directly for an up-to-date price sheet and catalog on their extensive line-up of high quality competition pistols and related components. Custom revolvers, rifles, and shotguns are also available in addition to various handgun competition parts, related gunsmithing services, and a firearms training facility called The Shootout.

The legendary James E. Clark, Sr. passed away during 2000. In 1958, he became the first and only full-time civilian to win the National Pistol Championships.

HANDGUNS

Clark Custom Guns manufactures a wide variety of M1911 style pistols and revolvers. Current models include: Premium Bullseye Pistol (MSR $2,685-$2,785), Custom 1911 Bianchi Open Pistol (MSR $4,000), Custom Combat Hardball Pistol (P.O.R.),Custom Combat SWAR/SWCAT Revolver (MSR $1,291-$1,412), Custom Optical Heavy Slide Pistol ($2,535), 1911 Custom Race Gun Pistol (MSR $3,295-$3,695), Game Master Revolver (MSR $1,291-$1,412), Lightweight Revolver (MSR $1,595), Meltdown Pistol (P.O.R.), and the SSR Revolver (MSR $1,595-$1,744). Previous models include: Bullseye Pistol (last MSR in 2013 was $1,695-$3,100), Millennium Meltdown (damascus slide, only 50 mfg. during 2000 - last MSR $3,795), .460 Rowland Hunter LS (last MSR $2,640), and the Unlimited (last MSR $3,395-$3,790). Clark will also build the above configurations on a customer supplied gun - prices are less. Please contact the company directly regarding more information on its wide variety of pistols and revolvers, including availability and pricing.

RIFLES: SEMI-AUTO

Clark Custom Guns manufactures or customizes various rifles including the AR-15 platform (detailed below in the Custom Gator) or the venerable Ruger 10/22, 77/17, or 77/22 rifles. Features of these firearms usually include custom barrels, stocks, actions, and tuned or custom internal components such as triggers. Pricing for Clark Cusom Guns' 10/22s or other Ruger rifle derivatives starts at MSR $885 plus the cost of the customers chosen stock for the gun. Clark Custom Guns will also build the above configurations or services on a customer supplied gun - prices are less. Please contact the company directly regarding more information on its wide variety of custom rifle options, including availability and pricing.

CUSTOM GATOR - 5.56 NATO or .223 Wylde chamber cal., GIO, 20 in. heavy barrel, 1-9 twist 4 groove rifling, JP Enterprises adj. gas block with Picatinny rail, Jerry Miculek muzzle brake, uses AR-15 mags, A3 style forged aluminum upper receiver w/flat-top Picatinny rail, forged lower receiver, JP adj. trigger, free floating Clark Custom carbon fiber handguard, laser engraved Gator logo on mag. well, black hardcoat anodized finish with Teflon coating.

Current base MSR on this model is $1,925.

CLASSIC DOUBLES

Previous trademark manufactured in Tochigi City, Japan until 1987. Previously imported and distributed by Classic Doubles International, Inc. located in St. Louis, MO.

The factory closed in 1987, and all Classic Doubles remaining in inventory were sold to GU Wholesalers located in Omaha, NE in 1990. To date, there has been little collectibility in the Classic Doubles trademark. As a result, values are determined by the shooting value each model has to offer against other competing models in the same configuration. Also, in some regions of the country, 98% condition or less specimens may be priced lower than values shown in this section.

In late 1987, Winchester/Olin discontinued importation of their Japanese shotgun models (Models 101 and 23). At that point, Classic Doubles International, Inc. became the sole importer of these shotguns. There were very few changes made during this changeover of importation. The late manufacture Classic Double shotguns (Models 101 and 201) do not have the Winchester trademark or definitive Winchester proofmark stamped on the barrels. The Model 201 was a new model designation.

SHOTGUNS: O/U, MODEL 101 - FIELD MODELS

The late manufacture Classic Doubles have an interchangeable choke tube system compatible with the older Winchester manufactured models. Prices listed include a luggage style carrying case.

100% values listed below for the Classic Doubles Shotguns assume NIB condition - subtract 10%-15% if without box, warranty card, and original shipping container (with packing materials).

CLASSIC FIELD GRADE I - 12 or 20 ga., 3 in. chambers, vent. rib, 25 1/2 or 28 in. vent. barrels with choke tubes, blue receiver with moderate scroll engraving, ejectors, checkered pistol grip or English stock and forearm, 6 1/4-7 lbs.

	100%	98%	95%	90%	80%	70%	60%	LAST MSR
	$1,400	$1,250	$1,100	$1,000	$900	$825	$750	*$1,905*

GRADING - PPGS™	100%	98%	95%	90%	80%	70%	60%	LAST MSR

CLASSIC FIELD GRADE II – 12, 20, 28 ga., or .410 bore, 28 in. VR barrels with choke tubes, deluxe walnut with round knob pistol grip stock and forearm with fine fleur-de-lis checkering, coin finished receiver (different sizes) with game scene engraving featuring hunting motifs on receiver sides and bottom, .410 bore bored M/F only, 6 1/4-7 lbs.

	$1,795	$1,475	$1,275	$1,100	$1,000	$900	$795	*$2,190*

Add 15% for .410 bore (baby frame).
Add 50% for 28 ga. (baby frame).

The lack of supply of the Winchester/Olin Model 101 28 ga. small frame has caused a significant increase in demand for the .410 bore or 28 ga. The Grade II .410 bore is the only round knob pistol grip produced in both Winchester and Classic Doubles manufacture.

CLASSIC FIELD GRADE II TWO BARREL SET – 12 and 20 ga. barrels, both with Winchokes, 26 in. barrels - 20 ga., 28 in. barrels - 12 ga., coin finished receiver with game scene engraving and borders, 6 1/2 (20 ga.) or 7 (12 ga.) lbs.

	$2,695	$2,175	$1,825	$1,550	$1,375	$1,200	$1,075	*$3,420*

CLASSIC SPORTER – 12 ga. only, made for Sporting Clays competition, 28 or 30 in. vent. barrels and rib with choke tubes, quick detachable stock system, border engraved coin finished receiver with non-reflective matte surface on top frame and lever, checkered walnut stock and forearm, 7 3/4 lbs.

	$1,995	$1,500	$1,295	$1,150	$1,000	$900	$775	*$1,980*

Add $965 for extra barrel.

WATERFOWL MODEL – 12 ga. only, 3 in. chambers, 30 in. barrels with vent. rib and choke tubes, matte blue receiver with moderate engraving, low gloss walnut stock with vent. recoil pad, 7 3/4 lbs.

	$1,300	$1,125	$950	$825	$700	$650	$600	*$1,520*

SHOTGUNS: O/U, MODEL 101 - TARGET MODELS

CLASSIC TRAP SINGLE – 12 ga. only, over single 32 or 34 in. VR barrel with choke tubes, blue receiver with light engraving, choice of Monte Carlo or regular stock, recoil pad, 8 1/2 lbs.

	$1,200	$1,100	$1,000	$900	$825	$750	$600	*$2,070*

CLASSIC TRAP – 12 ga. only, 30 or 32 in. vent. barrels and rib with choke tubes, choice of Monte Carlo or standard stock with recoil pad, blue finish receiver with light engraving, 8 3/4 or 9 lbs.

	$1,300	$1,125	$1,000	$900	$825	$750	$675	*$1,905*

CLASSIC TRAP COMBO – includes one set of O/U barrels (30 or 32 in.) and one over single barrel (32 or 34 in.), choke tubes, choice of Monte Carlo or standard stock, 8 3/4 or 9 lbs.

	$2,400	$2,100	$1,875	$1,600	$1,475	$1,300	$1,175	*$2,825*

CLASSIC SKEET – 12 or 20 ga., 27 1/2 in. vent. barrels and rib, choke tubes on 12 ga. only, smaller gauges are bored SK/SK, similar metal finish to Classic Trap models, 7 1/4 or 7 3/4 lbs.

	$1,695	$1,375	$1,175	$1,025	$900	$825	$750	*$1,905*

* ***Classic Skeet 4 ga. Set*** – 12, 20, 28 ga. or .410 bore, has four 27 1/2 in. VR barrels, 12 ga. has choke tubes, smaller gauges are bored SK/SK, similar metal finish to Classic Trap models, 7 1/4 or 7 3/4 lbs.

	$4,300	$3,875	$3,500	$3,100	$2,875	$2,600	$2,300	*$4,765*

SHOTGUNS: SxS

MODEL 201 CLASSIC – 12 or 20 ga., 3 in. chambers, forged steel monobloc with improved lug design, 26 in. choke tube barrels with vent. rib, high lustre bluing, no engraving, SST, ejectors, premium walnut stock and beavertail forearm with fancy checkering pattern, solid red rubber recoil pad, 6 3/4-7 lbs.

	$2,500	$2,150	$1,875	$1,650	$1,400	$1,200	$995	*$2,190*

Add $120 for 20 ga.

The 12 ga. could be ordered with choke tubes at no extra charge. Only 63 were mfg. with choke tubes and slight premiums are being asked.

* ***Model 201 Classic Small Bore Set*** – 28 ga. and .410 bore two barrel set, similar to Model 201 Classic except has smaller frame and overall dimensions, 28 in. VR barrels only bored IC/M on 28 ga. and M/F on .410 bore, very limited importation, 6 or 6 1/2 lbs.

	$4,250	$3,650	$3,250	$2,800	$2,400	$1,950	$1,475	*$3,675*

GRADING - PPGS™	100%	98%	95%	90%	80%	70%	60%	LAST MSR

CLERKE ARMS, LTD.

Previous manufacturer located in Raton, New Mexico 1997-2001.

PISTOLS: SINGLE SHOT

COMPETITOR PISTOL – available in 16 centerfire and 2 rimfire cals., 10, 12, 14, 16, or 20 (.410 bore only) in. barrel, features new uplifting C Breech gun system, Xtender slide can be fitted to all Colt .45 ACPs and replicas with no frame modification, matte finish, checkered wood grips. Mfg. 1998-2001.

	100%	98%	95%	90%	80%	70%	60%	LAST MSR
	$300	$285	$265	$240	$220	$200	$185	*$325*

Add $135-$155 per interchangeable barrel, depending on length.

CLERKE PRODUCTS

Previous manufacturer located in Santa Monica, CA.

REVOLVERS: DOUBLE ACTION

DOUBLE ACTION REVOLVER – .22 S, L, LR, or .32 S&W Long cal., inexpensive double action revolvers, which sold to dealers for $15 in 1971.

RIFLES: SINGLE SHOT

HI-WALL – available in most modern calibers, single shot, falling block replica of Winchester 1885 High Wall rifle, lever operated, case hardened receiver, 26 in. barrel, no sights, checkered walnut pistol grip stock, Schnabel forearm. Mfg. 1972-74.

	100%	98%	95%	90%	80%	70%	60%	LAST MSR
	$250	$225	$185	$175	$150	$140	$125	

DELUXE HI-WALL – available in most modern calibers, falling block replica of Winchester 1885 High Wall rifle, lever operated, 26 in. half octagon barrel, no sights, select wood and recoil pad, case hardened receiver.

	100%	98%	95%	90%	80%	70%	60%	LAST MSR
	$300	$275	$235	$210	$180	$160	$145	

CLIFTON ARMS

Previous manufacturer of custom rifles from 1992-1997 located in Medina, TX.

Clifton Arms manufactured composite, hand laminated stocks (with or without integral, retractable bipod), which were patterned after the Dakota 76 stock configuration.

RIFLES: BOLT ACTION

CLIFTON SCOUT RIFLE – .243 Win. (disc. 1993), .30-06, .308 Win., .350 Rem. Mag., .35 Whelen, 7mm-08 Rem. (disc. 1993), or .416 Rem. Mag. cal., choice of Dakota 76, pre-64 Winchester Model 70, or Ruger 77 MK II (standard) stainless action with bolt face altered to controlled round feeding, Shilen stainless premium match grade barrel, Clifton synthetic stock with bipod, many other special orders were available. Mfg. 1992-97.

	100%	98%	95%	90%	80%	70%	60%	LAST MSR
	$3,000	$2,350	$1,650	$1,455	$1,195	$1,010	$835	

This model was available as a Standard Scout (.308 Win. cal. with 19 in. barrel), Pseudo Scout (.30-06 cal. with 19 1/2 in. barrel), Super Scout (.35 Whelen or .350 Rem. Mag. with 20 in. barrel), or African Scout (.416 Rem. Mag. with 22 in. barrel).

COACH GUNS

A coach gun is a SxS shotgun with short barrels, which was used extensively in the American West for the protection of horse-drawn coach passengers, hence the name. They were also called guard guns, as they were used for guard duty and other security purposes.

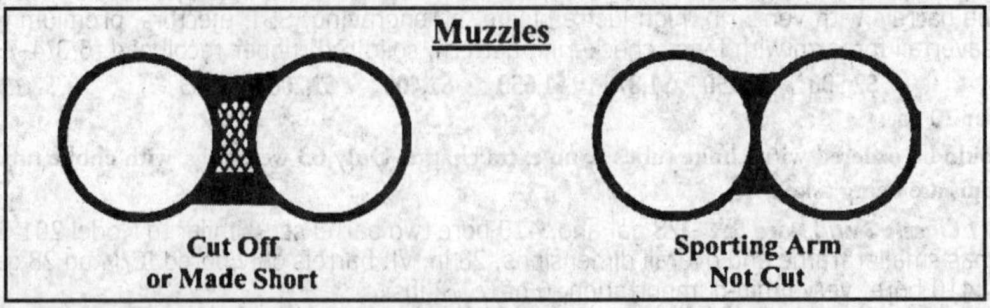

SHOTGUNS: SxS, COACH/GUARD GUNS

The author wishes to express his thanks to Jon Vander Bloomen for compiling the following information.

Extensive research indicates that three American gun companies made coach guns in the late 1800s and

early 1900s - Colt, Parker, and Ithaca. Remington and Whitney may also have produced some, but there are no factory records to prove it. W.W. Greener of Birmingham, England may have made some short double barrel shotguns for guard use, but no one has seen any factory documentation to support this.

An "original" coach gun, properly called a guard gun, is a double barrel (SxS) shotgun originally manufactured with short barrels, not a long barreled sporting gun, which was cut off (see muzzle diagram). However, the muzzles of an original coach gun and a gun whose barrels have been cut off look the same. On both, there is a gap between the muzzles, which is filled in with lead. The reason for this is because shotgun barrels are tapered. In order for the muzzles to touch on a 26 inch or shorter gun, the barrel walls would need to be thicker at the muzzle to eliminate the gap.

Some original coach guns may also have original factory markings, identification letters/numerals on the stock and other distinguishing features, which indicate that the gun was originally made and marked to identify it as company property. However, don't think that there's "safety in numbers." There are a lot more Wells Fargo marked guns today than there were 85 years ago.

The real question is, how can you tell an original coach gun from a sporting arm whose barrels have been cut down to potentially "enhance" its desirability factor? Hopefully, by obtaining factory documentation. To find out if a coach gun is an original or a "cut" gun, it is recommended that you contact the factory for documentation (if possible), giving the serial number of the gun and asking for the actual barrel length at the time the gun left the factory. Unfortunately, no Remington records exist. Parker records can be found in Vols. I & II of *The Parker Story*. W.W. Greener is still in business, and will look up a serial number, but it will take some time.

Colt records show that several double barrel shotguns left the factory with short barrels. Most of them were the Model 1878 hammer guns with 18 inch barrels. There where only three Model 1883 hammerless, boxlock guns made with short barrels; the lengths are as follows, 18, 22, and 24 inches. All of the Colt Damascus barrels were made in Belgium and shipped to the Colt factory in an unfinished state, so they were just Damascus tubes. Therefore when Colt got an order for a coach/guard gun, the barrels were custom made to length just as the longer barreled guns. These short barreled Colts are "original coach/guard guns". The extreme rarity of a Colt factory coach gun precludes accurate pricing evaluation.

Parker records show that several guns were made with short barrels. Not all short Parkers were made for guard use however, since some hunters preferred short barrels in the field (for fast upland birds). Parker purchased different grades of steel tubes and made their own barrels. When Parker received an order for a guard gun, the barrels were custom made to length. It would have been more costly for Parker to cut a long barreled choked gun, except in the case of used sporting arms that were cut for guard use. It is likely that the lower grade 10 and 12 ga. guns, which left the Parker factory with short barrels are "original" coach/guard guns. The extreme rarity factor of a Parker factory coach gun precludes accurate pricing evaluation.

Ithaca records show that 750 hammer doubles were made for Wells Fargo between 1909 and 1917. The first 200 guns had 26 in. barrels, and the remaining 550 had 24 in. barrels. Wells Fargo, as well as other express companies, used various makes of shotguns, mostly used lower grade models that were cut to a shorter length. There is no proof that any company other than Ithaca made guard guns for Wells Fargo. Buyers are cautioned to obtain original documentation when considering a purchase of a Wells Fargo coach gun or any other gun, which is claimed to have been used by a famous person. Average condition Wells Fargo coach guns are typically priced in the $4,000-$7,000 range, regardless if they are manufactured by Ithaca or are another trademark with cut barrels. What's important to the buyer is that the gun is a documented Wells Fargo gun, and should have some paperwork specifying that.

What's important to remember is that if there is no original documentation, there's no proof. And if there's no proof, the shotgun may or may not be an original coach gun. When buying, selling, or trading coach guns, the price tag should be proportional to the gun's originality and provenance. Anything less could result in an unwarranted premium for a tired out, "reconfigured" SxS plain Jane shotgun, with some added non-original markings/carvings.

Older sawed-off double barrel shotguns with no documentation that they were an express company gun, or a gun used by a famous person are valued in the $200 to $2,000 range, depending on trademark and condition, condition being most important. A good guide for pricing sawed-off doubles is to check the value of the same gun that has not been cut and then deduct 5% to 50%. If no price guide is available for that particular make, then consider availability. For example, tens of thousands of Belgian doubles were made in the 1800s. Because of the increase in collectibility of American western artifacts, original coach guns and all express company guns are highly prized and sought after, but the buyer must always be wary.

GRADING - PPGS™	100%	98%	95%	90%	80%	70%	60%	LAST MSR

COBALT KINETICS

Current manufacturer of AR-15 style rifles and pistols beginning circa 2015. Currently located in Saint George, UT. Previously located in Washington, UT from 2015- 2020.

Please refer to BlueBookOfGunValues.com to order the *Blue Book of AR-15s & Variations*, available as a book or online subscription.

COBB MANUFACTURING, INC.

Previous bolt action and AR-15 style rifle manufacturer located in Dallas, GA until 2007.

Please refer to BlueBookOfGunValues.com to order the *Blue Book of AR-15s & Variations*, available as a book or online subscription.

COBRA

Current trademark imported by Tristar, located in Kansas City, MO. Please refer to Tristar in the T section.

COBRA FIREARMS (COBRA ENTERPRISES OF UTAH, INC.)

Current pistol manufacturer established in 2001, with headquarters in Salt Lake City, UT. During 2004, the name was changed from Cobra Enterprises to Cobra Enterprises of Utah, Inc.

DERRINGERS

Beginning 2008, all models come equipped with a lockable plastic case and cable gun lock.

COBRA DERRINGER – .22 LR, .22 WMR, .25 ACP, .32 ACP, .32 H&R Mag., .38 Spl., .380 ACP, or 9mm Para. cal., SFO, 2.4 (Standard Series), 2 3/4 (Big Bore Series), or 3.5 (Long Bore Series) in. barrel, tip-up action, fixed sights, spur trigger, internal hammer block safety, pearl, black, or laminated wood grips, chrome, black powder coat, or satin chrome standard finish.

* ***Standard Series*** – .22 LR, .22 WMR, .25 ACP, or .32 ACP cal., SAO, 2.4 in. barrel, 2 shot, sheathed spur trigger, fixed sights, pearl or laminated wood grips, crossbolt safety, chrome, black powder coat, or satin nickel standard finish, custom colored finishes also available. 9 1/2 oz.

MSR $169	$140	$125	$100	$95	$75	$65	$50	

Add $69 for custom colored finishes, including Black Chrome, Royal Blue, Ruby Red, Majestic Pink, Imperial Purple, or King Cobra Copper (special order).

Add $363 for a multi-barrel Derringer set (includes frame, 4 barrels, storage pouch and all necessary components).

* ***Big Bore Series*** – .22 WMR, .32 H&R Mag., .38 Spl., .380 ACP, or 9mm Para. cal., SAO, larger frame than Standard Series, 2 3/4 in. barrel, sheathed spur trigger, fixed sights, black, white, or pink molded plastic or laminated rosewood grips, crossbolt safety, chrome, satin nickel, or black powder coat standard finish, custom colored finishes also available. 14 oz.

MSR $187	$160	$140	$120	$110	$90	$75	$55	

Add $63 for custom colored finishes, including Black Chrome, Royal Blue, Ruby Red, Majestic Pink, Imperial Purple, or King Cobra Copper (special order).

Add $383 for a multi-barrel Derringer set (includes frame, 4 barrels, storage pouch and all necessary components).

* ***Long Bore Series*** – .22 WMR, .38 Spl., or 9mm Para. cal., SAO, 3 1/2 in. barrel, 2 shot, sheathed spur trigger, fixed sights, laminated rosewood, black, white, or pink grips, crossbolt safety, chrome, satin nickel, or black powder coat standard finish, custom colored finishes also available. 16 oz.

MSR $187	$160	$140	$120	$110	$90	$75	$55	

Add $63 for custom colored finishes, including Black Chrome, Royal Blue, Ruby Red, Majestic Pink, Imperial Purple, or King Cobra Copper (special order).

TITAN DERRINGER – .45 LC/.410 shotshell or 9mm Para. cal., SAO, 3 1/2 in. VR rifled barrels, 2 shot, stainless steel frame, rebounding hammer, removable trigger guard, rosewood grips, polished stainless, brushed stainless, or black stainless, custom molded case (disc. 2011). Mfg. 2010-disc.

MSR $399	$340	$285	$250	$225	$200	$185	$170	

Add $40 for custom molded case (disc. 2011).

PISTOLS: SEMI-AUTO

Beginning 2008, all models come equipped with a lockable plastic case and cable gun lock.

CA (COBRA) SERIES – .32 ACP (CA32 Model) or .380 ACP (CA380 Model) cal., blowback operated, SAO, 2.8 in. barrel, 5 or 6 shot mag., fixed sights, chrome, black powder coat, or satin chrome finish, 22 oz. Disc. 2013.

	$110	$100	$90	$80	$65	$55	$40	*$129*

Add $121 for custom colored finishes, including black chrome, royal blue, ruby red, majestic pink, imperial purple, or King Cobra copper (special order).

GRADING - PPGS™	100%	98%	95%	90%	80%	70%	60%	LAST MSR

FS (FREEDOM) SERIES – .32 ACP (FS32 Model) or .380 ACP (FS380 Model) cal., blowback operated, SAO, alloy frame 3 1/2 in. steel barrel, 7 (.380 ACP) or 8 (.32 ACP) shot mag., fixed sights, bright chrome, black powder coat, satin nickel, two-tone (mfg. 2012-2013), or tri-colored (mfg. 2012-2013) finish, 2.1 lbs. Mfg. 2004-disc.

MSR $138	$120	$100	$90	$80	$65	$55	$40	

Add $15 for chrome finish.

Add $112 for custom colored finishes, including Black Chrome, Royal Blue, Ruby Red, Majestic Pink, Imperial Purple, or King Cobra Copper (special order).

PATRIOT SERIES – .380 ACP or 9mm Para. cal., DAO, 3.3 in. barrel, black polymer frame, stainless steel slide, 10 shot mag., fixed sight, loaded indicator, Brushed stainless, Polished stainless, or Black stainless finish, 18 oz.

MSR $349	$275	$240	$200	$185	$150	$125	$100	

* ***Patriot 45*** – .45 ACP cal., DAO, black polymer frame with stainless steel slide, 3.3 in. barrel, ergonomic grip, non-slip trigger guard, brushed stainless, polished stainless, or black stainless, 6 or 7 shot mag., 20 oz.

MSR $395	$300	$265	$225	$200	$165	$140	$110	

DENALI – .380 ACP cal., SA, lightweight polymer frame, alloy slide, extended magazine base, push-button mag. release, ergonomical grip, extended finger grip, black, Satin, Tactical Tan, or OD Green Cerakote finish. New 2014.

MSR $139	$120	$100	$90	$80	$65	$55	$40	

REVOLVERS

SHADOW – .38 Spl. +P cal., DAO, 1.9 in.stainless steel barrel, 5 shot, stainless steel cylinder, concealed hammer, fixed sights, black rubber, rosewood, ebony (disc. 2010), or Crimson Trace Laser (new 2010) grips, brushed satin, black titanium, or pink finish, 15 oz. New 2009.

MSR $369	$315	$265	$235	$215	$200	$185	$165	

Add $40 for rosewood grips.

Add $256 for Crimson Trace Lasergrips (new 2010).

Styled after Smith & Wesson's J. frame revolver.

COBRAY INDUSTRIES

Please refer to S.W.D. Inc. in the S section.

COGSWELL & HARRISON (GUNMAKERS), LTD.

Current manufacturer established in 1770 and located in County Louth, Ireland. Previously located in London, England until 2012. Previously imported by British Game Guns located in Kent, WA. No current U.S. importation.

In 1993, Cogswell & Harrison came under new management and have concentrated on building best quality Beesley or Purdey type sidelocks, Woodward styled O/Us, and a round action boxlock. The company also provides a serialization service (free of charge), that provides the exact date of manufacture. A Certificate of Origin is also available for a fee, and indicates the original specifications and configuration - weights, dimensions, materials, points of choke, and original owner (including price paid). Cogswell & Harrison also offers a full repair and restoration service.

RIFLES: BOLT ACTION

Cogswell & Harrison has manufactured best quality bolt action rifles for over 90 years in very limited quantities using various actions. All guns were special ordered per individual consumer, and values today are based on the caliber, configuration, and condition. Average condition guns in medium sized calibers typically range from $1,500-$2,250. Rifles in .375 H&H or larger cals. can range from $2,650-$6,000+ depending on the quality of wood, features, and original condition. Original trunk cases will add an additional $400-$800, depending on condition and how many accessories are included.

Currently, the company is offering a Certus Model available in either centerfire or rimfire configuration. The centerfire variation has a black synthetic stock, detachable 3 shot mag., and stainless steel or blue frame and barrel. The rimfire variation has a checkered wood stock and blued frame and barrel w/o sights. Please contact the company directly for current availability and information/pricing on this model.

GRADING - PPGS™ 100% 98% 95% 90% 80% 70% 60% LAST MSR

RIFLES: SxS

Please contact the company directly for an up-to-date quotation on the current models listed below. All new prices do not include VAT. Values for used rifles in 98%-60% condition factors are priced in U.S. dollars. Allow 12-14 months for delivery on boxlocks, 18-24 months on sidelocks.

BOXLOCK MODEL – various cals. from .300 H&H - .600 NE, boxlock action, custom order only. New 1999.

Please contact the company directly for an up-to-date quotation on this model.

* ***Boxlock Model, Early Ejector Models*** – .400 or larger cals., mfg. circa 1900.

Original guns under .450 cal. are generally priced in the $20,000-$40,000 range depending on condition. On calibers .450-.600 NE, values are typically in the $40,000-$60,000 range depending on condition. A Certificate of Origin or individual appraisal is highly recommended.

SIDELOCK MODEL – standard cals. include .300 H&H, .375 H&H, .465, .470 NE, .577, and .600 NE, Beesley or Purdey type action standard, also available with H&H type system, individually made per customer specifications, 8 lbs. 10 oz.-14 lbs. 6 oz., depending on caliber. New 1999.

MSR POR N/A $60,000 $50,000 $43,000 $36,000 $29,000 $21,500

.375 H&H, .450 No. 2 NE, .450 NE, .465, and .470 NE cals. will command premiums over values listed above for both used and new guns.

* ***Sidelock Model Cals. .577 & .600 NE***

MSR POR N/A $72,000 $60,000 $50,000 $43,000 $36,000 $28,000

SHOTGUNS: O/U, SIDELOCK

In addition to the sidelock model listed below, Cogswell & Harrison also offers an imported Windsor boxlock game model available in 12, 20, or 28 ga. in addition to a 12 ga. sporting clays variation. Please contact the company directly for current availability and information/pricing on this model.

WOODWARD TYPE – Woodward style action, finest materials, each gun custom-built for individual specifications, delivery time approx. 18-23 months.

MSR POR N/A $47,250 $41,000 $36,000 $29,500 $22,350 $16,750

Please contact the company directly for an up-to-date quotation on this model.

SHOTGUNS: SxS, OLDER MFG.

REGENCY – 12, 16, or 20 ga., 26, 28, or 30 in. barrels, any choke combination, hammerless Anson & Deeley system, boxlock, double triggers, auto ejectors, straight English stock.

$4,275 $3,750 $3,450 $3,125 $2,750 $2,500 $2,250 *$3,200*

AMBASSADOR MODEL – 12, 16, or 20 ga., 26, 28, or 30 in. barrels, boxlock with ornamental strengthening sideplates, auto ejectors, double triggers, engraved game scene or scroll rose motif, English stock.

$5,500 $4,950 $4,450 $3,950 $3,500 $3,100 $2,850 *$4,000*

MARKOR – 12, 16, or 20 ga., 27 1/2 or 30 in. barrel and choke, boxlock, double trigger, English stock. Disc.

$1,675 $1,475 $1,300 $1,050 $975 $825 $700

Add 20% for auto ejectors.

HUNTIC MODEL – 12, 16, or 20 ga., 25, 27, or 30 in. barrels, any choke, sidelock, auto ejectors, English style stock. Disc.

$3,900 $3,500 $3,200 $3,000 $2,800 $2,500 $2,175

Add $400 for SST.

AVANT TOUT SERIES – 12, 16, or 20 ga., 25, 27 1/2, or 30 in. barrels, boxlock, ornamental strengthening sideplates, straight English stock, auto ejectors, series disc.

$2,550 $2,250 $1,925 $1,700 $1,495 $1,350 $1,200

REX OR AVANT TOUT III – no sideplates.

$2,150 $1,800 $1,650 $1,500 $1,350 $1,200 $1,075

SANDHURST OR AVANT TOUT II

$2,800 $2,500 $2,300 $2,150 $2,000 $1,750 $1,500

KONOR OR AVANT TOUT I

$3,275 $2,850 $2,500 $2,250 $2,000 $1,750 $1,500

Add $400 for SST.
Add 20% for 20 ga.
Subtract 10% for 16 ga.

GRADING - PPGS™	100%	98%	95%	90%	80%	70%	60%	LAST MSR

BEST QUALITY – 12, 16, or 20 ga., 25, 26, 28, or 30 in. barrels, any choke, hand detachable sidelock, auto ejectors, double triggers standard, English stock.

GRADING - PPGS™	100%	98%	95%	90%	80%	70%	60%	LAST MSR
* ***Best Quality Primic Model*** – disc.								
	$6,200	$5,750	$4,650	$4,150	$3,650	$3,050	$2,500	
* ***Best Quality Victor Model***								
	$9,250	$8,500	$7,250	$6,250	$5,000	$4,350	$3,740	

Add $400 for SST.
Add 20% for 20 ga.

Note: Degree of engraving and grade of wood are the basic differences among models.

SHOTGUNS: SxS, BOXLOCK & SIDELOCK - CURRENT MFG.

Please contact the company directly for an up-to-date quotation on current models. All new prices do not include VAT. Values for used guns in 98%-60% condition factors are priced in U.S. dollars. Allow 9-12 months for delivery on boxlocks, 18-23 months on sidelocks.

All models below are available in 12, 20, or 28 ga.

REGENCY – scalloped boxlock action, DTs, 100% large scroll engraving coverage on receiver and tangs, light barrel engraving, checkered straight grip stock with teardrop. Introduced 1970 to commemmorate C&H's bicentennial.

GRADING - PPGS™	100%	98%	95%	90%	80%	70%	60%	LAST MSR
MSR POR	N/A	$14,750	$12,250	$10,000	$8,000	$6,500	$4,950	

VICTORIA – features scalloped round body boxlock action with 100% medium scroll engraving coverage on receiver and tangs, moderate barrel engraving, select checkered stock and forearm.

GRADING - PPGS™	100%	98%	95%	90%	80%	70%	60%	LAST MSR
MSR POR	N/A	$16,950	$14,500	$12,250	$10,000	$7,800	$6,100	

EXTRA QUALITY VICTORIA – similar to Victoria Model, except has better quality wood and more engraving.

GRADING - PPGS™	100%	98%	95%	90%	80%	70%	60%	LAST MSR
MSR POR	N/A	$18,750	$16,250	$14,000	$11,750	$8,900	$7,350	

Add £440 for 20 ga.
Add £890 for 28 ga.

EXTRA QUALITY (SPECIAL) VICTORIA – top-of-the-line round boxlock action with best quality walnut and chopperlump barrels, removable crosspin, and other refinements.

GRADING - PPGS™	100%	98%	95%	90%	80%	70%	60%	LAST MSR
MSR POR	N/A	$22,350	$19,450	$16,350	$13,150	$10,250	$8,400	

SELF-OPENING SLE SxS – sidelock action, best quality Beesley action and engraving, each gun custom-built per individual specifications, delivery time approx. 18-23 months.

GRADING - PPGS™	100%	98%	95%	90%	80%	70%	60%	LAST MSR
MSR POR	N/A	$41,000	$36,000	$29,500	$22,350	$16,750	$12,500	

COLE ARMS INC.

Previous manufacturer of custom trap shotguns from 1991 to 2012 and located in McMinnville, OR.

Cole Arms manufactured custom trap shotguns built per individual customer's specifications. Base guns started at $8,500 and went up depending on wood, engraving, and other customer choices.

COLT'S MANUFACTURING COMPANY, LLC

Current manufacturer with headquarters located in West Hartford, CT.

Manufactured from 1836-1842 in Paterson, NJ; 1847-1848 in Whitneyville, CT; 1854-1864 in London, England; and from 1848-date in Hartford, CT. Colt Firearms became a division of Colt Industries in 1964. In March 1990, the Colt Firearms Division was sold to C.F. Holding Corp. located in Hartford, CT, and the new company was called Colt's Manufacturing Company, Inc. The original Hartford plant was closed during 1994, the same year the company was sold again to a new investor group headed by Zilkha Co., located in New York, NY. During 1999, Colt Archive Properties LLC, the historical research division, became its own entity.

In late 1999, Colt discontinued many of their consumer revolvers, but reintroduced both the Anaconda and Python Elite through the Custom Shop. Production on both models is now suspended. The semi-auto pistols remaining in production are now referred to as Model "O" Series.

In November 2003, Colt was divided into two separate companies, Colt Defense LLC (military/law enforcement) and Colt's Manufacturing Company LLC (handguns and match target rifles). The largest portion of Colt Defense's business is now in sporting rifles, a line of business the company got back into during 2011. Military orders have been on the decline since 2009.

100%	98%	95%	90%	80%	70%	60%	50%	40%	30%	20%	10%

During 2013, Colt Defense LLC acquired Colt's Manufacturing LLC for $60.5 million and reunited Colt's military and civilian handgun businesses. By combining the two companies after a decade long split, Colt Defense has eliminated the risk that its contract with Colt's Manufacturing to sell commercial firearms to civilian sportsmen and hunters under its namesake brand wouldn't be extended beyond March 2014. The company plans to remain in West Hartford. In February 2021, CZ's parent company CZG announced that is was buying Colt.

For more information and current pricing on both new and used Colt airguns, please refer to the *Blue Book of Airguns* - also available as an online subscription. For more information and current pricing on both new and used Colt black powder reproductions and replicas, please refer to the *Blue Book of Modern Black Powder Arms* (also available online).

REVOLVERS: PERCUSSION

Prices shown for percussion Colts are for guns only. Original cased guns with accessories will bring a healthy premium over non-cased models (200%-350% over a gun only is common). Be very careful when buying an "original" cased gun, as many fake cases have shown up in recent years.

If possible, it is advisable to procure a factory letter (available only within the following ser. no. ranges) before buying, selling, or trading Models 1851 Navy (ser. range 98,000-132,000), 1860 Army (ser. range 1,000-140,000), or 1861 Navy (ser. range 1-12,000). These watermarked letters are available by writing Colt Archive Properties LLC in Bloomfield, CT, with a charge of $300 or more per serial number (if they can research it). Some 1849 Pockets can also be researched for $200. Include your name and address, Colt model name, serial number, and check or credit card information to: COLT ARCHIVE PROPERTIES LLC, 1295 Blue Hills Avenue, Bloomfield, CT 06002. Please allow 90-120 days for a response.

Prices shown for extremely rare Colt's firearms might not include values in the 90%, 95%, 98%, and 100% condition columns. Prices are very hard to establish since these excellent to mint specimens are seldom seen or sold.

The author wishes to express his thanks to Greg Martin from Greg Martin Auctions for his pricing updates on Colt percussion revolvers, Conversions, Open Tops, Pocket models, and the New Line Series.

Revolvers: Percussion, Paterson Variations

PATERSON NO. 1 POCKET MODEL – also known as "Baby Paterson", .28 cal., single action with folding trigger, 2 1/2-4 3/4 in. octagon barrels, 5 shot, folding trigger, varnished walnut grips, Serial range 1 to approx. 500. Standard barrel marking "Patent Arms M'g Co. Paterson N.J.-Colt's Pt.", Centaur scene with four horse head trademark and "COLT" on 1 1/16 in. cylinder of round or square type., blue metal. Mfg. 1837-1838.

This and all other Paterson models have 5 shot cylinders and serial numbers are not commonly in evidence externally. Disassembly of the arm is usually necessary to determine the serial number.

The Pocket Model Paterson No. 1 (Baby Paterson) is the first production-made handgun in Colt's Paterson, N.J. facility. It is very small in size, almost appearing as a toy or miniature.

* ***Paterson No. 1 Pocket Model Standard Production Model*** – without attached loading lever.

N/A N/A $125,000 $100,000 $85,000 $72,500 $60,000 $55,000 $50,000 $45,000 $40,000 $35,000

* ***Paterson No. 1 Pocket Model Late Production Ehlers Model*** – with attached loading lever, 31/32 round back cylinder and recoil shield milled for ease of capping. Barrel marked "Patent Arms Paterson N.J.-Colt's Pt." Approx. 500 mfg. including the Ehlers Model under Belt Model No. 2 Mfg. 1840-1843.

N/A N/A $90,000 $75,000 $67,500 $60,000 $55,000 $50,000 $47,500 $45,000 $40,000 $35,000

PATERSON NO. 2 BELT MODEL – .31 or .34 cal., single action with folding trigger, 5 shot, 2 1/2-5 1/2 in. octagon barrels, blue metal, varnished walnut grips, serial range 1-approx. 850 which includes the Belt Model No. 3. All standard production Belt Models No. 2 have straight bottom style grips. Standard barrel markings "Patent Arms M'g Co. Paterson N-J. Colt's Pt." Centaur scene with four horse head trademark and "COLT" on cylinder of round or square backed type. Mfg. 1837-40. Somewhat heavier than the Pocket No. 1 revolver.

* ***Paterson No. 2 Belt Model Standard Production Model*** – without attached loading lever.

N/A N/A $80,000 $70,000 $65,000 $60,000 $55,000 $50,000 $47,500 $45,000 $40,000 $35,000

* ***Paterson No. 2 Belt Model Ehlers*** – with attached loading lever, 1 1/16 in. round back cylinder, recoil shield milled for ease of capping. Barrel marked "Patent Arms Paterson N-J. Colt's Pt." Approx. 500 mfg. including the Ehlers Model under Pocket Model No. 1. Mfg. 1840-43.

N/A N/A $125,000 $100,000 $85,000 $75,000 $70,000 $65,000 $57,500 $50,000 $45,000 $40,000

100%	98%	95%	90%	80%	70%	60%	50%	40%	30%	20%	10%

PATERSON NO. 3 BELT MODEL - .31 or .34 cal., single action with folding trigger, 5 shot, 3 1/2-5 1/2 in. octagon barrels, blue metal, a few having case hardened hammers, varnished walnut grips. Serial range 1-approx. 850 which includes the Belt Model No. 2. All standard production Belt Models No. 3 have the flared bottom style grips. Standard barrel markings "Patent Arms M'g Co. Paterson N-J. Colt's Pt." The square backed cylinder is seen less often than the more common round back, both bearing the Centaur scene with four horse head trademark and "COLT," with both Belt Models, revolvers exhibiting attached loading levers are less common than those without a lever. Mfg. 1837-1840.

* ***Paterson No. 3 Belt Model Standard w/o Lever*** - without attached loading lever.

N/A	N/A	$95,000	$85,000	$80,000	$75,000	$67,500	$60,000	$57,500	$55,000	$50,000	$45,000

* ***Paterson No. 3 Belt Model Standard With Lever*** - with attached loading lever and recoil shield milled for ease of capping (scarce).

N/A	N/A	$140,000	$110,000	$90,000	$75,000	$67,500	$60,000	$57,500	$55,000	$50,000	$45,000

PATERSON NO. 5 HOLSTER MODEL - also known as "Texas Paterson" - .36 cal., single action with folding trigger, 5 shot, 4 to 12 in. octagon barrels, blue metal with case hardened frame and hammer. All cylinders bear the stage coach hold-up scene. Varnished walnut grips of flared bottom style. Serial range 1 to approx. 1,000. As with all models of Patersons, the serial number usually cannot be seen without disassembly of the revolver. Very large and heavy compared to the other Paterson models. Enjoys more popularity with collectors because of its military and frontier use. Mfg. 1838-1840.

Many specimens encountered in this variation show extreme use. Consequently, fine to mint specimens are quite rare and highly prized by collectors. Values are given for non-military marked specimens. Any specimen bearing an authenticated martial marking is truly a rarity and should be appraised individually. NOTE: Watch for fakes here. There are now many times more faked martial markings, often times on non-original Patersons, than there are originals.

* ***Paterson No. 5 Holster Model Standard Production Model w/o Lever*** - without attached loading lever, round or square backed cylinder.

N/A	N/A	$160,000	$140,000	$125,0000	$110,000	$90,000	$85,000	$80,000	$75,000	$65,000	$60,000

* ***Paterson No. 5 Holster Model Standard Production Model With Lever*** - with attached loading lever, round backed cylinder and recoil shield milled for ease of capping.

N/A	N/A	$200,000	$175,000	$150,000	$125,000	$100,000	$95,000	$82,500	$75,000	$70,000	$65,000

Revolvers: Percussion, Walker Model

WALKER MODEL - .44 cal., single action, 9 in. part round/part octagon barrel, 6 shot cylinder, brass trigger guard, one-piece walnut grips, blue metal with case hardened frame, lever, and hammer, cylinder left in the white without finish, barrels marked "Address SamL Colt New-York City," found on right side of barrel lug is "US" over "1847," cylinder bears Texas Ranger/Indian fight scene, various metal parts and walnut grips stamped with Govt. Inspectors' marks, Ser. numbers beginning with no. 1 were applied for each of five different military companies (A,B,C,D, & E). The total for the military issue Walkers was approx. 1,000 revolvers; the remaining approx. 100 revolvers were produced for civilian distribution. Total production approx. 1,100 mfg. 1847.

Because of these arms being subjected to great extremes of use, they will exhibit high degrees of wear, often to the extent that most or all markings will be worn off. Replaced parts are common and many badly worn and damaged specimens have been extensively rebuilt and restored. NOTE: Use great caution when contemplating the purchase of a Walker. A multitude of out-and-out fakes and "antiqued" reproduction Walkers have been fed into the market over the past few decades. Some of these are old enough (and have aged enough naturally) to almost resemble an authentic specimen. Enlist the services of a qualified expert before your dollars are spent. Only 10%-12% of the original production of approx. 1,100 specimens have been accounted for. The acquisition of an authenticated Walker revolver is the ultimate goal of serious Colt handgun collectors.

* ***Walker Standard Military Issue Model***

N/A	N/A	N/A	N/A	N/A	N/A	$500,000	$400,000	$250,000	$150,00	$125,000	$100,000

* ***Walker Limited Civilian Issue Model*** - .44 cal., serial range 1001 to approx. 1100. Similar to military model except Govt. inspectors' marks were not applied.

N/A	N/A	N/A	N/A	N/A	N/A	$500,000	$400,000	$250,000	$150,00	$125,000	$100,000

Pricing is difficult on the civilian issue arms. They tend to be in considerably better condition than the much more common military specimens. The factors of scarcity and condition will often bring higher prices from the advanced collector of means, especially in the finer grades of condition. On the other hand, the collector appreciating military usage will pay more for military marked examples. This publication tries to reflect the latest trends on purchase of civilian models.

100%	98%	95%	90%	80%	70%	60%	50%	40%	30%	20%	10%

Revolvers: Percussion, Dragoon Series

WHITNEYVILLE HARTFORD DRAGOON – .44 cal., 6 shot, 7 1/2 in. part octagon/part round barrel, some of the left-over Walker parts were used in Dragoons, blue metal with case hardened frame, lever, hammer, brass trigger guard, and steel cylinder bears Texas Ranger and Indian battle scene. Total production approx. 240. Serial range approx. 1,100 to 1,340 in sequence following civilian Walkers. Mfg. 1847.

* ***Whitneyville Hartford Dragoon w/Rear frame cut out for grips***

100%	98%	95%	90%	80%	70%	60%	50%	40%	30%	20%	10%
N/A	N/A	$350,000	$175,000	$150,000	$100,000	$85,000	$75,000	$65,000	$50,000	$45,000	$40,000

* ***Whitneyville Hartford Dragoon w/Straight rear frame***

100%	98%	95%	90%	80%	70%	60%	50%	40%	30%	20%	10%
N/A	N/A	$250,000	$150,000	$125,000	$90,000	$75,000	$65,000	$55,000	$40,000	$30,000	$25,000

FIRST MODEL DRAGOON – .44 cal., 6 shot, 7 1/2 in. round and octagon barrel, blue metal with case hardened frame, lever, hammer, brass grip straps, silvered straps for civilian market, serial range numbered after Hartford Dragoon, 1341 to around 8000. Oval cyl. slots, square back trigger guard, Texas Ranger and Indian fight scene on cylinder. Total production approx. 7,000. Mfg. 1848-1850.

* ***First Model Dragoon Military Model***

100%	98%	95%	90%	80%	70%	60%	50%	40%	30%	20%	10%
N/A	N/A	$125,000	$80,000	$60,000	$45,000	$27,500	$25,000	$20,000	$15,000	$12,500	$10,000

* ***First Model Dragoon Civilian Model***

100%	98%	95%	90%	80%	70%	60%	50%	40%	30%	20%	10%
N/A	N/A	$80,000	$60,000	$50,000	$25,000	$22,500	$20,000	$17,500	$15,000	$12,500	$10,000

FLUCK MODEL DRAGOON – basically a First Model Dragoon, with 7 1/2 in. altered Walker barrels and fully martially marked, should be extensively checked over, used to replace defective Walkers. Mfg. 1848. Total production 300. Serial range approx. 2,216 to 2,515.

100%	98%	95%	90%	80%	70%	60%	50%	40%	30%	20%	10%
N/A	N/A	$85,000	$75,000	$65,000	$30,000	$25,000	$20,000	$17,500	$15,000	$13,500	$12,000

SECOND MODEL DRAGOON – .44 cal., 6 shot, 7 1/2 in. round and octagon barrel, serial range following the First Model Dragoon 8,000-10,700. Texas Ranger and Indian fight scene on cylinder. Mfg. 1850-1851.

* ***Second Model Dragoon Military Model***

100%	98%	95%	90%	80%	70%	60%	50%	40%	30%	20%	10%
N/A	N/A	$85,000	$70,000	$50,000	$30,000	$25,000	$20,000	$16,000	$12,000	$10,000	$7,500

* ***Second Model Dragoon Civilian Model***

100%	98%	95%	90%	80%	70%	60%	50%	40%	30%	20%	10%
N/A	N/A	$75,000	$60,000	$40,000	$35,000	$22,500	$20,000	$17,500	$15,000	$11,000	$6,000

* ***Second Model Dragoon New Hampshire or Massachusetts*** – notice state markings on front portion of trigger guard.

100%	98%	95%	90%	80%	70%	60%	50%	40%	30%	20%	10%
N/A	N/A	$80,000	$65,000	$52,500	$40,000	$37,500	$25,000	$20,000	$15,000	$12,500	$10,000

THIRD MODEL DRAGOON – .44 cal., 6 shot, 7 1/2 in. round and octagon barrel, same basic features as earlier models, but with round trigger guard and rectangular cylinder slots, Texas Ranger and Indian fight scene on cylinder, serial range approx. 10,200-19,600, some overlapping of numbers, with approx. 10,500 mfg. from 1851-1861.

* ***Third Model Dragoon Civilian***

100%	98%	95%	90%	80%	70%	60%	50%	40%	30%	20%	10%
N/A	N/A	$60,000	$45,000	$35,000	$30,000	$25,000	$17,500	$15,000	$12,000	$10,000	$7,500

* ***Third Model Dragoon Martially Marked U.S.***

100%	98%	95%	90%	80%	70%	60%	50%	40%	30%	20%	10%
N/A	N/A	$55,000	$40,000	$35,000	$25,000	$22,500	$20,000	$17,500	$15,000	$12,000	$8,500

* ***Third Model Dragoon Third Model*** – 8 in. barrel.

100%	98%	95%	90%	80%	70%	60%	50%	40%	30%	20%	10%
N/A	N/A	$65,000	$55,000	$40,000	$30,000	$25,000	$22,000	$21,000	$19,500	$14,000	$9,500

* ***Third Model Dragoon First and Second Variation*** – shoulder stock model.

100%	98%	95%	90%	80%	70%	60%	50%	40%	30%	20%	10%
N/A	N/A	$60,000	$45,000	$35,000	$25,000	$22,500	$20,000	$17,500	$15,000	$12,500	$9,500

* ***Third Model Dragoon Third Variation***

100%	98%	95%	90%	80%	70%	60%	50%	40%	30%	20%	10%
N/A	N/A	$60,000	$45,000	$35,000	$25,000	$20,000	$17,500	$15,000	$12,000	$10,000	$7,500

* ***Third Model Dragoon C.L. Dragoon***

100%	98%	95%	90%	80%	70%	60%	50%	40%	30%	20%	10%
N/A	N/A	$75,000	$65,000	$50,000	$35,000	$26,000	$22,500	$19,000	$15,000	$12,500	$10,000

ENGLISH HARTFORD DRAGOON – basically a Third Model Dragoon, assembled at Colt's London factory, with unique serial range 1-700, some were assembled from earlier parts inventories, easy to spot with British proofs of crown over V and crown over GP, the blue was of the English type, many were engraved.

100%	98%	95%	90%	80%	70%	60%	50%	40%	30%	20%	10%
N/A	N/A	$55,000	$40,000	$32,000	$22,500	$19,000	$15,000	$12,500	$10,000	$8,750	$7,500

100%	98%	95%	90%	80%	70%	60%	50%	40%	30%	20%	10%

1848 BABY DRAGOONS – .31 cal., 5 shot, 3, 4, 5, or 6 in. octagon barrels, most without loading lever, serial range 1-15,500, a scaled down version of the .44 caliber Dragoons, early ones with Texas Ranger scene and later ones with the holdup scene.

* ***1848 Baby Dragoon Type I*** – left-hand barrel stamping, Texas Ranger and Indian scene, approx. serial range 1-150.

100%	98%	95%	90%	80%	70%	60%	50%	40%	30%	20%	10%
N/A	N/A	$25,000	$15,000	$11,000	$7,500	$7,000	$6,5000	$6,000	$5,500	$5,000	$4,500

* ***1848 Baby Dragoon Type II*** – with Texas Ranger and Indian scene, 11,600 serial range, without loading lever.

100%	98%	95%	90%	80%	70%	60%	50%	40%	30%	20%	10%
N/A	N/A	$17,500	$12,000	$9,500	$6,500	$6,250	$6,000	$5,200	$4,500	$4,000	$3,500

* ***1848 Baby Dragoon Type III*** – with Stagecoach scene and oval cylinder slots, serial range 10,400-12,000.

100%	98%	95%	90%	80%	70%	60%	50%	40%	30%	20%	10%
N/A	N/A	$17,500	$12,000	$9,500	$6,500	$6,250	$6,000	$5,200	$4,500	$4,000	$3,500

* ***1848 Baby Dragoon Type IV*** – with Stagecoach holdup scene, rectangle cylinder slots, serial range 11,000-12,500.

100%	98%	95%	90%	80%	70%	60%	50%	40%	30%	20%	10%
N/A	N/A	$17,500	$12,000	$9,500	$6,500	$6,250	$6,000	$5,200	$4,500	$4,000	$3,500

* ***1848 Baby Dragoon Type V*** – with Stagecoach holdup scene, rectangle cylinder slots and loading lever, serial range 11,600-15,500.

100%	98%	95%	90%	80%	70%	60%	50%	40%	30%	20%	10%
N/A	N/A	$17,500	$12,000	$9,500	$6,500	$6,250	$6,000	$5,200	$4,500	$4,000	$3,500

Revolvers: Percussion, Models 1849, 1851, 1855, 1860, 1861, 1862, & 1865

1849 POCKET MODEL – .31 cal., 5 or 6 shot, 3, 4, 5, and 6 in. octagon barrels, most with loading levers, blue metal with case hardened frame, lever and hammer, grip straps of brass (silver plated), or steel (silver plated or blue), stagecoach hold-up scene on cylinder, serial range 12,000 to 340,000. Mfg. 1850-73.

* ***1849 Pocket Model First Type*** – 4, 5, or 6 in. barrel, loading lever and small or large brass trigger guard.

100%	98%	95%	90%	80%	70%	60%	50%	40%	30%	20%	10%
N/A	N/A	$5,000	$4,000	$3,000	$2,250	$1,750	$1,500	$1,200	$800	$625	$500

* ***1849 Pocket Model Second Type*** – 4, 5, or 6 in. barrel, loading lever and steel grip straps.

100%	98%	95%	90%	80%	70%	60%	50%	40%	30%	20%	10%
N/A	N/A	$4,500	$3,000	$2,500	$1,500	$1,200	$950	$850	$750	$625	$500

* ***1849 Pocket Model Wells Fargo Model*** – 3 in. barrel, without loading lever and with small round trigger guard.

100%	98%	95%	90%	80%	70%	60%	50%	40%	30%	20%	10%
N/A	N/A	$18,500	$15,000	$10,000	$8,500	$5,000	$4,000	$3,000	$2,500	$2,250	$2,000

1849 LONDON POCKET MODEL – London pistols were of the same general configuration, but of better finish, serial range 1-11,000. Mfg. 1853-57.

* ***1849 London Pocket Model Early Type*** – serial numbered under 1500, with small trigger guard and brass grip straps.

100%	98%	95%	90%	80%	70%	60%	50%	40%	30%	20%	10%
N/A	N/A	$7,500	$4,500	$4,000	$3,500	$2,900	$2,250	$1,750	$1,200	$1,075	$950

* ***1849 London Pocket Model Late Type*** – oval trigger guard and steel grip straps.

100%	98%	95%	90%	80%	70%	60%	50%	40%	30%	20%	10%
N/A	N/A	$4,750	$3,750	$3,000	$2,250	$1,500	$1,200	$1,075	$950	$850	$750

1851 NAVY – .36 cal., 6 shot, 7 1/2 in. octagon barrel and loading lever, blue metal with case hardened frame, lever, and hammer, one-piece walnut finished grips, cylinder scene of Texas Navy battle with Mexico, serial range 1-highest recorded number was 215,348, three barrel addresses 1-74,000 (ADDRESS SAML COLT, NEW YORK CITY), 74,000-101,000 (ADDRESS SAML COLT, HARTFORD, CT.) 101,000-215,348 (ADDRESS COL. SAML COLT, NEW YORK, U.S. AMERICA). Mfg. 1850-1873.

* ***1851 Navy First Model*** – square back trigger guard, bottom wedge screw, serial range 1-1,250.

100%	98%	95%	90%	80%	70%	60%	50%	40%	30%	20%	10%
N/A	N/A	$28,000	$24,000	$20,000	$17,500	$12,500	$10,000	$8,250	$6,500	$5,500	$4,500

* ***1851 Navy Second Model*** – square back trigger guard, top wedge screw, serial range 1,250-4,000.

100%	98%	95%	90%	80%	70%	60%	50%	40%	30%	20%	10%
N/A	N/A	$25,000	$20,000	$17,500	$12,000	$10,000	$7,500	$6,250	$5,000	$4,250	$3,500

* ***1851 Navy Third Model*** – small round brass trigger guard, serial range 4,200-85,000.

100%	98%	95%	90%	80%	70%	60%	50%	40%	30%	20%	10%
N/A	N/A	$7,500	$6,500	$5,000	$4,000	$3,000	$2,000	$1,600	$1,200	$1,100	$1,000

* ***1851 Navy Fourth Model*** – large round brass trigger guard, serial range 85,000-215,348.

100%	98%	95%	90%	80%	70%	60%	50%	40%	30%	20%	10%
N/A	N/A	$7,500	$6,500	$5,000	$4,000	$3,000	$2,000	$1,600	$1,200	$1,100	$1,000

* ***1851 Navy Iron Gripstrap Model*** – most often seen in fourth model.

100%	98%	95%	90%	80%	70%	60%	50%	40%	30%	20%	10%
N/A	N/A	$7,500	$6,500	$5,000	$4,000	$3,000	$2,200	$1,850	$1,500	$1,350	$1,200

100%	98%	95%	90%	80%	70%	60%	50%	40%	30%	20%	10%

* ***1851 Navy Martially Marked U.S. Navys*** – brass or iron gripstrap.

N/A N/A $22,500 $18,500 $15,000 $11,000 $8,500 $6,000 $4,750 $3,500 $3,000 $2,500

* ***1851 Navy Cut for shoulder stock*** – first and second type (like third model Dragoon).

N/A N/A $15,000 $10,000 $9,250 $8,500 $6,750 $5,000 $3,500 $2,000 $1,750 $1,500

* ***1851 Navy Third Type*** – four screw frame.

N/A N/A $7,500 $6,500 $5,000 $4,000 $3,000 $2,500 $2,250 $2,000 $1,750 $1,500

51 NAVY LONDON MODEL – basically the same gun as the Hartford piece with London barrel address, with British proof marks in serial range 1-42,000. Mfg. 1853-1857.

* ***51 Navy London Early First Model*** – serial range below 2000, brass grip straps and small trigger guard.

N/A N/A $7,500 $6,500 $5,000 $4,000 $3,000 $2,500 $2,250 $2,000 $1,750 $1,500

* ***51 Navy London Late Second Model*** – balance of production, large round trigger guard, steel grip straps, all London parts.

N/A N/A $8,000 $4,500 $4,000 $3,500 $3,000 $2,500 $2,000 $1,500 $1,350 $1,200

1855 SIDEHAMMER POCKET MODEL (ROOT MODEL) – .28 cal., had 3 1/2 in. octagon barrel, .31 cal. usually had 3 1/2 in. or 4 1/2 in. round barrel. Blue with case hardened lever and hammer, one-piece wraparound style walnut grips.

Commonly called the "Root" Model by collectors, manufactured 1855 through 1870. The .28 cal. model serial numbered 1 through approx. 30,000. The .31 cal. round barrel model serial numbered 1 through approx. 14,000. Total production approx. 44,000.

Easily recognizable by its side mounted hammer and cylinder rotation ratchet at rear of frame.

* ***1855 Sidehammer Pocket Model 1 and 1A*** – .28 cal., 3 7/16 in. octagonal bbl., oct. load lever, Indian/cabin cyl. scene, Hartford barrel address. Serial range 1 to 384.

N/A N/A $12,500 $8,000 $6,500 $5,000 $4,250 $3,500 $3,000 $2,500 $2,250 $2,000

* ***1855 Sidehammer Pocket Model 2*** – .28 cal., 3 1/2 in. oct. bbl., Indian/cabin cyl. scene, Hartford barrel address with pointed hand. Serial range 476 to 25,000.

N/A N/A $3,500 $2,000 $1,600 $1,200 $1,000 $950 $850 $750 $625 $500

* ***1855 Sidehammer Pocket Model 3*** – .28 cal., 3 1/2 in. oct. bbl., full fluted cylinder, Hartford barrel address with pointed hand. Serial range 25,001 to 30,000.

N/A N/A $4,250 $2,500 $2,000 $1,200 $1,075 $950 $850 $750 $625 $500

* ***1855 Sidehammer Pocket Model 3A*** – .31 cal., 3 1/2 in. oct. bbl., full fluted cylinder, Hartford barrel address. Serial range 1 to 1,350.

N/A N/A $3,500 $2,000 $1,600 $1,200 $1,000 $950 $850 $750 $625 $500

* ***1855 Sidehammer Pocket Model 4*** – .31 cal., 3 1/2 in. oct. bbl., full fluted cylinder, Hartford barrel address. Serial range 1,351 to 2,400.

N/A N/A $4,500 $3,500 $3,000 $2,250 $1,500 $1,200 $1,075 $950 $850 $750

* ***1855 Sidehammer Pocket Model 5*** – .31 cal., 3 1/2 in. round bbl., full fluted cylinder, "COL. COLT NEW-YORK" barrel address. Serial range 2,401 to 8,000.

N/A N/A $4,500 $3,500 $3,000 $2,250 $1,500 $1,200 $1,075 $950 $850 $750

* ***1855 Sidehammer Pocket Model 5A*** – .31 cal., 4 1/2 in. round bbl., included in same serial range as Model 5.

N/A N/A $4,500 $3,500 $3,000 $2,250 $1,875 $1,500 $1,350 $1,200 $1,075 $950

* ***1855 Sidehammer Pocket Model 6*** – .31 cal., 3 1/2 in. round bbl., stage coach hold-up cylinder scene, "COL. COLT NEW-YORK" barrel address. Serial range 8,001 through 11,074.

N/A N/A $4,500 $3,500 $3,000 $2,250 $1,800 $1,500 $1,350 $1,200 $1,075 $950

* ***1855 Sidehammer Pocket Model 6A*** – .31 cal., 4 1/2 in. round bbl., included in same serial range as Model 6.

N/A N/A $4,500 $3,500 $3,000 $2,250 $1,800 $1,500 $1,350 $1,200 $1,075 $950

* ***1855 Sidehammer Pocket Model 7*** – .31 cal., 3 1/2 in. round bbl., stage coach hold-up cylinder scene, "COL. COLT NEW-YORK" barrel address. Cylinder pin retained by screw-in cylinder. Serial range 11,075 through 14,000.

N/A N/A $5,500 $4,000 $3,500 $3,000 $2,750 $2,500 $2,000 $1,500 $1,350 $1,200

100%	98%	95%	90%	80%	70%	60%	50%	40%	30%	20%	10%

* ***1855 Sidehammer Pocket Model 7A*** – .31 cal., 4 1/2 in. round bbl., including same cylinder scene, barrel address and serial range as Model 7.

N/A N/A $5,000 $4,000 $3,500 $3,000 $2,750 $2,250 $1,750 $1,200 $1,100 $1,000

1860 MODEL ARMY – .44 cal., 6 shot, 7 1/2 and 8 in. round barrels with loading lever, blue metal with case hardened frame, lever and hammer, one-piece walnut grips, normally blue steel back strap and brass trigger guard, barrel markings were "ADDRESS SAM COLT, HARTFORD, CT." on early productions and "ADDRESS COL. SAM COLT, NEW YORK, U.S. AMERICA" on balance, serial range 1-about 200,500, Texas Navy scene on round cylinder model. Mfg. 1860-73.

* ***1860 Model Army Fluted Cylinder*** – full length cylinder flutes and no cylinder scene, 7 1/2 or 8 in. barrel, grips of Navy (very rare) or Army size, usually 4 screw frames.

N/A N/A $22,500 $15,000 $12,000 $7,500 $6,000 $5,000 $4,250 $3,500 $3,000 $2,500

* ***1860 Model Army Round Cylinder*** – roll engraved Texas Navy scene, some with early Hartford address, Army grips, four screw frame to about 50,000 range, most were sold to the U.S. Government and will be martially marked.

N/A N/A $13,500 $9,250 $8,000 $5,000 $4,250 $3,500 $3,000 $2,500 $2,000 $1,500

* ***1860 Model Army Civilian*** – same general configurations as Round Cylinder Model, but with 3 screw frame, no shoulder stock cuts and better blue finish than military pieces, late New York barrel address.

N/A N/A $7,500 $6,500 $5,000 $4,000 $3,000 $2,500 $2,000 $1,500 $1,350 $1,200

1861 MODEL NAVY – .36 cal., 6 shot, 7 1/2 in. round barrel with loading lever, blue metal with case hardened frame, lever and hammer, silver plated brass grip straps, the barrel address was "ADDRESS COL. SAM COLT, NEW YORK, U.S. AMERICA", serial range 1-38,843, cylinder scene of Texas Navy and Mexico Battle. Mfg. 1861-1873.

* ***1861 Model Fluted Cylinder Navy*** – in serial range 1-100, with fluted cylinder and without rolled cylinder scene.

N/A N/A $40,000 $35,000 $30,000 $25,000 $21,500 $17,500 $15,000 $12,000 $10,000 $7,500

* ***1861 Model Navy Regular Production model***

N/A N/A $20,000 $12,000 $10,000 $7,500 $6,000 $5,000 $4,250 $3,500 $2,750 $2,000

* ***1861 Model Martially Marked Navys*** – will bear the U.S. stamp and inspector's marks, those marked U.S.N. on butt were of a 650 piece order for the Navy.

N/A N/A $35,000 $22,500 $15,000 $8,500 $7,500 $6,000 $5,000 $4,000 $3,250 $2,500

* ***1861 Model London Marked Navy*** – with "ADDRESS COL. COLT, LONDON", for barrel address.

N/A N/A $22,500 $12,000 $10,000 $7,500 $6,000 $5,000 $4,750 $4,500 $3,250 $2,000

* ***1861 Model Shoulder Stock Cut Navy*** – 4 screw frames in serial range 11,000-14,000, made for third style stock (see Dragoon stocks).

N/A N/A $25,000 $15,000 $12,000 $9,000 $7,500 $6,500 $5,500 $4,500 $4,000 $3,500

1862 POLICE MODEL – .36 cal., 5 shot half fluted and rebated cylinder, 4 1/2, 5 1/2, and 6 1/2 in. round barrels (also 3 1/2 in. barrel but quite rare) and loading lever. Mfg. 1861-1873. Serial numbered with Model 1862 Pocket Navy, approx. 28,000 1862 Police Models were produced. Blue with case hardened frame, lever, and hammer, grip straps silver plated, one-piece walnut grips. Serial range 1 through approx. 47,000. Standard barrel marking "ADDRESS COL. SAML COLT NEW-YORK U.S. AMERICA" "COLTS/PATENT" on left side of frame, "PAT SEPT. 10TH 1850" stamped in cyl. flute.

Many Model 1862 Police and 1862 Pocket Navy revolvers were converted to cartridge with the advent of the metallic cartridge. Consequently these models in their original cap and ball chambering are quite desirable to collectors.

* ***1862 Police Early Model*** – "ADDRESS SAM COLT/HARTFORD CT" barrel address, silvered iron or brass grip straps.

N/A N/A $6,000 $5,000 $4,000 $3,000 $2,500 $2,250 $2,000 $1,750 $1,500 $1,200

* ***1862 Police Standard Production Model*** – with New York barrel address.

N/A N/A $4,750 $3,500 $3,000 $2,500 $2,000 $1,750 $1,500 $1,250 $1,100 $950

* ***1862 Police Export Production Model*** – with "L" below serial numbers (for export to England), steel grip straps. Most often but not always bearing British proofs.

N/A N/A $4,000 $3,000 $2,500 $2,250 $2,000 $1,750 $1,500 $1,250 $1,100 $950

100%	98%	95%	90%	80%	70%	60%	50%	40%	30%	20%	10%

* ***1862 Police London Marked Model*** – similar to above, except with "ADDRESS, COL. COLT/LONDON" address on barrel.

N/A	N/A	$17,500	$12,000	$9,000	$6,000	$5,000	$5,000	$4,000	$3,000	$2,500	$2,000

POCKET MODEL OF NAVY CALIBER (MODEL 1865) – .36 or .38 cal., 5 shot rebated cylinder, 4 1/2, 5 1/2, and 6 1/2 in. octagonal barrels with loading lever. Mfg. 1865-1882. Blue with case hardened frame, lever and hammer, grip straps silver plated brass, one-piece walnut grips. Standard barrel markings "ADDRESS COL. SAML COLT NEW-YORK U.S. AMERICA" "COLTS/PATENT" on left side of frame, stage coach hold-up scene on cylinder. Serial numbered with Model 1862 Police Model, approx. 19,000 produced. Serial range 1 through approx. 47,000. Mfg. began 1865.

This model has been identified for decades to collectors as the Model 1853 or the Model 1862 Pocket Model Navy. Recent research indicates that a more correct model name for this revolver is the Pocket Model of Navy Caliber.

Because of being produced during the advent of the metallic cartridge, the number remaining in the original cap and ball configuration is rather few; scarce with any serial number, but particularly so in numbers over approx. 19,800.

* ***Pocket Model of Navy Caliber Standard Model*** – 4 1/2, 5 1/2 or 6 1/2 in. barrel lengths.

N/A	N/A	$12,000	$9,000	$7,500	$5,000	$3,500	$3,000	$2,750	$2,500	$2,000	$1,500

* ***Pocket Model of Navy Caliber Export Production Model*** – with "L" below serial numbers (for export to England), steel grip straps. Often found with British proofs.

N/A	N/A	$10,000	$7,500	$6,000	$4,500	$3,500	$3,000	$2,750	$2,500	$2,000	$1,500

* ***Pocket Model of Navy Caliber London Marked Model*** – similar to above but "ADDRESS COL. COLT/ LONDON" address on barrel.

N/A	N/A	$17,500	$12,500	$10,000	$7,500	$6,000	$5,000	$4,250	$3,500	$3,250	$3,000

REVOLVERS: PERCUSSION CONVERSIONS

Colt Thuer Conversions

Subtract approx. 50% for factory nickel plating on models listed below.

COLT THUER CONVERSIONS (c. 1868-1872) – .31, .36, or .44 centerfire cal., less than 5,000 produced in all models. This was Colt's first commercial attempt at converting percussion revolvers to fire fixed ammo. Standard features: usually threaded inside rammer for a Thuer loading tool, a hardened flat face on hammer, deepened loading cutout on right side of lug, Thuer ring and back of cylinder have matching assembly numbers. Beware of fakes! Only non-experimental Colt models are listed. Rarity by barrel length will not be considered here. Serial numbers are often missing on cylinder.

Prices for Colt Conversions reflect values for blue and case hardened examples. Nickel plated specimens are rarely seen, but typically sell for 20%-40% less than blue finish.

Any defects, excessive wear, or dulled blue will affect value. Nickeled conversions that have lost their translucence (become cloudy) should be discounted more than usual 20%-40% from blue and case hardened examples, especially on near-mint to mint specimens.

* ***Colt Thuer Conversion 1849 Pocket***

N/A	N/A	$70,000	$40,000	$32,500	$25,000	$21,500	$18,000	$15,000	$12,000	$10,000	$7,500

* ***Colt Thuer Conversion 1851 Navy***

N/A	N/A	$30,000	$27,500	$25,000	$22,000	$18,500	$15,000	$11,500	$8,500	$7,250	$6,000

* ***Colt Thuer Conversion 1860 Army*** – the most common Thuer, but popular because it's a large frame model.

N/A	N/A	$35,000	$27,500	$23,750	$20,000	$18,750	$17,500	$15,500	$12,500	$10,750	$9,000

* ***Colt Thuer Conversion 1861 Navy***

N/A	N/A	$35,000	$25,000	$21,000	$17,500	$16,250	$15,000	$12,500	$10,000	$8,750	$7,500

* ***Colt Thuer Conversion 1862 Police***

N/A	N/A	$22,500	$18,500	$16,750	$15,000	$13,500	$12,000	$10,250	$8,500	$7,500	$6,500

* ***Colt Thuer Conversion 1862 Pocket Navy***

N/A	N/A	$30,000	$27,000	$22,500	$17,500	$16,250	$15,000	$12,500	$10,000	$8,750	$7,500

Richards Conversions: All Variations

Subtract approx. 50% for factory nickel plating on models listed below.

100%	98%	95%	90%	80%	70%	60%	50%	40%	30%	20%	10%

RICHARDS CONVERSION, COLT 1860 ARMY REVOLVER – .44 CF cal., produced circa 1870s, special machining to barrel and breech of cylinder for conversion to a cartridge weapon. Produced in three serial ranges: one numbered under 10,000, a separate group generally in the 190,000 to 200,000 range, and approx. 9,000 produced 1873-1878 in the 24,000-144,000 serial range.

* ***1860 Army First Model Richards*** – integral rear sight and floating firing pin on breech plate, front edge of barrel lug is same as 1860 Percussion Army. Breech plate extends over rear edge of cylinder.

N/A	N/A	$25,000	$15,000	$11,750	$8,500	$7,000	$5,500	$5,000	$4,500	$4,000	$3,500

* ***1860 Army Second Model Richards*** – standard Richards type barrel. A space between face of conversion ring and rear of cylinder when viewed from the side. No integral sight on breechplate, cut away at top allowing hammer to directly strike the cartridge.

N/A	N/A	$25,000	$20,000	$14,500	$8,500	$7,750	$7,000	$5,750	$4,500	$4,250	$4,000

* ***1860 Army Twelve Stop Cylinder Variation Richards*** – generally the same as the Second Model Richards except cylinder has extra "safety" notches between the locking notches. This variation was usually produced in the 100-300, 1,000-1,700 and 200,000 serial ranges. Cylinder locking notches over chambers often broken through. Watch for alterations.

N/A	N/A	$35,000	$25,000	$18,500	$12,000	$10,500	$9,000	$8,250	$7,500	$7,000	$6,500

* ***1860 Army U.S. Marked Richards*** – generally the same as 1st Model Richards (many minor differences). Has "U.S." stamped on left barrel lug and "A" (Ainsworth) inspector marks in several places. They are converted 1860 percussion Armys, so original numbers are typically in 23,000-144,000 range plus a second set of assembly numbers. Oiled grips, military soft blue finish.

N/A	N/A	$35,000	$25,000	$18,500	$12,000	$10,500	$9,000	$8,250	$7,500	$7,000	$6,500

Richards-Mason Conversions: All Variations

Subtract approx. 50% for factory nickel plating on models listed below.

1860 ARMY RICHARDS-MASON – .44 CF cal., overall, much rarer than Richards Army Conversions, circa 1870s, approximately 2100 produced. A rare variation has an 1860 Army rebated cylinder and a barrel with a lug shaped similar to 1861 Navy Conversion. breechplate without integral rear sight, cutout at top so hammer can strike primer directly. A space can be seen between breechplate and rear of cylinder. Rear of lug is a vertical line instead of the bullet shape cutout seen on Richards models.

N/A	N/A	$30,000	$20,000	$17,500	$15,500	$12,500	$9,500	$8,000	$6,500	$5,750	$5,000

1851 NAVY RICHARDS-MASON – .38 CF and RF cal., circa 1870s. Produced in two different serial ranges. Has improved Richards-Mason breechplate that is flush with diameter of recoil shield. Difficult to locate in prime condition.

* ***1851 Navy Civilian Model Richards-Mason*** – Richards-Mason breechplate which is same diameter as recoil shield, octagon barrel, mirrored civilian blue. Nickel finish commonly seen.

N/A	N/A	$17,500	$12,000	$9,500	$6,500	$5,500	$4,500	$4,000	$3,500	$2,500	$2,000

* ***1851 U.S. Navy Richards-Mason*** – Richards-Mason breechplate, oiled grips, soft blue military finish, produced in US. percussion range of 40,000-90,000. Inconsistent "U.S.N." and other inspector markings. Iron straps, "U.S." on frame.

N/A	N/A	$20,000	$15,000	$12,000	$8,500	$7,500	$6,500	$5,500	$4,500	$4,000	$3,500

1861 NAVY RICHARDS-MASON – produced in civilian and military versions, circa 1870s, made in RF and CF cal. in two serial ranges. Round 7 1/2 in. barrel.

* ***1861 Navy Civilian Model Richards-Mason*** – Richards-Mason breechplate, round 7 1/2 in. barrel with attached ejector housing, unrebated cylinder. When blue, has a commercial high gloss finish.

N/A	N/A	$25,000	$17,000	$13,750	$10,000	$8,750	$7,000	$6,250	$5,000	$4,000	$3,000

* ***1861 Navy U.S. Navy Richards-Mason*** – soft military blue finish, oiled grips, converted from percussion U.S. Navy revolvers, inconsistent military markings, centerfire, set of extra serial numbers often seen on cylinder.

N/A	N/A	$25,000	$20,000	$16,000	$12,000	$10,500	$8,000	$7,250	$6,000	$4,750	$3,500

COLT 1862 POLICE & POCKET NAVY RICHARDS-MASON CONVERSIONS (circa 1870s) – .38 RF and CF cal., parts for 1862 Police, Pocket Navy, as well as 1849 Pockets are often intermixed. As parts bins were depleted, Colt used whatever components that would fit, resulting in a tremendous amount of minor variations. Some barrels were converted from percussion models while others were newly made as cartridge barrels without rammer plugs and loading slots in the lug. There are five different serial ranges (1849, 1862 Police, Pocket Navy, Conversion). 3 1/2 to 6 1/2 in. barrels, again not all features available on all models.

Nickel plated conversions will bring 20%-40% less than blue and case hardened specimens.

100%	98%	95%	90%	80%	70%	60%	50%	40%	30%	20%	10%

* ***1862 Police & Pocket Navy Richards-Mason Conversion 4 1/2 in. Octagon Barrel Model*** – 4 1/2 in. octagon barrel without ejector. Rebated Pocket Navy Cylinder.

N/A	N/A	$9,500	$6,500	$5,000	$3,500	$2,600	$1,750	$1,350	$950	$850	$750

* ***1862 Richards-Mason Conversion Round (Percussion) Barrel Pocket Navy with Ejector*** – plug in rammer slot; ejector housing, loading cutout in right side of lug, barrel remachined from Pocket Navy percussion barrel, Pocket Navy rebated cylinder. Similar appearance to cartridge barrel variation.

N/A	N/A	$10,000	$8,000	$6,750	$5,000	$4,000	$3,000	$2,250	$1,500	$1,200	$850

1862 POLICE AND POCKET (1865 POCKET MODEL) NAVY CONVERSION – 4 1/2, 5 1/2, or 6 1/2 in. barrels with 1862 Police percussion profile and added ejector housing. Has rebated Pocket Navy cylinder or rarer half fluted 1862 Police cylinder. 6 1/2 in. barrel will bring a premium.

* ***1862 Police/Pocket Navy with Rebated Pocket Navy Cylinder*** – 1862 Police profile barrel with ejector housing and rebated 1862 Pocket Navy cylinder.

N/A	N/A	$9,500	$6,000	$5,250	$4,000	$3,100	$2,250	$1,550	$850	$750	$650

* ***1862 Police/Pocket Navy with Half Fluted Cylinder*** – 1862 Police profile barrel with ejector housing and 1/2 fluted Police cylinder.

N/A	N/A	$12,000	$8,500	$6,750	$5,000	$4,000	$3,000	$2,250	$1,500	$1,175	$850

Conversions with Round Cartridge Barrel

Subtract approx. 50% for factory nickel plating on models listed below.

ROUND CARTRIDGE BARREL WITH EJECTOR

See Baby Open Top listing under Revolvers:"Open Top" models.

3 1/2 IN. ROUND CARTRIDGE BARREL CONVERSION – .38 RF or CF cal., sometimes seen with serial numbers that are from 1849 Pocket Model (300,000 range). Barrel newly made for cartridges, not converted from a percussion barrel, only type conversion with 3 1/2 in. barrel. No ejector, no loading lever slot or loading cutout in lug area. Pocket Navy rebated cylinder.

N/A	N/A	$6,000	$4,000	$3,250	$2,500	$2,000	$1,500	$1,250	$1,000	$875	$750

REVOLVERS: "OPEN TOP" MODELS

If possible, it is advisable to procure a factory letter before buying/selling this Open Top Revolver. These watermarked letters are available by writing Colt Archive Properties LLC in Bloomfield, CT, with a charge of $200 or more per serial number (if they can research it). Send your name and address, Colt model name, serial number, and check or credit card information to: COLT ARCHIVE PROPERTIES LLC, 1295 Blue Hills Avenue, Bloomfield, CT 06002. Please allow 90-120 days for a response.

1871-72 OPEN TOP MODEL RIMFIRE – .44 RF cal., 6 shot, 7 1/2 in. barrel, without frame top strap, blue metal with case hardened hammer, serial range 1-approx. 7,000, barrel address "ADDRESS COL. SAM COLT, NEW YORK, U.S. AMERICA", forerunner of the single action Army, quite desirable. Mfg. 1871-72.

Add 20% for blue finish on models listed below.

* ***Baby Open Top Prototype*** – .38 RF and CF cal., 4 1/2, 5 1/2, or 6 1/2 in. barrels produced as a cartridge component without rammer slots and lug cutouts inherent to a percussion barrel, much shorter lug area than similar model converted from percussion barrel, no slots or loading cutouts on barrel, with ejector housing and Pocket Navy rebated cylinder, only unnumbered and single digit serial numbers have been observed, very scarce.

N/A	N/A	$10,000	$6,000	$4,750	$3,500	$3,000	$2,500	$2,000	$1,500	$1,350	$1,200

* ***1871-72 Open Top Model Rimfire Regular Production Model*** – 7 1/2 in. barrel, New York address, Navy grips.

N/A	N/A	$45,000	$27,000	$24,000	$20,000	$16,500	$12,000	$10,000	$7,500	$6,250	$5,000

* ***1871-72 Open Top Model Rimfire Regular Production*** – with Army grips.

N/A	N/A	$45,000	$27,000	$24,000	$20,000	$16,500	$12,000	$10,000	$7,500	$6,250	$5,000

* ***1871-72 Open Top Model Rimfire Late Production*** – with address "COLT PT. F. A. MANUFACTURING CO., HARTFORD, CT., U.S.A."

N/A	N/A	$45,000	$25,000	$21,500	$17,500	$13,750	$10,000	$8,250	$6,500	$5,500	$4,000

Add 40% for models with 8 in. barrel or COLTS/PATENT frame markings.

100%	98%	95%	90%	80%	70%	60%	50%	40%	30%	20%	10%

REVOLVERS: PERCUSSION, 2ND & 3RD GENERATION BLACK POWDER SERIES

To learn more about the 2nd & 3rd Generation Percussion Black Powder Series, it is recommended to purchase the *Blue Book of Modern Black Powder Arms*. The latest edition contains more information on the Colt 2nd Generation Black Powder Series than anything else previously published. These definitive books are available from Blue Book Publications, Inc. To order visit BlueBookOfGunValues.com.

DERRINGERS

FIRST MODEL DERRINGER - .41 RF cal., single shot, 2 1/2 in. barrel, all steel construction, scroll engraving standard, blue, nickel, or silver plated barrel, downward pivoting barrel, no grips, serial numbered 1-6,500. Mfg. approx. 1870-1890.

100%	98%	95%	90%	80%	70%	60%	50%	40%	30%	20%	10%
$3,750	$2,850	$2,450	$2,200	$2,000	$1,600	$1,200	$1,075	$875	$750	$675	$650

SECOND MODEL DERRINGER - .41 RF or CF cal., single shot, 2 1/2 in. barrel, scroll engraving standard, blue, nickel, or silver plated barrel, downward pivoting barrel, checkered and varnished walnut grips, "No 2" marked on top of barrel, serial numbered 1-9,000. Mfg. approx. 1870-1890.

100%	98%	95%	90%	80%	70%	60%	50%	40%	30%	20%	10%
$1,775	$1,475	$1,275	$1,100	$950	$850	$750	$650	$585	$550	$500	$475

* ***Second Model Derringer .41 Centerfire cal.***

100%	98%	95%	90%	80%	70%	60%	50%	40%	30%	20%	10%
$3,850	$2,950	$2,550	$2,200	$2,000	$1,750	$1,500	$1,300	$1,175	$1,000	$975	$950

THIRD MODEL DERRINGER (THUER MODEL) - .41 RF or CF (rare) cal., single shot, side pivoting 2 1/2 in. barrel, varnished walnut grips, blue barrels, bronze frames, engraving optional, Colt barrel address, spur trigger, serial numbered approx. 1-45,000. Mfg. approx. 1875-1912.

100%	98%	95%	90%	80%	70%	60%	50%	40%	30%	20%	10%
$1,750	$1,500	$1,250	$1,100	$1,000	$800	$650	$575	$500	$450	$400	$350

Add 30%-50% for .41 centerfire cal. Early models are worth considerably more.

GRADING - PPGS™	100%	98%	95%	90%	80%	70%	60%	LAST MSR

FOURTH MODEL DERRINGER (FIRING) - .22 Short cal., single shot similar in appearance to the 3rd Model, 2 1/2 in. barrel, approx. 112,000 mfg. 1959-1963 with either D or N suffix. A few were put in books (sometimes as pairs), picture frames, penholders, bookends, etc. (these will command premiums).

	100%	98%	95%	90%	80%	70%	60%
Gun only	$100	$90	$75	$70	$55	$45	$35
Gun w/accessories	$375	$330	$280	$255	$205	$170	$130

* ***Fourth Model Derringer (non-firing)*** - this variation was normally used for decoration and is normally encountered in books, picture frames, penholders, bookends, etc. Values below assume all factory materials intact - if not, prices are reduced to $50-$75 for gun only.

100%	98%	95%	90%	80%	70%	60%
$375	$330	$280	$255	$205	$170	$130

Non-firing guns usually do not have the barrel notch, thus preventing the hammer from striking the cartridge.

LORD DERRINGER - .22 Short cal. only, side pivoting Thuer action, gold plated with black chrome barrel and walnut grips. Mfg. 1970-76 by Colt, cased.

100%	98%	95%	90%	80%	70%	60%
$175	$155	$130	$120	$95	$80	$60

LADY DERRINGER - .22 Short cal. only, side pivoting Thuer action, full gold plated finish with pearlite grips. Mfg. 1970-76 by Colt, cased.

100%	98%	95%	90%	80%	70%	60%
$175	$155	$130	$120	$95	$80	$60

LORD & LADY CASED SET - one each of the Lord & Lady Derringers or combinations, consecutive serial numbers, numbered 1,001-up, with DER suffix.

100%	98%	95%	90%	80%	70%	60%
$495	$435	$370	$335	$270	$225	$175

LADY CASED SET - cased pair of Lady Derringers. Approx. 12,000 pairs shipped first year.

100%	98%	95%	90%	80%	70%	60%
$495	$435	$370	$335	$270	$225	$175

LORD CASED SET - cased pair of Lord Derringers. Approx. 3,000 pairs shipped first year.

100%	98%	95%	90%	80%	70%	60%
$495	$435	$370	$335	$270	$225	$175

BOOKCASE DERRINGER PAIR - .22 Short cal., consecutively numbered Derringers with synthetic ivory grips and nickel finish, cased inside unique hardcover "Colt Derringers" labeled book with red velvet lining, limited mfg. in early 1960s.

100%	98%	95%	90%	80%	70%	60%
$350	$300	$265	$240	$195	$160	$125

100%	98%	95%	90%	80%	70%	60%	50%	40%	30%	20%	10%

REVOLVERS: POCKET MODELS

If possible, it is advisable to procure a factory letter before buying/selling this variation (open top only). These watermarked letters are available by writing Colt Archive Properties LLC in Bloomfield, CT, with a charge of $200 or more per serial number (if they can research it). Send your name and address, Colt model name, serial number, and check or credit card information to: COLT ARCHIVE PROPERTIES LLC, 1295 Blue Hills Avenue, Bloomfield, CT 06002. Please allow 90-120 days for a response.

CLOVERLEAF HOUSE PISTOL – .41 Short or long RF cal., cloverleaf configured 4 shot cylinder, spur trigger, 1 1/2 or 3 in. barrel, blue or nickel plated, approx. 7,500 mfg. in ser. no. range 1-8,300 during 1871-76.

$2,550	$2,300	$1,850	$1,600	$1,400	$1,200	$1,100	$925	$825	$725	$650	$600

Add 30% for blue finish.
Add 80% for 1 1/2 in. barrel.

This model is sometimes referred to as the Jim Fisk model, as he was murdered by Edward Stokes with a Cloverleaf.

* ***5-shot Cloverleaf*** – similar to 4 shot model, except has round 5 shot cylinder and 2 5/8 in. barrel only, approx. 2,500 mfg. in ser. no. range 6,160-9,950 during 1871-76.

$2,175	$1,900	$1,600	$1,325	$1,150	$975	$850	$750	$650	$600	$550	$500

OPEN TOP REVOLVER (OLD LINE) – .22 Short or long RF cal., 2 3/8 or 2 7/8 in. barrel, 5 variations with a variety of finishes, engraving, and grips, first model has cone shaped firing pin that drops through frame (up to approx. ser. no. 125), without topstrap on frame, with or without integral ejector, varnished walnut grips were standard. Approx. 114,200 mfg. 1871-1877.

$1,450	$1,250	$1,150	$950	$850	$750	$700	$600	$550	$450	$375	$325

Add 30% for blue finish.

This model is also known as the Open Top .22 seven shot revolver, the Old Line .22, and the Open Top .22 Pocket. After 1873, Colt referred to this model as the O.M., or Old Model.

* ***Open Top Revolver (Old Line, Early Model)*** – has ejector and high hammer spur.

$3,195	$2,750	$2,525	$2,100	$1,875	$1,650	$1,550	$1,325	$1,200	$995	$825	$725

REVOLVERS: NEW LINE SERIES & VARIATIONS

If possible, it is advisable to procure a factory letter before buying/selling New Line Revolvers. These watermarked letters are available by writing Colt Archive Properties LLC in Bloomfield, CT, with a charge of $100 or more per serial number (if they can research it). Send your name and address, Colt model name, serial number, and check or credit card information to: COLT ARCHIVE PROPERTIES LLC, 1295 Blue Hills Avenue, Bloomfield, CT 06002. Please allow 90-120 days for a response.

Add 30% for blue finish on models listed below.

1ST MODEL – .22, .30, .32, .38, or .41 RF and CF cal., mfg. 1873-1876, 7 (.22 cal. only) or 5 shot, short cylinder flutes, cylinder stop slots cut on exterior of cylinder, 1 3/4, 2 1/4, or 4 in. barrel, full nickel or blue/case hardened finish, spur trigger. Many thousands mfg. 1873-1884.

$1,250	$1,050	$925	$825	$750	$675	$600	$550	$450	$350	$300	$250

2ND MODEL – similar to 1st Model, except has longer cylinder flutes and cylinder stop slots are on the back of cylinder, may or may not have loading gate. Mfg. 1876-1884.

$1,125	$995	$875	$800	$725	$650	$575	$500	$400	$325	$275	$225

Caliber rarity on both models from highest mfg. to lowest is: .22, .32, .30, .41, and .38.

NEW HOUSE MODEL – .38 or .41 CF cal., 5 shot, 2 1/4 in. barrel, spur trigger, checkered hard rubber grips. Approx. 4,000 mfg. 1880-1886 starting at ser. no. 10,300.

$1,475	$1,150	$1,000	$875	$800	$675	$600	$500	$425	$375	$350	$325

NEW POLICE MODEL – .32, .38, or .41 CF cal., 5 shot, 2 1/4, 4 1/2, 5, or 6 in. barrel, spur trigger, with or without ejector, stamped or etched "NEW POLICE" on barrel. Approx. 4,000 mfg. 1882-1886.

N/A	N/A	$1,950	$1,750	$1,500	$1,100	$725	$650	$600	$550	$525	$475

REVOLVERS: SAA, 1873-1940 MFG. (SER. NOS. 1-357,000)

The author wishes to express thanks to Charles Layson for making the following information available and reformatting the Colt 1st Generation SAA section.

The Colt SAA was produced in 36 calibers with many special order features or combinations available directly from the Colt factory. These factory special order features can greatly enhance the value of the revolver. The Single Action Colt, or "Peacemaker," as it is often called, is undoubtedly the most collectible handgun in the world, and as such, can command very high prices.

Standard barrel markings include the "short" two-line address on 4 3/4 in. or shorter barrels, or "long" one-line address on all other barrel lengths.

It is prudent to secure several professional opinions as to originality when contemplating an expensive purchase, since many SAAs have been altered or "improved" over the decades. Before he died, Keith Cochran, author of the

Colt Peacemaker Encyclopedia, Vol. II, guesstimated that over 1/2 of all pre-WWII revolvers were no longer factory original. Because of this, it is advisable to procure a factory letter when buying or selling older or recently manufactured Colt Single Actions (hence guaranteeing original configuration and value credibility). These watermarked letters are based on the original factory handwritten shipping ledgers and are available by contacting Colt Archive Properties LLC in Bloomfield, CT. While not totally infallible, these letters are normally very accurate. The cost to document a 1st Generation SAA is $100. This research can be expedited by phone service for either $100 (2nd and 3rd Generation SAA), or $150 (First Generation SAA through ser. number 343,000). The expedite service provides a verbal report over the phone within 24 hours and a documentation letter follows in 2-3 weeks. Single actions shipped during the time period of 1933-1945 cannot be documented due to lost records. The serial number range typically affected is 354,000-357,859. Documentation letters for .44 rimfire SAA require a $200 research fee.

Additionally, historical research premium charges apply for factory engraving ($100-150, depending on if standard, expert, or master engraving with no gold inlays), and unique shipping destinations such as company executives, famous Western personalities or Colt family members ($50-$200). To contact the Archive Department for assistance call 1-800-962-2658, Ext. 1343. Once contacted, they can advise you what the exact historical research charge will be for the service you are requesting. The address to write to is COLT ARCHIVE PROPERTIES LLC, 1295 Blue Hills Avenue, Bloomfield, CT 06002. For a complete Archive Services price list, please refer to the Colt website at coltsmfg.com.

Values shown are for guns without special order features. Factory engraving, ivory grips, very rare special order barrel lengths, and special finishes would add considerably to the values shown below. One final word on single action Colts: Black Powder Colts (pre 165,000 serial range) should be scrutinized carefully for potential problems, including refinishing (including aging), replacement parts, restamped serial numbers, and added, non-factory special order features. This makes a major difference in pricing the SAA, since a genuine, original SAA's price tag will vary immensely from a non-original, made-up "parts gun."

SAA 1st Generation Civilian/Commercial (Mfg. 1873-1940)

One of the most well known handguns, and certainly the most collected revolver in the world, the Colt Single Action Army has been produced almost continuously since 1873, with only a minor interruption between 1940 and 1955. It is without a doubt, the most copied revolver with over fifteen clones currently in production.

Better known as the "Peacemaker", this firearm has appreciated in value at an accelerated rate over the last fifty years. Spurred by the popularity of television westerns in the 1950s and 60s, a standard pre-war, 1st generation single action in excellent condition has gone from $250 in 1960 to approximately $10,000 today, and in some cases much higher.

Not every Colt Peacemaker, however, is worth thousands of dollars. While many factors determine the actual value, the single most important has to be the overall condition of the gun now, compared to the day it left the factory. Because of the demand for Peacemakers in excellent condition many have been reworked and/or reblued, both by private gunsmiths and by the Colt factory itself. Unfortunately only the factory marked its refinished guns, while private individuals normally did not.

The Colt company has used at least three different methods of marking handguns that are to be reworked and/or refinished, and while there is some disagreement among collectors as to exactly what these marks indicate, e.g., refinishing, major parts replacement, or both, it is the opinion of this writer that the first to be used was a six pointed star stamped on the rear right bow of the trigger guard, from approximately 1890 to 1920. The second was a small ampersand placed in the same location, from approximately 1920 to 1945. The third was completely different, and is occasionally found in addition to the ampersand. It was a series of three numbers stamped on most major parts. Called "bin" numbers, they correspond to the numbers on small boxes or "bins" in the custom shop, into which are placed all the parts of a disassembled handgun destined

100%	98%	95%	90%	80%	70%	60%	50%	40%	30%	20%	10%

to be reworked and /or refinished. On the Single Action Army, these numbers were placed on the rear flat of the loading gate, visible when it is open (not to be confused with the assembly number stamped on the rear curve of the loading gate), on the front of the cylinder, on the left side of the grip straps, and on the bottom of the barrel, near the frame.

Any reworking or refinishing has a negative effect on the value of a gun to the collector, and the amount varies depending upon the age of the gun, what was actually done and the quality of the workmanship. For example, an early black powder single action that has been expertly refinished by the factory or a qualified restorer is worth only 10 to 20% of what the same gun would be worth in original, mint condition. A late smokeless powder Single Action similarly redone, however, is still worth 30%-40% of one in near new condition. In many cases, the factory had an irritating habit of adding then current markings to an earlier gun, e.g., a caliber designation added to the barrel of a pre-1890 Single Action, or a rampant Colt to the frame.

Values quoted relate only to original, unaltered examples.

SINGLE ACTION ARMY (SAA) - STANDARD MFG. – over 30 cals., six shot single action revolver, three standard barrel lengths. The 4 3/4 in. barrel had a two line address, while the 5 1/2 in. and 7 1/2 in. had a one line address. Blue with color case hardened frame or full nickel finish were both available. Of the many (36) calibers offered, .45 Colt was by far the most popular, accounting for 42% of total production, followed by .44/.40 (18%), .38-40 (11%), .32-20 (8%) and .41 (4.5%). One-piece, varnished walnut grips were standard for the first ten years, then gradually replaced with two-piece hard rubber. When grips are "not listed" on Colt historical letters, you should assume that they were the standard for their time period, either wood or rubber; not the pearl or ivory that someone added at a later date.

* ***Pinch Frame SAA (ser. no. range 1-160)*** – very rare and seldom found with any original finish, .44 S&W American and .45 Colt calibers, 7 1/2 in. barrel, blue and case hardened finish, one-piece varnished wood grips, distinctive rear sight situated one-half inch in front of hammer notch, which gives the impression that the top strap has been "pinched." Mfg. 1873.

100%	98%	95%	90%	80%	70%	60%	50%	40%	30%	20%	10%
N/A	N/A	N/A	N/A	N/A	N/A	$150,000	$130,000	$100,000	$75,000	$50,000	$25,000

Add 50% for original .44 S&W American caliber (it is estimated that only 20-25 were produced in this caliber, and most were later converted).

Be aware! There are many counterfeits in this variation.

* ***Early Black Powder SAA (Mfg. 1873-1876, ser. no. range 160-22,000)*** – .45 LC cal., 7 1/2 in. barrel standard, blue or nickel finish, rear sight changed to standard "V" notch, first few hundred have German silver front sight, distinctive italic script style lettering used in barrel address, two line, two date patent marking on frame, one-piece varnished wood grips has more distinctive flair at bottom rear on early guns, serial numbers shared with early martial production, 5 1/2 in. barrels introduced in 1875 in guns for export. Mfg. 1873-76.

» **Ser. Nos. 160-999 (Mfg. 1873)**

100%	98%	95%	90%	80%	70%	60%	50%	40%	30%	20%	10%
N/A	N/A	$80,000	$74,000	$55,000	$52,000	$44,000	$38,000	$30,000	$24,000	$18,000	$13,000

» **Ser. Nos. 1,000 - 9,999 (Mfg. 1873-1874)**

100%	98%	95%	90%	80%	70%	60%	50%	40%	30%	20%	10%
N/A	N/A	$67,000	$60,000	$50,000	$44,000	$35,000	$31,000	$24,000	$19,000	$14,000	$11,000

» **Ser. Nos. 10,000 - 22,000 (Mfg. 1874 - 1876)**

100%	98%	95%	90%	80%	70%	60%	50%	40%	30%	20%	10%
N/A	$55,000	$51,000	$45,000	$35,000	$30,000	$24,000	$21,000	$16,000	$13,000	$11,000	$8,000

Subtract 20%-40% for nickel finish, depending on original condition.

* ***Intermediate Black Powder SAA (Mfg. 1876-1890, ser. no. range 22,000-130,000)*** – the italic style of lettering in the barrel address is changed to a block letter style in the 22,000 range, the first two-piece hard rubber grips with eagle motif appear in 1882 and became the standard by 1888, the .44-40 (.44WCF) caliber is introduced in 1878, the round head ejector is changed to oval shape in the 52,000 serial range, 4 3/4 in. to 5 1/2 in. barrels are becoming more popular, and Colt gradually abandons the practice of placing serial numbers on the cylinders and barrels of civilian revolvers. Nickel plated single actions seldom have numbered barrels and cylinders after the 60,000 serial range. Blue guns normally have numbers on both up to the 110,000 range, and occasionally thereafter up to 125,000. Two line, two date patent markings change to three line, three dates by 1878.

Subtract 25% for nickel finish.
Add 30% for original box.
Add 10% for 4 3/4 in. barrel.
One-piece wood grips are more desirable than two-piece rubber grips.

100%	98%	95%	90%	80%	70%	60%	50%	40%	30%	20%	10%

» **Ser. Nos. 22,000 - 54,000 (Mfg. 1876 - 1880)**

N/A	$40,000	$35,000	$30,000	$23,000	$20,000	$15,000	$12,000	$9,000	$7,000	$5,500	$4,500

» **Ser. Nos. 54,000 - 130,000 (Mfg. 1880 - 1890)**

N/A	$38,000	$33,000	$27,000	$21,000	$16,000	$13,000	$9,500	$8,000	$6,500	$5,500	$4,500

* ***Late Black Powder SAA (Mfg. 1890 - 1896, ser. no. range 130,000-165,000)*** – three line patent date format changes to two lines with three dates, circled rampant Colt trademark is added to left side of frame, grips transition from wood and rubber with eagle to plain two-piece rubber by 1892, and caliber designation is added to the barrel and eliminated from trigger guard.

N/A	$30,000	$25,000	$20,000	$15,000	$12,000	$9,500	$8000	$6,000	$5,600	$4,800	$4,000

Subtract 40% for nickel finish.
Add 25% for original box.
Add 10% for 4 3/4 in. barrel.
Add 20% for wood or rubber with eagle grips.

* ***Early Smokeless Powder SAA (Mfg. 1896 - 1908)*** – several important physical characteristics were changed during this transition period. Most notably, in 1896 the vertical screw retaining the cylinder pin was eliminated in favor of the horizontal latch. This was identical to what had already been used on the double action models since 1877. This change coincided with the introduction of ammunition loaded with white or smokeless powder, which was more powerful and less corrosive than black powder. It was necessary for firearms manufacturers, therefore, to modify and strengthen their products to safely use the new ammunition. By adopting the more modern and tool-free horizontal latch for the Single Action at this time, Colt gave its customers an easy way to tell the new from the old, the stronger from the weaker, and a good excuse to purchase a new Peacemaker! As a result, sales boomed and more Single Actions were sold in the next ten years, than any other ten year period in Colt's history.

* ***The knurling pattern on the hammer spur began a two step revision in 1906. Up until this time, the knurling was enclosed in a border with a line underneath. Beginning in 1906, for approximately two years, the border remained, but the line underneath was eliminated. By late 1908, the border was also eliminated, and thereafter, the knurling ran to the very edges of the hammer spur. Although Colt advertised their improved smokeless powder Single Actions as early as 1897, they did not add the "VP" proof mark (verified proof, Colt's guarantee for smokeless powder use) to the trigger guard until 1904. While the highest production and sales figures were reached during this period, quality did not suffer. Many collectors feel that the fitting, polishing and finishing work performed during this period was superior to any other.***

» **Ser. Nos. 165,000 - 182,000 (Mfg. 1896 - 1899)** – the first three years of this period, 1896 to 1899, have recently become known as the "blackpowder transition" period, to distinguish Single Actions made with the modern, stronger frame and yet still considered "antique" by federal law that uses January 1st, 1899 as the beginning of the modern gun era.

N/A	$25,000	$21,000	$13,000	$11,000	$8,000	$6,500	$5,300	$4,000	$3,100	$2,800	$2,400

» **Ser. Nos. 182,000 - 300,000 (Mfg. 1899 - 1908)**

N/A	$20,000	$17,000	$11,000	$7,500	$6,200	$4,800	$4,400	$4,000	$3,200	$2,500	$2,000

Add 25% for original box.
Subtract 10% for nickel finish.

* ***Intermediate Smokeless Powder SAA (Mfg. 1908 - 1920, ser. no. range 300,000-339,000)*** – physical changes continued to occur during this period. Rampant Colt medallions were inserted into pearl, ivory, and checkered walnut grips in 1909, the .44 Special caliber was introduced circa 1912, the blueing process was gradually changed, and the circled rampant Colt on the frame began to lose its circle as the die stamps wore. The company, however, did not quickly give up the use of black powder rifling (wide grooves and narrow lands) completely until 1914, although an experimentation and transition period with narrower grooves and wider lands had begun about 1910. Similarly, the small and low black powder front sight did not change to the larger and higher smokeless profile until 1914. WWI came and went, and SAA sales began to decline. The year 1920 is very significant to Single Action collectors since this was the year that the serial number relocation was completed. Those numbers on the trigger guard and backstrap were moved under the grips beginning in the late 338,000 serial range (1919), leaving only the number on the frame visible from exterior. This brought to a close a practice which had begun in the 1840s with the percussion revolvers. Many collectors regard this as the end of the "cowboy" period.

100%	98%	95%	90%	80%	70%	60%	50%	40%	30%	20%	10%

» **Ser. Nos. 300,000 - 328,000 (Mfg. 1908 - 1914)**

N/A	$18,000	$13,000	$9,000	$7,500	$5,700	$5,000	$3,800	$3,200	$2,800	$2,400	$2,100

Add 20% for original box.
Add 10% for smooth, two-piece walnut grips.
Add 25% for checkered, varnished walnut grips with deep set medallions.
Subtract 25% for nickel finish.

» **Ser. Nos. 328,000 - 339,000 (Mfg. 1914 - 1920)**

N/A	$15,000	$12,000	$9,000	$6,500	$5,000	$4,300	$3,600	$3,100	$2,700	$2,300	$2,000

Add 20% for original box.
Add 15% for smooth, two-piece walnut grips.
Add 25% for checkered, varnished walnut grips with deep set medallions.
Subtract 30% for nickel finish.

* ***Late Smokeless Powder SAA (ser. no. range 339,000-357,000)*** – single action sales continued to diminish after 1920, as sales of semi-automatics increased. Only 19,000 SAAs were sold in the twenty year period, with only 100 being produced in 1936. The complete serial number is visible only on the frame, but many cylinders are stamped on the rear with the last two or three digits. In 1928, the caliber marking on the left side of the barrel was changed to read "Colt Single Action Army," followed by the caliber. In 1930, the "V" notch rear sight was replaced with a square groove to match the wider front sight, and in 1935, the finish on the hammer was changed from color case hardened to blue with polished sides. Colt special order grip medallions also made a three step, transitional change by 1923. Since 1909, deep set bronze medallions on pearl, ivory or checkered walnut grips had been recessed into the grips and both horses faced forward. They were first changed to a less expensive, flush mount design, still facing forward and then within the same year to a flush mount, with one facing forward and one backward, a cost cutting measure which required only one die. The finish on the checkered wood grips was also changed from a varnish to an oil finish in 1924.

It is important to remember that while special order grips such as pearl, ivory, or checkered wood may add as much as 25% to an SAA's value, they must be factory original to that particular gun, and be recorded as such in the factory records.

» **Ser. Nos. 339,000 - 350,000 (Mfg. 1920 - 1928)**

$13,000	$11,000	$9,000	$7,000	$5,000	$4,000	$3,500	$3,000	$2,800	$2,600	$2,400	$2,000

Add 20% for original box in good condition.
Add 25% for original checkered wood, pearl, or ivory grips.
Add 10% for original stag horn grips (very rare!).

» **Ser. Nos. 350,000 - 355,000 (Mfg. 1928 - 1935)**

$12,000	$10,000	$8,000	$6,000	$4,500	$4,000	$3,200	$2,800	$2,600	$2,500	$2,200	$2,000

Add 20% for original box in good condition.
Add 25% for original checkered wood, pearl, or ivory grips.

» **Ser. Nos. 355,000 - 357,000 (Mfg. 1935 - 1940)**

$11,000	$8,500	$6,500	$5,500	$4,000	$3,200	$2,700	$2,400	$2,200	$2,000	$1,900	$1,800

Add 20% for original box in good condition.
Add 25% for original checkered wood, pearl, or ivory grips.

SAA 1st Generation Commercial, Non-Standard Mfg.

SINGLE ACTION ARMY (SAA) - NON-STANDARD MFG. – between 1873-1940, Colt mfg. approx. 327,000 Commercial SAA revolvers. There were several distinct types or configurations of SAAs that varied from the standard and therefore, have special significance to the collector.

* ***.44 Rimfire SAA*** – .44 Henry rimfire cal., 7 1/2 in. barrel, blue and nickel finishes, most were shipped to the southwest and saw hard use, rare with any original finish remaining, many barrels shortened during their period of use, serial numbered in their own range, 1 - 1,863, mfg. from 1875 to 1880.

N/A	N/A	N/A	N/A	$75,000	$60,000	$47,000	$35,000	$27,000	$22,000	$18,000	$15,000

Beware! Many have been found with cut and/or stretched barrels.
A factory letter on this model is available for $200.

100%	98%	95%	90%	80%	70%	60%	50%	40%	30%	20%	10%

* ***.22 Rimfire SAA*** – blue or nickel finish, 5 1/2 in. and 7 1/2 in. barrels, manufactured in two distinct runs, slightly less than 100 converted from unsold .44 RF still in inventory in the late 1880s, and approximately 20 mfg. new in 1891.

100%	98%	95%	90%	80%	70%	60%	50%	40%	30%	20%	10%
N/A	$45,000	$40,000	$35,000	$28,000	$25,000	$22,000	$20,000	$18,000	$15,000	$12,000	$9,000

Add 10% for rare 5 1/2 in. barrel.
Subtract 50% for factory refinished models.
Subtract 10% for those converted from .44 rimfire.

* ***Buntline Special Model SAA*** – .45 LC cal., long barrel model named after Ned Buntline, author of dime novels in the late 19th century. Only 28 believed to be mfg. with folding adjustable rear sight and extended hammer screw for attachment of nickel-plated metal skeleton shoulder stock, all in the 28,800 serial range, most with 10, 12, or 16 in. barrel. Very rare.

100%	98%	95%	90%	80%	70%	60%	50%	40%	30%	20%	10%
N/A	N/A	$125,000	$110,000	$85,000	$75,000	$62,000	$55,000	$50,000	$40,000	$30,000	$20,000

Add 50% if with original shoulder stock.

Individual appraisals are highly recommended for this model.

* ***Etched Panel .44-40 SAA*** – the most desirable of all Commercial black powder era SAAs, this variant has the words "Colt Frontier Six Shooter" acid etched in a panel on the left side of the barrel. This marking was the result of a request in January 1878 by J. P. Moore's and Sons, one of Colt's largest distributors in New York. to help them market the new .44-40 Winchester chambered SAA. Colt agreed and shipped the first "etched panels" to Moore's and Sons in February 1878. The lowest serial numbered known etched panel .44-40 is in the 41,000 serial range (1878) and the highest in the 129,000 range circa 1890.

100%	98%	95%	90%	80%	70%	60%	50%	40%	30%	20%	10%
N/A	$55,000	$48,000	$35,000	$25,000	$18,000	$15,000	$12,000	$9,000	$8,000	$7,000	$6,000

Subtract 30% for nickel finish.
Add 20% for one-piece wood grips.
Add 20% for 4 3/4 in. barrel.
Add 30% for 5 1/2 in. barrel.

* ***Ejectorless (Sheriff's Model) Model SAA*** – this term denotes Single Actions without ejectors and ejector housings. Most were produced in .45 LC and .44-40 WCF cal., with 3 1/2 in. or 4 in. barrels, but 2 1/2 in., 3 in., 4 3/4 in., and 7 1/2 in. were made. According to collector and researcher Wynn Paul, the first ejectorless Sheriff's or Storekeeper's models were shipped from the factory on February 22, 1882 to Hibbard, Spencer, Bartlett & Co., Chicago, IL, in two shipments of ten each, one group with 3 1/2 in. barrels, one group with 4 in. barrels. At least 1,500 were produced, most in the latter part of the 19th century.

Factory nomenclature never referred to the Ejectorless Model SAA's as Sheriff's or Storekeepers Models.

» **Ejectorless (Sheriff's Model) Smokeless Powder Frame SAA**

100%	98%	95%	90%	80%	70%	60%	50%	40%	30%	20%	10%
N/A	$67,000	$56,000	$46,000	$30,000	$27,000	$21,000	$18,000	$16,000	$13,000	$11,000	$8,000

Add 30% for .44-40 cal. w/etched panel.
Add 30% for original special order grips.
Add 50% for 2 1/2 in. or 7 1/2 in. barrel.
Subtract 15% for nickel finish below 70% condition.

Factory nomenclature never referred to the Ejectorless Model SAA's as Sheriff's or Storekeepers Models.

» **Ejectorless (Sheriff's Model) Black Powder Frame SAA** – pre-1896 mfg. with old style black powder frame.

100%	98%	95%	90%	80%	70%	60%	50%	40%	30%	20%	10%
N/A	$85,000	$75,000	$60,000	$47,000	$33,000	$27,000	$22,000	$19,000	$15,000	$11,500	$9,000

Add 20% for .44-40 cal. w/etched panel.
Add 30% for original special order grips.
Add 50% for 2 1/2 in. or 7 1/2 in. barrel.
Subtract 15% for nickel finish below 70% condition.

Beware of fakes! The *Blue Book of Gun Values* strongly recommends getting a historical letter from Colt, then checking the authenticity of the serial numbers. Many guns have had numbers altered to match records.

* ***Flat-Top Target Model SAA*** – many calibers from .22 RF to .476 Eley were available, target version of the SAA with flat-top frame and adj. sights, approximately 925 were manufactured from 1888-1896, both in 5 1/2 and 7 1/2 in. barrel and full blue finish, two-piece smooth walnut, two-piece rubber, or two-piece checkered walnut grips are known.

100%	98%	95%	90%	80%	70%	60%	50%	40%	30%	20%	10%
N/A	$28,000	$22,000	$19,000	$15,000	$12,000	$9,000	$8,000	$7,000	$6,000	$5,000	$4,500

Add 10% for 5 1/2 in. barrel.

Beware! Many target models were returned to the factory for refinishing.

* ***Long Flute Series SAA*** – in 1913, Colt decided to make use of approximately 1500 cylinders left over from the model 1878 double action production. Since it was necessary to add a bolt lock notch and a lead-in groove on these long flute cylinders, a block of serial numbers, 330,000 to 331,480, was set aside to be used for this special production. Manufactured in 1913 and 1914, specimens are known in .32 WCF, .38 WCF, .41 LC, .44 S&W Spl., .44 WCF, and .45 LC cals.

According to researchers Hull and Rowcliffe, whose survey includes 114 long flute Single Actions, no .44 WCF have been noted. The actual total mfg. may possibly exceed 1,500, and while quite rare, these long flute variations sell for only 5% to 10% more than other Single Actions of this period.

* ***Pre-war/Post-war Mfg. SAAs*** – made from pre WWII parts remaining in inventory after production of the Single Action Army had ended in 1940, many of these post-war guns were given as gifts to dignitaries and retiring Colt employees, known calibers include .30 Carbine, .357 Mag., .38 Spl., .44 Spl., .44-40 WCF and .45 Colt. Most are found with 5 1/2 in. barrels and blue and case hardened finish; nickel is rare. Shipping cartons vary from pre-war dark maroon and brown, hinged top, circa 1950, to black 2nd generation style. Approximately 338 were assembled and shipped between 1947-1961.

Add 10% for nickel finish.

Add 20% plus for important or well known recipient.

Most of these guns are found in 95% or better condition, and are valued like the last of the pre-war 1st generation Single Actions.

* ***Factory Engraved SAAs*** – slightly less than 1% (approximately 3,400) Single Actions are thought to have been engraved at the factory or elsewhere by authority from Colt between 1873 and 1940. Between 1873-circa 1929 Colt offered three basic grades of engraving with alphabetical designations - A (least coverage), B, and C (most coverage). Circa 1929-1936 Colt changed these alphabetical engraving designations to numerical, and became No. 1 (least coverage), 2, and 3 (most coverage). Many of these early SAA's also carried special inscriptions, initials, grips, etc., and because of this, the value ranges are very wide. Condition also plays a huge role here. Factory engraved black powder SAAs typically sell in the $10,000 to $100,000 range, while factory engraved smokeless powder SAAs usually peak in the $50,000 range. Very special or one-of-a-kind pieces, such as the six known "panel" engraved guns, or one carried by a famous outlaw or lawman may bring upward of $300,000, depending on condition and particulars. Most factory work is documented in the records.

* ***Special Order SAAs*** – Included in the approximate 3,400 factory engraved SAAs, there are a small number of one of a kind, custom special ordered guns. These are, of course, well documented in the Colt held factory archives by serial number and can be accessed through the office of Beverly Haynes, Colt Firearms Historian. While most of these special order guns were factory engraved, some were not, and their orders include request such as initials, monograms, inscriptions, trigger pulls, alternate sights, stocks and special targeting requirements. On handguns made between 1889 and 1914, it is possible to access some of these special order details. The original Colt Special Order and Repair Ledgers and now the property of the Colt Collectors Association Historian, Don Jones, and he is available to all members of the CCA. To quote Mrs. Haynes and Mr. Jones, "As a supplement to the Colt Factory letter, the Colt Special Order Ledger entries dovetail nicely in corroborating the original configuration detailed in the Factory letter. In effect the special order entry is the build order for the Colt firearm, tracing the order from receipt through production. As such they will document configuration details and changes that are sometimes left silent in the Colt shipping based production record. In addition, the Colt Repair Ledgers that are available are very limited in scope, but they do stand alone in their serial number based, period documentation or repairs, factory refinishing, and ownership of certain Colt handguns and rifles." Obviously, the information contained in these Colt Special Order and Repair ledgers is very important to Colt collectors, as it may seriously affect the value of certain guns.

* ***Non-Factory Engraved SAAs*** – value depends on when and where the engraving was done. Early "New York" or "dealer" engraved Single Actions done outside the factory were usually shipped from Colt in the "soft" and w/o finish. The majority of these were done in the 1870s or 1880s, and condition being equal, are generally priced at 25% to 50% of factory original specimens. 1st generation guns attributed to L.D. Nimschke, usually done in NY, either under contract from the Colt company or one of the large NY retailers, will bring up to 50% more than a standard NY engraved gun. Later guns, well done by a known contemporary artist, are usually priced by adding the value of the gun to the cost of the engraving. Poor execution may actually lower the value of a plain, but original gun, much as refinishing would. The notation of "soft" in the factory records is desirable, since the large wholesalers in the northeast used many of the same engravers as Colt. There are and have been some 20th century engravers who stand out, however, and their work commands higher prices, e.g. Lynton McKenzie, Ben Lane, Leonard Francolini, Mike Dubber,

100%	98%	95%	90%	80%	70%	60%	50%	40%	30%	20%	10%

Howard Dove, Cole Agee, and Weldon Bledsoe - the two latter being famous for their "cattle brand" style, and Ben Lane for his meticulous duplication of the patterns of Cuno Helfricht, the most famous of all Colt factory engravers.

* ***Bisley Model SAA*** – numbered in the same serial range as the standard Single Action Army, the Bisley model featured a more curved forward and longer grip strap and a smaller, raked back hammer. It was designed with the target shooter in mind and named after Bisley, England, the location of the international shooting matches during the late 19th and early 20th century. It was offered in the same barrel lengths, the same finishes and most all of the more popular Single Action calibers, .32 WCF (.32-20) being the most popular. It was advertised from 1896 (approx. ser. no. 165,900) to 1912 (approx. ser. no. 323,000). The highest number known (331,916) was assembled in 1915, but not shipped until November, 1919. Slightly over 45,000 were produced.

100%	98%	95%	90%	80%	70%	60%	50%	40%	30%	20%	10%
N/A	$14,000	$9,500	$7,500	$6,200	$5,000	$4,200	$3,500	$2,800	$2,200	$1,800	$1,500

Add 30% for nickel finish above 70% condition.
Add 50% for original box.
Add 25% for pre-1899 serial number.

Only approx. one dozen black powder Bisley boxes known.

* ***Flat-Top Target Bisley SAA*** – a target version similar to the flat-top target Single Action with adj. sights. Available in all standard calibers with a 7 1/2 in. barrel, blue finish and either walnut or rubber grips. Offered from 1894 to 1912, the most popular caliber was .455 Eley followed closely by .32 WCF. Only 976 were manufactured.

100%	98%	95%	90%	80%	70%	60%	50%	40%	30%	20%	10%
N/A	$20,000	$18,000	$15,500	$12,500	$10,000	$8,000	$7,200	$6,700	$6,000	$5,000	$4,000

Add 30% for any barrel length other than 7 1/2 in.

* ***Battle of Britain SAA*** – late 1st generation Single Action Armys purchased by the British government in anticipation of invasion from Germany in 1940. A total of 163, mostly .38 and .45 cal. in both blue and nickel finish were sent to England by Colt. These guns were fully inspected and proofed by the British, in many cases showing the exact specifications of the cartridge on the bottom of the barrel. Most, if not all, were unissued, and remain today in 90% plus condition.

100%	98%	95%	90%	80%	70%	60%	50%	40%	30%	20%	10%
$14,000	$11,000	$9,500	$8,500	$6,500	$5,500	$4,700	$4,200	$3,500	$3,000	$2,500	$2,000

Add 10% for blue and color case hardened finish.
Add 20% for original shipping carton.

* ***London Agency SAA*** – as with percussion revolvers and derringers, Colt shipped Single Action Army revolvers to England for sale through its London Agency. John Kopec, co-author of *A Study of the Colt Single Action Army Revolver*, estimates that 18% of production during the first 2 1/2 years went to England. These early guns were marked with the standard Hartford address, and most were chambered in either .450 Eley or Boxer caliber, with a 7 1/2 or 5 1/2 in. barrel. A small number were shipped with 4 3/4 in. barrels in May of 1877. According to Kenneth Moore, author of *Single Action Army Revolvers and the London Agency*, and co-author of *A Study of the Colt SAA Revolver*, Baron Von Oppen, head of Colt's London Agency, requested in Oct. 1875 that Colt change the barrel address to "14 PALL MALL, LONDON" only, in an effort to increase his sales and to prevent English customers from ordering direct from Hartford. Colt complied and sent 150 revolvers with the new barrel address in early 1876. This created a problem with English customs officials, since the guns were not made in England, they could not be marked "LONDON" only, and would not pass inspection. The London address could not be used. It is believed by Moore that these 150 Colt SAAs were the only ones marked with the London barrel address. By Jan. 1877, a compromise was reached and English customs authorized the use of the dual Hartford/London address to read "COLT'S PT. F.A. MFG. CO. HARTFORD, CT USA DEPOT 14 PALL MALL LONDON". The London proofed SAAs were usually stamped at the bottom of the barrel, and in each flute of the cylinder, and had a high quality nickel or blue finish with case hardened frame, although some all-blue examples are known. Through 1890, several thousand SAAs were sold through the London Agency.

Values for the more common English proofed SAAs with the combined Hartford/London address are approx. 40% less than those SAAs sold during the same period in the United States. A gun with the Hartford only address would be more desirable, and one of the 150 with the London only address command substantially more than a model with the dual Hartford/London address, and perhaps more than an American counterpart. An original model with 4 3/4 in. barrel would also bring a premium. Many were reblued by the London Agency.

SAA U.S. Military, Mfg. 1873-1903

Since many of the military models listed below are frequently encountered with no original finish remaining, prices for original no condition specimens will be approx. three quarters of the 10% prices

100%	98%	95%	90%	80%	70%	60%	50%	40%	30%	20%	10%

listed below. With original specimens getting harder and harder to find, many guns are now observed with major parts replacements, including barrels, cylinders, grips, etc.

Beware of restorations that are purported to be original! One expert believes that as many as 90% of Colt SAA Cavalry & Artillery models currently offered for sale, especially at gun shows, have been intentionally faked, or "enhanced" in some way. Likewise, many "questionable" guns have been consigned to the auction houses for disposal. Many have been altered in the last 40 years in all inspector serial ranges. Some have now been skillfully "aged" to look more original. When making a substantial purchase, a letter of authentication from a reliable source is suggested in addition to a factory historical letter. Also ask for a guarantee of originality in writing from the seller. No factory information is available on U.S. Cavalry revolvers below ser. no. 30,600.

Blue Book Publications, Inc. would be happy to refer you to a credible source for authenticating the military revolvers listed below (very important). While a factory letter (if possible) verifies the configuration when shipped, it does not verify originality and/or authenticity. All inquiries are treated confidentially.

Notice: Values listed on the following models in this category are for original unaltered examples only.

SINGLE ACTION ARMY (CAVALRY) - U.S. MILITARY CONTRACT – the Colt SAA was the primary sidearm of the U.S. military forces between 1873 and 1892. While frequently called the "cavalry" model, this revolver was carried by commissioned officers in the regular army and the state militias, and issued to each man in the mounted units. A total of 37,063 were purchased by the U.S. government at an average cost of $12.50 each. Contract specifications called for 7 1/2 in. barrel, .45 Colt caliber, government blue and color case hardened finish (a softer blue color compared to the darker and more brilliant civilian finish, which required a higher polish and was therefore more expensive), and one-piece, oil finished walnut grips. Each gun was stamped with the initial(s) of a U.S. ordnance principal sub-inspector and finally, with the letters "U.S." on the frame after being approved for delivery to the National Armory at Springfield, MA.

Examples displaying their original inspector's grip cartouches will command a premium. Beware of fakes! All inspector's cartouche stamps are being replicated today.

* ***Early U.S. Model SAA (Mfg. 1873 - 1875)*** – principal sub-inspectors of this early period used only the first letter of their last name to mark the revolvers which they inspected. Chronologically, they were O.W. Ainsworth (A), S.B. Lewis (L), W.W. Johnson (J), and A.P. Casey (C).

While the lower serial numbers are generally the most desirable, the small number of guns inspected by Lewis, Johnson and Casey make them harder to find and perhaps more valuable than a higher numbered Ainsworth. These guns are in the same number sequence as guns made for the civilian market up to #20,000. There are no known "U.S." marked Single Actions between serial numbers 20,000 and 30,000. According to John Kopec, arguably the most knowledgeable and authoritative U.S. Single Action researcher and co-author of the widely respected work,

A Study of the Single Action Army Revolver, **the earliest known complete Ainsworth inspected Single Action is serial number "179". (Earlier numbered Ainsworth components are found on Artillery revolvers).**

Those examples displaying their original inspector's grip cartouches will command a premium. Beware of fakes! All inspector's cartouche stamps are being replicated today.

» **Ainsworth Serial Range 179 - 999 (1873)**

100%	98%	95%	90%	80%	70%	60%	50%	40%	30%	20%	10%
N/A	N/A	$112,000	$90,000	$85,000	$65,000	$60,000	$45,000	$35,000	$25,000	$18,000	$15,000

» **Ainsworth Serial Range 1,000 - 9,999 (1873-1874) (Prime Indian Wars Period)**

100%	98%	95%	90%	80%	70%	60%	50%	40%	30%	20%	10%
N/A	N/A	$100,000	$90,000	$72,000	$60,000	$48,000	$36,000	$28,000	$24,500	$19,500	$14,500

Add 25% - 50% for Ainsworth inspected guns between ser. nos. 4,516 and 5,521 possibly issued to George Custer's 7th Cavalry. Probable (not proven) historical connotation will usually trump condition.

» **Ainsworth Serial Range 10,000 - 14,500 (1874)**

100%	98%	95%	90%	80%	70%	60%	50%	40%	30%	20%	10%
N/A	N/A	$90,000	$70,000	$52,000	$35,000	$25,000	$20,000	$18,000	$15,000	$9,000	$8,000

Many nickel-plated examples found.

» **Lewis Serial Range 15,000-16,500 (1875)**

100%	98%	95%	90%	80%	70%	60%	50%	40%	30%	20%	10%
N/A	N/A	$85,000	$80,000	$56,000	$45,000	$31,000	$25,000	$17,000	$15,000	$14,000	$13,000

» **Johnson Serial Range 16,800-18,450 (1875)**

100%	98%	95%	90%	80%	70%	60%	50%	40%	30%	20%	10%
N/A	N/A	$90,000	$80,000	$56,000	$45,000	$30,000	$20,000	$15,000	$14,000	$13,000	$12,000

100%	98%	95%	90%	80%	70%	60%	50%	40%	30%	20%	10%

» **Casey Serial Range 16,400 - 19,530 (1875)**

N/A	N/A	$90,000	$75,000	$50,000	$35,000	$25,000	$18,000	$16,000	$14,000	$13,000	$12,000

More than a few Casey range guns are dual inspected, most with a "C" and a "J", but while interesting, this does not necessarily add a premium.

* ***Mid-Range U.S. Model SAA (1876 - 1887)*** – when military production resumed in the 30,000 serial range, the principal sub-inspectors during this eleven-year period were John T. Cleveland (J.T.C.), Henry Nettleton (H.N.), and David F. Clark (D.F.C.). Starting in 1876, the marking procedure changed from one last name initial to two or all three of the sub-inspector's initials. Also in 1876, the third patent date was added to the left side of the frame in a third line, and three very significant models were produced.

» **Cleveland Serial Range 30,690 to 35,570 (1876 - 1877)** – these are the very first of the U.S. Cavalry models to be recorded in the Colt records and the first ones that can be lettered by the factory. Slightly more than 2,000 were delivered under government contract, and were inspected by John T. Cleveland. A small group of these guns show the initials of Lewis Draper "L.D." stamped on the frames, instead of the normal "J.T.C." There is also an unusually high ratio of Civilian SAAs in this serial range with the condemned "C" mark on the frame, and there is existing correspondence from Colt and to the U.S. Ordnance Dept. complaining that Inspector Lt. David A. Lyle was being unduly hard to please. Lewis Draper was a temporary replacement during this period. Regardless, this small group of "L.D." marked Single Action Cavalrys are an interesting variation and may command a slight premium.

N/A	N/A	$55,000	$50,000	$40,000	$25,000	$20,000	$16,000	$13,000	$11,000	$9,500	$8,500

Add 10% for "L.D." marked frames.

» **Early Henry Nettleton Serial Range 36,800 - 39,880 Civilian U.S. Models (1877)** – according to John Kopec's "Cavalry and Artillery Revolvers" there are a small group of known cavalry revolvers which were part of a large surplus of civilian SAAs which were inspected and accepted by the government. While some are Henry Nettleton inspected, most are marked with the "W" of E.C. Wheeler. It is known that Wheeler substituted for Nettleton during an illness. Regardless, this is a very small and desirable group of Cavalry SAAs and a premium is probably justified.

N/A	N/A	$65,000	$60,000	$44,000	$34,000	$28,000	$24,000	$20,000	$18,000	$15,000	$13,000

» **Early David F. Clark Serial Range 41,000-42,300 (1878)** – "The Civilian U.S." Series. All are stamped "45 cal." on trigger guard.

N/A	N/A	$49,500	$38,500	$27,500	$22,000	$19,750	$16,500	$14,750	$13,250	$11,000	$10,000

» **Standard Henry Nettleton Serial Range 47,000-50,600 U.S. Models (1878)**

N/A	N/A	$49,500	$38,500	$27,500	$22,000	$19,750	$16,500	$14,750	$13,250	$12,000	$11,000

» **Later David F. Clark Serial Range 53,000-121,000 (Mfg. 1880-1887)**

N/A	N/A	$44,000	$33,000	$27,500	$19,750	$17,500	$16,500	$14,250	$11,000	$9,750	$8,750

* ***Rinaldo A. Carr, Serial Range 131,187-140,361 (Mfg. 1890 - 1891)*** – this was the last of U.S. Single Action production. Four thousand were inspected by Rinaldo A. Carr during this sixteen month period. As hostilities in the west subsided, demand decreased and many revolvers of this group went to state militias or were left in storage. Consequently, a higher percentage of R.A.C. inspected SAAs are found in excellent condition than those of other inspectors, and this is reflected in their value. The last of this group was shipped from the factory on April 29, 1891.

N/A	$60,000	$50,000	$30,000	$25,000	$18,000	$15,000	$13,000	$11,000	$9,000	$7,200	$5,600

* ***Artillery Model SAAs*** – refers to U.S. government model SAA revolvers with 5 1/2 in. barrels, which were reworked and refinished between 1896 and 1903. In response to growing dissatisfaction with the stopping power of the newly adopted M1892 .38 LC cal. double action revolvers, the U.S. Ordnance Dept. directed Springfield Armory to recall all remaining quantities of .45 Colt Cavalry revolvers during 1893. The Colt Company refurbished approximately 1,200 of these during 1896, while the other 16,300 were reconditioned at Springfield Armory. During 1898, all of these Springfield refurbished revolver serial numbers became mixed and barrels were shortened. During this first re-work at Colt's in 1896, care was taken to match serial numbered parts, and in some instances, parts were even renumbered to match. After seeing hard use in the Spanish American War and the Philippine Insurrection, approximately 5,294 of these same guns were returned to Colt between 1900 and 1903 for refurbishing, and total refinishing. Our source estimates that 85% of these 1896 Colt refurbished revolvers were initially issued to the Rough Riders.

100%	98%	95%	90%	80%	70%	60%	50%	40%	30%	20%	10%

* ***Standard Mixed Numbers Variation***

N/A	$12,000	$10,000	$8,800	$8,250	$7,700	$6,000	$5,000	$4,600	$4,400	$3,850	$3,300

Add 100% documented "Rough Rider" association.
Add 10% for Custer period frames (under #6500).

Only rarely will one be found with all the matching serial numbers (except the barrel), indicating that it had been refurbished at Colt's during 1896. (Factory letter advised). These guns will bring a premium price, and must be authenticated, as they may have been recently altered, or are simply shortened Cavalry revolvers.

A few artillery models are believed to have been redone at various government arsenals, and this could explain the existence of several known artillery revolvers with blue frames. In fact, new information recently discovered by noted Single Action specialist Dave Lanara seems to confirm that some U.S. Artillery and Cavalry models were indeed refinished at the Manila Arsenal in the Philippines with blue frames, this was due to the lack of color case hardening capabilities at that location. Regardless, the artillery model is very popular with collectors and has become one of the most studied and interesting variants of the Colt Single Action revolver.

* ***Matching Numbers in Late Inspector Ranges (DFC & RAC)***

N/A	$17,000	$15,000	$12,000	$10,500	$8,000	$7,000	$6,000	$5,200	$4,600	$4,000	$3,400

Must be authenticated and confirmed by 1896 Colt factory letter.

* ***Matching Numbers in Early Inspector Ranges (A, C, J, LD, JTC, HN)***

N/A	$23,000	$21,500	$18,000	$15,000	$13,500	$11,000	$9,500	$8,000	$6,500	$5,200	$4,000

Add 20% for SAA's in the Custer ser. no. range (ser. no. 4516 - 6500).

Must be authenticated and confirmed by 1896 Colt factory letter.

* ***Blued Frame Variation With Mixed Number*** – must be authenticated.

N/A	$10,000	$8,500	$7,200	$6,000	$4,600	$4,100	$3,600	$3,200	$2,800	$2,500	$2,200

* ***New York State Militia SAA*** – in 1895 before work began on the artillery models, Colt refurbished 800 SAA revolvers supplied by Springfield Armory, especially for the New York State Militia. These guns retained their 7 1/2 inch barrels and all original parts wherever possible. Replacement parts were serial numbered to match, and strangely, barrels and cylinders were given the missing first and second digits of the whole serial number where they had never before been applied. In addition to receiving a high polish blue and case hardened civilian finish, their hammers were "fire-blued" instead of being color case hardened. Since most other Cavalry models in the government's possession were cut to 5 1/2 inches shortly thereafter, these 800 are quite possibly the only remaining 7 1/2 inch SAAs that could actually have seen service on the American frontier against hostiles. Most other 7 1/2 inch Cavalry revolvers that are seen today were likely issued to state militias rather than the U.S. Army. Some are found with unit markings on their buttstraps and/or grips or with lanyard swivels. These 800 Colt revolvers therefore may have played a very significant role in the history of the Indian wars.

N/A	$28,000	$24,000	$20,000	$15,000	$13,000	$10,000	$8,000	$6,750	$5,500	$4,800	$4,000

Since New York Militia revolvers are frequently encountered with a mismatched part, the question is often asked if the mismatched part affects value. If the serial number of the mismatched part can be attributed to another known New York Militia revolver, then the answer is "only slightly". Since the serial numbers of all 800 refurbished 1895 New York Militia models are recorded in the Colt ledgers, the serial number of the mismatched part should always belong to another documented New York example. In many cases, cylinders had been inadvertently switched by a New York Trooper, or back straps were refitted onto an incorrect revolver when the New York Militia armorer fitted the lanyard swivel.

CAUTION: Unscrupulous fakers have been known to restamp the (correctly) mismatched part with the "host" revolver's primary serial number.

* ***Condemned U.S. Cavalry*** – throughout military contract production, a small percentage of SAAs did not pass inspection and were condemned, receiving a large "C" stamped on the frame, just over the serial number. These guns were set aside, and later completed as civilian revolvers. They are often found with the Ordnance sub-inspector's initials, such as J.T.C., on the bottom of the frame, but will not have a "U.S." on the left side. This does not have a negative effect on the value of these guns to the collector, and they should be regarded as normal civilian revolvers with an interesting history. Beware of re-stamped "US" markings.

REVOLVERS: SAA, 2ND GENERATION: 1956-1975 MFG.

The author wishes to express his thanks to Charles Layson, and Carol and the late Don Wilkerson for their generous contributions to the 2nd & 3rd Generation Colt SAA information.

GRADING - PPGS™	100%	98%	95%	90%	80%	70%	60%	LAST MSR

Popular demand brought back the Single Action Army in 1956 with minor modifications, most not detectable except to experts. Serial numbers began at 0001SA, and continued to 73,000SA before the "New Model" was introduced in 1976 (ser. no. 80,000SA). Premiums are paid for rare production variances in NIB condition. It should be noted "premium niches" exist in this model as collectors are establishing premiums paid for rarer production variances (the interrelation of barrel length, caliber, frame type, finish quality, year of manufacture, and other special features). The order of desirability on standard 2nd Generation SAAs is as follows: 4 3/4 in. barrels are the most desirable, followed by 7 1/2 in., and then 5 1/2 in. Caliber desirability is as follows: .45 LC has the most demand, followed by .44 Spl., .38 Spl., and then .357 Mag. It follows that desirable calibers found with desirable barrel lengths will command healthy premiums if production was unusually low for a particular configuration. Reference books specifically on the post-war SAA are a must when determining the rarity factors on these multiple production combinations. Buntlines, Sheriff's Models, and special orders through the Custom Gun Shop are in a class by themselves and have to be evaluated one at a time.

It is advisable to procure a factory letter when buying or selling older or recently manufactured Colt single actions (hence, guaranteeing authenticity and value credibility). These watermarked letters are based on the original factory shipping records and are available by contacting Colt Archive Properties LLC in Bloomfield, CT. While not totally infallible, these letters are normally very accurate. The cost to document 2nd generation SAA's is $100. This research can be expedited for an additional $100. This expedited service provides a verbal report within 24-48 hours and a documentation letter follows in 2-3 weeks. Additionally, premium charges apply for factory engraved guns ($50-$150), or unique shipping destinations ($50-$200). To contact the Archive Department for assistance, call 1-800-962-2658, Ext. 1343. Once contacted, they will tell you what the exact historical research charge will be for the service you are requesting. The address to write to is COLT ARCHIVE PROPERTIES LLC, 1295 Blue Hills Avenue, Bloomfield, CT 06002. For a complete Archive Services price list, please refer to the Colt website at coltsmfg.com.

SINGLE ACTION ARMY (SAA, 2ND GENERATION) – .357 Mag., .38 Spl., .44 Spl., or .45 LC cal., denoted by SA suffix, 3 (Sheriff's Model), 4 3/4, 5 1/2, 7 1/2, or 12 (Buntline) in. barrel length - 5 1/2, 7 1/2, and 12 in. barrels have the one-line barrel address, and are all blue, blue/case hardened, or nickel finished. 2nd Generation SAAs have been grouped into the following 3 categories.

* ***SAA Early 2nd Generation*** – ser. no. range 0001SA to approx. 39,000SA, shipped in one-piece black box similar to pre-war box. Mfg. from 1956-65.

.45 LC cal.	$3,100	$2,500	$2,250	$1,800	$1,600	$1,350	$1,100
.44 Spl. cal.	$2,900	$2,300	$2,100	$1,600	$1,500	$1,200	$1,000
.38 Spl. cal.	$2,700	$2,100	$1,900	$1,500	$1,400	$1,100	$1,000
.357 Mag. cal.	$2,300	$1,800	$1,600	$1,400	$1,300	$1,000	$900

Add 30% for original black box in good condition.

Add 20% for original nickel finish.

Add 15% for original 4 3/4 in. barrel.

Subtract 10% for rounded "fanning, quick draw" hammer configuration, where sharp corners above the firing pin were removed so as not to scratch the shooter's palm or thumb when trying to cock and fire quickly. Guns with this type of hammer fall between serial #26,500SA (1959) and #61,900SA (1972) approximately.

The very earliest models of this group, with serial numbers under 10,000 SA, have become more desirable when found in 100% new condition, with perfect black box, brush and papers - this configuration may bring an additional 30%.

* ***SAA Mid-Range 2nd Generation*** – approx. ser. no. range 39,000SA to 70,055SA, most were shipped in a red and white, two-piece, stagecoach box, but at approx. serial range 65,XXXSA a light wood grain box was used followed by a dark wood grain box. Mfg. 1965-1973.

.45 LC cal.	$2,200	$2,000	$1,800	$1,600	$1,350	$1,150	$950
.44 Spl. cal.	$2,000	$1,850	$1,600	$1,400	$1,250	$1,000	$850
.357 Mag. cal.	$1,900	$1,700	$1,500	$1,300	$1,100	$900	$800

Add 30% for original stagecoach box.

Add 20% for original light or dark grain wood box with styrofoam inserts.

Add 20% for original nickel finish.

Add 25% for original 4 3/4 in. barrel.

GRADING - PPGS™	100%	98%	95%	90%	80%	70%	60%	LAST MSR

* ***SAA Late 2nd Generation*** – approx. ser. no. range 70,055SA to 73,205SA, shipped in a brown, wood grain cardboard shell with 2 styrofoam inserts. Mfg. 1973-1976.

.45 LC cal.	$2,000	$1,850	$1,650	$1,400	$1,250	$1,000	$900	
.357 Mag. cal.	$1,800	$1,650	$1,450	$1,250	$1,050	$900	$800	

Add 20% for original brown/Styrofoam box.
Add 20% for original nickel finish.
Add 20% for original 4 3/4 in. barrel.

2nd Generation SAAs in stagecoach box w/o eagle black grips (ser. numbered under approx. 52,000SA) are more desirable than those with eagle. Also, flat-top hammers are more desirable than round top hammers found between ser. no. range 27,012SA-61,575SA (mfg. mid-1959-1972).

Colt manufactured approximately 100 screwless frames during the 1970s and assembled approximately 50 guns at the time. The other 50 sat in the warehouse until Colt started assembling the screwless frames again during the 1990s. Most of these recent guns are engraved and in .38-40 WCF or .45 LC cal., and have either a 4 3/4 or 5 in. barrel. Typically, the engraver's name is part of the serial number. Bangor's distributed most of these guns, and in today's marketplace they are priced in the $7,500-$25,000 range.

SHERIFF'S MODEL SAA (1961 MODEL) – .45 LC cal., distinictive configuration with 3 in. barrel and no ejector rod housing, ser. no. followed by SM suffix, 503 were mfg. for Centennial Arms Corp. - 478 had a blue/case hardened finish and 25 were done in nickel.

Blue/cc finish	$2,750	$2,000	$1,750	$1,550	$1,300	$1,100	$900	
Nickel finish	$7,850	$4,850	$4,200	$3,600	$3,000	$2,400	$2,100	

Add 25% for original two-piece box.

Original nickel finish is very rare on this model, watch for refinishing.

BUNTLINE SPECIAL SAA (2ND GENERATION) – .45 LC cal. only, 12 in. barrel, blue/case hardened finish, rubber (early mfg.) or walnut grips. Over 3,900 mfg. 1957-1975.

	$2,000	$1,750	$1,500	$1,450	$1,350	$1,200	$1,000	
Nickel finish	$3,850	$2,900	$2,500	$2,250	$1,950	$1,800	$1,650	

Add 10% for black hard rubber grips.
Add 40% for nickel finish w/original later tan box.
Add 100% for nickel finish with early black box.

Original nickel finish is very rare on this model, watch for refinishing and get a factory letter to verify.

NEW FRONTIER SAA (2ND GENERATION) – .357 Mag., .38 Spl. (rare), .44 Spl., or .45 LC cal., denoted by flat-top frame, adj. rear sight, and "NF" after the serial number, 4 3/4 (scarce), 5 1/2 (scarce), or 7 1/2 (most common) in. barrel, case hardened frame/blue finish and smooth walnut grips were standard. Approx. 4,200 mfg. 1961-1975.

	$1,400	$1,200	$1,100	$950	$850	$750	$650	
.38 Spl., 5 1/2 in. bbl.	$3,750	$2,850	$2,600	$2,400	$2,200	$2,000	$1,800	

Add 20% for later brown/styrofoam box.
Add 25% for stagecoach or black box (must be in correct ser. no. range).
Add 35% for early black and gold box.
Add 50% for 4 3/4 in. barrel.
Add 25% for 5 1/2 in. barrel.

NEW FRONTIER BUNTLINE SAA (2ND GENERATION) – .45 LC cal. only, 12 in. barrel, flat-top frame and adj. rear sight. Approx. 72 mfg. 1962-67.

	$2,500	$2,190	$1,875	$1,700	$1,375	$1,125	$875	

Add 50% for original black or tan box (must be serial numbered to the gun).

FACTORY ENGRAVED 2ND GENERATION SAAs – approx. 350 revolvers were factory engraved with 90% being in .45 LC cal. Values range from 75%-100% higher than non-engraved specimens, with additional premiums paid for rare styles and configurations and/or for the notoriety of the engraver. Those SAAs done by Albert Herbert, A.A. White, Robert Burt, Leonard Francolini, and Dennis Kies are probably the highest-priced examples. Always check authenticity when buying, selling, or trading engraved 2nd Generation SAAs with the Colt Archive Dept. The charge for a factory letter per engraved gun is $150. $50 will be refunded if Colt cannot provide historical documentation.

Factory engraved 2nd Generation SAAs are at least 10 times rarer than engraved 3rd Generation pistols.

REVOLVERS: SAA, 3RD GENERATION: 1976-CURRENT MFG.

After a short break in production, Colt Firearms announced the resumption of full-scale production of the Single Action on Feb. 4th, 1976, at the N.S.G.A. (National Sporting Goods Association) Bi-

GRADING - PPGS™	100%	98%	95%	90%	80%	70%	60%	LAST MSR

Centennial show in Chicago.

The "New Model Colt Single Action Army" or the "Colt Post-War Single Action Army - New Model", as it was commonly referred to at the time, is known today to collectors as the "3rd Generation Colt Single Action Army". The most significant change in the new 3rd Generation guns was the elimination of the full length, removable cylinder bushing which was no longer considered necessary with the use of modern, smokeless powder. This removal reduced the cost of manufacturing of each unit.

Production began with ser. no. 80,000SA, and reached 99,999SA in 1978. At this point, the SA suffix changed to a prefix beginning with SA01,001. Serialization reached SA99,999 during 1993, and began over, this time separating the letters SA, and starting with S02,001A.

Many collectors note that the fit and workmanship suffered greatly in the period of the 1980s and early 1990s. It was a period when the fine art of case coloring was much neglected and many 3rd SAA were simply all blue - since the men that made the old case color had retired. However, Colt started showing more care in case colored guns and the fitting of grips after 1996 in the Colt Custom Shop issues.

Starting at approximately ser. no. S34,000A, Colt reintroduced the full length cylinder bushing which had been eliminated in 1976, making these current 3rd Generation Single Actions essentially the same as the 1st and 2nd Generation guns. The factory still refers to these as 3rd Generation however, and not 4th Generation, as some collectors are now calling them. For a listing of Colt's "P-Codes" (referring to the factory's model number designations specifying frame type, caliber, finish, and barrel length), please refer to the Colt Single Action Model Numbers section in the back of this book (located in Colt Serialization). As with 1st and 2nd Generation Single Actions, a factory letter authenticating configuration and shipping destination can be obtained by writing to: COLT ARCHIVE PROPERTIES LLC, 1295 Blue Hills Avenue, Bloomfield, CT 06002.

All 100% values on currently manufactured revolvers in this section assume NIB condition.

Please contact the Colt Custom Shop for a written quotation ($25) regarding a custom built SAA with special options/features. Their address is: Colt Manufacturing Company, Inc. P.O. Box 1868, Hartford, CT 06101, ATTN: Custom Shop.

STANDARD/CUSTOM SINGLE ACTION ARMY SAA (3RD GENERATION) – .32-20 WCF (mfg. 2005-2011), .357 Mag. (disc. approx. 1983, reintroduced 2005-2019), .38 Spl. (reintroduced 2005-2011), .38-40 WCF (reintroduced 2005-2011), .44 Spl. (disc. approx. 1983), .44-40 WCF (disc. 2011), or .45 LC cal., 4 (disc. 1988), 4 3/4, 5 (disc. 1987), 5 1/2, or 7 1/2 in. barrel, 5 1/2 and 7 1/2 in. barrels have the one-line barrel address, fixed sights, standard finishes include full blue (disc.), color case hardened/blue or nickel (disc. 2018), plastic black eagle or walnut grips (used mostly during 1991-92) standard, current mfg. of black powder frames are available in .45 LC cal. only (see separate listing for current mfg.), most recent mfg. has blue shipping box with white slip cover. Mfg. 1976 to date. Original 1976 issue price was approx. $242.

MSR $1,799	**$1,799**	**$1,500**	**$1,295**	**$1,195**	**$995**	**$895**	**$795**

Add $200 nickel finish (disc. 2018).
Add 25% for original .38 Spl. cal. (disc.)
Add 10% for black powder frame mfg. pre-1996.
Add $700 for original two-piece ivory grips with screw.
Add $700 for original one-piece ivory grips w/o screw.
Add 5% for original brown box with styrofoam inserts (mfg. 1976-93).
Add approx. 15% over the 100% value per gun for a matched pair (w/consecutive ser. nos.).
Typically, the engraver's name is part of the serial number. Bangor's originally distributed most of these guns. In today's marketplace price range from $8,500-$25,000, depending on configuration and engraving.

The following calibers .32-20 WCF, .38 Spl., .38-40 WCF, .44-40 WCF, and .44 Spl. are available through special order from the Colt Custom Shop. Please contact the Custom Shop for availability of options and pricing.

Some Colt SAA dealers and collectors have recently commented that current NIB 3rd Generation SAAs are bringing premiums over the 100% values listed due to the custom shop not producing SAAs per individual order like it used to. This has resulted in a decrease in supply (especially nickel-finished SAAs), and the result is that values on these NIB specimens have gone up accordingly.

Through 2001, Colt offered the SAA as both Standard and Custom Models. The difference is that single actions, which are further customized with engraving, special barrel lengths, stocks, etc., are packaged more elaborately because of the added value of the customizing.

GRADING - PPGS™	100%	98%	95%	90%	80%	70%	60%	LAST MSR

Beginning 2001, all orders for SAA models are processed through the Colt Custom Shop. The 2001 Custom Shop MSR for the Custom SAA was $2,100.

Various custom order barrel lengths have been available on this model for some time.

The .357 Mag. and .44 Spl. cals. were mostly discontinued by 1983.

Colt manufactured approximately 100 screwless frames during the 1970s, and assembled approximately 50 guns at the time. The other 50 sat in the warehouse until Colt started assembling the screwless frames again during the 1990s. Most of these recent guns are engraved and in .38-40 WCF or .45 LC cal., and have either a 4 3/4 or 5 in. barrel.

To reference factory coding for the various Standard Model P (SAA) configurations, please refer to the Colt Single Action Model Numbers within the Colt Serialization section in the back of this text.

BLACK POWDER FRAME SAA (3RD GENERATION) – .45 LC cal., 4 3/4, 5 1/2, or 7 1/2 in. barrel, features old style black powder frame, standard finish is case colored frame and blue barrel/cylinder. Mfg. 1984-1995, reintroduced 2008-2018.

	100%	98%	95%	90%	80%	70%	60%	LAST MSR
	$2,000	$1,700	$1,395	$1,195	$995	$895	$795	*$1,799*

Add 30% with original box and instructions.

COLT COWBOY SAA – .45 LC cal., 4 3/4 (disc. 1999, reintroduced 2002), 5 1/2, or 7 1/2 (disc. 1999) in. barrel marked "COLT COWBOY .45 COLT" on left side, transfer bar safety, all steel construction, frame assembly done in the U.S., charcoal case colors on frame with blue metal parts, rampant Colt black composition grips similar in design to those used on 1st generation SAAs, 40 oz. Not mfg. in U.S. While advertised beginning 1998, this model was not manufactured until 1999-2003.

	100%	98%	95%	90%	80%	70%	60%	LAST MSR
	$1,700	$1,300	$950	$850	$650	$550	$450	*$670*

Add 30% for original box and instructions.

* ***Cowboy SAA Collection Set*** – includes SAA in .45 LC cal., with 5 1/2 in. barrel, stag (very limited) or imitation ivory (more common) grips, blue/color case hardened finish, accessories include collector's Bowie knife, silver medallion and collector's case, marked "1 of 1,000". Limited mfg. 2000 only.

	100%	98%	95%	90%	80%	70%	60%	LAST MSR
Faux ivory	$1,650	$1,250	$825	$675	$575	$475	$400	
Stag	$1,850	$1,625	$1,375	$1,100	$875	$700	$550	*approx. $1,600*

SHERIFF'S MODEL SAA (3RD GENERATION, MFG 1980-1985) – .44-40 WCF, .44 Spl., or .45 LC cal., 3 in. barrel w/o ejector rod, blue/case colored, nickel, or royal blue finish. Approx. 4,560 guns mfg. 1980-85.

	100%	98%	95%	90%	80%	70%	60%	LAST MSR
.45 LC cal. (blue/CH)	$1,800	$1,350	$1,050	$900	$750	$600	$550	
.44 Spl./.44-40 WCF	$1,700	$1,275	$975	$850	$725	$625	$525	

Add 30% for original box and instructions.
Add 10% for extra convertible cylinder.
Add 10% for original nickel finish.
Add $550 for original ivory grips.
Subtract 20% for all blue finish.

* ***Sheriff's Model SAA (3rd Generation - Recent Mfg.)*** – .44-40 WCF or .45 LC (most popular) cal., 3 or 4 in. barrel w/o ejector rod, blue/case colored (disc. 2009) or nickel finish, black plastic grips. Mfg. 2008-2010.

	100%	98%	95%	90%	80%	70%	60%	LAST MSR
Blue/cc finish (2008-09)	$1,600	$1,250	$975	$825	$725	$650	$575	
Nickel finish (2009-2010)	$1,700	$1,300	$1,025	$850	$750	$675	$600	

Add 30% for original box and instructions.

Last MSR was $1,490 (nickel finish) in 2010.

BUNTLINE SPECIAL MODEL SAA (3RD GENERATION) – .44-40 WCF or .45 LC cal. only, 12 in. barrel, blue/case hardened finish, walnut grips.

	100%	98%	95%	90%	80%	70%	60%	LAST MSR
	$1,695	$1,050	$850	$750	$650	$600	$550	

Add 10% for original nickel finish.

Add 30% for original box and instructions.
Add $550 for original ivory grips.

NEW FRONTIER SAA (3RD GENERATION - 1978-1981 MFG.) – .357 Mag. (rare), .44-40 WCF (rare), .44 Spl., or .45 LC cal., denoted by "NF" serial suffix, 4 3/4, 5 1/2, or 7 1/2 in. barrel, blue/case hardened finish, flat-top frame, adj. rear sight, plain two-piece walnut grips. Mfg. 1978-1983.

	100%	98%	95%	90%	80%	70%	60%	LAST MSR
	$1,700	$1,350	$1,025	$850	$750	$675	$600	

Subtract 10% for 5 1/2 in. barrel.
Subtract 15% for 7 1/2 in. barrel.
Add 30% for original box with styrofoam inserts.

GRADING - PPGS™	100%	98%	95%	90%	80%	70%	60%	LAST MSR

Add 50% for all-nickel issue of 509 in .357 Mag. cal. and 7 1/2 in. barrel (model P4671). Rarest of New model New Frontiers. Ser. range 14100NF to 15000NF (1981).

Add 50% for issue of 519 in in .44-40 WCF cal. and 4 3/4 in. barrel (model P4940). Rarest of New model New Frontiers. Ser. range 15000NF to 15700 NF. (1981-83).

Serial numbers on the New Frontier started at 01001NF, but during 1980 a few New Frontiers with 5 1/2 in. barrels were produced in the 7000NF serial range, where 2nd Generation New Frontiers left off. Therefore, a 3rd Generation New Frontier will either have a ser. no. starting with "O" or will have a higher number than 7288NF with no "O" prefix.

FRONTIER SIX SHOOTER SAA (3RD GENERATION) – .44-40 WCF cal., black powder frame, 4 3/4, 5 1/2, or 7 1/2 in. barrel with "Colt Frontier Six Shooter" acid etched in a panel on the left side of barrel, similar to 1st Generation SAAs, blue (disc. 2009) or nickel finish. Mfg. 2008-2010.

	100%	98%	95%	90%	80%	70%	60%	LAST MSR
Blue finish (2008-09)								
	$2,000	$1,500	$1,275	$1,100	$900	$800	$700	
Nickel finish (2008-2010)								
	$2,000	$1,500	$1,275	$1,100	$900	$800	$700	*$1,547*

Add 20% for original box and instructions.

NEW FRONTIER SAA (3RD GENERATION - RECENT MFG.) – .357 Mag. (disc. 2011), .44 Spl., or .45 LC cal., 4 3/4 (.45 LC cal. only), 5 1/2, or 7 1/2 in. barrel, royal blue/case hardened finish, flat-top frame, adj. rear sight, two-piece smooth walnut grips with medallions. Mfg. 2011-2018.

	100%	98%	95%	90%	80%	70%	60%	LAST MSR
	$1,500	$1,250	$975	$850	$725	$625	$575	*$1,899*

Add 20% for original box and instructions.

The following calibers .32-20 WCF, .38 Spl., .38-40 WCF, .44-40 WCF, and .44 Spl. are available through special order from the Colt Custom Shop. Please contact the Custom Shop for availability of options and pricing.

NEW FRONTIER BUNTLINE SPECIAL SAA (3RD GENERATION) – .45 LC cal. only, 12 in. barrel, flat-top frame, adj. rear sight, limited mfg. as the New Buntline Commemorative during 1979. Please refer to the Colt Commemorative section for value information.

STOREKEEPER'S MODEL SAA (3RD GENERATION - 1984-85 MFG.) – .45 LC cal. only, black powder frame, 4 in. barrel w/ejector rod, full nickel or royal blue/case hardened finish, ivory grips. Approx. 280 mfg. 1984-1985.

	100%	98%	95%	90%	80%	70%	60%	LAST MSR
Blue/cc finish	$1,900	$1,650	$1,500	$1,250	$1,000	$850	$650	
Nickel finish	$2,000	$1,700	$1,600	$1,300	$1,100	$900	$800	

* ***Storekeeper's Model SAA (3rd Generation - 2008-2010 Mfg.)*** – .44-40 WCF or .45 LC cal., 4 in. barrel w/ejector rod, blue/case hardened (disc. 2009) or nickel (mfg. 2010) finish. Mfg. 2008-2010.

	100%	98%	95%	90%	80%	70%	60%	LAST MSR
Blue/cc finish (2008-09)								
	$1,700	$1,300	$1,025	$850	$750	$675	$600	
Nickel finish (2008-2010)								
	$1,800	$1,350	$1,050	$900	$750	$600	$525	*$1,490*

Add 20% for original box and instructions.

COLT CLASSIC SAA – .45 LC cal., 5 1/2 in. barrel only, all blue finish, uncheckered wood grips with Colt medallions, twin gold barrel bands on back of cylinder and front of barrel. Limited mfg. 2010 only.

	100%	98%	95%	90%	80%	70%	60%	LAST MSR
	$1,800	$1,350	$1,050	$900	$750	$600	$525	*$1,620*

Add 20% for original box and instructions.

HUGH O'BRIAN-WYATT EARP LIMITED EDITION – .45 LC cal., set includes one 4 3/4 in. and one 12 in. barreled Buntline SAA models, smooth walnut grips, case colored frame and hammer with polished blue barrel and cylinder, barrels are etched "Hugh O'Brian - Wyatt Earp Tribute" and backstrap features Hugh O'Brian's signature, set includes French fitted walnut case with hinged glass top and removable drawer, includes replica marshall badge, certificates signed by Hugh O'Brian and double holster Buntline special gun belt, mfg. by Frontier Gunleather, total mfg. determined by orders taken by Dec. 31, 2010.

	100%	98%	95%	90%	80%	70%	60%	LAST MSR
	$4,500	$4,100	$3,600	$3,100	$2,750	$2,350	$1,900	*$4,712*

Add 30% for original box and instructions.
Add $150 for holster set.

COLT 175th ANNIVERSARY LIMITED EDITION SAA – .45 LC cal., Colt royal blue finish only, 175th Anniversary (1836-2011) Limited Edition with selective 24Kt. gold plated scroll on frame, backstrap, barrel and cylinder, black powder frame, left side of barrel is marked "1836 - 175th Anniversary - 2011", 4 3/4, 5 1/2, or 7 1/2 in. barrel, black eagle plastic grips, 175 manufactured in each barrel length 2011 only.

	100%	98%	95%	90%	80%	70%	60%	LAST MSR
	$2,250	$1,575	$1,325	$1,100	$950	$825	$700	*$1,580*

Add 30% for original box and instructions.

GRADING - PPGS™	100%	98%	95%	90%	80%	70%	60%	LAST MSR

COLT CUSTOM SHOP ENGRAVING, SAA & SEMI-AUTO, 1976-PRESENT

Prior to 1976, Colt had three factory engraving patterns - A, B, and C coverage. During 1976, they expanded the Custom Shop and a new class D pattern was added. To inaugurate the Custom Gun shop in 1976, Colt created a "Custom Edition" of deluxe engraved Model P revolvers. This custom edition was the first of many custom editions to be produced by the Custom Gun Shop over the years. The term "Custom Edition" is defined by Don Wilkerson as a group of identical revolvers assembled under the direction of the Custom Gun Shop and sold through Colt's normal distribution system. A "Custom Edition" differs from a "Special Edition" in that a special edition is a group of revolvers made per customer specifications, sold to one purchaser, and not through Colt's normal distribution system. An example of a custom edition: Twenty-five P-1970 revolvers were assembled on Custom Shop order #2622. All twenty-five .44-40 cal. Royal Blue and casehardened revolvers were assembled with unfluted cylinders and ivory stocks. This custom edition was shipped to the various Colt distributors in early 1984.

An example of a special edition: Two hundred P-1970 revolvers were ordered by the Powder Horn Gun Shop in Bozeman, Montana to commemorate the founding of the Bozeman trail. Each revolver in the edition was assembled with an unfluted cylinder and acid etched with gold leaf. All two hundred revolvers were contracted by and sold to the Powder Horn Gun Shop.

A large number of custom editions have been assembled by the Custom Gun Shop since 1976. The great majority of revolvers coming from the Custom Gun Shop are associated with either a "factory order" number or a "Custom shop" number. The end label of the shipping carton is the place where these two terms are most likely to be encountered. Custom Shop orders have varied from as few as a single revolver to as many as 100 revolvers.

The listings below represent both current and discontinued Custom Shop engraving prices for the various frame sizes, amount of engraving coverage (A = 25% coverage, B = 50% coverage, C = 75% coverage, and D = 100% coverage), and the three levels of engraving execution (i.e., Standard, Expert, and Master levels). SAAs are considered large frame, revolvers and full-size Government Models are considered medium frame, and Government Model 380s are considered small frame. Most buyers of engraved Colt SAAs today are very knowledgeable, and many of them are no longer satisfied with Standard types of patterns and styles. As a result, those engraved guns with the rarest production variances coupled with unique engraving done at an Expert or better level are currently more desireable than their counterparts with Standard engraving patterns. Colt currently employs three full-time engravers at the factory, in addition to several outside sources (at all engraving levels).

The name of the engraver is available only when ordering either the Expert or the Master level of engraving.

CUSTOM & SPECIAL ENGRAVED SAA EDITIONS (3RD GENERATION) - beginning in 1976, with the introduction of the "New Model" SAA (3rd Generation), the Colt Custom Shop produced many custom and special edition engraved Single Army Action revolvers. According to Mr. Don Wilkerson, author of *The Post-War Single Action Revolver 1976-1986*, "the term custom edition is defined as a group of identical revolvers assembled under the direction of the Custom Gun Shop at Colt's and sold through the normal distribution system. A custom edition differs from a special edition in that special editions are a group of revolvers made up to a customer's unique specifications, and sold as a group to one purchaser...." While the exact number is not known, it is thought that approx. 3,500 SAAs have been engraved since 1976. Since each edition is unique, values vary widely, depending upon the notability of the engraver, the amount and type of coverage, and the number produced. Models listed below are recent Colt Custom Editions.

* ***SAA Engraved European Model*** - 9mm Para. cal., nickel finish only, 4 3/4 (110 mfg.), 5 1/2 (110 mfg.), or 7 1/2 (50 mfg.) in. barrel, rosewood grips with silver medallions, 40-43 oz. Mfg. 1991-92 only.

$2,600	$1,900	$1,475	$1,225	$1,075	$875	$750	*$1,990*

* ***SAA Engraved U.S. Model*** - .45 ACP cal., royal blue finish only, 4 3/4, 5 1/2, or 7 1/2 in. barrel, walnut grips, 40-43 oz. Mfg. 1991-92 only.

$1,950	$1,325	$1,100	$985	$795	$675	$565	*$1,960*

* ***SAA Old World Engravers Sampler*** - .45 LC cal., 5 1/2 in. barrel, nickel finish, buffalo horn grips, includes four unique styles of engraving. Mfg. 1997-98, reintroduced 2001-2002.

$2,975	$2,450	$2,000	$1,740	$1,495	$1,215	$1,000	*$3,445*

* ***Legend Rodeo/Legend Rodeo II SAA*** - disc. 1998.

$1,950	$1,500	$1,250	$1,100	$895	$785	$630	*$2,450*

GRADING - PPGS™	100%	98%	95%	90%	80%	70%	60%	LAST MSR

* ***125th Anniversary Edition SAA*** – beveled cylinder, fire blue finish, "45 COLT" on left side of barrel and address on top of barrel. 1,000 mfg. 1997-2002.

	$1,600	$1,150	$825	N/A	N/A	N/A	N/A	*$2,070*

* ***Model P w/Unsigned B Coverage Engraving*** – choice of cals. and barrel lengths, blue or nickel finish, features unsigned standard American scroll B engraving coverage. Disc. 2010.

	$2,250	$2,000	$1,750	$1,500	$1,250	$1,000	$875	*$2,319*

Add $231 for nickel finish.

* ***Modern Masters Model P w/Signed B Coverage Engraving*** – choice of cals. and barrel lengths, blue or nickel finish, features signed standard American scroll B engraving coverage. Mfg. 2009-disc.

Last MSR on this model was $6,528.

SAA CUSTOM SHOP ENGRAVING PRICES - PRE-1997 – values below represent 1995 published SAA Custom Shop A-D engraving options before the company started separate Standard, Expert, and Master level pricing during 1997. For current Colt Custom Shop engraving prices, please refer to the "Colt Custom Shop Engraving - Current Mfg." section below.

Add $1,163 for Class "A" engraving (25% metal coverage).
Add $2,324 for Class "B" engraving (50% metal coverage).
Add $3,487 for Class "C" engraving (75% metal coverage).
Add $4,647 for Class "D" engraving (100% metal coverage).
Add an additional 13% (approx.) for Buntline engraving.

Standard Engraving was performed mostly by standard level factory engravers and engraving options generally included A-D style coverage. Typically, gold work was not performed by these engravers and specimens are mostly unsigned. Expert Engravers executed classic American style scroll, w/o gold work, and may have signed their work.

FACTORY ENGRAVED SAAs (3RD GENERATION) – the rarity of the SAA configuration in addition to the notability of the engraver will make the difference on the premiums commanded. 3rd Generation factory engraved SAAs were produced in much greater numbers than were 2nd Generation SAAs. Over 80% of engraved 3rd Generation SAAs are .45 LC caliber, the majority have 7 1/2 in. barrels, and some variation of blue finish. Grade "C" (41% of engraved mfg.) and Grade "D" (24% of engraved mfg.) dominate production.

Current MSR on a Colt SAA with signed Master Level Engraving "B" coverage is $7,061.
Use the following add-ons as general guidelines for values on factory engraved recently manufactured 3rd Generation SAAs.
Add approx. 10% for original nickel finish.
Add 25% for 4 3/4 in. barrel.
Add 15% for 5 1/2 in. barrel.
Add 10% for calibers other than .45 LC.
Add 30% for factory ivory grips.
Add 10% for original blue cardboard or plastic box.
Unfortunately, the quality of the engraving on some early Third Generation SAAs has been substandard, and as a result, these guns usually cap at approx. $2,000.

During 1978-79, Colt engraved as many as 300-500 guns on a single factory order. If the level of quality is similar to today's SAAs, the price will also be similar.

Large Frame Size: Current SAAs and M1911s

The following is a listing of current Custom Shop engraving for both SAAs and M1911s. Other Custom Shop options are priced on request, including a wide variety of gold/silver inlays, panel scenes, color enamel inlays, gold/silver frame outlines, etc.

Add $1,130 for A Standard engraving.
Add $1,300 for B Standard, $2,075 for B Expert (signed), or $3,725 for B Master (signed) level engraving.
Add $1,700 for C Standard, $2,878 for C Expert (signed), or $5,415 for C Master (signed) level engraving.
Add $2,000 for D Standard, $4,280 for D Expert (signed), or $6,900 for D Master (signed) level engraving.
Add 20% to large frame pricing for Buntline Models (disc.).

Medium Frame Size

Medium frame engraving was discontinued circa 1998.

Values listed reflect last published MSRs.
Add $900 for Standard A level engraving.
Add $1,200 for B Standard, $1,700 for B Expert, or $3,150 for B Master level engraving.
Add $1,400 for C Standard, $2,500 for C Expert, or $4,538 for C Master level engraving.
Add $1,600 for D Standard, $3,600 for D Expert, or $6,300 for D Master level engraving.

GRADING - PPGS™	100%	98%	95%	90%	80%	70%	60%	LAST MSR

Small Frame Size

Factory small frame engraving was disc. 1998.

Values listed reflect last published MSRs. Subtract 20% from small frame pricing for Mustang Models.
Add $400 for A Standard, $600 for A Expert, or $800 for A Master level engraving.
Add $600 for B Standard, $800 for B Expert, or $1,000 for B Master level engraving.
Add $800 for C Standard, $1,100 for C Expert, or $1,500 for C Master level engraving.
Add $1,100 for D Standard, $1,300 for D Expert, or $1,900 for D Master level engraving.

POPULAR SAA CUSTOM SHOP SPECIAL ORDER OPTIONS

Add $329 for special barrel length, for "45 Colt" or two line address on barrel add $95, add $450 for caliber change, for custom-tuned action most recent MSR was $197, add $275 (available in .45 LC only beginning 2000) for extra regular fluted or unfluted cylinder, for extra long fluted cylinder most recent MSR was $308, add $152 for beveled front of cylinder, add $180 for fire blue package (screws, base pin, and ejector rod head), add $200 for mirror brite finish (disc.), add $1,618 for nickel finish, add $1,390 for blue/color case finish, add $1,390 for full blue finish, add $425, for gold or silver plating, last published MSR was $425, currently it's POR), add $105 for black eagle grips, add $305 for smooth walnut grips with medallions, add $275 for North American elkhorn grips (disc.), add $400 for red stag grips (disc.), add $450 for sambar stag grips (disc.), add $625 for stag grips, add $425 for buffalo horn grips, add $375 for mother-of-pearl grips (disc.), add $840 for one or two piece plain ivory grips, $425 for imitation ivory, approx. 10% for grip checkering, add $350 for scrimshaw engraving (3 initials only), add $65 for consecutive serial numbers, add $350 for individual unique serial number, add $105 to modify and shorten ejector housing, add $55 for bullseye ejector rod head, add $359 for birdshead grips, add $400 for extra long backstrap, for extended butt frame last MSR was $400, for special length barrel add $329, to regulate barrel for accuracy add $225, for qualify screws add $84, for wide spur hammer with blue finish add $225, for wide spur hammer with nickel or hard chrome finish add $255.
While a few screwless frame SAAs have been mfg. to date (approx.100), the Custom Shop now lists this option as a standard custom order feature. Price is POR.

REVOLVERS: SAA, SCOUT MODEL

100% values below assume NIB condition. Subtract 10% without box.

FRONTIER SCOUT (Q or F SUFFIX) – .22 LR or .22 WMR (introduced after 1960) cal., "Q" or "F" suffix, blue or bright alloy frame, all blue, or duotone (bright alloy frame disc. 1961), 4 3/4 or 9 1/2 (Buntline, blue only) in. barrel, available with interchangeable cylinders after 1964, black composition or walnut grips, approx. 246,000 mfg. 1957-1970.

	100%	98%	95%	90%	80%	70%	60%
	$600	$475	$400	$325	$250	$200	$150

Add 20% for extra cylinder.
Add 20% for Buntline model (marked "BUNTLINE SCOUT .22 CAL.")
Add 25% for "Q" suffix with duo-tone finish (mfg. 1957-58 only).
Add 20% for original box.
Add 50% for walnut grips (must have factory box or letter).

FRONTIER SCOUT (K SUFFIX) – Zamac alloy frame version of "Q" Model with "K" suffix, nickel finish with walnut stocks, approx. 44,000 mfg. 1960-1970.

	100%	98%	95%	90%	80%	70%	60%
	$600	$475	$400	$325	$250	$200	$150
Scout cased pair	$1,300	$1,050	$850	$650	$525	$425	$325
Buntline cased pair	$1,600	$1,325	$1,050	$825	$675	$525	$400

Add 20% for Buntline model (marked "BUNTLINE SCOUT .22 CAL.")
Add 10% for original box.

This model used the alloy Zamac for manufacture (as opposed to aluminum in the "Q" and "F" suffix models), and specimens are 6 oz. heavier as a result.

FRONTIER SCOUT '62 (P SUFFIX) – blue finish version of "K" Model, except has "P" suffix, Staglite grips, approx. 68,000 mfg. 1962-1970.

	100%	98%	95%	90%	80%	70%	60%
	$600	$475	$400	$325	$250	$200	$150
Scout cased pair	$1,300	$1,050	$850	$650	$525	$425	$325
Buntline cased pair	$1,600	$1,325	$1,050	$825	$675	$525	$400

Add 20% for original box.
Add 20% for Buntline model (marked "BUNTLINE SCOUT .22 CAL.")

PEACEMAKER 22 SCOUT – .22 LR/.22 WMR cal., color case hardened steel frame, 4.4, 4 3/4, 6, or 7 1/2 (nicknamed Buntline Model but may be marked Peacemaker or Buntline) in. barrel, black composition grips, furnished with interchangeable .22 LR/.22 WMR cylinders, approx. 190,000 mfg. 1970-1977.

	100%	98%	95%	90%	80%	70%	60%
	$750	$600	$475	$375	$300	$225	$175

GRADING - PPGS™	100%	98%	95%	90%	80%	70%	60%	LAST MSR

Add 20% for 4.4 in. barrel.
Add 50% for 4 3/4 in. barrel (first year of production).
Add 20% for original box.
Add 25% for single cylinder model (must have original box with model number).
Subtract 10% if without extra cylinder.

This model can be identified by its "G" or "L" ser. no. prefix.

NEW FRONTIER 22 SCOUT - similar features as Peacemaker Model, except with flat-top frame, ramp front and adj. rear sight, mfg. 1970-1977, reintroduced in 1982 without convertible .22 WMR cylinder and added crossbolt safety, all blue finish became standard in 1985, models with safety are .22 LR only, G or L (1974 only) ser. no. prefix. Mfg. disc. 1986.

$600	$475	$400	$325	$250	$200	$150	*$181*

Add 50% for 4 3/4 in. barrel (first year of production).
Add 25% for single cylinder model w/o safety (must have original box with model number).
Add 20% for 4.4 in. barrel.
Add 20% for original box.
Subtract 10% if w/o extra cylinder (model w/o safety only).

PISTOLS: SEMI-AUTO, DISC.

Most of the semi-auto pistol models listed in the various pistol categories can have their original configuration confirmed with a Colt factory letter. To receive a letter, write: COLT ARCHIVE PROPERTIES, LLC, 1295 Blue Hills Avenue, Bloomfield, CT 06002. The research fee for these pistols is typically either $75 or $100, depending on the model. If they cannot obtain additional information on the variation you request, they will refund $50.

Until several years ago, the Single Action Army revolver commanded the most attention among Colt handgun collectors. Since 1987, Colt Semi-Autos have been in tremendous demand and have out-accelerated many other areas of Colt collecting. Because condition and originality play such a key role in determining Colt Semi-Auto prices, many variations have had their values pushed upward to the point where it is difficult to accurately determine a realistic price, especially on those models in 98% original condition or better. As a result, some of the rarer models rarely encountered in true 100% original condition have had their values deleted since extreme rarity precludes accurate price evaluation. As always, the hardest prices to ascertain when firearms market conditions are bullish are the 98-100% values.

MODEL 1900 - .38 ACP cal., 6 in. barrel, blue, plain walnut grips - checkered hard rubber grips after S/N 2,450, high spur hammer, sight safety. Mfg. 1900-03.

N/A	$15,000	$11,000	$7,600	$5,500	$4,000	$3,000

Add 100% for U.S. marked 1st Army contracts (100 guns serial numbered 11-207).
Add 75% for U.S. marked Navy contracts (250 guns serial numbered 1,001-1,250).
Add 60% for U.S. marked 2nd Army contracts (200 guns serial numbered 1,501-1,700).
Subtract 30%-50% for altered sight safety (factory refinished).

This model is serial numbered approx. between 1-4,274.

Somewhere between serial number 2,200 and 2,450, Colt began altering the sights to fixed sights in the production process, shipping both types. By approx. serial number 3,300, most guns shipped were altered during production. Guns altered during production are not refinished. Altered guns below serial number 2,200 were refinished, or at least had the slides refinished.

MODEL 1902 SPORTING - .38 ACP, 6 in. barrel, blue, fixed sights, checkered hard rubber grips, no safety, high spur hammer or round hammer. Mfg. 1902-08.

N/A	$5,750	$4,250	$3,250	$2,500	$1,750	$900

This model is serial numbered approx. 4,275-11,000 and 30,000-30,190.

MODEL 1902 MILITARY - .38 ACP cal., 6 in. barrel, blue, similar to 1902 Sporting, round hammer changed to spur type in 1908, checkered black hard rubber grips, lanyard swivel on bottom rear of left grip. Mfg. 1902-29.

N/A	$5,750	$4,500	$3,500	$2,500	$1,500	$900

Add 30% for front slide serrations.
Add 20% with original box and instructions.

This model is serial numbered approx. 11,000-16,000 and 30,200-43,266.

GRADING - PPGS™	100%	98%	95%	90%	80%	70%	60%	LAST MSR

MODEL 1902 MILITARY-U.S. ARMY MARKED – similar specifications to 1902 Military, only serial number range 15,001-15,200.

	N/A	$18,000	$15,000	$12,500	$10,000	$8,750	$6,000	

MODEL 1903 POCKET HAMMER (.38 ACP) – .38 ACP cal., 4 1/2 in. barrel, blue finish standard, round or spur hammer, checkered black hard rubber grips, similar to 1902 Sporting, but 4 1/2 in. barrel, 7 1/2 in. overall. Mfg. 1903-29.

	$5,000	$4,000	$2,750	$2,000	$1,250	$900	$750	

Add 30% for early round hammer.
Add 20% with original box and instructions.

This model is serial numbered approx. 16,000-47,226.

MODEL 1903 POCKET (MODEL M .32 ACP) – .32 ACP cal., 3 3/4 (Types II-IV) or 4 (Type I) in. barrel, charcoal blue, checkered hard rubber grips, hammerless, slide lock and grip safeties, barrel bushing. Mfg. 1903-1946.

	$1,650	$1,200	$900	$700	$500	$375	$325	

Add 20% for nickel finish (mostly w/pearl grips).
Add 60% for first model (Type I) mfg. 1903-1911 if in 100%-98% condition. If lower than 98%, add 20%.
Add 30% for Type II if in 100%-98% condition.
Add 30% with original box and instructions.

Type I - 32 ACPs have a 4 in. barrel, barrel bushing, no magazine safety, and are serial numbered 1-71,999.

Type II - 32 ACPs still retain their barrel bushing but have a 3 3/4 in. barrel and were mfg. from 1908-1910. They are serial numbered 72,000-105,050.

Type III - 32 ACPs do not have a barrel bushing and were mfg. from 1910-1926. They are serial numbered 105,051-468,096.

Type IV - 32 ACPs have the added magazine safety (of which there are both the commercial and "U.S. Property" variations). They are serial numbered 468,097-554,446.

* ***Model 1903 Parkerized*** – U.S. Property, 3 1/4 in. barrel, no barrel bushing, magazine safety, serial numbered 554,447-572,214.

	$2,400	$1,950	$1,200	$1,000	$850	$650	$600	

Add 50% for blue U.S. Property S/N 554,447 - approx. 562,000.
Add 20% with original box and instructions.

The 100% value on this model assumes NIB condition.

* ***Model 1903 Pocket General Officer's Pistol*** – .32 ACP cal., blue (mfg. until 1942) or parkerized (mfg. started 1942) finish.

Parkerized	N/A	$3,000	$2,000	$1,700	$1,300	$1,050	$900	
Blue finish	N/A	$3,400	$2,700	$2,300	$1,850	$1,550	$1,250	

Values assume issue to a General, and there must be paperwork to link the gun to the recipient. Otherwise, these values do not apply - see U.S. Property above for applicable values.

MODEL 1905 – .45 ACP cal., 5 in. barrel, blue, fixed sights, checkered walnut grips, similar to the Model 1902 Sporting. Mfg. 1905-1911.

	N/A	$7,500	$5,000	$3,800	$3,000	$2,000	$1,500	
1907 U.S. Military Contract								
	N/A	$25,000	$17,500	$13,250	$10,000	$7,000	$5,000	

Add 50% for factory slotted specimens (500 manufactured).
Add $7,500-$10,000 for an authentic should stock, depending on original condition - exceedingly rare.

Only 205 military variations were manufactured - very rare.

MODEL 1908 POCKET (MODEL M .380 ACP) – .380 ACP cal., first issue, 3 3/4 in. barrel only, similar to Model M .32 ACP, except chambered for .380 ACP. Mfg. 1908-1940.

	$2,250	$1,750	$1,200	$900	$800	$700	$450	

Add $100 for nickel finish.
Add 50% for factory pearl grips.
100% values assume NIB condition. Subtract 15% if without cardboard box. Pearl grips are normally encountered with nickel finish on this model.

Type II - 380 ACPs with barrel bushing and were mfg. 1908-1910 (6,251 mfg.). They are serial numbered 1-6,251.

Type III - 380 ACPs do not have a barrel bushing and were mfg. 1910-1926. They are serial numbered 6,252-92,893.

Type IV - 380 ACPs have the added magazine safety (of which there are both the commercial and "U.S. Property" variations). They are serial numbered 92,894-134,499.

GRADING - PPGS™	100%	98%	95%	90%	80%	70%	60%	LAST MSR

* ***Model 1908 "U.S. Property"*** – blue finish only, U.S. Property marking. Serial numbered 134,500-138,000.

	100%	98%	95%	90%	80%	70%	60%
	N/A	$3,250	$2,500	$1,750	$1,300	$950	$750

* ***Model 1908 General Officer's Pistol*** – .380 ACP cal., blue finish only.

	100%	98%	95%	90%	80%	70%	60%
	N/A	$4,000	$3,250	$2,700	$2,300	$1,950	$1,550

Values assume issue to a General, and there must be paperwork to link the gun to the recipient. Otherwise, these values do not apply - see U.S. Property above for applicable values.

VEST POCKET MODEL 1908-HAMMERLESS – .25 ACP cal., 2 in. barrel, fixed sights, checkered hard rubber grips on early models, walnut on later, 6 shot mag., magazine disconnect added on guns made after 1916. Mfg. 1908-1946.

* ***Vest Pocket Model 1908 Blue finish***

	100%	98%	95%	90%	80%	70%	60%
	$850	$750	$600	$500	$425	$350	$275

Add 50% for factory pearl grips.
Add 50% for NIB condition if in 95% or better condition only.

* ***Vest Pocket Model 1908 Nickel finish***

	100%	98%	95%	90%	80%	70%	60%
	$1,200	$1,000	$850	$650	$550	$450	$375
U.S. Property marked	$3,750	$3,000	$2,750	$2,400	$2,100	$1,800	$1,500

Add 50% for factory pearl grips.
Add 50% for NIB condition if in 95% or better condition only.
This model was also supplied with a suede purse. Add $150-$200, depending on condition.

MODEL 1909 – .45 ACP cal., straight handle design, 5 in. barrel, checkered walnut grips, approx. 22 mfg., ultra rare.

Extreme rarity factor precludes accurate price evaluation by individual condition factors. Specimens that are original and over 90% have sold for over $35,000 recently.

MODEL 1910 – .45 ACP cal., while not a production model, this gun is probably the most desirable semi-auto Colt pistol.

PISTOLS: SEMI-AUTO, GOVT. MODEL 1911 COMMERCIAL VARIATIONS

MODEL 1911 COMMERCIAL – .45 ACP cal., 5 in. barrel, fixed sights, 7 shot mag., flat main spring housing, polished blue finish only, checkered walnut grips. Denoted by "C" preceding serial number, approx. ser. no. range C1-C138,532. Watch for fakes. Colt licensed other companies to manufacture the military variation under government contracts, 39 oz. Mfg. 1912-1925.

Most M1911 variations listed below are not as collectible if under 60% original condition. However, they are still very desirable as shooters, and values (if in original condition) will approximate the 60% prices if in good mechanical condition.

Colt Model 1911s continue to enjoy high demand as of this writing and prices continue to be strong in the 95%-100% condition factors. Be careful on the 98%+ condition specimens, especially the rarer variations. Some collectors are now requiring a potential high-dollar Model 1911 to pass a metallurgical X-ray examination before purchasing.

* ***Model 1911 High Polish Blue*** – mfg. 1912 through ser. no. 4,500.

	100%	98%	95%	90%	80%	70%	60%
	N/A	$15,000	$12,000	$9,000	$6,500	$4,000	$2,000

* ***Model 1911 Regular Finish*** – pistols mfg. after ser. no. 4,500.

	100%	98%	95%	90%	80%	70%	60%
	N/A	$4,100	$3,250	$2,100	$1,350	$1,100	$850

Approx. 138,532 were mfg. between 1912-1925.

BRAZILIAN NAVY CONTRACT – Brazilian Navy first procured M1911 pistols in 1921 when a first batch of 200 pistols (scattered through serial numbers C129000 to C131000) were delivered to the Minas Geraes battleship then docked at Brooklyn Naval Yard. Another order was made in 1922 for 500 guns (scattered among serials C128000-C129500). These first guns do not bear any specific markings and can only be identified by a factory letter and are extremely rare in the U.S. as these had not been released to the surplus dealers by the Brazilian Navy.

	100%	98%	95%	90%	80%	70%	60%
	N/A	$6,200	$4,500	$3,500	$2,200	$1,300	$1,000

PISTOLS: SEMI-AUTO, GOVT. MODEL 1911 MILITARY VARIATIONS

All pistols in this section are .45 ACP (11.25mm) cal., unless otherwise noted. Values for original 98%+ M1911 Military Models have risen considerably in recent years, and as a result, values for original mint guns can double and even sometimes triple the values of 98% condition.

GRADING - PPGS™	100%	98%	95%	90%	80%	70%	60%	LAST MSR

Over 2,550,000 M1911 pistols were ordered for WWI and WWII by the U.S. Government, but approx. 650,000 were mfg. between 1911-1925. Those pistols with a parkerized finish will indicate post-WWI reworking, usually marked with an arsenal code (ie. AA-AUGUSTA ARSENAL, SA-SPRINGFIELD ARSENAL, RIA-ROCK ISLAND ARSENAL, etc.). Please check individual listings for values of arsenal refinished pistols.

COLT MFG. MODEL 1911 MILITARY – right side of slide marked "MODEL OF 1911 U.S. ARMY", blue finish only (NOT parkerized unless reworked).

Recent sales for original mint examples of the Model 1911 Military are as follows: $14,000 for 1912 mfg., depending on the variation (there are three), $7,000 for 1913-1915 mfg., $7,500 for 1916 mfg., $6,000 for 1917-1918 mfg. and $6,000 for 1918 later mfg. (black Army finish).

* ***Model 1911 (1912 mfg.)*** – includes three variations.

	100%	98%	95%	90%	80%	70%	60%
	N/A	$10,000	$7,750	$6,000	$5,000	$4,000	$3,000

* ***Model 1911 (1913-1915 mfg.)***

	100%	98%	95%	90%	80%	70%	60%
	N/A	$5,400	$4,750	$3,850	$3,100	$2,350	$1,600
Ser. no. range 115-2400	N/A	$13,000	$11,750	$9,600	$8,750	$6,000	$4,000
Ser. no. range 1-114	N/A	$21,000	$17,000	$14,000	$11,000	$8,750	$6,000

Initial 114 pistols are marked "United States Property".

* ***Model 1911 (1916 mfg.)*** – only 4,200 produced.

	100%	98%	95%	90%	80%	70%	60%
	N/A	$5,700	$5,000	$4,200	$3,650	$2,050	$1,500

* ***Model 1911 (1917-1918 early mfg.)*** – early blue finish.

	100%	98%	95%	90%	80%	70%	60%
	N/A	$4,750	$3,200	$2,050	$1,500	$1,200	$1,000

* ***Model 1911 (1917-1918 mfg.)*** – can be determined by black Army finish.

	100%	98%	95%	90%	80%	70%	60%
	N/A	$4,750	$3,200	$2,050	$1,500	$1,200	$1,000

* ***Model 1911 (1919-1925 mfg.)***

	100%	98%	95%	90%	80%	70%	60%
	N/A	$4,750	$3,500	$3,000	$2,000	$1,500	$1,200

NORTH AMERICAN ARMS COMPANY – less than 100 mfg. in Quebec, Canada during 1918 only, blue finish. Be very aware of fakes, as this variation is perhaps the most desirable Colt WWI Govt. semi-auto.

	100%	98%	95%	90%	80%	70%	60%
	N/A	N/A	$35,000	$30,000	$25,000	$20,000	$16,000

Note: a characteristic of the North American is the poor finish. The very best condition specimens will be in the 80%-90% range. All mint 100% specimens encountered in this model appear to have been refinished.

REMINGTON - UMC – over 21,500 mfg. (ser. numbered 1-21,676) in 1918-1919 only, blue finish.

	100%	98%	95%	90%	80%	70%	60%
	N/A	$8,550	$5,500	$3,850	$3,000	$2,500	$2,000

Most mint 100% specimens encountered in this model have been refinished - be careful. Mint original pistols are currently selling as high as $8,500.

SPRINGFIELD ARMORY – approx. 30,000 mfg. 1914-1915, blue finish.

	100%	98%	95%	90%	80%	70%	60%
	N/A	$7,550	$5,750	$3,750	$3,000	$2,500	$2,000

Mint original pistols are currently selling in the $7,500 range.

Serialization is 72,751-83,855, 102,597-107,596, 113,497-120,566, and 125,567-133,186.

Most mint 100% specimens encountered in this model have been refinished - be careful.

U.S. NAVY – over 31,000 mfg. for U.S. Navy contract between 1911-1914 in defined serial ranges, blue finish. Marked "MODEL OF 1911 U.S. NAVY" on right slide side.

	100%	98%	95%	90%	80%	70%	60%
	N/A	$10,500	$6,000	$4,500	$3,200	$2,200	$1,500

Add 100% for specimens under ser. no. 3,500.

U.S. Navy specimens are seldom found in over 80% original condition because of the corrosive conditions encountered while at sea.

U.S. MARINE CORPS. – approx. 13,500 mfg. between 1911-13 and 1916-18 in defined serial ranges, blue finish, right side of slide marked "MODEL OF 1911 U.S. ARMY".

	100%	98%	95%	90%	80%	70%	60%
	N/A	$7,500	$5,500	$4,500	$3,500	$3,000	$2,250

Mint original specimens are currently selling in the $13,000-$15,000 range.

WWI BRITISH SERIES – .455 cal., serialized W19,000-W110,695, marked "CALIBRE 455", blue finish, proofed with broad arrow British Ordnance stamp. Mfg. 1915-19.

	100%	98%	95%	90%	80%	70%	60%
	N/A	$5,750	$4,750	$2,950	$2,000	$1,200	$1,000

Subtract 30% if converted to .45 ACP cal.

Mint original specimens in this model have been selling in the $7,500 - $8,500 range.

GRADING - PPGS™	100%	98%	95%	90%	80%	70%	60%	LAST MSR

Many WWI British-series M1911s were exported back to the U.S. following WWI and were converted to .45 ACP. Usually, a "5" has been crossed out of the original cal. designation. This model also had reworks purchased for Royal Air Force. All Government Model Colts sold in England prior to July 1915 were .45ACP with "C" serial number prefix - approx. 4200 with British War Office purchases of these being 2,200 pistols (most likely issued to Royal Flying Corps (RFC), Royal Navy Air Service, Royal Navy, Royal Horse Artillery). British Ministry of Munitions contracts for the RFC and RAF Colt Government Model .455 in. Webley & Scott Self Loading Calibre pistols with "W" prefix - total 10,500. These were marked RAF.

A.J. SAVAGE MUNITIONS CO. – mfg. slides only, blue finish, marked in middle on left side of slide with flaming ordnance bomb with "S" in center.

	N/A	$3,000	$2,250	$1,750	$1,250	$1,000	$800

Mint original specimens have been selling in the $3,250 - $3,500 range.

NORWEGIAN TRIAL MODEL 1911 COLT – 11.25mm cal., approx. 300 mfg. with "C" prefix in 1913-14 and 1917, usually encountered in 90% or less condition.

	N/A	$4,500	$3,750	$2,750	$2,000	$1,200	$800

These guns were ordered for Norwegian service evaluation and were mfg. by Colt in Hartford, CT.

NORWEGIAN MODEL 1912 11.25MM – 11.25mm cal., mfg. under license from Colt's during 1917, "M1912" slide designation. Approx. 95 mfg.

	N/A	$8,500	$7,500	$6,000	$5,000	$4,000	$3,200

NORWEGIAN 1914 11.25MM – this model has a distinctive extended slide release, all parts should be serial numbered and have numerous matching numbers, approx. 32,850 mfg. 1918-1947, mostly military contract, commercial production was very limited, Waffenamt Nazi mfg. 1945 only. Most have been refinished.

	N/A	$2,350	$1,800	$1,550	$1,300	$900	$700
Nazi mfg. (mfg. 1945 only)	N/A	$8,200	$6,250	$5,450	$4,500	$3,100	$2,500

Serial ranges with corresponding year of manufacture on this model are as follows: 96-600 - 1918, 601-1,150 - 1919, 1,151-1,650 (Naval Artillery) - 1920, 1,651-2,200 - 1921, 2,201- 2,950 - 1922, 2,951-4,610 - 1923, 4,611-6,700 - 1924, 6,701-8,940 - 1925, 8,941-11,820 - 1926, 11,821-15,900 - 1927, 15,901-20,100 - 1928, 20,101-21,440 - 1929, 21,441-21,940 - 1932, 21,941-22,040 - 1933, 22,041-22,141 - 1934, 22,142-22,211 - 1936, 22,212-22,311 - 1939, 22,312-22,361 - 1940, 22,362-26,460 - 1941, 26,461-29,614 - 1942, 29,615-32,335 (Waffenamt Nazi proofed) - 1945, 32,336-32,854 - (last original production) 1947.

Nazi production of the M1914 began in 1941. Between 1941-42, approx. 7,000 pistols were mfg. without Waffenamt stampings. Nazi proofed guns (all 1945 dated) began in the mid- 29,000 serial range, and 920 were mfg. with the Nazi Eagle (ser. no. range 29615-30,534). Also, three guns were produced as prototypes for further German pistol production - they are marked M1-M2, and M3.

ARGENTINE CONTRACT MODEL 1916 – identified by the Argentine seal on top of slide, with C prefix 5 digit ser. no., from 1914-1919, Colt delivered approx. 1,000 pistols to Argentina, with the ser. no. range approx. 20001-21000.

	N/A	$3,850	$3,500	$3,150	$2,750	$2,250	$1,800

Most specimens of this model have been refinished.

RUSSIAN CONTRACT – approx. 51,000 mfg. in U.S. as commerical guns with random serial numbers approx. C23000-C89000, blue finish, identified by cyrillic inscription on left side of frame (translates to English Order). Mfg. 1916-17.

	N/A	$8,750	$4,500	$4,000	$3,250	$2,500	$2,000

Mint original specimens have been selling in the $12,500 - $15,000 range.

This contract is seldolm encountered - beware of fakes.

1911 MILITARY REWORKS – .45 ACP cal., these are pistols that the government sent back to various military arsenals for reworking, arsenals include Augusta Arsenal (AA), Springfield Armory (SA), and Rock Island Arsenal (RIA), pistols may have original parts (matching) or parts from other manufacturers (mismatched), parkerized (most common), or arsenal blue finish.

Colt Mfg.	$1,400	$1,225	$1,050	$950	$770	$625	$495
Remington UMC Mfg.	$1,800	$1,575	$1,350	$1,225	$995	$815	$625
Springfield Mfg.	$1,800	$1,575	$1,350	$1,225	$995	$815	$625

Add 15% for box and DCM papers.
Add 15% for arsenal blue finish.
Subtract 40% if mismatched.

GRADING - PPGS™	100%	98%	95%	90%	80%	70%	60%	LAST MSR

BRAZILIAN NAVY 1911 CONTRACT – .45 ACP cal., commercial checkered walnut grips, blue finish. Approx. 1,000 mfg. for the Brazilian Navy between 1921-1925, approx. serial range C129000-C179000.

	N/A	$4,950	$4,300	$3,700	$3,250	$2,600	$2,200	

PISTOLS: SEMI-AUTO, GOVT. MODEL 1911A1 COMMERCIAL VARIATIONS

All pistols in this section are .45 ACP cal., unless otherwise noted.

GOVERNMENT MODEL 1911A1 – commercial blue finish or parkerized, checkered walnut grips, checkered arched mainspring housing relief cuts in frame for improved trigger reach, and longer grip safety spur. As in the Model 1911, Colt licensed other companies to produce under govt. contract during WWII. Mfg. 1925-1970.

Most M1911A1 variations listed below are not as collectible if under 60% original condition. However, they are still very desirable as shooters, and values (if in original condition) will approximate the 60% prices if in good mechanical condition.

MODEL 1911A1 PRE-WWII COLT COMMERCIAL – "C" preceding serial number, mfg. 1925-1942. Approx. ser. no. range C138,533-C215,000.

	N/A	$4,500	$3,500	$3,000	$2,500	$1,800	$1,000	

Add 50% for nickel finish.
Add 30% with original box and instructions.
Add 30% for Swartz safety.

MODEL 1911A1 1946-1970 COLT COMMERCIAL – 5 in. barrel, fixed sights, "C" prefix until 1950 when changed to "C" suffix. Approx. 196,000 mfg. 1946-1970.

* ***Model 1911A1 1946-1950 Mfg.*** – "C" Prefix with serial numbers C221,000-C240,227.

	$2,800	$2,450	$2,150	$1,750	$1,100	$950	$700	

Add 30% for original box and instructions.

* ***Model 1911A1 1950-1970 Mfg.*** – "C" Suffix with serial numbers 240,228C-336,169C.

	$2,700	$2,300	$2,050	$1,650	$1,000	$900	$700	

Add 20% for nickel finish.
Add 30% for original box and instructions.

SUPER .38 AUTOMATIC PISTOL – identical to Govt. Model .45, except chambered for .38 Super cal., blue or nickel finish. Mfg. 1928-70.

* ***Super .38 Automatic Pistol Pre-War***

	N/A	$6,000	$5,750	$3,500	$2,250	$1,700	$1,200	

Add 30% for original box and instructions.

* ***Super .38 Automatic Pistol 2nd Model***

	$3,200	$2,750	$2,400	$1,800	$1,400	$1,100	$900	

Add 30% for original box and instructions.

* ***Super .38 Automatic Pistol 3rd Model***

	$2,800	$2,200	$1,800	$1,200	$900	$750	$600	

Add 30% for original box and instructions.

* ***Super .38 Automatic Pistol 4th Model***

	$2,200	$1,800	$1,600	$1,000	$800	$700	$600	

Add 30% for original box and instructions.

* ***Super .38 Automatic Pistol CS Prefix***

	$2,200	$1,800	$1,600	$1,000	$800	$700	$600	

Add approx. 50% for nickel finish.

Pre-war variations are serialized below approx. 37,000.

The 2nd Model may be differentiated by noticing the heavier barrel and Rampant Colt on right side. The 3rd Model has a fat barrel with Rampant Colt on left side. The 4th Model has a thin barrel and Rampant Colt on left side.

SUPER MATCH .38 – similar to Super .38, but hand honed action, match grade barrel, recent research indicates that 2,392 had adj. sights, 857 were supplied with fixed sights, and on 557 models the type of sights was not indicated. 4,001 mfg. 1934-1947. Examine carefully for fakes.

Buyer beware - fakes are known to exist!

The first Super Match noted is ser. no. 15550, a fixed sight model, and was shipped on Feb. 9, 1934.

GRADING - PPGS™	100%	98%	95%	90%	80%	70%	60%	LAST MSR

The lowest serial number is 14310 and was shipped on July 10, 1934. However, two serial numbers were much lower than the expected serial number ranges. Ser. no. 2253 was shipped on June 18, 1940 and ser. no. 10312 was shipped on Sept. 25, 1935. It is unknown if these guns were roll marked Super Match, but they were noted in the Colt Records as Super Match models.

The first adj. sight Super Match is ser. no. 17091, and was shipped on Feb. 7, 1935.

The last adj. sight Super Match noted is ser. no. 35731, and was shipped on Jan. 17, 1947.

The highest ser. no. Super Match is ser. no. 35999, a fixed sight model, and was shipped on Oct. 20, 1939.

Approx. 40 were mfg. with match barrels and/or hand fitted actions, w/o mention of the Super Match markings.

Total .38 Super Match pistols recorded in the Colt shipping records is 3,961. 2,250 were noted as having adj. sight, and 831 were noted as having fixed sights.

* ***Super Match .38 Fixed Sights***

N/A $10,000 $7,500 $6,000 $4,500 $3,000 $2,000

Add 30% for original box and instructions.

* ***Super Match .38 Adj. Sights***

N/A $11,500 $9,000 $7,000 $5,500 $4,000 $3,000

For adj. sight values to apply, the sight must be an original factory installed Stevens sight. After market adj. sights are not applicable. Be cautious of fixed sight Super Matches converted to adj. sight. A Colt historical letter is available for this model for $100.

There were 3,909 .38 Super Matches manufactured from Feb. 16, 1934 - Jan. 17, 1947. 998 had fixed sights and 2,911 had adj. sights.

MATCH .38 AMU – .38 AMU cal. (semi-rimless .38 Spl., mfg. by Win.), this variation was mfg. by Colt from a .38 Super frame (and has .38 Super serialization) with a .38 AMU conversion kit slide, the Army took .45 frames and assembled their guns using .38 AMU kits, blue finish.

* ***Match .38 AMU Colt Mfg. (Unmodified)***

N/A $3,500 $2,700 $2,200 $1,900 $1,675 $1,400

Add 30% for original box and instructions.

* ***Match .38 AMU Army Modified***

N/A $2,250 $1,850 $1,275 $1,000 $800 $700

* ***Match .38 AMU Kit Only***

$1,850 $1,700 $1,450 $1,150 $900 $700 $500

On this configuration, the barrel, slide, and mag. were marked ".38 AMU".

SUPER MATCH .38 MS – .38 Super cal., 1961 mfg., serial numbered 101MS - 855MS, 754 total mfg, same configuration as the .38 AMU.

$5,500 $4,500 $3,500 $2,700 $2,000 $1,500 $1,300

1968-1969 BB TRANSITIONAL – denoted by BB prefix on serial number.

$3,100 $2,750 $2,100 $1,500 $1,000 $800 $700

Add 30% for original box and instructions.

.45 ACP TO .22 LR CONVERSION UNIT – consists of slide assembly, barrel, bushing, floating chamber, ejector, recoil spring and guide, fitted with Stevens adj. rear sight from 1938 to 1947 and Colt Master adj. sight from 1947 to 1954.

$650 $600 $550 $425 $350 $275 $200

Add 30% for original box and instructions.

* ***.45 ACP to .22 LR Conversion Unit U Prefix*** – has "U" prefix on top of slide.

$2,000 $1,800 $1,650 $1,275 $1,050 $825 $600

Add 30% for original box and instructions.

* ***.45 ACP to .22 LR Conversion Unit Marine Corps*** – should have pre-war Marine Corps documentation.

$2,500 $2,275 $2,100 $1,925 $1,475 $1,225 $950

.22 LR TO .45 ACP CONVERSION UNIT – converted service Ace .22 to .45 ACP cal. Mfg. 1938-1942. Very rare - 112 mfg.

$6,500 $5,000 $4,000 $3,000 $2,250 $1,500 $1,100

Add 50% for original box and instructions.

These units have "U" prefixed serial numbers on top of slide. Watch for fakes!

GRADING - PPGS™	100%	98%	95%	90%	80%	70%	60%	LAST MSR

PISTOLS: SEMI-AUTO, GOVT. MODEL 1911A1 MILITARY VARIATIONS

All pistols in this section are .45 ACP (11.25mm) cal., unless otherwise noted. Values for original 98%+ M1911A1s have risen considerably in recent years, and as a result, values for original mint guns can double and even sometimes triple the values of 98% condition. Inspect carefully for arsenal reworks (so marked by proofing, normally on left side of frame above or behind trigger), and reparkerizing.

COLT MFG. MODEL 1911A1 MILITARY - approx. 438,527 mfg. between 1924- 1945, ser. nos. 700,000 - on up, right side of frame marked "M1911A1 U.S. ARMY", bright blue finish up to approx. ser. no. 740,000, parkerized finish after that. - standard military finish (WWII mfg.).

N/A $4,500 $3,850 $2,950 $2,200 $1,500 $1,000

Blue finish (outside military ser. ranges)

N/A $10,250 $8,500 $6,550 $5,500 $3,750 $2,500

Bright blue finish (military ser. ranges)

N/A $10,000 $8,550 $6,500 $5,000 $4,000 $2,750

1937 Navy variations with blue finish are currently selling in the $4,500 - $20,000 range (S/N 710001 - 712345), depending on original condition.

1938 Army variations with blue finish are currently selling in the $3,250 - $15,000 range (S/N 712350 - 713645), depending on original condition.

1939 Navy variations with blue finish are currently selling in the $4,500 - $20,000 range (S/N 713646 - 717281), depending on original condition.

1942 Navy w/parkerized finish are currently selling in the $1,500 - $10,000 range (S/N 793658 - 797639), depending on condition.

Add 25-50% for Schwartz safety variation depending on condition.

A large grouping of over 7,000 Commercial 1911A1s was transferred to the U.S. government. These pistols had their commercial serial numbers crudely removed (in ser. range 860,000 - 866,000) and re-stamped with a new military serial number. Some of these guns are unusual as the frames and slides have been cut for the Schwartz safety.

*** Model 1911A1 General Officer's Pistol***

N/A $7,000 $6,000 $4,500 $3,500 $2,100 $1,600

Values above assume issue to a General, and there must be paperwork to link the gun to the recipient.

DRAKE NATIONAL MATCH - Drake made slides only for use by the U.S. Army Marksmanship Unit to allow assembly of match guns.

N/A $2,000 $1,700 $1,400 $1,000 $850 $700

GOVERNMENT NATIONAL MATCH REWORKS - assembled by government armorers, all parts marked "NM", parkerized finish. Most will be "S.A." marked.

N/A $2,000 $1,700 $1,400 $1,000 $850 $700

Add 25% for Air Force pistols marked "AFPG" on slide.

These pistols were made specifically for the U.S. shooting team at Camp Perry.

ITHACA - .45 ACP cal., 7 shot mag., 5 in. barrel, parkerized finish, approx. 369,129 mfg. 1943-1945 in Ithaca, NY, ser. no. ranges 856,405-916,404, 1,208,674-1,279,673, 1,441,431-1,471,430, 1,743,847-1,890,503, 2,075,104-2,134,403, and 2,619,014-2,693,613.

N/A $3,000 $2,500 $1,750 $1,200 $1,100 $800

Add 20% for original shipping carton.

UNION SWITCH AND SIGNAL - approx. 55,000 mfg. 1943 only in Swissvale, PA, ser. no. range 1,041,405-1,096,404. Sandblast and blue finish.

$10,000 $7,500 $5,700 $4,000 $3,300 $2,200 $1,600

REMINGTON RAND - approx. 1,086,624 mfg. 1943-1945 in Syracuse, NY, ser. no. ranges 916,405-1,041,404, 1,279,649-1,441,430, 1,471,431-1,609,528, 1,743,847-1,816,641, 1,890,504-2,075,103, 2,134,404-2,244,803, and 2,380,014-2,619,013. Parkerized finish.

$2,500 $2,250 $2,000 $1,650 $1,200 $1,000 $900

Add 20% for original shipping carton (watch for fakes).

SINGER MFG. CO. - 500 mfg. 1941 in Elizabeth, NJ, ser. no. range S800,001-S800,500. Blue finish with plastic grips.

N/A $100,000 $85,000 $60,000 $45,000 $38,500 $24,000

The Singer 1911A1 variation is one of the most sought-after Colt models. In recent years, values have increased significantly, and as a result, some fakes have emerged. Most specimens are now recognized by ser. no. and be very cautious when contemplating a purchase. Some collectors unsure of authenticity are now requiring X-ray testing to determine originality (slide restampings, ser. no. changes, etc.).

GRADING - PPGS™	100%	98%	95%	90%	80%	70%	60%	LAST MSR

GENERAL OFFICER'S PISTOL (M15) – standard military finish, issued by Rock Island Arsenal to Generals.

	$7,500	$6,500	$5,500	$4,000	$3,200	$2,800	$2,200	

MEXICAN CONTRACT – mfg. approx. 1921-27 with "C" prefix ser. nos., frames marked "EJERCITO MEXICANO", most surviving examples show much use.

	N/A	$3,800	$2,900	$1,900	$1,400	$1,100	$900	

BRAZILIAN ARMY CONTRACT - .45 ACP cal., Brazilian Army first procured M1911A1 pistols in 1932 when 1,000 were purchased (dispersed in serial number C154000 to C164000 range). These first guns do not bear any specific markings and can only be identified by a factory letter. A larger contract followed in 1937, comprising 14,500 pistols (scattered through serial numbers C188000-C209000), with the right side of the slide bearing the Brazil Coat of Arms, the inscription "EXERCITO BRASILEIRO", and an inventory number (ranging from 0001-14500); a second line presents a date, corresponding to the delivery date to the Brazilian Army. Dates observed: "1937" (common), "1938" (very rare), and "1940" (very scarce). These guns are extremely rare in the U.S. as these had not been released to the surplus dealers by the Brazilian Army.

	$7,500	$6,500	$5,000	$4,000	$2,500	$1,500	$1,000	

Add 20% for "1940" dated guns.

Add 50% for "1938" dated guns

BRAZILIAN NAVY CONTRACT – in addition to the purchases made in 1921-1922, the Brazilian Navy procured 300 M1911A1 pistols in 1925 (scattered through serial numbers C139000 to C141000) and again in 1935 when another 200 guns (dispersed among serials C178000-C179000) were sent to the Navy General Command in Rio de Janeiro. These guns do not bear any specific markings and can only be identified by a factory letter and are extremely rare in the U.S. as these had not been released to the surplus dealers by teh Brazilian Navy.

	N/A	$6,200	$4,500	$3,500	$2,200	$1,300	$1,000	

ARGENTINE CONTRACT MODEL 1927 – serial numbered 1-10,000 under the mainspring housing and on the top of slide (should be matching), must have Argentine crest and "Model 1927" on right side of slide, external serial number applied to top of slide by the Argentine Arsenal, most have been Arsenal refinished.

	$2,000	$1,300	$1,100	$900	$800	$600	$500	

Add 75% if original finish.

Add 30% with original box and instructions.

ARGENTINE MFG. – in 1927, the Argentina Arsenal "DGFM-FMAP" began manufacturing the Model 1911A1. The slide marking is two lines and reads "EJERCITO ARGENTINO SIST.COLT.CAL. 11.25mm MOD.1927", these guns were made in Argentina under license from Colt, with Colt machinery, and with help from Colt engineers, and are known as Model 1927 Systema Colt.

	$2,400	$2,200	$1,700	$1,000	$700	$600	$500	

Add 50% if original finish.

Add 30% with original box and instructions.

Add 20% for Argentine Navy "ARMADA NACIONAL" (small shipments between 1912-1948). Markings vary on different types.

Add 30% for Air Force markings ("AERONAUTICA ARGENTINA" and winged crest).

This variation is not to be confused with the Ballester Molina/Rigaud Models (sold by Hispano Argentino Fábrica de Automóviles S.A., in Buenos Aires, Argentina - also known as the HAFDASA). Please refer to the Hispano Argentino Fábrica de Automóviles S.A. section.

ARGENTINE SERVICE MODEL ACE – .22 LR cal., conversion of the 1927 Argentine Contract Model, bottom right side of slide is marked "TRANSE A CAL .22 POR EST. VENTURINI S.A." Originally imported during 1996, this model was arsenal refinished and most pistols were in the 70%-95% condition range.

	$1,800	$1,200	$900	$650	$600	$550	$525	

1911A1 MILITARY REWORKS – .45 ACP cal., these are pistols that the government sent back to various military arsenals for reworking, arsenals include Augusta Arsenal (AA), Springfield Armory (SA), and Rock Island Arsenal (RIA), pistols may have original parts (matching) or parts from other manufacturers (mismatched), finish is generally parkerized, but some pistols will have original finish with arsenal markings.

Colt Mfg.	$2,200	$1,825	$1,650	$1,250	$775	$625	$495	
Remington Mfg.	$2,000	$1,750	$1,400	$1,200	$675	$550	$425	
Ithaca Mfg.	$1,800	$1,650	$1,200	$1,000	$675	$550	$425	
US & S Mfg.	$2,400	$2,000	$1,750	$1,525	$995	$815	$625	
Singer Mfg.	N/A	$20,000	$17,000	$12,500	$10,000	$8,000	$6,500	

Add 15% for box and DCM papers.

Add 100% if arsenal marked but with original finish.

Subtract 20% for mismatched slide and frame.

GRADING - PPGS™	100%	98%	95%	90%	80%	70%	60%	LAST MSR

PISTOLS: SEMI-AUTO, ACE MODELS, 1931-1947 MFG.

COMMERCIAL ACE – .22 LR cal., similar to Government .45 ACP, but in .22 LR cal., 4 3/4 in. barrel, blue, adj. sights, checkered walnut grips, almost 11,000 mfg. (ser. no. range 1-10,935) 1931-41 and 1947.

	N/A	$4,500	$3,500	$2,500	$2,000	$1,500	$1,200	

Add 20% for original box and instructions.

SERVICE MODEL ACE – .22 LR cal., 5 in. barrel, blue finish until serial number 3864, then parkerized finish, similar to .45 ACP National Match except for caliber, has floating chamber to simulate .45 ACP recoil. Limited mfg. 1935-1945.

	N/A	$7,500	$6,000	$4,500	$3,250	$2,500	$2,000	

Add 20% for original box and instructions.
Subtract 30% for parkerized finish.
Add 25% for models shipped to the U.S. Coast Guard (short production run, rarely seen).

This variation is marked "SERVICE MODEL" on left frame, serial numbers have "SM" prefix and have ranges to approx. 13,800. Other markings such as "U.S. PROP'Y" or "R.S." (inspectors' marks) have also been observed on this model, and can add a premium if original condition is 95% or more.

PISTOLS: SEMI-AUTO, NATIONAL MATCH MODELS - PRE-WWII

NATIONAL MATCH – .45 ACP cal., similar to Government Model, except has hand-honed action, match grade barrel, blue or nickel finish, stamped "National Match" on right side of slide. There were a total of 4,813 National Matches manufactured between Feb. 9, 1932 - Sept. 16, 1941, serial numbered C162997-C204640. 3,339 had fixed sights, and 1,474 had adj. sights.

Add 20% with original box and instructions.

The first National Match and lowest ser. no. C162997, a fixed sight model, was shipped on Jan. 7, 1932.

The last National Match, ser. no. C200288, a fixed sight model, was shipped on Feb. 22, 1942.

The highest ser. no. is C204671, an adj. sight model, and was shipped on Aug. 20, 1941.

Of the total 4,813 National Match pistols, 1,474 were noted as having adj. sights, and 3,339 were noted as having fixed sights.

There were 45 nickel National Match models, four were engraved and two were inscribed.

There were 47 engraved National Match models, four of them nickel and eight with gold inlays.

There were fifteen inscribed National Match models, two of them nickel.

* ***National Match Fixed sights***

	N/A	$13,500	$11,000	$9,000	$7,000	$4,750	$3,650	

* ***National Match Adj. sights***

	N/A	$16,500	$14,000	$11,500	$8,750	$5,750	$3,950	

For adj. sight values to apply, the sight must be an original factory installed Stevens sight. After market adj. sights are not applicable. Be cautious of fixed sight National Match models that have been converted to adj. sight.

A Colt historical letter is available for this model for $100.

PISTOLS: SEMI-AUTO, NATIONAL MATCH MODELS - WWII & POST-WWII

Add 10% for NIB condition on discontinued models listed below.
Unless noted otherwise, all National Match models listed in this section will have "National Match" stamped on the left side of the slide.

NATIONAL MATCH – .45 ACP cal., match grade barrel, royal blue finish, new design bushing, beveld barrel bushing and recoil spring plug, flat or arched (mfg. approx. 1959-64) mainspring housing, long trigger w/adj. overtravel stop, hand fitted slide with enlarged ejection port, adj. target sights, gold medallions in grips, "NM" suffix. Mfg. 1957-1970.

	$3,000	$2,300	$1,700	$1,125	$800	$650	$600	

Note: This model was the first Gold Cup National Match Model manufactured following WWII.

MKII/MKIII NATIONAL MATCH MID-RANGE – .38 Spl. Mid-Range Wadcutter cal., similar to National Match, except chambered for .38 Spl. Mid-Range Wadcutter, "MR" suffix. Mfg. 1961-1971.

	$2,000	$1,600	$1,200	$1,000	$800	$700	$600	

Colt had problems with the original barrels of the Gold Cup .38 Mid-Range. The MKII was the first revision (very scarce), and the MKIII was the final revision.

GRADING - PPGS™	100%	98%	95%	90%	80%	70%	60%	LAST MSR

MKIV/SERIES 70 GOLD CUP NATIONAL MATCH – 9mm Para. (rare) or .45 ACP cal., flat mainspring housing, Colt blue finish accurizer barrel and bushing, adj. trigger, target hammer, solid rib, Colt-Elliason rear sight. Mfg. 1970-1983.

	$2,100	$1,750	$1,550	$1,050	$800	$700	$600	

Add 25% for satin nickel if in 98% or better condition.

MKIV/SERIES 70 GOLD CUP 75TH ANNIVERSARY NATIONAL MATCH – similar to Gold Cup, except was mfg. as a Camp Perry commemorative, 200 mfg. 1978 only.

	$1,650	$1,400	$1,200	$1,000	$750	$650	$550	

MKIV SERIES 80 GOLD CUP NATIONAL MATCH – .45 ACP cal., 5 in. barrel, flat mainspring housing, 7 or 8 shot mag., accurizer barrel and bushing, wide grooved adj. target trigger, target hammer, solid rib, Colt-Elliason rear sight, 39 oz. Mfg. 1983-1996.

	$1,200	$1,000	$850	$700	$600	$550	$500	*$937*

In 1992, this model was updated to accept an 8 shot mag. During 1997, this updated model was designated the Gold Cup Trophy.

* ***MKIV Series 80 Stainless Gold Cup National Match*** – similar to Gold Cup, only manufactured from stainless steel, matte finish. Mfg. late 1986-1996.

	$1,100	$950	$800	$650	$600	$550	$500	*$1,003*

Add $200 for "Ultimate" bright stainless steel finish.
Add 10% for NIB condition.

* ***Gold Cup MKIV Series 80 Elite IX Gold Cup National Match*** – 9mm Para. cal., stainless steel and blue, marked "GCNM" on right side, and "ELITE IX - 9mm Luger" on left side, "IX" prefix in ser. no. Approx. 750 mfg. in 1989.

	$2,500	$1,900	$1,500	$1,150	$900	$700	$675	

Add 10% for NIB condition.

* ***Gold Cup MKIV Series 80 .38 Super Elite National Match*** – two-tone gun (stainless steel frame and blue slide), special edition by AcuSport. Mfg. 1987.

	$1,800	$1,400	$1,100	$900	$675	$550	$400	

* ***Gold Cup MKIV Series 80 .45 ACP Super Elite National Match*** – Mfg. circa 1987.

	$1,800	$1,400	$1,100	$900	$675	$550	$400	

* ***Gold Cup MKIV Series 80 Bullseye National Match*** – .45 ACP cal., hand-built, tuned, and adjusted by Colt's custom gunsmiths for precise match accuracy, includes factory-installed Bo-Mar sights, equipped with carrying case and 2 extra mags. Mfg. 1991-92.

	$1,700	$1,400	$1,200	$950	$800	$700	$650	*$1,500*

* ***Gold Cup MKIV Series 80 National Match Presentation*** – .45 ACP cal., similar to regular Gold Cup Series 80 National Match, except has a deep blue mirror bright finish accented by custom jeweled hammer, trigger, and barrel hood. Supplied with oak and velvet custom case. Mfg. 1991-92.

	$1,500	$1,200	$1,000	$900	$850	$750	$550	*$1,195*

GOLD CUP TROPHY NATIONAL MATCH (MODEL O) – .45 ACP cal., flat mainspring housing, 7 (disc.) or 8 shot mag., accurizer barrel and bushing, flat-top slide, adj. aluminum trigger, target hammer, Bo-Mar rear sight, checkered black wrap-around rubber grips, shipped with test target, 39 oz. Mfg. 1997-2010.

	$1,200	$1,000	$800	$700	$600	$500	$450	*$1,053*

This model replaced the MKIV/Series 80 Gold Cup National Match in 1997, and is only available from the Colt Custom Shop.

GOLD CUP NATIONAL MATCH O SERIES 70 – 9mm Para. (new 2018), .38 Super (new 2020), or .45 ACP cal., 5 in. National Match barrel, fully adj. Bomar style rear sight, spur hammer, drilled wide target trigger, lowered and flared ejection port, rounded slide top, blue finish, wrap-around rubber grips with Colt medallions, 37 oz. New 2015.

MSR $1,299	$1,250	$1,050	$900	$800	$700	$600	$550	

Add 5% (MSR $1,349) for .38 Super cal. (new 2020).

GOLD CUP NATIONAL MATCH O SERIES 80 – .45 ACP cal., 5 in. National Match barrel, features fully adj. Bomar style rear sight, spur hammer, drilled wide target trigger, lowered and flared ejection port, rounded slide top, blue finish, wrap-around rubber grips with Colt medallions, 37 oz. Mfg. 2012-mid-2015.

	$1,075	$975	$875	$800	$700	$600	$550	*$1,217*

PISTOLS: SEMI-AUTO, CUSTOM SHOP ENGRAVING PRICING, PRE-1991

Values below represent pre-1991 factory semi-auto Custom Shop A-D engraving options, before they started separate Standard, Expert, and Master level pricing (1997). It should also be understood that, in most cases, the quality of the engraving and notoriety of the engraver can be as important as the amount of coverage. Small Frame Engraving Options: includes Mustang, .380 ACP Government, Detective Special, and Diamondback models. Medium Frame Engraving Options: includes .45 ACP Gold Cup, Government Model, Officer's ACP, Python, Combat Commander, King Cobra, Trooper MKV, Lawman MKV, and Delta Elite models. Special engraving/options include inlays, seals, custom grips, and lettering. Prices were quoted upon request. Smooth ivory grips were $215 extra (1990 retail). Beginning in 1991, Colt began shipping all models in a distinctive blue plastic carrying case/shipping container. Please refer to the "SAA & Semi-Auto Colt Custom Shop Engraving - 1976-Present" listing earlier in this section for current semi-auto engraving options and pricing. Semi-auto custom-order quotations from Colt are available at $25 each (deductible from work order).

Add $776-$969 for Class "A" Engraving (1/4 Metal Coverage) depending on frame size.
Add $959-$1,199 for Class "B" Engraving (1/2 Metal Coverage) depending on frame size.
Add $1,426-$1,783 for Class "C" Engraving (3/4 Metal Coverage) depending on frame size.
Add $1,814-$2,289 for Class "D" Engraving (Full Metal Coverage) depending on frame size.
Add 7% for 6 in. barrel, 14% for 8 in. barrel, or 25% for stainless steel construction.

PISTOLS: SEMI-AUTO, CURRENT CUSTOM SHOP ENGRAVING PRICING

The following Colt Custom Shop engraving options apply to M1911 variations only.

Add $1,130 for A Standard engraving.
Add $1,300 for B Standard, $2,075 for B Expert (signed), or $3,725 for B Master (signed) level engraving.
Add $1,700 for C Standard, $2,878 for C Expert (signed), or $5,415 for C Master (signed) level engraving.
Add $2,000 for D Standard, $4,280 for D Expert (signed), or $6,900 for D Master (signed) level engraving.

PISTOLS: POPULAR 1911 CUSTOM SHOP SPECIAL ORDER OPTIONS

Many custom shop feature options are available for the Model 1911 and variations, and the following list contains many of them. Add $325 for matte blue or stainless matte (sand blast) finish. Add $425 for blue or brushed stainless finish. Add $525 for National Match blue finish. Add $675 for royal blue finish. Add $475 for black, stainless, or grey Cerakote finish. Add $575 for black or M45 Brown IonBond finish. Add $35-$65 for Novak front sight (various configurations). Add $45-$130 for Novak rear sight (various configurations). Add $85 for adj. rear sight. Add $75-$150 for thumb safety installation. Add $145 for blued enhanced grip safety (requires refinishing). Add $150 for stainless enhanced grip safety. Add $150 for street trigger tune (4-5 lbs.). Add $250 for National Match trigger w/tune (3-4 lbs.). Add $300 for National Match barrel. Add $75-$165 for slide modification (requires refinishing). Add $275 for Enhanced Reliability Series 70 package. Add $175 for Enhanced Reliability Series 80 package. Add $50-$100 for ejection port modifications. $50 for recoil system upgrades. Add $185-$345 for serrated or checker front grip strap. Add $85 for full magazine well bevel. Add $230 for front slide cocking serrations. Add $1,150 for tactical package w/undercut trigger guard. Add $1,750 for tactical package w/o undercut trigger guard.

PISTOLS: SEMI-AUTO, SINGLE ACTION, RECENT/CURRENT MFG.

Factory Colt abbreviations used on its price sheets are as follows: B - blue, BPF - black powder frame, BRS - Bomar rear sights, BSTS - bright polished stainless steel, CARS - Colt adjustable rear sight, CC/B - colored case/blue, CCBS - Colt Champion Bomar style sight, CCES - Colt Champion Elliason style sights, CER - Cerakote, FDE - Flat Dark Earth, F-H - Front Heinie sight, FOA - Fiber optic front, adj. rear, FOB - Fiber Optic Front, Bomar Style Rear, FXS - fixed sights, GE - gold enhancement, HC - hard chrome, IBFDE - Ion Bond FDE finish, L/W - lightweight, M - matte black, MP - Magpul accessories, NBRFFO - Novak Black Rear Front Fiber Optic, NM - National Match, NNS - Novak Night Sights, R - accessory rail, SE - semi-automatic enhanced, STS - stainless steel, TT - Two Tone, WDS - white dot sights, WDC - white dot carry, and WDCN - white dot carry Novak sights.

Some Series 80 pistols, including Gold Cups and Defenders with slanted slide serrations, polished ejection port, and beavertail safety are more desirable than standard models without these features. See individual models for pricing.

GRADING - PPGS™	100%	98%	95%	90%	80%	70%	60%	LAST MSR

JUNIOR COLT POCKET MODEL – .22 S or .25 ACP cal., 2 1/4 in. barrel, blue, checkered walnut grips, made by Astra in Spain 1958-1968.

.22 Short	$550	$400	$325	$325	$200	$180	$150	
.25 ACP	$450	$375	$300	$225	$175	$160	$140	

Add 10% for nickel finish.

A very few conversion kits were offered for this model. They are rare and asking prices are $250-$325 if in mint condition.

COLT AUTOMATIC CALIBER .25 – .25 ACP cal., mfg. by Firearms International for Colt 1970-1973.

	$400	$350	$300	$225	$175	$160	$140	

COMMANDER (PRE-70 SERIES) – 9mm Para., .38 Super, or .45 ACP cal., 4 1/4 in. barrel, full size grips, Colt alloy frame and mainspring housing. Mfg. 1950-1969.

9mm Para.	$1,850	$1,425	$1,125	$1,000	$900	$700	$600	
.38 Super/.45 ACP	$1,800	$1,400	$1,125	$1,000	$900	$700	$600	

Add 10% if NIB.

* ***Commander General Officer's Pistol M1969*** – there were two shipments of the M1969 pistol. One was on 3/18/1969 to the Arsenal and were serialized 327248C, 327337C, 327338C, and 327673C. The second shipment was sent to military exchange in care of Robert Tremont on 5/2/1969, and were serialized CS-001868, CS-002019, CS-002023, CS-002027, CS-02248, and CS-002770.

	$8,000	$7,500	$7,000	$6,000	$5,000	$4,000	$3,250	

.38 SPECIAL/.45 ACP KIT GUNS – .38 Spl. or .45 ACP cal., left side slide marking includes either "COLT .38 SPEC. KIT", or "COLT .45 ACP KIT", these kit guns were designed to be used for competitive target shooting, and many of the guns were shipped without sights, with the buyer providing the sights of his/her choice, kit guns can be found with a myriad of various target sights. Approx. serial no. range is 00100-01164. Production began in 1964, and fewer than 400 of the .38 Spl. Kit Guns were mfg. by 1970. It is estimated that approx. 1,050 .45 ACP Kit Guns were mfg. by the end of 1970.

	$2,300	$2,000	$1,500	$1,100	$800	$650	$550	

This model is also known as the Gil Hebard Model and is basically a .38 AMU.

SERIES 70 LIGHTWEIGHT COMMANDER – 7.65mm (.30 Luger), 9mm Para., .38 Super, or .45 ACP cal., 4 1/4 in. barrel, full size grips, this model is denoted by a "CLW" prefix. Mfg. 1970-1983.

9mm Para.	$1,650	$1,100	$800	$700	$600	$500	$450	
.38 Super/.45 ACP	$1,600	$1,300	$1,000	$675	$575	$500	$450	
7.65mm	$2,600	$2,000	$1,575	$1,250	$995	$875	$750	

Add 10% for NIB condition.

500 Lightweight Commanders were mfg. in 7.65mm cal. during 1971. While most of these were mfg. for export trade, 5 were sold in the U.S.

SERIES 70 COMBAT COMMANDER – 9mm Para., .38 Super, or .45 ACP cal., similar to Series 70 Lightweight (LW) Commander, except has steel frame, blue or satin nickel (scarce) finish. Mfg. 1971-1980.

	$1,400	$1,225	$1,000	$800	$675	$610	$500	

Add 10% for NIB condition.

Add 10% for satin nickel finish if in 98% condition or better.

Editor's Note: **A study of 1970s and 1980s Colt catalogs revealed that only two finishes were offered for the Combat Commander. These were Colt Blue and Satin Nickel. However, it is known that a third finish was also available; Royal Coltguard (also known as Coltguard, Electroless Nickel & E-Nickel). Satin Nickel and Royal Coltguard have a similar texture to their finish but vary slightly in color, with the Royal Coltguard finish having a slightly yellow/gold cast. Order of scarcity beginning with the most common finish is Colt Blue-Satin Nickel-Royal Coltguard.**

GOVERNMENT MODEL MKIV/SERIES 70 – .45 ACP, .38 Super, 9mm Para., or 9mm Steyr cal., 5 in. barrel, checkered walnut grips/medallion. Series 70 models were serial numbered with "SM" prefixes (approx. 3,000 mfg.), "70G" prefixes 1970-76, "70L" and "70S" prefixes also (see Serialization section for more information), "G70" suffixes 1976-80, "B70" suffixes 1979-81, and "70B" prefixes 1981-83. Mfg. 1970-83.

Blue finish	$1,450	$1,200	$995	$800	$650	$525	$425	
Nickel finish	$1,800	$1,550	$1,200	$900	$775	$600	$500	

Add 10% if in NIB condition, 20% for NIB with early two-piece box.

Add 10% for .38 Super, 9mm Para., or 9mm Steyr cal. if in 100% condition.

Add 10% for satin nickel finish if in 98% condition or better.

9mm Steyr was made for export to Europe only. However, a few specimens have found their way into the United States. Prices for NIB specimens are in the $1,000 range.

GRADING - PPGS™	100%	98%	95%	90%	80%	70%	60%	LAST MSR

* ***Series 70 Combat Govt.*** – .45 ACP cal., bluish-black metal finish, features modifications for combat shooting, forerunner to the Combat Elite.

	$1,400	$1,200	$1,000	$850	$775	$700	$650	

Add 10% for NIB condition.

* ***Government Model MKIV/Series 70 Conversion Unit*** – converts .45 ACP to .22 LR, mfg. 1954-84 with either Accro adj. rear or fixed sight.

Adj. Sight	$600	$550	$400	$350	$300	$250	$200	
Fixed Sight	$700	$600	$450	$375	$300	$250	$200	

Add 50% for conversion units in bright nickel finish (very scarce). Must be accompanied by original box w/nickel label.

GOVERNMENT MODEL SERIES 70 (NEW MFG.) – .45 ACP cal., patterned after the original Series 70 pistol, 5 in. barrel, various configurations. Introduced 2018.

* ***Government Model Series 70*** – .45 ACP cal., single action, patterned after the original Series 70 pistol, 5 in. barrel, spur hammer, high-profile fixed sights, checkered diamond pattern rosewood grips, arched mainspring housing, high polish blue finish, 37 oz. New 2018.

MSR $899	$1,050	$850	$700	$500	$450	$415	$375	

* ***Government Model Classic 1911 Series 70*** – .38 Super or .45 ACP cal., patterned after the original Series 70 pistol, 5 in. National Match barrel, 7 shot mag., spur hammer, high-profile fixed sights, double diamond checkered rosewood grips, carbon steel blue finish, 35 oz. New 2019.

MSR $799	$725	$600	$500	$400	$350	$325	$295	

1991 SERIES GOVERNMENT MODEL SERIES 70 MODEL O – .45 ACP cal., patterned after the original Series 70 pistol, 5 in. barrel, high polish blue finish, fixed sights. Mfg. from the Custom Shop 2002-2016.

	$875	$750	$650	$575	$500	$375	$325	*$899*

* ***1991 Series Government Model Series 70 Model O Stainless*** – .45 ACP cal., similar to Series 70 Model O except is stainless steel. Mfg. 2005-2016.

	$1,050	$850	$700	$525	$450	$395	$350	*$979*

POST-WAR ACE SERVICE MODEL – .22 LR cal., similar specifications to previous pre-WWII manufacture, blue (most common) or electroless nickel Custom Shop finish, "SM" prefix (most common) or "B 70" suffix, approx. 30,000 mfg. between 1978-1989.

Blue finish	$2,400	$1,950	$1,450	$1,000	$650	$525	$425	

Add 10% for NIB condition.

This model is serial numbered approx. SM14,001-SM43,830.

GOVERNMENT MODEL MKIV/SERIES 80 – .38 Super, 9mm Para. (disc. 1992), 9x23mm Win. (mfg. 1997 only), or .45 ACP (disc. 1996) cal., single action, 5 in. barrel, 7 or 8 (new 1992) shot mag. in .45 ACP, approx. 38 oz., firing pin safety, checkered walnut (pre-1991 mfg.) or rubber combat style grips with medallion (new 1991). Production started in 1983 with ser. no. FG01000.

* ***Government Model MKIV/Series 80 Blue Finish*** – this finish was disc. in 1997.

	$975	$825	$675	$600	$525	$500	$450	*$600*

Add 10% for 9mm Para. (disc. 1992) cal.
Add 10% for NIB condition.
Add 10% for 9X23 Win.

* ***Government Model MKIV/Series 80 Nickel Finish*** – .45 ACP (disc. 1986) or .38 Super (disc. in 1987) cal.

	$1,000	$775	$725	$625	$550	$500	$450	*$735*

Add 10% for NIB condition.

* ***Government Model MKIV/Series 80 Satin Nickel & Blue Finish*** – with Colt-Pachmayr grips. Disc. 1986.

	$1,000	$850	$750	$650	$575	$500	$450	*$557*

Add 10% for NIB condition.

* ***Government Model MKIV/Series 80 Stainless Steel*** – 9mm Para. (mfg. 1991-92), .38 Super (new 1990), .40 S&W (new 1992), or .45 ACP cal. Disc. 1998.

	$995	$875	$725	$650	$575	$525	$475	*$813*

Add 10% for 9mm Para. (disc. 1992) cal.
Add 10% for NIB condition.

* ***Government Model MKIV/Series 80 "Ultimate" Bright Stainless Steel*** – .38 Super (new 1991) or .45 ACP cal., high polish stainless finish. Mfg. 1986-96.

	$1,400	$1,200	$1,000	$800	$700	$625	$550	*$863*

Add 10% for NIB condition.

GRADING - PPGS™	100%	98%	95%	90%	80%	70%	60%	LAST MSR

* ***Government Model MKIV/Series 80 Limited Class Model .45 ACP*** – .45 ACP cal., designed for tactical competition, includes parkerized matte finish, lightweight composite trigger, ambidextrous safety, upswept beavertail grip safety, beveled magwell, accurized, includes signed target. Mfg. 1994-97.

	$1,000	$850	$750	$650	$575	$500	$450	*$936*

* ***Government Model MKIV/Series 80 Custom Compensated Model .45 ACP*** – .45 ACP cal., designed for serious competitive shooting, blue slide with full profile BAT Compensator, Bo-Mar rear sight, flared funnel magwell. Mfg. by Custom Shop 1994-98.

	$2,000	$1,600	$1,350	$1,100	$975	$850	$725	*$2,428*

MODEL M1911A1 CUSTOM TACTICAL GOV'T - LEVEL I – .45 ACP cal., designed for tactical competition, Commander style hammer, beveled/contoured magwell, nylon flat mainspring housing, ambidextrous safety, long nylon trigger with overtravel stop, available in Officer's or Commmander's length. Mfg. 1998-2001.

	$995	$900	$800	$600	$525	$450	$400	*$730*

In late 1999, this model was redesignated the Model O Custom Tactical Gov't.

* ***Model M1911A1 Custom Tactical Gov't. Model - Level II*** – similar to Level I, except has Videcki long aluminum trigger with overtravel stop, Heinie fixed combat sights, Colt match grade barrel bushing, high-ride grip safety with palm swell, double diamond stocks. Mfg. 1998-2001.

	$1,100	$950	$825	$625	$550	$475	$425	*$935*

* ***Model M1911A1 Custom Tactical Gov't. Model - Level III*** – similar to Level II, except has Bo-Mar adj. rear sight, super match hammer. Mfg. 1998-2001.

	$1,250	$995	$875	$675	$595	$525	$450	*$1,350*

COMBAT GOVERNMENT SERIES 80 – .45 ACP cal., dark matte metal finish, features modifications for combat shooting, successor to the Series 70 Combat Govt. Mfg. 1983-1998.

	$950	$800	$650	$550	$475	$450	$400	

Add 10% for NIB condition.

* ***Combat Elite Series 80*** – .38 Super or .45 ACP cal., similar to Gold Cup, only with wraparound rubber grips, beveled magwell, stainless steel frame with carbon steel slide, and Accro adj. sighting system. Mfg. 1986-1996.

	$1,300	$1,100	$875	$750	$575	$525	$450	*$895*

Note: Colt has issued a factory recall on the safety for this model sold after March 2007 in the following ser. no. range: CG10000E-CG11293E. These pistols must be returned to Colt's factory for part(s) replacement.

COMBAT GOVERNMENT SERIES 80 CONVERSION UNIT – converts Series 80 Govt. Model only to .22 LR or 9mm Para., mfg. 1984-86, 1995, and 1998, with Accro adj. rear sight.

9mm Para.	$725	$650	$500	$400	$325	$250	$200	
.22 LR (mfg. 1984-86)	$750	$650	$500	$400	$325	$250	$200	
.22 LR (mfg. 1995, rare)	$775	$675	$525	$425	$325	$250	$200	

Last MSR was $305 for .22 LR (mfg. 1984-86).

* ***Colt Ace II Conversion Unit*** – similar to above, except features an aluminum slide and barrel w/o floating chamber, does not have hold open feature. Mfg. 1998.

	$350	$295	$275	$225	$190	$175	$150	

Add 75% for all steel model (very rare).

COMBAT TARGET MODEL SERIES 80 – .45 ACP cal. only, 5 in. barrel, adj. sights, matte finish. Mfg. 1997 only.

	$1,000	$875	$750	$650	$450	$425	$400	*$768*

* ***Combat Target Model Stainless Series 80*** – similar to Combat Target Model, except stainless steel finish. Mfg. 1997 only.

	$995	$900	$800	$650	$525	$450	$400	*$820*

SPECIAL COMBAT GOVERNMENT MODEL O (COMPETITION SERIES 80) – .38 Super (mfg. 2005-2017) or .45 ACP cal., competition model, blue (disc.), two-tone (new 2004), or hard chrome (disc. 2017) slide and frame, 5 in. throated barrel, supplied with two 8 shot mags., flared magwell, flared ejection port, cut-out hammer, skeletonized trigger, Bo-Mar rear and Clark dovetail front sight, custom tuning, polished ramp, shipped with certified target. Mfg. by the Custom Shop. Mfg. 1992-2019.

	$1,925	$1,700	$1,450	$1,300	$1,100	$900	$700	*$2,199*

SPECIAL COMBAT GOVERNMENT CARRY MODEL O (SERIES 80) – .45 ACP cal., 5 in. throated barrel, flared ejection port, skeletonized trigger, custom tuning, blue or royal blue (disc.), hard chrome (disc.), or two-tone (disc.) finish, bar-dot-bar (disc. 2000) or Novak (new 2009) night sights, and ambidextrous safety. Mfg. 1992-2000, reintroduced 2009-2019.

	$1,775	$1,450	$1,125	$950	$775	$675	$575	*$2,099*

GRADING - PPGS™	100%	98%	95%	90%	80%	70%	60%	LAST MSR

SPECIAL COMBAT GOVERNMENT CMC MARINE MODEL O – .45 ACP cal., full size with 5 in. National Match stainless steel barrel, front and rear slide serrations (features Desert Tan Cerakote finish), stainless steel frame and slide, Novak night sights with Trijicon inserts, serrated grip straps with lanyard loop, aluminum trigger, unique patterned grips, G10 composite grips, lower Picatinny rail, includes Pelican case with two 7 shot mags, cleaning kit, and test target. Mfg. to Marine Corps specification by the Custom Shop, limited civilian availability. Mfg. 2013-2015.

	100%	98%	95%	90%	80%	70%	60%	LAST MSR
	$2,600	$2,100	$1,750	$1,200	$775	$675	$575	*$2,149*

SPECIAL COMBAT GOVERNMENT – .45 ACP cal., 5 in., 8 shot, 3-hole aluminum trigger, Bomar adj. rear sight, Novak front sight, lowered and flared ejection port, 38 1/2 oz. Mfg. 2017 only.

	100%	98%	95%	90%	80%	70%	60%	LAST MSR
	$1,850	$1,650	$1,450	$1,300	$1,100	$900	$700	*$2,099*

LIGHTWEIGHT COMMANDER – 9mm Para. (disc. 2018, reintroduced 2020) or .45 ACP cal., 4 1/4 in. barrel, 8 or 9 (disc. 2018) shot, dual spring recoil system, black anodized aluminum receiver, blued carbon steel slide, vertical front strap serrations, white dot carry Novak sights, undercut trigger guard, upswept beavertail grip safety, custom Colt logo Black Cherry G10 grips, 29.4 oz. New 2016.

	100%	98%	95%	90%	80%	70%	60%	LAST MSR
MSR $999	$975	$750	$600	$475	$425	$400	$375	

COMMANDER LIGHTWEIGHT SERIES 80 – 9mm Para., .38 Super, or .45 ACP cal., 4 1/4 in. barrel, similar to Government Model, except shorter and lighter alloy frame, fixed sights, round spur hammer, 27 1/2 oz. Mfg. 1983-97.

	100%	98%	95%	90%	80%	70%	60%	LAST MSR
	$1,050	$800	$650	$575	$525	$475	$450	*$735*

Add 10% for .38 Super or 9mm Para. (disc.) cals.

Some pistols are marked "Super Lite Commander - .38 Super - " on left side, and "Lightweight Commander Model" on right side. There may be an "M" on magazine floorplate, with the Colt logo.

COMBAT COMMANDER SERIES 80 – .38 Super (disc.), 9mm Para. (disc. 1992), or .45 ACP cal., similar to Lightweight, except has steel frame.

* ***Combat Commander Series 80 Blue Finish*** – disc. 1996.

	100%	98%	95%	90%	80%	70%	60%	LAST MSR
	$1,050	$800	$650	$500	$450	$425	$400	*$735*

Add 10% for 9mm Para. (disc.) or .38 Super (disc.) cal.

* ***Combat Commander Series 80 Blue Slide/Stainless Steel Receiver*** – .45 ACP cal., two-tone matte finish, upswept grip safety, lightweight perforated trigger, black Hogue grips, 8 shot mag., 35 oz. Mfg. 1998 only.

	100%	98%	95%	90%	80%	70%	60%	LAST MSR
	$800	$650	$550	$525	$500	$475	$450	*$813*

* ***Combat Commander Series 80 Stainless Steel*** – .38 Super (mfg. 1992-97) or .45 ACP cal. Mfg. 1990-98.

	100%	98%	95%	90%	80%	70%	60%	LAST MSR
	$850	$675	$550	$475	$450	$425	$400	*$813*

* ***Combat Commander Series 80 Satin Nickel*** – disc. 1986.

	100%	98%	95%	90%	80%	70%	60%	LAST MSR
	$975	$800	$675	$625	$575	$550	$475	*$550*

* ***Combat Commander Series 80 Gold Cup Commander*** – .45 ACP cal., features custom shop alterations including heavy duty adj. target sights, beveled magwell, serrated front strap, checkered mainspring housing, wide grip safety, and Palo Alto wood grips. Mfg. 1991-93.

	100%	98%	95%	90%	80%	70%	60%	LAST MSR
	$2,200	$1,950	$1,500	$1,050	$825	$700	$600	*$936*

* ***Combat Commander Series 80 Gold Cup Commander Stainless*** – stainless variation of the Gold Cup Commander. Mfg. 1992-disc.

	100%	98%	95%	90%	80%	70%	60%	LAST MSR
	$2,200	$1,950	$1,500	$1,050	$825	$700	$600	*$949*

COMMANDING OFFICER'S LIGHTWEIGHT – 9mm Para. cal., 3 1/2 in. barrel, Officer slide, lightweight commander frame, three-dot sights, Officer's Model extended grip safety, round combat commander hammer, matte black finish, black pebble rubber grips with gold medallions, 500 mfg. by the Custom Shop.

	100%	98%	95%	90%	80%	70%	60%	LAST MSR
	$1,395	$1,075	$825	$700	$575	$500	$450	

COMPETITION PISTOL – 9mm Para. (disc. 2018), .38 Super (limited mfg.), or .45 ACP cal., full size Government model, 5 in. National Match barrel, 8 or 9 shot, dual spring recoil system, Novak adj. rear and fiber optic front sights, undercut trigger guard, upswept beavertail grip safety, custom blue Colt logo G10 grips, 36 oz. New 2016.

	100%	98%	95%	90%	80%	70%	60%	LAST MSR
MSR $949	$925	$700	$575	$450	$400	$375	$350	

Add $50 for .38 Super cal. (disc.).

GRADING - PPGS™	100%	98%	95%	90%	80%	70%	60%	LAST MSR

* ***Competition Pistol Stainless Steel*** – 9mm Para., .38 Super, or .45 ACP cal., full size Government model, 5 in. National Match barrel, 8 or 9 shot, stainless steel construction, undercut trigger guard, Novak adj. rear and fiber optic front sights, G10 checkered blue grips, upswept beavertail grip safety became available in 2018 (not available in .38 Super cal.), dual spring recoil system, stainless steel or blue titanium finish, 36 oz. New 2016.

MSR $999	$975	$750	$600	$475	$425	$400	$375	

Add 5% (MSR $1,049) for .38 Super cal.

* ***Competition Plus (Two-Tone)*** – .45 ACP cal., SA, full size Government model, 5 in. National Match barrel, 8 shot, stainless steel construction, undercut trigger guard, Novak adj. rear and fiber optic front sights, black and grey G10 grips, upswept beavertail grip safety, dual spring recoil system, 25 LPI checkering on front strap, blued slide, brushed stainless steel frame (two-tone finish), 36 oz. New 2020.

MSR $1,199	$1,175	$950	$775	$625	$525	$425	$375	

CONCEALED CARRY GOLD CUP COMMANDER – .45 ACP cal., 4 1/4 in. barrel, stainless steel with hard chrome finish, gold cup features including adj. sights, trigger, and match barrel, rosewood grips, designed by Joe Pittenger for the Colt Custom Shop during 2001. 15 pistols were mfg. with serial numbers CC001JP-CC015JP. Mfg. 2001 only.

	$3,000	$2,700	$2,250	$1,500	$900	$750	$650	

OFFICER'S ACP MODEL SERIES 80 – .45 ACP cal. only, 3 1/2 in. barrel, 34 oz., 6 shot mag., short version of the Government Model. Mfg. 1985-disc.

* ***Officer's ACP Model Series 80 Blue Finish*** – disc. 1996.

	$1,250	$900	$700	$500	$400	$350	$300	*$735*

* ***Officer's ACP Model Series 80 Matte Blue Finish*** – disc. 1991.

	$850	$750	$650	$550	$450	$425	$400	*$625*

* ***Officer's ACP Model Series 80 Stainless Steel*** – matte stainless steel finish. Mfg. 1986-97.

	$1,050	$850	$700	$550	$450	$425	$400	*$813*

Add $200 for "Ultimate" bright stainless steel finish (mfg. 1987-1996).

* ***Officer's ACP Model Series 80 Lightweight*** – similar to Officer's ACP, except has alloy frame and weighs 24 oz. Mfg. 1985-1997.

	$900	$800	$700	$600	$500	$475	$425	*$735*

* ***Officer's ACP Model Series 80 Concealed Carry*** – .45 ACP cal., features matte stainless steel slide with matte blue aluminum alloy receiver, 7 shot mag., black contoured Hogue grips, upswept beavertail grip safety, lightweight perforated trigger, 26 oz. Mfg. 1998 only.

	$1,200	$1,000	$800	$700	$500	$450	$400	*$813*

* ***Officer's ACP Model Series 80 Satin Nickel*** – disc. 1985.

	$950	$850	$750	$650	$550	$500	$450	*$513*

* ***General Officer's ACP Model Series 80*** – bright stainless steel with rosewood grips, special edition. Disc. 1996.

	$1,750	$1,500	$1,250	$900	$675	$550	$425	*$750*

DEFENDER SERIES MODEL O – 9mm Para., .40 S&W (mfg. 1999 only) or .45 ACP cal., 3 in. barrel with 3-dot (disc.) or white dot carry Novak sights, 7 shot mag., rubber wrap-around grips with finger grooves, lightweight perforated trigger, blue or stainless steel slide and frame - frame finished in matte stainless, firing pin safety, 22 1/2 oz. New 1998.

MSR $999	$975	$750	$600	$475	$425	$375	$325	

Note: Colt has issued a factory recall on the safety for this model sold after March 2007 in the following ser. no. range: DR33036 - DR35948 X. Colt will send you a new recoil spring assembly kit that includes the Guide Pad to replace in your pistol.

DEFENDER PLUS – .45 ACP cal., similar to Defender Model O, except has aluminum frame and 8 shot mag. Mfg. 2002-2003.

	$875	$775	$700	$625	$575	$550	$475	*$876*

COLT CONCEALED CARRY – .45 ACP cal., 3 in. barrel, aluminum frame with steel slide, Series 80 firing pin safety system, checkered double diamond walnut grips, front strap serrations, 25 oz. Mfg. 2007.

	$800	$725	$650	$575	$500	$450	$400	*$885*

GRADING - PPGS™	100%	98%	95%	90%	80%	70%	60%	LAST MSR

XSE (XS) SERIES MODEL O – .45 ACP cal., 4 1/4 or 5 in. barrel, stainless brushed finish, front and rear slide serrations, checkered double diamond rosewood grips, 3-dot (disc.) or white dot carry Novak sights, new roll marking and enhanced tolerances, extended ambidextrous thumb safeties. New 2000.

* ***XSE Series Model O Government*** – 9mm Para. (new 2015) or .45 ACP cal., 5 in. barrel, blue (new 2002) or stainless brushed (SS Model) finish, 8 shot mag., 36 oz. Disc. mid-2015.

	$925	$775	$675	$575	$475	$400	$350	*$1,104*

* ***XSE Series Model O Lightweight Government*** – .45 ACP cal., 5 in. barrel, features lightweight aluminum alloy frame, blue finish, carbon steel slide, 8 shot mag., 27 oz. Mfg. 2012-mid 2015.

	$925	$775	$675	$575	$475	$400	$350	*$1,104*

* ***XSE Series Model O Combat Elite*** – .45 ACP cal., 5 in. barrel, two-tone finish (brushed stainless steel receiver/blued carbon steel slide), 8 shot, combat hammer with elongated slot, white dot carry Novak sights, skeletonized trigger, checkered rosewood grips with Colt logo. Mfg. 2009-2017.

	$935	$795	$675	$575	$475	$425	$375	*$1,099*

Note: Colt has issued a recall for ser. nos. CG10000E - CG11293E X due to a problem with the safety and/or guide pad. Improper hardness may cause the safety or guide pad to crack and might not prevent the gun from an accidental firing. Please contact Colt directly if you have one of the pistols - recall@colt.com.

* ***XSE Series Model O Concealed Carry Officers SS*** – features lightweight aluminum alloy frame, 4 1/4 in. barrel and 7 shot mag. Limited mfg. 2000 only.

	$1,000	$900	$700	$600	$500	$450	$400	*$750*

* ***XSE Series Model O Commander SS*** – .45 ACP cal., features 4 1/4 in. barrel, 8 shot mag., brushed stainless steel receiver and slide, 33 1/2 oz. Disc. mid-2015.

	$925	$775	$675	$575	$475	$400	$350	*$1,104*

* ***XSE (XS) Series Model O Lightweight Commander SS*** – .38 Super (disc. 2011), 9mm Para. (new 2015), or .45 ACP cal., features lightweight aluminum alloy frame, 4 1/4 in. barrel, brushed stainless steel slide, cerakote, 8 shot mag., 27 oz. Disc. mid-2015.

	$925	$775	$675	$575	$475	$400	$350	*$1,104*

Early production first series XS Series Lightweight Commander pistols manufactured during 2000 became the XSE Series Lightweight Commander SS pistols during 2001.

RAIL GUN SERIES MODEL O – 9mm Para. (mfg. 2016-2017) or .45 ACP cal., dual recoil spring system, 5 in. National Match stainless steel barrel, 8 or 9 (disc. 2017) shot mag., 3-hole aluminum trigger, Novak white dot sights, diamond checkered rosewood grips, upswept beavertail grip safety, Series 80 firing pin safety, Picatinny rail underneath frame in front of trigger guard, wide slide serrations, stainless, two-tone (disc.), or Cerakote (mfg. 2011-2016) finish, 40 oz. Mfg. 2009-2018.

	$1,025	$895	$725	$625	$525	$450	$395	*$1,199*

Add $50 for Cerakote finish (mfg. 2011-2016).

* ***Rail Gun Model O Cerakote Stainless*** – .45 ACP cal., 5 in. barrel, 7 shot mag., Desert Tan Cerakote finish, includes blue plastic pistol case. Mfg. 2015-2016.

	$1,475	$1,225	$1,025	$875	$775	$675	$575	*$1,699*

* ***Rail Gun M45A1 Close Quarter Battle*** – .45 ACP cal., SA, 1911-style, Decobond Brown coated stainless steel slide and frame, 5 in. National Match barrel, 7 shot mag., 3-hole aluminum trigger, Novak Tritium front and rear 3-dot night sights, G10 checkered Desert Camo grips, ambi thumb safety, grip safety, Picatinny rail, Zinc Brown Ion Bond finish, includes blue plastic pistol case, 40 oz. New 2016.

MSR $1,699	$1,650	$1,325	$1,075	$875	$775	$675	$575	

* ***Rail Gun Model O Commander Stainless Steel*** – .45 ACP cal., features 4 1/4 in. barrel, 8 shot mag., brushed stainless steel receiver and slide, features Picatinny rail in front of trigger guard, 33 1/2 oz. Limited mfg. 2015 only.

	$1,025	$895	$725	$625	$525	$450	$395	*$1,198*

* ***Rail Gun Model O Lightweight Commander Stainless Steel*** – .45 ACP cal., features 4 1/4 in. barrel, 8 shot mag., black anodized frame with blue steel slide, diamond patterned checkered walnut grips, features Picatinny rail in front of trigger guard and skeletonized trigger, 33 1/2 oz. Limited mfg. 2015 only.

	$1,025	$895	$725	$625	$525	$450	$395	*$1,198*

* ***Rail Gun Model O Lightweight*** – .45 ACP cal., 5 in. barrel, 8 shot mag., black anodized frame with blue steel slide, diamond patterned checkered walnut grips, features Picatinny rail in front of trigger guard and skeletonized trigger, 33 1/2 oz. Limited mfg. 2015 only.

	$1,025	$895	$725	$625	$525	$450	$395	*$1,198*

GRADING - PPGS™	100%	98%	95%	90%	80%	70%	60%	LAST MSR

M45A1 MARINE CORPS (DECOMMISSIONED) – .45 ACP cal., originally issued to U.S. Marine Corps Forces Special Operations Command (MARSOC) Marine Raiders and the Corp's Force Reconnaissance Marines, Tritium Novak sights, G10 grips, marked "USMC" on left side of slide w/laser etched "X" over it, includes original cardboard box, Wilson Combat mag., matte light tan Cerakote finish, approx. 1,000 pistols decommissioned late 2018.

	$6,000	$4,500	$4,000	$3,750	$3,500	$3,000	$2,500	

GOLD CUP NATIONAL MATCH MKIV/SERIES 80/MODEL O – please refer to the listings for Gold Cup National Match models under Pistols: Semi-Auto, National Match Models - WWII and Post-WWII.

GOLD CUP TROPHY STAINLESS – 9mm Para. (new 2018), .38 Super (new 2019), or .45 ACP cal., stainless steel, 5 in. barrel, Bomar style sights, round top slide and wraparound black synthetic grips, matte finish, 39 oz. New 1997.

MSR $1,699	$1,650	$1,325	$1,075	$875	$650	$475	$375	

Add 2.5% (MSR $1,749) for .38 Super cal.

GOLD CUP – 9mm Para., .45 ACP, or .38 Super cal., Series 70 firing system, 5 in. National Match barrel, 8 shot mag., perforated trigger, fiber optic front sight and Bomar rear sight, blue checkered G10 scalloped grips, manual thumb safety, brushed stainless steel finish, 38 oz. New 2019.

MSR $1,199	$1,175	$950	$775	$625	$525	$425	$375	

Add 2.5% (MSR $1,249) for .38 Super cal.

GOVERNMENT 1911A1 GOLD CUP ACE .22 LR CAL. – .22 LR cal., 5 in. barrel, SA, fully adj. rear sight, w/o rail, 12 shot mag. only, Commander-style hammer, black checkered rubber wrap-around grips with diamond patterns, black anodized zinc alloy finish, manual and beavertail grip safeties, checkered front grip strap, skeleton trigger, 36 oz. Mfg. by Umarex GmbH in Germany under license from Colt beginning 2012, and currently distributed by Walther Arms.

MSR $499	$425	$365	$325	$295	$260	$230	$200	

GOVERNMENT MODEL O (1991 SERIES/MKIV SERIES 80) – 9mm Para. (disc. 2001, reintroduced 2015-2016), .38 Super (New 2020), or .45 ACP cal., 5 in. barrel, similar to original WWII issue pistols with government issue parkerized matte (disc.) or blue finish, fixed sights, checkered rosewood double diamond wood (blue only) or checkered black composite grips, 7 shot mag., early guns were marked Colt M1991A1 on left side of slide, 38 oz., includes brown molded case. New 1991.

MSR $799	$775	$625	$500	$400	$350	$325	$295	

Add 5% (MSR $849) for .38 Special cal.

Add $93 for Custom Government Model in .45 ACP cal. with blue steel and low profile combat sights (mfg. 2013 only).

Add 15% for 9mm Para. cal.

This model is serialized consecutively with the last batch of Govt. military models manufactured during 1945.

* ***Government Model O Stainless*** – 9mm Para. (disc. 2001, reintroduced 2015-2016), .38 Super (New 2020), or .45 ACP cal., 5 in. barrel, similar to original WWII issue pistols with government issue parkerized matte (disc.) or blue finish, fixed sights, checkered rosewood double diamond wood (blue only) or checkered black composite grips, 7 shot mag., early guns were marked Colt M1991A1 on left side of slide, 38 oz., includes brown molded case. New 1991.

MSR $799	$775	$625	$500	$400	$350	$325	$295	

Add 5% (MSR $849) for .38 Special cal.

Add $93 for Custom Government Model in .45 ACP cal. with blue steel and low profile combat sights (mfg. 2013 only).

Add 15% for 9mm Para. cal.

This model is serialized consecutively with the last batch of Govt. military models manufactured during 1945.

* ***Government Model O Stainless Steel (1991 Series)*** – .38 Special (new 2020),.45 ACP or 9mm Para. (disc.) cal., 5 in. barrel, matte stainless steel frame and slide, black checkered grips, white dot sights. Mfg. 1996-2016, reintroduced 2020.

MSR $899	$850	$700	$575	$450	$395	$350	$325	

Add 5% (MSR $949) for .38 Special cal.

GOVERNMENT MODEL O (1991 SERIES) – .38 Super cal., 5 in. barrel, M1911 (bright stainless only) or M1911A1 style frame, Govt. Model, blue, 3-dot sights, checkered rubber or double diamond walnut (bright stainless only) grips, 9 shot mag., beveled magwell. Mfg. 2003-2009, reintroduced 2011-2016.

	$850	$725	$625	$550	$495	$450	$350	*$849*

* ***Government Model O .38 Super Stainless*** – similar to Government Model O .38 Super, except is available in stainless steel. Disc. 2009, reintroduced mid-2015-2016.

	$925	$825	$700	$600	$425	$400	$375	*$929*

GRADING - PPGS™	100%	98%	95%	90%	80%	70%	60%	LAST MSR

* ***Government Model O Super Bright Stainless*** – .38 Super or .45 ACP (new 2018) cal., bright polished stainless steel only. Mfg. by Colt Custom Shop. New 2003.

MSR $1,499	$1,450	$1,200	$1,000	$850	$700	$600	$450	

Add 2.5% (MSR $1,549) for .38 Super cal.

CQB GOVERNMENT MODEL O – .45 ACP cal., 5 in. National Match barrel, 8 shot mag., stainless steel construction with grey Cerakote frame finish and black Cerakote slide finish or FDE Cerakote frame and black DLC slide finish (new 2019), custom tune trigger, Novak low mount carry night sights, G10 grips, lower Picatinny rail, dual recoil spring system, 42 oz. Current Mfg.

MSR $1,999	$1,950	$1,700	$1,450	$1,325	$1,075	$875	$675	

CUSTOM CARRY LIMITED – 9mm Para. or .45 ACP cal., 4 1/4 in. barrel, 8 shot mag., Gen 2 magwell, stainless steel construction w/Decobond Ionbond smoke gray finish, full custom rear sights, beavertail grip safety, New 2021.

MSR $2,599	$2,500	$2,175	$1,875	$1,700	$1,375	$1,125	$875	

CUSTOM COMPETITION O SERIES – 9mm Para. (new 2020), .38 Super (new 2020), or .45 ACP cal., 5 in. National Match target barrel, 8 shot mag., fully blended magwell, stainless steel construction w/ grey Cerakote frame finish and black Cerakote slide finish, competition trigger, green fiber optic front sight, adj. Bomar style rear sights, gray/black G10 grips, front and rear slide serrations, 25 LPI front strap checkering, 42. oz. New 2018.

MSR $2,299	$2,250	$1,900	$1,625	$1,400	$1,150	$950	$700	

Add 2.5% (MSR $2,349) for .38 Super cal. (new 2020).

COMBAT COMMANDER MODEL O (1991 SERIES COMMANDER/MKIV SERIES 80) – 9mm Para. (disc., reintroduced 2015) or .45 ACP cal., 4 1/4 in. barrel, full size grip, 7 shot mag., parkerized finish, blued carbon steel receiver and slide, 36 oz. Mfg. 1993-2005, reintroduced 2007.

MSR $999	$975	$750	$600	$475	$425	$400	$375	

* ***Combat Commander Stainless Steel (1991 Series Commander SS)*** – .45 ACP cal., similar to Combat Commander Model O, except is stainless steel. Mfg. 1999-2005, reintroduced 2007-2016.

	$800	$675	$550	$475	$425	$400	$375	*$929*

COMBAT ELITE COMMANDER – 9mm Para. or .45 ACP cal., steel Commander frame, 4 1/4 in. barrel, 9 shot mag., Novak night sights, G10 half checkered black grips with scallop, Series 80 upswept beavertail grip safety, 25 LPI checkering, Two-Tone Elite (stainless steel and black) finish. New late 2018.

MSR $1,399	$1,350	$1,100	$950	$825	$725	$625	$525	

COMBAT ELITE DEFENDER – 9mm Para. or .45 ACP cal., stainless steel frame and slide, 3 in. barrel, 7 shot mag., Novak night sights, G10 half checkered black grips with scallop, Series 80 upswept beavertail grip safety, 25 LPI checkering, polished slide flats, Two-Tone (stainless steel and black) Elite finish. New late 2018.

MSR $1,399	$1,350	$1,100	$950	$825	$725	$625	$525	

COMBAT ELITE GOVERNMENT – 9mm Para. or .45 ACP cal., steel frame, 5 in. National Match barrel, 7 shot mag., Novak night sights, G10 half checkered black grips with scallop, Series 80 upswept beavertail grip safety, 25 LPI checkering, dual recoil spring system, Two-Tone (stainless steel and black) Elite finish. New late 2018.

MSR $1,399	$1,350	$1,100	$950	$825	$725	$625	$525	

COMBAT UNIT RAIL GUN (OLDER MFG) – 9mm Para. or .45 ACP cal., 5 in. National Match barrel, 8 or 9 shot, blackened stainless steel receiver and slide, undercut trigger guard, Novak night sights, custom Gray Colt logo G10 grips, upswept beavertail grip safety, dual spring recoil system, checkered front strap, 40 oz. Limited mfg. 2016 only.

	$1,295	$1,050	$900	$775	$650	$550	$450	*$1,499*

COMBAT UNIT CCO/CCU SERIES – 9mm Para. or .45 ACP cal., Colt Series 80 firing system, various tactical configurations and finishes, 4 1/4 or 5 in. National Match barrel. New 2019.

* ***Combat Unit Officers Model*** – 9mm Para. or .45 ACP cal., SA, Colt Series 80 firing system, steel frame, 4 1/4 in. National Match barrel, 7 shot mag., Novak front and rear sight, G10 gray grips w/25 LPI checkering, ambi extended thumb safety, front and rear slide serrations and recoil control, anodized black DLC finish, 32 oz. New 2019.

MSR $1,499	$1,450	$1,200	$1,000	$850	$700	$600	$450	

* ***Combat Unit Government*** – 9mm Para. or .45 ACP cal., SA, Colt Series 80 firing system, steel frame, 5 in. National Match barrel, 8 shot mag., Novak front and rear sight, G10 gray grips w/25 LPI checkering, ambi extended thumb safety, front and rear slide serrations and recoil control, matte black DLC finish, 40 oz. New 2019.

MSR $1,499	$1,450	$1,200	$1,000	$850	$700	$600	$450	

GRADING - PPGS™	100%	98%	95%	90%	80%	70%	60%	LAST MSR

* ***Combat Unit Rail Gun (Current Mfg.)*** – 9mm Para. or .45 ACP cal., Colt Series 80 firing system, 5 in. National Match barrel, 9 shot, blackened stainless steel receiver and slide, undercut trigger guard, Novak night sights, custom gray checkered G10 scallop grips, ambi extended thumb safety, dual spring recoil system, checkered front strap, matte black DLC finish, 40 oz. New 2019.

MSR $1,599	$1,550	$1,275	$1,050	$875	$725	$575	$500	

WILEY CLAPP CCO – 9mm Para. or .45 ACP cal., Series 70 firing system, alloy frame and carbon steel Commander slide, 4 1/4 in. barrel, 6 shot mag., long black trigger, ramp w/brass bead front sight, Novak w/wide notch rear sight, rounded butt, brown fingerprint checkered wood grips w/"Colt" on top, thumb safety, grip safety, Pete Single 25lpi checkered front strap, Commander size slide, blue finish, special serialization. Talo exclusive, new mid-2017.

MSR $1,299	$1,125	$1,025	$925	$825	$725	$625	$495	

WILEY CLAPP GOVERNMENT 1911 - .45 ACP cal., Series 70 firing system, carbon steel frame, 5 in. barrel, 8 shot mag., long black trigger, Novak brass bead front sights and plain black extra wide notch rear sights, oval brown laminate grips w/scalloped checkering on lower half w/"Colt" on top, beavertail grip safety, original 1911 small safety lock, Pete Single 25lpi checkered front strap, blue finish, special serialization. Talo exclusive, new mid-2017.

MSR $1,299	$1,125	$1,025	$925	$825	$725	$625	$495	

WILEY CLAPP LIGHTWEIGHT COMMANDER - 9mm Para. or .45 ACP cal., Series 70 firing system, lightweight aluminum frame, 4 1/4 in. barrel, 8 shot mag., long black trigger, Novak brass bead front sights and plain black extra wide notch rear sights, oval brown laminate grips w/scalloped checkering on lower half w/"Colt" on top, upswept beavertail grip safety, original 1911 small safety lock, Pete Single 25lpi checkered front strap, blue finish, special serialization. Talo exclusive, new mid-2017.

MSR $1,299	$1,125	$1,025	$925	$825	$725	$625	$495	

WILEY CLAPP STAINLESS COMMANDER - .45 ACP cal., Series 70 firing system, steel frame, 4 1/4 in. barrel, 8 shot mag., long black trigger, Novak brass bead front sights and plain black extra wide notch rear sights, oval brown laminate grips w/scalloped checkering on lower half w/"Colt" on top, upswept beavertail grip safety, original 1911 small safety lock, Pete Single 25lpi checkered front strap, stainless finish, special serialization. Talo exclusive, new mid-2017.

MSR $1,399	$1,195	$1,050	$950	$850	$725	$625	$500	

1991 SERIES OFFICER'S COMPACT (MKIV SERIES 80) – similar to Model M1991 Commander, except has 3 1/2 in. barrel, 6 shot mag., 34 oz. Mfg. 1992-1999.

	$600	$500	$425	$400	$375	$350	$325	*$556*

* ***1991 Series Officer's Stainless Compact*** – similar to Model M1991A1 Officer's Compact, except is stainless steel. Mfg. 1999 only.

	$800	$725	$650	$500	$475	$450	$400	*$610*

NEW AGENT SA MODEL O – 9mm Para. (disc. 2012) or .45 ACP cal., 3 in. barrel, Series 80 firing pin safety system, hammerless, 7 shot mag., double diamond slim fit or Crimson Trace (new 2012) grips, black anodized aluminum frame, blue finish, beveled magwell, skeletonized trigger, snag free trench style sights, front strap serrations, captive recoil spring system. Mfg. 2008-mid-2015.

	$925	$795	$650	$550	$450	$400	$350	*$1,078*

Add $288 for Crimson Trace Lasergrips (new 2012).
Add 10% for 9mm Para. cal. (disc. 2012).

Note: Colt has issued a factory recall on the safety for this model sold after March 2007 in the following ser. no. range: GT01001-GT04505 XX. These pistols must be returned to Colt's factory for part(s) replacement.

GUNSITE MODEL O - .45 ACP cal., M1911 style frame, Series 70 firing pin safety system, 4 1/4 (Commander configuration) or 5 in. barrel, checkered thin rosewood grips, blue or stainless steel, many shooting features are included, such as serrated flat mainspring housing, Gold Cup front strap serrations, Heinie front and Novak rear sights, two 8 shot Wilson mags., McCormick hammer and sear, slide marked with Gunsite logo. Mfg. 2003-2005.

	$1,300	$1,100	$900	$775	$700	$625	$575	*$1,400*

M1911 MODEL O SERIES 70 - .45 ACP cal., 5 in. barrel, accurate reproduction of the Model 1911 U.S. military sidearm, original style checkered walnut grips, carbonia blue finish, 7 shot mag., original WWI roll marks, original style packaging (cardboard box with wax paper), 4,400 were scheduled for mfg. by the Custom Shop, 38 oz. Mfg. 2003-2009.

	$1,400	$1,250	$900	$750	$575	$475	$425	*$990*

Note: Colt has issued a recall for ser. nos. 4597WMK - 5414WMK X due to a problem with the safety and/or guide pad. Improper hardness may cause the safety or guide pad to crack and might not prevent the gun from an accidental firing. Please contact Colt directly if you have one of the pistols - recall@colt.com.

GRADING - PPGS™	100%	98%	95%	90%	80%	70%	60%	LAST MSR

M1911A1 WWII REPLICA MODEL O – .45 ACP cal., 5 in. barrel, incorporates pre-Series 70 firing pin safety system, accurate reproduction of the Model 1911A1 U.S. military sidearm, original style composite grips, parkerized finish or stainless steel construction, 7 shot mag., original WWII roll marks, lanyard loop on arched serrated mainspring housing, wide spur hammer, safety and slide stop with original serrations, 38 oz., original style packaging (cardboard box with wax paper), approx. 4,000 mfg. by the Custom Shop. Mfg. 2001-2004.

	100%	98%	95%	90%	80%	70%	60%	LAST MSR
	$1,400	$1,250	$900	$750	$575	$500	$450	*$940*

Colt has issued a factory recall on the safety for this model sold after March 2007 in the following ser. no. range: 4597WMK-5414WMK. These pistols must be returned to Colt's factory for part(s) replacement.

M1911 SERIES 70 WWI MODEL 1918 REPLICA – .45 ACP cal., 5 in. barrel, accurate reproduction of the Model 1911 U.S. military sidearm manufactured during 1918, featuring black finish, original WWI roll marks, limited mfg. by the Custom Shop. Mfg. 2008-2009.

	100%	98%	95%	90%	80%	70%	60%	LAST MSR
	$1,400	$1,100	$950	$825	$600	$525	$450	*$990*

Colt also offered this model in a Presentation Grade with blue or nickel finish and unsigned A engraving coverage - MSRs ranged from $2,278 - $2,378.

Note: Colt has issued a factory recall on the safety for this model sold after March 2007 in the following ser. no. range: 1001WW1-3431WW1X. These pistols must be returned to Colt's factory for part(s) replacement.

GOVERNMENT MODEL 1911A1 .22 CAL. – .22 LR cal., patterned after the Colt Post War Ace Service Model, features 5 in. barrel, checkered diamond patterned rubber grips, half-cock mechanism, all steel construction, 10 or 12 shot mag., standard 1911A1 model with removable front and drift adj. rear sight, single slide serrations, 36 oz. Mfg. by Umarex in Germany beginning 2011 and distributed by Walther Arms.

	100%	98%	95%	90%	80%	70%	60%	LAST MSR
MSR $399	$350	$300	$265	$225	$200	$185	$175	

This model is also available in a Gold Cup variation - please refer to the listing in the Pistols: Semi-Auto, National Match Models - WWII & Post-WWII category.

GOVERNMENT MODEL 1911A1 .22 CAL. RAIL GUN – .22 LR cal., similar to Government Model 1911 .22 cal., except has lower Picatinny rail on frame, double slide serrations, skeleton trigger, low mount 3-dot combat style sights, beavertail grip safety and Commander style hammer, black or FDE (new 2013) finish, 36 oz. Mfg. by Umarex in Germany beginning 2011 and imported/distributed by Walther Arms.

	100%	98%	95%	90%	80%	70%	60%	LAST MSR
MSR $449	$385	$325	$285	$240	$215	$195	$185	

Add $50 for FDE finish (new 2013).

This model is also available in a Gold Cup variation - please refer to the listing in the Pistols: Semi-Auto, National Match Models - WWII & Post-WWII category.

M1911ANVII 100th ANNIVERSARY – .45 ACP cal., features 100th Anniversary of the M1911 with gold accents including slide banners, "Colt" and prancing stallion on rear sides of slide, royal blue metal finish, smooth cocobolo grips with 100th Anniversary gold plated medallions, includes walnut display case, serial numbers beginning with 19110001. 750 mfg. 2011 only.

	100%	98%	95%	90%	80%	70%	60%	LAST MSR
	$1,750	$1,550	$1,325	N/A	N/A	N/A	N/A	*$2,295*

M1911ANVIII 100th ANNIVERSARY – .45 ACP cal., based on Colt 1911A1 mfg. in 1918, custom military roll marks on frame and slide, brushed blue finish, walnut double diamond grips, special edition 100th Anniversary packaging, serialization begins with 00011911. Mfg. limited to all orders placed by Nov. 30, 2011.

	100%	98%	95%	90%	80%	70%	60%	LAST MSR
	$1,300	$1,150	$900	N/A	N/A	N/A	N/A	*$1,150*

M1911 100th ANNIVERSARY CUSTOM SHOP – .45 ACP cal., 4 variations featuring either A, B, C, or D coverage standard engraving, gold inlaid serial number and "1911-2011" on slide, blue finish. 100 mfg. total in all four engraving patterns, mfg. 2011 only.

* ***M1911 100th Anniversary Custom Shop w/A Engraving*** – .45 ACP cal., featuring Custom Shop A coverage standard engraving. Mfg. 2011 only.

	100%	98%	95%	90%	80%	70%	60%	LAST MSR
	$2,450	$2,100	$1,750	N/A	N/A	N/A	N/A	*$2,640*

* ***M1911 100th Anniversary Custom Shop w/B Engraving*** – .45 ACP cal., featuring Custom Shop B coverage standard engraving. Mfg. 2011 only.

	100%	98%	95%	90%	80%	70%	60%	LAST MSR
	$2,675	$2,275	$1,875	N/A	N/A	N/A	N/A	*$2,900*

* ***M1911 100th Anniversary Custom Shop w/C Engraving*** – .45 ACP cal., featuring Custom Shop C coverage standard engraving. Mfg. 2011 only.

	100%	98%	95%	90%	80%	70%	60%	LAST MSR
	$2,995	$2,550	$2,100	N/A	N/A	N/A	N/A	*$3,265*

GRADING - PPGS™	100%	98%	95%	90%	80%	70%	60%	LAST MSR

* ***M1911 100th Anniversary Custom Shop w/D Engraving*** – .45 ACP cal., featuring Custom Shop D coverage standard engraving. Mfg. 2011 only.

	$3,200	$2,875	$2,475	N/A	N/A	N/A	N/A	*$3,535*

DELTA ELITE (1987-1996 MFG.) – 10mm cal., 5 in. barrel, black neoprene grips, high profile 3-dot sights, blue finish, 8 shot mag., 38 oz. Mfg. 1987-96.

	$1,450	$1,150	$850	$600	$500	$475	$450	*$807*

* ***Delta Elite First Edition (1991 Mfg.)*** – features laser engraving with gold-fill, smooth wood grips, includes presentation case. 500 mfg. 1991 only.

	$1,650	$1,350	$1,050	$750	$525	$500	$450	

* ***Delta Elite Stainless Steel*** – matte stainless steel finish. Mfg. 1989-96.

	$925	$725	$625	$600	$575	$550	$525	*$860*

Add 30% for "Ultimate" brite stainless steel finish (disc. 1993).

* ***Delta Elite First Edition (1988 Mfg.)*** – features stamped lettering on slide, ebony grips, and do not have display case. 1,000 mfg. 1988 only.

	$1,150	$900	$725	$650	$550	$500	$450	

DELTA ELITE (CURRENT MFG.) – 10mm cal., single action, 5 in. barrel, 8 shot mag., stainless steel or two-tone (TT suffix, new 2018) frame, Novak (new 2016) white dot sights, diamond laser cut cocobolo grips with trademark Colt logo on both grips, upswept beavertail grip safety (new 2016), extended thumb safety (new 2016). New 2008.

MSR $1,199	$1,175	$950	$775	$625	$525	$425	$375	

Add 7.5% (MSR $1,299) for lower Picatinny rail (new 2017).

DELTA GOLD CUP STAINLESS – 10mm cal., target variation, includes Accro adj. rear sight and trigger (serrated also), wraparound combat grips. Mfg. 1989-93, re-released 1995-96.

	$1,550	$1,200	$900	$700	$650	$575	$525	*$1,027*

* ***Delta Gold Cup Blue*** – similar to Delta Gold Cup Stainless, except has blue finish. Mfg. 1991 only.

	$1,250	$950	$750	$675	$600	$550	$500	*$870*

.380 GOVERNMENT MODEL SERIES 80 – .380 ACP cal. only, single action, 3 1/4 in. barrel, 7 shot mag., fixed sights, composition stocks, 21 3/4 oz. Mfg. 1983-1997.

* ***.380 Government Model Series 80 Blue Finish*** – finish disc. in 1997.

	$725	$600	$550	$500	$450	$400	$350	*$474*

* ***.380 Government Model Series 80 Nickel Finish*** – bright polish nickel finish with white composite grips. Disc. 1994.

	$900	$750	$600	$500	$450	$400	$350	*$504*

* ***.380 Government Model Series 80 Coltguard Finish*** – employs a high-strength electroless matte nickel finish. Mfg. 1986-89.

	$750	$650	$575	$500	$450	$400	$350	*$406*

* ***.380 Government Model Series 80 Stainless Steel*** – mfg. 1989-97.

	$700	$600	$500	$450	$425	$400	$350	*$508*

GOVT. POCKETLITE L.W. – similar to .380 Series 80 Govt. Model, except frame is mfg. with alloy, blue or nickel/stainless (mfg. 1992-93) finish only, black composition grips, 14 3/4 oz. Mfg. 1991-97.

	$750	$650	$525	$450	$400	$350	$325	*$462*

Add 15% for nickel/stainless finish (disc. 1993).

* ***Govt. Pocketlite Teflon Nickel/Stainless*** – similar to Govt. Pocketlite L.W., except has combination of Teflon nickel, stainless steel finish. Mfg. 1997-98.

	$725	$600	$500	$400	$350	$300	$275	*$508*

MUSTANG – similar to .380 Series Govt., except has 2 3/4 in. barrel, single action, 5 or 6 (new 1992) shot mag., blue finish only, 18 1/2 oz. Mfg. 1986-1998.

	$825	$700	$575	$475	$375	$300	$275	*$462*

* ***Mustang Nickel finish*** – bright polish nickel finish with white composite grips. Mfg. 1987-94.

	$900	$750	$650	$525	$425	$350	$300	*$504*

* ***Mustang Stainless Steel*** – stainless steel variation of the Mustang. Mfg. 1990-97.

	$700	$650	$600	$550	$500	$395	$295	*$508*

* ***Mustang Coltguard finish*** – employs a high-strength electroless matte nickel finish. Mfg. 1987.

	$975	$825	$700	$600	$500	$400	$350	*$406*

GRADING - PPGS™	100%	98%	95%	90%	80%	70%	60%	LAST MSR

MUSTANG LITE - .380 ACP cal., SA only, 2 3/4 in. barrel, 6 shot mag., black tactical polymer grip frame with ribbed grip straps and tactical profile, brushed stainless steel slide, firing pin safety block, Commander style hammer, solid aluminum trigger, lowered ejection port, 12 1/2 oz. Mfg. 2015-19.

	$500	$425	$360	$315	$275	$235	$200	*$599*

MUSTANG PLUS II - .380 ACP cal. only, 2 3/4 in. barrel, blue finish, black composition grips, 7 shot mag., 20 oz. Mfg. 1988-96.

	$775	$650	$550	$475	$400	$350	$275	*$462*

This model has the full grip length of the .380 Government Model.

* ***Mustang Plus II Stainless Steel*** - stainless steel variation of the Mustang Plus II. Mfg. 1990-1998.

	$700	$600	$550	$475	$400	$350	$275	*$508*

MUSTANG POCKETLITE L.W. - similar to Mustang, except has aluminum alloy receiver and stainless slide, blue (disc. 1997) or nickel/stainless finish, black composite grips, 12 1/2 oz. Introduced 1987.

	$775	$650	$525	$450	$375	$325	$300	*$462*

* ***Mustang Pocketlite L.W. Nickel/Stainless Steel Finish*** - similar to Mustang Pocketlite, except has nickel finish frame and stainless steel slide. Mfg. 1991-96.

	$800	$700	$550	$450	$375	$325	$300	*$493*

* ***Mustang Pocketlite Teflon Nickel/Stainless*** - similar to Mustang Pocketlite L.W., except has combination of Teflon nickel, stainless steel finish. Mfg. 1997-99.

	$775	$650	$525	$450	$375	$325	$300	*$508*

* ***Mustang Pocketlite L.W. Lady Elite*** - features hard chrome receiver, blue slide with silver painted rollmark, finger extension mag., soft carrying case, limited mfg. 1995-96.

	$775	$650	$525	$450	$375	$325	$300	*$612*

* ***Mustang Pocketlite L.W. Nite Lite .380*** - .380 ACP cal., features bar-dot night sight, Teflon coated alloy receiver with stainless slide, finger extension mag., includes carrying case. Mfg. 1994 only.

	$775	$650	$525	$450	$375	$325	$300	*$577*

MUSTANG POCKETLITE, RECENT MFG. - .380 ACP cal., SA only, 2 3/4 in. barrel, 7 shot mag., firing pin safety block, commander style hammer, solid aluminum trigger, lowered ejection port, brushed stainless steel slide with electroless nickel finished frame, black composite grips with Colt medallions, 12 1/2 oz. Mfg. 2012-19.

	$595	$475	$415	$325	$275	$225	$200	*$699*

MUSTANG XSP - .380 ACP cal., 2 3/4 in. barrel, 6 shot mag., textured polymer grip frame with ribbed front and back straps, ambidextrous safety, black stainless steel slide, fixed front and rear sights, wide slide serrations, squared off trigger guard, lower 3/8 in. integrated accessory rail, hard chrome small parts, matte black finish, 12 oz. Mfg. mid-2013-mid 2015.

	$575	$475	$425	$350	$295	$250	$225	*$672*

Add $125 for Mustang XSP First Edition.

PISTOLS: SEMI-AUTO, DOUBLE ACTION - RECENT MFG.

DOUBLE EAGLE SERIES 90 I & II - 9mm Para. (mfg. 1991 only), .38 Super (mfg. 1991 only), .45 ACP, or 10mm (disc. 1993) cal., double action semi-auto that operates on the Browning/Colt short recoil, pivoting link locking system used by the Govt. Model, 5 in. barrel, matte stainless steel only, 3-dot sighting system or Accro adj. rear sight (disc. 1994), checkered synthetic Xenoy grips, 8 shot mag. (9 shot in 9mm Para. or .38 Super cal.), decocking lever, squared off combat trigger guard, 39 oz. Mfg. 1990-96.

	$850	$650	$500	$430	$375	$315	$270	*$727*

Add $100 for 9mm Para. or .38 Super cal.
Add $20 for 10mm cal.
Add 10% for NIB condition.

The first edition (1,000 mfg. in 1989) on this model did not have a decocking lever - MSR was $916.

* ***Double Eagle Combat Commander*** - .40 S&W (new 1992) or .45 ACP cal., 4 1/4 in. barrel, 8 shot mag., white dot sights, 36 oz. Mfg. 1991-96.

	$850	$650	$500	$430	$375	$315	$270	*$727*

Add 100-200% for X serial number guns.

* ***Double Eagle Officer's Model*** - .45 ACP cal., 3 1/2 in. barrel, 8 shot mag., 35 oz. Mfg. 1991-disc.

	$850	$650	$500	$430	$375	$315	$270	*$727*

GRADING - PPGS™	100%	98%	95%	90%	80%	70%	60%	LAST MSR

* ***Double Eagle Officer's Lightweight Model*** – .45 ACP cal. only, 3 1/2 in. barrel, alloy frame with blue finish only, white dot sights, 25 oz. Mfg. 1991-93.

$850	$650	$500	$400	$365	$330	$295	*$696*

ALL AMERICAN MODEL 2000 – 9mm Para. cal. only, double action semi-auto, roller-bearing mounted trigger allowing double action only trigger pull every shot, recoil operated rotary action featuring integral locking lugs similar to the military M16 rifle, hammerless, 4 1/2 in. barrel, matte finished steel slide and polymer receiver, 15 shot mag., 3-dot sighting system, ambidextrous mag. release, black synthetic checkered grips, internal striker block safety, checkered trigger guard and front grip strap, 29 oz. Manufacturing difficulty forced discontinuance and design and tooling were returned to Reed Knight. Mfg. 1991-93.

* ***Model 2000 - Polymer Frame***

$650	$550	$500	$450	$375	$325	$275	*$575*

Add 10% for NIB condition.

This model could also be converted to a shorter version using a 3 3/4 in. barrel/bushing kit (no tools or other components were needed - $75 retail during 1993 only).

* ***Model 2000 - Aluminum Frame*** – similar to polymer Model 2000, except frame is aluminum, serial numbered RK00001-RK03000 to commemorate the designer (Reed Knight). Mfg. 1993.

$850	$700	$550	$465	$375	$325	$275	*$575*

Add 10% for NIB condition.

PONY SERIES 90 – .380 ACP cal., double action only, 2 3/4 in. barrel, bobbed hammer, 6 shot mag., stainless construction, brushed finish, fixed sights, black composition grips, 19 oz. Mfg. 1997-1998.

$725	$650	$550	$450	$350	$300	$275	*$529*

* ***Pony Series 90 Pocketlite Lightweight*** – .380 ACP cal., similar to Pony Series 90, except utilizes aluminum and stainless steel construction, brushed finish, 13 oz. Mfg. 1997-1999.

$750	$675	$550	$450	$350	$300	$275	*$529*

POCKET NINE – 9mm Para. cal., double action only, 2 3/4 in. barrel, aluminum frame, ultra slim profile, 6 shot mag., matte/brushed stainless steel, wraparound rubber grips, 3-dot sights, 17 oz. Mfg. 1999 only.

$1,000	$925	$800	$700	$600	$500	$400	*$615*

COLT Z40 – .40 S&W cal., DAO, alloy frame, double column mag., firing pin safety, 3-dot sights, blue finish with black checkered synthetic grips and silver trigger, straight backstrap, marked "Colt Z40" on top of slide, while approx. 750-800 pieces were mfg. 1998-99 by CZ for a Colt subcontract, they were never shipped, and as a result, very few have made it into the U.S. to date from the Czech Republic.

$1,050	$900	$750	$600	$550	$525	$500	

NEW AGENT DAO MODEL O – .45 ACP cal., DAO, 3 in. barrel, Series 80 firing pin safety system, hammerless, 7 shot mag., double diamond slim fit grips, black anodized aluminum frame, blue finish, beveled magwell, snag free trench style sights, front strap serrations, captive recoil spring system. Mfg. 2008-2013.

$900	$775	$675	$550	$450	$400	$350	*$1,041*

Note: Colt has issued a recall for ser. nos. GT01001 - GT04505 X X due to a problem with the safety and/or guide pad. Improper hardness may cause the safety or guide pad to crack and might not prevent the gun from an accidental firing. Please contact Colt directly if you have one of the pistols - recall@colt.com.

1991 SERIES GOVERNMENT MODEL O LIGHTWEIGHT – .45 ACP cal., 5 in. barrel, DAO, features black anodized aluminum receiver with blued carbon steel slide, checkered double diamond slim fit grips, 7 shot mag., blue finish, white dot sights. Mfg. 2011-2013.

$925	$800	$700	$600	$500	$425	$375	*$1,068*

PISTOLS: SEMI-AUTO, .22 CAL. - WOODSMAN SERIES & VARIATIONS

The publisher wishes to once again express his thanks to Major (ret.) Robert J. Rayburn for his continued generous contributions of information regarding the Colt Woodsman Series.

The Colt Woodsman was made for 62 years, and included a multitude of variations/options in models, sights, barrels, grips, markings, etc. Many of the variations are quite scarce and desirable, but generally known only to specialized collectors. The following price guidelines are for standard production models, and only for those specimens in unmodified, factory original condition.

Internally at Colt the pre-Woodsman, Woodsman, Challenger, Huntsman, and Targetsman are collectively referred to as the "Model S", since they are all built on the S frame. Casually "Woodsman" is often used to include all the various models.

GRADING - PPGS™	100%	98%	95%	90%	80%	70%	60%	LAST MSR

Over 690,000 Woodsmans with variations were mfg. 1915-1977.

Factory engraved and special order Woodsmans are relatively rare and very desirable. Prices can fluctuate greatly, and auctions can sometimes be the only source of supply for these rarely encountered pistols. Note: 100% "as new" 1st Series Colt Woodsmans with box and accessories are almost always locked up in existing collections and are not sold except when an entire collection is liquidated. Since the demand exceeds the supply, the price of such pristine items has been rising rapidly. The older or rarer versions in such condition can sell for double or even triple the price of a 98% gun. In the listings in this section, 100% means exactly that - absolutely perfect in every way, without a single blemish or the slightest trace of blue wear or thinning on the pistol itself. Such perfect examples can still be found for some versions. For others, where such condition is rarely, if ever, encountered, market values are too volatile to be listed in the 100% column.

In this section the condition percentage does not consider accoutrements such as box, papers, or tools. Such items have grown in importance in recent years and the value assigned by collectors varies greatly depending on age, rarity and condition. For a common variety late model, the original box might add $40-$50. For a relatively rare and early Pre-WWII model, a pristine factory original box with original papers and tools might add $1,000 or even more.

BEWARE: With the Internet and the online auction sites that cater to collectors, recently manufactured fake boxes and papers have proliferated. These are sometimes advertised as modern reproductions, but all too often they are not honestly described. The unscrupulous sellers often obscure the truth by strongly implying that their product is original "new old stock" without ever actually saying that it is factory original or "correct" for the pistol listed on the label.

Three different barrel profiles were used with the 1st Series pre-Woodsman and Woodsman. Those manufactured between 1915-1922 had a thin, lightweight barrel commonly referred to as a pencil barrel (approx. serial range 1-31,000). The medium barrel, with a somewhat larger diameter, was introduced in 1922 and was retained until the 90,000 serial range (approx. mfg. 1922-1934). The pencil barrel and medium barrel both had a step-down just forward of the receiver to reduce the barrel diameter. The tapered barrel, used from 1934 until the end of production in 1947 (serial range approx. 90,000-187,423), did not have the step-down. Instead, it was gradually tapered down for the full length of the barrel.

PRE-WOODSMAN – .22 LR cal., 6 5/8 in. barrel, 10 shot mag., blue only, bottom mag. release, checkered wood grips, adj. front and rear sights, this model was officially named "Colt Automatic Pistol, Caliber .22 Target Model", magazine base has 2-line legend "CAL .22" "COLT". Standard velocity ammo. only. Approx. 54,000 mfg. 1915-1927.

100%	98%	95%	90%	80%	70%	60%
$2,450	$1,775	$1,050	$675	$450	$325	$300

Add 10% for pencil barrels (1915-1922 mfg. only, ser. nos. below 31000).

BEWARE: Because the early guns were used with corrosive ammo, many of them developed bad bores and have since been refitted with later barrels.

This model was manufactured to use standard velocity ammunition only (not high speed). Colt did offer a conversion kit for high velocity ammunition after the transition to high velocity in 1931.

WOODSMAN 1ST SERIES – .22 LR cal., 10 shot mag., blue only, bottom mag. release, checkered wood grips, marked "The Woodsman" on receiver, adj. sights, mfg. from 1927-1947, total production was approx. 112,000.

Note: Guns made prior to 1931 were designed for standard velocity .22 LR ammunition only. The new style main spring housing, designed for high velocity ammunition, began appearing at approx. ser. no. 80,000 and was completely phased in by approx. ser. no. 85,000. Later guns, INCLUDING ALL PISTOLS MADE AFTER WWII, were designed for high velocity ammunition.

151 factory engraved First Series Woodsmans were manufactured pre-WWII. The breakdown is 126 Target models, 14 Sport models, and 11 Match Target models. Values depend on engraving type/coverage and original condition.

* ***Woodsman Sport Model*** – 4 1/2 in. barrel, this model was introduced in 1933.

100%	98%	95%	90%	80%	70%	60%
$2,200	$1,700	$1,100	$650	$450	$350	$300

Add 10% for adj. front sight (available beginning 1937).

Add 50% for medium weight barrel (1933-34 mfg. only), and an additional 50% for semi-circular "half moon" front sight (1933 mfg. only).

The vast majority of this model came with a fixed front sight, rounded at the front and serrated ramp at the rear.

Approx. serial range of the First Series Sport is 86,105-187,423 from 1933 to 1947.

GRADING - PPGS™	100%	98%	95%	90%	80%	70%	60%	LAST MSR

* ***Woodsman Target Model*** – 6 5/8 in. barrel.

	$2,100	$1,400	$800	$450	$325	$300	$275

Note: Colt discontinued the 1st series in 1947. These guns are quite different from the 2nd series started later in 1947. Both the front and rear sights are adjustable.

WOODSMAN 1ST SERIES MATCH TARGET – .22 LR cal. only, 6 5/8 in. heavy barrel, commonly called "Bullseye" Match Target, mfg. 1938-44, production totaled around 16,000. Difficult to find in mint condition. Values listed assume original one-piece extended walnut grips.

	$3,800	$2,900	$1,800	$1,100	$950	$900	$850

In the lower conditions, much of the value derives from the original walnut "Elephant Ear" stocks. The value of the stocks, in excellent original condition, can actually exceed the value of a lower condition gun. The extended plastic stocks, as used on the military version of the Match Target, will fit on any 1st Series Colt Woodsman. Because the plastic military stocks are readily available and inexpensive, they are often used as replacements for lost or broken original stocks. They are not to be confused with the one piece "Elephant Ear" stocks.

The correct magazine on this model has a 3-line legend "COLT WOODSMAN", "CAL. 22 L.R.", and "MATCH TARGET MOD".

* ***Woodsman 1st Series Match Target "U.S. Property" Marked*** – approx. 4,000 Match Target Woodsmans were sold to the U.S. Army and U.S. Navy during WWII. Most have serial numbers above MT12500, although some were shipped out of sequence with lower numbers. The wartime guns had elongated plastic stocks and standard blue finish, although some of them are now parkerized as the result of arsenal refinishing or other non-factory modifications. They are marked with either "US PROPERTY" or the ordnance wheel with crossed cannon, as well as the initials of the govt. inspector. Some also have additional markings.

	N/A	$3,000	$2,100	$1,200	$925	$750	$575

Since the military models have two-piece plastic grips, rather than the "Elephant Ear" stocks, the values in the lower condition categories are lower than those for the standard civilian model.

Check parkerized finish carefully for originality on this variation, as some "recent parkerizing" has been observed.

WOODSMAN 2ND SERIES – .22 LR cal. only, automatic slide stop and hold open, push-button mag. release on this model is located on the left side of frame, ColtMaster rear sight was introduced during 1953, Coltwood plastic grips (mfg. 1947-1950) or injection molded plastic grips (mfg. 1950-1955), total production on all 2nd Series (not including the Challenger) was approx. 146,000, serialization has "S" suffix. Mfg. 1947-1955.

* ***Woodsman 2nd Series Sport Model*** – 4 1/2 in. barrel.

	$1,500	$1,300	$1,000	$800	$600	$500	$350

* ***Woodsman 2nd Series Target Model*** – 6 in. barrel.

	$1,400	$1,120	$1,000	$750	$500	$400	$325

* ***Woodsman 2nd Series Match Target Model*** – this model is not marked Woodsman on the gun. It is marked MATCH TARGET.

4 1/2 in. heavy bbl.	$1,950	$1,600	$1,050	$850	$700	$450	$425
6 in. heavy bbl.	$1,600	$1,400	$900	$700	$600	$400	$375

CHALLENGER MODEL – similar to Woodsman 2nd Series, only with fixed sights, without automatic hold open, and bottom mag. release, plastic grips, 4 1/2 and 6 in. barrels, mfg. 1950-1955 with total production reaching approx. 77,000.

	$895	$750	$550	$375	$325	$250	$225

WOODSMAN 3RD SERIES – .22 LR cal. only, automatic slide stop and hold open, black plastic grips (mfg. 1955-60) or walnut grips (1960-77), 3rd Models can be differentiated from 2nd Models by their bottom mag. release. Total production of all 3rd series Woodsman models (not including the Huntsman or Targetsman) exceeded 100,000, serialization has "S" suffix. Mfg. 1955-1977.

* ***Woodsman 3rd Series Sport Model*** – 4 1/2 in. barrel.

	$995	$895	$700	$450	$350	$300	$275

* ***Woodsman 3rd Series Target Model*** – 6 in. barrel.

	$895	$795	$550	$400	$350	$300	$275

* ***Woodsman 3rd Series Match Target Model*** – 4 1/2 or 6 in. heavy barrel. This model is not marked Woodsman on the gun.

	$1,450	$1,275	$875	$500	$400	$350	$325

Add $200 for a 4 1/2 in. barrel if condition is 95% or better.

GRADING - PPGS™	100%	98%	95%	90%	80%	70%	60%	LAST MSR

HUNTSMAN MODEL – .22 LR cal. only, 4 1/2 and 6 in. barrels, fixed sights and no automatic hold open, black plastic grips to serial number 141094-C; walnut grips after that cutoff. Mfg. 1955-1977 with total production reaching over 100,000.

	$795	$650	$500	$350	$275	$250	$225	

The Huntsman is very similar to the Challenger Model, except is built on a 3rd series frame.

* ***Huntsman Model S Master Series*** – approx. 400 Model S Masters were sold in 1983. This was a parts clean-up by Colt, using Huntsman frames leftover from the last days of production. They were equipped with automatic slide stop and Elliason rear sight, gold etching on the slide, and a French fitted walnut case marked "1 of 400". Approx. 285 had straight, non-tapered Huntsman barrel, while the remainder had the tapered Woodsman Sport barrel with pinned front sight.

Huntsman barrel	$1,600	$995	$600	N/A	N/A	N/A	N/A	
Woodsman barrel	$1,800	$900	$700	N/A	N/A	N/A	N/A	

Above values assume original walnut case included. Values for this model in 98%-60% original condition are hard to compute, as most are mint or new.

TARGETSMAN MODEL – similar to the Huntsman, except has adj. rear sight and thumbrest on left grip, 6 in. barrel only, approx. 65,000 mfg. 1959-1977.

	$850	$695	$495	$395	$275	$250	$225	

CADET – .22 LR cal., 4 1/2 in. barrel, stainless steel, 10 shot mag., predecessor to the Colt 22 Model, originally introduced in 1994, fixed sights, this model was disc. by 1995 because of litigation involving the trademarked model name and only protypes are known to exist, 33 1/2 oz.

Extreme rarity precludes acurrate pricing on this model.

COLT 22 FIRST EDITION – .22 LR cal., 4 1/2 inch VR barrel, stainless steel or black anodized stainless steel, 10 shot mag., one-piece black Pachmary rubber grips, 33 1/2 oz. Mfg. 1994

	$600	$450	$400	$300	$225	$180	$155	

An early version of the COLT 22 was called the "First Edition" Colt 22. It was available with either stainless steel or black hard chromed barrel. Marked First Edition 22 on slide. All had low serial numbers and could be ordered as matching serial number cased pairs, for example "00005PH" and "PH00005". A very small number were Colt Custom Shop engraved.

COLT 22 – .22 LR cal., 4 1/2 in. VR barrel, stainless steel, fixed sights, 10 shot mag., one-piece black Pachmayr rubber grips, 33 1/2 oz. Mfg. 1994-1998.

	$550	$425	$350	$275	$165	$140	$120	*$248*

COLT 22 TARGET – .22 LR cal., 6 in. VR barrel with full length grooved sight rib, adj. rear sight, 40 1/2 oz. Mfg. 1995-1999.

	$600	$450	$400	$300	$165	$140	$120	*$377*

100%	98%	95%	90%	80%	70%	60%	50%	40%	30%	20%	10%

REVOLVERS: DOUBLE ACTION

Most of the double action revolvers listed can have their original configuration confirmed with a Colt factory letter. To receive a letter, write: COLT ARCHIVE PROPERTIES, LLC, 1295 Blue Hills Avenue, Bloomfield, CT 06002. The research fee for these revolvers is typically either $75 or $100, depending on the model. If they cannot obtain additional information on the variation you request, they will refund $50. The Models 1877 and 1878 were the only fixed cylinder DA models made by Colt.

Prices on top condition Colt DAs have continued to rise steadily, particularly for correctly boxed/cased guns. Be aware of ill-matched, wrong, or fake vintage boxes or grips being mated to an unmatched gun. Original boxes and grips will enhance the values of all Colt DAs.

MODEL 1877 (RAINMAKER) – .32 Colt cal., otherwise similar to the Model 1877 Lightning. Approx. 300 mfg. from 1877-1909. Rare.

$4,800	$3,600	$2,400	$2,200	$1,800	$1,200	$1,075	$925	$850	$775	$675	$575

Ejectorless versions, fitted also with a long, knurled cylinder pin will bring a 10%-15% premium, depending on condition.

This model has a fragile mechanism - values are for working guns.

The "Rainmaker" name was used by dealers in period promotions, not by Colt.

100%	98%	95%	90%	80%	70%	60%	50%	40%	30%	20%	10%

MODEL 1877 (LIGHTNING) – .38 Colt cal., 1 1/2, 2, 2 1/2, 3, 3 1/2, 4, 4 1/2, 5, or 6 in. barrels without ejector, 4 1/2, 5, 6, 7, or 7 1/2 in. barrels with ejector, 6 shot double action, long cylinder fluting, blue finish with case hardened frame and hammer, full nickel plating also available. Over 166,000 mfg. from 1877-1909.

$4,500	$3,500	$2,000	$1,800	$1,600	$1,000	$900	$775	$700	$650	$575	$500

Subtract approx. 10% for nickel plating.

Ejectorless versions, fitted also with a long, knurled cylinder pin will bring a 10%-15% premium, depending on condition.

Also, an etched barrel will command a 10%-15% over a roll marked barrel, depending on condition.

Add 10% for 1st and 2nd year production examples or others with factory special or carved grips.

This model has a fragile mechanism - values are for working guns.

The "Lightning" and Thunderer names were used by dealers in period promotions, not by Colt.

MODEL 1877 (THUNDERER) – .41 Colt cal. only, otherwise same general specifications as Model 1877 Lightning.

$4,750	$3,750	$2,250	$2,100	$1,675	$1,125	$975	$850	$750	$700	$600	$500

Add 10% for 1st and 2nd year production examples or others with factory special grips.

MODEL 1878 DA – .32-20 WCF (scarce), .38 Colt (approx. 40 mfg.), .38-40 WCF, .41 LC (scarce, 308 mfg.), .44 Russian, .44 S&W, .44-40 WCF (Colt Frontier Six Shooter), .45 LC, .450 Eley, .455 Eley, or .476 Eley cal., 2 1/2 (scarce), 3, 3 1/2, or 4 in. barrels without ejector, 4 3/4, 5 1/2, 7 1/2, 8, 8 1/2, 9, 10, or 12 in. with ejector. Mfg. 1878-1905. Over 51,000 made.

$6,000	$5,500	$5,000	$4,250	$3,750	$2,950	$2,150	$1,500	$950	$850	$750	$700

Add 15% for 3 1/2 or 4 in. barrel. Front of frame must be checked to verify authenticity of a Sheriff's Model.

Approximately 80% of production for this model was in .44-40 WCF and .45 cals.

This model in .44-40 WCF was called the Colt Frontier Six Shooter, and this inscription is either acid etched or roll marked on the barrel.

On the acid etched variation of the .45 LC cal., fewer than 200 were marked "Omnipotent" - serial numbers can range from approx. 200-8,265. The Omnipotent marked 1878s were available in either nickel or blue finished and were manufactured between 1878-1882. The large majority of these were shipped Colt's distributor at the time, B. Kittredge. An authentic "Omnipotent" marked Model 1878 particularly in blue finish will bring approx. a 30%-50% premium over a gun in the same condition without the acid etched marking. It highly recommended that a Colt factory letter verifies this configuration.

This model has an action that is weaker than that of the SAA, and should be carefully inspected to make sure the cylinder turns and locks up properly. Since original parts are scarce, at least $750 must be deducted for a non-working action.

Many original 1878 barrels have "found their way" on the front end of a SAA frame since the barrels are interchangeable. Because of this, many "original" Model 1878 DAs may have an incorrect and/or later SAA Colt barrel attached. Watch yourself here! Also, scarce calibers should be verified with factory letter.

MODEL 1902/1904 (PHILIPPINE CONSTABULARY) – .45 LC cal., a variation of the Model 1878, except has oversized trigger guard and long trigger, 6 shot standard 1878 type cylinder with long flutes, pinched frame, 6 in. barrel, blue finish, hard rubber grips, many have been arsenal refinished.

* ***1902 Constabulary*** – 5,000 mfg., with a smaller number actually issued by the U.S. Army to the Philippine Constabulary (Police) Force (not to be confused with the Philippine Scouts, which were part of the U.S. Army), markings: "R.A.C." on left side of frame, 1902 date on right side of frame near grips, large "U.S." on right side of frame below cylinder, hard rubber grips, but some examples also show period correct wooden grips, perhaps from confirmed arsenal or Colt reworks.

N/A	N/A	$4,650	$3,650	$2,900	$2,200	$1,900	$1,800	$1,700	$1,600	$1,400	$1,300

Subtract 50% for arsenal or Colt refinish.

* ***1904 Constabulary Purchase*** – rare variation, approx. 50 more revolvers were delivered to the Army in 1904 within the 51,000 ser. no. range, use unknown, but assumed as Constabulary replacements with same overall configuration as 1902 version, last four digits of ser. no. are on the loading gate and cylinder, military inspection marks.

Price at approx. 10% above the equivalent 1902 production model.

This is a gun sold to the military that was not assigned a U.S. model number, so technically it is a 'contract purchase' variation, not a unique model.

100%	98%	95%	90%	80%	70%	60%	50%	40%	30%	20%	10%

REVOLVERS: DOUBLE ACTION, SWING OUT CYLINDER

Most of the double action revolvers listed can have their original configuration confirmed with a Colt factory letter. To receive a letter, write: COLT ARCHIVE PROPERTIES, LLC, 1295 Blue Hills Avenue, Bloomfield, CT 06002. The research fee for these revolvers is typically either $75 or $100, depending on the model. If they cannot obtain additional information on the variation you request, they will refund $50.

In Oct. of 1999, Colt announced that all double action revolvers would be discontinued, including any custom shop manufacture. After over 120 years of continuous production, the series of swing out double action revolvers finally ended. As a result, interest and prices for this discontinued revolver configuration have increased greatly in recent years, even on recently discontinued models/configurations. For a few years starting in 2002, the Colt Custom Shop produced both the Anaconda and the Python Elite, but both have also since been discontinued. Prices on top condition Colt DAs have continued to remain strong, particularly for correctly boxed/cased guns.

The Snake guns - Pythons, Diamondbacks, Cobras, Boas, Anacondas, and Vipers are currently undergoing so much demand that N/As have replaced many 100% condition factors due to volatile and unpredictable pricing/sales. On most of these recently manufactured Snake guns, NIB or nearly new examples are more readily available compared to Colt Pre-WWII revolvers. It is highly recommended that on short barreled snake guns with nickel finishes a factory letter be procured before buying/selling. Be wary/cautious of ill-matched/wrong vintage boxes and/or non-original grips. Also, reproduction box end labels and convincing repro boxes for Colt revolvers are now being made. Original, correct boxes and grips will enhance the values of all Colt DAs.

2 or low 3 digit serial number revolvers will always carry a substantial premium, regardless of condition.

MODEL 1889 "NAVY" (NEW NAVY DA, MODEL OF 1889) – .38 Short and Long Colt, and .41 Short and Long Colt cal., 3, 4 1/2, and 6 in. barrel, blue (military and civilian) or nickel (civilian only) finish, wood (U.S.Navy) or hard rubber (civilian) grips with the world "Colt" in oval at top. The first solid frame, swing out cylinder - recognizable by no visible locking latches - unless later converted to 1895 action. Cylinder rotates counter-clockwise, sideplate is also on the right-hand side of frame, Colt produced approx. 31,000 mfg. 1889-1894, 1st 5,000 were ordered by U.S. Navy, with some additional Navy orders later in production - hence name. Serial number is on the butt. US Navy versions (6 in. bbl. ONLY), also include Navy markings.

N/A	**$2,750**	**$2,250**	**$1,950**	**$1,550**	**$1,250**	**$850**	**$700**	**$550**	**$425**	**$350**	**$300**

Add 40% for 3 in. barrel (civilian models only). Subtract $100-$200 for broken hard rubber grips or broken action.

Add 65%-100% for U.S. Navy Contract (ser. no. 1-5,000, and in some later ser. no. blocks), U.S.N. on butt (.38 LC cal. only), depending on condition. Beware of fakes.

Note: Nearly all US Navy Military 1889 Navy issues were later converted to 1895 type actions. Unconverted Navy-marked specimens w/o notched cylinders will bring a premium, but must be authenticated by an expert - Fakes and re-assembled guns are common.

There was also no mass updating of civilian 1889 revolvers. Real, unmolested civilian 1889 Colt DAs should appear with the older and original 1889 action, not with any modified actions or updated features.

For later (post 1884) US Navy DA 38s, see below under civilian New Navy Guns.

US ARMY MODELS 1892, 1894, 1896, 1901, 1903 (DA 38 "NEW ARMY" - US ARMY ISSUED MODELS) – The US Army then followed Navy in adopting a modern 38 DA revolver. Based on Navy use, Army model has 2nd set of locking notches added to cylinder. 1892 and later DAs all look similar to 1889 Navy, except with double cylinder notches, double locking bolts, and shorter flutes, more square cyl. release thumb catch. Plain uncheckered wood grips (Army contract military issue models only). All Military models are all cal. 38 only and blue only.

US Army military issue models include Model of 1892, Model of 1894, Model of 1896, Model of 1901, and Model of 1903. 1903 and 1901 models were made and survived in greater quantity and so are worth less than earlier models. Most military models have been altered, refinished, reworked or otherwise altered, which reduces value. Technical alterations by the Army itself - such as cylinder-open lock bolt and lanyard rings added later were part of this evolution. Most alterations reduce value, but a few are sought after (similar to finding a correct SAA Artillery model) . Unaltered examples of Models of 1892, 1894 and 1896 bring a premium. US Models 1901 and 1903 are common.

Values below are only for US issued specimens marked on butt "US ARMY MODEL OF xxxx"; with original wood military grips, original barrel and with US Army military markings on the butt completely intact.

N/A	**$2,150**	**$1,750**	**$1,350**	**$900**	**$650**	**$500**	**$425**	**$350**	**$225**	**$195**	**$175**

Add 100% for unaltered Models of 1892 or 1894 (consult expert). Add 20% for Model of 1896 if w/o lanyard ring.

100%	98%	95%	90%	80%	70%	60%	50%	40%	30%	20%	10%

Subtract 90% for guns with butt markings removed. (very common - it seems a lot of these were "borrowed" from the government, and the butt or entire gun then reblued-usually very poorly.)
Subtract 75% for late factory/armory rebuilt versions of early models. Consult expert sources for details.
Subtract 90% on any U.S. marked gun if the barrel length is other than 6 in., or for altered/damaged sights, target sights added, etc. All U.S. Army issue models had 6 inch barrels, standard fixed sights, and are .38 caliber only.
Subtract 25% for Army military models if original U.S. Army wood grips with cartouche are missing.

MODEL 1892 & 1895 "NEW ARMY & NEW NAVY" - CIVILIAN & US NAVY VERSIONS – similar to 1889 Navy, but double cylinder notches, double locking bolts, and shorter flutes, square cyl. release thumb catch, hard rubber grips, .32-20 WCF (uncommon) added in 1905, .38 Short and Long Colt, and .41 Short and Long Colt cal., 3, 4 1/2, and 6 in. barrel, blue or nickel finish. Mfg. 1892-1907.

N/A	$1,650	$1,150	$700	$500	$400	$300	$275	$250	$225	$195	$175

Add $100-$750 for U.S.N. markings, depending on condition.
Add 40% for 3 in. barrel (civilian only).
Subtract $100-$200 for broken hard rubber grips or broken action.

After about 1894, US Navy Colt 38 DA models were based on standard civilian (1895) Colt models with 6 in. barrels (only), and include civilian style serial numbers and hard rubber "Navy" grips; also with Navy marks, and both civilian and Navy numbers on the butt. Models made before 1898 will bring a premium. Late models of all types made after about 1903 begin to show transitional details moving towards the later Army Special model. Serial numbers for all New Army DA & New Navy DA are on the butt, not in the yoke. Numbers on yoke, latch etc. are always assembly numbers. Civilian New Navy grips have "COLT" in oval. Civilian New Army grips have the Rampant Colt.

NEW ARMY & NEW NAVY DA38 models after about 1894:

Much confusion ensues after about 1894 since in commercial production, both "NEW NAVY" civilian & NEW ARMY" civilian arms also have the dual notch system. The only difference between commercial examples was the type of hard rubber grips. "NEW NAVY" grips have only the word COLT, but no image of the rampant colt.

To add confusion, while the US Army continued to contract for special production with wooden grips and serial number markings different from commercial guns, the US NAVY after about 1894 simply purchased batches of specially produced and inspected commercial style guns. These include normal commercial markings and the regular hard rubber "New Navy" grips. Colt then included the Navy inspection markings (tridents or stars at various times) and US Navy markings on the butt. So US Issue Navy guns from about 1894 until 1903 have a commercial serial number in the commercial location on the butt, but are clearly marked as US Navy Models as well. (Because of this similarity to commercial prod'n, US Navy fakes are known to exist. Consult references and note the orientation of US Navy markings).

* ***Models 1892, 1894, 1895, 1896, 1901, 1903*** – these were all civilian variations of the Model 1892, military model (.38 Long Colt only) and values are shown above for these civilian guns.

OFFICER'S MODEL (FIRST ISSUE) – .38 Spl. or .38 Long Colt cal., 6 in. barrel, cylinder rotates counter-clockwise and sideplate is on right-hand side of frame, adj. front - adj. rear sights, high luster blue, flat-top, last patent date 1901. Mfg. 1904-08.

N/A	$1,700	$1,350	$950	$775	$625	$550	$495	$395	$325	$275	$250

OFFICER'S MODEL (SECOND ISSUE) – .32 Colt or .38 Spl. cal., 4, 4 1/2, 5, 6, or 7 1/2 in. barrel, cylinder rotates clockwise, high luster blue through 1916, adj. front - adj. rear sights, checkered walnut grips, deep set medallions in grips were standard from 1913-1923. Mfg. 1908-1926. Last patent date July 4, 1905.

N/A	$1,700	$1,350	$900	$775	$600	$525	$495	$395	$325	$275	$250

Add 100% for .32 Colt cal. in 6 or 7 1/2 in. barrel in .32 Colt cal. (rare).
Add 100% for rare 4, 4 1/2, or 5 in. barrels.

Beware of "cut-offs" and check patent date locations and the front sight and its location carefully.

OFFICER'S MODEL TARGET (THIRD ISSUE) – similar design to the Second Issue, .22 LR cal. was added beginning 1930, heavy barrel was introduced in 1935. Mfg. 1927-1949. Last patent date Oct. 5, 1926.

N/A	$1,300	$1,000	$700	$550	$475	$400	$325	$300	$275	$250	$225

Add 10% for .22 LR cal. (mfg. started 1930).
Add 50% for .32 Colt cal. (mfg. 1939-1941, w/heavy barrel, and production estimates are 800-1,500 units).
Add 100% for 4 or 5 in. barrel.

For all short barrel Officers Models, beware of "cut-offs", and check patent date locations and the front sight and its location carefully.

100%	98%	95%	90%	80%	70%	60%	50%	40%	30%	20%	10%

MODEL 1905 MARINE CORPS – .38 Short or Long cal., similar to New Navy Second Issue, except has a round butt, checkered wood grips w/o medallion, and 6 in. barrel only. Mfg. 1905-1909 in approx. ser. no. range 10,001-10,926, about 926 mfg., 812 were for government contract, and 114 were commercial.

N/A	$3,500	$3,000	$2,000	$1,800	$1,425	$1,250	$1,000	$895	$795	$695	$595

Add 30% for Military issue marked "USMC" on butt (ser. nos. 1-812). Beware of fake USMC markings.

ARMY SPECIAL MODEL – .32-20 WCF, .38 (various), or .41 Colt cal., 4, 4 1/2, 5, and 6 in. barrels, hard rubber grips standard through 1923 - checkered wood with medallions beginning about 1924, blue finish, fixed sights, rounded checkered cylinder release thumb catch, smooth trigger, has heavier frame than New Navy, approx. ser. no. range 291,000-540,000, last patent date on barrel was July 4, 1905. Mfg. 1908-27.

N/A	$1,150	$950	$700	$575	$425	$295	$275	$250	$225	$200	$175

Add 35% for nickel finish.
Subtract $75-$200 if hard rubber grips are chipped or badly worn.

NEW SERVICE MODEL – .38 Spl., .357 Mag., .38-40 WCF, .44-40 WCF, .44 Russian, .44 Spl., .45 ACP, .45 LC, .450 Eley, .455 Eley, or .476 Eley cal., 4, 5, or 6 in. barrels in .357 Mag. and .38 Spl., 4 1/2, 5 1/2, and 7 1/2 in. barrel in all others, blue or nickel finish, bright blue finish was used through circa 1916, originally hard rubber grips (until approx. late '20s), with later guns having walnut grips with medallions. Mfg. 1898-1942.

Rare cals. (.450 and .476 Eley cals.) and 4 in. barrels will command premiums over values listed below.
Subtract $150 for broken, damaged, or heavily worn grips.
New Service revolvers with smoothbore barrel prices can range $6,500-$10,000+, depending on original condition.

New Service Models marked "NEW SERVICE 45 COLT" in .45 ACP cal. with shorter cylinder for rimmed cartridge are rare. All early New Service models (first type) have flat latches. Later models (second type) have rounded cylinder latches.

Approx. 356,000 Colt New Service revolvers were mfg., but only approx. 122,800 were Commercial variations. 95% were mfg. with blue finish, while 5% were nickel plated (approx. 6,140 revolvers). Colt also mfg. a very limited number (probably less than 10) of New Service revolvers with smoothbores. When encountered, it is important to get a Colt factory letter confirming the smoothbore barrel.

* ***New Service Model Commercial***

N/A	$2,950	$2,750	$2,200	$1,800	$1,525	$1,150	$900	$775	$675	$500	$400

Add 35% for nickel finish.
Add 10%-15% for "Early Model" (aka First Variation) with flat cylinder latch and non-tapered barrel profile; made up to approximately sn 21,000 to 23,000.
Add 40% for factory pearl, ivory, or FDL walnut grips, if in perfect condition.
Add 15% for some less common calibers/markings such as "44 Russian" or .44 Russian and Special.
Add 15% or more for short barrel length of 4 1/2 inches or other short lengths; each if documented by factory letter.

* ***New Service Model 1909 Army Model***

N/A	$3,400	$2,900	$2,450	$1,850	$1,700	$1,100	$900	$800	$700	$575	$500

* ***New Service Model RNWMP & RCMP Model*** – .45 LC or .455 Eley cal., contract for Royal Canadian Northwest Mounted Police.

N/A	$1,750	$1,375	$1,200	$925	$850	$775	$680	$590	$510	$435	$375

* ***New Service British Contract*** – .455 Webley cal., 5 1/2 in. barrel. Approx. 55,000 mfg.

N/A	$1,750	$1,375	$1,200	$925	$850	$775

* ***New Service Model 1909 Navy Model*** – shortest production run of the Model 1909 variations.

N/A	$3,500	$2,900	$2,450	$1,850	$1,700	$1,100	$900	$800	$725	$650	$525

* ***New Service Model 1909 Transition*** – a steel block was installed between the hammer and firing pin. The steel block would lower when the pistol is cocked, when not cocked the steel block is in the up position to block the hammer from striking the firing pin if dropped. Old Model serial numbers 0-21000. Mfg. 1898-1909. New Model added the "positive lock", serial numbers 21000-348000. Mfg. 1909-1943.

Current values are pending on this model.

* ***New Service Model 1909 - USMC***

N/A	$3,650	$3,200	$2,750	$2,250	$1,875	$1,525	$1,250	$975	$850	$775	$675

*** New Service Model 1917 Army**

100%	98%	95%	90%	80%	70%	60%	50%	40%	30%	20%	10%
$1,900	$1,600	$1,400	$1,125	$925	$775	$625	$525	$455	$390	$335	$295

*** New Service Model 1917 Civilian/Commercial (1917 C/CM)** – .45 ACP cal., 5 1/2 in. barrel only, last patent date is Oct. 5, 1926, checkered walnut grips with medallions, left side of barrel marked "COLT MODEL 1917 AUTO CTGE". Approx. 1,000 mfg. during 1932, serialized 335,000-336,000.

100%	98%	95%	90%	80%	70%	60%	50%	40%	30%	20%	10%
$1,500	$1,275	$1,050	$850	$650	$525	$450	$415	$385	$350	$325	$295

*** New Service Model 1917 Civilian/Commercial (Parts Model)** – .38-40 WCF, .44-40 WCF, or .45 LC cal., 4 1/2 or 5 1/2 in. barrel, hard rubber grips, or checkered walnut with medallions, last patent date is July 4, 1905, approx. 1,000 mfg. serialized 336,450- 337,500.

100%	98%	95%	90%	80%	70%	60%	50%	40%	30%	20%	10%
$1,375	$1,050	$925	$800	$625	$495	$415	$380	$360	$330	$300	$275

*** New Service Model Target** – similar to New Service Model, flat-top frame, hand-honed action and adj. front - adj. rear sights, 6 (scarce) or 7 1/2 in. barrel, square butt, round butt available after 1930, checkered grip straps, checkered walnut grips with medallion after 1913, blue or nickel (scarce) finish. Approx. 3,400 mfg. 1900-1940.

100%	98%	95%	90%	80%	70%	60%	50%	40%	30%	20%	10%
N/A	$3,300	$2,775	$2,300	$1,850	$1,500	$1,250	$900	$750	$635	$550	$460

Add 40% - 60% for 6 in. barrel, depending on original condition.
Add 25% for flat latch "Old Models" with original high polish finish.

Approx. 1,000 were mfg. in .45 LC, 960 in .455 Eley, 700 in .44 Russian, 500 in .44 Spl., and 80 in .45 ACP cal.

*** New Service Model Shooting Master** – various cals. from 38 Spl. through .45 LC, 6 in. barrel, checkered walnut grips with Colt Medallion, machined grip straps, trigger, hammer, and ejector rod head, round or square butt, approx. 3,500 mfg. in ser. no. range 333,000-350,000.

» **New Service Model Shooting Master .38 Spl.** – approx. 2,500 mfg.

100%	98%	95%	90%	80%	70%	60%	50%	40%	30%	20%	10%
N/A	$2,500	$1,950	$1,750	$1,500	$1,150	$950	$650	$550	$525	$500	$475

» **New Service Model Shooting Master .357 Mag.** – approx. 500 mfg.

100%	98%	95%	90%	80%	70%	60%	50%	40%	30%	20%	10%
N/A	$3,000	$2,800	$1,950	$1,700	$1,475	$1,300	$1,100	$995	$850	$750	$650

» **New Service Model Shooting Master .45 ACP or .45 LC cals.** – approx. 156 mfg. in .45 LC and 250 mfg. in .45 ACP cal.

100%	98%	95%	90%	80%	70%	60%	50%	40%	30%	20%	10%
N/A	N/A	$4,850	$3,750	$3,250	$2,500	$2,050	$1,675	$1,350	$1,000	$750	$600

» **New Service Model Shooting Master .44 Spl. cal.** – approx. 94 mfg.

100%	98%	95%	90%	80%	70%	60%	50%	40%	30%	20%	10%
N/A	N/A	$4,900	$4,050	$3,500	$3,000	$2,500	$2,000	$1,575	$1,250	$1,000	$850

The Shooting Master could be ordered with a square butt after 1933.

OFFICIAL POLICE PRE-WAR – .32-20 WCF (disc. 1942), .38-200 (British), .41 Long (disc. 1930), .38 Spl., or .22 LR (introduced 1930 - 4 or 6 in. barrel only, 4 in. scarce) cal., blue finish, 6 shot, round (very scarce) or square butt, 2, 4, 5, or 6 in. barrels, checkered walnut grips, fixed sights, last patent date on barrel was Oct. 5, 1926. Mfg. 1927-1946.

100%	98%	95%	90%	80%	70%	60%	50%	40%	30%	20%	10%
$1,150	$950	$750	$525	$465	$425	$285	$250	$225	$200	$185	$165

Add 100% for round butt with factory verified letter (very rare).
Add 15% for nickel finish.
Add 20% for .22 LR cal.

OFFICIAL POLICE POST-WAR – .22 LR or .38 Spl. cal., 2, 4, 5, or 6 in. barrel, Coltwood plastic grips 1947-1954 - checkered walnut thereafter, fixed sights, no patent dates on barrel. Mfg. 1947-69.

100%	98%	95%	90%	80%	70%	60%	50%	40%	30%	20%	10%
$950	$800	$625	$500	$335	$275	$215	$195	$175	$165	$145	$125

Add 25% for nickel finish.
Add 100% for .22 LR cal.

The 2 in. barrel in .38 Spl. cal. is scarce. .22 LR cal. was available with 4 or 6 in. barrel only.

MARSHAL MODEL – .38 Spl. cal., 2 (less common) or 4 in. barrel, round butt, differentiated by "M" suffix and "COLT MARSHAL" on barrel, about 2,500 mfg. 1954-1956 in approx. ser. no. range 833350-M through 845320-M.

100%	98%	95%	90%	80%	70%	60%	50%	40%	30%	20%	10%
N/A	$1,950	$1,750	$1,000	$850	$600	$475	$425	$385	$360	$275	$250

Add 60% for 2 in. barrel.
Add 50% for nickel finish.

GRADING - PPGS™ 100% 98% 95% 90% 80% 70% 60% LAST MSR

COMMANDO MODEL – .38 Spl. cal., 2 in. (less common), 4 in. (standard) barrel, the majority of wartime issued guns had Coltwood (plastic) grips, checkered walnut is also observed on post-war shipped guns, Parco-Lubrite (parkerized) finish, about 50,000 mfg. 1942-1945, marked "COLT COMMANDO/.38 SPECIAL" on barrel, last patent date on barrel was Oct. 5, 1926, a variety of proofmarks and/or agency markings may be encountered, many thousand shipped in the immediate post-war era to police departments, national parks, etc.

N/A $1,575 $1,375 $1,150 $900 $750 $650 $525 $450 $350 $300 $275

Add 15% for 2 in. barrel.

OFFICIAL POLICE MKIII – .38 Spl. cal., 4, 5, or 6 in. barrels, no patent dates on barrel. Mfg. 1969-75.

* ***Official Police MKIII Blue finish***

$650 $550 $500 $475 $385 $350 $325 $300 $285 $270 $150 $125

* ***Official Police MKIII Nickel finish***

$950 $800 $700 $550 $400 $350 $325 $300 $285 $270 $150 $125

METROPOLITAN MK III – .38 Spl. cal., similar to Official Police, except heavier 4 in. barrel only, blue finish. Mfg. 1969-72.

$750 $550 $450 $350 $275 $250 $225 $210 $190 $175 $165 $155

OFFICER'S MODEL SPECIAL (FOURTH ISSUE) – .22 LR or .38 Spl. cal., 6 in. barrel, blue, similar to Third Issue, only heavier non-tapered barrel, new style hammer and "Coltmaster Sight", checkered plastic grips, no patent dates on barrel. Mfg. 1949-52.

$1,525 $1,225 $1,125 $750 $625 $475 $400 $325 $275 $250 $225 $195

Add $75 for .22 LR cal.

OFFICER'S MODEL MATCH (FIFTH ISSUE) – .22 LR, .22 WMR (approx. 850 mfg.), or .38 Spl. cal., 6 in. barrel, single (rare) or double action, tapered heavy barrel, nickel finish is scarce in this model, wide spur hammer, Accro sight, large target grips (walnut). Mfg. 1953-1969.

$1,350 $1,175 $975 $750 $650 $500 $400 $350 $300 $275 $250 $225

Add $75 for .22 LR cal.

Add 50% for nickel finish verified with factory letter.

* ***Officer's Model Match (Fifth Issue) .22 Mag.*** – .22 WMR cal., approx. 850 mfg.

N/A $2,400 $1,900 $1,750 $1,500 $1,100 $800 $700 $600 $550 $500 $450

* ***Officer's Model Match Single Action Only*** – limited mfg., must have accompanying factory letter.

$1,925 $1,900 $1,250 $1,100 $950 $900 $700 $650 $600 $550 $475 $475

OFFICER'S MODEL MATCH MK III (SIXTH ISSUE) – .38 Spl. cal. only, 6 in. shrouded VR barrel, wide spur hammer, Accro sights, target grips. 496 mfg. 1969-1971 only.

N/A $2,450 $1,950 $1,600 $1,200 $775 $700 $650 $600 $550 $475 $475

NEW POCKET – .32 Short and LC, or .32 Colt New Police cal., 2 1/2, 3 1/2, 5, or 6 in. barrel, first modern swing out DA, rubber grips, blue or nickel finish, round butt, last patent date on barrel was Nov. 6, 1888. Mfg. 1893-1905.

$1,450 $1,300 $975 $725 $525 $400 $300 $250 $215 $190 $170 $165

Subtract $75-$100 for chipped hard rubber grips (commonly found on this model).

POCKET POSITIVE (FIRST ISSUE) – similar to New Pocket, except has round butt and positive lock feature, also chambered for .32 Colt, .32 S&W, or .32 Colt New Police cal., last patent date on barrel was July 4, 1905. Mfg. 1905-27.

$1,950 $1,700 $1,250 $1,000 $650 $350 $325 $295 $275 $210 $185 $175

Add 20% for NIB.

Add 15%-20% for nickel finish.

Add 15% for 90%+ condition early transitional guns that are double marked with "NEW POCKET" on frame.

Subtract $75-$100 for chipped hard rubber grips (commonly found on this model).

POCKET POSITIVE (SECOND ISSUE) – similar to Pocket Positive First Issue, except available in 2 in. barrel, stippled and matted top strap, last patent date on barrel was Oct. 5, 1926. Mfg. 1927-1940.

$1,950 $1,700 $1,250 $1,000 $650 $350 $325 $295 $275 $210 $185 $175

Add 20% for NIB.

Add 15%-20% for nickel finish.

Add 15%-20% for 2 in. barrel.

Subtract $75-$100 for chipped hard rubber grips (commonly found on this model).

100%	98%	95%	90%	80%	70%	60%	50%	40%	30%	20%	10%

NEW POLICE – .32 Colt and .32 Colt New Police cal., 2 1/2, 4, and 6 in. barrels, fixed sights, same frame as New Pocket, except larger square butt gripstraps, rubber grips, last patent date on barrel was Nov. 6, 1888. Mfg. 1896-1907.

$1,350	$975	$750	$525	$400	$300	$225	$200	$175	$160	$150	$145

Add 25% for nickel finish.

Subtract $25-$50 for chipped hard rubber grips (commonly found on this model).

NEW POLICE TARGET – .32 Colt cal., 6 in. barrel, blue, late models use New Police frame, but include transitional improvements from later Police Positive Target Model (First Issue), last patent date on barrel was Nov. 6, 1888. Approx. 5,000 mfg. 1897-1907.

N/A	$1,950	$1,650	$1,200	$925	$725	$625	$450	$375	$350	$300	$275

POLICE POSITIVE (FIRST ISSUE) – .32 Colt, .32 New Police, .38 New Police, or .38 S&W cal., 2 1/2 in. (.32 cal., only), 4, 5, or 6 in. barrel, improved "positive lock" version of the New Police, hard rubber grips standard through 1923, square butt, checkered walnut grips became standard 1924, denoted by 1905 last patent date and smooth top strap. Mfg. 1907-27.

$1,000	$750	$650	$450	$375	$300	$275	$250	$225	$170	$165	$160

Add 15%-20% for nickel finish.

Add 10% for 90%+ condition early transitional guns that are double marked with "NEW POLICE" on frame.

Subtract $75-$100 for chipped grips.

POLICE POSITIVE (SECOND ISSUE) – similar to Police Positive First Issue, except has 1926 last patent date, serrated top strap, and slightly heavier frame, walnut grips standard. Mfg. 1928-1947.

$1,000	$750	$650	$455	$375	$300	$275	$250	$200	$170	$165	$160

Add 10% for .38 cal.

POLICE POSITIVE TARGET MODEL (FIRST ISSUE, MODEL "G") – .22 LR, .22 WRF, .32 Colt, or .32 New Police cal., 6 in. barrel, blue, adj. sight, hard rubber grips standard through 1923, checkered walnut grips thereafter, last patent date on barrel was July 4, 1905, 22 oz. Mfg. 1907-1925.

$1,300	$1,100	$850	$575	$475	$425	$395	$375	$350	$325	$295	$275

Add 40% for .32 cal.

POLICE POSITIVE TARGET MODEL (SECOND ISSUE, MODEL "C") – similar to First Issue, except has slightly heavier frame and a last patent date of Oct. 5, 1926, blue finish, but a few were also mfg. in nickel, 26 oz. Mfg. 1926-41.

$1,200	$1,000	$775	$575	$475	$425	$395	$375	$350	$300	$270	$250

Add 40% for .32 cal.

Add 100% for nickel - extremely rare - must be verified by factory letter.

POLICE POSITIVE SPECIAL (FIRST ISSUE) – .32-20 WCF, .32 New Police, .38 New Police, or .38 Spl. cal., 4, 5, or 6 in. barrels, has a square butt and longer frame and cylinder to handle .38 Special and .32-20 WCF, fixed sights, frame longer to permit longer cylinder, denoted by 1905 last patent date on top of barrel, longer frame and smooth top strap, rubber grips. Mfg. 1907-27.

$900	$850	$550	$450	$375	$275	$250	$225	$200	$185	$175	$165

POLICE POSITIVE SPECIAL (SECOND ISSUE) – similar to Police Postitive Special (First Issue), except has 1926 last patent date on top of barrel, wood grips only, smooth (early mfg.) or checkered (later mfg.) trigger, and serrated top strap. Mfg. 1928-46.

$900	$850	$550	$450	$375	$275	$250	$225	$200	$185	$175	$165

CAMP PERRY MODEL – .22 LR cal., 8 in. (less common) or 10 in., Officer's Model frame modified to accept a flat single shot chamber. The model name was stamped on the left side of the chamber, the only single shot Colt on a revolver frame, last patent date on barrel was Oct. 5, 1926. 2,488 mfg. 1926-1941.

N/A	$3,250	$2,850	$2,100	$1,350	$975	$815	$745	$650	$495	$425	$365

Add 35% for 8 in. barrel.

BANKER'S SPECIAL – 2 in. barrel, blue, square butt standard through 1933, round butt standard 1934-40, last patent date on barrel was Oct. 5, 1926. Mfg. 1926-40.

* ***Banker's Special .38 cal.*** – available in .38 Colt Police Positive (New Police) or .38 S&W cal.

N/A	$2,500	$2,000	$1,500	$1,200	$900	$700	$600	$500	$400	$300	$250

Add 45% for nickel finish.

100%	98%	95%	90%	80%	70%	60%	50%	40%	30%	20%	10%

* ***Banker's Special .22 LR cal.***

N/A	$3,500	$3,000	$2,500	$2,000	$1,500	$1,000	$800	$600	$500	$400	$300

Add 30%-50% for nickel finish, depending on original condition.

COURIER - .22 S, L, or LR or .32 New Police (S&W) cal., double action, 6 shot, 3 in. barrel. Approx. 3,053 mfg. 1953-1956.

$1,500	$1,200	$950	$750	$550	$475	$425	$395	$350	$325	$295	$260

Add 10% for .22 cal.

Even though fewer .22 cal. Couriers were mfg. than Banker's Specials, the Banker's Specials are still more desirable, as they are of pre-war quality, and are less frequently encountered in 95-100% condition.

Some .32 New Police (S&W) cal. models can be found with alloy or steel cylinders.

AIRCREWMAN - .38 Spl. cal., double action, aluminum frame and cylinder, 2 in. barrel, 11 oz., fixed sights, checkered walnut grips overlapping at top of frame, inset with silver Air Force medallions, mfg. 1951 mostly.

N/A	$6,500	$4,500	$3,500	$2,500	$2,000	$1,500	$1,000	$800	$700	$600	$500

Approx. 1,200 mfg. within ser. no. range 2,900LW-7,775LW. Most were ordered destroyed. Perhaps less than 25 have survived.

BORDER PATROL (FIRST ISSUE) - .38 Spl. cal., double action, 6 shot, 4 in. heavy barrel, should have plastic grips, 400 mfg. during 1952 only in 823,000 ser. no. range.

N/A	$2,500	$1,500	$1,400	$1,125	$995	$875	$775	$675	$595	$525	$475

This model is built on the Official Police Model frame.

DETECTIVE SPECIAL PRE-WAR (FIRST ISSUE) - .38 Spl. cal., 2 in. barrel, blue, wood grips, square butt standard through 1932, round butt standard beginning 1933, last patent date on barrel was Oct. 5, 1926. Mfg. 1927-1946.

$3,250	$2,875	$2,100	$1,600	$1,300	$975	$795	$575	$400	$300	$250	$225

Add 20% for nickel finish.
Add 20% for square butt (early production only). Must be verified by factory letter and by ejector rod, since Police Positive Special (Second Issue) looks like a Detective Special.

DETECTIVE SPECIAL POST-WAR (SECOND ISSUE) - .32 NP, .38 NP, or .38 Spl. cal., 2 or 3 (scarce) in. barrel, can be distinguished from First Issue by 1/8 in. deeper frame (measured from hammer to bottom of frame behind trigger guard), plastic grips 1947-1954, wood grips 1955-1965, wraparound wood grips 1966-1972. Mfg. 1947-1972.

$1,550	$1,350	$1,050	$800	$550	$400	$275	$225	$210	$200	$190	$180

Add 20% for nickel finish.
Add 15% for 3 in. barrel.

There are four variations of the model - a pre-war design with post-war ser. nos., a "Transition" variation (late 1947-1952, with blue pre-war frame, late 1948-1952 have Coltwood grips), polished long grip frame (mfg. 1953-1966, round grip frame), and short grip frame (mfg. 1966-1972, walnut grip panels).

COBRA (FIRST ISSUE) - .22 LR, .32 Colt N.P., .38 Colt N.P., or .38 Spl. cal., first issue, 2, 3 (.22 LR cal. only), or 4 (square butt on early model, later models had round butt) in. barrel, blue or nickel finish, similar to Detective Special, only alloy frame and available in .22 LR, very early guns had plastic grips with silver medallions, changed to plastic w/o medallions, and finally changed to wood grips. Mfg. 1950-1972.

100% values on the following Cobra models have been intentionally omitted, as ascertaining accurate values is very difficult and not predictable.

For definitive information on Cobras and variations, please refer to *Seven Serpents - The History of Colt's Snake Guns* by Gurney Brown. Visit bluebookofgunvalues.com for more information, sample pages, and how to order. A few were shipped with factory installed hammer shroud.

* ***Cobra First Issue Blue Finish***

N/A	$1,450	$1,150	$800	$650	$450	$375	$325	$300	$275	$250	$200

Add 20%-40% for .22 LR cal.
Add 15%-25% for .38 cal. with 3 in. barrel.

* ***Cobra First Issue Nickel Finish***

N/A	$1,350	$1,050	$850	$750	$650	$575	$500	$425	$375	$300	$250

Add 30% for .22 LR cal.
Add 25% for .38 cal. with 3 in. barrel.

100%	98%	95%	90%	80%	70%	60%	50%	40%	30%	20%	10%

AGENT (FIRST ISSUE) – .38 Spl. cal., similar to Cobra first issue, except shorter grip frame. Mfg. 1962-1972.

$1,000	$900	$700	$550	$375	$235	$200	$190	$180	$170	$160	$150

COBRA (SECOND ISSUE) – .38 Spl. cal., similar to Cobra first issue, except shrouded ejector rod. Mfg. 1973-81.

100% values on the following Cobra models have been intentionally omitted, as ascertaining accurate values is very difficult and not predictable.

For definitive information on Cobras and variations, please refer to the book *Seven Serpents - The History of Colt's Snake Guns* by Gurney Brown. Visit bluebookofgunvalues.com for more information, sample pages, and how to order. A few were shipped with factory installed hammer shroud.

* ***Cobra Second Issue Blue Finish***

N/A	$850	$750	$600	$525	$450	$375	$325	$300	$275	$250	$200

Add 30% for .22 LR cal.
Add 25% for .38 cal. with 3 in. barrel.

* ***Cobra Second Issue Nickel Finish***

N/A	$1,150	$850	$800	$750	$650	$575	$500	$425	$375	$300	$250

Add 20%-40% for .22 LR cal.
Add 15%-25% for .38 cal. with 3 in. barrel.

COMBAT COBRA – .357 Mag. cal., 2 1/2 in. barrel, special edition for Lew Horton with "CC" prefix and stainless steel construction. Mfg. 1986-1987.

GRADING - PPGS™	100%	98%	95%	90%	80%	70%	60%	LAST MSR
	N/A	$4,150	$3,750	$2,450	$1,950	$1,800	$1,500	

100% values have been intentionally omitted, as ascertaining accurate values is very difficult and not predictable.

For definitive information on Cobras and variations, please refer to *Seven Serpents - The History of Colt's Snake Guns* by Gurney Brown. Visit bluebookofgunvalues.com for more information, sample pages, and how to order.

COBRA SERIES (NEW MFG.) – .38 Spl. +P cal., 6 shot, various configurations. Introduced 2017.

* ***Cobra*** – .38 Spl.+P cal., 2 in. barrel, 6 shot, matte finished stainless steel, red fiber optic front sight, Hogue stippled custom rubber grips with finger grooves, linear leaf main spring design allows smooth trigger pull, 25 oz. New 2017.

GRADING - PPGS™	100%	98%	95%	90%	80%	70%	60%	LAST MSR
MSR $699	$675	$600	$525	$450	$400	$350	$300	

* ***Cobra Classic*** – .38 Spl. cal., matte polished cylinder, 2 in. barrel, 6 shot mag., leaf spring trigger, brass bead front sight, checkered wooded combat grips w/Colt medallion, matte polished stainless steel finish. New mid-2018-2019.

GRADING - PPGS™	100%	98%	95%	90%	80%	70%	60%	LAST MSR
	$650	$575	$515	$450	$400	$350	$300	*$749*

* ***Cobra TT (Two-Tone)*** – .38 Spl.+P cal., 2 in. barrel, black DLC cylinder, 6 shot, brass bead front sight and Frame Trench rear sight, Hyena Brown G10 grips, LL2 Linear Leaf mainspring design, matte stainless steel two-tone finish. Mfg. 2019 only.

GRADING - PPGS™	100%	98%	95%	90%	80%	70%	60%	LAST MSR
	$650	$575	$515	$450	$400	$350	$300	*$749*

* ***Bright Cobra*** – .38 Spl.+P cal., steel frame, 2 in. barrel, 6 shot, brass bead front sight, Frame Trench rear sight, black composite grips with Colt logo, LL2 Linear Leaf mainspring design, bright stainless finish. New 2019.

GRADING - PPGS™	100%	98%	95%	90%	80%	70%	60%	LAST MSR
MSR $1,299	$1,250	$1,025	$875	$750	$650	$550	$450	

* ***Night Cobra*** – .38 Spl. +P cal., DAO, 2 in. barrel, 6 shot, stainless steel construction w/matte black DLC coating, bobbed hammer, Tritium front night sight, black synthetic VC G10 grips, linear leaf main spring design allows smooth trigger pull, 25 oz. Mfg. 2018-2019.

GRADING - PPGS™	100%	98%	95%	90%	80%	70%	60%	LAST MSR
	$775	$650	$550	$475	$415	$375	$325	*$899*

KING COBRA (OLDER MFG.) – .357 Mag. cal., 2 1/2 (new 1990), 4, or 6 in. solid rib barrel only, white outline rear sight, black neoprene round butt grips, blue metal finish, approx. 42 oz. (4 in. barrel). Mfg. 1986-1992.

GRADING - PPGS™	100%	98%	95%	90%	80%	70%	60%	LAST MSR
4 or 6 in. barrel	N/A	$1,950	$1,700	$1,450	$1,200	$950	$800	
2 1/2 in. barrel	N/A	$3,500	$2,650	$2,000	$1,500	$1,100	$900	*$410*

100% values have been intentionally omitted, as ascertaining accurate values is very difficult and not predictable.

For definitive information on Cobras and variations, please refer to *Seven Serpents - The History of Colt's Snake Guns* by Gurney Brown. Visit bluebookofgunvalues.com for more information, sample pages, and how to order.

GRADING - PPGS™	100%	98%	95%	90%	80%	70%	60%	LAST MSR

KING COBRA STAINLESS (OLDER MFG.) – .357 Mag. cal., DA revolver, 2 (mfg. 1988-1994), 4, 6, or 8 (mfg. 1990-1994) in. solid rib barrel, 6 shot cylinder, stainless steel construction, white outline rear sight, black neoprene round butt grips, approx. 36 oz. (2 1/2 in. barrel), Mfg. late 1986-1992, production resumed 1994, disc. 1998.

	100%	98%	95%	90%	80%	70%	60%	LAST MSR
4 or 6 in. barrel	N/A	$2,100	$1,750	$1,450	$1,150	$950	$825	
2 1/2 or 8 in. barrel	N/A	$2,500	$2,250	$1,975	$1,450	$1,050	$850	*$485*

100% values have been intentionally omitted, as ascertaining accurate values is very difficult and not predictable.

For definitive information on Cobras and variations, please refer to *Seven Serpents - The History of Colt's Snake Guns* by Gurney Brown. Visit bluebookofgunvalues.com for more information, sample pages, and how to order. A collector's note from Gurney Brown's research: There were approx. 200 8 in. vent rib barreled King Cobra revolvers assembled using left over barrels from the Whitetailer production run with standard King Cobra markings. These revolvers WILL NOT letter from Colt as having a VR barrel. Small premiums may exist.

* ***King Cobra "Ultimate" Bright Stainless (Older Mfg.)*** – similar to King Cobra, except for bright stainless steel, 2 1/2 (new 1990), 4, 6, or 8 (new 1991) in. barrel. Mfg. 1988-92.

100%	98%	95%	90%	80%	70%	60%	LAST MSR
N/A	$2,850	$2,650	$2,200	$1,700	$1,300	$925	*$470*

KING COBRA (CURRENT MFG). – .357 Mag. cal., heavy-duty stainless steel frame, 3 in. full underlug barrel, 6 shot, DA/SA trigger, elongated trigger guard, brass bead front sight, Hogue overmolded grips, brushed stainless steel finish, 28 oz. New 2019.

MSR	100%	98%	95%	90%	80%	70%	60%
MSR $899	$875	$725	$600	$500	$425	$375	$325

* ***King Cobra Carry*** – .357 Mag. cal., heavy-duty stainless steel frame, 2 in. full underlug barrel, 6 shot, bobbed hammer, DA/SA or DAO (new 2020) trigger, elongated trigger guard, brass bead front sight, Hogue overmolded grips, brushed stainless steel finish, 26 oz. New 2019.

MSR	100%	98%	95%	90%	80%	70%	60%
MSR $899	$875	$725	$600	$500	$425	$375	$325

* ***King Cobra Target*** – .357 Mag. cal., DA, LL2 linear mainspring design, 4 1/4 in. full underlug barrel, 6 shot, elongated trigger guard, elevated fiber optic front sight, adj. rear sight, Altamont wood medallion grips, matte stainless steel finish, 28 oz. New mid-2019.

MSR	100%	98%	95%	90%	80%	70%	60%
MSR $999	$975	$825	$700	$575	$475	$400	$350

100%	98%	95%	90%	80%	70%	60%	50%	40%	30%	20%	10%

AGENT L.W. (SECOND ISSUE) – .38 Spl. cal., similar to First Issue, except shrouded ejector rod, matte finish since 1982. Mfg. 1973-1991.

100%	98%	95%	90%	80%	70%	60%	50%	40%	30%	20%	10%
$800	$625	$525	$425	$325	$275	$230	$200	$190	$180	$170	$160

Last MSR was $260.

DETECTIVE SPECIAL (THIRD ISSUE) – .38 Spl. cal., similar to Second Issue, shrouded ejector rod, 2 or 3 (scarce) in. barrel, integral long serrated ramp front sight, wraparound wood grips. Mfg. 1973-1986.

100%	98%	95%	90%	80%	70%	60%	50%	40%	30%	20%	10%
$975	$850	$750	$550	$475	$385	$350	$295	$200	$195	$185	$175

Last MSR was $429.

Add $200 for nickel finish.
Add 15% for 3 in. barrel.
Add $1,000 for Class A engraving if in 98% condition or better.

COMMANDO SPECIAL – .38 Spl. cal., similar to Detective Special with steel frame, shrouded ejector rod, 2 in. barrel, matte parkerized finish, rubber grips. Mfg. 1984-86.

100%	98%	95%	90%	80%	70%	60%	50%	40%	30%	20%	10%
N/A	$750	$500	$400	$325	$295	$265	$235	$200	$190	$170	$150

Last MSR was $260.

POLICE POSITIVE SPECIAL (THIRD ISSUE) – .38 Spl. cal., similar to Detective Special Second Issue, except 4, 5, or 6 in. barrel. Mfg. 1947-76.

100%	98%	95%	90%	80%	70%	60%	50%	40%	30%	20%	10%
$750	$500	$400	$295	$250	$225	$200	$190	$180	$170	$160	$150

POLICE POSITIVE SPECIAL (FOURTH ISSUE) – .38 Spl. cal., shrouded ejector rod housing, steel frame, blue or nickel finish. Mfg. 1977-78.

100%	98%	95%	90%	80%	70%	60%	50%	40%	30%	20%	10%
$800	$600	$450	$300	$235	$210	$200	$190	$180	$170	$160	$150

Last MSR was $400.

Add 15% for nickel finish.

GRADING - PPGS™	100%	98%	95%	90%	80%	70%	60%	LAST MSR

POLICE POSITIVE MK V (FIFTH ISSUE) – .38 Spl. cal., full shrouded 4 in. barrel, steel frame, blue finish, rubber grips. Mfg. 1994-1995.

	100%	98%	95%	90%	80%	70%	60%	LAST MSR
	$650	$500	$400	$250	$195	$180	$165	

100%	98%	95%	90%	80%	70%	60%	50%	40%	30%	20%	10%

VIPER MODEL – .38 Spl. cal., similar to Police Positive Special (Fourth Issue), alloy frame, 4 in. barrel, shrouded ejector rod housing. Mfg. 1977 only - rare.

100%	98%	95%	90%	80%	70%	60%	50%	40%	30%	20%	10%
N/A	$4,000	$3,650	$2,950	$2,450	$1,825	$1,550	$1,350	$1,100	$995	$850	$750

Add 50% for nickel finish.

100% values have been intentionally omitted, as ascertaining accurate values is very difficult and not predictable.

While this model was manufactured in 1977, some "clean up" guns were also produced in 1993 using leftover parts.

For definitive information on Vipers and variations, please refer to *Seven Serpents - The History of Colt's Snake Guns* by Gurney Brown. Visit BlueBookOfGunValues.com for more information, sample pages, and how to order.

DIAMONDBACK .22 CAL. – .22 LR or .22 WMR (rare) cal., 2 1/2 (scarce in .22 LR), 4, or 6 in. VR barrel, blue or nickel (more desireable) finish, adj. sights, steel frame, checkered walnut grips. Mfg. 1966-1991.

100% values on the following Diamondback models have been intentionally omitted, as ascertaining accurate values is very difficult and not predictable.

Note: .22 WMR cal. is rare, and values are difficult to accurately ascertain. Buyer beware - fakes do exist! Diamondbacks have risen in value so much that higher value guns based upon finishes, barrel length, etc. should be accompanied by a factory letter verifying details. Some guns were manufactured in electroless nickel also.

For definitive information on Diamondbacks and variations, please refer to *Seven Serpents - The History of Colt's Snake Guns* by Gurney Brown. Visit bluebookofgunvalues.com for more information, sample pages, and how to order.

* ***Diamondback .22 cal. Blue w/2 1/2 In. Barrel***

100%	98%	95%	90%	80%	70%	60%	50%	40%	30%	20%	10%
N/A	$4,000	$3,200	$2,000	$1,825	$1,550	$1,350	$1,100	$995	$850	$750	$650

A factory letter is now advisable on this configuration.

* ***Diamondback .22 cal. Nickel w/2 1/2 In. Barrel***

100%	98%	95%	90%	80%	70%	60%	50%	40%	30%	20%	10%
N/A	$3,500	$3,150	$2,750	$2,250	$1,825	$1,550	$1,350	$1,100	$995	$850	$750

Extreme rarity factor precludes accurate pricing on this model. Currently, values can range from $4,000-$9,000 depending on condition, and if the gun will letter.

A factory letter is now advisable on this configuration.

* ***Diamondback .22 cal. Blue w/4 in. Barrel***

100%	98%	95%	90%	80%	70%	60%	50%	40%	30%	20%	10%
N/A	$2,750	$1,900	$1,350	$1,100	$995	$850	$750	$650	$550	$475	$350

* ***Diamondback .22 cal. Nickel w/4 in. Barrel***

100%	98%	95%	90%	80%	70%	60%	50%	40%	30%	20%	10%
N/A	$2,850	$2,400	$1,950	$1,700	$1,475	$1,300	$1,100	$995	$850	$750	$650

* ***Diamondback .22 cal. Blue w/6 in. Barrel***

100%	98%	95%	90%	80%	70%	60%	50%	40%	30%	20%	10%
$2,400	$1,800	$1,450	$1,300	$1,100	$995	$850	$750	$650	$550	$475	$350

* ***Diamondback .22 cal., Nickel w/6 in. Barrel*** – approx. 2,200 mfg. circa 1979.

100%	98%	95%	90%	80%	70%	60%	50%	40%	30%	20%	10%
$2,750	$2,500	$2,300	$1,950	$1,700	$1,475	$1,300	$1,100	$995	$850	$750	$650

DIAMONDBACK .38 SPL. – .38 Spl. cal., 2 1/2 (scarce), 4, or 6 in. VR barrel, blue or nickel finish, adj. sights, steel frame, checkered walnut grips. Mfg. 1966-1991.

For definitive information on Diamondbacks and variations, please refer to *Seven Serpents - The History of Colt's Snake Guns* by Gurney Brown. Visit bluebookofgunvalues.com for more information, sample pages, and how to order.

* ***Diamondback .38 Spl. 4 or 6 in. Barrel***

100%	98%	95%	90%	80%	70%	60%	50%	40%	30%	20%	10%
$1,950	$1,650	$1,350	$1,100	$995	$850	$750	$650	$550	$475	$350	$275

Last MSR was $461.

Add 20% for nickel finish.

* ***Diamondback .38 Spl. 2 1/2 in. Barrel***

100%	98%	95%	90%	80%	70%	60%	50%	40%	30%	20%	10%
$2,250	$2,000	$1,750	$1,450	$1,300	$1,100	$995	$850	$750	$650	$550	$475

Add 20% for nickel finish.

100%	98%	95%	90%	80%	70%	60%	50%	40%	30%	20%	10%

COLT .357 MAG – 4 or 6 in. barrel, heavy frame, Accro rear sight, blue or nickel finish, checkered walnut grips. Mfg. 1953-1961.

* ***Colt .357 Mag. Standard hammer***

100%	98%	95%	90%	80%	70%	60%	50%	40%	30%	20%	10%
N/A	$1,000	$850	$775	$625	$475	$450	$350	$285	$270	$255	$240

Add 35% for nickel.

* ***Colt .357 Mag. Wide hammer w/target grips***

100%	98%	95%	90%	80%	70%	60%	50%	40%	30%	20%	10%
N/A	$1,050	$900	$825	$675	$525	$475	$350	$300	$250	$225	$215

Add 35% for nickel.

In 1962, this model was absorbed into the Trooper line.

TROOPER – .22 LR (4 in. only, scarce), .357 Mag., or .38 Spl. cal., 4 or 6 in. barrel, blue or nickel finish, quick draw ramp front sight, adj. rear sight, checkered walnut grips. Mfg. 1953-69.

Add $100-$200 for .22 LR cal. (4 in. barrel only), depending on condition.
Add 25% for nickel finish.
Add 15% for .38 Spl. cal. only.

* ***Trooper Standard hammer***

100%	98%	95%	90%	80%	70%	60%	50%	40%	30%	20%	10%
$1,350	$1,100	$750	$675	$525	$350	$325	$295	$225	$195	$185	$175

* ***Trooper Wide hammer and target grips***

100%	98%	95%	90%	80%	70%	60%	50%	40%	30%	20%	10%
$1,450	$1,250	$950	$800	$550	$400	$350	$300	$250	$200	$190	$180

Add 35% for nickel.

GRADING - PPGS™	100%	98%	95%	90%	80%	70%	60%	LAST MSR

TROOPER MK III – .22 LR, .22 WMR, .357 Mag., or .38 Spl. cal., 4, 6, or 8 in. solid rib barrel, adj. rear sight, walnut target grips, redesigned lock work to reduce amount of hand fitting needed on earlier Trooper versions. Mfg. 1969-1983.

GRADING - PPGS™	100%	98%	95%	90%	80%	70%	60%	LAST MSR
Blue finish	$1,000	$950	$775	$575	$450	$325	$225	
Nickel finish	$1,150	$850	$650	$525	$400	$300	$250	

Add 30% for .22 LR cal.
Add 50% for .22 WMR cal.
Ad 30% for 8 in. barrel.
Add $300 for Custom Shop Model w/rosewood grips and factory tuned action.

TROOPER MK V – .357 Mag. cal. only, 4, 6, or 8 in. barrel, adj. rear sight, walnut target grips, improved version of Mark III action, vent. rib barrel, a few made with solid rib, redesigned 1982. Disc. 1986.

GRADING - PPGS™	100%	98%	95%	90%	80%	70%	60%	LAST MSR
Blue finish	$1,000	$950	$775	$575	$450	$325	$225	*$362*
Nickel finish	$1,150	$850	$650	$525	$400	$300	$250	*$396*

Add 30% for 8 in. barrel.

LAWMAN SKY MARSHAL – .38 Spl. cal., 2 in. barrel, experimental revolver with a replaceable plastic cylinder preloaded with plastic bullets, blue finish, checkered walnut grips, this model was designed to be carried on airliners by Federal Marshals during the 1970s.

100%	98%	95%	90%	80%	70%	60%	LAST MSR
N/A	$925	$850	$775	$700	$625	$550	

Be wary of non-original alterations on this model as it can be modified very easily.

LAWMAN MK III – .357 Mag. cal., 2 in. and 4 in. barrel, unshrouded or shrouded ejector rod for 2 in. barrel, fixed sights, checkered walnut grips. Mfg. 1969-83.

GRADING - PPGS™	100%	98%	95%	90%	80%	70%	60%	LAST MSR
Blue finish	$850	$750	$550	$450	$375	$300	$180	
Nickel finish	$900	$850	$650	$550	$450	$350	$250	

LAWMAN MK V – .357 Mag. cal., 2 or 4 in. barrel, shrouded ejector rod for 2 in. barrel, fixed sights, checkered walnut grips, improved version of MK III action. Mfg. 1984 and 1991 only.

GRADING - PPGS™	100%	98%	95%	90%	80%	70%	60%	LAST MSR
Blue finish	$850	$750	$550	$450	$375	$325	$180	*$309*
Nickel finish	$900	$850	$650	$550	$450	$350	$250	*$328*

BORDER PATROL (SECOND ISSUE) – .357 Mag. cal., 4 in. heavy barrel, similar to Trooper Mark III frame, less polishing of frame. Limited mfg. 1970-75.

* ***Border Patrol Blue Finish*** – 5,356 mfg.

100%	98%	95%	90%	80%	70%	60%	LAST MSR
$975	$700	$600	$450	$375	$325	$275	

* ***Border Patrol Nickel Finish*** – 1,152 mfg.

100%	98%	95%	90%	80%	70%	60%	LAST MSR
$1,150	$850	$650	$525	$400	$300	$250	

GRADING - PPGS™	100%	98%	95%	90%	80%	70%	60%	LAST MSR

PEACEKEEPER – .357 Mag. cal. only, similar to Trooper MK V, 4 or 6 in. barrel w/Python type rib, matte blue finish, rubber combat grips, adj. rear sight, about 42 oz. Mfg. 1985-1989.

	$1,000	$950	$775	$575	$450	$325	$225	*$330*

BOA – .357 Mag. cal., deep blue polish, Python type barrel w/full length ejector shroud and rib fitted to a Mark V action, 600 each mfg. in 4 and 6 in. barrel lengths. Entire production run was purchased by Lew Horton Distributing Co., Inc. located in Southboro, MA. 1985 retail was $525.

	N/A	$9,500	$8,500	$6,500	$5,500	$4,500	$3,500	

100% values on the following Boa models have been intentionally omitted, as ascertaining accurate values is very difficult and not predictable.

For definitive information on Boas and variations, please refer to *Seven Serpents - The History of Colt's Snake Guns* by Gurney Brown. Visit bluebookofgunvalues.com for more information, sample pages, and how to order.

* ***Boa Set*** – 100 sets mfg. including 4 and 6 in. barrels with Python type fully shrouded ejector rod housing and rib, consecutive serial numbers, cases were supplied by Lew Horton. 1985 retail was $1,200.

	N/A	$22,500	$18,500	$15,000	$12,500	$10,000	$8,500	

DETECTIVE SPECIAL (FOURTH ISSUE) – .38 Spl. cal., 6 shot, 2 in. shrouded barrel, steel frame, blue finish, black composition grips with gold medallions, 21 oz. Mfg. 1993-1995.

	$1,050	$800	$600	$400	$375	$300	$200	*$400*

* ***Bobbed Detective Special*** – .38 Spl. cal., double action only with bobbed hammer, front night sight, honed action, choice of hard chrome or standard blue finish. Mfg. 1994-1995.

	$1,850	$1,250	$800	$500	$375	$300	$250	*$599*

Add $30 for hard chrome finish.

COLT .38 SF-VI – .38 Spl. cal., 6 shot, 2 or 4 in. barrel, transfer bar safety, choice of matte (2 in.), bright polished (4 in.), or black (4 in.) finish, stainless steel, regular or bobbed (4 in. barrel only) hammer, fixed sights, black composition combat grips, 21 oz. Mfg. 1995-96.

	$850	$725	$600	$500	$375	$300	$250	*$408*

* ***Colt .38 Special Lady*** – while advertised during 1996, this model had very limited mfg.

Extreme rarity factor precludes accurate values on this model.

COLT .38 DSII – .357 Mag. (new 1998) or .38 Spl. cal., 6 shot, 2 or 3 in. barrel, stainless steel, service hammer, rubber combat style checkered grips, 21 oz. Mfg. 1997-1998.

Nickel finish	$1,800	$1,250	$800	$550	$450	$350	$250	*$435*

This model featured a redesigned trigger fire control group and is capable of shooting .38+P ammo.

COLT MAGNUM CARRY – .357 Mag. cal., 6 shot, 2 in. barrel, transfer bar safety, satin stainless steel, wraparound rubber grips with finger grooves, ramp front sight, 21 oz. Mfg. 1999 only.

	$2,450	$2,100	$1,750	$1,450	$1,150	$925	$725	*$460*

PYTHON & VARIATIONS – .357 Mag. cal., 2 1/2 (disc. 1994), 3 (a.k.a Combat Python, disc., very scarce), 4, 6, or 8 in. barrel with vent. rib, Royal blue, polished nickel, or Electroless Nickel (known as Royal Coltguard) satin nickel finish, fully shrouded ejector rod, adj. rear sight, checkered walnut grips (standard prior to 1991, and fitted on some SKUs much later), rubber Hogue monogrips (2 1/2 or 4 in. barrel), or rubber target (6 or 8 in. barrel) grips, 38-48 oz. A few late production guns included both a wood and rubber grip set. Mfg. 1955-1996.

As one of the few hand fitted revolvers ever produced, Python values have risen dramatically in recent years, especially early revolvers and any that remain in NIB or near NIB condition. 100% values on the following Python models have been intentionally omitted, as ascertaining accurate values is very difficult and not predictable. Over time, the value distinctions group the Python into 4 overall groups by period. These four groups are as follows: Early (circa 1950s) production with full checkered grips and high polish Royal blue, other early pre-suffix serial numbers up to about 1969, other production up to about 1990, and finally, 1990s production. In general, the older the Python, the higher the value.

For definitive information on all Pythons and variations, please refer to *COLT'S PYTHON - King of the Seven Serpents* by Gurney Brown and *Seven Serpents - The History of Colt's Snake Guns* by Gurney Brown. Visit bluebookofgunvalues.com for more information, sample pages, and how to order.

GRADING - PPGS™	100%	98%	95%	90%	80%	70%	60%	LAST MSR

* **Python Blue or Royal Blue Finish (Mfg. 1955-1969)** - first letter prefix or suffix used in ser. no., began in mid-1969 with the letter "E".

4 or 6 in. barrel	N/A	$3,100	$2,450	$1,850	$1,400	$1,100	$900	
2 1/2 in.	N/A	$4,250	$3,750	$2,675	$2,250	$1,750	$1,200	

Add 50% for 3 in. barrel - purchase only with factory letter. 3 in. barreled Pythons were first (but not exclusively) mfg. for Lew Horton with "K" prefix.

Early production Pythons (serial numbered without letter prefix or suffix) with 4 or 6 in. barrels, fully checkered walnut grips with gold Colt medallions, and Accro flat-top sights will command a substantial premium.

* **Python Blue or Royal Blue Finish (Mfg. circa 1970-1996)**

4 or 6 in. barrel	N/A	$2,750	$2,250	$1,850	$1,400	$1,100	$900	
2 1/2 in.	N/A	$3,750	$3,250	$2,675	$2,250	$1,750	$1,200	
8 in.	N/A	$3,350	$2,750	$2,150	$1,750	$1,250	$975	

Last MSR was $815.

Add 50% for 3 in. barrel with factory letter.

Beware of loose 3 in. barrel models sold by GPC and others during the 1990s.

The standard Python was manufactured 1955-1996, and 1997-recent production was through the Colt Custom Shop by special order only (see Python Elite listing).

During 2001-2002, Colt shipped some Pythons to dealers with prices in $1,100 - $1,200 retail range. These guns had a slightly different (rougher) line checkering pattern on the cylinder release and hammer parts.

There also exist a few Pythons mfg. in calibers other than .357 Mag., including .22 LR, .22 WMR, and .256 Win. Mag. (circa 1961), .41 Mag., and .44 Spl. cals. While the .22 LR and the .22 WMR (.22 Mag.) were advertised in earlier factory catalogs, they were never mass-produced - only a few prototypes exist. At least one known example of a .22 cal. Python was found at an auction, but it had only a special factory barrel sleeve for photographic purposes, and was not a shootable gun. The amount of premium on these cals. depends if the gun factory letters and how serious (and deep-pocketed) the Python collector is.

A California distributor special ordered a quantity of the first 3 in. barreled Pythons, which at the time were not available directly from the factory. This variation is called the California Combat Python, with the words "CALIFORNIA COMBAT" underneath the "PYTHON 357" marking on the left side of the barrel. Later, Colt made a special limited edition of 500 Combat Pythons, so marked for Lew Horton. These Lew Horton 3 inch Pythons are referred to as "Combat Pythons". A small number of the Combat Pythons were mfg. in nickel finish, and are very rare.

* **Combat Python** - .357 Mag cal., 3 in. barrel marked "COMBAT PYTHON." Rare.

	N/A	$9,500	$8,500	$6,500	$5,500	$4,500	$3,500	

* **California Combat Python** - .357 Mag cal., 3 in. barrel marked "PYTHON 357 MAG" over "CALIFORNIA COMBAT", made up from Python Targets with 8 in. barrels.

	N/A	$6,500	$5,500	$4,500	$3,250	$2,500	$1,750	

* **Python Nickel Finish** - available in traditional polished nickel or a satin nickel, called both Electroless Nickel and Royal Coltguard by Colt. Disc. 1985.

4 or 6 in. barrel	N/A	$3,550	$3,250	$2,750	$2,250	$1,550	$1,250	
4 or 6 in. Electroless Nickel	N/A	$5,050	$4,500	$4,150	$3,350	$2,750	$2,100	
2 1/2 in. barrel	N/A	$4,400	$3,850	$2,950	$2,500	$1,950	$1,500	
2 1/2 in. Electroless Nickel	N/A	$6,500	$5,650	$5,150	$4,750	$3,375	$2,600	
3 in. barrel	N/A	$9,500	$8,500	$6,500	$5,500	$4,500	$3,500	
8 in. barrel	N/A	$4,000	$3,500	$2,650	$2,150	$1,500	$1,250	
8 in. Electroless Nickel	N/A	$5,500	$4,750	$4,350	$3,450	$2,850	$2,200	

Last MSR was $693.

Satin nickel finish is so designated on original boxes as "Royal Coltguard" or "E NICK" (electroless nickel).

A Colt factory letter for the 3 in. barrel is mandatory if purchasing.

* **Python Stainless Steel** - stainless steel construction, matte or high polish finish, neoprene target or combat stocks, 2 1/2 (disc. 1994), 4, 6, or 8 (new 1989) in. barrel. Mfg. 1983-96.

4 or 6 in. barrel	N/A	$3,500	$3,150	$2,500	$1,950	$1,350	$950	
2 1/2 in. barrel	N/A	$7,500	$4,650	$3,150	$2,350	$1,600	$1,350	

GRADING - PPGS™	100%	98%	95%	90%	80%	70%	60%	LAST MSR
8 in. barrel	N/A	$3,950	$3,500	$3,000	$2,500	$2,000	$1,500	

Last MSR was $904.

Add 100% for 2.5 inch ported barrel, Lew Horton edition of 1995.

Add 100% for Python Silver Snake (Factory Model #13060ESS), from Colt Custom Shop, 1982, laser etched.

Later production of the 6 in. barrel includes neoprene target stocks.

* ***Python "Ultimate" Bright Stainless Steel*** – deluxe, highly polished stainless model, 2 1/2 (disc.), 4, 6, or 8 in. VR barrel. Mfg. 1985-disc.

4 or 6 in. barrel	N/A	$3,950	$3,500	$3,000	$2,500	$2,000	$1,500	
2 1/2 in. barrel	N/A	$4,950	$4,500	$3,950	$3,250	$2,500	$1,750	
8 in. barrel	N/A	$4,500	$4,000	$3,500	$2,750	$2,000	$1,500	

Last MSR was $935.

PYTHON (CURRENT MFG.) – .357 Mag. or .38 Spl. cal., 4 1/4 or 6 in. barrel, 6 shot mag., stainless steel construction, interchangeable front sight and re-designed adj. rear target sight, walnut target grip w/ Colt medallion, semi-bright finish, 46 oz. New 2020.

MSR $1,499	$1,450	$1,250	$1,050	$900	$750	$600	$475	

PYTHON ELITE – .357 Mag. cal., 4 or 6 in. VR barrel, choice of Royal Blue or stainless steel, adj. rear sight, rubber service style (disc.) or smooth walnut finger groove grips, roll-marked "PYTHON ELITE" on barrel, 38 or 43 1/2 oz. Mfg. 1997-1998, reintroduced 1999, again during 2002-2006.

This model was available by custom order only through the Colt Custom Shop.

Some early production models have Colt-Elliason rear sights, and recent production used Colt Accro sights.

Some guns were shipped with both wood and hard rubber grips until 1999.

* ***Python Elite Blue***

	N/A	$3,750	$3,250	$2,750	$2,250	$1,750	$1,250	*$1,150*

* ***Python Elite Stainless*** – similar to Python Elite, except is stainless steel. Mfg. 1997-99, reintroduced 2002-2006.

	N/A	$3,950	$3,500	$3,000	$2,500	$2,000	$1,500	*$1,150*

A few examples from the first production run of Python Elite revolvers with "PN" serial number prefix are in Bright Stainless. Box end labels on these revolvers are marked "Stainless Steel Finish".

ULTIMATE PYTHON – .357 Mag. cal., 6 in. barrel only, specially tuned by the custom shop, supplied with both Colt-Elliason target and Accro white outline sighting systems, walnut and rubber grips also included, choice of Colt Royal Blue or Ultimate Stainless finish. Mfg. 1991-1993.

Royal Blue	N/A	$3,950	$3,500	$3,000	$2,500	$2,000	$1,500	
Ultimate Stainlesss	N/A	$4,500	$3,950	$2,750	$2,250	$1,950	$1,625	

Last MSR was $1,140.

Guns were delivered with 2 sets of Colt Python factory grips. Prices assume guns include both sets and accessories at time of resale.

PYTHON HUNTER – .357 Mag. cal., 8 in. barrel, includes Leupold 2x scope, Halliburton aluminum case, and accessories. Mfg. 1980-1981.

	N/A	$3,500	$3,050	$2,550	$2,250	$1,950	$1,625	*$995*

Subtract 10% if missing luggage case and accessories.

Values assume undamaged Halliburton case, scope and accessories including plastic cartridge box. Carefully observe the finish on this model as the foam rubber insert inside the Halliburton case can react with the metal finish if the revolver is left unprotected inside over a long period of time.

PYTHON SILHOUETTE – .357 Mag. cal., 8 in. barrel, includes Leupold 2x scope, similar to Python Hunter, except barrel is roll marked with Silhouette name and scope position has been moved rearward, black luggage-type case. Mfg. circa 1983.

	N/A	$4,000	$3,650	$2,450	$1,950	$1,800	$1,500	

Subtract 10% if missing luggage case and accessories.

Values assume undamaged black luggage case, scope and accessories.

PYTHON STALKER – .357 Mag. cal., 8 in. barrel, stainless steel, black combat style rubber grips with finger grooves and Colt medallions, left side of barrel marked "Silhouette", includes Leupold 2x scope, unfluted cylinder. Cased.

	N/A	$3,950	$3,500	$2,200	$1,800	$1,650	$1,500	

GRADING - PPGS™	100%	98%	95%	90%	80%	70%	60%	LAST MSR

PYTHON TARGET - .38 Spl. cal., 8 in. barrel, blue (3,489 mfg.) or nickel (251 mfg.) finish, marked "PYTHON TARGET" on the barrel, sometimes referred to as "California Target Model." Disc.

Blue	N/A	$3,150	$2,600	$1,950	$1,700	$1,475	$1,300	
Nickel	N/A	$3,950	$3,500	$2,200	$1,800	$1,650	$1,500	

PYTHON TEN POINTER - .357 Mag. cal., 8 in. barrel, includes 3x Burris scope, wooden grips, extra set of neoprene composite grips, carrying case. Disc.

	N/A	$3,750	$3,250	$2,750	$2,250	$1,750	$1,250	

Deduct 15% if missing original case.

GRIZZLY - .357 Mag. cal., 6 in. Magna-Ported barrel, non-fluted cylinder, Pachmayr Decelerator rubber grips with Colt medallions, matte stainless, 999 mfg. 1994-1995.

	N/A	$4,500	$3,950	$2,750	$2,250	$1,950	$1,625	

This model was mfg. by the Colt Custom Shop using a King Cobra frame with a Python barrel and shipped in a blue box.

WHITETAILER - .357 Mag. cal., 8 in. barrel, blue or matte stainless finish, black plastic case, Burris 1.5-4x scope. 500 issued by Outdoor Sports Headquarters 1987.

	N/A	$3,500	$2,650	$2,000	$1,500	$1,100	$900	

Deduct 15% if original factory case is missing.

The Whitetailer Model was mfg. by the Colt Custom Shop using a Trooper MK V Model revolver.

* ***Whitetailer II*** - .357 Mag. cal., 8 in. barrel, matte stainless finish, Burris 1.5-4x scope and Colt soft case.

	N/A	$3,250	$2,500	$1,750	$1,350	$1,000	$800	

The Whitetailer II Model was mfg. by the Colt Custom Shop using a King Cobra Model revolver.

KODIAK - .357 Mag. (rare), or .44 Mag. cal., 4 or 6 in. Mag-na-ported barrel with non-fluted cylinder, stainless steel, Pachmayr grips, built on Anaconda frame, "Colt Kodiak .44 Magnum" with outline of bear's footprint on left side of barrel, ser. nos. start with CKA. Approx. 2,000 mfg. in 1993 by Custom Shop.

.44 Mag. cal.	N/A	$3,950	$3,500	$2,200	$1,800	$1,650	$1,500	
.357 Mag. cal. (rare)	N/A	$4,500	$3,950	$2,750	$2,250	$1,950	$1,625	

ANACONDA - .44 Mag. or .45 LC (mfg. 1992-1999) cal., 4 (new 1991), 5 (not factory cataloged, special edition only, mfg. 1998), 6, or 8 in. VR barrel, transfer bar safety system, 6 shot, choice of matte (disc. 2003), Realtree Grey camo (.44 Mag. with 8 in. barrel only, mfg. 1996 only) finish, or stainless steel, black neoprene combat grips with Colt medallion, red ramp front sight, full length ejector rod housing, white outline rear adj. sight, approx. 47-59 oz. Mfg. 1990-99, reintroduced 2002-2006.

100% values on the following Anaconda models have been intentionally omitted, as ascertaining accurate values is very difficult and not predictable.

For definitive information on Anacondas and variations, please refer to *Seven Serpents - The History of Colt's Snake Guns* by Gurney Brown. Visit BlueBookOfGunValues.com for more information, sample pages, and how to order.

* ***Anaconda 1st Edition*** - .44 Mag. cal., Ultimate Stainless finish, special rollmark on left side of barrel reads "Colt Anaconda First Edition", with aluminum carrying case, ser. no. range MM00001-MM01000, 1,000 mfg. 1990 only.

	N/A	$3,500	$3,000	$2,500	$2,000	$1,500	$1,000	

* ***Anaconda 1990-1999 Mfg.*** - standard production, not mfg. by the Colt Custom Shop.

6 or 8 in. barrel	N/A	$2,400	$1,950	$1,500	$1,250	$1,000	$750	
4 in. barrel	N/A	$2,700	$2,200	$1,750	$1,500	$1,250	$1,000	

Add 20% for .45 LC cal.

Add 30% for Custom Shop factory porting.

* ***Anaconda 2002-2006 Mfg.*** - from 2002-2006, the Anaconda was only available through the Colt Custom Shop.

6 or 8 in. barrel	N/A	$2,400	$1,900	$1,500	$1,250	$1,000	$750	
4 in. barrel	N/A	$2,600	$1,950	$1,750	$1,500	$1,250	$1,000	

Last MSR was $1,000.

Add 30% for Custom Shop porting. Beware of fakes!

* ***Anaconda Camo*** - .44 Mag. cal. only, 8 in. barrel, Realtree Grey camo finish on gun and Redfield 2.5-7x scope, Hogue rubber grips w/Serpentine Colt logo, barrel marked "COLT-REALTREE" over "44 magnum". Mfg. 1996 only.

	N/A	$2,500	$2,250	$1,900	$1,600	$1,225	$800	*$999*

Revolver shipped with Realtree Gray camo soft case marked in yellow embroidery "TEAM COLT REALTREE".

GRADING - PPGS™	100%	98%	95%	90%	80%	70%	60%	LAST MSR

* ***Anaconda Hunter*** – .44 Mag. cal., supplied with Leupold 2x scope, carrying case, cleaning accessories, and both walnut and rubber grips, 8 in. barrel only. Mfg. 1991-93.

N/A	$2,250	$2,100	$1,750	$1,350	$1,100	$750	*$1,200*

* ***Anaconda Custom Ported*** – .44 Mag. cal., features 6 (disc.) or 8 in. Mag-na-ported barrel and Colt-Elliason rear sight, contoured trigger, and Pachmayr rubber grips, brushed stainless steel. Mfg. 1992-93, re-released 1995-96, again in 2002-2003.

N/A	$4,800	$3,850	$2,800	$1,900	$1,225	$800	*$1,050*

100%	98%	95%	90%	80%	70%	60%	50%	40%	30%	20%	10%

RIFLES/CARBINES: PRE-1904

A Colt letter of provenance for the Colteer, Courier, and Stagecoach models listed below is $75.00 per gun. The charge for Lightning models listed below is $100 per gun (limited records). Colt-Burgess model factory letters are also available at $100 per gun.

The author wishes to express his thanks to Mr. Wilmer Kellogg and Mr. Michael Kelly for providing much of the information on Colt-Burgess and Lightning rifles in this section.

FIRST MODEL RING LEVER – .34, .36, .38, .40, or .44 cal., 8 or 10 shot revolving cylinder, 30 in. octagon barrel, walnut stock, no forend, 200 mfg., percussion. Mfg. 1837-1838.

* ***First Model Ring Lever Standard Model***

N/A	N/A	N/A	$38,000	$28,500	$22,000	$17,000	$14,000	$11,500	$9,500	$8,000	$7,000

* ***First Model Ring Lever Improved Model*** – attached loading lever.

N/A	N/A	N/A	$41,500	$30,150	$23,250	$18,000	$15,000	$12,500	$10,500	$9,000	$8,000

SECOND MODEL RING LEVER – similar to First Model, w/o top strap over cylinder, .44 caliber only, percussion, 500 mfg., 1838-1841.

* ***Second Model Ring Lever Standard Model***

N/A	N/A	N/A	$34,000	$30,000	$20,000	$15,000	$13,000	$11,000	$10,000	$7,800	$6,150

* ***Second Model Ring Lever Improved Model***

N/A	N/A	N/A	$34,000	$30,000	$20,000	$15,000	$13,000	$11,000	$10,000	$7,800	$6,150

MODEL 1839 CARBINE – .52 smoothbore cal., 6 shot cylinder, 24 in. barrel, exposed hammer for cocking, blue finish, walnut stock, percussion, approx. 950 mfg. 1838-1841.

* ***Model 1839 Carbine Early Model*** – no loading lever.

N/A	N/A	N/A	$41,000	$39,000	$29,500	$22,500	$18,000	$15,250	$12,000	$9,850	$8,250

* ***Model 1839 Carbine Standard Model***

N/A	N/A	N/A	$35,000	$31,500	$21,000	$16,000	$14,000	$11,000	$10,000	$7,800	$6,150

MODEL 1855 REVOLVING – .36, .44, or .56 cal., various barrel lengths and stock styles, 5 or 6 shot cylinder, blue with walnut buttstock, no forend, percussion. Mfg. 1856-1864.

* ***Model 1855 Revolving First Model w/o Forearm Wood*** – 15, 18, 21, 24, 27, or 30 in. barrel, no forearm wood, non-fluted roll engraved cylinder, ser. no. range 1-1,000, approx. 1,000 mfg.

N/A	N/A	N/A	$12,000	$9,500	$8,350	$7,500	$7,000	$6,500	$6,000	$5,600	$5,250

* ***Model 1855 Revolving 1/2 Stock Sporter*** – 24, 27, or 30 in. barrel, approx. 1,500 mfg.

N/A	N/A	N/A	$12,000	$9,500	$8,350	$7,500	$7,000	$6,500	$6,000	$5,600	$5,250

* ***Model 1855 Revolving Full Stock Sporter*** – 21, 24, 27, 30, or 31 in. barrel, approx. 2,000 mfg.

N/A	N/A	N/A	$14,000	$12,000	$9,650	$9,000	$8,000	$7,450	$7,000	$6,600	$6,250

* ***Model 1855 Revolving Military Model, U.S.*** – martially marked, 21-37 in. barrel, 9,310 mfg.

N/A	N/A	N/A	$18,000	$15,000	$12,400	$11,000	$10,300	$9,550	$9,000	$8,400	$8,000

* ***Model 1855 Revolving .36 Caliber Carbine Model*** – 15, 18, or 21 in. barrel, 4,400 mfg.

N/A	N/A	N/A	$18,000	$15,000	$12,400	$11,000	$10,300	$9,550	$9,000	$8,400	$8,000

* ***Model 1855 Revolving .56 Caliber Artillery Carbine*** – 5 shot, 21 in. barrel with bayonet lug and forestock, approx. 64 mfg.

N/A	N/A	N/A	$19,500	$17,000	$14,000	$11,375	$10,350	$9,600	$8,900	$8,450	$8,000

100%	98%	95%	90%	80%	70%	60%	50%	40%	30%	20%	10%

BERDAN – .42 bottle-necked CF cal., breechloading, approx. 30,000 mfg. 1866-circa 1870. Scarce since most were sent to Russia and have Russian barrel markings, approx. 50-100 are Hartford marked.

* ***Berdan Rifle*** – 32 1/2 in. barrel, approx. 10 lbs.

N/A	N/A	N/A	$6,300	$5,300	$4,300	$3,800	$3,550	$3,300	$2,300	$1,650	$1,300

* ***Berdan Carbine*** – half stock, 18 1/4 in. barrel, approx. 50 mfg., both Russian and Hartford marked.

N/A	N/A	N/A	$8,600	$7,900	$7,025	$6,400	$5,800	$5,050	$4,250	$3,575	$3,050

MODEL 1861 MUSKET – .58 cal., percussion, muzzle loader, 40 in. barrel, with 3 bands, white metal parts, white walnut stock. 75,000 mfg., 1861-65.

N/A	N/A	N/A	$7,300	$5,300	$4,300	$3,800	$3,550	$3,300	$2,300	$1,650	$1,300

COLT-BURGESS LEVER ACTION – .44-40 WCF cal., 25 1/2 in. barrel, 15 shot tube mag., blue with case hardened lever and hammer, walnut stock. 6,403 mfg., 1883-1885.

N/A	N/A	N/A	$12,900	$9,775	$6,600	$5,600	$4,500	$4,000	$3,450	$2,950	$1,890

COLT-BURGESS CARBINE – similar to Rifle, with 20 in. barrel.

N/A	N/A	N/A	$19,200	$16,500	$12,900	$10,800	$8,700	$7,150	$5,600	$4,000	$2,950

COLT-BURGESS LIGHT CARBINE – lightened version of Carbine.

N/A	N/A	N/A	$22,575	$19,425	$16,275	$14,175	$12,075	$9,975	$7,875	$4,725	$3,675

LIGHTNING SLIDE ACTION RIFLE (CLMR) - SMALL FRAME – .22 S or L cal., 24 in. barrel, open sights, walnut straight stock, round or octagon barrel. Approx. 90,000 mfg. 1887-1904.

N/A	N/A	N/A	$5,700	$4,275	$3,800	$3,325	$2,850	$2,550	$2,150	$1,600	$950

Add 25% for deluxe model.

LIGHTNING SLIDE ACTION RIFLE (CLMR) - MEDIUM FRAME – .32 CLMR (.32-20 WCF), .38 CLMR (.38-40 WCF), or .44 CLMR (.44-40 WCF) cal., similar to Small Frame, except with 26 in. barrel and larger frame. Serial range 1-23,000, id not have a dust cover. Approx. 90,000 mfg. 1884-1902.

N/A	N/A	N/A	$6,175	$5,500	$4,850	$4,500	$3,325	$2,850	$2,500	$1,900	$1,700

Add 25% for deluxe model.

23 Medium Frame rifles were shipped to A.G. Spalding and Brothers during 1897, a major sporting goods supplier located in Chicago. Most of these guns are factory engraved, and were probably used for display during the Chicago Exposition. These deluxe rifles represent some of the finest Colt rifles ever manufactured.

LIGHTNING CARBINE MEDIUM FRAME – similar to Medium Frame Rifle, with 20 in. barrel.

N/A	N/A	N/A	$8,075	$7,125	$6,175	$5,225	$4,275	$3,800	$3,325	$2,850	$1,900

LIGHTNING BABY CARBINE MEDIUM FRAME – lightened version of Medium Frame Carbine, one pound lighter.

N/A	N/A	N/A	$9,250	$7,125	$6,175	$5,225	$4,275	$3,800	$3,325	$2,850	$2,375

Add 50% for .50-95 Express cal.

LIGHTNING SLIDE ACTION RIFLE (CLMR) - LARGE FRAME – .38-56 WCF, .40-60 Marlin (most common), .45-60 WCF (rarest), .45-85 Marlin, or .50-95 Express (rare) cal., large version of previously described Lightnings, approx. 4,600 mfg. 1887-1894.

N/A	N/A	N/A	$11,000	$9,000	$7,600	$6,650	$5,225	$4,275	$3,325	$2,375	$1,900

Add 25% for .50-95 Express cal.
Add 25% for deluxe model.
Add 25% for .45-60 cal. (approx. 8% mfg. in this cal.).

There may be a gap in the serial range of this model from ser. no. 2435 to 4444.

LIGHTNING CARBINE LARGE FRAME – similar to Large Frame Rifle, 22 in. barrel.

N/A	N/A	N/A	$13,000	$10,150	$8,250	$6,350	$5,425	$4,450	$3,750	$3,500	$3,050

LIGHTNING BABY CARBINE LARGE FRAME – lightened version of Large Frame Carbine, one pound lighter.

N/A	N/A	N/A	$13,000	$10,165	$8,250	$6,350	$5,400	$4,450	$3,750	$3,500	$3,050

Add 50% for .50-95 Express cal.

LIGHTNING MILITARY STYLE MUSKET – similar to Medium Frame Rifle, with bayonet lug.

N/A	N/A	N/A	N/A	N/A	N/A	$5,225	$4,275	$3,325	$2,375	$1,900	$1,425

Approximately 250 of these rifles with 27 in. round barrels, swivels, and carbine buttstocks, in serial ranges 50,000 and 51,000 were shipped to Costa Rica.

100%	98%	95%	90%	80%	70%	60%	50%	40%	30%	20%	10%

LIGHTNING SAN FRANCISCO POLICE – .44 CLMR (.44-40 WCF) cal., 26 in. round barrel Medium Frame rifle, with S.F.P. Police and rack numbers on lower tang. Ser. no. range S.F.P. 1-S.F.P. 401.

N/A	$9,975	$8,800	$7,350	$6,500	$5,000	$4,000	$3,550	$3,000	$2,500	$1,875	$1,500

DOUBLE RIFLE SxS – various cals. in the .45 range, hammers, very limited production between 1878-1880. Most guns were owned by friends of Caldwell Colt - Sam Colt's son, the original designer. Colt Double Rifles are extremely rare and desirable, and should be examined carefully.

Prices typically range between $80,000-$110,000, if all original.

GRADING - PPGS™	100%	98%	95%	90%	80%	70%	60%	LAST MSR

RIFLES: BOLT ACTION, CENTERFIRE

COLT "57" – .243 Win. or .30-06 cal., FN Mauser action, mfg. by Jefferson Mfg. Co. in N. Haven, CT during 1957, approx. 5,000 mfg. starting at ser. no. 1, checkered American Monte Carlo walnut stock, rear aperture and wraparound front sight, drilled and tapped for scope.

$695	$650	$600	$550	$500	$450	$400	

This model was also available in a deluxe version with deluxe hand checkered walnut stock - add 15%.

COLTSMAN STANDARD RIFLE – .223 Rem., .243 Win., .264 Win. Mag., .30-06, .300 Win. Mag., or .308 Win. cal., mfg. by Kodiak, Mauser or Sako action, 22 or 24 (.300 Win. Mag.) in. barrel, 5 or 6 shot mag. Approx. 10,000 (both models) mfg. 1958-66.

$495	$450	$425	$400	$350	$325	$300	

COLTSMAN CUSTOM RIFLE – deluxe variation including deluxe walnut stock with skipline checkering and rosewood forearm cap.

$695	$650	$600	$550	$500	$450	$400	

COLT SAUER RIFLE (STANDARD ACTION) – .25-06 Rem., .270 Win., or .30-06 cal., non-rotating bolt action, manufactured in Germany by J. P. Sauer & Sohn, 24 in. barrel, 4 shot detachable mag., no sights, checkered walnut stock with rosewood forend tip and pistol grip cap, recoil pad. Mfg. 1974-1985.

$2,175	$1,875	$1,650	$1,475	$1,325	$1,075	$850	*$1,257*

Add 20% for .25-06 Rem. cal.

COLT SAUER SHORT ACTION – similar to the standard except in .22-250 Rem., .243 Win., or .308 Win. cal. Mfg. 1976-1985.

$2,750	$2,375	$1,975	$1,750	$1,425	$1,150	$875	*$1,257*

Add 30% for .22-250 Rem. or .308 Win. cal. in high condition.

COLT SAUER MAGNUM – similar to the standard except in 7mm Rem. Mag., .300 Win. Mag., or .300 Weatherby Mag. cal. Mfg. 1974-1985.

$2,695	$2,350	$2,025	$1,835	$1,475	$1,225	$950	*$1,300*

Subtract 20% for 7mm Rem. Mag. cal.

COLT SAUER GRADE III – similar to Grade IV, except scroll engraved nitride/nickel receiver w/o game scenes, "Colt" stamped on flat knob or standard round knob.

$4,995	$4,375	$3,750	$3,395	$2,750	$2,250	$1,750	

Add 10% for Magnum cals.

COLT SAUER GRADE IV – similar to the Magnum except has silver receiver, each caliber featured a different engraved animal.

$5,995	$5,250	$4,495	$4,075	$3,295	$2,700	$2,100	

Add 10% for Magnum cals.

COLT SAUER GRAND ALASKAN – heavier version in .375 H&H cal., adj. sights. Mfg. 1978-1985.

$2,895	$2,535	$2,175	$1,975	$1,595	$1,300	$1,050	

COLT SAUER GRAND AFRICAN – .458 Win. Mag. cal., 4 round capacity, 9 lb. 12 oz. Mfg. 1974-1985.

$2,895	$2,535	$2,175	$1,975	$1,595	$1,300	$1,050	*$1,400*

COLT LIGHT RIFLE – .243 Win., .260 Rem., .270 Win., .280 Rem., .25-06 Rem., .30-06, .308 Win., 7x57mm, .300 Win. Mag., 7mm-08 Rem., or 7mm Rem. Mag. cal., short or long action, matte black synthetic stock, matte metal finish, adj. trigger, 3-position side-swing safety, approx. 5.4 lbs. in short action. Mfg. by Saco Defense in the U.S. 2000-disc.

$675	$550	$500	$450	$400	$350	$295	*$779*

GRADING - PPGS™	100%	98%	95%	90%	80%	70%	60%	LAST MSR

COLT PRECISION RIFLE (M2012SA308) – .308 Win. cal., tactical configuration featuring 22 in. heavy match grade spiral fluted stainless steel barrel with muzzle brake, skeletonized adj. forged aluminum stock, pistol grip, vent. aluminum handguard with 2/3 length Picatinny rail, 5 or 10 shot mag., black finish, Timney single stage adj. trigger, 13.2 lbs. Mfg. by Cooper Firearms of Montana 2013-2015.

$3,300	$2,950	$2,600	$2,300	$2,000	$1,850	$1,625	*$3,799*

COLT M2012LT260G/308G – .260 Rem. or .308 Win. cal., 22 in. 6-groove button rifled medium heavy match grade chrome moly fluted barrel with Cooper Firearms muzzle brake, 5 or 10 shot mag., Timney adj. single stage trigger, custom grey laminated wood stock, 8 1/2 lbs. Mfg. 2013-2015.

$2,375	$2,075	$1,775	$1,625	$1,300	$1,075	$825	*$2,799*

COLT M2012MT308T – .308 Win. cal., 22 in. 6-groove button rifled heavy match grade stainless fluted barrel with Cooper Firearms muzzle brake, 5 or 10 shot mag., Timney adj. single stage trigger, custom Manners composite stock, Coyote Tan finish, 10 1/4 lbs. Mfg. mid-2013-2015.

$2,775	$2,400	$2,050	$1,850	$1,500	$1,225	$950	*$3,199*

RIFLES: BOLT/SEMI-AUTO ACTION, RIMFIRE

COLTEER 1-22 – .22 LR or .22 WMR cal., single shot bolt action, 20, 22, or 24 (.22 WMR only, w/o sights) in. round barrel, adj. rear sight (20 or 22 in. barrel), plain walnut stock. Approx. 50,000 mfg. 1957-66.

$400	$325	$265	$225	$200	$175	$150

Add 10% for .22 WMR cal.

STAGECOACH – .22 LR cal., semi-auto, 16 1/2 in. barrel, 13 shot mag., deluxe walnut stock, saddle ring w/leather thong, roll-engraved hold-up scene. Over 25,000 mfg. 1965-mid 1970s.

$400	$325	$265	$225	$200	$175	$150

Subtract 5% if wood and finish are scratched in front of the barrel/forearm band.
Subtract 5-10% if w/o the front sight hood.
Subtract 10% if gold color is missing in stagecoach scene.

This model has a soft aluminum alloy painted receiver which was very easily scratched. It is quite common to find these guns in 80 to 85% condition with very little market interest. It is becoming common place to find these guns with the receiver repainted. There is a limited market interest in guns that are 98% condition and better. On the models that have the band around the barrel and forearm, it is common to see the wood and finish scratched where the band has been slid forward.

COLTEER – .22 LR cal., similar to Stagecoach, except 19 3/8 in. barrel, 15 shot mag., no engraving and plain walnut stock. Over 25,000 mfg. 1965-mid 1970s.

$375	$325	$265	$225	$200	$175	$150

Subtract 5% if wood and finish are scratched in front of the barrel/forearm band.
Subtract 5-10% if w/o the front sight hood.

This model has a soft aluminum alloy painted receiver which was very easily scratched. It is quite common to find these guns in 80 to 85% condition with very little market interest. It is becoming common place to find these guns with the receiver repainted. There is a limited market interest in guns that are 98% condition and better. On the models that have the band around the barrel and forearm, it is common to see the wood and finish scratched where the band has been slid forward.

COURIER – similar to Colteer semi-auto, except pistol-grip stock and enlarged forearm. Mfg. 1970-mid-1970s.

$400	$325	$265	$225	$200	$175	$150

Subtract 5% if wood and finish are scratched in front of the barrel/forearm band.
Subtract 5-10% if w/o the front sight hood.

This model has a soft aluminum alloy painted receiver which was very easily scratched. It is quite common to find these guns in 80 to 85% condition with very little market interest. It is becoming common place to find these guns with the receiver repainted. There is a limited market interest in guns that are 98% condition and better. On the models that have the band around the barrel and forearm, it is common to see the wood and finish scratched where the band has been slid forward.

RIFLES: SINGLE SHOT, CENTERFIRE

COLT-SHARPS STANDARD OR DELUXE RIFLE – .17 Rem., .222 Rem. (Mfg. 1), .22-250 Rem. (Mfg. 106), .243 Win. (Mfg. 103), .25-06 Rem. (Mfg. 79), .270 Win. (Mfg. 1), 7mm Rem. Mag. (Mfg. 86), .30-06 (Mfg. 120), .375 H&H (Mfg. 2), .50-70 Govt. (two known) cal., 26 or 28 in. heavy (rare) barrel, Sharps falling block action with Timken roller bearings, high-gloss bluing, Canjar set trigger, deluxe Fleur-De-Lis checkered Monte Carlo walnut stock and forearm with cheekpiece and choice of beavertail or standard forearm, engraved cartridge trap door (Deluxe Models) in stock and trigger guard, wood case

GRADING - PPGS™	100%	98%	95%	90%	80%	70%	60%	LAST MSR

with accessories, all guns were shipped with a Leupold VARI-X II 3-9x40mm scope with a special scope mount, supplied with either a full length wood and leather case (most desirable) or a green fiberglass case. Approx. 502 were mfg. 1970-1977 serial numbered CS000-CS502.

$6,250	$5,500	$5,000	$4,500	$3,750	$3,250	$2,750	

Add 10% for 28 in. heavy barrel.

Subtract 10% for missing case and accessories or Leupold scope and mount.

Subtract 10% for Standard model (approx. 50 mfg. without Monte Carlo stock, cartridge trap, engraving, or case) - serial range starts at CS2000.

Above values are for the standard calibers .22-250 Rem., .243 Win., .25-06 Rem., .30-06, or 7mm Rem. Mag. with case, accessories, and Leupold scope and mount.

DRILLINGS

COLT SAUER DRILLING – 12 ga./.30-06, 16 ga./.30-06 (rare), or .243 Win. cal., 25 in. barrels, engraved receiver, 8 lbs. Disc. 1985.

$4,850	$4,300	$3,600	$3,100	$2,675	$2,200	$1,800	*$4,228*

RIFLES: SEMI-AUTO, CENTERFIRE, AR-15 & VARIATIONS

The AR-15 rifle and variations are the civilian versions of the U.S. armed forces M-16 model, which was initially ordered by the U.S. Army in 1963. Colt's obtained the exclusive manufacturing and marketing rights to the AR-15 from the ArmaLite division of the Fairchild Engine and Airplane Corporation in 1961.

Factory Colt AR-15 receivers are stamped with the model names only (Sporter II, Government Model, Colt Carbine, Sporter Match H-Bar, Match Target), but are not stamped with the model numbers (R6500, R6550, R6521, MT6430, CR6724). Because of this, if an AR-15 rifle/carbine does not have its original box, the only way to determine whether the gun is pre-ban or not is to look at the serial number and see if the configuration matches the features listed below within the two pre-ban subcategories.

AR-15 production included transition models, which were made up of obsolete and old stock parts. These transition models include: blue label box models having large front takedown pins, no internal sear block, 20 in. barrel models having bayonet lugs, misstamped nomenclature on receivers, or green label bolt assemblies.

Rifling twists on the Colt AR-15 have changed throughout the years, and barrel twists are stamped at the end of the barrel on top. They started with a 1:12 in. twist, changed to a 1:7 in. twist (to match with the new, longer .223 Rem./5.56mm SS109-type bullet), and finally changed to a 1:9 in. twist in combination with 1:7 in. twist models as a compromise for bullets in the 50-68 grain range. Current mfg. AR-15s/Match Targets have rifling twists/turns incorporated into the model descriptions.

Colt's never sold pre-ban lower receivers individually. It only sold completely assembled rifles.

A Colt letter of provenance for the following AR-15 models is $100 per gun.

AR-15, Pre-Ban, 1963-1989 Mfg. w/Green Label Box

Common features of 1963-1989 mfg. AR-15s are bayonet lug, flash hider, large front takedown pin, no internal sear block, and no reinforcement around the magazine release button.

AR-15 boxes during this period of mfg. had a green label with serial number affixed on a white sticker. Box is taped in two places with brown masking tape. NIB consists of the rifle with barrel stick down the barrel, plastic muzzle cap on flash hider, factory tag hanging from front sight post, rifle in plastic bag with ser. no. on white sticker attached to bag, cardboard insert, accessory bag with two 20 round mags., manual, sling, and cleaning brushes. Cleaning rods are in separate bag.

Pre-ban parts rifles are rifles which are not assembled in their proper factory configuration. Counterfeit pre-ban rifles are rifles using post-ban receivers and assembled into a pre-ban configuration (it is a felony to assemble or alter a post-ban rifle into a pre-ban configuration).

Add $100 for NIB condition.

Add $300 for early green label box models with reinforced lower receiver.

SP-1 (R6000) – .223 Rem. cal., GIO, original Colt tactical configuration without forward bolt assist, 20 in. barrel with 1:12 in. twist, identifiable by the triangular shaped handguards/forearm, no case deflector, A1 sights, finishes included parkerizing and electroless nickel, approx. 6 3/4 lbs. Ser. no. range SP0001-SP16000 through 1976. Mfg. 1963-1984.

$2,450	$2,150	$1,850	$1,650	$1,500	$1,350	$1,200	

Add 40%-60% for mint original models with early two and three digit serial numbers.

Pre-ban serialization is ser. no. SP360,200 and lower.

Early SP-1s were packaged differently than later standard green box label guns.

GRADING - PPGS™	100%	98%	95%	90%	80%	70%	60%	LAST MSR

* ***SP-1 Carbine (R6001)*** – .223 Rem. cal., similar to SP-1, except has 16 in. barrel, ribbed handguards, collapsible buttstock, high gloss finish.

	$3,000	$2,600	$2,250	$1,950	$1,800	$1,500	$1,350	

Mint original condition models with early two and three digit serial numbers are selling in the $3,500-$5,000 range.

Pre-ban serialization is ser. no. SP360200 and lower.

Early SP-1s were packaged differently than later standard green box label guns.

SP-2 (R6400) – .223 Rem. cal., GIO, original Colt tactical upper receiver configuration without forward bolt assist or case deflector, slabside lower receiver, 20 in. A2 profile barrel with 1:7 in. twist, birdcage style flash hider, round A2 style handguards/forearm, A1 sights, finishes included anodizing and parkerizing, approx. 6 3/4 lbs. Mfg. circa 1984.

More research is pending to determine accurate values on this model.

SPORTER II (R6500) – .223 Rem. cal., GIO, various configurations, receiver stamped "Sporter II", 20 in. barrel, 1:7 twist, A1 sights and forward assist, disc.

	$1,850	$1,650	$1,450	$1,250	$1,100	$950	$850	

Serial numbers SP360200 and below are pre-ban.

* ***Sporter II Carbine (R6420)*** – .223 Rem. cal., similar to Sporter II, except has 16 in. barrel, A1 sights and collapsible buttstock.

	$2,500	$2,200	$1,900	$1,750	$1,600	$1,400	$1,250	

Serial numbers SP360200 and below are pre-ban.

GOVERNMENT MODEL (R6550) – .223 Rem. cal., GIO, receiver is stamped Government Model, 20 in. barrel with 1:7 in. twist and bayonet lug, A2 sights, forward assist and brass deflector, very desirable because this model has the closest configurations to what the U.S. military is currently using.

	$2,250	$1,950	$1,800	$1,650	$1,400	$1,200	$950	

In 1987, Colt replaced the AR-15A2 Sporter II Rifle with the AR-15A2 Govt. Model. This new model has the 800 meter rear sighting system housed in the receiver's carrying handle (similar to the M-16 A2).

Serial numbers GS008000 and below with GS prefix are pre-ban.

* ***Government Model (6550K)*** – .223 Rem. cal., similar to R6550, except does not have bayonet lug, originally supplied with .22 L.R. cal. conversion kit.

	$2,100	$1,900	$1,750	$1,600	$1,450	$1,250	$1,000	

Subtract $300 w/o conversion kit.

Serial numbers GS008000 and below with GS prefix are pre-ban.

* ***Government Model (R6550CC)*** – .223 Rem. cal., similar to R6550, except has Z-Cote tiger striped camo finish, very scarce (watch for cheap imitation paint jobs).

	$3,500	$3,350	$3,100	$2,800	$2,600	$2,400	$2,000	

Serial numbers GS008000 and below with GS prefix are pre-ban.

H-BAR MODEL (R6600) – GIO, HBAR model with 20 in. heavy barrel, 1:7 twist, forward assist, A2 sights, brass deflector, 8 lbs. New 1986.

	$2,100	$1,900	$1,750	$1,600	$1,450	$1,250	$1,000	

Serial numbers SP360200 and below are pre-ban.

* ***H-Bar (R6600K)*** – similar to R6600, except has no bayonet lug, supplied with .22 LR cal. conversion kit.

	$1,850	$1,650	$1,450	$1,250	$1,100	$950	$850	

Subtract $300 if w/o conversion kit.

Serial numbers SP360200 and below are pre-ban.

* ***Delta H-Bar (R6600DH)*** – similar to R6600, except has 3-9x rubber armored scope, removable cheekpiece, adj. scope mount, and black leather sling, test range selected for its accuracy, aluminum transport case. Mfg. 1987-1991.

	$2,500	$2,200	$1,900	$1,750	$1,600	$1,400	$1,250	*$1,460*

Serial numbers SP360200 and below are pre-ban.

GRADING - PPGS™	100%	98%	95%	90%	80%	70%	60%	LAST MSR

AR-15, Pre-Ban,1989-Sept. 11,1994 Mfg. w/Blue Label Box

Common features of 1989-1994 AR-15 production include a small front takedown pin, internal sear block, reinforcement around the mag. release button, flash hider, no bayonet lug on 20 in. models, A2 sights, brass deflector, and forward bolt assist. Models R6430 and 6450 do not have A2 sights, brass deflector, or forward bolt assist.

Blue label boxed AR-15s were mfg. between 1989-Sept. 11, 1994. Please refer to box description under Pre-1989 AR-15 mfg.

Pre-ban parts rifles are rifles which are not assembled in their proper factory configuration. Counterfeit pre-ban rifles are rifles using post-ban receivers and assembled into a pre-ban configuration.

Add $100 for NIB condition.

AR-15A3 TACTICAL CARBINE (R-6721) – .223 Rem. cal., GIO, M4 flat-top with 16 in. heavy barrel, 1:9 twist, A2 sights, pre-ban configuration with flash hider, bayonet lug, and 4-position, collapsible stock, removable carry handle, 134 were sold commercially in the U.S., most collectible AR-15. Mfg. 1994 only.

	100%	98%	95%	90%	80%	70%	60%	LAST MSR
S/N 134 and lower	$3,000	$2,500	$2,275	$2,050	$1,900	$1,775	$1,600	
S/N 135 and higher	$2,000	$1,850	$1,700	$1,450	$1,225	$1,050	$900	

On the R-6721, serial numbers BD000134 and below are pre-ban.

Please note the serial number cutoff on this model, as Colt shipped out a lot of unstamped post-ban law enforcement only "LEO" rifles before finally stamping them as a restricted rifle.

GOVERNMENT CARBINE (R6520) – .223 Rem. cal., GIO, receiver is stamped Government Carbine, two-position collapsible buttstock, 800 meter adj. rear sight, 16 in. barrel with bayonet lug, 1:7 twist, shortened forearm, 5 lbs. 13 oz. Mfg. 1988-94.

100%	98%	95%	90%	80%	70%	60%	LAST MSR
$2,275	$2,125	$2,000	$1,850	$1,650	$1,500	$1,250	*$880*

Add $200 for green label box.

On the R6520, serial numbers GC018500 and below are pre-ban.

Please note the serial number cutoff on this model, as Colt shipped out a lot of unstamped post-ban law enforcement only "LEO" rifles before finally stamping them as a restricted rifle.

This model was manufactured in both green and blue label configurations.

COLT CARBINE (R6521) – receiver is stamped Colt Carbine, similar to R6520, except has no bayonet lug, 16 in. barrel, 1:7 twist. Disc. 1988.

100%	98%	95%	90%	80%	70%	60%	LAST MSR
$2,275	$2,125	$2,000	$1,850	$1,650	$1,500	$1,250	*$770*

Serial numbers CC001616 and below are pre-ban.

SPORTER LIGHTWEIGHT (R6530) – .223 Rem. cal., GIO, receiver is stamped Sporter Lightweight, 16 in. barrel, 1:7 twist, similar to R6520, except does not have bayonet lug or collapsible stock.

100%	98%	95%	90%	80%	70%	60%	LAST MSR
$2,000	$1,850	$1,700	$1,450	$1,225	$1,050	$900	*$740*

Serial numbers SI027246 and below are pre-ban.

9MM CARBINE (R6430) – 9mm Para. cal., similar to R6450 Carbine, except does not have bayonet lug or collapsible stock. Mfg. 1992-1994.

100%	98%	95%	90%	80%	70%	60%	LAST MSR
$2,150	$2,050	$1,950	$1,800	$1,600	$1,450	$1,150	

Serial numbers NL004800 are pre-ban.

9MM CARBINE (R6450) – 9mm Para. cal., GIO, carbine model with 16 in. barrel, 1:10 twist, bayonet lug, w/o forward bolt assist or brass deflector, two-position collapsible stock, 20 shot mag., 6 lbs. 5 oz.

100%	98%	95%	90%	80%	70%	60%	LAST MSR
$2,250	$2,100	$2,000	$1,800	$1,600	$1,500	$1,250	*$696*

On the R6450, serial numbers TA010100 are pre-ban.

Please note the serial number cutoff on this model, as Colt shipped out a lot of unstamped post-ban law enforcement only "LEO" rifles before finally stamping them as a restricted rifle.

This model was manufactured with either a green or blue label.

7.62X39MM CARBINE (R6830) – 7.62x39mm cal., GIO, 16 in. barrel w/o bayonet lug, 1:12 twist, fixed buttstock. Mfg. 1992-1994.

100%	98%	95%	90%	80%	70%	60%	LAST MSR
$1,850	$1,700	$1,550	$1,400	$1,200	$1,025	$875	

Serial numbers LH011326 are pre-ban.

GRADING - PPGS™	100%	98%	95%	90%	80%	70%	60%	LAST MSR

TARGET COMPETITION H-BAR RIFLE (R6700) – .223 Rem. cal., GIO, flat-top upper receiver for scope mounting, 20 in. H-Bar barrel (1:9 in. twist), quick detachable carry handle with a 600-meter rear sighting system, dovetailed upper receiver grooved to accept Weaver style scope rings, 8 1/2 lbs.

	$1,850	$1,700	$1,550	$1,400	$1,200	$1,025	$875	

Serial numbers CH019500 and below are pre-ban.

COMPETITION H-BAR CUSTOM SHOP (R6701) – .223 Rem. cal., similar to the R6700, but with detachable scope mount, custom shop enhancements added to trigger and barrel, 2,000 mfg. from Colt Custom Shop.

	$1,950	$1,800	$1,650	$1,500	$1,350	$1,200	$1,000	

MATCH H-BAR (R6601) – .223 Rem. cal., GIO, heavy 20 in. HBAR barrel with 1:7 twist, fixed buttstock, 8 lbs.

	$1,850	$1,700	$1,550	$1,400	$1,200	$1,025	$875	

* ***Delta H-Bar (R6601DH)*** – similar to R6601, except has 3-9x rubber armored variable scope, removable cheekpiece, adj. scope mount, black leather sling, test range selected for its accuracy, aluminum transport case. Mfg. 1987-91.

	$2,500	$2,300	$2,150	$2,000	$1,800	$1,600	$1,450	*$1,460*

Serial numbers MH086020 and below are pre-ban.

SPORTER TARGET (R6551) – similar to R6601, except had 20 in. barrel with reduced diameter underneath handguard, 7 1/2 lbs.

	$1,850	$1,700	$1,550	$1,400	$1,200	$1,025	$875	

On the R6551, serial numbers ST038100 and below are pre-ban.

AR-15, Post-Ban, Mfg. Sept. 12, 1994-2019

During 2007, Colt released the M-5 Military Carbine and the LE 10-20, with 11 1/2, 14 1/2, or 16 in. barrel. These guns were only available for military and law enforcement.

During 2013, production began on a series of competition rifles released under the brand "Colt Competition" and manufactured under license by Bold Ideas, located in Breckenridge, TX. Every rifle/carbine comes with a 100 yard target.

State compliant variations are not listed in this text. Values are typically similar to the models from which they were derived.

In 2017, "Colt Competition" ceased production entirely.

Add $368 for Colt Scout C-More Sight (disc.).
Add $444 for Colt Tactical C-More Sight (disc.).

COMPETITION CRP-18 WITH GUNGODDESS TOUCH – .223 Rem. cal., GIO, 18 in. match grade stainless steel fluted barrel with triple port muzzle brake, 30 shot Magpul mag., enlarged trigger guard, Geissele two-stage match trigger, Magpul CTR 6-pos. adj. stock with locking adjustments, Magpul MOE grip, matched bolt and carrier with H-buffer, GunGoddess 15 in. free float handguard, one 2 in. accessory rail, Colt Competition charging handle with extended tactical latch, black finish, 7.22 lbs. Mfg. 2015-2019.

	$1,800	$1,600	$1,400	$1,200	$1,050	$850	$700	*$1,995*

Add $130 for Robin Egg Blue, Pink, Bright Purple, Snow White, Crimson, Zombie Green, Brushed Nickel, or Crushed Silver furniture.

COMPETITION PRO – .223/5.56 Wylde chamber, GIO, 18 in. match grade stainless steel fluted barrel, fully adj. gas block, triple chamber or SureFire muzzle brake, forged upper and lower receiver, flat-top with Picatinny rail, 30 shot mag., matte black finish, Geissele two-stage match trigger, Magpul adj. stock, grip, and forend, approx. 7 lbs. Mfg. 2013 only.

	$1,850	$1,600	$1,400	$1,250	$1,000	$850	$650	*$2,029*

EXPERT CRE-16 – 5.56 NATO cal., similar to Expert CRE-18, except has 16 in. barrel. Mfg. 2014-2015.

	$1,400	$1,200	$1,050	$950	$750	$650	$500	*$1,599*

EXPERT CRE-16T GEN2 – .223 Rem. cal., mid-length gas system, 16 in. stainless steel HBAR contour match grade barrel, steel muzzle brake, Magpul 30 shot PMAG, Magpul enlarged trigger guard, no sights, Hogue overmolded collapsible stock, Hogue rubber beavertail grip, low profile fixed gas block, extended charging handle, M-LOK 12 in. aluminum-alloy float tube handguard, matte black finish, 6.66 lbs. Mfg. 2019 only.

	$1,450	$1,250	$1,100	$975	$850	$675	$550	*$1,599*

EXPERT CRE-16T GEN3 PRECISION CARBINE – .223/5.56 Wylde chamber, fixed gas block, 16 in. stainless steel HBAR midweight barrel, 3-chamber muzzle brake, 30 shot mag., Hogue stock with buttpad, Hogue grip, 15 in. M-LOK float-tube handguard with sling swivel mount. Mfg. 2017-2019.

	$1,550	$1,350	$1,200	$1,050	$900	$725	$600	*$1,699*

GRADING - PPGS™	100%	98%	95%	90%	80%	70%	60%	LAST MSR

EXPERT CRE-18/CRE-18 RR – 5.56 NATO cal., GIO, low profile gas block, forged and precision fitted upper and lower receivers, matte black finish, 18 in. midweight match grade air gauged polish stainless steel barrel, 10 or 30 shot Magpul mag., competition nickel Teflon coated match target trigger, enlarged Magpul trigger guard, Magpul MOE four position adj. stock or CTR adj. stock (Model CRE-18 RR, new 2014), Expert Brake (CRE-18) or ProBrake (CRE-18 RR, mfg. 2014-2015), 15 in. vented modular float tube handguard, 5 1/2 in. top mounted Picatinny handguard rail with 11 slots, two 3 in. accessory rails with five slots each or quad rails (CRE-18 RR, disc. 2015), Hogue rubber finger groove grip, competition charging handle with extended tactical latch, matched bolt and bolt carrier with H-buffer, 13 slot Picatinny rail on flat-top upper receiver. Mfg. 2013-2019.

$1,450 $1,250 $1,100 $975 $850 $675 $550 *$1,599*

Add $100 for CRE-18 RR model with quad rails and ProBrake (mfg. 2014-2015).

EXPERT CRE-18T GEN2 - .223 Rem. cal., rifle length gas system, 18 in. stainless steel HBAR contour match grade barrel, steel muzzle brake, Magpul 30 shot PMAG, Magpul enlarged trigger guard, no sights, Hogue overmolded collapsible stock, Hogue rubber beavertail grip, low profile fixed gas block, extended charging handle, M-LOK 15 in. aluminum-alloy float tube handguard, matte black finish, 7 lbs. Mfg. 2019 only.

$1,450 $1,250 $1,100 $975 $850 $675 $550 *$1,599*

EXPERT CRE-18T GEN3 LONG RANGE RIFLE – .223/5.56 Wylde chamber, fixed gas block, 18 in. stainless steel HBAR midweight barrel, 3-chamber muzzle brake, 30 shot mag., Hogue stock with buttpad, Hogue grip, 15 in. M-LOK float-tube handguard with sling swivel mount. Mfg. 2017-2019.

$1,550 $1,350 $1,200 $1,050 $900 $725 $600 *$1,699*

MARKSMAN CRX-16/CRX-16E – .223 Rem. cal., GIO, low profile gas block, 16 in. midweight match grade manganese phosphate chrome moly steel barrel, Expert brake, 10 or 30 shot Magpul mag., competition match target nickel Teflon coated trigger, enlargd Magpul trigger guard, carbine style four position adj. buttstock or Magpul MOE fixed rifle stock (CRX-16E), checkered A2 style finger groove grip, forged and precision fitted upper and lower receivers, 12 in. vented modular float tube handguard, 5 1/2 in. top mounted Picatinny handguard rail with 11 slots, two 3 in. accessory rails with five slots each, matched bolt and bolt carrier with H-buffer, 13 slot Picatinny rail on flat-top upper receiver, matte black finish. Mfg. 2013-2015.

$1,250 $1,100 $950 $850 $700 $550 $450 *$1,399*

MARKSMAN CRX-16 GEN2 – 5.56 NATO cal., carbine length fixed gas system, blackened 16 in. HBAR contour barrel, triple chamber steel muzzle brake, Magpul 30 shot PMAG, Magpul enlarged trigger guard, no sights, Hogue overmolded collapsible stock, Hogue beavertail grip, extended charging handle, M-LOK 12 in. aluminum alloy float tube handguard, matte black finish, 6.65 lbs. Mfg. 2016-2019.

$1,100 $950 $825 $725 $625 $525 $425 *$1,199*

MARKSMAN CRX-16 GEN3 LIGHT CARBINE – 5.56 NATO cal., fixed gas block, 16 in. chrome moly, midweight barrel, 3-chamber muzzle brake, 30 shot mag., Hogue stock with buttpad, Hogue grip, 15 in. M-LOK float-tube handguard with sling swivel mount. Mfg. 2017-2019.

$1,100 $1,000 $875 $775 $675 $525 $425 *$1,249*

MARKSMAN CRZ-16 GEN2 – 5.56 NATO cal., low profile fixed gas block, blackened 16 in. HBAR contour barrel, twin chamber steel muzzle brake, Magpul 30 shot PMAG, Magpul enlarged trigger guard, no sights, M4 collapsible stock, A2 grip, extended charging handle, M-LOK 10 in. aluminum-alloy float tube handguard, matte black finish, 6 lbs. Mfg. 2016-2019.

$900 $800 $700 $600 $525 $425 $350 *$999*

PRO CRB-16 – .300 AAC Blackout or .300 Whisper (new 2014) cal., GIO, patented low profile adj. gas block, forged and precision fitted upper and lower receivers, matte black finish, 16 in. match grade air gauged stainless steel barrel with Colt competition triple port muzzle brake, 10 or 30 shot aluminum mag., Geissele two-stage match trigger, Magpul enlarged trigger guard, Magpul STR six position adj. stock with locking adjustments, Magpul MOE grip with extended backstrap, Hogue 12 in. multi-piece slotted free floated tubular handguard, Competition charging handle with extended tactical latch, matched bolt and bolt carrier with H-buffer, 13 slot Picatinny rail on flat-top upper receiver, 6.7 lbs. Mfg. 2013-2015.

$1,600 $1,400 $1,200 $1,100 $900 $700 $550 *$1,799*

PRO CRC-22 – 6.5 Creedmoor cal., 22 in. fluted stainless steel HBAR+ match barrel, ProBrake, 20 shot Magpul mag., PRS adj. stock, 3 rails, 15 in. float tube modular handguard. Mfg. 2014-2015.

$2,675 $2,350 $2,000 $1,800 $1,450 $1,200 $950 *$2,979*

PRO CRC-22 GEN2 – 6.5 Creedmoor cal., rifle length adj. gas system, 22 in. polished HBAR contour heavy fluted stainless steel barrel, triple chamber steel muzzle brake, Magpul 20 shot PMAG, enlarged integral trigger guard, no sights, Luth-AR stock, Ergo tactical beavertail grip, extended charging handle, M-LOK 15 in. aluminum alloy float tube handguard, matte black finish, 11.2 lbs. Mfg. 2016-2019.

$2,600 $2,300 $2,000 $1,750 $1,550 $1,250 $1,000 *$2,899*

GRADING - PPGS™	100%	98%	95%	90%	80%	70%	60%	LAST MSR

PRO CRG-20 – 6.5 Grendel cal., GIO, patented low profile adj. gas block, forged and precision fitted upper and lower receivers, matte black finish, 20 in. match grade air gauged chrome moly steel custom barrel with black Nitride finish, 10 or 25 shot aluminum mag., Colt competition match target trigger, nickel Teflon coated, 15 in. vented modular free floated tubular handguard, 10 in. top mounted Picatinny handguard rail with 23 slots and 2-3 accessory rails, oversized trigger guard, Magpul CTR 6-position adj. buttstock with locking adjustments, Magpul MOE pistol grip with extended backstrap, competition charging handle with extended tactical latch, matched bolt and bolt carrier with H-buffer, 13 slot Picatinny rail on flat-top upper receiver. Limited mfg. 2013 only.

$1,450	$1,300	$1,100	$1,000	$800	$650	$500	*$1,649*

PRO CRL-16 – .308 Win. cal., GIO, low profile adj. gas block, CNC machined and precision fitted upper and lower receivers, matte black finish, 16 in. tapered midweight match grade air gauged polished stainless steel custom barrel with triple port muzzle brake, 10 or 20 shot Magpul mag., integral enlarged trigger guard, Geissele two-stage SSA-E match trigger, Magpul CTR six position adj. stock with locking adjustments, Magpul MOE pistol grip with extended backstrap, 12 1/2 in. free floated tubular handguard, top mounted Picatinny handguard rail, two 3 in. accessory rails, competition charging handle with extended tactical latch, matched bolt and bolt carrier, 18 slot Picatinny rail on flat-top upper receiver. Mfg. 2013-2015.

$2,100	$1,850	$1,600	$1,450	$1,150	$950	$750	*$2,339*

PRO CRL-16 GEN2 – .308 Win. cal., adj. mid-length gas system, 16 in. polished HBAR contour heavy tapered stainless steel barrel, triple chamber vented muzzle brake, Magpul 20 shot PMAG, SST, enlarged integral trigger guard, no sights, Hogue overmolded 6-pos. collapsible stock, Hogue rubber beavertail grip, M-LOK 12 in. aluminum-alloy float tube handguard, extended charging handle, matte black finish, 8.67 lbs. Mfg. 2016-2019.

$2,050	$1,800	$1,550	$1,400	$1,150	$900	$700	

PRO CRL-20 – .308 Win. cal., adj. rifle length gas system, 20 in. match barrel with six flutes, 3-chamber muzzle brake, 20 shot Magpul mag., Geissele match trigger, Magpul PRS stock, 15 in. float tube handguard, 3 rails. Mfg. 2013-2015.

$2,675	$2,350	$2,000	$1,800	$1,450	$1,200	$950	*$2,979*

PRO CRL-20 GEN2 – .308 Win. cal., rifle length adj. gas system, 20 in. polished HBAR contour heavy fluted stainless steel barrel, triple chamber steel muzzle brake, Magpul 20 shot PMAG, enlarged trigger guard, no sights, Luth-AR stock, Ergo tactical beavertail grip, extended charging handle, M-LOK 15 in. aluminum alloy float tube handguard, matte black finish, 10.8 lbs. Mfg. 2016-2019.

$2,600	$2,300	$1,950	$1,750	$1,450	$1,150	$900	*$2,899*

PRO CRP-16 – 5.56 NATO cal., GIO, low profile adj. gas block, forged and precision fitted upper and lower receivers, matte black finish, 16 in. two-diameter heavy weight match grade air gauged polished stainless steel barrel, triple port muzzle brake, 10 or 30 shot Magpul mag., Geissele two-stage match trigger, Magpul enlarged trigger guard, Magpul CTR 6-position adj. stock with locking adjustments, Magpul MOE grip with extended backstrap, competition 12 in. vented modular float tube handguard, 5 1/2 in. top mounted Picatinny handguard rail with 11 slots, two 3 in. accessory rails, competition charging handle with extended tactical latch matched bolt and bolt carrier with H-buffer, 13 slot Picatinny rail on flat-top upper receiver. Mfg. 2013-2019.

$1,700	$1,500	$1,300	$1,150	$1000	$825	$650	*$1,899*

PRO CRP-18 THREE-GUN MATCH RIFLE – 5.56 NATO cal., similar to CRP-16, except has 18 in. custom fluted midweight barrel, 15 in. vented modular float tube handguard, and full length Picatinny top handguard rail with one 2 in. accessory rail. Mfg. 2013-2015.

$1,850	$1,600	$1,400	$1,250	$1,000	$850	$650	*$2,019*

PRO CRP-18LV (LIGHT VARMINT RIFLE) – .223 Rem. cal., adj. rifle length gas system, 18 in. stainless steel HBAR match barrel, 3-chamber muzzle brake, 30 shot Magpul mag., Geissele match trigger, Magpul CTR 6-pos. stock, 15 in. float tube modular handguard, 4 rails. Disc. 2015.

$1,700	$1,500	$1,300	$1,150	$950	$750	$600	*$1,899*

PRO CRP-18 GEN2 – .223 Rem. cal., rifle length adj. gas system, 18 in. polished HBAR stainless steel barrel, triple chamber muzzle brake, Magpul 30 shot PMAG, Magpul enlarged trigger guard, no sights, Luth-AR stock, Ergo tactical beavertail grip, extended charging handle, M-LOK 15 in. aluminum alloy float tube handguard, matte black finish, 7 lbs. Mfg. 2016-2019.

$1,800	$1,550	$1,350	$1,200	$1,000	$800	$650	*$1,999*

PRO CRP-18 GEN3 3-GUN COMPETITION – .223/5.56 Wylde chamber, fully adj. gas block, 18 in. stainless steel HBAR midweight barrel, 3-chamber fluted muzzle brake, 30 shot mag., Hogue stock with buttpad, Hogue grip, 15 in. M-LOK float-tube handguard with sling swivel mount. Mfg. 2017-2019.

$1,800	$1,600	$1,400	$1,200	$1,050	$850	$700	*$1,999*

GRADING - PPGS™	100%	98%	95%	90%	80%	70%	60%	LAST MSR

PRO CRP-20/20L/22RR – .223 Rem. cal., adj. rifle length gas system, 20 in. stainless steel extra heavy match barrel, 3-chamber vented muzzle brake, 30 shot Magpul mag., Geissele match trigger, Magpul CTR 6-position (CRP-20) or Magpul PRS adj. sniper (CRP-20L or CRP-20RR) stock, forged receivers, 15 in. float tube modular handguard with 3 rails, polished barrel (CRP-20 or CRP-20L) or blackened barrel (CRP-20RR) finish. Mfg. 2013-2015.

$1,700	$1,500	$1,300	$1,150	$950	$750	$600	*$1,899*

Add $100 for CRP-20L or CRP-20SS model.

PRO CRP-20VR (VARMINT RIFLE) – .223 Rem. cal., adj. rifle length gas system, 20 in. stainless steel HBAR match barrel, 3-chamber muzzle brake, 30 shot Magpul mag., Geissele match trigger, Magpul MOE fixed stock, forged receivers, 15 in. float tube modular handguard, 4 rails. Mfg. 2013-2019.

$1,700	$1,500	$1,300	$1,150	$1,000	$825	$650	*$1,899*

SPORTING RIFLE CSR-1516/CSR-1518 – .223 Rem. or 5.56 NATO cal., GIO, 16 (CSR-1516) or 18 (CSR-18) in. midweight match grade chrome moly black manganese phosphate threaded steel barrel with standard flash suppressor, 10 or 30 shot mag., nickel Teflon coated match target trigger, adj. 6-position carbine (CSR-16) or rifle stock with wide cheekpiece (CSR-18), rubber over-molded finger groove grip with integral beavertail, solid steel machined low profile gas block, forged alloy upper and lower receivers, 12 in. float tube handguard, standard charging handle, bolt, and bolt carrier, top mounted seven slot accessory rail, matte black finish. Mfg. 2013-2015.

$900	$800	$700	$600	$500	$400	$325	*$990*

Add $59 for CSR-18.

TACTICAL PATROL CARBINE CRX-16 RR – 5.56 NATO cal., low pro gas system, 16 in. chrome moly M4 contour barrel, ProBrake, quad rails, CTR stock, 6 lb. trigger, 30 shot mag. Mfg. 2014-2015.

$1,250	$1,100	$950	$850	$700	$550	$450	*$1,379*

COLT ACCURIZED RIFLE (CR6720/CR6724) – .223 Rem. cal., GIO, 20 (CR6720) or 24 (CR6724, disc. 2012, reintroduced 2014) in. stainless match barrel, matte finish, accurized AR-15, 8 (disc. 1998) or 9 (new 1999) shot mag., 9.41 lbs. Mfg. 1997-2019.

$1,250	$1,100	$950	$850	$725	$600	$475	*$1,374*

MATCH TARGET COMPETITION H-BAR RIFLE (MT6700/MT6700C) – .223 Rem. cal., GIO, features flat-top upper receiver for scope mounting, 20 in. barrel (1:9 in. twist), quick detachable carry handle which incorporates a 600-meter rear sighting system, counterbored muzzle, dovetailed upper receiver is grooved to accept Weaver style scope rings, supplied with two 5 (disc.), 8 (disc.), or 9 (new 1999) shot mags., cleaning kit, and sling, matte black finish, 8 1/2 lbs. Mfg. 1992-2013.

$1,125	$1,000	$850	$750	$600	$500	$400	*$1,230*

Add $57 for compensator (MT6700C, mfg. 1999-disc).

MATCH TARGET COMPETITION H-BAR II (MT6731) – .223 Rem. cal., GIO, flat-top, 16.1 in. barrel (1:9 in.), 9 shot mag., matte finish, 7.1 lbs. Mfg. 1995-2012.

$1,050	$900	$800	$700	$600	$475	$375	*$1,173*

MATCH TARGET LIGHTWEIGHT (MT6430, MT6530, or MT6830) – .223 Rem. (MT6530, 1:7 in. twist), 7.62x39mm (MT6830, disc. 1996, 1:12 in. twist), or 9mm Para. (MT6430, disc. 1996, 1:10 in. twist) cal., GIO, features 16 in. barrel (non-threaded per C/B 1994), initially shorter stock and handguard, rear sight adjustable for windage and elevation, includes two detachable 5, 8, or 9 (new 1999) shot mags., approx. 7 lbs. Mfg. 1991-2002.

$1,000	$850	$750	$700	$550	$450	$350	*$1,111*

Add $200 for .22 LR conversion kit (disc. 1994).

MATCH TARGET M4 CARBINE (MT6400/MT6400R) – .223 Rem. cal., GIO, similar to current U.S. armed forces M4 model, except semi-auto, 9 or 10 shot mag., 16.1 in. barrel, 1:7 in. twist, matte black finish, fixed tube buttstock, A3 detachable carrying handle, 7.3 lbs. Mfg. 2002-2013.

$1,100	$950	$800	$750	$600	$500	$375	*$1,211*

Add $341 for quad accessory rail (MT6400R).

MATCH TARGET 6400001 – 5.56 NATO cal., GIO, 16.1 in. M4 barrel with flash suppressor, 10 shot mag., flat-top receiver, fixed tube stock, Magpul Gen. II rear backup sight, two-piece ribbed handguard with post front sight, black finish, 7 lbs. Mfg. 2013 only.

$1,325	$1,150	$1,000	$900	$750	$600	$475	*$1,461*

MATCH TARGET 6400R001 – 5.56 NATO cal., 16.1 in. M4 barrel with flash suppressor, 10 shot mag., flat-top receiver with Picatinny rail integrated with quad rail handguard, Magpul Gen. II rear sight and flip-up adj. post front sight, black finish, 7.2 lbs. Mfg. 2013 only.

$1,650	$1,450	$1,250	$1,100	$900	$750	$600	*$1,825*

GRADING - PPGS™	100%	98%	95%	90%	80%	70%	60%	LAST MSR

MATCH TARGET H-BAR RIFLE (MT6601/MT6601C) - .223 Rem. cal., GI, heavy 20 in. HBAR barrel, 1:7 in. twist, A2 sights, 8 lbs. Mfg. 1986-2010.

$1,100 $950 $800 $750 $600 $500 $375 *$1,218*

Add $200 for .22 LR conversion kit (mfg. 1990-94). Add $1 for compensator (MT6601C, new 1999).

TACTICAL ELITE MODEL (TE6700) - .223 Rem. cal., GIO, 20 in. heavy barrel, 1:8 in. twist, Hogue finger groove pistol grip, Choate buttstock, fine tuned for accuracy, scope and mount included, approx. 1,000 rifles made by the Custom Shop circa 1996-97.

$2,450 $2,150 $1,850 $1,650 $1,350 $1,100 $850

TARGET GOVT. MODEL RIFLE (MT6551) - .223 Rem. cal., GIO, semi-auto version of the M16 rifle with forward bolt assist, 20 in. barrel (1:7 in.), straight line black nylon stock, aperture rear and post front sight, 5, 8, or 9 (new 1999) shot mags., 7 1/2 lbs. Disc. 2002.

$1,050 $900 $800 $700 $600 $475 $375 *$1,144*

Add $200 for .22 LR conversion kit (mfg. 1990-94).

SPORTER CARBINE (SP6920) - .223 Rem. cal., GIO, has M-4 features including flat-top receiver with A3 removable carry handle, 16.1 in. barrel with flash hider, 4-position collapsible buttstock, ribbed oval handguard, matte black finish, 5.95 lbs. Mfg. 2011 only.

$1,050 $900 $800 $700 $600 $475 $375 *$1,155*

Add 15% for the legal LE6920 variation that were sold to civilians.

The last 100 carbines of the Model LE6920 marked "Law Enforcement Carbine" and "Restricted" were sold as commercial guns to FFL dealers. Each of these has a factory letter stating as such.

COLT SPORTER (SP6940) - .223 Rem. cal., GIO, 16.1 in. fully floated barrel, 20 shot mag., flip-up adj. sights, 4-position collapsible stock, one-piece monolithic upper receiver, flat-top receiver with full-length quad Picatinny rails, matte black metal finish, 6.1 lbs. Mfg. 2011 only.

$1,350 $1,200 $1,000 $900 $750 $600 $475 *$1,500*

Add 15% for the legal LE6940 variation that were sold to civilians.

The last 100 carbines of the Model LE6940 marked "Law Enforcement Carbine" and "Restricted" were sold as commercial guns to FFL dealers. Each of these has a factory letter stating as such.

SP901 RIFLE - .308 Win. cal., GIO, 16 in. full floated heavy chrome-lined barrel, direct gas system, locking bolt, matte black finish, one-piece monolithic upper receiver with rail, upper receiver can be swapped out for .223, ambidextrous operating controls, flip-up post sights, bayonet lug and flash hider.

While advertised in 2011, this model never went into production (see LE901-16S).

COLT CARBINE AR6450 - 9mm Para. cal., GIO, 16.1 in. barrel with flash suppressor, A3 detachable carrying handle, 32 shot mag., grooved aluminum handguard, A2 post front sight, adj. Rogers Super-Stoc, matte finish, 6.35 lbs. Mfg. 2012 only.

$1,050 $900 $800 $700 $600 $475 $375 *$1,176*

COLT CARBINE AR6520TRI - 5.56 NATO cal., GIO, 16.1 in. barrel, matte black finish, 30 shot mag., adj. sights. Mfg. 2013 only.

$1,125 $1,000 $850 $750 $600 $500 $400 *$1,223*

LIGHTWEIGHT CARBINE (AR6720) - 5.56 NATO cal., GIO, 16.1 in. light barrel with flash hider and A2 front sight, 30 shot PMAG, ribbed aluminum forearm, A3 detachable carrying handle, MBUS Gen 2 rear sight, matte black finish, adj. stock, 6.2 lbs. Mfg. 2012-2018.

$900 $800 $700 $600 $500 $400 $325 *$999*

COLT CARBINE AR6720LECAR - 5.56 NATO cal., GIO, 16.1 in. barrel, Magpul Gen. II rear sight with adj. post front sight, 30 shot mag., matte black finish, 6 lbs. Mfg. 2013 only.

$1,325 $1,150 $1,000 $900 $750 $600 $475 *$1,468*

TACTICAL CARBINE (AR6721) - 5.56 NATO cal., GIO, 16.1 in. heavy barrel with flash hider and A2 front sight, 30 shot PMAG, MBUS Gen 2 rear sight, ribbed aluminum forearm, A3 detachable carrying handle, matte black finish, adj. stock, 7.3 lbs. Mfg. 2012 - 2017.

$825 $700 $600 $550 $450 $375 $300 *$929*

9MM CARBINE (AR6951) - 9mm Para. cal., GIO, 16.1 in. barrel with flash suppressor, 32 shot mag., folding rear sight, adj. Rogers Super-Stoc, flat-top receiver, A3 detachable carrying handle, grooved aluminum handguard, choice of matte black or Muddy Girl (AR6951MPMG, limited mfg. 2015 only) finish, 6.4 lbs. Mfg. 2012-2018.

$975 $850 $750 $650 $550 $450 $350

Last MSR for Muddy Girl finish was $1,567 in 2015.
Last MSR in 2018 was $1,099.

Add $319 for Muddy Girl camo finish (limited mfg. 2015 only).

GRADING - PPGS™	100%	98%	95%	90%	80%	70%	60%	LAST MSR

AR15 A4 RIFLE – 5.56 NATO cal., GIO, 20 in. barrel with flash suppressor, 30 shot mag., flat-top receiver with removable carry handle, A2 style buttstock and front sight, ribbed handguard, black finish, 7.7 lbs. Mfg. 2013-2019.

	$975	$875	$775	$675	$575	$475	$375	*$1,099*

AR15 A4MP-FDE – 5.56 NATO cal., GIO, 20 in. barrel with flash suppressor, FDE furniture, 30 shot mag., 2/3 quad rail with cover, A2 front sight with Magpul Gen. II rear sight, fixed stock, matte black barrel, matte black or FDE (new 2014) receiver finish, 7 1/2 lbs. Mfg. 2013-2014.

	$1,175	$1,050	$900	$800	$650	$550	$400	*$1,304*

Add $35 for FDE receiver finish.

COLT CARBINE AR-6821/AR-6821MP-R – .300 AAC Blackout cal., AR-6821 is similar to AR-6720, AR-6821MP-R has Magpul furniture and accessory rail. Mfg. 2015 only.

	$1,050	$900	$800	$700	$600	$475	$375	*$1,155*

Add $113 for Magpul furniture and accessory rail.

COLT CARBINE CR6724001 – 5.56 NATO cal., GIO, 24 in. stainless barrel without sights, one-piece flat-top upper receiver with integrated 2/3 length quad Picatinny rail, fixed non-adj. stock, 10 shot mag., black finish, 8.8 lbs. Mfg. 2013-2015.

	$1,500	$1,350	$1,150	$1,050	$850	$700	$550	*$1,653*

AR-15 SCOPE (3X/4X) AND MOUNT – initially offered with 3x magnification scope, then switched to 4x. Disc.

	$395	$300	$240	$185	$160	$130	$115	*$344*

LE901-16S (SP901) – .308 Win. cal., GIO, 16.1 in. heavy full floated barrel with bayonet lug and flash hider, flat-top with Picatinny rail, one-piece upper receiver with BUIS, ambidextrous controls, flip-up adj. front sight post, flip-up adj. rear sight, 20 shot mag., fixed stock, matte black finish, 9.4 lbs. Mfg. 2012-2015.

	$2,350	$2,050	$1,750	$1,600	$1,300	$1,050	$800	*$2,544*

M.A.R.C.901 MONOLITHIC – .308 Win. cal., GIO, 16.1 or 18 (LE901-18SE, mfg. 2015 only) in. heavy full floated barrel with bayonet lug and flash hider, 20 shot mag., one-piece monolithic flat-top upper receiver with Picatinny rail, BUIS, ambidextrous controls, adj. VLTOR buttstock, matte black or FDE (LE901FDE-16SE) finish, 9.4 lbs. Mfg. 2015-17.

	$1,800	$1,550	$1,350	$1,200	$1,000	$800	$650	*$1,999*

Add $100 for FDE finish (model LE901FDE-16SE), disc. 2015.

M.A.R.C.901 CARBINE (AR901-16S) – .308 Win. cal., 16.1 in. heavy free floating barrel with muzzle brake, 20 shot mag., retractable B5 Bravo buttstock, flat-top receiver with full length Picatinny rail, vent tubular handguard with 3 Picatinny rails. Mfg. 2015 -2016.

	$1,250	$1,100	$950	$850	$700	$550	$450	*$1,399*

LE6900 – 5.56 NATO cal., GIO, 16.1 in. barrel, no sights, 30 shot mag., matte black finish, 6 lbs. Mfg. 2012-mid-2013.

	$800	$700	$600	$550	$450	$350	$275	*$899*

LE6920 M4 CARBINE – 5.56 NATO cal., GIO, 16.1 in. barrel with bayonet lug and flash hider, 30 shot mag., adj. front sight post, ribbed handguard, Magpul Gen2 backup rear sight, flat-top receiver with Picatinny rail, collapsible stock, matte black finish, 6.9 lbs. Mfg. 2012-2019.

	$975	$875	$775	$675	$575	$475	$375	*$1,099*

LE6920AE – 5.56 NATO cal., 16.1 in. barrel, ambidextrous mag. release, bolt catch and fire selector, 30 shot PMAG, MBUS rear Gen. 2 sights, collapsible stock, matte black finish, 6.38 lbs. Mfg. 2014-2016.

	$1,250	$1,100	$950	$850	$700	$550	$450	*$1,374*

LE6920-OEM1/OEM2 M4 – 5.56 NATO cal., 16.1 in. barrel with muzzle brake, includes pistol grip and rear buffer tube, flat-top receiver with Picatinny rail, no furniture, OEM1 (disc. 2016) includes A2 style front sight. Mfg. 2015-2018.

	$765	$650	$600	$500	$425	$350	$275	*$849*

LE6920 SOCOM – 5.56 NATO cal., GIO, 16.1 in. barrel with bayonet lug and flash hider, 30 shot mag., flat-top receiver with BUIS, Knights Armament rail system, adj. front sight post, flip-up adj. rear sight, non-adj. tube stock, matte black finish, 7.2 lbs. Mfg. 2012-2014.

	$1,450	$1,300	$1,100	$1,000	$800	$650	$500	*$1,602*

LE6920MP-R – 5.56 NATO cal., 16.1 in. barrel, 30 shot PMAG, MBUS rear Gen. 2 sight, Troy rail, Magpul MOE furniture, black finish, 7.11 lbs. Mfg. 2014-2015.

	$1,150	$1,000	$850	$800	$650	$500	$400	*$1,268*

GRADING - PPGS™	100%	98%	95%	90%	80%	70%	60%	LAST MSR

LE6920MP & VARIATIONS – 5.56 NATO cal., GIO, 16.1 in. barrel with bayonet lug and flash hider, 30 shot PMAG, adj. front sight post, MBUS Gen2 backup rear sight, Magpul MOE carbine collapsible stock with MOE handguard and pistol grip, flat-top receiver with Picatinny rail, MOE trigger guard, Magpul MOE furniture in black (LE6920MP-B), A-TACS Foliage/Green (LE6920MPFG, new 2013), Olive Drab (LE6920MP-OD), USA One Nation Hydro-dipped (LE6920MP-USA, new 2014), ATAC camo hydro-dipped (LE6920MPATAC, new 2014), or Steel Gray (LE6920MP-STG, new 2015), 6.9 lbs. Mfg. 2012-mid-2015.

$1,125 $1,000 $850 $750 $600 $500 $400 *$1,229*

Add $87 for USA One Nation Hydro-Dipped Magpul furniture (LE6920-USA, new 2014).
Add $166 for ATACS Foliage/Green finish (LE6920MPFG).
Add $247 for ATAC camo Hydro-Dipped Magpul furniture (LE6920MPATAC, new 2014).

* ***LE6920MPG*** – 5.56 NATO cal., similar to LE6920MP, except features OD Green upper and lower receivers, OD Green Magpul furniture (LE6920MPG-OD) or black Magpul furniture (LE6920MPG-B, new 2014), vertical grip. Mfg. 2012-mid-2015.

$1,225 $1,050 $900 $850 $700 $550 $425 *$1,361*

* ***LE6920MPFDE*** – 5.56 NATO cal., similar to LE6920MP, except features FDE Magpul MOE furniture with vertical grip, FDE finish. Mfg. 2012-mid-2015.

$1,225 $1,050 $900 $850 $700 $550 $425 *$1,361*

* ***LE6920MPFDE-R*** – 5.56 NATO cal., similar to LE6920MP, except features FDE coated upper and lower receivers, FDE Troy Rail, FDE Magpul furniture. Mfg. 2014-mid-2015.

$1,400 $1,200 $1,050 $950 $750 $650 $500 *$1,572*

LE6920MPS-B/FDE – 5.56 NATO cal., 16.1 in. barrel, 30 shot round PMAG, MBUS Gen 2 rear sight, Magpul MOE SL carbine vertical pistol grip stock, Magpul MOE SL handguard, black or FDE (disc. 2018) furniture. Mfg. 2019 only.

$1,100 $950 $825 $725 $625 $525 $425 *$1,199*

LE6920-R TROOPER – 5.56 NATO cal., GIO, 16.1 in. barrel, 30 shot mag., single stage trigger, milled aluminum receiver, full-length top Picatinny rail, anodized black finish, 6 1/2 lbs. Mfg. 2018 only.

$925 $800 $700 $650 $500 $425 $325 *$1,049*

LE6940 M4 MONOLITHIC – 5.56 NATO cal., GIO, 16.1 in. full floated barrel with bayonet lug and flash hider, 1-piece upper receiver, 30 shot mag., flip-up adj. front sight post, Magpul Gen2 backup rear sight, collapsible stock, matte black finish, 6.9 lbs. Mfg. 2012-2019.

$1,250 $1,100 $975 $850 $750 $600 $475 *$1,399*

LE6940P – 5.56 NATO cal., GPO, 16.1 in. full floated barrel with bayonet lug and flash hider, one-piece upper receiver, 30 shot mag., flip-up adj. front sight post, Magpul Gen2 backup rear sight, collapsible stock, matte black finish, 6.9 lbs. Mfg. 2012-mid-2015.

$1,950 $1,700 $1,450 $1,300 $1,100 $900 $700 *$2,105*

* ***LE6940MPFG*** – 5.56 NATO cal., similar to LE6940P, except features A-TACS Forest Green Camo. Mfg. 2012-2013.

$1,250 $1,100 $950 $850 $700 $550 $450 *$1,395*

LE6940AE-3G – 5.56 NATO cal., 16.1 in. barrel, 30 shot PMAG, Colt articulating piston system, lower receiver features ambidextrous operating controls and 3 operating controls on both sides, monolithic upper is fully modular with smooth handguard allowing for different rail locations, A2 grip, M4 buttstock, MBUS rear Gen. 2 sight, black furniture, 7.2 lbs. Mfg. 2014-2015.

$1,750 $1,550 $1,300 $1,200 $950 $800 $600 *$1,945*

LE6960-CCU (COMBAT UNIT CARBINE) – 5.56 NATO cal., GIO, 16 in. chrome-lined barrel, 30 shot mag., SST, optic ready, Magpul MOE SL buttstock, Magpul MOE SL pistol grip, ambidextrous safety, aluminum receiver, mid-length gas system, hardcoat anodized black finish, 6.47 lbs. Mfg. 2016-2017.

$1,150 $1,000 $850 $800 $650 $500 $400 *$1,299*

LT6720-R – 5.56 NATO cal., 16.1 in. barrel, 30 shot PMAG, MBUS front and rear Gen 2 sights, Troy rail, Magpul ACS telescoping stock, black Magpul furniture, matte black finish, 6.48 lbs. Mfg. 2014-2016.

$1,175 $1,050 $900 $800 $650 $550 $400 *$1,321*

* ***LT6720MPMG*** – 5.56 NATO cal., 16.1 in. light contour barrel with birdcage flash hider, 30 shot mag., Magpul MBUS sights, Magpul ACS Muddy Girl camo telescoping stock, trigger guard, and pistol grip, Muddy Girl camo finish, 6.2 lbs. Mfg. 2014-mid-2015.

$1,300 $1,150 $1,000 $900 $700 $600 $450 *$1,448*

EXPANSE M4 – 5.56 NATO cal., GIO, 16.1 in. barrel, 30 shot round aluminum mag., adj. front sight post, flat-top Picatinny rail, matte black finish, 6.44 lbs. Mfg. 2016-2017.

$700 $650 $550 $500 $400 $325 $275 *$799*

GRADING - PPGS™	100%	98%	95%	90%	80%	70%	60%	LAST MSR

CRM 16A1 CLASSIC SERIES – 5.56 NATO cal., 20 in. barrel, 20 shot mag., single stage trigger, A1 style fixed sights, gray furniture (including triangular forearm), A1 style buttstock, A1 style grips, semi-auto reproduction of the Vietnam era M16A1, left side of magwell marked "COLT AR-15/PROPERTY OF U.S. GOVT./M16A1/CAL. 5.56 MM", 6.37 lbs. Mfg. mid-2016-2019.

$2,200	$2,000	$1,750	$1,550	$1,350	$1,050	$875	*$2,499*

M4A1 SOCOM – 5.56 NATO cal., gas operated, 14 1/2 in. heavy SOCOM barrel with extended A2 flash hider pinned and welded to make non-NFA 16.1 in. barrel length, 30 shot mag., A2 front and Matech folding rear sights, 4-pos. collapsible stock, ambi safety selector, lower receiver features PROPERTY OF THE US GOVT, M4A1 CARBINE, and CAL. 5.56 MM, includes KAC RAS rail, side sling swivel, matte black finish, 6.95 lbs. Mfg. mid-2018-2019.

$1,350	$1,200	$1,050	$925	$800	$650	$525	*$1,499*

CM65 MODULAR CARBINE – 6.5 Creedmoor cal., 18 in. stainless chrome-lined barrel w/muzzle brake, 20 shot mag., no sights, collapsible/folding stock, 15 in. M-LOK rail system, ambi features, matte black finish, 9 lbs. Mfg. 2019 only.

$1,350	$1,200	$1,050	$925	$800	$650	$525	*$1,499*

CM762 MODULAR CARBINE – 7.62 NATO cal., 16.1 in. heavy chrome-lined barrel w/muzzle brake, 20 shot mag., flip-up front and adj. rear sights, telescoping VLTOR stock, 15 in. M-LOK rail system, matte black finish. Mfg. 2019 only.

$1,350	$1,200	$1,050	$925	$800	$650	$525	*$1,499*

XM177E2 RETRO CARBINE – 5.56 NATO cal., 11 1/2 in. barrel with extended flash hider (to make legal 16 in. length), 20 shot USGI mag., A1 fixed front and rear sights, Vinyl-Acetate coated aluminum synthetic stock, safety selector switch, Retro Classic Carbine built to the original Colt Model 629 specifications from the 1960s, matte black finish, 6 1/2 lbs. Mfg. 2019 only.

$2,300	$2,100	$1,800	$1,600	$1,400	$1,100	$900	*$2,599*

RIFLES: SEMI-AUTO, RIMFIRE, AR-15 & VARIATIONS

The following models were manufactured by Carl Walther, located in Ulm, Germany, under license from New Colt Holding Corp., and imported/distributed by Walther Arms.

M4 CARBINE – .22 LR cal., GIO, 16.2 in. shrouded barrel, flat-top receiver, 10 or 30 shot mag., detachable carry handle, single left-side safety lever, four position retractable stock, ribbed aluminum handguard, black finish, approx. 6 lbs. Mfg. by Umarex under license from Colt and imported by Walther Arms. Imported 2009-2016.

$475	$400	$350	$315	$285	$250	$225	*$569*

* ***M4 Ops*** – .22 LR cal., GIO, 16.2 in. barrel, 10 or 30 shot mag., aluminum upper and lower receiver, black finish, quad tactical rail interface system with elongated Picatinny rail on top of barrel and frame, inline barrel/stock design, cartridge case deflector, muzzle compensator, detachable rear sight, four position collapsible stock, ejection port cover, approx. 6 1/2 lbs. Mfg. by Umarex under license from Colt and imported by Walther Arms. Imported 2009-2016.

$515	$435	$375	$340	$310	$285	$250	*$599*

M16 – .22 LR cal., GIO, 21.2 in. barrel, 10 or 30 shot mag., flat-top receiver with detachable carry handle, fixed stock, elongated ribbed aluminum handguard, removable rear sight, ejection port cover, single left-side safety lever, black finish, approx. 6 1/4 lbs. Mfg. 2009-2010.

$575	$525	$475	$425	$395	$375	$350	*$599*

* ***M16 SPR (Special Purpose Rifle)*** – .22 LR cal., GIO, 21.2 in. barrel, 30 shot mag., black finish, fixed stock, aluminum upper and lower receiver, quad tactical rail interface system with Picatinny rail, flip-up front and rear sights, inline barrel/stock design, cartridge case deflector, muzzle compensator. Mfg. 2009-2010.

$625	$575	$525	$475	$450	$415	$395	*$670*

RIFLES: SEMI-AUTO, MISC. CENTERFIRE

COLT 1918 SELF LOADING RIFLE – .30-06 cal., gas operated w/three position regulator, 20 shot staggered mag., uncheckered walnut stock and forearm w/horizontal finger grooves, lock breech, closed bolt, hammer fired, sling swivels, includes leather display case, blue metal finish, 16 lbs. Mfg. by Ohio Ordnance Works under license from Colt Manufacturing Company.

MSR $8,799	$8,500	$7,750	$7,000	$6,250	$5,500	$4,750	$4,000

100%	98%	95%	90%	80%	70%	60%	50%	40%	30%	20%	10%

SHOTGUNS: O/U

ARMSMEAR – 12 ga. only, 2 3/4 in. chambers, a few prototypes were mfg. by Worshipful Co. Gunmakers of London, boxlock action with engraved sideplates, checkered high-grade European walnut stock and forearm, 28 (HE) or 30 (LE) in. VR barrels with screw-in chokes, choice of light (Armsmear 12 LE) or heavy (Armsmear 12 HE) engraving, 7 1/2 lbs. This model was originally advertised in 1995.

While advertised, only several prototypes of this model were manufactured.

SHOTGUNS: PERCUSSION

MODEL 1855 REVOLVING SHOTGUN MODEL – 16 gauge or .60 cal., 10 ga. or .75 cal., smoothbore, 27, 30, 33, or 36 in. barrels, 1,100 mfg.

100%	98%	95%	90%	80%	70%	60%	50%	40%	30%	20%	10%
N/A	N/A	N/A	$17,500	$15,000	$12,000	$9,000	$8,000	$7,500	$6,800	$6,500	$6,100

PATERSON MODEL 1839 SHOTGUN – 16 gauge, percussion, center hammer, revolving, 6 shot cylinder with scene, browned finished in a Damascus pattern 24 or 32 in. barrel marked on right side of lug "-Patent Arms M'g. Co. Paterson, NJ.-Colt's Pt. -" in one line, front pin and either dovetailed block or brazed half moon shape on breech end with U-shaped notch, blue finish, walnut buttstock with minor crescent shaped buttplate, 9 1/4 lbs. Approx. 225 mfg. circa 1839-1841.

100%	98%	95%	90%	80%	70%	60%	50%	40%	30%	20%	10%
N/A	N/A	N/A	N/A	$35,000	$30,000	$25,000	$20,000	$15,000	$11,500	$10,000	$8,500

SHOTGUNS: SxS, DISC.

Strong, original case colors and vivid damascus barrel patterning will make the difference when determining values on the Models 1878 and 1883. Remember, the models listed below were designed to shoot black powder loads only, not smokeless powder.

A Colt letter of provenance for the models listed below is $100 per gun.

MODEL 1878 HAMMER SHOTGUN – 10 or 12 ga., 28-32 in. blue or browned damascus barrels, double triggers, sideplates, case hardened breech, extractors, semi-pistol grip stock, 22,683 mfg. between 1878-89. Many of these guns were ordered with special features - these original guns command premiums above the prices listed below.

100%	98%	95%	90%	80%	70%	60%	50%	40%	30%	20%	10%
$12,500	$10,000	$8,000	$4,500	$3,000	$2,600	$2,300	$1,975	$1,600	$1,275	$750	$600

MODEL 1883 HAMMERLESS – 8, 10, or 12 ga., 28-32 in. damascus barrels, many deluxe custom orders mfg. in this model from 1883-1895. Approx. serial range is 1-3,050 and 4,055-8,365. Seldom encountered in mint condition. Most guns were custom ordered.

100%	98%	95%	90%	80%	70%	60%	50%	40%	30%	20%	10%
$17,500	$15,000	$11,500	$7,500	$3,500	$3,000	$2,500	$1,650	$1,475	$1,200	$750	$450

Subract 15% for 10 ga.

This model was generally a custom order gun with no standard grades being designated. Quality was extremely high, and the high cost of manufacture is a large reason why the gun never sold in large numbers commercially. The Model 1883 was discontinued after only 12 years of manufacture (it was one of the most expensive shotguns during its day). Values above assume moderate engraving and above average walnut.

* ***Model 1883 Hammerless 8 Ga.*** – 8 ga.

Rarity precludes accurate pricing for this model. Extremely rare.

SxS SHOTGUN MFG. 1961-62 – 12 or 16 ga., various barrel lengths, DTs, checkered stock and forearm, mfg. in France 1961-62 by Fabrication Mechanique, estimated total between 25-50 guns in serial range 467,000-469,000.

GRADING - PPGS™	100%	98%	95%	90%	80%	70%	60%	LAST MSR
	$675	$595	$525	$450	$400	$360	$320	

SHOTGUNS: SEMI-AUTO

STANDARD AUTO SHOTGUN – 12 or 20 ga. (also available in Magnum), aluminum frame, 26, 28, 30, or 32 in. plain or VR barrel. Almost 5,300 mfg. (both models) mfg. by Franchi of Italy 1962-66.

GRADING - PPGS™	100%	98%	95%	90%	80%	70%	60%	LAST MSR
	$375	$350	$325	$295	$260	$230	$200	

Add $50 for VR barrel.

CUSTOM AUTO SHOTGUN – similar to Standard Model, except deluxe walnut, hand engraved receiver. Mfg. 1962-1966.

GRADING - PPGS™	100%	98%	95%	90%	80%	70%	60%	LAST MSR
	$475	$425	$375	$350	$325	$295	$260	

GRADING - PPGS™	100%	98%	95%	90%	80%	70%	60%	LAST MSR

SHOTGUNS: SLIDE ACTION

COLTSMAN PUMP SHOTGUN - 12, 16, or 20 ga., Manufrance frame assembled by both Kodiak and Montgomery Wards, 26 or 28 in. plain barrel, aluminum frame. Approx. 2,000 mfg. 1961-1965.

	100%	98%	95%	90%	80%	70%	60%	LAST MSR
	$325	$295	$260	$230	$200	$180	$165	

Add 30% for Riot model with extended magazine and 20 in. barrel (not cataloged).

FACTORY COMMEMORATIVES & SPECIAL/LIMITED EDITIONS

During the course of a year, we receive many phone calls and letters on Colt non-factory special editions and limited editions that do not appear in this section. It should be noted that Colt factory commemoratives and special/limited editions are guns that has been manufactured, marketed, and sold through the auspices of the specific trademark (in this case Colt). There have literally been hundreds of non-factory special and limited editions which, although mostly made by Colt (some were subcontracted), were not marketed or retailed by Colt. These guns are NOT factory Colt commemoratives or special/limited editions and for the most part, do not have the desirability factor that the factory commemoratives and special/limited editions have. Your best alternative to find out more information about the multitude of these special/limited editions is to write: COLT ARCHIVE PROPERTIES, LLC, 1295 Blue Hills Avenue, Bloomfield, CT 06002. If anyone could have any information, it will be the factory. Their research fee is $100 per gun, with a premium charge for factory engraving. If they cannot obtain additional information on the variation you request, they will refund $50. Unfortunately, in some cases, a special/limited edition may not be researchable. In situations like this, do not confuse rarity with desirability.

Typically, non-factory special and limited editions are made for distributors. These sub-contracts seem to be mostly made to signify/commemorate an organization, state, special event or occasion, personality, etc. These are typically marketed and sold through a distributor to dealers, or a company/individual to those people who want to purchase them. These non-factory special/limited editions may or may not have a retail price and often times, since demand is regional, values may decrease rapidly in other areas of the country. In some cases, if the distributor/wholesaler who ordered the initial non-factory special/limited edition is known (and still in business), you may be able to find more information by contacting them directly (i.e. Lew Horton (disc. 2019), Davidson's, etc.). Overall desirability is the key to determining values on these non-factory special/limited editions.

The word commemorative as it applies to firearms is almost an obsolete term - kind of like calling a flight attendant a stewardess these days. The last factory gun Colt designated a "Colt Commemorative" was manufactured back in the mid-1980s. One of the biggest reasons Colt dropped its commemorative program was because during this time period, it became more advantageous for Colt to sell large domestic distributors special order guns with the features these distributors wanted. This way Colt did not have to inventory, market, and sell these guns through the company. In today's marketplace, Colt is now producing factory special/limited editions which are marketed and sold through the auspices of Colt, so a line in the sand has now been drawn between factory Colt commemoratives and special/limited editions versus non-factory special/limited editions. The word commemorative has never applied to non-factory guns. In this text, recent Colt factory special/limited editions will appear as listings in those sections where their standard models are listed. Older factory special/limited editions will appear in this section.

Because the commemorative consumer is now more in charge (consumers now own most of the guns since distributor/dealer inventories are depleted) than during the 1980s, commemorative firearms are possibly as strong as they have ever been. When the supply side of commemorative economics has to be purchased from knowledgable collectors or savvy dealers and demand stays the same or increases slightly, prices have no choice but to go up. If and when the manufacturers crank up the commemorative production runs again (and it won't be like the good old days), the old marketplace characteristics may reappear. Until then, however, the commemorative marketplace remains steady, with values having become more predictable.

As a reminder on commemoratives, I would like to repeat a few facts, especially for the beginning collector, but applicable to all manufacturers of commemoratives. Commemoratives are current production guns designed as a reproduction of an historically famous gun model, or as a tie-in with historically famous persons or events. They are generally of very excellent quality and often embellished with select woods and finishes such as silver, nickel, or gold plating. Obviously, they are manufactured to be instant collectibles and to be pleasing to the eye. As with firearms in general, not all commemorative models have achieved collector status, although most enjoy an active market. Consecutive-numbered pairs as well as collections based on

GRADING - PPGS™	100%	Issue Price	Qty. Made

the same serial number may bring a premium. Remember that handguns usually are in some type of wood presentation case, and that rifles may be cased or in packaging with graphics styled to the particular theme of the collectible. The original factory packaging and papers should always accompany the firearm, as they are necessary to realize full value at the time of sale, and get more important every year.

NIB commemorative firearms should be absolutely new, unfired, and as issued, since any obvious use or wear removes it from collector status and lowers its value significantly. Many owners have allowed their commemoratives to sit in their boxes while encased in plastic wrappers for years without inspecting them for corrosion or oxidation damage. This is risky, especially if stored inside a plastic wrapper for long periods of time, since any accumulated moisture cannot escape. Periodic inspection should be implemented to ensure no damage occurs - this is important, since even light "freckling" created from touching the metal surfaces can reduce values significantly. A mint or unfired gun without its original packaging can lose as much as 50% of its normal value - many used commemoratives get sold as "fancy shooters" with little, if any, premiums being asked.

A final note on commemoratives: One of the characteristics of commemoratives/special editions is that over the years of ownership, most of them stay in the same NIB condition. Thus, if supply always is constant and in one condition, demand has to increase before price appreciation can occur. After 47 years of commemorative/special edition production, many model's performance records can be accurately analyzed and the appreciation (or depreciation) can be compared against other purchases of equal vintage. You be the judge.

1961 GENESEO, ILLINOIS 125TH ANNIVERSARY DERRINGER - ser. no. range, 87150D-87253D.

	$650	$28	104

1961 125TH ANNIVERSARY MODEL SAA - ser. no. range, 1AM-7390AM.

	$1,495	$150	7,390

1961 CIVIL WAR CENTENNIAL PISTOL .22 SHORT - ser. no. range, 50W-24189W (numbers 1W-49W and 124W-149W were not mfg.).

	$250	$33	24,114

1961 KANSAS STATEHOOD CENTENNIAL FRONTIER SCOUT - ser. no. range, 001G-6201G.

	$595	$75	6,201

1961 PONY EXPRESS CENTENNIAL FRONTIER SCOUT - ser. no. range, 1W-550W, 1E-500E.

	$695	$80	1,007

1961 SHERIFF'S MODEL - blue and case hardened, 3 in. barrel, "SM" suffix, w/two-piece box.

	$4,000	$130	478

1961 SHERIFF'S MODEL NICKEL - nickel, 3 in. barrel, "SM" suffix, w/two-piece box.

	$9,500	$140	25

1962 COLUMBUS, OHIO SESQUICENTENNIAL SCOUT - ser. no. range, 001CS-200CS.

	$750	$100	200

1962 FORT FINDLAY CASE PAIR - .22 LR and .22 WMR cals., ser. no. range, FF0001-FF0150, one hundred revolvers shipped as singles, forty shipped as cased pairs.

	$2,750	$185	20

1962 FORT FINDLAY, OHIO SESQUICENTENNIAL SCOUT - ser. no. range, FF0001-FF0150, 110 revolvers shipped as singles, 40 shipped as cased pairs.

	$750	$90	110

1962 FORT MCPHERSON, NEBRASKA CENTENNIAL DERRINGER - ser. no. range, 001McP-300McP.

	$595	$29	300

1962 NEW MEXICO GOLDEN ANNIVERSARY SCOUT - ser. no. range, 001NMA-1000NMA.

	$695	$80	1,000

1962 ROCK ISLAND ARSENAL CENTENNIAL MODEL - ser. no. range, 1RIA-550RIA.

	$250	$39	550

1962 WEST VIRGINIA STATEHOOD CENTENNIAL SCOUT - ser. no. range, WV5, WV8, WV9, WV50, and WV100-WV3546, not all shipped.

	$595	$75	3,452

GRADING - PPGS™	100%	Issue Price	Qty. Made

1963 WEST VIRGINIA STATEHOOD CENTENNIAL SAA .45 – ser. no. range, 25WVC-624WVC, not all shipped.

	$1,595	$150	600

1963 ARIZONA TERRITORIAL CENTENNIAL SCOUT – ser. no. range, AT001-AT5355.

	$695	$75	5,355

1963 ARIZONA TERRITORIAL CENTENNIAL SAA .45 – ser. no. range, 100AT-129AT, and 24AC-1273AC.

	$1,595	$150	1,280

1963 BATTLE OF GETTYSBURG CENTENNIAL SCOUT – ser. no. range, 0001GC-1019GC.

	$695	$90	1,019

1963 CAROLINA CHARTER TERCENTENARY SCOUT – ser. no. range, 001CT-300CT.

	$595	$75	300

1963 CAROLINA CHARTER TERCENTENARY 22/45 COMBO – ser. no. range, Scout: 301CT-550CT and SAA: 301CCT-550CCT.

	$2,195	$240	251

1963 FORT STEPHENSON, OHIO SESQUICENTENNIAL SCOUT – ser. no. range, 001FS-200FS, records indicate 150 cased singles and 25 cased doubles.

	$695	$75	200

1963 GEN. JOHN HUNT MORGAN INDIANA RAID SCOUT – ser. no. range, 1JHM-100JHM.

	$795	$75	100

1963 H. COOK "1 OF 100" 22/45 COMBO – ser. no. range, Scout: 001HCK-100HCK and SAA: 001HC-100HC.

	$2,750	$275	100

1963 IDAHO TERRITORIAL CENTENNIAL SCOUT – ser. no. range, 0001TC-0902TC.

	$695	$75	902

1964 CALIFORNIA GOLD RUSH SCOUT – ser. no. range, 0001GR-0500GR.

	$695	$80	500

1964 CHAMIZAL TREATY SCOUT – ser. no. range, 0001CS-0500CS, 350 singles and 50 cased pairs.

	$695	$85	450

1964 CHAMIZAL TREATY SAA .45 – ser. no. range, 0001CP-0100CP, 50 singles and 1 cased pair.

	$1,795	$170	50

1964 CHAMIZAL TREATY 22/45 COMBO – ser. no. range, Scout: 0001CS-0500CS and SAA: 0001CP-0100CP.

	$2,500	$280	50

1964 CHERRY'S SPORTING GOODS 35TH ANNIVERSARY 22/45 COMBO – ser. no. range, Scout: REC1-REC100 and SAA: EPC1-EPC100.

	$2,500	$275	100

1964 COL. SAM COLT SESQUI. PRESENTATION SAA .45 – ser. no. range, 0001SC-5000SC.

	$1,495	$225	4,750

1964 COL. SAM COLT SESQUI. DELUXE PRES. SAA .45 – ser. no. range, 2000SC-2200SC.

	$3,500	$500	200

1964 COL. SAM COLT SESQUI. SPEC. DELUXE PRES. SAA .45 – ser. no. range, 0001SC-5000SC, only numbers ending with 00 or 000.

	$5,500	$1,000	50

1964 GENERAL HOOD CENTENNIAL SCOUT – ser. no. range, 0001GH-1503GH.

	$695	$75	1,503

1964 MONTANA TERRITORIAL CENTENNIAL SCOUT – ser. no. range, 0001MF-2300MF.

	$695	$75	2,300

1964 MONTANA TERRITORIAL CENTENNIAL SAA .45 – ser. no. range, 0001MA-0850MA.

	$1,650	$150	851

Approx. 100-200 sets (including the Scout) were sold with matching ser. numbers.

GRADING - PPGS™	100%	Issue Price	Qty. Made

1964 NEVADA STATEHOOD CENTENNIAL SCOUT – ser. no. range, 0001NS-1752NS, 1846NS, 1964NS, and 2001NS-4996NS.

	$595	$75	3,984

1964 NEVADA STATEHOOD CENTENNIAL SAA .45 – ser. no. range, 0001NC-1752NC, 1864NC, 1964NC, and 2001NC-2700NC.

	$1,595	$150	1,688

1964 NEVADA STATEHOOD CENTENNIAL 22/45 COMBO – ser. no. range, Scout: 0001NS-1752NS, 1846NS, 1964NS, and 2001NS-4996NS, SAA: 0001NC-1752NC, 1864NC, 1964NC, and 2001NC-2700NC.

	$2,195	$240	189

1964 NEVADA ST. CENT. 22/45 COMBO W/EXTRA ENGR. CYLS. – ser. no. range, Scout 0001NS-1752NS, 1846NS, 1964NS, and 2001NS-4996NS, SAA 0001NC-1752NC, 1864NC, 1964NC, and 2001NC-2700NC, records do not indicate how revolvers were cased.

	$2,395	$350	577

1964 NEVADA "BATTLE BORN" SCOUT – ser. no. range, 001BB-1001BB.

	$695	$85	981

1964 NEVADA "BATTLE BORN" SAA .45 – ser. no. range, 001NB-100NB, .45 cal., cased singles and cased pairs shipped.

	$1,895	$175	80

1964 NEVADA "BATTLE BORN" 22/45 COMBO – ser. no. range, Scout: 001BB-100BB and S.A.A.: 001NB-100NB.

	$2,595	$265	20

1964 NEW JERSEY TERCENTENARY SCOUT – ser. no. range, 0001NJ-1001NJ.

	$595	$75	1,001

1964 NEW JERSEY TERCENTENARY SAA .45 – ser. no. range, 0001JT-0250JT.

	$1,495	$150	250

1964 PONY EXPRESS PRESENTATION SAA .45 – ser. no. range, 1W-500W and 1E-500E also 0E, 00E, 0W, 00W, X1-W, X1-E, and CAL-1.

	$1,750	$250	1,004

100% value assumes all accessory items included.

1964 ST. LOUIS BICENTENNIAL SCOUT – ser. no. range, 0251SL-1051SL.

	$595	$75	802

1964 ST. LOUIS BICENTENNIAL SAA .45 – ser. no. range, 0251SB-0450SB.

	$1,595	$150	200

1964 ST. LOUIS BICENTENNIAL 22/45 COMBO – ser. no. range, Scout: 0001SL-0250SL and SAA: 0001SB-0250SB.

	$2,195	$240	250

1964 WYATT EARP BUNTLINE SAA .45 – ser. no. range, 0001WE-0150WE.

	$2,995	$250	150

1964 WYOMING DIAMOND JUBILEE SCOUT – ser. no. range, 001DJ-2357DJ.

	$695	$75	2,357

1965 APPOMATTOX CENTENNIAL SCOUT – ser. no. range, 1000AK-2000AK.

	$595	$75	1,001

1965 APPOMATTOX CENTENNIAL SAA .45 – ser. no. range, 1000AP-1249AP.

	$1,595	$150	250

1965 APPOMATTOX CENTENNIAL 22/45 COMBO – ser. no. range, Scout: 0001AK-0250AK and SAA: 0001AP-0250AP.

	$2,195	$240	250

1965 FORTY-NINER MINER SCOUT – ser. no. range, 0001FN-0500FN.

	$695	$85	500

GRADING - PPGS™	100%	Issue Price	Qty. Made

1965 GENERAL MEADE CAMPAIGN SCOUT – ser. no. range, 1GM-1197GM.

	$595	$75	1,197

1965 JOAQUIN MURIETTA 22/45 COMBO – ser. no. range, Scout: 001JMK-100JMK and SAA: 001JMP-100JMP.

	$2,500	$350	100

1965 OREGON TRAIL SCOUT – ser. no. range, 0001OT-1995OT.

	$695	$75	1,995

1965 OLD FT. DES MOINES RECONSTRUCTION SCOUT – ser. no. range, 0101DM-0800DM.

	$695	$90	700

1965 OLD FT. DES MOINES RECONSTRUCTION SAA .45 – ser. no. range, 0101FD-0200FD.

	$1,695	$170	100

1965 OLD FT. DES MOINES RECONSTRUCTION 22/45 COMBO – ser. no. range, Scout: 0001DM-0100DM and SAA: 0001FD-0100FD.

	$2,195	$290	100

1965 ST. AUGUSTINE QUADRACENTENNIAL SCOUT – ser. no. range, 1AQ-500AQ.

	$695	$85	500

1965 KANSAS COWTOWN SERIES – Wichita Scout, ser. no. range, 1KW-500KW.

	$595	$85	500

1966 ABERCROMBIE & FITCH "TRAILBLAZER" CHICAGO – Chicago, ser. no. range, 201AF-300AF.

	$1,495	$275	100

1966 ABERCROMBIE & FITCH "TRAILBLAZER" NEW YORK – New York, ser. no. range, 001AF-200AF.

	$1,495	$275	200

1966 ABERCROMBIE & FITCH "TRAILBLAZER" SAN FRANCISCO – San Francisco, ser. no. range, 301AF-400AF.

	$1,495	$275	100

1966 CALIFORNIA GOLD RUSH SAA .45 – ser. no. range, 0001GP-0500GP, not all shipped.

	$1,695	$175	130

1966 COLORADO GOLD RUSH SCOUT – ser. no. range, 0CG-1350CG.

	$695	$85	1,350

1966 DAKOTA TERRITORY SCOUT – ser. no. range, 1DT-1000DT.

	$695	$85	1,000

1966 GENERAL MEADE SAA .45 – ser. no. range, 0001MC-0200MC.

	$1,595	$165	200

1966 INDIANA SESQUICENTENNIAL SCOUT – ser. no. range, 1IS-1745IS.

	$695	$85	1,500

1966 KANSAS COWTOWN SERIES ABILENE – Abilene Scout, ser. no. range, 1KA-500KA.

	$595	$95	500

1966 KANSAS COWTOWN SERIES – Dodge City Scout, ser. no. range, 1KD-500KD.

	$595	$85	500

1966 OKLAHOMA DIAMOND JUBILEE – ser. no. range, 1OK-1343OK.

	$695	$85	1,343

1966 PONY EXPRESS .45 SAA 4-SQUARE SET (4 GUNS) – ser. no. range with backstrap marking, PE001E-PE250E "SACRAMENTO TO FRIDAY'S STATION", PE251E-PE500E "SALT LAKE CITY TO FORT LARAMIE", PE001W-PE250W "ST. JOSEPH TO MARYSVILLE"' PE251W-PE500W "FORT KEARNEY TO JULESBURG".

	$7,500	$1,400	unknown

1967 ALAMO SCOUT – ser. no. range, cased single 1051A22-4500A22 and cased pairs 251A22-1050A22.

	$595	$85	4,250

1967 ALAMO SAA .45 – ser. no. range, 251A45-1000A45, 450 singles and 300 cased pairs.

	$1,595	$165	750

GRADING - PPGS™	100%	Issue Price	Qty. Made

1967 ALAMO 22/45 COMBO – ser. no. range, 1A22-250A22 and 1A45-250A45.

	$2,095	$265	250

1967 KANSAS COWTOWN SERIES – Coffeyville Scout, ser. no. range, 1KC-500KC.

	$595	$95	500

1967 KANSAS TRAIL SERIES – Chisolm Trail Scout, ser. no. range, 1CH-500CH.

	$595	$100	500

1967 LAWMAN SERIES SAA – Bat Masterson SAA .45, ser. no. range, 1LMP-500LMP.

	$1,995	$180	500

1967 LAWMAN SERIES SCOUT – Bat Masterson Scout, ser. no. range, 1LM-3000LM.

	$750	$90	3,000

1967 WWI SERIES – .45 ACP cal., Chateau Thierry, ser. no. range, 101CT-7500CT.

	$995	$200	7,400

1967 WWI SERIES DELUXE – Chateau Thierry Deluxe, ser. no. range, 26CT-100CT.

	$1,995	$500	75

1967 WWI SERIES SPECIAL DELUXE – Chateau Thierry Spec. Deluxe, ser. no. range, 1CT-25CT.

	$3,000	$1,000	25

1968 GEN. NATHAN BEDFORD FORREST SCOUT – ser. no. range, 1NBF-3000NBF.

	$595	$110	3,000

1968 KANSAS TRAIL SERIES PAWNEE TRAIL – Pawnee Trail Scout, ser. no. range, 1PT-500PT.

	$595	$110	501

1968 KANSAS TRAIL SERIES SANTA FE TRAIL – Santa Fe Trail Scout, ser. no. range, 1SF-500SF.

	$595	$120	501

1968 LAWMAN SERIES SAA – Pat Garrett .45 SAA, ser. no. range, 1PGP-500PGP.

	$1,795	$220	500

1968 LAWMAN SERIES SCOUT – Pat Garrett Scout, ser. no. range, 1PG-3000PG.

	$750	$110	3,000

1968 NEBRASKA CENTENNIAL SCOUT – ser. no. range, 1NEB-7000NEB.

	$595	$100	7,001

1968 WWI SERIES – .45 ACP cal., Belleau Wood, ser. no. range, 1BW-100BW and 201BW-7500BW.

	$995	$200	7,400

1968 WWI SERIES DELUXE – Belleau Wood Deluxe, ser. no. range, 126BW-200BW.

	$1,995	$500	75

1968 WWI SERIES SPECIAL DELUXE – Belleau Wood Special Deluxe, ser. no. range, 101BW-125BW.

	$3,000	$1,000	25

1968 WWI SERIES BATTLE OF THE MARNE – .45 ACP cal., 2nd Battle of the Marne, 1M2-200M2 and 301M2-7500M2.

	$995	$220	7,400

1968 WWI SERIES BATTLE OF THE MARNE DELUXE – 2nd Battle of the Marne Deluxe, ser. no. range, 226M2-300M2.

	$1,995	$500	75

1969 ALABAMA SESQUICENTENNIAL SCOUT – ser. no. range, 1AS-3098AS, not all shipped.

	$595	$110	3,001

1969 ALABAMA SESQUICENTENNIAL .45 SAA – ser. no. ALA1P.

	$17,500	unknown	1

1969 ARKANSAS TERRITORIAL SESQUICENTENNIAL SCOUT – ser. no. range, 1ARK-3500ARK.

	$595	$110	3,500

1969 CALIFORNIA BICENTENNIAL SCOUT – ser. no. range, 1CBI-5000CBI.

	$595	$135	5,000

1969 GOLDEN SPIKE SCOUT – ser. no. range, 1GS-11000GS.

	$695	$135	11,000

GRADING - PPGS™	100%	Issue Price	Qty. Made

1969 KANSAS TRAIL SERIES – Shawnee Trail Scout, ser. no. range, 1ST-500ST.

	$595	$120	501

1969 LAWMAN SERIES SAA – .45 SAA Wild Bill Hickok, ser. no. range, 1WBH-500WBH.

	$1,795	$220	500

1969 LAWMAN SERIES SCOUT – Wild Bill Hickok Scout, ser. no. range, 1WB-3000WB.

	$750	$117	3,000

1969 WWI SERIES BATTLE OF THE MARNE DELUXE – 2nd Battle of the Marne Spec. Deluxe, ser. no. range, 201M2-225M2.

	$3,000	$1,000	25

1969 WWI SERIES MEUSE-ARGONNE – .45 ACP cal., Meuse-Argonne, ser. no. range, 1MA-300MA and 401MA-7500MA.

	$995	$220	7,400

1969 WWI SERIES MEUSE-ARGONNE DELUXE – Meuse-Argonne Deluxe, ser. no. range, 326MA-400MA.

	$1,995	$500	75

1969 WWI SERIES MEUSE-ARGONNE SPECIAL DELUXE – Meuse-Argonne Spec. Deluxe, ser. no. range, 301MA-325MA.

	$3,000	$1,000	25

1970 KANSAS FORT HAYS – Ft. Hays Scout, ser. no. range, 1FH-500FH.

	$595	$130	500

1970 KANSAS FORT LARNED – Ft. Larned Scout, ser. no. range, 1FL-500FL.

	$595	$120	500

1970 KANSAS FORT RILEY – Ft. Riley Scout, ser. no. range, 1FR-500FR.

	$595	$130	500

1970 LAWMAN SERIES SAA – Wyatt Earp .45 SAA, ser. no. range, 1WYE-500WYE.

	$2,995	$395	500

1970 LAWMAN SERIES SCOUT – Wyatt Earp Scout, ser. no. range, 1LWE-3000LWE.

	$750	$125	3,000

1970 MAINE SESQUICENTENNIAL SCOUT – ser. no. range, 1MES-3000MES.

	$595	$120	3,000

1970 MISSOURI SESQUICENTENNIAL SCOUT – ser. no. range, 1MOS-3000MOS.

	$595	$125	3,000

1970 MISSOURI SESQUICENTENNIAL .45 SAA – ser. no. range, P1MOS-P900MOS.

	$1,595	$220	900

1970 TEXAS RANGER SAA .45 – ser. no. range, N/A.

	$2,500	$650	1,000

1970 TEXAS RANGER GRADE I (95% ENGRAVING COVERAGE) – ser. no. range, N/A.

	$6,000	N/A	90

1970 TEXAS RANGER GRADE II (75% ENGRAVING COVERAGE) – ser. no. range, N/A.

	$5,500	$2,250	80

1970 TEXAS RANGER GRADE III (50% ENGRAVING COVERAGE) – ser. no. range, N/A.

	$5,000	$2,950	90

1970 WWII SERIES EUROPEAN THEATRE – European Theatre, ser. no. range, 0001ETO-9959ETO, not all shipped.

	$995	$250	11,500

1970 WWII SERIES PACIFIC THEATRE – Pacific Theatre, ser. no. range, 0001PTO-9960PTO, not all shipped.

	$995	$250	11,500

Note: A complete set of the WWI and WWII Series standard grade models (6 guns) with matching serial numbers in NIB condition is currently selling in the $4,750-$5,500 range.

1971 KANSAS SERIES – Ft. Scott Scout, ser. no. range, 1FSC-500FSC.

	$595	$130	500

1971 NRA CENTENNIAL GOLD CUP .45 ACP – ser. no. range, 1NRA-2500NRA, not all shipped.

	$1,495	$250	2,500

GRADING - PPGS™	100%	Issue Price	Qty. Made

1971 NRA CENTENNIAL .45 SAA – ser. no. range, NRA1-NRA7000, not all shipped.

	$1,495	$250	5,000

1971 NRA CENTENNIAL .357 SAA – ser. no. range, NRA1-NRA7000, not all shipped.

	$1,495	$250	5,000

1971 1851 NAVY LEE-GRANT – Lee-Grant Set, ser. no. range, 1LGP-250LGP.

	$1,595	$500	250

1971 1851 NAVY U.S. GRANT – U.S. Grant, ser. no. range, 251USG-4398USG, not all shipped.

	$795	$250	4,750

1971 1851 NAVY ROBERT E. LEE – Robert E. Lee, ser. no. range, 251REL-4900REL.

	$795	$250	4,750

1972 ARIZONA RANGER SCOUT – ser. no. range, 1AR-3000AR.

	$695	$135	3,001

1972 FLORIDA TERRITORY SESQUICENTENNIAL SCOUT – ser. no. range, 1FLA-2000FLA.

	$695	$125	2,001

1975 PEACEMAKER CENTENNIAL .45 – ser. no. range, PC501-PC2000.

	$1,795	$300	1,500

1975 PEACEMAKER CENTENNIAL 44.40 – ser. no. range, 501PC-2000PC.

	$1,795	$300	1,500

1975 PEACEMAKER CENT. CASED PAIR – ser. no. range, .44-40 cal.: 1MPC-500MPC and .45 cal.: MPC1-MPC500.

	$3,250	$625	500

USS TEXAS BATTLESHIP SPECIAL EDITION (1975) – .45 ACP cal., Model 1911A1 with special embellishments, nickel finish, this model is not a factory commemorative, ser. no. range N/A.

	$1,250	unknown	500

USS ARIZONA BATTLESHIP SPECIAL EDITION (1975) – .45 ACP cal., Model 1911A1 with special embellishments, nickel finish, this model is not a factory commemorative, ser. no. range N/A.

	$1,250	unknown	500

1976 U.S. BICENTENNIAL SET – ser. no. range, SAA .45: 0001PM-1776PM, Python .357 Mag.: 0001PY-1776PY, and black powder Dragoon: 0001DG-1776DG, in walnut display case with drawers.

	$4,995	$1,695	1,776

1976 BICENTENNIAL SAA FREEDOM COLTS – consisted of A, B, and C sets, set As were engraved, Bs had gold work and accessories, Cs were similar to Bs, but had shoulder stock. Set A prices averaged $1,500-$3,000 in 1976, set B prices varied between $3,500-$20,000, and set C prices started at $5,000. Total mfg. was 4 set As, 6 set Bs, and 1 set C. These sets in today's marketplace are too rare to accurately evaluate and pricing is literally "what the market will bear."

These guns were all engraved by Dwain Wright located in Applegate, OR.

1977 2ND AMENDMENT .22 – ser. no. range, G0001RB-G3020RB.

	$595	$195	3,020

1977 U.S. CAVALRY 200TH ANNIVERSARY SET – ser. no. range, US0001-US3020 and 0001US-3020US, not all shipped.

	$1,450	$995	3,000

1978 STATEHOOD 3RD MODEL DRAGOON – ser. no. range, N/A.

	$7,500	$12,500	52

1979 NED BUNTLINE .45 SAA – ser. no. range, NB0001-NB3000.

	$1,395	$895	3,000

OHIO PRESIDENT'S SPECIAL EDITION (1979) – .45 ACP cal., Model 1911A1 with special Ohio embellishments, this is not a factory commemorative, ser. no. range N/A.

	$1,250	unknown	250

1979 TOMBSTONE CENTENNIAL .45 SAA – .45 LC cal., 7 1/2 in. barrel, nickel finish, two-piece walnut stocks, P-1876 Model, etched with scroll engraving and Western scenes. 300 mfg. (200 singles and 50 pairs), ser. no. range N/A.

	$2,500	$995	300

This model was not sold retail through the auspices of Colt.

GRADING - PPGS™	100%	Issue Price	Qty. Made

1980 DRUG ENFORCEMENT AGENCY (DEA) .45 AUTO - ser. no. range N/A.

	$1,250	$550	910

This model was not sold at retail through the auspices of Colt.

1980 OLYMPICS ACE MODEL SPECIAL EDITION - ser. no. range N/A.

	$1,600	$1,000	200

This model was not sold at retail through the auspices of Colt.

1980 HERITAGE-WALKER .44 PERCUSSION - ser. no. range, 0001 C CO-1850 C CO.

	$850	$1,475	1,847

1981 "JOHN M. BROWNING" .45 ACP SEMI-AUTO - ser. no. range, CJMBC0001-CJMBC3000.

	$995	$1,100	3,000

1980-81 .45 ACP GOVT. SIGNATURE SERIES - .45 ACP cal., blue finished Govt. with gold auroplated or nickel finish. 250 mfg. in both finishes, ser. no. range N/A.

	$1,250	$833	250

Add $50 for blue finish.

1980-81 ACE SIGNATURE SERIES - .22 LR cal., cocobolo grips with medallions, blue finish with photo engraving, cased. 1,000 mfg., ser. no. range N/A.

	$1,500	$955	1,000

1981 BUFFALO BILL SPECIAL EDITION - .44-40 WCF cal., 7 1/2 in. barrel, gold and silver plating, Class C engraved, scrimshaw ivory grips featuring Buffalo Bill and his TE Wyoming Ranch brand, leather cased, 250 mfg. serialized 1BB-250BB.

	$4,975	$3,750	250

This model was a special edition (not commemorative), which was made specifically for the Buffalo Bill Historical Center.

1982 JOHN WAYNE SAA STANDARD - ser. no. range, CJWC0001-CJWC3100.

	$2,250	$2,995	3,100

While advertising literature indicated 3,100 were mfg., 3,041 were sold.

1982 JOHN WAYNE SAA DELUXE - ser. no. range, JWD001-JWD500.

	$8,000	$10,000	500

While advertising literature indicated 500 were mfg., only 90 were sold.

1982 JOHN WAYNE SAA PRESENTATION - ser. no. range, JWP001-JWP100.

	$13,500	$20,000	100

While advertising literature indicated 100 were mfg., only 47 were sold.

1983 BUFFALO BILL WILD WEST SHOW CENTENNIAL SAA .45 - ser. no. range, CBC0001-CBBC1236, not all shipped.

	$1,695	$1,350	500

1983 CCA LIMITED EDITION SAA - .44-40 WCF cal., 4 3/4 in. barrel, nickel finish, fleur-de-lis checkered walnut grips, two line barrel address and Colt Frontier Six Shooter roll marking. 250 mfg. in 1983 to commemorate Colt Collector's Assn., ser. no. range N/A.

	$1,995	$825	250

This model was not sold at retail through the auspices of Colt.

1983 "ARMORY MODEL" SAA .45 ACP - this model had limited production, and should not be considered a commemorative. So-called because it was shipped with extra .45 LC cylinder and the "Colt Armory Edition" book by E. Grant. 250 mfg. with nickel finish, 250 mfg. with blue finish, presentation cased, smooth ivory grips, ser. no. range N/A.

	$2,500	$1,125	500

20 Armory Models were available with class A engraving - $2,995, B engraving - $3,500, C engraving - $3,995, D engraving - $4,500.

1983 PYTHON SILVER SNAKE SPECIAL EDITION - .357 Mag. cal., 6 in. barrel, stainless steel with black chrome finish, Pachmayr grips with custom shop pewter medallions, etched engraving, includes custom gun pouch, ser. no. range N/A.

	$10,500	$1,150	250

GRADING - PPGS™	100%	Issue Price	Qty. Made

1984 1ST EDITION GOVT. MODEL .380 ACP – ser. no. range, RC00000-RC01000.

	$850	$425	1,000

1984 JOHN WAYNE "DUKE" FRONTIER .22 – ser. no. range N/A.

	$895	$475	5,000

1984 COLT/WINCHESTER SET – 1 ea. of the Model 1894 Winchester carbine and Colt Peacemaker, serial numbered 1WC-4440WC, .44-40 WCF cal., elaborate gold etching, cased. Pistol became available for sale individually in 1986 - see individual listing below for values.

	$3,500	$3,995	2,300

Approx. 2,300 sets were actually put together in this combination. Some sets were split up with individual prices being discounted.

1984 COLT SAA ONLY FROM SET – .44-40 WCF cal., 7 1/2 in. barrel, gold etching, this commemorative was originally made as part of the 1984 Winchester/Colt rifle-pistol set, but was later able to be purchased individually. Originally mfg. 1984, ser. no. range N/A.

	$1,495	N/A	4,000

1984 USA EDITION SAA – .44-40 WCF cal., 7 1/2 in. barrel, old style black powder frame, bullseye ejector rod head, 3 line patent date, high polished blue with gold line engraving. 100 guns total mfg. - 1 for each state and its capitol, ser. no. range N/A.

	$2,995	$4,995	100

1984 KIT CARSON .22 NEW FRONTIER – 6 in. barrel, color case hardened frame, gold artwork, serial numbered KCC0001-KCC1000, cased.

	$695	$550	1,000

1984 SECOND EDITION GOVT. MODEL .380 ACP – serial numbered 00000RC- 01000RC.

	$850	$525	1,000

1984 OFFICER'S COMMENCEMENT ISSUE – Officer's ACP with Marine Corps emblem, rosewood grips, silver plated oak leaf scroll, cased, ser. no. range N/A.

	$995	$700	1,000

This model was not sold retail through the auspices of Colt.

1984 THEODORE ROOSEVELT COMMEMORATIVE SAA – .44-40 WCF cal., 7 1/2 in. barrel, black powder frame, case colored receiver, factory "B" hand engraving, ivory stocks, cased, ser. no. range, TRC001-TRC500.

	$2,250	$1,695	500

1984 NORTH AMERICAN OILMEN SAA BUNTLINE – .45 LC cal., 12 in. barrel, non-fluted cylinder, elaborate gold etching, ebony grips with ivory inlays, stand-up glass case, ser. nos. 1-100 mfg. for Canada, 101-200 for the U.S.

	$3,250	$3,900	200

This model was not sold retail through the auspices of Colt.

1985 TEXAS 150th SESQUICENTENNIAL SAA – .45 cal., Sheriff's model, 4 3/4 in. barrel, mirror bright blue, gold etching, 24Kt. gold plated backstrap and trigger guard, smooth ivory grips, French fit oak presentation case. Mfg. 1985 only.

* ***1985 Texas 150th Sesquicentennial SAA Standard Model*** – 1,000 mfg., ser. no. range TX0001-TX1000.

	$1,695	$1,836	1,000

* ***1985 Texas 150th Sesquicentennial SAA Premier Model*** – elaborate engraving, 75 mfg., ser. no. range TEXAS0001-TEXAS0096, not all shipped.

	$5,000	$7,995	75

1986 150th ANNIVERSARY SAA – .45 LC cal., 10 in. barrel, 50% coverage engraving, royal blue finish, Goncalo Alves smooth grips, 150th anniversary logo in stocks, cherrywood case. 490 mfg. 1986 only, ser. no. range AM0001-AM1000, not all shipped.

	$1,995	$1,595	490

1986 150th ANNIVERSARY ENGRAVING SAMPLER SAA – various cals. and barrel lengths, 4 different engraving styles featuring Nimschke, Helfricht, Henshaw, and Contemporary (these names are scrimshawed on the ivory grips), approx. 75% coverage signed by the engraver, available in either blue or nickel finish, no special serialization. Mfg. 1986.

	$3,500	$1,613	unknown

GRADING - PPGS™	100%	Issue Price	Qty. Made

1986 150th ANNIVERSARY ENGRAVING SAMPLER .45 M1911A1 – .45 ACP cal., 4 different engraving styles on metal surfaces, 75% coverage, ivory grips, signed by the engraver, available with either blue or nickel finish. New 1986, ser. no. range N/A.

	$2,500	$1,155	unknown

Add $60 for nickel.

1986 MUSTANG FIRST EDITION – .380 ACP cal., 1,000 manufactured serialized MU00001-MU01000 (the first thousand of production), rosewood stocks, walnut presentation case. Mfg. 1986 only.

	$850	$475	1,000

OFFICER'S ACP HEIRLOOM EDITION – .45 ACP cal., personalized with individual's choice for serial number (ie. John Smith 1), mirror brite bluing, jeweled barrel, hammer, and trigger, ivory grips, with historical letter and mahogany case. New 1986, ser. no. range N/A.

	$1,550	$1,643	open

1986 DOUBLE DIAMOND SET – Python Ultimate .357 Mag. revolver and Officer's Model .45 ACP, both guns in stainless steel, smooth rosewood grips, presentation cased. 1,000 sets mfg. 1986 only, serial numbered 1-1,000 (matched).

	$7,500	$1,575	1,000

DELTA MATCH H-BAR RIFLE – AR-15 A2 H-Bar rifle selectively chosen and equipped with 3-9x variable power rubber armored scope, leather sling, shoulder stock cheekpiece, cased. Mfg. 1987, ser. no. range N/A.

	$1,500	$1,425	open

12TH MAN-'SPIRIT OF AGGIELAND' – .45 ACP cal., mfg. to commemorate Texas A&M University, serial numbered TAM001-TAM999, 24Kt gold plating including wreaths on left frame and inscription on right, cherrywood glass top presentation case, includes personalized class graduation inscription. Available 1987 only.

	$1,150	$950	999

This model was not sold retail through the auspices of Colt.

COMBAT ELITE CUSTOM EDITION – .45 ACP cal., with ambidextrous thumb safety, wide grip safety, hand tuned action, and carrying case, ser. numbered CG00001-CG00500. Mfg. 1987.

	$1,150	$900	500

1987 SHERIFF'S EDITION – set of 5 SAA Sheriff's configuration revolvers in .45 LC cal., barrel lengths include 2, 2 1/2, 3, 4, and 5 1/2 in., royal blue finish, smooth rosewood grips with medallions, supplied with glass top case which displays the revolvers in a circle around a brass sheriff's badge. Serialization has 3 numeral prefix (which is the same in each set), followed by the letters "SE", followed by 1 or 2 numerals (indicating barrel length) - i.e. serial number 002SE25 indicates the second set built, Sheriff's Edition (SE), and a barrel length of 2 1/2 inches.

	$6,995	$7,500	200 sets

1989 SNAKE EYES LIMITED EDITION – includes two Python revolvers (2 1/2 in. barrels), one finished in brite stainless steel and the other in Royal Blue finish, grips are ivory-like with scrimshaw "snake eyes" dice on left side and royal flush poker hand on right, includes chips and playing cards, 500 sets only of consecutive serial numbers. New 1989, ser. no. range N/A.

	$14,000	$3,500	500

1990 SAA HEIRLOOM II EDITION – .45 LC cal., 7 1/2 in. barrel, color case hardened frame and hammer, balance of metal finished in Colt Royal Blue, one-piece American Walnut grips with cartouche on lower left side, personalized inscription on backstrap, walnut cased. Available 1990 only, ser. no. range N/A.

	$1,795	$1,600	open

1990 JOE FOSS LIMITED EDITION .45 ACP GOVT. MODEL – .45 ACP cal., first limited edition in Colt's All American Hero Series, commemorates Joe Foss, famous American WWII Marine Fighter Pilot, gold etched scenes on slide sides, smooth walnut grips. While 2,500 were advertised, only 300+ were mfg. Serial numbered beginning with JF 0001. French fitted walnut presentation case, 38 oz. Mfg. 1990 only.

	$1,650	$1,375	300+

1911A1 50th ANNIVERSARY BATTLE OF THE BULGE – .45 ACP cal., special edition commemorating the Battle of the Bulge, silver plated with gold inlays, 100 mfg. serialized BB001-BB100.

	$1,595	$1,250	100

Add $150 for deluxe presentation case.

This special edition was sold exclusively by Cherry's located in Greensboro, NC.

GRADING - PPGS™	100%	Issue Price	Qty. Made

1993 CCA LIMITED EDITION SAA – .38-40 WCF cal., 4 3/4 in. barrel, nickel finish, walnut grips, CCA markings on grip strap. 150 mfg. in 1993, ser. no. range N/A.

	$1,750	$1,165	150

This model was not sold at retail through the auspices of Colt.

2014 SAA SAM COLT 200TH BIRTHDAY COMMEMORATIVE – .45 LC cal., 7 1/2 in. barrel with front and rear gold barrel bands and engraving, 100% Royal Blue finish, unfluted cylinder with gold-etched Sam Colt on left side and Colt dome on the right, scroll engraved frame and top strap, gold-plated hammer, trigger, and screws, hand-carved ivory grips, while advertised during 2014, Colt never manufactured this commemorative outside of prototypes.

COMANCHE

Current trademark manufactured in Argentina beginning 2001. Currently distributed (master distributor) beginning 2002 by Eagle Imports, located in Wanamassa, NJ. Distributor sales.

GRADING - PPGS™	100%	98%	95%	90%	80%	70%	60%	LAST MSR

PISTOLS: SINGLE SHOT

SUPER COMANCHE – .45 LC cal./.410 bore or .22 WMR (mfg. 2011-2013) cal., 6 (new 2014) or 10 in. rifled barrel, blue, duo-tone (mfg. 2004-2005, reintroduced 2011-2013), camo (mfg. 2006-2007), or satin nickel finish, black rubber grips and forearm, barrel release lever on front of trigger guard, adj. rear sight, transfer bar and manual safeties, 47 oz. New 2002.

MSR $240	$200	$175	$150	$135	$110	$90	$70	

Add $15 for 6 in. barrel with satin nickel finish (new 2014) or $20 for 10 in. barrel with satin nickel finish.
Add $33 for camo (disc. 2007). Add $5 for duo-tone finish (disc. 2013).
Add $10 for .22 WMR cal. (mfg. 2011-2013).

This model is not available for sale in some states.

REVOLVERS: SA

COMANCHE I – .22 LR cal., 6 in. full lug barrel, 9 shot, blue, stainless, or alloy, adj. sights, rubber grips, 39 oz. Mfg. 2002-2009.

	$225	$195	$170	$155	$125	$100	$80	*$274*

Add $25 for stainless steel construction.
Subtract $66 for alloy (disc.).

COMANCHE II-A – .38 Spl. +P cal., 2 (mfg. 2006-disc.), 3 (new 2004), or 4 in. full lug barrel, steel (disc. 2010) or alloy frame, 6 shot, blue, nickel (new 2014), or stainless (disc. 2010) finish, adj. rear sight, approx. 30 oz. Mfg. 2002-2019.

	$190	$165	$145	$125	$110	$90	$70	*$220*

Add $15 for stainless steel construction (disc. 2010).
Add $9 for 2 in. barrel (disc.).

COMANCHE III – .357 Mag. cal., 2 (mfg. 2006), 3, 4, or 6 in. full lug barrel, 6 shot, blue or stainless, adj. rear sight, 29-39 oz. Mfg. 2002-2009.

	$240	$210	$180	$165	$130	$110	$85	*$289*

Add $27 for stainless steel construction.
Add $8 for 2 in. barrel.

COMANCHE IV – .44 Mag. cal., 6 in. barrel only with adj. rear sight, blue or stainless steel. Mfg. 2004.

	$250	$220	$185	$170	$135	$110	$85	*$308*

Add $25 for stainless steel construction.

COMBINATION GUNS

A two-barrel long gun configuration of either SxS or O/U design, consisting of a rifle and a shotgun barrel. Combination guns originated in Europe.

Many imported combination guns designed for the U.S. have been known as turkey guns in the past, typically with a .22 rimfire/medium cal. centerfire rifle barrel over a 12 ga., 20 ga., or .410 bore shotgun barrel. European guns typically have metric rifle cals., and the shotgun barrel is usually 12 or 16 ga., with the shotgun barrel over the rifle barrel. The rifle barrel typically is provided with a single set trigger. European combination guns (see configurations below) need to be evaluated individually, since values will depend on the desirability of the gun's configuration in the U.S. (i.e., metric vs. American cals., gauge, type of lock, engraving, quality of wood, etc.). The most desirable combination gun configuration is the one shown in the middle below where the shotgun barrel is above the rifle barrel. This allows the rifle barrel to be in line with a shooter's shoulder and the center

GRADING - PPGS™	100%	98%	95%	90%	80%	70%	60%	LAST MSR

of gravity for better accuracy and less muzzle rise during shooting. Most European boxlock combination guns with metric cals. in average condition are currently priced in the $1,500-$3,500 range. A premium can be added for factory or custom-order quick detach mounted scope. Newly-constructed, custom-ordered, top quality major trademark European combination guns with profuse engraving and best-quality wood can sell for $25,000+ or more. Typical American combination guns (the Savage Model 24 and others) are priced in the $400-$700 range, depending on condition.

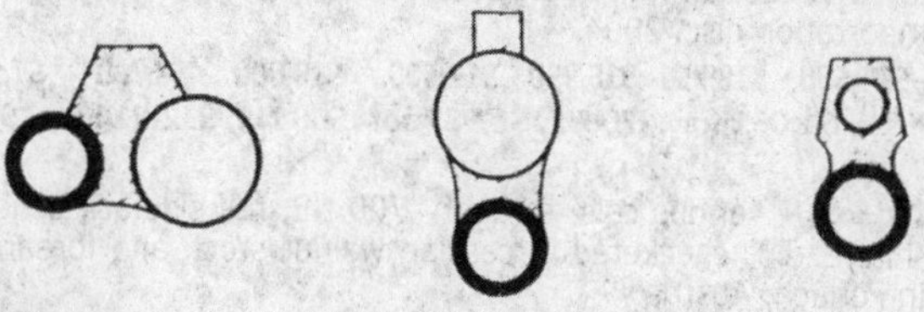

COMMANDO ARMS

Previous manufacturer located in Knoxville, TN.

Commando Arms became the new name for Volunteer Enterprises in the late 1970s.

CARBINES: SEMI-AUTO

MARK 45 - .45 ACP cal., carbine styled after the Thompson submachine gun, 16 1/2 in. barrel.

	100%	98%	95%	90%	80%	70%	60%	LAST MSR
MARK 45	$495	$425	$350	$315	$280	$225	$195	

COMMANDO ARMS (NEW MFG.)

Current trademark of shotguns manufactured in Balikesir, Turkey. Previously located in Konya, Turkey. Currently imported under private label Dickinson LLC, located in Moorpark, CA. Previously imported by Webley & Scott and SKB Shotguns.

SHOTGUNS

Current SxS models include the Estate, Prestige, Plantation, and the Classic (disc.). Current O/U models include the Classic (disc.), Elite, Estate (disc.), Gold, Hunter, Royal, Osso, Trap and Skeet, and the Ultra (disc.). Current semi-auto models include the Gold and Classic Series. Current single barrel models include the Century III and Star Series (disc.). Slide action defense guns include the Pump Series. Please contact the company directly for more information, including U.S. availability and pricing on non-Webley & Scott, SKB, and/or Dickinson labeled models.

COMPETITIVE EDGE GUNWORKS LLC

Previous rifle manufacturer located in Bogard, MO until 2013.

RIFLES: BOLT ACTION

Competitive Edge Gunworks LLC built custom order bolt action rifles based on its patented action. Tactical, Hunting, Varmint, and Competition configurations were available.

COMPETITOR CORPORATION

Competitor

Previous manufacturer established in 1988 and located in Jaffrey, NH until 2014. Previously located in New Ipswich, NH until 2001, and in West Groton, MA from 1988-1995.

PISTOLS: SINGLE SHOT

COMPETITOR - available in over 400 cals. from .17 LR - .50 AE, ranging from small rimfire to large belted Magnums, 14 in. barrel standard, rotary cannon action, cocks on opening, dual sliding thumb and trigger safety, rotary style ejector, click adj. sights, matte blue or optional electroless nickel finish, choice of synthetic, laminated, or natural wood grips (ambidextrous), extractor or ejector. Approx. 59-73 oz. Mfg. 1988-2014.

	100%	98%	95%	90%	80%	70%	60%	LAST MSR
COMPETITOR	$575	$500	$425	$375	$300	$245	$190	*$660*

Add $30 for laminated wood stock.
Add approx. $50 for walnut grips (disc.).
Add $60 for electroless nickel finish (barreled action only, disc.).
Add $195 for extra 14 in. standard cal. barrel with sights.
Add $40 for less than 16 in. standard cal. barrel with sights.
Add $70 for 16-23 in. barrel.
Add $60-$80 for factory-installed muzzle brake.
Add $275 for rimfire or centerfire conversion kit.

GRADING - PPGS™	100%	98%	95%	90%	80%	70%	60%	LAST MSR

CONCO ARMS

Previous importer of Hambrusch rifles located in Emmaus, PA.

RIFLES: SxS

PRO HUNTER BOXLOCK SxS - various cals. through .700 NE, Anson & Deeley action with double underlocking lugs and scalloped frame, ejectors, standard scroll engraving, H&H style frame reinforcement, checkered Circassian walnut stock and forearm, custom order only, mfg. by Hambrusch in Ferlach, Austria. Importation disc. 2004.

	$21,500	$18,750	$15,950	$12,500	$10,000	$8,700	$7,500	*$23,611*

Add $673 for .375 H&H, $1,061 for .470 NE, $1,987 for .500 NE, $12,816 for .577/.600 NE or $30,318 for .700 NE cal.

PRO HUNTER SIDELOCK SxS - various cals. through .700 NE, full sidelock action with standard scroll engraving, ejectors, hinged DT, checkered Circassian walnut stock and forearm, custom order only, mfg. by Hambrusch in Ferlach, Austria.

	N/A	$26,000	$20,500	$16,750	$14,000	$11,000	$9,995	

Premiums exist for .375 H&H cal. and above.

CONNECTICUT SHOTGUN MANUFACTURING CO.

Current rifle and shotgun manufacturer established during 1995, and located in New Britain, CT. Consumer direct sales.

Connecticut Shotgun Manufacturing Co. has established itself as one of America's premier gunmakers, specializing in best quality O/U and SxS shotguns, in addition to a SxS double rifle. Please contact the company directly for more information, including pricing and availability.

RIFLES: SxS

MODEL 21 RIMFIRE - .22 LR or .22 WMR cal., based on a special order small frame, everything is scaled and proportioned to the caliber, open sights, base price is for Model 21-1 w/light scroll engraving and A fancy wood. New mid-2006.

MSR $25,000	$23,750	$20,000	$17,000	$13,500	$10,500	$8,750	$7,750	

MSR for Grade 21-5 is $30,000, Grade 21-6 is $32,000, and Grand American is $34,000.

MODEL 21 CENTERFIRE - various centerfire calibers, based on the Model 21 action, Grand American styling and features, 4 game animals inlaid in 24Kt. gold, frame scaled proportionately to the caliber, iron sights, SST. Limited mfg. beginning 2002.

Each gun is custom-built to the customer's exact specifications and prices start at $35,000.

CHRISTIAN HUNTER SxS - 12, 16, 20, 28 ga., or .410 bore, Anson & Deeley boxlock action, scalloped frame, 26-30 in. barrels, choke tubes or fixed chokes, single or double trigger, hard rubber buttplate or recoil pad, straight grip, long tang pistol grip, or semi-pistol grip, automatic safety, drop plate, rose and scroll engraving with case hardening or deluxe grade ornamental engraving, custom made to customer's specifications. New 2016.

Current MSR is $12,500 for rose and scroll engraving or $13,500 for deluxe grade ornamental engraving.

SHOTGUNS: O/U

A. GALAZAN MODEL - 12, 16, 20, 28 ga., or .410 bore, low profile sidelock action with Boss-style metal reinforced forearm, top-of-the-line model utilizing best quality materials and U.S. workmanship, wide choice of custom features and engraving options. Less than 20 are made per year.

Each gun is custom-built to the customer's exact specifications, base MSR is POR.

A. GALAZAN ROUND BODY MODEL - 12, 16, 20, 28 ga., or .410 bore, round body, wide choice of custom features and engraving options.

Each gun is custom-built to the customer's exact specifications and base MSR is POR.

A-10 AMERICAN - 12, 20, or 28 ga., choice of 26, 28, 30, or 32 in. VR barrels, 12 ga. frame (20 and 28 ga. small frame available by request), five TruLock choke tubes, XX grade American black walnut pistol or straight grip checkered stock and forearm, steel (standard A-10), platinum, or stainless steel receiver with light (not full coverage) rose and scroll engraving standard, SST, ejectors, hidden hand detachable sidelock with four exposed pins on each side, includes case. New 2010.

MSR $7,995	$7,500	$6,250	$5,250	$4,500	$3,750	$3,000	$2,500	

Add $1,000 for the Deluxe Model with higher grade wood and more engraving coverage.
Add $2,000 for rose and scroll engraving, or add $7,000 for platinum engraving and wood upgrade.
Add $350 for 3X, $600 for 4x, $900 for exhibition, or POR quotation for Turkish wood walnut upgrades.

This model is available by contacting the company directly or can be ordered through Galazan Premium

GRADING - PPGS™	100%	98%	95%	90%	80%	70%	60%	LAST MSR

Galleries which include: Cook-Winston, Steve Barnett Fine Guns, Puglisi Gun Imporium, and John Foster Gunmakers, UK.

* ***A-10 American Sporting Clays*** – 12 ga. only, 3 in. chambers, sidelock action with choice of engraving and finish, 30 or 32 in. ported VR barrels with 5 extended choke tubes, adj. point of impact high top rib, weight distribution system under forend, XX American black walnut stock features adj. recoil pad and comb with stock weight balance system and target palm swell pistol grip, SST, ejectors, non-automatic safety, approx. 8 1/2 lbs. New 2012.

MSR $14,950	$12,700	$11,100	$9,500	$8,650	$7,000	$5,700	$4,450

INVERNESS – 20 ga., 28 or 30 in. file cut VR barrels with 5 choke tubes, ejectors, SST, checkered walnut straight or pistol grip stock with Galazan recoil pad, elongated top and bottom tangs, case colored rounded boxlock frame with fine scroll engraving, case colored frame, 6 lbs. 5 oz. New late 2011.

MSR $8,995	$8,500	$7,450	$6,375	$5,775	$4,675	$3,825	$2,975

* ***Inverness Deluxe*** – 20 ga. only, 3 in. chambers, rounded action with trigger plate, 28 or 30 in. VR cryo-pattern barrels with 5 choke tubes, SST, AE, long tang straight or pistol grips, checkered forearm, highly figured Turkish walnut stock, engraved coin finished receiver, 6 lbs. 5 oz. New late 2012.

Current MSR is $12,500.

MODEL 21 – 20 ga., 3 in. chamber, 26-32 in. VR barrel with five choke tubes, gold plated single selective trigger, red front bead, American walnut checkered stock and forearm, Winchester recoil pad, automatic safety, available in Standard, Pigeon Grade, or Grand American configuration, optional wood upgrades and engraving is available, approx. 6 lbs. 5 oz.

* ***Model 21 Standard Grade***

Current MSR is $3,995.
Add $350 for AA Grade, $600 for AAA Grade, or $900 for Exhibition Grade American walnut upgrade.

* ***Model 21 Pigeon Grade*** – engraved with hunting dogs, game birds, and intricate English scroll, AAA fancy American walnut with gold oval, "A" style checkering on stock and forend.

Current MSR is $7,500.
Add $300 for Exhibition Grade wood upgrade.

* ***Model 21 Grand American*** – Exhibition full fancy feather crotch American walnut with gold oval, magnificently executed scroll engraving with solid gold inlaid dogs and birds in the panel scene, "B" carved stock and forend, includes leather covered impact case.

Current MSR is $12,500.

REVELATION – 20 ga., 2 3/4 or 3 in. chamber, round action, 26, 28, or 30 in. VR barrels, multi-chokes (SK, IC, M, IM, F), ejectors, SST, straight or pistol grip walnut stock, hard rubber buttplate, automatic safety, traditional bone and charcoal case hardened receiver, available in several wood upgrades and configurations, approx. 6 lbs. New 2018.

MSR $1,995	$1,825	$1,725	$1,600	$1,450	$1,200	$925	$725

Add $350 for wood upgrade.

SHOTGUNS: SxS

Connecticut Shotgun Manufacturing Company will custom make a "Winchester" Model 21, with Winchester appearing on the barrel address. Please contact the factory directly for details and a price quotation.

Add $3,250 for extra set of 12, 16, or 20 ga. barrels on same gun, $4,500 for extra 28 ga. or .410 bore barrels on standard frame.

MODEL 21 – 12, 16, 20, 28 ga., or .410 bore, 4 frame sizes (12, 16, 20, and 28/.410 bore), various barrel lengths up to 32 in. with either matte solid or vent. rib and fixed chokes, best quality checkered wood, wide choice of custom features and engraving options, new mfg. not associated with Winchester production. Limited mfg. beginning 2002.

Each gun is custom-built to the customer's exact specifications.

* ***Model 21-1*** – features frame light scroll engraving patterned after Winchester's No. 1 style, A fancy wood. New 2002.

MSR $15,000	$15,000	$12,500	$9,995	$8,750	$7,250	$6,500	$5,750

Add $3,000 for 28 ga. or $3,500 for .410 bore.
Add $11,500 for 28 ga. or .410 bore on baby frame.

GRADING - PPGS™	100%	98%	95%	90%	80%	70%	60%	LAST MSR

* ***Model 21-5*** – features both scroll and three hunting scenes engraving patterned after Winchester's No. 5 style on frame and barrels, AA fancy wood. New 2002.

MSR $18,000	$18,000	$14,500	$12,500	$9,950	$8,750	$7,250	$6,500	

Add $2,000 for 28 ga. or $3,000 for .410 bore.
Add $11,500 for 28 ga. or .410 bore on baby frame.

* ***Model 21-6*** – features both tight scroll and dog/game bird engraving patterned after Winchester's No. 6 style on frame and barrels, AAA fancy wood. New 2002.

MSR $21,500	$21,500	$17,500	$13,750	$11,250	$9,250	$8,250	$7,000	

Add $2,000 for 28 ga. or $3,500 for .410 bore.
Add $9,500 for 28 ga. or .410 bore on baby frame.

* ***Model 21 Small Frame*** – 28 ga., or .410 bore, 30% smaller frame, approx. 5 1/2 lbs.

MSR $25,000	$25,000	$21,875	$18,750	$17,000	$13,750	$11,250	$8,750	

* ***Model 21 Grand American*** – top-of-the-line standard model with 2 sets of barrels, elaborate scroll engraving on barrels and frame, 5 gold inlays, including dogs and birds, B carved stock and forearm, AAA full fancy feather crotch American walnut. New 2002.

Current MSR starting at $24,500.
Add $2,000 for 28 ga. or $5,500 for .410 bore.
Add $9,500 for 28 ga. or .410 bore on baby frame.

* ***Model 21 Royal Exhibition*** – top-of-the-line model with 2 sets of barrels, numerous engraving and gold inlay options, best quality wood. New 2002.

This model is built to customer's specifications and is POR only.

A. GALAZAN ROUND BODY MODEL – 12, 16, 20, 28 ga., or .410 bore, round body, top-of-the-line model utilizing best quality materials and U.S. workmanship, no visible pins or screws, wide choice of custom features and engraving options.

Each gun is custom built to the customer's exact specifications and price is POR depending on order.

RBL EDITIONS – 12, 16, 20, 28 ga. or .410 (new late 2011) bore, rounded boxlock action, barrels with 5 choke tubes or fixed chokes, ejectors, DT or ST, XX walnut, choice of pistol or straight grip stock, case colored receiver, hammer, sears and triggers are treated in Hard Gold, recoil pad, canvas and leather cased with all accessories, choice of 14 1/4 or 14 3/4 LOP, approx. 5 1/2 (28 ga.) or 6 1/8 lbs. This series was introduced 2006.

Add $350 for XXX walnut, $600 for XXXX or $900 for Exhibition wood upgrade.
Add $400 for beavertail forearm.
Add $175 for SST (disc.)
Add $450 for assisted opening action (disc.)

* ***RBL 12 ga.*** – 12 ga., 26, 28, 30, or 32 in. barrels with 5 TruLock chokes, raised rib, case colored receiver with light scroll and three ducks in flight on right and two pheasants on left, 2X premium walnut, two quick change recoil pads, metal grip cap, designed by Paul Lantuch. Mfg. 2009-2010, reintroduced 2012.

MSR $3,795	$3,350	$2,950	$2,650	$2,350	$2,000	$1,800	$1,600	

» ***RBL 12 ga. Sporting Clays*** – 12 ga., 30 or 32 in. raised VR barrels, exhibition grade checkered walnut stock with adj. comb, weight balancing system, and interchangeable recoil pads, case colored receiver with gold inlaid pigeons, non-automatic safety, beavertail forearm, 9 lbs. New 2011.

MSR $6,995	$6,650	$6,000	$5,250	$4,500	$3,750	$3,000	$2,250	

* ***RBL 16 ga.*** – 16 ga., scaled frame, 29 in. barrels, case colored receiver with light scroll engraving, features game scenes of a pointer and a setter, quick change recoil pad available in two lengths. Mfg. 2009-2010, reintroduced 2012.

MSR $3,795	$3,350	$2,950	$2,650	$2,350	$2,000	$1,800	$1,600	

* ***RBL 20 ga. Special*** – 20 ga., DT or SST, Exhibition grade checkered walnut stock and forearm, straight or pistol grip, case colored receiver with light scroll and gold pheasant inlays, custom built to order. New 2014.

MSR $7,995	$7,500	$6,575	$5,625	$5,100	$4,125	$3,375	$2,625	

* ***RBL 20 ga. Launch Edition*** – 20 ga., 28 in. barrels with 5 chokes, case colored receiver with scroll engraving by Richard Roy (launch edition) or French greyed receiver, metal grip cap, hard rubber buttplate, also available with fully rifled bore and open sights (Slug). Mfg. 2005-2010.

	$3,995	$3,500	$2,995	$2,500	$2,100	$1,750	$1,550	*$2,795*

Add approx. $650 for fully rifled barrels with open sights - mfg. approx. 2009-2010.

GRADING - PPGS™	100%	98%	95%	90%	80%	70%	60%	LAST MSR

* ***RBL 28 ga.*** – 28 ga., 26, 28, or 30 in. barrels with choke tubes, case colored receiver features pointer and setter games scenes designed by James Demunk, splinter forend. Disc. 2010.

	$4,500	$4,150	$3,650	$3,150	$2,750	$2,350	$2,050	*$4,995*

* ***RBL .410 Bore*** – .410 bore, 28 in. barrels with fixed chokes, case colored true baby frame, J. Purdey style rose and scroll engraving, 5 lbs. Only 500 to be mfg. New 2012.

MSR $6,995	$6,650	$6,000	$5,250	$4,500	$3,750	$3,000	$2,250

* ***RBL Galleria*** – built to customer order, DT, stainless steel choke tubes, Exhibition black, English, or Turkish walnut, high gloss or rubbed oil finish, color case hardened or French greyed receiver, includes special leather case with canvas cover, RBL special label.

This model was POR.

* ***RBL NRA Special Wayne LaPierre Signature Edition*** – 20 ga., case colored receiver, straight or pistol grip stock, DT, splinter forend, 5 choke tubes, includes gold embossed NRA logo and gold Wayne LaPierre signature on trigger guard, many other options and upgrades available, includes leather case and accessories. Mfg. 2008-disc.

Base price on this model started at $4,350.

RBL GALLERY EDITION – 20 ga. only, many options and special orders are available per individual customer order. Mfg. 2011-2013.

The price range on this model was $10,000-$40,000 depending on special order options and features.

* ***RBL Launch Edition Gallery Gun*** – 20 ga., 28 in. barrel with choke tubes, many options and special orders were available. Mfg. 2011-2013.

Base price for this model started at $12,000.

RBL 20 GA. PROFESSIONAL SLUG GUN – 20 ga., 3 in. chambers, 24 in. fully rifled barrels with quarter rib and iron sights, walnut straight or pistol grip stock with splinter forearm, double triggers, ejectors, includes sling swivels. New 2011.

MSR $4,995	$4,500	$3,950	$3,375	$3,050	$2,475	$2,050	$1,750

RBL SPORTING COMPEITION S SERIES – 12 ga., raised VR Tuff Bore barrels with Trulock interchangeable choke tubes, exhibition grade checkered walnut stock with adj. comb and competition beavertail forend with push-button release, weight balancing system, and interchangeable recoil pad, SST, case colored receiver with gold inlaid pigeons, non-automatic safety. New 2014.

MSR $6,995	$6,650	$6,000	$5,250	$4,500	$3,750	$3,000	$2,250

RBL RESERVE EDITIONS – 12, 16, 20, or 28 ga., these editions were made at the end of the standard RBL production run. They can be distinguished by their special bluing, case colors, wood finish, and engraving. All are marked "Reserve" on the top rib, many options are available.

* ***RBL Reserve 12 ga.*** – 12 ga., case colored receiver with light scroll and three ducks in flight on right and two pheasants on left. Introduced 2010.

MSR $4,150	$3,950	$3,600	$3,250	$2,800	$2,400	$2,000	$1,650

* ***RBL Reserve 16 ga.*** – 16 ga., scaled frame, 29 in. barrels, case colored receiver with light scroll engraving, features game scenes of a pointer and a setter, quick change recoil pad available in two lengths. New 2010.

MSR $4,150	$3,950	$3,600	$3,250	$2,800	$2,400	$2,000	$1,650

* ***RBL Reserve 20 ga.*** – 20 ga., 28 or 30 in. barrels with 5 choke tubes, XX American black walnut stock and splinter forend with Classic 2 point checkering pattern, ejectors, double rolled edge trigger guard, metal grip cap, hard rubber buttplate, ornamental engraving standard, many options and special orders are available.

MSR $3,795	$3,500	$3,075	$2,625	$2,375	$1,925	$1,575	$1,225

Add $705 for rose and scroll engraving.

* ***RBL Reserve 28 ga.*** – 28 ga., 26, 28, or 30 in. barrels with choke tubes, double rolled edge trigger guard, splinter forend, 2X premium walnut, hard rubber buttplate, case colored receiver features dogs on point surrounded by full coverage scroll engraving. New 2010.

MSR $4,995	$4,500	$3,950	$3,375	$3,050	$2,475	$2,050	$1,750

* ***RBL Reserve Launch Edition*** – 20 ga., 28 in. barrels with choke tubes, similar to RBL 20 ga. Launch Edition, XXX American black walnut stock and forearm, many options and special orders are available. New 2011.

MSR $3,299	$3,000	$2,650	$2,300	$2,000	$1,700	$1,400	$1,100

GRADING - PPGS™	100%	98%	95%	90%	80%	70%	60%	LAST MSR

RBL RESERVE SPECIAL EDITION – available in most gauges, this model typically has deeper engraving with gold inlays. Mfg. 2011-2013.

Base price on this model started at $12,999.

RBL RESERVE CAMBRIDGE SPECIAL – 20 ga. This model was released at the end of RBL 20 production, and features rose and scroll pattern engraving, model name is engraved on trigger guard, many options are available, including wood upgrades, engraving, etc. Mfg. 2011-2013.

Base price on this model started at $4,000.

CONNECTICUT VALLEY ARMS

Current importer of firearms, muzzleloaders, and muzzleloading accessories established during 1971 and located in Lawrenceville, GA.

CVA is well known for their muzzleloading rifles and related black powder accessories. Please refer to the *Blue Book of Modern Black Powder Arms* (also available online) for more information on these products - visit BlueBookOfGunValues.com.

PISTOLS: SINGLE SHOT

SCOUT PISTOL – .357 Mag., .44 Mag., .45 LC/.410 shotshell cal., includes DuraSight scope mount. Mfg. 2010-2013.

	$300	$260	$225	$200	$180	$160	$140	*$370*

SCOUT V2 PISTOL – .243 Win. (new 2014), .357 Mag. (disc. 2017), .300 Blackout (disc. 2016), or .44 Mag. (disc. 2017) cal., single shot pistol, 11 1/2 (threaded, .300 AAC Blackout only, disc. 2016) or 14 in. stainless steel barrel, DuraSight Z2 scope rail, black grips, 3.7 lbs. Mfg. 2013-2018.

	$350	$300	$265	$240	$195	$160	$125	*$405*

Add $151 for Konus dot sight and soft case (mfg. 2016-2017).
Add $63 for 11 1/2 in. threaded barrel in .300 AAC Blackout cal. only (disc. 2016).

RIFLES: BOLT ACTION

CASCADE – .243 Win. (new 2020), 6.5 Creedmoor, 6.5 PRC (new 2020), 7mm-08 Rem., .308 Win., .300 Win. Mag (new 2020), .450 Bushmaster (new 2020), .350 Legend (new 2020), .22-250 Rem. (new 2020), 6.5 PRC (new 2021), or 7mm Rem. Mag. (new 2021) cal., 22 or 24 in. blued carbon steel barrel with threaded muzzle, 4 shot detachable mag., fiberglass reinforced charcoal grey or Veil Camo (new 2020) synthetic stock with SoftTouch and adj. LOP, 1 in. spacer and Crushzone recoil pad, dual front sling swivel studs, two-position safety, blued or Cerakote finish, approx. 7 lbs. New 2019.

MSR $567	$500	$445	$375	$345	$275	$225	$175	

Add $101 for Cerakote finish options.

RIFLES: SINGLE SHOT

APEX – .22 LR (disc. 2013), .22-250 Rem., .222 Rem., .223 Rem., 243 Win., .270 Win., .30-06, .45-70 Govt., 7mm-08 Rem., .35 Whelen (new 2010), .300 Win. Mag., or .308 Win. cal., break open action, 25 in. stainless steel standard contoured or full contoured fluted barrel, Black or Realtree APG HD camo stock, DuraSight Z2 scope rail, 7 1/2 lbs. Mfg. by Bergara in Spain. Imported 2009-2016.

	$575	$500	$425	$375	$325	$250	$200	*$651*

Add $80 for Realtree APG HD camo coverage.

ELITE STALKER – .35 Whelen, .444 Marlin, or .45-70 Govt. cal., blue or stainless steel barrel, black or camo finish, DuraSight Dead-On intergral mount. Mfg. 2012-2016.

	$285	$250	$215	$195	$150	$125	$100	*$331*

Add $40 for stainless steel.
Add $72 for camo.

HUNTER – .35 Whelen, .35 Rem. (disc. 2015), .45-70 Govt., .450 Bushmaster (new 2018), .444 Marlin (mfg. 2018 only), .300 AAC Blackout (disc. 2015), or .44 Mag. cal., break-action centerfire, 16 1/2 (threaded, .300 AAC Blackout only, disc. 2015), 22, or 25 in. blued steel barrel, 100% ambi black composite stock, CrushZone recoil pad, DuraSight DEAD-ON one-piece scope mount, 14 in. LOP, 38-41 in. OAL, 5.8-8 lbs. Mfg. 2013-2020.

	$250	$220	$190	$170	$140	$115	$90	*$287*

Add $40 for 16 1/2 in. threaded barrel in .300 Blackout cal. only (disc. 2015).
Add $82 for Konus 3-9x32 scope, DuraSight DEAD-ON Z2 mounts and soft case (scope is mounted and bore sighted).

GRADING - PPGS™	100%	98%	95%	90%	80%	70%	60%	LAST MSR

* ***Hunter Compact*** – .223 Rem. (disc. 2017), .243 Win., .35 Rem. (disc. 2015), or 7mm-08 cal. (disc. 2017), similar to Hunter model, except features 20 in. barrel, 13 in. LOP, 35 in. OAL, 5 1/2 lbs. Mfg. 2013-2020.

	$215	$190	$160	$145	$120	$95	$75	*$247*

Add $97 for Konus 3-9x32 scope, DuraSight DEAD-ON Z2 mounts and soft case (scope is mounted and bore sighted).

SCOUT (2010-2013 MFG.) – .243 Win., .270 Win. (disc. 2011), .30-06 (disc. 2011), .35 Whelen, .44 Mag. (new 2011), .45-70 Govt., or 7mm-08 Rem. cal., similar to Apex model, 20 in. compact or 22 in. fluted stainless steel or blued barrel, black synthetic stock with Fibergrip, open sights (.243 Win. or 7mm-08 Rem. cal. only) or DuraSight scope mount, CrushZone recoil pad, reversible hammer spur, 5.8 lbs. Mfg. 2010-2013.

	$285	$240	$210	$185	$165	$150	$135	*$341*

Add $42 for stainless steel barrel.
Add $9 for mounted and bore sighted KonusPro scope with engraved reticle (various powers), DuraSights mounts, and soft case.
Subtract $10 for Scout Model with open sights.

SCOUT (CURRENT MFG.) – .243 Win. (new 2020), 7mm-08 Win. (new 2020), 6.5 Creedmoor (new 2020), .350 Legend, .45-70 Govt., .450 Bushmaster, .35 Whelen, or .44 Mag cal., break open action, 20, 22, or 25 in. blued/black steel barrel, DuraSight scope rail, ambi stock, CrushZone recoil pad, reversible cocking spur, 6.3-7.5 lbs. New 2020.

MSR $349	$300	$250	$225	$200	$175	$125	$100

* ***Scout Compact*** – .243 Win., 7mm-08, or 6.5 Creedmoor cal., 20 in. blued/black steel barrel, DuraSight scope rail, ambidextrous stock, CrushZone recoil pad, reversible cocking spur, 6.3-7.5 lbs. New 2020.

MSR $349	$300	$250	$225	$200	$175	$125	$100

SCOUT V2 – .35 Whelen, .35 Rem. (disc. 2016), .300 AAC Blackout (disc. 2016), .444 Marlin, .450 Bushmaster (new 2018), .45-70 Govt. (new 2017) or .44 Mag. cal., 16 1/2 in. threaded (.300 AAC Blackout cal. only, disc. 2016), 22, or 25 in. fluted stainless steel barrel, reversible hammer spur, 100% ambidextrous stock in Black or Extra Green camo (.444 Marlin cal. only), CrushZone recoil pad, DuraSight DEAD-ON one-piece scope mount, 14 in. LOP, 38-41 in. OAL, 5.8-8 lbs. Mfg. 2013-2018.

	$350	$300	$275	$250	$200	$150	$125	*$394*

Add $25 for 25 in. barrel with DEAD-ON mount and muzzle brake.
Add $131 for Extra Green camo finish.
Add $132 for KonusPro scope with engraved reticle, DuraSight DEAD-ON Z-2 mounts, and soft case.
Add $42 for .300 AAC Blackout cal. (disc. 2016).

* ***Scout V2 Compact*** – .243 Win., .300 AAC Blackout (new 2019), .35 Rem., or 7mm-08 Rem. cal., 20 in. compact stainless steel barrel, otherwise similar to Scout V2 model, 5.8 lbs. Mfg. 2013-2016, reintroduced 2019 only.

	$375	$325	$275	$250	$200	$175	$150	*$406*

Add $64 for Extra Green camo finish.
Add $95 for KonusPro 1.5-5x32 scope with engraved reticle, DuraSight DEAD-ON Z-2 mounts, and soft case.

SCOUT TD (TAKEDOWN) – .35 Whelen, .450 Bushmaster, .45-70 Govt., .44 Mag., or .444 Marlin cal., 22 or 25 in. stainless steel fluted barrel with muzzle brake (not included on 22 in. model) and rail base, reversible cocking spur, trigger guard actuated breech system, 100% ambidextrous black stock, CrushZone recoil pad, 14 in. LOP, quick takedown capability, disassembles with no tools for easy storage and transport, DuraSight scope rail, 5.8 lbs. New 2016.

MSR $394	$350	$300	$275	$250	$200	$150	$125

Add $25 for 25 in. barrel with muzzle brake.
Add $89 for KonusPro 1.5-5 scope with engraved reticle, DuraSight DEAD-ON Z-2 mounts, and soft case (disc.).

* ***Scout Compact TD*** – .223 Rem. (disc. 2017), .243 Win., .300 AAC Blackout (new 2020), .350 Legend (new 2020), or .44 Mag. (disc. 2017) cal., 16 1/2 (new 2019) or 20 in. threaded stainless steel black barrel, reversible hammer spur, DuraSight DEAD-ON one-piece scope mount, 100% ambidextrous black composite stock, CrushZone recoil pad, 13 in. LOP, disassembles with no tools for easy storage and transport.

MSR $406	$350	$300	$265	$240	$195	$160	$125

GRADING - PPGS™	100%	98%	95%	90%	80%	70%	60%	LAST MSR

SHOTGUNS: SINGLE SHOT

HUNTER – .410 bore or 20 ga. 24 in. smoothbore barrel with fixed mod. choke or rifled blued barrel, reversible cocking spur, bead front sight or DuraSight Z2 scope rail, black finish, CrushZone® recoil pad, 13-14 in. adj. LOP, 39 in. OAL, 5.8 lbs. Mfg. 2016-2018.

	$195	$175	$150	$135	$110	$95	$75	*$214*

Add $47 for rifled barrel with DuraSight Z2 scope rail.
Add $90 for Konus 3-9x32 scope.

* ***Hunter Compact*** – 20 ga. or .410 bore, 24 in. smoothbore barrel with fixed full choke or rifled (20 ga. only) blued barrel, reversible cocking spur, bead front sight or DuraSight Z2 scope rail, black finish, CrushZone® Recoil Pad, 13-14 in. adj. LOP, 38-39 in. OAL, 5.8 lbs. Mfg. 2016-2018.

	$195	$175	$150	$135	$110	$95	$75	*$215*

Add $47 for rifled barrel with DuraSight Z2 scope rail.
Add $90 for Konus 3-9x32 scope.

SCOUT (2011-2012 MFG.) – 12 ga., 22 in. rifled barrel with scope mount, choice of blued or stainless steel barrel. Mfg. 2011-2012.

	$275	$240	$210	$185	$165	$150	$135	*$330*

Add $40 for stainless steel barrel.

SCOUT (CURRENT MFG.) – .410 bore, 22 in. blued barrel w/JEBS X-Full turkey choke, DuraSight scope rail, Realtree Timber ambidextrous stock. New 2020.

MSR $397	$325	$300	$250	$225	$175	$150	$125	

CONNECTICUT VALLEY CLASSICS, INC.

Previous trademark manufactured by Cooper Arms, located in Stevensville, MT 1996-1998. CVC, Inc. was a division of CVC Sports, Inc. Previous sales and marketing offices were located in Holyoke, MA until 1996 and in Westport, CT 1993-95.

SHOTGUNS: O/U

The models listed below have receiver dimensions built to the exact specifications of the original Classic Doubles Model 101. The only difference is that the tang spacer has been made an integral part of the frame.

Add $1,350 for each additional barrel set.

CLASSIC 101 SPORTER – 12 ga. only, boxlock action, monobloc, 28, 30, or 32 in. VR barrels with multi-chokes, SST, ejectors, nickel finished receiver with light engraving, checkered American black walnut stock and forearm with low luster finish, approx. 7 3/4 lbs.

	$1,875	$1,550	$1,225	$1,000	$825	$700	$600	*$2,195*

CLASSIC SPORTER SB – 12 ga. only, boxlock action, entry level sporter model. Mfg. 1997-98.

	$2,250	$1,875	$1,575	$1,175	$950	$775	$650	*$2,495*

GRADE I CLASSIC SPORTER – 12 ga. only, boxlock action, monobloc, 28, 30, or 32 in. vented barrels with VR, lengthened forcing cones, and 2 3/8 in. multi-chokes, SST, ejectors, stainless steel receiver with light engraving, checkered 20 LPI AA American black walnut stock and forearm with low luster finish, approx. 7 3/4 lbs. Disc. 1998.

	$2,695	$2,100	$1,675	$1,250	$1,000	$825	$700	*$2,995*

* ***Women's Classic Sporter*** – similar to Grade I Classic Sporter, except has smaller stock dimensions and 28 in. barrels only, 7 1/2 lbs. Mfg. 1996-98.

	$2,695	$2,100	$1,675	$1,250	$1,000	$825	$700	*$2,995*

This model was also available in Grade II or Grade III Women's Classic Sporter.

* ***Grade II Classic Sporter*** – similar to Grade I Classic Sporter, except has AAA American or Claro walnut with 22 LPI hand-checkering, 30 in. barrels only.

	$3,100	$2,350	$1,800	$1,325	$1,050	$850	$725	*$3,595*

* ***Grade III Classsic Sporter*** – similar to Grade II Classic Sporter, except has fleur-de-lis checkering patterns and gold accents. Disc. 1998.

	$3,600	$2,750	$1,975	$1,450	$1,175	$925	$750	*$4,195*

GRADE I CLASSIC FIELD – 12 ga. only, similar to Grade I Classic Sporter, except has solid rib and standard flush-mounted choke-tubes, 27 1/2 in. barrels, 7 1/2 lbs. Mfg. 1996-98.

	$2,695	$2,100	$1,675	$1,250	$1,000	$825	$700	*$2,995*

GRADING - PPGS™	100%	98%	95%	90%	80%	70%	60%	LAST MSR

* ***Classic Waterfowler*** – 12 ga. only, 30 or 32 (disc. 1995) in. VR barrels, non-reflective surfaces, bird scene engraving, overbored barrels with lengthened forcing cones and four standard CVC chokes, 8 lbs. Mfg. 1993-98.

$2,495	$2,000	$1,575	$1,175	$950	$775	$650	*$2,795*

* ***Grade II Classic Field*** – similar to Grade I Classic Field, except has AAA American or Claro walnut with 22 LPI hand-checkering.

$3,025	$2,250	$1,750	$1,300	$1,050	$850	$725	*$3,495*

* ***Grade III Classic/English Field*** – similar to Grade II Classic Field, except has fleur-de-lis checkering patterns and gold accents, choice of straight English (25 1/2 in. VR barrels only) or pistol grip stock. Disc. 1998.

$3,575	$2,850	$2,025	$1,500	$1,200	$925	$750	*$4,195*

Add $100 for straight English stock.

* ***Classic Skeet*** – 12 ga. only, 29 in. vented barrels with 9mm VR, otherwise similar to Grade I Classic Sporter, 7 1/2 lbs. Mfg. 1996-98.

$2,695	$2,100	$1,675	$1,250	$1,000	$825	$700	*$2,995*

* ***Classic Flyer*** – 12 ga. only, live bird gun featuring AAA walnut and 22 LPI checkering, oil finish, 30 in. vented overbored barrels with 11mm tapered top rib and lengthened forcing cones, scroll engraving with pigeon scene on receiver bottom, 8 lbs. Mfg. 1996-98.

$3,100	$2,350	$1,800	$1,325	$1,050	$850	$725	*$3,595*

CONQUEST

Previous trademark of guns manufactured by various companies in Spain, Turkey, Germany, and Italy.

The Conquest trademark included shotguns in O/U, SxS, slide action, and semi-auto configuration. These models had little or no importation into the U.S.

CONSTITUTION ARMS

Current palm pistol and carbine manufacturer located in Maplewood, NJ.

PISTOLS: SEMI-AUTO

PALM PISTOL – 9mm Para. cal., single shot, DAO, thumb operated trigger, polymer/metal frame, short barrel, may be fired by using either hand, 3-pos.combination lock, grip safeties, optional Picatinny rail.

Please contact the company directly for pricing, options, and availability.

CARBINES/RIFLES: BOLT ACTION

PALM CARBINE – .38 Spl. cal., easy breech access and loading, dual operable grip safeties, latch safety, cocked striker, indicator, handguard, grip assist ramp, striker safety ramp, spring loaded trigger covers, black finish. Limited mfg. of 100.

Please contact the company directly for pricing, options, and availability.

CONTENTO/VENTURA

Previously imported by Ventura Imports in Seal Beach, CA. Ventura also imported Bertuzzi and Piotti.

For individual model listings, please go to BlueBookOfGunValues.com/overflow.

CONTINENTAL ARMS CORPORATION

Previous importer of high quality shotguns and rifles (usually Belgian), circa mid-1950s-mid-1970s.

RIFLES

BOLT ACTION – mostly large cals., typically custom Mauser action, makers include Defourney and Dumoulin.

Specimens should be evaluated individually due to the many configurations and embellishments encountered. This model is rarely seen in today's marketplace.

DOUBLE RIFLE – .270 Win., .303 British, .30-40 Krag, .348 Win., .30-06, .375 H&H, .400 Jeffery, .470, .475, .500, or .600 Nitro Express cal., 24 or 26 in. barrels, Anson & Deeley boxlock system, although some sidelocks were mfg., double triggers, checkered stock.

$5,750	$5,000	$4,425	$3,800	$3,425	$3,150	$2,875

Add 10% for boxlock with sideplates.
Add 15% for ejectors.
Add 30%-50% for .375 H&H and larger cals., depending on the size of the cal.

GRADING - PPGS™	100%	98%	95%	90%	80%	70%	60%	LAST MSR

SHOTGUNS: O/U

Most grades and models came in gauges from .410 bore up to 10 gauge dictated by customer preference.

Add 20% for .410 bore.
Add 30% for 28 ga.
Add 10% for Defourney mfg.

CENTAURE BOXLOCK – 10, 12, 20, 28 ga., or .410 bore, ejectors, light engraving, chopper lump barrels with crossbolt, double underlocks, SST, 3-piece forearm.

	100%	98%	95%	90%	80%	70%	60%	LAST MSR
	$2,500	$2,100	$1,875	$1,550	$1,275	$1,100	$925	

CENTAURE LIEGE ROYAL CROWN GRADE – similar to Centaure Boxlock, except has game scene engraving, better figured wood and silver crown inlay.

	100%	98%	95%	90%	80%	70%	60%	LAST MSR
	$3,925	$3,575	$3,250	$2,825	$2,375	$2,000	$1,750	

CENTAURE IMPERIAL CROWN GRADE – similar to Royal Crown Grade, except has higher grade wood, extensive game scene engraving, oak leaf engraving on barrels, and gold inlay on top lever.

	100%	98%	95%	90%	80%	70%	60%	LAST MSR
	$5,625	$5,275	$4,675	$4,375	$4,000	$3,625	$3,375	

SHOTGUNS: SxS

Add 20% for .410 bore.
Add 30% for 28 ga.
Add 10% for Defourney mfg.

CENTAURE – all gauges, basic boxlock action with double triggers and extractors.

	100%	98%	95%	90%	80%	70%	60%	LAST MSR
	$1,300	$1,175	$1,125	$1,050	$875	$625	$500	

Add 35% for ejectors.

CENTAURE ROYAL CROWN GRADE – all gauges, single trigger, ejectors, checkered stock and forearm, game scene engraving, can be identified by silver crown inlaid on top lever.

	100%	98%	95%	90%	80%	70%	60%	LAST MSR
	$4,250	$3,925	$3,500	$3,250	$2,900	$2,625	$2,425	

CENTAURE IMPERIAL CROWN GRADE – similar to Royal Crown, except gold inlay on top lever, extensive game scene engraving on receiver and barrels.

	100%	98%	95%	90%	80%	70%	60%	LAST MSR
	$5,350	$4,800	$4,375	$3,925	$3,575	$3,275	$2,875	

CONTROLLED CHAOS ARMS

Current custom AR-15 style firearm manufacturer located in Baxter, IA.

Please refer to BlueBookOfGunValues.com to order the *Blue Book of AR-15s & Variations*, available as a book or online subscription.

COOEY, H.W., MACHINE & ARMS CO. LTD.

Previous manufacturer located in Cobourg, Ontario, Canada 1903-1979. During 1961, Cooey was sold to the Olin Corporation and placed under the supervision of the Winchester Western Division. At that point, the manufacture of Winchesters (primarily for Winchester Canada) began and continued through the mid-1970s (see Iver Johnson).

COOEY MODEL 84 MADE IN CANADA

To date, there has been limited collector interest domestically for most models in this trademark and values should be based on the shooting utility rather than collector premiums due to rarity. Values for average condition single shot shotguns and rimfire bolt actions will typically range between $100-$325, depending on the desirability of the configuration.

RIFLES

Cooey manufactured a wide number of rifles, including bolt actions, single shots, and semi-autos. During the late 1920s-early 1930s, Cooey manufactured the Model X and 2X for Iver Johnson (please refer to Iver Johnson section).

Pre-1961 Cooey mfg. models include: 25, 35, 39, 55, 60, 62, 75, 78, 82, Ace, Ace 1, Ace 2, Ace 3, Ace Repeater, Ace Special, Bisley Sport, Canuck, Canuck 25, Canuck Junior, Canuck Western, Cooey Repeater, HWC, Mohawk, and several unnumbered single shot and repeating sporter rifles. Post-1961 Cooey firearms made for Winchester include: Model 10, Model 39, Model 60, Model 600, Model 64, Model 64 Deluxe, Model 64A, 64B, Model 71, 71 Carbine, Model 75, 750, and 750 Deluxe, Model 710, and Ranger.

GRADING - PPGS™	100%	98%	95%	90%	80%	70%	60%	LAST MSR

SHOTGUNS

Cooey manufactured both double and single barrel shotguns for Iver Johnson (Hercules and Champion) during the late 1920s-early 1930s (see Iver Johnson section). Cooey also manufactured single shot shotguns. Pre-1961 Cooey mfg. models include: .22 rimfire smoothbore, 37A, 410, 84, Canuck 25, and Canuck 410. Post-1961 Cooey firearms made for Winchester include: Models 84 and 840.

COONAN ARMS

Previously manufactured by Dan Coonan, and distributed from November 1994-September 1998 by JS Worldwide Distribution Co. located in Maplewood, MN. Previously located in St. Paul, MN, approx. 1983-1996.

During 1985, Dan Coonan sold Coonan Arms to Bill Davis. In 1990, Dan Coonan left the company, and during July 1994, the company filed for Chapter 11. Coonan Arms was incorporated by JS Worldwide Distribution in November 1994. On Sept. 25, 1998, Coonan Arms and JS Worldwide Distribution was dissolved by the state of MN.

PISTOLS: SEMI-AUTO

COONAN .357 MAG. MODEL B – .357 Mag. cal. only, stainless steel and alloy construction, single action, semi-auto, design based on the Colt Model 1911, 7 shot mag., 5 or 6 (new 1989) in. barrel, smooth or checkered (new 1996) walnut grips, Teflon finish options (new 1996), 42 oz. Mfg. 1983-1998.

$795	$725	$650	$475	$400	$350	$295	*$735*

Add $40 for checkered walnut grips.
Add $33 for 6 in. barrel (new 1989).
Add $140 for Millett adj. rear sight.
Add $165 for Bo-Mar sight.
Add $45 for .38 Spl. conversion kit (new 1986).

This model could be differentiated from the Model A in that it had an extended grip safety lever, linkless barrel system, enclosed trigger bar slot, and recontoured rear grip strap. This model became standard in 1985.

* ***Coonan .357 Mag. Cadet Model*** – similar to .357 Mag. Model B, except is compact variation with 3.9 in. barrel and 6 shot mag., 39 oz. Mfg. 1993-98.

$850	$775	$675	$500	$425	$375	$315	*$855*

Options were similar to those listed for the Model B.

* ***Coonan .357 Mag. Cadet II*** – features standard grip with 7/8 shot mag. Mfg. 1996-98.

$850	$775	$675	$500	$425	$375	$315	*$855*

Options were similar to those listed for the Model B.

* ***Coonan .357 Mag. Model B Compensated*** – 6 in. barrel with compensator. Mfg. 1990-98.

$1,000	$900	$800	$650	$540	$465	$385	*$1,015*

Options were similar to those listed for the Model B.

* ***Coonan .357 Mag. Model Classic Compensated*** – features 5 in. barrel with integral compensator, Millett white/orange outline sights, checkered black walnut grips, Teflon black and matte stainless two-tone finish, 42 oz. Mfg. 1996-98.

$1,275	$1,025	$825	$675	$595	$525	$450	*$1,400*

COONAN .357 MAG. MODEL A – original model without above listed improvements, special order only, inventory depleted in 1991. Serialization is under 2,000 for this model (less than 1,200 were mfg.).

$1,150	$775	$550	$460	$395	$335	$285	*$625*

Add approx. $350 for early variations with engraved slide.

This variation will also shoot .38+P loads. The first 25 Model As were engraved on both sides of slide.

COONAN .41 MAGNUM – .41 Mag. cal., 5 in. barrel, smooth or checkered walnut grips. Only 1 mfg. circa 1997-1998.

Last MSR was $825.

Extreme rarity factor precludes accurate pricing.

Options were similar to those listed for the .357 Mag.

GRADING - PPGS™	100%	98%	95%	90%	80%	70%	60%	LAST MSR

COONAN, INC.

Previous manufacturer of pistols, located in Blaine, MN circa 2009-2020.

PISTOLS: SEMI-AUTO

COONAN CLASSIC .357 MAGNUM AUTOMATIC – .357 Mag. cal., single action, 1911 style, 5, 5.7 (threaded), or 6 in. barrel, linkless barrel system, compensated barrel became optional 2013, 7 shot mag., stainless steel, pivoting trigger, dovetail front and rear fixed or adj., white dot or night sights, smooth or textured black walnut or aluminum grips, extended grip safety, includes case, satin (new 2018) or straight line stainless, black or digital camo DuraCoat (new 2013) finish, 48 oz. Mfg. 2010-disc.

$1,300	$1,140	$1,025	$875	$750	$625	$525	*$1,540*

Add $78 for 5.7 or 6 in. barrel.
Add $20 for fixed white dot or $162 for adj. white dot sights.
Add $232 for fixed night sights or $268 for adj. night sights.
Add $400 for compensator pkg.
Add $100 for satin stainless (new 2018).

* ***Coonan Classic .357 Magnum Automatic Camo*** – .357 Mag. cal., 5 in. linkless barrel, 2 or 3 shot mag., pivoting trigger, recoil operated, fixed black (standard), white dot, or fixed night sights, or adj. white dot or adj. night sights, smooth wood or black or silver Alumagrips, smooth or textured mainspring housing, extended slide catch and thumb lock, ACU camo, Desert camo (w/smooth wood grips), Pink camo, Purple camo (with silver Alumagrips), or Urban camo finish, includes custom carry case and lock. Mfg. 2013-disc.

$1,795	$1,575	$1,350	$1,225	$985	$825	$650	*$2,107*

Add $19 for fixed white dot sights or $162 for adj. white dot sights.
Add $232 for fixed night or $268 for adj. night sights.

COONAN COMPACT .357 MAGNUM – .357 Mag. cal., 4 in. stainless steel linkless bull barrel, 6 shot mag., external extractor, Commander-style hammer, pivoting trigger, fixed white dot or night sights, smooth black walnut grip panels with the Coonan symbol engraved into the wood, extended slide catch and thumb lock, full length guide rod, includes custom carry case, takedown wrench, and two mags., satin (new 2018), straight line stainless steel, or black Duracoat finish, 39 oz. Mfg. 2016-disc.

$1,450	$1,265	$1,115	$985	$840	$725	$590	*$1,725*

Add $250 for satin finish.
Add $150 for fixed night sights.
Add $459 for black Duracoat finish with black aluminum grips.

COONAN MOT .45 ACP – .45 ACP cal., 5 in. stainless steel linkless barrel, 7 shot mag., external extractor, pivoting trigger, Novak style sights in fixed black, white dot, or night sights, or adj. white dot or night sights, fiber optic also available, smooth walnut grips, includes custom carry case, satin (new 2018) or straight line stainless finish. Mfg. 2017-disc.

$1,160	$1,030	$900	$750	$685	$585	$485	*$1,399*

Add $19 for fixed white dot or $129 for adj. white dot sights.
Add $198 for fixed night sights or $234 for adj. night sights.
Add $206 for fiber optic sights.
Add $75 for satin stainless finish.

COONAN MOT 10 – .45 ACP cal., 5 in. stainless or satin stainless steel linkless barrel, 7 shot mag., external extractor, pivoting trigger, Novak rear and blade front sights, fixed black (standard) or white dot, fixed night sights, or adj. white dot or night sights, smooth walnut or black aluminum grips, includes custom carry case. Mfg. 2017-disc.

$1,160	$1,030	$900	$750	$685	$585	$485	*$1,399*

Add $19 for fixed white or $129 for adj. white dot sights.
Add $198 for fixed night or $234 for adj. night sights.
Add $75 for satin stainless finish.
Add $69 for fixed white dot or $179 for adj. white dot sights w/satin stainless steel barrel.
Add $248 for fixed night or $284 for adj. night sights w/satin stainless steel barrel.

COONAN .45 ACP 1911 PISTOL – .45 ACP cal., 5 in. stainless steel linkless barrel, 7 shot mag., external extractor, pivoting trigger, Novak rear and blade front sights, fixed night sights, or adj. rear sights, smooth walnut grips, extended slide catch and thumb lock, includes custom carry case, 40 oz. Mfg. 2016-disc.

$1,160	$1,030	$900	$750	$685	$585	$485	*$1,399*

Add $18 for fixed or $129 for adj. white dot sights
Add $198 for fixed or $234 for adj. night sights.

GRADING - PPGS™	100%	98%	95%	90%	80%	70%	60%	LAST MSR

COOPER FIREARMS OF MONTANA, INC.

Current manufacturer located in Stevensville, MT since 1991. Available through Cooper Firearms registered dealers only.

RIFLES: BOLT ACTION

Various options and upgrades are available for most of the following models unless otherwise noted. Please contact the manufacturer directly for custom orders, options, price, and availability.

Add $200 for left-hand action (custom order only) on the following models, except for Model 51, Model 52, Model 54, and Model 58 - add $250.

Add $375-$1,950 for wood upgrade.

MODEL 21 SINGLE SHOT - various medium size cals., 3 front locking lugs.

* ***Model 21 Classic*** – various cals., single shot, 24 in. chrome moly match grade barrel, AA Claro walnut stock with 20 LPI hand checkering and hand rubbed oil finish, machined aluminum trigger guard, matte metal finish, approx. 7-7 1/4 lbs. New 1999.

MSR $2,795	$2,400	$2,100	$1,800	$1,600	$1,300	$1,050	$850	

* ***Model 21 Custom Classic*** – single shot, blued match barrel, AAA Claro walnut stock, Shadow line cheekpiece, Brownell No. 1 checkering pattern (disc.) or western fleur wrap-around hand checkering, ebony forend tip, steel grip cap, high polish metal finish.

MSR $3,855	$3,300	$2,850	$2,450	$2,250	$1,800	$1,500	$1,150	

* ***Model 21 Western Classic*** – various cals., features octagon blued match barrel, AAA+ Claro walnut, raised comb cheekpiece, ebony forend tip, vertical pistol grip and stock, wrap around western-fleur hand checkering, case hardened action and metal work, options available. New 1997.

MSR $4,395	$3,750	$3,250	$2,800	$2,550	$2,050	$1,700	$1,300	

* ***Model 21 Varminter*** – various cals., 24 in. stainless steel match grade barrel, AA Claro walnut stock with 20 LPI hand checkering and hand rubbed oil finish, machined aluminum trigger guard, approx. 7-7.25 lbs. New 1999.

MSR $2,795	$2,400	$2,100	$1,800	$1,600	$1,300	$1,050	$850	

* ***Model 21 Varmint Extreme*** – various cals. between .17 Rem.-.223 Rem. (including metric cals.), stainless barrel, checkered stock, Benchrest Model with Jewell trigger (mfg. 1995-96). New 1994.

MSR $3,595	$3,050	$2,700	$2,300	$2,100	$1,700	$1,400	$1,050	

Add $465 for Benchrest Model with Jewell trigger (mfg. 1995-96).

* ***Model 21 Varmint Extreme 25th Anniversary Limited Edition*** – .223 Rem. cal., AAA Claro walnut stock, custom hand engraved, silver inlaid "25" in the grip cap. Only 25 mfg. 2015-disc.

Retail pricing wasn't available on this model.

* ***Model 21 Varmint Laminate*** – similar to Varminter, except has laminated stock. Mfg. 2009-2014, reintroduced 2016-2020.

	$2,100	$1,850	$1,600	$1,450	$1,150	$950	$750	*$2,495*

* ***Model 21 Jackson Varmint*** – various cals., 22 in. stainless steel match grade barrel, oil finished hand checkered AA select walnut stock with rollover cheekpiece, steel grip cap, matte metal finish. Disc.

	$2,200	$1,950	$1,650	$1,500	$1,200	$1,000	$750	*$2,595*

* ***Model 21 Montana Varminter*** – various cals., 24 in. stainless steel barrel, oil finished hand checkered AA select Claro walnut stock, steel grip cap, cooling vent, high polish metal finish. New 2000.

MSR $3,095	$2,650	$2,300	$2,000	$1,800	$1,450	$1,200	$900	

* ***Model 21 Mannlicher*** – various cals., steel match grade barrel, high polish bone charcoal finish, oil finished hand checkered full length AAA Claro walnut stock with ebony tip, steel grip cap. New 2012.

MSR $5,355	$4,550	$4,000	$3,400	$3,100	$2,500	$2,050	$1,600	

* ***Model 21 Phoenix*** – 24 in. stainless match barrel, flat black or brown spider web synthetic stock, aluminum bedding block, matte metal finish. New 2005.

MSR $2,795	$2,400	$2,100	$1,800	$1,600	$1,300	$1,050	$850	

* ***Model 21 TRP-3*** – various cals., 26 in. stainless steel match barrel, wood or laminate stock, "bench rest style", matte metal finish, limited additional options.

MSR $3,395	$2,900	$2,500	$2,150	$1,950	$1,600	$1,300	$1,000	

* ***Model 21 Var-Tac*** – various cals., 24 in. stainless matte match barrel, hand rubbed oil finish, AA+ Claro walnut vertical pistol grip and stock, raised comb cheekpiece, western-fleur hand checkering, high polish metal finish.

MSR $2,995	$2,550	$2,200	$1,900	$1,750	$1,400	$1,150	$900	

GRADING - PPGS™	100%	98%	95%	90%	80%	70%	60%	LAST MSR

MODEL 22 – various mid-length action cals., larger-sized version of the Model 21.

* ***Model 22 Classic*** – various mid-action cals., 24 in. chrome moly match grade barrel, AA Claro walnut stock with 20 LPI hand checkering and hand rubbed oil finish, machined aluminum trigger guard, matte metal finish, approx. 7-7.25 lbs. New 1999.

MSR $2,795	$2,400	$2,100	$1,800	$1,600	$1,300	$1,050	$850	

* ***Model 22 Custom Classic*** – various cals., 24 in. chrome moly match grade barrel, ebony forend tip, AA (disc.) or AAA Claro walnut stock, Brownell No. 1 checkering pattern (disc.), western-fleur wrap-around hand checkering, steel grip cap, high polish metal finish.

MSR $3,855	$3,300	$2,850	$2,450	$2,250	$1,800	$1,500	$1,150	

* ***Model 22 Western Classic*** – various cals., 24 in. blued octagon barrel, AAA+ Claro walnut stock, Shadowline cheekpiece, ebony tip, steel grip cap and bottom metal, wrap-around western-fleur hand checkering, high polish metal finish, case hardened action and bolt. New 1997.

MSR $4,395	$3,750	$3,250	$2,800	$2,550	$2,050	$1,700	$1,300	

* ***Model 22 Varminter*** – various cals., otherwise similar to the Model 21 Varminter. New 2000.

MSR $2,795	$2,400	$2,100	$1,800	$1,600	$1,300	$1,050	$850	

* ***Model 22 Montana Varminter*** – various cals., 24 in. stainless steel barrel, oil finished hand checkered AA+ Claro walnut stock, steel grip cap, cooling vents, western-fleur hand checkering, high polish metal finish. New 2000.

MSR $3,095	$2,650	$2,300	$2,000	$1,800	$1,450	$1,200	$900	

* ***Model 22 Varmint Extreme*** – .220 Swift, .22 BR (new 1996), .22-250 Rem., .243 Win., .25-06 Rem., .308 Win., 6mm PPC, 6.5x55mm (new 1996), or 7.62x39mm (new 1996) cal., available in either Pro-Varmint (disc.), Benchrest (disc. 2011), or Black Jack (black synthetic stock) configuration, 26 in. stainless (matte) match barrel, AAA Claro walnut stock, Shadowline cheekpiece, steel grip and stock, western-fleur hand checkering, matte metal finish. New 1995.

MSR $3,595	$3,050	$2,700	$2,300	$2,100	$1,700	$1,400	$1,050	

Add $400 for Benchrest Model (disc. 2011).

* ***Model 22 Varmint Laminate*** – similar to Varminter, except has laminated stock. Mfg. 2009-2014, reintroduced 2016-2020.

	$2,100	$1,850	$1,600	$1,450	$1,150	$950	$750	*$2,495*

* ***Model 22 Mannlicher*** – various cals., steel blued match grade barrel, oil finished hand checkered full length AAA Claro walnut stock with ebony tip, steel grip cap, high polish bone charcoal (disc.) or metal finish. New 2012.

MSR $5,355	$4,550	$4,000	$3,400	$3,100	$2,500	$2,050	$1,600	

* ***Model 22 Phoenix*** – similar to the Montana Varminter, 24 in. stainless match barrel, flat black, brown (disc.), or red spider web synthetic stock, no grip cap, aluminum bedding block, matte metal finish, other options limited. New 2005.

MSR $2,795	$2,400	$2,100	$1,800	$1,600	$1,300	$1,050	$850	

* ***Model 22 TRP-3*** – various cals., 26 in. stainless steel match barrel, wood or laminate stock, "bench rest style", matte metal finish, limited additional options.

MSR $3,595	$3,050	$2,700	$2,300	$2,100	$1,700	$1,400	$1,050	

* ***Model 22 Var-Tac*** – various cals., 24 in stainless matte match barrel, hand rubbed oil finish, AA+ Claro walnut vertical pistol grip stock, raised comb cheekpiece, western-fleur hand checkering, high polish metal finish.

MSR $2,595	$2,200	$1,950	$1,650	$1,500	$1,200	$1,000	$750	

MODEL 22 CLASSIC REPEATER – .22-250 Rem., .243 Win., .308 Win., or 7mm-08 Rem. cal., 3 shot mag. While advertised during 1996 only at $2,400 retail, this model was never mfg.

MODEL 22R – various cals. New 2018.

* ***Model 22R Excalibur*** – various cals., bolt action rifle, 23 in. fluted steel barrel, 3 shot mag., fully adj. single stage trigger, synthetic stock, spiral fluted bolt, matte metal finish. Mfg. 2019 only.

	$2,200	$1,950	$1,650	$1,500	$1,200	$1,000	$750	*$2,595*

* ***Model 22R Jackson Game*** – similar to Squirrel rifle, stainless steel match grade barrel, AA select Claro walnut stock with rollover cheekpiece, semi-beavertail forearm, VE hand checkered grip, Pachmayr recoil pad, steel grip cap, sling swivels, limited options available on this model. New 2019.

MSR $2,595	$2,200	$1,950	$1,650	$1,500	$1,200	$1,000	$750	

GRADING - PPGS™	100%	98%	95%	90%	80%	70%	60%	LAST MSR

* ***Model 22R Jackson Hunter*** – 22 in. match blue barrel, camo synthetic stock with aluminum bedding block, matte metal finish. Mfg. 2019 only.

	$2,200	$1,950	$1,650	$1,500	$1,200	$1,000	$750	*$2,595*

* ***Model 22R Montana Varminter*** – various cals., 24 in. stainless steel match grade barrel, oil finished hand checkered AA select Claro walnut stock. steel grip cap, cooling vents, matte metal finish. New 2019.

MSR $2,595	$2,200	$1,950	$1,650	$1,500	$1,200	$1,000	$750	

* ***Model 22R Phoenix*** – 24 in. stainless match barrel, flat black or brown spider web synthetic stock, aluminum bedding block, matte metal finish. Mfg. 2019-2020.

	$2,100	$1,850	$1,600	$1,450	$1,150	$950	$750	*$2,495*

* ***Model 22R Raptor-M*** – various cals., 22 (new 2021) or 24 in. heavy varmint stainless fluted match barrel, Cooper muzzle brake, 5 shot AICS-style mag., tactical synthetic stock, spiral fluted bolt, Picatinny rail, tan finish, limited options available. New late 2018.

MSR $2,995	$2,550	$2,200	$1,900	$1,750	$1,400	$1,150	$900	

* ***Model 22R Schnabel*** – various cals., barrel in various lengths, machined aluminum trigger guard, checkered AA+ select Claro walnut stock with high comb and slim tapered forearm, multi-point Southwestern hand checkering, machined steel grip cap, other options available, matte metal finish, 6 1/4 lbs. Mfg. 2019 only.

	$2,200	$1,950	$1,650	$1,500	$1,200	$1,000	$750	*$2,595*

* ***Model 22R Varminter*** – various cals., single shot, 24 in. stainless steel match grade barrel, stock is AA Claro walnut with 20 LPI hand checkering and hand rubbed oil finish, machined aluminum trigger guard, approx. 7-7 1/4 lbs. Mfg. 2019 only.

	$2,100	$1,850	$1,600	$1,450	$1,150	$950	$750	*$2,495*

* ***Model 22R Varmint Laminate*** – similar to Varminter, except has laminated stock. Disc. 2014, reintroduced 2016-2020.

	$2,100	$1,850	$1,600	$1,450	$1,150	$950	$750	*$2,495*

MODEL CUSTOM CLASSIC – .22 LR, .22 WMR, .22 Hornet, or .222 Rem. cal., features Anschutz Match 54 action with deluxe walnut stock with American features and smaller trigger guard. Mfg. 1996-99.

	$1,750	$1,530	$1,310	$1,190	$960	$785	$610	*$1,995*

MODEL CUSTOM MANNLICHER – .22 LR, .22 WMR, .22 Hornet, or .222 Rem. cal., features newest Anschutz Match 54 action with deluxe Mannlicher walnut stock and other special features. Mfg. 1996-99.

	$1,975	$1,730	$1,480	$1,345	$1,085	$890	$690	*$2,195*

MODEL 36 SPORTSMAN – .22 LR, .17 CCM, or .22 Hornet cal., without Shilen barrel, standard wood with rubber recoil pad. Mfg. 1994 only.

	$675	$590	$505	$460	$370	$305	$235	*$750*

MODEL 36 MARKSMAN – .22 LR, .17 CCM, or .22 Hornet cal., 4 shot mag., 23 in. chrome moly barrel, AA Claro walnut with 22 LPI checkering, 45 degree bolt lift, sling swivels, hand rubbed oil finish, 7 lbs. Mfg. 1992-94.

	$975	$855	$730	$665	$535	$440	$340	*$1,125*

* ***Model 36 Montana Trail Blazer*** – .22 LR cal. only, lightweight field gun with sporter barrel. Mfg. 1996 only.

	$1,300	$1,135	$975	$885	$715	$585	$455	*$1,475*

* ***Model 36 Classic*** – .22 LR cal. only, features choice of AAA Claro or AA French walnut with Monte Carlo cheekpiece. Disc. 1996.

	$1,500	$1,310	$1,125	$1,020	$825	$675	$525	*$1,695*

* ***Model 36 Varmint Extreme*** – various cals., stainless heavy bull barrel, checkered stock. Mfg. 1997 only.

	$1,525	$1,335	$1,145	$1,035	$840	$685	$535	*$1,695*

* ***Model 36 Western Classic*** – various cals., features octagon barrel and case hardened action and bolt. Mfg. 1997-99.

	$1,900	$1,660	$1,425	$1,290	$1,045	$855	$665	*$2,195*

* ***Model 36 Custom Classic*** – includes Brownell No. 1 checkering pattern, ebony forend tip, and steel grip cap. Disc. 1999.

	$1,625	$1,420	$1,220	$1,105	$895	$730	$570	*$1,850*

GRADING - PPGS™	100%	98%	95%	90%	80%	70%	60%	LAST MSR

* ***Model 36 TRP-1*** – target variation of the Model 36 with ISU synthetic stock and adj. cheekpiece, 23 in. Wiseman/McMillan stainless steel or chrome moly barrel, single shot, fully adj. single stage trigger, vent. forearm. Mfg. 1992-93.

	$950	$830	$710	$645	$520	$425	$330	*$1,095*

* ***Model MS-36 (TRP-1S)*** – silhouette variation of the Model 36 TRP-1, clear epoxy finish, silhouette style stock, Pachmayr buttpad. Mfg. 1992-93.

	$895	$785	$670	$610	$490	$405	$315	*$995*

* ***Model 36 BR-50*** – .22 LR cal., benchrest variation featuring black synthetic stock and heavy stainless barrel. Mfg. 1993-99.

	$1,675	$1,465	$1,255	$1,140	$920	$755	$585	*$1,950*

* ***Model 36 IR-50/50*** – .22 LR cal. only, lightweight sporter style competition rifle with heavy 20 in. barrel. Mfg. 1996-99.

	$1,675	$1,465	$1,255	$1,140	$920	$755	$585	*$1,950*

* ***Model 36 Featherweight*** – .17 CCM, .22 LR, or .22 Hornet cal., features matte black synthetic stock and metal, Jewell trigger. Mfg. 1994-99.

	$1,600	$1,400	$1,200	$1,090	$880	$720	$560	*$1,795*

MODEL 38 SPORTER – .17 CCM, or .22 CCM cal., 3 shot mag., 24 in. chrome moly barrel, AA Claro walnut with 22 LPI checkering, 45 degree bolt lift, sling swivels, hand rubbed oil finish, 8 lbs. Mfg. 1992-93.

	$965	$845	$725	$655	$530	$435	$340	*$1,095*

Add $100 for Standard Grade (AA Claro walnut).
Add $200 for Custom Grade.
Add $300 for Custom Classic Grade.

The custom grade includes choice of AAA Claro or AA French walnut with Monte Carlo cheekpiece.

The .17 CCM and .22 CCM cartridges are Cooper Centerfire Magnums. Basically, the .22 CCM is a centerfire derivative of the .22 WMR cal., and the .17 CCM is simply a necked down variation.

* ***Model 38 Repeater (Deluxe)*** – deluxe variation of the Model 38 Sporter. 650 mfg. 1992-1994.

	$1,750	$1,530	$1,310	$1,190	$960	$785	$610	

MODEL 38 SINGLE SHOT – small, mostly rimmed cals., 3 front locking lugs. New 1998.

* ***Model 38 Classic*** – various cals., single shot, 20 in. chrome moly match grade barrel, stock is AA Claro walnut with 20 LPI hand checkering and hand rubbed oil finish, machined aluminum trigger guard, matte metal finish, approx. 7-7 1/4 lbs. Mfg. 1999-2018.

	$1,895	$1,660	$1,425	$1,290	$1,050	$875	$725	*$2,225*

* ***Model 38 Custom Classic*** – blued match barrel, Brownell No. 1 checkering pattern (disc.) or western fleur wrap-around hand checkering, AAA Claro walnut, Shadow line cheekpiece, ebony forend tip, and steel grip cap, all options available. Disc. 2018.

	$2,200	$1,925	$1,650	$1,500	$1,225	$1,000	$850	*$2,595*

* ***Model 38 Western Classic*** – various cals., octagon barrel, case hardened action and bolt. Mfg. 1997-2018.

	$2,950	$2,575	$2,225	$2,000	$1,625	$1,325	$1,150	*$3,455*

* ***Model 38 Varminter*** – various cals., single shot, 24 in. stainless steel match grade barrel, stock is AA Claro walnut with 20 LPI hand checkering and hand rubbed oil finish, machined aluminum trigger guard, approx. 7-7 1/4 lbs. Mfg. 1999-2018.

	$1,895	$1,660	$1,425	$1,290	$1,050	$875	$725	*$2,225*

* ***Model 38 Varmint Extreme*** – various cals. including the new .19-223, heavy stainless steel barrel w/o sights, checkered stock. Mfg. 1997-2018.

	$2,065	$1,800	$1,550	$1,400	$1,150	$950	$775	*$2,425*

* ***Model 38 Montana Varminter*** – various cals., 24 in. stainless steel match grade barrel, oil finished hand checkered AA select Claro walnut stock. steel grip cap, cooling vents, matte metal finish. Mfg. 2000-2018.

	$1,950	$1,700	$1,475	$1,325	$1,075	$875	$750	*$2,275*

* ***Model 38 Varmint Laminate*** – similar to Varminter, except has laminated stock. Mfg. 2009-2014, reintroduced 2016-2018.

	$1,895	$1,660	$1,425	$1,290	$1,050	$875	$725	*$2,225*

GRADING - PPGS™	100%	98%	95%	90%	80%	70%	60%	LAST MSR

* ***Model 38 Jackson Varmint*** – various cals., 22 in. stainless steel match grade barrel, oil finished hand checkered AA select walnut stock with rollover cheekpiece, steel grip cap, matte metal finish. Disc. 2018.

	$2,000	$1,750	$1,500	$1,360	$1,100	$900	$775	*$2,355*

* ***Model 38 Mannlicher*** – various cals., steel match grade barrel, high polish bone charcoal finish, oil finished hand checkered full length AAA Claro walnut stock with ebony tip, steel grip cap. Mfg. 2012-2018.

	$3,750	$3,275	$2,825	$2,550	$2,075	$1,700	$1,450	*$4,395*

* ***Model 38 Phoenix*** – 24 in. stainless match barrel, flat black or brown spider web synthetic stock, aluminum bedding block, matte metal finish. Mfg. 2005-2018.

	$1,895	$1,660	$1,425	$1,290	$1,050	$875	$725	*$2,225*

MODEL 40 – .17 CCM (disc. 1995), .17 Ackley Hornet, .22 CCM (disc. 1995), .22 Hornet, or .22 K Hornet cal., 3 lug action, incorporates Anschütz mag., choice of Classic, Custom Classic, or Classic Varminter configuration. Mfg. 1995-96.

	$1,600	$1,400	$1,200	$1,090	$880	$720	$560	*$1,825*

Add $200 for Custom Classic or Classic Varminter (disc.) Model.

MODEL 51 REPEATER – .17 Rem., 19-223, Tactical 20, .204 Ruger, .222 Rem., .222 Rem. Mag., .223 Rem., .223 Rem. AI, 6x45, 6x47, or .300 AAC Blackout cal., matte black metal finish, 20, 22, or 24 in. stainless steel or blue barrel, 4 shot mag., Sako style extraction machined from solid bar stock, plunger style ejector machined from solid bar, fully adjustable single stage trigger, machined steel or aluminum trigger guard, checkered walnut stock and forearm, machined steel pistol grip cap, Pachmayr rubber buttpad, 6 1/4 to 7 1/2 lbs. New late 2013.

* ***Model 51 Classic*** – 22 in. blue barrel, matte metal finish, machined aluminum trigger guard, AA select Claro 4-panel Cooper Southwestern style checkered walnut stock and forearm, machined steel grip cap, 6 1/4 lbs.

MSR $3,095	$2,650	$2,300	$2,000	$1,800	$1,450	$1,200	$900

* ***Model 51 Custom Classic*** – 22 in. blue steel barrel, machined steel trigger guard, AAA Claro walnut Len Brownell wrap-around Western fleur checkered stock and forearm, ebony tip, Shadowline cheekpiece, machined steel grip cap, hand polished high gloss metal finish, additional options available, 6 1/2 lbs.

MSR $3,995	$3,400	$2,950	$2,550	$2,300	$1,850	$1,550	$1,200

* ***Model 51 Western Classic*** – 24 inch octagon blue barrel, Machined steel trigger guard, machined steel grip cap, AAA Claro Brownell wrap-around western fleur checkered walnut stock and forearm, ebony tip, Shadowline cheekpiece, screw-in sling swivels, bone charcoal case colored high gloss metal finish, 6 1/2 lbs.

MSR $4,595	$3,900	$3,400	$2,950	$2,650	$2,150	$1,750	$1,350

* ***Model 51 Varminter*** – 24 (disc.) or 26 in. stainless steel barrel, matte metal finish, machined aluminum trigger guard, AA Claro 2-panel on grip checkered walnut stock and forearm, 7 1/4 lbs.

MSR $2,895	$2,450	$2,150	$1,850	$1,700	$1,350	$1,100	$850

* ***Model 51 Varmint Laminate*** – 24 in. stainless steel barrel, matte metal finish, machined aluminum trigger guard, laminate stock, 7 1/4 lbs. Disc. 2014, reintroduced 2016-2020.

	$2,100	$1,850	$1,600	$1,450	$1,150	$950	$750	*$2,495*

* ***Model 51 Montana Varminter*** – matte metal finish, 24 in. stainless steel barrel, machined aluminum trigger guard, AA+ select walnut stock with 2-panel on a grip checkering and vented forearm, machined steel grip cap, 7 1/4 lbs.

MSR $3,195	$2,700	$2,400	$2,050	$1,850	$1,500	$1,200	$950

* ***Model 51 Varmint Extreme*** – 24 in. stainless steel barrel, hand polished matte metal finish, machined steel trigger guard, AAA Claro walnut stock with 2-panel multi-point on grip checkering, machined steel grip cap, 7 1/2 lbs.

MSR $3,695	$3,150	$2,750	$2,350	$2,150	$1,700	$1,400	$1,100

* ***Model 51 Varmint Extreme 25th Anniversary Limited Edition*** – .223 Rem. cal., AAA Claro walnut stock, custom hand engraved, silver inlaid "25" in the grip cap, only 25 mfg. 2015 only.

Retail pricing was not available for this model.

* ***Model 51 Excalibur*** – 22 inch fluted steel blue barrel, 4 shot mag., synthetic stock and forearm, spiral fluted bolt, all metal matte finish.

MSR $2,795	$2,400	$2,100	$1,800	$1,600	$1,300	$1,050	$850

GRADING - PPGS™	100%	98%	95%	90%	80%	70%	60%	LAST MSR

* ***Model 51 Jackson Game*** – 22 in. stainless steel barrel, matte metal finish, machined aluminum trigger guard, AA+ select Claro checkered walnut stock and forearm with rollover cheekpiece, machined steel grip cap, 6 1/4 lbs.

MSR $3,295	$2,800	$2,450	$2,100	$1,900	$1,550	$1,250	$1,000

* ***Model 51 Jackson Hunter*** – 22 in. stainless steel match barrel, matte metal finish, synthetic stock and forearm.

MSR $2,895	$2,450	$2,150	$1,850	$1,700	$1,350	$1,100	$850

* ***Model 51 Mannlicher*** – 20 in. blue steel barrel, hand polished high gloss finish, machined steel trigger guard and grip cap, multi-point hand checkered oil finished AAA Claro Mannlicher walnut stock and forearm with Shadowline cheekpiece and ebony tip, 6 1/2 lbs.

MSR $5,595	$4,750	$4,150	$3,550	$3,250	$2,600	$2,150	$1,650

* ***Model 51 Phoenix*** – 24 in. stainless steel match barrel, aluminum bedding block, matte metal finish, black and brown spiderweb finished synthetic stock and forearm with cooling vents.

MSR $2,795	$2,400	$2,100	$1,800	$1,600	$1,300	$1,050	$850

* ***Model 51 Schnabel*** – 22 or 24 in. blue barrel, machined aluminum trigger guard, checkered AA+ select Claro walnut stock with high comb and slim tapered forearm, multi-point Southwestern hand checkering, machined steel grip cap, matte metal finish, 6 1/4 lbs.

MSR $3,255	$2,750	$2,400	$2,100	$1,900	$1,500	$1,250	$950

* ***Model 51 Var-Tac*** – various cals., 24 in stainless matte match barrel, hand rubbed oil finish, AA+ Claro walnut vertical pistol grip stock, raised comb cheekpiece, western-fleur hand checkering, high polish metal finish.

MSR $2,995	$2,550	$2,200	$1,900	$1,750	$1,400	$1,150	$900

MODEL 52 – .25-06 Rem., .30-06, .270 Win. .280 Rem., .35 Whelen, .338-06, and may other cals., variety of stock options and barrel lengths, available in Classic, Jackson Game, Custom Classic, Western Classic, or Jackson Hunter configurations. New 2007.

* ***Model 52 Classic*** – oil finished AA Claro walnut stock, steel grip cap, 4-panel hand checkering, matte metal finish, limited options available.

MSR $2,495	$2,100	$1,850	$1,600	$1,450	$1,150	$950	$750

* ***Model 52 Custom Classic*** – steel blued match barrel, AAA Claro walnut, Shadowline cheekpiece, ebony forend tip, Brownell No. 1 checkering pattern, steel grip cap, high polish metal finish, additional options available.

MSR $3,995	$3,400	$2,950	$2,550	$2,300	$1,850	$1,550	$1,200

* ***Model 52 Western Classic*** – various cals., octagon barrel, case hardened action and metal work.

MSR $4,595	$3,900	$3,400	$2,950	$2,650	$2,150	$1,750	$1,350

* ***Model 52 Excalibur*** – 23 in. fluted steel barrel, synthetic version of the Classic with spiral fluted bolt and 3 shot mag.

MSR $2,795	$2,400	$2,100	$1,800	$1,600	$1,300	$1,050	$850

* ***Model 52 Jackson Game*** – similar to Squirrel rifle, stainless steel match grade barrel, AA select Claro walnut stock with rollover cheekpiece, semi-beavertail forearm, VE hand checkered grip, Pachmayr recoil pad, steel grip cap, sling swivels.

MSR $3,295	$2,800	$2,450	$2,100	$1,900	$1,550	$1,250	$1,000

* ***Model 52 Jackson Hunter*** – 22 in. blue match barrel, camo synthetic stock with aluminum bedding block, matte metal finish.

MSR $2,895	$2,450	$2,150	$1,850	$1,700	$1,350	$1,100	$850

* ***Model 52 Mannlicher*** – various cals., steel match grade barrel, oil finished hand checkered full length AAA Claro walnut stock with ebony tip, Shadowline cheekpiece, steel grip cap, high polish bone charcoal finish. New 2012.

MSR $5,595	$4,750	$4,150	$3,550	$3,250	$2,600	$2,150	$1,650

* ***Model 52 Montana Varminter*** – various cals., 24 in. stainless steel barrel, oil finished hand checkered AA+ Claro walnut stock, steel grip cap, cooling vents, western-fleur hand checkering, high polish metal finish, other options available. New late 2018.

MSR $3,195	$2,700	$2,400	$2,050	$1,850	$1,500	$1,200	$950

* ***Model 52 Schnabel*** – various cals., matte metal finish, AA select hand checkered walnut stock with raised comb, slim tapered forearm. New 2012.

MSR $3,255	$2,750	$2,400	$2,100	$1,900	$1,500	$1,250	$950

GRADING - PPGS™	100%	98%	95%	90%	80%	70%	60%	LAST MSR

* ***Model 52 Varminter*** – 26 inch stainless steel barrel, machined aluminum trigger guard, AA Claro checkered walnut stock and forearm, matte metal finish, limited options available, 7 1/4 lbs. New 2018.

MSR $2,895 $2,450 $2,150 $1,850 $1,700 $1,350 $1,100 $850

* ***Model 52 Varmint Extreme*** – 24 in. stainless steel barrel, hand polished matte metal finish, machined steel trigger guard, AAA Claro walnut stock with 2-panel multi-point on grip checkering, machined steel grip cap, 7 1/2 lbs.

MSR $3,695 $3,150 $2,750 $2,350 $2,150 $1,700 $1,400 $1,100

* ***Model 52 Open Country LR*** – select cals. only, 26 in. lightweight fluted barrel, 3 or 5 shot mag., Cooper designed muzzle brake, fully adj. SST, Cooper Firearms synthetic stock, Raptor style bolt handle and bolt shroud, Ken Farrell 10 or 20 in. MOA Picatinny rail, limited options available, left-hand option, 9 lbs. New late 2018.

MSR $3,995 $3,400 $3,000 $2,550 $2,300 $1,850 $1,550 $1,200

* ***Model 52 Timberline*** – various cals., 24 in. stainless steel fluted barrel, threaded muzzle and knurled thread protector, fully adj. SST, Cooper Firearms synthetic stock, raised comb cheekpiece, semi-vertical grip, dual palm swell, spiral fluted bolt, limited options available, available in left-hand. New late 2018.

MSR $2,795 $2,400 $2,100 $1,800 $1,600 $1,300 $1,050 $850

Add $250 for left-hand.

MODEL 54 – .22-250 Rem., .243 Win., .243 Win. AI, .250 Savage, .250 Savage AI, .220 Swift, 6mm Rem., .257 Roberts, .257 Roberts AI, 6.5 Creedmoor, 6.5x47 Lapua, .338 Federal, .358 Win., .260 Rem., .308 Win., or 7mm-08 Rem. cal., short action repeater, various configurations and options. New 2010.

* ***Model 54 Classic*** – AA Claro walnut oil finished stock, 4-panel hand checkering, steel grip cap, matte metal finish, limited options available.

MSR $2,795 $2,400 $2,100 $1,800 $1,600 $1,300 $1,050 $850

* ***Model 54 Custom Classic*** – various cals., short action, steel blued match barrel, AAA+ Claro, Shadowline cheekpiece, multi-wrap around hand checkering, Brownell No. 1 checkering pattern, ebony forend tip, and steel grip cap, high polish metal finish, options available.

MSR $3,995 $3,400 $2,950 $2,550 $2,300 $1,850 $1,550 $1,200

* ***Model 54 Western Classic*** – various cals., steel blued match octagon barrel, oil finish, AAA+ Claro walnut, Shadowline cheekpiece, steel grip cap and metal bottom, ebony tip, western-fleur hand checkering, bone charcoal case hardened action and metal work, options available.

MSR $4,595 $3,900 $3,400 $2,950 $2,650 $2,150 $1,750 $1,350

* ***Model 54 Excaliber*** – .22-250 Rem., .243 Win., .250 Savage, .260 Rem., .308 Win., or 7mm-08 Rem. cal., 24 in. fluted steel barrel, 3 shot mag., fully adj. single stage trigger, synthetic stock, spiral fluted bolt, matte metal finish.

MSR $2,795 $2,400 $2,100 $1,800 $1,600 $1,300 $1,050 $850

* ***Model 54 Varmint Extreme*** – various cals., premium match grade barrel, checkered grip in crossover Western fleur pattern, oil finish wood, Pachmayr pad, steel grip cap, sling swivel studs, blued steel w/high gloss finish, all options available.

MSR $3,695 $3,150 $2,750 $2,350 $2,150 $1,700 $1,400 $1,100

* ***Model 54 Var-Tac*** – various cals., repeater, 26 in. matte stainless match barrel, 4 shot detachable mag., fully adj. SST, AA+ Claro walnut stock, raised comb cheekpiece, western-fleur hand checkering, hand rubbed oil finish, vertical pistol grip, 7.5 lbs. New 2021.

MSR $2,995 $2,550 $2,200 $1,900 $1,750 $1,400 $1,150 $900

* ***Model 54 Varmint Laminate*** – similar to Varminter, except has laminated stock. Disc. 2014, reintroduced 2016.

MSR $3,195 $2,700 $2,400 $2,050 $1,850 $1,500 $1,200 $950

* ***Model 54 Varminter*** – various cals., 26 in. stainless steel straight taper premium match barrel, 3 shot detachable mag., fully adj. SST, AA Claro walnut stock, hand rubbed oil finish, Pachmayr recoil pad, hand checkered pistol grip, stainless or matte metal finish, 7.5-9 lbs. New 2021.

MSR $2,895 $2,450 $2,150 $1,850 $1,700 $1,350 $1,100 $850

* ***Model 54 Jackson Game*** – similar to Squirrel rifle, stainless steel match grade barrel, AA select Claro walnut stock with rollover cheekpiece, semi-beavertail forearm, VE hand checkered grip, sling swivels, Pachmayr recoil pad, steel grip cap.

MSR $3,295 $2,800 $2,450 $2,100 $1,900 $1,550 $1,250 $1,000

GRADING - PPGS™	100%	98%	95%	90%	80%	70%	60%	LAST MSR

* ***Model 54 Jackson Hunter*** – 22 in. blue match barrel, camo synthetic stock with aluminum bedding block, matte metal finish.

MSR $2,895 $2,450 $2,150 $1,850 $1,700 $1,350 $1,100 $850

* ***Model 54 Mannlicher*** – various cals., steel match grade barrel, high polish bone charcoal finish, oil finished hand checkered full length AAA Claro walnut stock with ebony tip, steel grip cap, other options available. New 2012.

MSR $5,595 $4,750 $4,150 $3,550 $3,250 $2,600 $2,150 $1,650

* ***Model 54 Phoenix*** – 24 in. stainless match barrel, flat black or brown spider web synthetic stock, aluminum bedding block, matte metal finish.

MSR $2,795 $2,400 $2,100 $1,800 $1,600 $1,300 $1,050 $850

* ***Model 54 Montana Varminter*** – various cals., 24 in. stainless steel match grade barrel, oil finished hand checkered AA select Claro walnut stock. steel grip cap, cooling vents, matte metal finish. New 2000.

MSR $3,195 $2,700 $2,400 $2,050 $1,850 $1,500 $1,200 $950

* ***Model 54 Schnabel*** – various cals., matte metal finish, AA select hand checkered walnut stock with raised comb, slim tapered forearm. New 2012.

MSR $3,255 $2,750 $2,400 $2,100 $1,900 $1,500 $1,250 $950

* ***Model 54 Raptor-M*** – various cals., 24 in. heavy varmint stainless fluted match barrel, Cooper muzzle brake, 5 shot AICS-style mag., tactical synthetic stock, spiral fluted bolt, Picatinny rail, tan finish, limited options available. New late 2018.

MSR $2,755 $2,350 $2,050 $1,750 $1,600 $1,300 $1,050 $800

MODEL 56 – various cals., 26 in. barrel, machined aluminum trigger guard with fully adj. trigger, matte metal finish, AA Claro walnut stock with Cooper multi-point checkering pattern, Pachmayr Decelerator pad, 3 shot mag., Sako style extraction, 8 1/4 lbs. New 2012.

* ***Model 56 Classic*** – AA Claro walnut, steel grip, four panel hand checkering, oil finished stock, matte metal finish, no options. Disc. 2013.

$2,375 $2,075 $1,775 $1,615 $1,300 $1,075 $825 *$2,795*

* ***Model 56 Custom Classic*** – includes Brownell No. 1 checkering pattern, ebony forend tip, and steel grip cap. Disc. 2013.

$2,975 $2,600 $2,225 $2,025 $1,625 $1,325 $1,025 *$3,495*

* ***Model 56 Western Classic*** – various cals., features octagon barrel and case hardened action and metal work. Disc. 2013.

$3,725 $3,250 $2,795 $2,525 $2,050 $1,675 $1,300 *$4,395*

* ***Model 56 Excaliber*** – 23 in. fluted steel barrel, synthetic version of the Classic with spiral fluted bolt and 3 shot mag. Disc. 2013.

$2,450 $2,150 $1,825 $1,675 $1,350 $1,100 $850 *$2,895*

* ***Model 56 Jackson Game*** – similar to Squirrel rifle, stainless steel match grade barrel, AA select Claro walnut stock with rollover cheekpiece, semi-beavertail forearm, VE hand checkered grip, sling swivels, Pachmayr recoil pad, steel grip cap. Disc. 2013.

$2,550 $2,225 $1,900 $1,725 $1,400 $1,150 $895 *$2,995*

* ***Model 56 Jackson Hunter*** – 22 in. blue match barrel, camo synthetic stock with aluminum bedding block, matte metal finish. Disc. 2013.

$2,375 $2,075 $1,775 $1,600 $1,300 $1,075 $825 *$2,795*

* ***Model 56 Schnabel*** – various cals., matte metal finish, AA select hand checkered walnut stock with raised comb, slim tapered forearm. Mfg. 2012-2013.

$2,625 $2,295 $1,975 $1,775 $1,450 $1,175 $925 *$3,095*

* ***Model 56 Mannlicher*** – various cals., steel match grade barrel, high polish bone charcoal finish, oil finished hand checkered full-length AAA Claro walnut stock with ebony tip, steel grip cap. Mfg. 2012-2013.

$5,095 $4,450 $3,825 $3,475 $2,800 $2,295 $1,775 *$5,995*

MODEL 57M – .17 Mach 2, .17 HMR (new 2002), .22 LR, or .22 WMR (new 2001) cal., 3 rear locking lugs, 3 (.22 WMR or .17 HMR), or 4 (.17 Mach 2 and .22 LR cal.) shot mag., various configurations, barrel lengths, and features. New 2000.

* ***Model 57M Classic*** – steel grip, 4-panel hand checkering, AA Claro walnut stock, oil finished wood, matte metal finish, limited options. New 2000.

MSR $2,795 $2,400 $2,100 $1,800 $1,600 $1,300 $1,050 $850

GRADING - PPGS™	100%	98%	95%	90%	80%	70%	60%	LAST MSR

* ***Model 57M Custom Classic*** – blued match barrel, AAA Claro walnut stock, western fleur wrap-around hand checkering, Shadow line cheekpiece, ebony forend tip, steel grip cap, Brownell No. 1 checkering pattern, ebony forend tip, and steel grip cap, high polish metal finish, all options available. New 2000.

MSR $3,855	$3,300	$2,850	$2,450	$2,250	$1,800	$1,500	$1,150	

* ***Model 57M Western Classic*** – various cals., octagon barrel, AAA+ Claro walnut, shadow line cheekpiece, steel grip cap and bottom metal, wrap around western fleur hand checkering, ebony tip, Bone Charcoal case color metal, high polish metal finish, wrap around western fleur hand checkering, oil finish, other options available. New 2000.

MSR $4,395	$3,750	$3,250	$2,800	$2,550	$2,050	$1,700	$1,300	

* ***Model 57M Jackson Squirrel*** – bolt action rifle, 22 in. stainless match barrel, fluted forearm, oil finished hand checkered AA Claro walnut with roll over cheekpiece, steel grip cap, matte metal finish, other options available, 6 1/2 lbs. New 2005.

MSR $3,195	$2,700	$2,400	$2,050	$1,850	$1,500	$1,200	$950	

* ***Model 57M Jackson Hunter*** – 22 in. blue match barrel, camo synthetic stock with aluminum bedding block, matte metal finish. New 2005.

MSR $2,695	$2,300	$2,000	$1,700	$1,550	$1,250	$1,050	$800	

* ***Model 57M LVT*** – 24 in. stainless match barrel, oil finished AA select Claro hand checkered walnut, matte metal finish. Mfg. mid-2005-2014.

	$1,875	$1,650	$1,400	$1,275	$1,025	$850	$700	*$2,195*

* ***Model 57M Mannlicher*** – various cals., 20 in. steel match grade barrel, oil finished hand checkered full-length AAA Claro walnut stock with ebony tip, steel grip cap, Shadowline cheekpiece, high polish bone charcoal finish. New 2012.

MSR $5,355	$4,550	$4,000	$3,400	$3,100	$2,500	$2,050	$1,600	

* ***Model 57M Schnabel*** – various cals., AA+ select hand checkered walnut stock with raised comb, slim tapered forearm, multi-point Southwestern hand checkering, matte metal finish, options available. New 2012.

MSR $3,255	$2,750	$2,400	$2,100	$1,900	$1,500	$1,250	$950	

* ***Model 57M TRP-3*** – .22 LR cal. only, 24 in. stainless match barrel, single shot, bench rest style, synthetic stock, matte metal finish, not available in left-hand. New 2009.

MSR $2,695	$2,300	$2,000	$1,700	$1,550	$1,250	$1,050	$800	

* ***Model 57M Varminter*** – various cals., short action, single shot, 24 (disc.) or 26 in. stainless steel match grade barrel, machined aluminum trigger guard, stock is AA Claro walnut with 20 LPI hand checkering and hand rubbed oil finish, Pachmayr pad, standard sling swivel studs. New 2015.

MSR $2,795	$2,400	$2,100	$1,800	$1,600	$1,300	$1,050	$850	

* ***Model 57M Montana Varminter*** – various cals., 24 in. stainless steel barrel, oil finished hand checkered AA select Claro walnut stock, steel grip cap, Pachmayr pad, standard sling swivel studs, cooling vents, matte metal finish. New 2015.

MSR $3,095	$2,650	$2,300	$2,000	$1,800	$1,450	$1,200	$900	

* ***Model 57M Varmint Extreme*** – 24 in. stainless steel straight taper barrel with matte finish, hand rubbed oil finished AAA Claro walnut stock, hand checkered grip in a crossover Western fleur pattern, Pachmayr pad, steel grip cap, standard sling swivel studs, all blued steel is high gloss finish. New 2015.

MSR $3,595	$3,050	$2,700	$2,300	$2,100	$1,700	$1,400	$1,050	

MODEL 58 DANGEROUS GAME – .375 H&H (mfg. 2015 only), .416 Rigby, .416 Rem. (mfg. 2015 only), .404 Jeffery, .458 Win. Mag. (mfg. 2015 only), .458 Lott, or .505 Gibbs cal., 2 front locking lug bolt action repeater, 24 in. premium match grade barrel, hinged floorplate single stack mag., controlled round feed extraction, mechanical ejection, Timney trigger. Mfg. 2015-2016.

* ***Model 58 Classic*** – various cals., chrome moly premium match grade barrel, AA Claro walnut stock with hand-rubbed oil finish, Pachmayr pad, steel grip cap, sling swivel studs, 4-panel hand checkering, matte finish metal work. Mfg. 2015-2016.

	$2,630	$2,300	$1,975	$1,785	$1,450	$1,200	$950	*$3,095*

* ***Model 58 Custom Classic*** – various cals., chrome moly premium match grade barrel, AAA Claro walnut stock with shadowline beaded cheekpiece and hand-rubbed oil finish, African ebony tip, Western fleur wrap around hand checkering, steel grip cap, sling swivel studs, high gloss finish on all metal work. Mfg. 2015-2016.

	$3,625	$3,175	$2,725	$2,465	$1,995	$1,650	$1,300	*$4,255*

GRADING - PPGS™	100%	98%	95%	90%	80%	70%	60%	LAST MSR

* ***Model 58 Western Classic*** – various cals., chrome moly premium match grade octagon barrel, AAA+ Claro walnut stock with shadowline beaded cheekpiece and hand-rubbed oil finish, African ebony tip, Western fleur wrap-around hand checkering, Pachmayr pad, steel grip cap, sling swivel studs, selected metal work is highighted with case coloring. Mfg. 2015-2016.

	$3,900	$3,415	$2,925	$2,650	$2,150	$1,775	$1,385	*$4,595*

* ***Model 58 Jackson Game*** – various cals., stainless steel premium match grade barrel, AA+ Claro walnut stock, rollover cheekpiece, semi-beavertail forearm, VE hand checkered grip in a crossover multi-point pattern, hand-rubbed oil finished wood, Pachmayr pad, steel grip cap, standard sling swivel studs, matte finish metal work. Mfg. 2015-2016.

	$2,725	$2,385	$2,050	$1,850	$1,500	$1,225	$1,065	*$3,195*

* ***Model 58 Mannlicher*** – various cals., chrome moly premium match grade barrel, AAA+ Claro walnut stock with shadowline beaded cheekpiece and hand-rubbed oil finish, African ebony tip, multi-point wrap-around hand checkering, Pachmayr pad, steel grip cap, sling swivel studs, high gloss finish on all metal work. Mfg. 2015-2016.

	$4,850	$4,250	$3,650	$3,300	$2,675	$2,185	$1,700	*$5,695*

* ***Model 58 Schnabel*** – various cals., chrome moly premium match grade barrel, AA+ Claro walnut stock with raised comb and hand-rubbed oil finish, slim taper forearm, multi-point two panel hand checkering, Pachmayr pad, steel grip cap, sling swivel studs, matte finish metal work. Mfg. 2015-2016.

	$2,725	$2,385	$2,050	$1,850	$1,500	$1,225	$1,065	*$3,195*

MODEL 92 BACKCOUNTRY – various cals., 24 in. Wilson Arms fluted barrel w/muzzle brake, detachable 3 shot mag., fully adj. trigger, hand-laid composite w/Kevlar reinforced stock, standard long action and belted mag. (up to .338 cals. available), 5 lbs. 12 oz.

MSR $3,295	$2,800	$2,450	$2,100	$1,900	$1,550	$1,250	$1,000	

Add $250 for left-hand option.

RIFLES: SINGLE SHOT

MODEL 7 PEREGRINE FALLING BLOCK – various cals., falling block action with under lever, choice of varmint extreme or custom sporter configuration, 24 in. barrel, deluxe checkered walnut stock, tang mounted safety, approx. 6 lbs. Limited production 2001 only.

	$1,750	$1,400	$1,100	$925	$800	$675	$550	*$1,995*

Add $300 for custom sporter variation.

MODEL 16 – WSSM cals., 24 in. stainless match grade barrel, hand checkered, oil finished walnut stock, available in varmint styles only. Mfg. 2005-disc.

	$1,225	$975	$825	$725	$625	$550	$450	*$1,395*

Add $200 for Montana Varminter.
Add $400 for Varmint Extreme.

MODEL 72 MONTANA PLAINSMAN – various cals., single shot featuring case colored Win. Model 1885 action with heavy octagon barrel, double set triggers, deluxe checkered straight grip stock and forearm, no sights.

While advertised during 1997 at a retail price of $2,195, this model never went into production.

COP

Previous derringer manufacturer located in Torrance, CA.

DERRINGERS

COP DERRINGER – .22 WMR or .357 Mag. cal., double action, 3 in. barrel, 4 shot, stainless steel, wood grips, COP stands for Compact Off-Duty Police, 28 oz. Disc.

	$895	$785	$670	$610	$490	$400	$310	

Add 10% for box in 98%+ condition.

CORCIL

Current trademark of shotguns manufactured by the Hedef Arms Company, located in Konya, Turkey. No current U.S. importation.

A wide variety of semi-auto, slide action, and O/U shotguns are manufactured. Many configurations are available, including wood, synthetic, and carbon fiber stocks, various finishes, engraving, and gold inlays. Please contact the manufacturer for more information, including domestic availability and pricing.

GRADING - PPGS™	100%	98%	95%	90%	80%	70%	60%	LAST MSR

CORE RIFLE SYSTEMS

Current trademark of AR-15 style carbines, rifles, and pistols manufactured by Good Time Outdoors, Inc. (GTO), located in Ocala, FL.

Please refer to BlueBookOfGunValues.com to order the *Blue Book of AR-15s & Variations*, available as a book or online subscription.

CORONADO ARMS

Previous bolt action and AR-15 style rifle manufacturer located in Dixon, CA until circa 2016.

RIFLES: BOLT ACTION

AKANDO – .25-06 Rem., .264 Win. Mag., or .300 Win. Mag. cal., 26 in. fluted barrel, 4 shot mag., 24 LPI premium ribbon scroll pattern, single piece dual swivel mount for sling and bipod usage, wide beavertail forend, AA Claro walnut stock, 9 lbs. Disc.

	100%	98%	95%	90%	80%	70%	60%	LAST MSR
	$4,795	$4,300	$3,850	$3,300	$2,850	$2,350	$1,700	*$5,300*

COLOMA – .25-06 Rem., .30-06, .264 Win. Mag., .300 Win. Mag., or .338 Win. Mag. cal., 26 in. Sporter barrel, 4 shot mag., 24 LPI basic ribbon scroll pattern, AAA Claro walnut stock with ebony tip, 8 1/2 lbs. Disc.

	100%	98%	95%	90%	80%	70%	60%	LAST MSR
	$5,350	$4,750	$4,100	$3,500	$2,975	$2,500	$1,800	*$5,900*

DESPERADO – .30-06, .300 Win. Mag., or .338 Win. Mag. cal., 26 in. Sporter barrel, 4 shot mag., 22 LPI basic multi point pattern with single line border, Grade A Claro walnut stock, matte finish, 8 1/2 lbs. Disc.

	100%	98%	95%	90%	80%	70%	60%	LAST MSR
	$3,600	$3,200	$2,800	$2,400	$2,000	$1,750	$1,325	*$3,937*

PALISADE – .25-06 Rem., .30-06, .270 Win., .264Win., .or 300 Win. Mag. cal., 24 in. lightweight barrel, 4 shot mag., 24 LPI premium ribbon scroll with engraved fleur de lis pattern, AA Claro walnut stock with Schnabel forearm, 7 1/4 lbs. Disc.

	100%	98%	95%	90%	80%	70%	60%	LAST MSR
	$5,100	$4,500	$3,975	$3,400	$2,925	$2,400	$1,750	*$5,600*

RIFLES/CARBINES: SEMI-AUTO

CA-15 CARBINE – 5.56 NATO or 6.8 SPC cal., AR-15 style, GIO, Lothar Walther button rifled barrel, 10 shot mag., Geissele trigger, extended upper and lower receivers, flared and broached magwell, Magpul MOE grip, Magpul STR stock, black hardcoat anodized finish, 7 1/4 lbs. Disc.

	100%	98%	95%	90%	80%	70%	60%	LAST MSR
	$1,250	$975	$875	$775	$725	$675	$600	*$1,650*

CA-15 COMPETITION CARBINE – .223/5.56 Wylde chamber, GIO, 16 in. stainless steel barrel with Crosshill Technologies X-Comp Compensator or muzzle brake, 10 shot mag., Gunfighter Industries Mod 4 charging handle, Geissele 3-gun trigger, KeyMod rifle length handguard, extended upper receiver, adj. gas block, Magpul STR stock, Magpul MOE grip, approx. 8 lbs. Mfg. 2015-disc.

	100%	98%	95%	90%	80%	70%	60%	LAST MSR
	$1,500	$1,175	$1,050	$925	$875	$800	$725	*$1,995*

CA-15 RIFLE – 5.56 NATO or 6.8 SPC cal., AR-15 style, GIO, Lothar Walther button rifled and fluted bull barrel, 10 shot mag., mid-length gas system, Geissele two-stage trigger, extended upper and lower receivers, flared and broached magwell, Magpul MOE grip, Magpul PRS stock, black hardcoat anodized finish. Mfg. 2014-disc.

	100%	98%	95%	90%	80%	70%	60%	LAST MSR
	$1,850	$1,450	$1,300	$1,150	$1,075	$1,000	$900	*$2,450*

CA-15 COMPETITION RIFLE – .223/5.56 Wylde chamber, GIO, 18 in. button rifled barrel, competition muzzle brake, adj. gas block, 10 shot mag., Gunfighter Industries Mod 4 charging handle, Geissele two-stage trigger, KeyMod rifle length handguard, Magpul MOE+ grip, Magpul PRS stock, 9 1/2 lbs. Mfg. 2016-disc.

	100%	98%	95%	90%	80%	70%	60%	LAST MSR
	$1,925	$1,525	$1,350	$1,200	$1,125	$1,025	$950	*$2,550*

CORTONA

Previous trademark of shotguns manufactured exclusively by F.A.I.R. Techni-Mec, located in Marcheno, Italy for the Kalispel Case Line, an Indian tribe in Idaho. Previously imported until 2010 by Kalispel Case Line, located in Cusick, WA.

SHOTGUNS: O/U

Cortona shotguns utilized boxlock actions with a 3-lug system and Boss style frames in both aluminum and steel. Many variations are possible, and the lineup included the Legend Series with engraved sideplates (last MSR $3,085-$3,285), the Prestige Series with case colored and engraved sideplates and deluxe Turkish walnut stock and forearm (last MSR $3,610-$4,210) (also available in 16 ga.), the Grande Series (last MSR $2,095-$3,995), and the Alumino Series (last MSR $2,665-$2,800). A GR Series was also available in 12, 20, and 28 ga. MSRs ranged from $1,785 - $2,585 (disc. 2007).

COSMI, AMERICO & FIGLIO

Current semi-auto shotgun manufacturer established during 1930, and located in Ancona, Italy. Current U.S. agent is Pacific Sporting Arms, located in Azuza, CA. Previously distributed exclusively late 2005-2008 by Dewing's Fly & Gun Shop, located in West Palm Beach, FL. Previously imported 2005-2008 by Pacific Sporting Arms, located in Azuza, CA, from 2003-2004 by Old Friends Hunting & Shooting Co., from 1985-2003 by New England Arms Co., and from 2001-2002 by Autumn Sales, Inc., located in Fort Worth, TX. Please contact the factory directly for more information and model availability.

Approximately 8,200 Cosmi shotguns have been manufactured since 1930 (the design dates back to 1925). They are known for their unique mechanism and high-quality fabrication techniques. Since each gun's parts are made separately (and individually serial numbered), most components are not interchangeable from one gun to another.

SHOTGUNS: SEMI-AUTO

STANDARD DELUXE MODEL – 12, 16, 20, or 28 (new 2014) ga., 2 3/4 (16 ga. only) or 3 in. chamber, unique pivoting break open action loads cartridges into stock chamber from inside of receiver, 8 shot mag. with 3 shot reducer option, steel, alloy, or titanium frame, Boehler Antinit or stainless steel barrel (moves when shooting) available with or without choke tubes, all internal parts are mfg. from special chrome-nickel steel or titanium (new 1990), custom order gun only with dimensions specified by individual customer (approx. 6 month delivery time on 12 and 20 ga.).

* ***Standard DeLuxe Model*** – barrel and attached receiver assembly are blue, frame is chromed-nickel steel, w/o engraving, current importation is with best quality wood only and deluxe case.

Please contact the manufacturer directly for pricing and availability.
Subtract approx. 25% for older mfg. w/o fancy wood and choke tubes.

* ***DeLuxe Engraved Models***

Please contact the manufacturer directly for a price quotation on the many Deluxe models it offers with a wide variety of engraving options.

* ***Standard Aluminum Model*** – 12 or 20 ga., receiver made out of machined aluminum, approx. 7 lbs. in 12 ga., approx. 5.9 lbs. in 20 ga., very limited mfg.

Please contact the manufacturer directly for pricing, options, and availability.

* ***Standard DeLuxe Titanium Model*** – 12 or 20 ga., receiver made out of machined titanium, approx. 6.8 lbs. in 12 ga., approx. 5.7 lbs. in 20 ga., MSR and 100% values are listed in euros, but used pricing is in dollars. New 1990.

Please contact the manufacturer directly for pricing, options, and availability.

» **DeLuxe Titanium Grade Engraved Models**

Please contact the manufacturer directly for a price quotation on the many Deluxe models it offers with a wide variety of engraving options.

COSMOS

Current trademark of bolt action rifles manufactured by Balistik Suvanma located in Istanbul, Turkey. No current U.S. importation.

COSTER, GEORGE & SON

Previous custom longarm maker circa 1920-1930, located in Glasgow, Scotland.

George Coster was the son of a German-born gunmaker, George Ernest Julius Coster, who left Germany to work for Alex Henry in 1869. Both Julius and George were talented gunmakers who worked for Alex Henry, and in 1886, Julius formed a partnership with a Mr. Hunter, trading as Coster & Hunter in Edinburgh until 1890. Julius continued to work independently until the late 1890s, when he moved to Glasgow and worked for Charles Ingram. Around 1920, father and son worked together as George Coster & Son. Julius died in 1927, and George carried on until 1930, when he went to work for Alex Martin. He stayed there until his retirement.

In 1993, the Coster name was obtained by Glasgow Gunmakers Ltd. (now trading as Graham Mackinlay & Co Gunmakers). Since Mackinlay states that no company records have survived, it is highly recommended that an independent evaluation be done on any Coster firearm before purchase/selling.

Some information courtesy of David Grant and Vic Venters.

COUNTY, S.A.L.

Previous shotgun manufacturer located in Eibar, Spain.

SHOTGUNS: O/U

County manufactured a wide variety of both boxlock and sidelock O/Us, which had very limited U.S. importation.

GRADING - PPGS™	100%	98%	95%	90%	80%	70%	60%	LAST MSR

CRESCENT FIRE ARMS CO. & CRESCENT-DAVIS ARMS CORP.

Previous manufacturers and trademarks manufactured circa 1888-1931 in Norwich, CT.

In 1888, George W. Cilley bought out the defunct Bacon Arms Co. of Norwich, CT. He then formed an alliance with Frank Foster, and borrowed enough money to form the Crescent Fire Arms Company. Cilley and Foster each held several firearms patents, and both were highly qualified in firearms design and manufacture. Production began with single shot tip-up shotguns, which had an external side hammer. Double barrel shotgun production was started in 1891. In 1893, they began making bicycle chains, and that same year, H&D Folsom took over the company's financial control. Early in the 1890s, Crescent built a rifle that resembled the Remington No. 4. A very rare Crescent was the .410 bore shotgun pistol, which was introduced in the 1920s. In 1929, N.R. Davis Firearms Co., then owned by Warner Arms Corp., merged with Cresent to become Crescent-Davis Arms Corp. Because of financial crisis, business continued to decline, and they were forced to sell out. Savage Arms Co. acquired Cresent-Davis in 1931, assembled guns from the remaining parts, and these guns were sold under the Crescent name only. In 1932, the city of Norwich, CT, took over the Crescent property for non-payment of back taxes. After the Norwich facility was closed, manufacture was moved to Chicopee Falls.

It is unknown whether or not Crescent did any high grade or custom work. However, a very well engraved SxS, with the Crescent logo, is known to exist in a private collection.

Crescent Fire Arms Company remains best known as a manufacturer of "house brand" shotguns (i.e., Crescent private labeled guns for retailers, distributors, mail-order houses, etc.). Over 100 different trademarks have been observed to date, manufactured by Crescent. Almost all the remaining specimens today are priced as shooters and have no collector value.

SHOTGUNS

Certain models may be considered Curios or Relics by the BATFE (subject to change). Other models fall under 1934 NFA legislation, and are subject to seizure w/o proper paperwork and registration. Please contact your local BATFE branch for clarification.

SINGLE SHOT MODEL – 12, 16, 20, 28 ga., or .410 bore, exposed hammer, various barrel lengths, walnut stock and forearm. Disc.

12 ga.	$140	$115	$100	$85	$75	$65	$50
16 or 20 ga.	$170	$140	$115	$100	$85	$75	$65
28 ga.	$225	$185	$160	$135	$115	$90	$75
.410 bore	$350	$300	$275	$250	$215	$185	$160

SxS MODEL – values below assume standard models with double triggers, extractors, original finish, and 100% working order. Most shotguns feature sidelock actions. Shotguns with exposed hammers can equal their hammerless counterparts if condition is 80% or better.

12 ga.	$375	$325	$295	$265	$230	$210	$185
16 ga.	$335	$295	$265	$210	$185	$165	$145
20 ga.	$375	$325	$295	$265	$230	$210	$185
28 ga./.410 bore	$1,000	$875	$750	$675	$550	$450	$350

KNICKERBOCKER – 20 ga., 14 in. nickel-plated barrels, case-hardened receiver, pistol grip, mfg. circa 1900s.

Extreme rarity factor precludes accurate pricing information.

Guns not currently registered with the BATFE cannot be legally owned and are subject to seizure.

VICTOR EJECTOR – .410 bore, 12 in. single barrel, total production unknown, possibly prototype for Crescent Certified Shotgun.

Extreme rarity factor precludes accurate pricing information.

Guns not currently registered with the BATFE cannot be legally owned and are subject to seizure.

NEW EMPIRE – hammerless .410 bore or 20 ga., 12 1/4 in. barrels, extremely rare firearm whose total production and years of manufacture are unknown at this time (only known documentation is an "Auto Burglar Gun" in an advertisement by "Saul Ruben, The Gun Store, 68 E. Long St., Columbus, OH" of the October 1932 issue of *Hunter-Trader-Trapper,* which lists a $14.75 retail price). The receiver is marked "New Empire". At this time, 5 specimens are known in .410 bore, with ser. nos. scattered throughout the S-1 to S-19 range. The ser. no. appears on the metal under the forearm. The Crescent Auto & Burglar Gun may have been distributed by the H.& D. Folsom Arms Co. of New York City through its manufacturing division, the Crescent Firearms Co., Norwich, CT. Crescent's sellers included the Belknap Hardware Co., Louisville, KY and Hibbard-Spencer-Bartlett Co., Chicago, IL.

	$1,425	$1,200	$1,000	$900	$800	$700	$600

Guns not currently registered with the BATFE cannot be legally owned and are subject to seizure.

GRADING - PPGS™	100%	98%	95%	90%	80%	70%	60%	LAST MSR

CRESCENT CERTIFIED SHOTGUN – .410 bore, 12 1/2 in. barrel, approx. 4,000 mfg. from approx. 1930-32 by the Crescent-Davis Arms Corp., and possibly thereafter until 1934 by the J. Stevens Arms Co., left receiver side is stamped "Crescent Certified Shotgun/Crescent-Davis Arms Corp./Norwich, Conn. U.S.A." Also termed the "Ever-Ready" Model 200 and advertised with a blue frame, but specimens with "tiger stripe" and regular case coloring have been observed.

	$1,425	$1,200	$1,000	$900	$800	$700	$600	

Add $100-$300 for original cardboard box.

Guns not currently registered with the BATFE cannot be legally owned and are subject to seizure.

CRICKETT RIFLE

Current trademark manufactured by Keystone Sporting Arms, located in Milton, PA.

PISTOLS: BOLT ACTION, SINGLE SHOT

CRICKETT SYNTHETIC HUNTER – .22 LR or .22 WMR cal., 10 1/2 in. forged blue steel or stainless steel fluted and threaded barrel with machined low scope bolt handle, Williams Fire sights or scope base, black, pink (disc.), or leaf camo (disc.) synthetic stock, ergonomic target grip, integral Picatinny rail, drilled and tapped receiver, 2 1/2 lbs. New 2014.

MSR $159	$125	$110	$100	$80	$70	$60	$50	

Add $10 for .22 WMR cal. (MSR $169).
Add $20 for stainless steel (MSR $179).
Add $22 for leaf camo (disc.).
Add $70-$80 for black synthetic package including scope, bipod, and hard case (last MSR was $229/$239), disc. 2020.

RIFLES: BOLT ACTION

CRICKETT ADULT RIFLE – .22 WMR (disc. 2019) or .22 Short, Long, or LR cal., manually cocking single shot, 16 1/8 in. barrel, EZ load feed ramp (except .22 WMR), fixed front or adj. rear peep sight, drilled and tapped for scope mounts, American walnut or pink laminate (disc. 2020) stock, 13 1/2 in. LOP, swivel screws, blued or stainless steel (disc. 2019) barrel and receiver, 3.4 lbs.

MSR $249	$215	$190	$160	$145	$120	$95	$80	

Add $18 for .22 WMR cal. (disc. 2019).
Add $25 for stainless steel (disc. 2019).

CRICKET ALLOY MODEL 6061 – .22 LR cal., manually cocking single shot bolt action, 16 1/8-31 3/4 in. blued barrel, fixed front and adj. rear peep sight, drilled and tapped for scope mounts, black Alum 6061T-6 anodized stock, 11.5-14.5 in. LOP, Magpul Picatinny rail (new 2020), right or left (new 2020) hand configuration, 4 lbs.

MSR $269	$230	$200	$175	$155	$125	$110	$90	

CRICKETT AMENDMENT RIFLE – .22 LR cal., single shot, 16 1/8 in. blued or stainless steel barrel, adj. peep sights, synthetic custom amendment flag stock, manual safety, blued or black metal finish, 3 lbs.

MSR $219	$190	$165	$145	$130	$105	$85	$70	

Add $19 for stainless steel finish (MSR $238).
Add $190 for package (blued barrel only) which includes bipod, muzzle break, scope with Sunshade, and Crickettinny rail (MSR $409).

CRICKETT EXTREME TARGET RIFLE – .22 WMR or .22 LR cal., manually cocking single shot, 16 1/8 in. straight tapered bull blued or stainless steel barrel, 3/8 in. dovetail mount, alloy nickel plated steel construction, no sights, walnut, black, blue, brown (disc. 2020), camo, pink (disc. 2020), pink/black (new 2021), purple, red/white/blue, or orange/black (disc. 2020) ergonomic thumbhole extreme stock with raised cheekpiece, 12 1/4 in. LOP, 3.6 lbs.

MSR $219	$190	$165	$145	$130	$105	$85	$70	

Add $10 for .22 WMR cal. (MSR $229).
Add $10 for black, blue, brown (disc. 2020), camo, pink (disc. 2020), pink/black (new 2021), purple, red/white/blue, or orange/black (disc. 2020) stock (MSR $229).
Add $20 for stainless steel (MSR $239).

CRICKETT GRAND UNION (ONE NATION) – .22 LR cal., 16 1/8 in. barrel, open rifle sights, synthetic stock, synthetic grips, two-position crossbolt, blued finish, 2.8 lbs. New 2018.

MSR $219	$190	$165	$145	$130	$105	$85	$70	

Add $20 for stainless steel finish (MSR $239).

In 2021, the One Nation model underwent design changes and the model name changed to Grand Union.

GRADING - PPGS™	100%	98%	95%	90%	80%	70%	60%	LAST MSR

CRICKETT PRECISION RIFLE – .22 LR or .22 WMR (FDE only) cal., single shot, 16 1/8 in. blued or stainless steel threaded bull barrel with muzzle brake, integrated rails on buttstock and forend, adj. cheek comb, includes Crickettinny scope mount (will accept Weaver or Picatinny style rings), adj. LOP 10 3/8-11 7/8 in., adj. cheekpiece, EZ loader feed ramper, adj. bipod, package includes 4x28 combat scope with sunshade, black, Tariis Camo (Sports Inc. Exclusive, disc. 2020), Multi Cam (NBS Exclusive, disc. 2020), Muddy Girl, Serenity, FDE, Kryptek, or Digital Camo (Worldwide Exclusive, disc. 2020) finish.

MSR $316	$275	$240	$215	$185	$150	$125	$100	

Add $63 for gun package (MSR $379).
Add $73 for .22 WMR cal. w/FDE finish (MSR $389).
Add $83 for stainless steel in .22 LR cal. (MSR $399).
Add $93 for Tariis Camo (disc. 2020), Multi Cam (disc. 2020), Muddy Girl, Serenity, Kryptek, or Digital Camo (disc. 2020) finish available as a package only (MSR $409).

CRICKETT SPORTER – .22 Short (disc. 2008), .22 LR or .22 WMR (mfg. 2001-2004, reintroduced) cal., manually cocked single shot, 16 1/8 in. barrel with adj. rear aperture sight, steel or stainless steel (new 1999) construction, 11 1/2 in. LOP (youth dimension), choice of beech hardwood, walnut, colored laminate, camo, pink, desert tan, orange or black synthetic stock, stainless or blue barrel and receiver, 30 in. overall length, 2 1/2 lbs. Mfg. 1997-2018.

	$135	$110	$90	$75	$70	$55	$50	*$163*

Add $36 for deluxe walnut or beech stock.
Add $41 for color laminated stock (various colors).
Add $37 for stainless steel, and $47 for bull barrel.
Add $10 for .22 WMR cal.

* ***Crickett Sporter Custom/Deluxe*** – .22 Short, .22 LR, or .22 WMR cal., features deluxe hand checkered stock. Mfg. 1998-2000.

	$225	$195	$175	$150	$135	$120	$105	*$250*

Add $10 for deluxe configuration.

CRICKETT STANDARD RIFLE – .22 LR cal., threaded bull barrel with cap, walnut or laminated stock in black, camo, or red/white/blue (new 2021).

MSR $239	$200	$180	$155	$140	$115	$90	$80	

Add $10 for black, camo, or red/white/blue (new 2021) laminated stock (MSR $249).

CRICKETT SYNTHETIC RIFLE – .22 LR or .22 WMR cal., manually cocking single shot, 16 1/8 in. blued or stainless steel barrel, fixed front and adj. rear peep sight, drilled and tapped for scope mounts, synthetic stock in Black, Blue, Desert Tan, Pink, Purple, Gen 1 Pink, Gen 1 Desert Tan, Gen 1 Black, or Gen 1 Blue finish, 11.5 in. LOP ("My First Rifle" youth model), Generation 2 models include EZ load feed ramp (except .22 WMR) and swivel screws, 3 lbs.

MSR $169	$145	$125	$110	$100	$80	$65	$55	

Add $10-$30 for .22 WMR cal. depending on blued or stainless steel barrel (black synthetic stock only, MSR $179/$199).
Add $20 for stainless steel (MSR $189).
Subtract $30 for Gen 1 Pink, Gen 1 Deset Tan, Gen 1 Black, or Gen 1 Blue finish (beginning in 2021, available through big box retailers with no feed ramp or swivel studs, MSR $139).

* ***Crickett Hydro-Dipped Synthetic*** – .22 LR or .22 WMR cal., similar to Crickett Synthetic, except has Hydro-Dipped stock in Kryptec camo (with threaded handle), Muddy Girl, Mossy Oak Pink Blaze, Mossy Oak Shadow Grass Blades Camo, Mossy Oak Break-Up Country, Muddy Girl Serenity, or Mossy Oak Overwatch NRA (new 2020).

MSR $219	$190	$165	$145	$130	$105	$85	$70	

Add $10 for .22 WMR cal. (MSR $229).
Add $20 for stainless steel (MSR $239).
Add $30 for Kryptec Camo with threaded handle and stainless steel barrel (MSR $249).

CRICKETT TARGET RIFLE – .22 LR cal., blued or stainless steel (walnut stock only), thumbhole stock in walnut (disc. 2020), Black, Blue, Brown (disc. 2020), Orange/Black (disc. 2020), or Purple (disc. 2020).

MSR $269	$230	$200	$175	$155	$125	$110	$90	

Add $20 for stainless steel (MSR $286).

CRICKETT XBR – .22 LR cal., blued or stainless steel barrel, slotted muzzle brake, birch or black laminate stock, knurled grooved handle. Mfg. 2019 only.

	$325	$275	$250	$225	$175	$150	$115	*$379*

Add $29 for stainless steel barrel with black laminate stock (MSR $399).

GRADING - PPGS™	100%	98%	95%	90%	80%	70%	60%	LAST MSR

SHOTGUNS

"MY FIRST SHOTGUN" BREAK ACTION – .410 bore, 3 in. chamber, break action, youth model, recoil reducing chamber, 18 1/2 in. blued barrel, fixed modified choke, foldable Turkish walnut stock, soft rubber recoil pad. 11 in. LOP. New 2020.

MSR $179	$150	$130	$115	$100	$85	$70	$60	

"MY FIRST SHOTGUN" SLIDE ACTION – .410 bore, 2 3/4 or 3 in. chamber, slide action, 18 1/2 in. barrel with MC-1 choke, 4 or 5 shot, aluminum receiver, blade sights, Turkish walnut stock. New 2021.

MSR $399	$340	$300	$255	$230	$185	$155	$130	

CROSS CANYON ARMS

Current bolt action rifle manufacturer located in Ogden, UT. Previously located in West Haven, UT.

For individual model listings, please go to BlueBookOfGunValues.com/overflow.

CROSSFIRE LLC

Previous manufacturer located in La Grange, GA 1998-2001.

COMBINATION GUNS

CROSSFIRE MK-I – 12 ga. (3 in. chamber) over .223 Rem. cal., unique slide action O/U design allows stacked shotgun/rifle configuration, 18 3/4 in. shotgun barrel with invector chokes over 16 1/4 in. rifle barrel, detachable 4 (shotgun) and 5 (rifle) shot mags., open sights, Picatinny rail, synthetic stock and forearm, choice of black (MK-I) or RealTree 100% camo (MK-1RT) finish, single trigger with ambidextrous fire control lever, 8.6 lbs. Limited mfg. mid-1998-2001.

	$1,295	$1,150	$995	$895	$795	$695	$595	*$1,895*

Add $100 for camo finish.

CROWN CITY ARMS

Previous pistol and pistol frame manufacturer located in Cortland, NY circa 1970s-1981.

PISTOLS: SEMI-AUTO

M1911 A1 – 9mm Para., .38 Super, or .45 ACP cal., patterned after the Colt MKIV Series 70 Govt. and Commander Models, 4 1/4 or 5 in. barrel, 7 shot mag., carbon steel, alloy, or stainless steel frame, smooth or checkered walnut grips, matte black oxide finish or brushed stainless steel, fixed or adj. sights, 27-39 oz. Disc. circa 1981.

	$675	$600	$525	$450	$375	$325	$275	

The last MSR was approx. $200 for the base model.

CRUSADER WEAPONRY

Previous firearms manufacturer (including AR-15 style rifles) located in Murray, UT until 2015.

For individual model listings, please go to BlueBookOfGunValues.com/overflow.

CUMBERLAND MOUNTAIN ARMS, INC.

Previous manufacturer located in Winchester, TN early 1993-99.

RIFLES: SINGLE SHOT

PLATEAU RIFLE – .40-65 or .45-70 Govt. cal., patterned after the Browning High Wall single shot, various barrel lengths up to 32 in., manual safety, blue receiver and barrel, Marble's style buckhorn rear sight, receiver drilled for scope mounts. Mfg. 1993-99.

	$1,075	$825	$675	$575	$500	$450	$400	*$1,295*

Add approx. $200-$350 for deluxe wood.

CUSTOM GUN GUILD

Previous manufacturer located in Doraville, GA.

FIREARMS

WOOD'S MODEL IV SINGLE SHOT – various cals., custom manufactured, falling block type single shot, lightweight, only 5 1/2 lbs. Mfg. 1984 only.

	$2,975	$2,500	$2,000	$1,850	$1,700	$1,500	$1,250	

GRADING - PPGS™	100%	98%	95%	90%	80%	70%	60%	LAST MSR

CYLINDER & SLIDE, INC.

Current pistol manufacturer located in Fremont, NE. Direct consumer sales only through FFL.

PISTOLS: SEMI-AUTO

William Laughridge has been making M1911 style custom pistols for decades. Currently he manufactures a historical Pocket Model based on the 1903/1908 Colt Pocket Model (MSR $4,000), the Trident Series (MSR $4,202), in addition to building a new series - 100th Anniversary Limited Edition 1911 Government models based on the 1st 500 1911's ever produced. Models include the U.S. Army, U.S. Navy, and U.S. Marine Corp. William Laughridge went through an exhaustive research project to make sure every component is exactly produced as the 1st 500 1911's (MSR $5,000).

CZECHPOINT, INC.

Current partner and sole distributor for Czech Small Arms. Czechpoint Inc. was established in 2008, and is located in Knoxville, TN.

For individual model listings, please go to BlueBookOfGunValues.com/overflow.

CZECH SMALL ARMS (CSA)

Current manufacturer of rifles and pistols located in Jablunka, Czech Republic. Currently imported by CzechPoint, Inc. located in Knoxville, TN.

Czech Small Arms currently manufactures the very popular Sa. Vz. 58 Rifle (mfg. started circa 1960s) in a variety of configurations for North American and European distributors. Additionally, the factory also manufactures a semi-auto copy of the Skorpion semi-auto pistol in .32 ACP, .380 ACP, and 9mm Makarov, vz.15 pistol in 9mm Luger, and the Sa vz. 61 pistol in .22 LR cal. Please refer to the Czechpoint Inc. section for information on CSA models, or contact Czechpoint Inc. directly for information regarding U.S. availability.

150
YEARS
STRONG
NRA
1871~2021
WE ARE
STRONGER
TOGETHER
Join or
Renew
Today
NRA.ORG
NRA

D SECTION

D&L SPORTS, INC.

Current manufacturer located in Chino Valley, AZ.

Gunsmith Dave Lauck manufactures a complete line of 1911 style custom pistols, AR-15 style semi-auto carbines, and precision bolt action rifles. A wide variety of options and accessories are available. Additionally, D&L offers custom gunsmithing services. Please contact the company directly for more information, including pricing, options, and delivery time.

D.A.R. GmbH (DYNAMICS ARMS RESEARCH)

Current AR-15 style rifle and carbine manufacturer located in Fraureuth, Germany (previously located in Lichentanne, Germany). No current U.S. importation.

D.A.R. currently manufactures a variety of good quality AR-15 style carbines and rifles in various configurations. Additionally, the company also manufactures a variety of AR-15 style components and mounts. Please contact the company directly for U.S. availability and pricing.

DDI ARMS (DESTRUCTIVE DEVICES INDUSTRIES, LLC)

Previous AK-47 design manufacturer located in Knoxville, TN.

For individual model listings, please go to BlueBookOfGunValues.com/overflow.

DGS, INC.

Custom rifle gunsmith and machinest located in Casper, WY. During late 2013, DGS, Inc. combined its business with RGS, LLC. For current listings, please refer to RGS, LLC in the "R" section.

Master gunsmith Dale A. Storey and custom machinist Robert J. Stone have a total over seventy-five years of experience in fine rifles and precision machining. DGS, Inc. offers a variety of rifles built per individual specification. Custom machining of octagon barrels in various configurations from assorted name brand blanks is also available. Please contact the company directly for more information and current prices on these quality custom rifles.

DNO FIREARMS

Current firearms manufacturer specializing in unique AK-design modular rifles and receivers located in Aston, PA. Previously located in Flagstaff, AZ.

RIFLES: SEMI-AUTO

DX-7 – 7.62 NATO/.308 Win., 5.56 NATO, or .300 AAC Blackout cal., AK design, accepts standard AK mags., ambi AR-15 safety lever, Tapco G2 trigger, Picatinny rail, milled billet aluminum upper and lower receiver, Magpul components, iron sights, left-side charging handle, black finish.

Please contact the manufacturer directly for pricing and availability on this model.

DP-12

Current trademark of Double Pump Repeater manufactured by Standard Manufacturing Co. LLC beginning late 2013, and located in New Britain, CT. Please refer to the Standard Manufacturing Co. LLC listing in the S section.

DPMS FIREARMS (LLC)

Previous trademark by Remington Arms Co. located in Huntsville, AL late 2014-2020. Previous manufacturer established in 1986 and located in St. Cloud and Becker, MN. Previous company name was DPMS, Inc. (Defense Procurement Manufacturing Services, Inc.) DPMS Firearms assembled high quality AR-15 style rifles, in addition to related parts and components.

In December 2007, Cerberus Capital Management acquired the assets of DPMS. The new company name became DPMS Firearms, LLC, then later DPMS Firearms. In 2015, the Freedom Group became Remington Outdoor Company. In January 2020, Remington Outdoor Company announced they had made the decision to focus on their core hunting and shooting brands so DPMS Firearms would no longer be produced. The DPMS website (www.dpmsinc.com) will redirect you to the Remington parent company for consumer questions, parts, repairs, and owner manuals.

GRADING - PPGS™	100%	98%	95%	90%	80%	70%	60%	LAST MSR

PISTOLS: SEMI-AUTO

DPMS .45 – .45 ACP cal., patterned after the Colt M1911A-1, 7 shot mag., 5 in. barrel, 38 oz. Limited mfg. 2001 only.

	$475	$425	$360	$330	$300	$275	$250	*$519*

GRADING - PPGS™	100%	98%	95%	90%	80%	70%	60%	LAST MSR

PANTHER .22 LR PISTOL – .22 LR cal., blowback action, 8 1/2 in. heavy chrome moly steel barrel, 10 shot mag., black aircraft aluminum flat-top upper receiver, black forged aircraft aluminum lower receiver, phosphate and hard chrome finished bolt and carrier, aluminum trigger guard, ribbed aluminum tubular handguard, no sights, 4 1/4 lbs. Limited mfg. 2006-2007.

	$700	$625	$550	$475	$425	$375	$325	*$850*

PISTOLS: SLIDE ACTION

PANTHER PUMP PISTOL – .223 Rem. cal., 10 1/2 in. threaded heavy barrel, aluminum handguard incorporates slide action mechanism, pistol grip only (no stock), carrying handle with sights, 5 lbs. Disc. 2007.

	$1,200	$1,025	$925	$825	$700	$575	$495	*$1,600*

RIFLES: BOLT ACTION

DPMS also distributed Evolution USA bolt action rifles until 2006. Please refer to the Evolution USA section for current models and pricing.

RIFLES: SEMI-AUTO

Each new DPMS rifle/carbine came equipped with two mags. (high cap where legal), a nylon web sling, and a cleaning kit. Post-crime bill manufactured DPMS rifles may have pre-ban features, including collapsible stocks, high capacity mags, and a flash hider/compensator. Models with these features are not available in certain states.

The Panther AR-15 Series was introduced in 1993 in various configurations, including semi-auto GIO and slide action, and feature a tactical design in various barrel lengths and configurations, with a 10 or 30 shot mag.

300 AAC BLACKOUT – .300 AAC Blackout cal., 16 in. heavy chrome-lined barrel, Blackout suppressor adapter or an inert slipover mock suppressor, AP4 stock, A2 pistol grip, choice of carbine or mid-length handguard (disc. 2016) or DPMS M111 modular free float tube (new 2017), 7-7 1/2 lbs. Mfg. 2012-2019.

	$850	$675	$600	$550	$500	$475	$425	*$1,149*

COMPACT HUNTER – .308 Win. cal., 16 in. Teflon coated stainless steel barrel, B5 Systems SOPMOD stock, two-stage match trigger, carbon fiber free float handguard, Hogue rubber pistol grip, 7 3/4 lbs. Mfg. 2012-2014.

	$1,250	$825	$575	$475	$425	$375	$350	*$1,499*

A1 LITE 20 (PANTHER LITE A1/A3) – 5.56 NATO cal., 16 (disc.) or 20 (new 2007) in. post-ban chrome moly barrel with A2 birdcage flash hider (new 2007), 1:9 in. twist, non-collapsible fiberite CAR (disc.) or A2 fixed pistol grip stock, choice of forged A1 upper with forward bolt assist or A3 (disc.) carry handle, black Teflon finish, 6-7.3 lbs. Mfg. 2002-2014.

	$725	$500	$435	$375	$335	$315	$295	*$829*

LITE 16 A2 – 5.56 NATO cal., 16 in. lightweight barrel with A2 birdcage flash hider, forged upper and lower receivers, GlacierGuard handguard, Pardus stock, A2 sights, 6 lbs. Disc. 2019.

	$550	$425	$400	$350	$325	$300	$275	*$729*

LITE 16M A2 – 5.56 NATO cal., 16 in. lightweight barrel with A2 birdcage flash hider, A2 sights, Pardus stock, forged upper and lower receivers, M-111 modular free floating handguard, 6 lbs. Mfg. 2018-2019.

	$650	$525	$450	$400	$375	$350	$325	*$869*

LITE HUNTER (PANTHER LITE 308/338) – .243 Win., .260 Rem., .308 Win., or .338 Federal cal., 18 (disc. 2012) or 20 (new 2012) in. free floating barrel, no sights, carbon fiber free floating handguard, bipod stud, A3 style flat-top, Picatinny rail, A2 stock (new 2012), Hogue rubber grips, various accessories and options available. Mfg. 2009-2014.

	$1,250	$825	$575	$475	$425	$375	$350	*$1,499*

LONG RANGE LITE – .308 Win. cal., 24 in. stainless steel barrel, A2 fixed stock, two-stage match trigger, carbon fiber free float handguard, Hogue rubber pistol grip, 10 1/4 lbs. Mfg. 2012-2014.

	$1,250	$825	$575	$475	$425	$375	$350	*$1,499*

MOE SL CARBINE – 5.56 NATO cal., 16 in. chrome-lined barrel with AAC Blackout flash hider, enhanced trigger guard, backup sights, Magpul MOE SL furniture, Picatinny rail, matte black or FDE finish, approx. 6.5 lbs. Mfg. 2018-2019.

	$825	$650	$575	$525	$475	$450	$400	*$1,099*

MOE WARRIOR – 5.56 NATO cal., 16 in. heavy barrel, supressor adapter, enhanced trigger guard, backup sights, Magpul MOE stock, MOE handguard and pistol grip, sling adapter, black or Dark Earth finish, 7.3 lbs. Mfg. 2012-2014.

	$975	$595	$495	$425	$365	$335	$300	*$1,159*

GRADING - PPGS™	100%	98%	95%	90%	80%	70%	60%	LAST MSR

TAC2 – 5.56 NATO cal., 16 in. barrel with Panther flash hider, Magpul ACS stock, MOE pistol grip, M111 modular handguard system (disc. 2018) or Midwest Industries M-LOK handguard (new 2019), utilizes a full rifle length gas system, A2 front and Magpul rear sights, 8 1/2 lbs. Mfg. 2012-2019.

$925 $750 $675 $575 $550 $500 $450 *$1,249*

TAC20 – .308 Win. cal., 20 in. heavy chrome moly barrel, A2 fixed stock, detachable carry handle, Panther flash hider, 11 1/2 lbs. Mfg. 2012-2015.

$975 $775 $700 $600 $575 $525 $475 *$1,299*

TPR (TACTICAL PRECISION RIFLE) – 5.56 NATO cal., AR-15 style, 20 in. heavy stainless steel barrel with AAC flash hider, two-stage trigger, B5 Systems SOPMOD (disc. 2017) or Magpul MOE (new 2018) stock, Magpul MOE pistol grip, M111 modular handguard (disc. 2018) or Midwest Industries M-LOK handguard (new 2019), 7 3/4 lbs. Mfg. 2012-2019.

$925 $750 $675 $575 $550 $500 $450 *$1,249*

PANTHER A2/A3 CLASSIC – 5.56 NATO cal., 16 (disc.) or 20 in. heavy barrel, ribbed barrel shroud, A3 stock with detachable carrying handle with sights, or A2 fixed stock, 9 lbs. Disc. 2015.

$725 $575 $525 $450 $425 $400 $350 *$980*

Add $76 for left-hand variation (Southpaw Panther, disc.).

* ***Panther Classic Bulldog*** – 5.56 NATO cal., 20 in. stainless fluted bull barrel, flat-top, adj. buttstock, vented free float handguard, 11 lbs. Disc. 1999.

$1,025 $625 $495 $450 $395 $350 $325 *$1,219*

PANTHER CARBINE 16 – 5.56 NATO cal., 16 in. heavy barrel with A2 birdcage flash hider, A3 flat-top upper, Pardus 6-position collapsible stock, GlacierGuard handguard, A2 pistol grip, 7.1 lbs. Disc. 2015.

$725 $575 $525 $450 $425 $400 $350 *$979*

PANTHER 7.62x39mm CARBINE/RIFLE – 7.62x39mm Russian cal., 16 or 20 in. heavy barrel, black Zytel buttstock with trapdoor assembly, A2 flash hider, A2 pistol grip, 7-9 lbs. Mfg. 2000-2011.

$725 $500 $435 $375 $335 $315 $295 *$850*

Add $10 for 20 in. barrel.

PANTHER DCM – .223 Rem. cal., 20 in. stainless steel heavy barrel, National Match sights, two-stage trigger, black Zytel composition buttstock, 9 lbs. Mfg. 1998-2003, reintroduced 2006-2012.

$875 $550 $465 $395 $350 $325 $300 *$1,129*

PANTHER CLASSIC SIXTEEN – 5.56 NATO cal., 16 in. lightweight chrome moly (new 2012) or heavy (disc. 2011) barrel with A2 birdcage flash hider, adj. sights, black Zytel composition buttstock (disc.) or A2 fixed pistol grip stock, 7.1 lbs. Mfg. 1998-2014.

$745 $500 $435 $375 $335 $315 $295 *$859*

Add $55 for Panther Free Float Sixteen with free floating barrel and vent. handguard (disc. 2008).

PANTHER LO-PRO CLASSIC – 5.56 NATO cal., 16 in. bull barrel, A2 fixed stock, flat-top lo-pro upper receiver with push pin, 7 3/4 lbs. Mfg. 2002-2012.

$665 $500 $415 $375 $335 $315 $295 *$769*

PANTHER TUBER – 5.56 NATO cal., 16 in. post-ban heavy free float barrel with full-length 2 in. diameter aluminum free float handguard, adj. A2 rear sights. Mfg. 2002-2008.

$665 $500 $415 $375 $335 $315 $295 *$754*

PANTHER A2 TACTICAL – 5.56 NATO cal., 16 in. heavy manganese phosphate barrel, standard A2 handguard, 9 3/4 lbs. Mfg. 2004-2013.

$745 $500 $435 $375 $335 $315 $295 *$859*

PANTHER AP4 CARBINE – 5.56 NATO cal., 16 in. M4 contour barrel with A2 flash hider, with or w/o attached Miculek compensator, fixed fiberglass reinforced polymer M4 stock, 7 1/4 lbs. Mfg. 2004-2012.

$825 $535 $450 $385 $340 $325 $295 *$959*

Add $54 for Miculek compensator.

* ***Panther AP4 Carbine (Disc.)*** – 6.8x43mm SPC or 5.56x45mm cal., 16 in. barrel, collapsible stock, includes carrying handle, 6 1/2 lbs. Disc.

$785 $525 $450 $385 $340 $325 $295 *$904*

PANTHER AP4 A2 CARBINE – 5.56 NATO cal., 16 in. chrome moly steel heavy barrel with A2 flash hider, standard A2 front sight assembly, A2 fixed carry handle and adj. rear sight, forged aircraft aluminum upper and lower receiver, hardcoat anodized Teflon coated black finish, AP4 6-pos. telescoping fiber reinforced polymer stock, GlacierGuard handguard, 7.1 lbs. Mfg. 2006-2019.

$700 $550 $500 $450 $425 $375 $350 *$945*

GRADING - PPGS™	100%	98%	95%	90%	80%	70%	60%	LAST MSR

PANTHER A2 CARBINE "THE AGENCY" – 5.56 NATO cal., 16 in. chrome moly steel barrel with A2 flash hider, two 30 shot mags., A3 flat-top forged receiver, two-stage trigger, EoTech and "Mangonel" rear sights, Ergo SureGrip forearm and collapsible stock, A3 flat-top forged receiver, two-stage trigger, tactical charging handle, package includes SureFire quad rail and flashlight, 7 lbs. Mfg. 2007-2012.

$1,675 $1,000 $825 $625 $550 $475 $425 ***$2,069***

LR-6.5 (PANTHER 6.5) – 6.5 Creedmoor cal., 24 in. stainless steel free float bull barrel, single rail gas block, no sights, ribbed aluminum free float tube handguard, bipod stud, A3 style flat-top, black Teflon coated, standard A2 black Zytel Mil-Spec stock, A2 pistol grip, 11.3 lbs. Mfg. 2009-2014.

$1,050 $650 $495 $450 $395 $350 $325 ***$1,239***

PANTHER 6.8mm CARBINE/RIFLE – 6.8x43mm Rem. SPC cal., 16 (new 2007) or 20 in. chrome moly manganese phosphate steel barrel with A2 flash hider, two 25 shot mags., standard A2 front sight assembly, A3 flat-top upper receiver with detachable carry handle and adj. rear sight, aluminum aircraft alloy lower receiver, black standard A2 Zytel Mil-Spec stock with trap door assembly, A2 handguard, approx. 9 lbs. Mfg. 2006-2011.

$865 $550 $465 $395 $350 $325 $300 ***$1,019***

Add $10 for 20 in. barrel.

PANTHER 6.8 SPCII HUNTER – 6.8x43mm Rem. SPC cal., 18 in. steel barrel with Miculek compensator, aluminum A3 flat-top with forward assist, black Zytel skeletonized A2 stock, mid-length carbine fiber free floating forearm tube, 7.65 lbs. Mfg. 2011-2012.

$1,065 $650 $500 $450 $395 $350 $325 ***$1,269***

PANTHER RECON MID-LENGTH CARBINE – 5.56 NATO or 7.62 NATO (mfg. 2012-2014) cal., 16 in. stainless steel heavy barrel with AAC blackout flash hider, flat-top aluminum upper receiver with Magpul BUIS front and rear sights, mid-length quad rail free floating forearm tube (disc. 2018) or Midwest Industries M-LOK handguard (new 2019), Magpul MOE stock and pistol grip, 7.7 lbs. Mfg. 2011-2019.

$900 $700 $625 $550 $525 $475 $450 ***$1,197***

PANTHER LBR CARBINE – 5.56 NATO cal., 16 in. lightweight stainless barrel with A2 flash hider, muzzle brake, flat-top receiver with integral Picatinny rail, Magpul MOE stock with A2 pistol grip, vent. free floating handguard with front upper Picatinny rail, choice of matte black or Muddy Girl camo (new 2018) finish, 7 1/4 lbs. Mfg. 2011-2019.

$725 $575 $525 $450 $425 $400 $350 ***$979***

* ***Panther LBR DIVA Edition*** – 5.56 NATO cal., similar to Panther LBR, except has 16 in. chrome moly barrel and Leopard print especially for women. Mfg. 2012-2014.

$850 $550 $465 $395 $350 $325 $295 ***$979***

PRAIRIE PANTHER – 5.56 NATO cal., 20 in. heavy fluted free float barrel, flat-top, vented handguard, 8 3/4 lbs. Disc. 1999.

$825 $535 $450 $385 $340 $325 $295 ***$959***

PRAIRIE PANTHER (RECENT MFG.) – .223 Rem. or 6.8 SPC (black finish only, disc. 2014) cal., 20 in. stainless steel fluted heavy barrel, target crown, carbon fiber free float tube, no sights, hard anodized finish, choice of black with carbon fiber handguard (mfg. 2011-2015), King's Desert Shadow (disc.), King's Snow Shadow (mfg. 2011-2015), Mossy Oak Brush (disc. 2018), TrueTimber Strata (new 2019), or Kuiu Verde (new 2019) camo coverage, A3 Picatinny rail flat-top, tactical charging handle assembly, Magpul winter trigger guard, skeletonized black Zytel Mil-Spec stock with trapdoor assembly, A2 pistol grip stock, two-stage trigger, approx. 7.1 lbs. Mfg. 2010-2019.

$925 $750 $675 $575 $550 $500 $450 ***$1,249***

Subtract approx. $60 for black finish (disc. 2015).

ARCTIC PANTHER – .223 Rem. cal., 20 in. barrel, similar to Prairie Panther, except has white powder coat finish on receiver and aluminum handguard, railed gas block, 9 lbs. Mfg. 1997-2015.

$900 $700 $625 $550 $525 $475 $450 ***$1,197***

PANTHER BULL/SWEET 16 – .223 Rem. cal., features 16 (Sweet 16), 20, or 24 in. stainless free float bull barrel, flat-top, aluminum forearm, A2 fixed stock, aluminum pistol grip, A2 handguard, railed gas block/optics ready, 7 3/4-9 1/2 lbs. Disc. 2019.

$725 $575 $525 $450 $425 $400 $350 ***$979***

Add $10 for 20 in. barrel (Panther Bull 20).
Add $20 for 24 in. barrel (Panther Bull 24).

* ***Panther Bull Classic*** – .223 Rem. cal., 20 in. long 1 in. bull barrel, adj. sights, 10 lbs. Mfg. 1998-2008.

$785 $525 $450 $385 $340 $325 $295 ***$910***

Add $200 for SST lower.

GRADING - PPGS™	100%	98%	95%	90%	80%	70%	60%	LAST MSR

* ***Panther Bull Twenty-Four Special*** – 5.56 NATO cal., 24 in. stainless fluted barrel, adj. A2 buttstock with sniper pistol grip, JP trigger, 10 1/4 lbs. Mfg. 1998-2015.

$1,000 $800 $725 $625 $600 $550 $500 ***$1,348***

* ***Panther Super Bull*** – .223 Rem. cal., 16, 20, or 24 in. extra heavy free float bull barrel, flat-top receiver, handguard, approx. 11 lbs. Mfg. 1997-98, 24 in. model reintroduced reintroduced late 2004-2006.

$995 $625 $495 $450 $395 $350 $325 ***$1,199***

* ***Panther Super Bull 24*** – .223 Rem. cal., 24 in. extra heavy stainless steel bull barrel (1 1/8 in. diameter barrel), flat-top, hi-rider upper receiver, skeletonized A2 buttstock, 11 3/4 lbs. Mfg. 1999-2004.

$995 $625 $495 $450 $395 $350 $325 ***$1,199***

PANTHER PARDUS – .223 Rem. cal., 16 in. stainless steel free float bull barrel, integrated compensator, titanium Nitride plated steel bolt and carrier, three rail extruded upper receiver, aluminum alloy upper and lower receiver, Teflon coated tan or black 6-position telescoping fiber reinforced polymer stock, curved and serrated buttplate, four-rail aluminum handguard, no sights, includes two 30 shot mags., 8.1 lbs. Mfg. 2006-2008.

$1,315 $850 $625 $500 $435 $375 $350 ***$1,600***

PANTHER MK-12 5.56 NATO – 5.56 NATO cal., 18 in. stainless heavy free float barrel with flash hider, one-piece four rail tube and six long rail covers, A3 flat-top receiver, 5-position SOPMOD collapsible stock with tactical pistol grip, two-stage trigger, two 30 round mags., Midwest Industry flip-up sights, 8 3/4 lbs. Mfg. 2007-2014.

$1,350 $875 $650 $525 $450 $385 $350 ***$1,649***

PANTHER MK-12 7.62 NATO – 7.62 NATO cal., 18 in. stainless steel heavy barrel, flash hider, Midwest Industries flip-up rear sight, gas block with flip-up front sight, A3 Picatinny rail flat-top, aluminum lower receiver, integral trigger guard, Magpul CTR adj. stock, Hogue rubber grip with finger grooves, two-stage match trigger, hardcoat anodized black finish, four rail free float tube, six rail covers, approx. 9.6 lbs. Mfg. 2010-2014.

$1,475 $950 $725 $550 $475 $395 $350 ***$1,799***

PANTHER SDM-R – .223 Rem. cal., 20 in. heavy stainless free float barrel with A2 flash hider, four rail aluminum tube, pistol grip stock, National Match front sight, Harris bipod with rail adapter, two 30 shot mags., 8.85 lbs. Mfg. 2007-2008.

$1,175 $775 $550 $465 $415 $375 $350 ***$1,404***

PANTHER 20TH ANNIVERSARY – .223 Rem. cal., 20 in. stainless steel fluted bull barrel, phosphated steel bolt and carrier, hi-rider forged high polished chrome upper and lower receiver with commemorative engraving, chrome plated charging handle, semi-auto trigger group, aluminum trigger guard and mag. release button, A2 black Zytel Mil-Spec stock with trap door assembly and engraved DPMS logo, no sights, vented aluminum handguard, includes two 30 shot mags., approx. 9 1/2 lbs. Limited mfg. of 100 rifles in 2006.

$1,650 $1,000 $795 $595 $495 $425 $395 ***$1,995***

PANTHER RACE GUN – .223 Rem. cal., 24 in. stainless steel barrel with Hot Rod handguard, IronStone steel and aluminum stock with rubber buttplate and brass weights, 16 lbs. Mfg. 2001-2008.

$1,425 $925 $700 $550 $475 $395 $350 ***$1,724***

PANTHER SINGLE SHOT – 5.56 NATO cal., 20 in. barrel, A2 black Zytel stock and handguard, single shot only w/o magazine, 9 lbs. Disc. 2008.

$695 $500 $425 $375 $335 $315 $295 ***$819***

AP4 CARBINE .22 LR – .22 LR cal., 16 in. barrel, GlacierGuard M4 handguard, A2 pistol grip and flash hider, AP4 stock with detachable carry handle, 6 1/2 lbs. Disc. 2014.

$800 $700 $600 $545 $445 $345 $275 ***$935***

BULL CARBINE .22 LR – .22 LR cal., 16 in. bull barrel, aluminum handguard, A2 pistol grip and flash hider, fixed A2 stock, no sights, 7.3 lbs. Disc. 2015.

$700 $550 $500 $450 $400 $375 $350 ***$935***

PANTHER .22 LR RIFLE – .22 LR cal., AR-15 style receiver, 16 in. bull barrel, black Teflon metal finish, Picatinny rail, black Zytel A2 buttstock, 7.8 lbs. Mfg. 2003-2008.

$695 $615 $525 $475 $375 $315 $245 ***$804***

PANTHER DCM .22 LR RIFLE – .22 LR cal., 20 in. fluted stainless steel HBAR barrel with 1:16 in. twist, A2 upper receiver with National Match sights, black Teflon finish, A2 stock and handguards, also available with optional DCM handguard system. Mfg. 2004-2008.

$850 $745 $645 $575 $475 $385 $300 ***$994***

GRADING - PPGS™	100%	98%	95%	90%	80%	70%	60%	LAST MSR

PANTHER AP4 .22 LR RIFLE – .22 LR cal., 16 in. M4 contoured barrel, M4 handguards and pinned carstock, A3 flat-top upper receiver, detachable carry handle with A2 sights and black Teflon finish, 6 1/2 lbs. Mfg. 2004-2008.

$765 $675 $575 $525 $425 $345 $275 *$894*

PANTHER LR-.308 – .308 Win. cal., 24 in. free float bull barrel with 1:10 in. twist, ribbed aluminum forearm tube, aircraft alloy upper/lower, A2 fixed pistol grip stock, black Teflon finish, 11 1/4 lbs. Mfg. mid-2003-2014.

$995 $625 $495 $450 $395 $350 $325 *$1,199*

* ***Panther LR-.308B*** – .308 Win. cal., similar to Long Range Rifle, except has 18 in. chrome moly bull barrel and carbine length aluminum handguard. Mfg. late 2003-2012.

$995 $625 $495 $450 $395 $350 $325 *$1,189*

* ***Panther LR-.308T*** – 7.62 NATO cal., similar to .308B, except has 16 in. HBAR. Mfg. 2004-2012.

$995 $625 $495 $450 $395 $350 $325 *$1,189*

* ***Panther LR-.308 AP4*** – 7.62 NATO cal., similar to Panther .308 Long Range, except has AP4 6-position telescoping fiber reinforced polymer stock. Disc. 2012.

$1,075 $675 $500 $450 $400 $350 $325 *$1,299*

* ***Panther LR-.308 Classic*** – 7.62 NATO cal., similar to Panther LR-.308, except has 20 in. barrel, A3 style flat-top receiver and removable carry handle. Mfg. mid-2008-2014.

$995 $625 $495 $450 $395 $350 $325 *$1,199*

PANTHER LR-308C – .308 Win. cal., 20 in. heavy steel free float barrel, features A3 flat-top receiver with detachable carrying handle, standard A2 front sight assembly, four rail standard length tube, two 19 shot mags., 11.1 lbs. Mfg. 2007-2008.

$1,065 $650 $500 $450 $395 $350 $325 *$1,254*

PANTHER LRT-SASS – 7.62 NATO cal., 18 in. stainless steel contoured barrel with Panther flash hider, A3 style flat-top upper receiver solid aluminum lower receiver, AR-15 trigger group, ambi-selector, JP adj. trigger, black waterproof VLTOR Clubfoot carbine 5-position (disc.) or Magpul stock, vented handguard and Panther tactical pistol grip, Magpul sights, approx. 11 1/2 lbs. Mfg. 2006-2014.

$1,725 $1,050 $850 $625 $550 $475 $425 *$2,179*

PANTHER MINI-SASS – 5.56 NATO cal., 18 in. stainless steel fluted barrel with Panther flash hider, forged A3 flat-top upper receiver, aircraft aluminum alloy lower receiver, aluminum trigger guard, Magpul PRS stock, tactical pistol grip, Magpul sights, includes Harris bipod, 10 1/4 lbs. Mfg. 2008-2019.

$1,200 $950 $850 $750 $700 $650 $600 *$1,599*

PANTHER LR-30S – .300 RSUM cal., 20 in. stainless steel free float fluted bull barrel, aluminum upper and lower receiver, hardcoat anodized Teflon coated black skeletonized synthetic stock, integral trigger guard, ribbed aluminum tube handguard, includes two 4 shot mags., nylon web sling and cleaning kit. Mfg. 2004-2008.

$1,065 $650 $500 $450 $395 $350 $325 *$1,255*

PANTHER LR-204 – .204 Ruger cal., 24 in. fluted stainless steel bull barrel, no sights, A3 flat-top forged upper and lower receiver, semi-auto trigger group, standard A2 black Zytel Mil-Spec stock with trapdoor assembly, includes two 30 shot mags., 9 3/4 lbs. Mfg. 2006-2015.

$900 $725 $650 $574 $525 $500 $450 *$1,213*

PANTHER LR-243 – .243 Win. cal., 20 in. chrome moly steel heavy (disc. 2012) or lightweight (Lite Hunter) free float barrel, no sights, raised Picatinny rail, aluminum upper and lower receiver, standard AR-15 trigger group, skeletonized black Zytel Mil-Spec stock with trapdoor assembly, ribbed aluminum free float handguard, includes two 19 shot mags., 10 3/4 lbs. Mfg. 2006-2013.

$1,250 $825 $575 $475 $425 $375 $350 *$1,499*

PANTHER LR-260 SERIES – .260 Rem. cal., 18 (mfg. 2007-2012, LR-260L), 20 (LR-260H, Lite Hunter) or 24 (LR-260) in. stainless steel fluted bull barrel, no sights, raised Picatinny rail, thick walled aluminum upper receiver, solid lower receiver, standard AR-15 trigger group, integral trigger guard, A2 black Zytel stock with trapdoor assembly, includes two 19 shot mags., 11.3 lbs. Mfg. 2006-2014.

$1,050 $650 $495 $450 $395 $350 $325 *$1,239*

Add $260 for 18 in. barrel (LR-260L) with skeletonized stock, Miculek compensator and JRD trigger (disc. 2012).

ORACLE 5.56 NATO CAL. (PANTHER ORACLE) – 5.56 NATO cal., 16 in. stainless steel (mfg. 2010-2014) or chrome moly heavy barrel, A2 flash hider, integral trigger guard, optics ready, Pardus 6-pos. telescoping stock with cheekpiece, GlacierGuards oval carbine length handguard, curved and serrated

GRADING - PPGS™	100%	98%	95%	90%	80%	70%	60%	LAST MSR

buttplate, A2 pistol grip, Mil-Std A3 upper receiver, Picatinny rail, multiple sling slots, hard anodized black or ATACS camo (mfg. 2011-2014) finish, 6.64 lbs. Mfg. 2010-2019.

	$450	$375	$325	$295	$275	$250	$225	*$611*

Add $30 for stainless steel barrel (disc. 2014).
Add $80 for quad rail handguard (disc. 2014).
Add $110 for ATACS Oracle Carbine (includes ATACS camo coverage), mfg. 2011-2014.

ORACLE 7.62 NATO CAL. (PANTHER ORACLE) - 7.62 NATO cal., 16 in. chrome moly heavy barrel, A2 flash hider, gas block with single rail, integral trigger guard, optics ready, Pardus 6-pos. telescoping stock with cheekpiece, curved and serrated buttplate, multiple sling slots, A2 pistol grip, GlacierGuards oval carbine length handguard, A3 Picatinny flat-top, hard anodized black or ATACS camo (mfg. 2011-2015) finish, 8.3 lbs. Mfg. 2010-2015, reintroduced 2017-2019.

	$725	$575	$525	$450	$425	$400	$350	*$969*

Add $90 for ATACS Oracle Carbine (includes ATACS camo coverage) mfg. 2011-2015.

PANTHER SPORTICAL - 5.56 NATO or 7.62 NATO cal., 16 in. chrome moly heavy or light contour barrel, single rail gas block, A2 flash hider, various rails and accessories. Mfg. mid-2008-2015.

	$550	$450	$400	$350	$325	$300	$275	*$746*

PANTHER REPR - 7.62 NATO cal., 18 in. chrome moly (disc.) or 20 in. fluted stainless steel free float barrel, Gem Tech flash hider/suppressor, micro gas block, A3 style flat-top upper receiver, milled aluminum lower receiver, hardcoat anodized coyote brown finish, removable hinged trigger guard, Picatinny rail, four rail tube handguard, Magpul PRS stock, Hogue rubber grip with finger grooves, 9 1/2 lbs. Mfg. 2009-2014.

	$2,050	$1,250	$950	$650	$575	$495	$475	*$2,589*

PANTHER RAPTR CARBINE - 5.56 NATO cal., 16 in. chrome moly steel contoured barrel, 30 shot mag., flash hider, A2 front sight, Mangonel flip-up rear sight, Ergo Z-Rail two-piece four rail handguard, Crimson Trace vertical grip with integrated light and laser combination, A3 Picatinny rail flat-top, dust cover, aluminum trigger guard, AP4 6-position telescoping polymer stock, Ergo Ambi SureGrip, hardcoat anodized black finish, 8.2 lbs. Mfg. 2010-2011.

	$1,350	$875	$650	$525	$450	$385	$350	*$1,649*

PANTHER CSAT TACTICAL - 5.56 NATO cal., 16 in. chrome moly steel contoured barrel, 30 shot mag., A2 front sight assembly with A2 front sight post, detachable rear sight, four rail free float tube, A3 Picatinny rail flat-top, aluminum lower receiver, Magpul CTR adj. stock, Magpul MIAD pistol grip, 7.8 lbs. Mfg. 2010-2012.

	$1,475	$950	$725	$550	$475	$395	$350	*$1,799*

PANTHER CSAT PERIMETER - 5.56 NATO cal., similar to Tactical, except has 16 in. heavy barrel, approx. 8 lbs. Mfg. 2010-2011.

	$1,475	$950	$725	$550	$475	$395	$350	*$1,799*

PANTHER 3G1 - 5.56 NATO or 7.62 NATO (mfg. 2012-2014) cal., 18 in. stainless standard or heavy barrel, 30 shot mag., Miculek compensator, no sights, VTAC modular handguard, bipod stud, A3 Picatinny rail flat-top, black anodized finish, aluminum trigger guard, JP adj. trigger group, Magpul CTR adj. stock, Hogue rubber pistol grip, 7 3/4 lbs. Mfg. 2010-2019.

	$1,050	$825	$750	$650	$625	$575	$525	*$1,399*

PANTHER 3G2 - 5.56 NATO cal., 16 in. stainless lightweight barrel with Miculek compensator, Magpul STR buttstock, M111 modular handguard, Ergo rubber pistol grip, Magpul Gen. 2 BUIS sights, enhanced charging handle, two-stage trigger, 7 lbs. 2 oz. Mfg. 2013-2015.

	$1,075	$850	$750	$675	$625	$575	$525	*$1,420*

GII AP4 - .308 Win./7.62 NATO cal., 16 in. lightweight chrome-lined barrel with Cancellation Brake flash hider, forged anodized Teflon coated upper and lower receiver, F marked front sight base, Magpul BUIS rear sight, 6-position M4 collapsible stock, carbine length GlacierGuard handguard, A2 pistol grip, matte black finish, 7 1/4 lbs. Mfg. 2014-2019.

	$1,050	$825	$750	$650	$625	$575	$525	*$1,399*

GII AP4-OR - .308 Win./7.62 NATO cal., 16 in. lightweight barrel, A2 birdcage flash hider, railed gas block optics ready, AP4 stock, A2 pistol grip, DPMS carbine length GlacierGuard handguard, Teflon coated upper and lower receivers, 7 lbs. Mfg. 2017-2019.

	$925	$750	$675	$575	$550	$500	$450	*$1,249*

GII BULL 24 - 7.62 NATO/.308 Win. cal., 24 in. stainless steel bull barrel, A2 stock, aluminum free float handguard, and no flash hider, 10 lbs. Mfg. 2014-2019.

	$975	$775	$700	$600	$575	$525	$475	*$1,299*

GRADING - PPGS™	100%	98%	95%	90%	80%	70%	60%	LAST MSR

GII HUNTER – 7.62 NATO/.308 Win., .243 Win. (mfg. 2015, reintroduced 2018), .260 Rem. (mfg. 2015, reintroduced 2018), or .338 Federal (mfg. 2015 only) cal., 20 in. stainless steel barrel with target crown, no sights, Hogue pistol grip, carbon fiber free float tube handguard, Magpul MOE stock, 7.76 lbs. Mfg. 2014-2019.

$1,200 $950 $850 $750 $700 $650 $600 *$1,599*

GII COMPACT HUNTER – 7.62 NATO/.308 Win., .243 Win. (disc. 2016, reintroduced 2018), .260 Rem. (disc. 2016, reintroduced 2018 only), or .338 Federal (disc. 2016) cal., 16 (new 2017) or 18 (disc. 2016) in. stainless Teflon coated barrel, carbon fiber free float tube handguard, Magpul MOE (disc. 2016) or B5 SOPMOD (new 2017) stock, Hogue pistol grip, black finish, 6.9 lbs. Mfg. 2015-2019.

$1,200 $950 $850 $750 $700 $650 $600 *$1,599*

GII MOE – .308 Win./7.62 NATO cal., 16 in. lightweight chrome-lined barrel, Magpul BUIS sights, MOE carbine stock, Magpul MOE pistol grip, and carbine length MOE handguard, 7 1/4 lbs. Mfg. 2014-2019.

$1,125 $900 $800 $700 $650 $600 $550 *$1,499*

GII RECON – .308 Win./7.62 NATO cal., 16 in. stainless steel bead blasted mid-length barrel with Advanced Armament Blackout silencer adapter, mid-length gas system, forged anodized Teflon coated A3 type upper and lower receiver, Magpul front and rear BUIS sight, Magpul MOE 6-position collapsible stock, Magpul MOE pistol grip, four rail free float tube handguard, matte black finish, 8 1/2 lbs. Mfg. 2014-2019.

$1,250 $975 $875 $775 $725 $675 $625 *$1,659*

GII SASS – .308 Win./7.62 NATO cal., mid-length gas system, 18 in. Teflon coated stainless steel fluted bull barrel with Panther flash hider, forged anodized Teflon coated A3 type upper and lower receiver, Magpul front sight and rear BUIS sight, Magpul PRS rifle stock, Harris bipod and adapter, Panther tactical grip, four rail free float tube handguard, matte black finish, 10 1/2 lbs. Mfg. 2014-2019.

$1,700 $1,350 $1,200 $1,050 $1,000 $925 $850 *$2,279*

GEN I ORACLE – 7.62 NATO cal., compact, 16 in. heavy barrel, optics ready, GlacierGuard handguard, black finish. Mfg. 2016 only.

$725 $575 $500 $450 $425 $400 $350 *$954*

LCAR – 5.56 NATO cal., 16 in. barrel, F-marked carbine-height front sight, folding Magpul backup rear sight, Mil-Spec 6-pos. M4 stock, 8 1/2 lbs. Mfg. 2019 only.

$550 $450 $400 $350 $325 $300 $275 *$749*

RIFLES: SLIDE ACTION

PANTHER PUMP RIFLE – .223 Rem. cal., 20 in. threaded heavy barrel with flash hider, aluminum handguard incorporates slide action mechanism, carrying handle with sights, bayonet lug, designed by Les Branson, 8 1/2 lbs. Disc. 2009.

$1,350 $1,125 $995 $875 $725 $575 $495 *$1,700*

DRD TACTICAL

Current AR-15 style rifle manufacturer and previous manufacturer of semi-auto AR-15 style pistols located in Lyons Falls, NY. DRD Tactical was acquired by Otis Technology in 2019. Dealer and distributor sales.

For individual model listings, please go to BlueBookOfGunValues.com/overflow.

DS ARMS INC. (DSA INC.)

Current manufacturer, importer, and distributor of AR-15 style and FAL style semi-auto rifles, pistols, and related components established during 1987 and currently located in Barrington, IL. Previously located in Round Lake and Grayslake, IL.

DSArms (DSA Inc). is a manufacturer of FAL design and SA58 style rifles for both civilian and law enforcement purposes (L.E. certificates must be filled out for L.E. purchases). Until recently, DSA, Inc. also imported a sporterized SIG 550 rifle.

PISTOLS: SEMI-AUTO

SA58 PISTOL – 7.62 NATO cal., short stroke GPO, PARA operating system, 8 1/4 in. threaded barrel, 3-prong Trident or WarZ Series (new 2019) flash hider, 20 shot detachable box mag., enhanced ambi mag. release, enlarged winter trigger guard, adj. front sight, dual aperture PARA rear sight w/quick adjust windage knob, with or w/o folding SB Tactical arm brace, SAW style pistol grip, SA58 Type 1 steel upper receiver, aluminum lower trigger housing, pistol length military grade handguards, left side non-reciprocating folding charging handle, Extreme Duty ext. PARA scope mount, matte black DuraCoat finish.

MSR $1,695 $1,385 $895 $675 $525 $450 $385 $350

Add $100 for folding SB Tactical arm brace.

GRADING - PPGS™	100%	98%	95%	90%	80%	70%	60%	LAST MSR

SA58 TACTICAL PISTOL – 7.62 NATO cal., 8 in. barrel w/A2 flash hider, based on SA58 FAL design, detachable 10 or 20 shot mag., SAW pistol grip, Type 1 or 2 receiver, black glass filled nylon furniture, PARA. ext. scope mount, lightweight alloy lower receiver, folding cocking handle, includes sling and hard case, 9 1/2 lbs. Mfg. 2013-2017.

	$1,450	$1,275	$1,125	$1,000	$850	$735	$595	*$1,695*

Add $200 for folding SIG arm brace.

SA58 OSW PISTOL – 7.62 NATO cal., short stroke GPO, PARA operating system, 11 in. threaded barrel with 3-prong Trident flash hider, 20 shot mag., enhanced ambi mag. release, SA58 Type 1 steel upper receiver, 7075-T6 aluminum lower frame, enlarged winter trigger guard, adj. front sight, dual aperture PARA rear sight w/quick adjust windage knob, glass filled nylon reinforced handguards or Picatinny rail handguard (disc. 2020), available with or w/o SB Tactical arm brace, SAW style pistol grip, left side non-reciprocating folding charging handle, Extreme Duty ext. PARA scope mount, matte black DuraCoat finish.

MSR $1,695	$1,385	$895	$675	$525	$450	$385	$350	

Add $100 for folding SB Tactical arm brace.
Add $200 for folding SB Tactical arm brace and railed handguard (disc. 2020).

SA58 IMPROVED BATTLE PISTOL – 7.62 NATO cal., short stroke GPO, PARA operating system, 8 1/4 or 11 in. threaded barrel w/WarZ ext. length flash hider, 20 shot mag., enhanced ambi mag. release, SA58 Type 1 steel upper receiver, aluminum alloy lower frame, dual aperture PARA rear sight, adj. front sight, SB tactical SOB brace, DSA short M-LOK handguard, SAW style pistol grip, enlarged winter trigger guard, left side non-reciprocating charging handle, Extreme Duty ext. scope mount, matte black DuraCoat finish, 8.4 lbs. Mfg. 2019-2020.

	$1,625	$1,425	$1,225	$1,100	$875	$725	$575	*$1,895*

AR15-ZM4 WARZ M4 MIDWEST INDUSTRIES COMBAT RAIL – 5.56mm NATO cal., GIO, 10.3 in. M4 profile barrel w/A2 flash hider, stainless steel carbine length gas tube, low profile gas block, 30 shot mag., ALG Defense Advanced Combat Trigger, SB Tactical SBA3 brace, Midwest Industries 9.5 in. Combat Series M-LOK free float handguard, Magpul MOE K2 grip, Radian Weapons Talon short throw ambi selector, enhanced aluminum trigger guard, WarZ enhanced bolt catch, WarZ ext. latch charging handle, lightweight enhanced upper receiver, forged lower receiver, black anodized finish. Mfg. 2019-2020.

	$950	$825	$725	$650	$550	$450	$375	*$1,050*

AR15-ZM4 WARZ TI-V2 TITANIUM EDITION – 5.56mm NATO cal., GIO, 10.3 in. M4 profile barrel w/titanium A2 flash hider, stainless steel carbine length gas tube, 30 shot mag., forged aluminum receivers, ALG Defense Advanced Combat Trigger, SB Tactical SBA3 brace, Midwest Industries 10.5 in. Ultra Light Series M-LOK free float handguard, Magpul MOE K2 grip, Radian Weapons Talon short throw ambi selector, WarZ NTFE finished ext. latch charging handle, titanium parts suite including takedown pins, bolt catch, bolt catch plunger, recoil buffer retaining plunger, forward assist assembly, ejection port door pin and castle nut, black anodized finish, 5.6 lbs. Mfg. 2019-2020.

	$1025	$925	$800	$700	$600	$500	$400	*$1,150*

AR15-ZM4 SERVICE SERIES MK18-MOD 0, KAC UPGRADES – 5.56mm NATO cal., GIO, 10.3 in. chrome-lined M4 profile barrel w/A2 flash hider, stainless steel carbine length gas tube, 30 shot mag., forged aluminum receivers, MATECH back-up iron sights w/ranging, A2 front sight gas block, SB Tactical SBA3 brace, Knight's Armament Company M4 RAS carbine length handguard, A2 grip, PRI Gas Buster charging handle w/military latch, Mil-Spec M16 BCG, black anodized finish. Mfg. 2019-2020.

	$1,125	$1,000	$875	$775	$675	$525	$425	*$1,250*

RIFLES: BOLT ACTION

DS-MP1 – .308 Win. cal., 22 in. match grade barrel, Rem. 700 action w/Badger Ordnance precision ground heavy recoil lug, trued bolt face and lugs, hand lapped stainless steel barrel w/recessed target crown, black McMillan A5 pillar bedded stock, Picatinny rail, includes test target guaranteeing 1/2 MOA at 100 yards, black or camo DuraCoat finish, 11 1/2 lbs. Mfg. 2004-2009.

	$2,500	$2,150	$1,800	$1,550	$1,250	$1,000	$850	*$2,800*

RIFLES: SEMI-AUTO

The SA-58 and ZM-4 rifles listed are available in a standard DuraCoat solid or camo pattern finishes. Patterns include: ACU, Advanced Tiger Stripe, Afghan, AmStripe, Belgian, Belgian Digital, Belgian Advanced Tiger Stripe, Black Forest MirageFlage, Desert MirageFlage, MultiColor, OD MirageFlage, Mossy Oak Breakup (disc.), Rhodesian, Thailand Marine, Tiger Stripe (disc.), Underbrush (disc.), Urban MirageFlage, Urban Tiger Stripe, Vietnam Tiger stripe (disc.), Wilderness MirageFlage, Winter Twig (disc.), or Woodland Prestige. DSA Inc. makes three types of forged steel receivers, and they are

distinguished by the machining cuts on Types I and II, and no cuts on Type III.

Add $50 for MK16 fluted M4 barrel.
Add $65 for stainless steel M4 barrel.
Add $90 for Magpul MOE furniture.

DS-AR SERIES – .223 Rem. cal., GIO, available in a variety of configurations including carbine and rifle, standard or bull barrels, various options, stock colors, and features. Mfg. 2006-2008.

$900 $800 $700 $600 $525 $425 $350 *$1,000*

Add $243 for SOPMOD Carbine. Add $30 for 1R Carbine. Add $150 for 1V Carbine. Add $130 for S1 Bull rifle. Add $500 for DCM rifle. Add $30 for XM Carbine.
Add $1,395 - $1,515 for monolithic rail platform. Add $675 for Z4 GTC Carbine with corrosion resistant operating system.

DS-CV1 CARBINE – 5.56 NATO cal., GIO, 16 in. chrome moly D4 barrel with press on mock flash hider, fixed Shorty buttstock, D4 handguard and heat shield, forged front sight base, forged lower receiver, forged flat-top upper receiver, variety of DuraCoat solid or camo finishes available, 6 1/4 lbs. Mfg. 2004-2005.

$775 $675 $600 $525 $450 $375 $300 *$850*

DS-LE4 CARBINE – 5.56 NATO cal., GIO, 16 in. chrome moly D4 barrel with threaded A2 flash hider, collapsible CAR buttstock, D4 handguard with heat shield, forged lower receiver, forged front sight base with bayonet lug, forged flat-top upper receiver, DuraCoat solid or camo finish, 6.15 or 6 1/4 lbs. Mfg. 2004-2012.

Retail pricing was not available for this model.

DS-S1 – .223 Win. cal., GIO, 16, 20, or 24 in. match chamber stainless steel free float bull barrel, A2 buttstock, aluminum handguard, Picatinny gas block sight base, forged lower receiver, NM two-stage trigger, forged flat-top upper receiver, optional fluted barrel, variety of DuraCoat solid or camo finishes available, 8-10 lbs. Mfg. 2004-2005.

$850 $750 $650 $575 $500 $400 $325 *$950*

DSA CUSTOM MANCOW EDITION RIFLE – 5.56 NATO cal., 16 in. HBAR barrel, A2 flash hider, Magpul PMAG, steel low profile gas block, 13 1/2 in. Diamondhead USA VRS-T handguard, forged aluminum charging handle, Mil-Spec 6-pos. buffer tube, B5 Systems SOPMOD stock, CCA pistol grip, cow camo finish. Limited mfg. 2017-2018.

Retail pricing was not available for this model.

IMBEL 58 – .308 Win. cal., Imbel FAL standard rifle with 21 in. original Imbel barrel, DSA Type 1 carry handle cut receiver, original flash hider, U.S. humpback stock and handguard. Mfg. 2011-2012.

$900 $750 $650 $600 $475 $400 $300 *$995*

RPD CARBINE – 7.62x39mm cal., 17 1/2 in. fluted barrel, billet machined receiver, belt fed, quad rail handguard, SAW style pistol grip, fully adj. AR-15 style stock, lightweight alloy lower trigger frame, includes two 100 shot belt and drum sets, carry bag, sling, and hard case, approx. 14 lbs. Mfg. 2013-2018.

$2,400 $2,100 $1,800 $1,625 $1,300 $1,075 $825 *$2,850*

RPD TRADITIONAL RIFLE – 7.62x39mm cal., 20 1/2 in. barrel, billet machined receiver, belt fed, wood stock, includes two 100 shot belt and drum sets, carry bag, sling, hard case, approx. 17 lbs. Mfg. 2013-2018.

$1,875 $1,625 $1,400 $1,275 $1,025 $875 $675 *$2,200*

SA58 STANDARD RIFLE/CARBINE – .308 Win/7.62x51mm cal., FAL design using high precision CNC machinery, 16 (carbine, disc.), 18 (carbine, disc.), 19 (disc. 2012), 21 (rifle), or 24 (bull only, disc. 2009) in. steel or stainless steel (disc.) barrel, Belgian flash hider, black synthetic (disc.), X-Series, or Humpback stock, pistol grip (standard 2001) attached to frame, 10 or 20 shot mag., lightweight alloy lower receiver, Type 1 or 2 receiver, includes sling and hard case, 8.7-11 lbs.

MSR $1,700 $1,450 $1,250 $1,075 $975 $800 $650 $500

Add $150 for bull barrel (disc. 2009).
Add $250 for stainless steel barrel (disc.).

* ***SA58 Standard Rifle Predator*** – .243 Win., .260 Rem., or .308 Win. cal., Type 1 or Type 3 receiver, 16 or 19 in. barrel w/target crown, green fiberglass furniture, Picatinny rail, 5 or 10 shot mag., approx. 9 lbs. Mfg. 2003-2012.

  $1,425 $925 $700 $550 $475 $395 $350 *$1,750*

* ***SA58 Standard Rifle Gray Wolf*** – .300 WSM (disc. 2005) or .308 Win. cal., Type 1 or Type 3 receiver, 21 in. bull barrel w/target crown, gray aluminum handguard, synthetic stock and adj. pistol grip, Picatinny rail, 5 or 10 shot mag., approx. 13 lbs. Mfg. 2003-2010.

  $1,795 $1,050 $875 $625 $550 $475 $425 *$2,295*

GRADING - PPGS™	100%	98%	95%	90%	80%	70%	60%	LAST MSR

* ***SA58 Standard Rifle Collectors Series*** – .308 Win. cal., models included the Congo ($1,970 - last MSR), Para. Congo ($2,220 - last MSR), and the G1 ($2,000 - last MSR). Mfg. 2003-2010.

Add $230 for DuraCoat finish.

* ***SA58 Standard Rifle T48 Replica*** – .308 Win. cal., 10 or 20 shot fixed mag., stripper clip top cover, cryogenically treated barrel, wood furniture, replica Browning flash hider. Imported 2002-2008.

	$1,475	$950	$725	$550	$475	$395	$350	*$1,795*

* ***SA58 Tactical Carbine*** – .308 Win. cal., similar to SA58 Standard Rifle, except has 16 1/4 in. barrel, 8 1/4 lbs. Mfg. 1999-2012.

	$1,385	$895	$675	$525	$450	$385	$350	*$1,700*

Add $275 for Para. folding stock.
Add $200 for SA58 Lightweight Carbine with aluminum receiver components (disc. 2004).
Add $250 for SA58 Stainless Steel Carbine (included scope mount through 2000).
Subtract 5% if w/o fluted barrel (became standard 2009).

SA58 TRADITIONAL CARBINE/RIFLE – .308 Win./7.62x51mm cal., short-stroke GPO, 16, 16 1/4, 18, or 21 (disc. 2020) in. traditional profile barrel w/Belgian style combo flash hider, 20 shot mag., steel SA58 Type I or II receiver (with or w/o carry handle cut), stamped steel top cover, lightweight aluminum lower frame, front sight post, rear ramp sight, fixed X-Series (disc.) or humpback buttstock, glass filled nylon reinforced full length handguards, glass filled nylon FAL style grip, metric-style non-reciprocating charging handle, includes adj. sling and hard gun case, matte black DuraCoat finish, 8.35-8.75 lbs. New 2011.

MSR $1,700	$1,450	$1,250	$1,075	$975	$800	$650	$500	

SA58 DMR (DESIGNATED MARKSMAN RIFLE) – .308 Win./7.62 NATO cal., 16 1/2 in. fluted barrel, Type 1 receiver, detachable 10 or 20 shot mag., lightweight aluminum A2 Hampton lower, VLTOR CAS-V short rail handguard/bipod, front sight post, M16A2 adj. rear sight, Magpul PRS fixed buttstock, SAW pistol grip, SA58 extended Extreme Duty scope mount, 12.4 lbs. Mfg. 2015-2018

	$1,650	$1,500	$1,250	$1,100	$950	$825	$675	*$1,995*

SA58 CLASSIC EDITION FIXED STOCK CARBINE/RIFLE – .308 Win./7.62x51mm cal., short-stroke GPO, 16, 18, or 21 in. traditional profile barrel w/Belgian style combo flash hider, 20 shot mag., steel SA58 Type II receiver (w/carry handle cut), lightweight aluminum lower frame, front sight post, ramp style rear sight, glass filled nylon humpback fixed stock, glass filled nylon reinforced full length handguards, attached bipod, glass filled nylon FAL pistol grip, sand cut BCG, metric-style non-reciprocating charging handle, includes adj. sling and hard gun case, matte black DuraCoat finish, 8.75 lbs. New 2019.

MSR $1,725	$1,475	$1,275	$1,100	$1,000	$800	$675	$525	

SA58 FALO – 7.62x51 NATO cal., stainless steel gas piston, 21 in. chrome-lined FN heavy barrel, flash hider/bipod design, 20 shot Belgian style mag., elevation adj. front sight, glass filled nylon reinforced humpback buttstock, metric pistol grip, fully adj. gas system, left-side non-reciprocating fixed knob, American black walnut handguard, R-marked selector switch, horizontal frame lock lever, matte black Duracoat finish. New 2020.

MSR $1,995	$1,650	$1,000	$795	$595	$495	$425	$395	

SA58 FLUTED TACTICAL RIFLE – .308 Win./7.62x51mm cal., short-stroke GPO, 16 in. fluted medium contour threaded barrel, 3-prong Trident flash hider, 10 or 20 shot mag., steel SA58 Type I or II receiver (with or w/o carry handle cut), lightweight aluminum lower frame, front sight post, ramp style rear peep sight, standard stamped steel top cover, fixed stock, short military grade handguard, SAW style pistol grip, winter trigger guard, ext. metric-style non-reciprocating charging handle, includes adj. sling and hard gun case, matte black DuraCoat finish, 8.25 lbs.

MSR $1,700	$1,450	$1,250	$1,075	$975	$800	$650	$500	

SA58 GAME RANGER SPECIAL EDITION – 7.62 NATO cal., 18 in. threaded barrel, Belgian style combo flash hider, bipod cut and front sling swivel, 20 shot mag., forged alloy lower trigger frame, nylon humpback buttstock, nylon pistol grip, Type 2 non-carry handle cut receiver, full-length handguard, custom engraved with rhino emblem, includes hard case and sling, KG Gun Kote Green finish, 9.75 lbs. Mfg. 2016-2017.

	$1,315	$1,200	$1,075	$950	$815	$700	$575	*$1,595*

SA58 IMPROVED BATTLE CARBINE – 7.62 NATO cal., short stroke GPO, 16 or 18 in. fluted medium contour threaded barrel, WarZ Series ext. length flash hider, 20 shot mag., steel Type I receiver w/o carry handle cut, aluminum lower frame, ext. winter trigger guard, elevation adj. front sight post, Para. rear sight w/quick-adj. windage knob, side folding DS Arms fully adj. Battle Rifle Stock, M-LOK short handguard, SAW-style pistol grip, Extreme Duty ext. PARA scope mount, ext. charging handle, matte black Duracoat finish. New 2019.

MSR $2,245	$1,900	$1,675	$1,400	$1,275	$1,050	$850	$675	

GRADING - PPGS™	100%	98%	95%	90%	80%	70%	60%	LAST MSR

SA58 PARA CTC (PARA COMPACT TACTICAL CARBINE) – .308 Win./7.62 NATO cal., short-stroke GPO, 16 in. fluted medium contour barrel w/WarZ ext. flash hider, detachable 10 or 20 shot mag., steel SA58 Type I or II receiver (with or w/o carry handle cut), lightweight aluminum lower frame, front sight post, dual aperture rear peep sight, DS Arms Extreme Duty Picatinny scope mount, folding Magpul CTR Para. stock w/ medium cheek riser, short military grade handguard, synthetic SAW style pistol grip, winter trigger guard, ext. metric-style non-reciprocating charging handle, includes adj. sling and hard gun case, matte black DuraCoat finish, 8.83 lbs.

MSR $2,175	$1,850	$1,625	$1,400	$1,275	$1,025	$850	$650	

SA58 RANGE READY COMPACT TACTICAL CARBINE – .308 Win./7.62x51mm cal., short-stroke GPO, 16 in. fluted medium contour threaded barrel, 3-prong Trident flash hider, 10 or 20 shot mag., steel SA58 Type I or II receiver (with or w/o carry handle cut), lightweight aluminum lower frame, front sight post, ramp style rear peep sight, DS Arms Extreme Duty Picatinny scope mount, fixed stock, short military grade handguard, SAW style pistol grip, winter trigger guard, ext. metric-style non reciprocating charging handle, includes adj. sling and hard gun case, matte black DuraCoat finish, 8.25 lbs.

MSR $1,845	$1,575	$1,375	$1,175	$1,075	$850	$700	$550	

SA58 RANGE READY TRADITIONAL CARBINE/RIFLE – .308 Win./7.62x51mm cal., short-stroke GPO, 16, 18, or 21 in. traditional profile barrel w/Belgian style combo flash hider, 20 shot mag., ambi mag. release, steel SA58 Type I or II receiver (with or w/o carry handle cut), lightweight aluminum lower frame, front sight post, adj. tactical Para. rear sight, DS Arms Extreme Duty Picatinny scope mount, glass filled nylon humpback fixed stock and reinforced full length handguards, SAW style pistol grip, winter trigger guard, ext. metric-style non-reciprocating charging handle, includes adj. sling and hard gun case, matte black DuraCoat finish, 8.35 lbs. New 2019.

MSR $1,845	$1,575	$1,375	$1,175	$1,075	$850	$700	$550	

SA58 RANGE READY PARA CARBINE/RIFLE – .308 Win./7.62x51mm cal., short-stroke GPO, 16 or 18 in. traditional profile barrel w/Belgian style combo flash hider, 20 shot mag., ambi mag. release, steel SA58 Type I or II receiver (with or w/o carry handle cut), lightweight aluminum lower frame, front sight post, adj. tactical Para. rear sight, DS Arms Extreme Duty Picatinny scope mount, FAL PARA folding buttstock, glass filled nylon reinforced full length handguards, SAW style pistol grip, winter trigger guard, ext. metric-style non-reciprocating charging handle, includes adj. sling and hard gun case, matte black DuraCoat finish, 8.76 lbs. New 2019.

MSR $2,095	$1,775	$1,550	$1,325	$1,200	$975	$800	$625	

SA58 TRADITIONAL PARA CARBINE/RIFLE – .308 Win./7.62x51mm cal., short-stroke GPO, 16, 18 (disc. 2019), or 21 in. traditional profile barrel w/Belgian style combo flash hider, 20 shot mag., steel SA58 Type I or II receiver (with or w/o carry handle cut), lightweight aluminum lower frame, front sight post, adj. tactical Para. rear sight, FAL Para. folding buttstock, glass filled nylon reinforced full length handguards, glass filled nylon FAL style grip, metric-style non-reciprocating charging handle, includes adj. sling and hard gun case, matte black DuraCoat finish, 8.76 lbs. (16 in.) 9.10 lbs. (21 in.). New 2011.

MSR $1,975	$1,675	$1,450	$1,250	$1,150	$925	$750	$575	

SA58 MEDIUM CONTOUR – .223 Rem. (disc.) or .308 Win./7.62 NATO cal., standard configuration, 21 in. medium contour barrel w/Belgian short flash hider, detachable 10 or 20 shot mag., Type I or II receiver, lightweight alloy (disc.) or aluminum lower, injection molded fiberglass reinforced handguard, front sight post, rear peep sight, standard synthetic or X-Series buttstock, synthetic pistol grip. New 2011.

MSR $1,700	$1,450	$1,250	$1,075	$975	$800	$650	$500	

Add $150 for .223 Rem. cal. (disc.).

SA58 PREDATOR – .308 Win./7.62 NATO cal., standard configuration, 16 or 19 in. medium contour barrel w/target crown, detachable 5 or 10 shot mag., SA58 Type 1 receiver, lightweight aluminum lower, injection molded fiberglass reinforced handguard w/OD Green finish, adj. front sight post, rear peep sight, standard synthetic or X-Series buttstock and synthetic pistol grip in OD Green finish, SA58 Extreme Duty scope mount, also includes adj. sling and hard gun case. Mfg. 2015-2016.

Retail pricing was not available for this model.

SA58 SPARTAN – .308 Win. cal., 16 or 18 in. barrel w/Steyr short flash hider (disc.) or YHM Phantom flash hider, Type 1 non-carry handle cut receiver w/Spartan Series logo, aluminum lower receiver, DSA custom shop speed trigger, tactical Para. rear sight, post front sight, standard synthetic buttstock, SAW pistol grip, military grade handguard, Black DuraCoat finish or Black w/OD Green finish, three detachable 20 shot mags., adj. sling and case. Mfg. 2009-2015.

	$2,050	$1,250	$950	$650	$575	$495	$475	*$2,595*

* ***SA58 Spartan Tactical*** – 7.62 NATO cal., 16 in. fluted medium contour barrel w/Trident flash hider, Type 1 Spartan marked receiver, short gas system handguards, DSA speed trigger, three 20 shot mags., SOCOM Para. folding stock, SAW pistol grip, all black or black/green DuraCoat finish. Disc. 2015.

	$2,225	$1,395	$1,050	$675	$595	$525	$475	*$2,795*

GRADING - PPGS™	100%	98%	95%	90%	80%	70%	60%	LAST MSR

SA58 SPR (SPECIAL PURPOSE RIFLE) – .308 Win./7.62 NATO cal., 19 in. fully fluted premium barrel, Trident (disc.) or SilencerCo trifecta (new 2015) flash hider, Type I forged receiver, detachable 10 or 20 shot mag., match grade speed trigger, long rail interface handguard, ext. Extreme Duty scope mount, SPR side folding adj. stock, SAW pistol grip, Magpul PRO sights, ambi safety, BT Industries vertical front grip (disc. 2020) and adj. monopod (new 2015) or DSA Modular Vertical Combat Foregrip (new 2020), rail mounted Atlas bipod, DuraCoat finish, includes adj. sling, hard case, and Leupold 3.5x10x40 MK4 optic (mfg. 2015-2020) or Leupold VX-3I LRP 4.5-14x50 SF FFP TMR scope (new 2020), 13.8 lbs. New 2009.

MSR $5,495	$4,950	$4,325	$3,725	$3,375	$2,725	$2,225	$1,725	

SA58 TARGET – .308 Win./7.62 NATO cal., 21 in. premium medium contour barrel w/target crown, Type 1 receiver, lightweight aluminum lower, alloy free float tube with textured finish, elevated front sight post, rear peep sight, detachable 10 or 20 shot mag., standard synthetic or X-Series buttstock, synthetic pistol grip, includes hard gun case, 11.1 lbs. Mfg. 2015-2016.

Retail pricing was not available for this model.

SA58 VOYAGER – .308 Win./7.62 NATO cal., 21 in. premium threaded barrel w/Belgian short flash hider, detachable 10 or 20 shot mag., Type 1 non-carry handle cut cast receiver, lightweight aluminum lower, injection molded fiberglass reinforced military grade handguard, Holland style rear sight, adj. post front sight, standard synthetic buttstock and pistol grip, includes adj. sling and hard gun case, 9.75 lbs. Mfg. 2014-2017.

	$995	$925	$800	$685	$595	$515	$440	*$1,200*

STG58 AUSTRIAN FAL – .308 Win. cal., DSA Type I or Type II upper receiver, carry handle, steel lower receiver, rifle has long flash hider, carbine has Steyr short flash hider, steel handguard with bipod cut, metric FAL buttstock and pistol grip, adj. front and rear sight, 10 or 20 shot detachable mag., 10-10.4 lbs. Imported 2006-2008 and 2011-2012.

	$1,050	$900	$800	$700	$600	$475	$375	*$1,150*

Add $50 for carbine.
Add $290 for rifle with folding stock (disc. 2008).
Add $340 for carbine with folding stock (disc. 2008).

SA58 PARA CONGO EDITION RIFLE – .308 Win./7.62x51mm cal., short-stroke GPO, 18 in. traditional profile barrel w/Belgian style combo flash hider, 20 shot mag., steel SA58 Type I or II receiver (with or w/o carry handle cut), lightweight aluminum lower frame, front sight post, adj. tactical para rear sight, FAL Para. folding buttstock, glass filled nylon reinforced full length handguards, glass filled nylon FAL style grip, non-reciprocating folding charging handle, includes Belgian carry handle, adj. sling and hard gun case, matte black DuraCoat finish, 8.76 lbs. New 2019.

MSR $1,975	$1,650	$1,475	$1,225	$1,100	$950	$825	$675	

SA58 WARRIOR SERIES – .308 Win./7.62x51mm cal., short-stroke GPO, 16 (Jungle Warrior), 18 (Bush Warrior), or 21 (Cold Warrior) in. traditional profile barrel w/Belgian style combo flash hider, 20 shot mag., steel SA58 Type 3 receiver w/carry handle cut, stamped steel top cover, lightweight aluminum lower frame, front sight post, Holland style rear sight assembly w/windage adjustment click screw, Para. (16 or 18 in. barrel only.) or fixed humpback stock, glass filled nylon reinforced full length handguard and FAL style grip, sand-cut enhanced BCG, non-reciprocating folding charging handle, includes adj. sling and hard gun case, matte black DuraCoat finish, 8.5-8.75 lbs. New late 2019.

MSR $1,450	$1,225	$1,075	$925	$850	$675	$550	$425	

Add $275 for Para. stock.

SA58 ISRAELI LIGHT BARREL/SA58 ISRAELI LIGHT BARREL OFFICER GRADE – .308 Win./7.62x51mm cal., short-stroke GPO, 21 in. Israeli light profile barrel, Belgian style combo flash hider (Officer Grade model only), 20 shot Israeli FAL mag., steel SA58 Type 1 receiver w/carry handle cut and Israeli markings, stamped steel top cover, Israeli steel lower frame w/Israeli internals, Israeli safety lever, front sight post, ramp style rear sight, Israeli wooden buttstock and handguards, U.S. made glass filled nylon FAL style grip, Israeli carry handle and forward assist charging handle, includes adj. sling, extra polymer handguards and stock (Officer Grade model only), and hard gun case, Battle Worn Original or matte black DuraCoat (Officer Grade model only) finish, 10.4 lbs. Mfg. 2019-2020.

	$1,250	$1,100	$950	$850	$700	$550	$450	*$1,395*

Add $100 for SA58 Israeli Light Barrel Officer Grade model).

WARZ M-4 COMBAT COMPANION – 5.56 NATO cal., GIO, 16 in. M4 profile barrel, stainless steel carbine length gas tube, MK12 style low profile gas block, A2 style flash hider, 30 shot Magpul mag., forged receivers, Magpul SL Series adjustable stock, Midwest Industries 14 in. Combat Series free float handguard, Magpul K2 pistol grip, 6-pos. Mil-Spec buffer tube, Mil-Spec BCG, WarZ ext. latch charging handle, black anodized finish. New 2019.

MSR $865	$775	$700	$600	$525	$450	$375	$300	

GRADING - PPGS™	100%	98%	95%	90%	80%	70%	60%	LAST MSR

WARZ M-4 CUSTOM FDE – 5.56 NATO cal., GIO, 16 in. lightweight barrel, stainless steel mid-length gas tube, low profile titanium gas block, Surefire ProComp compensator, custom two-tone 30 shot Magpul mag., forged lightweight enhanced upper receiver, forged lower receiver, ALG Defense Advanced Combat Trigger, FDE enhanced alloy trigger guard, FDE two-tone B5 Systems SOPMOD stock, Midwest Industries 15 in. Combat Series M-LOK free float handguard, two-tone Magpul MOE MIAD grip, Noveske STS Short Throw Selector, black Magpul M-LOK handguard panel set, WarZ ext. latch tactical charging handle, WarZ enhanced bolt catch, low mass enhanced sand cut BCG, Mil-Spec 6-pos. buffer tube, B5 Systems QD endplate, two-tone FDE DuraCoat/black hardcoat anodized finish, 6.9 lbs. New 2019.

MSR $1,150	$1,025	$925	$800	$700	$600	$500	$400	

WARZ M-4 RIFLE – 5.56 NATO cal., GIO, 16 in. lightweight stainless steel barrel, SureFire ProComp muzzle device, Magpul PMAG, steel micro gas block, A.R.M.S. sights, 15 in. Midwest Industries Gen III stainless steel handguard, forged lightweight enhanced upper receiver, BCM Ambi Gunfighter charging handle, Mil-Spec 6-pos. buffer tube, enhanced trigger guard, B5 Systems SOPMOD stock, Magpul MIAD pistol grip, Seekins Precision ambi selector switch. Mfg. 2016-2020.

	$1,350	$1,200	$1,025	$925	$800	$650	$525	*$1,495*

WARZ M-4 GM EDITION – 5.56 NATO cal., 16 in. fluted mid-length barrel, titanium birdcage flash hider, Magpul PMAG, nickel Teflon coated ejection port door, enhanced alloy trigger guard, ALG Defense Advanced Combat Trigger, Magpul SL Series buttstock and pistol grip, M4 feed ramps, Geissele 13 in. Super MK4 modular M-LOK handguard, Magpul M-LOK rail panel set, or Magpul M-LOK rail hand stop, forged A3M4 upper receiver, forged enhanced lower, Bravo Company Mod4 Gunfighter charging handle, ambi sling mount endplate, 6-pos. buffer tube, Seekins Precision ambi selector. Mfg. 2017-2018.

	$1,225	$1,075	$950	$825	$725	$575	$475	*$1,365*

* ***WarZ M-4 GM Edition (Recent Mfg.)*** – 5.56 NATO cal., GIO, 16 in. straight fluted barrel w/M4 feed ramps, titanium birdcage flash hider, stainless steel mid-length gas tube, low profile titanium gas block, 30 shot Magpul PMAG, forged aluminum receivers, ALG Defense Advanced Combat Trigger, enhanced trigger guard, Magpul SL Series buttstock, Magpul MOE K2 grip, Noveske STS Short Throw Ambi Selector Switch, HGTi titanium metal parts, enhanced bolt catch, Geissele 13 in. Super MK4 modular M-LOK handguard, Magpul M-LOK rail panel set, or Magpul M-LOK rail hand stop, WarZ forged charging handle w/tactical latch, Bravo Company QD sling mount, Mil-Spec 6-pos. buffer tube. Mfg. 2019-2020.

	$1,025	$925	$800	$700	$600	$500	$400	*$1,150*

WARZ M-4 TITANIUM EDITION – 5.56 NATO cal., 16 in. lightweight mid-length stainless steel barrel, Griffin Armament titanium Minimalist muzzle brake, M4 feed ramps, Magpul 30 shot PMAG, FDE enhanced alloy trigger guard, Geissele SSA-E trigger, A.R.M.S. folding sight set, FDE Seekins Precision ambi selector, stainless steel mid-length gas tube, Midwest Industries SS G3 15 in. free float handguard and two-tone handguard panel set, forged lightweight enhanced receivers, Bravo Company ambi Gunfighter charging handle, nickel Teflon coated BCG and 6-pos. buffer tube, black B5 Systems SOPMOD stock, two-tone Magpul MIAD modular pistol grip, HGTi titanium metal parts, includes plastic hard case. Mfg. 2017-late 2018.

	$1,525	$1,350	$1,175	$1,050	$900	$725	$600	*$1,695*

* ***WarZ M-4 Titanium Edition (Current Mfg.)*** – 5.56 NATO cal, GIO, 16 in. lightweight mid-length stainless steel barrel, titanium A2 flash hider, M4 feed ramps, Magpul 30 shot PMAG, forged lightweight enhanced receivers, ALG Advanced Combat Trigger, two-tone B5 Systems SOPMOD stock, Midwest Industries 15 in. Combat Series M-LOK free float handguard and FDE handguard panel set, two-tone Magpul MIAD modular pistol grip, Radian Weapons Talon ambi selector, WarZ series ext. latch tactical charging handle, WarZ enhanced low mass sand cut BCG, 6-pos. Mil-Spec buffer tube, enhanced alloy trigger guard, stainless steel mid-length gas tube, titanium low profile gas block, HGTi titanium metal parts, black anodized finish, includes plastic hard case, 6.9 lbs. New 2019.

MSR $1,150	$1,025	$925	$800	$700	$600	$500	$400	

WARZ M-4 TITANIUM V2 EDITION – 5.56 NATO cal., 16 in. lightweight mid-length stainless steel barrel, titanium enhanced birdcage flash hider, M4 feed ramps, Magpul 30 shot PMAG, enhanced alloy trigger guard, Geissele Super Dynamic Combat trigger, Seekins Precision ambi selector, stainless steel mid-length gas tube, Midwest Industries 12 1/2 in. free float M-LOK lightweight handguard, Magpul rubber M-LOK rail, forged lightweight enhanced receivers, Bravo Company Mod4 Gunfighter charging handle, nickel Teflon coated BCG and 6-pos. buffer tube, B5 Systems Bravo stock w/HGTi titanium buttstock metal, Magpul SL pistol grip, HGTi titanium metal parts, includes plastic hard case. Mfg. 2017-2018.

	$1,200	$1,000	$900	$800	$750	$700	$625	*$1,695*

GRADING - PPGS™ 100% 98% 95% 90% 80% 70% 60% LAST MSR

* ***WarZ M-4 Titanium V2 Edition (Current Mfg.)*** – 5.56 NATO cal., GIO, 16 in. lightweight mid-length stainless steel barrel, titanium enhanced A2 flash hider, M4 feed ramps, stainless steel mid-length gas tube, low profile titanium gas block, Magpul 30 shot PMAG, forged lightweight enhanced receivers, ALG Defense Advanced Combat Trigger, B5 Systems Bravo stock w/HGTi buttstock metal, Midwest Industries 14 in. Ultra Light Series free float M-LOK handguard, Magpul MOE K2 grip, Radian Weapons Talon ambi selector, HGTi titanium parts throughout, enhanced low mass sand cut BCG, WarZ NTFE coated charging handle with extended latch, enhanced bolt catch, and Mil-Spec 6-pos. buffer tube, enhanced alloy trigger guard, black anodized finish, 6.2 lbs. New 2019.

MSR $1,150 $1,050 $925 $800 $700 $600 $500 $400

WARZ M-4 TITANIUM X EDITION – 5.56 NATO cal., 16 in. chrome-lined M4 profile barrel, HGTi titanium birdcage flash hider, X Products X-15 skeletonized 50 round drum mag., enhanced alloy trigger guard, Geissele Automatics SSA-E trigger, A.R.M.S. front and rear backup sights, Noveske short throw ambi selector, M4 feed ramps, steel micro gas block, stainless steel carbine gas tube, X Products 14 1/2 in. Cobra free float M-LOK handguard and G10 M-LOK handguard panels, forged lightweight enhanced upper and forged lower receiver, Bravo Company ambi Gunfighter charging handle, nickel Teflon coated BCG and 6-pos. buffer tube, BufferLoc System, B5 Systems Bravo stock, X Products modular pistol grip, HGTi titanium metal parts, includes plastic hard case. Mfg. 2017-2018.

$1,700 $1,500 $1,325 $1,150 $1,000 $800 $650 *$1,895*

Z-IAR RIFLE – 5.56 NATO cal., GIO, 16 in. chrome moly fluted barrel, A2 flash hider, detachable mag., VLTOR collapsible stock, forged lower w/ambi safety switch, forged flat-top upper w/steel charging handle, VLTOR rail interface handguard system w/customizable rails, VLTOR collapsible stock, incorporates new features such as Bufferloc and Keyloc technologies, includes hard gun case, 8.4 lbs. Mfg. 2015 only.

Retail pricing was not available for this model.

ZM-4 SERIES – .223 Rem./5.56 NATO or .300 AAC Blackout (disc. 2015) cal., GIO, 16 or 20 in. barrel, forged upper and lower receiver, various configurations, black finish, detachable magazine, hard case. New 2004.

* ***ZM-4 .300 Blackout*** – .300 AAC Blackout cal., GIO, 16 in. blue or stainless steel barrel w/Trident flash hider, A3 flat-top alloy receiver, forged front sight base w/bayonet lug, M4 handguard w/heat shield, Hogue pistol grip, 6-pos. collapsible M4 stock, matte black finish. Mfg. 2013-2015.

$775 $675 $600 $525 $450 $375 $300 *$853*

Add $20 for stainless steel barrel.

* ***ZM-4 A2 Carbine*** – 5.56 NATO cal., 16 in. M4 barrel w/A2 flash hider, alloy receivers, A2 carry handle receiver, forged front sight base w/bayonet lug, M4 handguard w/heat shield, 6-pos. collapsible M4 stock. Disc. 2015.

$750 $650 $575 $500 $450 $350 $300 *$831*

* ***ZM-4 A2 Rifle*** – 5.56 NATO cal., 20 in. M4 barrel w/A2 flash hider, alloy receivers, A2 carry handle receiver, forged front sight base w/bayonet lug, rifle length handguard w/heat shield, fixed A2 stock, Hogue pistol grip. Disc. 2015.

$750 $675 $575 $525 $450 $350 $300 *$844*

* ***ZM-4 Flat-Top Carbine With Rail*** – 5.56 NATO cal., 16 in. M4 barrel w/A2 flash hider, alloy lower and A3 flat-top upper receiver, forged front sight base w/bayonet lug, folding detachable rear sight, carbine length quad rail handguard, 6-pos. collapsible M4 stock, Hogue pistol grip. Mfg. 2015 only.

$950 $825 $725 $650 $550 $450 $375 *$1,050*

* ***ZM-4 Gas Piston CQB*** – .223 Rem. cal., GPO, 16 in. chrome-lined free floating barrel, A2 flash hider, 30 shot mag., Mil-Spec forged lower receiver, CQB forged upper receiver, one-piece bolt carrier, quick change barrel system, collapsible CAR stock. Disc. 2010.

$2,575 $2,275 $2,000 $1,750 $1,525 $1,225 $1,000 *$2,870*

* ***ZM-4 Midfal*** – 5.56 NATO cal., 16 in. chrome moly barrel w/FAL Belgian style flash hider, detachable mag., forged alloy lower and flat-top upper receiver, forged front sight base w/bayonet lug, enhanced steel charging handle and Delta ring, ambi selector switch, folding rear iron sight, Magpul enhanced trigger guard, Magpul MOE mid-length handguard, Magpul MOE pistol grip, Magpul or ACE fixed skeleton stock, includes hard gun case. Mfg. 2013-2015.

$850 $750 $650 $575 $500 $400 $325 *$936*

* ***ZM-4 Mid-Length Carbine*** – 5.56 NATO cal., 16 in. fluted or non-fluted mid-length barrel w/A2 flash hider, M4 A3 flat-top receiver, forged front sight base w/bayonet lug, mid-length handguards w/heat shield, alloy receivers, 6-pos. collapsible M4 stock, Hogue pistol grip. Disc. 2020.

$750 $675 $575 $500 $450 $350 $300 *$834*

Add $13 for fluted barrel.

GRADING - PPGS™	100%	98%	95%	90%	80%	70%	60%	LAST MSR

* ***ZM-4 MK16 (Enhanced Carbine)*** – 5.56 NATO cal., GIO, 16 in. enhanced MK16 fluted M4 barrel w/ YHM muzzle brake, alloy lower and A3 flat-top upper receiver, forged front sight base w/bayonet lug, ambi selector switch, enhanced Delta ring, Magpul MOE handguard, 6-pos. MOE stock, Magpul MOE pistol grip, matte black finish. Mfg. 2013-2015.

$825 $750 $650 $575 $500 $400 $325 ***$929***

* ***ZM-4 M.R.C. (Multi-Role Carbine)*** – 5.56 NATO cal., GIO, 16 in. chrome-lined heavy barrel, 3-prong Trident flash hider, steel low profile gas block, Magpul PMAG, Magpul MBUS sights, 13 1/2 in. Diamondhead USA VRS-T handguard, BCM Ambi Gunfighter charging handle, Mil-Spec 6-pos. buffer tube, B5 Systems SOPMOD stock, Hogue pistol grip. Mfg. 2016-2020.

$1,150 $1,025 $875 $775 $675 $550 $450 ***$1,275***

* ***ZM-4 Spartan*** – .223 Rem. cal., GIO, 16 in. fluted chrome moly barrel, YHM Phantom flash hider, Mil-Spec forged lower and flat-top upper receiver, forged front sight base with lug, Magpul trigger guard, Robar NP3 BCG and charging handle, Hogue pistol grip, SOPMOD collapsible stock, two-piece rail system became standard 2013, 6.65 lbs. Disc. 2014.

$1,300 $1,150 $1,000 $900 $775 $625 $500 ***$1,455***

» **ZM-4 Spartan Leo** – 5.56 NATO cal., 16 in. fluted chrome moly barrel w/YHM Phantom flash hider, detachable mag., forged lower w/Spartan Series logo, forged flat-top upper w/mid-length gas system and forged front sight base, Rock River Arms competition trigger, Magpul trigger guard, YHM two-piece rail system and plastic handguard, LMT SOPMOD collapsible stock, Hogue pistol grip, includes hard gun case, 7 lbs. Disc. 2015.

$1,225 $825 $575 $475 $425 $375 $350 ***$1,455***

* ***ZM-4 Standard Flat-Top Carbine*** – .223 Rem./5.56 NATO cal., GIO, 16 in. chrome moly M4 barrel w/A2 flash hider, detachable mag., Mil-Spec forged lower and A3 flat-top upper receiver, forged front sight base w/bayonet lug, M4 handguard w/heat shield, 6-pos. collapsible M4 stock, Hogue pistol grip, includes hard gun case, 6 1/4 lbs. Disc. 2020.

$750 $675 $575 $525 $450 $350 $300 ***$845***

Subtract $11 if without chrome-lined barrel.

* ***ZM-4 Standard Flat-Top Rifle*** – 5.56 NATO cal., 20 in. barrel w/A2 flash hider, alloy lower and A3 flat-top upper receiver, forged front sight base w/bayonet lug, rifle length handguard w/heat shield, fixed A2 stock, Hogue pistol grip. Disc. 2020.

$725 $650 $575 $500 $425 $350 $275 ***$820***

* ***ZM-4 Standard MRP*** – .223 Rem. cal., GIO, 16 or 18 in. chrome-lined (16 in.) or stainless steel free float barrel, Mil-Spec forged lower receiver, LMT MRP forged upper receiver w/20 1/2 in. full-length quad rail, LMT enhanced bolt, dual extractor springs, collapsible CAR stock, detachable 30 shot mag., A2 flash hider. Disc. 2010.

$2,425 $2,150 $1,875 $1,650 $1,425 $1,150 $925 ***$2,695***

Add $100 for stainless steel barrel.

* ***ZM-4 WerkerZ V1 Rifle*** – 5.56 NATO cal., GIO, 16 in. fluted steel barrel, 3-prong Trident flash hider, Magpul PMAG, Magpul MOE M-LOK handguard, enhanced contour Delta ring, Picatinny gas block, forged lightweight enhanced upper receiver, Mil-Spec forged alloy charging handle, enhanced trigger guard, B5 Systems SOPMOD stock, Magpul MOE pistol grip. Mfg. 2016-2020.

$875 $775 $675 $600 $500 $425 $325 ***$965***

* ***ZM-4 WerkerZ V2 Rifle*** – 5.56 NATO cal., GIO, 16 in. fluted heavy chrome-lined barrel, 3-prong Trident flash hider, Magpul PMAG, Magpul SL Series M-LOK handguard, enhanced contour Delta ring, Picatinny gas block, forged lightweight enhanced upper receiver, forged steel charging handle, Mil-Spec 6-pos. buffer tube, enhanced trigger guard, B5 Systems SOPMOD stock, Magpul MOE pistol grip. Mfg. 2016-2018.

$950 $850 $750 $650 $575 $450 $375 ***$1,065***

* ***ZM-4 WerkerZ V2 Rifle (Recent Mfg.)*** – 5.56 NATO cal., GIO, 16 in. chrome-lined, custom knurled fluted barrel, stainless steel carbine length gas tube, rail height steel Picatinny gas block, WarZ ext. length flash hider, 30 shot Magpul mag., forged lightweight enhanced upper receiver, forged lower, Magpul SL Series collapsible buttstock, Magpul MOE M-LOK SL Series carbine handguards, Magpul MOE K2 grip, NTFE coating on 6-pos. buffer tube, enhanced sand cut BCG, and charging handle w/ext. tactical latch, black anodized finish. Mfg. 2019-2020.

$775 $700 $600 $525 $450 $375 $300 ***$865***

GRADING - PPGS™	100%	98%	95%	90%	80%	70%	60%	LAST MSR

ZM-4 SERVICE SERIES M4A3 FLAT-TOP CARBINE – 5.56 NATO cal., GIO, 16 in. M4 profile chrome-lined barrel, stainless steel carbine length gas tube, front sight gas block, A2 flash hider, 30 shot mag., forged receivers, M4 style collapsible stock, 6-pos. Mil-Spec buffer tube, round M4 style handguard with heat shield, A2 grip, black anodized finish, 6.3 lbs. New 2019.

MSR $665	$600	$525	$450	$400	$350	$275	$225	

ZM-4 SERVICE SERIES M4A3 FLAT-TOP CARBINE IDF CLONE CONFIGURATION – 5.56 NATO cal., GIO, 14.7 in. M4 profile chrome-lined barrel w/permanently attached A2 flash hider, stainless steel carbine length gas tube, front sight gas block, two 30 shot mags. w/contract overrun mag. coupler, forged receivers, Samson Mfg. IDF contract folding rear sight, M4 style collapsible stock w/o rear sling loop, 6-pos. Mil-Spec buffer tube, CAR style tapered carbine handguard w/heat shield, A2 grip, Zahal IDF sling and web gear kit including elastic bands and adaptor, black anodized finish, 6.3 lbs. New 2020.

MSR $795	$725	$625	$550	$475	$425	$350	$275	

ZM-4 SERVICE SERIES M4 BLOCK 1 CARBINE KAC UPGRADED – 5.56 NATO cal., GIO, 14.5 in. barrel w/ permanently attached A2 flash hider, carbine length gas system, 30 shot ASC grey alloy mag., forged receivers, MATECH rear back-up sight with ranging, front sight gas block, M4 style collapsible stock, 6-pos. Mil-Spec buffer tube, Knights Armament M4 RAS carbine length handguard assembly, A2 grip, stainless steel gas tube, Knights Armament Company forward vertical grip, Mil-Spec BCG and charging handle, black anodized finish, comes with standard 2 point sling, hard case. New 2019.

MSR $1,200	$1,075	$950	$825	$725	$625	$525	$425	

ZM-4 SERVICE SERIES A4 RIFLE KAC UPGRADED – 5.56 NATO cal., 20 in. HBAR profile barrel, rifle length gas system, A2 flash hider, 30 shot ASC grey alloy mag., forged receivers, MATECH rear back-up sight with ranging, front sight gas block, A2 style rifle stock, Knights Armament M4 RAS rifle length handguard assembly, A2 grip, stainless steel gas tube, Knights Armament Company forward vertical grip, Mil-Spec BCG and charging handle, black anodized finish, comes with standard 2 point sling, hard case. New 2019.

MSR $1,200	$1,075	$950	$825	$725	$625	$525	$425	

DSP ARMORY

Current AR-15 style semi-auto rifle manufacturer located in Fulton, MS.

Please refer to BlueBookOfGunValues.com to order the *Blue Book of AR-15s & Variations*, available as a book or online subscription.

DWM

Previous manufacturer located in Berlin, Germany circa 1900-1972. DWM (Deutsche Waffen und Munitionsfabriken) manufactured Lugers circa 1900-1930, and they are listed in the Luger section.

PISTOLS: SEMI-AUTO

POCKET AUTOMATIC – 7.65mm cal., 3 1/2 in. barrel, blue, hard rubber grips. Mfg. 1921-1931.

	$1,000	$850	$600	$500	$450	$400	$350	

D.Z. ARMS

Current custom rifle manufacturer established in 1991, located in Oklahoma City, OK.

D.Z. Arms manufactures replica Remington #3 Hepburn rifles, as well as bolt action benchrest and hunting rifles. The company also offers gunsmithing services. Please contact the company directly for more information, including pricing, options, and availability.

DAEWOO

Previous commercial firearms manufacturer located in Korea. Previous limited importation by Century International Arms, located in Delray Beach, FL. Previous importation included Kimber of America, Inc. until 1997, Daewoo Precision Industries, Ltd., until mid-1996, located in Southampton, PA, and previously distributed by Nationwide Sports Distributors 1993-96. Previously imported by KBI, Inc. and Firstshot, Inc., both located in Harrisburg, PA, and B-West located in Tucson, AZ.

Daewoo made a variety of firearms available for commercial use, and most of these were never imported into the U.S.

PISTOLS: SEMI-AUTO

DH380 – .380 ACP cal., DA/SA, styled after the Walther PPK. Imported 1995-96.

	$330	$285	$260	$235	$210	$185	$165	*$375*

GRADING - PPGS™	100%	98%	95%	90%	80%	70%	60%	LAST MSR

DH40 - .40 S&W cal., otherwise similar to DP51, 32 oz. Imported 1995-disc.

$325 $270 $245 $225 $200 $185 $170

DP51 STANDARD/COMPACT - 9mm Para. cal., "fast action" allows lowering hammer w/o depressing trigger, 3 1/2 (DP51 C or S, disc.) or 4.1 (DP51) in. barrel, 10 (C/B 1994), 12* (.40 S&W), or 13* (9mm Para.) shot mag., 3-dot sights, tri-action mechanism (SA, DA, or fast action), ambidextrous manual safety, alloy receiver, polished or sand-blasted black finish, 28 or 32 oz., includes lockable carrying case with accessories. Imported in various configurations circa 1991-2009.

$450 $265 $240 $220 $200 $185 $170

Add 10% for DP51 Compact (disc.).

DP52 - .22 LR cal., DA/SA, similar to DH380, 3.8 in. barrel, alloy receiver, 10 shot mag., blue finish, 23 oz. Imported 1994-96.

$320 $275 $225 $200 $180 $165 $150 *$380*

RIFLES: SEMI-AUTO

MAX I (K1A1) - .223 Rem. cal., 18 in. barrel with integrated flash hider, uses STANAG (AR-15, M16) style nags., forged aluminum upper and lower receivers, dual aperture rear sight, front post sight guarded in wings, 3-pos. retractable wire stock, triangular heat shield handguard, black plastic pistol grip, 180 degree safety throw, light grey finish. Importation disc. 1986.

$2,200 $2,000 $1,825 $1,600 $1,350 $1,100 $850 *$592*

MAX II (K2) - .223 Rem cal., long stroke gas piston operation, 18 in. barrel with flash hider, uses STANAG (AR-15, M16) style magazines, forged aluminum upper and lower receivers, shrouded rear sight assembly, hooded front sight post/gas block assembly, right side folding fiberglass stock, polymer handguards, black plastic pistol grip, 180 degree safety throw, light grey finish, 7 lbs. importation disc. 1986.

$1,900 $1,700 $1,525 $1,300 $1,100 $875 $700 *$609*

DR200 - .223 Rem. cal., similar to Daewoo Max II/K2 except has an AWB compliant thumbhole stock, 10 shot mag. Imported 1995-96.

$1,400 $1,250 $1,125 $1,000 $800 $675 $550 *$535*

DR300 - 7.62x39mm cal., similar to Daewoo Max II/K2, except has AWB compliant thumbhole stock. Importation disc.

$1,300 $1,100 $1,000 $900 $700 $600 $500

DAISY

Current airgun manufacturer with headquarters located in Rogers, AR. Daisy manufactured firearms 1968-1991.

For more information and current pricing on both new and used Daisy airguns, please refer to the *Blue Book of Airguns* - also available as an online subscription.

RIFLES: SINGLE SHOT, DISC.

As the V/L ammunition availability diminishes, the following values may fluctuate.

V/L STANDARD RIFLE - .22 V/L cal. (caseless air ignited cartridge), 1,100 FPS, 18 in. barrel, plastic stock, not particularly accurate. Approx. 19,000 mfg. 1968-69.

$400 $350 $300 $275 $225 $180 $140

V/L PRESENTATION - similar to Collector's Kit, except does not have owner's name inscribed on buttplate, walnut stock. 4,000 mfg. for dealers.

$495 $425 $375 $325 $275 $225 $175 *$125*

V/L COLLECTOR'S KIT - comes with case, gun cradles, 300 rounds of ammo, and a gold plated brass buttplate with owner's name and serial number of gun. Approx. 4,000 mfg., available only by direct factory order.

$700 $625 $525 $475 $375 $300 $250 *$125*

Note: The Daisy .22 V/L was discontinued because the BATFE ruled that the gun constituted a firearm, and since Daisy was federally licensed to manufacture air weapons only, the factory decided to discontinue manufacture.

RIFLES: BOLT ACTION, DISC.

All Legacy models have a removable trigger, slings and swivels, takedown barrel, dovetail receiver for scope mounting, rifled inner steel barrel with 12 lands and grooves, and an adj. rear sight. Weight is between 6 1/2-7 lbs.

GRADING - PPGS™	100%	98%	95%	90%	80%	70%	60%	LAST MSR

MODEL 8 - .22 S or LR cal., single shot, 16 in. barrel, black synthetic stock, 30,000 mfg. for Wal-Mart only 1987-88.

	100%	98%	95%	90%	80%	70%	60%	LAST MSR
	$275	$250	$200	$175	$150	$125	$95	

During 1987, Daisy assembled this model using left-over Iver Johnson parts.

LEGACY MODELS 2201/2211 - .22 LR cal., single shot, plastic (2201) or walnut finished hardwood (2211) stock, models vary in features. Mfg. 1988-1991.

	100%	98%	95%	90%	80%	70%	60%	LAST MSR
	$275	$250	$200	$175	$150	$125	$95	

LEGACY MODELS 2202/2212 - .22 LR cal., bolt action repeater, 10 shot rotary mag., plastic (2202) or walnut finished hardwood (2212) stock, models vary in features. Mfg. 1988-1991.

	100%	98%	95%	90%	80%	70%	60%	LAST MSR
	$325	$275	$250	$225	$175	$150	$125	

Model 2202 has copolymer stock with adj. buttplate.

RIFLES: SEMI-AUTO

LEGACY MODELS 2203/2213 - .22 LR cal., 7 shot box mag., models vary in features. Mfg. 1988-1991.

	100%	98%	95%	90%	80%	70%	60%	LAST MSR
	$350	$300	$275	$250	$200	$150	$125	

Model 2203 has copolymer stock with adj. buttplate. Model 2213 has American hardwood stock.

DAIWA

Previous U.S. firearms importer and distributor.

Daiwa imported various firearms circa 1960s-early 1970s. Configurations included semi-auto shotguns mfg. by Nikko, Ltd. of Japan, and bolt action rifles. Values are based on the current utilitarian value, since there is little collectibility on these guns.

DAKIN GUN CO.

Previous importer located in San Francisco, CA, and Kansas City, MO, circa 1960s.

SHOTGUNS: O/U

MODEL 170 - 12, 16, 20 ga., or .410 bore, boxlock, light engraving, double triggers, vent. rib.

	100%	98%	95%	90%	80%	70%	60%	LAST MSR
	$495	$400	$325	$275	$245	$220	$195	

SHOTGUNS: SxS

MODEL 100 - 12 or 20 ga., boxlock, engraved, double trigger.

	100%	98%	95%	90%	80%	70%	60%	LAST MSR
	$425	$350	$275	$240	$205	$190	$170	

MODEL 147 - 12 or 20 ga., boxlock, engraved, vent. rib, double trigger.

	100%	98%	95%	90%	80%	70%	60%	LAST MSR
	$495	$385	$300	$265	$235	$215	$195	

MODEL 160 - 12 or 20 ga., boxlock, single trigger, ejectors, vent. rib.

	100%	98%	95%	90%	80%	70%	60%	LAST MSR
	$825	$700	$595	$495	$450	$395	$360	

MODEL 215 - 12 or 20 ga., sidelock, heavy engraving, special walnut, single trigger, ejectors, vent. rib.

	100%	98%	95%	90%	80%	70%	60%	LAST MSR
	$2,250	$1,900	$1,675	$1,300	$1,100	$925	$775	

SHOTGUNS: SINGLE BARREL

Dakin imported a single barrel trap gun manufactured by Miroku while the company was located in Kansas City, MO.

DAKOTA ARMS, INC.

Current manufacturer and previous importer established in 1986, located in Sturgis, SD. Dealer and direct sales through manufacturer only.

This company is not affiliated with Dakota Single Action Revolvers. On June 5, 2009, Remington Arms Company purchased Dakota Arms, Inc.

Dakota Arms Inc. also owned the rights to Miller Arms and Nesika actions. Please refer to these individual sections for more information.

Dakota Arms models listed below are also available with many custom options - please contact the factory directly for availability and pricing. Left-hand actions are available on all bolt action rifles at no extra charge. Actions (barreled or unbarreled) may also be purchased separately. Please contact the manufacturer directly for individual quotations.

GRADING - PPGS™	100%	98%	95%	90%	80%	70%	60%	LAST MSR

RIFLES: BOLT ACTION

DAKOTA .22 RIFLE – .17 HMR (new 2004), .22 LR, .22 Win Mag. (new 2004), or .22 Hornet (disc.) cal., full sized receiver, 22 in. chrome moly barrel, 5 shot mag., trigger and striker block safety similar to Dakota 76, no sights, checkered XX walnut stock, combines features of the Win. Model 52 Sporter and Dakota 76, 6 1/2 lbs. Mfg. 1992-98, reintroduced 2003-2004.

	100%	98%	95%	90%	80%	70%	60%	LAST MSR
	$2,650	$2,325	$1,985	$1,800	$1,450	$1,195	$925	*$3,000*

DAKOTA 76 TRAVELER – various cals. between .25-06 Rem.-.450 Dakota, in addition to Dakota proprietary calibers, 23 or 24 (African only) in. barrel, almost seamless take down rifle based on the Dakota 76 design, threadless disassembly ensuring scope stability and accuracy, in addition to no possibility of increasing the head space during repeated disassembly, checkered wood stock, available in Classic (XX grade walnut), Safari (XXX grade walnut, Magnum cals.), or African (XXX grade walnut, ebony forend tip and plugs, 24 in. barrel), approx. 7 1/2 lbs. New 1999.

	100%	98%	95%	90%	80%	70%	60%	LAST MSR
MSR $9,995	$9,000	$7,800	$6,750	$6,000	$5,000	$4,000	$3,250	

Add $2,000 for Safari Traveler.
Add $3,500 for African Traveler.
Add $2,490 (standard cals.) or $2,720 (Safari cals.) per interchangeable barrel.
Add $2,950 for African barrel (disc.).

DAKOTA 76 CLASSIC GRADE – available in various cals. (short, standard, or long action), custom frame incorporating many Win. Model 70 features, 21 (disc.) or 23 in. match grade barrel, Mauser type extractor, checkered XX grade English walnut stock, swivel studs, deluxe recoil pad, matte blue finish, 7 1/2 lbs. New 1987.

	100%	98%	95%	90%	80%	70%	60%	LAST MSR
MSR $6,295	$5,700	$4,900	$4,250	$3,800	$3,150	$2,500	$2,050	

This Model was previously available with a composite stock at no extra charge.

* ***Model 76 Classic Deluxe*** – various cals. between .22-250 Rem-.416 Rem., 23 in. barrel, barrel band and inletted Ken Howell swivel stud, custom trigger guard, front ramp sight with rear island single blade, right or left-hand configuration, XXX grade walnut stock, wrap-hand checkering, cheekpiece, ebony tip, custom serial number.

	100%	98%	95%	90%	80%	70%	60%	LAST MSR
MSR $8,995	$8,100	$7,000	$6,150	$5,400	$4,500	$3,600	$2,900	

DAKOTA 76 .30-06 100TH ANNIVERSARY – .30-06 cal., 100 year banner on floorplate, Exhibition walnut with limited edition checkering pattern, stainless steel Model 76 Classic action and receiver, custom LOP, only 100 mfg. 2006-2007.

	100%	98%	95%	90%	80%	70%	60%	LAST MSR
	$8,350	$7,300	$6,250	$5,675	$4,595	$3,750	$2,925	*$8,945*

DAKOTA 76 VARMINT GRADE – available in 9 cals. between .17 Rem. and 6mm PPC, single shot, heavy barrel. Mfg. 1994-1997.

	100%	98%	95%	90%	80%	70%	60%	LAST MSR
	$2,275	$1,995	$1,700	$1,550	$1,250	$1,025	$795	*$2,500*

DAKOTA 76 PROFESSIONAL HUNTER – .375 H&H, .404 Jeffery, .416 Rem., .416 Rigby, .458 Lott, .450 Dakota, or .450 Rigby cal., 23 in. Douglas premium stainless steel barrel with matte black Cerakote finish, custom pillar bedded fiberglass stock with cheekpiece, barrel band swivel stud, quarter rib with one fixed blade and banded/hooded front sight with optic bead and window hood, black decelerator pad. New 2013.

	100%	98%	95%	90%	80%	70%	60%	LAST MSR
MSR $6,995	$6,300	$5,450	$4,750	$4,200	$3,500	$2,800	$2,250	

DAKOTA 76 SAFARI GRADE – available in various cals., 23 in. barrel, one-piece drop trigger guard assembly with hinged floorplate, checkered XXX English walnut stock with ebony forearm tip, barrel band, and inletted swivel studs, black recoil pad, cheekpiece, right or left-hand action, 8 1/2 lbs. New 1987.

	100%	98%	95%	90%	80%	70%	60%	LAST MSR
MSR $8,995	$8,100	$7,000	$6,150	$5,400	$4,500	$3,600	$2,900	

Subtract $400 (retail) if ordered with composite stock (disc.).

DAKOTA 76 AFRICAN GRADE – various cals from .257 Roberts to .450 Dakota cal., 24 in. barrel, barrel band and inletted Ken Howell swivel, 4 shot mag., point wrap hand checkering on forend, ebony tip, recoil reducer, XXX grade walnut stock, cheekpiece with shadowline, two crossbolts with ebony plugs, "R" prefix on serial number, 9 1/2 lbs. New 1989.

	100%	98%	95%	90%	80%	70%	60%	LAST MSR
MSR $9,995	$9,000	$7,800	$6,750	$6,000	$5,000	$4,000	$3,250	

DAKOTA 76 ALPINE GRADE – .22-250 Rem., .243 Win., 6mm Rem., .250-3000 Savage, 7mm-08 Rem., .308 Win., or .358 Win. cal., short action variation of the Classic Grade, 21 (disc. 2013) or 23 in. barrel, lighter weight model featuring a blind 4 shot mag., XX walnut streamline stock with two panel checkering, barrel band with Ken Howell swivel stud, Schnabel forearm tip, 1/2 in. black recoil pad, serial numbered with a "K" prefix, 6 1/2 lbs. Mfg. 1989-1992, reintroduced 2008.

	100%	98%	95%	90%	80%	70%	60%	LAST MSR
MSR $6,995	$6,300	$5,450	$4,750	$4,200	$3,500	$2,800	$2,250	

Other calibers are available on a special order basis.

GRADING - PPGS™	100%	98%	95%	90%	80%	70%	60%	LAST MSR

* ***Dakota 76 Alpine Deluxe*** – various cals., 23 in. barrel, Exhibition grade English wood stock, wrap checkering, Schnabel forearm tip, case colored finish, Talley bases and rings, custom serial number, gold oval. Mfg. 2011-disc.

	$7,500	$6,850	$5,650	$4,650	$4,100	$3,350	$2,725	*$8,010*

DAKOTA 76 MANNLICHER – .22-250 Rem. or .30-06 cal., 20 in. barrel, Mannlicher stock w/two panel stock checkering, XX grade walnut stock, talley bases and rings, case colored finish.

MSR $7,595	$6,850	$6,000	$5,100	$4,650	$3,750	$3,100	$2,400	

DAKOTA LONGBOW T-76 TACTICAL – .300 Dakota Mag., .300 Win. Mag. (new 2006), .330 Dakota Mag., .308 Win. (new 2006), .338 Lapua Mag., or .338 Dakota Mag. cal., 28 in. stainless barrel, long range tactical design, black synthetic stock with adj. comb, includes Picatinny optical rail, Model 70 style trigger, matte finish metal, controlled round feeding, and deployment kit, 13.7 lbs. Mfg. 1997-2009.

	$4,300	$3,760	$3,225	$2,925	$2,365	$1,935	$1,505	*$4,795*

DAKOTA SCIMITAR TACTICAL – .308 Win. or .338 Lapua cal., 24 or 27 in. match grade chrome moly barrel, 2nd generation Longbow with solid top receiver, long and short action, one-piece bolt handle, oversized claw extraction system, true controlled round feed, three postition safety, non-glare matte black finish, synthetic stock, optical rail. Mfg. 2008-2009.

	$5,850	$5,120	$4,385	$3,980	$3,215	$2,630	$2,045	*$6,295*

DAKOTA MODEL 97 CLASSIC – various cals. between .22-250 and .375 H&H, 24 or 26 in. match grade barrel, blind box magazine, black synthetic stock, deluxe recoil pad, pillar and glass bedding, controlled round feed, right or left-hand, black finish. Current Mfg.

MSR $4,295	$3,900	$3,350	$2,900	$2,575	$2,150	$1,725	$1,400	

DAKOTA MODEL 97 LIGHTWEIGHT HUNTER – available in most popular cals. between .22-250 Rem. and .308 Win., features fiberglass stock with black recoil pad, right-hand only, 6 lbs. Mfg. 1998-2004.

	$1,925	$1,685	$1,445	$1,310	$1,060	$865	$675	*$2,195*

Add $300 for Wood Hunter 97 (includes semi-fancy wood and blind mag.).

* ***Dakota Model 97 Lightweight Hunter Deluxe*** – available in short or long action, matte blue finish, checkered AAA Claro stock with cheekpiece, controlled round feed, three position safety, cloverleaf tang, 24 or 26 in. precision match chrome moly blue or stainless barrel. Disc. 2010.

	$3,750	$3,280	$2,810	$2,550	$2,060	$1,685	$1,310	*$4,295*

Add $200 for stainless barrel.

* ***Dakota Model 97 Lightweight Hunter All Weather Outfitter*** – available in short or long action, 24 or 26 in. precision match chrome moly stainless barrel, precision sand-colored composite stock, three position safety, aluminum pillar bedding, controlled round feed, cloverleaf tang, right or left-hand, matte blue finish. Limited mfg. 2005.

	$2,650	$2,320	$1,985	$1,800	$1,455	$1,190	$925	*$2,995*

DAKOTA MODEL 97 OUTFITTER TAKEDOWN – various cals., 24 in. barrel, barrel assembly has ramped rear sight and hooded front sight, barrel band, drilled and tapped, tan or grey finish on barrel, textured tan or grey synthetic stock, deluxe recoil pad. New 2010.

MSR $5,495	$4,950	$4,275	$3,700	$3,300	$2,750	$2,200	$1,750	

DAKOTA MODEL 97 LONG RANGE HUNTER – available in 13 popular cals. between .25-06 Rem. and .375 Dakota Mag., 26 in. barrel, matte blued finish, adj. match trigger, Model 76 ejector system, composite black H-S Precision stock, swivel studs, deluxe recoil pad, approx. 7.7 lbs. Mfg. 1997-disc.

	$3,350	$2,800	$2,400	$1,925	$1,750	$1,475	$1,250	*$3,720*

Add $300 for Wood Hunter 97 (includes semi-fancy wood and blind mag., disc. 2004).

* ***Dakota Model 97 Long Range Hunter Deluxe*** – available in 13 popular cals. between .25-06 Rem. and .375 Dakota Mag., similar to Model 97 Long Range Hunter, except features Triple A checkered Claro walnut stock with recoil pad and chrome moly matte blued action/barrel, small aperture rear sight. Disc.

	$4,400	$3,950	$3,500	$3,000	$2,500	$2,000	$1,600	*$4,820*

DAKOTA MODEL 97 ALL WEATHER HUNTER (STAINLESS) – available in short or long action, 24 in. precision match chrome moly stainless barrel, blind box magazine, black synthetic stock, deluxe recoil pad, aluminum pillar bedding, controlled round feed, three position safety, cloverleaf tang, right or left-hand, matte stainless steel. New mid-2008.

MSR $4,695	$4,250	$3,650	$3,150	$2,800	$2,350	$1,875	$1,525	

GRADING - PPGS™	100%	98%	95%	90%	80%	70%	60%	LAST MSR

DAKOTA MODEL 97 VARMINTER – available in 14 cals. between .117 Rem.-6.8 SPC, short or long action, 24 or 26 in. barrel w/o sights, XX Claro uncheckered walnut stock with semi-beavertail forend, deluxe recoil pad, swivel studs, pillar bedded, blind box magazine, custom straddle floorplate assembly, drilled and tapped, right or left-hand configuration, blue finish on barrel and receiver. Mfg. mid-2014-disc.

	$4,400	$3,950	$3,500	$3,000	$2,500	$2,000	$1,600	*$4,820*

* ***Dakota Model 97 Varminter Stainless*** – similar to Model 97 Varminter, except features stainless steel barrel and receiver. Mfg. mid-2014-disc.

	$4,625	$4,000	$3,400	$2,850	$2,400	$1,900	$1,700	*$5,120*

DAKOTA CLASSIC PREDATOR – various cals., special select checkered Claro walnut sporter style stock with cheekpiece, 22 in. match grade stainless steel barrel, swivel studs. Mfg. 2005-2009.

	$3,650	$3,200	$2,800	$2,400	$2,000	$1,600	$1,375	*$4,295*

* ***Dakota Classic Predator Series*** – similar to Classic Predator, except has varmint type stock with semi-beavertail forend.

	$2,850	$2,495	$2,135	$1,940	$1,565	$1,280	$995	*$3,295*

* ***Dakota Classic Predator All-Weather*** – similar to Predator Series, except has precision composite varmint type stock with semi-beavertail forend. Disc.

	$2,275	$1,990	$1,705	$1,545	$1,250	$1,025	$795	*$2,595*

RIFLES: SxS

DOUBLE RIFLE – .470 NE, .500 NE, .570 NE, and most rimmed cals., round boxlock action similar to Dakota shotgun, 25 in. chopper lump barrels, selective ejectors, supplied with Americase, limited mfg. by Ferlib circa 2001-2005.

	$25,500	$21,250	$17,250	$14,000	$11,250	$9,500	$8,250	*$28,500*

RIFLES: SINGLE SHOT

DAKOTA MODEL 10 – available in most rimmed and rimless commercially loaded standard and Mag. cals., falling block standard or enlarged Magnum (new 1994) action designed by Don Allen, 23 in. round precision match barrel, ambidextrous tang safety, panel wrap hand cut checkered XX English walnut stock and forearm with hand-rubbed oil finish, black recoil pad, rear swivel stud and front barrel band, Talley bases, 6-7 lbs. New 1990.

MSR $5,395	$4,850	$4,200	$3,675	$3,250	$2,700	$2,150	$1,750	

* ***Dakota Model 10 Deluxe*** – various cals., similar to Dakota Model 10, except has case colored action and exhibition grade wood.

MSR $6,995	$6,300	$5,450	$4,750	$4,200	$3,500	$2,800	$2,250	

* ***Dakota Model 10 Mannlicher*** – various cals., similar to Dakota Model 10, except has Mannlicher full-length stock.

MSR $6,595	$5,950	$5,150	$4,450	$3,950	$3,300	$2,650	$2,150	

MODEL 10 .30-06 100TH ANNIVERSARY – .30-06 cal., 100 year banner on floorplate, Exhibition walnut with limited edition checkering pattern, custom LOP, color case hardened frame, jewelled bolt, only 100 mfg. 2006-2007.

	$7,600	$6,650	$5,700	$5,170	$4,180	$3,420	$2,660	*$8,195*

DAKOTA MODEL 97 VARMINT HUNTER – various varmint cals., rounded short action, 24 in. chrome moly barrel, adj. trigger, black fiberglass stock standard, right-hand only, approx. 8 lbs. Mfg. 1998-2013.

	$1,600	$1,400	$1,200	$1,090	$880	$720	$560	*$1,795*

Add $700 for Wood Varmint Hunter 97 (includes semi-fancy wood and blind mag.).

Add $1,200 for Deluxe Varmint Hunter 97 (includes semi-fancy wood and point panel checkering with floorplate).

DAKOTA VARMINTER (STANDARD PREDATOR) – various cals., 24 in. match grade stainless steel barrel w/o sights, pillar bedded, right or left-hand acton, XX walnut stock, matte stainless receiver. New 2008.

MSR $2,495	$2,250	$1,950	$1,700	$1,500	$1,250	$1,000	$825	

* ***Dakota Varminter Deluxe (Predator Deluxe)*** – various cals., similar to Dakota Varminter, except features upgraded wood and hand cut checkering.

MSR $3,295	$2,975	$2,575	$2,225	$1,975	$1,650	$1,325	$1,075	

* ***Dakota Varminter Heavy Barrel (Predator Heavy Varmint)*** – various cals, 24 in. match grade stainless steel barrel w/o sights, choice of Claro walnut wood or green synthetic stock with beavertail forearm, matte stainless steel finish. New 2010.

MSR $3,295	$2,975	$2,575	$2,225	$1,975	$1,650	$1,325	$1,075	

Add $500 for All Weather with deluxe synthetic stock (Predator Heavy Varmint All Weather).

GRADING - PPGS™	100%	98%	95%	90%	80%	70%	60%	LAST MSR

DAKOTA SHARPS RIFLE – various cals. between .22 LR and .38-55 WCF, features scaled-down frame for smaller cals. (20% smaller than original Sharps), 25 or 26 in. octagon barrel, tang rear sight with front bead combinations, XX walnut stock with straight grip, steel buttplate, matte blue metal finish, approx. 8 lbs. New 1998.

MSR $4,995	$4,500	$3,900	$3,350	$3,000	$2,500	$2,000	$1,625	

MILLER CLASSIC – Please refer to the listing under the Miller Arms section.

SHOTGUNS: SxS

CLASSIC GRADE – 20 ga. only, case colored round boxlock action, 27 in. barrels with fixed chokes, DTs, straight grip checkered English walnut stock and splinter forearm, no engraving, 6 lbs. Mfg. 1996-98.

	$7,450	$6,520	$5,585	$5,065	$4,095	$3,350	$2,600	*$7,950*

PREMIER GRADE – 20, 28 ga. (new 2000), or .410 bore (new 2000), similar to Dakota Classic Field Grade, 27 in. barrels, exhibition grade English walnut, French grey metal finish, 50% engraving coverage, straight grip, splinter forend, DT, hand-rubbed oil finish stock, game rib with gold bead, ejectors, choice of chokes. Mfg. in conjunction with Ferlib.

	$13,950	$12,200	$10,460	$9,485	$7,670	$6,275	$4,880	*$14,950*

Add 10% for 28 ga. or .410 bore.

DAKOTA AMERICAN LEGEND – 20, 28 ga., or .410 bore, fully scroll-engraved coin finish round boxlock action with gold inlays, French grey metal finish, special select English walnut mfg. to customer dimensions, 27 in. barrels with game rib and gold bead, straight grip, DT, round action, ejectors, choice of chokes, oak and leather trunk case, 6 lbs., mfg. by Ferlib 1996-2005.

	$16,000	$14,000	$12,000	$10,880	$8,800	$7,200	$5,600	*$19,000*

Add 10% for 28 ga. or .410 bore.

Only 100 guns were scheduled to be mfg. Also offered in a 12 ga. and .410 bore/28 ga. set.

DAKOTA CLASSIC FIELD GRADE SUPERLIGHT KNOCKABOUT – 12, 16, 20, 24 (new 2005), 28, 32 (new 2005) ga., or .410 bore, Anson & Deeley boxlock action, monobloc (12, 20, or 28 ga.) or chopper lump (16 ga. or .410 bore only) 28 or 30 in. barrels, ejectors, DT, custom dimensions, checkered Turkish walnut stock and splinter forearm with oil finish, includes scroll and border engraving. Mfg. 2004-2007.

	$4,200	$3,675	$3,150	$2,855	$2,310	$1,890	$1,470	*$4,600*

Add $600 for 16, 32 ga. or .410 bore.

Add $1,501 for Express Gun with rifled 24 1/2 in. barrels with quarter rib and folding leaf express sights (12 or 20 ga. only, disc. 2004).

DAKOTA CLASSIC GRADE II – similar to Field Grade, except has extra fancy Turkish walnut and game scene engraving. Mfg. 2004-2007.

	$5,100	$4,460	$3,825	$3,470	$2,800	$2,295	$1,785	*$5,600*

Add $700 for 16, 32 ga. or .410 bore.

Add $1,501 for Express Gun with rifled 24 1/2 in. barrels with quarter rib and folding leaf express sights (12 or 20 ga. only, disc. 2004).

DAKOTA CLASSIC GRADE III – similar to Grade II, except has XXX Turkish walnut and scroll and gold game scene engraving. Mfg. 2004-2007.

	$6,100	$5,335	$4,575	$4,150	$3,355	$2,745	$2,135	*$6,600*

Add $800 for 16, 32 ga. or .410 bore.

Add $1,501 for Express Gun with rifled 24 1/2 in. barrels with quarter rib and folding leaf express sights (12 or 20 ga. only, disc. 2004).

DAKOTA SINGLE ACTION REVOLVERS

DAKOTA®

Previous trademark of revolvers imported until mid-2008 by E.M.F. Company, Inc. located in Santa Ana, CA.

Dakota trademarked revolvers imported by E.M.F. company Inc. were initially manufactured by Armi Jager, located in Val Trompia, Italy circa mid 1970s-mid 1980s. Armi San Marco then began manufacturing Dakotas circa mid 1980s-early 1990s. Uberti was the last manufacturer to make this trademark, and it produced Dakota revolvers from the early 1990s until 2008.

Great Western II and Hartford revolvers (previously listed in this section) imported by E.M.F. can be found listed alphabetically under separate listings. Other firearms imported by E.M.F. Co., Inc. will be found in the E section.

REVOLVERS: REPRODUCTIONS

Add $125 for combo cylinder on the models listed (.45 ACP cal. only on Remingtons, .44-40 WCF, .44 Spl., or .45 ACP on Peacemaker SAAs).

GRADING - PPGS™	100%	98%	95%	90%	80%	70%	60%	LAST MSR

OLD MODEL SAA – .22 LR, .32-20 WCF, .357 Mag., .38-40 WCF, .44 Spl., .44-40 WCF, or .45 LC cal., copy of the Colt SAA, 4 5/8, 5 1/2, or 7 1/2 in. barrels, blue finish, case hardened frame, 1-piece walnut grips, solid brass backstrap and trigger guard. Importation disc. 1991.

$400	$350	$295	$265	$235	$200	$185	*$600*

Add $100 for nickel finish (disc.).
Add $110 for convertible cylinders.

* ***Old Model SAA Engraved Old Model*** – .32-20 WCF, .357 Mag., .38-40 WCF, .44-40 WCF, or .45 cal., 4 3/4, 5 1/2, or 7 1/2 in. barrel. Disc. 1993, reintroduced 1996-98.

$775	$695	$500	$425	$350	$325	$300	*$840*

Add $160 for nickel finish (disc).

* ***Old Model SAA Cattlebrand Engraved*** – .44-40 WCF or .45 LC cal., 5 1/2, or 7 1/2 in. barrel, patterned after the famous Colt Cattlebrand variation (features various cattlebrands engraved on the barrel, frame and cylinder). Imported 1992-93, reintroduced 1996-98.

$775	$695	$500	$425	$350	$325	$300	*$840*

Add $140 for silver-plating.

NEW DAKOTA SAA – .357 Mag., .44-40 WCF, or .45 LC cal., features forged steel frame, black nickel backstrap and trigger guard, 4 (.45 LC cal. with standard grips), 4 3/4, 5 1/2, or 7 1/2 in. barrel, choice of case hardened or nickel frame, one-piece walnut grips, original Colt type hammer (without transfer bar safety). Imported 1991-2004.

$400	$350	$295	$265	$235	$200	$185	*$375*

Add $85 for combo. cylinder (disc. 2002).
Add $135 for satin nickel (disc.) or $175 for bright satin nickel finish.

* ***New Dakota SAA Sheriff Model*** – cals. similar to New Model, 3 1/2 in. barrel. Imported 1997-99.

$395	$350	$295	$250	$220	$180	$160	*$435*

DAKOTA PREMIER SAA – .45 LC cal., black powder frame, initial mfg. was with 4 5/8 or 5 1/2 in. barrel, set screw cylinder pin release, steel backstrap and trigger guard, one-piece grips. This model was the predecessor to the New Hartford Model.

$450	$375	$295	$250	$190	$170	$160	*$520*

FRONTIER MARSHAL SA – .357 Mag., .44-40 WCF (disc. 2004), or .45 LC cal., 4 3/4, 5 1/2, or 7 1/2 in. barrel, case colored frame, brass backstrap and trigger guard, blue barrel/cylinder. Imported 2003-2008.

$395	$350	$295	$250	$220	$180	$160	*$450*

SHERIFF'S OLD/NEW MODEL SAA – .32-20 WCF (disc.), .357 Mag. (disc. 2000), .38-40 WCF (disc.), .44 Spl. (disc.), .44-40 WCF (disc. 2000), or .45 LC cal., 3 1/2 in. barrel only. Imported 1991, 1994-2000, and 2003-disc..

$415	$335	$300	$265	$225	$175	$150	*$480*

U.S. ARMY SAA – variety of cals., premium quality construction. Disc. 1985.

$400	$350	$295	$265	$235	$200	$185	*$395*

* ***U.S. Army SAA Commemorative*** – .45 LC cal., 7 1/2 in. barrel, serial numbered 1-500, blue finish, case hardened frame, steel backstrap and trigger guard, 1-piece walnut grips. Importation disc. 1987.

$450	$375	$275	N/A	N/A	N/A	N/A	*$495*

CONVERTIBLE MODEL SAA – available with .22 LR/.22 WMR, .32-20 WCF/.32 H&R Mag., .357 Mag./9mm Para., .44-40 WCF/.44 Spl. cal., or .45 LC/.45 ACP double cylinders. Imported 1986-1990.

$495	$450	$395	$350	$310	$275	$250	*$580*

FAST DRAW MODEL SAA – .22 LR, .22 WMR, .32-20 WCF, .32 H&R Mag., .357 Mag., .38-40 WCF, 9mm Para., .44 Spl., .44-40 WCF, .45 ACP, or .45 LC cal., case hardened frame, 4 5/8 in. barrel. Importation disc. 1990.

$385	$340	$295	$225	$165	$150	$135	*$480*

BISLEY MODEL SAA – .22 LR (disc.), .22 WMR (disc.), .32-20 WCF (disc.), .32 H&R Mag. (disc.), .38-40 WCF (disc.), .357 Mag. (disc. 1999), 9mm Para. (disc.), .44 Spl. (disc.), .44-40 WCF (disc.), .45 ACP (disc.), or .45 LC (current mfg.) cal., 4 3/4 (disc. 1994, reintroduced 2001-2003 in .44-40 WCF cal. only), 5 1/2, or 7 1/2 in. barrel lengths. Imported 1986-1991, 1993-1995, and 1997-2008.

$435	$385	$350	$315	$280	$250	$215	*$490*

Add $200 for bright or satin (disc.) nickel finish.
Add $112 for combo. cylinder (.45 ACP - disc.).

GRADING - PPGS™	100%	98%	95%	90%	80%	70%	60%	LAST MSR

* ***Bisley Model SAA Engraved*** – .32-20 WCF, .38-40 WCF, .357 Mag., .44-40 WCF, or .45 LC cal. (disc. 1990), 4 3/4, 5 1/2, or 7 1/2 in. barrel, action engraved throughout. Imported 1987-91.

	$600	$525	$450	$400	$350	$300	$275	*$570*

Add $100 for nickel finish.

1873 FRONTIER MODEL SAA – .22 LR cal., 4 3/4 in. barrel, case colored frame, black nickel backstrap and trigger guard. Mfg. by IAR, imported 1999-2002.

	$325	$275	$250	$225	$175	$150	$135	*$315*

Add $125 for bright nickel finish.

DALVAR OF USA

Previous importer of recently manufactured Radom pistols located in Henderson, NV. Please refer to the Radom listing in the R section.

DALY, CHARLES

Charles Daly is a registered trademark that has been manufactured by various companies and countries, including Prussia, England, Belgium, U.S., Japan, and most recently, Turkey. Please refer to the various Charles Daly listings in the C section.

DAMKO / DK PRECISION OUTDOOR LLC

Current firearms and accessories manufacturer located in White City, OR.

RIFLES: SINGLE SHOT

Damko also offers a custom shop Martini rifle. Current base MSR is $1,854. Please contact the manufacturer directly for additional options, pricing, and availability.

MARTINI RIFLE – .25-35 Win., .30-30 Win., .30-40 Krag, .303 British, .357 Mag., or .44 Rem. Mag. cal., falling block action, polished blued Krieger 20 in. barrel or 22 (scoped version only, disc.), 24, or 26 (scoped version only) in. chrome moly Pac-Nor barrel, blued steel receiver, available with bead front sight and flat-top rear sight, peep sights, or DAMKO scope mount base (accepts dovetail type scope rings), walnut straight grip stock with DAMKO steel buttplate, floating forearm, cocking indicator, high polish finish, 6 lbs.

MSR $1,854	$1,675	$1,460	$1,255	$1,135	$920	$750	$600

Add $103 for peep sights.
Add $206 for scope version.

DAN ARMS OF AMERICA

Previous trademark of shotguns manufactured in Italy by Silma. Previously imported by Dan Arms of America located in Allentown, PA and by Dan Arms of North America (previously called Sportsman's Emporium Ltd.) located in Fort Washington, PA.

All shotguns listed below were discontinued in early 1988.

SHOTGUNS: O/U

LUX GRADE I – 12 or 20 ga., 3 in. Mag. chambers, 26, 28, or 30 in. barrels, vent. rib, extractors, pistol grip, double trigger, European walnut.

	$280	$220	$210	$200	$190	$180	$170	*$350*

LUX GRADE II – 12 ga. only, 3 in. Mag. chambers, 26, 28, or 30 in. barrels, vent. rib, extractors, pistol grip, single trigger, European walnut.

	$320	$250	$240	$230	$215	$200	$190	*$395*

LUX GRADE III – 12 or 20 ga., 3 in. Mag. chambers, 26, 28, or 30 in. barrels, vent. rib, ejectors, pistol grip, single trigger, checkered European walnut.

	$375	$300	$285	$270	$255	$240	$220	*$450*

LUX GRADE IV – 12 ga. only, 3 in. Mag. chambers, 28 in. barrels, vent. rib, ejectors, pistol grip, single trigger, checkered European walnut, multi-chokes with 5 tubes.

	$460	$390	$350	$310	$285	$265	$245	*$550*

SKEET MODEL – 12 ga. only, 26 1/2 in. barrels, 10mm vent. rib, anatomical pistol grip.

	$550	$450	$400	$355	$320	$300	$285	*$650*

TRAP MODEL – 12 ga. only, 30 in. barrels, 10mm vent. rib, anatomical pistol grip.

	$550	$450	$400	$355	$320	$300	$285	*$650*

SILVERSNIPE – 12 or 20 ga., made to customer specifications, sideplates, select high grade walnut, name engraving upon request.

	$1,300	$1,200	$1,050	$900	$800	$700	$600	*$1,475*

GRADING - PPGS™	100%	98%	95%	90%	80%	70%	60%	LAST MSR

SHOTGUNS: SxS

FIELD MODEL – 12, 16, 20, 28 ga., or .410 bore, double triggers, extractors, 26 or 28 in. barrels.

	$285	$220	$210	$200	$190	$180	$170	*$350*

DELUXE FIELD MODEL – 12 or 20 ga., single triggers, ejectors, 26 or 28 in. barrels.

	$440	$375	$340	$310	$290	$260	$230	*$500*

DAN WESSON

Current trademark manufactured by Dan Wesson Firearms beginning 2005, located in Norwich, NY. Distributed beginning 2005 by CZ-USA, located in Kansas City, KS. Previously manufactured by New York International Corp. (NYI) located in Norwich, NY 1997-2005. Distributor and dealer sales.

DAN WESSON / WESSON FIREARMS CO. TIMELINE HISTORY

1968-1978 Dan Wesson Arms Inc. located in Monson, MA (owner D.B. Wesson).

1978-1990 Dan Wesson Arms Inc. located in Monson, MA. In late 1990, ownership of Dan Wesson Arms changed (within the family), and the new company was renamed Wesson Firearms Co. Inc.

1991-1992 Wesson Firearms Co. located in Monson, MA.

1992-1995 Wesson Firearms Co. located in Palmer, MA.

1997-2005 Wesson Firearms manufactured by New York International Corp. (NYI) located in Norwich, NY.

2005-present Dan Wesson Firearms located in Norwich, NY.

PISTOLS: SEMI-AUTO

Until 2005, Dan Wesson manufactured a complete line of .45 ACP 1911 style semi-auto pistols. Previously manufactured models include: Seven (last MSR was $999), Seven Stainless (last MSR was $1,099), Guardian (last MSR was $799), the Guardian Deuce (last MSR was $799), the Dave Pruit Signature Series (last MSR was $899), and the Hi-Cap (last MSR was $689).

50TH ANNIVERSARY LIMITED EDITION – .45 ACP cal., 5 in. barrel, 8 shot mag., stainless steel frame, brass bead front sights, G10 grips with DW logo medallions, slide and frame engraving, grip safety and recoil spring plug are engraved and gold-inlaid with "DW" and "50th", high-polish Nitride finish, 40.4 oz. Limited mfg. 2018 only.

	$2,675	$2,325	$2,050	$1,875	$1,600	$1,375	$1,050	*$2,999*

A2 – .45 ACP cal., forged steel frame and slide, 5 in. stainless steel match barrel, 8 shot mag., lowered and flared ejection port, combat sights, double diamond walnut grips, extended thumb safety, tactical beavertail, matte blue or parkerized (mfg. 2018-2019) finish, 40 oz. Limited mfg. 2017-2020.

	$1,150	$1,000	$875	$775	$650	$550	$450	*$1,363*

A2 COMMANDER – .45 ACP cal., Commander size frame, 4.25 in. stainless steel match barrel, 8 shot mag., forged steel frame and slide, lowered and flared ejection port, modern combat sights, double diamond walnut grips, tactical beavertail and extended thumb safety, matte blue finish, 37.3 oz. Limited mfg. 2017-2019.

	$1,150	$1,000	$875	$775	$650	$550	$450	*$1,363*

BRUIN – 10mm or .45 ACP (disc. 2020) cal., 6.03 in. barrel, 8 shot mag., stainless steel long slide, adj. Tritium sights/fiber optic combo front sight, red/black or black (Bronze model) G10 grips, two-tone black/bronze duty or black duty finish, 43.9 oz. New 2016.

MSR $2,235	$1,900	$1,660	$1,425	$1,290	$1,045	$850	$745	

Subtract approx. $232 for .45 ACP cal. (disc. 2020).

CCO BOBTAIL – .45 ACP cal., SA, Commander slide on an Officer frame, 4 1/4 in. barrel, 7 shot, anodized black aluminum frame, stainless steel slide, undercut trigger guard, Tritium sights, wood stipled shadow grips, black ceramic coat (disc.) or black duty finish, 26 oz. Mfg. 2009-2017.

	$1,350	$1,075	$950	$825	$650	$550	$475	*$1,558*

COMMANDER CLASSIC BOBTAIL – .45 ACP (mfg. 2005-2009, reintroduced 2016) or 10mm (mfg. 2005-2009) cal., 4 1/4 in. barrel, stainless steel frame and slide, Colt Series 70 design, Ed Brown bobtail mainspring housing, many target features, diamond checkered cocobolo grips, brushed/bead blasted finish, 34 oz. Mfg. 2005-2009, reintroduced 2016.

MSR $1,689	$1,435	$1,250	$1,075	$975	$790	$650	$560	

Last MSR in 2009 was $1,191.

Add $33 for 10mm cal. (disc. 2009).
Add $339 for two-tone finish and black ceramic coated slide (10mm cal. only, mfg. 2009 only).

GRADING - PPGS™	100%	98%	95%	90%	80%	70%	60%	LAST MSR

DWX – 9mm Para. or .40 S&W cal., 1911 style, SA, full size stainless steel frame, 4.95 in. match grade barrel, 10, 15, or 19 shot double stack mag. w/flush bases, square hammer, flat K-style long trigger, fiber optic dovetail front and CZ Shadow 2 adj. rear sight, red CZ 75 aluminum grips, ambi thumb safety, front strap checkering, lower 1913 Picatinny rail, serrated top rib, Black Duty finish, 43 oz. New 2020.

MSR $1,810	$1,540	$1,350	$1,150	$1,045	$850	$700	$600	

* ***DWX Compact*** – 9mm Para. cal., 1911 style, SA, compact aluminum frame, 4 in. match grade barrel, 10 or 15 shot double stack mag. w/flush bases, square hammer, red flat K-style long trigger, fiber optic dovetail front and CZ Shadow 2 adj. rear sight, CZ 75 aluminum grips, ambi thumb safety, front strap and backstrap has Frag pattern checkering (inspired by Ned Christiansen), with light rail or dustcover, Black Duty finish, 28.5 oz. New 2020.

MSR $1,810	$1,540	$1,350	$1,150	$1,045	$850	$700	$600	

DISCRETION – 9mm Para. or .45 ACP cal., 5 3/4 in. extended match grade stainless steel threaded barrel, suppressor ready, 8 or 10 shot mag., light rails, competition-inspired hammer, serrated trigger, adj. night sights, G10 grips, manual thumb and grip safety, Black Duty finish. Mfg. 2016-2020.

	$1,850	$1,625	$1,390	$1,250	$1,000	$875	$700	*$2,181*

* ***Discretion Commander*** – 9mm Para. or .45 ACP cal., stainless steel frame, 5 in. barrel, 8 or 10 shot mag., high night sights, black G10 grips, Black Duty finish, 41.7 oz. Mfg. 2018-2020.

	$1,850	$1,625	$1,390	$1,250	$1,000	$875	$700	*$2,181*

ECO MODEL – 9mm Para. or .45 ACP cal., Officer sized model with 3 1/2 in. ramped bull barrel with target crown, SA, single stacked mag., G10 grips, black duty or OD Green (mfg. 2018-2019) finish on aluminum frame and steel slide, Tritium night sights, 25 oz. Mfg. 2012-2020.

	$1,385	$1,210	$1,040	$940	$750	$625	$525	*$1,623*

Add $39 for .45 ACP cal.
Add $39 for OD Green finish (mfg. 2018-2019).

ECP – 9mm Para. or .45 ACP cal., forged aluminum frame, 4 in. heavy match grade bull barrel, compact stainless steel slide, 8 shot, brass bead front and u-notch rear sight, G10 grips, tri-tipped slide with side serrations, Black Duty finish, 29 oz. New mid-2018.

MSR $1,575	$1,340	$1,175	$1,015	$925	$750	$625	$525	

Add $30 for .45 ACP cal.

ELITE SERIES CHAOS – 9mm Para. cal., SA, stainless frame, 5 in. barrel, 21 shot double stack mag., adj. sights, G10 grips, ambi thumb/grip safety, 1913 rail, front and rear serrations, matte black finish, 3.2 lbs. Mfg. 2014-2019.

	$3,250	$2,850	$2,450	$2,210	$1,800	$1,500	$1,325	*$3,829*

ELITE SERIES FURY – 9mm Para. or 10mm cal., 5 1/2 in. extended, threaded barrel, 14 or 18 shot mag., Trijicon RMR, G10 grips, ambidextrous thumb safety, matte black finish. Mfg. 2017-2019.

	$4,175	$3,650	$3,150	$2,825	$2,300	$1,950	$1,625	*$4,899*

ELITE SERIES HAVOC – .38 Super or 9mm Para. cal., 4 1/4 (disc.) or 5 in. barrel with compensator, SA, all steel construction, designed for Open IPSC/USPSA Division, C-More red dot sights, 21 shot mag., matte black finish, 38 oz. Mfg. 2011-2019.

	$3,650	$3,200	$2,750	$2,475	$2,000	$1,650	$1,400	*$4,299*

ELITE SERIES MAYHEM – .40 S&W cal., SA, Limited IPSC/USPSA, stainless steel frame, 6 in. bull barrel with tactical rail, 18 shot mag., adj. fiber optic sights, G10 grips, ambi thumb/grip safety, matte black finish, 38 3/4 oz. Mfg. 2011-2019.

	$3,325	$2,925	$2,500	$2,250	$1,825	$1,500	$1,325	*$3,899*

ELITE SERIES TITAN – 10mm cal., 4 3/4 in. bull barrel, SA, 13 shot mag., all steel construction, lower frame tactical rail, matte black finish, Tritium sights, G10 grips, snake scale serrations on the slide, 26 oz. Mfg. 2011-2019.

	$3,250	$2,850	$2,450	$2,210	$1,800	$1,500	$1,325	*$3,829*

GLOBAL – .45 ACP or 10mm cal., 5 or 6 in. barrel, full size frame, steel or stainless steel, choice of accessory light rail or full-length dust cover. Disc. 2005.

	$1,000	$900	$800	$700	$600	$475	$350	*$1,149*

GUARDIAN – 9mm Para., .38 Super (new 2014), or .45 ACP (new 2011) cal., SA, forged aluminum Commander frame, 4 1/4 in. barrel, 8 or 9 shot mag., Commander-length slide, bobtail mainspring housing, Tritium sight/fixed night sights, checkered cocobolo grips, Black Duty finish, 28.5 oz. New 2010.

MSR $1,589	$1,350	$1,175	$1,015	$925	$750	$625	$530	

Add $60 for .45 ACP cal. (new 2011).

GRADING - PPGS™	100%	98%	95%	90%	80%	70%	60%	LAST MSR

HEIRLOOM – .45 ACP cal., SA, steel frame, 5 in. barrel with blue finish, 8 shot mag., brass front and U-notch rear sights, smooth French walnut grips, manual thumb and grip safety, engraved slide with scrollwork (mfg. 2020 only), 25 LPI front and backstrap checkering, color case hardened finish, 40.1 oz. New 2020.

MSR $1,589	$1,350	$1,175	$1,015	$925	$750	$625	$530	

KO3 PANTHER SERIES – .45 ACP cal., full size, 5 in. barrel, Series 70 pistol with cast alloy frame, external extractor, Chip McCormick beavertail with Commander style hammer, forged conventional round top slide, fixed rear sight, matte bead blasted frame and slide top, slide sides are polished, blue or stainless, Hogue rubber grips. Disc.

	$595	$525	$450	$415	$385	$350	$325	

Add $20 for stainless steel.

KODIAK – 10mm cal., SA, stainless steel frame, 6 in. bushing-less barrel, 8 shot mag., fiber optic front and adj. rear sights, G10 grips, manual thumb and grip safety, bead blasted with matte gray slide or Black Duty finish with bronze controls, 47.1 oz. New 2019.

MSR $2,299	$1,950	$1,700	$1,465	$1,325	$1,075	$890	$765	

Add $50 for bead blasted finish with matte gray slide.

MARKSMAN – .45 ACP cal., stainless steel frame, 5 in. barrel, similar to Pointman, except slimmer design, 38 1/2 oz. Mfg. 2009.

	$1,225	$1,000	$900	$775	$650	$550	$475	*$1,391*

PATRIOT 1911 SERIES – .45 ACP or 10mm (Commander slide and frame only) cal., 4 1/4 (Commander) or 5 in. stainless steel match barrel, 1911 Series 70 action, external extractor, fitted parts, and many high-end components by McCormick, Ed Brown, Nowlin, etc., each gun shipped with test target, variations include Patriot Expert (blue or stainless, Bo-Mar style target sights), Patriot Marksman (blue or stainless, fixed sights), AAA cocobolo double diamond checkered grips with gold medallions, 2.3 lbs. Mfg. 2001-2005.

	$825	$750	$650	$550	$475	$425	$375	*$929*

Add $20 for 5 in. Patriot with blued action.
Add $70 for 5 in. barrel in stainless steel.
Add $30 for checkered front grip strap.
Add $70 for bobtail frame.

PM3-P MINOR SERIES – .45 ACP cal., full size, 5 in. barrel, Series 70 pistol with cast alloy frame, Chip McCormick beavertail with Commander style hammer, forged conventional round top slide, fixed rear sight, matte bead blasted frame and slide top, slide sides are polished, blue or stainless, checkered exotic hardwood grips. Disc.

	$515	$450	$415	$385	$350	$325	$295	

PM POINTMAN SERIES – .45 ACP or 10mm cal., full size, 5 in. target barrel, features Chip McCormick beavertail with Commander style hammer, forged conventional round top slide, high target rib or low profile Clark style sights with adj. white outline or Bo-Mar rear sight, blue or stainless, PM1-S is standard gun, checkered exotic hardwood grips. Disc. 2005.

	$725	$650	$575	$500	$425	$385	$350	*$809*

Add $50 for checkered front grip strap.
Add $50 for high or Ausi rib (Model PMA-S).
Add $100 for blue finish with Clark/Bo-Mar rib and sights (Model PMA-B, disc.).

POINTMAN CARRY (PM-C) – 9mm Para. (mfg. 2017-2019), .38 Super (mfg. 2018-2019), or .45 ACP (new 2018) cal., stainless steel Commander length slide with Officer frame, 4.25 in. stainless steel barrel, 8 shot mag., fixed night sights, double diamond wood grips, manual thumb and grip safety, matte stainless steel finish, 36.7 oz. Mfg. 2017-2020.

	$1,375	$1,200	$1,025	$925	$750	$625	$525	*$1,597*

POINTMAN SEVEN – .40 S&W (new 2009), .45 ACP or 10mm cal., 5 in. barrel, features stainless steel frame and slide, patterned after the Colt Series 70 semi-auto, 7 shot mag., double slide serrations, many target features, diamond checkered cocobolo grips, 38 oz. Mfg. 2005-2009.

	$1,050	$900	$775	$700	$600	$500	$400	*$1,158*

Add $33 for 10mm cal.
Add $31 for .40 S&W cal.
Add $111 for desert tan Teflon finish with black grips and controls (.45 ACP cal. only, new 2009).

POINTMAN SEVEN PM-7 – .45 ACP cal., 5 in. barrel, forged stainless steel frame, 8 shot, undercut trigger guard, front strap checkering, serrated rib on top of forged slide, adj. rear and fiber optic front sights, double diamond cocobolo grips, 38 1/2 oz. New 2015.

MSR $1,599	$1,360	$1,190	$1,020	$925	$750	$625	$530	

GRADING - PPGS™ 100% 98% 95% 90% 80% 70% 60% *LAST MSR*

POINTMAN NINE PM-9 – 9mm Para. cal., forged stainless steel frame, 5 in. barrel, 9 shot, undercut trigger guard, fiber optic front and adj. target rear sight, double diamond cocobolo grips, serrated rib on top of forged slide, front and rear cocking serrations, 25 LPI front strap checkering, brushed/bead blasted stainless finish, 38 1/2 oz. New 2009.

MSR $1,629 $1,385 $1,210 $1,040 $940 $750 $625 $540

POINTMAN 38 PM-38 – .38 Super cal., forged stainless frame with undercut trigger guard and front strap checkering, 5 in. barrel, 9 shot mag., adj. rear target and fiber optic front sights, double diamond cocobolo grips, manual thumb and grip safety, forged slide, front and rear cocking serrations, soft brushed finish, 2.42 lbs. Mfg. 2016-2019.

$1,375 $1,200 $1,025 $925 $750 $625 $525 ***$1,597***

POINTMAN 45 (PM-45) – .45 ACP cal., forged stainless steel frame and slide with brushed finish, 5 in. barrel, 8 shot mag., undercut trigger guard, adj. rear target and fiber optic front sight, double diamond cocobolo grips, 25 LPI front strap checkering, front and rear cocking serrations, 41.3 oz. New 2018.

MSR $1,629 $1,385 $1,210 $1,040 $940 $750 $625 $540

RZ-10 RAZORBACK SPECIAL EDITION – 10mm cal., full size, 5 in. barrel, Colt Series 70 design with forged stainless frame and slide, Bo-Mar adj. rear sight, match barrel, bushing, and link, match grade trigger, sear, hammer, and beavertail, checkered synthetic or rubber (new 2006) grips, limited mfg. 2002-2004, and resumed 2006-2009.

$1,050 $900 $775 $700 $600 $500 $450 ***$1,191***

Add $257 for Sportsman Model with VZ G10 black operator grips, FO front sights and adj. sights (new 2009).

RZ-10 RAZORBACK – 10mm cal., SA, forged stainless steel frame, 5 in. match grade ramped barrel, 9 shot mag., undercut trigger guard, fixed Tritium (disc.) night sights, double diamond cocobolo grips, smooth front strap, serrated Clark-style target rib, brushed slide finish, approx. 38-1/2 oz. New 2012.

MSR $1,589 $1,350 $1,175 $1,015 $925 $750 $625 $530

RZ-45 HERITAGE – .45 ACP cal., SA, stainless steel frame, 5 in. barrel, 8 shot mag., fixed night sights (disc. 2019) or fiber optic front and tactical rear sights (new 2020), rubber grips, manual thumb safety, polished flats, 25 LPI front strap and backstrap checkering, brushed/bead blasted stainless finish, 38 1/2 oz. New 2009.

MSR $1,589 $1,350 $1,175 $1,015 $925 $750 $625 $530

SILVERBACK – 9mm Para. (new 2016), .45 ACP, or 10mm cal., stainless steel slide and frame, 5 in. barrel, 8 or 9 shot mag., adj. target style Tritium sights, G10 grips, serrated top rib, Black Duty finish, 2.38 lbs. Mfg. 2015-2017.

$1,600 $1,400 $1,200 $1,090 $880 $725 $575 ***$1,883***

Add $181 for 10mm cal.

SPECIALIST/SPECIALIST BLACK – 9mm Para. (new 2016), 10mm (new 2020), or .45 ACP cal., SA, 5 in. barrel, forged stainless steel slide, 8, 9 (new 2016), or 10 shot mag., extended magazine release, undercut trigger guard, Tritium night sights, G10 VZ Operator II grips, ambidextrous thumb safety, serrated rib, frame has lower Picatinny rail, recessed slide stop, upgraded in 2020 to include a new style light rail frame as well as forward cocking serrations and inset slide serrations, bead blasted matte stainless or black duty finish. New 2012.

MSR $1,735 $1,475 $1,290 $1,100 $1,000 $825 $675 $580

Add $120 for 10mm cal. (new 2020).

Add $250-$380 for Black Duty finish, depending on caliber.

* ***Specialist Distressed*** – .45 ACP cal., forged stainless frame, 5 in. stainless barrel, two 8 shot mags., extended mag. release and magwell, forged stainless steel slide, Clark-style serrated rib, undercut trigger guard, amber Tritium dot rear and green lamp with white target ring front sight, G10 grips, ambi thumb safety, integral Picatinny rail, 25 LPI front strap checkering, recessed slide stop, upgraded in 2020 to include a new style light rail frame, as well as forward cocking serrations, and inset slide serrations, Distressed Duty finish over stainless steel, 42.3 oz. Mfg. 2018-2020.

$1,740 $1,525 $1,300 $1,185 $950 $775 $625 ***$2,049***

SPECIALIST COMMANDER – 9mm Para. (mfg. 2017-2019) or .45 ACP cal., 4 1/4 in. stainless barrel, two 8 shot mags., extended mag. release and magwell, forged stainless steel slide with Clark-style serrated rib, undercut trigger guard, amber Tritium dot in the rear sight and a green lamp with white target ring in front sight, G10 grips, ambidextrous thumb safety, integral Picatinny rail, front strap checkering, recessed slide stop, upgraded in 2020 to include a new style light rail frame, forward cocking serrations, and inset slide serrations, matte stainless or Black Duty finish, 40 oz. New 2017.

MSR $1,735 $1,475 $1,290 $1,100 $1,000 $825 $675 $580

Add $314 for Black Duty finish.

GRADING - PPGS™	100%	98%	95%	90%	80%	70%	60%	LAST MSR

* ***Specialist Commander Distressed*** – .45 ACP cal., 4 1/4 in. barrel, 8 shot mag., extended mag. release and magwell, forged stainless steel slide, undercut trigger guard, amber tritium dot rear sight and green lamp with white target ring front sight, G10 grips, ambidextrous thumb safety, integral 1913 Picatinny rail, 25 LPI front strap checkering, recessed slide stop, matte stainless or black Distressed Duty finish. Mfg. 2018-2019.

	$1,715	$1,500	$1,285	$1,165	$950	$775	$625	*$2,012*

SS CUSTOM – .40 S&W cal., stainless steel construction, fiber optic front sight, ambidextrous safety, shark grips. Mfg. 2008-2009.

	$1,225	$1,000	$900	$775	$650	$550	$475	*$1,389*

TCP – 9mm Para. or .45 ACP cal., forged aluminum frame, 4 in. match grade bull barrel, 8 or 9 shot, one-piece magwell, compact stainless tri-topped slide with aggressive slide serrations, square hammer, flat K-style trigger, brass bead front and U-notch rear sight, G10 grips, Black Duty finish, 32 oz. New mid-2018.

MSR $1,705	$1,450	$1,275	$1,090	$985	$800	$650	$570	

Add $20 for .45 ACP cal.

VALKYRIE – 9mm Para. (new 2016) or .45 ACP cal., 4 1/2 in. barrel, 7 or 8 (new 2016) shot mag., fixed Tritium night sights, slim G10 grips, features the latest upgrades to the CCO platform including the ECO frame with recessed slide stop hole, black duty finish, 1.62 lbs. Mfg. 2015-2017.

	$1,715	$1,500	$1,285	$1,165	$950	$775	$625	*$2,012*

VALKYRIE COMMANDER – 9mm Para. or .45 ACP cal., aluminum Commander-length frame, 4 1/4 in. barrel, 7 or 9 shot mag., fixed Tritium night sights, G10 grips, Black Duty finish, 1.62 lbs. Mfg. 2016-2017.

	$1,715	$1,500	$1,285	$1,165	$950	$775	$625	*$2,012*

VALOR – 9mm Para. (new 2016), 10mm (new 2017), or .45 ACP cal., SA, 5 in. barrel, 8 or 9 (9mm, new 2016) shot mag., adj. (disc.) or Heinie Ledge Straight 8 (new 2010) Tritium night sights, VZ slimline G10 grips, manual thumb and grip safety, choice of black ceramic coated (disc.), Black Duty finish, or matte stainless steel (new 2010), 38 oz. Mfg. 2008-2018.

	$1,450	$1,275	$1,100	$985	$825	$675	$525	*$1,701*

Add $259 for 10mm cal. (new 2017).
Add $311 for Black Duty finish.

VALOR/VALOR BLACK (CURRENT MFG.) – .45 ACP cal., forged stainless steel frame and slide, 5 in. barrel, 8 shot mag., serrated U-notch rear sight and front Tritium sight with large orange ring, tapered G10 grips, tactical ambi thumb safety, Stan Chen SI magwell, new style recessed slide stop, GI-style cocking serrations and inset serrations, bead blasted or Black Duty finish, 39.7 oz. New 2020.

MSR $1,865	$1,585	$1,385	$1,190	$1,080	$875	$725	$620	

Add $320 for Black Duty finish.

VALOR BLUE – 9mm Para. or .45 ACP cal., steel frame, 5 in. steel barrel, 8 or 9 shot mag., fixed night sight, double diamond G10 grips, polished/matte blue finish. Mfg. 2017 only.

	$1,490	$1,315	$1,150	$1,025	$875	$750	$615	*$1,766*

VALOR COMMANDER – 9mm Para. or .45 ACP cal., SA, 4 1/4 in. barrel, 8 or 9 shot mag., stainless steel, fixed Tritium night sights, G10 grips, manual thumb and grip safety, bead blasted or Black Duty finish, 2.2 lbs. Mfg. 2016-2018.

	$1,450	$1,275	$1,100	$985	$825	$675	$525	*$1,701*

Add $311 for Black Duty finish.

V-BOB/V-BOB BLACK – .45 ACP cal., Commander size stainless steel frame, 4 1/4 in. match grade barrel, 8 shot mag., serrated U-notch rear sight and Tritium front sight with large orange ring, black tapered G10 grips, ambi safety, bobbed mainspring housing, new style recessed slide stop, inset serrations, bead blasted or Black Duty finish, 36.5 oz. New 2020.

MSR $1,855	$1,575	$1,380	$1,180	$1,075	$865	$725	$620	

Add $250 for Black Duty finish.

V-BOB TWO-TONE – .45 ACP cal., matte stainless steel Commander-size frame, 4 1/4 in. barrel, 8 shot mag., u-notch rear sight and Tritium front with large orange ring, tapered G10 grips, ambi thumb and grip safety, bobbed mainspring housing, GI-style rear slide serrations, inset serrations, recessed slide stop, blued slide finish, 36.5 oz. Limited mfg. beginning 2020.

MSR $1,865	$1,585	$1,385	$1,190	$1,080	$875	$725	$620	

GRADING - PPGS™	100%	98%	95%	90%	80%	70%	60%	LAST MSR

V-BOB BLACK/V-BOB STAINLESS (VALOR BOBTAIL COMMANDER) – 9mm Para. (new 2016) or .45 ACP cal., 4 1/4 in. barrel, 8 or 9 (new 2016) shot mag., fixed Tritium night sights, double diamond black/gray G10 grips and Black Duty finish or black G10 grips with matte stainless finish, manual thumb and grip safety, Ed Brown bobtail Commander style features, 35.2 oz. Mfg. 2010-2018.

	$1,500	$1,315	$1,125	$1,025	$825	$675	$525	*$1,766*

Add $311 for Black Duty finish.

VIGIL – 9mm Para. or .45 ACP cal., forged aluminum frame, 5 in. barrel, 8 or 9 shot mag., stainless steel slide, skeletonized aluminum trigger, Tritium front and serrated tactical rear sight, cocobolo Shadow grips, 25 LPI front strap checkering, Black Duty finish, 32.8 oz. New 2018.

MSR $1,299	$1,105	$975	$825	$750	$600	$500	$435	

* ***Vigil Commander*** – 9mm Para. or .45 ACP cal., forged aluminum frame, 4 1/4 in. barrel, 8 or 9 shot mag., stainless steel slide, Tritium front and serrated tactical rear sight, cocobolo Shadow grips, front strap checkering, Black Duty finish. New 2018.

MSR $1,299	$1,105	$975	$825	$750	$600	$500	$435	

* ***Vigil Suppressor-Ready*** – 9mm Para. or .45 ACP cal., forged aluminum frame, 5 3/4 in. extended threaded barrel, 8 or 9 shot mag., stainless steel slide, skeletonized aluminum trigger, suppressor height Tritium front and serrated tactical rear sight, cocobolo Shadow grips, 25 LPI front strap checkering, Black Duty finish, 33.6 oz. Mfg. 2018-2020.

	$1,200	$1,050	$900	$815	$660	$540	$420	*$1,397*

VIGIL CCO – 9mm Para. or .45 ACP cal., sub-compact forged aluminum Officer frame, 4 1/4 in. barrel, 7 or 8 shot mag., compact Commander slide, tactical rear sight and Tritium night sights in front, cocobolo Shadow grips, 25 LPI front strap checkering, round-top slide, Black Duty finish. New 2018.

MSR $1,299	$1,105	$975	$825	$750	$600	$500	$435	

WRAITH – 9mm Para., 10mm, or .45 ACP cal., Government sized 1911, stainless steel frame, 5 3/4 in. threaded barrel, 8, 9, or 10 shot mag., high night sights, grippy stippled G10 grips, forward slide serrations, Distressed Duty finish. Mfg. 2018-2020.

	$1,465	$1,280	$1,100	$995	$800	$675	$525	*$1,720*

Add $65 for 10mm cal.

REVOLVERS: DOUBLE ACTION, 1970-1995 MFG.

As a guideline, the following information is provided on Wesson Firearms frames. The smallest frames are Models 738P and 38P. Small frame models include 22, 722, 22M, 722M, 32, 732, 322, 7322, 8-2, 708, 9-2, 709, 14-2, 714, 15-2, and 715-2. Large frames include 41, 741, 44, 744, 45, and 745. SuperMag frame models include 40, 740, 375 (disc.), 414 (new 1995), 7414 (new 1995), 445, and 7445. Small frames are sideplate design, while large frames are solid frame construction. Dan Wesson revolvers were mfg. with solid rib barrels as standard equipment.

MODEL 8 SERVICE DA – .38 Spl. cal., similar to Model 14, recessed barrel nut. Mfg. 1971-75.

	$550	$475	$425	$375	$300	$250	$200	

MODEL 8-2 SERVICE DA – similar to Model 14, except .38 Spl. cal., recessed barrel nut. Mfg. 1975-1995.

	$550	$475	$425	$350	$300	$250	$200	*$274*

Add approx. $6 for each additional barrel length.

* ***Model 8-2 Service DA PPC*** – .38 Spl. cal., extra heavy shrouded 6 in. bull barrel with removable underweight, Hogue Gripper grips, Aristocrat sights, recessed barrel nut. Mfg. 1992 only.

	$1,000	$875	$750	$675	$550	$450	$350	*$780*

MODEL 9 TARGET DA (1970S MFG.) – similar to Model 15, except .38 Spl. cal., recessed barrel nut. Mfg. 1971-75.

	$550	$475	$425	$350	$300	$250	$200	

MODEL 9-2 TARGET DA – similar to Model 15, except .38 Spl. cal. Use same add-ons as in Model 15. Mfg. 1975-1995.

	$650	$575	$500	$450	$350	$275	$225	*$346*

This model was also available in a Pistol Pac - same specifications and values as the Model 15 Pistol Pac.

MODEL 11 SERVICE DA – .357 Mag. cal., 6 shot, 2 1/2, 4, or 6 in. interchangeable barrels, fixed sights, blue, interchangeable grips, exposed barrel nut. Mfg. 1970-71 only.

	$550	$475	$425	$350	$300	$250	$200	

Add $60 per extra barrel.

GRADING - PPGS™	100%	98%	95%	90%	80%	70%	60%	LAST MSR

MODEL 12 SERVICE DA – similar to Model 11, with adj. sights, exposed barrel nut. Mfg. 1970-71 only.

	$625	$550	$475	$425	$325	$265	$215	

MODEL 14 SERVICE DA (1970S MFG.) – .357 Mag. cal., similar to Model 11, with recessed barrel nut. Mfg. 1971-75.

	$625	$550	$475	$425	$325	$265	$215	

MODEL 14-2 SERVICE DA – .357 Mag. cal., 2 1/2, 4, 6, or 8 (disc. 1994) in. interchangeable barrels, fixed sights, blue. Mfg. 1975-1995.

	$550	$475	$425	$350	$300	$250	$200	*$274*

Add approx. $7 for each additional barrel length.

* ***Model 14-2 Service DA Fixed Barrel*** – .357 Mag. cal., 2 1/2 or 4 in. (fixed sight Service Model) barrel, satin blue finish. Mfg. 1993-95.

	$525	$450	$400	$325	$275	$225	$175	*$289*

Add $7 for 4 in. barrel.

* ***Model 14-2 Service DA PPC*** – .357 Mag. cal., extra heavy shrouded 6 in. bull barrel with removable underweight, Hogue Gripper grips, Aristocrat sights. Mfg. 1992 only.

	$1,000	$875	$750	$675	$550	$450	$350	*$780*

* ***Model 14-2 Service DA Pistol Pac*** – includes 2 1/2, 4, and 6 in. barrel assemblies, extra grip and aluminum case. Disc. 1994.

	$1,200	$1,050	$900	$825	$650	$525	$425	*$463*

MODEL 15 TARGET DA (1970S MFG.) – similar to Model 14, with adj. sights. Mfg. 1971-75.

	$625	$550	$475	$425	$325	$265	$215	

MODEL 15-2 TARGET DA – similar to Model 14, except adj. sights, available with 2, 4, 6, 8, 10, 12, or 15 in. barrels. Disc. 1995.

* ***Model 15-2 Target DA 2 in. barrel***

	$550	$475	$425	$350	$300	$250	$200	*$346*

Add approx. $8-$13 for each additional barrel length over 2 inches, $22 for VR barrel (Model 15V), or $60 for VR heavy barrel shroud (Model 15HV).

* ***Model 15-2 Target DA Fixed Barrel*** – .357 Mag. cal., 3, 4, 5, or 6 in. barrel, high bright blue finish. Mfg. 1993-95.

	$550	$475	$425	$350	$300	$250	$200	*$322*

Add approx. $9 for each barrel length over 3 in.
Add approx. $80 for compensated barrel (4, 5, or 6 in. - new 1994).

* ***Model 15-2 Target DA Gold Series*** – .357 Mag. cal., 6 or 8 in. VR heavy slotted barrel, "Gold" stamped shroud with Dan Wesson signature, smoother action (8 lb. double action pull), 18Kt. gold-plated trigger, white triangle rear sight with orange-dot Patridge front sight, exotic hardwood grips. Mfg. 1989-94.

	$800	$700	$600	$550	$450	$350	$275	*$544*

* ***Model 15-2 Target DA Pistol Pac*** – includes 2 1/2, 4, 6, and 8 in. barrel assemblies, extra grip, 4 additional front sight blades, and aluminum case. Disc. 1995.

	$1,350	$1,200	$1,000	$900	$750	$600	$450	*$629*

Add $104 for full shroud VR barrels.
Add $214 for heavy full shroud VR barrels.

MODEL 22 – .22 LR cal., double action, 6 shot, adj. sights, 2 1/2, 4, 6, 8, or 10 in. (disc. 1987) barrel, disc. 1995.

	$625	$550	$475	$425	$325	$265	$215	*$357*

Add approx. $9 for each additional barrel length, $21 for VR, $57 for vent. heavy rib shroud.

* ***Model 22 Pistol Pac*** – includes 2 1/2, 4, 6, and 8 in. barrel assemblies, extra grip, 4 additional front sight blades, and aluminum case. Disc. 1995.

	$1,500	$1,325	$1,125	$1,000	$825	$675	$525	*$653*

Add $103 for full shroud VR barrels.
Add $227 for heavy full shroud VR barrels.

* ***Model 22 Silhouette*** – .22 LR cal., choice of 10 in. vent. or heavy vent. barrel, single action only, combat style grip, narrow rear sight blade and Patridge front. Mfg. 1992-95.

	$650	$575	$500	$450	$350	$275	$225	*$474*

Add $18 for vent. heavy barrel.

GRADING - PPGS™	100%	98%	95%	90%	80%	70%	60%	LAST MSR

MODEL 22M – .22 WMR cal., otherwise similar to Model 22. Disc. 1994.

	$650	$575	$500	$450	$350	$275	$225	*$349*

* ***Model 22M Pistol Pac*** – includes 2 1/2, 4, 6, and 8 in. barrel assemblies, extra grip, 4 additional front sight blades, and aluminum case. Disc. 1994.

	$2,250	$1,975	$1,650	$1,525	$1,250	$1,000	$750	*$637*

Add $101 for full shroud VR barrels.
Add $191 for heavy full shroud VR barrels.

MODEL 32 – .32 H&R Mag. cal., 2 1/2, 4, 6, or 8 in. barrel, adj. rear sight, interchangeable colored front sight blades, blue finish, checkered target grips. Mfg. 1986-95.

	$800	$700	$600	$550	$450	$350	$275	*$357*

Add $21 for VR barrel shroud (Model 32-V), $57 for VR heavy barrel shroud (Model 32-VH), approx. $9 for each additional barrel length over 2 1/2 in.

* ***Model 32 Pistol Pac*** – includes 2 1/2, 4, 6, and 8 in. barrel assemblies, extra grip, 4 additional front sight blades, and aluminum case. Disc. 1995.

	$2,250	$1,975	$1,650	$1,525	$1,250	$1,000	$750	*$653*

Add $103 for full shroud VR barrels.
Add $227 for heavy full shroud VR barrels.

MODEL 38P – .38 +P cal., 5 shot, 6 1/2 in. barrel, fixed sights, wood or rubber grips, 24.6 oz. Mfg. 1992-93.

	$550	$475	$425	$350	$300	$250	$200	*$285*

MODEL 322 – .32-20 WCF cal., 2 1/2, 4, 6, or 8 in. barrel, adj. rear sight, interchangeable colored front sight blades, blue finish, checkered target grips. Mfg. 1991-95.

	$550	$475	$425	$350	$300	$250	$200	*$357*

Add $21 for VR barrel shroud (Model 322-V), $57 for VR heavy barrel shroud (Model 322-VH), approx. $9-$30 for each additional barrel length over 2 1/2 in.

* ***Model 322 Pistol Pac*** – includes 2 1/2, 4, 6, and 8 in. barrel assemblies, extra grip, 4 additional front sight blades, and aluminum case. Disc. 1995.

	$2,250	$1,975	$1,650	$1,525	$1,250	$1,000	$750	*$653*

Add $103 for full shroud VR barrels.
Add $227 for heavy full shroud VR barrels.

MODEL 375 SUPERMAG – .375 Super Mag. cal., 4, 6, 8, or 10 in. VR barrel, adj. rear sight, interchangeable front and rear sight blades, bright blue finish, smooth target grips. Mfg. 1986-94.

	$1,000	$875	$750	$675	$550	$450	$350	*$498*

Add approx. $15 for each barrel length after 6 in., $39 for slotted shroud (Model 375-V8S, 8 in. barrel only), $10-$12 for VR heavy shroud (Model 375-VH).

MODEL 40 (.357 SUPERMAG) – .357 Super Mag. cal. (.357 Max.), double action, 6 shot, 4, 6, 8, or 10 in. barrel VR. Disc. 1995.

	$1,000	$875	$750	$675	$550	$450	$350	*$502*

Add $87 for slotted barrel shroud (8 in. barrel only), $22-$129 for heavy VR barrel, approx. $33 for each additional barrel length.

MODEL 41 – .41 Mag. cal., double action, 6 shot, 4, 6, 8, or 10 in. barrel VR. Disc. 1995.

	$800	$700	$600	$550	$450	$350	$275	*$447*

Add approx. $20 for heavy barrel shroud, approx. $15 for each additional barrel length.

* ***Model 41 Pistol Pac*** – includes 6 and 8 in. VR barrel assemblies, extra grip, 2 additional front sight blades, and aluminum case. Disc. 1995.

	$2,250	$1,975	$1,650	$1,525	$1,250	$1,000	$750	*$678*

Add $53 for full shroud VR barrels.

MODEL 414 SUPERMAG – .414 Super Mag. cal., 4, 6, 8, or 10 in. VR barrel, adj. rear sight, interchangeable front and rear sight blades (optional), bright blue finish, smooth target grips. Mfg. 1995 only.

	$1,200	$1,050	$900	$825	$650	$525	$425	*$519*

Add approx. $14 for each barrel length after 4 in., $58 for slotted shroud (Model 414-V8S, 8 in. barrel only), approx. $23 for VR heavy rib shroud.

MODEL 44 – .44 Mag. cal., double action, similar to Model 41, adj. sights. Disc. 1995.

	$650	$575	$500	$450	$350	$275	$225	*$447*

Add approx. $20 for heavy barrel shroud, approx. $15 for each additional barrel length.

GRADING - PPGS™	100%	98%	95%	90%	80%	70%	60%	LAST MSR

* ***Model 44 Target Fixed Barrel*** – .44 Mag. cal., 4, 5, 6, or 8 in. barrel, high bright blue finish. Mfg. 1994-95.

$550 $475 $425 $350 $300 $250 $200 *$447*

Add approx. $4 for each barrel length over 3 in.

* ***Model 44 Pistol Pac*** – includes 6 and 8 in. VR barrel assemblies, extra grip, 4 additional front sight blades, and aluminum case. Disc. 1995.

$2,250 $1,975 $1,650 $1,525 $1,250 $1,000 $750 *$678*

Add $53 for full shroud VR barrels.

MODEL 45 – .45 LC cal., 4, 6, 8, or 10 in. VR barrel, same frame as Model 44V, blue finish. Mfg. 1988-95.

$650 $575 $500 $450 $350 $275 $225 *$447*

Add $20 for VR heavy barrel shroud, approx. $15 for each additional barrel length.

* ***Model 45 Pistol Pac*** – includes 6 and 8 in. VR barrel assemblies, extra grip, 2 additional front sight blades, and aluminum case. Disc. 1995.

$2,250 $1,975 $1,650 $1,525 $1,250 $1,000 $750 *$678*

Add $53 for full shroud VR barrels.

* ***Model 45 Pin Gun*** – .45 ACP cal., competition pin gun model with 5 in. vent. or heavy vent. barrel configuration, blue steel, two-stage Taylor forcing cone, 54 oz. Mfg. 1993-95.

$800 $700 $600 $550 $450 $350 $275 *$654*

Add $9 for VR heavy shroud barrel.

MODEL 445 SUPERMAG – .445 Super Mag. cal., 4, 6, 8, or 10 in. VR barrel, adj. rear sight, interchangeable front and rear sight blades (optional), bright blue finish, smooth target grips. Mfg. 1991-95.

$1,000 $875 $750 $675 $550 $450 $350 *$519*

Add approx. $14 for each barrel length after 4 in., $58 for slotted shroud (Model 445-V8S, 8 in. barrel only), approx. $23 for VR heavy rib shroud.

HUNTER SERIES – .357 Super Mag., .41 Mag., .44 Mag., or .445 Super Mag. cal., 7 1/2 in. barrel with heavy shroud, Hogue rubber finger grooved and wood presentation grips, choice of Gunworks iron sights or w/o sights with Burris base and rings, non-fluted cylinder, with or w/o compensator, approx. 4 lbs. Mfg. 1994-95.

$800 $700 $600 $550 $450 $350 $275 *$805*

Add $32 for compensated barrel.
Add $33 for scope mounts (w/o sights).

REVOLVERS: STAINLESS STEEL, 1986-1995 MFG.

Models 722, 722M, 709, 715, 732, 7322, 741V, 744V, and 745V were available in a pistol pack including 2 1/2, 4, 6, and 8 in. solid rib barrel assemblies, extra grip, 4 additional sight blades, and fitted carrying case. Last published retail prices were $712 and $785 for the standard and stainless steel models, respectively. VR or full shroud barrels were optional and were approx. priced $103 and $210, respectively.

MODEL 722 – .22 LR cal., stainless version of Model 22, use same add-ons for various barrel options. Disc. 1995.

$550 $475 $425 $375 $300 $250 $200 *$400*

* ***Model 722 Silhouette*** – .22 LR cal., choice of 10 in. vent. or heavy vent. barrel, single action only, combat style grip, narrow rear sight blade and Patridge front. Mfg. 1992-95.

$650 $575 $500 $450 $350 $275 $225 *$504*

Add $28 for heavy vent. barrel.

MODEL 722M – .22 WMR cal., otherwise similar to Model 722, use same add-ons for various barrel options. Disc. 1994.

$650 $575 $500 $450 $350 $275 $225 *$391*

MODEL 708 – .38 Spl. cal., similar to Model 8. Add approx. $6 for each additional barrel length. Disc. 1995.

$550 $475 $425 $375 $300 $250 $200 *$319*

* ***Model 708 Action Cup/PPC*** – .38 Spl. cal., extra heavy shrouded 6 in. bull barrel with removable underweight, Hogue Gripper grips, mounted Tasco Pro Point II on Action Cup, Aristocrat sights on PPC. Mfg. 1992 only.

$850 $750 $650 $575 $475 $375 $300 *$857*

Add $56 for Action Cup Model with Tasco Scope.

GRADING - PPGS™ 100% 98% 95% 90% 80% 70% 60% LAST MSR

MODEL 709 – .38 Spl. cal., target revolver, adj. sights. Also available in special order 10, 12 (disc.), or 15 (disc.) in. barrel lengths. Disc. 1995.

$550 $480 $415 $375 $305 $250 $195 *$376*

Add approx. $10 for each additional longer barrel length, approx. $19 for VR, approx. $56 for heavy VR.

MODEL 714 (INTERCHANGEABLE OR FIXED) – .357 Mag. cal., fixed sight Service Model with 2 1/2, 4, or 6 in. barrel, brushed stainless steel. Mfg. 1993-95.

$550 $480 $415 $375 $305 $250 $195 *$319*

Add approx. $6 for 4 or 6 in. barrel.

Subtract $6 for fixed barrel (2 1/2 or 4 in. barrel only).

* ***Model 714 Action Cup/PPC*** – .357 Mag. cal., extra heavy shrouded 6 in. bull barrel with removable underweight, Hogue Gripper grips, mounted Tasco Pro Point II on Action Cup, Aristocrat sights on PPC. Mfg. 1992 only.

$850 $750 $650 $575 $475 $375 $300 *$857*

Add $56 for Action Cup Model with Tasco Scope.

MODEL 715 INTERCHANGEABLE – .357 Mag. cal., 2 1/2, 4, 6, 8, or 10 in. barrel with adj. rear sight, brushed stainless steel. Mfg. 1993-95.

$550 $480 $415 $375 $305 $250 $195 *$376*

Add approx. $10 for each additional longer barrel length, approx. $19 for VR, approx. $56 for heavy VR.

* ***Model 715 Fixed Target*** – .357 Mag. cal., 3, 4, 5, or 6 in. fixed barrel, adj. rear sight. Mfg. 1993-95.

$550 $480 $415 $375 $305 $250 $195 *$345*

Add approx. $70 for compensated barrel (4, 5, or 6 in. - new 1994).

MODEL 732 – .32 H&R Mag. cal., similar to Model 32, except is stainless steel. Mfg. 1986-95.

$650 $575 $500 $450 $350 $275 $225 *$400*

Add $22 for VR barrel shroud (Model 732-V), $53 for VR heavy barrel shroud (Model 732-VH), approx. $9 for each additional barrel length over 2 1/2 in.

MODEL 738P – .38 +P cal., 2, 4, or 6 1/2 in. barrel, 5 shot cylinder, stainless steel, groove in top strap rear and ramp front fixed sights, rubber or wood grips, 24.6 oz. Mfg. 1992-95.

$550 $480 $415 $375 $305 $250 $195 *$340*

MODEL 7322 – .32-20 WCF cal., similar to Model 322, except is stainless steel. Mfg. 1991-95.

$650 $575 $500 $450 $350 $275 $225 *$400*

Add $22 for VR barrel shroud (Model 7322-V), $53 for VR heavy barrel shroud (Model 7322-VH), approx. $9 for each additional barrel length over 2 1/2 in.

MODEL 740V - .357 SUPERMAG – .357 Max. cal., 4, 6, 8, or 10 in. barrel, adj. rear sight with interchangeable front and rear blades, high polished finish, smooth target grips. Mfg. 1986-95.

$850 $750 $650 $575 $475 $375 $300 *$567*

Add approx. $20 for each additional barrel length after 4 in., $78 with vent. slotted shroud (only avail. with 8 in. barrel), $20 for VR heavy barrel shroud (Model 740-VH).

MODEL 741V – .41 Mag. cal., similar to Model 41V. Disc. 1995.

$800 $700 $600 $550 $450 $350 $275 *$524*

Add approx. $20 for heavy VR, approx. $13 for each barrel length over 4 in.

MODEL 744V – .44 Mag. cal., similar to Model 44V. Disc. 1995. - limited mfg.

$800 $700 $600 $550 $450 $350 $275 *$524*

Add approx. $20 for heavy VR, $13 for each barrel length over 4 in.

* ***Model 744V Target Fixed Barrel*** – .44 Mag. cal., 4, 5, 6, or 8 in. barrel, brushed stainless steel. Mfg. 1994-95.

$700 $600 $550 $500 $400 $300 $250 *$493*

Add approx. $4 for each barrel length over 3 in.

* ***Model 744 Commemorative***

$800 $700 $600 $550 $450 $350 $275

MODEL 745V – .45 LC cal., similar to Model 45, except in stainless steel. Disc. 1995.

$800 $700 $600 $550 $450 $350 $275 *$524*

Add $20 for heavy full shroud VR barrels, $13 for each additional barrel length.

MODEL 745 PIN GUN – .45 ACP cal., similar to Model 45 Pin Gun, except is stainless steel. Mfg. 1993-95.

$800 $700 $600 $550 $450 $350 $275 *$713*

Add $49 for VR heavy rib shroud.

GRADING - PPGS™	100%	98%	95%	90%	80%	70%	60%	LAST MSR

MODEL 7414 SUPERMAG – .414 Super Mag. cal., 4, 6, 8, or 10 in. VR barrel, adj. rear sight, interchangeable front and rear sight blades (optional), bright blue finish, smooth target grips. Mfg. 1995 only.

$1,000 $875 $750 $675 $550 $450 $350 *$596*

Add approx. $14 for each barrel length after 4 in., $74 for slotted shroud (Model 7414-V8S, 8 in. barrel only), approx. $25 for VR heavy rib shroud.

MODEL 7445 SUPERMAG – .445 Super Mag. cal., 4, 6, 8, or 10 in. VR barrel, adj. rear sight, interchangeable front and rear sight blades (optional), high polished finish, smooth target grips. Mfg. 1991-95.

$1,000 $875 $750 $675 $550 $450 $350 *$596*

Add approx. $17 for each barrel length after 6 in., $74 for slotted shroud (Model 7445-VH8S, 8 in. barrel only), approx. $25 for VR heavy rib shroud, approx. $40 for VR heavy shroud and interchangeable sights (Model 7445-VH).

SUPER RAM SILHOUETTE – .357 Max., .414 Super Mag., or .44 Mag. cal., silhouette variation featuring modified Iron Sight Gun Works rear sight, Allen Taylor throated barrel, factory trigger job, 4 lbs. Mfg. 1995 only.

$1,000 $875 $750 $675 $550 $450 $350 *$807*

Add $43 for .414 Super Mag. cal.

HUNTER SERIES – .357 Super Mag., .41 Mag., .44 Mag., or .445 Super Mag. cal., 7 1/2 in. barrel with heavy shroud, Hogue rubber finger grooved and wood presentation grips, choice of Gunworks iron sights or w/o sights with Burris base and rings, non-fluted cylinder, with or w/o compensator, approx. 4 lbs. Mfg. 1994-95.

$1,000 $875 $750 $675 $550 $450 $350 *$849*

Add $32 for compensated barrel.
Add $32 for scope mounts (w/o sights).

REVOLVERS: DOUBLE ACTION, CURRENT/RECENT MFG.

Dan Wesson has also manufactured a variety of revolver packages that were available by special order only.

MODEL 44-AGS (ALASKAN GUIDE SPECIAL) – .445 SuperMag. cal., 6 shot, stainless steel, compensated 4 in. heavy barrel with VR and full ejector shroud, black Teflon metal finish, rubber wraparound finger groove grips, fully adj. sights. Mfg. 2002-2004, resumed 2006-2007.

$1,075 $950 $850 $725 $650 $550 $475 *$1,295*

MODEL 715 SMALL FRAME SERIES – .357 Mag. cal., 6 shot, stainless steel, 2 1/2, 4, 6, 8, or 10 in. heavy barrel with VR and full ejector shroud, rubber wraparound finger groove grips, interchangeable barrels. Mfg. 2002-2004.

$625 $550 $475 $425 $375 $325 $275 *$709*

Add $50 for 4 in., $90 for 6 in., $150 for 8 in., or $190 for 10 in. barrel.

This model was also available as a pistol pack with four barrels and case. MSR was $1,699.

MODEL 715 – .357 Mag. cal., 6 shot, SA/DA, 6 in. heavy VR barrel with full shroud, stainless steel, adj. target rear sight with interchangeable front sight, Hogue finger grooved rubber grips, includes hard case, 38 oz. Mfg. 2011-2012.

$1,025 $900 $775 $650 $525 $425 $325 *$1,168*

Barrel assemblies and grips for this model are interchangeable with those on the older Dan Wesson Model 15-2 and later variations.

MODEL 715 (RECENT MFG.) – .357 Mag. cal., DA/SA, 6 in. stainless steel barrel, stainless frame, 6 shot, adj. sights, transfer bar safety, heavy vent. shroud profile (HV6), black rubber grips, shipped in a custom Dan Wesson hardcase, includes three additional barrel assemblies and factory supplied barrel wrench kit, 2.36 lbs. Mfg. 2015-2019.

$1,325 $1,150 $995 $900 $725 $625 $525 *$1,558*

Barrel assemblies and grips for this model are interchangeable with those on the older Dan Wesson Model 15-2 and later variations.

MODEL 715 PISTOL PACK – .357 Mag./.38 Spl. cal., DA/SA, stainless frame, includes 4, 6, and 8 in. barrel/shroud assemblies (heavy vent. shroud profile), adj. sights, black rubber grips, transfer bar safety, shipped in a custom Dan Wesson hardcase with compartments for additional barrel assemblies and a factory-supplied barrel wrench kit, brushed stainless finish. Mfg. 2016-2020.

$1,700 $1,500 $1,275 $1,150 $925 $750 $650 *$1,999*

MODEL 741 LARGE FRAME SERIES – .41 Mag. cal., 6 shot, stainless steel, 4, 6, 8, or 10 in. heavy barrel with VR and full ejector shroud, rubber wraparound finger groove grips, raked hammer, interchangeable barrels. Mfg. 2002-2004.

$725 $650 $575 $500 $450 $400 $350 *$829*

Add $30 for 6 in., $110 for 8 in., or $170 for 10 in. barrel.

GRADING - PPGS™	100%	98%	95%	90%	80%	70%	60%	LAST MSR

MODEL 7445 SUPERMAG FRAME SERIES – .445 SuperMag. cal., 6 shot, stainless steel, 4, 6, 8, or 10 in. heavy barrel with VR and full ejector shroud, rubber wraparound finger groove grips, interchangeable barrels. Mfg. 2002-2004, resumed 2006-2007.

	$965	$875	$775	$675	$600	$525	$450	*$1,070*

MODEL 7460 – .45 ACP, .45 Auto Rim., .445 Super Mag., .45 Win. Mag., or .450 Rowland cal., Mfg. 1999-disc.

	$800	$725	$650	$575	$500	$450	$400	

RIFLES: BOLT ACTION

COYOTE CLASSIC – .22 LR or .22 WMR cal., 22 3/4 in. tapered barrel, 6 or 10 shot mag., checkered hardwood stock and forend, adj. rear sight. Limited mfg. 2002 only.

	$200	$180	$160	$145	$130	$115	$100	*$239*

COYOTE TARGET – .22 LR or .22 WMR cal., 18 3/8 in. heavy bull barrel, 6 or 10 shot mag., uncheckered target hardwood stock with high cheekpiece, w/o sights. Limited mfg. 2002 only.

	$230	$200	$175	$155	$145	$135	$125	*$279*

DANE ARMORY LLC

Previous AR-15 style rifle manufacturer located in Mesa, AZ until 2013.

Please refer to BlueBookOfGunValues.com to order the *Blue Book of AR-15s & Variations*, available as a book or online subscription.

DANIEL DEFENSE

Current AR-15 style rifle, pistol, and bolt action rifle manufacturer located in Black Creek, GA, with facilities also located in Ridgeland, SC.

PISTOLS: SEMI-AUTO

DDMK18 – 5.56 NATO cal., GIO, 10.3 in. CHF Govt. profile barrel with DD improved flash suppressor, flared magwell, pistol receiver extension, SB Tactical SBA3 pistol stabilizing brace, ambi QD swivel point, glass filled polymer pistol grip with Soft Touch overmolding, MK18 RIS II rail system, ambi GRIP-N-RIP charging handle, includes DD full-latch impact plastic case, black or FDE hardcoat anodized finish, 5.4 lbs. New 2015.

MSR $1,967	$1,725	$1,550	$1,425	$1,300	$1,100	$850	$675	

Add $281 for Law Tactical Gen3M folding adaptor w/SB Tactical SOB brace (new 2016).

DDM4300 – .300 AAC Blackout cal., 10.3 in. CHF S2W barrel with DD improved flash suppressor, pistol length gas system, pinned low profile gas block, 30 shot Magpul PMAG, polymer pistol grip with Soft Touch overmolding, black finish, 5.3 lbs. Mfg. 2015-2018.

	$1,625	$1,450	$1,325	$1,200	$1,025	$800	$625	*$1,836*

DDM4 PDW – .300 AAC Blackout cal., 7 in. CHF S2W profile barrel, DD linear compensator, flared magwell, Maxim Defense CQB pistol brace, 6 in. MFR XL flat front M-LOK handguard, SLR M-LOK MOD2 plain front handstop, pistol grip, ambi safety selector, black finish, 5.7 lbs. New 2020.

MSR $1,940	$1,700	$1,525	$1,400	$1,275	$1,075	$850	$675	

DDM4V7P – 5.56 NATO or .300 AAC Blackout cal., GIO, 10.3 in. CHF Govt. profile barrel with DD improved flash suppressor, carbine length gas system, low profile gas block, AR pistol receiver extension w/SB Tactical SOB (disc. 2019) or SBA3 (new 2020) pistol stabilizing brace, MFR9.0 M-LOK handguard, Daniel Defense pistol grip with integral trigger guard and Soft Touch overmolding, Type III hardcoat anodized black or Mil-Spec+ Cerakote finish, 5.4 lbs. New 2018.

MSR $1,798	$1,575	$1,425	$1,300	$1,175	$1,000	$775	$625	

Add $173 for "Mil-Spec +" Cerakote finish.
Add $281 for Law Tactical Gen3M folding adaptor.

RIFLES: BOLT ACTION

DELTA 5 – 7mm-08 Rem. (disc. 2020), 6.5 Creedmoor, or .308 Win. cal., stainless steel action with integral recoil lug, 20 or 24 in. stainless steel CHF interchangeable barrel, 5 shot PMAG, accepts AICS pattern mags., Timney Elite Hunter single stage adj. trigger, carbon fiber reinforced polymer ergonomic stock with adj. comb and LOP, removable bolt knob, Picatinny scope base, 14 total M-LOK points along forend with one point on bottom of buttstock, three M-LOK QD sling points, black or FDE (mfg. 2020 only) finish, 8.9-9.5 lbs. New 2019.

MSR $1,799	$1,550	$1,350	$1,150	$1,050	$850	$700	$550	

Add $1,596 for Accuracy Package (includes 6.5 Creedmoor, 24 in. barrel w/Nightforce SHV 4-14x50 rifle scope and Atlas bipod w/Picatinny rail mount). New late 2019.

GRADING - PPGS™	100%	98%	95%	90%	80%	70%	60%	LAST MSR

DELTA 5 PRO – .308 Win., 6.5 Creedmoor, or 6mm Creedmoor cal., stainless steel action w/integral recoil lug, 20, 24, or 26 in. CHF Heavy Palma or Varmint profile barrel w/Cerakote finish, Area 419 Hellfire muzzle brake, 10 shot Magpul PMAG, adj. single stage Timney Elite Hunter trigger, user configurable aluminum chassis w/fully adj. stock, integrated M-LOK, QD sling attachment points, integral ARCA lock rail, Daniel Defense grip, uses AR-15 grips, 2-pos. safety, 3-lug bolt and floating bolt head, Picatinny scope base, thumb rest, includes plastic case, black, Olive Drab, or Coyote Tan finish, approx. 11 lbs. New 2021.

MSR $2,499 $2,100 $1,850 $1,600 $1,450 $1,150 $950 $750

RIFLES/CARBINES: SEMI-AUTO

In addition to the models listed below, Daniel Defense can build a custom rifle based on customer specifications. Please contact the company directly for this service. Daniel Defense also offers a complete line of tactical accessories and parts. All carbines and rifles come with a limited lifetime warranty. For information on Daniel Defense's Ambush line of hunting rifles please refer to Ambush Firearms in the "A" section.

DDM4 CARBINE SERIES – 5.56 NATO cal., GIO, 16 in. chrome-lined barrel, A2 birdcage flash hider, 10, 20, or 30 shot mag., Mil-Spec enhanced magwell, A4 feed ramp, A1.5 BUIS sight, pinned "F" marked front sight base, Omega X rails, Magpul 5-position collapsible buttstock (disc.) or Daniel Defense pistol grip and buttstock with Soft Touch overmolding, A2 vertical grip, includes plastic case.

* ***DDM4V1*** – 5.56 NATO cal., GIO, 16 in. chrome-lined M4 standard or lightweight (new 2012) barrel, curved and serrated front sight, Magpul MOE stock (disc.) or DD buttstock w/Soft Touch overmolding, DDM4 rail, QD swivel attachment points, A2 grip (disc.) or DD pistol grip w/Soft Touch overmolding, original Daniel Defense rifle, black anodized finish, 6.7 lbs.

MSR $1,946 $1,725 $1,525 $1,400 $1,275 $1,075 $850 $675

* ***DDM4V2*** – 5.56 NATO cal., GIO, 16 in. chrome-lined barrel, similar to DDM4V1, except lightweight configuration with Omega X 7.0 rail system, also available with lightweight carbine barrel (DDM4V2LW). Mfg. 2011-2013.

$1,550 $1,400 $1,275 $1,150 $975 $775 $600 ***$1,759***

* ***DDM4V3*** – 5.56 NATO or 6.8 SPC (mfg. 2012-2015) cal., GIO, 16 in. chrome-lined Government profile barrel or lightweight carbine barrel (DDM4V3LW, disc. 2015) with flash suppressor, curved and serrated front sight, 9 in. free float Omega quad rail, black finish, 6 1/2 lbs. Disc. 2016.

$1,575 $1,425 $1,300 $1,175 $1,000 $775 $625 ***$1,799***

* ***DDM4V4*** – 5.56 NATO cal., GIO, 16 in. CHF carbine barrel, pinned low profile gas block, Omega X 9.0 rail system, available in lightweight profile (disc. 2011), no sights, fixed sights, or flip-up sights. Disc. 2013.

$1,450 $1,300 $1,175 $1,075 $900 $700 $550 ***$1,639***

Add $120 for fixed sights.
Add $299 for flip-up sights (disc. 2011).

* ***DDM4V5*** – 5.56 NATO or .300 AAC Blackout (mfg. mid-2012-2014) cal., GIO, 16 in. CHF Govt. or lightweight barrel, DD improved flash suppressor, 30 shot mag., no sights, fixed sights, or flip-up sights (disc. 2011), pinned low profile gas block, Omega X (disc.) or DD M4 12.0 rail system, DD pistol grip buttstock with Soft Touch overmolding, Type III hardcoat anodized black, Daniel Defense Tornado, or Mil-Spec+ Cerakote (disc. 2016) finish, 6.4 or 6.15 (lightweight) lbs. Disc. 2019.

$1,575 $1,400 $1,275 $1,175 $975 $775 $600 ***$1,773***

Add $168 for Daniel Defense Tornado or Mil-Spec+ Cerakote (disc. 2016) finish.
Add $299 for flip-up sights (disc. 2011).

» **DDM4V5S** – 5.56 NATO cal., GIO, 14 1/2 in. (16.1 w/muzzle) Govt. profile chrome moly barrel w/ permanently attached ext. DD improved flash suppressor, Daniel Defense buttstock, vertical grip and pistol grip, DDM4 Rail 12.0 with Mil-Std Picatinny rail with QD swivel attachment points, Type III hardcoat anodized black or Mil-Spec+ Cerakote finish, 6.23 lbs. Mfg. 2016-2017.

$1,650 $1,475 $1,350 $1,225 $1,025 $800 $625 ***$1,857***

Add $67 for Mil-Spec+ Cerakote finish.

* ***DDM4V7/DDM4V7 LW*** – 5.56 NATO or 6.8 SPC (disc. 2014) cal., GIO, 16 (5.56 NATO) or 18 (6.8 SPC, disc. 2014) in. Govt. or lightweight barrel with flash hider (disc.) or DD improved flash suppressor (new 2017), 30 shot mag., with or w/o sights, DD pistol grip and buttstock with Soft Touch overmolding, flat-top receiver, full-length top Picatinny rail, forearm features three modular Picatinny rails that are moveable (disc.) or free floating MFR XS 15.0 M-LOK handguard (new 2017), Type III hardcoat anodized black, Mil-Spec+, Tornado (new 2017), Rattlecan (new 2019), or Deep Woods (new mid-2017) Cerakote finish, 6 1/2 lbs. New 2012.

MSR $1,798 $1,575 $1,425 $1,300 $1,175 $1,000 $775 $625

GRADING - PPGS™	100%	98%	95%	90%	80%	70%	60%	LAST MSR

Add $110 for fixed sights.
Add $173 for Mil-Spec+, Tornado (new 2017), Rattlecan (new 2019), or Deep Woods (new mid-2017) Cerakote finish.

* ***DDM4V7 PRO*** – 5.56 NATO cal., GIO, low profile gas block, 18 in. S2W profile CHF steel barrel, Daniel Defense Muzzle Climb Mitigator, 30 shot Magpul PMAG, flared magwell, Geissele Automatics Super Dynamic 3 Gun trigger, Daniel Defense polymer buttstock and pistol grip with Soft Touch overmolding, Mil-Spec upper and lower receivers, M4 feed ramps, M16 profile bolt carrier group, 15 in. MFR XS M-LOK rail, full-length top Picatinny rail, VLTOR Gunfighter Mod 4 charging handle, 6-position Mil-Spec aluminum receiver extension, includes full latch impact plastic case, Type III hardcoat anodized black, Rattlecan (new 2019), or Gun Metal Gray Cerakote (new 2021) finish, 7.4 lbs. New mid-2016.

MSR $2,079	$1,825	$1,650	$1,500	$1,375	$1,150	$900	$700	

Add $173 for Rattlecan finish (new 2019).
Add $180 for Gun Metal Gray Cerakote finish (new 2021).

* ***DDM4V7 SLW*** – 5.56 NATO cal., GIO, 14 1/2 in. CHF lightweight profile barrel, mid-length gas system, low profile gas block, permanently attached ext. flash suppressor, 32 shot mag., polymer buttstock and pistol grip w/Soft Touch overmolding, DD free floating MFR 13.5 in. M-LOK handguard, full-length top Picatinny rail, Type III hardcoat anodized black or Daniel Defense Deep Woods finish, 31 1/2 - 34 3/4 in. OAL, 5.9 lbs. New 2019.

MSR $1,877	$1,650	$1,475	$1,350	$1,225	$1,050	$825	$650	

Add $173 for Daniel Defense Deep Woods finish.

* ***DDM4V9*** – 5.56 NATO cal., GIO, 16 in. Govt. profile chrome moly barrel, low profile gas block, mid-length gas system, Daniel Defense flash suppressor, 30 shot PMAG, CNC machined aluminum upper and lower receiver, glass filled polymer adj. buttstock with Soft Touch overmolding, flared magwell, vertical grip and pistol grip, 15 in. quad rail aluminum handguard, 3 low profile rail ladders, 6-position receiver extension, no sights, M16 chrome-lined bolt carrier group, H buffer, hardcoat anodized finish, 6.6 lbs. New 2014.

MSR $1,899	$1,675	$1,500	$1,375	$1,250	$1,050	$825	$650	

» **DDM4V9 S2W (Strength to Weight)** – 5.56 NATO cal., similar to DDM4V9, except has 18 in. CHF S2W profile barrel, black finish, 7 1/2 lbs. Mfg. 2014-2015.

	$1,500	$1,325	$1,225	$1,100	$925	$725	$575	*$1,689*

» **DDM4V9 Lightweight** – 5.56 NATO cal., similar to DDM4V9, except has 16 in. lightweight profile barrel and Daniel Defense Tornado Cerakote finish, 6.34 lbs. Mfg. 2014-2016.

	$1,625	$1,450	$1,325	$1,200	$1,025	$800	$625	*$1,840*

* ***DDM4V11/DDM4V11 LW*** – 5.56 NATO cal., GIO, 16 in. CHF Govt. or lightweight (disc.) barrel, iron sights, DD improved flash suppressor, 15 in. KeyMod SLiM rail, top Picatinny rail, iron sights, DD pistol grip and buttstock with Soft Touch overmolding, Type III hardcoat anodized black, Cerakote finish in Mil-Spec+ (mfg. 2015-2019), Tornado (mfg. 2015-2019), Deep Woods (mfg. mid-2017-2018), or Kryptek Typhon (mfg. 2016-2019), 6.28 lbs. New 2015.

MSR $1,798	$1,575	$1,425	$1,300	$1,175	$1,000	$775	$625	

Add $52 for Kryptek Typhon finish (mfg. 2016-2019).
Add $168 for Deep Woods Cerakote finish (mfg. mid-2017-2018).
Add $223 for Mil-Spec+ or Tornado Cerakote finish (mfg. 2015-2019).

* ***DDM4V11 PRO*** – 5.56 NATO cal., GIO, 18 in. CHF S2W barrel with DD Gen II Muzzle Climb Mitigator, 30 shot Magpul PMAG, Geissele Super Dynamic 3-Gun trigger, machined aluminum upper and lower receivers with M4 feed ramps and enhanced flared magwell, 15 in. SLiM rail, VLTOR BCM Gunfighter Mod 4 charging handle, top Picatinny rail with KeyMod attachment, 6-pos. aluminum receiver extension, polymer pistol grip buttstock with Soft Touch overmolding, black hardcoat anodized or Daniel Defense Tornado Cerakote (2016-2017) finish, 7 1/2 lbs. New 2015.

MSR $2,079	$1,825	$1,650	$1,500	$1,375	$1,150	$900	$700	

Add $158 for Daniel Defense Tornado Cerakote finish (mfg. 2016-2017).

* ***DDM4V11 SLW*** – 5.56 NATO cal., AR-15 style, GIO, 14 1/2 in. (16 in. with muzzle) CHF lightweight profile barrel, permanently attached ext. flash suppressor, polymer pistol grip and buttstock with Soft Touch overmolding, free floating SLiM Rail 12.0 KeyMod handguard, full-length top Picatinny rail, Type III hardcoat anodized black, Cerakote finishes in Mil-Spec+, Daniel Defense Tornado (mfg. 2016-2017) or Deep Woods (new 2018), 6.09 lbs. Mfg. 2016-2018.

	$1,550	$1,375	$1,275	$1,150	$975	$750	$600	*$1,752*

Add $168 for Mil-Spec+, Daniel Defense Tornado (disc. 2017), or Deep Woods Cerakote finish.

GRADING - PPGS™	100%	98%	95%	90%	80%	70%	60%	LAST MSR

* ***DDM4V11 300*** – .300 AAC Blackout cal., GIO, free floating 16 in. CHF chrome moly S2W profile barrel, DD improved flash suppressor, carbine length gas system, polymer pistol grip and buttstock with Soft Touch overmolding, 15 in. free float SLiM rail KeyMod handguard, Picatinny upper rail, forged aluminum receivers, M16 BCG, Mil-Spec+ Cerakote finish, 6 3/4 lbs. Mfg. 2016-2019.

	$1,675	$1,500	$1,375	$1,250	$1,050	$825	$650	*$1,902*

DDM4 HUNTER (DDM4V7 HUNTER) – 5.56 NATO, 6.8 SPC, or .300 AAC Blackout cal., 16 (.300 AAC Blackout) or 18 in. chrome-lined heavy phosphate-coated S2W profile barrel, thread protector, two-stage Geissele trigger, free floating MFR 15.0 M-LOK rail system, Kryptek Highlander finish, 6.55-7 lbs. New 2020.

MSR $1,946	$1,725	$1,525	$1,400	$1,275	$1,075	$850	$675	

DDM4 ISR (INTEGRALLY SUPPRESSED RIFLE) – .300 AAC Blackout cal., GIO, 16.1 in. S2W barrel (9 in. barrel with permanently attached suppressor), integral suppressor, 30 shot Magpul PMAG, pistol length gas system, 12 in. modular float rail with three modular Picatinny rail sections, 6-pos. aluminum receiver extension, enhanced flared magwell, rear receiver QD swivel, M4 feed ramps, polymer pistol grip buttstock with Soft Touch overmolding, black anodized or Mil-Spec+ (new 2017) or Deep Woods (new 2018) Cerakote finish, 7 1/2 lbs. Mfg. 2015, reintroduced 2017.

MSR $3,135	$2,775	$2,475	$2,275	$2,075	$1,725	$1,350	$1,075	

Add $159 for Mil-Spec+ (new 2017) or Deep Woods (new 2018) finish.

Note: This firearm is integrally suppressed and is subject to all relevant NFA regulations. Failure to comply with these regulations may result in fines/imprisonment.

DD5V1 – .308 Win. cal., 16 in. CHF S2W profile barrel, mid-length gas system, extended DD Superior suppression device, flared magwell, integral oversized trigger guard, Geissele SSA two-stage trigger, DD pistol grip and buttstock with Soft Touch overmolding and two buttpads, ambi safety selector, 15 in. KeyMod handguard, Picatinny top rail, configurable modular charging handle, Type III hardcoat anodized black, Mil-Spec+, Deep Woods (new mid-2017), Kryptek Typhon (disc.), or Tornado (new 2017) Cerakote finish, 8.3 lbs. Mfg. 2016-2019.

	$2,675	$2,400	$2,200	$2,000	$1,675	$1,325	$1,050	*$3,044*

Add $154 for Mil-Spec+, Deep Woods (new mid-2017) or Tornado (new 2017) Cerakote finish.
Add $150 for Kryptek Typhon finish (mfg. 2016 only).

* ***DD5V1M*** – .308 Win. cal., 16 in. CHF S2W profile barrel with integral DD improved flash suppressor, mid-length gas system, flared magwell, integral oversized trigger guard, Geissele SSA two-stage trigger, DD pistol grip and buttstock with Soft Touch overmolding and two buttpads, ambi safety selector, 15 in. Picatinny top rail, M-LOK handguard, configurable modular charging handle, Type III hardcoat anodized black or Deep Woods Cerakote finish, 8.3 lbs. Mfg. 2018-2019.

	$2,675	$2,400	$2,200	$2,000	$1,675	$1,325	$1,050	*$3,044*

Add $154 for Deep Woods Cerakote finish.

DD5V2 – .308 Win. cal., free floating 18 in. CHF S2W profile barrel, extended DD superior suppression device, rifle length gas system, DD pistol grip and buttstock with Soft Touch overmolding and two buttpads, 15 in. KeyMod handguard, top Picatinny rail, ambi safety selector, mag. catch, bolt release, and configurable modular charging handle, black or Daniel Defense Deep Woods (new 2018) finish, 8.6 lbs. Mfg. 2016-2019.

	$2,675	$2,400	$2,200	$2,000	$1,675	$1,325	$1,050	*$3,044*

Add $154 for Daniel Defense Deep Woods finish (new 2018).

* ***DD5V2M*** – .308 Win. cal., free floating 18 in. CHF S2W profile barrel, ext. DD superior suppression device, rifle length gas system, DD pistol grip and buttstock with Soft Touch overmolding and two buttpads, 15 in. M-LOK handguard, top Picatinny rail, ambi safety selector, mag. catch, bolt release, and configurable modular charging handle, hardcoat anodized black or Deep Woods finish, 8.6 lbs. Mfg. 2018-2019.

	$2,675	$2,400	$2,200	$2,000	$1,675	$1,325	$1,050	*$3,044*

Add $154 for Deep Woods finish.

DD5V3 – 7.62x51mm NATO or .308 Win. cal., 16 in. CHF chrome-lined S2W profile barrel, intermediate gas system, adj. gas block, 20 shot Magpul PMAG, enhanced flared magwell, Mil-Spec trigger, glass-filled polymer buttstock and pistol grip w/soft touch overmolding, safety selector, aluminum upper and lower receiver, 4-bolt connection system, 15 in. DD5 M-LOK rail, fully ambi controls, Grip-N-Rip charging handle, QD swivel attachment, Type III hardcoat anodized black finish, 8.3 lbs. New mid-2019.

MSR $2,499	$2,200	$1,975	$1,800	$1,650	$1,375	$1,075	$850	

DD5V4 – 6.5 Creedmoor or 7.62x51mm NATO cal., GIO, 18 in. CHF chrome-lined S2W profile barrel, rifle length gas system, pinned user-adj. gas block, 20 shot Magpul PMAG, enhanced flared magwell, Mil-Spec trigger, glass-filled polymer buttstock and pistol grip w/soft touch overmolding, safety selector,

GRADING - PPGS™	100%	98%	95%	90%	80%	70%	60%	LAST MSR

aluminum upper and lower receiver, 15 in. DD5 M-LOK rail, fully ambi controls, Grip-N-Rip charging handle, QD swivel attachment, includes full-latch impact plastic case, Type III hardcoat anodized black or Mil-Spec+ Cerakote finish, 8.6 lbs. New mid-2019.

MSR $2,499	$2,200	$1,975	$1,800	$1,650	$1,375	$1,075	$850	

Add $173 for Mil-Spec+ Cerakote finish.

DD5V4 HUNTER – .308 Win., 6.5 Creedmoor, or .260 Rem. cal., GIO, 18 in. CHF S2W profile barrel, rifle length gas system, adj. gas block, DD Superior Suppression muzzle device, 5 shot Magpul PMAG, two-stage Geissele SSA trigger, Daniel Defense buttstock with Soft Touch overmolding, polymer pistol grip, GRIP-N-RIP ambi charging handle, 7075-T6 aluminum receivers, enhanced flared magwell, QD swivel attachment point, 15 in. DD5 M-LOK Rail, 6-pos. Mil-Spec receiver extension, includes Daniel Defense Full-Latch Impact plastic case, 8.6 lbs. New 2019.

MSR $2,933	$2,575	$2,325	$2,125	$1,925	$1,625	$1,275	$1,000	

DD5V5 – 6.5 Creedmoor or .260 Rem. cal., GIO, 20 in. CHF chrome-lined S2W profile barrel, 20 shot Magpul PMAG, enhanced flared magwell, Mil-Spec trigger, glass-filled polymer buttstock and pistol grip w/soft touch overmolding, safety selector, aluminum receivers, 6-pos. Mil-Spec receiver extension, 4-bolt connection system, M-LOK 15 in. DD5 rail, fully ambi controls, Grip-N-Rip charging handle, QD swivel attachment, includes full-latch impact plastic case, Type III hardcoat anodized black or Mil-Spec+ Cerakote finish, 8.9 lbs. New mid-2019.

MSR $2,499	$2,200	$1,975	$1,800	$1,650	$1,375	$1,075	$850	

Add $173 for Mil-Spec+ Cerakote finish.

DD5V5 HUNTER – 6.5 Creedmoor or .260 Rem. cal., GIO, 20 in. CHF S2W profile barrel, DD Superior Suppression muzzle device, 10 shot PMAG, two-stage Geissele SSA trigger, DD buttstock with Soft Touch overmolding, polymer pistol grip, adj. gas block, GRIP-N-RIP ambi charging handle, 7075-T6 aluminum receivers, enhanced flared magwell, QD swivel attachment point, 15 in. DD5 M-LOK Rail, 6-pos. Mil-Spec receiver extension, includes Daniel Defense Full-Latch Impact plastic case, Kryptek Highlander finish, 8.9 lbs. New 2019.

MSR $2,933	$2,575	$2,325	$2,125	$1,925	$1,625	$1,275	$1,000	

DDXV/XV EZ – 5.56 NATO cal., GIO, 16 in. CHF barrel, "F" marked fixed front sight base, flared magwell on lower receiver, Magpul enhanced trigger guard, M16 BCG, rear receiver QD sling swivel attachment, with (XV EZ) or w/o (XV, disc. 2011) EZ CAR 7.0 rail system and A1 fixed rear sight, Mil-Spec buttstock. Mfg. 2010-2013.

	$1,250	$1,125	$1,025	$925	$775	$625	$475	*$1,419*

Add $68 for EZ CAR 7.0 rail system.
Add $129 for XVM model with mid-length barrel.

DDV6.8 – 6.8 SPC cal., GIO, 16 in. CHF mid-length barrel, Omega X 9.0 VFG and A1.5 fixed rear sight. Disc. 2011.

	$1,350	$1,225	$1,125	$1,000	$850	$675	$525	*$1,537*

M4A1 – 5.56 NATO cal., GIO, 14 1/2 in. CHF M4 profile barrel with permanently attached DD improved flash suppressor, carbine length gas system, pinned low profile gas block, M4A1 RIS II rail system, Type III hardcoat anodized FDE or Mil-Spec+ Cerakote finish, 6 3/4 lbs. New 2016.

MSR $2,046	$1,800	$1,625	$1,475	$1,350	$1,125	$900	$700	

Add $111 for Deep Woods Cerakote finish (mfg. mid-2017-2019).
Add $173 for Mil-Spec+ Cerakote finish.

MK12 – 5.56 NATO cal., GIO, 18 in. CHF stainless steel MK12 barrel, DD improved flash suppressor, rifle length gas system, 20 shot Magpul PMAG, upper receiver with 12 in. M4 free floating rail, Geissele SSA two-stage trigger, 6-pos. aluminum receiver extension, VLTOR Mod 4 charging handle, polymer pistol grip and buttstock with Soft Touch overmolding, Type III hardcoat anodized black, DD Tornado Cerakote (disc. 2019), DD Deep Woods (mfg. 2018-2019), or Kryptek Typhon (mfg. 2016-2017) finish, 7.41 lbs. New mid-2014.

MSR $2,248	$1,975	$1,775	$1,625	$1,475	$1,250	$975	$775	

Add $50 for Kryptek Typhon finish (mfg. 2016-2017).
Add $105 for Daniel Defense Tornado (disc. 2019) or DD Deep Woods Cerakote (mfg. 2018-2019) finish.

DARDICK

Previous manufacturer located in Hamden, CT.

CARBINES

DARDICK CARBINE CONVERSION – .22 or .38 Dardick Tround cal., 23 in. barrel (interchangeable), walnut stock. Limited mfg.

	$1,895	$1,650	$1,350	$975	$875	$750	$700	

GRADING - PPGS™	100%	98%	95%	90%	80%	70%	60%	LAST MSR

PISTOLS: SEMI-AUTO

SERIES 1100 – .38 Dardick Tround cal., double action, 11 shot mag., black finish.

	100%	98%	95%	90%	80%	70%	60%	LAST MSR
	$3,750	$3,300	$2,600	$1,975	$1,650	$1,395	$1,100	

Add 10% for original box.

Dardick ammunition in itself is collectible - currently, individual "Trounds" are selling in the $5-$10 range.

SERIES 1500 – .22, .30, or .38 Dardick Tround cal., double action, 15 shot mag., black finish.

	100%	98%	95%	90%	80%	70%	60%	LAST MSR
	$2,950	$2,495	$1,875	$1,525	$1,275	$1,000	$975	

Add 10% for original box.

D'ARCY ECHOLS & CO.

Current manufacturer beginning 1996, and located in Millville, UT.

RIFLES: BOLT ACTION

Current models include the Classic Light Sporter ($36,000 MSR), Classic Scope Sighted Heavy Sporter (MSR $37,600), Classic Iron Sighted Heavy Sporter ($37,600 MSR), Legend Standard Sporter in either right or left-hand configuration ($15,700 MSR), Legend Standard Sporter in Stainless Steel ($15,950 MSR), Legend Heavy Sporter scoped or iron sight version in right or left-hand configuration ($15,700 MSR), or Legend Heavy Sporter Stainless Steel ($15,950 MSR). Previously manufactured models include: Legend Long Range Sporter (last MSR was $15,650), and Long Range (disc. 2010, last MSR was $13,700). Additionally, many special orders and options are also available. Please contact the company directly for more information.

RIFLES: SINGLE SHOT

A new single shot rifle with Farquharson action in various calibers was released during 2012. Please contact the company directly for more information and a price quotation on this model.

DARK STORM INDUSTRIES LLC (DSI)

Current AR-15 style rifle manufacturer as well as AR-15 parts and accessories manufacturer/distributor established in late 2012, located in Oakdale, NY.

Please refer to BlueBookOfGunValues.com to order the *Blue Book of AR-15s & Variations*, available as a book or online subscription.

DARNE S.A.

Current manufacturer producing shotguns 1881-1979 and 1990 to date in Saint Etienne, France. Darne also began making double rifles circa 1996. No current U.S. importation. Previously imported until 2013 by Geoffroy Gournet, located in Easton, PA. Previously imported by The Drumming Stump, Inc. located in Circle Pines, MN circa 1996-2005, and by Wes Gilpin located in Dallas, TX until 1992.

For F. Darne Fils Ainé please refer to the F Section. Also, please refer to the Bruchet section for 1982-1990 mfg. utilizing the Darne action.

RIFLES: DOUBLE

Please contact the manufacturer directly for a current price quotation on the following models.

DARNE DAMON PETRIK O/U – 8x57R, 9.3x74R, or .30R Blaser cal.

MODEL R EXPRESS SxS – 8x57 JRS or 9.3x74R cal., double rifle version of the Darne Model R Series shotgun, many options available, including style of rib, sights, stock configuration, etc. Importation began 1996.

EXPRESS SUPERPOSEÉ – .30-06, 8x57 JRS, or 9.3.74R cal., double rifle version of the Darne O/U shotgun, boxlock with false sideplates, straight grip stock, many options available. Importation began 1996.

MODEL V EXPRESS SxS – 8x57R, 9.3x74R, .30R Blaser, or .375 H&H cal., no obturators discs.

SHOTGUNS: SxS, PRE-1980 MFG.

DARNE SLIDING BREECH SHOTGUN – 12, 16, 20, or 28 ga., SxS, unique action utilizes sliding breech lock-up, high quality mfg., 27 1/2 in. barrel standard with other lengths available, any choke combination, either straight grip or pistol grip stock, checkered, models differ in amount of engraving and grade of wood.

* ***Darne Sliding Breech Shotgun Bird Hunter Model R11***

	100%	98%	95%	90%	80%	70%	60%	LAST MSR
	$1,500	$1,350	$1,100	$950	$825	$700	$600	

GRADING - PPGS™	100%	98%	95%	90%	80%	70%	60%	LAST MSR
* ***Darne Sliding Breech Shotgun Pheasant Hunter Model R15***								
	$2,250	$2,000	$1,800	$1,625	$1,500	$1,425	$1,300	
* ***Darne Sliding Breech Shotgun Magnum Model R16***								
	$3,500	$3,150	$2,650	$2,300	$2,000	$1,750	$1,500	
* ***Darne Sliding Breech Shotgun Quail Hunter Model V19***								
	$4,500	$4,150	$3,700	$3,350	$2,850	$2,400	$1,950	
* ***Darne Sliding Breech Shotgun Model V22***								
	$5,750	$5,300	$4,600	$4,150	$3,650	$3,000	$2,500	
* ***Darne Sliding Breech Shotgun Hors Series No. 1 Model V***								
	$6,350	$5,750	$5,250	$4,500	$3,850	$3,150	$2,600	

SHOTGUNS: 1989-CURRENT MFG.

In 1990, Paul Bruchet (the old Darne plant superintendent) obtained permission to once again use the Darne trademark. Hence, all 1990 and later mfg. has been produced by Paul Bruchet.

All new manfuctured Darnes can be choked to the customer's choice. All models listed have automatic ejectors, are oil finished by hand, and may be barreled to any length (except for Models R 11, 12, and 13).

O/U Models

SB1 – similar to SB3, traditional European O/U, DT, extractors, straight or semi-pistol grip stock. Importation began 1998.

MSR POR	N/A	N/A	$2,000	$1,650	$1,450	$1,100	$950

SB2 – similar to SB3, except has scroll engraving, wood upgrade, and 28 in. barrels. Importation began 1996.

MSR POR	N/A	N/A	$2,400	$1,975	$1,625	$1,250	$1,000

SB3 – 12 or 20 ga., scalloped boxlock action, extractors, 26 in. barrels, DTs, choice of English straight grip stock or semi-pistol grip. Importation began 1996.

MSR POR	N/A	N/A	$2,900	$2,300	$1,925	$1,800	$1,650

DARNE DAMON PETRIK – 12, 16, 20 ga. or .410 bore (special order only), boxlock action, with or w/o ejectors.

This model is POR.

SxS Sliding Breech Models

Every R Model is a custom order per individual customer specifications. Current delivery time is approximately four months. The Basic R model starts at $12,000 and the Basic V Model starts at $19,000. Please contact the manufacturer directly for current price quotations on the following R and V models.

R 11 – 12, 16, 20, 28 ga., or .410 bore, half pistol grip stock, light engraving.

R 12 – similar to R 11, except with better engraving.

R 13 – 12, 16, or 20 ga., straight or pistol grip stock, traditional action with bouquet engraving and obturator discs.

R 14 – 12, 16, or 20 ga., slug gun, choice of forearms, light engraving, and optional cheek rest pistol grip stock was optional. Importation disc. circa 2002.

N/A	$3,225	$2,675	$2,250	$1,950	$1,750	$1,200	*$6,600*

R 15 – 12, 16, 20, 24, 28 ga., or .410 bore, select walnut stock and forearm with fine checkering, large scroll engraving, obturator discs.

R 16 – same as R 15, except has 3 in. chambers. Importation disc. circa 2002.

N/A	$3,450	$2,800	$2,350	$2,000	$1,750	$1,200	*$7,800*

R 17 – 12 (including Mag.), 16, 20, 24, 28 ga., or .410 bore, Magnum model (3 in. chambers), customer's choice engraving patterns, superior quality wood finish. Importation disc. circa 2002.

N/A	$5,125	$4,600	$3,625	$2,900	$2,450	$1,975	*$8,900*

RHS – all gauges, top-of-the-line model incorporating customer's choice of engraving style, type of inlays, and checkering pattern, best quality wood. Due to the unique nature of this model, each specimen must be appraised individually. New guns are priced per individual customer order.

V 19 – all gauges, easy opening large key action, top quality walnut and checkering, full coverage rose and scroll engraving with chiseled fences.

GRADING - PPGS™	100%	98%	95%	90%	80%	70%	60%	LAST MSR

V 20 - similar to V 19, except has deep relief rose engraving and chiseled fences. Importation disc. circa 2002.

	N/A	$6,600	$5,500	$4,400	$3,200	$2,550	$2,000	*$12,300*

V 21 - similar to V 19, except has 100% coverage English rose and scroll engraving and chiseled fences. Importation disc. circa 2002.

	N/A	$7,600	$6,500	$5,500	$4,400	$3,200	$2,550	*$14,400*

V 22 - similar to V 21, except has 100% engraving coverage featuring bouquet patterns and deeply chiseled fences, sculpted shoulders, best quality walnut.

V 28 - top-of-the-line V model with elaborate engraving and best quality wood.

	N/A	$8,500	$7,250	$6,000	$4,750	$3,500	$2,950	

VHS - all gauges, top-of-the-line model incorporating customer's choice of engraving style, type of inlays, and checkering pattern, best quality wood. Due to the unique nature of this model, each specimen must be appraised individually. New guns are priced per individual customer order.

DASAN

Trademark of AR-15s and semi-auto pistols manufactured by Dasan Machineries located in South Korea. Currently imported (parts and accessories only) by Dasan USA beginning in 2019, located in Duluth, GA.

DAUDSONS ARMOURY

Current manufacturer located in Peshawar, Pakistan. No current U.S. importation.

Daudsons Armoury's origins stretch back over two centuries dealing in the sporting arms and defense firearms trade. The company provides firearms for the armed forces of Pakistan as well as the Defense Ministry.

Daudsons Armoury manufactures the DSA line of 12 ga. shotguns. Basic models include: DSA Royal, DSA Regal, DSA Super Deluxe, DSA Shooter, DSA Commando, DSA Sure Shot, and the DSA Security. All are manufactured from high grade alloy steel, with black synthetic stocks and forearms, and all parts are completely interchangeable. Daudsons also manufactures double barrel rifles and a semi-auto .22 cal. rifle. For more information on these guns, including pricing and U.S. availability, please contact the company directly.

DAVID MILLER CO.

Current custom rifle manufacturer located in Tucson, AZ since 1973.

The David Miller Co., composed of David Miller and Curt Crum, is a custom rifle shop building best quality bolt action rifles only. All guns are built per individual custom order and the company should be contacted directly for more information and price quotations.

All currently crafted rifles from the David Miller Co. are made using highly modified and finished Winchester Model 70 Classic actions or, on rare occasion, a Weatherby Mark V action. Three models of rifles are crafted in the Miller shop, the Classic, the Marksmen, and the GraGun. The Classic is the top-of-the-line in custom bolt action rifles available today and is priced starting at $61,000. The Marksmen is equally well constructed, but without many of the very labor-intensive features and is standard with a laminated wood stock rather than top quality walnut. The Marksmen is intended as a serious hunting rifle and has a starting price of $35,000. The latest model is the GraGun, with a base price starting at $35,000 and features a Bansner synthetic stock in two colors. The waiting period for any of the models is about 2-1/2 years. Please contact the David Miller Co. directly for a quotation on a new rifle.

Used rifles should be individually appraised to ascertain current values. Very few genuine Miller rifles ever appear on the used gun market. Used Miller rifles can be authenticated by the David Miller Co.

DAVIDSON FIREARMS

Previously manufactured by Fábrica de Armas, located in Eibar, Spain.

SHOTGUNS: SxS

MODEL 63B - 12, 16, 20, 28 ga., or .410 bore, 25, 26, 28, or 30 in. barrels, Anson & Deeley boxlock, engraved and nickel plated frame, various chokes, walnut checkered stock. Mfg. 1963-disc.

	$350	$315	$275	$250	$225	$200	$175	

Add 30% for 28 ga. or .410 bore.

* ***Model 63B Magnum*** - similar to 63B, except 10 ga. Mag., 12, or 20 ga. Mag., 32 in. barrel.

12 or 20 ga.	$395	$360	$325	$275	$230	$195	$165	
10 ga.	$425	$375	$330	$300	$275	$250	$225	

MODEL 69SL - 12 or 20 ga., true detachable sidelock action, engraved nickel plated action, 26 in. and 28 in. barrels, imp. cyl. and mod., mod. and full, checkered walnut stock. Mfg. 1963-76.

	$415	$395	$375	$340	$320	$290	$260	

GRADING - PPGS™	100%	98%	95%	90%	80%	70%	60%	LAST MSR

MODEL 73 STAGECOACH – 12 or 20 ga., detachable sidelock, exposed hammers, 3 in. chambers, 20 in. mod. and full barrels, checkered walnut stock. Mfg. 1976-disc.

	$275	$260	$220	$200	$175	$165	$155	

DAVIDSON'S

Current distributor located in Prescott, AZ.

For individual model listings, please go to BlueBookOfGunValues.com/overflow.

DAVIS INDUSTRIES

Previous manufacturer located in Chino, CA 1995-2001. Previously located in Mira Loma, CA until 1995.

Davis Industries provided a lifetime warranty on all products, which is now void.

DERRINGERS

D-SERIES DERRINGER – .22 LR, .22 WMR, .25 ACP, .32 ACP, .32 H&R Mag. (new 1995), .38 Spl. (new 1992), or 9mm Para. cal., O/U steel construction, 2.4 or 2 3/4 (.38 Spl. only) in. vent. rib barrel, 9 1/2 or 11 1/2 oz., black Teflon or chrome finish. Disc. 2001.

	$150	$125	$100	$80	$65	$55	$45	*$75*

Add $23 for Big-Bore series (larger frame) in .22 WMR, .32 H&R Mag., .38 Spl., or 9mm Para. cal.
Add $29 for Long-Bore cals. (.22 WMR, .32 H&R Mag. - disc., .38 Spl., or 9mm Para.).

In this series, the .25 ACP cal. is the Model D-25 and the .32 ACP cal. is the Model D-32.

LONG BORE DERRINGER – .22 WMR, .32 H&R Mag. (disc. 1998), .38 Spl., or 9mm Para. cal., similar to D Series, except has 3 3/4 in. barrel, 13 oz. Mfg. 1995-2001.

	$185	$150	$125	$100	$85	$75	$65	*$104*

PISTOLS: SEMI-AUTO

P-32 – .32 ACP cal., single action, 6 shot mag., 2.8 in. barrel, black Teflon or chrome finish, laminated wood grips, 22 oz. Mfg. 1987-2001.

	$125	$100	$75	$65	$55	$50	$45	*$88*

P-380 – .380 ACP cal., single action, similar to P-32, 5 shot mag., 2.8 in. barrel, bright chrome or black Teflon finish, internal recoil buffer, wood (disc.) or black synthetic grips, 22 oz. Mfg. 1989-2001.

	$150	$125	$100	$85	$75	$65	$60	*$98*

DAVIS N.R.

Please refer to the Crescent Fire Arms Co. listing in the C section.

DEAD FOOT ARMS LLC

Current AR-15 and accessories manufacturer located in Brooklyn, WI, and established circa 2018.

Please contact the company directly for more information on models, pricing, and availability.

DEFOURNEY

Previous long gun manufacturer located in Belgium.

Defourney specialized in both quality sidelock and boxlock (with or w/o sideplates) shotguns in both SxS and O/U configuration. Prices range from $750-$3,250 for boxlock shotguns and start in the $3,500 range for sidelock models, assuming 80% or better original condition.

DEHAAN SHOTGUNS LTD.

Previous shotgun importer, repair center, and gunsmith for various Turkish shotgun manufacturers established 1999-2008, and located in Rigby, ID.

SHOTGUNS

DeHaan Shotguns made high-quality O/U and SxS models, with a wide variety of engraving and wood options. Guns were built per customer order.

DEL-TON INCORPORATED

Current AR-15 style rifle and pistol manufacturer located in Elizabethtown, NC. Previously distributed until 2011 by American Tactical Imports, located in Rochester, NY.

Please refer to BlueBookOfGunValues.com to order the *Blue Book of AR-15s & Variations*, available as a book or online subscription.

DEMAS, ETS (L'ATELIER VERNEY-CARRON)

Current manufacturer of custom shotguns and rifles located in St. Etienne, France since 1967. Currently imported by Kebco LLC, located in Hanover, PA. Previously imported by Verney-Carron USA, Inc., located in Clay Center, KS until 2008, and by The Drumming Stump, located in Circle Pines, MN.

During 2004, Verney-Carron S.A., located in St. Etienne, France (please refer to separate listing) purchased Demas, which manufactures a full line of custom O/U and SxS rifles and shotguns. Prices vary according to configuration, engraving options, and quality of wood. Please contact the importer (or Verney-Carron directly) for more information, including current model availability and U.S. pricing regarding these fine firearms.

In December 2008, Verney-Carron legally absorbed its subsidiary and physically moved its facility to the Verney-Carron factory. The custom workshop is now known as "L'Atelier Verney-Carron".

Please refer to Verney-Carron in the V section listing for current models.

DEMRO

Previous manufacturer located in Manchester, CT.

RIFLES: SEMI-AUTO

T.A.C. MODEL 1 RIFLE – .45 ACP or 9mm Luger cal., blowback operation, 16 7/8 in. barrel, open bolt firing system, lock-in receiver must be set to fire, also available in carbine model.

100%	98%	95%	90%	80%	70%	60%	LAST MSR
$650	$595	$525	$475	$425	$395	$360	

XF-7 WASP CARBINE – .45 ACP or 9mm Luger cal., blowback operation, 16 7/8 in. barrel.

100%	98%	95%	90%	80%	70%	60%	LAST MSR
$650	$595	$525	$475	$425	$395	$360	

Add $45 for case.

DEMYAN

Previous manufacturer located in Moscow, Russia.

Demyan manufactured good quality target pistols, including the SP-08 Khaydurov in .22 LR cal. Demyan also manufactured target rifles, including the T4 Bullpup, and the T4 Karbine. Demyan manufactured target air rifles and these models were not imported into the U.S.

DEPAR

Previous manufacturer located in Istanbul, Turkey.

Depar manufactured both semi-auto and O/U shotguns.

SHOTGUNS

ATAK O/U – 12 ga. only, 2 3/4 in. chambers, ejectors, SST.

100%	98%	95%	90%	80%	70%	60%	LAST MSR
$425	$350	$295	$250	$225	$200	$185	*$350*

Add approx. 30% with scroll engraving and walnut stock and forearm.

ATILGAN SEMI-AUTO – 12 ga. only, 3 in. chamber, gas operated, includes multi-chokes.

100%	98%	95%	90%	80%	70%	60%	LAST MSR
$200	$175	$150	$135	$125	$115	$105	*$195*

* ***Atilgan Semi-Auto De Luxe*** – 12 ga. only, 3 in. chamber, gas operated, multi-chokes, deluxe walnut stock and forearm, engraved receiver.

100%	98%	95%	90%	80%	70%	60%	LAST MSR
$350	$295	$250	$225	$200	$185	$170	*$350*

SAFARI SLIDE ACTION – 12 ga. only, 3 in. chamber, synthetic stock standard.

100%	98%	95%	90%	80%	70%	60%	LAST MSR
$170	$150	$135	$125	$115	$105	$95	*$170*

Add 10% for walnut stock and forearm.

Add approx. 50% for nickel chrome receiver finish and light scroll engraving.

DERYA INTERNATIONAL ARMS COMPANY (DERYA HUNTING ARMS)

Current manufacturer established in 2000, located in Konya, Turkey. Distributed in the U.S. since 2012 by Advanced Tactical Imports, located in Huntsville, AL.

Derya International Arms Company currently manufactures semi-auto, slide action, O/U, and single shot shotguns in various configurations, in addition to air rifles and tactical accessories. Please contact the importer directly for more information, including prices and availability.

DESENZANI

Previous manufacturer located in Italy circa 1929-2010.

Desenzani manufactured approximately ten best quality shotguns per year, utilizing top quality wood and customer's choice of engraver.

GRADING - PPGS™	100%	98%	95%	90%	80%	70%	60%	LAST MSR

DESERT EAGLE

Please refer to the Magnum Research, Inc. listing in the M section.

DESERT INDUSTRIES, INC.

Previous manufacturer located in Las Vegas, NV 1991-1996. See listing under Steel City Arms, Inc. for older models.

In 1990, Desert Industries, Inc. was created - this new company was the same as Steel City Arms, Inc. More recently manufactured guns will have the Las Vegas slide address.

PISTOLS: SEMI-AUTO

THE DOUBLE DEUCE - .22 LR cal., double action, 2 1/2 in. barrel, matte stainless steel construction, 6 shot mag., rosewood grips, 15 oz. Limited mfg. 1991-1996.

	100%	98%	95%	90%	80%	70%	60%	LAST MSR
	$350	$295	$275	$225	$195	$165	$140	*$400*

TWO BIT SPECIAL - .25 ACP cal., double action, 2 1/2 in. barrel, 5 shot mag., matte stainless steel construction, rosewood grips, 15 oz. Approx. 12 protoypes mfg. 1991-1996.

	100%	98%	95%	90%	80%	70%	60%	LAST MSR
	$375	$350	$295	$235	$205	$175	$150	*$400*

DESERT ORDNANCE

Current manufacturer of bolt action rifles and AR-15 style rifles located in McCarran, NV. Current distributor for U.S. Ordnance.

For individual model listings, please go to BlueBookOfGunValues.com/overflow.

DESERT TECH (DESERT TACTICAL ARMS)

Current rifle manufacturer located in West Valley City, UT beginning 2014. Previously named Desert Tactical Arms located in Salt Lake City, UT from 2007-2013.

For individual model listings, please go to BlueBookOfGunValues.com/overflow.

DESERT TOYS

Previous rifle manufacturer located in Mesa, AZ.

For individual model listings, please go to BlueBookOfGunValues.com/overflow.

DETONICS DEFENSE TECHNOLOGIES, LLC

Previous semi-auto pistol manufacturer located in Millstadt, IL from 2007 until circa 2020.

During 2013, Detonics changed its name to Detonics Defense Technologies, LLC.

PISTOLS: SEMI-AUTO

COMBAT MASTER HT - .40 S&W cal., 3 1/2 in. barrel, SAO, 7 shot mag., two-tone Cerakote finish, stainless steel frame, low profile sights, aluminum/dymondwood grips, 30 oz. Mfg. 2010-2016.

	100%	98%	95%	90%	80%	70%	60%	LAST MSR
	$1,575	$1,385	$1,185	$1,065	$915	$785	$635	*$1,849*

DTX - 9mm Para. or .40 S&W cal., DAO, 4 1/4 in. barrel, two-tone Cerakote finish, aluminum/polymer frame, 14 (.40 S&W) or 16 (9mm Para.) shot, low profile sights, aluminum/polymer grips, 25 1/2 oz. Mfg. mid-2011-2014.

	100%	98%	95%	90%	80%	70%	60%	LAST MSR
	$925	$850	$725	$625	$550	$475	$425	*$1,099*

MTX - .45 ACP cal., DAO, 4 1/4 in. match barrel, black over black or black over silver finish, 10 shot mag., aluminum frame with steel receiver, fixed combat sights, 27 oz. Limited mfg. 2014-disc.

	100%	98%	95%	90%	80%	70%	60%	LAST MSR
	$850	$750	$650	$600	$475	$375	$300	*$1,000*

NEMESIS HT - .40 S&W cal., SA, 5 in. barrel, 9 shot mag., low profile sights, aluminum/diamondwood grips, two-tone Cerakote finish, 38 oz. Mfg. 2011-2014.

	100%	98%	95%	90%	80%	70%	60%	LAST MSR
	$1,915	$1,685	$1,425	$1,225	$1,035	$885	$735	*$2,249*

STX - striker fired, full or compact size aluminum frame, accepts 4 barrel/slide lengths, 14 (sub-compact) or 17 (full) shot mag., SA, low profile adj. Tritium night sights, textured polymer grip, internal drop safety, Mil-Std 1913 lower Picatinny rail, matte black ceramic coating, 20-23 oz. Limited mfg. 2014-disc.

	100%	98%	95%	90%	80%	70%	60%	LAST MSR
	$850	$750	$650	$600	$475	$375	$300	*$1,000*

DETONICS FIREARMS INDUSTRIES

Previous manufacturer located in Bellevue, WA 1976-1988. Detonics was sold in early 1988 to the New Detonics Manufacturing Corporation, a wholly owned subsidiary of "1045 Investors Group Limited."

Please refer to the New Detonics Manufacturing Corporation listing in the N section for complete model listings of both companies.

GRADING - PPGS™	100%	98%	95%	90%	80%	70%	60%	LAST MSR

DETONICS USA

Previous manufacturer located in Pendergrass, GA circa 2004-mid-2007.

PISTOLS: SEMI-AUTO

COMBATMASTER – .45 ACP cal., 3 1/2 in. barrel, 6 shot, fixed sights (stainless steel model), stainless steel, black bonded, two-tone, or mirror polish finish, 34 oz.

$1,050	$875	$750	$650	$575	$500	$425	*$1,200*

Add $40 for two-tone finish, $100 for black bonded finish, $375 for mirror polish finish, or $550 for mirror polish finish w/stag grips.

9-11-01 – .45 ACP cal., 5 in. barrel, 7 shot, logo engraved checkered rosewood grips, low profile fixed combat sights, available in black bonded, two-tone, or mirror polish finish.

$1,050	$875	$750	$650	$575	$500	$425	*$1,200*

Add $40 for two-tone finish, $100 for black bonded finish, or $375 for mirror polish finish.

STREETMASTER – .45 ACP cal., 5 in. barrel, 6 shot, low profile fixed combat sights, stainless steel construction, logo engraved checkered rosewood grips.

$1,050	$875	$750	$650	$575	$500	$425	*$1,200*

SERVICEMASTER – .45 ACP cal., choice of Standard or Compact frame, 4 1/4 in. barrel, 7 shot, stainless steel construction, low profile fixed combat sights, logo engraved checkered rosewood grips, 39 oz.

$1,050	$875	$750	$650	$575	$500	$425	*$1,200*

SCOREMASTER – .45 ACP cal., stainless steel construction, 5 in. barrel, SAO, 7 shot, MMC adj. rear sight, logo engraved checkered rosewood grips, available in Tactical (adj. sights and rail) or Target (Bo-Mar adj. sights, ext. slide stop, mag. release, and ambidextrous safety) configuration, 43 oz.

$1,475	$1,250	$1,050	$925	$800	$775	$625	*$1,650*

MILITARY TACTICAL – .45 ACP cal., SAO, black bonded finish, adj. sights, includes rail, forward serrations, checkered front strap, and lanyard ring.

$1,750	$1,525	$1,350	$1,125	$950	$800	$675	*$1,975*

DEVIL DOG ARMS LLC

Current manufacturer of 1911-style pistols and AR-15-style rifles located in Geneva, IL since 2016.

Please refer to BlueBookOfGunValues.com to order the *Blue Book of AR-15s & Variations*, available as a book or online subscription.

DEVIL DOG ARMS INC.

Previous handgun and AR-15 style rifle, parts, and accessories manufacturer located in Lake Zurich, IL until 2015.

Please refer to BlueBookOfGunValues.com to order the *Blue Book of AR-15s & Variations*, available as a book or online subscription.

DEZ TACTICAL ARMS, INC.

Current AR-15 style rifle manufacturer located in Wisconsin Dells, WI since 2012.

Please refer to BlueBookOfGunValues.com to order the *Blue Book of AR-15s & Variations*, available as a book or online subscription.

DIAMOND

Trade name on shotguns manufactured by Matsan A.S. located in Istanbul, Turkey since 1962. Previously imported by Adco Arms Co., Inc. until 2015, located in Woburn, MA.

For individual model listings, please go to BlueBookOfGunValues.com/overflow.

DIAMOND SHOTGUNS

Please refer to Diamond and the Vega listing in the V section.

DIAMONDBACK FIREARMS

Current pistol and AR-15 style firearm manufacturer established during 2009 and located in Cocoa, FL.

Please refer to BlueBookOfGunValues.com to order the *Blue Book of AR-15s & Variations*, available as a book or online subscription.

DIAMONDHEAD

Current manufacturer of AR-15 style pistols, rifles, parts, and accessories based in West Springfield, MA.

Please refer to BlueBookOfGunValues.com to order the *Blue Book of AR-15s & Variations*, available as a book or online subscription.

DIARM S.A.

Previous manufacturing conglomerate (25 companies) located in Deba, Spain 1986-1989. Previously imported and distributed by American Arms, Inc. located in North Kansas City, MO. Older Diarm models can be found under the American Arms, Inc. section.

DICKINSON, LLC

Current trademark of shotguns manufactured by Akdas in Huglu, Turkey. Imported exclusively by Dickinson, LLC located in Moorpark, CA.

For individual model listings, please go to BlueBookOfGunValues.com/overflow.

DICKSON & MACNAUGHTON

Previous trading company located in Edinburgh, Scotland 1999-2017.

In 1999, the directors of James MacNaughton & Sons acquired the whole share capital of John Dickson & Son, from whom they purchased the MacNaughton manufacturing rights in 1996. The two companies traded under the name of Dickson & MacNaughton, alongside the other trademarks: Daniel Fraser, Alexander Henry, Alex Martin, and Thomas Mortimer. See also listing for John Dickson & Son Ltd.

JOHN DICKSON & SON, LTD.

Current trademark purchased during 1999 by James MacNaughton & Sons, located in Edinburgh, Scotland. During mid-2010, the company began making guns under the name John Dickson & Son, Ltd.

Currently, John Dickson & Son, Ltd. manufactures a round action O/U shotgun based on the original 1879 James MacNaughton design.

JOHN DICKSON & SON, LTD. COMPANY HISTORY

The business of John Dickson and Son was founded in Edinburgh, Scotland in 1820 and is Scotlands oldest gunmaker. Over generations, the Dickson's established themselves as premier makers of breech loading guns and rifles in the capital but it was not until 1880 that they filed the patent for the iconic "Round-Action" gun - a gun which through clever design is attractive, strong, light, and fast-handling. With under 2,000 "Round-Actions" made since 1880, the gun has gained qite a following and become very collectible. Today, the business operates in Dunkled, Scotland from the workshop and showroom that they established in 2001. The "Round-Action" is still produced on the classic design and completely bespoke built in Scotland. The company also continues to provide a full repair, restoration, and record enquiry service for the vintage Dickson guns. Over the last century, John Dickson and Son has acquired a number of other iconic Scottish gun and rifle makers, including James MacNaughton - Gun and Rifle Makers, Alexander Henry - Rifle Makers, Daniel Fraser - Rifle Makers, Alex Martin - Gun Makers, and Thomas W. Mortimer & Sons - Gun Makers. For more information on these companies, please see individual listings in their respective sections.

SHOTGUNS

ROUND-ACTION SHOTGUN – based on the 1880 triggerplate design. Bespoke specification and build.

Current MSR starts at $65,000.
Please contact the company directly for options, availability, and delivery time.

DISSIDENT ARMS

Current manufacturer of highly customized competition and tactical firearms, located in Conroe, TX.

Dissident Arms is known for customizing Kalashnikov variations, most notably Molot firearms including the VEPR-12 shotgun. They also tune and customize other factory firearms from Arsenal Inc., Israeli Weapon Industries (IWI), Kalashnikov USA, Benelli, and Breda. Please contact the manufacturer for current availability and pricing.

DIXIE GUN WORKS

Current importer, distributor, and catalog retailer established 1954, and located in Union City, TN.

For individual model listings, please go to BlueBookOfGunValues.com/overflow.

DLASK ARMS CORP.

Current manufacturer and distributor located in British Columbia, Canada. Direct sales.

For individual model listings, please go to BlueBookOfGunValues.com/overflow.

GRADING - PPGS™	100%	98%	95%	90%	80%	70%	60%	LAST MSR

DOLPHIN GUN COMPANY

Current rifle manufacturer located in Lincolnshire, United Kingdom. No current U.S. importation.

Dolphin Gun Company was founded circa 2006 by competitive shooters Mik Maksimovic and Pete Hobson. The company builds custom competition "F Class" and tactical style rifles, utilizing Accuracy International or tactical style stocks. Many calibers and options are available. Please contact the company directly for more information, including pricing, delivery time, availability, gun services, etc.

DOMINGO, ACHA

Please refer to the Acha listing in the A section.

DOMINION ARMS

Previous trademark of slide action shotguns manufactured by Rauch Tactical, located in Blaine, WA.

Rauch manufactured 12 ga. tactical style slide action shotguns until circa 2010.

DOMINO, IGI

Previous Italian company absorbed during 1990 by FAS (see separate listing in F section). Previously imported by Mandall Shooting Supplies located in Scottsdale, AZ.

PISTOLS: SEMI-AUTO

MODEL OP 601 MATCH PISTOL – .22 Short cal., 5 shot, 5.6 in. barrel, match sights, full target grips, vent. barrel and slide to reduce recoil, adj. and removable trigger.

$1,300	$1,000	$715	$635	$550	$495	$440	*$1,495*

MODEL SP 602 MATCH PISTOL – .22 LR cal., 5 1/2 in. barrel, similar to 601, but .22 LR and slightly different trigger.

$1,300	$1,100	$800	$700	$600	$550	$495	*$1,495*

DOUBLE D ARMORY, LTD

Previous AR-15 style rifle manufacturer located in Greenwood Village, CO 2012-2018.

Please refer to BlueBookOfGunValues.com to order the *Blue Book of AR-15s & Variations*, available as a book or online subscription.

DOUBLESTAR CORP.

Current AR-15 style rifle, pistol, and accessories manufacturer located in Winchester, KY. Distributed by J&T Distributing.

For individual model listings, please go to BlueBookOfGunValues.com/overflow.

DOUBLETAP DEFENSE, LLC

Previous trademark of O/U derringers with headquarters located in St. Louis, MO, and manufactured by Azimuth Technology, LLC located in Florida late 2013-circa 2018.

DERRINGERS: O/U

DOUBLETAP – 9mm Para. or .45 ACP cal., tip-up action with ambidextrous thumb latch for ejecting fired rounds, 3 in. ported or non-ported stainless steel barrels, DA trigger for two consecutive shots, design allows to carry two spare rounds in grip, choice of titanium (disc.) or aluminum frame, checkered integral grips, only 5/8 in. wide, 12 (aluminum) or 14 (titanium, disc.) oz. Mfg. late 2012-circa 2018.

$450	$415	$385	$350	$325	$295	$275	*$499*

Add $70 for ported barrels.
Add $230 for titanium construction (disc.).
Add $199 per non-ported barrel assembly or $269 for ported barrel assembly.

DORKAS FOREIGN TRADE

Current exporter of Turkish-made shotguns located in Konya, Turkey. No current U.S. importer.

Dorkas currently distributes and exports hunting and tactical shotguns manufactured in Turkey by Özkanlar (Akrep, Kobra, Bavyer and Lupus trademarks), Turkuaz, and Mertmak. Please contact the company directly for current information, including U.S. availability and pricing.

DORUK SILAH CO.

Current manufacturer of Eternal branded shotguns located in Konya, Turkey. Please refer to the Eternal section for more information on this trademark.

GRADING - PPGS™	100%	98%	95%	90%	80%	70%	60%	LAST MSR

DOWNSIZER CORPORATION

Previous pistol manufacturer located in Santee, CA circa 1994-2007.

DERRINGERS

MODEL WSP (WORLD'S SMALLEST PISTOL) – 9mm Para. (disc. 1999), .357 Mag., .357 SIG (disc. 1999), .40 S&W (disc. 1999), or .45 ACP cal., single shot pistol, tip-up 2.1 in. barrel with push-button release, internal firing pin block, double action only, synthetic grips, stainless steel, overall size is smaller than a playing card, 11 oz. Mfg. 1997-circa 2007.

	100%	98%	95%	90%	80%	70%	60%	LAST MSR
	$415	**$300**	**$235**	**$185**	**$150**	**$135**	**$110**	*$499*

DRAGON

Current trademark of shotguns manufactured by Aziz Silah, located in Konya, Turkey. No current U.S. importation.

Aziz Silah manufactures a line of good quality slide action and semi-auto shotguns under the Dragon trademark. Currently, this trademark has had little or no importation into the U.S. Please contact the company directly for more information, including domestic availability and pricing.

DRAKE ASSOCIATES

Current rifle manufacturer located in Shelter Island, NY. Dealer, law enforcement/military, and civilian sales.

RIFLES: BOLT ACTION

A17/A22 – .17 HMR or .22 LR cal., 16 in. heavy barrel, custom fitted A17/A22 monolithic design rifle chassis allows ability to switch from AR style pistol trip to traditional rifle stock design, Magpul M-LOK attachments, various color options in Cerakote or Mil-Spec finishes. New 2018.

Please contact the company directly for pricing and availability.

DRAKE 06 PREDATOR – .300 Win. Mag. cal., Savage 110BA long action, 26 in. 5R 3006 heavy profile fluted barrel, AICS pattern mag., monolithic chassis w/adj. PRS buttstock or optional shock mitigating buttstock and enlarged cheekpiece, integrated bubble level system for M1913 scope rail, M1913 night vision hood/rail w/additional Mil-Std 1913 rails at 9,3, and 6 o'clock positions.

Please contact the company directly for pricing and availability.

STALKER ASR-3 MULTICALIBER TACTICAL – .308 Win, .30-06, .300 Win Mag., .300NM, .338NM, or .338 Lapua Mag. cal., Stalker ASR-3 long or short action w/integrated recoil lug system, Drake fluted heavy tactical cut barrel, threaded OSS muzzle brake, detachable mag. base, adj. match trigger, 2 (secondary) or 4 in. 3, 6, or 9 o'clock rail system, accuracy truing, Strike Dual 30 or 33 chassis, optional ASR tool kit and cleaning kit, or a second detachable magazine base.

Base pricing on this model starts at $6,999, depending on the configuration, features, and options.

STALKER STRIKE DUAL – .223 Rem., .308 Win., .300 Win. Mag., 30-06, right or left-hand action, long or short Remington 700 action (2 lug action), 26 in. M24E profile benchmark or Satern threaded barrel, AAC Blackout 51T, Surefire 7.62, or Drake 3 port removable muzzle brake w/Hex, Remington X-Mark Pro adj. trigger, Cadex strike dual 30 chassis, 20 in. MOA long rail, 2 and 4 in. 3, 6, or 9 o'clock rail systems, black Cerakote or stainless steel bead blast finish.

Base pricing on this model ranges from $3,995-$5,159, depending on the configuration, features, and options.

TIER 1 HUNTER STALKER SYSTEM – .223 Rem., .30-06, 7mm Rem. Mag., .308 Win. or .300 Win. Mag. cal., short or long action, super match chamber, right or left-hand Rem. 700 action, 16 1/2 or 20 in. single point cut competition barrel with target crown, AAC Blackout 51T muzzle brake or DRAKE 3 port removable muzzle brake with Hex, Remington X-Mark Pro adj. trigger, Hunter Stalker LWSS Universal Chassis in black, FDE, or OD Green, bipod attachment point, FAB Defense GL SHOCK CP with cheek riser kit, Hogue pistol grip, 20 MOA long rail, 3 or 9 o'clock Picatinny rails with QD Swivel hard point, Mil-Spec tube, Cerakote barrel and action finish, includes case.

Base pricing on this model is $3,336, depending on the configuration, features, and options.

* ***Tier 1 Hunter Stalker SOCOM Elite System*** – .223 Rem., .30-06, 7mm Rem. Mag., .308 Win. or .300 Win. Mag. cal., super match chamber, right or left-hand Rem. 700 or Savage action, match competition barrel, option of AAC Blackout 51T, Surefire 7.62, or Drake 3 port removable muzzle brake w/hex, AICS pattern mag., adj. trigger, Hunter Stalker SOCOM Universal chassis, bipod attachment point, FAB Defense GL SHOCK CP with cheek riser kit, Hogue pistol grip, target crown, 20 MOA long rail, 5 in. 3 or 9 o'clock Picatinny rails with QD Swivel hard point, Mil-Spec tube, includes case, black, FDE, or OD Green Cerakote barrel and action.

Base pricing on this model is $3,336, depending on the configuration, features, and options.

GRADING - PPGS™	100%	98%	95%	90%	80%	70%	60%	LAST MSR

TIER 1 STALKER M24E – .223 Rem., .30-06, 7mm Rem. Mag., .308 Win. or .300 Win. Mag. cal., super match chamber, right-hand only Rem. 700 short or long action, 26 in. single point cut competition barrel with target crown, AAC Blackout 51T muzzle brake or DRAKE 3 port removable muzzle brake with Hex, Remington X-Mark Pro adj. trigger, 20 MOA long rail, three 9 o'clock Picatinny rails with QD Swivel hard point, Mil-Spec tube, choice of Strike Dual 30 or Strike Dual 33 Chassis in black, FDE, or Pink Warrior finish, Cerakote barrel and action finish, includes case.

Base pricing on this model ranges from $3,995-$5,159, depending on the configuration, features, and options.

TIER 2 STALKER – .223 Rem., .30-06, 7mm Rem. Mag., .308 Win. or .300 Win. Mag. cal., right-hand only Rem. 700 action, 16 1/2, 20, or 26 in. SPS or varmint barrel, Remington X-Mark Pro adj. trigger, 20 MOA long rail, three 9 o'clock Picatinny rails with QD Swivel hard point, Hogue pistol grip, Mil-Spec tube, choice of Cadex Field Strike, Strike Dual 30 or Strike Dual 33 Chassis in black, FDE, ODG, or Pink Warrior finish, bipod attachment point, Cerakote barrel and action finish, includes case.

MSR $2,995	$2,550	$2,225	$1,925	$1,750	$1,400	$1,150	$895

Add $1,000 for Strike Dual 30 or 33 Chassis.

This model comes with an SPS barrel in 16 1/2 or 20 inches only with flash hider, and the varmint barrel is only available in .300 Win Mag., .30-06, or 7mm Rem. Mag.

TIER 3 HUNTER STALKER SYSTEM – .223 Rem., .30-06, 7mm Rem. Mag., .308 Win., .300 AAC Blackout, or .300 Win. Mag. cal., short or long, right or left-hand action, 16 1/2, 20, or 26 in. SPS or varmint barrel, Remington X-Mark Pro adj. trigger, Hunter Stalker LWSS Universal Chassis in black, FDE, or ODG finish, bipod attachment point, FAB Defense GL SHOCK CP with cheek riser kit, Hogue pistol grip, 20 MOA long rail, three 9 o'clock Picatinny rails with QD Swivel hard point, Mil-Spec tube, includes case.

Base pricing on this model ranges from $2,295 depending on the configuration, features, and options.

TIER 4 SPECIAL APPLICATION STALKER – .300 Win. Mag., .338 Lapua, .416 Rem. Mag., or .50 BMG cal., super match chamber, right-hand McMillan G30 or TAC50 action, 26 in. M24 profile single cut competition fluted or non-fluted barrel with target crown, AAC Blackout or Drake 3 port removable muzzle brake with Hex (MK13 only) or Rangemaster Precision Arms removable muzzle brake (MK15 only), Timney (MK13), Huber (MK15), or X-Treme (MK15) adj. trigger, Strike Dual 33 or Dual 50 Chassis in black, FDE, OD Green or Pink Warrior finish, 20 (MK13) or 40 (MK15) MOA long rail, 2 and 4 in. 3/6/9 o'clock Picatinny rail kits, QD Swivel hard point, Cerakote action and barrel finish.

MSR $6,495	$5,525	$4,850	$4,150	$3,750	$3,050	$2,485	$2,000

Add $2,200 for Tac 50 MK15 configuration in .416 Rem. Mag. or .50 BMG cal.

TITANIUM TACTICAL STALKER – .308 Win., .30-06, or .300 Win. Mag. cal., short or long action, Stalker Remington 700 Series or Savage M10/M110BA, Drake Titan titanium heavy M24E profile barrel, RPA muzzle brake, AICS mag., adj. trigger, Cadex Strike Dual 30 or 33 chassis, rail system, black Cerakote finish. New 2016.

Base pricing on this model ranges from $5,999-$6,159 depending on the configuration, features, and options.

TITANIUM TITAN HUNTER STALKER SWS – .308 Win., .243 Mag., 7mm-08, .300 AAC Blackout, or .223 Rem. cal., right or left hand Savage action, single point cut competition barrel, 5R rifling, tactical profile .820 muzzle, port removable muzzle brake w/Hex, AICS pattern mag., Hogue pistol grip, Hunter Stalker LWSS Universal chassis, target crown, Mil-Spec tube, bipod attachment point, 20 in. MOA long rail, Super Match chamber, includes case, black, FDE, or OD Green Cerakote finish.

Base pricing on this model ranges from $3,496-$3,769 depending on the configuration, features, and options.

RIFLES: SEMI-AUTO

ATHENA PRECISION CHASSIS TACTICAL/TIER 1 PREMIER RIFLE – 5.56 NATO cal., GIO, 16, 18, or 20 in. Satern Heavy Profile Match barrel with button or cut (Tier 1 Premier) rifling, mid-length (16 in. barrel) or rifle length gas system, low profile gas block, 11 degree target crown, A2 flash hider, Magpul 20 shot mag., uses AR-15 style mags., billet aluminum lower "chassis" receiver, forged aluminum A3 Mil-Spec or billet aluminum (Tier 1 Premier) trued upper receiver, Drake Match Competition two-stage trigger, collapsible multi-position stock or FAB Defense RAPS adj. buttstock with adj. LOP and cheek riser (Tier 1 Premier), integrated chassis handguard with four QD sling sockets, 6 o'clock bottom Picatinny rail, ergonomic pistol grip with finger grooves, M16 bolt assembly, long Picatinny top rail system with 11/1 o'clock M-LOK slots, black, FDE or OD Green anodized finish, 9 lbs. New 2020.

MSR $1,776	$1,575	$1,400	$1,275	$1,175	$975	$775	$600

GRADING - PPGS™	100%	98%	95%	90%	80%	70%	60%	LAST MSR

DREYSE

Previously manufactured by Rheinische Metallwaren und Machinenfabrik, located in Sommerda, Germany.

PISTOLS: SEMI-AUTO

MODEL 1907 AUTOMATIC – 7.65mm/.32 ACP cal., 8 shot, 3 1/2 in. barrel, blue, fixed sights, hard rubber grips. Mfg. 1907-14.

$650	$575	$450	$400	$325	$200	$100	

MODEL 1910 – 9mm Para. cal., mfg. 1912-1915. Production estimated at 1,000 pistols, usually found in the 12xx-13xx ser. no. range. Seldom encountered.

$7,850	$6,875	$5,900	$5,350	$4,325	$3,525	$2,750	

VEST POCKET AUTOMATIC – .25 ACP cal., 6 shot, 2 in. barrel, blue, fixed sights, hard rubber grips. Mfg. 1912-15.

$425	$375	$325	$275	$225	$175	$125	

Add 100% for early version with double extractors.

RIFLES: SEMI-AUTO

1907 LIGHT RIFLE – 7.65mm (.32 ACP) cal., 18 3/4 in. barrel, staggered box 6-9 shot mag., used mostly for small game hunting, earlier rifles can be found with full "Rheinmetall" and "Dreyse" markings, and later rifles do not have markings, most have sporter stocks, some have military type stocks with cheekpieces and full forends to near the muzzle, other markings may include European sporting goods dealers and various police agencies, including the South American police. Mfg. 1907-circa 1913.

$2,500	$2,200	$2,000	$1,800	$1,400	$1,000	$600	

Values shown are for the sporter type stock.

DRILLINGS

A Drilling is a three-barrel combination gun (two shotgun barrels and a rifle barrel, vice versa, or three shotgun barrels). Most Drillings have two triggers (a very few have three triggers). The front trigger usually fires the right shotgun barrel, and the rear fires the left shotgun barrel. The rifle barrel is most often fired with the front trigger when it is selected. Most selectors are on top of the grip, but quite a few other designs can be found.

It is very important that owners familiarize themselves with a Drilling before shooting it.

The author would like to express his thanks to the German Gun Collectors Association, including members Dietrich Apel, Dick Hummel, Steve Meyer, and Hal Hamilton for helping to compile the following information on Drillings.

Most well-made Drillings in above-average condition are surprisingly accurate when using the rifle barrel(s), because of the stiffness gained with three barrels fixed together.

DRILLING CONFIGURATIONS & EXPLANATIONS

Please refer to illustrations below depicting the most commonly encountered Drilling barrel configurations. These various types are designed to accomodate the firing mechanism, which makes the Drilling slimmer, lighter, and more practical.

Illustration No. 1 – Normal Drilling configuration with 2 shotgun barrels over a rimmed, centerfire rifle (most are 16 ga. x 16 ga. by either 9.3x72R or 8x57JR cal.).

Illustration No. 2 – Two rifle barrels over a shotgun. This configuration will normally command twice the price as No. 1. German designation is "Doppelbüchsdrilling".

Illustration No. 3 – Three barrels with no two being the same gauge or caliber. This configuration is very collectible, especially if the smallest caliber is .22 LR. Again, price will be double (or more) of No. 1.

Illustration No. 4 – Sometimes called a Bock Drilling with one shotgun and two rifle barrels of different calibers. This variation brings a good premium over No. 1.

Illustration No. 5 – Rib Drilling with rifle caliber generally small (.22 LR or .22 Hornet). German designation is "Schienendrilling".

Illustration No. 6 – Three shotgun barrels with the same gauge or three rifle barrels with different calibers. This configuration is quite rare and healthy premiums are charged over No. 1.

Illustration No. 7 – A variation of No. 3, this configuration features shotgun O/U barrels with a rifle barrel on the side. German designation is "Bock-Doppelflinte mit seitlichem Kleinkaliberlauf".

Illustration No. 8 – Very unusual - a 3-barrel Drilling in vertical design - two rifle barrels under a shotgun barrel. This configuration is seldom encountered.

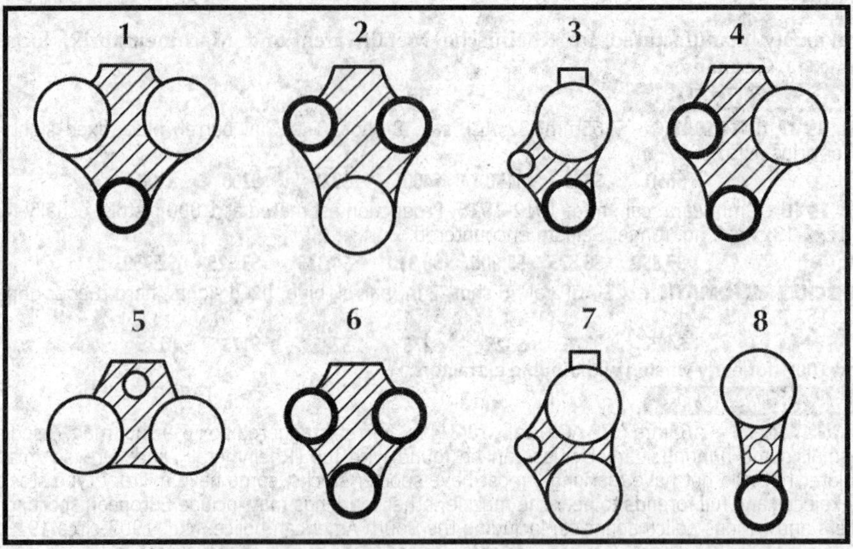

The following German nomenclatures apply as follows: single barrel rifle = *Büchse;* **SxS double rifle =** *Doppelbüchse;* **O/U double rifle =** *Bock-Doppelbüchse;* **SxS double shotgun =** *Doppelflinte;* **O/U double shotgun =** *Bock-Doppelflinte;* **SxS double shotgun, rifle bbl. under =** *Drilling;* **SxS double shotgun, rifle bbl. on top =** *Schienendrilling;* **single shotgun, rifle bbl. under =** *Bock-Büchsflinte;* **single shotgun, rifle bbl. at side =** *Büchsflinte;* **single shotgun, rifle bbl. under and at side =** *Bock-Drilling;* **double rifle, shot bbl. under =** *Doppelbüchsdrilling;* **O/U double shotgun, rifle bbl. at side =** *Bock-Doppelflinte mit seitlichem Kleinkaliberlauf;* **SxS double shotgun, plus two rifle bbls. =** *Vierling.*

DRILLING HISTORY

For over 150 years, Drillings have been the classic hunting gun of many European countries, especially Germany and Austria. Because a single hunting trip might require shooting both wildfowl and animals (often times within several hours), Europeans have long favored a single long-arm that could afford both rifle and shotgun shooting, be reliable, and not wear the hunter out while transporting it in the field. Another big reason the Europeans like the Drilling is that in recent years, ownership of firearms has become severely regulated and limited, thus making a versatile single firearm like the Drilling more desirable.

In order to save weight, Hubertus Gewehrfabrik of Suhl was the first company to use light alloy metal for receiver construction during 1933. Meffert was the first company to make a Drilling action from aluminum (Dural) with steel reinforcements. Aluminum receivers were somewhat weaker than steel, but sufficient for their limited use on a hunting gun. This weight savings made the Drilling even more popular in Europe, because it could be carried all day with little fatigue.

Americans, on the other hand, have not placed as much emphasis on this combination gun principle, and more often than not have chosen to buy both a rifle and shotgun for each specific hunting application. Since Drillings are becoming more popular now that metric rifle ammunition is more prevalent and affordable in the U.S., collectability has improved in this country for those collectors who see the utility and functionality of these mostly hand-assembled weapons.

DRILLING CALIBERS

Some Americans may be confused as to how the European metric calibers compare to domestic cartridges in terms of overall performance. This comparison has been added to assist you when contemplating what type of field performance, velocity, and killing power you can expect in these European calibers: 9.3x74mm is similar to .375 H&H, 9.3x72Rmm is similar to .35 Rem., 8x57RmmJS is similar to .300 Savage, .30-30 Win. and 7.62x51Rmm; 8x57RmmJ is similar to .30-06; 7x65Rmm is similar to .280 Rem.; 7x57R is similar to .30-40 Krag; 6.5x57R is similar to .260 Rem.; 5.6x52Rmm is a .22 Savage Hi-Power; 5.6x35Rmm (Vierling) is similar to .22 Hornet. Drillings can also be encountered in American calibers such as .270 Win., .30-06, .30-30 Win., .38-55 WCF, or .32-20 WCF.

DRILLING VALUES AND CONDITION FACTORS

Rather than list the various manufacturers of Drillings (there are hundreds), it should be noted that guns with major trademarks and established provenances (i.e. Charles Daly, Colt Sauer, Ferlach-addressed, Heym, Krieghoff, Merkel, J.P. Sauer, Simpson, Berlin [rare] and Suhl-addressed, etc.) will usually be more collectible than other, lesser-known brands, even if the quality of workmanship is similar. The overall quality, condition, engraving, wood type/fanciness, and carving all have to be taken into consideration when evaluating a Drilling. Some Drillings were assembled from manufactured parts by skilled self-employed gunsmiths and are sometimes better quality than factory specimens. Many Drillings are marked with the names of retailers who had their names added to units manufactured by major makers such as Simpson, J.P. Sauer, etc. Pre-war specimens are generally more desirable to collectors, if the quality and engraving are better than post-war specimens. Many older pre-war specimens were designed for rimmed cartridges with lower breech pressures and should not be re-bored or reloaded for the "hotter" cartridges/loads available today.

Many pre-war guns have safeties that block only the triggers. Set triggers, also called hair triggers, can be dangerous when set, and a good working knowledge of any Drillings operation is essential for maintaining proper safety.

Post-war guns have more functional designs which can be manufactured more efficiently with today's CNC equipment. Most modern Drillings now have hand cocking mechanisms for the rifle barrel, and set triggers, which unset themselves when the gun is opened.

It should be noted that since Drillings are more complex than a typical shotgun, most of the manufacture has been done by hand; some guns have taken individual craftsmen over a year to fabricate!

Ordering a new Drilling today is a very expensive proposition, and buying a good used specimen will save you thousands of dollars (and maybe a year's wait). For these reasons, many collectors feel Drillings today are under-priced since they can be purchased at a fraction of the cost of a new one (and may be better quality also).

Condition is another major consideration. A gun that shows much use and is not operationally intact/correct may bring several thousand dollars less than another similar specimen showing little wear and excellent original finish (including the case colors or coin finish).

Most above-average condition boxlock Drillings in the above mentioned trademarks start in the $2,750-$3,250 range and can go to $20,000 and higher if the configuration, features, and condition are all desirable. Average-condition boxlock Drillings not made by a famous trademark usually sell in the $1,850-$3,250 range, assuming moderate engraving, metric calibers, and some popular options. Sidelock Drillings typically start in the $3,500-$4,000 range, and can go well past $25,000, depending on the trademark, engraving, and desirable features. One of the most important accessories on any Drilling is the original detachable factory scope mounts and especially the scope. These will increase the value of any Drilling at least $1,500-$2,500, depending on condition and desirability.

Also, while not many Drillings are available in the secondary marketplace, they have become increasingly popular due to shooting sports magazines and other gun publications. For these reasons, Drillings have to be evaluated one at a time and a COMPETENT appraisal/evaluation should be procured before buying or selling a specimen.

FEATURES THAT ADD VALUE TO DRILLINGS

Drillings with American calibers and smaller gauges will sometimes be more desirable (depending on engraving, case colors, or coin finish) than the European metric calibers (i.e. a gun configured 20 ga. x 20 ga. by .243 Win. will sell for more than a similar gun in 16 ga. x 16 ga. by an obscure metric cal.). In recent years, some firearms distributors are once again importing older metric cartridges in limited quantities - this helps the value of those Drillings chambered for those previously obsolete cartridges. Some suppliers of reloading supplies offer modern brass in the more common obsolute calibers: 8X57R, 9.3X72R, etc. The most commonly encountered gauges and calibers are the 16 ga. (most pre-war guns are chambered for 2 9/16 in. shotshells). In addition, a sidelock action will be more desirable than a boxlock, and a lot more expensive if the locks are also detachable (exceptionally rare!).

Drilling aficionados will mention there are four main things to look for when contemplating a Drilling purchase - beauty or eye appeal, condition, quality, and features. Features and embellishments become very critical in ascertaining Drilling values also. A gun with deep relief engraving, carved stock, claw

GRADING - PPGS™	100%	98%	95%	90%	80%	70%	60%	LAST MSR

mounts w/scope, buffalo horn trigger guard and buttplate, cocking indicators, two position front sight (i.e. night sight), middle set of express sights, adj. trigger, concealed upper tang peep sight, a non-Greener safety system, lightweight (under 6 1/2 lbs.), separate rifle cocking, shotgun-barrel inserts in .22 LR or .22 WMR cal. (approx. 8 or 11 in. long), cartridge trap, etc. is going to be A LOT more collectible than a plain-Jane hammer model with a loose action.

Drillings with original, detachable claw-mounted scopes, rail-mount, or swing-off are worth a 20% to 50% premium, depending on overall desirability of the gun. Original Drilling scopes for pre-war Drillings are rare, as most were removed when the guns were turned in after WWII.

FEATURES THAT DETRACT VALUE FROM DRILLINGS

If a Drilling is worn out and/or needs some service work or parts replaced, its eye appeal is compromised; values decrease significantly, and can end up in the three low digits. Make sure that any Drilling is mechanically inspected thoroughly, especially if it shows a lot of use, before contemplating a purchase.

DRULOV

Current trademark of pistols and rifles manufactured by PPK s.r.o., and located in Holice, Czech Republic. No current U.S. importation.

PISTOLS: SINGLE SHOT

Please contact the manufacturer directly for U.S. availability and pricing.

PAV – .22 LR cal., single shot, 9 3/4 in. barrel, all steel construction. Imported 1986 only.

	100%	98%	95%	90%	80%	70%	60%	LAST MSR
	$175	$150	$125	$110	$90	$75	$50	*$105*

DRULOV 70 – .22 LR cal., single shot, wood grip with thumb rest.

	100%	98%	95%	90%	80%	70%	60%	LAST MSR
	$375	$325	$275	$250	$200	$175	$125	

DRULOV 75 – .22 LR cal., single shot, set trigger, micrometer sights, short or long (with wood forearm) barrel. Also available in left-hand.

DRULOV 78 – .22 LR cal., similar to Drulov 75. Imported 1986 only.

	100%	98%	95%	90%	80%	70%	60%	LAST MSR
	$375	$325	$275	$250	$200	$175	$125	*$180*

DRULOV 90 – .22 LR or .22 Hornet cal., single shot, target model with ergonomic thumb rest grip and wood forearm, target sights.

DRULOV 97 MSP – .22 LR, .22 WMR, or .22 Hornet cal., short or long barrel, target model with weaver rail attached, micrometer sights, ergonomic grip with thumb rest and wood forearm.

RIFLES: SINGLE SHOT

DRULOV RIFLE – .22 LR, .22 WMR, or .22 Hornet cal., single shot action, wood Monte Carlo stock with ergonomic pistol grip and grooved forearm, 16 in. barrel, micrometer target sights.

Please contact the manufacturer directly for U.S. availability and pricing on this model.

DUBIEL ARMS COMPANY

Previous custom bolt action rifle manufacturer located in Sherman, TX from 1975-approximately 1990.

RIFLES: BOLT ACTION

BOLT ACTION RIFLE – .22-250 Rem.-.458 Win. Mag. cals., custom made, barrel length and weight to order, no sights, Canjar trigger, all steel parts, custom made rifle stocks available in five styles. Disc.

	100%	98%	95%	90%	80%	70%	60%	LAST MSR
	$2,000	$1,750	$1,500	$1,275	$1,125	$975	$825	*$2,500*

DUCKS UNLIMITED, INC.

National wildlife organization established in 1937, with headquarters located in Memphis, TN.

For individual model listings, please go to BlueBookOfGunValues.com/overflow.

DUMOULIN, ERNEST S.P.R.L.

Current manufacturer located in Herstal, Belgium. Previously imported until 2011 by Empire Rifle Company, LLC, located in Meriden, NH. Previously imported from 1998-2000 by Armes De Chasse LLC, located in Hertford, NC, and on a very limited basis by Midwest Gun Sport located in Zebulon, NC until 1990 (formerly from Ellisville, MO). Older importation was by Abercrombie & Fitch located in New York, NY.

For individual model listings, please go to BlueBookOfGunValues.com/overflow.

GRADING - PPGS™	100%	98%	95%	90%	80%	70%	60%	LAST MSR

DUMOULIN, FRANCOIS

Previous shotgun manufacturer located in Liege, Belgium circa 1950s-1960s.

While Francois Dumoulin was well known for his shotguns, his company had no connection with any other Dumoulin family or trademark.

DUMOULIN, HENRI & FILS

Current manufacturer established circa 1950s and located in Herstal, Belgium. No current importation. Previously imported and distributed by New England Arms Corp. located in Kittery Point, ME.

Henri Dumoulin was the grandfather of the current owner of the Ernest Dumoulin and Dumoulin Herstal company. He began Henri Dumoulin & Fils during the late 1950s and worked with his 2 sons, Ernest and Noël. They were famous for their bolt action rifles based on k98 actions.

During the 1980s, Henri sold the company to Mr. Aukes from the Netherlands and worked with him until the early 1990s when his uncle died. Mr. Aukes continues the production of rifles under the name Henri Dumoulin & Fils. The company specializes in big-bore, high quality rifles, generally built on Mauser 98 or commercial Mauser actions. The improved double square bridge Imperial Magnum action was developed and introduced in 1987.

RIFLES: BOLT ACTION

GRAND LUXE BOLT ACTION – .300 Wby. Mag., .338 Win. Mag., .375 H&H, .378 Wby. Mag., .404 Jeffery, .416 Rigby, .460 Wby. Mag., or .505 Gibbs cal., 24, 25.6, or 26 in. barrel, European walnut stock with ebony forend tip and pistol grip cap, folding leaf rear sight, hooded front sight, custom made on the Dumoulin Imperial Magnum double square bridge action. Many engraving options are available.

MSR N/A	N/A	$7,995	$7,525	$6,700	$5,750	$5,100	$4,400

Add $750 for left-hand action.
Add $1,150 for extended top and bottom tang.
Add $1,000 for claw mounts.
Add $1,000 for .505 Gibbs cal.

SOVEREIGN – available in same cals. as Grand Luxe Bolt Action, except with a higher quality finish, knurled bolt handles, gold inlaid lettering. Many engraving options are available.

Values on this model depend on engraving, wood and other options.

Imperial Magnum was also available in various stages of completion, barreled actions, actions in the white, etc.

RIFLES: SxS, CUSTOM

Henri Dumoulin manufactures best quality boxlock and sidelock double rifles custom ordered to customer's specifications. Many options are available, including high quality wood and engraving. Prices start between $15,000 - $20,000. All guns should be individually appraised before buying or selling to determine accurate value.

SHOTGUNS: SxS, CUSTOM

Henri Dumoulin manufactured best quality boxlock and sidelock shotguns individually built to customer's specifications. Many options were available, including high quality wood and engraving. All guns should be individually appraised before buying or selling to determine accurate value.

DUMOULIN HERSTAL S.A.

Current company established in 1997 and located in Herstal, Belgium. This manufacturer's sister company is Ernest Dumoulin.

Dumoulin Herstal SA and Ernerst Dumoulin are two branches of the same company. Dumoulin-Hersal SA specializes in mechanical works and the production of parts for Ernest Dumoulin manufactured firearms.

E SECTION

84 GUN CO.

Previous manufacturer located in Eighty Four, PA. Circa early 1970s.

GRADING - PPGS™	100%	98%	95%	90%	80%	70%	60%	LAST MSR

RIFLES: BOLT ACTION

CLASSIC RIFLE – various calibers. Grades 1-4.

Grade 1	$420	$315	$275	$235	$210	$190	$170	
Grade 2	$780	$585	$512	$430	$390	$355	$315	
Grade 3	$860	$645	$560	$475	$430	$390	$345	
Grade 4	$1,580	$1,185	$1,030	$870	$790	$715	$640	

LOBO RIFLE – various calibers. Grades standard, 1-4.

Standard	$415	$315	$270	$230	$210	$190	$170	
Grade 1	$540	$405	$355	$300	$270	$245	$220	
Grade 2	$795	$600	$520	$440	$400	$360	$320	
Grade 3	$1,600	$1,200	$1,040	$880	$800	$720	$640	
Grade 4	$2,350	$1,765	$1,530	$1,295	$1,175	$1,060	$940	

PENNSYLVANIA RIFLE – various calibers. Grades standard, 1-4.

Standard	$420	$315	$275	$235	$210	$190	$170	
Grade 1	$540	$405	$355	$300	$270	$245	$220	
Grade 2	$795	$600	$520	$440	$400	$360	$320	
Grade 3	$1,600	$1,200	$1,040	$880	$800	$720	$640	
Grade 4	$2,350	$1,765	$1,530	$1,295	$1,175	$1,060	$940	

E. ARTHUR BROWN COMPANY INC.

Current manufacturer of falling block single shot rifles and pistols located in Garfield, MN. E. Arthur Brown also sells a wide variety of parts and shooting accessories including custom barrels and accessories for the T/C Encore, Contender AR-15, Savage, and Ruger 10-22.

PISTOLS: SINGLE SHOT

BF FALLING BLOCK SPORTING PISTOL – .22 LR, 6.5 BRM, or .44 Mag. cal., falling block action built on small frame, 10 (disc.), 10.75, 12, or 15 in. fixed barrel 2 or 3 ring KeyLock Mag. scope mount, w/rings, w/o scope, Harrett grooved right handed target grips with smooth forearm, Custom options engraving, premium wood and checkering, color case hardening, French gray, and more were available, but have since been discontinued, standard models are still available.

MSR $1,395	$1,180	$1,030	$890	$800	$650	$530	$470

Add $50 for grooved left or ambi target grips.

LTD ED BF ULTIMATE SILHOUETTE PISTOL – 7mm-08 or .284 Win. cal., ram head etched receiver, 10.75 in. heavy barrel, ScopeRib III Silhouette sight system, Harrett Walnut target grips, French Gray finish.

MSR $1,695	$1,440	$1,260	$1,080	$980	$790	$650	$560

RIFLES: SINGLE SHOT

MODEL 97D – 6.5 cal.BRM falling block action, 24 in. heavy contour blue or stainless steel barrel, no sights, uncheckered walnut stock and forearm, French grey receiver, includes Weaver rail, discontinued special features offered were 97D engraving, premium wood and checkering, color case hardening, French Gray finish, muzzle break and more, only standard models available, 6 lbs.

MSR $1,695	$1,500	$1,300	$1,100	$900	$700	$600	$550

Add $200 Camo stock.

* ***Deluxe Model 97D*** – 6.5 BRM or .17 Hornet cal., falling block, 24 in. blue steel barrel, KeyLock Mag. scope base and 1 in. rings, walnut stock, French Gray receiver finish and gold anodized stock transition, 6 lbs.

MSR $1,895	$1,610	$1,410	$1,210	$1,090	$880	$725	$630

Add $50 for ambi stock.

EAA CORP.

Please refer to European American Armory Corp. listing in this section.

E.D.M. ARMS

Previous manufacturer established in 1997, located in Hurricane, UT from 2008-2017. Previously located in Redlands, CA 1997-2008.

For individual model listings, please go to BlueBookOfGunValues.com/overflow.

GRADING - PPGS™	100%	98%	95%	90%	80%	70%	60%	LAST MSR

E.M.F. CO., INC.

Current importer and distributor established 1956, located in Santa Ana, CA. Distributor and dealer sales. E.M.F. stands for Early & Modern Firearms Inc.

For information on Great Western, Dakota Single Action and Hartford revolvers, rifles, and carbines imported by E.M.F., please refer to these individual sections. EMF previously imported Accu-Tech, Citadel, Excel, Howa, and ISSC pistols, rifles and shotguns from 2014-2015. Please refer to their individual sections for these listings. Please refer to the *Blue Book of Modern Black Powder Arms* (also online) for more information and prices on E.M.F.'s lineup of modern black powder models.

DERRINGERS: REPRODUCTIONS

STANDARD MODEL – .22 Short cal., copy of Colt Model Lord or Lady Derringer, blue, nickel, gold (disc.), or silver (disc.) gold finish. Importation disc. 1992.

$95	$80	$70	$60	$55	$50	$45	*$125*

1872 STANDARD MODEL – .22 Short cal., copy of Colt Model Lord or Lady Derringer, hardwood grips, nickel or silver/gold frame finish, 7 oz. Disc. 2005.

$75	$65	$60	$55	$50	$45	$40	*$90*

Add $30 for case, $95 for cased set with two Derringers.

PISTOLS: REPRODUCTIONS

REMINGTON ROLLING BLOCK PISTOL – .357 Mag. cal., rolling block design. Disc. 1992.

$300	$225	$185	$165	$155	$145	$135	*$395*

1892 "RANCH HAND" LEVER ACTION PISTOL – .45 LC cal., 12 in. barrel, gold bead front sight, adj. buckhorn rear sight, uncheckered straight grip walnut stock, saddle ring, large loop lever, barrel band, blue finish, 4 lbs. Mfg. by Rossi. Imported 2013-2014.

$495	$435	$375	$335	$275	$225	$175	*$580*

PISTOLS: SEMI-AUTO

All current semi-auto pistols are manufactured in the U.S.

HARTFORD 1911-A1 – .45 ACP cal., SA, patterned after original 1911, 5 in. barrel, 7 shot mag., fixed sights, black ergo, brown plastic military, ultra stag, or checkered hardwood grips, flat or arched mainspring housing, includes two mags., parkerized finish. Mfg. 2009-2013.

$515	$465	$400	$360	$330	$300	$275	*$585*

HARTFORD 1911 COMBAT MODEL – .45 ACP cal., 7 shot mag., similar to 1911-A1 model except has choice of fixed Tritium low profile, or adj. sights with Tritium inserts, black ergo or checkered hardwood grips, includes two mags., lock, and hard case, parkerized, blue, Duracoat, or nickel finish. Mfg. 2009-2013.

$595	$525	$450	$395	$360	$330	$300	*$685*

HARTFORD 1911 CCC MODEL – .45 ACP cal., 4 1/4 in. barrel, SA, 8 shot mag., choice of fixed low profile, Novak style fixed night, or Bo-Mar adj. sights, parkerized, blue, stainless, Duracoat, or nickel finishes, includes two mags., lock, and hard case. Mfg. 2009-2013.

$950	$825	$700	$575	$475	$425	$375	*$1,075*

Add $710 for night sights and skip checkered grips.

HARTFORD 1911-A1 COMMEMORATIVE MODEL – .45 ACP cal., 5 in. barrel, ultra ivory grips with Army, Navy, Air Force, or Marines insignia, includes medallion and deluxe presentation case, black finish with scrolled embellishments. Disc. 2013.

$895	$775	$650	N/A	N/A	N/A	N/A	*$999*

REVOLVERS: REPRODUCTIONS

Please refer to the Dakota Single Action Revolvers section in this text for previously imported revolvers under the Dakota trademark. Please also refer to the Great Western Arms and Hartford listings for trademarked guns imported by E.M.F.

1851 CONVERSION – .38 Spl. cal., color case hardened frame, walnut grips, 5 1/2 or 7 1/2 in. barrel. Imported 2007-2008.

$395	$340	$280	$235	$200	$180	$160	*$450*

1860 CONVERSION – .38 Spl. cal., 5 1/2 or 8 in. barrel, color case hardened frame, walnut grips. Imported 2007-2008.

$415	$370	$340	$300	$270	$240	$210	*$475*

1871 OPEN TOP – .38 Spl. or .45 LC cal., 5 1/2 or 7 1/2 in. barrel, color case hardened frame, walnut grips. Imported 2007-2008.

$375	$330	$280	$235	$200	$180	$160	*$440*

GRADING - PPGS™	100%	98%	95%	90%	80%	70%	60%	LAST MSR

1873 DAKOTA II – .357 Mag. or .45 LC cal., 4 3/4 or 5 1/2 in. barrel, antique brass backstrap and trigger guard, smooth walnut grips, matte black finish. Mfg. by Pietta, imported 2010-2020.

$475 $400 $350 $325 $250 $200 $175 *$520*

1873 DAKOTA III – .357 Mag. or .45 LC cal., 5 1/2 in. barrel, antique brass backstrap and trigger guard, smooth walnut grips, all blue finish. Mfg. by Pietta, imported 2018-2020.

$475 $425 $375 $325 $275 $225 $175 *$540*

1873 STALLION STANDARD – includes .22 LR and .22 WMR 10 shot cylinders, 5 1/2 in. barrel, patterned after the Colt SAA, case colored frame, brass backstrap and trigger guard. Mfg. by Uberti. Imported 2009-2013.

$350 $315 $285 $260 $240 $220 $200 *$480*

1873 STALLION TARGET – .22 LR cal., 10 shot cylinder, 5 1/2 in. barrel with ramp front sight and adj. rear sight, otherwise similar to 1873 Stallion Standard. Mfg. by Uberti. Imported 2009-2013.

$350 $315 $275 $240 $215 $195 $175 *$530*

RUSSIAN TOP-BREAK MODEL 1875 – .44 Russian (3rd Model only), or .45 LC cal., configurations include 2nd Model Hideout (3 1/2 in. barrel), Wells Fargo (5 in. barrel), 3rd Model Russian (6 1/2 in. barrel), or Cavalry (7 in. barrel), walnut grips, blue finish. Imported 2006-2008.

$795 $675 $600 $525 $450 $400 $350 *$900*

REMINGTON 1875 SA ARMY/FRONTIER – .357 Mag., .44-40 WCF (disc. 2003, reintroduced 2006) or .45 LC (disc. 2003, reintroduced 2006) cal., available in either 5 1/2 (Frontier) or 7 1/2 (Army, disc. 2003, reintroduced 2006) in. barrel, blue and case colored metal finishes, walnut grips. Mfg. by A. Uberti. Disc. 2013.

$450 $385 $335 $275 $240 $200 $175 *$520*

Add $280 for laser engraving with custom patina finish.
Add $220 for nickel finish or case coloring (disc. 2010).
Add $15 for steel trigger guard (disc.).
Add $200 for bright or satin (disc. 2000) nickel plating.
Add $250 for engraving (disc.).
Add $85 for convertible cylinder (.45 LC/.45 ACP, disc.).

REMINGTON MODEL 1890 SA POLICE – .45 LC cal., standard blue or engraved frame with custom patina finish, 5 1/2 in. barrel, lanyard ring in buttstock, blue frame, walnut grips. Mfg. by A. Uberti. Imported 1986-2009.

$425 $365 $315 $260 $230 $200 $175 *$480*

Add $210 for laser engraving with custom patina finish (disc.).
Add $10 for steel trigger guard (disc.).
Add $200 for bright or satin (disc. 2000) nickel plating.
Add $85 for convertible cylinder (.45 LC/.45 ACP, disc.).
Add $260 for engraving (disc.).

SCHOFIELD MODEL – .45 LC cal., replica of the original S&W Schofield, choice of 3 1/2 (Hideout), 5 (Wells Fargo), or 7 in. (Civilian/Cavalry) barrel, blue finish. Mfg. by Uberti. Imported 1999-2003.

$575 $500 $450 $415 $385 $360 $340 *$625*

RIFLES: SxS

CLASSIC 92 – 9.3x74mm or .45-70 cal., 24 in. barrels, extractor, single trigger, engraving on polished receiver. Disc.

$2,775 $2,550 $2,300 $2,000 $1,750 $1,475 $1,050 *$3,110*

KODIAK MARK IV DOUBLE EXPRESS – .45-70 Govt. cal., back action, browned 24 in. barrels with triple leaf express sights, color case hardened frame, trigger guard and hammers. Imported until 2020.

$5,750 $5,000 $4,250 $3,500 $2,750 $2,000 $1,750 *$6,361*

RIFLES: SEMI-AUTO

J R CARBINE – 9mm Para., .40 S&W, or .45 ACP cal., blowback operation, utilizes standard M4/AR-15 furniture and trigger components, right or left-hand action, Glock magazine, can be converted to other popular pistol mags., flat-top receiver, quad rail forend, black adj. stock, extended pistol grip, tri-flatted barrel design, patented ejection and extraction features, compatible with AR-15 accessories. Mfg. in U.S.A. by J R Carbines, LLC mid-2010-2013.

$675 $600 $525 $475 $425 $400 $350 *$750*

Please refer to Just Right Carbines listing for current manufacture.

GRADING - PPGS™	100%	98%	95%	90%	80%	70%	60%	LAST MSR

J R CARBINE 12 – 9mm Para., .40 S&W, or .45 ACP cal., blowback operation, utilizes standard M4/AR-15 furniture and trigger components, right or left-hand action, Glock magazine, can be converted to other popular pistol mags., flat-top receiver, quad rail forend, black adj. stock, extended pistol grip, tri-flatted barrel design, patented ejection and extraction features, compatible with AR-15 accessories. Mfg. in U.S.A. by J R Carbines, LLC mid-2010-2013.

	$675	$600	$525	$475	$425	$400	$350	*$750*

Please refer to Just Right Carbines listing for current manufacture.

KRONOS (CHRONOS) – .30-06 or .308 Win. cal., 20 in. round barrel, checkered wood stock and forend, matte black finish. Mfg. by Pietta. Importation began 2016.

MSR $1,390	$1,200	$1,050	$900	$825	$675	$550	$425	

RIFLES: SEMI-AUTO, REPRODUCTIONS

These models are authentic shooting reproductions previously manufactured in Italy.

AP 74 – .22 LR or .32 ACP cal., copy of the Colt AR-15, 15 shot mag., 20 in. barrel, 6 3/4 lbs. Importation disc. 1989.

	$350	$295	$250	$200	$175	$155	$145	*$295*

Add $25 for .32 ACP cal.

* ***AP74 Sporter Carbine*** – .22 LR cal. only, wood sporter stock. Importation disc. 1989.

	$375	$325	$275	$225	$195	$175	$160	*$320*

* ***AP74 Paramilitary Paratrooper Carbine*** – .22 LR cal. only, folding wire, black nylon, or wood folding stock. Importation disc. 1987.

	$395	$350	$300	$260	$215	$175	$165	*$325*

Add $10 for wood folding stock.

* ***AP74 "Dressed" Military Model*** – Cyclops scope, Colt bayonet, sling, and bipod. Disc. 1986.

	$395	$350	$300	$265	$240	$220	$200	*$450*

GALIL – .22 LR cal. only, reproduction of the Israeli Galil. Importation disc. 1989.

	$350	$295	$250	$200	$175	$155	$145	*$295*

KALASHNIKOV AK-47 – .22 LR cal. only, reproduction of the Russian AK-47, semi-auto. Importation disc. 1989.

	$350	$295	$250	$200	$175	$155	$145	*$295*

FRENCH M.A.S. – .22 LR cal. only, reproduction of the French bullpup combat rifle, with carrying handle, 29 shot mag. Importation disc. 1989.

	$375	$325	$265	$240	$220	$200	$185	*$320*

M1 CARBINE – .30 cal. only, copy of the U.S. Military M1 Carbine. Disc. 1985.

	$295	$250	$225	$200	$175	$150	$125	*$205*

Add 50% for Paratrooper variation.

RIFLES/CARBINES: COLT REPRODUCTIONS

LIGHTNING STANDARD – .357 Mag. (new 2009), .44-40 WCF or .45 LC cal., patterned after the Colt Lightning rifle, blue finish, 20 in. round or octagon, 24 in. octagon, or 26 in. octagon (disc. 2009) barrel, straight grip uncheckered walnut stock, drilled and tapped, semi-buckhorn rear sight. Mfg. by Pedersoli 2008-2013.

	$1,300	$1,175	$1,050	$925	$800	$675	$550	*$1,450*

Add $100 for rifle configuration with 20 in barrel, or $150 for 24 or 26 (disc.) in. barrel.

* ***Lightning Deluxe*** – .357 Mag., .44-40 WCF or .45 LC cal., patterned after the Colt Lightning rifle, 20, 24, or 26 in. barrel, color case hardened finish, checkered semi-fancy walnut stock, drilled and tapped, semi-buckhorn rear sight. Mfg. by Pedersoli 2008-2013.

	$1,450	$1,250	$1,050	$925	$800	$650	$525	*$1,670*

Add $20 for 24 in. or $40 for 26 in. barrel.

Add $280 for Super Deluxe Model with engraved coin finished frame and fine checkered fancy walnut stock.

RIFLES: REMINGTON REPRODUCTIONS

ROLLING BLOCK CARBINE/RIFLE – .45-70 Govt. cal., authentic reproduction of the Remington Rolling Block Rifle, standard (disc. 2003) or target model, 26 (carbine) or 30 (disc.) in. octagon barrel. Mfg. by Pedersoli. Imported 1991-2006, reintroduced 2009-2013.

	$825	$725	$625	$550	$475	$400	$325	*$930*

Subtract approx. $100 for standard model.

GRADING - PPGS™	100%	98%	95%	90%	80%	70%	60%	LAST MSR

* ***Rolling Block Rifle Target Deluxe*** – .45-70 Govt. cal., similar to Rolling Block Rifle, except has 30 or 32 (disc. 2013) in. barrel, checkered pistol grip stock, case hardened finish, and German silver forearm cap. Imported 2000-2002, reintroduced 2009-2014.

$1,150	$1,000	$865	$775	$635	$525	$400	*$1,350*

ROLLING BLOCK SILHOUETTE – .45-70 Govt. cal., color case hardened finish, 30 in. blue octagon barrel. Mfg. by Pedersoli 2013-2015.

$1,295	$1,125	$975	$875	$710	$585	$450	*$1,520*

ROLLING BLOCK SUPER MATCH – .45-70 Govt. cal., color case hardened finish, 34 in. blue octagon barrel, unchecked pistol grip walnut stock and forearm. Mfg. by Pedersoli 2013-2014.

$1,395	$1,225	$1,050	$950	$775	$625	$495	*$1,635*

ROLLING BLOCK "JOHN BODINE" MODEL – .45-70 Govt. cal., color case hardened finish, 30 or 34 in. blue octagon barrel, unchecked pistol grip walnut stock and forearm, DT. Mfg. by Pedersoli 2013-2014.

$1,650	$1,450	$1,250	$1,125	$910	$750	$575	*$1,950*

Add $100 for 34 in. barrel.

BABY ROLLING BLOCK CARBINE/RIFLE – .357 Mag. cal., 22 or 26 in. barrel, color case hardened frame. Importation began 1992, reintroduced 2006 and 2009.

$595	$525	$450	$375	$325	$275	$225	*$665*

Add $25 for 26 in. rifle configuration.

REVOLVING CARBINE – .357 Mag., .44-40 WCF (disc.), or .45 LC cal., 18 in. barrel, case colored frame, walnut grips, Model 1875 Army Single Action design, 5 lbs. Importation disc. 1995, reintroduced 2003.

$450	$375	$315	$265	$230	$200	$185	*$560*

TEXAS CARBINE (1858 REMINGTON) – .22 LR cal., action patterned after Remington revolving carbine, 21 in. octagon barrel, wood stock and forearm, brass frame. Also available with extra .22 WMR cal. cylinder. Importation disc. 1998.

$295	$225	$175	$150	$135	$125	$110	*$400*

RIFLES: SHARPS REPRODUCTIONS

1874 SHARPS SPORTING OR MILITARY RIFLE – .45-70 Govt., .45 LC (mfg. 2004-2006), or .45-120 cal., copy of the Sharps Single Shot, 28 or 30 in. octagonal barrel, case hardened frame, single or double set triggers. Importation disc. 1999, reintroduced 2003-2008.

$900	$800	$700	$625	$550	$475	$395	*$1,025*

Add $120 for checkered stock.
Add $180 for in-the-white (no metal finish, disc.).
Add $120 for brown finish (disc.)
Add $45 for target variation with 1/2 round, 1/2 octagon barrel (disc.)

* ***1874 Sharps Deluxe Rifle*** – .45-70 Govt. or .45-120 (disc.) cal., blue or brown finish, 32 in. tapered octagon barrel, double set triggers, checkered pistol grip and forearm, case hardened frame, silver forend tip. Disc. 2008.

$1,325	$1,200	$1,025	$875	$775	$695	$625	*$1,500*

An engraved version of this model was available for $2,500, and Super Deluxe with gold inlays was $3,150.

* ***1874 Sharps Silhouette*** – .45-70 Govt. cal., 32 in. tapered octagon barrel, double set triggers, checkered pistol grip stock and forearm, case colored frame. Mfg. 2009-2013.

$1,525	$1,375	$1,225	$1,050	$900	$775	$625	*$1,700*

Add $200 for Billy Dixon variation with straight grip stock.
Subtract $400 for 1874 Business Rifle configuration in .45-70 Govt. cal. only.

* ***1874 Sharps Sporting Rifle (Recent Mfg.)*** – .45-70 Govt. cal., copy of the Sharps Single Shot, 32 in. octagonal barrel, case hardened frame, adj. front and rear sights, oil finished checkered straight grip walnut stock and forearm, double set trigger, drilled and tapped, 11 lbs. Mfg. by Pedersoli. Imported 2013-2020.

$1,375	$1,200	$1,025	$935	$750	$625	$475	*$1,615*

* ***1874 Sharps Military Carbine*** – saddle ring carbine with 22 in. round barrel, single trigger. Disc. 2005.

$695	$625	$550	$495	$450	$425	$400	*$760*

QUIGLEY SHARPS MODEL 1874 SPORTING RIFLE – .45-70 Govt., .45-90 (disc.), .45-110 (new 2007), or .45-120 (disc. 2003, reintroduced 2006) cal., 34 in. heavy octagon barrel with storage compartment in stock. Imported 2000-2020.

$2,075	$1,775	$1,500	$1,350	$1,075	$875	$750	*$2,405*

Add $100 for .45-110 or .45-120 cal.(disc.).

GRADING - PPGS™	100%	98%	95%	90%	80%	70%	60%	LAST MSR

1874 SHARPS BUSINESS RIFLE - .45-70 Govt. cal., 32 in. octagonal barrel, case hardened frame, adj. front and rear sights, oil finished checkered straight grip walnut stock and forearm, double set trigger, drilled and tapped, 11 lbs. Mfg. by Pedersoli. Imported 2013-2020.

	$1,350	$1,175	$975	$875	$725	$575	$450	*$1,585*

1874 SHARPS COMPETITION RIFLE - .45-70 Govt. cal., 34 in. octagonal barrel, satin finished frame, interchangeable front sight, oil finished checkered pistol grip walnut stock and forearm, double set trigger, drilled and tapped, German silver grip cap, Hartford collar, 13 lbs. Mfg. by Pedersoli. Importation began 2013.

MSR $2,200	$1,850	$1,600	$1,325	$1,175	$950	$775	$625	

1874 SHARPS "BILLY DIXON" RIFLE - .45-70 Govt. cal., 32 in. octagonal barrel, case hardened frame, checkered straight grip walnut stock and forearm, double set trigger, German silver grip cap, mfg. by Pedersoli, 10.8 lbs. Imported 2013-2020.

	$1,850	$1,600	$1,325	$1,175	$950	$775	$625	*$2,215*

EMF SILHOUETTE RIFLE - .45-70 Govt. cal., 32 in. tapered octagonal barrel, case hardened frame, checkered pistol grip walnut stock and forearm, double set trigger, mfg. by Pedersoli exclusively for EMF. Imported 2013-2014.

	$1,525	$1,325	$1,150	$1,025	$840	$685	$535	*$1,800*

RIFLES: SPENCER REPRODUCTIONS

1865 SPENCER CARBINE - .44-40 WCF or .56-50 cal., 20 in. barrel with barrel band, case colored receiver and hammer, includes sling swivels, 8 lbs. Mfg. by Armi Sport 2006-2008.

	$1,095	$950	$825	$700	$600	$500	$400	*$1,280*

RIFLES: SPRINGFIELD REPRODUCTIONS

SPRINGFIELD 1873 TRAPDOOR CARBINE/RIFLE - .45-70 Govt. cal., trapdoor single shot action, 22 (carbine), 26 (Officer's Model), or 32 (Rifle) in. barrel, blue action, walnut stock. Mfg. by Pedersoli. Disc. 2015.

	$1,225	$1,075	$925	$835	$675	$550	$450	*$1,430*

Add $190 for Rifle (disc. 2009) or $460 for Officer's Model.

RIFLES: WINCHESTER REPRODUCTIONS

DELUXE 1860 HENRY RIFLE - .44-40 WCF or .45 LC cal. only, brass or case colored steel frame, deluxe walnut, reproduction of New Haven Arms Co.'s Henry Rifle, 24 in. blue or white barrel. Mfg. 1987-2008.

	$925	$750	$525	$400	$350	$300	$275	*$1,050*

Add $135 for in-the-white barrel or for case colored steel (.45 LC cal. only) frame.

* ***Deluxe 1860 Henry Rifle Engraved*** - similar to deluxe Henry Rifle except has hand engraved receiver. Imported 1987-90.

	$1,350	$975	$700	$525	$400	$340	$295	*$1,598*

1866 YELLOWBOY CARBINE - .22 LR (disc. 2002), .22 WMR (mfg. 2000-2002), .32-20 WCF (mfg. 2000-2002), .38 Spl., .38-40 WCF (mfg. 2000-2002, reintroduced 2005), .44-40 WCF, or .45 LC (new 1993) cal., 19 in. barrel, brass frame, saddle ring carbine. Disc. 2003, reintroduced 2005-2008.

	$725	$600	$475	$350	$275	$235	$200	*$870*

Add $330 for laser engraved Indian model (.45 LC cal. only).

* ***1866 Yellowboy Rifle*** - same cals. as 1866 Yellowboy Carbine, 20 (Border model short rifle, new 1999) or 24 1/4 (Sporting) in. barrel. Disc. 2008.

	$775	$625	$495	$350	$275	$235	$200	*$920*

Add $50 for in-the-white barrel.

* ***1866 Yellowboy Border Rifle*** - .38 Spl. or .45 LC cal., 20 in. octagon barrel, brass frame. Mfg. by Uberti. Imported 2010-2013.

	$1,000	$875	$750	$675	$550	$450	$350	*$1,175*

Add $200 for "Jim Bowie" action job.

* ***1866 Yellowboy Carbine Engraved*** - .38 Spl. or .44-40 WCF cal. Importation disc. 1990.

	$875	$575	$440	$330	$295	$260	$230	*$1,080*

1873 CARBINE - .22 WMR (disc.), .32-20 WCF (mfg. 1999-2000, reintroduced 2005-2006), .357 Mag. (disc. 2000, reintroduced 2003, and again in 2005), .38-40 WCF (mfg. 2000, reintroduced 2005-2006), .44 Spl. (mfg. 2000, reintroduced 2005-2006), .44-40 WCF (disc. 2000, reintroduced 2005), or .45 LC cal., 16 (Trapper model) or 19 in. round barrel, copy of the Winchester Model 1873 Carbine, blue (disc. 2000) or case hardened steel receiver. Disc. 2003, reintroduced 2005-2008.

	$875	$700	$525	$425	$325	$275	$235	*$1,040*

GRADING - PPGS™	100%	98%	95%	90%	80%	70%	60%	LAST MSR

* ***1873 Carbine/Rifle*** – .32-20 WCF, .357 Mag., .38-40 WCF, .44-40 WCF, or .45 LC cal., 20 (Border model short rifle, new 1999), 24 1/4, or 30 (limited importation 2000, reintroduced 2007) in. barrel, case hardened receiver. Disc. 2008.

	$880	$700	$525	$425	$325	$275	$235	*$1,050*

Add $30 for 30 in. barrel.
Add $50 for Deluxe Border model.
Add $120 for Deluxe model with checkered pistol grip stock (.357 Mag. or .45 LC cal. only, disc. 2003).

* ***1873 Border Rifle*** – .357 Mag. or .45 LC cal., 20 in. octagon barrel, brass frame, mfg. by Uberti. Imported 2010-2013.

	$1,050	$925	$795	$715	$575	$475	$375	*$1,250*

Add $200 for "Jim Bowie" action job.

* ***1873 Carbine/Rifle Youngboy*** – .22 LR cal., blue steel, 19 or 24 1/4 in. barrel. Imported 1995-96.

	$800	$600	$450	$330	$295	$260	$230	*$1,050*

Add $50 for rifle barrel.

* ***1873 Carbine Rifle Engraved*** – .357 Mag. or .44-40 WCF cal. only. Importation disc. 1987.

	$895	$635	$500	$450	$400	$360	$325	*$850*

PREMIER 1873 CARBINE & RIFLE – .45 LC cal., case hardened frame, uncheckered walnut stock and forearm, full mag., rifle has 24 1/4 in. barrel, carbine has 19 in. barrel. Imported 1988-1989 only.

	$850	$595	$450	$330	$295	$260	$230	*$1,160*

1876 RIFLE – .40-60 or .45-75 cal., patterned after the Model 1876 Winchester, case hardened frame with 28 in. octagon barrel with open sights. Imported 2006-2008.

	$1,050	$875	$750	$625	$500	$450	$400	*$1,265*

1885 HIGH WALL RIFLE (UBERTI MFG.) – .38-55 WCF (new 2000), .40-65 (mfg. 2005-2006), .45-70 Govt., or .45-90 (mfg. 2005-2006) cal., action patterned after the Winchester Model 1885 High Wall, 30 or 32 (mfg. 2003 only) in. barrel, checkered walnut stock. Mfg. by Uberti. Imported 1998-2003, reintroduced 2005-2008.

	$925	$800	$675	$550	$500	$465	$435	*$900*

Add approx. 15% for deluxe model with checkered pistol grip stock.

1885 HIGH WALL RIFLE (PEDERSOLI MFG.) – .38-55 WCF (disc. 2014) or .45-70 Govt. cal., case hardened frame, 30 (disc. 2014) or 32 in. blued octagon barrel, deluxe wood with cheekpiece. Imported 2009-2015, reintroduced 2018-2020.

	$1,885	$1,650	$1,395	$1,250	$1,025	$835	$650	*$2,220*

MODEL 1886/71 LEVER ACTION – .45-70 Govt. cal., inertia firing pin, 24 in. round barrel, adj. rear sight, checkered pistol grip walnut stock and forend, drilled and tapped, blue finish, 7 lbs. Mfg. by Pedersoli. Imported 2013-2020.

	$1,550	$1,350	$1,150	$1,025	$850	$695	$575	*$1,850*

MODEL 1892 LEVER ACTION – .357 Mag., .44 Mag., or .45 LC cal., 16 or 20 in. round or 20 or 24 in. octagonal barrel, 8, 10, or 12 shot, uncheckered straight grip hardwood stock and forend with buttplate, blue, color case hardened, or stainless, 5-7 lbs. Mfg. by Rossi. Imported 2013-2020.

	$485	$425	$365	$325	$265	$225	$175	*$575*

Add $25 for saddle ring.
Add $10 for stainless.
Add $55 for octagonal barrel.

SHOTGUNS

1878 HARTFORD SXS – 12 or 20 ga., Colt style coach gun, 20 in. barrel, external hammers, select wood stock. Mfg. by Pietta.

MSR $1,150	$1,000	$850	$750	$650	$550	$450	$350

CHALLENGE SEMI-AUTO SERIES – 12 or 20 ga., inertia or gas, configurations include Zephyrus (12 ga., inertia), Ghibli (20 ga., inertia), or Mistral (gas operated) models. Mfg. by Pietta. Importation began 2016.

GHIBLI – 20 ga., inertia operated, 28 in. matte blue barrel, matte black receiver, black synthetic stock. Mfg. by Pietta. Importation began 2016.

MSR $970	$825	$725	$625	$575	$450	$375	$300

* ***Ghibli Camo*** – 20 ga., inertia operation, 28 in. barrel, synthetic stock, 100% camo finish. Mfg. by Pietta. Importation began 2016.

MSR $1,195	$1,025	$900	$775	$700	$575	$475	$375

GRADING - PPGS™	100%	98%	95%	90%	80%	70%	60%	LAST MSR

* ***Ghibli Wood*** – 20 ga., inertia operation, 28 in. blued barrel, blued or nickel receiver, varnished wood stock. Mfg. by Pietta. Importation began 2016.

MSR $1,120	$950	$825	$725	$650	$525	$425	$325	

Add $140 for nickel receiver with gold plated engraved birds and fiber optic sight.

MARK V CONQUEST SEMI-AUTO – 12 ga. only, 28 in. barrel with choke tubes. Limited importation 2003.

	$385	$325	$275	$240	$220	$200	$185	*$460*

MISTRAL – 12 or 20 ga., gas operated, 28 in. barrel, blued or nickel receiver, synthetic or wood stock, black or 100% camo finish. Mfg. by Pietta. Importation began 2016.

MSR $915	$775	$675	$575	$525	$425	$350	$275	

MODEL 1878 SxS – 12 ga. only, exposed hammers, 20 in. barrels, patterned after the Colt Model 1878 shotgun. Imported 2006-2013.

	$425	$385	$340	$300	$260	$230	$195	*$475*

MODEL 1878 "WYATT EARP" SxS HAMMER GUN – 12 ga. only, exposed hammers, 20 1/8 in. barrels, patterned after the Colt Model 1878 shotgun, color case hardened frame with "Wyatt Earp" engraved on receiver, checkered pistol grip walnut stock and forearm. Mfg. by Pedersoli. Imported 2013-2020.

	$1,350	$1,175	$1,000	$925	$750	$610	$475	*$1,590*

MODEL 1897 SLIDE ACTION – 12 ga. only, 20 in. barrel, patterned after the Winchester Model 1897, exposed hammer. Imported 2006-2008.

	$440	$395	$350	$300	$260	$230	$195	*$515*

STAGECOACH SxS MODEL – 12 ga. only, features exposed hammers and 20 in. brown barrels, mfg. by S.I.A.C.E. Imported 2000-2002.

	$1,175	$900	$700	$500	$450	$400	$365	*$1,375*

ZEPHYRUS – 12 ga., inertia operated, 28 in. matte blue barrel, matte black receiver, black synthetic stock. Mfg. by Pietta. Importation began 2016.

MSR $965	$825	$725	$625	$575	$450	$375	$300	

* ***Zephyrus Camo*** – 12 ga., inertia operation, 28 in. barrel, synthetic stock, 100% camo finish. Mfg. by Pietta. Importation began 2016.

MSR $1,190	$1,025	$900	$775	$700	$575	$475	$375	

* ***Zephyrus Wood*** – 12 ga., inertia operation, 28 in. blued barrel, blued or nickel receiver, varnished wood stock. Mfg. by Pietta. Importation began 2016.

MSR $1,115	$950	$825	$725	$650	$525	$425	$325	

Add $140 for nickel receiver with gold plated engraved birds and fiber optic sight.

E.R. SHAW INC.

Current rifle and barrel manufacturer established circa 1913 and located in Bridgeville, PA. Consumer direct sales through FFL dealers.

RIFLES: BOLT ACTION

E.R. Shaw's website offers a "custom online rifle builder," allowing the customer to choose exactly what they want with an instant price quotation. Current built time is approx. 4-5 months. Please contact the company directly for a quotation based on individual specifications and special orders.

MK X CS/MK VII CS RIFLE – various cals., short action, right-hand only, heavy varmint contour barrel, target crown or threaded muzzle, optional Shaw Ti muzzle brake, one AI style mag., Magpul PRS Gen III stock, MDT LSS XL Gen II chassis, includes soft case, choice of steel or Woodland, Urban, or Desert Camo finish, 12-14 lbs. New 2019.

Current MSR on these models are $1,595 (Mk. VII CS model) and $1,860 (Mk. X CS model).

MK VII CUSTOM RIFLE – various cals., choice of stainless or chrome moly barrel, laminate wood, walnut, or synthetic stock, as well as many other special features may be ordered. Mfg. 2012-circa 2017.

Last base MSR on this model was $775.

* ***MK VII Gen II Custom Rifle*** – over 80 cals. available ranging from .17 Rem. to .450 Marlin cal., long or short action, up to 26 in. stainless or chrome moly barrel w/heavy Sporter or light Varmint contour, triple-honed trigger, Timney trigger and Warne bases available up on request, checkered or laminate wood stock w/Pachmayr recoil pads, glass pillar bedded actions w/full free float barrels, polished feed ramp and rail, drilled and tapped for Savage round receiver scope bases, tear drop bolt handles, 7 1/2 -8 1/2 lbs. New 2019.

Current base MSR on this model ranges from $990-$1,600.

GRADING - PPGS™ 100% 98% 95% 90% 80% 70% 60% LAST MSR

MK VII TS CUSTOM RIFLE – over 80 cals. available ranging from .17 Rem. to .450 Marlin cal., #5 heavy barrel in chrome moly or stainless steel in multiple barrel lengths, helical and straight fluting, long or short actions, aluminum bedding block, bottom rail, sling swivels, right or left-hand configuration, non-gloss matte black tactical synthetic stock with adj. spacers, polished or matte finishes. New 2015.

Since this model can be built to individual customer specifications, please contact the company directly for more information including price, options, and delivery time.

MK VII VS CUSTOM RIFLE – various cals., single shot receiver in stainless steel, choice of steel, stainless or chrome moly barrel with or w/o fluting, choice of barrel length from 18 to 26 inches, choice of two stocks in pepper laminate (fully adj. cheekpiece and separately adj. buttplate, or a cheekpiece that can be set at two heights), fully adjustable bottom rail. Mfg. 2013-2017.

Last base MSR on this model was $1,282.

MK X CUSTOM RIFLE – over 80 cals. available ranging from .17 Rem. to .450 Marlin cal., stainless steel or blued chrome moly steel barrel, heavy Sporter or light Varmint, bolt and barrel fluting, muzzle brake or muzzle threads, detachable magazine or hinged floorplate, fixed ejector, licensing agreement for the Savage AccuTrigger, Timney trigger upgrade available, select grade walnut stock, Shaw's proprietary advanced receiver, integral bases, controlled round push feed bolt, integral 1/4 in. recoil lug, 7 1/2-8 1/2 lbs. Initially advertised during 2013, mfg. started 2017.

Current base MSR is $1,400.

RIFLES: SEMI-AUTO

E.R. Shaw's website offers a "custom online rifle builder," allowing the customer to choose exactly what they want with an instant price quotation. Current built time is approx. 4-5 months. Please contact the company directly for a quotation based on individual specifications and special orders.

Previous AR-15 style models include: ERS M4 (last MSR $830), ERS15 22LR (last MSR $695), SPG ERS-15 (last MSR $1,046), and SPG ERS-15 (last MSR $1,046 -$1,183).

ERS-15 – 5.56 NATO or .300 AAC Blackout cal., 16, 18 (M4 or H-Bar), or 20 (bull barrel only) in. stainless steel, matte, or polish finish, choice of straight, staggered, or Shaw Helical fluting, optics ready, Magpul stock, aluminum forged upper and lower receiver, NiB bolt, one-piece T-MOD or two-piece Magpul MOE rail, laser engraved T-Marks, hardcoat anodized or Cerakote finish. New 2017.

Please contact the manufacturer directly for custom order specifications and pricing on this model.

ERS15 SPC – 5.56 NATO cal., GIO, 18 in. stainless steel helical fluted barrel, flash hider, single stage trigger, Magpul MOE stock, 15 in. free floating APF handguard. Disc.

$650 $575 $510 $440 $385 $340 $325 *$756*

ERS-10 – .308 Win. or 6.5 Creedmoor cal., 20-24 in. Precision button rifled, stainless steel barrel, Shaw Custom muzzle brake, Magpul stocks, aluminum forged upper and lower receiver, 15 in. free float handguard, wire EDM magwells.

Current base MSR on this model is $1,200.

EAGLE ARMS, INC.

Previous trademark of AR-15 style pistols and carbines/rifles manufactured by ArmaLite, Inc. from 2017-2020. Eagle Arms, Inc. was a previous manufacturer located in Geneseo, IL until they became a division of ArmaLite, Inc. 1995-2002. In 2003, Eagle Arms became a separate company, and no longer a division of ArmaLite. Manufacture of pre-1995 Eagle Arms rifles was in Coal Valley, IL.

PISTOLS: SEMI-AUTO

EAGLE-15 – .223 Rem./5.56x45mm cal., 6 or 11 in. chrome moly/chrome-lined barrel with flash suppressor, 20 shot Magpul PMAG, single stage trigger, front sight base, SIG pistol brace, Magpul K2 grip, carbine length gas system, 5 or 10 in. tactical KeyMod handguard, forged aluminum lower and flat-top upper with full-length Mil-Std 1913 rail, black hard anodized aluminum finish, 6 lbs. Mfg. 2018-disc.

$750 $600 $525 $475 $425 $400 $375 *$996*

RIFLES: SEMI-AUTO, CURRENT

EAGLE-15 – .223 Rem./5.56x45mm cal., 16 in. chrome moly straight taper barrel with flash suppressor, 30 shot Magpul PMAG, single stage trigger, A2 front sight base or gas block with Picatinny rail (ORC model), 6-pos. collapsible stock, carbine length gas system, 6 in. standard handguard, forged aluminum lower and flat-top upper with Picatinny rail, hard anodized finish, 6 1/2 lbs. Mfg. 2017-disc..

$450 $350 $325 $275 $250 $235 $225 *$599*

GRADING - PPGS™	100%	98%	95%	90%	80%	70%	60%	LAST MSR

EAGLE-15 MISSION FIRST TACTICAL – .223 Wylde chamber, GIO, gas block rail, 16 in. straight taper heavy barrel, flash suppressor, 30 shot MFT mag., A2 front sight, polymer backup sight, 6 in. standard handguard, 6-pos. MFT BMS stock, forged aluminum lower and flat-top upper receiver, Picatinny rail, SST, charging handle, black anodized finish, 6 1/2 lbs. Mfg. 2017-disc.

$500 $375 $350 $300 $275 $250 $225 *$650*

EAGLE-15 OPTICS READY CARBINE – .223 Wylde chamber, GIO, gas block rail, 16 in. straight taper heavy barrel with Cerakote finish, flash suppressor, 30 shot Magpul PMAG, SST, 6 in. standard handguard, forged aluminum lower and flat-top upper receiver with Picatinny rail, charging handle, 6-pos. collapsible stock, 6 1/2 lbs. Mfg. 2017-disc.

$475 $375 $325 $300 $275 $250 $225 *$623*

EAGLE-15 VERSATILE SPORTING RIFLE (VSR) – .223 Rem./5.56x45mm cal. (.223 Wylde chamber), 16 in. chrome moly barrel with flash suppressor and knurled thread protector, 30 shot Magpul PMAG, SST, 6-pos. collapsible stock, rubberized Ergo grip, free float rail system, carbine length gas system, 15 in. VSR handguard with KeyMod attachments, forged aluminum lower and flat-top upper with Picatinny rail, hard anodized aluminum finish, 6.6 lbs. Mfg. 2018-disc.

$625 $475 $425 $375 $350 $325 $300 *$818*

RIFLES: SEMI-AUTO, RECENT MFG.

On the following M-15 models manufactured 1995 and earlier, A2 accessories included a collapsible carbine type buttstock (disc. per 1994 C/B) and forward bolt assist mechanism. Accessories are similar, with the addition of National Match sights. The A2 suffix indicates the rifle is supplied with carrying handle, A4 designates a flat-top receiver, some are equipped with a detachable carrying handle.

AR-10 MATCH RIFLE - .308 Win. cal., AR-15 style, GIO, very similar to the Armalite AR-10 A4 rifle, 20 or 24 (Match rifle) in. chrome moly barrel, 10 shot mag., no sights, black stock with pistol grip and forearm, A2 (Service rifle) or A4 style flat-top upper receiver, 9.6 lbs. Mfg. 2001-2005.

$850 $550 $465 $395 $350 $325 $295 *$1,000*

Add $65 for Service rifle with A2 front/rear sights.
Add $480 for 24 in. barrel and aluminum free floating handguard.

MODEL M15 A2/A4 RIFLE (EA-15 E-1) – .223 Rem. or .308 Win. cal., GIO, patterned after the Colt AR-15A, 20 in. barrel, A2 sights or A4 flat-top, with (pre 1993) or w/o forward bolt assist, 7 lbs. Mfg. 1990-1993, reintroduced 2002-2005.

$675 $500 $425 $375 $335 $315 $295 *$795*

Add $40 for .223 cal. flat-top (Model E15A4B).
Add $205 for .308 Win. cal. flat-top.

* ***Model M15 A2/A4 Rifle Carbine (EA9025C/EA9027C)*** – .223 Rem. or .308 Win. cal., GIO, 16 in. barrel, collapsible (disc. per C/B 1994) or fixed (new 1994) buttstock, 5 lbs. 14 oz. Mfg. 1990-1995, reintroduced 2002-2005.

$675 $500 $425 $375 $335 $315 $295 *$795*

Add $40 for flat-top (Model E15A4CB).
1997 retail for the pre-ban models was $1,100 (EA9396).

Beginning 1993, the A2 accessory kit became standard on this model.

* ***Model M15 A2 H-BAR Rifle (EA9040C)*** – .223 Rem. or .308 Win. cal., GIO, heavy target barrel, includes E-2 accessories, 8 lbs. 14 oz. Mfg. 1990-1995.

$765 $515 $440 $375 $335 $315 $295 *$895*

1997 retail for this pre-ban model was $1,100 (EA9200).

* ***Model M15 A4 Rifle Eagle Spirit (EA9055S)*** – .223 Rem. or .308 Win. cal., GIO, designed for IPSC shooting, 16 in. premium air gauged National Match barrel, fixed stock, full-length tubular aluminum handguard, includes match grade accessories, 8 lbs. 6 oz. Mfg. 1993-1995, reintroduced 2002 only.

$725 $500 $435 $375 $335 $315 $295 *$850*

The 1995 pre-ban variation of this model retailed at $1,475 (EA9603).

* ***Model M15 A2 Rifle Golden Eagle (EA9049S)*** – .223 Rem. or .308 Win. cal., GIO, 20 in. extra heavy barrel, two-stage trigger, National Match accessories, 12 lbs. 12 oz. Mfg. 1991-1995, reintroduced 2002 only.

$935 $575 $475 $415 $350 $325 $300 *$1,125*

The 1997 pre-ban variation of this model retailed at $1,300 (EA9500).

GRADING - PPGS™ 100% 98% 95% 90% 80% 70% 60% LAST MSR

* ***Model M15 A4 Rifle Eagle Eye (EA9901)*** – .223 Rem. or .308 Win. cal., GIO, designed for silhouette matches, 24 in. free floating barrel, weighted buttstock, tubular aluminum handguard, 14 lbs. Mfg. 1993-1995.

$1,250 $825 $575 $475 $425 $375 $350 *$1,495*

* ***Model M15 Rifle Action Master (EA9052S)*** – .223 Rem. or .308 Win. cal., GIO, match rifle, free floating 20 in. barrel with compensator, fixed stock, flat-top, solid aluminum handguard tube, National Match accessories, 8 lbs. 5 oz. Mfg. 1992-1995, reintroduced 2002 only.

$725 $500 $435 $375 $335 $315 $295 *$850*

The 1995 pre-ban variation of this model retailed at $1,475 (EA5600).

* ***Model M15 A4 Rifle Special Purpose (EA9042C)*** – .223 Rem. or .308 Win. cal., GIO, 20 in. barrel, flat-top (A4) or detachable handle receiver. Disc. 1995.

$825 $535 $450 $385 $340 $325 $295 *$955*

The 1995 pre-ban variation of this model retailed at $1,165 (EA9204).

* ***Model M15 A4 Rifle Predator (EA9902)*** – .223 Rem. or .308 Win. cal., GIO, post-ban only, 18 in. barrel, National Match trigger, flat-top (A4) or detachable handle receiver. Mfg. 1995 only.

$1,125 $700 $525 $450 $400 $350 $325 *$1,350*

EAST RIDGE/STATE ARMS GUN COMPANY, INC.

Current rifle manufacturer located in Bancroft, WI.

For individual model listings, please go to BlueBookOfGunValues.com/overflow.

ED BROWN CUSTOM, INC.

Ed Brown
Custom Rifles

Previous rifle manufacturer circa 2000-2014, located in Perry, MO. During 2009, the rifle division was transferred to Ed Brown Products, Inc.

Please refer to Ed Brown Products, Inc. for currently manufactured rifles.

RIFLES: BOLT ACTION

702 DENALI – various short and long action cals., designed as lightweight mountain hunting rifle, 22, 23 (disc.), or 24 in. lightweight barrel, glass bedded McMillian sporter stock with checkering and recoil pad, 3-position safety, 7 3/4 lbs. Mfg. 2002-2004.

$2,895 $2,535 $2,170 $1,970 $1,590 $1,305 $1,015 *$2,895*

702 OZARK – various cals., lightweight hunting rifle utilizing Ed Brown custom short action, steel trigger guard and floorplate, 3-position safety, checkered lightweight fiberglass stock, match grade, hand lapped 21 in. barrel, approx. 6 1/2 lbs. Disc. 2003.

$2,800 $2,450 $2,100 $1,905 $1,540 $1,260 $980 *$2,800*

702 LIGHT TARGET (TACTICAL) – .223 Rem. or .308 Win. cal., features Ed Brown short repeater action, aluminum trigger guard and floorplate, 21 in. match grade barrel, includes Talley scope mounts, approx. 8 3/4 lbs. Disc. 2005.

$2,495 $2,185 $1,870 $1,695 $1,370 $1,125 $875 *$2,495*

A3 TACTICAL – various cals., top-of-the-line sniper weapon, 26 in. heavyweight match grade hand lapped barrel, Shilen trigger, McMillan fiberglass A-3 tactical stock, 11 1/4 lbs. Disc. 2008.

$2,995 $2,620 $2,245 $2,035 $1,645 $1,350 $1,050 *$2,995*

ED BROWN PRODUCTS, INC.

Ed Brown
Products

Current manufacturer established during 1988, located in Perry, MO. Consumer direct sales.

PISTOLS: SEMI-AUTO

All the models in this category except the Classic Custom are available with Gen. 4 black coating at no extra charge.

The following MSRs represent each model's base price, with many options available at additional charge.

Add $75 for ambidextrous safety on certain models.

ALPHA CARRY – .45 ACP cal., single stack Commander bobtail frame, 4 1/4 in. Commander model slide, stainless steel, fixed dovetail 3-dot night sights, square cut serrations on rear of slide, Chainlink I treatment on forestrap and bobtail housing or optional Gen4 coating (AC-SS-G4), approx. 35 oz. Mfg. 2016-2017.

$2,425 $2,100 $1,750 $1,525 $1,300 $1,100 $900 *$2,695*

GRADING - PPGS™	100%	98%	95%	90%	80%	70%	60%	LAST MSR

ALPHA ELITE – .45 ACP cal., single stack Govt. model frame, 5 in. Govt. model slide, stainless steel, fixed dovetail 3-dot night sights, Black or Black/Sand G10 grips, square cut serrations on rear of slide only, with or w/o integral light rail (AE-SS-G4-LR), Chainlink I treatment on forestrap and mainspring housing or optional Gen4 coating (AE-SS-G4), approx. 38 oz. Mfg. 2016-2017.

	100%	98%	95%	90%	80%	70%	60%	LAST MSR
	$2,425	$2,100	$1,750	$1,525	$1,300	$1,100	$900	*$2,695*

Add $100 for integral light rail with Gen4 coating and Black/Sand grips (Alpha Elite Light Rail, AE-SS-G4-LR).

CCO – 9mm Para., .38 Super, or .45 ACP cal., 4 1/4 in. barrel, Commander slide, single stack compact (Officer sized) frame, Snakeskin treatment on forestrap and mainspring housing, Snakeskin rear cocking serrations, fixed black rear and red fiber optic front sight (disc. 2018) or orange HD XR front night sight (new 2019), 34 oz.

	100%	98%	95%	90%	80%	70%	60%	LAST MSR
MSR $3,145	$2,825	$2,475	$2,125	$1,925	$1,550	$1,275	$1,000	

* ***CCO Lightweight*** – 9mm Para., .38 Super, or .45 ACP cal., aluminum compact frame, 4 1/4 in. barrel, Commander slide, single stack compact (Officer sized) frame, Snakeskin treatment on forestrap and mainspring housing, rear cocking serrations, fixed black rear and red fiber optic (disc. 2018) or orange HD XR front night sight (new 2019), 29 oz. New 2017.

	100%	98%	95%	90%	80%	70%	60%	LAST MSR
MSR $2,495	$2,125	$1,875	$1,600	$1,450	$1,175	$950	$750	

CHAMPION MOLON LABE 1911 – .45 ACP cal., 5 in. barrel, designed by certified law enforcement instructor Dave Champion, hand fitted and assembled, "Molon Labe" in Greek letters is laser engraved on the left side of the frame, "Champion" is laser engraved on the right side of the slide, custom G10 grips with engraved Spartan battle helmet, custom Snakeskin metal treatment on front and back grip straps, wide notch rear sight with Tritium front night sight, solid aluminum trigger, black Gen. III coating. Limited mfg. 2011 only.

	100%	98%	95%	90%	80%	70%	60%	LAST MSR
	$2,595	$2,250	$1,900	$1,500	$1,250	$1,100	$950	*$2,595*

CLASSIC CUSTOM – .45 ACP cal., M1911 style, top-of-the-line model with highest level of cosmetic finishing, 5 in. barrel, incorporates all custom Ed Brown features, including slide and frame, choice of blue/blue, stainless/blue, or stainless/stainless frame and slide, exotic checkered cocobolo wood grips, adj. Ed Brown rear sight, 39 oz.

	100%	98%	95%	90%	80%	70%	60%	LAST MSR
MSR $3,695	$3,325	$2,900	$2,495	$2,250	$1,825	$1,485	$1,200	

CLASSIC CUSTOM CENTENNIAL EDITION – .45 ACP cal., 5 in. barrel, hand relief engraved package, "Centennial Edition 1911-2011" special laser engraving on left hand side of slide, custom rib on top of slide, adj. sights, Tru-Ivory grips, special serial number starting with JMB prefix (signifies John Moses Browning). Limited mfg. 2010-2011.

	100%	98%	95%	90%	80%	70%	60%	LAST MSR
	$6,995	$6,250	$5,500	$4,500	$3,500	$2,750	$2,250	*$6,995*

CLASSIC CUSTOM SIGNATURE EDITION – .45 ACP cal., marked "Signature Edition" on left side of slide and "Custom by Ed Brown" on right side of slide, hand engraved on frame and slide, custom rib, blue/blue or stainless/stainless. New 2012.

	100%	98%	95%	90%	80%	70%	60%	LAST MSR
MSR $7,695	$7,250	$6,000	$5,750	$4,650	$3,600	$2,800	$2,250	

Add $2,300 for stainless slide and frame.

CLASSIC CUSTOM ENHANCED EDITION – .45 ACP cal., stainless steel frame and blue slide, oversize mag. release button, Ed Brown adj. sights, skipline checkering on frame and mainspring housing, hand relief engraving on slide, flattened and serrated top of slide, serrated back of slide, two-piece guide rod. New 2014.

	100%	98%	95%	90%	80%	70%	60%	LAST MSR
MSR $5,195	$4,650	$4,025	$3,400	$3,100	$2,475	$2,025	$1,575	

CLASS A LIMITED – available in 8 cals., M1911 style, basic custom pistol and features all custom Ed Brown accessories, including slide and frame, 7 shot mag., 4.25 (Commander) or 5 in. barrel length, Hogue exotic grips, 34 or 39 oz. Disc. 2003.

	100%	98%	95%	90%	80%	70%	60%	LAST MSR
	$2,250	$1,970	$1,685	$1,530	$1,235	$1,010	$785	*$2,250*

Add $100 for stainless steel frame and all lower parts.
Add $100 for Novak night sights.

COMMANDER BOBTAIL – various cals., M1911 style, SA, carry configuration, features round butt variation of the Class A Limited frame, incorporating frame and grip modifications, including a special housing w/o checkering, 4 1/4 in. barrel, Hogue exotic wood grips, 34 oz. Disc. 2003.

	100%	98%	95%	90%	80%	70%	60%	LAST MSR
	$2,350	$2,055	$1,760	$1,600	$1,290	$1,055	$820	*$2,350*

ED BROWN 2ND AMENDMENT 1911 – .45 ACP cal., single stack Govt. model frame, 5 in. Govt. model slide, recessed slide stop, Ed Brown magwell, 3-hole aluminum trigger, ledge style rear sight paired with a green fiber optic front sight, VZ Operator II black G10 grips, square cut rear cocking serrations, "Don't Tread on Me" image is engraved on the right side of slide, left features the 2nd Amendment text, "Freedom" is engraved on the barrel bushing, Snakeskin treatment on the front strap and magwell housing, approx. 41 oz. Mfg. 2016-2017.

	100%	98%	95%	90%	80%	70%	60%	LAST MSR
	$2,725	$2,350	$1,950	$1,650	$1,400	$1,100	$975	*$2,970*

GRADING - PPGS™	100%	98%	95%	90%	80%	70%	60%	LAST MSR

EVO CCO9 LIGHTWEIGHT – 9mm Para. cal., 1911 style, single stack aluminum compact Officer frame, 4 in. bull barrel, external extractor, three hole trigger, HDXR front sight and "Tactical Edge" u-notch rear sight, checkered wood grips, guide rod w/flat wire recoil spring system, Snakeskin treatment forestrap and mainspring housing, 7-top slide w/front and rear serrations, black finish, 27 oz. New 2019.

MSR $2,295	$1,950	$1,700	$1,450	$1,300	$1,100	$900	$700	

EVO-E9 – 9mm Para. cal., full size single stack frame, 4 in. bull barrel, external extractor, easy to change black front sight, ledge-style U-notch rear sight, 7-top custom cut slide with special front and rear serrations, 25 LPI checkering on forestrap, 35 oz. New 2019.

MSR $2,495	$2,125	$1,875	$1,600	$1,450	$1,175	$950	$750	

* ***EVO-E9-LW*** – 9mm Para. cal., lightweight single stack aluminum frame, 4 in. bull barrel, external extractor, 3-hole aluminum trigger, Vortex Venom red dot sight (6 MOA dot rear sight), Labyrinth grips, single side or ambi thumb safety, 7-top custom cut slide w/special front and rear serrations, guide rod w/flat wire recoil spring system, flushed barrel w/recessed crown, 25 LPI checkering, fitted Chen Gen2 magwell, 35 oz. New mid-2019.

MSR $3,095	$2,625	$2,300	$1,975	$1,790	$1,450	$1,175	$925	

Add $200 for ambi thumb safety.

EVO-KC9 – 9mm Para. cal., single stack Bobtail frame, 4 in. bull barrel, redesigned slide shortened to 4 in. and thinned substantially for weight reduction, external extractor, orange HD XR front night sight and ledge style U-notch rear sight, flat wire recoil spring system, slide includes unique 7-top custom cut, special front and rear serrations, recessed slide stop, snakeskin treatment on forestrap and Bobtail housing, 34 oz. New late 2018.

MSR $2,195	$1,875	$1,625	$1,400	$1,275	$1,025	$840	$650	

* ***EVO-KC9-LW*** – 9mm Para. cal., single stack Bobtail frame, 4 in. bull barrel, redesigned slide shortened to 4 in. and thinned substantially for weight reduction, external extractor, orange HD XR front night sight and ledge style U-notch rear sight, flat wire recoil spring system, slide includes unique 7-top custom cut, special front and rear serrations, recessed slide stop, snakeskin treatment on forestrap and Bobtail housing, custom options include: slim grips and conceal carry grip safety, 27 oz. New 2019.

MSR $2,495	$2,125	$1,875	$1,600	$1,450	$1,175	$950	$750	

* ***EVO-KC9-G4/G4-VTX*** – 9mm Para. cal., single stack Bobtail stainless steel frame, 4 in. bull barrel, redesigned slide shortened to 4 in., thinned substantially for weight reduction, 9 shot mag., external extractor, U notch rear and HD XR front night sights or Vortex venom red dot rear and black front sights (VTX model only, new 2020), flat wire recoil spring system, slide includes unique 7 top custom cut, special front and rear serrations, recessed slide stop, snakeskin treatment on forestrap and Bobtail housing, black Gen4 finish, 34 oz.

MSR $2,495	$2,125	$1,875	$1,600	$1,450	$1,175	$950	$750	

EXECUTIVE COMMANDER – 9mm Para. (stainless slide only) or .45 ACP cal., single stack Government frame, 4 1/4 in. Commander slide, 25 LPI checkering on front strap and mainspring housing, black fixed rear and red fiber optic front sight, approx. 35 oz. New 2017.

MSR $3,395	$2,995	$2,575	$2,150	$1,825	$1,525	$1,200	$1,050	

EXECUTIVE ELITE – 9mm Para., .38 Super, or .45 ACP cal., M1911 style, 5 in. barrel, SA, choice of all blue/blue, stainless blue (disc.), stainless/stainless, or stainless/stainless with black Gen4 slide/barrel, features Hardcore components, flared and lowered ejection port, Commander style hammer, 25 LPI checkering on front and rear grip strap, beveled magwell, fixed black rear sight, red fiber optic front sight, checkered cocobolo (disc.) or laminate wood grips, 34 oz. New 2004.

MSR $3,295	$2,850	$2,500	$2,050	$1,775	$1,475	$1,175	$1,025	

EXECUTIVE ELITE CENTENNIAL EDITION – .45 ACP cal., 5 in. barrel, traditional blue matte finish, "Centennial Edition 1911-2011" special laser engraving on left hand side of slide, Tru-Ivory grips, fixed sights, special serial number starting with JMB prefix (signifies John Moses Browning). Limited mfg. 2010-2011.

	$2,495	$2,175	$1,750	$1,675	$1,350	$1,100	$950	*$2,495*

EXECUTIVE CARRY – .45 ACP cal., similar to Executive Elite, except has 4 1/4 in. barrel and Bobtail grip, 34 oz. Mfg. 2004-2017.

	$2,425	$2,100	$1,750	$1,525	$1,300	$1,100	$900	*$2,695*

EXECUTIVE TARGET – .38 Super (limited mfg. 2014 only), .45 ACP cal., 1911 style, Government model frame, modified for target and range shooting, 5 in. Govt. model slide, single stack mag., Ed Brown adj. rear and cross dovetail front sight, cocobolo diamond checkered grips, 25 LPI checkering on front strap and mainspring housing, matte stainless or matte black Gen. 4 stainless finish, approx. 38 oz. Mfg. 2006-disc., reintroduced 2016-2017.

	$2,475	$2,150	$1,750	$1,600	$1,325	$1,150	$925	*$2,845*

GRADING - PPGS™	100%	98%	95%	90%	80%	70%	60%	LAST MSR

2018 EXECUTIVE TARGET – 9mm Para., .38 Super, or .45 ACP cal., single stack Government frame, 5 in. barrel, 25 LPI checkering on frame, French border and ball endmill cuts on slide, flattened and serrated top of slide, square cut rear cocking serrations, Ed Brown RMR mount with Trijicon RMR sight, 40 oz. New 2018.

MSR $3,880	$3,500	$2,950	$2,500	$2,100	$1,675	$1,475	$1,275	

FUELED MP-F1/MP-F2/MP-F3 – polymer frame, black DLC or stainless (MP-F3) slide and frame pins, stainless button rifled match barrel, target crown, Ed Brown tread flutes in black DLC (MP-F1 and MP-F3) or Spectrum multi-colored (MP-F2) finish, custom thread protector and extractor, Apex Tactical black DLC or FDE (MP-F2) trigger, with (black RMR, black SRO, or Coyote Brown RMR Trijicon options available) or w/o sights, low profile magwell, aluminum baseplate, custom serrations available, Ed Brown Accuracy Rail. New 2020.

MSR $1,995	$1,800	$1,550	$1,350	$1,200	$1,000	$800	$650	

Add $500 for black Trijicon RMR sights.
Add $520 for Coyote Brown Trijicon RMR sights.
Add $549 for black Trijicon SRO sights.

FX1/FX1 RMR – 9mm Para., .38 Super, or .45 ACP cal., 1911 style, Commander slide, single stack Government frame with integral light rail, 4 1/4 in. barrel, u-notch rear with red fiber optic front or Trijicon RMR with tall night sights, FX1 Snakeskin on forestrap, American flag serrations on right side of slide, square cut cocking serrations on left side, brushed stainless or Dirty Olive Gen 4 finish, 40 oz. New late 2017.

MSR $3,875	$3,500	$2,950	$2,500	$2,100	$1,675	$1,475	$1,275	

Add $760 for Trijicon RMR with tall night sights.

FX2 – 9mm Para. or .45 ACP cal., Commander Bobtail frame, 4 1/4 in. barrel w/recessed crown, 7 shot mag., stainless steel construction, 3-hole trigger, Trijicon RMRcc sight with Ed Brown co-witness rear and Ameriglo orange front sight, black G10 grips, snakeskin on frontstrap, American flag serrations on both sides of slide, Industrial stainless finish, 37 oz. New 2020.

MSR $4,295	$3,650	$3,200	$2,750	$2,500	$2,000	$1,650	$1,300	

Add $100 for 9mm Para. cal.

IPSC EDITION – .45 ACP cal., single stack Govt. model frame, 5 in. Govt. model slide, Ed Brown magwell, 3-hole aluminum trigger, black fixed rear sight with green fiber optic front, double diamond black G10 grips, IPSC logo engraved on right side of slide behind cocking serrations, "40th Anniversary" engraved under ejection port and DVC engraved on the bushing, Chainlink I treatment on forestrap and mainspring housing, approx. 41 oz. Limited edition mfg. Dec. 2015-Dec. 2016.

	$2,475	$2,150	$1,750	$1,600	$1,325	$1,150	$925	*$2,695*

A portion of the proceeds from the sale of every pistol went to IPSC (International Practical Shooting Confederation) to help fund their mission.

JEFF COOPER COMMEMORATIVE LIMITED EDITION (OLDER MFG.) – .45 ACP cal., 5 in. barrel, SA, Govt. style, forged frame and slide, matte finish, square cut serrations on rear of slide, Jeff Cooper signature on slide, fixed Novak Lo-mount dovetail rear sight, dovetail front sight, 7 shot mag., exhibition grade cocobolo grips with Jeff Cooper pen and sword logo, includes limited edition leather bound copy of *Principles of Self Defense*, 38 oz. Limited mfg. 2008.

	$2,295	$2,000	$1,700	$1,550	$1,250	$1,050	$800	*$2,295*

JEFF COOPER COMMEMORATIVE LIMITED EDITION (CURRENT MFG.) – .45 ACP cal., SA, Govt. style, forged frame and high polish slide, 5 in. barrel, two 7 shot mags., solid long trigger, smooth cocobolo grips w/engraved Jeff Cooper logo of pen and sword, concealed carry grip safety, square cut serrations on rear of slide, Cooper's signature inlayed in gold on ejection port side of slide, right side of slide inlayed "DVC" in 24 kt. gold, 38 oz. Limited mfg. began 2019.

MSR $3,170	$2,850	$2,500	$2,150	$1,950	$1,550	$1,300	$1,000	

Add $250 for gun and package.

JIM WILSON SPECIAL LIMITED EDITION – .45 ACP cal., SA, features black frame with Jim Wilson signature on slide, smooth Tru-Ivory grips, 7 shot mag., 38 oz. Limited mfg. 2007.

	$2,295	$2,000	$1,700	$1,550	$1,250	$1,050	$800	*$2,295*

KOBRA – .45 ACP cal., 1911 style, SA, 5 in. barrel, 7 shot mag., fixed black rear and red fiber optic front sights, checkered laminate grips, features "snakeskin" metal treatment on frame, mainspring housing and slide, matte stainless or matte black Gen. 4 stainless finish, 39 oz. Mfg. 2002-2017.

	$2,475	$2,150	$1,750	$1,600	$1,325	$1,150	$925	*$2,695*

KOBRA CARRY – .45 ACP cal., 1911 style, SA, 4 1/4 in. barrel, black rear, red fiber optic front sight (disc. 2018), or orange HD XR front night sight (new 2019), features bobtail and "snakeskin" metal treatment on frame, mainspring housing and slide, matte stainless or matte black Gen. 4 stainless finish, 34 oz. New 2002.

MSR $2,995	$2,695	$2,350	$2,025	$1,835	$1,475	$1,225	$950	

GRADING - PPGS™	100%	98%	95%	90%	80%	70%	60%	LAST MSR

* ***Kobra Carry Lightweight*** - 9mm Para., .38 Super, or .45 ACP cal., 1911 style, 4 1/4 in. barrel, 7075 aluminum single stack commander frame and bobtail housing, orange HD XR (new 2019) front night sight, ledge style U-notch black rear (new 2019) or 10-8 black sight (disc. 2018), slim cocobolo (disc.) or laminate wood grips, black Gen. 4 coating, 27 oz. New 2010.

MSR $3,510	$3,150	$2,750	$2,365	$2,150	$1,735	$1,425	$1,100	

KRYPTEIA EDITION - .45 ACP cal., single stack Government model frame, 5 in. Government model slide, oversized Ed Brown magwell, Ledge style U-notch plain black rear sight and fixed dovetail front, VZ Operator II black grips, front and rear serrated slide, Krypteia shield logo engraved on right side of slide and "Krypteia Edition" engraved on left, Chainlink II treatment on forestrap and mainspring housing, Gen4 bronze coating, 38 oz. Limited mfg. Aug. 2014-Aug. 2015 only.

2014/2015 MSR was $3,095.

LS10 - 10mm cal., single stack Government model frame, 6 in. barrel with long slide, Trijicon RMR sight with adj. tall night sights, wood checkered grips, 25 LPI checkering on forestrap and mainspring housing, solid recoil plug, traditional "square cut" front and cocking serrations, French border, 43 oz. New mid-2017.

MSR $3,995	$3,575	$3,100	$2,650	$2,175	$1,725	$1,550	$1,275	

MASSAD AYOOB SIGNATURE EDITION - .45 ACP cal., 4 1/4 in. barrel, Commander bobtail stainless steel frame, SA, 25 LPI checkering on frame and mainspring housing, Massad Ayoob signature on right side of slide, ambidextrous safety, fixed 3-dot sights, black G10 checkered grips, 4 1/2 lb. trigger pull, includes a copy of *Gun Digest Book of Concealed Carry* by Massad Ayoob. Limited mfg. 2009-2010.

	$2,700	$2,325	$1,925	$1,650	$1,400	$1,100	$975	*$2,700*

SPECIAL FORCES - .45 ACP cal., 1911 style, SA, 5 in. barrel, 7 shot mag., Commander style hammer, fixed black rear and red fiber optic front sight, checkered diamond pattern cocobolo (disc.) or G10 grips, special Chainlink treatment on front and rear grip straps, Gen. 4 black coating applied to all metal surfaces, 38 oz. New 2006.

MSR $2,900	$2,625	$2,225	$1,925	$1,475	$1,250	$1,200	$950	

Add $100 for Stealth Gray or Bronze Gen. III (disc.) or Gen4 finish and carbon fiber grips (new 2011).

SPECIAL FORCES LIGHT RAIL - .45 ACP cal., 1911 style, SA, forged Government style frame with integral light rail, 5 in. barrel, fixed black rear, red fiber optic front sights, diamond cut wood (disc. 2012) or Black Sand G10 grips, Chainlink treatment on forestrap and mainspring housing, traditional square cut cocking serrations on rear of slide, beginning 2016 Gen4 color options include black, Stealth Gray, or bronze, approx. 38 oz. Mfg. 2009-2012, reintroduced 2016-2017.

	$2,550	$2,250	$1,825	$1,725	$1,375	$1,125	$875	*$2,695*

Add $1,200 for suppressor ready barrel and Trijicon RMR sights (new 2016).

SPECIAL FORCES CARRY/CARRY II - .45 ACP cal., SA, single stack Commander bobtail frame, 4 1/2 in. Commander style barrel, 8 shot, stainless steel construction, low profile combat rear sights, fixed dovetail 3-dot night front sights, diamond cut wood (disc.) or black G10 grips, Chainlink treatment on forestrap and mainspring housing, square cut serrations on rear of slide, optional Gen III (disc.) or Gen4 coating available in black, stealth gray, or bronze, approx. 35 oz. Mfg. 2009-2017.

	$2,150	$1,800	$1,625	$1,325	$1,075	$850	$725	*$2,695*

Add $100 for Stealth Gray or bronze Gen4 coating with carbon fiber grips (new 2016).

SPECIAL FORCES MOLON LABE - .45 ACP cal., single stack Govt. model frame, match grade barrel, flush barrel crown, recessed slide stop, 5 in. Govt. model slide, fully blended magwell, 3-hole aluminum trigger, Ledge style U-notch rear sight and red fiber optic front sight, VZ Operator II Marsoc grips with a Spartan helmet and Molon Labe engraving, slide features "Molon Labe" engraving on left side, Chainlink III treatment on forestrap and magwell housing, Black, Stealth Gray, or Battle Bronze Gen4 coating, approx. 40 oz. Mfg. 2016-2017.

	$2,775	$2,350	$1,950	$1,650	$1,400	$1,100	$975	*$3,095*

SPECIAL FORCES SOCOM EDITION - .45 ACP cal., SA, Govt. model frame, 5 in. barrel, two 8 shot mags., Trijicon SOCOM Coyote Brown RMR sight w/tall night sights, VZ Alien Grips, integrated light rail, one-piece magwell, square-cut American Flag serrations on rear of slide, front cocking serrations front of slide, Chainlink III treatment on forestrap and mainspring housing, black Nitride finished suppressor and FDE Gen4 on frame w/thread protector finish, 43 oz. New 2019.

MSR $4,495	$4,050	$3,550	$3,050	$2,750	$2,200	$1,800	$1,400	

SPECIAL FORCES SR - 9mm Para. or .45 ACP cal., Government frame with integral light rail, 5 in. threaded suppressor ready barrel with thread protector, blended magwell, front and rear cocking serrations, Trijicon RMR sight, Trijicon tall iron night sights, Chainlink III pattern, 42 oz. New 2017.

MSR $4,275	$3,850	$3,400	$2,950	$2,450	$2,000	$1,750	$1,450	

GRADING - PPGS™	100%	98%	95%	90%	80%	70%	60%	LAST MSR

SPECIAL FORCES SRC – 9mm Para. or .45 ACP cal., lightweight single stack aluminum frame, 4 1/4 in. threaded suppressor ready barrel with thread protector, front and rear cocking serrations, Trijicon RMR sight, Trijicon tall iron night sights, Chen Gen2 one-piece magwell with Chainlink III treatment, square cut front and rear cocking serrations, approx. 38 oz. New 2018.

MSR $4,675	$4,200	$3,700	$3,250	$2,700	$2,200	$1,900	$1,575	

ZEV 1911 RMR – 9mm Para. cal., single stack Government frame with integral light rail, 4 1/4 in. dimpled and threaded suppressor-ready barrel, ZEV thread protector, Trijicon RMR with tall night sights, VZ Alien G10 grips, match profile ambi thumb safety, ZEV Orion slide cuts package, Alien on front strap, 41 oz. New 2019.

MSR $4,995	$4,495	$3,950	$3,375	$3,050	$2,475	$2,025	$1,575	

2018 ZEV 1911 – 9mm Para. cal., 4 1/4 in. dimpled and threaded suppressor-ready barrel, ZEV thread protector, single stack Government frame with integral light rail, ZEV designed Commander slide with side and top ports, FX1 Snakeskin on front strap, Trijicon RMR with tall night sights, VZ Alien black G10 grips, tactical profile ambi thumb safety, 40 oz. Limited mfg. 2018 only.

	$4,400	$3,950	$3,500	$2,950	$2,400	$2,100	$1,750	*$4,995*

2019 ZEV 1911 – 9mm Para. cal., single stack Government frame, 4 1/4 in. dimpled barrel, Chen Magwell Gen2, VZ Alien G10 grips, tactical profile single side thumb safety, ZEV Orion slide cuts package, Alien on front strap, 37 oz. New 2019.

MSR $3,995	$3,575	$3,100	$2,650	$2,175	$1,725	$1,550	$1,275	

RIFLES: BOLT ACTION

In August of 2010, Ed Brown Products announced that all bolt action rifle production had been put on hold indefinitely. The following last MSRs represent each model's base price, and many options were available at additional cost. Beginning 2006, all M-702 actions were disc. in favor of Ed Brown's new Model 704 controlled feed action with spring-loaded extractor integral with the bolt. All recently manufactured rifles have stainless steel barrels and the entire rifle is coated with Generation III black coating (new 2007).

BUSHVELD – various short and long action cals., dangerous game rifle utilizing Ed Brown custom action, match grade 24 in. medium or heavyweight barrel, McMillan fiberglass stock with cheekpiece and recoil pad, approx. 8 1/2-9 lbs. Disc. 2008.

	$2,995	$2,620	$2,245	$2,035	$1,645	$1,350	$1,050	*$2,995*

Add $300 for .416 Rem. Mag or .458 Lott cals. (disc. 2005).

EXPRESS – .375 H&H, .416 Rem. Mag., or .458 Lott cal., dangerous game rifle utilizing Ed Brown custom M-704 fully controlled feed action, 4 shot internal mag, 24 in. barrel with iron sights and barrel band, Shilen trigger, hand-bedded McMillan fiberglass stock with Monte Carlo cheekpiece and Pachmayer Decelerator recoil pad, approx. 9-10 lbs. Mfg. 2006-2010.

	$4,995	$4,370	$3,745	$3,395	$2,745	$2,250	$1,750	*$4,995*

SAVANNA – various long and short action cals., hunting rifle utilizing Ed Brown custom action, McMillan checkered fiberglass stock with steel trigger guard and floorplate, Talley rings and bases, 24 or 26 in. match grade barrel, approx. 7.5-8 lbs. Disc. 2010.

	$3,895	$3,410	$2,925	$2,650	$2,150	$1,750	$1,350	*$3,895*

Add $100 for muzzle brake.

DAMARA – various cals., lightweight hunting rifle with Ed Brown repeater action, 23 in. barrel and ultra-lightweight McMillan graphite stock with Pachmayr Decelerator pad, 6.1 lbs. Mfg. 2004-2010.

	$3,995	$3,475	$3,000	$2,650	$2,200	$1,850	$1,350	*$3,995*

Add $100 for Mag. cals. with muzzle brake.

VARMINT/COMPACT VARMINT – various varmint cals., features Ed Brown action with steel trigger guard and adj. Jewell trigger, match grade 22 (mfg. 2006-2008, compact variation), 24 (Varmint), or 26 (optional, disc.) in. barrel, hand-bedded McMillan fiberglass stock and recoil pad, approx. 9 lbs. Disc. 2010.

	$3,895	$3,410	$2,920	$2,650	$2,140	$1,755	$1,365	*$3,895*

A5 TACTICAL – .300 Win. Mag. or .308 Win. cal., features adj. McMillan A-5 tactical stock, 5 shot detachable mag., black finish, Shilen trigger, 12 1/2 lbs. Mfg. 2008-2010.

	$4,495	$3,935	$3,370	$3,055	$2,470	$2,025	$1,575	*$4,495*

M40A2 MARINE SNIPER – .30-06 or .308 Win. cal., 24 in. match grade barrel, special McMillan GP fiberglass tactical stock with recoil pad, Woodlands camo is molded into stock, this model is a duplicate of the original McMillan Marine Sniper rifle used in Vietnam, except for the Ed Brown action, 9 1/4 lbs. Mfg. 2002-2010.

	$3,695	$3,235	$2,770	$2,515	$2,030	$1,665	$1,295	*$3,695*

GRADING - PPGS™	100%	98%	95%	90%	80%	70%	60%	LAST MSR

EDGE ARMS

Previous semi-auto pistol manufacturer circa 2013-2015, and located in Gallatin, TN. Current manufacturer of the Reliant pistol is Signal 9 Defense (see listing in S section).

EDWARD ARMS COMPANY

Current manufacturer located in Phoenix, AZ.

Please refer to BlueBookOfGunValues.com to order the *Blue Book of AR-15s & Variations*, available as a book or online subscription.

EFFEBI SRL

Current manufacturer established in 1994 and located in Concesio, Italy. Previously imported and distributed 2004-2006 by American Outdoor Adventures, located in Leesburg, GA. Previously named Dr. Franco Beretta until 1994. Also refer to the Dr. Franco Beretta listing.

Effebi manufactures a variety of good quality shotguns in O/U, SxS, and single barrel configurations. Effebi also manufactures both SxS and O/U barrel assemblies. These models have limited importation into the U.S.

EGE SPORTING ARMS

Previous shotgun manufacturer located in Izmir, Turkey.

EGE Sporting Arms manufactured good quality O/U, slide action, and semi-auto shotguns that had limited importation into the U.S.

EGEMEN

Previous trademark of shotguns manufactured by Vatan Hunting Firearms Co., located in Konya, Turkey. Please refer to Vatan Hunting Firearms Company listing in the V section.

EGO ARMAS, S.A.

Previous manufacturer circa 1953-2006 and located in Eibar, Spain.

Ego Armas manufactured high quality sidelock double rifles ranging in price from approx. €5,000-€8,850 in cals. up to .375 H&H, and €13,100 for the .416 Rigby or .470 NE., in addition to a boxlock express model for €3,000. Mounted scopes were also available. Boxlock and sidelock shotguns were also available ranging in price from €770-€1,050 for a boxlock (hammer model also available), and €1,475-€2,200 for sidelock action with ejectors and English wood finish.

EGYPTIAN MILITARY

For more information on Egyptian designed models, please refer to individual listings under the Helwan, Hakim, and Rasheed sections.

EMPEROR ARMS

Current shotgun manufacturer established circa 1962 in Turkey and currently imported by Emperor Arms located in Fort Myers, FL.

For individual model listings, please go to BlueBookOfGunValues.com/overflow.

EMPIRE RIFLE COMPANY LLC

Previous trademark of rifles manufactured by various independent gunmakers and located in Meriden, NH until 2011.

For individual model listings, please go to BlueBookOfGunValues.com/overflow.

EMTAN KARMIEL LTD.

Current rifle manufacturer and parts supplier located in Karmiel, Israel. No current U.S. importation.

For individual model listings, please go to BlueBookOfGunValues.com/overflow.

ENFIELD AMERICA, INC.

Previous manufacturer located in Atlanta, GA.

PISTOLS: SEMI-AUTO

MP-9 – 9mm Para. cal., design similar to MP-45. Mfg. 1985.

	100%	98%	95%	90%	80%	70%	60%	LAST MSR
	$550	$475	$425	$350	$295	$260	$240	

Add $150 for carbine kit.

MP-45 – .45 ACP cal., 4 1/2, 6, 8, 10, or 18 1/2 in. shrouded barrel, parkerized finish, 10, 30, 40, or 50 shot mag., 6 lbs. Mfg. 1985 only.

	100%	98%	95%	90%	80%	70%	60%	LAST MSR
	$550	$475	$425	$350	$295	$260	$240	*$350*

GRADING - PPGS™	100%	98%	95%	90%	80%	70%	60%	LAST MSR

ENFIELDS

Originally manufactured by the Royal Small Arms Factory at Enfield on the northern outskirts of London, in Middlesex, England. Various Enfield rifles, carbines and revolvers were produced and/or converted by other British factories (B.S.A., L.S.A., S.S.A., N.R.F., P. Webley & Son, Webley & Scott Ltd., Albion Motors, W.W. Greener, Westley Richards, Vickers (VSM), ROF Fazakerley, ROF Maltby, BSA Shirley (M47C), as well as at Lithgow, Australia (from 1913), Canada at Long Branch (from 1941), the United States by Stevens-Savage (also from 1941), RFI Ishapore, India (from 1905), Nakhu, Pyuthan and Sundrijal in Nepal (from 1911), and at Wah Cantt in Pakistan (from the late 1950s).

The publisher would like to thank Mr. Bob Maze and Mr. Ian Skennerton for making the following information available.

REVOLVERS

ENFIELD REVOLVER MK I & II - .450 Adams or .455 Enfield cal., often called the ".476", which was a commercial ammunition designation. A 6 shot, hinged barrel with exposed knuckle-joint axis at front, a top break action with forward-sliding chamber for extraction. Mk I model (checkered grips) introduced in 1880 with a Mk II variant (plain wooden grips) in 1882. Designed by American Owen Jones and made at Enfield R.S.A.F., it was not liked due to its sliding chamber extraction and cumbersome proportions.

	$2,900	$2,600	$2,250	$1,850	$1,450	$1,100	$900

Add 10% for early Mk. I revolvers with nickel plated grip frames.

Add 10% for Australian colonial MK. II revolvers with 3 3/4 in. barrels shortened during WW II.

ENFIELD MARK VI - .455 Webley cal., 6 shot, made by the Royal Small Arms Factory at Enfield Lock, approx. 27,600 of its version of the Webley Mk. VI (the No.1 Mk. VI) were produced for the British military from 1921-1926, with a serial number range: 1-9,999, A1-A9,999, and B1-B7,600.

	$1,900	$1,600	$1,400	$1,200	$900	$750	$650

NO. 2 MK I REVOLVER - .380 Enfield (based on .38 S&W with 200 gr. bullet), double action, 6 shot, fixed sights, blued or black finish, wood or composition grips, top break action, essentially an Enfield copy of .380 Webley Mk IV, introduced circa 1929.

	$1,300	$1,100	$950	$800	$700	$600	$500

NO. 2 MK I*/MK I REVOLVER** - .380 Enfield with hammer spur removed and other manufacturing concessions applied. Wartime production by Albion in England with very few by Howard Auto Cultivators (H.A.C.) in Australia which bring a huge premium due to a short run of only 355 revolvers. Enfield & Albion production only.

	$1,100	$950	$850	$750	$600	$500	$400
H.A.C Production	$5,000	$4,500	$4,000	$3,500	$3,000	$1,900	$1,400

N.B. - rare Webley MK IV variant with sideplate, the Enfield No.2 Mk.I design was taken from this model, very rare - only a few examples exist.

	$5,500	$5,000	$4,750	$4,250	$4,000	$3,750	$3,500

RIFLES & CARBINES

In 1926 there was an overhaul of the nomenclature for weapons, for example: SMLE Mk III became the Rifle No.1 Mk III, and the Pistol, Revolver, Webley Mk VI became the Revolver No.1 Mk VI, etc.

.577 ENFIELD PATTERN 1853/1856/1858 RIFLE/CARBINE/MUSKET - adopted from 1853 as the general service issue rifle, percussion lock marked Tower, Enfield, B.S.A., L.S.A., or Windsor on the lockplate, available in 3-band long rifle (Model 1853), 2-band short rifle, engineer (Lancaster), artillery, and cavalry carbine configurations, many were supplied to the Confederacy during America's Civil War.

	$2,400	$2,100	$1,950	$1,700	$1,400	$1,100	$900

Add 20% for Civil War provenance.

Add 10% for 2-band short rifle (most desirable) or carbine (most rare).

LANCASTER OVAL BORE ENGINEER'S CARBINE - Lancaster's Sappers' and Miners'/Engineers' carbine has a 2-groove oval bore, rather than Enfield type. These models are less common than the Pattern 1853 rifle-musket.

	$2,750	$2,500	$2,250	$1,900	$1,750	$1,400	$1,000

.577 SNIDER-ENFIELD RIFLE/CARBINE - adopted in 1866 as a breech-loading conversion of the .577 Enfield, a single shot, swing-over breechblock, modified percussion lock, the Mk III improved locking breech in 1869 was new manufacture, safer to shoot.

	$1,700	$1,600	$1,450	$1,250	$1,000	$850	$650

Add 10% for 2-band short rifle or artillery carbine. Add 15% for cavalry carbine or naval pattern short rifle.

Subtract 10% for Indian issue.

Naval pattern short rifle has a brass trigger guard.

GRADING - PPGS™	100%	98%	95%	90%	80%	70%	60%	LAST MSR

.450 MARTINI-HENRY – Britain's first purpose built breech-loader in 1871, hinged falling block action with internal lock mechanism, early Mk I rifle had a safety catch, Mk II rifle introduced in 1876, Cavalry Carbine in 1877, Artillery Carbine in 1879, Mk III rifle in 1879, and the long lever "humpback" Mk IV in 1887 which was sent to India & Nepal.

	100%	98%	95%	90%	80%	70%	60%	LAST MSR
	$1,800	$1,650	$1,500	$1,300	$1,100	$900	$700	

Mk I & Mk II rifles are more sought after variants because of an association with the 1879 Zulu War. Mk III and IV models are commonly found in better condition.
Add 10% for Artillery or Cavalry carbines.

.303 MARTINI-METFORD – conversion of .450 M.-H. with Metford rifling, converted markings are stamped on left side of receiver. Artillery & Cavalry carbines are more prolific than the rifles, Artillery models are marked "A.C." with Mark number on left side of the receiver, Cavalry models are marked "C.C." followed by the Mark number. Metfords are much rarer than ensuing Martini-Enfield models, only made between 1889 and 1895, with more carbines converted than rifles. A small number of rifles were converted only for the colonies of Natal, South Australia, Western Australia, and Canada. Most Martini-Metfords are marked "M.M. .303" on the left side of the action body whereas Martini-Enfields are marked "M.E. .303".

	100%	98%	95%	90%	80%	70%	60%	LAST MSR
	$2,200	$1,950	$1,600	$1,450	$1,200	$1,000	$800	

Add 20% for Cavalry carbines marked "C.C."
Add 10% for Artillery Carbines (A.C.).
Subtract 10% for commercial patterns.
One thousand Martini-Metford Mk. VI rifles (and bayonets) purchased for the Royal Reg't. of Canadian Infantry have the Royal Cipher, and are usually found in excellent to new condition, therefore quite desirable and should be 30% higher than baseline values.

.303 MARTINI-ENFIELD – conversion of .450 M.-H., the conversion markings are stamped on the left side of the receiver. Artillery and Cavalry carbines are more prolific than the rifles, Artillery models are marked "A.C." with the Mark number on the left side of the receiver while Cavalry models are marked "C.C.", followed by the Mark designation.

	100%	98%	95%	90%	80%	70%	60%	LAST MSR
	$1,600	$1,400	$1,250	$1,100	$900	$750	$550	

Add 20% for Cavalry carbines marked "C.C."
Subtract 10% for commercial patterns.
A Royal Cypher will indicate service issue and should command a premium price.

.303 MAGAZINE LEE-METFORD RIFLE – introduced in 1888 with 7-groove Metford segmental rifling and 8-round detachable magazine, rifles proceeded through Marks I, I*, II, and II* which is marked on the right side of the action body below the factory and year, underneath the closed bolt handle, rifles have 30.2 in. barrels, carbines have 20 3/4 in. barrels. Mk I and I* rifle have single-row 8 round magazine, carbines are 6 round, Mk II and II* rifles are 10 round staggered box. Mfg. by Enfield, BSA, LSA, Nepal, and Sparkbrook.

	100%	98%	95%	90%	80%	70%	60%	LAST MSR
Mk. I	$4,500	$4,000	$3,800	$3,200	$3,000	$2,800	$2,600	
Mk. I*	$3,500	$3,000	$2,600	$2,450	$2,350	$2,200	$1,950	
Mk. II	$2,800	$2,500	$2,250	$2,100	$1,750	$1,500	$1,300	
Mk. II*	$3,000	$2,800	$2,600	$2,400	$2,000	$1,750	$1,500	

Original Cavalry carbines with the 'D' ring on the left butt socket bring values in the Mk. I* range.
Subtract 10% from Mk. I* rifle values for later modified Cavalry Carbines with 'D' ring removed.
Subtract 50% for Nepal mfg.

The Mk. I Lee-Metford has Lewes sights and has a safety catch on the left side of the receiver, later removed on the Mk. I*. The Mk. II* Lee-Metford was mfg. for approx. 6 months circa 1895 as a transition between the Lee-Metford and Lee-Enfield rifles only differing in the type of rifling used. The difference between the Lee-Metford Mk. II and the Mk. II* is a safety catch on the cocking piece and the II* designation on the right side of the butt socket.

.303 MAGAZINE LEE-ENFIELD RIFLE – introduced in 1895 with 5-groove Enfield rifling for cordite loads, fitted with safety catch on the cocking piece, rifles and carbines went through Marks I and I*, Mk I* has no cleaning rod provision in forend or nosecap. Few cleaning rods are seen as they were withdrawn in 1895. Mfg. by Enfield, BSA, LSA, and Sparkbrook, repaired at Ishapore.

	100%	98%	95%	90%	80%	70%	60%	LAST MSR
	$2,400	$2,200	$1,950	$1,700	$1,500	$1,250	$1,000	

Add 25% for early Mk. I Cavalry Carbines.
Add 10% for Mk. I* Cavalry Carbines or RIC (Royal Irish Constabulary) variants.
Add $25%-30% for Lee-Enfield New Zealand carbine.

Commercial models were produced and used primarily by volunteer units and for target competitions. The Lee-Enfield New Zealand carbine is similar to the Lee-Enfield RIC carbine, fitted for the Pattern 1888 bayonet, approx. 1,500 mfg. circa 1901-1903.

GRADING - PPGS™	100%	98%	95%	90%	80%	70%	60%	LAST MSR

.303 CHARGER LOADING LEE-ENFIELD – M.L.M. and M.L.E. rifles with 30.2 in. barrels, modified for clip charger loading, after 1909 fitted with improved sights and foresight protector, conversions marked on left of receiver butt socket with factory and year (i.e., Enfield, BSA, LSA, VSM).

$2,400 $2,200 $2,000 $1,750 $1,500 $1,300 $950

Add 10% for .303 Charger Loading Lee-Enfield examples manufactured with Metford-rifled barrels.

Commercially models were produced, used primarily by volunteer units and for target competitions.

.22 LEE-ENFIELD LONG RIFLE – .22 LR cal., 30.2 in. new manufacture or sleeved barrel for rimfire cartridge, Mk I, Mk I*, and MK II variations, only a few were converted at Enfield and by the Royal Navy, some commercial models may be encountered. In the colonies, the .297/.230 CF round was used in Long Rifle conversions, these were locally converted.

Mks. I/I*/II $3,200 $2,850 $2,600 $2,300 $1,900 $1,600 $1,100

.303 S.M.L.E. MK I (SHORT MAGAZINE, LEE-ENFIELD) – features a sliding charger guide on the bolthead, bone inserts on the rear sight slide and incurving protector wings on nosecap, 10 round staggered row detachable mag. with magazine cut-off provision in the receiver, also Mks. I*, I**, I***, and "ConD" Mks. II, II*, II**, II***, and IV upgrades and conversions. Introduced 1903, mfg. at Sparkbrook until 1906, Enfield, BSA, and LSA until 1907.

$2,150 $1,950 $1,750 $1,500 $1,300 $1,100 $950

Add 20% for an original unaltered Mk I S.M.L.E.

Add 25% for converted MK II/II*/IV variations.

Prices for the SMLE MK.1 can also be used for the scarce Mks. I* and I IP (India Pattern) conversions to the MK.III specification.**

.303 S.M.L.E. MK III (RIFLE NO. 1 MK III, POST 1926) – improved solid charger guide, rear sight and rear handguard over the S.M.L.E. Mk I, still retains the magazine cut-off and volley sights of the Mk I S.M.L.E. Model, approved in 1907, also made by Lithgow, Ishapore, and Nepal.

SMLE Mk. III $1,300 $1,150 $1,000 $850 $750 $600 $500

Subtract 50% for Nepal mfg.

Subtract 20% for restocked Mk. III rifles mfg. during the interwar years w/o long range sights.

.303 S.M.L.E. MK III* (RIFLE NO.1 MK III*, POST 1926) – later model that incorporates production shortcuts, no magazine cut-off, long range volley sights, or backsight windage adjustment. Made by Enfield, BSA, SSA, NRF, Lithgow, Ishapore, and Nepal, introduced in 1915.

$1,000 $850 $700 $600 $500 $400 $350

Subtract 50% for Nepal mfg.

.303 RIFLE NO. 1 MK III* H.T. LITHGOW SNIPER – factory fitted telescopic sight and heavy barrel, converted at Lithgow, Australia at the end of WWII, special bedding of furniture, some were also fitted with a cheekpiece, British and Lithgow actions. Over 1600 mfg. circa 1917-1921.

$7,000 $6,500 $6,000 $5,500 $5,000 $4,250 $3,500

Add 20% for low mounted scopes, approx. 480 mfg.

Subtract 20% for non-matching no. scopes.

Buyer beware - check for authentic serial numbers, as there have been some fakes on this model.

.303 S.M.L.E. MK V – features a folding aperture backsight on upper rear part of action body, reinforcing outer band at the base of the nosecap, full-length top handguards, magazine cut-off, "V" marked safety catch with angled thumb grooves, limited production at Enfield in 1922-1924 of 20,000 rifles.

$1,900 $1,700 $1,500 $1,300 $1,100 $950 $800

Many found with damaged rear sight or wanting the upper reinforcing band - check for replacement parts. This reduces the value up to 30%.

.22 SHORT RIFLE MK I, I*, & II – conversions from 1907 of M.L.M. and M.L.E. long rifles to short rifle configuration, 25.2 in. barrel, service conversions by R.S.A.F. Enfield for the War Office.

$1,850 $1,700 $1,500 $1,250 $1,000 $850 $700

Add 10% for Mk I and Mk I*, scarce.

.22 SHORT RIFLE MK III – converted from .303 Cd. Mk II & II* SMLE for miniature range practice, external resemblance to SMLE Mk I, service conversions done at Enfield as well as by BSA and LSA.

$1,750 $1,600 $1,400 $1,250 $1,000 $800 $600

Add $750 for Parker-Hiscock magazine.

.22 PATTERN 1914 SHORT RIFLES NOS. 1 & 2 – single shot WW1 conversions by the British gun trade. No. 1 model is from SMLE Mk I, No. 2 is from SMLE Mk III. Converted by A.G. Parker and Westley Richards.

$1,600 $1,400 $1,200 $1,000 $850 $700 $550

The .22 Patt. 1914 No. 1 can bring a 30%+ premium due to its earlier S.M.L.E. Mk I configuration.

GRADING - PPGS™	100%	98%	95%	90%	80%	70%	60%	LAST MSR

.22 PATTERN 1918 SHORT RIFLE – a short-lived WWI training rifle that utilized mock cartridges ("Conveyors") to feed .22 RF cartridges from a .303 magazine into a .303 chamber, to be subsequently fired through a lined .22 cal. barrel. W.W. Greener manufactured only 975, so this is a scarce trainer. This pattern was declared obsolete in 1920. Chamber areas on top of the receiver are marked: "PARKER-HALE .303 CUM .22 SYSTEM".

	$2,200	$2,000	$1,750	$1,500	$1,300	$1,150	$950

Add $80 for each Enfield (EFD) marked conveyor that resembles a steel .303 cartridge.

.22 NO. 2 MK IV* – converted No. 1 rifle (S.M.L.E.) to single-loading trainer, modified in Britain, Lithgow (Australia), and Ishapore (India).

	$1,000	$900	$750	$600	$500	$425	$375

.276 PATTERN 1913 TRIALS RIFLE – 1,200 of these rifles, with bayonets, were produced in 1913 at Enfield for troop trials using a modified Mauser bolt design, the rifle chambered the very high velocity rimless .276 caliber cartridge, WWI arrived before the completion of the trials, but the P1913's design was used for the basis of the U.S. manufacture Patt. 1914 and M1917 rifles.

	$9,950	$8,000	$7,000	$6,250	$5,500	$5,000	$4,750

Subtract 20% for later upgrade or test modifications.

.303 NO. 3 MK I* (PATTERN 1914 RIFLE) – U.S. manufactured British modified Mauser action during WWI, made by Winchester, Remington, and Eddystone, very similar to the U.S. .30 Model 1917, and shares many interchangeable component parts.

	$1,400	$1,200	$1,000	$900	$750	$600	$450

Add $500 for original fine adj. rear sight.

Add 20% for Pattern 1914 rifles refurbished to No.3 Mk II.

Subtract 10% for Eddystone mfg.

H. Morris & Co. was contracted to restock 11,000 Pattern 1914 rifles in Britain during WWII to the No.3 Mk II standard configuration. The 'new' stocks are stamped 'No.3 Mk.II' on right side of butts and N-over-49 on bottom of forends below the muzzle cap.

.303 NO. 3 MK I* (T) (PATTERN 1914 SNIPER) – converted in England by Periscope Prism Co. (1918) & B.S.A. (1938) from Winchester rifles, the Pattern 1918 telescope on clawfoot mounts was fitted.

	$9,500	$8,500	$7,000	$6,000	$5,000	$4,250	$3,750

Rifles converted to Pattern 1914 Snipers by B.S.A. circa 1938 were for Ireland.

.303 NO. 3 MK I* (T) A SNIPER – converted in England by Alex Martin in WWII from Winchester MK I* (F) rifles, Great War Aldis and P.P. Co. telescopes (ex-SMLE snipers) were fitted, original SMLE rifle engraved number is usually visible, scope is offset (left) of the bore line. 421 mfg. beginning of WWII.

	$7,500	$6,500	$5,500	$4,500	$4,000	$3,750	$2,900

.410 MUSKET (INDIA) – conversion of the SMLE rifle after 1927 to single loader, smoothbore barrel, uses straight sided .303 cartridge equating to .410 medium length case. The .410 shot shell will not chamber.

	$900	$800	$700	$600	$500	$400	$300

Subtract 10% for rifles converted to chamber standard .410 ga. 3 in. ammo.

.303 SINGLE LOADER (S.L.) INDIA – similar configuration to .410 Musket, converted at Ishapore from 1923, but has rifled barrel and chambers the service .303 round, less common than the .410 Musket.

	$950	$850	$750	$650	$550	$450	$350

NO. 1 MK VI TRIALS RIFLE – the No.1 Mk.VI rifle is the earliest direct predecessor of the No.4 Mk.1 rifle, produced between 1929-1933 at RSAF Enfield for troop trials. Serial numbers, with many gaps, overlap those of the No.4 Mk.I trials rifle (A001-A1700), with many of both types of rifles being renumbered, with an "A" suffix in 1941-2 to designate their limited interchangeability of parts with the then new No.4 Mk.I production rifles. Many Mk.VIs were lost with the Fall of France and the evacuation from Dunkirk in 1940. An as yet unestablished number (probably a few hundred) of unfinished Mk.VI receivers were supplied to the ROF Fazakerly during 1941-2 to be made into complete rifles to supplement No.4 Mk.I production. The range of serial numbers for these hybrid variants is between 24000A-27000A; again note the "A" suffix. A complete original No.1 Mk.VI trials rifle can instantly be recognized by a coarsely checkered walnut forend and a brass marking disk near the toe on the right side of its butt, whereas the later Fazakerly-produced rifles, for all intents and purposes, are stocked with early (usually beech) No.4 Mk.I woodwork and lack a marking disk. Also, the left wall of the receiver of the Mk.VI appears to be scooped-out in front of the charger bridge, thus making it much lower than those found on the subsequent No. 4 trials and production rifles.

	$8,500	$7,500	$6,500	$5,750	$4,750	$4,250	$3,750
Fazakerly mfg.	$3,000	$2,750	$2,250	$2,000	$1,750	$1,500	$1,250

GRADING - PPGS™	100%	98%	95%	90%	80%	70%	60%	LAST MSR

NO. 4 MK I TRIALS RIFLE – the No.4 Mk.I trials rifle more closely resembles the wartime No.4 Mk.I than the No.1 Mk.VI, but was better finished and stocked-up in walnut. It was made from 1930-1935 at the RSAF Enfield. In 1941, roughly 1,400 of their production were used as the basis for the initial No.4 Mk.1(T) sniping rifles (see comments below on No.4 Mk.I (T) sniping rifles). In 1935, 50-60 trials rifles that were fitted with aluminum butt-plates, and a modified rear sight were designated the "C" Pattern. This pattern of trials rifle possesses a small "c" on the left of its butt socket, just below its "No.4 Mk.I" designation. Original rifles of this pattern are obviously exceedingly rare, and should attain roughly the same price as a No.1 Mk.VI. However, many of the "C" Pattern receivers were later (1941-2) used on standard production No.4 rifles, so without an aluminum buttplate, and Enfield-inspected woodwork and rear sights, these rifles should have only a 30-50% markup over the wartime produced No.4 Mk.I rifles.

Trials	$7,000	$6,250	$5,000	$4,000	$3,250	$2,750	$2,000	
"C" Pat.	$9,000	$8,000	$7,250	$6,500	$5,500	$4,500	$3,750	

.303 NO. 4 MK I & I* – WWII production Lee-Enfield, British R.O.F. Fazakerley, Maltby, and BSA Shirley (M47C) from 1941, Britain only made the Mk I model, wartime U.S. Lend-Lease production marked "US PROPERTY", serial number contains letter "C", many components are marked with a squared "S", while Canadian Long Branch rifles contain an "L" (for Long Branch), U.S. and Canada made both Mk I and Mk I* models.

	$1,400	$1,200	$1,100	$1,000	$875	$750	$650	

Rare 1933 trials No. 4 rifles made at Enfield will bring a 50%+ premium.
Add 10% for Pakistan Wah Cantt (POF) made with machinery from the BSA Shirley plant in the late 1950s.
Add 20% for early 1941 Long Branch MK I rifles in the 0L ser. no. range.

.303 NO. 4 MK 2, MK 1/2 & 1/3 – postwar Fazakerley [ROF(F)] production with the "hung" trigger and better quality fittings than wartime production, Mk 1/2 and 1/3 converted from Mk I and Mk I* rifles respectively, the No. 4 Mk 2 was of new manufacture, also made in the early 1970s at Wah Cantt, Pakistan on ex-Fazakerley machinery. Irish contracts imported during the early 1990s had waxed gauze wrapping and matching bayonets.

	$1,200	$1,100	$950	$800	$675	$500	$400	

Subtract 10% if w/o matching bayonet.
Subtract 10% for Mk 1/3 and Mk 1/2.

.303 NO. 4 MK I (T) SNIPING RIFLES – while BSA Shirley, with Holland & Holland, produced the majority of these weapons (roughly 26,000 by 1945), four other manufacturers were also involved in setting up No.4 Mk.I/I* (T) sniping rifles during the war. These [other] makes are quite sought after by both the Lee-Enfield and sniping rifle collectors.

	$8,500	$7,500	$6,500	$5,500	$4,750	$4,250	$3,500	
w/scope mounts only	$3,000	$2,750	$2,500	$2,250	$2,000	$1,750	$1,250	

Due to their limited production, or other peculiarities, rifles from the following manufactories should be able to attain a 20% premium over the more common BSA examples.
Add 20% for the following variations:
1. ROF Maltby, No.4 Mk.I (T) only, early war, with only 600 produced. Set up at Enfield in 1941-1942.
2. Enfield No.4 Mk.I trials rifle, approx. 1400 No.4 Mk.I (T) rifles were set up at Enfield in 1941-1942.
3. Long Branch, Ontario, Canada produced approx. 900 No.4 Mk.I*(T) sniping rifles during WWII. Rifles were set up at Long Branch and the optics were supplied by R.E.L., Canada. A few of these rifles were later converted (in 1970-1971) at Enfield to the (7.62mm X 51mm NATO) L42A1 configuration.
4. A small number (as many as 1200) of Savage Arms Co., Chicopee, MA - produced No.4 Mk.I and I* rifles were converted to the "T" sniping configuration in England by Holland & Holland during the mid-war period along side those No.4 Mk.I (T)s supplied by BSA, Shirley, and are therefore marked "S51" at the base of their pistol-grips. As above, a very few of these Savage rifles were made into L42A1s.
Add 30% for the following variants:
Long Branch No. 4 Mk I* (w/Lyman Alaskan scopes on Griffin & Howe mounts) and the No. 4 MK I* T fitted with the REL No. 69 scope and a sporter style buttstock (w/high comb, pistol grip, and recoil pad).

Buyers should beware of fakes with newly manufactured mounts and No. 32 Mk I scopes.

.303 NO. 5 MK I JUNGLE CARBINE – 20 1/2 in. barrel with flash hider, lightened action body and shortened furniture. From 1944, for service in the Far East.

	$1,250	$1,000	$850	$700	$600	$500	$400	

Add 50% for BSA Shirley (M47C) rifle grenade trials rifles with serial numbers beginning with "BB" and a hung trigger.
Add $1,500 for "Paratrooper" prototypes.
Add approx. $2,500 for the .22 No. 5 Mk I rifle produced during 1945 in limited quantities for trials.
Subtract 20% for Indian service issues that have a transverse wood screw in the forend which is less desirable.

Beware of recently imported (circa 1990s) No. 4 rifles converted to appear as Jungle Carbines. These models do not have the lightning cuts on the receiver, barrel, and trigger guard. Paratrooper prototypes were mfg. with dismountable butts removed by a dovetail fitting or a screw-knob attachment circa Feb. - June 1944.

GRADING - PPGS™	100%	98%	95%	90%	80%	70%	60%	LAST MSR

.22 NO. 7 MK I – postwar rimfire trainer on No. 4 action, British model has magazine feed, the Long Branch is designated "C No. 7" but is single shot only, originally issued in chest. Mfg. in England by BSA and in Canada by Long Branch.

$1,900 $1,750 $1,500 $1,350 $1,100 $950 $750

Add $250-$350 for original marked Canadian chest.
Subtract 40% if w/o bolthead.

.22 NO. 8 MK I – postwar rimfire trainer, half-stock target rifle style made by BSA (M47C) and Fazakerley on a modified No. 4 action body.

$1,750 $1,600 $1,350 $1,200 $950 $750 $600

.22 NO. 9 MK I – single shot only, full-length rifle resembling the No. 4, British conversion of the No. 4 Mk I rifle by Parker Hale for the Royal Navy.

$1,400 $1,200 $1,000 $850 $750 $650 $550

SKELETON ARMOURER & TRAINING ACTIONS – with shortened barrel, sometimes serial no. with SKN prefix. Models from MLM thru' to No.4. Some made at Enfield, others at Ordnance Depots. Beware of fakes.

$1,100 $950 $850 $750 $675 $475 $425

Note: these actions with shortened barrels under 16 inches are classified as short barreled rifles (SBR) and fall under the National Firearms Act (NFA) classifications. They cannot be imported, bought, or sold if not registered, and if registered, not without the appropriate federal paperwork. Some legitimate actions were imported in the 1990s in rebarreled to 16 inches, thus allowing for their general ownership.

* ***Skeleton Armourer & Training Actions Full Length Models*** – full-length models of SMLE made at Lithgow in short production run. Beware of fakes.

$3,500 $2,800 $2,200 $1,900 $1,750 $1,600 $1,500

These models are also considered firearms by the Gun Control Act for importation or sale.

LONG BRANCH TRAINING RIFLE & SWIFT TRAINER – non-guns with needle pointed striker at front of barrel, Canadian & British variants used with panoramic target in a frame.

$1,400 $1,300 $1,000 $900 $750 $600 $450

Subtract 10% for Swift trainers. Subtract 20% if missing case and accessories.

.303 SHORTENED & LIGHTENED NO. 1 RIFLE – Lithgow trials full-stock carbines, 20.2 in. barrel, serial numbered XP followed by 1-100 number, came with 10 inch bayonet. Rare. Late WWII production.

$7,500 $7,000 $6,500 $6,000 $5,000 $4,000 $3,500

.303 NO. 6 MK I & I/I – Lithgow trials jungle carbines, Mk I has bed backsight, Mk I/I has aperture sight at rear of body, carbine length, marked XP followed by serial number. Rare.

$8,500 $7,500 $6,500 $5,750 $5,000 $4,500 $4,000

.303 LONG BRANCH LIGHT RIFLE – wartime short-run test rifle, one-piece stock, grooved forend with recess in butt and rubber recoil pad, rifle length, marked J5550 followed by serial number. Very rare.

$9,950 $9,000 $8,500 $7,750 $7,000 $6,250 $5,000

.303 EAL (EX-CAL LONG BRANCH) SURVIVAL RIFLES – sporter style survival, Ranger and surplus sale model, variations in sights, depending upon variant and applications, originally with orange color recoil pad. Mfg. late 1950s.

$1,800 $1,600 $1,500 $1,300 $1,100 $1,000 $950

Subtract 10% for non-Canadian service rifles with a Williams leaf rear sight.

.22 HORNET SLAZENGER SPORTER – made at Lithgow under contract for Slazengers, Sporter model with modified 400 yd. leaf rear sight, ramp front sight, pistol grip buttstock, 5 shot mag.

$1,000 $900 $800 $700 $600 $500 $400

.410 SLAZENGER SPORTER – sporter with short 'bobbed' forend, single loader, no rear sight, grooved top of action body for sighting, bead foresight, made at Lithgow under contract for Slazengers.

$800 $750 $600 $500 $400 $325 $250

7.62MM RIFLE 2A & 2A1 (INDIA) – new manufacture SMLE rifle in NATO cal., higher quality steel, 2A1 upgrade has metric rear sight graduated to 800m, and angled ramp on sight bed. Production from the mid-1960s.

$850 $775 $700 $600 $500 $500 $300

7.62MM L42A1 SNIPER – Enfield conversion and extensive rebuild of the No. 4 Mk I(T) sniper rifle, fitted with an upgraded No. 32 telescopic sight to L1A1, half-stocked furniture, 7.62mm magazine with integral ejector, with heavy target barrel.

$9,950 $9,000 $8,250 $7,500 $7,000 $6,500 $5,500

Add 30% for Iraq war issue with 6x Schmidt & Bender scope (beware of non-originals!)

GRADING - PPGS™	100%	98%	95%	90%	80%	70%	60%	LAST MSR

7.62mm L1A1 SELF LOADING RIFLE (SLR) – Enfield, CAL, and Lithgow manufacture along with ensuing imports from South America and some domestic market action bodies (receivers) and parts, values can vary considerably, depending on the source of component parts, country of origin and markings, ATF and import restrictions apply to safety sear action bodies, as on original British, Canadian and Australian service models.

$4,000 $3,500 $2,750 $2,250 $2,000 $1,750 $1,400

Values assume NFA compliant upper receivers fitted to original British and Commonwealth parts kits imported during the early 1990s.

Add 50%-75% for original Lithgow SAF Model L1A1 made for U.S. market (limited production).

Add 10% for a Trilux L2A2 optical sight.

.230 FRANCOTTE CADET MARTINI – turn of the century British empire trainer with Belgian Francotte patent, small size modular Martini action.

$1,200 $1,000 $900 $800 $700 $550 $450

Add 30% for takedown model.

Add 10% for colonial markings.

.310 CADET MARTINI – later production small Francotte action on Australian contract by W.W. Greener and BSA, circa 1910.

$1,000 $900 $800 $700 $600 $500 $400

RIFLES: U.S. MILITARY

Add 10% for Winchester mfg.

Add 10% for Type I guns.

Add 10% for British service models with red painted band around stock.

U.S. MODEL 1917 ENFIELD – .30-06 cal., bolt action, 6 shot (5 shot mag.), 26 in. barrel, original finish was high polish blue, although wartime and post war refurbished rifles may be parkerized or black matte, adj. sights, military stock, derived from English P14 Enfield, production run continued at Winchester, Remington, and Eddystone after British .303 cal. pattern contracts concluded, over two million mfg. 1917-18, but original guns in 90%+ condition are rare, some used in British service have red-painted band around stock to differentiate them from .303 Patt. '14.

* ***U.S. Model 1917 Enfield Rifle Original High Polish Blue***

$2,000 $1,800 $1,600 $1,400 $1,200 $1,000 $800

This model was manufactured primarily by Remington at the Eddystone plant in Eddystone, PA (Eddystone marked), the Ilion Remington plant, and by Winchester in New Haven, CT.

* ***U.S. Model 1917 Enfield Rifle Matte Blue Or Parkerized Reworks*** – most frequently encountered variation, many differences in the reworked matte blue and parkerized finishes, barrels marked "JA" are on rifles rebarreled during WWII using Johnson Automatics original barrels.

$1,400 $1,200 $1,000 $900 $800 $700 $600

RIFLES: LEE-ENFIELD

THE ENFORCER – a commercial heavy barreled sniping rifle of a similar configuration to the British Army's L42A1 purpose-built for law enforcement agencies in the U.K. However, as a commercial rifle [though produced at Enfield Royal Small Arms Factory (RSAF)] its woodwork is finished to a much higher standard than most military arms. The woodwork is commonly a blonde beech hardwood, with a similarly shortened forestock to that of the L42A1 sniping rifle. However, its trigger, unlike the L42A1, pivots (is "hung") on the rear of the action body (rather than on the trigger guard), and its butt is "sporterized" with a cheek rest, pistol grip, and a recoil pad. Parker-Hale commercial scope bases and rings were utilized to mount a German Pecar 4-10x variable power scope. Also fitted were provisions for a tunnel foresight and a Parker-Hale PH5E micrometer adj. rear sight.

$6,500 $6,000 $5,250 $4,750 $4,250 $3,000 $2,250

NO. 4 7.62MM CONV. – the No. 4 7.62mm Conv. (converted) is somewhat of a mysterious companion to the L39A1 series of military target rifles. It was produced as a commercial rifle, primarily in 1968-69, concurrent with the early XL39E1, L39A1, and Envoy rifles. It is rarer than the L39A1, though encountered to a similar degree as the experimental/prototype XL39E1.

$3,500 $3,250 $3,000 $2,750 $2,250 $1,700 $1,300

XL39E1 TRIALS RIFLE – a transient variant for a brief troop trials period before the almost immediate introduction of the L39A1. It also served alongside of the L39A1 in subsequent service use.

$4,500 $4,000 $3,500 $3,000 $2,600 $2,250 $1,750

L39A1 – the standard target rifle of the British Services from the late 1960s until 1990s.

$4,250 $3,975 $3,250 $2,750 $2,250 $2,000 $1,500

GRADING - PPGS™	100%	98%	95%	90%	80%	70%	60%	LAST MSR

ENVOY – a commerical match rifle finished to a much higher standard than its military cohorts. The furniture is a polished blonde beech, with a widened forend and a "sporter" style butt. It used a 10 shot Enfield 7.62mm mag., and was mounted with an A.J. Parker "Matchmaker" tunnel foresight and a 4/47 TZ micrometer rear sight. The British 1970 Palma Match team used these rifles to triumph at Bisley Camp. These particular rifles are engraved on the body, above the left boltway: "PALMA MATCH BISLEY 1970", and stamped on the receiver ring: "REGULATED BY FULTON". Only approximately 70 of these rifles were made, as such, and should command a clear 50% premium over the standard Envoy.

	$3,750	$3,500	$3,000	$2,500	$2,250	$1,950	$1,750	

L8 SERIES OF 7.62x51MM SERVICE RIFLES – converted from primarily, No. 4 Mks. 2, 1/2, and 1/3 rifles by rebarreling, headspacing and reproving .303" rifles to the new caliber. Additionally, a new extractor with a lengthened claw, charger guide, and a 10 round Enfield 7.62 magazine with an integral ejector were fitted. Actions, barrels, bolts, and boltheads are engraved with the "19T" (19 tons per square inch) proofmark. Barrels were produced in the UK, Belgium, and Canada; with the bayonet lugs being omitted in Canadian production. The original full-length No. 4 woodwork was maintained. Enfield converted rifles were originally intended to be a reserve arm and for sales to foreign militaries. Sterling Engineering also produced a kit for converting the No. 4, differing fundamentally from the Enfield version by the use of an external ejector and a Sterling-made magazine. In reality, few legitimate Enfield (or Sterling) convered L8 rifles exist, though hundreds of No. 4s (of all marks) were converted for military match competiion by Canadian Arsenals Limited (CAL) and various UK gunsmiths in the 1960s and 1970s. The Canadian rifles have, of course, the CAL stylized broad arrow proofmark in place of 19T. Of the small number of original Enfield L8 rifles in existence, an even smaller number were converted to the L8(T) sniping variant; these should consequently be priced 100% above the baseline.

Enfield L8	$5,000	$4,500	$4,250	$4,000	$3,500	$2,750	$2,250	
CAL* or UK L8-type	$2,500	$2,000	$1,750	$1,500	$1,250	$1,000	$900	

Add $200 if fitted with a Parker Hale PH5C micrometer-adj. rear sight.

ENGLISH SHOTGUNS

Shotguns manufactured by various British makers.

Unlike American shotguns such as Parker, L.C. Smith, and A.H. Fox, the critical aspect of finish originality is not of premier importance with English shotguns. There are many English gunsmiths in both Britain and the U.S. who are capable of refinishing English guns on a level with the Old World masters. Of course, original guns with 100% original finish have the greatest desirability, but, when done properly, restored guns closely approach the same value of original guns. Do not confuse this with restored American guns, which are only worth a fraction of their "original" finish value.

Percentage of case colors on receivers and blue on barrels is not as critical in determining values, which diminish less drastically than with American guns. Tremendous fluctuations in value do occur in smaller gauges (20, 28 ga. and .410 bore). The rarity and value of gauges, as they descend, are prodigious in English shotguns. However, the opposite is true in regard to double rifles, where bigger is better. A vintage English double with the original inside labeled trunk style case increases the gun's value $1,000 - $5,000+ depending on style, inclusive tools and accessories, and case materials. Cases with exotic leathers such as crocodile, elephant and ostrich are also very valuable.

A fine old English double, tastefully engraved and stocked with exhibition Turkish walnut by a master craftsman, is a work of art that is highly treasured by collectors, and should be appropriately valued. The same application can apply to American guns, but again, is subject to narrower limitations.

Also unlike most other shotguns, English guns are more delicate and sleek in design, eliminating any excess metal and wood, resulting in minimum weight and better balance. Because of this, there is far less margin for error in retaining necessary strength after modification such as chamber lengthening and back boring of barrels. Therefore, the importance of proof or reproofing after modification is a serious consideration. In Britain, it is serious enough to be a matter of law.

After years of hard use and sometimes neglect, rust pits appear in the bores which require back boring to restore them. Barrels can be cut and back bored to simulate chokes which are actually cylinder bore. This back boring must not result in more than a .015 in. increase in bore diameter from that of the original. Barrels more than .015 in. over original are considered "out of proof" and potentially dangerous. In any case, the barrel thickness should always exceed a minimum. Most authorities consider the minimum to be no less than .022 to .025 inch in wall thickness w/o a British reproof. The foregoing only applies to fluid steel barrels. Many consider "nitro proofed" damascus barrels safe to shoot - however, this is a dangerous crapshoot.

The above limitations are critical to overall value and their presence or absence must be established to buyer satisfaction prior to purchase. Bore micrometers and barrel thickness gauges are relatively inexpensive compared to the purchase of a $25,000 Purdey that has a true market value of only $10,000 because its aesthetically beautiful barrels are dangerously out of proof. New best English made chopper lump barrels currently cost at least $10,000, and

GRADING - PPGS™	100%	98%	95%	90%	80%	70%	60%	LAST MSR

original Purdey made barrels are about three times as much. Remember, the most important criterion for purchasing an English shotgun is the barrels.

Somewhat of a paradox is the later serial numbered guns. Albeit generally of lesser quality than early guns, they are generally more valuable on a sliding scale due to the ever increasing cost of currently manufactured guns.

The publisher would like to thank Mr. Larry Baer for providing the above information.

ENTRÉPRISE ARMS INC.

Previous manufacturer located in Irwindale, CA, circa 1996-2009.

For individual model listings, please go to BlueBookOfGunValues.com/overflow.

ERA

Previous manufacturer located in Brazil.

SHOTGUNS

ERA O/U – 12 or 20 ga., 28 in. vent. rib barrel, full and mod., double triggers, extractors, checkered hardwood stock.

	100%	98%	95%	90%	80%	70%	60%	LAST MSR
	$275	$250	$225	$200	$170	$150	$125	
Trap version	$300	$275	$250	$225	$200	$175	$150	
Skeet version	$300	$275	$250	$225	$200	$175	$150	

ERA SxS – 12, 20 ga., or .410 bore, 26, 28, or 30 in. barrels, various chokes, double triggers, extractors, checkered pistol grip stock.

100%	98%	95%	90%	80%	70%	60%	LAST MSR
$165	$150	$135	$125	$110	$100	$85	

ERA RIOT SxS – 12 or 20 ga., 18 in. barrels.

100%	98%	95%	90%	80%	70%	60%	LAST MSR
$185	$175	$150	$140	$125	$110	$95	

ERA QUAIL SxS – 12 or 20 ga., 20 in. barrels.

100%	98%	95%	90%	80%	70%	60%	LAST MSR
$185	$175	$150	$140	$125	$110	$95	

ERHARDT, DENNIS

Current custom manufacturer and gunsmith located in Helena, MT.

Dennis Erhardt is a custom maker specializing in modern classic and European style custom rifles and shotguns. Many options and configurations are available. Please contact the company directly for more information and pricing.

ERMA SUHL, GmbH

Previous manufacturer located in Suhl, Germany January 1998 - circa 2004. Erma Suhl purchased the remaining assets of Erma-Werke.

RIFLES: BOLT ACTION

SR100 SNIPER RIFLE – .300 Win. Mag., .308 Win., or .338 Lapua Mag. cal., tactical rifle featuring brown laminated wood stock with thumbhole, adj. buttplate/cheekpiece, and vent. forend, forged aluminum receiver, 25 1/2 or 29 1/2 in. barrel, muzzle brake, adj. match trigger, approx. 15 lbs. Limited importation 1997-98 only.

100%	98%	95%	90%	80%	70%	60%	LAST MSR
$6,500	$5,750	$5,000	$4,350	$3,750	$3,000	$2,350	*$8,600*

This model was imported exclusively by Amtec 2000, Inc., located in Gardner, MA.

Most recent importation was in .300 Win. Mag., and included a Steyr scope mount.

ERMA-WERKE

Previous manufacturer located in Dachau, Germany (Erma-Werke production) until bankruptcy occurred in October of 1997. Pistols were previously imported and distributed by Precision Sales International, Inc. located in Westfield, MA, Nygord Precision Products located in Prescott, AZ, and Mandall's Shooting Supplies, Inc. located in Scottsdale, AZ. Previously distributed by Excam located in Hialeah, FL.

Erma-Werke also manufactured private label handguns for American Arms Inc. (refer to their section for listings).

PISTOLS: SEMI-AUTO

MODEL LA 22 – .22 LR cal., similar action and styling as the Luger. Mfg. 1964-1967.

100%	98%	95%	90%	80%	70%	60%	LAST MSR
$395	$335	$275	$240	$200	$175	$140	

GRADING - PPGS™	100%	98%	95%	90%	80%	70%	60%	LAST MSR

ERMA KGP68A/BEEMAN MP-08 - .32 ACP or .380 ACP cal., Luger type toggle action, 3 1/2 (Beeman) or 4 in. barrel, 6 shot mag., blue, 1.4 lbs. Mfg. 1968-disc.

	$450	$400	$335	$275	$240	$185	$145	*$500*

This model was imported exclusively by Mandall's Shooting Supplies, Inc. located in Scottsdale, AZ. From 1988-90, Beeman took over importation of this model in .380 ACP cal. only with new Luger style checkered walnut grips and 3 1/2 in. barrel. Previous models had plastic grips.

ERMA KGP69/BEEMAN P-08 - .22 LR cal., Luger type toggle action, 8 shot mag., 3 3/4 in. barrel, blue, plastic (disc.) or checkered walnut grips. Mfg. 1969-disc.

	$335	$275	$240	$185	$145	$115	$95	*$390*

Beeman was the sole importer of this model between 1988-90.

MODEL ESP 85A SPORT/MATCH PISTOL - .22 LR or .32 S&W Long Wadcutter cal., blowback semi-auto, 6 in. barrel, 5 or 8 (.32 S&W only) shot mag., choice of sporting or adj. stippled match grips with thumbrest, fully adj. and interchangeable sights, gun is supplied with 1 extra weight, extra mag., sights, disassembly tools, and attaché style case ($134 option) with foam rubber cut-outs, 2 1/2 lbs. Imported 1989-97.

	$1,225	$925	$800	$650	$550	$495	$450	*$1,785*

Subtract $315 for Junior Model.
Add $215 for .32 S&W cal.
Add $110 for Match Model (with anatomical grips).
Add $980-$1,390 for conversion unit.
Add approx. $215 for chrome finish.
Add $24 for left-hand action (Match Model only - disc. 1994).

ESP 85 refers to Junior Model (new 1995). The ESP 85 series was distributed by Precision Sales International, Inc. and Mandall Shooting Supplies, Inc.

* ***Model ESP 85A Sport/Match Pistol Set*** - includes both .22 LR and .32 S&W Long Wadcutter barrels and mags., cased with accessories, complete set was disc. 1991.

	$1,525	$1,350	$1,125	$950	$825	$750	$625	*$1,995*

EP-22 - similar to Model LA 22.

	$395	$335	$275	$240	$200	$175	$140	

ET-22 LUGER CARBINE - .22 LR cal., 11 3/4 in. barrel, blue rear ramp sight, checkered walnut grips and uncheckered forearm, adj. artillery type rear sight, rarely seen.

	$500	$400	$350	$300	$250	$200	$175	

Add 20% for leatherette case.

EP-25 - .25 ACP cal., 7 shot, 2 3/4 in. barrel, blue finish, fixed sights with grips.

	$395	$335	$275	$240	$200	$175	$140	

REVOLVERS: DOUBLE ACTION

These models were distributed by Precision Sales International, Inc. only.

ER-772 STANDARD/MATCH - .22 LR cal., standard or match gun with special adj. contoured grips with stippling, 6 in. barrel, action similar to ER-777, fully adj. and extended rear sight, interchangeable front sight, 3 lbs. Imported 1990-94.

	$1,100	$875	$725	$625	$550	$495	$450	*$1,371*

ER-773 STANDARD/MATCH - .32 S&W Long Wadcutter cal., otherwise similar to ER-772 Match, 2.9 lbs. Imported 1990-95.

	$925	$825	$695	$525	$475	$425	$385	*$1,068*

ER-777 STANDARD - .357 Mag. cal., 6 shot, 4 or 5 1/2 in. barrel, solid rib and full barrel shroud, adj. target rear sight, blue steel, checkered sport grips, 2 3/4 lbs. Imported 1990-95.

	$875	$775	$650	$475	$425	$385	$350	*$1,019*

RIFLES

Models listed were available from Mandall Shooting Supplies, unless otherwise noted.

EM-1 .22 CARBINE - .22 LR cal., M1 copy, 10 or 15 shot mag., 18 in. barrel, rear adj. aperture sight, 5.6 lbs. Mfg. 1966-97.

	$365	$295	$250	$215	$190	$175	$160	*$400*

EGM-1 - similar to EM-1 except for unslotted buttstock, 5 shot mag.

	$260	$230	$195	$175	$150	$125	$100	*$295*

GRADING - PPGS™	100%	98%	95%	90%	80%	70%	60%	LAST MSR

EG-72 PUMP – .22 LR cal., outside hammer, 15 shot mag., 18 1/2 in. barrel. Mfg. 1970-76.

	$125	$95	$90	$75	$70	$65	$60	

EG-712 LEVER-ACTION – .22 LR cal., Win. Model 94 copy, tube mag., 18 1/2 in. barrel. Mfg. 1976-97.

	$260	$230	$195	$175	$150	$125	$100	*$295*

EG-73 – .22 WMR cal., similar to EG-712 12 shot mag. Mfg. 1973-97.

	$265	$230	$195	$175	$150	$125	$100	*$300*

ERN, MAX

Current custom rifle and shotgun manufacturer located in Leverkusen-Schlebusch, Germany. Direct sales through importer/FFL. Previously imported on a limited basis by New England Custom Gun Service, located in Claremont, NH until 2012.

Max Ern builds high quality double (SxS and O/U) rifles, bolt action rifles, and boxlock shotguns. Current models include bolt action Model 98, takedown bolt action Model 98, sidelock single barrel rifle, sidelock SxS double rifle, O/U sidelock double rifle, O/U shotgun, and SxS boxlock shotgun (20 ga.).

A variety of options and special orders are available. Please contact Max Ern directly for more information, including an individualized price quotation, availability, and delivery time.

ESCALADE

Previous trademark of slide action shotguns imported until circa 2008 by Mitchell's Mausers, located in Fountain Valley, CA.

SHOTGUNS: SLIDE ACTION

ESCALADE MODEL – 12 ga. only, 18 1/2, 22, or 28 in. chrome-lined barrel with choke tubes (except Home Defense model), dual action bars, Turkish walnut checkered stock and grooved forearm, available in Home Defense (18 1/2 in.) or Hunting (22 or 28 in.) configurations. Imported from Turkey 2004-2007.

	$360	$295	$260	$220	$175	$150	$125	*$395*

ESCORT

Current trademark of rifles and shotguns manufactured by Hatsan Arms Co. located in Izmir, Turkey. Hatsan shotguns are currently imported and distributed by Hatsan USA located in Bentonville, AR beginning 2011. Previously imported by Legacy Sports International, located in Reno, NV 2002-2018.

RIFLES: BOLT ACTION

ESCORT RIMFIRE RIFLE – .22 LR cal., 25 in. barrel, 10 shot detachable mag., chrome plated steel receiver and barrel, fiber optic sights, Turkish walnut stock with checkered grip and forearm, vent. rubber buttpad, manual safety and cocking indicator, 6.4 lbs. New 2017.

MSR $299	$250	$225	$195	$175	$160	$145	$125	

SHOTGUNS: O/U

ESCORT – 12 ga. only, 3 in. chambers, 28 in. VR barrels with five choke tubes, boxlock action with choice of blue (disc. 2010) or silver finished receiver, Turkish walnut (disc., reintroduced 2011-2013) or black synthetic stock and forearm with Cobblestone grip inserts, adj. comb, and Trio recoil pad (vent recoil pad became standard during 2009) with three adj. spacers, ST, extractors, fiber optic front sight, 7-8.2 lbs. Imported 2007-2015.

	$550	$475	$425	$350	$315	$275	$250	*$641*

Add $53 for hardshell case.

Add $186 for AAA select walnut stock and silver finished receiver (disc.) or $17 for standard checkered walnut stock and forearm (disc. 2013).

* ***Escort Shorty Home Defense*** – 12 ga. only, 3 in. chambers, 18 in. VR barrels with choke tubes, fiber optic front sight, accessory rail on lower barrel, nickel plated receiver, black synthetic stock with adj. comb and vent recoil pad, 7 lbs. Mfg. 2011-2015.

	$575	$500	$450	$365	$325	$285	$265	*$663*

OPTIMA D12 – 12 ga., 3 in. chambers, 28 in. VR barrels, multi-chokes (F, IM, CYL), white chrome steel finish, ejector or extractor, SST, brass bead front sight, select Turkish walnut stock and forend w/matte finish, rubber recoil pad, black chrome finished barrel, 7.2 lbs.

Please contact the importer directly for pricing and availability on this model.

GRADING - PPGS™	100%	98%	95%	90%	80%	70%	60%	LAST MSR

SHOTGUNS: SEMI-AUTO

Beginning 2004, all models have a round back receiver with 3/8 in. dovetail milled along top for mounting sights. Beginning in 2009, all Escort semi-auto shotguns use a bottom feed system similar to a Remington 11-87.

ESCORT AS/ESCORT AS 20 – 12 or 20 ga., 2 3/4 or 3 in. Mag. chamber, SMART Valve self-regulating gas piston, 28 in. chrome plated VR barrel, multi-choke system with 5 chokes (F, IM, M, IC, CYL), 2 or 4 shot mags. w/migratory plug, Ni-Cr-Mo steel construction, brass bead front sight, Turkish walnut stock and forend, recoil pad, DynaComb cheekpiece, manual cross-button trigger safety, steel receiver, detachable sling swivels, black finish, 6.8 lbs.

Please contact the importer directly for price and availability.

ESCORT DF12 – 12 ga., 3 in. Mag. chamber, modern sporting style, gas operated, 18 in. hard chrome barrel, multi-chokes (F, IC, CYL), two 5 shot mags. (optional 2 shot mag. available), aircraft alloy receiver, adj. and rear carry handle sight (adj. flip-up front and rear sight also included), fixed tactical stock w/integrated pistol grip, angled foregrip, manual trigger switch safety, reversible bolt cocking handle (ambi operations), rubber recoil pad, fitted Picatinny rail, sling swivels, elevated adj. comb, matte black finish, 8.9 lbs.

Please contact the importer directly for pricing and availability on this model.

ESCORT DYNAMAX – 12 ga., 3 in. Mag. chamber, kinetic/gas hybrid cycling system (HCS), two-piece modular design, 28 in. chrome plated VR barrel, multi-choke system with 5 chokes (F, IM, M, IC, CYL), 4 shot mag., Ni-Cr-Mo steel construction, Hi-Viz Spark sight, synthetic single piece stock and forend, rubber recoil pad, DynaComb cheekpiece, manual cross-button trigger safety, steel receiver, detachable sling swivels, black finish, 7 lbs. New 2019.

Please contact the importer directly for price and availability.

ESCORT MPA – 12 ga., 3 in. Mag. chamber, SMART Valve self-regulating gas piston, 18 in. chrome plated VR barrel, fixed cylinder, 5 shot mag. w/migratory plug, Ni-Cr-Mo steel construction, adj. fiber optic front sight, ghost ring adj. rear sight, polymer pistol grip stock and forend, recoil pad, manual cross-button trigger safety, steel receiver, sling swivels on stock and mag. cap, Picatinny rail, shotshell holder, black finish, 7.9 lbs.

MSR $349	$300	$265	$225	$200	$165	$135	$115

ESCORT PS/ESCORT PS 20 – 12 or 20 ga., 3 in. Mag. chamber, SMART Valve self-regulating gas piston, 28 in. chrome plated VR barrel, multi-choke system with 5 chokes (F, IM, M, IC, CYL), 2 or 4 shot mag. w/migratory plug, Ni-Cr-Mo steel construction, brass bead front sight, synthetic polymer stock and forend, recoil pad, checkered grip, manual cross-button trigger safety, steel receiver, detachable sling swivels, black finish, 6.2-7 lbs.

Please contact the importer directly for pricing and availability on this model.

* ***Escort PS Youth*** – 20 ga., 3 in. Mag. chamber, SMART Valve self-regulating gas piston, 28 in. chrome plated VR barrel, multi-choke system w/5 chokes (F, IM, M, IC, CYL), 2 or 4 shot mag. w/migratory plug, Ni-Cr-Mo steel construction, brass bead front sight, synthetic polymer stock and forend, TrioPad rubber buttpad, checkered grip, manual cross-button trigger safety, steel receiver, detachable sling swivels, availalbe in black, Realtree APG, Realtree MAX5, or Mossy Oak Bottomland finish, 6 lbs.

Please contact the importer directly for pricing and availability on this model.

ESCORT RAIDER/RAIDER 20 – 12 or 20 ga., 3 in. Mag. chamber, SMART Valve self-regulating gas piston, 18 in. hard chrome barrel, multi-chokes (F, IC, CYL), 2 or 5 shot mag. (optional 2 shot mag. available), aircraft alloy receiver, adj. front sight w/fiber optic sights, ghost ring adj. rear sight, polymer pistol grip stock w/shotshell holder, elastic buttpad, angled foregrip, manual cross-trigger switch safety, rubber recoil pad, fitted Picatinny rail, sling swivels, elevated adj. comb, matte black finish, 7.7-8.6 lbs.

Please contact the importer directly for pricing and availability on this model.

ESCORT SD-X SERIES – 12 ga. or .410 bore, 3 in. chamber, sporting style, 18 or 20 in. hard chrome plated barrel w/removable chokes or fixed cylinder, two detachable 5 shot mags., optional flip-up front and rear sights included, soft rubber pistol grip, manual safety selector switch, alloy upper receiver w/integrated Picatinny rail and synthetic ThermoDefend handguard, mounting sling loops, reversible cocking handle, detachable carry handle, optional storage for mags., matte black or FDE Cerakote finish, 7.8-9 lbs. New 2020.

MSR $619	$500	$450	$400	$350	$300	$225	$175

Add $70 for .410 bore.

GRADING - PPGS™	100%	98%	95%	90%	80%	70%	60%	LAST MSR

ESCORT SERIES - 3 IN. – 12 or 20 (new 2005) ga., 3 in. chamber, gas operated action with 2 position adj. screw (disc. 2003), 20 (disc. 2008), 22 (AS Youth and PS Slug, new 2005), 24 (disc. 2008), 26 (new 2005), or 28 in. VR barrel with 3 multi-chokes, blue finish, vent recoil pad, gold trigger, checkered walnut (Model AS) or polymer (Model PS) black or 100% camo coverage Mossy Oak Break-Up (disc. 2004), Mossy Oak Obsession (mfg. 2005-2008), Shadowgrass (disc. 2008), King's Woodland (mfg. 2009-2010), King's Desert (mfg. 2009-2010), King's Snow (mfg. 2009-2010), or Muddy Girl (new 2013) camo stock and forearm, 6.4-7 lbs. Imported 2002-2013.

	$400	$350	$315	$280	$250	$230	$215	*$489*

Add $169 for AS Supreme model with gloss finished walnut stock and forearm (disc.). Add $99 for Model PS Slug with rifled slug barrel and cantilever mount (disc. 2011).

Add $182 for AS Select Model with select walnut (mfg. 2007-2008). Add $100 for 100% camo coverage (disc. 2010). Add $74 for HiViz Spark front sight and King's Field metal finish (mfg. 2009). Add $175 for Model PS Slug Combo (mfg. 2006-2008). Add $81 for 24 in. barrel with Model PS TriViz sights and Mossy Oak Break Up camo coverage (disc. 2004).

* ***Escort Series - 3 in. - Aimguard*** – similar to Escort model, except has black chrome finish, black polymer stock, 18 (new 2006) or 20 (disc. 2005) in. barrel, cylinder bore. Imported 2004-2007.

	$340	$295	$275	$250	$230	$215	$195	*$392*

* ***Escort Series - 3 in. - Waterfowl/Tukey Combo*** – includes camo stock and forearm, 24 in. barrel with HiViz and TriViz sights and 28 in. barrel with HiViz Spark sight, hard case. Imported 2003-2008, reintroduced 2010-2011.

	$565	$500	$445	$395	$335	$295	$280	*$659*

* ***Escort MP Tactical (Escort Series 3 In. Home Defense)*** – 12 or 20 ga., 3 in. chamber, gas operated action, 18 in. barrel with cyl. bore choke, muzzle brake, aluminum alloy receiver, adj. ghost ring rear sight and adj. fiber optic front sight, black MP TacStock2 with built-in 2-round shell holder and cushioned pistol grip, low density recoil pad, sling swivel studs, Picatinny rail on extended forend and top of receiver, 6.9 lbs. New 2011.

MSR $559	$475	$415	$350	$325	$260	$215	$185	

ESCORT SERIES - 3 1/2 IN. – 12 ga., 3 1/2 in. chamber, polymer stock and forearm, blued steel or Mossy Oak Obsession (disc. 2008), Shadowgrass (mfg. 2007-2008), or King's (new 2009) camo coverage, 24 or 28 in. barrel with choke tubes, standard or choice of Spark front sight or TriViz sights, 7.6 lbs. Imported 2005-2010.

	$415	$365	$310	$280	$230	$185	$160	*$489*

Add $100 for King's Field model with Spark front sight. Add $64 for 24 in. barrel with Model PS TriViz sights and camo coverage (disc. 2008).

ESCORT STANDARD MAGNUM – 12 or 20 ga., 2 3/4 and 3 in. chamber, FAST loading system, SMART valve self-regulating gas piston, 26 or 28 in. chrome moly lined barrel, 3 chokes, raised vent. rib, single round mag. cut-off, fiber optic sight, black synthetic stock, sling swivel studs, 3/8 in. dovetail accessory rail on top of receiver, 5.8-7 lbs. New 2014.

MSR $499	$425	$375	$325	$295	$235	$195	$165	

* ***Escort Standard Magnum Youth (Escort Series 3 in. Youth)*** – 20 ga., 3 in. chamber, gas operated action, right or left-hand action, 22 in. barrel with 3 chokes, single round magazine cut-off, choice of black synthetic, walnut hardwood (disc. 2017), Muddy Girl (mfg. 2013-2015), Realtree Max-4 (disc. 2015), Realtree Max-5 (mfg. 2016-2017), Realtree APHD (disc. 2017), or Foxy Woods (mfg. 2016-2017) 100% camo coverage, Trio recoil pad and shim system, includes sling swivel studs, 13 in. LOP.

MSR $499	$425	$375	$325	$295	$235	$195	$165	

Add $36 for walnut stock (disc. 2017).

Add $45 for Foxy Woods (mfg. 2016-2017) or $49 for Realtree Max-5 (mfg. 2016-2017), or Realtree APHD camo finish (disc. 2017).

Add $58 for select wood (disc. 2011).

ESCORT SUPREME MAGNUM – 12 or 20 ga., 3 in. Mag. chamber, SMART Valve self-regulating gas piston, aluminum alloy receiver, 26 or 28 in. nickel chrome moly barrel with raised vent. rib and 5 choke tubes, right or left-hand action, FAST loading system, premium Turkish walnut stock with two adjustment shims, sling swivels, fiber optic front sight, 7.4 lbs. New 2013.

MSR $699	$600	$525	$450	$425	$350	$275	$225	

ESCORT XTREME/XTREME 20 – 12 or 20 ga., 2 3/4 or 3 in. Mag. chamber, SMART Valve self-regulating gas piston, 28 in. chrome plated VR barrel, multichoke system w/5 chokes (F, IM, M, IC, CYL), 4 shot w/migratory plug, mag., Ni-Cr-Mo steel barrel construction, Hi-Viz Spark sight, synthetic single piece

GRADING - PPGS™	100%	98%	95%	90%	80%	70%	60%	LAST MSR

stock and forend, rubber inlays and recoil pad, DynaComb cheekpiece, rubber grips, manual cross-button trigger safety, steel receiver, mounted sling studs, 4 stock shims to adj. stock drop and cast, black anodized aircraft alloy receiver, black or RealTree APG, RealTree MAX5 camo finish, 6-7 lbs.

Please contact the importer directly for pricing and availability on this model.

ESCORT XTREMEMAX – 12 ga., 3 1/2 in. Dbl. Mag. chamber, SMART Valve self-regulating gas piston, 28 in. chrome plated VR barrel, multi-choke system w/5 chokes (F, IM, M, IC, CYL), 2 or 4 shot w/ migratory plug, mag. cut for single shot, Ni-Cr-Mo steel construction, Hi-Viz Spark sight, synthetic single piece stock and forend, rubber inlays and recoil pad, DynaComb cheekpiece, manual cross-button trigger safety, steel receiver, mounted sling studs, 4 stock shims to adj. stock drop and cast, Realtree APG or Realtree Max5 camo finish, 7 1/2 lbs.

Please contact the importer directly for price and availability.

EXTREME MAGNUM 3 IN. – 12 or 20 (new 2013) ga., 3 in. chamber, SMART valve self regulating gas system, 28 in. VR nickel chrome moly lined barrel with 5 Hevi-Shot choke tubes, raised Soft Touch inserts on forend and pistol grip, sling swivel studs, black synthetic stock and forearm, Hi-Viz sights, right or left-hand action, approx. 7.4 lbs. Mfg. 2012-2017.

$500 $435 $385 $345 $295 $265 $250 ***$565***

* ***Extreme Magnum 3 In. Turkey*** – 12 ga. only, 24 in. barrel with extended turkey choke tube, pistol grip stock, receiver Picatinny rail, 100% Realtree APHD camo coverage, raised Hi-Viz sights, 7.4 lbs. Mfg. 2012-2017.

$615 $545 $485 $435 $375 $335 $295 ***$675***

* ***Extreme Magnum 3 In. Waterfowl*** – 12 ga., 28 in. nickel chrome moly lined barrel, multichokes, Hi-Viz Magni fiber optic front sight, sling swivel studs, raised vent. rib, 100% Avery Buckbrush (disc.), Killer Weed (disc.), Realtree Max-4 (mfg. mid-2011-2015), Realtree Max-5 (new 2016), or Realtree APHD (new mid-2011) camo coverage, also available in left-hand, 7.4 lbs. Mfg. 2011-2017.

$665 $595 $525 $465 $415 $350 $310 ***$763***

* ***Extreme Magnum 3 In. Youth*** – 20 ga., 3 in. chamber, 22 in. barrel with 3 chokes, 13 in. LOP, Foxy Woods finish, 6.4 lbs. Mfg. 2016-2017.

$500 $435 $385 $345 $295 $265 $250 ***$565***

EXTREME MAGNUM 3 1/2 IN. – 12 ga., 3 1/2 in. chamber, 28 in. VR barrel with choke tubes, black synthetic stock and forearm, 5 Hevi-Shot choke tubes, right or left-hand action, Hi-Viz sights, non-slip grip pads on forend and pistol grip, approx. 7.4 lbs. Mfg. 2012-2017.

$590 $525 $465 $415 $355 $315 $275 ***$655***

* ***Extreme Magnum 3 1/2 In. Waterfowl*** – 12 ga., 28 in. nickel chrome moly lined barrel, multichokes, Hi Viz Magni fiber optic front sight, sling swivel studs, raised vent. rib, 100% Avery Buckbrush (disc.), Killer Weed (disc.), Realtree Max-4 (mfg. mid-2011-2015), Realtree Max-5 (new 2016), or Realtree AP (new mid-2011) camo coverage, also available in left hand, 7.4 lbs. Mfg. 2011-2017.

$735 $645 $550 $500 $435 $375 $325 ***$825***

GLADIUS HOME DEFENSE – 12 (disc.) or 20 ga., 18 in. cyl. bore barrel with muzzle brake, aluminum alloy receiver, adj. ghost ring rear and fiber optic front sights, upper Picatinny rail, extended length forend with Picatinny rail, black or Marine (disc.) finish, forend pistol grip, black synthetic stock with cushioned pistol grip, recoil pad, adj. cheek pad, built-in holder for 2 extra shells, sling swivel studs, 6.8 lbs. Mfg. 2014-2017.

$525 $460 $405 $365 $315 $285 $265 ***$590***

Add $27 for Marine finish (disc.).

TURKEY/COYOTE TACTICAL – 12 ga., FAST loading system, 24 in. chrome moly barrel, extended full choke Turkey tube, fiber optic ghost ring sights, 100% Realtree AP camo stock with cushioned pistol grip, built-in shell storage in the stock, upper and lower Picatinny rails, mag. cut off, sling swivel studs included, 7.4 lbs. Mfg. 2013-2015.

$595 $525 $465 $415 $355 $315 $275 ***$659***

YOTE – 12 or 20 (disc. 2016) ga., 2 3/4 or 3 in. chamber, SMART valve regulating system, 28 in. chrome moly ported VR barrel, three chokes, fiber optic sight, synthetic stock, Thunder Mountain camo on barrel and stock, 7 lbs. Mfg. 2015-2017.

$500 $435 $385 $345 $295 $265 $250 ***$565***

* ***Yote Youth*** – 20 ga., 2 3/4 or 3 in. chamber, SMART valve regulating system, 22 in. chrome moly ported VR barrel, three chokes, fiber optic sight, synthetic stock, Trio recoil pad, 12 1/2 in. LOP, Thunder Mountain camo on barrel and stock, 6.4 lbs. Disc. 2017.

$500 $435 $385 $345 $295 $265 $250 ***$569***

GRADING - PPGS™	100%	98%	95%	90%	80%	70%	60%	LAST MSR

SHOTGUNS: SLIDE ACTION

ESCORT M87 PUMP – 12 or 20 ga., 3 in. chambers, 26 or 28 in. barrel with 3 interchangeable chokes, raised ventilated rib, 4 shot, fiber optic sights, Turkish walnut stock with satin finish, sling swivel studs, 3/8 in. dovetail accessory rail on top of receiver, enlarged slide release button, 5.8-6.8 lbs. Importation 2015-disc.

	$300	$250	$225	$200	$175	$150	$125	*$359*

* ***Escort M87 Youth Pump*** – 20 ga., 3 in. chambers, 22 in. barrel with 3 interchangeable chokes, 4 shot, 13 1/2 in. LOP, fiber optic front sights, Turkish walnut stock with satin finish, includes sling swivel studs, 6.2 lbs. Importation 2015-disc.

	$300	$250	$225	$200	$175	$150	$125	*$359*

ESCORT SERIES – 12 or 20 (new 2005) ga., 3 in. chamber, matte blue finish, black synthetic or 100% camo (disc.) stock and forearm, 18 (Aimguard or MarineGuard Model), 22 (Field Slug, mfg. 2005-2011), 24 (Turkey, includes extra turkey choke tube and FH TriViz sight combo with Mossy Oak Break Up [disc. 2004] or Obsession camo coverage, disc. 2008), 26 (new 2005, Field Hunter), or 28 (Field Hunter) in. barrel, alloy receiver with 3/8 in. milled dovetail for sight mounting, trigger guard safety, 4 or 5 shot mag. with cut off button, two stock adj. shims, 6.4-7 lbs. Importation began 2003.

* ***Escort Series Field Hunter (Recent Mfg.)*** – 12 or 20 ga., 24 (disc. 2008), 26 (new 2009), or 28 in. barrel, black synthetic stock, 100% Mossy Oak Obsession (disc. 2008), Shadowgrass (disc. 2008), or King's Woodland (mfg. 2009-2010) camo coverage or matte blue finish, includes 3 choke tubes, 6-7.4 lbs. Disc. 2015.

	$325	$275	$250	$225	$200	$175	$150	*$379*

Add $40 for Slug with rifled barrel and cantilever mount (disc. 2011).
Add $80 for 100% camo coverage and Spark front sight (disc. 2010). Add $23 for combo in 12 ga. (disc. 2006). Add $100 for FH TriViz sights in Obsession camo finish with extra Turkey choke tube (disc. 2008).
Add $144 for Slug Combo (disc. 2006).

* ***Escort Series Field Hunter (Current Mfg.)*** – 12 or 20 ga., 3 in. chamber, 28 in. barrel w/5 choke tubes (F, IM, M, IC, CYL), 4 shot mag. with cut off button, anodized alloy construction, brass bead front sight, black polymer stock and forend w/textured grip surfaces, rubber buttpad, adj. shims, manual cross-button trigger safety, mounted sling studs, black finish, available as Slug Pump combo w/raised rib barrel and cantilever scope mount w/adj. rear TruGlo sight, 6.2-6.8 lbs.

Please contact the importer directly for pricing and availability on this model.

* ***Escort Series Field Hunter Youth*** – 20 ga. only, 3 in. chamber, 22 in. barrel, 5 chokes (F, IM, M, IC, CYL), 2 or 4 shot mag. w/migratory plug, anodized aircraft alloy construction, brass bead front sight, synthetic stock and forend w/textured grip, TrioPad rubber buttpad, manual cross-button safety, black finish, 6.2 lbs.

Please contact the importer directly for pricing and availability on this model.

* ***Escort Series Field Youth*** – 20 ga. only, 3 in. chamber, 22 in. barrel, black synthetic stock and forearm with Trio recoil pad, choice of blued metal or 100% King's Woodland (disc. 2010) camo coverage, 5.8 lbs. Mfg. 2009-2015.

	$350	$295	$275	$250	$225	$200	$175	*$393*

Add $23 for Youth Slug model with 22 in. rifled barrel (mfg. 2011 only).
Add $80 for camo (disc. 2010).

* ***Escort Series Aimguard*** – 12 or 20 ga., 3 in. chamber, 18 in. barrel, fixed cyl. bore choke, 4 (disc.) or 5 shot mag. with cut off button, alloy receiver, fiber optic front sight, matte black synthetic stock, 14 in. LOP, sling swivel studs, manual cross-button trigger safety, 3/8 in. milled dovetail accessory rail on top of receiver, enlarged slide release button, mounted sling studs, black or marine finish, 5.5 -6.4 lbs.

MSR $299	$250	$220	$195	$175	$150	$135	$115	

* ***Escort Series Marine Guard*** – 12 or 20 ga., 3 in. chamber, 18 in. barrel, fixed cyl. bore choke, 5 shot mag., white nickel receiver, brass bead front sight, black synthetic stock, sling swivel studs, 14 in. LOP, manual cross-button safety, rubber recoil pad, 5.5-6.3 lbs.

MSR $439	$375	$325	$300	$250	$225	$200	$185	

* ***Escort MP Tactical (Home Defense, Tactical Entry/Special Ops)*** – 12 ga. only, 3 in. chamber, 18 in. barrel, synthetic stock, cushioned vertical pistol grip, available in a variety of configurations, forearm features upper and lower Picatinny rail, current mfg. features the MP-P/A TacStock2 with pistol grip and built in holder for two extra shells, fiber optic front sight, fully adj. ghost ring rear, 6.85 lbs. Mfg. 2009-2017.

	$350	$295	$275	$250	$225	$200	$175	*$400*

Subtract approx. 15% if w/o TacStock2 (new 2010).

GRADING - PPGS™	100%	98%	95%	90%	80%	70%	60%	LAST MSR

ESCORT STANDARD MAGNUM – 12 or 20 ga., 2 3/4 and 3 in. chamber, 26 or 28 in. chrome moly lined and ported barrel, 3 chokes, raised and ventilated rib, fiber optic sight, black synthetic stock with three adjustment shims, sling swivel studs, 3/8 in. dovetail accessory rail on top of receiver, enlarged slide release button, 6-7.4 lbs. Disc. 2017.

	$335	$285	$265	$235	$215	$185	$165	*$385*

* ***Escort Standard Magnum Youth*** – 20 ga., 2 3/4 and 3 in. chamber, 22 in. chrome moly lined and ported barrel, 3 chokes, raised ventilated rib, fiber optic sight, black synthetic stock with three adjustment shims, TRIO recoil pad, sling swivel studs, 12 1/2 in. LOP, enlarged slide release button, 3/8 in. dovetail accessory rail on top of receiver. Disc. 2017.

	$350	$295	$275	$250	$225	$200	$175	*$399*

GLADIUS HOME DEFENSE – 20 ga., 18 in. cyl. bore barrel with muzzle brake, aluminum alloy receiver, adj. ghost ring rear and fiber optic front sights, black synthetic stock with built-in 2-round shell holder, cushioned rear and forend pistol grip, low density recoil pad, adj. cheek pad, sling swivel studs, Picatinny rail on extended forend and top of receiver, 6.8 lbs. Mfg. 2014-2017.

	$435	$385	$365	$325	$300	$265	$225	*$485*

ESCORT BM12 – 12 ga., 3 in. Mag. chamber, SMART Valve self-regulating gas piston, 18 in. hard chrome barrel, fixed cylinder, 2 or 5 shot mag. (optional 2 shot mag. available), aircraft alloy receiver, adj. front sight w/fiber optic sights, ghost ring adj. rear sight, polymer pistol grip stock w/shotshell holder, elastic buttpad, ergonomic forend, manual cross-trigger switch safety, rubber recoil pad, 3 Picatinny rails, mounted sling studs, matte black or A-TACS tactical camo finish, 8.3 lbs.

Please contact the importer directly for price and availability.

ESCORT WS – 12 or 20 ga., 3 in. chamber, 28 in. VR barrel, multi-chokes (F, IM, M, IC, CYL), 4 shot mag., brass bead front sight, checkered Turkish walnut stock and forend, manual cross-button trigger safety, mounted sling studs, rubber recoil, 4 stock shims, black chrome finished barrel, 7-7 1/2 lbs.

Please contact the importer directly for price and availability.

ESCORT SLUGGER SERIES – 12 ga., 2 3/4 or 3 in. chamber, 18 in. black chrome plated barrel, fixed cylinder chokes, 5 shot mag., black anodized aircraft alloy construction, fiber optic front sight, synthetic stock and rubber buttpad, manual cross-button safety, approx. 6.5 lbs. New 2020.

MSR $210	$175	$150	$125	$125	$100	$75	$50	

* ***Escort Slugger Tactical*** – 12 ga., 2 3/4 or 3 in. chamber, 18 in. black chrome plated barrel, fixed cylinder chokes, 5 shot mag., black anodized aircraft alloy construction, fiber optic front sight, synthetic stock and rubber buttpad, soft rubber pistol grip w/finger grooves, manual cross-button safety, extra sling mounting point, Picatinny rail, approx. 6.5 lbs. New 2020.

MSR $220	$175	$175	$150	$125	$100	$75	$75	

ETERNAL

Current trademark of shotguns and air rifles manufactured by the Doruk Silah Co. located in Konya, Turkey. No current U.S. importation.

Currently, Doruk shotgun configurations include semi-auto, slide action, single barrel, and O/U. Semi-auto and slide action firearms are available in both sporting and tactical configurations.

EUROARMS ITALIA Srl

Previous black powder replica manufacturer and current importer/exporter located in Concesio, Italy.

Euroarms Italia was the new name for Armi San Paolo, and was established during 2002. Euroarms Italia exported its black powder reproductions and accessories through Euroarms of America, Dixie Gun Works, Cabela's, and Navy Arms. It ceased operation during late 2011.

EUROARMS OF AMERICA

Previous black powder replica importer and distributor located in Winchester, VA circa 1970-2011. Manufactured by Euroarms Italia Srl, established 1970, and located in Concesio, Italy. The factory was named Armi San Paolo until 2002.

Euroarms imported a variety of firearms, including revolvers and rifles, mfg. by Armi San Paolo between 1970-1996. Values were determined by other similar competitive makes and models, and the condition factor.

Please refer to the *Blue Book of Modern Black Powder Arms* (also online) for more information and prices on Euroarms of America's quality lineup of modern black powder reproductions and replicas.

GRADING - PPGS™	100%	98%	95%	90%	80%	70%	60%	LAST MSR

EUROPEAN AMERICAN ARMORY CORP.

Current importer and distributor established in late 1990, located in Cocoa, FL. Previously located in Rockledge, FL and Sharpes, FL 1990-2006. Distributor and dealer sales.

EAA currently imports: Tanfoglio Witness series of semi-auto pistols, located in Italy, H. Weihrauch revolvers, located in Germany, Husan shotguns, located in Turkey, Girsan pistols and shotguns, located in Turkey, Akkar shotguns, located in Turkey, and previously imported select models for Zastava and ATA Arms (2018 only). All guns are covered by EAA's lifetime limited warranty. EAA has also imported various trademarks of long guns including Saiga and Izhmash. Please refer to these individual sections for model listings.

Zastava Z98 and Z5 bolt actions, Sarpa slide action shotguns manufactured by Sarzilmaz, and Sabatti double rifles are currently imported by U.S. Sporting Goods Inc. Please refer to individual listings for more information and current pricing.

PISTOLS: SEMI-AUTO

EAA has issued a safety upgrade notice regarding any Witness style semi-auto pistol bearing a serial number between AE00000 - AE700000. Owners are requested to field strip the pistol and send the slide assembly directly to EAA. EAA will replace the firing pin and return it to you. Please refer to Witness model listings under Tanfoglio.

F.A.B. 92 – 9mm Para. or .40 S&W cal., double action featuring hammer drop safety and decocker (Witness style), 4 1/2 in. barrel, 16* (9mm Para.), 12* (.40 S&W), or 10 (C/B 1994) shot mag., all steel construction, blue, chrome (disc. 1993), or Duo-Tone (disc. 1993) finish, smooth wood grips, 33 oz. Imported 1992-95.

$335 $295 $250 $225 $185 $150 $115 *$386*

Add $40 for chrome or Duo-Tone finish.
Add $29 for .40 S&W cal.

F.A.B. designates Foreign American Brands.

* ***F.A.B. 92 Compact*** – similar to F.A.B. 92, except has 3 5/8 in. barrel, 13* (9mm Para.), 10 (9mm only, C/B 1994), or 9 (.40 S&W) shot mag., 30 oz. Imported 1992-95.

$335 $295 $250 $225 $185 $150 $115 *$386*

Add $40 for chrome or Duo-Tone finish.
Add $29 for .40 S&W cal.

SAR B6 COMPETITOR – 9mm Para. cal., SA, polymer frame, 4 3/4 in. barrel, 17 shot mag., extended mag. release, stainless steel, competition hammer and magwell, fully adj. sight, aluminum grips and front/backstrap, full length dust cover, 44 oz., mfg. by Sarsilmaz. Imported 2017 only.

$700 $600 $550 $475 $400 $325 $250 *$837*

SAR B6P – 9mm Para. cal., 3.8 (Compact) or 4 1/2 in. barrel, blue steel or stainless, polymer frame, 13 (Compact) or 16 shot mag., matte black finish, checkered polymer grips, 22-24 oz. Mfg. by Sar Arms. Imported mid-2013-2017.

$340 $300 $285 $260 $240 $220 $200 *$371*

SAR B6PL PAVONA COMPACT LADY – 9mm Para. cal., SA, polymer frame, blue steel or stainless, pink or violet with blue or stainless steel (disc. 2016) slide, 3.8 in. barrel, 13 shot mag., checkered polymer grips, 22 oz. Mfg. by Sarsilmaz. Importation began 2014.

MSR $383 $350 $300 $285 $260 $240 $220 $200

Add $68 for stainless steel (disc. 2016).

SAR K2 – 9mm Para., .40 S&W (disc. 2013), 10mm (disc. 2013) or .45 ACP cal., 4 1/2 in. barrel, DA/SA, 14 (.45 ACP), 16 (9mm Para.), 17 (.40 S&W and 10mm), or 18 (9mm Para.) shot mag., all steel frame, steel or stainless steel slide, ergonomic grip, accessory rail, extended beavertail, elongated squared trigger guard with serrations, removable dovetail front sight, fully adj. rear sight assembly, blue finish, mfg. by Sarsilmaz for Turkish military, 40 oz. Imported mid-2011-2017.

$390 $335 $285 $250 $225 $200 $185 *$459*

Add $104 for stainless steel.
Add $277 for .45 ACP cal.
Add $354 for Sport Configuration in .45 ACP cal.
Add $521 for stainless steel in .45 ACP cal.

SAR K2P – 9mm Para. cal., 3.8 in. barrel, blue or stainless, lower accessory rail, 16 shot mag., ambidextrous safety, full size grip, compact slide, polymer frame, 24 oz. Mfg. 2013 only.

$365 $325 $275 $250 $200 $165 $125 *$433*

Add $98 for stainless.

GRADING - PPGS™	100%	98%	95%	90%	80%	70%	60%	LAST MSR

SAR ST10 – 9mm Para. cal., 4.4 in. barrel, blue or two-tone finish, ergonomic polymer grips, steel frame and slide, adj. rear sights, lower accessory rail, 16 shot mag., removable dovetail front sight, includes carry case, holster, two-pocket mag. pouch, two mags., lock and cleaning tools, 34 oz., mfg. by Sarsilmaz. Imported mid-2013-disc.

$650	$575	$495	$450	$400	$365	$335	*$754*

Add $69 for stainless steel.

SARGUN – 9mm Para., .40 S&W, or .45 ACP cal., 4 1/2 in. barrel, polymer frame, blue or stainless steel slide, 15 or 17 shot mag., matte black finish, ambidextrous controls, loaded chamber indicator, adj. front and rear sights, integral accessory rail, includes case, holster, and other shooting accessories, 20 oz., mfg. by Sarsilmaz. Imported mid-2013-disc.

$540	$475	$425	$360	$325	$295	$250	*$613*

Add $26 for 9mm Para. or $64 for .40 S&W cal. Add $101 for stainless.

ZASTAVA EZ – 9mm Para., .40 S&W, or .45 ACP (disc. 2010) cal., DA/SA, ambidextrous controls, 10 (.45 ACP), 11 (.40 S&W), or 15 (9mm Para.) shot mag., 4 in. barrel, aluminum frame, accessory rail, spur hammer, blue or chrome finish, 33 oz. Imported 2007-2011.

$495	$435	$375	$335	$285	$250	$215	*$573*

Add $47 for chrome finish (disc. 2010).

* ***Zastava EZ Compact*** – similar to Zastava EZ Model, except has compact frame, 7 (.45 ACP), 8 (.40 S&W), or 12 shot mag., 3 1/2 in. barrel. Imported 2007-2010.

$495	$435	$375	$335	$285	$250	$215	*$573*

Add $47 for chrome finish (disc. 2010).
Subtract 10% if without ported barrel (disc. 2010).

ZASTAVA M88 – 9mm Para. or .40 S&W (disc. 2010) cal., SA, 6 or 8 shot mag., 3.6 in. barrel, blue finish, compact frame, 28 oz. Imported 2008-2011.

$265	$225	$190	$170	$135	$110	$85	*$309*

Add $16 for .40 S&W cal. (disc. 2010).

ZASTAVA EZ CARRY – 9mm Para. or .40 S&W cal., full size frame, 3 1/2 in. ported barrel, DA/SA, 10 or 14 shot mag. Imported 2010-2011.

$550	$495	$450	$395	$350	$300	$250	*$619*

PISTOLS: SEMI-AUTO, EUROPEAN SERIES

MODEL EA220 – .22 LR cal., 3.88 in. barrel, 10 shot mag., single action, steel frame, 26 oz., blue, chrome or blue/chrome, wood grips. Importation disc. 1992.

$185	$160	$140	$125	$100	$85	$65	*$225*

Add approx. $20 for chrome or blue/chrome finish.

MODEL EA22-T – .22 LR cal., 6 in. barrel, cocking indicator and grip safety, 5 or 12 shot mag., adj. trigger and grip, single action, steel frame, target model, 40 oz. Imported 1991-93.

$375	$330	$280	$255	$205	$170	$130	*$450*

EUROPEAN 32 (320) – .32 ACP cal., 3.88 in. barrel, 7 shot mag., single action, steel frame, 26 oz., blue, chrome or blue/chrome, wood grips. Imported 1991-95.

$130	$115	$95	$90	$70	$60	$45	*$161*

Add $14 for chrome finish.

EUROPEAN 380 – .380 ACP cal., single (new 1994) or double (disc. 1994) action, 3 7/8 in. barrel, blue, brushed chrome (disc. 1996), Wonder (new 1997), matte blue/chrome (disc. 1993), or blue/gold plated Duo-Tone (European Lady, disc. 1995) finish, 7 shot bottom release mag., steel construction, firing pin safety, external hammer, smooth wood or ivory rose polymer (European Lady) grips, 26 oz. Imported 1992-2001.

$145	$125	$110	$100	$80	$65	$50	*$179*

Add $9 for Wonder finish (new 1997).
Add $67 for European Lady model (disc. 1995).
Add $32 for double action design (disc. 1994).
Add $14 for brushed chrome or matte blue/chrome (disc. 1993) finish.

This model employed a unique patented magazine gun lock system.

PISTOLS: SINGLE SHOT

THOR RAPTOR – .223 Rem., .270 Win., .30-06, .300 Win. Mag., .308 Win., .375 Win., .44 Mag., .45-70 Govt., .500 S&W, 7mm-08 Rem., or 7mm Rem. cal., blue steel frame, 14 in. barrel with polygonal rifling, single action, rubber grips, auto ejector, integral sight base, 5 lbs. Imported 2005 only.

$895	$785	$670	$610	$490	$405	$315	*$1,099*

GRADING - PPGS™	100%	98%	95%	90%	80%	70%	60%	LAST MSR

RIFLES

Some EAA rifles were manufactured by Sabatti in Italy (est. 1674), Lu-Mar in Italy, and H. Weihrauch in Germany (see separate listing in the H. Weihrauch section). Imported 1992-96.

SP1822 SEMI-AUTO SPORTER – .22 LR cal., semi-auto, 18 1/2 in. barrel, wood stock and forearm, adj. sights, 10 shot box mag., 5 1/4-6 1/2 lbs. Imported 1994-96.

$180 $145 $120 $100 $90 $80 $70 ***$206***

* ***SP1822 Semi-Auto Sporter Thumbhole*** – similar to Sporter, except has one-piece Bell & Carlson green synthetic thumbhole stock, without sights. Importation disc. 1995.

$310 $260 $230 $200 $175 $150 $135 ***$358***

ZASTAVA PAP 762 SEMI-AUTO – 7.62x39mm cal., patterned after the AK-47, blonde hardwood thumbhole stock and furniture, 10 shot mag., 16 3/4 in. barrel, removable accessory rail, 10 lbs. Imported 2008-2013.

$435 $375 $335 $295 $265 $240 $220 ***$488***

ROVER 870 BOLT ACTION – .22-250 Rem., .243 Win., .25-06 Rem., .270 Win., .30-06, .308 Win., 7mm Rem. Mag., .300 Win. Mag., or .338 Win. Mag. cal., bolt action rifle featuring all-steel construction with 22 in. hammer forged rifled barrel, staggered 5 shot internal mag., open sights. Imported 1993 only.

$795 $695 $600 $550 $495 $450 $395 ***$995***

M-93 BLACK ARROW BOLT ACTION – .50 BMG cal., Mauser action, 36 in. fluted heavy barrel with muzzle brake, adj. folding bipod, iron sights, detachable 5 shot mag., carry handle, detachable scope mount, wood case, 35 lbs., mfg. by Zastava. Imported 2007-2011

$6,400 $5,800 $5,000 $4,250 $3,500 $2,900 $2,300 ***$6,986***

Z5 BOLT ACTION – .17 HMR (disc. 2010), .22 LR, or .22 WMR cal., 16 (Youth) or 20 in. blue barrel, 5 shot mag., checkered pistol grip walnut stock and forearm, mfg. by Zastava. Imported 2009-2011.

$240 $210 $185 $170 $155 $140 $125 ***$276***

Add $12 for .17 HMR (disc. 2010) or .22 WMR cal.

Z98 BOLT ACTION – .243 Win., .25-06 Rem. (Mfg. 2009), .270 Win., .30-06, .308 Win., 7mm Rem. Mag., .300 Win. Mag., .375 H&H, or .458 Win. Mag. cal., 22 or 24 in. blue or stainless (mfg. 2009) steel barrel, black synthetic pistol grip stock, controlled round feeding, steel floorplate, large claw extractor, drilled and tapped, non-glare finish, mfg. by Zastava. Imported 2009-2011.

$450 $400 $375 $350 $325 $295 $275 ***$522***

Add $21 for 7mm Rem. Mag. or .308 Win. Mag. cal.
Add $192 for .375 H&H or .458 Win. Mag. cal.
Add $22 for 7mm Rem. Mag. or .300 Win. Mag.

* ***Z98 Bolt Action Target*** – .270 Win., .30-06, .308 Win., 7mm Rem. Mag., or .300 Win. Mag. cal., 22 or 24 in. blue barrel, walnut thumbhole stock with raised cheekpiece, machined steel receiver, scope rail, short extractors, 3 or 4 shot detachable box mag., mfg. by Zastava. Imported 2009-2011.

$925 $825 $725 $625 $525 $450 $375 ***$1,070***

PAVONA ISIDE SxS – .45-70 Govt. cal., blue frame with feather engraving, ejectors, SST, blue trigger guard, fiber optic sights, luxury oil finished checkered walnut stock and forearm, vent. recoil pad, automatic safety, 6 lbs. Mfg. by F.A.I.R of Italy. Limited importation 2014-2015.

$4,750 $4,150 $3,575 $3,250 $2,625 $2,150 $1,675 ***$5,576***

SHOTGUNS: O/U

SCIROCCO BASIC – 12 ga. only, single trigger, extractors, 26 or 28 in. fixed choke VR barrels, boxlock action, nickel engraved frame. Imported 1994-95.

$425 $370 $320 $290 $235 $190 $150 ***$478***

This model was mfg. by Lu-Mar located in Italy.

SCIROCCO SPORTING CLAYS – 12 ga. only, 28 or 30 in. barrels with 5 choke tubes and wide VR, SST, ejectors, Raybar front sight, nickel engraved frame. Imported 1994-95.

$650 $570 $485 $440 $355 $290 $225 ***$734***

This model was mfg. by Lu-Mar located in Italy.

FALCON – 12, 20 ga., or .410 bore, 3 in. chambers, 26, 28, or 30 in. fixed choke VR barrels, boxlock action, single or double trigger, extractors or ejectors, checkered pistol grip and forend. Imported 1993 only.

$650 $570 $485 $440 $355 $290 $225 ***$795***

Add $80 for .410 bore.
Add $100 for SST and ejectors.

GRADING - PPGS™	100%	98%	95%	90%	80%	70%	60%	LAST MSR

SPORTING CLAYS PRO GOLD – 12 ga. only, 2 3/4 in. chambers, 28 or 30 in. screw-in choke barrels with wide VR, boxlock action, SST, ejectors, blue frame with engraving, recoil pad with custom carry case. Imported 1993-94.

	$850	$745	$635	$580	$465	$380	$295	*$978*

PAVONA PATHOS – 12, 20 ga. or .410 bore, boxlock action, blued frame with feather engraving, 26 or 28 in. barrels with choke tubes, ejectors, SST, blued trigger guard, brass sight, luxury oil finished checkered walnut stock and forearm, vent. recoil pad, automatic safety, 6-7.2 lbs. Mfg. by F.A.I.R. of Italy. Limited importation began 2014-2015.

	$2,575	$2,250	$1,925	$1,750	$1,425	$1,160	$900	*$3,026*

Add $95 for .410 bore.

SP – 12 ga., 28 or 30 in. VR barrel, 2 shot mag., aluminum alloy construction, auto ejectors, SST, Turkish walnut stock and forend, steel insert, blued metal finish, 7-7.2 lbs., mfg. by ATA Arms. Imported 2018 only.

	$595	$500	$450	$400	$325	$275	$200	

SHOTGUNS: SxS

MP220/MP220F – Please refer to listing in the Baikal section.

PAVONA ISIDE – 12, 20 ga., or .410 bore, break boxlock action, blue frame with Pavona feather engraving, 26 or 28 in. barrels with choke tubes, SST, blued trigger guard, brass sight, luxury oil finish checkered walnut stock and forearm, vent. recoil pad, automatic safety, approx. 6 lbs. Mfg. by F.A.I.R. of Italy. Limited importation 2014-2015.

	$2,785	$2,435	$2,095	$1,895	$1,525	$1,250	$975	*$3,281*

Add $96 for .410 bore.

SABA – 12, 20, 28 ga., or .410 bore, 3 in. chambers, boxlock action with scrolled nickel finish, DT or SST, 26 or 28 in. fixed choke barrels with raised matted rib, ejectors, checkered stock and forearm with sling swivels. Imported 1993 only.

	$950	$830	$710	$645	$520	$425	$330	*$1,195*

Add $100 for SST.

SHOTGUNS: SEMI-AUTO

BUNDA SERIES – 12 ga. only, 2 3/4 or 3 in. chamber (depending on barrel) gas operated, 19, 26, 28 or 30 in. barrel with 4 choke tubes, choice of black synthetic or Turkish walnut stock and forearm, aluminum receiver. Limited importation 1998 only.

	$360	$315	$270	$245	$200	$160	$125	*$406*

Add $9 for Turkish walnut stock and forearm.

MKA 1919 AP – 12 ga., AR-15 style, 18 1/2 in. barrel, enlarged mag. release, forend w/split rails, AR grip, ambi safety, skeletonized aluminum receiver, bolt release, left-side charging handle, Picatinny rail, black finish. Mfg. by Husan Arms, importation began 2019.

MSR $895	$650	$525	$475	$425	$400	$375	$325	

MKA 1919 MATCH – 12 ga., 2 3/4 or 3 in. chamber, 20 in. barrel, internal thread chokes, 5 shot detachable mag. enlarged mag. release, adj. rear sight, forend w/split rails, AR grip, ambi safety, fully machined aluminum receiver, extended bolt handle, Picatinny rail, removable carry handle, black finish, includes two mags. and three internal choke tubes (CYL, M, F), 8.2 lbs. Mfg. by Husan Arms.

MSR $563	$400	$325	$300	$275	$250	$225	$200	

* ***MKA 1919 Match Pro*** – 12 ga., 2 3/4 or 3 in. chamber, AR-15 style, 20 in. barrel, internal thread chokes, 5 shot detachable mag., enlarged mag. release, adj. rear sight, railed aluminum forearm, AR grip, ambi safety, fully machined aircraft aluminum receiver, extended bolt handle, Picatinny rail on top of receiver, black finish, 8.7 lbs. Mfg. by Husan Arms.

MSR $605	$425	$350	$325	$275	$250	$225	$200	

MKA 1923 – 12 ga., 20 in. barrel, removable sights, fully adj. rear sight, reinforced nylon stock, rubber buttpad, trigger block safety, Picatinny rail, 9.7 lbs. Mfg. by Husan Arms, importation began 2019.

MSR $769	$550	$450	$400	$350	$325	$300	$275	

NEO – 12, 20, or 28 ga., bolt body, inertia spring, and rotating bolt head, 28 in. VR barrel, 4 shot mag., synthetic stock, steel receiver, blued/black metal finish, 6.75 lbs., mfg. by ATA Arms. Imported 2018 only.

	$315	$275	$225	$225	$175	$150	$100	

GRADING - PPGS™	100%	98%	95%	90%	80%	70%	60%	LAST MSR

SHOTGUNS: SLIDE ACTION

MODEL PM2 – 12 ga. only, unique 7 shot detachable mag., 20 in. barrel, black wood stock and composite forearm, dual action bars, crossbolt safety on trigger guard, available in matte blue or chrome finish, 6.81 lbs. Imported 1992 only.

$550	$480	$410	$375	$300	$245	$190	*$695*

Add $200 for night sights.
Add $75 for matte chrome finish.

EVANS MACHINING SERVICE (EVANS ARMS)

Current firearms and components manufacturer located in Clairton, PA. Evans Machine Service is also the current manufacturer and trademark holder of New Order Firearms (formerly Nite Owl Firearms) since 2015. Evans Machining Service also specializes in manufacturing parts and components for M249 and M240 machine guns.

For individual model listings, please go to BlueBookOfGunValues.com/overflow.

EVANS, WILLIAM, GUN & RIFLE MAKERS

Please refer to the William Evans Limited listing in the W section.

EVOLUTION USA

Current rifle manufacturer located in White Bird, ID since 1984.

Evolution USA formerly manufactured AR-15 style rifles.

RIFLES: BOLT ACTION

Evolution USA uses nine different types of actions for its rifles. Some actions include the MSR-10 that is a faceted and highly customized Remington M700 receiver, the MSX-10 that uses a Post-64 Classic Win. Model 70 with claw extractor, the Pre-64 Win. Model 70 action, and the Mauser Express 98 action manufactured by CZ USA. Most models can be ordered by selecting one of the previous receivers.

ARGALI – most short action cals., trued Rem. Model 700 action, Krieger ultra light barrel, synthetic stock, 5 1/2 lbs. Mfg. 2000-2004.

$2,000	$1,700	$1,450	$1,225	$950	$775	$675	*$2,450*

BOLT ACTION SNIPER/VARMINT SERIES – various cals., 3 different configurations include Sniper, Informal Target Varmint, and Field Grade Varmint, features match barrel, action, and tuned trigger. Disc. 2000.

Prices for the Sniper rifle started at approx. $3,000 while the Varmint guns started at approx. $2,000.

BREAKDOWN – various cals., two-piece light to medium rifle, available as "break in the middle" or "unscrew the barrel" variation, choice of wood or synthetic stock. Disc.

Retail pricing was not available for this model.

COYOTE – available in various cals., blue printed Rem. Model 700 action, Grand Master (disc. 1999) or Kreiger match barrel with cryogenic treatment, Kevlar/graphite stock. Mfg. 1996-2004.

$1,900	$1,600	$1,325	$1,100	$900	$825	$725	*$2,296*

COYOTE II – various cals., trued Remington M 700 action and customized trigger, matte black metal parts, HS Precision Kevlar graphite tactical stock with aluminum and fiberglass reinforced bedding. Mfg. 2001-2006.

$1,900	$1,600	$1,325	$1,100	$900	$825	$725	*$2,295*

IMPALA – most popular cals., Rem. Model 700 trued action w/o floorplate, lightweight sporter, Kevlar graphite stock. Mfg. 1998-99.

$1,275	$1,050	$950	$750	$650	$575	$500	*$1,456*

KUDU – most standard length cals., Winchester Pre-64 Model 70 action, stainless steel match barrel, sporter style Kevlar graphite stock. Mfg. 1998-2006.

$2,150	$1,850	$1,650	$1,350	$1,050	$875	$725	*$2,579*

Add $2,500 for presentation walnut stock.

MBOGO – .375 H&H, .416 Rem., .458 Win. Mag., or .505 Gibbs cal., choice of Sako (disc.), Dakota (disc.), Rem. Model 700, CZ (new 2007), Win. Pre-64 Model 70 (disc. 2006), or stainless steel Evolution M1000 action, Krieger stainless steel match barrel, express style Kevlar graphite stock. New 1998.

This rifle with Evolution action requires 11% federal excise tax.

* ***Mbogo Recent Mfg.*** – Disc.

$1,550	$1,325	$1,100	$925	$750	$650	$575	*$1,828*

GRADING - PPGS™	100%	98%	95%	90%	80%	70%	60%	LAST MSR

* ***Mbogo (Recent Mfg.)*** – Evolution M-1000 action. Disc.

	$3,625	$3,000	$2,500	$2,050	$1,750	$1,575	$1,300	*$4,050*

Add $1,768 for exhibition grade walnut stock (disc. 2013).
Add $150 for calibers from .404 Jeffery to .416 Rigby.

* ***Mbogo Dakota Action*** – Disc.

	$2,775	$2,400	$2,000	$1,750	$1,500	$1,250	$1,000	*$3,142*

PHANTOM – sniper-style rifle, ultra match grade barrel, McMillan A5 stock, 10-12 lbs.

Please contact the manufacturer for pricing and availability on this model.

PHANTOM II – various cals. from .22 -.408, trued and blue printed custom Evolution (disc.) or choice of repeater action, Krieger match stainless steel barrel, Timney match trigger, McMillan A2 or A3 tactical stock, matte black metal, 1,000 yard competition rifle, 12-30 lbs. (depending on customer's gun preference). Mfg. beginning 1999-disc.

	$3,400	$2,975	$2,650	$2,300	$1,900	$1,700	$1,400	*$3,695*

PHANTOM III – .50 BMG cal., Magnum single shot bolt action rifle, very large version of Phantom II, 29 lbs. Mfg. 2012-disc.

	$5,500	$4,995	$4,500	$3,950	$3,500	$3,000	$2,750	*$5,800*

SHI-AWELA – various cals., medium weight sporter, Evolution M1000 stainless action, stainless match barrel, Kevlar graphite stock. Mfg. 1999-2002.

	$2,600	$2,000	$1,750	N/A	N/A	N/A	N/A	*$3,052*

YELLOW WOLF SPORTER – available in various cals., designed for big game, blue printed Rem. Model 700 or Evolution M-1000 action, Kreiger match barrel, Kevlar graphite stock, available in Standardweight (7.8 lbs.), Lightweight (7.2 lbs.), Superlight (6.8 lbs.), and Ultralight (5.9 lbs.). Mfg. 1996-disc.

	$3,250	$2,750	$2,300	$2,175	$1,750	$1,450	$1,125	*$3,475*

Add $20 for Lightweight, $315 for Superlight, or $1,235 for Ultralight configuration.
Add $435 for McMillan Glass stock with Pre-64 Classic receiver or $615 with MSX-10 receiver.
Add $500 for McMillan Edge stock with Pre-64 Classic receiver or $710 with MSX-10 receiver.
Add $875 for Super Deluxe stock with Pre-64 Classic receiver or $975 with MSX-10 receiver.
Add $2,575 for Exhibition stock with Pre-64 Classic receiver or $2,675 with MSX-10 receiver.

RIFLES: SxS

CHAPUIS DOUBLE RIFLE BROUSSE/PH/UGEX – many calibers available, built to customer specification, various sight and trigger options, choice of wood grade and metal finish, with or w/o engraving, lighter weight model available (UGEX model).

This model is POR.

DOUBLE RIFLE (NYATI) – various cals. from .30-06 to .500 NE, reinforced Chapuis Anson & Deeley action, choice of color case hardened or coin finished engraved receiver, blue chrome moly barrels, various wood grades available, express sights. Mfg. 1999-2013. Custom order only.

Last MSRs on this model were as follows: .30-06 - $6,000, .375 H&H - $9,500, .450/400 NE - $11,500, .470 NE - $11,800, .500 NE - $13,500.

NYALA – various standard cals., including .300 Win. Mag., 3 grades available, 7 lbs., 9 oz. Mfg. 2001-2006.

	$4,500	$4,000	$3,600	$3,150	$2,750	$2,350	$2,000	*$4,895*

RIFLES: SEMI-AUTO

DESERT STORM – .223 Rem. cal., paramilitary design based on the AR-15, GIO, 21 in. stainless steel match barrel with integral muzzle brake, NM trigger, flat-top upper receiver. Disc. 2003.

	$995	$625	$495	$450	$395	$350	$325	*$1,189*

GRENADA – .223 Rem. cal., GIO, design based on the AR-15 with flat-top upper receiver, 17 in. stainless steel match barrel with integral muzzle brake, NM trigger. Disc. 2000.

	$995	$625	$495	$450	$395	$350	$325	*$1,195*

IWO JIMA – GIO, A2 HBAR action, 20 in. stainless steel match barrel, carrying handle incorporating iron sights, tubular handguard. Limited mfg.

	$1,350	$875	$650	$525	$450	$385	$350	

WOLVERINE – .22 LR cal., Grand Master barrel, Kevlar graphite stock. Mfg. 1996-2000.

	$550	$495	$450	$400	$365	$335	$295	*$850*

GRADING - PPGS™	100%	98%	95%	90%	80%	70%	60%	LAST MSR

RIFLES: SINGLE SHOT

IMPALA – various standard cals. including .300 Win. Mag., similar appearance and handling to the Nyala model, 5 grades available. Mfg. 2001-disc.

This model was POR.

PHANTOM III SINGLE SHOT – .50 BMG or .700 NE cal., Evolution M-2000 stainless single shot action, 28 in. Lilja match barrel with flutes and muzzle brake, approx. 30 lbs. Mfg. 2000-2011.

| | $4,700 | $4,300 | $3,850 | $3,500 | $2,950 | $2,400 | $2,250 | *$4,700* |

Add $1,700 for Delta Model (50-80 lbs.) or .700 NE cal. (24-30 lbs.), disc.

EXCAM

Previous importer and distributor located in Hialeah, FL, which went out of business late 1990. Excam distributed Dart, Erma, Tanarmi, Targa, and Warrior exclusively in the U.S. These trademarks will appear under Excam. All importation of Excam firearms ceased in 1990.

For individual model listings, please go to BlueBookOfGunValues.com/overflow.

EXCEL ARMS

Current trademark of pistols and rifles manufactured by Excel Industries, Inc., located in Ontario, CA. Previously located in Chino, CA.

PISTOLS: SEMI-AUTO

ACCELERATOR MP – .17 HMR (MP-17), .17 Mach 2 (new 2007, SP-17), .22 LR (new 2007, SP-22), or .22 WMR (MP-22) cal., 6 1/2 (new 2007) or 8 1/2 in. barrel, SA, polymer frame with stainless steel slide, adj. sights, 9 shot mag., 45 or 54 oz. Mfg. 2005-2009.

| | $385 | $325 | $285 | $260 | $240 | $220 | $195 | *$433* |

Add $63 for red/green dot optic sight or $87 for 4x32mm scope with illuminated crosshairs.
Add $87 for choice of Realtree Hardwoods HD Green or Digital Desert camo coverage (new 2008).

MP-17 – .17 HMR cal., SA, 8 1/2 in. barrel, 9 shot mag., stainless steel, adj. sights, available with red dot optic or scope and rings, polymer grip, matte black, Digital Desert, or Realtree Hardwoods HD camo. Mfg. late 2008-2010.

| | $375 | $325 | $285 | $260 | $240 | $220 | $195 | *$433* |

Add $63 for red dot optic front sight.
Add $87 for scope and rings.
Add $87 for camo.

MP-22 (ACCELERATOR PISTOL-CURRENT MFG) – .22 WMR cal., blowback action, SA, 6 1/2 (disc.) or 8 1/2 in. stainless steel bull barrel, 9 shot mag., stainless steel construction, adj. sights, integral Weaver base, available with red dot optic (disc.) or scope and rings (disc.), polymer grip, stainless steel, black Cerakote, Digital Desert (disc. 2010), or Realtree Hardwoods HD camo (disc. 2010) finish, 12 7/8 in. OAL, 3 3/8 lbs. New late 2008.

| MSR $540 | $475 | $415 | $350 | $325 | $275 | $225 | $175 | |

Add $71 for red dot optic front sight (disc.).
Add $87 for camo (disc. 2010).
Add $97 for scope and rings (disc.).

MP-5.7 – 5.7x28mm cal., blowback action, SA, 8 1/2 in. bull barrel, 9 shot mag., stainless steel construction, fully adj. target sights, available with red dot optic (disc.) or scope and rings (disc.), polymer grip, integrated Picatinny rail, LRBHO, stainless steel or black Cerakote finish, 3 3/8 lbs. New 2011.

| MSR $694 | $625 | $550 | $475 | $425 | $350 | $275 | $225 | |

Add $70 for red dot optic sights (disc.).
Add $96 for scope and rings (disc.).

X-5.7P – 5.7x28mm cal., blowback action, SA, 8 1/2 in. barrel, 10, 20, or 25 (disc.) shot mag., CNC machined billet aluminum and stainless steel construction, no sights or adj. iron sights (25 shot mag. only, disc.), Picatinny rail, threaded holes in the handguard allow for accessory mounting, black Cerakote finish, 4 1/2 lbs. New 2011.

| MSR $753 | $675 | $600 | $500 | $475 | $375 | $300 | $250 | |

Add $121 for adj. iron sights (25 shot mag. only). Disc.

X-9P – 9mm Para. cal., blowback action, 8 1/2 in. barrel, 10 or 17 shot mag., CNC machined billet aluminum and stainless steel construction, with or w/o adj. sights, black finish, 4 1/2 lbs. New 2016.

| MSR $753 | $675 | $600 | $500 | $475 | $375 | $300 | $250 | |

Add $121 for adj. iron sights.
Add $280 for adj. iron sights, pistol brace, and one 30 shot Glock compatible mag. (X-9P B).

GRADING - PPGS™	100%	98%	95%	90%	80%	70%	60%	LAST MSR

X-22P - .22 LR cal., SA, blowback action, 4 1/2 in. barrel, 10 or 25 shot mag., adj. sights, black synthetic stock, Picatinny rail, 12 in. OAL, 40 oz. Mfg. 2009-2020.

	$400	$335	$290	$250	$225	$200	$185	*$455*

X-30P - .30 Carbine cal., aluminum frame with integral Picatinny rail, 8 1/2 in. partially shrouded barrel, delayed blowback action, tilted black synthetic pistol grip with finger grooves, 10 or 20 shot mag., no sights or adj. iron sights (20 shot mag. only), black finish, 4 1/2 lbs. Mfg. 2011-circa 2019.

	$650	$575	$500	$450	$400	$350	$295	*$715*

Add $121 for adj. iron sights (20 shot mag. only).

SP-17 - .17 Mach 2 cal., 6 1/2 or 8 1/2 in. barrel, SA, 10 shot, stainless steel, polymer grip, adj. sights, available with red dot optic or scope and rings, matte black, Digital Desert, or Realtree Hardwoods HD camo. Mfg. late 2008-2010.

	$375	$325	$285	$260	$240	$220	$195	*$433*

Add $63 for red dot optic front sight. Add $87 for scope and rings. Add $87 for camo.

SP-22 - .22 LR cal., 6 1/2 or 8 1/2 in. barrel, SA, 10 shot, stainless steel, polymer grip, adj. sights, available with red dot optic or scope and rings, matte black, Digital Desert, or Realtree Hardwoods HD camo. Mfg. late 2008-2010.

	$375	$325	$285	$260	$240	$220	$195	*$433*

Add $63 for red dot optic front sight. Add $87 for scope and rings. Add $87 for camo.

RIFLES: SEMI-AUTO

CR-9 - 9mm Para. cal., stainless steel construction, 18 in. stainless bull barrel, full-length Weaver rail and two side rails, adj. and detachable sights, 10 shot mag., nylon sling and detachable swivels. Mfg. 2008.

	$550	$480	$415	$375	$305	$250	$195	*$635*

MR/SR SERIES - .17 HMR (MR17), .17 Mach 2 (SR17, new 2007), .22 LR (SR22, new 2007), or .22 WMR (MR22) cal., black composite stock with large thumbhole, fluted 18 in. stainless steel barrel and receiver with shroud, black, silver, or camo finish, fully adj. sights, 9 shot mag., standard package is supplied with red dot optic and hard sided case, 8 lbs. Mfg. 2004-2009.

	$435	$380	$325	$295	$240	$195	$150	*$488*

Add $195 for choice of Realtree Hardwoods HD Green or Digital Desert camo coverage (new 2008).
Add $35 for red dot optical sight.
Add $147 for iron sights or 3-9x40mm scope.
Add $231 for iron sights and 6x9 in. bipod.

MR-17 - .17 HMR cal., 18 in. bull barrel, 9 shot mag., silver or black shroud, available options include no sights, red dot optic, iron sights, scope and rings, sling, bipod, side rails, and flashlight, black, Digital Desert, or Realtree Hardwoods HD Green camo. Mfg. late 2008-2010.

	$425	$370	$320	$290	$235	$190	$150	*$488*

Add $35 for red dot optic sights. Add $147 for iron sights or 3-9x40mm scope. Add $84 for bipod (iron sights or scope only). Add $257 for side rails and flashlight. Add $195 for camo.

The no sight model is only available with one magazine - all other variations include two.

MR-22 - .22 WMR cal., blowback action, 18 in. bull barrel, 9 shot mag., silver or black shroud, full-length top Picatinny rail, black synthetic thumbhole stock, available options include no sights, red dot optic, iron sights, scope and rings, sling, bipod, side rails, and flashlight, black, Digital Desert (disc. 2010), or Realtree Hardwoods HD Green camo (disc. 2010) finish, 8 lbs. New late 2008.

MSR $605	$450	$385	$335	$300	$250	$195	$150

Add $39 for red dot optic sights.
Add $162 for iron sights or 3-9x40mm scope.
Add $183 for P2 package including nylon sling, swivels, and 3-9x40 Scope w/rings.
Add $195 for camo (disc. 2010).
Add $255 for bipod (iron sights or scope only).
Add $446 for side rails and flashlight.
Add $504 for P-5 package with red dot optic, detachable iron sights, side rails, flashlight, and bipod.

The no sight model is only available with one magazine - all other variations include two.

* ***MR-22 Camo*** - .22 WMR cal., similar to MR-22, except has Desert Digital or Timbers Edge camo stock and shroud, no sights. Mfg. 2014 only.

	$510	$450	$385	$350	$275	$225	$185	*$600*

GRADING - PPGS™	100%	98%	95%	90%	80%	70%	60%	LAST MSR

MR-22 TIM WELLS SIGNATURE RIFLE - .22 LR or .22 WMR cal., 18 in. stainless steel fluted bull barrel, 9 shot mag., full-length Weaver rail integrated into the aluminum shroud, polymer composite pistol grip stock, Kryptek Highlander camo finish, includes 3-9x40 scope and sling studs, Relentless Pursuit TV logo on buttstock, 8 lbs. Mfg. 2015-2016.

	$625	$545	$470	$425	$350	$285	$225	*$732*

MR-5.7 - 5.7x28mm cal., 18 in. fluted bull barrel, 9 shot mag., black or silver shroud, full-length upper Picatinny rail, no sights, black synthetic thumbhole stock, LRBHO, 8 lbs. New 2011.

MSR $755	$595	$515	$460	$400	$350	$300	$275	

Add $163 for 3.9x40mm scope.

SR-17 - .17 Mach 2 cal., 18 in. bull barrel, 10 shot mag., silver or black shroud, available options include no sights, red dot optic, iron sights, scope and rings, sling, bipod, side rails, and flashlight, black, Digital Desert or Realtree Hardwoods HD Green camo. Mfg. 2008-2010.

	$425	$370	$320	$290	$235	$190	$150	*$488*

Add $35 for red dot optic sights. Add $147 for iron sights or 3-9x40mm scope. Add $84 for bipod (iron sights or scope only). Add $257 for side rails and flashlight. Add $195 for camo.

The no sight model is only available with one magazine - all other variations include two.

SR-22 - .22 LR cal., 18 in. bull barrel, 10 shot mag., silver or black shroud, available options include no sights, red dot optic, iron sights, scope and rings, sling, bipod, side rails, and flashlight, black, Digital Desert or Realtree Hardwoods HD Green camo. Mfg. late 2008-2010.

	$425	$370	$320	$290	$235	$190	$150	*$488*

Add $35 for red dot optic sights. Add $147 for iron sights or 3-9x40mm scope. Add $84 for bipod (iron sights or scope only). Add $257 for side rails and flashlight. Add $195 for camo.

The no sight model was only available with one magazine - all other variations included two.

X-9R - 9mm Para. cal., 16 in. barrel, 10 or 17 shot mag., compatible with Glock magazines, with or w/o adj. sights, collapsible stock, top Picatinny rail, manual bolt hold open feature, black finish, 6 1/4 lbs. New 2016.

MSR $837	$725	$650	$575	$500	$450	$400	$350	

Add $121 for adj. iron sights (17 shot mag. only).

X-22R - .22 LR cal., 18 in. barrel, fixed (mfg. 2011-2015) or collapsible black synthetic stock, blowback action, no sights, 10 or 25 shot mag., drilled and tapped, accepts Ruger 10/22 mags., 4 3/4 lbs. Mfg. 2009-Disc.

	$450	$400	$350	$300	$250	$200	$175	*$504*

Add $90 for 3-9x40 scope.
Add $15 for fixed stock (mfg. 2011-2015).

X-30R - .30 Carbine cal., blowback action, 18 in. partially shrouded barrel, aluminum receiver with integral Picatinny top rail, fixed or collapsible stock, no sights or adj. iron sights (20 shot mag. only), 10 or 20 shot mag., approx. 6 1/4 lbs. Mfg. 2011-Disc.

	$725	$650	$575	$500	$450	$400	$350	*$795*

Add $15 for fixed stock (10 shot mag. only).
Add $121 for adj. iron sights (20 shot mag. only).

X-5.7R - 5.7x28mm cal., blowback action, otherwise similar to the X-30R, 10 or 25 shot mag. New 2011.

MSR $837	$725	$650	$575	$500	$450	$400	$350	

Add $15 for fixed stock (10 shot mag. only).
Add $121 for adj. iron sights (25 shot mag. only).

EXEL ARMS OF AMERICA, INC.

Previous importer located in Gardener, MA. Exel Arms previously imported Lanber (Series 100), Ugartechea (Series 200), and Laurona (Series 300) shotguns. Please refer to the appropriate sections for more information on this series.

F SECTION

57 CENTER LLC

Please refer to AR57 LLC listing in the A section.

F-1 FIREARMS

Current AR-15 style pistol and rifle manufacturer located in Spring, TX beginning 2012.

Please refer to BlueBookOfGunValues.com to order the *Blue Book of AR-15s & Variations*, available as a book or online subscription.

F4 DEFENSE

Current AR-15 style firearms and related accessories manufacturer located in Lexington Park, MD.

Please refer to BlueBookOfGunValues.com to order the *Blue Book of AR-15s & Variations*, available as a book or online subscription.

F. DARNE FILS AINÉ

Previous manufacturer located in St. Etienne, France.

Francisque Darne was the eldest son of Regis Darne, who developed the sliding breech gun. In 1910, Francisque left his father's company to form his own, "F. Darne Fils Ainé," producing high quality versions of the original 1894 patent R model Darne. Regis Darne updated most of his designs in 1909 and allowed the older patents to become public domain.

Francisque Darne died in 1917, but his company remained in production until 1955 under at least four different owners. SIFARM, a combination of the manufacturers Berthon Freres, Francisque Darne, Didier-Drevet, Gerest, and Ronchard-Cizeron, was absorbed in 1963 by Verney-Carron, along with the famous Canonnerie (barrel makers) Jean Breuil.

As is usually the case, the earlier production guns are by far the highest quality. Wide variations in quality exist in this marque, depending on the financial health of the owners at the time of production.

GRADING - PPGS™	100%	98%	95%	90%	80%	70%	60%	LAST MSR

SHOTGUNS: SxS, PRE-WAR MODELS

CLASSIC MODEL – 12 or 16 ga., an exact copy of the first Darne patent of 1894. Available in four grades.

* ***Classic Model Type A*** – 12 or 16 ga., no quality stamps on barrel flats, standard French proof barrels, very light engraving, color case hardened.

	100%	98%	95%	90%	80%	70%	60%	LAST MSR
	$1,200	$1,000	$800	$700	$600	$500	$450	

* ***Classic Model Type B*** – 12 or 16 ga., one quality stamp on barrel flats, somewhat more engraving, French gray hardened or color case hardened.

	100%	98%	95%	90%	80%	70%	60%	LAST MSR
	$1,700	$1,400	$1,200	$900	$700	$600	$500	

* ***Classic Model Type C*** – 12 or 16 ga., double proofed barrels with two quality stamps on barrel flats, French gray hardening over modern or old English engraving.

	100%	98%	95%	90%	80%	70%	60%	LAST MSR
	$2,000	$1,650	$1,350	$1,000	$800	$650	$550	

* ***Classic Model Type E*** – 12 or 16 ga., double proof barrels with four quality stamps on barrel flats, better quality wood in either English or semi-pistol grip, French gray hardening over elaborate engraving.

	100%	98%	95%	90%	80%	70%	60%	LAST MSR
	$2,400	$2,000	$1,600	$1,300	$1,000	$900	$800	

MODEL T – 12 or 16 ga., barrels removed by holding a button on forend, two-piece stock, stylistic improvements to the 1894 patent R model, 4 grades, all were originally color case hardened, never blue.

Both the T 32 and T 34 were available in 10 ga. with 70mm or 75mm chambers and 72cm or 76cm barrels on special order. The barrels would carry triple proof in 10 ga.

* ***Model T 32 Type*** – 10, 12, or 16 ga., 3 quality stamps on barrel flats, lightly engraved.

	100%	98%	95%	90%	80%	70%	60%	LAST MSR
	$1,950	$1,700	$1,250	$950	$700	$600	$500	

Add 30% for 10 ga.

* ***Model T 34*** – 10, 12, or 16 ga., 5 quality stamps on barrel flats, higher quality wood stock, better engraving and wood.

	100%	98%	95%	90%	80%	70%	60%	LAST MSR
	$2,100	$1,800	$1,500	$1,100	$850	$675	$575	

Add 30% for 10 ga.

* ***Model T 35*** – 12 or 16 ga., 6 quality stamps on barrel flats, monobloc barrels of superior French proof steel, better engraving and wood.

	100%	98%	95%	90%	80%	70%	60%	LAST MSR
	$2,500	$2,200	$1,800	$1,400	$1,200	$1,000	$800	

* ***Model T 36*** – 12 or 16 ga., 7 quality stamps on barrel flats, monobloc barrels of superior French proof steel, top-of-the-line T model.

	100%	98%	95%	90%	80%	70%	60%	LAST MSR
	$2,800	$2,500	$2,100	$1,700	$1,400	$1,200	$850	

GRADING - PPGS™	100%	98%	95%	90%	80%	70%	60%	LAST MSR

MODEL FIXED – 12 or 16 ga., further tinkering with the 1894 R model, these located the barrels in a rectangular block cut near the flats. Two grades.

* ***Model Fixed Type No. 3*** – 12 or 16 ga., wood stock, good quality engraving and wood, color case hardened or French gray hardened.

For pricing, see Type T 34.

* ***Model Fixed Type No. 4*** – 12 or 16 ga., better wood and engraving.

For pricing, see Type T 35.

MODEL PLATINUM – 12 or 16 ga., based on the Model Fixed, these were top-of-the-line sliding breech guns in four grades.

* ***Model Platinum Type No. 5*** – 12 or 16 ga., monobloc barrels, English or art nouveau style engraving, chisled fences.

	100%	98%	95%	90%	80%	70%	60%
	$3,100	$2,800	$2,500	$2,200	$1,700	$1,400	$1,100

* ***Model Platinum Type No. 6*** – 12 or 16 ga., monobloc barrels, high grade wood stock, English rose and scroll engraving or game scene or art nouveau style.

	100%	98%	95%	90%	80%	70%	60%
	$3,400	$2,900	$2,600	$2,350	$1,900	$1,600	$1,200

* ***Model Platinum Type No. 7*** – 12 or 16 ga., Pigeon model, monobloc barrels of top quality French proof steel, superior wood stock, engraved in English rose and scroll or deep chiseled art nouveau style.

	100%	98%	95%	90%	80%	70%	60%
	$3,800	$3,500	$3,000	$2,800	$2,200	$1,900	$1,500

* ***Model Platinum Type No. 8*** – monobloc barrels of top quality French proof steel. Top-of-the-line model with all details to customer's wishes. Very rare in any condition.

Rarity precludes accurate pricing.

SHOTGUNS: SxS, POST-WAR MODELS

Note: the model name of the following post-war guns is usually engraved on the side of the gun in front of the safety lever.

CLASSIC MODEL – 12 or 16 ga., modified and full choke on 70 cm barrels, semi-pistol grip or straight stock, simple case colored gun with no engraving and plain wood, two quality stamps.

	100%	98%	95%	90%	80%	70%	60%
	$1,250	$1,000	$850	$700	$600	$525	$400

BARONNET-BROUSSARD – 12, 16, or 20 ga. with 70 cm barrels (two-piece stock on 12 and 16 ga.), lightly engraved with satin chrome receiver finish, Broussard model featured 80 cm barrels but was essentially the same, 3 quality stamps.

	100%	98%	95%	90%	80%	70%	60%
	$1,400	$1,200	$1,000	$800	$675	$550	$475

Add 20% for Broussard model.

GOUVERNEUR MODEL – 12, 16, or 20 ga., better engraving and one-piece stock of select walnut, French gray receiver, choice of barrel lengths in 12 ga. (70 cm, 72 cm, or 74 cm.) classic or modern style engraving, 5 quality stamps.

	100%	98%	95%	90%	80%	70%	60%
	$1,800	$1,650	$1,200	$1,000	$750	$600	$550

GOUVERNEUR PLUME AND PLUME MAGNUM – 12, 16, or 20 ga., choice of barrel lengths in 12 ga. (70 cm, 72 cm, or 74 cm), plume (swamped rib) on Plume Model, plume rib and 76mm chambers included on Plume Magnum Model, one-piece stock of select walnut, classic or modern style engraving, 6 quality stamps, French grey receiver.

Values are about 10% higher than previous models due to these having six quality stamps on flats of barrels, in spite of being the same basic gun.

RAMBOUILLET MODEL – 12 or 16 ga., choice of rib, straight grip or semi-pistol grip one-piece stock of select walnut, double sears in a large key action somewhat similar to the Darne V models stylistically, light engraving, 8 quality stamps, color case hardening.

	100%	98%	95%	90%	80%	70%	60%
	$1,500	$1,300	$1,100	$900	$700	$650	$575

AMBASSADEUR MODEL – 12 or 16 ga., large key model with double sears. French gray finish on breech with excellent engraving, one-piece stock of good quality walnut, top-of-the-line production model, 10 quality stamps.

	100%	98%	95%	90%	80%	70%	60%
	$2,700	$2,400	$2,200	$1,800	$1,500	$1,100	$850

PRESTIGE MODEL – top-of-the-line custom gun, 72 cm barrels, monobloc barrels of Jacob Holtzer steel with plume swamped rib, straight grip one-piece stock of best quality walnut, large key action with silent operation and double sears, excellent full coverage engraving, 12 quality stamps.

	100%	98%	95%	90%	80%	70%	60%
	$3,500	$3,100	$2,900	$2,600	$2,200	$1,700	$1,200

GRADING - PPGS™	100%	98%	95%	90%	80%	70%	60%	LAST MSR

F&D DEFENSE

Current manufacturer located in Seminole, OK. Previously located in New Braunfels, TX.

For individual model listings, please go to BlueBookOfGunValues.com/overflow.

F.A.I.R. Srl

Current manufacturer established during 1971 (F.A.I.R. stands for Fabbrica Armi Isidoro Rizzini, owned by Isidoro Rizzini) and located in Marcheno, Italy. Select models are currently imported by IFG (Italian Firearms Group), located in Amarillo, TX. In 2003, the name changed from F.A.I.R. Tecni-Mec I. Rizzini to F.A.I.R. s.r.l. Previously imported and distributed exclusively by New England Arms Corp. located in Kittery Point, ME.

For individual model listings, please go to BlueBookOfGunValues.com/overflow.

F.A.V.S. di FRANCESCO GUGLIELMINOTTI

Current manufacturer established in 1957, located in Villar Focchiardo, Italy. No current U.S. importation. F.A.V.S. is an abbreviation for Fabbrica Armi Valle Susa.

RIFLES: SINGLE SHOT

STRADIVARI – various cals., unique "shorty" bullpup configuration utilizing a break open single shot action and pivoting wood buttstock that opens/closes breech, 19 3/4, 24, or 29 in. barrel with muzzleweight, finger grooved pistol grip wood stock with short forend, standard walnut stock, 100% camo coverage, laminated birch/red stock, or deluxe finished wood stock, four variations are currently being mfg. - K, M, L, and MK, scope is mounted on front portion of barrel, approx. 6.8 lbs.

Current European MSRs on this model range from €2,400-€3,065, please contact the manufacturer directly for U.S. availability.

FAS

Previous pistol and current air pistol manufacturer located in Lainate, Italy. Previously located in Milan, Italy. Air pistols currently imported by Airguns of Arizona, located in Gilbert, AZ. No current U.S. importation of firearms. Previously imported and distributed by Nygord Precision Products located in Prescott, AZ, Mandall Shooting Supplies, located in Scottsdale, AZ, Beeman Precision Arms, Inc. located in Santa Rosa, CA, and Osborne's located in Cheboygan, MI.

PISTOLS: SEMI-AUTO

MODEL OP601 – .22 Short cal. only, competition pistol, 5.9 in. barrel, 5 shot mag., wraparound match wood grips, 41 1/2 oz.

100%	98%	95%	90%	80%	70%	60%	Last MSR
$1,025	$875	$695	$640	$565	$500	$450	

MODEL 602 – .22 LR cal. only, competition pistol, 5.6 in. barrel, 5 shot mag., ergonomically designed match wood grips, 40 oz. Importation disc. 1994.

100%	98%	95%	90%	80%	70%	60%	Last MSR
$895	$800	$625	$600	$525	$475	$425	*$1,100*

MODEL CF603 – .32 S&W Wadcutter cal. only, competition pistol, 5.3 in. barrel, 5 shot mag., ergonomically designed adj. or non-adj. match wood grips, 40 oz.

100%	98%	95%	90%	80%	70%	60%	Last MSR
$975	$875	$695	$640	$565	$500	$450	

MODEL SP607 (LADY) – .22 LR cal., competition pistol, 5.6 in. barrel, removable barrel weights, 5 shot mag., ergonomically designed match wood grips.

100%	98%	95%	90%	80%	70%	60%	Last MSR
$975	$875	$695	$640	$565	$500	$450	

FEG

Previous manufacturer located in Hungary (FÉG stands for Fegyver és Gépgyár) since 1891. Arms manufacturing ceased with FÉG closure in 2005. Surplus firearms previously imported 2007-2010 by SSME Deutsche Waffen, Inc., located in Plant City, FL. A few models were imported by Century International Arms located in Delray Beach, FL (see additional information under the Century International Arms in this text). Previously imported and distributed by K.B.I., Inc. located in Harrisburg, PA, and distributed until 1998 by Interarms located in Alexandria, VA. (Not all importers may be listed).

PISTOLS: SEMI-AUTO, INTERARMS IMPORTED

All FEG pistols were supplied with two mags.

MARK II AP22 – .22 LR cal., double action, 3.4 in. barrel, 8 shot mag., blue finish, black plastic grips, 23 oz. Imported 1997-98.

100%	98%	95%	90%	80%	70%	60%	Last MSR
$325	$285	$250	$225	$175	$150	$125	*$269*

GRADING - PPGS™	100%	98%	95%	90%	80%	70%	60%	LAST MSR

MARK II AP – .32 ACP or .380 ACP cal., double action, patterned after the Walther PP, 3.9 in. barrel, 7 or 8 shot mag., blue finish, black plastic grips, 27 oz. Imported 1997-98.

$235	$200	$175	$160	$145	$130	$115	$269

MARK II APK – .380 ACP cal., patterned after the Walther PPK/S, 3.4 in. barrel, 7 shot mag., black plastic grips, blue finish, 25 oz., Imported 1997-98.

$235	$200	$175	$160	$145	$130	$115	$269

PISTOLS: SEMI-AUTO, RECENT MFG./ IMPORTATION

In addition to the following imported models, FÉG also makes additional models available mostly in Europe. Currently, these pistols include the RL61 (.22 LR cal.), the AP9/APK9 (.380 ACP cal.), P9RZ Compact (9mm Para. cal.), and the AC/ACK (.45 ACP cal.).

TOKAGYPT 58 – 9mm Para. cal., slide marked "Tokagypt 58", brown plastic grips, FÉG 58 Model with crest of Egypt, numbered mags., blue finish.

$900	$800	$650	$525	$400	$350	$295	

Add 10% for NIB.

FIREBIRD (TOKAGYPT) – 9mm Para. cal., commercial version, some from cancellation of Egyptian contract, left side of slide marked "Firebird" over "Kal 9mm" followed by three small circles inside a large circle, followed by "West Germany" over "Parabellum" or "Parabellum 9mm" or blank slide, numbered mags., black plastic grips, blue finish, ser. nos. start with E, F, or H prefix.

$525	$425	$360	$320	$260	$220	$175	

Add 10% for NIB.

SUPER 12 (TOKAGYPT) – 9mm Para. or 7.62x25mm cal., left side of slide marked with hammer and sickle stamp and "Parabellum Cal. 9mm", "7.62x25mm, "Kit TT", black plastic grips, ser. no. prefix HF.

$475	$425	$360	$320	$260	$220	$175	

MODEL PMK-380 – .380 ACP cal., patterned after Walther PP, alloy frame, double action, 4 in. barrel, plastic grips with thumbrest, blue finish, 21 oz. Importation by K.B.I. 1992-2003.

$205	$180	$160	$135	$120	$110	$100	$239

MODEL SMC-380 – .380 ACP cal., double action semi-auto, patterned after Walther PPK, alloy frame, 3 1/2 in. barrel, 6 shot mag., plastic grips with thumbrest, blue finish, 18 1/2 oz. Importation by K.B.I. 1993-2003.

$205	$180	$160	$135	$120	$110	$100	$239

* ***Model SMC-22*** – .22 LR cal., 8 shot mag., otherwise similar to Model SMC-380. Importation disc. 1997.

$210	$195	$180	$165	$150	$135	$115	$235

MODEL SMC-918 – 9x18mm Makarov cal., double action, semi-auto, 7 shot mag. Importation disc. 1997.

$175	$150	$130	$110	$95	$85	$75	$235

MODEL PA-63 – 9x18mm Makarov cal., single or double action, 3.93 in. barrel, blue or bright aluminum anodized frame with blued steel slide, fixed sights, plastic grips, decocking safety. Previously imported by Century International Arms.

$235	$190	$150	$125	$95	$85	$75	

MODEL PPH – .380 ACP cal., patterned after Walther PP, alloy frame, double action, plastic grips with thumbrest, blue finish. Imported 1986-87 only.

$200	$170	$140	$125	$115	$105	$95	$225

MODEL B9R – .380 ACP cal., little importation into the U.S., many are encountered with "Turkce Polis" (Turkish Police) on the slide, blue finish. Disc.

$250	$225	$200	$175	$150	$125	$100	

MODEL P9R (MBK-9HP OR R-9) – 9mm Para. cal., patterned after Browning Hi-Power, double action, 4 2/3 in. barrel, 14 shot mag., blue finish, steel construction, checkered wood grips, 36 oz. Imported 1992 only, reimported 2007-2011.

$450	$395	$350	$315	$275	$250	$225	$499

* ***Model MBK-9HPC*** – 9mm Para. cal., double action, compact variation of the Model MBK-9HP, 4 in. barrel, steel construction, blue finish, 34 oz. Imported 1992 only.

$325	$275	$250	$225	$200	$185	$170	$359

MODEL P9M (PJK-9HP) – 9mm Para. cal., patterned after Browning Hi-Power, single action, all steel construction, 4 3/4 in. barrel, thumb safety, 10 (C/B 1994) or 13* shot mag., cleaning rod, 32 oz. Importation by K.B.I. 1992-2003, reimported 2007-2011.

$550	$375	$335	$300	$275	$250	$225	$475

GRADING - PPGS™ 100% 98% 95% 90% 80% 70% 60% LAST MSR

Add $175 for .40 cal. conversion kit.
Add 30% for PM9 Lithuania-Police matching numbered mags.
Add approx. $60 for industrial hard chrome finish (Model PJK-9HPC - includes Uncle Mike's rubber grips, disc. 1999).

* ***Model P9L*** – similar to P9M, except has 6 in. barrel and resembles the Browning HP. Imported 2007-2011.

$695 $600 $525 $450 $400 $365 $335 *$799*

MODEL P9RK (GKK-92C) – 9mm Para. cal., double action semi-auto, 4 in. barrel, 14 shot mag., improved variation of MBK models, includes same accessories as PJK-9H, 34 oz. Importation disc. 1993, reimported 2007-2011.

$450 $395 $350 $315 $275 $250 $225 *$499*

MODEL GKK-40C – .40 S&W cal., double action, 4 in. barrel, 9 shot mag., all steel, checkered walnut grips, blue or chrome finish. Imported 1995-1996.

$300 $265 $230 $200 $180 $160 $145 *$349*

MODEL GKK-45 – .45 ACP cal., double action, 4 1/4 in. barrel, 8 shot mag., all steel, checkered walnut grips, blue (disc. 1994) or chrome (Model GKK-45C) finish, approx. 37 oz. Imported 1993-96.

$300 $265 $230 $200 $180 $160 $145 *$349*

WALAM 48 – .380 ACP cal., DA/SA, blowback operation, patterned after the Walther PP, 3.9 in. barrel, 8 shot mag., steel slide and frame, round hammer, fixed sights, red-brown bakelite grips with or without Hungarian crests, slide mounted decocker safety, blued finish, approx. 26 oz., Mfg. by FEG for the Egyptian government circa 1957-1960, imported sporadically appearing circa 2011, again circa 2019.

RIFLES: SEMI-AUTO

MODEL SA-85M – 7.62x39mm cal., sporter rifle utilizing AKM action, 16.3 in. barrel, 6 shot detachable mag., thumbhole stock, 7 lbs. 10 oz. Imported 1991, banned 1998.

$550 $480 $410 $375 $300 $245 $190 *$429*

SA-85 S (SA-2000M) – .223 Rem. (disc. 2000) or 7.62x39mm cal., 16.3 (new 2007) or 17 3/4 (disc. 2000) in. barrel with muzzle brake, 6, 10, or 30 shot detachable mag., skeletonized Choate synthetic stock. Imported 1999-2000, reimported 2007-2011.

$950 $830 $710 $645 $520 $425 $330 *$1,075*

FIAS

Previous long gun and related components manufacturer located in Brescia, Italy. FIAS is an abbreviation for Fabbrica Italiana Armi Sabatti.

FIAS became part of the Sabatti Armi group circa 2002, and is based in Gardone VT, Brescia. Please refer to Sabatti s.p.a. for current information, including any domestic importation.

F.I.E.

Previous importer (F.I.E. is the acronym for Firearms Import & Export) located in Hialeah, FL until 1990.

For individual model listings, please go to BlueBookOfGunValues.com/overflow.

FK BRNO

Current semi-auto pistol manufacturer located in Brno, Czech Republic. Currently imported by FK Brno US, located in Gainesville, FL.

PISTOLS: SEMI-AUTO

7.5 FK FIELD PISTOL – 7.5 FK cal., SAO, 6 in. barrel, 16 shot mag., slender steel frame and slide, butterfly sight, 3-point target sights, or optional reflex optics, slim red or FDE aluminum grips, left side safety, Nitride Dark Gray finish. Importation began 2019.

MSR $7,500 $6,375 $5,575 $4,775 N/A N/A N/A N/A

PSD MULTI CALIBER PISTOL (7.5 FK PSD) – 7.5 FK, 9mm Para., 10mm Auto, or .40 S&W cal., SAO, 5.3 in. barrel, 10 shot (10mm Auto), 15 shot (7.5 FK) or 17 shot (9mm Para.) mag., slender polymer frame, steel slide, butterfly sights, 3-point target sights, or FK Ring sight, various reflex optics can also be mounted, pistol brace optional, polymer grip, left side safety, frame mounted Picatinny rail, Nitride Dark Gray finish. Importation began 2019.

MSR $1,650 $1,475 $1,300 $1,100 $1,000 $825 $675 $525

Pricing reflects package sold with a spare auxiliary barrel.

GRADING - PPGS™	100%	98%	95%	90%	80%	70%	60%	LAST MSR

FM (FOXTROT MIKE) PRODUCTS

Current AR-15 style pistol, rifle, and parts manufacturer located in Boise, ID.

Please refer to BlueBookOfGunValues.com to order the *Blue Book of AR-15s & Variations*, available as a book or online subscription.

FMJ

Previous manufacturer located in Copperhill, TN, until circa 1998.

Little information is available regarding FMJ firearms (including short barrel derringers and pistols), except they were inexpensive shooters and have little collectibility, other than some oddball configurations. Their production records were turned in to the BATF during 1998.

FMK FIREARMS

Current pistol manufacturer located in Placentia, CA. Dealer direct sales beginning 2014. Previously distributed by American Tactical Imports, located in Rochester, NY until 2013.

For individual model listings, please go to BlueBookOfGunValues.com/overflow.

FMR

Current rifle manufacturer located in Pantin, France. No current U.S. importation.

RIFLES: BOLT ACTION

FMR owns the rights to the French trademark Unique, and manufactures a line of bolt action rifles based on the original Unique design. All rifles have an aluminum ERGAL or stainless steel action, interchangeable barrels, and fully adjustable stocks. The RS1 Sniper is available as a single shot or a repeater, and has a base MSR of €2,990. The RS1 Commando has a heavy barrel and muzzle brake and has an MSR of €2,490. The RS1 Micro has an MSR of €2,690. The RS1 .22 LR has an MSR of €890. Various options are also available, including an unmodified adjustable stock for the CZ22. Please contact the company directly for more information, including options, pricing, and U.S. availability.

FN AMERICA LLC (FNH USA)

Current manufacturer and importer established in 1998, located in McLean, VA. Dealer and distributor sales.

In the U.S., FN (Fabrique Nationale) is represented by two entities - FNH USA, which is responsible for sales, marketing, and business development, and FNM, which stands for FN Manufacturing, which handles manufacturing. FNH USA has two separate divisions - commercial/law enforcement, and military operations. FN Manufacturing is located in Columbia, SC. Design, research and development are conducted under the authority of FN Herstal S.A. In mid-2014, it was announced that the consolidation of FN Manufacturing LLC and FNH USA LLC would be called FN America LLC, and headquarters would remain in McLean.

Some of the firearms that FNM currently produces for the U.S. government are M16 rifles, M249 light machine guns, and M240 medium machine guns. FNM also produces the FNP line of handguns for the commercial, military, and law enforcement marketplaces. FNM is one of only three small arms manufacturers designated by the U.S. government as an industry base for small arms production. In November 2004, the FN model was chosen by the U.S. Special Operations Command (USSOCOM) for the new SCAR military rifle.

FN America LLC manufactures a full suite of firearms for civilian sales, including handguns, shotguns, bolt action rifles, and AR-15 style rifles and pistols.

PISTOLS: SEMI-AUTO

In addition to the models listed, FNH USA also imported the HP-SA ($800 last MSR), and the HP-SFS until 2006.

All FNP guns come standard with three magazines and a lockable hard case.

FNP-9 – 9mm Para. cal., 4 in. barrel, 10 or 16 (disc. 2010) shot mag., polymer frame, matte black or matte stainless steel slide, DA/SA, matte black or FDE finish (mfg. 2010 only) finish, ambidextrous frame mounted decocker, underframe rail, interchangeable backstrap inserts, 25.2 oz. Disc. 2011.

$575	$495	$435	$380	$340	$300	$275	*$649*

Add $125 for night sights (disc. 2009).

Add $50 for USG operation (DA/SA, ambidextrous frame mounted decocker/manual safety), disc. 2010.

FNP-9M – 9mm Para. cal., 3.8 in. barrel, DA/SA, 10 or 15 shot mag., polymer frame, similar to the FNP-9, except is smaller frame, 24.8 oz. Disc. 2008.

$525	$450	$400	$365	$335	$300	$275	*$593*

Add $118 for night sights.

GRADING - PPGS™	100%	98%	95%	90%	80%	70%	60%	LAST MSR

FNP-357 – .357 SIG cal., similar to FNP-9, black finish only, 14 shot mag., 27.2 oz. Mfg. 2009.

$565 $475 $425 $375 $335 $300 $275 *$629*

Add $65 for USG operation (features ambidextrous frame mounted decocker/manual safety levers).

FNP-40 – .40 S&W cal., 4 in. barrel, 10 or 14 (disc. 2010) shot mag., DA/SA, black or FDE (mfg. 2010 only) polymer frame, optional stainless steel slide, underframe rail, interchangeable backstrap, external hammer, 25.2 or 26.7 oz. Disc. 2011.

$575 $495 $435 $380 $340 $300 $275 *$649*

Add $125 for night sights (disc. 2009).

Add $50 for USG operation (features ambidextrous frame mounted decocker/manual safety levers), disc. 2010.

FNP-45 – .45 ACP cal., 4 1/2 in. barrel, DA/SA, 10 (disc. 2011), 14, or 15 (new 2011) shot mag., polymer frame, matte black finish with optional stainless steel slide, or FDE (new 2010) finish, external extractor, underframe rail, interchangeable backstraps, 33.2 oz. Disc. 2013.

$725 $625 $575 $525 $450 $400 $350 *$795*

Add $125 for night sights (disc.).

Subtract approx. 5% if without USG operation (features ambidextrous frame mounted decocker/manual safety levers).

Add approx. $186 for pistol package, which includes three mags., molded polymer holster, double mag. pouch, and training barrel (mfg. 2009 only).

* ***FNP-45 Competition*** – .45 ACP cal., DA/SA, matte black finish, 15 shot mag., lower accessory rail, interchangeable arched and flat backstrap inserts with lanyard holes, 33.2 oz. Mfg. 2011-2012.

$1,075 $925 $825 $725 $625 $550 $475 *$1,239*

* ***FNP-45 Tactical*** – .45 ACP cal., 5.3 in. threaded barrel, 15 shot mag., DA/SA, polymer frame with Mil-Std 1913 mounting rail and interchangeable backstraps with lanyard eyelets, serrated trigger guard, ambidextrous mag. release, manual safety and slide stop, fixed combat sights, black or FDE finish, stainless steel slide, includes fitted soft case. Mfg. 2010-2012.

$1,200 $1,025 $875 $775 $675 $575 $495 *$1,395*

FNS-9 – 9mm Para. cal., DAO, SFO, 4 in. cold hammer forged stainless steel barrel, 10 or 17 shot mag., matte black or matte silver slide finish, fixed 3-dot sights or night sights, external extractor with loaded chamber indicator, front and rear cocking serrations, black or FDE (disc.) finished polymer frame, lower accessory rail, two interchangeable backstraps with lanyard eyelets, serrated trigger guard, fully ambidextrous slide stop lever and mag. release, 25.2 oz. Mfg. 2012-2018.

$525 $465 $400 $340 $300 $265 $250 *$599*

Add $50 for night sights or for left-hand action.

Add $66 for 10 shot mag. with left-hand action.

FNS-9 COMPACT – 9mm Para. cal., DAO, striker fired, polymer frame, 3.6 in. cold hammer forged stainless steel barrel, 10, 12, or 17 shot mag., external extractor with loaded chamber indicator, fixed 3-dot sights or night sights, lower accessory rail, front and rear cocking serrations, matte black or matte silver slide finish, matte black, FDE (new 2016), or grey (mfg. 2017-2019) frame finish, 23.4 oz. Mfg. 2015-2020.

$575 $500 $435 $365 $325 $280 $265 *$639*

Add $50 for night sights.

FNS-9 LONGSLIDE (COMPETITION) – 9mm Para. cal., DAO, SFO, 5 in. hammer forged stainless steel barrel, stainless steel slide, fixed 3-dot sights, loaded chamber indicator, front and rear cocking serrations, 17 shot mag., Mil-Std 1913 accessory mounting rail, serrated trigger guard, black frame finish, 27.2 oz. Mfg. 2013-2018.

$575 $500 $435 $365 $325 $280 $265 *$649*

FNS-40 – .40 S&W cal., DAO, SFO, 4 in. cold hammer forged stainless steel barrel, 14 shot mag., matte black or matte silver slide finish, black or FDE (disc.) finished polymer frame, fixed 3-dot sights or night sights, external extractor with loaded chamber indicator, front and rear cocking serrations, lower accessory rail, two interchangeable backstraps with lanyard eyelets, serrated trigger guard, fully ambidextrous slide stop lever and mag. release, 27.5 oz. Mfg. 2012-2018.

$525 $465 $400 $340 $300 $265 $250 *$599*

Add $50 for night sights or for left-hand action.

Add $66 for 10 shot mag. with left-hand action.

* ***FNS-40 Compact*** – .40 S&W cal., similar to FNS-40, except has 3.6 in. barrel, 10 or 14 shot mag., stainless steel slide with matte black finish, matte black polymer frame, 25.8 oz. Mfg. 2015-2018.

$525 $465 $400 $340 $300 $265 $250 *$599*

Add $50 for night sights.

GRADING - PPGS™	100%	98%	95%	90%	80%	70%	60%	LAST MSR

FNS-40 LONGSLIDE – .40 S&W cal., striker fired, DAO, SFO, 5 in. hammer forged stainless steel barrel, stainless steel slide, fixed 3-dot sights, loaded chamber indicator, front and rear cocking serrations, 14 shot mag., Mil-Std 1913 accessory mounting rail, serrated trigger guard, black frame finish, 29.5 oz. Mfg. 2013-2018.

	$575	$500	$435	$365	$325	$280	$265	*$649*

FNX-9 – 9mm Para. cal., DA/SA, polymer frame, 4 in. stainless steel barrel, 10 (new 2012) or 17 shot mag., serrated trigger guard, deep V fixed combat sights, two or four (disc.) interchangeable backstrap inserts, ambidextrous mag. release and manual safety, front and rear cocking serrations, Mil-Std mounting rail, black/black or black/stainless finish, 21.9 oz. New 2010.

MSR $699	$615	$540	$470	$400	$350	$310	$295	

Add $50 for night sights (disc.).

FNX-40 – .40 S&W cal., DA/SA, polymer frame, 4 in. barrel, 10 (new 2012) or 14 shot mag., serrated trigger guard, deep V fixed combat sights, four interchangeable backstrap inserts, ambidextrous mag. release and manual safety, front and rear cocking serrations, Mil-Std mounting rail, stainless steel slide with matte black finish, 24.4 oz. Mfg. 2010-2018.

	$615	$540	$470	$400	$350	$310	$295	*$699*

Add $50 for night sights (disc. 2013).

FNX-45 – .45 ACP cal., DA/SA, 4 1/2 in. stainless steel barrel, 10, 12 (disc. 2013), or 15 shot mag., matte black or stainless steel slide, low profile fixed 3-dot sights, external extractor with loaded chamber indicator, matte black polymer frame, front and rear cocking serrations, two interchangeable backstrap inserts, lower accessory rail, ambidextrous decocking levers, ring style external hammers, black/black, black/stainless steel, or black/FDE finish, 33.2 oz. New 2012.

MSR $824	$695	$615	$550	$475	$420	$365	$335	

* ***FNX-45 Tactical*** – .45 ACP cal., similar to FNX-45, except has threaded barrel, 10 or 15 shot mag., high profile night sights, includes fitted Cordura nylon soft case, black, FDE, or grey (mfg. 2017) finish, available with Vortex Venom 6-MOA miniature red-dot (mfg. late 2019-2020) or Vortex Viper optic (new 2021), 33.6 oz. New 2012.

MSR $1,349	$1,135	$1,015	$885	$740	$675	$575	$475	

Add $100 for Vortex Venom red-dot optic (mfg. 2019-2020).
Add $100 for Vortex Viper optic (new 2021).

FIVE-SEVEN – 5.7x28mm cal., SA, polymer frame, 4 3/4 in. cold hammer forged stainless steel barrel with hard chrome chamber and bore, polymer encased steel slide, USG (disc. 2012) or MK2 variation, 10 or 20 shot mag., reversible mag. release, internal hammer, textured grip, black, OD Green (disc. 2011) or FDE finish, Mil-Std mounting, ambi manual safety, magazine disconnect safety, choice of fixed 3-dot (standard mfg.), adj. (USG model), C-More fixed (disc.), or C-More fixed night sights (disc.), underframe rail, includes three mags., hard case and cleaning kit, 20.8 oz.

MSR $1,199	$1,025	$900	$775	$700	$575	$450	$350	

Add 20% for early mfg. that incorporated a larger trigger guard than current mfg.

FN 503 – 9mm Para. cal., striker fired autoloader, slim frame, 3.1 in. barrel, recessed target crown, 6 shot mag. w/pinky extender and 8 shot mag. with grip sleeve, all-metal trigger, low profile iron sights, textured grips, loaded chamber indicator, rear cocking slide serrations, includes locking device and soft gun case, black finish, 21 oz. New 2020.

MSR $549	$475	$400	$350	$325	$250	$200	$175	

FN 509 – 9mm Para. cal., striker fire autoloader, DA, polymer frame, 4 or 4 1/4 (new 2020) in. cold hammer forged stainless steel barrel w/polished chamber and feed ramp, 10 or 17 shot mag., external extractor, fixed 3-dot luminescent combat-style sights, enhanced all-condition grips, front and rear cocking serrations, ambidextrous slide stop lever and mag. release, Mil-Std 1913 mounting rail, interchangeable backstraps, black or FDE (new 2019) finish, 26.9 oz. New 2017.

MSR $679	$600	$525	$450	$375	$325	$280	$265	

FN 509 COMPACT MRD – 9mm Para. cal., striker fire autoloader, DA, compact frame, 3.7 in. cold hammer forged stainless steel barrel w/polished chamber and feed ramp, recessed target crown, 12 shot mag. w/pinky extender and 15 shot mag. w/grip sleeve, external extractor, flat face trigger, fixed 3-dot luminescent combat-style iron sights, low profile optics mounting system plate kit, enhanced all condition grips, front and rear cocking serrations, ambidextrous controls, slide stop lever, and mag. release, Mil-Std 1913 mounting rail, interchangeable backstraps, black or FDE finish, 25.0 oz. New late 2019.

MSR $799	$700	$650	$550	$500	$400	$325	$300	

GRADING - PPGS™	100%	98%	95%	90%	80%	70%	60%	LAST MSR

FN 509 COMPACT TACTICAL – 9mm Para. cal., striker-fired autoloader, polymer frame w/replaceable steel frame/slide rails, 4.3 in. cold hammer forged threaded barrel, recessed target crown, three 10 shot or one 12, 15 (mfg. 2020 only), or 24 shot mag., external extractor, compatible w/FN Low Profile Optics-Mounting System, enhanced textured grips, fully ambi stop slide stop lever and mag. release, Mil-Std 1913 Picatinny rail, includes soft case, black or FDE finish, 26.2 oz. New 2020.

MSR $1,049	$900	$800	$650	$600	$500	$400	$300	

FN 509 LS EDGE – 9mm Para. cal., double action, striker fired, 5 in. hammer forged barrel, 10 or 17 shot mag., compatible w/24 shot FN 509 mag, knurled mag. release, graphite anodized floorplates and magwell, ambi optimized long slide, flat face trigger, fiber optic front, blackout rear notch sights, ballistics case, 3 mags., 4 MRD mounting plates, 2 frame backstraps included, graphite PVD type III anodizing, 31 oz. New 2021.

MSR $1,499	$1,350	$1,175	$1,025	$925	$750	$600	$475	

FN 509 MIDSIZE – 9mm Para. cal., striker fire autoloader, DA, polymer frame, 4 in. cold hammer forged stainless steel barrel w/polished chamber, feed ramp, and recessed target crown, two 10 or 15 shot mags., external extractor, loaded chamber indicator, flat-face trigger, fixed 3-dot luminescent combat-style sights, enhanced all condition grips, offered as non-manual safety, improved front and rear cocking serrations, ambi slide stop lever and mag. release, Mil-Std 1913 mounting rail, interchangeable backstraps, fully ambi controls, includes soft pistol case and locking device, also available with optics mounting package (FN-509 Midsize MRD, new mid-2019), black finish, 7.4 in. OAL, 26.5 oz. New 2019.

MSR $679	$600	$525	$450	$375	$325	$280	$265	

Add $120 for optics mounting package (FN-509 Midsize MRD, new mid-2019).

FN 509 MIDSIZE MRD – 9mm Para. cal., striker fire autoloader, DA, polymer frame, 4 in. cold hammer forged stainless steel barrel, recessed target crown, 10 or 15 shot mag., external extractor, low profile optics mounting system plate kit, combat style iron sights, enhanced grip textures, loaded chamber indicator, front and rear cocking serrations, ambi controls, Mil-Std 1913 mounting rail, interchangeable backstraps, black or FDE finish, 26.5 oz. New 2020.

MSR $799	$700	$650	$550	$500	$400	$325	$300	

FN 509 TACTICAL – 9mm Para. cal., striker fire autoloader, DA, polymer frame, 4 1/2 in. cold hammer forged stainless steel threaded barrel with O-ring retention thread cap, polished chamber, and feed ramp, 10, 17, or 24 shot mag., external extractor, loaded chamber indicator, low profile optics mounting system, suppressor height night sights, sight protecting slide cap, enhanced all condition grips, front and rear cocking serrations, ambi slide stop lever and mag. release, Mil-Std 1913 mounting rail, interchangeable backstraps, black, Battle Gray (Limited Ed., mfg. 2019 only), or Desert Tan finish, includes soft pistol case and locking device, 7.9 in. OAL, 27.9 oz. New late 2018.

MSR $1,049	$900	$800	$650	$600	$500	$400	$300	

FN 15 PISTOL 5.56 – 5.56x45mm cal., GIO, 10 1/2 in. cold hammer forged chrome-lined free floating barrel, stainless steel pinned gas block, A2 flash hider, 30 shot Magpul PMAG, SBX-K pistol stabilizing brace, Magpul MOE grip, ergonomic safety lever and mag. release, hard anodized aluminum flat-top receiver, Mil-Std 1913 rail, 9 in. Midwest Industries rail with M-LOK, carbine length gas system, forward assist, pistol buffer kit, 5.2 lbs. Mfg. 2018-2019.

	$1,400	$1,275	$1,150	$1,050	$875	$700	$550	*$1,599*

FN 15 PISTOL .300 BLACKOUT – .300 AAC Blackout cal., GIO, 12 in. cold hammer forged chrome-lined free floating barrel, stainless steel pinned gas block, SureFire ProComp 762 muzzle brake, 30 shot Magpul PMAG, SBX-K pistol stabilizing brace, Magpul MOE grip, ergonomic safety lever and mag. release, hard anodized aluminum flat-top receiver, Mil-Std 1913 rail, 10 in. Midwest Industries rail with M-LOK, pistol length gas system, forward assist, pistol buffer kit, 5.56 lbs. Mfg. 2018-2019.

	$1,400	$1,275	$1,150	$1,050	$875	$700	$550	*$1,599*

RIFLES: BOLT ACTION

FNH USA imports a wide range of tactical rifle systems for military and law enforcement only. FNH USA also imported a line of modular system rifles, including the Ultima Ratio Intervention, the Ultima Ratio Commando II, and the .338 Lapua Model. Please contact the company directly for more information, including availability and pricing.

BALLISTA – .308 Win. (mfg. 2013 only), .300 Win. Mag. (mfg. 2013 only), or .338 Lapua Mag. cal., 26 in. fluted barrel, ambidextrous fully adj. folding stock, 5 or 8 shot detachable box mag., aluminum alloy receiver with top mounted Mil-Std 1913 rail plus multiple rail segments for other accessories, fully adj. single or two-stage trigger, FDE or Desert Tan finish, 14 1/2 lbs. Mfg. by Unique Alpine AG. Mfg. 2013-2020.

	$6,950	$6,400	$5,800	$5,200	$4,500	$3,650	$2,875	*$7,499*

GRADING - PPGS™	100%	98%	95%	90%	80%	70%	60%	LAST MSR

PBR (PATROL BOLT RIFLE) – .300 WSM (XP Model) or .308 Win. cal., 22 in. heavy free floating barrel standard, stippled black Hogue overmolded stock, Picatinny rail, four shot fixed or removable box mag., some models may be marked "FN Herstal", later production marked "FNH", approx. 9 1/2 lbs.

	$1,075	$925	$825	$750	$625	$500	$425	*$1,075*

Add $170 for XP Model in .300 WSM cal.

SPR A1/A1a – .308 Win. cal., 20 in. fluted (A1/A1a) or 24 (A1) in. non-fluted cold hammer forged free floating barrel, recessed target crown, 4 shot detachable box mag., pre-'64 Model 70 action, external claw extractor, matte black McMillan fiberglass stock with adj. comb and LOP, textured gripping surfaces, premium recoil pad, multiple steel sling swivel studs, knurled bolt handle, 3-pos. safety, blade ejector, 1-piece steel 1913 optics rail, matte black finish, 11.8-12.4 lbs. Disc. 2017.

	$2,000	$1,775	$1,575	$1,375	$1,175	$975	$750	*$2,245*

Subtract $246 for A1 model with non-fluted barrel.

SPR A2 – .308 Win. cal., similar to A1, 20 in. fluted or 24 in. non-fluted barrel, 11.6 or 12.2 lbs. Disc. 2009.

	$2,500	$2,185	$1,875	$1,700	$1,375	$1,125	$875	*$2,745*

SPR A3 G (SPECIAL POLICE RIFLE) – .308 Win. cal., 24 in. fluted barrel with hard chromed bore, hinged floorplate, one-piece steel Mil-Std 1913 optical rail, A3 fiberglass tactical stock with adj. comb and LOP, steel sling studs, designed to achieve 1/2 MOA accuracy standard, 14.3 lbs. Disc. 2016.

	$3,175	$2,750	$2,350	$2,125	$1,700	$1,395	$1,075	*$3,495*

SPR A5M – .308 Win. or .300 WSM cal., steel construction, 20 or 24 in. non-fluted free floating barrel, target crown, 4 or 5 shot mag., controlled round feed with external claw extractor, blade ejector, one-piece steel Mil-Std 1913 optics rail, 2-lever adj. trigger, 3-position safety, McMillan fiberglass stock with adj. LOP and cheekpiece, textured gripping surfaces, multiple sling/bipod studs, matte black finish, 11.3-11.8 lbs. Disc. 2017.

	$2,625	$2,325	$1,975	$1,750	$1,475	$1,250	$950	*$2,899*

Add $100 for traditional hinged floorplate in .300 WSM cal. or $200 for hinged floorplate in .308 Win. cal. (both disc. 2013).

SPR A5M XP – .308 Win. cal., steel construction, 20 or 24 in. chrome-lined free floating heavy fluted barrel, threaded muzzle, recessed target crown, 5 shot box mag., controlled round feed with external claw extractor, blade ejector, one-piece 20 MOA optics rail, McMillan fiberglass stock with adj. LOP and cheekpiece, textured gripping surfaces, multiple sling/bipod studs, 6 integral quick detach sling mounts, premium recoil pad, 2-lever adj. trigger, 3-pos. safety, oversized bolt handle, ambidextrous mag. release, matte black finish, 11 1/2-11 3/4 lbs. Mfg. 2013-2018.

	$2,625	$2,325	$1,975	$1,750	$1,475	$1,250	$950	*$2,899*

Add $200 for TBM (tactical box mag.) with 20 or 24 in. fluted barrel (mfg. 2011-2013).

PSR I – .308 Win. cal., 20 in. fluted or 24 in. non-fluted barrel, 3, 4, or 5 shot internal mag., FN tactical sport trigger system, hinged floorplate, matte black McMillan sporter style fiberglass stock, raised comb, recoil pad, steel sling studs, 7.7 or 8.7 lbs. Disc. 2009.

	$2,000	$1,750	$1,500	$1,360	$1,100	$900	$700	*$2,253*

PSR II/III – .308 Win. or .300 WSM (PSR II) cal., 22 in. fluted or 24 in. non-fluted barrel, 3, 4 (PSR III), or 5 shot internal or detachable box mag., FN tactical sport trigger system, matte olive drab McMillan sporter style fiberglass stock, raised comb, recoil pad, steel sling studs, 8.7-9.8 lbs. Disc. 2009.

	$2,000	$1,750	$1,500	$1,360	$1,100	$900	$700	*$2,253*

TSR XP/XP USA (TACTICAL SPORT RIFLES) – .223 Rem. (XP USA), 7.62x39mm (XP USA, disc. 2009), .300 WSM (disc. 2013), or .308 Win. (disc. 2013) cal., Model 70 short (XP) or ultra short (XP USA) action, 20 in. fluted (disc. 2010), 20 or 24 (disc. 2013) in. non-fluted barrel, 3, 4 (detachable box mag., XP Model only), 5, or 6 shot mag., one-piece steel Mil-Std 1913 optical rail, full aluminum bedding block molded into FN/Hogue synthetic stock, Olive Drab overmolded surface, recoil pad, steel sling studs, 8.7-10.1 lbs. Disc. 2015.

	$1,050	$925	$800	$700	$600	$500	$400	*$1,199*

Add $100 for .300 WSM cal. with floorplate (disc. 2013).

RIFLES/CARBINES: SEMI-AUTO

FN 15 1776 – 5.56x45mm cal., GIO, 16 in. alloy steel button-broached barrel, A2 style compensator, 30 shot Magpul PMAG Gen 3, optics ready Mil-Std 1913 flat-top rail, 6-pos. collapsible stock, two-piece single heat shield, oval handguard, sling attachments, matte black finish, 6.6 lbs. Mfg. 2015-2016.

	$800	$700	$650	$600	$500	$400	$300	*$899*

GRADING - PPGS™	100%	98%	95%	90%	80%	70%	60%	LAST MSR

FN 15 CARBINE – 5.56x45mm cal., GIO, 16 in. barrel with A2 style compensator, 30 shot aluminum mag., A2 style front sights, removable M4 style rear carrying handle, flat-top upper receiver with rail, two-piece oval handguard, 6-pos. collapsible stock, matte black finish, 6.94 lbs. Mfg. 2014-2016.

	$1,025	$900	$825	$750	$625	$500	$400	*$1,149*

FN 15 COMPETITION – 5.56x45mm cal., GIO, 18 in. cold hammer forged barrel, SureFire ProComp 556 muzzle brake, steel low profile gas block, 30 shot mag., Timney trigger, Magpul MOE-SL collapsible buttstock, Magpul MOE black pistol grip, rifle length gas system, H2 buffer, nickel boron bolt carrier group, extended rifle length M-LOK 16 in. handguard, ambidextrous bolt release, billet aluminum upper and lower receiver with anodized blue finish, 8.1 lbs. Mfg. 2016-2020.

	$1,975	$1,775	$1,625	$1,475	$1,250	$975	$775	*$2,249*

Add $1,550 for Leupold scope package (new 2019).

FN 15 DMR – 5.56x45mm cal., GIO, 18 in. chrome-lined free floating barrel with SureFire ProComp 556 muzzle brake, 30 shot Magpul PMAG, Magpul MBUS Pro sights, Timney competition trigger, Midwest Industries SSM M-LOK 15 in. handguard, flat-top receiver with rail, Magpul STR buttstock, Magpul MOE grip, matte black finish, 7.2 lbs. Mfg. 2015-2016.

	$1,675	$1,500	$1,375	$1,250	$1,050	$825	$650	*$1,899*

FN 15 DMR II – 5.56x45mm cal., GIO, 18 in. cold hammer forged chrome-lined free floating barrel with pinned gas block, SureFire ProComp 556 muzzle device, 30 shot Magpul PMAG, 3.5 lb. Timney match trigger, Magpul MOE STR buttstock, Magpul MOE grip, ergonomic safety lever and mag. release, FN Rail System with M-LOK technology, hard anodized aluminum flat-top upper receiver with 1913 Mil-Spec rail, upgraded Mil-Spec lower receiver, forward assist, 7.03 lbs. Mfg. 2017-2020.

	$1,775	$1,575	$1,450	$1,325	$1,100	$875	$675	*$1,999*

FN 15 MD HEAVY BARREL CARBINE – 5.56x45mm cal., GIO, 16 in. cold hammer forged chrome-lined free floating heavy profile barrel, pinned gas block, PWS muzzle brake, 10 shot Magpul PMAG, FN combat trigger, collapsible 6-pos. stock with sling mount, A2 pistol grip, ergonomic safety lever and mag. release, 12 in. free float Midwest Industry rail with M-LOK, hard anodized aluminum flat-top receiver with Mil-Spec rail, 7.1 lbs. Mfg. 2018-2020.

	$1,225	$1,100	$1,025	$925	$775	$600	$475	*$1,399*

FN 15 MD HEAVY BARREL RIFLE – 5.56x45mm cal., GIO, 20 in. cold hammer forged chrome-lined free floating heavy barrel with pinned gas block and muzzle thread protector, 15 in. free float Samson evolution rail, 10 shot Magpul PMAG, hard anodized aluminum flat-top receiver, Mil-Spec rail, FN combat trigger, fixed A2 buttstock, A2 pistol grip, ergonomic safety lever and mag. release, forward assist, 8.7 lbs. Mfg. 2018-2020.

	$1,225	$1,100	$1,025	$925	$775	$600	$475	*$1,399*

FN 15 MILITARY COLLECTOR M4 – 5.56x45mm cal., GIO, 16 in. button-broached barrel, 30 shot AR style mag., A2 style front and adj. rear sights, 6-pos. stock with sling mount, M4 pistol grip, ambi safety lever, Knights Armament M4 RAS adapter rail with rail covers, hard anodized aluminum flat-top receiver with Picatinny rail, matte black finish, 6.6 lbs. New 2015.

MSR $1,749	$1,550	$1,375	$1,275	$1,150	$975	$750	$600	

FN 15 MILITARY COLLECTOR M16 – 5.56x45mm cal., GIO, 20 in. button-broached barrel, A2 compensator, 30 shot aluminum AR style mag., A2 style front and adj. rear sights, fixed A2 buttstock, M16 pistol grip, ambi selector, Knights Armament M5 RAS adaptor rail with rail covers, hard anodized aluminum flat-top receiver with Picatinny rail, matte black finish, 8.2 lbs. New 2015.

MSR $1,749	$1,550	$1,375	$1,275	$1,150	$975	$750	$600	

FN 15 MOE SLG – 5.56x45mm cal., GIO, 16 in. alloy steel button-broached barrel, A2 compensator, 30 shot Magpul PMAG, Magpul MBUS rear and A2 style front sights, Magpul MOE SL gray buttstock and grip, hard anodized aluminum receiver, Magpul MOE SL gray M-LOK carbine handguard, forward assist, matte black/gray finish, 6.8 lbs. Mfg. 2015-2016.

	$1,050	$950	$875	$800	$675	$525	$400	*$1,199*

FN 15 RIFLE – 5.56x45mm cal., GIO, 20 in. barrel with A2 compensator, 30 shot mag., flat-top receiver with rail, A2-style front sights, removable carrying handle, two-piece ribbed round handguard with heat shields, fixed stock with sling mount and storage compartment, matte black finish, 7.97 lbs. Mfg. 2014-2016.

	$1,025	$900	$825	$750	$625	$500	$400	*$1,149*

FN 15 SPORTING – .223 Rem. cal., GIO, 18 in. match grade cold hammer forged free floating barrel with SureFire ProComp 556 muzzle brake, 30 shot mag., Timney competition trigger, flat-top receiver with rail, Samson Evolution 15 in. handguard, Magpul CTR buttstock, Magpul MOE grip, matte black finish, 7.7 lbs. Mfg. 2015-2020.

	$1,550	$1,375	$1,275	$1,150	$975	$750	$600	*$1,749*

GRADING - PPGS™	100%	98%	95%	90%	80%	70%	60%	LAST MSR

FN 15 SRP TACTICAL – 5.56x45mm cal., GIO, 16 in. button-broached barrel with pinned and welded A2 style flash hider, 30 shot mag., FN combat trigger, A2 style grip, 6-pos. buttstock, hard anodized aluminum flat-top receiver, Mil-Std 1913 rail, Midwest Rail System with M-LOK technology, mid-length gas system, Precision Reflex low profile gas block with magnesium phosphate finish, Mil-Spec buffer tube, ergonomic safety lever and mag. release, forward assist, 6 lbs. Mfg. 2017-2019.

	100%	98%	95%	90%	80%	70%	60%	LAST MSR
	$1,050	$950	$875	$800	$675	$525	$400	*$1,199*

FN 15 TACTICAL – 5.56x45mm cal., GIO, 16 in. match grade free floating barrel with FNH USA 3-prong flash hider, 30 shot Magpul PMAG, aluminum flat-top receiver with rail, Magpul MBUS sights, Midwest Industries LWM 12 in. handguard with M-LOK accessory mounting system, Magpul MOE grip, enhanced combat trigger, Magpul MOE SL buttstock, matte black finish, 6.6 lbs. Mfg. 2015-2016.

	100%	98%	95%	90%	80%	70%	60%	LAST MSR
	$1,300	$1,175	$1,075	$975	$825	$650	$500	*$1,479*

FN 15 TACTICAL II – 5.56x45mm cal., GIO, 16 in. cold hammer forged chrome-lined free floating barrel with pinned gas block, FN 3-prong flash hider, 30 shot Magpul PMAG, FN combat trigger, Magpul MOE SL buttstock, Magpul MOE grip, ergonomic safety lever and mag. release, hard anodized aluminum flat-top upper receiver with 1913 Mil-Spec rail, enhanced Mil-Spec lower receiver, FN Rail System with M-LOK technology, forward assist, black or FDE finish, 6.7 lbs. New 2017.

	100%	98%	95%	90%	80%	70%	60%	LAST MSR
MSR $1,599	$1,400	$1,275	$1,150	$1,050	$875	$700	$550	

FN 15 TACTICAL .300 BLK – .300 AAC Blackout cal., GIO, 16 in. match grade hammer forged, free floating barrel, SureFire ProComp 762 muzzle brake, low profile gas block, 30 shot mag., Magpul front and rear sight assembly, Magpul MOE-SL buttstock and MOE pistol grip, carbine length gas system, H buffer, lightweight 12 in. M-LOK rail, 6 3/4 lbs. Mfg. 2016 only.

	100%	98%	95%	90%	80%	70%	60%	LAST MSR
	$1,300	$1,175	$1,075	$975	$825	$650	$500	*$1,479*

FN 15 TACTICAL .300 BLK II – .300 AAC Blackout cal., GIO, 16 in. cold hammer forged chrome-lined free floating barrel with pinned gas block, SureFire ProComp 762 muzzle device, 30 shot Magpul PMAG, FN combat trigger, Magpul MOE SL buttstock, Magpul MOE grip, ergonomic safety lever and magazine release, hard anodized aluminum flat-top receiver with 1913 Mil-Spec rail, FN Rail System with M-LOK technology, forward assist, carbine length gas system, 6.91 lbs. Mfg. 2017-2020.

	100%	98%	95%	90%	80%	70%	60%	LAST MSR
	$1,400	$1,275	$1,150	$1,050	$875	$700	$550	*$1,599*

FN 15 TACTICAL CARBINE FDE P-LOK – 5.56x45mm cal., 16 in. cold hammer forged chrome-lined barrel, FN 3-prong flash hider, 30 shot Magpul PMAG, 16 in. cold hammer forged chrome-lined barrel, FN combat trigger, B5 Systems buttstock and grip, ergonomic safety lever and mag. release, mid-length gas block, P-LOK handguard with M-LOK technology, hard anodized aluminum flat-top receiver with Picatinny rail, forward assist, FDE finish, 7.2 lbs. New 2018.

	100%	98%	95%	90%	80%	70%	60%	LAST MSR
MSR $1,499	$1,325	$1,175	$1,075	$975	$825	$650	$525	

FNAR COMPETITION – 7.62x51mm cal., gas operated, 20 in. fluted barrel, target crowned, front barrel mounted sight rail for aftermarket sights, 20 shot detachable box mag., aluminum alloy receiver with one-piece Mil-Std 1913 optics rail, hard anodized blue receiver finish with Team FNH USA markings, blue/grey laminated stock assembly with checkered gripping surfaces, adj. for cheekpiece, non-slip recoil pad, crossbolt safety, 8.9 lbs. Mfg. 2013-19.

	100%	98%	95%	90%	80%	70%	60%	LAST MSR
	$1,550	$1,400	$1,275	$1,175	$975	$775	$600	*$1,767*

FNAR STANDARD – .308 Win. cal., gas operated, 16 (new 2010) or 20 in. light or heavy fluted contoured barrel, 10 or 20 shot detachable box mag., one-piece M-1913 optical rail, three accessory rails attached to forearm, matte black synthetic pistol grip stock with soft cheekpiece, adj. comb, ambidextrous mag. release, 8.8-9 lbs. Mfg. 2009-2013.

	100%	98%	95%	90%	80%	70%	60%	LAST MSR
	$1,500	$1,350	$1,225	$1,125	$950	$750	$575	*$1,699*

FN M249S MILITARY COLLECTOR – 5.56x45mm cal., GPO, closed bolt operation, formed steel frame, 18 1/2 in. cold hammer forged steel barrel, quick change barrel capability, 30 shot mag., ergonomic polymer buttstock, crossbolt safety, removable heat shield, folding steel bipod, folding carry handle, flip-up feed tray cover and feed mechanism, top cover integrated Mil-Std 1913 rail system, non-reciprocating charging handle, 17 lbs. Mfg. 2016-2019.

	100%	98%	95%	90%	80%	70%	60%	LAST MSR
	$7,750	$6,775	$5,825	$5,275	$4,275	$3,485	$2,725	*$8,499*

FN M249S PARA – 5.56x45mm cal., GPO, closed bolt operation, formed steel frame, 16 in. cold hammer forged barrel, quick change barrel capability, 30 shot mag., ergonomic polymer buttstock, crossbolt safety, removable heat shield, folding steel bipod, folding carry handle, flip-up feed tray cover and feed mechanism, top cover integrated Mil-Std 1913 rail system, non-reciprocating charging handle, black or FDE finish, 17 lbs. New 2017.

	100%	98%	95%	90%	80%	70%	60%	LAST MSR
MSR $8,799	$7,750	$6,950	$6,375	$5,800	$4,875	$3,825	$3,000	

Add $400 for FDE finish.

GRADING - PPGS™	100%	98%	95%	90%	80%	70%	60%	LAST MSR

FN PS90 – 5.7x28mm cal., blowback operation, bullpup configuration, 16 in. barrel, 10 or 30 shot box mag. runs horizontally along the top, empty cases are ejected downward, integrated muzzle brake, Olive Drab or black finish, configurations include PS90 RD with reflex sight module (mfg. 2009), PS90 USG with non-magnifying black reticle optical sight, and the PS90 TR with three M-1913 rails for optional optics, 6.3 lbs. Disc. 2011.

	$1,925	$1,675	$1,450	$1,295	$1,075	$925	$800	*$2,199*

Add $391 for red-dot sights.

FN PS90 STANDARD – 5.7x28mm cal., blowback operation, 16 in. hammer forged barrel with ported muzzle brake, 10 (new 2012) or 30 shot mag., alloy upper receiver, bottom ejection port, forward handstop, 1913 accessory rail and backup iron sight, molded-in rear sling attachment point, ambidextrous charging handles, synthetic thumbhole bullpup design, sliding trigger, enlarged trigger guard, black or OD Green (disc. 2016) finish, 6.28 lbs. New 2010.

MSR $1,679	$1,475	$1,325	$1,175	$1,050	$875	$700	$550	

FS2000 STANDARD/TACTICAL – .223 Rem. cal., bullpup configuration, 17.4 in. barrel, gas operated with rotating bolt, 10 or 30 shot AR-15 style mag., empty cases are ejected through a forward port, includes 1.6x optical sighting package on Standard Model (disc. 2010), Tactical Model features emergency backup folding sights, CQB model features lower accessory rail, ambidextrous polymer stock, top mounted 1913 rail, ODG or black finish, 7.6 lbs. Disc. 2013.

	$2,425	$2,100	$1,825	$1,675	$1,450	$1,250	$995	*$2,779*

FN SCAR 16S – .223 Rem. cal., GPO, semi-auto only version of U.S. SOCOM's newest service rifle, gas operated short stroke piston system, free floating 16 1/4 in. barrel with hard chrome bore, 10 or 30 shot detachable box mag., folding open sights, fully ambidextrous operating controls, three optical rails, side folding polymer stock, A2 pistol grip, fully adj. comb and LOP, black or FDE finish on receiver and stock, 7 1/4 lbs. New 2009.

MSR $3,399	$2,975	$2,550	$2,075	$1,875	$1,575	$1,275	$1,050	

FN SCAR 17S – .308 Win. cal., semi-auto rifle, GPO, 16 1/4 in. hammer forged free floating barrel, compensator, 10 or 20 shot mag., enlarged trigger guard, adj. folding front and folding/removable rear iron sights, telescoping side folding polymer stock, adj. cheekpiece, A2-style pistol grip, ambi safety lever and mag. release, hard anodized monolithic aluminum receiver, Mil-Std 1913 accessory rails, black or FDE finish, 8 lbs. New 2009.

MSR $3,569	$3,050	$2,675	$2,295	$2,075	$1,680	$1,375	$1,075	

FN SCAR 20S (CURRENT MFG.) – 7.62x51mm or 6.5 Creedmoor (new 2020) cal., GPO, 20 in. cold hammer forged heavy free floating barrel with muzzle device, 10 shot mag., two-stage Geissele Super SCAR trigger, enlarged trigger guard, fixed buttstock with adj. LOP and comb, adj. cheekpiece, Hogue rugger grips with finger grooves, ambi safety lever and mag. release, extended aluminum monolithic receiver, top Picatinny rail, matte black (new 2020) or FDE finish. New 2019.

MSR $4,499	$3,825	$3,350	$2,875	$2,600	$2,100	$1,725	$1,350	

FN SCAR 20S (RECENT MFG.) – 7.62x51mm cal., GPO, 20 in. cold hammer forged free floating barrel, 10 shot mag., factory-installed, double-stage Geissele Super SCAR trigger, enlarged trigger guard, adj. folding front and rear sights, adj. non-folding polymer stock, adj. cheekpiece, A2 black pistol grip, ambidextrous safety lever and mag. release, Monolithic receiver, top Picatinny rail, FDE finish, 42 1/2 in. OAL. Limited mfg. 2016 only.

Retail pricing was not available for this model.

SHOTGUNS

FNH USA manufactured tactical style shotguns, including the FN Police Shotgun ($500 last MSR) and the FN Tactical Police Shotgun (with or w/o fixed stock, $923 last MSR).

FN SLP STANDARD (MODEL SLP - SELF LOADING POLICE) – 12 ga., 3 in. chamber, semi-auto, gas system, 18 in. barrel with standard Invector chokes, 6 shot extended tube mag., high profile adj. rear sights, two-piece bolt, aluminum alloy receiver, top mounted one-piece 1913 rail, two steel sling swivel studs, crossbolt safety, matte black synthetic stock with checkered gripping panels on forearm and grip, non-slip recoil pad, matte black finish, 7.7 lbs. Mfg. 2008-2020.

	$1,150	$1,030	$900	$750	$685	$585	$485	*$1,379*

FN SLP COMPETITION – 12 ga., 3 in. chamber, semi-auto, gas operated with one interchangeable gas piston, 22 (disc. 2014) or 24 (new 2015) in. VR barrel with IC Invector Plus extended choke tubes, crossbolt safety, flip-up rear and fiber optic front sights, 8 shot extended tube mag. with blue aluminum tube cover, aluminum alloy receiver with enlarged loading port and blue hard anodized finish, matte black synthetic stock with checkered gripping panels on forearm and grip, non-slip recoil pad, sling swivel studs, 7 1/2 lbs. Mfg. 2013-2020.

	$1,235	$1,100	$985	$835	$725	$615	$515	*$1,449*

GRADING - PPGS™	100%	98%	95%	90%	80%	70%	60%	LAST MSR

FN SLP TACTICAL – 12 ga., 3 in. chamber, semi-auto, gas operated, 18 in. barrel with standard Invector choke tubes, 6 shot extended tube mag., high profile adj. ghost ring rear and wing protected front sights, aluminum alloy receiver, top mounted rail, crossbolt safety, two steel sling swivel studs, forward mounted 1913 tri-rail mount, matte black synthetic pistol grip stock with 3 interchangeable cheekpieces and 3 interchangeable recoil pads, checkered gripping surfaces on forearm and grip, matte black finish, 7.4 lbs. Disc. 2020.

$1,250	$1,100	$985	$835	$725	$615	$515	*$1,479*

FN SLP MK1 – 12 ga., 3 in. chamber, semi-auto, active valve gas system, 22 in. barrel with standard Invector chokes, 8 shot extended mag. tube with aluminum tube cover, low profile adj. rear and red fiber optic front sights, two-piece bolt, aluminum alloy receiver, top mounted Cantilever Weaver-pattern accessory rail, two steel sling swivels, matte black synthetic stock with checkered gripping surfaces on forearm and grip, non-slip recoil pad, crossbolt safety, matte black finish, 8.2 lbs. Disc. 2020.

$1,125	$1,000	$875	$735	$650	$550	$465	*$1,324*

FN SLP MK1 TACTICAL – 12 ga., 3 in. chamber, semi-auto, active valve gas system, 18 in. barrel with standard Invector interchangeable choke tubes, 6 shot extended tube mag. with aluminum mag. tube cover, forward mounted 1913 tri-rail mount, low profile adj. folding rear and red fiber optic front sights, two-piece bolt, matte black synthetic pistol grip stock with interchangeable comb inserts and recoil pads, crossbolt safety, matte black finish, 7.9 lbs. Disc. 2020.

$1,225	$1,100	$950	$800	$700	$600	$495	*$1,429*

MODEL SC1 O/U – 12 ga., 2 3/4 in. chambers, 28 (disc. 2013) or 30 in. VR barrel with Invector plus choking, silver receiver, blue/gray, black, or green adj. comb laminate stock with recoil pad. Mfg. 2011-2018.

$2,150	$1,850	$1,625	$1,400	$1,175	$940	$815	*$2,449*

P-12 SLIDE ACTION – 12 ga., 2 3/4 or 3 in. chrome-lined chamber, 18 in. cantilever barrel, matte black finish, aluminum alloy receiver, checkered synthetic stock, recoil pad, Invector cylinder choke Weaver rail pattern, sling swivels, 7 lbs. 7 oz. Mfg. 2013-2020.

$595	$525	$450	$395	$360	$330	$295	*$669*

FTL

Previously manufactured by Wilkinson Arms located in Covina, CA for the FTL Marketing Corp. located in N. Hollywood, CA.

PISTOLS: SEMI-AUTO

FTL AUTO NINE – .22 LR cal., single action, hammerless, blowback action, 8 shot mag., checkered plastic grips, fixed sights. Disc.

$200	$160	$125	$105	$95	$85	$75

FABARM, S.p.A.

Current manufacturer established in 1900, located in Brescia, Italy. Currently imported by Fabarm USA beginning 2012, located in Cambridge, MD. Previously imported by Tristar, located in Kansas City, MO circa 2007-2009. Select models previously retailed until 2012 by Bill Hanus Birdguns, LLC, located in Newport, OR. Previously imported by SIG Arms during 2005, located in Exeter, NH, and by Heckler & Koch, Inc. 1998-2004. Certain models had limited importation by Ithaca Acquisition Corp. located in King Ferry, NY during 1993-1995. Previously imported and distributed (1988-1990) by St. Lawrence Sales, Inc. located in Lake Orion, MI. Previously imported until 1986 by Beeman Precision Arms, Inc. located in Santa Rosa, CA.

For individual model listings, please go to BlueBookOfGunValues.com/overflow.

FABBRI s.n.c.

Current manufacturer established during 1965, currently located in Nave (Brescia), Italy since 2007. Previously located in Concescio. Fabbri shotguns are sold directly worldwide, but exclusive agent located in Oxfordshire, UK is Callvert Sporting.

Ivo Fabbri and Daniele Perazzi were partners in a shotgun manufacturing business beginning in 1960 - these guns are ser. no. 5001-5339. Circa 1965, Fabbri and Perazzi split up and formed their own individual companies. "Armi Fabbri" relocated from Brescia to Concesio during 1969 and underwent a name change from Armi Fabbri to Fabbri s.n.c. during 1989. The first CNC machine was installed during 1974. Currently, Fabbri s.n.c. engravers include Creative Art, Pedersoli, Torcoli, and Fracassi. In-house engravers include Mario Terzi, Laura Vibrioni, Luisa Garlasche, and Erika Pedretti. Fabbri manufactures perhaps the highest quality shotguns available in today's marketplace - approx. 20-30 guns are manufactured annually. Delivery times range from 2-4 years.

SHOTGUNS: CUSTOM

O/U SHOTGUN – 12, 20, 28 (disc.) ga. or .410 bore (disc.), top-of-the-line quality with advanced CNC metal fabrication, steel, stainless steel (new 2002), or titanium construction, any combination of

GRADING - PPGS™	100%	98%	95%	90%	80%	70%	60%	LAST MSR

engraving, wood, and other options. Unique full laser welded stainless steel barrels. Both the type/style of engraving and the engraver will make a big difference on the current value of a custom ordered Fabbri O/U shotgun. Because engraving alone can add $50,000+ to the cost of a new shotgun, a qualified appraisal from a reputable dealer/collector is advised when buying or selling recently manufactured Fabbri O/U shotguns.

Current retail on the Classic model starts at approx. €100,000, Full Stainless Steel model is €110,000, and Titanium/Stainless Steel model is €125,000. All prices are Export Base Price (not including taxes), w/o engraving. Please contact Fabbri directly for a firm price quotation and delivery times.

O/U guns mfg. 1967-1983 (typically marked Ivo Fabbri) are currently priced in the $40,000-$80,000 range, depending on condition and engraving. O/U guns mfg. 1983-1989 (typically marked Ivo Fabbri) are priced in the $75,000-$110,000 range, depending on condition, notoriety of engraver, and amount of engraving coverage. Guns mfg. within the last 10 years are currently priced in the $100,000-$150,000 range, depending on condition, notoriety of engraver, and amount of engraving coverage. Add 25% for matched pair.

SxS SHOTGUN – 12 or 20 ga., one of the world's best sidelock SxS shotguns, ejectors, full engraving, "E" prefix ser. no., two types of back action. Disc.

Older Fabbri SxS shotguns manufactured with type II actions and in mint condition are priced in the $65,000 range. Subtract $10,000 for scroll engraving, and/or approx. 50% for type I action.

FABRIQUE NATIONALE

Current manufacturer located in Herstal, near Liege, Belgium. The current company name is "Group Herstal." However, the company is better known as "Fabrique Nationale" or "Fabrique Nationale d'Armes de Guerre". FN entered into their first contract with John M. Browning in 1897 for the manufacture of their first pistol, the FN 1899 Model. Additional contracts were signed and the relationship further blossomed with the manufacture of the A-5 shotgun. FN was acquired by GIAT of France in 1992. In late 1997, the company was purchased by the Walloon government of Belgium. Additional production facilities are located in Portugal, Japan, and the U.S.

Also see: Browning Arms under Rifles, Shotguns, and Pistols, and FN AMERICA LLC (FNH USA) for current offerings in the U.S.

PISTOLS: SEMI-AUTO

For FN Models 1899, 1900, 1903, 1905, 1910, 1922 (10/22), Baby Model, Model 10/71, and BAC marked Hi-Powers (post 1954 mfg.), please refer to the Browning Pistol section in this text.

PISTOLS: SEMI-AUTO, HIGH POWER VARIATIONS

The F.N. High Power (also known as P-35) was John Browning's last pistol design. A 9mm Para., single action, semi-auto pistol, it was the first to incorporate a staggered high capacity magazine. It has a 4 2/3 in. barrel, 13 shot mag., hammer and mag. safeties, a wide variety of finishes and sight options. It's probably the most widely used military pistol in the world.

For information on post-WWII BAC marked Hi-Powers, including model codes and identification, please refer to the Browning section under Serialization.

1933 BELGIAN MILITARY TRIALS: HIGH EFFICIENCY PISTOL – similar to the Pre-War Commercial and Military High Power model, this was the last variant of developments that led to the High Power. Officially named Grand Rendement or High Efficiency, about 1,100 were produced in 1933 as trials guns (1,000) and sales samples (approximate 100). These can easily be distinguished by the oval ejection port but otherwise share the appearance of the later High Power. Serial range 1-1100.

	100%	98%	95%	90%	80%	70%	60%
	N/A	$6,500	$5,000	$4,000	$3,500	$3,000	$2,400

PRE-WAR COMMERCIAL AND MILITARY HIGH POWER – 9mm Para. cal., single action, blue, wood grips, slotted for stock with tangent rear sight (fixed rear sight with unslotted rear grip strap not encountered in this model), 13 shot mag., commercial pistols display Liege proofs only, Belgian military pistols display Liege proofs and Belgian military acceptance markings. Mfg. 1935-1940.

	100%	98%	95%	90%	80%	70%	60%
Tangent Sight & Slotted	$2,750	$2,200	$1,700	$1,250	$950	$750	$650

Add $1,200-$1,500 for original prewar Belgian military or Finnish Air Force flat board stock w/o attached holster. Check stock for small Belgian military acceptance marking. Beware of fakes and reproductions!

Add $1,250 for correct Belgian military combination shoulder-stock - pistol holster. Beware of reproductions!

GRADING - PPGS™	100%	98%	95%	90%	80%	70%	60%	LAST MSR

PRE-WAR FOREIGN MILITARY CONTRACTS – mfg. under military contract for various countries.

Lithuanian Crest	N/A	$3,600	$2,950	$1,900	$1,350	$1,000	$900	
Estonian Contract ("E.V." or "K.L.")	N/A	$3,700	$3,100	$2,500	$1,800	$1,350	$1,000	
Finnish Contract ("SA" marked)	N/A	$2,800	$2,300	$1,900	$1,600	$1,100	$800	
Paraguayan Crest	N/A	$3,750	$3,000	$2,500	$2,250	$1,900	$1,750	
Chinese, Original Finish	N/A	$2,400	$1,850	$1,500	$1,000	$850	$750	

Add $1,200 for original (Finnish contract) pre-war flat board stock with attached holster.
Add $1,000 for original Finnish contract stock (ser. no. 11,000-15,000) with removed holster.
Add $200 for period Chinese inventory marking on Chinese contract pistols.
Subtract 50% for refinished Chinese contract pistols or reworks with Inglis parts.

Note: Finnish contract guns can be identified by the "SA" marking on frame, and/or slide, and/or mag. 2,400 pistols were shipped to Finland in 1940, all are in ser. no. range: 11,000 - 15,000.

Most Chinese contract pistols were refinished or reworked to include Inglis parts. Chinese contract pistols fall in the 6,000 - 11,000 and 20,000 - 21,000 ser. no. range.

Paraguayan contract guns are rare in the U.S. Numerous counterfeits have surfaced - check crest and slide markings for originality. Check bluing carefully, as most were refinished. Beware of matching numbered shoulder stocks as most are counterfeits or recently renumbered.

WWII PRODUCTION: WAFFENAMT PROOFED – There is a range of finishes during Nazi production that varies from the excellent pre-war commercial finish on early guns assembled from captured parts to the roughly milled, poorly finished specimens mfg. late in the war. Values listed assume all major parts (slide, barrel, and frame) are matching with original magazine.

In recent years, some Nazi production Hi-Powers have had the rear grip strap milled out and slotted to accept a shoulder stock. Careful observation is advised before purchasing a "rare" (and expensive) slotted and tangent sight specimen. Many HPs have been restored, since the restoration is easily accomplished by professionals.

* ***WWII Production: Waffenampt Proofed Type I*** – tangent sights, slotted, taken from existing pre-war Belgian production, quality is excellent, correct ser. range is quite limited, approx. 42,000-46,000+. Ser. range for production under German occupation is 50,001-52,500. All are proofed WaA 613.

N/A	$5,500	$4,500	$4,000	$3,000	$2,500	$2,000	

Beware of fakes and restorations. A large percentage of WaA613 pistols in the U.S. are counterfeits.

* ***WWII Production: Waffenampt Proofed Type II*** – tangent sights, not slotted, approx. 90,000 mfg. with last ser. no. approx. 145,000, generally good quality finish, pistols are proofed WaA613, WaA103, some are WaA140.

N/A	$2,500	$2,000	$1,500	$1,000	$900	$800	

Add 25% if pistol is marked WaA613.
Add 15% if pistol is marked WaA103.

* ***WWII Production: Waffenampt Proofed Type III Standard Fixed Sights*** – not slotted, most common HP pistol produced during the war.

$1,500	$1,100	$850	$600	$500	$450	$400	

Add 15% for late war Bakelite/synthetic grips.
Add 20% for eagle N proof instead of WaA140 proof, or for no WaA140 proof.

POST-OCCUPATION PRODUCTION – commercial assembly began September 1944 from wartime parts. Complete manufacturing from raw materials started in 1946. First imported with BAC markings in 1954 (see Browning HP section). Early (1944-1945) models are identifiable by an "A" serial number prefix and are not fitted with a magazine safety. Starting in 1947, the rear slide bushing was hardened by a new heat treatment process. Other design modifications were added in 1950. Many thousands manufactured for various government contracts.

Add $200-$2,000 for military pistols with crests, depending on condition and variation.

* ***Post-Occupation Production Tangent Sight Only***

$1,300	$1,100	$900	$700	$650	$550	$500	

Add $100 for "T" prefix.

GRADING - PPGS™	100%	98%	95%	90%	80%	70%	60%	LAST MSR

* ***Post-Occupation Production Tangent sight*** – slotted for stock, military or commercial mfg.

	$1,500	$1,350	$1,100	$900	$750	$600	$500	

Add 90% for "T" prefix, circa 1975, 300,000+ serial, high polished.
Add $50 for internal extractor.

* ***Post-Occupation Production Fixed sight*** – most common variation.

	$650	$525	$450	$400	$350	$325	$300	

Add $100 for ring hammer.
Add 40% for "A" prefix, but only in 98%+ condition.

SULTAN OF MUSCAT AND OMAN CONTRACT

* ***Sultan Of Muscat And Oman Contract First Model*** – matte finish, reverse crest, scarce.

	$4,500	$3,500	$2,500	$2,200	$2,000	$1,600	$1,300	

* ***Sultan Of Muscat And Oman Contract Second Model*** – high polish finish, standard crest.

	$4,000	$2,950	$1,750	$1,540	$1,265	$1,055	$875	

INGLIS MANUFACTURED HI-POWERS – SEE INGLIS SECTION.

REVOLVERS

BARRACUDA – .357 Mag./9mm Para. cal., 4 in. barrel, blue finish, includes two cylinders chambered for .357 Mag. and 9mm Para. cal. Very limited importation.

	$875	$775	$675	$600	$525	$450	$375	

Add $175 for original styrofoam box, moon clips and documents.
Subtract $250 if sold with only one cylinder.

RIFLES: BOLT ACTION

FN MAUSER SPORTER DE LUXE – available in popular American and European calibers, 24 in. barrel, checkered pistol grip stock. Sold in the U.S. 1947-1963. Sold in the U.S. without rear sight installed or with a choice of Armstrong sights. No engraving. Note that barreled actions were also sold in the U.S.

	$900	$750	$500	$450	$400	$350	$300	

Add $100 for original FN box.
Prices assume original FN rifles with FN stock and FN buttplate, prices do not apply to FN barreled actions assembled by independent gunsmiths.

FN MAUSER SPORTER DE LUXE SCROLL ENGRAVED – available in popular American and European calibers, 24 in. barrel, checkered pistol grip stock. Introduced shortly after the standard De Luxe model. Sold in the U.S. without rear sight installed or with a choice of Armstrong sights. FN scroll engraving in floral motif on receiver, buttplate and trigger guard. Note that scroll engraved barreled actions were also sold in the U.S.

	$2,400	$1,700	$1,000	$750	$500	$450	$350	

Prices assume original FN rifles with FN stock and FN buttplate, prices do not apply to scroll engraved FN barreled actions assembled by independent gunsmiths.
Add $100 for original FN box
Subtract $350 (95% or better) if the top of the engraved receiver is drilled and tapped for a scope.

FN MAUSER SPORTER (DE LUXE) PRESENTATION RIFLE – .30-06 or .270 Win. cal., other calibers only available on special order, 24 in. barrel, checkered pistol grip stock, rear sight installed on barrel, elaborate FN presentation grade engraving with dragon motifs on receiver, buttplate, trigger guard and barrel, engraved receiver and trigger guard are polished white and not blued, engraving design created and first executed by FN's Master Engraver Felix Funken. Note that presentation grade barreled actions were also sold in the U.S. Introduced 1954.

	$4,800	$3,500	$2,400	$1,600	$900	$800	$700	

Prices assume original FN rifles with FN stock and FN buttplate, prices do not apply to presentation grade FN barreled actions assembled by independent gunsmiths.
Add $100 for original FN box
Subtract $1,000 (95% or better) if the top of the engraved receiver is drilled and tapped for a scope.

FN SUPREME – .243 Win., .270 Win., 7mm Rem. Mag., .308 Win. or .30-06 cal., 24 in. barrel, peep sight, checkered pistol grip stock. Sold in the U.S. 1957-1975.

	$850	$725	$500	$450	$400	$350	$300	

FN SUPREME MAGNUM – .264 Win. Mag., 7mm Rem. Mag., .300 Win. Mag., or .375 H&H cal. Mfg. beginning circa 1957.

	$975	$850	$700	$550	$475	$425	$375	
.375 H&H cal.	$1,950	$1,700	$1,400	$1,100	$950	$850	$750	

GRADING - PPGS™	100%	98%	95%	90%	80%	70%	60%	LAST MSR

FN SNIPER RIFLE (MODEL 30) – .308 Win. cal., this model was a Mauser actioned Sniper Rifle equipped with 20 in. extra heavy barrel, flash hider, separate removable diopter sights, Hensoldt 4x scope, hardcase, bipod, and sling. 51 complete factory sets were imported into the U.S., with additional surplus rifles that were privately imported.

	$4,750	$4,250	$4,000	$3,500	$3,000	$2,750	$2,500	

Subtract 15% if removable diopter sights or bipod is missing.

Subtract 10% if scope is not marked with F.N. logo.

Values assume complete factory outfit with all accessories.

RIFLES: SEMI-AUTO

BROWNING PATENT 1900 – .35 Rem. cal. only, usually features matted rib barrel and checkered stock and forearm, similar to Remington Model 8 auto-loading rifle. 4,913 mfg. 1910-1929 by FN, and not officially exported to the U.S.

	N/A	$3,500	$3,250	$3,000	$2,500	$2,000	$1,500	

Add 15% if rifle has plain barrel with tangent leaf rear sight.

Factory engraved rifles are very rare and will command substantial premiums.

MODEL 1949 – 7x57mm Mauser, 7.65mm Mauser, 7.92mm Mauser, or .30-06 cal., (.308 Win. cal. for Argentine conversion rifles), gas operated, 10 shot box mag. (20 round detachable mag. for Argentine conversions), 23 in. barrel, military rifle, tangent rear sight.

Columbia	$2,000	$1,850	$1,400	$1,000	$900	$750	$700	
Luxembourg	$2,500	$2,000	$1,500	$1,100	$1,000	$850	$700	
Venezuela	$2,200	$1,850	$1,400	$1,000	$700	$600	$550	
Argentina	N/A	$1,250	$1,100	$950	$850	$750	$650	
Egyptian	$2,200	$1,850	$1,400	$1,000	$895	$725	$675	

Add $100 for detachable grenade launcher.

Subtract 30% for U.S. rebuilt, non-matching rifles with reproduction stocks.

Original FN-49 sniper rifles are extremely rare and may add $3,500+.

Beware of U.S. assembled "sniper" configurations, and Belgian military "ABL" scopes mounted on other contract rifles and sold as original sniper configurations.

FN-49 contract rifles not listed above are very rare in the U.S. and will demand a premium.

Carefully inspect black paint finish for factory originality, as all FN-49s were factory painted.

RIFLES: SEMI-AUTO, FAL/LAR/CAL/FNC SERIES

After tremendous price increases between 1985-88, Fabrique Nationale decided in 1988 to discontinue this series completely. Not only are these rifles not exported to the U.S. any longer, but all production has ceased in Belgium as well. The only way FN will produce these models again is if they are given a large military contract - in which case a "side order" of commercial guns may be built. 1989 Federal legislation regarding this type of tactical design also helped push up prices to their current level. FAL rifles were also mfg. in Israel by I.M.I.

F.N. FAL – semi-auto, French designation for the F.N. L.A.R. (light automatic rifle), otherwise similar to the L.A.R.

	$4,175	$3,950	$3,750	$3,475	$3,150	$3,100	$2,750	

*** *F.N. FAL G***

Standard	$6,250	$5,500	$4,500	$3,500	$3,000	$2,500	$2,000	
Paratrooper	$5,200	$4,400	$3,900	$3,350	$2,850	$2,550	$2,400	
Heavy Barrel	$6,800	$6,250	$4,950	$4,400	$3,750	$3,250	$2,750	
Lightweight	$5,200	$4,250	$3,750	$3,100	$2,600	$2,350	$2,100	

Values listed assume inclusion of factory bipod.

The Standard G Series was supplied with a wooden stock and wood or nylon forearm. The Heavy Barrel variant had all wood furniture and was supplied with a bipod. The Lightweight Model had an aluminum lower receiver, piston tube and magazine.

G Series FALs were imported between 1959-1962 by Browning Arms Co. This rifle was declared illegal by the GCA of 1968, and was exempted 5 years later. Total numbers exempted are: Standard - 1,822, Heavy Barrel - 21, and Paratrooper - 5.

F.N. L.A.R. COMPETITION (50.00, LIGHT AUTOMATIC RIFLE) – .308 Win. (7.62x51mm) cal., semi-auto, competition rifle with match flash hider, 21 in. barrel, adj. 4 position fire selector on automatic models, wood stock, aperture rear sight adj. from 100-600 meters, 9.4 lbs. Mfg. 1981-83.

	$4,250	$4,025	$3,850	$3,625	$3,450	$3,175	$2,950	

This model was designated by the factory as the 50.00 Model.

GRADING - PPGS™	100%	98%	95%	90%	80%	70%	60%	LAST MSR

Mid-1987 retail on this model was $1,258. The last MSR was $3,179 (this price reflected the last exchange rate and special order status of this model).

* ***FN L.A.R. Competition Heavy Barrel Rifle (50.41 & 50.42)*** – barrel is twice as heavy as standard L.A.R., includes wood or synthetic stock, short wood forearm, and bipod, 12.2 lbs. Importation disc. 1988.

$4,495 $4,275 $4,150 $4,000 $3,675 $3,500 $3,250

Add $500 for walnut stock.
Add $350 for match sights.

There were 2 variations of this model. The Model 50.41 had a synthetic buttstock while the Model 50.42 had a wood buttstock with steel buttplate incorporating a top extension used for either shoulder resting or inverted grenade launching.

Mid-1987 retail on this model was $1,497 (Model 50.41) or $1,654 (Model 50.42). The last MSR was $3,776 (this price reflected the last exchange rate and special order status of this model).

* ***FN L.A.R. Competition Paratrooper Rifle (50.63 & 50.64)*** – similar to L.A.R. model, except has folding stock, 8.3 lbs. Mfg. 1950-88.

$4,275 $3,700 $3,300 $3,000 $2,550 $2,300 $2,150

There were 2 variations of the Paratrooper L.A.R. Model. The Model 50.63 had a stationary aperture rear sight and 18 in. barrel. The Model 50.64 was supplied with a 21 in. barrel and had a rear sight calibrated for either 150 or 200 meters. Both models retailed for the same price.

Mid-1987 retail on this model was $1,310 (both the Model 50.63 and 50.64). The last MSR was $3,239 (this price reflected the last exchange rate and special order status of this model).

CAL – originally imported in 1980, FN's .223 CAL military rifle succeeded the .308 FAL and preceeded the .223 FNC, at first declared illegal but later given amnesty, only 20 were imported by Browning and most remain in NIB condition.

$8,500 $7,500 $6,500 $5,500 $4,750 $4,100 $3,600

FNC MODEL – .223 Rem. (5.56mm) cal., lightweight combat carbine, 16 or 18 1/2 in. barrel, NATO approved, 30 shot mag., 8.4 lbs. Disc. 1987.

$2,950 $2,700 $2,550 $2,100 $1,900 $1,650 $1,500

Add $350 for Paratrooper model (16 or 18 1/2 in. barrel).

While rarer, the 16 in. barrel model incorporated a flash hider that did not perform as well as the flash hider used on the standard 18 1/2 in. barrel.

Mid-1987 retail on this model was $749 (Standard Model) and $782 (Paratrooper Model). The last MSR was $2,204 (Standard Model) and $2,322 (Paratrooper Model) - these prices reflected the last exchange rate and special order status of these models.

SHOTGUNS: SxS

FN ANSON STANDARD GRADE – 12 or 16 ga., 26, 28, or 30 (most common) in. barrels, boxlock action, with or w/o ejectors, DT, checkered walnut stock, Greener style crossbolt, FN legend roll engraved on bottom of boxlock, minor engraving on and around screws. Mfg. circa 1910-1940.

$1,500 $1,300 $950 $625 $550 $375 $325

Add $150 for factory checkered stock options or semi-pistol grip option.
Add $200+ for more elaborate engraving. FN offered six luxury engraving styles.
Subtract $50-$100 if w/o ejectors.
Subtract approx. $250 for replacement buttplate (not original), if in 95%+ original condition.

FN NEW ANSON STANDARD GRADE – 12 or 16 ga., 26, 28, or 30 (most common) in. barrels, boxlock action, with or w/o ejectors, DT, checkered walnut stock, FN legend hand engraved on top of the barrels, minor engraving on and around screws. Mfg. circa 1930-1968.

$1,400 $1,150 $850 $550 $475 $350 $300

Add $150 for factory checkered stock options or semi-pistol grip option.
Add $200+ for more elaborate engraving. FN offered six luxury engraving styles.
Subtract approx. $250 for replacement buttplate (not original), if in 95%+ original condition.

FN SIDELOCK STANDARD GRADE – 12 or 16 ga., 26, 28, or 30 (most common) in. barrels, sidelock action, ejectors, DT, checkered walnut stock, minor engraving on sideplates Mfg. 1921-1950. Improved in 1930, and often referred to as the Model 1930.

$1,500 $1,300 $950 $625 $550 $375 $325

Add $200+ for more elaborate engraving. FN offered six luxury engraving styles.
Subtract approx. $250 for replacement buttplate (not original), if in 95%+ original condition.

GRADING - PPGS™	100%	98%	95%	90%	80%	70%	60%	LAST MSR

FABRYKA BRONI LUCZNIK - RADOM SP.ZO.O

Current manufacturer of commercial and military firearms located in Radom, Poland beginning circa 1923. Currently imported by Arms of America (AOA) beginning 2021. Previously imported by Inter Ordnance (I.O.) circa 2013-2017.

PISTOLS: SEMI-AUTO

MODEL .223 S MINI BERYL M1 (MINI BERYL PISTOL) – 5.56 NATO cal., GPO, 9.375 in. CHF barrel w/ pinned flash hider, 30 shot FB Radom Beryl mag., stamped receiver, hybrid iron sight/optics mount rail on rear sight block, shortened polymer upper and lower handguard, ergonomic pistol grip, right side safety lever, rear trunnion angled sling loop, black finish, 6 lbs. Importation beginning 2021.

MSR $1,389	$1,250	$1,100	$950	$850	$700	$575	$450	

Add $50 for spare FB Radom rear trunnion.

RIFLES: SEMI-AUTO

BERYL "ARCHER" – 5.56 NATO cal., GPO, based on the Polish military wz. 96 "Beryl" rifle, 16.25 or 18 in. CHF barrel w/flash hider, 30 shot ProMag or Beryl mag., stamped reciever, adj. front and rear sights, detachable optics rail over the dust cover, choice of collapsible or fixed stock, tactical pistol grip, RH safety lever with bolt hold open, FB (Fabryka Broni) trademark on left side of the rear sight block, tactical sling swivels, Black polymer furniture, 7 lbs., Mfg. in Radom, Poland. Imported circa 2013-2017.

	$2,700	$2,375	$2,000	$1,825	$1,475	$1,225	$950	*$1,380*

FALCO, Srl

Current manufacturer established circa 1960, and located in Marcheno, Italy. Currently imported by Chiappa Firearms USA beginning in 2013, located in Dayton, OH. Previously imported by Accardi Importer, located in Vacaville, CA. Previously represented in Europe by Effebi, snc. Some models were imported by K.B.I. until 2002.

Falco manufactures a variety of good quality shotguns and rifles in various configurations, including O/U, SxS, combinations, and single shots. Falco is well-known for its folding action design. Falco also manufactures a single shot, SxS pistol in either 9mm Flobert or .410 bore with approx. 19 3/4 in. barrels. Please contact the U.S. importer directly for information on current availability and pricing.

FALCON FIREARMS

Previous manufacturer located in Northridge, CA from 1986-1990.

PISTOLS: SEMI-AUTO

PORTSIDER – .45 ACP cal., patterned after Colt M 1911 A-1, stainless steel, fixed sights, 5 in. barrel, 7 shot mag., available in left-hand only. Mfg. 1986-90.

	$500	$425	$375	$315	$270	$230	$200	*$580*

* ***Portsider Set*** – features right and left-hand models with matching serial numbers. Only 100 sets mfg. 1986-1987.

	$1,300	$1,100	$895	$785	$655	$550	$465	*$1,400*

GOLD FALCON – .45 ACP cal., machined receiver made from solid 17 Kt. gold alloy, stainless steel slide, diamond sighting system, choice of grips, standard or personalized engraving options. Only 50 mfg.

	$25,000	$17,500	$11,500	N/A	N/A	N/A	N/A	*$30,500*

FALKOR DEFENSE

Current AR-15 style rifle and pistol manufacturer located in Kalispell, MT beginning 2016.

Please refer to BlueBookOfGunValues.com to order the *Blue Book of AR-15s & Variations*, available as a book or online subscription.

FAMARS di ABBIATICO & SALVINELLI Srl (CURRENT MFG.)

Current long gun and accessories manufacturer located in Gardone, Italy. Exclusively imported by Famars U.S.A., located in Coventry, RI.

For individual model listings, please go to BlueBookOfGunValues.com/overflow.

FAMARS di ABBIATICO & SALVINELLI Srl (MFG. 1967-2012)

Previous manufacturer from 1967-2012, established by Mario Abbiatico and Remo Salvinelli, and located in Gardone, Italy. Famars USA is currently selling the remaining Famars inventory, in addition to offering a new line of luxury knives and shooting accessories. Previously distributed and imported by Chris Batha, located in Okatie, SC, and by Robin Hollow Outfitters, located in Addieville, RI. Previously distributed by William Larkin Moore, located

GRADING - PPGS™	100%	98%	95%	90%	80%	70%	60%	LAST MSR

in Scottsdale, AZ, the First National Gun Banque, located in Colorado Springs, CO and by Fieldsport, located in Traverse City, MI. Previously imported by Dewing's Fly and Gun, located in West Palm Beach, FL, and by A&S of America, located in Jefferson Boro, PA.

For individual model listings, please visit the Online Only/Removed Manufacturer's List at BlueBookOfGunValues.com.

FANZOJ, JOHANN

Current long gun manufacturer established in 1790 and located in Ferlach, Austria. Consumer direct sales.

Johann Fanzoj is a nine-generations family business, and premium maker of fine arms and rifles, who brings new visions to an old craft. The company uses advanced materials and aerospace technology to build not only beautiful, but very precise long arms. Among their product range are single shot stalking rifles, bolt action rifles, double rifles and double shotguns, as well as combination guns in any possible configuration. All models are P.O.R., available for ultra-customization.

RIFLES

Fanzoj is capable of manufacturing almost any configuration of rifle, including SxSs, three-barrelled guns, bolt actions, double rifles, stalking rifles, and even combination guns. All models are P.O.R. with many options. In 2010, the company released the Mauser 98 Action made from titanium. They also offer a single shot stalking rifle with all parts made of titanium. Please contact the company directly for a customized quotation.

SHOTGUNS

Fanzoj currently manufactures classic double shotguns, SxS, and soon also O/U configurations. A specialty of Fanzoj is their Three-barreled game gun - a mechanical masterpiece available in 20, 28, and .410 bore. All models are currently P.O.R., with a wide variety of available options. Please contact the company directly for a customized quotation.

FARQUHARSON

Single shot rifle configuration designed by John Farquharson in 1871. The Farquharson was influential during the height of the British Empire, and was popular with sportsmen and soldiers alike.

Previously, Ballard Arms of Onsted, MI built a rifle based on this configuration until their closing in 2016. Please contact the company directly for more information, including pricing, availability and delivery time.

FAUSTI STEFANO Srl

Current manufacturer established in 1948 and located in Marcheno, Italy. Currently imported beginning 2009 by Fausti USA, located in Fredericksburg, VA.

For individual model listings, please go to BlueBookOfGunValues.com/overflow.

FAUSTI STEFANO s.r.l.

FAXON FIREARMS

Current AR-15 style rifle, pistol, and parts/components manufacturer located in Cincinnati, OH since 2012.

Please refer to BlueBookOfGunValues.com to order the *Blue Book of AR-15s & Variations*, available as a book or online subscription.

FEATHER INDUSTRIES, INC.

Previous manufacturer located in Boulder, CO until 1995.

DERRINGERS

GUARDIAN ANGEL CENTERFIRE – 9mm Para. or .38 Spl. cal., O/U design, stainless steel, double action backup derringer. Mfg. 1988-89 only.

	100%	98%	95%	90%	80%	70%	60%	LAST MSR
	$225	$190	$160	$130	$100	$80	$60	*$140*

This model has interchangeable loading blocks that allow shooting 9mm Para. or .38 Spl. There is no exposed hammer and trigger is totally enclosed.

GUARDIAN ANGEL RIMFIRE – .22 LR or .22 WMR cal., design is similar to 9mm Para./.38 Spl. model, loading block breech, 2 in. barrel, fixed sights, 12 oz. Mfg. 1990-95.

	100%	98%	95%	90%	80%	70%	60%	LAST MSR
	$150	$125	$100	$75	$60	$55	$50	*$120*

Add $30 for individual extra loading blocks.

This model has interchangeable loading blocks that allow shooting .22 LR or .22 WMR. There is no exposed hammer and the trigger is totally enclosed.

GRADING - PPGS™	100%	98%	95%	90%	80%	70%	60%	LAST MSR

PISTOLS: SEMI-AUTO

MINI-AT – .22 LR cal., pistol variation of the AT-22, 5 1/2 in. shrouded barrel, 20 shot mag., approx. 2 lbs. Mfg. 1986-89.

$300 $265 $235 $195 $165 $145 $135 *$220*

RIFLES: SEMI-AUTO

AT-9 – 9mm Para. cal., blowback action, 16 in. barrel, available with 10 (C/B 1994), 25*, 32 (disc.), or 100 (disc. 1989) shot mag., 5 lbs. Mfg. 1988-1995.

$850 $775 $700 $650 $600 $550 $500 *$500*

Add $250 for 100 shot drum mag.

AT-22 – .22 LR cal., semi-auto blowback action, 17 in. detachable shrouded barrel, collapsible metal stock, adj. rear sight, with sling and swivels, 20 shot mag., 3 1/4 lbs. Mfg. 1986-1995.

$325 $275 $250 $240 $230 $220 $215 *$250*

F9 – 9mm Para. cal., blowback action, 16 in. barrel, fixed polymer buttstock. Mfg. 1992-1995.

$725 $675 $600 $550 $485 $450 $375 *$535*

F2 – .22 LR cal., blowback action, 17 in. detachable shrouded barrel, 20 shot mag., adj. rear sight, fixed polymer buttstock, sling swivels. Mfg. 1992-1995.

$295 $240 $215 $200 $185 $175 $160 *$280*

KG-9 – 9mm Para. cal., blowback action, 25 or 50 shot mag., tactical configuration. Mfg. 1989 only.

$850 $775 $700 $650 $600 $550 $500 *$560*

Add $100 for 50 shot mag.

KG-22 – .22 LR cal., blowback action, 20 shot mag., tactical configuration. Mfg. 1989 only.

$395 $350 $300 $275 $255 $245 $235 *$300*

SAR-180 – .22 LR cal., blowback action, 17 1/2 in. barrel, 165 shot drum mag., fully adj. rear sight, walnut stock with combat style pistol grip and forend, 6 1/4 lbs. Mfg. 1989 only.

$695 $625 $575 $525 $475 $440 $400 *$500*

Add $250 for 165 shot drum mag.
Add $200 for retractable stock.
Add $395 for laser sight.

This variation was also manufactured for a limited time by ILARCO (Illinois Arms Company), previously located in Itasca, IL.

SATURN 30 – 7.62x39mm Kalashnikov cal., gas operated, 19 1/2 in. barrel, composite stock with large thumbhole pistol grip, 5 shot detachable mag., drilled and tapped for scope mounts, adj. rear sight, 8 1/2 lbs. Mfg. 1990 only.

$800 $700 $625 $575 $525 $450 $425 *$695*

FEATHER USA/AWI LLC

Previous firearms and current parts manufacturer established 1996, located in Eaton, CO.

For individual model listings, please go to BlueBookOfGunValues.com/overflow.

FEDERAL

Current trademark of shotguns manufactured by Kale Silah, located in Konya, Turkey. No current U.S. importation.

SHOTGUNS

Federal branded shotguns manufactured in Turkey are currently available in both O/U and semi-auto configurations. Please contact the manufacturer directly for U.S. availability and pricing.

FEDERAL ENGINEERING CORPORATION

Previous manufacturer located in Chicago, IL.

RIFLES: SEMI-AUTO

XC-220 – .22 LR cal., 16 5/16 in. barrel, 28 shot mag., machined steel action, 7 1/2 lbs. Mfg. 1984-89.

$495 $450 $400 $350 $320 $295 $275

XC-450 – .45 ACP cal. only, 16 1/2 in. barrel length, 30 shot mag., fires from closed bolt, machined steel receiver, 8 1/2 lbs. Mfg. 1984-89.

$950 $825 $750 $675 $600 $550 $500

XC-900 – 9mm Para. cal., 16 1/2 in. barrel length, 32 shot mag., fires from closed bolt, machined receiver action, 8 lbs. Mfg. 1984-89.

$950 $825 $750 $675 $600 $550 $500

GRADING - PPGS™ 100% 98% 95% 90% 80% 70% 60% LAST MSR

FEDERAL ORDNANCE, INC.

Previous manufacturer, importer, and distributor located in South El Monte, CA from 1966-1992. Briklee Trading Co. bought the remaining assets of Federal Ordnance, Inc. in late 1992, and continued to import various firearms until circa 1998.

For individual model listings, please go to BlueBookOfGunValues.com/overflow.

FEINMECHANISCHE ENTWICKLUNGEN GmbH

Current bolt action rifle company located in Koln, Germany. No current U.S. importation.

Also known as Steel Action Gmbh. Please contact the company directly for more information on their models including price, options, and availability.

FEINWERKBAU

Current manufacturer established circa 1951, and located in Oberndorf, Germany. Currently imported beginning 2005 by Brenzovich Firearms Training Center (B.F.T.C.), located in Fort Hancock, Texas. Previously imported until 2004 by Nygord Precision, located in Prescott, AZ.

Feinwerkbau manufactures some of the world's finest quality target rifles and pistols (.22 LR rimfire and airgun). Target rifles and pistols have had limited importation into the U.S.

Feinwerkbau also manufactures world championship winning airguns and a black powder pistol. For more information and current pricing on both new and used Feinwerkbau airguns, please refer to the *Blue Book of Airguns* - also available as an online subscription. For more information on the black powder pistol, please refer to the *Blue Book of Modern Black Powder Arms* (also available online).

PISTOLS: SEMI-AUTO, RIMFIRE

MODEL AW-93 - .22 LR cal., 6 in. barrel, 5 shot mag., ergonomically designed stippled walnut grips with adj. heel, unique damper prevents muzzle jump and recoil, satin nickel receiver finish, bolt burnished, top-of-the-line Target pistol, adj. two-stage trigger, adj. rear sight, right or left-hand grip, current mfg. includes plastic case, approx. 2 1/2 lbs. New 1993.

MSR $2,443 $2,275 $1,925 $1,600 $1,400 $1,150 $950 $850

* ***Model AW-93 Lightweight*** - similar to standard Model AW-93, except has lightened frame, blue aluminum damper/weight underneath slide, 2 1/3 lbs. Limited importation began 2004.

MSR $2,527 $2,350 $1,975 $1,650 $1,425 $1,175 $975 $850

RIFLES: BOLT ACTION, RIMFIRE

MODEL 2000 - .22 LR cal. only, single shot, match target bolt action rifle, fully adj. trigger, walnut stocks, four variations featuring different specifications. Importation disc. 1988.

* ***Model 2000 Universal Model*** - 26 3/8 in. barrel, aperture sights, stippled pistol grip and forearm, 9 3/4 lbs.

$1,150 $925 $850 $735 $650 $595 $550 ***$1,395***

Add $350 for electronic trigger.
Add $160 for left-hand variation.

* ***Model 2000 Mini (Junior)*** - 22 in. barrel, aperture sights, stippled pistol grip, 9 1/8 lbs.

$1,025 $875 $825 $700 $625 $575 $525 ***$1,225***

Add $350 for electronic trigger.
Add $150 for left-hand variation.

* ***Model 2000 Match Model*** - 26 1/4 in. barrel, adj. cheekpiece on stock, stippled pistol grip and forearm, aperture sights.

$1,075 $895 $825 $700 $625 $575 $525 ***$1,285***

Add $390 for electronic trigger.
Add $113 for left-hand variation.

* ***Model 2000 Running Target*** - adj. cheekpiece on stock, thumbhole stippled pistol grip, no sights, for running boar competition.

$1,150 $925 $850 $735 $650 $595 $550 ***$1,398***

Add $142 for left-hand variation.

MODEL 2600 UNIVERSAL - .22 LR cal. only, similar design to Model 600 air rifle, single shot, 26.3 in. barrel, aperture sights, 10.6 lbs. Imported 1986-94.

$1,425 $1,125 $925 $850 $735 $650 $595 ***$1,695***

Add $160 for left-hand variation.

MODEL 2600 ULTRA MATCH FREE RIFLE – .22 LR cal., single shot match gun based on Model 2600 action, 26.1 in. barrel, laminated stock with thumbhole, fully adj. aperture sights, 14 lbs. 1 oz. Mfg. 1986-94.

$2,175 $1,750 $1,400 $1,150 $925 $850 $735 *$2,498*

Add $250 for electronic trigger (disc. 1988).
Add $152 for left-hand variation.

MODEL 2602 UNIVERSAL (UIT) RIFLE – .22 LR cal., designed for Match competition, state-of-the-art Target rifle with different color wood laminations possible, adj. cheekpiece, short or long barrel, two-stage trigger. Mfg. 1997-2003.

$1,450 $1,275 $1,125 $975 $850 $725 $600 *$1,615*

Add $125 for left-hand action.

MODEL 2602 FREE RIFLE – .22 LR cal., standard Match rifle with red and blue anodized aluminum stock with adj. cheekpiece and buttplate, and adj. hand rest, 16 3/4 or 26 1/2 in. barrel with unique 13 3/4 in. squared-off barrel sleeve with sight, diopter sights, top-of-the-line competition rifle, approx. 13.86 lbs. Mfg. 1997-2003.

$2,035 $1,800 $1,575 $1,350 $1,175 $1,000 $850 *$2,365*

Add $155 for left-hand action.

MODEL 2602 SUPER MATCH – .22 LR cal., Super Match variation featuring state- of-the-art design, adj. stock, comb, LOP, and trigger pull. Disc. 2003.

$2,550 $2,175 $1,800 $1,575 $1,350 $1,175 $1,000 *$2,995*

Add $130 for left-hand action.
Subtract $130 for Model 2602 Sport RT.

MODEL 2602 SPORT – .22 LR cal., sporter variation of the Model 2602, short or long barrel, right or left-hand action, two-stage trigger, laminated wood stock with red stripes and thumbhole, adj. cheekpiece and buttplate, approx. 12 3/4 lbs. Mfg. 2000-2003.

$1,950 $1,750 $1,525 $1,325 $1,175 $1,000 $850 *$2,240*

MODEL 2700 UNIVERSAL – .22 LR cal., competition rifle, single shot, features laminate stock and adj. cheekpiece, right or left-hand action, adj. two-stage trigger, adj. aluminum buttplate, muzzle brake, approx. 12 lbs. Imported 2004-disc.

$2,300 $1,900 $1,575 $1,275 $1,075 $875 $750 *$2,484*

MODEL 2700 FREE RIFLE SUPER MATCH – .22 LR cal., current top-of-the-line rifle, 27 in. barrel, single shot, right or left-hand action, adj. two-stage trigger, features blue or silver aluminum stock, pivoting anatomical grip and interior sliding weight, adj. cheekpiece, adj. buttplate, sling holder with anatomical handstop, 12 1/4-13 1/2 lbs. Imported 2004-disc.

$3,275 $2,850 $2,500 $2,225 $1,875 $1,575 $1,375 *$3,601*

MODEL 2800 – right or left-hand, adj. single stage or two-stage match trigger, marked "W" on wood stock, adj. cheekpiece, ergonomic grip, standard with hook plate X-line, approx. 12 lbs. Importation began 2019.

Please contact the importer directly for information on this model.

* ***Model 2800 ALU*** – right or left-hand, adj. barrel dampener, adj. single stage or two-stage match trigger, full aluminum chassis construction, adj. cheekpiece, ergonomic grip, standard with hook plate X-line stock, approx. 12 lbs. Importation began 2021.

Please contact the importer directly for information on this model.

FELIXTEAM

Current trademark of 1911-style pistols manufactured by Felix Mogdans, located in Vaihingen/Enz, Germany. No current U.S. importation.

PISTOLS: SEMI-AUTO

M1911 – .45 ACP cal., 6 in. competition match barrel, double slide serrations, 7 shot mag., blue steel construction, left or right-hand ejection port, adj. rear sight, beavertail safety.

Please contact the company directly for pricing and U.S. availability on this model.

FELK TRAILERS PTY LTD.

Previous pistol manufacturer located in Australia circa 1998-2000.

PISTOLS: SEMI-AUTO

MTF919 – 9mm Para. cal., designed similar to a compact Glock with trigger safety, striker fire, black polymer frame, metal slide, 3 in barrel, 10 shot clear plastic mag., limited importation during the late 1990s.

$395 $275 $225 $200 $175 $150 $135

GRADING - PPGS™	100%	98%	95%	90%	80%	70%	60%	LAST MSR

FEMARU

Previously manufactured by Femaru-Fegyver és Gépgyár R.T. located in Budapest, Hungary.

PISTOLS: SEMI-AUTO

MODEL 1929 (29M) - .380 ACP cal., 3.93 in. barrel, 8 shot mag., identifiable by squared-off rear slide with vertical serrations, two-piece walnut grips, approx. 50,000 mfg.

$795	$600	$400	$300	$200	$165	$145	

MODEL 1937 (37M) - .32 ACP or .380 ACP cal., 3.93 in. barrel, 8 shot mag., commercial blue finish, left slide marking "FEMARU FEGYVER ES GEPGYAR RT. 37M", vertically grooved 2-piece walnut grips, approx. 200,000 mfg. (.380 ACP cal.) for Hungarian service before Nazi variations began (dubbed "Pistole Modell 37 (ung)," circa 1941), Nazi marked "jhv 41" or "jhv 44", 27 oz.

$625	$550	$475	$350	$275	$225	$175	

Add 50% for Waffenamt proofing (.32 ACP only).
Add another 100% if with holster and 2 matching mags.

FROMMER STOP POCKET AUTO - .32 ACP or .380 ACP cal., 6 or 7 shot, 3 7/8 in. barrel, fixed sights, blue, rubber grips, locked breech, external hammer. Mfg. 1912-1920.

$650	$500	$400	$350	$300	$250	$200	

Add 50% for .380 ACP cal.

FROMMER BABY POCKET AUTO - .32 ACP or .380 ACP cal., 2 in. barrel, 5 or 6 shot, external hammer, fixed sights, rubber grips, locked breech, blue finish.

$400	$350	$300	$250	$200	$150	$100	

FROMMER LILIPUT AUTO - .25 ACP cal., blowback action, 6 shot, 2.14 in. barrel, blue, hard rubber grips. Mfg. in early 1920s.

$400	$300	$200	$160	$140	$125	$90	

FROMMER MODEL 1910 - 7.65mm Roth/Steyr cal., rare and only infrequently encountered. Estimated serial range 1-10,000.

$3,000	$2,500	$2,000	$1,500	$1,250	$1,000	$750	

FERLACH GUNS

Includes those firearms manufactured in Ferlach, Austria from 1558 to present. The Ferlach Guild (Genossenschaft) represented most of Ferlach's gunmakers until it was dissolved in 2004.

Many people mistakenly believe that Ferlach is a trademark - it is not. Rather, it is a small village in Austria where a gun guild was started as early as 1558. At that time, it was absolutely necessary that all the people involved in fabricating a firearm were located together in close proximity. This enabled the barrel maker, the stock maker, and the lock mechanism maker to work together closely to ensure that everyone was performing their task(s) correctly, effectively and efficiently. As the individual skills became better and more refined, more and more firearms were manufactured. Eventually, individual gunsmiths began to put their name on the barrel or frame of those guns which they had either manufactured solely or with the help of their fellow Ferlach craftsmen. Since all Ferlach firearms are essentially hand made per individual special order, very few are exactly alike. In the past, the gunsmiths of Ferlach have produced almost every type of shoulder arm imaginable, including such modern firearms as superposed and juxtaposed rifles and shotguns, hammerless drillings, repeating rifles, 3 barrel rifles, combination guns, 4 barrel rifles/shotguns/combination guns (called Vierlings), hammer guns of every type, etc. Some of these specimens represent the highest refinement in the gunmakers trade. Because of the almost unlimited variety of Ferlach variations, it is recommended that a COMPETENT appraisal is procured before buying or selling a specimen.

As is the case with many other European firearms, those models with desirable American features will generally outperform those with European specifications (i.e. a Ferlach sidelock combination gun that is 20 ga. x .243 Win. will be more desirable than a similar specimen chambered for 16 ga. w/ 2 1/2 in. chambers x 5.6 by 50Rmm), even though metric caliber ammunition is now more afforadable in the U.S. than it used to be. Original condition and overall beauty are the primary factors to consider when contemplating buying or selling a Ferlach longarm. Other considerations include: type of action, difficulty of fabrication (Vierlings are very complicated to construct), caliber/gauge desirability, notoriety of gunsmith on barrel legend, elaborateness of embellishments, condition, rarity, accessories, and any provenance a specimen might have.

Today's master gunsmiths of Ferlach carry on the Old World tradition of quality in every respect. Most guns manufactured today are by individual special order with a wide range of calibers/gauges and other special features and options. As of this writing, these gunsmiths in alphabetical order are: Ludwig Borovnik, Johann Fanzoj, Wilfried Glanznig, Josef Hambrusch, Karl Hauptmann, Gottfried Juch, Josef Just, Jakob Koschat, Peter Michelitsch, Johann & Walter Outschar, Herbert Scheiring, Benedikt Winkler, and Josef Winkler. Anyone wishing to contact these master gunmakers should contact the individual gunmaker.

GRADING - PPGS™	100%	98%	95%	90%	80%	70%	60%	LAST MSR

FERLACHER WAFFEN PRÄZISIONSTECHNIK PRODUCTIONS GmbH & CO. KG.

Previous organization located in Ferlach, Austria.

When the Ferlach Guild was dissolved in 2004, gunmakers Fanzoj and Schiering bought the remaining assets and reopened the facility. The original function, namely to represent the gunmakers of Ferlach, did not change.

Please refer to the Ferlach Guns listing for a complete explanation and list of gunmakers.

FERLIB

Previous manufacturer and trademark established circa late 1940s-2005, and located in Gardone V.T., Italy. During 2005-2009, Ferlib entered into a partnership with B. Rizzini, and the new company was called Rizzini & Tanfoglio srl (see separate listing). SxS rifles were imported and distributed by Dakota Arms, Inc. 1999-2005. Previously distributed until 1999 by Hi-Grade Imports located in Gilroy, CA.

For individual model listings, please go to BlueBookOfGunValues.com/overflow.

FERRELL, ROGER

Please refer to Roger's Gun Works, Inc. in the R section for up-to-date information.

FIALA ARMS AND EQUIPMENT CO.

Previous manufacturer located in New Haven, CT. Fiala Arms and Equipment Co. was founded circa 1920, and went bankrupt shortly thereafter. Fiala Outfits, Inc. of New York City, NY reportedly bought the remaining guns, parts, and inventory and sold them between 1922 until approximately 1930. Also see Schall & Co.

PISTOLS: SLIDE ACTION

FIALA REPEATING PISTOL – .22 LR cal., Fiala Arms and Equipment Co., manual operation, blue finish, interchangeable 3, 7 1/2 (fixed or smoothbore), or 20 (smoothbore optional) in. barrel, optional detachable walnut buttstock early dovetail or screw to frame connection, smooth or ribbed vertical striation walnut grips, rear sight is square notched blade that tips up into an elevated adj. aperture sight, marked "Fiala Arms and Equipment Co. Inc./New Haven Conn./Patents Pending" on right side of frame behind the grip, and "MODEL 1920/Made in U.S.A." on the right side of the frame above the trigger guard, left side of frame marked "FIALA ARMS" above the image of a polar bear with "TRADE MARK" below polar bear in area above the trigger guard. Most Fialas have serial numbers between 1 and 5566 with a few outliers in the 8000 range. The Columbia marked guns are scattered in the lower Fiala serial number range between 1059 and 2837.

* ***Fiala Repeating Pistol cased with all 3 barrels and screw attached stock***

	100%	98%	95%	90%	80%	70%	60%
	$3,000	$2,750	$2,500	$2,000	$1,500	$1,250	$1,000

Add 15% for dovetail frame attachment.
Add $100 for smoothbore 20 in. barrel.

This model was available with three different case variations - canvas roll up, black or tan leatherette cased (purple velvet lined and fitted with a keyed lock). Some pistols are also marked "Columbia Arms Company" or "Botwinik Brothers".

This model has been classified by the ATF as a Curio or Relic, and is collectible when complete with all accoutrements.

* ***Fiala Repeating Pistol (gun only)***

	100%	98%	95%	90%	80%	70%	60%
	$800	$700	$600	$475	$400	$350	$300

Add $200 for uncased pistol with screw attached stock. Add $300 for uncased pistol with dovetail attached stock. Add $150 for extra 3 in. barrel, $150 for extra 7 1/2 in. barrel, $200 for extra 20 in. rifled barrel, or $300 for extra 20 in. smoothbore barrel.

FIERCE FIREARMS, LLC

Current custom manufacturer located in Gunnison, UT.

Fierce Firearms manufactures custom bolt action rifles in various calibers to customer specifications with many options to choose from including stainless steel or titanium action, stainless steel or carbon barrels, stock dipping, paint jobs, and various finishes.

RIFLES: BOLT ACTION

Fierce Firearms offers Long Range Rifle packages for the Edge ($3,360 base MSRP) and Fury ($3,350 base MSRP). Packages include: caliber choice, removable e-brake, Talley steel rings & bases, rifle sling, baseball cap, one year subscription to Hunting Illustrated magazine, and Americase aluminum airline rifle case. Additional upgrades are available. Please contact the manufacturer directly for availability and pricing on these packages.

GRADING - PPGS™	100%	98%	95%	90%	80%	70%	60%	LAST MSR

EDGE/CARBON EDGE – .22-250, 6.5 Creedmoor, 6.5 PRC, 7mm-08, .308 Win., 7mm Rem., .28 Nosler, .300 Win. Mag., .300 PRC, .300 RUM, .338 Lapua, or .375 H&H cal., 24 or 26 in. carbon fiber bull (Carbon Edge) or stainless steel fluted barrel (Edge), detachable speed box mag., mini claw extractor with control round feed, adj. trigger, black/gray carbon fiber stock, Limbsaver recoil pad, 3-pos. True Lock safety, Armor Black, Armor Bronze, or Titanium Grey Cerakote action finish, 6.9 lbs. New 2014.

MSR $2,785	$2,370	$2,075	$1,780	$1,610	$1,300	$1,065	$930	

Add $100 for stainless steel radial break (Edge). Add $150 for muzzle brake w/cap (Carbon Edge). Add $150 for Midnight, Urban, Blackout, Phantom, or Blaze patterned stock. Add $160 for Kuiu or Kuiu Verde patterned stock. Add $200 (Carbon Edge) or $250 (Edge) for thumbhole custom stock, bedded and fitted. Add $200 (Carbon Edge) or $250 (Edge) for custom LOP on stock. Add $585 for Carbon Edge model. Add $325 for left-handed model.

* ***CT Edge*** – .22-250, 6.5 Creedmoor, 6.5 PRC, 7mm Rem. Mag., .28 Nosler, .300 WSM, .300 Win., .300 RUM, .300 PRC, .338 Lapua, or .375 H&H cal., titanium action, 23, 24, or 26 in. carbon fiber barrel, target crown, speed detachable box mag., mini claw extractor with control round feed, adj. trigger, black/gray carbon fiber Monte Carlo stock, 3-position True Lock safety, Bronze, Titanium Grey, or Armour Black Cerakote finish, 5.9 lbs. New 2014.

MSR $3,975	$3,380	$2,950	$2,535	$2,300	$1,860	$1,520	$1,185	

Add $150 for Midnight, Urban, Blackout, Phantom, or Blaze patterned stock.
Add $160 for Kuiu or Kuiu Verde patterned stock.

* ***Edge LR*** – 6.5 Creedmoor, 6.5 PRC, 7mm Rem. Mag., .28 Nosler, .300 Win., .300 RUM, .300 PRC, or .338 Lapua cal., stainless steel action, 24 or 26 in. stainless steel fluted match grade barrel, Last Guard coating, 3 shot, carbon fiber stock, 3-position safety. Mfg. 2020 only.

	$2,370	$2,075	$1,780	$1,610	$1,305	$1,065	$930	*$2,785*

* ***Tactical Edge*** – 6.5 Creedmoor, .308 Win., .300 Win., or .338 Lapua, 24 or 26 in. carbon fiber match grade fluted bull barrel, target crown, speed detachable box mag., mini claw extractor w/control round feed and extended bolt handle, McMillan A3 tactical adj. stock or Manners PRS-2 tactical stock, 3-pos. True Lock safety, 20 MOA one-piece, black/gray carbon fiber stock, 7.1 lbs. Disc. 2019.

	$3,550	$3,100	$2,650	$2,400	$1,950	$1,600	$1,250	*$4,175*

Add $500 for C3 carbon barrel.
Add $200 for custom trigger.
Add $195 for titanium e-brake.

* ***TI Edge*** – .22-250, 6.5 Creedmoor, 6.5 PRC, 7mm Rem. Mag., .28 Nosler, .300 WSM, .300 in., .300 RUM, .300 PRC, .338 Lapua, or .375 H&H cal., 24 or 26 in. stainless steel match grade fluted barrel, target crown, speed detachable box mag., titanium action, mini claw extractor with control round feed, adj. trigger, carbon fiber stock, cheekpiece, 3-pos. True Lock safety, black & gray, camo, or True Timber finish, various finishes available, 6.4 lbs. Mfg. 2014-2019.

	$3,100	$2,700	$2,300	$2,100	$1,700	$1,400	$1,100	*$3,650*

FURY/CARBON FURY – 6.5 Creedmoor, 6.5 PRC (new 2019), 7mm Rem., .28 Nosler, .300 WSM (disc. 2020), .300 Win. Mag., .300 PRC or .300 RUM cal., 24 or 26 in. stainless steel or carbon fiber barrel, adj. trigger, black/gray carbon fiber stock, 3-pos. safety, Tungsten, black, bronze, or gray Cerakote finish, 6.9 lbs. New 2016.

MSR $2,385	$2,030	$1,775	$1,525	$1,380	$1,110	$910	$795	

Add $100 for muzzle brake w/cap (Carbon Fury). Add $150 for Midnight, Urban, Blackout, Phantom, or Blaze carbon fiber patterned stock.
Add $160 for Kuiu or Kuiu Verde patterned carbon fiber stock.
Add $250 thumbhole custom stock, bedded and fitted.
Add $250 for custom LOP on stock. Add $510 for Carbon Fury model.

* ***Fury LR (Long Range)*** – .22-250, 6.5 Creedmoor, 6.5 PRC, 7mm-08, .308 Win., 7mm Rem., .28 Nosler, .300 Win. Mag., .300 PRC, .300 RUM, .338 Lapua or .375 H&H cal., 24 or 26 in. match grade stainless steel barrel w/target crown, detachable speed box mag., adj. match grade custom trigger tan w/black or black w/gray web custom carbon fiber stock, ergonomic vertical pistol grip, 3-pos. True Lock safety, Tungsten, black, gray or bronze Cerakote finish, 7.2 lbs. New 2017.

MSR $2,785	$2,365	$2,075	$1,775	$1,610	$1,300	$1,065	$930	

Add $150 for Midnight, Urban, Blackout, Phantom, or Blaze patterned carbon stock. Add $160 Kuiu or Kuiu Verde patterned carbon stock.

RIVAL/CARBON RIVAL LR – 6.5 Creedmoor, 6.5 PRC, 7mm Rem., .28 Nosler, .300 Win. Mag., .300 PRC, or .300 RUM cal., 20, 22, 24, or 26 in. carbon or stainless steel spiral fluted barrel, optional radial or directional muzzle brake, 3 shot, dual plunger system w/mini claw extractor, TriggerTech special trigger, carbon fiber LR stock in Carbon Phantom, Blaze, Blackout, or Forest pattern, built-in bipod rail,

GRADING - PPGS™	100%	98%	95%	90%	80%	70%	60%	LAST MSR

Armor Black, Midnight Bronze, or Titanium Grey Cerakote finish w/Last Guard coating, 6.5 (carbon) or 6.9 (steel) lbs. Mfg. 2020 only.

	$1,990	$1,740	$1,490	$1,355	$1,095	$895	$695	*$2,340*

Add $160 for Kuiu Vias or Kuiu Verde stock.
Add $150 for steel barrel radial or directional muzzle brake.
Add $125 for carbon barrel radial or $195 for NIX directional muzzle brake.
Add $470 for Carbon Rival LR model.

* ***Carbon Rival/CT Rival*** – 6.5 Creedmoor, 6.5 PRC, 7mm Rem., .28 Nosler, .300 Win. Mag., .300 PRC, or .300 RUM cal., stainless steel (Carbon Rival) or titanuim (CT Rival) action, 20 (CT Rival only), 22, 24, 26 in. spiral fluted carbon barrel with or w/o muzzle brake, dual plunger system w/mini claw extractor, Bix'n Andy Dakota trigger, C3 carbon fiber patterned stock w/ integrated bipod rail, Tungsten, black, gray, or bronze Cerakote finish, 5.8-6.8 lbs. New 2021.

MSR $ 2,665	$2,265	$1,980	$1,700	$1,540	$1,250	$1,025	$890

Add $125 for radial or $195 for NIX directional brake.
Add $160 for Kuiu Vias or Kuiu Verde patterned carbon stock.
Add $385 for CT Rival.

* ***Twisted Rival*** – 6.5 Creedmoor, 6.5 PRC, 7mm Rem., .28 Nosler, .300 Win. Mag., .300 PRC, or .300 RUM cal., 24 or 26 in., spiral fluted, match grade stainless steel, cyro treated barrel, Bix'n Andy adj. trigger, C3 carbon patterned stock w/integral bipod rail, Tungsten, gray, black, or bronze Cerakote finish, 6.5-6.7 lbs. New 2021.

MSR $2,355	$2,000	$1,750	$1,500	$1,360	$1,100	$900	$790

RIFLES: SEMI-AUTO

F-15 SIDEWINDER – .223 Wylde chamber or .22 Nosler cal., sporting side-charger, no forward assist and side charging handle, 16 in. match grade stainless steel hand lapped or C3 carbon barrel, Precision Velocity (mfg. 2020 only) or TriggerTech trigger, carbon pistol grip and handguard, full-length Picatinny rail, M-LOK design compatible w/bottom rails and accessories, ambi controls, black finish, 5.9-6.2 lbs., New 2019.

MSR $2,595	$2,200	$1,925	$1,650	$1,500	$1,210	$990	$865

Add $400 for C3 carbon barrel.

SHOTGUNS: SEMI-AUTO

MAYHEM FX – 12 ga., 3 1/2 in. chamber, 28 in. barrel, 3 Fierce flush chokes and one extended Fierce KO Custom extended choke, vented rib, Fierce XL trigger guard, High-VIS fiber optic front bead sight (green), Ergo slim contour forearm, Limbsaver recoil pad, swivel studs, rubberized pistol grip, MAX-GRIP contact points, oversized bolt release and handle, 100% True Timber Prairie or Strata camo pattern finish, 7.7 lbs. New 2021.

MSR $825	$700	$615	$525	$475	$385	$325	$275

FIGHTLITE INDUSTRIES (ARES DEFENSE SYSTEMS INC.)

Current semi-auto rifle and accessories manufacturer established in 1997, located in Melbourne, FL.

Please refer to BlueBookOfGunValues.com to order the *Blue Book of AR-15s & Variations*, available as a book or online subscription.

FINNCLASSIC

Current trademark owned and manufactured by Marocchi CD Europe, located in Brescia, Italy. Currently imported by Whitworth Arms LLC, located in May, TX since 2014. Previously imported by Network Retailing LLC, located in Canby, OR.

For individual model listings, please go to BlueBookOfGunValues.com/overflow.

FINNISH LION

Previous trademark manufactured by Valmet (now Tikka) located in Sweden. Limited importation into the U.S. by Mandall's Shooting Supplies, Inc. in Scottsdale, AZ.

RIFLES: BOLT ACTION

MATCH MODEL – .22 LR cal., single shot, 29 in. barrel, extended aperture sight, globe front sight, thumbhole stock, adj. hook butt. Mfg. 1937-72.

$495	$415	$360	$305	$250	$210	$195

GRADING - PPGS™	100%	98%	95%	90%	80%	70%	60%	LAST MSR

CHAMPION FREE MODEL – .22 LR cal., single shot, 29 in. barrel, double set trigger, full target stock and accessories. Mfg. 1965-72.

	100%	98%	95%	90%	80%	70%	60%	LAST MSR
	$580	$495	$440	$385	$330	$290	$265	

STANDARD ISU TARGET MODEL – .22 LR cal., single shot, 27 in. barrel, full target stock and accessories. Mfg. 1966-1977.

	100%	98%	95%	90%	80%	70%	60%	LAST MSR
	$330	$275	$250	$205	$180	$165	$150	

TARGET MODEL – .22 LR cal., target rifle with adj. stock and trigger, bolt action, single shot, aperture sights.

	100%	98%	95%	90%	80%	70%	60%	LAST MSR
	$725	$595	$495	$440	$385	$340	$295	*$795*

FIOCCHI OF AMERICA, INC.

Previous firearms importer and distributor located in Ozark, MO.

Fiocchi of America imported Pardini target pistols until 1990, and continues to manufacture a wide variety of ammunition both domestically and internationally. Fiocchi also imported Antonio Zoli shotguns until 1988. These trademarks can be found in their respective sections of this text.

FIREARMS INTERNATIONAL CORP. (F.I.C.)

Previous importer and assembler located in Washington, D.C.

F.I.C. manufactured and imported various pistols, rifles, and shotguns, including AYA, Astra (mostly Star D models), Bronco (.22 LR cal. single shot rifles and .410 bore single shot shotguns - see listings under Bronco), FN Supreme Mauser bolt action rifles, Iver Johnson Pony handguns, Rossi .22 cal. rifles, Sako rifles, Star pistols, and Unique pistols and rifles.

F.I.C. sold less than 100 Pony .380 ACPs, which were marked Colt before the Mustang was introduced - these are rare. While some models are relatively rare, collectability to date has been minimal and most models sell in the $150-$295 range, depending on overall desirability and condition.

Please look under individual manufacturer listings for values on similar models.

FIREARMS INTERNATIONAL, INC.

Previous manufacturer established in 1998, located in Houston, TX. Dealer sales.

For individual model listings, please go to BlueBookOfGunValues.com/overflow.

FIREBIRD PRECISION

Current AR-15 style rifle and shotgun manufacturer located in Mountainair, NM.

Firebird Precision builds custom made AR-15 style firearms in a variety of configurations and calibers. Each gun is built to individual customer specifications, and a wide variety of options and features are available. Please contact the company directly for options, delivery time, and an individualized price quotation.

FIREPOWER XTREME

Current trademark of pistols and rifles imported by American Tactical Imports located in Summerville, SC. Please refer to American Tactical Imports in the A section for listings.

FIRESTORM

Previous trademark of pistols and revolvers manufactured by Industria Argentina, Fabrinor, S.A.L., and Armscor. Distributed (master distributor) and imported from late 2000-2011 by SGS Imports, International Inc., located in Wanamassa, NJ.

PISTOLS: SEMI-AUTO

Beginning 2004, all Firestorm pistols were available with an integral locking system (ILS).

FIRESTORM SERIES – .22 LR, .32 ACP (disc. 2007), or .380 ACP cal., DA/SA, 3 1/2 or 6 (.22 LR cal. only, Sport Model) in. barrel, matte or duo-tone finish, 7 (.380 ACP) or 10 (.22 LR or .32 ACP) shot mag., 3-dot combat sights, anatomic rubber grips with finger grooves, 23 oz. Imported 2001-2011.

	100%	98%	95%	90%	80%	70%	60%	LAST MSR
	$280	$235	$185	$155	$145	$135	$125	*$329*

Add $6 for duo-tone finish.

MINI-FIRESTORM – 9mm Para., .40 S&W, or .45 ACP (new 2002) cal., DA/SA, 3 1/2 in. barrel, nickel, matte or duo-tone finish, 7 (.45 ACP cal.), 10, or 13 (9mm Para. only) shot mag., 3-dot sights, polymer grips, safeties include manual, firing pin, and decocking, 24 1/2-27 oz. Imported 2001-2009.

	100%	98%	95%	90%	80%	70%	60%	LAST MSR
	$365	$315	$275	$230	$195	$180	$165	*$425*

Add $10 for duo-tone finish.

Add $20 for nickel finish.

GRADING - PPGS™	100%	98%	95%	90%	80%	70%	60%	LAST MSR

FIRESTORM 45 GOVERNMENT – .45 ACP cal., SA, 5 1/8 in. barrel, matte or duo-tone finish, 7 shot mag., anatomic rubber grips with finger grooves, 36 oz. Imported 2001-2005.

$260	$230	$200	$180	$165	$150	$135	*$309*

Add $8 for duo-tone finish.

* ***Firestorm 45 Government Compact*** – .45 ACP cal., 4 1/4 in. barrel, otherwise similar to Firestorm 45 Government, 34 oz. Imported 2001-2005.

$260	$230	$200	$180	$165	$150	$135	*$309*

Add $8 for duo-tone finish.

* ***Firestorm 45 Government Mini Compact*** – .45 ACP cal., 3 1/8 in. barrel, chrome, matte, or duo-tone finish, 10 shot staggered mag., polymer grips, 31 oz. Imported 2001 only.

$280	$245	$215	$195	$180	$170	$155	*$324*

Add $17 for chrome finish.

FIRESTORM 45 GOVT. 1911 – .45 ACP cal., SA, patterned after the M1911, choice of matte or deluxe blue finish, 7 shot mag., current mfg. has skeletonized hammer, forward slide serrations, Novak style sights, diamond checkered walnut grips, and flared ejection port, 36 oz. Imported 2006-2007, reintroduced 2009.

$395	$360	$330	$295	$275	$250	$200	*$460*

Add $39 for deluxe blue finish.

REVOLVERS

FIRESTORM .38 SPL. – .38 Spl. cal., 6 shot, 2 in. barrel, choice of satin nickel, polished nickel, or parkerized metal finish. Mfg. by Armscor. Imported 2011.

$285	$235	$185	$155	$145	$135	$125	*$349*

Add $10 for satin nickel finish or $20 for polished nickel finish.

FIRESTORM .380 – .380 ACP cal., 7 shot, double action, blue finish with nickel accents. Imported by Ellet Brothers 2011. Mfg. by Armscor.

$265	$235	$195	$175	$150	$125	$100	*$335*

FLAVIO FARÈ

Current custom bolt action rifle manufacturer located in Vinzaglio, Italy. No current U.S. importation.

Flavio Farè manufactures high quality custom bolt action rifles. All guns are built per customer specifications. Please contact him directly for pricing, available options, and delivery time.

FLINT RIVER ARMORY LLC

Current AR-15 style pistol and rifle manufacturer located in Huntsville, AL.

Please refer to BlueBookOfGunValues.com to order the *Blue Book of AR-15s & Variations*, available as a book or online subscription.

FLODMAN GUNS

Current manufacturer established in 1978 and located in Järsta, Sweden. In 1992, Skullman Enterprise AB took over Flodman Guns. No current U.S. importation.

For individual model listings, please go to BlueBookOfGunValues.com/overflow.

FORBES RIFLE, LLC

Previous bolt action rifle manufacturer located in Westbrook, ME 2011-2015.

RIFLES: BOLT ACTION

M20B – .243 Win. (disc.), .260 Rem., .308 Win., or 7mm-08 Rem. cal., CNC machined action, #1 Forbes custom contour profile 21 in. alloy or stainless steel barrel, Sporter type crown, 3 shot internal mag., Timney adj. trigger, no sights, two-position safety, Carbon fiber Kevlar straight comb stock with integral cheek rest, Hunter Green, Coyote Brown, Charcoal Gray, or 8 camo finishes, right or left-hand, approx. 4 3/4 lbs. Mfg. 2011-2015.

$1,350	$1,150	$975	$875	$700	$575	$450	*$1,499*

Add $68 for stainless steel barrel or $100 for stainless steel barrel and action.
Add $85 for left-hand action.

M24B – .25-06 Rem., .270 Win., .280 Rem., .30-06, .35 Whelen (disc.), 6.5x55mm, .300 Win. Mag. (disc.), or 7mm Rem. Mag. (disc.) cal., CNC machined action, #2 Forbes custom contour profile 24 in. barrel with black oxide finish, Sporter-type crown, black composite (disc.) or carbon fiber Kevlar straight comb stock with integral cheek rest, no sights, Timney adj. trigger, two position safety, 3 shot internal mag., Hunter Green, Coyote Brown, Charcoal Gray, or 8 camo pattern finishes, approx. 5 1/2 lbs. Mfg. 2011-2015.

$1,350	$1,150	$975	$875	$700	$575	$450	*$1,499*

Add $68 for stainless steel barrel or $100 for stainless steel barrel and action.
Add $85 for left-hand action.

GRADING - PPGS™	100%	98%	95%	90%	80%	70%	60%	LAST MSR

M28B – .300 Win. Mag. or 7mm Rem. Mag. cal., CNC machined action, #2.5 Forbes custom contour profile 24 in. barrel with black oxide finish, Sporter-type crown, carbon fiber Kevlar straight comb stock with integral cheek rest, Pachmayr Decelerator buttpad, no sights, Timney adj. trigger, two-position safety, 3 shot internal mag., Hunter Green, Coyote Brown, Charcoal Gray, or 8 camo pattern finishes, approx. 6 lbs. Mfg. 2015 only.

	100%	98%	95%	90%	80%	70%	60%	LAST MSR
	$1,350	$1,150	$975	$875	$700	$575	$450	*$1,499*

Add $85 for left-hand action.

Add $68 for stainless steel barrel or $100 for stainless steel barrel and action.

FORT DISCOVERY, INC.

Current AR-15 style manufacturer located in Port Townsend, WA. Previously located in Sequim, WA.

Please refer to BlueBookOfGunValues.com to order the *Blue Book of AR-15s & Variations*, available as a book or online subscription.

FORT SOE SIA

Current trademark manufactured by the Science Industrial Association Fort of the Ministry of Internal Affairs of Ukraine, located in Vinnitsa, Ukraine. No current U.S. importation.

The Ministry manufactures a line of semi-auto pistols, semi-auto rifles, shotguns, and various military weapons with a wide variety of options. Currently, these guns are not imported into the U.S. Please contact the company directly for more information, including pricing and availability.

FORT WORTH FIREARMS

Previous manufacturer located in Fort Worth, TX 1995-2000.

For individual model listings, please go to BlueBookOfGunValues.com/overflow.

FOSTECH MFG.

Current AR-15 style pistol, rifle, semi-auto shotgun, and accessories manufacturer located in Seymour, IN.

Please refer to BlueBookOfGunValues.com to order the *Blue Book of AR-15s & Variations*, available as a book or online subscription.

FOX, A.H.

Current registered trademark manufactured by Connecticut Shotgun Manufacturing Company located in New Britain, CT. The A.H. Fox trademark was brought to life once again during 1993 when the Connecticut Shotgun Manufacturing Company began producing an A.H. Fox 20 gauge in 5 different grades. Previously manufactured in Philadelphia, PA 1903-1930, and in Utica, NY from 1930-approx. 1946. Manufactured by Savage 1930-1988.

Depending on the remaining A.H. Fox factory data, a factory letter authenticating the configuration of a particular Fox shotgun (not to be confused with the more recent Savage/Stevens designed Fox doubles) may be obtained by contacting the Cody Firearms Records Office at the Buffalo Bill Center of the West (www.centerofthewest.org) or through the A.H. Fox Gun Collectors Association (foxcollectors.com). Contact the Cody Firearms Records Office for more information and current factory letter pricing.

Mr. Ansley H. Fox first started manufacturing shotguns in circa 1896. This first company was called the Fox Gun Co. and was located in Baltimore, MD. Relatively few guns were made and surviving specimens today are very rare. After this venture, Mr. Fox was employed by the Baltimore Gun Co. for several years (circa 1900-1903). Following this period, he formed the Philadelphia Gun Co. where the predecessors to the A.H. Fox Gun Co. models were manufactured. These Philadelphia Gun Co. models (circa 1904) were the same as the newer Fox shotguns except that the hinge pin was removed. Sources indicate that the lowest grade was an A with the highest being an E (fully engraved and ultra rare). Mr. Fox went on to form the A.H. Fox Gun Co. in 1906. In addition to being an entrepreneur and trend setter, Mr. Fox also had the reputation of being an expert shot in his own right, winning more than a few events on the East Coast around the turn of the century.

The A.H. Fox Gun Company of Philadelphia, Pennsylvania, began production in 1905 and produced high quality double barrel shotguns until 1930. The Savage Arms Company, then of Utica, New York, acquired the Fox Company and produced these guns until 1942, when all but the utilitarian model B series guns were discontinued.

A.H. Fox guns are considered an American classic comparable to L.C. Smith, Parker, and others. Collector interest is high and will undoubtedly grow. The guns do not command quite as high a price as the Smith and Parker guns, but represent a fine investment collectible value.

Savage-made guns from 1930-1942 are usually valued similarly to the early A.H. Fox guns. The recent production B series are just not in the same class and are obviously not intended to be. They are lower priced by today's standards and are designed as a utility grade hunting gun. It is extremely important to note that prices listed below for the Philadelphia and Utica produced guns are for strictly original guns only. Values will vary widely for guns that have been altered or restored. Original case coloring on A.H. Fox shotguns did change throughout the course of the company's production and colors can vary widely. When dealing with higher graded guns, it is advised to seek professional guidance as there have been numerous upgrades and spurious examples in circulation. Just because a gun has a Factory letter does not neccessarily mean the gun is authentic.

The publisher would like to express his thanks to Mr. Josh Lowensteiner for his contributions in this section.

FOX COMPANY CHRONOLOGY

1906 - Company formed January 1906, A, B & C Grades introduced in 12 ga. only. D and F Grades introduced in 12 ga. in 1907. Ejector guns introduced in 1908. 1910 saw the introduction of the 12 ga. Sterlingworth - William H. Gough takes over as Chief of Engraving. Ansley Fox resigns in 1911 - first catalog showing Sterlingworth Model (called Model 1911). A-F Grades released in 16 and 20 ga. during 1912, as well as the addition of a 20 ga. Sterlingworth. 16 ga. Sterlingworth introduced in 1913. Fox/Kautsky single trigger introduced in 1914 - engineering transition complete. During 1915, the XE Grade was introduced. The B Grade was dropped in 1918. Single barrel trap guns (J, K, and L Grades) were introduced in 1919. 1920 saw the introduction of the M Grade single barrel trap. In 1922, both the G and HE Grades were released. Beavertail forend and vent. rib were introduced in 1927. 1929 was the Savage buy-out (November), GE Grade dropped. Company moved from Philadelphia, PA to Utica, NY in 1930. Skeeter Grade introduced in 1931 while the 20 ga. HE Grade was disc. 1932 saw the introduction of both the Trap Grade Double and SP Grade. Wildfowl Grade was introduced in 1934. 1935 was the last year of the K and L single barrel trap guns. 1937 was the last year for the J Grade single barrel trap gun. The last 16 and 12 ga. Sterlingworths were built in 1939. The outbreak of the war in 1941 saw the last FE Grade shipped, the Wildfowler Grade dropped, and the introduction of the Model B. 1942 was the last retail catalog. Factory records indicate that the last 12 ga. was shipped in 1945 and the last 20 ga. was shipped during 1946 (SP Grade shipped in December, 1946). However, guns continued to be assembled from left-over parts as late as the 1960s.

FOX SERIAL NUMBER ASSIGNMENTS

The publisher wishes to express his thanks to Mr. John Callahan and Mr. Gurney Brown for providing the model serialization and years of mfg. in this section.

Ser. # range 1-35,285 - 12 ga. Grades A-F
Ser. # range 200,000-203,975 - 20 ga. Grades A-F
Ser. # range 300,000-303,875 - 16 ga. Grades A-F
Ser. # range 50,000-161,556 - 12 ga. Sterlingworth
Ser. # range 250,000-271,304 - 20 ga. Sterlingworth
Ser. # range 300,000-378,481 - 16 ga. Sterlingworth
Ser. # range 400,000-450,568 - 12 ga. Single Barrel Traps, Grades J,K,L,M

FOX MODELS BY YEARS IN MFG.

Sterlingworth - 1910-1942 mfg.
Wildfowler - 1934-1940 mfg.
Trap Double - 1932-1936 mfg.
Skeeter - 1931 mfg.
SP - 1932-1946 mfg.
A - 1906-1942 mfg.
B - 1905-1918 mfg.
C - 1905-1942 mfg.
D - 1907-1942 mfg.
F - 1907-1940 mfg.
G - 1922-1929 mfg.
H - 1923-1942 mfg.
J - 1919-1939 mfg.
K - 1919-1934 mfg.
L - 1919-1934 mfg.
M - 1919-1936 mfg.
X - 1915-1942 mfg.

SHOTGUNS: SxS, CURRENT MFG.

Delivery time for custom orders is currently 10-14 months, depending on gauge and grade. The following models are manufactured by the Connecticut Manufacturing Co. located in New Britain, CT. These finely made shotguns have the following standard features: automatic safety, auto ejectors, DTs, Chromox 26, 28, or 30 in. barrels, individual barrel chokings, 2 3/4 in. chambers, scalloped receiver, Turkish Circassian walnut with hand-rubbed oil finish, choice of straight, semi-pistol, or full-pistol grip stock with custom dimensions, splinter forearm, ivory bead sights. Special order options are as follows: Krupp steel barrels ($350), Fox SST ($2,400), walnut upgrades ($800-$3,500), custom initials ($450-$1,000), personalized gold inlays on barrel ($1,000), skeleton steel buttplate ($900), beavertail forearm ($750), vent. rib ($1,000), and traditional leather trunk case with accessories ($650-$850). Multi-barrel sets (same or multi-gauge) are also available with prices ranging from $5,250-$9,000, depending on the

GRADING - PPGS™	100%	98%	95%	90%	80%	70%	60%	LAST MSR

grade. For additional information, please visit http://connecticutshotgun.com/A-H-Fox.

28 ga. and .410 bore guns on the following models (except Exhibition Grade) are by quotation only.

CE GRADE – 16 (new 1995), 20, 28 ga. (new 1995), or .410 bore (new 1995), engraved with fine scroll and game scenes, Grade I Turkish Circassian walnut. New 1993.

MSR $19,500	$19,500	$14,000	$12,000	$10,500	$9,750	$8,525	$6,250	

XE GRADE – gauges similar to CE Grade, scroll work and engraved game scenes, Grade II Turkish Circassian walnut. New 1993.

MSR $22,000	$22,000	$15,500	$12,750	$11,300	$10,500	$9,350	$7,250	

DE GRADE – gauges similar to CE Grade, intricate and extensive engraving, Grade III highly figured Turkish Circassian walnut. New 1993.

MSR $25,000	$25,000	$17,500	$14,750	$13,250	$11,750	$10,500	$9,000	

FE GRADE – gauges similar to CE Grade, gold inlays surrounded by different types of scroll work, Grade IV highly figured Turkish Circassian walnut with finest checkering. New 1993.

MSR $30,000	$30,000	$25,500	$21,500	$19,125	$15,000	$13,500	$11,475	

EXHIBITION GRADE – gauges similar to CE Grade, individually built per customer specifications on a "cost-no-object" basis, includes best-quality leather trunk case with full accessories, Exhibition Grade Turkish Circassian walnut. New 1993.

This model is a special order only, and is POR. Please contact the company directly for an individual price quotation and available options.

FOX A GRADE – 12 ga., case colored boxlock receiver, carbon steel barresl, DT, deluxe straight grip checkered walnut stock and forearm, currently manufactured by Connecticut Shotguns. Made by CSMC for Savage Arms.

MSR $4,999	$4,500	$3,850	$3,400	$2,950	$2,400	$1,900	$1,500	

100%	98%	95%	90%	80%	70%	60%	50%	40%	30%	20%	10%

SHOTGUNS: SxS & SINGLE SHOT, DISC.

Prices listed below are for factory original guns. Guns with alterations or restoration will bring 25-75% less.

STERLINGWORTH – 12, 16, or 20 ga., 26, 28, or 30 in. barrels, various chokes, boxlock, extractors, double trigger, checkered pistol grip stock. Mfg. 1910-1942.

$1,750	$1,600	$1,200	$1,100	$900	$750	$695	$650	$475	$375	$300	$250

Add 33% for auto ejectors.
Add 100% for 20 ga. or 50% for 16 ga.
Add 33% for single trigger.

Ser. no. range on 12 ga. Sterlingworths is 50,000-161,556, 16 ga. is 300,000-378,481, and 20 ga. is 250,000-271,304.

STERLINGWORTH DELUXE – similar to Sterlingworth, with recoil pad and ivory bead front sight, 32 in. barrel available.

$2,200	$1,800	$1,400	$1,200	$1,000	$850	$800	$750	$650	$550	$375	$300

Add 33% for auto ejectors.
Add 100% for 20 ga. or 50% for 16 ga.

A single trigger was not an option on this model.

STERLINGWORTH SKEET – similar to Sterlingworth, with 26 or 28 in. skeet boring, straight grip stock, beavertail forearm. Mfg. 1935-1945.

This model is very scarce (only several are known) and the extreme rarity factor precludes accurate price evaluation.

SUPER HE GRADE – 12 ga., 2 3/4 (very rare) or 3 in. chambered long range gun, 30 and 32 in. full choke, auto ejectors, otherwise similar to Sterlingworth.

N/A	$14,000	$10,000	$9,500	$9,000	$8,750	$6,500	$5,750	$5,500	$4,800	$3,250	$2,500

Add 10% for SST.

Original 3 in. chambered HE grades are marked "not warranteed, see instruction tag" on barrel flats. The HE grade was also manufactured in 20 ga. but is extremely rare. 2 3/4 in. chambers are rarer than 3 in. guns in this model. In recent years, these guns have become highly sought after by collectors and are very hard to find in higher original condition as most were used for heavy waterfowl hunting.

100%	98%	95%	90%	80%	70%	60%	50%	40%	30%	20%	10%

HIGHER GRADE MODELS (A-F) – 12, 16, or 20 ga., the following higher grade Fox shotguns are similar to the Sterlingworth in configuration. The grades differ in engraving and inlays, grade of wood and general workmanship. The E designation means auto ejectors.

Add 50% for 16 ga. (made on same frame as 20 ga.).
Add 100% for 20 ga.
Add $200-$1,000 for SST, depending on grade.
Add $200-$1,000 for beavertail forearm, depending on grade.
Deduct 10% for Savage Era guns except in 95% value or better condition.
Prices below are for guns with modern shootable dimensions (length of pull greater than 13.5 in. and drop of less than 3 in. at heel). Guns with unusual stock dimensions will generally bring 24-40% less than the prices quoted below except in 95% or better original condition.

Early A and B grades have very little engraving and are much less desirable than later models. The following values are for later guns.

Note: These guns were disc. in 1942 by Savage Arms after they mfg. them for 12 years. Pre-1930 guns were made by A.H. Fox Company.

* ***Higher Grade Model: A Grade***

$3,500	$3,000	$2,250	$1,875	$1,625	$1,375	$1,075	$700	$675	$550	$400	$350

* ***Higher Grade Model: AE Grade (ejectors)***

$3,700	$3,400	$2,900	$2,500	$1,900	$1,550	$1,275	$975	$825	$650	$475	$400

* ***Higher Grade Model: BE Grade (ejectors)***

N/A	$5,000	$4,750	$4,000	$3,775	$3,150	$2,450	$2,500	$1,700	$1,200	$975	$600

This model is rarely encountered.

* ***Higher Grade Model: CE Grade (ejectors)***

N/A	$8,500	$6,000	$4,750	$4,000	$3,500	$3,000	$2,750	$2,500	$2,275	$2,000	$1,750

* ***Higher Grade Model: XE Grade (ejectors)***

N/A	$17,000	$14,000	$11,750	$9,000	$7,950	$6,700	$5,250	$4,000	$3,500	$3,000	$2,250

* ***Higher Grade Model: DE Grade (ejectors)*** – Prices below are for 1st Generation style engraving.

N/A	$27,000	$21,500	$19,000	$14,000	$11,000	$7,500	$6,000	$5,500	$5,000	$4,500	$3,500

Add 10% for 2nd Generation style engraving.

* ***Higher Grade Model: FE Grade (ejectors)*** – top-of-the-line model, only infrequently encountered.

N/A	$90,000	$85,000	$67,500	$52,500	$40,000	$36,000	$32,500	$28,000	$23,000	$17,000	$12,750

Beware of upgrades on this model. It is prudent to seek professional advice when considering the purchase of an FE Grade Fox as there are several known counterfeits.

SINGLE BARREL TRAP – 12 ga., 30 or 32 in. vent. rib barrels, full choke, boxlock, auto ejector, checkered trap style stock with recoil pad. The grades differ in wood, engraving, and overall quality. ME grade is custom built and extremely high quality with gold inlays. These models were disc. 1942. 568 single barrel trap guns were mfg. between 1932-42 and have a ser. range of 400,000-400,568, with Monte Carlo stock.

Even though trap guns may be rarer than their SxS counterparts, to date their desirability is less since there are simply fewer collectors.

* ***Single Barrel Trap JE Grade***

$10,500	$8,000	$5,500	$4,250	$3,700	$3,200	$2,400	$2,200	$1,600	$1,400	$975	$650

* ***Single Barrel Trap KE Grade***

$14,500	$11,500	$9,000	$6,500	$5,250	$4,300	$2,950	$2,800	$2,175	$2,000	$1,625	$1,225

* ***Single Barrel Trap LE Grade***

N/A	$19,000	$16,750	$12,250	$9,850	$7,250	$4,950	$4,000	$3,300	$2,800	$2,100	$1,500

* ***Single Barrel Trap ME Grade***

Extreme rarity factor precludes accurate percentage pricing on this model.

GRADING - PPGS™	100%	98%	95%	90%	80%	70%	60%	LAST MSR

MODEL B DOUBLE BARREL – 12, 16, 20 ga., or .410 bore, 24-30 in. barrels, various chokes, vent. rib on newer models, boxlock, extractors, double triggers, handcut or pressed checkered pistol grip stock and forearm. Mfg. 1940-86.

12 or 16 ga.	$450	$395	$350	$295	$265	$235	$200	
20 ga.	$650	$575	$500	$450	$400	$365	$335	
.410 bore	$1,100	$975	$850	$750	$675	$600	$550	*$250*

GRADING - PPGS™	100%	98%	95%	90%	80%	70%	60%	LAST MSR

MODEL B-ST – similar to model B, with single trigger. Mfg. 1955-66.

12 or 16 ga.	$575	$475	$425	$350	$315	$275	$250	
20 ga.	$725	$650	$600	$550	$500	$425	$350	
.410 bore	$1,300	$1,075	$925	$800	$700	$600	$500	

MODEL B-DL – similar to model B-ST, with satin chrome frame, select wood. Mfg. 1962-65.

12 or 16 ga.	$600	$475	$425	$350	$315	$275	$250	
20 ga.	$750	$675	$600	$550	$500	$425	$350	
.410 bore	$1,350	$1,100	$925	$800	$700	$600	$500	

MODEL B-DE – similar to B-DL, with less checkering. Mfg. 1965-66.

12 or 16 ga.	$575	$475	$425	$350	$315	$275	$250	
20 ga.	$725	$650	$600	$550	$500	$425	$350	
.410 bore	$1,300	$1,075	$925	$800	$700	$600	$500	

MODEL B-SE – 12, 20 ga., or .410 bore, single trigger, selective ejectors, vent. rib, beavertail forearm, select walnut with pressed checkering. Mfg. 1966-88.

12 ga.	$850	$750	$675	$600	$550	$475	$400	
20 ga.	$1,000	$900	$800	$700	$625	$550	$475	
.410 bore	$1,850	$1,375	$1,125	$950	$850	$750	$650	*$525*

Even though there were multiple series designations assigned to this model, there seems to be little difference in desirability. For that reason, other designations will be priced similarly to values shown above.

FOX CARBINE

Previous rifle trademark manufactured by FoxCo Products Inc., located in Manchester, CT, and by Tri-C Corporation, located in Meridan, CT circa 1974-1976.

CARBINES: SEMI-AUTO

FOX CARBINE – 9mm Para. (mfg. by FoxCo Products) or .45 ACP (mfg. by Tri-C Corp.) cal., patterned after the Tommy Gun, 16 in. barrel with muzzle brake, grip safety, open bolt with fixed firing pin, removable wood rear stock and grooved forearm, uses M-3 30 shot mags., three safeties including a three-digit combination lock on left side of frame, loaded chamber indicator, adj. rear sight, matte metal finish, approx. 8 lbs.

	$995	$875	$750	$625	$550	$500	$450	

In 1977, the rights to manufacture the FoxCo carbine were sold to Demro Products Inc., which continued to manufacture this configuration until the mid-1980s.

FRANCHI, LUIGI

Current manufacturer established during 1868, located in Brescia, Italy. In 1987, Franchi was sold to Socimi, then to Beretta, and most recently to Benelli. This trademark has been imported for approximately the past 50 years. Currently imported exclusively by Benelli USA, located in Accokeek, MD, since 1998. Previously imported and distributed by American Arms, Inc. located in North Kansas City, MO. Some models were previously imported by FIE firearms located in Hialeah, FL.

Also see Sauer/Franchi heading in the S section.

RIFLES: BOLT ACTION

MOMENTUM RIFLE – .243 Win. (disc. 2020), 6.5 Creedmoor, .270 Win. (disc. 2020), .308 Win., .30-06, .300 Win. Mag., or .350 Legend (new 2021) cal., 22 or 24 in. CHF free floating threaded or plain (mfg. 2018 only) barrel, 4 shot mag., no sights, black synthetic ergonomic stock with TSA recoil pad and recessed swivel attachments, one-piece three lug fluted bolt, 60 degree bolt handle, receiver top has Picatinny rails, hinged floorplate, black (disc. 2020), FDE (new 2020), or Hunter Gray (new 2021) finish, 6.6-7.8 lbs. New 2018.

MSR $609	$550	$495	$450	$400	$365	$335	$295	

Add $120 for Burris Fullfield II 3-9x40mm rifle scope (mfg. 2018-2019).

MOMENTUM ELITE RIFLE – 6.5 Creedmoor, .223 Rem. (disc. 2020), .308 Win., .300 Win. Mag. (new 2021), 6.5 PRC (new 2021), or .350 Legend (new 2021) cal., 22 or 24 in. threaded barrel with Cobalt, Burnt Bronze, or Midnight Bronze Cerakote finish, muzzle brake, detachable mag., hinged floorplate, ergonomic stock, TSA recoil pad, one-piece Picatinny top rail, Hunter Gray (disc. 2020), Realtree Excape camo, True Timber Strata camo, or Optifade Elevated II (new 2021) finish on stock, 7.1-7.5 lbs. New 2020.

MSR $899	$765	$670	$575	$520	$420	$375	$325	

Subtract approx. $50 for Hunter Gray stock (mfg. 2020 only).

GRADING - PPGS™	100%	98%	95%	90%	80%	70%	60%	LAST MSR

MOMENTUM VARMINT RIFLE – .223 Rem., .22-250 Rem., or .224 Valkyrie cal., 24 in. threaded barrel with Midnight Bronze Cerakote finish, muzzle brake, removable box mag., Optifade Subalpine stock, 9.4 lbs. New 2021.

MSR $999	$850	$750	$650	$575	$475	$385	$325	

RIFLES: SEMI-AUTO

CENTENNIAL MODEL – .22 LR cal., 21 in. barrel, open sight, commemorates Franchi's 100th anniversary. Mfg. 1968 only.

	$330	$250	$220	$195	$165	$150	$140	

* ***Centennial Model Engraved Deluxe***

	$415	$330	$305	$275	$240	$200	$165	

* ***Centennial Model Gallery***

	$220	$195	$160	$120	$100	$80	$60	

SHOTGUNS: O/U

Currently manufactured Franchi O/U shotguns are supplied with a custom-fitted hard case, and use choke tubes that are compatible with both Beretta and Benelli shotguns.

ALCIONE 2000 SX (FIELD MODEL) – 12 ga., 3 in. chambers, 28 in. barrels, SST, separated barrels, ejectors, single trigger, engraved silver finished frame with gold accents, with case, 7 lbs. 4 oz. Imported 1997 only.

	$1,675	$1,495	$1,275	$1,025	$875	$750	$650	*$1,895*

ALCIONE CLASSIC – 12 ga., 3 in. chambers, 26 or 28 in. VR barrels with choke tubes, blue non-engraved receiver, SST, ejectors, checkered satin finished walnut stock and forearm. 7 1/2 lbs. Mfg. 2004-2005.

	$1,125	$960	$825	$725	$600	$500	$425	*$1,320*

Add $475 for extra set of 12 or 20 ga. barrels.

ALCIONE FIELD – 12 ga., 3 in. chambers, right or left-hand action, blue (Classic Field, new 2004) or polished steel (silver) alloy frame with game bird etching, 26 or 28 in. interchangeable barrels with choke tubes, ejectors, SST, checkered satin finished walnut stock and forearm, 7.4 lbs. Mfg. 1998-2005.

	$1,125	$960	$825	$725	$600	$500	$425	*$1,310*

Add $90 for Classic Field Model with blue receiver, gold trigger, and Schnabel forearm.

This model was previously designated 97-12 IBS.

* ***Alcione Field LF*** – 12 or 20 ga., 3 in. chambers (20 ga. only), lightweight alloy receiver with etching and gold fill, approx. 6.8 lbs. Mfg. 2000-2002.

	$1,150	$975	$875	$775	$650	$550	$425	*$1,305*

ALCIONE MODEL – 12 ga., 28 in. barrels, less engraving than Alcione SL, separated barrels. Importation disc. 1989.

	$675	$550	$495	$460	$430	$380	$335	*$800*

Previously designated Diamond Model.

This model was imported exclusively by FIE Firearms located in Hialeah, FL.

ALCIONE SL – 12 ga., 27 or 28 in. separated barrels, ejectors, single trigger, silver finished frame engraved with luggage case, 6 lbs. 13 oz. Importation disc. 1986.

	$1,200	$1,050	$900	$850	$775	$650	$550	*$1,595*

ALCIONE SL SPORT – 12 ga. only, 2 3/4 in. chambers (can also be fitted for barrels with 3 in. chambers), polished stainless steel receiver, blue barrels, SST, manual safety, ejectors, 30 in. target rib ported barrels with choke tubes, detachable sideplates, available in left-hand, 7.7 lbs. Disc. 2005.

	$1,435	$1,200	$950	$850	$725	$625	$475	*$1,700*

This model was previously designated SL IBS.

ALCIONE SP – 12 ga., 3 in. chambers, boxlock action, 28 in. VR barrels with choke tubes, 20 ga. barrels can be ordered without additional gunsmithing, gloss finished AA Grade checkered walnut pistol grip stock and Schnabel forearm, engraved sideplates including mallard and pheasant gold inlays, satin silver finish, 7 1/2 lbs. Imported 2003-2005.

	$2,400	$2,100	$1,800	$1,650	$1,350	$1,150	$1,000	*$2,780*

Add $490 for extra set of 20 ga. barrels.

GRADING - PPGS™	100%	98%	95%	90%	80%	70%	60%	LAST MSR

ALCIONE SX – 12 ga., 3 in. chambers, 26 or 28 in. interchangeable barrels with VR and 3 choke tubes, gold plated trigger, deluxe walnut stock, removable sideplates with etched game scenes, approx. 7.4 lbs. Imported 2001-2005.

$1,650 $1,450 $1,250 $1,100 $900 $750 $600 *$1,855*

Add $490 for extra set of barrels.
Add $125 for Alcione Classic SX with blued receiver (new 2004).

ALCIONE TITANIUM (T) – 12 or 20 ga., 3 in. chambers, 26 or 28 in. interchangeable vent. barrels with VR and 3 choke tubes, receiver manufactured from aluminum alloy coupled with titanium inserts, gold plated trigger with selector switch, deluxe walnut stock, removable sideplates with etched game scenes, selector switch, approx. 6.8 lbs. Imported 2002-2005.

$1,260 $1,050 $950 $875 $800 $750 $695 *$1,470*

Add $460 for 2 barrel set (includes extra 20 ga. barrels).

ARISTOCRAT DELUXE – finer wood, more engraving. Mfg. 1960-66.

$990 $870 $835 $810 $770 $715 $660

ARISTOCRAT FIELD – 12 ga., 26, 28, or 30 in. barrels, various chokes, vent. rib, auto ejectors, boxlock, selective single trigger, checkered pistol grip stock. Mfg. 1960-1969.

$660 $470 $440 $395 $375 $340 $310

ARISTOCRAT IMPERIAL – high grade wood, more engraving. Mfg. 1967-69.

$2,640 $2,200 $2,090 $1,925 $1,815 $1,650 $1,430

ARISTOCRAT MAGNUM – 12 ga., 3 in. chambers, 32 in. barrels, full choke, ejectors, SST, checkered pistol grip stock. Mfg. 1962-1965.

$660 $470 $440 $395 $375 $340 $310

ARISTOCRAT MONTE CARLO – highest grade wood, elaborate engraving and inlay. Mfg. 1967-1969.

$3,520 $3,080 $2,915 $2,640 $2,420 $2,090 $1,870

ARISTOCRAT SILVER KING – select wood, engraved coin finished frame. Mfg. 1962-69.

$750 $560 $535 $485 $470 $430 $400

ARISTOCRAT SKEET – 12 ga., boxlock, 26 in. vent. rib barrels, bored skeet no. 1 and no. 2, SST, checkered pistol grip stock. Mfg. 1960-1969.

$715 $525 $495 $450 $430 $395 $365

ARISTOCRAT SUPREME – gold inlaid game birds. Mfg. 1960-66.

$1,430 $1,265 $1,155 $1,075 $990 $935 $880

ARISTOCRAT TRAP – 30 in. vent. rib barrels, bored mod. and full, trap stock. Mfg. 1960-1969.

$745 $550 $525 $480 $455 $415 $380

ASPIRE ROUND ACTION – 28 ga. or .410 bore, 2 3/4 or 3 in. chambers, 28 in. barrels with five chokes, vent. rib, oil finished pistol grip walnut stock, beavertail forearm, mechanical triggers, color case hardened frame, automatic safety, 5.8 lbs. Mfg. 2013-2015.

$1,950 $1,700 $1,475 $1,325 $1,075 $875 $675 *$2,299*

BLACK MAGIC SPORTING HUNTER – 12 ga., 3 in. chambers, 28 in. separated barrels with VR and Franchokes, black frame with gold accents and gold plated trigger, SST, ejectors, checkered walnut stock and forearm, 7 lbs. Imported 1989-91.

$995 $875 $800 $725 $650 $575 $495 *$1,249*

The Black Magic Model Series was imported exclusively by American Arms, Inc. located in North Kansas City, MO.

* ***Black Magic Sporting Hunter Lightweight*** – 12 ga., 2 3/4 in. chambers, alloy frame, 26 in. separated barrels with VR and Franchokes, checkered walnut stock and forearm, 6 lbs. Imported 1989-91.

$975 $850 $775 $700 $625 $550 $475 *$1,209*

DE LUXE MODEL PRITI – 12 or 20 ga., boxlock action, ST, ejectors, 26 or 28 in. VR barrels with fixed chokes. Imported 1988-89 only.

$395 $350 $315 $285 $240 $215 $185 *$460*

This model was imported exclusively by FIE Firearms located in Hialeah, FL.

FALCONET 97-12 IBS – 12 ga., 2 3/4 in. chambers, ultra light alloy frame with gold inlays, scroll engraving, and nickel finish, SST, ejectors, 26 in. barrels with Franchokes, checkered walnut stock and forearm, includes hard case. Imported 1998-2000.

$875 $750 $625 $550 $500 $450 $400 *$965*

GRADING - PPGS™	100%	98%	95%	90%	80%	70%	60%	LAST MSR

FALCONET 2000 – 12 ga., boxlock with alloy frame featuring silver finish with gold plated game scenes, 26 in. separated barrels with VR and choke tubes, SST, ejectors, select checkered walnut stock and forearm, hard case, 6 lbs. Imported 1992-1997.

	$1,245	$975	$850	$725	$650	$575	$500	*$1,375*

FALCONET FIELD – 12, 16, 20, 28 ga., or .410 bore, 24-30 in. barrels, various chokes, auto ejectors, SST, engraved alloy frame, checkered walnut stock. Mfg. 1968-75.

Buckskin (light)	$550	$495	$470	$440	$415	$385	$360
Ebony (black)	$550	$495	$470	$440	$415	$385	$360
Silver	$605	$550	$525	$495	$470	$415	$385

Add 25% for 28 ga. or .410 bore.

FALCONET INTERNATIONAL SKEET – higher grade wood, more engraving. Mfg. 1970-74.

	$1,045	$935	$865	$825	$770	$745	$700

FALCONET INTERNATIONAL TRAP – higher grade wood, more engraving. Mfg. 1970-74.

	$1,045	$935	$865	$825	$770	$745	$700

FALCONET S – 12 ga., lightweight model of the Alcione SL, 27 or 28 in. separated barrels, moderate engraving on silver finish frame, 6 lbs. 1 oz. Disc. 1985.

	$895	$765	$660	$560	$510	$460	$410	*$1,015*

FALCONET SKEET – 26 in. barrels, bored skeet no. 1 and no. 2, wide vent. rib, case hardened steel frame. Mfg. 1970-74.

	$935	$855	$825	$770	$715	$690	$650

FALCONET STANDARD TRAP – 12 ga., 30 in. mod. and full, wide vent. rib, trap stock, pad. Mfg. 1970-74.

	$935	$855	$825	$770	$715	$690	$650

INSTINCT CATALYST – 12 (disc. 2020) or 20 (new 2020) ga., 2 3/4 or 3 in. chambers, 26 (new 2020) or 28 in. barrels, choke tubes, color case hardened steel or brushed aluminum (new 2021), auto ejectors, red fiber optic front sights, A Grade satin finished walnut stock, auto safety, drop, cast, LOP, and grip length have all been designed to fit a woman's body, 5.4-7.2 lbs. New 2016.

MSR $1,469	$1,295	$1,100	$975	$850	$750	$625	$500

Add $230 for brushed aluminum (Instinct Catalyst SL, new 2021).

INSTINCT L – 12, 20, 28 (mfg. 2016-2020) ga., or .410 bore (mfg. 2016-2020), 3 in. chambers, 26 (mfg. 2012-circa 2014) or 28 in. barrels, 5 choke tubes, color case hardened receiver, auto ejectors, SST, red fiber optic front bead sights, checkered A Grade satin walnut stock and forearm, includes custom fitted hard case, 6.1-6.4 lbs. New 2012.

MSR $1,369	$1,175	$1,025	$875	$800	$650	$550	$450

Add $100 for 28 ga. or .410 bore (mfg. 2016-2020).

INSTINCT LX – 12, 20, or 28 (new 2021) ga., 2 3/4 or 3 in. chambers, 28 in. gloss blued barrels, extended choke tubes, auto ejectors, red fiber optic bead sight, AA Grade checkered satin walnut stock, Schnabel forend, auto safety, color case hardened steel receiver engraved with hunting scene and gold inlaid highlights, includes hard case. New 2019.

MSR $1,699	$1,450	$1,270	$1,095	$985	$800	$650	$525

Add $100 for 28 ga. (new 2021).

INSTINCT SL – 12, 16 (new 2018), 20, 28 (new 2020) ga., or .410 bore (new 2020), 3 in. chambers, 26 or 28 in. barrels, 5 extended choke tubes, coin finished aluminum alloy receiver, auto ejectors, red fiber optic front bead sights, checkered AA Grade satin walnut stock and forearm, includes custom fitted hard case, 5.3-5.7 lbs. New 2012.

MSR $1,599	$1,395	$1,150	$1,000	$900	$800	$675	$575

Add $100 for 28 ga. or .410 bore (new 2020).
Add $130 for 16 ga. (new 2018).

INSTINCT SLX – 12, 16, 20, or 28 (new 2021) ga., 2 3/4 or 3 in. chambers, 28 in. barrels, five extended choke tubes, auto ejectors, gold trigger, AA Grade satin walnut stock with checkering, Schnabel forend, Prince of Wales grip, traditional floral engraving on receiver, 5.6-6.3 lbs. New 2020.

MSR $1,999	$1,700	$1,495	$1,275	$1,150	$935	$775	$650

Add $100 for 16 or 28 (new 2021) ga.

INSTINCT SPORTING – 12 ga., 3 in. chambers, 30 in. VR barrels with extended choke tubes, checkered satin finished "A" Grade walnut stock with square pistol grip and Schnabel forearm, nickel finished receiver with gold trigger, includes fitted hard case, 7 1/2 lbs. Mfg. 2014-2018.

	$1,685	$1,400	$1,175	$995	$850	$725	$625	*$1,919*

GRADING - PPGS™	100%	98%	95%	90%	80%	70%	60%	LAST MSR

INSTINCT SPORTING II – 12 or 20 (new 2020) ga., 2 3/4 or 3 in. chambers, 30 in. ported barrels with wide vented rib, extended choke tubes, polished steel receiver, auto ejectors, fiber optic sights, satin walnut stock with adj. comb and right-hand palm swell. New 2019.

MSR $1,999	$1,700	$1,495	$1,275	$1,150	$950	$775	$600	

MODEL 2003 TRAP – 12 ga., boxlock, 30 or 32 in. barrels, imp. mod. and full or full and full, auto ejectors, SST, high vent. rib, trap style stock, buttpad, cased. Mfg. 1976-disc.

	$1,205	$1,090	$1,045	$910	$855	$770	$660	

MODEL 2004 TRAP – 12 ga., similar to Model 2003 Trap, except single barrel, cased. Mfg. 1976-diisc.

	$1,205	$1,090	$1,045	$910	$855	$770	$660	

MODEL 2005 COMBINATION TRAP – two sets of barrels, one single, one O/U, cased. Mfg. 1976-disc.

	$1,815	$1,595	$1,515	$1,320	$1,210	$1,075	$935	

MODEL 2005/3 COMBINATION TRAP – three sets of barrels, cased. Mfg. 1976-disc.

	$2,425	$2,095	$1,985	$1,715	$1,525	$1,495	$1,325	

PEREGRINE MODEL 400 – 12 ga., steel frame, 26-28 in. barrels, various chokes, vent. rib, auto ejectors, SST, checkered pistol grip stock. Mfg. 1975.

	$660	$605	$570	$540	$495	$460	$385	

PEREGRINE MODEL 451 – 12 ga., 26-28 in. barrels, various chokes, vent. rib, auto ejectors, alloy frame, SST, checkered pistol grip stock. Mfg. 1975.

	$600	$550	$525	$495	$440	$415	$360	

RENAISSANCE CLASSIC – similar to Renaissance Field, except has gold plated trigger, A Grade walnut and gold bird inlays. Imported 2006-2010.

	$1,575	$1,350	$1,125	$975	$875	$775	$650	*$1,820*

Add $70 for 28 ga.

* ***Renaissance Classic Combo*** – includes 26 in. 20 and 28 ga. barrels. Mfg. 2008-2010.

	$2,325	$1,925	$1,700	$1,500	$1,325	$1,150	$1,000	*$2,729*

RENAISSANCE ELITE – similar to Renaissance Classic, except has AA Grade walnut, deep relief engraving, gold game scene inlays. Imported 2006-2010.

	$2,000	$1,750	$1,475	$1,225	$995	$825	$700	*$2,329*

Add $110 for 28 ga.

RENAISSANCE FIELD – 12, 20, or 28 ga., 3 in. chambers (2 3/4 in. on 28 ga.), boxlock action with polished blue finish, 26 or 28 in. VR barrels with choke tubes, ejectors, SST, oil finished walnut stock and forearm, Twin Shock absorber recoil pad with gel insert, 5.5-6.2 lbs. Imported 2006-2010.

	$1,425	$1,200	$1,000	$875	$750	$650	$575	*$1,659*

Add $40 for 28 ga.

RENAISSANCE SPORTING – 12 ga., 3 in. chambers, 30 in. VR ported barrels with extended choke tubes, A Grade walnut stock with adj. comb, engraving, approx. 8 lbs. Imported 2007-2010.

	$1,925	$1,675	$1,450	$1,250	$995	$825	$700	*$2,219*

SPORTING 2000 – 12 ga. only, design for sporting clays or hunting, 28 in. vent. ported (disc. 1993) or unported (new 1997) barrels with target VR and choke tubes, SST, ejectors, select walnut with checkering, solid pad, hard case, 7 3/4 lbs. Imported 1992-1993, resumed 1997, disc. 1998.

	$1,275	$1,025	$875	$750	$650	$575	$500	*$1,495*

UNDERGUN MODEL 3000 – radical competition trap, very high rib separated barrels, under single and O/U, drop in set screw chokes (hex drive), set aluminum cased. Disc.

	$2,750	$2,530	$2,310	$2,090	$1,980	$1,870	$1,760	

VELOCE – 20 or 28 ga., 3 in. chambers on 20 ga., 26 or 28 (20 ga. only) in. vent. barrels with 3 choke tubes, aluminum frame with steel reinforcement, etched game scene receiver with gold filled inlays, skeletonized opening lever, deluxe oil finished checkered pistol grip or English (new 2002) stock and forearm, mechanical gold plated SST, 5.5 (28 ga.) or 5.8 (20 ga.) lbs. Imported 2001-2005.

	$1,260	$1,050	$950	$875	$800	$750	$695	*$1,470*

Add $75 for 28 ga.

* ***Veloce Grade II*** – 20 or 28 ga., 3 in. chambers, similar to Veloce Model, except has semi-pistol grip deluxe walnut stock. Limited importation 2004 only.

	$1,750	$1,500	$1,250	$1,050	$925	$825	$725	*$2,000*

Add $75 for 28 ga.

GRADING - PPGS™	100%	98%	95%	90%	80%	70%	60%	LAST MSR

* ***Veloce Squire Limited Edition*** – includes one set of 26 in. 20 ga. and one set of 26 in. 28 ga. barrels, cased, 5.7 lbs. Imported 2003-2005.

	$2,050	$1,750	$1,450	$1,125	$975	$875	$775	*$2,470*

VELOCE SP – 20 ga., 26 in. barrel, checkered oil finished AA walnut stock and forearm, deep relief engraving with gold game bird inlays, gold plated trigger, 5 1/2 lbs. Available from World Class dealers only. U.S. importation 2007-2012.

	$2,525	$2,250	$1,975	$1,750	$1,525	$1,300	$1,100	*$2,889*

SHOTGUNS: SxS

AIRONE – 12 ga., choice of barrel length and chokes, Anson & Deeley box lock action, auto ejectors, double triggers, checkered English style stock, engraved. Mfg. 1940-50.

	$1,320	$1,100	$935	$825	$745	$715	$660	

ASTORE – 12 ga., Anson & Deeley boxlock action, extractors, double triggers, checkered English style stock, engraved. Mfg. 1937-1960.

	$990	$910	$770	$715	$635	$580	$550	

ASTORE 5 – 12 ga., similar to Astore, except higher grade wood, more engraving, auto ejectors. Disc.

	$2,200	$1,925	$1,650	$1,540	$1,460	$1,375	$1,320	

ASTORE II – 12 ga., similar to Astore 5, except less elaborate. Mfg. in Spain for Franchi.

	$1,210	$1,045	$935	$880	$800	$715	$660	

DESTINO – 20 ga., 3 in. chambers, boxlock action with satin nickel finish and game scene engraving with gold inlays, SST, extractors, checkered straight grip AAA English walnut stock, fitted rubber buttpad, limited production of 250 during 2007-mid-2008.

	$3,100	$2,700	$2,300	$1,950	$1,575	$1,375	$1,150	*$3,495*

HIGHLANDER – 12, 20, or 28 ga., 3 in. chambers except for 28 ga., English style straight grip walnut stock and splinter forearm, scalloped coin finished boxlock receiver, SST, extractors, 26 in. barrels with fixed chokes, includes fitted hardcase, 5.7-6.4 lbs. Limited importation 2003.

	$1,575	$1,275	$1,075	$950	$825	$700	$600	*$1,800*

HIGHLANDER (RECENT MFG.) – 12 or 20 ga., 3 in. chambers, scalloped boxlock action, SST, blued or case colored (20 ga. only) frame, 26 in. VR barrels with choke tubes, straight grip A Grade oil finished walnut stock and splinter forearm. Imported 2007-2009.

	$2,400	$2,100	$1,800	$1,500	$1,250	$1,000	$850	*$2,799*

SIDELOCK DOUBLE BARREL – 12, 16, or 20 ga., barrels and choke custom order, stock to order, hand detachable side lock, self-opening action, auto ejectors, six grades offered, they differ only in overall quality and ornamentation, and grade of wood used.

Condor	$7,700	$6,600	$6,050	$5,720	$5,500	$4,620	$3,960	
Imperial	$10,450	$9,350	$8,800	$8,250	$7,480	$6,600	$5,720	
Imperiales	$10,670	$9,570	$9,020	$8,470	$7,700	$6,820	$5,940	

SIDE-LOCK DOUBLE BARREL – the following models are available through the Beretta Galleries and selected premium dealers only.

* ***Side-Lock Double Barrel No. 5 Imperial Monte Carlo***

	$30,000	$20,000	$16,000	$12,000	$10,000	$8,000	$6,500	*$35,000*

* ***Side-Lock Double Barrel No. 17 Imperial Monte Carlo***

	$37,500	$30,000	$25,000	$20,000	$15,000	$10,000	$7,500	*$42,500*

* ***Side-Lock Double Barrel Imperial Monte Carlo Extra*** – 12 or 20 ga., limited importation.

Imperial Monte Carlo Extra is currently being mfg. by Beretta. Prices are $145,000 for single guns, and $325,000 - $345,000 for pairs.

SHOTGUNS: SEMI-AUTO & SLIDE ACTION

48 AL FIELD MODEL – 12 (disc. 2001), 20, or 28 (new 1996) ga., 2 3/4 in. chamber, semi-humpback design, long recoil operation, 24, 26, 28, or 30 (disc. in 1990) in. VR barrel with (beginning 1989) or w/o choke tubes, standard choke tubes became available in 1989, alloy receiver, checkered pistol grip satin walnut stock and forearm, 6 lbs. 9 oz. (12 ga.) and 5 lbs. 6 oz. (20 ga.). Mfg. 1950-2016.

	$850	$725	$650	$600	$550	$500	$450	*$999*

Add $150 for 28 ga.
Add $30 for 12 ga. 24 in. slug barrel (disc. 1994).
Subtract 10% if without choke tubes.

GRADING - PPGS™	100%	98%	95%	90%	80%	70%	60%	LAST MSR

* ***48 AL Field Youth Model*** – 20 ga., 2 3/4 in. chamber, 24 in. barrel with choke tubes (became standard 1990), 4 shot, black receiver, bead sights, satin walnut stock and forearm, 12 1/2 in. LOP, matte blue finish, 5.4 lbs. Disc. 2016.

	$850	$725	$650	$600	$550	$500	$450	*$999*

* ***48 AL Field Model Deluxe*** – 20 or 28 ga., 2 3/4 in. chamber, 26 in. barrel, 4 shot, gold trigger, bead sights, A Grade satin walnut, English (mfg. 2002-disc.) or Prince of Wales (new 2012) stock and forearm, receiver accents, high polish blue finish, approx. 5 1/2 lbs. New 2000-2016.

	$995	$800	$650	$525	$425	$375	$350	*$1,199*

Add $50 for Prince of Wales stock (20 ga. only).
Add $150 for 28 ga.

STANDARD MAGNUM (48/AL) – similar to 48 AL Field, except has 3 in. chamber with 28 in. (disc. 1988) or 32 in. VR barrel, recoil pad. Mfg. 1954-1990.

	$415	$360	$300	$270	$250	$230	$210	*$482*

This model was slated to be replaced with the Combo S/T - however, while advertised, the Combo S/T was never mfg.

HUNTER MODEL (48/AL) – similar to 48 AL Field, except etched receiver, better wood, VR standard, Franchokes became available in 1989. Mfg. 1950-1990.

	$415	$360	$300	$270	$250	$230	$210	*$482*

Add $35 for internal Franchokes (3).

This model was imported exclusively by FIE Firearms located in Hialeah, FL.

AFFINITY 3 150TH ANNIVERSARY – 12 or 20 ga., 2 3/4 or 3 in. chamber, 26 or 28 in. barrel, 4 shot mag., engraved silver receiver, AA-Grade satin walnut stock. Limited mfg. 2018 only.

	$1,275	$1,075	$950	$825	$700	$600	$500	*$1,469*

AFFINITY – 12 or 20 (disc. 2017) ga., 2 3/4 and 3 in. chamber, 26 (disc. 2017) or 28 in. barrel, 3 choke tubes, 4 shot mag., fiber optic red bar front sight, includes shim kit, walnut (disc. 2017) or black synthetic, Realtree Max-4 (disc.), Realtree Max-5 (disc. 2017), Mossy Oak Bottomland (disc. 2017), or Realtree APG (disc. 2016) 100% camo finish, right (disc. 2017) or left-hand configuration, 5.6-6 1/2 lbs. New 2012.

MSR $849	$725	$635	$550	$495	$415	$375	$325

Add $100 for walnut stock (disc. 2017).
Add $100 for Realtree Max-4 (disc.), Realtree Max-5 (disc. 2017), Realtree APG (disc. 2016), or Mossy Oak Bottomland (disc. 2017) 100% camo finish.
Add $50 for adj. shims (disc.).

* ***Affinity Sporting*** – 12 or 20 ga., 2 3/4 or 3 in. chambers, 28 or 30 in. barrel, nickel receiver, black synthetic stock and forearm. Mfg. 2013-2016.

	$1,025	$895	$750	$675	$550	$495	$450	*$1,159*

* ***Affinity Compact*** – 12 or 20 ga., 3 in. chamber, 24 or 26 in. VR barrel, fiber optic front sight, adj. shims, shorter dimensions, choice of black synthetic, Realtree Max-4 (disc. 2015), Realtree Max-5 (new 2016), or Realtree APG 100% camo finish, 5.8 lbs. Mfg. 2014-2017.

	$725	$650	$575	$525	$475	$425	$375	*$899*

Add $100 for camo finish.

AFFINITY CATALYST – 12 or 20 (new 2018) ga., 2 3/4 or 3 in. chamber, 26 (new 2018) or 28 in. barrel, choke tubes, A Grade satin finished walnut stock, the drop, cast, pitch, and LOP are all tailored to fit a woman's build, includes shim kit, 6.6 lbs. New 2016.

MSR $969	$825	$725	$625	$560	$450	$375	$300

AFFINITY 3 – 12 or 20 ga., 2 3/4 and 3 in. chamber, inertia driven action, 26 or 28 in. chrome-lined VR barrel, interchangeable chokes, 4 shot mag., red bar fiber optic front sight, A-Grade satin walnut stock (with black anodized receiver and barrel), or synthetic stock in black, Realtree Max-5, or Mossy Oak Bottomland camo, TSA recoil pad, sling attachment points on the mag. cap and buttstock, ergonomic pistol grip, ambidextrous safety, drilled and tapped receiver, oversized bolt handle and bolt release button, enlarged loading port, includes shim kit, 6.9 lbs. New 2017.

MSR $849	$725	$635	$550	$495	$415	$375	$325

Add $110 for A-Grade satin walnut stock.
Add $110 for Realtree Max-5 or Mossy Oak Bottomland camo.

GRADING - PPGS™	100%	98%	95%	90%	80%	70%	60%	LAST MSR

* ***Affinity 3 Compact*** – 12 (disc. 2018) or 20 ga., 3 in. chamber, 24 or 26 in. chrome-lined VR barrel with 3 chokes, 4 shot, fiber optic red bar front sight, black synthetic, Realtree Max-5, or Mossy Oak Bottomland (new 2019) camo stock and forend, includes four 1/4 in. spacers for LOP adjustment, 6.7 lbs. New 2017.

MSR $899 $765 $675 $575 $525 $425 $375 $325

Add $100 for camo finish.

* ***Affinity 3 Turkey*** – 20 ga., 3 in. chamber, Inertia Driven system, 24 in. barrel, extended choke tubes, drilled and tapped receiver, hooded dual color fiber optic front bar sight, Steadygrip pistol grip stock, TSA recoil pad, two sling attachment points, 100% Mossy Oak Bottomland camo finish, 6.7 lbs. New 2021.

MSR $959 $815 $715 $610 $555 $450 $365 $320

AFFINITY 3 COMPANION – 12 or 20 ga., 2 3/4 or 3 in. chamber, 26 or 28 in. chrome-lined VR barrel, Mobil chokes, 4 shot mag., gold trigger, black trigger guard, AA Grade satin walnut stock and forend with cut checkering, TSA recoil pad, nickel-colored receiver with etched game scene engraving featuring the Labrador Retriever. Mfg. 2019 only.

$1,350 $1,180 $1,015 $925 $750 $625 $500 *$1,599*

AFFINITY 3 COMPANION-GSP – 12 or 20 ga., 2 3/4 or 3 in. chamber, inertia driven, 26 or 28 in. chrome-lined VR barrel, 3 Mobil chokes, 4 shot mag., gold trigger, black trigger guard, AA Grade satin walnut stock and forend with cut checkering, TSA recoil pad, nickel-colored receiver with engraving featuring a German Shorthaired Pointer, 6-6.9 lbs. New 2020.

MSR $1,699 $1,450 $1,275 $1,095 $985 $800 $675 $550

AFFINITY 3 ELITE – 12 or 20 ga., 2 3/4 or 3 in. chamber, 26 or 28 in. barrel, 4 shot mag., synthetic stock with Optifade Waterfowl Marsh or Optifade Waterfowl Timber finish, Burnt Bronze or Cobalt Cerakote receiver finish. New 2019.

MSR $1,249 $1,075 $950 $800 $725 $595 $485 $375

* ***Affinity 3 Elite - Upland*** – 12 or 20 ga., 2 3/4 or 3 in. chamber, 26 or 28 in. barrel, extended chokes, 4 shot mag., TruGlo dual color fiber optic front sight, A Grade satin walnut stock, TSA recoil pad, Gun Metal Gray Cerakote finish on receiver, 6-6.9 lbs. New 2020.

MSR $1,249 $1,075 $950 $800 $725 $595 $485 $375

AFFINITY 3.5 – 12 ga., 2 3/4, 3, or 3 1/2 in. chamber, inertia driven action, 26 or 28 in. chrome-lined VR barrel with three choke tubes, 4 shot mag., red fiber optic front sight, Midnight Bronze (new 2021) or Patriot Bronze (new 2021) Cerakote finish on receiver, synthetic stock in black, Realtree Max-5, or Mossy Oak Bottomland camo, TSA recoil pad, sling attachment points on the mag. cap and buttstock, ergonomic pistol grip, ambi safety, drilled and tapped receiver, oversized bolt handle and bolt release button, enlarged loading port, includes shim kit, 6.9 lbs. New 2017.

MSR $999 $850 $750 $650 $585 $475 $395 $325

Add $130 for camo coverage.

Add $250 for Midnight Bronze or Patriot Bronze Cerakote finish on receiver (new 2021).

* ***Affinity 3.5 Turkey*** – 12 ga., 2 3/4 in. chamber, 24 in. barrel, extended choke tubes, hooded dual color fiber optic front bar sight, Steadygrip pistol grip stock, TSA recoil pad, two sling attachment points, 100% Mossy Oak Bottomland Camo finish, 7.5 lbs. New 2021.

MSR $1,129 $950 $825 $700 $635 $515 $425 $350

AFFINITY 3.5 ELITE – 12 ga., 3 or 3 1/2 in. chamber, 28 in. barrel, 4 shot mag., synthetic stock with Optifade Waterfowl Marsh or Optifade Waterfowl Timber finish, Burnt Bronze or Cobalt Cerakote receiver finish. New 2019.

MSR $1,419 $1,200 $1,050 $900 $815 $650 $550 $425

AFFINITY 3 SPORTING II – 12 or 20 (new 2020) ga., 2 3/4 or 3 in. chamber, 28 (new 2020) or 30 in. chrome-lined ported barrel with matte blued finish, raised rib, three extended choke tubes, 4 shot mag., A Grade satin walnut stock, TSA recoil pad, polished chrome bolt with oversized handle, white anodized finished receiver. New 2019.

MSR $999 $850 $750 $650 $575 $475 $385 $300

BLACK MAGIC GAME – 12 ga., 3 in. chamber with gas metering system, interchangeable shell handling without gas system adjustments, two-tone black alloy receiver with gold plated accents and trigger, 24, 26, or 28 in. VR barrel with Franchokes, checkered walnut stock and forearm, 7 lbs. Imported 1989-91.

$550 $450 $395 $330 $300 $270 $240 *$659*

* ***Black Magic Game Skeet*** – skeet variation of the Black Magic Game, 2 3/4 in. chamber, 26 in. ported VR barrel with fixed Tula skeet choke, skeet dimensioned stock, 7 1/4 lbs. Imported 1989-91.

$580 $475 $425 $350 $325 $295 $265 *$699*

GRADING - PPGS™	100%	98%	95%	90%	80%	70%	60%	LAST MSR

* ***Black Magic Game Trap*** – trap variation of the Black Magic Game, 2 3/4 in. chamber, 30 in. VR barrel with Franchoke system, trap dimensioned stock, 7 1/2 lbs. Imported 1989-91.

	$615	$495	$430	$350	$325	$295	$265	*$739*

FENICE – 20 or 28 ga., 26 or 28 in. barrel, checkered oil finished AA walnut stock and forearm, 5 shot mag., silver receiver with light scroll and gold game bird inlays, gold plated trigger, 5.4-5.7 lbs., available from World Class dealers only. Imported 2007-2016.

	$1,240	$1,050	$900	$775	$650	$575	$475	*$1,399*

HUNTER MAGNUM – mfg. 1954-1973.

	$430	$380	$370	$340	$315	$290	$275	

INTENSITY – 12 ga. only, 3 1/2 in. chamber, 26, 28, or 30 (disc.) in. VR barrel with 3 choke tubes and fiber optic front sight, choice of black synthetic, RealTree Max-4 (disc.), RealTree Max-5, RealTree APGX (disc.), or Mossy Oak Bottomlands camo coverage, includes shim kit, approx. 6.8 lbs. Mfg. 2014-2017.

	$950	$850	$750	$650	$575	$500	$450	*$1,099*

Add $100 for 100% camo finish.

PRESTIGE MODEL – 12 ga. only, gas operated, vent. rib, various barrel lengths, alloy receiver, Franchokes became available in 1989. Imported 1985-89.

	$575	$475	$395	$325	$310	$295	$275	*$720*

Add $40 for internal Franchokes (3).

This model was imported exclusively by FIE Firearms located in Hialeah, FL.

* ***Prestige Model Turkey*** – similar to Prestige Model except has dull matte black finish, Franchokes standard. Imported 1989 only.

	$615	$515	$425	$350	$320	$300	$280	*$760*

This model was imported exclusively by FIE Firearms located in Hialeah, FL.

ELITE MODEL – same general specifications as the Prestige Model, only etched receiver, Franchokes became available in 1989. Imported 1985-89.

	$595	$500	$425	$350	$320	$300	$280	*$740*

Add $45 for internal Franchokes (3).

This model was imported exclusively by FIE Firearms located in Hialeah, FL.

MODEL 610 VS – 12 ga., incorporates gas-operated Variopress System, adjusts for both 2 3/4 and 3 in. shells, 4 lug rotating breech bolt, alloy receiver, non-glare finish, 26 or 28 in. VR barrels with Franchokes, checkered walnut stock and forearm. Imported 1997 only.

	$650	$550	$425	$325	$275	$250	$225	*$750*

Add $45 for engraved receiver and bolt (Model 610 VSL).

MODEL 612/620 (VS) – 12 (Model 612) or 20 (Model 620) ga., 3 in. chamber, features VarioSystem/Variomax gas operation utilizing reversible gas adjustment collar on mag. tube, advanced safety system, black receiver with (disc. 2001) or w/o gold borders (new 2002), 24, 26, or 28 in. barrel with choke tubes, last shot hold open, choice of checkered satin walnut, black synthetic (not available in 20 ga.) stock and forearm, 100% Realtree X-tra brown (disc. 1999), Realtree HD Timber (new 2002), Max-4 HD (new 2004, not available in 20 ga.), or Advantage (mfg. 2000-2002) camo coverage, 5.9-7 lbs. Mfg. 1998-2004.

	$550	$475	$415	$350	$325	$300	$275	*$660*

Add $15 for satin finished walnut stock and forearm.
Add $105 for 100% camo coverage (Models 612/620 VS Camo).
Add $15 for 20 ga. or for Youth Model (20 ga. only, 12 1/2 LOP stock).

This model was previously designated the Variopress 612/620.

MODEL 612 SPORTING – 12 ga., blue receiver with gold logo (new 2002), or silver receiver with black border and gold small parts (disc. 1998), matte black receiver with green logo (mfg. 2000-2002), or matte black top/polished sides receiver with gold lettering (new 2003), 28 (disc. 1998) or 30 (new 2000) in. ported target rib barrel with extended 4 in. forcing cone and elongated Franchokes, select checkered walnut stock and forearm, 7.1 lbs. Limited mfg. 1998, reintroduced 2000-2004.

	$825	$750	$625	$525	$450	$375	$325	*$975*

This model was previously designated the Variopress 612 Sporting.

MODEL 612 DEFENSE – 12 ga. only, 18 1/2 in. barrel with cyl. bore, matte finish metal with black synthetic stock and forearm, 6 1/2 lbs. Imported 2000-2002.

	$525	$450	$375	$325	$285	$265	$245	*$635*

This model was previously designated the Variopress 612 Defense.

GRADING - PPGS™	100%	98%	95%	90%	80%	70%	60%	LAST MSR

MODEL 712 – 12 ga. only, 3 in. chamber, Benelli inertia recoil system with rotating bolt head, aluminum receiver, 24, 26, or 28 in. VR barrel, 5 shot mag., choice of synthetic, Weathercoat walnut, or 100% Advantage Timber HD or Max-4 HD camo coverage, recoil pad, approx. 7 lbs. Limited importation 2004 only.

$650 $575 $500 $450 $375 $325 $275 *$750*

Add $65 for walnut stock and forearm with Weathercoating.
Add $105 for camo finish.

* ***Model 712 Raptor*** – features 30 in. ported VR barrel with extended choke tubes, satin nickel receiver with green Franchi logo insert on right side, checkered Weathercoat pistol grip stock with recoil pad, blue finish, 5 shot mag., Benelli rotary bolt design, approx. 7 lbs. Mfg. 2005-2007.

$845 $700 $575 $500 $440 $395 $350 *$999*

MODEL 720 – 20 ga. only, 3 in. chamber, 26 or 28 in. barrel, similar to Model 712, except is not available with synthetic stock, also available with short LOP, blue or 100% Advantage Timber HD (disc. 2007) or Max 4-HD camo coverage, approx. 6 lbs. Mfg. 2004-2011.

$875 $725 $600 $500 $425 $375 $325 *$999*

Subtract $60 for short LOP.

* ***Model 720 Raptor*** – features 28 in. barrel with Weathercoat stock, blue finish, 5 shot mag. Mfg. 2005-2007.

$845 $700 $575 $500 $440 $395 $350 *$999*

* ***Model 720 Competition*** – 20 ga. only, 3 in. chamber, nickel finished receiver, 28 in. VR barrel with extended choke tube, Weathercoat stock and forearm, 6.2 lbs. Mfg. 2008-2011.

$950 $800 $700 $600 $525 $450 $400 *$1,109*

MODEL 912 – 12 ga. only, 3 1/2 in. chamber, VarioSystem/Variomax gas operation utilizing reversible gas adjustment collar on mag. tube, lightweight alloy receiver, 24, 26, 28, or 30 in. VR barrel with 3 choke tubes, choice of satin walnut stock (new 2002), black synthetic or 100% Advantage Timber HD or Max-4 HD (new 2004) camo coverage, magazine cutoff, includes hard case, 7.5-7.8 lbs. Imported 2001-2005.

$665 $575 $500 $450 $375 $325 $275 *$790*

Add $110 for camo coverage.
Add $60 for satin finished walnut stock and forearm.
Add $60 for Model 912 steady-grip with 24 in. barrel and 100% Timber HD camo coverage.

This model was previously designated the Variopress 912.

I-12 INERTIA – 12 ga. only, 3 in. chamber, 24, 26, or 28 in. VR barrel, inertia operating system with free floating bolt which compresses an inertia spring upon recoil, choice of synthetic or satin walnut stock and forearm, blued, matte blue, Max-4 HD, APG HD (new 2007), or Timber HD (disc. 2007) camo coverage, Twin Shock Absorber recoil pad with gel insert, approx. 7 1/2 lbs. Mfg. 2005-2011.

$695 $575 $475 $400 $350 $325 $285 *$839*

Add $100 for 100% camo coverage.
Add $100 for walnut stock and forearm.

I-12 LIMITED WHITE GOLD – 12 ga. only, similar to I-12 Inertia, except has AA Grade checkered walnut stock and forearm, 28 in. barrel only, engraved matte nickel receiver, includes hard case. Imported 2006-2011.

$1,425 $1,150 $975 $825 $725 $625 $525 *$1,699*

I-12 UPLAND HUNTER – 12 ga. only, 3 in. chamber, 26 in. VR barrel with choke tubes, Weathercoat straight grip stock and forearm. Mfg. 2008-2009.

$1,075 $925 $800 $700 $600 $500 $400 *$1,169*

I-12 SPORTING – 12 ga., 30 in. VR barrel with extended choke tubes, satin finished walnut stock and forearm, 7.8 lbs. Mfg. 2008-2011.

$1,175 $1,000 $875 $750 $650 $550 $475 *$1,329*

SAS-12 – 12 ga. only, 3 in. chamber, slide action only, synthetic stock with built-in pistol grip, 8 shot tube mag., 21 1/2 in. barrel, 6.8 lbs. Imported 1988-90 only.

$600 $525 $450 $395 $350 $295 $250 *$473*

This model was imported exclusively by FIE Firearms located in Hialeah, FL.

SPAS-12 – 12 ga., 2 3/4 in. chamber, tactical shotgun, slide action or semi-auto operation, 5 (new 1991) or 8 (disc.) shot tube mag., alloy receiver, synthetic stock with built-in pistol grip (limited quantities were also mfg. with a folding stock or metal fixed stock), one-button switch to change operating mode, 21 1/2 in. barrel, 8 3/4 lbs. Importation disc. 1994.

$1,500 $1,300 $1,175 $1,000 $900 $800 $700 *$769*

This model was imported exclusively by FIE Firearms located in Hialeah, FL until 1990.

GRADING - PPGS™	100%	98%	95%	90%	80%	70%	60%	LAST MSR

SPAS-15 – 12 ga. only, 2 3/4 in. chamber, tactical shotgun, slide action or semi-auto operation, 6 shot detachable box mag., 21 1/2 in. barrel, lateral folding skeleton stock, carrying handle, one button switch to change operating mode, 10 lbs. Limited importation 1989 only.

Even though the retail was in the $700 range, demand and rarity have pushed prices up dramatically, with NIB examples in the $5,000 - $7,500 range.

This model had very limited importation (less than 200) as the BATFE disallowed further importation almost immediately.

LAW-12 – 12 ga. only, 2 3/4 in. chamber, gas operated semi-auto, synthetic stock with built-in pistol grip, 5 (new 1991) or 8 (disc.) shot tube mag., 21 1/2 in. barrel, 6 3/4 lbs. Imported 1988-94.

	100%	98%	95%	90%	80%	70%	60%	LAST MSR
	$570	$485	$400	$360	$320	$300	$280	*$719*

TURKEY GUN – 12 ga., similar to Standard Mag., 3 in. chamber only, turkey scene engraved. Mfg. 1963-65.

	100%	98%	95%	90%	80%	70%	60%
	$415	$385	$370	$340	$315	$290	$275

SLUG GUN – 22 in. plain barrel, rifle sights.

	100%	98%	95%	90%	80%	70%	60%
	$360	$330	$315	$295	$275	$255	$240

SKEET GUN – 26 in. skeet choke vent. rib barrel, select wood. Mfg. 1972-1974.

	100%	98%	95%	90%	80%	70%	60%
	$385	$370	$350	$330	$310	$285	$265

ELDORADO – fancy wood and gold filled engraved receiver. Mfg. 1954-75.

	100%	98%	95%	90%	80%	70%	60%
	$450	$420	$395	$380	$360	$340	$320

CROWN GRADE – engraved hunting scene. Mfg. 1954-75.

	100%	98%	95%	90%	80%	70%	60%
	$1,540	$1,320	$1,210	$1,045	$965	$910	$855

DIAMOND GRADE SILVER INLAID SCROLL – mfg. 1954-75.

	100%	98%	95%	90%	80%	70%	60%
	$1,980	$1,735	$1,540	$1,430	$1,210	$1,045	$965

IMPERIAL GRADE – gold inlaid hunting scene.

	100%	98%	95%	90%	80%	70%	60%
	$2,420	$2,090	$1,925	$1,760	$1,595	$1,485	$1,320

Note: Standard, Skeet and Slug with steel frame mfg. 1965-1972, designated "Dynamic" 12 ga., values are the same.

MODEL 500 STANDARD – 12 ga., 26 or 28 in. barrel, various chokes, vent. rib, gas operated, checkered pistol grip stock. Mfg. 1976-disc.

	100%	98%	95%	90%	80%	70%	60%
	$330	$310	$305	$265	$230	$195	$165

MODEL 520 DELUXE – engraved receiver.

	100%	98%	95%	90%	80%	70%	60%
	$385	$365	$330	$290	$260	$220	$195

MODEL 520 ELDORADO GOLD – fine wood, engraved gold, inlaid receiver. Mfg. 1977-disc.

	100%	98%	95%	90%	80%	70%	60%
	$990	$770	$715	$660	$580	$525	$470

MODEL 530 AUTO TRAP – 12 ga., similar to 500, except 30 or 32 in. full choke barrel, very high rib, special trap stock, recoil pad.

	100%	98%	95%	90%	80%	70%	60%
	$660	$550	$525	$440	$415	$385	$330

FRANCOLIN INTERNATIONAL ARMS CO.

Current shotgun manufacturer established in 1994, located in Konya, Turkey. No current U.S. importation.

Francolin International Arms was founded under Lazer Arms in 1994 with the brand starting in 2012. Francolin manufactures a complete line of good quality shotguns in a variety of configurations, including: O/U, revolving, slide action (including tactical models), semi-auto (including tactical models), and single barrel. For current U.S. availability and pricing, please contact the company directly.

FRANCOTTE, AUGUSTE & CIE. S.A.

Current trademark owned by Connecticut Shotgun Manufacturing Company beginning 2011. Previous manufacturer located in Leige, Belgium 1805-2002. Previously imported until 1999 by Armes De Chasse located in Hertford, NC, Von Lengerke & Detmold between 1900-1930s, and Abercrombie & Fitch until approx. 1962.

It is important to note that original A. Francotte SxS rifles and shotguns should exhibit the "crown over AF" maker's mark amongst the proof marks.

GRADING - PPGS™	100%	98%	95%	90%	80%	70%	60%	LAST MSR

PISTOLS: SEMI-AUTO

FRANCOTTE AUTOMATIC (SEMI-AUTO PISTOL) - 6.35mm cal., 6 shot mag., frame marked "Francotte Liege." Mfg. 1912-1914.

	$495	$450	$395	$335	$295	$260	$230

REVOLVERS

Francotte manufactured Pryse-type revolvers at the end of the 19th century, and these revolvers bore the name of the well-known British retailer. Encountered only infrequently domestically, these specimens found overseas are usually priced in the $250-$800 range.

RIFLES

All recently mfg. rifles in this section were custom made to the purchaser's individual specifications. Francotte took advantage of 5 different frame sizes for its double rifles.

Add 20%-50% for P. Grifnee engraving, depending on coverage and amount of detail.

BOLT ACTION MODEL - many calibers between .18 Bee and .505 Gibbs Mag., select checkered walnut stock, engraved mag. floorplate, gold inlays optional, the following values assume engraving.

* ***Bolt Action Model Short*** - cals. with shorter cartridges.

	$9,400	$8,225	$7,050	$6,390	$5,170	$4,230	$3,290

Subtract $3,250 if without engraving.

* ***Bolt Action Model Standard*** - cals. with medium cartridge lengths.

	$7,825	$6,845	$5,870	$5,320	$4,305	$3,520	$2,740

Subtract $2,675 if without engraving.

* ***Bolt Action Model Magnum Action*** - cals. with longer cartridge lengths.

	$13,750	$12,030	$10,315	$9,350	$7,565	$6,190	$4,815

Subtract $7,850 if without engraving.

SINGLE SHOT MOUNTAIN RIFLE - variety of cals., boxlock or sidelock action, custom order only.

* ***Single Shot Mountain Rifle Boxlock*** - 6.5x50Rmm, 7x57Rmm, or 7x65Rmm cal.

	$13,900	$12,165	$10,425	$9,450	$7,645	$6,255	$4,865

Subtract $4,800 if without engraving.
Add 10% for optional sideplates.

* ***Single Shot Mountain Rifle Sidelock*** - 7x65Rmm or 7mm Rem. Mag. cal.

	$24,800	$21,700	$18,600	$16,865	$13,640	$11,160	$8,680

Subtract $5,725 if without engraving.

BOXLOCK SxS RIFLE - .30-06, .375 H&H, .470 NE, .500-3 in., or 9.3x62mm cal., ejectors, case colored frame with border engraving (including screws), quarter rib on barrel, deluxe checkered pistol grip walnut stock and forearm. Mfg. 1997-disc.

	$13,750	$12,030	$10,315	$9,350	$7,565	$6,190	$4,815

Add 50% for .375 H&H cal.
Add 100% for .470 NE or .500-3 in. cal.

SIDELOCK SxS RIFLE - .30-06, .375 H&H, .470 NE, .500-3 in., or 9.3x62mm cal., ejectors, case colored frame with border engraving (including screws), quarter rib on barrel, deluxe checkered pistol grip walnut stock and forearm. Mfg. 1997-disc.

	$26,000	$22,750	$19,500	$17,680	$14,300	$11,700	$9,100
.470 NE or .500-3 in. cal.	$52,000	$45,500	$39,000	$35,360	$28,600	$23,400	$18,200

Add 50% for .375 H&H, .470 NE, or .500 cal.

SHOTGUNS: SxS

Please contact CT Shotgun Manufacturing Company directly for availability and pricing on any new releases.

All recently manufactured shotguns in this section were custom made to purchaser's individual specifications. Basic types listed were also available in 24 or 32 ga. upon special order. Francotte took advantage of 5 different action sizes, one for each gauge. Auguste Francotte did not manufacture guns by model - all guns were custom order. Original A. Francotte SxS shotguns must have the "Francotte Choke Bore" marking on the water table. Be wary of fake barrel and frame markings, as some guns have recenty surfaced that are not Francotte, but have the Francotte name.

Add 50% for 20 ga.
Add 100% for 28 ga. or .410 bore, on the following models (except Jubilee), depending on condition.
Add 20%-50% for P. Grifnee engraving, (post-1970 mfg.) depending on coverage and amount of detail.

GRADING - PPGS™	100%	98%	95%	90%	80%	70%	60%	LAST MSR

BOXLOCK MODEL – 12, 16, 20, 28 ga., or .410 bore, premium grade Belgium side-by-side, double triggers standard, auto ejectors, English scroll engraving, Anson & Deeley boxlock action.

	$15,450	$11,250	$8,000	$6,250	$5,000	$4,000	$3,250	

Subtract approx. 30% if without engraving.

Add approx. 15% for sideplates with engraving.

* ***Boxlock Model Deluxe Anson & Deeley*** – gold inlaid game scenes, and engraving was by customer's personal preference.

	$17,500	$14,250	$11,000	$8,750	$7,250	$6,000	$4,750	

SIDELOCK MODEL (OLDER MFG.) – 12, 16, 20, 28 ga., or .410 bore, true sidelock action, Arabesque scroll engraving, various chokes and barrel lengths, custom order only.

	$27,300	$22,000	$18,750	$15,150	$12,000	$9,000	$7,750	

Subtract approx. 15% if without engraving.

* ***Sidelock Model Deluxe (Older Mfg.)*** – gold inlaid game scenes and engraving were by customer's personal preference.

	$32,500	$27,500	$22,000	$18,750	$15,000	$12,000	$9,500	

SIDELOCK MODEL (CURRENT MFG.) – 12, 16, 20, 28 ga., or .410 bore, full sidelock action, case colored receiver with rose and scroll engraving, various chokes and barrel lengths, DT, custom order only, approx. 12 month delivery time.

Base price on this model is $25,000.

JUBILEE MODEL – case colored frame with hand engraving, Von Lengerke & Detmold or Abercrombie & Fitch import. Mfg. circa 1920-1970.

Knockabout	$3,300	$2,950	$2,600	$2,100	$1,650	$1,450	$1,200	
No. 14	$4,100	$3,600	$3,000	$2,550	$2,200	$2,050	$1,750	
No. 18	$4,625	$4,000	$3,400	$2,950	$2,525	$2,075	$1,875	
No. 20	$5,500	$4,800	$4,100	$3,400	$2,925	$2,550	$2,100	
No. 25	$6,000	$5,500	$4,700	$4,100	$3,500	$2,850	$2,375	
No. 30	$7,800	$6,950	$6,100	$5,600	$5,050	$4,400	$3,850	
No. 45 Eagle Grade	$11,000	$9,900	$8,800	$7,700	$6,600	$5,500	$4,750	

Add 100%-150% for 20 ga., depending on condition.

Add approx. 300%-350% for 28 ga. or .410 bore, depending on condition.

Jubilee Models No. 20, 25, 30, and 45 Eagle Grade are boxlocks with sideplates.

FRANKLIN ARMORY

Current manufacturer of AR-15 style firearms located in Morgan Hill, CA and Minden, NV.

Please refer to BlueBookOfGunValues.com to order the *Blue Book of AR-15s & Variations*, available as a book or online subscription.

FRASER, DANIEL (FRASER, DANL. & CO.)

Current rifle maker located in Edinburgh, Scotland. Previously imported and distributed by Flying G Ranch, located in Carrizo Springs, TX.

The business of Daniel Fraser was founded in 1873 in Edinburgh, Scotland. After serving his apprenticeship with Alexander Henry, Fraser would go on to receive a number of patents relating to design and improvement of guns and rifles of the period, but specializing in rifle building as his master had taught him. The Fraser name is long associated with high quality sporting single and double rifles and became part of John Dickson and Son in 1918. Fraser continues to build these rifles in Scotland in the same manner, utilising the renowned Mauser 98 action to produce a functional and practical lightweight stalking rifle in the smaller calibers and Double Square bridge Mauser 98 actions for Magnum calibers.

RIFLES

AFRICAN EXPRESS RIFLE – based on the Mauser 98 style action. Bespoke specification and build.

Current base price starts at $24,000.

HIGHLANDER SINGLE SHOT – .22 LR or .22 Hornet cal., underlever falling block action (color case hardened), 24 in. (1/2 round, 1/2 octagon) barrel, folding express-style sights, pistol grip walnut stock with fine checkering. Disc.

	$415	$335	$300	$280	$260	$240	$220	*$475*

* ***Highlander Single Shot Royal*** – .22 LR or .22 Hornet cal., mfg. in Scotland, rose and scroll engraving with 18Kt. inlays. This model was available through special order only. Disc.

STALKING RIFLE – based on the Mauser 98 style action. Bespoke specification and build.

Current base price starts at $12,000.

GRADING - PPGS™	100%	98%	95%	90%	80%	70%	60%	LAST MSR

FRASER FIREARMS CORP.

Previously manufactured by R.B. Industries, Ltd. until 1990. Previously distributed by Fraser Firearms Corp. located in Fraser, MI.

PISTOLS: SEMI-AUTO

FRASER 25 CAL. – .25 ACP cal. only, copy of the Bauer semi-auto pocket model, 6 shot mag., 2 1/4 in. barrel, stainless steel construction.

	100%	98%	95%	90%	80%	70%	60%	LAST MSR
	$120	$100	$90	$85	$80	$75	$70	*$133*

Add $17 for Model 2 (black nylon grips).
Add $115 for Model 3 (24Kt. gold plated).

FREEDOM ARMS

Current manufacturer established during 1983, and located in Freedom, WY. Distributor and dealer sales.

PISTOLS: SINGLE SHOT

MODEL 2008 SINGLE SHOT HANDGUN – .223 Rem., 6.5 Creedmoor, .243 Win., .260 Rem., 7 BR Rem., 7-08 Rem., .308 Win., .338 Federal, .357 Mag., .357 Max., .375 Win., .41 Mag., .454 Casull, .460 Casull, .460 S&W, or .45-70 Govt. cal., single shot pistol, SA, 10 or 15 in. interchangeable barrel, positive extractor, impregnated hardwood grips and forend, stainless steel, matte finish, approx. 3.94 lbs.

	100%	98%	95%	90%	80%	70%	60%	LAST MSR
MSR $1,566	$14,095	$12,330	$10,570	$9,585	$7,750	$6,340	$4,935	

REVOLVERS: MINI, STAINLESS STEEL

Because Freedom Arms' manufacturing capacity has been maximized due to the success of the .454 Casull revolver, the mini-revolver series was discontinued beginning 1989.

FA-S-22LR (PATRIOT) – .22 LR cal., 5 shot, 1, 1 3/4 (disc. 1988), or 3 (disc. 1988) in. barrel, Hi-Gloss finish. Disc. 1989.

	100%	98%	95%	90%	80%	70%	60%	LAST MSR
	$175	$135	$100	$90	$80	$75	$70	*$153*

Add $15 for 3 in. barrel model (FA-BG-22LR, Minute-Man, disc. 1988).

FA-S-22M (IRONSIDES) – .22 WMR cal., 4 shot, 1, 1 3/4 (disc. 1988), or 3 in. barrel, Hi-Gloss finish. Disc. 1989.

	100%	98%	95%	90%	80%	70%	60%	LAST MSR
	$200	$150	$110	$95	$85	$80	$75	*$177*

Add $43 for 3 in. barrel model (Bostonian).

FA-S-22-LR BUCKLE/REVOLVER COMBINATION – .22 LR cal., 1 in. barrel, pistol is housed in belt buckle. Disc. 1989.

	100%	98%	95%	90%	80%	70%	60%	LAST MSR
	$350	$295	$225	$185	$145	$120	$105	*$193*

* ***FA-S-22-LR Buckle/Revolver Combination .22 Mag. cal.***

	100%	98%	95%	90%	80%	70%	60%	LAST MSR
	$395	$350	$250	$200	$150	$125	$110	*$216*

REVOLVERS: SA, STAINLESS STEEL

Freedom Arms also offers a complete line of accessories and factory installed options. The factory should be contacted directly for an up-to-date listing and prices. Beginning in 1999, all revolvers are equipped with a locking safety device which slides into the muzzle and locks into the chamber under the firing pin, making it impossible to either load the top chamber or turn the cylinder.

Add $363 per interchangeable cylinder in different cals. on most of the following centerfire models.
Add $578 for octagon barrel.
Add $104 for non-standard barrel length.

MODEL 83 FIELD GRADE – .22 LR (w/match chamber), .357 Mag., .41 Mag., .44 Mag., .45 LC (disc. 1990), .454 Casull, .475 Linebaugh, .50 AE (disc. 2004) or .500 Wyoming Express (new 2006) cal., 5 shot, 4 3/4, 6, 7 1/2, 9 (.357 Mag. only), or 10 (not available in .500 Wyoming Express) in. barrel, fixed (disc.) or aluminum base adj. rear sight, replaceable blade front sight, matte stainless steel construction, manual sliding-bar safety system, Pachmayr presentation (disc.) or impregnated hardwood grips, 56 oz. (.454 Casull cal. with 7 1/2 in. barrel). New 1988.

	100%	98%	95%	90%	80%	70%	60%	LAST MSR
MSR $2,406	$2,150	$1,900	$1,600	$1,450	$1,200	$1,000	$750	

Add $92 for .454 Casull, .475 Linebaugh, .50 AE (disc. 2004), or .500 Wyoming Express cal.
Add $312 for .22 LR cal. with match chamber and 10 in. barrel.

MODEL 83 HUNTER PAK FIELD GRADE – .357 Mag., .44 Rem. Mag., or .454 Casull cal., 7 1/2 in. barrel, plastic grips, field grade low profile adj. rear sight or no front sight base, sling and studs, locking aluminum carrying case with cleaning kit and tool. Mfg. 1990-93.

	100%	98%	95%	90%	80%	70%	60%	LAST MSR
	$1,150	$975	$875	$775	$700	$625	$550	*$1,333*

Add $76 for low profile adj. sight and Pachmayr grips.

GRADING - PPGS™	100%	98%	95%	90%	80%	70%	60%	LAST MSR

* ***Model 83 Hunter Pak Field Grade Premier*** – .357 Mag., .44 Rem. Mag., or .454 Casull cal., 7 1/2 in. barrel, ebony Micarta grips, no sights or premier grade adj. sights, sling and studs, locking aluminum carrying case with cleaning kit and tool. Mfg. 1990-93.

	$1,395	$1,125	$925	$825	$750	$675	$500	*$1,611*

Add $100 for adj. sights.

MODEL 83 PREMIER GRADE – .357 Mag., .41 Mag., .44 Mag., .454 Casull, .475 Linebaugh, .50 AE (disc.), .500 Wyoming Express (new 2006) cal., 5 shot, 4 3/4, 6, 7 1/2, 9 (.357 Mag. only) or 10 (not available in .500 Wyoming Express) in. barrel, fixed or steel base adj. rear sight and replaceable blade front sight, stainless steel construction, bright brushed finish, manual sliding-bar safety system, and impregnated hardwood grips, 52.8 oz. New 1983.

MSR $2,825	$2,550	$2,200	$1,900	$1,750	$1,400	$1,150	$900	

Add $5 for adj. sights.
Add $114 for .454 Casull, .475 Linebaugh, .500 Wyoming Express, or .50 AE (disc.) cal. with adj. sights.

MODEL 83 VARMINT GRADE – .22 LR cal., 5 shot, dual firing pins, choice of 5 1/8 or 7 1/2 in. barrel, steel base adj. V notch rear sight and replaceable brass bead front sight, stainless steel construction, matte finish, manual sliding-bar safety system, pre-set trigger overtravel stop, impregnated hardwood grips, 58 oz. Disc. 2005.

	$1,525	$1,275	$950	$850	$775	$700	$650	*$1,828*

Add $264 for extra .22 WMR cylinder.

MODEL 83 CENTERFIRE SILHOUETTE – .357 Mag., .41 Mag., or .44 Mag. cal., 5 shot, 9 (.357 Mag. only) or 10 in. barrel, Pachmayr presentation (disc.) or wood grips, Iron Sight Gun Works silhouette rear sight and replaceable adj. front sight blade with hood, stainless steel construction, matte finish, manual sliding-bar safety system.

MSR $2,538	$2,350	$2,050	$1,750	$1,600	$1,300	$1,050	$800	

* ***Model 83 Centerfire Silhouette (.454 Casull Silhouette Model)*** – .454 Casull cal., includes 10 in. barrel, Pachmayr grips, field grade finish, silhouette competition sights, and trigger overtravel stop.

	$1,600	$1,275	$1,075	$925	$825	$750	$675	*$1,958*

* ***Model 83 Centerfire Silhouette Pak*** – .44 Mag. cal., includes 10 in. barrel, silhouette competition sight, honed action with 3 lb. trigger pull, plastic grips, locking aluminum carrying case with cleaning kit and tool. Mfg. 1990 only.

	$1,750	$1,450	$1,100	$950	$850	$775	$700	*$1,242*

* ***Model 83 Centerfire Silhouette .454 Casull Pak*** – .454 Casull cal., includes 10 in. barrel, silhouette competition sight, honed action with 3 lb. trigger pull, hardwood grips, locking aluminum carrying case with cleaning kit and tool. Mfg. 1990 only.

	$1,750	$1,450	$1,100	$950	$850	$775	$700	*$1,522*

MODEL 83 .22 CAL. SILHOUETTE CLASS – .22 LR cal., 5 shot, 10 in. barrel, wood (standard), black Micarta (standard, disc.), or Pachmayr (disc.) grips, Iron Sight Gun Works silhouette rear sight and replaceable adj. front sight blade with hood, stainless steel construction, matte finish, manual sliding-bar safety system, dual firing pins, lightened hammer for fast lock time, pre-set trigger overtravel stop, 63 oz. New 1991.

MSR $2,850	$2,550	$2,250	$1,900	$1,750	$1,400	$1,150	$900	

MODEL 97 PACKER – .357 Mag., .44 Spl., or .45 Colt/ACP cal., small frame size, 2 1/2 in. barrel, 5 shot, no ejection rod, transfer bar in hammer, fixed sights front blade and rear groove, black Micarta grips, stainless steel finish. New 2019.

Please contact the manufacturer directly for pricing and availability on this model.

MODEL 97 PREMIER GRADE – .17 HMR (new 2004), .22 LR (new 2002), .224-32 F.A. (new 2009), .327 Federal (new 2010), .357 Mag., .32 H&R Mag. (mfg. 2004-2009), .41 Rem. Mag. (new 2000), .44 Spl. (new 2003), .45 LC (new 1999) cal., 5 (.41 Mag., .44. Spl., or .45 LC cal.) or 6 (.17 HMR, .22 LR or .357 Mag. cal.) shot, 3 1/2 (mfg. 2004-2005), 4 1/4, 4 1/2 (mfg. 2000-disc.), 5 1/2, 7 1/2, or 10 in. barrel, fixed or steel base adj. rear sight and replaceable blade front sight, stainless steel construction, bright brushed finish, automatic transfer bar safety system, optional round butt grip, impregnated hardwood grips. New 1997.

MSR $2,255	$2,050	$1,800	$1,500	$1,400	$1,100	$900	$700	

Add $166 for .17 HMR or .22 LR cal. with sporting chambers.
Add $141 for adj. sights on most calibers.
Add $215 for optional round butt grip (disc.).
Add $215 for 3 1/2 in. barrel (disc.).

U.S. DEPUTY MARSHAL – 3 in. barrel only with no ejector, fixed or adj. sights, U.S. Marshal medallion in left hardwood grip. Mfg. 1990-93.

	$1,325	$900	$750	$640	$535	$450	$390	*$1,475 (fixed sights)*

Add approx. $80 for adj. sights (last MSR was $1,558).

GRADING - PPGS™	100%	98%	95%	90%	80%	70%	60%	LAST MSR

SIGNATURE EDITION – .454 Casull cal., high polish stainless steel, 7 1/2 in. barrel only, rosewood grips, cased with accessories, only 93 of 100 were actually mfg.

	$2,300	$1,750	$1,300	$1,150	$935	$815	$650	*$2,684*

PRIMUS INTER PARES – 1 of every 1,000 guns were made in this variation, includes octagonal barrel, ivory grips, 7 1/2 in. barrel, and cased. Disc. 1993.

Rarity factor precludes accurate pricing.

FREEDOM ORDNANCE

Current AR-15 style manufacturer of pistols and rifles located in Chandler, IN.

Please refer to BlueBookOfGunValues.com to order the *Blue Book of AR-15s & Variations*, available as a book or online subscription.

FRENCH MILITARY

Various configurations manufactured in several locations in France.

REVOLVERS: DOUBLE ACTION

MODEL 1892 SERVICE REVOLVER – 8mm Lebel cal., primary French Service revolver used through WWI until replaced by the M1935-A. Chambering similar to the smaller U.S. .32-20 cartridge, blued with checkered walnut grips and a lanyard loop on the frame.

	$600	$500	$450	$400	$350	$300	$225

PISTOLS: SEMI-AUTO

MODEL 1935-A (1935A AUTO PISTOL) – 7.65mm French Long cal., 4.3 in. barrel, 8 shot, fixed sights, checkered wood grips, locking mechanism similar to U.S. M1911A1, blue finish, Designed and mfg. for the French military (about 10,000 were issued). Approx. 24,000 were mfg. under German occupation. Mfg. 1935-1945.

Standard Model	$575	$475	$300	$250	$225	$200	$175

Add 50% if Nazi proofed.

MODEL 1935-S (MODEL 1935S AUTO PISTOL) – 7.65mm French Long cal., 4.1 in. barrel, 8 shot, distinct raised area at rear of slide, uses a slightly modified locking system similar to the M1935A, enamel finish, 26 oz. Approx. 85,000 were produced between 1939 and 1953. Issued to the French foreign legion fighting in Indo China 1953-1954.

	$550	$500	$425	$375	$300	$250	$200

M.A.B. MODEL C – .380 ACP (mfg. 1933-1963) or 7.65mm cal., design based on FN Browning Model 1910 7.65mm cal., 6.1 in. barrel. Mfg. 1933-1967.

Standard prod. 7.65mm	N/A	$425	$375	$350	$300	$250	$200
Standard prod. .380 ACP	N/A	$450	$400	$350	$325	$275	$250

Add 10% for prewar 7.65mm or 15% for prewar .380 ACP cal.

The Model C was intended mostly for civilian use. The MAB facility in Bayonne, France was under German control from June 1940-1942.

M.A.B. MODEL D – .380 ACP or 7.65mm cal., enlarged version of the Model C (similar to Browning Model 1922 in size), steel (early versions) or alloy (later versions) frame, lanyard loop, longer grip area, intended primarily for police use. Mfg. 1933-1964.

Standard Prod. 7.65mm	N/A	$425	$375	$325	$300	$275	$200
Standard Prod. .380 ACP	N/A	$500	$425	$400	$375	$350	$275

Add 10% for prewar 7.65mm or 15% for prewar .380 ACP cal.

Add 50% for German acceptance stamped (WaA 251).

Add 60% for prewar Navy marked.

During German occupation from June 1940-1942, approx. 53,000 Model Ds were procured by the German military. These examples contain Waffenamt proof and acceptance stamps and are considered rare.

PISTOLS: SEMI-AUTO; POST WAR OCCUPATION PRODUCTION

French Forces continued production of German P.38 pistols at the occupied Mauser factory located in Oberndorf, Germany after the end of WWII, 1945.

P.38 svw-45 – 9mm Para. cal., blue or grey phosphate finish, French five pointed star proof located on right side of slide, some parts may contain E/WaA135 Garman acceptance stamps, ser. no. range approx. 1g-4500k. Mfg. by Mauser, late 1945.

Standard Model	$825	$775	$725	$550	$480	$425	$325

Add 20% for French assembly with FN manufactured slide (marked ac-43 or ac-44 with E/WaA135 stamps).

GRADING - PPGS™	100%	98%	95%	90%	80%	70%	60%	LAST MSR

P.38 svw-46 – 9mm Para. cal., grey phosphate finish, French five pointed star proof located on right side of the slide, some parts may contain E/WaA135 German acceptance stamps, pressed steel grips are common, ser. no. range approx. 4501k-9999k. Mfg. by Mauser, 1946.

$850 $800 $775 $725 $600 $525 $500

P.38 svw-46 (With L SERIAL SUFFIX) – 9mm Para. cal., black/blue finish, French five pointed star proof located on right side of the slide, ser. no. located on left side of slide (early) or under the rear tang of the frame, pressed steel grips common, ser. no. range 1L-500L. Mfg. by Mauser, 1946.

$1,350 $1,225 $1,125 $1,000 $875 $800 $725

MODEL 1950 – 9mm Para. cal., SA, 9 shot, most models saw heavy use, 221,900 mfg. by de Armes Chatellerault (MAC) from circa 1953-1963.

$2,250 $1,750 $1,250 $1,000 $800 $600 $400

Add 15% for rig/holster, belt, and cleaning rod.

MODEL M.A.B. PA-8 – 9mm Para. cal., single action, 8 shot, blued finish, formerly used by French military.

$475 $450 $400 $350 $300 $225 $200

MODEL M.A.B. PA-15 – 9mm Para. cal., single action, 15 shot staggered row mag., blued finish, formerly used by French military.

$850 $600 $475 $400 $365 $335 $300

MODEL M.A.B. PAP Mle F 1 TARGET (M.A.B. PA-15 TARGET) – rare target variation of PA-15, adj. rear sight, 6 in. barrel, parkerized finish, cased.

$7,000 $5,000 $3,000 $2,500 $2,000 $1,500 $1,000

Add 20% if cased with accessories.

RIFLES: BOLT ACTION

MODEL 1886 LEBEL – 8mm Lebel rimmed smokeless cartridge (first modern small bore magazine fed rifle to utilize this cartridge), 31 or 32 in. barrel, 8 shot tubular mag., adj. sight, military stock. Mfg. 1886-WWII.

N/A $750 $675 $625 $550 $500 $450

This model was made in a shortened version and used by the French as late as WWII. Also known as "Fusil Mle 1886 M93". An estimated 2,900,000 were produced. It was made obsolete by the introduction of the Berthier rifle in the 1890s.

RIFLES/CARBINES: BERTHIER BOLT ACTION

Berthier bolt action rifles and carbines were adopted as French service rifles beginning in 1890. They were chambered for the 8mm Lebel rimmed cartridge. These rifles and carbines were initially produced with a three shot clip-fed mag. During WWI and later, many were modified to accept a five shot magazine similar to the Mannlicher style. These firearms were produced at three French arsenals: Manufacture d'Armes de Chatellerault (MAC), Manufacture d'Armes de St. Etienne (MAS), and Establissement Delaunay-Belleville (EDB). Remington Arms-Union Metallic Cartridge Company (RAC-UMC) produced the model and contract in 1914 and 1915. Only 20,000 of 250,000 were manufactured prior to contract cancellation.

MODEL 1890 CARBINE – 8mm Lebel cartridge, 17.7 in. carbine barrel, marked on left side of receiver, sling swivels mounted to left side of the stock, no bayonet lug. Mfg. at the Chatellerault and St. Etienne Arsenals.

N/A $700 $650 $600 $550 $500 $450

MODEL 1892 CARBINE – 8mm Lebel cartridge, 17,5 in. barrel, no upper handguard (later variations may have had handguards), marked "MLE. 1892" on left side of receiver.

N/A $875 $825 $775 $700 $625 $550

MODEL 1902 CARBINE – 8mm Lebel cartridge, based on the Models of 1890 and 1892 carbines. Designed especially for the Indo-China troops. Contained a long bolt and one-piece stock with straight grip. French artillery personnel were issued a variant as the model 1892 Artillery Short Rifle.

N/A $750 $675 $625 $575 $525 $450

MODEL 1907 RIFLE – 8mm Lebel cartridge, similar to the Model 1902, except has 31.5 in. barrel and no upper handguard.

N/A $700 $650 $600 $550 $475 $400

GRADING - PPGS™	100%	98%	95%	90%	80%	70%	60%	LAST MSR

MODEL 1907/1915 RIFLE – 8mm Lebel cartridge, similar to Model 1907, except for a straight bolt action design and 31.5 in. barrel. Some were made by RAC-UMC under a 1914-1915 contact. Manufacturer marking on the left side of the receiver.

N/A	$900	$825	$750	$675	$600	$525	

Add 100% for RAC-UMC produced rifles.

MODEL 1916 RIFLE – 8mm Lebel cartridge, similar to the Model 1907/1915, except it was fitted with a 5 shot extended mag.

N/A	$875	$800	$750	$700	$600	$525	

1936 MAS BOLT ACTION – 7.5x54mm MAS rimless cartridge, 21 3/4 in. barrel, adj. sights, military stock, bayonet in forearm, distinguishable by forward bolt handle, housing machined from one-piece forging, integral box. mag., loaded with stripper clips, no safety, 8 1/2 lbs. Mfg. 1936-1949.

$550	$400	$300	$275	$200	$175	$150	

MODEL 45 RIFLE – .22 LR cal., trainer configuration, may have Mauser parts, aperture rear sight, post-war mfg.

$450	$375	$350	$300	$250	$200	$175	

RIFLES: SEMI-AUTO

MAS 49 – 7.54mm MAS, gas operated (direct impingement), 22.8 in. barrel with grenade launcher and adj. grenade sight on left front side of forend, no provision for bayonet, 10 shot detachable mag., scope rail, two-piece military stock, gray finish, approx. 9 lbs. Estimated total production of 20,600.

$825	$775	$725	$675	$650	$600	$550	

MAS 49/56 SEMI-AUTO – 7.5x54mm MAS cal., gas operated (direct impingment), 20 1/2 in. barrel w/NATO standard 22mm rifle grenade launcher and adj. grenade sight on top of barrel, gas cut-off, provision for 7.9 in. blade bayonet, 10 shot detachable mag., scope rail, two-piece military stock with shortened forend, gray finish, approx. 8.6 lbs. Estimated total production of 275,240. Many MAS 49/56 rifles were imported to the U.S. by Century Arms Internatonal (CAI) and rechambered to 7.62x51mm NATO.

$800	$700	$625	$550	$450	$350	$300	

FRIGON GUNS, INC.

Previously manufactured by Marocchi in Italy. Previously imported by Frigon Guns, Inc. located in Clay Center, KS.

SHOTGUNS

FT-I – 12 ga. only, single barrel trap gun, blue finish, 32 or 34 in. VR barrel, quick-change stock. Mfg. 1986-94.

$925	$675	$525	$435	$375	$350	$295	*$1,100*

FT-C – 12 ga. only, quick-change stock, trap combination gun includes 1 single barrel and 1 set of O/U barrels, cased. Mfg. 1986-94.

$1,700	$1,325	$1,050	$875	$775	$685	$620	*$1,975*

FS-4 – 4-barrel skeet set including 12, 20, 28 ga., or .410 bore, individual forearms, quick-change stock, vent. barrels (except for .410 bore), cased. Mfg. 1986-94.

$2,575	$1,975	$1,675	$1,475	$1,350	$1,250	$1,150	*$2,890*

FROMMER PISTOLS

Previously manufactured by Femaru-Fegyver és Gépgyár R.T., Budapest, Hungary.

Please refer to the Femaru listing in this section.

FUCHS FINE GUNS GmbH

Current long gun manufacturer established in 1986, and located in Innsbruck, Austria. Currently imported into North America by Beale's Guns located in Windsor, Canada.

For individual model listings, please go to BlueBookOfGunValues.com/overflow.

FULTON ARMORY

Current rifle manufacturer and parts supplier located in Savage, MD. Dealer sales.

Please refer to BlueBookOfGunValues.com to order the *Blue Book of AR-15s & Variations*, available as a book or online subscription.

FURR ARMS

Current manufacturer located in Orem, UT.

Please refer to the Gatling Gun listing in the G section.

FUSION FIREARMS

Current 1911-style semi-auto pistol manufacturer established in 2007, located in Venice, FL.

For individual model listings, please go to BlueBookOfGunValues.com/overflow.

G SECTION

G2 PRECISION, LLC

Current AR-15 style manufacturer located in Porter, TX.

Please refer to BlueBookOfGunValues.com to order the *Blue Book of AR-15s & Variations*, available as a book or online subscription.

GA PRECISION

Current manufacturer of bolt action rifles and AR-15 style rifles, established in 1999, located in N. Kansas City, MO.

For individual model listings, please go to BlueBookOfGunValues.com/overflow.

G.A.C. RIFLES Srl

Current rifle manufacturer established in 1993, located in Corner Spa, Brescia, Italy. No current U.S. importation.

RIFLES: BOLT ACTION

G.A.C. Rifles manufactures top quality target rifles for a variety of shooting disciplines. Guns are individually ordered. Please contact the company directly for potential U.S. importation/availability, pricing, and length of delivery time.

G.A.R. ARMS

Previous AR-15 style firearm manufacturer located in Fairacres, NM from 2012-late 2014.

Please refer to BlueBookOfGunValues.com to order the *Blue Book of AR-15s & Variations*, available as a book or online subscription.

GWACS ARMORY

Previous manufacturer of AR-15 style carbines/rifles, receivers, and accessories, located in Tulsa, OK.

Please refer to BlueBookOfGunValues.com to order the *Blue Book of AR-15s & Variations*, available as a book or online subscription.

GALAZAN

Current trademark established in 1995, and manufactured by Connecticut Shotgun Manufacturing Co., located in New Britain, CT. Consumer direct sales.

The Galazan trademark has established itself as one of the premier names in best quality O/U shotguns and double rifles. All guns are custom order. For more information regarding current firearms, please refer to the Connecticut Shotgun Manufacturing Co. listing in the C section.

GALEF SHOTGUNS

Previous importer of Zabala Hermanos (Spanish) and Antonio Zoli (Italian) shotguns.

GRADING - PPGS™	100%	98%	95%	90%	80%	70%	60%	LAST MSR

SHOTGUNS

COMPANION FOLDING SINGLE BARREL – 12, 16, 20, 28 ga., or .410 bore, 28 in. barrel, full choke, 30 in. full, 12 ga. only, hammerless, underlever, checkered pistol grip stock.

	100%	98%	95%	90%	80%	70%	60%	LAST MSR
	$155	$125	$100	$85	$75	$65	$55	

MONTE CARLO TRAP SINGLE BARREL – 12 ga., 32 in. full vent. rib, hammerless, underlever, recoil pad, checkered pistol grip Monte Carlo stock. Disc.

	100%	98%	95%	90%	80%	70%	60%	LAST MSR
	$225	$185	$175	$150	$135	$125	$100	

SILVER SNIPE O/U – 12 or 20 ga., 3 in. chambers, 26, 28, or 30 in. barrels, imp. cyl. and mod. or full and mod. vent. rib, checkered pistol grip stock, boxlock, extractors, single trigger. Mfg. by Angelo Zoli, disc.

	100%	98%	95%	90%	80%	70%	60%	LAST MSR
	$525	$500	$475	$400	$375	$325	$275	

GOLDEN SNIPE O/U – similar to Silver Snipe, except has auto ejectors.

	100%	98%	95%	90%	80%	70%	60%	LAST MSR
	$595	$525	$500	$475	$375	$350	$300	

SILVER HAWK SxS – 12 or 20 ga., 3 in. chambers, 26, 28, or 30 in. barrels, imp. cyl. and mod. or mod. and full, boxlock, extractors, checkered pistol grip and beavertail forearm. Mfg. by Angelo Zoli, 1968-72.

	100%	98%	95%	90%	80%	70%	60%	LAST MSR
	$450	$400	$375	$350	$300	$275	$250	

GALEF ZABALA SxS – 10, 12, 16, or 20 ga., 22, 26, 28, or 30 in. barrels, boxlock, extractors.

	100%	98%	95%	90%	80%	70%	60%	LAST MSR
10 gauge	$250	$230	$200	$175	$150	$140	$125	
Other gauges	$200	$175	$150	$130	$120	$110	$100	

GALENA INDUSTRIES INC.

Please refer to the AMT and Automag listings in the A section.

GRADING - PPGS™	100%	98%	95%	90%	80%	70%	60%	LAST MSR

GALIL

Current trademark manufactured by Israel Weapon Industries Ltd. (IWI), formerly Israel Military Industries (IMI). Currently imported by IWI US, Inc. located in Middletown, PA beginning late 2014. Galil semi-auto sporterized rifles and variations with thumbhole stocks were banned in April, 1998. Beginning late 1996, Galil rifles and pistols were available in selective fire mode only (law enforcement, military only). Previously imported by UZI America, Inc. (a subsidiary of O.F. Mossberg & Sons, Inc.), Action Arms, Ltd., located in Philadelphia, PA until 1994, Springfield Armory located in Geneseo, IL, and Magnum Research, Inc., located in Minneapolis, MN.

Magnum Research importation can be denoted by a serial number prefix "MR". Action Arms imported rifles have either "AA" or "AAL" prefixes.

PISTOLS: SEMI-AUTO

GALIL ACE PISTOL (GAP39) – 7.62x39mm cal., closed rotating bolt, long stroke GPO, milled steel receiver, 8.3 in. barrel, 2-piece Picatinny Tri-Rail forearm system w/removable covers and protected pressure switch area, 30 shot standard AK-style mag., adj. rear and Tritium post front sights, 18 in. OAL, parkerized finish, 6 lbs. Imported late 2014-2015.

	100%	98%	95%	90%	80%	70%	60%	LAST MSR
	$1,500	$1,300	$1,100	$1,000	$800	$700	$500	*$1,749*

On December 28, 2015, IWI US, Inc. conducted a recall of all Galil ACE (GAP39) pistols that have a receiver with a 3-pin (3-hole) fire control group construction. There are no safety issues involved with this recall. FFL Dealers and Consumers should contact IWI US, Inc. at (717) 695-2081, or email recall@iwi.

GALIL ACE PISTOL (GAP39SB/GAP39-II) – 7.62x39mm cal., closed rotating bolt, long stroke GPO, milled steel receiver, 8.3 in. chrome-lined CHF barrel, 30 shot standard AK-style mag., fully adj. sights with Tritium front post, with or w/o side folding stabilizing brace, two-piece Picatinny top rail, Tri-Rail forearm system w/removable covers and protected pressure switch area, black parkerized finish, 6-6.5 lbs. Importation began 2016.

	100%	98%	95%	90%	80%	70%	60%	LAST MSR
MSR $1,749	$1,485	$1,300	$1,110	$1,010	$815	$675	$580	

Add $100 for GAP39SB (side stabilizing brace) model.

GALIL ACE PISTOL (GAP51/GAP51SB) – 7.62 NATO cal., closed rotating bolt, long stroke gas system, 11.8 in. chrome-lined CHF barrel, 20 shot mag. (Magpul LR/SR25 mag. compatible), fully adj. sights w/Tritium front post and two-dot Tritium rear aperture, full-length two-piece Picatinny top rail, slide on/off rail covers, reciprocating charging handle on left side, milled steel receiver, optional side folding stabilizer brace, black finish, 6 lbs.

	100%	98%	95%	90%	80%	70%	60%	LAST MSR
MSR $1,949	$1,700	$1,500	$1,300	$1,150	$950	$750	$650	

Add $100 for side folding stabilizer brace.

GALIL ACE PISTOL (GAP545SB) – 5.45X39mm cal., closed rotating bolt, long stroke gas piston, 8.3 in. chrome-lined CHF CrMoV steel barrel, 30 shot Magpul PMAG 30 AK74 MOE mag., adj. Tritium front post and two-dot Tritium rear sights, black finish, 6 lbs. Limited mfg. of 545 units w/matching custom serial number beginning 2021.

	100%	98%	95%	90%	80%	70%	60%	LAST MSR
MSR $1,849	$1,575	$1,380	$1,180	$1,075	$875	$725	$615	

GALIL ACE PISTOL (GAP556/GAP556SB) – 5.56 NATO cal., long stroke gas system, 8.3 in. chrome-lined CHF barrel, 30 shot Magpul PMAG Gen. M3 w/window, fully adj. sights with Tritium front post and two-dot Tritium rear aperture, full-length two-piece Picatinny top rail, closed rotating bolt, milled steel receiver, with or w/o side folding stabilizing brace, charging handle on left side, black finish, 7.6 lbs. Importation began late 2018.

	100%	98%	95%	90%	80%	70%	60%	LAST MSR
MSR $1,749	$1,485	$1,300	$1,110	$1,010	$815	$675	$580	

Add $100 for side folding stabilizer brace.

GALIL ACE SBR PISTOL – 5.56 NATO or 7.62 NATO, or 7.62x39mm cal., closed rotating bolt, long stroke gas piston, 8.3 (5.56 NATO or 7.62x39mm) or 11.8 (7.62 NATO) in. chrome-lined CHFCrMoV steel barrel, 20 or 30 shot MAGPUL GEN M3 (20) or MOE AK/AKM PMAG (30) mag., adj. Tritium front post and two-dot Tritium rear sights, black finish, 6.72 lbs. New 2021.

	100%	98%	95%	90%	80%	70%	60%	LAST MSR
MSR $1,899	$1,615	$1,415	$1,225	$1,100	$900	$725	$630	

Add $200 for 7.62 NATO cal.

RIFLES: SEMI-AUTO

Models 329, 330 (Hadar II), 331, 332, 339 (sniper system with 6x40 mounted Nimrod scope), 361, 372, 386, and 392 all refer to various configurations of the Galil rifle.

GRADING - PPGS™	100%	98%	95%	90%	80%	70%	60%	LAST MSR

MODEL AR – .223 Rem. or .308 Win. cal., gas operated, rotating bolt, 16.1 (.223 Rem. cal. only) or 19 (.308 Win. cal. only) in. barrel, parkerized, folding stock, flip-up Tritium night sights, 8.6 lbs.

	100%	98%	95%	90%	80%	70%	60%	LAST MSR
	$3,150	$2,650	$2,475	$2,150	$1,925	$1,750	$1,625	*$950*

Add $500 for .308 Win. cal.

MODEL ARM – .223 Rem. or .308 Win. cal., similar to Model AR, except includes folding bipod, vented hardwood handguard, and carrying handle.

	100%	98%	95%	90%	80%	70%	60%	LAST MSR
	$3,450	$3,100	$2,850	$2,600	$2,300	$2,100	$1,900	*$1,050*

Add $500 for .308 Win. cal.

GALIL SPORTER – .223 Rem. or .308 Win. cal., gas operated, rotating bolt, 16.1 or 19 in. barrel, parkerized, one-piece thumbhole stock, 4 (.308 Win.) or 5 (.223 Rem.) shot mag., choice of wood (disc.) or polymer handguard, 8 1/2 lbs. Imported 1991-93.

	100%	98%	95%	90%	80%	70%	60%	LAST MSR
	$1,650	$1,525	$1,375	$1,200	$1,100	$1,000	$950	*$950*

Add $400 for .308 Win. cal.

HADAR II – .308 Win. cal., GPO, tactical type configuration, 18 1/2 in. barrel, 4 (standard) or 25 shot mag., adj. rear sight, one-piece walnut thumbhole stock with pistol grip and forearm, recoil pad, 10.3 lbs. Imported 1989 only.

	100%	98%	95%	90%	80%	70%	60%	LAST MSR
	$1,575	$1,375	$1,275	$1,050	$950	$825	$750	*$998*

SNIPER OUTFIT – .308 Win. cal., limited production, sniper model built to exact I.D.F. specifications for improved accuracy, 20 in. heavy barrel, hardwood folding stock (adj. recoil pad and adj. cheekpiece) and forearm, includes Tritium night sights, bipod, detachable 6x40mm Nimrod scope, two 25 shot mags., carrying/storage case, 14.1 lbs. Imported 1989 only.

	100%	98%	95%	90%	80%	70%	60%	LAST MSR
	$6,500	$5,750	$5,000	$4,350	$3,750	$3,250	$2,850	*$3,995*

GALIL ACE RIFLE (GAR1639) – 7.62x39mm cal., closed rotating bolt, long stroke GPO, milled steel receiver, 16 in. barrel, two-piece Picatinny top rail, Tri-Rail forearm system w/removable covers and protected pressure switch area, 30 shot standard AK-style mag., fully adj. iron sights w/Tritium front post, side folding adj. telescoping buttstock w/two position removable comb, 34 1/2 in. OAL, parkerized finish, 7 1/2 lbs. w/o mag. New 2016.

	100%	98%	95%	90%	80%	70%	60%	LAST MSR
MSR $1,899	$1,615	$1,415	$1,225	$1,100	$900	$725	$630	

GALIL ACE RIFLE (GAR1651) – 7.62x39mm cal., closed rotating bolt, long stroke GPO, milled steel receiver, 16 1/2 in. barrel, 20 shot standard AK-style mag., fully adj. sights with Tritium front post and 2-dot Tritium rear aperture, 2-piece Picatinny top rail, Tri-Rail forearm system w/removable covers and protected, side folding adj. telescoping buttstock w/two position removable comb, black finish, 36 in. OAL, 8.7 lbs.

	100%	98%	95%	90%	80%	70%	60%	LAST MSR
MSR $2,099	$1,785	$1,550	$1,324	$1,200	$950	$800	$700	

GALIL ACE RILFE (GAR1654) – 5.45x39mm cal., closed rotating bolt, long stroke gas piston, 16 in. chrome-lined CHF CrMoV steel barrel, 30 shot Magpul PMAG 30 AK74 MOE mag., adj. Tritium front post and two-dot Tritium rear sights, side folding buttstock, black finish, 7.5 lbs. Limited mfg. of 545 units w/matching custom serial number beginning 2021.

	100%	98%	95%	90%	80%	70%	60%	LAST MSR
MSR $1,899	$1,615	$1,415	$1,225	$1,100	$900	$725	$630	

GALIL ACE RIFLE (GAR16556) – 5.56 NATO cal., closed rotating bolt, long stroke GPO, milled steel receiver, 16 in. chrome-lined, cold hammer forged barrel, 30 shot standard AK-style mag., fully adj. sights with Tritium front post and 2 dot Tritium rear aperture, 2 piece Picatinny top rail, Tri-Rail forearm system w/removable covers and protected, side folding adj. telescoping buttstock w/two position removable comb, black finish, 34 1/2 in. OAL, 7.8 lbs.

	100%	98%	95%	90%	80%	70%	60%	LAST MSR
MSR $1,899	$1,615	$1,415	$1,225	$1,100	$900	$725	$630	

GAMBA, RENATO

RENATO GAMBA

Current trademark established in 1748, located in Gardone V.T., Italy. Gamba firearms are currently manufactured by Bre-Mec srl beginning 2007, and are not currently being imported into the U.S. Previously imported in limited quantities circa 2005-2010 by Renato Gamba U.S.A., located in Walnut, CA. The U.S. service center is located in Bernardsville, NJ. Gamba of America, a subsidiary of Firing Line, located in Aurora, CO, was the exclusive importer and distributor for Renato Gamba long guns from 1996-2000. Pistols were previously imported and distributed (until 1990) by Armscorp of America, Inc. located in Baltimore, MD. Shotguns were previously (until 1992) imported by Heckler & Koch, Inc. located in Sterling, VA.

For individual model listings, please go to BlueBookOfGunValues.com/overflow.

GRADING - PPGS™	100%	98%	95%	90%	80%	70%	60%	LAST MSR

GARBI, ARMAS

Current manufacturer located in Eibar, Spain. Imported and distributed exclusively by William Larkin Moore & Co. located in Scottsdale, AZ.

For individual model listings, please go to BlueBookOfGunValues.com/overflow.

GARRAY RIFLES LTD.

Previous rifle manufacturer with headquarters located in Kelowna, British Columbia, Canada until 2008.

For individual model listings, please go to BlueBookOfGunValues.com/overflow.

GASTINNE RENETTE

Previous manufacturer and retailer 1812-2003, and located in Paris, France.

For individual model listings, please go to BlueBookOfGunValues.com/overflow.

GATEWAY PRECISION ARMS

Previous manufacturer located in Affton, MO.

Current model information can be found under the RPM listing.

PISTOLS: SINGLE SHOT

XL HUNTER – over 40 cals., tip-up action, stainless steel frame, 5 1/16 in. underlug, 12 or 14 in. Douglas chrome moly (new 2004) or stainless steel barrel, ISGW rear and Patridge or hooded front sight, with (became standard 2000) or w/o external positive extractor. Mfg. 1995-2008.

	100%	98%	95%	90%	80%	70%	60%	LAST MSR
XL HUNTER	$1,375	$1,250	$995	$800	$700	$600	$500	*$1,500*

Add $250 for stainless steel barrel or integral muzzle brake.
Add $50 for left-hand action.
Add approx. $400-$550 per extra barrel, depending on length.

GATLING GUNS (OLDER MFG.)

For more information and up-to-date values on older Gatling Guns manufactured circa 1862-1906, please refer to the *Blue Book of Antique American Firearms & Values*, also available as an online subscription - please visit BlueBookOfGunValues.com for ordering information and viewing sample pages.

GATLING GUNS (RECENT MFG.)

Gatling Gun refers to a rifle configuration utilizing multiple barrels and box magazine, which is operated by a rotating hand crank. Original full size Gatling guns were manufactured by Colt and some British manufacturers.

Full size Gatling reproductions are currently manufactured by Battery Gun Company.

Model Gatling guns include various models and scales of original Gatlings made from 1874 to 1893. Model cannons include the British Naval Cannon and the James Six Pounder. Prices vary according to the complexity of each model and are available by contacting Battery Gun Company.

For space considerations, no individual manufacturer/model listings or values are listed, but please check for more information on currently produced full size and scale replica reproductions.

GAUCHER

Current manufacturer established in 1834, and located in St. Etienne, France. No current U.S. importation. Previously imported and distributed by Mandall Shooting Supplies located in Scottsdale, AZ. Gaucher merged with Bretton in 2000, and the new company name is Bretton-Gaucher.

During 1997, Gaucher released four shooting rifles with unique sound suppression (approx. 71 dB) in 9mm Para., 12mm cal., or .410 bore. Additionally, Gaucher manufactures rifles (O/U and SxS double, bolt action rimfire, and semi-auto rimfire), shotguns (SxS, single shot), and 22 LR cal. target pistols. To date, there has been little importation of Gaucher firearms. Please contact the Bretton-Gaucher factory directly for more information and up-to-date pricing regarding their current lineup of firearms.

PISTOLS: SINGLE SHOT, TARGET

MODEL GN1 – .22 LR cal., single shot silhouette pistol, 10 in. barrel, adj. sights, anatomically shaped grips, monobloc lever cocking, 2.42 lbs. Limited importation.

	100%	98%	95%	90%	80%	70%	60%	LAST MSR
MODEL GN1	$360	$325	$290	$260	$230	$200	$185	*$380*

MODEL GP – similar to Model GN1, except has forearm integrated into grip. Limited importation.

	100%	98%	95%	90%	80%	70%	60%	LAST MSR
MODEL GP	$300	$275	$250	$225	$200	$185	$160	*$323*

GRADING - PPGS™	100%	98%	95%	90%	80%	70%	60%	LAST MSR

GAZELLE ARMS

Previous trademark circa 1970-2008, and manufactured by Hisar Avcilik & Doga Sporlasi San Ve Tic. Ltd. Sti., located in Konak-Izmir, Turkey. Previously imported by EMA Distributors, LLC, located in Pineville, NC.

Gazelle Arms manufactured a line of good quality, inexpensive shotguns, including semi-autos, SxSs, single shots, and O/Us. Last MSRs on the semi-auto shotguns ranged from $345-$390, while the O/U was priced at $500.

GAZELLE SHOTGUNS

Current trademark of shotguns manufactured by Koc Arms, located in Konya, Turkey. No current U.S. importation.

Koc Arms manufactures a complete line of good quality semi-auto and slide action shotguns under the Gazelle trademark. A wide variety of configurations are available, including camo, carbon fiber, various receiver finishes, grip and stock options, as well as engraving. Koc Arms also manufactures air rifles under the Gazelle trademark. Please contact the company directly for more information, including domestic availability and pricing.

GAVAGE

Previous manufacturer located in Liege, Belgium circa 1936-1943.

PISTOLS: SEMI-AUTO

GAVAGE PISTOL – .32 ACP/7.65mm cal., patterned after the Clement, fixed barrel, limited mfg.

	100%	98%	95%	90%	80%	70%	60%	LAST MSR
	$650	$550	$450	$400	$350	$300	$250	
Waffenamt proofmarks	$1,750	$1,350	$1,100	$800	$700	$600	$500	

This pistol is very rare with Waffenamt proofmarks.

GEAR HEAD WORKS

Current manufacturer of bolt action pistols and firearms parts and accessories, established in 2012, located in Murfreesboro, TN.

PISTOLS: BOLT ACTION

ONE PISTOL – .300 AAC Blackout cal., 9 in. fluted or non-fluted barrel, threaded 5/8x24 with muzzle thread protector, detachable AICS pattern 10 shot mag., Remington 700 style steel receiver with Savage style barrel nut, billet aluminum chassis, Tailhook Mod 1 brace with side folding adapter or telescoping Tailhook Mod 2 black, Magpul or Venom Defense Carbon Fiber inlaid grip, grips come in various colors, M-LOK compatible chassis, front sling/bipod swivel stud, Black, FDE, Gear Head Grey, or OD Green Cerakote finish, various camo patterns such as Bracken, Fragment, Desolate, Debris, Meltdown, Abyss, or Hellfire also available, 5.7 lbs. New 2018.

Please contact the manufacturer directly for pricing and availability on this model.

GEISSELE AUTOMATICS

Current AR-15 pistol, rifle, and accessories manufacturer established in 2004, located in North Wales, PA.

Please refer to BlueBookOfGunValues.com to order the *Blue Book of AR-15s & Variations*, available as a book or online subscription.

GELAN TRANSFORMER

Current rifle manufacturer located in Al Ajban, Abu Dhabi. Previously located in Bernau a. Chiemsee, Germany.

RIFLES

Gelan Transformer currently manufactures a straight pull, bolt-action rifle - current MSR € 2,717 and a semi-auto rifle with rear bolt handle and top tang safety - current MSR is € 2,941.

GENTRY CUSTOM LLC

Current custom rifle maker located in Belgrade, MT. Previous company name was David Gentry - Custom Gunmaker.

David Gentry was a custom rifle builder who fabricated rifles to individual custom order requests. His son Dennis took over the business after David's death in 2007. The company continues to build custom rifles, proprietary muzzle brakes, as well as three position safeties for the Mauser 98 in right or left-hand, as well as a variety of rifle accessories. Mr. Gentry should be contacted directly for more information on options/prices.

GERMAN P.38 MILITARY & COMMERCIAL PISTOLS

Please refer to the P.38 listings in the P section.

GRADING - PPGS™ 100% 98% 95% 90% 80% 70% 60% *LAST MSR*

GERMAN SPORT GUNS GmbH

Current firearms and air soft manufacturer and distributor established in 2002, located in Ense-Höingen, Germany. Currently imported by American Tactical Imports, located in Summerville, SC. Previously located in Rochester, NY.

For individual model listings, please go to BlueBookOfGunValues.com/overflow.

GEVARM

Previous manufacturer located in Saint Etienne, France.

RIFLES: SEMI-AUTO

E-1 AUTOLOADING RIFLE - .22 LR cal., 19 in. barrel, open sights, walnut pistol grip stock.

$300 $250 $225 $195 $180 $165 $150

GIANI, VITTORIO

Please refer to MAG Custom Rifles listing in the M section.

GIB

Previous trademark manufactured in Spain.

SHOTGUNS: SxS

10 GAUGE MAGNUM - 10 ga., 3 1/2 in. chambers, 32 in. full choke barrels, case hardened frame, matted rib, rubber pad, checkered pistol grip walnut stock. Disc.

$275 $250 $235 $220 $200 $175 $150

GIBBS, GEORGE

Current trademark established 2007, and located in Wiltshire, U.K. Previous gunmaker circa 1830-1929, located in Bristol, U.K.

George Gibbs began manufacturing guns in Bristol circa 1830. He built a new factory in 1873, and became famous for big game rifles popular during the Victorian and Edwardian eras. The .505 Gibbs cartridge became widely known. In 1874, the maker patented the Gibbs & Pitt gun - sometimes dubbed the first commercially successful hammerless shotgun - a triggerplate design that cocked via its underlever (later a toplever-cocking variant was also produced). In 1906, Gibbs moved to 35 Savile Row. The firm's founder, George C. Gibbs, died in 1918, and company ownership passed out of family hands and into a partnership. By 1929, the firm went bankrupt, but survived for a time in smaller quarters off Baldwin Street in Bristol. During 1964, Gibbs was purchased by Bath gunmaker I.M. Crudgington and Norman Harper. In 2007, Crudgington's son, stockmaker Mark Crudgington, purchased the name and continues to make guns under the Gibbs name.

Information courtesy of David Grant and Vic Venters.

GIBBS GUNS, INC.

Previously manufactured by Volunteer Enterprises in Knoxville, TN and previously distributed by Gibbs Guns, Inc. located in Greenback, TN.

CARBINES

MARK 45 CARBINE - .45 ACP cal. only, based on M6 Thompson machine gun, 16 1/2 in. barrel, 5, 15, 30, or 90 shot mag. U.S. mfg. Disc. 1988.

$750 $625 $525 $450 $375 $330 $300 *$279*

Add $200 for 90 shot mag.
Add 10% for nickel plating.

GIBBS RIFLE COMPANY, INC.

Current manufacturer, importer, and distributor located in Martinsburg, WV. Gibbs manufactured rifles with the Gibbs trademark in Martinsburg, WV 1991-1994, in addition to importing Mauser-Werke firearms until 1995. Dealer and distributor sales.

In the past, Gibbs Rifle Company, Inc. imported a variety of older firearms, including British military rifles and handguns (both original and refurbished condition), a good selection of used military contract pistols and rifles, in addition to other shooting products and accessories, including a bipod patterned after the Parker-Hale M-85.

Gibbs Rifle Company, Inc. has imported and manufactured military collectibles, historical remakes, and special sporting rifles. All rifles are carefully inspected, commercially cleaned and boxed to ensure their quality, and all have a limited lifetime warranty. Gibbs Rifle Company, Inc. also offered membership in the Gibbs Military Collectors Club, an organization dedicated to military firearms collectors.

GRADING - PPGS™	100%	98%	95%	90%	80%	70%	60%	LAST MSR

RIFLES: BOLT ACTION

M-71/84 MAUSER - 11mm Mauser cal., 31 1/2 in. barrel, available in good original or refurbished condition, 10 lbs. Imported 1999-2004.

	$450	$400	$365	$335	$300	$275	$250	*$190*

Add $110 for refurbished condition (all parts are historically correct and have been cleaned and hand inspected).

This rifle cannot be safely shot with modern ammunition.

M1871/84 "SAMURAI" MAUSER - built on original Mauser action, replica wood stock, gold trigger guard, designed by Robert "Rock" Galotti for the movie *"The Last Samurai"*. Mfg. 2002-2003.

	$600	$550	$500	$450	$400	$375	$350	*$550*

M-1888 MAUSER - 8mm Mauser (7.92x57mm) cal., good original condition, 30 in. barrel, 10 lbs. Imported 1999-2004.

	$85	$75	$65	$55	$45	$40	$35	*$100*

This rifle cannot be safely shot with modern ammunition.

M-98K ISRAELI MAUSER - .308 Win. cal., rebarreled by the Israeli Arsenal Ha'as, various makers, 23.6 in. barrel, original condition (offered in 3 grades), 9 lbs. Imported 1999-2003.

	$500	$450	$400	$365	$335	$300	$275	*$170*

Add 10% for Grade 2, or 20% for Grade 1.

M-98 MAUSER SPORTER - .270 Win. or .30-06 cal., Mauser M-98 type action, blue finish, sporterized checkered hardwood stock and forend, 24 in. Wilson barrel. Mfg. in Martinsburg, WV 1998-99.

	$350	$295	$265	$245	$225	$210	$195	*$330*

2A HUNTER RIFLE/CARBINE - .308 Win. cal., sporterized action features black enamel refinish, synthetic stock, 12 shot mag, and choice of 18 (carbine) or 22 1/2 (rifle) in. barrel with Parker-Hale muzzle brake, approx. 10 lbs. Mfg. 1999 only.

	$325	$285	$260	$23,	$195	$175	$150	*$275*

ENFIELD NO. 5 JUNGLE CARBINE - .303 British cal., older No. 4 Enfield barreled action with newly manufactured stock, bayonet lug and flash hider have been added, 20 in. barrel, 7 3/4 lbs. Imported 1999-2004, reintroduced 2010 with camo synthetic stock. Disc.

	$400	$350	$300	$265	$235	$200	$175	

A bayonet and scabbard were also available for this model.

ENFIELD NO. 7 JUNGLE CARBINE - .308 Win. cal., older 2A action with reconfigured original wood, flash hider and bayonet lug have been added, 20 in. barrel, 8 lbs. Imported 1999-2004.

	$375	$325	$285	$265	$250	$225	$200	*$200*

QUEST EXTREME CARBINE - .303 British cal., updated No. 5 Enfield action, 20 in. barrel with compensator/flash hider, electroless nickel metal finish, new buttstock with survival kit packaged in butt trap, 7 3/4 lbs. Imported 2000-2004.

	$375	$325	$285	$265	$250	$225	$200	*$250*

QUEST II - .308 Win. cal., modern 2A Enfield barreled action, mfg. from chrome vanadium steel, 20 in. barrel with compensator/flash hider and adj. rear sight, front sight protector, pre-fitted see-through scope mount accepts all Weaver based optics and accessories, electroless nickel finish, hardwood stock with survival kit included, 12 shot mag., 8 lbs. Imported 2001-2004.

	$375	$325	$265	$235	$200	$185	$170	*$280*

QUEST III - .308 Win. cal., similar to Quest II, except has black synthetic stock, w/o survival kit. Imported 2002-2004.

	$395	$345	$280	$240	$200	$185	$170	*$300*

SUMMIT FRONTIER .45-70 CARBINE - .45-70 Govt. cal., remanufactured No. 4 Enfield action, new 21 in. button rifled barrel with front sight, blue action and barrel, checkered hardwood sporting stock, 3 shot mag., 8 1/2 lbs. Imported 2000-2005.

	$650	$600	$550	$500	$450	$400	$375	*$385*

GIBBS ECONOMY SPORTER - 8mm Mauser cal., sporterized military action with good barrel and sporting sights, walnut finished checkered hardwood stock. Mfg. 1993-94.

	$275	$225	$185	$150	$135	$120	$100	*$205*

GIBBS MAUSER SPORTER - .243 Win., .270 Win., .30-06, or .308 Win. cal., features M-98 action, walnut finished checkered hardwood stock, action is drilled and tapped, flip-up rear sight and ramp front. Mfg. 1993-94.

	$375	$325	$275	$225	$195	$175	$150	*$295*

GRADING - PPGS™	100%	98%	95%	90%	80%	70%	60%	LAST MSR

MODEL 81 CLASSIC – available in 11 cals. between .22-250 Rem. and 7mm Rem. Mag., 24 in. barrel, open sights, 4 shot mag., select checkered walnut with sling swivels, 7 3/4 lbs.

$795 $595 $475 $395 $340 $300 $280 *$900*

* ***Model 81 Classic African*** – .375 H&H or 9.3x62mm cal., similar specifications as Model 81 Classic with quarter rib and express sights, engraved action, Pachmayr recoil pad, 9 lbs.

$925 $725 $600 $500 $425 $360 $330 *$1,050*

MODEL 85 SNIPER RIFLE – .308 Win. cal., 24 in. heavy barrel, 10 shot mag., camo green synthetic McMillan stock with stippling, built in adj. bipod and recoil pad, enlarged contoured bolt, adj. sights, 12 lbs. 6 oz.

$3,950 $3,650 $3,250 $2,850 $2,400 $2,000 $1,650 *$2,050*

MODEL 87 TARGET – .243 Win., 6.5x55mm, .308 Win., .30-06, or .300 Win. Mag. cal., target stock, aperture sights. Mfg. disc. 1992.

$2,150 $1,800 $1,500 $1,250 $1,050 $900 $750 *$1,500*

MODEL 1000 STANDARD – .22-250 Rem., .243 Win., 6mm Rem., 6.5x55mm, 7x57mm, 7x64mm, .270 Win., .30-06, or .308 Win. cal., 22 in. barrel, 4 shot built in mag., checkered walnut stock with cheekpiece, open sights, 7 1/4 lbs.

$425 $375 $325 $290 $260 $240 $220 *$495*

* ***Model 1000 Standard Clip*** – similar to Model 1000 Standard, except has detachable 4 shot mag.

$460 $395 $350 $300 $270 $240 $220 *$535*

MODEL 1100 LIGHTWEIGHT – available in 9 cals. between .22-250 Rem. and .308 Win., 22 in. barrel, open sights, 4 shot mag., 6 1/2 lbs.

$435 $380 $325 $290 $260 $240 $220 *$510*

* ***Model 1100M Lightweight African*** – .375 H&H, or .458 Win. Mag. cal., 24 in. barrel, 4 shot mag., 9 1/2 lbs.

$825 $650 $575 $500 $450 $425 $400 *$930*

MODEL 1200 SUPER – .22-250 Rem., .243 Win., 6mm, 6.5x55mm, 7x64mm, .270 Win., .30-06, or .308 Win. cal., bolt action, Mauser type action, 24 in. barrel, folding sight, skip checkered walnut stock, pad swivels, rosewood pistol grip cap and forend tip.

$495 $400 $350 $325 $285 $270 $255 *$595*

* ***Model 1200 Super Clip*** – similar to Model 1200 Super, except has detachable 4 shot box mag.

$525 $425 $375 $350 $300 $280 $265 *$640*

MODEL 1300S SCOUT – .243 Win. or .308 Win. cal., 20 in. barrel with muzzle brake, internal 5 shot or detachable 5/10 shot mag., laminated checkered birchwood stock, sling swivels, 8 1/2 lbs. Disc.

$425 $375 $325 $290 $260 $240 $220 *$495*

Add $30 for detachable mag. (Model 1300C).

MODEL 1500S SURVIVOR – .308 Win. cal., matte stainless construction, black composite (Kevlar/fiberglass) stock, 22 in. barrel, 4 shot mag., 7 lbs. Mfg. 1993-disc.

$395 $350 $300 $270 $240 $210 $185 *$450*

Add $30 for detachable mag. (Model 1500C).

This model was made for the Gibbs Rifle Co. by Bell & Carlson, Inc.

M1903-A4 SPRINGFIELD SNIPER MODEL – .30-06 cal., replica of original M1903-A3 Springfield, drilled and tapped, Redfield replica rings and mounts, new C stock, barrel marked with modern dates of mfg., includes U.S. issue leather sling and OD Green canvas carrying case. M73G2 scope became standard during 2012. Mfg. 2009-2015.

$1,100 $975 $875 $775 $675 $575 $475 *$1,250*

M1903-A4-82 SPRINGFIELD SNIPER MODEL – .30-06 cal., similar to M1903, except has improved M82 rifle scope and 7/8 in. rings. While advertised for $1,200, this model was never manufactured.

M1903-A4-84 SPRINGFIELD SNIPER MODEL – .30-06 cal., similar to M1903A4-82, except has improved M84 rifle scope and 7/8 in. rings. Mfg. 2010-2012.

$1,100 $950 $825 $700 $600 $500 $400 *$1,250*

MODEL 1916 MAUSER – 7x57 Mauser cal., includes 3x9x32 sun optic scope, checkered black synthetic stock, small ring 1916 Mauser barreled action. New late 2017.

MSR $300 $275 $250 $225 $215 $195 $185 $175

PIG BUSTER – .30-06 cal., 1903A3 Springfield action, new 19 in. barrel with No. 5 Jungle Carbine flash hider, camo finished fully synthetic stock. Limited quantities. Mfg. 2012-2014.

MSR $750 $650 $525 $450 $400 $350 $300 $275

GRADING - PPGS™	100%	98%	95%	90%	80%	70%	60%	LAST MSR

RIFLES: BOLT ACTION, MIDLAND SERIES

MODEL 2100 MIDLAND DELUXE – similar to Model 2600 Midland, except has checkered walnut stock and pistol grip cap. Disc. 1997.

$375	$325	$275	$235	$210	$190	$180	*$390*

MODEL 2600 MIDLAND – .22-250 Rem., .243 Win., 6mm Rem. (disc. 1994), 6.5x55mm (disc. 1994), 7x57mm (disc. 1994), 7x64mm (disc. 1994), .270 Win., .30-06, or .308 Win. cal., 22 in. barrel, 4 shot mag., checkered hardwood stock with Monte Carlo cheekpiece, open sights, drilled and tapped action, 7 lbs. Disc. 1997.

$400	$360	$310	$260	$220	$185	$165	*$400*

This model was re-introduced during late 1996, utilizing a 1903 Springfield action with choice of 5 shot fixed mag. with hinged floorplate or 3 shot detachable mag.

MIDLAND 2700 LIGHTWEIGHT – lightweight variation of the Model 2100 Midland Deluxe featuring tapered barrel, anodized aluminum trigger housing and lightened stock with full pistol grip and recoil pad, Schnabel forend, 6 1/2 lbs. Disc. 1997.

$400	$360	$310	$260	$220	$185	$165	*$415*

MIDLAND 2800 – similar to Model 2600 Midland, except has laminated birchwood stock, reintroduced during late 1996, utilizing a 1903 Springfield action, 7 lbs. Disc. 1997.

$385	$325	$265	$215	$195	$185	$175	*$430*

SHOTGUNS: SINGLE SHOT

MIDLAND STALKER – 12 ga., trigger bar safety, unique squeeze break open action and cocking system, 28 1/2 in. barrel bored F, hardwood stock and forearm, 6 lbs.

$90	$65	$55	$45	$35	$30	$25	*$110*

GIL, ANTONIO & CO.

Please refer to GYC Armas located within this section.

GILA RIVER GUN WORKS

Previous custom rifle manufacturer located in Pocatello, ID. Previously located in Yuma, AZ.

RIFLES: CUSTOM

Michael Scherz specialized in high-quality, bolt action rifles in .550 Magnum caliber. During late 2011 Gila River Tactical was formed and was a division of Gila River Gun Works. This tactical division offered a wide variety of long range precision tactical rifles.

GILBOA

Current trademark manufactured by Silver Shadow Advanced Security Systems Ltd., located in Kiryat Ono, Israel. Currently imported by Gilboa-USA located in Dayton, OH. Previously imported and distributed by LDB Supply, located in Dayton, OH.

Please refer to BlueBookOfGunValues.com to order the *Blue Book of AR-15s & Variations*, available as a book or online subscription.

GILL ARMS

Current pistol manufacturer located in Lakewood, WA.

PISTOLS: SEMI-AUTO

GILL GPR 9M – 9mm Para. cal., full size aluminum frame, 4 1/2 in. barrel, 17 shot mag. w/asymmetrical sides, stainless steel construction, SafeSet ergonomic trigger w/lock safety, low profile metal sights, dual textured grips, DLC coated slide, 3 ergonomically sized grip straps w/side panels, full Picatinny rail and bullnoze, aft slide extensions and serration, ambi slide stop, black Cerakote finish. New 2019.

Please contact the manufacturer directly for pricing and availability on this model.

This model's design is comprised of only 25 component parts. Low ser. no. is available upon reservation.

* ***Gill GPR 9M Metal Frame Limited Edition*** – 9mm Para. cal., full size metal frame, 4 1/2 in. barrel, 17 shot mag. w/asymmetrical sides, stainless steel construction, SafeSet ergonomic trigger w/ lock safety, low profile metal sights, dual textured grips, DLC coated slide, 3 ergonomically sized grip straps w/side panels, full Picatinny rail and bullnoze, aft slide extensions and serration, ambi slide stop, 4 built-in safeties, black Cerakote finish, low serialization and limited mfg. New 2019.

MSR $795	$700	$600	$550	$475	$400	$325	$250

This model's design is comprised of only 25 component parts.

GRADING - PPGS™	100%	98%	95%	90%	80%	70%	60%	LAST MSR

GIRSAN MACHINE & LIGHT WEAPON INDUSTRY COMPANY

Current handgun and shotgun manufacturer established in 1994, located in Giresun, Turkey. Currently imported by European American Armory (EAA) Corp., located in Cocoa, FL. Previously imported by Zenith Firearms until 2017, located in Afton, VA.

PISTOLS: SEMI-AUTO

Girsan manufactures a complete line of good quality semi-auto pistols in a variety of configurations, calibers, frame sizes, and finishes. Many options are available. Currently only select models are being imported. Please contact the importer directly for more information on models not listed here, including U.S. availability and pricing.

All models include a rugged plastic carry case, factory cleaning kit, keyed cable lock, three magazines, and a 5-year warranty unless otherwise listed.

MC9/MC9-TV – 9mm Para. cal., polymer frame, 4.2 in. threaded barrel, 17 shot mag., integral trigger safety, low profile 3-dot system, dovetail front sight or FAR-DOT Optics (MC9-TV only), 3 grip panels, accessory rail, blue/black (BL) finish, 1.4 lbs. Importation began 2021.

MSR $430 $365 $320 $275 $250 $200 $165 $145

Add $138 for FAR-DOT optics (MC9-TV).

MC9 MATCH TV – 9mm Para. cal., SA, polymer frame, 4.7 in. barrel, 17 shot mag., integral trigger safety, FAR-DOT optics, dovetail front sight, 3 grip panels, accessory rail, blue/black (BL) finish, 1.6 lbs. New 2021.

MSR $661 $560 $490 $420 $380 $310 $260 $215

MC 14 – .380 ACP cal., SA/DA, 3.43 in. cold forged barrel, 13 shot, dovetailed sights, ambidextrous thumb safety, black or bright white finish, 1.4 lbs. Importation by EAA Corp. disc.

$315 $275 $235 $215 $175 $145 $115 *$370*

Add $52 for bright white finish.

MC 39 – 9mm Para. cal., SA/DA, 4.33 in. cold forged barrel, 15 shot, dovetailed sights, black or white finish, 1.7 lbs. Disc. 2020.

$365 $325 $275 $250 $200 $165 $135 *$422*

Add $51 for white finish.

MC28 SA/MC 28 SA-TV/MC28 SA-TV BX – 9mm Para. cal., polymer frame, 4.25 or 4.7 (MC28 SA-TV BX) in. standard or threaded (MC28 SA-TV BX only) barrel, 15 shot, integral trigger safety, Novak style rear sight, low profile 3-dot sight system, Dot Carry optics (MC28 SA-TV only), 3 grip panels, accessory rail, blue/black (BL), two-tone (TT, not available in MC28 SA-TV BX), or Dark Earth (DE) finish, 28.8 oz. Importation began 2020.

MSR $365 $325 $300 $250 $225 $175 $150 $125

Add $22 for Dark Earth (DE) finish (MSR $387).

Add $89 for MC28 SA-TV model with Dot Carry optics (MSR $454).

Add $134 for MC28 SA-TV BX model with threaded barrel (MSR $499).

MC1911 S MATCH – .45 ACP cal., 5 in. barrel, 8 shot, steel construction, long hole hammer, target fully adj. rear sight, checkered laminated grips, extended beavertail, extended ambi safety, blue/black (BL), two-tone (TT), or nickel (NI) finish, 2.55 lbs. Importation began 2020.

MSR $753 $635 $550 $475 $425 $350 $285 $250

Add $20 for two-tone or nickel finish.

MC1911 S MATCH ELITE – .45 ACP cal., 5 in. Competition barrel, cone barrel lockup, 8 shot, long hole hammer, Competition trigger, fully adj. sight and competition rear sight, G10 grips, ambi safety, extended beavertail safety, competition trigger and barrel, deep slide serrations, matte hard chrome finish, 2.55 lbs. Importation began 2020.

MSR $856 $725 $635 $550 $500 $400 $325 $280

MC1911 C/MC1911 C-TV – 9mm Para. or .45 ACP cal., steel frame and slide, 4.4 in. barrel, 8 or 9 shot, long hole hammer, Novak sights or Dot Carry Optics (MC1911 C-TV), checkered grips, extended ambi safety and beavertail, accessory rail, deep slide serrations, blue/black (BL), two-tone (TT), or Dark Earth (DE) finish, 2.35 lbs. Importation began 2020.

MSR $567 $475 $415 $350 $325 $260 $215 $185

Add $23 for two-tone or Dark Earth finish. Add $89 for Dot Carry Optics (MC1911 C-TV).

MC1911 S/MC1911 S-TV – .45 ACP or 9mm Para. cal., Govt. size frame, 5 in. barrel, 8 shot, steel construction, long hole hammer, Novak sights or Dot Carry optics (MC 1911 S-TV), checkered grips, extended beavertail and ambi safety, accessory rail, deep slide serrations, blue/black (BL), two-tone (TT), or Dark Earth (DE) finish, 2.55 lbs. New 2020.

MSR $567 $475 $415 $350 $325 $260 $215 $185

Add $23 for two-tone or Dark Earth finish.

Add $112 for Dot Carry optics (MC1911 S-TV only).

GRADING - PPGS™	100%	98%	95%	90%	80%	70%	60%	LAST MSR

MC1911 SC – .45 ACP or 9mm Para. cal., Officer size frame, 3.4 in. barrel, 6 or 7 shot, steel construction, fully adj. rear sight, checkered grips, extended beavertail, ambi safety, deep slide serrations, blue/black (BL), two-tone (TT), or Dark Earth (DE) finish, 25.6 oz. Importation began 2020.

MSR $618	$525	$460	$395	$355	$290	$240	$200	

Add $21 for two-tone or Dark Earth finish.

MC1911 SC ULTIMATE – .45 ACP or 9mm Para. cal., fully melded Officer size frame and slide, 3.4 in. cone barrel, 6 or 7 shot window mag., steel construction, lone hole hammer, low profile iron sights, optional optics, G10 grips with capacity windo, enlarged grip safety, extended beavertail and rounded ambi safety, deep slide serrations, blue/black (BL) or Dark Earth (DE) finish, 1.6 lbs. Importation began 2020.

MSR $710	$610	$525	$450	$410	$325	$275	$225	

Add $22 for Dark Earth finish.

MC1911 S HUNTER – 10mm cal., steel frame and slide, 6 in. barrel, 8 shot, long hole hammer, fully adj. super sight, checkered grip, ambi safety, extended beavertail, deep slide serrations, accessory rail, ambi safety, 3.2 lbs. Importation began 2021.

MSR $699	$600	$525	$450	$410	$325	$275	$225	

MC1911 S LUX/MC1911 S GOLD LUX – .45 ACP cal., 5 in. Competition barrel, heavy duty slide barrel bushing, 8 shot, long hole hammer, competition trigger, fully adj. competition rear sight, checkered ivory Lite grips, extended ambi safety, extended beavertail, deep front and rear slide serrations, includes leather bound custom carry case, black hard chrome or gold frame and slide finish, 2.55 lbs. Importation began 2021.

MSR $1,101	$935	$825	$700	$635	$515	$425	$365	

Add $157 for gold frame and slide finish (MC1911 S Gold Lux)

MC1911 S NOEL – 9mm Para. or .45 ACP cal., stainless steel frame and slide, 5 in. Competition barrel, heavy duty slide barrel bushing, 8 or 10 shot, long hole hammer, competition trigger, fully adj. competition rear sight, checkered G10 grips, super extended thumb shield ambi safety, extended beavertail, deep front and rear slide serrations, 2.55 lbs. Importation began 2021.

MSR $924	$790	$690	$595	$535	$435	$355	$300	

REGARD MC/REGARD MC DELUXE – 9mm Para. cal., SA/DA, 4.9 in. barrel, 15 shot, fixed front and dovetailed rear sights, ambi thumb safety, accessory rail, hand engraved (Regard MC Deluxe model only), black (mfg. 2019 only), white (mfg. 2019 only), white/gold (mfg. 2019 only), blue/black (BL, new 2020), two-tone (TT, new 2020), Dark Earth (DE, new 2020), or Gold-Plated (new 2020, Regard MC Deluxe only) finish, 1.94 lbs. Importation began mid-2019.

MSR $454	$385	$335	$290	$260	$210	$175	$150	

Add $23 for two-tone or Dark Earth finish (new 2020).
Add $270 Gold-Plated finish (Regard MC Deluxe, new 2020).
Add $51 for white finish (mfg. 2019 only)
Add $118 for white/gold finish (mfg. 2019 only).

REGARD MC BX – 9mm Para. cal., lightweight design, 5 in. threaded barrel, 18 shot, drift adj. sight, G10 grips, ambi thumb safety, accessory rail, decocker, protective nut, blue/black or Dark Earth finish, 2.15 lbs. Importation began 2020.

MSR $550	$470	$410	$350	$325	$260	$215	$185	

Add $21 for Dark Earth finish.

REGARD MC COMPACT – 9mm Para. cal., SA/DA, 4.33 in. cold forged barrel, 15 shot, ambidextrous thumb safety, fixed front and dovetailed rear sights, black, bright white, white/gold, or engraved white finish, 1.81 lbs.

MSR $422	$365	$325	$275	$250	$200	$165	$135	

Add $58 for bright white finish.
Add $118 for white/gold finish.
Add $190 for engraved white finish.

REGARD MC SPORT GEN 3/GEN 4 – 9mm Para. cal., lightweight design (Gen 4), 4.9 in. barrel, 18 shot, adj. sights, G10 grips, ambi frame safety (Gen 3) or slide safety and windowed mag. and grip (Gen 4), accessory rail, decocker, blue/black (BL) finish, 2.15 lbs. Importation began 2020.

MSR $578	$495	$435	$375	$335	$275	$225	$195	

Add $35 for frame safety (Gen 3 model).

SHOTGUNS: SEMI-AUTO

In 2012, the company expanded its line into the 312 series of semi-auto hunting and tactical shotguns. Select models are currently imported by EAA Corp and listed below.

GRADING - PPGS™	100%	98%	95%	90%	80%	70%	60%	LAST MSR

MC312 – 12 ga., 2 3/4, 3, or 3 1/2 in. chamber, inertia operated, 28 in. VR barrel with screw-in choke tubes, high visible front sight, polymer stock and forend, rubber buttpad, sling swivel attachments, rotating bolt, blue/black (BL) or or camo finish, 6.95 lbs. Importation began 2019.

MSR $413	$350	$300	$265	$240	$195	$160	$135

Add $61 for camo finish.

MC312 GOBBLER – 12 ga., 2 3/4, 3, or 3 1/2 in. chamber, inertia operated, 24 in. VR barrel w/screw choke tubes, fiber optic front sight, straight or pistol grip stock, rubber butt pad, semi-enhanced loading port, rotating bolt, sling swivel attachments, Picatinny rail, camo + Cerakote combo finish, 6.75 lbs. Importation began 2019.

MSR $613	$520	$455	$390	$355	$285	$235	$200

MC312 SPORT – 12 ga., inertia operated, 24 or 28 in. raised VR barrel, 5 screw in chokes, red mag. tube follower, mid bead, large fiber optic front sight (optics not included on MC312 Sport Wood model), straight or pistol grip wood or polymer stock, rubber buttpad, Picatinny rail, enhanced loading port, rotating bolt, blue/black (BL), red, or blue anodized finish, 6.75-6.95 lbs. Importation began 2020.

MSR $619	$525	$460	$395	$355	$290	$240	$200

Add $15 for red or blue anodized finish.
Add $60 for 28 in. barrel with 14.25 in. LOP (blue/black finish only).

MC312 TACTICAL – 12 ga., inertia operated, 18 1/2 in. barrel, 5 screw-in chokes, red mag. tube follower, raised front rifle sight, red-dot optics, polymer pistol grip stock and forend, rubber buttpad, pistol grip stock, Picatinny rail, enhanced loading port, rotating bolt, blue/black (BL) finish, 6.75 lbs. Importation began 2020.

MSR $561	$475	$415	$350	$325	$260	$215	$185

GLANZIG PRÄZISIONS-UND SPORTWAFFEN JAGDZUBEHÖR

Previous custom long gun manufacturer located in Ferlach, Austria.

Glanzig manufactured custom long guns, built per individual customer specifications. Guns should be individually evaluated by a knowledgeable expert.

GLENFIELD

Previous trademark of promotional rifles sold by the Marlin Firearms Company circa 1960-1983.

Please refer to the Marlin Firearms Company listing in the M section.

GLISENTI

Please refer to the Italian Military Arms listing in the I section.

GLOCK

Currently manufactured by Glock GmbH in Austria beginning 1983. Sales in the U.S. began in 1986. Glock also opened a production facility for manufacturing its polymer frames and assembling complete pistols in Smyrna, GA during late 2005. Exclusively imported and distributed by Glock, Inc. USA, located in Smyrna, GA. Distributor and dealer sales.

All Glock pistols have a "safe action" constant operating system (double action mode) which includes trigger safety, firing pin safety, and drop safety. Glock pistols have only 35 parts for reliability and simplicity of operation. With approximately 170 or more variations, over 10 million Glock semi-auto pistols have been manufactured since 1983.

In 1995 the Glock Collector's Association was formed. To date Glock has manufactured commemoratives (see Pistols: Semi-Auto, Commemoratives in this section), specially marked, and engraved models, plus the agency and police marked variations. By joining the Glock Collector's Association, members can find out the history of the most desirable G17-G48 civilian models. Please refer to Firearms/Shooting Organizations for more information on the Glock Collector's Association, including how to join.

PISTOLS: SEMI-AUTO

To date, there have been five generations of Glock pistols. Generation 1 (Gen 1), circa 1986-1988 features a pebbled finish frame without horizontal grooves on the front or back strap. Generation 2 (Gen 2), circa 1988-1997 can be identified by a checkered grenade finish with horizontal grooves on both the front and rear grip straps. Generation 3 (Gen 3), circa 1995-current started out with transition finger grooves and no front rail with thumb rests, then transitioned into finger grooves, an accessories rail with recessed thumb rest, and checkered finished frame. This was followed by Variant 2 which is identified by an (extreme polymid traction) Rough Textured Frame (RTF-2), finger grooves, accessories rail with recessed thumb rests. During 2010, Glock introduced Generation 4 (Gen 4, RTF-4) Rough Textured

GRADING - PPGS™	100%	98%	95%	90%	80%	70%	60%	LAST MSR

Frame, this enables standard frame Glock pistols to adopt the new short frame technology, which can be almost instantly fitted to any hand size, and features the (less polymid traction) Rough Textured Frame with recessed thumb rests, finger grooves, accessories rail, and interchangeable frame back straps. It also includes a reversible enlarged magazine catch, dual recoil spring assembly, and a new trigger system, and in 2014, the first model Generation 4 (Gen4) features slim frame (less than 1 inch width), sub-compact "Less Aggressive" "Rough Textured Frame" (RTF) with thumb rest, reversible enlarged magazine catch, dual recoil spring assembly and new trigger system with no finger grooves and accessories rail, single stack magazine. Glock began transitioning its pistols to Gen 4 beginning 2010.

In 2017-2018, Glock released its initial Gen 5 offerings available in Model 17 (Sport/Service), Model 19 Compact, Model 19X Compact, Model 26 Sub-Compact, and Models G17 MOS, G19 MOS, Model G34 MOS, and G45 Compact. Gen 5 features include a new Glock Marksman barrel (GMB w/hexagonal rifling), grips w/o finger groups, ambidextrous slide stop levers, nDLC black finish, with accessories rails, recessed thumb rest, a flared magwell housing, "FS" Front Slide serrations, interchangeable frame backstraps, and beavertail system (MBS), Model 26 Sub-Compact w/o magwell, LE with magwell.

In 2018-2019, Glock released its Gen 5 slimline series, (Sub-Compact G43X or Compact G48 pistols), thus creating a perfect slim fit for a wide variety of hand sizes. They both have a silver slide nPVD finish which has withstood rigorous military testing. GMB Glock Marksman barrel, no flared magwell, no finger grooves and accessories rail, with "FS" Front Slide serrations, single stack magazine, a comfortable built-in beavertail, reversible enlarged magazine catch, recessed thumb rest, short trigger distance, "Less Aggressive" Polymid Traction Rough Textured Frame (RTF). Also, Gen 5 Compact; G45 MOS and full size; G47 (Law Enforcement only) pistol. Model 17M Full size (Sport Service). Model G19M Compact (Sport Service) and Compact Model G46 for German Police. In 2020, the new compact model G44 LR cal. a generation in itself, Gen 5 slimline series (Sub-Compact G43X MOS or Compact G48 MOS), and P80 1st Generation "pebbled frame" Classic Edition in itself. Also Glock rebooted the .40 Auto in Gen 5 pistols. The Model G22 Full size, Model G23 Compact, and Model 27 Sub-Compact with flared magwell, Model G22 MOS Full size and Model G23 MOS Compact pistols.

Add $18 for adj. rear sight, $22 for Glock steel sights (new 2004), or $47 for Glock night sights (new 2004).
Add $80 for fixed Meprolight sight or $105 for fixed Trijicon sight (disc. 2003-2004, depending on model).
Add $25 for internal locking system (ILS) on most currently manufactured models listed below (new 2004).
Add $95 for tactical light or $284 for tactical light with laser for most currently manufactured pistols listed below.

MODEL 17/17C GEN 1, GEN 2, GEN 3 (SPORT/SERVICE) – 9mm Para. cal., striker fired constant double action mode, polymer frame, mag., trigger and other pistol parts, 4.48 in. hexagonal rifled barrel, Gen1 (new 1986), Gen2 (new 1989), Gen3 (new 1998),Gen4 (new 2010), or Gen5 (new 2017), with (Model 17C, Gen2 checkered grip, new 1997) (Model 17, 17C Gen3 ported non-ported (new 1997-98), steel slide and springs, 5 1/2 lb. trigger pull, 10 (C/B 1994), 17* (reintroduced late 2004), or 19* (reintroduced late 2004) shot mag., adj. (Sport Model) or fixed (Service Model) rear sight, standard black or optional OD Green (Gen3 only 2004-current, limited mfg.), or FDE (Light Brown) (Gen3 2012-current limited mfg.) finish, includes a lockable pistol box, cable lock, cleaning rod, and other accessories, extra mag. and a spare rear sight, 24 3/4 oz. Importation began late 1985.

MSR $599	$550	$475	$400	$350	$300	$240	$190	

Add 65% for Gen 1 variation if in mint/NIB condition.
Add $22 for Model 17C with fixed rear sight (new 1997).
Add $119 for competition model w/adj. sights (Model 17CC, mfg. 2000-2003).

This model is still available with the RTF-2 finish (extreme polymid traction) Rough Textured Frame (Model 17 RTF-2 mfg. 2009).

During 2011, Glock released its 25th Silver Anniversary Limited Edition of the Model 17 Gen4. It featured a 25 year marking on the top of the slide in addition to a special 25th year silver medallion inletted in polymer frame - only 2,500 were produced.

All Gen3-4 models have recessed thumb rests and finger grooves mounting accessories rail, except Gen3 standard, compact, sub-compact Transition models (mfg. 1995-1998) have finger grooves, but no mounting accessories rail. Gen4 sub-compact slim frame (less than 1 in. width) "Less Aggressive" Rough Textured Frame (RTF) with thumb rests, reversible enlarged mag. catch, dual recoil spring assembly and new trigger system with no finger grooves and accessories rail. New 2014.

GRADING - PPGS™	100%	98%	95%	90%	80%	70%	60%	LAST MSR

MODEL 17L GEN 1, GEN 2, GEN 3 (SPORT/SERVICE COMPETITION) – 9mm Para. cal., 6.02 in. ported/non-ported barrel, slotted relieved slide, recalibrated trigger pull (4 1/2 lb. pull), adj. rear sight, 26.3 oz. mfg. Gen1 pebbled grip (new 1988), Gen2 non-ported checkered grip, has no mounting accessories rail (new 1990), Gen3 non-ported has thumb rests, finger grooves, mounting accessories rail (new 1998).

MSR $750 $680 $575 $500 $425 $375 $300 $240

Add 65% for Gen1 variation if in mint/NIB condition.
Add $28 for adj. sight.
Early Gen1 production with barrel ports, will command a high premium (new 1988).

This model is a long barreled competition version of the Model 17 "pebbled frame".

MODEL 17 TB GEN 3 (SPORT/SERVICE) – 9mm Para. cal., similar to Model 17, except features the new TB "Threaded Barrel" for a suppressor-ready design, roughly .5 in. longer than the 4.48 in. barrel, finger grooves, mounting accessories rail and elevated sights. New 2014.

MSR $649 $590 $515 $450 $375 $325 $265 $205

MODEL 17 GEN 4 25TH SILVER ANNIVERSARY LIMITED EDITION – 9mm Para. cal., Glock steel sights only, features 25th year silver medallion inletted in polymer frame and special inscription in back of slide on top, includes silver case. 2,500 to be mfg. during 2011.

$700 $600 $500 $450 $375 $350 $295 *$850*

MODEL 17 GEN 4 30TH ANNIVERSARY LIMITED EDITION – 9mm Para. cal., Glock steel sights only, features engraved slide with American Flag on the side of slide. Through careful craftsmanship of 5 Master USA Engravers, 30 pistols have been custom engraved for 30 Organizations to commemorate this momentous occasion. To our loyal customers, employees and fans alike, we thank you in celebrating this crowning achievement in the company's history. 30 pistols to be manufactured during 2016. Learn how you can win an engraved G17 Gen 4 at 30th.glock.com.

MODEL 17/17C GEN 4 – 9mm Para. cal., similar to Model 17, except features (less polymid traction) Rough Textured Frame (RTF-4) with recessed thumb rests, finger grooves, accessories rail, and interchangeable frame back straps, includes a reversible enlarged magazine catch, dual recoil spring assembly, and a new trigger system, Model 17C Gen 4 ported (new 2017), fixed rear, adj. rear Glock steel, or Glock night sights, Model 17 Gen 4 optional "FS" Front Slide Serrations (2017), standard black or optional FDE (light brown) (2012-current, limited mfg.) or gray (2015-current, limited mfg.), OD (green) (2016-current limited mfg.) finish. All Gen4 and Gen5 models shipped with 3 magazines, except Sub-Compact Models have 2 mags. New 2010.

MSR $599 $550 $475 $400 $350 $300 $240 $190

MODEL 17 MOS GEN 4 COMPETITION (SPORT/SERVICE) – 9mm Para. cal., adj. rear sight, similar to Model 17 Gen 4, except has Glock MOS (Modular Optic System), and lower rail for mounting accessories. New 2015.

MSR $679 $620 $550 $465 $415 $340 $280 $215

MODEL 17M GEN 5 (SPORT/SERVICE) – 9mm Para. cal., includes all of the standard model Gen 5 features with a (4.49 in. GMB-Glock Marksman Barrel), AmeriGlo Agent sights, 10 or 17 shot mag. standard; 19 or 33 shot mag optional, special extended ambidextrous slide stop lever and unique rounded "FBI" magazine catch, flared magazine well, nDLC finish, 25 oz. New 2019

MSR $745 $680 $575 $500 $425 $375 $300 $240

MODEL 17 GEN 5 (SPORT/SERVICE) – 9mm Para. cal., similar to Model 43 except has 4.49 in. "match crown" barrel w/hexagonal rifling, (GMB - Glock Marksman Barrel), w/less aggressive polymid traction, shipped w/three mags. 10 or 17 shot mag. standard, 19 or 33 shot mag. optional, 5 1/2 lb. trigger pull, new trigger system, choice of standard plastic sights, 3-dot night sights or Ameriglo bold operator sights, grip w/o finger grooves, redesigned firing pin and safety, Rough Textured Frame (RTF), SF (Short Frame) includes interchangeable frame backstraps, ambidextrous slide stop levers, flared mag. well, recessed thumb rests and rails, reversible enlarged mag. catch, nDLC black finish, 25 oz. New 2017.

MSR $699 $640 $560 $480 $435 $350 $290 $225

MODEL G17 MOS GEN5 COMPETITION (SPORT/SERVICE) – 9mm Para. cal., similar to Model 17 Gen5, except has GLOCK MOS (Modular Optic System), "FS" (Front Slide Serrations) and lower rail for mounting accessories, also available in 10, 19, 24, or 31 shot mag. New late 2018.

MSR $745 $680 $575 $500 $425 $375 $300 $240

MODEL 18/18C GEN 1, GEN 2, GEN 3 SELECTIVE FIRE CONTROL – 9mm Para. cal., similar to Model 17, except has Selective Fire Control with non interchangeable parts, with hexagonal rifled barrels. Gen1 pebbled finish frame has ported/non-ported barrel. New 1988. Gen2 checkered grip has ported/non-ported barrel. New 1996. Model 18C Gen3 finger grooves, recessed thumb rest, mounting accessories rail has ported/non-ported barrel, 19 shot mag., optional 33 shot mag., 24oz. New 1997.

Available for law enforcement and military units only (USA).

GRADING - PPGS™	100%	98%	95%	90%	80%	70%	60%	LAST MSR

MODEL 19/19C COMPACT GEN 1, GEN 2, GEN 3 (SPORT/SERVICE) – 9mm Para. cal., compact size to the Model 17, 4.01 in. barrel with hexagonal rifling ported (Model 19C, Gen2 checkered grip, new 1997), or unported barrel and checkered grip Gen2 has no accessories rail, (new 1988). 10 (C/B 1994), 15* (reintroduced late 2004), or 17* (reintroduced late 2004) shot mag., fixed (Service Model) or adj. (Sport Model) rear sight, 23 1/2 oz., Gen1 cut-down pebbled grip, has no mounting accessories rail (new 1988), Gen3 early transition model has finger grooves, thumb rests, no mounting accessories rail, (new 1997), standard black or optional OD (green) (Gen3 only 2004-current, limited mfg.) or FDE (light brown) (Gen3 2012-current, limited mfg.) finish. Later Gen3 models ported/non-ported barrel have thumb rests, finger grooves, mounting accessories rail, (new 1997-98).

MSR $649 $590 $515 $450 $375 $325 $265 $205

Add 65% for Gen 1 variation if in mint/NIB condition.
Add $22 for Model 19C with fixed sight only (new 1997).
Add $119 for competition model w/adj. sights (Model 19CC, mfg. 2000-2003).

This model is still available with RTF-2 finish (extreme polymid traction, Rough Textured Frame, Model 19 RTF-2, mfg. 2009).

This model is similar to Model 17, except has scaled down dimensions.

During 1996, AccuSport Corp. commissioned Glock to make a special production run of matching 9mm Para. cal. sets. Each set consists of a Model 19 and 26 with serialization as follows: Model 19 (ser. prefix AAA0000-AAA0499) and Model 26 (ser. prefix AAB0000-AAB0499).

MODEL 19 TB COMPACT GEN 3 (SPORT/SERVICE) – 9mm Para. cal., compact size to the Model 17, except features the new TB "Threaded Barrel" for a suppressor-ready design, roughly .5 in. longer than the 4.01 in. barrel, finger grooves, mounting accessories rail and elevated sights. New 2014.

MSR $649 $590 $515 $450 $375 $325 $265 $205

MODEL 19/19C GEN 4 – 9mm Para. cal., similar to Model 19, except features (less polymid traction) Rough Textured Frame (RTF-4) with recessed thumb rests, finger grooves, accessories rail, and interchangeable frame back straps, includes a reversible enlarged magazine catch, dual recoil spring assembly, and a new trigger system, Model 19C Gen 4 ported (new 2017), fixed rear, adj. rear Glock steel, or Glock night sights, Model 19 Gen 4 optional "FS" Front slide serrations (2017), standard black or optional FDE (light brown) (2012-current, limited mfg.), gray (2015-current, limited mfg.), or OD (green) (2016-current limited mfg.) finish. New 2010.

MSR $599 $550 $475 $400 $350 $300 $240 $190

MODEL 19 MOS GEN 4 COMPETITION (SPORT/SERVICE) – 9mm Para. cal., adj. rear sight, similar to Model 19 Gen 4, except has Glock MOS (Modular Optic System), and lower rail for mounting accessories. New 2015.

MSR $750 $680 $575 $500 $425 $375 $300 $240

MODEL 19M GEN 5 (SPORT/SERVICE) – 9mm Para. cal., includes all of the standard model Gen 5 features with a (4.01 in. GMB-Glock Marksman barrel) compact size comparable to the model 17 Gen 5, AmeriGlo Agent Sights, 10 or 15 shot mag. standard, 17 or 33 shot mag. optional, special extended ambidextrous slide stop lever and unique rounded "FBI" magazine catch, flared magwell, nDLC finish, 24 oz. New 2019.

MSR $699 $640 $560 $480 $435 $350 $290 $225

MODEL 19 COMPACT GEN 5 (SPORT/SERVICE) – 9mm Para. cal., compact size to the Model 17 Gen 5, 4.01 in. "match crown" barrel w/hexagonal rifling, (GMB - Glock Marksman Barrel), w/less aggressive polymid traction, shipped w/three mags. 10 or 15 shot mag. standard, 17 or 33 shot mag. optional, 5 1/2 lb. trigger pull, new trigger system, choice of standard plastic sights, 3-dot night sights or Ameriglo bold operator sights, grip w/o finger grooves, redesigned firing pin and safety, Rough Textured Frame (RTF), SF (Short Frame) includes interchangeable frame backstraps, ambidextrous slide stop levers, flared mag. well, recessed thumb rests, accessories rail, and reversible enlarged mag. catch, nDLC black finish, 24 oz. New 2017.

MSR $699 $640 $560 $480 $435 $350 $290 $225

MODEL G19 MOS GEN 5 COMPETITION (SPORT/SERVICE) – 9mm Para. cal., similar to Model 19 Gen5, except has GLOCK MOS (Modular Optic System), "FS" (Front slide serrations) and lower rail for mounting accessories, also available in 15, 24, or 31 shot mag. New late 2018.

MSR $745 $675 $590 $500 $440 $375 $300 $235

MODEL G19 X – 9mm Para. cal., similar features to Gen 5 models, Marksman 4.02 in. barrel, first ever factory colored Coyote Tan, 17 and 19 shot mag., slide, frame, and box, has Model 17 size grip and Model 19 size slide, approx. 25 oz., this model was developed for the military, no finger grooves and flared magwell, ambidextrous slide stop levers, reversible enlarged mag. catch, recessed thumb rest, mounting accessories rail, interchangeable frame backstraps, new trigger system, lanyard loop, and also comes with nDLC black finish. New 2017.

MSR $749 $675 $590 $500 $440 $375 $300 $235

GRADING - PPGS™	100%	98%	95%	90%	80%	70%	60%	LAST MSR

MODEL 20/20C GEN 2, GEN 3 (SPORT/SERVICE) – 10mm Norma cal., similar to Model 17 features except has 4.61 in. barrel ported/non-ported Model 20-20C, Gen3 with hexagonal rifling, optional 6 in. "Hunting Barrel" factory available. Early transition model has recessed thumb rests, finger grooves, no mounting accessories rail (new 1997), 10 (C/B 1994) or 15* (reintroduced late 2004) shot mag., larger slide and receiver, fixed (Service Model) or adj. (Sport Model) rear sight, Gen3 ported/non-ported barrel have recessed thumb rests, finger grooves, mounting accessories rail, (new 1997-98), Gen2 non-ported barrel, checkered grip, has no mounting accessories rail, standard black or optional OD (green) (Gen3 only 2004-current, limited mfg.) or FDE (light brown) (Gen3 2012-current, limited mfg.) finish, 30 oz. New 1990.

MSR $637	$580	$500	$425	$375	$325	$260	$205

Add $39 for compensated barrel (Model 20C, fixed sight only, new 1997).
Add $145 for competition model w/adj. sights (Model 20CC, mfg. 2000-2003).

* ***Model 20SF Gen 3*** – 10mm Norma cal., similar to Model 20, except has Gen3 (short frame), have recessed thumb rests, finger grooves, mounting accessories rail, 4.61 in. barrel with hexagonal rifling, 15 shot mag., all Glock sight options available, new trigger position, 30.7 oz. New 2009.

MSR $637	$580	$500	$425	$375	$325	$260	$205

MODEL 20 GEN 4 – 10mm Norma cal., similar to Model 20 except features (less polymid traction) Rough Textured Frame (RTF-4) with recessed thumb rests, finger grooves, accessories rail, and interchangeable frame back straps, includes a reversible enlarged magazine catch, dual recoil assembly and new trigger system, fixed rear, adj. rear Glock steel or Glock night sights, standard black or optional FDE (light brown) (2013-current, limited mfg.) or gray (2015-current, limited mfg.) finish. New 2012.

MSR $687	$625	$550	$475	$400	$340	$280	$220

MODEL 21/21C GEN 2, GEN 3 (SPORT/SERVICE) – .45 ACP cal., similar to Model 17, except has 4.61 in. barrel with octagonal rifling ported/non-ported Model 21-21C, Gen3 early transition model has recessed thumb rests, finger grooves, no mounting accessories rail (new 1997), 10 (C/B 1994) or 13* (reintroduced late 2004) shot mag., larger slide and receiver, Gen3 ported/non-ported barrel, have recessed thumb rests, finger grooves, mounting accessories rail (new 1997-98), Gen2 non-ported barrel, checkered grip, has no mounting accessories rail, standard black, optional OD (green) (Gen3 only 2004-current, limited mfg.) or FDE (Gen3 2012-current, limited mfg.) finish, 29 oz. New 1990.

MSR $637	$580	$500	$425	$375	$325	$260	$205

Add $39 for compensated barrel (Model 21C, fixed rear sight only, new 1997).
Add $145 for competition model w/adj. sights (Model 21CC, mfg. 2000-2003).

MODEL 21SF GEN 3 – .45 ACP cal., similar to Model 21, except has Gen3 (short frame), new trigger position, recessed thumb rests, finger grooves, mounting accessories rail, 4.61 in. barrel with octagonal rifling, 13 shot mag., 29 oz. (new 2007). Gen3 RTF-2 (extreme polymid traction) Rough Textured Frame (new 2009).

MSR $637	$580	$500	$425	$375	$325	$260	$205

MODEL 21SF TB GEN 3 (SPORT/SERVICE) – .45 ACP cal., similar to Model 21, except has Gen 3 (short frame), new trigger position, recessed thumb rests, finger grooves, mounting accessories rail, elevated sights, features the new TB "Threaded Barrel" for a suppressor-ready design, roughly .5 in. longer than the 4.61 in. barrel. New 2014.

MSR $649	$590	$515	$450	$375	$325	$265	$205

MODEL 21 GEN 4 – .45 ACP cal., similar to Model 21, except features (less polymid traction) Rough Textured Frame (RTF-4) with recessed thumb rests, finger grooves, accessories rail, and interchangeable frame back straps, includes a reversible enlarged magazine catch, dual recoil spring assembly, and a new trigger system, fixed rear, adj. rear Glock steel, or Glock night sights, standard black, optional FDE (light brown) (2012-current, limited mfg.) or gray (2015-current, limited mfg.) finish. New 2011.

MSR $687	$625	$550	$475	$400	$340	$280	$220

MODEL 22/22C GEN 2, GEN 3 (SPORT/SERVICE) – .40 S&W cal., similar to Model 17, except has 4.48 in. barrel with hexagonal barrel ported Model 22C Gen2 checkered grip (new 1997), 10 (C/B 1994), 15* (reintroduced late 2004), 16, or 22 shot mag., all Glock sight variations available, Gen3 has ported/non-ported barrel, have recessed thumb rests, finger grooves mounting accessories rail (new 1997-98), Gen2 has non-ported barrel, checkered grip has no mounting accessories rail, standard black, optional OD (green) (Gen3 only 2004-current, limited mfg.) or FDE (light brown) (Gen3 2012-current, limited mfg.) finish, 25 1/2 oz. New 1990.

MSR $599	$550	$475	$400	$350	$300	$240	$190

Add $22 for Model 22C with compensated barrel (fixed rear sight only, new 1997).
Add $119 for competition model with adj. sights (Model 22CC, mfg. 2000-2003).

This model is still available with RTF-2 finish (extreme polymid traction, Rough Textured Frame, Gen 3 Model 22 RTF-2, mfg. 2009) and also Gen 3 Model 22C RTF-2, mfg. 2009); Gen 4 Model 22c (RTF-2) mfg. 2016; also Gen 3 Model 22C RTF-2 mfg. (Law Enforcement only). USA.

GRADING - PPGS™	100%	98%	95%	90%	80%	70%	60%	LAST MSR

MODEL 22 GEN 4 – .40 S&W cal., 4.48 in. barrel, similar to Model 22, except features (less polymid traction) Rough Textured Frame (RTF-4) with recessed thumb rests, finger grooves, accessories rail, and interchangeable frame back straps, includes a reversible enlarged magazine catch, dual recoil spring assembly, and a new trigger system, fixed rear, adj. rear Glock steel, or Glock night sights, standard black, optional FDE (light brown) (2012-current, limited mfg.) or gray (2015-current, limited mfg.) finish. New 2010.

MSR $599	$550	$475	$400	$350	$300	$240	$190	

MODEL 22 GEN 5 (SPORT/SERVICE) – .40 S&W cal., similar to Model 17 Gen 5, 4.49 in. "match crown" barrel w/hexagonal rifling (GMB - Glock Marksman barrel), w/less aggressive polymid traction, ships with three mags., 10 or 15 shot mag. (standard), 16 or 22 shot mag. is optional, 5 1/2 lb. trigger pull, new trigger system, choice of standard plastic sights, 3-dot night sights or Ameriglo bold operator sights, grip w/o finger grooves, redesigned firing pin and safety, Rough Textured Frame (RTF), SF (Short Frame) includes interchangeable frame backstraps, beavertail system (MBS), ambidextrous slide stop levers, FS (Front Slide serrations), flared magwell, recessed thumb rests and accessories rails, reversible enlarged mag. catch, nDLC black finish, 25 1/2 oz. New 2020.

MSR $599	$550	$475	$400	$350	$300	$240	$190	

MODEL 22 MOS GEN 5 COMPETITION (SPORT/SERVICE) – .40 S&W cal., similar to Model 22 Gen5, except has Glock MOS (Modular Optic System), "FS" (Front Slide Serrations), and lower rail for mounting accessories, also available in 10 or 15 shot mag. (standard), 16 or 22 shot mag. is optional. New 2020.

MSR $599	$550	$475	$400	$350	$300	$240	$190	

MODEL 23/23C GEN 2, GEN 3 COMPACT (SPORT/SERVICE) – .40 S&W cal., compact variation of the Model 22, 4.01 in. barrel with hexagonal rifling ported (Model 23C), Gen2 checkered grip (new 1997), 10 (C/B 1994), 13* (reintroduced 2004), or 14 shot mag., available in all Glock sight variations, Gen3 ported/non-ported barrel have recessed thumb rests, finger grooves, mounting accessories rail (new 1997-98), Gen2 non-ported barrel, checkered grip has no mounting accessories rail, standard black, optional OD (green) (Gen3 only 2004-current, limited mfg.) or FDE (light brown) (Gen3 2012-current, limited mfg.) finish, 23 1/2 oz. New 1990.

MSR $599	$550	$475	$400	$350	$300	$240	$190	

Add $22 for compensated barrel Model 23C (fixed rear sight only, new 1997).
Add $145 for competition model w/adj. sights (Model 23CC, mfg. 2000-2003).

This model is still available with RTF-2 finish (extreme polymid traction) Rough Textured Frame (Gen 3 Model 23 RTF-2 mfg. 2009; also Gen 3 Model 23C RTF-2 mfg. 2010).

During 1996, AcuSport Corp. commissioned Glock to make a special production run of matching .40 S&W cal. sets. Each set consists of a Model 23 and 27 with serialization as follows: Model 23 (ser. prefix AAC0000-AAC1499) and Model 27 (ser. prefix AAD0000-AAD1499).

MODEL 23 TB GEN 3 COMPACT (SPORT/SERVICE) – .40 S&W cal., similar to Model 22, except compact size, features the new TB "Threaded Barrel" for a suppressor-ready design, roughly .5 in. longer than the 4.01 in. barrel, finger grooves, mounting accessories rail, and elevated sights. New 2014.

MSR $649	$590	$515	$450	$375	$325	$265	$205	

MODEL 23 GEN 4 – .40 S&W cal., similar to Model 23 Compact, except features (less polymid traction) Rough Textured Frame (RTF-4) with recessed thumb rests, finger grooves, accessories rail, and interchangeable frame back straps, includes a reversible enlarged magazine catch, dual recoil spring assembly, and a new trigger system, fixed rear, adj. rear Glock steel, or Glock night sights, standard black, optional FDE (light brown) (2012-current, limited mfg.) or gray (2015-current, limited mfg.) finish. New 2010.

MSR $599	$550	$475	$400	$350	$300	$240	$190	

MODEL 23 GEN 5 (COMPACT SPORT/SERVICE) – .40 S&W cal., similar to Model 19 Gen5, 4.02 in. "match crown" barrel w/hexagonal rifling (GMB-Glock Marksman barrel) w/less aggressive polymid traction, "FS" (Front Slide Serrations), shipped with three mags, 10 or 13 shot (standard), 14, 15, 16, or 22 shot mag. (optional), 24 oz. New 2020.

MSR $599	$550	$475	$400	$350	$300	$240	$190	

MODEL 23 MOS GEN 5 COMPETITION (COMPACT SPORT/SERVICE) – .40 S&W cal., similar to Model 23 Gen5, except has Glock MOS (Modular Optic System), "FS" (Front Slide Serrations), and lower rail for mounting accessories, available in 10 or 13 shot mag. (standard), 14, 15, 16, or 22 shot mag. is optional. New 2020.

MSR $599	$550	$475	$400	$350	$300	$240	$190	

GRADING - PPGS™	100%	98%	95%	90%	80%	70%	60%	LAST MSR

MODEL 24/24C GEN 2, GEN 3 COMPETITION (SPORT/SERVICE) – .40 S&W cal., Gen3, similar to Model 22, except has 6.02 in. barrel with hexagonal rifling, internally compensated, recessed thumb rest, finger grooves, accessories rail ported (Model 24C, new 1999), adj. rear sight, 10, 15, 16, or 22 shot mag., recalibrated trigger pull (4 1/2 lb. pull), Gen2 checkered grip has no rail, "P" ported/non-ported series, 29 1/2 oz. New 1994.

MSR $750	$680	$575	$500	$425	$375	$300	$240

Add $40 for compensated barrel (Model 24C).

MODEL 25 COMPACT GEN 3 (SPORT/SERVICE) – .380 ACP cal., similar to Model 19 Compact, except has 4.02 in. barrel, 15 or 17 shot mag., recessed thumb rest, finger grooves, accessories rail, 22.5 oz. New 2008.

This model is available for law enforcement only (USA).

MODEL 26 GEN 3 SUB-COMPACT – 9mm Para. cal., sub-compact variation of the Model 19 Compact, except has shortened grip, 3.42 in. barrel with hexagonal rifling, 10 or 12 shot mag., available with all Glock sight variations, thumb rest, finger grooves, no mounting rail, first Gen3 production run Transition model, standard black or optional OD/Olive Drab (green) (Gen3 only 2004-current, limited mfg.) or FDE/Flat Dark Earth (light brown) (Gen3 2012-current, limited mfg.) finish, 21 3/4 oz. New 1995.

MSR $599	$550	$475	$400	$350	$300	$240	$190

MODEL 26 GEN 4 – 9mm Para. cal., similar to Model 26 Sub-Compact, except features (less polymid traction) Rough Textured Frame (RTF-4) with recessed thumb rests, finger grooves, no mounting accessories rail, and interchangeable frame back straps, includes a reversible enlarged magazine catch, dual recoil spring assembly, and a new trigger system, fixed rear, adj. rear Glock steel, or Glock night sights, standard black or optional FDE/Flat Dark Earth (light brown) (2012-current, limited mfg.) or gray (2015-current, limited mfg.) finish. New 2010.

MSR $599	$550	$475	$400	$350	$300	$240	$190

MODEL 26 GEN 5 SUB-COMPACT – 9mm Para. cal., 3.43 in. "match crown" barrel w/hexagonal rifling, (GMB - Glock Marksman Barrel), w/less aggressive polymid traction, 10 shot mag. standard, 5 1/2 lb. trigger pull, choice of standard plastic sights, 3-dot night sights or Ameriglo bold operator sights, grip w/o finger grooves, redesigned firing pin and safety, Rough Textured Frame (RTF), SF (Short Frame) includes interchangeable frame backstraps, ambidextrous slide stop levers, recessed thumb rests, no mounting accessories rail and magwell, reversible enlarged mag. catch, nDLC black finish, 21 oz. New 2018.

MSR $647	$590	$515	$450	$375	$325	$265	$205

MODEL 27 GEN 3 SUB-COMPACT – .40 S&W cal., sub-compact variation of the Model 23 Compact, except has shortened grip, 3.42 in. barrel with hexagonal rifling, 9 or 10 shot mag., all Glock sight variations available, recessed thumb rest, finger grooves, no mounting accessories rail, standard black or optional OD/Olive Drab (green) (Gen3 only, 2004-current, limited mfg.) or FDE/Flat Dark Earth (light brown) (Gen3 2012-current, limited mfg.) finish, 21 3/4 oz. New 1995.

MSR $599	$550	$475	$400	$350	$300	$240	$190

MODEL 27 GEN 4 – .40 S&W cal., similar to Model 27 Sub-Compact, except features (less polymid traction) Rough Textured Frame (RTF-4) with recessed thumb rests, finger grooves, no mounting accessories rail, and interchangeable frame back straps, includes a reversible enlarged magazine catch, dual recoil spring assembly, and a new trigger system, fixed rear, adj. rear Glock steel, or Glock night sights, standard black or optional FDE/Flat Dark Earth (light brown) (2012-current, limited mfg.) or gray (2015-current, limited mfg.) finish. New 2010.

MSR $599	$550	$475	$400	$350	$300	$240	$190

MODEL 27 GEN 5 SUB-COMPACT – .40 S&W cal., similar to Model 27 Gen4, except features 3.42 in. "match crown" barrel w/hexagonal rifling (GMB - Glock Marksman Barrel) w/less aggressive polymid traction, shipped with three mags., 10 shot (standard), 13, 14, 15, 16, or 22 shot mag. (optional), 5 1/2 lb. trigger pull, new trigger system, choice of standard plastic sights, 3-dot night sights or Ameriglo bold operator sights, grip w/o finger grooves, redesigned firing pin and safety, Rough Textured Frame (RTF), SF (Short Frame) includes interchangeable frame backstraps, beavertail system (MBS), ambidextrous slide stop levers, "FS" (Front Slide serrations), flared magwell, recessed thumb rests, no rails, reversible enlarged mag. catch, nDLC black finish, 21 3/4 oz. New 2020.

MSR $599	$550	$475	$400	$350	$300	$240	$190

MODEL 28 GEN 3 SUB-COMPACT – .380 ACP cal., similar to Model 26/27/33/39 Sub-Compact, except has scaled down dimensions with 3.42 in. barrel, recessed thumb rests, finger grooves, no mounting accessories rail, 10 shot mag., approx. 20 oz. New 1998.

This model is available for law enforcement only (USA).

GRADING - PPGS™	100%	98%	95%	90%	80%	70%	60%	LAST MSR

MODEL 29 GEN 3 SUB-COMPACT – 10mm Norma cal., sub-compact variation of the Model 20, featuring 3.77 in. barrel with hexagonal rifling, 10 shot mag., all Glock sight variations are available, recessed thumb rests, finger grooves, with or w/o (early mfg.) accessories rail, standard black or optional OD/Olive Drab (green) (Gen3 only 2004-current, limited mfg.) finish, 27 oz. New 1996.

MSR $637	$580	$500	$425	$375	$325	$260	$205

MODEL 29SF GEN 3 – 10mm Norma cal., 3.77 in. barrel, Gen3, short frame, all Glock sight options available, new trigger position, recessed thumb rests, finger grooves, mounting accessories rail, otherwise similar to Model 29. New 2009.

MSR $637	$580	$500	$425	$375	$325	$260	$205

MODEL 29 GEN 4 – 10mm Norma cal., similar to Model 29 Sub-compact except features (less polymid traction) Rough Textured Frame (RTF-4) with recessed thumb rests, finger grooves accessories rail, and interchangeable frame back straps, reversible enlarged magazine catch, dual recoil spring assembly, and new trigger system, fixed rear, adj. rear Glock steel, or Glock night sights. New 2012.

MSR $687	$625	$550	$475	$400	$340	$280	$220

MODEL 30 GEN 3 SUB-COMPACT – .45 ACP cal., sub-compact variation of the Model 21 featuring 3.77 in. barrel with octagonal rifling, mag. extension, 10 shot mag., all Glock sight options available, thumb rest, finger grooves, with or w/o (early mfg.) rail, standard black or optional OD Green (Gen3 only 2004-current, limited mfg.) finish, 26 1/2 oz. New 1996.

MSR $637	$580	$500	$425	$375	$325	$260	$205

MODEL 30SF GEN 3 – .45 ACP cal., 3.77 in. barrel, Gen3 short frame, all Glock sight options available, new trigger position, recessed thumb rests, finger grooves, mounting accessories rail, otherwise similar to Model 30. New 2008.

MSR $637	$580	$500	$425	$375	$325	$260	$205

MODEL 30S GEN 3 – .45 ACP cal., 3.78 in. barrel, Gen3 short frame, all Glock sight options available, new trigger position, recessed thumb rests, finger grooves, accessories rail, otherwise similar to Model 30SF. Model 36 slim style slide. New 2012.

MSR $637	$580	$500	$425	$375	$325	$260	$205

MODEL 30 GEN 4 – .45 ACP cal, similar to Model 30 Sub-compact except features (less polymid traction) Rough Textured Frame (RTF-4) with recessed thumb rests, finger grooves, accessories rail, and interchangeable frame back straps, reversible enlarged magazine catch, dual recoil spring assembly, and new trigger system, fixed rear, adj. rear Glock steel, or Glock night sights. New 2012.

MSR $687	$625	$550	$475	$400	$340	$280	$220

MODEL 31/31C GEN 2, GEN 3 (SPORT/SERVICE) – .357 SIG cal., similar to Model 22, 4.48 in. barrel with hexagonal rifling, ported/non-ported (Model 31-31C Gen3) recessed thumb rests, finger grooves, mounting accessories rail (new 1997-98), all Glock sight options available, 10, 15, or 16 shot mag., Model 31 Gen2 non-ported barrel, checkered grip has no mounting accessories rail, standard black or optional OD/Olive Drab (green) (Gen3 only 2004-current, limited mfg.) finish, 26 oz. New 1997.

MSR $599	$550	$475	$400	$350	$300	$240	$190

Add $22 for compensated barrel (Model 31C, fixed rear sight only, new 1998).
Add $119 for competition model w/adj. sights (Model 31CC, mfg. 2000-2004).

MODEL 31 GEN 4 – .357 SIG cal., similar to Model 31, except features (less polymid traction) Rough Textured Frame (RTF-4) with recessed thumb rests, finger grooves, accessories rail, and interchangeable frame back straps, includes a reversible enlarged magazine catch, dual recoil spring assembly, and a new trigger system, fixed rear, adj. rear Glock steel, or Glock night sights. New 2010.

MSR $599	$550	$475	$400	$350	$300	$240	$190

MODEL 32/32C COMPACT GEN 2, GEN 3 (SPORT/SERVICE) – .357 SIG cal., similar to Model 23, 4.01 in. barrel with hexagonal rifling ported/non-ported (Model 32-32C Gen3), recessed thumb rests, finger grooves, mounting accessories rail (new 1997-98), Model 32 Gen2 non-ported barrel checkered grip, has no mounting accessories rail, all Glock sight options are available, 10, 13, or 14 shot mag., standard black or optional OD/Olive Drab (green) (Gen3 only 2004-current, limited mfg.) finish, 24 oz. New 1997.

MSR $599	$550	$475	$400	$350	$300	$240	$190

Add $22 for compensated barrel (Model 32C, fixed rear sight only, new 1998).
Add $119 for competition model w/adj. sights (Model 32CC, mfg. 2002-2004).

MODEL 32 GEN 4 – .357 SIG cal., similar to Model 32 Compact, except features (less polymid traction) Rough Textured Frame (RTF-4) with recessed thumb rests, finger grooves, accessories rail, and interchangeable frame back straps, includes a reversible enlarged magazine catch, dual recoil spring assembly, and a new trigger system, fixed rear, adj. rear Glock steel, or Glock night sights. New 2012.

MSR $599	$550	$475	$400	$350	$300	$240	$190

GRADING - PPGS™	100%	98%	95%	90%	80%	70%	60%	LAST MSR

MODEL 33 GEN 3 SUB-COMPACT – .357 SIG cal., sub-compact variation of the Model 32 Compact, shortened grip, 3.42 in. barrel with hexagonal rifling, 9 or 10 shot mag., recessed thumb rests, finger grooves, no mounting accessories rail, standard black or optional OD/Olive Drab (green) (Gen 3 only 2005-current, limited mfg.) finish, 22 oz. New 1997.

MSR $599	$550	$475	$400	$350	$300	$240	$190

MODEL 33 GEN 4 – .357 SIG cal., similar to Model 33 Sub-compact, except features (less polymid traction) Rough Textured Frame (RTF-4) with recessed thumb rests, finger grooves, no accessories rail, and interchangeable back straps, includes a reversible enlarged magazine catch, dual recoil spring assembly, and a new trigger system, fixed rear, adj. rear Glock steel, or Glock night sights. New 2012.

MSR $599	$550	$475	$400	$350	$300	$240	$190

MODEL 34 GEN 3 COMPETITION (SPORT/SERVICE) – 9mm Para. cal., similar features as the Model 17, except has 5.31 in. barrel, recalibrated trigger pull (4 1/2 pull), relieved slide, with hexagonal rifling, extended slide stop lever and magazine catch, adj. rear sights, target grips have recessed thumb rests, mounting accessories rail, standard 10, 17, or optional 19 or 33 shot mag., standard black or optional OD/Olive Drab (green) (Gen3 only 2004-current, limited mfg.) or FDE/Flat Dark Earth (light brown) (Gen3 2012-current, limited mfg.) finish, 25.75 oz. New 1998.

MSR $679	$620	$550	$465	$415	$340	$280	$215

MODEL 34 GEN 4 – 9mm Para. cal., 5.31 in. barrel, similar to Model 34, except features (less polymid traction) Rough Textured Frame (RTF-4) with recessed thumb rests, finger grooves, accessories rail, and interchangeable frame back straps, includes a reversible enlarged magazine catch, dual recoil spring assembly, and a new trigger system, adj. rear sight only, standard black or optional FDE/Flat Dark Earth (light brown) (2012-current, limited mfg.) or gray (2015-current, limited mfg.) finish, 25.95 oz. New 2011.

MSR $840	$760	$650	$575	$500	$425	$340	$265

MODEL 34 MOS GEN 4 COMPETITION (SPORT/SERVICE) – 9mm Para. cal., similar to Model 34, except has Glock MOS (Modular Optic System), adjustable rear sights, finger grooves, mounting accessories rail. New 2015.

MSR $840	$760	$650	$575	$500	$425	$340	$265

MODEL 34 MOS GEN 5 COMPETITION (SPORT/SERVICE) – 9mm Para. cal., similar to the Model 17 Gen 5, except has 5.31 in. "match crown" barrel w/hexagonal rifling, (GMB - Glock Marksman Barrel), w/less aggressive polymid traction, 10 or 17 shot mag. standard, 19 or 33 shot mag. optional, 4 1/2 lb. trigger pull, modular optic system (MOS) and adj. rear sight, grip w/o finger grooves, redesigned firing pin and safety, Rough Textured Frame (RTF), SF (Short Frame) includes interchangeable frame backstraps, ambidextrous slide stop levers, flared magwell, recessed thumb rests, accessories rail, reversible enlarged mag. catch, optional "FS" Front slide serrations, nDLC black finish, approx. 26 oz. New 2017.

MSR $899	$820	$725	$625	$550	$450	$375	$285

MODEL 35 GEN 3 COMPETITION (SPORT/SERVICE) – .40 S&W cal., standard 10, 15, or optional 16, or 22 shot mag., recessed thumb rest, finger grooves, accessories rail, otherwise similar to Model 34, standard black or optional OD/Olive Drab (green) (Gen3 only 2004-current, limited mfg.) or FDE/Flat Dark Earth (light brown) (Gen3 2012-current, limited mfg.) finish, 27.5 oz. New 1998.

MSR $679	$620	$550	$465	$415	$340	$280	$215

MODEL 35 GEN 4 – .40 S&W cal., 5.31 in. barrel, similar to Model 35, except features (less polymid traction) Rough Textured Frame (RTF-4) with recessed thumb rests, finger grooves, accessories rail, and interchangeable frame back straps, includes a reversible enlarged magazine catch, dual recoil spring assembly, and a new trigger system, adj. rear sight only, standard black or optional FDE/Flat Dark Earth (light brown) (2012-current, limited mfg.) or gray (2015-current, limited mfg.) finish. New 2010.

MSR $679	$620	$550	$465	$415	$340	$280	$215

MODEL 35 MOS GEN 4 COMPETITION (SPORT/SERVICE) – .40 S&W cal., similar to Model 35 Gen 4, except has Glock MOS (Modular Optic System), adjustable rear sight, finger grooves, mounting accessories rail. New 2015.

MSR $840	$760	$650	$575	$500	$425	$340	$265

MODEL 35 MOS GEN 5 COMPETITION (SPORT/SERVICE) – .40 S&W cal., similar to Model 35 Gen 4, except has Glock MOS (Modular Optic System), adjustable rear sight, finger grooves, mounting accessories rail, 28.29 oz. New 2021.

MSR $840	$760	$650	$575	$500	$425	$340	$265

MODEL 36 GEN 3 SUB-COMPACT – .45 ACP cal., similar to Model 30 Sub-compact, except has single column 6 shot mag., 3.77 in. barrel with octagonal rifling, recessed thumb rest, finger grooves, with or w/o (early mfg.) rail, all Glock sight options are available, slimmest Glock .45 ACP cal. for concealment, standard black or optional OD/Olive Drab (green) (Gen3 only 2004-current, limited mfg.) finish, 22 1/2 oz. New 1999.

MSR $637	$580	$500	$425	$375	$325	$260	$205

GRADING - PPGS™	100%	98%	95%	90%	80%	70%	60%	LAST MSR

MODEL 37 GEN 3 (SPORT/SERVICE) – .45 G.A.P. (Glock Automatic Pistol) cal., 4.48 in. barrel with octagonal rifling, all Glock sight options are available, similar to Model 17, except has extended slide stop lever, wider and heavier slide, improved locking block and ejector, 10 shot semi-staggered column mag., recessed thumb rest, finger grooves, accessories rail, standard black or optional OD/Olive Drab (green) (Gen3 only 2004-current, limited mfg.) finish, 28 3/4 oz. New 2003.

MSR $614 $535 $450 $375 $325 $295 $260 $225

MODEL 37 GEN 4 – .45 G.A.P. (Glock Automatic Pistol) cal. similar to Model 37, except features (less polymid traction) Rough Textured Frame (RTF-4) with recessed thumb rests, finger grooves, accessories rail, and interchangeable frame back straps, includes a reversible enlarged magazine catch, dual recoil spring assembly, and a new trigger system, fixed rear, adj. rear Glock steel, or Glock night sights. New 2010.

MSR $664 $600 $525 $450 $375 $325 $270 $210

MODEL 38 GEN 3 COMPACT (SPORT/SERVICE) – .45 G.A.P. cal., compact variation to the Model 37, except has 4.01 in. barrel with octagonal rifling, 8 shot semi-staggered column mag., recessed thumb rests, finger grooves, accessories rail, all Glock sight options are available, standard black or optional OD Green (Gen3 only 2005-current, mfg. limited) finish, 26 oz. New 2005.

MSR $614 $535 $450 $375 $325 $295 $260 $225

MODEL 39 GEN 3 SUB-COMPACT – .45 G.A.P. cal., sub-compact variation of the Model 38 Compact, except has shortened grip, 6 shot semi-staggered column mag., 3.42 in. barrel with octagonal rifling, all Glock sight options are available, recessed thumb rests, finger grooves, no accessories rail, standard black or optional OD Green (Gen3 only 2005-current, limited mfg.) finish, 22 oz. New 2005.

MSR $614 $535 $450 $375 $325 $295 $260 $225

MODEL 40 MOS GEN 4 COMPETITION (SPORT/SERVICE) – 10mm Norma cal., similar to the Model 20 Gen 4, except has 6.01 in. hexagonal rifled barrel recalibrated trigger pull (4 1/2 lb. pull) with Glock MOS (Modular Optic System) adjustable rear sight, 10 or 15 shot mag., lower rail for mounting accessories, 31.32 oz. New 2015.

MSR $840 $760 $650 $575 $500 $425 $340 $265

MODEL 41 GEN 4 COMPETITION (SPORT/SERVICE) – .45 ACP cal., similar to Model 21 Gen 4, except has 5.31 in. barrel, recalibrated 4 1/2 lb. trigger pull, (less polymid traction) Rough Textured Frame (RTF-4), recessed thumb rests, finger grooves, accessories rail, interchangeable frame backstrap, reversible enlarged magazine catch, dual recoil spring assembly, new trigger system, octagonal rifling, adj. rear Glock sights, 10 or 13 shot mag., standard black or optional FDE/Flat Dark Earth (light brown) or gray (2015-current, limited mfg.) finish, 27 oz. New 2013.

MSR $729 $625 $550 $495 $440 $375 $325 $250

MODEL 41 MOS GEN 4 COMPETITION (SPORT/SERVICE) – .45 ACP cal., similar to Model 41, except has Glock MOS (Modular Optic System), adjustable rear sight, lower rail for mounting accessories. New 2015.

MSR $840 $760 $650 $575 $500 $425 $340 $265

MODEL 42 GEN 4 SUB-COMPACT – .380 ACP cal., (Gen4) features "Less Aggressive" Polymid Traction Rough Textured Frame (RTF) single column, fires from standard Glock locked breech, 3.25 in. barrel with hexagonal rifling, 6 shot mag., measures less than 1 inch width, slimmest Glock frame for concealment, reversible enlarged magazine catch, dual recoil spring assembly, new trigger system, recessed thumb rests, no finger grooves, no accessories rail, 5 1/2 lb. trigger pull, adj. rear Glock sights, standard black, FDE/Flat Dark Earth (light brown) (2015-current, limited mfg.), or gray (2016-current, limited mfg.) finish, 13 3/4 oz. New 2013.

MSR $480 $435 $375 $325 $285 $240 $195 $150

This model is manufactured in the U.S.

MODEL 43 GEN 4 SUB-COMPACT – 9mm Para. cal., (Gen4) features "Less Aggressive" Polymid Traction Rough Textured Frame (RTF) single column, fires from standard Glock locked breech, 3.39 in. barrel with hexagonal rifling, 6 shot mag., measures 1.02 inch width, slimmest Glock 9mm frame for concealment, reversible enlarged magazine catch, dual recoil spring assembly, new trigger system, recessed thumb rests, no finger grooves, noaccessories rail, 5 1/2 lb. trigger pull, adj. rear Glock sights, standard black, FDE/Flat Dark Earth (light brown) (2016-current, limited mfg.), OD/Olive Drab (green) (2017-current, limited mfg.), or gray (2016-current, limited mfg.), 18 oz. Mfg. in Austria. New 2015.

MSR $580 $530 $475 $400 $360 $290 $240 $185

MODEL 43X GEN 5 SUB-COMPACT – 9mm Para. cal., similar features to Model 43, except has a fuller size grip length with a minimal profile width of approx. 1 in. for a comfortably balanced, versatile grip. 3.41 in. Glock Marksman barrel (GMB), single column 10 rd. mags., similar height as the compact Model 19 with front slide serrations, a comfortable built-in beavertail, reversible enlarged magazine catch, recessed thumb rests, no flared magwell, no finger grooves, no accessories rail, all Glock sight options available, silver nPVD or nDLC black slide finish, 18.7 oz. New 2019.

MSR $538 $490 $425 $375 $325 $275 $225 $175

GRADING - PPGS™	100%	98%	95%	90%	80%	70%	60%	LAST MSR

MODEL 43X MOS GEN 5 SUB-COMPACT – 9mm Para. cal., features Glock MOS (Modular Optic System), 3.41 in. match grade Glock Marksman Barrel (GMB), match grade hexagonal rifling, single column 10 shot mag., flared magwell, reversible enlarged mag. catch, precision-milled front serrations, built-in beavertail, recessed thumb rests, Shield RSMc mini red dot sight, versatile compact-size grip with a minimal profile, Glock Slim Mounting Rail, nDLC black finish on slide, approx. 18.7 oz. New 2020.

MSR $582	$530	$475	$400	$360	$290	$240	$185

MODEL 44 COMPACT (SPORT/SERVICE) – .22 LR cal., Gen 5 grip (w/o finger grooves), mounting accessories rail, interchangeable frame backstraps, "FS" Front Slide serrations, ambidextrous slide stop lever and reversible enlarged magazine catch, recessed thumb rests, flared magwell, similar size to Model 19, 4.02 in. Glock Marksman Barrel (GMB) for increased accuracy and precision, adj. rear sights, 10 shot mag., hybrid steel-polymer lightweight slide featuring low recoil and optimal control, approx. 14.64 oz. Mfg. in Austria. New 2020.

MSR $430	$390	$340	$295	$265	$215	$175	$135

MODEL 45 GEN 5 COMPACT (SPORT/SERVICE) – 9mm Para. cal., similar features to the Model 19X Gen5 compact crossover pistol with Safe Action System, 4.02 in. "match Crown" barrel with hexagonal rifling, (GMB - Glock Marksman Barrel), has Model 17 size grip and Model 19 size slide, interchangeable frame backstraps, ambidextrous slide stop levers, reversible enlarged magazine catch, no finger grooves with flared magwell (FS) Front slide serrations, recessed thumb rests, new trigger system, and mounting accessories rail, modular backstrap system (MBS), shipped with three mags., 10, 17, 19, 24, 31, or 33 shot mag. standard (19 or 33 shot mag. optional), 5 1/2 lb. trigger pull. "Less Aggressive" Polymid Traction Rough Textured Frame (RTF) nDLC black finish, all Glock sight options available, approx. 25 oz. New late 2018.

MSR $699	$640	$560	$480	$435	$350	$290	$225

MODEL 45 MOS GEN 5 COMPACT (SPORT/SERVICE) – 9mm Para. cal., similar to Model 45 Gen5 has Glock MOS (Modular Optic System) all sight options available, no finger grooves w/mounting accessories rail, and flared magwell, (FS) Front Slide Serration. New 2019.

MSR $745	$680	$575	$500	$425	$375	$300	$240

MODEL 46 GEN 5 COMPACT (SPORT/SERVICE) – 9mm Para. cal., similar features to the Model 19 Gen 5 and was designed for the German Police. Straight front grip strap with no finger groves, mounting accessories rail, integral beavertail, ambidextrous slide stop lever, reversible magazine catch, enlarged trigger housing and trigger that is thinner and flatter than the typical Glock trigger. Has a different operating system, cam-actuated rotating barrel. The rotating barrel system dissipates recoil energy for a reduction in felt recoil, a muzzle rise also increases accuracy, 24 oz. Mfg. in Austria for the German police. New 2017.

This model is available for law enforcement only.

MODEL 47 GEN 5 (SPORT/SERVICE) – 9mm Para. cal., similar features to the Gen 5 Model 17 MOS style slide with a G45 frame, 4.5 in. Glock Marksman Barrel (GMB), Ameriglo Bolt sights, extended mag. floorplates. G47 has full parts interchangeability with the Model Gen 5 G19, G19X, G34 and G45 17 rd. mag and optional 19, 24, 31, or 33 shot mag. should the need arise. Interchangable frame backstraps, ambidextrous slide stop levers, reversible enlarged magazine catch, no finger grooves with flared magwell (FS) Front slide serrations, recessed thumb rests, new trigger system and mounting accessory rail, "Less Aggressive" Polymid Traction Rough Textured Frame (RTF) nDLC black finish. Gen 5 G19 and G26 were also selected by law enforcement with all three Model Gen 5 G47, G19 and G26 pistols with flared magwell. New 2019.

This model is available for law enforcement only (USA).

MODEL 48 GEN 5 COMPACT (SPORT/SERVICE) – 9mm Para. cal., similar features to the Model 43, except has a fuller-size grip length with a minimal profile width of approx. 1-inch for a comfortably balanced, versatile grip. The slide has the silver nPVD finish which has withstood rigorous military testing. Similar height as the compact Model 19 with front slide serrations, a comfortable built-in beavertail, reversible enlarged magazine catch, recessed thumb rests, no flared magwell and accessories rail, no finger grooves, no rail, a match grade hexagonal rifling, GMB Glock Marksman 4.17 in. barrel. Also comes with single column 10 rd. mags., "Less Aggressive" Polymid Traction Rough Textured Frame (RTF), short trigger distance 5 1/2 trigger pull. All Glock sight options available, slide also comes in nDLC black finish, approx. 20.47 oz. New 2019.

MSR $538	$490	$425	$375	$325	$275	$225	$175

MODEL 48 MOS GEN 5 COMPACT – 9mm Para. cal., features Glock MOS (Modular Optic System), 4.17 in. match grade Glock Marksman Barrel (GMB), match grade hexagonal rifling, single column 10 shot mag., flared magwell, reversible enlarged mag. catch, precision-milled front serrations, built-in beavertail, recessed thumb rests, Shield RSMc mini red dot sight, versatile compact-size grip with a minimal profile, Glock Slim Mounting Rail, nDLC black finish on slide, 20.74 oz. New 2021.

MSR $582	$530	$475	$400	$360	$290	$240	$185

GRADING - PPGS™	100%	98%	95%	90%	80%	70%	60%	LAST MSR

MODEL G44 – .22 LR cal., Safe Action System, compact size and features similar to the Model 19 Gen 5, hybrid steel polymer slide, 4.02 in. GMB - Glock Marksman Barrel, two 10 shot load assist mags., reversible mag. catch, adj. rear sights, textured grips, ambi slide stop lever, adj. backstraps, ghost hole loaded chamber indicator, black finish, 12.63 oz. New 2020.

MSR $430	$390	$340	$295	$265	$215	$175	$135

MODEL P80 GEN1 (SPORT/SERVICE) – 9mm Para. cal., similar to Model 17 Gen1 (pebbled frame), has single pin frame, P80 marking on slide, flat extractor, smooth trigger, polymer front and rear sights, no front slide serrations, "Tupperware" Peel Top Box, includes collectable packaging and Certificate of Authenticity. It is a pistol generation in itself. New 2020.

MSR $699	$640	$560	$480	$435	$350	$290	$225

PISTOLS: SEMI-AUTO, COMMEMORATIVES, ENGRAVED, & SPECIAL/LIMITED EDITIONS 1991-CURRENT

For detailed information on Commemoratives and Special/Limited Edition models from 1991-current, please visit our website at BlueBookOfGunValues.com/overflow.

GOLAN

Please refer to the KSN Industries Ltd. listing in the K section.

GOLDEN EAGLE

Previous trademark of rifles/shotguns produced by Nikko Limited located in Tochigi, Japan, circa 1975-1981.

Please refer to the Nikko Firearms Limited listing in this text for a complete chronological history of Nikko - Japan's previous long gun manufacturer.

RIFLES: BOLT ACTION

MODEL 7000 GRADE I – all popular American calibers, including .270 Win., and .300 Wby. Mag., 24 or 26 in. barrel, select skipline checkered walnut stock, rosewood forend tip, golden eagle head engraved in pistol grip cap, recoil pad. Mfg. 1976-1981.

	$650	$575	$525	$450	$375	$340	$290

MODEL 7000 GRADE I AFRICAN – .375 H&H and .458 Win. Mag. cal., similar to 7000, open sights.

	$975	$850	$725	$625	$575	$495	$450

MODEL 7000 GRADE II – scroll engraving, better grade wood.

	$775	$650	$575	$500	$425	$385	$350

SHOTGUNS: O/U

MODEL 5000 GRADE I (FIELD) – 12 or 20 ga., 26, 28, or 30 in. barrels, various chokes, vent. rib, engraved frame, gold eagle head inlay, auto ejectors, SST, checkered pistol grip beavertail stock. Mfg. 1975-81.

	$850	$775	$700	$625	$560	$510	$440

MODEL 5000 GRADE I SKEET – similar to 5000 Field, except 26 or 28 in. skeet bored, wide rib.

	$875	$800	$725	$650	$580	$510	$440

MODEL 5000 GRADE I TRAP – similar to 5000 Field, except 30 or 32 in. barrel, mod. and full, imp. mod. and full, or full and full choke, wide rib, trap stock with pad.

	$875	$800	$725	$650	$580	$510	$440

MODEL 5000 GRADE II – available in Field, Trap, and Skeet, more engraving, better grade wood, with screaming eagle on frame in gold.

	$950	$875	$790	$710	$630	$540	$460
Skeet	$975	$895	$810	$725	$640	$540	$460
Trap	$975	$895	$810	$725	$640	$540	$460

GRANDEE GRADE III – similar to 5000 Grade II, except elaborate engraving, inlays, and better grade wood.

	$2,500	$2,200	$1,900	$1,575	$1,250	$1,000	$850

GOLDEN STATE ARMS

Previous importer located in Pasadena, CA. Golden State Arms imported and subcontracted various firearms constructed by European and Japanese manufacturers - achieving private label status on some guns.

Most firearms previously imported by Golden State Arms (including private labels) are not that collectible. In many cases, the shooting value will determine the price of a specimen. In some models or configurations which are currently desirable, however, premiums may exist.

GRADING - PPGS™	100%	98%	95%	90%	80%	70%	60%	LAST MSR

GONCZ ARMAMENT, INC.

Previous manufacturer located in North Hollywood, CA circa 1984-1990.

While advertised, BATF records indicate very few Goncz pistols or carbines were actually produced. All of these guns were prototypes or individually hand-built and none were ever mass produced through normal fabrication techniques.

In 1990, Claridge Hi-Tec, Inc. purchased Goncz Armament, Inc.

GRAHAM BROTHER RIFLEWORKS

Current manufacturer of bolt action pistols and accessories established in 2019, located in East Hampton, MA.

Graham Brothers Rifleworks is a sub-division of Yankee Hill Machine. They also manufacture the MARC chassis and long range accessories.

PISTOLS: BOLT ACTION

MARC SPORT BOLT ACTION PISTOL – .308 Win. or .300 AAC Blackout cal., Remington 700 action, 9 or 12 1/2 in. barrel, YHM slant muzzle brake, Accurate-Mag steel mag., GBR-0 MOA scope rail, AR style pistol grip, folding SB Tactical arm brace, MARC Sport chassis system and handguard, black finish. New 2020.

MSR $2,018	$1,700	$1,500	$1,300	$1,150	$950	$750	$600

Add $37 for .308 Win. cal.

GRAND POWER s.r.o.

Current manufacturer established in 2002, located in Slovakia. Currently imported by Global Ordnance LLC, located in Sarasota, FL. Previously imported by Eagle Imports, located in Wanamassa, NJ, Century International Arms from 2013-2015, located in Delray Beach, FL, and by STI International, located in Georgetown, TX until 2007.

For individual model listings, please go to BlueBookOfGunValues.com/overflow.

GRANGER, G.

Current manufacturer established during 1902, located in Saint Etienne, France. Current U.S. importer is JJ Perodeau Gunmaker, located in Sand Springs, OK.

SHOTGUNS: SxS, SIDELOCK

All guns are made on a custom order basis. For more information on model options, price, availability, and delivery time, please contact the importer directly.

GRANGER SxS – 12, 16, 20, or 28 ga., case hardened receiver, Granger sidelock mechanism and plates, DT or SNT, choice of pistol or straight grip, deluxe French walnut stock and forearm, prices will vary per older customer specifications and appointments, delivery time is 12-36 months. Limited mfg.

Engraving is available by request.

Please contact the importer directly for pricing and availability.

GRANITE MOUNTAIN ARMS, INC.

Current action/related components and previous firearms manufacturer located in Phoenix, AZ. Previously located in Prescott, AZ.

Granite Mountain Arms, Inc. currently manufactures precision rifle actions based on the Mauser 98, in addition to related components. Various custom gun makers utilize Granite Mountain Arms' actions for their custom rifles. Granite Mountain Arms previously manufactured a double square bridge Mauser magnum rifle and action, available in four sizes, in both left and right-hand. Sizes ranged from Short Magnum, Standard Magnum, Express Magnum, and the African Express Magnum for the largest of calibers such as the .505 Gibbs and the .585 cal. All prices are curently POR, depending on features, caliber, and other specifications. Additionally, custom rifle manufacturers also use Granite Mountain Arms, Inc. actions to build their own bolt action rifles. Please contact the company directly for more information, including availability and pricing.

GRANT, STEPHEN

Current trademark manufactured by Atkin, Grant & Lang, established in 1867, and located in Hertfordshire, England.

For individual model listings, please go to BlueBookOfGunValues.com/overflow.

GREAT WESTERN

Current trademark of revolvers manufactured by Pietta of Italy. Currently imported by E.M.F. Company, Inc., located in Santa Ana, CA.

Please refer to Pietta F.LLI in the P section for a current listing of Great Western revolvers.

GRADING - PPGS™	100%	98%	95%	90%	80%	70%	60%	LAST MSR

GREAT WESTERN ARMS COMPANY

Previous manufacturer located in Los Angeles, CA circa 1954-1964.

Most firearms enthusiasts are more or less familiar with Great Western Arms Co., an enterprise initially organized in Los Angeles through the efforts of Hy Hunter and established by three partners; Dr. Hassam, a prominent surgeon, Dan Reeves, owner of the L.A. Rams, and Dan Fortmann. Bill Wilson, a former production engineer at North American Aviation, served as president.

Wilson established his shop in a tin covered building on Minor Street in Southgate, CA and staffed it with a small group of employees, some taken from Weatherby. As time went by, as many as fifty workers were busy producing guns.

Hy Hunter's American Weapons Corp. in Burbank was chosen by the partners to be the exclusive distributor. Hunter so aggressively marketed the Frontier Six Shooter that his name became synonymous with Great Western and many believed that he was the owner of the company.

With Bob Green as financial officer and Bill Hensley as plant superintendent, machining of parts to manufacture exact copies of the original Colt Model P began in early 1954. Fitting, de-burring, polishing, finishing and assembly began slowly in the spring, with initial production and sales generated by notoriety of the proprietary .357 Atomic cartridge.

Great Western Arms Co. operated for approximately ten years, during which time they were reorganized by at least five different owners. Even though the company was well funded with $250,000 initially, it was never stable, lacking in manufacturing expertise and management skills. But the employees made up for it with enthusiasm and a genuine desire to accommodate their customers.

Appearing in early Great Western brochures and catalogues were spokesmen John Wayne and Audie Murphy. Exhibition shooters Dee Woolem and Sam Toole represented the company with their fast draw talents.

The Great Western revolver line-up offered a well-rounded variety of models with sub-variants. A good selection of barrel lengths, finishes, decoration and calibers were available. They offered interchangeable auxiliary cylinders and a variety of other special and innovative accessories.

The author would like to thank Mr. John Dougan for providing information and values for this section.

ADDITIONAL HISTORY & INFORMATION

Additional Great Western Arms Company percentages and model production totals can be found in the back of this text in the Serialization section listed under Great Western Arms Company.

Examination and survey of approximately four hundred Great Western revolvers and derringers revealed the following.

- A small quantity of smoothbore guns were shipped.

- Single-actions with a through the frame firing pin hole and a full radius to the front of the cylinder frame have Colt frames. Many of the earliest revolvers were made with the Colt cylinder frame; serial numbers 73, 95, 111, 245, 332, 348, and 367.

- Serial number GW5543 is roll marked on the side of the cylinder frame "GREAT WESTERN LOS ANGELES".

- Occasionally an example will be found that has a letter T stamped on the trigger guard oval. Assembler Toni Rimerez hand stamped the guns that she assembled until she was instructed to stop.

- Some revolvers feature chrome lined barrels.

- Standard finishes were cyanide case colored, blued, chrome, nickel, silver, gold, bead blasted, and blued.

- A specially fabricated Great Western revolver was built to be used by Don Knotts in the Disney production, *The Shakiest Gun in the West*, it was designed to fall apart upon cocking.

DERRINGERS

GREAT WESTERN DERRINGER – .38 S&W or .38 S&W Spl. cal. (not interchangeable). Basically an improved version of the Remington Double Derringer frame.

$600	$550	$500	$400	$350	$300	$250	

Add a premium for engraving, plating and presentation case.

One verified .22 WRM prototype is known.

Some derringers were shipped with plated finishes and several are known to have been engraved. One cased salesman sample, serial number 1838 was engraved by Carl Courts, it is gold & silver plated and fitted with pearl grip panels.

GRADING - PPGS™	100%	98%	95%	90%	80%	70%	60%	LAST MSR

Derringer serial number 25 was given to Elvis.

There were two distinct frame configurations specific to the hinge, at first the hinge was in identical proportion to the original Remington, and like the originals many failed. A more robust hinge was introduced and is visually discernable. The original configuration was referred to in Great Western catalogs and parts lists as the Old Model and the guns with the larger hinge lug were of course referred to as the New Model. The change occurred at approximately serial number 1800.

REVOLVERS: SINGLE ACTION

FRONTIER SIX SHOOTER – chambered for .22 LR/WMR and a variety of centerfire calibers, 4 3/4, 5 1/2, 7 1/2, or 12 in. barrel, plastic faux stag (standard), walnut, stag, pearl, or ivory grips, cyanide case colored, blue, chrome, or nickel plated finish, Christy Gun Works firing pin mounted in recoil shield.

Centerfire	$800	$750	$600	$550	$400	$350	$300	
Rimfire	$600	$550	$450	$400	$350	$300	$250	

Add a premium for plating or presentation case.

Add $300 for 12 in. Buntline model.

A .22 LR/.22 WMR convertible model was listed in the catalog.

SHERIFF'S MODEL – .45 LC cal., nickel, blue, cyanide case colored finish, plastic faux stag grips standard.

	$1,000	$950	$900	$850	$800	$750	$700	

Add a premium for plating or presentation case.

Aside from the definitive short barrel, Sheriffs Models were made with three features which distinguished them from the rest of the guns. Oral history is that Great Western purchased Colt's existing inventory of single-action parts, cylinder frames, and some tools when they began operations.

When viewed from the bottom, the Sheriffs Model offers strong evidence of this; all Sheriffs Models examined feature a full radius to the front of the cylinder frame, whereas the Great Western frames exhibit a pinched and elliptical appearance. Further, all of the Sheriffs Models examined feature a Colt hammer with the firing pin and a hole through the recoil shield. It is believed that these cylinder frames were actually made by Colt. To make a Sheriffs Model, the ejector rod housing lug was simply removed. It has been noted that Sheriffs Models are serial numbered below 400.

The words "GREAT WESTERN" were roll marked on the side of the barrel, there was not enough space on top of the barrels.

FAST DRAW MODEL – solid brass backstrap and trigger guard, 4 3/4 in. barrel, blue finish, plastic faux stag grips.

	$750	$700	$650	$600	$550	$500	$450	

Dee Woolem initiated the Fast Draw project and personally fitted and set-up each gun. Based on the Frontier Six Shooter, these revolvers came from the factory fitted with a solid brass back-strap and trigger-guard. The hammer spur was slightly longer and turned upward. The action was smoothed-up.

TARGET MODEL – most .22 LR cal., blue or case colored finish.

	$700	$650	$600	$500	$450	$400	$350	

Again, based on the Frontier Six Shooter, this model was fitted with a MICRO front blade and adjustable rear sights. The top strap was planed or milled flat and the rear sight mounted with two screws. Various calibers and barrel lengths were shipped, most were .22 LR cal. Blue or case colored examples are known.

DEPUTY MODEL – .22 LR, .38 Spl., or .357 Mag. cal., 4 in. barrel, deluxe blue finish, walnut grips.

	$1,000	$950	$900	$850	$800	$750	$700	

Announced in 1956, the first of these special revolvers were intended only for Great Western Arms Co. distributors and dealers. The accepted quantity is sixty guns. They all feature a 4" barrel with a full length sight rib with adjustable rear sight. These are the rarest of the cataloged Great Western revolvers, according to Great Western's service manager John McCormick, they number less than 100 and until recent years, many believed that only prototype Deputy Models were made. They appear in the 17XXX - 19XXX serial number range.

ENGRAVED MODEL

Values will vary depending on the configuration, engraver, case, provenance, and verification of authenticity. Verified factory engraved guns can bring $1,500+. For guns with factory plating, cases, or fancy grip panels, add a negotiated premium.

Offered from the beginning, this model could be ordered with any amount of coverage in any style of engraving and inlay. Cattle brand engraving was popular. Finishes were gold, silver, nickel, and blue.

Carl Courts was Great Western's primary artist and engraved most of the verifiable revolvers, including the following cased presentation pairs - serial numbers GW1 & GW2 for Bill Wilson, serial numbers GW3 & GW4 for Dan Fortmann and serial numbers GW9828 & GW9737 for Mel Torme, and a brace with 4 3/4 in. barrels for John Wayne which were later used in *The Shootist*, his last movie in 1976.

Special engraved single examples were: serial number, GW73 factory sales sample, GW5000 for President Eisenhower, and A.A. White engraved serial number 17694. Carl Courts engraved another for the Duke. George Montgomery received GW5571 & GW5572 and 17856 & 17857, the officers and crew of the USS Taluga presented Capt. R.H. Caldwell with serial numbers 12250 & 12251. Nickel plated serial number 12838 was received by film actor Arvo Ojala. Exhibition shooters Sam Toole and Dee Woolem were presented with cased pairs. Dozens of other notable personalities were presented revolvers and Derringers. Ruger engraver Charles H. Jerred completed at least one gun, serial number 11390 in November 1955 and the correspondence between Wilson and Jerred suggest that he may have engraved others.

Cole Agee was a well-known and popular engraver at the time and according to John McCormick, engraved the pair of 5 1/2 in. Frontier Models, which John Wayne is pictured holding in the photograph on the back of Great Western catalogs. Agee is also credited with engraving a Derringer for the Duke.

KIT GUNS

Unassembled in box - $1,000.
Unassembled with no box - $750.
Assembled - depending on quality of fit and finish - $350-$400.

Unthinkable in today's climate of litigation, Great Western sold guns which could be assembled and completed at the kitchen table with a few basic tools and average skills. The kit guns came with all machining complete, all holes were drilled and tapped and the final contours roughed out. To finish the gun, the customer would de-burr and final polish all surfaces. Of course the lock-work had to be cleaned-up and honed and the preferred finish applied.

According to service manager John McCormick there could have been as many as 1,000 Kit Guns shipped.

Typically, the first digit of the serial number on Kit Guns is zero, followed by five numbers, i.e. 020173. The Kit Guns first made their debut in the 1956 catalog and were priced at $59.95. Unassembled Kit Guns in the original box with assembly instructions are extremely rare.

GREAT WESTERN MYTHS

For access more information on myths involving Great Western Arms Company, please go to BlueBookOfGunValues.com/overflow.

GREEN, ROGER

Current custom gun maker located in Brewster, WA. Previously located in Evansville, WY.

Roger Green builds high quality custom made rifles and shotguns to order per customer's specifications. He is an importer of firearms and firearms accessories. In particular he is the sole importer of the newly manufactured FZH Mauser Actions of Germany and the Mayfair Engineering Action of England. Please contact him directly for more information, including pricing, availability, and custom order options.

GREENER, W.W., LIMITED

Please refer to W.W. Greener Limited in the W section.

GREIFELT AND COMPANY

Previous manufacturer located in Suhl, Germany (formerly East Germany).

For individual model listings, please go to BlueBookOfGunValues.com/overflow.

GRENDEL, INC.

Previous manufacturer located in Rockledge, FL, circa 1990-1995.

PISTOLS: SEMI-AUTO

MODEL P-10 SERIES – .380 ACP cal., blowback double action, 10 shot mag., small dimensions, hammerless, matte blue finish, 15 oz. Disc. 1991.

100%	98%	95%	90%	80%	70%	60%	Last MSR
$250	$215	$175	$165	$155	$145	$140	*$155*

Add $15 for electroless nickel finish.
Add $15 for nickel green finish.

Green finish was available at no extra charge.

GRADING - PPGS™	100%	98%	95%	90%	80%	70%	60%	LAST MSR

MODEL P-12 – .380 ACP cal., double action only, 3 in. barrel, steel construction with polymer grip area, no external safety, 11 shot Zytel mag., blue or electroless nickel finish, 11 lb. trigger pull, 13 oz. Mfg. 1992-95.

	$250	$215	$175	$165	$155	$145	$140	*$175*

Add $20 for nickel finish.
Add $50 for threaded barrel with muzzle brake parts option.

MODEL P-30 – .22 WMR cal., blowback action, 5 in. barrel, hammerless, matte black finish, 10 (C/B 1994) or 30* shot mag., 21 oz. Mfg. 1990-95.

	$350	$300	$250	$225	$200	$185	$175	*$225*

Add $25 for electroless nickel finish (disc. 1991).
Add $35 for scope mount (Weaver base).

* ***Model P-30M*** – similar to Model P-30, except has 5.6 in. barrel with removable muzzle brake. Mfg. 1990-95.

	$350	$300	$250	$225	$200	$185	$175	*$235*

Add $25 for electroless nickel finish (disc. 1991).

MODEL P-30L – similar to Model P-30, except has 8 in. barrel with removable muzzle brake, 22 oz. Mfg. 1991-92.

	$395	$350	$325	$285	$250	$230	$220	*$280*

Add $15 for Model P-30LM that allows for fitting various accessories.

MODEL P-31 – .22 WMR cal., same action as P-30, except has 11 in. barrel, enclosed synthetic barrel shroud and flash hider, 48 oz. Mfg. 1990-95.

	$450	$400	$365	$325	$290	$265	$235	*$345*

RIFLES & CARBINES

MODEL R-31 – .22 WMR cal., similar design to Model P-31 pistol, except has 16 in. barrel and telescoping stock, 64 oz. Mfg. 1991-1995.

	$495	$450	$425	$375	$335	$310	$285	*$385*

SRT-20F COMPACT – .243 Win. or .308 Win. cal., bolt action based on the Sako A2 action, 20 in. match grade finned barrel with muzzle brake, folding synthetic stock, integrated bipod rest, no sights, 9 shot mag., 6.7 lbs. Disc. 1989.

	$775	$725	$675	$595	$565	$540	$520	*$525*

Grendel previously manufactured the SRT-16F, SRT-20L, and SRT-24 - all were disc. 1988. Values are approx. the same as the SRT-20F.

GREYBULL PRECISION

Previous rifle manufacturer located in Loveland, CO.

For individual model listings, please go to BlueBookOfGunValues.com/overflow.

GREY GHOST PRECISION

Current AR-15 style rifle manufacturer established in circa 2015, located in Lakewood, WA.

Please refer to BlueBookOfGunValues.com to order the *Blue Book of AR-15s & Variations*, available as a book or online subscription.

GRIFFIN & HOWE

Griffin & Howe

Current custom gunsmith, rifle manufacturer, and importer established in 1923, with store locations in Bernardsville, NJ (gunsmithing also), and Greenwich, CT. Griffin & Howe also had a New York City store location until April, 2003.

Founded in 1923 by Seymour Griffin and James Howe, Griffin & Howe continues to build its custom rifles as well as providing the full spectrum of gunsmithing services and importation of fine English guns.

Griffin & Howe has been building custom rifles since 1923. Prices may vary greatly depending on configuration, desirability, condition, quality of wood, and special features. Most used Griffin & Howe Custom Rifles in average condition and without special engraving start at $4,500+ and rise according to condition and nature of the individual gun. Since 1923, fewer than 2,800 have been made, not including rifles that have been re-barreled by G&H and are so marked. In 1930, Griffin & Howe became a subsidiary of Abercrombie & Fitch and remained with them until 1976, when it became a privately held company. Because all Griffin & Howe rifles are essentially special ordered, accurate pricing can be ascertained only by examining each individual gun. Low production, coupled with the amount of experienced sportsmen who prefer to hunt using a vintage bolt action have resulted in values climbing in recent years. Very few show up at gun shows or auctions. Elaborate specimens by this

GRADING - PPGS™	100%	98%	95%	90%	80%	70%	60%	LAST MSR

maker/trademark will command over $10,000. Engraving by Joseph Fugger, Winston Churchill, Robert Swartley, or Rudolph Kornbrath will add multiples to the value.

During 2011, Griffin & Howe acquired the sales records of Von Lengerke & Detmold and Abercrombie & Fitch. These records cover the recording sales and inventory between 1901-1976. Within the records, most of the "new sales" are grouped by make and model. Please visit www.griffinhowe.com for more information on how to access these older records.

Pricing on new custom rifles, with a wide selection of options, is available directly from Griffin & Howe.

RIFLES: BOLT ACTION

Values represent a standard gun with no upgrades or options.

G&H ALL-AMERICAN RIFLE - .22-250 Rem., .243 Win., 6.5 Creedmoor, .270 Win., 7mm Rem. Mag., .308 Win., or .300 Win. Mag. cal., Proof Research double stress or turned down stainless steel carbon fiber barrel, Mauser 98 claw extractor, Springfield inertial ejector, black or polished stainless steel Huber two-stage trigger w/Staged-Break technology, American walnut stock w/oil finish, ergonomically designed bolt knob, integral lug, titanium recessed floorplate and trigger guard, 3-piece titanium rings w/dovetail and rail locking design, leather wrapped recoil. New late 2018.

Please contact the company directly for pricing and availability.

G&H CUSTOM SPORTER - most popular cals., custom honed action with lapped lugs, Douglas premium barrel, hand engraving, French walnut sporter stock with ebony forend tip, G&H pistol grip cap, "Griffin & Howe, New York" barrel address, custom order.

Current MSR on this model is $13,500-$18,000.

G&H HIGHLANDER MOUNTAIN RIFLE - .22-250 Rem., .243 Rem., 6.5 Creedmoor, .308 Win., or .300 Win. Mag. cal., right or left-hand configuration, Proof Research Sendero light carbon fiber wrapped stainless steel or Bartlein stainless steel barrel, polished stainless steel or black Huber two-stage trigger, Classic Sporter, High Monte Carlo, or Vertical grip stock, low or medium profile with 20 MOA built in, olive, grey, green/tan camo, Three Color Desert, Desert Camo, or Sitka Open Country Optifade finish, 7 lbs. 2 oz. New 2017.

Please contact the company directly for pricing and availability for this model.

G&H LONG RANGE PRECISION RIFLES - .22-250 Rem., .243 Win., 6.5 Creedmoor, .308 Win., .300 Win Mag., or .338 Lapua cal., right or left-hand configuration, Proof Research carbon fiber wrapped stainless steel or Bartlein stainless steel barrel, polished stainless steel or black Huber two-stage trigger, short or long open rail forend, fixed lightweight buttstock, low or medium profile with 20 MOA built in, black anodized, Cerakote black, Poly-T2 Tan, Dark OD Green, or Gunmetal Grey finish, Sitka Optifade Open Country. New 2017.

Please contact the company directly for pricing and availability for this model.

G&H PRE-'64 MODEL 70 CLASSIC SYNTHETIC STOCK - most popular cals., features glass bedded synthetic classic sporter stock in black or woodgrain finish, Douglas premium barrel, "Griffin & Howe, New York" barrel address, custom order. Disc. 2002.

	100%	98%	95%	90%	80%	70%	60%	LAST MSR
	$4,750	$4,450	$4,000	$3,700	$3,500	$3,300	$3,100	*$2,250*

WIN M70 STANDARD ACTION - .243 Win., .270 Win., .30-06, or .308 Win. cal.

	100%	98%	95%	90%	80%	70%	60%
	$5,750	$5,000	$4,500	$4,250	$3,750	$3,300	$2,750

WIN M70 MEDIUM - .300 Win. Mag., 7mm Rem. Mag., or .338 Win. Mag. cal.

	100%	98%	95%	90%	80%	70%	60%
	$6,750	$6,250	$5,500	$4,750	$4,000	$3,450	$2,950

WIN M70 MAGNUM - .375 H&H or .416 Rigby cal.

	100%	98%	95%	90%	80%	70%	60%
	$7,000	$6,500	$5,650	$4,850	$4,100	$3,550	$3,000

WIN M52 - .22 LR cal.

	100%	98%	95%	90%	80%	70%	60%
	$5,750	$5,000	$4,500	$4,250	$3,100	$2,700	$2,400
WIN HIGHWALL	$4,500	$4,150	$3,800	$3,500	$3,150	$2,850	$2,500
SPRINGFIELD 1903	$4,950	$4,400	$3,750	$3,450	$3,150	$2,800	$2,550
SPRINGFIELD 1922	$4,500	$4,100	$3,650	$3,350	$3,000	$2,750	$2,500
MAUSER STANDARD	$5,750	$5,000	$4,500	$4,250	$3,750	$3,300	$2,750
MAUSER MAGNUM	$11,000	$10,000	$8,500	$7,850	$6,850	$6,250	$5,250
SAVAGE 99	$3,500	$3,175	$2,850	$2,550	$2,250	$2,000	$1,850

GRADING - PPGS™ 100% 98% 95% 90% 80% 70% 60% LAST MSR

SHOTGUNS: O/U

MADISON – 12, 20, 28 ga., or .410 bore, case hardened frame, 26 1/2, 28, or 30 in. VR barrels, scroll engraved with gold accents. Mfg. by the Belgian Browning custom shop using a B25 action, 1999-2006.

$9,000 $8,250 $7,750 $7,150 $6,450 $5,500 $4,500 *$9,750*

CLAREMONT – 12 ga. only, case hardened frame, shallow frame BOSS style lock-up, 30 in. VR barrels standard, scroll engraving with gold accents. Mfg. by Gamba beginning 1999.

MSR $8,750 $8,000 $7,500 $7,100 $6,250 $5,750 $5,000 $4,300

EXTRA FINISH CLAREMONT – similar to Claremont, except has coin finished frame with full coverage acanthus scroll engraving and drop out trigger group. Importation began 1999.

MSR $11,500 $10,800 $9,950 $8,500 $7,300 $6,500 $5,700 $5,200

CLAREMONT LUSSO – similar to Extra Finish Claremont, except has fully engraved sideplates. Importation began 2000.

MSR $18,000 $17,250 $16,750 $14,800 $12,000 $10,250 $9,000 $8,000

BROADWAY – 12 or 20 ga., case hardened frame, 26, 28, or 30 in. VR barrels, scroll engraving with gold accents. Mfg. by the Belgian Browning custom shop using a B125 action, 1999-2003.

$5,750 $5,250 $4,600 $4,150 $3,650 $2,950 $2,550 *$5,750*

SUPERBRITTE – 12 or 16 ga., unique side opening design, built by Britte company in Liege, Belgium before WWII, purchased by G&H in 2001.

$32,000 $29,000 $25,750 $23,500 $21,250 $18,500 $16,750 *$25,000*

BLACK RAM – 12 or 20 ga., boxlock action, inertial cocking system, single bolt locking system, SST, 30 or 32 in. barrels with Briley chokes, traditional checkered Turkish walnut stock with pistol grip and recoil pad, 8 1/4 lbs. Mfg. by Zoli, importation began 2007.

MSR $5,450 $4,950 $4,500 $4,000 $3,500 $3,000 $2,500 $2,000

SILVER RAM – 12 or 20 ga., boxlock action, inertial cocking system, single bolt locking system, SST, 30 or 32 in. barrels with Briley chokes, traditional checkered Turkish walnut stock with pistol grip and recoil pad, game scene engraving, 8 1/4 lbs. Mfg. by Zoli, importation began 2007.

MSR $8,450 $7,750 $6,700 $5,900 $5,100 $4,300 $3,600 $2,950

SHOTGUNS: SxS

ROUND BODY GAME GUN – 12, 16, 20, 28 ga., or .410 bore, case colored round frame with sidelock action, "SAFE" in gold, H&H style selective ejectors, 25-30 in. barrels, double triggers, checkered straight grip stock and splinter forearm, G&H name inlaid in gold, cased (optional 2004). Mfg. by Arrieta, importation began 1989.

MSR $5,950 $5,500 $5,100 $4,750 $4,150 $3,600 $3,100 $2,500

Add $500 for 20 ga., $900 for 28 ga. or .410 bore.
Add $1,150 for single trigger.

* ***Round Body Game Guns Pair*** – 12, 16, 20, 28 ga. or .410 bore, scroll engraved with case colored hardened finish, "SAFE" in gold, round sidelock action, H&H style selective ejectors, 25-30 in. barrels, double triggers, checkered straight grip and splinter forearm, G&H name inlaid in gold, built as a pair, and gold numbered 1 & 2 on barrels, forend, and top lever. Mfg. by Arrieta.

MSR $12,950 $11,950 $10,500 $9,500 $8,500 $7,650 $6,850 $6,000

Add $1,000 for pair of 20 ga.
Add $3,000 for assisted opening.

EXTRA FINISH ROUND BODY GAME GUN – same action as Round Body Game Gun, except has coin finished frame and game scene engraving with gold accents, upgraded wood. Importation began 1999.

MSR $8,950 $8,300 $7,850 $7,200 $6,400 $5,600 $4,900 $4,000

Add $800 for 20 ga. or $1,000 for 28 ga. or .410 bore.
Add $1,150 for single trigger.

* ***Extra Finish Round Body Game Guns Pair*** – built as a pair, gold numbered 1 & 2 on barrels, forend, and top lever.

MSR $19,750 $18,500 $16,500 $14,750 $13,500 $11,500 $9,750 $8,500

Add $1,250 for pair of 20 ga.
Add $3,000 for assisted opening.

BRITTE – 12 ga. only, best quality sidelock ejector, built by Britte company in Liege, Belgium before WWII, purchased by G&H in 2001.

$13,750 $12,900 $11,700 $10,500 $9,250 $8,400 $7,500 *$15,000*

GRADING - PPGS™	100%	98%	95%	90%	80%	70%	60%	LAST MSR

CONTINENTAL SIDELOCK – 12 ga. only, best quality Britte action, finished by Belgian gunmakers such as Lebeau-Courally, various scroll patterns, case colored or bright finish, finest European walnut stock. Disc. 2006.

	$17,000	$15,000	$13,100	$11,000	$9,250	$8,300	$6,900	*$18,500*

* ***Continental Sidelocks Pair*** – 12 ga. only, built as a pair, gold numbered 1 & 2 on barrels, forend, and top lever. Disc. 2006.

	$35,500	$31,400	$28,750	$26,750	$23,500	$19,500	$17,750	*$38,500*

TRADITIONAL GAME GUN – 12, 16, 20, 24, 28 ga., or .410 bore, square body action, color case hardened with bright brush finish, DT, seven pin lock assemblies, 29 in. barrels with IC/Mod chokes, English style straight checkered Turkish walnut stock, available with optional game scene engraving, 6 3/4 lbs. Importation began 2007.

MSR $7,500	$6,750	$5,900	$5,100	$4,300	$3,600	$3,100	$2,650

Add $750 for 20 ga.
Add $825 for 28 ga. or .410 bore.
Add $3,000 for game scene engraving.

* ***Traditional Game Gun Pair*** – 12 and 16 ga.

MSR $16,000	$14,500	$13,250	$12,000	$10,000	$8,950	$7,750	$7,000

Add $3,000 for assisted opening.
Add $1,500 for 20 ga.
Add $6,000 for game scene engraving.

GRIFFIN ARMAMENT

Current AR-15 style pistol, rifle, and accessories manufacturer established in 2005, located in Dousman, WI.

Please refer to BlueBookOfGunValues.com to order the *Blue Book of AR-15s & Variations*, available as a book or online subscription.

GRIFFON

Previously manufactured until 2003 by Continental Weapons (Pty) Ltd. established in 1996, and located in Midrand, Johannesburg, South Africa. Previously imported and distributed by Griffon USA, Inc., a subsidiary of 21st Century Technologies, Inc., located in Ft. Worth, TX, and by First Defense International located in San Clemente, CA.

PISTOLS: SEMI-AUTO

GRIFFON 1911 A1 COMBAT – .45 ACP cal., patterned after the Colt M1911, single action, 4.13 in. barrel, 7 shot mag., ported barrel/slide, black Teflon finish, Commander hammer, Tritium sights, 36.5 oz. Mfg. 1997-2003.

	$445	$375	$335	$300	$275	$250	$225

GRIFFON CW 11 – 9mm Para. cal., 4 in. barrel without porting, 8 shot mag., perforated trigger, 3-dot sighting system, combo blue/chrome finish, limited importation. Mfg. 1997-2003.

	$475	$375	$335	$300	$275	$250	$225

GRISEL, H.L.

Previous custom rifle manufacturer located in Bend, OR.

H.L. "Pete" Grisel co-founded Dakota Arms in 1986, and was a founding member of the American Custom Gunmakers Guild. He built many custom rifles using actions of various types, including six using his own proprietary action. Grisel designed the Dakota 76 action and built some of Dakota's early guns, including the Leupold 40th anniversary rifle. Grisel also designed the Kimber Model K770 bolt action prototype, which Kimber never put into production. Grisel retired from gunmaking circa 2006-2007 and passed away on Dec. 1, 2017. Since Grisel guns were essentially custom made, each gun should be evaluated individually in order to determine value and shootability.

GRULLA ARMAS

Current manufacturer located in Eibar, Spain since 1932. Currently imported by Chris Batha located in Okatie, SC and Griffin & Howe located in Andover, NJ. Previously imported by Harry Marx Hi-Grade Imports, located in Los Banos, CA, imported and distributed until 2009 by Merkel USA, located in Trussville, AL, Fieldsport, located in Traverse City, MI, Lion Country Supply, located in Port Matilda, PA, and by Dale's Decoy Den, located in Nelsonville, OH.

For individual model listings, please go to BlueBookOfGunValues.com/overflow.

GRADING - PPGS™	100%	98%	95%	90%	80%	70%	60%	LAST MSR

GRUND, KARL

Current rifle manufacturer located in Ferlach, Austria. No current U.S. importation.

Karl Grund manufactures high quality custom double rifles in a variety of configurations, including drillings and express rifles. Please contact him for more information, including pricing, U.S. availability, or a price quotation.

GRÜNIG & ELMIGER AG

Current rifle manufacturer located in Malters, Switzerland. Currently represented in the U.S. by Brenzovich Firearms Training Center, located in Ft. Hancock, TX. Previously represented by Gunsmithing, Inc., located in Colorado Springs, CO, and Champion's Choice, located in Lavergne, TN until 2012.

Grünig & Elmiger AG is a third generation Swiss company that manufactures both rimfire and centerfire high quality competition and sporter rifles in various configurations. Numerous options and accessories are available. Please contact the U.S. representatives directly for current U.S. availability and pricing.

GUERINI, CAESAR

Please refer to the Caesar Guerini, s.r.l. listing in the C section.

GUN 1

Previous trademark owned by Savage Arms, Inc.

RIFLES

GUN 1 SERIES – .22 LR cal., 16 (Junior) or 19 (Youth) in. barrel, short LOP, AccuTrigger. Mfg. 2008.

$180	$165	$150	$140	$130	$120	$110	*$213*

Add $9 for 19 in. barrel.

* ***Gun 1 Series Youth Centerfire*** – .243 Win. cal., 22 in. barrel, AccuTrigger, similar to Gun 1 Series, short LOP. Mfg. 2008.

$550	$495	$450	$400	$350	$300	$250	*$605*

GUNCRAFTER INDUSTRIES

Current pistol manufacturer located in Huntsville, AR.

PISTOLS: SEMI-AUTO

Add $95 for ambi safety.
Add $125 for fluted chamber.
Add $225 for tactical light rail option.
Add $275 for optics cut slide option.

.50 GI COMPLETE GLOCK PISTOL – .50 GI cal., SFO, 4 1/2 or 6 in. barrel, 9 shot mag., black polymer Glock Gen 3 or Gen 4 frame, steel slide, Glock style sights, Trijicon RMR optics cut, stainless, Melonite, or Cerakote finish.

MSR $1,095	$975	$850	$725	$675	$525	$450	$350

Add $65-$105 for Cerakote finish.
Add $175 for RMR optics cut or 6 in. barrel

CZ75 GUNCRAFTER EXECUTIVE SERIES PISTOL – 9mm Para. cal., DA/SA, built from select models of CZ75 variants including the CZ75B, CZ75 Compact, CZ75 SP01/Shadow/Accushadow, flush cut and crowned, DLC coated barrel, color case hardened frame w/clear Cerakote overcoat and a hot salt blued slide with polished flats, factory sights or upgraded fiber optic sights, Guncrafter Slim-Tac G10 grips.

MSR $1,675	$1,500	$1,325	$1,125	$1,025	$825	$675	$525

Add $75 for CZ75 SP01 model.
Add $165 for upgraded fiber optic sights.
Add $340 For Cajun Gun Works Defensive Carry Internals Package.
Add $426 for Cajun Gun Works Pro Internals Package.

MODEL NO. 1 – .45 ACP (disc.) or .50 GI cal., 1911 style, SA, 7 shot mag., 5 in. heavy match grade barrel, parkerized or hard chrome finish, front strap checkering, Heinie Slant Pro Tritium sights, Aluma checkered grips, includes two mags. and cordura case, 41.3 oz.

MSR $3,595	$3,250	$2,850	$2,400	$2,200	$1,800	$1,450	$1,150

MODEL NO. 2 – .45 ACP (disc. 2015) or .50 GI cal., 1911 style, 7 shot mag., 5 in. heavy match grade barrel, full profile slide with dust cover frame, integral light rail, parkerized or hard chrome finish, front strap checkering, Heinie Slant Pro Tritium sights, Aluma checkered grips, includes two mags. and cordura case, 45.9 oz. Disc., reintroduced 2019.

MSR $ 3,695	$3,300	$2,900	$2,500	$2,250	$1,850	$1,500	$1,150

GRADING - PPGS™	100%	98%	95%	90%	80%	70%	60%	LAST MSR

MODEL NO. 3 – .50 GI cal., similar to Model No. 1, except has Commander style frame. New 2010.

MSR $3,595	$3,200	$2,800	$2,400	$2,175	$1,765	$1,440	$1,125	

MODEL NO. 4 – .50 GI cal., 1911 style, similar to Model No. 3, 6 in. barrel, 7 shot mag., matte black finish, longer sight radius, hard anodized machine checkered aluminum G.I. grips, checkered front and back grip strap, rear slide serrations, 43 oz. New mid-2013.

MSR $4,595	$4,150	$3,635	$3,115	$2,825	$2,285	$1,875	$1,450	

MODEL NO. 5 – .50 GI cal., Officer size round-butt forged steel frame, 4 1/2 in. heavy match grade stainless steel barrel, solid match grade trigger, fully machined hammer, sear, and disconnector, thin black fully checkered Alumagrips, GI Tritium sights, checkering on front strap and mainspring housing, beveled magwell, fully dehorned, includes black GI logo Cordura case, black Melonite finish, 33 oz. New 2017.

MSR $3,895	$3,500	$3,065	$2,625	$2,385	$1,925	$1,575	$1,225	

MODEL NO. 5 CUSTOM – .50 GI cal., Officer size round-butt forged chamfered steel frame, 4 1/2 in. heavy match grade IonBond, flush cut and deep crown stainless steel barrel, flush cut slide stop, solid match grade trigger, ambi thumb safety, fully machined hammer, sear, and disconnector, thin black fully checkered Alumagrips, GI Tritium sights with gold bead front, checkering on front strap and mainspring housing, beveled magwell, slide top serrations, fully dehorned, includes black GI logo Cordura case, black Melonite finish, 33 oz. New 2018.

MSR $4,414	$3,975	$3,485	$2,985	$2,700	$2,185	$1,795	$1,395	

NO NAME CCO – 9mm Para. or .45 ACP cal., Commander size slide over Officer frame, 4 1/2 in. match grade barrel, beveled magwell, solid match trigger, G.I. Tritium sights, slim grips, two-tone, reverse two-tone, or hard chrome finish, includes GI Logo Cordura case, 33 oz. New 2015.

MSR $2,995	$2,700	$2,365	$2,025	$1,835	$1,485	$1,215	$945	

NO NAME COMMANDER – 9mm Para., 10mm (new 2017), .38 Super, or .45 ACP cal., Commander frame, 4 1/2 in. match grade barrel, beveled magwell, solid match trigger, G.I. Tritium sights, Shredder grips, checkered front strap and mainspring housing, slide stop serrations, two-tone, reverse two-tone, or hard chrome finish, includes GI Logo Cordura case, 35 oz. New 2015.

MSR $2,795	$2,500	$2,195	$1,875	$1,700	$1,375	$1,125	$875	

Add $300 for 9mm Para. or .38 Super cal.
Add $400 for 10 mm cal.

NO NAME GOVERNMENT (PISTOL WITH NO NAME) – 9mm Para., 10mm, .38 Super, or .45 ACP cal., available with 4 1/2 (either Commander size, or with Officer size frame, Commander size slide/barrel), or 5 in. Match Grade barrel and Government full size frame, single side thumb safety, beveled magwell, solid match trigger, shredder grips, slide top serrations, G.I. Tritium sights, fully dehorned, black melonite finish, includes two mags. and GI logo cordura case, 38 oz. New 2010.

MSR $2,795	$2,500	$2,200	$1,900	$1,700	$1,400	$1,150	$900	

Add $300 for 9mm Para. or .38 Super cal. or $400 for 10mm cal.
Add $500 for No Name Longslide variation.

CCO (CONCEALED COMMANDER OFFICER) – 9mm Para. or .45 ACP cal., SA, 4 1/4 in. match grade stainless steel barrel, black anodized aluminum or steel frame with black Melonite or matte finished stainless steel slide, 7 shot mag., reverse duotone, all stainless or hard chrome finish, ambi-cut checkered Slimline Alumagrips with GI logo, GI sights, includes 2 mags. and a case, 36 oz. Mfg. 2013-2020.

	$2,650	$2,325	$1,995	$1,800	$1,465	$1,195	$935	*$2,939*

Add $250 9mm Para. cal.

THE AMERICAN – 9mm Para. (new mid-2016) or .45 ACP cal., full size frame, 5 in. match grade stainless steel barrel, black Melonite finish, heavy duty bushing with extra thick flange, integral light rail, high grade steel hammer, sear, and disconnector, ambi thumb safety, one-piece magwell with integral lanyard loop, 15 LPI checkered front strap, "Shredder" extra coarse patterned grips, Heine Ledge Slant Pro Tritium sights, includes two mags. and black GI logo Cordura case, approx. 47 oz.

MSR $3,095	$2,750	$2,400	$2,065	$1,875	$1,525	$1,245	$965	

Add $200 for 9mm Para. cal.

THE BC-17 HELLCAT – .45 ACP, 9mm Para., 10mm, or .38 Super cal., forged steel full size frame with 4 1/4 (Commander) or 5 (Government) in. match grade stainless steel barrel, flush cut and deep crown, BattleCrown Super Heavy Duty bushing, one-piece magwell, two fitted and tuned mags., flat match grade trigger, GI Tritium sights, black Shredder grips, slide top serrations, GI 15 LPI checkering on front strap and mainspring housing, fully dehorned, heavy bevel on bottom of slide, ball end mill cuts, flush cut slide stop and chamfered frame, includes black GI logo Cordura case, Guncrafter Gray Cerakote over our Melonite finish. New 2018.

MSR $3,695	$3,300	$2,900	$2,500	$2,250	$1,850	$1,500	$1,150	

Add $300 for 9mm Para. or .38 Super cal. Add $400 for 10mm cal.

GRADING - PPGS™	100%	98%	95%	90%	80%	70%	60%	LAST MSR

THE BC-17 HELLCAT CCO – .45 ACP, 9mm Para., or .38 Super cal., forged steel Officer size frame, 4 1/4 in. match grade stainless steel barrel, flush cut and deep crowned barrel, two fitted and tuned mags., flat match grade trigger, GI Tritium sights, black Shredder grips, slide top serrations, GI 15 LPI checkering on front strap and mainspring housing, fully dehorned, heavy bevel on bottom of slide, ball end mill cuts, flush cut slide stop and chamfered frame, includes black GI logo Cordura case, Guncrafter Gray Cerakote over our Melonite finish. New 2018.

MSR $3,525 $3,175 $2,785 $2,385 $2,165 $1,745 $1,435 $1,125

THE HELLCAT GOVERNMENT/COMMANDER – .45 ACP, 10mm, 9mm Para., or .38 Super cal., forged steel Officer size frame with 4 1/4 (Commander) or 5 (Government) in. match grade stainless steel barrel, flush cut and deep crowned barrel, two fitted and tuned mags., flat match grade trigger, GI Tritium sights, black Shredder grips, slide top serrations, GI 15 LPI checkering on front strap and mainspring housing, fully dehorned, heavy bevel on bottom of slide, ball end mill cuts, flush cut slide stop and chamfered frame, includes black GI logo Cordura case, Guncrafter Gray Cerakote over our Melonite finish. New 2018.

MSR $3,695 $3,325 $2,925 $2,500 $2,275 $1,825 $1,500 $1,175

Add $75 for Commander slide.

Add $300 for 9mm Para. or .38 Super cal, or $400 for 10mm cal.

THE HELLCAT X2 GOVERNMENT/COMMANDER – 9mm Para., .40 S&W, .45 ACP, or .38 Super cal., 4 1/4 (Commander) or 5 (Government) in. match grade stainless steel barrel, flush crowned and deep crowned, two fitted and tuned mags., match grade trigger, GI Tritium (Commander) or fiber optic front or Bomar adj. rear sights (Government), frag pattern grip and mainspring housing, fully dehorned, slide stop serrations, BattleCrown super heavy-duty bushing, ball end mill cuts, includes black GI logo Cordura case, black Cerakote over melonite finish (other custom finishes available), approx. 28 oz. New mid-2019.

MSR $3,895 $3,500 $3,065 $2,625 $2,385 $1,925 $1,575 $1,225

THE FRAG – 9mm Para., 10mm (new 2015), .38 Super, or .45 ACP cal., 4 1/4 (Commander) or 5 in. barrel, matte black finish, 8 (.45 ACP) or 9 (9mm Para.) shot mag., U-notch rear and brass bead front sight, unique frag pattern treatments on front and backstrap as well as the grips, 35-38 oz. New mid-2013.

MSR $3,295 $2,950 $2,550 $2,150 $1,900 $1,575 $1,350 $1,075

THE FRAG LONG SLIDE – 9mm Para. or .45 ACP cal., 6 in. match grade barrel, matte black finish, two 8 (.45 ACP) or 9 (9mm Para.) shot mags., Bomar adj. rear and fiber optic front sight, unique frag pattern treatments on front and backstrap as well as the grips, 35-38 oz. New mid-2018.

MSR $3,795 $3,400 $2,975 $2,550 $2,315 $1,875 $1,535 $1,195

THE FRAG SQUARED – 9mm Para. or .45 ACP cal., forged steel frame and slide, 5 in. match grade IonBond black barrel, two sets of Tech-Well magazine wells, fully machined hammer, sear, and disconnector, squared black trigger guard, Bomar adj. rear and ultra bright fiber optic front sight post, FRAG pattern Alumagrips, ambi thumb safety, fully dehorned, slide top serrations, FRAG pattern front and backstrap, includes black GI logo Cordura case, black Melonite finish.

MSR $3,325 $3,000 $2,600 $2,250 $2,050 $1,650 $1,350 $1,050

Add $96 for 9mm Para. cal.

THE H.O.S.S. CUSTOM 1911 (HEAVY OPERATING SHOOTING SYSTEM) – 9mm Para. cal., 5 in. slide, HOSS heavy barrel, two fitted and tuned mags., HOSS extractor, fully machined hammer, sear, and disconnector, match grade trigger, GI Tritium sights, black Alumagrips with full checkering, single sided thick safety, HOSS slide stop, slide top serrations, front strap and mainspring housing checkering, fully dehorned, includes black GI logo Cordura case, Melonite finish. New 2018.

MSR $3,895 $3,500 $3,065 $2,625 $2,385 $1,925 $1,575 $1,225

THE RENAISSANCE CUSTOM 1911 – full size forged steel frame and slide, 5 in. flush cut and deep crown match grade stainless steel barrel, fluted chamber, two fitted and tuned mags., beveled magwell, tool steel fully machined hammer, sear, and disconnector, solid match grade trigger, gold bead front and U-notch rear sight, top quality wood grips, "B" Type hand engraving on slide, slide top and rear serrations, fully dehorned, Chain Link checkering on front strap and mainspring housing, includes black GI logo Cordura case, Hot Salt blue or stainless steel finish. New 2018.

MSR $5,195 $4,700 $4,100 $3,500 $3,200 $2,550 $2,100 $1,650

GUN ROOM CO., LLC

Please refer to the Noreen Firearms LLC listing in the N section.

GRADING - PPGS™	100%	98%	95%	90%	80%	70%	60%	LAST MSR

GUNSMOKE

Previous gun customizer and gunshop with gunsmithing services located in Wheat Ridge, CO., circa 1996-2015.

Rich Wyatt and his talented family/staff at Gunsmoke Enterprises (featured in the Discovery Channel's recent American Guns series) customized firearms per individual customer specifications. Additionally, Gunsmoke offered a complete line of gunsmithing services, including engraving.

GUNWERKS, LLC

Current custom rifle and ammunition manufacturer established in 2006, located in Cody, WY. Previously located in Burlington, WY.

RIFLES: BOLT ACTION

Many options are available, including caliber, muzzle brakes, left-hand action, etc. Please contact the manufacturer for availability on some of the models listed in this section.

Values below are for the base rifles only. Gunwerks offers various packages with these firearms that include choice of optics, premium ammo, custom calibration, and other optical/ballistics equipment that can severely increase or affect pricing. Gunwerks also has a custom division known as Skunkwerks. Please contact the manufacturer directly for more information on these packages.

CARBONX - 6XC or 6.5 Creedmoor cal., stainless steel LR-1000 precision action, 24 in. stainless steel match grade barrel wrapped in carbon fiber with muzzle brake, Accuracy International double stack 5 shot detachable mag., molded long range hunting stock with aluminum bedding block, Jewell trigger, Ti Cerakote metal finish, includes all-weather double rifle case, 9.9 lbs. Mfg. 2013-2018.

	100%	98%	95%	90%	80%	70%	60%	LAST MSR
	$5,375	$4,725	$4,000	$3,600	$2,925	$2,395	$1,850	*$5,850*

CLYMR RIFLE SYSTEM (CLYMR) - customer's choice of caliber, 18, 20, 21, 22, or 23 in. stainless steel or carbon fiber wrapped barrel in customer specified contour, barrel fluting and muzzle devices optional, GW floorplate integral mag., stainless steel or titanium GRB or GLR action, ultra light carbon fiber composite or fiberglass stock, Gunwerks recoil pad, spacer system for LOP adjustments, thumb safety, aluminum bedding block, flush Picatinny bipod rail, integrated flush QD sling sockets. New 2019.

	100%	98%	95%	90%	80%	70%	60%	LAST MSR
MSR $3,995	$3,675	$3,225	$2,750	$2,500	$2,000	$1,650	$1,275	

Add $500 for GLR action.
Add $500 for carbon fiber stock
Add $750 for titanium action.
Add $750 for carbon fiber wrapped barrel.

CO-PILOT - 6mm Creedmoor cal., 16 1/2 in. Proof Research carbon fiber wrapped stainless steel barrel, SilencerCo. Omega suppressor (where legal), 5 shot mag., TriggerTech trigger, EH1 Manner collapsible composite stock, recoil pad, sling studs, Tungsten Cerakote finish, 9.8-10.6 lbs. Limited mfg. 2018 only.

	100%	98%	95%	90%	80%	70%	60%	LAST MSR
	$12,650	$11,000	$10,750	$9,500	$8,250	$7,000	$6,000	*$13,995*

HAMR 2.0 RIFLE SYSTEM - .375 Cheytac cal., 30 in. stainless steel or carbon fiber wrapped barrel, Cadex Defense MX1 muzzle brake, detachable AICS mag, stainless steel action, Timney trigger, Cadex Defense Dual Strike chassis system available in Black, Sniper Grey, or FDE finish, folding stock with adj. LOP and cheek riser, Ergo grip, 40 MOA Unitized Picatinny top rail, Elite Iron bipod, Graphite Black Cerakote finish, 21.25 lbs. New 2020.

	100%	98%	95%	90%	80%	70%	60%	LAST MSR
MSR $9,150	$8,400	$7,350	$6,300	$5,725	$4,625	$3,775	$2,950	

Add $750 for carbon fiber wrapped barrel.

HELIOS - 6XC, 6.5 SLRM, 6.5-284 Norma, 6.5 Creedmoor (disc.), 7 WSM (disc.), 7 LRM (new 2014), or .300 RCM (new 2014) cal., features LR-1000 titanium action, 21 1/2 in. match grade stainless steel barrel with 8 flutes and no sights, Jewell target trigger, Ti Cerakote metal finish, molded black Gunwerks mountain hunting stock with aluminum bedding block, approx. 7 lbs. Mfg. 2013-2018.

	100%	98%	95%	90%	80%	70%	60%	LAST MSR
	$5,295	$4,650	$3,975	$3,600	$2,925	$2,395	$1,850	*$5,750*

LITE SABR - .338 RCM cal., titanium GLR action, 22 in. integrally suppressed barrel, 5 shot detachable mag., TriggerTech set, XLR Industries 3D printed titanium grip, XLR Industries Element 3 Magnesium chassis w/ARCA rail, custom hard case with laser cut Skunkwerks art, includes soft carry case, matte black finish, 8.5 lbs. New 2020.

	100%	98%	95%	90%	80%	70%	60%	LAST MSR
MSR $12,900	$10,950	$9,600	$8,200	$7,450	$6,050	$4,950	$3,850	

LR LIGHTWEIGHT (LR-800) - various cals., custom action, one-piece bolt and side bolt release, target trigger, match grade contoured lightweight stainless steel barrel, synthetic stock with recoil pad, includes case. Disc. 2012.

	100%	98%	95%	90%	80%	70%	60%	LAST MSR
	$4,750	$4,250	$3,750	$3,400	$3,000	$2,500	$2,150	*$5,250*

GRADING - PPGS™	100%	98%	95%	90%	80%	70%	60%	LAST MSR

LR-1000 – 6XC, 6.5-284 Norma, 7mm Rem. Mag., 7mm LRM, .300 Win. Mag., or .300 RUM cal., precision action, spiral cut bolt stainless steel fluted match grade barrel with integral muzzle brake, positive extractor, side bolt release, Jewell trigger, long range style stock in black or grey synthetic, includes all-weather case, 9.7 lbs. Disc. 2017.

	$5,295	$4,650	$3,975	$3,600	$2,925	$2,395	$1,850	*$5,750*

MAGNUS RIFLE SYSTEM (MAGNUS) – .300 Norma. (disc.), .338 Norma (disc.), .300 Win. Mag., .338 Edge Wildcat (disc.), .300 RUM, 7mm LRM, or other customer specified caliber., stainless steel or carbon fiber wrapped barrel with integral (disc.) or detachable muzzle brake or thread cap, GW floorplate mag., GW AICS detachable mag., or Wyman double stack detachable mag. (disc.)., stainless steel or titanium GRB or GLR action, Jewell (disc.) or TriggerTech Primary trigger, textured black synthetic or tan camo (disc.), fiberglass, or carbon fiber stock, spacer system for LOP adjustments, integrated flush cup QD sling mounts, spiral bolt, tactical bolt knob, aluminum bedding block, includes all-weather double rifle case, Cerakote metal finish, 12.9 lbs. New 2013.

MSR $4,250	$3,925	$3,425	$2,950	$2,675	$2,150	$1,775	$1,375	

Add $200 for muzzle brake.
Add $300 for AICS detachable mag.
Add $500 for GLR action or carbon fiber stock.
Add $750 for titanium action or carbon fiber wrapped barrel.

MOUNTAIN X – various cals., spiral cut bolt, 24 in. stainless steel 2G fluted barrel, w/o sights, lightweight black textured LR100 carbon stock with built in bipod, 6.9 lbs. Mfg. 2015-2017.

	$6,150	$5,500	$4,850	$4,395	$3,550	$2,900	$2,275	*$6,550*

REV X - .22-250 Rem., .28 Nosler, .30 Nosler, 6.5 Creedmoor, 6.5 PRC, 7mm Rem. Mag., .300 Win. Mag., or .300 Rem. Ultra Mag., improved GRB action (new 2017), 25 in. fluted Shilen barrel w/o sights, Gunwerks radial brake, composite stock w/molded recoil pad, integrated, flush-mounted Picatinny rail on forend, improved bedding chassis w/o glass bedding compounds, dark grey, forest, orange, tan, Cerakote Sand, Cerakote Tungsten, or Cerakote Graphite Black finish, approx. 8 lbs. Mfg. 2017-2018.

Retail pricing wasn't available for this model.

SKUHL RIFLE SYSTEM – .338 Remington Ultra Mag., .375 Ruger, or .416 Ruger cal., 21 in. G3 stainless steel barrel, Gunwerks Radial muzzle brake, stainless steel GLR Push Feed action, TriggerTech trigger, Gunwerks Carbon Fiber Fusion stock with Flax Fiber inlay (mimics wood grain appearance), adj. LOP set by customer preference, Picatinny rail on forearm, laser engraved action, bolt, recoil lug, barrel, and hinged floorplate, Battle Worn Tungsten finish, 8.9-9.9 lbs. New 2020.

MSR $6,995	$6,425	$5,625	$4,825	$4,375	$3,525	$2,900	$2,250	

Add $100 for .416 Ruger cal.
Add $100 for left-hand configuration.

SPECTR – 26 in. 7G stainless steel or carbon barrel, titanium Thunderbeast suppressor (where legal), accepts Accuracy International magazine boxes, JA Enterprises stock, adj. cheek rest with thumb wheel, adaptable chassis, 13 1/4-14 3/4 lbs. Mfg. 2016-2018.

	$5,800	$5,200	$4,500	$4,000	$3,350	$2,700	$2,100	*$6,250*

THUMPR – 6mm Creedmoor cal., titanium GLR action, 16 1/2 in. carbon wrapped threaded barrel, tactical box mag., includes two bottom metals (interchangeable), standard hinged floorplate, includes one ultralight carbon fiber ClymR stock and one short LOP fiberglass ClymR stock with custom hand-painted finish, Gunwerks recoil pad, integrated flush cup QD sling mounts, integrated aluminum bedding block, includes Nightforce ATACR F2 4-16x50 scope with custom ballistic turret, waterproof travel hard case, flush-mount bipod rail, Tungsten Cerakote finish, 8.4 lbs. Limited mfg. late 2018-2019.

	$9,600	$8,400	$7,200	$6,525	$5,285	$4,325	$3,700	*$11,302*

VERDICT RIFLE SYSTEM (VERDICT) – .300 Norma, .338 Norma, .338 Lapua, or other customer specified cal., 20-26 in. stainless steel or carbon fiber wrapped barrel with integrated (disc.) or directional muzzle brake or thread cap, GW floorplate integral mag. or detachable AICS mag., stainless steel or titanium GRB, GLR, or LR-1500 (magnum length cals.) action, Jewell target trigger (disc.) or TriggerTech Primary trigger, tan textured McMillan A5 stock with adj. cheekpiece (disc.), fully adj. fiberglass stock or fully adj. carbon fiber stock, spiral fluted or unfluted bolt, forearm Picatinny rail, tactical bolt knob, includes case, black or other customer specified finish. New 2013.

MSR $5,250	$4,825	$4,225	$3,625	$3,275	$2,650	$2,175	$1,700	

Add $200 for muzzle brake.
Add $300 for AICS detachable mag.
Add $350 for LR-1500 action.
Add $500 for GLR action or carbon fiber stock.
Add $750 for titanium action or carbon fiber wrapped barrel.

GRADING - PPGS™	100%	98%	95%	90%	80%	70%	60%	LAST MSR

GUN WORKS, LTD.

Previous manufacturer and distributor located in Buffalo, NY. Early guns were made in Tonawanda, NY.

HANDGUNS

X-CALIBER – .44 Mag. cal., single shot, tip up pistol, 8 in. barrel, matte type blue finish, ergonomic hardwood grips, probably used older Sterling Arms parts and restamped the barrel address. Limited mfg.

$350	$300	$260	$230	$200	$175	$150	

MODEL 9 – .357 Mag., 9mm Para., .38 Super, or .38 Spl. cal., O/U derringer, electroless nickel finish, 2 1/2 in. barrel, wood grips, Millett sights, 15 oz. Disc. 1986.

$135	$120	$105	$95	$65	$55	$50	*$149*

GUSTAF, CARL

Please refer to Carl Gustaf listing in the C section.

GYROJET

Please refer to the MBA Associates (Gyrojet) listing in the M section.

GYC ARMAS (GIL, ANTONIO & CO.)

Current manufacturer located in Eibar, Spain. Limited U.S. importation. Previously imported and distributed exclusively late 2000-2004 by New England Arms Corp., located in Kittery Point, ME.

All GYC Armas/Antonio Gil shotguns are handmade, and can be built to each customer's exact measurements at no extra cost. All models are equipped with chopper lump barrels as a standard feature. Please contact the company directly for more information, including current U.S. pricing and availability.

SHOTGUNS: SxS

All models are sidelock only.

Add 10% for 20, 28 ga. or .410 bore.
Add $500-$1,500 for wood upgrade.
Add $1,000-$1,250 per extra set of barrels.
Add $500 for non-selective trigger.

ALHAMBRA – 12, 16, 20, 28 ga., or .410 bore, sidelock action, features elaborate full coverage floral scroll engraving on coin finished receiver and wood upgrade. Imported 2001-disc.

$3,625	$3,150	$2,575	$2,250	$1,750	$1,500	$1,350	

DIAMOND – 12, 16, 20, 28 ga., or .410 bore, sidelock action, top-of-the-line model with best engraving and best quality wood. Imported 2001-disc.

$5,475	$4,650	$4,125	$3,625	$3,050	$2,500	$2,000	

LAGA – 12, 16, 20, 28 ga., or .410 bore, sidelock action with color case hardened receiver and scroll engraving, demi-bloc barrels, DT, deluxe checkered walnut stock and forearm. Imported 2001-disc.

$2,250	$1,750	$1,500	$1,350	$1,200	$1,100	$995	

OLIMPIA – 12, 16, 20, 28 ga., or .410 bore, sidelock action, features traditional rose and scroll engraving on coin finished receiver. Imported 2001-disc.

$2,575	$2,250	$1,750	$1,500	$1,350	$1,200	$1,050	

NOTES

H SECTION

HHF

Please refer to the Huglu listing in the H section.

H.J.S. INDUSTRIES, INC.

Previous manufacturer located in Brownsville, TX.

GRADING - PPGS™	100%	98%	95%	90%	80%	70%	60%	LAST MSR

DERRINGERS

FRONTIER FOUR – .22 LR cal., 4 shot derringer, stainless steel construction, 5 1/2 oz.

$115	$90	$80	$75	$70	$60	$50	

LONE STAR – .38 S&W cal., single shot derringer, stainless steel construction, 6 oz.

$140	$105	$95	$80	$75	$65	$50	

HM DEFENSE & TECHNOLOGY

Current AR-15 style pistol and rifle manufacturer located in Mount Orab, OH.

Please refer to BlueBookOfGunValues.com to order the *Blue Book of AR-15s & Variations*, available as a book or online subscription.

HMS PRÄZISIONSTECHNIK GmbH

Current straight pull bolt action rifle manufacturer located in Eugendorf, Austria. Currently imported by International Firearms Corp. (IFC) located in Midwest City, OK.

RIFLES: BOLT ACTION

STRASSER RS 05 – .243 Win., 6.5x55mm, .270 Win., .30-06, 7x64Rmm, .308 Win., 8x57Rmm, 8.5x63mm, 9.3x62mm, 7mm Rem. Mag. or .300 Win. Mag. cal., 22 or 24 in. barrel, 2 or 3 shot mag., Dr. Horst J.E. Blaser's latest straight pull design featuring ultra short bolt action, with or w/o deep relief engraved sideplates, front sling swivel, interchangeable barrels, silent firing pin block safety, breech bolt locks directly into the barrel, ergonomic mag. release, right or left-hand ejection, removable trigger group, all metal open sights, integral scope mount, dust cover, available in Standard, Premium, Deluxe (all with sideplates), Consul I, II, or III (non-sideplates) configurations, 7-7 1/4 lbs. Importation disc.

Strasser models range in price from €1,841 - €17,963, depending on the model, features, engraving, and quality of the wood.

STRASSER RS 14 STANDARD STRAIGHT PULL – .222 Rem., .223 Rem., .300 AAC Blackout, .22-250 Rem., .243 Win., 6 XC, 6.5 Creedmoor, 6.5-284 Norma, 6.5x55 SE, 6.5x65 RWS, .270 Win., 7x64, 7mm Rem. Mag., 7mm-08 Rem., .300 Win. Mag., 308 Win., 30-06, 8x57 IS, 8.5x63, or 9.3x62 cal., available as standard, mini, or magnum cal., 22 (standard or mini) or 24 (magnum) in. threaded Walther barrel, 6 shot detachable box mag., adj. trigger pull, removable trigger group, adj. iron sights, Class 1 wood stock w/black sideplates, interchangeable bolt face, quick detach scope base.

Please contact the company directly for more information, including pricing, delivery time, and U.S. availability.

* ***Strasser Solo Straight Pull*** – .222 Rem., .223 Rem., .300 AAC Blackout, .22-250 Rem., .243 Win., 6 XC, 6.5 Creedmoor, 6.5-284 Norma, 6.5x55 SE, 6.5x65 RWS, .270 Win., 7x64, 7mm Rem. Mag., 7mm-08 Rem., .300 Win. Mag., 308 Win., 30-06, 8x57 IS, 8.5x63, or 9.3x62 cal., similar to the RS 14 Standard Straight Pull, except has fixed barrel, 22 (standard or mini) or 24 (magnum) in. threaded Walther barrel, 6 shot detachable box mag., adj. trigger pull, removable trigger group, adj. iron sights, Class 1 wood stock w/black sideplates, interchangeable bolt face, quick detach scope base.

Please contact the company directly for more information, including pricing, delivery time, and U.S. availability.

STRASSER TAC 1 PRECISION RIFLE – various cals., fluted threaded barrel, secondary mag. holder, adj. LOP, folding stock, adj. cheekpiece, heel, and toe for recoil pad, Picatinny rail, carry handle, folding monopod and bipod, equipped w/universal tool.

Please contact the company directly for more information, including pricing, delivery time, and U.S. availability.

H & R 1871, LLC. (HARRINGTON & RICHARDSON)

Current trademark with headquarters located in Madison, NC, beginning 2008. Currently manufactured by Remington in Ilion, NY beginning early 2011. Previous manufacturer with production facilities and corporate headquarters located in Gardner, MA 1991-2008. During 2000, Marlin Firearms Co. purchased the assets of H&R 1871, Inc., and the name was changed to H&R 1871, LLC.

H & R 1871, LLC utilizes the original H & R trademark and does not accept warranty work for older (pre-1986 mfg.) Harrington & Richardson, Inc. firearms. Distributor sales only.

GRADING - PPGS™	100%	98%	95%	90%	80%	70%	60%	LAST MSR

The use of the original Harrington & Richardson trademark was permitted during 1991. All new manufacture will use this trademark, but older H & Rs manufactured by Harrington & Richardson, Inc. are not the responsibility of H & R 1871, LLC.

REVOLVERS

Additional revolvers using the New England Firearms trademark may be located in the N section. During 1997-1999, all H & R 1871, Inc. revolvers were supplied with a lockable plastic case.

929 SIDEKICK – .22 LR cal., 9 shot, blue metal, swing-out cylinder, 4 in. heavy barrel, square butt with brown laminate grips, fixed sights, 30 oz. Mfg. 1996-99.

$300	$250	$205	$175	$145	$120	$100	*$173*

* ***929 Sidekick Trapper Edition*** – similar to 929 Sidekick, except has grey laminate grips and special barrel markings, limited mfg. 1996 only, distributed through 1996.

$300	$250	$205	$175	$145	$120	$100	*$175*

939 PREMIER WESTERN TARGET – .22 LR cal., 9 shot, blue metal, swing-out cylinder, target model with ribbed 6 in. heavy barrel and adj. rear sight, hardwood grips, 36 oz. Mfg. 1995-99.

$325	$270	$220	$185	$155	$130	$105	*$190*

FOURTY-NINER (WESTERN 949) – .22 LR cal., 9 shot fixed cylinder, case colored frame, 5 1/2 or 7 1/2 in. barrel, hardwood grips, fixed sights, approx. 37 oz. Mfg. 1995-99.

$325	$270	$220	$185	$155	$130	$105	*$190*

SPORTSMAN 999 – .22 LR cal., single or double action, top break action with auto shell ejection, 9 shot, 4 or 6 in. barrel with fluted solid rib, smooth hardwood stocks, transfer bar safety, blue finish, adj. sights, 30-34 oz. Mfg. 1991-99.

$400	$325	$270	$230	$190	$160	$130	*$285*

RIFLES: SINGLE SHOT

H&R 1871 began providing the Trigger Guardian trigger locking system beginning Dec. 1, 1999 at no extra charge. During 2008, H&R 1871 reintroduced its Ultragon rifling on its rifled slug barrels, which feature six oval lands and grooves w/o sharp corners. All H&R models are built in the U.S.A.

ULTRA HUNTER MODEL – .22 WMR (mfg. 2002-2007), .22-250 Rem. (disc. 1994), .223 Rem. (disc. 1997, reintroduced 2002-2008), .25-06 Rem. (mfg. 1995-2008), .243 Win. (disc. 2008), .270 Win. (mfg. 2005-2006), .30-06 (mfg. 2005-2007), .308 Win. (mfg. 1995-2008), .357 Rem. Max. (mfg. 1996-98), .450 Marlin (mfg. 2001-2004), .45-70 Govt. (new 2008), 7x57mm (mfg. 1997 only), or 7x64mm (mfg. 1997 only) cal., single shot break-open action with ejector, side-lever release, 22 in. heavy (.22-250 Rem. or .223 Rem.), 22 in. normal (.22 WMR, .308 Win. or .450 Marlin), 24 in. bull (.223 Rem. or .243 Win. cal., new 2006) or 26 in. (.25-06 Rem.) steel or stainless (new 2008) barrel with scope mount rail, checkered curly maple (disc. 1994), laminated cinammon hardwood Monte Carlo stock with black line recoil pad (disc. 2008), or thumbhole stock (new 2008), sling swivel studs, 7-8 lbs. Mfg. 1993-2013.

.45-70 cal.	$445	$375	$325	$265	$230	$195	$160	
Cals. other than .45-70	$325	$275	$235	$200	$175	$150	$125	*$517*

Subtract approx. 10% for metric cals.

This model featured a scope rail on .25-06 Rem. and .308 Win. cals.

* ***Ultra Model .22 Mag.*** – .22 WMR cal. only, 22 standard or 24 in. heavy (disc.) in. barrel. Disc. 2008.

$150	$125	$105	$90	$85	$80	$75	*$183*

* ***Ultra Model Varmint*** – .204 Ruger (mfg. 2005-2009), .22-250 Rem. (new 2005), .223 Rem., .243 Win. (disc. 2004, reintroduced 2006), .25-06 Rem., or .308 Win. cal., features heavy 24 in. fluted (mfg. 2005-2009) or unfluted barrel, blue finish, natural finish cinnamon laminate Monte Carlo stock with (new 2008) or w/o thumbhole, or skeletonized black synthetic stock (new 2005, fluted barrel only, disc. 2010), includes scope mount rail, 7 lbs. Mfg. 1998-2013.

$330	$275	$240	$210	$185	$160	$140	*$381*

Add $74 for thumbhole stock (.22-250 Rem., .223 Rem., or .243 Win. cal. only).

Add $44 for fluted barrel and skeletonized stock (disc. 2010).

Subtract approx. 15% if w/o fluted barrel.

* ***Ultra Model Comp.*** – .270 Win. or .30-06 cal., features 23 in. barrel with integral compensator, blue finish, multi-color checkered laminate wood stock and forearm. Approx. 7-8 lbs. Mfg. 1997-2003.

$340	$260	$225	$175	$140	$125	$100	*$376*

GRADING - PPGS™	100%	98%	95%	90%	80%	70%	60%	*LAST MSR*

* ***Ultra Model Rocky Mountain Elk Foundation Commemorative 1st Ed.*** – .280 Rem. cal., 26 in. blue barrel, features RMEF medallion in stock, high gloss bluing, 7-8 lbs. Mfg. 1995-96.

$225 $175 $135 $100 N/A N/A N/A *$270*

* ***Ultra Model Rocky Mountain Elk Foundation Commemorative 2nd Ed.*** – .35 Whelen cal., 26 in. blue barrel, features RMEF medallion in multi-color laminate stock and forearm, high gloss bluing, 7-8 lbs. Mfg. 1996-97.

$275 $225 $175 $150 N/A N/A N/A *$300*

HANDI-MAG – 7mm Rem. Mag. or .300 Win. Mag. cal., blued receiver, 26 in. stainless barrel w/o sights, black polymer synthetic Monte Carlo stock, includes scope mount rail, approx. 7 1/2 lbs. Mfg. 2008.

$265 $225 $165 $135 $120 $110 $100 *$319*

WHITETAILS UNLIMITED COMMEMORATIVE RIFLE – .30-30 (new 1998) or .45-70 Govt. cal., Topper style break-open action, 22 in. barrel, blue frame with special etching, checkered American walnut stock (with medallion) and forearm. 7 lbs. Mfg. 1997-98.

$250 $210 $170 N/A N/A N/A N/A *$290*

BUFFALO CLASSIC – .45 LC (new 2007) or .45-70 Govt. cal., top lever break open action, 20 (.45 LC cal.) in. barrel with carbine front sights or 32 in. barrel with Williams rear receiver and Lyman front target sights with aperture inserts, case hardened frame, checkered walnut stock and forearm, 8 lbs. Mfg. 1995-2018.

$420 $365 $315 $265 $230 $200 $180 *$479*

This model was also produced under the Wesson & Harrington trademark.

TARGET RIFLE – .38-55 WCF cal., 28 in. heavy barrel, target sights, blue finish, 7 1/2 lbs. Mfg. 1998-2007.

$345 $280 $230 $180 $145 $125 $105 *$395*

This model was also produced under the Wesson & Harrington trademark.

HANDI-RIFLE – .204 Ruger, .22-250 Rem., .223 Rem., .243 Win. (new 2009), .25-06 Rem., .270 Win. (disc.), .280 Rem. (disc. 2011), .30-30 Win., .30-06, .35 Whelen (new 2010), .308 Win., .444 Marlin, .45-70 Govt., 7mm-08 Rem., or .500 S&W cal., break open single shot action, 22 or 26 in. regular or bull barrel, blue receiver, regular or Monte Carlo walnut stained hardwood stock, scope mount rail or ramp front and adj. rear sights, sling swivels, 7 lbs. Mfg. 2008-2013.

$270 $235 $200 $165 $140 $120 $100 *$314*

Add $46 for 3-9x32mm scope (.223 Rem. or .243 Win. cal. only).

* ***Handi-Rifle Compact*** – .243 Win. or 7mm-08 Rem. cal., break open single shot action, 22 in. blue barrel, blue receiver, walnut stained hardwood stock, no sights, hammer extension, scope mount rail, sling swivels, 7 lbs. Mfg. 2008-2013.

$270 $235 $200 $165 $140 $120 $100 *$314*

Add $46 for 3-9x32mm scope (.243 Win. cal. only).

* ***Handi-Rifle Synthetic*** – .22 Hornet, .223 Rem., .243 Win., .270 Win., .30-06, .35 Whelen (new 2010), .357 Mag., .44 Rem. Mag., .444 Marlin, or .45-70 Govt. cal., 22 in. barrel, blue finish, features black synthetic stock and forearm, adj. sights on some cals., drilled and tapped, scope base mount only on others, 7 lbs. Mfg. 2008-2014.

$280 $240 $200 $165 $140 $120 $100 *$323*

* ***Handi-Rifle Synthetic Compact*** – .223 Rem. or .243 Win. cal., 20 or 22 in. barrel, blued finish, ramp adj. sights, features black synthetic stock and forearm, drilled and tapped. Disc. 2014.

$280 $240 $200 $165 $140 $120 $100 *$323*

Add $36 for 3-9x32 scope (.243 Win. cal. only). Disc. 2013.

* ***Handi-Rifle Synthetic Handi-Grip*** – .204 Ruger, .22-250 Rem., .223 Rem., .25-06 Rem., .243 Win., .45-70 Govt., or .308 Win. cal., 22, 24 (heavy), or 26 in. barrel, ambidextrous synthetic thumbhole stock, black finish. Mfg. 2010-2013.

$290 $245 $205 $170 $150 $135 $120 *$341*

* ***Handi-Rifle Synthetic Stainless*** – .270 Win., .30-06, 7mm Rem. Mag. or .300 Win. Mag. cal., similar to Handi-Rifle Synthetic, features 22 or 26 in. matte stainless steel barrel with matte blue or nickel finished receiver, 7 lbs. Mfg. 2008.

$255 $200 $160 $120 $80 $70 $60 *$319*

HANDI-GUN COMBINATION – .22 Hornet, .223 Rem., .243 Win., .30-30 Win., .30-30 Win., .30-06, or .45-70 Govt. cal., also includes either 12 or 20 ga. shotgun barrel, 22 in. barrels, side lever opening, ejector, brass bead or ramp front and adj. folding rear sights, tapped for scope mounts, nickel finished receiver and rifle barrel with blue or nickel finished shotgun barrel, walnut finished hardwood or synthetic PG buttstock and forend, 6 1/2 lbs. or 9 1/2 lbs. with both barrels.

$335 $295 $265 $215 $185 $160 $140

GRADING - PPGS™	100%	98%	95%	90%	80%	70%	60%	LAST MSR

HANDI-RIFLE/SLUG COMBO SERIES – includes 12 (disc.) or 20 ga. Slug barrel with 3 in. chamber and choice of 22 in. .243 Win., .270 Win., or .30-06 barrel, 22 (available with compact stock and .243 Win. only), 24 (disc.) or 26 (new 2010) in. rifled slug barrel, black synthetic stock, blue finish, hammer extension. Mfg. 2009-2011.

$315 $260 $225 $200 $170 $150 $135 ***$350***

SUPERLIGHT HANDI-RIFLE – .223 Rem. or .243 Win. cal., break open single shot, 20 or 22 in. barrel, black synthetic stock and forearm, drilled and tapped, blue finish, Compact model with 11 3/4 in. LOP became standard during 2010. Mfg. 2008-2012.

$280 $240 $200 $165 $140 $120 $100 ***$323***

Add $37 for 3-9x32mm mounted and bore sighted scope (.243 Win. cal., Youth only).

SPORTSTER – .17 HMR (new 2002), .17 Mach 2 (mfg. 2005-2007), .22 LR, or .22 WMR (new 2001) cal., 20 (midweight) or 22 (.17 HMR cal. only, heavy) in. barrel with Weaver style scope rail, no iron sights, available in either adult or youth (.22 LR cal. only) dimensions, black polymer stock and forearm. Mfg. 1999-2013.

$300 $265 $225 $205 $165 $135 $105 ***$217***

SURVIVOR – .223 Rem. or .308 Win. cal., similar in design to the Survivor Series shotgun, 22 or 24 in. bull barrel, blue finish, removable forearm for ammo storage, thumbhole design with storage compartment, no iron sights, scope mount rail, 6 lbs. Mfg. 2008-2014.

$275 $235 $190 $160 $135 $110 $100 ***$327***

SHOTGUNS: O/U

PINNACLE – 12 or 20 ga., 3 in. chambers, boxlock action, 26 (12 ga.) or 28 (20 ga.) in. vent. rib barrels with choke tubes, SST, ejectors, checkered walnut pistol grip stock with fluted comb, vent. recoil pad, bead front sight, 6 3/4 lbs. Limited importation 2005 only.

$775 $625 $550 $500 $465 $400 $350 ***$886***

SHOTGUNS: SEMI-AUTO

During 2008-2010, H&R 1871 decided to import all semi-auto shotguns under its New England Firearms trademark. Please refer to this section for 2008-2010 imported semi-auto shotguns.

EXCELL AUTO – 12 ga., 3 in. chamber, gas operated, 28 in. VR barrel with 4 choke tubes, matte black finish, black synthetic stock with recoil pad and forearm, 7 lbs. Mfg. 2014-2015.

$450 $395 $335 $300 $275 $250 $225 ***$499***

* ***Excell Auto Tactical*** – 12 ga., 3 in. chamber, 18 1/2 in. VR barrel with fixed cyl. choke, black oxide finish, 5 shot, bead front sight, black synthetic stock, 6 lbs. Mfg. 2014-2015.

  $450 $395 $335 $300 $275 $250 $225 ***$499***

* ***Excell Auto Turkey*** – 12 ga., 3 in. chamber, 22 in. VR barrel with 4 screw-in Rem Choke tubes, fiber optic front and rear sights, 100% Realtree Hardwoods camo finish, 6 1/4 lbs. Mfg. 2014-2015.

  $525 $500 $450 $400 $350 $300 $235 ***$579***

* ***Excell Auto Waterfowl*** – 12 ga., 28 in. VR barrel with 4 screw-in Rem Choke tubes, bead front sight, 100% Realtree Advantage Wetlands camo finish, 7 lbs. Mfg. 2014-2015.

  $525 $500 $450 $400 $350 $300 $235 ***$579***

EXCELL AUTO 5 – 12 ga., 3 in. chamber, 28 in. VR barrel with choke tubes, 5 shot mag., black synthetic, walnut, or Realtree Advantage Wetlands 100% camo covered pistol grip stock with fluted comb, vent. recoil pad, bead front sight, approx. 7 lbs. Mfg. 2005-2007.

$300 $250 $210 $180 $160 $140 $120 ***$374***

Add $29 for walnut stock or $82 for 100% camo coverage (Waterfowl model).

* ***Excell Auto 5 Turkey*** – 12 ga., 3 in. chamber, 5 shot mag., 22 in. vent. rib barrel with choke tubes and fiber optic sights, Realtree Advantage Hardwoods camo covered pistol grip stock and barrel, 7 lbs. Mfg. 2005-2007.

  $395 $345 $300 $265 $230 $195 $170 ***$456***

* ***Excell Auto 5 Combo*** – includes 24 in. rifled slug barrel and 28 in. regular barrel, synthetic stock only. Mfg. 2005-2007.

  $425 $380 $330 $290 $260 $230 $200 ***$512***

SHOTGUNS: SINGLE SHOT

H&R 1871 began providing the Trigger Guardian trigger locking system beginning Dec. 1, 1999 at no extra charge.

TOPPER (098) – 12, 16 (mfg. 1992-2007), 20, 28 (mfg. 1992-95, reintroduced 1998-2005) ga., or .410 bore, 2 3/4 (16 and 28 ga.) or 3 in. chamber, 26 or 28 in. fixed choke barrel, break open side lever release action, transfer bar safety, ejector, satin nickel frame with blue barrel, black finish hardwood stock with full pistol grip and forearm, 5-6 lbs. Mfg. 1991-2011.

$140 $110 $95 $80 $70 $60 $50 ***$161***

Add $24 for screw-in choke on 12 ga. only (Topper Deluxe).

GRADING - PPGS™	100%	98%	95%	90%	80%	70%	60%	LAST MSR

* ***Topper 3 1/2 in.*** – 12 ga. only, 3 1/2 in. chamber, satin nickel frame with blue barrel, 28 in. barrel with 1 choke tube, black finish hardwood stock (with recoil pad) and forearm, 5-6 lbs. Mfg. 1991-2008.

$125	$110	$90	$75	$60	$50	$40	*$164*

* ***Topper Deluxe Classic*** – 12 or 20 (new 2005) ga., 3 in. chamber, 26 (20 ga. only, mfg. 2005-2010) or 28 (12 ga. only) in. VR barrel with Mod. choke tube, matte nickel plated receiver, checkered American walnut pistol grip stock and forearm with recoil pad, 6-7 lbs. Mfg. 2004-2011.

$200	$175	$145	$120	$95	$80	$70	*$238*

* ***Topper Deluxe Rifled Slug Gun*** – 12 ga. only, 3 in. chamber, 24 in. compensated barrel, rifle sights, dark American hardwood stock and forearm, satin nickel frame, approx. 5 1/2 lbs. Mfg. 1996-99.

$150	$120	$100	$90	$80	$65	$55	*$170*

* ***Topper Jr.*** – 20 ga. or .410 bore, smaller variation of the Topper 098 with youth dimensions including 22 in. fixed choke barrel and shortened hardwood stock with recoil pad, satin nickel frame with blue barrel, 12 1/2 in. LOP, 5-6 lbs. Mfg. 1991-2011.

$145	$120	$100	$80	$70	$60	$50	*$169*

* ***Topper Jr. Classic*** – 20, 28 (disc. 2004) ga., or .410 bore, 22 in. fixed choke barrel, checkered American black walnut stock and forearm, recoil pad, 12 1/2 in. LOP, 5-6 lbs. Mfg. 1991-2011.

$175	$150	$125	$100	$90	$80	$70	*$208*

* ***Topper Trap*** – 12 ga., 3 in. chamber, 30 in. VR barrel with IM extended choke tube, checkered walnut stock and forearm with decelerator recoil pad, nickel finished receiver with blue barrel, 7 lbs. Mfg. 2008-2011.

$365	$315	$265	$225	$200	$180	$160	*$416*

* ***Topper NWTF Turkey Mag.*** – 10 (mfg. 1996 only) or 12 (mfg. 1991-95) ga., 3 1/2 in. chamber, 24 in. drilled and tapped barrel with 1 choke tube, entire gun is covered in Mossy Oak camo, includes sling and swivels, 6 lbs. Mfg. 1991-96.

$150	$120	$100	$90	$80	$65	$55	*$180*

This model was part of the National Wild Turkey Federation (NWTF) sponsorship program.

* ***Topper 1994 NWTF Youth Turkey Gun*** – 20 ga., 3 in. chamber, 22 in. full choke barrel, features Realtree camo finish and sling, limited mfg. 1994-95.

$150	$120	$100	$90	$80	$65	$55	*$160*

* ***Topper 2000 NWTF/Youth Edition*** – 12 or 20 ga., 3 in. chamber, 20 ga. is NWTF Youth Edition with 22 in. barrel, camo finished laminate stock and forend with NWTF laser engraved frame, includes sling and swivels. Mfg. 2000-2004.

$175	$130	$115	$95	$80	$70	$60	*$207*

Add $9 for NWTF Edition - 12 ga. with 24 in. barrel.

THE TAMER – 20 ga. (new 2007) or .410 bore, 3 in. chamber, synthetic thumbhole stock is designed to hold 3 or 4 shells, transfer bar system, 19 or 20 (20 ga. only) in. full choke barrel, electroless nickel finish, 6 lbs. Mfg. 1994-2014.

$185	$150	$125	$100	$85	$75	$65	*$223*

SB1-920 ULTRA SLUG HUNTER – 20 ga. only, utilizes 12 ga. action and barrel that has been under-bored to 20 ga. and fully rifled, hardwood Monte Carlo stock and forearm, matte black frame. Mfg. 1996-disc.

$190	$155	$125	$100	$85	$75	$65	*$225*

ULTRA SLUG HUNTER – 12 or 20 ga., 3 in. chamber, 22 (20 ga., Youth Model) or 24 in. fully rifled heavy barrel, side-release lever, black Monte Carlo hardwood stock with recoil pad, matte finished frame, 8-9 lbs. Mfg. 1995-2014.

$250	$215	$175	$140	$110	$90	$80	*$291*

Add $46 for 3-9x32mm scope (new 2007).
Add $3 for 20 ga. (standard stock or Youth model).

* ***Ultra Slug Hunter Deluxe*** – similar to Ultra Slug Hunter, except has checkered camo laminate wood and scope mount rail (scope optional), adj. rear sight. Mfg. 1997-2014.

$320	$280	$230	$200	$175	$150	$125	*$359*

Add $3 for 20 ga.

* ***Ultra Light Slug Hunter*** – 12 or 20 ga., 3 in. chamber, 24 in. rifled barrel w/o sights, blue finish, walnut stained hardwood stock and forearm, 5 1/4 lbs. Mfg. 2008-2014.

$240	$195	$170	$150	$125	$100	$85	*$291*

Add $3 for 20 ga.

GRADING - PPGS™	100%	98%	95%	90%	80%	70%	60%	LAST MSR

* ***Ultra Slug Hunter Thumbhole*** – 12 or 20 ga., 3 in. chamber, 24 in. rifled barrel w/Weaver rail type scope base, blue finish, features colored laminate thumbhole stock and forearm, 8 1/2 lbs. Mfg. 2008-2014.

	$355	$295	$265	$230	$200	$180	$160	*$401*

PARDNER – 12, 20, 28 ga., or .410 bore, 2 3/4 (28 ga.) or 3 in. chamber, single shot, break open action, safety transfer bar mechanism on hammer, side lever release, color case hardened receiver, 14 in. LOP, 26, 28, or 32 (12 ga. only, new 2009) in. barrel, fixed or mod. choke tube (12 or 20 ga. only, with black synthetic stock and forearm), extractor, walnut stained hardwood or black synthetic (disc., 12 or 20 ga. only) stock and forearm, 5-6 lbs. Mfg. 2008-2014.

	$175	$150	$130	$120	$95	$80	$60	*$206*

Add $19 for 32 in. barrel (12 ga. only).
Add $23 for modified choke tube with black synthetic stock and forearm (12 or 20 ga. only, disc. 2009).

* ***Pardner Compact (Youth)*** – 20, 28 (disc. 2011) ga., or .410 bore, similar to Pardner, except has 22 in. barrel and straight grip stock with recoil pad, 12 1/2 in. LOP, 5-5 1/2 lbs. Mfg. 2008-2014.

	$190	$165	$145	$130	$100	$85	$65	*$225*

Add $12 for modified choke tube (20 ga. only with black synthetic stock and forearm, disc. 2009).

* ***Pardner Turkey Gun*** – 10, 12, or 20 (Youth only) ga., 3 (20 ga.) or 3 1/2 in. chamber, 22 (20 ga.) or 24 in. barrel with fixed or full choke tube, Realtree Hardwoods camo or matte black (disc. 2013) wood finish, recoil pad, sling swivel studs and sling, 5 1/2 - 9 lbs. Mfg. 2008-2014.

	$235	$200	$175	$160	$130	$100	$80	*$277*

Add $45 for 10 ga. with camo wood finish.
Add $10 for Mossy Oak Break-Up camo in 12 ga. with full choke bore (disc. 2009).

* ***Pardner Waterfowl*** – 10 ga., 3 1/2 in. chamber, 30 or 32 in. barrel, blue barrel and receiver, walnut or Mossy Oak Break Up camo (disc.) finish on stock and forearm, recoil pad, 9 1/2 lbs. Mfg. 2008-2009.

	$185	$150	$125	$100	$85	$65	$55	*$228*

SURVIVOR – .410 ga./.45 LC cal., 3 in. chamber, 20 in. barrel with screw-in modified choke, blue or nickel finish, black synthetic stock with open pistol grip, 6 lbs. Disc. 2014.

	$250	$210	$180	$160	$135	$115	$100	*$327*

Add $20 for nickel finish.

TRACKER II SLUG MODEL – 12 or 20 ga., 3 in. chamber, 24 in. rifled slug barrel, 14 in. LOP, walnut finished hardwood stock, adj. iron sights, 5 1/4 lbs. Mfg. 2008-2014.

	$240	$195	$165	$130	$110	$90	$80	*$291*

Add $3 for 20 ga.
Add $44 for Tracker II 12 ga. Slug Gun/Huntsman .50 cal. black powder muzzleloader (disc. 2002).

WHITETAILS UNLIMITED RIFLED SLUG GUN – 12 ga., 3 in. chamber, 24 in. fully rifled heavy barrel, hand checkered Monte Carlo black laminate stock and forend, Whitetails medallion, hammer extension, swivels and sling. Mfg. 1998-99.

	$220	$185	$145	$120	$100	$85	$75	*$255*

SHOTGUNS: SLIDE ACTION

PARDNER PUMP – 12 or 20 ga., 3 in. chamber, 26 or 28 in. VR barrel with modified screw-in choke, brass bead front sight, drilled and tapped, grooved forend, vent. recoil pad, choice of American walnut stock or black synthetic stock with molded checkering, matte black metal finish, 7 1/2 lbs. New 2008.

MSR $235	$185	$165	$145	$130	$120	$110	$100

Add $28 for walnut stock and forearm.

* ***Pardner Pump Compact*** – 20 ga. only, 3 in. chamber, 21 in. VR threaded barrel with choke tube, 13 in. LOP, black synthetic stock with grooved forend and vent. recoil pad, molded checkering, matte black metal finish, 6 1/2 lbs. New 2008.

MSR $215	$175	$165	$145	$130	$120	$110	$100

* ***Pardner Pump Protector*** – 12 ga., 3 in. chamber, 18 1/2 in. cylinder bore barrel, black synthetic stock with grooved forend, vent. recoil pad, molded checkering swivel studs, bead front sights, 7 1/2 lbs. New 2008.

MSR $215	$175	$165	$145	$130	$120	$110	$100

H-S PRECISION, INC.

Current custom pistol and rifle manufacturer located in Rapid City, SD since 1990. H-S Precision, Inc. also manufactures synthetic stocks and custom machine barrels. Dealer and consumer direct sales.

H-S Precision introduced the aluminum bedding block for rifle stocks in 1981, and has been making advanced

GRADING - PPGS™	100%	98%	95%	90%	80%	70%	60%	LAST MSR

composite synthetic stocks and custom ballistic test barrels for more than two decades.

In addition to the following models, H-S Precision, Inc. also built rifles using a customer's action (mostly Remington 700 or Winchester Post-'64 Model 70). 2004 MSRs ranged from $1,520-$1,830.

PISTOLS: SINGLE SHOT

PRO-SERIES 2000 VP/SP – various cals., stainless steel receiver, 15 in. fluted stainless steel barrel, 3-position safety, laminated composite Pro-Series stock, Teflon coated receiver and barrel, choice of Varmint (VP, no sights) or Silhouette (SP, drilled and tapped for sights) model configurations, choice of stock colors, 4.7-5 1/2 lbs. Mfg. late 1997-2018.

	100%	98%	95%	90%	80%	70%	60%	LAST MSR
	$2,785	$2,435	$2,095	$1,900	$1,575	$1,275	$1,050	*$3,095*

RIFLES: BOLT ACTION, PRO-SERIES 2000

All H-S Precision rifles feature Kevlar/graphite laminate stocks, cut rifle barrels, and other high tech innovations including a molded aluminum bedding block system. Beginning in 1999, H-S Precision began utilizing their H-S 2000 action, and model nomenclature was changed to begin with Pro-Series 2000.

For most rifles, depending on specifications, you can add the following options.
Add $30-$55 for special stock colors.
Add $175 for Cerakote colors excluding Teflon.
Add $200 for left-handed models (Add $250 for left-hand Pro-Hunter Long Range Carbon)
Add $2,599 for additional takedown barrel with same bolt face diameter (for Pro-Hunter or Tactical Takedown)
Add $2,999 for additional takedown barrel with different bolt face diameter (for Pro-Hunter or Tactical Takedown)
Please contact the company directly for any other additional options or accessories.

PRO-SERIES 2000 BENCHREST (BCR) – various cals from .204 Ruger-.325 WSM cal., 16.5 (new 2020), 20-26, or 28 (new 2020) in. fluted barrel, right-hand short action only, yellow/black stock. Mfg. 2012-2020.

	100%	98%	95%	90%	80%	70%	60%	LAST MSR
	$3,780	$3,310	$2,835	$2,575	$2,080	$1,700	$1,400	*$4,199*

PRO-SERIES 2000 CLASSIC HUNTING RIFLE (CHR) – .25-06 Rem., .264 Win., .270 Win., .280 Rem., .300 H&H, .300 Win., or 7mm Mag. cal., 20-26 in. fluted barrel, w/o sights, right-hand action only, internal blind box magazine, tan/black stock, approx. 7.1 lbs. Mfg. 2012-2018.

	100%	98%	95%	90%	80%	70%	60%	LAST MSR
	$3,475	$3,100	$2,675	$2,300	$2,075	$1,675	$1,375	*$3,895*

PRO-SERIES 2000 F CLASS RIFLE (FCR) – 6.5x284 Norma cal., 20-26 in. fluted barrel, short or long action, black/red stock, approx. 9.3 lbs. Mfg. 2012-2018.

	100%	98%	95%	90%	80%	70%	60%	LAST MSR
	$3,400	$3,050	$2,675	$2,295	$2,075	$1,675	$1,375	*$3,795*

PRO-SERIES 2000 HEAVY TACTICAL HTR (HEAVY TACTICAL MARKSMAN) – .204 Ruger-.458 Lott cal., Remington BDL (disc. 1999) or Pro-Series 2000 (new 2000) action, 16 1/2 (new 2020), 20-26, 28 (new 2020), or 30 (new 2021) in standard or cut-rifled heavy contour fluted (disc. 2020) barrel, detachable box mag., composite stock w/adj. LOP and cheekpiece, full-length aluminum bedding block, left-hand action available, 10.8-12.1 lbs. New 1990.

	100%	98%	95%	90%	80%	70%	60%
MSR $3,999	$3,600	$3,150	$2,700	$2,450	$1,975	$1,625	$1,330

PRO-SERIES 2000 PRO-HUNTER LIGHTWEIGHT (PHL) – various cals., .204 Ruger-.300 WSM, short action only, 20, 22, or 24 (new 2021) in. fluted barrel, green/tan camo stock, other colors and patterns available, Teflon coated action and barrel, 5.5 lbs. New 2004.

	100%	98%	95%	90%	80%	70%	60%
MSR $3,999	$3,600	$3,150	$2,700	$2,450	$1,975	$1,625	$1,330

PRO-SERIES 2000 PRO-HUNTER LONG RANGE (PLR) – available in various cals. from .204 Ruger-.458 Lott cal., 16.5-26 or 28 (disc. 2020) in. fluted (disc. 2020) or non-fluted (new 2021), stainless steel barrel with cut rifling, detachable mag., adj. trigger, fixed sporter stock with vertical grip and small dual palm swell, full-length aluminum bedding block, Kevlar, fiberglass, carbon fiber, reaction injection molded polyurethane foam, two front swivel studs, single rear swivel stud, various Cerakote finishes optional, left-hand action available, 5.7-5.9 lbs. New mid-2013.

	100%	98%	95%	90%	80%	70%	60%
MSR $3,799	$3,425	$3,000	$2,575	$2,330	$1,875	$1,540	$1,260

* ***Pro-Series 2000 Pro-Hunter Long Range Carbon (PLC)*** – available in various cals. from .204 Ruger-.458 Lott cal., short or long action, 20-26 in. carbon fiber barrel, adj. cheekpiece, vertical grip. New 2020.

	100%	98%	95%	90%	80%	70%	60%
MSR $4,750	$4,275	$3,740	$3,200	$2,900	$2,350	$1,925	$1,580

PRO-SERIES 2000 PRO-HUNTER RIFLE (PHR) – available in various cals. from .204 Ruger-.458 Lott cal., long or short action, 16.5-26, 28 (disc. 2020) in. fluted (disc. 2020) or non-fluted (new 2021) stainless steel barrel with cut rifling, optional muzzle brake, optional iron sights, Pro-Series sporter stock with cheekpiece and built-in mercury recoil reduction system, Teflon finish, 7.25-8.25 lbs.

	100%	98%	95%	90%	80%	70%	60%
MSR $3,799	$3,425	$3,000	$2,575	$2,330	$1,875	$1,540	$1,260

GRADING - PPGS™ 100% 98% 95% 90% 80% 70% 60% LAST MSR

PRO-SERIES 2000 PRO-HUNTER TAKEDOWN (PTD) – .204 Ruger-.458 Lott cal., short or long takedown action, right hand only, 20-26 in. fluted (disc. 2020) or non-fluted (new 2021) barrel with muzzle brake, detachable mag., sand finish, approx. 9.4 lbs. New 2012.

MSR $5,999 $5,400 $4,725 $4,050 $3,675 $2,975 $2,425 $2,000

PRO SERIES 2000 RAPID DEPLOYMENT RIFLE (RDR) – .204 Ruger-.325 WSM cal., Pro-Series 2000 stainless steel short action only, 16.5-20 in. fluted barrel, compact and lightweight, black synthetic stock with or w/o thumbhole (right hand only, new 2006), short forend, black teflon metal finish, approx. 7.5 lbs. New 2000.

MSR $3,999 $3,600 $3,150 $2,700 $2,450 $1,975 $1,625 $1,330

Add $125 for PST60A Long Range stock (disc.).

PRO-SERIES 2000 SHORT TACTICAL (STR) – available in various cals., .204 Ruger-.325 WSM cal., short action only, 16.5-20 in. fluted barrel with standard porting, detachable mag. box, Pro Series Tactical adj. stock, matte Teflon finished action and barrel. New 2004.

MSR $3,999 $3,600 $3,150 $2,700 $2,450 $1,975 $1,625 $1,330

PRO-SERIES 2000 TAKEDOWN TACTICAL LONG RANGE (TTD) – .204 Ruger-.458 Lott cal., Remington BDL takedown action, 20-26 in. stainless steel barrel, matte blue finish, 11.25-11.75 lbs. Mfg. 1990-2005, reintroduced 2008.

MSR $6,499 $5,850 $5,125 $4,390 $3,975 $3,225 $2,635 $2,160

Add $100 for extended barrel port (Model TTD EP, disc.).

PRO-SERIES 2000 SPORTER (SPR) – various cals. available, .204 Ruger-.338 Win. Mag., Remington ADL (disc.) or stainless steel action only, fluted barrel became standard 2006, 16.5-26 in. stainless steel barrel, detachable mag. system, synthetic stock in choice of standard colors, each rifle is built per individual specifications, black teflon metal finish, 7.5-7.75 lbs. New 1990.

MSR $3,799 $3,425 $3,000 $2,575 $2,330 $1,875 $1,540 $1,260

Add $100 for extended barrel port (Model SPR EP, disc.).

Add $880 for extra stainless barrel (disc.).

* ***Pro-Series 2000 Sporter Lightweight (SPL)*** – similar to Pro-Series 2000 Sporter, available in various cals., .204 Ruger-.338 Win. Mag., short or long action, 16.5-26 in. 10X cut-rifled fluted barrel, detachable mag. system, synthetic stock, 7.1-7.6 lbs. New 1990.

MSR $3,799 $3,425 $3,000 $2,575 $2,330 $1,875 $1,540 $1,260

PRO-SERIES 2000 VARMINT (VAR) – available in various cals., .204 Ruger-.458 Lott cal., short or long stainless steel action, 16.5-26 in. fluted stainless steel match grade barrel, detachable box mag., synthetic stock vertical grip stock and beavertail forend, ambi palm swell, each rifle is built per individual specifications, 8-8.5 lbs.

MSR $3,799 $3,425 $3,000 $2,575 $2,330 $1,875 $1,540 $1,260

Add $200 for 28 in. barrel.

PRO-SERIES 2000 VARMINT TAKEDOWN (VTD) – various cals., accurized Remington Model 700 receiver (disc. 1999) or H-S 2000 action (new 2000), 20-26 in. H-S stainless steel cut rifled and fluted barrel, 5 or 10 shot detachable mag., Teflon coated metal Urban camo finish, approx. 8.9 lbs. Mfg. 1997-2018.

$5,025 $4,650 $4,225 $3,600 $3,200 $2,750 $2,250 *$5,595*

Add $100 for extended barrel port (Model VTD EP, disc.).

TAKEDOWN LONG RANGE (TACTICAL MARKSMAN) – .223 Rem., .243 Win., .30-06, .308 Win., 7mm Rem. Mag., .300 Win. Mag., or .338 Win. Mag. cal., includes "kwik klip" and stainless fluted barrel. Mfg. 1990-1997.

$2,495 $2,050 $1,675 $1,350 $995 $850 $750 *$2,895*

A complete rifle package consisting of two calibers (.308 Win. and .300 Win. Mag.), scope and fitted case was available for $5,200 retail.

TOM HOUGHTON SR. TRIBUTE RIFLE (LTD. ED.) – available in various cals., short or long action, 16.5-26 in. 10X cut-rifled fluted barrel, detachable mag., red, white, and blue stock, elevated cheek weld, full length aluminum bedding block, right-handed availability only, "Limited Edition" and number out of 50 are engraved on the rifle, special limited edition TOMSR serial number. Limited mfg. of 50 beginning 2017.

MSR $5,000 $4,500 $3,950 $3,375 $3,060 $2,475 $2,025 $1,660

HWP INDUSTRIES

Previous manufacturer located in Milwaukee, WI circa 1989.

GRADING - PPGS™	100%	98%	95%	90%	80%	70%	60%	LAST MSR

REVOLVERS

THE SLEDGEHAMMER – .500 HWP Mag. cal., 5 shot revolver, double action, stainless steel, full shrouded 4 in. barrel (quick change), Pachmayr grips. Limited mfg. 1989 only.

$1,150	**$895**	**$750**	**$640**	**$535**	**$450**	**$390**	*$1,295*

HAENEL, C.G. (OLD MFG.)

Previous firearms and airguns manufacturer located in Suhl, Germany 1840-1946.

For individual model listings, please go to BlueBookOfGunValues.com/overflow.

HAENEL, C.G., GmbH (NEW MFG.)

Current trademark established during 2006 and manufactured by various gunmakers/craftsmen from the Suhl Arms Alliance, located in Suhl, Germany. Select models currently imported on a limited basis by Steyr Arms or B&T USA.

During 2006, the Suhl Arms Alliance was founded by a group of industrial manufacturers and gunsmithing craftspeople located in Suhl, Germany. All guns manufactured by this alliance are proofed in the Suhl firearms proof house.

Currently manufactured Haenel trademarked guns include a Jaeger 8.10 bolt action rifle (various configurations and finishes), Model SLB2000+ semi-auto rifle, Jaeger 9 single shot rifle, Jaeger 8.10 O/U combination gun, Jaeger 8.11 O/U shotgun, Jaeger 11 O/U shotgun, RS8 or RS9 tactical rifle utilizing a modular design, and CR 223 semi-auto rifle. Please contact the company directly for more information including U.S. availabilty and pricing.

HAGELBERG ARMS DESIGN

Current manufacturer located in Denmark. No current U.S. importation.

For individual model listings, please go to BlueBookOfGunValues.com/overflow.

HAHN TACTICAL

Previous AR-15 style rifle and parts manufacturer located in Winchester, VA 2015-2020.

Please refer to BlueBookOfGunValues.com to order the *Blue Book of AR-15s & Variations*, available as a book or online subscription.

HAILEY ORDNANCE CO.

Previous AR-15 style rifle manufacturer located in Oklahoma City, OK.

Please refer to BlueBookOfGunValues.com to order the *Blue Book of AR-15s & Variations*, available as a book or online subscription.

HAKIM

Previous trademark of rifle adopted by the Egyptian army during the early 1950s.

For individual model listings, please go to BlueBookOfGunValues.com/overflow.

HALO ARMS, LLC

Previous rifle manufacturer located in Phoenixville, PA from 2003-2013.

For individual model listings, please go to BlueBookOfGunValues.com/overflow.

HAMBRUSCH JAGDWAFFEN GmbH

Current manufacturer established in 1752, located in Ferlach, Austria. Previously imported and distributed exclusively by CONCO Arms, located in Emmaus, PA.

Hambrusch Jagdwaffen was a member of the Ferlach Gun Guild until it was dissolved in 2004. This company manufactures many types of high-grade long arms, including SxS shotguns, combination guns, Drillings, double rifles, and single shot rifles. The combinations of these configurations are almost endless. During 2002, Hambrusch introduced a new proprietary big game cartridge, the .600/538 MM (Mega Magnum with 722 grain bullet). All guns are built per customer specifications. Please contact the company directly for more information, availability, and current pricing.

HÄMMERLI AG

Current trademark purchased during 2006 by Walther, and firearms are currently manufactured in Ulm/Donau, Germany beginning 2008. Previous manufacture was located in Lenzburg, Switzerland circa 1863-late 2005. Firearms are currently distributed by Brenzovich Firearms, located in Fort Hancock, TX and Champion's Choice, located in LaVergne, TN. Previously distributed by Larry's Guns, located in Gray, ME until 2019. Airguns are currently imported by Umarex USA, located in Ft. Smith, AR. Previously imported by SIG Arms Inc. located in Exeter, NH, Gunsmithing Inc.,

GRADING - PPGS™	100%	98%	95%	90%	80%	70%	60%	LAST MSR

located in Colorado Springs, CO, Hämmerli Pistols USA, located in Groveland, CA, and by Beeman Precision Arms located in Santa Rosa, CA.

For more information and current pricing on both new and used Hämmerli airguns, please refer to the *Blue Book of Airguns* - also available as an online subscription.

PISTOLS: SINGLE SHOT, RIMFIRE

Values listed below for recently manufactured pistols reflect older mfg. by Hämmerli in Lenzburg, Switzerland.

FP-10 FREE PISTOL – .22 LR cal., top-of-the-line Hämmerli pistol. Imported 2000-2004.

$1,525	$1,200	$950	$850	$750	$650	$575	*$1,749*

MODEL 33MP – .22 LR cal., similar to the Model 100, except not available in a deluxe model. Mfg. 1933-49.

$925	$725	$650	$550	$470	$440	$385

MODEL FP 60 – .22 LR cal., refined ergonomic design from the FP-10, 12 3/4 in. barrel, increased stability, adj. rear sight with integral front sight, many accessories available, approx. 2 1/2 lbs. Importation began 2005. Disc.

$2,068	$1,675	$1,450	$1,275	$1,050	$875	$750

MSR was not available for this model.

MODEL 100 FREE PISTOL – .22 LR cal., 11 1/2 in. octagon barrel, blue, martini action single shot, set trigger, micro rear sight, walnut stock and forearm. Mfg. 1950-56.

$880	$660	$605	$550	$470	$440	$385

Add 15%-20% for Olympic rings, "London", and "1948" markings (indicative of Swiss shooting team).

* ***Model 100 Free Pistol Deluxe Model*** – carved stock.

$990	$770	$715	$660	$580	$550	$495

MODEL 101 – similar to Model 100, but heavy round barrel, improved action and sights, matte finish. Mfg. 1956-60.

$880	$660	$605	$550	$470	$440	$385

MODEL 102 – similar to Model 101, except high polished finish. Mfg. 1956-60.

$880	$660	$605	$550	$470	$440	$385

* ***Model 102 Deluxe Model***

$990	$770	$715	$660	$580	$550	$495

MODEL 103 FREE PISTOL – similar to Model 101, except lighter octagon polished barrel. Mfg. 1956-60.

$935	$715	$660	$605	$580	$550	$495

MODEL 104 MATCH PISTOL – similar to Model 103, except lighter round barrel, redesigned stock, mfg. 1961-65.

$760	$660	$550	$495	$470	$440	$385

MODEL 105 MATCH PISTOL – similar to Model 103, except redesigned action and stock, octagon barrel. Mfg. 1962-65.

$935	$715	$660	$605	$580	$550	$495

MODEL 106 MATCH PISTOL – similar to Model 105, except improved trigger.

$910	$690	$580	$525	$495	$470	$415

MODEL 107 MATCH PISTOL – similar to Model 105, except improved trigger.

$990	$770	$660	$550	$525	$495	$440

* ***Model 107 Match Pistol Deluxe model*** – engraved and carved wood.

$1,320	$990	$880	$660	$635	$605	$550

MODEL 120-1 SINGLE SHOT FREE PISTOL – .22 LR cal., bolt action, 9.9 in. barrel, blue barrel and receiver, side lever operated, anodized aluminum lever and frame, walnut checkered grips.

$625	$550	$475	$425	$375	$325	$295

MODEL 120-2 – similar to 120-1, except stocks hand contoured.

$700	$600	$550	$475	$425	$375	$325

MODEL 120 HEAVY BARREL – similar to 120-1, with 5.7 in. bull barrel, 1,000 mfg.

$800	$700	$600	$550	$475	$425	$375

This model was cased with test target and tools.

MODEL 150 FREE PISTOL – .22 LR cal., 11.3 in. barrel, improved Martini-type action, set trigger, innovative design incorporating many unusual features. Disc. 1989.

$1,850	$1,495	$1,275	$1,120	$980	$900	$850	*$1,980*

Add $113 for left-hand variation.

The Model 150 was replaced by the Model 151.

GRADING - PPGS™	100%	98%	95%	90%	80%	70%	60%	LAST MSR

MODEL 151 FREE PISTOL – replacement for the Model 150 Free Pistol. Imported 1990-93.

$1,850	$1,495	$1,275	$1,120	$995	$900	$800	*$1,980*

MODEL 152 FREE PISTOL – .22 LR cal., 11.3 in. barrel. improved Martini-type action, electronic trigger release, innovative design incorporating many unusual features. State-of-the-art target pistol. Disc. 1992.

$1,995	$1,600	$1,350	$1,195	$1,090	$990	$895	*$2,105*

Add $57 for left-hand variation.

MODEL 160 FREE PISTOL – .22 LR cal., similar to Model 150, except has poly-carbon fiber forend, includes carrying case. Mfg. 1993-2002.

$1,725	$1,475	$1,175	$900	$800	$700	$595	*$1,850*

Add $290 for smaller adj. grips.

MODEL 162 FREE PISTOL – .22 LR cal., replacement for the Model 152 Free Pistol, includes poly-carbon fiber forend, includes carrying case. Imported 1993-2000.

$2,150	$1,700	$1,375	$1,125	$900	$800	$700	*$2,410*

Add $290 for smaller adj. grips.

PISTOLS: SEMI-AUTO

Values listed below are for both pistols manufactured by Hämmerli in Lenzburg, Switzerland, and by Walther in Ulm/Donau, Germany (beginning 2008).

MODELS 200-205 – see Hämmerli-Walther.

INTERNATIONAL MODEL 206 – .22 Short or .22 LR cal., 7 1/16 in. barrel with muzzle brake, adj. sights, walnut grips, blue. Mfg. 1962-69.

$675	$625	$525	$450	$395	$365	$330	

INTERNATIONAL MODEL 207 – similar to 206, except adj. grip heel.

$725	$650	$550	$475	$425	$375	$350	

INTERNATIONAL MODEL 208 – .22 LR cal., 9 shot, 6 in. barrel, blue, adj. sights, checkered walnut grips with adj. heel. Mfg. 1966-88.

$1,500	$1,250	$950	$850	$750	$650	$550	*$1,755*

This model was replaced by the Model 208S.

* ***International Model 208S*** – .22 LR cal., similar to Model 208, except has redesigned trigger guard and safety with interchangeable rear sight element. Imported 1988-2000.

$1,750	$1,500	$1,250	$1,000	$900	$800	$700	*$2,021*

Add $125 for factory scope mount. Add $180 for smaller adj. grips.

* ***International Model 208 Deluxe*** – similar to Model 208, except has carved grips and elaborate engraving. Importation disc. 1988.

$2,995	$2,500	$1,995	$1,735	$1,495	$1,215	$1,000	*$3,250*

* ***International Model 208C (Commemorative)*** – limited edition commemorative. Disc. 1987.

$2,100	$1,750	$1,400	N/A	N/A	N/A	N/A	*$2,225*

INTERNATIONAL MODEL 209 – .22 Short cal., 5 shot, 4 3/4 in. barrel, muzzle brake, adj. sights, blue, walnut stock. Mfg. 1966-70.

$800	$690	$635	$550	$525	$485	$440	

INTERNATIONAL MODEL 210 – similar to 209, but grips have adj. heel. Mfg. 1966-70.

$800	$715	$660	$590	$540	$525	$495	

MODEL 211 – .22 LR cal., 9 shot, 6 in. barrel, adj. sights, blue, similar to Model 208 except non-adj. walnut stocks. Importation disc. 1990.

$1,550	$1,275	$1,050	$950	$880	$835	$770	*$1,669*

MODEL 212 HUNTER – .22 LR cal., hunter's pistol, 9 shot, 5 in. barrel, adj. sights, blue, walnut stocks. Importation disc. 1993.

$2,000	$1,800	$1,650	$1,400	$1,200	$850	$675	*$1,395*

MODEL 215 – .22 LR cal., commercial target version with Model 208 specifications, 9 shot, 5 in. barrel, adj. sights, blue, walnut stocks. Importation disc. 1990.

$2,300	$1,950	$1,775	$1,550	$1,300	$1,150	$995	*$1,505*

Add $300 for Model 215S.

MODEL 230 RAPID FIRE PISTOL – .22 S cal., 5 shot, 6.3 in. barrel, blue, adj. sights, smooth walnut grips. Mfg. 1970-83.

$705	$635	$580	$530	$485	$450	$415	

MODEL 230-2 – similar to 230, except checkered grips with adj. heel. Mfg. 1970-83.

$735	$655	$605	$570	$515	$485	$470	

GRADING - PPGS™	100%	98%	95%	90%	80%	70%	60%	LAST MSR

MODEL 232-1 RAPID FIRE PISTOL – .22 S cal., 6 shot, 5.1 in. barrel, blue, adj. sights, contoured walnut grips. Importation disc. 1993.

	$1,395	$1,125	$950	$850	$750	$700	$650	*$1,505*

Add $25 for wraparound grips sizes S-M-LG (Model 232-2).

MODEL 280 – .22 LR or .32 S&W Wadcutter cal., new modular pistol design utilizing carbon fiber synthetic material to replace frame and other critical parts, adj. grips, trigger, and rear sight, 4.6 in. barrel, 5 or 6 shot mag., approx. 2.2 lbs. Imported 1988-2000.

	$1,450	$1,125	$900	$800	$675	$575	$475	*$1,643*

Add $200 for .32 S&W Wadcutter cal.
Add $765 (.22 LR) or $965 (.32 S&W Wadcutter) for conversion kit.
Add $200 for smaller adj. grips.

A package was also available with both calibers, magazines, and hard case for $2,595.

MODEL SP 20 – .22 LR or .32 S&W Wadcutter cal., replacement for Model 280, features low-level sight line, colored alloy receiver (blue, red, gold, violet, or black), adj. "JPS" buffer system that varies recoil characteristics per individual preference, black Hi-Grip anatomical grips. Imported 1998-circa 2008.

	$1,749	$1,500	$1,325	$1,075	$925	$800	$700	

Add $246 for .32 S&W Wadcutter cal.
Add $499 for .22 LR conversion (disc.), $599 for .32 S&W Wadcutter conversion (disc.).

MODEL SP 20 RRS – .22 LR or .32 S&W Wadcutter cal., state-of-the-art target pistol featuring composite frame with redesigned ergonomic grips, RRS designates recoil reducing system, fully hand adj. rear sight, various slide colors available. Mfg. 2002-2005.

	$1,430	$1,250	$1,125	$1,025	$925	$825	$725	

Add $113 for .32 S&W Wadcutter cal.
Add $795 for .22 LR conversion, or $850 for .32 Wadcutter conversion.

This model is currently manufactured by Walther. Please refer to the current listings in the Walther section.

MODEL P-240 – see SIG-Hämmerli for this model.

TRAILSIDE PL 22 – .22 LR cal., single action, 4 1/2 or 6 in. barrel, two-tone finish, choice of ultralight polymer composite grips or target variation which includes wood grips and adj. rear sight, 10 shot mag., cased with trigger lock, lower cost variation of the X-Esse, 28 or 30 oz. Imported exclusively by SigArms. Mfg. 1999-2006.

	$395	$350	$300	$275	$250	$225	$200	*$455*

Add $79 for 4 1/2 in. barrel with target sights, or $95 for 6 in. barrel with target sights.

This model was also available as one of SIG Arms' limited editions in Jan. 2004 - it included a BSA 30mm red dot optical sight with integrated mount and 6 in. barrel. Last MSR was $709.

* ***Trailside Competition*** – includes 6 in. barrel with blue anatomical stippled grips and adj. bottom rest, cased with trigger lock, 37.2 oz. Limited importation 2000-2005.

	$580	$500	$400	$350	$300	$265	$225	*$710*

X-ESSE – .22 LR cal., available in Sport, Long, and Short configurations, 4 1/2 or 6 in. barrel, polymer or anatomic stippled polymer target (Competition model) grips, adj. hand rest, 10 shot mag. Mfg. in the Walther factory located in Ulm beginning 2008. Importation began 2009.

MSR $850	$750	$650	$575	$500	$450	$400	$365	

Add $250 for Competition (Sport) Model with anatomic grips, adj. front and rear sights, and barrel weight (disc.).
Add $125 for IPSC variation with 6 in. barrel (standard grips).

RIFLES: BOLT ACTION, TARGET

OLYMPIC 300 METER – .30-06 cal., bolt action, single shot free rifle, U.S.A. import, 7x57mm overseas, 29 1/2 in. heavy barrel, double set trigger, aperture rear and globe front sight, free rifle stock with thumbhole pistol grip, beavertail forearm, Swiss style target butt. Mfg. 1945-59.

	$880	$745	$605	$550	$470	$440	$415	

HÄMMERLI-TANNER 300 METER FREE RIFLE – similar to Olympic 300, except 7.5x55mm standard, also was available in other calibers. Mfg. 1962-disc.

	$895	$825	$770	$715	$660	$580	$520	*$935*

MODEL 45 SMALLBORE MATCH RIFLE – .22 LR cal., single shot, 27 1/2 in. heavy barrel, same sights and stock type as Hämmerli-Tanner. Mfg. 1945-1957.

	$660	$550	$470	$440	$385	$360	$330	

GRADING - PPGS™	100%	98%	95%	90%	80%	70%	60%	LAST MSR

MODEL 54 SMALLBORE MATCH RIFLE – similar to 45 Smallbore, except adj. butt. Mfg. 1954-57.

	$670	$560	$480	$450	$395	$370	$340	

MODEL S 205 – 6mm BR, 7.5x55mm, or .308 Win. cal., designed for 300 meter competition, adj. blue aluminum or wood stock, 5 shot mag., Hammerli aperture rear sight, Sauer produced 205 action with 26 in. heavy free floating barrel, 12 lbs. Mfg. 2004-2005.

	$3,995	$3,650	$3,300	$3,000	$2,650	$2,300	$1,850	

Add $723 for adj. aluminum stock.

MODEL 503 SMALLBORE FREE RIFLE – similar to 54 Smallbore, except free style stock.

	$660	$550	$470	$440	$385	$360	$330	

MODEL 505 MATCH RIFLE – match stock with aperture sights.

	$690	$580	$495	$470	$415	$385	$360	

MODEL 506 SMALLBORE MATCH RIFLE – similar to 503 Smallbore. Mfg. 1963-66.

	$690	$580	$495	$470	$415	$385	$360	

SPORTING RIFLE – various calibers, set triggers, Mauser repeating action.

	$725	$650	$490	$425	$360	$325	$300	

RIFLES: SEMI-AUTO

MODEL 22SA SPORT – .22 LR cal., 21 1/4 in. barrel, 17 shot tube mag., pistol grip uncheckered wood or synthetic stock, ambidextrous manual safety, adj. rear fiber optic sight, rubber recoil pad, 3.3 lbs.

While advertised, this model has yet to go into production.

HÄMMERLI-WALTHER

Previously manufactured semi-auto target pistols made under joint effort from Hämmerli and Walther.

PISTOLS: SEMI-AUTO, RIMFIRE

MODEL 200 OLYMPIA – .22 Short or LR cal., 7 1/2 in. barrel, 1952 type, adj. sights, barrel weight, blue, checkered walnut grips. Mfg. 1952-58.

	$660	$605	$550	$440	$415	$385	$360	

MODEL 200 OLYMPIA – 1958 type, similar to 1952 type, except has muzzle brake. Mfg. 1958-63.

	$715	$605	$550	$495	$470	$415	$385	

MODEL 201 – similar to 200, 1952 type, except has 9 1/2 in. barrel. Mfg. 1955-57.

	$660	$605	$550	$440	$415	$385	$360	

MODEL 202 – similar to 201, except adj. heel grips. Mfg. 1955-57.

	$715	$605	$550	$495	$470	$415	$385	

MODEL 203 – similar to 200, except has adj. heel grip.

* ***Model 203 1955 Type*** – no muzzle brake.

	$715	$605	$550	$495	$470	$415	$385	

* ***Model 203 1958 Type*** – muzzle brake.

	$770	$660	$605	$550	$525	$470	$440	

MODEL 204 – similar to 200, except .22 LR cal. only.

* ***Model 204 1956 Type*** – no muzzle brake.

	$745	$635	$580	$525	$495	$470	$440	

* ***Model 204 1958 Type*** – muzzle brake.

	$800	$690	$635	$550	$525	$495	$470	

MODEL 205 – .22 LR cal., similar to 204, except has adj. heel grips.

* ***Model 205 1956 Type*** – no muzzle brake.

	$800	$690	$635	$550	$525	$495	$470	

* ***Model 205 1958 Type*** – muzzle brake.

	$855	$745	$715	$635	$580	$525	$495	

HARDENED ARMS

Previous manufacturer of custom AR-15 style firearms, parts, and accessories located in Friday Harbor, WA circa 2012-2019.

Please refer to BlueBookOfGunValues.com to order the *Blue Book of AR-15s & Variations*, available as a book or online subscription.

GRADING - PPGS™	100%	98%	95%	90%	80%	70%	60%	LAST MSR

HARDY

Current manufacturer of bolt action rifles located in New Zealand. Importation began 2020 by Legacy Sports International, LLC, located in Reno, NV.

RIFLES: BOLT ACTION

THE HYBRID – 6.5 PRC cal., switch barrel rifle, 24 in. carbon barrel, adj. trigger, square trigger guard, pistol grip, includes bolt and mag., black finish, 6.7 lbs. Importation began 2020.

MSR $6,600	$5,600	$4,900	$4,200	$3,800	$3,100	$2,500	$2,200	

HARRINGTON & RICHARDSON, INC.

Previous manufacturer located in Gardner, MA - formerly from Worcester, MA. Successors to Wesson & Harrington, manufactured from 1871 until January 24, 1986. H & R 1871, LLC was formed during 1991 (an entirely different company). H & R 1871, LLC is not responsible for the warranties or safety of older pre-1986 H & R firearms.

A manufacturer of utilitarian firearms for over 115 years, H & R ceased operation on January 24, 1986. Even though new manufacture (under H & R 1871, LLC) is utilizing the H & R trademark, the discontinuance of older models in either NIB or mint condition may command slight asking premiums, but probably will not affect values on those handguns only recently discontinued. Most H & R firearms are still purchased for their shooting value rather than collecting potential. In recent years, pre-1950s examples have become increasingly more collectible.

Further recent research indicates that many H&R frames were manufactured and stamped with serial numbers in the mid-1930s, but not assembled as complete guns until the WWII era. Therefore, H&R serial numbers alone will not always indicate the variation number.

Please refer to H & R listing in the Serialization section online at BlueBookOfGunValues.com for alphabetical suffix information on how to determine year of manufacture for most H & R firearms between 1940-1982.

The author would like to thank the late Mr. Jim Hauff and the late Mr. W.E. "Bill" Goforth for providing pricing and information on many of the H&R models.

PISTOLS: SEMI-AUTO

H&R SELF LOADING .25 ACP – .25 ACP cal., 6 shot mag. (magazines may be either blue, nickel, or in-the-white), 2 in. barrel, blue finish, markings on right side of slide "HARRINGTON & RICHARDSON ARMS CO. WORCESTER, MASS. U.S.A. PAT. AUG.20.'07. APRIL 13, 1909" in three lines on left side of slide, "H&R SELF-LOADING CALIBER 25" in two lines on left side of frame at rear ser. no., the ser. no. is in its own series numbered from 01 to about 16,500. One source lists manufacture date between 1912 and 1916, however, it was featured in the catalogs until 1920. Mfg. 1912-1920.

First Variation	$565	$485	$415	$355	$300	$250	$225	
Second Variation	$525	$465	$395	$340	$295	$250	$220	

The First Variation is serial numbered from 01 to approx. 10,000, with 12 slide serrations, magazine follower is flat and straight, right side of slide markings middle line is stretched out.

The Second Variation is serial numbered from approx. 10,000 to 16,500+, 16 slide serrations, magazine follower is curved and stepped at rear, right side of slide markings middle line compacted and in line with other markings.

H&R SELF LOADING .32 ACP – .32 ACP cal., 8 shot mag. (magazines with either be blue, nickel, or in-the-white), 3 1/2 in. barrel, blue finish, marking on right side of slide: "HARRINGTON & RICHARDSON ARMS CO. WORCESTER, MASS. U.S.A. PAT. AUG.20.'07. APRIL 13, 1909" in three lines, left side of slide "H&R SELF-LOADING CALIBER 32" in two lines at rear ser. no., the ser. no. is in its own series numbered 01 to approx. 34,500. Mfg. 1914-1924.

First Variation	$525	$465	$395	$340	$295	$250	$220	
Second Variation	$495	$435	$370	$320	$275	$235	$200	

The First Variation is serial numbered 01 to approx. 2,000, 12 slide serrations, magazine follower is flat and straight, on right side of slide markings, the middle line is stretched out.

The Second Variation is serial numbered approx. 2,000 to 34,500+, 16 slide serrations, magazine follower is curved and stepped at rear, on the right side of slide markings the middle line is compacted and in line with other markings.

In order to take advantage of the wartime shortage of handguns, H&R offered the remaining inventory of the .32 Self-Loader in the 1939 and 1940 catalogs. Since this model was not sold in ser. no. sequence, it is impossible to tell when any one pistol was shipped between 1914-1924 or 1939-1940.

HK-4 – please refer to listings under Heckler & Koch section.

GRADING - PPGS™	100%	98%	95%	90%	80%	70%	60%	LAST MSR

PISTOLS: SINGLE SHOT

HANDY GUN SMOOTH BORE – 28 ga. or .410 bore, smoothbore pistol with shotgun type break open action, blue finish, color case hardened frame, built on H&R's small frame Model 1915 Single Barrel Shotgun action, 28 ga. standard factory loads (early production 2 1/2 inch and late production 2 3/4 inch chamber), black and smokeless powder, .410 bore chambered for 2 1/2 inch shells, 8 and 12 1/4 inch barrel lengths, oversized uncheckered one-piece walnut saw handle grips, detachable wire stock offered after 1932. Serial number in a separate series from 01 up to about 54,000 with both gauges in the same series classified by the government as NFA Curio & Relic, if registered with the ATF. Guns not already registered are illegal to own and subject to seizure. Mfg. 1924-1934.

Legal smooth bore Handy Guns are typically priced between $1,200-$2,500, depending on original condition.

After 1930 listed in catalogs as HANDY GUN No. 141 SINGLE SHOT SMOOTH BORE .410 BORE. After 1930 listed in catalogs as HANDY GUN No. 128 SINGLE SHOT SMOOTH BORE .28 GAUGE.

HANDY GUN RIFLED BARREL – .22 LR or .32-20 WCF cal., blue finish with color case hardened frame, shotgun type break open action, built on H&R's small frame Model 1915 Single Barrel Shotgun action, 12 1/4 in. barrel, oversized one-piece checkered rounded walnut grips, short uncheckered walnut forend, .22 LR is serial numbered in a separate series 1 (or 101) to approx. 300, and .32-20 in same series as smoothbores. Mfg. 1931-1934.

This model is rarely seen, and legal original specimens are typically valued in the $1,250-$2,250 range.

Listed in catalog as HANDY GUN No. 122 SINGLE SHOT RIFLED BARREL .22 RF CALIBER, and as HANDY GUN No. 132 SINGLE SHOT RIFLED BARREL .32-20 WCF CALIBER.

MODEL 195 H&R SINGLE SHOT PISTOL TOP BREAK (aka U.S.R.A. MODEL) – .22 LR cal., large frame, blue finish, oversized checkered walnut grips, adj. sights, automatic ejector, serial number location is on the front of the grip strap or on the left side of the grip frame under the grips and on the bottom of the breech block, original production has a 10 inch barrel only, later production could be ordered with a 7 or 8 in. barrel, plastic, walnut, or birds-head grips (this model is referred to by collectors as "Rice Frame"), serial numbered in its own series from 01 up to about 40,000, after 1930 this model is known as the U.S.R.A. Model. Mfg. 1928-1942.

	100%	98%	95%	90%	80%	70%	60%
	N/A	N/A	$1,800	$1,475	$1,000	$775	$625

Add 25% for rare square plate type ejector.
Add $300 for fitted case and accessories.

There are many sub-variations of this model due to special orders and factory reworks.

First Variation; two piece walnut grips, round ribbed barrel with non-adj. front sight, 10 inch barrel only - 1928.

Second variation; features a plunger type (round head) ejector, one-piece walnut grips - 1928-1929.

Third Variation; grooved trigger, name and model markings changed to U.S.R.A. Model 195 -1930.

Fourth Variation; 7 inch barrel length added, new front & rear sight and different shaped rib - 1931-1932.

Fifth Variation; grooved trigger, new barrel shape - 1933-1934.

Sixth variation; lever type automatic ejector - 1935-1942.

REVOLVERS: SINGLE ACTION SPUR TRIGGER, 1871-1883

WESSON & HARRINGTON MARKED SINGLE ACTION SPUR TRIGGER (BLACK POWDER) – .22 Short, .32 rimfire, .38 rimfire, or .41 rimfire cal., 5 or 7 shot, 2 1/2 (Third type), 3 3/16 (First type, No. 3), or 3 1/2 in. octagon barrel, First type has brass frame silver-plated, patented cartridge ejector, bird's head grip frame, rosewood grips, Second type has iron frame nickel-plated patented cartridge ejector, bird's head grip frame, rosewood grips, Third type has iron frame nickel-plated bird's head grip frame, no cartridge ejector pull pin cylinder release. No. 2 is 7 shot, .22 Short, small frame, 3 3/16 in. octagon barrel, No. 3 is 5 shot, .32 rimfire cal., medium frame, 3 3/16 octagon barrel, No. 4 is 5 shot, .38 rimfire cal., large frame, 3 1/2 in. octagon barrel. Both First and Second type will be marked with Feb.7 and June 13, 1871 patent dates. Mfg. 1871-1876.

	100%	98%	95%	90%	80%	70%	60%
First Type (rare)	$1,200	$1,000	$865	$765	$660	$575	$495
Second Type No. 2, 3, & 4	$600	$520	$440	$390	$340	$285	$245
Third Type	$400	$350	$300	$265	$225	$190	$165

Add 50% for late production with Harrington & Richardson barrel markings.

H&R MODEL 1 SPUR TRIGGER SINGLE ACTION (BLACK POWDER) – .32 or .38 rimfire cal., 5 or 7 shot, pull pin cylinder release, 3 inch octagon barrel, bird's head grip frame, hard rubber grip panels, only slightly changed version of the Wesson & Harrington Third Type marked with patent date May 23, 1876. Mfg. 1876-1883.

	100%	98%	95%	90%	80%	70%	60%
	$500	$440	$375	$325	$275	$235	$200

GRADING - PPGS™	100%	98%	95%	90%	80%	70%	60%	LAST MSR

H&R SPUR TRIGGER SINGLE ACTION (BLACK POWDER) - pull pin cylinder release, nickel finish only, most will be marked with patent date May 23, 1876 and company name and address on left side of barrel, sometimes called "New Design of 1878", saw handle grip. Mfg. 1878-1883.

Subtract 50%-70% for models not marked H&R.

The above model as well as modified Wesson & Harrington Models can be found marked with the following Brand Names: AETNA, VICTOR, BANGUP, CROWN, EAGLE, ELY & WRAY, GREAT WESTERN, PANTHER, SMOKY CITY and maybe more names.

* ***Model 1 1/2*** - .32 rimfire cal. 5 shot, 2 1/2 in. octagon barrel (actual barrel length may vary slightly), medium frame.

  $400 $350 $300 $265 $225 $190 $165

* ***Model 2 1/2*** - .32 rimfire cal., 7 shot, 3 1/4 in. octagon barrel (actual barrel length may vary slightly), large frame.

  $400 $350 $300 $265 $225 $190 $165

* ***Model 3 1/2*** - .38 rimfire cal., 5 shot, 3 1/2 in. octagon barrel (actual barrel length may vary slightly), large frame.

  $400 $350 $300 $265 $225 $190 $165

* ***Model 4 1/2*** - .41 rimfire cal., 5 shot, 3 1/2 in. octagon barrel (actual barrel length may vary slightly), large frame, rare.

  $700 $600 $525 $450 $385 $340 $285

REVOLVERS: SOLID FRAME, 1880-1952

MODEL 1880 MEDIUM DOUBLE ACTION, (BLACK POWDER) - .32 or .38 centerfire cal., 5 or 6 shot, 2 1/2 in. round barrel, nickel finish, pull pin cylinder release, side plate on left side of frame, hard rubber grip panels with floral design, marked with patent date January 20, 1880 and company name and address on left side of barrel. Mfg. 1880-1883.

$550 $475 $415 $360 $315 $265 $230

AMERICAN DOUBLE ACTION FIRST MODEL, (BLACK POWDER) - .32, .38, or .44 cal., 5 (.38 or .44) or 6 (.32 cal.) shot, 2 1/2, 4 1/2, or 6 in. barrel, nickel (standard) or blue (rare) finish, pull pin cylinder release, marked on top strap "THE AMERICAN DOUBLE ACTION", first variation has round barrel and nickel trigger guard with rear retaining pin offset to rear slightly (1884 only), second variation has round barrel and nickel trigger guard (1884-1887), third variation has octagon barrel and nickel trigger guard (1888-1897), fourth variation has octagon barrel, blue trigger guard and company name and address on left side of barrel (1898-1904). Mfg. 1884-1904.

$225 $195 $170 $140 $125 $110 $95

Add 50% for first variation (rare).
Add 15% for blue finish.
Add 10% for 4 1/2 or 6 in. barrel.
Add 5%-10% for nickel trigger guard (pre-1898 mfg.).

BULLDOG FIRST MODEL LARGE FRAME (BLACK POWDER) - .32 or .38 rimfire cal., 5 (.38 cal.) or 6 (.32 cal.) shot, 2 1/2, 4 1/2, or 6 in. barrel, variation of the American Double Action First Model marked on the top strap "H&R BULL DOG". Mfg. 1888-1904.

$235 $200 $180 $150 $125 $110 $95

SAFETY HAMMER DOUBLE ACTION FIRST MODEL (BLACK POWDER) - .32, .38, or .44 cal., 5 (.38 or .44) or 6 (.32 cal.) shot, 2 1/2, 4 1/2, or 6 in. barrel, nickel (standard) or blue (rare) finish, patented spurless hammer, marked on top strap "SAFETY HAMMER DOUBLE ACTION". Mfg. 1888-1904.

$235 $200 $180 $150 $125 $110 $95

AMERICAN DOUBLE ACTION SECOND MODEL (SMOKELESS POWDER) - .32, .38, or .44 Webley (disc. 1921) cal., 5 (.38 or .44 cal.) or 6 (.32 cal.) shot, 2 1/2, 4 1/2, or 6 in. barrel, nickel or blue finish, pull pin cylinder release, the difference between First Model and Second Model is the caliber markings on the left side of the barrel, .44 Webley has a larger frame, after 1930 this model was listed in catalogs as: AMERICAN DOUBLE ACTION No. 60 .32 Caliber 6 shot, and AMERICAN DOUBLE ACTION No. 65 .38 Caliber 5 shot. Mfg. 1905-1941.

$225 $195 $170 $140 $125 $110 $95

Add 15% for blue finish or 10% for 4 1/2 or 6 in. barrel.

BULLDOG SECOND MODEL LARGE FRAME (SMOKELESS POWDER) - .32 or .38 rimfire cal., 5 (.38 cal.) or 6 (.32 cal.) shot, 2 1/2, 4 1/2, or 6 in. barrel, nickel or blue finish, variation of the American Double Action Second Model, except the top strap is marked "H&R BULL DOG". Mfg. 1905-1923.

$235 $200 $180 $150 $125 $110 $95

GRADING - PPGS™	100%	98%	95%	90%	80%	70%	60%	LAST MSR

SAFETY HAMMER DOUBLE ACTION SECOND MODEL (SMOKELESS POWDER) - .32, .38, or .44 Webley (disc. 1921) cal., 5 (.38 or .44 cal.) or 6 (.32 cal.) shot, 2 1/2, 4 1/2, or 6 in. barrel, nickel or blue finish, patented spurless hammer, patent date may be marked on hammer, and the top strap is marked "SAFETY HAMMER DOUBLE ACTION". Mfg. 1904-1940.

	$235	$200	$180	$150	$125	$110	$95

VEST POCKET FIRST MODEL MEDIUM FRAME (BLACK POWDER) - .32 S&W cal., 5 shot, 1 1/4 in. round or 2 in. octagon barrel (rare), double action, pull pin cylinder release, spurless hammer, blue (rare) or nickel finish, markings on top strap are "VEST POCKET SELF COCKER" "VEST POCKET SAFETY HAMMER" or "VEST POCKET". The First Variation has 1 1/4 in. round or 2 in. octagon barrel, nickel finish and nickel trigger guard (mfg. 1891-1897), the Second Variation has 1 1/4 in. round or 2 in. octagon barrel, nickel finish, and a blue trigger guard (mfg. 1897-1904). Mfg. 1891-1904.

	$215	$195	$165	$135	$120	$100	$90

Add 50% for 2 in. octagon barrel or 15% for blue finish.

VEST POCKET SECOND MODEL SMALL FRAME (SMOKELESS POWDER) - .22 rimfire cal., 7 shot, 1 1/4 in. round barrel, spurless hammer, nickel or blue finish, pull pin cylinder release, top strap markings are "VEST POCKET SAFETY HAMMER" or "VEST POCKET". The company name and address is marked on bottom of butt. After 1930 the catalog listing is "VEST POCKET No. 77", .22 rimfire caliber, 7 shots. Mfg. 1905-1941.

	$220	$190	$165	$140	$125	$110	$95

Add 5% for blue finish.

See American Double Actions for the differences between the First and Second models.

VEST POCKET SECOND MODEL MEDIUM FRAME (SMOKELESS POWDER) - .32 S&W cal., 5 shot, 1 1/4 in. round barrel, spurless hammer, medium frame, nickel or blue finish. Mfg. 1905-1941.

	$195	$175	$155	$125	$110	$95	$85

Add 15% for blue finish.

This model is similar to the Small Frame model.

YOUNG AMERICA DOUBLE ACTION FIRST MODEL (BLACK POWDER) - .22 rimfire or .32 S&W cal., 2, 4 1/2, or 6 in. round or octagon barrel, small (.22 cal.) or medium (.32 cal.) frame, pull pin cylinder release, nickel or blue (rare) finish, marking on top strap only "YOUNG AMERICA DOUBLE ACTION" or "YOUNG AMERICAN DOUBLE ACTION". The First Variation has a round barrel and nickel trigger guard (mfg. 1884-1887), the Second Variation has an octagon barrel and nickel trigger guard (mfg. 1888-1897), Third Variation has octagon barrel, blue trigger guard and company name and address on left side of barrel (mfg. 1897-1904). Mfg. 1884-1904.

First Variation	$300	$275	$245	$210	$170	$145	$120
Second & Third Variations	$250	$225	$195	$170	$140	$125	$110

Add 15% for blue finish or 10% for 4 1/2 or 6 in. barrel.

YOUNG AMERICA SAFETY HAMMER FIRST MODEL (BLACK POWDER) - .22 rimfire or .32 S&W cal., 2, 4 1/2, or 6 in. round or octagon barrel, small (.22 cal.) or medium (.32 cal.) frame, nickel or blue (rare) finish, spurless hammer, pull pin cylinder release, top strap only is marked "YOUNG AMERICA DOUBLE ACTION" or "YOUNG AMERICAN DOUBLE ACTION". Mfg. 1884-1904.

	$235	$200	$180	$150	$125	$110	$95

YOUNG AMERICA BULLDOG FIRST MODEL MEDIUM FRAME (BLACK POWDER) - .32 Short rimfire cal., 5 shot. Mfg. 1888-1904.

	$235	$200	$180	$150	$125	$110	$95

YOUNG AMERICA DOUBLE ACTION SECOND MODEL SMALL FRAME (SMOKELESS POWDER) - .22 Short cal., 7 shot, 2, 4 1/2, or 6 in. barrel, pull pin cylinder release, nickel or blue finish, caliber and company name and address marked on side of barrel, top strap will be marked "YOUNG AMERICA DOUBLE ACTION" or "YOUNG AMERICAN DOUBLE ACTION". After 1930 listed in catalogs as: YOUNG AMERICA No. 70 DOUBLE ACTION. Mfg. 1905-1941.

	$250	$235	$200	$180	$150	$125	$110

Add 15% for blue finish or 10% for 4 1/2 or 6 in. barrel.

See American Double Actions for the differences between the First and Second models.

YOUNG AMERICA DOUBLE ACTION SECOND MODEL MEDIUM FRAME (SMOKELESS POWDER) - .32 S&W cal., 5 shot, 2, 4 1/2 or 6 in. barrel, pull pin cylinder release, nickel or blue finish, caliber and company name and address marked on side of barrel, top strap will be marked "YOUNG AMERICA

GRADING - PPGS™	100%	98%	95%	90%	80%	70%	60%	LAST MSR

DOUBLE ACTION" or "YOUNG AMERICAN DOUBLE ACTION". After 1930 listed in catalogs as: YOUNG AMERICA No. 73 DOUBLE ACTION .32 Rimfire short 5 shot and YOUNG AMERICA No. 74 DOUBLE ACTION .32 S&W 5 shot. Mfg. 1905-1941.

	$250	$225	$195	$170	$140	$125	$110

Add 15% for blue finish or 10% for 4 1/2 or 6 in. barrel.

See American Double Actions for the differences between the First and Second models.

YOUNG AMERICA BULLDOG MEDIUM FRAME SECOND MODEL (SMOKELESS POWDER) – .32 Rimfire cal., 5 shot. Mfg. 1905-1923.

	$225	$195	$170	$140	$125	$110	$95

This model was only advertised as a separate model until 1923.

YOUNG AMERICA SAFETY HAMMER MEDIUM FRAME SECOND MODEL (SMOKELESS POWDER) – .32 S&W cal., 5 shot. Mfg. 1905-1939.

	$205	$185	$165	$130	$120	$100	$90

This model was only advertised as a separate model until 1939.

VICTOR (BRAND NAME VERSION OF AMERICAN DOUBLE ACTION AND YOUNG AMERICA DOUBLE ACTION SERIES, SMOKELESS POWDER) – .32 S&W Long or .38 S&W cal., 5 (.38 cal.) or 6 (.32 cal.) shot, 2 1/2 or 4 1/2 in. round barrel (Large Solid Frame), .32 S&W cal., 5 shot, 2 or 4 in. barrel (Medium Solid Frame Double Action), or .22 rimfire cal., 7 shot, 2 or 4 in. barrel (Small Solid Frame Double Action), marked "VICTOR DOUBLE ACTION" and have a round barrel and unfluted cylinder, pull pin cylinder release, and may have company name and address marked on frame or bottom of the butt (not listed in any H&R catalogs). Mfg. 1913-1936.

	$195	$175	$155	$125	$110	$95	$85

MODEL 1904 LARGE SOLID FRAME DOUBLE ACTION (SMOKELESS POWDER) – .38 S&W cal., 5 shot, 2 1/2, 4 1/2 or 6 in. barrel, hard rubber target logo grips, pull pin cylinder release, blue or nickel finish, marked with company name and address on left side of the barrel and on top strap in two lines "H&R DOUBLE ACTION MODEL 1904 .38 CAL.", after 1930 listed in catalogs as: H&R MODEL 4 DOUBLE ACTION No. 83 .38 S&W CALIBER 5 shot. Mfg. 1905-1941.

	$230	$195	$175	$150	$125	$110	$95

MODEL 04 LARGE SOLID FRAME DOUBLE ACTION – .32 S&W cal., 6 shot, 2 1/2, 4 1/2 or 6 in. barrel, pull pin cylinder release, blue or nickel finish, hard rubber target logo grips, marked with company name and address on left side of barrel and on top strap in two lines "H&R DOUBLE ACTION MODEL 04 .32 6 SHOT". After 1930 listed in catalogs as: H&R MODEL 4 DOUBLE ACTION No. 80 .32 S&W Long Caliber 6 shot. Mfg. 1905-1941.

	$220	$190	$165	$140	$125	$110	$95

MODEL 1905 MEDIUM SOLID FRAME DOUBLE ACTION – .32 S&W cal., 5 shot, 2 1/2, 4 1/2, or 6 in. barrel, pull pin cylinder release, hard rubber target logo grips, blue or nickel finish, marked with company name and address on left side of barrel and on top strap in two lines "H&R DOUBLE ACTION MODEL 1905 .32 CAL." After 1930 listed in catalogs as: H&R MODEL 5 DOUBLE ACTION No. 90 .32 S&W CALIBER 5 shot. Mfg. 1905-1941.

	$225	$195	$170	$140	$125	$110	$95

MODEL 1906 SMALL SOLID FRAME DOUBLE ACTION – .22 rimfire cal., 7 shot, 2 1/2, 4 1/2, or 6 in. barrel, hard rubber target logo grips, blue or nickel finish, marked with the company name and address on left side of barrel and on top strap in two lines "H&R MODEL 1906 22 CAL. R.F." After 1930 listed in catalogs as: H&R MODEL 6 DOUBLE ACTION No. 96 .22 RF CALIBER 7 shot. Mfg. 1905-1941.

	$185	$165	$140	$120	$100	$90	$80

TRAPPER SMALL SOLID FRAME DOUBLE ACTION – .22 rimfire cal., 7 shot, 6 in. octagon barrel, two-piece oversize walnut grips, pull pin cylinder release, blue finish only, marked "H&R TRAPPER" on the top strap. After 1930 listed in catalogs as: TRAPPER MODEL 722 SMALL SOLID FRAME DOUBLE ACTION .22 RIMFIRE 7 shot. Mfg. 1924-1941.

	$365	$315	$275	$225	$200	$165	$140

HUNTER SMALL SOLID FRAME DOUBLE ACTION – .22 rimfire cal., 2 1/2 (rare) or 10 in. octagon barrel, 7 shot, also mfg. with round frame (rare), two-piece oversize walnut or small two-piece target logo hard rubber (2 1/2 in. barrel only) grips, pull pin cylinder release, blue finish only, marked "H&R HUNTER" on the top strap, some with the "HUNTER" marking were assembled late in production with short 2 1/2 inch barrel and the small two-piece Target Logo hard rubber grips. Mfg. 1926-1929.

	$475	$425	$355	$300	$260	$220	$195

GRADING - PPGS™	100%	98%	95%	90%	80%	70%	60%	LAST MSR

HUNTER LARGE SOLID FRAME DOUBLE ACTION – .22 rimfire cal., 9 shot, (built on the M922 frame), 10 in. octagon barrel only, pull pin cylinder release, blue finish only, two-piece oversize walnut grips, marked on top strap "H&R HUNTER" or just "HUNTER". After 1930 catalogs listed as: MODEL 933 DOUBLE ACTION. Mfg. 1929-1939.

	$565	$485	$415	$360	$310	$260	$225	

MODEL 922 DOUBLE ACTION FIRST MODEL LARGE SOLID FRAME – .22 rimfire cal., 6 in. octagon barrel, pull pin cylinder release, 9 shot, two-piece oversize walnut saw handle grips, marked with company name and address on top of barrel, right side of barrel marked H&R 922 and caliber marked on left side of barrel, blue finish. Mfg. 1927-1952.

	$195	$175	$150	$125	$110	$95	$85	

Add 40% for First Variation, or 20% for Second, Third, Fourth, or Fifth Variations.

First Variation 1927-1930, approx. serial number range 124,270-143,000.

Second Variation 1931, Difference: new grip shape (saw handle shape eliminated) approx. serial number range 144000-160000.

Third Variation 1932-1937, Difference: new safety cylinder, approx. serial number range 160000-171000.

Fourth Variation 1938-1939, Difference: new grip frame and round barrel, approx. serial number range 171000-192000.

Fifth Variation 1940- 1947, Difference: same as 4th variation except letter code prefix to serial number A thru H.

Sixth Variation 1948-1949, Difference: a new barrel length, serial number letter codes I and J.

Seventh Variation 1949-1952, Difference: all-in-one cartridge extraction system, serial number letter codes J thru M.

Eighth Variation 1952, models for M922 Camper and M922 Bantam weight (see Revolvers: Recent Mfg.).

MODEL 923 DOUBLE ACTION FIRST MODEL LARGE SOLID FRAME – .22 rimfire cal., 6 in. barrel, similar to Model 922 Sixth and Seventh Variations, except has chrome finish. Mfg. 1949-1952.

	$205	$185	$165	$135	$120	$100	$90	

The Model 923 Sixth Variation has serial number letter codes I and J (mfg. 1948-1949), and the Seventh Variation features an all-in-one cartridge extraction system, and has serial number letter codes J thru M (mfg. 1949-1952).

REVOLVERS: TOP BREAK, 1885-1952

MANUAL EJECTING MODEL (MANUAL SHELL EXTRACTOR, BLACK POWDER) – .32 S&W or .38 S&W cal., 5 (.38 cal.) or 6 (.32 cal.) shot, 3 1/4 in. barrel, manual ejector rod under barrel, hard rubber grip panels with floral design, nickel finish, modified American Double Action mechanism and frame, first variation marked on top of barrel with company name and address only, and two guide rods for ejector (1885-1887), second variation has patent date 10-4-87 marked on top of barrel along with company name and address, extractor does not have guide rods (1887-1889). Mfg. 1885-1889.

	$525	$465	$395	$340	$295	$250	$220	

MANUAL EJECTING SECOND MODEL BLACK POWDER – .32 S&W or .38 S&W cal., 5 or 6 shot, new frame (same as Second Model Auto Ejecting), 3 1/4 in. barrel, hard rubber grips with Target Logo, nickel or blue finish, one patent date marking, very rare. Mfg. 1890 - disc.

	$600	$520	$440	$390	$340	$285	$245	

AUTOMATIC EJECTING FIRST MODEL (BLACK POWDER) – .32 S&W or .38 S&W cal., 5 (.38 cal.) or 6 shot cylinder, hard rubber grip panels with floral design, 3 1/4 in. barrel, modified American Double Action mechanism and frame, nickel finish, First Variation marked on top of barrel with company name and address only and two guide rods for ejector (1885-1886), Second Variation patent date 10-4-87 marked on top of barrel along with company name and address, extractor does not have extra guide rods (1887-1889). Mfg. 1885-1889.

	$325	$285	$250	$200	$175	$150	$125	

Add 30% for First Variation.

Factory 2, 5, and 6 inch barrel examples were seen in 2011.

AUTOMATIC EJECTING MODEL 1 1/2 (BLACK POWDER) – .32 S&W or .38 S&W cal., different double action mechanism, trigger, trigger guard and hammer, 5 (.38 S&W cal.) or 6 (.32 S&W cal.) shot, new frame, nickel or blue finish, hard rubber grips with Target Logo, 3 1/4 in. barrel, marked with two patent date 10-04-87 and 12-25-88 (only revolver to use this date), rare. Mfg. 1889-1890.

	$600	$520	$440	$390	$340	$285	$245	

A second variation was found in 2011 with a new frame and Target Logo grips, rare. Mfg. 1890-unknown.

GRADING - PPGS™	100%	98%	95%	90%	80%	70%	60%	LAST MSR

AUTOMATIC EJECTING SECOND MODEL (BLACK POWDER) – .32 S&W or .38 S&W cal., 5 (.38 S&W cal.) or 6 (.32 S&W cal.) shot, new frame shape and new hard rubber grip panels with target logo, nickel or blue finish, 2 1/2 (rare), 3 1/4 (standard), 4, 5, or 6 in. barrel, if there is no caliber marking on the left side of the barrel, then it was manufactured for black powder, top of barrel markings include company name and address and patent dates. Mfg. 1890-1904.

$300 $195 $170 $140 $125 $110 $95

Add 75% for 2 1/2 in. barrel or 25% for 4, 5, or 6 in. barrels.
Add 15% for blue finish.
Add 10% for First, Second, Third, or Fourth Variations with nickel trigger guard and nickel finish.

First Variation; one patent date OCT-4-87 only (1890-1892).

Second Variation one patent date marked OCT-4-1887 (year marked in full) (1890-1892*).

Third Variation three patent dates, Oct-4-1887, May 14 & Aug-6-89 (1893-Only*).

Fourth Variation three patent dates Oct-4-87, May-14 & Aug-6-89 (note 87 date does not have full year markings) (1894-1896*).

Fifth Variation five patent dates Oct-4-87, May 14 & Aug-6-89, April-2-95, April-7-96 (1897-1904*).

*Serial numbers found on the bottom side of the top strap will have letter codes.

AUTOMATIC EJECTING POLICE SECOND MODEL (BLACK POWDER) – similar to Auto-Ejecting Second model except has a patented spurless Hammer, the Police Model will be found in all variations and calibers of the Second Model. Mfg. 1890-1904.

$235 $200 $180 $150 $125 $110 $95

AUTOMATIC EJECTING THIRD MODEL (SMOKELESS POWDER) – .32 S&W Long or .38 S&W cal., 5 (.38 cal.) or 6 (.32 cal.) shot, hard rubber grip panels with target logo, blue or nickel finish, 2 1/2 (rare), 3 1/4 (standard), 4, 5 or 6 in. barrel, top of barrel markings include company name, address, and early production has patent dates, the one recognizable difference in the Second and Third Models is the caliber marking on the left side of the barrel on the Third Model, which indicates it was manufactured for smokeless powder. Mfg. 1905-1940.

$235 $200 $180 $150 $125 $110 $95

Add 75% for 2 1/2 in. barrel, or 25% for 4, 5, or 6 in. barrel.
Add 15% for blue finish.

First Variation 4 patent dates (5-14 & 8-6-89, 4-2-95, 4-7-97) model name and caliber on left side of barrel (1905-1908).

Second Variation 2 patent dates (8-6-89 and 10-8-95) model name and caliber on left side of barrel (1909-1912).

Third Variation no patent dates the name of the state is marked as MASS (1913-1915).

Fourth Variation no patent dates the state name of Massachusetts is spelled out (1916-1924).

Fifth Variation new grip frame, it is now the same size as the rest of the frame with no step down for the grip panel (1925-1941).

After 1931 listed in Catalogs as: AUTOMATIC EJECTING No. 10 .32 S&W LONG CALIBER 6 shots.

After 1931 listed in Catalogs as: AUTOMATIC EJECTING No. 25 .38 S&W CALIBER 5 shots.

After 1932 listed in Catalogs as: AUTOMATIC EJECTING No. 20. .38 S&W CALIBER 5 shots.

AUTOMATIC EJECTING POLICE THIRD MODEL (SMOKELESS POWDER) – similar to Auto-Ejecting Third Model except has a patented spurless hammer, Police Model will be found in all variations and calibers of the Third Model until 1939. Mfg. 1905-1939.

$275 $215 $185 $150 $125 $110 $95

AUTOMATIC EJECTING KNIFE MODEL – similar to regular Auto-Ejector Model except 4 in. barrel with a 2 1/4 inch double edge knife attached under the barrel, 6 (.32 S&W) and 5 (.38 S&W) shot, only finish listed in catalogs was nickel but some blue finish examples have been observed, Second Model Black Powder mfg. 1901-1904, Third Model Smokeless Powder mfg. 1905-1917.

$2,000 $1,700 $1,500 $1,150 $850 $700 $625

Add 10% for blue finish.
Subtract 60% if knife is missing.

.22 SPECIAL LARGE FRAME TOP BREAK – .22 rimfire or .22 WRF cal., 6 in. barrel, 7 or 9 shot, blue finish, two-piece walnut grips (after 1932 one-piece grips). Mfg. 1925-1941.

$330 $290 $255 $200 $175 $150 $125

Add 50% for .22 WRF cal., 15% for First Variation, or 10% for Fourth and Fifth Variation.

First Variation, 7 shot, .22 rimfire only, oversized 2 piece saw handle shaped walnut grips (serial number range above 490000*) (1926-1928).

GRADING - PPGS™	100%	98%	95%	90%	80%	70%	60%	LAST MSR

Second Variation, 9 shot, .22 rimfire and 7 shot, 22WRF, (serial number range 497000-559100*) (1928-1930).

Third Variation, new rounded two-piece grip (saw handle grip eliminated) (serial number range unknown) (1931-1932).

Fourth Variation, safety cylinder and new grip frame (RICE FRAME) (serial number range 559100-590000*) (1933-1938).

Fifth Variation, automatic cylinder stop (serial number range above 590000*) (1939-1942).

After 1930 listed in catalogs as: MODEL 944 LARGE FRAME TOP BREAK .22 RIMFIRE CALIBER 9 shots.

After 1930 listed in catalogs as: MODEL 945 LARGE FRAME TOP BREAK .22 Winchester Rim Fire CALIBER 7 shots.

22 EXPERT LARGE FRAME TOP BREAK – similar to .22 Special Large Frame Top Break, except has 10 in. barrel. Mfg. 1927-1941.

	$430	$370	$320	$275	$235	$195	$175

Add 50% for .22 WRF cal.

After 1930 listed in catalogs as: MODEL 955 LARGE FRAME TOP BREAK .22 RIMFIRE CALIBER 9 shot, or MODEL 956 LARGE FRAME TOP BREAK .22WRF CALIBER 7 shot.

H&R BOBBY LARGE FRAME TOP BREAK – .32 or .38 centerfire cal., double action, 5 or 6 shot, round ribbed 4 inch barrel, fixed sights, blue finish, one-piece oversize checkered walnut grips (some furnished with one-piece plastic grips), free wheeling cylinder, only the .32 caliber seems to have been purchased by London's Metropolitan Police, these will be marked MK-II, on the top strap as well as having the company name and address on the top of the barrel rib, No. 15 model is .32 cal. 6 shot, No. 25 model is .38 cal. 5 shot, own serial number range, OAL. 9 inches, 23 oz. Mfg. 1939-1942.

	$300	$255	$220	$175	$150	$125	$115

Add 100% for Metropolitan Police marked model (MK-II on top strap, M.P. P on front of grip frame.
Subtract $25 for plastic grips.

H&R HAMMERLESS FIRST MODEL LARGE FRAME TOP BREAK (BLACK POWDER) – .38 S&W cal., 5 shot, double action, double top post barrel latch, nickel or blue finish, hard rubber grips with a Target Logo at the top, 3 1/4 (standard), 4, 5 or 6 in. barrel, rebounding hammer; automatic cylinder stop, top of barrel is marked with the same 5 patent dates as the Auto-Ejector Second Model 5th Variation, no caliber markings on left side of barrel means designed for black powder cartridge pressures only. Mfg. 1899-1904.

	$295	$260	$220	$180	$160	$140	$120

Add 10% for blue finish or 20% for 4, 5, or 6 in. barrel.

Serial number range is approximately 01* to 45000* (No letter codes): Highest known 43308 (* Estimate).

H&R HAMMERLESS SECOND MODEL LARGE FRAME TOP BREAK (SMOKELESS POWDER) – .38 S&W cal., 5 shot, double top post barrel latch, nickel or blue finish, grips are hard rubber with a target logo at the top; 3 1/4 (standard), 4, 5, or 6 in. barrel, rebounding hammer, automatic cylinder stop, cylinder was lengthened to take the .32 S&W long cartridge and the catalogs now listed the calibers as: 6 shot .32 S&W, .32 S&W Long, .32 Colt New Police cartridges, also offered in 5 shot .38 S&W and .38 Colt New Police, caliber marked on left side of barrel, designed for smokeless powder cartridge. Mfg. 1905-1941.

	$325	$285	$250	$200	$175	$150	$125

Add 10% for blue finish. Add 20% for 4, 5, or 6 in. barrel.

First variation, 5 patent dates same as First model with caliber marked on left side of barrel, serial number range 45000*-55000* (estimate) - 1905.

Second Variation, patent dates, 5-14 & 8-6-89, 4-2-95, 4-7-96, serial number range: 55000*- 100000*(estimate) - 1906-1908.

Third Variation, patent dates 8-6-1889, 10-8-1895, serial number range: 100000*-120000*(estimate) - 1909-1912.

Fourth Variation, no patent dates, state in address not spelled out (MASS.), serial number range: 120000*-160000*(estimate) - 1913-1915.

Fifth Variation, no patent dates, state name in address is spelled out (MASSACHUSETTS), serial number range: 160000*-190000*(estimate) - 1916-1924.

Sixth Variation, new grip frame same as Auto-Ejector, serial number range: unknown - 1925-1940.

There is some indication production of the hammerless model stopped somewhere in the early 1920's but it was carried in catalogs until 1941.

After 1930 listed in Catalogs as: H&R HAMMERLESS No. 50 TOP BREAK .32 S&W LONG 6 shot.

After 1930 listed in Catalogs as: H&R HAMMERLESS No. 55 TOP BREAK .38 S&W 5 shot.

GRADING - PPGS™	100%	98%	95%	90%	80%	70%	60%	LAST MSR

H&R HAMMERLESS FIRST MODEL SMALL FRAME TOP BREAK (BLACK POWDER) – .32 S&W cal., 5 shot, double top post barrel latch, nickel or blue finish, hard rubber grips with a Target Logo at the top, 3 1/4 (standard), 4, 5, or 6 in. barrel, rebounding hammer, automatic cylinder stop, no caliber markings on left side of barrel, designed for black powder cartridge pressures. Mfg. 1899-1904.

	$255	$225	$195	$155	$130	$115	$100	

Add 10% for blue finish. Add 20% for 4, 5, or 6 in. barrel.

First Variation, patent dates 10-4-87, 4-2-95, 4-7-96, serial number range: 01*-82000* (Estimate) - 1899-1903.

Second Variation, patent dates 5-14-89,4-2-95, 4-6-96, serial number range: 82000*-90000* (Estimate) - 1904.

H&R HAMMERLESS BICYCLE FIRST MODEL – .32 S&W cal., 5 shot, similar to H&R Hammerless First Model, except has 2 in. barrel only. Mfg. 1899-1904.

	$275	$245	$210	$170	$145	$120	$110	

Add 10% for blue finish.

H&R HAMMERLESS SECOND MODEL SMALL FRAME TOP BREAK (SMOKELESS POWDER) – .22 rimfire or .32 S&W cal., 5 (.32 cal.) or 7 (.22 cal.) shot, double top post barrel latch, nickel or blue finish, hard rubber grips with Target Logo at the top, 3 (standard), 4, 5, or 6 in. barrel, rebounding hammer, automatic cylinder stop, caliber marking on left side of barrel, designed for smokeless powder cartridge pressures only. Mfg. 1905-1941.

	$265	$235	$200	$160	$135	$110	$100	

Add 10% for blue finish. Add 20% for 4, 5, or 6 in. barrel, or 20% for .22 rimfire cal.

First Variation, patent dates 5-14-89, 4-2-95, 4-7-96, serial number range: 90000*-100000* (estimate) - 1905-1906.

Second Variation, patent dates 4-2-95, 4-7-96, serial number range: 100000*-120000* (estimate) - 1907-1909.

Third Variation, patent date 10-8-95, serial number range: 120000*-180000* (estimate) - 1910-1913.

Fourth Variation, no patent dates, small font used for company name, serial number range: 180000*-190000* (estimate) - 1914.

Fifth variation, large font used in company name and state not spelled out (MASS), serial number range: 190000*-200000* (estimate) - 1915.

Sixth Variation, state name in address spelled out (MASSACHUSETTS), serial number range: 200000*-220000* (estimate) - 1916-1924.

Seventh Variation, new grip frame, it is now same width as rest of frame, no step down for grips, serial number range: unknown - 1925-1942.

After 1930 listed in catalogs as: HAMMERLESS No. 40 TOP BREAK .22 Rimfire 7 shot.

After 1930 listed in catalogs as: HAMMERLESS No. 45 TOP BREAK .32 S&W 5 shot.

H&R HAMMERLESS BICYCLE SECOND MODEL – .22 rimfire or .32 S&W cal., 5 or 7 shot, similar to H&R Hammerless Second Model, except has 2 in. barrel only, not listed as a separate model after 1920 but 2 inch barrel was still available. Mfg. 1905-1920.

	$295	$260	$225	$185	$160	$140	$120	

Add 10% for blue finish or 20% for .22 rimfire cal.

H&R PREMIER FIRST MODEL SMALL FRAME TOP BREAK (BLACK POWDER) – .22 rimfire or .32 centerfire cal., 5 or 7 shot, double top post barrel latch, free wheeling cylinder (no automatic cylinder stop), nickel with case hardened hammer and barrel latch, 3 (standard), 4, 5, or 6 in. barrel, features a scaled down version of the new frame and double action mechanism introduced in 1890 on the Auto-Ejecting Second Model, does not have caliber marking on left, manufactured for black powder cartridge pressures. Mfg. 1895-1904.

	$285	$255	$220	$175	$150	$125	$115	

Add 10% for blue finish, 20% for 4, 5, or 6 in. barrel, or 20% for .22 rimfire cal.

First Variation, patent dates 10-4-87, 5-14-89, 2-23-92, serial number range 01*-15,000 (estimate) - 1895-April 1896.

Second Variation, patent dates 10-4-87, 5-14-89, 4-2-95, 4-7-96, serial number range 15,000*-20,000* (estimate) - May 1896.

Third Variation, patent dates 10-4-87, 4-2-95, 4-7-96, serial number range 20,000* to 100,000* (estimate) - 1897-1898.

Fourth Variation, automatic cylinder stop, same patent dates as 3rd variation several different serial number series that may have letter codes - 1899-1903.

Fifth Variation, use different font in barrel markings and may have an A letter code in the serial number - 1904.

GRADING - PPGS™	100%	98%	95%	90%	80%	70%	60%	LAST MSR

H&R PREMIER BICYCLE MODEL FIRST MODEL TOP BREAK (BLACK POWDER) – similar to Premier First Model, except has 2 in. barrel only. Mfg. 1895-1904.

$295	$260	$220	$180	$160	$140	$120	

Add 10% for blue finish or 20% for .22 rimfire caliber.

H&R PREMIER POLICE (SPURLESS HAMMER, BLACK POWDER) – similar to Premier First Model, except has patented spurless hammer. Mfg. 1895-1904.

$300	$265	$225	$185	$160	$140	$120	

Add 10% for blue finish, 20% for .22 rimfire caliber, or 20% for 4, 5, or 6 in. barrel.

H&R PREMIER POLICE BICYCLE FIRST MODEL (BLACK POWDER) – similar to Premier First Model, except has 2 in. barrel and patented spurless hammer. Mfg. 1895-1904.

$315	$280	$235	$190	$165	$145	$125	

Add 10% for blue finish or 20% for .22 rimfire caliber.

H&R PREMIER SECOND MODEL SMALL FRAME TOP BREAK R.F. & C.F. – .22 rimfire or .32 S&W cal., double top post barrel latch, 5 or 7 shot, automatic cylinder stop, nickel finish with case hardened hammer and barrel latch, 2, 3 (standard), 4, 5, and 6 in. barrel, caliber markings on left side of barrel, manufactured for smokeless powder cartridge pressures. Mfg. 1905-1941.

$265	$235	$200	$160	$135	$110	$100	

Add 10% for blue finish, 20% for 4, 5, or 6 in. barrel, 20% for .22 rimfire cal., or 10% for Seventh Variation.

There has not been enough data gathered on serial number ranges for the different variations.

First Variation, model name & caliber marked on left side of barrel, patent dates 5-14-89, 4-2-95, 4-7-96; 1905.

Second Variation, model name & caliber marked on left side of barrel, patent dates 4-2-95, 4-7-96; 1906-1908.

Third Variation, caliber only marked on left side of barrel, patent date 10-8-95; 1909-1913.

Fourth Variation, caliber only marked on left side of barrel, no patent date, state not spelled out in address (MASS); 1914-1915.

Fifth Variation, caliber only marked on left side of barrel, same as 4th except different font used in barrel markings; 1914-1915.

Sixth Variation, caliber only marked on left side of barrel. State name in barrel marking spelled out (MASSACHUSETTS); 1916-1924.

Seventh Variation, new grip frame, there is no step down for the grip panels to fit into - 1925-1942.

After 1930 listed in catalogs as: PREMIER No. 30 .22 Rimfire 7 shot or PREMIER No. 35 .32 S&W 5 shot.

H&R PREMIER BICYCLE SECOND MODEL (SMOKELESS POWDER) – similar to Premier Second Model, except has 2 in. barrel, not listed as a separate model after 1919. Mfg. 1905-1920.

$285	$255	$220	$175	$150	$125	$115	

Add 10% for blue finish or 20% for .22 rimfire caliber.

H&R PREMIER POLICE SECOND MODEL (SMOKELESS POWDER) – similar to Premier Second Model, except has spurless hammer, not listed as a separate model after 1938. Mfg. 1905-1939.

$275	$245	$210	$170	$145	$120	$110	

Add 10% for blue finish, 20% for .22 rimfire caliber, or 20% for 4, 5, or 6 in. barrel.

H&R PREMIER POLICE BICYCLE SECOND MODEL (SMOKELESS POWDER) – similar to Premier Second Model, except has 2 in. barrel and patented spurless hammer, not listed as a separate model after 1919. Mfg. 1905-1920.

$285	$255	$220	$175	$150	$125	$115	

Add 10% for blue finish or 20% for .22 rimfire caliber.

H&R TARGET SMALL FRAME TOP BREAK (AKA MODEL 766) – .22 rimfire cal., 7 shot, blue finish, 6 in. barrel, double action, oversized two-piece walnut grips, marked on left side of barrel "H&R TARGET", 22 rimfire on the right side of the barrel, company name and address on the top of the barrel rib. Mfg. 1925-1934.

$325	$285	$250	$200	$175	$150	$125	

After 1930 listed in the catalogs as: MODEL 766 TARGET SMALL FRAME TOP BREAK REVOLVER 7 SHOT.

MODEL 299 NEW DEFENDER LARGE FRAME TOP BREAK – .22 rimfire cal., 9 shot, 2 in. barrel, large frame top break revolver, adj. sights, one-piece walnut grips, pocket size, marked on right side of barrel with model name and caliber, modified "Rice Frame", automatic cylinder stop, finger rest trigger guard, OAL 6 1/4 inches, serial number range unknown, but believed to be in the same series as the Model 999 Sportsman. Mfg. 1935-1939.

$525	$465	$395	$340	$295	$250	$220	

GRADING - PPGS™	100%	98%	95%	90%	80%	70%	60%	LAST MSR

H&R DEFENDER SPECIAL MODEL 299 LARGE FRAME TOP BREAK – .38 S&W cal., 5 shot, 2 and 4 in. flat sided barrel, large frame double action top break revolver, adj. front and rear sight, blue finish, finger rest trigger guard, bird's head grip frame shortened for special one-piece pocket size checkered walnut grips, automatic cylinder stop, OAL 6 1/4 in., serial number range unknown. Mfg. 1935-1939, limited production from 1939-1949.

$600	$520	$440	$390	$340	$285	$245

DEFENDER NO MODEL NUMBER LARGE FRAME TOP BREAK – .38 S&W cal., 5 shot, large frame double action, 4, 5 or 6 inch flat sided barrel, fixed sights, blue finish, no finger rest on trigger guard, bird's head grip frame, one-piece oversized checkered walnut grips, automatic cylinder stop, hammer mounted firing pin, top of barrel marked with company name and address, left side of barrel is marked "DEFENDER 38" and right side is marked "38 S&W CTGE". Mfg. 1939-1942.

$400	$285	$250	$200	$175	$150	$125

Add 20% for 5 or 6 (scarce) in. barrel.

Most likely this is the beginning of the Defender 38 Model 25, but the literature for the Model 25 shows a slightly different revolver. The literature for this revolver refers to it as the Defender 38. Believed to be in a separate serial number range and possibly have letter code prefixes. Early examples will not be marked "Defender".

DEFENDER NO. 25 LARGE FRAME TOP BREAK – .38 S&W cal., 5 shot, 4 in. flat sided barrel, double action, adj. front and rear sights, blue finish, no finger rest on trigger guard, bird's head grip frame, one-piece oversized checkered black plastic grips, automatic cylinder stop, cylinder release via push-button on left side of barrel lug, right side of barrel is marked with company name and address and caliber, left side of barrel marked "DEFENDER 38", serial numbers is believed to be a separate range. Mfg. 1943-1945.

$350	$300	$265	$210	$180	$150	$125

DEFENDER MODEL 925 LARGE FRAME TOP BREAK – .38 S&W cal., 5 shot, 4 in. flat sided barrel, adj. front and rear sights, blue finish, no finger rest on trigger guard, bird's head grip frame, one-piece oversized checkered black plastic grips, automatic cylinder stop, cylinder release via push-button on left side of barrel lug, 9 in. OAL, 25 oz. Mfg. 1946-1947.

$325	$285	$250	$200	$175	$150	$125

Add 50% for manual ejecting model.

There has been one model 925 that is a factory manual ejection revolver with a serial number low enough that it actually may be a Model 25. It has company name and address on top of the barrel, "DEFENDER" on right side of barrel and the caliber on the left side of the barrel.

ULTRA SPORTSMAN MODEL 777 LARGE FRAME TOP BREAK – .22 rimfire cal., 9 shot, large frame single action top break, 6 in. flat-top oval shaped barrel (same as the Model 199), adj. front and rear sight, elevation screw on front of barrel just above muzzle, oversized one-piece checkered walnut grips (eleven different styles available), straight trigger, arched hammer spur, cylinder release is a vertical lever on the right side of barrel lug, rear of cylinder has the patented H&R safety rim, finger rest trigger guard, trigger pull factory set 2 1/2 to 3 pounds, hammer mounted firing pin, serial numbered in its own series U01 to at least U954, top of barrel markings in two lines: "HARRINGTON & RICHARDSON ARMS CO. WORCESTER, MASS. U.S.A.", left side of barrel in three lines: "H&R NO. 777 ULTRA SPORTSMAN", right side of barrel, one line: ".22 LONG RIFLE CTCG." Mfg. 1938-1939.

$800	$685	$600	$535	$475	$325	$275

EUREKA SPORTSMAN MODEL 196 – .22 rimfire cal., 6 shot, large frame single action top break, cylinder chambers individually recessed, 6 in. flat-top oval heavy barrel, adj. front and rear sight (has a different configuration than found on any other H&R adj. rear sight), oversized one-piece checkered walnut grips (eleven different styles available), trigger guard is heaver and wider than Model 777, trigger pull factory set 2 1/2 to 3 pounds, with over travel adjustment, curved trigger and heavy straight hammer spur, hammer mounted firing pin, bird's head shaped grip frame, top of barrel markings in two lines: "HARRINGTON & RICHARDSON ARMS CO., WORCESTER, MASS U.S.A.", left side of barrel in three lines: "H&R NO. 196 EUREKA SPORTSMAN", right side of barrel, one line: "22 LONG RIFLE CTGE", OAL approx. 10 3/4 inches, 30-32 oz. Mfg. 1940 only.

$1,000	$860	$770	$680	$525	$450	$395

Add $250 for fitted case (rare).

SPORTSMAN SINGLE ACTION MODEL 199 LARGE FRAME TOP BREAK – .22 LR cal., 9 shot, safety rim cylinder, blue finish, 6 in. round heavy rib barrel, automatic cylinder stop, adj. front and rear sights, finger rest trigger guard, one-piece oversized checkered walnut grips, birds-head grip frame, top of barrel marked with company name and address, left side of barrel marked in two lines: "H & R SPORTSMAN SINGLE ACTION", right side of barrel marked: "22 LONG RIFLE CTGE", serial numbered in series from 01 up and early production will have S letter code denoting single action. Mfg. 1932-1951.

$575	$495	$415	$340	$285	$250	$210

GRADING - PPGS™	100%	98%	95%	90%	80%	70%	60%	LAST MSR

Add 15% for First Variation or 10% for Fifth Variation.

First Variation; heavy ribbed barrel with non-adjustable front sight - Oct. 1932-April 1933.

Second Variation; oval shaped barrel with flat top, fully adjustable sights - May 1933-disc.

Third Variation; very small lettering on cylinder patent date - unknown-1936.

Fourth Variation; firing pin moved to the hammer - 1937-1941.

Fifth Variation; limited production (1949=J101-J148, 1950=K101-K265, 1951=L111-L112) - 1949-1951.

SPORTSMAN DOUBLE ACTION MODEL 999 LARGE FRAME TOP BREAK - .22 LR or .22 WRF cal., 7 (.22 WRF cal.) or 9 shot, blue finish, 6 in. ribbed barrel, safety rim cylinder, automatic cylinder stop, adj. rear sight, three different front sights - fixed full blade, Partridge type, and Partridge type pinned to barrel top rib, finger rest trigger guard, one-piece oversized checkered walnut grips, birds-head grip frame (Rice frame), frame mounted firing pin, hammer face is flat, cylinder release is long pivoting lever on right side of frame (there are two different version of this), serial numbered in its own series from 01 up to at least 89761 by the end of 1939, starting in 1940 letter codes were used. Mfg. 1932-1952.

$525	$450	$375	$300	$265	$225	$195	

Add 15% for First Variation, 50% for 7 shot, .22 WRF cal. variation, or 30% for 3 in. barrel (scarce).

Early production until about 1933 the letter code "D" was used to denote double action.

First Variation; round heavy weight ribbed barrel with non-adjustable front sight blade - 1932- to before April 18,1933.

Second Variation; adjustable front sight - 1933 (after 4-18-1933).

Third Variation; firing pin moved to hammer - 1934.

Fourth Variation; three inch barrel was offered - 1935.

Fifth Variation; two patent dates marked on cylinder (before there was only one) - 1936 (after 3-17)-1937.

Sixth Variation; top of barrel markings moved to right side of barrel - 1937-1939.

Seventh Variation; .22 WFR caliber dropped, 3 inch barrel dropped - 1940-1941.

Eighth Variation; one piece over size plastic grips are standard, limited production during WWII years - 1942-1952.

REVOLVERS: RECENT MFG.

MODEL 504 SQUARE BUTT - .32 H&R Mag. cal., 5 shot, blue finish, 3, 4, or 6 in. barrel, transfer bar ignition, solid frame, DA, swing out cylinder, square butt. Mfg. 1984-1986.

$235	$200	$175	$140	$125	$110	$95	*$185*

Add 10% for 3 in. barrel, or 15% for 6 in. barrel.

* ***Model 504 Round Butt*** - compact design available with 3 or 4 in. barrel only. Disc. 1985.

$165	$145	$135	$120	$110	$100	$90	*$185*

MODEL 532 - .32 H&R Mag. cal., blue finish, 2 1/2 or 4 in. barrel, case colored hardened frame, 5 shot, DA, solid frame, transfer bar ignition, pull pin cylinder release. Mfg. 1983-1986.

$165	$145	$125	$110	$90	$80	$70	*$115*

MODEL 586 - .32 H&R Mag. cal., 5 shot, similar to Model 686, Western-style revolver, double action, 4 1/2, 5 1/2, 7 1/2, or 10 in. barrels, adj. rear sight, antique finish frame with blue cylinder and barrel, black plastic or walnut grips. Mfg. 1983-1985.

$275	$245	$210	$170	$145	$120	$110	*$195*

Add 30% for 10 in. barrel.

MODEL 600 FORTY-NINER - .22 LR cal., 9 shot, 5 1/2 in. barrel, DA, solid frame, rod ejection, blue finish, Western style grips. Mfg. 1960 only.

$275	$225	$185	$150	$125	$100	$90	

MODEL 603 - .22 WMR cal., similar to Model 903 but is 6 shot, 6 in. full round bull barrel, DA, transfer bar ignition, swing out cylinder. Mfg. 1980-83.

$300	$245	$195	$160	$125	$100	$90	

MODEL 604 - .22 WMR cal., 6 shot, blue finish, 6 in. flat sided bull barrel, DA, solid frame, swing out cylinder, square butt. Mfg. 1980-1983.

$300	$245	$195	$160	$125	$100	$90	

MODEL 622 - .22 S, L, or LR cal., solid frame, DA, 6 shot, 2 1/2, 4, 6, or 10 in. barrels, blue finish, round or square butt, plastic grips, pull pin cylinder release. Mfg. 1957-1973.

$200	$165	$130	$110	$90	$75	$65	*$104*

GRADING - PPGS™	100%	98%	95%	90%	80%	70%	60%	LAST MSR

* ***Model 622 Second Model*** – similar to Model 622, except round butt only, 2 1/2 or 4 in. barrel, transfer bar ignition system. Mfg. 1974-1986.

$250	$185	$145	$120	$95	$85	$70	

MODEL 623 – similar to Model 622, chrome/nickel finish only. Mfg. 1957-1964.

$260	$195	$155	$130	$110	$95	$80	

* ***Model 623 Second Model*** – similar to Model 622 Second Model, except electroless nickel finish, transfer bar ignition system. Mfg. 1977-1979.

$250	$155	$130	$115	$95	$85	$75	

MODEL 632 – .32 S&W cal., 6 shot, blue finish, large solid frame, DA, round or square butt, 2 1/2 or 4 in. barrel, pull pin cylinder release. Mfg. 1952-1959.

$165	$145	$125	$110	$90	$80	$70	

* ***Model 632 Second Model*** – .32 S&W Long cal., 2 1/2 or 4 in. barrel, blue finish, 6 shot, transfer bar ignition system, DA, solid frame, pull pin cylinder, round or square butt. Mfg. 1973-1986.

$175	$155	$130	$115	$95	$85	$75	

MODEL 633 – similar to the Model 632, except chrome/nickel finish, 2 1/2 in. barrel only, round butt. Mfg. 1953-1959.

$185	$165	$140	$120	$100	$90	$80	

* ***Model 633 Second Model*** – similar to Model 632 Second Model, except nickel finish, 2 1/2 in. barrel only, transfer bar ignition system. Mfg. 1977-1979.

$195	$175	$150	$125	$110	$95	$85	

MODEL 642 – .22 WMR cal., 2 1/2 or 4 in. barrel, 6 shot, blue finish, DA, solid frame, pull pin cylinder release, round butt, transfer bar ignition. Mfg. 1980-1983.

$195	$175	$150	$125	$110	$95	$85	

MODEL 649 CONVERTIBLE – .22 LR or .22 cal., furnished with extra cylinder, similar to Model 949, Western style, double action, side loading, 5 1/2 or 7 1/2 in. barrel, 6 shot, walnut grips, blue finish, transfer bar ignition system. Mfg. 1976-1985.

$290	$235	$185	$150	$125	$100	$90	*$160*

MODEL 650 CONVERTIBLE – similar to Model 649, except with nickel finish and only available with 5 1/2 in. barrel. Mfg. 1975-1986.

$295	$240	$190	$155	$130	$110	$100	*$175*

MODEL 660 GUNFIGHTER – .22 LR cal., 6 shot, blue finish, 6 in. barrel, DA, solid frame, Western style grip. Mfg. 1960-1961.

$325	$285	$250	$200	$175	$150	$125	

MODEL 666 CONVERTIBLE – .22 LR or .22 WMR cal., 6 shot, 6 in. barrel, blue finish, plastic grips, square butt, extra cylinder, transfer bar ignition system. Mfg. 1975-1979.

$145	$125	$110	$90	$80	$75	$70	

MODEL 676 CONVERTIBLE – .22 LR/.22 WMR cal., similar to the Model 649, except has finger spur on trigger guard, blue/case colored finish, 6 shot, 4 1/2, 5 1/2, 7 1/2, or 12 in. barrel, side load and eject, one-piece walnut stock, fixed sights. Mfg. 1975-1980.

$300	$260	$215	$170	$145	$120	$110	

Add 20% for 12 in. barrel.
Subtract $35 if with only one cylinder.

MODEL 686 CONVERTIBLE – .22 LR or .22 WMR cal., similar to Model 676 except with adj. target sights, larger frame, 4 1/2, 5 1/2, 7 1/2, or 12 in. barrel, transfer bar ignition. Mfg. 1980-1986.

$315	$270	$225	$175	$150	$125	$110	

Add 20% for 12 in. barrel.
Subtract $35 if with only one cylinder.

MODEL 732 GUARDSMAN – .32 S&W cal., similar to Model 929, 6 shot, 2 1/2 and 4 in. barrels, DA, fixed sights, swing out cylinder, blue finish, round or square butt, black plastic grips. Mfg. 1957-1973.

$185	$165	$140	$120	$100	$90	$80	

* ***Model 732 Guardsman Second Model*** – similar to Model 732 Guardsman, except with transfer bar ignition. Mfg. 1974-1986.

$195	$175	$150	$125	$110	$95	$85	

GRADING - PPGS™	100%	98%	95%	90%	80%	70%	60%	LAST MSR

MODEL 733 GUARDSMAN – similar to the Model 732, except chrome/nickel finish, 2 1/2 in. barrel, round butt. Mfg. 1957-1986.

$195 $175 $150 $125 $110 $95 $85

* ***Model 733 Guardsman Second Model*** – .32 S&W Long cal., 6 shot, nickel finish, 2 1/2 or 4 (rare) in. barrel, transfer bar ignition, solid frame, DA, swing out cylinder, round butt. Mfg. 1973-1986.

$195 $175 $150 $125 $110 $95 $85

Add 10% for 4 in. barrel.

MODEL 826 – .22 WMR cal., 6 shot, 3 in. barrel, adj. rear sight, solid frame, DA, swing out cylinder, transfer bar ignition. Mfg. 1981-1983.

$190 $175 $150 $125 $110 $95 $85

MODEL 829 – .22 LR cal., 9 shot, blue finish, 3 in. barrel, adj. rear sight, solid frame, DA, swing out cylinder, transfer bar ignition. Mfg. 1981-1983.

$190 $175 $150 $125 $110 $95 $85

MODEL 830 – similar to Model 829, but with nickel finish. Mfg. 1982-1983.

$195 $175 $150 $125 $110 $95 $85

MODEL 832 – .32 S&W Long cal., similar to Model 830. Mfg. 1981-1983.

$190 $175 $150 $125 $110 $95 $85

MODEL 833 – similar to Model 832, but with nickel finish. Mfg. 1982-1983.

$195 $175 $150 $125 $110 $95 $85

MODEL 900 – .22 S, L, or LR cal., 9 shot, 2 1/2, 4, or 6 in. barrels, snap out cylinder, DA, blue finish, black plastic grips, solid frame. Mfg. 1962-1973.

$180 $150 $125 $90 $85 $70 $65

MODEL 901 – similar to Model 900, but chrome finish with white Tenite grips. Mfg. 1962-1964.

$185 $155 $125 $110 $90 $80 $70

MODEL 903 – .22 LR cal., successor to the Model 939, 6 in. heavy barrel with raised rib, 9 shot, blue finish, adj. sights, DA, solid frame, swing out cylinder, transfer bar ignition. Mfg. 1980-1983.

$300 $195 $170 $140 $125 $110 $95

MODEL 904 – .22 S, L, or LR cal., SA, similar to Model 903 except has 4 or 6 in. round bull barrel, target grade, 9 shot, adj. sights. Mfg. 1980-1985.

$300 $260 $215 $170 $145 $120 $110 *$168*

MODEL 905 – similar to Model 904, except with nickel finish and 4 in. round bull barrel only. Mfg. 1980-1986.

$300 $260 $215 $170 $145 $120 $110 *$185*

MODEL 922 BANTAM WEIGHT – .22 LR cal., blue finish, 2 1/2 in. barrel, 9 shot, DA, solid frame, pull pin cylinder release, round butt. Mfg. 1952-1961.

$215 $195 $165 $135 $120 $100 $90

MODEL 922 CAMPER – .22 LR cal., similar to Model 922 Bantam Weight, except has 4 in. barrel. Mfg. 1952-1955.

$215 $195 $165 $135 $120 $100 $90

MODEL 922 THIRD MODEL – .22 LR cal., features new frame, 2 1/2, 4, or 6 in. barrel, 9 shot, blue finish, solid frame, DA, pull pin cylinder release, round or square butt. Mfg. 1953-1961.

$195 $175 $150 $125 $110 $95 $85

MODEL 922 FOURTH MODEL – .22 LR cal., similar to Model 922 Second Model, except has transfer bar ignition. Mfg. 1973-1979.

$200 $180 $160 $130 $120 $100 $90

MODEL 923 FIRST MODEL BANTAM WEIGHT – .22 LR cal., 9 shot, chrome finish, 2 1/2 in. barrel, DA, solid frame, pull pin cylinder release, round butt. Mfg. 1953-1961.

$215 $195 $170 $135 $120 $100 $90

MODEL 923 FIRST MODEL CAMPER – .22 LR cal., similar to Model 923 Bantam Weight, except has 4 in. barrel. Mfg. 1952-1955.

$215 $195 $165 $135 $120 $100 $90

MODEL 923 SECOND MODEL – .22 LR cal., features new frame. Mfg. 1953-1961.

$205 $185 $165 $135 $125 $100 $90

MODEL 923 THIRD MODEL – .22 LR cal., similar to 922 Third Model. Mfg. 1977-1979.

$210 $190 $165 $135 $120 $100 $90

GRADING - PPGS™	100%	98%	95%	90%	80%	70%	60%	LAST MSR

MODEL 925 DEFENDER SECOND MODEL TOP BREAK – .22 LR or .38 S&W cal., new frame version of pre-1953 Model 925, blue or matte black finish, 2 1/2 or 4 (disc. 1969) in. barrel, top break, DA, 5 (.38 cal.) or 9 (.22 cal.) shot, birds-head grip, square butt (4 in. barrel 1968-69). Mfg. 1964-1972.

$265 $215 $180 $140 $125 $110 $95

Add 10% for 4 in. barrel.
Add 75% for 4 in. barrel (.22 cal.).
Add 15% for matte black finish.

MODEL 925 DEFENDER THIRD MODEL TOP BREAK – .38 S&W cal., similar to Second Model, except 2 1/2 in. barrel only, 5 shot, transfer bar ignition. Mfg. 1973-1978.

$265 $215 $180 $140 $125 $110 $95

MODEL 926 MANUAL EJECTOR TOP BREAK – .22 LR or .38 S&W cal., 5 (.38 S&W) or 9 (.22 LR) shot, 4 in. barrel, blue finish, DA, square butt, manual ejection, adj. rear sight, top break, walnut grips. Mfg. 1968-1972.

$265 $215 $180 $140 $125 $110 $95

Add 10% for .22 LR cal.

MODEL 926 MANUAL EJECTOR SECOND MODEL TOP BREAK – .22 LR or .38 S&W cal., 5 (.38 S&W) or 9 (.22 LR) shot, 4 in. barrel, blue finish, DA, square butt, manual ejection, adj. rear sight, top break, walnut grips, transfer bar ignition. Mfg. 1973-1978.

$265 $215 $185 $150 $125 $110 $95

MODEL 929 SIDEKICK – .22 LR cal., 9 shot, 2 1/2, 4, or 6 in. barrels, swing out cylinder, plastic grips, blue finish, DA, round or square solid frame, DA, round or square butt. Mfg. 1956-1973.

$200 $165 $135 $115 $95 $85 $75 *$127*

MODEL 929 SIDEKICK SECOND MODEL – .22 LR cal., 9 shot, 2 1/2, 4, or 6 in. barrels, swing out cylinder, plastic grips, blue finish, DA, round or square butt, transfer bar ignition. Mfg. 1974-1986.

$210 $175 $150 $125 $110 $95 $85 *$127*

MODEL 930 SIDEKICK – similar to 929 Sidekick Second Model, except chrome/nickel finish and not available with 6 in. barrel. Mfg. 1957-1986.

$215 $195 $170 $135 $120 $100 $90 *$140*

MODEL 930 SIDEKICK SECOND MODEL – similar to Model 930 Sidekick, except has transfer bar ignition, nickel finish. Mfg. 1974-1986.

$220 $190 $165 $135 $120 $95 $80

MODEL 935 DEFENDER TOP BREAK – similar to Model 925 Third Model, top break, DA, nickel finish, transfer bar ignition. Mfg. 1977-1978.

$275 $245 $210 $170 $145 $120 $110

MODEL 939 ULTRA SIDEKICK – .22 S, L, or LR cal., 9 shot, 6 in. flat sided bull barrel, swing out cylinder, vent. rib, adj. sights, blue finish, solid frame, DA, square butt. Mfg. 1957-1972.

$310 $265 $220 $180 $155 $135 $115

In 1962, the hammer mounted cylinder release button was discontinued. A key lock for safety was added in 1962, and discontinued in 1972. This model was H&R's second most expensive revolver.

MODEL 939 ULTRA SIDEKICK SECOND MODEL – similar to Model 939 Ultra Sidekick, except has transfer bar ignition. Mfg. 1973-1980.

$300 $265 $225 $185 $160 $140 $120

MODEL 940 ULTRA SIDEKICK – similar to Model 939, except has 6 in. full round bull barrel. Mfg. 1970-1972.

$300 $265 $225 $185 $160 $140 $120

MODEL 940 ULTRA SIDEKICK SECOND MODEL – similar to Model 940 Ultra Sidekick, except has transfer bar ignition. Mfg. 1973-1980.

$275 $225 $175 $150 $125 $100 $90

MODEL 949 "FORTY NINER" – .22 S, L, or LR cal., 5 1/2 in. barrel, DA, solid frame, 9 shot, side load and Western style ejection, adj. rear sight, walnut grips. Mfg. 1961-1972.

$275 $225 $175 $150 $125 $100 $90 *$127*

MODEL 949 "FORTY NINER" SECOND MODEL – .22 S, L, or LR cal., similar to Model 949 Forty Niner, except has transfer bar safety. Mfg. 1973-1986.

$285 $235 $200 $160 $140 $115 $100

MODEL 950 – similar to Model 949, except with nickel finish. Mfg. 1974-1986.

$290 $245 $210 $170 $145 $120 $110 *$145*

GRADING - PPGS™	100%	98%	95%	90%	80%	70%	60%	LAST MSR

MODEL 976 – .22 LR cal., 9 shot, 7 1/2 in. barrel, rod ejection, solid frame, DA, Western style grips, blue finish, case colored hardened frame, fixed sights, transfer bar ignition, catalog number 97603, in 1978 catalog advertised as a 6 in. barrel. Mfg. 1978-1981.

$310	$265	$220	$180	$155	$135	$115	

Subtract $35 if with only one cylinder.

MODEL 976 DELUXE – .22 LR cal., 9 shot, 7 1/2 in. barrel, rod ejection, solid frame, DA, Western style grips, blue finish, case colored hardened frame, adj. sights, transfer bar ignition, catalog number 97602. Mfg. 1978-1981.

$325	$280	$225	$185	$160	$140	$120	

Subtract $35 if with only one cylinder.

MODEL 999 ENGRAVED – similar to 999, only engraved throughout, 6 in. barrel only. Disc. 1985.

$600	$500	$425	$365	$325	$285	$225	*$525*

MODEL 999 SPORTSMAN SECOND MODEL (NEW FRAME, TOP BREAK) – .22 LR cal., 9 shot, 6 in. barrel, adj. sights, top break, DA, blue finish. Mfg. 1953-1972.

$575	$475	$410	$350	$210	$170	$150	

MODEL 999 SILVER SPORTSMAN TOP BREAK – .22 LR cal., 9 shot, 6 in. barrel, top break, DA, chrome finish, serial number letter codes Z, AA, AB, AC only. Mfg. 1963-1966.

$600	$500	$425	$365	$325	$285	$225	

MODEL 999 SPORTSMAN THIRD MODEL TOP BREAK – .22 LR cal., 9 shot, 4 (new 1979) or 6 in. barrel, top break, DA, blue finish, adj. sights. Mfg. 1973-1986.

$575	$475	$410	$350	$210	$170	$150	

In 1979, this model was advertised as the Model 999 Automatic Ejecting and was offered as a 6 shot in .32 S&W Long cal.

MODEL 999 SPORTSMAN 1 of 999 TOP BREAK – .22 LR cal., top break, DA, 9 shot, 6 in. barrel, adj. sights, engraved, fitted wood case. Mfg. 1979-1986.

$750	$625	$525	$450	$385	$340	$285	

Values are only for unfired models with all original tags, manuals, commemorative medallion, wooden presentation case and cardboard box. Use Model 999 Third Model values if not intact.

RIFLES

MODEL 12 TARGET BOLT ACTION – .22 LR cal., single shot, 28 in. heavy barrel, high polish blue finish, no sights, drilled and tapped, walnut stained birch target stock, bolt cocks on closing, adj. trigger, accessory rail, palm rest, same military specs as the Winchester Model 52, internal company model name is M12 JROTC, 11 lbs. Mfg. 1981-1986.

$850	$700	$600	$500	$425	$365	$310	

Subtract 25% if w/o sights.

MODEL 58 (058) COMBO SINGLE SHOT – .22 Hornet or .30-30 Win. cal., or 20 ga., single shot side lever action, 22 in. rifle barrel and 24 in. smoothbore barrel, drilled and tapped, modified choke, blade front sight, adj. folding rear sight (rifle barrel only), color case frame with blue barrels, walnut stained pistol grip buttstock, 6 1/2 lbs. Mfg. 1975-1986.

$225	$195	$170	$140	$125	$110	$95	

While marked Model 58, the catalogs listed this gun as the Model 058.

MODEL 58C SEMI-AUTO – .22 LR cal., military designation for the H&R Model 65, early models marked "USMC Property" and late models (approx. 300 mfg.) marked "U.S. Property", 23 in. heavy barrel, 10 shot detachable box mag., protected front blade sight, buttstock dimensions same as M-1 Garand, safety on inside of trigger guard, manual bolt hold open, sling swivels, 9 lbs. Approx. 3,250 mfg. 1958-1959.

$2,500	$2,200	$1,800	$1,400	$1,000	$750	$575	

MODEL 60 REISING SEMI-AUTO – .45 ACP cal., delayed blowback action, 18 1/4 in. barrel, parkerized finish, 10 or 20 shot detachable box mag., front post and adj. rear sight, pistol grip walnut stock, sling swivels, semi-auto version of the Model 50. Mfg. 1944-1946.

$2,800	$2,400	$1,925	$1,575	$1,275	$1,050	$900	

MODEL 65 H&R REISING SEMI-AUTO – .22 LR cal., blow back action, civilian version of the Model 58C, 23 in. heavy barrel, manual bolt hold open, 10 shot detachable box mag., front blade sight, rear adj. aperture sight, buttstock dimensions same as M-1 Garand, sling swivels, 9 lbs. Mfg. 1944-1945.

$650	$600	$525	$450	$350	$275	$200	

The Model 65 H&R was originally a marine corp training rifle (mfg. circa 1943-1945), and then commercially produced (in limited quantity) around the approx. serial no. of 10000.

GRADING - PPGS™	100%	98%	95%	90%	80%	70%	60%	LAST MSR

MODEL 150 LEATHERNECK SEMI-AUTO – .22 LR cal., blow back action, 22 in. heavy barrel, blue finish, 5 or 10 shot detachable box mag., adj. rear open sight, ramped front blade sight, plain walnut stock, 7 1/4 lbs. Mfg. 1948-1952.

$300 $265 $225 $185 $160 $140 $120

MODEL 151 LEATHERNECK SEMI-AUTO – .22 LR cal., blow back action, 22 in. heavy barrel, blue finish, 5 or 10 shot detachable box mag., Redfield M70 rear aperture sight, ramped front blade sight, plain walnut buttstock, 7 1/4 lbs. Mfg. 1948-1952.

$375 $325 $285 $235 $210 $175 $150

MODEL 155 SHIKARI SINGLE SHOT – .45-70 Govt. or .44 Mag. cal., single shot side lever break action, 24 or 28 in. blue barrel, drilled and tapped, blade front sight, adj. folding rear sight, case colored frame, walnut stained hardwood straight grip buttstock, brass cleaning rod, 7 - 7 1/4 lbs. Mfg. 1973-1981.

$275 $225 $190 $155 $130 $115 $100

Add 10% for .45-70 Govt. cal.

MODEL 157 SINGLE SHOT – .22 Hornet (mfg. 1976-1977), .22 WMR (1976-1977), or .30-30 Win. cal., single shot side lever break action, 22 in. blue barrel, drilled and tapped, blade front sight, adj. folding rear sight, case colored hardened frame, walnut stained hardwood pistol grip stock with Mannlicher-style forearm with nose cap, sling swivels, 6 1/2 lbs. Mfg. 1975-1983.

$295 $260 $225 $185 $160 $140 $120

MODEL 158

* ***Model 158 Topper 30/Topper Jet*** – .22 S&W Jet or .30-30 Win. cal., side lever break action, 22 in. blue barrel, case colored hardened frame, drilled and tapped, walnut stained hardwood pistol grip stock, blade front sight, folding rear sight, 6 1/2 lbs. Mfg. 1963 only.

$225 $195 $170 $140 $125 $110 $95

Add 25% for extra .22 Jet barrel.

* ***Model 158 Topper 4 in 1*** – standard with four barrels in .30-30 Win., .22 Jet, 20 ga. (mod. choke), and .410 bore (full choke). Mfg. 1964-1967.

$450 $395 $335 $285 $245 $210 $180

* ***Model 158 Topper Combo*** – standard with one rifled and one smoothbore barrel in .22 Jet (1968-1975), .22 Hornet (new 1975), or .30-30 Win., and 20 ga., straight grip stock. Mfg. 1968-1975.

$350 $320 $275 $225 $200 $165 $140

* ***Model 158 Rifle*** – 20 ga. shotgun barrel was disc. and model became rifle only in .22 Hornet, .30-30 Win., .357 Mag., or .44 Mag. cal. Mfg. 1976-1984.

$225 $195 $170 $140 $125 $110 $95

MODEL 163 MUSTANG SINGLE SHOT – .30-30 Win. cal., 22 in. blue barrel, side lever break action, drilled and tapped, blade front sight, adj. folding rear sight, blue finished frame, gold plated trigger, straight grip walnut stock with contoured forearm, 6 1/2 lbs. Mfg. 1965-1966.

$225 $195 $170 $140 $125 $110 $95

MODEL 164 SINGLE SHOT – similar to Model 163 Mustang, except nickel finished frame. Mfg. 1966.

$225 $195 $170 $140 $125 $110 $95

MODEL 165 LEATHERNECK SEMI-AUTO – .22 LR cal., blow back action, 23 in. round tapered blue barrel, 10 shot detachable box mag., Redfield M79 rear aperture sight, ramped blade front sight, plain walnut stock, sling swivels. Mfg. 1946-1947 and 1959-1961.

$250 $225 $195 $170 $140 $125 $110

MODEL 171 SPRINGFIELD CAVALRY CARBINE – .45-70 Govt. cal., replica of Model 1873 Springfield Trapdoor Cavalry carbine, heavy 22 in. blue barrel, plain walnut stock with metal buttplate, adj. rear sight, blade front sight, color case hardened receiver, lock plate and buttplate, 7 lbs. Mfg. 1972-1986.

$650 $600 $525 $450 $395 $325 $275

MODEL 171 SPRINGFIELD CAVALRY RIFLE – similar to Carbine, except has 26 in. barrel. Mfg. 1972-1973.

$675 $585 $500 $435 $375 $325 $275

MODEL 171 DELUXE SPRINGFIELD CAVALRY CARBINE – similar to Model 171 Carbine, except has engraved receiver and lock plate, extra fancy walnut stock, original style rear sight. Mfg. 1974-1986.

$750 $645 $560 $485 $420 $365 $310

GRADING - PPGS™	100%	98%	95%	90%	80%	70%	60%	LAST MSR

MODEL 172 SILVER PLATE CARBINE – .45-70 Govt. cal., 22 in. heavy barrel, similar to Model 171 Carbine, except hand checkered select walnut stock with metal buttplate and grip adaptor, adj. tang mounted aperture rear sight, blade front sight, silver plated engraved receiver and lock plate, 7 1/4 lbs. Mfg. 1975 and 1977-1980.

	$1,650	$1,495	$1,250	$1,050	$875	$750	$625	

MODEL 173 OFFICER MODEL RIFLE – .45-70 Govt. cal., 26 in. heavy blue barrel, plain walnut stock, metal buttplate and grip adaptor, adj. tang mounted aperture rear sight, blade front sight, color case hardened receiver, lock plate, and buttplate, cleaning rod mounted under barrel, 7 lbs. Mfg. 1975-1981.

	$800	$675	$550	$495	$425	$375	$325	

MODEL 178 SPRINGFIELD RIFLE – .45-70 Govt. cal., 32 in. heavy blue barrel, full-length American walnut stock, metal buttplate, ladder type rear sight, blade front sight, color case hardened receiver, lock plate, and buttplate, cleaning rod mounted under barrel, available in three variations - a Commemorative (ser. no. SPR-1 to SPR-1000, mfg. 1973-1975), Rifle (unknown ser. nos. and quantity, mfg. 1976), and the Infantry Rifle (unknown ser. nos. and quantity, mfg. 1977). Mfg. 1973-1977.

	$700	$600	$525	$450	$385	$340	$285	

Add 50% for Commemorative model.

MODEL 250 SPORTSTER BOLT ACTION REPEATER – .22 LR cal., 23 in. round blue barrel, 5 shot detachable mag., plain walnut grip stock, ramped blade front sight, step adj. rear sight, 6 1/2 lbs. Mfg. 1948-1950.

	$195	$175	$150	$125	$110	$95	$85	

MODEL 251 SPORTSTER BOLT ACTION REPEATER – similar to Model 250 Sportster, except has Lyman No. 55H adj. aperture rear sight. Mfg. 1948-1950.

	$225	$195	$170	$140	$125	$110	$95	

MODEL 258 HANDY GUN II SINGLE SHOT COMBO – .22 Hornet, .30-30 Win., .357 Mag., .357 Max., or .44 Mag. and 20 ga. smoothbore, side lever break action, 22 in. rifled barrel, drilled and tapped, electroless nickel finish, walnut stained hardwood pistol grip buttstock, includes fitted canvas carrying case, 6 1/2 lbs. Mfg. 1982-1986.

	$250	$220	$190	$155	$130	$115	$100	

MODEL 264 TARGETEER BOLT ACTION REPEATER – .22 LR cal., 22 in. round blue barrel, 10 shot detachable box mag., plain walnut pistol grip stock, ramped blade front sight, step adj. rear sight, 6 3/4 lbs. Mfg. 1947-1948.

	$185	$165	$140	$120	$100	$90	$80	

MODEL 265 TARGETEER BOLT ACTION REPEATER – similar to Model 264, except has adj. Lyman rear aperture sight. Mfg. 1946-1950.

	$285	$250	$215	$170	$145	$120	$110	

* ***Model 265 Targeteer Jr.*** – .22 LR cal., similar to Model 265, except has shortened LOP stock. Mfg. 1948-1950.

	$250	$220	$190	$155	$130	$115	$100	

MODEL 300 ULTRA BOLT ACTION – .22-250 Rem., .243 Win., .270 Win., .30-06, .308 Win., 7mm Rem. Mag., or .300 Win. Mag. cal., Mauser (mfg. by FN 1965-1972), Sako (mfg. 1973-1977), or Mauser Mark X (Mfg. by Zastava 1978-1983) repeater action, 3 or 5 shot internal mag., 22 in. blue barrel, drilled and tapped, ramped front blade sight, adj. rear sight, hinged floorplate, adj. trigger, checkered American walnut Monte Carlo stock with rollover cheekpiece and pistol grip stock, contrasting wood on pistol grip cap and forend, recoil pad, sling swivels, 7 3/4 lbs. Mfg. 1965-1981.

	$700	$525	$425	$350	$295	$250	$220	

MODEL 301 ULTRA BOLT ACTION CARBINE – .22-250 Rem., .243 Win., .270 Win., .30-06, or .308 Win. cal., repeater action similar to Model 300, 3 or 5 shot internal mag., 18 in. blue barrel, drilled and tapped, ramped front blade sight, adj. rear sight, hinged floorplate, adj. trigger, checkered Mannlicher American walnut Monte Carlo stock with rollover cheekpiece and pistol grip, contrasting wood on pistol grip cap and forend, recoil pad and sling swivels, 7 1/4 lbs. Mfg. 1967-1981.

	$650	$495	$400	$325	$275	$225	$200	

MODEL 317 ULTRA WILDCAT BOLT ACTION – .17/223 H&R Wildcat, .17 Rem., .222 Rem., or .223 Rem. cal., 6 shot internal mag., 20 in. blue barrel, hinged floorplate, no sights, drilled and tapped, hand checkered American walnut stock with cheekpiece and pistol grip, recoil pad, early mfg. used leftover inventory of the O'Brien Rifle Co. of Las Vegas, NV, which H&R purchased in the late 1960s, early production barrels were mfg. by Ackley and Shilen, later mfg. used Sako actions, 5 1/4 lbs. Mfg. 1968-1976.

	$600	$520	$440	$390	$340	$285	$245	

GRADING - PPGS™	100%	98%	95%	90%	80%	70%	60%	LAST MSR

* ***Model 317P Presentation Grade Ultra Wildcat*** – similar to Model 317, except has basket weave pattern hand checkered American walnut stock with contrasting wood pistol grip cap and forend tip. Mfg. 1968-1976.

	$675	$585	$500	$435	$375	$325	$275	

MODEL 322 BOLT ACTION REPEATER – .222 Rem. cal., 5 shot mag., Sako short action, 24 in. medium weight barrel, adj. trigger, hand checkered European walnut Monte Carlo stock with cheekpiece, sling swivels, no sights. Mfg. 1973.

	$415	$350	$315	$275	$235	$195	$175	

MODEL 330 BOLT ACTION REPEATER – .243 Win., .270 Win., .30-06, or .308 Win. cal., 22 in. blue barrel, drilled and tapped, Mauser action, ramped front blade sight, adj. rear sight, hinged floorplate, adj. trigger, plain American walnut Monte Carlo stock with pistol grip, recoil pad, sling swivels, 7 1/8 lbs. Mfg. 1968-1972.

	$400	$350	$300	$265	$225	$190	$165	

MODEL 340 BOLT ACTION REPEATER – .22-250 Rem., .243 Win., .270 Win., .30-06, .308 Win., or 7x57mm cal., 3 shot internal mag., 22 in. blue barrel, blue finish, no sights, drilled and tapped, hinged floorplate, adj. trigger, American walnut Classic style stock, vent. recoil pad, sling swivels, 7 1/4 lbs. Mfg. 1981-1983.

	$400	$350	$300	$265	$225	$190	$165	

MODEL 360 ULTRA SEMI-AUTO – .243 Win. or .308 Win. cal., gas operated, side ejection, manual bolt stop, 3 shot detachable box mag., 22 in. blue barrel, drilled and tapped, ramped front sight, adj. open rear sight, checkered American walnut Monte Carlo stock with cheekpiece and pistol grip, contrasting wood on forearm tip and pistol grip cap, 7 1/2 lbs. Mfg. 1965-1977.

	$500	$440	$375	$325	$275	$235	$200	

MODEL 361 ULTRA DELUXE SEMI-AUTO – similar to Model 360, except has extra fancy American walnut stock with full rollover cheekpiece for right or left-hand. Mfg. 1970-1973.

	$525	$465	$395	$340	$295	$250	$220	

MODEL 365 REG'LAR (A.K.A. ACE) – .22 LR cal., bolt action single shot, 22 in. round blue barrel, bolt cocks on closing, plain full size walnut pistol grip stock, ramped blade front sight, Lyman No. 55 rear sight, 6 1/2 lbs. Mfg. 1946-1947.

	$145	$125	$110	$100	$85	$75	$65	

MODEL 370 ULTRA MEDALIST BOLT ACTION – .22-250 Rem., .243 Win., 6mm Rem. Mag., repeater Mauser action, blue finish, 5 shot internal mag., 24 in. bull barrel with recessed muzzle crown, no sights, hinged floorplate, drilled and tapped, adj. trigger, target style American walnut oil finished stock with rollover cheekpiece, semi-beavertail forend, recoil pad, adj. sling swivels, 9 1/2 lbs. Mfg. 1968-1973.

	$515	$450	$395	$340	$295	$250	$220	

MODEL 422 SLIDE ACTION – .22 LR cal., repeater action, 21 shot tube mag., 24 in. barrel, ramped front sight, step adj. rear sight, blue finish, plain walnut stock, grooved slide handle, 6 lbs. Mfg. by Noble Firearms Co. 1956-1958.

	$325	$285	$250	$200	$175	$150	$125	

MODEL 424 BOLT ACTION – .22 LR cal., single shot, 22 in. round barrel, manual cocking, shortened plain walnut pistol grip stock, ramped blade front sight, step adj. rear sight, beginner's or boy's model, mfg. by Nobel Firearms Co. 1960-1961.

	$135	$120	$100	$85	$75	$65	$50	

MODEL 450 MEDALIST BOLT ACTION – .22 LR cal., 26 in. round barrel, 5 shot detachable mag., repeater action, plain walnut pistol grip stock, no sights, blue finish, 9 1/2 lbs. Mfg. 1948.

	$375	$325	$285	$235	$210	$175	$150	

MODEL 451 MEDALIST BOLT ACTION – similar to Model 450, except has Lyman No. 524 extension rear aperture sight. Mfg. 1948-1950 and 1959-1961.

	$400	$350	$300	$265	$225	$190	$165	

MODEL 550 PAL BOLT ACTION – .22 LR cal., single shot, 22 in. round tapered barrel, bolt cocks on closing, plain full size walnut pistol grip stock, blade front sight, step adj. rear sight, blue finish, 5 lbs. Mfg. 1947-1948.

	$145	$125	$110	$100	$85	$75	$65	

MODEL 565 PAL BOLT ACTION – .22 LR cal., single shot, 22 in. round tapered barrel, bolt cocks on closing, plain full size walnut pistol grip stock, blade front sight, Lyman adj. rear sight, blue finish, 5 lbs. Mfg. 1947.

	$175	$155	$130	$115	$95	$85	$75	

GRADING - PPGS™	100%	98%	95%	90%	80%	70%	60%	LAST MSR

MODEL 700 SEMI-AUTO – .22 WMR cal., blow back action, 22 in. round blue barrel, 5 or 10 shot detachable box mag., open adj. folding rear sight, ramped blade front sight, full size Monte Carlo style pistol grip walnut stock, high polish blue finish, composite buttplate, 6 1/2 lbs. Mfg. 1975-1986.

$425 $365 $315 $275 $235 $195 $175

* ***Model 700 DL Deluxe*** – similar to Model 700, except has extra fancy checkered Monte Carlo walnut stock. Mfg. 1978-1986.

$475 $425 $355 $300 $260 $220 $195

MODEL 749 SLIDE ACTION – .22 LR cal., 15 shot tube mag., 19 in. barrel, bead front sight, step adj. rear sight, walnut stained straight grip stock, grooved slide handle, 4 1/2 lbs. Mfg. 1970-1971.

$150 $130 $115 $100 $85 $75 $65

This model was manufactured by Rossi and imported from Brazil. It was not listed in any H&R catalog.

MODEL 750 BOLT ACTION – .22 LR cal., 22 (mfg. 1966-1969) or 24 in. round barrel, bolt cocks on closing, plain full size sporter walnut pistol grip, rounded (mfg. 1978-1986) or Monte Carlo comb (mfg. 1963-1964) stock, finger grooved forend (mfg. 1965), bead front sight, step adj. rear sight, blue finish. Mfg. 1953-1986.

$125 $110 $100 $85 $75 $65 $50

MODEL 751 BOLT ACTION – similar to Model 750, except has Mannlicher stock, 5 1/4 lbs. Mfg. 1971-1972.

$155 $130 $115 $100 $85 $75 $65

MODEL 755 SAHARA SINGLE SHOT – .22 S, L, or LR cal., blow back action, automatic ejection, 18 in. blue barrel, walnut stained hardwood Mannlicher pistol grip stock, blade front sight, step adj. rear sight, 4 lbs. Mfg. 1963-1970.

$145 $125 $110 $100 $85 $75 $65

MODEL 760 SINGLE SHOT – similar to Model 755, except has regular Monte Carlo style stock. Mfg. 1965-1970.

$165 $145 $125 $110 $90 $80 $70

MODEL 765 PIONEER BOLT ACTION – .22 S, L, or LR cal., single shot, 24 in. blue barrel, pistol grip walnut stock, "RED DEVIL" hooded front (designed by Walter Roper) or dovetailed bead sight (mfg. 1950-1952), step adj. rear sight, safety on right side of receiver, "redi-feed" loading platform, 5 lbs. Mfg. 1948-1952.

$175 $155 $130 $115 $95 $85 $75

MODEL 766 PIONEER BOLT ACTION – similar to Model 765, except has nickel finish. Mfg. 1949-1950.

$200 $180 $160 $130 $120 $100 $90

MODEL 800 LYNX SEMI-AUTO – .22 LR cal., blow back action, 22 in. round barrel, blue finish, 10 shot detachable box mag., full size plain pistol grip walnut stock, bead front sight, open step adj. rear sight, 6 lbs. Mfg. 1958-1961.

$300 $265 $225 $185 $160 $140 $120

MODEL 880 LYNX DELUXE – similar to Model 800, except has nickel finish. Mfg. 1958-1959.

$375 $325 $285 $235 $210 $175 $150

MODEL 852 FIELDSMAN BOLT ACTION – .22 LR cal., repeater action, 21 shot tube mag., 24 in. tapered barrel, full size pistol grip walnut stained hardwood stock, blue finish, bead front sight, step adj. rear sight, 5 1/2 lbs. Mfg. 1952-1954.

$175 $155 $130 $115 $95 $85 $75

MODEL 865 PLAINSMAN BOLT ACTION – .22 LR cal., repeater action, 22 (mfg. 1966-1969) or 24 in. round tapered barrel, 5 shot detachable box mag., full size oil finished or satin (mfg. 1959-1961) walnut, blonde Monte Carlo (mfg. 1962-1964), or walnut stained hardwood (mfg. 1970-1975) pistol grip stock, ramped white bead front sight, step adj. rear sight, blue finish, single claw extractor, stamped steel trigger guard, 5 lbs. Mfg. 1949-1986.

$135 $120 $100 $85 $75 $65 $50

Add 10%-50% for stock options, depending on grade.

MODEL 866 BOLT ACTION – similar to Model 865, except has Mannlicher stock. Mfg. 1971-1972.

$175 $155 $130 $115 $95 $85 $75

MODEL 5200 TARGET BOLT ACTION – .22 LR cal., single shot, bolt cocks on closing, 28 in. heavy barrel, no sights, drilled and tapped, full size walnut stained birch target stock, accessory rail, palm stop, adj. trigger, high polish blue finish, fluid feed loading platform, similar to Mil-Spec version of the Winchester Model 52. Mfg. 1981-1986.

$550 $475 $415 $360 $315 $265 $230

GRADING - PPGS™	100%	98%	95%	90%	80%	70%	60%	LAST MSR

MODEL 5200S SPORTER BOLT ACTION – .22 LR cal., repeater action, 24 in. bull barrel, 5 shot detachable box mag., hand checkered American walnut pistol grip stock, adj. trigger, hooded ramped blade front sight, adj. Lyman aperture sight, blue finish, 6 1/2 lbs. Limited mfg. 1982-1983.

	$650	$565	$485	$425	$360	$310	$265	

MODEL M-4 SURVIVAL – .22 Hornet cal., 5 shot mag., 14 or 16 in. barrel, wire collapsible stock. Mfg. for U.S. military during the 1950s.

	$2,000	$1,650	$1,425	$1,125	$965	$855	$750	

Add $400 for barrels less than 16 in. (sales restricted).

This model was packaged in survival kits for U.S. pilots, and is usually encountered with a replacement barrel of 16 inches or more.

MODEL M-1 GARAND – refer to U.S. Military Long Arms in the U section.

MODEL T-48 FAL/T223 (H&R MFG. FAL) – .308 Win. cal., 20 shot mag., selective fire. Approx. 200 mfg. for U.S. military during the 1960s.

Recent values are approx. $10,000 for 98% condition.

Since sales of this rifle are restricted, it is not often encountered in the used marketplace.

M-14 RIFLE/GUERILLA GUN – .308 Win. cal., selective fire, 20 shot mag., Guerilla gun mfg. in prototype only. Mfg. for the U.S. military during the 1960s.

Recent values are approx. $20,000 for 98% condition.

Since sales of this rifle are restricted, it is not often encountered in the used marketplace.

M-16 AUTOMATIC BATTLE RIFLE – 5.56 NATO cal., selective fire, 20 or 30 shot mag. Mfg. for the U.S. military during the 1960s-1970s.

Recent values are approx. $15,000 for 98% condition.

Since sales of this rifle are restricted, it is not often encountered in the used marketplace.

T-223 (H&R MFG. H&K 93) – .223 Rem. or .308 Win. cal., selective fire, 20 shot mag. Approx. 200 mfg. for the U.S. military during the 1960s.

Recent values are approx. $15,000 for 98% condition.

Since sales of this rifle are restricted, it is not often encountered in the used marketplace.

SLIDE ACTION CENTERFIRE RIFLE – .300 Sav. cal., prototype, only 2 known to exist, one complete firing model, and one non-firing model, based on Eugene Reising's patent. Mfg. during the 1940s-1950s.

Extreme rarity precludes accurate pricing on this model.

SHOTGUNS: BOLT ACTION

MODEL 120 – 16 ga., 2 3/4 in. chamber, 5 shot tube mag., blue finish, 26 in. barrel with choke tubes, safety on right side of receiver, oil finished walnut pistol grip stock, vent. rubber recoil pad, 7 1/2 lbs. Mfg. 1941-1942.

	$145	$125	$110	$95	$85	$75	$65	

H&R sold the rights to this shotgun to Sears Roebuck & Co, and it was mfg. by High Standard.

MODEL 121 – 20 ga., 2 3/4 in. chamber, otherwise similar to Model 120. Mfg. 1941-1942.

	$145	$125	$110	$95	$85	$75	$65	

H&R sold the rights to this shotgun to Sears Roebuck & Co, and it was mfg. by High Standard.

MODEL 348 GAMESTER – 12 or 16 ga., 28 in. barrel, 3 shot tube mag., blue finish, safety located on the right side of the receiver, oil finished pistol grip walnut stock with fluted comb, hard rubber recoil pad, 7 1/2 lbs. Mfg. 1949-1954.

	$165	$145	$125	$110	$90	$80	$70	

MODEL 349 GAMESTER DELUXE – 12 or 16 ga., 26 in. barrel, 3 shot tube mag., H&R's "VARI-CHOKE" adj. choke, oil finished pistol grip walnut stock with fluted comb, 7 1/2 lbs. Mfg. 1952-1955.

	$175	$155	$130	$115	$95	$85	$75	

MODEL 351 HUNTSMAN – similar to the Model 349 Deluxe, except has new model number and walnut stained hardwood stock. Mfg. 1956-1958.

	$175	$155	$130	$115	$95	$85	$75	

SHOTGUNS: DOUBLE

ANSON & DEELEY DOUBLE BARREL SxS – 10 or 12 ga., 28, 30, or 32 in. damascus barrels, hammerless boxlock action, 4 grades of European walnut stock and forend, 4 levels of engraving, Anson & Deeley markings on lockplate, H&R markings on barrels, ser. no. 01-3000+. Mfg. 1883-1887.

	N/A	$1,000	$865	$765	$660	$495	$450	

GRADING - PPGS™	100%	98%	95%	90%	80%	70%	60%	LAST MSR

SMALL BORE DOUBLE BARREL HAMMER GUN - 20, 28 ga., or .410 bore, 26 or 28 in. barrels, SxS, sidelock action with exposed hammers, English checkered walnut pistol grip stock, DT, crossbolt barrel locking, forged steel case hardened frame, 5 1/4-6 1/4 lbs. Mfg. 1909-1919.

N/A	$1,500	$1,225	$1,050	$875	$675	$550	

MODEL 404 DOUBLE BARREL SxS - 12, 20 ga., or .410 bore, hammerless boxlock action, DT, 26 or 28 in. barrels, walnut stained Brazilian hardwood stock with beavertail forend, with (Model 404) or w/o (Model 404C) machine checkering. Mfg. by Rossi 1970-1971.

$250	$220	$190	$155	$130	$115	$100	

Add 15% for Model 404C.

HARRICH #1 O/U - 12 ga., 2 3/4 in. chambers, hammerless boxlock action, single barrel mfg. on O/U frame from Ferlach, Austria, raised vent. rib, 30 or 32 in. barrel, blue finish, engraved receiver, European walnut buttstock and beavertail forearm, Anson & Deeley crossbolt with double locking lugs. Mfg. 1971-1975.

$1,950	$1,635	$1,425	$1,125	$965	$855	$750	

MODEL 1212 O/U - 12 ga., 2 3/4 in. chambers, boxlock hammerless action, European walnut stock and beavertail forearm, SST, extractors, 28 in. barrels with vent. rib, gold bead front sight, 7 lbs. Mfg. by Lanber 1975-1980.

$400	$365	$325	$285	$250	$200	$175	

* ***Model 1212WF*** - similar to Model 1212, except has 3 in. chambers, 30 in. barrels, 7 1/2 lbs. Mfg. by Lanber 1975-1980.

$350	$320	$275	$225	$200	$165	$140	

SHOTGUNS: SINGLE BARREL, 1900-1942 MFG.

MODEL 1900 - 12, 16, or 20 ga., 28, 30, or 32 in. barrel, top lever break action, two-piece takedown via removable hinge pin, full choke, case hardened frame, walnut pistol grip stock with short forearm, hard rubber buttplate, 5 3/4 - 6 3/8 lbs. Mfg. 1901-1916.

$175	$155	$130	$115	$95	$85	$75	

This model may have been available under a store brand name through mail order catalogs.

MODEL 1905 - many gauges, small frame version of the Model 1900. Mfg. 1906-1916.

$175	$155	$130	$115	$95	$85	$75	

Add 25% for auto-ejector model in .44 cal., 14mm, and .410 Eley chambering (mfg. 1911-1916).

This model may have been available under a store brand name through mail order catalogs.

MODEL 1908 - 12, 16, 20, 24 (disc. 1923), 28 (disc. 1923) ga., or .410 bore (new 1925), top lever break action, case hardened frame, 26, 28, 30, or 32 in. barrel, three piece takedown (non-removable hinge pin), non-adj. barrel lock, walnut pistol grip stock and forearm, hard rubber buttplate, 5 3/4 - 6 3/8 lbs. Mfg. 1909-1942.

$195	$175	$150	$125	$110	$95	$85	

Add 25% for 24 or 28 ga.
Subtract 25% for store brand model.

The first variation (mfg. 1909-1921) has a 2 1/2 in. chamber and short forearm, the second variation (mfg. 1922-1930) has a 2 3/4 in. chamber and slim, long forearm, third variation (mfg. 1925-1942) featured .410 bore, and the fourth variation (mfg. 1931-1942) had a wider forearm and was known as the No. 8 Standard, and "STANDARD" is marked on the left side of frame.

This model was available under a store brand name through mail order catalogs.

MODEL 1915 - 24, 28 ga., or .410 bore, top lever break action, 26, 28, or 30 in. barrel, small frame, non-adj. barrel lock, three piece take down (non-removable hinge pin), case hardened frame, walnut pistol grip stock and forearm, hard rubber buttplate, 4 - 4 3/4 lbs. Mfg. 1916-1942.

$375	$325	$285	$235	$210	$175	$150	

The .410 bore can be dated by its markings: 410-44 (mfg. 1916-1921), 410-12MM (mfg. 1922-1936), and 410 (mfg. 1937-1941 - only pre-WWII model chambered for the 3 in. shell).

This model was available under a store brand name through mail order catalogs.

The first variation (mfg. 1916-1921) has a short forearm, the second variation (mfg. 1922-1930) has a long forearm and squared off pistol grip, the third variation (mfg. 1931-1936) was known as the No. 5 Standard (may be marked on the frame), and the fourth variation (mfg. 1937-1942) is a .410 bore chambered for 3 in. shells.

GRADING - PPGS™	100%	98%	95%	90%	80%	70%	60%	LAST MSR

BAY STATE & COLUMBIA BRAND NAME – 12, 16 ga., or .410 bore, top lever break action, blue finish, 26, 28, 30, or 32 in. barrel, three piece takedown (non-removable hinge pin), walnut pistol stock and forearm, hard rubber buttplate, 5 3/4 - 6 3/8 lbs. Mfg. 1916-1942.

$200 $180 $160 $130 $120 $100 $90

This model was a brand name shotgun and can be found under the following trade names: No. 7 Bay State, No. 7 Bay State Lightweight Gun, No. 9 Columbia, No. 9 Bay State, No. 9 Bay State Lightweight and others.

H&R FOLDING MODEL – 12, 16, 20 ga., or .410 bore, 26 in. barrel, top lever break action, case hardened frame, blue finish, walnut pistol grip stock and forearm, 5 3/4 - 6 1/2 lbs. Mfg. 1928-1942.

$375 $325 $285 $235 $210 $175 $150

The .410 bore model was available with a 3 in. chamber after 1937. This model was known after 1931 as the No. 4 Folding Model.

H&R LIGHTWEIGHT FOLDING MODEL – 28 ga. or .410 bore, 26 in. barrel, top lever break action, case hardened small frame, blue finish, walnut pistol grip stock and forearm, 5 3/4 - 6 1/2 lbs. Mfg. 1925-1930.

$400 $350 $300 $265 $225 $190 $165

The .410 bore model was available with a 3 in. chamber after 1937. This model was known after 1931 as the No. 4 Folding Lightweight Model.

H&R HAMMERLESS – 12, 16, 20 ga., or .410 bore, top lever break action, 26, 28, 30, 32, 34, or 36 in. barrel, three piece take down (non-removable hinge pin), snap-on forearm, walnut pistol grip stock, 6 1/4 - 7 1/4 lbs. Mfg. 1925-1941.

$400 $350 $300 $265 $225 $190 $165

The .410 bore model was available with a 3 in. chamber after 1937. After 1931, this model was listed in catalogs as the No. 3 Hammerless Model.

H&R RE-ENFORCED BREECH (A.K.A. HEAVY BREECH) – 10 (new 1931), 12, 16, or 20 (new 1933) ga., large heavy frame, top lever break action, 30, 32, 34, or 36 in. barrel, case hardened frame, walnut pistol grip stock and forearm, hard rubber buttplate, 7 - 7 3/8 lbs. Mfg. 1913-1941.

$385 $330 $285 $235 $210 $175 $150

Add 15% for 10 ga.

After 1931 this model is known as the No. 6 Heavy Breech Model, and is marked "RE-ENFORCED" on the frame.

H&R TOP RIB MODEL – 12, 16, or 20 ga., top lever break action, 28 or 30 in. barrel with chokes, case hardened frame, three piece take down (non-removable hinge pin), non-adj. barrel lock, walnut pistol grip stock, hard rubber buttplate, 5 1/4 - 6 1/4 lbs. Mfg. 1926-1932.

$325 $285 $250 $200 $175 $150 $125

After 1931, this model was listed in catalogs as the No. 2 Top Rib Model.

SHOTGUNS: SINGLE BARREL, 1943-1986 MFG.

TOPPER MODEL HISTORY – the Topper name was applied to a large series of single barrel shotguns, therefore there were several different models that used the Topper name starting with the Model 48 in 1943 and continuing through the early Model 058/098. All other single barrel shotguns are variations of these basic models except for the Hammerless Model manufactured between 1925 and 1942. The Topper name was last used in the 1974 catalog. The Model 088 was actually introduced in 1979 but did not become the main line model until 1982. The Topper name has also been used by New England Firearms and H&R 1871 after the purchase by Marlin, but these models are not considered true H&R Topper single barrel shotguns.

MODEL 47 TOPPER DELUXE – similar to Model 48 Topper, except has all chrome finish. Mfg. 1947.

$165 $145 $125 $110 $90 $80 $70

MODEL 48 TOPPER – 12, 16, 20 ga., or .410 bore, 26 to 32 in. barrel with chokes, case hardened frame, top lever break open action, rebounding hammer, self-adj. barrel latch, auto-ejector, three-piece takedown (snap on forearm), oil finished walnut pistol grip stock, semi-beavertail forearm, hard rubber buttplate, this model was the first to use the Topper name. Mfg. 1943-1956.

$150 $130 $115 $100 $85 $75 $60

MODEL 058 TOPPER – 12, 16, 20 ga., or .410 bore, 26 to 36 in. barrel with chokes, case hardened frame, side lever break open action, self-adj. barrel latch, walnut stained pistol grip hardwood stock, semi-beavertail forearm, hard rubber buttplate, 13 3/4 in. LOP, rebounding hammer (mfg. 1974-1976) or transfer bar ignition system (mfg. 1977-1981). Mfg. 1974-1981.

$165 $145 $125 $110 $90 $80 $70

Guns are marked Model 58.

GRADING - PPGS™	100%	98%	95%	90%	80%	70%	60%	LAST MSR

MODEL 088 AMERICAN CLASSIC – 12, 16, 20, 28 ga., or .410 bore, 25 to 36 in. barrel with chokes, side lever break open action, transfer bar ignition system, case colored frame, walnut stained semi-pistol grip hardwood stock and semi-beavertail forearm, hard rubber buttplate, 13 3/4 in. LOP, 5 - 6 1/2 lbs. Mfg. 1979-1986.

$165 $145 $125 $110 $90 $80 $70

The name "American Classic" was not added until the 1982 catalog.

Guns are marked Model 88.

* ***Model 088 American Classic Junior*** – similar to Model 088 American Classic, except only 20 ga. or .410 bore, 12 3/4 in. LOP, 5 lbs. Mfg. 1979-1986.

$165 $145 $125 $110 $90 $80 $70

MODEL 098 TOPPER DELUXE – 12 (new 1977), 20 ga., or .410 bore, deluxe version of the Model 058, 26 in. barrel with chokes, nickel frame, black hardwood pistol grip stock, 5 1/2 lbs. Mfg. 1974-1981.

$185 $165 $140 $120 $100 $90 $80

Guns are marked Model 98.

MODEL 099 AMERICAN CLASSIC DELUXE – 12, 16, 20 ga., or .410 bore, deluxe version of the Model 088, 25 to 28 in. barrel with choke, electroless nickel frame, walnut stained pistol grip hardwood stock, semi-beavertail forearm, transfer bar ignition system, hard rubber buttplate, 5 1/4 - 6 1/2 lbs. Mfg. 1982-1986.

$185 $165 $140 $120 $100 $90 $80

Guns are marked Model 99.

MODEL 148 TOPPER – 12, 16, 20 ga., or .410 bore, similar to Model 48 Topper, except has vent. rubber recoil pad. Mfg. 1957-1958.

$150 $130 $115 $100 $85 $75 $65

* ***Model 148A Topper*** – similar to the Model 148 Topper, except has a side lever break open action. Mfg. 1958-1961.

$155 $135 $120 $100 $85 $75 $65

MODEL 158 TOPPER – 12, 16, 20 ga., or .410 bore, 28 to 36 in. barrel with chokes, side lever break open action, rebounding hammer, self-adj. barrel latch, three piece takedown with snap on forearm, case hardened frame, blue finish, glossy-satin finished pistol grip walnut stock, semi-beavertail forearm, vent. rubber recoil pad. Mfg. 1962-1973.

$155 $135 $120 $100 $85 $75 $65

MODEL 158 COMBO RIFLE/SHOTGUN – please refer to the Rifle section.

MODEL 159 GOLDEN SQUIRE – 12 or 20 ga., side lever break open action, 28 (20 ga.) or 30 (12 ga.) in. barrel with chokes, rebounding hammer, self-adj. barrel latch, three piece takedown, snap on forearm, case hardened frame, high polish blue finish, glossy satin finished straight grip walnut stock, Schnabel forearm, custom recoil pad, gold hammer, trigger, gold filled lettering. Mfg. 1964-1966.

$225 $195 $170 $140 $125 $110 $95

MODEL 162 TOPPER BUCK – 12 or 20 (mfg. 1973-1978) ga., side lever break open action, 22 or 24 in. barrel, rebounding hammer, self-adj. barrel latch, case hardened frame, blue finish, three piece takedown, screw retained forearm, pistol grip walnut stained hardwood stock, semi-beavertail forearm, vent. rubber recoil pad, adj. rear aperture sight. Mfg. 1968-1986.

$185 $165 $140 $120 $100 $90 $80

MODEL 176 MAGNUM – 10, 12, 16, or 20 ga., heavy frame, 32 or 36 in. barrel, chokes, side lever break open action, self-adj. barrel latch, three piece takedown, case hardened frame, blue finish, walnut stained pistol grip hardwood stock, semi-beavertail forearm, vent. rubber recoil pad, approx. 9 1/2 lbs. Mfg. 1975-1986.

$350 $320 $275 $225 $200 $165 $140

Add 15% for 10 ga. with 36 in. barrel.

MODEL 176 SLUG GUN – 10 ga., 3 1/2 in. chamber, 28 in. barrel, heavy frame, side lever break open action, cylinder bore choke, three piece takedown, bored special for rifled slugs, case hardened frame, walnut stained pistol grip hardwood stock, semi-beavertail forearm, vent. rubber recoil pad, 9 1/4 lbs. Mfg. 1982-1986.

$375 $325 $285 $235 $210 $175 $150

MODEL 188 TOPPER DELUXE – .410 bore, 3 in. chamber, 28 in. barrel with chokes, chrome frame, top lever break open action, rebounding hammer, deluxe variation of the Model 148, black lacquer pistol grip stock, semi-beavertail forearm, vent. rubber recoil pad. Mfg. 1957-1958.

$175 $155 $130 $115 $95 $85 $75

GRADING - PPGS™ 100% 98% 95% 90% 80% 70% 60% LAST MSR

* ***Model 188A Topper Deluxe*** – similar to Model 188 Topper Deluxe, except has multi-colored lacquered stock. Mfg. 1958-1961.

$185 $165 $140 $120 $100 $90 $80

MODEL 198 TOPPER DELUXE – 20 ga. (mfg. 1970-1973) or .410 bore, 3 in. chamber, 26 or 28 in. barrel, side lever break open action, deluxe variation of the Model 158, rebounding hammer, chrome finish, three piece takedown, snap-on forearm, glossy satin finished ebony painted pistol grip stock, semi-beavertail forearm, approx. 5 1/2 lbs. Mfg. 1962-1973.

$185 $165 $140 $120 $100 $90 $80

MODEL 459 GOLDEN SQUIRE JR. – 20 ga. or .410 bore, side lever brake open action, gold hammer, trigger, and gold filled lettering, rebounding hammer, 26 in. barrel with chokes, three piece takedown, snap on forearm, case hardened frame, high polish blue finish, straight grip walnut stock with Schnabel forearm, custom recoil pad, short LOP. Mfg. 1964.

$235 $200 $175 $145 $125 $110 $95

MODEL 480 TOPPER JR. – 20 ga. or .410 bore, Junior version of the Model 148, 12 1/2 in. LOP, 26 in. barrel with chokes, satin lacquered stock and forearm, hard rubber buttplate, approx. 5 lbs. Mfg. 1958-1961.

$155 $135 $120 $100 $85 $75 $65

MODEL 488 DELUXE SPORTER – 12, 16, 20 ga., or .410 bore, 28 or 30 in. barrel with chokes, deluxe edition of the Model 48, top lever break open action, rebounding hammer, chrome finished frame, hard rubber buttplate, pistol grip walnut stock and semi-beavertail forearm, approx. 6 lbs. Mfg. 1951-1957.

$195 $175 $150 $125 $110 $95 $85

MODEL 490 TOPPER JR. – 20, 28 ga., or .410 bore, side lever break open action, junior verson of the Model 158, 26 in. barrel, rebounding hammer, three-piece takedown, case hardened frame, walnut stained pistol grip hardwood stock, semi-beavertail forearm, vent. rubber recoil pad, short LOP, 5 lbs. Mfg. 1961-1983.

$155 $135 $120 $100 $85 $75 $65

MODEL 490 GREENWING – 20, 28 ga., or .410 bore, based on the Model 158, transfer bar ignition system, 26 in. barrel, high polished blue frame, walnut stained pistol grip hardwood stock, semi-beavertail forearm, hard rubber buttplate, gold trigger, gold markings, short LOP, 5 lbs. Mfg. 1978-1983.

$185 $165 $140 $120 $100 $90 $80

MODEL 580 TOPPER JR. DELUXE – 20 ga. (new 1959) or .410 bore, junior version of the Model 148, 26 in. barrel, chrome frame finish, ebony painted pistol grip stock, satin lacquered semi-beavertail forearm, short LOP, 5 lbs. Mfg. 1958-1960.

$195 $175 $150 $125 $110 $95 $85

MODEL 590 TOPPER JR. DELUXE – 20 ga. or .410 bore, junior version of the Model 158, similar to Model 580 Topper Jr. Deluxe, except has satin finished forearm. Mfg. 1961-1963.

$165 $145 $125 $110 $90 $80 $70

SHOTGUNS: SEMI-AUTO

MODEL 403 – .410 bore, gas operated, hammerless small size receiver, 3 in. chamber, 6 shot tube mag., 26 in. barrel, blue finish, walnut pistol grip stock, vent. rubber recoil pad, 5 3/4 lbs. Mfg. by Noble Firearms Corp. 1964.

$200 $180 $160 $130 $120 $100 $90

H&R MANUFRANCE – 12 ga., 3 in. chamber, 4 shot tube mag., recoil operated, takedown model with interchangeable barrels, checkered walnut buttstock. Mfg. by Manufrance 1969.

$250 $220 $190 $155 $130 $115 $100

SHOTGUNS: SLIDE ACTION

MODEL 400 – 12 or 16 ga., 2 3/4 in. chamber, 6 shot tube mag., hammerless standard size receiver, 28 in. barrel, blue finish, vent. rubber recoil pad, walnut pistol grip stock, 7 1/4 lbs. Mfg. by Noble Firearms Corp. 1958-1967.

$165 $145 $125 $110 $90 $80 $70

MODEL 401 – 12 or 16 ga., similar to Model 400, except has fancy checkered walnut, adj. "VARI-CHOKE", 7 1/4 lbs. Mfg. by Noble Firearms Corp. 1958-1963.

$185 $165 $140 $120 $100 $90 $80

MODEL 402 – similar to Model 400, except is .410 bore, small frame, 26 in. barrel, 5 1/2 lbs. Mfg. by Noble Firearms Corp. 1959-1967.

$200 $180 $160 $130 $120 $100 $90

GRADING - PPGS™	100%	98%	95%	90%	80%	70%	60%	LAST MSR

MODEL 440 – 12, 16 (2 3/4 in. chamber), or 20 ga., 4 shot tube mag., 26 or 28 in. barrel, hammerless standard size receiver, push-button safety at rear of trigger, bolt release at front of trigger, side ejecting, blue finish, walnut pistol grip stock and semi-beavertail forearm, vent. rubber recoil pad, 6 1/4 - 6 1/2 lbs. Mfg. by Manufrance 1968-1973.

$165 $145 $125 $110 $90 $80 $70

MODEL 442 – similar to Model 440, except has extra fancy checkered walnut stock and forearm. Mfg. 1969-1972.

$195 $175 $150 $125 $110 $95 $85

MODEL 500 – 12, 16, or 20 ga., 2 3/4 in. chamber, 3 or 4 shot detachable box mag., 28 or 30 in. barrel, oil finished walnut stock, 6 1/4 - 6 3/4 lbs. Mfg. 1946.

This model never appeared in any H&R catalog, and likely exists in prototype form only. Design appears to be based on a Eugene Reising patent.

COMMEMORATIVES

CHISHOLM TRAIL MODEL 999 – 300 mfg., not listed in catalogs. Mfg. 1967.

$495 $435 $370 $320 $270 $230 $195

NEBRASKA CENTENNIAL – letter coded "NE" serial numbers, presentation case, unknown number mfg. 1967.

$1,000 $865 $765 $660 $575 $495 $450

MODEL 926 ABILENE KANSAS CENTENNIAL – .22 LR cal., barrel is marked "Abilene Kansas" and "1869 Centennial 1969", not listed in catalogs, 300 mfg. 1969 only.

$350 $320 $275 $225 $200 $165 $140

MODEL 999 1 of 999 – similar to previous Model 999 1 of 999, except listed in 1981 catalog, values are for complete set. Mfg. 1981-1986.

$700 $600 $525 $450 $385 $340 $285

MODEL 171 AND 171 DELUXE – please refer to listings under Rifles section.

MODEL 172 SILVER CARBINE – please refer to listing under Rifles section.

CUSTER MEMORIAL ISSUE (MODEL 177) – .45-70 Govt. cal., limited production, deluxe walnut stock, highly engraved, gold inlaid, mahogany display case and two volumes on Custer history - *Reno Court of Inquiry* and *Men with Custer*. Each weapon bears the name of one who fell at Little Big Horn, originally 25 Officer models and 243 Enlisted Men models were scheduled to be mfg., but only 100 total were actually made. Total number made of each model is unknown.

* ***Custer Memorial Issue Officer's Model*** – 26 in. heavy barrel, tang mounted rear sight, box and accessories, 8 lbs.

  $3,995 $3,150 $2,400 $2,100 $1,900 $1,500 $1,200 *$3,000 (1973)*

* ***Custer Memorial Issue Enlisted Men's Model*** – 22 in. heavy barrel, original ladder style rear sight, box and accessories, 7 lbs.

  $1,995 $1,400 $900 $785 $655 $550 $465 *$2,000 (1973)*

MODEL 174 LITTLE BIG HORN CARBINE – .45-70 Govt. cal., replica of Model 1873 Springfield Trapdoor Cavalry Carbine, heavy 22 in. blue barrel, plain walnut stock with metal buttplate and grip adaptor, adj. rear sight, blade front sight, color case hardened receiver, lock plate and buttplate, engraved lock and receiver, includes box with the book *In the Valley of the Little Big Horn*, 7 lbs., 4 oz. Mfg. 1972-1983.

$850 $725 $640 $550 $490 $425 $375

MODEL 178 SPRINGFIELD COMMEMORATIVE RIFLE – please refer to Rifles section.

MODEL 1871-1971 H&R CENTENNIAL COMMEMORATIVE OFFICERS RIFLE – .45-70 Govt. cal., 26 in. heavy blue barrel, select hand checkered walnut stock, metal buttplate, forend cap, and grip adaptor, tang mounted adj. rear sight, blade front sight, cleaning rod mounted under barrel, color case hardened receiver, lock plate, and buttplate, original production was going to be 10,000, but number actually mfg. is unknown. Mfg. 1971.

$1,250 $995 $825 $725 $675 $600 $500

Subtract $225 for ser. nos. 1501-3000 or $300 for ser. nos. 3001-10000.

HARRIS GUNWORKS

Previous firearms manufacturer located in Phoenix, AZ 1995-March 31, 2000. Previously named Harris-McMillan Gunworks and G. McMillan and Co., Inc.

GRADING - PPGS™	100%	98%	95%	90%	80%	70%	60%	LAST MSR

RIFLES: BOLT ACTION

BENCHREST COMPETITOR – .222 Rem. (disc.), .243 Win., 6mm Rem., 6mm PPC, 6mm BR, or .308 Win. cal., benchrest configuration. Mfg. 1993-2000.

$2,675 $2,425 $1,950 $1,675 $1,425 $1,200 $1,025 *$3,050*

NATIONAL MATCH COMPETITOR – .308 Win., or 7mm-08 Rem. cal. Mfg. 1993-2000.

$3,125 $2,675 $2,300 $1,875 $1,650 $1,325 $1,100 *$3,500*

LONG RANGE TARGET MODEL – .300 Win. Mag., .300 Phoenix, .30-378 Wby. Mag., .30-416 Rigby, .338 Lapua, or 7mm Rem. Mag. cal., black synthetic fully adj. stock, w/o sights, grey barrel finish. Mfg. 1996-2000.

$3,225 $2,700 $2,325 $1,900 $1,650 $1,325 $1,100 *$3,620*

TALON SPORTER – available in various cals. between .22-250 Rem. and .416 Rem., receiver available in either 4340 chrome molybdenum or 17-4 stainless steel, drilled and tapped, match grade barrel. Mfg. 1992-2000.

$2,600 $2,075 $1,725 $1,375 $1,050 $895 $800 *$2,900*

The Talon action was patterned after the Winchester pre-64 Model 70. It featured a coned breech, controlled feed, claw extractor, and 3 position safety.

SIGNATURE CLASSIC SPORTER – various cals. available between .22-250 Rem. and .416 Rem., premium wood stock, matte metal finish, buttoning used on rifling for 22 or 24 in. stainless steel barrel, McMillan action made from 4340 chrome moly steel (either left- or right-handed), 3 or 4 shot mag. supplied with 5 shot test target. Mfg. 1988-2000.

$2,450 $2,000 $1,675 $1,325 $1,000 $895 $800 *$2,700*

SIGNATURE VARMINTER – similar to Signature Model, except is available in 12 cals. between .22-250 Rem. and .350 Rem. Mag., hand bedded fiberglass stock, adj. trigger, 26 in. heavily contoured barrel. Mfg. 1988-2000.

$2,450 $2,000 $1,675 $1,325 $1,000 $895 $800 *$2,700*

SIGNATURE TITANIUM MOUNTAIN RIFLE – .270 Win., .280 Rem., .30-06, .300 Win. Mag., .338 Win. Mag., or 7mm Rem. Mag. cal., lighter weight variation with shorter stainless steel or graphite/steel composite barrel, 5 3/4 (w/graphite barrel), or 6 1/2 lbs. Mfg. 1990-2000.

$2,950 $2,575 $2,300 $1,925 $1,650 $1,325 $1,100 *$3,300*

Add $400 with graphite barrel.

SIGNATURE ALASKAN – available in many cals. between .270 Win. and .458 Win. Mag. Mfg. 1990-2000.

$3,425 $2,725 $2,275 $1,650 $1,250 $1,125 $900 *$3,800*

TALON SAFARI – available in many cals. between .300 Win. Mag. and .460 Wby. Mag., hand bedded fiberglass stock, 4 shot mag., 24 in. stainless steel barrel, matte black finish, 9 1/2 lbs. Mfg. 1988-2000.

$3,650 $2,850 $2,500 $2,150 $2,000 $1,850 $1,700 *$3,900*

Add $300 for .300 Phoenix, .30-416 Rigby, .30-378 Wby. Mag., .338 Lapua, .335-378, .338-378, .378 Wby. Mag., .416 Wby. Mag. or Rigby, or .460 Wby. Mag. cal.

The Talon action was patterned after the Winchester pre-64 Model 70. It featured a coned breech, controlled feed, claw extractor, and 3 position safety. Older Signature action rifles do not have this new Talon action.

M-40 SNIPER RIFLE – .308 Win. cal., Remington action with McMillan match grade heavy contour barrel, fiberglass stock with recoil pad, 4 shot mag., 9 lbs. Mfg. 1990-2000.

$1,825 $1,450 $1,125 $925 $800 $700 $600 *$2,000*

M-86 SNIPER RIFLE – .300 Phoenix (disc. 1996), .30-06 (new 1989), .300 Win. Mag., or .308 Win. cal., fiberglass stock, variety of optical sights. Mfg. 1988-2000.

$2,450 $2,000 $1,675 $1,325 $1,000 $895 $800 *$2,700*

Add $300 for .300 Phoenix cal. with Harris action (disc. 1996).
Add $200 for takedown feature (mfg. 1993-96).

.300 PHOENIX – available in most popular .30 cals., special fiberglass stock with adj. cheekpiece and buttplate, right or left-hand action, 12 1/2 lbs. Mfg. 1997-2000.

$3,025 $2,650 $2,325 $1,925 $1,675 $1,325 $1,100 *$3,380*

M-87 LONG RANGE SNIPER RIFLE – .50 BMG cal., stainless steel bolt action, 29 in. barrel with muzzle brake, single shot, camo synthetic stock, accurate to 1,500 meters, 21 lbs. Mfg. 1988-2000.

$3,450 $2,800 $2,375 $2,000 $1,850 $1,700 $1,575 *$3,885*

GRADING - PPGS™	100%	98%	95%	90%	80%	70%	60%	LAST MSR

* ***M-87R Long Range Sniper Rifle*** – similar to Model 87, except has 5 shot fixed box mag. Mfg. 1990-2000.

	$3,725	$2,950	$2,550	$2,200	$2,000	$1,850	$1,700	*$4,000*

M-88 U.S. NAVY – .50 BMG cal., reintroduced U.S. Navy Seal Team shell holder single shot action with thumbhole stock (one-piece or breakdown two-piece), 24 lbs. Mfg. 1997-2000.

	$3,250	$2,600	$2,200	$1,625	$1,250	$1,125	$900	*$3,600*

Add $300 for two-piece breakdown stock.

M-89 SNIPER RIFLE – .308 Win. cal., 28 in. barrel with suppressor (also available without), fiberglass stock adj. for length and recoil pad, 15 1/4 lbs. Mfg. 1990-2000.

	$2,875	$2,525	$2,250	$1,875	$1,650	$1,325	$1,100	*$3,200*

Add $425 for muzzle suppressor (disc. 1996).

M-92 BULL PUP – .50 BMG cal., bullpup configuration with shorter barrel. Mfg. 1993-2000.

	$4,300	$3,250	$2,750	$2,300	$2,050	$1,850	$1,700	*$4,770*

M-93 – .50 BMG cal., similar to M-87, except has folding stock and detachable 5 or 10 shot box mag. Mfg. 1993-2000.

	$3,800	$3,250	$2,750	$2,300	$2,000	$1,850	$1,700	*$4,150*

Add $300 for two-piece folding stock or dovetail combo quick disassembly fixture.

M-95 TITANIUM/GRAPHITE – .50 BMG cal., features titanium alloy M-87 receiver with graphite barrel and steel liner, single shot or repeater, approx. 18 lbs. Mfg. 1997-2000.

	$4,650	$4,175	$3,475	$2,875	$2,300	$2,050	$1,850	*$5,085*

Add $165 for fixed mag.
Add $315 for detachable mag.

RIFLES: SxS

BOXLOCK MODEL – various cals. from .270 Win. - .500 NE, engraved boxlock action, 3 leaf express rear sights, AAA wood, high polish barrel blue, equipped with aluminum case and chain, custom order. Mfg. 1998-2000.

	$12,000	$10,000	$8,500	$7,000	$6,000	$5,000	$4,000	*$12,000*

Add $1,000 for quick detachable claw scope mounts.
Add $6,000 for additional set of rifle barrels.
Add $5,000 for additional set of shotgun barrels.

SIDELOCK MODEL – various cals. from .375 H&H - .577 NE, engraved sidelock action, 3 leaf express rear sights, AAA wood, high polish barrel blue, equipped with aluminum case and chain, custom order. Mfg. 1998-2000.

	$18,200	$15,750	$12,000	$10,000	$8,500	$7,000	$6,000	*$18,200*

Add $1,000 for quick detachable claw scope mounts.
Add $6,000 for additional set of rifle barrels.
Add $5,000 for additional set of shotgun barrels.

RIFLES: SEMI-AUTO

M-96 – .50 BMG cal., gas-operated with 5 shot detachable mag., carry handle scope mount, steel receiver, 30 lbs. Mfg. 1997-2000.

	$6,200	$5,625	$5,075	$4,650	$4,175	$3,475	$2,875	*$6,800*

HARRISON & HUSSEY LTD.

Current trademark founded in 1919 and currently owned by Cogswell & Harrison, located in Slough, England.

Harrison & Hussey Ltd. was founded in 1919 and purchased by Stephen Grant & Joseph Lang Ltd. in 1930. Boss & Co. took over Harrison & Hussey's original 41 Albermarle Street location and remained there until 1961.

Harrison & Hussey guns are best quality English longarms. It is recommended that an appraisal be obtained before purchase. Harrison & Hussey records have remained intact, and Cogswell & Harrison can provide owners with a date of manufacture free of charge, providing there is a serial number. A full repair and restoration service is also offered. Please contact Cogswell & Harrison for more information about these services.

HARTFORD

Current trademark of reproductions manufactured in Italy and Brazil, and imported by E.M.F., located in Santa Ana, CA. Previously manufactured by Armi San Marco.

For individual model listings, please go to BlueBookOfGunValues.com/overflow.

GRADING - PPGS™	100%	98%	95%	90%	80%	70%	60%	LAST MSR

HARTFORD ARMORY

Previous manufacturer located in Collinsville, CT circa 2003-2006.

REVOLVERS: REPRODUCTIONS

MODEL 1875 – .357 Mag., .44 Mag., .44-40 WCF, or .45 LC cal., reproduction of original Remington Model 1875 with reinforced barrel, 5 3/4 or 7 1/2 in. barrel, blue metal finish standard (optional frame case colors by Doug Turnbull), or stainless steel construction, includes wooden presentation box with six brass snap caps. Limited mfg. 2004-2005.

100%	98%	95%	90%	80%	70%	60%	LAST MSR
$1,325	$1,100	$875	$700	$600	$500	$450	*$1,495*

Add $325 for stainless steel.
Add $325 for case colored frame.

MODEL 1890 – .357 Mag., .44 Mag., .44-40 WCF, or .45 LC cal., reproduction of original Remington Model 1890, 5 3/4 or 7 1/2 in. barrel, blue metal or stainless steel, includes wooden presentation box with six brass snap caps. Limited mfg. 2004-2005.

100%	98%	95%	90%	80%	70%	60%	LAST MSR
$1,325	$1,100	$875	$700	$600	$500	$450	*$1,495*

Add $325 for stainless steel.
Add $325 for case colored frame.

HARTFORD ARMS AND EQUIPMENT COMPANY

Previous manufacturers of sporting arms, target pistols, both automatic and single shot pistols, located at 618 Capital Avenue, Harford, CT 1925-1932. Established in 1925 and purchased by High Standard Manufacturing Company in 1932. The company made the four rimfire pistols listed and a .22 caliber bolt action rifle.

PISTOLS: SEMI-AUTO, RIMFIRE

HARTFORD AUTOMATIC TARGET MODEL 1925 – .22 LR cal., frame marked "MANFD. BY THE HARTFORD ARMS & EQUIP. CO HARTFORD, CONN. PATENTED 22 CAL. LONG RIFLE", 6 3/4 in. barrel, 10 shot mag. double pinned at base plate, fixed sights, checkered black hard rubber or ribbed vertical striation walnut grips, there are three slight variations of this pistol. Highest known serial number is 4991. A few pistols have an "S" prefix. Approx. 5,000 mfg. 1926-1930.

100%	98%	95%	90%	80%	70%	60%
$825	$725	$625	$525	$425	$350	$300

Add $300 for guns in original Hartford Arms box with paperwork (Type 1-95) numbered to gun. (Pistol illustrated with text on box).
Add $400 for guns in original Hartford Arms box with paperwork (Type 2-95) numbered to the gun Late production box. (Text only on box).

HARTFORD AUTOMATIC TARGET MODEL 1925 .22 SHORT – .22 Short cal., frame marked "MANFD. BY THE HARTFORD ARMS & EQUIP. CO HARTFORD, CONN. PATENTED 22 CAL. LONG RIFLE", with SHORT stamped on left side in front of breech, 6 3/4 in. barrel, 10 shot mag. numbered to pistol, fixed or adj. sights, checkered black hard rubber or ribbed/vertical striation walnut grips. Approx. 50 mfg. late limited production/scarce.

100%	98%	95%	90%	80%	70%	60%
$3,500	$3,000	$2,500	$2,000	$1,750	$1,500	$1,250

Add $400 for guns in original Hartford Arms box with paperwork (Type 2-95) numbered to the gun. (Text only on box) 22 Short penciled on top of lid.

All known examples are between serial number 1 and 36. Serial #36 resides in the British War Museum collection & serial #18 in the Cody Firearm Museum. The .22 short pistols can have mottled/case colored frames or blued frames, mottled/case colored slides or blued slides. The barrels have a machined band around the front sight then the barrel tapers concentrically towards the frame.

HARTFORD REPEATING PISTOL – The existence of this pistol is in doubt. If encountered, please have the gun checked for authenticity by an expert. The interrelationship of Hartford, Fiala, and Schall through the common gun design of Lucius N. Diehm suggests that if this gun exists, then it is probably a Hartford marked repeater like the Fiala and Schall. Numerous examples of unmarked Schall pistols exist, and some have confused the Schall as a Hartford repeater. None of the factory advertisements or documents mention a repeating pistol.

PISTOLS: SINGLE SHOT, RIMFIRE

HARTFORD SINGLE SHOT TARGET – .22 LR cal., frame marked "MANFD. BY THE HARTFORD ARMS & EQUIP. CO HARTFORD, CONN. PATENTED 22 CAL. LONG RIFLE", on the left side in front of the breech, 6 3/4 in. barrel, single shot manual operation, fixed sights, ribbed/vertical striation walnut, resembles a semi-auto but no provisions for a magazine.

100%	98%	95%	90%	80%	70%	60%
$925	$800	$700	$625	$500	$425	$375

GRADING - PPGS™	100%	98%	95%	90%	80%	70%	60%	LAST MSR

Add $500 for guns in original Hartford Arms box with paperwork (Type 1-SS) numbered to gun. (Has not been encountered by the collecting community).

Add $400 for guns in original High Standard box with paperwork (Type 2-SS) numbered to gun. (Written text only on box these were the High Standard assembled Hartford single shots).

High Standard assembled the pistols with slight improved modifications a number of these models in 1932 and 1933 with the majority sold by J.L. Galef & Son, Inc. These guns were manufactured from Hartford parts and carried the Hartford Arms roll mark. Boxes for High Standard manufactured guns carry on the box top label both the High Standard and Hartford names. Hartford production is unknown, but probably less than 800. High Standard production was less than 900 pistols. Early models have an "S" prefix serial number. The highest serial number known with the "S" prefix is S439. It is not currently known if this was a separate series.

HARTFORD SINGLE SHOT TARGET 10 IN. BARREL - .22 LR cal., frame marked "MANFD. BY THE HARTFORD ARMS & EQUIP. CO HARTFORD, CONN. PATENTED 22 CAL. LONG RIFLE", on the left side in front of the breech. 10 in. barrel, single shot manual operation, adjustable sights, ribbed/vertical striation walnut or unique custom grips, mottled/case colored frames or blued frames, mottled/case colored slides or blued slides, the adjustable rear sight sits forward on top of the slide that has been machined flat towards the rear for an unobstructed sight picture. Barrels have a machined band around the front sight then the barrel tapers concentrically towards the frame. One example serial #5 resides in the Cody Firearm Museum. Approx. 10 mfg. late limited production/very scarce.

	100%	98%	95%	90%	80%	70%	60%	LAST MSR
	$4,000	$3,500	$3,000	$2,700	$2,300	$2,000	$1,800	

Add $500 for guns in original Hartford Arms box numbered to gun. (Has not been encountered by the collecting community and doubt that a larger box was fabricated for this limited production pistol).

HARTMANN & WEISS GmbH

Current manufacturer established during 1965 and located in Hamburg, Germany.

Hartmann and Weiss, previously employed by James Purdey & Sons, Ltd., manufactures only top quality longarms, including sidelock SxS shotguns and rifles, O/U shotguns and rifles, falling block single shot rifles (including the Heeren and Hagn action), and bolt action rifles with three lengths of action. Please contact the manufacturer directly for more information and/or a price quotation.

HASKELL MANUFACTURING

Previous manufacturer of .45 ACP cal. semi-auto pistols located in Lima, OH. Previously distributed by MKS Supply located in Mansfield, OH.

Refer to listing under Hi-Point Firearms in the H section.

HATCHER GUN COMPANY

Current custom pistol, rifle, and shotgun manufacturer established in 1983, located in Elsie, NE.

Hatcher Gun Company manufactures custom pistols, rifles, and shotguns for both the civilian and law enforcement marketplaces. Rifles include a series of AR-15 style firearms in various barrel lengths and configurations, pistols include a bolt action model based on the Remington XP-100, and shotguns include modified Saiga semi-autos. NFA items include short barreled Saigas and SxS shotguns. Please contact the company directly for more information, availability, and pricing.

RIFLES: SEMI-AUTO

Hatcher Gun Company also manufactures custom AR-15 style rifles per customer specifications. As such, not all offerings may be listed here. Please contact the company directly for options, pricing, and availability.

HGC AR08 RAPTR GEN 2 - .308 Win. cal., 18 in. stainless steel or carbon fiber (new 2021) fluted bull barrel, M2-72 muzzle brake, 25 shot Magpul PMAG, Elftmann match trigger, flip-up sights, Magpul PRS stock, Hogue grip, billet lower and A3 billet left side charging upper, checkering on magwell, low profile gas block, 12 1/2 in. KeyMod handguard, adj. bipod, includes black nylon sling and tactical soft case, Coyote Tan or black Cerakote finish, 8-10 lbs. New 2016.

	100%	98%	95%	90%	80%	70%	60%
MSR $2,500	$2,200	$1,975	$1,800	$1,650	$1,375	$1,075	$850

HGC AR08 RAPTR GEN 2 CARBON FIBER - .308 Win. cal., 18 in. Christensen carbon fiber barrel, M2-72 muzzle brake, 25 shot Magpul PMAG, Elftmann match trigger, flip sights, Luthar adj. stock, Hogue grip, ODIN 15 1/2 in. KeyMod handguard, billet lower and A3 billet left side charging upper, low profile gas block, checkering on front of magwell, includes adj. bipod, sling swivel, one 3 in. KeyMod rail section, black nylon sling and tactical soft case, Cerakote Coyote tan and black finish, 8.4 lbs. New 2016.

	100%	98%	95%	90%	80%	70%	60%
MSR $2,895	$2,550	$2,275	$2,100	$1,900	$1,600	$1,250	$1,000

GRADING - PPGS™	100%	98%	95%	90%	80%	70%	60%	LAST MSR

HGC AR08 RECON - .308 Win. cal., 16 in. HBAR threaded barrel, flash suppressor, 25 shot Magpul PMAG, standard Mil-Spec trigger, flip sights, 6-pos. collapsible stock, 12 1/2 in. KeyMod handguard, billet lower and A3 billet upper receiver, low profile gas block, checkering on front magwell, steel bolt carrier, includes sling swivel, one 3 in. KeyMod rail section, black nylon sling and tactical soft case, Coyote Tan/Black Cerakote finish, 8.5 lbs. Current mfg.

MSR $1,675	$1,475	$1,325	$1,225	$1,100	$925	$725	$575

HGC AR15HB .204 LEFT HAND - .204 Ruger cal., 20 in. Lilja stainless steel fluted bull barrel, target crown muzzle, Gemtech QD flash suppressor, 30 shot mag., checkering on front of magwell, Jewell two-stage AR trigger, Magpul PRS buttstock, ambi mag. release and safety selelctor, Gen 4 billet lower and A3 left-hand upper receiver, DPMS free float vented handguard, drilled and tapped for swivel stud and bipod, engraved pictograph of SAFE and FIRE on each side of receiver, single rail gas block, tactical latch, includes sling swivel, black nylon sling and tactical soft case, custom Leupold VX-3 SF 30mm 6.5x20x50 scope, and TPS TSR 30mm low rings, Cerakote Magpul Dark Earth finish, 10.75 lbs. Current mfg.

MSR $3,675	$3,250	$2,900	$2,650	$2,425	$2,025	$1,600	$1,250

HGC AR15HB BULL - 5.56 NATO/.223 Rem. cal., 24 in. SS bull barrel, 30 shot mag., standard semi-auto trigger group, flip-up sight set, A2 standard stock, single rail gas block drilled and tapped with swivel stud, checkering on front of magwell, round free float handguard, engraved pictograph of "SAFE" and "FIRE" on each side of receiver, round forward assist, solid machined trigger guard, includes black nylon sling and tactical case, black hardcoat anodized finish, 9.75 lbs. Current mfg.

MSR $1,240	$1,100	$975	$900	$825	$675	$550	$425

HGC AR15HB CAR HBAR - 5.56 NATO/.223 Rem. cal., 16 in. HBAR barrel, 30 shot mag., standard semi-auto trigger group, flip-up sight set, M4 6-pos. collapsible stock, single rail gas block drilled and tapped with swivel stud, checkering on front of magwell, custom Gen 4 billet lower and A3 octagon upper receiver, CAR quad rail handguard, engraved pictograph of "SAFE" and "FIRE" on each side of receiver, includes black nylon sling and tactical case, hardcoat anodized black finish, 6 1/2 lbs.

MSR $1,070	$950	$850	$775	$700	$600	$475	$375

HGC AR15HB HBAR - 5.56 NATO/.223 Rem. cal., 20 in. HBAR barrel, 30 shot mag., standard semi-auto trigger group, flip-up sight set, A2 standard stock, single rail gas block drilled and tapped with swivel stud, checkering on front of magwell, rifle length quad rail handguard, engraved pictograph of "SAFE" and "FIRE" on each side of receiver, includes black nylon sling and case, black hardcoat anodized finish, 8 lbs. Current mfg.

MSR $1,070	$950	$850	$775	$700	$600	$475	$375

HGC AR15HB CAR M4 - 5.56 NATO/.223 Rem. cal., AR-15 style, 16 in. M4 barrel, 30 shot mag., standard semi-auto trigger group, flip-up sight set, M4 6-pos. collapsible stock, single rail gas block, CAR quad rail handguard, Gen 4 billet lower and A3 upper receiver, sling swivel, checkering on front of magwell, engraved pictograph marked "SAFE" and "FIRE" on each side, black Type III hardcoat anodized finish, 6 1/2 lbs. Current mfg.

MSR $1,070	$950	$850	$775	$700	$600	$475	$375

HGC AR15HB SIDEWINDER GEN 2 - 5.56 NATO/.223 Rem. cal., 16 in. stainless steel fluted HBAR barrel, A2 flash suppressor, 30 shot aluminum mag., flip sight set, standard grip, 6-pos. collapsible stock, Gen 4 billet lower and A3 billet left side charging upper receiver, 12 1/2 in. KeyMod handguard, low profile gas block, checkering on front of magwell, includes one 3 in. KeyMod rail section, QD sling swivel, black nylon sling, and tactical soft case, black or Magpul Dark Earth/black finish, 7 1/2 lbs. Current mfg.

MSR $1,450	$1,275	$1,150	$1,050	$950	$800	$625	$500

Add $200 for Magpul Dark Earth/black finish.

HATFIELD GUN CO., INC.

Previous manufacturer located in St. Joseph, MO. The following shotguns were previously manufactured until 1996 by the Hatfield Gun Co., Inc. (designated Hatfield Rifle Works until 1986).

For individual model listings, please go to BlueBookOfGunValues.com/overflow.

HATFIELD GUN COMPANY LLC

Current importer of sidelock O/U and SxS shotguns manufactured in Turkey, established 2005, located in Des Plains, IL. Previously located in Sagle, ID.

For individual model listings, please go to BlueBookOfGunValues.com/overflow.

GRADING - PPGS™	100%	98%	95%	90%	80%	70%	60%	LAST MSR

HATFIELD'S

Current manufacturer established during 2003, located in Amazonia, MO. Previously located in St. Joseph, MO.

SHOTGUNS: O/U

HATFIELD 1 OF 100 – 28 ga., small frame O/U, 28 in. barrels with five choke tubes, vent. rib, chrome-lined bores, SST, extractors, matte blue finish, checkered Circassian pistol grip stock and forend. New 2007.

MSR $1,695	$1,550	$1,375	$1,175	$975	$825	$700	$600

SHOTGUNS: SxS

UPLANDER 28 – 28 ga., small scalloped boxlock frame, extractors, SST or DT, 26 in. monobloc barrels with matte rib, checkered Circassian walnut straight grip stock and splinter forearm, case colored frame, 4 lbs. New 2004.

MSR $1,499	$1,350	$1,200	$1,000	$875	$700	$550	$475

Add $100 for single trigger.

HATSAN ARMS COMPANY

Current shotgun manufacturer established in 1976, located in Izmir, Turkey. Hatsan shotguns are currently imported and distributed by Hatsan USA located in Bentonville, AR beginning 2011. Previously imported by Legacy Sports International LLC, located in Reno, NV until 2018.

Hatsan Arms Company manufactures the Escort line of shotguns. Please refer to the Escort section for current model availability and pricing.

KARL HAUPTMANN JAGDWAFFEN

Current long arm manufacturer established in 1939 and located in Ferlach, Austria. Consumer direct sales through licensed dealers/collectors.

Karl Hauptmann II was a member of the Ferlach Guild until it was dissolved in 2004. His son Gerd Hauptmann is currently the managing director of the company. Hauptmann Jagdwaffen manufactures high quality shotguns, combination guns, and double rifles, and a very unique three barrel SxSxS rifle. Since every gun is custom made according to each customer's specifications, please contact the factory directly for an individual price quotation and delivery time.

HAUSMANN & CO. GmbH

Current long gun manufacturer located in Ferlach, Austria.

Hausmann & Co. manufactures high quality rifles and shotguns in various configurations. Since every gun is manufactured per individual customer specifications, please contact the company directly for a price quotation and availability.

HAWES FIREARMS

Previously manufactured by J.P. Sauer & Sohn in Eckernforde, Germany. Previously imported by Hawes Firearms in Van Nuys, CA.

Hawes Firearms was created after Hy Hunter discontinued their gun line in the early 1960s.

REVOLVERS

Rather than give an individual listing of the various single action and double action (including Medallion models) revolvers that have been imported, a generalized price range is as follows: centerfire single actions usually are in the $225-$450 range, centerfire double actions are $175-$325, while .22 rimfire models are typically valued between $100-$200.

HAWK GROUP CO LTD.

Current shotgun manufacturer located in Qiqihar City, China, established circa 1950s. No current U.S. importation.

Hawk Group manufactures a variety of shotguns including slide action and drum fed semi-autos with folding or fixed stock configuration for commercial, military, and law enforcement use. Please contact the company directly for more information, including pricing and availability.

HEAD DOWN FIREARMS (HEAD DOWN PRODUCTS, LLC)

Current AR-15 style semi-auto rifle manufacturer located in Lawrenceburg, TN beginning 2018.

Please refer to BlueBookOfGunValues.com to order the *Blue Book of AR-15s & Variations*, available as a book or online subscription.

GRADING - PPGS™	100%	98%	95%	90%	80%	70%	60%	LAST MSR

HECKLER & KOCH

Current manufacturer established in 1949, and located in Oberndorf/Neckar, Germany. Currently imported and distributed beginning mid-2008 by H & K USA, located in Columbus, GA. .22 LR cal. pistols and rifles are currently imported by Walther Arms, located in Fort Smith, AR. Previously imported by Merkel USA, located in Trussville, AL, by Heckler & Koch, Inc. located in Sterling, VA (previously located in Chantilly, VA). During 2004, H & K built a new plant in Columbus, GA, primarily to manufacture guns for American military and law enforcement. During 2017, H&K consolidated all existing American manufacturing in a new production facility also located in Columbus, GA.

In early 1991, H & K was absorbed by Royal Ordnance, a division of British Aerospace (BAE Systems) located in England. During December 2002, BAE Systems sold Heckler & Koch to a group of European investors. Heckler & Koch, Inc. and HKJS GmbH are wholly owned subsidiaries of Suhler Jag und Sportwaffen Holding GmbH and the sole licensees of Heckler & Koch commercial firearms technology.

PISTOLS: SEMI-AUTO

USP and USP Compact (with bobbed hammer) Models are divided into 10 variants. They include: USP Variant 1 (DA/SA with control safety decocking lever on left), USP Variant 2 (DA/SA with control safety decocking lever on right), USP Variant 3 (DA/SA with control safety decocking lever on left), USP Variant 4 (DA/SA with control safety decocking lever on right), USP Variant 5 (DAO with control safety decocking lever on left), USP Variant 6 (DAO with control safety decocking lever on right), USP Variant 7 (DAO with no control lever), USP Variant 9 (DA/SA with safety control lever on left), and USP Variant 10 (DA/SA with safety control lever on right).

Current H&K pistol model suffixes include the following: D (decocking/ambidextrous safety), DA (Double Action), L (lengthen barrel/slide), S (short slide), SK (sub-compact), SKS (sub-compact w/ambidextrous safety), SL (lengethen barrel/slide and ambidextrous extrernal safety lever) Please contact your H&K dealer for pricing on these variants.

LEM refers to Law Enforcement Modification (enhanced DAO and conventional SA/DA with serrated decocking button on rear of frame).

All currently manufactured H&K pistols feature a patented lock-out safety device which blocks the hammer strut and slide.

Add $65 for variant change or night sights prior to shipping on currently manufactured USP and USP Compact models.

Add $387 for laser sighting device BA-6 (mfg. 2002-2005).

HK-4 - First and Second Variations. Mfg. 1968-1973.

* ***HK-4 First Variation*** - .22 LR, .25 ACP, .32 ACP, or .380 ACP cal. DA, blowback action, 8 (.380 ACP), 9 (.32 ACP), or 10 (.22 LR or .25 ACP) shot mag., fixed front sight, adj. rear sight, brown checkered plastic grips with HK logo, firing pin block safety mounted on the left side of the slide, high polished blue finish on slide, matte black finish, 18 oz. Mfg. 1967-1970.

	$550	$475	$395	$350	$295	$250	$225

An early four barrel set in all calibers with recoil springs, 4 mags., .22 cal. ejector, bolt tool and four plastic fitted cases is currently priced in the $2,000 range.

A late four barrel set in all calibers with recoil springs, 4 mags., .22 cal. ejector, bolt tool and two cardboard fitted cases is currently priced in the $2,500 range.

* ***HK-4 Second Variation*** - .380 ACP cal., DA, blowback action, 8 shot mag., adj. rear sight, fixed front sight, firing pin block safety mounted on the left side of the slide, blue finish, 22 LR cal. conversion kit offered as optional 10 round magazine, 18 oz. Mfg. 1971-1973.

	$575	$495	$400	$350	$295	$250	$225

Add approx. 10%-15% for .22 LR cal. conversion kit.

HK-4 COMMEMORATIVE COMBO - includes one .22 LR cal. and one .380 ACP cal. barrel, in wooden presentation with gold plating for H&R. Mfg. 1971.

	$1,750	$1,500	$1,250	$1,000	$800	$700	$600

MARK 23 SPECIAL OPERATIONS PISTOL - .45 ACP cal., DA/SA, 5.87 in. threaded barrel with O-Ring and polygonal rifling, 10 or 12 (optional beginning late 2004) shot mag., polymer frame, squared off trigger guard, 3-dot sights, ribbed integral grips, lower frame is grooved for mounting accessories, lock-out safety device, extended slide release, mechanical recoil reduction system, 39 oz. Limited availability. New 1996.

MSR $2,499	$2,200	$1,900	$1,650	$1,300	$1,100	$925	$800

The "MK23" is the official military design that is not available to civilians.

A Desert Tan finish became available during 2005-2006 at no extra charge (includes matching nylon carrying case).

GRADING - PPGS™	100%	98%	95%	90%	80%	70%	60%	LAST MSR

P9/P9S – .45 ACP or 9mm Para. cal., SAO (P9 - only 485 mfg.) or DA/SA (P9S), roller lock delayed blowback action, combat model, 4 in. barrel, fixed sights, sculptured plastic grips, blue (early mfg.) or phosphate finish. Although production ceased in 1984, limited quantities were available until 1989.

P9	$3,000	$2,500	$2,000	$1,600	$1,400	$1,200	$1,000	
P9S	$1,500	$1,250	$1,000	$800	$700	$600	$500	*$1,299*

Add 50% for .45 ACP cal.

P9S TARGET – .45 ACP or 9mm Para. cal., DA/SA, 4 in. barrel, adj. trigger, adj. sights, phosphate finish. Although production ceased in 1984, limited quantities were available until 1989.

	$1,950	$1,575	$1,200	$995	$850	$750	$650	*$1,382*

Add 20% for .45 ACP cal.

P9S COMPETITION KIT SPORT MODEL – 9mm Para. or .45 ACP (rare) cal., similar to P9S Target, except extra 5 1/2 in. barrel and weight, 2 slides, competition walnut grip, factory case. Disc. 1984.

Sport 1	$4,000	$3,250	$2,650	$2,300	$1,950	$1,650	$1,450	
Sport 2	$5,000	$4,000	$3,450	$2,650	$2,100	$1,775	$1,575	
Sport 3	$7,000	$5,750	$4,750	$4,000	$3,400	$2,950	$2,400	*$2,250*

PSP – 9mm Para. cal., gas delayed blowback operation, SFO, 8 shot mag., fixed sights, unmarked plastic grips, engraved "Mod. PSP" on the left side of the slide with serial numbers on the right side of the slide and frame., blued finish, Mfg. 1976-1978 w/limited importation, serial numbers range 001-239.

	$5,000	$4,375	$3,750	$3,400	$2,750	$2,250	$1,750	

P7 PSP – 9mm Para. cal., SFO, older variation of the P7 M8, w/o extended trigger guard, ambi. lever mag release, or heat shield. Features a heel style mag. release (coloquially referred to as "European Style" mag. release). Standard production ceased 1986. A reissue of this model was mfg. in 1990, with approx. 150 produced. Limited quantities remained through 1999.

	$2,500	$2,200	$1,875	$1,700	$1,375	$1,125	$875	*$1,111*

Subtract 20%-50% for police marked imports, depending on condition.

The PSP is serial numbered 001-239. The PSP/P7 is serial numbered 240-251, and the P7 serialization starts at 252. See PSP model for more information.

P7 M8 – 9mm Para. cal., unique squeeze cocking single action, SFO, extended square combat type trigger guard with heat shield, 4.13 in. fixed barrel with polygonal rifling, 8 shot mag., ambidextrous mag. release, fixed 3-dot sighting system, stippled black plastic grips, black phosphate or nickel (mfg. 1992-2000) finish, includes 2 mags., 28 oz. Disc. 2005.

	$2,500	$2,200	$1,875	$1,700	$1,375	$1,125	$875	*$1,515*

Add 30% for nickel/hard chrome finish.
Add $100 for Tritium sights (various colors, new 1993).
Add $1,200 for .22 LR conversion kit (barrel, slide, and two mags., disc. 1999).

P7 M13 – similar to P7 M8, only with staggered 13 shot mag., SFO, 30 oz. Disc. 1994.

	$3,700	$3,250	$2,775	$2,500	$2,100	$1,675	$1,300	*$1,330*

Add 20% for nickel/hard chrome finish.
Add $85 for Tritium sights (various colors, new 1993).
Add $150 for factory wood grips.

P7 M10 – .40 S&W cal., similar specifications as P7 M13, except has 10 shot mag., SFO, 39 oz. Mfg. 1991-1994.

	$3,450	$2,825	$2,500	$2,250	$1,875	$1,475	$1,250	*$1,315*

Add 20% for nickel/hard chrome finish.
Add $85 for Tritium sights (various colors, new 1993).

P7 K3 – .22 LR or .380 ACP cal., uses unique oil-filled buffer to decrease recoil, 3.8 in. barrel, matte black or nickel (less common) finish, 8 shot mag. (includes 2), 26 1/2 oz. Mfg. 1988-94.

	$3,800	$3,325	$2,850	$2,575	$2,100	$1,725	$1,350	*$1,100*

Add $1,500 for .22 LR conversion kit.
Add $1,000 for .32 ACP conversion kit.
Add $85 for Tritium sights (various colors, new 1993).

HK45 – .45 ACP cal., DA/SA and variant (1), 4.53 in. O-ring barrel with polygonal rifle, 10 shot mag., black polymer frame, spur hammer, also available with LEM trigger, low profile 3-dot sights, finger groove grips, interchangeable grip panels, integrated Picatinny rail, twin slide serrations, internal mechanical recoil reduction system reduces recoil 30%, ambidextrous controls, includes one additional backstrap and two 10 shot mags., black, OD Green (new 2015), or tan (new 2015) Cerakote slide, 27.7 oz. New 2008.

MSR $849	$700	$625	$525	$475	$400	$350	$300	

Add $100 for night sights.

GRADING - PPGS™	100%	98%	95%	90%	80%	70%	60%	LAST MSR

* ***HK45 Tactical*** – .45 ACP cal., choice of DA/SA with safety decocking lever on left or LEM trigger, or DAO with no safety/decocking lever, with threaded barrel, high profile Tritium three-dot sights (new 2015), choice of black, tan, or green frame, includes one additional backstrap. New 2013.

MSR $1,029	$825	$725	$625	$500	$425	$375	$350	

HK45 COMPACT – .45 ACP cal., small grip frame, 3.9 in. O-ring barrel with polygonal rifling, 8 or 10 shot mag. w/finger grip floorplate, bobbed hammer, LEM trigger, 3-dot sights, finger groove grips, adj. backstrap, ambidextrous slide release levers, integrated Picatinny rail, black, OD Green (new 2015), or tan (new 2015) Cerakote slide and matching polymer frame, includes 2 magazines and one additional backstrap, 28.5 oz. New 2008.

MSR $849	$700	$625	$525	$475	$400	$350	$300	

Add $100 for three mags. with night sights.

* ***HK45 Compact Tactical*** – .45 ACP cal., similar to HK45 Compact, except has 4.57 in. threaded barrel, safety/decocking lever on left side, spur hammer, high profile Tritium three-dot sights (new 2015), includes 2 magazines, and one additional backstrap, 29 oz. New 2011.

MSR $1,029	$825	$725	$625	$500	$425	$375	$350	

Add $100 for decocking lever on left side, LEM trigger, or for two 10 shot mags. and one 8 shot mag.

HK-416 – .22 LR cal., blowback action, 9 in. barrel, 10 or 20 shot mag., aluminum receivers, diopter adj. rear sight, fixed front sight (Walther mfg.), folding adj. front and rear sights (Umarex mfg.), external safety, quad Picatinny rail (Walther mfg.), M-LOK Rail Interface System (Umarex mfg.), black finish. Mfg. by Carl Walther in Ulm, Germany, and imported by Walther Arms. Mfg. mid-2009-2016. Reintroduced early 2019, mfg. by Umarex.

MSR $479	$420	$350	$325	$300	$250	$200	$150	

MP5 – .22 LR cal., blowback action, 9 in. barrel, 10 or 25 shot mag., aluminum receivers, Mfg. by Carl Walther in Ulm, Germany, and imported by Walther Arms. New 2021.

MSR $479	$420	$350	$325	$300	$250	$200	$150	

P30 – 9mm Para. or .40 S&W (new 2011) cal., 3.86 in. barrel w/polygonal rifling, 10, 13 (.40 S&W) or 15 (9mm Para.) shot mag., self decocking DA spur hammer, multiple trigger variants including DA/SA, standard (disc. 2012), or lightened LEM DAO (new 2012) trigger, 3-dot sights, ergonomic grips w/interchangeable side panels and backstraps, firing pin block safety, lower Picatinny rail, loaded chamber indicator, double slide serrations, internal recoil reduction system, approx. 23 oz. Importation began mid-2007.

MSR $789	$650	$550	$475	$425	$375	$325	$275	

Add $110 for three extra magazines and night sights (new 2014).

* ***P30L*** – similar to P30, except has 4 1/2 in. barrel and 1/2 in. longer slide, 27.5 oz. New 2009.

MSR $789	$650	$550	$475	$425	$375	$325	$275	

Add $110 for three 10 (new 2020) or 15 shot magazines and night sights (new 2014).

» **P30LS** – DA/SA, similar to P30L, except has ambidextrous safety lever/rear decocking button, and includes two 15 shot magazines.

MSR $789	$650	$550	$475	$425	$375	$325	$275	

Add $110 for three 15 shot mags. and night sights.

* ***P30S*** – 9mm Para. or .40 S&W cal., DA/SA, 3.85 in. barrel with polygonal rifling, two 10 (new late 2018), 13, or 15 (9mm Para., disc.) shot mag., spur hammer with rear decocking lever on back of frame, 3-dot sights, ergonomic grips with interchangeable side panels and backstraps, firing pin block safety and ambidextrous safety lever, lower Picatinny rail, double slide serrations, internal recoil reduction system, loaded chamber indicator.

MSR $789	$650	$550	$475	$425	$375	$325	$275	

Add $110 for three 13 or 15 (disc.) shot magazines and night sights (new 2014).

* ***P30SK Sub Compact*** – 9mm Para. cal., ergonomic polymer frame with lower Picatinny rail, with or w/o ambidextrous dual magazine release and manual safety levers, 3.27 in. barrel with polygonal rifling, 10 shot mag., trigger variants include conventional DA/SA with spur hammer and serrated decocking button on rear of frame or LEM enhanced DAO with "light strike V1" trigger setup and bobbed hammer, 3-dot sights, grips with interchangeable side panels and backstraps, firing pin block safety, loaded chamber indicator, double slide serrations, HK Lock-Out safety device, approx. 24 oz. Importation began 2016.

MSR $789	$650	$550	$475	$425	$375	$325	$275	

Add $110 for three extra mags. and night sights.

» **P30SKS Sub Compct** – similar to the P30SK Sub Compact, except has ambidextrous safety lever/rear decocking button, and includes two 10 shot magazines.

MSR $789	$650	$550	$475	$425	$375	$325	$275	

Add $110 for three mag's and night sights.

GRADING - PPGS™	100%	98%	95%	90%	80%	70%	60%	LAST MSR

P2000 – 9mm Para., .357 SIG (mfg. 2005-2012), or .40 S&W cal., SA/DA or LEM (Law Enforcement Modification) DAO (w/o control lever), patterned after USP Compact Model, 3.66 in. barrel w/polygonal rifling, 10, 12 shot mag. w/finger extension, or 13 shot mag. (new late 2004), pre-cocked hammer system w/short trigger reset distance, features pre-cocked hammer system w/very short trigger reset distance, 3-dot sights, interchangeable rear grip panels, lockout safety device, with or w/o decocker, black finish, approx. 25 oz.

MSR $879	$725	$625	$550	$475	$400	$350	$300	

Add $100 for three mags. and night sights (new 2014).
Add up to 100% for special Swiss police markings.
Subtract approx. $50 for .357 SIG cal. (mfg. 2005-2012).

* ***P2000 SK Sub Compact*** – 9mm Para., .357 SIG (disc. 2012), or .40 S&W cal., similar to P2000, choice of LEM (Law Enforcement Modification) or regular DA/SA trigger system, 3.26 in. barrel, 9 (.357 SIG, disc. 2012) or .40 S&W cal. or 10 (9mm Para.) shot mag., with or w/o rear decocking button, approx. 24 oz. Importation began 2005.

MSR $879	$725	$625	$550	$475	$400	$350	$300	

Add $100 for three mags and night sights (new 2014).
Subtract approx. $50 for .357 SIG cal. (disc. 2012).

SP5 – 9mm Para. cal., pistol caliber carbine platform, roller-delayed blowback operating system, patterned after the MP5, 8.86 in. Navy barrel, 6 grooves, threaded tri-lug adaptor, two 10 or 30 shot mags., paddle mag. release, smooth pistol grip, elastic bungee sling, black finish, optional 15 shot mag., 5.1 lbs. New late 2019.

MSR $2,949	$2,800	$2,450	$2,100	$1,800	$1,550	$1,250	$975	

Add $80 for 15 shot or additional mags.

SP5K – 9mm Para. cal., 4.53 in. barrel, 10 or 30 shot mag., MP5K type sights, semi-auto civilian version of the MP5K machine gun, roller bearing operation, top Picatinny rail, includes hard-shell case, black finish, 4 3/4 lbs. Mfg. 2016-2019.

	$2,450	$2,200	$2,000	$1,800	$1,600	$1,400	$1,200	*$2,699*

SP 89 – 9mm Para. cal., roller lock delayed blowback, 4 1/2 in. barrel, 15 shot mag., adj. aperture rear sight (accepts HK claw-lock scope mounts), 4.4 lbs. Mfg. 1990-1993.

	$4,950	$4,500	$4,150	$4,000	$3,750	$3,625	$3,500	*$1,325*

USP CUSTOM COMBAT – 9mm Para. or .40 S&W cal., DA/SA, Variant 1, two 16 (.40 S&W cal.) or 18 (9mm Para. cal.) shot mags., Novak combat sight system, jet funnel kit. Mfg. 2009 only.

	$1,150	$975	$875	$775	$675	$550	$450	*$1,295*

USP COMBAT COMPETITION – 9mm Para. or .40 S&W cal., DA/SA OR LEM TRIGGER (became standard mid-2008), 4 1/4 in. barrel, jet funnel kit w/two 16 (.40 S&W) or 18 (9mm Para.) mags., LEM trigger became standard mid-2008, Novak combat sight system, lower accessory rail on frame, 26 1/2 oz. Importation 2007-2010.

	$1,250	$1,025	$925	$825	$700	$600	$500	*$1,450*

Subtract approx. $100 if w/o LEM trigger.

USP COMPETITION – similar to USP Combat Competition, except features LEM match trigger system. Imported 2007-2008.

	$1,125	$975	$850	$750	$625	$500	$450	*$1,279*

USP 9 – 9mm Para. cal., available in 9 variants of DA/SA/DAO, 4 1/4 in. barrel with polygonal rifling, Browning-type action with H & K recoil reduction system, polymer frame, all metal surfaces specially treated, can be carried cocked and locked, stippled synthetic grips, bobbed hammer, 3-dot sighting system, multiple safeties, 10 (C/B 1994), 15 (new late 2004), or 16* shot polymer mag., 26.5 oz. New 1993.

MSR $1,059	$925	$800	$700	$600	$500	$425	$350	

Add $90 for LEM trigger, DAO and two 10 or 15 shot mags.
Add $120 for three 10 or 15 shot magazines and night sights (new 2014).
Add $107 for Tritium sights (various colors, disc. 2010).

* ***USP 9 SD*** – similar to USP 9, except has adj. target sights and 4.7 in. threaded barrel, approx. 27 oz. Imported 2004-2006, reintroduced 2011-importation disc. 2018.

	$1,225	$1,050	$925	$800	$675	$550	$475	*$1,399*

* ***USP 9 Stainless*** – similar to USP 9, except has satin finished stainless steel slide. Mfg. 1996-2001.

	$850	$725	$625	$550	$475	$375	$300	*$817*

GRADING - PPGS™	100%	98%	95%	90%	80%	70%	60%	LAST MSR

USP 9 COMPACT – 9mm Para. cal., compact variation of the USP 9 featuring 3.58 in. barrel, 10 or 13 (new late 2004) shot mag., LEM trigger became available 2003, 25.5 oz. New 1997.

MSR $1,089	$950	$825	$725	$625	$525	$450	$375	

Add $110 for three extra magazines with night sights (new 2014).
Add $210 for LEM trigger, DAO, three 13 shot mags., and night sights.

* ***USP 9 Compact Stainless*** – similar to USP 9 Compact, except has satin finished stainless steel slide. Mfg. 1997-2004.

	$850	$725	$625	$550	$475	$375	$300	*$849*

* ***USP 9 Compact LEM*** – 9mm Para. cal., DAO, blue finish only, LEM trigger mechanism decreases trigger pull to 7 1/2 - 8 1/2 lbs., 24 1/2 oz. Imported 2003-2004.

	$900	$775	$675	$575	$500	$400	$325	*$799*

USP 9 TACTICAL – 9mm Para. cal., DA/SA, 4.86 in. threaded O-ring barrel, match grade trigger, adj. target sights, fixed grips, safety/decocking lever on left, two 10 or 15 shot mags., black finish, 28 oz. New 2015.

MSR $1,479	$1,325	$1,150	$975	$850	$725	$600	$500	

Add $100 for three 15 shot mags. and adj. night sights.

USP 9x19 TACTICAL – 9mm Para. cal. enhanced variation of the USP 9, 4.92 in. threaded barrel with rubber o-ring, 10 or 15 shot mag., adj. target type sights and trigger, approx. 28 1/2 oz. Mfg. 2007-2010.

	$975	$850	$750	$625	$525	$450	$400	*$1,112*

USP 357 – .357 SIG cal., available in 4.25 (Standard, disc. 2004) or 3.58 (Compact) in. barrel, 10 or 12 (optional beginning 2004) shot mag., black finish, approx. 24.5 oz. Imported 2001-2005.

	$695	$560	$500	$450	$395	$350	$300	*$799*

Subtract $30 for Standard Model (disc. 2004).

USP 40 – .40 S&W cal., similar to USP 9, 9 variants of DA/SA/DAO, 10 (C/B1994), 13* (reintroduced late 2004), or 16 (optional, new 2005, needs jet funnel modification) shot mag., LEM trigger (new 2013), 27.75 oz. New 1993.

MSR $1,059	$925	$800	$700	$600	$500	$425	$350	

Add $90 for LEM trigger and two mags. (new 2013).
Add $120 for three 10 or 13 shot mags. and night sights.
Add $200 for LEM trigger, three 10 mags. and night sights.
Add $107 for Tritium sights (various colors, disc.).

A Desert Tan finish became available during 2005 at no extra charge (includes matching nylon carrying case). Limited mfg. 2005-2006.

* ***USP 40 Stainless*** – .40 S&W cal., similar to USP 40, except has satin finished stainless steel slide. Mfg. 1996-2003.

	$850	$725	$625	$550	$475	$375	$300	*$817*

USP 40 COMPACT – .40 S&W cal., compact variation of the USP 40 featuring 3.58 in. barrel, 10 or 12 (new late 2004) shot mag., LEM trigger became available 2002, 27 oz. New 1997.

MSR $1,089	$950	$825	$725	$625	$525	$450	$375	

Add $110 for LEM trigger, DAO, and two 10 or 12 shot mags.
Add $220 for three 10 or 12 shot magazines with night sights (new 2014).

A Desert Tan finish became available during 2005-2006 at no extra charge (includes matching nylon carrying case). Grey was also available in limited quantities during 2005 only.

* ***USP 40 Compact Stainless*** – .40 S&W cal., similar to USP 40 Compact, except has satin finished stainless steel slide. Mfg. 1997-2004.

	$850	$725	$625	$550	$475	$375	$300	*$849*

* ***USP 40 Compact LEM*** – .40 S&W cal., DAO, blue finish only, LEM trigger mechanism decreases trigger pull to 7 1/2 - 8 1/2 lbs., 24 1/2 oz. Imported 2002-2005.

	$900	$775	$675	$575	$500	$400	$325	

USP 40 TACTICAL – .40 S&W cal., enhanced variation of the USP 40, 4.92 in. threaded barrel with rubber O-Ring, 10 (standard) or 13 shot mag., adj. target type sights and match trigger, 30 1/2 oz. Mfg. 2005-2019.

	$1,150	$995	$850	$750	$625	$550	$495	*$1,349*

Add $100 for three 13 shot mags. and adj. night sights (Mfg. 2014-2019).

GRADING - PPGS™	100%	98%	95%	90%	80%	70%	60%	LAST MSR

USP 45 – .45 ACP cal., similar to USP 9, 9 variants of DA/SA/DAO, 10 (C/B 1994), 12 (new late 2004) or 13* shot mag., 27 3/4 oz. New 1995.

MSR $1,089	$950	$825	$725	$625	$525	$450	$375	

Add $110 for LEM trigger, DAO (new 2011).
Add $220 for three 12 shot mags. and night sights.
Add $107 for Tritium sights (various colors, disc. 2010).

A desert tan or green finish became available during 2005-2006 at no extra charge (includes matching nylon carrying case). Grey was also available in limited quantities during 2005 only.

* ***USP 45 Stainless*** – .45 ACP cal., similar to USP 45, except has satin finished stainless steel slide. Mfg. 1996-2003.

	$850	$725	$625	$550	$475	$375	$300	*$888*

* ***USP 45 Match Pistol*** – .45 ACP cal., features 6.02 in. barrel with polygonal rifling, micrometer adj. high relief and raised rear sight, raised target front sight, 10 shot mag., barrel weight, fluted, and ambidextrous safety, choice of matte black or stainless steel slide, supplied with additional o-rings and setup tools, 38 oz. Mfg. 1997-98.

	$2,150	$1,850	$1,575	$1,300	$1,050	$900	$800	*$1,369*

Add $72 for stainless steel slide model.

USP 45 COMPACT – .45 ACP cal., compact variation of the USP 45, featuring 3.8 in. barrel, 8 shot mag., 28 oz. New 1998.

MSR $1,149	$1,025	$875	$750	$700	$575	$475	$375	

Add $110 for LEM trigger, DAO (new 2011).
Add $210 for three magazines and night sights.

* ***USP 45 Compact Stainless*** – .45 ACP cal., similar to USP 45 Compact, except has satin finished stainless steel slide. Mfg. 1998-2004.

	$850	$725	$625	$550	$475	$375	$300	*$894*

* ***USP 45 Compact 50th Anniversary*** – .45 ACP cal., commemorates the 50th year of H & K (1950-2000), 1 of 1,000 special edition featuring high polish blue slide with 50th Anniversary logo engraved in gold and silver, supplied with presentation wood case and commemorative coin. Limited mfg. 2000 only.

	$1,150	$895	$795	N/A	N/A	N/A	N/A	*$999*

USP 45 TACTICAL PISTOL – .45 ACP cal., enhanced variation of the USP 45, 5.09 in. threaded barrel with rubber o-ring, 10 or 12 (new late 2004) shot mag., adj. 3-dot target type sights and match trigger, limited availability, 36 oz. New 1998.

MSR $1,479	$1,325	$1,150	$975	$850	$725	$600	$500	

Add $100 for three 12 shot magazines and adj. night sights.

A Desert Tan finish became available during 2005-2006 at no extra charge (includes matching nylon carrying case).

* ***USP45CT Compact Tactical (USP 45 Tactical Pistol Compact)*** – .45 ACP cal., 3.78 in. barrel, 8 shot mag., 28 oz. Imported 2006-2012.

	$1,100	$950	$850	$750	$650	$550	$450	*$1,242*

USP ELITE – 9mm Para. (disc. 2005) or .45 ACP cal., long slide variation of the USP Expert, 6.2 in. barrel, match trigger parts, target sights, ambidextrous control levers, blue finish, includes two 10 shot mags. or 12 (.45 ACP) or 15 (9mm Para.) shot mag. Imported 2003-2009.

	$1,375	$1,150	$1,000	$900	$800	$700	$600	*$1,406*

USP EXPERT – 9mm Para. (mfg. 2003-2005, reintroduced 2013), .40 S&W (mfg. 2002-2009), or .45 ACP (disc. 2009) cal., features new slide design with 5.2 in. barrel, 10 (standard), 12 (.45 ACP, disc. 2009), 13 (.40 S&W, disc. 2009), 15 (9mm Para.) or 18 (new 2013) shot mag., match grade SA or DA trigger pull, recoil reduction system, reinforced polymer frame, adj. rear sight, approx. 30 oz. Imported 1999-2009, reintroduced 2013.

MSR $1,529	$1,375	$1,175	$1,000	$875	$750	$625	$525	

Add $110 for jet funnel frame and two 18 shot mags. (new 2013).

VP 70Z – 9mm Para. cal., 18 shot, DAO, SFO, 4 1/2 in. barrel, parkerized finish, plastic receiver/grip assembly. Disc. 1984.

	$750	$675	$600	$550	$500	$450	$400	

Add 300% if frame cut for shoulder stock (Model VP 70M, NFA Class III).

The majority of pistols that were cut for shoulder stock are the Model VP 70M, and are subject to NFA Class III regulation. A complete M stock with sear is also considered NFA.

GRADING - PPGS™	100%	98%	95%	90%	80%	70%	60%	LAST MSR

VP9 – 9mm Para. cal., SFO, polymer frame, 4.09 in. cold hammer forged barrel, 10 or 15 shot steel mag., machined steel slide, enhanced HK "light pull" trigger, fixed 3-dot luminous sights, optics ready (new 2020), ergonomic handgun grip that includes three changeable backstraps and six side panels, molded finger grooves, trigger has safety latch, ambidextrous controls, extended Picatinny rail, cock firing pin indicator, features patented charging supports (components mounted on each side of slide to provide better gripping leverage), front and rear slide serrations, black, FDE (new mid-2016), OD Green (mfg. 2017-2019), Grey (mfg. 2017-2019), or Midnight Bronze (new 2020) finish, 1.6 lbs. Mfg. in Oberndorf, Germany beginning mid-2014.

MSR $789	$650	$550	$475	$425	$375	$325	$275	

Add $110 for three 10 or 15 shot mags. and night sights.
Add $60 for optics ready mounting plates (new 2020).

Beginning 2019, the VP Series is available with Crimson Trace Laserguard attached to the front of the trigger guard. Contact the importer directly for availability and pricing.

* ***VP9L*** – similar to the VP9, except has a 5 in. barrel and 1/2 in. longer slide, optics ready. New 2021.

MSR $949	$850	$750	$650	$575	$475	$375	$300	

Add $110 for three 10 or 20 shot mags. and night sights.

VP9 SK – 9mm Para. cal., striker fired, sub-compact, 3.39 in. cold hammer forged steel barrel, two or three steel 10 shot mags. with flat or extended polymer floorplate, ambidextrous "paddle style" mag. release, steel slide with carbon nitride finish, extended heavy duty extractor with loaded chamber indicator, large recurved trigger guard, 3-dot or Tritium night sights, optional Crimson Trace Laserguard (new 2019), ergonomic grip profile with finger contours and changeable grip panels, Picatinny rail for mounting lights and aimers, firing pin block, disconnector, drop safety, interchangeable backstraps, right and left side slide release, front slide serrations, 36.4 oz, black, FDE (new 2018), grey (new 2018), or OD/NATO Green (new 2018) finish. Mfg. in Oberndorf, Germany beginning 2017.

MSR $789	$650	$550	$475	$425	$375	$325	$275	

Add $110 for three mags and night sights.

VP TACTICAL – 9mm Para. or .40 S&W cal., SFO, polymer frame, 4.09 in. cold hammer forged threaded barrel, 10 or 15 shot steel mag., machined steel slide, 3-dot sights, ergonomic grip that includes three interchangeable backstraps and six side panels, molded finger grooves, trigger has safety latch, ambidextrous controls, extended Picatinny rail, cock firing in indicator, front and rear slide serrations, optics ready (new 2021), black finish. Mfg. in Oberndorf, Germany beginning mid-2016.

MSR $999	$900	$775	$675	$575	$500	$400	$325	

Beginning in 2021, this model was only available optics ready and came with three mags standard.

VP40 – .40 S&W cal., SFO, polymer frame, 4.09 in. cold hammer forged barrel, 10 or 13 shot mag., machined steel slide, enhanced HK "light pull" trigger, fixed 3-dot luminous sights, ergonomic handgun grip that includes three changeable backstraps and six side panels, molded finger grooves, trigger has safety latch, cocked firing pin indicator, ambidextrous controls, extended Picatinny rail, front and rear slide serrations, black, FDE (new mid-2016), OD Green (new 2017), or grey (new 2017) finish, 1.8 lbs. Mfg. in Oberndorf, Germany. New 2016.

MSR $789	$650	$550	$475	$425	$375	$325	$275	

Add $110 for three 10 or 13 shot mags. and night sights.

RIFLES: BOLT ACTION

BASR – .22 LR, .22-250 Rem., 6mm PPC, .300 Win. Mag., .30-06, or .308 Win. cal., Kevlar stock, stainless steel barrel, limited production. Special order only. Mfg. 1986 only.

	$5,750	$5,000	$4,500	$4,000	$3,650	$3,300	$2,600	*$2,199*

Less than 135 of this variation were manufactured and they are extremely rare. Contractual disputes with the U.S. supplier stopped H & K from receiving any BASR models.

RIFLES: SEMI-AUTO

Most of the models listed, being of a tactical design, were disc. in 1989 due to Federal legislation. Sporterized variations mfg. after 1994 with thumbhole stocks were banned in April, 1998.

In 1991, the HK-91, HK-93, and HK-94 were discontinued. Last published retail prices (1991) were $999 for fixed stock models and $1,199 for retractable stock models.

In the early '70s, S.A.C.O. importers located in Virginia sold the Models 41 and 43 which were the predecessors to the Model 91 and 93, respectively. Values for these earlier variations will be higher than values listed.

GRADING - PPGS™	100%	98%	95%	90%	80%	70%	60%	LAST MSR

G3 SEMI-AUTO – .308 Win. cal., patterned after the H&K G3 select-fire military rifle, two variations were imported by Golden State Arms circa 1962.

	$20,000	$17,500	$16,000	$14,500	$13,000	$11,500	$10,000	

MODEL G36 – .22 LR cal., blowback action, 18.1 in. barrel with flash suppressor, 20 shot detachable mag., aluminum frame with black synthetic hardware, fixed front and adj. rear sight, skeletonized folding stock with black synthetic vent. handguard, black synthetic pistol grip, elevated Picatinny rail over receiver incorporating open sights, matte black finish, 6 3/4 lbs. Mfg. by Walther in Ulm, Germany under contract from H&K. Mfg. 2015-disc.

	$550	$495	$450	$395	$350	$300	$275	*$599*

MP5 – .22 LR cal., 10 or 25 shot mag., aluminum receivers, Mfg. by Carl Walther in Ulm, Germany, and imported by Walther Arms. New 2021.

MSR $479	$420	$350	$325	$300	$250	$200	$150	

SR-9 – .308 Win. cal., semi-auto sporting rifle, 19.7 in. barrel, Kevlar reinforced fiberglass thumbhole stock and forearm, 5 shot mag., diopter adj. rear sight, accepts H & K claw-lock scope mounts. Mfg. 1990-93.

	$2,075	$1,725	$1,400	$1,225	$1,075	$950	$850	*$1,199*

While advertised again during 1998, this model was finally banned in April, 1998.

SR-9T – .308 Win. cal., precision target rifle with adj. MSG 90 buttstock and PSG-1 trigger group, 5 shot mag. Mfg. 1992-93.

	$2,795	$2,375	$2,050	$1,775	$1,375	$1,295	$1,050	*$1,725*

While advertised again during 1998, this model was finally banned in April, 1998.

SR-9TC – .308 Win. cal., similar to SR-9T except has PSG-1 adj. buttstock. Mfg. 1993 only.

	$3,350	$2,925	$2,600	$2,275	$1,925	$1,475	$1,250	*$1,995*

While advertised again during 1998, this model was finally banned in April, 1998.

PSG-1 – .308 Win. cal. only, high precision marksman's rifle, 5 shot mag., adj. buttstock, includes accessories (Hensholdt illuminated 6x42mm scope) and case, 17.8 lbs. Importation disc. 1998.

	$13,950	$12,500	$10,950	$9,500	$8,500	$7,500	$7,000	*$10,811*

MODEL 41 A-2 – .308 Win. cal., predecessor to the Model 91 A-2, originally imported by Golden State Arms.

	$5,200	$4,600	$4,000	$3,600	$3,350	$3,200	$3,000	

MODEL 43 A-2 – predecesor to the Model 93 A-2. Disc.

	$4,500	$4,000	$3,750	$3,500	$3,350	$3,200	$3,000	

MODEL 91 A-2 – .308 Win. cal., roller lock delayed blowback action, attenuated recoil, black cycolac stock, 17.7 in. barrel, 20 shot mag., 9.7 lbs. Importation disc. 1989.

* ***Model 91 A-2 Fixed Stock Model***

	$2,350	$2,000	$1,800	$1,600	$1,400	$1,250	$1,000	*$999*

Add $200 for Desert camo finish.
Add $275 for NATO black finish.

* ***Model 91 A-2 SBF (Semi-Beltfed)*** – supplied with bipod and M60 link (200 shot with starter tab) and MG42 modified belt (49 shot with fixed starter tab), limited mfg. Disc.

	$10,500	$9,500	$8,500	N/A	N/A	N/A	N/A	

* ***Model 91 A-3*** – with retractable metal stock.

	$3,100	$2,900	$2,700	$2,500	$2,150	$2,000	$1,895	*$1,114*

Add $775 for .22 LR conversion kit.

* ***Model 91 A-2 Package*** – includes A.R.M.S. mount, B-Square rings, Leupold 3-9x compact scope with matte finish. Importation disc. 1988.

	$3,150	$2,750	$2,400	$2,150	$1,900	$1,700	$1,475	*$1,285*

Add 30% for retractable stock.

MODEL 93 A-2 – .223 Rem. cal., smaller version of the H & K 91, 25 shot mag., 16.14 in. barrel, 8 lbs.

* ***Model 93 A-2 Fixed Stock Model***

	$2,500	$2,250	$2,000	$1,750	$1,500	$1,250	$1,000	*$946*

Add 10% for desert camo finish.
Add 15% for NATO black finish.

* ***Model 93 A-3*** – with retractable metal stock.

	$3,400	$3,250	$3,000	$2,800	$2,650	$2,500	$2,250	*$1,114*

GRADING - PPGS™	100%	98%	95%	90%	80%	70%	60%	LAST MSR

* ***Model 93 A-2 Package*** – includes A.R.M.S. mount, B-Square rings, Leupold 3-9x compact scope with matte finish. Importation disc. 1988.

	$3,500	$3,100	$2,850	$2,550	$2,400	$2,100	$1,895	*$1,285*

Add 10% for retractable stock.

MODEL 94 CARBINE A-2 - 9mm Para. cal., 16.54 in. barrel, aperture rear sight, 15 shot mag. Mfg. 1983-1988.

* ***Model 94 Carbine A-2 Fixed Stock Model***

	$3,950	$3,750	$3,500	$3,400	$3,000	$2,600	$2,500	*$946*

* ***Model 94 Carbine A-3*** – retractable metal stock.

	$4,150	$3,900	$3,700	$3,550	$3,200	$2,800	$2,700	*$1,114*

* ***Model 94 Carbine A-2 Package*** – includes A.R.M.S. mount, B-Square rings, Leupold 3-9x compact scope with matte finish. Importation disc. 1988.

	$4,300	$3,875	$3,650	$3,300	$3,000	$2,800	$2,500	*$1,285*

Add 10% for retractable stock.

* ***Model 94 Carbine A-2 SGI*** – 9mm Para. cal., target rifle, aluminum alloy bipod, Leupold 6X scope, 15 or 30 shot mag. Imported 1986 only.

	$3,950	$3,750	$3,500	$3,000	$2,750	$2,500	$2,150	*$1,340*

MODEL 270 - .22 LR cal., sporting rifle, 19.7 in. barrel with standard or polygonal rifling, 5 or 20 shot mag., high luster blue, plain walnut stock, approx. 5.7 lbs. Disc. 1985.

	$975	$895	$725	$675	$525	$400	$350	*$200*

MODEL 300 - .22 WMR cal., 5 or 15 shot, polygonal rifling standard, otherwise similar to H & K 270 with checkered walnut stock. Importation disc. 1989.

	$1,350	$1,050	$925	$775	$700	$600	$550	*$608*

Add $350-$400 for factory H & K scope mount system.

* ***Model 300 Package*** – includes A.R.M.S. mount, B-Square rings, Leupold 3-9x compact scope with matte finish. Importation disc. 1988.

	$1,625	$1,275	$1,075	$900	$800	$700	$650	*$689*

MODEL HK 416 - .22 LR cal., blowback action with last shot bolt hold open, 16.1 in. barrel with muzzle brake, 10 or 20 shot mag., H&K style diopter sight, H&K style 5-position buttstock with storage compartment and recoil pad, black ergonomic pistol grip with storage compartment, manual safety, steel flat-top receiver with quad Picatinny rail, black finish. Mfg. mid-2010-2011. Mfg. by Carl Walther in Ulm, Germany. Reintroduced early 2019, mfg. by Umarex.

MSR $479	$420	$350	$325	$300	$250	$200	$150	

MODEL 416 D145RS - .22 LR cal., blowback action, 16.1 in. barrel, fixed front sight, adj. rear sight, external safety, 10 or 20 shot mag., metal receiver, black finish, upper and lower rail interface system, pistol grip with compartment, adj. buttstock, functional dust cover, 6.8 lbs., mfg. by Carl Walther in Ulm, Germany, and imported by Umarex USA. New late 2009.

MSR $599	$550	$495	$450	$395	$350	$300	$275	

MODEL 630 - .223 Rem. cal., roller lock delayed blowback action, 17.7 in. barrel with or w/o muzzle brake (early mfg.), reduced recoil, checkered walnut, 4 or 10 shot mag., 7.04 lbs. Importation disc. 1986.

	$1,650	$1,400	$1,200	$1,100	$1,000	$850	$750	*$784*

Add $350-$400 for factory H & K scope mount system.

The .222 Rem. cal. was also available in this model. Most were French contracts.

MODEL 770 - .308 Win. cal., 3 or 10 shot mag., 19.7 in. barrel with or w/o muzzle brake (early mfg.), otherwise similar to Model 630, 7.92 lbs. Importation disc. 1986.

	$2,150	$1,900	$1,650	$1,375	$1,150	$1,000	$900	*$797*

Add $350-$400 for factory H & K scope mount system.

Significant price increases stopped the importation of this model.

Approx. 6 Model 770s were imported in .243 Win. cal. during 1984. Values for the .243 Win. cal. will be considerably higher than listed for the .308 Win. cal.

MODEL 911 - .308 Win. cal., earlier importation. Disc.

	$1,900	$1,700	$1,500	$1,275	$1,050	$900	$775	

GRADING - PPGS™	100%	98%	95%	90%	80%	70%	60%	LAST MSR

MODEL 940 – .30-06 cal., 21.6 in. barrel with or w/o muzzle brake (early mfg.), otherwise same as Model 770, 8.62 lbs. Importation disc. 1986.

	$1,950	$1,750	$1,500	$1,250	$995	$875	$750	*$917*

Add $350-$400 for factory H & K scope mount system.

Cals. 7x64mm and 9.3x62mm were also available in this model.

Significant price increases stopped the importation of this model.

* ***Model 940K*** – similar to Model 940, except has 16 in. barrel and higher cheekpiece. Two imported 1984 only.

Rarity precludes accurate price evaluation.

SLB 2000 – .30-06 or .308 Win. (new 2003) cal. (bolt head dimension allows cartridge interchangeability), short stroke piston actuated gas operating system, alloy receiver with black weather resistant coating, gold accents on receiver, 19.69 in. barrel (interchangeable), checkered walnut stock and specially angled pistol grip, tang mounted safety blocks hammer and trigger, 2, 5, or 10 shot mag., iron sights, 7.28 lbs. Imported 2001-2003.

	$1,150	$995	$895	$825	$775	$700	$650	*$1,299*

MODELS SL6 & SL7 CARBINE – .223 Rem. (HK-SL6) or .308 Win. (HK-SL7) cal., roller lock delayed blowback action, 17.71 in. barrel, reduced recoil, vent. wood handguard, 3 or 4 shot mag., matte black metal finish, 8.36 lbs. Importation disc. 1986.

	$1,650	$1,450	$1,250	$1,050	$925	$800	$650	

Add $250-$300 for factory H & K scope mount system.
Add $200 for .308 Win. cal.

These models were the last sporter variations H & K imported into the U.S. - no U.S. importation since 1986.

MODEL SL8-1 – .223 Rem. cal., short stroke piston actuated gas operating system, advanced grey carbon fiber polymer construction based on the German Army G36 rifle, thumbhole stock with adj. cheekpiece and buttstock, 10 shot mag., modular and removable Picatinny rail, removable sights, 20.8 in. cold hammer forged heavy barrel, adj. sights, 8.6 lbs. Imported 2000-2003, reimported 2007-2010.

	$1,950	$1,650	$1,500	$1,350	$1,200	$1,000	$900	*$2,449*

Add $338 for carrying handle with 1.5X-3x optical sights (disc. 2009).
Add $624 for carrying handle with 1.5X-3x optical sights and red dot reflex sight (disc. 2009).

MODEL SL8-6 – .223 Rem. cal., similar to SL8-1, except has elevated Picatinny rail that doubles as carrying handle. Mfg. 2010-2011.

	$1,950	$1,650	$1,500	$1,350	$1,200	$1,000	$900	*$2,388*

MODEL USC .45 ACP CARBINE – .45 ACP cal., blowback action, 16 in. barrel, includes two 10 shot single stack mags., steel reinforced polymer receivers, patterned after the H&K UMP SMG, hooded front sight, aperture or notch rear sight, grey or black polymer skeletonized buttstock, thumb safety, left side charging handle above the forearm, bolt catch on left side of receiver, 6 lbs. Imported 2000-2003, reimported beginning 2007-2011, reimported again in limited quantities beginning 2018.

	$1,500	$1,275	$1,050	$925	$825	$725	$625	*$1,788*

MR556A1 RIFLE – 5.56 NATO cal., GPO, 10 or 30 shot steel mag., 16 1/2 in. heavy barrel with muzzle brake, free floating rail system handguard with four Mil-Std 1913 Picatinny rails, Picatinny rail machined into top of upper receiver, two-stage trigger, diopter sights, black anodized finish, adj. buttstock with (disc. 2013) or w/o (new 2014) storage compartment, HK pistol grip with optional configurations, 7.6 lbs. Mfg. in the U.S. using American and German made components. New 2009.

MSR $3,499	$3,075	$2,775	$2,525	$2,300	$1,925	$1,525	$1,200	

* ***MR556A1 Competition*** – 5.56 NATO cal., GPO, 16 1/2 in. cold hammer forged barrel with compensator, 10, 20, or 30 shot mag., two-stage trigger, 14 in. lightweight modular rail system, extended magazine release button, upper receiver with charging handle with extended latch, collapsible and locking Magpul CTR stock, no sights, HK grip, 8.8 lbs. Mfg. 2014-19.

	$2,825	$2,525	$2,325	$2,100	$1,775	$1,400	$1,100	*$3,199*

* ***MR556A1-SD*** – 5.56 NATO cal., GPO, 16 1/2 in. cold hammer forged barrel, OSS suppressor which comprises two modules - a Back Pressure Regulator (BRM) and a Signature Reduction Module (SRM), 10, 20, or 30 shot mag., two-stage trigger, HK black grip, HK 6-position adj. stock, black finish, 9 1/2 lbs. Mfg. 2014-disc.

Last MSR was $4,995.

Note: This firearm is integrally suppressed and is subject to all relevant NFA regulations. Failure to comply with these regulations may result in fines/imprisonment.

GRADING - PPGS™	100%	98%	95%	90%	80%	70%	60%	LAST MSR

MR762A1 RIFLE – 7.62x51mm cal., GPO, 16 1/2 in. barrel, 10 or 20 shot polymer mag., flip-up front and diopter rear sights, adj. buttstock with storage compartment, pistol grip with optional configurations, free floating rail system, upper and lower accessory rails, optics ready (new 2021), black anodized or FDE finish, 9.84-10.4 lbs. New 2009.

MSR $4,129	$3,725	$3,250	$2,800	$2,550	$2,200	$1,725	$1,375	

* ***MR762A1 LRP (Long Rifle Package)*** – 7.62x51mm cal., GPO, 16 1/2 in. cold hammer forged barrel, 20 shot mag., two-stage trigger, collapsible stock with adj. cheekpiece, Ergo SureGrip, Blue Force Gear sling and Manta rail covers, tan finish, features a 3-9x40mm Leupold VX-R Patrol rifle scope perched in a set of Leupold rings on a Leupold Pic-rail mount, Tan finish, includes LaRue Tactical BRM-6 bipod, cleaning kit, two mags., and Pelican case, 10.42 lbs. Mfg. 2013-2016.

	$6,075	$5,450	$5,000	$4,550	$3,825	$3,000	$2,350	*$6,899*

* ***MR762A1 LRP II (Long Rifle Package II)*** – 7.62x51mm NATO cal., GPO, 16 1/2 in. cold hammer forged barrel with 14.7 in. modular rail system, 10 or 20 shot mag., two-stage trigger, G28 collapsible stock with adj. cheekpiece, buttpad, and LOP, FDE pistol grip with storage, accessory Picatinny rail, integrated quick detachable sling attachment points, 3-9x40mm Leupold VX-R Patrol rifle scope and mount/base, Leupold rings and Picatinny rail mount, LaRue/Harris Tactical BRM-S bipod, cleaning kit, and Pelican case, black and tan finish, 13.46 lbs. Mfg. in the USA beginning 2016.

MSR $7,249	$6,500	$5,700	$4,875	$4,400	$3,550	$2,925	$2,200	

MODEL MP5 A5 – .22 LR cal., blowback action, 10 or 25 shot mag., 16.1 in. barrel with compensator, black finish, metal receiver, Navy pistol grip, H&K adj. front and rear sights, 3 lug, standard forearm, retractable stock, external safety, 5.9 lbs., mfg. by Carl Walther in Ulm, Germany, imported by Umarex USA. Imported 2009-disc.

	$450	$395	$360	$330	$300	$275	$250	*$499*

MODEL MP5 SD – .22 LR cal., blowback action, 10 or 25 shot mag., 16.1 in. barrel with compensator, black finish, metal receiver, adj. rear sights, interchangeable front post sight, 3 lug imitation, SD type ribbed forearm, Navy pistol grip, retractable stock, external safety, 5.9 lbs. Mfg. by Carl Walther in Ulm, Germany, imported by Umarex USA. Imported 2009-disc.

	$525	$475	$425	$395	$360	$330	$300	*$599*

SHOTGUNS: SEMI-AUTO

Benelli shotguns previously imported by H&K can be found under Benelli.

MODEL 512 – 12 ga. only, mfg. by Franchi for German military contract, rifle sights, matte finished metal, walnut stock, fixed choke pattern diverter giving rectangular shot pattern. Importation disc. 1991.

	$1,500	$1,300	$1,100	$925	$800	$700	$600	

Last Mfg.'s Wholesale was $1,895.

SLS 2002 – 12 ga. only, 3 in. chamber, IQ-port gas operation (excess gas is vented forward through forearm cap), various barrel lengths, including slug barrel, double slide rails, deluxe checkered walnut stock and forearm, phosphate black finish, prototypes only in Europe, approx. 6 3/4 lbs.

While advertised during 2002, this gun was never manufactured past the prototype stage.

HEDEF ARMS COMPANY

Current shotgun manufacturer established in 2005, located in Konya, Turkey. No current U.S. importation.

Hedef Arms Company manufactures good quality shotguns under the Army Serra, Azra 16, Corcil, and Scorpion trademarks. Please refer to these individual listings for more information.

HEGMANS, THEO

Current custom manufacturer located in Kerken, Germany. No current U.S. importation.

Master craftsman Theo Hegmans creates one-of-a-kind unusual custom firearms, in addition to unique airguns, percussion replicas, cross bows, compound bows, as well as interesting items in woodworking and metal. Please visit his website and contact him directly for more information on a custom designed firearm.

N.L. HEINEKE, INC.

Current custom bolt action rifle and shotgun manufacturer located in Laramie, WY.

N.L. Heineke also specializes in turn-of-the-past military and single shot rifle restorations and repairs. Please contact the manufacturer directly for more information, including pricing, delivery time, and availability.

GRADING - PPGS™	100%	98%	95%	90%	80%	70%	60%	LAST MSR

RIFLES: BOLT ACTION, CUSTOM

Nathan Heinke manufactures high quality bolt action rifles on a custom order basis only. The base price is $16,000, and many options and accessories are available, including engraving. Please contact the company directly for more information, including delivery time (approx. 16 months), custom options, and availability.

HEINIE SPECIALTY PRODUCTS

Previous pistol manufacturer established in 1973, located in Quincy, IL. Heinie currently manufactures sights only.

Heinie manufactured both scratch built personal defense and tactical/carry 1911 packages in a wide variety of chamberings.

HEIRLOOM PRECISION

Current 1911-style custom pistol manufacturer established in 2005, located in Mesa, AZ.

J. Burton manufactures custom made 1911-style pistols built to customer specifications. Please contact Mr. Burton directly for more information, including pricing, delivery time, and availability.

HEIZER DEFENSE

Current pistol manufacturer established in 2011, located in Pevely, MO.

PISTOLS: SEMI-AUTO

PKO 9 – 9mm Para. cal., single action/blowback, aluminum frame, 2 3/4 in. stainless steel slide/barrel, 7 (flush mag.) or 10 (extended mag.) shot, ambi manual rear safety, front strap grip safety, pistol is .8 in. wide, loaded chamber indicator, chambered round disconnect, 20 oz. Mfg. 2017-Circa 2020.

Retail pricing was not available for this model.

PKO 45 – .45 ACP cal., single action/blowback, 2 3/4 in. stainless steel fixed barrel is under the guide rod, 5 (flush mag.) or 7(extended mag.) shot, stainless steel or optional titanium slide/frame, internal hammer, HiViz Light wave and TruGlo night sights, ambi manual rear safety, front strap grip safety, pistol is only .8 in. wide, loaded chamber indicator, Blaze, Ghost Gray, Tactical Black, Copperhead, Champagne Chrome, or Titanium finish, 26 oz. New 2016.

MSR $899	$825	$750	$650	$550	$500	$495	$450

Add $100 for TruGlo night sights. Add $300 for titanium frame.

PISTOLS: SINGLE SHOT

HEDY JANE POCKET SHOTGUN PISTOL – .45 ACP/.410 ga., stainless steel construction, snag free design, radius grip, trigger is on roller bearings for a smooth action, storage compartment in handle holds 2 extra rounds, available in aqua/stainless, pink/stainless, purple/stainless, Zombie Green/ stainless, or Zombie Green/black finish. New 2015.

MSR $449	$380	$340	$280	$260	$200	$175	$140

PAK1 "POCKET AK" PISTOL – 7.62x39mm cal., single shot, 3 3/4 in. barrel with "Progressive" porting, small, flat, snag-free design, case/shell extractor, recessed ambi operating latches, black Isonite or stainless finish, 23 5/8 oz. New 2017.

MSR $399	$340	$300	$250	$225	$180	$150	$125

Add $199 for additional barrel.

PAR1 "POCKET AR" PISTOL – .223 Rem. cal., 3 3/4 in. ported (new 2016) or unported barrel, case/shell extractor, ergonomic grip, small/flat design, snag free with recessed ambi-operating latches, black Isonite or stainless finish, 23 oz. New 2015.

MSR $399	$340	$300	$250	$225	$180	$150	$125

Add $20 for ported barrel (new 2016).

PS1 POCKET SHOTGUN PISTOL – .45 ACP/.410 ga., 3 1/4 in. pivoted tip-up stainless steel barrel, stainless steel frame, snag free design, case shell extractor, storage compartment in handle for 2 additional rounds, available in Black Isonite or stainless finish, 21 oz. New late 2013.

MSR $399	$340	$300	$250	$225	$180	$150	$125

Add $159 for additional AR barrel.

HELLIS, CHARLES

Previous trademark of shotguns, located in London, England circa 1884-1986.

SHOTGUNS: CUSTOM

Charles Hellis manufactured high quality traditional SxS and O/U shotguns with a unique spring assisted opening mechanism. All guns were entirely handmade to custom order. The most recent SxS prices began at £32,500, and O/U prices started at £39,950.

GRADING - PPGS™	100%	98%	95%	90%	80%	70%	60%	LAST MSR

HELWAN

Previous trademark imported by Navy Arms Co. and Interarms until 1995.

PISTOLS: SEMI-AUTO

BRIGADIER – 9mm Para. cal., single action, 4 1/2 in. barrel, all steel construction, 8 shot mag. with finger extension, black plastic grips, 32.6 oz. Imported 1988-94.

	100%	98%	95%	90%	80%	70%	60%	LAST MSR
	$450	$375	$300	$250	$225	$200	$175	*$260*

Add 20% for early mfg. with better finish.

This model is patterned after the Beretta Model 1951. They were manufactured at the Helwan arsenal in Egypt.

MODEL 920 – 9mm Para. cal., patterned after the Beretta M92, blue finish, bottom mag. release. Mfg. in Egypt, limited importation in 1997 by Intrac Arms.

	100%	98%	95%	90%	80%	70%	60%	LAST MSR
	$500	$375	$325	$275	$250	$225	$195	

Add 10% for NIB condition.

HENDRY, RAMSAY & WILCOX

Previous manufacturer located in Perth, Scotland.

Hendry, Ramsay & Wilcox manufactured top quality shotguns and rifles which were priced per individual quotation. The company, now called Hendry, Ramsay & Waters, Ltd., is a hunting and sporting outfitter.

HENRY, ALEXANDER

Previous trademark currently managed and operated by John Dickson & Son, located in Edinburgh, Scotland.

After an apprenticeship to Thomas Mortimer in Edinburgh, Alexander Henry set up on his own in 1852. Although only in business a short while, (forty-two years), but in that time rose to become the pre-eminent rifle maker in the world. In 1860, he took out one of the most famous patents of the nineteenth century, his rifling system that created the world famous Henry rifling. When breech-loading rifles made their appearance in the 1860s, he invented a falling block action in 1865 that became the most popular and successful of all such actions. Currently, the business is manaaged and operated by John Dickson and Son. Although no new guns or rifles are currently produced under the Henry name, a full repair, restoration, and record enquiry service are offered for vintage Henry guns and rifles.

HENRY REPEATING ARMS COMPANY

Current rifle and shotgun manufacturer established during 1997, located in Bayonne, NJ beginning 2008, with manufacturing facilities in Rice Lake, WI beginning in 2014. Previously located in Brooklyn, NY. Distributor and dealer sales.

HENRY® Made in America and Priced Right

PISTOLS: LEVER ACTION

HENRY MARE'S LEG CENTERFIRE – .357 Mag./.38 Spl. (new 2013), .44 Mag./.44 Spl. (new 2013), or .45 LC cal., 12.9 in. barrel, brass barrel band, 5 shot, fully adj. semi-buckhorn rear with reversible white diamond insert and brass bead front sights, cut-down American walnut stock, large loop lever, left-side saddle ring, hardened brass receiver and buttplate, transfer bar safety, blued barrel and lever, 5.8 lbs. New 2011.

	100%	98%	95%	90%	80%	70%	60%	LAST MSR
MSR $1,079	$915	$800	$685	$620	$500	$410	$360	

HENRY MARE'S LEG RIMFIRE – .22 S/L/LR or .22 WMR (new 2015) cal., 12 1/2 or 12 7/8 in. round blued barrel with barrel band, 8 or 10 shot, hooded front sights, fully adj. rear with semi-buckhorn, cut-down American walnut stock with or w/o checkering and forearm, plastic buttplate, includes saddle ring, large loop lever, approx. 4 1/2 lbs. New 2011.

	100%	98%	95%	90%	80%	70%	60%	LAST MSR
MSR $484	$410	$360	$310	$280	$225	$185	$160	

Add $17 for .22 WMR cal. (new 2015).

RIFLES: BOLT ACTION

HENRY ACU-BOLT – .17 HMR, .22 LR, or .22 WMR cal., scaled down action, single shot, 20 in. stainless steel barrel and receiver, checkered black fiberglass stock, Williams Fire Sights, includes 4X scope with cantilever mount, 4 1/4 lbs. Mfg. 2004-2013.

	100%	98%	95%	90%	80%	70%	60%	LAST MSR
	$335	$285	$225	$185	$160	$140	$120	*$400*

HENRY MINI-BOLT – .22 S & LR cal., single shot, 16 1/4 in. stainless steel barrel, stainless steel receiver, Williams Fire Sights (green fiber optic dot sights), black, Instant Orange (mfg. 2009-2014, reintroduced 2017), or Muddy Girl (new 2014) synthetic stock, plastic buttplate, pistol grip, manual safety, 11 1/2 in. LOP, 3 1/4 lbs. New 2002.

	100%	98%	95%	90%	80%	70%	60%	LAST MSR
MSR $304	$260	$230	$195	$175	$145	$115	$100	

GRADING - PPGS™	100%	98%	95%	90%	80%	70%	60%	LAST MSR

RIFLES: LEVER ACTION

HENRY CLASSIC LEVER ACTION – .17 HMR (disc. 2010), .22 S-L-LR, or .22 WMR (new 2000) cal., side ejection, blue steel receiver, 18 1/4 (.22 LR only), 19 1/4 (.22 WMR only) in. round or 20 in. octagon (mfg. 2006-2010) barrel, 11 (.22 WMR) or 15 (.22 LR) shot mag., deluxe American walnut stock and forearm, adj. rear and hooded front sights, 5 1/4 lbs. New 1997.

MSR $386	$325	$285	$245	$220	$180	$150	$125	

Add $166 for .22 WMR (new 2000) cal.
Add $100 for octagon barrel (disc. 2010).
Add $225 for .17 HMR cal. with octagon barrel (disc. 2010).

* ***BSA Venturing Edition*** – .22 S, L, LR cal., lever action rifle, 18 1/4 in. round blue barrel, 15 (.22 LR), 16 (.22 Long), or 21 (.22 Short) shot mag., hooded front sight, adj. rear sight, straight grip American walnut stock, "10th Anniversary Venturing" logo on receiver, 5 1/4 lbs. Mfg. 2008.

	$385	$340	$300	$265	$235	$200	$175	*$430*

* ***Carbine Lever Action (Carbine Large Loop)*** – .17 HMR (disc. 2010), .22 S, L, LR, or .22 WMR (mfg. 2000-disc.) cal., 16 1/8 in. barrel and large loop lever, 11 or 15 shot mag., side ejection, adj. rear sight and hooded front, American walnut stock and forearm, 4 1/2 lbs. New 1998.

MSR $415	$350	$300	$265	$240	$195	$160	$135	

* ***Lever Action Youth*** – .22 S-L-LR cal., 16 1/8 in. barrel, blued barrel and receiver, adj. rear and hooded front sights, American walnut stock, 12 (.22 LR), 17 (.22 L), or 18 (.22 S) shot mag., 13 in. LOP, 4 1/4 lbs.

MSR $397	$340	$300	$255	$230	$185	$155	$130	

* ***Octagon Frontier*** – .17 HMR, .22 S/L/LR, or .22 WMR cal., 20 or 24 (new 2017) in. blue octagon barrel, 11, 12, 16 or 21 shot, American walnut stock, Marbles adj. semi-buckhorn rear sight, brass bead front sight, 6 1/4 lbs.

MSR $500	$425	$375	$325	$295	$235	$195	$165	

Add $27 for 24 in. barrel in .22 S/L/LR or $129 for 24 in. barrel in .22 WMR cal. (new 2017).
Add $104 for .22 WMR or .17 HMR cal.

* ***Octagon Frontier Suppressor Ready*** – .22 S/L/LR or .22 WMR cal., 24 in. threaded octagon barrel, 8 or 10 shot, fully adj. semi-buckhorn rear sight with adj. white diamond insert and brass beaded front sight, American walnut stock, 7 lbs. New 2017.

MSR $522	$445	$390	$335	$300	$245	$200	$175	

Add $134 for .22 WMR cal.

* ***Varmint Express*** – .17 HMR cal., 20 in. round barrel, 11 shot tube mag., Williams Fire Sights, checkered Monte Carlo high comb American walnut stock, includes cantilever scope mount, 5 3/4 lbs. New 2003.

MSR $605	$515	$450	$385	$350	$285	$230	$200	

HENRY ALL-WEATHER SIDE GATE (HENRY ALL-WEATHER) – .30-30 or .45-70 cal., 18 1/2 or 20 in. round barrel, 4 or 5 shot mag., side loading gate (became standard 2021), hard chrome plating on all metal surfaces, fully adj. semi-buckhorn rear and brass beaded front sights, straight (.30-30) or pistol (.45-70) grip stained hardwood stock w/industrial coating, rubber buttpad, drilled and tapped receiver, 7 lbs. New 2016.

MSR $1,141	$970	$850	$730	$660	$535	$435	$380	

HENRY AMERICAN BEAUTY – .22 S, L, LR cal., 20 in. octagon blued barrel, nickel barrel band, 16 shot, Marbles fully adj. semi-buckhorn rear with reversible white diamond insert and brass bead front sights, American walnut stock, nickel buttplate, drilled and tapped, main panel features a rose and floral scroll pattern above an AMERICAN BEAUTY banner, nickel finished receiver displays mechanically transferred rose and embellishments enhanced with 14Kt. gold plating, 6 3/4 lbs. New 2015.

MSR $994	$845	$740	$635	$575	$465	$380	$330	

HENRY AMERICAN EAGLE – .22 S, L, LR cal., 20 in. octagon blued steel barrel, 16 shot mag., brass bead front sight and fully adj. semi-buckhorn rear with diamond insert, ivory colored American walnut stock and forend with engraving, drilled and tapped, nickel plated receiver finish, 6.75 lbs. New 2019.

MSR $1,020	$865	$750	$650	$590	$475	$400	$340	

HENRY BIG BOY ALL-WEATHER SIDE GATE (BIG BOY ALL-WEATHER) – .44 Mag./.44 Spl., .45 LC, or .357 Mag./.38 Spl. cal., 20 in. round barrel, 10 shot mag., with (new 2021) or w/o (disc. 2020) side gate, fully adj. semi-buckhorn rear with adj. white diamond insert and brass bead front sights, straight grip stained hardwood stock with rubber buttpad, industrial hard chrome satin finish, 7 lbs. New 2017.

MSR $1,141	$975	$850	$725	$675	$550	$450	$380	

Subtract $51 for All Weather w/o side gate.

GRADING - PPGS™	100%	98%	95%	90%	80%	70%	60%	LAST MSR

HENRY BIG BOY AMERICAN OILMAN TRIBUTE EDITION – .44 Mag. or .44 Spl. cal., 20 in. octagonal barrel, 10 shot, fully adj. semi-buckhorn rear with adj. diamond insert and brass beaded front sight, straight grip American walnut stock, hardened brass receiver, buttplate, and barrel band, 8.68 lbs. New 2014.

MSR $1,580 $1,340 $1,175 $1,000 $910 $735 $600 $525

HENRY BIG BOY BSA VENTURING EDITION – .44 Mag. cal., 20 in. octagon blue barrel with brass barrel band, 10 shot mag., solid brass receiver, Marbles adj. semi-buckhorn rear with reversible diamond insert and brass bead front sights, straight grip American walnut stock, brass buttplate. Mfg. 2008.

$875 $750 $675 $600 $525 $475 $400 *$1,000*

HENRY BIG BOY CARBINE – .38 Spl./.357 Mag., .45 Colt, .44 Mag./.44 Spl., .327 Fed. Mag. (new 2017), or .41 Mag. (new 2017) cal., 16 1/2 in. blued barrel with brass barrel band, 7 shot, fully adj. semi-buckhorn rear and brass bead front sights, American walnut stock, brass buttplate, large loop lever, hardened brass receiver, 7.76 lbs. New 2015.

MSR $1,001 $850 $750 $650 $575 $475 $385 $330

HENRY BIG BOY CLASSIC LEVER ACTION – .38 Spl./.357 Mag. (new 2008), .44 Mag./.44 Spl., .45 LC (new 2004), .327 Fed. Mag. (new 2017), or .41 Mag. (new 2017) cal., 20 in. octagon barrel, 10 shot tube mag., brass receiver, buttplate, and barrel band, fully adj. semi-buckhorn rear with adj. white diamond insert and brass beaded front sight, straight grip American walnut stock and forearm, 8.68 lbs. New 2003.

MSR $1,001 $850 $750 $650 $575 $475 $385 $330

HENRY BIG BOY COLOR CASE HARDENED CARBINE/RIFLE – .44 Mag/.44 Spl., .357 Mag./.38 Spl., or .45 LC cal., steel frame, 16 1/2 or 20 in. barrel, adj. buck and bead sights, clean checkering on forend and straight-wrist stock, rubber recoil pad, automatic in-hammer transfer bar safety, large loop lever, traditional tube loading, drilled and tapped for scope mounts, color case hardened finish. New 2018.

MSR $1,141 $970 $850 $730 $660 $535 $435 $380

HENRY BIG BOY COWBOY EDITION II – .44 Mag. (disc. 2013) or .45 LC cal., 20 in. octagon blued barrel w/brass barrel band, 10 shot mag., solid top brass receiver, Marbles adj. semi-buckhorn rear and brass bead front sights, straight grip American walnut stock, cowboy motif embedded in stock, brass buttplate. New 2011.

MSR $1,525 $1,300 $1,140 $975 $885 $715 $585 $510

This model was made in two editions - the original first edition of the one of 1,000 (disc.), and the second edition of one of 1,000 (recent mfg.).

HENRY BIG BOY DELUXE II – .38 Spl./.357 Mag. (new 2008), .44 Mag. (disc. 2013), or .45 LC cal., features hand engraved brass frame and barrel band, deluxe uncheckered walnut stock and forearm, 1,000 mfg. 2007-2014.

$1,725 $1,500 $1,225 $995 $850 $700 $575 *$1,995*

This model has been made in two editions - the original first edition of the one of 1,000 (disc.), and the second edition of one of 1,000 (current mfg.).

HENRY BIG BOY DELUXE ENGRAVED 3RD EDITION – .357 Mag./.38 Spl., .45 Colt, or .44 Mag./.44 Spl. cal., 20 in. octagon barrel, 10 shot tube-loading mag., fully adj. semi-buckhorn rear and brass bead front sights, American walnut stock, drilled and tapped, hand engraved, 1 of 1,000, hardened brass receiver, barrel band, and buttplate, 8.68 lbs. Limited mfg. beginning 2015.

MSR $2,096 $1,780 $1,560 $1,335 $1,210 $980 $800 $700

HENRY BIG BOY EAGLE SCOUT CENTENNIAL TRIBUTE EDITION – .44 Mag./.44 Spl. cal., 20 in. octagon blued steel barrel, 10 shot, hardened brass receiver, buttplate, and barrel band, fully adj. semi-buckhorn rear with adj. white diamond insert and brass beaded front sights, straight grip American walnut stock and forearm, etched with eagle scout award medal, nickel plated receiver with an American style scroll pattern w/words "THIS I PLEDGE MY SACRED HONOR", left side etched with the Official BSA Eagle Scout 100th Anniversary logo and banner with words below "BOY SCOUTS OF AMERICA", 8.68 lbs.

MSR $1,641 $1,395 $1,225 $1,050 $950 $775 $625 $530

HENRY BIG BOY GOD BLESS AMERICA EDITION – .44 Mag./.44 Spl. cal., 20 in. blued octagon barrel with nickeled barrel band, 10 shot, adj. buck and bead sights, transfer bar safety, hardened brass receiver with highly polished nickel plating with floral scroll engraving, 24K gold "God Bless America" banner below a gold outline of the 48 contiguous states on right side, left has the Liberty Bell in raised gold relief, fancy American walnut stock with painted mural above a gold banner reading "O Say Can You See", nickeled brass buttplate. New 2018.

MSR $1,641 $1,395 $1,225 $1,050 $950 $775 $625 $530

GRADING - PPGS™	100%	98%	95%	90%	80%	70%	60%	LAST MSR

HENRY BIG BOY ORDER OF THE ARROW CENTENNIAL EDITION - .44 Mag./.44 Spl. cal., 20 in. octagon barrel, 10 shot, fully adj. semi-buckhorn rear with adj. white diamond insert and brass bead front sights, straight grip American walnut stock, features distinctive Order of the Arrow totem, motto, and scout emblem etchings on receiver and Centennial stock markings, hardened brass receiver, buttplate, and barrel band, 8.68 lbs. New 2015.

MSR $1,641	$1,395	$1,225	$1,050	$950	$775	$625	$530	

HENRY BIG BOY SILVER - .44 Mag./.44 Spl., .45 LC, or .357 Mag./.38 Spl. cal., 20 in. octagon barrel, 10 shot tube mag., polished aluminum brass receiver, buttplate, and barrel band, fully adj. semi-buckhorn rear with adj. white diamond insert and brass bead front sights, straight grip American walnut stock, transfer bar safety, 8.68 lbs. New 2016.

MSR $1,105	$940	$825	$705	$640	$515	$425	$370	

* ***Henry Big Boy Silver Deluxe Engraved*** - .44 Mag., .45 LC, or .357 Mag. cal., 20 in. blued octagon barrel, 10 shot tube mag., polished aluminum brass receiver, buttplate, and barrel band, fully adj. semi-buckhorn rear with adj. white diamond insert and brass bead front sights, straight grip, fancy American walnut stock, transfer bar safety, features extensive floral engraving pattern, silver receiver, 8.68 lbs. Only 1,000 mfg. beginning 2016.

MSR $2,116	$1,800	$1,575	$1,350	$1,225	$990	$810	$700	

HENRY BIG BOY STEEL CARBINE/RIFLE - .357 Mag. (disc. 2020), .32 H&R Mag. (disc. 2020), .44 Mag. (disc. 2020), .45 Colt (disc. 2020), .41 Mag. (new 2016), or .327 Fed. Mag. (new late 2016) cal., matte finished blued steel frame, 16 1/2 (Carbine only, new 2016) or 20 in. round barrel, 7 or 10 shot, sliding transfer bar safety, fully adj. semi-buckhorn rear and brass bead front sights, checkered American walnut stock with ventilated rubber recoil pad and forend cap, swivel studs, oversized lever (Carbine only), drilled and tapped, matte-finished blued steel receiver, barrel, and lever, 6 1/2-7 lbs. New 2015.

MSR $950	$810	$710	$610	$550	$445	$365	$315	

HENRY BIG BOY TRUCKER'S TRIBUTE EDITION - .44 Mag. cal., 20 in. octagonal barrel, 10 shot, fully adj. semi-buckhorn rear with adj. diamond insert and brass bead front sights, brass barrel band and receiver, right side features 18-wheeler and banner that reads "TRUCKERS MOVE AMERICA", left side features convoy of trucks and banner that reads "BOUND FOR GLORY", straight grip American walnut stock, 8.68 lbs. Mfg. 2014-disc.

	$1,340	$1,175	$1,000	$910	$735	$615	$525	*$1,575*

HENRY BIG BOY "WILDLIFE" EDITION I/"WILDLIFE EDITION II - .44 Mag. or .45 LC cal., 20 in. octagon barrel, 10 shot mag., Marbles adj. semi-buckhorn rear and brass bead front sights, straight grip American walnut stock with wildlife scenes painted on stock and forearm.

MSR $1,525	$1,300	$1,140	$975	$885	$715	$585	$510	

This model has been made in two editions - the original first edition of the one of 1,000 (disc.), and the second edition of one of 1,000 (current mfg.).

HENRY .30-30/.45-70 BRASS OCTAGON - .30-30 Win. or .45-70 (new 2016) cal., 20 (.30-30) or 22 (.45-70) in. round (disc. 2020) or octagon blued steel barrel with or w/o barrel band, 5 (.30-30) or 4 (.45-70) shot, blue steel (.30-30 only, disc. 2020) or brass receiver, Marbles semi-buckhorn rear and brass bead front sight or XS Ghost ring sights (steel frame only), straight grip American checkered walnut stock and forearm with rubber buttpad (disc.) or brass buttplate, drilled and tapped, sling swivels and large loop lever (.45-70 only), 7-8.3 lbs. New 2008.

MSR $1,036	$880	$765	$650	$595	$475	$400	$325	

Subtract approx. $95 for round barrel and blued steel receiver (disc. 2020).

HENRY .30-30/.45-70 BRASS WILDLIFE EDITION - .30-30 or .45-70 cal., 20 (.30-30) or 22 (.45-70) in. octagon blued steel barrel, 5 (.30-30) or 4 (.45-70) shot, brass receiver, drilled and tapped, fully adj. semi-buckhorn rear and brass beaded front sight, straight grip American walnut stock with brass buttplate, transfer bar safety, black-filled highly engraved frames featuring American vine scroll and braided borders surrounding the portrait of a buck's head on the right and leaping buck on the left, high polished metalwork, larger loop lever (.45-70 only), 8.1-8.3 lbs. New 2016.

MSR $1,406	$1,195	$1,045	$895	$815	$655	$540	$475	

Add $170 for .45-70 cal.

HENRY COLOR CASE HARDENED SIDE GATE (COLOR CASE HARDENED) - .30-30 or .45-70 cal., 20 (.30-30) or 22 (.45-70) in. blued octagon barrel, 4 or 5 shot tube mag., with (new 2021) or w/o (disc. 2020) side gate, drilled and tapped case hardened steel receiver, fully adj. semi-buckhorn rear and brass beaded front sight, checkered American walnut stock with ventilated rubber recoil pad, straight or pistol grip, transfer bar safety, sling swivel studs, 8.1-8.5 lbs., New 2016.

MSR $1,141	$975	$850	$725	$675	$550	$450	$380	

Subtract $51 for color case hardened w/o side gate (disc. 2020).

GRADING - PPGS™	100%	98%	95%	90%	80%	70%	60%	LAST MSR

HENRY FRONTIER CARBINE "EVIL ROY" EDITION – .22 S, L, LR or .22 WMR (new 2016) cal., 16 1/2 in. octagon barrel, nickel plated barrel band, 9 (.22 WMR), 12, or 16 shot, fully adj. semi-buckhorn w/ diamond insert rear sights and brass bead front sights, American walnut stock, 13 in. LOP, Evil Roy logo and large loop lever, brushed finish grooved receiver, 5 1/2 lbs. New 2015.

MSR $552	$470	$410	$350	$325	$260	$215	$185

Add $122 for .22 WMR cal. (new 2016).

HENRY GOLDEN EAGLE/SILVER EAGLE 2ND EDITION – .22 S, L, or LR cal., 20 in. blued octagon barrel, nickel barrel band, 16 or 21 shot, nickel receiver, fully adj. buckhorn rear and brass bead front sights, American walnut stock, nickel buttplate, receiver depicts American eagle in flight in high relief with (Golden Eagle) or w/o (Silver Eagle) 24K gold, surrounded by scroll engraving patterns and the words "Golden Eagle" in banners in engraved panel on both sides of receiver, 6 3/4 lbs., New 2016.

MSR $925	$790	$690	$595	$535	$435	$355	$310

Add $55 for Golden Eagle model.

HENRY LEVER ACTION SIDE GATE – .30-30, .38-55, .35 Rem., or .45-70 Govt. (new late 2019) cal., 5 shot mag., 20 in. round blued steel barrel, ivory bead front sight w/ramp and fully adj. semi-buckhorn rear sight, Weaver 63B scope mount, drilled and tapped, American walnut stock, transfer bar safety, regular level swivel studs, polished brass receiver, 7 1/2 lbs. New mid-2019.

MSR $1,100	$935	$825	$700	$635	$515	$425	$365

HENRY LONG RANGER – .223 Rem., .243 Win., 6.5 Creedmoor (new 2019), or .308 Win. cal., 20 in. round blued free floated sporter barrel, 4 or 5 shot, hard anodized aircraft aluminum receiver, with or w/o fully adj. folding rear and ramp with ivory bead front sights (new 2017), straight grip checkered American walnut stock with black rubber recoil pad, sling swivel studs, 7 lbs. New 2016.

MSR $1,138	$975	$850	$725	$675	$550	$450	$380

* ***Henry Long Ranger Deluxe Engraved*** – .223 Rem./5.56 NATO, .243 Win., or .308 Win./7.62 NATO cal., 20 in. round blued steel barrel, 4 or 5 shot detachable mag., ivory bead front and fully adj. rear sights, checkered American walnut stock with solid black rubber recoil pad, nickel plated receiver with 24K gold inlay, scroll engraving, 7 lbs. New late 2018.

MSR $1,973	$1,675	$1,465	$1,250	$1,140	$925	$750	$660

* ***Henry Long Ranger Wildlife Engraved Edition*** – .223 Rem./5.56 NATO (Coyote), .243 Win. (Antelope), or .308 Win. (Elk) cal., 20 in. round blued steel barrel, 5 shot detachable mag., ivory bead front and folding fully adj. rear sight, American walnut stock, black solid rubber recoil pad, nickel plated receiver with 24K gold inlay, drilled and tapped, Wildlife Coyote features a single coyote head on the left flat and a pair of full-figured coyotes on the right, the Wildlife Antelope shows a single antelope head against a background of rolling hills on the left, and a full-figured pair on the prairie on the right, and the Wildlife Elk depicts a majestic bull elk in a mountain setting on its left and a grazing pair on its right flat, 7 lbs. New 2019.

MSR $1,973	$1,675	$1,465	$1,250	$1,140	$925	$750	$660

HENRY SILVER EAGLE – .17 HMR (new 2015), .22 S, L, LR, or .22 WMR (new 2015) cal., 20 or 20 1/2 (.22 WMR only) in. octagon blued barrel with silver barrel band, 11 (.17HMR), 12 (.22 WMR), or 16 (.22 S, L, LR) shot, nickel receiver, Marbles fully adj. semi-buckhorn rear sight with reversible white diamond insert and brass beaded front sight, fancy American walnut buttstock, silver buttplate, 6 3/4 lbs. New 2014.

MSR $925	$790	$690	$595	$535	$435	$355	$310

Add $34 for .22 WMR cal. (new 2015).
Add $55 for .17 HMR cal. (new 2015).

HENRY SMALL GAME CARBINE/RIFLE – .22 S/L/LR, or .22 WMR cal., 16 1/4 (disc.) 17 (carbine), 20 (rifle, .22 S/L/LR), or 20.5 (rifle, .22 WMR) in. blued steel octagon barrel, 7 (disc.) , 9, 12, 16 or 21 shot mag., fully adj. Skinner peep sight with brass beaded front sight, American walnut stock, 1/4 cock safety, black finish, 5.75-6.5 lbs. New 2015.

MSR $552	$470	$410	$350	$325	$260	$215	$185

Add $96 for .22 WMR cal.

HENRY STEEL LEVER SIDE GATE – .45-70 or .30-30 Win. cal., 18.43 (.45-70) or 20 (.30-30) in. round blued steel barrel, 4 (.45-70) or 5 (.30-30) shot mag., brass bead front and semi-buckhorn rear sight w/diamond insert, American Walnut stock, black solid rubber recoil pad, transfer bar safety, drilled and tapped, swivel studs, side gate, optional large loop, 7 lbs. New 2020.

MSR $969	$825	$720	$620	$560	$455	$375	$325

Add $15 for 20 in. barrel w/large loop lever.

GRADING - PPGS™	100%	98%	95%	90%	80%	70%	60%	LAST MSR

HENRY STEEL OCTAGON – .45-70 cal., 18 1/2 in. barrel, 4 shot mag., blued steel receiver drilled and tapped for scope mounting, fully adj. semi-buckhorn rear and brass beaded front sight, checkered American walnut stock with buttplate, pistol grip, rubber recoil pad, approx. 7 lbs. Disc. 2020.

	$785	$685	$590	$535	$425	$350	$275	*$922*

HENRY STEEL WILDLIFE EDITION – .45-70 or .30-30 cal., 18.43 (.45-70) or 20 (.30-30) in. round blued steel barrel, 4 (.45-70) or 5 (.30-30) shot mag., fully adj. semi-buckhorn rear and brass beaded front sight, checkered pistol grip (.45-70) or straight grip (.30-30) American walnut stock, black rubber recoil pad, sling swivel studs, buck head or moose head portrait in 24K gold relief on right side and leaping buck or bear adorns on the left, 7 lbs. Mfg. 2016-2020.

	$1,325	$1,160	$995	$900	$725	$600	$500	*$1,553*

HENRY STEEL WILDLIFE EDITION SIDE GATE – .30-30 Win. or .45-70 cal., steel frame, 18.43 or 20 in. round blued steel barrel, 4 or 5 shot removable tube mag., side loading gate, drilled and tapped receiver, brass bead front and fully adj. semi-buckhorn rear sights with diamond insert, straight or pistol grip fancy American walnut stock with checkering, solid or ventilated black rubber recoil pad, swivel studs, engraved steel receiver with 24K gold inlay, blued finish, 7 lbs. New 2021.

MSR $1,572	$1,340	$1,175	$1,000	$910	$735	$600	$525	

MAGNUM EXPRESS – .22 WMR cal., 19 1/4 in. round blued steel barrel, no sights, checkered American walnut Monte Carlo buttstock with high comb, soft rubber buttpad, Picatinny rail pre-installed on receiver cover, 5.5 lbs. New 2021.

MSR $622	$525	$460	$395	$355	$290	$240	$200	

MODEL X – .45-70 Govt., .30-30 cal., 19.8 (.45-70) or 21.38 (.30-30) in. round blued steel threaded barrel, removable thread protector, 4 (.45-70) or 5 (.30-30) shot removable tube mag., side loading gate, drilled and tapped receiver, fiber optic front and adj. fiber optic sights, black synthetic stock, solid rubber recoil pad, in-line swing swivel studs, transfer bar safety, Picatinny rail, M-LOK accessory slots, 8.07 lbs. New 2020.

MSR $1,020	$865	$750	$650	$590	$475	$400	$325	

NEW ORIGINAL HENRY RIFLE – .44-40 WCF or .45 LC (new 2017) cal., 24 1/2 in. blued steel barrel, 13 shot, folding ladder rear and blade front sights, fancy American walnut buttstock w/polish hardened brass buttplate and receiver, 9 lbs. New 2014.

MSR $2,590	$2,200	$1,925	$1,650	$1,495	$1,210	$1,000	$860	

* ***New Original B.T. Henry 200th Anniversary Edition*** – .44-40 WCF cal., 24 1/2 in. octagon blued steel barrel, 13 shot mag., blade front and folding ladder rear sight, fancy American walnut stock, half cock safety, polished brass engraved receiver, 9 lbs. Limited mfg. of 200 beginning 2020.

MSR $4,286	$3,650	$3,200	$2,750	$2,480	$2,000	$1,650	$1,425	

* ***New Original Henry Deluxe Engraved Limited Edition*** – .44-40 cal., 24 in. barrel, 13 shot, folding ladder rear and blade front sights, fancy American walnut buttstock with hardened brass crescent buttplate, features deluxe scroll engraving, hardened brass receiver, 9 lbs. Limited edition 1 of 1,000. Mfg. 2014 only.

	$3,150	$2,750	$2,375	$2,150	$1,750	$1,425	$1,100	*$3,495*

* ***New Original Henry Deluxe Engraved Limited 2nd Edition*** – .44-40 WCF cal., 24 1/2 in. barrel, 13 shot, folding ladder rear and blade front sights, fancy American walnut buttstock with hardened brass crescent buttplate, features deluxe scroll engraving, polished hardened brass receiver, 9 lbs. Serial number range from BTH0001D2 to BTH1000D2. Limited edition of 1,000. Mfg. late 2018-2020.

	$3,125	$2,735	$2,350	$2,125	$1,725	$1,450	$1,225	*$3,670*

* ***New Original Henry Deluxe Engraved Limited 3rd Edition*** – .44-40 WCF cal., 24 1/2 in. octagon blued steel barrel, 13 shot, folding ladder rear and blade front sights, fancy American walnut stock with brass buttplate, engraved receiver, polished brass receiver finish, 9 lbs., serial number range from BTH0001D3 to BTH1000D3. Limited edition of 1,000. New 2018.

MSR $3,810	$3,240	$2,835	$2,430	$2,205	$1,780	$1,460	$1,275	*$3,739*

* ***New Original Henry Rare Carbine*** – .44-40 WCF cal., Lever Toggle Link System, 20.4 in. blued octagon barrel, 10 shot, folding ladder rear and blade front sights, fancy American walnut buttstock with hardened brass buttplate, hardened brass receiver, 8.49 lbs. New 2016.

MSR $2,590	$2,200	$1,925	$1,650	$1,495	$1,210	$990	$865	

* ***New Original Henry Rifle Iron Framed*** – .44-40 WCF cal., 24 1/2 in. octagon barrel, 13 shot, case color receiver, folding ladder rear and blade front sights, fancy American walnut buttstock with case color hardened steel crescent buttplate, half cock safety hammer notch, 8.62 lbs. New 2016.

MSR $3,023	$2,570	$2,250	$1,930	$1,750	$1,415	$1,150	$1,010	

GRADING - PPGS™	100%	98%	95%	90%	80%	70%	60%	LAST MSR

* ***New Original Henry Silver Deluxe Engraved Edition*** – .44-40 WCF cal., Lever Toggle Link System, 24 1/2 in. blued steel octagon barrel, 13 shot, folding ladder rear and blade front sights, fancy American walnut buttstock, nickel plated hardened brass receiver with engraving, nickel plated crescent buttplate with cleaning rod trapdoor, 9 lbs. Limited mfg. of 1,000 beginning 2017.

MSR $4,078	$3,465	$3,030	$2,600	$2,350	$1,900	$1,560	$1,360	

PHILMONT SCOUT RANCH RIFLE SPECIAL EDITION – .22 S, L, LR cal., 20 in. octagon barrel, 16 or 21 shot, American walnut stock, Marbles fully adj. rear and bead front sights, blue finish, Black Bull logo with 18K gold plate on right side of receiver cover, right side of stock laser etched and painted with mountain slope with "TOOTH OF TIME" underneath, Philmont scripted emblem burned into forearm, licensed by the Boy Scouts of America commemorating the oldest national high-adventure base and youth camp.

MSR $744	$625	$545	$475	$425	$345	$275	$225	

RIFLES: LEVER ACTION, GOLDEN BOY MODELS

GOLDEN BOY – .17 HMR (new 2005), .22 S, L, LR, or .22 WMR (new 2002) cal., 20 or 20 1/2 (.22 WMR cal. only) in. blue octagon steel barrel, 11, 12, 16, or 21 shot mag., drilled and tapped (beginning 2011), brasslite barrel band, receiver, and buttplate, fully adj. semi-buckhorn rear with adj. white diamond insert and brass bead front sights, American walnut stock, 6 3/4 lbs. New mid-1999.

MSR $589	$500	$440	$375	$340	$275	$225	$195	

Add $67 for .22 WMR cal. (new 2002).
Add $85 for .17 HMR cal. (new 2005).
Add $150 for personalized 20-word inscription on right side of receiver.

* ***Golden Boy 2nd Amendment Tribute Edition*** – .22 S, L, or LR cal., 20 in. octagon blued barrel, brasslite barrel band, 16 shot, fully adj. semi-buckhorn rear sight with reversible white diamond insert and brass beaded front sight, American walnut stock, brass buttplate, nickel finished receiver with floral engraving and 24K gold plating, 6 3/4 lbs. Limited mfg. of 2,000 for Friends of the NRA to salute the organization's contributions. New 2017.

MSR $1,209	$1,025	$900	$775	$700	$575	$475	$400	

* ***Golden Boy Abraham Lincoln Bicentennial*** – .22 S, L, LR cal., replica of Lincoln's ser. no. 6 Henry rifle, 20 in. barrel, 16 or 21 shot mag., brasslite receiver, brass bead front sight, Marbles adj. semi-buckhorn rear sight, straight grip American walnut stock, brass buttplate, brass replica of Lincoln memorial embedded in stock, 6 3/4 lbs. Mfg. 2009-2016.

	$1,075	$925	$800	$700	$600	$500	$400	*$1,200*

* ***Golden Boy American Farmer Tribute Edition*** – .22 S, L, or LR cal., 20 in. barrel, brasslite barrel band, 16 or 21 shot, Marbles fully adj. semi-buckhorn rear sights with reversible white diamond insert and brass bead front sight, American walnut stock, brass buttplate, nickel receiver, left side of receiver features image of farmer working behind horse-drawn plow, 24K gold selective plate, front and rear panels have agriculture scroll pattern, right side features "American Farmers feeding the World" on a swirling banner washed in 24K gold, 6 3/4 lbs. New 2014.

MSR $1,122	$950	$825	$700	$635	$515	$425	$350	

* ***Golden Boy American Railroad Tribute Edition*** – .22 S, L, LR cal., 20 in. barrel, 16 or 21 shot, fully adj. semi-buckhorn rear with reversible white diamond insert and brass bead front sights, nickel receiver, barrel band, and buttplate, blued lever and barrel, American walnut stock, scrollwork surrounds 24K gold plated No. 119 behind a bannered "THE LAST RAIL IS LAID", forward panel features golden spike next to banner marked "THE LAST SPIKE IS DRIVEN", Promontory ceremonial image on stock, forend marked "AMERICAN RAILROAD TRIBUTE", 6 3/4 lbs. New 2015.

MSR $1,122	$950	$825	$700	$635	$515	$425	$350	

* ***Golden Boy American Rodeo Tribute Edition*** – .22 S, L, LR cal., 20 in. octagon blued steel barrel, silver barrel band, 16 (LR cal.) or 21 (S cal.) shot, brass bead front and fully adj. semi-buckhorn rear sight with diamond insert, American walnut engraved stock, nickel plated buttplate, drilled and tapped, receiver engraving with 24Kt. gold plating, nickel plated receiver finish, 6.75 lbs. New 2019.

MSR $1,296	$1,100	$965	$825	$750	$600	$500	$425	

* ***Golden Boy BSA Centennial Edition*** – .22 S, L, LR cal., 20 in. round/octagon blue barrel and barrel band, 16 or 21 (.22 S cal.) shot mag., brass bead front sight, adj. buckhorn rear sight, straight grip American walnut stock, "100 Years of Scouting" medallion on stock, brass buttplate, brasslite receiver with Scout Law engraved on right side, Scout oath on left side, 6 3/4 lbs. Mfg. 2009-2016.

	$795	$700	$625	$550	$475	$400	$325	*$900*

GRADING - PPGS™	100%	98%	95%	90%	80%	70%	60%	LAST MSR

* ***Golden Boy BSA Venturing Edition*** – .22 S, L, LR cal., 20 in. octagon blue barrel, 16 or 21 shot mag., straight grip American walnut stock, "10th Anniversary Venturing" logo in buttstock, Marbles adj. semi-buckhorn rear sight with reversible diamond insert, brass bead front sight, brasslite receiver, buttplate, and barrel band. Mfg. 2008.

	$575	$500	$425	$350	$300	$265	$235	*$650*

* ***Golden Boy Coal Miner Tribute Edition I/II/Limited Edition*** – .22 S, L, or LR cal., 20 in. octagonal barrel, blued barrel and metal barrel band, 16 or 21 shot, Marbles fully adj. semi-buckhorn rear and beaded front sights, American walnut stock with right side featuring laser scroll of the Coal Miners' prayer (first edition) or outline of the United States of America and "AMERICA IS COAL COUNTRY" (second edition), 24K gold plated engravings, American style scroll with nickel plated receiver, black, laser etch of Coal Miners United image, gold banners with words below "Faces of Coal", and "Hearts of Gold" and shovel and pick axe (first edition) or 2 coal miners working, "working hands of a miner holding the results of his labor", and coal crane images, brasslite receiver, brass buttplate, 6 3/4 lbs.

MSR $1,122	$950	$825	$700	$635	$515	$425	$350	

Historical Armory made 1,000 Golden Boy American Coal Miner Exclusive Limited Editions w/coal miner engravings on a golden receiver and stock, numbered to 1,000 w/engraved wooden box. In 2019, different engravings were put on the receiver and stock, making the Golden Boy Coal Miner Tribute Edition II.

* ***Golden Boy Deluxe II*** – .17 HMR (new 2006), .22 S, L, LR (disc. 2013), or .22 WMR (new 2014) cal., features hand engraved gold and silver brasslite receiver, deluxe uncheckered walnut stock and forearm, Marbles fully adj. semi-buckhorn rear and brass bead front sights. Mfg. 2004-2014.

	$1,400	$1,225	$1,035	$900	$750	$600	$525	*$1,577*

Add $29 for .17 HMR (new 2006) cal.

This model has been made in two editions - the original first edition of the one of 1,000 (disc.), and the second edition of one of 1,000.

* ***Golden Boy Deluxe Engraved 3rd Edition*** – .17 HMR, .22 S, L, LR, or .22 WMR cal., 20 or 20 1/2 in. barrel, 11, 12, or 16 shot mag., fully adj. semi-buckhorn rear and brass bead front sights, American walnut stock, scrollwork engraving pattern on receiver, serial numbered 1-1000, brasslite receiver and barrel band, brass buttplate, blued lever and barrel, 6 3/4 lbs. Limited mfg. beginning 2015.

MSR $1,641	$1,395	$1,225	$1,050	$950	$775	$625	$545	

Add $52 for .22 WMR or $76 for .17 HMR cal.

* ***Golden Boy Eagle Scout Tribute Edition*** – .22 S, L, or LR cal., 20 in. blued barrel, brasslite barrel band, 16 or 21 (.22 S cal.) shot mag., nickel receiver, Marbles adj. semi-buckhorn rear with reversible white diamond insert and brass bead front sights, American walnut stock with Eagle Scout embedded logo, brass buttplate, 6 3/4 lbs. New 2011.

MSR $1,193	$1,020	$895	$765	$695	$560	$460	$395	

* ***Golden Boy EMS Tribute Edition*** – .22 S, L, or LR cal., 20 in. blued barrel with metal barrel band, 16 or 21 shot, brasslite receiver, Marbles fully adj. semi-buckhorn rear with reversible white diamond insert and brass bead front sights, American walnut stock is laser etched and hand painted with various iconic images such as medivac helicopter, EMS ambulance, emergency technician, etc., wood forearm features the EMS blue Star of Life emblem, 6 3/4 lbs. New 2015.

MSR $1,122	$950	$825	$700	$635	$515	$425	$350	

This rifle was created in honor of all those who help to preserve life, prevent injury, and promote recovery.

* ***Golden Boy Firefighter Tribute Edition*** – .22 S, L, LR cal., 20 in. octagonal barrel, 16 or 21 shot, 24K gold plated engravings, nickel plated receiver, right side shows American flag, image of firefighter rescuing a child, and banner with words "IN TRIBUTE TO AMERICA'S BRAVEST", left side depicts Saint Florian cross and words "SERVICE VALOR COURAGE" below a firefighter's helmet, aerial truck laser etched and hand painted on American walnut stock, adj. buckhorn rear and brass bead front sights, brasslite receiver, brass buttplate, blued barrel and metal barrel band, 6 3/4 lbs. New 2013.

MSR $1,122	$950	$825	$700	$635	$515	$425	$350	

* ***Golden Boy Fraternal Order of Eagles Tribute Edition*** – .22 S, L, LR cal., 20 in. barrel, brasslite barrel band, 16 or 21 shot, fully adj. semi-buckhorn rear with reversible white diamond insert and brass bead front sights, engraved and painted American walnut stock, 24Kt. gold plated engraving on nickel receiver, brass buttplate, blued lever and barrel, 6 3/4 lbs. New 2017.

MSR $1,173	$995	$870	$745	$675	$545	$450	$390	

GRADING - PPGS™	100%	98%	95%	90%	80%	70%	60%	LAST MSR

* ***Golden Boy Freemasons Tribute Edition*** – .22 S, L, LR cal., 20 in. barrel, 16 shot, fully adj. semi-buckhorn rear with reversible white diamond insert and brass bead front sights, painted and engraved American walnut stock, 24K gold engraving on receiver, nickel plated finish, 6 3/4 lbs. New 2017.

MSR $1,122	$950	$825	$700	$635	$515	$425	$350

* ***Golden Boy God Bless America Edition*** – .22 S, L, LR cal., 20 in. blued oct. barrel with barrel band, engraved nickeled receiver with floral scrollwork background, right side displays 24Kt. gold banner with words "Home of the Free Because of the Brave", and the American flag with stars and strips in gold accents, left side features gold Liberty Bell and Bald Eagle, adj. buckhorn rear sight, brass bead front, American walnut stock with 3-color painting of the Statue of Liberty's torch, "God Bless America" engraved and painted in two colors on the forend, bright brass buttplate, 6.75 lbs. New 2018.

MSR $1,296	$1,100	$965	$825	$750	$600	$500	$425

* ***Golden Boy Law Enforcement Tribute Edition*** – .22 S-L-LR cal., 20 in. octagonal barrel, 16 or 21 shot, American walnut stock, adj. buckhorn rear and brass bead front sights, blued and metal barrel bands, brasslite receiver, brass buttplate, 24K gold plated engravings, left side of receiver has engraving of Michael the Archangel - patron of police, laser etched on the stock is an American bald eagle with the words GOD BLESS AMERICA'S FINEST, 6 3/4 lbs.

MSR $1,122	$950	$825	$700	$635	$515	$425	$350

* ***Golden Boy Military Service Tribute Edition I/II*** – .22 S, L, LR cal., 20 in. blued barrel with brasslite barrel band, 16 or 21 shot mag., nickel receiver, fully adj. semi-buckhorn rear with reversible white diamond insert and brass bead front sights, seals of United States Army, Navy, AirForce, Marine Corps, and Coast Guard (first edition) or "SALUTING OUR MILITARY HEROS" (second edition) evgraved forearm, American walnut stock with American flag and "God Bless America" embedded logo, brass buttplate, drilled and tapped, 6 3/4 lbs. New 2011.

MSR $1,296	$1,100	$965	$825	$750	$600	$500	$425

Forearm engravings were changed, creating Golden Boy Military Service Tribute 2nd Edition.

A portion of the proceeds from each gun will benefit the American Legion, VFW, Wounded Warrior Project, and the Fisher House for military families.

* ***Golden Boy Salute To Scouting Edition*** – .22 S, L, LR cal., 20 in. octagon barrel, fully adj. semi-buckhorn rear with reversible white diamond insert and brass bead front sights, American walnut stock, 19th century style engraving, features 24K gold-plated "BOY SCOUTS OF AMERICA" banner on right hand side of the receiver and Universal Emblem with eagle and shield, displays "I WILL DO MY BEST" laser etched into left of buttstock and "DUTY TO GOD AND COUNTRY, DUTY TO OTHERS, DUTY TO SELF" laser etched into forearm, nickel receiver, barrel band, and buttplate, blued lever and barrel, 6 3/4 lbs. New 2015.

MSR $1,252	$1,065	$930	$800	$725	$585	$480	$415

* ***Golden Boy Shriner International Tribute Edition*** – .22 S, L, or LR cal., 20 in. blued steel octagon barrel and barrel band, 16 or 21 shot, nickel-plated receiver with 24K gold plating and engraving, semi-buckhorn rear and brass bead front sights, engraved/painted American walnut stock with Shriner Tribute, nickel-plated buttplate, 6.75 lbs. New 2018.

MSR $1,296	$1,100	$965	$825	$750	$600	$500	$425

* ***Golden Boy Silver*** – .17 HMR, .22 S, L, LR, or .22 WMR cal., 20 or 20 1/2 in. octagon blued barrel, nickel barrel band, 11, 12, 16, or 21 shot, fully adj. semi-buckhorn rear with reversible white diamond insert and brass bead front sights, American walnut stock, nickel buttplate, 6 3/4 lbs. New 2015.

MSR $663	$565	$495	$425	$380	$310	$250	$225

Add $53 for .22 WMR or $73 for .17 HMR cal.

Add $150 for personalized receiver cover.

* ***Golden Boy Silver Youth*** – .22 S, L, or LR cal., 17 in. blued octagon barrel, 16 shot mag., adj. semi-buckhorn w/Diamond insert, brass bead front sight, American walnut straight grip stock, 13 in. LOP, nickel plated finish, 6 lbs. New 2020.

MSR $663	$560	$490	$420	$380	$310	$260	$215

* ***Golden Boy Stand for the Flag Edition*** – .22 S/L/LR cal., 20 in. barrel, nickeled barrel band, 16 or 21 shot, brightly polished nickel receiver features 3-color depiction of the Star Spangled Banner applied in a Cerakote formulation by Baron Technology, walnut stock with "O Say Can You See" on right rear side, nickeled carbine-style buttplate. New 2018.

MSR $1,296	$1,100	$965	$825	$750	$600	$500	$425

GRADING - PPGS™	100%	98%	95%	90%	80%	70%	60%	LAST MSR

* ***Golden Boy Texas Tribute Edition*** – .22 S, L, or LR cal., 20 in. blued steel octagon barrel, brass barrel band, 16 (LR) or 21 (S) shot, brass bead front and fully adj. semi-buckhorn rear w/diamond insert sights, American walnut stock, brass buttplate, 24K gold inlay stars on forearm and buttstock, brasslite receiver, "Lone Star Flag" motif surrounded by Texas outline, 6 3/4 lbs. New late 2019.

MSR $1,020	$865	$750	$650	$590	$475	$400	$325

* ***Golden Boy Trucker's Tribute Edition*** – .22 S, L, LR cal., 20 in. octagonal blued barrel, 16 or 21 shot, brasslite receiver, fully adj. semi-buckhorn rear with adj. diamond insert and brass bead front sights, American walnut stock, brass buttplate, right side features 18-wheeler and banner in 24K gold that reads "TRUCKERS MOVE AMERICA", left side features convoy of trucks and banner that reads "BOUND FOR GLORY" engraved in 24K gold, 6 3/4 lbs. New 2014.

MSR $1,122	$950	$825	$700	$635	$515	$425	$350

* ***Golden Boy Youth*** – .22 S, L, LR cal., 17 in. blued octagon barrel, 16 shot mag., fully adj. semi-buckhorn rear with adj. white diamond insert and brass bead front sights, American walnut stock, 13 in. LOP, 6 3/4 lbs., brasslite receiver and buttplate, 6-6.75 lbs. New mid-1999.

MSR $605	$510	$450	$385	$350	$275	$225	$200

RIFLES: SEMI-AUTO

U.S. SURVIVAL AR-7 – .22 LR cal., patterned after the Armalite AR-7 with improvements, 16.125 in. steel covered, ABS plastic coated barrel, two 8 shot mags., peep rear and blade front sights, ABS plastic stock, rubber buttpad, 14 in. LOP, switch safety, takedown design enables receiver, 16.5 in. long when stowed, weather resistant silver (disc.), black (new 1999), 100% Mossy Oak Break-Up camo (mfg. 2000-disc.), True Timber Kanati Camo, or True Timber Viper Western Camo finish, 3.5 lbs. New 1997.

MSR $319	$275	$240	$200	$185	$150	$125	$100

Add $66 for Mossy Oak Camo finish (mfg. 2000-disc.).
Add $69 for True Timber Camo finishes.
Add $258 for U.S. Survival AR-7 black kit w/survival gear and bag.

RIFLES: SINGLE SHOT

Henry announced that it is voluntarily recalling all H015-series Single Shot Rifles and Single Shot Shotguns manufactured prior to July 1, 2020. Henry has recently discovered a potential safety issue wherein, under certain conditions, it is possible that some of these models may discharge without the trigger being pulled if the hammer is partially cocked and released. Please contact the manufacturer directly for more information.

HENRY SINGLE SHOT STEEL RIFLE – .223 Rem., .243 Win., .45-70 Govt., .308 Win., .44 Mag./.44 Spl., .30-30 Win. (new 2019), .357 Mag./.38 Spl. (new 2019), .350 Legend (new late 2020), or .450 Bushmaster (new late 2020) cal., 22 in. round blued steel barrel, steel frame, non-ejecting case extractor, rebounding hammer, brass bead front sight, fully adj. folding leaf rear sight, American walnut stock, curved or straight pistol grip wrist, drilled and tapped for optional scope, matte blue finish, 6.96-7.18 lbs. New 2017.

MSR $525	$450	$400	$340	$300	$250	$200	$175

* ***Henry Single Shot Youth Rifle*** – .243 Win. cal., steel frame, 22 in. round blued steel barrel, rebounding hammer, brass bead front sight, fully adj. folding leaf rear sight, American walnut stock, black solid rubber recoil pad, 13 in. LOP, non-ejecting case extractor, drilled and tapped for optional scope, matte blue finish, 6.95 lbs. New 2017.

MSR $525	$450	$400	$340	$300	$250	$200	$175

HENRY SINGLE SHOT BRASS RIFLE – 44 Mag./.44 Spl., .45-70 Govt., or .357 Mag./.38 Spl. (new 2019) cal., 22 in. round blued steel barrel, non-ejecting case extractor, rebounding hammer, fully adj. folding leaf rear and brass bead front sights, straight grip American walnut stock with brass buttplate, drilled and tapped for Weaver 82 mount, polished brass receiver finish, 7-7.14 lbs. New 2017.

MSR $646	$550	$480	$410	$375	$300	$250	$210

RIFLES: SLIDE ACTION

HENRY PUMP ACTION – .22 S, L, LR or .22 WMR (new 2006) cal., 18 1/4 in. round (disc. 2005), 20, or 20 1/2 in. blued octagon (new 2006) barrel, 12 (.22 WMR), 15 (disc.), 16 (.22 S or LR), or 21 (S) shot mag., blue grooved receiver, adj. semi-buckhorn w/diamond insert rear and brass beaded front sights, walnut straight grip stock and forearm, 6 lbs. New 1999.

MSR $605	$515	$450	$385	$350	$285	$230	$200

Add $43 for .22 WMR cal.

GRADING - PPGS™	100%	98%	95%	90%	80%	70%	60%	LAST MSR

SHOTGUNS

GARDEN GUN SMOOTHBORE .22 – .22 LR shotshell, smooth action, 18 1/2 in. round blued steel barrel and hammer, 15 shot, fully adj. rear and blade front sights, black ash stock, 14 in. LOP, black finish, 5.25 lbs. New 2019.

MSR $446	$380	$335	$285	$260	$210	$175	$150	

LEVER ACTION SIDE GATE (HENRY LEVER ACTION) – .410 bore, 19.75 (new 2020), 20 (disc. 2020), or 24 in. round blued barrel w/screw-in invector choke (24 in.) or cylinder bore (19.75 or 20 in.), 5 shot, side loading gate (became standard 2020), brass beaded front and adj. semi buckhorn rear w/diamond insert (19.75 or 20 in.) rear sights, pistol grip American walnut stock with ventilated rubber buttpad, sling swivel studs, approx. 7.5 lbs. New 2017.

MSR $969	$825	$725	$625	$560	$450	$375	$325	

Add $43 for rare models (19.75 or 20 in. barrel).

* ***Lever Action Brass Side Gate*** – .410 bore, 2 1/2 in. chamber, polished brass receiver, 19.8 in. round blued steel barrel, standard removable tube mag., side loading gate, ivory bead ramp front and fully adj. semi-buckhorn w/diamond insert rear sights, Weaver 63B scope mount, American walnut stock, brass buttpad, transfer bar safety, drilled and tapped, regular lever, swivel studs, polished brass receiver finish, New late 2019.

MSR $1,100	$935	$825	$700	$635	$515	$425	$365	

SINGLE SHOT/SINGLE SHOT BRASS SHOTGUN – 12, 20 ga., or .410 bore, 3 or 3 1/2 in. chamber, 26 or 28 in. round barrel, brass beaded front sight, American walnut pistol (std.) or staight (brass) grip stock, black solid rubber recoil pad (std.) or brass buttplate (brass), blued steel (std.) or polished hardened brass (brass) receiver, 6.62-6.83 lbs. New 2017.

MSR $525	$450	$400	$340	$300	$250	$200	$175	

Add $121 for brass model.

Henry announced that it is voluntarily recalling all H015-series Single Shot Rifles and Single Shot Shotguns manufactured prior to July 1, 2020. Henry has recently discovered a potential safety issue wherein, under certain conditions, it is possible that some of these models may discharge without the trigger being pulled if the hammer is partially cocked and released. Please contact the manufacturer directly for more information.

* ***Henry Single Shot Youth*** – 20 ga., 3 in. chamber, 26 in. round barrel, rebounding hammer, brass bead front sight, American walnut stock, black rubber recoil pad, 13 in. LOP, blued steel receiver finish, 6.74 lbs. New 2019.

MSR $525	$450	$395	$340	$300	$250	$200	$175	

Henry announced that it is voluntarily recalling all H015-series Single Shot Rifles and Single Shot Shotguns manufactured prior to July 1, 2020. Henry has recently discovered a potential safety issue wherein, under certain conditions, it is possible that some of these models may discharge without the trigger being pulled if the hammer is partially cocked and released. Please contact the manufacturer directly for more information.

* ***Single Shot Slug Shotgun*** – 12 ga., 3 in. shells, 24 in. round blued barrel and receiver, fiber optic rear and front sights, American walnut stock, black solid rubber recoil pad, 14 in. LOP, rebounding hammer safety, 6.88 lbs. New 2020.

MSR $560	$475	$415	$350	$325	$260	$215	$185	

* ***Single Shot Turkey Camo Shotgun*** – 12 ga., 3 1/2 in. chamber, 24 in. round barrel, fiber optic sights, American walnut stock, black solid rubber recoil pad, swivel studs, rebounding hammer, Weaver 82 scope mount, Mossy Oak Obsession camo finish, 6.78 lbs. New 2021.

MSR $687	$585	$510	$440	$400	$325	$275	$230	

X MODEL SHOTGUN – .410 bore, 19.8 in. round steel barrel, threaded invector style chokes, 6 shot, fiber optic front sight, M-LOK Picatinny rail, black synthetic stock, solid rubber recoil pad, 14 in. LOP, transfer bar safety, blued steel finish, 7.5 lbs. New 2020.

MSR $1,000	$850	$750	$640	$580	$470	$380	$330	

HENRY RIFLE

Please refer to the Winchester listing in the W section for this model.

HERA ARMS

Current firearms manufacturer located in Triefenstein, Germany. Currently imported (parts and accessories only) by Hera USA located in Draper, UT.

Hera Arms manufactures a complete line of AR-15 style semi-auto rifles in .223 Rem. cal., as well as several styles of conversions for SIG, Glock, Walther, CZ, H&K, and S&W pistols. Hera Arms also manufactures a variety of tactical accessories geared towards military, law enforcement, and sport shooters. Please contact the company directly for more information, including options, U.S. availability, and pricing.

GRADING - PPGS™	100%	98%	95%	90%	80%	70%	60%	LAST MSR

HERITAGE MANUFACTURING, INC.

Current manufacturer established 1992, located in Bainbridge, GA. Previously located in Miami Lakes and Opa Locka, FL.

For individual model listings, please go to BlueBookOfGunValues.com/overflow.

HERMANN WEIHRAUCH REVOLVER GmbH

Current revolver manufacturer located in Mellrichstadt, Germany. Some models are currently imported exclusively by E.A.A. Corp., located in Cocoa, FL.

REVOLVERS

The Windicator and Bounty Hunter private label models are currently imported by EAA Corp. Recently manufactured Weihrauch revolvers with no U.S. importation are not individually listed, including the Arminius Series (refer to the Arminius section for previously imported models). There are, however, many models, including combat, sport, and target variations. Calibers include .22 LR, .22 WMR, .32 S&W Wadcutter, .357 Mag., and .38 Spl. Please contact the company directly for pricing and availability on these currently manufactured revolvers.

BIG BORE BOUNTY HUNTER – .357 Mag., .44-40 WCF (mfg. 2005-2008, 7 1/2 in. barrel only), .44 Mag., or .45 LC cal., 4 1/2 (new 1994), 5 1/2 (disc. 1993), or 7 1/2 in. barrel, 6 shot, choice of blue, chrome (mfg. 1994-95), nickel (new 1998), or case colored finish, gold plated trigger guard/gripstraps (disc. 1994), or gold (disc.) finish, 32-41 oz. New 1992.

MSR $519 $440 $385 $330 $300 $240 $200 $175

Add $17 for case colored finish.
Add $72 for nickel finish.
Add $20 for chrome finish (disc.).
Add $15 for gold-plated grip strap and trigger guard (disc.).
Add approx. $100 for gold plated finish (disc.)

* ***Small Bore Bounty Hunter Combo*** – .22 LR/.22 WMR cal. cylinders, 4 3/4 or 6 3/4 in. barrel, half cock mechanism and transfer bar safety, choice of 6, 8, or 10 (disc. 2020) shot, blue or nickel (new 1998) finish. New 1997.

MSR $373 $315 $270 $230 $200 $160 $135 $125

Add $46 for nickel finish.
Add $142 for steel frame with 10 shot cylinder (disc. 2015).

MODEL EASAB – .22 LR cal., single action revolver, 6 shot, 4 3/4 in. barrel, blue or chrome (disc. 1991) finish, wood grips. Importation disc. 1995.

$70 $60 $50 $45 $40 $30 $25 *$85*

Add $20 for chrome finish.

* ***Model EASAMB Combo*** – includes .22 LR and .22 WMR cal. cylinders, 4 3/4 (standard), 6, or 9 in. barrel, blue finish, wood grips. Importation disc. 1995.

$85 $75 $65 $55 $45 $40 $30 *$100*

Add $14 for 9 in. barrel. Add $40 for gold plated gripstrap and trigger guard (disc.).

WINDICATOR STANDARD GRADE – .22 LR (disc.), .22LR/.22 WMR combo. (disc.), .22 WMR (disc.), .32 H&R (disc. 1993), .357 Mag. (new 1994), or .38 Spl. (alloy frame only) cal., 2 (.32 H&R, .357 Mag., or .38 Spl. only), 4 (new 1997), or 6 (disc., reintroduced 2019 in .357 Mag. only) in. squared off barrel, 6 (.38 Spl. or .357 Mag.), 7 (.32 H&R, disc.), or 8 (.22 LR/.22 WMR, disc.) shot, steel (disc. 2020), or alloy frame, finger grooved rubber grips., blue, chrome (.38 Spl. only, new 1994-disc.), or nickel finish. Importation from Germany began 1992.

MSR $351 $300 $265 $225 $200 $165 $135 $120

Add $22 for 4 in. barrel.
Add $25 for .357 Mag. cal.
Add $79 for .357 Mag. cal., 4 in. bbl.
Add $91 for 4 in. or $106 for 6 in. nickel bbl.
Add $88 for nickel finish.
Add $90 for steel frame in .357 Mag. cal (disc. 2020).
Add $78 for .22 LR/.22 WMR combo. (disc.).

WINDICATOR TACTICAL GRADE – .38 Spl. cal. only, fixed sights, 6 shot, 2 in. (bobbed hammer) or 4 in. compensated barrel, blue finish only. Imported 1992-93.

$220 $190 $165 $150 $120 $100 $75 *$295*

Add $80 for 4 in. compensated barrel.

GRADING - PPGS™	100%	98%	95%	90%	80%	70%	60%	LAST MSR

WINDICATOR TARGET GRADE – .22 LR, .357 Mag., or .38 Spl. cal., 6 or 8 (.22 LR) shot, 6 in. squared off barrel, finger grooved hardwood stocks, adj. trigger pull and rear sight, blue finish only, 3.1 lbs. Imported 1992-1993.

	$425	$370	$320	$290	$235	$190	$150	*$550*

HERO GEAR (HERO GUNS) INC.

Previous semi-auto pistol manufacturer located in Winchester, TN from 2010-2017.

PISTOLS: SEMI-AUTO

Hero Gear previously manufactured custom 1911-style semi-auto pistols. Last MSRP started at $2,400.

HEROLD RIFLE

Previously manufactured by Franz Jaeger, located in Suhl, Germany.

RIFLES: BOLT ACTION

SPORTING RIFLE – .22 Hornet cal., miniature Mauser action, 24 in. barrel, leaf sight, double set trigger, select checkered stock, imported by Daly & Stoeger, pre-WWII.

	$990	$880	$825	$770	$660	$550	$495	

HERTERS

Previous importer, distributor, and retailer headquartered in Waseca, MN from early 1960s - 1979. Herters also had additional retail stores scattered throughout the upper Midwest.

Herters subcontracted various manufacturers (mostly European) to fabricate Powermag revolvers, U-9/J-9 rifles, and shotguns, which were mostly patterned after more famous original models. Most of these copies were designed to undersell the competition at the time and while quality in most cases was quite good, consumer sales were not strong enough to continue production. While many Herters models are relatively rare, collectibility to date has been minimal. Herters model values are usually under the original trademarks from which they were derived and to date have been based more on the shooting utility than the collector potential.

HESSE ARMS

Previous manufacturer located in Inver Grove Heights, MN.

Please refer to BlueBookOfGunValues.com to order the *Blue Book of AR-15s & Variations*, available as a book or online subscription.

HEUBERG JAGDWAFFEN

Current custom long gun manufacturer located in Mosbach, Germany. No current U.S. importation.

Thomas Heuberg manufactures custom SxS rifles and shotguns. Since all guns are special order, please contact the company directly for a price quotation and delivery information.

HEYM AG

Current manufacturer established in 1865 and located in Gleichamberg, Germany since 1995. Currently imported beginning 2006 by Double Gun Imports LLC, located in Dallas, TX. Limited importation 1999-2005 by New England Custom Gun Service, Ltd., located in Plainfield, NH. During 1998, Heym underwent a management change. The company name was changed from Heym Waffenfabrik AG to Heym AG during mid-2007. Previously manufactured in Muennerstadt, Germany circa 1952-1995 and Suhl, Germany between 1865-1945. Originally founded in 1865 by F.W. Heym. Previously imported by JagerSport, Ltd. located in Cranston, RI 1993-94 only, Heckler & Koch, Inc. (until 1993) located in Sterling, VA, Heym America, Inc. (subsidiary of F.W. Heym of W. Germany) located in Fort Wayne, IN, and originally by Paul Jaeger, Inc. 1970-1986.

Please contact the importer for more information, current pricing and domestic model availability. Pre-war guns in 95%+ original condition will bring a premium over values listed.

COMBINATION GUNS

MODEL 22 S2 O/U – rifle/shotgun combination, 12, 16, or 20 ga. (3 in.), under rifle (17 cals. available), single set trigger, takedown feature (standard 1990), coin finish with engraving, 5 1/2 lbs.

	$3,675	$3,000	$2,450	$1,875	$1,575	$1,250	$995	*$4,125*

Subtract $380 without engraving.

This model featured a dampened rifle barrel which prevents the "climbing" of groups, thereby enhancing accuracy.

MODEL 25 O/U – rifle/shotgun combination, 12, 16, or 20 ga. over various rifle cals., 23 3/4 in. barrels with iron sights, checkered walnut stock and forearm, 5.9 lbs.

	$2,425	$1,725	$1,350	$1,125	$950	$750	$650	

Add $800 for deluxe game scene engraving.

GRADING - PPGS™	100%	98%	95%	90%	80%	70%	60%	LAST MSR

MODEL 55 BF O/U – rifle/shotgun combination, popular U.S. and European cals., shotgun barrels interchangeable in 12 (disc.), 16, or 20 ga., 25 or 28 in. barrels, boxlock, auto ejectors, silver finish, fine German engraving, folding leaf sight, checkered pistol grip stock.

	$6,500	$5,400	$4,950	$4,525	$3,950	$3,500	$3,100	*$7,485*

Add $3,250 for O/U rifle and $2,250 for O/U shotgun or shotgun/rifle combination extra barrels.

MODEL 88 BF SxS – 2 barrel set with 20 ga. barrels and an extra set of rifle barrels available in cals. .375 H&H Mag., .458 Win. Mag., .470 N.E., or .500 N.E.

	$13,100	$10,750	$9,600	$8,150	$6,900	$5,600	$4,575	*$15,060*

This model is a larger frame variation of the Model 88 B.

* ***Model 88B/F SxS Safari*** – includes set of rifle and shotgun barrels, choice of .375 H&H, .458 Win. Mag., .470 NE, or .500 NE cal. and extra set of 20 ga. 3 in. chamber barrels.

	$16,150	$14,100	$11,950	$10,250	$8,950	$6,450	$4,995	*$18,530*

MODEL 88 F SxS – available in various cals. and 20 ga. with 2 3/4 or 3 in. chambers.

	$13,300	$11,250	$10,100	$9,400	$8,000	$6,100	$4,750	*$14,650*

DRILLINGS

MODEL 33 BOXLOCK STANDARD – 16 or 20 ga., boxlock, Arabesque engraving, shotgun barrels over popular European cals., and .222 Rem., .243 Win., .270 Win., .308 Win., and .30-06 cal. rifle barrel, 25 in. full and mod. barrels, set trigger on rifle, checkered pistol grip stock.

	$6,075	$5,300	$4,525	$3,950	$3,350	$2,750	$2,150	

* ***Model 33 Boxlock Standard Deluxe*** – similar to Standard Model, except has hunting scene engraving.

	$6,450	$5,425	$4,650	$4,025	$3,400	$2,750	$2,150	

MODEL 35 STANDARD – 3 barrels, (two rifle and one shotgun), choice of cals. with top barrel either 16 or 20 ga., light border engraving, 8 1/4 lbs.

	$13,650	$11,000	$9,250	$8,000	$6,850	$5,700	$4,600	*$15,100*

Add $2,430 for hunting scene engraving.

MODEL 37F SIDELOCK STANDARD – 12, 16, or 20 ga. 25 in. SxS barrels over rifle barrel in .22 Hornet, .30 Blaser, 5.6x50R, 5.6x52R, 5.6x57R, 6x70R, 6.5x57R, 6.5x65RWS, 7x57R, 7x65R, 8x57JRS, 8x75RS, or 9.3x74, (other chamberings available by request), sidelock action with Greener crossbolt, cocking indicators, non-automatic safety, set front trigger, hand engraved, case colored or coin finished, other barrel lengths available by request, select French walnut stock, approx. 8 lbs.

MSR N/A	$21,750	$18,250	$15,000	$12,500	$10,500	$8,500	$6,950	

* ***Model 37B Sidelock Standard Deluxe*** – 12, 20, 16, 28 ga. or .410 bore over same rifle cals. as the Model 37, available in right or left hand, more engraving.

MSR N/A	$24,000	$20,500	$16,500	$13,250	$11,000	$9,000	$7,500	

MODEL 37 B STANDARD – rifle barrels over shotgun (20 ga.), sidelock, border engraved, about 8.6 lbs.

	$13,250	$10,875	$9,500	$8,400	$7,550	$6,500	$5,650	*$15,065*

* ***Model 37 B Standard Deluxe*** – similar to Model 37 B Standard, except has large hunting scene engraving.

	$15,600	$12,750	$10,700	$9,450	$8,200	$7,050	$5,750	*$17,620*

RIFLES: BOLT ACTION

On most of the models listed, the "N" suffix in the model denotes standard calibers, whereas "G" refers to Mag. cals.

MODEL SR 10 SPORTER – various cals., originally mfg. by H & K. Limited mfg.

	$1,325	$1,100	$950	$850	$750	$650	$550	

MODEL SR 20N & CLASSIC – available in 18 cals., Mauser type bolt action, single trigger, French walnut, 24 in. Krupp steel barrel except Mag. (25 in.). Importation disc. 2001.

	$1,825	$1,425	$1,100	$900	$800	$700	$600	*$2,100*

Subtract $70 without iron sights.
Add $430 for left-hand variation.
Add $300 for Mag. cals. (G suffix).
Add $1,140 for .375 H&H cal. (Model SR20 G Etoscha).
Add $260 for Classic Model.
Add $300 for Carbine Classic Model.

* ***Model SR 20 Hunter*** – similar to Model SR 20N, except has classic style fiberglass stock with either matte blue or parkerized metal finish. Imported 1988-90.

	$1,500	$1,225	$1,050	$900	$800	$700	$600	*$1,750*

GRADING - PPGS™	100%	98%	95%	90%	80%	70%	60%	LAST MSR

* ***Model SR 20L*** – Mannlicher style stock, European configuration, 18 in. barrel, 7 lbs.

	$1,475	$1,225	$985	$895	$785	$720	$650	*$1,700*

SR 20 TROPHY – available in all SR 20 cals., bolt action, 22 or 24 (Mag. cals. only) in. octagonal barrel, classic stock configuration with cheekpiece and recoil pad. Importation began 1989.

	$2,550	$2,100	$1,800	$1,500	$1,250	$985	$895	*$2,815*

Add $120 for Mag. cals.

This model was also available in either right-hand or left-hand action.

SR 20G CLASSIC SPORTER – available in various cals., bolt action, 22 or 24 in. round barrel, steel grip cap. Importation began 1989.

	$1,875	$1,600	$1,300	$1,050	$900	$785	$720	*$2,235*

Subtract $70 without iron sights.

This model was also available in either right-hand or left-hand action.

SR 20 ALPINE – available in standard cals. between .243 Win. and 9.3x62mm, mountain style rifle with Mannlicher forend and classic buttstock, supplied with mounted open sights. Importation began 1989.

	$1,900	$1,650	$1,325	$1,075	$925	$800	$750	*$2,165*

This model was also available in either right-hand or left-hand action.

SR 20 MATCH – .308 Win. cal., 24 in. heavy barrel, target stock with accessory rail, large bolt handle, supplied without sights, 9 lbs. Imported 1991-94.

	$1,860	$1,600	$1,300	$1,050	$900	$785	$720	*$2,200*

SR 20 CLASSIC SAFARI – .375 H&H, .404 Jeffery (disc.), .425 Express, or .458 Win. Mag. cal., 24 in. barrel only, express rear sight and large front post sights, tight grained walnut stock. Imported 1989-94.

	$2,150	$1,650	$1,250	$1,050	$875	$800	$700	*$2,530*

This model was also available in either right-hand or left-hand action.

SR 21 CLASSIC (N) – 24 standard and metric cals., 22 or 24 in. barrel, traditional bolt action that is bascially a Mauser M90 design with modern extractor recessed in the bolt face, set or standard trigger, unique interchangeable barrel/receiver, detachable mag., 3-position side safety, right or left-hand action, with or w/o open sights, approx. 7 lbs. New 2001.

Add $325 for carbine (disc.)
Add $1,325 for Model SR 21 N Concorde (disc.)
Add $110 for Model SR 21 N Keiler (disc.)
This model is POR.

SR 30 CLASSIC (N) – various cals., 22 or 24 in. barrel, straight pull bolt which locks in the receiver head, with or w/o open sights, deluxe checkered walnut stock with rosewood pistol grip cap and forend tip, sling swivels, set or standard trigger, detachable mag., 7-7 1/2 lbs. Current Mfg.

Add $264 for carbine (disc.).
Add $1,505 for SR 30 N Concorde Model (disc.).
Add $155 for SR 30 N Wild Boar Model (disc.).
This model is POR.

EXPRESS SERIES RIFLE – .338 Lapua Mag. (disc.), .375 H&H, .378 Wby. Mag. (disc.), .404 Jeffery (disc. 1992, reintroduced), .416 Rigby, .450 Ackley (disc.), .450 Rigby, .458 Win. Mag., .458 Lott, .460 Wby. Mag., .500 NE (new 1994), .500 A-Square (disc.), or .505 Gibbs (disc.) cal., double square bridge Mauser action, express sights, Timney single trigger, available in right or left hand. New 1989.

MSR N/A	$9,995	$8,750	$7,500	$6,250	$5,000	$4,000	$3,250	

Add $525 for .460 Wby. Mag. - .505 Gibbs cal.
Add $375 for muzzle brake (included installation, disc.).
Add $555 for left-hand action (disc. 1992).

* ***Express Series Rifle .577 NE & .600 NE Cals.*** – .577 NE (disc.) or .600 NE cal., 24 in. barrel, reinforced action, 2 shot mag. New 1991.

MSR N/A	$18,950	$16,500	$14,500	$12,500	$10,500	$8,500	$6,500	

RIFLES: O/U

MODEL 26 B – .223 Rem., 7x65R, .30R Blaser, .30-30 Win., .30-06, 8x57RJS, or 9.3x74R cal., double lock system, manual cocking, ST, buttstock with slightly curved stock comb and Bavarian cheekpiece, game scene engraving with stag and boar, extractors, other calibers available by request. New 2006.

MSR N/A	$4,875	$4,400	$3,900	$3,450	$3,000	$2,650	$2,300	

Add $550 for Luxus model (disc.).

GRADING - PPGS™	100%	98%	95%	90%	80%	70%	60%	LAST MSR

This model was also available in Luxus variation, with higher grain wood, wild boar sights, and hunting scene engraving.

MODEL 55 BOXLOCK – various cals. up to .500 NE, boxlock action, Greener crossbolt, double Purdey underbite, right or left hand, case colored or coin finish, 26 in. barrels standard, other lengths available by request, ejectors, steel grip cap, express sights, intercepting sears, cocking indicators, non-automatic safety, articulated front trigger, hand engraved. Current Mfg.

MSR $22,000	$19,995	$17,500	$15,500	$13,500	$11,500	$9,500	$7,500

Add $1,500 for NE calibers.

* ***Model 55BF*** – similar to Model 55 Boxlock, except has shotgun barrel on bottom in 12, 16, 20, 28 ga. or .410 bore. Current Mfg.

MSR N/A	$16,000	$14,000	$12,000	$10,000	$8,000	$6,750	$5,500

MODEL 55 SIDELOCK – O/U rifle only with different caliber for each barrel, double set triggers, "Bergstutzen" design. Disc.

	$9,350	$8,000	$6,850	$5,950	$5,125	$4,500	$3,975

Add $1,000 for Deluxe Model.

* ***Model 55 SS Sidelock*** – various cals. up to .500 NE, pinless sidelock action, Greener crossbolt, double Purdey underbite, right or left hand, case colored or coin finish, 26 in. barrels standard, other lengths available by request, ejectors, steel grip cap, express sights, intercepting sears, cocking indicators, non-automatic safety, articulated front trigger, hand engraved.

MSR N/A	$25,000	$22,250	$19,250	$17,000	$15,000	$12,750	$9,250

RIFLES: SxS

MODEL 80 B – various cals., modified boxlock action with top sear bars, small frame, regular or manual cocking, 23 3/4 in. barrels with quarter rib and iron sights, DT or ST, deluxe checkered walnut stock and forearm, extractors, available with splinter or semi-beavertail forend with interchangeable rifle or shotgun barrels, hand made, limited production, 6.6 lbs. Current Mfg.

MSR N/A	$10,750	$9,500	$8,250	$7,000	$5,750	$4,750	$3,950

Add $600 for ST with hand cocking (disc.), $700 for DT with hand cocking (disc.).

MODEL 88 B – available in most safari cals. between .300 Win. Mag. - .458 Win. Mag. boxlock action, 25 in. Krupp steel barrels, double underlocking lugs with Greener crossbolt, ejectors, checkered Circassian walnut stock and forearm, built to customer specifications, hand engraved with case colored or coin finish, splinter or semi-beavertail forend, interchangeable rifle or shotgun barrels available by request, steel grip cap., express sights, 7 1/2 lbs.

MSR N/A	$15,250	$13,500	$11,500	$9,500	$7,750	$6,500	$5,500

Add $550 for .416 Rigby - .500 NE cal. (disc.)

* ***Model 88 B SS*** – similar cals. as Model 88B, pinless sidelock model with interceptor sears. Current Mfg.

MSR N/A	$19,995	$17,500	$15,500	$13,500	$11,500	$9,500	$7,500

This model was also available in both .577 NE and .600 NE cal. Prices started at $28,575 for the .577 NE, and $32,500 for .600 NE.

* ***Model 88 B PH Boxlock*** – available in various safari cals., boxlock action, 26 in. barrels, Greener crossbolt, right or left hand, ejectors, cocking indicators, intercepting sears, non-automatic safety, articulated front trigger, no engraving, case colored or coin finish, steel grip cap, short trigger guard, express sights, splinter or semi-beavertail forend with interchangeable rifle or shotgun barrels to order, other barrel lengths available by request. New 2007.

MSR N/A	$15,250	$13,500	$11,500	$9,500	$7,750	$6,500	$5,500

* ***Model 88 B Safari*** – similar to PH Model, except has more detailed hand shaping on action and action bolsters, long trigger guard extending to steel grip cap, higher grade of wood and hand engraved to order. Current Mfg.

MSR N/A	$19,995	$17,500	$15,500	$13,500	$11,500	$9,500	$7,500

* ***Model 88 B Safari Sidelock*** – similar to Safari Model, except has pinless sidelock action. Current Mfg.

MSR N/A	$25,000	$22,250	$19,250	$17,000	$15,000	$12,750	$9,250

* ***Model 88 B Jumbo*** – .470 NE, .500 NE, .577 NE, or .600 NE cal., large frame, 26 in. barrels, best grade pinless sidelock action with hidden Purdey fastener, ejectors, cocking indicators, non-automatic safety, case colored or coin finished with hand engraving, express sights, intercepting sears, articulated front trigger, steel grip, other barrel lengths available by request, splinter or semi-beavertail forend with interchangeable rifle or shotgun barrels available by request. Current Mfg.

MSR N/A	$45,000	$38,500	$33,000	$27,000	$23,000	$19,000	$16,500

GRADING - PPGS™	100%	98%	95%	90%	80%	70%	60%	LAST MSR

MODEL 89 B – .300 Win Mag., .375 H&H Belted Mag., .375 H&H Flanged Mag., .416 Rigby, .416/500 NE, .450/400 NE, .450 NE, .470 NE, .500 NE, or .577 NE cal., 20 ga., A&D boxlock w/triple lockup (Purdey double underbite w/Greener crossbolt), 26 in. Krupp steel barrels, automatic ejectors, extractors available by request, articulated front trigger, European walnut stock (right or left hand), non-automatic safety, additional stock upgrades available, 9-13 lbs. New late 2016.

Please contact the factory directly for a price quotation and availability on this model.

IVORY HUNTER – large dangerous game cals. only, sidelock model, Purdey locking system, custom engraving, steel pistol grip cap, steel trigger guard, Classic stock with German cheekpiece, rubber recoil pad, custom order only, 12.8 lbs. Disc.

This model was POR.

RIFLES: SINGLE SHOT

MODEL HR 30N – available in many cals., Ruger No. 1 falling block action, 24 in. round barrel, Sporter or full-length carbine style French walnut stock with Bavarian cheekpiece, engraved coin finished receiver, 6.6 lbs. Disc.

	100%	98%	95%	90%	80%	70%	60%	LAST MSR
	$3,500	$2,975	$2,350	$1,950	$1,675	$1,350	$1,175	*$4,040*

Add $440 for Mag. cals.
Add $1,710 for Mannlicher stocked Carbine Model.
Add $850 for hunting scene engraving (minimum extra charge).

MODEL HR 38 N – available in many cals., Ruger No. 1 falling block action, 24 in. octagon barrel, Sporter, or full-length carbine style French walnut stock with Bavarian cheekpiece, engraved coin finished receiver, 6.6 lbs. Disc.

	100%	98%	95%	90%	80%	70%	60%	LAST MSR
	$4,150	$3,450	$2,875	$2,300	$1,950	$1,675	$1,350	*$4,835*

Add $235 for Mag. cals.
Add $2,400 for sideplates with engraved large game hunting scenes.

MODEL 44 B – various standard and metric cals., single lock action with thumbpiece and sideplates, open sights with barrel quarter rib, deluxe checkered stock and forearm, 6.6 lbs. Disc.

	100%	98%	95%	90%	80%	70%	60%	LAST MSR
	$4,900	$4,350	$3,550	$3,025	$2,350	$2,000	$1,750	

Add $1,100 for Deluxe Model.

SHOTGUNS: O/U

MODEL 55 F – 12, 16, or 20 ga., boxlock action, Greener crossbolt, various barrel lengths up to 28 in., non-automatic safety, case colored or coin finished receiver, cocking indicators, extractors or ejectors, right or left hand, hand made, limited production. Importation disc. 1992, reintroduced 2009.

	100%	98%	95%	90%	80%	70%	60%	LAST MSR
MSR N/A	$10,750	$9,500	$8,250	$7,000	$5,750	$4,750	$3,950	

MODEL 55 SS – sidelock version of Model 55 F, large engraved hunting scenes. Current Mfg.

	100%	98%	95%	90%	80%	70%	60%	LAST MSR
MSR N/A	$16,000	$14,000	$12,000	$10,000	$8,000	$6,750	$5,500	

MODEL 200 – 20 ga., 3 in. chambers, boxlock action, DTs, 28 in. VR barrels, light engraving, previous importation. Disc.

	100%	98%	95%	90%	80%	70%	60%	LAST MSR
	$895	$795	$700	$650	$600	$550	$500	

VIERLINGS

MODEL 37 V – 4 barrel configuration, various cals. and gauges, special order only. Limited mfg.

	100%	98%	95%	90%	80%	70%	60%	LAST MSR
MSR N/A	$37,500	$32,000	$28,000	$24,000	$21,000	$18,000	$15,000	

HIENDLMAYER, KLAUS

Please refer to Waffen Hiendlmayer listing in the W section.

HI-POINT FIREARMS

Current trademark marketed by MKS Supply, Inc. located in Dayton, Ohio. Currently manufactured by Beemiller Inc. located in Mansfield, OH since 1988 and Strassells Machine. Dealer and distributor sales.

Prior to 1993, trademarks sold by MKS Supply, Inc. (including Beemiller, Haskell Manufacturing, Inc., Iberia Firearms, Inc., and Stallard Arms, Inc.) had their own separate manufacturers' markings. Beginning in 1993, Hi-Point Firearms eliminated these individualized markings and chose instead to have currently manufactured guns labeled "Hi-Point Firearms". All injection molding for Hi-Point Firearms is done in Mansfield, OH.

CARBINES: SEMI-AUTO

Beginning January 2016, all Hi-Point .45 ACP and .40 S&W caliber carbines are being manufactured by Strassells Machine, located in Mansfield, OH.

GRADING - PPGS™	100%	98%	95%	90%	80%	70%	60%	LAST MSR

MODEL 995TS – 9mm Para. cal., 16 1/2 in. barrel, 10 shot mag., aperture rear (disc.) or fully adj. sights, internal recoil buffer in stock, Weaver style rails, LRBHO, one-piece camo (disc.) or black polymer skeletonized stock features pistol grip (target stock became standard 2013), parkerized or chrome (disc. 2007), FDE (new 2017), or OD Green (new 2017) finish, 31 in. OAL, 6 1/4 lbs. New 1996.

MSR $315	$285	$250	$225	$200	$150	$125	$100

Add $27 for forward grip (995TS FG) or $60 for forward grip and flashlight (995TS FGFL).
Add $49 for 4x32 scope (995TS 4X) or $41 for red dot scope (995TS RD).
Add $53 for Pro Pack Kit with target stock (new 2011, 995TS PRO).
Add $53 for forward grip and 2 Redball mags. (new 2017, 995TS FG 2xRB).
Add $110 for laser sight (995TS LAZ).
Add $166 for forward grip, flashlight, and laser sight (new 2011, 995TS FGFL-LAZ).
Add $143 for 4x RGB scope (disc. 2015, 995TS 4xRGB).
Add $10 for chrome finish (disc. 2007).
Add $15 for camo stock (mfg. 2002-disc.).
Add $34 for OD Green (mfg. 2017-2019, OD 995TS) or FDE (mfg. 2017-2019, FDE 995) finish.
Add $85 for detachable compensator, laser, and mount (mfg. 1999-2010).

This model is manufactured by Beemiller, located in Mansfield, OH.

* ***Model 995TS Camo*** – 9mm Para. cal., 16 1/2 in. barrel, 10 shot mag., Weaver style rails, internal recoil buffer in stock, LRBHO, fully adj. sights, sling, swivels, and scope base, all-weather polymer skeletonized stock, Hydro dipped Desert Digital Camo (995TS Camo DD), Pink Camo (995TS Camo PI), or Woodland Style Camo (995TS Camo WC) finish, 6 1/4 lbs. New 2015.

MSR $373	$325	$280	$250	$225	$180	$150	$125

MODEL 1095TS – 10mm Auto cal., 17 1/2 in. threaded barrel, 10 shot mag., fully adj. post front and rear peep sight, all-weather black polymer skeletonized stock, rubber cheekpiece, pistol grip, quick on/off thumb safety, flat receiver cover, sling swivels and scope base, internal recoil buffer in stock, Weaver style rails, trigger lock, black or FDE (new 2019) finish. 7 lbs. New 2018.

MSR $390	$350	$300	$260	$240	$200	$160	$125

Add $55 for FDE finish (new 2019).

* ***Model 1095TS Edge (Camo)*** – 10mm Auto cal., 17 1/2 in. threaded barrel, 10 shot mag., fully adj. post front and rear peep iron sights, all-weather black polymer skeletonized stock, rubber cheekpiece, pistol grip, quick on/off thumb safety, flat receiver cover, sling swivels and scope base, internal recoil buffer in stock, weaver style rails, trigger lock, Realtree Edge hyrdro-dipped finish, 7 lbs. New 2018.

MSR $439	$400	$350	$300	$275	$225	$180	$140

* ***Model 1095TS White Camo*** – 10mm Auto cal., 17 1/2 in. threaded barrel, 10 shot mag., fully adj. post front and rear peep sight, all-weather polymer skeletonized stock, rubber cheekpiece, pistol grip, quick on/off thumb safety, flat receiver cover, sling swivels and scope base, internal recoil buffer in stock, Weaver style rails, trigger lock, Kryptek Yeti or Mothwing Winter Mimicry camo finish. 7 lbs. New 2020.

MSR $449	$400	$350	$300	$275	$225	$180	$140

MODEL 4095TS – .40 S&W cal., 17 1/2 in. barrel, 10 shot mag., Weaver style rails, aperture rear (disc.) or fully adj. sights (Ghost ring rear peep and post front), one-piece camo (disc.) or black polymer skeletonized stock features pistol grip (target stock became standard 2013), parkerized or chrome (disc. 2007) finish, sling, swivels, and scope base, 7 lbs. Mfg. 2003-2008, reintroduced 2011.

MSR $325	$285	$250	$220	$200	$150	$130	$100

Add $27 for forward grip (4095TS FG) or $60 for forward grip and flashlight (4095TS FGFL).
Add $49 for 4x32 scope (4095TS 4X) or $41 for red dot scope (4095TS RD).
Add $54 for Pro Pack Kit with target stock (new 2011, 4095TS PRO).
Add $110 for laser (4095TS-LAZ).
Add $170 for forward grip, flashlight, and laser (new 2011, 4095TS FGFL-LAZ).
Add $137 for 4x RGB scope (4095TS 4xRGB, mfg. 2013-2015).
Add $85 for detachable compensator, laser, and mount (mfg. 1999-2010).

* ***Model 4095TS Camo*** – .40 S&W cal., 16 1/2 in. barrel, 10 shot mag., Weaver style rails, sling, swivels, and scope base, fully adj. sights, all-weather polymer skeletonized stock, Hydro dipped Desert Digital Camo (4095TS DD), Pink Camo (4095TS PI), or Woodland Style Camo (4095TS WC) finish, 6 1/4 lbs. New 2015.

MSR $385	$350	$300	$275	$240	$200	$160	$125

GRADING - PPGS™	100%	98%	95%	90%	80%	70%	60%	LAST MSR

MODEL 4595TS – .45 ACP cal., 17 1/2 in. barrel, 9 shot mag., adj. peep sight, black polymer stock (target stock became standard 2013), Weaver style rails, sling, swivels, and scope base, black, OD Green (new 2017), or FDE (new 2017) finish, 7 lbs. New 2011.

MSR $349	$320	$280	$240	$225	$175	$150	$120	

Add $20 for OD Green (new 2017, OD 4595TS) or FDE (new 2017, 4595TS) finish.
Add $20 for forward grip (4595TS FG) or $50 for forward grip and flashlight (4595TS FGFL).
Add $48 for 4x32 scope (4595TS 4x32) or $39 for red dot scope (4595TS RD).
Add $105 for laser sight (4595TS-LAZ).
Add $50 for Pro Pack Kit with target stock (new 2011, 4595TS PRO).
Add $89 for forward grip and two Redball mags. (4595TS FG 2xRB).
Add $170 for forward grip, flashlight, and laser sight (new 2011, 4595TS FGFL-LAZ).
Add $142 for 4x RGB scope (mfg. 2013-2015).

* ***Model 4595TS Camo*** – .45 ACP cal., 16 1/2 in. barrel, 9 shot mag, fully adj. sights, all-weather polymer skeletonized stock, Weaver style rails, sling, swivels, and scope base, Hydro dipped Desert Digital Camo (4595TS DD), Pink Camo (4595TS PI), or Woodland Style Camo (4595TS WC) finish, 6 1/4 lbs. New 2015.

MSR $406	$360	$325	$275	$250	$200	$160	$125	

* ***Model 4595TS Winter Camo*** – .45 ACP cal., 17 1/2 in. barrel, 9 shot mag., adj. peep sight, polymer stock (target stock became standard 2013), Weaver style rails, sling, swivels, and scope base, finish, 7 lbs. Kryptek Yeti or Mothwing Winter Mimicry camo finish. New 2020.

MSR $415	$350	$300	$275	$250	$200	$175	$125	

MODEL 3895TS – .380 ACP cal., 16 1/2 in. barrel, 10 shot mag., fully adj. Ghost Ring rear peep and post front sights, all-weather black molded polymer stock, grip-mounted mag. release, forward folding grip (optional), quick on/off thumb safety, sling swivels and scope base, Weaver style rails, 6 1/4 lbs. New 2016.

MSR $315	$280	$250	$220	$200	$150	$125	$100	

Add $27 for forward grip (3895TS FG).
Add $53 for Pro Pack 9 Kit (3895TS PRO).

* ***Model 3895TS Camo*** – .380 ACP cal., 16 1/2 in. barrel, 10 shot mag., fully adj. Ghost Ring rear peep and post front sights, all-weather polymer skeletonized stock, internal recoil buffer in stock, grip-mounted clip release, quick on/off thumb safety, sling swivels and scope base, Weaver style rails, forward folding grip (optional), pink camo finish, 6 1/4 lbs. New 2016.

MSR $373	$340	$300	$250	$225	$180	$150	$125	

HUNTER SERIES – 9mm Para., .45 ACP, or .40 S&W cal., 16 1/2 (9mm Para. only) or 17 1/2 in. barrel, 9 (.45 ACP only) or 10 shot mag., free trigger lock, fully adj. sights, all-weather, hydro-dipped molded polymer skeletonized stock, grip-mounted mag. release, quick on/off thumb safety, Weaver style rails, Konus scope, sling swivels and scope base, Desert Digital or Woodland camo finish, 31-32 in. OAL, 6 1/4 - 7 lbs. New 2019.

MSR $459	$425	$375	$320	$280	$225	$200	$150	

Add $12 for .40 S&W cal.
Add $27 for .45 ACP cal.

PISTOLS: SEMI-AUTO

Beginning 2000, all compact models feature magazine disconnect safety and last shot hold open (or LRBHO), and all pistols are shipped with a rear adj. aperture sight (which can replace the standard rear adj. sight).

Beginning January 2016, all Hi-Point .380 ACP and 9mm pistols are being manufactured by Strassells Machine, located in Mansfield, OH.

CF-380 – .380 ACP cal., single action, high impact polymer frame and grips, 3 1/2 or 4 (mfg. 2002-2007) in. barrel, 8 shot mag. with thumb activated release, 3-dot adj. sights, chrome slide (disc.), two-tone black satin (disc.), black powder coat with chrome rail or Hydro dipped Pink Camo (mfg. 2015-2016) finish, 29 oz. New 1995.

MSR $179	$160	$140	$120	$110	$90	$70	$60	

Add $10 for hard case (CF-380 HC).
Add $16 for Hydro Dipped Pink Camo finish (CF-380 PI, new 2015).
Add $90 for Laserlyte trigger guard mount laser (CF380LLTGM, new 2017).

* ***CF-380 Comp*** – .380 ACP cal., polymer frame, 4 in. barrel, includes two mags. (8 and 10 shot), plastic grip, integral compensator, black/silver finish. New 2002-2007, reintroduced.

MSR $204	$180	$160	$140	$120	$100	$80	$65	

GRADING - PPGS™	100%	98%	95%	90%	80%	70%	60%	LAST MSR

C9 (JS-9 COMPACT) – 9mm Para. cal., 3 1/2 in. barrel, 8 shot mag., choice of alloy (disc.) or high impact polymer (new 1994, various slide/frame finishes) frame, high impact polymer grips, LRBHO, mag. disconnect safety, 3-dot adj. sights became standard in 2000, black powder coat finish, 29 oz. New 1993.

MSR $199	$180	$160	$140	$120	$100	$80	$65	

Add $10 for hard case (916HC).
Add $11 for nylon holster (916NYL).
Add $36 for Galco leather holster (916G).
Add $36 for hard case and Kershaw knife (916HCKN).
Add $90 for Laserlyte trigger guard mount laser (916LLTGM, new 2017).

* ***C9 Camo*** – 9mm Para. cal., 3 1/2 in. barrel, high impact polymer frame and grips, 8 shot mag., fully adj. 3-dot sights, Hydro dipped Desert Digital camo (916 DD), Pink Camo (916 PI), or Woodland Style camo (916 WC) finish, 29 oz. New 2015.

MSR $213	$190	$165	$150	$130	$100	$85	$65	

JS-9 – 9mm Para. cal., single action, 4 1/2 in. barrel, thumb safety, fixed (disc. 1999) or adj. (new 2000) sights, 8 shot mag., non-glare military blue finish (early mfg.) or black satin finish (new 1991), copolymer synthetic grips, 39 oz. Mfg. 1990-2000.

	$135	$115	$100	$90	$80	$70	$60	*$159*

Add 10% for nickel finish (disc.).

This model was manufactured by Beemiller, Inc. located in Mansfield, OH.

* ***JS-9 Comp*** – 9mm Para. cal., 4 in. barrel with compensator, 10 shot mag., with (new 1999) or w/o laser sight package, adj. sights. Mfg. 1998-2006.

	$135	$115	$100	$90	$80	$70	$60	*$159*

Add $61 for laser sights and mount.

JCP-40 – .40 S&W cal., single action, 4 1/2 in. barrel, 10 shot mag., high impact polymer frame and grips, 3-dot adj. sights, accessory rail (new 2004), mag. disconnect safety, black powder coat finish or OD Green slide with camo grips (mfg. 2009-2014), 35 oz. New 2002.

MSR $219	$200	$175	$150	$140	$110	$90	$70	

Add $10 for hard case (34013).
Add $16 for Galco Matrix M5X (34010M5X).
Add $66 for Laserlyte trigger guard mount laser (34010LLTGM).

This model is manufactured by Iberia Firearms, Inc. located in Iberia, OH.

* ***JCP-40 Camo*** – .40 S&W cal., single action, 4 1/2 in. barrel, 10 shot mag., high impact polymer frame and grips, 3-dot adj. sights, accessory rail, mag. disconnect safety, Hydro dipped Desert Digital (34010 DD), Pink Camo (34010 PI), or Woodland Style Camo (34010 WC) finish, 35 oz. New 2015.

MSR $235	$210	$185	$160	$150	$115	$95	$75	

JS-40 – .40 S&W cal., single action, steel frame, black or nickel (disc. 1994) finish, 4 1/2 in. barrel, 3-dot adj. sights, 8 shot mag., 39 oz. Mfg. 1992-2002.

	$135	$115	$100	$90	$80	$70	$60	*$159*

Add $7 for nickel finish (disc. 1994).

This model was manufactured by Iberia Firearms, Inc. located in Iberia, OH.

JHP-45 – .45 ACP cal., single action, 4 1/2 in. barrel, 9 shot mag., high impact polymer frame and grips, accessory rail (new 2004), fully adj. 3-dot sights, LRBHO, mag. disconnect safety, black powder coat finish with polished sides or OD Green slide with camo grips (mfg. 2009-2014), 35 oz. New 2003.

MSR $219	$200	$175	$150	$140	$110	$90	$70	

Add $10 for hard case (34513).
Add $16 for Galco Matrix M5X holster (34510M5X).
Add $66 for Laserlyte trigger guard mount laser (34510LLTGM).

This model is manufactured by Haskell Mfg., Inc. located in Lima, OH.

* ***JHP-45 Camo*** – .45 ACP cal., 4 1/2 in. barrel, 9 shot mag., high impact polymer frame and grips, accessory rail, fully adj. 3-dot sights, LRBHO, mag. disconnect safety, Hydro dipped Desert Digital Camo (3510 DD), Pink Camo (34510 PI), or Woodland Style Camo (34510 WC) finish, 35 oz. New 2015.

MSR $235	$210	$185	$160	$150	$115	$95	$75	

JS-45 – .45 ACP cal., single action, steel frame, similar to JS-9, except has 7 shot mag. and 4 1/2 in. barrel, adj. sights, 39 oz. Mfg. 1991-2002.

	$135	$115	$100	$90	$80	$70	$60	*$159*

Add $10 for nickel finish (disc. 1994).

This model was manufactured by Haskell Mfg., Inc. located in Lima, OH.

HIGGINS, J.C.

Please refer to the J.C. Higgins listing in the J section.

HIGH STANDARD

Previous manufacturer located in New Haven, Hamden, and East Hartford, CT. High Standard Mfg. Co. was founded in 1926. They entered the firearms business when they purchased Hartford Arms and Equipment Co. in 1932. The original plant was located in New Haven, CT. During WWII High Standard operated plants in New Haven and Hamden. After the war, the operations were consolidated in Hamden. In the late 1940s and early 1950s the pistol plant was located in East Haven but the guns continued to be marked New Haven. In 1968, the company was sold to the Leisure Group, Inc. A final move was made to East Hartford, CT in 1977 where they remained until the doors were closed in late 1984. In early 1978, the Leisure Group sold the company to the management and the company became High Standard, Inc.

Many collectors have realized the rarity and quality factors this trademark has earned. 13 different variations (Models C, A, D, E, H-D, H-E, H-A, H-B First Model, G-380, GD, GE, and Olympic, commonly called the GO) had a total production of less than 28,000 pistols. For these reasons, top condition High Standard pistols are getting more difficult to find each year.

As a final note on High Standard pistols, they are listed under the following category names: Letter Series, Letter Series w/Hammer, Lever Letter Series, Lever Name Series, 100 Series, 101 Series, 102 Series, 103 Series, 104 Series, 105 Series, 106 Series - Military Models, 107 Series, Conversion Kits, and SH Series.

Note: catalog numbers were not always consistent with design series, and in 1966-1967 changed with accessories offered, but not design series.

The approx. ser. number cut-off for New Haven, CT marked guns is 442,XXX.

The approx. ser. number range for Hamden, CT marked guns is 431,XXX-2,500,811, G 1,001-G 13,757 (Shipped) or G15,650 (Packed) or ML 1,001-ML 23,065. One exception is a 9211 Victor serial number 3,000,000 shipped 1 March, 1974.

The first gun shipped 16 June, 1977 from E. Hartford was a Victor 9217 serial number EH0001.

The approx. ser. number ranges for E. Hartford, CT manufacture is ML 25,000-ML 86,641 and SH 10,001-SH 34,034. One exception is a single gun numbered ML90,000.

All "V" marked guns were shipped during June 1984 or later independent of serial number.

Original factory boxes have become very desirable. Prices can range from $50-$100 for a good condition Model 106 or 107 factory box to over $150 for an older box of a desirable model.

DERRINGERS

DERRINGER MODELS – .22 or .22 WMR cal., double action only O/U, 2 shot, 3 1/2 in. barrels.

The first derringer was mfg. about 1962, at the approximate serial number 1,261,903 in Hamden, CT. The serial numbers continued in the handgun serial number series until serial number 2,500,464 in 1975, when the derringers were put into a separate serial number group with a D prefix, D 1,001 through D 96,098 V. Serial number D 12,047 was the last Hamden made gun, with E. Hartford production beginning with D 13,000. After 1976, the guns were made in East Hartford.

Three different styles of roll marking methods were used during production.

The First style is marked with the caliber and "D-100" or "DM-101" on left side of frame, "Hi-Standard Derringer" with eagle logo on left side of barrel.

The Second style is marked with the caliber and "D-100", "D-101", or "DM-101" on left side of frame, "Hi-Standard Derringer" with trigger logo on left side of barrel. Both the first and second types were marked "HIGH STANDARD MFG. CORP./-HAMDEN, CONN. U.S.A.-"

The Third style is marked with the caliber and "D-101" or "DM-101" on left side of frame, "Derringer" on left side of barrel. The third style was marked with different addresses and company names on the right side of the barrel. Style 3A is marked on the right side of the barrel the same as types one and two. Type 3B is marked with "HIGH STANDARD MFG. CORP./-E. HARTFORD, CONN. US.A.-" and type 3C is marked "HIGH STANDARD INC./-E. HARTFORD, CONN. U.S.A.-" Later third style is not marked with the "D-101" or "DM-101". The early derringers had a grooved back grip strap, which changed to a smooth grip strap just before the move to E. Hartford.

Near the end of production, a "V" suffix was added to some visually impaired guns, which were sold at

GRADING - PPGS™	100%	98%	95%	90%	80%	70%	60%	LAST MSR

discount. These guns were guaranteed to function properly, but the company would not allow them to be returned for appearance reasons. Numerous guns' earlier serial numbers, held back because of visual flaws, were also marked with the "V" and were shipped in 1984. The earliest V suffix gun found to date is D 25,945V.

* ***Derringer Model Blue Finish*** – .22 LR or .22 WMR cal ., blue, white or black grips.

$325	$280	$240	$215	$195	$180	$170

Add $25 for hinged maroon case.
Add 15% for .22 WMR cal.

* ***Derringer Model Nickel Finish*** – .22 LR or .22 WMR cal., nickel, black grips, ivory grips were used on some early models, introduced 1970.

$375	$325	$275	240	$215	$195	$175

Add 15% for .22 WMR cal.

* ***Derringer Model Gold Plated*** – .22 LR or .22 WMR cal., with black grips, includes presentation case, introduced 1964.

$595	$525	$450	$295	$250	$200	$175

Add $85 for derringers with 1-3 digit serial numbers.
Add 10% for .22 WMR cal.
Subtract $75 if w/o presentation case.

* ***Derringer Model Electroless Nickel Finish*** – . 22 LR or .22 WMR cal., checkered walnut grips.

$395	$350	$315	$270	$240	$210	$185

Add 15% for .22 WMR cal.

PRESIDENTIAL DERRINGER – .22 WMR cal., gold plated, smooth walnut grips, includes walnut case marked "PRESIDENTIAL DERRINGER".

$595	$525	$450	$375	$300	$250	$215

Subtract $100 if w/o presentation case.

Serial numbers DM1 through DM 416 (353 guns) and HDM153 through HDM160 (7 guns) and a few special prefixes on about 10 guns.

PRESENTATION DERRINGER

* ***Presentation Derringer Gold Plated*** – .22 WMR cal., smooth walnut grips, includes presentation case marked "PRESENTATION DERRINGER", ser. no GP0 through GP1000, approx. 917 produced in 1980 in E. Hartford.

$550	$495	$425	$350	$275	$225	$195

Subtract $75 if w/o presentation case.

* ***Presentation Derringer Silver Plated*** – .22 WMR cal., faux mother-of-pearl grips, includes presentation case marked "PRESENTATION DERRINGER", ser. nos. SP0 through SP500, 501 were mfg. 1981.

$595	$525	$450	$375	$300	$225	$200

Subtract $100 if w/o presentation case.

PISTOLS: SEMI-AUTO, LETTER SERIES

These were the first models made and used letters to designate the various models. A few guns from this series were sold after WWII. Catalog numbers for this series were assigned after the war in order to utilize the record keeping system of that time. This design series utilized three different takedowns. Types I-A and I-B takedowns have the takedown lever on the left side of the frame. Type I-A takedown has a round retracting rod protruding through the rear of the slide off center to the left side. Type I-B takedown is an improved, more durable design with a rectangular retracting rod. Type II takedown has the takedown lever in the right side of the frame with a round pick-up button on the top of the slide. Type I-A takedown was utilized from 1932 to February 1938 and the type I-B takedown was utilized from that time until August 1939. Models B and C are the only models with the Type I-A takedown. The Model B and other Letter Models utilized type I-B and II takedowns. Guns with original boxes and original papers can add significant premiums but, like the guns, the condition is very important as is the requirement that the box be numbered to the gun. Those guns listed as a Curio or Relic by BATFE are noted in this text with a C-R abbreviation at the end of the model description. Serial number ranges are best estimates as of this printing and may change with further research. All serial numbers are located on the front gripstrap.

Add approx. 15% for original box with papers in the same condition as gun on the following models.

GRADING - PPGS™	100%	98%	95%	90%	80%	70%	60%	LAST MSR

MODEL B - .22 LR cal., original High Standard pistol, basically the same gun as Hartford Arms 1925 Automatic, small frame, 4 1/2 or 6 3/4 in. lightweight barrel (approx. 63" diameter at frame), fixed Patridge type front and rear sights, checkered hard rubber grips (later production versions have checkered grips impressed with the High Standard monogram), 10 shot mag. Beginning ser. no. 5,000. Approx. 65,000, early production utilized Hartford front sight, safety and takedown levers. Post War models have the frame contour of the B-US. C-R.

	100%	98%	95%	90%	80%	70%	60%
	$625	$495	$395	$325	$250	$200	$125

Add $75 for I-B Type takedown.
Add $75 for early models with Hartford Arms parts.
Add $50 for post-war versions (ser. nos. greater than 146,000).

4 1/2 in. barrel #9000 1932-1942 & 1946. 6 3/4 in. barrel #9001 1932-1942 & 1946. Most guns found in serial number ranges from 5,000 to about 95,894 and from about 148,198 to about 151,021.

MODEL B-US – a version of the Model B with slight contour modification to the back of the frame. 4 1/2 in. barrel only. 14,000 made for the US government during 1942-1943. Most are marked "PROPERTY OF U.S." on the top of the barrel and on the right side of the frame above trigger guard. Crossed cannon ordnance stamp usually found on the right side of the frame. Monogrammed hard rubber grips. Type II takedown only. Note the early Model Bs shipped to the government and marked "PROPERTY OF U.S." had the original frame contour with transition to the B-US contour between ser. no. 99,261 and 100,972, .22 LR cal., 10 shot mag.

	100%	98%	95%	90%	80%	70%	60%
	$850	$725	$595	$475	$370	$270	$195

Most guns found in serial number range from about 92,344 to about 111,631.

MODEL S - .22 LR cal., chambered for .22 LR shot shell cartridge, essentially a Model B with a 6 3/4 in. smoothbore barrel only without choke, ivory bead front sight, left side of slide is stamped "HI-STANDARD MODEL S .22 LR SHOT ONLY", this variation was never a production model, ten are registered as Model S. Additional five with Model C slides are registered, Model C/S. Others may exist but only 15 are registered with BATFE (see serial numbers below). Manufactured in 1939 and 1940. Values for both variations are equal. 6 3/4 in. barrels. C-R.

	100%	98%	95%	90%	80%	70%	60%
	$4,750	$4,320	$3,900	$3,325	$2,850	$2,450	$2,100

Serial numbers: Model S - 48,142, 48,143, 48,144, 48,145, 48,146, 59,474, 59,496, 59,458, 59,459, 59,493, Model C/S: 59,279, 59,460, 59,469, 59,473, 59,478. S/N 59,484 is listed as a Model S in the factory records but is not currently registered with the BATFE.

MODEL C - .22 Short cal. only, identical to Model B in appearance, small frame, 4 1/2 or 6 3/4 in. lightweight barrel, fixed rear sight, checkered hard rubber grips with or without H.S. monogram, this action was adapted for the decreased power of the .22 Short cartridge. Early production in separate serial number series beginning with 500 and continuing through 3,116. Joined regular serial number series at 42,806. There are numerous Model Cs in the regular serial number series earlier than 42,806 around 25,600 which shipped a date later than the Model Bs in the same serial number range. C-R.

	100%	98%	95%	90%	80%	70%	60%
	$925	$750	$550	$425	$305	$215	$175

Add $75 for I-A takedown.
Add $175 for I-B takedown.

Most guns found in serial number ranges from 500 to 3,116 and from about 42,806 to about 86,249. This model was used primarily for plinking and gallery shooting. The Model C was made in all 3 variations of takedowns - I-A, I-B, and Type II. 4 1/2 in. barrel #9061 1936 -1942. 6 3/4 in. barrel #9062 1936 -1942.

MODEL A - .22 LR cal., similar to Model B, except grip part of frame is lengthened with a squared-off butt, 4 1/2 or 6 3/4 in. lightweight barrel, adj. rear sight, checkered walnut grips, checkered thumb rest walnut grips optionally available separately, automatic slide lock, 10 shot mag. Approx. 7,300 mfg. C-R.

	100%	98%	95%	90%	80%	70%	60%
	$795	$695	$550	$440	$310	$230	$180

Add $175 for I-B takedown.

Most guns found in serial number range from about 33,209 to about 97,734. A very few guns found in serial number range between 500 and 555. 4 1/2 in. barrel #9005 1938 - 1942. 6 3/4 in. barrel #9006 1938 - 1942.

MODEL D - .22 LR cal., identical to Model A except 4 1/2 or 6 3/4 in. medium weight barrel (approx. 79 in. diameter at frame), adj. sights, walnut grips, checkered thumb rest walnut grips optionally available separately, slide lock, trigger stop, 10 shot mag. Approx. 2,500 mfg. C-R.

	100%	98%	95%	90%	80%	70%	60%
	$995	$825	$600	$455	$330	$230	$190

Add $175 for I-B takedown.

4 1/2 in. barrel #9063 1938-1942. 6 3/4 in. barrel #9064 1938-1942. Most guns found in serial number range from about 33,216 to about 95,206. A very few guns found in serial number range between 500 and 555.

GRADING - PPGS™	100%	98%	95%	90%	80%	70%	60%	LAST MSR

MODEL E – .22 LR cal., high quality, deluxe model of the hammerless series, adj. sight, 4 1/2 or 6 3/4 in. heavy bull barrel (approx. 90 in. diameter at frame), checkered walnut target grips with thumb rest, automatic slide lock, trigger stop, 10 shot mag. Approx. 2,600 mfg. C-R.

	$1,225	$995	$825	$675	$500	$370	$245

Add $175 for I-B takedown.

4 1/2 in. barrel #9067 1938-1942. 6 3/4 in. barrel #9068 1938-1942. Most guns found in serial number range from about 34,419 to about 98,306.

PISTOLS: SEMI-AUTO, LETTER SERIES W/HAMMER

Second series of models made, like the letter models with external hammers. Letters were still used to designate the various models. Most were produced before the war, but a few models were produced after the war. Catalog numbers for this series were assigned after the war in order to utilize the record keeping system of that time. Type II takedown only. Guns with original boxes and original papers can add significant premiums but, like the guns, condition is very important, as is the requirement that the box be numbered to the gun. Those guns listed as a Curio or Relic by BATFE are noted - C-R. Serial number ranges are best estimates as of this printing and may change with further research. All ser. numbers are located on forestrap of frame.

Add approx. 15% for original box with papers in the same condition as the gun on the following models.

MODEL H-D – .22 LR cal., first exposed hammer model, similar to Model D, 4 1/2 or 6 3/4 in. medium weight barrel, adj. sight, trigger stop, slide lock, checkered walnut grips, (checkered thumb rest walnut grips optionally available separately), no external safety, 10 shot mag, pistols in the 135,990 to 145,439 range have a safety and are marked "Model HD" but do not have the adjustable sight or trigger overtravel screw. Fewer than 700 mfg. C-R.

	$1,225	$1,050	$825	$600	$450	$325	$235

Most guns found in serial number ranges from about 45,463 to about 93,164 and from about 135,990 to about 145,439. 4 1/2 in. barrel #9065 1940 - 1941 & 1945. 6 3/4 in. barrel #9066 1940 - 1941.

USA-MODEL-HD – .22 LR cal., this model was developed because the government needed a training pistol similar to the Colt Model 1911 .45 ACP, the result was a Model HD with external safety and fixed sight, 4 1/2 in. medium weight barrel, the barrel is marked "Property of USA", black checkered hard rubber grips, first models mfg. had high gloss blue finish, changed to a parkerized finish around ser. no. 128,000 to 130,000. Approx. 34,000 mfg. 1943-1945. C-R.

	$1,075	$925	$750	$650	$525	$400	$325

Add 20% for early blue finish.
Add $150 for box.

Most guns found in serial number range from about 103,863 to about 145,700.

MODEL USA-HD-MS – .22 LR cal., variation of the USA-Model-HD with integral silencer, mfg. for U.S. Government for the OSS during 1944 and 1945, ownership requires NFA transfer, approx. 2,000 mfg. Only a few registered with BATFE for civilian ownership.

	$6,000	$5,600	$5,250	$4,875	$4,540	$4,250	$3,750

Most guns found in serial number range from about 110,074 to about 130,040.

MODEL H-D MILITARY – .22 LR cal., though called H-D Military, this model was not mfg. for the government, essentially a Model H-D with an external safety, 4 1/2 or 6 3/4 in. barrel, plastic (early mfg.) or checkered walnut grips (later mfg,) trigger stop (later manufacture), 10 shot mag. Approx. 143,000 mfg. C-R.

	$650	$525	$450	$375	$275	$195	$135

4 1/2 in. barrel #9050 1945 - 1950. 6 3/4 in. barrel #9051 1945 - 1950. Most guns found in serial number range from about 145,196 to about 334,751.

MODEL H-E – .22 LR cal., deluxe model of exposed hammer series, 4 1/2 or 6 3/4 in. heavy barrel, adj. sight, trigger stop, slide lock, deluxe hand checkered walnut grips with thumb rests, no external safety, 10 shot mag. Rare - approx. 1,000 mfg. 1941-42. C-R.

	$2,200	$1,875	$1,550	$1,000	$725	$575	$450

4 1/2 in. barrel #9026 1940-1942. 6 3/4 in. barrel #9027 1940-1942. Most guns found in serial number range from about 51,802 to about 90,588.

MODEL H-A – .22 LR cal., similar to Model A, 4 1/2 or 6 3/4 in. lightweight barrel, adj. sight, slide lock, plain checkered walnut grips, no external safety, 10 shot mag. Rare - approx. 1,000 mfg. C-R.

	$1,325	$1,125	$950	$725	$500	$350	$225

4 1/2 in. barrel #9007 1940 - 1942. 6 3/4 in. barrel #9008 1940 - 1942. Most guns found in serial number range from about 53,176 to about 92,816.

GRADING - PPGS™	100%	98%	95%	90%	80%	70%	60%	LAST MSR

MODEL H-B – .22 LR cal., duplicate of Model B with external hammer, 4 1/2 or 6 3/4 in. lightweight barrel, fixed sight, checkered hard rubber grips with or w/o H.S. monogram, no external safety, 10 shot mag. Approx. 2,200 mfg. C-R.

$775 $650 $510 $385 $275 $225 $175

4 1/2 in. barrel 1940 - 1941. 6 3/4 in. barrel 1940 - 1941. Most guns found in serial number range from about 52,405 to about 86,155.

* ***Model H-B Second Model*** – reintroduced as the H-B second model similar to first model, except with external safety. C-R.

$675 $595 $450 $325 $225 $185 $150

4 1/2 in. barrel #9003 1948 - 1949 274,197 - 311,535. 6 3/4 in. barrel #9004 1948 - 1949 274,996 - 311,520.

PISTOLS: SEMI-AUTO, LEVER LETTER SERIES

These were the third design models made, which incorporate interchangeable barrels with a lever takedown. The .22 caliber guns evolved from the Model G-380, High Standard's first production removable barrel gun which is included in this section. Like the letter models with external hammers, these .22 caliber models still use letters to designate the various models. New to this series was the adjustable Davis sight. Also introduced in this series was a breech face shrouded by the slide. Significant premiums can be asked for guns with the combination of both barrels, if verified by factory records that the gun shipped as a combination. (Buyer beware - many "combinations" have been created after leaving the factory). Non-factory combinations should have additional value equal to the value of an extra barrel. Guns with original boxes and papers can add significant premiums but, like the guns, the condition is very important, as is the requirement that the box be numbered to the gun. Those guns listed as a Curio or Relic by BATFE are noted - C-R. Serial number ranges are best estimates, and may change with further research. Ser. numbers are on the right side of slide and rear right side of frame. Mfg. 1949-1950.

Add approx. 15% for original box with papers in the same condition as gun on the following models.

MODEL G-380 CENTERFIRE – .380 ACP cal., only in-house production of a center-fire pistol, transition model to the G-series using a lever takedown, exposed hammer, fixed sights, checkered black plastic grips, external safety, 5 in. barrel only, 6 shot mag. Approx. 7,400 mfg. in a serial number series of its own but a few examples exist in the regular serial number range around 329,337. C-R.

$650 $550 $450 $350 $250 $225 $185

5 in. barrel #9060 1947 - 1950 123 - 7,551

MODEL G-B – .22 LR cal., similar to Model B with light barrel, small frame, external safety, fixed sight, monogrammed checkered brown plastic grips, interchangeable 4 1/2 or 6 3/4 in. barrel with lever takedown, 10 shot mag., last short frame model produced. Approx. 4,900 mfg. C-R.

$650 $550 $400 $325 $245 $210 $180

Add $225 for factory combination.

4 1/2 in. barrel #9010 1949 - 1950 310,449 - 335,278. 6 3/4 in. barrel #9011 1949 - 1950 309,578 - 335,095. Combination with both barrels #9012 1949 - 1950 311,001 - 335,066.

MODEL G-D – .22 LR cal., large frame, medium weight, interchangeable 4 1/2 or 6 3/4 in. barrel with lever takedown, adj. Davis sight (named for designer G.F. Davis), sight is adj. for both windage and elevation, trigger stop, slide lock, grips avail. in plain checkered walnut or deluxe with thumb rest, 10 shot mag. Approx. 3,300 mfg. C-R.

$1,025 $900 $750 $535 $400 $300 $225

Add $325 for factory combination. Add $75 for factory target grips.

4 1/2 in. barrel standard walnut grips #9020 1949 - 1950 315,445 - 335,279. 6 3/4 in. barrel standard walnut grips #9021 1949 - 1950 311,804 - 335,300. Combination with both barrels and standard walnut grips #9022 1949 - 1950 312,001 - 335,247. 4 1/2 in. barrel thumb rest walnut grips #9023 1949 - 1950 316,623 - 326,850. 6 3/4 in. barrel thumb rest walnut grips #9024 1949 - 1950 311,804 - 335,222. Combination with both barrels and thumb rest walnut grips #9025 1949 - 1950 317,914 - 335,278.

MODEL G-E – .22 LR cal., deluxe top-of-the-line model, large frame, interchangeable 4 1/2 or 6 3/4 in. heavy bull barrel with lever takedown, Davis adj. sight, deluxe walnut hand checkered grips with thumb rest, trigger stop, slide lock, 10 shot mag. Approx. 2,900 mfg. C-R.

$1,425 $1,225 $875 $740 $465 $350 $250

Add $375 for factory combination.

4 1/2 in. barrel #9030 1949 - 1950 314,050 - 335,275. 6 3/4 in. barrel #9031 1949 - 1950 314,027 - 335,198. Combination with both barrels #9032 1949 - 1950 312,002 - 335,200.

GRADING - PPGS™	100%	98%	95%	90%	80%	70%	60%	LAST MSR

OLYMPIC (G-O) – .22 Short cal., adaptation of Model GE in .22 Short cal., also known as First Model Olympic, deluxe top-of-the-line quality, interchangeable 4 1/2 or 6 3/4 in. heavy bull barrel with lever takedown, Davis adj. sight, deluxe hand checkered walnut grips with thumb rests, trigger stop, slide lock, grooved fore and rear strap, first High Standard production gun with aluminum slide. special curved magazine, about 32 early guns exist which utilized a curved magazine with a straight back, the majority of these Olympics use the curved magazine with a humped back, grooved surface on top of barrel and slide. Rare - approx. 1,250 mfg. C-R.

	100%	98%	95%	90%	80%	70%	60%	LAST MSR
	$1,725	$1,425	$1,150	$825	$550	$525	$425	

Add $375 for factory combination.
Add $500 for the straight back magazine variation.

4 1/2 in. barrel #9040 1949 - 1950 325,929 - 334-735. 6 3/4 in. barrel #9041 1949 - 1950 307,734 - 334,979. Combination with both barrels #9012 1949 - 1950 329,590 - 334,399.

PISTOLS: SEMI-AUTO, LEVER NAME SERIES

These models were the fourth design evolving from the lever letter series with slight changes. This series followed the precedent set by the Olympic (G-O) of naming the models instead of utilizing letters. The upscale models, the Supermatic and Olympic, incorporated a rib dovetailed to the top of the barrel and a dovetail slot on the bottom of the barrel for mounting balance weights. This series continued the breech face shrouded by the slide design. Significant premiums can be asked for combination guns which have both barrels, if verified by factory records that the gun shipped as a combination. (Buyer beware - many "combinations" have been created after leaving the factory). Non-factory combinations should have additional value equal to the value of the extra barrel. Adjustable sight models continued to use the Davis sight. No guns in this series were offered with barrels incorporating the integral stabilizer but stabilizer barrels were offered in 1954 after the series ended. Most guns in this series utilized a single screw to retain the grips. However, the earliest Olympics used a screw for each side before changing to a single screw. Guns with original boxes and original papers can add significant premiums but, like the guns, the condition is very important, as is the requirement that the box be numbered to the gun. Serial number ranges are best estimates, and may change with further research. Those guns which have Curio or Relic status by virtue of being over 50 years old are noted C-R.

Add approx. 15% for original box with papers in the same condition as gun on the following models.

SPORT-KING (FIRST MODEL) – .22 LR cal., 10 shot mag., similar to Field-King except has fixed sight and lightweight interchangeable 4 1/2 or 6 3/4 in. barrel featuring lever takedown, early models did not have a slide hold back when the magazine became empty, early variation w/o hold back was produced in about twice the quantity as the later models incorporating this feature. C-R.

	100%	98%	95%	90%	80%	70%	60%	LAST MSR
	$450	$375	$325	$250	$200	$150	$100	

Add $25 for guns with hold back.
Add $200 for factory combination.

4 1/2 in. barrel #9080 1950 - 1954 335,001 - 442,605. 6 3/4 in. barrel #9081 1950 - 1954 335,012 - 442,572. Combination with both barrels #9082 1951 - 1953 337,699 - 442,574.

FIELD-KING (FIRST MODEL) – .22 LR cal., plain version of Supermatic, 10 shot mag., interchangeable 4 1/2 or 6 3/4 in. barrels with lever takedown, Davis adj. sight, trigger stop, slide lock, 10 shot mag., no rib on barrels or provisions for weights. C-R.

	100%	98%	95%	90%	80%	70%	60%	LAST MSR
	$650	$575	$475	$350	$275	$225	$175	

Add $225 for factory combination.

4 1/2 in. barrel #9090 1951 - 1953 342,703 - 439,658. 6 3/4 in. barrel #9091 1951 - 1953 341,751 - 439,665. Combination with both barrels #9092 1951 - 1953 348,762 - 439,660.

SUPERMATIC (FIRST MODEL) – .22 LR cal., 4 1/2 or 6 3/4 in. interchangeable barrel with lever takedown, Davis adj. sight, trigger stop, 10 shot mag., slide lock, grooved front and back straps, brown plastic thumb rest grips, serrated rib between front and rear sight, adj. 2 oz. and 3 oz. weights which dovetail into and beneath barrel, a filler strip was provided for when the weights were not used. C-R.

	100%	98%	95%	90%	80%	70%	60%	LAST MSR
	$825	$675	$550	$415	$320	$225	$175	

Add $250 for factory combination.
Add $30 for each weight and $25 for filler strip if present with gun.

Price is for pistol without both weights and filler strip. 4 1/2 in. barrel with provisions for weights #9070 1951 - 1953 340,103 - 438,698. 6 3/4 in. barrel with provisions for weights #9071 1951 - 1953 338,210 - 438,726. Combination with both barrels #9072 1951 - 1953 340,101 - 438,714.

GRADING - PPGS™	100%	98%	95%	90%	80%	70%	60%	LAST MSR

OLYMPIC (SECOND MODEL) – .22 Short cal., identical in all respects to the Supermatic, except has aluminum slide for rapid recoil, 10 shot mag., interchangeable 4 1/2 or 6 3/4 in. barrel with lever takedown, also available as combination with both barrels, Davis adj. sight, ribbed barrels and provisions for weights, 2 oz. and a 3 oz. weight were provided with this model, as was a filler strip for when the weights were not used, grooved front and back straps on frame. Some, perhaps a few hundred, of the early guns exist which utilize the hump back curved magazine from the previous series, but the majority of these Olympics use a newly developed straight magazine. C-R.

	$1,250	$995	$795	$600	$500	$400	$300	

Add $250 for factory combination.
Add a slight premium for curved magazine version.
Add $30 for each weight and $25 for filler strip if present with gun.
Price is for pistol without both weights and filler strip.

Note: Conversion kits for converting from .22 LR to .22 Short became available in 1956 (see the information at the end of the 101 section).

4 1/2 in. barrel with provisions for weights #9043 1951 - 1953 341,795 - 428,989. 6 3/4 in. barrel with provisions for weights #9044 1951 - 1953 341,788 - 428,982. Combination with both barrels #9045 1951 - 1953 348,505 - 428,990.

PISTOLS: SEMI-AUTO, 100 SERIES

The 100 Series firearms were the fifth design models evolving from the Lever Name Series designs. This series introduced the small, push button barrel release takedown, and deleted the shrouded breech. This series featured slanted plastic grips as standard issue. The upscale models continued with the ribbed barrel and a dovetail slot on the bottom of the barrel for mounting balance weights. Adjustable sight models continued to use the Davis sight. New to this series was the introduction of an aluminum frame on the Flite King and the Sport King Lightweight. Significant premiums can be asked for guns with the combination of both barrels, if verified by factory records that the gun shipped as a combination. Buyer beware - many "combinations" (over 50% of those researched) have been created after leaving the factory. Non-factory combinations should have additional value equal to the value of the extra barrel. Guns with original boxes and original papers can add significant premiums but, like the guns, the condition is very important, as is the requirement that the box be numbered to the gun. There are some pistols that represent a transition between the 100 Series in the Field King, Supermatic, and Olympic models where the slides are marked with the 100 Series, but the barrels are from the 101 Series. These transistion pistols are generally listed as 101 Series pistols and only the factory records will tell the tale. Serial number ranges starting points are best estimates, and may change with further research. Those guns which have Curio or Relic status by virtue of being over 50 years old are noted C-R.

Add approx. 15% for original box with papers in the same condition as gun on the following models.

SPORT-KING (SECOND MODEL) – .22 LR cal., similar to Flite-King but with steel slide and frame, SK 100 stamped on right side of slide, front and rear grip straps on this model are smooth, slide lock, fixed rear sight. C-R.

	$425	$375	$295	$200	$175	$150	$100	

Add $200 for factory combination.
Add $350 for ARMAMEX version.

In late 1958, Col. Rex Applegate imported about three hundred into Mexico. These guns are marked with his company's name, ARMAMEX. Marked "ARMAMEX, MEXICO" on the right side of the barrel and "SPORT KING / CAL. 22 L.R." on the left side of the barrel. Customary "HI-STANDARD" marking on the left side of the slide. Serial numbers around 870,084-870,383. Note that the Applegate guns were made after the 102 series was in production. Armamex catalog number 1910.

4 1/2 in. barrel #9100 1954 - 1957 436,311 - 804,081. 6 3/4 in. barrel #9101 1954 - 1957 436,308 - 804,080. Combination with both barrels #9102 1954 - 1957 443,651 - 804,075.

SPORT-KING LIGHTWEIGHT – .22 LR cal., similar to standard Sport-King, except has forged aluminum alloy frame, "Lightweight" is inscribed in script on the left side of frame, also available in nickel.

	$550	$425	$350	$250	$175	$150	$100	

Add $150 for nickel finish. Add $200 for factory combination.

4 1/2 in. barrel blue #9156 1955 - 1964 506,248 - 1,333,056. 6 3/4 in. barrel blue #9157 1955 - 1964 506,243 - 1,333,043. Combination with both barrels blue #9158 1956 - 1959 506,320 - 1,030,619. C-R. 4 1/2 in. barrel nickel #9166 1957 - 1960 726,752 - 1,136,533. C-R. 6 3/4 in. barrel nickel #9167 1957 - 1960 726,745 - 1,136,534. C-R. Combination with both barrels nickel #9168 1957 - 1959 726,909 - 1,025,505. C-R.

GRADING - PPGS™	100%	98%	95%	90%	80%	70%	60%	LAST MSR

FLITE-KING (FIRST MODEL) – .22 Short cal., 10 shot mag., blued finish with black anodized aluminum frame and slide, 4 1/2, 6 3/4 in. barrel, or a combination with both barrel lengths, brown plastic checkered thumb rest grips, fixed sights. C-R.

	$625	$500	$425	$340	$260	$180	$135

Add $200 for factory combination.

4 1/2 in. barrel #9103 1953 - 1957 431,297- 1,090,206. 6 3/4 in. barrel #9104 1953 - 1957 431,286 - 1,131,844. Combination with both barrels #9105 1954 - 1957 431,532 - 1,039,917.

FIELD-KING (SECOND MODEL) – .22 LR cal., 4 1/2 or 6 3/4 in. interchangeable barrel with push-button takedown, FK 100 stamped on right side of slide, 10 shot mag., front and rear grip straps on this model are smooth, slide lock, trigger stop, adj. rear sight. Mfg. briefly in 1954. C-R.

	$800	$675	$550	$425	$350	$250	$150

Add $325 for factory combination.

4 1/2 in. barrel #9106 1954 - 1954 446,645. 6 3/4 in. barrel #9107 1954 - 1954 446,595. Combination with both barrels #9108 1954 - 1954 446,601.

SUPERMATIC (SECOND MODEL) – .22 LR cal., 4 1/2 or 6 3/4 in. interchangeable barrel with push-button takedown, "S-100" stamped on right side of slide, 10 shot mag., adj. 2 oz. or 3 oz. weights, slide lock, trigger stop, adj. rear sight, grooved front and back straps on frame, a 2 oz. and a 3 oz. weight were provided with this model as was a filler strip for when the weights were not used. Mfg. briefly in 1954. A few were sold to the U.S. government. C-R.

	$875	$750	$650	$500	$350	$250	$150

Add $350 for factory combination.
Add $30 for each weight and $25 for filler strip if present with gun.
Price is for pistol without both weights and filler strip.

4 1/2 in. barrel with provisions for weights #9109 1954 - 1954 446,516. 6 3/4 in. barrel with provisions for weights #9110 1954 - 1954 446,445. Combination with both barrels #9111 1954 - 1954 446,705.

OLYMPIC (THIRD MODEL) – .22 Short cal., 4 1/2 or 6 3/4 in. interchangeable barrel with push-button takedown, 10 shot mag., "O-100" stamped on right side of alloy slide, adj. 2 oz. or 3 oz. weights, adj. rear sight, slide lock, trigger stop, grooved front and back straps on frame, a 2 oz. and a 3 oz. weight were provided with this model as was a filler strip for when the weights were not used. Mfg. briefly in 1954. C-R.

	$1,175	$925	$750	$575	$425	$300	$200

Add $350 for factory combination.
Add $30 for each weight and $25 for filler strip if present with gun.
Price is for pistol without both weights and filler strip.

Note: Conversion kits for converting from .22 LR to .22 Short became available in 1956 - see the information at the end of the 101 section.

4 1/2 in. barrel with provisions for weights #9112 1954 - 1954 447,209. 6 3/4 in. barrel with provisions for weights #9113 1954 - 1954 447,210. Combination with both barrels #9114 1954 - 1954 447,205.

PISTOLS: SEMI-AUTO, 101 SERIES

The 101 Series were the sixth design models evolving from the 100 Series. This series continued the small push button barrel release takedown. The ribbed barrel was dropped from the upscale models, but the dovetail slot on the bottom of the barrel for mounting balance weights continued. Adjustable sight models continued to use the Davis sight (Note: the Flite-King, Sport King, and Sport King Lightweight did not upgrade to this series). Significant premiums can be asked for guns with the combination of both barrels, if verified by factory records that the gun shipped as a combination. Buyer beware - many "combinations" (over 50% of those researched) have been created after leaving the factory. Non-factory combinations should have additional value equal to the value of the extra barrel. Guns with original boxes and papers can add significant premiums, but like the guns, the condition is very important, as is the requirement that the box be numbered to the gun. Serial number ranges are best estimates and may change with further research.

Add approx. 13% for original box with papers in same condition as gun on the following models.

FIELD-KING (THIRD MODEL) – .22 LR cal., 4 1/2 or 6 3/4 in. interchangeable barrel with push-button takedown, FK 101 stamped on right side of slide, 10 shot mag., front and rear grip straps on this model are smooth, adj. rear sight, slide lock, trigger stop, brown plastic thumb rest grips, 6 3/4 in. barrel incorporates a muzzle brake with one slot either side of the front sight. A few shipped in 1959 around ser. no. 1,039,1XX. C-R.

	$650	$550	$475	$425	$350	$235	$175

Add $300 for factory combination.

4 1/2 in. barrel #9115 1954 - 1957 447,149. 6 3/4 in. barrel #9116 1954 - 1957 447,146 - 799,260. Combination with both barrels #9117 1954 - 1957 - 799,259.

GRADING - PPGS™	100%	98%	95%	90%	80%	70%	60%	LAST MSR

SUPERMATIC (THIRD MODEL) – .22 LR cal., 4 1/2 or 6 3/4 in. interchangeable barrel with push-button takedown, "S 101" stamped on right side of slide, 10 shot mag., adj. 2 oz. or 3 oz. weights and a filler strip for when the weights were not used, 6 3/4 in. barrel incorporates a muzzle brake with one slot either side of the front sight, slide lock, trigger stop, adj. rear sight, brown plastic thumb rest grips, grooved front and back straps on frame, about 3,700 were produced with U.S. marking for the military and another approx. 1,600 made for the USMC which typically are not US marked. C-R.

$750 $675 $550 $475 $350 $235 $175

Price is for pistol without both weights and filler strip.
Add $350 for factory combination.
Add $30 for each weight and $25 for filler strip if present with gun.

4 1/2 in. barrel with provisions for weights #9118 1954 - 1957 447,586 -. 6 3/4 in. barrel with provisions for weights and integral stabilizer #9119 1954 - 1957 446,511 -. Combination with both barrels #9120 1954 - 1957 447,595.

OLYMPIC (FOURTH MODEL) – .22 Short cal., 4 1/2 or 6 3/4 in. interchangeable barrel with push-button takedown, "O-101" stamped on right side of alloy slide, 10 shot mag., adj. 2 oz. or 3 oz. weights and a filler strip for when the weights were not used, 6 3/4 in. barrel incorporates a muzzle brake with one slot either side of the front sight, adj. rear sight, slide lock, trigger stop, brown plastic thumb rest grips, grooved front and back straps on frame. A very small number were sold to the U.S. government. C-R.

$1,150 $950 $750 $595 $450 $325 $200

Price is for pistol without both weights and filler strip.
Add $350 for factory combination.
Add $30 for each weight and $25 for filler strip if present with gun.

4 1/2 in. barrel with provisions for weights #9121 1954 - 1957 447,230 -. 6 3/4 in. barrel with provisions for weights and integral stabilizer #9122 1954 - 1957 447,214 -.Combination with both barrels #9123 1954 - 1957 447,227.

* ***Olympic (Fourth Model) Conversion Kits*** – kits for converting .22 LR guns to .22 Short were announced in both the 1956 catalog and in a 1956 brochure. Kits include a barrel, an aluminum slide, and magazine (.22 short to .22 LR conversion had a steel slide).

$525 $435 $375 $315 $270 $230 $200

Values are for kits in original boxes - subtract 20% if w/o box.

Cat.# 9150 Supermatic/Field King to 22 Short, 4 1/2 Bbl. Cat.# 9151 Supermatic/Field King to 22 Short, 6 3/4 Bbl. Cat.# 9152 Olympic to Supermatic 22 LR, 4 1/2 Bbl. Cat.# 9153 Olympic to Supermatic 22 LR, 6 3/4 Bbl. Cat.# 9154 Olympic to Field King 22 LR, 4 1/2 Bbl. Cat.# 9155 Olympic to Field King 22 LR, 6 3/4 Bbl. Kits were also offered for the earlier lever name series and the 100 Series guns. Catalog numbers are unknown for conversion kits for lever name series or the 100 series guns.

PISTOLS: SEMI-AUTO, DURA-MATIC SERIES

The Dura-Matic pistols are a striker fired design that was designed and patented by O.O. Sunderland, a former designer for High Standard. The design was shopped around, and High Standard became the producer of this low cost plinker. The basics of this design can also be found in the Colt Cadet, Colt 22 and the Beretta U22 Neos.

Add approx. 10% for original box with papers in same condition as gun on the following models.

DURA-MATIC SEARS M-80

4 1/2 in. barrel #9133 1955-1962 477,292. 6.5 in. barrel #9134 1955-1962 477,649. Combination with both barrels #9135 1955-1962 477,303.

DURA-MATIC M-100 – .22 LR cal., 4 1/2 or 6 1/2 in. barrels, fixed sight, striker fired, oversized plastic grips, M-100 stamped on right side of slide, unique thumb screw takedown, push button release for the thumb screw, push button mag. release and oversized trigger guard. Mfg. 1954.

$350 $295 $235 $175 $150 $125 $100

Add $150 for factory combination.

4 1/2 in. barrel #9124 1954-1954 458,801 - 47X,XXX. 6 1/2 in. barrel #9125 1954-1954 458,802 - 47X,XXX. Combination with both barrels #9126 1954-1954 459,675 - 47X,XXX.

DURA-MATIC M-101 – .22 LR cal., 4 1/2 or 6 1/2 in. barrel, fixed sight, oversized plastic grips, "M-101" stamped on right side of slide (mfg. 1954 to 1970), later appeared renamed "Plinker" M-101 during 1971 to 1973.

$325 $250 $200 $160 $125 $100 $80

Add $150 for factory combination.
Add $80 for Plinker with case in original box.

The Plinker was not available with both barrel combination. During the first year, the Plinker came with a

GRADING - PPGS™	100%	98%	95%	90%	80%	70%	60%	LAST MSR

zippered carrying case. The Dura-matic was sold by Sears Roebuck & Co. as the J.C. Higgins Model 80. This Sears variation had some minor exterior differences but, mechanically it was the same - including a unique thumb screw takedown, push-button mag. release and oversized trigger guard. A slightly modified version was sold by Sears Roebuck & Co. as the J. C. Higgins M-80.

* ***Dura-Matic M-101***

4 1/2 in. barrel #9124 1955-1970 47X,XXX. 6.5 in. barrel #9125 195 1970 47X,XXX. Combination with both barrels #9126 1955-1959 47X,XXX - 1,030,956.

* ***Dura-Matic M-101 Plinker***

4 1/2 in. barrel #9214 1971-1973. 6 3/4 in. barrel #9215 1971-1973.

PISTOLS: SEMI-AUTO, 102 SERIES

The 102 Series was a major design change, incorporating a new frame with a large push button takedown release, and a superb adjustable sight. There is little difference between the two series. Pistols in this series are marked Model 102 on right side of the slide. Three variations of ejectors were utilized during the 102 Series. No premiums exist for these variations. Significant premiums can be asked for guns with the combination of both barrels, if verified by factory records that the gun shipped as a combination. Buyer beware - many "combinations" have been created after leaving the factory. Non-factory combinations should have additional value equal to the value of the extra barrel. The 102 Series was produced from 1958 to 1960, ending at approx. ser. no. 1,12X,XXX. Guns with original boxes and papers can add significant premiums but, like the guns, the condition is very important as is the requirement that the box be numbered to the gun.

Original cased 102 Series Trophy, Olympic Citation models, and Special Presentation combinations in 98%+ condition are currently in great demand and are bringing asking prices in the $1,700-$2,600 range.

Add approx. 15% for original box with papers in same condition as gun on the following models.

SPORT-KING – .22 LR cal., 10 shot mag., 4 1/2 or 6 3/4 in. lightweight, round and tapered barrels, blued finish, fixed sights, checkered plastic grips, smooth grip straps, also available as a combination with both barrel lengths. C-R.

$395	$325	$275	$215	$160	$120	$90	

Add $200 for factory combination.

4 1/2 in. tapered barrel blued #9200 1958 - 1960 778,028. 6 3/4 in. tapered barrel blued #9201 1958 - 1960 778,021. Combination with both barrels #9202 1958 - 1959 778,026.

FLITE-KING – .22 Short cal., otherwise similar to the Sport King Models 102 and 103, steel frames with an alloy slide. C-R.

$525	$450	$365	$310	$240	$170	$120	

Add $200 for factory combination.

4 1/2 in. tapered barrel blued #9220 1958 - 1960 791,149. 6 3/4 in. tapered barrel blued #9221 1958 - 1960 791,150. Combination with both barrels #9222 1958 - 1959 791,169.

SUPERMATIC TOURNAMENT – .22 LR cal., 10 shot, 4 1/2 or 6 3/4 in. tapered barrel, brown diamond checkered plastic slant grips, adj. sight, push-button takedown, smooth front and back grip straps. C-R.

$695	$595	$495	$375	$300	$220	$150	

Add $200 for factory combination.

Add $50 for factory guns marked U.S.

4 1/2 in. tapered barrel #9270 1958 - 1960 796,555. 6 3/4 in. tapered barrel #9271 1958 - 1960 796,536. Combination with both barrels #9272 1958 - 1959. The U.S. Govt. ordered the Model 102 Tournaments to use for training. These models were marked "U.S." on left side of frame.

SUPERMATIC CITATION – .22 LR cal., 10 shot, 6 3/4, 8, and 10 in. tapered barrels, diamond checkered plastic slant grips, adj. sight, push-button takedown, one grade above Tournament, grooved front and back grip straps, trigger stop, trigger pull adjustment, adj. sight located on 8 and 10 in. barrel, detachable stabilizer and 2 or 3 oz. barrel weights available. C-R.

$850	$700	$600	$450	$340	$250	$180	

Price is for pistol without both weights and muzzle brake.

Add $150 for 8 in. barrel.

Add $200 premium for 10 in. barrel.

Add $50 for each weight and $90 for muzzle brake if present with gun.

Add $50 for factory guns marked U.S.

6 3/4 in. tapered barrel with provisions for weights and stabilizer #9260 1958 - 1960 803,303. 8 in. tapered

GRADING - PPGS™	100%	98%	95%	90%	80%	70%	60%	LAST MSR

barrel with provisions for weights and stabilizer #9261 1958 - 1960 795,726. 10 in. tapered barrel with provisions for weights and stabilizer #9262 1958 - 1960 771,275. The U.S. Govt. ordered a quantity of Model 102 Citations to be used for training, marked "U.S." on left side of frame.

SUPERMATIC TROPHY – .22 LR cal., 10 shot, 6 3/4 in., 8 in. and 10 in. tapered barrels, high gloss "Trophy" finish, detachable barrel weights and stabilizer also available, walnut checkered thumb rest grips, grooved front and back grip straps, trigger stop, trigger pull adjustment, gold trigger, gold safety button and gold inlaid lettering, adj. sight and push-button takedown. The U.S. government ordered a small number of the Model 102 Trophys. C-R.

	$1,250	$995	$800	$615	$445	$325	$215

Price is for pistol without both weights and muzzle brake.
Add $175 for 8 in. barrel.
Add $225 for 10 in. barrel.
Add $60 for each weight and $120 for muzzle brake if present with gun.

6 3/4 in. tapered barrel with provisions for weights and stabilizer #9250 1958 - 1960 812,641. 8 in. tapered barrel with provisions for weights and stabilizer #9251 1958 - 1960 791,247. 10 in. tapered barrel with provisions for weights and stabilizer #9252 1958 - 1960 791,246.

OLYMPIC – .22 Short cal., similar to Citation, adj. sight located on 8 and 10 in. barrel and on the slide of the 6 3/4 in barrel, early models marked "Olympic Citation", then changed to "Olympic" only about 1960, grooved front and back straps on frame, checkered plastic grips, trigger stop, trigger pull adjustment. C-R.

	$1,250	$995	$800	$615	$445	$325	$215

Add $175 for 8 in. barrel.
Add $225 for 10 in. barrel.
Add $350 for "Olympic Citation" marked guns.
Add $50 for each weight and $90 for muzzle brake if present with gun.

6 3/4 in. tapered barrel with provisions for weights and stabilizer #9280 1958 - 1960 812,365. 8 in. tapered barrel with provisions for weights and stabilizer #9281 1958 - 1960 796,924. 10 in. tapered barrel with provisions for weights and stabilizer #9282 1958 - 1960 796,930.

PISTOLS: SEMI-AUTO, 103 SERIES

The 103 Series is much the same as the later 102 Series pistols. There is little difference between the two Series. This Series is marked Model 103 on right side of the slide. Significant premiums can be asked for guns with the combination of both barrels, if verified by factory records that the gun shipped as a combination. Buyer beware - many "combinations" have been created after leaving the factory. Non-factory combinations should have additional value equal to the value of the extra barrel. The 103 Series was produced 1960 to 1963, except for the Sport King, the Flite King, the Supermatic Tournament, and the Sharpshooter - see date ranges of the individual models below. After mid-1975, the Sport King and the Sharpshooter appeared in the "G" prefix serial numbered series - see serial number chart. Guns with original boxes and papers can add significant premiums but, like the guns, the condition is very important as is the requirement that the box be numbered to the gun.

Original cased 103 Series Trophy, Olympic Trophy, Olympic Citation models, and Special Presentation combinations in 98%+ condition are currently in great demand, with asking prices in the $1,700-$2,600 range.
Add approx. 15% for original box with papers in the same condition as gun on the following models.

SPORT-KING – .22 LR cal., 4 1/2 or 6 3/4 in. lightweight, round and tapered barrel, 10 shot mag., blue finish, fixed sights, checkered plastic grips, smooth grip straps, available as a combination with both barrel lengths.

	$350	$300	$250	$200	$150	$120	$90

Add $100 for nickel finish.

4 1/2 in. tapered barrel blued #9200 1960 - 1970 & 1973 - 1977. 6 3/4 in. tapered barrel blued #9201 1960 - 1970 & 1973 - 1978. 4 1/2 in. tapered barrel nickel #9208 1973 - 1977. 6 3/4 in. tapered barrel nickel #9209 1973 - 1977. Note that later production models were not marked 103. 254 Sport Kings (#9200 & #9201) shipped in May, 1977 with serial numbers between G160,000 - G162,590. 116 guns, #9201 Sport Kings, shipped April and May 1978 serial numbers G20,106 - G20,223.

FLITE-KING – .22 Short cal., similar to Sport King Model 103, steel frame with an alloy slide. There were 44 specials with 6 3/4 in. barrels made with adjustable sights for export in April 1962. There were two export only models made in 1966 and 1967, catalog numbers 9224 and 9225. The export models were

GRADING - PPGS™	100%	98%	95%	90%	80%	70%	60%	LAST MSR

made in relative small numbers and to date none have been reported in the US.

	$525	$425	$360	$310	$240	$170	$120	

Add $200 for factory combination.

4 1/2 in. bull tapered barrel #9220 1960 - 1965. 6 3/4 in. fluted tapered barrel #9221 1960 - 1965.

SUPERMATIC TOURNAMENT – .22 LR cal., 4 1/2, 5 1/2 bull (avail. 1963), or 6 3/4 in. tapered barrel, 10 shot mag., brown diamond checkered plastic slant grips, adj. sight, push-button takedown, smooth front and back grip straps.

	$675	$575	$475	$375	$300	$220	$150	

Add $50 for factory guns marked U.S.

4 1/2 in. tapered barrel #9270 1960 - 1962. 6 3/4 in. tapered barrel #9271 1960 - 1965. 5 1/2 in. bull barrel with provisions for weights and stabilizer #9275 1962 - 1965.

SHARPSHOOTER – .22 LR cal., 5 1/2 in. bull barrel, 10 shot mag., blue finish, adj. sights, checkered plastic grips, smooth grip straps, some mfg. with Model 103 marked slides.

	$550	$450	$350	$240	$200	$160	$125	

Add $25 for "SPORT KING" marked guns.

5 1/2 in. bull barrel #9205 1971 - 1977. Although the Model 103 marked guns have 1969 and later serial numbers, they were shipped after the introduction of the Sharpshooter in 1971, and were probably converted from unsold Sport Kings. Some early Sharpshooters have "Sport King" on the left side of the frame.

SUPERMATIC CITATION – .22 LR cal., 6 3/4, 8, or 10 in. tapered barrels, 10 shot, diamond checkered plastic slant grips, adj. sight, push-button takedown, one grade above Tournament, grooved front and back grip straps, trigger stop, trigger pull adjustment, adj. sight located on 8 and 10 in. barrel (a 5 1/2 in. target bull barrel became avail. in 1962), detachable stabilizer and 2 or 3 oz. barrel weights available.

	$825	$650	$525	$430	$340	$250	$180	

Add $150 for 8 in. barrel.
Add $200 for 10 in. barrel.
Add $50 for each weight and $90 for muzzle brake if present with gun.
Add $50 for factory guns marked U.S.
Add $125 for extra magazine (#9263 only).
Price is for pistol without weights and muzzle brake.

6 3/4 in. tapered barrel with provisions for weights and stabilizer #9260 1960 - 1964. 8 in. tapered barrel with provisions for weights and stabilizer #9261 1960 - 1964. 10 in. tapered barrel with provisions for weights and stabilizer #9262 1960 - 1963. 5 1/2 in. bull barrel #9263 1962 - 1963. The U.S. Govt. ordered a quantity of Model 103 Citations to be used for training, marked "U.S." on left side of frame.

SUPERMATIC TROPHY – .22 LR cal., 6 3/4 in., 8 or 10 in. tapered barrels, 5 1/2 bull and 7 1/4 in. fluted barrels became avail. in 1962, high gloss "Trophy" finish, 10 shot, detachable barrel weights and stabilizer were also available, walnut checkered thumbrest grips, grooved front and back grip straps, trigger stop, trigger pull adjustment, gold trigger, gold safety button and gold inlaid lettering, adj. sight and push-button takedown.

	$1,175	$975	$800	$650	$475	$350	$225	

Values are for pistol w/o weights and muzzle brake.
Add $175 for 8 in. barrel.
Add $225 for 10 in. barrel.
Add $60 for each tapered barrel weight, $30 for each fluted or bull barrel weight, and $120 for muzzle brake if present with gun.

6 3/4 in. tapered barrel with provisions for weights and stabilizer #9250 1960 - 1962. 8 in. tapered barrel with provisions for weights and stabilizer #9251 1960 - 1962. 10 in. tapered barrel with provisions for weights and stabilizer #9252 1960 - 1962.

ISU OLYMPIC – .22 Short cal., 6 3/4 in. barrel with integral stabilizer, 10 shot, grooved grip straps, checkered walnut thumbrest grips, trigger stop, trigger pull adjustment, alloy slide.

	$1,250	$995	$825	$525	$475	$350	$225	

Price is for pistol without weights and muzzle brake.
Add $1,000 for Model 9289 marked "Olympic Trophy" if in 98% or better condition.
Add $50 for each weight if present with gun.

6 3/4 in. tapered barrel with integral stabilizer - with accessories #9299 1961 - 1963. 6 3/4 in. tapered barrel with integral stabilizer - with accessories #9289 1961 - 1962. 5 1/2 in. bull barrel #9294 1963 - 1963. There was also an Olympic ISU with a Supermatic Trophy finish (catalog number 9289) - fewer than 500 were produced.

GRADING - PPGS™	100%	98%	95%	90%	80%	70%	60%	LAST MSR

OLYMPIC – .22 Short cal., similar to Citation, adj. sight located on 8 in and 10 in. barrel and on the slide of the 6 3/4 in barrel, grooved front and back straps on frame, checkered plastic grips, trigger stop, trigger pull adjustment.

	$1,250	$995	$825	$525	$475	$350	$225	

Values are for pistol w/o weights and muzzle brake.
Add $175 for 8 in. barrel.
Add $225 for 10 in. barrel.
Add $50 for each weight and $90 for muzzle brake if present with gun.

6 3/4 in. tapered barrel with provisions for weights and stabilizer #9280 1960 - 1963. 8 in. tapered barrel with provisions for weights and stabilizer #9281 1960 - 1963. 10 in. tapered barrel with provisions for weights and stabilizer #9282 1960 - 1963.

PISTOLS: SEMI-AUTO, 104 SERIES

The 104 Series is the last of the slant grip gun designs. Early production marked "Model 104". Later production is unmarked. The trigger stop screw moved from the right side of the frame to the trigger on the up scale models with that feature. During the production of this series, the accessories were deleted in lieu of a price increase. The serial numbers of later guns produced after mid-1975 utilized a new serial numbering system with the slant grip models utilizing a "G" prefix on the serial number. This series was produced from 1963 to 1978. Guns with original boxes and papers can add significant premiums but, like the guns, the condition is very important as is the requirement that the box be numbered to the gun.

Add approx. 12% for original box with papers in same condition as gun on the following models.

SUPERMATIC CITATION – .22 LR cal., similar to Model 102/103 Series, 10 shot mag., blue finish, adj. sights, brown plastic grips were standard on the 6 3/4, 8, and 10 in. guns, or thumbrest walnut checkered grips standard on the 5 1/2 in. model, grooved front and back straps.

	$775	$650	$525	$430	$340	$250	$180	

Values are for pistol w/o weights and muzzle brake.
Add $150 for 8 in. barrel.
Add $250 for 10 in. barrel.
Add $50 for each tapered barrel weight, $30 for each bull barrel weight, and $90 for muzzle brake if present with gun.
Add $125 for extra magazine (#9263 only).

103 guns, #9244 Citations, shipped March-May, 1978 serial numbers G20,000-G-20,105. 6 3/4 in. tapered barrel with provisions for weights and stabilizer #9260 1963 - 1965. 8 in. tapered barrel with provisions for weights and stabilizer #9261 1963 - 1965. 10 in. tapered barrel with provisions for weights and stabilizer #9262 1963 - 1963. 5 1/2 in. bull barrel with extra magazine #9263 1963 - 1966. 5 1/2 in. bull barrel w/o extra magazine #9244 1967 - 1978.

SUPERMATIC TROPHY – .22 LR cal., similar to Model 102/103 Series, top-of-the-line target model, 5 1/2 in. bull, or 7 1/4 in. fluted barrel, extra mag., muzzle brake and weights were supplied with gun, grooved front and back straps, super polished blue finish, adjustable sights, 2 and 3 oz. adjustable weights, checkered walnut thumb rest grips, grooved front and back straps on frame. Mfg. 1964-65.

	$1,100	$1,000	$750	$375	$325	$240	$170	

Price is for pistol without weights and muzzle brake.
Add $150 for high polish blue finish.
Add $40 for each weight and $120 for muzzle brake if present with gun.

5 1/2 in. bull barrel with accessories #9254 1963 - 1965. 7.25" fluted barrel with accessories #9255 1963 - 1965.

OLYMPIC – .22 LR cal., similar to Model 102, grooved front and back straps, checkered plastic grips.

	$1,100	$1,000	$750	$465	$325	$240	$170	

Price is for pistol without weights and muzzle brake.
Add $50 for each weight and $90 for muzzle brake if present with gun.

8 in. barrel #9281 1963 - 1963.

ISU OLYMPIC – .22 Short cal., similar to Model 102, grooved front and back straps, 6 3/4 in. barrel with integral muzzle brake, the 5 1/2 in. bull barrel was supplied with muzzle brake and weights, walnut checkered thumbrest grips standard, 5 1/2 in. barrel introduced 1964.

	$1,150	$1,025	$775	$475	$325	$240	$170	

Values are for pistol w/o weights and muzzle brake.
Add $50 for each weight and $90 for muzzle brake on bull barrel if present with gun.
Add $125 for extra magazine (#9299 only).

GRADING - PPGS™	100%	98%	95%	90%	80%	70%	60%	LAST MSR

5 1/2 in. barrel w/accessories #9295 1964 - 1965. 6 3/4 in. tapered barrel with integral stabilizer - with accessories #9299 1963 - 1966. 6 3/4 in. tapered barrel with integral stabilizer - w/o accessories #9237 1967 - 1977. Catalog and price lists refer to #9295 as both the Olympic and Olympic ISU. This model met ISU regulations and included a removable muzzle brake and weights.

THE VICTOR (SLANT GRIP) - .22 LR cal., 10 shot mag. 4 1/2 in. or 5 1/2 in. slab sided barrels with either ventilated or solid ribs, adj. sights are integral with the rib, blue finish, barrel tapped for weight, checkered walnut thumb rest grips, grooved front and back straps on frame, trigger is adj. for both pull force and over travel, probably 600 of these slant grip Victors were mfg. in all configurations, and probably fewer than 40 each of the 4 1/2 in. guns. Most guns are in the ser. no. range above 2,401,860 to 2,460,614, with a possible few in the ML serial number series. All but a few of the just over 200 guns produced in 1974 were exported, making finding one in the U.S. more difficult.

$3,200 $2,650 $1,975 $850 $550 $250 $200

Add $75 for steel rib.
Add $200 for solid rib.
Add $300 for 4 1/2 in. barrel.
Add $30 for original weight if present with gun.

4 1/2 in. slabbed barrel with ventilated steel rib #9218 1973 - 1973. 5 1/2 in. slabbed barrel with ventilated steel rib #9219 1973 - 1973. 4 1/2 in. slabbed barrel with solid aluminum rib #9226 1973 - 1974. 5 1/2 in. slabbed barrel with solid aluminum rib #9229 1973 - 1974. 4 1/2 in. slabbed barrel with ventilated aluminum rib #9218 1974 - 1974. 5 1/2 in. slabbed barrel with ventilated aluminum rib #9219 1974 - 1974.

Note the early vent. rib. barrels were steel, and the later ones were aluminum - w/o a change in the catalog numbers. Buyer beware - fakes exist.

CONVERSION KITS MODEL 102/103/104

$500 $450 $400 $325 $275 $200 $150

Add $250 for Trophy Conversions.
Add $125 for 8 in. barrel.
Add $225 for 10 in. barrel.

Cat. # 9266 Olympic to Supermatic Citation, 6 3/4 Bbl., Cat. # 9264 Olympic to Supermatic Citation, 8 Bbl., Cat. # 9265 Olympic to Supermatic Citation, 10 Bbl., Cat. # 9283 Supermatic Citation to Olympic, 6 3/4 Bbl., Cat. # 9284 Supermatic Citation to Olympic, 8 Bbl., Cat. # 9285 Supermatic Citation to Olympic, 10 Bbl., Cat. # 9286 Supermatic Trophy to Olympic, 6 3/4 Bbl., Cat. # 9287 Supermatic Trophy to Olympic, 8 Bbl., Cat. # 9288 Supermatic Trophy to Olympic, 10 Bbl.

PISTOLS: SEMI-AUTO, 105 SERIES

Note: High Standard designed the Model 105 but did not produce it. The 105 Series was to have been a 104 Series gun with the bridge style sight that appeared on the 106 series.

PISTOLS: SEMI-AUTO, 106 SERIES, MILITARY MODELS

Referred to as military models, this series was designed to provide same grip angle and feel of the Colt Military Model 1911. This design was introduced in 1965, and continued through most of 1968. The design utilized the tooling of the 104 Series guns, which resulted in the occasional appearance of a bullet shaped brass design in the rear grip strap when the spring hole was not properly plugged. This design appears as both a full bullet shape or only the outline. There is no premium for this feature. The magazines in this series have a red plastic bottom. The right side of the frame is marked "MODEL 106"/"MILITARY". During the production of this series, the accessories were deleted in lieu of a price increase. This resulted in two catalog numbers for each model. Guns with original boxes and papers can add significant premiums but, like the guns, the condition is very important as is the requirement that the box be numbered to the gun.

Add approx. 12% for original box with papers in same condition as gun on the following models.

SUPERMATIC TOURNAMENT MILITARY - .22 LR cal., entry level target pistol, early guns had smooth front and back straps and no trigger stop, later models had stippled grip straps and a trigger stop, slide mounted rear sight instead of bridge sight, 5 1/2 in. bull or 6 3/4 in. tapered barrel with military grips.

$650 $495 $375 $250 $200 $150 $125

Add $125 for guns with boxes and accessories if factory records verify model numbers.

5 1/2 in. bull barrel with accessories #9230 1965 - 1966 1,484,801 - 1,602,XXX. 6 3/4 in. barrel with accessories #9231 1965 - 1966 1,484,817 - 1,599,XXX. 5 1/2 in. bull barrel w/o accessories #9232 1967 - 1968 1,594,XXX - 1,93X,XXX. 6 3/4 in. barrel w/o accessories #9233 1967 - 1968 1,598,XXX - 1,94X,XXX.

GRADING - PPGS™	100%	98%	95%	90%	80%	70%	60%	LAST MSR

SUPERMATIC CITATION MILITARY – .22 LR cal., 5 1/2 in. bull or 7 1/4 in. fluted barrel, mid-level target pistol, trigger stop, trigger pull adjustment, stippled front and back straps, new rear bridge type sight.

	$750	$625	$495	$375	$275	$200	$175	

Add $150 for guns with boxes and accessories if factory records verify model numbers.
Add $30 for each weight and $90 for muzzle brake if present with gun.

5 1/2 in. bull barrel with accessories #9240 1965 - 1966 1,465,195 - 1,595,XXX. 7.25" fluted barrel with accessories #9241 1965 - 1966 1,467,353 - 1,595,XXX. 5 1/2 in. bull barrel w/o accessories #9242 1967 - 1968 1,595,XXX - 1,98X,XXX. 7.25" fluted barrel w/o accessories #9243 1967 - 1968 1,592,XXX - 1,98X,XXX.

SUPERMATIC TROPHY MILITARY – .22 LR cal., 5 1/2 bull or 7 1/4 in. fluted barrel, high gloss "Trophy" finish on early guns, top-of-the-line target pistol, trigger stop, trigger pull adjustment, stippled front and back straps, gold plated trigger, safety and magazine release, gold filled lettering, new rear bridge type sight.

	$1,050	$875	$675	$500	$375	$225	$175	

Add $100 for high polish blue finish.
Add $200 premium for guns with boxes and accessories if factory records verify model numbers.
Add $30 for each weight and $90 for muzzle brake if present with gun.
Add $10 per weight or $20 for muzzle brake with high gloss Trophy finish.

5 1/2 in. bull barrel with accessories #9245 1965 - 1966 1,436,172 - 1,595,XXX. 7.25" fluted barrel with accessories #9246 1965 - 1966 1,436,170 - 1,595,XXX. 5 1/2 in. bull barrel w/o accessories #9247 1967 - 1968 1,595,XXX - 1,97X.XXX. 7.25" fluted barrel w/o accessories #9248 1967 - 1968 1,595,XXX - 1,97X,XXX.

OLYMPIC MILITARY – listed in catalog but not in shipping records.

Catalog number #9235 for 5 1/2 in. barrel.

OLYMPIC ISU MILITARY – .22 Short cal., target pistol, 6 3/4 in. tapered barrel with integral stabilizer, trigger stop, trigger pull adjustment, stippled front and back straps, rear bridge type sight, military grips, supplied with extra mag. and weights.

	$1,100	$875	$700	$500	$375	$225	$175	

Add $50 for each weight if present with gun.
Add $200 if w/box and accessories and factory records can verify model.

6 3/4 in. tapered barrel with integral stabilizer - with accessories #9238 1966 - 1966. 6 3/4 in. tapered barrel with integral stabilizer - w/o accessories #9236 1967 - 1968 1,511,284.

PISTOLS: SEMI-AUTO, 107 SERIES

The 107 Series was the evolutionary successor to the 106 Series. This Series had the frame redesigned to eliminate the plugging of the spring hole produced with the old tooling. During the time of this series' production, the "MODEL 107" and the "MILITARY" marking on the frame was removed at about serial number 2,330,000. Then later the "MILITARY" marking reappeared at about serial number 2,4XX,XXX and remained until the end of the traditional serial number series. The "MILITARY" marking is absent from the guns with the "ML" prefixed serial numbers. There is no premium associated with these variations. These marking changes were not a change in design series, but rather only a change in markings. The traditional serial number series ran until August of 1975. The serial numbers on guns produced beginning July 1975 utilized a new serial numbering system. The Military models utilized an "ML" prefix on the serial number. Early production utilized the red bottomed magazines. Later guns had magazines with blued steel bottoms. The 107 Series was produced from 1968 until Sept 1981. Production was at Hamden, CT from 1968 to 1976 (S/N ML23,065), and at East Hartford 1977 (S/N ML25,000) to 1981 (S/N ML 86,641). Note that early E. Hartford pistols used up old stock of Hamden marked barrels.

The desirability factor for Hamden guns is higher than for East Hartford guns. Guns with original boxes and papers can add significant premiums, but like the guns, the condition is very important as is the requirement that the box be numbered to the gun.

Add approx. 12% for original box with papers in same condition as gun on the following models.
Subtract about 10% for East Hartford mfg.
Use 106 Series pricing for weights and muzzle brakes if present with gun.

SPORT KING – .22 LR cal., similar to previous Sport-Kings, except has military grips, labeled "SPORT KING-M." Mfg. in East Hartford only.

	$325	$250	$200	$175	$150	$125	$100	

4 1/2 in. barrel #9258 1978 - 1981 ML35,454 - ML86,493. 6 3/4 in. barrel #9259 1978 - 1981 ML35,453 - ML86,488. 6 3/4 in. barrel (123 guns) #9259 1980 - 1980 MLG20,224 - MLG20,408.

GRADING - PPGS™	100%	98%	95%	90%	80%	70%	60%	LAST MSR

SHARPSHOOTER – .22 LR cal., early models were marked "SHARPSHOOTER", later models were labeled "SHARPSHOOTER-M." Mfg. in East Hartford only.

	$425	$365	$300	$250	$200	$150	$125	

5 1/2 in. bull barrel #9210 1977 - 1981 ML29,215 - ML86,641.

* ***Sharpshooter Survival Pack*** – introduced 1981, includes Sharpshooter-M pistol, electroless nickel, 5 1/2 in. bull barrel, push-button takedown, packaged in canvas carrying case with extra nickel magazine.

	$625	$550	$450	$350	$250	$200	$150	

Subtract $100 for guns without the case.

Subtract $65 for guns without the extra magazine for guns in exc. condition.

5 1/2 in. bull barrel #9424 1981 - 1981 ML 85,635 - ML86,044.

SUPERMATIC TOURNAMENT MILITARY – .22 LR cal., similar to Model 106 Series, last of the Tournament pistols, adj. sight mounted on slide, smooth front and back straps on frame. About 1,600 are U.S. marked on the right side and were sold to the U.S. government.

	$550	$475	$375	$300	$250	$150	$125	

5 1/2 in. bull barrel #9232 1968 - 1971. 6 3/4 in. barrel #9233 1968 - 1971.

SUPERMATIC CITATION MILITARY – .22 LR cal., similar to Model 106 Series, 7 1/4 fluted and 5 1/2 in. bull barrel available, mid-level target pistol.

	$595	$575	$460	$340	$280	$230	$175	

5 1/2 in. bull barrel #9242 1968 - 1981. 7.25" fluted barrel #9243 1968 - 1981.

SUPERMATIC TROPHY MILITARY – .22 LR cal., similar to Model 106 Series, top-of-the-line target pistol.

	$900	$750	$575	$450	$325	$250	$175	

5 1/2 in. bull barrel #9247 1968 - 1981. 7.25" fluted barrel #9248 1968 - 1981.

1972 OLYMPIC COMMEMORATIVE – .22 LR cal., highly engraved version of a Supermatic Trophy Military Model 107, high polish blue finish, 5 1/2 in. bull barrel, has 5 Olympic gold rings on right side of receiver, ser. no. has a "T" prefix, came with a lined presentation case, early models were marked "MODEL 107", and were not high polished. C-R.

	$6,500	$5,000	$4,000	N/A	N/A	N/A	N/A	*$605*

Values assume guns in original presentation cases.

5 1/2 in. bull barrel #9207 1972 - 1975 T0,000,000 - T0,000,999

This model was a limited edition with 1,000 guns planned, but only 108 guns were listed in the shipping records, plus one frame manufactured due to their high price. A couple of prototypes are believed to exist in the regular serial number series. The original issue price was $550. One fully engraved gun is known. Buyer beware - fakes may exist.

OLYMPIC ISU MILITARY – .22 Short cal., target pistol for Olympic Style Rapid Fire Events, 6 3/4 in. fluted barrel with integral stabilizer and two detachable weights.

	$1,050	$875	$675	$575	$475	$325	$250	

Add $50 for each weight if present with gun.

6 3/4 in. barrel #9238 1968 - 1977

1980 OLYMPIC COMMEMORATIVE – engraved, right side of slide has the five gold ring Olympic logo, "USA" prefix on serial numbers from 0001 to 1000, lined presentation case, a limited edition of the Model 107 Olympic ISU with 1000 being produced. C-R.

	$1,500	$1,200	$975	N/A	N/A	N/A	N/A	

Values assume complete guns with box, papers, and presentation case - subtract $250 for guns in exc. condition w/o box, papers and presentation case. Subtract $100 for guns with presentation case but w/o box and papers.

6 3/4 in. barrel #9239 1980 - 1980 USA 0001 - USA 1000

THE VICTOR – .22 LR cal., 4 1/2 or 5 1/2 in. slab sided barrels with either ventilated or solid ribs, 10 shot mag., adjustable sights are integral with the rib, blue finish, barrel tapped for weight, checkered walnut thumb rest grips, stippled front and back straps on frame, earliest ventilated steel ribs (1971) were smooth on top, later steel ventilated ribs were grooved, aluminum replaced the steel on later ventilated ribs, still later a clearance groove was added for spent shell ejection behind the barrel, solid aluminum ribs introduced 1973, early models marked "THE VICTOR" on the left side of the barrel, later guns marked simply "VICTOR" on the left side of the frame, a few transition guns are marked in both locations, early weights are rectangular with round bottoms, later weights were flat bottomed with three grooves.

	$795	$650	$550	$425	$300	$200	$150	

Add $35 if weight is present with gun.

Add $100 for 4 1/2 in. barrel.

Add $125 for steel ribs, $150 for solid rib guns, or $150 for smooth topped vent. steel rib from first year

GRADING - PPGS™	100%	98%	95%	90%	80%	70%	60%	LAST MSR

of production.

Add $140 for Hamden guns (7 digit serial numbers and ML prefix serial numbers below ML 23,066).

4 1/2 in. slabbed barrel with ventilated steel rib #9216 1971 - 1973. 5 1/2 in. slabbed barrel with ventilated steel rib #9217 1971 - 1973. 4 1/2 in. slabbed barrel with solid aluminum rib #9206 1973 - 1977. 5 1/2 in. slabbed barrel with solid aluminum rib #9211 1973 - 1977. 4 1/2 in. slabbed barrel with ventilated aluminum rib #9216 1973 - 1979. 5 1/2 in. slabbed barrel with ventilated aluminum rib #9217 1973 - 1981.

10X – .22 LR cal., 5 1/2 in. bull barrel, push-button takedown. Specifically designed for top flight shooting, hand-picked parts and precisely assembled by one of only five High Standard Master Gunsmiths (with his initials under the left grip of each gun), black matte finish, black painted checkered walnut grips, stippled front and back straps. Mfg. in East Hartford.

$2,800	$2,300	$1,950	$1,300	$950	$725	$575	

Values are for guns with box and papers including test target - subtract $150 if missing.

5 1/2 in. bull barrel #9372 1980 - 1981 ML71,116 - ML86,123.

PISTOLS: SEMI-AUTO, CONVERSION KITS

These kits for the conversion of .22 LR cal. to .22 Short cal. contained an aluminum slide, the barrel and accessory listed below, and two Short mags., and comes in "gun size box" set in styrofoam. Manufactured in E. Hartford 1979-1982.

VICTOR KIT – includes 5 1/2 in. barrel with aluminum vent. rib and barrel weight, designated #9370 when mfg.

$550	$450	$350	$285	$250	$215	$185	

TROPHY/CITATION KIT – includes a 5 1/2 in. bull barrel and a stabilizer, designated #9371 when mfg.

$550	$450	$350	$285	$250	$215	$185	

SILHOUETTE KIT – includes a .22 LR cal., 10 in. bull barrel with front sight and rear sight adapter for adj. rear sights, barrel will work with either large push-button takedown or socket head screw takedown.

$550	$450	$350	$285	$250	$215	$185	

PISTOLS: SEMI-AUTO, SH SERIES

This was the final series of High Standard pistols and can be differentiated from the 107 Series by the new barrel release in place of the push button takedown. An allen head screw attached the frame to the barrel. This was a cost reduction design change. Shipped from late May 1981- October 1984. Serial No. range was SH10,001-SH34,034. Near the end of production, a "V" suffix was added to some visually impaired guns which were sold at discount. These guns were guaranteed to function properly, but the company would not allow them to be returned for appearance reasons. A few guns were made in this Series with an "SH" prefix serial number with the Model 107 pushbutton takedown. Serial number ranges are best estimates, and may change with further research.

Add approx. 10% for original box with papers in same condition as gun on the following models.

Add $25 for push button takedown.

Use 106 Series pricing for weights or muzzle brakes if present with gun.

SPORT KING - M – .22 LR cal., similar to ML series, except has allen screw takedown, 4 1/2 or 6 3/4 in. barrel, electroless nickel finish also available, also called the "SPORT KING-M."

$275	$235	$215	$185	$150	$125	$100	

Add 15% for the electroless nickel guns.

Values are for the blued guns.

4 1/2 in. barrel blued #9258 1981 - 1984 SH10,889 - SH33,964. 6 3/4 in. barrel blued #9259 1981 - 1983 SH10,001 - SH28,232. 4 1/2 in. barrel electroless nickel #9450 1983 - 1983 SH27,003 - SH31,436. 6 3/4 in. barrel electroless nickel #9451 1983 - 1983 SH27,004 - SH31,054.

SHARPSHOOTER - M – .22 LR cal., "SH" prefix serial no. with allen screw takedown, military grips, electroless nickel version utilized in some survival kits.

$350	$285	$240	$200	$175	$150	$125	

5 1/2 in. bull barrel #9210 1981 - 1982 SH10,8XX - SH25,074

SUPERMATIC CITATION MILITARY – .22 LR cal., similar to previous Citation model, except with allen screw takedown and military grips.

$500	$435	$350	$275	$225	$175	$150	

5 1/2 in. bull barrel #9242 1981 - 1982 SH10,550 - SH25,166. 7.25" fluted barrel #9243 1981 - 1982 SH10,513 - SH25,167.

GRADING - PPGS™	100%	98%	95%	90%	80%	70%	60%	LAST MSR

CITATION II – .22 LR cal., 10 shot, new variation of the Supermatic Citation, 5 1/2 or 7 1/4 in. slab sided barrel, checkered military-type wood grips, allen screw takedown, SH prefix serial no., slab sided barrel, rear sight mounted on slide, electroless nickel model also available in the survival pack, this model replaced the Sharpshooter and the Supermatic Citation.

$475	$400	$325	$275	$225	$175	$150	

5 1/2 in. slab sided barrel #9348 1982 - 1984 SH25,326 - SH31,495. 7.25" slab sided barrel #9349 1982 - 1984 SH25,575 - SH31,496.

SUPERMATIC TROPHY MILITARY – .22 LR cal., similar to previous Trophy Model with "SH" prefix, except has allen screw takedown, military grips.

$650	$525	$375	$300	$250	$200	$150	

5 1/2 in. bull barrel #9247 1981 - 1984 SH10,865 - SH32,630. 7.25" fluted barrel #9248 1981 - 1984 SH10,492 - SH33,828.

VICTOR – .22 LR cal., similar to previous Victor, new allen screw takedown, "SH" prefix, military grips, 5 1/2 in. vent. barrel only mfg. in this Victor Series, some Victor ser. numbers had a "V" suffix.

$525	$465	$375	$275	$180	$140	$120	

Add $35 if weight is present with gun.

5 1/2 in. slabbed barrel with vent. aluminum rib 9217 1984 - 1984 SH10,321 - SH34,034

10-X – .22 LR cal., top-of-the-line model similar to previous 10-X, but with allen screw takedown, also available with 7 1/4 in. fluted barrel and a 5 1/2 in. ribbed barrel like a Victor.

$2,125	$1,795	$1,450	$1,025	$795	$675	$575	

Add $1000-$900 for ribbed barrel model.
Add $500-$600 for fluted barrel.
Values are for guns with box and papers including test target - subtract $150 if missing.

5 1/2 in. bull barrel #9372 1981 - 1983 SH10,200 - SH29,640. 7.25" fluted barrel #9249 1983 - 1983 SH27,536 - SH29,641. 5 1/2 in. Slabbed barrel w/vent. rib #9434 1983 - 1983 SH26,657 - SH29,601.

Buyer beware - fakes are known to exist.

SURVIVAL PACK – .22 LR cal., Sharpshooter "M" or Citation II electroless nickel, allen screw takedown, packaged in canvas carrying case with extra nickel magazine (two different fabrics utilized during production).

$550	$500	$375	$300	$250	$200	$175	

Subtract $100 for guns without the case and $65 for guns without the extra magazine for guns in exc. condition.

Sharpshooter version #9424 1981 - 1982 SH10,048 - SH25,XXX. Citation II version #9424 1982 - 1984 SH25,XXX - SH31,312.

REVOLVERS: POLICE STYLE

The Sentinel revolvers begin with the R-100 design series, and continue through the R-109 design series. Later steel framed Sentinels carry no design series markings. A change of design series designation indicates design changes to the guns. The R-105 has the fewest known survivors. The design series designations and the associated catalog numbers which follow are best estimates, and may require further research. Earliest Sentinels in 1955 were in a separate serial number series from 1 through approximately 45,000. Then they were included in a serial number series common to all handguns. In 1974, they were again put in a separate serial number series with a prefix - S101 through S79946. Many of the later guns had a "V" suffix which indicates it was visually impaired, but guaranteed to work properly. High Standard private labeled the aluminum framed Sentinels for both Sears and Western Auto. A few were also provided to Col. Rex Applegate for his ARMAMEX company in Mexico.

R-100, R-101, and R-102 models are all C-R.

Add 20% for extra convertible cylinder (.22 LR/.22 Mag.) on those models listed that apply.
Add 20% for original box in 95+% condition, unless otherwise specified.

SENTINEL – .22 S, L, or LR cal., aluminum frame, 9 shot, SA and DA, swing out cylinder, 2 3/8, 3, 4, 5, or 6 in. barrel, fixed sights, return spring on ejector beginning with R-102 Series, 2 3/8 in. barrel model with bobbed hammer (disc. 1960) then standard spur hammer (beginning 1961) w/o change of category number.

* ***Sentinel Blue finish***

$450	$400	$350	$300	$250	$200	$150	

GRADING - PPGS™	100%	98%	95%	90%	80%	70%	60%	LAST MSR

* ***Sentinel Nickel finish***

	$500	$450	$400	$350	$275	$225	$175	

Subtract $15 for early models without spring return ejector.
Add $50 for 5 in. barrel.
Add $200 for R-105.

R-100, R-101, R-102 Series 3 in. bbl., brown sq. butt, plastic grips, blue, #9127, mfg. 1955-1960. R-100, R-101, R-102 Series 3 in. bbl., brown sq. butt, plastic grips, nickel #9136, mfg. 1956-1960. R-100 Series 5 in. bbl., brown sq. butt, plastic grips, blue, #9128, mfg. 1955 only.

* ***Sentinel R-100, R-101, R-102 Series 6 in. bbl.***

Blue #9128 mfg. 1956-1964, brown square butt, plastic grips.

Nickel #9137 mfg. 1956-1964, white square butt, plastic grips.

* ***Sentinel R-102, R-103 Series 4 in. bbl.***

Blue #9159 mfg. 1957-1964, brown square butt, plastic grips.

Nickel #9160 mfg. 1957-1964, white square butt, plastic grips.

* ***Sentinel R-102, R-103 Series 2 3/8 in. barrel*** – faux ivory round butt, plastic grips.

Blue #9144 mfg. 1957-1966. Nickel #9145 mfg. 1957-1966.

* ***Sentinel w/Dura-Tone colors*** – 2 3/8 in. barrel, offered w/either turquoise, pink, or gold color anodized frames, featured nickel plated cylinders, triggers, and hammers, round butt ivory colored plastic grips, mahogany finished case.

Turquoise finish	$1,200	$1,100	$850	$700	$550	$400	$375	
Pink finish	$1,200	$1,100	$850	$700	$550	$400	$375	
Gold finish	$1,100	$1,000	$750	$600	$475	$350	$300	

Add $50 for R-102 models. Add $100 for R-103 models.
Subtract $50 if w/o wood presentation case.

Gold R-101, R-102 Series #9161 mfg. 1957-1962 710,397 - 1,221,102. Turquoise R-101, R-102 Series #9162 mfg. 1957-1962 710,463 - 1,221,101. Pink R-101, R-102 Series #9163 mfg. 1957-1962 710,393 - 1,160,442.

SENTINEL IMPERIAL – .22 S, L, or LR cal., swing out cylinder, aluminum frame, adj. sights, two-piece walnut grips. Mfg. 1962-1964.

* ***Sentinel Imperial Blue finish***

	$500	$450	$400	$350	$300	$250	$200	

* ***Sentinel Imperial Nickel finish***

	$550	$500	$450	$400	$350	$275	$225	

R-104 Series 4 in. bbl., blue #9187 mfg. 1962-1964. R-104 Series 6 in. bbl., blue #9188 mfg. 1962-1964. R-104 Series 4 in. bbl., nickel #9191 mfg. 1962-1964. R-104 Series 6 in. bbl., nickel #9192 mfg. 1962-1964.

SENTINEL DELUXE – .22 S, L, or LR cal., swing out cylinder, aluminum frame, wide trigger, fixed sights, two-piece plastic or walnut square butt grips, blue or nickel finish, 24 or 26 oz.

* ***Sentinel Deluxe Blue finish***

	$450	$400	$350	$300	$250	$200	$150	

* ***Sentinel Deluxe Nickel finish***

	$500	$450	$400	$350	$275	$225	$175	

R-106, R-107 Series 4 in. bbl., blue #9146 mfg. 1965-69, 1972-73. R-106, R-107 Series 4 in. bbl., nickel #9148 mfg. 1965-1973. R-106, R-107 Series 6 in. bbl., blue #9147 mfg. 1965-69, 1972-73. R-106, R-107 Series 6 in. bbl., nickel #9149 mfg. 1965-1973.

SENTINEL SNUB – .22 S, L, or LR cal., swing out cylinder, 2 3/8 in. barrel, aluminum frame, checkered bird's head grip, blue or nickel finish, 20 oz.

* ***Sentinel Snub Blue finish***

	$450	$400	$350	$300	$250	$200	$150	

* ***Sentinel Snub Nickel finish***

	$500	$450	$400	$350	$275	$225	$175	

R-108 Series, brown round butt, plastic grip. Blue #9344 mfg. 1967-69, 1972-73. Nickel #9345 mfg. 1967-69, 1972-73.

GRADING - PPGS™	100%	98%	95%	90%	80%	70%	60%	LAST MSR

KIT GUN – 22 LR cal., swing out cylinder, 9 shot, 4 in. barrel, adj. sights, blue finish, aluminum frame, round butt walnut grips.

	$500	$450	$400	$350	$300	$250	$200	

R-109 Series #9304 mfg. 1971-1973.

CAMP GUN – 22 LR or .22 WMR cal., 6 in. barrel, blue, adj. rear sight, checkered walnut grips, also available as a combination with both cylinders.

	$700	$625	$500	$425	$375	$300	$250	

Add $50 for combination with both cylinders.

R-109 Series, .22 S/L/LR #9342 mfg. 1976-77. R-109 Series, .22 WMR #9343 mfg. 1976-77. R-109 Series, Combination #9393 mfg. 1977-1984.

SENTINEL MARK I – .22 S, L, or LR cal., 2, 3, or 4 in barrel, steel frame, fixed sights, blue or nickel finish, adj. sights on 3 or 4 in. barrel, smooth wood, square butt grips.

* ***Sentinel Mark I Blue finish***

	$450	$400	$350	$300	$250	$250	$150	

* ***Sentinel Mark I Satin Nickel finish***

	$475	$425	$375	$325	$275	$225	$175	

$25 premium for adj. sights.

SENTINEL MARK IV – .22 WMR cal., 2, 3, or 4 in. barrel, steel frame, fixed or adj. sights, smooth wood square butt grips, blue or nickel finish.

* ***Sentinel Mark IV Blue finish***

	$450	$400	$350	$300	$250	$200	$150	

* ***Sentinel Mark IV Satin Nickel finish***

	$475	$425	$375	$325	$275	$225	$175	

Add $25 for adj. sights.

POWER PLUS – .38 Spl. cal., 5 shot, SA or DA, swing out cylinder, blue finish, steel frame, serial numbers between PG 1010 and PG1273, only 177 mfg. 1983-84.

	$1,000	$900	$775	$650	$550	$475	$400	

Catalog number 9438.

SENTINEL COMBO – similar to Mark I Sentinel, except without the Mark I markings, steel frame, blue finish, offered as a combination with cylinders for .22 LR and .22 WMR cal.

	$550	$500	$450	$400	$350	$300	$250	

Values are for guns with both cylinders.
Add $25 for adj. sights.
Subtract $50 for guns with only one cylinder.

2 in. bbl., fixed sights #9390 mfg. 1978-1984. 4 in. bbl., adj. sights #9392 mfg. 1978-1984.

SENTINEL MARK II – .357 Mag. cal., SA or DA, 6 shot, swing out cylinder, blue finish, steel frame, fixed sights, produced by Dan Wesson for High Standard from 1974-75.

	$400	$350	$300	$250	$200	$175	$150	

Serial numbers had an "H" prefix H10001 to H35100. A few preproduction guns were sold to employees (H1 to about H28). 2 1/2 in. bbl., #9401, 4 in. bbl., #9402. 6 in. bbl., #9403.

SENTINEL MARK III – .357 Mag. cal., swing out cylinder, 2 1/2, 4, or 6 in. barrel, 6 shot, steel frame, adj. sights, blue finish. Mfg. by Dan Wesson for High Standard 1974-1975.

	$425	$375	$325	$275	$225	$200	$175	

2 1/2 in. and 6 in. bbl. #9407. 4 in. bbl. #9408. 6 in. bbl. #9409.

CRUSADER – .44 Mag. or .45 Colt cal., swing-out cylinder, 6 shot, unique geared SA/DA, adj. sights.

Extreme rarity precludes accurate pricing.

CRUSADER 50TH ANNIVERSARY ENGRAVED – .44 Mag. or .45 LC cal., 51 mfg. for each cal. in 8 3/8 in. barrel with 1/3 coverage engraving (ser. no. 0-50), employing gear assembly, blue with a gold crusader figure on the sideplate and an anniversary rollmark to commemorate High Standard's 50th anniversary, cased.

* ***Crusader 50th Anniversary Standard Model w/o Engraving*** – 6 1/2 in. barrel.

	$1,100	$900	$800	$700	$600	$500	$400	

Add 20% for wood display case, shipping carton, and paper.

GRADING - PPGS™	100%	98%	95%	90%	80%	70%	60%	LAST MSR

* ***Crusader 50th Anniversary With Engraving, 8 3/8 in. barrel***

	$1,750	$1,500	$1,300	$1,100	$900	$850	$700	

Add 20% for wood display case, shipping carton, and paper.
Add 25% for single digit serial number.
Limited availability might affect asking prices considerably. Two gun sets with matching serial numbers were also available.

REVOLVERS: WESTERN STYLE

The Western style revolvers begin with the W-100 design series and continue through the W-106 design series. The changes of design series designations indicate design changes to the guns. All High Standard Western revolvers were single and double action with a 9 shot swing out cylinder. The design series designations and the associated catalog numbers which follow are best estimates. Early western revolvers were in the serial number series common to all handguns. In 1972, they were put in a separate serial number series with an "M" prefix - M 1001 through M90916. Many of the later guns had a "V" suffix which indicated the gun was visually impaired but guaranteed to work properly. All "V" marked guns were shipped during June 1984 or later independent of serial number. High Standard private labeled the aluminum frame Western style revolvers for both Sears and Western Auto.

Add 20% for original box in 95+% condition.

DURANGO – .22 S, L, or LR cal., SA/DA, 9 shot, blue or nickel finish, aluminum or steel frame, 4 1/2 or 5 1/2 in. barrel, fixed or adj. sights, square butt walnut grips, two models have their grip straps and trigger guard nickel plated.

* ***Durango Blue Finish***

	$500	$450	$400	$350	$300	$250	$200	

* ***Durango Nickel Finish***

	$575	$500	$450	$400	$350	$275	$225	

Add $40 for steel frame.
Add $25 for adj. sights.
Add $50 for 41/2 in. barrel.
Values assume aluminum frames.

HOMBRE – .22 S, L, or LR cal., SA/DA, 4 or 4 1/2 in. barrel, no ejector rod housing, aluminum frame, fixed sights, square butt walnut grips, blue or nickel finish.

Blue Finish	$550	$500	$450	$400	$350	$300	$250	
Nickel Finish	$600	$550	$500	$450	$400	$350	$300	

W-105 Series, blue #9300 mfg. 1970-1972. W-105 Series, nickel #9301 mfg. 1970-1972.

LONGHORN – .22 LR or .22 WMR cal., DA, 4 1/2, 5 1/2, or 9 1/2 in. barrel, 9 shot, swing out cylinder, fixed sights except for one model.

* ***Longhorn Aluminum Frame 1958-1970 Mfg.*** – .22 S, L, or LR cal., SA/DA, aluminum frame guns, blue finish, fixed sights, square butt grips, one model has grip straps and trigger guard with gold plating contrasting with the blue frame.

	$600	$550	$500	$450	$400	$350	$300	

Add $40 for gold trigger guard/grip strap.

These guns are found in the W-102 and W-104 design series.

* ***Longhorn Steel Frame W-106 Series, 1971-1984 Mfg.*** – .22 S, L, LR, or .22 WMR cal., steel frame, or a combination with both cylinders, 9 1/2 in barrel only.

	$600	$550	$500	$450	$400	$350	$300	

Add $25 for adj. sights.
Add $75 for combination models.

DOUBLE NINE SERIES

* ***Double Nine 1958-1970 Mfg.*** – .22 S, L, or LR cal., SA/DA, aluminum frame, 5 1/2 in. barrel, one model has grip straps and trigger guard with gold plating contrasting with the blue frame, return spring on ejector beginning with W-102 Series.

» **Double Nine 1958-1970 Mfg. Blue Finish**

	$500	$450	$400	$350	$300	$250	$200	

Subtract $15 for early models without spring return ejector.

GRADING - PPGS™	100%	98%	95%	90%	80%	70%	60%	LAST MSR

» **Double Nine 1958-1970 Mfg. Nickel Finish**

$525 $475 $425 $375 $325 $275 $225

Subtract $15 for early models without spring return ejector.

* ***Double Nine 1971-1984 Mfg.*** – steel frame, walnut grips.

» **Double Nine 1971-1984 Mfg. Blue Finish**

$550 $500 $450 $400 $350 $300 $275

» **Double Nine 1971-1984 Mfg. Nickel Finish**

$575 $525 $475 $425 $375 $325 $300

Add $65 for combination models.
Subtract $100 for "V" suffix guns.

THE GUN/HIGH SIERRA – .22 S, L, LR cal., SA/DA, 9 shot, available as a combination model with a second cylinder in .22 WMR, blue finish with gold plated grip straps and trigger guard, steel frame, 7 in. octagon barrel, fixed or adj. sights and square butt walnut grips, gold plated grip frame.

$625 $575 $525 $475 $425 $375 $325

Add $50 for presentation case.
Add $65 for combination models.
Add $25 for adj. sights.

This gun was introduced as "The Gun" in the February 1973 price list and the name changed to "High Sierra" by the November 1973 price list. Note that the early production had neither "High Sierra" markings nor any other name. Without a case #9379 mfg. 1984 only.

POSSE – .22 S, L, or LR cal., 3 1/2 in. barrel, brass grip frame, fixed sights, walnut grips, blue finish.

$650 $600 $525 $450 $400 $350 $300

NATCHEZ – .22 S, L, LR cal., SA/DA, 9 shot, blue finish, aluminum frame, 4 1/2 in. barrel, fixed sights, faux ivory bird's head grips.

$900 $850 $775 $650 $550 $475 $400

Add $100 for box and papers.

MARSHAL – .22 S, L, LR cal., SA or DA, 9 shot, blue finish, aluminum frame, fixed sights, 5 1/2 in. long barrel, square butt stag style plastic or faux ivory grips.

$475 $425 $375 $325 $275 $225 $175

Values are for gun alone. Add $70 if box, papers and accessories are present and in excellent condition.

Catalog number 9330 , mfg. 1971-73.

Offered in a special promotion package with a holster, trigger lock, and spray can of G-96 gun scrubber.

RIFLES/CARBINES

SPORT-KING FIELD SEMI-AUTO RIFLE – .22 S, L, or LR cal., 22 1/4 in. barrel, walnut stock, open sights, 15, 17, or 21 shot tube mag.

$200 $175 $150 $115 $90 $80 $65

A-100, A-103. Catalog number #8000 mfg. 1960-1965.

SPORT-KING SPECIAL – similar to Field Model, except has beavertail forearm and Monte Carlo stock.

$225 $195 $150 $125 $110 $95 $75

A-100, A-103. Catalog number #8001 mfg. 1960-1965.

SPORT-KING SEMI-AUTO CARBINE – .22 S, L, or LR cal., 18 1/4 in. barrel, straight grip walnut stock with barrel band and sling, open sights, 12, 14, or 17 shot tube mag.

$225 $200 $175 $150 $115 $100 $75

A-101, A-102. Catalog number #8002 mfg. 1962-1971.

SPORT-KING DELUXE/SPORT KING SEMI-AUTO RIFLE – revised nomenclature for the Sport-King Special, catalog number 6005 is also the same gun but called Sport-King, a special promotional package (catalog number 8007) was offered which included the Sport-King rifle, a zippered gun case, a plastic trigger lock, and G-96 gun lubricant.

$225 $195 $150 $125 $110 $95 $75

Add 10% for complete 8007 package in original box.

A-1041 Sport King Deluxe Catalog number #8005 mfg. 1966-1971. Sport King Catalog number #8007 mfg. 1971 only. Sport King Catalog number #6005 mfg. 1973-1976.

GRADING - PPGS™	100%	98%	95%	90%	80%	70%	60%	LAST MSR

HI-POWER FIELD CENTERFIRE BOLT ACTION – .270 Win. or .30-06 cal., Mauser type action, 4 shot mag., 22 in. barrel, folding rear sight, plain stock.

	$475	$425	$375	$350	$300	$250	$200	

H-100 .30-06 Catalog number #8507 mfg. 1962-1965. H-100 .270 Catalog number #8509 mfg. 1962-1965.

HI-POWER DELUXE – similar to Field, except has checkered Monte Carlo stock and sling swivels.

	$500	$450	$400	$350	$300	$250	$200	

H-100 .30-06 Catalog number #8506 mfg. 1962-1965. H-100 .270 Catalog number #8508 mfg. 1962-1965. H-100 .308 Catalog number #8511 mfg. 1965-1965. H-100 .243 Catalog number #8513 mfg. 1965-1965.

SPORT-KING/FLITE-KING SLIDE ACTION RIFLE – .22 S, L, or LR cal., 24 in. barrel, tube mag., hammerless, Patridge sight, Monte Carlo stock with pistol grip, semi beavertail forearm.

	$225	$195	$150	$125	$110	$95	$75	

P-100 Sport-King Catalog number #8004 mfg. 1963-1965. P-1011 Sport-King Catalog number #8006 mfg. 1966-1971. Flite-King Catalog number #6006 mfg. 1973-1976.

SHOTGUNS: BOLT ACTION

MODEL 514 – some of the Sears versions of this shotgun were recalled for safety considerations in the late 1990s.

	$135	$120	$90	$70	$60	$50	$40	

CATALOG NUMBERS: Series Barrel Full Choke Adj. Choke Single Shot Full Choke Date Range - 12 Ga. 514 Plain 8370 8373 8376 Unknown. 16 Ga. 514 Plain 8371 8374 8377 Unknown. 20 Ga. 514 Plain 8372 8375 8378 Unknown. The catalog numbers shown are from a parts book which does not provide production dates.

SHOTGUNS: SEMI-AUTO

High Standard began making shotguns for Sears Roebuck in the late 1940s. In 1960, High Standard began marketing shotguns under their own name and the approximately 200 models in the following listing is derived from the High Standard catalogs and price lists of that time. A redesign of the shotgun line occurred with new models introduced in 1966. In 1973, High Standard introduced their new "Trophy Line" of shotguns and this marked a change in catalog numbers from the number beginning with the numeral 8 to the number beginning with the numeral 6. At this time the previous catalog numbers were referred to as the "Regular Line". Some regular line guns were cataloged in 1973, but this was the last year for them except the Police models. The 12 gauge pumps in the Trophy line were the guns which had interchangeable barrels. Serial numbers began appearing on the High Standard shotguns during mid to late 1967. Beginning about 1958, many of the shotguns had a two letter date code.

Additionally, there are over 150 catalog numbers for both semi-auto and slide action shotguns not listed here which represent models with High Standard markings but with special roll marking or other features which High Standard produced for several large distributors. Many of these distributor specials had their own model names which included Point Right, Pointer, Birdwing, NATO Pintail Field Classic Mallard Model 200 (J.C. Penney 20 ga. semi-auto), Model 220, and Sport Deluxe. These distributor label guns are not listed in the following data.

The choke markings used by High Standard are: * Full, ** Modified, * Improved Cylinder, and **** Skeet Bore. Cylinder Bore has no mark.**

SUPERMATIC FIELD – 12 or 20 ga., 2 3/4 (12 ga.) or 3 (20 ga.) chambers, 28 or 30 in. barrel, full or modified choke, improved cylinder, gas operated, blue finish, plain pistol grip walnut stock and forearm, 4 shot mag. capacity.

	$225	$210	$185	$170	$150	$140	$120	

Add 10% for 20 gauge.

Supermatic Field models were superseded by models in the Supermatic Deluxe group beginning in 1966.

SUPERMATIC SPECIAL – 12 or 20 ga., similar to the Supermatic Field except has 27 in. barrel with 6-position click stop adjustable choke, 2 3/4 (12 ga.) or 3 in. (20 ga.) chambers.

	$230	$210	$195	$175	$150	$140	$120	

Add 10% for 20 ga.

Supermatic Special models were superseded by models in the Supermatic Deluxe group beginning in 1966.

GRADING - PPGS™	100%	98%	95%	90%	80%	70%	60%	LAST MSR

SUPERMATIC DELUXE – 12 or 20 ga., 2 3/4 (12 ga.) or 3 (20 ga.) in. chambers, gas operated, blue finish, 26, 27, 28, or 30 in. barrel, checkered pistol grip, walnut stock and forearm, 4 shot mag., recoil pad (new 1966).

$270	$245	$205	$175	$150	$140	$130	

Add $20 for vent. rib versions. Add 10% for 20 ga.

SUPERMATIC CITATION – similar to Supermatic Trophy model except w/o vent. rib, 2 3/4 in. chambers, 6 click stop adjustable choke.

$245	$230	$210	$190	$160	$140	$115	

SUPERMATIC TROPHY – 12 or 20 ga., 2 3/4 (12 ga.) or 3 (20 ga.) in. chamber, gas operated, blue finish, checkered walnut stock and forend, 4 shot mag., 6 click stop adjustable choke.

$255	$235	$210	$190	$165	$145	$120	

Add 10% for 20 ga.

SUPERMATIC DUCK – 12 ga., 3 in. magnum chamber, (also fits 2 3/4 in. shells), blue finish, checkered pistol grip walnut stock and forearm, 5 (2 3/4 in. shells) or 4 (3 in. shells) shot mag.

$285	$255	$205	$175	$145	$125	$110	

Add $20 for vent. rib.

SUPERMATIC DEER GUN – similar to Supermatic Deluxe, except has 22 in. cylinder bore barrel, rifle sights, checkered stock and forearm, recoil pad.

$250	$225	$195	$175	$150	$125	$115	

SUPERMATIC SKEET – similar to Supermatic Deluxe, except has select American walnut stock and forearm, 2 3/4 (12 ga.) or 3 (20 ga.) in. chamber.

$300	$275	$250	$225	$200	$175	$150	

Add 10% for 20 ga.

SUPERMATIC TRAP – similar to Supermatic Deluxe, except has select American walnut stock and forearm and recoil pad.

$300	$275	$225	$200	$180	$160	$140	

SHOTGUNS: SLIDE ACTION

FLITE-KING FIELD – 12, 16, 20 ga. or .410 bore, 2 3/4 (12 or 16 ga.) or 3 (20 ga. or .410 bore) in. chamber, blued finish, 4 or 5 shot mag., plain pistol grip walnut stock and forend.

$200	$175	$150	$130	$115	$105	$95	

Add 50% for .410 bore, add 5% for 16 ga., and 10% for 20 ga.

FLITE-KING SPECIAL – 12, 16, or 20 ga., 2 3/4 (12 or 16 ga.) or 3 (20 ga.) in. chamber, 5 shot mag., blued finish, 27 in. barrel, 6 click adj. choke, walnut stock and forend.

$200	$175	$150	$130	$115	$105	$95	

Add 5% for 16 ga., or 10% for 20 ga.

FLITE-KING DELUXE – 12, 16, 20, 28 ga., or .410 bore, 2 3/4 (12, 16, 28 ga.) or 3 (20 ga. or .410 bore) chamber, blued finish, checkered walnut pistol grip stock and forearm, 5 shot mag., 6 click adj. choke, available with and without a vent. rib, recoil pad beginning 1966 except .410 models.

$205	$185	$160	$140	$120	$100	$90	

Add 5% for 16 ga. or 10% for 20 ga.
Add $20 for vent. rib.
Add 50% for plain barrel in 28 ga. or .410 bore.
Add 70% for ribbed barrel in 28 ga. or .410 bore.
Add $25 for catalog numbers 6135-6142 with interchangeable barrels capability.

MODEL 200 – 12 ga., also sold as part of a promotional package beginning in 1971, which included the Model 200, a zippered gun case, a plastic trigger lock, and G-96 gun lubricant.

$175	$160	$140	$120	$105	$95	$90	

Add $20 premium for entire promotional package in original box.

FLITE-KING CITATION – 12 or 16 ga., 2 3/4 in. chamber, similar to Flite-King Trophy, except does not have vent. rib.

$210	$195	$175	$150	$120	$100	$90	

Add 5% for 16 ga.

FLITE-KING TROPHY – 12, 16, or 20 ga., 2 3/4 (12 or 16 ga.) or 3 (20 ga.) in. chamber, blued finish, walnut stock and forend, 5 shot mag, vent. rib.

$220	$210	$180	$160	$130	$110	$100	

Add 5% for 16 ga. or 10% for 20 ga.

GRADING - PPGS™	100%	98%	95%	90%	80%	70%	60%	LAST MSR

FLITE-KING BRUSH – 12, ga., 2 3/4 in. chamber, similar to the Flite-King Field, except has adjustable rifle sights, receiver is tapped for the Williams sight and provisions exist for sling swivels, deluxe models have Williams receiver sight, a leather sling and a recoil pad.

$325 $275 $250 $225 $135 $100 $90

Add $10 for deluxe model.

Add $25 for catalog no. 6166 with interchangeable barrel capability.

FLITE-KING SKEET – 12, 20, 28 ga. or .410 bore, 2 3/4 (12 or 28 ga.) or 3 (20 ga. or .410 bore) in. chamber, similar to Flite-King Deluxe except has select American walnut stock and forearm and no recoil pad.

$290 $260 $230 $185 $150 $120 $100

Add 50% for 28 ga. or .410 bore.

Add 10% for 20 ga.

FLITE-KING TRAP – 12 ga., 2 3/4 in. chamber, similar to Flite-King Deluxe, except has select American Walnut stock and forearm and recoil pad, 30 in. barrel.

$275 $225 $195 $175 $150 $130 $110

Add $25 for Fajen Monte Carlo stock.

SHOTGUNS: IMPORTED

SUPERMATIC SHADOW INDY O/U – 12 ga., boxlock, selective auto ejectors, single trigger, fully engraved receiver, skipline checkered walnut stock with pistol grip, vent. forearm, recoil pad, special "Airflow" rib. Imported from Nikko in Japan.

$860 $820 $770 $720 $625 $550 $500

SUPERMATIC SHADOW SEVEN – similar to Shadow Indy, except has a standard size vent. rib, conventional forearm, no recoil pad, standard checkering, and less engraving. Imported from Nikko in Japan.

$695 $660 $620 $575 $480 $430 $390

SUPERMATIC SHADOW AUTOMATIC – 12 or 20 ga., semi-auto, gas operated, interchangeable barrels, checkered walnut stock and forearm, special "Airflow" rib. Imported from Nikko in Japan.

$400 $370 $345 $270 $200 $175 $150

SHOTGUNS: DEFENSE & LAW ENFORCEMENT

SEMI AUTOMATIC MODEL – 12 ga., 20 in. cylinder bore barrel, 4 shot mag., recoil pad walnut stock and forearm.

$325 $300 $275 $250 $225 $200 $150

MODELS 10A/10B SEMI-AUTO – 12 ga., combat model, 18 in. barrel, unique bullpup design incorporates raked pistol grip in front of receiver and metal shoulder pad attached directly to rear of receiver, black Cycolac plastic shroud and pistol grip, very compact size (28 in. overall). Disc.

* ***Model 10-A Semi-Auto*** – 4 shot mag., fixed carrying handle and integral flashlight. Between 1,700 and 1,800 were produced beginning 1967.

  $875 $795 $725 $650 $575 $500 $425

* ***Model 10-B Semi-Auto*** – 12 ga., folding carrying handle, provisions made for attaching a Kel-lite flashlight to receiver top, extended blade front sight, 4 shot mag., carrying case.

  $850 $775 $715 $650 $575 $515 $450

Add 15% for flashlight.

SLIDE ACTION RIOT SHOTGUN – 12 ga. only on the Flite King Action, 18 or 20 in. barrel, police riot gun, available with or w/o rifle sights, plain pistol grip oiled walnut stock & forearm, changed to walnut stained and lacquered birch in the mid-1970s.

$325 $275 $250 $200 $175 $125 $115

HIGH STANDARD MANUFACTURING CO.

Previous trademark manufactured by Firearms International Inc. located in Houston, TX. from 1993-2018.

This company was formed during 1993, utilizing many of the same employees and original material vendors which the original High Standard company used during their period of manufacture (1926-1984). During 2004, Crusader Group Gun Company, Inc. was formed, and the new company included the assets of High Standard Manufacturing Co, Firearms International Inc., AMT-Auto Mag, Interarms, and Arsenal Line Products. High Standard Manufacturing closed its doors in 2018.

GRADING - PPGS™	100%	98%	95%	90%	80%	70%	60%	LAST MSR

PISTOLS: SEMI-AUTO

CRUSADER COMPACT – .45 ACP cal., SA, recoil operated, officer sized steel slide and frame, 3 1/2 in. barrel, 7 shot mag., fixed Novak front and rear sights, wood grips, thumb and grip safety, parkerized finish. Disc.

$475 $425 $350 $325 $250 $225 $175 *$555*

DURAMATIC PLINKER – .22 LR cal., 4 1/2 in. barrel, fixed sights, parkerized metal finish, black plastic grips, 10 shot mag., 44 oz. Mfg. 2013-disc.

$450 $400 $365 4335 $300 $275 $250 *$525*

GI 1911 – .45 ACP cal., SA, recoil operated, Govt. size steel slide and frame, 5 in. barrel, 8 shot mag., GI profile hammer, short GI trigger, fixed GI profile front and rear sights, checkered wood grips, left side thumb safety and GI profile beavertail safety, beveled magwell, flat mainspring housing, parkerized finish, 38 oz. Disc.

$475 $415 $350 $325 $260 $215 $165 *$559*

SPORT KING – .22 LR cal., 4 1/2 or 6 3/4 in. barrel, blue finish, military grips, fixed sights, 10 shot mag. Limited edition produced in small quantities. Disc. 2013.

$750 $665 $575 $500 $450 $395 $325 *$835*

LIMITED EDITIONS – during 1996, High Standard offered several limited editions. They included the Victor (fully engraved, 6 mfg., $1,862 MSR), the Tournament (non-engraved, 26 mfg., $608 MSR), and the engraved Tournament (50% engraved, 6 mfg. $1,062 MSR). Additionally, only 5 sets were mfg. with 4 guns included - the Olympic 8 in. Space Gun, Tournament, Flite King, and Victor. Retail was $3,200 (non-engraved) or $7,200 (engraved). A 3 gun set was also available (w/o Olympic) for $2,150 (non-engraved) or $5,150 (engraved).

Extreme rarity of these guns precludes accurate pricing.

OLYMPIC I.S.U. – .22 Short cal., 6 3/4 in. fluted barrel with integral muzzle brake, blue finish, military grips, 10 shot mag. Mfg. 1994-95 only.

$550 $450 $385 $315 $250 $200 $185 *$625*

OLYMPIC MILITARY – .22 Short cal., 5 1/2 in. fluted bull barrel with removable stabilizer, aluminum alloy slide with steel frame, scope base or open sights. Mfg. 1995-disc.

$895 $725 $600 $500 $400 $350 $325 *$1,050*

Subtract approx. $60 if w/o open sights.

OLYMPIC RAPID FIRE – .22 Short cal., 4 in. VR barrel with integral muzzle brake and forward mounted compensator, gold-plated small parts, matte finish, special grips with rear support, adj. trigger, 46 oz., custom shop only. New 1996-2003.

$925 $725 $625 $525 $425 $375 $325 *$1,027*

OLYMPIC TROPHY "SPACE GUN" – .22 LR cal., blue/black finish, updated version of 1960 Olympic gold medal pistol, 6 3/4, (disc. 2010) 8, or 10 in. barrel, 10 shot mag., checkered walnut grips with thumbrest, muzzle brake, 39 - 43 oz. Mfg. 2010-disc.

$1,150 $995 $875 $750 $625 $500 $400 *$1,350*

PLINKER – .17 High Standard (advertised but never mfg.) or .22 LR cal., same design as former Ram-Line pistol, 4, 6, or 8 in. barrel with adj. rear sight, uses many plastic materials, interchangeable barrels, 10 shot mag., 14 1/4 oz. Limited mfg. 2011 only.

$450 $400 $350 $300 $250 $200 $175 *$495*

SUPERMATIC CITATION – .22 LR cal., 5 1/2 or 7 1/4 (disc. 1995) in. barrel, matte blue (disc. 1996) or parkerized finish, military grips, open sights (disc. 2001) or universal scope base, 9 shot mag., 44 oz. Mfg. 1994-2003.

$650 $550 $475 $425 $325 $275 $200 *$490*

Add $317 for .22 Short conversion kit (includes barrel, slide, and 2 mags.).

SUPERMATIC CITATION MS – .17 High Standard (new 2003-disc.) or .22 LR cal., 10 in. barrel, mounting bracket with scope base, designed for the Metallic Silhouette shooter, 54 oz. Mfg. 1997-disc.

$850 $735 $575 $475 $375 $300 $275 *$975*

Add approx. $119 for RPM sights (scope base only, disc).

SUPERMATIC CITATION 10X – .22 LR cal., 5 1/2 in. barrel, blue finish, military grips, High Standard's most accurate pistol, choice of either factory or Shea custom tuning, 10 shot mag., approx. 45 oz., custom shop only. Mfg. 1994-disc.

* ***Supermatic Citation 10X Factory Tuned*** – Disc.

$1,150 $995 $850 $725 $600 $500 $400 *$1,375*

GRADING - PPGS™	100%	98%	95%	90%	80%	70%	60%	LAST MSR

* ***Supermatic Citation 10X Custom Shea*** – limited mfg. (approx. 150 pistols annually), hand-built by Bob Shea. Mfg. 1995-disc.

	$1,450	$1,225	$1,075	$875	$775	$650	$550	*$1,650*

SUPERMATIC TOURNAMENT – .22 LR cal., choice of 4 1/2 (disc. 1995), 5 1/2, or 6 3/4 (disc. 1995) in. barrel, matte blue, non-adj. trigger, approx. 44 oz. Mfg. 1995-97, reintroduced 2004 through the custom shop. Disc.

	$895	$750	$650	$550	$475	$375	$300	*$1,025*

SUPERMATIC TROPHY – .17 High Standard (mfg. 2003-2009) or .22 LR cal., 5 1/2 or 7 1/4 in. barrel, blue finish, scope base became standard on 5 1/2 in. barrel in 2000, 2002 for 7 1/4 in. barrel, fixed (disc.) or adj. iron sights, military grips, 10 shot mag., 44 or 46 oz. Mfg. 1994-disc.

	$940	$800	$700	$600	$500	$400	$300	*$1,100*

Add $85 for adj. sights.
Add $135 for 7 1/4 in. barrel.
Subtract approx. 10% if with fixed sights.
Add $450 for .22 Short conversion kit (includes barrel, slide, and 2 mags.). Disc.

VICTOR – .17 High Standard (mfg. 2003-2009) or .22 LR cal., 4 1/2 (disc.) or 5 1/2 in. barrel, blue or parkerized (new 1995, 5 1/2 in. barrel only) finish, military grips, fixed (disc.) or adj. sights, or universal scope base mount (HSUM, blue only, new 1996, standard mfg. currently), 10 shot mag., approx. 45 oz., custom shop only. Mfg.1994-disc.

	$840	$725	$650	$550	$475	$375	$300	*$965*

Add $85 for adj. sights and VR barrel.
Add $50 for open sights (5 1/2 in. barrel only, disc.).
Add $440 for .22 Short conversion kit (includes VR barrel, slide, and 2 mags.). Disc.

* ***Victor 10X*** – factory tuned and individually tested, includes test target signed by the gunsmith, 46 oz. Mfg. 1997-disc.

	$1,225	$1,075	$900	$800	$725	$625	$525	*$1,375*

* ***Victor 10X Shea*** – parkerized finish, 5 1/2 in. barrel only, 150 built by Bob Shea annually, 46 oz. Mfg. 1996-disc.

	$1,450	$1,175	$975	$850	$750	$650	$550	*$1,650*

RIFLES/CARBINES: SEMI-AUTO

HSA-15 – 5.56 NATO, 6x45mm (mfg. 2012-disc.), or .300 AAC Blackout cal., GIO, AR-15 style, A2 configuration, 16 (carbine), or 20 (rifle) in. barrel, A2 flash hider, A2 front sight base with sling swivel, fixed (rifle) or collapsible (carbine) stock, 30 shot mag. Disc.

	$600	$475	$425	$375	$350	$325	$300	*$785*

Add $40 for .300 AAC Blackout cal.
Add $115 for rifle configuration with 20 in. barrel and fixed stock.
Subtract $72 for 6x45mm cal. (mfg. 2012-disc.).

HSA-15 CRUSADER – 5.56 NATO cal., 16 in. M4 barrel with A2 flash hider, aluminum forged upper and lower receivers, 30 shot mag., quad rail in choice of carbine, mid, or rifle length, low profile gas block or Picatinny gas block, M4 style 6-position adj. stock, ambidextrous safety, Ergo pistol grip, ambidextrous single point sling adaptor, black or tan finish. Mfg. 2014-disc.

	$775	$600	$550	$475	$450	$425	$375	*$1,025*

HSA-15 ENFORCER – 5.56 NATO or .300 AAC Blackout cal., 16 in. M4 style barrel with A2 flash hider, 30 shot mag., aluminum forged upper and lower receivers with hardcoat anodized finish, quad rail in choice of carbine, mid, or rifle length, low profile gas block or Picatinny rail, M4 6-position adj. stock, Ergo pistol grip, front and rear flip-up rail mounted sights, ambidextrous single point sling adaptor, black or tan finish. Mfg. 2014-disc.

	$750	$600	$525	$475	$450	$400	$375	*$1,000*

Add $50 for .300 AAC Blackout cal.

HSA-15 NATIONAL MATCH – 5.56 NATO cal., AR-15 style, 20 (National Match) or 24 (Long Range Rifle) in. fluted barrel, includes Knight's military two-stage trigger. Mfg. 2006-2012.

	$1,050	$650	$495	$450	$395	$350	$325	*$1,238*

Add $12 for Long Range Rifle.

HSA - HUNTER COMBO – 5.56 NATO or .300 AAC Blackout cal., GIO, 16 in. barrel, A2 flash hider, interchangeable uppers, optic ready, low profile gas block, Magpul MOE handguard, Magpul polymer rail, 6-position stock, hard anodized black finish. Disc.

	$800	$625	$550	$500	$450	$425	$400	*$1,050*

GRADING - PPGS™	100%	98%	95%	90%	80%	70%	60%	LAST MSR

HSA - LONESTAR – 5.56 NATO, GIO, low profile gas block, 16 in. chrome-lined barrel, A2 flash hider, two-stage trigger, Magpul trigger guard, no sights, free floating 15 in. Diamondhead VRS T-556 handguard with Magpul rail attachment, 6-position Magpul stock. Disc.

	100%	98%	95%	90%	80%	70%	60%	LAST MSR
	$950	$750	$675	$575	$550	$500	$450	*$1,250*

M-4 CARBINE – 5.56 NATO or 9mm Para. cal., 16 in. barrel, fixed A2 (.223 Rem. cal. only, new 2010) or 6-position adj. stock, fixed or adj. sights. Mfg. 2009-disc.

	100%	98%	95%	90%	80%	70%	60%	LAST MSR
	$765	$515	$440	$375	$335	$315	$295	*$880*

Add $35 for adj. sight (disc.).

Add $65 for quad rail with Picatinny gas block.

Add $450 for chrome-lined barrel, free floating quad rails, flip-up sights, flash hider and two-stage match trigger (.223 Rem. cal. only, disc. 2009).

M-4 ENFORCER CARBINE – 5.56 NATO cal., 16 in. barrel with A2 flash hider, SOCOM style 6-position collapsible stock, flip-up battle sights, full-length flat-top receiver, YHM quad rail with smooth sides, Ergo grip, 30 shot mag. Mfg. 2012-2016.

	100%	98%	95%	90%	80%	70%	60%	LAST MSR
	$1,700	$1,350	$1,200	$1,075	$1,000	$925	$850	*$2,275*

HIGH TECH CUSTOMS (HIGH TECH CUSTOM RIFLES)

Current custom manufacturer of bolt action rifles and parts located in Colorado Springs, CO.

RIFLES: BOLT ACTION, CUSTOM

High Tech Custom Rifles manufactures a complete line of custom built, high quality bolt action rifles, including the Shadow (base price $2,200), Shadow II (POR), Falcon Series (base price $2,450), Varmint Hunter (base price $2,200), Alaskan Pro Hunter (base price $2,800), and Mountain Hunter (base price $2,200). They also manufacture and install their own proprietary muzzle brake (60%-80% recoil reduction). Please contact the company directly for more information, including pricing, availability, and a custom quotation.

HILL & MAC GUNWORKS (HMG STURMGEWEHR)

Current semi-auto rifle manufacturer established in 2012, located in Alpharetta, GA.

For individual model listings, please go to BlueBookOfGunValues.com/overflow.

HILL COUNTRY RIFLES (HILL COUNTRY RIFLE COMPANY)

Current custom bolt action rifle and previous pistol manufacturer established in 1996, and located in New Braunfels, TX. Consumer direct sales.

For individual model listings, please go to BlueBookOfGunValues.com/overflow.

HISPANO ARGENTINO FABRICADE AUTOMOVILES SA (HAFDASA)

Previous car manufacturer located in Buenos Aires, Argentina.

This company accepted and sold both commercial and military pistols manufactured by Ballester-Rigaud initially, followed by Ballester-Molina. Please refer to the Ballester-Molina/Rigaud (HAFDASA) listing.

HODGE DEFENSE SYSTEMS INC.

Current AR-15 style carbine and rifle manufacturer located in San Antonio, TX.

Please refer to BlueBookOfGunValues.com to order the *Blue Book of AR-15s & Variations*, available as a book or online subscription.

GEORGE HOENIG, INC.

Previous custom rifle builder located in Emmett, ID until circa 2019. Previously located in Boise, ID.

LONG GUNS

George Hoenig built unique patented rotary round action O/U rifle, shotgun, or combination guns. Opening is achieved by rotating barrels quarter turn to the right, then sliding barrel assembly forward. Because of this, there is no top opening lever. Standard features included double triggers, extractors, rotary safety on stock, and coin finished scroll engraved frame. Prices for a 20, 28 ga. or .410 bore game gun started at $22,500, while the double rifle had a base price of $27,500 (plus additional $2,000 for Mag. cals. up to .450 NE). Combination guns also had a base price of $27,500. During 2009, George Hoenig introduced a four-barrel Vierling (20 ga.x20 ga., .223 Rem., and .22 LR barrels), which had a base price of $50,000.

GRADING - PPGS™	100%	98%	95%	90%	80%	70%	60%	LAST MSR

HOFER-JAGDWAFFEN, PETER

Current custom gun manufacturer and master gunsmith located in Ferlach, Austria. No current U.S. importation.

Peter Hofer manufactures custom order only, best quality rifles (most configurations), combination guns, Drillings, and shotguns (O/U and SxS), all made per individual order. Prices usually start in the $20,000 range, and can go up to over $600,000! Information (including an individualized quotation) can be obtained by contacting Mr. Hofer directly.

HOGAN MANUFACTURING LLC

Previous AR-15 style carbine/rifle manufacturer located in Glendale, AZ from 2011-2016.

Please refer to BlueBookOfGunValues.com to order the *Blue Book of AR-15s & Variations*, available as a book or online subscription.

P.L. HOLEHAN, INC.

Current custom rifle manufacturer located in Tucson, AZ. Consumer direct sales.

P.L. Holehan, Inc. is a custom rifle maker fabricating best quality bolt action rifles only. The company is also known for its integral return to zero scope mounting system. All guns are essentially built per individual custom order and the company should be contacted directly for more information, including special order options/features.

RIFLES: BOLT ACTION

An additional fiberglass stock can be installed on all models except for the African Hunter.

Beginning in 2017, all rifles include a screwless grip cap and screw less sling studs, custom designed by PL Holehan.

AFRICAN HUNTER – various Safari cals., similar to Safari Hunter, except features Dakota Magnum action, 10 1/4 lbs. New 2002.

MSR $21,750	$21,750	$17,000	$14,000	$12,000	$9,250	$8,250	$6,250

Beginning in 2014, all African Hunter models come standard with a fully integral barrel, including quarter rib, barrel lug, barrel band, sling stud, and barrel band front sight.

ALPINE HUNTER – available in most popular hunting cals., features Win. M-70 controlled feed claw extractor, double square bridge action, blind box mag., fiberglass (disc.), Kevlar, or McMillian (new 2005) stock, approx. 6-6 3/4 lbs. New 2000.

MSR $8,250	$8,250	$6,900	$5,900	$5,300	$4,300	$3,500	$2,750

CLASSIC HUNTER – available in most popular hunting cals., No. 3 contour barrel, Win. M-70 controlled feed claw extractor, double square bridge action, premium grade walnut stock, hinged floorplate, blind box or standard box, 7 1/2-8 lbs.

MSR $18,500	$18,500	$15,500	$12,500	$11,000	$9,000	$7,750	$5,250

LIGHTWEIGHT CLASSIC HUNTER – available in most popular hunting cals., features Win. M-70 controlled feed claw extractor, double square bridge action, premium grade checkered walnut stock, customer choice of barrel weight and length, standard or blind box mag., 6 1/2-7 lbs.

MSR $18,500	$18,500	$15,500	$12,500	$11,000	$9,000	$7,750	$5,250

Add $750 for left hand with Dakota 76 short action.

LONG RANGE HUNTER – available in most popular hunting cals., choice of short or long action, features Win. M-70 controlled feed claw extractor, double square bridge action, 26 in. fluted barrel, satin blue or matte Teflon metal finish, laminated stock, 8 3/4 lbs.

MSR $15,500	$15,500	$12,950	$11,000	$9,950	$8,250	$6,700	$5,150

SAFARI HUNTER – various Safari cals., features Win. M-70 controlled feed claw extractor, double square bridge action, premium grade barrel, rear sight with one leaf standing and one leaf folding, front sight bead and detachable sight hood, satin blue metal finish, fiberglass (disc. 2005) or premium walnut stock finished in oil with ebony forend tip, Pachmayr Decelerator pad, hinged floorplate, 9 1/2 lbs.

MSR $21,000	$21,000	$16,500	$13,500	$11,500	$9,000	$8,000	$6,000

Beginning in 2014, all Safari Hunter models come standard with a fully integral barrel, including quarter rib, barrel lug, barrel band, sling stud, and barrel band front sight.

HOLLAND & HOLLAND LTD.

HOLLAND & HOLLAND
Established 1835

Current manufacturer established in 1835 and located in London, England since 1835, with gun showrooms currently located in Dallas, TX and London, England. In February 2021, Beretta Holding acquired Holland & Holland. Beretta Holding plans to preserve the heritage of Holland & Holland's luxury brand in the UK with a high dedication to skilled craftsmanship.

GRADING - PPGS™	100%	98%	95%	90%	80%	70%	60%	LAST MSR

Holland & Holland over the years has justly earned the reputation of producing some of the finest firearms ever manufactured, exhibiting outstanding quality and superior craftsmanship. Most of these fine arms were made to order for the famous, wealthy, or royalty of their day. Because of the individual nature of each firearm, these early guns, as with any high grade item, must be individually appraised.

All H&H long guns are built per individual special order. Orders may be placed directly with the office in England.

The early double rifles were proofed and regulated with the black powder ammunition of their day. These exposed hammer rifles were almost exclusively sold cased with accessories by Holland & Holland, and are seldom encountered today. Purchase of these as well as any high grade firearm should include trusted appraisal.

RIFLES: MODERN

During 2003, H&H released two new large proprietary cartridges. They are: .400 H&H Mag. Belted Rimless (400 grain bullet with 400 H&H headstamp), and .465 H&H Belted Rimless (480 grain bullet with 465 H&H headstamp).

All currently manufactured H&H rifles are priced in English pounds, and 98%-60% values are not included. All older and recently manufactured used rifles are priced in dollars.

BOLT ACTION MAGAZINE RIFLE (BEST QUALITY MAGAZINE RIFLE) – available in most modern cals., Mauser 98 (current mfg.) or Enfield (disc.) action, barrel band with sling loop, single stage trigger, standard wide-V rear sight, one folding leaf and a standard foresight with folding protector, oil finished selected walnut stock with traditional beaded-style cheekpiece, checkered grip, rubber recoil pad or horn buttplate, optional gold oval engraved with initials or crest, 8 lbs. 4 oz.-10 lbs. 4 oz.

The current MSR for all cals. below .375 H&H £49,000.
Add £1,000 for calibers .375 H&H and greater.
Add £4,000 for full length carbine stock.
Add £2,500+ for deluxe grade walnut.
Add £1,600 for takedown.
The values listed represent the standard model without additional options or engraving (of which there are a wide array).

*** *Best Quality Magazine Rifle Older & Recent Mfg.***

	N/A	$17,750	$15,530	$14,025	$11,185	$9,230	$7,100	

Subtract 25% for Enfield action.

CENTENARY MAGAZINE RIFLE – .375 H&H cal., limited mfg. beginning 2011 to commemorate the 100th year of the .375 H&H caliber. Disc.

Retail pricing was not available for this model.

DE LUXE MAGAZINE RIFLE – similar to Best Quality, except with deluxe grade walnut and various engraving options. Very limited mfg. Disc.

There was no standard base MSR on this model - rather, individual options were custom ordered and individually priced.

DOMINION GRADE NO. 2 MODEL DOUBLE RIFLE SxS – various British and American cals., 24-28 in. barrels, sidelock, folding leaf sight, checkered French walnut stock, auto ejectors.

	$22,500	$19,690	$16,875	$15,300	$12,375	$10,125	$7,875	
.400-.500 cal.	$33,750	$28,500	$24,000	$21,000	$18,000	$15,000	$13,125	
larger than .500 cal.	$45,000	$38,000	$32,000	$28,000	$24,000	$20,000	$17,500	

Subtract 25% for extractors.

ROOK RIFLE – .250, .295/.300, .360, .380 black powder cals., single shot, break-open action, various levels of embellishment - Royal Models were made but most Rook rifles were base models with few extra features. Disc.

Values today range from $1,000 (average condition, small cal.) to $3,000 (larger cal., engraving, better wood, perhaps cased).

ROYAL DOUBLE BARREL RIFLE (ROYAL DE LUXE SxS RIFLE) – .275 H&H (disc.), .300 H&H, 9.3mm, .240 H&H (disc.), 7mm, 8mm, .375 H&H, .500/.465 H&H, .577 NE, or .600 NE cal., flanged, belted, or rimless designs, back action and bolstered, hand detachable sidelock design, two triggers, 22-26 in. chopper lump barrels, traditional sling loop, wide V rear sight with one folding leaf, combined moon protector foresight, polished and oil finished select walnut stock, pistol grip and cap box, cheekpiece, recoil pad, optional gold oval engraved with initials or crest, traditional "Royal" scroll engraving pattern, rifle's serial number engraved or inlaid in gold, color hardened or bright finish, built to individual order only with almost any option possible, includes aluminum travel case, 8.75-13 lbs.

Current base MSR for 7mm or 8mm cal. is £153,000.
Current base MSR for .300 H&H or 9.3mm cal. is £154,000.
Current base MSR for .375 H&H or .500/.465 H&H cal. is £165,000.
Current base MSR for .577 NE or .600 NE cal. is £179,000.

GRADING - PPGS™	100%	98%	95%	90%	80%	70%	60%	LAST MSR

* ***H&H .700 Bore SxS Double Rifle (Royal De Luxe Model)*** – .700 H&H cal., similar to Royal De Luxe SxS rifle, except has 3 1/2 in. chambers, 1,000 grain jacketed bullet, 26 in. barrels, 18 lbs. This is the largest caliber rifle available in the world today, and a top-of-the-line model with every refinement.

Current base MSR is £245,000.

* ***SxS Double Rifle Royal Model*** – Disc. 1997.

Last MSR was $115,920.

ROYAL DOUBLE SxS RIFLE - OLDER & RECENT MFG. – similar to No. 2, except has deluxe finish and more engraving.

.300 H&H cal. or less	N/A	N/A	$52,250	$44,000	$39,600	$33,000	$27,500
Up to .375 H&H cal.	N/A	N/A	$65,000	$55,000	$48,000	$40,000	$36,000
Up to .577 NE cal.	N/A	N/A	$92,500	$82,500	$72,500	$60,000	$55,000
.577NE-.600 NE cal.	N/A	N/A	$135,000	$115,000	$100,000	$85,000	$72,500

Add 50% for self-opening action.
Subtract 25% if w/o ejectors.
Subtract 25% if w/o reinforced action.

ROUND ACTION SIDELOCK SxS DOUBLE RIFLE – available in standard flanged cals., rounded back action sidelock with DT, 24 in. chopper lump barrels, polished and oiled select walnut stock, fully rounded pistol grip, steel grip cap, cheekpiece, recoil pad or heelplate, English rose and fine scroll and border engraving, color case hardened or bright finish frame, 8-10 3/4 lbs. New 2004.

Current MSR on this model is £94,000.

SHOTGUNS: O/U

All currently manufactured H&H shotguns are priced in English pounds, and 98%-60% values are not included. All older and recently manufactured used rifles are priced in dollars.

ROYAL OLD MODEL – 12 ga., customer specifications as to barrel length and choke, hand detachable sidelocks, auto ejectors, checkered straight grip stock. Mfg. until 1951. Very rare, very few mfg., but not nearly as desirable as a newer model.

$37,500	$32,000	$28,000	$23,500	$20,000	$18,000	$16,500

Add 5% for single trigger.

ROYAL NEW MODEL – similar to Old Model, with improved narrow action. Mfg. until 1960, fewer than 30 mfg.

$50,000	$42,000	$36,000	$31,000	$27,000	$22,500	$19,000

ROYAL SIDELOCK GAME GUN – 12, 16, 20, 28 (new 1997) ga., or .410 bore (new 1997), 2 3/4 or 3 in. chambers, somewhat similar to New Model, with improved cocking, striking and ejection, slimmer action body, DT, 25 to 30 in. game or VR barrels, 2 3/4 in. chambers, finest checkered walnut straight hand or pistol grip stock, scroll engraved receiver with color case hardened or bright finish, gun's serial number engraved or inlaid in gold, includes aluminum case, 5-7 lbs. 8 oz.

Current base MSR for 12, 16, or 20 ga. is £130,000.
Current base MSR for 28 ga. or .410 bore is £136,000.
Add £27,000 per extra set of barrels.

ROYAL DE LUXE MODEL – similar to Royal Sidelock Game Gun, except choice of more elaborate engraving and exhibition wood.

This model is quoted per individual special order only.

SPORTING MODEL – 12, 16 (disc.), 20, or 28 ga., 2 3/4 or 3 in. chambers, designed with a trigger plate action, Game or Sporting Clays configuration featuring detachable SST mechanism, 25 to 32 in. game or VR barrels, medium scroll engraving, bright finish only. Options on specifications to include screw-in chokes, 12 ga.- 7 1/4-8 lbs., 28 ga.-6 lbs. New 1993.

Current MSR on this model is £55,000.
Add £18,500 per extra set of barrels.
Add £1,250 for color case hardened action with gold name inlay (disc.).

SPORTING DE LUXE MODEL – 12, 20, or 28 ga., 2 3/4 or 3 in. chambers, 25-32 in. game or VR barrels, polished and oil finished select walnut stock with choice of grip styles, finely checkered, optional gold oval engraved with initials or crest, recoil pad or buttplate, scroll and border engraving with Holland & Holland "gold name" inlay, color hardened or bright finish. New 1993.

Current base MSR on this model is £90,000.
Add £22,000 per extra set of barrels.

GRADING - PPGS™	100%	98%	95%	90%	80%	70%	60%	LAST MSR

SHOTGUNS: SxS

Holland & Holland currently manufactures the Royal De Luxe Game Gun and Royal Game Gun (limited mfg.) models in sidelock configuration. In addition to the sidelock models, H&H also manufactured the boxlock models Cavalier, Cavalier De Luxe, Northwood, and Northwood De Luxe until recently. The following values assume standard model with double triggers, game rib, standard walnut, or casing. Additional special order features will add considerable value to the price of a new custom order.

In 1988, Holland & Holland absorbed W & C Scott and manufactured the Chatsworth, Bowood, and Kinmount boxlock models until they were discontinued in late 1990. H&H has phased this trademark out, and more information can be found in the W & C Scott section of this text.

All currently manufactured H&H shotguns are priced in English pounds, and 98%-60% values are not included. All older and recently manufactured used rifles are priced in dollars.

CAVALIER SxS BOXLOCK – 12, 20, or 28 (disc. 1992) ga., best quality model boxlock with scalloped frame, double triggers, ejectors, and case colored receiver. Disc.

$9,500 $7,750 $6,350 $5,500 $4,850 $4,100 $3,500 *$11,175*

Add approx. 10% for 20 ga.
Add approx. 20% for 28 ga.

* ***Cavalier SxS Boxlock De Luxe*** – similar to Cavalier Model, except has deluxe walnut and better engraving. Disc. 1993.

$9,950 $8,000 $6,500 $5,600 $4,950 $4,200 $3,600 *$11,920*

Add approx. 10% for 20 ga.
Add approx. 20% for 28 ga.

CENTENARY SIDELOCK – 12 ga., 2 in. chambers, lightened version of Royal, Badminton, and Dominion grades, mfg. until 1962.

Add 35% over standard 12 ga. chambered guns.

DOMINION GAME GUN – 12, 16, or 20 ga., 25-30 in. barrels, any choke, sidelock, auto ejectors, double triggers, checkered straight grip stock. Disc. 1990.

$6,750 $6,150 $5,650 $4,750 $4,150 $3,650 $3,250

Add 50% for 20 gauge.
Add 100% ejector sidelock model with 2 in. chamber.

NORTHWOOD SxS BOXLOCK – 12, 16 (disc. 1992), 20, or 28 (disc. 1992) ga., 28 or 30 in. barrels, scalloped-case colored receiver, boxlock, auto ejectors, double triggers, border engraving, checkered pistol grip or straight stock. The values shown are for the standard model. Disc. 1993.

$5,950 $5,200 $4,450 $3,850 $3,300 $2,800 $2,300 *$6,705*

Add approx. 10% for 20 ga.
Add approx. 20% for 28 ga.

* ***Northwood SxS Boxlock De Luxe*** – 12, 16, 20, or 28 ga., scalloped-case colored receiver with moderate engraving and select walnut, double triggers. Disc. 1993.

$6,950 $5,950 $5,000 $4,250 $3,500 $3,000 $2,500 *$7,450*

Add approx. 10% for 20 ga.
Add approx. 20% for 28 ga.

ROUND ACTION SIDELOCK – 12 or 20 ga., 2 3/4 in. chambers, rounded frame with back action sidelock, DT, 25-30 in. chopper lump barrels with game rib, scroll and border engraving, polished and oiled select walnut stock with fully rounded straight hand grip, recoil pad or heelplate, color case hardened or bright finish. New 2004.

Current MSR on this model is £60,000.

ROUND ACTION SIDELOCK PARADOX – 12 ga., 2 3/4 or 3 (disc.) in. chambers, rounded back action sidelock design, DT, 28 in. chopper lump barrels with paradox rifled chokes, two-leaf folding rear sight, polished and oil finished select walnut stock with fully rounded straight hand grip, optional gold oval engraved with initials or crest, scroll and borders engraving, bright or case colored finish, approx. 7.25-8 lbs. New 2005.

Current MSR on this model is £115,000.

* ***Round Action Royal Sidelock Paradox*** – 12 ga., 2 3/4 or 3 in. chambers, rounded back action sidelock design, features Royal upgrades, DT, 28 in. chopper lump barrels with paradox rifled chokes, two-leaf folding rear sight regulated for 50 and 100 yards, bright or case colored finish, approx. 7 1/4 or 8 lbs. New 2005.

Current MSR on this model is £130,000.

GRADING - PPGS™	100%	98%	95%	90%	80%	70%	60%	LAST MSR

ROYAL HAMMERLESS EJECTOR SIDELOCK (OLDER & RECENT MFG.) – 12, 16, 20, 28 ga., or .410 bore, non-self (disc.) or self-opening (recent mfg.), customer specifications as to barrel length and chokes, hand detachable sidelocks, stocked in pistol grip or straight style to specifications. Mfg. 1885-disc.

12 ga.	N/A	$42,500	$37,500	$32,500	$27,750	$25,000	$23,000	
20 ga.	N/A	$50,000	$45,000	$40,000	$36,000	$33,000	$30,000	
28 ga.	N/A	$70,000	$65,000	$60,000	$55,000	$50,000	$45,000	
.410 bore	N/A	$85,000	$75,000	$65,000	$60,000	$57,500	$51,000	

Add 15% for self-opening action.
Add 10%-15% if cased with accessories.
Subtract approx. 10%-15% on 12 ga. with 2 1/2 in. chambers.

Values listed are for older, previously manufactured specimens.

ROYAL GAME GUN – 12, 16, 20, 28 ga., or .410 bore, 2 3/4 in. chambers, best quality sidelock self-opening game gun, hand detachable locks, two triggers, manual or automatic safety, 25-32 in. chopper lumb barrels, game rib, finely checkered select walnut stock with straight hand or semi-pistol grip, "Royal" scroll engraving pattern, color hardened or bright finish, gun's serial number engraved or inlaid in gold. Mfg. per individual customer specifications, includes aluminum travel case, 4 3/4-10 3/4 (12 ga.) lbs. The following values reflect most recent factory information. Mfg. 1922 to date.

Current MSR for 12, 16, or 28 ga. is £120,000.
Current MSR for 28 ga. or .410 bore is £125,000.
Add £3,500 for single trigger (mechanical type).
Add £28,600 per extra set of barrels.
Add $3,100 for VR (disc.).

ROYAL DE LUXE GAME GUN – 12, 16, 20, 28 ga., or .410 bore, top-of-the-line sidelock self-opening shotgun. Mfg. per individual customer specifications. Current production.

This model is quoted per individual special order only.

Older mfg. is sometimes referred to as the De Luxe Model.

BADMINTON SIDELOCK – 12, 16, or 20 ga., similar to Royal model, except has traditional rose and scroll engraving and does not have self-opening action. Disc.

12 or 16 ga.	N/A	$25,000	$22,000	$20,000	$18,000	$16,000	$14,000	
20 ga.	N/A	$34,500	$31,000	$28,000	$24,000	$22,000	$20,000	

Add $1,000 for SST.

* ***Badminton Sidelock Game Gun*** – 12 or 20 ga., double or single trigger. Disc. 1988.

	N/A	$31,000	$27,000	$24,000	$21,000	$18,000	$16,000	*$28,000*

RIVIERA SIDELOCK – similar to Badminton model, with two sets of barrels. Mfg. until 1967.

12 or 16 ga.	N/A	$31,000	$28,000	$25,000	$22,000	$19,000	$17,000	
20 ga.	N/A	$33,000	$29,500	$26,000	$23,000	$20,000	$18,000	

SHOTGUNS: SINGLE SHOT

SINGLE BARREL TRAP GUN – 12 ga., 30 or 32 in. full choke barrel, vent. rib, boxlock, auto ejector, Monte Carlo pistol grip stock, pad. Disc.

	N/A	$9,250	$8,000	$6,750	$5,800	$4,750	$3,950	*$28,420*

* ***Single Barrel Trap Guns - Older Mfg.***

Standard Grade	N/A	$4,500	$4,000	$3,250	$2,500	$2,250	$2,000	
De Luxe Grade	N/A	$7,000	$6,250	$5,000	$4,500	$3,750	$3,000	
Exhibition Grade	N/A	$8,950	$7,500	$6,000	$5,500	$5,000	$4,250	

HOLLENBECK GUN COMPANY

Previous manufacturer located in Wheeling, WV circa 1901-1903, and Moundsville, WV circa 1903-1910.

The Hollenbeck Gun Company began circa 1901, moved to Moundsville, WV in 1903 and stayed until they went out of business in 1910. The company name changed in 1905 to The Three Barrel Gun Company (circa 1905-1909), and then to The Royal Gun Company (circa 1909-1910). The company made a total of approx. 1,500 three barrel guns, as well as a few SxS models. After going out of business, an unknown Florida man bought the name and all the assets. He assembled and sold some three barrel guns as late as 1930.

Pricing on these three-barrel shotguns with unique, sculpted recoil shields in average original condition typically ranges from $950 - $1,500 for both damascus (most common) and steel barrels. There were two basic grades - 0 and 1, but there are also shotguns with more elaborate engraving which will command a premium.

Information appears courtesy of AntiqueGuns.com and the Gurnmeister.

GRADING - PPGS™	100%	98%	95%	90%	80%	70%	60%	LAST MSR

HOLLOWAY & NAUGHTON GUNMAKERS

Current trade name of long guns manufactured since 1909 in Leicestershire, England. Consumer direct sales.

For individual model listings, please go to BlueBookOfGunValues.com/overflow.

HOLLOWAY ARMS CO.

Previous manufacturer located in Fort Worth, TX.

Holloway made very few rifles or carbines before operations ceased and existing specimens are scarce.

RIFLES: SEMI-AUTO

HAC MODEL 7 RIFLE – .308 Win. cal., gas operated, 20 in. barrel, adj. front and rear sights, 20 shot mag., side folding stock, right or left-hand action. Mfg. 1984-1985 only.

	$3,750	$3,350	$3,100	$2,800	$2,650	$2,350	$2,000	*$675*

* ***HAC Model 7C Rifle Carbine*** – 16 in. carbine, same general specifications as Model 7. Disc. 1985.

	$3,750	$3,350	$3,100	$2,800	$2,650	$2,350	$2,000	*$675*

Also available from the manufacturer were the Models 7S and 7M (Sniper and Match models).

HOLMES FIREARMS

Previous manufacturer located in Wheeler, AR. Previously distributed by D.B. Distributing, Fayetteville, AR.

PISTOLS: SEMI-AUTO

These pistols were manufactured in very limited numbers, most were in prototype configuration and exhibit changes from gun to gun. These models were open bolt and subject to 1988 federal legislation regulations.

MP-83 – 9mm Para. or .45 ACP cal., 6 in. barrel, walnut stock and forearm, blue finish, 3 1/2 lbs.

	$700	$600	$500	$450	$400	$375	$350	*$450*

Add 10% for deluxe package.

Add 40% for conversion kit (mfg. 1985 only).

MP-22 – .22 LR cal., steel and aluminum construction, 6 in. barrel, similar appearance to MP-83, 2 1/2 lbs. Mfg. 1985 only.

	$395	$360	$320	$285	$250	$230	$210	*$400*

SHOTGUNS

COMBAT 12 – 12 ga., riot configuration, cylinder bore barrel. Disc. 1983.

	$795	$720	$650	$595	$550	$500	$450	*$750*

HONOR DEFENSE LLC

Previous manufacturer of concealed carry pistols located in Gainesville, GA from 2015-circa 2019.

All parts and materials for models manufactured by Honor Defense are 100% American made.

PISTOLS: SEMI-AUTO

Beginning late 2019, Honor Defense started shipping Mossy Oak Overwatch pistols in a limited quantity.

HONOR GUARD COMPACT – 9mm Para. cal., +P rated, 3.2 in. barrel, two 7 and 8 shot ambi magazines, short reset trigger, snag-free sights, custom designed textured grip, rail accessory, serrations that go over the top of slide, ambidextrous slide catch, two sizes of backstraps for a customized fit, various custom finishes, 25 oz. Disc.

Retail pricing was not available for this model.

* ***Honor Guard Compact w/Manual Safety*** – 9mm Para. cal., +P rated, 3.2 in. barrel, two 7 and 8 shot ambi magazines, short reset trigger, snag-free sights, custom designed textured grip, manual thumb safety, rail accessory, serrations that go over the top of slide, ambidextrous slide catch, two sizes of backstraps for a customized fit, various custom finishes, 25 oz. Disc.

Retail pricing was not available for this model.

HONOR GUARD SUB-COMPACT – 9mm Para. cal., +P rated, 3.2 in. barrel, two 7 and 8 shot ambi magazines, short reset trigger, snag-free sights, custom designed textured grip, serrations that go over the top of slide, ambidextrous slide catch, two sizes of backstraps for a customized fit, black, FDE (new 2017), OD Green (new 2017), or Mahogany (new 2017) finish, 22 oz. Mfg. late 2015-2016.

	$450	$395	$365	$335	$300	$275	$250	*$499*

Add $230 for Crimson Trace laser.

GRADING - PPGS™	100%	98%	95%	90%	80%	70%	60%	LAST MSR

* ***Honor Guard Sub-Compact Long Slide*** – 9mm Para. cal., +P rated, SFO, 3.8 in. barrel, ambidextrous slide catch and mag. release, stainless steel chassis system, short reset trigger, iron sights, custom textured grip with two backstrap options, manual thumb safety (optional), integrated rail for attachments, custom serrations. Mfg. late 2015-disc.

$450	$395	$365	$335	$300	$275	$250	*$499*

HONOR GUARD SUB-COMPACT WITH FIST FRAME – 9mm Para. cal., +P rated, FIST (Firearm with Integrated Standoff) frame, 3.2 in. barrel, two 7 and 8 shot ambi magazines, short reset trigger, snag-free sights, custom designed textured grip, serrations that go over the top of slide, ambidextrous slide catch, two sizes of backstraps for a customized fit, black, FDE (new 2017), OD Green (new 2017), or Mahogany (new 2017) finish, 22 oz. Mfg. late 2015-disc.

$450	$395	$365	$335	$300	$275	$250	*$499*

HONOR GUARD SUB-COMPACT WITH MANUAL SAFETY – 9mm Para. cal., +P rated, 3.2 in. barrel, two 7 and 8 shot ambi magazines, short reset trigger, snag-free sights, custom designed textured grip, manual safety, serrations that go over the top of slide, ambidextrous slide catch, two sizes of backstraps for a customized fit, black, Acid Green, Battleship Gray, FDE, Mahogany, OD Green, Electric Blue, Enigma Blue, or Turquois (all proprietary colors new late 2017), 22 oz. Mfg. late 2015-disc.

$450	$395	$365	$335	$300	$275	$250	*$499*

* ***Honor Guard Sub-Compact With Manual Safety Long Slide*** – 9mm Para. cal., similar to Honor Guard Sub-Compact with Manual Safety, +P rated, except also features a long slide. Mfg. late 2015-disc.

$450	$395	$365	$335	$300	$275	$250	*$499*

HOPKINS & ALLEN ARMS COMPANY, 1902-1914

Previous manufacturer located in Norwich, CT. H&A started their firearms business in 1867, manufacturing percussion revolvers.

Before 1870, they were producing rimfire cartridge guns and eventually centerfire handguns and long guns. Prior to 1896, H&A guns were marked "HOPKINS & ALLEN MANUFG. CO. NORWICH CONN." or other private trade names, including Merwin, Hulbert & Company. Hopkins & Allen guns are about equally priced with Stevens, N.R. Davis, Crescent Firearms Co., etc. There are many exceptions due to the numerous limited production guns, examples of which are the AA GRADE double shotgun and the "PARROT BEAK" Derringer. Hopkins & Allen also manufactured firearms which were not described in their catalogs. Compiled from Hopkins & Allen catalogs by Charles E. Carder.

HANDGUNS

Most H&A handguns were nickel plated, with blue finish originally costing $.50 extra, grips were hard rubber, wood or pearl. Some had engraving from low to very good quality. Revolver barrel lengths varied from 1 3/4-6 in. Calibers were .22 rimfire (.22 S, L, or LR) up to .38-40 WCF. Specific calibers have not been listed in this section.

FOREHAND MODEL TOP BREAK – .32 cal., top break, double action, five shot.

$190	$160	$140	$120	$100	$85	$75

FOREHAND MODEL TOP BREAK HAMMERLESS – similar to above except hammerless. (This model was offered in large and small frame).

$190	$160	$140	$120	$100	$85	$75

FOREHAND MODEL LARGE FRAME W/FULL HAMMER – large frame as above in .32 and .38 centerfire cal. with full hammer or "bobbed" hammer.

$190	$160	$140	$120	$100	$85	$75

FOREHAND MODEL SOLID FRAME – solid frame and hard rubber grips, otherwise as above in small frame.

$170	$140	$120	$100	$85	$75	$65

FOREHAND MODEL FOLDING HAMMER – similar to above models, with "folding hammer." .22 rimfires were 7 shot, while .32 and .38 centerfires were 5 shot. By 1909, the Forehand logo was dropped from these revolvers.

$295	$265	$235	$195	$170	$150	$130

H&A NEW MODEL AUTOMATIC HAMMER REVOLVER – similar to top break with hammer, produced in small and large frame, in .22 rimfire, .32 and .38 centerfire cal.

$170	$140	$120	$100	$85	$75	$65

H&A SOLID FRAME – .32 and .38 centerfire cal., 5 shot, double action, hammer or "bobbed" hammer.

$175	$140	$120	$100	$85	$70	$55

GRADING - PPGS™	100%	98%	95%	90%	80%	70%	60%	LAST MSR

H&A XL MODEL – similar to above in .22, .32 and .38 cal.

	$160	$140	$120	$100	$85	$70	$55	

H&A RANGE MODEL – .22, .32 and .38 cal., solid frame, loading gate on right side, wood target style grips, single or double action (two models, large and small frames).

	$200	$175	$140	$120	$100	$85	$70	

H&A TRIPLE ACTION SAFETY POLICE REVOLVER – .22, .32 and .38 cal., top break with newly designed locking mechanism, hard rubber or pearl grips (considered to be one of the best designed breaktops in its time). Other options for this model included hammerless, engraved, and wood target or pearl grips.

	$375	$340	$310	$275	$235	$200	$185	

H&A NEW VEST POCKET DERRINGER – .22 Short rimfire cal., single shot, tip up, single action, 3 1/2 in. overall length, folding trigger, blue or nickel finish, wood or pearl grips with golden monograms. This model was first listed about 1910 and known as the "Parrot Beak." It is estimated that less than one thousand were produced, and they are very rare.

	$2,375	$2,100	$1,800	$1,550	$1,250	$950	$650	

H&A NEW MODEL TARGET PISTOL – .22 rimfire cal., single shot top break with the same new locking mechanism as the Safety Police Revolver, wood target grips with golden monograms, blue finish and 6, 8, or 10 in. barrels.

	$565	$495	$440	$375	$325	$285	$250	

H&A NEW MODEL SKELETON STOCK TARGET PISTOL – similar to above, with rounded hard rubber grips with logo, detachable "skeleton metal stock", 18 in. barrel, and blue finish.

	$850	$775	$675	$600	$550	$500	$465	

RIFLES

Hopkins & Allen started building "falling block" rifles circa 1887-1914 with the buy-out of the Baystate Arms Company. Most commonly seen is the "Junior" model, known after 1902 as 922, 925, and 932. These numbers were in reference to the catalog numbers, not model numbers. In the very late 1890s or early 1900s, the Number 722, 822, and 832 rifles were added. In 1906, a "bolt action" repeater was added to their line, followed in 1909 by a "bolt action" single shot "military". Specific calibers have not been listed in this section.

Add $60-$75 for Lyman tang sights on the following models.

NUMBER 922 – .22 cal. rimfire, round barrel, falling block, lever operated.

	$310	$245	$195	$195	$165	$125	$110	

NUMBER 925 – similar to above in .25 cal. rimfire.

	$390	$310	$245	$195	$150	$110	$95	

NUMBER 932 – similar to above in .32 cal. rimfire.

	$310	$245	$195	$150	$110	$95	$80	

NUMBER 938 – similar to above in .38 S&W centerfire.

	$440	$350	$285	$225	$200	$175	$150	

NUMBER 1922 – similar to above in .22 cal. rimfire with octagon bbl.

	$310	$250	$200	$180	$165	$150	$125	

NUMBER 1932 – similar to above in .32 cal. rimfire.

	$310	$250	$200	$165	$125	$110	$90	

NUMBER 2922 – similar to above in .22 cal. rimfire, with checkering.

	$420	$335	$265	$225	$195	$175	$150	

NUMBER 2932 – similar to above in .32 cal. rimfire.

	$420	$335	$265	$225	$195	$175	$150	

NUMBER 3922 – similar to above in .22 cal. rimfire, "SCHUETZEN RIFLE", nickeled Swiss buttplate, octagon barrel (Schuetzen rifles in good cond. are somewhat rare).

	$775	$620	$495	$450	$400	$365	$325	

NUMBER 3925 – similar to above in .25-20 WCF (this caliber rifle is more rare than the .22 cal. rimfire).

	$1,010	$810	$650	$600	$550	$500	$450	

NUMBER 44XL – chambered for the .44XL shotshell, similar to Number 922, except has smoothbore (referred to as "TAXIDERMIST'S" or "LADIES GUN").

	$530	$430	$350	$325	$275	$235	$200	

NUMBER 722 – .22 cal. rimfire, rolling block, thumb operated.

	$300	$240	$195	$165	$125	$110	$90	

GRADING - PPGS™	100%	98%	95%	90%	80%	70%	60%	LAST MSR

SCOUT MILITARY RIFLE – similar to above with military style stock and with a "Bonneted Indian" stamped on the left side of frame (these are somewhat rare).

$505 $405 $325 $285 $250 $200 $175

NUMBER 822 – .22 cal. rimfire, rolling block, lever operated.

$300 $240 $195 $175 $150 $125 $100

NUMBER 832 – .32 cal. rimfire, otherwise similar to Model 822 (this model was offered first with "pig tail" type levers and later with "loop" type levers. The "loop" levers are somewhat rare).

$350 $280 $225 $200 $175 $150 $125

NUMBER 4922 – .22 rimfire cal., bolt action, repeater.

$260 $205 $165 $135 $120 $100 $80

NUMBER 5022 – similar to above with deluxe checkering.

$340 $270 $215 $175 $150 $135 $100

MILITARY RIFLE – similar to above, except single shot with military style stock and sling (in good condition, these are somewhat rare).

$490 $395 $315 $250 $225 $200 $185

NOISELESS – .22 rimfire, similar to the Number 922, except for checkered wood and the addition of a noise suppressor attached to the muzzle, by means of mating threads inside of suppressor and outside of barrel. The machining/threading is so precise that it is difficult to recognize the suppressor. The front sight is attached to a dovetail slot in the suppressor. These rifles are listed under the National Firearms Act of 1934 and must have proper licensing. Very rare.

$690 $625 $575 $500 $450 $395 $325

SHOTGUNS: SxS

Hopkins & Allen purchased Forehand Arms Co. and W.H. Davenport and continued to produce their line of firearms, and after a few years dropped the Forehand name. In 1902, they offered the Forehand double boxlocks with or without outside hammers. Most models were offered in 12, 16 & 20 gauge. Sidelocks were added 1906-09. In 1902, the AA GRADE, a very high quality boxlock, was offered for $100 to $125. It had fine damascus barrels, straight grip, plain or automatic ejectors, fine wood, and engraving, and was competitive with some Remingtons, L.C. Smiths, Bakers and other fine guns of that era. This gun was very short lived and today is rare. One feature found on all H&A double barrel guns is the "rib extension" or "doll's head."

BOXLOCK – Anson & Deeley type frame, damascus, twist, and steel barrels.

$315 $275 $235 $195 $160 $130 $95

BOXLOCK – similar to above, except with outside hammers.

$315 $275 $235 $195 $160 $130 $95

SIDELOCK – hammerless, damascus, twist, and steel barrels.

$315 $275 $235 $195 $160 $130 $115

SIDELOCK – similar to above, except with outside hammers.

$315 $275 $235 $195 $160 $130 $95

SHOTGUNS: SINGLE SHOT

H&A produced a "falling block" shotgun in most gauges circa 1887-early 1900s. Falling Blocks (FBs) in 12 ga. were built on heavy frames with the 20 and 16 gauges sharing a medium frame. Prior to 1902, some FBs were chambered for .45-70 shotshells and, today, these are rare if in good condition. From the 1890s through 1914, 38XL, 44XL shotshell guns were periodically offered in the Junior frame. After 1902, "tip-over" single shotguns were offered in Forehand designs and, later, the Davenport designs.

FALLING BLOCK – lever operated, outside hammer.

$275 $235 $210 $180 $160 $145 $125

BOXLOCK – with outside hammer, damascus, twist, and steel barrels.

$190 $170 $150 $130 $110 $95 $80

BOXLOCK – hammerless, top safety.

$190 $170 $150 $130 $110 $95 $80

GOOSE GUNS – outside hammer, 8, 10, or 12 ga., were offered with barrels up to 40 inches long.

$250 $225 $190 $170 $150 $135 $115

GRADING - PPGS™	100%	98%	95%	90%	80%	70%	60%	LAST MSR

"SAFETY SINGLE GUN" – engraved with outside hammer and top safety. Was offered in 1911 and recommended for trap shooting for $15.00.

	$250	$225	$195	$175	$155	$140	$125	

HORIZON FIREARMS

Current manufacturer of custom long range bolt action rifles, located in College Station, TX.

For individual model listings, please go to BlueBookOfGunValues.com/overflow.

HORSLEY, THOMAS

Previous gunmaker circa 1830-1956, and located in Doncaster and York, U.K.

Thomas Horsley began his business circa 1830 in his hometown of Doncaster, but returned to York circa 1834. York had a large army base, which offered great commercial opportunity for the company. By the 1860s, Horsley was making best long guns with distinctive patented features. By the 1880s, due to the advent of the hammerless gun and social changes, the guns became less distinctive, but there was production of an unusual hammerless gun. Thomas, who died in 1882, handed the business off to his son, also named Thomas, who ran the business until his death in 1915. Continuing economic pressures had the firm retailing bicycles in the 1890s, and at the turn-of-the-century, a brief flirtation with a motor car of their own design. After WWI, fewer guns were sold, and the ones that were made were no longer custom best guns. The company moved again before World War II, and moved to another location in York in 1933. Thomas Jr., who continued running the business almost until his death, also had a son named Thomas. Thomas III and three of his four brothers continued running the business between them until Thomas III's death in 1954. Tony Horsley briefly ran the business until it finally closed down in 1959. Records for the company have survived, but unfortunately, the quality of the ledger descriptions is not good and somewhat sparse.

Thomas Horsely guns, like many guns made by formerly bespoke manufacturers, should be evaluated individually for desirability, features/options, eye appeal, and collectibility. Most guns were bought by active sportsmen and women to be used in the field. Values of pre-WWI guns will be more than post-WWI manufacture.

Some information appears courtesy of David J. Baker, author of Thomas Horsley - Gunmaker of York, Boothroyd's Directory of British Gunmakers 1850-Present Day by Geoffrey Boothroyd & Susan M. Boothroyd, and British Gunmakers Volume Two by Nigel Brown.

HORTON, LEW, DIST. CO.

Please refer to the Lew Horton Dist. Co. listing in the L section.

HOULDING PRECISION FIREARMS

Previous AR-15 style firearm manufacturer located in Madera, CA until 2015.

Please refer to BlueBookOfGunValues.com to order the *Blue Book of AR-15s & Variations*, available as a book or online subscription.

HOUSTON ARMORY

Previous AR-15 style firearm and bolt action rifle manufacturer located in Stafford, TX until 2015.

RIFLES

Houston Armory manufactured a line of AR-15 style semi-auto rifles, including the .440 Hash (last MSR was $3,485), .50 Beowulf (last MSR was $3,485), H300IC (last MSR was $3,085), H16IC (last MSR was $3,085), H308IC (last MSR was $4,085), and HASPR16 (last MSR was $2,890). Houston Armory also offered a bolt action rifle (last MSR range was $1,900-$2,900), as well as a complete line of suppressors.

HOWA

Current manufacturer established in 1967, located in Tokyo, Japan. Howa sporting rifles are currently imported beginning Oct. 1999 by Legacy Sports International, LLC, located in Reno, NV. Previously located in Alexandria, VA. Previously imported until 1999 by Interarms/Howa, located in Alexandria, VA, Weatherby (Vanguard Series only), Smith & Wesson (pre-1985), and Mossberg (1986-1987).

RIFLES: BOLT ACTION

Howa also manufactures barreled actions in various configurations - these are available exclusively through Brownells. During mid-2011, detachable magazines became available for all Model 1500s.

GRADING - PPGS™	100%	98%	95%	90%	80%	70%	60%	LAST MSR

HOWA .300 BLACKOUT RIFLE – .300 AAC Blackout cal.,16 1/4 in. heavy threaded capped barrel, H.A.C.T. trigger, HTI synthetic stock in black or OD Green, ORYX chassis in FDE, grey, or OD green finish, 3-position safety, short bolt throw. New 2019.

MSR $639	$550	$475	$400	$375	$300	$250	$200	

HOWA/CHRISTENSEN CARBON FIBER RIFLE – .204 Ruger, .223 Rem., .22-250 Rem., .243 Win., or .308 Win. cal., 24 in. Christensen carbon fiber barrel, 4 or 5 shot mag., pepper colored TH Varminter stock, includes green Howa soft case, 8 lbs. Limited production and importation 2007-2008.

	$1,675	$1,465	$1,255	$1,140	$920	$755	$585	*$1,923*

Add $153 for Nikko Stirling Night Eater scope package.

LIGHTNING WOODGRAIN – .243 Win., .270 Win., .30-06, .308 Win., or 7mm Rem. Mag. cal., features lightweight Carbolite synthetic stock with simulated wood grain and checkering, 22 in. barrel, 5 shot mag., no sights, 7 1/2 lbs. Imported 1994 only.

	$450	$395	$335	$305	$245	$200	$155	*$537*

Add $19 for 7mm Rem. Mag. cal.

REALTREE CAMO RIFLE – .270 Win. or .30-06 (disc. 1993) cal., 22 in. barrel, 5 shot mag., monobloc receiver, drilled and tapped, thumb safety, entire rifle is coated with a Realtree brown leaf camo pattern, no sights, 8 lbs. Imported 1993-94.

	$495	$435	$370	$335	$270	$225	$175	*$620*

MODEL 1500+/1500 LIGHTNING – various cals., lightweight variation of the Model 1500 Hunter featuring heavy (new 2007) or lightweight regular or Carbolite (disc.) black synthetic stock with cheekpiece and pressed checkering or Realtree camo (new 2005), 22 or 24 in. barrel, no sights, 3 or 5 shot mag., blue or stainless steel, approx. 7-7.6 lbs. Imported 1988-1991, reimported 1993-2008.

	$435	$380	$325	$295	$240	$195	$150	*$506*

Add $21 for standard Mag. cals. or $27 for WSM cals.
Add $187 for camo stock and stainless steel barrel.
Add $77 for camo stock (scope not included).
Add $99 for heavy blue barrel w/camo stock.
Add $223 for heavy stainless barrel w/camo stock.
Add $156 for scope package with Leupold VX-I scope.

The Model 1500+ was introduced during 2005, and featured a three position safety.

During 2007, this model was supplied with a Nikko Sterling scope with rings and bases (black polymer stock only).

MODEL 1500+/1500 SUPREME – available in various standard and Mag. cals. between .22-250 Rem. - .338 Win. Mag., 22 or 24 in. barrel, 3 or 5 shot mag., choice of JRS Classic, black (Varminter only), Thumbhole Sporter, Varminter, or Thumbhole Varminter stock configuration available in either pepper or nutmeg finish, blue metal finish or stainless steel, 8-9.9 lbs. Importation began 2003.

The Model 1500+ was introduced during 2005, and features a three position safety.

* ***Model 1500+/1500 Supreme JRS Classic*** – standard stock configuration, w/o sights, 8 lbs. Imported 2003-2006.

	$515	$450	$385	$350	$285	$230	$180	*$646*

Add $109 for stainless steel. Add $29 for Mag. cals.

* ***Model 1500+/1500 Supreme Varminter*** – .204 Ruger (new 2006), .22-250 Rem., .223 Rem., .243 Win. (new 2005) or .308 Win. cal., 24 in. bull barrel, blue or stainless steel, nutmeg, pepper, or black synthetic (disc. 2008) stock with raised comb and rollover cheekpiece, vented beavertail forend, 9.3 lbs. Imported 2003-2009.

	$615	$540	$460	$420	$340	$275	$215	*$679*

Add $100 for stainless steel.

* ***Model 1500+/1500 Supreme Varminter Thumbhole*** – similar to Supreme Varminter, except has thumbhole stock configuration, nutmeg (disc. 2011) or woodland laminate stock, grooved forend, Picatinny rail, approx. 10 lbs. Imported 2003-2013.

	$695	$600	$525	$475	$375	$315	$250	*$813*

Add $105 for stainless steel.

* ***Model 1500+/1500 (Supreme) Thumbhole Sporter*** – similar to Thumbhole Varminter, except has 22 in. barrel, nutmeg (blue only, disc. 2010), woodland, or pepper (stainless only, disc. 2009) colored laminated stock, no sights or Picatinny rail, sporterized forend, 7.6 lbs. Imported 2003-2013.

	$650	$575	$495	$450	$350	$295	$225	*$773*

Add $126 for stainless steel. Add $66 for standard Mag. cals. or $60 for WSM (disc. 2008) cals.

GRADING - PPGS™	100%	98%	95%	90%	80%	70%	60%	LAST MSR

MODEL 1500+/1500 ULTRALIGHT – .22-250 Rem., .223 Rem., .243 Win., .308 Win. (new 2003), or 7mm-08 Rem. (new 2003) cal., 20 in. barrel, short bolt throw, non-glare blue, blue/black metal, or stainless steel finish, laminated hardwood stock with black textured coating, 5 shot mag., w/o sights, Youth model with 12 5/8 in. LOP introduced 2003, 6.4 lbs. Imported 2002-2008.

	$485	$425	$365	$330	$265	$220	$170	*$599*

Add $149 for stainless steel (.308 Win. or 7mm-08 cals. only).
Subtract $16 for Nikko scope package.

The Model 1500+ was introduced during 2005, and featured a three position safety.

MODEL 1500 ALPINE MOUNTAIN RIFLE/PACKAGE – .243 Win., .308 Win., 6.5 Creedmoor, or 7mm-08 Rem. cal., 20 in. barrel, H.A.C.T. two-stage trigger, Ammo Boost detachable magazine system, Pachmayr Decelerator buttpad, sling swivel studs, High Tech lightweight stock with OD Green/black finish, available with or w/out scope package, gray Cerakote treatment on all metal parts, 5.7-6.7 lbs. Imported 2015-2018.

	$1,000	$865	$725	$650	$525	$450	$350	*$1,188*

Add $44 for detachable magazine kit.
Add $116 for Nikko Stirling Panamax 3-9x40 scope (new 2016).
Add $456 for Vortex Viper 3-9x42 scope and Talley rings (Alpine Mountain Rifle Package), mfg. 2015 only.

MODEL 1500 ARCHANGEL – .223 Rem. or .308 Win. cal., 20 or 24 in. standard, fluted, or threaded barrel, 10 shot, two-stage H.A.C.T. trigger, Archangel AA1500 precision stock (ambidextrous gooseneck-style with palm swell), click adjustable cheek riser and LOP, secure grip storage compartment, 3-pos. safety, black finish. Imported 2016 only.

	$775	$680	$580	$525	$425	$350	$285	*$915*

Add $44 for threaded barrel or $60 for fluted barrel.
Add $215 for Diamond Long Range 30mm 4-16x50 scope and 10 shot detachable mag.

MODEL 1500 AUSTRALIAN PRECISION CHASSIS (APC) – .223 Rem. (disc. 2019), .243 Win. (disc. 2019), .308 Win. Mag., 6mm Creedmoor (disc. 2019), 6.5 Creedmoor, or .22-250 Rem. (disc. 2015) cal., 16 1/4 (new 2020), 20 (disc.), 24, or 26 (disc.) in. heavy threaded barrel, 10 shot detachable mag., LUTH-AR MBA-4 buttstock with LOP adjustment, adj. comb, 6-pos. buffer tube, two-stage H.A.C.T. trigger, Hogue overmolded grip, aluminum chassis with free floating M-LOK handguard, integrated Picatinny rail, 3-pos. safety, black, Multicam/FDE (disc.), American Flag Red/White/Blue (new 2018), or American Flag Grayscale (new 2018) finish, 10.5-12 lbs. New 2018.

MSR $1,549	$1,300	$1,150	$1,000	$900	$700	$600	$450	

Add $50 for 26 in. barrel (disc.).
Add $150 Multicam/FDE finish (disc.).
Add $290 for Nikko Stirling Diamond Long Range 4-16x50 scope combo package.

MODEL 1500 AXIOM STANDARD – .204 Ruger, .22-250 Rem., .223 Rem., .243 Win., .25-06 Rem., .270 Win., .308 Win., .300 Win. Mag., .338 Win. Mag., or 7mm Rem. Mag. cal., 22 blue barrel, 4 or 5 shot mag., choice of black aluminum (disc. 2008) or camo synthetic adj. Blackhawk/Knoxx stock (with cheekpiece allowing LOP to be adjusted from 11 1/2 to 15 1/2 in.), pistol grip, patented recoil reduction. Mfg. 2007-2009.

	$625	$545	$470	$425	$345	$280	$220	*$699*

Add $20 for Mag. cals.
Add $120 for rifle package with Nikko scope, rings and bases.
Add $360 for black aluminum stock (disc. 2008).

MODEL 1500 AXIOM VARMINTER – various cals., 20 or 24 in. heavy blue barrel, 4 or 5 shot mag., choice of black aluminum (disc. 2008), black, green (mfg. 2010-2012), Sand (mfg. 2010-2012), or Desert camo (new 2010) synthetic, or camo synthetic adj. Blackhawk/Knoxx stock (with cheekpiece allowing LOP to be adjusted from 11 1/2 to 15 1/2 in.), pistol grip, patented recoil reduction, Picatinny top rail, approx. 10 lbs. Mfg. 2007-2014.

	$775	$680	$580	$525	$425	$350	$285	*$915*

Add $150 for Kings Desert Shadow camo stock.
Add $360 for black aluminum stock (disc. 2008).

* ***Model 1500 Axiom Varminter Package*** – various cals., 20 or 24 in. heavy blue barrel, 4 or 5 shot mag., choice of black aluminum (disc. 2008), black, green (mfg. 2010-2012), Sand (mfg. 2010-2012), or King's Desert Shadow camo (new 2010) synthetic, or camo synthetic adj. Blackhawk/Knoxx stock (with cheekpiece allowing LOP to be adjusted from 11 1/2 to 15 1/2 in.), pistol grip, patented recoil reduction, Picatinny top rail, includes Nikko Stirling Nighteater 4-16x44 scope, rings, and a one-piece base, approx. 10 lbs. Mfg. 2007-2014.

	$900	$785	$665	$585	$475	$400	$325	*$1,065*

Add $153 for King's Desert Shadow camo finish.

GRADING - PPGS™	100%	98%	95%	90%	80%	70%	60%	LAST MSR

MODEL 1500 CLASSIC LAMINATE THUMBHOLE SPORTER – .22-250 Rem., .204 Ruger, .223 Rem., .243 Win., 6.5x55mm, .25-06 Rem., .270 Win., .30-06, .308 Win., .300 Win. Mag., or 7mm Rem. Mag. cal., blue finish, 22 or 24 in. #2 contour blue barrel, two-stage match trigger, nutmeg laminate stock with large thumbhole, full pistol grip with palm swell, raised cheekpiece, 3-pos. safety, forged one-piece bolt with two locking lugs, sling swivel studs, approx. 8 1/2 lbs. Mfg. mid-2013-2014.

	$650	$575	$495	$450	$360	$295	$225	*$773*

Add $28 for Mag. cals.

* ***Model 1500 Classic Laminate Thumbhole Sporter Stainless*** – .22-250 Rem., .204 Ruger, .223 Rem., .243 Win., 6.5x55mm, .25-06 Rem., .270 Win., .30-06, .308 Win., .300 Win. Mag., or 7mm Rem. Mag. cal., similar to Classic Laminate Thumhole Sporter, except features 22 or 24 in. #2 contour stainless steel barrel, pepper laminate stock with large thumbhole, 8 1/2 lbs. Mfg. mid-2013-2014.

	$750	$650	$575	$515	$415	$350	$275	*$900*

Add $18 for Mag. cals.

MODEL 1500 CLASSIC LAMINATE VARMINTER – .204 Ruger (disc. 2015), .22-250 Rem., .223 Rem., .243 Win., .308 Win., or 6.5 Creedmoor (new 2016) cal., short action, 24 in. blue, stainless steel (disc. 2015), or Cerakote Gray (new 2016) barrel, two-stage match trigger, nutmeg or pepper (stainless only) laminate stock with full pistol grip and palm swell, with or without thumbhole, dual sling swivel studs, 3-pos. safety, beavertail forend with large cooling vents, forged one-piece bolt with two locking lugs, approx. 10 lbs. Mfg. 2012-2016.

	$725	$615	$525	$475	$375	$315	$250	*$869*

Add $116 for Cerakote Gray finish on barrel (new 2016).
Add $105 for stainless steel barrel (disc. 2015).

MODEL 1500 CUSTOM – .300 Win. Mag. or .300 WSM cal., 22 or 24 (.300 Win. Mag. cal. only) in. barrel, black polymer or laminate wood in either the Classic JRS or thumbhole configuration, 3 shot mag., blue (.300 Win. Mag. cal. only) or stainless steel barrel and action, 7.6-8.1 lbs. Imported 2002-2004.

	$775	$680	$580	$525	$425	$350	$270	*$858*

Add $30 for JRS nutmeg finish stock and blued finish.
Add $102 for JRS laminate stock.
Add $131 for thumbhole laminate stock in pepper finish.

MODEL 1500 FOXY WOODS RIFLE – .204 Ruger (new 2017), .223 Rem., .22-250 Rem., .243 Win., .25-06 Rem., 6.5 Creedmoor (new 2017), .270 Win., .308 Win., or .30-06 cal., 22 in. standard barrel, 13.87 in. LOP, features Foxy Woods pink camo finish, 7.15 lbs. Mfg. 2015-2017.

	$560	$490	$420	$380	$310	$250	$200	*$667*

* ***Model 1500 Foxy Woods Rifle Lightweight*** – .204 Ruger (new 2017), .223 Rem., .22-250, .243 Win., 6.5 Creedmoor (new 2017), .308 Win., or 7mm-08 Rem. cal., 20 in. lightweight barrel, 13.87 in. LOP, Foxy Woods pink camo finish, 7.15 lbs. Mfg. 2015-2017.

	$585	$510	$440	$400	$325	$275	$215	*$695*

* ***Model 1500 Foxy Woods Youth Rifle*** – .223 Rem., .204 Ruger, .22-250, .243 Win., 6.5 Creedmoor, .308 Win., or 7mm-08 Rem. cal., 20 in. lightweight barrel, 12.62 in. LOP, features Foxy Woods Pink camo finish, 6.95 lbs. Mfg. 2015-2017.

	$600	$525	$450	$410	$325	$275	$210	*$724*

Add $58 for scope combo package.

MODEL 1500 FULL DIP – 6mm Creedmoor (mfg. 2019 only), 6.5 Creedmoor, or .308 Win. cal., 24 in. heavy threaded barrel, 10 shot mag., includes rings and Nikko Stirling Gamepro 4-16x44 scope, full dipped Favlos or Kratos camo on barrel and stock, also available with Kryptek Highlander finish, 10 lbs. Importation began 2019.

MSR $899	$765	$675	$575	$525	$425	$350	$275	

MODEL 1500 GRS – .223 Rem., .243 Win., .308 Win. Mag., 6mm Creedmoor., 6.5 Creedmoor, .22-250 Rem. cal., 20, 24, or 26 in. No. 6 threaded barrel, 10 shot detachable mag., ergonomic pistol grip, GRS Berserk stock with pillar bedded fiberglass Durethan w/adj. LOP and cheekpiece, black finish, 9.8 -10 lbs. Mfg. 2018-disc.

	$1,150	$925	$800	$700	$600	$500	$400	*$1,249*

Add $30 for 20 or 24 in. barrel.

MODEL 1500 GAMEKING – .223 Rem., .22-250 Rem., .243 Win., .25-06 Rem., .270 Win., .30-06, .308 Win., 6.5 Creedmoor, .300 Win. Mag., 7mm-08 Rem., or 7mm Rem. cal., short or long action, 22 or 24 in. No. 2 barrel, 3, 4, or 5 shot mag., includes Nikko Stirling 3.5-10x44mm scope, black or green finish, 9.4-9.6 lbs. Mfg. 2018 only.

	$595	$525	$450	$400	$365	$335	$295	*$669*

Add $20 for 24 in. barrel.

GRADING - PPGS™	100%	98%	95%	90%	80%	70%	60%	LAST MSR

MODEL 1500 HOGUE GAMEPRO 2 – 6.5 Creedmoor or .308 Win. cal., 22 in. stainless steel threaded barrel, Nikko Stirling Gamepro scope included, Hogue pillar bedded stock, recoil pad, pistol grip, 7.8 lbs. Importation began 2020.

MSR $769	$655	$570	$490	$445	$360	$295	$230	

MODEL 1500 HCR (HOWA CHASSIS RIFLE) – .223 Rem. (disc. 2017), .243 Win., 6mm Creedmoor (new 2018), 6.5 Creedmoor, .300 Win. Mag., or .308 Win. cal., Howa 1500 action, 20, 24, or 26 (6.5 Creedmoor and .308 only) in. standard (disc.) or heavy barrel (threading became standard during 2018), 5 (.300 Win. Mag. cal. only) or 10 shot mag., aluminum chassis with free float M-LOK forend, two-stage H.A.C.T. trigger, fully adj. LUTH-AR MBA-3 buttstock, adj. comb, Ergo grip, 3-position safety, black, Multicam, or Kryptek Highlander (new 2018) anodized chassis/forend, blue or Cerakote FDE barrel finish, black or FDE furniture, 9.6-10.2 lbs. New mid-2016.

MSR $1,379	$1,250	$1,000	$900	$800	$700	$600	$395	

Add $50 for 26 in. threaded barrel.
Subract $50 if w/o threaded barrel.
Add $170 for Multicam chassis/forend, Cerakote FDE or Kyrptek Highlander barrel finish and black furniture.
Add $210 for Multicam chassis/forend, Cerakote FDE barrel finish and FDE furniture.
Add $290 for Howa Package or $441 for Nikko Stirling Diamond Long Range 4-16x44 scope.

MODEL 1500 HS PRECISION – .223 Rem., .22-250 Rem., .243 Win., .25-06 Rem., .270 Win., .30-06, .308 Win., 6.5 Creedmoor, .300 Win. Mag., 7mm-08 Rem., 7mm Rem. Mag., .300 PRC (mfg. 2020 only), or 6.5 PRC (mfg. 2020 only) cal., short or long action, 22 or 24 in. standard barrel, 3, 4, or 5 shot mag., hand laminated stock w/Kevlar, fiberglass, and carbon fiber injected with a dense polyurethane foam, features CNC aluminum bedding block, available in gray/black, tan/black, or green/black finish, 7.6 or 7.8 lbs. Importation began 2018.

MSR $1,099	$925	$825	$725	$625	$525	$425	$375	

Add $20 for .300 Win. Mag. or 7mm Rem. Mag. cal.

* ***Model 1500 HS Precision Threaded Semi-Heavy Barrel*** – .308 Win. Mag., 6.5 Creedmoor, 6mm Creedmoor, .300 Win. Mag., or 7mm Rem. Mag. cal., short or long action, 26 in. No. 4 semi-heavy threaded barrel, 3, 4, or 5 shot mag., available in gray/black, tan/black, or green/black finish, 8.1 lbs. Importation began 2018.

MSR $1,119	$950	$850	$700	$650	$500	$425	$350	

Add $10 for 7mm Rem. Mag. or .300 Win. Mag. cal.

* ***Model 1500 HS Carbon Fiber*** – 6.5 Creedmoor, .308 Win., or 6.5 PRC (new 2021) cal., 24 in. heavy carbon barrel w/threaded cap, scope options available, full aluminum bed stock, HS Precision Gray, OD Green, Kratos, Kuiu Vias 2.0, or Kuiu Verde 2.0 finish, 7.8 lbs. Importation began 2020.

MSR $1,819	$1,550	$1,350	$1,150	$1,050	$850	$700	$600	

MODEL 1500 HOGUE LIGHTWEIGHT – .243 Win., .308 Win., or 6.5 Creedmoor cal., 20 in. lightweight No. 1 barrel, black or green Hogue overmolded stock, 13 7/8 in. LOP, 7 lbs. Importation began 2018.

MSR $529	$450	$415	$385	$350	$325	$250	$225	

MODEL 1500 HOWA HUNTER – various standard and Mag. cals., 20, 22, or 24 in. blue or stainless steel barrel, one-piece high grade checkered pistol grip walnut stock, rubber recoil pad, sling swivels, two-stage match trigger, approx. 7 1/2 lbs. Mfg. 2012-2015.

	$600	$525	$450	$410	$325	$275	$210	*$710*

Add $47 for Mag. cals.
Add $143 for stainless steel.
Add $63 for Gameking Package with 3.5-10x44 Nikko scope, rings, and one-piece base.

* ***Model 1500 Howa Hunter Zeiss Package*** – various standard or Mag. cals., 20, 22 or 24 in. blued or stainless steel barrel, forged one-piece bolt with two locking lugs, two-stage match trigger, three position safety, checkered pistol grip walnut stock, includes Zeiss Terra 3-9x42 scope, DNZ one-piece scope base with integral rings, approx. 9 lbs. Mfg. 2014-2015.

	$950	$825	$715	$650	$525	$425	$350	*$1,103*

Add $28 for Mag. cals. Add $138 for stainless steel.

MODEL 1500 HOWA WHITETAIL PACKAGE – .204 Ruger, .223 Rem., .243 Win., .22-250 Rem., 7mm-08 Rem., or .308 Win. cal., lightweight 20 in. barrel with #1 contour, Ammo Boost polymer detachable magazine kit converts the steel box magazine into a 5 round detachable for quick loads, M16 style extractor, two-stage trigger system, Hogue overmolded synthetic stock with pillar bedding, pebbled grip panels, pistol grip, three position safety, forged bolt with two locking lugs, Nikko Stirling Nighteater 3-10x42 scope with rings and one-piece Picatinny style base, Buffalo River tripod, blue barrel finish, Harvest Moon, Outshine, or Muddy Girl camo finish. Mfg. mid-2013-2014.

	$650	$575	$495	$440	$360	$295	$225	*$762*

GRADING - PPGS™	100%	98%	95%	90%	80%	70%	60%	LAST MSR

MODEL 1500 HOWA/HOGUE – .204 Ruger (disc. 2017), .223 Rem., .22-250 Rem., .243 Win., .25-06 Rem. (disc. 2018), .270 Win., .30-06, .308 Win., 6.5x55mm (mfg. 2010-2017), .300 Win. Mag., .338 Win. Mag. (disc.), .375 Ruger (mfg. 2009-2015), 7mm Rem. Mag., 7mm-08 Rem. (disc. 2018), 6mm Creedmoor (new 2018), 6.5 Creedmoor (new mid 2015), .300 WSM (disc. 2008), .270 WSM (disc. 2008), or 7mm WSM (disc. 2008) cal., short or long action, 20, 22, or 24 in. No. 2 barrel with blued or Cerakote Gray (mfg. 2016-2017) finish, fluted barrels were optional 2011-2015, 3, 4, or 5 shot mag., forged one-piece bolt with two locking logs, two-stage match trigger, Hogue overmolded stock with non-slip rubber skin, choice of black, Sand (disc.), OD Green, Harvest Moon (mfg. 2013-2014), Muddy Girl (mfg. 2013-2014), or Outshine (mfg. 2013-2014) finish, with or w/o HiViz (new 2009) sights, includes Gamepro 2.5-10x44 scope, 7 3/4 lbs. Importation began 2007.

MSR $529	$450	$415	$385	$350	$325	$250	$225	

Add $10 for standard Mag. cals. or approx. $60 for WSM cals. (disc.).
Add $116 for Cerakote gray finish (mfg. 2016-2017).
Add $174 for Kryptec Typhon camo stock (mfg. 2017 only).
Add $56 for Harvest Moon, Muddy Girl, or Outshine camo finish (mfg. 2013-2014) or $98 for Moonshine Nighteater Package w/scope (disc. 2014).
Add $108 for fluted barrel (disc. 2015).
Various scope packages are available for this model. Please contact the manufacturer directly for pricing and availability.

* ***Model 1500 Howa/Hogue Stainless*** – .204 Ruger, .223 Rem., .22-250 Rem., .243 Win., .25-06 Rem., .270 Win., .30-06, .308 Win., 6.5x55mm (new 2010), .300 Win. Mag., .338 Win. Mag., .375 Ruger (new 2009), 7mm Rem. Mag., .300 WSM (disc. 2008), .270 WSM (disc. 2008), or 7mm WSM (disc. 2008) cal., similar to Model 1500 Howa/Hogue, except features 20, 22, or 24 in. stainless standard or heavy varmint barrel, choice of black, Sand (disc.), OD Green, Harvest Moon (mfg. 2013-2014), or Muddy Girl (mfg. 2013-2014) camo Hogue overmolded stock, 7 3/4-8 1/2 lbs. Imported 2007-2015.

	$600	$525	$450	$410	$325	$275	$225	*$710*

Add $16 for Mag. cals. or heavy varmint barrel.
Add $26 for Harvest Moon or Muddy Girl camo finish (mfg. 2013-2014).

* ***Model 1500 Howa/Hogue Youth Lightweight*** – .243 Win., 6.5 Creedmoor, or .308 Win. cal., short LOP, 20 in. No. 1 standard barrel, black, Harvest Moon (mfg. 2013-2014), Muddy Girl (mfg. 2013-2014), or Yote (mfg. 2017) finish, 2-N-1 combo package with scope and extra adult sized OD Green stock became standard during 2011. Importation began 2009.

MSR $599	$525	$450	$395	$350	$300	$250	$200	

Add $70 for scope package (new 2017).
Add $33 for MoonShine Package (includes Harvest Moon, Muddy Girl, or Outshine camo finish with 3-9x42 scope), disc. 2014.
Add $130 for Yote full dip camo finish (mfg. 2017).

* ***Model 1500 Howa/Hogue Zeiss Package*** – various standard or Mag. cals., 20, 22, or 24 in. blued or stainless steel barrel, fluted barrel avail. on .270 Win., .300 Win. Mag., or 7mm Rem. Mag. cal. only, forged one-piece bolt with two locking lugs, two-stage match trigger, three position safety, Hogue overmolded stock in black or OD Green, includes Zeiss Terra 3-9x42 scope, DNZ one-piece scope base with integral rings, approx. 9 1/2 lbs. New 2014.

MSR $965	$820	$725	$625	$575	$450	$375	$300	

Add $55 for fluted barrel or Mag. cals.
Add $124 for stainless steel.

MODEL 1500 HOWA/HOGUE HEAVY BARREL (VARMINTER) – .22-250 Rem., .223 Rem., 6.5 Creedmoor (new mid-2015, 24 in. only), 6mm Creedmoor (new 2018), .204 Ruger (disc. 2017), .243 Win., .300 Win. Mag., or .308 Win. cal., short action, 20 or 24 (new mid-2015) in. fluted or non-fluted No. 6 contour heavy barrel, blue or Cerakote Gun Metal Gray (new 2017) finish, sling swivel studs, forged one-piece bolt with two locking lugs, two-stage match trigger, three position safety, Hogue overmolded stock in black or OD Green, Hogue recoil pad, 8 1/4-8 1/2 lbs.

MSR $569	$485	$435	$395	$350	$325	$295	$250	

Add $10 for 26 in. barrel.
Add $10 for .300 Win. Mag.
Add $50 if w/fluted barrel.
Subtract $45 for threaded barrel.
Add $87 for Cerakote Gun Metal Gray barrel finish (new 2017).
Various scope packages are available for this model. Please contact the manufacturer directly for pricing and availability.

GRADING - PPGS™	100%	98%	95%	90%	80%	70%	60%	LAST MSR

MODEL 1500 HOWA/HOGUE KRYPTEK CERAKOTE HIGHLANDER PACKAGE – various standard and Mag. cals., short or long action, 20, 22, or 24 in. lightweight, standard, or heavy barrel, 4 shot mag., two-stage match trigger, three position safety, forged one-piece bolt with two locking lugs, Austrian Brown Cerakote coating on barrel, action, and trigger group, Kryptek Highlander camo dip on the Hogue overmolded stock, with or w/o Nikko Stirling Gameking 4-16x44 scope with matching rings, one-piece base, and illuminated reticle, sling swivel studs, 7-10 lbs. New 2015.

MSR $782	$610	$525	$450	$410	$325	$275	$225	

Add $29 for lightweight barrel package or Mag. cals.
Add $58 for heavy barrel.
Add $203 for Nikko Stirling Gameking scope package (4-16x44 scope with matching rings, one-piece base, and illuminated reticle).

MODEL 1500 HOWA/HOGUE KRYPTEK HEAVY BARREL FULL DIP PACKAGE – .22-250 Rem., .223 Rem., or .308 Win. cal., 20 in. No. 6 contour heavy barrel (threading became standard 2018), one-piece scope rail, forged one-piece bolt with two locking lugs, two-stage match trigger, three position safety, illuminated reticle, Hogue recoil pad, Hogue overmolded stock in Kryptek Camo with Highlander, Typhon, and Raid (disc. 2015) patterns (everything is dipped except the bolt, trigger group, and recoil pad), includes sling swivel studs, Nikko Stirling Gameking 4-16x44 scope, rings, one-piece base, and Ammo Boost magazine conversion kit, 10 lbs. New 2014.

MSR $959	$795	$700	$600	$550	$450	$350	$285	

Subtract $50 if w/o barrel threading.

MODEL 1500 HOWA/HOGUE KRYPTEK RIFLE – .223 Rem., .204 Ruger, .22-250 Rem., .243 Win., .25-06 Rem., 6.5 Creedmoor, .270 Win., .30-06, .300 Win. Mag., .308 Win., .338 Win. Mag., .375 Ruger (disc.), 6.5x55 SW, or 7mm Rem. Mag. cal., short or long action, 20 (.375 Ruger only, disc.), 22 or 24 (Mag. cals. only) in. barrel with blued or Cerakote Gray (new 2016) finish, includes sling swivel studs, two-stage match trigger, forged one-piece bolt with two locking lugs, three position safety, Hogue overmolded stock in Kryptek Camo with Highlander, Raid (disc. 2015), or Typhon patterns, with (became standard 2017) or w/o Nikko Stirling Gameking 3.5-10x44 scope, 7 3/4 lbs. New 2014.

MSR $782	$610	$525	$450	$410	$325	$275	$225	

Subtract approx. $110 for rifle only (package with scope became standard in 2017).
Add $34 for Mag. cals.

* ***Model 1500 Howa/Hogue Kryptek Stainless*** – similar to Howa/Hogue Kryptek Rifle, except features stainless steel barrel, 7 3/4 lbs. Mfg. 2014-2015.

	$625	$550	$475	$425	$350	$275	$225	*$736*

Add $26 for Mag. cals.

MODEL 1500 HOWA/HOGUE RANCHLAND COMPACT – various cals., 20 in. free floating lightweight barrel, forged steel flat bottomed receiver, large recoil lug, one-piece bolt, two locking lugs, M16 style extractor, three position safety, Hogue fiberglass reinforced stock in black, Coyote Sand (disc. 2016), OD Green, King's Desert Shadow camo (mfg. 2009-2014, package only), Harvest Moon (mfg. 2013-2014), Muddy Girl (mfg. 2013-2014), Outshine (mfg. 2013-2014), or Yote (new 2015, package only) camo finish, 7 lbs. Mfg. 2008-2017.

MSR $652	$560	$490	$420	$380	$310	$250	$200	

Add $78 for Yote or Desert camo finish (available as a package only).
Add $110 for scope package with Nikko Stirling 3-10x42mm Night Eater scope, rings, and tactical rail.
Add $196 for scope package with King's Desert Shadow Camo finish (mfg. 2009-2014).
Add $72 for Harvest Moon, Muddy Girl, or Outshine camo finish (disc. 2014).

MODEL 1500 HUNTER – various cals., 3 (Mag. or WSM cals. only) or 5 shot mag., 22 or 24 in. barrel, adj. rear sight and trigger, checkered walnut stock, blue metal finish or stainless steel (new 1999) construction, approx. 7.6 lbs. Imported by Interarms 1988 only, reintroduced by Legacy 1999-2006.

	$460	$400	$345	$310	$255	$205	$160	*$574*

Add $21 for Mag. cals.
Add $108 for stainless steel.

MODEL 1500 HUNTER WALNUT SERIES – .22-250 Rem., .243 Win., 6.5 Creedmoor, 7mm-08 Rem., .308 Win., .270 Win., .30-06., 7mm Rem. Mag., .300 Win. Mag., .300 PRC., 6.5 PRC cal., 22 in. standard or stainless steel (6.5 Creedmoor or .308 Win.) barrel w/thread cap, two-stage HACT trigger, checkered walnut stock, pistol grip, 3-pos. safety, 7.2 lbs.

MSR $629	$550	$475	$400	$375	$300	$250	$175	

Add $70 for stainless steel barrel.

GRADING - PPGS™	100%	98%	95%	90%	80%	70%	60%	LAST MSR

* ***Model 1500 Walnut Hunter Mini Action*** – .223 Rem./6.5 Grendel, 7.62x39mm, .350 Legend, 16.25 (.350 Legend), 20, or 22 (.223 Rem./6.5 Grendel) in. barrel, two-stage HACT trigger, 3-pos. safety, 7 lbs. New 2020.

MSR $619	$525	$460	$395	$355	$290	$235	$200	

MODEL 1500 KUIU SERIES – .223 Rem. (disc. 2019), .22-250 Rem., .243 Win., 6mm Creedmoor (disc. 2019), 6.5 Creedmoor, 7mm-08 Rem. (new 2020), .308 Win., .270 Win., .30-06, 7mm Rem. Mag., .22-250 Rem. (new 2021), .243 (new 2021) or .300 Win. Mag. cal., short or long action, 20 (disc. 2019), 22, or 24 (Mag. cals. only) in. No. 2 barrel, 5 shot mag., Kulu Vias or Kulu Verde camo on Hogue pillar bedded stock, recoil pad, Cerakote Tactical Gray finish on barrel and action, 7-8 lbs. New 2017.

MSR $759	$650	$575	$495	$440	$360	$300	$250	

Add $10 for Mag. cals.

MODEL 1500 KRG BRAVO – .308 Win., 6mm Creedmoor, or 6.5 Creedmoor cal., 20, 24, or 26 in. No. 6 threaded barrel, 10 shot detachable mag., KRG stock upgrade, precision machined bedding area w/ full-length aluminum brace, black or FDE finish, 10.5-11 lbs. New 2018.

MSR $1,279	$1,050	$950	$825	$725	$625	$525	$475	

Add $60 for 26 in. barrel.

MODEL 1500 LONG RANGE RIFLE – 6.5 Creedmoor or .308 Win. cal., 26 in. heavy threaded barrel with thread cap protector, 5 shot mag., Bell and Carlson varmint/tactical style stock, vented forend, raised cheekpiece, dual sling studs, 1 in. Pachmayr Decelerator recoil pad, full aluminum bedding block, desert tan/black or green/black finish, 9 1/2 lbs. Mfg. 2017 only.

	$895	$695	$625	$550	$475	$400	$325	*$1,015*

Add $284 for Nikko Stirling Diamond FFP 4-16x44 scope.

MODEL 1500 M1100 RIMFIRE RIFLE – .22 LR, .22 WMR, or .17 HMR cal., 18 in. #4 barrel, two 10 shot detachable mags., beavertail forearm, Black or Green, package comes Kratos full dip w/Gamepro 4-12x40 scope, Walnut Hunter is also available as a Rimfire, 6.3 lbs., Importation began 2020.

MSR $699	$600	$500	$450	$400	$325	$275	$200	

MODEL 1500 MINI ACTION CHASSIS RIFLE – .223 Rem., 6.5 Grendel, or 7.62x39mm cal., short bolt cycling action, 20 in. No. 6 threaded barrel, 5 or 10 (.223 Rem. only) shot mag., fully adj. LOP stock and cheekpiece, modular construction, aluminum alloy billet chassis, black or Multicam/FDE finish, 7 lbs. New 2018.

MSR $1,199	$1,000	$865	$725	$650	$525	$450	$350	

Add $200 for Multicam/FDE finish.

MODEL 1500 MINI ACTION RIFLE – .204 Ruger (disc.), .222 Rem. (disc.), .223 Rem., .300 AAC Blackout (new 2019), 7.62x39mm (new 2017), .350 Legend (new 2020), or 6.5 Grendel (new 2016) cal., short action, 16 1/4 (new 2019, .300 AAC Blackout only) or 22 in. No. 2 hammer forged standard heavy barrel, chamber and bolt are 12% shorter than regular short actions, factory installed 5 shot synthetic detachable mag., three position safety, H.A.C.T. two-stage trigger, Hogue stock in black, OD Green, Kryptek Highlander, Yote (mfg. 2016-2017), or Multicam (new 2016) camo finish, available with or w/out Nikko Stirling Panamax 3-9x40 scope, 5.8-6 lbs. New 2015.

MSR $521	$450	$375	$325	$300	$250	$200	$150	

Add $50 for Kryptek Highlander, Yote (mfg. 2016-2017), or Multicam (new 2016) camo finish.
Add $110-$160 for Nikko Stirling Panamax 3-9x40 scope, depending on caliber.

* ***Model 1500 Mini Action Rifle Lightweight*** – .204 Ruger, .222 Rem., .223 Rem., 7.62x39mm (new 2017), or 6.5 Grendel (new 2016) cal., similar to Mini Action rifle, except has 20 in. lightweight barrel, black, OD Green, Kryptek Highlander, Yote (new 2016), or Multicam (new 2016) camo finish, available with or w/out Nikko Stirling Panamax 3-9x40 scope, 5.7 lbs. New 2015.

MSR $579	$495	$450	$395	$355	$295	$250	$200	

Add $50 for Kryptek Highlander, Yote (mfg. 2016-2017), or Multicam (new 2016) camo finish.
Add $110-$160 for Nikko Stirling Panamax 3-9x40 scope, depending on caliber.

* ***Model 1500 Mini Action Rifle Heavy*** – .204 Ruger, .222 Rem., .223 Rem., 7.62x39mm (new 2017), or 6.5 Grendel (new 2016) cal., similar to Mini Action rifle, except has 20 in. heavy barrel, black, OD Green, or Kryptek Highlander, Yote (new 2016), or Multicam (new 2016) camo finish, available with or w/out Nikko Stirling Panamax 3-9x40 scope, 7.15 lbs. New 2015.

MSR $629	$540	$475	$415	$375	$300	$250	$200	

Add $50 for Kryptek Highlander, Yote (mfg. 2016-2017), or Multicam (new 2016) camo finish.
Add $90-$140 for Nikko Stirling Panamax 3-9x40 scope, depending on caliber.

GRADING - PPGS™	100%	98%	95%	90%	80%	70%	60%	LAST MSR

MODEL 1500 MINI EXCL LITE – .223 Rem., .350 Legend (new 2020), .300 AAC Blackout (mfg. 2019 only), 7.62x39, or 6.5 Grendel cal., 16 1/4 (.350 Legend) or 20 in. heavy threaded barrel, suppressor ready, 5 or 10 shot mag., H.A.C.T. trigger, fully adj. LOP, Mil-Spec folding adaptor compatible, large pistol grip, black, Speed Flag, or Kratos finish, 7-7 1/2 lbs. Importation began 2019.

MSR $639	$550	$475	$400	$375	$300	$250	$200	

MODEL 1500 MULTICAM RIFLE/PACKAGE – various short, long, or magnum action cals., Howa 1500 barreled action, 20, 22, or 24 in. standard (disc. 2017) or heavy barrel (barrel threading became standard in 2018), two-stage H.A.C.T. trigger, MultiCam camo on Hogue stock, recoil pad, sling swivel studs, 3-pos. safety, Cerakote FDE finish on barrel and action. New 2016.

MSR $879	$750	$625	$525	$450	$375	$300	$250	

Subtract approx. $80 if w/o barrel threading.
Add $10 for Mag. cals. or $58 for heavy barrel.
Add $87 for threaded cap heavy barrel.
Add $400 for Diamond scoped package (includes Nikko Stirling 3-12x42 scope, disc. 2017).
Add $336 for Package (includes Nikko Stirling Targetmaster 4-16x44 scope with illuminated reticle (disc. 2017), one-piece base and rings, 5 round Ammo-Boost detachable magazine, and Buffalo River 6-9 in. adj. bipod).

MODEL 1500 ORYX – 6mm Creedmoor, 6.5 Creedmoor (short action), 6.5 PRC, or .300 PRC, or .308 Win. (short action) cal., 20, 24, or 26 in. threaded heavy barrel, 10 shot mag., full monolithic aluminum chassis with adj. LOP and comb height, green/black, FDE/black, or gray/black finish, 10.8-11.5 lbs. Importation began 2019.

MSR $1,189	$1,000	$900	$750	$700	$550	$450	$350	

Add $110 for short action.

* ***Model 1500 Mini Action Oryx*** – .300 AAC Blackout, .223 Rem., 7.62x39, or 6.5 Grendel cal., 16 1/4-22 in. threaded barrel, 5 or 10 shot mag., full monolithic aluminum chassis with adj. LOP and comb height, green/black, FDE/black, or gray/black finish, 8.2-8.8 lbs. Importation began 2019.

MSR $1,299	$1,100	$950	$850	$750	$600	$500	$375	

MODEL 1500 PCS – .308 Win. cal., police counter sniper rifle featuring 24 in. barrel, choice of blue metal or stainless steel, black synthetic or checkered walnut stock, no sights, approx. 9.3 lbs. Imported 1999-2000.

	$385	$335	$290	$260	$210	$175	$135	*$465*

Add $20 for wood stock.
Add $60 for stainless steel.

MODEL 1500 SCOUT RIFLE/PACKAGE – .308 Win. cal., Howa 1500 barreled action, 18 1/2 in. threaded barrel, A2 flash hider, 10 shot Ammo Boost detachable mag., two-stage H.A.C.T. trigger, Williams one-piece rail and peep sight, fiber optic front blade sight, Hogue stock and recoil pad, 3-pos. safety, Cerakote Tactical Gray finish on barrel, action, and original steel floorplate, black, OD Green, or Feral Hog Thunder Mountain camo (mfg. 2016 only) finish on stock and forend. Mfg. 2016-2017.

	$775	$680	$580	$525	$425	$350	$285	*$913*

Add $58 for Feral Hog Thunder Mountain camo (mfg. 2016 only).
Add $116 for Scout Package (Nikko Stirling Panamax 3-9x40 scope, one-piece base and rings).

MODEL 1500 TALON THUMBHOLE VARMINTER – various cals., 20, 22, or 24 in. standard or heavy barrel, fluted barrel became optional during 2011, black Axiom thumbhole stock with two-stage Knoxx recoil compensator, vent. and grooved cutaway forend, 8.3 - 9.7 lbs. Mfg. 2010-2016.

	$710	$600	$525	$475	$375	$315	$250	*$831*

Add $29 for Mag. cals.
Add $58 for fluted barrel or $84 for heavy barrel.
Add $134 for Nikko Stirling Nighteater 2.5-10x42 scope with Picatinny mounting rail.

MODEL 1500 TEXAS SAFARI – .270 Win. or .300 Win. Mag. cal., features Howa M-1500 barreled action with Bill Wiseman recontoured bolt sleeve and receiver, bolt release, and 3-position safety, 3 or 5 shot mag., non-glare blue Teflon metal finish, brown laminate glass bedded stock, individually test fired, approx. 7.8 lbs. Imported 2002-2003.

	$1,350	$1,180	$1,010	$920	$740	$605	$470	*$1,580*

Add $240 for .300 Win. Mag. cal.

This model was also available as a complete custom rifle with many options and special orders.

MODEL 1500 TROPHY – .22-250 Rem., .223 Rem., .243 Win., .270 Win., .308 Win., .30- 06, .300 Win. Mag., .338 Win. Mag., or 7mm Rem. Mag. cal., 3 (Mag. cals. only) or 5 shot, 22 or 24 in. barrel, adj. rear sight and trigger, select Monte Carlo stock with skipline checkering. Imported 1988-92.

	$528	$460	$395	$360	$290	$235	$185	*$528*

Add $20 for Mag. cals.

GRADING - PPGS™	100%	98%	95%	90%	80%	70%	60%	LAST MSR

MODEL 1500 TSP X FOLDING CHASSIS SYSTEM – 6.5 Creedmoor, .300 PRC, or 6.5 PRC cal., 24 in. heavy barrel, scope options available, skeletonized folding adj. buttstock, Southern Cross Small Arms chassis, A2 pistol grip, sling swivels, black or American Flag finish, 13 1/2 lbs. Importation began 2020.

MSR $1,189	$1,000	$900	$750	$700	$550	$450	$350	

MODEL 1500 VARMINT – .204 Ruger (new 2006), .22-250 Rem., .223 Rem., .243 Win. (new 2005), or .308 Win. (mfg. 1990-92, reintroduced 2001) cal., 24 in. heavy barrel without sights, 5 shot mag., blue steel or stainless steel (new 1999) construction, black polymer (new 1999), 100% Realtree camo (new 2005), or walnut stock, approx. 9.3 lbs. Imported 1988-92, and from 2001-2006.

	$450	$395	$335	$305	$245	$200	$155	*$546*

Add $64 for wood stock.
Add $36 for camo.
Add $118 for stainless steel.

HUDSON MFG.

Previous manufacturer of semi-auto pistols located in Temple, TX from 2016-2019.

PISTOLS: SEMI-AUTO

HUDSON H9 – 9mm Para. cal., striker fire design, 4.28 in. barrel, 15 shot mag., 1911 style trigger, Trijicon HD front sight, G10 VZ grips, G10 Hogue textured lower backstrap, lower bore axis, front and rear slide serrations, lower Picatinny rail, stainless steel slide, 34 oz. Mfg. 2017-2019.

	$1,000	$900	$800	$700	$600	$500	$400	*$1,147*

HUG-SAN

Previous shotgun manufacturer located in Huglu, Turkey until 2000.

Hug-San manufactured slide action, semi-auto, and O/U shotguns, in various configurations and gauges.

HUGLU

Current shotgun manufacturer established in 1962, located in Huglu, Turkey. Current exclusive importer beginning 2005 is CZ USA, located in Kansas City, KS. Previously imported 2002-2004 by Armsco Firearms Corp., located in Des Plaines, IL, and from 1999-2002 by Huglu USA, located in Rigby, ID.

Huglu makes a wide variety of quality O/U, semi-auto, and SxS shotguns available in all gauges, and are now imported by CZ USA. Please refer to the CZ section for models and pricing for guns imported by CZ USA.

Some Huglu models were imported 1999-2002 by Huglu USA, and are stamped "Huglu USA, Rigby, ID" on the barrel. Huglu USA Ltd. Co. was reorganized in January 2003 as H-Legacy Shotguns Ltd. Co., and is now a Huglu dealer. For more information, including current models, prices, and U.S. availability, please contact CZ USA directly.

SHOTGUNS: O/U

Armsco previously imported the 103 Series. Models with last MSRs included: 103D - $679, 103D Mini (28 ga. or .410 bore) - $849, 103DE (ejectors) - $849, 103C (case colored receiver) - $799, 103C Mini - $999, 103CE - $949, 103F - $949, 103F Mini - $1,199, 103FE - $1,099, 103FEC - $1,199, 103FC Mini - $1,299, 104A -$499, and 104A Mini - $699.

SHOTGUNS: SxS

Armsco's previous lineup of Huglu SxS shotguns through 2003 with last MSRs included: 201A - $899 MSR, 201AC (choke tubes) - $999 MSR, 201A Mini - $1,099, 201AC Mini - $1,199, 202B - $599 MSR, 202B Mini - $799 MSR, 202BCB - $599 MSR, and the 200ACB - $799 MSR. Other previous models include: Woodcock - disc. 2004, last MSR was $1,049, Woodcock Small Gauge - disc. 2004, last MSR was $1,299, Woodcock Deluxe - disc. 2004, last MSR was $1,199.

Current SxS models include: the Bobwhite - $699 MSR, Bobwhite Silver - $899 MSR, Ringneck - $999 MSR, Ringneck Small Gauge - $1,199 MSR, Amarillo - $699 MSR, and the Durango - $849 MSR.

SHOTGUNS: SEMI-AUTO

Armsco's previous lineup of Huglu's semi-auto shotguns through 2003 with last MSRs included: 501GA - $499 MSR, 501GB - $499 MSR, 601GA - $499 MSR, 601GB - $499 MSR, 601GM (3 1/2 in. chamber) - $599 MSR, 701GA - $499 MSR, and the 701GB - $499 MSR.

SHOTGUNS: SINGLE SHOT

Armsco imported the Model 301A. MSR was $199.

GRADING - PPGS™	100%	98%	95%	90%	80%	70%	60%	LAST MSR

HULDRA ARMS

Previous trademark of AR-15 style semi-auto rifles manufactured by Adams Arms and sold exclusively by Fleet Farm until mid-2016.

Please refer to BlueBookOfGunValues.com to order the *Blue Book of AR-15s & Variations*, available as a book or online subscription.

HUNTER ARMS COMPANY

Previous manufacturer located in Fulton, NY circa 1891-1945.

The Hunter Arms Company was formed to manufacture L.C. Smith shotguns circa 1891. During 1915, Hunter Arms began producing its own line of shotguns. Please refer to the L.C. Smith section in this text for further information regarding this manufacturer (including Fulton, Fulton Special, and Hunter Special models).

HUNT GROUP INTERNATIONAL ARMS & SECURITY

Current manufacturer established in 1992, located in Konya, Turkey. No current U.S. importation.

Hunt Group Arms manufactures good quality lever action, semi-auto, slide action, O/U, SxS, and single shot shotguns in various configurations as well as air rifles and blank pistols. Please contact the manufacturer directly for more information including pricing and availability.

HUSAN ARMS

Current manufacturer of semi-auto rifles and shotguns located in Konya, Turkey. Currently imported by European American Armory (EAA) Corp., located in Cocoa, FL. Shotguns previously imported by Century Arms (Century International Arms, Inc.), located in Delray Beach, FL, and by RAAC, located in Scottsburg, IN.

Husan Arms manufactures a complete line of AR-15 style semi-auto rifles with various stock options and receiver finishes. Currently, these models are not imported into the U.S. Husan also manufactures the MKA 1919 12 ga. AR-15 style shotgun. Please refer to the importers listings for more information.

HUSQVARNA

Previous manufacturer located in Husqvarna, Sweden.

Also see: Lahti Pistols.

PISTOLS: SEMI-AUTO

For information on the Finnish L-35 pistol refer to Lahti Pistol in the "L" section.

RIFLES: BOLT ACTION

HI-POWER – .220 Swift, .270 Win., or .30-06 cal., Mauser type action, open sights, checkered beech wood. Mfg. 1946-51, early models found in 6.5x55mm, 8x57Rmm, 9.3x57mm cals.

$625	$550	$500	$450	$400	$365	$335

MODEL 1951 – similar to Hi-Power, except high profile stock.

$500	$465	$425	$385	$340	$300	$270

SERIES 1100 DELUXE – similar to Model 1951, except has European walnut and jeweled bolt. Mfg. 1952-56.

$520	$480	$440	$360	$330	$310	$290

SERIES 1000 SUPER GRADE – similar to Model 1951, has walnut Monte Carlo stock. Mfg. 1952-56.

$520	$480	$440	$360	$330	$310	$290

SERIES 3100 CROWN GRADE – .243 Win., .270 Win., .30-06, 7x57mm, or .308 Win. cal., improved HVA Mauser action, 24 in. barrel, walnut stock, black forend tip and pistol grip cap. Mfg. 1954-72.

$575	$525	$475	$400	$360	$330	$315

SERIES 3000 CROWN GRADE – similar to 3100, except has Monte Carlo stock.

$660	$595	$525	$475	$400	$360	$330

SERIES 4100 LIGHTWEIGHT – .243 Win., .270 Win., .30-06, 7x57mm, or .308 Win. cal., HVA Mauser action, 20 1/2 in. barrel, open sights, lightweight walnut stock, pistol grip, Schnabel forend. Mfg. 1954-72.

$625	$525	$475	$400	$360	$330	$315

SERIES 4000 LIGHTWEIGHT – similar to 4100, except has Monte Carlo stock, no sights.

$900	$795	$675	$615	$495	$400	$315

MODEL 456 LIGHTWEIGHT – similar to 4000/4100, except full-length stock. Mfg. 1959-70.

$675	$600	$550	$495	$415	$385	$330

GRADING - PPGS™	100%	98%	95%	90%	80%	70%	60%	LAST MSR

SERIES 6000 IMPERIAL GRADE – similar to 3100, except has select wood, 3 leaf folding rear sight. Mfg. 1968-70.

	$795	$695	$625	$575	$495	$470	$440

SERIES 7000 IMPERIAL LIGHTWEIGHT – similar to 6000 Imperial, except 20 1/2 in. barrel, lightweight stock.

	$850	$775	$695	$625	$575	$495	$470

SERIES P-3000 PRESENTATION – similar to Crown, except engraved action, special wood. Mfg. 1968-70.

	$1,100	$1,000	$925	$850	$775	$675	$575

MODEL 9000 CROWN GRADE – .243 Win., .270 Win., .30-06, 7x57mm, .300 Win. Mag., or .308 Win. cal., Husqvarna action, 23 1/2 in. barrel, adj. trigger, adj. sight, walnut stock. Mfg. 1971-72.

	$575	$525	$475	$400	$360	$330	$315

MODEL 8000 IMPERIAL – similar to 9000, but jeweled bolt, engraved floorplate, no sights and deluxe stock. Mfg. 1971-1972.

	$750	$675	$595	$525	$495	$470	$415

SHOTGUNS

Husqvarna also manufactured limited quantities of SxS and underlever shotguns in various configurations, including a Model 20 SxS in 12 or 16 ga. with exposed hammers (popular with cowboy action shooting). Most of these shotguns are currently selling in the $375-$1,200 range, depending on the desirability of the configuration and original condition.

HY-HUNTER INC. FIREARMS MANUFACTURING CO.

Previous trademark imported by Hy-Hunter Inc., located in Hollywood, CA.

Hy-Hunter Inc. imported single action revolvers in various calibers and O/U derringers manufactured in West Germany. Typically, prices are determined by their shooting value rather than their collector value. Prices generally range from $100-$175 depending on caliber and finish.

HYPER

Previous manufacturer located in Jenks, OK.

RIFLES: SINGLE SHOT

SINGLE SHOT RIFLE – all calibers, all standard lengths and contours, falling block trigger guard lever activated, adj. trigger, no sights, stocked to customer specifications, in AA grade walnut. Disc. 1984.

	$2,200	$1,980	$1,925	$1,870	$1,650	$1,540	$1,375

Add $75 for stainless barrel.
Add $85 for octagon barrel.

I.A.B. Srl

Previous manufacturer (Industria Armi Bresciane) of modern firearms, black powder replicas and historical Sharps rifles located in Gardone, Val Trompia, Brescia, Italy. Previously imported by E.M.F., located in Santa Ana, CA, Dixie Gun Works, located in Union City, TN, Kiesler's, located in Jeffersonville, IN, American Arms, located in Kansas City, MO, and Tristar Sporting Arms, located in Kansas City, MO. Previously distributed by Sporting Arms International, Inc. located in Indianola, MS.

I.A.B. also manufactured shotguns (O/U and single barrel trap or skeet) in various styles and configurations including combo sets. These guns employed a boxlock action, had ejectors, and various amounts of engraving. Prices for 100% condition usually started in the $650-$1,000 price range. Values for older models will be determined by their shooting value, not collector value, as there are very few I.A.B. collectors.

IAC

Please refer to Interstate Arms Corp. listing in this section.

IAI

Please refer to Intrac Arms International LLC listing.

Derya Hunting Arms (Derya Arms Industry) currently manufactures air rifles and tactical accessories in addition to semi-auto, slide action, and single shot shotguns in various configurations. Please contact the factory directly for more information, values, and availability.

IAI INC. - AMERICAN LEGENDS

Previous manufacturer, importer, and distributor located in Houston, TX. Firearms were manufactured by Israel Arms International, Inc., located in Houston, TX. IAI designates Israel Arms International, and should not be confused with Irwindale Arms, Inc. (also IAI).

The models listed were part of an American Legend Series that are patterned after famous American and Belgian military carbines/rifles and semi-auto pistols.

GRADING - PPGS™	100%	98%	95%	90%	80%	70%	60%	LAST MSR

PISTOLS: SEMI-AUTO

MODEL 2000 – .45 ACP cal., patterned after the Colt Govt. 1911, 5 or 4 1/4 (Commander configuration, Model 2000-C) in. barrel, SA, parkerized finish, plastic or rubber finger groove grips, 36-38 oz. Mfg. in South Africa 2002-2004.

$415	$365	$325	$295	$275	$250	$225	*$465*

RIFLES/CARBINES: SEMI-AUTO

MODEL 888 M1 CARBINE – .22 LR or .30 Carbine cal., 18 in. barrel, mfg. from new original M1 parts and stock by IAI (barrel bolt and receiver) and unused GI parts, 10 shot mag., choice of birch or walnut stock, parkerized finish, metal or wood handguard, 5 1/2 lbs. Mfg. by IAI in Houston, TX 1998-2004.

$675	$595	$565	$435	$395	$315	$295	*$556*

Add $11 for .22 LR cal.

Add $31 for walnut/metal forearm or $47 for walnut/wood forearm.

MODEL 333 M1 GARAND – .30-06 cal., patterned after the WWII M1 Garand, 24 in. barrel, internal magazine, 8 shot en-bloc clip, parkerized finish, 9 1/2 lbs. Mfg. 2003-2004.

$950	$875	$775	$625	$525	$400	$350	*$972*

I A I

Please refer to the Irwindale Arms, Inc. listing in this section.

IAR, Inc.

Previous importer and distributor since 1995 located in San Juan Capistrano, CA. During late 2009, E.M.F. bought the remaining assets of IAR and discontinued any importation under the IAR name.

IAR, Inc. (International Antique Reproductions, Inc.) imported and distributed a wide variety of firearms, including SA revolvers, rolling block pistols, rolling block target rifles, Henry rifle reproductions, baby rolling block carbines, exposed hammer shotguns, and reproduction rifles and carbines. IAR, Inc. also imported black powder reproductions and replicas, plus a complete lineup of blank firing arms and ammunition, including pistols, revolvers, and rifles.

Black Powder Revolver Reproductions & Replicas and *Black Powder Long Arms & Pistols - Reproductions & Replicas* by Dennis Adler are also invaluable sources for most black powder reproductions and replicas, and include hundreds of color images on most popular makes/models, provide manufacturer/trademark histories, and up-to-date information on related items/accessories for black powder shooting - BlueBookOfGunValues.com.

GRADING - PPGS™	100%	98%	95%	90%	80%	70%	60%	LAST MSR

I.F.G.

Current importer (Italian Firearms Group) established during 2011 for the importation of select Italian makes/models into the U.S., and currently located in Amarillo, TX. The Italian Firearms Group is a partnership between the following Italian firearms manufacturers: F.A.I.R., Pedersoli, Sabatti, and Tanfoglio (FT Italia trademark). It also has a U.S.A. partner, Canyon Arms, LLC. Please refer to these individual listings for more information.

I G A

Current trademark with manufacturing facilities located in Veranopolis, Brazil (O/U and SxS shotguns only), and by Vursan Manufacturing (semi-auto shotguns only) beginning in 2000, located in Istanbul, Turkey. Currently imported by Stoeger Industries, Inc. located in Accokeek, MD. Previously located in Wayne, NJ.

For individual model listings, please go to BlueBookOfGunValues.com/overflow.

IMI

Please refer to the Israel Military Industries listing in this section.

I.O., INC. (INTER ORDNANCE)

Current AR-15 and AK style rifle and pistol manufacturer and importer established in 2008, located in Palm Bay, FL. Previously located in Monroe, NC until mid-2013.

For individual model listings, please go to BlueBookOfGunValues.com/overflow.

ISSC HANDELSGESELLSCHAFT

Current manufacturer of semi-auto firearms located in Ried, Austria. Previously imported by American Tactical Imports located in Summerville, SC (2015-2016), by Legacy Sports International located in Reno, NV (late 2011-2014), and by Austrian Sporting Arms located in Ware, MA (2010-2011).

PISTOLS: SEMI-AUTO

M22 - .22 LR cal., patterned after the Glock semi-auto, 4, 4 3/4 (new 2012), or 5 1/2 (new 2012) in. threaded (new 2012), standard, or target (new 2012) barrel, SA, 10 shot mag., white dot front and adj. rear sights, lower accessory rail, loaded chamber indicator, safety decocker, magazine disconnect, black polymer frame with contoured grip, adj. rear sight, black, two-tone Desert Tan, OD Green, pink, Harvest Moon camo (new 2013), Outshine camo (new 2013), or Muddy Girl camo (new 2013) finish, with or w/o brushed chrome slide (new 2012), 21 oz. Imported 2009-2014.

$365 $325 $285 $265 $245 $225 $200 *$429*

Add $72 for Harvest Moon camo, Outshine camo, or Muddy Girl camo (new 2013) stock.
Add $110 for 4 3/4 in. threaded barrel.
Add $38 for 5 1/2 in. target barrel.

M22 GEN2 - .22 LR cal., 4 in. barrel, two 10 shot mags., five safeties. Imported 2015-2016.

$195 $175 $150 $135 $100 $90 $75 *$220*

RIFLES: BOLT ACTION

SPA STRAIGHT PULL ACTION - .17 HMR, .22 LR, or .22 Mag. cal., 10 shot detachable box mag., straight pull Biathlon Style action, 20 in. match barrel w/o sights, black synthetic or Hunter wood stock with raised cheekpiece, 7.84 lbs. Imported 2013-2014.

$460 $410 $350 $315 $275 $250 $225 *$532*

Add $15 for .17 HMR or .22 Mag. cal.
Add $139 for wood stock.

* ***Spa Target Straight Pull Action*** - .17 HMR, .22 LR, or .22 Mag. cal., similar to Spa Straight Pull Action Rifle, except features a Target adj./folding thumbhole stock, adj. cheekpiece, and butt spike, 7.84 lbs. Imported 2013-2014.

$685 $600 $525 $475 $375 $310 $250 *$804*

Add $7 for .17 HMR or .22 Mag. cal.

SPA 22/17 - .17 HMR or .22 LR cal., 20 in. barrel, straight pull action, 10 shot mag., black synthetic or wood stock, black finish. Imported 2015-2016.

$375 $330 $280 $255 $200 $175 $150 *$420*

Add $70 for wood stock.

GRADING - PPGS™	100%	98%	95%	90%	80%	70%	60%	LAST MSR

RIFLES: SEMI-AUTO

MK22 – .22 LR cal., 10 or 22 shot mag., 16.6 in. Lothar Walther match barrel with muzzle brake, multiple charge bar locations on right and left side of receiver, ambidextrous safety and mag. release, black or Desert tan (new 2012) finish, variable and folding adj. open sight, Picatinny quad rail, fixed, folding or collapsible stock with adj. cheekpiece, features UCAS (Universal Cocking Adaptation System), 6 1/2 lbs. Imported 2011-2014.

	$575	$500	$450	$400	$365	$335	$300	*$665*

Add $37 for Desert Tan finish.

MK22 GEN2 – .22 LR cal., 16 in. barrel, 22 shot mag., adj. folding stock, black finish. Imported 2015-2016.

	$425	$365	$315	$275	$240	$220	$195	*$470*

IWI

Please refer to the Israel Weapon Industries Ltd. lising in this section.

IBERIA FIREARMS

Current manufacturer of .40 S&W cal. pistols located in Iberia, OH. Distributed by MKS Supply located in Dayton, OH. Distributor sales only.

Please refer to the Hi-Point listing in the H section.

IDAHO ARMORY

Previous custom rifle manufacturer located in Rigby, ID, circa 2010-2015.

RIFLES: BOLT ACTION

Idaho Armory manufactured the IA 1R long range modular rifle system in various calibers and configurations, including plinking, varminting, hunting, or tactical competition. Each rifle was essentially built per individual custom order, and came with either a 5 or 10 shot magazine that was compatible with Accuracy International magazines.

IMPALA PLUS

Current trademark of semi-auto shotguns manufactured by Istanbul Silah. No current U.S. importation. Please refer to the Istanbul Silah listing in the I section for more information.

IMPALA PRECSION

Previous rifle manufacturer located in London, England.

IMPERIAL GUN CO. LTD

Previous manufacturer located in Surrey, Great Britain circa 1992-1995. The Imperial Gun Co. Ltd. had limited importation into the U.S.

Imperial Gun secondary marketplace values must be based realistically on their competitive shooting value, not collectibility.

INDIAN ARMS

Previous trademark manufactured by Indian Arms Corporation located in Detroit, MI.

PISTOLS: SEMI-AUTO

INDIAN ARMS .380 – .380 ACP cal., patterned after Walther PPK, stainless steel, 3 1/4 in. barrel, 6 shot mag., natural or blue finish, with (early specimens) or without key lock safety, with or without VR barrel, walnut grips, 20 oz. Mfg. 1975-77.

	$395	$350	$300	$275	$250	$225	$195	

This model had limited manufacture with approx. 1,000 guns being made.

INDUSTRIA ARMI GALESI

Previous manufacturer located in Brescia, Italy.

PISTOLS: SEMI-AUTO

GALESI MODEL 6 POCKET AUTO – .22 LR or .25 ACP cal., 6 shot, 2 1/4 in. barrel blue, fixed sights, plastic grips. Mfg. 1930-disc.

	$165	$145	$125	$110	$90	$75	$60	
Chrome engraved	$330	$290	$250	$225	$180	$150	$115	

GALESI MODEL 9 POCKET AUTO – .22 LR, .32 ACP, or .380 ACP cal., 8 shot, 3 1/4 in. barrel, blue, fixed sights, plastic grips. Mfg. 1930-disc.

	$195	$170	$145	$135	$105	$90	$70	
Chrome engraved	$395	$345	$295	$270	$215	$180	$140	

GRADING - PPGS™	100%	98%	95%	90%	80%	70%	60%	LAST MSR

INDUSTRY ARMAMENT

Previous manufacturer of AR-15 style pistols and rifles, located in Mesa, AZ, 2015-2017.

Please refer to BlueBookOfGunValues.com to order the *Blue Book of AR-15s & Variations*, available as a book or online subscription.

INFALLIBLE

Previous trademark manufactured by Warner Arms Corp. located in Norwich, CT, and Davis-Warner Arms Corp. located in Assonet, MA.

PISTOLS: SEMI-AUTO

INFALLIBLE PISTOL – .32 ACP cal., 3.2 in. barrel, 7 shot mag., 24.7 oz.

* ***Infallible Pistol Type I*** – mfg. and marked "Warner Arms Corp., Norwich, Conn.", serial range is 501-2,299.

$450	$325	$295	$270	$250	$225	$200	

* ***Infallible Pistol Type II*** – marked "Davis-Warner Arms Corporation, Assonet, Massachusetts", serial range is 2,300-5,299.

$400	$300	$250	$225	$195	$170	$150	

* ***Infallible Pistol Type III*** – marked "Warner Arms Corporation, Norwich, Connecticut", serial range is 5,300-7,400.

$400	$300	$250	$225	$195	$170	$150	

INFINITY FIREARMS

Current trademark manufactured by Strayer-Voight Inc. since 1994 and located in Gordon, TX. Previously located in Grand Prairie, TX. Previously distributed on a limited basis by JP Enterprises, located in Hugo, MN. Distributor and dealer sales.

PISTOLS: SEMI-AUTO

Strayer-Voight manufactures a complete line of custom high quality M1911-based semi-auto pistols in a wide variety of finishes, materials (including titanium), options, and special orders. Some models have included the Tiki, Titanium Model, Bushing, Comp. Gun, Hybricomp, IED 1911, Duotone 1911, PPC Masterpiece, and Competition Gun. Please contact the manufacturer directly for more information on pricing and availability regarding Infinity Firearms.

INGLIS HI-POWERS

Previously manufactured by John Inglis Co. Limited of Toronto, Canada. Over 151,000 Inglis Hi-Powers were manufactured between February 1944 and September 1945 under military contractual agreements.

PISTOLS: SEMI-AUTO

For more information on Inglis serialization and model coding, please refer to the Serialization section.

CHINESE CONTRACT PATTERN 35

* ***Chinese Contract Pattern 35 No. 1*** – 9mm Para. cal., large Chinese characters (2-6) on left slide, slotted for stock and tangent sights, can be denoted by no numerical prefix before the "CH" in serial number.

$4,000	$3,750	$3,175	$2,600	$2,000	$1,450	$1,150	

Add approx. $500 for original wood holster stock. Beware of reproductions.

Add $400-$500 for early front sight (approx. first 100 pistols only).

CH SERIES MILITARY

* ***CH Series Military MK 1-No. 1 Inglis*** – 9mm Para. cal., tangent sight, slotted, contracts included Canadian, Chinese, and other countries.

$1,600	$1,275	$1,000	$825	$750	$625	$525	

Add 10%-20% for decal on front strap.

Add approx. $500 for original wood holster stock. Beware of reproductions.

This model has been recently imported again. Most recent imports have been painted black or refinished, and are priced in the $350-$575 range.

T SERIES CANADIAN MILITARY

* ***T Series Canadian Military MK 1-No. 2 Inglis*** – 9mm Para. cal., fixed sight, without slot, numerical ser. no. prefix (0-10) references the sequence of guns in increments of 10,000. Scarcer variations include: 0, 9, and 10.

$1,300	$1,075	$875	$750	$625	$525	$425	

GRADING - PPGS™	100%	98%	95%	90%	80%	70%	60%	LAST MSR

Add 10%-20% for original decal on front strap.
Add 15% for 0 variation prefix.
Add 10% for 9 variation prefix.
Add 30% for 10 variation (ser. no.) prefix.
Most recent imports are priced $350-$650.

Since the original decals are very fragile, most are observed with approx. 10%-90% of the decal remaining.

This model has been recently imported again.

* ***T Series Canadian Military Inglis "DIAMOND" logo*** – refers to Inglis trademark in diamond shaped logo on left side of slide, only a few prototypes were mfg. 1946-47.

	$4,000	$3,750	$3,175	$2,600	$2,000	$1,450	$1,150

Add 50% for polished steel (parkerized finish is more common).
Add 50% for 5 CH Series.

All Inglis diamond variations are in the 5CH or 9T ser. no. range.

Be careful of fakes!

* ***T Series Canadian Military MK 1-No. 2 Inglis*** – fixed sight, slotted. Inspect slot very carefully, and provenance verification is advised.

	$2,250	$1,850	$1,525	$1,300	$1,075	$900	$725

INGRAM

Previously manufactured until late 1982 by Military Armament Corp. (MAC) located in Atlanta, GA.

PISTOLS: SEMI-AUTO

MAC 10 – .45 ACP or 9mm Para. cal., open bolt, semi-auto version of the submachine gun, 10 (.45 ACP cal.), 16 (9mm Para. cal.), 30 (.45 ACP cal.), or 32 (9mm Para. cal.) shot mag., compact all metal welded construction, rear aperture and front blade sight. Disc. 1982.

	$950	$875	$800	$700	$650	$575	$525

Add approx. $160 for accessories (barrel extension, case, and extra mag.).

MAC 10A1 – similar to MAC 10 except fires from a closed bolt.

	$395	$375	$350	$280	$265	$225	$210

MAC 11 – similar to MAC 10 except in .380 ACP cal.

	$750	$695	$650	$575	$550	$535	$485

INLAND MANUFACTURING (NEW MFG.)

Current semi-auto rifle, pistol, and shotgun manufacturer established during late 2014, located in Dayton, OH. Marketed by MKS Supply, LLC.

CARBINES: SEMI-AUTO

M1 1944 CARBINE – .30 Carbine cal., patterned after the 1944 M1 carbine, 18 in. barrel, Type 2 barrel band, 10 shot mag., adj. rear sights, "low wood" walnut stock, push-button safety, round bolt, includes cloth and oiler, 5 lbs. 3 oz. New late 2014.

MSR $1,139	$900	$785	$685	$600	$535	$465	$415

M1 1944 1ST INFANTRY COMMEMORATIVE CARBINE – .30 Carbine cal., patterned after the 1944 M1 carbine, 18 in. barrel, Type 2 barrel band, 10 shot mag., adj. rear sights, "low wood" walnut stock, hand rubbed w/oil, push-button safety, round bolt, includes cloth and boiler, embellished w/engraving of the 1st Infantry Div. shoulder patch, accomplishments, and recognition of 100 year anniversary, 5 lbs. 3 oz. Limited Mfg. beginning 2017, disc.

	$975	$825	$725	$625	$550	$475	$425	*$1,179*

M1 1945 CARBINE – .30 Carbine cal., patterned after the 1945 produced carbine, 18 in. barrel, Type 3 bayonet lug/barrel band, 15 shot mag., adj. rear sight, low wood walnut stock, push-button safety, round bolt, includes cloth and oiler, 5 lbs. 3 oz. New late 2014.

MSR $1,139	$900	$785	$685	$600	$535	$465	$415

M1A1 PARATROOPER – .30 Carbine cal., modeled after a late production 1944 M1A1 Paratrooper, 18 in. barrel, Type 2 barrel band, 15 shot mag., adj. rear sight, "low wood" walnut forend, folding heavy wire stock, push-button safety, round bolt, includes cloth sling and oiler, 5 lbs. 3 oz. New late 2014.

MSR $1,279	$1,075	$925	$800	$700	$600	$500	$450

M1 "JUNGLE" CARBINE – .30 Carbine cal., 16 in. threaded barrel with conical flash hider, Type 2 barrel band, 15 shot mag., adj. rear sights, "low wood" walnut stock, push button safety, round bolt, 5 lbs. 3 oz. New 2016.

MSR $1,159	$950	$800	$700	$600	$525	$450	$395

GRADING - PPGS™	100%	98%	95%	90%	80%	70%	60%	LAST MSR

M1 "SCOUT" CARBINE – .30 Carbine cal., 16 in. threaded barrel with conical flash hider, 15 shot mag., adj. rear sights, black textured stock, push-button safety, round bolt, aluminum tactical handguard with Picatinny top rail, 5 lbs. 3 oz. New 2016.

MSR $1,295	$1,075	$965	$825	$725	$625	$535	$450	

MODEL T30 CARBINE – .30 Carbine cal., 18 in. barrel, clamp-on style conical flash hider, 10 shot mag., "low wood" walnut stock, push-button safety, integrated T30 scope mount utilizing Redfield style rings, round bolt, 5 lbs. 3 oz. New 2017.

MSR $1,279	$1,075	$925	$800	$700	$600	$500	$450	

Add $416 for Hi-Lux M82 Vintage sniper scope.

M30-C – .30 Carbine cal., 16 1/2 in. threaded barrel, birdcage flash hider, 10 shot mag., adj. ghost ring aperture rear sight, Inland/Sage Mil-Spec black anodized aluminum chassis w/Ergo collapsible stock, Ergo SureGrip, 6 lbs. New 2018.

MSR $1,559	$1,300	$1,150	$1,000	$900	$750	$600	$475	

DERRINGERS

The models in this section were manufactured in collaboration with Bond Arms.

LIBERATOR – .45 ACP cal., 3 in. double barrel, 6 groove, 2 shot, patented rebounding hammer, wood grips w/Inland cartouche, crossbolt safety, retracting firing pins, spring-loaded cammed locking lever, stainless steel w/bead blasted anti-glare finish, 18 oz. New 2017.

MSR $495	$425	$375	$325	$295	$235	$195	$150	

FIREARMS: OTHER

Per the manufacturer: these firearms are legally classified as "Firearm/Other", they are not considered a shotgun, nor are they NFA classified as an "Any Other Weapon" (AOW).

STAKEOUT II – 12 ga. 3 in. chamber, pump action operation, 14 in. cylinder bore barrel, 4 shot tubular magazine, bottom load and ejection, steel receiver, brass bead front sight, wooden forearm, wooden pistol grip with brass buttplate, parkerized finish, 6.7 lbs. 26.5 in. OAL, New 2018.

MSR $749	$650	$575	$500	$425	$350	$300	$225	

PISTOLS: SEMI-AUTO

1911A1 1ST INFANTRY COMMEMORATIVE PISTOL – .45 ACP cal., original "G.I." configuration, precision machined frame and slide, 7 shot mag., fixed combat sights, GI-style wood grip panels, thumb safety, vertical slide serrations, lanyard loop, engraving on slide (right side) of 1st Infantry Div. shoulder patch, accomplishments, and recognition of the 1917-2017 100th year anniversary, matte metal finish, 39 oz. Limited Mfg. beginning 2017, disc.

	$725	$650	$550	$475	$425	$375	$325	*$829*

1911A1 GOVERNMENT MODEL – .45 ACP cal., original "G.I." configuration, precision machined frame and slide, 7 shot mag., fixed combat sights, checkered brown plastic grips, thumb safety, vertical slide serrations, lanyard loop, Parkerized finish.

MSR $949	$800	$700	$600	$550	$450	$375	$275	

1911A1 ITHACA HARDBALL 70 PISTOL – .45 ACP cal., Pre-Series 70 action Government Model, 5 in. National Match barrel, ext. aluminum trigger, adj. sights, overtravel adjustment, black finish, 2 lbs. 8 oz. Mfg. 2017-2018.

	$2,500	$2,200	$1,800	$1,425	$1,150	$1,000	$875	*$2,849*

1911A1 NATIONAL MATCH – .45 ACP cal., National Match barrel and bushing, ext. aluminum trigger w/ overtravel adjustment, adj. sights, checkered brown plastic grips, matte metal finish. Mfg. 2016 only.

	$1,275	$1,115	$950	$865	$700	$575	$475	*$1,499*

1911 CUSTOM CARRY – .45 ACP cal., stainless steel frame and slide, 5 in. barrel, 7 shot detachable box mag., skeletonized combat hammer, adj. target trigger, Novak sights, Ergo XTR grip panels, ext. thumb safety, beavertail grip safety, aggressive slide serrations, ext. full-length recoil guide rod, checkering on grip and mainspring housing, 2 1/2 lbs.

MSR $1,219	$1,050	$900	$800	$700	$550	$475	$375	

1911 PRE-SERIES 70 CUSTOM CARRY – .45 ACP cal., 5 in. barrel, skeletonized combat hammer, adj. target trigger, Novak sights, Ergo XTR grip panels, ext. thumb safety, beavertail grip safety, aggressive slide serrations, checkering on grip and mainspring housing, 2 lbs. 8 oz. Mfg. 2017-2018.

	$1,950	$1,750	$1,500	$1,250	$1,000	$850	$725	*$2,149*

1911 ITHACA 70 PISTOL – .45 ACP cal., original "GI" configuration, precision machined frame, 5 in. barrel, 7 shot, fixed combat sights, wood grip panels, thumb and grip safety, vertical slide serrations, lanyard loop, also features markings from the Ithaca Gun Company, black finish, 2 lbs. 8 oz. Mfg. 2017-2018.

	$1,950	$1,750	$1,500	$1,250	$1,000	$850	$725	*$2,149*

GRADING - PPGS™	100%	98%	95%	90%	80%	70%	60%	LAST MSR

M30-IMP (MOTOR PATROL PISTOL) – .30 Carbine cal., 7 1/2 in. threaded barrel with thread protector, 10 shot mag., adj. ghost ring aperture rear sight, Inland/Sage Mil-Spec black anodized aluminum chassis, Ergo SureGrip, 4 1/2 lbs. New late 2017.

MSR $1,439	$1,200	$1,050	$900	$850	$700	$550	$425	

M30-P – .30 Carbine cal., 12 in. threaded barrel with thread protector, 10 shot mag., adj. ghost ring aperture rear sight, Inland/Sage EBR chassis w/Gear Head Works Mod II Tail Hook Arm Brace, Ergo SureGrip, black Mil-Spec anodized finish, 5 lbs. New late 2017.

MSR $1,729	$1,500	$1,300	$1,100	$1,000	$800	$650	$500	

M1 ADVISOR (M1 CARBINE PISTOL "ADVISOR MODEL") – .30 Carbine cal., modeled after the modified M1 carbine, 12 in. threaded barrel with conical flash hider, 15 shot mag., modified "Paratrooper" walnut stock w/folding stock and mechanism omitted, wooden pistol grip w/sling swivel, sling swivel on barrel band, parkerized finish, 4 lbs. 5 oz. New 2016.

MSR $1,259	$1,025	$900	$800	$700	$600	$500	$450	

SHOTGUNS: SLIDE ACTION

M37 TRENCH GUN – 12 ga., 3 in. chamber, based on the original Ithaca Model 37 Trench gun, 20 in. barrel, bayonet lug, 4 shot mag., bottom load and ejection, bead sight, oiled stock, ventilated heat shield handguard, parkerized finish, 6.7 lbs. Mfg. in conjunction with Ithaca Gun Company beginning 2016.

MSR $1,279	$1,075	$925	$775	$700	$575	$475	$375	

INLAND (PREVIOUS MFG.)

Previous WWII subcontractor of M1 carbines. Former division of General Motors, located in Dayton, OH.

Please refer to U.S. M1 Carbines/Rifles listings under U.S. Military.

INNOGUN

Current long gun manufacturer located in Obersfeld, Germany. No current U.S. importation.

InnOGun makes two models currently. The InnOGun Hybrid is a unique O/U interchangeable two-barrel gun with a box magazine feeding the lower barrel which has a slide action operation. The top barrel is a single shot rifle, and the gun has a break-open style action with top opening lever. This allows it to be a combination gun in shotgun/rifle, rimfire/centerfire, or centerfire/centerfire configurations. The InnOGun Impulse model is a single shot repeater available in various cals. Additionally, the company also offers a Pulse Tac bolt-action rifle in 7x64mm, 30-06, .308 Win., 7x57mm IS, and an Integral bolt action model. Please contact the manufacturer directly for more information on its unique offerings, current U.S. availability, and pricing.

INTACTO ARMS

Previous manufacturer of AR-15 style firearms located in Boise, ID 2008-circa 2017.

Please refer to BlueBookOfGunValues.com to order the *Blue Book of AR-15s & Variations*, available as a book or online subscription.

INTEGRITY ARMS & SURVIVAL

Current custom AR-15 style rifle manufacturer located in Jefferson, GA. Previously located in Watkinsville, GA.

Please refer to BlueBookOfGunValues.com to order the *Blue Book of AR-15s & Variations*, available as a book or online subscription.

INTERARMS

Previous importer and distributor located in Alexandria, VA, from circa 1956-1999.

Interarms imported a multitude of trademarks and models since the early 1960s. Most of the models listed were recent imports. The FÉG, Howa, Rossi, and Walther trademarks will be found in their own sections listed alphabetically in this text.

PISTOLS: SEMI-AUTO, FÉG & HELWAN MFG.

Please refer to the FÉG & HELWAN sections in this text.

REVOLVERS: SA, VIRGINIAN SERIES

Virginian Revolvers were previously manufactured in Europe by various manufacturers (including Hämmerli of Switzerland). They were also manufactured in Midland, VA from 1976-1984. Older models with exceptional quality (including Hämmerli guns) are worth a premium over values listed.

GRADING - PPGS™	100%	98%	95%	90%	80%	70%	60%	LAST MSR

VIRGINIAN DRAGOON STANDARD – .41 Mag., .44 Mag., or .45 LC (mfg. 1982-84) cal., improved action patterned after Colt SAA design, 6 shot, 6, 7 1/2, 8 3/8, or 12 (Buntline) in. barrel, blue finish, smooth walnut grips, adj. rear sight, 51 oz. with 7 1/2 in. barrel.

	$450	$295	$255	$225	$205	$190	$180	*$315*

Add 15% for Buntline Model.

* ***Virginian Dragoon Standard Stainless*** – .41 Mag., .44 Mag., or .45 LC cal., 6 (disc.), 7 1/2 (disc.), or 8 3/8 in. barrel, same general specifications as Standard Dragoon.

	$450	$325	$275	$235	$215	$190	$180	*$315*

DRAGOON SILHOUETTE – .357 Mag. or .44 Mag. cal., stainless steel, 7 1/2, 8 3/8, or 10 1/2 in. (standard on .357 Mag.) barrel, special sights and grips.

	$475	$325	$365	$320	$275	$225	$195	*$425*

DRAGOON ENGRAVED – .44 Mag. cal. only, choice of stainless steel or blue finish, 6 or 7 1/2 in. barrel., "Sic Semper Tyrannis" inscription on butt with a 5 point star.

	$650	$575	$500	$450	$395	$360	$320	*$625*

Add $75 for presentation case.

DRAGOON "DEPUTY" – .357 Mag. or .44 Mag. cal., blue barrel, case hardened frame, 5 in. barrel only.

	$340	$295	$255	$225	$205	$190	$180	*$295*

* ***Dragoon "Deputy" Stainless*** – similar to Dragoon "Deputy", except .44 Mag. available in 6 in. barrel only, stainless steel.

	$375	$325	$275	$235	$215	$190	$180	*$295*

VIRGINIAN .22 CONVERTIBLE – .22 LR/.22 WMR cal. cylinders, 5 1/2 in. barrel only, adj. rear sight, 38 oz.

	$250	$185	$155	$145	$135	$125	$115	*$219*

* ***Virginian .22 Convertible Stainless*** – stainless steel fabrication, otherwise similar to above.

	$250	$200	$170	$155	$125	$110	$95	*$239*

RIFLES: BOLT ACTION, DISC.

MODEL JW-15 – .22 LR cal., 5 shot detachable mag., 23.8 in. barrel, open sights, blue finish, Model 70 style safety, patterned after the Brno Model ZKM, 5 1/2 lbs. Mfg. by Norinco. Imported 1990-96.

	$135	$115	$85	$70	$60	$50	$40	*$109*

ENFIELD NO. 4 – .303 British cal., genuine British Commonwealth issue, 25 1/4 in. barrel, 10 shot box mag., 9 lbs. Importation disc. 1996.

	$495	$450	$400	$350	$300	$275	$250	*$86*

RIFLES: BOLT ACTION, HOWA MFG.

Please refer to the Howa section.

RIFLES: BOLT ACTION, MAUSER ACTIONS

Whitworth rifles were mfg. in England. Mark X rifles were mfg. in Yugoslavia by Zastava Arms until late 1997.

MARK X VISCOUNT – .22-250 Rem. (disc. 1993), .243 Win. (disc. 1993), .25-06 Rem. (disc. 1993), .270 Win. (disc. 1993), 7x57mm (disc. 1993), 7mm Rem. Mag. (disc. 1994), .308 Win. (disc. 1994), .30-06, or .300 Win. Mag. (disc. 1994) cal., 5 shot, 3 shot mag., 24 in. barrel, adj. rear sight and trigger, classic style Monte Carlo stock. Disc. 1983, reintroduced 1985, disc. 1996.

	$425	$375	$300	$265	$240	$225	$205	*$471*

Add $15 for 7mm Rem. Mag. or .300 Win. Mag. cal.

This model is often referred to as the Viscount. Early manufacture was done in Manchester, England. Recent manufacture was in Yugoslavia. Earlier Manchester guns (before approx. 1980) will bring a slight premium over the values listed.

* ***Mark X Viscount Mini*** – .223 Rem. or 7.62x39mm (new in 1990) cal., miniature M98 Mauser System action, 20 in. barrel with iron sights, checkered hardwood stock, 5 shot mag., adj. trigger, 6.35 lbs. Imported 1987-94.

	$410	$360	$295	$265	$240	$225	$205	*$455*

* ***Mark X Viscount Lightweight*** – .22-250 Rem. (new 1994), .270 Win. (disc.), .30-06 (disc. 1994), or 7mm Rem. Mag. (disc.) cal., similar to Mark X Viscount, except has Carbolite (synthetic) stock and 20 in. barrel, 7 lbs. Imported 1988-90, reintroduced 1994-97.

	$395	$350	$290	$265	$240	$225	$205	*$438*

CAVALIER – similar to Viscount, except modern style stock, roll-over cheekpiece, rosewood pistol grip cap and forend tip, recoil pad. Disc.

	$425	$375	$335	$305	$290	$265	$230	

GRADING - PPGS™	100%	98%	95%	90%	80%	70%	60%	LAST MSR

MANNLICHER STYLE CARBINE – similar to Cavalier, except 20 in. barrel, full-length stock, no Magnum or varmint calibers. Disc.

	$550	$500	$450	$395	$350	$300	$275	

CONTINENTAL CARBINE – similar to Mannlicher Style, except with double set trigger. Disc.

	$600	$550	$495	$440	$400	$325	$295	

THE MARQUIS – .243 Win., .270 Win., .308 Win., 7x57mm, or .30-06 cal., 20 in. barrel, adj. trigger. Mannlicher style carbine. Disc. 1984.

	$550	$500	$450	$395	$350	$300	$275	

ALASKAN – similar to Mark X, except .375 H&H or .458 Win. Mag. cal., recoil pad and extra stock crossbolt. Disc. 1984.

	$650	$595	$550	$500	$450	$395	$350	

MARK X REALTREE – .270 Win. or .30-06 cal., features Realtree Camo finish. Imported 1994-96.

	$460	$390	$365	$320	$275	$250	$225	*$549*

MARK X WHITWORTH – .270 Win., .30-06, and .300 Win. Mag. cals., Mauser action, 24 in. barrel, open sights, 5 shot mag. (.300 Win. Mag. is only 3), checkered deluxe walnut stock with ebony forearm tip, thumb safety, sling swivels, adj. trigger, rubber recoil buttplate, 7 lbs. Imported 1984-96.

	$475	$400	$365	$320	$275	$250	$225	*$565*

Add $19 for 7mm Rem. Mag. (disc.) or .300 Win. Mag. cal.

This model was the Whitworth American Field Series until 1987. Early manufacture was done in Manchester, England. Later manufacture was by Zastava located in Yugoslavia. Earlier Manchester guns (before approx. 1980) will bring a slight premium over the values listed.

WHITWORTH MANNLICHER STYLE CARBINE – .243 Win., .270 Win., .308 Win., 7x57mm, or .30-06 cal., bolt action with full-length walnut Mannlicher style stock, open sights, sling swivels, thumb safety, 20 in. barrel, 5 shot mag., 7 lbs. Imported 1984-87.

	$675	$600	$525	$450	$415	$375	$340	*$675*

WHITWORTH EXPRESS RIFLE – .375 H&H (disc. 1993) or .458 Win. Mag. cal., 3 shot, 24 in. barrel, 3 leaf express sight, English style walnut stock, checkered pistol grip and forend, 8 1/2 lbs. Imported 1974-96.

	$995	$895	$825	$750	$650	$550	$450	*$703*

RIFLES: SEMI-AUTO

22-ATD – .22 LR cal. only, patterned after the Browning Semi-Auto, 19.4 in. barrel, 11 shot mag. in stock, blue finish, checkered hardwood stock, takedown design, adj. rear sight, 4.6 lbs. Mfg. by Norinco 1987-96.

	$250	$225	$195	$175	$150	$125	$100	*$121*

Add $16 for camo case (disc.).

INTERARMS ARSENAL

Previous trademark of AR-15 style firearms imported and distributed by High Standard Manufacturing Company, located in Houston, TX.

Please refer to BlueBookOfGunValues.com to order the *Blue Book of AR-15s & Variations*, available as a book or online subscription.

INTERCONTINENTAL ARMS INC.

Previous importer located in Los Angeles, CA circa 1970s.

Intercontinental Arms Inc. imported a variety of SA revolvers, an AR-15 type semi-auto rifle, a derringer, a rolling block single shot rifle, and a line of black powder pistol reproductions and replicas. While these firearms were good, utilitarian shooters, they have limited desirability in today's marketplace. The single action revolvers manufactured by Hämmerli are typically priced in the $200-$395 range, the derringer is priced in the $115-$175 range, the AR-15 copy is priced in the $425-$675 range, and the single shot rolling block rifle is priced in the $150-$200 range, depending on original condition.

INTERDYNAMIC OF AMERICA, INC.

Previous distributor located in Miami, FL 1981-84.

PISTOLS: SEMI-AUTO

KG-9 – 9mm Para. cal., 3 in. barrel, SA, open bolt, tactical design pistol. Disc. approx. 1982.

	$850	$800	$700	$675	$650	$600	$575	

KG-99 – 9mm Para. cal., 3 in. barrel, SA, tactical design pistol, closed bolt, 36 shot mag., 5 in. vent. shroud barrel, blue only, a stainless steel version of the KG-9. Mfg. by Interdynamic 1984 only.

	$425	$375	$325	$275	$250	$225	$195	

* ***KG-99M Mini Pistol***

	$495	$450	$400	$325	$275	$250	$225	

GRADING - PPGS™	100%	98%	95%	90%	80%	70%	60%	LAST MSR

INTERNATIONAL BUSINESS MACHINE CORP. (IBM)

Previous WWII subcontractor of M1 carbines located in Poughkeepsie, NY.

Please refer to U.S. M1 Carbines/Rifles listings under U.S. Military.

INTERNATIONAL FIREARMS CORP. (IFC)

Current importer located in Midwest City, OK.

International Firearms Corp. currently imports pistols from Arsenal Firearms located in Italy, rifles from Strasser located in Austria, shotguns from Iron Armi located in Italy, and shotguns from Yazicilarav (YAZ) located in Turkey. Pistols were also previously imported from Bul Armory/Bul Ltd. located in Israel until 2019.

INTERNATIONAL HARVESTER CORP.

Previous Post-WWII subcontractor of M1 Garand rifles.

Please refer to U.S. M1 Carbines/Rifles listings under U.S. Military.

INTERSTATE ARMS CORP.

Previous importer and current wholesale distributor located in Billerica, MA. Interstate Arms Corporation closed its doors in January 2019 and the business is now owned by Witmer Public Safety Group out of Coatesville, PA. Interstate Arms Corp. retained their name and is now operating as a DBA.

Interstate Arms Corp. imported a variety of Chinese made cowboy action shotguns and reproductions, as well as pistols from Turkey.

PISTOLS: SEMI-AUTO

REGENT R100 1911 – .45 ACP cal., 5 in. stainless steel barrel, matte black finish, 7 shot mag., checkered brown plastic grips, mfg. by Tisas in Turkey. Imported 2010-2011.

$495	$450	$395	$365	$335	$300	$275	*$560*

Current production imported by Umarex can be found under the Regent listing.

SHOTGUNS: SxS

MODEL 99 COACH GUN – 12 or 20 ga., 3 in. chambers, exposed hammers, 20 in. barrels with cyl./cyl. fixed chokes, blue finish with checkered stock and forearm, 7.2 lbs. Importation began 1999, manufactured by SD2 Linyi. Disc. 2009.

$325	$275	$250	$225	$200	$175	$160	*$340*

SHOTGUNS: LEVER ACTION

MODEL 87W – 12 ga. only, 2 3/4 in. chamber, patterned after the Winchester Model 1887, 20 in. barrel, walnut stock and forearm, previous mfg. by SD1 Rizhou, current mfg. by Sun City Machinery Ltd. Imported mid-2003-2010.

$675	$600	$500	$450	$375	$300	$250	*$560*

SHOTGUNS: SLIDE ACTION

MODEL 97W HAMMER – 12 ga. only, patterned after the Win. Model 97, hammer, 20 or 26 (new 2008) in. plain barrel with cylinder bore fixed choke, solid frame, oil finish American walnut (new 2005) or hardwood (disc. 2004) stock with grooved "corn cob" forearm, previous mfg. by SD1 Rizhou, current mfg. by Sun City Machinery Ltd. Imported 2001-2010.

$850	$750	$650	$575	$475	$375	$300	*$425*

MODEL 97T WWI TRENCH GUN – 12 ga. only, authentic reproduction of the original Winchester WWI Trench Gun, complete with shrouded barrel, proper markings, finish, and wood. Imported mid-2002-2006, reintroduced 2010. Mfg. by Sun City Machinery Ltd. Importaton disc. circa 2018.

$1,000	$875	$750	$675	$550	$450	$350	*$465*

MODEL 372 – 12 ga., 3 in. chamber, 18 1/2 in. barrel with heat shield and ghost ring sights, bottom ejection port, cylinder choke, black synthetic stock and forearm. Limited importation 2007-2009.

$200	$175	$150	$135	$110	$90	$70	*$250*

MODEL 1893/97 – similar to Model 97, except built on receiver patterned after Winchester Model 1893, mfg. by SD1 Rizhou. Limited importation mid-2006-2007.

$575	$500	$425	$400	$325	$250	$200	*$399*

HAWK FIELD – 12 ga., steel receiver, 26 or 28 in. VR barrel with modified choke, bead sight, black synthetic stock and forearm. Imported 2014-circa 2018.

$280	$245	$210	$190	$180	$170	$160	*$310*

GRADING - PPGS™	100%	98%	95%	90%	80%	70%	60%	LAST MSR

HAWK 981R DEFENSE – 12 ga. only, 3 in. chamber, defense configuration with 18 1/2 in. cylinder bore barrel, black synthetic stock and forearm, matte black steel receiver, bead sight with 4 1/2 in. Picatinny rail. Imported 2013-circa 2018.

$250 $225 $200 $185 $170 $160 $150 ***$277***

HAWK 982 – 12 ga. only, 3 in. chamber, defense configuration with 18 1/2 in. cylinder bore barrel with fixed choke, black synthetic stock and forearm, matte black metal finish, current mfg. uses ghost ring sights. Imported 2001-circa 2018.

$260 $230 $200 $185 $170 $160 $150 ***$293***

HAWK 982 T – 12 ga., steel receiver, cyl. bore, ghost ring sights, black synthetic pistol grip stock. Imported 2014-circa 2018.

$270 $240 $210 $190 $180 $170 $160 ***$300***

INTRAC ARMS INTERNATIONAL INC.

Previous importer located in Knoxville, TN. Intrac imported trademarks manufactured by Arsenal Bulgaria, and by IM Metal Production facility in Croatia late 2000-2004. Previously imported by HS America, located in Knoxville, TN.

For individual model listings, please go to BlueBookOfGunValues.com/overflow.

INTRATEC

Previous manufacturer located in Miami, FL circa 1985-2000.

PISTOLS: SEMI-AUTO

PROTEC-25 – .25 ACP. cal., double action only, 2 1/2 in. barrel, 8 shot mag., 13 oz. Disc. 2000.

$110 $80 $65 $45 $35 $30 $25 ***$137***

Add $5 for Tec-Kote finish or black slide/frame finish (disc.).

TEC-DC9 – 9mm Para. cal., 5 in. shrouded barrel, SA, matte black finish, 10 (C/B 1994) or 32* shot mag. Mfg. 1985-1994.

$475 $425 $375 $300 $275 $225 $200 ***$269***

* ***TEC-9DCK*** – similar to TEC-9, except has new durable Tec-Kote finish with better protection than hard chrome. Mfg. 1991-94.

$495 $465 $425 $375 $325 $295 $260 ***$297***

* ***TEC-DC9S*** – matte stainless version of the TEC-9. Disc. 1994.

$550 $500 $450 $400 $350 $300 $250 ***$362***

Add $203 for TEC-9 with accessory package (deluxe case, 3-32 shot mags., tactical design grip, and recoil compensator).

TEC-DC9M – mini version of the Model TEC-9, including 3 in. barrel and 20 shot mag. Disc. 1994.

$495 $465 $425 $375 $325 $295 $260 ***$245***

* ***TEC-DC9MK*** – similar to TEC-9M, except has Tec-Kote rust resistant finish. Mfg. 1991-94.

$525 $450 $400 $350 $300 $250 $200 ***$277***

* ***TEC-DC9MS*** – matte stainless version of the TEC-9M. Disc. 1994.

$575 $500 $450 $400 $350 $300 $275 ***$339***

TEC-22 "SCORPION" – .22 LR cal., 4 in. barrel, SA, ambidextrous safety, military matte finish, or electroless nickel, 30 shot mag., adj. sights, 30 oz. Mfg. 1988-1994.

$375 $325 $275 $225 $200 $175 $160 ***$202***

Add $20 for Tec-Kote finish.

* ***TEC-22N*** – similar to TEC-22, except has nickel finish. Mfg. 1990 only.

$395 $345 $300 $275 $250 $230 $220 ***$226***

Add $16 for threaded barrel (Model TEC-22TN).

TEC-22T – threaded barrel variation of the TEC-22 "Scorpion." Mfg. 1991-94.

$395 $350 $300 $250 $225 $195 $175 ***$161***

Add $23 for Tec-Kote finish.

SPORT-22 – .22 LR cal., 4 in. non-threaded barrel, 10 shot Ruger styled rotary mag., matte finish, adj. rear sight, 29 1/2 oz. New 1995.

$195 $175 $150 $125 $100 $85 $75 ***$170***

Add $15 for stainless steel barrel.

GRADING - PPGS™	100%	98%	95%	90%	80%	70%	60%	LAST MSR

CAT-9, CAT-45, CAT-380 – .380 ACP (new 1995), 9mm Para., or .45 ACP (new 1995) cal., double action only, black finish, polymer frame, sight channel, in slide, only 27 parts, blowback action on 9mm Para., locked breech on .45 ACP, 6 (.45 ACP cal.) or 7 (.380 ACP or 9mm Para.) shot mag., 3 or 3 1/4 (.45 ACP only) in. barrel, 18-21 oz. Mfg. 1993-2000.

$235	$200	$175	$150	$125	$100	$90	*$260*

Subtract $25 for .380 ACP cal.
Add $20 for .45 ACP cal.
Add $15 for Fire Sights.

This series was designed by N. Sirkis of Israel.

AB-10 – 9mm Para. cal., design similar to Luger, 2 3/4 in. non-threaded barrel, SA, choice of 32* (limited supply) or 10 shot mag., black synthetic frame, firing pin safety block, black or stainless steel finish, 45 oz. Mfg. 1997-2000.

$325	$275	$235	$200	$180	$160	$150	*$225*

Add $20 for stainless steel (new 2000).
Add $100 for 32 shot mag.

INTRATEC U.S.A., INC.

Previous manufacturer located in Miami, FL.

CARBINES

TEC-9C – 9mm Para. cal., carbine variation with 16 1/2 in. barrel, 36 shot mag.

Only 1 gun mfg. 1987 - extreme rarity precludes accurate pricing.

DERRINGERS

TEC-38 DERRINGER – .22 WMR, .32 H&R Mag., .357 Mag., or .38 Spl. cal., O/U, 3 in. blue barrel, synthetic black frame, double action, 13 oz. Mfg. 1986-1988.

$110	$95	$85	$75	$65	$60	$55	*$125*

PISTOLS: SEMI-AUTO

PROTEC-22 – while advertised for $112 MSR during 1993, this model never went into production.

TEC-9 – 9mm Para. cal., 5 in. shrouded barrel, SA, 32 shot mag. Disc.

$550	$495	$450	$395	$350	$295	$250	

INVESTARM, Srl

Current manufacturer located in Marcheno, Italy. Previously distributed by Kimber until 2005, located in Yonkers, NY.

Investarm manufactures a wide variety of competition shotguns in various configurations, including folding single shot and folding O/Us, which are not currently imported into the U.S. The company also manufactures a single shot folding rifle, in addition to muzzleloading black powder rifles and pistols. Please contact the company directly for more information, including pricing and U.S. availability.

INVESTMENT ARMS INC.

Previous company specializing in limited/special editions located in Fort Collins, CO.

Investment Arms Inc. subcontracted with various gun manufacturers to produce their own limited editions/special editions. These guns were typically marketed within a limited geographic area (usually county or state), and featured various engraving motifs, configurations, and other embellishments. Secondary marketplace liquidity is difficult to determine, based on relative desirability and limited collectibility.

INVINCIBLE ARMS LLC

Previous AR-15 style rifle, parts, and accessories manufacturer located in Willoughby, OH circa 2013-2016.

Please refer to BlueBookOfGunValues.com to order the *Blue Book of AR-15s & Variations*, available as a book or online subscription.

IRON ARMI Srl

Current manufacturer of hunting, sporting, and tactical/defensive shotguns, located in Flero (Brescia), Italy. Currently imported by International Firearm Corp. located in Midwest City, OK.

Iron Armi manufactures good quality semi-automatic, slide action, SxS, and O/U shotguns. Please contact the importer directly for U.S. availability and pricing.

GRADING - PPGS™	100%	98%	95%	90%	80%	70%	60%	LAST MSR

SHOTGUNS: SEMI-AUTO

SPORTING SHOTGUN – 12 ga., 3 in. chamber, GIO, raised rib w/mid-bead and choke tubes, compatible w/JEBS Precision choke tubes, carbon fiber stock and forend, adj. buttstock and cheekpiece, milled receiver, billet receiver, matte black barrel and receiver (red also available). Importation began 2016.

Please contact the importer for availability and pricing on this model.

COMPETITION SHOTGUN – 12 ga., 3 in. chamber, GIO, high polished blued barrel, operational w/choke tubes or compensator (compatible w/JEBS Precision choke tubes), adj. fiber optic sights, carbon fiber stock, adj. buttstock, milled, billet aluminum receiver, oversized charging handle and bolt stop.

This model was built in partnership with Toni Systems.

IRON BRIGADE ARMORY

Previous rifle manufacturer located in Jacksonville, NC 1979-2016.

Iron Brigade Armory closed its doors shortly following the passing of owner Roy Chandler passed away December 2015.

RIFLES: BOLT ACTION

Iron Brigade Armory previously manufactured the following bolt action rifles: XM-3 Rifle - last MSR was $8,295, Chandler M40 Long Range Precision Rifle - last MSR was $5,995, M40 USM Chandler Urban Model - last MSR was $6,900, TAC-100 Tactical Standard Grade (rifle only) - last MSR was $2,295, TAC-200 Tactical Standard Grade (with optics) - last MSR was $3,195, TAC-300 Tactical Standard Grade (complete) - last MSR was $3,595, TAC-400 Tactical Super Grade (rifle only) - last MSR was $2,850, TAC-500 Tactical Super Grade (with optics) - last MSR was $3,750, and TAC-600 Tactical Super Grade (complete) - last MSR was $4,150. Several options and upgrades were available on each model.

IRON RIDGE ARMS CO.

Current AR-15 style rifle manufacturer located in Longmount, CO.

Please refer to BlueBookOfGunValues.com to order the *Blue Book of AR-15s & Variations*, available as a book or online subscription.

IRWIN PEDERSON ARMS CO.

Previous WWII subcontractor of M1 carbines located in Grand Rapids, MI.

Please refer to U.S. M1 Carbines/Rifles listings under U.S. Military.

IRWINDALE ARMS, INC. (IAI)

Previous manufacturer located in Irwindale, CA 1988-1991.

PISTOLS: SEMI-AUTO

In June, 1991, AMT reacquired the manufacturing rights to all IAI models. Please refer to the AMT section for recent models.

AUTOMAG III – .30 Carbine or 9mm Win. Mag. (mfg. 1990-92) cal., stainless steel only, 6 3/8 in. barrel, patterned after Colt Govt. Model, Millett adj. sights with white outline, grooved Lexan grips, 8 shot mag., 43 oz. Mfg. 1989-91.

$2,300	$2,000	$1,625	$1,400	$1,275	$1,000	$800	*$606*

AUTOMAG IV – .45 Win. Mag., or 10mm cal., 6 1/2 or 8 5/8 (mfg. 1991) in. barrel, 7 shot mag., Millett adj. sights, stainless steel only, 46 oz. Mfg. 1990-1991.

$2,000	$1,750	$1,500	$1,325	$1,100	$900	$700	*$630*

JAVELINA – 10mm cal., 5 (disc. 1991) or 7 in. barrel, 8 shot mag., Millett adj. sights, wraparound Neoprene grips, stainless steel, wide adj. trigger, long grip safety, 48 oz. Mfg. 1990-1991.

$1,475	$1,300	$1,100	$1,000	$825	$675	$525	*$570*

BACKUP PISTOL – .380 ACP cal., semi-auto action, 2 1/2 in. barrel, stainless steel, Lexan grips, 5 shot mag., 18 oz. Older disc. walnut grip models are worth a slight premium. Disc. 1989.

$380	$330	$275	$250	$220	$175	$140	*$243*

ISRAEL ARMS INTERNATIONAL, INC.

Previous importer and manufacturer located in Houston, TX, 1997-2004. Please refer to IAI Inc. - American Legend listing in this section.

ISRAEL ARMS LTD.

Previous manufacturer located in Kfar Saba, Israel. Imported and distributed exclusively by Israel Arms International, Inc. located in Houston, TX 1997-2001.

GRADING - PPGS™	100%	98%	95%	90%	80%	70%	60%	LAST MSR

PISTOLS: SEMI-AUTO

MODEL 1500 HI POWER – 9mm Para. cal., single action, 3.85 (Compact) or 4.64 (Standard, disc. 1998) in. barrel, two-tone finish, rubberized grips, regular or Meprolite sights, 10 shot mag., 33.6 oz. Imported 1997-98 only.

$360 $305 $255 $225 $200 $185 $170 *$413*

Add approx. $160 for two-tone finish with Meprolite sights.

* ***Model 1500/1501 Hi-Power Compact*** – 9mm Para. or .40 S&W cal., compact variation with 3.85 in. barrel, choice of two-tone (Model 1500) or blue (Model 1501) finish, 32.2 oz. Imported late 1999-2000.

$360 $305 $255 $225 $200 $185 $170 *$412*

MODEL 2500 – 9mm Para. or .40 S&W cal., single or double action, ambidextrous safety with decocking feature, steel slide with alloy frame, 3 7/8 in. barrel, 10 shot mag., matte black finish, 34 oz. While advertised during 1999, this model had very limited importation.

MODEL 3000 – 9mm Para. cal., double action. Limited importation 2000-2001.

$335 $295 $260 $230 $200 $175 $150 *$374*

MODEL 4000 – .40 S&W cal., double action. Limited importation 2000-2001.

$335 $295 $260 $230 $200 $175 $150 *$374*

MODEL 5000/5001 COMBAT – .45 ACP cal., single action, 4 1/4 in barrel, combat configuration with ambidextrous safety, competition trigger, hammer, and slide stop, front and rear slide serrations, blue (Model 5001) or two-tone (Model 5000) finish, wraparound rubber grips, 42 oz. Mfg. in Philippines. Imported 1999-2001.

$395 $365 $330 $295 $265 $235 $210 *$448*

MODEL 6000/6001 STANDARD – .45 ACP cal., single action, 5 in. stainless steel barrel, features beveled feed ramp, extended slide stop, safety and magazine release, ambidextrous safety, beavertail grip safety, combat style hammer, blue (Model 6001) or two-tone (Model 6000, disc. 2000) finish, 38 oz. Mfg. in Philippines. Imported 1999-2001.

$395 $365 $330 $295 $265 $235 $210 *$448*

MODEL 7000/7001 WIDE FRAME – .45 ACP cal., single action, similar to Model 6000/6001, except has double stack mag., blue (Model 7001) or two-tone (Model 7000) finish, 40 oz. Imported 1999-2000.

$445 $395 $350 $300 $255 $225 $200 *$490*

RIFLES: SEMI-AUTO

MODEL 333 M1 GARAND – .30-06 cal., 24 in. barrel, parts remanufactured to meet GI and Mil-Specs, parkerized finish, 8 shot en bloc clip, 9 1/2 lbs. Mfg. 2000-2001.

$895 $850 $800 $700 $600 $500 $400 *$852*

MODEL 444 FAL – .308 Win. cal., patterned after the FN FAL model. Mfg. by Imbel, located in Brazil, 2000-2001.

$925 $850 $795 $725 $675 $595 $550 *$897*

ISRAEL MILITARY INDUSTRIES (IMI)

Previous manufacturer established 1933-circa 2009, and located in Israel.

IMI manufactured guns (both new and disc. models) include Galil, Jericho, Magnum Research, Timberwolf, Uzi, and others, and can be located in their respective sections.

ISRAEL WEAPON INDUSTRIES LTD. (IWI)

Current manufacturer established circa 2009, located in Israel. Currently imported beginning 2013 by IWI US, Inc. located in Middletown, PA. Previously located in Harrisburg, PA.

For individual model listings, please go to BlueBookOfGunValues.com/overflow.

ISTANBUL SILAH

Current manufacturer located in Istanbul, Turkey since 2003. No current U.S. importation. Istanbul Silah manufactures semi-auto shotguns under the Impala Plus trademark. Please contact the manufacturer directly for more information on their current line-up including price, options, and availability.

ITALIAN MILITARY ARMS

Previous Italian popular military models mfg. since 1891.

PISTOLS: SEMI-AUTO

GLISENTI MODEL 1910 – 9mm Glisenti cal., 4 in. barrel, 7 shot mag., checkered wood grips, official Italian service pistol of both WWI and WWII, 32 oz.

$1,750 $1,500 $1,200 $1,000 $800 $600 $500

Warning: 9mm Para. ammunition (9x19mm) cannot be used in this pistol - only 9mm Glisenti, as it is approx. 25% less powerful than the 9mm Para.

GRADING - PPGS™	100%	98%	95%	90%	80%	70%	60%	LAST MSR

BRIXIA – similar to Glisenti Model 1910, except utilizes simplified mfg. techniques, mostly sold to civilians.

	$2,250	$1,750	$1,250	$1,000	$750	$600	$500	

SOSSO – 9mm Para. cal., large experimental semi-auto, early pistols were double action and marked "Sosso", late guns were single action and built by FNA. All Sosso pistols feature a unique continuous "chain link" 19 or 21 shot mag. Approx. 5 guns mfg.

Extreme rarity factor precludes accurate price evaluation.

RIFLES/CARBINES: BOLT ACTION

MODEL 1891 MANNLICHER-CARCANO – 6.5x52mm Carcano cal., integrated 6 shot mag. that forms front part of trigger guard housing, 18 (carbine) or 31 (rifle) in. barrel, straight bolt handle, adj. sight, military stock, carbine has either folding or detachable bayonet, mfg. in Italian Govt. Arsenals, located in Terni, Brescia, Torre Annuziata, and Torino circa 1891-1918. Approx. 3.5-4 million mfg.

	$225	$175	$150	$125	$100	$85	$70	

MODEL 38 TERNI MILITARY RIFLE – 7.35x52mm Carcano cal., similar to 1891, except turned down bolt handle, 21 in. barrel and folding bayonet.

	$225	$175	$150	$125	$100	$85	$70	

ITHACA CLASSIC DOUBLES

Previous importer and SxS shotgun manufacturer 1998-2003, and located in Victor, NY from 1999-2003 and Mendon, NY until 1999.

RIFLES: SxS

DOUBLE RIFLE – many popular cals., including .45-70 Govt., also available in 20 ga. with 26 in. fully rifled barrels, express sights, German claw type scope mounts, DT, ejectors, exhibition walnut standard, many options were available. Limited importation only.

Advertised MSR was $8,500, w/o engraving or other special orders/features.

SHOTGUNS: SxS

All Ithaca Classic Doubles shotguns were handmade to order in the U.S. Frames were made from the traditional forgings and internal parts from solid steel. Barrels were hammer forged from geniune Krupp steel. Metal finishing, checkering, oil finish, and engraving were done completely by hand. All guns were fitted to customer's specifications and wood selection. Guns were available in .410 bore through 12 ga., with full rifle barrels available in 12 or 20 ga. and .45-70 Govt. cal. Each gauge has its own frame size, and serial numbers were continued from the last gun Ithaca manufactured in 1948 (ser. no. 469,999).

The Ithaca custom shop manufactured custom orders, including special options and features.

For Special Combination Sets - add $3,000 (4E, 5E, 6E) and $3,750 (Grades 7E & Sousa) for extra set of 16 (20 ga. frame) or 28 (.410 bore frame) ga. barrels.
Add $600-$2,150 for canvas, canvas and leather, leather, or oak and leather cases.
Add $1,125 for SST and vent. rib.
Add $950 for VR.

SKEET GRADE (SPECIAL FIELD) – 16 (new 2001), 20, 28 ga., or .410 bore, designed for field and clay shooting, DT, ejectors, 26, 28, or 30 in. barrels with fixed chokes, light perimeter hand engraving with metal stippling on shoulders and in front of top opening lever, Turnbull bone and charcoal case colors, checkered pistol grip or English feather crotch walnut stock and forearm, 5 lbs. 5 oz.-6 lbs. 6 oz. Mfg. late 1998-2002.

	$5,500	$4,750	$3,750	$3,250	$2,650	$2,175	$1,775	*$5,999*

Add 20% for SST or vent. rib option.

CLASSIC COMPETITION GRADE – all gauges, competition features. Mfg. 2002-2003.

	$5,500	$4,750	$3,750	$3,250	$2,650	$2,175	$1,775	*$5,995*

GRADE 4E CLASSIC – 16 (new 2001), 20, 28 ga., or .410 bore, features gold plated triggers, jewelled barrel flats, hand tuned locks, hand engraved three game scenes with floral scroll, deluxe walnut stock and forearm with fleur-de-lis pattern and 22 LPI checkering, other specifications similar to Special Field/Skeet Grade. Mfg. 1998-2003.

	$6,750	$5,750	$4,900	$4,100	$3,300	$2,500	$1,850	*$7,500*

STAR MODEL COMPETITION – competition model. Limited mfg. 2003.

	$6,750	$5,750	$4,900	$4,100	$3,300	$2,500	$1,850	*$7,500*

GRADE 5E CLASSIC – step up from Grade 4E, with more elaborate frame engraving and gold inlays on frame sides, upgraded walnut. Mfg. 2002-2003.

	$7,500	$6,500	$5,750	$4,850	$4,100	$3,500	$2,500	*$8,500*

GRADING - PPGS™	100%	98%	95%	90%	80%	70%	60%	LAST MSR

GRADE 6E CLASSIC – step up from Grade 5E, with fine scroll engraving and gold dog inlays on frame sides, upgraded walnut. Mfg. 2002-2003.

	$8,500	$7,500	$6,500	$5,750	$4,950	$4,150	$3,250	*$9,999*

GRADE 7E CLASSIC – 16 (new 2001), 20, 28 ga., or .410 bore, features hand engraved oak leaf scroll on frame and barrels, and 24Kt. flat gold game scene inlays, including a bald eagle on floorplate, exhibition grade American walnut with 12 checkered panels in fleur-de-lis pattern, other specifications similar to Special Field/Skeet Grade. Mfg. 1998-2003.

	$9,250	$8,250	$7,250	$6,150	$5,350	$4,450	$3,500	*$11,000*

SOUSA SPECIAL – 16 (new 2001), 20, 28 ga., or .410 bore, top-of-the-line model with every possible refinement, each gun individually hand fitted, jewelled, and polished, includes famous 24Kt. Sousa mermaid on trigger guard, other specifications similar to Special Field/Skeet Grade. Special order only, limited mfg. 1998-2003.

	$16,750	$14,000	$12,000	$10,000	$8,250	$7,000	$5,750	*$18,000*

SUPERLATIVE CLASS – custom order, best quality model with a wide choice of engraving options and inlays, exhibition grade walnut, approx. 10-15 guns were mfg. annually. Limited mfg. 2002-2003.

Prices for this model started at $20,000.

SHOTGUNS: SINGLE SHOT

KNICKERBOCKER SINGLE BARREL TRAP – limited mfg. of 100 guns during 2003.

Prices for this model started at $9,000, w/o engraving.

ITHACA GUN COMPANY (NEW MFG.)

Current manufacturer established in 2006, located in Upper Sandusky, OH, with facilities in Aynor, SC, beginning 2014.

During December of 2007, Ithaca Gun Company bought out the remaining assets and equipment of Ithaca Gun Company LLC and moved production to Upper Sandusky, OH.

PISTOLS: SEMI-AUTO

MODEL 1911 – .45 ACP cal., hand lapped frame and slide, 4 1/4 (Carry Model, new 2015) or 5 in. stainless match grade barrel (Standard Model), 7 shot mag., rear slide serrations, blue or chrome (new 2014) finish, skeletonized trigger, extended beavertail, double diamond checkered walnut grips, includes case. New mid-2011.

MSR $1,575	$1,375	$1,150	$1,000	$875	$725	$575	$425	

Add $50 for adj. sights or $150 for adj. sights and ambidextrous safety.
Add $951 for chrome finish (new 2015).
Add $800 for hand-fit construction.

RIFLES: BOLT ACTION

GUARDIAN – .308 Win. cal., short action platform, competition grade barrel and trigger, chrome moly steel billet receiver, maple, synthetic, or walnut stock. Mfg. 2015-2018.

	$1,375	$1,150	$1,000	$875	$725	$575	$425	*$1,575*

Add $300 for maple stock.

PROTECTOR – .300 Win. Mag. cal., long action platform, competition grade barrel and trigger, chrome moly steel billet receiver, maple, synthetic, or walnut stock. Mfg. 2015-2018.

	$1,450	$1,250	$1,100	$1,000	$800	$650	$500	*$1,650*

Add $300 for maple stock.

SAVIOR – .308 Win., .300 Win. Mag., or .338 Lapua cal., long action platform, competition grade barrel and trigger, chrome moly steel billet receiver, aluminum chassis. Mfg. 2015-2017.

	$2,750	$2,400	$2,050	$1,850	$1,500	$1,250	$950	*$3,173*

Add $80 for .300 Win. cal.
Premium added for .338 Lapua cal.

SHOTGUNS: SLIDE ACTION

MODEL 37 CLASSIC FEATHERLIGHT – 12, 20, or 28 ga., 2 3/4 in. chamber, 24, 26, or 28 in. VR barrel, three choke tubes, 5 shot, bottom ejection, gold plated trigger, fancy AAA walnut stock, Pachmayr recoil pad, right or left-hand configuration, matte blue or hard chrome (disc.) finish, 6 lbs. New 2007.

MSR $895	$795	$725	$650	$575	$500	$400	$300	

Add $250 for 28 ga. w/engraving and deluxe wood.
Add $300 for hard chrome (disc.).

GRADING - PPGS™	100%	98%	95%	90%	80%	70%	60%	LAST MSR

MODEL 37 CLASSIC FEATHERLIGHT TRAP – 12 ga., 3 in. chamber, 30 in. with (60/40 or 70/30) VR or field (disc.) barrel, three Briley choke tubes, 5 shot, bottom ejection, gold plated trigger, TruGlo front sight (VR barrel) or brass bead front (Field barrel) sight, classic game scene engraving, fancy A, AA, or AAA walnut Monte Carlo stock, Pachmayr recoil pad, matte blue finish, 7.6 lbs.

MSR $1,020	$875	$725	$625	$500	$400	$350	$295	

Add $350 for Grade AAA walnut stock.

* ***Model 37 Classic Featherlight Trap Combo*** – 12 or 20 ga., 3 in. chamber, 24, 26, 28, or 30 in. VR or Field barrel, three choke tubes, 5 shot, bottom ejection, gold plated trigger, TruGlo front sight (VR barrel) or brass bead front (Field barrel) sight, classic game scene engraving, fancy AAA walnut stock, Pachmayr recoil pad, matte blue finish, includes 24 in. rifled Deerslayer barrel with customer choice of fiber optic rifle sights or cantilever scope mounts.

MSR $1,180	$1,000	$875	$750	$625	$500	$400	$350	

* ***Model 37 Classic Featherlight Trap Youth Stock*** – 12 or 20 ga., 3 in. chamber, 24, 26, 28, or 30 in. VR or Field barrel, three choke tubes, 5 shot, bottom ejection, gold plated trigger, TruGlo front sight (VR barrel) or brass bead front (Field barrel) sight, classic game scene engraving, fancy AAA walnut ATI adj. youth stock, Pachmayr recoil pad, matte blue finish.

MSR $895	$765	$675	$575	$520	$420	$350	$300	

MODEL 37 CLASSIC FEATHERLIGHT LADIES STOCK – 20 ga., Solderless Barrel System (SBS) with 26, 28, or 30 in. VR barrel, three Briley choke tubes, 5 shot, bottom ejection, lengthened forcing cone, gold plated trigger, classic game scene engraving, features unique drop of comb, drop of heel, cast pitch, and toe out, 14 1/4 in. LOP, TruGlo front sight, fancy black walnut semi-pistol buttstock, slim grip checkered forend, black Pachmayr Decelerator recoil pad, matte blued steel receiver, barrel, and trigger group, 6.8 lbs. New 2014.

MSR $895	$765	$675	$575	$520	$420	$350	$300	

MODEL 37 DEERSLAYER II – 12 or 20 ga., 3 in. chamber, 24 in. fixed barrel, 5 shot, bottom ejection, gold plated trigger, fiber optic rifle sight, drilled and tapped for scope mounts, fancy Grade A, AA, or AAA walnut stock, with or without thumbhole, Pachmayr recoil pad, sling swivel studs, Weaver scope base, matte blue finish, 6.8-7 1/2 lbs.

MSR $1,150	$985	$875	$750	$625	$500	$400	$350	

Add $350 for Grade AAA walnut stock.

MODEL 37 DEERSLAYER III – 12 or 20 ga., 3 in. chamber, 26 in. fluted fixed barrel, 5 shot, bottom ejection, gold plated trigger, fancy Grade A, AA, or AAA walnut stock, with or without thumbhole, Pachmayr recoil pad, sling swivel studs, Weaver scope base, matte blue finish, 8-9 1/2 lbs. Current Mfg.

MSR $1,350	$1,175	$1,000	$875	$775	$675	$575	$475	

Add $350 for Grade AAA walnut stock.

MODEL 37 DEFENSE – 12 or 20 ga., 3 in. chamber, 18 1/2 or 20 in. fixed barrel with standard cylinder bore, 5 or 8 shot, brass bead front sight, matte blued finish, walnut or synthetic buttstock and forend, black Pachmayr Decelerator pad, available in tactical configuration w/adj. pistol grip stock (disc.), 6.8-7.1 lbs. Current Mfg.

MSR $784	$695	$625	$525	$425	$350	$300	$250	

Add $71 for walnut stock.
Add $151 for tactical configuration w/adj. pistol grip stock (disc.).

MODEL 37 HOG SLAYER – 12 ga., 20 in. rifled barrel, 5 shot, rifled sights, synthetic stock, matte blue or camo finish, 7 lbs. Disc. 2016.

	$775	$650	$550	$475	$400	$350	$295	*$895*

Add $55 for camo finish.

MODEL 37 TACTICAL – 12 ga., 18 1/2 or 20 in. barrel, 5 or 8 shot, synthetic Mark 5, pistol grip adj., or side folding stock, 6-7.7 lbs.

MSR $799	$695	$625	$525	$425	$350	$300	$250	

MODEL 37 TURKEY SLAYER – 12 or 20 ga., 3 in. chamber, 23 in. free floating fixed barrel, extended extra-full turkey choke, 5 shot, bottom ejection, fiber optic sights, camo, synthetic or thumbhole stock, sling swivel studs, drilled and tapped for scope mounts, weather-resistant matte finish, 7.6-8.2 lbs.

MSR $899	$765	$675	$575	$520	$420	$350	$300	

MODEL 37 WATERFOWL – 12 or 20 ga., 3 in. chamber, 28 or 30 in. VR barrel, three choke tubes, 5 shot, bottom ejection, synthetic stock, steel shot compatible, PermaGuard matte black or 100% camo finish, 7.2 lbs.

MSR $865	$750	$650	$550	$475	$400	$350	$295	

GRADING - PPGS™ 100% 98% 95% 90% 80% 70% 60% LAST MSR

ITHACA GUN COMPANY LLC (OLDER MFG.)

Previous manufacturer located in Ithaca, NY from 1883-1986, King Ferry, NY circa 1989-2005, and Auburn, NY right before it closed in June, 2005.

Ithaca Gun Company, LLC resumed production on the Model 37 slide action shotgun and variations during 1989 and absorbed companies including Syracuse Arms Co., Lefever Arms Co., Union Fire Arms Co., Wilkes-Barre Gun Co., and others.

The Cody Firearms Records office offers Ithaca Gun Company research letters for some models, which have been donated to the museum by Ithaca Authority and author, Walt Snyder. Factory letters are available for approximate productions years 1886-1939, late 1950s, early 1960s, and mid 1980s. The collection includes Lefever Arms Company, Inc (1921-1939) and Western Arms Corporation (1930-1939). For more information, please visit: centerofthewest.org/explore/firearms/firearms-records/ithaca/

COMBINATION GUNS

LSA-55 TURKEY GUN – O/U shotgun-rifle combo, 12 ga., .222 Rem., 24 1/2 in. ribbed barrel, exposed hammer, folding rear sight, checkered Monte Carlo stock. Mfg. by Tikka, Finland 1970-81.

$650 $575 $475 $450 $425 $385 $330

MODEL M-6 SURVIVAL – .22 Hornet cal. over .410 bore, 14.5 in. barrels, skeletonized stock with cartridge block inside, marked on the left side of the receiver "U.S.A.F. PROPERTY/ 128304/ RIFLE-SHOTGUN. SURVIVAL/CAL. .22/410, M6" and on the right side "ITHACA GUN CO., INC. ITHACA N.Y.", with the crossed cannon ordnance stamp, mfg. for U.S. military during the 1950s.

$4,000 $3,500 $3,000 $2,720 $2,200 $1,800 $1,400

This model was packaged in survival kits for U.S. pilots, and is usually encountered with a replacement barrel of 16 inches or more. These are restricted as a National Firearms Act (NFA), AOW, (Any Other Weapon) that is currently registered with the Bureau of Alcohol, Tobacco, Firearms and Explosives (BATF&E) that has been classified as a "Curio or Relic" as defined in 27 CFR, 478.11. These weapons are still subject to the provisions of 18 U.S.C. Chapter 44 and 27 CFR part 478.

HANDGUNS

ITHACA WWII MILITARY MFG.

For more information on other WWI and WWII M1911/A1 military contracts, please refer to the Colt's Manufacturing section Pistols: Semi-Auto, Govt. M1911/1911A1 Military Variations.

ITHACA 50TH SEMI-AUTO ANNIVERSARY MODEL – .45 ACP cal., 5 in. match barrel with bushing, blue polished or tactical matte finish, checkered diamond pattern walnut grips, extended beavertail grip safety, includes plastic case and certificate, only 125 mfg. with special serialization 1995-97. Disc.

$695 $625 $550 $500 $450 $400 $360 *$795*

This model was offered exclusively by All American Sales, Inc. located in Memphis, TN.

X-CALIBER SINGLE SHOT – .22 LR or .44 Mag. (advertised only) cal., break open action with contoured wood grip and forearm, 8, 10 or 15 in. barrel, unique dual firing pin detonates both rimfire and centerfire cartridges. While advertised in 1988, the Models 20 & 30 were never retailed. Approx. 300 units were mfg. in 22 cal. only.

$1,200 $950 $825 $695 $550 $425 $300

RIFLES: BOLT ACTION

The LSA Model designation stands for Light, Strong, Accurate.

LSA-55 STANDARD – .222 Rem., .22-250 Rem., 6mm Rem., .243 Win., or .308 Win. cal., Mauser type action, 22 in. barrel, leaf sight, 3 shot mag., checkered Monte Carlo stock. Mfg. in Finland by Tikka from 1969-77.

$500 $425 $375 $325 $275 $225 $175

LSA-55 DELUXE – similar to LSA-55 Standard, except has rollover cheekpiece, rosewood pistol grip cap and forend tip, skipline checkering, no sights, scope mounts furnished.

$700 $600 $525 $450 $375 $325 $250

LSA-55 HEAVY BARREL – similar to LSA-55, except in .222 Rem. or .22-250 Rem. cal. only, target heavy barrel, special beavertail stock, 8 1/2 lbs.

$600 $525 $450 $375 $325 $275 $225

LSA-65 – similar to LSA-55, except long action for calibers .25-06 Rem., .270 Win., or .30-06 cal. Mfg. 1969-77.

$500 $425 $375 $325 $275 $225 $175

GRADING - PPGS™	100%	98%	95%	90%	80%	70%	60%	LAST MSR

LSA-65 DELUXE – similar to LSA-55, except has deluxe checkered walnut stock, .25-06 Rem., .270 Win., or .30-06 cal.

	$700	$600	$525	$450	$375	$325	$250	

RIFLES: LEVER ACTION

MODEL 49 SADDLEGUN – .22 LR or .22 WMR cal., Martini-style action, single shot. Mfg. 1961-1978.

	$250	$220	$190	$165	$140	$115	$90	

Add 15% for .22 WMR cal.
Add 20% for Deluxe Model.

MODEL 49R – .22 LR cal., similar to Model 49 Saddlegun, except is a repeater with 15 shot tube magazine. Mfg. 1965-1971.

	$300	$250	$215	$190	$165	$135	$100	

Add 15% for .22 WMR cal.

MODEL 49 PRESENTATION – .22 LR or .22 WMR cal., similar to Model 49 Saddlegun, except has gold-plated trigger, hammer, engraved receiver, fancy walnut stock. Mfg. 1962-1974.

	$350	$300	$265	$230	$195	$160	$125	

MODEL 49 ST. LOUIS BICENTENNIAL – like Deluxe Model 49, except has inscription on receiver. 200 mfg. 1964.

	$450	$390	$340	$300	$250	$200	$160	*$35*

MODEL 72 SADDLEGUN – .22 or .22 WMR cal., 18 1/2 in. barrel, hooded front sight. Mfg. 1973-78 by Erma Werke, W. Germany.

	$375	$325	$275	$200	$175	$145	$125	

MODEL 72 DELUXE – .22 or .22 WMR, similar to Model 72 Saddle Gun, except has silver finished engraved receiver, deluxe walnut, octagon barrel. Mfg. 1974-1976.

	$450	$400	$300	$250	$225	$175	$145	

RIFLES: SEMI-AUTO

MODEL X5 LIGHTNING – .22 LR cal., 7 shot mag., grooved forearm, Model X5-T Lightning has tube mag., Model X5-C has box mag. Mfg. 1958-1964.

	$350	$300	$265	$235	$195	$160	$130	

MODEL X-15 LIGHTNING – .22 LR cal., similar to X5-C, except forearm is not grooved. Mfg. 1964-1967.

	$350	$300	$265	$235	$195	$160	$130	

RIFLES: SINGLE SHOT

MODEL 89 – .243 Win., .30-06, .375 H&H, .416 Rigby, or 7x57mm cal., falling block action, 26 or 28 in. Shilen barrel, full-length uncheckered walnut stock.

While advertised at $658 MSR during 1994, this model never went into production.

SHOTGUNS: O/U, PREVIOUS IMPORTATION

Note: Ithaca was the sole importer for Perazzi in the '70s. All new and used models will be in the P section under Perazzi. Perazzi currently distributes their own firearms.

Note: Please refer to the Fabarm section in this text for those models previously imported by Ithaca (imported 1994-95).

Note: Previously imported SKB O/U shotguns can be found under the SKB heading.

SHOTGUNS: SxS, PREVIOUS IMPORTATION

Note: Previously imported SKB SxS shotguns can be found under the SKB heading.

SHOTGUNS: SxS, 1880-1948 MFG.

AUTO & BURGLAR SxS – 20 ga., 10 in. barrels, case hardened finish, pistol grip, Model A (approx. 2,500 mfg.) has grip spur, Model B (approx. 2,000 mfg.) has squared grip; both were mfg. in lots of about 100, according to demand, and serial numbers are mixed with those of regular Ithaca shotguns. Guns not currently registered with BATFE cannot be legally owned and are subject to seizure. Mfg. 1922-34.

* ***Auto & Burglar SxS Model A*** – serial no. range is 343,336-398,365.

	$8,500	$7,750	$6,500	$5,000	$3,750	$3,000	$2,500	

* ***Auto & Burglar SxS Model B*** – serial no. range is 425,000-464,699.

	$7,500	$7,000	$6,000	$4,500	$3,500	$2,750	$2,100	

Add $300-$500 for original holster (very rare). Prototype or special order guns (in 16, 28 ga., or .410 bore) are extremely rare and command premiums of 100%+.

100%	98%	95%	90%	80%	70%	60%	50%	40%	30%	20%	10%

ITHACA HAMMERLESS – 12, 16, 20, 28 ga., or .410 bore, 26-32 in. fluid steel or damascus barrels, boxlock, extractors, double triggers, any standard choke, checkered pistol grip stock and forearm, grades shown differ in overall quality, ornamentation, grade of wood, and style of checkering. In 1925, the rotary bolt and stronger frame were adapted (ser. numbers after 400,000 - commonly referred to as NID or New Ithaca Double). Values are the same as for pre-400,000 serial range shotguns. Ithaca doubles incorporated a number of design changes made on the action - they are referred to as the Lewis, Crass, Flues, and Minier frame variations.

Add $200 for SST.
Add $150 for SNT.
Add $350 for VR on Grades 4, 5, 7, and $2,000 Grade.
Add $200 for VR - lower grades.
Add $175 for beavertail forearm.
Add 33% for auto ejectors on Grades No. 1, 2, and 3.
Subtract 20% if without ejectors on Grades 4E-7E.
Early hammer doubles in average condition are approx. valued between $175-$450. However, if 60%+ condition remains (including original case colors), values can approximate those listed.
Deduct 20% for models other than NID (example: Flues, Lewis, Crass, etc.).

FIELD GRADE

* ***Field Grade 10 ga. Mag.***

N/A	$3,000	$2,100	$1,800	$1,600	$1,1150	$975	$800	$675	$600	$500	$450

3 1/2 in. chambered 10 ga. Mags. are serial numbered over 500,000. Total mfg. was approx. 850 guns for all grades. 2 7/8 in. chambered 10 gauges are priced the same as a 12 ga. A 12 ga., 3 in. model was also made on the 10 ga. frame - only 87 were mfg. and specimens are noted in the 500,000 serial range.

* ***Field Grade 12 ga.***												
	$1,800	$1,500	$1,200	$1,000	$800	$500	$459	$350	$325	$300	$190	$150
* ***Field Grade 16 ga.***												
	$1,500	$1,200	$1,000	$800	$700	$650	$600	$550	$500	$425	$375	$340
* ***Field Grade 20 ga.***												
	$1,600	$1,300	$1,100	$1,000	$850	$800	$750	$700	$600	$550	$500	$440
* ***Field Grade 28 ga.***												
	N/A	N/A	$3,000	$2,700	$2,400	$2,300	$2,250	$2,200	$2,100	$1,700	$1,400	$1,250
* ***Field Grade .410 bore***												
	$5,750	$4,800	$3,500	$3,000	$2,500	$2,300	$2,250	$2,200	$2,100	$1,800	$1,550	$1,400

GRADE NO. 1 – manufactured in both Flues and NID models, similar to Field Grade.

* ***Grade No. 1 12 ga.***												
	$2,100	$1,850	$1,600	$1,200	$850	$550	$450	$415	$380	$350	$325	$315
* ***Grade No. 1 16 ga.***												
	$2,400	$2,100	$2,000	$1,600	$1,200	$950	$750	$700	$650	$600	$550	$500
* ***Grade No. 1 20 ga.***												
	$3,000	$2,800	$2,500	$2,000	$1,500	$1,000	$850	$800	$750	$700	$600	$450
* ***Grade No. 1 28 ga.***												
	N/A	N/A	$4,200	$3,900	$3,600	$3,000	$2,725	$2,400	$2,100	$1,900	$1,600	$1,300
* ***Grade No. 1 .410 bore***												
	$9,500	$6,500	$5,250	$4,500	$4,000	$3,200	$2,900	$2,500	$2,200	$2,000	$1,725	$1,500

GRADE NO. 2

* ***Grade No. 2 10 ga. Mag.***

$4,800	$4,500	$4,000	$3,750	$3,250	$2,500	$1,750	$1,400	$1,250	$1,150	$1,000	$600

3 1/2 in. chambered 10 ga. Mags. are serial numbered over 500,000. Total mfg. was approx. 850 guns for all grades. 2 7/8 in. chambered 10 gauges are priced the same as a 12 ga.

* ***Grade No. 2 12 ga.***

$2,700	$2,400	$2,100	$1,900	$1,150	$925	$825	$750	$700	$650	$600	$550

100%	98%	95%	90%	80%	70%	60%	50%	40%	30%	20%	10%
* ***Grade No. 2 16 ga.***											
$3,450	$3,100	$2,750	$2,300	$1,700	$1,200	$700	$650	$600	$550	$500	$475
* ***Grade No. 2 20 ga.***											
$3,750	$3,400	$2,800	$2,500	$2,000	$1,300	$900	$850	$800	$750	$700	$600
* ***Grade No. 2 28 ga.***											
N/A	N/A	$5,500	$5,000	$4,400	$4,000	$3,600	$3,200	$2,800	$2,400	$2,000	$1,725
* ***Grade No. 2 .410 bore***											
N/A	N/A	$5,750	$5,150	$4,500	$4,000	$3,600	$3,200	$2,800	$2,400	$2,000	$1,725
GRADE NO. 3											
* ***Grade No. 3 10 ga. Mag.***											
$4,250	$3,500	$3,200	$2,900	$2,000	$1,400	$1,300	$1,200	$1,100	$950	$825	$735
3 1/2 in. chambered 10 ga. Mags. are serial numbered over 500,000. Total mfg. was approx. 850 guns for all grades. 2 7/8 in. chambered 10 gauges are priced the same as a 12 ga.											
* ***Grade No. 3 12 ga.***											
$3,600	$3,050	$2,700	$2,200	$1,700	$1,000	$800	$750	$700	$650	$600	$550
* ***Grade No. 3 16 ga.***											
N/A	N/A	$1,950	$1,700	$1,400	$1,200	$1,000	$900	$850	$800	$750	$700
* ***Grade No. 3 20 ga.***											
N/A	N/A	$2,150	$1,950	$1,700	$1,400	$1,200	$1,000	$900	$850	$800	$750
* ***Grade No. 3 28 ga.*** – only 5 mfg.											
Extreme rarity factor precludes accurate pricing evaluation. Recent prices have ranged from $15,000-$25,000.											
* ***Grade No. 3 .410 bore*** – only 7 mfg.											
Extreme rarity factor precludes accurate pricing evaluation.											
GRADE NO. 4E – auto ejectors.											
* ***Grade No. 4E 10 ga. Mag.***											
$5,800	$5,350	$4,650	$4,100	$3,350	$2,650	$2,100	$1,975	$1,875	$1,750	$1,650	$1,550
3 1/2 in. chambered 10 ga. Mags. are serial numbered over 500,000. Total mfg. was approx. 850 guns for all grades. 2 7/8 in. chambered 10 gauges are priced the same as a 12 ga.											
* ***Grade No. 4E 12 ga.***											
N/A	$3,750	$3,325	$3,000	$2,500	$2,100	$1,700	$1,550	$1,325	$1,200	$1,100	$995
* ***Grade No. 4E 16 ga.***											
N/A	N/A	$4,100	$3,750	$3,325	$3,000	$2,400	$2,000	$1,875	$1,650	$1,550	$1,450
* ***Grade No. 4E 20 ga.***											
N/A	N/A	$5,000	$4,625	$4,250	$3,725	$3,525	$3,300	$3,100	$2,950	$2,700	$2,300
* ***Grade No. 4E 28 ga.***											
Extreme rarity factor precludes accurate pricing evaluation.											
* ***Grade No. 4E .410 bore***											
Extreme rarity factor precludes accurate pricing evaluation.											
GRADE NO. 5E – auto ejectors.											
* ***Grade No. 5E 10 ga.*** – only 9 mfg.											
Extreme rarity factor precludes accurate pricing evaluation.											
* ***Grade No. 5E 12 ga.***											
N/A	N/A	$4,750	$4,200	$3,750	$3,325	$3,000	$2,700	$2,200	$1,875	$1,650	$1,325
* ***Grade No. 5E 16 ga.***											
N/A	N/A	$5,400	$4,750	$4,200	$3,750	$3,325	$3,000	$2,700	$2,200	$1,875	$1,650
* ***Grade No. 5E 20 ga.***											
N/A	N/A	$6,000	$5,400	$4,750	$4,200	$3,750	$3,325	$3,000	$2,700	$2,200	$1,875

100%	98%	95%	90%	80%	70%	60%	50%	40%	30%	20%	10%

* ***Grade No. 5E 28 ga.***

Extreme rarity factor precludes accurate pricing evaluation.

* ***Grade No. 5E .410 bore***

Extreme rarity factor precludes accurate pricing evaluation.

GRADE NO. 6E – auto ejectors, mfg. in all gauges.

Rarity factor precludes accurate price evaluation on this model.

GRADE NO. 7E – auto ejectors, only 22 mfg. in all gauges.

Extreme rarity factor precludes accurate pricing evaluation on this model.

$2,000 GRADE – 12 ga., top-of-the-line model, auto ejectors, single selective trigger.

100%	98%	95%	90%	80%	70%	60%	50%	40%	30%	20%	10%
N/A	N/A	$8,450	$7,400	$6,500	$5,650	$4,750	$4,000	$3,250	$2,600	$2,100	$1,700

PRE-WAR $1,000 GRADE – 12 ga., top-of-the-line models, auto ejectors, single selective trigger.

100%	98%	95%	90%	80%	70%	60%	50%	40%	30%	20%	10%
N/A	N/A	$9,500	$8,450	$7,400	$6,500	$5,650	$4,750	$4,000	$3,250	$2,600	$2,250

SOUSA GRADE – has mermaids on trigger guard in gold, only 11 manufactured (including one .410 bore). This model is very rare and prices are hard to establish. Recently, the price range has been approx. $15,000-$40,000, depending on gauge and original condition.

The famous band director and composer, John Phillip Sousa, assisted in the development of this model. Recent prices have been in the $40,000 to $75,000 range. Use caution when considering this model as there are a number of upgrades.

GRADING - PPGS™	100%	98%	95%	90%	80%	70%	60%	*LAST MSR*

SHOTGUNS: SEMI-AUTO

MODEL 51A FEATHERLIGHT STANDARD – 12 or 20 ga., 30 in. full, 28 in. full or mod., 26 in. imp. cyl., gas operated, autoloading, checkered pistol grip stock. Vent. rib became standard during late production. Mfg. 1970-1985.

	100%	98%	95%	90%	80%	70%	60%	LAST MSR
Older models w/o VR	$300	$250	$215	$190	$165	$135	$100	
Vent. rib	$350	$300	$265	$230	$195	$160	$125	

Last MSR with VR was $477.

MODEL 51A MAGNUM – similar to 51 Standard, except 3 in. shells only, blue finish, recoil pad, VR became standard in 1984. Disc. 1985.

	100%	98%	95%	90%	80%	70%	60%	LAST MSR
Older models w/o VR	$325	$275	$240	$210	$180	$145	$115	
Vent. rib	$400	$350	$300	$260	$220	$180	$140	

MODEL 51A MAGNUM WATERFOWLER – similar to 51 Standard, except 3 in. shells only, matte finished metal, flat finished walnut, recoil pad. Vent. rib standard. Mfg. 1984-86.

100%	98%	95%	90%	80%	70%	60%	LAST MSR
$400	$350	$300	$260	$220	$180	$140	*$625*

Add $40 for camouflaged exterior finish (mfg. 1986 only).

MODEL 51A SUPREME TRAP – similar to 51 Standard, except 12 ga. only, 30 in. barrel, 7 post rib, full choke, select wood, pad, trap style stock. Add $36 for Monte Carlo. Mfg. 1970-86.

100%	98%	95%	90%	80%	70%	60%	LAST MSR
$500	$425	$375	$325	$275	$225	$175	*$869*

MODEL 51A SUPREME SKEET – similar to 51 Standard, except 26 in. VR barrel, skeet choke, select wood, 20 ga. was available 1983. Mfg. 1970-1986.

100%	98%	95%	90%	80%	70%	60%	LAST MSR
$550	$475	$400	$350	$300	$250	$200	*$858*

MODEL 51A DEERSLAYER – similar to 51 Standard, with 24 in. slug barrel, rifle sights, recoil pad, no rib. Mfg. 1972-83.

100%	98%	95%	90%	80%	70%	60%	LAST MSR
$400	$350	$300	$260	$220	$180	$140	*$477*

MODEL 51A TURKEY GUN – 12 ga. Mag. only, 26 in. barrel, matte finish, sling and swivels included. Mfg. 1984-86.

100%	98%	95%	90%	80%	70%	60%	LAST MSR
$360	$305	$275	$265	$250	$230	$210	*$625*

MODEL 51 DUCKS UNLIMITED – similar to 51 Deluxe, with D/U emblem on receiver.

100%	98%	95%	90%	80%	70%	60%	LAST MSR
$425	$375	$335	$300	$280	$260	$230	

MODEL 51 PRESENTATION – 12 ga., blue, engraved, gold engraved receiver with deluxe walnut. Mfg. 1984-86.

100%	98%	95%	90%	80%	70%	60%	LAST MSR
$1,325	$1,050	$875	$700	$575	$450	$325	*$1,658*

MODEL XL 300 – 12 or 20 ga., gas operated, various barrel lengths with or w/o VR. Mfg. 1973-76.

100%	98%	95%	90%	80%	70%	60%	LAST MSR
$250	$230	$200	$180	$165	$150	$130	

Add 15% for VR barrel.

GRADING - PPGS™	100%	98%	95%	90%	80%	70%	60%	LAST MSR

MODEL XL 900 – 12 or 20 ga., gas operated, various barrel lengths with VR. Mfg. 1973-78.

	$295	$275	$245	$210	$185	$170	$150	

Add 10% for skeet, trap, or slug variations.

Shotguns: Semi-Auto, Mag-10 Series

All Ithaca Mag-10s were disc. 1986.

MAG-10 – 10 ga., 3 1/2 in. Mag., various barrel lengths, stainless steel breechblock assembly, gas operated, various chokes, plain barrel, 11 lbs. Mfg. 1975-1986.

100% values assume NIB condition - if without, subtract 10%.

* ***Mag-10 Standard Grade*** – dull finished, plain uncheckered walnut stock, plain barrel, matte finished metal.

	$675	$600	$550	$500	$460	$430	$395	*$726*

* ***Mag-10 Standard Grade with VR*** – available in 22, 26, 28, or 32 in. barrel lengths - otherwise similar to Standard Grade.

	$750	$650	$550	$495	$450	$400	$360	*$781*

Add $60 for camouflaged exterior finish.
Add $60 for interchangeable choke tubes (3) - became available in 1986.

* ***Mag-10 Deluxe Vent*** – select checkered walnut stock and forearm with sling swivels, 22, 26, 28, or 32 in. barrels, high lustre wood finish.

	$800	$700	$600	$550	$495	$450	$400	*$924*

* ***Mag-10 Supreme Grade*** – extra-select checkered walnut stock and forearm with sling swivels, otherwise similar to Deluxe Vent.

	$995	$800	$725	$675	$595	$550	$495	*$1,124*

* ***Mag-10 Mag. 10 Roadblocker*** – 22 in. cylinder bored ribless barrel, parkerized finish.

	$750	$625	$575	$500	$460	$430	$400	*$741*

* ***Mag-10 National Wild Turkey Fed. Special Edition*** – mfg. in 1985 only.

	$950	$795	$625	N/A	N/A	N/A	N/A	

MAG-10 PRESENTATION OR CENTENNIAL – 10 ga. Mag., blue, engraved, gold inlaid receiver, extra fancy walnut. Limited production. Approx. 200 mfg. in Presentation Grade 1983-86.

	$1,875	$1,550	$1,300	$1,050	$915	$830	$745	*$1,727*

This configuration was also offered as a 3 gun set - a NIB set is currently selling in the $4,750 range.

SHOTGUNS: SINGLE SHOT, LEVER ACTION

MODEL 66 – 12, 20 ga., or .410 bore single shot lever action, field gun only. Mfg. 1963-78.

	$150	$125	$100	$75	$70	$65	$55	

Add 33% to .410 bore.
Add 25% for VRs that were also available on special order.

* ***Model 66 RS*** – 20 ga. slug gun with 22 in. barrel and rifle type sights, recoil pad.

	$195	$165	$135	$115	$90	$80	$70	

Add 25% for special order VR.

SHOTGUNS: SINGLE BARREL, TRAP

CENTURY TRAP – please refer to the SKB section.

CENTURY II TRAP – please refer to the SKB section.

SINGLE BARREL TRAP – 12 ga., 30, 32, or 34 in. barrels, VR, boxlock, auto ejector, checkered pistol grip and forearm, grades differ in engraving, overall workmanship, and grade or wood and checkering. Values on these models sometimes vary greatly depending on originality of finish, customer alterations, and other variations trap shooters might use to alter dimensions for their particular shooting requirements. Values represent trap guns in original, unaltered condition.

Note: Flues model mfg. prior to 1921 with serial numbers under 400,000 generally have better engraving than NID (New Ithaca Double) models over serial number 400,000 (also referred to as Knick models).

Trap guns under 60% original condition will be within 25% of the value shown in the 60% column.

* ***Single Barrel Trap Victory Grade*** – disc. 1938.

	$1,250	$995	$850	$775	$675	$575	$495	

* ***Single Barrel Trap No. 4E*** – disc. 1976.

	$2,950	$2,675	$2,450	$2,200	$2,000	$1,825	$1,625	

GRADING - PPGS™	100%	98%	95%	90%	80%	70%	60%	LAST MSR

* ***Single Barrel Trap No. 5E*** – 12 ga., 32 or 34 in. barrel, custom order only, elaborate engraving, quality worksmanship throughout. Originally mfg. 1925-86, mfg. resumed 1988-91.

	$4,000	$3,500	$3,000	$2,550	$2,175	$1,900	$1,725	*$7,500*

* ***Single Barrel Trap No. 6E*** – this model was available by special order only. Rarity factor precludes accurate pricing.

* ***Single Barrel Trap No. 7E*** – disc. 1964.

	$6,500	$5,500	$4,700	$4,000	$3,500	$3,000	$2,500	

* ***Single Barrel Trap Dollar Grade*** – 12 ga., 32 or 34 in. barrel. Top-of-the-line model custom built to customer specifications. Original mfg. was stopped 1986 and resumed 1988-91.

	$6,750	$5,950	$5,200	$4,600	$3,850	$3,250	$2,775	*$10,000*

* ***Single Barrel Trap $5,000 Grade*** – similar to Pre-War $1,000 grade.

	$9,500	$8,900	$8,175	$7,650	$6,725	$5,825	$4,950	

* ***Single Barrel Trap Sousa Grade*** – extremely rare.

Extreme rarity factor precludes accurate pricing evaluation. Prices will be higher than the $5,000 Grade.

SHOTGUNS: SLIDE ACTION

In 1987, Ithaca Acquisition Corp. reintroduced the Model 37 as the Model 87. Recently manufactured Model 87s are listed in addition to both new and older Model 37s (produced pre-1986). During late 1996, Ithaca Gun Co., LLC resumed manufacture of the Model 37, while discontinuing the Model 87.

Over 2 million Model 37s have been produced.

Model 37s with ser. nos. above 855,000 will accept both 2 3/4 and 3 in. chambered barrels interchangeably. Earlier guns have incompatible threading for the magnum barrels.

MODEL 37 TRENCH AND RIOT GUNS – see separate listing under Trench Guns in the T Section.

MODEL 37 DS POLICE SPECIAL – 12 ga. only, 18 1/2 in. barrel with rifle sights, Parkerized finish on metal, oil finished stock, typically subcontracted by police departments or law enforcement agencies, with or without unit code markings.

	$325	$275	$235	$200	$185	$170	$160	

MODEL 37 $1000 GRADE – all gauges, deluxe engraving and checkering, gold inlaid, select figured walnut, hand-finished parts. Mfg. 1937-40.

	$5,750	$5,200	$4,750	$4,250	$3,750	$3,250	$2,650	

MODEL 37 $5000 GRADE – similar to $1000 Grade, post-war designation. Mfg. 1947-67.

	$5,250	$4,850	$4,250	$3,850	$3,250	$2,850	$2,250	

MODEL 37V – similar to 37, except VR. Mfg. 1962-disc.

	$415	$260	$240	$195	$180	$170	$165	

All recently manufactured Model 37s have the Featherlight designation. Prices are for older manufactured Model 37s.

MODEL 37D – similar to Model 37 Standard, except recoil pad, beavertail forearm, checkered wood. Mfg. 1954-1981.

	$395	$275	$235	$200	$185	$175	$160	

MODEL 37DV – similar to 37D, except VR. Mfg. 1962-1981.

	$475	$325	$265	$225	$200	$185	$170	

MODEL 37 AMERICANA – 12 ga., 28 in. VR barrel with modified choke, uncheckered walnut stock, corncob forearm, roll engraved eagle on a banner with "Heritage. The Ithaca Gun Company, Pride." Approx. 2,200 mfg. circa 1972 with ser. nos. A0001-A2200.

	$275	$250	$225	$185	$165	$145	$125	

MODEL 37 ULTRA FEATHERLIGHT – 20 ga. only, bottom ejection, 4 shot mag., 26 or 28 in. VR barrel, standard choke, approx. 4 3/4 lbs. Disc.

	$495	$350	$275	$235	$210	$190	$175	

MODEL 37 ULTRA FEATHERLIGHT RUFFED GROUSE SOCIETY SPECIAL EDITION – 20 ga. only, bottom ejection, aluminum receiver, 22 or 24 in. barrel, English style American walnut stock. Limited mfg. 2003-2004.

	$715	$565	$435	$375	$300	$260	$230	*$840*

GRADING - PPGS™	100%	98%	95%	90%	80%	70%	60%	LAST MSR

MODEL 37 FIELD GRADE MAGNUM – 12 or 20 ga., 3 in. chambers, VR, walnut stock and corncob forearm, supplied with three choke tubes. Mfg. 1984-86.

	$300	$240	$195	$180	$170	$165	$150	*$428*

MODEL 37 FIELD GRADE STANDARD – 12 or 20 ga., economy model, corncob style forearm, 26, 28, or 30 in. barrel. Mfg. 1983-1985 only.

	$245	$225	$195	$175	$160	$140	$120	*$298*

MODEL 37 ULTRALIGHT – 12 (disc.) or 20 ga., new manufacture features checkered pistol grip (with Sid Bell red grip cap) and forearm, most recent mfg. was in deer configuration, 20 ga. only with 20 or 25 in. smoothbore barrel. Mfg. 1996-2002.

	$475	$380	$340	$300	$275	$250	$225	*$600*

MODEL 37 ENGLISH ULTRALIGHT DELUXE – 12 (disc.), 16 or 20 ga., 24, 25 (disc.), 26 or 28 in. barrels, choice of English straight grip stock with checkered forearm or pistol grip stock and grooved forearm, aluminum receiver, world's lightest pump, 20 ga. weighs 4 3/4 lb., 12 ga. weighs 5 1/2 lbs. Mfg. 1983-1986, reintroduced 1999-2005.

	$520	$410	$300	$250	$225	$200	$185	*$659*

* ***Model 37 English Ultralight Deluxe Classic*** – 16 or 20 ga., choice of pistol grip or English straight grip deluxe checkered walnut stock and forearm, 24, 26, or 28 in. VR barrel with three choke tubes, 5 1/4 lbs.

	$700	$555	$425	$375	$300	$260	$230	*$834*

MODEL 37/37R STANDARD – 12, 16, or 20 ga., solid rib, checkered walnut stock and forearm (mfg. 1937-1946), smooth pistol grip and grooved forearm (mfg. 1946-1952). Mfg. 1937-1952.

Plain stock	$395	$275	$225	$145	$130	$110	$90	
Checkered stock	$435	$320	$250	$175	$165	$145	$120	

Add 20% for 16 or 20 ga.

MODEL 37R DELUXE – similar to 37R, except fancy wood. Mfg. 1937-1955.

	$600	$550	$475	$400	$325	$250	$200	

MODEL 37R FEATHERLIGHT – 12, 16, or 20 ga., bottom ejection, 4 shot mag., 26, 28, or 30 in. barrel, hammerless, take down, any standard choke. Mfg. 1952-1985.

	$600	$550	$475	$400	$325	$250	$200	

Add 25% for 16 or 20 ga.

MODEL 37 PROTECTION SERIES – 12 ga. only, 18 1/2 or 20 in. smoothbore barrel w/o chokes, 5 or 8 shot tube mag., approx. 6 3/4 lbs. Limited mfg. 2005.

	$425	$375	$325	$275	$250	$225	$195	*$482*

Add $27 for 20 in. barrel.

TURKEYSLAYER – 12 (Storm) or 20 (new 2000, Storm Light)) ga., 3 in. chamber, choice of matte blue or 100% camo coverage in Realtree Hardwoods (disc. 2002), Realtree Hardwoods HD (new 2003), Realtree Timber (disc. 2002), or Advantage (disc. 2001) pattern, 22 (disc. 2002) or 24 in. barrel with extended choke tube, TruGlo fiber optic sights standard beginning 2003, 7 lbs. Mfg. 1996-2004.

	$375	$335	$300	$275	$250	$225	$200	*$459*

Add $20 for ported choke tube (disc.).

* ***Turkeyslayer Youth*** – 20 ga. only, features 22 in. barrel and shortened youth dimension stock. Mfg. 1998-2003.

	$500	$375	$295	$225	$175	$160	$145	*$615*

TURKEYSLAYER II GUIDE SERIES – 12 ga. only, 3 in. chamber, 20 in. interchangeable barrel with turkey choke, choice of Realtree Hardwoods Green or 100% Mossy Oak Break Up camo coverage, pistol grip stock, includes 30mm red dot scope and sling, fiber optic sights. Limited production 2005 only.

	$500	$425	$365	$330	$300	$275	$250	*$599*

WATERFOWLER – 12 (Storm) or 20 (Storm Light) ga., features black finish or Wetlands (disc.), Realtree Hardwoods HD green, or Realtree Max 4 camo treatment, 24, 26, 28 (standard) or 30 in. barrel designed for shooting steel shot. Mfg. 1998-2004.

	$425	$375	$335	$300	$275	$250	$225	*$499*

Add $50 for Realtree Max 4 camo.

MODEL 37 DELUXE W/VR – 12, 16 (Featherlight, new 1999), or 20 ga., similar to Model 87 Field Grade except has cut checkering, 26, 28, or 30 (disc. 2002) in. VR barrel, high gloss lacquer finish, and gold trigger, newer mfg. includes 3 choke tubes. Mfg. 1996-2005.

	$500	$380	$285	$230	$175	$160	$145	*$627*

Add $30 for 20 ga. Youth Model.

GRADING - PPGS™	100%	98%	95%	90%	80%	70%	60%	LAST MSR

* ***Model 37 Deluxe W/VR English*** – 12 (new 2000) or 20 ga., features 24, 26, or 28 in. English style vent. rib barrel, approx. 7 lbs. Mfg. 1998-2003.

	$485	$365	$275	$225	$175	$160	$145	*$600*

Add $30 for 20 ga.

MODEL 37 CLASSIC – 12, 16 (Featherlight, new 1999), or 20 ga., features knuckle cut receiver, corncob style forearm, hand checkering, and Sunburst recoil pad, 26 or 28 in. VR barrel with choke tubes, choice of pistol grip or English straight grip deluxe checkered walnut stock and forearm, 6 1/2 - 7 lbs. Limited production 1998-2005.

	$680	$540	$425	$375	$300	$260	$230	*$812*

* ***Model 37 Classic NRA Women's*** – 16 or 20 ga., 24 in. VR barrel with three choke tubes, 5 1/4 or 6 1/2 lbs. Mfg. 2003-2004.

	$715	$565	$435	$375	$300	$260	$230	*$840*

MODEL 37 SUPREME – 12, 16, or 20 ga., deluxe checkered walnut stock and forearm, 28 or 30 in. VR barrel, engraved receiver, approx. 7 3/4 lbs. Originally mfg. 1967-1986, reintroduced late 1996, disc. 1997, reintroduced 2003-2004.

	$895	$650	$550	$450	$400	$350	$425	
1967-1997 Mfg.	$675	$575	$495	$425	$375	$325	$295	*$1,185*

MODEL 37S SKEET GRADE – features Knicker VR, large forearm, deluxe wood. Mfg. 1937-55.

	$1,000	$875	$750	$650	$550	$450	$350	

Add 20% for 16 or 20 ga.

MODEL 37 SPORTING CLAYS – 12 ga. only, 24 (disc.), 26 (disc.), 28, or 30 (disc.) in. VR ported (standard 2001) or unported (disc. 2000) barrel with 3 Briley choke tubes, similar in appearances and features to Model 37 Trap. Mfg. 2000-2004.

	$1,275	$1,075	$925	$800	$650	$525	$450	*$1,495*

MODEL 37T TRAP GRADE – similar to 37S, except trap stock, select walnut, recoil pad. Mfg. 1937-55.

	$475	$425	$375	$325	$295	$275	$250	

Add 20% for early models with fleur-de-lis checkering.

MODEL 37 TRAP – 12 ga. only, 30 in. VR ported (standard 2001) or unported (disc. 2000) barrel with 3 Briley choke tubes, antique silver finished receiver with scroll style engraving and gold inlays on receiver sides, optional adj. cheekpiece stock. Mfg. 2000-2004.

	$1,275	$1,075	$925	$800	$650	$525	$450	*$1,495*

MODEL 37T TARGET GRADE – replaced 37S and 37T. Mfg. from 1955-1961.

	$575	$475	$375	$325	$295	$275	$250	

MODEL 37 DEERSLAYER – 12, 16, or 20 ga., original Deerslayer, smoothbore with fixed choke only, rifle sights. Mfg. circa 1959-1986.

	$400	$350	$300	$260	$220	$180	$140	

MODEL 37 SUPER DELUXE DEERSLAYER – 12, 16, or 20 ga., similar to Model 37 (87) Deerslayer, except Williams aperture rear sight and fancy wood. Mfg. 1962-1985.

	$450	$390	$340	$300	$250	$200	$160	*$447*

MODEL 37 DEERSLAYER DELUXE – 12, 16 (new 1999 - smoothbore only, rifled beginning 2000) or 20 ga., 20, 24, or 25 (disc.) in. smoothbore (disc.) or rifled barrel, 100% Realtree Hardwoods 20/200 camo (mfg. 2000-2002, 12 ga. only) or walnut stock and forearm with cut checkering, light receiver engraving. Mfg. 1959-2005.

	$550	$475	$400	$350	$300	$250	$200	*$591*

Add $50 for Hardwoods camo (disc.).

DEERSLAYER II – 12, 16 (new 2001), or 20 ga., 20, 24 (new 2003) or 25 (disc.) in. barrel with 1:34 rifling (also available with fast twist 1:25 rifling, 12 ga. only, disc.), Monte Carlo stock and forearm with cut checkering, receiver is drilled and tapped for scope mounting, 6.25-7 lbs. Mfg. 1996-2005.

	$520	$390	$310	$230	$175	$160	$145	*$642*

* ***Deerslayer II Model 37 Storm*** – 12 or 20 (Storm Light) ga., 24 in. smoothbore barrel with choke tube and open rifle sights, 100% DSS treatment on stock, approx. 6 1/2 lbs. Mfg. 2003-2004.

	$350	$300	$275	$250	$225	$200	$185	*$399*

DEERSLAYER II GUIDE SERIES – 12 or 20 ga., 20 or 24 in. rifled barrel with fiber optic sights, 3 in. chamber, blued metal, grey camo laminate pistol grip stock and forearm. Limited production 2005.

	$500	$415	$330	$285	$240	$210	$185	*$599*

GRADING - PPGS™	100%	98%	95%	90%	80%	70%	60%	LAST MSR

DEERSLAYER III – 12 ga., 26 in. smoothbore barrel with DSR-1 choke tube, 11 lbs. Mfg. 2003-2004.

$750	$675	$600	$525	$450	$375	$300	*$900*

MODEL 37 BICENTENNIAL – 12 ga., engraved, fancy wood, cased with pewter buckle, 1,776 mfg. 1976, 100% value assumes NIB condition with case and belt buckle.

$595	$450	$325	$265	$230	$195	$170	

MODEL 37 2500 SERIES CENTENNIAL – 12 ga., customized version of the Model 37 commemorating Ithaca's 100th year anniversary, silver plated, etched antique finish receiver, deluxe walnut. Mfg. 1980-84.

$775	$625	$450	$385	$335	$280	$235	*$919*

MODEL 37 60TH ANNIVERSARY LIMITED EDITION – 20 ga., scroll engraving by A&A Engraving on both sides of nickel receiver with dog game scene/eagle motif, supreme grade wood, includes case. 200 mfg. 1997 only.

$1,450	$850	$475	$415	$360	$300	$255	*$2,000*

MODEL 37 PRESENTATION – 12 ga., blue, engraved, gold mounted receiver with extra-fancy walnut, cased, limited production. Mfg. 1981-86.

$1,500	$1,245	$1,080	$915	$830	$745	$665	*$1,658*

A 3 gun set was also available - an NIB set is currently priced in the $4,500 range.

MODEL 37 DUCKS UNLIMITED – 12 ga., VR. Please refer to the Ducks Unlimited section.

MODEL 37 60TH ANNIVERSARY – 20 ga., 3 in. chamber, 26 in. VR barrel, checkered Supreme wood, engraved, cased. 200 mfg. 1997 only.

$1,750	$1,250	$850	$740	$620	$515	$440	

MODEL 87 FIELD (BASIC) – 12 or 20 ga., 3 in. chamber, economy model, walnut stock and forearm with pressed checkering, 26, 28, or 30 (disc.) in. barrel with 3 choke tubes standard. Reintroduced 1987-96.

$360	$290	$240	$195	$170	$160	$145	*$477*

* ***Model 87 Field Basic Combo*** – 12 or 20 ga., includes 20/25 in. deer barrel with special bore and 28 in. VR multi-choke field barrel, uncheckered walnut stock and corncob forearm, 7 lbs. Mfg. 1989-92.

$400	$315	$275	$235	$210	$190	$170	*$459*

Add $32 for rifled bore barrel.
Add $104 for laminated wood (includes rifle bored barrel).

* ***Model 87 Field Camo*** – 12 ga. only, 3 in. chamber, 24, 26, or 28 in. VR barrel, camo-seal rust resistant finish on exterior parts. Available in either green or brown camo finish. Mfg. began 1986, resumed 1988, disc. 1996.

$425	$315	$260	$200	$175	$160	$145	*$542*

* ***Model 87 Field Turkey*** – 12 ga. only, 24 in. VR barrel with choice of fixed full choke or full choke tube, camo or matte blue finish. Mfg. 1989-96.

$365	$285	$235	$190	$170	$160	$145	*$466*

Add $85 for camo finish. Add $43 for full choke tube.

MODEL 87 ULTRALITE FIELD – 12 or 20 ga., 3 in. chamber, aluminum receiver, 20 (disc. 1988), 24, 25 (disc. 1988), or 26 in. barrel. 20 ga. weighs 5 lbs., 12 ga. weighs 5 3/4 lbs, multi-chokes (3) became standard in 1989. Originally mfg. 1985-86, reintroduced 1988-90.

$445	$375	$295	$240	$210	$190	$170	*$481*

Add $50 for slim grip model (12 1/2 in. stock - disc. 1985).
Subtract $42 if without multiple choke feature.

The 20 and 25 in. barrels were disc. when mfg. was resumed 1988.

* ***Model 87 Ultralite Field Deluxe*** – similar to Model 87 Ultralite Field except has cut checkering, high gloss lacquer finish, and gold trigger. Mfg. 1989-1991.

$425	$360	$300	$250	$220	$190	$170	*$514*

MODEL 87 ENGLISH – 20 ga. only, 3 in. chamber, 24 or 26 in. VR barrel with 3 choke tubes, steel receiver, checkered walnut stock and forearm, recoil pad, 6 3/4 lbs. Mfg. 1991-96.

$425	$315	$260	$200	$175	$160	$145	*$545*

MODEL 87 DELUXE – similar to Model 87 Field Grade except has cut checkering, 26, 28, or 30 in. VR barrel, high gloss lacquer finish, and gold trigger, newer mfg. includes 3 choke tubes. Mfg. 1989-96.

$415	$310	$255	$200	$175	$160	$145	*$533*

Add $54 for combo package (includes 20 in. special bore deer barrel, disc. 1992).
Add $87 for combo package with 20 or 25 in. rifled bore deer barrel, disc. 1992.

GRADING - PPGS™	100%	98%	95%	90%	80%	70%	60%	LAST MSR

* ***Model 87 Deluxe Magnum*** – 12 or 20 ga., 3 in. chambers, VR, deluxe wood with checkered forearm. Mfg. 1981-86, production resumed 1988 only.

	$320	$270	$230	$210	$200	$185	$165	*$395*

Add $77 for Combo package (extra 28 in. barrel).

Recent mfg. 20 ga. shotguns were available with a 25 in. barrel only (with choke tubes).

MODEL 87 SUPREME GRADE – 12 or 20 ga., presentation walnut, high luster blue, limited production, previously available in either trap, skeet, or field models, fixed chokes. Mfg. 1988-96.

	$640	$475	$395	$325	$295	$270	$250	*$809*

MODEL 87 BASIC DEERSLAYER – 12 ga. only, 20 or 25 in. special bore or rifled barrel, oil finished stock and corncob style forearm with no checkering, iron sights, matte metal finish, 7 lbs. Mfg. 1989-1996.

	$375	$325	$275	$235	$200	$170	$130	*$425*

Add $40 for rifled barrel.

MODEL 87 FIELD DEERSLAYER – 12 or 20 ga., rifle slug barrel, 20 or 25 in. special smoothbore barrel with open sights. Mfg. 1959-86, reintroduced 1988-1993.

	$300	$250	$210	$180	$160	$150	$140	*$364*

MODEL 87 DELUXE DEERSLAYER – similar to Field Deerslayer except stock has cut checkering and high gloss lacquer finish, gold trigger. Mfg. 1989-96.

	$365	$285	$235	$190	$170	$160	$145	*$465*

Add $34 for rifled bore.
Add $120 for combo package (28 in. multi-choke barrel).

* ***Model 87 Deluxe Deerslayer Ultra*** – similar to Deluxe Deerslayer except has aluminum frame. Mfg. 1989-90 only.

	$350	$285	$245	$200	$175	$160	$145	*$444*

MONTE CARLO DEERSLAYER II – 12 ga. only, 20 or 25 in. barrel with rifling, Monte Carlo stock and forearm with cut checkering, receiver is drilled and tapped for scope mounting, 7 lbs. Mfg. 1989-96.

	$445	$335	$270	$210	$175	$160	$145	*$567*

DEERSLAYER II FAST TWIST – 12 ga. only, 25 in. rifled permanently fixed barrel, Monte Carlo stock with checkering, receiver is drilled and tapped. Mfg. 1992-93.

	$440	$385	$325	$275	$235	$200	$180	*$550*

MODEL 87 MILITARY & POLICE – 12 (3 in.) or 20 (new 1989) ga., short barrel Model 37 w/normal stock or pistol grip only, 18 1/2, 20, or 24 3/4 (scarce) in. barrel, choice of front bead or rifle sights, front blade was usually a fluorescent orange plastic, 5, 8, or 10 shot. Originally disc. 1983, reintroduced 1989-95.

	$265	$230	$200	$180	$170	$160	$150	*$323*

Add $104 for nickel finish (mfg. 1991-92 only).

IVER JOHNSON ARMS, INC. (NEW MFG.)

Current manufacturer and importer established during 2004, located in Rockledge, FL. Dealer and distributor sales.

Select shotgun models are currently being private labeled by Armed Guns, located in Turkey.

DERRINGERS

POCKET ACE - .22 LR cal., 4 barrel single action pistol, 2 in. stainless steel barrel, light oak Dymondwood, black Dymondwood, or rosewood Dymondwood grips, integrated, ambidextrous safety/takedown lever, rotating firing pin to shoot 4 individual shots, 7 oz. While advertised beginning 2017, models became available mid-2019.

MSR $351	$300	$265	$225	$200	$165	$135	$100	

In 2017, the black Dymondwood Model was advertised as the "Maverick" and the rosewood Dymondwood was advertised as the "Quad Ace" before becoming commercially available in 2019.

PISTOLS: 1911 STYLE

Iver Johnson Arms, Inc. previously manufactured the Raven Series in both .22 LR and .45 ACP cals. until 2009, and the last MSR was $532. Also discontinued during 2009 was the Frontier Four Derringer and the Model PM 30G M1 Carbine. The Trojan was discontinued in 2012 (last MSR was $574). The 1911 A1 Thrasher was disc. in 2013, last MSR was $608-$817.

1911A1 – 9mm Para., .38 Super (new 2021), or .45 ACP cal., GI-style parts, Government size frame, 5 in. barrel, forged slide, 8 shot mag., GI rear sight with fixed blade front sight, vertical rear serrations, finger relief cut near trigger, flat, serrated metal mainspring housing, walnut logo engraved or Black Dymondwood dual texture (new 2014, Digital finish models only) grips, matte blue, Pink Duracoat (disc.

GRADING - PPGS™	100%	98%	95%	90%	80%	70%	60%	LAST MSR

2016), Muddy Girl (mfg. 2015-disc.), Kryptek Grey/Black hydrographic (mfg. 2016-2017), OD Green Cerakote, Coyote Tan Cerakote, Digital Navy (new 2014), or Digital Snow (new 2014) finish, 2.5 lbs.

MSR $560	$475	$415	$350	$325	$265	$215	$185	

Add $79 for OD Green, Muddy Girl (mfg. 2015-disc.), or Coyote Tan Cerakote finish.
Add $170 for Pink Duracoat finish (disc. 2016).
Add $123 for Kryptek Grey/Black hydrographic (mfg. 2016-2017), Digital Navy (new 2014), or Digital Snow (new 2014) finish.

* ***1911A1 Boa*** - .45 ACP cal., similar to 1911A1, except features Boa snakeskin hydrographic finish and black Dymondwood snakeskin grips. New 2014.

MSR $689	$585	$510	$440	$400	$325	$275	$230	

* ***1911A1 Copperhead*** - .45 ACP cal., similar to 1911A1, except features high grade epoxy base coat with hydrographic snakeskin printing in tan, black Dymondwood grips with snakeskin texture and logo. New 2014.

MSR $689	$585	$510	$440	$400	$325	$275	$230	

* ***1911A1 Water Moccasin*** - .45 ACP cal., similar to 1911A1, except features high grade epoxy base coat with hydrographic snakeskin printing in dark green, synthetic white pearlized grips with black engraved owl logo. New 2014.

MSR $689	$585	$510	$440	$400	$325	$275	$230	

* ***1911A1 Zombie*** - .45 ACP cal., similar to 1911A1, except features fixed sights, Zombie green slide with hydrographic zombie print, black frame and parts, and Zombie engraved pearlized green Hogue grips. New 2014.

MSR $668	$565	$495	$425	$385	$320	$270	$220	

1911A1 CHROME - .38 Super or .45 ACP cal., Government size frame, 5 in. barrel, dovetail front sight, black Dymondwood grips, black, or white (new 2021) pearl synthetic grips with medallion, GI-style parts, polished chrome finish. New 2017.

MSR $824	$700	$615	$525	$475	$385	$315	$275	

Add $22 for black pearl grips.

EAGLE - 9mm Para. or .45 ACP cal., Government size frame, 5 or 5 3/4 (Eagle Special, mfg. 2019 only) in. barrel, lowered and flared ejection port, skeleton hammer, 3-hole trigger, Millet white outline fully adj. rear sight with dovetail front sight, walnut large diamond wood or Rosewood double border/diamond with engraved logo (polished models only) grips, extended slide stop and thumb safety, high luster polished blue (.45 ACP), all matte blue (9mm Para.), OD Green Cerakote, or Coyote Tan Cerakote finish, 2.4 lbs.

MSR $713	$615	$540	$460	$425	$345	$275	$225	

Add $57 for high luster polished blue finish.
Add $77 for ported slide.
Add $89 for OD Green or Coyote Tan Cerakote finish.
Add $317 for Eagle Special with 5 3/4 in. threaded barrel (mfg. 2019 only).

* ***Eagle Stainless Steel*** - 10mm cal., Deluxe 1911 style, Government size frame, stainless steel construction, standard or ported barrel, adj. sight, walnut grips. Mfg. 2017 only.

	$825	$725	$625	$550	$475	$375	$295	*$912*

Add $73 for ported barrel.

EAGLE LR - .45 ACP cal., deluxe 1911 style, Government size frame, forged slide, 5 in. barrel, beveled magwell, lowered and flared ejection port, skeleton hammer, 3-hole trigger, Millett white outline fully adj. rear sight with dovetail front sight, black Dymondwood grips with dual texture, beavertail grip safety w/memory cut, extended slide stop and thumb safety, angled rear and front serrations, matte blue finish, 2 1/2 lbs.

MSR $850	$725	$635	$550	$500	$400	$325	$280	

* ***Eagle LR MB/Eagle LR Special*** - .45 ACP cal., deluxe 1911 style, Government size frame, forged slide, 5 in. barrel, with or w/o threading (Eagle LR Special), beveled magwell, lowered and flared ejection port, skeleton hammer, 3-hole trigger, dovetail front sight and fully adj. 3-dot sight or night sights, black Dymondwood grips with dual texture, beavertail grip safety w/memory cut, extended slide stop and thumb safety, angled rear and front serrations, light rail, Midnight Bronze Cerakote finish w/black slide, 2.5-2.69 lbs.

MSR $899	$765	$670	$575	$520	$420	$350	$300	

Add $131 for threaded barrel (Eagle LR Special).

GRADING - PPGS™	100%	98%	95%	90%	80%	70%	60%	LAST MSR

* ***Eagle LR Zombie*** – .45 ACP cal., similar to Eagle LR, except features Zombie engraved pearlized green Hogue grips, Zombie green slide with hydrographic zombie print, black frame and parts, 2 1/2 lbs. New 2014.

MSR $938	$800	$700	$600	$545	$440	$360	$310	

EAGLE XL – .45 ACP or 10mm (new 2016) cal., 6 in. barrel, with or without ported slide, lowered and flared ejection port, skeleton hammer, 3-hole trigger, fully adj. rear sight with dovetail front sight, walnut or Dymondwood (10mm only, new 2016) grips, beavertail grip safety with memory cut, extended slide stop and thumb safety, front and rear angled thin line serrations, matte black finish, 2 lbs. 10 oz. New 2015.

MSR $844	$715	$625	$535	$485	$395	$320	$280	

Add $20 for 10mm cal.
Add $88 for magna ported barrel and slide.

* ***Eagle XL CH*** – .45 ACP or 10mm cal., 1911 style, 6 in. barrel with ported slide, lowered and flared ejection port, skeleton hammer, 3-hole trigger, fully adj. rear sight with dovetail front sight, black wood or white pearl grips, beavertail grip safety with memory cut, extended slide stop and thumb safety, front and rear angled thin line serrations, case hardened finish, 2 lbs. 10 oz. New 2018.

MSR $1,700	$1,450	$1,275	$1,095	$985	$800	$650	$550	

* ***Eagle XL Stainless*** – 10mm cal., deluxe 1911, 6 in. stainless steel barrel and slide, adj. sight. Mfg. 2017 only.

	$900	$800	$700	$600	$495	$415	$340	*$1,020*

* ***Golden Eagle XL*** – .45 ACP or 10mm cal., 1911 style, 6 in. barrel with ported slide, lowered and flared ejection port, skeleton hammer, 3-hole trigger, fully adj. rear sight with dovetail front sight, black wood or white pearl grips, beavertail grip safety with memory cut, extended slide stop and thumb safety, front and rear angled thin line serrations, 24K high polished gold plated finish, 2 lbs. 10 oz. New 2018.

MSR $1,750	$1,500	$1,300	$1,120	$1,015	$820	$675	$580	

EAGLE XLC – 10mm or .45 ACP cal., 6 in. barrel, slightly beveled magwell, lowered and flared ejection port, skeletonized hammer, 3-hole trigger, LPA fully adj. 3-dot sight made by Kensight, Dymondwood walnut dual textured grips with engraved logo, extended slide stop and thumb safety, beavertail grip safety with memory cut, front and rear-angled serrations, satin chrome finish on steel construction, 44 oz. New late 2017.

MSR $1,099	$935	$825	$700	$635	$515	$425	$365	

Add $59 for ported barrel and slide.

FALCON – .45 ACP cal., Series 70 1911, Commander size frame, 4 1/4 in. barrel, combat style round hammer, GI rear sight w/fixed blade front sight, vertical rear serrations, walnut logo engraved grips, matte blue finish, 2.2 lbs.

MSR $560	$475	$415	$350	$325	$265	$215	$185	

HAWK – 9mm Para. or .45 ACP cal., Commander size frame, 4 1/4 in. barrel, forged slide, Novak style LoMount fixed rear sight with dovetail front sight, beveled magwell, skeleton hammer and 3-hole trigger, lowered and flared ejection port, beavertail grip safety with memory cut, extended slide stop and thumb safety, angled front and rear serrations, walnut large diamond wood or rosewood double border/diamond with engraved logo (polished models only) grips, high luster polished blue (.45 ACP), all matte blue (9mm Para.), OD Green Cerakote, Coyote Tan Cerakote finish, 2.2 lbs.

MSR $668	$565	$495	$425	$385	$320	$270	$220	

Add $77 for high luster polished blue finish.
Add $89 for OD Green or Coyote Tan Cerakote finish.
Add $131 for LoMount Trijicon night sights.

* ***Hawk Digital Navy/Digital Snow*** – .45 ACP cal., similar to Hawk, except features Digital Navy or Digital Snow (disc. 2020) hydrographic finish and black Dymondwood dual texture grips, 38 oz. New 2018.

MSR $817	$700	$615	$525	$475	$385	$315	$275	

Add $149 Trijicon/AmeriGlo night sights.

THRASHER – 9mm Para. or .45 ACP cal., Officer size 1911, 3.12 in. bull barrel, two-stage recoil spring system, fixed GI-style sights, lowered and flared ejection port, GI-style trigger, thumb safety, and slide stop, round combat style hammer, beavertail grip safety, walnut, large diamond checkered grips with engraved owl logo, matte blue finish, includes one magazine, 1.9 lbs.

MSR $647	$550	$480	$415	$375	$310	$260	$215	

GRADING - PPGS™	100%	98%	95%	90%	80%	70%	60%	LAST MSR

* ***Thrasher Chrome*** – 9mm Para. or .45 ACP cal., Officer frame, 3.18 in. barrel, slightly beveled magwell, polished chrome, round combat style hammer, 3-hole trigger, Novak rear sight w/dovetail front sight, Trijicon/AmeriGlo night sights, black Dymondwood grips with Spanish checkering, beavertail grip safety, front and rear angled serrations, polished chrome finish. New 2017.

MSR $950	$810	$710	$610	$550	$445	$365	$315	

Add $130 Trijicon/AmeriGlo night sights.

* ***Thrasher Polished*** – 9mm Para., .40 S&W, or .45 ACP cal., Officer size 1911, 3.12 in. barrel, two-stage recoil spring system, LoMount Novak style rear and Dovetail front sight, lowered and flared ejection port, front and rear serrations, 3-hole trigger and extended thumb safety, round, combat style hammer, beavertail grip safety, rosewood double border, large diamond checkered grips with engraved logo, polished matte blue finish, includes one magazine, 1.9 lbs.

MSR $745	$635	$550	$475	$425	$350	$285	$250	

Add $130 for Trijicon night sights (disc. 2019).

* ***Thrasher Stainless*** – .45 ACP cal., 3 1/8 in. polished bull barrel, 7 shot, slightly beveled magwell, stainless steel frame and slide, lowered and flared ejection port, round combat hammer, low profile Novak style rear sight with dovetail front sight or Trijicon night lamps on front and rear sight, rosewood double diamond double border grips with owl head logo, beavertail grip safety with memory cut, two-stage recoil spring system, thin line angled serrations on slide, polished stainless finish on sides of frame and slide, 34 oz.

MSR $851	$725	$635	$550	$500	$400	$325	$280	

Add $105 for Trijicon night sights.

* ***Thrasher TB9*** – 9mm Para. cal., Officer size frame, 3 1/8 in. polished bull barrel, 8 shot, slightly beveled magwell, lowered and flared ejection port, round combat style hammer, skeleton trigger, low profile Novak style rear sight with dovetail white dot front sight, white pearl synthetic grips with silver Iver Johnson logo, beavertail grip safety with memory, extended thumb safety, two-stage recoil spring system, thin line angled serrations in front and rear of the slide, Tiffany Blue Cerakote frame, silver Cerakote slide and external parts, 36 oz. New 2018.

MSR $857	$725	$635	$550	$500	$400	$325	$280	

* ***Thrasher TT9*** – 9mm Para. cal., Officer size frame, 3 1/8 in. polished bull barrel, 8 shot, slightly beveled magwell, lowered and flared ejection port, round combat style hammer, skeleton trigger, low profile Novak style rear sight with dovetail white dot front sight, beavertail grip safety with memory, extended thumb safety, two-stage recoil spring system, thin line angled serrations in front and rear of the slide, black frame, silver Cerakote slide and external parts, 36 oz. Mfg. 2019-2020.

	$635	$550	$475	$425	$350	$285	$250	*$756*

RIFLES

1911A1 CARBINE – .45 ACP cal., 1911A1 military style, 16 in. GI-style barrel, includes one 8 shot mag., detachable walnut stock, walnut double diamond grips with engraved logo, 1911 style military style external parts, black oxide finish, 4 lbs. New 2017.

MSR $728	$625	$550	$475	$400	$350	$300	$275	

During 2013, Iver Johnson Arms produced a 1911A1 Carbine/Rifle with Mech-Tech Systems upper and Iver Johnson lower (last MSR $775).

SHOTGUNS: O/U

IJ600 – 12, 20, 28 ga. (new 2019), or .410 bore, 28 in. VR barrel with internal chokes, with (12 ga. or .410 only, new 2021) or w/o ejectors, bead front sight, walnut stock and forend with checkering, selector switch on safety, engraved receiver in black or silver, 7 lbs. 5 oz. New 2015.

MSR $527	$450	$400	$340	$300	$250	$200	$175	

Add $48 for ejectors (new 2021).

SHOTGUNS: SXS

IJ800 – 12 ga., 20 or 28 in. smoothbore barrel, 5 Mobil chokes, extractors, internal hammers, single trigger w/selector switch, bead front sight, walnut stock and forend w/sling swivels. New 2020.

MSR $555	$475	$415	$350	$325	$260	$215	$185	

SHOTGUNS: SEMI-AUTO

HP18 – 12 or 20 ga., 18 in. barrel with muzzle brake, Picatinny rail with adj. rear sight, fiber optic front sight, two-piece pistol grip full stock (removable leaving pistol grip), rubber buttpad, matte black or digital tan camo (new 2017) finish, 6 lbs. 6 oz. New 2015.

MSR $379	$350	$300	$250	$225	$200	$150	$125	

Add $96 for digital tan camo finish (new 2017).

GRADING - PPGS™	100%	98%	95%	90%	80%	70%	60%	LAST MSR

IJ500 – 12 or 20 ga., 2 3/4 or 3 in. chamber, 28 in. VR barrel with bead sight and internal chokes, walnut stock and forend with checkering, black receiver and barrel, 7 lbs. 2 oz. New 2015.

MSR $385	$350	$300	$250	$225	$200	$150	$125	

Add $96 for Max-4 camo finish (new 2017).

15 SA – 12 ga., 2 3/4 or 3 in. chamber, AR-15 style, 20 in. barrel, three removable chokes, 5 shot mag., fully adj. rear sight, synthetic stock with rubber buttpad, top and bottom rail, detachable carry handle, black finish, 7 lbs. 12 oz. Mfg. 2016 only.

	$395	$350	$310	$285	$255	$225	$195	*$445*

STRYKER – 12 ga. or .410 bore (new 2020), 2 3/4 and 3 in. chamber, AR-15 style, 20 in. smoothbore barrel with muzzle brake, MKA 1919 5 shot box mag. (includes two), A2 style detachable carry handle with adj. sight, fiber optic front sight, synthetic forend with light rails on sides and bottom, two-piece pistol grip stock, push-button releases the stock and leaves the pistol grip, thick rubber buttpad, 14 1/4 in. LOP, cross trigger safety, standard AR-15 bolt release and mag. release, black or satin nickel/black (new 2020) finish, 7 lbs. 10 oz. New 2018.

MSR $459	$395	$340	$295	$265	$215	$175	$150	

* ***Stryker Bullpup*** – 12 ga., 2 3/4 or 3 in. chamber, AR-15 style, 18 1/2 in. smoothbore barrel with muzzle brake, two MKA 1919 5 shot box mags., fiber optic front sight, two-piece pistol grip, standard AR-15 bolt and mag. release, black finish. Mfg. 2020 only.

	$450	$400	$325	$300	$250	$200	$150	*$525*

SHOTGUNS: SINGLE BARREL

IJ700 – 20 ga. or .410 bore, 2 3/4 and 3 in. chamber, 18 1/2 or 26 in. barrel with fixed full choke, blade front sight, black synthetic or wood stock and forend, folds in half for easy storage or transport, silver receiver with black barrel, 4 lbs. 15 oz. New 2017.

MSR $165	$145	$125	$110	$100	$80	$65	$55	

Add $15 for wood stock.

* ***IJ700 Youth*** – 20 ga. or .410 bore, 2 3/4 and 3 in. chamber, 18 1/2 or 24 in. barrel with fixed full choke, blade front sight, youth size black synthetic or wood stock and forend, folds in half for easy storage or transport, silver receiver with black barrel, 4 lbs. 15 oz. New 2017.

MSR $165	$145	$125	$110	$100	$80	$65	$55	

Add $15 for wood stock.

SHOTGUNS: SLIDE ACTION

PAS12 – 12 ga., 2 3/4 or 3 in. chamber, 18 in. smoothbore barrel, 4 shot mag., aluminum lightweight receiver with machined top rails for ring mounts, polymer stock in black, Cerakote OD Green (disc. 2020), Cerakote Coyote Tan (disc. 2020), Duracoat Pink (disc. 2016), Boa (disc. 2018), Copperhead, Water Moccasin, Digital Navy (disc. 2020), Digital Snow (disc. 2020), or Muddy Girl (disc. 2018) finish, black polymer medium length forend with deep ribbing, sling swivels, extended bolt release latch, cross trigger block safety, blade front sight, avail. with or w/o muzzle brake, includes gun lock and manual, 6 lbs. Mfg. by Armed in Turkey.

MSR $257	$220	$195	$165	$150	$120	$100	$85	

Add $6 for muzzle brake (disc. 2020).

Add $87 for Cerakote OD Green (disc. 2020), Cerakote Coyote Tan (disc. 2020), or Duracoat Pink (disc. 2016) finish.

Add $144 for Digital Navy (disc. 2020), Digital Snow (disc. 2020), Muddy Girl (disc. 2018), Boa (disc. 2018), Copperhead, or Water Moccasin Hydrographic snake print finish.

* ***PAS12 Adj. Sight*** – 12 ga., similar to PAS12, except has white dot fully adj. rear sight with fiber optic front sight, available with muzzle brake, 6 lbs. Mfg. by Armed in Turkey.

MSR $277	$240	$210	$180	$165	$130	$110	$90	

Add $7 for muzzle brake.

* ***PAS12 Combo*** – 12 ga., similar to PAS12, except has either 28 or 30 in. VR barrel with bead sight, includes 3 internal chokes for long barrel, black finish. Mfg. by Armed in Turkey. Disc. 2020.

	$325	$285	$250	$225	$190	$165	$140	*$350*

* ***PAS12 PG*** – 12 ga., similar to PAS12, except features two-piece pistol grip stock, no muzzle brake available, 6 lbs. Mfg. by Armed in Turkey.

MSR $277	$240	$210	$180	$165	$130	$110	$90	

GRADING - PPGS™	100%	98%	95%	90%	80%	70%	60%	LAST MSR

* ***PAS12 PG-R/C*** – 12 ga., 2 3/4 or 3 in. chamber, 18 in. smoothbore barrel with muzzle brake, 4 shot mag., Picatinny rail on aluminum lightweight receiver, two-piece pistol grip stock with rubber pad, black, Digital Navy (new 2014) or Digital Snow (new 2014) finish, black polymer medium length forend with deep ribbing, sling swivels, extended bolt release latch, crossbolt trigger block safety, fiber optic sight, includes gun lock and manual, 6 lbs. Mfg. by Armed in Turkey.

MSR $290	$250	$220	$190	$170	$140	$115	$95	

Add $149 for Digital Navy or Digital Snow finish (new 2014).

* ***PAS12 Rail*** – 12 ga., similar to PAS12, except features Picatinny rail on top of receiver with fiber optic front sight, 6 lbs. Mfg. by Armed in Turkey. Importation disc. 2020.

	$230	$200	$175	$155	$125	$115	$90	*$270*

Add $7 for muzzle brake.

* ***PAS12 Satin*** – 12 ga., similar to PAS12, except features all satin finish and no muzzle brake, 6 lbs. Mfg. by Armed in Turkey.

MSR $297	$255	$225	$190	$175	$140	$115	$100	

Add $41 for two-piece PG stock (new 2019).

PAS20 – 20 ga., 18 in. barrel, blade front sight, straight stock, scaled down synthetic forend, 14 1/2 in. LOP, black or Muddy Girl (new 2017) finish, 5 lbs. 6 oz. New 2015.

MSR $257	$215	$190	$160	$145	$120	$95	$80	

Add $135 for Muddy Girl finish (new 2017).

* ***PAS 20 PG-R/C*** – 20 ga., 18 in. barrel with muzzle brake, fiber optic front sight, two-piece pistol grip stock, rubber buttpad, scaled down synthetic forend, Picatinny rail on receiver, black finish, 5 lbs. 10 oz. New 2015.

MSR $290	$250	$220	$190	$170	$140	$115	$95	

IVER JOHNSON ARMS & CYCLE WORKS

Previously located in Worcester, MA, 1883-1890, Fitchburg, MA, 1890-1975, Middlesex, NJ 1975-1983 (name changed to Iver Johnson Arms Inc.) and Jacksonville, AR 1984-1993. Formerly Johnson Bye & Co. 1871-1883. Renamed Iver Johnson's Arms & Cycle Works mid-year 1894-1975 (incorporated as Iver Johnson's Arms & Cycle Works Inc. in 1915). Renamed Iver Johnson's Arms & Cycle Works in 1891 with manufacturing moving to Fitchburg, MA. In 1975 the name changed to Iver Johnson's Arms, Inc., and two years later, company facilities were moved to Middlesex, NJ. In 1982, production was moved to Jacksonville, AR under the trade name Iver Johnson Arms, Inc. In 1983, Universal Firearms, Inc. was acquired by Iver Johnson Arms, Inc.

The author and publisher would like to thank the late Mr. Bill Goforth for providing much of the information on Iver Johnson Arms & Cycle Works.

IVER JOHNSON HISTORY & DATES OF INTEREST

1841: Iver Johnson born in Nordjford, Norway. 1857: Became apprentice gunsmith in Bergen, Norway. 1862: Opened gunshop in Christiania, Norway. 1863: Immigrated to the United States (Boston) went to work for Allen & Wheelock Co. in Worcester Mass. Married Mary Elizabeth Speirs, children: Fredrick Iver, John Lovell, Walter Clof and Mary Louise. 1871: Formed partnership with Martin Bye as Johnson & Bye Gunsmith in Worcester, Mass. 1873: Company moved to new five-story building on Central St. in Worcester, Mass. First bicycles introduced. 1883: Partnership with Martin Bye ended: became Iver Johnson & Co. some firearms marked "Iver Johnson Maker" or "Iver Johnson's Arms Co." Company remained at the central street location in Worcester. 1888: Iver Johnson becomes a U.S. citizen. 1890: Company moved to Fitchburg, Mass. Owl's head first appeared on revolver's grips. 1894: Company became Iver Johnson's Arms & Cycle Works of Fitchburg, Mass. Purchased bicycle shop in Fitchburg, Mass. and opened first retail sporting goods store in Fitchburg. 1895: August 3rd, Iver Johnson dies (age 54) eldest son Fred became president of company. 1896: First catalog issued, opened retail stores in Worchester, Boston and Keene, New Hampshire. 1900: Purchased J.P. Lovell Co. (wholesale and retail store in Boston). 1903: Opened sales offices in New York City, Chicago, San Francisco, Hamburg (Germany), Paris (France), London (England), and Constantinople (Turkey). 1904: Slogan "Hammer the Hammer" first used. 1909: All firearms manufactured for smokeless powder pressure. John L., second eldest son, became president of company. 1910: First Patent for semi-automatic pistol issued to Fred I. Johnson (no prototype). 1911: Motorcycles introduced. L.H. Cobb received a patent for a semiautomatic pistol (no prototype built). 1915: Mary Elizabeth Johnson dies (Iver's wife). Company incorporated as

100%	98%	95%	90%	80%	70%	60%	50%	40%	30%	20%	10%

Iver Johnson's Arm's & Cycle Works Inc. Family retains control of the majority of stock. 1916: William Barnes received patent for .25 ACP pistol (one prototype known). 1935: Walter O., youngest of Iver's sons, becomes president. 1953: Luther M. Otto III becomes president of company (Iver's grandson and son of Mary Louise, Iver's daughter). 1971: Company celebrates its 100th birthday. 1973: Company sold to Louis Imperato (owner of John Jovine Company of New York City). 1975: Purchased Plainsfield Machine Co. (makers of M-1 carbine), moved to Middlesex, New Jersey. Name changed to Iver Johnson's Arms Co. 1978: First semi-automatic pistol manufactured. 1980: Company sold to Interstate Dist. Co. of Little Rock, Arkansas. 1983: Company moved to Jacksonville, Arkansas. 1985: Purchased Universal Firearms Co. (Universal Carbines appeared in 1986 catalog only). 1986: October 22 - company filed for Chapter 11 bankruptcy, production ceased and plant closed in December. 1987: Louis Imperato re-assumed control, renamed Iver Johnson Arms by AMAC. 1988: Resumed limited production of M-1 carbine and semiautomatic pistols. A few new prototype firearms were designed by AMAC but none of them ever reached full production. 1993: Doors shut for good, auction held and equipment sold.

HANDGUNS: SOLID FRAME, DOUBLE ACTION MODELS MFG. 1878-1978

AMERICAN EAGLE (EAGLE/LION/OLD HICKORY) - .22 rimfire (small frame) or .32 rimfire (medium frame) cal., saw handle grip frame with eagle design on hard rubber grip panels, 2 1/4 (small) or 2 7/16 (medium) in. round rifled barrel, 5 (medium) or 7 (small) shot, usually marked with the model name and patent dates "June 4, 1878" or "Feb. 25, 1879", 9 1/4 or 11 7/8 oz. Mfg. 1878-1881.

$425	$365	$315	$275	$235	$195	$175	$155	$130	$115	$95	$85

AMERICAN BULLDOG FIRST MODEL (LION/OLD HICKORY) - .22 rimfire (small frame), .32 rimfire and centerfire (medium frame), .38 rimfire and centerfire (extra large frame), .44 Webley or .44 Bulldog cal., nickel finish, 2 1/2 in. round, 2 7/16 in. octagon (extra large frame), 4 1/2, 5, or 6 in. half-octagon/half-round barrel (extra large frame, 5 or 7 (small frame) shot, saw handle shaped grip frame, eagle design on hard rubber grip panels, model name marked on top strap, 9 5/8-19 7/8 oz., sold under the brand names Lion, Old Hickory, Navy Favorite and Ajax Army. Mfg. 1882-1884.

$425	$365	$315	$275	$235	$195	$175	$155	$130	$115	$95	$85

Add 25% for .22 cal. small frame or .44 cal. extra large frame.

AMERICAN BULLDOG SECOND MODEL - .22 rimfire (small frame), .32 rimfire or centerfire (medium frame), .38 rimfire or centerfire (extra large frame), .44 Webley, or .44 Bulldog cal., nickel finish, 2 1/4 (small frame), 2 1/2 (medium frame), or 2 7/16 (extra large frame) in. octagon barrel, longer barrel lengths of 4 1/2 or 6 were available on medium, rounded grip frame with square butt, hard rugger grip panels with dog's head design on large and extra large frame, small and medium frame have eagle design, 5 (large and extra large frames) or 7 shot, model name marked on top of barrel, sold under the brand names Lion, Old Hickory, Navy Favorite, and Ajax Army, 9 5/8 - 19 5/8 oz. Mfg. 1885-1899.

$350	$320	$275	$225	$200	$165	$140	$120	$100	$85	$75	$65

Add 25% for small .22 cal. frame or extra large .44 cal. frame.

AMERICAN BRITISH BULLDOG - similar to the American Bulldog First Model, except has bird's head grip frame shape and checkered hard rubber grip panels. Mfg. 1882-1887.

$450	$395	$335	$285	$245	$210	$180	$160	$140	$120	$100	$85

Variations of the American Bulldog First Model have also been marked "BRITISH BULL DOG".

BOSTON BULLDOG - .22 rimfire (small frame), .32 centerfire (medium frame), or .38 centerfire (large frame) cal., nickel finish, 2 1/4 (small frame) or 2 15/32 in. octagon barrel, nickel finish, 5 (medium or large) or 7 shot, hard rubber grip panels, small and medium frames have floral design, large frame has dog's head design, 8 3/8 - 16 oz. Mfg. 1887-1899.

$435	$370	$320	$275	$235	$195	$175	$155	$130	$115	$95	$85

LOVELL SAFETY DOUBLE ACTION REVOLVER (MODEL 1879) - .38 centerfire cal., 2 7/8 in. ribbed barrel, hard rubber grip panels with dog's head design, nickel finish, one-piece frame and barrel, not marked with model name, only marked "Iver Johnson Co. Maker", cylinder swings to the right, 17 oz. Mfg. 1883-1889.

$600	$520	$440	$390	$340	$285	$245	$220	$190	$155	$130	$115

This model was the first double action revolver manufactured in the U.S. with a side swing cylinder for loading and unloading.

GRADING - PPGS™	100%	98%	95%	90%	80%	70%	60%	LAST MSR

I.J. MODEL 1900 - .22 rimfire (small frame), .32 rimfire or centerfire (medium frame), or .38 centerfire (large frame) cal., 2 1/4 (small frame), 2 1/2 (medium/large frame) in. octagon barrel or various optional barrel lengths, nickel or blue finish, hard rubber grips panels with owl's head logo, 7 (.22 cal.), 5 (.32/.38 cal.), or 6 (.32 cal. large frame only after 1930) shot, does not have hammer the hammer action, pull pin cylinder release, 11 - 18 oz. Mfg. 1900-1941.

	100%	98%	95%	90%	80%	70%	60%	LAST MSR
	$150	$135	$125	$100	$85	$75	$65	

The large frame model was introduced in 1903.

* ***I.J. Model 1900 Target Small Frame*** - .22 rimfire cal., built on the small frame Model 1900, blue finish, 6 or 9 in. octagon barrel, oversize two-piece checkered wood grips, 7 shot, does not have hammer the hammer action, pull pin cylinder release, 12 7/8 - 14 3/8 oz. Mfg. 1925-1928.

	100%	98%	95%	90%	80%	70%	60%	LAST MSR
6 in. barrel	$200	$180	$160	$130	$120	$100	$90	
9 in. barrel (rare)	$250	$220	$190	$155	$130	$115	$100	

* ***I.J. Model 1900 Target Large Frame*** - .22 rimfire cal., built on the large frame Model 1900, 6 or 10 in. octagon barrel, oversize saw-handle shape checkered grips, 7 or 9 shot, does not have hammer the hammer action, pull pin cylinder release, 24 -27 oz. Mfg. 1921-1941.

	100%	98%	95%	90%	80%	70%	60%	LAST MSR
6 in. barrel	$200	$180	$160	$130	$120	$100	$90	
10 in. barrel (rare)	$250	$220	$190	$155	$130	$115	$100	

In the 1938 Iver Johnson Arms & Cycle Works catalog, this revolver was given a model number - Model 69 (6 in. barrel) or Model 79 (10 in. barrel).

I.J. PETITE - .22 rimfire cal., 6 shot, 1 1/4 in. barrel, folding trigger, pull pin cylinder release, hard rubber grip panels with large IJAC molded into them, 4 7/8 oz. Ltd. production run of less than 1,000, most likely 500 to 600. Mfg. 1909 only.

	100%	98%	95%	90%	80%	70%	60%	LAST MSR
	$600	$520	$440	$390	$340	$285	$245	

This model is one of the smallest double action revolvers ever built in the U.S.

U.S. REVOLVER CO. DOUBLE ACTION - .22 rimfire (small frame), .32 centerfire (medium or large frame), or .38 centerfire (large frame), 5 (.32 or .38 cal.), 6 (.32 cal.), or 7 (.22 cal.) shot, 2 1/2 in. round barrel with unfluted cylinder, hard rubber grip panels with U.S. on top or optional two-piece oversized hard rubber grips, does not have hammer the hammer action, approx. 17 oz. Mfg. 1911-1935.

	100%	98%	95%	90%	80%	70%	60%	LAST MSR
	$135	$120	$100	$85	$75	$65	$50	

This model was manufactured for sale through mail order catalogs, and it was never listed in any Iver Johnson catalog.

I.J. TARGET SEALED 8 FIRST MODEL (LARGE FRAME OCTAGON BARREL) - .22 rimfire cal., 8 shot, 6 or 10 in. octagon barrel, does not have hammer the hammer action, large solid frame, double action with pull in cylinder release, cylinder features recessed chambers that fully enclose the cartridge case head, one-piece checkered wood grips, 24-27 oz. Mfg. 1932-1941.

	100%	98%	95%	90%	80%	70%	60%	LAST MSR
	$250	$220	$190	$155	$130	$115	$100	

This model is the first major improvement of the solid frame double action model since its introduction in 1900. The 1938 catalog refers to the 6 in. model as the Model 68, and the 10 in. barrel as the Model 78.

I.J. TARGET SEALED 8 SECOND MODEL (LARGE FRAME ROUND BARREL) - .22 rimfire cal., 8 shot, 4 1/2 or 6 in. round barrel, blue finish, does not have hammer the hammer action, but does have recessed chambers in the cylinder, pull pin cylinder release, oversized checkered wood or plastic grips, 24-27 oz. Mfg. 1947-1954.

	100%	98%	95%	90%	80%	70%	60%	LAST MSR
	$240	$215	$190	$155	$130	$115	$100	

This model was introduced after WWII with only minor modifications, and the model number continued to be the Model 68.

I.J. SEALED 8 SNUB MODEL 68S (LARGE FRAME ROUND BARREL) - .22 rimfire cal., 8 shot, 2 1/2 in. round barrel, blue finish, does not have hammer the hammer action, but does have recessed chambers in the cylinder, pull pin cylinder release, two-piece wood pocket-size grips, 20 1/2 oz. Mfg. 1952-1954.

	100%	98%	95%	90%	80%	70%	60%	LAST MSR
	$265	$235	$210	$190	$155	$130	$115	

I.J. TARGET MODEL 55 - .22 rimfire cal., 8 shot, blue finish, 4 1/2 or 6 in. barrel, pull pin cylinder release, recessed chambers and flash control front rim (unfluted cylinder until 1958), oversized one-piece Tenite plastic grips, does not have hammer the hammer action, 26-27 oz. Mfg. 1955-1960.

	100%	98%	95%	90%	80%	70%	60%	LAST MSR
	$225	$195	$170	$140	$125	$110	$95	

Beginning in 1955, Iver Johnson Arms & Cycle Works introduced a newly designed solid frame double action revolver. Over the next few years, IJ introduced at least one new model a year, and during the first year, two new models were introduced.

GRADING - PPGS™	100%	98%	95%	90%	80%	70%	60%	LAST MSR

* ***I.J. Target Model 55A (Iver Johnson Sportman)*** – .22 rimfire cal., similar to I.J. Target Model 55, except has a loading gate on right side of frame, approx. 29-30 oz. Mfg. 1961-1978.

	$225	$195	$170	$140	$125	$110	$95	

This model was also called the Iver Johnson Sportman from 1974-1978.

I.J. CADET MODEL 55S – .22 rimfire cal., 8 shot, blue finish, 2 1/2 in. barrel, two-piece walnut or Tenite grips, does not have hammer the hammer action, recessed chambers with flash control front rim (unfluted cylinder until 1958), similar to the Model 55, 24 oz. Mfg. 1955-1960.

	$225	$195	$170	$140	$125	$110	$95	

* ***I.J. Cadet Model 55SA*** – .22 rimfire, .22 WMR, .32 S&W, .38 S&W, or .38 Spl. cal., 8 shot, blue finish, similar to Cadet Model 55A, except has loading gate on right side of frame, approx. 27 oz. Mfg. 1961-1978.

	$225	$195	$170	$140	$125	$110	$95	

I.J. MODEL 56 STARTER REVOLVER – .22 rimfire blank cal., built on the older Model Target Sealed 8 frame, half-length cylinder, 8 shot, pull pin cylinder release, 2 1/2 in. barrel, hard rubber or wood grips, does not have hammer the hammer action, 10 oz. Mfg. 1956-1960.

	$120	$100	$85	$75	$65	$60	$50	

* ***I.J. Starter Model 56A*** – .22 rimfire or .32 centerfire blank cal., 5 (.32) or 8 (.22) shot, similar to the Model 56 Starter Revolver, except has loading gate on right side of frame, approx. 12 oz. Mfg. 1961-1978.

	$120	$100	$85	$75	$65	$60	$50	

I.J. TARGET MODEL 57 – .22 rimfire cal., 8 shot, 2 1/2, 4 1/2, or 6 in. barrel, similar to the Model 55, except has adj. front and rear sights, oversize molded plastic grips with thumb rest, 27-30 1/2 oz. Mfg. 1957-1960.

	$235	$200	$175	$140	$125	$110	$95	

* ***I.J. Target Model 57A (Sportsman Deluxe)*** – .22 rimfire blank cal., similar to the Model 57, except has loading gate on right side of frame. Mfg. 1961-1978.

	$235	$200	$175	$140	$125	$110	$95	

This model was also called the Iver Johnson Sportsman Deluxe between 1974-1978.

I.J. SIDEWINDER MODEL 50/50A – .22 rimfire cal. (.22 WMR combo new 1974), blue or nickel (new 1974) finish, oversize western style wood or plastic imitation stag (new 1968) grips, 8 shot, recessed chambers, flash control, 4 3/4 (new 1974) or 6 in. barrel, fixed front sight, adj. rear sight (new 1974), does not have hammer the hammer action, 30-31 oz. Mfg. 1961-1978.

	$250	$220	$190	$155	$130	$115	$100	

During 1963, this model's nomenclature changed to Model 50A. After 1974, this model had different model numbers for different finishes, barrel lengths, calibers, and rear sight combinations.

NEW AMERICAN BULLDOG SERIES – .22 rimfire, .22 WMR, or .38 Spl. cal., blue or satin nickel finish, 2 1/2 or 4 in. barrel, 5 or 6 shot, large oversize plastic one-piece or small pocket two-piece grips, ramp front sight, adj. rear sight, pull pin cylinder release, does not have hammer the hammer action, heavy full-length rib, 26-30 oz. Mfg. 1973-1978.

	$275	$240	$215	$190	$155	$130	$115	

I.J. ROOKIE – .38 Spl. cal., 5 shot, blue finish, 4 in. barrel, pull pin cylinder release, oversized one-piece plastic grips with molded thumb rest, fixed sight, does not have hammer the hammer action, 29 oz. Mfg. 1973-1978.

	$235	$200	$175	$140	$125	$110	$95	

I.J. SWINGOUT CYLINDER PROTOTYPE – .22 rimfire, .32 S&W Long, or .38 Spl. cal., blue finish, hammer the hammer action, large frame, (modified Model 55), ramp front sight, fixed or adj. rear sight, only five models known, each is different, .22 rimfire cal. has 6 in. barrel, full-length vent. rib and under lug, 8 shot, two-piece oversized wood grips, .32 S&W Long cal. has 2 1/2 in. barrel, full-length solid rib and under lug, 5 shot, two-piece combat wood grips, second .32 S&W Long model (tool room model) has plain round barrel, 5 shot, no sights, no grips, and no finish, .38 Spl. cal. has 4 in. barrel, half under lug, no top rib, fixed rear sight, (groove in top strap), two-piece service style composite grips, third .32 S&W Long cal. model is 5 shot, similar to .38 Spl., except has homemade grips. Mfg. 1976.

Values range from $600 for 100% condition to $400 for 60% condition.

This model is rare and only three have shown up in the used marketplace.

GRADING - PPGS™	100%	98%	95%	90%	80%	70%	60%	LAST MSR

PISTOLS: SEMI-AUTO

.25 ACP PROTOTYPE – .25 ACP cal., only one example known to exist, patent #1173161 issued on Feb. 29, 1916 to William O. Barnes, who assigned it to Mary E. Spears Johnson, Iver's widow. Mfg. 1916.

Extreme rarity factor precludes accurate pricing.

An individual appraisal would be recommended if this specimen is ever encountered. One other early semi-auto pistol patent was assigned to Iver Johnson - #992854, issued to L.H. Cobb. No known examples of this patent exist.

MODEL X300 PONY MEDIUM FRAME SINGLE ACTION – .380 ACP cal., blue, nickel, or matte blue finish, checkered wood grips, front blade sight, adj. rear sight, 3 in. barrel, 6 shot mag., no mag. safety, 20 oz. Mfg. in Middlesex, NJ 1978-1982, Jacksonville, AR 1983-1988, and Jacksonville, AR by AMAC 1989-1991.

	100%	98%	95%	90%	80%	70%	60%
	$385	$335	$290	$260	$210	$175	$135

Add 10% for nickel finish.

I.J. SUPER ENFORCER (M1 CARBINE) – .30 Carbine cal., gas operated pistol version of the M1 Carbine, 5, 10, or 15 shot mag., walnut stock, fires from closed bolt, 9 1/2 in. barrel, 4 lbs. Mfg. 1978-1993.

	100%	98%	95%	90%	80%	70%	60%
	$850	$745	$640	$580	$470	$385	$300

TP SERIES 25 – .25 ACP cal., double action, small frame, 2.85 in. barrel, black plastic wraparound grips, blue or nickel finish, fixed sights, hammer block safety mounted on slide, 7 shot mag., does not have slide hold open device, designed by Erma Werke in Germany, 14 1/2 oz. Mfg. 1981-1982.

	100%	98%	95%	90%	80%	70%	60%
	$250	$220	$190	$170	$140	$115	$90

TP SERIES 22 – .22 LR cal., double action, black plastic wraparound grips, 2.85 in. barrel, 7 shot, blue or nickel finish, fixed sights, hammer block safety and patented firing pin block safety, does not have a slide hold open or mag. safety, designed by Erma Werke. Mfg. 1982-1989.

	100%	98%	95%	90%	80%	70%	60%
	$275	$240	$205	$185	$150	$125	$95

NEW TRAILSMAN – .22 LR cal., large frame, single action, copy of Colt Woodsman, blue finish, plastic or wood grip panels, 4 1/2 or 6 in. barrel, 10 shot mag., sear block safety, internal hammer mechanism, fixed sights, slide hold open latch, push-button mag. release, 64 oz. First 500 mfg. in Argentina and assembled in the USA (not all of these 500 were assembled). Mfg. 1985-1991.

	100%	98%	95%	90%	80%	70%	60%
	$275	$240	$205	$185	$150	$125	$95

9MM PROTOTYPE – redesigned .380 ACP Pony model chambered for 9mm Luger cal., never put into production, but one prototype is known to exist, double action, medium frame. Mfg. 1986.

Extreme rarity factor precludes accurate pricing.

UNIVERSAL ENFORCER (M1 CARBINE) – .30 Carbine cal., gas operated, blue finish, single action, pistol version of the M1 carbine, 5, 10, or 15 shot mag., 9 1/2 in. barrel, hardwood stock, fires from close bolt, trigger block safety, 4 lbs. Mfg. 1986.

	100%	98%	95%	90%	80%	70%	60%
	$850	$745	$640	$580	$470	$385	$300

COMPACT 25/COMPACT ELITE – .25 ACP cal., 6 shot, single action, 2 in. barrel, checkered plastic grips, matte blue finish, bright blue slide, trigger block safety, packaged in jewelry presentation case, also available as a Compact Elite with 24Kt. gold finish and Ivorex grips, 9.3 oz. Mfg. 1991-1993.

	100%	98%	95%	90%	80%	70%	60%
Compact 25	$250	$220	$190	$170	$140	$115	$90
Compact Elite	$500	$440	$375	$340	$275	$225	$175

100%	98%	95%	90%	80%	70%	60%	50%	40%	30%	20%	10%

PISTOLS: SINGLE SHOT MFG. 1871-1899

UNCLE SAM PERCUSSION DERRINGER – .28, .30, or .36 cal., 2 1/4 in. barrel, smoothbore, muzzle loading, spur trigger, center mounted hammer, brown finish, one-piece frame and barrel, 4 1/2 oz. Mfg. 1871-1873.

100%	98%	95%	90%	80%	70%	60%	50%	40%	30%	20%	10%
$400	$350	$320	$275	$225	$200	$150	$140	$120	$110	$100	$90

Add 25% for engraved "Prince" model.

A deluxe engraved version with detachable barrel and nickel finish was called the "Prince" model.

ECLIPSE CARTRIDGE DERRINGER – .22 (small frame), .32, or .38 (large frame) rimfire cal., smoothbore, 2 in. half-round, half-octagon barrel, swings to side for loading, nickel frame, brown barrel, spur trigger, center mounted hammer, wood, hard rubber, or mother-of-pearl grips. Mfg. 1871-1899.

100%	98%	95%	90%	80%	70%	60%	50%	40%	30%	20%	10%
$350	$325	$285	$250	$200	$175	$150	$125	$110	$100	$90	$80

Add 25% for the engraved "Star" model.

A deluxe engraved version was called the "Star" model, featuring a fully engraved frame and fancy grips.

100%	98%	95%	90%	80%	70%	60%	50%	40%	30%	20%	10%

GEM BLANK PISTOL – .22 rimfire blank cal., spur trigger, Flobert type action. Mfg. 1880-1890.

100%	98%	95%	90%	80%	70%	60%	50%	40%	30%	20%	10%
$250	$200	$180	$160	$130	$120	$100	$90	$80	$75	$70	$65

REVOLVERS: SA, MFG. 1873-1899

Model names for these guns included: Defender, Eagle, Encore, Enterprise (Enterprise Gun Works), Eureka, Favorite, Invincible, J.T. Johnson, J.S.T. Co., Lion, Navy Favorite, Old Hickory, Red Hot, Smoker, Tiger, and Tycoon.

SQUARE BUTT MODELS – .22 (small frame), .32 (medium frame), .38, or .41 (large frame) rimfire cal., 2 1/16 in. smoothbore (small frame), 2 15/16 in. (medium frame) with three straight grooves, or 2 3/8 in. octagon rifled bore (large frame) barrel, 5 (medium or large frame) or 7 shot, 7-14 oz. Mfg. 1873-1888.

100%	98%	95%	90%	80%	70%	60%	50%	40%	30%	20%	10%
$250	$220	$200	$190	$175	$155	$130	$115	$100	$90	$75	$60

Barrel lengths as long as 10 inches have been seen.

BIRD'S HEAD GRIP MODELS – .22 (small frame), .32 (medium frame), .38 or .41 (large frame) rimfire cal., 2 1/2 in. smoothbore (small or medium frame) or 2 7/16 in. rifled bore (large frame) barrel, 5 or 7 shot. Mfg. 1873-1888.

100%	98%	95%	90%	80%	70%	60%	50%	40%	30%	20%	10%
$250	$220	$200	$190	$175	$155	$130	$115	$100	$90	$75	$60

Barrel lengths as long as 10 inches have been seen.

Not all spur trigger single action revolvers marked with the Defender name were manufactured by Iver Johnson (Johnson & Bye Gunsmith). All of these brand names were actually owned by J.P. Lovell Co. Before Iver Johnson (Johnson & Bye) started manufacturing revolvers, J.P. Lovell Co. had Hopkins & Allen manufacture the Defender (and quite possibility some of the other names associated with Iver Johnson). The main difference in these Hopkins & Allen Defenders is that the cylinder locking notches are at the front of the cylinder. The era of manufacture for the Hopkins & Allen manufactured Defenders was 1868 - 1872.

DEFENDER 89 SERIES – .22 (small frame), .32 (medium frame), .38 or .41 (large frame) rimfire cal., 2 1/16 (small frame), 2 7/16 (medium frame), or 2 3/8 (large frame) in. round or octagon barrel, improved version of the older Defender series, square butt and bird's head grip variations, wood or hard rubber grips, 5 or 7 shot, frame sizes are similar to earlier Defender series, may also be found with same names as the earlier series of single action spur trigger revolvers. Mfg. 1889-1899.

100%	98%	95%	90%	80%	70%	60%	50%	40%	30%	20%	10%
$265	$240	$220	$200	$175	$160	$140	$120	$100	$90	$75	$60

GRADING - PPGS™	100%	98%	95%	90%	80%	70%	60%	LAST MSR

REVOLVERS: SA

Between 1973-1978, Iver Johnson imported single action revolvers, as well as a line of black powder reproductions and replicas manufactured by Uberti in Italy.

CATTLEMAN SERIES – .357 Mag., .44 Mag., or .45 LC cal., 4 3/4, 5 1/2, or 7 1/4 in. barrel, blue finish, case hardened large frame, rod ejection, brass trigger guard and backstrap, one-piece European walnut grips, fixed (Magnum) or adj. (Buckhorn Magnum) sights, 6 shot, automatic hammer block safety, some very early Buckhorn models were imported with a 12 in. barrel and shoulder stock attachments, 41-44 oz. Mfg. by Uberti, imported 1973-1978.

GRADING - PPGS™	100%	98%	95%	90%	80%	70%	60%	LAST MSR
	$350	$320	$275	$225	$200	$160	$140	

Add 25% for 12 in. barrel.

Subtract approx. 10% for Cattleman Magnum model.

* ***Cattleman Buckhorn Buntline*** – similar to Cattleman Buckhorn Magnum, except has 18 in. barrel with detachable stock, front blade sight, rear sight dovetailed into frame top strap.

GRADING - PPGS™	100%	98%	95%	90%	80%	70%	60%	LAST MSR
	$400	$350	$300	$265	$225	$190	$165	

* ***Cattleman Trailblazer*** – .22 LR or .22 WMR cal., 5 1/2 or 6 1/2 in. barrel, medium frame, otherwise similar to Cattleman Magnum, 40 oz.

GRADING - PPGS™	100%	98%	95%	90%	80%	70%	60%	LAST MSR
	$350	$320	$275	$225	$200	$160	$140	

100%	98%	95%	90%	80%	70%	60%	50%	40%	30%	20%	10%

REVOLVERS: TOP BREAK, MFG. 1887-1978

LOVELL SAFETY HAMMERLESS AUTOMATIC – .38 centerfire cal., 5 shot, nickel finish, 3 1/4 in. barrel, hard rubber grip panels with dog's head design, does not have hammer the hammer action, not marked with model name or number, "Iver Johnson & Co." on the barrel top rib, 18 1/8 oz. Mfg. 1887-1889.

100%	98%	95%	90%	80%	70%	60%	50%	40%	30%	20%	10%
$600	$520	$440	$390	$340	$285	$245	$220	$190	$155	$130	$115

100%	98%	95%	90%	80%	70%	60%	50%	40%	30%	20%	10%

LOVELL SWIFT REVOLVER HAMMER & HAMMERLESS MODELS – .38 centerfire cal., 5 shot, 3 1/4 in. barrel, nickel finish, hard rubber grip panels with owl's head at top, marked on barrel top rib with patent dates and "Iver Johnson Co. Worcester Mass." marked on barrel top strap, with model name "SWIFT", does not have hammer the hammer action, only sold through J.P. Lovell Co., 16 7/8 - 17 7/8 oz. Mfg. 1890-1894.

$450	$395	$335	$285	$245	$210	$180	$160	$140	$120	$100	$85

Add $50 for hammerless model.

FIRST MODEL SAFETY AUTOMATIC HAMMER (BLACK POWDER CARTRIDGE) – .22 rimfire, .32 centerfire, or .38 centerfire cal., nickel (standard) or blue finish, hard rubber grips with owl's head design, small or large frame, 5 or 7 shot, 3 (small) or 3 1/4 in. barrel, single top post barrel latch (release lever mounted on left side of top strap), flat leaf hammer spring, first revolver marked "Iver Johnson's Arms & Cycle Works", some early models were marked "Iver Johnson & Co.", uses hammer the hammer action, main ser. no. location on left side of grip frame, 12-17 1/4 oz. Mfg. 1894-1895.

$290	$260	$180	$160	$140	$120	$110	$100	$90	$80	$70	$60

Add 10% for models marked "Iver Johnson & Co."

SECOND MODEL SAFETY AUTOMATIC HAMMER (BLACK POWDER CARTRIDGE) – .22 rimfire, .32 centerfire, or .38 centerfire cal., 5 or 7 shot, 3 or 3 1/4 in. barrel, nickel (standard) or blue finish, hard rubber grips with owl's head at top, double top post latch, flat leaf hammer spring, two cross pins in lower frame, uses hammer the hammer action, main ser. no. located on left side of grip frame, 12-17 1/4 oz. Mfg. 1896-1908.

$275	$245	$220	$200	$175	$160	$140	$120	$100	$90	$75	$60

Add 100% for Bourne Knuckleduster.

FIRST MODEL SAFETY AUTOMATIC HAMMERLESS (BLACK POWDER CARTRIDGES) – .32 centerfire, or .38 centerfire cal., small or large frame, 5 shot, 3 (small) or 3 1/4 in. barrel, nickel (standard) or blue finish, hard rubber grips with owl's head logo at top, single top post barrel latch (release lever mounted on left side of top strap), flat leaf hammer spring, two cross pins in lower frame, uses hammer the hammer action, main ser. no. location on left side of grip frame, 12-17 1/4 oz. Mfg. 1895-1896.

$300	$265	$185	$160	$140	$120	$110	$100	$90	$80	$70	$60

SECOND MODEL SAFETY AUTOMATIC HAMMERLESS (BLACK POWDER CARTRIDGE) – .32 centerfire, or .38 centerfire cal., small or large frame, 5 shot, 3 (small) or 3 1/4 in. barrel, nickel (standard) or blue finish, hard rubber grips with owl's head at top, double top post latch, flat leaf hammer spring, two cross pins in lower frame, uses hammer the hammer action, main ser. no. located on left side of grip frame, 12 1/2-17 1/4 oz. Mfg. 1896-1908.

$285	$250	$225	$200	$175	$160	$140	$120	$100	$90	$75	$60

Add 100% for Bourne Knuckleduster.

GRADING - PPGS™	100%	98%	95%	90%	80%	70%	60%	LAST MSR

THIRD MODEL SAFETY AUTOMATIC HAMMER (SMOKELESS POWDER CARTRIDGE) – .22 rimfire, .32 centerfire, or .38 centerfire cal., 5 or 7 shot, small or large frame, 3 or 3 1/4 in. barrel, hard rubber grips with owl's head on top, optional oversized wood or hard rubber grips, all coil springs, redesigned model for smokeless powder, double top post barrel latch, hammer the hammer action, coil hammer spring, four cross pins in lower frame, main ser. no. located on left side of grip frame, 13-19 oz. Mfg. 1909-1941.

	$250	$220	$200	$190	$175	$155	$130	

THIRD MODEL SAFETY AUTOMATIC HAMMERLESS (SMOKELESS POWDER CARTRIDGE) – .22 rimfire, .32 centerfire, or .38 centerfire cal., 5 or 7 shot, small or large frame, 3 or 3 1/4 in. barrel, hard rubber grips with owl's head on top, optional oversized wood or hard rubber grips, all coil springs, redesigned model for smokeless powder, double top post barrel latch, hammer the hammer action, coil hammer spring, four cross pins in lower frame, main ser. no. located on left side of grip frame, 13 1/2 - 19 1/4 oz. Mfg. 1909-1941.

	$260	$225	$200	$190	$175	$155	$130	

U.S. REVOLVER CO. AUTOMATIC HAMMER – .22 rimfire, .32 or .38 centerfire cal., large or small frame, blue or nickel finish, 5 or 7 shot, 3 or 3 1/4 in. barrel (5 in. barrels have been seen), does not have hammer the hammer action, safety notch on hammer, hard rubber grips with U.S. at top, oversized two-piece hard rubber grips optional, brand name revolver mfg. by Iver Johnson's Arms & Cycle Works sold through the wholesale trade, never listed in any IJ catalog, although it was listed in some European catalogs as an original Iver Johnson product, main ser. no. located on left side of grip frame, 12-17 3/4 oz. Mfg. 1910-1935.

	$225	$195	$170	$140	$125	$110	$95	

GRADING - PPGS™	100%	98%	95%	90%	80%	70%	60%	LAST MSR

U.S. REVOLVER AUTOMATIC HAMMERLESS – .32 or .38 centerfire cal., similar to Hammer model, except has rebounding hammer, 12 1/2-18 oz. Mfg. 1910-1935.

$225	$195	$170	$140	$125	$110	$95	

SECRET SERVICE SPECIAL HAMMER – same model as the U.S. Revolver Co., except for markings on the barrel, large and small frame, does not have hammer the hammer action, top of barrel marked for .38 SMITH & WESSON cartridge" (or .32 for small frame), and "SECRET SERVICE SPECIAL" on left side of barrel, main ser. no. location on left side of grip frame, mfg. for Fred Biffar Co. of Chicago., four other companies also manufactured this gun - Meriden Firearms Co., Hopkins & Allen Firearms Co., H&R Arms Co., and an unknown Spanish company. Mfg. 1912-disc.

$225	$195	$170	$140	$125	$110	$95	

Subtract 10% for H&R Arms Co., 15% for Hopkins & Allen Co., 20% for Meriden Firearms Co., or 25% for Spanish mfg.

SECRET SERVICE SPECIAL HAMMERLESS – same model as the U.S. Revolver Co. hammerless, except for markings on the barrel and grips, mfg. for Fred Biffar Co. of Chicago., four other companies also manufactured this gun - Meriden Firearms Co., Hopkins & Allen Firearms Co., H&R Arms Co., and an unknown Spanish company. Mfg. 1912-disc.

$225	$195	$170	$140	$125	$110	$95	

Subtract 10% for H&R Arms Co., 15% for Hopkins & Allen Co., 20% for Meriden Firearms Co., or 25% for Spanish mfg.

SECRET SERVICE MODEL W/HAMMER BLOCK SAFETY – similar to U.S. Revolver Automatic Hammer, except has patented hammer block safety, patented by Prospero Donaldo and assigned to Fred Biffar Co. of Chicago. Mfg. 1917-disc.

$250	$220	$200	$190	$175	$155	$130	

.22 SUPERSHOT AUTOMATIC (LARGE FRAME) – .22 rimfire cal., blue finish, 6 in. barrel, one-piece checkered wood grips, features hammer the hammer action, Model 70 (7 shot) or Model 90 (9 shot), built on the Safety Automatic Hammer Third Model large frame with similar specs, left side of barrel marked "22 SUPERSHOT", 24 oz. Mfg. 1928-1941.

$250	$220	$200	$190	$175	$155	$130	

.22 SUPERSHOT SEALED EIGHT FIRST MODEL (LARGE FRAME) – .22 rimfire cal., blue finish, 8 shot, 6 in. barrel, oversized checkered wood grips, hammer the hammer action, cylinder with recessed chambers that full enclose the cartridge case head, large frame top break, left side of barrel marked "22 SUPERSHOT SEALED EIGHT", main ser. no. located on left side of grip frame, ser. nos. below L26601, 24 oz. Mfg. 1932-1941.

$275	$245	$220	$200	$175	$160	$140	

Add 20% for adj. sight model.

The 1938 catalog identifies this model as the Model 88 (fixed sights), the Model 833 (adj. rear sight), and the Model 834 (adj. rear sight and adj. finger rest).

.22 SUPERSHOT SEALED EIGHT SECOND MODEL (LARGE FRAME) – .22 rimfire cal., blue finish, similar to First Model, except has altered grip frame, and was also available in 4 1/2 in. barrel, ser. nos. above L26600, 26 3/4-28 3/4 oz. Mfg. 1947-1954.

$275	$245	$220	$200	$175	$160	$140	

.22 SUPERSHOT THIRD MODEL (MODEL 844) – .22 rimfire cal., blue finish, similar to Second Model, except has unfluted cylinder, known and marked as the Model 844, 24-27 oz. Mfg. 1955-1957

$300	$275	$245	$220	$200	$175	$160	

PROTECTOR SEALED EIGHT LARGE FRAME – .22 rimfire cal., blue finish, 2 1/2 in. barrel, hammer the hammer action, cylinder has 8 recessed chambers, pocket size one-piece checkered wood grips, marked on left side "PROTECTOR SEALED EIGHT", listed as the Model 84 in the 1938 catalog, 20 oz. Mfg. 1932-1941.

$415	$350	$315	$275	$235	$195	$175	

Add 10% for serial numbers above L26600.

MODEL 36T TRIGGER COCKING, LARGE FRAME SINGLE ACTION – .22 rimfire cal., 8 shot, blue finish, 6 in. barrel, oversize checkered wood grips with finger rest, adj. rear sight, patented trigger cocking action, first pull of trigger cocks the hammer and next pull releases it, main ser. no. located on left side of grip frame, scarce, 24 oz. Mfg. 1938-1941.

$495	$425	$375	$325	$275	$225	$200	

This model Iver Johnson's was first attempt at a true adj. sight target revolver. The patent rights to the action were obtained early in the 1900s and experimented with for many years.

GRADING - PPGS™ 100% 98% 95% 90% 80% 70% 60% LAST MSR

I.J. CHAMPION MODEL 822 SINGLE ACTION TARGET – .22 rimfire cal., blue finish, 6 in. barrel, 8 shot, based on .22 Supershot Sealed Eight frame, oversize fancy checkered wood grips with finger rest, does not have hammer the hammer action, large frame, design for target shooting, recessed chambers in the cylinders, 24 oz. Mfg. 1939-1947.

$450 $400 $350 $300 $275 $210 $195

ARMSWORTH MODEL 855 – .22 rimfire cal., 6 in. barrel, flat side with round bottom, full-length top rib, adj. sights, does not have hammer the hammer action, combination of earlier Champion single action and .22 Supershot Third Model, has Champion single action mechanism and barrel, grips, and cylinder of the .22 Supershot, unfluted cylinder with recessed chambers and flash control front rim, 30 oz. Mfg. 1955-1957.

$425 $365 $315 $275 $235 $195 $175

I.J. TRAILSMAN MODEL 66 LARGE FRAME – .22 rimfire cal., 4 1/2 or 6 in. barrel, blue finish, double action, oversized plastic Tenite grips with molded thumbrest, adj. rear and front sight, manual ejection, hammer mounted firing pin, 8 shot, cylinder has recessed chambers and flash control front rim, main ser. no. located on front of the grip strap until 1961, then on right side of frame below cylinder, 31-34 oz. Mfg. 1958-1978.

$225 $195 $170 $140 $125 $110 $95

* ***I.J. Trailsman Model 66S Snub Large Frame*** – .22 rimfire, .32 centerfire (new 1962), or .38 centerfire (new 1962) cal., similar to the Trailsman Model 66, except has two-piece plastic grips, 2 3/4 in. barrel, manual extractor, 5 or 8 shot, main ser. no. located on front of grip strap until 1961, then moved to right side of frame below cylinder, 25 oz. Mfg. 1959-1963.

$235 $200 $175 $140 $125 $110 $95

HIJO QUIK BREAK LARGE FRAME – similar to Trailsman Model 66, nickel finish, 2 3/4 in. barrel, double action, does not have hammer the hammer action, small two-piece pocket size grips, mfg. for sale through NYC mail order companies, 25 oz. Mfg. 1961.

$235 $200 $175 $140 $125 $110 $95

MODEL 67 VIKING LARGE FRAME – .22 rimfire cal., 8 shot, blue finish, 4 1/2 or 6 in. chrome-lined barrel, redesigned Model 66 double action incorporating the hammer the hammer feature, oversized plastic grips with molded thumb rest, adj. rear and front sight, cylinder has recessed chambers and flash control front rim, main ser. no. located on right side of frame below cylinder, 31-34 oz. Mfg. 1964-1978.

$250 $220 $200 $190 $175 $155 $130

* ***Model 67S Viking Snub Large Frame*** – .22 rimfire, .32 or .38 centerfire cal., similar to Model 67 Viking, except has small two-piece plastic grips, 2 3/4 in. barrel, 5 or 8 shot, 25 oz. Mfg. 1964-1978.

$260 $225 $200 $190 $175 $155 $130

MODEL 69 STARTER DELUXE LARGE FRAME – .22 rimfire blank or .32 centerfire blank, double action, 2 3/4 in. solid barrel, does not have hammer the hammer action, fixed sights, action similar to Trailsman Model 66, small two-piece plastic pocket size grips, 5 or 8 shot, blue finish, manual ejection, main ser. no. located on right side of frame below cylinder, 22 oz. Mfg. 1964-1978.

$125 $100 $85 $75 $65 $60 $50

RIFLES

Iver Johnson's first rifle was manufactured in 1928 and remained the only rifle manufactured entirely within the Iver Johnson factory in Fitchburg. The later .22 cal. rifles were all imported from either Canada or Germany, except the Lil Champ Model, which was manufactured in Jacksonville, AR. The M1 Carbine models were manufactured in either Middlesex, NJ or Jacksonville, AR.

I.J. X BOLT ACTION EARLY MODEL – .22 rimfire cal., bolt action, single shot, fixed open rear sight, blade front sight, 22 in. round tapered barrel, thumb screw take down, solid block gum or walnut stock with large knob at front of forend, patented automatic safety, steel buttplate, 4 lbs. Mfg. 1928-1941.

$250 $220 $190 $155 $130 $115 $100

I.J. X BOLT ACTION LATE MODEL – .22 rimfire cal., bolt action, similar to Early model, except larger, heavier stock, 4 1/2 lbs.

$250 $220 $190 $155 $130 $115 $100

I.J. 2X BOLT ACTION – .22 rimfire cal., single shot, adj. rear sight, post front sight, round tapered 24 in. barrel, blue finish, thumb screw take down, checkered full pistol grip stock with finger grooves in forend, steel buttplate, chromium plated bolt and trigger, patented automatic safety, 4 1/2 lbs. Mfg. 1930-1955.

$285 $250 $215 $175 $145 $120 $110

GRADING - PPGS™	100%	98%	95%	90%	80%	70%	60%	LAST MSR

* ***I.J. 2XA Bolt Action*** – .22 rimfire cal., single shot, similar to Model 2X, except has Lyman #55 adj. rear sight, Lyman #3 bead front sight, sling swivels, leather sling strap, tapered 24 in. proofed and targeted barrel, 4 5/8 lbs. Mfg. 1930-1941.

$325 $300 $275 $250 $200 $175 $150

I.J. LIL CHAMP BOLT ACTION – .22 rimfire cal., single shot, 16 1/4 in. blue barrel, blue receiver, nickel bolt and trigger, step adj. rear sight, ramp front sight, black plastic molded shortened stock, designed for smaller shooters, 3 1/8 lbs. Mfg. 1985-1990.

$175 $155 $130 $115 $95 $85 $75

I.J. TRAILBLAZER SEMI-AUTO – .22 LR cal., recoil operated, blue finish, 10 shot detachable mag., Monte Carlo style hardwood stock, post front sight, step adj. rear sight, plastic buttplate, 18 1/2 in. barrel, imported from Canada. Mfg. 1984-1986.

$150 $130 $115 $100 $85 $75 $65

I.J. WAGONMASTER LEVER ACTION – .22 Rimfire or .22 WMR cal., 12 (.22 WMR), 15, 17, or 21 shot mag., tubular mag. under the barrel, 18 1/2 in. barrel, hooded ramp front sight, step adj. rear sight, walnut finished hardwood stock and forend, plastic buttplate, imported from Germany, 5 3/4 lbs. Mfg. 1985-1990.

$325 $300 $275 $250 $200 $175 $150

* ***I.J. Wagonmaster Junior*** – .22 rimfire cal., similar to I.J. Wagonmaster, except has 16 1/4 in. barrel, 14, 15, or 18 shot mag., imported from Germany, 5 1/4 lbs. Mfg. 1985-1990.

$325 $300 $275 $250 $200 $175 $150

I.J. TARGETMASTER SLIDE ACTION – .22 rimfire cal., 12, 15, or 19 shot mag., tubular magazine under the barrel, 18 1/2 in. barrel, hooded ramp front sight, step adj. rear sight, blue finish, walnut finished hardwood stock, plastic buttplate, imported from Germany, 5 3/4 lbs. Erma Mfg. 1985-1990.

$325 $300 $275 $250 $200 $175 $150

I.J. SEMI-AUTO CARBINE – .22 LR cal., 15 shot mag., recoil operated, blue finish, copy of the M1 carbine, 18 1/2 in. barrel, military type front sight protected by wings, rear aperture adj. sight, walnut finished hardwood stock and handguard, sling swivels, imported from Germany, 5 3/4 lbs. Mfg. 1985-1990.

$425 $365 $315 $275 $235 $195 $175

I.J. MAGNUM SEMI-AUTO CARBINE – .22 WMR cal., gas operated, otherwise similar to Semi-Auto Carbine, imported from Germany. Mfg. 1985-1990.

$525 $465 $395 $340 $295 $250 $220

I.J. PLAINSFIELD SEMI-AUTO CARBINE – .30 Carbine, 9mm Para. (new 1986), or 5.7mm (disc. 1986) cal., gas operated, copy of WWII U.S. Military Carbine, 5, 10, 15, or 30 shot detachable mag., stainless steel or blue finish, 18 in. barrel, American walnut or hardwood stock, model names and numbers changed several times, M2 full auto model available during the 1980s, 6 1/2 lbs. Mfg. 1978-1993.

$450 $395 $335 $285 $245 $210 $180

Add 10% for walnut stock.
Add 20% for stainless steel.
Add 35% for 5.7mm cal. (Spitfire Model) or 9mm Para. cal.

I.J. PARATROOPER SEMI-AUTO CARBINE – .30 Carbine cal., gas operated, copy of WWII U.S. Military Carbine, 5, 10, 15, or 30 shot detachable mag., stainless steel or blue finish, 18 in. barrel, American walnut or hardwood stock, with collapsible stock extension, model names and numbers changed several times, M2 full auto model available with 12 in. barrel, 4 1/2 lbs. Mfg. 1978-1989.

$595 $550 $500 $460 $430 $395 $360

Add 10% for walnut stock.
Add 20% for stainless steel.

I.J. SURVIVAL CARBINE SEMI-AUTO – .30 Carbine or 5.7mm cal., gas operated, copy of WWII military carbine, 5, 10, 15, or 30 shot detachable mag., stainless steel or blue finish, Zytel black plastic pistol grip stock, 6 1/2 lbs.

$450 $395 $335 $285 $245 $210 $180

Add 20% for stainless steel.
Add 35% for 5.7mm cal. (Spitfire Model).

* ***I.J. Survival Carbine Semi-Auto w/Folding Stock*** – .30 Carbine or 5.7mm cal., similar to Survival Carbine, except has folding stock. Mfg. 1983-1989.

$585 $500 $425 $375 $325 $275 $235

Add 20% for stainless steel.
Add 35% for 5.7mm cal. (Spitfire Model).

GRADING - PPGS™	100%	98%	95%	90%	80%	70%	60%	LAST MSR

I.J. UNIVERSAL CARBINE SEMI-AUTO – .30 Carbine or .256 Win. Mag. cal., gas operated, GI military type carbine, 5 or 10 shot detachable mag., 18 in. barrel, stainless steel or blue finish, walnut stained hardwood, sling swivel, drilled and tapped, known as Model 1003 (.30 Carbine) or Model 1256 (.256 Win. Mag., 5 shot only). Mfg. 1986.

	$450	$395	$335	$285	$245	$210	$180

Iver Johnson marked models are rare.

I.J. UNIVERSAL PARATROOPER SEMI-AUTO CARBINE – .30 Carbine cal., similar to Universal Carbine model, except has Schmeisser-type hardwood folding stock, 5 or 10 shot detachable mag., drilled and tapped. Mfg. 1986.

	$550	$475	$415	$360	$315	$265	$230

Iver Johnson marked models are rare.

MODEL 5100 BOLT ACTION SNIPER – .338 Win., .416 Win., or .50 BMG cal., single shot, free floating 29 in. barrel, no sights, drilled and tapped, marketed with Leupold Ultra M1 20X scope, adj. composite stock, adj. trigger, two different model numbers, 36 lbs. Limited mfg. 1985-1993.

	$4,550	$3,775	$3,375	$3,000	$2,600	$2,300	$2,000

SHOTGUNS: O/U

IVER JOHNSON SILVER SHADOW O/U – 12 ga., 3 in. chambers, boxlock action, 26, 28, or 30 in. barrels with chokes, full-length vent. rib, extractors, DT or non-SST, checkered European pistol grip walnut stock and forend, plastic buttplate, pistol grip cap, imported from Italy, 7 1/2 lbs. Mfg. 1973-1977.

	$600	$500	$400	$350	$300	$235	$200

SHOTGUNS: SxS

There are two basic double barrel designs - the early monobloc breech models (mfg. 1913-1923) and one piece barrel/breech models originally called the Hercules Grade (mfg. 1924-1935), and later called Hammer Forged (mfg. 1936-1941). These are mass produced high quality field grade guns. The later Skeeter (mfg. 1933-1943) doubles were specially built high quality with excellent fit and finish. However, there is no difference in the internal mechanism of any of these guns.

HAMMERLESS MONOBLOC – 12 ga., boxlock, 28, 30, or 32 in. browned barrels with chokes, case hardened receiver, breech sleeve area is solid one-piece (monobloc), dropped forged, hammers can be lowered w/o snapping them on empty chambers, automatic safety, extractors, DT, checkered pistol grip American black walnut stock and forend, hard rubber buttplate, 7 1/2 lbs. Mfg. 1914-1923.

	$600	$525	$440	$390	$340	$285	$245

HAMMERLESS HERCULES GRADE – 12, 16, 20, or 28 ga., boxlock action, case hardened receiver with hunting dog etched on left side, 26, 28, or 30 in. blued barrels and lug forged as one-piece and joined together, hand checkered American black walnut stock and forend with pistol grip cap, plain extractor model has slim forend, D&E fastener, hard rubber buttplate, automatic safety, DT, some seen with Canadian markings, most likely mfg. by Cooey, approx. 7 3/4 lbs. Mfg. 1924-circa 1935.

	$1,100	$900	$795	$695	$595	$495	$450
28 ga.	$2,200	$1,800	$1,575	$1,395	$1,175	$995	$900

Add 15% for ejectors or 25% for single trigger.

A special run of this model was manufactured in the 1930s for Montgomery Wards and marked "Western Field Model 53".

HAMMERLESS HERCULES GRADE .410 BORE – .410 bore, boxlock action, hammerless design, top lever break open (cocks on opening), small case colored frame, straight grip American black walnut stock and forend, extractors or ejectors (ejector model has D&E fastener), 26 in. fully choked blue barrels, barrels and lug forged as one-piece, hunting dog etched on left side of frame, approx. 5 3/4 - 6 lbs. Mfg. 1924-circa 1935.

	$2,600	$2,250	$1,850	$1,350	$995	$895	$800

HAMMERLESS SUPERTRAP HERCULES GRADE – 12 ga., boxlock action, 32 in. fully choked barrels and lug forged as one-piece then joined together after proof test, full-length raised vent. rib, selective ejectors, DT, two Lyman ivory sights, hunting dog etched on left side of frame, automatic safety, hand checkered American black walnut stock and beavertail forend, D&E fastener, hard rubber pistol grip cap and anti-flinch recoil pad, approx. 7 3/4 lbs. Mfg. 1924-circa 1935.

	$1,600	$1,375	$1,050	$925	$825	$725	$625

HAMMERLESS HAMMER FORGED MODEL – similar to Hercules Grade, except left side of frame is marked "IVER JOHNSON HAMMER FORGED" in two lines and right side of frame marked with company name and address, blued receiver. Mfg. circa 1936-1943.

	$1,100	$900	$795	$695	$595	$495	$450

GRADING - PPGS™	100%	98%	95%	90%	80%	70%	60%	LAST MSR

HAMMERLESS SUPERTRAP (HAMMER FORGED BARREL) – similar to Hammerles Hercules Grade, except left side of frame is marked "IVER JOHNSON HAMMER FORGED" in two lines and right side of frame is marked with company name and address. Mfg. circa 1936-1941.

	100%	98%	95%	90%	80%	70%	60%
	$1,600	$1,375	$1,050	$925	$825	$725	$625

HAMMERLESS HAMMER FORGED MODEL .410 BORE/28 GA. – 28 ga. or .410 bore, boxlock action, similar to Hercules Grade, except left side of frame marked "IVER JOHNSON HAMMER FORGED" in two lines and right side of frame marked with company name and address, blued receiver. Mfg. circa 1936-1941.

	100%	98%	95%	90%	80%	70%	60%
	$2,800	$2,400	$2,000	$1,500	$1,100	$950	$850

Add 50% for 28 ga.

SKEET-ER – 12, 16, 20, or 28 ga., 26 or 28 in. special skeet bored barrels, boxlock action, barrel and lug forged as one-piece, proofed, then joined together, select fancy figured hand checkered lacquer finished high grade American black walnut pistol grip or straight grip stock and large beavertail forend, D&E fastener, extractors or ejectors, automatic or manual safety, Lyman #10 front sight, Jostam anti-flinch recoil pad, Miller single selective or non-selective trigger, 8 1/2 lbs. Mfg. 1933-1943.

	100%	98%	95%	90%	80%	70%	60%
	$2,300	$1,960	$1,600	$1,300	$1,150	$900	$800
16 or 28 ga.	$4,400	$3,600	$3,000	$2,300	$1,100	$1,650	$1,550

Add 30% for ejectors, 30% for U.S. Navy marked, 50% for SST, 20% for non-selective trigger, 100% for factory VR, 30% for 20 ga., 200% for rare factory engraving (be wary of upgrades) and 50% for scarce factory case colors (be wary of new colors).

SKEET-ER .410 BORE – .410 bore, boxlock action, 3 in. chambers, 26 or 28 in. special skeet choked barrels, high grade American black walnut straight grip or pistol grip stock with beavertail forend, extractors or ejectors (w/D&E fastener), hard rubber buttplate, Lyman #10 ivory front sight, SST, single non-selective trigger or DT, same small frame as .410 Hammerless Hercules Grade, 6 lbs. Mfg. 1931-1943.

	100%	98%	95%	90%	80%	70%	60%
	$4,000	$3,500	$3,000	$2,500	$2,000	$1,800	$1,500

Add 25% for Miller NST or 40% for Miller SST.
Add 25% for scare 30 in. barrels.
Add 200% for rare factory engraving.

.410 bore is the most commonly encountered gun and was made on a special small frame. This model was probably responsible for more Skeet records than any other American .410 bore SxS shotgun.

* ***Skeet-er Italian Mfg.*** – .410 bore, straight grip, DT, Arkansas address, extractors, figured wood, a few were imported during the late 1970s-early 1980s as a possible reintroduction of the Skeet-er Model, not cataloged, rare.

	100%	98%	95%	90%	80%	70%	60%
	$2,500	$2,150	$1,825	$1,600	$1,300	$1,100	$875

100%	98%	95%	90%	80%	70%	60%	50%	40%	30%	20%	10%

SHOTGUNS: SINGLE BARREL

Some single barrel shotguns may have Canadian markings, as parts were probably shipped to Canada and assembled there.

On the following models where applicable, add 10% for 16 ga., 20% for 20 ga., 50% for 24, 28, or 32 ga., and 100% for .410 bore.

CHAMPION TOP SNAP – 12 ga., 30 in. plain twist steel barrel, top lever break open mechanism, rebounding hammer, double locking bolt, extractors, American black walnut stock and forend, nickel frame, browned barrel (imported from Belgium), marked "Champion" on top of barrel and possibly with patent date of July 27, 1880. Mfg. 1880-1900.

100%	98%	95%	90%	80%	70%	60%	50%	40%	30%	20%	10%
$300	$275	$250	$200	$175	$150	$125	$110	$100	$90	$80	$70

CHAMPION SIDE SNAP – 12 ga., 30 in. plain twist steel choked browned barrel (imported from Belgium), side lever opening mechanism, double locking bolts, rebounding hammer, extractors, American black walnut stock and forend, nickel frame, marked with Champion name on top of barrel and patent date of July 27, 1880, 6 1/2 lbs. Mfg. 1880-1900.

100%	98%	95%	90%	80%	70%	60%	50%	40%	30%	20%	10%
$300	$275	$250	$200	$175	$150	$125	$110	$100	$90	$80	$70

CHAMPION SIDE SNAP HAMMERLESS – 12 ga., concealed hammer, 30 or 32 in. plain twist steel choke barrel (imported from Belgium), side lever break open mechanism, cocks on opening, double locking bolt, extractors, American black walnut stock and forend, nickel frame, marked with Champion name on top of barrel and patent date of July 27, 1880, 6 1/2 lbs. Mfg. 1880-1900.

100%	98%	95%	90%	80%	70%	60%	50%	40%	30%	20%	10%
$325	$300	$275	$250	$200	$175	$150	$125	$110	$100	$90	$80

100%	98%	95%	90%	80%	70%	60%	50%	40%	30%	20%	10%

IVER JOHNSON EJECTOR SEMI-HAMMERLESS (RING TRIGGER) - 12 ga., semi-hammerless (does not have spur), ring trigger break open mechanism (ring in front of trigger opens action), 28, 30, or 32 in. plain twist steel choked brown barrel, rebounding hammer, ejector, American black walnut stock and forend, case hardened frame, 7 lbs. Mfg. 1897-1899.

100%	98%	95%	90%	80%	70%	60%	50%	40%	30%	20%	10%
$325	$300	$275	$250	$200	$175	$150	$125	$110	$100	$90	$80

GRADING - PPGS™	100%	98%	95%	90%	80%	70%	60%	LAST MSR

IVER JOHNSON EJECTOR SEMI-HAMMERLESS IMPROVED MODEL 1900 (RING TRIGGER) - 12 or 16 ga., 28, 30, 32, or 34 in. browned barrel, semi-hammerless break open, ring in front of trigger opens action, rebounding hammer, ejector, improved barrel take down, American black walnut stock and forend, case hardened frame, 6 1/4 lbs. Mfg. 1900-1908.

	100%	98%	95%	90%	80%	70%	60%	LAST MSR
	$300	$275	$250	$200	$175	$150	$125	

IVER JOHNSON EJECTOR SEMI-HAMMERLESS JUNIOR MODEL (RING TRIGGER) - 12 or 16 ga., 26 or 28 in. browned barrel, semi-hammerless break open, ring in front of trigger opens action, rebounding hammer, single locking bolt, shortened American black walnut stock and forend, case hardened frame, hard rubber buttplate, 5 1/2 - 6 lbs. Mfg. 1901-1908.

	100%	98%	95%	90%	80%	70%	60%	LAST MSR
	$300	$275	$250	$200	$175	$150	$125	

IVER JOHNSON TOP SNAP IMPROVED MODEL 1901 - 12 or 16 ga., 28, 30, 32, or 34 in. steel choke bored browned barrel, hammer top lever operated break open mechanism, ejectors, American black walnut pistol grip stock and forend, case hardened frame, hard rubber buttplate, pistol grip cap, approx. 6 lbs. Mfg. 1901-1904.

	100%	98%	95%	90%	80%	70%	60%	LAST MSR
	$300	$275	$250	$200	$175	$150	$125	

This model is also know as the New White Powder Wonder or White Powder Wonder, and was manufactured for Sears, Roebuck & Co.

(IVER JOHNSON) CHAMPION TOP SNAP - 12 or 16 ga., similar to Iver Johnson Top Snap Improved Model 1901, top lever opening, 28, 30, or 32 in. browned steel barrel, with chokes, case hardened receiver, ejectors, rebounding hammer, American black walnut stock and forend, hard rubber buttplate, marked "CHAMPION", approx. 6 lbs. Mfg. 1905-1908.

	100%	98%	95%	90%	80%	70%	60%	LAST MSR
	$300	$275	$250	$200	$175	$150	$125	

IVER JOHNSON TRIGGER ACTION SINGLE GUN - 12 ga., 28, 30, or 32 in. brown barrel with full choke, trigger action break open mechanism, when hammer is in rebound position, a pull on it will release the barrel locking bolt, fired by manually cocking the hammer, then pressing a small trigger insert into main trigger, American black walnut stock and forend, case hardened frame, ejector, hard rubber buttplate, pistol grip cap, approx. 6 lbs. Mfg. 1905-1908.

	100%	98%	95%	90%	80%	70%	60%	LAST MSR
	$325	$300	$275	$250	$200	$175	$150	

There are two different version of the trigger action and not enough information has turned up to give details as to when each version was manufactured.

IVER JOHNSON TRIGGER ACTION JUNIOR MODEL - 12 or 16 ga., 26 or 28 in. browned barrel with full choke, similar to Trigger Action Model, except has shortened American black walnut stock and forend, approx. 5 1/2 lbs. Mfg. 1905-1908.

	100%	98%	95%	90%	80%	70%	60%	LAST MSR
	$325	$300	$275	$250	$200	$175	$150	

CHAMPION MODEL 36 - 10, 12, 16, 20, 24 (new 1913), 28 (new 1913), 32 ga., or .410 bore, 28, 30, or 32 in. barrel (barrel and lug forged into one-piece), rebounding center mounted hammer, top lever operated break open design, full choke, case hardened or nickel receiver, extractors or ejectors, American black walnut stock and forend, name changed to Champion Single Barrel in 1923, approx. 6 3/4 lbs. Mfg. 1909-1922.

	100%	98%	95%	90%	80%	70%	60%	LAST MSR
	$250	$220	$190	$155	$130	$115	$100	

Add 20%-40% for 10, 20, 28, 32 ga., or .410 bore.

CHAMPION SINGLE BARREL - 10, 12, 16, 20, 24 (new 1913), 28 (new 1913), 32 ga., or .410 bore, 28, 30, or 32 in. barrel (barrel and lug forged into one-piece), same model as Champion Model 36, except smaller gauges are built on same frame as large gauges, exact year production stopped not determined, some seen with Canadian markings, most likely because they were shipped to Canada, as there is no evidence that Iver Johnson ever had a production facility in Canada. Mfg. 1923-approx. 1978.

	100%	98%	95%	90%	80%	70%	60%	LAST MSR
	$250	$220	$190	$155	$130	$115	$100	

Add 50%-75% for 24, 28, 32 or .410 ga.

CHAMPION MODEL 36 JUNIOR - 12, 16, or 20 ga., 26 or 28 in. barrel, similar to Champion Model 36, except has shortened buttstock and forend, 6 1/4 lbs. Mfg. 1909-1916.

	100%	98%	95%	90%	80%	70%	60%	LAST MSR
	$300	$250	$220	$190	$155	$130	$115	

GRADING - PPGS™	100%	98%	95%	90%	80%	70%	60%	LAST MSR

CHAMPION MODEL 39 – 24, 28 ga., .410 bore (mfg. 1911-1915), or .44 cal. (mfg. 1911-1915), smaller frame than the Model 36, center mounted rebounding hammer, top lever break open mechanism, 28 or 30 in. plain full choke barrel, extractors or ejectors, case hardened or nickel frame, American black walnut stock and forend, pistol grip cap, hard rubber buttplate, 5 3/4 lbs. Mfg. 1909-1916.

	$325	$300	$275	$250	$200	$175	$150	

CHAMPION MODEL 39 JUNIOR – 24, 28 ga., .410 bore (mfg. 1911-1915), or .44 cal. (mfg. 1911-1915), similar to Model 39, except has shortened stock, 26 or 28 in. barrel, extractors, 5 1/4 lbs. Mfg. 1909-1916.

	$325	$300	$275	$250	$200	$175	$150	

CHAMPION JACKETED BREECH – similar to Champion Model 36, except has reinforced barrel breech to accept heavier loads that were available for waterfowl hunting. Mfg. 1912-1918.

	$300	$275	$250	$200	$175	$150	$125	

CHAMPION MATTED RIB MODEL – 12, 16, 20 ga., or .410 bore (new 1928), 28, 30, or 32 in. fully choked blue barrel, center mounted rebounding hammer, top lever break open, solid raised full-length rib, finely matted, extractors or ejectors, case hardened frame, American black walnut full checkered pistol grip stock and forend, may also be marked with the Western Field brand name, 7 1/4 lbs. Mfg. 1912-1941.

	$315	$285	$260	$200	$175	$150	$125	

Add 50% for .410 bore.

CHAMPION SEMI-OCTAGON – 12 or 16 ga., 28, 30, or 32 in. blue full choke barrel, center mounted rebounding hammer, top lever break open, top half of barrel is octagon, matted top surface, case hardened frame, American walnut stock and forend with or w/o (later production) pistol grip cap, hard rubber buttplate, extractors or ejectors, 6 1/2 - 6 3/4 lbs. Mfg. 1912-1920.

	$300	$275	$250	$200	$175	$150	$125	

I.J. SPECIAL TRAP – 12 ga., 32 in. full choke brown barrel with full-length raised vent. rib, finely matted, top lever break open, two Lyman ivory sights, blue frame, hand checkered American black walnut stock and forend with pistol grip cap and hard rubber buttplate, ejectors, anti-flinch recoil pad optional, approx. 7 lbs. Mfg. 1927-1941.

	$400	$350	$300	$265	$225	$190	$165	

EXCEL – 12, 16, 20 ga., or .410 bore, 26, 28, 30, or 32 in. fully choked blue barrel (barrel and lug forged in one-piece), blue or nickel receiver, rebounding center mounted hammer, top lever operated break open design, extractors, walnut stock and forend, approx. 6 3/4 lbs. Mfg. 1910-1935.

	$175	$155	$130	$115	$95	$85	$75	

This was the economy model of the Champion single barrel that was offered to mail order houses and other wholesalers, and can also be found under the following brand names: T. Barker (H&D Folsum CO., NY), Blackfield (Hibbard-Spencer & Bartlett Co., Chicago), Blackimp K-S-CO (Keith Simmons Co, San Francisco), Challenger (George Worthington Co, Cleveland), Diamond Arms Co. (Shapleigh Hardware Co., St. Louis), Eastern Arms Co. (Sears, circa pre and post WWII), Famous (Hirch Mercantile Co., San Francisco), Falcon (National Lead Co., San Francisco), Hermitage K-S-CO (Keith Simmons Co., Nashville), Ideal (Charles Williams Stores, Brooklyn), King Nitro (Shapleigh Hardware Co., St. Louis), Marshfield (could also be Marshwood, Charles Williams Stores, Brooklyn), Moniter (Paxton & Gallager Co., Omaha), Newport (Hibbard-Spencer & Bartlett Co., Chicago), Olympic Arms Co. (Morley & Murphy Hardware, Green Bay or Morley Brothers, Saginaw), Ranger (Sears, circa pre and post WWII), Revonoc (Rev-o-noc, Richardson & Conover Hardware Co, Kansas City, or Hibbard-Spencer & Bartlett), Scout (Frankfurth Hardware Co., Milwaukee), Sioux (Larson Hardware Co., SD), Triumph (Montgomery Wards), True Blue (Shapleigh Hardware Co., St. Louis), Volunteer (Belknap Hardware Co., St. Louis), Western Field (Montgomery Wards), XLCR (W. Bingham Co., Cleveland). Some of these names will also be found on guns manufactured by other makers, as some names were the property of the wholesaler/retailer.

GRADING - PPGS™	100%	Issue Price	Qty. Made

COMMEMORATIVES

100TH YEAR COMMEMORATIVE FOUR GUN CASE SET – set contains one each of the following models: Model 50A Sidewinder (E code), Model 55A Target (H code), Model 57A Target (J code), Model 67 Viking (A code), all serial numbered the same except for the letter code, ser. nos. 1-450, all were bright blue finish, white plastic grips with gold owl's head on top, ser. no. marked on lower right side of frame and 1871-1971 on upper right frame. Mfg. 1971.

	$1,000	$299	450

GRADING - PPGS™	100%	Issue Price	Qty. Made

100TH YEAR COMMEMORATIVE SINGLE CASED GUN – an unknown number of cased single guns were mfg. using the same models and letter codes as the four gun case set, finish and grips were the same, included a metal box with vinyl covering, ser. nos. starting at 451. Mfg. 1971.

	$300	N/A	N/A

The issue price of each gun were as follows: Model 67 was $85, Model 50A was $73, Model 57A was $72.50, and the Model 55A was $69.50.

U.S. BORDER PATROL COMMEMORATIVE – .380 ACP Pony model with engraving, some sold as match pairs, wooden presentation case, 500 mfg.

	$650	N/A	500

D-DAY COMMEMORATIVE CARBINE – includes carbine model with two 15 shot mags., double magazine pouch, web sling, oiler, full color poster depicting invasions, one set of dog tags (could be returned to have original owner's name stamped on them), special edition of Bill Mauldin's book *Up Front*, brown cardboard box encased in a color sleeve depicting the invasion. Mfg. 1980.

	$1,500	N/A	N/A

Subtract $500 for non-NIB.
Subtract 50% if w/o accessories.

WWII COMMEMORATIVE CARBINE – engraved with gold filled markings, packaged in special wood and glass display case, includes papers, mfg. for American Historical Foundation circa mid-1980s.

	$1,500	N/A	2,500

Subtract $500 for non-NIB.
Subtract 50% if w/o display case and papers.

50th ANNIVERSARY CARBINE – did not include accessories, production number unknown. Mfg. 1991-1993.

	$700	N/A	N/A

Subtract 40% for non-NIB.

NATIONAL GUARD CARBINE – did not include accessories, production number unknown. Mfg. 1991-1993.

	$700	N/A	N/A

Subtract 40% for non-NIB.

IZHMASH

Current manufacturer located in Izhevsk, Russia. Previously imported exclusively beginning 2012 by RWC Group LLC, located in Tullytown, PA. Previously imported and distributed by Russian American Armory, located in Scottsburg, IN, and until 2004 by European American Armory (certain models only), located in Sharpes, FL. Other models were also imported by Kalashnikov USA, located in Port St. Lucie, FL. Previously distributed by Interstate Arms Corp., located in Billerica, MA, and by L.A. Austin International, Inc., located in Surprise, AZ.

Current Izhmash trademarks include Saiga (see separate listing in S section), Hesse-Saiga, Krebs-Saiga, Romak, Sobol, Korshun, LOS, Maral (not imported), and Dragunov (not imported). On July 16, 2014, economic sanctions were placed against Russian firearms imports, and they are currently no longer allowed to be imported into the U.S. As a result, quantities of Izhmash firearms may be in short supply. Legion Ltd. was the custom shop of the Izhmash factory in Russia and Arsenal Inc. in Las Vegas, NV.

GRADING - PPGS™	100%	98%	95%	90%	80%	70%	60%	LAST MSR

RIFLES: BOLT ACTION

URAL 5.1 MATCH RIFLE – .22 LR cal., single shot, competition model with eccentric bolt, adj. cheekpiece, trigger, and buttplate, 26 1/2 in. barrel with aperture sights, 11.3 lbs. Imported 2000.

	$1,075	$950	$825	$700	$600	$500	$425	

URAL 6-1 MATCH RIFLE – .22 LR cal., U.I.T. configuration with adj. buttplate and 26 3/4 in. barrel, aperture sights, various accessories included, 10 2/3 lbs. Imported 2000-2002.

	$550	$500	$450	$400	$360	$330	$300	*$625*

URAL 6-2 MATCH RIFLE – .22 LR cal., features laminated stock. Imported 2000-2002.

	$1,000	$875	$750	$650	$550	$450	$350	*$1,125*

BIATHLON BASIC – .17 HMR (new 2003), 22 LR, or .22 WMR (new 2003) cal., entry level biathlon model, beech stock, heavy barrel with Weaver rail, 6.1 lbs. Imported 2002-2004.

	$315	$275	$240	$195	$175	$160	$145	

Add $10 for .22 WMR or $20 for .17 HMR cal. Add $50 for adj. sights.

GRADING - PPGS™	100%	98%	95%	90%	80%	70%	60%	LAST MSR

BIATHLON 7-4 – .22 LR cal., features pivoting crank right or left-hand action, extra mags. that can be stored on the stock, 19.7 in. barrel with aperture sights, includes biathlon harness, spare mags., and counter weights, safety slings, cased, with or w/o chrome barrel exterior, 9.1 lbs. Imported 2000-2004, reimportation began 2012.

MSR $1,543	$1,350	$1,150	$1,000	$875	$750	$625	$550

Add $95 for left-hand action.
Add $392 for Version 8 Model or $524 for Version 10 Model w/chrome barrel exterior.

CM-2 – .22 LR cal., light match rifle, similar overall to Ural 6-1, 19.8 in. (Youth) or 26.7 in. barrel. Imported 2000-2002, reintroduced 2003.

	$365	$325	$285	$250	$225	$200	$180

LOS 7-1 SPORTER – .223 Rem. (disc.), .308 Win., or 7.62x39mm (disc.) cal., 21.8 in. hammer forged barrel with two lug bolt lockup, detachable 5 shot mag., adj. trigger, checkered hardwood stock with vent. recoil pad, includes scope, 7.3 lbs. Imported 2000-2002, reimported beginning 2012.

MSR $1,200	$1,050	$950	$850	$750	$650	$550	$450

Subtract 10% if w/o scope.

BARS 4-1 – .223 Rem., 5.6x39mm, or 7.62x39mm cal., birch stock, 21 in. barrel. Importation began 2012.

MSR $1,130	$1,000	$900	$800	$700	$600	$500	$450

RECORD – 7.62x54R, .308 Win., or .338 Lapua cal., hardwood stock, monopod, bipod. Importation began 2012.

MSR $8,330	$7,500	$6,500	$5,500	$4,750	$4,000	$3,250	$2,650

Add $1,410 for 7.62x54R or .338 Lapua cal.

KORSHUM – .22 LR cal., 19 in. heavy barrel, birch stock. Importation began 2012.

MSR $1,040	$950	$850	$750	$650	$550	$500	$400

SM-2 – .22 LR cal., adj. birch target stock, optional Cadet configuration. Importation began 2012.

MSR $955	$850	$725	$600	$500	$400	$350	$300

Add $103 for Cadet configuration.

BI-7-2-KO BASIC – .22 LR cal., birch stock. Importation began 2012.

MSR $1,035	$950	$850	$750	$650	$550	$500	$400

SABLE (SOBOL) – .22 LR cal., birch stock. Importation began 2012.

MSR $925	$825	$700	$600	$500	$400	$350	$300

SHOTGUNS

Please refer to the Saiga section for more information about these models.

IZMIRLIOGLU

Current manufacturer located in Izmir, Turkey, producing the following brand name, Armed Guns (see listing in the A section).

J SECTION

J.B. CUSTOM INC.

Current manufacturer and restorer located in Blue Ridge, TX. Previously located in Huntertown, IN. Originated in Fort Wayne, IN. Consumer direct sales.

For individual model listings, please go to BlueBookOfGunValues.com/overflow.

J.C. HIGGINS

Previous trademark used on Sears & Roebuck rifles and shotguns manufactured between 1946-1962.

The J.C. Higgins trademark has appeared literally on hundreds of various models (shotguns and rifles) sold through the Sears & Roebuck retail network. Most of these models were manufactured through subcontracts with both domestic and international firearms manufacturers. Typically, they were "spec." guns made to sell at a specific price to undersell the competition. Most of these models were derivatives of existing factory models (i.e., Browning, High Standard, Marlin, Mossberg, Savage, Stevens, Winchester, etc.) with less expensive wood and perhaps missing the features found on those models from which they were derived.

To date, there has been minimal interest in collecting J.C. Higgins guns, regardless of rarity. Rather than list J.C. Higgins models, a general guideline is that values generally are less than models of their "1st generation relatives" (listed above). The Ranger trademark was also used by Sears & Roebuck - it is not any more desirable than those guns marked "J.C. Higgins". As a result, prices are ascertained by the shooting value of the gun, rather than its collector value.

To find the original manufacturer of a J.C. Higgins model, please refer to the Store Brand Crossover List.

J.C SHOTWELL & SONS

Current rifle manufacturer established in 1962 and located in Versailles, France. U.S. agent is located in Chicago, IL.

RIFLES: SxS

J.C Shotwell & Sons manufactures a hammer back action double rifle chambered in .450 NE-3 1/4 in. (MSR €5,990-€7,590). Please contact U.S. agent for more information regarding availability and pricing.

J.L.D. ENTERPRISES, INC.

Previous rifle manufacturer located in Farmington, CT. In 2006, the company name was changed to PTR 91, Inc. The company was re-organized circa 2012 and the name was changed to PTR Industries, Inc.

Please refer to PTR Industries, Inc. listing in the P section for value information on models produced untill circa 2016.

J.O. ARMS

Previous importer of KSN Industries, Ltd. pistols until 1997.

J. ROBERTS & SON (GUNMAKERS) LTD.

Current manufacturer, import agent, and dealer established during 1950, and located in West Sussex, U.K. since 2013. Previously located in London.

Please contact J. Roberts & Son (Gunmakers) Ltd. directly for more information on their current inventory of custom rifles and shotguns, in addition to other services.

J. Roberts & Son also owns the trademark W.J. Jeffery & Co. Please refer to this section for more information.

JMC FABRICATION & MACHINE, INC.

Previous manufacturer located in Rockledge, FL 1997-99.

GRADING - PPGS™	100%	98%	95%	90%	80%	70%	60%	LAST MSR

RIFLES: BOLT ACTION

MODEL 2000 M/P – .50 BMG cal., rapid takedown, 30 in. barrel, matte black finish, cast aluminum stock with Pachmayr pad, fully adj. bipod, 10 shot staggered mag., two-stage trigger, includes 24X U.S. Optics scope, prices assume all options included, 29 1/2 lbs. Limited mfg. 1998-99.

	100%	98%	95%	90%	80%	70%	60%	LAST MSR
	$7,950	$7,400	$6,800	$6,150	$5,500	$4,900	$4,200	*$8,500*

Subtract $2,800 if w/o options.

JO. LO. AR.

Previous semi-auto pistol manufacturer circa 1924-disc. and located in Eibar, Spain.

GRADING - PPGS™	100%	98%	95%	90%	80%	70%	60%	LAST MSR

PISTOLS: SEMI-AUTO

SEMI-AUTO PISTOL – .25 ACP, .32 ACP, .380 ACP, 9mm Largo, or .45 ACP (rare) cal., designed for one handed cocking, presumably for the cavalry, features rotating lever on the right side of the slide, most sales were commercial but a few pistols in 9mm Largo were purchased by the Peruvian military, available in four frame sizes.

.25 ACP cal.	$3,500	$2,950	$2,500	$2,000	$1,500	$1,250	$1,000	
.32 ACP cal.	$1,500	$1,250	$1,000	$800	$600	$500	$400	
.380 ACP cal.	$1,995	$1,795	$1,495	$1,000	$900	$800	$700	
9mm Largo cal.	$1,500	$1,250	$1,000	$800	$600	$500	$400	
.45 ACP cal. (rare)	$7,500	$6,500	$5,000	$4,250	$3,500	$2,750	$2,000	

JP ENTERPRISES, INC.

Current manufacturer of custom AR-15 rifles and pistols established in 1978, located in Hugo, MN beginning 2010. Previously located in White Bear Lake, MN 2000-2009, Vadnais Heights, MN 1998-2000, and in Shoreview, MN 1995-98. Distributor, dealer, and consumer sales.

JP Enterprises previously customized Remington shotgun Models 11-87, 1100, and 870, the Remington bolt action Model 700 series, Glock pistols, and the Armalite AR-10 series. JP Enterprises also manufactures a complete line of high quality parts and accessories for AR-15 style rifles, including upper and lower assemblies, sights and optics, machined billet receivers, barrels/barrel kits, fire control kits, handguards, etc. and gunsmithing services. Please contact the company directly for more information and pricing regarding these parts, accesssories, and services.

PISTOLS: SEMI-AUTO

Level I & Level II custom pistols were manufactured 1995-97 using Springfield Armory slides and frames. Only a few were made and retail prices were $599 (Level I) and $950 (Level II). Take note, JP Enterprises may offer many factory options on these firearms that are not listed here.

The following options are available for most current models.

Add $50 for Black Teflon barrel finish. Add $60 for solid Cerakote handguard only. Add $70 for Competition side-charging handle. Add $100 for bead blasted barrel finish. Add $75-$179 for Thermal Dissipator (depending on color). Add $225 for solid Cerakote upper and handguard only. Add $350 for solid Cerakote finish. Add $400 for solid Gun Candy finish. Add $420 for Chameleon Gun Candy finish. Add $450 for Color-Shift Prismatic finish. Add $550 for Distressed Cerakote finish. Add $700 for Presentation Grade high polish finish.

ASF-20 PISTOL – 5.56 NATO or .300 Blackout cal., GIO, 10 1/2, 13 1/2, or 14 1/2 in. JP Supermatch cryo treated light or ultralight profile polished stainless steel or black Teflon finished barrel, JP adj. gas block, Tactical or Competition compensator, ASF-20 fully ambi billet lower receiver, JP-15 forged upper, JP Fire Control Package, Phase 5 pistol buffer tube, MKIII or M-LOK series handguard system, JP Hand Guard Brace, Hogue grip, fully ambi controls, matte black hardcoat anodized finish. New 2020.

MSR $2,399	$2,150	$1,950	$1,750	$1,575	$1,350	$1,150	$950	

Add $25 for M-LOK handguard system.

CTR-02 PISTOL – .223 Rem./5.56 NATO cal., GIO, 10 1/2, 13 1/2, or 14 1/2 in. JP Supermatch stainless steel light or ultralight contour barrel with polished stainless, Black Teflon, or bead blasted finish, low profile adj. gas block, JP 3-port Comp, Tactical Comp, or flash hider muzzle device, CTR-02 billet upper and lower receiver, standard JP trigger, Phase 5 pistol buffer tube or SIG pistol brace, 7 or 9 1/4 in. handguard, A2 or Hogue pistol grip, ambi safety, Mil-Spec charging handle, forward handguard brace, matte black hardcoat anodized finish. New 2015.

MSR $2,499	$2,250	$2,025	$1,825	$1,625	$1,400	$1,175	$1,000	

GMR-13 – 9mm Para. cal., blowback action, 10 1/2 in. JP Supermatch button rifled barrel with standard profile compensator, JP modular handguard, Phase 5 buffer tube, matte black receiver finish. Disc. 2019.

	$1,350	$1,200	$1,100	$975	$850	$700	$600	*$1,499*

GMR-15 PISTOL – 9mm Para. cal., direct blowback operation, 10 1/2 or 14 1/2 in. JP stainless steel light contour barrel with polished stainless, black Teflon, or bead blasted finish, 9mm 3-port comp or 9mm Tactical Comp muzzle device, accepts Glock 9mm mags., JP15 forged upper or PSC-17 billet dual-charging upper receiver, GMR-15 billet lower receiver, standard JP trigger, Phase 5 pistol buffer tube or SIG pistol brace, 7 or 9 1/4 in. handguard, A2 or Hogue grip, ambi safety, Mil-Spec top-charging handle and low profile or competition side-charging handle, forward handguard brace, matte black hardcoat anodized finish.

MSR $1,749	$1,600	$1,450	$1,300	$1,175	$1,000	$850	$725	

Add $70 for Competition side-charging handle. Add $200 for CTR-02 billet lower receiver. Add $600 for PSC-17 upper receiver.

GRADING - PPGS™	100%	98%	95%	90%	80%	70%	60%	LAST MSR

* ***GMR-15 Ready Pistol*** – 9mm Para. cal., direct blowback operation, 10 1/2 in. JP stainless steel light contour barrel with black Teflon finish, JP 9mm Tactical Compensator, accepts Glock 9mm mags., forged JP-15 upper receiver, GMR-15 billet lower receiver, JP trigger, SBA3 brace, 9 1/8 in. MK III Rapid Configuration handguard, Hogue grip, ambi safety, standard top-charging handle, forward handguard brace, QD sling swivel, hardcoat anodized matte black finish. New 2020.

MSR $2,009	$1,800	$1,625	$1,450	$1,300	$1,125	$950	$800	

JP-15 PISTOL – .223 Rem./5.56 NATO cal., GIO, 10 1/2, 13 1/2, or 14 1/2 in. JP Supermatch stainless steel light or ultralight contour barrel with polished stainless, black Teflon, or bead blasted finish, low profile adj. gas block, JP 3-port Comp, Tactical Comp, or flash hider muzzle device, JP-15 forged upper receiver and small frame lower receiver, standard JP trigger, Phase 5 pistol buffer tube or SIG pistol brace, 7 or 9 1/4 in. JP handguard, A2 or Hogue pistol grip, ambi safety, Mil-Spec charging handle, forward handguard brace, matte black hardcoat anodized finish. New 2015.

MSR $1,699	$1,525	$1,375	$1,250	$1,125	$950	$800	$675	

PSC-11 PISTOL – .223 Rem./5.56 NATO cal., GIO, 10 1/2, 13 1/2, or 14 1/2 in. JP Supermatch stainless steel light contour barrel with polished stainless, black Teflon, or bead blasted finish, low profile adj. gas block, JP 3-port Comp, Tactical Comp, or flash hider muzzle device, PSC-11 billet dual-charging upper receiver, JP-15 forged or CTR-02 billet lower receiver, standard JP trigger, Phase 5 Pistol Buffer Tube or SIG Pistol Brace, 7 or 9 1/4 in. JP handguard, A2 or Hogue pistol grip, ambi safety, Mil-Spec top-charging handle and low profile or Competition side-charging handle, forward handguard brace, matte black hardcoat anodized finish. Disc. 2020.

	$2,375	$2,150	$1,925	$1,725	$1,475	$1,250	$1,050	*$2,639*

Add $70 for Competition side-charging handle. Add $200 for CTR-02 billet lower receiver.

SCI-20 PISTOL – 5.56 NATO or .300 AAC Blackout cal., GIO, 10 1/2, 13 1/2, or 14 1/2 in. Supermatch polished stainless steel or black Teflon finished barrel, JP adj. gas block, Tactical or Competition compensator, SCI-20 billet side charge upper receiver w/integral barrel nut, SCR-11 billet lower receiver, JP Fire Control Package, Phase 5 pistol buffer tube, MK III handguard system, Hogue pistol grip, matte black hardcoat anodized finish. New 2020.

MSR $2,699	$2,425	$2,175	$1,975	$1,775	$1,500	$1,275	$1,075	

SCR-11 PISTOL – .223 Rem./5.56 NATO cal., GIO, 10 1/2, 13 1/2, or 14 1/2 in. JP Supermatch stainless steel light or ultralight contour barrel with polished stainless, black Teflon, or bead blasted finish, low profile adj. gas block, JP 3-port Comp, Tactical Comp, or flash hider muzzle device, SCR-11 billet side-charging upper and lower receiver, standard JP trigger, Phase 5 Pistol Buffer Tube or SIG Pistol Brace, 7 or 9 1/4 in. JP handguard, A2 or Hogue pistol grip, ambi safety, low profile or competition side-charging handle, forward handguard brace, matte black hardcoat anodized finish.

MSR $2,699	$2,425	$2,175	$1,975	$1,775	$1,500	$1,275	$1,075	

RIFLES: BOLT ACTION

The following options are available for most current models.

Add $50 for Black Teflon barrel finish. Add $100 for Presentation Grade Thermal Dissipator. Add $400 for solid Cerakote finish. Add $520 for solid Gun Candy finish. Add $520 for Chameleon Gun Candy finish.

MOR-07 – .260 Rem., 7mm WSM (new 2009), or .308 Win. cal., 24 in. stainless steel cryo-treated bull barrel, benchrest quality bolt action, Picatinny rail, JP Tactical Chassis system, Timney trigger, benchrest or tactical style forend, Precision grip system, matte black hardcoat anodized finish, 10 shot detachable mag., includes hard case. Mfg. 2007-2010.

	$4,250	$3,850	$3,350	$2,925	$2,500	$2,000	$1,600	*$4,499*

MR-10 – .260 Rem. (new 2012), 7mm WSM (mfg. 2012-2016), .308 Win., .300 WSM (disc. 2016), or 6.5 Creedmoor (disc. 2016) cal., 3 lug short-throw bolt action with upper Picatinny rail, spiral fluted bolt, 24 in. JP Supermatch fluted stainless steel barrel with large profile JP compensator, folding Magpul stock with tactical grip including palmrest, benchrest style forend or JP modular handguard system. Mfg. 2010-2019.

	$3,400	$2,975	$2,550	$2,325	$1,875	$1,525	$1,200	*$3,999*

MR-19 – 6mm Creedmoor, 6.5 Creedmoor, or .308 Win. cal., 20 (.308 Win.) or 26 (6mm, 6.5 Creedmoor) in. JP Supermatch or Proof Research medium contour stainless steel barrel with polished stainless or Black Teflon finish, threaded muzzle fitted with JP 2-Port comp, 3-Port comp, JP Recoil Eliminator muzzle brake, or thread protector, 10 shot Magpul PMAG AICS Mag., Ultimatum Precision "Deadline" short action left or right-handed receiver, TriggerTech Diamond Series Trigger, JP APAC Chassis with fully adj. folding stock, MKIII forearm with Picatinny or Arca-Swiss mounting package, Hogue or Magpul MIAD grip, Dark Grey Teflon Hardcoat finish standard, other finishes such as Chameleon Gun Candy, Solid Gun Candy, and Cerakote available. New 2019.

MSR $5,000	$4,250	$3,725	$3,200	$2,875	$2,325	$1,900	$1,500	

GRADING - PPGS™	100%	98%	95%	90%	80%	70%	60%	LAST MSR

RIFLES: SEMI-AUTO

JP Enterprises may offer many factory options on these firearms that are not listed here. If necessary, please contact the manufacturer for a complete list of factory options for the models in this section.

The following options are available for most current models.

Add $50 for Black Teflon barrel finish. Add $60 for solid Cerakote handguard only. Add $70 for Competition side-charging handle. Add $100 for bead blasted barrel finish. Add $75-$179 for Thermal Dissipator (depending on color). Add $225 for solid Cerakote upper and handguard only. Add $350 for solid Cerakote finish. Add $400 for solid Gun Candy finish. Add $420 for Chameleon Gun Candy finish. Add $450 for Color-Shift Prismatic finish. Add $550 for Distressed Cerakote finish. Add $700-$800 for Presentation Grade finish (non-engraved). All models featuring 14 1/2 in. barrels will have permanently attached muzzle devices.

ASF-20 RIFLE – 5.56 NATO, .300 AAC Blackout, or 6.5 Grendel cal., GIO, 14 1/2, 16, 18, 20, or 22 (6.5 Grendel only) in. JP Supermatch cryo treated ultralight, light, or medium profile polished stainless steel or black Teflon finished barrel, JP adj. gas block, Tactical or Competition compensator, ASF-20 fully ambi billet lower receiver, JP-15 forged upper, JP Fire Control Package, Hogue, MFT, Magpul, LUTH-AR, or other stock options available, MKIII or M-LOK series hand guard system, Hogue grip, other grip options available, fully ambi controls, Matte black hardcoat anodized finish. New 2020.

MSR $2,399 $2,150 $1,950 $1,750 $1,575 $1,350 $1,150 $950

Add $50 for M-LOK handguard system.

Add $100 for 6.5 Grendel cal.

A-2 MATCH – .223 Rem. cal., GIO, JP-15 lower receiver with JP fire control system, 20 in. JP Supermatch cryo-treated stainless barrel, standard A2 stock and pistol grip, DCM type free float forend, Mil-Spec A2 upper assembly with Smith National Match rear sight. Mfg. 1995-2003.

$1,385 $895 $675 $525 $450 $385 $350 *$1,695*

AR-10T – .243 Win. or .308 Win. cal., GIO, 24 in. cryo treated stainless barrel, uses Armalite AR-10 profile mags., features Armalite receiver set w/flat-top upper receiver, JP fire control group, laminated wood thumbhole stock (optional), vent. free floating tubular handguard, black finish. Mfg. 1998-2004.

$2,150 $1,950 $1,750 $1,575 $1,350 $1,150 $950 *$2,399*

Add $150 for anodized upper assembly in custom color.

Add $350 for laminated wood thumbhole stock.

* ***AR-10LW*** – .243 Win. or .308 Win. cal., lightweight variation of the Model AR-10T, GIO, 16-20 in. cryo treated stainless barrel, uses Armalite AR-10 profile mags., features flat-top upper receiver, detachable sights (optional), composite fiber tubular handguard, black finish, 7-8 lbs. Mfg. 1998-2004.

$2,150 $1,950 $1,750 $1,575 $1,350 $1,150 $950 *$2,399*

Add $200 for detachable sights.

BARRACUDA 10/22 – .22 LR cal., features customized Ruger 10/22 action with reworked fire control system, choice of stainless bull or carbon fiber superlight barrel, 3 lb. trigger pull, color laminated "Barracuda" skeletonized stock. Mfg. 1997-2003.

$1,025 $900 $750 $650 $550 $475 $375 *$1,195*

CTR-02 COMPETITION TACTICAL RIFLE – .223 Wylde chamber, 5.56 NATO (new 2017), .204 Ruger (mfg. 2012-2015), .22 LR (new 2016), .300 AAC Blackout (new 2016), .223 Rem. (disc. 2016), .224 Valkyrie (disc. 2020), or 6.5 Grendel (new 2012) cal., GIO, 14 1/2, 16, 18, or 20 in. JP Supermatch polished stainless steel ultralight, light, or medium contour barrel, low profile or low profile adj. gas block, threaded muzzle fitted with JP Tactical Comp, JP 3-Port comp, flash Hider, or Recoil Eliminator muzzle device, billet CTR-02 lower and upper receiver with flat-top Picatinny rail and ACOG interface, JP trigger, choice of A2, ACE ARFX, Hogue Overmold, Magpul, LUTH-AR, or MFT stock, rifle or mid-length JP modular handguard system, A2 or Hogue grip, beveled magwell, hardcoat anodized black finish. New 2002.

MSR $2,499 $2,250 $2,025 $1,825 $1,625 $1,400 $1,175 $1,000

6.5 Grendel (new 2012) or .224 Valkyrie (disc. 2020) cal.

CTR-02 ENGRAVED EDITION RIFLE – .223 Rem. cal., GIO, 20 in. JP Supermatch medium contour barrel with polished stainless finish, JP large profile compensator, T6 billet upper and lower receivers with black hardcoat anodizing on aluminum components and Presentation Grade finish with hand engraving, JP MK III 2XL Signature handguard system, JP adj. minimized gas block, Ace ARFX buttstock, Hogue pistol grip, includes polished JP scope mount and accessory pack. New 2015.

MSR $4,839 $4,350 $3,925 $3,525 $3,175 $2,700 $2,300 $1,925

GRADING - PPGS™	100%	98%	95%	90%	80%	70%	60%	LAST MSR

CTR-02 MATCH READY RIFLE – .223 Wylde chamber, GIO, 18 in. light contour JP Supermatch barrel, 3-port compensator, ACE-ARFX skeletonized stock, Hogue grip, 15 1/2 in. XL MK III signature handguard, JP LMOS BCG, JP Enhanced Bolt, QD sling swivel, matte black hardcoat anodized finish.

MSR $2,829	$2,525	$2,275	$2,050	$1,850	$1,575	$1,350	$1,125	

GMR-15 RIFLE – 9mm Para. cal., blowback operation, JP Supermatch cryo-treated barrel, JP tactical or competition compensator, flared magwell, enhanced reliability fire control package, billet lower and forged upper receiver, Hogue overmolded, Mission First Tactical, Magpul MOE, Magpul CTR, or Magpul ACS-L stock, Hogue pistol grip, forged JP-15 or PSC-17 dual-charging upper (new 2019), MK III handguard system, matte black finish, accessory pack includes backpack soft case. New 2017.

MSR $1,749	$1,575	$1,425	$1,275	$1,150	$975	$825	$700	

Add $600 for PSC-17 dual charging upper (new 2019).

* ***GMR-15 All Purpose Carbine*** – 9mm Para. cal., blowback operation, 14.5 in. JP Supermatch cryo-treated light contour barrel with black Teflon finish, permanently attached JP tactical compensator for 16 in. overall length, uses Glock 9mm mags., flared magwell, forged JP15 upper receiver, billet GMR-15 lower receiver, JP EZ Trigger, Hogue overmolded stock, 12.5 in. MKIII Rapid Configuration handguard, Hogue pistol grip, ambi safety, matte black finish, 6.6 lbs. New 2019.

MSR $1,799	$1,625	$1,450	$1,325	$1,175	$1,000	$850	$725	

* ***GMR-15 Match PCC (PCC Competition Ready)*** – 9mm Para. cal., blowback operation, 14.5 in. JP Supermatch cryo-treated light contour barrel with polished stainless finish, permanently attached JP Competition Series compensator for 16 in. overall length, uses Glock 9mm mags., flared magwell, forged JP15 upper receiver, billet GMR-15 lower receiver, JP EZ Trigger, Hogue overmolded stock, 12.5 in. MKIII Rapid Configuration handguard, Hogue pistol grip, ambi safety, matte black finish, 6.8 lbs. New 2019.

MSR $1,819	$1,625	$1,475	$1,325	$1,200	$1,025	$875	$725	

* ***GMR-15 Ultralight PCC*** – 9mm Para. cal., blowback operation, 5.5 in. JP Supermatch cryo-treated ultralight contour barrel with permanently attached aluminum barrel sleeve (with integral compensator cuts) for 16.5 in. overall length, uses Glock 9mm mags., flared magwell, forged JP15 upper receiver, billet GMR-15 lower receiver, JP EZ Trigger, Hogue overmolded stock, 12.5 in. MKIII Rapid Configuration handguard, Hogue pistol grip, ambi safety, matte black finish, barrel finished in clear hard anodizing, 6.2 lbs. New 2020.

MSR $1,799	$1,625	$1,450	$1,325	$1,175	$1,000	$850	$725	

GRADE II – .223 Rem. cal., GIO, 18-24 in. cryo-treated stainless barrel, Mil-Spec JP lower receiver with upper assembly finished in a special two-tone color anodizing process, JP fire control, composite skeletonized stock, Harris bipod, choice of multi-color or black receiver and forend, includes hard case. Mfg. 1998-2002.

	$1,600	$1,400	$1,200	$1,000	$850	$700	$550	*$1,895*

Add $200 for laminated wood thumbhole stock.

GRADE III (THE EDGE) – .223 Rem. cal., GIO, 18-24 in. barrel (cryo-treated beginning 1998) with recoil eliminator, RND machined match upper/lower receiver system, two-piece free floating forend, standard or laminated thumbhole wood stock, includes Harris bipod, top-of-the-line model, includes hard case. Mfg. 1996-2002.

	$2,375	$2,000	$1,750	$1,600	$1,300	$1,000	$825	*$2,795*

Add $250 for laminated thumbhole stock.

JP-15 & VARIATIONS (GRADE I A-3 FLAT-TOP) – .204 Ruger (mfg. 2012-2015), .223 Rem. (disc. 2016), .22 LR, .300 AAC Blackout, or 6.5 Grendel (new 2012) cal., GIO, 18 or 24 in. JP Supermatch cryo-treated stainless barrel, JP Compensator muzzle treatment, 10 shot mag., synthetic modified thumbhole (disc. 2011), synthetic A2 or ACE ARFX buttstock (new 2012), Magpul MOE, or laminated wood thumbhole (disc. 2002) stock, JP vent. two-piece free float forend, Hogue pistol grip, Eagle Arms (disc. 1999), DPMS (disc. 1999) or JP15 lower assembly with JP fire control system, Mil-Spec A3 type upper receiver, gas system and recoil eliminator, black Teflon hardcoat anodized finish. New 1995.

MSR $1,999	$1,800	$1,625	$1,450	$1,300	$1,125	$950	$800	

Add $400 for NRA Hi-Power version with 24 in. bull barrel and sight package (disc. 2002).
Add $200 for laminated wood thumbhole stock (disc. 2002).
Subtract $300 for Duty Defense rifle (JP-15D), disc.
Subtract $500 for .22 LR cal.

GRADING - PPGS™	100%	98%	95%	90%	80%	70%	60%	LAST MSR

* ***JP-15 Essentials Carbine*** – .223 Wylde chambering, GIO, 18 in. JP Supermatch light contour barrel with Black Teflon finish, rifle length gas system, low profile detent adj. gas block, JP Competition Series Compensator, forged JP15 upper and lower receiver set, JP Trigger, Magpul CTR stock, 15 1/2 in. JP MK III Rapid Configuration handguard, Hogue grip, ambi safety, FMOS (Full Mass Operating System) black QPQ finished BCG, QD sling adapter, matte black hardcoat anodized finish, 7 lbs. New 2019.

MSR $1,749	**$1,575**	**$1,425**	**$1,275**	**$1,150**	**$975**	**$825**	**$700**	

* ***JP-15 Essentials Rifle*** – .223 Wylde chambering, GIO, 18 in. JP Supermatch light contour barrel with Black Teflon finish, rifle length gas system, low profile detent adj. gas block, JP Competition Series Compensator, forged JP15 upper and lower receiver set, JP Trigger, Magpul MOE fixed rifle stock, 15 1/2 in. JP MK III Rapid Configuration handguard, Hogue grip, ambi safety, FMOS (Full Mass Operating System) black QPQ finished BCG, QD sling adapter, matte black hardcoat anodized finish, 7.2 lbs. New 2019.

MSR $1,749	**$1,575**	**$1,425**	**$1,275**	**$1,150**	**$975**	**$825**	**$700**	

* ***JP-15 Gladiator*** – .223 Rem. cal., GIO, 16 in. Supermatch barrel with Black Teflon finish, Tactical compensator with crush washer, Mil-Spec forged upper and lower receivers, 2 and 4 in. full-length top rail, extra long JP Rapid Configuration handguard, Magpul BUIS sights, Magpul CTR stock, Magpul MIAD grips, VTAC sling, matte black hardcoat anodized finish, includes accessory pack. Mfg. 2015-2016.

	$1,850	**$1,650**	**$1,500**	**$1,350**	**$1,150**	**$975**	**$825**	*$2,049*

* ***JP-15 Grade I IPSC Limited Class*** – .223 Rem. cal., GIO, similar to Grade I, except has quick detachable match grade iron sights, Versa-pod bipod. Mfg. 1999-2004.

	$1,625	**$1,450**	**$1,300**	**$1,175**	**$1,000**	**$850**	**$725**	*$1,795*

* ***JP-15 Grade I Tactical/SOF*** – .223 Rem. cal., GIO, similar to Grade I, all matte black non-glare finish, 18, 20, or 24 in. Supermatch barrel. Mfg. 1999-2003.

	$1,315	**$850**	**$625**	**$500**	**$435**	**$375**	**$350**	*$1,595*

Add $798 for Trijicon ACOG sight with A-3 adapter.

* ***JP-15 Hunter Ready Rifle*** – .223 Wylde chamber, GIO, 18 in. light contour JP Supermatch barrel with Black Teflon finish, thread protector, small profile 3-port compensator, Magpul ACS-L buttstock, Magpul MIAD grip, forged upper and lower receiver with matte black finish, 15 1/2 in. XL MKIII RC handguard with FDE Cerakote finish, QD sling swivel, JP flat-top scope mount, Red Rock 2-point sling, JP accessory pack, 6.8 lbs. Disc.

	$2,225	**$2,000**	**$1,800**	**$1,625**	**$1,400**	**$1,175**	**$1,000**	*$2,479*

* ***JP-15 Hunter Ready Rifle 224*** – .224 Valkyrie cal., GIO, 20 in. Supermatch light contour barrel with Black Teflon finish, low profile detent adj. gas block, Competition Series Comp., forged JP15 upper and lower receiver, JP trigger, Magpul ACS-L stock, 17 1/4 in. MK III Signature Series handguard, Hogue grip, ambi safety, VMOS stainless steel BCG with black QPQ finish, Radian Raptor LT charging handle, QD sling swivel, matte black hardcoat anodized finish, 7.6 lbs. Disc. 2020.

	$2,250	**$2,025**	**$1,825**	**$1,650**	**$1,400**	**$1,200**	**$1,000**	*$2,509*

* ***JP-15 Match Ready Rifle*** – .223 Wylde chamber, GIO, 16 (disc.) or 18 in. light contour JP Supermatch barrel with polished finish, low profile detent adj. gas block, small profile 3-port compensator, forged JP15 upper and lower receiver, JP trigger, Magpul CTR (disc.) or Hogue Overmolded buttstock, 15 1/2 in. MK III Rapid Configuration handguard, Hogue grip, ambi safety, LMOS (Low Mass Operating System) polished stainless steel BCG, Radian Raptor LT charging handle, QD sling swivel, matte black hardcoat anodized finish, 7 lbs.

MSR $2,269	**$2,050**	**$1,850**	**$1,650**	**$1,475**	**$1,275**	**$1,075**	**$900**	

* ***JP-15 ORRC*** – .223 Rem. cal., GIO, 16 or 18 in. JP Supermatch barrel with black Teflon finish, tactical profile JP compensator, extra long JP Rapid Configuration handguard, forged upper and lower receivers, MOE trigger guard, TI-7 (disc.) or A2 fixed stock, Hogue pistol grip, matte black hardcoat anodized finish, includes accessory pack, 6.8-7 lbs. Mfg. 2013-2017.

	$1,525	**$1,375**	**$1,250**	**$1,125**	**$950**	**$800**	**$675**	*$1,699*

* ***JP-15 Patrol Rifle (Patrol Ready Rifle)*** – .223 Rem. cal. (disc. 2018) or .223 Wylde chambering, GIO, 16 in. JP Supermatch light contour barrel with Black Teflon finish, mid-length gas system, low profile detent adj. gas block, tactical compensator (disc. 2018) or flash hider, forged JP15 upper and lower receiver set, TI-7 (disc. 2018) or Hogue Overmolded buttstock, rifle length rapid configuration handguard, A2 grip, ambi safety, Magpul MOE trigger guard, FMOS (Full Mass Operating System) BCG, matte black hardcoat anodized finish, 6.7 lbs. New 2016.

MSR $1,549	**$1,400**	**$1,250**	**$1,125**	**$1,025**	**$875**	**$725**	**$625**	

GRADING - PPGS™	100%	98%	95%	90%	80%	70%	60%	LAST MSR

* ***JP-15 Professional Rifle*** - .223 Wylde chambering, GIO, 16 in. JP Supermatch light contour barrel with Black Teflon finish, mid-length gas system, low profile detent adj. gas block, black JP Thermal Dissipator, JP Tactical Compensator, forged JP15 upper and lower receiver set, front and rear BUIS, Magpul CTR stock, 15 1/2 in. MK III Rapid Configuration handguard, Magpul MIAD grip, ambi safety, FMOS (Full Mass Operating System), Radian Raptor LT charging handle, Red Rock (disc. 2020) or JP 2-point sling, matte black hardcoat anodized finish, 7.4 lbs. New 2019.

MSR $2,109	$1,900	$1,700	$1,550	$1,375	$1,175	$1,000	$850	

* ***JP-15 Ultralight Rifle*** - .223 Wylde chamber, GIO, 14.5 in. Supermatch ultralight contour barrel with polished finish, low profile detent adj. gas block, black JP Thermal Dissipator, permanently attached JP Competition Series Compensator, forged JP15 receivers, JP trigger, MFT Minimalist stock, 12 1/2 in. MK III Rapid Configuration handguard, Hogue grip, ambi safety, LMOS polished stainless steel BCG, Radian Raptor LT charging handle, QD sling swivel, matte black hardcoat anodized finish, 6 lbs.

MSR $2,359	$2,125	$1,900	$1,725	$1,550	$1,325	$1,125	$950	

Add $50 for Ladies Ultralight Rifle with pink JP Thermal Dissipator, handguard brace, and safety selectors.

* ***JP-15/VTAC Kyle Lamb Signature Rifle*** - .223 Rem. cal., GIO, 16 in. JP Supermatch barrel with Black Teflon finish, JP Tactical Compensator with crush washer, Mil-Spec forged upper/lower receiver, Magpul CTR buttstock, rifle-length JP Rapid Configuration handguard, Hogue pistol grip, FMOS (Full Mass Operating System) BCG, accessory pack included, matte black hardcoat anodized finish, 6.4 lbs. Disc. 2016.

	$1,700	$1,550	$1,375	$1,250	$1,075	$900	$750	*$1,899*

JP-22R - .22 LR cal., blowback operation, 18 in. Supermatch light contour stainless steel barrel, A2 or ACE ARFX buttstock, Hogue pistol grip, extra long JP rapid configuration handguard system, matte black finish. New mid-2014.

MSR $1,449	$1,300	$1,175	$1,050	$950	$800	$700	$575	

Add $150 for polished compensator (Model JP-15/22LR-C).
Add $600 for PSC-17 dual charge upper receiver (disc. 2020).
Add $650 for CTR-02 billet upper and lower receivers.
Add $850 for SCR-11 side charge billet upper and lower receivers.

LRI-20 - .308 Win., .260 Rem., 6mm Creedmoor, or 6.5 Creedmoor cal., GIO, 14 1/2, 16, 18, 20, or 22 in. JP Supermatch stainless or Proof Research carbon fiber barrel, adj. gas system, JP compensator, Recoil Eliminator, or flash hider muzzle device, billet LRI-20 side charging mono upper, billet LRP-07 lower receiver, Hogue overmolded, Magpul MOE, Magpul CTR, Luth-AR "Skullaton", or MFT Battlelink stock, Signature or Rapid configuration MK III handguard, A2 or Hogue pistol grip, ambi safety, low profile or competition side charging handle, matte black anodized finish. New late 2019.

MSR $3,499	$3,150	$2,825	$2,550	$2,300	$1,950	$1,650	$1,400	

Add $70 for Competition side-charging handle.
Add $70 for .260 Rem., 6mm Creedmoor, or 6.5 Creedmoor cal.
Add $500 for Proof Research carbon fiber barrel.

* ***LRI-20 Long Range Competition Rifle (LRCR)*** - 6.5 Creedmoor cal., GIO, 22 in. JP Supermatch medium contour barrel with black Teflon finish, thread protector, XL gas system, detent adj. low profile gas block, black JP Thermal Dissipator, JP Large Profile compensator, 20 shot Magpul mag., billet LRI-20 side charging monolithic upper, billet LRP-07 lower receiver, JP EZ Trigger, Magpul PRS Gen 3 stock, 17.25 in. MKIII Rapid Configuration handguard, Magpul or Hogue grip, ambi safety, low profile side charging handle, QD sling swivel, 2 in. modular rail section, Red Rock 2-point sling, matte black anodized finish, 11 lbs. New 2020.

MSR $4,149	$3,725	$3,350	$3,025	$2,725	$2,325	$1,975	$1,650	

LRP-07 - .260 Rem., .308 Win., 6mm Creedmoor, 6.5 Creedmoor (new 2012), or .338 Federal (mfg. 2012) cal., GIO, 14 1/2, 16, 18, 20, or 22 in. Supermatch stainless steel cryo-treated barrel, adj. gas block, JP Compensator, Recoil Eliminator, or Flash Hider muzzle device, billet LRP-07 lower receiver and side charging upper, choice of A2, ACE ARFX black synthetic, Hogue OverMolded, Magpul MOE, Magpul CTR, Luth-AR "Skullaton", or MFT Battlelink stock, JP MKIII Signature or Rapid Configuration handguards, A2 or Hogue pistol grip, left side charging system (new 2009), JP low, full, or variable mass BCG operating systems available, matte black hardcoat anodized finish.

MSR $3,299	$2,975	$2,675	$2,400	$2,150	$1,850	$1,575	$1,325	

Add $70 for .260 Rem., 6mm Creedmoor, or 6.5 Creedmoor cal.
Add $295 for Bench Rest variation with 22 in. barrel.

GRADING - PPGS™	100%	98%	95%	90%	80%	70%	60%	LAST MSR

* ***LRP-07H Long Range Precision Hunting Rifle (Hunter)*** – .308 Win. cal., GIO, 18 in. JP Supermatch cryo-treated barrel with black Teflon finish, JP adj. gas system, JP Competition Compensator, 10 shot mag., billet receivers, JP fire control package, Hogue OverMolded buttstock, MK III rapid configuration handguard system, Hogue grip, LMOS (Low Mass Operating System) BCG, includes JP 30mm/1 in. flat-top scope mount and Red Rock sling, matte black hardcoat anodized finish. Disc 2020.

	$3,300	$2,975	$2,675	$2,400	$2,050	$1,750	$1,475	*$3,659*

* ***LRP-07 Designated Marksman Rifle*** – .308 Win. cal., 20 in. medium contour JP Supermatch barrel with black Teflon finish, thread protector or large profile 2-port compensator, Magpul Gen3 PRS stock, Hogue grip, billet receivers, 15 1/2 in. XL MK III RC handguard, QD sling swivel, 2 in. modular rail, JP flat-top scope mount, Red Rock 2-point sling, JP accessory pack, matte black finish, 11 lbs. Disc.

	$3,525	$3,175	$2,850	$2,575	$2,200	$1,850	$1,575	*$3,919*

* ***LRP-07 SASS*** – .308 Win. cal., GIO, similar to LRP-07, except has SASS (Semi-Auto Sniper System) package that includes 20 in. Supermatch barrel, Magpul PRS buttstock, Magpul MIAD grip, scope mount, three 20 shot mags., and soft backpack case. Mfg. 2013-2014.

	$4,150	$3,725	$3,350	$3,025	$2,575	$2,175	$1,850	*$4,600*

Add $1,375 for Leupold Mark 4 scope.
Add $1,599 for Bushnell Elite Tactical scope.
Add $2,500 for U.S. Optics SN-3-T-PAL scope.

* ***LRP-07 Billet Beauty Special Edition Rifle*** – .308 Win. cal., GIO, 20 in. JP Supermatch medium contour barrel with custom Cerakote finish, adj. minimized gas block, JP large profile compensator, aluminum billet receivers, JP Fire Control Package, Magpul MOE fixed stock, extra long Rapid Configuration handguard system, Magpul MIAD grip, Low Mass Operating System (LMOS) BCG, JPSCS-10 buffer system, Custom Liberty Belle Bomber inspired Cerakote finish, the sides of the magwell have been fitted with plates displaying both the period Army Air Force logo and specially commissioned Billet Beauty nose art. Limited mfg. of 25 pieces beginning 2015.

MSR $4,649	$4,175	$3,775	$3,400	$3,050	$2,600	$2,200	$1,850	

This model pays special tribute to the B-17 bomber, and is in commemoration of American airmen who took to the skies in defense of liberty. It is styled after the iconic aircraft that carried America to victory in WWII.

* ***LRP-07 Long Range Competition Rifle*** – 6.5 Creedmoor cal., GIO, 22 in. JP Supermatch medium contour barrel, XL gas system, low profile detent adj. gas block, black JP Thermal Dissipator, large profile 2-port compensator, billet LRP-07 receivers, Magpul Gen3 PRS stock, 17 1/4 in. MK III Rapid Configuration handguard, Hogue grip, low profile side-charging handle, QD sling swivel, 2 in. modular rail, JP flat-top scope mount, Red Rock 2-point sling, JP accessory pack, matte black hardcoat anodized finish, 11.4 lbs. Disc.

	$3,600	$3,250	$2,925	$2,625	$2,250	$1,900	$1,600	*$3,999*

* ***LRP-07 MHI Cazador Special Edition Rifle*** – .308 Win. cal., GIO, 16 in. JP Supermatch light contour button rifled barrel w/black Teflon finish, JP adj. minimized gas block, silver Thermal Dissipator, JP standard profile compensator, billet receiver set with MHI logo, JP Fire Control Package, Magpul ACS adj. stock, JP XL MK III Rapid Configuration handguard, Hogue pistol grip, JP Low Mass Operating System (LMOS) BCG, QD sling attachment, 2 and 4 in. modular rail, silver barricade brace, soft case, custom distressed Burnt Bronze Cerakote finish over hardcoat anodized black finish on aluminum components. Limited Mfg.

MSR $4,499	$4,050	$3,650	$3,275	$2,950	$2,525	$2,125	$1,800	

* ***LRP-07 Suppressor Ready Precision Package*** – .308 Win. cal., 20 in. medium contour JP Supermatch barrel with Black Teflon finish, large profile 2-port compensator, Magpul Gen3 PRS stock with JPPRS-SM QD cup and AP-ABP adj. buttplate, Magpul MIAD grip, billet receiver, 15 1/2 in. XL MK III RC handguard, package includes JP flash hider, 34mm flat-top scope mount, four 2 in. modular rails, one 4 in. modular rail, 2-point JP Tactical sling, bipod, monopod, three 20 shot PMAGs, benchrest forearm adapter, matte black finish, 11.8 lbs. Mfg. 2017-Disc.

	$4,500	$4,050	$3,650	$3,275	$2,800	$2,375	$2,000	*$4,999*

LTC-19 LIGHT-WEIGHT PRECISION RIFLE – .308 Win., .260 Rem., 6mm Creedmoor, or 6.5 Creedmoor cal., GIO, 14 1/2, 16, 18, 20, or 22 in. Supermatch stainless steel cryo-treated barrel, adj. gas block, JP Compensator, Recoil Eliminator, or flash hider muzzle device, billet LTC-19 lightweight top charging upper receiver, modified lightweight billet LRP-07 lower receiver, choice of Hogue OverMolded, Magpul MOE, Magpul CTR, LUTH-AR MBA-2, or Mission First Tactical Battlelink stock, JP MKIII Signature or Rapid Configuration handguards, Hogue pistol grip, ambi safety, matte black hardcoat anodized finish. New 2019.

MSR $3,299	$2,975	$2,675	$2,400	$2,150	$1,850	$1,575	$1,325	

Add $70 for .260 Rem., 6mm Creedmoor, or 6.5 Creedmoor cal.

GRADING - PPGS™	100%	98%	95%	90%	80%	70%	60%	LAST MSR

* ***LTC-19 Designated Marksman Rifle*** – .308 Win. cal., GIO, 20 in. Supermatch medium contour stainless steel barrel with Black Teflon finish, rifle length gas system, low profile detent adj. gas block, large profile compensator, billet LTC-19 lightweight top charging upper receiver, modified lightweight billet LRP-07 lower receiver, Magpul PRS Gen2 stock, 17 1/4 in. JP MKIII Rapid Configuration handguard, Hogue grip, ambi safety, matte black hardcoat anodized finish, 11.2 lbs. New 2019.

MSR $3,569	$3,200	$2,900	$2,600	$2,350	$2,000	$1,700	$1,425	

* ***LTC-19 Essentials Carbine*** – .308 Win. cal., GIO, 16 in. Supermatch light contour stainless steel barrel with Black Teflon finish, mid-length gas system, low profile locking adj. gas block, threaded muzzle, thread protector, billet LTC-19 lightweight top charging upper receiver, modified lightweight billet LRP-07 lower receiver, JP trigger, Hogue Overmolded stock, 12 1/2 in. JP MKIII Rapid Configuration handguard, A2 grip, ambi safety, matte black hardcoat anodized finish, 7.3 lbs. New 2019.

MSR $2,999	$2,700	$2,425	$2,200	$1,975	$1,675	$1,425	$1,200	

* ***LTC-19 Essentials Rifle*** – .308 Win. cal., GIO, 18 in. Supermatch light contour stainless steel barrel with Black Teflon finish, rifle length gas system, low profile locking adj. gas block, threaded muzzle, thread protector, billet LTC-19 lightweight top charging upper receiver, modified lightweight billet LRP-07 lower receiver, JP trigger, Luth-AR "Skullaton" stock, 15 1/2 in. JP MKIII Rapid Configuration handguard, A2 grip, ambi safety, JP LMOS stainless steel BCG with black QPQ finish, matte black hardcoat anodized finish, 8.1 lbs. New 2019.

MSR $2,999	$2,700	$2,425	$2,200	$1,975	$1,675	$1,425	$1,200	

* ***LTC-19 Tactical Ready Rifle*** – .308 Win. cal., GIO, 18 in. Supermatch medium contour stainless steel barrel with Black Teflon finish, rifle length gas system, adj. gas block, Competition Series Compensator, billet LTC-19 lightweight top charging upper receiver, modified lightweight billet LRP-07 lower, JP trigger, Magpul UBR Gen2 stock, 17 1/4 in. MKIII Rapid Configuration handguard, Hogue grip, ambi safety, matte black hardcoat anodized finish, 8.8 lbs. New 2019.

MSR $3,519	$3,150	$2,850	$2,550	$2,300	$1,975	$1,675	$1,400	

NC-22 – .22 LR cal., blowback operation, precision machined Nordic Component upper receiver, 18 in. lightweight stainless steel barrel with JP Compensator, extra long JP modular handguard system, matte black anodized hardcoat finish. Mfg. 2013-2014.

	$1,350	$1,225	$1,100	$975	$850	$700	$600	*$1,499*

PSC-11 – .223 Wylde chamber (new 2017), .204 Ruger (mfg. 2012-2015), .223 Rem. (disc. 2016), .22 LR (new 2016), .224 Valkyrie (new 2019), .300 AAC Blackout (new 2016), 6.5 Grendel (new 2012), or 5.56 NATO (new 2017) cal., GIO, 16-20 in. JP Supermatch polished stainless barrel, ultralight, light, or medium contour, adj. gas system, JP Compensator, PSC-11 billet dual charging upper with Picatinny rail, JP-15 forged lower receiver, JP Fire Control trigger pack, A2 (disc.), ACE ARFX (disc.), Hogue, Magpul, LUTH-AR, or MFT Stock, JP MK III, JP Modular, or JP Rapid Configuration Hand Guard system, Hogue pistol grip, matte black hardcoat anodized finish on aluminum components. Mfg. 2011-2020.

	$2,300	$2,100	$1,900	$1,700	$1,450	$1,250	$1,050	*$2,599*

Add $100 for 6.5 Grendel (new 2012) or .224 Valkyrie (new 2019) cal.

PSC-12 – .260 Win. (disc.), .308 Win., 6.5 Creedmoor (disc.), or 6.5 Grendel (disc.) cal., GIO, large frame, JP Supermatch button rifled barrel with polished stainless finish, JP Compensator, adj. gas system, dual charging upper assembly compatible with DPMS lower receivers, MK III handguard system, A2 or ACE ARFX buttstock, A2 or Hogue grip, JP fire control trigger. Mfg. 2012-2018.

	$3,150	$2,825	$2,550	$2,300	$1,950	$1,650	$1,400	*$3,499*

SCI-20 RIFLE – 5.56 NATO, .300 AAC Blackout, or 6.5 Grendel cal., GIO, 14 1/2, 16, 18, 20, or 22 (6.5 Grendel only) in. Supermatch polished stainless steel or black Teflon finished barrel, JP adj. gas block, Tactical or Competition compensator, SCI-20 billet side charge upper receiver w/integral barrel nut, SCR-11 billet lower receiver, JP Fire Control Package, Phase 5 pistol buffer tube, MK III handguard system, Hogue pistol grip, matte black hardcoat anodized finish. New 2020.

MSR $2,699	$2,425	$2,175	$1,975	$1,775	$1,500	$1,275	$1,075	

Add $100 for 6.5 Grendel cal.

SCR-11 – .223 Wylde chamber, .22 LR (new mid-2014), .204 Ruger (disc. 2015), .224 Valkyrie (new 2019), .300 AAC Blackout (new 2016), .223 Rem. (disc. 2016), 6.5 Grendel, or 5.56 NATO (new 2017) cal., GIO, 16-20 in. JP Supermatch polished stainless barrel, ultralight, light, or medium contour, adj. gas system, JP Compensator, SCR-11 billet side charging flat-top upper with Picatinny rail, JP-15 forged lower or SCR-11 billet receiver, choice of A2 (disc.), ACE ARFX (disc.), Hogue, Magpul, LUTH-AR, or MFT buttstock, MKIII handguard system, Hogue pistol grip, matte black anodizing on aluminum components. Mfg. 2011-2020

	$2,425	$2,175	$1,975	$1,775	$1,500	$1,275	$1,075	*$2,699*

Add $100 for 6.5 Grendel or .224 Valkyrie (new 2019) cal.

GRADING - PPGS™	100%	98%	95%	90%	80%	70%	60%	LAST MSR

5.11 ALWAYS BE READY EDITION RIFLES/SCR-11 ABR – .223 Wylde chambering, GIO, 18 in. JP Supermatch medium contour barrel with Black Teflon finish, black or orange JP Thermal Dissipator, low profile gas block, JP Small Profile comp., billet side charging upper receiver, billet lower receiver, flip-up iron sights, Magpul UBR buttstock, JP Extra Long Modular Hand Guard, Hogue Overmold grip, JP ambi safety, JP Low Mass Operating System BCG in black QPQ finish, 5.11 Storm Grey Cerakote, comes with 2 and 4 in. modular rail pieces, optional 5.11 rifle case.

MSR $3,899	$3,500	$3,200	$2,800	$2,600	$2,200	$1,850	$1,550	

This rifle was created in collaboration with 5.11 Tactical.

* ***JP-15ABR*** – .223 Rem. cal., 16 in. medium contour JP Supermatch barrel with Black Teflon finish, tactical compensator with crush washer, Mil-Spec forged receivers, extra long JP Rapid Configuration handguard, TI-7 buttstock, MOE trigger guard, Hogue grip, 5.11 Storm Grey Cerakote finish, 7.2 lbs. Mfg. 2015-2016.

	$2,250	$2,025	$1,825	$1,625	$1,400	$1,175	$1,000	*$2,499*

* ***LRP-07 ABR*** – .308 Win. cal., 20 in. medium contour barrel with large profile compensator and Black Teflon finish, billet aluminum receivers with left-side charging system, minimized black JP adj. gas block, extra long JP modular handguard, black Magpul PRS stock, Magpul MIAD black grip, accessories include extra long 14 1/2 in. top rail, 2 and 4 in. modular rails, and JP swivel mount adaptor, 5.11 Storm Grey Cerakote over hardcoat anodized finish with 5.11 logo. Mfg. 2015-disc.

	$4,075	$3,675	$3,325	$2,975	$2,550	$2,150	$1,825	*$4,539*

J R CARBINES

Please refer to the Just Right Carbines listing in this section.

J R DISTRIBUTING

Previous manufacturer located in Moorpark, CA. J R Distributing was a division of J R Sports Distribution Corporation.

RIFLES: SEMI-AUTO

.22 MAG. CUSTOM RIFLE – .22 WMR cal., choice of Ruger 10/22 or AMT action, 20 in. bull barrel with laminate or synthetic stock, 9 shot rotary mag., supplied with hard case. Circa 1998-2012.

	$725	$650	$550	$500	$450	$400	$360	*$795*

JSL (HEREFORD)

Previous manufacturer located in Hereford, England. Imported until 1994 by Specialty Shooters Supply, Inc. located in Fort Lauderdale, FL.

PISTOLS: SEMI-AUTO

SPITFIRE (G1) – 9mm Para. or 9x21mm cal., patterned after the Czech CZ-75/85, 3.7 in. barrel, ambidextrous safety, commander style hammer, black non-slip rubberized grip panels, investment cast stainless steel fabrication, 10 (C/B 1994) or 15* shot mag., 2.2 lbs. Imported 1992-94.

* ***Spitfire Standard*** – includes fixed rear sight, 2 mags., presentation case, and allen key.

	$1,600	$1,100	$925	$810	$670	$565	$475	*$1,332*

Add $81 for adj. rear sight (Sterling Model).

JTS GROUP

Current semi-auto shotgun manufacturer located in Katy, TX. Previously located in Houston, TX.
For individual model listings, please go to BlueBookOfGunValues.com/overflow.

JACKSON HOLE FIREARMS

Previous manufacturer located in Jackson Hole, WY circa mid-70s.

RIFLES: BOLT ACTION

STANDARD RIFLE – various cals., Mauser 98 action utilizing patented system for interchangeable barrels, checkered walnut stock.

	$1,050	$875	$800	$725	$650	$575	$495	

Jackson Hole Firearms manufactured a limited quantity of their unique interchangeable barrel bolt action rifles. Collectibility to date has been minimal, and values are affected by the J.P. Sauer Models 90 and 200 which also feature the interchangeable barrel design.

GRADING - PPGS™	100%	98%	95%	90%	80%	70%	60%	LAST MSR

JACKSON RIFLES

Previous rifle manufacturer located in Castle Douglas, Scotland. Currently, the company manufactures and distributes parts for custom rifles.

Jackson Rifles manufactured high quality long-range competition rifles, including the J5-P (single shot) and the J5-T (bolt action repeater), available in both right and left-hand actions.

JAEGER, FRANZ

Previous manufacturer located in Suhl, Germany circa 1900-1945. Franz Jaeger firearms included pistols, rifles, and shotguns.

For individual model listings, please go to BlueBookOfGunValues.com/overflow.

JAGD-UND SPORTWAFFEN SUHL GmbH

Previous company name of Merkel, located in Suhl, Germany since 1535.

Currently, the famous Merkel trademark (mfg. by Merkel Jagd-Und Sportwaffen Suhl GmbH) is imported by Merkel USA, located in Trussville, AL. Previously imported by Heckler & Koch, located in Sterling, VA. Please refer to the Merkel listing in this text for current information regarding this older European trademark.

JAMES RIVER ARMORY

Current manufacturer and restoration company specializing in military firearms from WWI and WWII, located in Burgaw, NC. Previously located in Baltimore, MD.

Classic Firearms is the exclusive dealer for James River Armory. Please visit their website at www.classicfirearms.com for more details and availability.

RIFLES/CARBINES: SEMI-AUTO

James River Armory currently restores and manufactures (beginning 2013) selected military WWI and WWII rifles, and puts on new Criterion barrels and in some cases, new stocks. When completed, all rifles are test fired for safety. Please contact the company directly for current model availability and pricing on its restored military firearms.

Current offerings include the M1 Garand, Rockola M14 Carbine Model, Rockola M14 Original Military Configuration, BM-59 .308 Cal. Rifle (various configurations), AK-74 5.45x39 Original Military Style, AK-47 Rifle w/Quad Rail, Serbian Police SKS Rifle, and Hungarian AMD 65 AK-47 with Folding stock or Phoenix stock.

JANZ GmbH

Current revolver manufacturer established in 1999, and located in Malente, Germany. Currently imported by JANZ-Revolver USA beginning in 2015, located in Fort Worth, TX. Previously imported 2007-2009 by Brenzovich, located in Fort Hancock, TX. Previously imported 2003-2004 by Rocky Mountain Armoury, located in Silverthorne, CO.

PISTOLS

JANZ PISTOL – 9mm Para. cal., linear barrel, rotating bolt lock. Introduced 2018.

Please contact the importer directly for current pricing and availability on this model.

REVOLVERS

Please contact the importer directly for up-to-date pricing and availabilty for the following models.

TYPE E (JTL-E) – 9mm Para., .22 LR, .357 Mag., .44 Mag., .45 Win. Mag., .454 Casull, .45 LC (mfg. 2000-2016), or .500 S&W (mfg. 2005-2016) cal., SA/DA, 3-12 in. barrel, M-frame,6, 7, or 8 shot, 3-12 in. barrel, different surfaces available, cylinder exchangeable, fine tuned trigger, run with train-field profile, different grips available, micrometer adjustment of side and height, sight and front sight exchangeable, trigger weight adjustable, target sights available.

This model was originally called the JTL-E (mfg. 2000-2016).

TYPE EM – 9mm Para., .22 LR, .357 Mag., or .44 Mag. cal., 5, 6, or 7 shot, 3-10 in. barrel, SA/DA, small frame, different surfaces available, cylinder exchangeable, fine tuned trigger, run with train-field profile, different grips available, micrometer adjustment of side and height, sight and front sight exchangeable, target sights available, trigger weight adjustable.

TYPE EM-S – 9mm Para., .22 LR, .32, .38, .357 Mag., or .44 Mag. cal., SA/DA, 3-12 in. barrel, K/L-frame, 5, 6, or 7 shot, different surfaces available, cylinder and barrel exchangeable, fine tuned trigger, different grips available, run with train-field profile, micrometer adjustment of side and height, sight and front sight exchangeable, front sight undercut, trigger weight adjustable from outside and visualized with +/- scala, target sights available.

GRADING - PPGS™	100%	98%	95%	90%	80%	70%	60%	LAST MSR

TYPE MA – .460 S&W or .500 S&W cal., SA/DA, 3-12 in. barrel, large frame, fixed barrel, 5 shot, different surfaces available, cylinder exchangeable, triple lock, fine tuned trigger, different grips available, run with train-field profile, micrometer adjustment of side and height, sight and front sight exchangeable, front sight undercut, target sights available.

This model was originally the JTL 500 (prototype) but the frame and cylinder have been substantially enlarged.

TYPE S (JTL-S) – 9mm Para., .22 LR, .32, .357 Mag., .44 Mag., .45, or .454 Casull cal., SA/DA, N-frame, 3-12 in. barrel, 5, 6, 7, or 8 shot, different surfaces available, cylinder and barrel exchangeable, fine tuned trigger, different grips available, run with train-field profile, micrometer adjustment of side and height, sight and front sight exchangeable, front sight undercut, trigger weight adjustable from outside and visualized with +/- scala, target sights available. .22 LR, .357 Mag./.38 Spl., .44 Mag., .45 Win. Mag., or .454 Casull/.45 LC cal., DA, 6 or 7 (.357 Mag.) shot, unique interchangeable barrels and cylinders allow cals. to be changed rapidly, 4-12 in. barrel with full lug, ergonomic stippled wood grips, target sights. Mfg. 2003-2016.

This model was originally called the JTL-S (mfg. 2003-2016).

JAPANESE MILITARY

Previously manufactured prior to and during WWII in Japan by various manufacturers.

PISTOLS: SEMI-AUTO

Please refer to the Nambu section for further information on Nambus and variations.

HAMADA VARIATIONS

* ***Hamada Type 1*** – .32 ACP cal., striker fired, blowback operated, 3 1/2 in. fixed barrel, 9 shot mag., fixed serrated ramp front sight, fixed notched rear sight, checkered wooden grip panels, two pos. left sided thumb safety, salt blued finish. Mfg. estimated at 5,000 pistols but examples are scarce and usually in the 2000-3000 ser. range in the United States.

	$9,500	$8,500	$7,500	$6,250	$5,000	$4,000	$3,000	

Add 10% for early variation.

Pistols with original accoutrement such as a holster or spare magazine carry a premium.

* ***Hamada Type 2*** – 8mm Nambu cal., striker fired, blowback operated, 3 5/8 in. fixed barrel, 6 shot mag., fixed serrated ramp front sight, fixed notched rear sight, checkered wooden grip panels, two pos. left sided thumb safety, larger than Type 1 Hamada and with a more squared profile, all known examples are unfinished in the white. Known examples exist in the serial number range 1-50.

	$15,000	$12,500	$9,500	$8,500	$7,500	$6,500	$5,500	

Because every known example of these pistols has surfaced unfinished in the white, please consider surface finish and overall condition as the grading factor in appraising these types of pistols.

REVOLVERS

TYPE 26 REVOLVER (1893 REVOLVER) – 9mm Japanese Revolver (9×22mmR Type 26) cal., double action only, top break action, 4 3/4 in. barrel, 6 shot cylinder, automatic ejectors, bobbed hammer, notch rear sight, blade front sight, checkered wood grips, lanyard ring, blued finish. Approx. 59,000 mfg. 1893-1925.

	$1,500	$1,250	$1,000	$750	$500	$400	$300	

Subtract 50% for arsenal rework.

Add 100% for early mfg. with internal numbers (approx. first 300 revolvers), or final Kokura assembled pistols in 58,971-59,183 serial range.

RIFLES: MILITARY

Subtract 25% for Murata rifles missing their bolt head.

Subtract 20% if Imperial Seal (Chrysanthemum Flower or "Mum") has been ground off of the front receiver ring.

Subtract 20% if serial numbers are not matching (does not apply to sniper rifles, as they are only rarely found with matching scopes and mounts).

Subtract 10%-40% for training rifles of each type.

Rifles that feature original dust covers should carry a slight premium. Beware of fakes and reproduction dust covers!

MURATA TYPE 13 RIFLE – 11×60mmR Murata cal., black powder cartridges, 32 in. barrel, single shot capacity, steel receiver, barrel, and fittings, ladder rear sight, blade front sight, full length smooth contour wooden stock, short (Type 13) or long (Type 18) stock wrist receiver tangs, two barrel retaining bands, bayonet lug on right side of forward barrel retaining band, two sling swivels mounted on rear barrel band and bottom of stock, blued finish, approx. 9 lbs. Type 13 Murata mfg. began circa 1880, Type 18 Murata mfg. began circa 1885, mfg. of all Murata rifles ceased entirely by 1905.

	N/A	$2,800	$2,300	$1,500	$1,000	$700	$425	

Type 13 rifles can be easily distinguished from Type 18 rifles by the location of the bolt stop. Type 13 rifles have the bolt stop attached to the top of the bolt body, whereas the Type 18 rifle has a threaded cross-bolt on the left side of the stock that stops the bolt.

GRADING - PPGS™	100%	98%	95%	90%	80%	70%	60%	LAST MSR

MURATA TYPE 22 RIFLE – 8×53mmR Murata cal., 32 in. barrel for rifles, 19 1/2 in. barrel for carbine variant, 8 (rifle) or 5 (carbine) shot tubular mag., steel receiver, barrel, and fittings, ladder rear sight, blade front sight, full length wooden stock with deep finger grooves and checkering on the handguard, short upper handguard between rear sight and rear barrel band, magazine cut-off switch, blued finish, approx. 9 lbs. Mfg. circa 1889, Mfg. of all Murata rifles ceased entirely by 1905.

N/A	$2,800	$2,300	$1,500	$1,000	$700	$425

Rifles with original intact upper handguard carry a slight premium.

TYPE 30 ARISAKA RIFLE – 6.5x50SR Arisaka cal., Japanese type Mauser inspired action, 31 in. barrel, 5 shot internal box mag., two-piece bolt construction, adj. rear ladder sight, fixed front blade sight, full length wooden stock, bottom mounted sling swivels, metal buttplate, finger grooves on forearm, unique hook safety located on the rear of the bolt body, push-button style bolt release, brass-headed cleaning rod located under barrel, blued finish. Mfg. 1897-1905.

$700	$625	$525	$475	$375	$300	$225

A Type 30 Carbine variant was made, these are quite rare and command a strong premium.

Unlike its contemporaries, the Type 30 Arisaka Rifle used a wire coil spring in the magazine rather than a folded leaf spring.

TYPE 35 ARISAKA RIFLE – 6.5x50SR Arisaka cal., Mauser inspired bolt action, 31 in. barrel, 5 shot internal box mag., two-piece bolt construction, adj. rear tangent sight enclosed in tall guards w/range markings, fixed front blade sight, full length wooden stock, bottom mounted sling swivels, metal buttplate, finger grooves on forearm, unique enlarged hook safety located on the rear of the bolt body, manually operated sliding dust cover, push-button style bolt release, brass-headed cleaning rod located under barrel, blued finish. Mfg. 1902-1905.

$925	$825	$700	$625	$500	$425	$300

TYPE 38 ARISAKA RIFLE – 6.5x50SR Arisaka cal., Mauser inspired bolt action, 31 in. barrel, 5 shot internal box mag., one-piece bolt construction, controlled feed Mauser style extractor, adj. rear peep style ladder sight, fixed shrouded front blade sight, full length wooden stock, short length upper handguard, bottom mounted sling swivels, metal buttplate, finger grooves on forearm, knurled knob style safety located on the rear of the bolt body, action operated sliding dust cover, lever-style bolt release with integral ejector, blued finish. Mfg. 1905-1945.

$675	$600	$500	$450	$350	$275	$200

* ***Type 38 Cavalry Carbine (Type 38 A & B Cavalry Carbine)*** – 6.5x50R Arisaka cal., similar to Type 38 Arisaka Rifle, except has 19 in. barrel. Mfg. 1911-disc.

$700	$625	$525	$475	$375	$300	$225

TYPE 44 CAVALRY CARBINE (TYPE 44 CAVALRY ARISAKA CARBINE) – 6.5x50SR Arisaka cal., Mauser inspired bolt action, 19 in. barrel, 5 shot internal box mag., one-piece bolt construction, controlled feed Mauser style extractor, adj. rear ladder sight, fixed shrouded front blade sight, full length wooden stock, full length wooden upper handguard between front and rear sight, finger grooves on stock forearm, left side mounted sling swivels, metal buttplate with trapdoor for cleaning rod actuated by switch on right side of buttstock, knurled knob style safety located on the rear of the bolt body, action operated sliding dust cover, lever-style bolt release with integral ejector, underfolding integrated bayonet, integrated stacking hook on the right side of the bayonet housing, blued finish. Mfg. 1911-disc.

$2,200	$1,925	$1,650	$1,400	$1,000	$750	$550

TYPE 97 SNIPER RIFLE – 6.5x50SR Arisaka cal., Mauser inspired bolt action, based on the Type 38 Arisaka Rifle, 31 in. barrel, 5 shot internal box mag., controlled feed Mauser style extractor, adj. rear ladder sight, fixed shrouded front blade sight, integral scope mount rail on left side of receiver for mounting offset dedicated 2.5 power scope, full length wooden stock with relief cut on the left side to accommodate the scope mount, bottom mounted sling swivels, metal buttplate, finger grooves on forearm, knurled knob style safety located on the rear of the bolt body, down-turned bolt handle, action operated sliding dust cover, lever-style bolt release with integral ejector, blued finish. Mfg. 1937-1945.

$3,500	$3,000	$2,600	$2,400	$1,800	$1,600	$1,250

Add $1,000-$2,000 if complete with scope.

TYPE I CARCANO RIFLE – 6.5x50SR Arisaka cal., Italian Carcano style bolt action, 31 in. barrel, 5 shot internal box mag., adj. rear v-notch style ladder sight, fixed non-shrouded front blade sight, full length wooden stock, short length upper handguard, bottom mounted sling swivels, metal buttplate, finger grooves on forearm, knurled toggle safety located just behind the bolt handle, blued finish. Mfg.1938-1941.

$550	$525	$400	$300	$250	$200	$100

The nomenclature is not "Type 1" but rather the letter "I" for "Italian".

These rifles lacked any Japanese markings, including the Chrysanthemum.

These rifles also came in two different lengths of pull, one nearly identical to the Type 38 rifle, and one approximately 1 in. longer.

GRADING - PPGS™	100%	98%	95%	90%	80%	70%	60%	LAST MSR

TYPE 99 SERVICE RIFLE – 7.7x58mm Arisaka cal., Mauser inspired bolt action, 31 in. (initial production Long Rifle variant, rare) or 26 in. barrel length, 5 shot internal box magazine, one-piece bolt construction, controlled feed Mauser style extractor, adj. rear peep style ladder sight with folding anti-aircraft lead arms, fixed shrouded front blade sight, full length wooden stock, full length upper handguard, bottom mounted sling swivels, metal buttplate, finger grooves on forearm, knurled knob style safety located on the rear of the bolt body, straight bolt handle, action operated sliding dust cover, lever-style bolt release with integral ejector, folding monopod attached to rear barrel band, blued finish. Mfg. 1939-1945.

	$700	$625	$525	$475	$375	$300	$225

Add 20% for original monopod.
Add 75% for 31 in. long barrel.

* ***Type 99 Sniper Rifle*** – 7.7x58mm Arisaka cal., Mauser inspired bolt action, 26 in. barrel length, 5 shot internal box magazine, one-piece bolt construction, controlled feed Mauser style extractor, adj. rear peep style ladder sight with folding anti-aircraft lead arms, fixed shrouded front blade sight, integral scope mount rail on left side of receiver for mounting dedicated 2.5 or 4 power scope, full length wooden stock with relief cut on the left side to accommodate the scope mount, full length upper handguard, bottom mounted sling swivels, metal buttplate, finger grooves on forearm, knurled knob style safety located on the rear of the bolt body, straight or down-turned bolt handle, action operated sliding dust cover, lever-style bolt release with integral ejector, blued finish. Mfg. 1939-1945.

Sniper Rifle w/4X scope	$4,500	$4,000	$3,500	$3,000	$2,500	$2,000	$1,500

Add 50% for externally adjustable scope.

TERA RIFLE SERIES (PARATROOPER RIFLES) – Japan had introduced a series of paratrooper variants of their standard service rifles with various forms of takedown or folding mechanisms. The TERA name is based on the Japanese terms for the rifles, **Te**ishin **Ra**kkasan Shoju meaning "Parachute Rifle". These rifles were based on existing service rifles. The Type 1 was based on the Type 38 rifle, while the Type 2 and Type 100 were based on the Type 99 rifle. While all of these rifles are rare, the most common variant is the Type 2 Paratrooper Rifle.

* ***Type 1 Paratrooper Carbine*** – 6.5x50SR Arisaka cal., 19 in. barrel, 5 shot internal box mag., one-piece bolt construction, controlled feed Mauser style extractor, adj. rear V-notch style ladder sight, fixed shrouded front blade sight, full length hinged stock folds horizontally to the right at the wrist of the stock. Stock latch is located on the left side just behind the action, full length upper handguard, bottom mounted sling swivels, metal buttplate, finger grooved forearm, action operated sliding dust cover, lever-style bolt release with integral ejector, blued finish. Very limited production by Nagoya Arsenal.

	$6,000	$5,250	$4,500	$4,000	$3,300	$2,700	$2,100

* ***Type 2 Paratrooper Rifle (Type 99 Paratrooper Takedown Version)*** – 7.7x58mm Arisaka cal., 26 in. barrel length, 5 shot internal box magazine, one-piece bolt construction, two-piece takedown mechanism utilizing a locking lug on the bottom of the barrel and a wedge pin screwed into the right side of the gun, Mauser style extractor, adj. rear peep style ladder sight with folding anti-aircraft lead arms, fixed shrouded front blade sight, two-piece wooden stock, full length upper handguard, side mounted sling swivels, metal buttplate, finger grooved forearm, knurled knob style safety located on the bolt body, fixed straight bolt handle, action operated sliding dust cover, lever-style bolt release with integral ejector, folding monopod, blued finish. Mfg. circa. 1942-1945.

	$3,800	$3,325	$2,850	$2,600	$2,000	$1,700	$1,400

* ***Type 100 Paratrooper Rifle*** – 7.7x58mm Arisaka cal., 26 in. barrel length, 5 shot internal box magazine, one-piece bolt construction, two-piece takedown mechanism utilizing interrupted threads on the barrel, controlled feed Mauser style extractor, adj. rear peep style ladder sight with folding anti-aircraft lead arms, fixed shrouded front blade sight, two-piece wooden stock, full length upper handguard, side mounted sling swivels, metal buttplate, finger grooved forearm, knurled knob style safety on rear of bolt, detachable threaded bolt handle, action operated sliding dust cover, lever-style bolt release with integral ejector, folding monopod, blued finish. Limited production by Nagoya Arsenal. Mfg. 1940-Disc.

	$8,500	$7,400	$6,375	$5,775	$4,675	$3,800	$3,000

JARD, INC.

Current firearms and components manufacturer located in Sheldon, IA.

For individual model listings, please go to BlueBookOfGunValues.com/overflow.

JARRETT RIFLES, INC.

Current manufacturer established in 1979, located in Jackson, SC. Direct custom order sales only.

GRADING - PPGS™	100%	98%	95%	90%	80%	70%	60%	LAST MSR

HANDGUNS

CUSTOM XP-100 HUNTER – various cals., re-machined Remington XP-100 action, Jarrett match grade stainless steel barrel, McMillan fiberglass stock, various options. Limited mfg.

	$3,450	$2,650	$2,150	$1,750	$1,350	$1,050	$995	

ULTIMATE REDHAWK – .44 Mag. cal., features Hogue grips and muzzle brake. Mfg. 1995-2000.

	$1,150	$1,025	$850	$675	$575	$500	$450	*$1,150*

RIFLES: BOLT ACTION

Jarrett Rifles, Inc. is justifiably famous for its well-known Beanfield rifles (refers to shooting over a beanfield at long range targets). A Jarrett innovation is the Tri-Lock receiver, which has 3 locking lugs, and a semi-integral recoil lug. Jarrett blueprints every action for proper dimensioning and rigid tolerances, and this explains why their rifles have set rigid accuracy standards.

A wide variety of options are available for Jarrett custom rifles (holders of 16 world records in rifle accuracy). Jarrett also manufactures its own precision ammunition for discriminating shooters/hunters. The manufacturer should be contacted directly for pricing and availability regarding these special order options, and custom gunsmithing services.

Current pricing does not include 11% excise tax or scope.

STANDARD HUNTING RIFLE – various cals., Remington Model 700 right or left-hand action, McMillan fiberglass stock, blue receiver, Jarrett satin finish match grade barrel, sling studs and leather sling, rings and base, weights vary. Disc. 2003.

	$4,625	$4,150	$3,650	$3,150	$2,750	$2,150	$1,750	*$4,625*

WALK ABOUT – various cals. in short action only, features Remington Model 7 action (left-hand utilizes Rem. Model 700 short action), weights vary. Mfg. 1995-2003.

	$4,625	$4,150	$3,650	$3,150	$2,750	$2,150	$1,750	*$4,625*

TRUCK GUN – various small bore cals., 19-20 in. barrel, black synthetic stock. Mfg. 1999-2003.

	$4,625	$4,150	$3,650	$3,150	$2,750	$2,150	$1,750	*$4,625*

BENCHREST/YOUTH/TACTICAL – various cals., various configurations depending on application. Mfg. 1999-disc.

	$4,625	$4,150	$3,650	$3,150	$2,750	$2,150	$1,750	*$4,625*

SERIES RIFLE – various cals., various configurations, only 100 made of each series. Mfg. 1993-2003.

* ***Series Rifle Standard*** – various cals.

	$5,025	$4,450	$3,850	$3,250	$2,850	$2,250	$1,850	*$5,025*

* ***Series Rifle Coup de Grace*** – various cals. Mfg. 1996-99.

	$3,295	$2,750	$2,300	$1,800	$1,500	$1,250	$995	*$3,495*

* ***Series Rifle Nombre Unique*** – various cals., 100 mfg. 1999 only.

	$3,495	$2,900	$2,400	$1,850	$1,550	$1,250	$995	*$3,695*

SIGNATURE SERIES – various cals., Jarrett tri-lock stainless steel receiver, fiberglass, wood laminate, or deluxe walnut stock, helical fluted bolt with three lugs, built to special order only. New 2004.

MSR $8,320	$7,500	$6,850	$5,950	$5,000	$4,500	$3,600	$2,925	

WIND WALKER SERIES – various cals. up to .30 cal., Rem. M-700 ADL action only, lightweight design, 24 in. tapered barrel with muzzle brake, Brown Precision or carbon fiber stock, 7 1/4 lbs. New 1999.

MSR $8,320	$7,500	$6,850	$5,950	$5,000	$4,500	$3,600	$2,925	

Add $260 for carbon fiber stock.

RIDGE WALKER – various cals., various barrel lengths, Jarrett Tri-lock receiver, aluminum floorplate, with or w/o muzzle brake, Kevlar/fiberglass pistol grip stock available in a variety of colors, 8 lbs. New 2009.

MSR $8,320	$7,500	$6,850	$5,950	$5,000	$4,500	$3,600	$2,925	

CUSTOM RIFLE – various cals., features Jarrett short action.

MSR $7,000	$6,300	$5,515	$4,725	$4,285	$3,465	$2,835	$2,325	

LONG RANGER – .30 Jarrett cal., 26 in. (hunting) standard or 27 in. (target) heavy barrel, Jewell trigger, highly polished metal (choice of colors), Kevlar/fiberglass pistol grip stock (choice of colors), 8 (hunting) or 12 (target) lbs. New 2009.

MSR $7,640	$6,875	$6,015	$5,150	$4,675	$3,785	$3,100	$2,550	

Add $680 for Target model.

PRESTIGE SERIES – Limited mfg. 2013 only.

	$8,750	$8,195	$7,175	$6,150	$5,575	$4,500	$3,695	*$9,640*

GRADING - PPGS™	100%	98%	95%	90%	80%	70%	60%	LAST MSR

ORIGINAL BEANFIELD RIFLE – built on customer supplied action, choice of caliber, stock style, color, barrel length and finish, with or w/o muzzle brake, supplied with 20 rounds of ammo and test target. New 2005.

MSR $6,050	$5,500	$4,995	$4,500	$3,925	$3,400	$3,000	$2,600	

PROFESSIONAL HUNTER – Mag. cals. to customer's specifications, starting with .375 H&H, features Winchester controlled round feed Model 70 action with claw extractor and 3-position bolt shroud safety, Jarrett match grade stainless steel barrel, McMillan stock, quarter rib with iron sights, includes 2 sets of detachable rings and two 1.75-6x32mm Leupold scopes, takedown action, includes custom built Americase.

MSR $11,070	$10,000	$9,150	$8,000	$6,850	$6,200	$5,000	$4,000	

SHIKAR SERIES – various cals., aircraft aluminum frame, two-part epoxy barrier provides moisture impervious finish, hand lapped, free floated barrel, three separate stock patterns - English, Estate, and Ultimate Classic, hand checkered 28-year-old American black walnut stock, trapdoor floorplate, decelerator pad, Talley rings and bases. New mid-2013.

MSR $10,320	$9,350	$7,900	$6,500	$5,850	$4,650	$3,900	$3,500	

.50 CAL. – .50 BMG cal., McMillan custom receiver, choice of repeater or single shot, 30 or 34 in. barrel with muzzle brake, 28-45 lbs. Mfg. 1999-2003.

	$8,050	$6,500	$5,300	$4,350	$3,650	$3,000	$2,500	*$8,050*

Add $300 for repeater action.

CLASSIC SERIES – various cals., 100 mfg. 1989 only.

	$3,195	$2,650	$2,100	$1,650	$1,375	$1,150	$875	

INVESTOR SERIES – various cals., 100 mfg. 1989 only.

	$3,195	$2,650	$2,100	$1,650	$1,375	$1,150	$875	

ACCURACY LEGEND SERIES – various cals., similar to Jarrett Custom Rifle, except has many accuracy tune-ups incorporated as well as muzzle brake. 100 mfg. 1993 only.

	$3,495	$2,850	$2,300	$1,850	$1,500	$1,250	$995	*$3,495*

COUP de MAIM – various cals., similar to the Jarrett Custom Rifle, includes muzzle brake, matte black or Olive Drab finish, Model 70 style bolt release. 100 mfg. 1995 only.

	$2,750	$2,300	$1,800	$1,500	$1,250	$995	$775	*$3,495*

PRIVATE COLLECTION – various cals., similar quality as the Jarrett Custom Rifle, except many extra cost special order options are included, ser. numbered 1-100. Mfg. 1994 only.

	$3,495	$2,850	$2,300	$1,850	$1,500	$1,250	$995	*$3,495*

SILENT PARTNER SERIES – various cals., only 10 mfg. 1994 only.

	$3,495	$2,850	$2,300	$1,850	$1,500	$1,250	$995	

ULTIMATE HUNTER SERIES – various cals., 100 mfg. 1989 only.

	$3,495	$2,850	$2,300	$1,850	$1,500	$1,250	$995	

REVOLUTION SERIES RIFLE – various cals., Remington-style action, Jarrett hand-lapped barrel, adj. trigger, Jarrett custom stock, extended bolt knob, all-weather coating, muzzle brake, load development, and Picatinny rail (optional). New 2017.

Please contact the company directly for pricing and availability.

SHIKAR RIFLE – various cals., hand lapped barrel with 1/10th of 1/1000th deviation, muzzle brake, Shilen or Jewell trigger, checkered American black walnut stock, available in English, Estate, or Grand Classic stocks, trapdoor floorplate, Jarrett Tri-Lock left or right-hand receiver, decelerator recoil pad, rings and bases by Talley Mfg. Inc., 8 lbs.

Base price for this model is $10,320 (includes muzzle brake, decelerator pad, hand checkering, and trapdoor).

RIFLES: RIMFIRE, SEMI-AUTO

SQUIRREL KING – .22 LR cal., reworked Ruger 10/22 action, 18 in. barrel, McMillan or Brown Precision synthetic stock. Mfg. 1999-2003.

	$900	$700	$575	$475	$425	$375	325	*$1,800*

Add $195 for Target King variation.

SHOTGUNS: SLIDE ACTION

JARRETT ULTIMATE SHOTGUN – 12 ga., Remington Model 870 action with 21 in. hand lapped barrel with interchangeable chokes, 8 shot mag. extension, matte black or OD Green finish. Disc. 1999.

	$900	$825	$675	$550	$450	$350	$295	*$1,000*

JEAN-MARC STEVAUX, S.P.R.L.

Current custom gun manufacturer located in Malonne, Belgium.

Jean-Marc Stevaux builds high quality custom order long guns. Currently, he does not have a U.S. importer. For more information, including pricing, availability, delivery time and variety of options, please contact him directly.

JEFFERY, W.J. & CO. LTD

Current manufacturer/trademark established in 1888, and currently manufactured in the UK. During 2000-2010, Jeffery was exclusively manufactured by J. Roberts & Son (Gunmakers) Ltd., located in West Sussex, U.K. Currently imported by Buehler Custom Sporting Arms located in Medford, OR.

W.J. Jeffery currently manufactures shotguns, double rifles, and bolt action rifles. Many options are available, including calibers, special engraving, etc. Please contact the importer directly for more information, including pricing, delivery time and availability.

In addition to making a complete line of their own shotguns and rifles, W.J. Jeffery also was subcontracted by many other exporters, distributors, and retailers, including London's famous Army & Navy department store (see separate listing). Many models were produced and, rather than list them individually, a generalized format has been adopted for determining values on both discontinued rifles and shotguns.

Current MSRs do not include English VAT.

RIFLES: CURRENT MFG.

BOLT ACTION RIFLE – various cals. between .243 Win. - .500 Jeffery, manufactured with both original Mauser actions and recent production (non-Mauser mfg.) actions, other commercial actions are available upon request.

Please contact the importer directly for current availability and pricing.

SxS MODEL – standard cals. are 9.3x74R, .375 H&H, .470 NE, or .500 Jeffery, choice of boxlock or sidelock action, ejectors, includes deep scroll engraving and case.

Please contact the importer directly for current availability and pricing.

RIFLES: DISC.

SINGLE SHOT – various cals., falling block action, checkered walnut stock and forearm, usually multiple folding leaves rear sight (also tangent), excellent quality.

Prices start in the $750 range for poor condition specimens in obsolete or undesirable cals. and can go up to $6,500 for 100% condition in .600 Nitro Express.

Subtract substantially for the Martini action variation.

BOXLOCK DOUBLE RIFLE – many cals., various engraving patterns, top or under (usually large cals.) lever opening, multiple folding leaves rear sight, checkered walnut stock and forearm.

Prices usually start in the $1,750 range for poor condition in undesirable cals. and can exceed $10,000 if encountered with elaborate engraving in .475 Express or larger cals.

Subtract approx. 40% if with hammers, over 50% if with damascus barrels.

SIDELOCK DOUBLE RIFLE – various cals., available in No. 1 or No. 2 grade, top-lever opening, best quality engraving, deluxe checkered walnut stock and forearm, almost any custom order could be filled.

Prices start in the $7,500 range for 60% condition in smaller cals. and can easily go to $25,000+ when found in excellent condition in the larger cals.

Subtract approx. 40% if with hammers, over 50% if with damascus barrels.

SHOTGUNS: CURRENT MFG.

Please contact the company directly for more information on currently manufactured W.J. Jeffery shotguns, including the sidelock ejector models, and the London finished SxS and O/U Italian and Spanish shotguns manufactured under J. Roberts & Son patterns.

SXS SIDELOCK MODEL – 12 or 20 ga., choice of H&H self-opening style or Beesley/Purdey action, deep scroll engraving is standard.

Please contact the importer directly for current availability and pricing.

SHOTGUNS: SxS, DISC.

BOXLOCK SHOTGUN – most ga., many combinations of options available, top-lever opening, many ranges of engraving, high quality and worksmanship.

Values usually start in the $950 range if in poor condition and can go to $5,500+ if in a small ga. in near new condition.

Subtract approx. 40% if with hammers, over 50% if with damascus barrels.

GRADING - PPGS™	100%	98%	95%	90%	80%	70%	60%	LAST MSR

SIDELOCK SHOTGUN – most ga., many combinations of options available, top-lever opening, many ranges of engraving, high quality and worksmanship.

Values usually start in the $2,250 range if in poor condition and can go to $20,000+ if in a small ga. in near new condition.

JEFFERY SHARPS

Previous rifle configuration manufactured by Ballard Arms located in Onsted, MI until 2016. Previously located in Cody, WY 1996-2009.

The original Jeffery Sharps was crafted during the late 1880s by W.J. Jeffery of London, and was based on the Winchester Model 1885.

New guns built in Cody are based on the original design and will come in calibers from .400 Jeffery to .577 NE. Pricing is POR. Please contact Ballard Arms directly for more information, including a price quotation and delivery time.

JENNINGS FIREARMS

Previous trademark and distributor established 1978 and located in City of Industry, CA until 1985. Jennings was a brand name for Bryco Arms, and was also the exclusive distributor for Bryco. Jennings also distributed Sundance and Accu-Tek.

PISTOLS: SEMI-AUTO

MODEL J-22 – .22 LR cal., 6 shot, single action, 2 1/2 in. barrel, positive safety locks sear, satin nickel, bright chrome or black Teflon finish, 13 oz. Disc. 1985.

	100%	98%	95%	90%	80%	70%	60%	LAST MSR
	$75	$55	$45	$35	$30	$30	$30	*$79*

JERICHO (CURRENT MFG.)

Current trademark of pistols manufactured by IWI Ltd., and currently imported by IWI US, Inc., located in Middletown, PA. Dealer and distributor sales.

Please contact the importer for more information, availability, and pricing on current models.

PISTOLS: SEMI-AUTO

On the following models, add approx. $124 for pistol kit (includes hardshell case, Mepro Tritium sights, J-Gear Kit w/UpLula).

PL POLYMER FRAME 910/4010 SERIES – 9mm Para. or .40 S&W cal., DA/SA, blowback action, polymer frame, 4.4 in. barrel, 10 shot mag., adj. sights, black finger groove grips, features lower Picatinny rail in front of squared off trigger guard, matte black finish, includes carrying case, 28 oz. Imported 2016-disc.

	100%	98%	95%	90%	80%	70%	60%	LAST MSR
	$475	$425	$375	$325	$295	$275	$250	*$559*

* ***PSL-910/PSL-4010*** – 9mm Para. or .40 S&W cal., DA/SA, blowback action, medium frame, 3.8 in. barrel, 10 shot mag., adj. sights, black finger groove grips, features lower Picatinny rail in front of squared off trigger guard, matte black finish, includes carrying case, 28 oz. New 2016.

	100%	98%	95%	90%	80%	70%	60%
MSR $559	$475	$425	$375	$325	$295	$275	$250

* ***FS-910/FS-4010*** – 9mm Para., .40 S&W cal., DA/SA, blowback action, steel frame, 4.4 in. barrel, 10 shot mag., adj. sights, features lower Picatinny rail in front of squared off trigger guard, matte black finish, includes carrying case, approx. 36 oz. New 2016.

	100%	98%	95%	90%	80%	70%	60%
MSR $655	$575	$495	$450	$375	$325	$295	$275

PL POLYMER FRAME 941 SERIES

* ***PL-9/PL-40*** – 9mm Para. or .40 S&W cal., DA/SA, blowback action, polymer frame, 4.4 in. barrel, 12 or 16 shot mag., adj. sights, black finger groove grips, features lower Picatinny rail in front of squared off trigger guard, matte black finish, includes carrying case, 28 oz. New 2015.

	100%	98%	95%	90%	80%	70%	60%
MSR $559	$475	$425	$375	$325	$295	$275	$250

* ***PSL-9/PSL-40*** – 9mm Para. or .40 S&W cal., DA/SA, blowback action, polymer frame, 3.8 in. barrel, 12 or 16 shot mag., adj. sights, black finger groove grips, features lower Picatinny rail in front of squared off trigger guard, matte black finish, includes carrying case, 25.5 oz. New 2015.

	100%	98%	95%	90%	80%	70%	60%
MSR $559	$475	$425	$375	$325	$295	$275	$250

F STEEL FRAME 941 SERIES

* ***F-9/F-40*** – 9mm Para. or .40 S&W (disc.) cal., DA/SA, blowback action, short recoil, steel frame, 4.4 in. cold hammer forged barrel, 12 (.40 S&W cal., disc.) or 16 shot mag., adj. sights, features lower Picatinny rail in front of squared off trigger guard, matte black finish, includes carrying case, 2.3 lbs. New 2015.

	100%	98%	95%	90%	80%	70%	60%
MSR $655	$575	$495	$450	$375	$325	$295	$275

GRADING - PPGS™	100%	98%	95%	90%	80%	70%	60%	LAST MSR

* ***FS-9/FS-40/FS-45*** – 9mm Para., .40 S&W, or .45 ACP cal., DA/SA, blowback action, steel frame, 3.8 in. barrel, 10 (.45 ACP), 12 (.40 S&W) or 16 (9mm Para) shot mag., adj. sights, features lower Picatinny rail in front of squared off trigger guard, matte black finish, includes carrying case, approx. 36 oz. New 2015.

MSR $655	$575	$495	$450	$375	$325	$295	$275	

* ***F-910/F-4010*** – 9mm Para. or .40 S&W cal., DA/SA, blowback action, steel frame, 4.4 in. barrel, 10 shot mag., adj. sights, features lower Picatinny rail in front of squared off trigger guard, matte black finish, includes carrying case, 36.8 oz. New 2016.

MSR $655	$575	$495	$450	$375	$325	$295	$275	

JERICHO (PREVIOUS MFG.)

Previous trademark of Israel Military Industries (I.M.I.). Previously imported by K.B.I., Inc. located in Harrisburg, PA.

PISTOLS: SEMI-AUTO

JERICHO 941 – 9mm Para. cal. or .41 Action Express (by conversion only) cal., DA/SA, 4.72 in. barrel with polygonal rifling, all steel fabrication, 3-dot Tritium sights, 11 or 16 (9mm Para.) shot mag., ambidextrous safety, polymer grips, decocking lever, 38 1/2 oz. Imported 1990-1992.

	$625	$550	$475	$425	$375	$325	$295	*$649*

Add $299 for .41 AE conversion kit.

Industrial hard chrome or nickel finishes were also available for all Jericho pistols.

* ***Jericho 941 Pistol Package*** – includes 9mm Para. and .41 AE conversion kit, cased with accessories. Mfg. 1990-91 only.

	$850	$775	$700	$625	$575	$495	$450	*$775*

JESSE JAMES FIREARMS UNLIMITED

Current manufacturer/customizer of AR-15 style rifles and pistols, 1911 style pistols, bolt action rifles, and silencers located in Dripping Springs, TX.

For individual model listings, please go to BlueBookOfGunValues.com/overflow.

JIEFFECO

Please refer to the Melior - Robar & Co. listing in the M section.

JIMENEZ ARMS INC.

Previous manufacturer located in Henderson, NV until fall 2020. Previously located in Costa Mesa, CA until 2005. Distributed by Shining Star Investments, LLC, located in Lewisville, TX.

Paul Jimenez, former plant manager of Bryco Arms, bought the remaining assets of Bryco in 2004. In February 2020, Jimenez Arms filed for bankruptcy and all assests were transferred to JA Industries, which resumed operations.

SEMI-AUTO PISTOLS

JA-NINE – 9mm Para. cal., SA, 3 3/4 in. barrel, 10 or 12 shot mag., high visibility front sight, adj. rear sight, magazine out safety, thumb operated mag. release, red cocked indicator, 30 oz. Disc. 2020.

	$175	$150	$125	$110	$100	$90	$85	*$199*

JA-.22LR/JA-.25 AUTO – .22 LR or .25 Auto cal., SA, compact size, 2 1/2 in. barrel, 6 shot mag., manual safety, fixed sights, easy recoil, cocking indicator, 13 oz. Disc. 2020.

	$125	$110	$95	$85	$75	$65	$55	*$149*

JA-.32 – .32 ACP cal., compact size, 2 3/4 in. barrel, fixed sights, extended mag. base, cocking indicator, 19 oz. Disc.

Retail pricing was not available for this model.

JA-.380 – .380 ACP cal., compact size, 2 3/4 in. barrel, 6 shot mag., fixed sights, extended finger rest, extended mag. base, 19 oz. Disc. 2020.

	$130	$115	$100	$90	$80	$70	$60	*$159*

JA-.380LC – .380 ACP cal., compact, 3 3/4 in. barrel, 10 or 30 shot mag., high visibility red front sight, screw adj. rear sight, magazine out safety, thumb operated mag. release, cocking indicator, chamber indicator, 30 oz.

Retail pricing was not available for this model.

JOHANNSEN RIFLES

Please refer to Reimer Johannsen GmbH listing in the R section.

JOHNSON AUTOMATICS, INC.

Previous manufacturer located in Providence, RI. Johnson Automatics, Inc. moved many times during its history, often with slight name changes. M.M. Johnson, Jr. died in 1965, and the company continued production at 104 Audubon Street in New Haven, CT as Johnson Arms, Inc., mostly specializing in sporter semi-auto rifles with Monte Carlo stocks in .270 Win. or .30-06 cal.

RIFLES: SEMI-AUTO

MODEL 1941 – .30-06 or 7x57mm cal., 22 in. removable air cooled barrel, recoil operated, perforated metal handguard, aperture sight, military stock. Most were made for Dutch military, some used by U.S. Marine Paratroopers, during WWII all .30-06 and 7x57mm were ordered by South American governments.

100%	98%	95%	90%	80%	70%	60%
$7,350	$6,750	$6,000	$5,250	$4,500	$3,950	$3,250

MilTech offers a restored version of this model. Inspect this model carefully for originality before considering a possible purchase. Values are somewhat lower for restored guns.

J. JONGMANS ARMS COMPANY PTY. LTD.

Previous manufacturer established circa 1979-1980 through 1993, and located in Hikutaia, New Zealand from 1979-1986, and Ipswich, Queensland, Australia from 1987-1993.

J. Jongmans was founded by Dutch-born John Jongmans. He built custom rifles, and manufactured a line of high quality rifles, actions, and barrels. Early bolt action receivers, whether octagonal or round, were made from the same (octagonal) investment castings and had a high parts rejection rate. Later receivers and bolt bodies were fully machined on CNC equipment.

Jongmans also built Miller (formerly De-Haas Miller) single shot rifles and actions under license. The late Dean Miller had contracted with Jongmans to supply approx. 150 actions, but investment casting again proved to be a problem with quality. Miller only made approx. 10-15 rifles with Jongmans' actions. Approx. 200 actions were made under the Jongmans brand, and most ended up in New Zealand or Australia.

Jongmans also supplied Farquharson-type single shot actions to the Farquharson Rifle Company of Melbourne, Australia. One completed rifle was purchased by Holland and Holland of London.

During 2009-2010, John Jongmans assembled a few Miller-type rifles using leftover parts. Any Jongmans gun should be evaluated individually for its features and shootability.

J. JONGMANS ARMS COMPANY

Current rifle manufacturer established in 2014, located in Karana Downs, Queensland, Australia.

RIFLES

Jongmans currently offers bolt action rifles in both right and left-hand configurations in rimfire calibers ranging from .17 Mach 2 to .17 HMR and in centerfire calibers ranging from .17 Rem. to .458 Win. Mag. The company also manufactures De-Haas Miller-type falling block single shot and Farquharson-type falling block rifles.

Please refer to the J. Jongmans Arms Company Pty. Ltd. listing for information regarding older manufacture.

JUCH-GRUND JAGDWAFFEN INH. KARL GRUND

Please refer to Grund, Karl in the G section.

JUGGERNAUT TACTICAL

Current AR-15 style firearm and accessories manufacturer located in Orange, CA. Dealer and consumer direct sales through FFL.

Please refer to BlueBookOfGunValues.com to order the *Blue Book of AR-15s & Variations*, available as a book or online subscription.

JUNG, WAFFEN, GMBH

Please refer to the Waffen Jung GmbH listing in the W section.

JURRAS, LEE E.

Previous custom pistolsmith located in Hagerman, New Mexico. Howdah pistols were distributed by J & G Sales located in Prescott, AZ.

Ammunition for Jurras pistols was manufactured by Robert Davis, Jr. located in Athens, TN.

GRADING - PPGS™	100%	98%	95%	90%	80%	70%	60%	LAST MSR

Lee Jurras was the founder and president of Super Vel Cartridge Corporation. Mr. Jurras also made custom AutoMags (see AutoMag section). He established the Outstanding American Handgunner Awards, and was a pioneer of the first metallic silhouette shooting matches.

PISTOLS

100 LEJ Howdah pistols were custom built in the late 1970s. The action was based on the Thompson/Center Contender receiver. Almost any caliber, barrel length, finish, and stock was available by special order. Original MSR was approx. $800.

HOWDAH - most common in .375, .416, .460, .475, .500, or .577 Jurras cals., action based on Thompson/Center Contender receiver, 12 in. bull barrel, satin nickel, nickel, or blue finish, adj. rear sight, ebony, mesquite, or walnut stocks, special order serial number range from 001-100, limited mfg. (100).

* ***Howdah Custom Grade***

	100%	98%	95%	90%	80%	70%	60%	LAST MSR
Howdah Custom Grade	$1,150	$925	$800	$725	$650	$575	$500	

* ***Howdah Presentation Grade*** - .375 Jurras or .460 Jurras cals. standard, deluxe Claro walnut stock and forearm.

	100%	98%	95%	90%	80%	70%	60%	LAST MSR
Howdah Presentation Grade	$2,000	$1,750	$1,500	$1,250	$1,050	$950	$825	

Special order .416, .475, .500, or .577 Jurras calibers command a premium on this model.

JUST, JOSEF

Current custom long gun manufacturer and gunsmith established in 1790, located in Ferlach, Austria.

Josef Just was a member of the Ferlach Guild until it was dissolved in 2004, and manufactures a variety of high quality long gun configurations (including SxSs, O/Us, Drillings, vierlings, combination guns, and single shot), all to custom order. Delivery time is up to three years. Please contact Mr. Just directly for more information and an individual price quotation.

J. SIP & SONS (JUSTIN SIP CUSTOM GUNS)

Current custom rifle manufacturer established in 2008, located in Toquerville, UT.

J. Sip & Sons specializes in hand carved wood stocks. They also do custom Cerakote on firearms and fiberglass stocks. Please contact the company directly for information and availability.

RIFLES: CUSTOM

Justin Sip Custom Guns builds both single shot and bolt action rifles, including a takedown bolt action in various cals. The standard bolt gun has a base price of $12,900, the Safari bolt gun has a base price of $14,900, the large bore Safari bolt gun has a base price of $15,900, a barrel takedown option is $1,800, and additional barrels are $2,400 each, quarter rib and express sights are $1,250. Upgrade options are POR. Please contact the company directly for more information, a quotation, and delivery time.

JUST RIGHT CARBINES

Current trademark of pistols and carbines established in 2011, and manufactured in Canandaigua, NY. Dealer and distributor sales. Currently distributed by LDB Supply LLC located in Dayton, OH. Previously distributed by American Tactical Imports (ATI), located in Rochester, NY, and by E.M.F., located in Santa Ana, CA.

Please refer to BlueBookOfGunValues.com to order the *Blue Book of AR-15s & Variations*, available as a book or online subscription.

K SECTION

K.B.I., INC.

Previous importer and distributor located in Harrisburg, PA until Jan. 29, 2010. Distributor sales.

K.B.I., Inc. imported Charles Daly semi-auto pistols, Bul Transmark semi-auto pistols, SA revolvers, AR-15 style rifles, and shotguns in many configurations, including O/U, SxS, semi-auto, lever action, and slide action. K.B.I. also imported Armscor (Arms Corp. of the Philippines), FEG pistols, and Liberty revolvers and SxS coach shotguns. These models may be found within their respective alphabetical sections. K.B.I. previously imported the Jericho pistol manufactured by I.M.I. from Israel. Older imported Jericho pistols may be found under its own heading in this text, and more recently imported pistols are listed under the Charles Daly listing.

GRADING - PPGS™	100%	98%	95%	90%	80%	70%	60%	LAST MSR

RIFLES: BOLT ACTION

KASSNAR GRADE I – available in 9 cals., GIO, thumb safety that locks trigger, with or w/o deluxe sights, 22 in. barrel, 3 or 4 shot mag., includes swivel posts and oil finished standard grade European walnut with recoil pad, 7 1/2 lbs. Imported 1989-93.

	100%	98%	95%	90%	80%	70%	60%	LAST MSR
	$445	$385	$325	$275	$225	$195	$175	*$499*

NYLON 66 - .22 LR cal., GIO, patterned after the Remington Nylon 66. Imported until 1990 from C.B.C. in Brazil, South America.

	100%	98%	95%	90%	80%	70%	60%	LAST MSR
	$125	$110	$95	$85	$75	$70	$65	*$134*

MODEL 122 - .22 LR cal., GIO, bolt action design with mag. Imported from South America until 1990.

	100%	98%	95%	90%	80%	70%	60%	LAST MSR
	$125	$110	$95	$85	$75	$70	$65	*$136*

MODEL 522 - .22 LR cal., GIO, bolt action design with tube mag. Imported from South America until 1990.

	100%	98%	95%	90%	80%	70%	60%	LAST MSR
	$130	$115	$100	$85	$75	$70	$65	*$142*

BANTAM SINGLE SHOT - .22 LR cal., GIO, youth dimensions. Imported 1989-90 only.

	100%	98%	95%	90%	80%	70%	60%	LAST MSR
	$110	$90	$85	$75	$70	$65	$60	*$120*

SHOTGUNS

GRADE I O/U - 12, 20, 28 ga., or .410 bore, GIO, gold plated SST, extractors, vent. rib, checkered walnut stock and forearm. Imported 1989-93.

	100%	98%	95%	90%	80%	70%	60%	LAST MSR
	$525	$425	$350	$295	$265	$240	$220	*$599*

Add $70 for 28 ga. or .410 bore.
Add $50 for choke tubes (12 and 20 ga. only).
Add $150 for automatic ejectors (with choke tubes only).

GRADE II SxS - 10, 12, 16, 20, 28 ga., or .410 bore, boxlock action, GIO, case hardened receiver, English style checkered European walnut stock with splinter forearm, chrome barrels with concave rib, extractors, double hinged triggers. Imported 1989-90 only.

	100%	98%	95%	90%	80%	70%	60%	LAST MSR
	$515	$435	$375	$325	$275	$250	$225	*$575*

Add $95 for 28 ga. or .410 bore.
Add $85 for 10 ga.

KDF, INC.

Previous rifle manufacturer until circa 2007 and current custom riflesmith specializing in restocking and installing muzzle brakes, in addition to supplying specialized rifle parts. Located in Seguin, TX. KDF utilized Mauser K-15 actions imported from Oberndorf, Germany for many rifle models. Previously, KDF rifles were manufactured by Voere (until 1987) in Vöhrenbach, W. Germany.

For individual model listings, please go to BlueBookOfGunValues.com/overflow.

KE ARMS

Current manufacturer of complete AR-15 style pistols, rifles, and AR-15 accessories located in Phoenix, AZ.

Please refer to BlueBookOfGunValues.com to order the *Blue Book of AR-15s & Variations*, available as a book or online subscription.

K.F.C.

Previously manufactured by Kawaguchiya Firearms Co., Ltd. Previously imported and distributed by La Paloma Marketing, Inc. located in Tucson, AZ.

GRADING - PPGS™	100%	98%	95%	90%	80%	70%	60%	LAST MSR

SHOTGUNS

MODEL 250 SEMI-AUTO – 12 ga. only, incorporates a patented, cushioned piston assembly, 26, 28, or 30 in. barrel, matte blue finish, vent. rib standard, checkered premium walnut, 7 lbs. Manufactured 1980-86.

	$360	$290	$270	$250	$235	$220	$205	*$485*

Add $60 for multi-chokes.

* ***Model 250 Semi-Auto Deluxe*** – same specifications as Model 250, except has scrolled acid etching panels on both sides of normally black receiver. Disc. 1986.

	$395	$310	$290	$270	$250	$225	$210	*$520*

FIELD GUN O/U – 12 ga. only, VR, premium grade walnut, semi pistol grip stock, F&IC chokes. Disc. 1986.

	$645	$565	$530	$495	$470	$445	$410	*$748*

E-1 TRAP OR SKEET O/U – 12 ga. only, VR, oil finished premium grade walnut, semi pistol grip stock, engraved. Disc. 1986.

	$935	$800	$750	$700	$625	$550	$495	*$1,070*

E-2 TRAP OR SKEET O/U – 12 ga. only, VR, oil finished premium grade walnut, semi pistol grip stock, detailed engraving. Disc. 1986.

	$1,450	$1,250	$1,075	$950	$850	$750	$650	*$1,660*

K&M ARMS

Current firearms manufacturer located in Chandler, AZ.

For individual model listings, please go to BlueBookOfGunValues.com/overflow.

KSN INDUSTRIES LTD.

Previous distributor (1952-1996) located in Houston, TX. Previously imported until 1996 exclusively by J.O. Arms, Inc. located in Houston, TX. Currently manufactured Israel Arms, Ltd. pistols may be found under their individual listing.

PISTOLS: SEMI-AUTO

The pistols listed were mfg. by Israel Arms, Ltd.

KAREEN MK I – 9mm Para. cal., patterned after the Browning HP, round or spur hammer, blue finish, wood grips, limited importation by Jo Lo Arms.

	$725	$650	$575	$500	$425	$350	$275	

KAREEN MK II – 9mm Para. or .40 S&W (new late 1994) cal., SA, 4.64 in. barrel, two-tone finish, rubberized grips, regular or Meprolite sights, 10 (C/B 1994), 13*, or 15* shot mag., 33 oz. Imported 1993-1996.

	$400	$305	$255	$225	$200	$185	$170	*$411*

Add approx. $160 for two-tone finish with Meprolite sights.

* ***Kareen Mk II Compact*** – compact variation with 3.85 in. barrel. Imported 1993-96.

	$415	$360	$315	$255	$225	$200	$185	*$497*

GOLAN MODEL – 9mm Para. or .40 S&W cal., single or double action, ambidextrous safety with decocking feature, steel slide with alloy frame, 3 7/8 in. barrel, matte black finish, 29 oz. Imported 1994-96.

	$565	$515	$460	$410	$360	$330	$295	*$650*

Add $35 for .40 S&W cal.

K-VAR CORP.

Current importer located in Las Vegas, NV. MSR Distribution is the distributor for K-Var Corp.

K-VAR Corp. currently distributes Saiga rifles and shotguns, in addition to importing select Zastava bolt action rifles and pistols, Vepr rifles mfg. by Molot, Arsenal Inc. SLR series, AK-47 design rifles and an RPK milled rifle. Additionally, K-Var Corp. manufactures a Model SA M-7 SFK AK-47 design rifle in the U.S. See separate listings for Saiga rifles/shotguns, Zastava bolt action rifles, Vepr rifles, Arsenal, and the RPK model. Please contact the company directly for availability and pricing.

GRADING - PPGS™	100%	98%	95%	90%	80%	70%	60%	LAST MSR

KAHR ARMS

Current manufacturer established in 1993 with corporate headquarters located in Greeley, PA. Previously located in Blauvelt, NY. Manufacturing is also located in Greeley, PA. Previously located in Worchester, MA.

Kahr order number nomenclature is as follows:

M= Steel frame, 3-3.1 in. barrel, PM= Polymer frame, 3.1-3.24 in. barrel, KP= Polymer frame, 3.54-3.6, 2.53 in. barrel, K= Steel frame, 3.465-3.5 in. barrel, TP=Polymer frame, 3.965-4.04 in. barrel, KT= Steel frame, 3.965-4 in. barrel,CM= Polymer frame, 3-3.14 in. barrel, CW= Polymer frame, 3.65-3.64 in. barrel, CT= Polymer frame, 4-4.04 in. barrel.

First three numbers - 383= .380 ACP, 909= 9mm, 919= 9mm with External Safety, 404= .40 S&W, 414= .40 S&W with External Safety, 454= .45 ACP.

4th number - 0= Carbon steel, black oxide (disc.), 1= Carbon steel, nickel finish (disc.), 2= Carbon steel, black T finish (disc.), 3= Matte stainless steel, 4= Blackened stainless steel, 6= Polished stainless steel, Elite98 (disc.), 8= Polished stainless steel, Elite.

Letters at end - A= Required for certain older inventory items, N= Tritium night sights, NOVAK= Novak low profile Tritium night sights

PISTOLS: SEMI-AUTO

All premium Kahr pistols are supplied with three magazines, hard polymer case, trigger lock, and five-year warranty. The premium pistols feature Lothar Walther polygonal rifled match grade barrels.

All value series Kahr pistols (CM, CW, CT) are supplied with one magazine, trigger lock, are shipped in a cardboard box, and have a five-year warranty.

CM9 – 9mm Para. cal., DAO, compact design, polymer frame with black or Kryptek Camo (new 2017) finish, 3 in. barrel, 6 shot mag., matte stainless, Cerakote Burnt Bronze (mfg. 2017 only), or Cerakote Armor Black (Kryptek Camo frame only, new 2017) slide, adj. white bar-dot combat sights, adj. white bar-dot day rear and pinned in polymer front night sight (new 2016), or adj. white two-dot rear and pinned in polymer front sights, textured polymer grips, 14 oz. New 2011.

MSR $499 $425 $375 $325 $295 $235 $195 $165

Add $34 for rear day and front night sights (new 2016).
Add $39 for Cerakote Burnt Bronze slide (mfg. 2017 only).
Add $42 for Kryptek camo finished polymer frame and Cerakote Armor Black slide (new 2017).

* ***CM9 Tungsten*** – 9mm Para. cal., DAO, compact, black polymer frame, 3 in. barrel, 6 shot mag., stainless steel slide, white 3-dot sights, Pachmayr tactical grip glove, Pearce finger rest extension, Tungsten Cerakote finish on slide, trigger, and slide stop lever. Mfg. 2017 only.

$425 $375 $325 $295 $235 $195 $165 *$499*

CM40 – .40 S&W cal., 3 in. barrel, black polymer frame with matte stainless slide, CW configuration, includes one mag. Mfg. 2012-2020.

$395 $350 $300 $275 $215 $185 $150 *$460*

Add $39 for LaserMax optics (disc.).

CM45 – .45 ACP cal., DAO, 3.24 in. barrel, black polymer frame, 5 shot mag., matte stainless steel or Cerakote Armor Black (CM45 exclusive, mfg. 2018 only) slide, drift adj. white bar-dot combat rear sight, pinned in polymer front sight, black textured polymer grip, 17.3 oz. New 2013.

MSR $499 $425 $375 $325 $295 $235 $195 $165

Add $27 for Armor Black slide (mfg. 2018 only).

* ***CM45 Tungsten*** – .45 ACP cal., black polymer frame, 3 1/4 in. barrel, 5 shot mag., white 3-dot sights, Pachmayr Tactical Grip Glove, Pearce finger rest extension, Tungsten Cerakote finish on slide, trigger, and slide stop lever. Mfg. 2017 only.

$425 $375 $325 $295 $235 $195 $165 *$499*

CT380 – .380 ACP cal., DAO, 3 in. barrel, 7 shot mag., black polymer frame, matte stainless steel or gold (mfg. 2018-2020) slide, adj. combat rear sight, pinned in polymer front sight, textured black polymer grip, 11.44 oz. New 2015.

MSR $433 $365 $320 $275 $250 $200 $165 $145

Add $6 for gold slide and trigger (mfg. 2018-2020).

GRADING - PPGS™	100%	98%	95%	90%	80%	70%	60%	LAST MSR

* ***CT380 Tungsten*** – .380 ACP cal., DAO, black polymer frame, 3 in. barrel, 7 shot mag., matte stainless steel slide, white 3-dot sights, with or w/o Pachmayr Tactical Grip Glove, Pearce finger rest extension, Tungsten Cerakote finish on slide, trigger, and slide stop lever, 11.44 oz. Mfg. 2017, reintroduced 2019-2020.

	$350	$300	$265	$240	$195	$160	$135	*$419*

Add $20 for Pachmayr Tactical Grip Glove.

CT9 – 9mm Para. cal., DAO, 4 in. barrel, 8 shot mag., polymer frame with black, black carbon fiber print (mfg. 2017-2020), or Kryptek Camo (new 2017) finish, matte stainless steel or Cerakote Armor Black (with Kryptek camo only, new 2017) slide, "Browning-type" recoil lug, passive striker block, no magazine disconnect, black textured polymer grips, drift adj. white bar-dot combat rear and pinned in polymer front sights or rear day and front night sights (new 2016), 18.5 oz. New 2015.

MSR $465	$395	$350	$295	$275	$215	$180	$160	

Add $34 for rear day and front night sights (new 2016).
Add $42 for Kryptek Camo finished polymer frame and Cerakote Armor Black slide (new 2017).
Add $36 for polymer frame with black carbon fiber print finish (mfg. 2017-2020).

CT40 – .40 S&W cal., 4 in. barrel, black polymer frame, matte stainless steel slide, CW configuration, ships in cardboard box with one mag. Mfg. 2014-2020.

	$385	$335	$290	$260	$210	$175	$145	*$449*

CT45 – .45 ACP cal., 4.04 in. barrel, black polymer frame, matte stainless steel slide, CW configuration, ships in cardboard box with one mag. New 2014.

MSR $465	$395	$350	$295	$275	$215	$180	$160	

CW380 – .380 ACP cal., polymer frame with black, black carbon fiber print (mfg. 2017-2020), or Kryptek Camo (new 2017) finish, 2 5/8 in. barrel, 6 shot mag., matte stainless steel, Burnt Bronze, or Cerakote Armor Black (new 2017, Kryptek Camo frame only) slide, with or without rear day sight and front night sight (new 2016), 10.2 oz. New 2013.

MSR $433	$365	$320	$275	$250	$200	$165	$145	

Add $32 for rear day sight and front night sight (new 2016).
Add $42 for black carbon fiber print or Kryptek Camo (new 2017).
Add $20 for Cerakote Burnt Bronze slide, black trigger, and slide stop lever (mfg. 2017 only).

* ***CW380 Tungsten*** – .380 ACP cal., black polymer frame, 2 5/8 in. barrel, 6 shot mag., white 3-dot sights, with or w/o Pachmayr Tactical Grip Glove, Pearce finger rest extension, Tungsten Cerakote finish on slide, trigger, and slide stop lever. Mfg. 2017 only.

	$350	$300	$265	$240	$195	$160	$125	*$419*

Add $20 for Pachmayr Tactical Grip Glove.

CW9 – 9mm Para. cal., DAO, 3.6 in. barrel, polymer frame with black or Kryptek Camo (new 2017) finish, matte stainless steel, Cerakote Burnt Bronze (new 2017), or Cerakote Armor Black (w/Kryptek frame, new 2017) slide, 7 shot mag., textured polymer grips, adj. rear sight, pinned in polymer front sight, white dot combat sights or rear day and front night sights (new 2016), 15.8 oz. New 2005.

MSR $483	$410	$360	$310	$280	$225	$185	$160	

Add $32 for rear day and front night sights (new 2016).
Add $32 for Cerakote Burnt Bronze slide, black trigger, and slide stop lever (new 2017).
Add $40 for Kryptek Camo finish on polymer frame and Cerakote Armor Black slide (new 2017).

* ***CW9 Carbon Fiber*** – 9mm Para. cal., polymer frame with carbon fiber print with Soft Touch, 3.6 in. barrel, 7 shot, matte stainless slide, white 3-dot sights, 15.8 oz. New 2016.

MSR $515	$440	$385	$330	$300	$240	$195	$170	

CW40 – .40 S&W cal., DAO, 3.6 in. barrel, black polymer frame, matte stainless steel or Cerakote Burnt Bronze (mfg. 2017 only) slide, 6 shot mag., textured polymer grips, adj. rear sight, pinned in polymer front sight, white dot combat sights, 16.8 oz. Mfg. 2008-2020.

	$385	$335	$295	$260	$210	$175	$135	*$449*

Add $46 for Cerakote Burnt Bronze slide, black trigger, and slide stop lever (mfg. 2017 only).

CW45 – .45 ACP cal., DAO, 3.64 in. barrel, 6 shot mag., black polymer frame, matte stainless steel or Cerakote Burnt Bronze (mfg. 2017 only) slide, adj. rear sight, pinned in polymer front sight, white dot combat sights, textured polymer grips, 19.7 oz. New 2008.

MSR $483	$410	$360	$310	$280	$225	$185	$160	

Add $46 for Cerakote Burnt Bronze slide, black trigger, and slide stop lever (mfg. 2017 only).

E9 – 9mm Para. cal., economized version of the K9 Compact, matte black finish or duo-tone (new 2003), supplied with one mag. Mfg. 1997 only, reintroduced 2003 only.

	$425	$365	$335	$300	$280	$265	$250	*$490*

GRADING - PPGS™	100%	98%	95%	90%	80%	70%	60%	LAST MSR

K9 25TH ANNIVERSARY LIMITED EDITION – 9mm Para. cal., 3 1/2 in. brightly polished barrel w/ polygonal rifling, two 7 shot mags., one 8 shot mag., trigger-cocking DAO, TruGlo Tritium night sights, Hogue aluminum grips w/custom engraving, "Browning-type" recoil lug, passive striker block, no mag. disconnect, slide porting, includes matching custom 1791 leather holster and plastic case, engraved w/limited edition number, Sniper Grey Cerakote frame and slide, 23.1 oz. Only 500 mfg. 2019-2020.

	$1,500	$1,300	$1,100	$1,000	$825	$675	$550	*$1,649*

K9 COMPACT – 9mm Para. cal., trigger cocking, DAO with passive striker block, locked breech with "Browning-type" recoil lug, steel construction, 3 1/2 in. barrel with polygonal rifling, 7 shot mag., wraparound black polymer grips, matte black, black titanium (Black-T, mfg. 1997-98), or electroless nickel (mfg. 1996-99) finish, 25 oz. Mfg. 1993-2003.

	$560	$485	$435	$385	$340	$315	$285	*$648*

Add $74 for electroless nickel finish (disc.).
Add $126 for black titanium finish (Black-T, mfg. 1997-98).
Add $103 for Tritium night sights (new 1996).

* ***K9 Compact Economy*** – 9mm Para. cal., 3 1/2 in. barrel, black matte finish, shipped with one 7 shot mag. only. Limited mfg. 1999 only.

	$350	$300	$275	$250	$230	$210	$190	*$399*

* ***K9 Compact Stainless*** – 9mm Para. cal., 3 1/2 in. barrel, similar to K9 Compact, except is matte finished stainless steel, NYCPD specs became standard 2006 (trigger LOP is 1/2 in. compared to 3/8 in.). New 1998.

MSR $923	$790	$690	$595	$535	$435	$355	$300	

Add $39 for matte blackened stainless steel finish (new 2004).
Add $137 for Tritium night sights.

* ***K9 Compact Elite 98 Stainless*** – 9mm Para. cal., similar to K9 Compact, except has high polish stainless steel slide and specially designed combat trigger utilizing shorter trigger stroke, front strap checkering (new 2015). New 1998.

MSR $1,006	$850	$750	$640	$580	$470	$380	$330	

Add $128 for Tritium night sights.

* ***K9 Compact Wilson Custom Package*** – includes Wilson customizing with Metalloy hard chrome frame, black slide, checkered front strap and beveled magwell. Limited quantities mfg. 1998.

	$1,175	$995	$875	$775	$700	$625	$550	*$1,310*

* ***K9 Compact Kahr Lady*** – 9mm Para. cal., similar to K9 Compact, except has lightened recoil spring, not available in black titanium finish, 25 oz. Mfg. 1997-99.

	$480	$435	$395	$365	$315	$285	$250	*$545*

Add $74 for electroless nickel finish.
Add $85 for Tritium night sights.

KP9 GEN2 – 9mm Para. cal., black polymer frame, 3 1/2 in. barrel, 7 shot, matte stainless slide, short trigger with trigger safety, TruGlo TFX Tritium/fiber optic day/night sights, accessory rail, ships with three magazines and high impact polymer case. Mfg. 2015-2017.

	$825	$700	$625	$550	$485	$415	$370	*$976*

K40 COMPACT – .40 S&W cal., DAO, 3 1/2 in. barrel, 6 shot mag., locked breech with "Browning-type" recoil lug, wraparound black polymer grips, matte black or electroless nickel finish (disc. 1999), 26 oz. Mfg. 1997-2003.

	$560	$485	$435	$385	$340	$315	$285	*$648*

Add $103 for Tritium night sights.
Add $74 for electroless nickel finish (disc. 1999).
Add $126 for black titanium finish (Black-T, disc. 1998).

* ***K40 Compact Stainless*** – .40 S&W cal., DAO, 3 1/2 in. barrel, 6 shot mag., matte stainless steel, wraparound textured soft polymer black grips, drift adj. white bar-dot combat sights, "Browning-type" recoil lug, passive striker block, no magazine disconnect, 24.1 oz. Mfg. 1997-2020.

	$760	$650	$565	$510	$415	$340	$275	*$896*

Add $135 for Tritium night sights.
Add $37 for matte black stainless steel (new 2004).

* ***K40 Compact Elite 98 Stainless*** – .40 S&W cal., 3 1/2 in. barrel, similar to K40 Compact, except has high polish slide and specially designed combat trigger utilizing shorter trigger stroke, front strap checkering (new 2015). Mfg. 1998-2020.

	$835	$725	$625	$560	$450	$375	$300	*$976*

Add $125 for Tritium night sights.

GRADING - PPGS™ 100% 98% 95% 90% 80% 70% 60% LAST MSR

* ***K40 Compact Wilson Custom Package*** – .40 S&W cal., includes Wilson customizing with Metalloy hard chrome frame, black slide, checkered front strap, and beveled magwell. Limited quantities mfg. 1998.

$1,175 $995 $875 $775 $700 $625 $550 *$1,310*

* ***K40 Compact Covert Stainless (KS40 Small Frame)*** – .40 S&W cal., similar to Kahr Compact K40, except grip is 1/2 in. shorter, supplied with 5 and 6 shot mags., 25 oz. Mfg. 1998-2000.

$500 $440 $400 $335 $290 $245 $215 *$580*

Add $88 for Tritium night sights.

KP45 GEN2 – .45 ACP cal., 3 1/2 in. barrel, black polymer frame, 6 shot, matte stainless slide, accessory rail, short trigger with trigger safety, TruGlo TFX Tritium/fiber optic day/night sights. Mfg. 2015-2017.

$825 $700 $625 $550 $485 $415 $370 *$976*

KT9 (T9) – 9mm Para. cal., 4 in. barrel with polygonal rifling, matte stainless steel construction, checkered Hogue Pau Ferro wood grips, 8 shot mag., Elite 98 trigger, MMC (disc.), white bar-dot (new 2006), optional Novak low profile (disc.), or Tritium night sights, 28 oz. New 2002.

MSR $882 $750 $650 $550 $500 $400 $350 $285

Add $128 for Tritium night sights.

* ***KT9 Elite Stainless (T9 Elite Stainless)*** – 9mm Para. cal., DAO, 4 in. barrel, 8 shot, high polished stainless steel slide, Tritium night sights, checkered Hogue Pau Ferro wood grips, 26 oz. New 2018.

MSR $1,080 $915 $800 $685 $620 $500 $410 $360

MK9 MICRO SERIES – 9mm Para. cal., micro compact variation of the K9 Compact featuring 3 in. barrel, double action only with passive striker block, overall size is 4 in. H x 5 1/2 in. L, duo-tone finish with stainless frame and black titanium slide, includes two 6 shot flush floorplate mags. Mfg. 1998-99.

$650 $575 $515 $465 $425 $395 $375 *$749*

Add $85 for Tritium night sights.

* ***MK9 Micro Series Box*** – 9mm Para. cal., similar to MK9 Micro, except has matte stainless steel frame with steel matte black slide, duo-tone finish. Limited mfg. 2003-2005.

$400 $325 $285 $235 $200 $170 $145 *$475*

Add $100 for Tritium night sights (disc.).

* ***MK9 Micro Series Stainless*** – 9mm Para. cal., DAO, compact, 3 in. barrel, supplied with 6 and 7 shot mag., matte stainless steel, with or w/o Tritium night sights, 24 oz. New 1998.

MSR $938 $800 $700 $600 $545 $440 $360 $310

Add $109 for Tritium night sights.

* ***MK9 Micro Series Elite 98 Stainless*** – 9mm Para. cal., DAO, micro compact, 3 in. barrel, high polish stainless steel, specially designed combat trigger utilizing shorter trigger stroke, front strap checkering (new 2015), high polish slide, 24 oz. New 1998.

MSR $1,021 $870 $750 $650 $590 $475 $400 $340

Add $128 for Tritium night sights.

* ***MK9 Micro Series Elite 2000 Stainless*** – 9mm Para. cal., similar to MK9 Elite 98 Stainless, except features black stainless frame and slide, black Roguard finish. Mfg. 2001-2002.

$575 $485 $425 $360 $315 $260 $225 *$694*

MK40 MICRO – .40 S&W cal., micro compact variation of the Compact K40, featuring 3 in. barrel, matte stainless frame and slide, supplied with one 5 shot and one 6 shot (with grip extension) mag., wraparound textured hard nylon black grips, 25 oz. Mfg. 1999-2020.

$775 $680 $580 $525 $425 $350 $275 *$911*

Add $106 for Tritium night sights.

* ***MK40 Micro Elite Stainless*** – .40 S&W cal., 3 in. barrel, similar to MK40 Micro, except has high polish slide and specially designed combat trigger utilizing shorter trigger stroke, front strap checkering (new 2015). Mfg. 2000-2020.

$840 $735 $625 $560 $450 $375 $300 *$991*

Add $124 for Tritium night sights.

MP9 COMPACT POLYMER – 9mm Para. cal., lightweight polymer frame and matte stainless steel slide, 3 in. barrel, DAO with passive striker block, supplied with 6 and 7 shot mag. with grip extension, includes hard case and trigger lock, 15.9 oz. Mfg. 2002-2003.

$565 $485 $415 $380 $340 $300 $275 *$660*

Add $101 for Tritium night sights.

GRADING - PPGS™	100%	98%	95%	90%	80%	70%	60%	LAST MSR

P380 – .380 ACP cal., 2 1/2 in. barrel, black polymer frame, matte stainless or matte blackened stainless steel slide, 6 shot mag., with or w/out Tritum night sights, approx. 10 oz. New 2010.

MSR $710	$610	$510	$425	$370	$325	$285	$250	

Add $52 for mag. disconnector and loaded chamber indicator with night sights (new 2011).
Add $282 for black rose motif on matte stainless slide with Lothar Walther match grade barrel (mfg. 2018-2019).
Subtract approx. $115 if without Tritium night sights.
Add $150 for Crimson Trace trigger guard laser (mfg. 2011-2014).
Add $300 for custom engraved slide (Custom Shop only, mfg. 2012-2014).

P9 POLYMER COMPACT – 9mm Para. cal., DAO, 3.6 in. barrel, lightweight black polymer frame, 7 shot mag., matte stainless or matte blackened stainless (new 2004) slide, "Browning-type" recoil lug, passive striker block, no magazine disconnect, black textured polymer grips, drift adj. white bar-dot combat (disc.) or Tritium night (new 2000) sights, 17.9 oz. New 1999.

MSR $762	$650	$575	$500	$450	$360	$295	$250	

Subtract approx. $120 if without Tritium night sights (new 2000).
Add $114 for external safety and loaded chamber indicator with new enhanced trigger (mfg. 2012-disc.).

* ***P9 Polymer Compact Covert*** – 9mm Para. cal., similar to K9 Polymer Compact, except has 1/2 in. shorter frame, supplied with one 6 and one 7 (with grip extension) shot mag., 16.9 oz. Limited mfg. 1999, reintroduced 2002-2006.

	$595	$495	$430	$365	$325	$285	$250	*$697*

Add $111 for Tritium night sights (new 2000).

P9-2/TP-2 – 9mm Para. cal., black polymer frame w/accessory rail, blackened stainless steel slide with front serrations, 3.6 (P9-2) or 4 (TP-2) in. barrel, two 7 (P9-2) or 8 (TP-2) shot mags., TruGlo night sights. New 2021.

MSR $646	$550	$480	$415	$375	$310	$260	$215	

P40 COMPACT POLYMER – .40 S&W cal., DAO, 3.6 in. barrel w/polygonal rifling, black polymer frame, matte stainless or matte blackened stainless (new 2004) slide, 6 shot mag., "Browning-type" recoil lug, passive striker block, drift adj. white bar-dot combat (disc.) or Tritium night sights, textured polymer black grips, 18.9 oz. New 2001.

MSR $762	$650	$575	$500	$450	$360	$295	$250	

Subtract approx. $120 if without Tritium night sights.
Add $114 for external safety and loaded chamber indicator, and enhanced trigger (mfg. 2015-2018).

P45 POLYMER – .45 ACP cal., DAO, black polymer frame with matte stainless or blackened stainless (new 2006) steel slide, 3.54 in. barrel, 6 shot mag., ribbed grip straps, low profile white dot combat (disc. 2018) or Novak night sights, textured black polymer grips, 18 1/2 oz. New 2005.

MSR $762	$650	$575	$490	$440	$360	$300	$250	

Subtract approx. $120 if without Novak night sights.

PM9 COVERT – 9mm Para. cal., black polymer textured extended grip frame, 3.1 in. barrel w/polygonal rifling, 7 or 8 shot mag., blackened stainless slide with front slide serrations, TruGlo Tritium Pro night sights, accessory rail, 14.5 oz. New 2019.

MSR $762	$650	$575	$500	$450	$360	$295	$250	

PM9 MICRO POLYMER COMPACT – 9mm Para. cal., 3 in. barrel with polygonal rifling, black polymer frame, trigger cocking DAO, matte stainless or matte blackened stainless (new 2004) slide, 6 or 7 (with mag. grip extension, disc.) shot mag., current mfg. comes standard with Tritium night sights, 16 oz. New 2003.

MSR $762	$650	$575	$500	$450	$360	$295	$250	

Subtract approx. $125 if without Tritium night sights.
Add $18 for external safety, loaded chamber indicator (mfg. 2010-disc.), and enhanced trigger (mfg. 2012-disc.).
Add $263 for custom engraved slide (Custom Shop only, mfg. 2012-2015).
Add $168 for stainless slide with Crimson Trace trigger guard laser (mfg. 2010-2014).

PM9 THIN BLUE LINE – 9mm Para. cal., 3.1 in. barrel w/polygonal rifling, 6 or 7 shot mag., TruGlo night sights, textured polymer grip, black polymer frame, Armor Black Cerakote finish w/thin blue line down both sides of slide or blackened stainless steel slide, 14 oz. New 2019.

MSR $899	$765	$675	$575	$525	$425	$350	$300	

GRADING - PPGS™	100%	98%	95%	90%	80%	70%	60%	LAST MSR

PM40 COMPACT POLYMER – .40 S&W cal., black polymer frame, 3 in. barrel, supplied with one 5 shot and one 6 shot (with grip extension) mag., matte stainless (disc.) or matte blackened stainless (new 2005) slide, drift adj. white bar-dot combat (disc.) or Tritium night sights, textured polymer black grips, 17 oz. New 2004.

MSR $762	$650	$575	$500	$450	$360	$295	$230	

Subtract approx. $125 if w/o Tritium night sights.

Add $18 for external safety and loaded chamber indicator with enhanced trigger (mfg. 2012-disc.).

Add $168 for stainless slide and Crimson Trace trigger guard laser (mfg. 2010-2014).

* ***P40 Compact Polymer Covert*** – similar to P40 Compact Polymer, except has 1/2 in. shorter frame, matte stainless slide, supplied with one 6 and one 7 (with grip extension) shot mag., 16.9 oz. Mfg. 2002-2006.

	$600	$500	$425	$370	$325	$285	$250	*$697*

Add $111 for Tritium night sights.

PM45 POLYMER – .45 ACP cal., black polymer frame, 3.24 in. barrel, 5 shot mag., matte stainless (disc.) or blackened stainless (new 2008) slide, white bar dot combat (disc.) or Novak night sights, textured black polymer grips, Crimson Trace trigger guard laser (mfg. 2011-2014), approx. 19 oz. New 2007.

MSR $762	$650	$575	$500	$450	$360	$295	$250	

Subtract approx. $120 for Novak night sights.

Add $89 for Crimson Trace trigger guard laser (mfg. 2011-2014).

S9 – 9mm Para. cal., DAO, black polymer frame with accessory rail, 3.6 in. barrel, two 7 shot stainless mags., matte stainless steel slide with front serrations, lock breech, "Browning-type" recoil lug, passive striker block, no magazine disconnect, textured polymer grips with ID tag, white 3-dot sights, 5.9 in. OAL, 15.8 oz. Mfg. 2017-2020.

	$410	$350	$300	$275	$215	$185	$150	*$477*

ST9 – 9mm Para. cal., DAO, "Safe-Cam" action, black polymer frame with accessory rail, 4 in. barrel, two 8 shot stainless mags., matte stainless steel slide with front serrations, white 3-dot sights, textured polymer grips with ID tag, lock breech with "Browning-type" recoil lug and a passive striker block with no magazine disconnect, 6 1/2 in. OAL, 18.5 oz. Mfg. 2017-2020.

	$395	$350	$300	$275	$215	$185	$150	*$456*

ST9 TIG LIMITED EDITION – 9mm Para. cal., DAO, Kryptek Typhon print polymer frame with accessory rail, 4 in. rifled barrel, two 8 shot stainless mags., Black Armor Cerakote stainless steel slide with front serrations, engraved with the TIG logo, BTB logo, and John TIG Tiegen signature, white 3-dot sights, textured polymer grips with serial ID tag, 6 1/2 in. OAL, 18.5 oz. Limited mfg. of 1,000. Mfg 2018-2020.

	$460	$405	$345	$315	$255	$205	$160	*$541*

The first 50 guns were sold as three gun sets (Auto Ordnance, Kahr ST9 Tig, and Magnum Research Desert Eagle TIG models). The set also included the book *13 Hours: The Inside Account of What Really Happened in Benghazi,* **signed by American Hero, John "TIG" Tiegen.**

T40 – .40 S&W cal., 4 in. barrel with polygonal rifling, matte stainless steel construction, checkered Hogue Pau Ferro wood grips, 7 shot mag., Elite 98 trigger, MMC (disc. 2005), white bar dot (standard, new 2006), Novak low profile night sights (disc.), or Tritium night sights, 29 oz. Mfg. 2004-2020.

	$725	$635	$550	$500	$400	$325	$250	*$857*

Add $111 for Novak (disc.) or $123 for Tritium night sights (T40 Tactical).

TP9 – 9mm Para. cal., 4 in. barrel, 8 shot mag., black polymer frame, matte stainless slide, Elite 98 trigger, white bar dot sights (mfg. 2006-disc.), Novak, or Tritium night sights, textured black polymer grips, 20 oz. Mfg. 2004-2014, reintroduced 2017-2020.

	$700	$615	$525	$475	$385	$315	$250	*$838*

Subtract approx. $141 if without Novak or Tritium night sights (reintroduced 2017-2019).

TP9 GEN2 4 IN. – 9mm Para. cal., black polymer frame, 4 in. barrel, 8 shot, matte stainless slide, short trigger with trigger safety, TruGlo TFX Tritium/fiber optic day/night sights, accessory rail, ships with three magazines and high impact polymer case. Mfg. 2015-2017.

	$825	$700	$625	$550	$485	$415	$370	*$976*

TP9 GEN2 5 IN. – 9mm Para. cal., black polymer frame, 5 in. barrel, 8 shot, matte satinless slide with front slide serrations, short trigger with trigger safety, co-witness white 3-dot sights, mount for reflex sights, accessory rail, ships with three mags. in a high impact polymer case. Mfg. 2015-2017.

	$860	$725	$650	$585	$515	$450	$395	*$1,015*

TP9 GEN2 6 IN. – 9mm Para. cal., black polymer frame, 6 in. compensated barrel, 8 shot, short trigger with trigger safety, co-witness white 3-dot sights, Leupold Delta Point Reflex Sight, matte stainless slide with front slide serrations, accessory rail, matte finish. Mfg. 2015-2017.

	$1,315	$1,155	$1,040	$875	$750	$625	$525	*$1,566*

GRADING - PPGS™	100%	98%	95%	90%	80%	70%	60%	LAST MSR

TP40 – .40 S&W cal., DAO, "Browning-type" recoil lug, passive striker block, black polymer frame, 4 in. barrel with polygonal rifling, 7 shot mag., no magazine disconnect, matte stainless slide, white bar-dot sights, textured black polymer grips. Mfg. 2006-2014, reintroduced 2017-2020.

	100%	98%	95%	90%	80%	70%	60%	LAST MSR
	$600	$500	$425	$370	$325	$285	$250	*$697*

Add $141 for Novak or Tritium night sights (TP40 Tactical).

TP45 POLYMER – .45 ACP cal., DAO, black polymer frame, 4.04 in. barrel, 7 shot mag., matte stainless steel slide, white bar dot combat sights, textured black polymer grips, approx. 23 oz. Mfg. 2007-2014, reintroduced 2017-2020.

	100%	98%	95%	90%	80%	70%	60%	LAST MSR
	$600	$500	$425	$370	$325	$285	$250	*$697*

Add $142 for Novak or Tritium sights.

TP45 GEN2 – .45 ACP cal., 4 in. barrel, black polymer frame, 7 shot, matte stainless slide, accessory rail, short trigger with trigger safety, TruGlo TFX Tritium/fiber optic day/night sights. Mfg. 2015-2017.

	100%	98%	95%	90%	80%	70%	60%	LAST MSR
	$825	$700	$625	$550	$485	$415	$370	*$976*

TP45 GEN2 5 IN. – .45 ACP cal., black polymer frame, 5 in. barrel, 8 shot, matte stainless slide with front slide serrations, short trigger with trigger safety, co-witness white 3-dot sights, short trigger with trigger safety, accessory rail, mount for reflex sights. Mfg. 2015-2017.

	100%	98%	95%	90%	80%	70%	60%	LAST MSR
	$860	$725	$650	$585	$515	$450	$395	*$1,015*

TP45 GEN2 6 IN. – .45 ACP cal., 6 in. compensated barrel, 8 shot, short trigger with trigger safety, co-witness white 3-dot sights, Leupold Delta Point Reflex Sight, matte stainless slide with front slide serrations, accessory rail, matte finish. Mfg. 2015-2017.

	100%	98%	95%	90%	80%	70%	60%	LAST MSR
	$1,315	$1,155	$1,040	$875	$750	$625	$525	*$1,566*

KALASHNIKOV USA

Current manufacturer of Kalashnikov-type pistols, rifles, shotguns, and other firearms, located in Pompano Beach, FL. Kalashnikov USA (KUSA) is a subsidiary of the Russian Weapons Company (RWC Group) based in Tullytown, PA.

PISTOLS: SEMI-AUTO

KP-9 – 9mm Para. cal., blowback operated, based on Russian Vityaz-SN submachine gun, 9 1/4 in. barrel w/flash suppressor, 10 or 30 shot Vityaz style mag., stamped steel receiver, hinged stamped steel top cover with Picatinny rail, AK style polymer handguards, Vityaz style grip, right side safety lever, removable rear trunnion block with QD sling socket, SBR ready, Picatinny rail section under front sight block, black, Russian Tiger camo (new 2020), Urban Strike camo (new 2020), Digiteal camo (new 2020), Woodland Camo (new 2020), or American Edition Cerakote (new 2020) finish, 5.62 lbs.

	100%	98%	95%	90%	80%	70%	60%
MSR $999	$950	$825	$700	$650	$525	$425	$350

Add $250 for Russian Tiger camo, Urban Strike camo, Digiteal camo, or American Edition Cerakote finish.
Add $500 for Woodland Camo finish.

RIFLES: SEMI-AUTO

Previous rifles manufactured/imported by Kalashnikov USA/RWC Group include: US132, US132L, US132S, US132SS, US132W, US132Z, US132F1, and US109T.

KOMP9 COMPETITION RIFLE – 9mm Para. cal., blowback operated, based on Russian Vityaz-SN submachine gun, 16 1/4 in. barrel w/muzzle brake, 10 or 30 shot Vityaz style mag., Dissident Arms KR-9 magwell and thumb actuated mag. release, stamped steel receiver, hinged stamped steel top cover with Picatinny rail, Dissident Arms tuned trigger, Magpul CTR stock, KUSA 6-pos. receiver extension, Dissident Arms KR-9 MOD2 M-LOK handguard, Magpul MOE AK grip, Dissident Arms Adaptive Safety lever, ext. charging handle, black finish w/red accents. New 2020.

	100%	98%	95%	90%	80%	70%	60%
MSR $1,599	$1,500	$1,325	$1,125	$1,025	$825	$675	$525

KR-9 – 9mm Para. cal., blowback operated, based on Russian Vityaz-SN submachine gun, 16 1/4 in. barrel w/flash suppressor or faux suppressor (KR-9S), 10 or 30 shot Vityaz style mag., stamped steel receiver, hinged stamped steel top cover with Picatinny rail, stamped steel triangular side folding stock w/sling swivel, AK style polymer handguards, Vityaz style grip, right side safety lever, Picatinny rail section under front sight block, black or rose gold (mfg. 2020 only) finish, 34 1/2 (extended) or 24 1/4 (folded) in. OAL, 6.58 lbs.

	100%	98%	95%	90%	80%	70%	60%
MSR $1,059	$1,000	$875	$750	$675	$550	$450	$350

Add $56 for faux suppressor variant (KR-9S).

GRADING - PPGS™	100%	98%	95%	90%	80%	70%	60%	LAST MSR

KR103 – 7.62x39mm cal., long stroke GPO, based on Russian AK100 Series, 16.33 in. chrome-lined barrel w/bayonet lug, AK100 style muzzle brake, 30 shot AK mag., stamped steel receiver and top cover, fixed polymer stock, polymer handguards, polymer AK pistol grip, right side safety lever, right side optics mounting rail, cleaning rod under barrel, black finish, 27 3/4 (folded) or 37 (extended) in. OAL, 6.24 lbs.

MSR $1,059	$1,000	$875	$750	$675	$550	$450	$350

While advertised prior, this model did not reach commercial sale until 2020.

* ***KR-103SF (Side Folding)*** – 7.62x39mm cal., based on Russian AK100 Series, 16 1/4 in. barrel w/ bayonet lug, 30 shot mag., optics rail, side folding or fixed stock, modern muzzle brake, flash suppressor, black finish, 27 3/4 (folded) or 37 (extended) in. OAL, 6.24 lbs.

While advertised, this model has not been commercially available to date.

* ***KR-103W (Wood Rifle)*** – 7.62x39mm cal., based on Russian AK100 Series, 16 1/4 in. barrel w/ bayonet lug, 30 shot mag., side mounted optics rail, fixed wood stock, modern muzzle brake, flash suppressor, black finish, 27 3/4 (folded) or 37 (extended) in. OAL, 6.24-6.58 lbs.

While advertised, this model has not been commercially available to date.

* ***KR-103T (Tactical)*** – 7.62x39mm cal., based on Russian AK100 Series, 16 1/4 in. barrel w/bayonet lug, 30 shot mag., mounted optics rail, collapsible stock, modern muzzle brake, flash suppressor, black finish, 36 1/4 (folded) or 40 1/4 (extended) in. OAL, 6.58 lbs.

While advertised, this model has not been commercially available to date.

SHOTGUNS: SEMI-AUTO

Previous shotguns being manufactured/imported by Kalashnikov USA/RWC group include: US109T and US109L.

KOMP12 COMPETITION SHOTGUN – 12 ga., 2 3/4 or 3 in. chamber, long stroke GPO, based on Russian Saiga-12 shotgun, 18 1/4 in. barrel w/Dissident Arms Phoenix One Compensator, Dissident Arms tuned 12 shot SGM mag., Dissident Arms Polymer Magwell and Ext. Ambi Index mag. release, Dissident Arms Ultra Low Optics Base (ULOB), Magpul CTR stock, TDI Arms 6-pos. receiver extension, Dissident Arms MOD2 M-LOK handguard, Magpul MOE AK grip, ext. IPSC style safety, left side optics rail, black finish w/red and Sniper Grey accents. New 2020.

MSR $1,499	$1,425	$1,250	$1,075	$975	$775	$650	$500

KS-12 – 12 ga., 2 3/4 or 3 in. chamber, long stroke GPO, based on Russian Saiga-12 shotgun, 18 1/4 in. barrel, threaded for Saiga-12 pattern chokes or muzzle devices, 5 shot Saiga-12 pattern mag., stamped steel lower receiver and top cover, fixed stock, Kalashnikov USA pistol grip, right side safety lever, left side optics rail, black, FDE (disc.), or OD Green (disc.) finish, 38 in. OAL, 8 1/2 lbs.

MSR $805	$750	$650	$575	$500	$425	$350	$275

Add $130 for OD Green (disc.) or FDE (disc.) finish.

KS-12 TACTICAL – 12 ga., 2 3/4 or 3 in. chamber, long stroke GPO, based on Russian Saiga-12 shotgun, 18 1/4 in. barrel w/flash suppressor, 10 shot Saiga-12 pattern mag., 6-pos. collapsible stock, tri-rail forend, adj. pistol grip, right side safety lever, left side optics rail, black, FDE, or OD Green (disc.) finish, 38 1/2 (collapsed) or 42 1/4 (extended) in. OAL, 8.86 lbs.

MSR $845	$775	$675	$575	$525	$425	$350	$300

Add $20 for OD Green (disc.) finish.
Add $40 for FDE finish.
Add $70 dollars for black or FDE folding stock.

FIREARMS: OTHER

Per the manufacturer: these firearms are legally classified as "Firearm/Other". They are not considered a handgun, rifle, or shotgun, nor are they NFA classified as an "Any Other Weapon" (AOW) or "Short Barreled Shotgun/Rifle" (SBS/SBR).

KOMRAD – 12 ga., 2 3/4 or 3 in. chamber, long stroke GPO, based on Russian Saiga-12 shotgun, 12 1/2 in. barrel, threaded for Saiga-12 pattern chokes or muzzle devices, two 5 shot Saiga-12 pattern mags., stamped steel lower receiver and top cover, SBA3 brace, tri-rail forend, CAA ergonomic grip, right side safety lever, left side optics rail, vertical grip, black or Russian Tiger camo (new 2020) finish, 38 in. OAL, 8 1/2 lbs.

MSR $1,250	$1,175	$1,025	$875	$800	$650	$525	$425

Add $500 for Russian Tiger camo finish (new 2020).

GRADING - PPGS™ 100% 98% 95% 90% 80% 70% 60% LAST MSR

KASSNAR IMPORTS, INC.

Previous importer and distributor located in Harrisburg, PA. Kassnar Imports operations ceased April, 1989.

Kassnar also imported Churchill and Omega shotguns which can be found in their individual section.

PISTOLS: SEMI-AUTO

PJK-9HP – 9mm Para. cal., single action, patterned after the Browning Hi-Power, 4 3/4 in. barrel, 13 shot mag., cone hammer, checkered walnut grips, 32 oz.

$325 $295 $270 $250 $225 $200 $175

Add $25 for VR barrel.

This pistol was imported from Hungary. Approximately 18,000 (including the MBK-9HP) were imported until importation was discontinued because of federal ramifications.

MBK-9HP – 9mm Para. cal., double action, patterned after the Browning Hi-Power, 4 2/3 in. barrel, spur hammer, blue metal, checkered walnut grips, 14 shot mag., 36 oz. Limited importation was stopped in late 1985.

$425 $375 $325 $275 $225 $200 $185

PMK-380 – .380 ACP cal., double action, patterned after the Walther PP, plastic grips with thumbrest, 4 in. barrel, 7 shot mag., 21 oz. Limited importation.

$275 $235 $200 $185 $175 $165 $155

This model was imported in very limited quantities before Interarms began exclusive importation.

PSP-25 – .25 ACP cal., single action semi-auto pistol, patterned after the Baby Browning, 2 in. barrel, 6 shot mag., fixed sights, checkered black plastic grips, blue finish.

$375 $335 $285 $250 $200 $175 $150

KEBERST INTERNATIONAL

Previously manufactured and distributed by Kendall International, located in Paris, KY.

RIFLES: BOLT ACTION

KEBERST MODEL 1A – .338 Lapua Mag., .338-416 Rigby, or .338-06 cal., muzzle brake and unique recoil pad, camouflaged synthetic stock, package includes 3-9 power Leupold scope, stainless steel cleaning rod, custom designed case, built to special order only. Mfg. 1987-88 only.

$3,475 $2,850 $2,475 $2,100 $1,750 $1,400 $1,150 *$3,750*

Add $275 for 10X Ultra scope.

KEKKI

Current manufacturer of bolt action rifles located in Bologna, Italy. No current U.S. importation. Previously imported by Lewis Drake & Associates located in Murray, KY until 2015.

RIFLES: BOLT ACTION

Kekki manufactures high quality bolt action rifles. Current models include the Prestige Imperial, Professional Hunter, Long Range, and the Bench Rest. Base price for a Kekki bolt action rifle is $22,000-$24,000, depending on features. Please contact the manufacturer directly for more information including price, options, and U.S. availability.

KELBLY'S INC.

Current manufacturer of custom bolt action rifles as well as actions and other accessories, located in North Lawrence, OH.

For individual model listings, please go to BlueBookOfGunValues.com/overflow.

KEL-TEC CNC INDUSTRIES, INC.

Current manufacturer established in 1991, located in Cocoa, FL. Dealer sales.

PISTOLS: SEMI-AUTO

CP33 – .22 LR cal., competition, 5.5 in. threaded barrel, 33 shot quad-stack mag., adj. fiber optic sights, ambidextrous safety lever on both sides, Picatinny top rail, Magpul M-LOK slot built into dust cover, heel catch mag. release and charging handle, black, OD Green, or Coyote Tan finish, 10.6 in. OAL, 1.5 lbs. New 2019.

MSR $550 $500 $425 $375 $325 $275 $225 $175

GRADING - PPGS™	100%	98%	95%	90%	80%	70%	60%	LAST MSR

P11 – 9mm Para. cal., DAO, locked breech design, 3.1 in. barrel, composite frame with steel slide, transfer bar safety, matte blue, parkerized (new 1997), hard chrome (new 1999), or electroless nickel (disc. 1995) finish, black, grey, or green (disc. 1998) synthetic grips, 10 shot double column mag., 14.4 oz. Mfg. 1995-2019.

	$285	$230	$195	$175	$155	$135	$125	*$347*

Add $45 for parkerized finish (choice of grips).
Add $60 for hard chrome finish (new 1999).
Add $30 for electroless nickel finish (disc. 1995).
Add $85 for night sights (mfg. 1997-2003, reintroduced 2007).
Add $175 for 9mm Para. to .40 S&W cal. conversion kit (disc. 2002).

* ***P11 Stainless*** – similar to P11, except is stainless steel, available with black (P- 11SB), grey (P-11SGY), or green (P-11SGN) grips. Mfg. 1996-98.

	$350	$295	$240	$200	$175	$150	$135	*$408*

P17 – .22 LR cal., compact frame, 3.93 in. threaded barrel, three 16 shot mags., fiber optic front sight, adj. rear sight, textured grips, ambi safety, lower Picatinny rail, black, OD Green, or Coyote Tan finish, 12-14 oz. New late 2019.

MSR $199	$175	$150	$125	$125	$100	$75	$75	

P32 – .32 ACP cal., double action only with internal hammer block safety, 7 shot mag., composite frame with steel slide, 2.68 in. barrel, choice of parkerized, blue, black, OD Green, Coyote Tan, or hard chrome finish, choice of light blue, dark blue, grey, or green full ivory grips, 6.6-7 oz. New 1999.

MSR $360	$325	$275	$250	$225	$175	$150	$125	

Add $43 for parkerized finish.
Add $59 for hard chrome finish.

* ***P3AT*** – .380 ACP cal., developed from the P32, 2.76 in. barrel, 6 shot mag. 7 and 9 shot extended mag. options available, black composite frame with parkerized steel slide, black, OD Green, or Coyote Tan finish, 8.3 oz. New 2003.

MSR $340	$275	$225	$190	$170	$150	$135	$125	

Add $43 for parkerized finish.
Add $61 for hard chrome finish.

P40 – .40 S&W cal., double action only with internal hammer block safety, composite frame with steel slide, 3.3 in. barrel, choice of parkerized, blue, or hard chrome finish, 9 or 10 shot mag., 15.8 oz. Mfg. 1999-2001.

	$275	$225	$190	$175	$160	$140	$130	*$331*

Add $41 for parkerized finish.
Add $58 for hard chrome finish.

P50 – 5.7x28mm cal., 9.6 in. barrel, 50 shot mag., Picatinny rails, QD mounts, black finish, 3.2 lbs. New 2021.

MSR $995	$900	$800	$650	$600	$500	$400	$325	

PLR16 – 5.56 NATO cal., GPO, 9.2 in. threaded barrel, upper frame has integrated Picatinny rail, 10 shot detachable mag., adj. sights, black composite frame, 3.2 lbs. New 2006.

MSR $600	$550	$475	$400	$375	$300	$250	$200	

Add $119 for OD Green or Desert Tan Cerakote finish.

PLR22 – .22 LR cal., blowback action, 10.1 in. barrel, 26 shot mag., ejector, adj. sights, integrated Picatinny rail, composite frame with black or Cerakote finish in OD Green or Desert Tan, 2.8 lbs. New 2008.

MSR $440	$400	$350	$300	$275	$225	$175	$150	

Add $193 for OD Green or Desert Tan Cerakote finish.

PF9 – 9mm Para. cal., similar operating system as P11, DAO, 3.1 in. barrel, single stack 7 shot mag., includes lower accessory rail, adj. sights, black, grey, Coyote Tan (new 2021), or OD Green grips, blued, parkerized, or hard chrome finish, 12.7 oz. Limited mfg. 2006, reintroduced 2008.

MSR $358	$285	$230	$195	$175	$155	$135	$125	

Add $45 for parkerized finish.
Add $60 for hard chrome finish.

PMR30 – .22 WMR cal., blowback action, 4.4 in. steel barrel, 30 shot mag., aluminum frame, steel slide and barrel, Hi-Viz sights, Zytel grips, manual safety, lower Picatinny rail, black, titatnium, or Cerakote finish in Burnt Bronze (disc.), OD Green, Coyote Tan, or Desert Tan (disc.) finish, 7.9 in. OAL, 13.6-14 oz. New 2010.

MSR $545	$500	$425	$375	$325	$275	$225	$175	

Add approx. $125 for titanium barrel finish.

GRADING - PPGS™	100%	98%	95%	90%	80%	70%	60%	LAST MSR

RIFLES/CARBINES: SEMI-AUTO

All Kel-Tec firearms are available in black or Cerakote finishes in OD Green or Desert Tan. Other colors are available by special order.

CMR30 – .22 WMR cal., 16 in. threaded barrel, 30 shot mag., single action trigger, ambidextrous safety, Magpul flip-up sights, upper and lower Picatinny rail, collapsible stock with nylon buttplate, Zytel grips, 3.8 lbs. New 2015.

MSR $630	$550	$475	$425	$365	$295	$250	$200	

M43 BULLPUP – .223 Rem. cal., short stroke piston system, 17.4 in. barrel, downward brass ejection system, pistol grip, ambidextrous bolt release, manually locked back charging handle, heat shield over piston, accepts standard AR-15 magazines, integral folding sights, wood furniture, parkerized finish, approx. 7 lbs.

While advertised in late 2014 with an MSR of $1,900, this model never went into production.

SUB-9/SUB-40 CARBINE – 9mm Para. or .40 S&W cal., unique pivoting 16.1 in. barrel rotates upwards and back, allowing overall size reduction and portability (16 in. x 7 in.), interchangeable grip assembly will accept most popular double column high capacity handgun mags., including Glock, S&W, Beretta, SIG, or Kel-Tec, tube stock with polymer buttplate, matte black finish, 4.6 lbs. Mfg. 1997-2000.

	$350	$300	$265	$240	$220	$200	$180	

Add $25 for .40 S&W cal.

SUB-2000 CARBINE – 9mm Para. or .40 S&W (new 2004) cal., similar to Sub-9/Sub-40, but features a completely new design, 16.1 in. barrel, aperture rear and adj. front sights, internal keyed deployment lock, push bolt safety, choice of blued, parkerized, or hard chrome finish with black, OD Green, or tan grips, 4 lbs. Mfg. 2001-2015.

	$350	$300	$265	$240	$220	$200	$180	*$409*

Add $32 for parkerized finish.
Add $42 for hard chrome finish.
Add $9 for OD Green or tan grips with parkerized finish. Add $12 for OD Green or tan grips with blued or hard chrome finish.

This model accepts magazines from the Glock 17, 19, 22, or 23, Beretta 92 or 96, S&W Model 59, or Sig 226.

SUB-2000 GEN 2 – 9mm Para. or .40 S&W cal., updated version of the Sub-2000, blowback action, 16 in. threaded barrel, will accept most double column handgun mags. such as Beretta, Glock, or S&W, larger ejection port, front sight is now constructed of aluminum, sight can be removed to add a flash hider, stock is now adj. to three different positions, top and bottom integral Picatinny rails are standard, includes 5 Magpul M-LOK slots per side, grip updated with ergonomic groove, "Gator Grip" texturing was added to grip, stock, and forend for better control, includes single point sling attachment and webbing sling loop, folding buttstock, black, OD Green, or Coyote Tan finish, 4 1/4 lbs. New 2016.

MSR $578	$500	$450	$400	$350	$275	$225	$175	

SU16 SERIES CARBINE/RIFLE – 5.56 NATO cal., unique downward folding stock, forearm folds down to become a bipod, 16 (new 2005) or 18 1/2 in. barrel, Picatinny receiver rail, M16 breech locking and feeding system, choice of black, OD Green (new 2012), or tan (new 2012) synthetic stock (stores extra mags.) and forearm, approx. 4.7 lbs. New 2003.

* ***SU16A*** – 5.56 NATO cal., 18 1/2 in. barrel that doubles as a bipod, 10 shot AR-15 compatible mag., right-hand reciprocating bolt handle and mag. catch, adj. sights, buttstock can store two 10 shot mags., Picatinny style rail, black or Cerakote finish in OD Green or tan, 37.4 in. OAL, 5 lbs.

MSR $575	$500	$450	$400	$350	$275	$225	$175	

Add $140 for OD Green or Desert Tan Cerakote finish.

* ***SU16B*** – 5.56 NATO cal., similar to SU16, except has lightened 16 in. barrel, 4 1/2 lbs.

MSR $600	$550	$475	$400	$375	$300	$250	$200	

* ***SU16C (Charlie Model)*** – .300 AAC Blackout (new 2013) or 5.56 NATO cal., similar to SU16A, except has 16 in. barrel, front sight is integrated into the gas block, integrated bipod, Picatinny rail, and also has a true folding stock, parkerized finish with black polymer components, 4.7 lbs.

MSR $625	$550	$500	$425	$375	$300	$250	$200	

* ***SU16CA*** – 5.56 NATO cal., hybrid of the SU16A and SU16B models, 16 in. barrel with chrome-lined bore and chamber and threads, front sight is integrated into the gas block, buttstock can store two 10 shot mags., Picatinny rail for mounting, parkerized finish with black polymer components, folding buttstock. New 2016.

MSR $625	$550	$500	$425	$375	$300	$250	$200	

GRADING - PPGS™	100%	98%	95%	90%	80%	70%	60%	LAST MSR

* ***SU16E*** – 5.56 NATO, .223 Rem., or .300 AAC Blackout (disc.) cal., GPO, 16 in. threaded barrel, 10 shot (or more) AR-15 compatible mags., adj. sights, 6-position collapsible stock, pistol grip, flat-top Picatinny receiver, small quad rail, black or Cerakote finish in OD Green or Desert Tan, 4.7 lbs. New 2012.

MSR $904	$825	$725	$625	$525	$450	$395	$350	

Add $138 for OD Green or Desert Tan Cerakote finish.

* ***SU16F*** – 5.56 NATO cal., similar to SU16A, except has Canadian black or choice of Cerakote finish in OD Green or Desert. Mfg. 2012-2014.

	$585	$515	$465	$415	$360	$310	$285	*$682*

Add $140 for OD Green or Desert Tan Cerakote finish.

SU22 RIFLE SERIES – .22 LR cal., blowback action, 16 in. barrel, 15 (SU-22C, disc.) or 26 shot mag., adj. sights, ejectors, Picatinny rail on top of receiver and bottom of aluminum quad forearm, crossbolt safety, black synthetic stock ,under folding stock (SU22 CA) or pistol grip style 4-pos. AR stock (SU-22E), parkerized finish, 4 lbs. New 2008.

MSR $425	$375	$325	$275	$250	$200	$175	$125	

Add $75 for 4-position stock (SU-22E).
Add $10 for under folding stock with 15 shot mag. (SU-22C, disc.).
Add $126 for OD Green or Desert Tan Cerakote finish (disc.).

RFB CARBINE – .308 Win. or 7.62 NATO. cal., GPO, bullpup configuration with pistol grip and rear detachable mag., 18 (Carbine), or 32 (Target, disc. 2012) in. barrel with A2 style flash hider, 10 or 20 shot mag., accepts FAL type mags., front ejection from tube located above barrel, adj. trigger, pistol grip stock, Picatinny rail, front ejection from tube located above barrel, tilting breechblock design, ambidextrous controls, black synthetic lower, adj. trigger, choice of black or Cerakote OD Green (disc. 2016) or Desert Tan (disc. 2016) finish, 8.1-11.3 lbs. Mfg. 2009-disc.

	$1,625	$1,400	$1,200	$1,075	$875	$725	$625	*$1,930*

Add $158 for OD Green or Desert Tan Cerakote finish (disc. 2016).

RFB RIFLE – 7.62 NATO cal., bullpup design, adj. gas piston system, 18 1/2 in. barrel, 20 shot, forward ejection system, dual bolt release, black, OD Green, Coyote Tan, 8.7 lbs.

MSR $1,800	$1,600	$1,400	$1,200	$1,100	$900	$750	$550	

* ***RFB Hunter*** – .308 Win./7.62 NATO cal., GPO, 24 in. threaded barrel, 10 or 20 shot mag., front ejection from tube located above barrel, adj. trigger, pistol grip, Picatinny rail, choice of Black, Canadian Green (disc.), or Tan (disc.) finish, 35.9 in. OAL, 8.7 lbs. New 2009.

MSR $2,000	$1,800	$1,600	$1,350	$1,200	$1,000	$800	$650	

Add $75 for OD Green or Desert Tan Cerakote finish (disc.).

RDB17/RDB HUNTER – .223 Rem. cal., adj. short stroke GPO, bullpup design, 17.3, 20 (new 2020), or 20 1/2 (RDB Hunter only) in. barrel with A2 flash hider, 10 shot mag., accepts standard AR-15 magazines, downward brass ejection system, Zytel forend, pistol grip, ambidextrous bolt release, manually locked back charging handle, polymer Picatinny top and bottom rail, matte black, OD green, or Coyote Tan finish, 6.7-6.9 lbs. New late 2014.

MSR $1,000	$900	$800	$700	$600	$500	$400	$325	

RDB-C – 5.56 NATO, .223 Rem. (disc.), or 6.5 Grendel cal., downward ejecting bullpup design, 20 or 24 in. barrel, 10 shot mag., push-button mag. release, polymer furniture, hunter-style fixed stock, grip, and forend, pistol grip, push-button safety, FDE or OD Green finish, 7 lbs. Mfg. 2016-2019.

	$1,050	$950	$815	$715	$625	$535	$450	*$1,273*

RDB DEFENDER – .223 Rem. cal., bullpup design, adj. gas piston system, 16 in. barrel, 20 shot mag., single-position collapsible stock and aluminum M-LOK forend, ergonomic textured pistol grip, top Picatinny rail, black, OD Green, or Coyote Tan finish, 6.7 lbs. New 2020.

MSR $1,300	$1,150	$1,000	$900	$800	$650	$500	$400	

RDB SURVIVAL (RDB-S) – .223 Rem. or 5.56x45mm cal., bullpup design, 16.1 in. lightweight barrel, 20 shot (or any AR-15) mag., downward shell ejection system, folding sights, collapsible stock, black or Cerakote finish in OD Green or Desert Tan, 26.1 in. OAL, 5.14 lbs.

MSR $1,150	$1,050	$900	$800	$700	$550	$475	$350	

SHOTGUNS: SLIDE ACTION

KSG – 12 ga., 3 in. chamber, unique bullpup configuration, utilizing an 18 1/2 in. cyl. bore barrel, twin mag. tubes under the barrel allow 12 or 14 shot capacity, steel and polymer construction, downward ejection, no sights, pistol grip stock, pistol grip, upper and lower Picatinny rails w/o sights, 26.1 in. OAL, 6.9 lbs. New 2011.

MSR $900	$800	$700	$600	$550	$450	$375	$275	

Add $50 for OD Green or Desert Tan Cerakote finish (disc. 2016).

GRADING - PPGS™	100%	98%	95%	90%	80%	70%	60%	LAST MSR

* ***KSG Compact*** – 12 ga., 3 in. chamber,18 1/2 in., 8 shot mag., built-in foregrip, 450 lumen Kel-Tec light, Picatinny style rail, black finish, 6.8 lbs. New 2018.

MSR $930	$850	$750	$650	$550	$450	$375	$300	

* ***KSG-NR*** – 12 ga., 3 in. chamber, unique bullpup configuration, utilizing an 18 1/2 in. cyl. bore barrel, twin mag. tubes under the barrel allow 10 shot capacity, downward ejection, steel and polymer construction, upper Picatinny rail w/o sights, pistol grip and folding forend grip, 26.1 in. overall length, 6.8 lbs. Mfg. 2015-disc.

	$1,100	$995	$875	$735	$650	$550	$465	*$1,299*

Add $50 for OD Green or Desert Tan Cerakote finish (disc. 2016).

* ***KSG-25*** – 12 ga., 3 in. chamber, unique bullpup configuration, utilizing an 30 1/2 in. cyl. bore shrouded barrel, twin mag. tubes under the barrel allow 20 or 24 shot capacity, steel and polymer construction, downward ejection, no sights, pistol grip stock, upper and lower Picatinny rails, M-LOK slots along heat shield for mounting lights, 30.5 in. OAL, 9 1/4 lbs. New 2016.

MSR $1,150	$1,050	$900	$800	$700	$550	$475	$350	

Add $50 for OD Green or Desert Tan Cerakote finish (disc. 2016).

KS7 – 12 ga., 3 in. chamber, bullpup design, 18 1/2 in. barrel, 6 or 7 shot mag., fiber optic bead sight, pistol grip, ambidextrous controls, carry handle, 26.1 in. OAL, 5.9 lbs. New 2019.

MSR $580	$500	$450	$400	$350	$275	$225	$175	

KEMEN

Current competition shotgun manufacturer established in 1990, located in Elgoibar, Spain. Currently imported exclusively by Fieldsport (all models), located in Traverse City, MI. Previously imported by Target Shotguns, located in Arden, NC, American Shooting Centers, located in Houston, TX, by Fly and Field, located in Bend, OR, and by New England Custom Gun Service (Model KM-4 only), located in Plainfield, NH. Gun service is available through Briley.

For individual model listings, please go to BlueBookOfGunValues.com/overflow.

KENDALL INTERNATIONAL

Previous importer and distributor located in Paris, KY. Kendall International also imported Australian Automatic Arms, and the Keberst Rifle. Air rifles can be found in the *Blue Book of Airguns* (also available online).

KENTUCKY RIFLES

U.S. flintlock/percussion long rifle configuration originated in Pennsylvania. Kentucky rifles are a field unto themselves, and should be evaluated by an experienced and known source for accurate identification and/or price evaluation.

KENTUCKY RIFLES IDENTIFICATION & PRICING

The author wishes to express his thanks, once again, to Mr. James Buelow for updating the following information.

The Kentucky rifle was the creation of early settlers from the Old Country. This new American configuration combined the architectural elements of the English Fowler with the ornamental features of the German Jaeger. The English Fowler (shotgun) was long and graceful, while the Jaeger was short and large caliber.

The Kentucky (American Long Rifle) played a major role in the settlement of the United States of America. It saw action in the French and Indian War, the American Revolution, the War of 1812, and the Texas War of Independence.

The earliest recorded use of the term "Kentucky rifle" was in a ballad written after the battle of New Orleans. The battle was won by the American Long Rifle, in the hands of 2,000 frontiersmen. During that period, the area west of the 13 colonies was known as Kentucky; hence the name Kentucky rifle.

Kentucky rifles began appearing around the middle of the 18th century and disappeared by the middle of the 19th century. Their origin is credited to eastern Pennsylvania, but soon spread to many other states, including Maryland, Virginia, Tennessee, North Carolina, and areas where the rifle maker found a market for his skills.

The styles vary, but they have two things in common: they are long, and most had curly maple stocks. The bores are found both rifled and smooth. The rifles most prized by the collector are the ones that have relief or incised carving. Original carved Kentucky rifles are now considered one of America's earliest art forms and have become a functional example of important early Americana. Present values may range from as low as $1,500 all the way up to almost $200,000! Non-carved or plain Kentuckys are most often encountered.

GRADING - PPGS™	100%	98%	95%	90%	80%	70%	60%	LAST MSR

The present value of an uncarved, original flintlock Kentucky rifle in average condition is approx. $3,500. An uncarved percussion specimen in average original condition is approx. $2,500. These prices diminish when the Kentucky rifle lacks a maker's name, usually found on the top of the barrel, or if it does not have a patch box. Kentucky rifle values vary greatly, due to maker popularity, quality of carving, condition, rifle style, and a multitude of other factors.

During the past several decades, many fine contemporary Kentucky rifles have been built by craftsmen who understand the trade. Many of these guns are now available in the secondary marketplace. A large percentage have outstanding craftsmanship, and are highly sought after. These specimens sell in the $2,000-$10,000 range, depending on the notoriety of the builder and the sophistication of the work. Because of this, these guns have to be evaluated one at a time.

The best way to find out the value of a Kentucky rifle is to seek out a knowledgeable Kentucky rifle collector. To find such a person in your area, contact Blue Book Publications Inc. at guns@bluebookinc.com and be specific as to the locality and type of Kentucky Rifle (good images will definitely help). For information regarding contemporary Kentucky rifles makers (with some contact information), visit the Contemporary Longrifle Association at longrifle.ws, or see their listing under Firearms Associations.

KEPPELER - TECHNISCHE ENTWICKLUNGEN GmbH

Current rifle manufacturer located in Fichtenberg, Germany. No current U.S. importation.

Keppeler manufactures a wide variety of top quality rifles in many target configurations (including UIT-CISM, Prone, Free, and Sniper Bullpup). Both metric and domestic calibers are available as well as a variety of special order options. Keppeler also manufactures precision caliber conversion tubes for the shotgun barrel(s) on combination guns and drillings. Please contact the factory directly for more information and current pricing.

KEPPLINGER, ING. HANNES

Please refer to the Kufsteiner Waffenstube listing in this section.

KESSLER ARMS CORPORATION

Previous manufacturer located in Silver Creek, NY.

SHOTGUNS

LEVERMATIC MODEL – 12, 16, or 20 ga., lever action, 26 or 28 in. full choke barrel, takedown, plain pistol grip stock. Disc. 1953.

$175	$150	$125	$100	$85	$65	$55	

BOLT ACTION MODEL – 12, 16, or 20 ga., 26 or 28 in. full choke barrel, takedown, plain stock. Mfg. 1951-53.

$90	$65	$50	$45	$35	$35	$35	

KESSLER, WAFFEN

Please refer to Waffen Kessler listing in the W section.

KEVIN'S

Current dealer and importer with store locations in Thomasville, GA and Tallahassee, FL.

SHOTGUNS

Kevin's has shotguns private labeled to its specifications. Currently, they have a line of Upland shotguns including an O/U Plantation Special Edition, Baby Frame SxS shotgun, and a Plantation Sporter O/U. Please contact Kevin's directly for more information, pricing, and current availability.

KEYSTONE SPORTING ARMS

Current manufacturer established 1996, located in Milton, PA. Distributor and dealer sales.

Keystone manufactures the Chipmunk and Crickett lines of youth bolt action rifles and pistols. In January 2007, Keystone purchased the remaining assets of Rogue Rifle Co., manufacturer of Chipmunk rifles. Please refer to the Crickett and Chipmunk sections for current models and pricing. In addition to Chipmunk and Crickett rifles and pistols, Keystone currently manufactures a Model 10 bolt action shotgun and a Hunter .22 caliber bolt action pistol. Additionally, the company makes a wide variety of conventional and thumbhole stocks and forearms in many different colors. Please contact the company directly for more information and pricing on these guns.

GRADING - PPGS™	100%	98%	95%	90%	80%	70%	60%	LAST MSR

RIFLES: BOLT ACTION

KPT KEYSTONE PRECISION TRAINER (MODEL 722 PT) – .22 LR cal., target chamber, 16 (disc.), 16 1/2 (new 2020), or 20 in. blued bull barrel, 7 shot mag. (one red shot mag. optional), A*B Arms MOD X aluminum chassis, optics ready, A*B Arms Urban Sniper shoulder stock, adj. LOP, Class III hardcoat anodized black or FDE (new 2019) finish, 6-6.3 lbs. New 2018.

MSR $549	$470	$410	$350	$325	$260	$215	$185	

KSA 91/30 MINI MOSIN – .22 LR cal., single shot, miniature version of classic Mosin-Nagant 91/30 rifle, 20 in. blued barrel, black walnut stock, 2.8 lbs. Special Edition version available w/limited mfg. of 500. New 2019.

MSR $399	$340	$300	$255	$230	$185	$155	$130	

Add $100 for Special Edition version.

MODEL 722 CLASSIC – .22 LR cal., 20 in. button rifled target barrel, 7 shot mag., billet aluminum trigger guard, fixed front sight, fiber optic adj. rear sight, high quality checkered walnut stock with raised cheekpiece, two sling studs, thumb trigger block safety, 13 1/2 in. LOP, short 5 in. receiver, Picatinny style rail, blued finish, 5.5 lbs.

MSR $449	$380	$335	$285	$260	$210	$175	$145	

MODEL 722 COMPACT DELUXE – .22 LR cal., 16 1/4 in. button rifled target barrel, 7 shot mag., fixed front sight, adj. rear sight, deluxe checkered walnut stock, raised cheekpiece, 12 5/8 in. LOP, Picatinny rail, blued finish, 4 lbs.

MSR $339	$300	$255	$220	$195	$160	$130	$110	

MODEL 722 COMPACT SPORTER – .22 LR cal., 16 1/4 in. button rifled target barrel, 7 shot mag., billet aluminum trigger guard, fixed front sight, adj. rear sight, walnut stock, thumb trigger block safety, 12 5/8 in. LOP, short 5 in. receiver, Picatinny rail, blued finish, 4 lbs.

MSR $299	$255	$225	$190	$175	$140	$115	$100	

MODEL 722 SPORTER – .22 LR cal., 20 in. blued, button rifled target barrel, 7 shot mag., billet aluminum trigger guard, fixed front sight, fiber optic adj. rear sight, walnut stock, thumb trigger block safety, 13 1/2 in. LOP, short 5 in. receiver, Picatinny rail, blued finish, 5.5 lbs.

MSR $355	$315	$275	$235	$215	$175	$140	$110	

MODEL 722 VARMINT – .22 LR cal., 20 in. heavy bull barrel, target chamber, 7 shot mag., billet aluminum trigger guard, thumbhole walnut stock, thumb trigger block safety, 13 1/2 in. LOP, short 5 in. receiver, Picatinny rail, adj. bipod included, 3 swivel studs, blued finish, hard case included, 8 lbs.

MSR $479	$400	$350	$300	$275	$225	$185	$155	

Add $120 for package including scope, rings, bipod, and hard case.

KHAN ARMS

Current trademark of shotguns established in 1985, and manufactured in Istanbul, Turkey. Previously imported by Tristar located in N. Kansas City, MO. Previously imported by Mossberg on a private label basis and Legacy Sports International, LLC, late 2004-2005, located in Alexandria, VA.

Current trademarks owned by Khan Arms include: Arista, A-Tac, Duo-Sys, K100 (disc.), K200 (disc.), K500, K213 (disc.), K226 (disc.), Kine-Sys (disc.), MXL, Matrix, SXL (disc.), Setter Premium, Stylox, VP, and Venator. These trade names are mostly marketed and sold throughout Europe. In 2016, Khan changed its name to Khan Arms.

SHOTGUNS: O/U

ARTHEMIS ELITE FIELD/DELUXE – 12, 20, 28 ga., or .410 bore, 3 in. chambers (except for 28 ga.), 26 or 28 in. VR barrels with multi-chokes (fixed chokes on .410 bore), extractors, SST, matte blue (Field) or bright blue (Deluxe) metal finish, light engraving, choice of satin finish (Field) or polished select finish (Deluxe) walnut stock, 5.7-7.9 lbs. Disc.

	$500	$450	$400	$350	$300	$265	$235	*$617*

Add $15 for 20 ga.
Add $22 for 28 ga. or .410 bore.
Add $174 for Deluxe Model with bright blue metal and polished select wood stock (12 or 20 ga. only).

* ***Arthemis Elite Field/Deluxe Sporting Clays*** – 12 ga., 2 3/4 in. chambers, ejectors, 28 in. barrels, ST, otherwise similar to Arthemis Field, 8 lbs. Disc.

	$925	$825	$725	$650	$575	$495	$425	*$1,104*

GRADING - PPGS™	100%	98%	95%	90%	80%	70%	60%	LAST MSR

SHOTGUNS: SxS

COACH GUN – 12 ga., 2 3/4 in. chambers, bright blue metal, hammerless boxlock action, extractors, polished select wood stock and forearm, 20 in. barrels with fixed cyl. bore chokes, 6.9 lbs.

$675	$595	$525	$450	$375	$300	$225	*$784*

KIFARU ARMS

Previous bolt action rifle and current outdoor gear manufacturer established circa 2013 and located in Wheat Ridge, CO.

Co-owner Ross Shelton teamed with Patrick Smith, long range backpack hunter and owner of outdoor gear manufacturer Kifaru International, to form Kifaru Arms in 2013. Kifaru continues to manufacturer a complete line of hunting gear, including backpacks in many configurations. Modular rifle production was limited to a few rifles and prototypes.

RIFLES: BOLT ACTION

RAMBLING RIFLE GEN II – .22-250 Rem., .220 Swift, .243 Win., .260 Rem., 6.5 Creedmoor, .284 Win., .308 Win., 7mm WSM, 7mm RSAUM, .270 WSM, .300 WSM, .300 RCM, .338 RCM, .270 WIn., .280 Rem., .30-06, 7mm Rem. Mag., .300 Win. Mag., or .338 Win. Mag. cal., short or long titanium right or left-hand action is glass embedded with aluminum pillars, all metal parts have Cerakote finish in choice of olive green, gray, black, or brown, with optional tan, black, or tan and black webbing custom micro-light stock, cryo-treated match grade stainless or chrome moly minimum contour carbon fiber fully floated barrel, optional titanium or aluminum micro-light muzzle brake, Timney lightweight trigger, adj. trigger pull, stock is aluminum pillar/glass bedded to individual action, fitted with decelerator recoil pad, includes Talley scope mount/ring, Kifaru soft carrying case, and microlight sling. New mid-2013-2015.

$5,750	$5,050	$4,325	$3,925	$3,175	$2,595	$2,015	*$6,749*

Add $650 for extra micro-light bolt.
Add $250 for aluminum muzzlebrake or $350 for titanium muzzle brake.
Add $111 for ultralight forend rail and $30 for angled fore grip.
Add $229 for aluminum travel case.
Add $1,250 for additional barrel.

KILIMANJARO RIFLES

Previous custom rifle manufacturer with headquarters located in Honolulu, HI and manufacturing facilities located in Kalispell, MT from 2010-circa 2019.

Kilimanjaro Rifles purchased the Serengeti name, model lines, and patents so it could continue making the Serengeti and Jaguar models, in addition to its flagship Kilimanjaro rifle.

RIFLES: CUSTOM

Kilimanjaro Rifles manufactured high quality custom rifles, including the bolt action Kilimanjaro (last MSR $15,000), The New Serengeti (last MSR $14,500), the Jaguar (last MSR in 2012 was $5,995), the Tigercat (last MSR $14,500), the Artemis (last MSR $14,500), and the Doctari (last MSR $16,000), as well as the Kilimanjaro lever action rifle (last MSR $9,995, special order only). Many options were available. Additionally, Kilimanjaro manufactured full custom versions of various historical rifles. These rifles were built to customer specifications and were POR.

KIMAR Srl

Current division of Chiappa Firearms Srl, located in Azzano Mella BS, Italy. Currently imported by Chiappa Firearms USA Ltd. located in Dayton, OH, and by Traditions located in Old Saybrook, CT. Previously imported by IAR, located in San Juan Capistrano, CA, and by Valor Corporation, located in Sunrise, FL.

Kimar is well known for its starter/signal revolvers and pistols in many popular configurations. Please contact the importer directly for more information and U.S. availability.

J. KIMBALL ARMS CO.

Previous manufacturer located in Detroit, MI circa 1958.

PISTOLS: SEMI-AUTO

AUTOMATIC PISTOL – .30 Carbine or .22 Hornet (very rare) cal., 7 shot, 3 in. (Combat Model) or 5 in. (Target Model) barrel, approx. 32 oz. Less than 300 mfg. in 1958 only.

$1,950	$1,875	$1,500	$1,325	$1,050	$875	$750

Add 50% for .22 Hornet cal.

Functional weaknesses of this pistol caused discontinuance. Surviving specimens should be checked carefully for slide failures and other potential problems. Values assume no operational damage to the pistol.

GRADING - PPGS™	100%	98%	95%	90%	80%	70%	60%	LAST MSR

KIMBER

Current trademark manufactured by Kimber Mfg., Inc., established during 1997. In 2019, Kimber expanded operations and now has a design engineering and manufacturing facility in Troy, AL. Previous company headquarters and manufacturing was located in Elmsford, NY. Previously located in Yonkers, NY until 2011. Previous rifle manufacture was by Kimber of America, Inc., located in Clackamas, OR circa 1993-1997.

PISTOLS: SEMI-AUTO

Kimber pistols, including the very early models marked "Clackamas, Oregon", have all been manufactured in the Yonkers, NY plant. Prior to the 1998 production year, the "Classic" model pistols were alternately roll-scrolled "Classic", "Classic Custom" or "Custom Classic". During 1997-98, the "Classic" moniker was dropped from Kimber pistol nomenclature as a specific model.

All Kimber 1911 pistols are shipped with a lockable high impact synthetic case with cable lock and one magazine, beginning 1999.

Beginning in 2001, the "Series II" pistol, incorporating the Kimber Firing Pin Safety System, was again phased into some centerfire models. All pistols incorporating the firing pin block have the Roman Numeral "II" following the name of the pistol presented on the slide directly under the ejection port. This conversion was completed by February 2002, and about 50% of subsequent Kimber 1911 pistol production have been Series II. There was no "Series I" pistol per se, but pre-series II models are often referred to in that manner.

During 2003, external extractors were phased out of many .45 ACP models. Due to consumer demand, production was phased back to traditional (internal) extractors during 2006.

All three changes (disuse of the term "Classic" for pistols, Series II safety system, and external extractor) were "phased in" throughout normal production cycles. Therefore, no distinctive cut-off dates or serial numbering series were established to identify specific product runs or identify when these features were incorporated.

Almost all Kimber pistols (exceptions are Royal II, Classic Carry Pro, rimfires and some pistols sold in California) have stainless steel match grade barrels beginning 2013.

Add $339 for .22 LR cal. or $344-$379 for .17 Mach 2 cal. (mfg. 2005-2006) conversion kit for all Mil-Spec 1911 pistols (includes complete upper assembly, lightweight aluminum slide, premium bull barrel, and 10 shot mag.). Available in satin black and satin silver. Kimber began manufacture of these kits in early 2003. Prior to that, they were manufactured by a vendor.

AEGIS ELITE CUSTOM – 9mm Para. or .45 ACP cal., serrated rounded heel stainless steel frame with satin silver finish, 5 in. stainless steel barrel, 8 shot, stainless steel slide with matte black KimPro II finish, green and red fiber optic or Vortex Venom red dot (OI model only) sights, G10 green/black/gray grips, AEX slide serrations, 38-39.6 oz. New 2018.

MSR $1,087	$915	$800	$685	$620	$500	$410	$360	

Add $21 for 9mm Para. cal.

Add $408-$429 for Aegis Elite Custom OI (Optics Installed) model, depending on caliber.

AEGIS ELITE PRO – 9mm Para. or .45 ACP cal., stainless steel frame with satin silver finish, 4 in. stainless steel barrel, 8 or 9 shot, stainless steel slide with KimPro II Gray finish, green and red fiber optic or Vortex Venom red dot (OI model) sights, G10 grips, two-position thumb safety on grip, rear and forward AEX slide serrations, 36.6 oz. New 2018.

MSR $1,087	$915	$800	$685	$620	$500	$410	$360	

Add $21 for 9mm Para. cal.

Add $408-$429 for Aegis Elite Pro OI (Optics Installed), depending on caliber.

AEGIS ELITE ULTRA – 9mm Para. or .45 ACP cal., aluminum frame with satin silver finish, 3 in. stainless steel barrel, 7 shot, stainless steel slide with matte black KimPro II finish, green and red fiber optic sights, G10 grips, rear and forward AEX slide serrations, front strap checkering, 25 oz. New 2018.

MSR $1,087	$915	$800	$685	$620	$500	$410	$360	

Add $21 for 9mm Para. cal.

AEGIS II SERIES – 9mm Para. cal., SA, 3 (Ultra), 4 (Pro), or 5 (Custom) in. stainless steel barrel, 8 or 9 shot mag., aluminum frame w/satin silver premium KimPro II finish, matte black slide, thin rosewood grips, 30 LPI front strap checkering, high relief cut under trigger guard, Tactical Wedge 3-dot (green) night sights, bumped and grooved grip safety, hammer, thumb safety and mag. release button are bobbed, Carry Melt treatment on both frame and slide, 25 oz. Mfg. 2006-2016.

	$1,125	$985	$850	$750	$625	$500	$400	*$1,331*

GRADING - PPGS™	100%	98%	95%	90%	80%	70%	60%	LAST MSR

CDP (CUSTOM DEFENSE PACKAGE) – 9mm Para. or .45 ACP cal., 3 (Ultra), 4 (Pro), or 5 (Custom) in. barrel, Tritium night sights, rosewood double diamond or Crimson Trace Lasergrips (Ultra CDP model only, disc. 2020), aggressive slide serrations, flat-top slide, front strap and under trigger guard checkering, Carry Melt treatment, Gray KimPro II finish on frame and slide, 25-31 oz. New 2017.

MSR $1,230	$1,050	$920	$790	$715	$580	$475	$400	

Add $21 for 9mm Para. cal.

Add $300 for Crimson Trace Lasergrips (Ultra CDP model only, disc. 2020).

CDP II (CUSTOM DEFENSE PACKAGE) SERIES – 9mm Para. (new 2008), .40 S&W (disc. 2007), or .45 ACP cal., Custom Shop pistol featuring Tritium night sights, stainless steel slide with black anodized aluminum frame, 3 in. (Ultra CDP II, 25 oz.), Ultra+ (3-in. barrel with full-length grip, new 2011), 4 in. (Pro CDP II and Compact CDP II, 28 oz.), or 5 in. (Custom CDP II, 31 oz.) barrel, SA, Carry Melt treatment, ambidextrous thumb safety, double diamond pattern checkered rosewood grips, 30 LPI checkered front strap and under trigger guard (new 2003), two-tone finish. Mfg. 2000-2016.

	$1,150	$1,000	$875	$775	$625	$525	$400	*$1,331*

Add $28 for 9mm Para. cal. (new 2008).

Add $300 for Crimson Trace Lasergrips (new 2010).

Add $40 for .40 S&W cal., available in either Ultra CDP II or Pro CDP II configuration (disc. 2007).

The Pro CDP II has a full-length grip frame.

This series' nomenclature added the Roman numeral "II" during 2001.

COMBAT CARRY – .40 S&W or .45 ACP cal., 4 in. barrel, SA, carry model featuring aluminum frame and trigger, stainless steel slide, Tritium night sights, and ambidextrous thumb safety, 28 oz. Limited mfg. 1999 only.

	$885	$775	$675	$625	$500	$425	$325	*$1,044*

Add $30 for .40 S&W cal.

COMPACT II – .45 ACP cal., SA, 4 in. barrel, .4 in. shorter aluminum or steel frame, 7 shot mag., Commander style hammer, single recoil spring, low profile combat sights, checkered black synthetic grips, 28 (aluminum) or 34 (steel) oz. Mfg. 1998-2001.

	$635	$555	$475	$430	$350	$285	$220	*$764*

* ***Compact Stainless II*** – .40 S&W (mfg. 1999-2001) or .45 ACP cal., stainless steel slide, 4 in. bull barrel, 4 in. shorter aluminum (disc., reintroduced 2009) or stainless (mfg. 2002-2008) frame, 7 shot mag., Commander style hammer, single recoil spring, low profile combat sights, black synthetic grips, 34 oz. Mfg. 1998-2013.

	$895	$785	$675	$625	$500	$425	$325	*$1,052*

Add $32 for .40 S&W cal. (disc. 2001).

This model's nomenclature added the Roman numeral "II" during 2001.

COVERT SERIES – .45 ACP cal., 3 (Ultra), 4 (Pro), or 5 (Custom) in. barrel, 3-hole trigger, Tactical Wedge Tritium 3-dot night sights, digital camo Crimson Trace Lasergrips, bumped and grooved beavertail grip safety, 30 LPI front strap checkering, Carry Melt treatment, gray KimPro II finish on frame and slide, matte black small parts, 25-31 oz. New 2017.

MSR $1,495	$1,275	$1,115	$950	$865	$700	$600	$500	

COVERT II SERIES – .45 ACP cal., SA, 3 (Ultra Covert II), 4 (Pro Covert II), or 5 (Custom Covert II) in. bushingless barrel, aluminum frame, lanyard ring and magazine with extended bumper (Pro Covert or Custom Covert only), Carry Melt treatment, 30 LPI front strap checkering, bumped and grooved beavertail grip safety, Tactical Wedge 3-dot (green) night sights, digital camo Crimson Trace Lasergrips, desert tan KimPro II finish on frame, matte black oxide slide, approx. 25-30 oz. Mfg. 2007-2016.

	$1,495	$1,300	$1,100	$1,025	$900	$775	$650	*$1,657*

CRIMSON CARRY II – .45 ACP cal., SA, satin silver aluminum frame, 3 (Ultra), 4 (Pro), or 5 (Custom) in. stainless steel barrel, matte black slide with black sights, shortened slide stop pin, beveled frame, extended thumb safety, rosewood Crimson Trace Lasergrips (red or green laser) with double diamond checkering and Kimber logo, 25-31 oz. Mfg. mid-2008-2019.

	$1,000	$875	$750	$680	$550	$455	$390	*$1,180*

Add $41 for green laser.

CUSTOM II/CUSTOM II TWO-TONE – .45 ACP or 9mm Para. (mfg. 2016-2020) cal., patterned after the Colt Government Model 1911, SA, steel frame, 5 in. match grade steel (disc.) or stainless steel (two-tone model) barrel, matte black (disc. 2015) or two-tone (new 2016) slide and frame finish, front slide serrations, 7 shot mag., lowered and flared ejection ports, three-hole trigger, dovetail mounted (disc.)

GRADING - PPGS™	100%	98%	95%	90%	80%	70%	60%	LAST MSR

or fixed low profile sights, high ride beavertail grip safety, choice of rubber (disc.), laminated wood (disc.), walnut (disc. 2015), or smooth/checkered rosewood grips, 38 oz. New 1995.

MSR $1,136	$965	$845	$725	$655	$530	$435	$350	

Add $20 for 9mm Para. cal. (mfg. 2016-2020).
Add $34 for walnut grips (disc.).
Add $117 for night sights (disc. 2015).
Add $185 for Royal II finish (polished blue and checkered rosewood grips, disc. 2010 and replaced by new Custom Shop version with same name).

This series' nomenclature added the Roman numeral "II" during 2001. Beginning 2020, this model is only available in two-tone finish so the model nomenclature changed to Custom II Two-Tone.

* ***Custom II Target*** – .45 ACP cal., similar to Custom II, except features Kimber adj. rear sight. Mfg. 1998-2015.

	$825	$725	$625	$575	$450	$375	$300	*$974*

CUSTOM STAINLESS II – .38 Super (advertised in 1999, mfg. late 2005-2008), 9mm Para. (advertised in 1999, new 2008), .40 S&W (mfg. 1999-2007), or .45 ACP cal., 5 in. barrel, 7 or 9 shot mag., stainless steel slide and frame, three-hole trigger, fiber optic night sights (became standard 2017, .45 ACP and 9mm only), black synthetic (disc. 2015) or rosewood with Kimber logo (new 2016) grips, beavertail grip safety.

MSR $891	$750	$650	$565	$510	$425	$350	$275	

Add $21 for 9mm Para. or $11 for .40 S&W (disc. 2007) cal.
Add $143 for high polish stainless in .38 Super cal. only (mfg. late 2005-2008).
Subtract $27 for Stainless Limited Edition marked "Stainless LE" (disc. 1998).

* ***Custom Stainless Target II*** – .38 Super (mfg. 2002-2015), 9mm Para., 10mm (mfg. 2003-2015), or .45 ACP cal., similar to Custom Stainless II, except features Kimber adj. rear sight, black synthetic (disc. 2015) or rosewood with Kimber logo (new 2016) grips, fiber optic sight became standard 2017. New 1998.

MSR $1,033	$875	$765	$650	$595	$475	$400	$325	

Add $20 for 9mm Para. cal.
Add $84 for .38 Super or 10mm cal. (disc. 2015).
Add $100 for .40 S&W cal. (disc. 2002).
Add $130 for high polish stainless in .38 Super cal. only (mfg. late 2005-2008).

CUSTOM TLE II – 10mm (new 2012) or .45 ACP cal., 5 in. barrel, SA, tactical law enforcement pistol (TLE) with exactly the same features as the Kimber pistols carried by LAPD SWAT, black oxide coated frame and slide, same features as Custom II, except has 30 LPI front strap checkering and night sights, integrated mainspring lanyard slot (new 2016), flat-top slide (new 2016), aggressive G10 grips (new 2016), approx. 38 oz. New 2003.

* ***Custom TLE II*** – 9mm Para. (mfg. 2014-2016, TFS model only), 10mm (new 2013), or .45 ACP cal., 5 or 5 1/2 (mfg. 2014-2016, TFS model) in. stainless steel barrel, 7 or 9 shot mag., with (mfg. 2017-2020) or w/o extended magwell, full-length guide rod, steel frame and slide with matte black finish, front strap checkering, front serrations, Tritium 3-dot night sights, double diamond black synthetic (disc. 2015) or aggressively textured G10 (new 2016) grips, 38 oz.

MSR $1,060	$900	$790	$675	$610	$500	$410	$350	

Add $48 for 10mm cal.
Add $61 for extended magwell (Custom TLE II EM, mfg. 2017-2020).
Add $73 for TFS Model with threaded barrel (mfg. 2014-2016).
Add $274 for Crimson Trace Lasergrips (disc. 2010).

* ***Stainless TLE II*** – .45 ACP cal., 5 in. barrel, stainless steel flat-top slide and frame, match grade trigger, black synthetic double diamond (disc. 2015) or aggressively textured G10 (new 2016) grips, integrated mainspring lanyard slot (new 2016), 38 oz. New 2004.

MSR $1,203	$1,025	$900	$775	$700	$575	$475	$400	

CUSTOM TLE/RL II – 10mm (new 2013) or .45 ACP cal., 5 in. barrel, black synthetic (disc. 2015) or aggressive G10 (new 2016) grips, Picatinny rail machined into the frame to accept optics and other tactical accessories, with (mfg. 2017-2020) or w/o extended magwell, 39 oz. New 2003.

MSR $1,162	$985	$850	$725	$675	$550	$450	$385	

Add $20 for 10mm cal.
Add $62 for extended magwell (Custom TLE/RL II EM, mfg. 2017-2020).

GRADING - PPGS™	100%	98%	95%	90%	80%	70%	60%	LAST MSR

* ***Custom TLE/RL II TFS*** – .45 ACP or 9mm Para. cal., 5 1/2 in. match grade threaded barrel, 7 or 9 shot mag., black synthetic (disc. 2015) or G10 (new 2016) grips, full-length guide rod, matte black finish, 39 oz.

MSR $1,244	$1,055	$925	$795	$715	$580	$475	$415	

Add $20 for 9mm Para.

* ***Stainless TLE/RL II*** – .45 ACP cal., similar to Custom TLE/RL II, except is stainless, double diamond black synthetic (disc. 2015) or G10 (new 2016) grips, 39 oz. New 2004.

MSR $1,298	$1,100	$965	$825	$750	$600	$500	$425	

CUSTOM LW OI, NIGHTSTAR – 9mm Para. or .45 ACP cal., aluminum frame, 5 in. match grade stainless steel barrel, 8 or 9 shot mag., steel slide with front serrations, 3-hole aluminum trigger, 6MOA Vortex Venom red dot optic, black/gray laminate grips with checkered gripping area, black finish, 31 oz.

MSR $992	$850	$740	$635	$575	$465	$380	$325	

ECLIPSE II SERIES – .38 Super (new 2016, Eclipse Target II only), 10mm (Eclipse Custom II, new 2004) or .45 ACP cal., SA, stainless steel slide and frame, black matte finish with brush polished flat surfaces for elegant two-tone finish, Tritium night sights, target models have adj. bar/dot sights, silver/grey laminated double diamond grips or Crimson Trace Lasergrips (new 2015), black small parts, 30 LPI front strap checkering, include Eclipse Ultra II (3 in. barrel, short grip), Eclipse Pro II and Eclipse Pro-Target II (4 in. barrel, standard grip, disc. 2012), Eclipse Custom II, and Eclipse Target II (full size). Mfg. 2002-2016.

	$1,165	$1,025	$875	$800	$650	$525	$425	*$1,351*

Add $42 for Eclipse Target II in .45 ACP cal. or Eclipse Pro-Target II (disc. 2012).
Add $238 for Crimson Trace Lasergrips (new 2015).

The initial Custom Shop version of these pistols was mfg. during late 2001, featuring an ambidextrous thumb safety, and "Custom Shop" markings on left side of slide, 7,931 were mfg.

ECLIPSE CUSTOM – 10mm or .45 ACP cal., 5 in. barrel, all steel construction, brush polished slide, charcoal gray frame, Premium Aluminum Trigger, TruGlo Tritium Pro sights, black and gray G10 "Cyclone" grips, front strap checkering, 38 oz. New 2017.

MSR $1,252	$1,075	$930	$800	$725	$585	$480	$415	

Add $21 for 10mm cal.

ECLIPSE PRO – .45 ACP cal., 4 in. barrel, 8 shot, all steel construction, brush polished slide, Premium Aluminum Trigger, Tritium night sights, black and gray G10 "Cyclone" grips, front strap checkering, charcoal gray finish, 35 oz. Mfg. 2017-2018.

	$1,075	$930	$800	$725	$585	$480	$415	*$1,252*

ECLIPSE TARGET – .38 Super or .45 ACP cal., 5 in. barrel, all steel construction, brush polished slide, charcoal gray frame, Premium Aluminum Trigger, adj. target sights, black and gray G10 "Cyclone" grips, front strap checkering, 35 oz. Mfg. 2017-2018.

	$1,165	$1,025	$875	$800	$650	$525	$425	*$1,361*

Add $32 for .45 ACP cal.

EVO SP (CDP - CUSTOM DEFENSE PACKAGE) – 9mm Para. cal., striker fired, aluminum frame with KimPro Charcoal Gray finish, 3.16 in. stainless steel match grade barrel with deep crown, 7 shot, beveled magwell, stainless steel slide with FNC black finish, premium aluminum trigger, Tritium night sights, red/black G10 grips with diamond checkering, 30 LPI front strap checkering, carry melt treatment, 19 oz. New 2019.

MSR $883	$750	$650	$550	$500	$400	$350	$285	

EVO SP (CS - CUSTOM SHOP) – 9mm Para. cal., striker fired, aluminum frame with KimPro II Charcoal Gray finish, 3.16 in. match grade stainless steel barrel with deep crown, 7 shot extended mag., Ferritic Nitrocarburizing (FNC) stainless steel slide with black finish, TruGlo Tritium Pro sights, gray/black G10 grips, Stiplex inspired serrations on slide, front strap, and grips, 18 oz. Mfg. by the Custom Shop beginning 2019.

MSR $965	$820	$720	$615	$560	$450	$370	$320	

EVO SP RAPTOR (COLLECTOR'S EDITION) – 9mm Para. cal., aluminum frame, 3.16 in. stainless steel match grade barrel w/deep crown, bushingless design, 7 shot, stainless steel slide, aluminum trigger, standard Tritium night sights, black/tan G10 (half smooth/half scale) grips, Collector Series marking on left side of slide and special serial no. prefixes, black KimPro and Tru-Tan finish, 19 oz. New 2020.

MSR $999	$850	$750	$625	$575	$475	$385	$300	

GRADING - PPGS™	100%	98%	95%	90%	80%	70%	60%	LAST MSR

* ***EVO SP Stainless Raptor*** – 9mm Para. cal., striker fire, KimPro Silver aluminum frame, stainless steel slide w/KimPro Silver over FNC finish, 3.16 in. stainless steel match grade barrel w/Deep Crown and bushingless design, 7 shot mag., aluminum trigger, Tritium night sights, Millennium wood grips w/scale pattern, checkering on front strap, 19 oz. New 2019.

MSR $883	$750	$650	$550	$500	$400	$350	$285	

EVO SP SELECT BLACK/STAINLESS – 9mm Para. cal., aluminum frame, 3.16 in. stainless steel match grade barrel w/deep crown, bushingless design, 7 shot, silver KimPro finish over FNC (Ferritic Nitro-Carburizing) slide, aluminum trigger, white 3-dot sights, medium sized brown or black nylon grips w/ diamond checkering, regular size backstrap, black or silver KimPro II finish, 19 oz. New 2020.

MSR $638	$540	$475	$400	$365	$300	$250	$210	

EVO SP (TLE) – 9mm Para. cal., striker fired, aluminum frame with KimPro black finish, 3.16 in. stainless steel match grade barrel with deep crown, 7 shot, beveled magwell, stainless steel slide, TruGlo Tritium Pro sights, green/black G10 TLE style grips with slant checkering, backstrap with diamond checkering, 19 oz. Mfg. 2019-2020.

	$790	$690	$595	$535	$435	$355	$300	*$925*

EVO SP (TWO-TONE) – 9mm Para. cal., striker fired, aluminum frame with KimPro silver finish, 3.16 in. stainless steel match grade barrel with deep crown, 7 shot, stainless steel slide with black finish, aluminum trigger, TruGlo Tritium Pro sights, nylon grips with diamond checkering, front strap checkering, 19 oz. New 2019.

MSR $795	$680	$600	$500	$450	$375	$300	$265	

GOLD MATCH II – .45 ACP cal., SA, 5 in. stainless steel match barrel and bushing, premium aluminum match grade trigger, ambidextrous thumb safety became standard in 1998, 8 shot mag., Kimber adj. sight, fancy checkered rosewood grips in double diamond pattern, high polish blue, 30 LPI on flat-top slide (new 2016), hand fitted barrel by Kimber Custom Shop, 38 oz. Disc.

	$1,190	$1,050	$900	$815	$675	$550	$450	*$1,393*

This series' nomenclature added the Roman numeral "II" during 2001.

* ***Gold Match Stainless II*** – .38 Super (advertised in 1999, never mfg.), 9mm Para. (advertised in 1999, mfg. 2008-2015), .40 S&W (mfg. 1999-2007), or .45 ACP cal., similar to Gold Match, except is stainless steel, 38 oz. Disc.

	$1,340	$1,175	$1,000	$910	$735	$600	$525	*$1,574*

Add $75 for 9mm Para. (disc. 2015) or $100 for .40 S&W (disc. 2007) cal.

KHX CUSTOM – 9mm Para. or .45 ACP cal., stainless steel slide and frame, 5 in. stainless steel barrel, 8 shot, green and red fiber optic ledged sights, Hogue enhanced MagGrip G10 grips with red laser and mainspring housing, Stiplex front strap texture, hexagonal serrations on slide and top strap, full-length guide rod, KimPro II gray finish with black small parts, 38 oz. New 2018.

MSR $1,325	$1,125	$985	$850	$765	$625	$500	$440	

Add $48 for 9mm Para. cal.

* ***KHX Custom (OI)*** – .45 ACP, 9mm Para., or 10mm cal., stainless steel frame, 5 in. stainless steel match grade barrel, 8 shot mag., milled slide, premium aluminum trigger, Trijicon 3.25 MOA Type 2 RMR, Hogue G10 Magrip, stiplex front strap stippling, Gray KimPro II finish, 38 oz. New 2020.

MSR $1,971	$1,675	$1,465	$1,255	$1,140	$920	$755	$650	

Add $27 for 9mm Para. or 10mm cal.

* ***KHX Custom OR (Optics Ready)*** – 9mm Para. or .45 ACP cal., stainless steel frame and slide, 5 in. stainless steel match grade barrel, milled slide that accepts optics plates, Hogue MagGrip G10 grips, Stiplex front strap stippling, matte black KimPro II finish, 38 oz. New 2018.

MSR $1,162	$985	$850	$725	$675	$550	$450	$385	

Add $20 for 9mm Para. cal.

* ***KHX Custom/RL*** – 9mm Para., 10mm, or .45 ACP cal., stainless steel frame and slide, 5 in. stainless steel match grade barrel, 8 shot, aluminum trigger, Trijicon 3.25 MOA Type 2 RMR red dot optic, white dot co-witness sights, Hogue G10 Magrip, Picatinny accessory rail, Stiplex front strap stippling, Gray KimPro II finish, 39 oz. New 2019.

MSR $2,039	$1,735	$1,520	$1,300	$1,180	$955	$780	$680	

Add $61 for 9mm Para. or 10mm cal.

KHX PRO – 9mm Para. or .45 ACP cal., stainless steel frame and slide, 4 in. stainless steel match grade barrel, 7 shot, green and red fiber optic sights, Hogue enhanced MagGrip G10 grips with red laser and mainspring housing, matte black KimPro II finish, 35 oz. New 2018.

MSR $1,352	$1,150	$1,000	$865	$780	$635	$525	$450	

Add $21 for 9mm Para. cal.

GRADING - PPGS™	100%	98%	95%	90%	80%	70%	60%	LAST MSR

* ***KHX Pro OR (Optics Ready)*** – 9mm Para. or .45 ACP (disc. 2020) cal., stainless steel frame, 4 in. stainless steel match grade barrel, 8 shot mag., solid aluminum trigger, optic ready, fiber optic, Hogue G10 Magrip, Gray KimPro II finish, 35 oz. New 2018.

MSR $1,182	$1,000	$875	$750	$680	$550	$455	$390	

Subtract approx. $21 for .45 ACP cal. (disc. 2020).

KHX ULTRA – 9mm Para. or .45 ACP cal., stainless steel frame and slide, 3 in. stainless steel match grade barrel, 7 shot, green and red fiber optic sights, Hogue enhanced MagGrip G10 grips with red laser and mainspring housing, matte black KimPro II finish, 25 oz. New 2018.

MSR $1,352	$1,150	$1,000	$865	$780	$635	$525	$450	

Add $21 for 9mm Para. cal.

KPD – while advertised during 2006-2007, this model never went into production.

LTP II – .45 ACP cal., designed for Limited Ten competition, Tactical Extractor, steel frame and slide, KimPro finish, 20 LPI front strap checkering, 30 LPI checkering under trigger guard, tungsten guide rod, flat-top serrated slide, beveled magwell, ambidextrous thumb safety, adj. rear sight. Mfg. by Custom Shop 2002-2006.

	$1,850	$1,620	$1,385	$1,260	$1,015	$830	$645	*$2,106*

MASTER CARRY SERIES – 9mm Para. (new 2017, Pro only) or .45 ACP cal., SA, 3 (Ultra), 4 (Pro), or 5 (Custom) in. stainless steel barrel, aluminum frame on Carry Pro and Carry Ultra models, stainless steel frame on Carry Custom, black KimPro II finish on slide and satin finish frame, skeletonized trigger, includes Crimson Trace master series Lasergrips with red beam, round heel frame, tactical wedge night sights, 25-30 oz. Mfg. 2013-2019.

	$1,250	$1,095	$940	$850	$685	$575	$490	*$1,477*

Add $20 for 9mm Para. cal. (new 2017, Pro only).

MICRO 9 AMETHYST – 9mm Para. cal., aluminum frame w/silver KimPro II finish, 3.15 in. stainless steel barrel, 7 shot, solid aluminum trigger, standard night sights, purple/black G10 grips, three vertical serrations, border engraving, purple PVD finish, 15.6 oz. New 2020.

MSR $1,114	$950	$825	$700	$635	$515	$425	$350	

MICRO 9 BEL AIR – 9mm Para. cal., aluminum frame with Bel Air Blue finish, 3.15 in. stainless steel barrel, 6 shot mag., stainless steel slide with mirror-polished finish, aluminum trigger, white dot sights, ivory G10 grips, 15.6 oz. New 2018.

MSR $864	$750	$650	$550	$500	$400	$325	$250	

MICRO 9 CDP – 9mm Para. cal., round aluminum frame, 3.15 in. stainless steel barrel, 7 shot, stainless steel slide, bobbed hammer, Tritium night sights or TruGlo TFX Pro day/night sights with rear cocking ledge and orange front sight ring (DN Model only), rosewood, Crimson Trace Lasergrips (LG Model), or Hogue wrap around black (DN Model) grips, ambidextrous thumb safety, Carry Melt treatment, front strap checkering, KimPro II gray finish, 15.6 oz. Mfg. 2018-2020.

	$790	$690	$595	$535	$435	$355	$300	*$924*

Add $104 for Hogue wrap around black grips (DN Model).
Add $117 for Crimson Trace Lasergrips (LG Model).

MICRO 9 COVERT – 9mm Para. cal., round heel aluminum frame, 3.15 in. stainless steel barrel, 7 shot mag., stainless steel slide, bobbed hammer, solid aluminum trigger, Tritium night sights, Crimson Trace Lasergrips in gray urban camo, checkered front strap, KimPro II gray finish, 15.6 oz. Mfg. 2018-2019.

	$830	$725	$625	$565	$455	$375	$325	*$973*

MICRO 9 CRIMSON CARRY – 9mm Para. cal., satin aluminum frame, 3.15 in. stainless steel barrel, 6 shot, steel slide with matte black finish, white dot sights, rosewood with Crimson Trace Lasergrips, full-length guide rod, 15.6 oz. Mfg. 2016-2019.

	$765	$670	$575	$520	$420	$350	$300	*$894*

MICRO 9 (LG) – 9mm Para. cal., aluminum frame, 3.15 in. barrel, 6 shot mag., steel slide, white dot sights, Crimson Trace Lasergrips in tan, matte black finish, 15.6 oz. Mfg. 2018-2019.

	$675	$595	$500	$450	$375	$300	$265	*$790*

MICRO 9 DESERT NIGHT – 9mm Para. cal., aluminum frame with Desert Tan finish, 3.15 in. barrel, 6 shot, stainless steel slide with KimPro II black finish, solid aluminum trigger, white dot sights (LG Model) or TruGlo TFX Pro day/night sights with rear cocking ledge and orange front sight ring (DN Model), black Crimson Trace Lasergrips (LG Model, disc. 2019) or Hogue wrap around grips in black (DN Model), 15.6 oz. New mid-2017.

MSR $795	$680	$600	$500	$450	$375	$300	$265	

Add $35 for Crimson Trace Lasergrips (LG Model, disc. 2019).

GRADING - PPGS™	100%	98%	95%	90%	80%	70%	60%	LAST MSR

MICRO 9 DESERT TAN (LG) – 9mm Para. cal., matte black aluminum frame, 3.15 in. stainless steel barrel, 6 shot mag., stainless steel slide with KimPro II Desert Tan finish, white dot sights, Crimson Trace Lasergrips in tan, 15.6 oz. New 2018.

MSR $808	$680	$600	$500	$450	$375	$300	$265	

MICRO 9 ECLIPSE – 9mm Para. cal., round heel aluminum frame, 3.15 in. stainless steel barrel, 7 shot, stainless steel slide with brushed polished flats, bobbed hammer, solid aluminum trigger, Tritium night sights, gray and black cyclone G10 grips, thumb safety and mag. release, contrast serrations, checkered front strap, KimPro II gray finish, 15.6 oz. New 2018.

MSR $822	$700	$615	$525	$475	$385	$315	$275	

MICRO 9 ESV – 9mm Para. cal., aluminum frame, 3.15 in. stainless steel match grade barrel coated in Titanium Nitride (TiN) or rose copper, ported stainless steel slide, aluminum trigger, standard night sights, Altamont G10 black grips with Kimber logo, ball mill cocking serrations, KimPro II black or gray finish, 15.35 oz. New 2019.

MSR $856	$725	$635	$550	$500	$400	$325	$280	

MICRO 9 KHX – 9mm Para. cal., aluminum frame, 3.15 in. stainless steel match grade barrel, 7 shot, stainless steel slide, aluminum trigger, red fiber optic front and green fiber optic rear sights, Hogue G10 grips, hexagonal pattern slide serrations, Stiplex front stap texture for positive grip, KimPro II gray finish, 15.6 oz. New 2019.

MSR $856	$725	$635	$550	$500	$400	$325	$280	

MICRO 9 NIGHTFALL (DN) – 9mm Para. cal., round heel aluminum frame with serrations, 3.15 in. stainless steel barrel, 7 shot, stainless steel slide, bobbed hammer, solid aluminum trigger, TruGlo TFX Pro day/night sights with rear cocking ledge and orange front sight ring, black Hogue wrap around grips, thumb safety, KimPro II black finish, 15.6 oz. New 2018.

MSR $795	$680	$600	$500	$450	$375	$300	$265	

MICRO 9 RAPIDE (BLACK ICE) – 9mm Para. cal., 3.15 in. stainless steel match grade barrel with DLC coating, 7 shot mag., aluminum frame, stainless steel slide, premium aluminum trigger, Tru-Glo TFX pro day/night sights, black G10 grips, front serrations, silver KimPro II finish, 15.6 oz. New 2020.

MSR $883	$750	$650	$550	$500	$400	$350	$285	

MICRO 9 RAPTOR COLLECTOR'S EDITION – 9mm Para. cal., aluminum frame, 3.15 in. stainless steel match grade barrel, 7 shot, aluminum trigger, Tritium night sights, G10 (half smooth/half scale) grips, Collector Series markings on left side of slide and special serial no. prefixes, black KimPro II and Tru-Tan finish, 15.6 oz. Limited mfg. 2020 only.

	$810	$710	$610	$550	$445	$365	$315	*$951*

MICRO 9 ROSE GOLD – 9mm Para. cal., aluminum frame, 3.15 in. stainless steel barrel, 7 shot, steel slide with rose gold PVD coating, Tritium night sights, G10 grips, ambidextrous thumb safety, mirror-polished slide and small parts, 15.6 oz. New mid-2017.

MSR $1,114	$950	$825	$700	$635	$515	$425	$350	

MICRO 9 SAPPHIRE – 9mm Para. cal., aluminum frame with satin silver finish, 3.15 in. stainless steel barrel, 6 shot, stainless steel slide, solid aluminum match grade trigger, Tritium night sights, blue/black G10 grips, ambidextrous thumb safety, delicately engraved scroll accents, mirror polished slide and small parts, bright blue PVD color finish, 15.6 oz. New 2018.

MSR $1,114	$950	$825	$700	$635	$515	$425	$350	

MICRO 9 STAINLESS – 9mm Para. cal., aluminum frame with satin silver finish, 3.15 in. stainless steel barrel, stainless steel slide, white dot sights or TruGlo TFX Pro day/night sights with rear cocking ledge and orange front sight ring (new 2018, DN model), rosewood or black Hogue wrap around (new 2018, DN model) grips, 15.6 oz. New 2016.

MSR $679	$580	$510	$435	$395	$320	$265	$225	

Add $116 for TruGlo TFX sights and Hogue grips (DN model), new 2018.

MICRO 9 STAINLESS RAPTOR – 9mm Para. cal., aluminum frame with KimPro silver finish, 3.15 in. stainless steel barrel, 6 shot, solid aluminum match grade trigger, Tritium night sights, Zebrawood grips with scale pattern and Kimber logo, ambidextrous thumb safety, patented scaled accents on slide and front strap, scalloped accents on mainspring housing and slide top, 15.6 oz. New 2018.

MSR $944	$800	$700	$600	$545	$440	$360	$310	

MICRO 9 TEXAS EDITION – 9mm Para. cal., matte black aluminum frame, 3.15 in. stainless steel match grade barrel, stainless steel slide with hot blue finish and polished flats features Western leaf and scroll engraving with saw tooth border, fixed low profile sights, bonded ivory grips with 1836 motto "Come and Take It" on left panel and state of Texas with state flag insert on right panel, 15.6 oz. Limited mfg. of 1,836 units 2017-2018.

	$850	$750	$650	$585	$475	$385	$325	*$987*

GRADING - PPGS™	100%	98%	95%	90%	80%	70%	60%	LAST MSR

MICRO 9 TLE – 9mm Para. cal., aluminum frame, 3.15 in. stainless steel barrel, 7 shot, stainless steel slide, bobbed hammer, solid aluminum trigger, Tritium night sights, green and black G10 grips, checkered front strap, KimPro II black finish, 15.6 oz. Mfg. 2018-2019.

	$675	$595	$500	$450	$375	$300	$250	*$788*

MICRO 9 TRIARI – 9mm Para. cal., aluminum frame with black KimPro II finish, 3.15 in. stainless steel match grade barrel, 7 shot mag., stainless steel slide with black oxide finish, aluminum trigger, red front and green rear fiber optic sights w/u-notch and cocking ledge, stacked cube pattern Black Linen Micarta grips, deep relief laser engraving, Stiplex front strap, black KimPro II finish, 15.6 oz. New 2020.

MSR $822	$700	$615	$525	$475	$385	$315	$275	

MICRO 9 TWO-TONE – 9mm Para. cal., 3.15 in. stainless steel ramped barrel, 6 shot, steel slide with black finish, solid aluminum match grade trigger, white dot sights or TruGlo TFX Pro day/night sights with rear cocking ledge and orange front sight ring (new 2018), rosewood grips with Kimber logo, black Hogue wrap around grips (mfg. 2018-2020), or Crimson Trace Lasergrips (new 2020), full-length guide rod, two-tone slide and frame finish, 15.6 oz. New 2016.

MSR $679	$580	$510	$435	$395	$320	$260	$225	

Add $143 for Crimson Trace Lasergrips (new 2020).
Add $101 for Hogue grips and TruGlo TFX sights (mfg. 2018-2020).

MICRO 9 WOODLAND NIGHT (LG) – 9mm Para. cal., aluminum frame with gray KimPro II finish, 3.15 in. stainless steel barrel, 6 shot, stainless steel slide with KimPro II black finish, white dot sights, Crimson Trace Lasergrips in OD Green, 15.6 oz. New mid-2017.

MSR $815	$700	$615	$525	$475	$385	$315	$275	

MICRO ADVOCATE – .380 ACP cal., 2 3/4 in. barrel, extended 7 shot mag., Tritium night sights, purple/black or brown/black G10 grips, matte black slide finish, 13.4 oz. Mfg. mid-2015-2018.

	$615	$525	$475	$425	$375	$325	$275	*$714*

MICRO AMETHYST – .380 ACP cal., 2 3/4 in. barrel, Tritium night sights, purple and black G10 grips, ambi thumb safety, engraved scroll accents, amethyst purple PVD finish. New 2017.

MSR $1,060	$900	$790	$675	$610	$500	$410	$350	

MICRO BEL AIR – .380 ACP cal., aluminum frame, 2.75 in. stainless steel barrel, 7 shot, stainless steel slide with mirror-polished finish, solid aluminum triger, fixed low profile 3-dot Tritium night sights, ivory Micarta grips, two-position safety, Bel Air Blue finish, 13.04 oz. New 2016.

MSR $904	$765	$670	$575	$520	$420	$350	$300	

MICRO CARRY – .380 ACP cal., SA, 2 3/4 in. stainless steel barrel, aluminum frame, stainless steel slide, satin silver, black (disc. 2015), or two-tone (new 2016) frame finish, 6 shot mag., steel or white dot (new 2016) sights, black synthetic double diamond grips or rosewood grips with Kimber logo (new 2016), 15.4 oz. Mfg. 2013-2017.

	$510	$450	$385	$350	$275	$225	$200	*$597*

* ***Micro Crimson Carry NS (Micro Crimson Carry)*** – .380 ACP cal., aluminum frame with satin silver finish, 2 3/4 in. stainless steel barrel, 7 shot mag., steel slide with matte black finish, white dot (disc.) or fixed night sights, rosewood Crimson Trace Lasergrips, 13.4 oz. Mfg. 2015-2019.

	$725	$635	$550	$500	$400	$325	$250	*$839*

MICRO CDP – .380 ACP cal., SA, 2 3/4 in. barrel, 6 shot mag., stainless steel slide and barrel, aluminum frame, 30 LPI front strap checkering, steel dovetail mounted 3-dot night sights, ambidextrous thumb safety, high cut under the trigger guard, double diamond checkered rosewood grips, matte black finish, checkered mainspring housing, 13.4 oz. Built in Kimber Custom Shop. Mfg. late 2012-2020.

	$740	$650	$550	$500	$400	$350	$285	*$869*

Add $218 for Crimson Trace Lasergrips (LG Model).

MICRO COVERT – .380 ACP cal., stainless steel round heel frame, 2.75 in. stainless steel barrel, 7 shot mag., stainless steel slide, bobbed hammer, aluminum trigger, Tritium night sights, Gray Urban camo Crimson Trace Lasergrips, checkered front strap and mainspring housing, Carry Melt treatment on slide and frame, KimPro II gray finish, 13.4 oz. Mfg. 2018-2019.

	$785	$685	$595	$550	$450	$375	$300	*$919*

MICRO DC – .380 ACP cal., 2 3/4 in. carbon steel barrel, extended 7 shot mag., Tritium night sights, textured G10 grips or black Crimson Trace Lasergrips, KimPro II black finish, 13.4 oz. Mfg. 2016-2018.

	$650	$575	$500	$450	$350	$300	$250	*$769*

Add $150 for Crimson Trace Lasergrips (Micro DC LG).

GRADING - PPGS™	100%	98%	95%	90%	80%	70%	60%	LAST MSR

MICRO DESERT NIGHT – .380 ACP cal., 2 3/4 in. barrel, aluminum frame with desert tan KimPro II finish, stainless steel slide with matte black KimPro II finish, white dot sights, brown and black G10 grips, 13.4 oz. New 2017.

MSR $659	$560	$490	$420	$380	$310	$260	$215	

MICRO DESERT TAN (LG) – .380 ACP cal., aluminum frame with matte black finish, 2.75 in. stainless steel barrel, 6 or 7 shot mag., steel slide with KimPro II Desert Tan finish, aluminum match grade trigger, fixed low profile 3-dot Tritium night sights, Desert Tan Crimson Trace Lasergrips, 13.4 oz. New mid-2017.

MSR $754	$635	$550	$475	$425	$350	$285	$250	

MICRO ECLIPSE – .380 ACP cal., 2.75 in. stainless steel match grade barrel, 8 shot, stainless steel frame and slide, brushed polished flats, Premium Aluminum trigger, Tritium night sights, gray and black Cyclone G10 grips, checkered front strap, KimPro II gray finish, 13.4 oz. New 2018.

MSR $768	$655	$575	$490	$450	$360	$300	$250	

MICRO RAPTOR – .380 ACP cal., 2 3/4 in. stainless steel barrel, aluminum or steel frame, stainless steel slide, 6 shot mag., full-length guide rod, high cut under trigger guard, solid aluminum match grade trigger, side and top slide scaling, front strap scale serrations, Carry Melt treatment, Tritium 3-dot night sights, Zebra wood grips with scale pattern and Kimber logo, black or satin silver finish, 13.4 oz. New 2015.

MSR $856	$725	$635	$550	$500	$400	$325	$280	

Add $27 for stainless steel slide, frame, and Satin Silver finish (Micro Raptor Stainless).

MICRO RCP – .380 ACP cal., aluminum frame, 2 3/4 in. stainless steel barrel, 6 shot, trench-cut sight, rosewood or Crimson Trace Lasergrips, matte black finish. Mfg. 2016-2018.

	$650	$575	$500	$450	$375	$310	$250	*$775*

Add $150 for Crimson Trace Lasergrips.

MICRO ROSE GOLD – .380 ACP cal., 2 3/4 in. stainless steel barrel, Tritium night sights, rose gold and black G10 grips, ambidextrous thumb safety, engraved scroll accents, mirror polished slide and small parts, PVD rose gold colored finish, 13.4 oz. New mid-2017.

MSR $1,060	$900	$790	$675	$610	$500	$410	$350	

MICRO SAPPHIRE – .380 ACP cal., 2 3/4 in. stainless steel barrel, 6 shot, mirror-polished slide and small parts, Tritium night sights, Micarta (disc.) or blue/black G10 grips, ambidextrous thumb safety, bright polished blue PVD accents and engraved stainless steel slide, 13.4 oz. New 2015.

MSR $1,060	$900	$790	$675	$610	$500	$410	$350	

MICRO STAINLESS ROSEWOOD – .380 ACP cal., aluminum frame, 2 3/4 in. barrel, 6 shot, stainless steel slide, aluminum match grade trigger, fixed low profile sights, rosewood grips with Kimber logo, satin silver slide and frame finish, 13.4 oz.

MSR $625	$525	$460	$395	$355	$290	$240	$200	

MICRO TLE (TACTICAL LAW ENFORCEMENT) – .380 ACP cal., stainless steel round heel frame, 2.75 in. stainless steel barrel, 7 shot, bobbed hammer, aluminum trigger, Tritium night sights, green and black G10 grips, thumb safety and mag. release, checkered front strap, full-length guide rod, KimPro II black finish, 13.4 oz. Mfg. 2018-2019.

	$625	$550	$475	$425	$350	$285	$225	*$734*

MICRO TWO-TONE – .380 ACP cal., aluminum frame with satin silver finish, 2 3/4 in. stainless steel barrel, 7 shot, stainless steel slide with matte black finish, solid aluminum match grade trigger, fixed low profile 3-dot Tritium night sights, checkered rosewood grips or Crimson Trace Lasergrips (new 2020), full-length guide rod, 13.4 oz.

MSR $625	$530	$465	$400	$360	$295	$240	$200	

Add $143 for Crimson Trace Lasergrips (new 2020).

POLYMER – .45 ACP cal., SA, widened black polymer frame offering larger mag. capacity, choice of fixed (Polymer) or adj. Kimber target (Polymer Target, disc. 1999) rear sight, matte black slide, 10 shot mag., 34 oz. Mfg. 1997-2001.

	$675	$595	$500	$450	$375	$300	$225	*$795*

Add $88 for Polymer Target.

All Polymer models were disc. in 2002 in favor of the new "Ten" Series with improved Kimber made frame. Magazines are interchangeable.

GRADING - PPGS™	100%	98%	95%	90%	80%	70%	60%	LAST MSR

* ***Polymer Stainless*** – .38 Super (advertised in 1999, never mfg.), 9mm Para. (advertised in 1999, never mfg.), .40 S&W (mfg. 1999 only), or .45 ACP cal., similar to Polymer, except has satin finish stainless steel slide. Mfg. 1998-2001.

	$745	$650	$550	$500	$410	$335	$250	*$856*

Add $88 for Polymer Stainless Target (disc. 1999).

* ***Polymer Gold Match*** – .45 ACP cal. only, similar to Gold Match, except has polymer frame, supplied with 10 shot double stack mag., 34 oz. Mfg. 1999-2001.

	$925	$810	$695	$630	$510	$415	$325	*$1,041*

» **Polymer Gold Match Stainless** – similar to Gold Match, except has polymer frame and stainless steel slide, 34 oz. Mfg. 1999-2001.

	$1,025	$895	$770	$695	$565	$460	$360	*$1,177*

* ***Polymer Pro Carry*** – .45 ACP cal. only, 4 in. bushingless bull barrel, steel slide, 32 oz. Mfg. 1999-2001.

	$725	$635	$545	$495	$400	$325	$255	*$814*

» **Polymer Pro Carry Stainless** – similar to Polymer Pro Carry, except has stainless steel slide. Mfg. 1999-2001.

	$755	$660	$565	$515	$415	$340	$265	*$874*

* ***Polymer Ultra Ten II*** – .45 ACP cal., black polymer frame with aluminum frame insert, stainless slide, 3 in. barrel, 10 shot staggered mag., low profile sights, lighter version of the Polymer Series frame, Kimber Firing Pin Safety, 24 oz.

While advertised during 2001 with an MSR of $896, this model was manufactured in prototypes only.

PRO CARRY II – 9mm Para. (new mid-2005), .40 S&W (disc. 2001) or .45 ACP cal., SA, 4 in. barrel, 7 or 8 shot mag., full-length guide rod, aluminum frame, steel slide, aluminum match grade trigger, fixed low profile sights, full-length black synthetic double diamond (disc. 2015) or rosewood (new 2016) grips, matte black (disc. 2015) or two-tone (new 2016) finish, 28 oz. New 1999.

MSR $883	$750	$650	$550	$500	$400	$350	$285	

Add $21 for 9mm Para. cal.
Add $35 for .40 S&W cal. (disc.).
Add $120 for night sights (.45 ACP cal. only).

This series' nomenclature added the Roman numeral "II" during 2001.

* ***Pro Carry II Stainless*** – .40 S&W (disc. 2007), .45 ACP, or 9mm Para. cal., similar to Pro Carry, except has stainless steel slide, black synthetic (disc. 2015) or rosewood with Kimber logo (new 2016) grips, fiber optic sights became standard 2017, 28 oz. New 1999.

MSR $938	$800	$700	$600	$545	$440	$360	$310	

Add $20 for 9mm Para. cal.
Subtract approx. $112 if without night sights (became standard 2017).
Add $38 for .40 S&W (disc. 2007) cal.
Add $295 for Crimson Trace grips (.45 ACP cal. only, disc. 2009).

* ***Pro Carry II HD*** – .38 Super (mfg. 2002-2015) or .45 ACP cal., similar to Pro Carry Stainless, except has heavier stainless steel frame, 4 in. barrel, 7 or 9 shot mag., black synthetic (disc. 2015) or rosewood with Kimber logo (new 2016) grips, 35 oz. Mfg. 2001-2016.

	$895	$785	$675	$610	$500	$425	$325	*$1,046*

Add $48 for .38 Super cal. (disc. 2015).

* ***Pro Carry II Two-Tone*** – 9mm Para. or .45 ACP cal., aluminum frame, 4 in. stainless steel match grade bushing barrel, 7 shot mag., steel slide, aluminum three hole standard trigger, fixed low profile sights, smooth checkered laser rosewood grips, matte black brush polished slide and satin silver frame finish, 28 oz. New 2020.

MSR $1,189	$1,010	$885	$760	$685	$550	$455	$355	

Add $21 for 9mm Para. cal.

PRO TLE/RL II – .45 ACP cal., 1911 style, 4 in. bushingless barrel, 7 shot mag., stainless steel, fixed low profile 3-dot Tritium night sights, double diamond black synthetic grips, 30 LPI front strap checkering, Picatinny rail, matte black finish, 36 oz. Mfg. 2004-2018.

	$935	$825	$700	$635	$515	$425	$365	*$1,102*

* ***Stainless Pro TLE/RL II*** – .45 ACP cal., 4 in. bushingless barrel, 7 shot mag., stainless steel construction, black synthetic (disc. 2015) or G10 (new 2016) grips, Picatinny rail, satin silver finish. Mfg. 2004-2018.

	$1,050	$920	$790	$715	$580	$475	$400	*$1,232*

GRADING - PPGS™	100%	98%	95%	90%	80%	70%	60%	LAST MSR

PRO TLE II (LG) – .45 ACP cal., 1911 style, 4 in. stainless steel bushingless barrel, 7 shot mag., fixed low profile 3-dot Tritium night sights, double diamond checkered black synthetic (disc. 2015), Crimson Trace laser (disc. 2008 only), or G10 (new 2016) grips, full-length guide rod, with (mfg. 2017-2020) or w/o extended magwell, matte black finish, 35 oz. Mfg. 2006-2008, reintroduced 2010.

MSR $1,060	$900	$790	$675	$610	$500	$410	$350	

Add $61 for extended magwell (Pro TLE II EM, mfg. 2017-2020).
Subtract $240 if w/o Crimson Trace Lasergrips (mfg. 2008 only).

* ***Stainless Pro TLE II*** – .45 ACP cal., 1911 style, 4 in. barrel, 7 shot mag., stainless steel construction, fixed low profile 3-dot Tritium night sights, double diamond checkered black synthetic grips, full-length guide rod, front strap checkering, satin silver finish. Disc. 2018.

	$975	$850	$725	$675	$550	$450	$375	*$1,136*

Add $265 for Crimson Trace Lasergrips (disc. 2015).

* ***Pro TLE II TFS*** – .45 ACP cal., 4 in. stainless steel threaded barrel, 7 shot mag., fixed low profile 3-dot Tritium night sights, black synthetic (disc. 2015) or G10 (new 2016) grips, full-length guide rod, Picatinny rail, matte black finish. Mfg. 2015-2016.

	$975	$850	$725	$625	$500	$425	$350	*$1,079*

RAPTOR II – .45 ACP cal., 1911 style, SA, full size carbon steel frame with "scales" on front strap, continuing on slide in lieu of standard serrations, 5 in. stainless steel barrel with or w/o engraved "Raptor II" and "Custom Shop", 8 shot mag., black anodized trigger, fixed slant night sights, scaled Zebra wood grip panels with Kimber logo, ambi thumb safety, back cut flat-top, matte black finish with brush polished flats, 38 oz. New mid-2004.

MSR $1,414	$1,200	$1,050	$900	$815	$660	$540	$475	

* ***Grand Raptor II*** – .45 ACP cal., SA, 5 in. barrel, full size stainless steel frame, blued slide, flats on frame and slide polished, two-tone finish, scale rosewood grips with Kimber logo, extended ambidextrous thumb safety, bumped beavertail grip safety, night sights, 38 oz. Mfg. by Custom Shop 2006-disc.

	$1,285	$1,125	$975	$875	$700	$585	$500	*$1,512*

* ***Pro Raptor II*** – 9mm Para. (new 2016, stainless only) or .45 ACP cal., SA, 4 in. stainless barrel with engraved "Pro Raptor II" and "Custom Shop", full size stainless steel frame with "scales" on front strap, continuing on carbon steel slide in lieu of standard serrations, flats on frame and slide polished, black oxide finish, back cut flat-top, black anodized trigger, ambidextrous safety, scaled Zebra wood grip panels with Kimber logo, fixed slant night sights, 38 oz. New mid-2004.

MSR $1,192	$1,025	$900	$775	$700	$575	$475	$375	

Add $101-$121 for Stainless Pro Rapter II (new 2009), depending on caliber.

* ***Ultra Raptor II*** – 9mm Para. (new 2016, stainless only) or .45 ACP cal., SA, 3 in. ramped match grade bushingless barrel, lightweight aluminum frame, scale serrations on flat-top slide and front strap, feathered logo zebra wood grips, flats on frame and slide polished, night sights, all-matte black finish, 25 oz. Mfg. by Custom Shop. New 2006.

MSR $1,257	$1,075	$930	$800	$725	$585	$480	$415	

Add $102-$123 for Stainless Ultra Raptor II, depending on caliber.

RIMFIRE SUPER – .22 LR cal., 5 in. barrel, 10 shot mag., aluminum frame with satin silver KimPro II finish, front strap checkering, aluminum flat-top slide with matte black KimPro II finish and aggressive fluting on upper sides, full-length guide rod, premium aluminum trigger, ambidextrous safety, rosewood grips with logo inserts, 23 oz. Mfg. by Kimber Custom Shop 2004-2016.

	$1,075	$925	$800	$700	$600	$500	$425	*$1,220*

RIMFIRE TARGET – .17 Mach 2 (mfg. 2004-2005) or .22 LR cal., 5 in. barrel, SA, 10 shot mag., aluminum frame with satin silver or matte black finish (black anodized finish was disc. in 2006), black oxide steel or satin stainless slide (.17 Mach 2 cal. only), black synthetic double diamond grips, Kimber adj. rear sight, 28 oz. Mfg. 2003-2015.

	$775	$675	$575	$500	$400	$325	$275	*$871*

Add $339 for black or silver conversion kit.
Add $75 for .17 Mach 2 cal. (disc. 2005).

SIS SERIES – .45 ACP cal., SA, stainless steel slide, frame, and serrated mainspring housing, 7 or 8 shot mag., 3 (Ultra), 4 (Pro), or 5 (Custom or Custom RL) in. barrel, SIS night sights, cocking shoulder for one-hand cocking, lightweight hammer, solid trigger, slide serrations, gray KimPro II finish, beavertail grip safety, stippled black laminate logo grips, ambidextrous thumb safety, choice of rounded frame and mainspring housing (SIS Ultra), Picatinny rail (SIS Pro & Custom RL), standard length guide rod (Custom & Custom RL), 31-39 oz. Mfg. 2008-2009.

	$1,250	$1,095	$935	$850	$685	$560	$435	*$1,427*

Add $95 for SIS Custom RL model with standard length guide rod and Picatinny rail.

GRADING - PPGS™	100%	98%	95%	90%	80%	70%	60%	LAST MSR

SOLO CARRY – 9mm Para. cal., DA, SFO, micro-compact aluminum frame, 2.7 in. stainless steel barrel, 6 or 8 (extended mag.) shot, matte black (Solo Carry) or satin silver (Solo Carry Stainless) KimPro II finish, stainless steel slide, amidextrous thumb safety, black synthetic removable grips, rosewood grips with special logo (new 2015), or Crimson Trace Lasergrips (new 2015), ambidextrous mag. release, 3-dot sights, 17 oz. Mfg. 2011-2017.

	$695	$610	$525	$475	$385	$325	$250	*$815*

Add $34 for rosewood grips with special logo (new 2015).
Add $258 for Crimson Trace Lasergrips (new 2015).

* ***Solo CDP (LG)*** – 9mm Para. cal., SFO, 2.7 in. barrel, matte black aluminum frame with satin stainless steel slide, 6 or 8 shot mag., checkered front and backstrap, fixed 3-dot Tritium night sights and rosewood Crimson Trace Lasergrips, 17 oz. Mfg. late 2011-2017.

	$1,050	$875	$750	$675	$550	$450	$350	*$1,223*

* ***Solo Carry DC*** – 9mm Para. cal., SA, SFO, 2.7 in. barrel, black DLC finished slide and barrel, night sights, Carry Melt treatment, 6 shot mag., 17 oz. Mfg. 2012-2017.

	$775	$675	$575	$525	$425	$375	$300	*$904*

Add $300 for Crimson Trace Lasergrips (Solo Carry DC-LG).

* ***Solo Sapphire*** – 9mm Para. cal., DA, SFO, 2.7 in. stainless steel barrel, ambidextrous thumb safety, bright polished blue PVD accents and engraved stainless steel slide, night sights, Micarta grips, 17 oz. Mfg. 2015-2017.

	$1,100	$975	$825	$750	$600	$500	$400	*$1,291*

STAINLESS RAPTOR II – 9mm Para. cal., 1911 style, SA, stainless steel frame, 5 in. stainless steel match grade barrel, 9 shot mag., stainless steel slide with front serrations, aluminum trigger, Tactical Wedge 3-dot Tritium night sights, Zebrawood grips with scale pattern and Kimber logo, ambi thumb safety, satin silver finish with brush polished flats, 38 oz. New mid-2004.

MSR $1,543	$1,310	$1,150	$985	$890	$725	$590	$510	

* ***Stainless Raptor II (Collectors Edition)*** – .45 ACP cal., full size stainless steel frame with KimPro black finish, 5 in. stainless steel match grade barrel, 8 shot mag., stainless slide with Black and Tru-Tan KimPro finish, Raptor scales with scaled flat-top, 3-hole aluminum black trigger, fixed low profile wedge Tritium rear night sight and Tritium front night sight, full size G10 smooth/scaled Collector Edition Raptor grip, Collector Series marking on left side of slide, special serial number prefix, two-tone finish, 38 oz. Limited mfg. beginning 2020.

MSR $1,524	$1,295	$1,135	$975	$880	$710	$585	$500	

STAINLESS TARGET (LS) – 10mm or .45 ACP cal., stainless steel slide and rounded heel frame, 6 in. stainless steel barrel, 7 shot, bobbed hammer, match grade 3-hole trigger, adj. rear target and red fiber optic front sight, rosewood grips with Kimber logo, 24 LPI front strap checkering, satin silver finish, 42 oz. New 2018.

MSR $1,101	$935	$825	$700	$635	$515	$425	$365	

Add $20 for 10mm cal.

STAINLESS TEN II – .45 ACP cal., SA, high capacity polymer frame, stainless steel slide with satin finish, impressed front grip strap checkering and serrations under trigger guard, textured finish, polymer grip safety and mainspring housing, 10 or 13 (new 2005) round double stack mag., includes Ultra Ten II (3 in. barrel, short grip, disc. 2003), Pro Carry Ten II (4 in. barrel, standard grip), Stainless Ten II (full size), and Gold Match Ten II (stainless steel barrel, polished stainless steel slide flats, hand fitted barrel/bushing to slide, adj. sight), 14 (pre-ban) round mags. also available, accepts magazines from older Kimber mfg. polymer pistols. Mfg. 2002-2007.

	$715	$625	$535	$485	$395	$320	$250	*$812*

Add $9 for Pro-Carry Ten II, $35 for Ultra Ten II (disc. 2003), or $294 for Gold Match Ten II.

* ***BP Ten II*** – similar to Stainless Ten II, except has black oxide carbon steel slide, and aluminum frame for lighter weight. Mfg. 2003-2007.

	$570	$500	$425	$385	$315	$255	$200	*$652*

* ***Pro BP Ten II*** – similar to Pro Carry Ten II, except has black oxide carbon steel slide, and aluminum frame for lighter weight. Mfg. 2003-2007.

	$570	$500	$425	$385	$315	$255	$200	*$666*

SUPERAMERICA LIMITED EDITION – .45 ACP cal., Presentation Grade 1911 with matching knife, 5 in. stainless steel match grade barrel, Premium Aluminum trigger, dovetail mounted adj. sight, mammoth ivory grips on pistol and knife, fine English scroll pattern engraving set against a gold border, each model bears a sequential serial number beginning with KSA, and each knife is serialized to match, set

GRADING - PPGS™	100%	98%	95%	90%	80%	70%	60%	LAST MSR

comes in a wood presentation case topped with the Kimber and SuperAmerica marks, highly polished blue on the flats and matte blue finish over the curves. Limited mfg. 2007 only.

	$3,200	$2,800	$2,400	$2,175	$1,760	$1,450	$1,185	*$3,570*

SUPER CARRY SERIES – .45 ACP cal., SA, 3 (Ultra), 4 (Pro), or 5 (Custom) in. barrel, stainless steel slide, aluminum frame, KimPro II finish, night sights, rounded edges, checkered double Dymondwood or Micarta (Ultra+, new 2011) grips, recessed slide stop pin with surrounding bevel, rear slide serrations, 25-31 oz. Mfg. 2010-2018.

	$1,360	$1,190	$1,020	$925	$750	$625	$530	*$1,596*

* ***Super Carry HD Series*** – .45 ACP cal., 3 (Ultra), 4 (Pro), or 5 (Custom) in. barrel, similar to Super Carry, except has matte black finish and G10 checkered blue/black Micarta grips, 32 oz. Mfg. 2011-2016.

	$1,525	$1,315	$1,100	$1,025	$900	$775	$650	*$1,699*

TACTICAL II SERIES – 9mm Para. (Tactical Pro II, new 2004) or .45 ACP cal., SA, lightweight tactical pistol, gray anodized (disc. 2008) or gray KimPro II finished frame with black steel slide, fixed Tritium 3-dot night sights, extended magwell, 30 LPI front strap checkering, black/gray laminated logo grips, 7 shot mag. with bumper pad, available in Tactical Ultra II (3 in. barrel, short grip, 25 oz.), Tactical Pro II (4 in. barrel, standard grip, 28 oz.), Tactical Custom II (5 in. barrel, standard grip, 31 oz.). Tactical Custom HD II (.45 ACP only, new 2009), or Tactical Entry II (.45 ACP only, includes integral rail and night sights). Mfg. 2003-2016.

	$1,125	$975	$850	$725	$600	$525	$400	*$1,317*

Add $34 for Tactical Pro II in 9mm Para. cal.
Add $70 for Tactical Custom HD II.
Add $173 for Tactical Entry II.

A Custom Shop version of the Pro Tactical II was manufactured in 2002, but without checkering and night sights.

TEAM MATCH II – 9mm Para. (new 2009), .45 ACP, or .38 Super (limited mfg. 2003-2004, reintroduced 2006-2010) cal., same pistol developed for USA Shooting Team (2004 Olympics Rapid Fire Pistol Team) competition, satin finish stainless steel frame and slide, 5 in. match grade barrel, SA, 30 LPI front strap checkering, match grade trigger, Tactical Extractor system (disc.) or internal extractor, extended magwell, 8 shot mag., laminated red/white/blue grips, 38 oz. Total production just over 10,000 units. Later mfg. had a gold logo on slide, red/blue grips and black DLC coating on slide. Mfg. 2003-2012.

	$1,315	$1,150	$975	$775	$725	$575	$450	*$1,563*

Add $13 for 9mm Para. cal.
Add $48 for .38 Super cal. (disc. 2010).

A $100 donation was made to the U.S.A. Shooting Team for every Team Match II sold.

* ***Team Match II (Recent Mfg.)*** – 9mm Para. or .45 ACP cal., SA, same pistol developed for USA Shooting Team (2004 Olympics Rapid Fire Pistol Team) competition, 5 in. match grade barrel and bushing, front serrations, satin finish stainless steel frame, stainless steel slide with black diamond-like coating finish and 24Kt. gold USA shooting team logo, 30 LPI front strap checkering, full-length guide rod, ambidextrous thumb safety, match grade trigger, extended magwell, 8 shot mag., laminated red and blue G10 grips, 38 oz. Mfg. 2014-2018.

	$1,425	$1,250	$1,075	$975	$785	$650	$550	*$1,674*

Add $20 for 9mm Para. cal.

A $100 donation was made to the U.S.A. Shooting Team for every Team Match II sold.

ULTRA CARRY II – .40 S&W (disc. 2001), 9mm Para. (new 2016) or .45 ACP cal., SA, 3 in. barrel, aluminum frame, 7 shot mag., full-length guide rod, steel slide, fixed low profile sights, black synthetic double diamond (disc. 2015) or rosewood (new 2016) grips, matte black (disc. 2015) or two-tone (new 2016) finish, 25 oz. New 1999.

MSR $883	$750	$650	$550	$500	$400	$350	$285	

Add $21 for 9mm Para. cal. (new 2016).
Add $120 for night sights (disc. 2015).
Add $39 for .40 S&W cal. (disc. 2001).
Add $375 for Crimson Trace grips (disc. 2009).

This series' nomenclature added the Roman numeral "II" during 2001.

* ***Stainless Ultra Carry II*** – 9mm Para. (new 2008), .40 S&W (disc. 2007), or .45 ACP cal., stainless steel construction, 3 in. barrel, fixed low profile or fiber optic (became standard 2017) sights, black synthetic (disc. 2015) or rosewood with Kimber logo (new 2016) grips. New 1999.

MSR $938	$800	$700	$600	$545	$440	$360	$310	

Add $20 for 9mm Para. (new 2008) or $45 for .40 S&W cal. (disc. 2007).
Add $109 for night sights (.45 ACP cal. only, disc. 2009).

GRADING - PPGS™	100%	98%	95%	90%	80%	70%	60%	LAST MSR

* ***Ultra Carry II Two-Tone*** – 9mm Para. or .45 ACP cal., aluminum frame with in silver finish, 3 in. stainless stteel match grade ramped barrel, 7 shot mag., steel slide with matte black brush-polished finish, aluminum 3-hole trigge, fixed low profile sights, smooth/checkered rosewood grips, 25 oz. New 2020.

MSR $883 $750 $650 $550 $500 $400 $350 $285

Add $21 for 9mm Para. cal.

ULTRA TEN CDP II – .45 ACP cal., SA, 3 in. barrel, stainless steel slide with black polymer frame, Tritium night sights, carry bevel treatment, standard manual safety, 10 shot mag., 24 oz. Mfg. 2003 only.

$825 $720 $620 $560 $455 $370 $290 *$926*

ULTRA TLE II – .45 ACP cal., SA, 3 in. bull barrel, 7 shot mag., aluminum frame, dovetail mounted night sights, double diamond checkered black synthetic (disc. 2015), Crimson Trace laser (disc. 2015), or G10 (new 2016) grips, matte black finish, 25 oz. New 2010.

MSR $1,060 $900 $790 $675 $610 $500 $410 $350

Add $243 for Crimson Trace Lasergrips (disc. 2015).

* ***Stainless Ultra TLE II*** – .45 ACP cal., similar to Ultra TLE II, except is stainless steel, black synthetic (disc. 2015) or G10 (new 2016) grips, satin silver finish, 25 oz. Mfg. 2010-2018.

$975 $850 $725 $675 $550 $450 $375 *$1,136*

Add $265 for Crimson Trace Lasergrips (disc. 2015).

WARRIOR – .45 ACP cal., SA, production began following adoption of this pistol by the Marine Expeditionary Unit (MEU) Special Operations Capable (SOC), Detachment 1 (Det. 1), civilian version with 5 in. barrel, Series I (no firing pin block), carbon steel slide and frame, integral Picatinny light rail, 24 LPI front strap checkering (new 2017), internal extractor, lanyard loop, bumped grip safety, G10 material grip (coyote brown), wedge night sights, ambidextrous safety, GI length (standard) guide rod, black KimPro II finish, 38 oz. Mfg. mid-2004-2018.

$1,190 $1,050 $900 $815 $675 $550 $450 *$1,392*

WARRIOR II – .45 ACP cal., steel frame with Picatinny rail, 5 in. carbon steel match grade barrel, 7 shot mag., steel slide with front serrations, aluminum match grade trigger, Tactical Wedge Tritium night sights, Kimber G10 tactical grips, ambi thumb safety, matte black KimPro II finish, 39 oz.

MSR $1,510 $1,285 $1,125 $965 $875 $700 $580 $500

WARRIOR SOC – .45 ACP cal., 5 in. barrel, tan/green KimPro II finish, lower front rail with removable Desert Tan Crimson Trace Rail Master laser sight, ambidextrous thumb safety, lanyard ring, 24 LPI front strap checkering (new 2017), textured G10 grips, 40 oz. Mfg. 2013-disc.

$1,300 $1,150 $975 $885 $725 $585 $450 *$1,533*

* ***Warrior SOC TFS*** – .45 ACP cal., similar to the Warrior SOC, except has 5 1/2 in. barrel threaded for suspension (TFS) and a thread protector cap, 40 oz. Mfg. 2015-disc.

$1,450 $1,275 $1,100 $985 $800 $675 $525 *$1,605*

DESERT WARRIOR – .45 ACP cal., 5 in. stainless steel barrel, 7 shot mag., steel frame and slide, Tactical Wedge Tritium night sights, light tan G10 grips, ambidextrous thumb safety, Kimber tactical rail, steel mainspring housing with lanyard ring, 24 LPI front strap checkering (new 2017), dark earth KimPro II metal finish, 40 oz. New mid-2005.

MSR $1,495 $1,275 $1,115 $950 $865 $700 $600 $500

* ***Desert Warrior TFS*** – .45 ACP cal., similar to Desert Warrior, except has 5 1/2 in. stainless steel barrel threaded for suspension (TFS), and thread protector cap, 40 oz. New 2015.

MSR $1,563 $1,325 $1,160 $995 $900 $730 $600 $525

Pistols: Kimber Non-Cataloged Models

Over the years, Kimber has manufactured a number of models that did not appear in their catalog. To help identify non-cataloged models, pistols are listed in two categories: Custom Shop/Special Edition Pistols and Limited Edition Pistols.

Pistols: Kimber Custom Shop/Special Editions, Single Action

Beginning in 1998, the Kimber Custom Shop began producing special edition pistols. Special edition models have been issued in either fixed numbers, or time limited. Where available, time limited models show the actual number produced. All models are .45 ACP caliber unless otherwise specified.

25th ANNIVERSARY CUSTOM LIMITED EDITION – .45 ACP cal., black oxide frame and slide, 5 in. barrel, premium aluminum trigger, fancy walnut anniversary logo grips, "1979-2004" engraving on slide, Series I safeties and traditional extractor, ser. no. range is KAPC0001-KAPC1911. Limited production of 1,911 during 2004-2005.

$825 $725 $650 $575 $500 $425 $350 *$923*

GRADING - PPGS™	100%	98%	95%	90%	80%	70%	60%	LAST MSR

* ***25th Anniversary Custom Limited Edition Gold Match*** – blued frame and slide, deep polish on flats, 5 in. stainless barrel, premium aluminum trigger, ambidextrous safety, adj. sights, fancy walnut anniversary logo grips, "1979-2004" engraving in slide, Series I safeties and traditional extractor, ser. no. range KAPG0001-KAPG0500, 38 oz. Limited production of 500 during 2004-2005.

	$1,175	$995	$875	$775	$700	$625	$550	*$1,357*

* ***25th Anniversary Custom Limited Edition Pistol Set*** – includes one Custom (ser. no. range KMSC0001-KMSC250) and one Gold Match (ser. no. range KMSG0001 - KMSG250), matched ser. nos., wood presentation case. Limited production of 250 during 2004-2005.

	$2,250	$2,000	$1,775	$1,525	$1,300	$1,100	$900	*$2,620*

AMETHYST ULTRA II – 9mm Para. or .45 ACP cal., round heel frame, 3 in. barrel, Tactical Wedge night sights, G10 grips, ambidextrous safety, highly polished stainless steel slide with amethyst purple PVD coating and cut scroll engraving and border, amethyst purple PVD-coated small parts, 25 oz. Special Edition mfg. by the Custom Shop beginning 2016.

MSR $1,754	$1,490	$1,300	$1,120	$1,015	$820	$675	$580	

Add $20 for 9mm Para. cal.

CAMP GUARD 10 – 10mm cal., round heel frame, 5 in. barrel, 8 shot mag., stainless steel construction, Tactical Wedge Tritium 3-dot night sights, custom RMEF carved rosewood grips, KimPro II finish, 38 oz. New 2017.

MSR $1,298	$1,100	$965	$825	$750	$600	$500	$425	

CENTENNIAL EDITION – .45 ACP cal., steel frame with finish by Turnbull Restoration, ivory grips, adj. target sights, light scroll engraving, aluminum trigger, includes presentation case, Limited mfg. of 250 during 2010.

	$3,995	$3,650	$3,275	N/A	N/A	N/A	N/A	*$4,352*

CLASSIC CARRY ELITE – .45 ACP cal., round heel steel frame with highly polished flats, 5 in. barrel, fine line engraving on stainless slide, 24 LPI front strap checkering, bi-tone gunmetal/rose gold PVD finish, 38 oz. Mfg. 2015-2017.

	$2,175	$1,850	$1,600	$1,390	$1,125	$925	$800	*$2,495*

CLASSIC CARRY PRO – .45 ACP cal., steel frame and slide, 4 in. bushingless match grade bull barrel, round heel frame, charcoal blue metal finish, G10 ivory grips, night sights, front strap checkering, 35 oz. Mfg. 2012-disc.

	$1,575	$1,340	$1,100	$1,025	$900	$775	$650	*$1,785*

CUSTOM TLE II 200TH ANNIVERSARY ALABAMA – .45 ACP cal., stainless steel frame with KimPro II Tru-Tan finish, 5 in. match grade stainless steel barrel, 7 shot mag., extended magwell, stainless steel slide with black satin KimPro II finish, front serrations, 3-hole aluminum trigger, fixed Tritium night sights, cherry/black G10 magwell grips, full length guide rod, features the Troy, Alabama Kimber location markings, special serial number run prefix (KALxxxxxx) for Kimber Alabama, Alabama state flag with the dates 1819-2019 are engraved on the right side, state motto "We Dare Defend our Rights" in Latin engraved on left of slide, engravings filled with red KimPro II finish to make the engraving stand out, 38 oz. Limited mfg. 2019 only.

	$1,000	$875	$750	$680	$550	$455	$390	*$1,183*

CUSTOM TLE II TROY ALABAMA EDITION – .45 ACP cal., stainless steel frame with KimPro II Tru-Tan finish, 5 in. stainless steel match grade barrel, 7 shot mag., extended magwell, stainless steel slide with KimPro II black satin finish, front serrations, 3-hole aluminum trigger, fixed Tritium night sights, cherry/black G10 magwell grips, full length guide rod, 30 LPI front strap checkering, features special serial number run prefix (KTAxxxxxx) for Kimber Troy Alabama, Spartan helmet with "Troy" and the town established date of 1843 are engraved on the right side, "SWEET HOME" and "ALABAMA" is engraved on the left side of the slide, red KimPro II finish fills the engravings to make them stand out, 38 oz. Limited mfg. 2019 only.

	$1,000	$875	$750	$680	$550	$455	$390	*$1,183*

DIAMOND ULTRA II – 9mm Para. or .45 ACP cal., aluminum round heel frame, 3 in. barrel, mirror-polished stainless steel slide and small parts, cut scroll engraving and border, Tactical Wedge night sights, G10 grips, ambidextrous safety, satin silver finish, 25 oz. Mfg. mid-2015-2016.

	$1,495	$1,300	$1,100	$1,025	$900	$775	$650	*$1,652*

ELITE CARRY – black anodized compact aluminum frame, stainless slide, 4 in. barrel, meltdown treatment on slide and frame, Tritium night sights, 20 LPI checkered front strap, ambidextrous safety, aluminum match trigger, hand checkered rosewood grips, 28 oz. 1,200 mfg. 1998.

Last MSR was $1,019.

GRADING - PPGS™	100%	98%	95%	90%	80%	70%	60%	LAST MSR

GOLD COMBAT II – .45 ACP cal. only, 5 in. barrel (bushingless bull became standard 2008), SA, full size carry pistol based on the Gold Match, steel frame and slide, stainless steel match grade barrel and bushing, serrated flat-top and scalloped French shoulders also became standard 2008, Tritium night sights, checkered walnut (disc. 2008) or 24 LPI herringbone pattern Micarta grips, ambidextrous thumb safety, extended and beveled magwell, full-length guide rod, matte black KimPro II finish, 38 oz, mfg. by Custom Shop. Mfg. 1994-2008, reintroduced 2011-2018.

	100%	98%	95%	90%	80%	70%	60%	LAST MSR
	$2,075	$1,800	$1,575	$1,375	$1,100	$900	$750	*$2,307*

This series' nomenclature added the Roman numeral "II" during 2001.

* ***Gold Combat Stainless II*** – .45 ACP cal., similar to Gold Combat, except is all stainless steel. Mfg. 1994-2008, reintroduced 2011-2018.

	100%	98%	95%	90%	80%	70%	60%	LAST MSR
	$2,000	$1,775	$1,550	$1,375	$1,100	$900	$700	*$2,251*

* ***Gold Combat RL II*** – .45 ACP cal., similar to Gold Combat, except has Picatinny rail machined into the lower forward frame to accept optics and other tactical accessories, 40 oz. Mfg. 1994-2008, reintroduced 2011-2018.

	100%	98%	95%	90%	80%	70%	60%	LAST MSR
	$2,100	$1,800	$1,575	$1,375	$1,125	$925	$800	*$2,405*

GOLD GUARDIAN – highly polished stainless steel slide and frame, hand fitted 5 in. match barrel and bushing, Tritium night sights, ambidextrous safety, extended magwell, skeletonized match trigger, hand checkered rosewood grips, 38 oz. 300 mfg. 1998.

Last MSR was $1,350.

HERITAGE EDITION – black oxide steel frame and slide, 30 LPI front strap checkering,ambidextrous safety, premium aluminum trigger, NSSF Heritage medallion and special markings on slide, ser. no. begins with KHE, 38 oz. 1,041 mfg. 2000.

Last MSR was $1,065.

HERO CUSTOM – .45 ACP cal., stainless steel frame with Desert Tan KimPro II finish, 5 in. stainless steel match grade barrel, 7 shot mag., stainless steel slide with matte black KimPro II finish, front serrations, and tan U.S. flag engraving, aluminum 3-hole trigger, fiber optic sights, Kryptek Highlander patterned grips, full-length guide rod, Boot Campaign logo engraved on topstrap, integrated lanyard loop, 38 oz. New 2018.

	100%	98%	95%	90%	80%	70%	60%	LAST MSR
MSR $1,019	$865	$750	$650	$590	$475	$400	$325	

ONYX ULTRA II – 9mm Para. or .45 ACP cal., 3 in. stainless steel barrel, 7 or 8 shot mag., solid aluminum match grade trigger, Tactical Wedge night sights, black Micarta thin grips, ambidextrous thumb safety, full-length guide rod, aluminum frame with satin silver finish, PVD coating on small parts, stainless steel slide with high polish deep black PVD coating and cut scroll engraving and border, 25 oz. Mfg. 2015-2016.

	100%	98%	95%	90%	80%	70%	60%	LAST MSR
	$1,495	$1,300	$1,100	$1,025	$900	$775	$650	*$1,652*

PRO ELITE – aluminum frame with silver KimPro finish, stainless slide with black KimPro finish, full meltdown treatment on slide and frame, 4 in. barrel, 30 LPI front strap checkering, 3-dot Tritium night sights, hand checkered rosewood grips, 28 oz. 2,500 mfg. 1999.

Last MSR was $1,140.

PRO SHADOW II – black steel slide and anodized aluminum frame, 4 in. barrel, fixed Tritium night sights, 30 LPI front strap checkering, grey laminate grips, silver grip and thumb safeties and mainspring housing, ser. no. begins with KPSLE, 28 oz.

Last MSR was $949.

RAPIDE – 10mm or .45 ACP cal., stainless steel frame, 5 in. stainless steel match grade barrel, 8 shot mag., stainless steel slide with front serrations, V-cut aluminum trigger, TruGlo TFX Pro day/night sights, gray/black WavZ G10 grips, black KimPro II finish, 38 oz. New 2019.

	100%	98%	95%	90%	80%	70%	60%	LAST MSR
MSR $1,597	$1,360	$1,190	$1,020	$925	$750	$625	$530	

Add $21 for 10mm cal.

* ***Rapide Black Ice*** – 9mm Para., 10mm, or .45 ACP cal., stainless steel frame, 5 in. stainless steel match grade barrel with DLC coating, 8 shot mag., stainless steel slide with front serrations, V-cut aluminum trigger, TruGlo TFX Pro day/night sights, black Rapide G10 grips w/matching accents, Kimber Stiplex TM front strap stiplling, Silver/Gray KimPro II finish, 38 oz. New 2020.

	100%	98%	95%	90%	80%	70%	60%	LAST MSR
MSR $1,597	$1,360	$1,190	$1,020	$925	$750	$625	$530	

Add $21 for 10mm or 9mm Para. cal.

ROSE GOLD ULTRA II – 9mm Para. or .45 ACP cal., round heel aluminum frame, 3 in. stainless steel barrel, 7 or 8 shot mag., highly polished stainless steel slide with rose gold PVD coating and scroll engraving and border, TW night sights, G10 grips, ambi safety, rose gold PVD-coated small parts, 25 oz. New 2017.

	100%	98%	95%	90%	80%	70%	60%	LAST MSR
MSR $1,754	$1,490	$1,300	$1,120	$1,015	$820	$675	$580	

Add $20 for 9mm Para. cal.

GRADING - PPGS™	100%	98%	95%	90%	80%	70%	60%	LAST MSR

ROYAL CARRY – compact aluminum frame, 4 in. bushingless barrel, highly polished blue, night sights, ambidextrous safety, hand checkered rosewood grips, 28 oz. 600 mfg. 1998.

Last MSR was $903.

ROYAL II – .45 ACP cal., 5 in. barrel, steel frame and slide, fixed low profile sights, aluminum match grade trigger, charcoal blue finish, solid bone grips, 38 oz. Mfg. by the Custom Shop 2010-disc.

	$1,575	$1,340	$1,100	$1,025	$900	$775	$650	*$1,785*

SAPPHIRE PRO II – 9mm Para. cal., 4 in. stainless steel barrel, 9 shot mag., aluminum frame with Satin Silver KimPro II finish, polished blue PVD finish on slide and small parts, stainless steel slide with engraving, full-length guide rod, ambidextrous safety, Tactical Wedge 3-dot green Tritium night sights, blue/black G10 thin grips, 28 oz. Mfg. 2015-2018.

	$1,495	$1,300	$1,100	$1,025	$900	$775	$650	*$1,652*

SAPPHIRE ULTRA II – 9mm Para. or .45 ACP cal., 1911 style, round heel frame, 3 in. barrel, stainless steel slide, Tactical Wedge nightsights., G10 grips, ambidextrous thumb safety, highly polished stainless steel slide and small parts feature a bright blue PVD finish with fine engraved border accents, 25 oz. New 2012.

MSR $1,754	$1,490	$1,300	$1,120	$1,015	$820	$675	$580

Add $20 for 9mm Para. cal.

STAINLESS COVERT – meltdown stainless slide and frame finished in silver KimPro, 4 in. barrel, 30 LPI front strap checkering, 3-dot Tritium night sights, hand checkered rosewood grips, 34 oz. 1,000 mfg. 1999.

Last MSR was $1,135.

STAINLESS GOLD MATCH SE II – .38 Super or .45 ACP cal., stainless steel frame and slide, 5 in. barrel, serrated flat-top slide, 30 LPI front strap checkering, hand checkered rosewood grips, ambidextrous safety, polished flats, ser. no. begins with KSO, 38 oz. 260 (.38 Super) and 294 (.45 ACP) mfg. 2001.

Last MSR was $1,487.

Add $88 for .38 Super cal.

STAINLESS II (CLASSIC ENGRAVED EDITION) – .45 ACP cal., 5 in. stainless steel barrel, stainless steel frame and slide, high grade walnut grips with ivory Micarta checkered inlay, accent-engraved mainspring housing, full coverage vine and leaf tool engraving with stipple relief on frame and slide, satin silver finish, 38 oz. Mfg. mid-2015-2018.

	$1,700	$1,500	$1,300	$1,100	$900	$700	$550	*$1,905*

STAINLESS II TEXAS EDITION – .45 ACP cal., stainless steel frame, 5 in. match grade stainless steel barrel, 7 shot mag., stainless steel slide with highly polished flats and Western leaf and scroll engraving with saw tooth border, aluminum match grade trigger, fixed low profile sights, bonded ivory grips with 1835 motto "Come and Take It" on left panel and State of Texas with state flag insert on right panel, special serial number range with TXE prefix, 38 oz. Limited mfg. of 500 units beginning 2017.

MSR $1,633	$1,395	$1,225	$1,050	$950	$775	$625	$550

SUPER JAGARE – 10mm cal., ported 6 in. barrel and slide, stainless steel slide and frame, two-hole trigger, Leupold DeltaPoint pro-rear mounted red dot sight, green and black G10 grips with black checkered inlay and serrated front strap, ambi thumb safety, 42 oz. New 2017.

MSR $2,869	$2,450	$2,150	$1,850	$1,650	$1,350	$1,100	$950

SUPER MATCH II – .45 ACP cal., SA, 5 in. barrel, extended flush magwell, stainless steel construction, match grade trigger, ambi thumb safety, serrated flat-top slide with aggressive serrations, top-of-the-line model, Custom Shop markings, two-tone KimPro finish on slide, 38 oz. New 1999.

MSR $2,801	$2,380	$2,085	$1,785	$1,625	$1,325	$1,125	$925

This series' nomenclature added the Roman numeral "II" during 2001.

ULTRA ELITE – aluminum frame with black KimPro finish, satin stainless slide, full meltdown treatment on slide and frame, 3 in. barrel, 30 LPI front strap checkering, 3-dot Tritium night sights, hand checkered rosewood grips, 25 oz. 2,750 mfg. 1999.

Last MSR was $1,085.

ULTRA CDP ELITE II – .45 ACP cal., first Kimber .45 pistols with ramped match grade barrels, black anodized aluminum frame, black oxide carbon steel slide, 3 in. barrel, Carry Melt treatment for rounded and blended edges, Meprolight 3-dot Tritium night sights, 30 LPI checkering on front strap and under trigger guard, ambidextrous thumb safety and charcoal/ruby laminated logo grips, 25 oz. Mfg. 2002-Jan. 2003.

Last MSR was $1,216.

GRADING - PPGS™	100%	98%	95%	90%	80%	70%	60%	LAST MSR

* ***Ultra CDP Elite STS II*** – .45 ACP cal., first Kimber .45 pistols with ramped match grade barrels, silver anodized aluminum frame, satin stainless steel slide, 3 in. barrel, Carry Melt treatment for rounded and blended edges, Meprolight 3-dot Tritium night sights, 30 LPI checkering on front strap and under trigger guard, ambidextrous thumb safety and charcoal/ruby laminated logo grips, 25 oz. Mfg. 2002-Jan. 2003.

Last MSR was $1,155.

ULTRA RCP II – .45 ACP cal., SA, (Refined Carry Pistol), 3 in. stainless steel barrel, 7 shot mag., black anodized frame (disc.) or aluminum frame with Matte Gray KimPro II finish, Carry Melt treatment, steel slide with Matte Black KimPro II finish, no sights, bobbed mag. release, hammer, beavertail grip safety and thumb safety, round mainspring housing and rear of frame, thin black Micarta grip panels (disc. 2014), Rosewood double diamond Crimson Trace lasergrips with Kimber logo became standard 2015, older mfg. had distinctive "hook" on hammer, new mfg. has straight hammer, 25 oz. Mfg. 2003-2005 by Custom Shop, reintroduced 2007-2018.

$1,495	$1,300	$1,100	$1,025	$900	$775	$650	*$1,652*

Subtract approx. $300 if without Crimson Trace Lasergrips.

ULTRA SHADOW II – black steel slide and anodized aluminum frame, 3 in. barrel, fixed Tritium night sights, 30 LPI front strap checkering, grey laminate grips, silver grip and thumb safeties and mainspring housing, ser. no. begins with KUSLE, 25 oz.

Last MSR was $949.

ULTRA SP II – special anodized frame colors (black/blue, black/red, and black/silver) with black oxide slide, 7 shot mag., 3 in. bushingless barrel, 3-dot sights, Carry Melt treatment, ball milled Micarta grips, standard fixed sights, 25 oz. Mfg. 2003-2005.

$1,025	$900	$800	$725	$625	$575	$495	*$1,175*

Pistols: Kimber Limited Editions, Single Action

Kimber has produced limited runs of pistols for dealer groups, NRA, sporting goods stores, law enforcement agencies, special requests, etc. Limited run pistols can be as small as 25 mfg.

THE BOSS II – limited edition to commemorate Blythe Sports 50th anniversary, stainless steel slide and frame, Carry Melt treatment, fixed white dot sights, premium aluminum 2 hole trigger, 5 in. barrel, engraved "The BOSS II" on ejection port side, and "SPECIAL EDITION", black and sliver laminate grips with Blythe 50th anniversary logo in center on white insert, ser. no. KBSS000-KBSS024, 25 mfg.

This model had no established MSR.

CLASSIC TARGET II – .45 ACP cal., two-tone stainless steel frame, matte black oxide slide, no cocking serrations, adj. sights, premium match grade trigger, smooth/stippled logo grips, match grade chamber, barrel, and barrel bushing, 38 oz. Sold exclusively through Gander Mountain. Mfg. 2006-2008.

$825	$675	$555	$460	$395	$350	$300	*$999*

CUSTOM DEFENDER II – two-tone stainless frame and slide, black oxide coating on frame, slide natural stainless, fixed low profile rear sight, double diamond rosewood grips, sold only through stores affiliated with National Buying Service, 38 oz. 290 mfg. 2001.

Last MSR was $839.

CUSTOM ECLIPSE II – stainless slide and frame, 5 in. barrel, black oxide finish brush polished on the flats, 30 LPI front strap checkering, adj. night sights, laminated grey grips, ser. no. begins with KEL, 38 oz. 4,522 mfg. 2001.

Last MSR was $1,121.

ECLIPSE CLE II – 5 in. barrel, Eclipse Custom II finish on slide with black over stainless frame (no front strap checkering), charcoal/ruby Kimber logo grips, sold only through stores affiliated with National Buying Service, 38 oz. 271 mfg. 2003.

Last MSR was $917.

* ***Eclipse PLE II*** – similar to Eclipse CLE II, except has 4 in. bushingless barrel, sold only through stores affiliated with Sports Inc. buying group, 35 oz. 232 mfg. 2003.

Last MSR was $877.

* ***Eclipse ULE II*** – Eclipse Ultra II finish on slide with black over stainless frame (no front strap checkering), 3 in. bushingless barrel, charcoal/ruby Kimber logo grips, sold only through stores affiliated with National Buying Service, 34 oz. 227 mfg. 2003.

Last MSR was $890.

FRANKLIN CUSTOM II – similar to Custom II, silver finished slide stop, bushing, mag. release, grip safety and mainspring housing, red, white and blue laminate grips with Franklin's Gun Shop logo, commemorates 44th anniversary of Franklin's Gun Shop, ser. no. KFGS01 - KFGS50, 50 mfg. 2006.

This model had no established MSR.

GRADING - PPGS™	100%	98%	95%	90%	80%	70%	60%	LAST MSR

LAPD SWAT – black oxide coated stainless frame and slide, 5 in. barrel, low profile Meprolight 3-dot night sights, 30 LPI front strap checkering, black rubber double diamond grips, 38 oz. 300 mfg. 2002.

Following extensive testing to select a duty pistol, LAPD SWAT chose a Kimber Stainless Custom II and had it enhanced to their specifications. This model was made strictly for law enforcement and not sold to the public. A civilian version called the Tactical law Enforcement (TLE) Series went into production in 2003. Pistols marked "LAPD SWAT" were not sold to the public.

MCSOCOM ICQB (2004) – .45 ACP cal., at the request of the Marine Corps Special Operations Command (MCSOCOM) Detachment 1 (Det. 1), Kimber produced Interim Close Quarters Battle (ICQB) 1911 patterned pistols in accordance with very high specific requirements: steel frame and slide finished in matte black, internal extractor, GI length guide rod and plug, light rail, bumped grip safety and ambidextrous manual safety, lanyard loop, Simonich G10 "Gunner" grips, and Novak Lo-Mount night sights.

There was no MSR on this model, as it was not available for sale to the general public.

The civilian version of this pistol is called the Warrior.

NRA EPOCH II – stainless slide and frame, 5 in. barrel, black oxide finish brush polished on flats, 30 LPI front strap checkering, standard safety, fixed Tritium night sights, laminated grey grips, ser. no. begins with KNRAE, Friends of NRA pistol available only at NRA banquets, 38 oz. 58 mfg. 2002.

This model had no established MSR.

PRO CARRY SLE – all stainless steel slide and frame, 4 in. barrel, identical to Stainless Pro Carry Model, except has stainless frame, mfg. for Kimber Master Dealers, cataloged in 2001, later production known as Pro Carry HD II, 1,329 mfg. during 2000.

Last MSR was $815.

PRO COMBAT – black oxide stainless steel frame and slide, 4 in. barrel, ambidextrous safety, Tritium 3-dot night sights, match grade aluminum trigger, 30 LPI front strap checkering, hand checkered rosewood grips, 35 oz. Marketed by RGuns. 52 mfg. 2000.

Last MSR was $860.

PRO ECLIPSE II – stainless steel frame and slide, 4 in. barrel, black oxide finish brush polished on the flats, 30 LPI front strap checkering, fixed 3-dot night sights, laminated grey grips, ambidextrous safety, ser. no. begins with KRE, 35 oz. 2,207 mfg. 2001.

Last MSR was $1,065.

STRYKER TEN II – Ultra Ten II with black polymer frame and frame insert and small parts, natural stainless slide, 25 oz. 200 mfg. 2002.

Last MSR was $850.

TARGET ELITE II – two-tone stainless frame and slide, black oxide coating on frame, slide natural stainless, adj. rear sight, rosewood double diamond grips, sold through stores affiliated with Sports Inc. buying group, 38 oz. 220 mfg. 2001.

Last MSR was $950.

TARGET MATCH – .45 ACP cal., oversized 5 in. stainless steel barrel, matte black frame and slide with brush polished flats, high relief cut under trigger guard, wide cocking serrations, solid match trigger, engraved bullseye inlaid burl walnut logo grips, 30 LPI checkering on front strap and under trigger guard, special ser. no. starting with "KTM", 38 oz. 1,000 mfg. 2006-2009.

	$1,215	$1,025	$875	$775	$700	$600	$500	*$1,427*

TEAM MATCH II 38 SUPER – .38 Super cal., identical to original Team Match II, with .38 Super ramped barrel, match grade chamber, bushing and trigger group, special Team Match features including 30 LPI checkered front strap, adj. sight, extended magwell, premium aluminum trigger and red, white, and blue USA Shooting Team logo grips, 38 oz. Mfg. 2003-2004.

	$1,150	$995	$875	$775	$675	$575	$475	*$1,352*

ULTRA ECLIPSE II – stainless steel frame and slide, 3 in. barrel, black oxide finish brush polished on the flats, 30 LPI front strap checkering, fixed 3-dot night sights, laminated grey grips, ambidextrous safety, 34 oz. 1,202 mfg. 2001.

Last MSR was $1,054.

REVOLVERS

K6s CDP (CUSTOM DEFENSE PACKAGE) – .357 Mag. cal., DAO, 2 in. brushed stainless steel barrel, 6 shot, match grade trigger, Tritium night sights, laminated checkered rosewood grips with (new 2019) or w/out Crimson Trace Lasergrips, serrated backstrap, two-tone black DLC finished frame over brushed stainless barrel, cylinder, and small parts, 23 oz. Mfg. 2018-2020.

	$985	$850	$750	$675	$550	$450	$375	*$1,155*

Add $355 for Crimson Trace Lasergrips (K6s CDP LG, new 2019).

GRADING - PPGS™	100%	98%	95%	90%	80%	70%	60%	LAST MSR

K6s DASA – .357 Mag., or .38 Spl. (new 2020) cal., DA/SA, stainless steel frame, 2 or 3 in. stainless steel barrel, 6 shot, enclosed or external hammer, non-stacking double action trigger and single action trigger, white 3-dot sights, walnut boot grips with diamond checkering, serrated backstrap, engraved over brushed stainless finish, 23 oz. New 2019.

MSR $1,030 $875 $765 $650 $600 $475 $400 $325

* ***K6s DASA Combat/Target/Target GFO*** – .357 Mag. cal., DA/SA, stainless steel frame, 4 in. stainless steel barrel, 6 shot, white 3-dot (combat), compact target adj. sights, or green fiber optic (Target GFO model only, new 2021), standard (combat) or extended (target) 3-finger combat grips w/ diamond checkering, serrated backstrap, engraved over brushed stainless finish, 25.5 oz. New 2020.

MSR $1,046 $900 $785 $675 $600 $495 $425 $350

K6s DASA TEXAS EDITION – .357 Mag. cal., 2 in. stainless steel barrel and frame, 6 shot, non-stacking double action and single action trigger, white 3-dot sights, ivory G10 grips w/Texas motif, serrated backstrap, vintage Western scroll work, engraved over smooth satin finish, 23 oz. New 2020.

MSR $1,454 $1,230 $1,075 $925 $835 $675 $550 $450

K6s DC (DEEP COVER) – .357 Mag. cal., DAO, stainless steel frame, 2 in. stainless steel barrel, 6 shot, match grade trigger, Tritium night sights, black and gray G10 grips with (new 2019) or w/out Crimson Trace Lasergrips, serrated backstrap, black DLC over brushed stainless finish, 23 oz. Mfg. 2018-2020.

$975 $850 $725 $675 $550 $450 $375 *$1,155*

Add $330 for Crimson Trace Lasergrips (K6s DC LG, new 2019).

K6s DCR (DELUXE CARRY REVOLVER) – .357 Mag. cal., DAO, stainless steel frame, 2 in. stainless steel barrel, 6 shot, red fiber optic front and black rear sights, checkered Millenium rosewood grips with Kimber logo, serrated backstrap, satin silver finish, 23 oz. New 2017.

MSR $1,189 $1,000 $875 $750 $680 $550 $455 $390

K6s FIRST EDITION – .357 Mag. cal., 2 in. barrel, 6 shot, high grade mirror-polished stainless steel, Pau Ferro wood grips, limited range serial number, 23 oz. Mfg. 2016-2017.

$1,795 $1,550 $1,325 $1,100 $900 $775 $675 *$2,039*

K6s ROYAL SPECIAL EDITION – .357 Mag. cal., stainless steel frame with serrated backstrap, 2 in. stainless steel barrel, smooth no-stack trigger, dovetailed white dot rear sight, brass bead front sight, ivory G10 grips, Dark Oil DLC over high polished stainless steel, 23 oz. Mfg. 2020 only.

$1,450 $1,275 $1,095 $985 $800 $650 $550 *$1,699*

K6s STAINLESS – .357 Mag. cal., DAO, recessed chambers, stainless steel frame, 2 or 3 (new 2018) in. stainless steel barrel, 6 shot, internal hammer, white 3-dot or Tritium night (mfg. 2017-2020) sights, black rubber grips, black laminate and rubber Crimson Trace Master Series Lasergrips (mfg. 2017-2020), or laminated walnut (new 2018, 3 in. model) grips, checkered push-button cylinder release, serrated back strap, low glare brushed stainless finish, 23 oz. New 2016.

MSR $938 $800 $700 $600 $545 $440 $360 $310

Add $27 for 3 in. barrel (new 2018).

Add $41 for Tritium night sights (K6s Stainless NS, mfg. 2017-2020).

Add $299 for Crimson Trace Lasergrips (K6s Stainless LG, mfg. 2017-2020).

K6s TLE – .357 Mag. cal., DAO, stainless steel frame, 2 or 3 in. stainless steel barrel, 6 shot, non-stacking double action trigger, Tritium 3-dot sights, green G10 3-finger grip with scallop texturing, serrated backstrap, matte black finish, 23 oz. Mfg. 2019-2020.

$850 $750 $650 $575 $475 $385 $325 *$1,000*

RIFLES: BOLT ACTION, RIMFIRE MODELS/REPEATING & SINGLE SHOT

A three position Win. Model 70 type safety became a standard feature on all Kimber .22 LR and .17 Mach 2 caliber rifles in early 2004.

HUNTER – .17 Mach 2 (new 2007) or .22 LR cal., similar to Classic, except has grade A walnut, clear stock finish, straight barrel contour, 6.7 lbs. Mfg. 2002-2007.

$850 $595 $515 $455 $400 $350 $300 *$863*

Add $40 for .17 Mach 2 cal.

YOUTH – .22 LR cal., similar to Hunter, except has 12 1/4 in. LOP.

While this model was cataloged during 2002-2003 with an MSR of $746, it never went into production.

CLASSIC – .22 LR cal., Mauser claw extractor with 2 position Model 70 type safety, unique eccentric bolt that allows a "centerfire-type" firing pin for faster lock time and greater strength, AA walnut sporter stock with 20 LPI 4-point panel checkering and hand rubbed oil finish, 22 in. match grade sporter barrel

GRADING - PPGS™	100%	98%	95%	90%	80%	70%	60%	LAST MSR

with match chamber and Custom Sporter contour, 5 shot mag., steel grip cap, pillar bedding, bead blasted blue finish, adj. trigger, approx. 6 1/2 lbs. Mfg. 1999-2007.

$1,100	$875	$765	$655	$550	$450	$350	*$1,223*

Through 2002, all Kimber .22 cal. Classic rifles had an A grade claro walnut stock, 2-point checkering pattern, urethane finish, and straight barrel taper contour.

* ***Classic Varmint*** – .17 Mach 2 (new mid-2004) or .22 LR cal., similar to Classic, except has A Grade walnut and 20 in. stainless fluted barrel in a heavy sporter contour. Mfg. 2003-2007.

$1,200	$825	$725	$600	$500	$425	$375	*$1,125*

* ***Classic Pro Varmint*** – .17 Mach 2 (new mid-2004) or .22 LR cal., similar to Classic Varmint, except has grey laminate uncheckered stock, brush polished stainless 20 in. barrel with black flutes. Mfg. 2004-2007.

$995	$850	$760	$655	$550	$450	$350	*$1,182*

Add $46 for .17 Mach 2 cal.

* ***Custom Classic*** – .22 LR cal., similar to Classic, except has 24 LPI wrap checkering, ebony forend tip and AAA walnut stock, 6 1/2 lbs. Mfg. 2003-2007.

$1,650	$1,375	$1,075	$925	$775	$650	$575	*$1,607*

SUPERAMERICA MODEL – .22 LR cal., top-of-the-line model with AAA Claro walnut with 24 LPI full wrap checkering, highly polished blue finish, hand rubbed oil finish, Custom Sporter barrel contour, ebony forend tip, cheekpiece and black recoil pad, 5 shot mag., 6 1/2 lbs. Limited mfg. 2001-2007.

$2,000	$1,650	$1,325	$1,100	$1,000	$850	$725	*$1,988*

Through 2001, all Superamerica rifles had urethane finish and straight taper barrel contour.

* ***SuperAmerica Model Custom Match 25th Anniversary Ltd. Ed.*** – .22 LR cal., similar to SuperAmerica model, except has AAA French walnut stock, black oxide matte finish barrel and receiver, steel buttplate, engraved grip cap, specially marked barrel and jeweled bolt. Limited production of 300 sequentially numbered rifles during 2004-2005.

$2,750	$2,000	$1,700	$1,400	$1,100	$900	$750	*$2,852*

SVT (SHORT VARMINT/TARGET) MODEL – .17 Mach 2 (new mid-2004) or .22 LR cal., 18 in. fluted stainless steel bull barrel, uncheckered grey laminate wood stock with high comb target design, matte blue action and satin stainless steel barrel, 5 shot mag., no sights, 7 1/2 lbs. Mfg. 1999-2007.

$945	$800	$700	$575	$475	$375	$300	*$1,073*

Add $52 for .17 Mach 2 cal.

HS (HUNTER SILHOUETTE) MODEL – .22 LR cal., 24 in. half-fluted medium sporter match grade barrel w/o sights, checkered walnut high comb Monte Carlo stock with clear stock finish, adj. trigger, matte blue finish, 7 lbs. Mfg. 1999-2007.

$850	$700	$585	$515	$425	$350	$275	*$976*

Through 2001, all HS Models had urethane finish.

MODEL 82C CLASSIC – .22 LR cal., 22 in. barrel, drilled and tapped receiver, repeater with 4 shot mag., checkered A Claro walnut stock, polished and blue metal, 6 1/2 lbs. Mfg. 1995-1999.

$975	$775	$690	$590	$500	$450	$425	*$917*

The C suffix on this model designates manufacture by Kimber of America.

* ***Model 82C Classic Stainless*** – .22 LR cal., stainless steel barrel with matte blue action. Approx. 600 mfg. 1997-98.

$1,000	$825	$700	$600	$500	$425	$375	*$968*

* ***Model 82C Classic Stainless Varmint*** – .22 LR cal., 20 in. fluted stainless steel barrel, Grade A Claro walnut stock with 18 LPI side panel checkering. Approx. 1,000 mfg. 1995-1998.

$1,025	$850	$725	$625	$525	$450	$350	*$1,002*

MODEL 82C SVT – .22 LR cal., single shot, features 18 in. fluted heavy stainless barrel with uncheckered high comb target style walnut stock, matte blue action, 7 1/2 lbs. Mfg. 1997 only.

$800	$550	$495	$425	$375	$315	$270	*$825*

SVT designates Short Varmint/Target.

MODEL 82C HS – while advertised during 1997, this model never went into production.

MODEL 82C SUPERAMERICA – .22 LR cal., 22 in. drilled and tapped barrel, 4 shot mag., AAA Claro checkered walnut stock with steel pistol grip cap, polished and blue metal, 6 1/2 lbs. Mfg. 1993-99.

$1,750	$1,250	$1,100	$925	$800	$725	$500	*$1,488*

GRADING - PPGS™	100%	98%	95%	90%	80%	70%	60%	LAST MSR

MODEL 82C CUSTOM MATCH – .22 LR cal., features AA French walnut with 22 LPI wraparound checkering, steel Neidner-style buttplate, matte rust blue finish. Mfg. 1995-99.

	$3,000	$1,900	$1,525	$1,225	$975	$800	$650	*$2,158*

MODEL 82C SUPER CLASSIC – .22 LR cal., features AAA Claro walnut with 18 LPI side panel checkering, polished and blue metal. Mfg. 1995-96.

	$1,500	$1,100	$975	$850	$750	$675	$550	*$1,090*

RIFLES: BOLT ACTION, CENTERFIRE MODELS

The models listed feature a Mauser style action with controlled round feeding and extraction.

MODEL 84C SINGLE SHOT CLASSIC – while advertised during 1996-97, this model never went into production.

MODEL 84C SINGLE SHOT SUPERAMERICA – while advertised during 1996-97, this model never went into production.

MODEL 84C SINGLE SHOT VARMINT STAINLESS – while advertised during 1997, this model never went into production.

MODEL 84C SINGLE SHOT VARMINT – .17 Rem. or .223 Rem. cal., 24 (first 200 rifles only) or 25 in. stainless match grade fluted barrel with recessed crown, matte blue receiver finish, checkered A Claro walnut stock with beavertail forend, 7 1/2 lbs. Mfg. 1997-99.

	$895	$785	$675	$610	$495	$400	$315	*$1,032*

Add $150 for .17 Rem. cal. (less than 100 mfg.).

MODEL 84L CLASSIC – .270 Win., .25-06 Rem. (disc.) or .30-06 Springfield cal., 24 in. Sporter barrel with matte blue finish, 5 shot mag., Mauser claw extractor, adj. trigger, 3-position safety, A Grade walnut stock with hand-rubbed oil finish, 1 in. Pachmayr Decelerator pad, sling swivel studs, 6 lbs. 2 oz. Mfg. 2010-2015.

	$1,025	$875	$750	$650	$550	$450	$395	*$1,223*

* ***Model 84L Classic Select Grade*** – .25-06 Rem. (disc.), .270 Win., .280 Ack. Imp. (mfg. 2011-2018), .30-06 Springfield, or .35 Whelen (mfg. 2012-2013) cal., 24 in. Sporter barrel with matte blue finish, 5 shot mag., 3-pos. safety, Mauser claw extractor, adj. trigger, A Grade French walnut stock with hand-rubbed oil finish, ebony forend tip, sling swivel studs, 1 in. Pachmayr Decelerator pad, steel grip cap, 6.2 lbs. Disc. 2020.

	$1,250	$1,050	$900	$800	$700	$600	$500	*$1,427*

* ***Model 84L Classic Stainless Select Grade*** – .25-06 Rem., .270 Win., .280 Ack. Imp., or .30-06 Springfield cal. Mfg. 2012-2014.

	$1,250	$1,050	$900	$800	$700	$600	$500	*$1,495*

* ***Model 84L Hunter*** – .270 Win., .280 Ack. Imp., or .30-06 cal., 24 in. stainless steel barrel, 3 shot detachable mag., adj. match grade trigger, reinforced synthetic stock, satin or KimPro II black (Black model, mfg. 2018-2020) finish. New 2017.

MSR $951	$810	$710	$610	$550	$450	$395	$350	

Add $54 for Hunter Black model (mfg. 2018-2020).

* ***Model 84L Hunter Boot Campaign*** – .25-06 Rem. (disc. 2019), .270 Win., .280 Ack. Imp., or .30-06 cal., 22 in. stainless steel Sporter barrel with KimPro II black finish, 3 shot removable box mag., controlled round feed, Mauser claw extractor, adj. trigger, reinforced synthetic stock in Kryptek Highlander patterned finish, 5.5 lbs. New 2018.

MSR $1,046	$895	$785	$675	$600	$495	$425	$350	

* ***Model 84L Hunter Camo*** – .270 Win. or .30-06 cal., 22 in. stainless steel barrel, detachable mag., controlled round feed, reinforced synthetic stock with Realtree Edge camo finish, KimPro II black finish. Mfg. 2018-2020.

	$825	$725	$625	$560	$450	$375	$325	*$973*

* ***Model 84L Montana*** – .25-06 Rem. (disc. 2018), .270 Win. (disc. 2019), .280 Ack. Imp., or .30-06 Springfield cal., 24 in. stainless steel Sporter threaded (new 2016) barrel with satin silver finish, adj. trigger, 4 shot mag., 3-pos. safety, Kevlar/carbon fiber stock with Grey Epoxy finish and 1 in. Decelerator pad, 5 lbs. 10 oz. Mfg. 2011-2020.

	$1,300	$1,135	$975	$885	$700	$600	$500	*$1,522*

* ***Model 84L Mountain Ascent*** – .270 Win. (disc. 2020), .280 Ack. Imp., or .30-06 cal., 24 in. stainless steel fluted barrel with muzzle brake, 4 shot mag., adj. trigger, Kevlar/carbon fiber stock with 1 in. Decelerator pad, Gore Optifade Open Country or Moss Green (mfg. 2017-2019) finish, 5 lbs. 5 oz. New 2012.

MSR $2,175	$1,850	$1,625	$1,390	$1,260	$1,020	$835	$725	

GRADING - PPGS™	100%	98%	95%	90%	80%	70%	60%	LAST MSR

* ***Model 84L Subalpine*** – .280 Ack. Imp. or .30-06 cal., 24 in. stainless steel fluted and threaded barrel, 4 shot mag., full-length Mauser claw extractor, reinforced carbon fiber stock in soft touch Gore Optifade Subalpine. New 2017.

MSR $2,175	$1,850	$1,625	$1,390	$1,260	$1,020	$835	$725	

MODEL 84M – .22-250 Rem., .204 Ruger (new 2004), .223 Rem. (new 2004), .243 Win. (new 2004), .260 Rem., .308 Win., or 7mm-08 Rem. cal., true Mauser action, much improved version of the Model 84C, longer and stronger receiver, 2 position Model 70 type safety, match grade barrel and trigger, 3-5 shot mag., walnut or laminated stock with sculpted steel floorplate. New 2001.

A three position Win. Model 70 type safety became a standard feature on all Kimber 84M rifles in early 2004.

* ***Model 84M Adirondack*** – 7mm-08 Rem., .308 Win., .300 AAC Blackout (mfg. 2015-2019), 6.5 Creedmoor (new 2015), or .338 Federal (mfg. 2016 only) cal., satin stainless steel barreled Mauser action, controlled round feeding, hollow bolt knob, 16 or 18 in. threaded stainless steel barrel, extraction, synthetic stock with black rubber recoil pad, 100% Gore Optifade Forest camo (disc. 2015) or Gore Optifade Elevated II (new 2016) coverage. New 2014.

MSR $1,883	$1,600	$1,400	$1,200	$1,090	$880	$725	$625	

* ***Model 84M Classic*** – .22-250 Rem. (disc.), .223 Rem. (mfg. 2009-2011), .243 Win. (disc. 2014), .260 Rem. (disc. 2009), .308 Win., 7mm-08 Rem., or .338 Federal (mfg. 2007-2011) cal., 22 in. light sporter barrel with matte blue finish, 5 shot mag., 3-position safety, adj. trigger, A Grade checkered walnut stock and forend with hand-rubbed oil finish, 1 in. Decelerator pad, sling swivel studs, 5 lbs. 13 oz. Mfg. 2001-2015.

	$1,025	$875	$750	$650	$550	$450	$395	*$1,223*

* ***Model 84M Classic Stainless*** – .243 Win., .308 Win., or 7mm-08 Rem. cal., stainless steel action and barrel.

	$1,025	$875	$750	$650	$550	$450	$395	*$1,223*

* ***Model 84M Classic Select Grade*** – .223 Rem. (disc.), .243 Win., .25-06 Rem. (disc.), .257 Roberts, 7mm-08 Rem. (disc. 2019), or .308 Win. cal., 22 in. steel Sporter barrel with matte blue finish, 6 shot, 3-position safety, Mauser claw extractor, checkered Claro or French walnut stock with hand-rubbed oil finish, ebony forend tip, sling swivel studs, 1 in. Pachmayr Decelerator pad, 5 lbs. 13 oz. Mfg. 2006-2020.

	$1,250	$1,050	$900	$800	$700	$600	$500	*$1,427*

Add $340 for Classic Select Grade with French walnut (mfg. 2006-2007, reintroduced 2015-disc.).

* ***Model 84M Classic Stainless Select Grade*** – .243 Win., 7mm-08 Rem., or .308 Win. cal., stainless steel action and barrel. Mfg. 2012-2014.

	$1,295	$1,075	$925	$825	$725	$625	$500	*$1,495*

* ***Model 84M Hunter*** – .243 Win., .257 Roberts, .270 Win. (new 2018), .308 Win., 6.5 Creedmoor, or 7mm-08 Rem. cal., Mauser-style controlled round feed, 22 in. stainless steel Sporter barrel with satin or KimPro II black (mfg. 2018-2020) finish, 4 shot detachable mag., stainless steel action, Mauser claw extractor, adj. trigger, FDE reinforced polymer stock with 1 in. Kimber recoil pad, sling swivel studs, 3-position safety, 6 1/2 lbs. New 2016.

MSR $951	$810	$710	$610	$550	$450	$395	$350	

Add $54 for Hunter Black model (mfg. 2018-2020).

* ***Model 84M Hunter Boot Campaign*** – .243 Win. (disc. 2019), 7mm-08 Rem. (disc. 2019), .308 Win., or 6.5 Creedmoor (new 2020) cal., 22 in. stainless steel Sporter barrel with KimPro II black finish, 3 shot removable box mag., controlled round feed, Mauser claw extractor, adj. trigger, reinforced synthetic stock in Kryptek Highlander patterned finish, 5.5 lbs. New 2018.

MSR $1,046	$895	$785	$675	$600	$495	$425	$350	

* ***Model 84M Hunter Camo*** – .243 Win., .270 Win., .30-06, .308 Win., or 6.5 Creedmoor cal., 22 in. stainless steel barrel, detachable mag., controlled round feed, reinforced synthetic stock with Realtree Edge camo pattern, KimPro II black finish, 5 lbs. 9 oz. Mfg. 2018-2020.

	$825	$725	$625	$560	$450	$375	$325	*$973*

* ***Model 84M LPT (Light Police Tactical)*** – .223 Rem. or .308 Win. cal., 22 in. matte blue heavy sporter contour fluted barrel, 5 shot mag., Picatinny rail, oversize bolt handle, sling swivels, recoil pad, full-length Mauser claw extractor, 3-position Model 70 style safety, adj. trigger, black laminate stock with panel stippling, 8 lbs., 7 oz. Mfg. 2008-2018.

	$1,295	$1,075	$925	$825	$725	$625	$500	*$1,495*

GRADING - PPGS™	100%	98%	95%	90%	80%	70%	60%	LAST MSR

* ***Model 84M Limited Edition*** – .257 Roberts or .308 Win. cal., Classic Select Grade French walnut stock and forearm, limited mfg. Mfg. 2010-2011.

	$1,575	$1,375	$1,175	N/A	N/A	N/A	N/A	*$1,767*

* ***Model 84M LongMaster Classic*** – .223 Rem., .243 Win. (disc. 2007), or .308 Win. cal., 24 in. heavy stainless steel fluted barrel, 6 shot, adj. trigger, A Grade checkered walnut stock with hand-rubbed oil finish, steel grip cap, recoil pad, sling swivel studs, 7 lbs. 5 oz. Mfg. 2002-2018.

	$1,125	$995	$875	$750	$650	$550	$425	*$1,291*

* ***Model 84M Longmaster Pro*** – .22-250 Rem. or .308 Win. cal., similar to Longmaster VT, except has synthetic stock, 24 (.308 Win. cal.) or 26 (.22-250 Rem. cal.) in. brush polished stainless bull barrel with black flutes.

While this model was cataloged during 2003 with an MSR of $1,189, it never went into production.

* ***Model 84M LongMaster VT*** – .22-250 Rem. cal. only, 26 in. stainless bull match grade barrel, match grade trigger, 5 shot mag. with sculpted steel floorplate, grey/black laminate target stock with high comb and extended pistol grip, 10 lbs. Mfg. 2001-2018.

	$1,175	$995	$850	$725	$600	$500	$450	*$1,427*

* ***Model 84M Montana*** – .204 Ruger (mfg. 2009-2014), .223 Rem. (mfg. 2009-2018), .22-250 Rem. (mfg. 2017-2018), .243 Win., .257 Roberts (mfg. 2008-2020), .260 Rem. (disc. 2009), 7mm-08 Rem., .308 Win., 6.5 Creedmoor (new 2017), or .338 Federal (mfg. 2007-2011) cal., 22 in. stainless steel Sporter threaded (new 2016) or standard barrel, 5 shot, synthetic stock and satin stainless steel barreled action, 5 lbs. 2 oz. New 2003.

MSR $1,522	$1,300	$1,135	$975	$885	$700	$600	$500	

Add $248 for Montana Black KimPro in .308 Win. cal. only (disc.).

* ***Model 84M Mountain Ascent*** – .308 Win., 7mm-08 (new 2016), or 6.5 Creedmoor (new 2016) cal., ultra lightweight model with 22 in. fluted barrel, satin stainless steel barreled action, 4 shot, reinforced carbon fiber stock with Gore Optifade Open Country or Moss Green (new 2017) finish, fluted bolt and bolt handle, hollow bolt knob, removable muzzle brake, Talley lightweight matte black one inch ring mounts, full-length Mauser claw extractor, 3-position safety, 4 lbs. 13 oz. New 2012.

MSR $2,175	$1,850	$1,625	$1,390	$1,260	$1,020	$835	$725	

* ***Model 84M Subalpine*** – .308 Win., .300 WSM, or .300 Win. Mag. cal., 22 in. stainless steel fluted and threaded barrel, 4 shot mag., full-length Mauser claw extractor, reinforced carbon fiber stock in soft touch Gore Optifade Subalpine. New 2017.

MSR $2,175	$1,850	$1,625	$1,390	$1,260	$1,020	$835	$725	

* ***Model 84M Superamerica*** – .223 Rem. (disc. 2009), .243 Win. (disc. 2009), .260 Rem. (disc. 2009), 7mm-08 Rem. (disc. 2015), .308 Win., or .338 Federal (disc. 2009) cal., 22 in. Sporter barrel with highly polished blue finish, 5 shot mag., stainless steel action, 24 LPI wrap checkering, ebony forend tip, AAA walnut stock with hand-rubbed oil finish, cheekpiece, Pachmayr Decelerator recoil pad, sling swivel studs, 5 lbs. 10 oz. New 2003.

MSR $2,386	$2,025	$1,775	$1,525	$1,375	$1,115	$925	$750	

* ***Model 84M SVT*** – .223 Rem. cal., 18 1/4 in. stainless steel bull barrel, 6 shot, adj. trigger, gray laminated stock with hand-rubbed oil finish, 8 lbs. 5 oz. Disc. 2018.

	$1,175	$995	$850	$725	$600	$500	$450	*$1,427*

* ***Model 84M Varmint*** – .204 Ruger or .22-250 Rem. cal., 24 in. heavy stainless steel fluted barrel, 6 shot, A Grade walnut stock with hand-rubbed oil finish, 7 lbs. 5 oz. New 2001.

MSR $1,400	$1,190	$1,050	$900	$815	$675	$550	$450	

* ***Model 84M Pro Varmint*** – .204 Ruger, .22-250 Rem., or .223 Rem. cal., 24 in. stainless steel bull barrel with black flutes, grey laminate uncheckered stock with 1 in. Pachmayr Decelerator pad, 8 lbs. Mfg. 2004-2020.

	$1,215	$1,065	$910	$825	$675	$550	$450	*$1,427*

MODEL 8400 ADVANCED TACTICAL II – .308 Win. (disc. 2016), .300 Win. Mag., or 6.5 Creedmoor (mfg. 2015-2016) cal., 22 (disc. 2016) or 27 in. match grade stainless steel threaded barrel with SureFire muzzle brake, full-length Mauser claw extractor, controlled round feeding, Manners MCS-TF4 folding stock with adj. comb, oversized bolt knob and extended bolt handle, upper and lower Picatinny rails, 5 or 10 shot detachable box mag., KimPro II desert tan finish. Mfg. 2014-2017.

	$3,695	$3,235	$2,775	$2,515	$2,025	$1,675	$1,295	*$4,351*

GRADING - PPGS™ 100% 98% 95% 90% 80% 70% 60% LAST MSR

* ***Model 8400 Advanced Tactical SOC*** – .308 Win., .300 Win. Mag. (disc. 2016), or 6.5 Creedmoor (new 2015) cal., 22 or 27 (disc. 2016) in. stainless steel threaded barrel with SureFire muzzle brake and matte KimPro II finish, 5 shot detachable box mag., Kimber modular chassis system, side folding stock with adj. comb, integral rear monopod, two Mil-Spec rails on forearm, Cerakote FDE finish, 11 lbs. 6 oz. Mfg. 2014-2017.

  $3,750 $3,275 $2,825 $2,550 $2,075 $1,695 $1,325 ***$4,419***

* ***Model 8400 Advanced Tactical SRC (Suppressor Ready Compact)*** – .308 Win. cal., 16 in. stainless steel threaded barrel with SureFire muzzle brake and matte KimPro II finish, 5 shot detachable mag., adj. trigger, Kimber modular chassis system, side folding stock with adj. comb, integral rear monopod, Mil-Spec rails on forearm, includes Harris bipod adapter, anodized black finish, 11 lbs. 6 oz. Mfg. 2015-2016.

  $3,750 $3,275 $2,825 $2,550 $2,075 $1,695 $1,325 ***$4,419***

MODEL 8400 CAPRIVI – .375 H&H, .416 Rem. Mag. (mfg. 2010-2019), or .458 Lott (disc. 2019) cal., 24 in. contoured blue barrel, 4 shot mag., Mauser claw extractor, 3-position Model 70 style safety, adj. trigger, oil finished checkered pistol grip AA Grade French walnut stock, pancake cheekpiece, ebony forend tip, swivel studs, three leaf express sight, double crossbolts, recoil pad, 8 lbs. 7 oz. New 2008.

MSR $3,481 $3,100 $2,600 $2,225 $2,015 $1,630 $1,330 $1,160

* ***Model 8400 Caprivi Special Edition*** – .375 H&H cal., similar to Caprivi, except has AAA grade French walnut stock and color case hardened receiver, approx. 9 lbs. While cataloged in 2011-2013, these rifles were never entered into production. Only one prototype, serial number KW24246, was ever produced.

  $4,500 $4,150 $3,600 N/A N/A N/A N/A ***$5,031***

MODEL 8400 CLASSIC – .25-06 Rem. (mfg. 2006-2009), .270 WSM (disc. 2014), .270 Win. (mfg. 2006-2009), 7mm Rem. Mag. (mfg. 2009-2011), 7mm WSM (disc. 2009), .300 WSM, .300 Win. Mag. (new 2006), .30-06 (mfg. 2006-2009), .325 WSM (mfg. 2005-2011), or .338 Win. Mag. (mfg. 2006-2011) cal., 24 or 26 in. sporter match grade blue barrel, match grade adj. trigger, 4 shot mag., A-Grade walnut stock with hand-rubbed oil finish, 20 LPI panel checkering, 3-position Model 70 type safety, 7 lbs. 4 oz. Mfg. 2003-2015.

  $1,025 $875 $750 $650 $550 $450 $395 ***$1,223***

While a left-hand version of this model was cataloged during 2003, they were never produced.

* ***Model 8400 Classic Stainless*** – .270 WSM, or .300 WSM cal., stainless steel action and slide. Disc. 2011.

  $1,025 $875 $750 $650 $550 $450 $395 ***$1,223***

* ***Model 8400 Classic Select Grade*** – .270 WSM (disc. 2019), .300 WSM (disc. 2019), .325 WSM (disc.), 7mm Rem. Mag. (disc.), .300 Win. Mag., or .338 Win. Mag. (disc.) cal., 26 in. steel Sporter barrel with matte blue finish, 4 shot mag., full-length Mauser claw extractor, Claro (disc.) or French walnut stock with hand-rubbed oil finish, ebony forend tip, 7 lbs. 4 oz. Mfg. 2006-2020.

  $1,250 $1,050 $900 $800 $700 $600 $500 ***$1,427***

* ***Model 8400 Classic Stainless Select Grade*** – .270 WSM, .300 WSM, .300 Win. Mag., or .338 Win. Mag. cal., stainless steel action and slide. Mfg. 2012-2013.

  $1,295 $1,075 $925 $825 $725 $625 $500 ***$1,495***

MODEL 8400 MONTANA – .223 Rem. (mfg. 2016-2017), .25-06 Rem. (mfg. 2006-2009, 2016-2017), .270 Win. (mfg. 2006-2009, 2016-2017), .270 WSM, .280 Ackley Improved (disc. 2009), 7mm WSM (disc. 2009), .300 WSM, .300 Win. Mag. (new 2006), .30-06 (mfg. 2006-2009, 2016-2017), .325 WSM (mfg. 2005-2011), or .338 Win. Mag. (mfg. 2006-disc.) cal., Mauser action, controlled round feeding, 24 or 26 in. satin stainless steel custom Sporter threaded (new 2016) barrel, 3 shot mag., adj. trigger, Kevlar/carbon fiber stock, 1 in. Pachmayr Decelerator recoil pad, 6 lbs. 3 oz. New 2003.

MSR $1,522 $1,300 $1,135 $975 $885 $700 $600 $500

Subtract $68 for .338 Win. Mag. cal. with non-threaded barrel (mfg. 2006-disc.).

MODEL 8400 MOUNTAIN ASCENT – .270 WSM, .300 WSM, .300 Win. Mag., or 7mm Rem. Mag. cal., 24 or 26 in. stainless steel barrel with muzzle brake and thread protector cap, fluted bolt handle, hollow bolt knob and fluted bolt body, carbon fiber stock with Gore Optifade Open Country finish. New 2015.

MSR $2,175 $1,850 $1,625 $1,390 $1,260 $1,025 $850 $725

MODEL 8400 PATROL/POLICE TACTICAL – .300 Win. Mag. or .308 Win. (new 2010) cal., 20 (Patrol), 24, or 26 in. match grade barrel, chamber, and trigger, trued bolt face, custom McMillan glass bedded stock, fixed Picatinny rail, enlarged bolt handle and knob, 8 3/4 lbs. Mfg. 2009-2013.

  $1,325 $1,160 $995 $900 $725 $595 $475 ***$1,495***

GRADING - PPGS™	100%	98%	95%	90%	80%	70%	60%	LAST MSR

MODEL 8400 PATROL TACTICAL – .308 Win. or .300 Win. Mag. cal., 24 or 26 in. match grade stainless steel fluted barrel, full-length Mauser claw extractor, controlled round feeding, Manners MCS-T6 reinforced carbon fiber black synthetic stock with squared forend and grooved forearm, vertical pistol grip, ambidextrous palm swell, oversized bolt knob and extended bolt handle, top rail, 5 or 10 shot detachable box mag., 8 lbs. 12 oz. Mfg. 2014-2018.

	$2,075	$1,825	$1,550	$1,400	$1,150	$935	$725	*$2,447*

MODEL 8400 SONORA – .25-06 Rem., .30-06 (disc. 2009), .300 Win. Mag., 7mm Rem. Mag., or .308 Win. (disc. 2009) cal., brown laminate stock, fluted stainless steel match grade barrel w/o sights, approx. 9 1/2 lbs. Mfg. 2008-2011.

	$1,100	$960	$825	$750	$600	$495	$385	*$1,359*

MODEL 8400 SUBALPINE – .300 WSM or .300 Win. Mag. (disc. 2019) cal., 24 or 26 in. stainless steel fluted and threaded barrel, 4 shot mag., full-length Mauser claw extractor, reinforced carbon fiber stock in soft touch Gore Optifade Subalpine. New 2017.

MSR $2,082	$1,775	$1,550	$1,325	$1,200	$975	$800	$685

MODEL 8400 SUPERAMERICA – .270 Win. (mfg. 2009), .30-06 (mfg. 2009), .270 WSM, 7mm WSM (disc. 2009), .300 WSM, .300 Win. Mag. (new 2006), .325 WSM (mfg. 2005-2009), or .338 Win. Mag. (mfg. 2006-2014) cal., 24 or 26 in. custom sporter barrel with highly polished blue finish, checkered AAA walnut stock with hand-rubbed oil finish, 24 LPI panel checkering, ebony forend tip, cheekpiece, Pachmayr Decelerator pad, sling swivel studs, 6 lbs. 10 oz. Mfg. 2003-2015.

	$1,925	$1,700	$1,450	$1,275	$1,025	$875	$750	*$2,240*

MODEL 8400 TACTICAL SERIES – .300 Win. Mag. or .308 Win. cal., matte blue (Tactical) or KimPro II dark earth (Advanced Tactical) finish, grey (Tactical) or desert camo (Advanced Tactical) McMillan synthetic stock, 24 in. fluted bull barrel, 5 shot mag., 9 lbs., 4 oz. Mfg. 2007-2013.

	$1,675	$1,450	$1,250	$1,125	$900	$750	$575	*$1,971*

Add $680 for Advanced Tactical with Desert Tan or black Pelican case.

MODEL K770 CLASSIC – while advertised during 1997, this model never went into production. Prototypes only.

MODEL K770 SUPER AMERICA – while advertised during 1997, this model never went into production. Prototypes only.

ADVANCED TACTICAL SOC II – .308 Win. or 6.5 Creedmoor cal., 22 in. stainless steel barrel with threaded muzzle and thread protector and KimPro II matte black finish, 5 shot detachable box mag., full-length Mauser claw extractor, controlled round feed, aluminum left-folding stock with 4 point adj. comb, oversized bolt handle, M-LOK slots, tripod mount, ships with night vision mount and stock pack, FDE or Sniper Gray (disc. 2020) finish, 11 lbs. 8 oz. New 2018.

MSR $2,556	$2,175	$1,900	$1,630	$1,475	$1,200	$1,000	$850

ADVANCED TACTICAL SRC II – .308 Win. cal., 16 in. stainless steel barrel with threaded muzzle and thread protector and KimPro II matte black finish, 5 shot detachable box mag., controlled round feed, Mauser claw extractor, aluminum folding stock with 4 point adj. comb, oversized bolt handle, M-LOK accessory rail, tripod mount, night vision mount, FDE finish, 10 lbs. 8 oz. New 2018.

MSR $2,556	$2,175	$1,900	$1,630	$1,475	$1,200	$1,000	$850

CLASSIC (TWO-TONE) LIMITED EDITION – 6.5 Creedmoor cal., 84M action, 22 in. stainless steel Sporter barrel with satin finish, 5 shot, front locking repeater, Mauser claw extractor, adj. trigger, hand checkered Claro walnut stock, Pachmayr Decelerator pad, sling swivel studs, steel grip cap, 3-pos. safety, KimPro II black receiver finish, 5 lbs. 13 oz. 1 of 1,000 Limited Edition with special serial number sequence, beginning 2021.

MSR $1,128	$950	$825	$700	$635	$515	$425	$350

OPEN COUNTRY (MODEL 84M OPEN COUNTRY) – 6.5 Creedmoor or .308 Win. (new 2018) cal., stainless steel action, 24 in. deep fluted heavy barrel, threaded muzzle with thread protector, 24 in. threaded heavy fluted barrel with Gray KimPro II finish, 4 shot mag., Mauser claw extractor, adj. trigger, reinforced carbon fiber stock with Gore Optifade Open Country pattern or pillar bedding in a textured granite color (new 2018), 1 in. recoil pad, 3-pos. Model 70-type wing safety, front and rear sling swivel studs, 6 lbs. 15 oz. New 2017.

MSR $2,420	$2,055	$1,800	$1,540	$1,395	$1,130	$925	$800

OPEN RANGE PRO CARBON (GRANITE) – 6.5 Creedmoor or .308 Win. (mfg. 2020 only) cal., 84M stainless steel action, 24 in. Proof Research carbon fiber wrapped stainless steel barrel with black KimPro II finish, thread protector and muzzle brake, 4 shot mag., Mauser claw extractor, adj. trigger, AG Composites carbon fiber stock in a textured granite color, 1 in. recoil pad, 3-pos. Model 70-type wing safety, Granite (mfg. 2020 only) or Tru-Timber 02 Octane pattern, 6 lbs. 3 oz. New 2020.

MSR $3,236	$2,750	$2,400	$2,065	$1,875	$1,515	$1,250	$1,075

GRADING - PPGS™	100%	98%	95%	90%	80%	70%	60%	LAST MSR

TALKEETNA (MODEL 8400 TALKEETNA) – .375 H&H cal., stainless steel action, controlled round feeding, 24 in. stainless steel barrel, front barrel band swivel stud, 4 shot mag., adj. trigger, single leaf express sight, Mauser claw extractor, Kevlar/carbon fiber pistol grip stock, Pachmayr Decelerator pad, satin stainless steel finish, 3-pos. Model 70-type wing safety, 7 3/4 lbs. New 2008.

MSR $2,175	$1,825	$1,595	$1,350	$1,225	$995	$850	$725	

RIFLES: BOLT ACTION, MAUSER 96 SPORTERS

MODEL 96 SPORTER – .308 Win. cal., features M-96 action with stainless steel fluted heavy barrel. Mfg. 1995-97.

	$450	$415	$365	$300	$260	$225	$200	*$520*

Retail prices ranged from $340-$415 for the Standard Sporter, while the Varmint/Heavy barrel variation was priced at approx. $510. Sporter variations were also available as a combo package with scope and hardshell case - add approx. $30.

During 1995-96, Kimber began sporterizing the Swedish Mauser Model 96 military surplus rifles. They featured stainless steel fluted barrels and a black synthetic Ramline stock, receivers were drilled and tapped to accept Weaver scope mounts, bead blasted bluing, and original reprofiled military bolt. The Sporter configuration included .243 Win., 6.5x55mm, or .308 Win. cal., while the heavy fluted barrel models were available in .22-250 Rem. or .308 Win. (Varmint or Heavy Barrel).

RIFLES: BOLT ACTION, MAUSER 98 SPORTERS

MODEL 98 SPORTER – .220 Swift (100 mfg.), .257 Roberts (100 mfg.), .270 Win., .280 Rem. (100 mfg.), .30-06, .300 Win. Mag., .338 Win. Mag., or 7mm Rem. Mag. cal., features Mauser M-98 action with stainless match grade fluted barrel, choice of synthetic or Claro walnut stock, and Warne bases, matte black finish receiver. Mfg. 1996-98.

	$465	$425	$375	$315	$270	$230	N/A	*$535*

Add $25 for Mag. cals.
Add $100 for Claro walnut stock.

* ***Mauser 98 Sporter Matte*** – .300 Win. Mag., .338 Win. Mag., or 7mm Rem. Mag. cal., features 25 in. non-fluted sporter barrel, synthetic stock, and Weaver style bases. Disc. 1998.

	$275	$250	$225	$200	$185	$170	$155	*$339*

SHOTGUNS: O/U

AUGUSTA SERIES – 12 ga., 2 3/4 (Trap & Skeet) or 3 (Sporting & Field) in. chambers, Boss type boxlock action with shallow frame, blue (Trap & Skeet) or polished metal (Field & Sporting) frame, ejectors, SST, tang safety with ejector, 26-34 in. vent. barrel lengths with VR backbored to .736 in., available in Field, Sporting, Skeet, and Trap variations, beavertail or Schnabel forend, Pachmayr Decelerator recoil pad, 7 lbs., 2 oz-7 lbs., 13 oz. Mfg. in Italy by Investarm 2002-2005, limited delivery 2003-2005.

	$4,750	$4,250	$3,750	$3,250	$2,750	$2,250	$1,850	*$5,676*

MARIAS SERIES – 12 or 20 ga., 3 in. chambers, 26, 28, or 30 in. VR barrels with 5 choke tubes, ejectors, charcoal case colored detachable sidelock action with engraving, deluxe checkered walnut English or pistol grip stock and forearm, available in Grade I with Grade III Turkish walnut or Grade II with Grade IV Turkish walnut, imported from Turkey. Imported 2006-2008.

	$4,995	$4,375	$3,750	$3,250	$2,700	$2,200	$1,825	*$5,799*

SHOTGUNS: SxS

VALIER SERIES – 16 (new 2006) or 20 ga., 26 or 28 in. barrels, hand engraved sidelock action with seven pins, hand checkered Turkish walnut straight grip English stock, DT, fixed chokes, hand engraved blue (20 ga. only), case colored, or optional bone charcoal case colored action, extractors, approx. 6 1/2 lbs., mfg. in Turkey 2005-2007.

	$3,525	$3,050	$2,675	$2,200	$1,850	$1,450	$1,100	*$3,999*

* ***Valier Grade II*** – similar to Grade I, except has ejectors, with or w/o (disc. 2007) charcoal case colored frame, mfg. in Turkey. Imported 2005-2008.

	$4,495	$3,995	$3,050	$2,675	$2,200	$1,850	$1,450	*$4,999*

Subtract approx. $600 if w/o bone charcoal case colors.

KIMBER OF OREGON, INC.

Previous manufacturer located in Clackamas, OR circa 1980-1991.

Kimber of Oregon went out of business with its final sale in 1991. In some models, magazines for these fine quality rifles are getting extremely hard to find with healthy premiums being asked. Once "B" suffix models were introduced, older manufacture started being referred to as "A" models.

GRADING - PPGS™	100%	98%	95%	90%	80%	70%	60%	LAST MSR

Kimber of Oregon, Inc. was started by Jack Warne, who was originally from Australia and moved to Oregon in 1969 as an executive for Omark Industries. The Warne's purchased all rimfire tooling from Omark Industries after the manufacture of Australian Sportcos ceased. Jack Warne, together with his son Greg, started Kimber in the late 1970s. By 1980, the first Model 82s in .22 rimfire were being shipped. The name Kimber was originally derived from the small town in South Australia named Kimba. The spelling was changed due to commercial considerations.

PISTOLS: BOLT ACTION

PREDATOR MODEL – .221 Fireball, .223 Rem., 6mm TCU (disc. 1987), 7mm TCU, or 6x45mm (disc. 1987) cal., single shot Model 84 action with shortened 14 7/8 in. barrel, scope use only, one-piece deluxe walnut stock with contoured pistol grip, 5 1/4 lbs., rare cals. will command a premium. Approx. 200 mfg. 1987-88 only.

* ***Predator Model Hunter Grade*** – AA Claro walnut without checkering. Disc. 1988.

	$1,995	$1,750	$1,500	$1,250	$950	$800	$700	*$995*

* ***Predator Model Super Grade*** – similar to Hunter Grade, except has select French walnut with ebony forend tip and 22 lines/in. checkering. Disc. 1988.

	$3,000	$2,650	$2,250	$2,000	$1,750	$1,400	$1,250	*$1,195*

RIFLES: BOLT ACTION

Note: No suffix in Kimber models denotes pre-1986 action design, "B" suffix models incorporate the new action with improved cocking system, faster lock time, swept-back bolt design, improved recoil lug, and are right-handed. Pre '83 rifles had no bolt release.

Add $175 for skeleton grip cap on models listed below.
Add $275 for skeleton buttplate on models listed below.
Add $100 for checkered bolt handle on models listed below.
Add $300 for raised quarter rib.
Add $100 for forend tip.
Extra fancy walnut on any Kimber will always command a premium.
10 shot mags. will typically bring $80-$100.

Model 82, .22 Cal. Series

Add $200-$500 for .22 Hornet or .22 WMR. cal. on the models listed, depending on the variation.

STANDARD MODEL 82 – .22 LR, .22 WMR, or .22 Hornet cal., Mauser type rear locking bolt action, 3 (.22 Hornet), 4 (.22 WMR), or 5 (.22 LR) shot mag., 22 in. (Sporter) or 24 in. (Varmint) barrel, deluxe Claro walnut, steel buttplate, rocker style safety, right or left-hand action, 6 1/2 lbs.

* ***Standard Model 82 Classic*** – disc. 1988.

	$1,250	$975	$825	$775	$625	$500	$425	*$750*

* ***Standard Model 82 Cascade*** – Monte Carlo cheekpiece, disc. 1988.

	$1,300	$975	$825	$700	$600	$500	$425	

Add 175% for Custom Cascade Model, with higher grade walnut, ebony forend tip, and Niedner style buttplate (34 mfg).

* ***Standard Model 82 Custom Classic*** – higher grade Claro walnut, ebony forearm tip, Niedner style steel buttplate. Disc. 1988.

	$2,100	$1,725	$1,100	$975	$850	$725	$625	
.218 Mashburn cal.	$2,650	$2,300	$1,925	$1,625	$1,475	$1,150	$950	*$995*

Add 30% for .218 Bee cal. (approx. 130 standard mfg.).
Add 10% for .22 WMR cal.

Also available in .25-20 (approx. 200 mfg. single shot only) cals. Mfg. 1985 only (retail price was $695).

* ***Standard Model 82 Deluxe Grade*** – .22 LR cal. only, similar to Custom Classic Model, AA walnut, 5 or 10 (optional) shot mag., 6 1/2 lbs. Mfg. 1989-90 only.

	$1,875	$1,725	$1,150	$825	$725	$625	$525	*$1,195*

A left-hand variation was also available at no extra charge, but had limited mfg. in 1990.

SPORTER MODEL – .17 Ackley Hornet (approx. 9 mfg.), .17 K. Hornet (approx. 88 mfg.), or .22 LR cal., includes Model 82A action, 22 in. sporter weight barrel, 4 shot mag., round top receiver with bases, checkered stock and forend, 6 1/2 lbs. Mfg. 1991 only.

	$995	$875	$775	$675	$550	$425	$330	*$995*

Add approx. 100% for .17 K Hornet or .17 Ackley Hornet cals.

GRADING - PPGS™	100%	98%	95%	90%	80%	70%	60%	LAST MSR

RIMFIRE VARMINTER – .22 LR cal. only, Model 82A action, free floating 25 in. medium heavy barrel, laminated stock, 5 or optional 10 shot mag., rubber buttpad, 8 1/4 lbs. Mfg. 1990-91 only.

$1,100 $995 $670 $610 $490 $400 $315 *$795*

The barrels were left over All-American Match rifle production, which had an accuracy guarantee of .3 @ 50 yards with match ammo.

HUNTER GRADE – .22 LR cal. only, similar to Rimfire Varminter with Super America configured barrel and action with low glare metal finish. Mfg. 1990 only.

$1,000 $925 $595 $535 $430 $350 $275 *$895*

MINI CLASSIC – .22 LR cal. only, Model 82 action, 18 in. barrel, steel buttplate, sling swivels. Mfg. 1988 only.

$1,050 $975 $675 $475 $385 $315 $245 *$795*

GOVERNMENT MODEL 82A TARGET – .22 LR cal. only, specifically designed for U.S. Army training, 25 in. heavy target barrel including scope blocks, oversized stock, some rifles are "star" marked indicating an accuracy guarantee, 10 3/4 lbs. Mfg. 1987-1991.

$725 $675 $550 $500 $400 $325 $250 *$595*

Add $300 for a "Star" marked rifle.

20,000 rifles were mfg. 1987-1989 to fill the initial U.S. government contract. These rifles were all transferred to the CMP for resale to the public and are all marked "US" over the serial number. Commercial guns were manufactured for the private sector pending an accuracy test of .3 @ 50 yards with match ammo. These guns were marked with a "Star" stamp over the serial number.

ALL AMERICAN MATCH – .22 LR cal. only, precision rifled 25 in. free floating target grade barrel, stock is adj. both vertically and for length of pull, fully adj. single stage trigger, approx. 9 lbs. Mfg. 1990-91 only.

$1,100 $995 $595 $535 $435 $355 $275 *$895*

CONTINENTAL – .22 LR, .22 WMR, or .22 Hornet cal., Sporter action only, full-length Mannlicher stock, open sights, deluxe walnut. Mfg. 1987-disc.

This model was only available as a special order with prices on request from the factory.
Add $200 for .22 WMR or .22 Hornet cal.

* ***Continental Super*** – .22 LR, .22 WMR, or .22 Hornet cal., similar to Continental, except has AAA Claro walnut with 22 lines/in. checkering. Mfg. 1987-1988.

$3,500 $2,950 $2,050 $1,350 $1,000 $850 $725 *$1,465*

Add 100% if model is one of three known laminated stock variations with cheekpieces that were mfg., all in .22 LR cal.

S SERIES – .22 LR (535 mfg.), .22 Hornet (354 mfg.), or .22 WMR (88 mfg.) cal., top-of-the-line limited production model, grooved for scope mounting, Neidner checkered steel buttplate, best quality walnut, continental cheekpiece, ebony forend tip, Sporter configuration only. Mfg. early 1980s.

$2,300 $2,250 $1,450 $950 $770 $630 $490

SUPER AMERICA – top-of-the-line model, includes detachable scope mounts, Niedner checkered steel buttplate and best quality walnut, cheekpiece and ebony forend tip added after 1983, available in Sporter configuration only. This model was disc. 1988, and reintroduced 1990-1991.

$2,900 $2,600 $1,375 $1,125 $900 $750 $600 *$1,295*

Extra fancy wood will command a premium on this model.

* ***Super America Super Grade*** – similar to Super America, AAA walnut, beaded cheekpiece, 5 or 10 (optional) shot mag., 6 1/2 lbs. Mfg. 1989 only.

$2,650 $2,395 $1,175 $1,090 $880 $720 $560 *$1,295*

CUSTOM MATCH – .22 LR or .22 WMR cal., limited edition of 217 rifles, match dimension chamber, French walnut stock with 22 L.P.I. checkering, rust blue finish, other custom rifle features. Mfg. 1984-disc.

$5,500 $4,500 $2,100 $1,850 $1,475 $1,250 $995

Add $500 for .22 WMR cal.

BROWNELL – .22 LR cal., only 500 mfg. to commemorate the late Leonard Brownell, Mannlicher style extra deluxe Claro walnut stock. Mfg. 1986 only.

$3,150 $2,725 $1,500 $1,325 $1,085 $930 $750 *$1,500*

CENTENNIAL – .22 LR cal. only, limited edition (100 rifles) to commemorate centennial of .22 LR cal., includes hand-picked checkered walnut, moderate engraving, special Wilson Arms match barrel, skeleton buttplate and other refinements, serial numbered C1-C100, shipped in a quality pine shipping container. Mfg. 1987 only.

$8,000 $7,550 $4,300 $2,450 $1,975 $1,625 $1,250 *$2,950*

GRADING - PPGS™	100%	98%	95%	90%	80%	70%	60%	LAST MSR

TENTH ANNIVERSARY ISSUE – .22 LR cal., limited edition, French walnut stock featuring slim forend design with shadowed cheekpiece, Neidner steel buttplate and other refinements. Mfg. 1989 only.

	$4,400	$3,995	$2,800	$1,550	$1,250	$1,085	$875	

Add $100 for matte finish.

Model 84 Centerfire Series

Model 84 caliber rarity is as follows: .222 Rem. and .223 Rem. are common. 6x45mm or 47mm, .221 Fireball, .17 Rem., and .17 Mach IV are less common and more desirable. .222 Rem. Mag. is rare, while 5.6x50mm is extremely rare.

Add $200-$375 for rare calibers.

Add $75 for forend tip - option A. Add $300 for iron sights - option B. Add $100 for checkered bolt handle - option C. Add $200 for skeleton grip cap - option D. Add $300 for skeleton buttplate - option G. Add $250-$300 for 3-position safety in this series.

STANDARD MODEL 84 – .17 Rem., .17 Mach IV (disc. 1987), 6x45 or 47mm (disc. 1987), 5.6x50mm (disc. 1987), .221 Fireball, .222 Rem., .222 Rem. Mag. (disc. 1987), or .223 Rem. cal., "Mini-Mauser" type head locking bolt action, 5 shot mag., 22 (Sporter) or 24 (Varmint) in. barrel, deluxe Claro walnut, steel buttplate, rocker style safety, 6 1/2 lbs.

* ***Standard Model 84 Classic*** – disc. 1988.

	$1,195	$1,050	$895	$815	$650	$540	$425	*$885*

Pricing for .222 and .223 calibers, others will bring a premium.

Add $55 for disc. Cascade Model (Monte Carlo cheekpiece).

Add 20% for left-hand action.

Also available in left-hand action in .22 Hornet, .222 Rem., .223 Rem., 6x45mm, 6x47mm, .17 Rem., and .17 Mach IV (very limited mfg.).

CUSTOM CLASSIC MODEL – higher grade Claro walnut, ebony forearm tip, Niedner style steel buttplate. Disc. 1988.

	$1,825	$1,525	$1,275	$1,100	$850	$700	$550	*$1,130*

* ***Custom Classic Model Deluxe Grade Sporter*** – .17 Rem., .221 Rem., or .223 Rem. cal., Mauser action, AA walnut, similar to Custom Classic Model, 6 1/4 lbs. Mfg. 1989-90.

	$1,775	$1,525	$1,275	$1,100	$850	$700	$550	*$1,295*

Also available in left-hand action (.223 Rem. cal. only), limited mfg.

CONTINENTAL – .221 Fireball (extremely rare, mfg. 1988 only) .222 Rem. or .223 Rem. cal., Sporter action only, full-length Mannlicher stock, open sights, deluxe walnut. Mfg. 1987-disc.

Extreme rarity precludes accurate price evaluation on this model.

* ***Continental Super*** – similar to Continental (same cals.), except has AAA Claro walnut with 22 lines/in. checkering. Mfg. 1987-88.

	$2,600	$2,350	$2,000	$1,250	$1,000	$800	$700	*$1,600*

Add 100% if model is one of three known laminated stocks that were mfg. in .223 Rem. cal.

HUNTER GRADE – .17 Rem., .222 Rem., or .223 Rem. cal., laminated stock, Super America configured action and barrel with low glare metal finish. Mfg. 1990 only.

	$995	$875	$750	$650	$550	$475	$400	*$995*

SPORTER – .17 Rem., .22 Hornet, .222 Rem., .22-250 Rem., or .223 Rem. cal., 22 in. sporter weight barrel, A grade Claro walnut, round top receiver with bases, 4 shot mag., hand checkering. Mfg. 1991 only.

	$1,020	$850	$725	$625	$550	$500	$450	*$1,095*

This model was available in either right or left-hand action.

* ***Sporter Big Bore*** – .250 Savage or .35 Rem. cal., similar action to Sporter Model, except has 3/4 in. red Pachmayr Decelerator recoil pad. Mfg. 1991 only.

Last MSR was $1,095.

Extreme rarity precludes accurate price evaluation on this model.

Consult an expert when buying/selling this model. This model was available in either right or left-hand action.

SUPER AMERICA/SUPER GRADE – .17 Rem., .17 MK IV, .221 Fireball, .22 Hornet, .222 Rem., .222 Rem. Mag., .22-250 Rem., .223 Rem., 5.6x56mm, or 6x47mm cal., 22 in. sporter weight barrel, top-of-the-line, with detachable scope mounts, available in Sporter configuration only, cheekpiece and ebony forend tip added after 1983, 4 shot mag., right or left-hand action. Disc. 1988, reintroduced 1990-1991.

	$2,850	$2,300	$1,925	$1,450	$1,125	$925	$725	*$1,495*

Extra fancy wood will command a premium on this model.

Base pricing is for .222/.223 calibers. Rare calibers will command a premium.

Be careful when buying rare cals. and/or options on this model.

GRADING - PPGS™	100%	98%	95%	90%	80%	70%	60%	LAST MSR

* ***Super America/Super Grade Big Bore*** – .250 Savage or .35 Rem. cal., similar action to Super America Model, except has 3/4 in. red Pachmayr Decelerator recoil pad. Mfg. 1991 only.

$4,200 $3,550 $2,850 $2,250 $1,850 $1,600 $1,400 *$1,495*

CUSTOM MATCH – .222 Rem. or .223 Rem. cal., limited edition of 200 rifles, match dimension chamber, French walnut stock with 22 L.P.I. checkering, rust blue finish, other custom rifle features. Introduced 1986.

$4,700 $4,000 $3,800 $3,000 $2,200 $2,000 $1,500

TENTH ANNIVERSARY ISSUE – .223 Rem. cal., limited edition, French walnut stock featuring slim forend design with shadowed cheekpiece, 22 in. barrel, roundtop receiver with mounts, Neidner steel buttplate and other refinements. Mfg. 1989 only.

$3,995 $3,650 $3,250 $2,200 $1,800 $1,575 $1,250

Add $100 for matte finish.

ULTRA VARMINTER – .17 Rem., .22 Hornet (rare, new 1991), .221 Rem. (disc. 1990), .222 Rem., .22-250 Rem. (rare), or .223 Rem. cal., 24 in. medium weight stainless steel barrel, laminated birch stock, plain buttstock, right or left-hand action, 7 3/4 lbs. Mfg. 1989-91 only.

$1,600 $1,300 $1,175 $1,000 $850 $750 $675 *$1,295*

* ***Ultra Varminter Super*** – similar to Ultra Varminter except has steel barrel, AAA walnut stock with beaded cheekpiece, 7 1/4 lbs. Mfg. 1989-91 only.

$2,500 $2,350 $2,000 $1,200 $975 $775 $675 *$1,495*

Model 89 Centerfire, Big Game Series

Fewer than 5,000 Model 89 BGRs were mfg. Note: fancy wood is harder to find in Model 89s.

MODEL 89 BGR – .270 Win., .280 Rem., 7mm Rem. Mag., .30-06, .300 Win. Mag., .338 Win. Mag., or .375 H&H cal., new action incorporates features from both Mauser 98 and Win. pre-64 Model 70, three position safety, 22 or 24 in. barrel, matte blue finish will command a premium. Introduced late 1988.

* ***Model 89 BGR Classic Model*** – deluxe Claro walnut checkered 18 lines/in. with steel buttplate. Disc. 1988.

$875 $725 $600 $500 $415 $350 $300 *$985*

Add $200 for .375 H&H cal.
Add $100 for matte finish.

* ***Model 89 BGR Custom Classic Model*** – higher grade Claro walnut, ebony forearm tip, Niedner style steel buttplate. Disc. 1988.

$1,250 $1,050 $850 $725 $625 $525 $425 *$1,230*

Add $200 for .375 H&H cal.

DELUXE GRADE – similar to Custom Classic Model, round top receiver with Model 70 scope mount hole configuration, AA walnut stock with ebony forend tip and rubber recoil pad (no cheekpiece), 22 or 24 in. barrel, 7 1/2-8 1/2 lbs. New 1989.

* ***Deluxe Grade Featherweight Barrel Model*** – .257 Roberts (rare), .25-06 Rem., 7x57mm (rare, disc. 1990), .270 Win., .280 Rem., or .30-06 cal., 5 shot mag., 22 in. Featherweight barrel, right-hand action only, 7 1/2 lbs. Disc. 1990.

$1,600 $1,225 $1,000 $850 $700 $600 $525 *$1,795*

Add 25% for 7x57mm cal.
Add $470 for Super America Grade with square bridge, dovetail receiver.
Add $100 for matte finish.

The Super America Grade will accept Kimber double lever scope mounts and has one grade better wood than the Deluxe Grade with beaded cheekpiece.

* ***Deluxe Grade Medium-weight Barrel Model*** – .300 Win. Mag., .300 H&H (rare, disc. 1990), .300 Wby. Mag. (very rare, new 1991), .338 Win. Mag., .35 Whelen (rare, disc. 1990), or 7mm Rem. Mag. cal., 3 shot mag., 24 in. medium-weight barrel, right-hand action only, 7 3/4-8 1/2 lbs. Disc. 1990.

$1,675 $1,250 $1,025 $875 $725 $625 $550 *$1,895*

Add a premium for rare cals.
Add $495 for Super America Grade with square bridge, dovetail receiver.
Add $100 for matte finish.

The Super America Grade will accept Kimber double lever scope mounts and has one grade better wood than the Deluxe Grade with beaded cheekpiece.

GRADING - PPGS™	100%	98%	95%	90%	80%	70%	60%	LAST MSR

* ***Deluxe Grade Heavy-weight Barrel Model*** – .375 H&H Mag. cal., 3 shot mag., 24 in. heavy weight barrel, right-hand action only, 9 lbs. Disc. 1990.

	$2,000	$1,750	$1,500	$1,250	$1,000	$800	$700	*$1,995*

Add $495 for Super America Grade with square bridge, dovetail receiver.
Add $100 for matte finish.

The Super America Grade will accept Kimber double lever scope mounts and has one grade better wood than the Deluxe Grade with beaded cheekpiece.

SPORTER MODEL – same cals. as Deluxe/Super America Models, 22 in. featherweight or 24 in. medium or heavy barrel, double square bridge dovetail receiver, A grade Claro walnut stock with 3/4 in. red Pachmayr Decelerator recoil pad (Mag. cals. only with 24 in. barrel). Mfg. 1991 only.

	$1,395	$1,050	$900	$775	$650	$500	$450	*$1,595*

Add $100 for medium Magnum action.
Add $200 for heavy Magnum action (.375 H&H and .458 Win. Mag. cals.).

HUNTER GRADE – .270 Win., .30-06, .300 Win. Mag., .338 Win. Mag., or 7mm Rem. Mag. cal., laminated stock, Super America configured action and barrel with low glare metal finish. Mfg. 1990-91 only.

	$1,325	$1,025	$895	$750	$625	$525	$450	*$1,495*

Add $100 for Mag. cals.

SUPER GRADE – similar to Super America Model, square top frame, AAA walnut, 22 or 24 in. barrel, plain buttstock, 7 1/2-8 1/2 lbs. Mfg. 1989 only.

	$1,575	$1,325	$995	$825	$695	$550	$500	*$1,495*

Add $100 for .375 H&H cal.
Add $100 for matte blue metal finish.

The 24 in. barrel was available in Mag. cals. only.

LIMITED WILDLIFE EDITION SERIES – series of 5 guns, includes .257 Roberts (Whitetail Deer Edition), .270 Win. (Mule Deer Edition), .338 Win. Mag. (Rocky Mt. Elk Edition), 7mm Rem. Mag. (Big Horn Sheep Edition), and .375 H&H (Grizzly Bear Edition) cals. included, hand select walnut, special Shilen Rifle barrel, gold plated trigger, receivers are stamped "Wildlife Edition", special prefix serialization, only 25 sets were to be manufactured in 1991 only, includes rings, swivels, and hard case.

Retail price was scheduled to be $3,595.

While advertised, only one .270 Win. Mule Deer model was mfg.

MODEL 89 AFRICAN – .375 H&H (rare), .416 Rigby (most common) cal., or .505 Gibbs (rare) cal., Magnum action, 24 in. heavy barrel, AA English walnut stock with beaded cheekpiece and rubber recoil pad, includes twin recoil crossbolts, express sights on quarter rib, drop box magazine, 10-10 1/2 lbs. Mfg. 1990-1991 only.

	$5,500	$4,500	$4,000	$3,500	$2,750	$2,250	$1,650	*$3,595*

.375 H&H or .505 Gibbs cal. will command a premium.

KIMEL INDUSTRIES, INC.

Previously manufactured until late 1994 by A.A. Arms located in Monroe, NC. Previously distributed by Kimel Industries, Inc. located in Matthews, NC.

CARBINES: SEMI-AUTO

AR-9 CARBINE – 9mm Para. cal., carbine variation of the AP-9 with 16 1/2 in. barrel, 20 shot mag., and steel rod folding stock. Mfg. 1991-94.

	$625	$550	$475	$425	$365	$315	$275	*$384*

PISTOLS: SEMI-AUTO

AP-9 PISTOL – 9mm Para. cal., SA, blowback operation, bolt knob on left side of receiver, 5 in. barrel with vent. shroud, front mounted 10 (C/B 1994) or 20* shot detachable mag., black matte finish, adj. front sight, 3 lbs. 7 oz. Mfg. 1989-1994.

	$475	$425	$375	$325	$300	$275	$250	*$279*

* ***AP-9 Pistol Mini*** – compact variation of the AP-9 Model with 3 in. barrel, blue or nickel finish. Mfg. 1991-94.

	$550	$500	$425	$375	$325	$300	$275	*$273*

* ***AP-9 Pistol Target*** – target variation of the AP-9 with 12 in. match barrel with shroud, blue finish only. Mfg. 1991-94.

	$600	$550	$475	$425	$375	$350	$325	*$294*

GRADING - PPGS™	100%	98%	95%	90%	80%	70%	60%	LAST MSR

* ***P-95 Pistol*** – similar to AP-9, except without barrel shroud and is supplied with 5 shot mag., parts are interchangeable with AP-9. Mfg. 1990-91 only.

	$395	$350	$300	$250	$200	$175	$150	*$250*

KING'S ARSENAL

Previous manufacturer of AR-15 style rifles, pistols, and bolt action rifles located in Abilene, TX, 2011-2018.

Please refer to BlueBookOfGunValues.com to order the *Blue Book of AR-15s & Variations*, available as a book or online subscription.

KING'S GUN WORKS, INC.

Previous custom handgun and accessories manufacturer 1949-circa 2011 located in Glendale, CA.

King's Gun Works manufactured a complete line of custom pistols patterned after Colt M-1911, in addition to many related accessories and/or after-market parts.

KINGSTON ARMORY

Previous rifle manufacturer located in Liberty, NY until circa 2017.

RIFLES: SEMI-AUTO

M1 .22 CAL. GARAND – .22 LR cal., National Match sights, American walnut stock, steel buttplate, .22 LR cal. variation of the M1-Garand. Mfg. 2016-2017.

	$850	$750	$650	$580	$475	$380	$300	*$699*

M14 .22 CAL. – .22 LR cal., National Match sights, American walnut stock, steel buttplate, .22 LR cal. semi-auto variation of the M14. Mfg. 2016-2017.

	$850	$750	$650	$580	$475	$380	$300	*$699*

KINTREK, INC.

Previous rifle manufacturer located in Owensboro, KY.

RIFLES: SEMI-AUTO

BULLPUP MODEL – .22 LR cal., bullpup configuration, hinged dust cover, clear Ram-Line type coil spring mag., black synthetic thumbhole stock, A2 style front/rear sight. Disc.

	$350	$300	$250	$225	$200	$175	$150	

KIRICI SILAH

Current manufacturer of shotguns located in Konya, Turkey. No current U.S. importation.

Kirici Silah manufactures a complete line of good quality O/U, single barrel, and slide action shotguns. A wide variety of options are available, including various receiver finishes, stocks, gold inlays and engraving. Please contact the company directly for more information, including pricing and domestic availability.

KLEINGUENTHER FIREARMS CO.

Previous custom rifle manufacturer located in Seguin, TX until circa 2001. The original KDF Co. was started by Mr. Robert Kleinguenther and sold in the early 1980s. Mr. Kleinguenther then started a new company called Kleinguenther Firearms Co.

RIFLES: BOLT ACTION

Values listed are for base models only with no additional customer special order options. Mr. Kleinguenther also custom built rifles utilizing customer actions.

BOLT ACTION RIFLE – various cals., individual customer special order rifle with a variety of options, guns are guaranteed to shoot 1/2 MOA, choice of actions, various weights.

* ***Bolt Action Rifle Winchester Model 70 Custom***

	$975	$800	$675	$575	$500	$450	$400	*$975*

* ***Bolt Action Rifle Sako Action*** – various cals., newer guns feature the ballistic recoil muzzle brake system (60-70% recoil reduction), most newer stocks are mfg. out of high tech laminated wood with 28-32 resin coated panels.

	$1,550	$1,325	$1,100	$950	$825	$725	$625	*$1,750*

Add $155 for ballistic recoil muzzle brake system.

* ***Bolt Action Rifle K-15***

	$1,375	$1,100	$950	$800	$675	$575	$500	*$1,375*

KNIGHT'S ARMAMENT COMPANY

Current AR-15 style rifle manufacturer established in 1983, located in Titusville, FL. Previously located in Vero Beach, FL. Dealer and consumer direct sales.

RIFLES: SEMI-AUTO

Some of the models listed were also available in pre-ban configurations. SR-25 Enhanced Match model has 10 or 20 shot mag. Some of the following models, while discontinued for civilian use, may still be available for military/law enforcement.

STONER SR-15 M-5 RIFLE – .223 Rem. cal., GIO, 20 in. standard weight barrel, flip-up low profile rear sight, two-stage target trigger, 7.6 lbs. Mfg. 1997-2008.

$1,525 $1,350 $1,150 $1,050 $850 $700 $550 *$1,837*

* ***Stoner SR-15 M-4 Carbine*** – .223 Rem. cal., similar to SR-15 rifle, except has 16 in. barrel, choice of fixed synthetic or non-collapsible buttstock. Mfg. 1997-2005.

$1,325 $1,150 $1,000 $900 $750 $600 $475 *$1,575*

Add $100 for non-collapsible buttstock (SR-15 M-4 K-Carbine, disc. 2001).

* ***SR-15 E3 Mod 2 URX 4 Keymod (Stoner SR-15 URX E3 Carbine)*** – 5.56 NATO cal., GIO, features 16 in. free floating barrel with URX forearm, E3 type rounded lug improved bolt. New 2004.

MSR $2,312 $2,000 $1,850 $1,650 $1,500 $1,300 $1000 $800

* ***SR-15 E3 Mod 2 URX 4 M-LOK*** – 5.56 NATO. cal., GIO, AR-15 style, 16 in. free floating barrel, E3 type rounded lug improved bolt, URX4 M-LOK handguard. New 2016.

MSR $2,450 $2,200 $1,950 $1,750 $1,600 $1,350 $1,050 $850

SR-15E IWS LIGHT PRECISION RIFLE – 5.56 NATO cal., 18 in. stainless steel match barrel with custom match chamber, URX (upper receiver extending) free floated barrel system, IWS lower, two-stage match trigger, ambidextrous controls, black furniture, 7.38 lbs.

$2,350 $2,050 $1,750 $1,600 $1,300 $1,050 $800

STONER SR-15 MATCH RIFLE – .223 Rem. cal., GIO, flat-top upper receiver with 20 in. match grade stainless steel free floating barrel with RAS forend, two-stage match trigger, 7.9 lbs. Mfg. 1997-2008.

$1,800 $1,550 $1,350 $1,200 $1,000 $800 $600 *$1,972*

SR-15 E3 LPR MOD 2 M-LOK – 5.56 NATO cal., 18 in. match stainless steel barrel with custom match chamber, free floated barrel system, two-stage match trigger, URX4 M-LOK handguard, IWS lower, ambidextrous controls, black furniture, 7.38 lbs. New 2016.

MSR $2,700 $2,400 $2,100 $1,950 $1,800 $1,500 $1,150 $925

SR-15 MOD 2 – 5.56 NATO cal., 16 in. hammer forged chrome-lined barrel, mid-length gas system, ambi bolt catch, selector, and mag. release, drop-in two-stage trigger, black finish, 6 3/4 lbs. New 2015.

Please contact the manufacturer directly for pricing and availability for this model.

SR-15 E3 LPR MOD 2 KEYMOD (LIGHT PRECISION RIFLE) – 5.56 NATO cal., Mod 2 Gas System, 18 in. match grade stainless steel barrel with a custom match chamber and QDC flash eliminator, adj. micro sights, two-stage match trigger, multi-lug improved E3 bolt, 6-pos. SOPMOD stock, URX 4 handguard with KeyMod mounting points, standard ambidextrous lower receiver, black finish, 7 1/2 lbs. New 2015.

MSR $2,700 $2,400 $2,100 $1,950 $1,800 $1,500 $1,150 $925

STONER SR-25 SPORTER – .308 Win. cal., GIO, 20 in. lightweight barrel, AR-15 configuration with carrying handle, 5, 10, or 20 (disc. per C/B 1994) shot detachable mag., less than 2 MOA guaranteed, non-glare finish, 8.8 lbs. Mfg. 1993-97.

$2,700 $2,350 $2,000 $1,850 $1,500 $1,200 $950 *$2,995*

* ***Stoner RAS Sporter Carbine (SR-25 Carbine)*** – .223 Rem. cal., GIO, 16 in. free floating barrel, grooved non-slip handguard, removable carrying handle, 7 3/4 lbs. Mfg. 1995-2005.

$3,150 $2,750 $2,350 $2,150 $1,750 $1,400 $1,100 *$3,495*

Subtract 15% if w/o RAS.

In 2003, the Rail Adapter System (RAS) became standard on this model.

SR-25 STANDARD MATCH – .308 Win. cal., GIO, free floating 24 in. match barrel, fiberglass stock, includes commercial gun case and 10 shot mag. Disc. 2008.

$3,500 $3,050 $2,600 $2,400 $1,900 $1,600 $1,200 *$3,918*

GRADING - PPGS™	100%	98%	95%	90%	80%	70%	60%	LAST MSR

SR-25 RAS MATCH – .308 Win. cal., similar to SR-25 Standard, except has 24 in. free floating match barrel and flat-top receiver, less than 1 MOA guaranteed, RAS became standard 2004, 10 3/4 lbs. Mfg. 1993-2008.

	$3,400	$3,000	$2,550	$2,300	$1,850	$1,550	$1,200	*$3,789*

Subtract approx. 15% if w/o Rail Adapter System (RAS).

Over 3,000 SR-25s were manufactured.

* ***SR-25 RAS Match Lightweight*** – .308 Win. cal., GIO, 20 in. medium contour free floating barrel, 9 1/2 lbs. Mfg. 1995-2004.

	$2,900	$2,550	$2,200	$1,950	$1,600	$1,300	$1,000	*$3,244*

Add approx. 15% for Rail Adapter System.

SR-25 E2 ACC KEYMOD (ADVANCED COMBAT CARBINE) – 7.62 NATO cal., 16 in. rifled chrome-lined barrel with 5-slot flash hider, ambi controls, carbon cutter bolt carrier, multi-lug improved E2 bolt, drop-in two-stage trigger, URX handguard, two-stage match trigger, black finish, 8.4 lbs. New 2015.

MSR $4,861	$4,300	$3,800	$3,500	$3,200	$2,700	$2,100	$1,650

SR-25 E2 ACC URX4 M-LOK – 7.62 NATO cal., 16 in. rifled chrome-lined barrel with 5-slot flash hider, ambi controls, carbon cutter bolt carrier, multi-lug improved E2 bolt, drop-in two-stage trigger, URX handguard, black finish, 8.4 lbs. New 2016.

MSR $4,861	$4,300	$3,800	$3,500	$3,200	$2,700	$2,100	$1,650

SR-25 E2 APC (ADVANCED PRECISION CARBINE) KEYMOD – 7.62 NATO cal., 16 in. barrel with QDC flash suppressor, URX 4 free floating barrel system, drop-in two-stage trigger, ambi bolt release, selector, and mag. release, black furniture, 9.12 lbs. New mid-2014.

MSR $4,861	$4,300	$3,800	$3,500	$3,200	$2,700	$2,100	$1,650

SR-25 E2 APC M-LOK – 7.62 NATO cal., 16 in. barrel with QDC flash suppressor, URX 4 free floating barrel system, drop-in two-stage trigger, ambi bolt release, selector, and mag. release, black furniture, 9.12 lbs. New 2016.

MSR $4,861	$4,300	$3,800	$3,500	$3,200	$2,700	$2,100	$1,650

SR-25 E2 APR (ADVANCED PRECISION RIFLE) KEYMOD – 7.62 NATO cal., 20 in. match barrel with QDC flash suppressor, ambi controls, drop-in two-stage trigger, E2 bolt and gas system, URX 4 handguard, black finish, 10 1/2 lbs. New 2015.

MSR $4,861	$4,300	$3,800	$3,500	$3,200	$2,700	$2,100	$1,650

SR-25 E2 APR M-LOK – 7.62 NATO cal., 20 in. match barrel with QDC flash suppressor, ambi controls, drop-in two-stage trigger, E2 bolt and gas system, URX 4 handguard, black finish, 10 1/2 lbs. New 2016.

MSR $4,861	$4,300	$3,800	$3,500	$3,200	$2,700	$2,100	$1,650

SR-25 ENHANCED MATCH RIFLE/CARBINE – .308 Win. cal., GIO, 16 or 20 in. barrel, 10 or 20 shot mag., URX rail system, two-stage trigger, ambidextrous mag. release, integrated adj. folding front sight, micro adj. folding rear sight, EM gas block, combat trigger guard, chrome plated multi-lug bolt and bolt carrier, fixed or nine position adj. stock, black anodized finish, flash hider (carbine only), approx. 8 1/2 lbs. Disc. 2013.

	$4,500	$3,950	$3,400	$3,050	$2,500	$2,000	$1,600	*$4,994*

Add $625 for 16 in. carbine.

SR-25 MK11 MOD O CIVILIAN DELUXE SYSTEM PACKAGE – .308 Win. cal., GIO, consumer variation of the Navy Model Mark Eleven, Mod O, w/o sound suppressor, includes Leupold 3.5-10X scope, 20 in. military grade match barrel, backup sights, cell-foam case and other accessories. Mfg. 2003-2008.

	$7,750	$6,700	$5,750	$5,200	$4,200	$3,450	$2,700	*$8,534*

SR-25 MK11 MATCH RIFLE – .308 Win. cal., GIO, includes MK11 Mod O features and 20 in. heavy barrel. Mfg. 2004-2008.

	$5,750	$5,050	$4,300	$3,900	$3,150	$2,600	$2,000	*$6,325*

SR-25 MK11 CARBINE – .308 Win. cal., GIO, includes MK11 Mod O features and 16 in. match grade stainless steel barrel with muzzle brake, URX 4x4 rail forend, 4-position buttstock. Mfg. 2005-2013.

	$6,000	$5,250	$4,500	$4,100	$3,300	$2,700	$2,100	*$6,636*

SR-25 BR CARBINE – .308 Win. cal., similar to SR-25 MK11 Carbine, except has chrome-lined steel barrel. Mfg. 2005-2008.

	$5,675	$4,950	$4,250	$3,850	$3,100	$2,550	$2,000	*$6,307*

GRADING - PPGS™	100%	98%	95%	90%	80%	70%	60%	LAST MSR

SR-30 - .300 AAC Blackout cal., 16 in. stainless steel barrel with QDC flash suppressor, URX 3.1 free floating rail system, micro front and rear iron sights, E3 bolt, ambi controls, two-stage trigger, fully adj. SOPMOD stock, black furniture, 6 1/2 lbs. Mfg. mid-2014-2015.

	$2,375	$2,100	$1,800	$1,600	$1,300	$1,050	$850	*$2,632*

SR-M110 SASS – 7.62x51mm cal., GIO, 20 in. military match grade barrel, full RAS treatment on barrel, civilian variation of the Army's semi-auto sniper rifle system, includes Leupold long-range tactical scope, 600 meter backup iron sights, system case and other accessories. Mfg. 2006-2009.

	$13,000	$11,350	$9,750	$8,850	$7,150	$5,850	$4,550	*$14,436*

"DAVID TUBB" COMPETITION MATCH RIFLE - .260 Rem. or .308 Win. cal., GIO, incorporates refinements by David Tubb, top-of-the-line competition match rifle, including adj. and rotating buttstock pad. Mfg. 1998 only.

	$5,450	$4,750	$4,100	$3,700	$3,000	$2,450	$1,900	*$5,995*

STONER SR-50 – .50 BMG cal., GIO, features high strength materials and lightweight design, fully locked breech and two lug rotary breech bolt, horizontal 5 shot box mag., tubular receiver supports a removable barrel, approx. 31 lbs. Limited mfg. 2000, non-commercial sales only.

Last MSR was $6,995.

Extreme rarity factor precludes accurate pricing on this model.

KOC ARMS

Current manufacturer of shotguns located in Konya, Turkey. No current U.S. importation.

Koc Arms manufactures good quality semi-auto, slide action, and single barrel shotguns under the trademarks Gazelle Shotguns and Prenses Arms. Please refer to these individual listings for more information.

KODIAK CO.

Previous manufacturer located in North Haven, CT circa 1963-66.

Kodiak Co. was in business for only a short time. They produced the first .22 WMR semi-auto rifle (Model 260), as well as a centerfire bolt action (Model 158 Deluxe), and a slide action shotgun (Model 458). While Kodiak long guns are rare and extremely well made, collectability to date has been minimal with most specimens selling at a slight premium over similar quality trade name counterparts of that era. Prior to 1963, Kodiak firearms were marketed under the trade name of Jefferson.

KODIAK DEFENCE, INC.

Current manufacturer of AR-15 style rifles located in Ontario, Canada. No current U.S. importation.

Please refer to BlueBookOfGunValues.com to order the *Blue Book of AR-15s & Variations*, available as a book or online subscription.

KOFS FIREARMS

Current shotgun manufacturer located in Isparta, Turkey. No current U.S. importation.

Kofs Firearms manufactures a complete line of good quality boxlock O/U and SxS shotguns - many grades and options are available. Current registered trademarks include: Cavalry, Coach, Eclipse, Impulse, Mono, Rampart, Sceptre, and Zenith. These trademarks are mostly marketed and sold throughout Europe. Please contact the company directly for more information including pricing and availability.

KOLAR ARMS

Current manufacturer located in Racine, WI. Dealer direct sales.

SHOTGUNS

Kolar Arms manufactures fine quality O/U and single barrel boxlock shotguns in Skeet, Sporting Clays, and Trap configurations. Many options are available including custom orders, wood upgrades, and engraving. Current models include: Max Trap T/S (MSR for nickel $8,995), Max Trap T/A (MSR for nickel $11,995), Max Lite Skeet (MSR for nickel $13,990), Max Lite Sporter (MSR for nickel $11,995), Max TA/TC All Around Combo (MSR for nickel $16,395). Prestige, Legend, Select, Gold Elite, Custom Select, and Custom Grade pricing is also available on each model. Please contact the company directly for more information, including model availability, delivery time, and pricing.

KOLIBRI

Previous trademark manufactured 1914-1925 by Georg Grabner located in Rehberg, Austria.

GRADING - PPGS™	100%	98%	95%	90%	80%	70%	60%	LAST MSR

PISTOLS: SEMI-AUTO

KOLIBRI PISTOL – 2.7 or 3mm centerfire cal., unrifled barrel, 5 shot box mag., world's smallest semi-auto centerfire pistol.

GRADING - PPGS™	100%	98%	95%	90%	80%	70%	60%	LAST MSR
	$2,500	$2,250	$1,950	$1,750	$1,500	$1,350	$1,175	

Add approx. $300 for original case.
Add approx. 20% for nickel finish (rare).

Individual rounds of 2.7 or 3mm (more rare) ammunition are currently trading in the $75 range as it has the distinction of being the world's smallest centerfire shell (shooting a 3 grain bullet at approx. 475 fps and generating 1.75 ft./lbs. of muzzle energy!).

KONGSBERG

Previous manufacturer circa 1814-1998 located in Kongsberg, Norway. Previously imported and distributed 1996-98, by Kongsberg America L.L.C. located in Fairfield, CT, and by Lew Horton Distributing Co., Inc. until 1996, located in Westboro, MA.

RIFLES: BOLT ACTION

Add $50 for iron sights on models listed below.

393 SERIES – .22-250 Rem., .243 Win., .270 Win., .30-06, .308 Win., 6.5x55 Swedish, 7mm Rem. Mag., .300 Win. Mag., or .338 Win. Mag. cal., available in either Classic, De Luxe, Thumbhole (.22-250 Rem. or .308 Win. only), or Select (Standard) configuration, checkered pistol grip, forend mounted recoil lug which connects to stock, 3-position rear safety, fixed rotary mag., fully adj. trigger. Imported 1994-98.

GRADING - PPGS™	100%	98%	95%	90%	80%	70%	60%	LAST MSR
*** 393 Series Classic Model**	$875	$750	$675	$575	$495	$440	$385	*$995*

Add $114 for Mag. cals.
Add $138 for left-hand action.

GRADING - PPGS™	100%	98%	95%	90%	80%	70%	60%	LAST MSR
*** 393 Series Select Model (Standard Model in Europe)**	$860	$735	$660	$560	$495	$440	$385	*$980*

Add $113 for Mag. cals.
Add $138 for left-hand action.

GRADING - PPGS™	100%	98%	95%	90%	80%	70%	60%	LAST MSR
*** 393 Series De Luxe Model**	$940	$795	$700	$595	$515	$450	$395	*$1,124*

Add $112 for Mag. cals.
Add $137 for left-hand action.

*** 393 Series Thumbhole Model** – .22-250 Rem. or .308 Win. cal., features thumbhole stock. Mfg. 1996-98.

GRADING - PPGS™	100%	98%	95%	90%	80%	70%	60%	LAST MSR
	$1,350	$1,175	$1,000	$875	$750	$625	$500	*$1,580*

Add $138 for left-hand action.

KORA BRNO

Current revolver/carbine trademark manufactured by Kroko a.s., located in Brno, Czech Republic. No current U.S. importation.

To date, the Kora Brno revolver/carbine line has had little or no importation into the U.S. Models include many configurations of both .22 LR, .22 WMR, and .38 Spl. cals. Please contact the factory directly for more information.

KORRIPHILA

Previous trademark manufactured until 2004 by Intertex, located in Eislingen, Germany. Previously imported 1999-2004 by Korriphila, Inc., located in Pineville, NC., and by Osborne's located in Cheboygan, MI until 1988.

PISTOLS: SEMI-AUTO

Less than 30 Korriphila pistols were made annually.

HSP 701 – 7.65 Luger, .38 Super, 9mm Para., 9mm Police, 9mm Steyr, .45 ACP, or 10mm Norma cal., DA/SA, Budischowsky delayed roller lock system assists in recoil reduction, 40% stainless steel parts, 4 or 5 in. barrel, blue or satin finish, walnut grips, 7 or 9 shot mag., based on earlier HSP 70, approx. 2.6 lbs. Very limited production.

GRADING - PPGS™	100%	98%	95%	90%	80%	70%	60%	LAST MSR
	$10,000	$7,000	$4,500	$3,250	$2,150	$1,850	$1,675	

GRADING - PPGS™	100%	98%	95%	90%	80%	70%	60%	LAST MSR

* ***HSP 701 Odin's Eye (Damascus)*** – similar to HSP 701, except is completely made from one block of Damascus stainless steel, rosewood grips with Manta skin inlays, custom order only.

	$15,500	$12,000	$9,500	N/A	N/A	N/A	N/A	

TP 70 – .22 LR or .25 ACP cal., designed by Edgar Budischowsky, compact frame, 6 shot, checkered wood grips.

	$450	$395	$350	$300	$250	$200	$160	

KORSTOG

Previous trademark of AR-15 style rifles manufactured by Adams Arms, previously retailed exclusively by Fleet Farm.

Please refer to BlueBookOfGunValues.com to order the *Blue Book of AR-15s & Variations*, available as a book or online subscription.

KORTH

Current manufacturer established 1954, located in Lollar, Germany. Previously located in Ratzeburg, Germany. Select models are currently being imported by Nighthawk Custom located in Berryville, AR. Also currently imported on a limited basis by Korth USA since 1994, a division of Earl's Repair Service, Inc., located in Tewksbury, MA. Previously imported 1997-99 by Keng's Firearms Specialty, Inc. located in Atlanta, GA. Previously imported by Mandall Shooting Supplies, Inc. located in Scottsdale, AZ, Beeman Precision Arms, located in Santa Rosa, CA and by Osborne's in Cheboygan, MI.

PISTOLS: SEMI-AUTO

KORTH PRS SEMI-AUTO – 9mm Para. or .45 ACP cal., roller locking system, 4, 5, or 6 in. Lothar Walther CHF precision fixed barrel, 7 or 8 shot mag., skeletonized trigger and hammer, squared off trigger guard, 3-dot fixed sights, walnut grips, blued, PVD, DLC, or Cerakote finish, 35-40 oz. New mid-2014.

This model is P.O.R.

KORTH SEMI-AUTO – 9mm Para., .357 SIG (disc. 2002), .40 S&W (disc. 2004), .45 ACP (Tactical Model, mfg. 2003-2004) or 9x21mm IMI (disc.) cal., double action, 4, 4 1/2 threaded, or 5 (disc.) in. barrel, all steel construction, 8 (.45 ACP cal.), 9 (.40 S&W and .357 SIG), or 10 (9mm Para. or 9x21mm IMI) shot mag., adj. sights, checkered walnut grips. Introduced 1986 with first guns shipped 1988, very limited mfg.

This model is POR.
Add $587 for .45 ACP Tactical Model (mfg. 2003-2004).
Add $285 for silver matte plasma finish.
Add $740 for silver polished plasma finish.
Add $845 for polished blue plasma finish.
Add $1,440 per interchangeable barrels.
Add $180 for extra mag.

JAEGER MODEL – 9mm Para. cal., 4 in. barrel, ivory grips with hunting scene, left side has hunter and dog, right side has deer in forest, gold inlaid, grey "pickled" finish, fully engraved in Arabesque style.

This model is POR.

WILLI KORTH "JUBILEE" 50th ANNIVERSARY MODEL – 9mm Para. cal., 4 in. barrel, combat trigger guard, gold inlaid with head of Willi Korth and dates (1954-2004), 50 Jahre oak leaf, and acorn engraving in high polish blue, deluxe hand engraved wood grips. Only 5 to be mfg. beginning 2004.

This model is POR. A special case which holds both the anniversary pistol and the revolver, as well as a matching commemorative knife is also available.

REVOLVERS

The crane of the main cylinder and of the extra cylinder (.22 LR/.22 WMR or .357 Mag./9mm Para.) are cut from the same billet of steel, and for reasons of smallest tolerance that Korth guarantees, once a gun is made with a single cylinder, the extra convertible cylinder cannot be ordered at a later date. 7,140 revolvers in 10 different configurations were manufactured between 1964-1981.

Add $255 for silver matte plasma finish, add $520 for silver polished plasma finish, and add $620 for bright blue polished plasma finish on Pre-Nighthawk models. Subtract approx. $550-$700 if w/o interchangeable different cal. cylinder on Combat, Sport, and Target Models. (Pre-Nighthawk models). Currently, most used Combat, Sport, and Target models encountered in the secondary marketplace are priced in the $2,500-$6,000 price range, depending on condition and configuration.

GRADING - PPGS™	100%	98%	95%	90%	80%	70%	60%	LAST MSR

COMBAT - .22 LR, .22 WMR, .38 Spl., or .357 Mag. cal., 3 (solid only), 4 VR, 5 1/4 VR, 6 VR, or 8 in. barrel, steel or stainless steel (disc., limited mfg.) construction, 6 shot, fixed or fully adj. combat sights, full-length shrouded or unshrouded ejector rod, adj. trigger, checkered and oil finished walnut grips, 2.6 lbs. Introduced circa early 1960s.

Base MSR on this model was $8,000.

Used specimens of this model are infrequently encountered, and secondary values are difficult to determine.

CLASSIC - .357 Mag. cal., 3, 4, 5 1/4, or 6 in. Lothar Walther barrel with polygonal rifling, 6 shot, interchangeable cylinder capability, adj. mainspring and trigger from the outside, high polish or matte blue finish, various configurations of grips, approx. 41 oz. Imported mid-2014-2019.

This model is P.O.R.

Used specimens of this model are infrequently encountered, and secondary values are difficult to determine.

MONGOOSE/SILVER MONGOOSE - .357 Mag./.38 Spl. cal. (extra 9mm cylinder is optional), 3, 4 (standard), 5 1/4, or 6 in. barrel with solid raised and grooved rib or vent. rib (Silver Mongoose, disc. 2019), 6 shot, billet steel, skeletonized high speed hammer, polished trigger, adj. rear and gold bead front sight, dimpled finger groove Hogue grip, black or silver DLC (disc. 2019) finish, 37.6 oz. Imported by Nighthawk Custom beginning 2017.

MSR $3,699	$3,375	$3,100	$2,875	$2,625	$2,400	$2,175	$1,875	

Add $1,850 for silver DLC finish and vent. rib (Silver Mongoose, disc. 2019).

MONGOOSE SILVER - .357 Mag./.38 Spl. cal. (extra 9mm cylinder is optional), 6 in. 416R stainless steel barrel with solid raised rib, 6 shot cylinder, billet steel construction, solid spur hammer, adj. rear and gold bead front sight, high grade Turkish walnut grip, silver DLC finish, 2.1 lbs. Imported by Nighthawk Custom beginning 2020.

MSR $5,199	$4,700	$4,100	$3,500	$3,200	$2,600	$2,100	$1,650	

NXA - .357 Mag. cal. (changeable cylinder in 9mm Para. cal. w/Moonclip cut), DA/SA, 4 or 6 in. CHF precision barrel, skeletonized red anodized aluminum barrel shroud with top and bottom Picatinny rails, 8 shot, classic back left cylinder release, steel frame, adj. rear sight, red/black laminate grips, removable side panels (front sight), DLC finish, 2.75 lbs. New 2020.

MSR $5,299	$4,775	$4,175	$3,575	$3,250	$2,625	$2,150	$1,675	

NXR - .44 Mag. cal., DA/SA, 4 or 6 in. CHF precision barrel, skeletonized steel barrel shroud with top and bottom Picatinny rails, removeable barrel weight, optional compensator, 6 shot, removable side panels on front sight and fully adj. rear sight, Turkish walnut grip, classic back left cylinder release, integrated Picatinny rail on frame, DLC finish, 48.8 lbs. Imported by Nighthawk Custom beginning 2020.

MSR $5,299	$4,775	$4,175	$3,575	$3,250	$2,625	$2,150	$1,675	

NXS 8-SHOT - .357 Mag. cal. (changeable cylinder in 9mm Para. cal. w/Mooncip cut), SA/DA, 4 or 6 in. CHF precision barrel, skeletonized steel barrel shroud with top and bottom Picatinny rails, 8 shot, classic back left cylinder release, steel frame, adj. rear sight, Jim Wilson Turkish walnut grip, removable side panels (front sight), DLC finish, 3.15 lbs. New 2020.

MSR $5,299	$4,775	$4,175	$3,575	$3,250	$2,625	$2,150	$1,675	

RANGER - .357 Mag. cal. (changeable cylinder in 9mm w/o clips), DA/SA, 4 in. CHF precision polished Lothar Walther barrel, skeletonized barrel shroud, high-speed hammer, adj. rear sight, Jim Wilson Turkish walnut grip, removable side panels (front sight), top Picatinny rail, DLC finish, 35.2 oz. Importation by Nighthawk Custom began circa 2018.

MSR $4,799	$4,300	$3,800	$3,250	$2,950	$2,400	$1,950	$1,500	

SPORT - .22 LR, .32 S&W Long, .38 Spl., or .357 Mag. cal., 2 1/2 (disc., scarce), 4, 5 1/4, 6 VR, or 8 in. barrel, 5 (early mfg.) or 6 shot, fixed or micro adj. sights, full-length shrouded or unshrouded ejector rod, adj. trigger, checkered and oil finished walnut grips, 2.6 lbs. Introduced circa early 1960s.

Current base MSR on this model is $8,000.

Subtract approx. 50% for 5 shot, depending on condition.

Used specimens of this model are infrequently encountered, and secondary values are difficult to determine.

SKY HAWK - 9mm Para. cal. (no moon clips), DA/SA, 2 or 3 in. barrel, 6 shot, billet steel barrel and aluminum frame, skeletonized hammer, polished trigger, adj. rear and gold bead front sight, dimpled Hogue rubber grips with finger grooves, marked "Sky Hawk" on left side of barrel, black DLC coated finish, 24 1/2 oz. Imported by Nighthawk Custom 2017-2019.

	$1,575	$1,400	$1,200	$1,000	$850	$750	$650	*$1,699*

GRADING - PPGS™	100%	98%	95%	90%	80%	70%	60%	LAST MSR

SUPER SPORT BLUE ALX/RED ULX – .357 Mag. cal., DA/SA, 6 in. Lothar Walther CHF barrel, polygonal rifling, high-speed hammer, 4-pos. multi-distance front sight, Hal Swaggert grip, top Picatinny rail, full length complete (Blue ALX) or skeletonized (Red ULX) Picatinny side rails and changeable barrel weights, removable side panels (front sight), anodized black/blue (ALX) or black/red (ULX) DLC/anodized finish, 43.5-46.5 oz. Imported by Nighthawk Custom beginning late 2019.

MSR $5,199	$4,700	$4,100	$3,500	$3,200	$2,600	$2,100	$1,650	

This model is also available with an optional 9mm Para./.38 Spl. conversion cylinder.

SUPER SPORT STX – .357 Mag. cal., DA/SA, 6 in. Lothar Walther CHF barrel, polygonal rifling, 6 shot, Roller trigger, fully adj. front/rear sights, dimpled Hogue grips with finger grooves or Jim Wilson wood grips, top Picatinny rail, full-length Picatinny rails on each side of barrel, 3.64 lbs. Importation by Nighthawk Custom began 2017.

MSR $5,199	$4,700	$4,100	$3,500	$3,200	$2,600	$2,100	$1,650	

This model is also available with an optional 9mm Para./.38 Spl. conversion cylinder.

TARGET – .22 LR, .32 S&W Long, .38 Spl., or .357 Mag. cal., 5 1/4 or 6 in. VR barrel, 6 shot, micro adj. sights, adj. trigger, stippled oversized target walnut grips, 2.6 lbs.

Base MSR on this model was $8,000.

Used specimens of this model are infrequently encountered, and secondary values are difficult to determine.

TROJA – .22 LR, .22 WMR, or .357 Mag. cal., 4 or 6 in. barrel, matte finish, smooth oversized walnut finger groove grips. Imported 2003-disc.

Base MSR on this model was $8,000.

WECHSEL – centerfire and .22 LR/.22 WMR cals., both cylinder and barrel can be changed. Mfg. 2003-2004.

Last MSR was $10,000.

Revolvers: Special/Limited Editions

MODEL EVEREST 40 YEARS KORTH SPECIAL EDITION – .357 Mag. cal., 5 1/4 in. barrel only, deeply engraved frame and barrel with gold inlays, smooth select walnut grips, cased, only 25 mfg. 1994 only.

	$8,950	$6,350	$4,500	N/A	N/A	N/A	N/A	*$8,500*

WILLI KORTH "JUBILEE" 50th ANNIVERSARY MODEL – .357 Mag. cal., 4 in. barrel, gold inlaid with head of Willi Korth and dates (1954-2004), 50 Jahre oak leaf, and acorn engraving in high polish blue, deluxe hand engraved wood grips. Only 5 to be mfg. beginning 2004.

Last MSR was $18,000.

A special case which holds both the anniversary pistol and the revolver, as well as a matching commemorative knife was also available.

ANNO DOMINI 2000 – .357 Mag. cal., 4 in. combat model, PVD gold plasma coating, deep relief engraving featuring thorns, includes black leather briefcase, only 10 mfg. during 2000.

Extreme rarity precludes accurate pricing on this model - manufacturer's suggested retail was $10,000.

PLATINUM MODEL – .357 Mag. cal., 6 shot, 4 in. barrel, platinum engraved model with deluxe grips, includes black leather briefcase. Mfg. 2002-disc.

Last MSR was $9,600.

ARABESQUE MODEL – .357 Mag. cal., 6 shot, 4 in. barrel, Arabesque engraved model with deluxe grips, includes black leather briefcase. Mfg. 2003-disc.

Last MSR was $9,600.

EICHENLAUB MODEL – .357 Mag. cal., 6 shot, 4 in. barrel, oak leaf engraved model with deluxe grips, includes black leather briefcase. Mfg. 2003-disc.

Last MSR was $12,000.

JAEGER MODEL – .357 Mag. cal., 4 in. barrel, ivory grips with hunting scene, left side has hunter and dog, right side has deer in forest, gold inlaid, grey "pickled" finish, fully engraved in Arabesque style. Disc.

Last MSR was $19,200.

MODEL BELLEZZA – .357 Mag. cal., 6 in. barrel, ruby and diamonds with palladium finish, special female figured grips, Arabesque engraving, includes case, very limited mfg. Disc.

Last MSR was $150,000.

"Bellezza" comes from a Handel opera, and means "the triumph over sorrow and disappointment."

CUSTOM PRESENTATION MODEL – deluxe variation of Sport/Combat model.

This variation is available with engraving and other special options that are priced per individual quotation from the factory.

GRADING - PPGS™	100%	98%	95%	90%	80%	70%	60%	LAST MSR

KOSCHAT, JAKOB

Current longarm manufacturer located in Ferlach, Austria. No current U.S. importation.

Jakob Koschat manufactures high quality shotguns and double rifles in a variety of sporting configurations. Many options are available. Please contact him directly for more information, including pricing, availability, and delivery time.

KRAG-JORGENSEN (30/40 KRAG)

Previous U.S. magazine fed military rifle. Official government designation is United States Magazine Rifle and Carbine, Caliber 30. First U.S. (.30-40 Krag) military repeating rifle to shoot smokeless powder ammunition. Approx. 475,000 mfg. by Springfield Armory 1894-1904.

There have been many alterations and conversions of Krag-Jorgensen rifles - some of which are hard to identify. As a rule, these alterations and conversions almost remove any collectibility, and pricing is determined mostly by its competitive shooter value. Since prices for upper condition (95%+), original Krag-Jorgensens have increased significantly in recent years, beware of non-original guns, conversions, and in some cases, fakes.

RIFLES: BOLT ACTION

MODEL OF 1892 RIFLE (DATED 1894) – 30 in. barrel, traditionally, these models have been categorized as either Type I (solid upper band) or Type II (double strap upper band), but this is too simple a definition - there were many variations. Ordnance documents list approx. 14 changes that were made during the production run, and examination of original rifles have found many more. 24,562 mfg.

$10,000	$8,000	$6,500	$5,000	$3,000	$2,000	$1,200

Early rifles in original condition will have numbered bolt parts (below S/N 500) and magazine parts (below S/N 1,500) - they will command a premium.

It is essential that anyone considering purchasing this model thoroughly research the sequence and scope of the changes.

Only one rifle that has all the appropriate bolt and magazine parts numbered to the receiver is known.

* ***Model of 1892 Rifle Carbine*** – 22 in. barrel, rare, only 2 known - one in a government museum, and the other in a private collection.

Extreme rarity precludes accurate pricing on this model.

MODEL 1892/1896 RIFLE (ARSENAL ALTERED) – numerous variations of Model 1892 rifles arsenal altered to Model 1896. 21,264 altered.

$1,200	$975	$875	$775	$700	$625	$575

Add a small premium for models upgraded in 1897 by being restocked but retaining the Model 1892 extractor, and a receiver with no notch.

MODEL 1892 CADET RIFLE – rare, 2 variations - 400 in the 18-19,000 serial number range, with 1894 dated receiver, 4 in the 35,XXX serial number range with 1896 receiver, both have 1896 dated cartouches, three of the 400 were surveyed or condemned, and the remainder were converted to service rifle configuration. 3 of the group of 4 are known - 2 are in private collections and one is at West Point. 404 mfg.

Extreme rarity precludes accurate pricing on this model.

MODEL 1895/1896 TRANSITION RIFLE – these rifles were produced prior to the official introduction of the Model 1896, receiver dates 1895 or 1896 with the MODEL prefix, cartouche dates will be 1896. 1,368 mfg.

$4,000	$3,000	$1,750	$950	$650	$500	$400

MODEL OF 1896 RIFLE – receivers marked Model 1896, cartouche dates are 1896, 1897, and 1898. 60,528 mfg. - receivers stamped "MODEL 1896", with 1896, 1897, 1898, or 1901 dated cartouches (rare), rear leaf sight, first type graduated for 700 to 2,000 yards, and 14,942 were mfg. with the second type sight graduated for 200 to 2,000 yards.

$4,000	$3,000	$1,750	$950	$650	$500	$400

Add a premium for rifles with 1897 dated cartouches impressed sideways.

Add a premium for rifles with 1901 dated cartouches.

* ***Model 1895/1896 Rifle Transition Carbine*** – a "crash" program was started in the spring of 1895 and completed in May, 1896 to arm the regular cavalry, receivers dated 1894 (rare) 1895, or 1896 with no MODEL prefix, 1896 cartouche date. 7,111 mfg.

$4,500	$3,200	$2,550	$1,850	$1,150	$825	$600

Add a premium for rare early version with two cleaning rod holes in the butt, stacked one above the other.

GRADING - PPGS™	100%	98%	95%	90%	80%	70%	60%	LAST MSR

* ***Model of 1896 Rifle Carbine*** – rear sight leaf graduated for 700 to 2,000 yards and will be stamped at the top right with a "C" and the base will have a "C" on the right side.

	$4,500	$3,500	$2,750	$1,850	$1,150	$825	$600	

Buyer beware - some models may have fake sights.

MODEL OF 1898 RIFLE – some 25 variations exist in this model. 342,526 mfg.

	$3,800	$3,200	$2,100	$1,400	$900	$750	$600	

Subtract 20%-40% for "as modified" guns.

Collectors must be aware of the correct combination of serial number, sight variation, and cartouche date of a rifle in original "as made" condition.

* ***Model of 1898 Rifle Carbine*** – scarce and rare in authentic original condition. 5,002 mfg.

	$4,500	$4,000	$3,500	$1,800	$1,500	$1,200	$1,000	

Beware of fakes.

* ***Model of 1898 Rifles with Parkhurst Device*** – scarce/rare, most were destroyed. 100 modified.

Extreme rarity precludes accurate pricing on this model.

MODEL OF 1899 CARBINE – numerous variations, sight and handguard changes. 36,052 mfg.

	$4,500	$4,000	$2,350	$1,450	$1,100	$850	$600	

Subtract 20% - 40% for "as modified" or parts guns.

Collectors must be aware of the correct combination of serial number, sight variation, handguard, and stock cartouche date.

* ***Model of 1899 Carbine with Parkhurst Device*** – scarce/rare, most were destroyed. 100 modified.

Extreme rarity precludes accurate pricing on this model.

BOARD OF ORDNANCE RIFLE – 26 in. barrel, rare. 100 mfg.

Extreme rarity precludes accurate pricing on this model.

PHILIPPINE CONSTABULARY RIFLE – records from the Bureau of Insular Affairs show that the civil government of the Philippines purchased Model of 1899 carbines, and had them modified by the U.S. military at the Manila Ordnance Facility. 4,980 converted.

The absence of an authenticated example of this model precludes accurate pricing.

SCHOOL GUN – officially known as the United States Magazine Carbine, Model of 1899, Modified for Use with Knife Bayonet and Gun Sling, these were carbines and stocks modified between 1906-1916 at both Springfield and Rock Island, examples of Springfield modification have been observed with a block J.F.C. cartouche. 3,371 carbines and 6,118 stocks converted.

	$4,500	$3,800	$1,800	$1,200	$1,000	$800	$600	

DCM/NRA CARBINE – original carbines and cut down rifles were sold by the DCM to NRA members and others during the 1930s-40s, widely imitated by commercial vendors.

	$1,500	$1,200	$1,000	$800	$600	$500	$400	

Buyer beware - this gun should have original documentation before considering a purchase.

KRAL AV

Current shotgun manufacturer established circa 1983, and located in Konya, Turkey. Kral Arms is the trademark of shotguns sold throughout Europe. Private label shotguns for TriStar Sporting Arms, Ltd., located in Kansas City, MO are currently being imported.

Kral AV manufactures a complete line of good quality O/U, SxS, single shot, semi-auto, and slide action shotguns. Current trademarks owned by KRAL AV include: A12 (disc.), A20 (disc.), Altes, Aria (disc.), Azarax, CaraCara, Compact, KRX, K12, KR-15, Kinematix, Kral Arms Raptor (disc.), Kral Arms Tactical, Kral Escord (disc.), XLM (disc.), Puncher, ST-500, Signature, Tundra, Volt-500, Queen (disc.), and XPS. The company also manufactures air rifles and blank pistols. Currently, TriStar Sporting Arms, Ltd. has a contract for importing private labeled Kral shotguns into the U.S. Please refer to the TriStar listing for current model offerings from Kral.

KRASSNIK, VALENTIN

Previous custom long gun manufacturer located in Ferlach, Austria.

Valentin Krassnik was a member of the Ferlacher Waffen Präzisionstechnik Produktions GmbH & Co KG, established after the Ferlach Guild was dissolved. Krassnik manufactured custom long guns, built per individual customer specifications. Guns should be evaluated individually by a knowledgeable expert.

GRADING - PPGS™	100%	98%	95%	90%	80%	70%	60%	LAST MSR

KRICO

Current trademark manufactured by Kriegeskorte Handels GmbH, located in Pyrbaum, Germany. No current U.S. importation. Previously imported exclusively mid-2005-2010 by Northeast Arms LLC, located in Fort Fairfield, ME. Previously distributed by Precision Sales, Int'l, located in Westfield, MA 1999-2002. Previously manufactured in Vohburg-Irsching, Germany 1996-1999, and in Fürth-Stadeln, Germany by Sportwaffenfabrik Kriegeskorte GmbH pre-1996.

For individual model listings, please go to BlueBookOfGunValues.com/overflow.

H. KRIEGHOFF GUN CO. (SHOTGUNS OF ULM)

Current manufacturer located in Ulm, Germany since circa 1954. Previous manufacture was in Suhl, Germany 1886-1947. Currently imported and distributed by Krieghoff International, Inc. located in Ottsville, PA. Dealer direct sales only.

Currently, Krieghoff manufactures 2,000 guns annually, in all configurations.

DRILLINGS

H. Krieghoff drillings can be ordered with a variety of cals. (.222 Rem., .243 Win., .270 Win., or .30-06) and special order features. The Universal Trigger System (UAS) and Combi-Cocking Device are standard on all Plus, Steingass, Optima, and Quadro drillings. A soft case is included with all guns. Prices shown below are for standard guns with no options. Better models will have a finer grade walnut and exhibit more elaborate deep relief engraving.

Add $1,290 for 3-claw scope mount system (disc.).

NEPTUN MODEL - various cals., 12, 16, or 20 ga., sidelocks, elaborate engraving, Mfg. began pre-WWII. Disc. 2011.

	100%	98%	95%	90%	80%	70%	60%	LAST MSR
	$13,250	$10,400	$9,000	$7,550	$6,200	$5,100	$4,150	*$16,500*

NEPTUN PRIMUS MODEL - 12, 16, or 20 ga., similar to Neptun Model, except has hand detachable sidelocks and elaborate deep relief engraving. Disc. 2011.

	100%	98%	95%	90%	80%	70%	60%	LAST MSR
	$18,500	$13,650	$10,450	$8,400	$7,100	$5,850	$4,950	*$24,500*

* ***Neptun Primus Model Dural*** - Dural aluminum frame variation at no extra charge. Disc. 2011.

	100%	98%	95%	90%	80%	70%	60%	LAST MSR
	$18,500	$13,650	$10,450	$8,400	$7,100	$5,850	$4,950	*$24,500*

OPTIMA - 6x70R, 6.5x57R, 6.5x65R, 7x57R, 7x65R, .308 Win., .30-06, .30R Blaser, 8x57JRS, 8x75RS, 8.5x63R, or 9.3x74R cal., 12 or 20 ga., 21 1/2 in. thermo stable barrels, universal trigger system, combi-cocking device, small Arabesque engraving on 20 ga., includes soft case.

	100%	98%	95%	90%	80%	70%	60%	LAST MSR
MSR $12,395	$11,000	$8,800	$7,750	$6,500	$5,500	$4,500	$3,500	

Add $1,595 for pivot scope mount.

* ***Optima Double Rifle Drilling*** - 7x57R, 7x65R, .308 Win., .30-06, .30R Blaser, 8x57JRS, 8x75RS, 8.5x63R, or .3x74R cal., 20 ga., 3 in. chambers, 21 1/2 in. barrels, universal trigger system, combi-cocking device, Arabesque engraving, includes soft case.

	100%	98%	95%	90%	80%	70%	60%	LAST MSR
MSR $15,495	$12,000	$9,600	$9,000	$8,000	$6,700	$5,700	$4,800	

Add $1,995 for pivot mount.

* ***Optima Big Five Double Rifle Drilling (African Drilling)*** - 20 ga. over .375 Flanged Mag. NE, .500/.416 NE, or .470 NE cal., 21 1/5 in. barrel, Universal Trigger System, combi-cocking device, includes soft case.

	100%	98%	95%	90%	80%	70%	60%	LAST MSR
MSR $25,295	$22,400	$17,900	$15,500	$13,000	$10,000	$8,000	$6,600	

Add $1,995 for pivot mount.

OPTIMUS TS MODEL - 12 or 20 ga. over 21 1/2 in. rifle barrel (various rifle cals.), features Thermo Stabil barrels, standard engraving is small Arabesque, includes soft case. Mfg. 2003-2009.

	100%	98%	95%	90%	80%	70%	60%	LAST MSR
	$9,350	$8,200	$7,100	$6,500	$5,500	$4,500	$3,500	*$10,950*

Add $2,800 for Quadro 20 Model with double rifle and 20 ga. shotgun barrel configuration.
Add $2,295 - $2,595 for KS full length rifled barrel insert, depending on caliber (up to 9.3x74R).
Add $1,975 for installed and sighted in pivot mount.
Add $975 for single trigger or $1,295 for single/double trigger.

During 2009, this model was dropped in favor of the new Optima Series.

GRADING - PPGS™	100%	98%	95%	90%	80%	70%	60%	LAST MSR

PLUS MODEL – 12, 16, or 20 ga. over rifle barrel (.222 Rem., .243 Win., .270 Win., or .30-06 cal.), boxlock action, choice of soldered or free floating rifle barrel with adj. point of impact (Thermo TS Stabil - Model Plus TS)., includes universal trigger system (UAS) as standard, light engraving. Mfg. 1988-2004.

	$5,125	$3,650	$2,800	$2,200	$1,825	$1,525	$1,200	*$6,275*

Add $1,700 for full length stock (Model Steingass, 20 ga. only).

QUADRO AFRICAN DRILLING – .20 ga. under rifle barrels (.375 Flanged Mag. NE, .500/.416 NE, or .470 NE), drilling frame with reinforced sidewalls, hinged front trigger, similar sights as the Classic Big 5 double rifle. Mfg. 2003-2009.

This gun was available by custom order only.

TRUMPF MODEL – 12, 16, or 20 ga., O/U or rifle shotgun combo., various cals., boxlock, 25 in. barrels, 7 1/2 lbs. Disc.

This model was POR.

Add $450 for free floating rifle barrels.

* ***Trumpf Model Dural*** – Dural aluminum frame variation of the Trumpf, 6.8 lbs., cased. Disc. 2003.

	$8,300	$6,300	$5,350	$4,250	$3,300	$2,750	$2,200	*$9,950*

Add $450 for free floating rifle barrels.

* ***Neptun Model Dural*** – Dural aluminum frame variation of the Neptun, cased. Disc. 2011.

	$13,250	$10,400	$9,000	$7,550	$6,200	$5,100	$4,150	*$16,500*

TRUMPF DRILLING (CURRENT MFG.) – 6x70R, 6,5x57R, 6,5x65R, 7x57R, 7x65R, .308 Win., .30-06, .30R Blaser, 8x57IRS, 8x75RS, 9.3x74R cal., 12 or 20 ga., combi-cocking device, 22 in. Krieghoff Thermo Stable barrel set, steel or dural aluminum, Universal Trigger System, steel trigger guard, right-handed stock with Bavarian style cheekpiece and Schnabel forearm, black rubber recoil pad, Arabesque engraving, Blitz locks, quick detachable sling swivels, front plate for pivot bridge mount, includes fitted hard case, nickel plated receiver finish, approx. 6 3/4-8 lbs. depending on wood density and caliber.

Please contact the importer directly for pricing and availability.

TRUMPF DOUBLE RIFLE DRILLING (CURRENT MFG.) – 7x57R, 7x65R, .308 Win., .30-06, .30R Blaser, 8x57IRS, 8x75RS, or 9.3x74R cal., 20 ga., steel action, combi-cocking device, 22 in. barrel, Universal Trigger System, steel trigger guard, right-handed stock with Bavarian style cheekpiece and Schnabel forearm, black rubber recoil pad, quick detachable sling swivels, small Arabesque engraving, Blitz locks, front plate for pivot bridge mount, includes fitted hard case, nickel plated receiver finish, approx. 8 1/2 lbs. depending on wood density and caliber.

Please contact the importer directly for pricing and availability.

PISTOLS: SEMI-AUTO

WWII Krieghoff Lugers will appear in the Luger section.

KRIEGHOFF LUGER – 9mm Para. cal., toggle lock action, 4 in. round barrel, 8 shot mag., based on the WWII production with Bakelite grips, blue finish. Only 200 mfg. beginning 2006, special ser. no. range 18001-18200. Disc.

	$15,995	$14,250	$12,000	$9,000	$7,000	$5,000	$4,000	*$17,545*

RIFLES: O/U & SxS

Various grades differ in style and amount of engraving, choice of walnut, and various options that can be special ordered.

Add $1,950 for 4-claw scope mount (standard or European).

TECK O/U – .30-06, .300 Win. Mag. (disc. 1994), .308 Win., 7x56R (disc. 1994), 7x65R (new 1995), 8x57JRS, 8x75RS (new 1995), 9.3x74R, .375 H&H (disc. 1988), or .458 Win. Mag. cal., boxlock action, O/U rifle, 25 in. barrels, cocking indicators, hard case included.

	$8,725	$6,475	$5,200	$4,300	$3,650	$3,300	$3,000	*$10,500*

Add $1,400 for .375 H&H or .458 Win. Mag. cal.

Add $990 for DTs with front set trigger.

* ***Teck-Handspanner O/U*** – 7x65R, .30-06, or .308 Win. cal. on 16 ga. receiver frame, manual cocking.

	$10,200	$7,950	$6,675	$5,175	$4,375	$3,950	$3,200	*$12,495*

ULTRA TS O/U – various cals. up to 9.3x74R, unique manual cocking/self cocking device and interchangeable muzzle wedge for adj. point of impact. New 1993.

MSR $10,195	$8,650	$7,600	$6,500	$5,900	$4,750	$3,900	$3,050	

Add $1,195 for single trigger.

GRADING - PPGS™	100%	98%	95%	90%	80%	70%	60%	LAST MSR

ULM O/U – similar to Teck Double Rifle, except has any combination of cals., with sidelocks and more elaborate engraving.

	$15,800	$13,400	$11,400	$9,700	$7,700	$6,200	$4,950	*$17,900*

Add $695 for hand detachable sidelocks.
Add $1,775 for single/double trigger.

* ***Ulm O/U Dekor*** – sidelock with light scroll engraving. Importation disc. 1991.

	$10,450	$9,150	$8,000	$6,750	$5,600	$5,000	$4,400	*$12,500*

* ***Ulm O/U Primus*** – deluxe sidelock. Disc. 2004.

	$19,750	$13,000	$10,250	$8,100	$6,550	$5,700	$5,300	*$26,000*

TRUMPF SxS – boxlock action, similar to Teck model, except in .30-06, 8x57JRS, or 9.3x74R cal. Disc. 1994.

	$13,200	$9,700	$8,350	$6,900	$6,100	$5,500	$4,950	*$16,150*

CLASSIC SxS STANDARD – current cals. include .30-06, .308 Win., 7x57R, 7x65R, .30R Blaser, 8.5x63R, 8x57JRS, 8x75RS, and 9.3x74R, boxlock action, UAS anti-doubling device, 21 1/2 (optional) or 23 1/2 in. regulated barrels, extractors, DT, steel trigger guard, removable wedge and integrated front sight in cals. up to .375 H&H, choice of standard or Bavarian style stock, combi-cocking device, small Arabesque engraving (standard), with or w/o sideplates, various engraving options, 7 1/2 - 11 lbs. New 1995.

MSR $11,995	$10,800	$9,450	$8,100	$7,350	$5,950	$4,850	$3,800	

Add $5,895 for a set of 20 ga., 3 in. chambered barrels.
Add $2,595 for ejectors.
Add $6,300 per set of interchangeable rifle barrels.
Add $3,995 for sideplates with standard scroll engraving or $2,250 for boxlock standard engraving.

* ***Classic SxS Standard Big Five (Big Bore)*** – .375 H&H, .375 Flanged Mag. NE (new 1996), .416 Rigby, .458 Win. Mag., .450/400 NE, .470 NE, .500/.416 NE (new 1996), or .500 NE cal., hinged front trigger, non-removable muzzle wedge, 23 1/2 in. barrels with express style quarter rib, 9 1/2 - 10 1/2 lbs. New 1995.

MSR $15,395	$13,900	$12,150	$10,400	$9,450	$7,650	$6,250	$4,850	

Add $2,595 for ejectors.
Add $5,895 for a set of 20 ga./3 in. barrels.
Add $6,300 per set of interchangeable rifle barrels.
Add $3,995 for sideplates with standard scroll engraving or $1,995 for boxlock standard engraving.
Add $4,400 for Big Game Grade II with small game scene engraving and best quality select wood (new 2012).

NEPTUN SxS – sidelock double rifle, same features as the Ulm model. Importation disc. 1991.

	$12,750	$10,400	$8,700	$7,350	$6,000	$5,450	$4,995	*$15,500*

RIFLES: SINGLE SHOT

HUBERTUS RIFLE – .22-250 Rem., .222 Rem., .243 Win., .270 Win., .30-06, .308 Win., .270 Wby. Mag. (disc.), .300 Win. Mag., 7mm Rem. Mag., or in 12 metric cals. between 5.6x50R Mag. - 9.3x74R, Arabesque engraved boxlock action, single shot stalking rifle, 23 1/2 in. barrel with quarter rib, extractor, steel trigger guard, Bavaria stock w/rounded cheekpiece and Schnabel forearm, Kickspanner (unique manual combi-cocking device), fast lock time, double underlugs, approx. 6 1/2 lbs. Importation began circa 1997.

MSR $7,495	$6,750	$5,900	$5,100	$4,600	$3,700	$3,050	$2,350	

Add $2,500 for Mag. cals.
Add $3,995 for sideplates with standard scroll engraving.
Add $1,125 for left-hand stock.
Add $3,795 per extra interchangeable barrel on standard U.S. or European cals.

RIFLES: SLIDE ACTION

SEMPRIO – .223 Rem., .243 Win., .270 Win., 7x64, 6.5x55mm, .30-06, .308 Win., 8x57IS, 9.3x62mm, 7mm Rem. Mag., .300 Win. Mag., .338 Win. Mag. (disc. 2009), or .375 Ruger cal., unique in-line action is operated by using the forearm to slide the barrel assembly forward (not backward), fluted bolt, full takedown capability, 21.7 or 25 (Mag. cals.) in. barrel, 3 (Mag. cals.) or 4 shot detachable mag., Universal Trigger System, open sights, walnut stock with Semprio cheekpiece or Next G1 Vista Forest Green or Blaze Orange camo stock, checkered pistol grip stock, combi-cocking Device, "Klick & Go" quick detachable sling swivels, black rubber recoil pad, black or nickel anodized finish, extra barrels, 7 1/2 lbs. New 2007.

MSR $4,695	$4,250	$3,400	$3,000	$2,750	$2,250	$1,775	$1,575	

Add $300 for Mag. cals.
Add $1,395 (standard cals) or $1,795 (Mag. cals.) per extra barrel, depending on configuration.
Add $2,800 for Semprio "Big Five" (.416 Ruger or .458 Win. Mag.). Disc.

GRADING - PPGS™	100%	98%	95%	90%	80%	70%	60%	LAST MSR

SHOTGUNS: O/U

Subtract 15% for 26 in. barrels on used models.
Subtract 25% for 26 in. barrels on used higher grade models.
Add $2,395 - $2,600 for "KS" full length rifle insert barrel, depending on caliber - available in 12, 16, or 20 ga. (new 2006).

MODEL 32 STANDARD - 12, 20, 28 ga., or .410 bore, O/U, 28-32 in. high rib barrels, ejectors, boxlock, single trigger, select wood. Disc. 1983.

	100%	98%	95%	90%	80%	70%	60%	LAST MSR
Standard	$3,000	$2,500	$2,250	$2,000	$1,900	$1,700	$1,500	
San Remo	$4,500	$4,000	$3,750	$3,400	$3,000	$2,250	$1,950	
Monte Carlo	$6,000	$5,250	$4,500	$3,750	$3,250	$3,000	$2,250	
Crown	$10,000	$8,000	$7,000	$6,000	$5,250	$4,000	$3,000	
Super Crown	$12,000	$10,000	$8,500	$7,000	$6,250	$5,500	$4,750	

* ***Model 32 Standard Low Rib*** - 28 ga. or .410 bore.

	100%	98%	95%	90%	80%	70%	60%	LAST MSR
	$3,750	$3,250	$2,875	$2,650	$2,200	$1,900	$1,600	

Add approx. 20% for two-barrel set.

MODEL 32 4-BARREL SKEET SET - 12, 20, 28 ga., or .410 bore, O/U, matched barrels in case, grades differ in engraving and wood quality. Disc. 1983.

	100%	98%	95%	90%	80%	70%	60%	LAST MSR
Standard	$5,250	$4,750	$4,250	$4,000	$3,500	$3,000	$2,775	
München Grade	$9,950	$8,450	$7,450	$6,500	$5,600	$4,650	$3,725	
San Remo Grade (unmarked)	$6,250	$5,750	$5,250	$4,750	$4,250	$3,500	$3,000	
Monte Carlo (Silver Crown 50 mfg.)	$8,500	$7,500	$6,750	$6,250	$5,750	$5,250	$4,750	
Crown Grade (400 mfg.)	$14,000	$13,000	$12,000	$11,000	$9,500	$8,500	$7,500	
Super Crown Grade (48 mfg.)	$16,000	$15,000	$14,000	$13,000	$11,500	$10,500	$9,500	

K-20 PARCOURS - 20 or 28 ga., 3 in. chambers, 30 or 32 in. barrels, fixed chokes, tapered rib, nickel plated steel action, SST, white pearl front bead and metal center bead sights, fine checkered Turkish walnut stock with oil finish, slim field style forearm, top tang push-button safety, light scroll engraving pattern, includes fitted hard case, approx. 7 lbs. New 2016.

	100%	98%	95%	90%	80%	70%	60%	LAST MSR
MSR $12,395	$11,150	$9,750	$8,350	$7,600	$6,150	$5,000	$3,900	

Add $5,195 for extra set of 20 or 28 gauge barrels.
Add $6,600 for engraving and wood upgrades (Parcours Special).

K-20 PRO SPORTER - 20, 28 ga., or .410 bore, 30 or 32 in. barrels, titanium choke tubes, single selective trigger, white pearl front bead and metal center bead sights, fine checkered select Turkish walnut stock with satin epoxy finish, Schnabel forearm, top tang safety, standard scroll engraving, case hardened, nickel plated steel receiver with satin grey finish, includes fitted hard case, 8 lbs.

	100%	98%	95%	90%	80%	70%	60%	LAST MSR
MSR $12,795	$11,500	$10,100	$8,650	$7,850	$6,350	$5,200	$4,100	

Add $5,595 for extra set of barrels with five choke tubes.
Add $6,030 for two gauge set with 10 choke tubes and two barrel hard case.
Add $11,225 for three gauge set with 15 choke tubes and three barrel hard case.

K-20 SPORTING AND FIELD - 20, 28 ga., or .410 bore, compact 20 ga. frame, incorporates all of the technical refinements of the K-80, nickel plated receiver with satin grey finish and classic scroll engraving, 28 (disc.), 30 or 32 in. separated barrels (28 ga. and .410 bore barrels can be purchased separately but must be fitted) with tapered flat rib, SST, AE, checkered walnut stock and Schnabel forearm, includes 5 choke tubes, approx. 7 1/4 lbs., includes fitted aluminum case. Importation began 2000.

	100%	98%	95%	90%	80%	70%	60%	LAST MSR
MSR $12,395	$11,150	$9,750	$8,350	$7,600	$6,150	$5,000	$3,900	

Add $5,195 for extra set of 20, 28 ga., or .410 bore barrels.
Add $5,230 for 20/28 ga. set with 10 choke tubes and hard case.
Add $10,425 for 3 ga. set of 20, 28 ga. and .410 bore with 15 choke tubes and hard case
Add $600-$4,500 for wood upgrades, depending on quality.

Additional options for the K-20 include case colors ($4,495), K-20 models with engraving options include K-20 Shadow (nickel or blued finish, $12,395), K-20 Logo (nickel or blued finish, $12,595), Vintage Scroll ($13,645), Super Standard ($15,195 MSR), Super Scroll ($17,495 MSR), Suhl Scroll ($19,195 MSR), Gold Super Scroll (nitride or blued finish, $22,495 MSR), Bavaria (disc. 2004), Bavaria Royale (new 2005, $20,695 MSR), Gold Bavaria Royale ($31,895 MSR), Gold Plantation Scroll (nitride or blued finish, $22,695 MSR), Plantation Scroll/Uplander (nickel or blued finish, $19,695 MSR), Millennium (last MSR was $28,695 in 2011), Waterfowl Medallion Nitride ($28,695, new 2005), and Bavaria Suhl ($27,395 MSR).

GRADING - PPGS™	100%	98%	95%	90%	80%	70%	60%	LAST MSR

K-20 VICTORIA – 20 or 28 ga., 30 or 32 in. Parcours barrels, M/IM fixed chokes, tapered flat rib, Ladies Victoria stock with adj. comb, tailored palm swell, oil finish with special Victoria checkering and elegant scroll, low profile receiver, standard grade engraving, includes Negrini case featuring cream colored exterior accented in tan leather with carrying strap, approx. 7 lbs. New 2019.

MSR $12,395	$11,150	$9,750	$8,350	$7,600	$6,150	$5,000	$3,900	

K-80 ACS COMBO – 12 ga., 3 in. chambers, 30, 32, or 34 (unsingle) in. floating rib barrels, with IC/M/IM or M/IM/F (unsingle) chokes, white pearl front bead and metal center bead sights, fine checkered select Turkish walnut Monte Carlo stock with adj. comb designed for floating rib, satin epoxy finish, top tang push-button safety, standard classic K-80 scroll engraving, includes fitted hard case, case hardened action, nickel plated steel receiver with silver Nitride finish, 8 3/4 lbs.

MSR $18,695	$16,800	$14,700	$12,600	$11,450	$9,250	$7,550	$5,900	

K-80 PARCOURS – 12 ga. only, 3 in. chambers, 28, 30, 32, or 34 (new 2020) in. non-separated (soldered rib) barrels with flat 6mm tapered VR, choice of fixed or optional Briley thin wall chokes, choice of case colored or nickel plated steel receiver with satin gray finish, SST, top tang safety, redesigned checkered adj. Monte Carlo stock and slim profile forearm, includes fitted aluminum case, 8 lbs. New 2013.

MSR $12,395	$11,150	$9,750	$8,350	$7,600	$6,150	$5,000	$3,900	

Add $680 for 28 in. barrels with Briley chokes.

Add $6,600 for engraving and wood upgrades (Parcours Special).

K-80 PIGEON – 12 ga., Standardweight configuration, 28 or 30 in. barrels, IM/F choking, standard tapered step rib.

Beginning 1992, the K-80 Pigeon Model became available by special order only. Rather than list the various Pigeon models separately, their current values will be approximately the same as the corresponding K-80 Trap/Skeet Models listed.

K-80 PRO SPORTER/PRO SKEET – 12 ga., 3 in. chambers, 30 or 32 in. barrels with extended choke tubes, bead sights, case hardened nickel plated receiver, optional SST, top tang push-button safety, choice of checkered Turkish walnut stock with adj. comb and choice of Pro Sporter #3/#7 Schnabel or Pro Skeet #3/#6 forend, approx. 8 3/4 lbs. New 2008.

MSR $12,795	$11,500	$10,100	$8,650	$7,850	$6,350	$5,200	$4,100	

Many engraving and wood upgrades are available, please contact the importer directly for more information.

K-80/S – limited edition model with standard K-80 or K-80 Parcours configuration, 32 in. Parcours barrel, hand rubbed Tru-Oil Exhibition Grade Turkish walnut stock, "Galapagos Islands" or "Summers End" image created by Master Engraver Hendrik Fruhauf, featuring pheasants, quail, and woodcock adorning the receiver, top latch, and trigger guard. Limited mfg. beginning 2018.

Please contact the importer directly for pricing, options, and availability.

K-80 SKEET/SKEET SPECIAL – 12 ga. only, available in Standardweight (8mm rib) or International (12mm rib) configuration, 28 (limited availability) or 30 in. barrels, approx. 8 3/4 lbs.

Beginning 2000, options for the K-80 Skeet include case colors ($4,295 MSR), and the following optional engraving choices with current MSRs: Vintage Scroll - $1,500, Celtic Scroll - $2,150, Gold Standard - $3,800, Super Standard - $3,000, Super Scroll - $5,300, Vintage Game I - $5,000, Parcours Special - $6,100, Suhl Scroll - $6,900, Plantation/Uplander/Plantation Scroll (nickel or blued finish) - $7,400, Bavaria Royale - $8,300, Gold Super Scroll (nitride or blued finish) $9,500, Vintage Game II - $10,500, Gold Plantation Scroll (nitride or blued finish) - $10,300, Gold Plantation/Uplander (nitride or blued finish)- $11,700, Heritage Scroll - $12,900, Highland Game I - $13,700, Bavaria Suhl - $14,700, San Remo - $16,800, Waterfowl Medallion Nitride - $16,400. Additionally, Krieghoff offers many more custom engraving options. Please contact Krieghoff International Inc. for current engraving options and pricing on the K-80 Series.

* ***K-80 Skeet/Skeet Special Standard Model*** – available in Standardweight frame, hard case optional.

MSR $11,295	$10,150	$8,300	$7,250	$6,000	$5,100	$4,350	$3,600	

Add $4,195 per extra set of barrels with fixed chokes.

Add $4,195 for Skeet Special with choke tubes (disc.) or $3,550 for heavy Skeet barrels (disc.).

Subtract 20% for receivers with "K-80" on side.

* ***K-80 Skeet Special Model*** – similar to Standard Model, except includes 5 choke tubes and tapered flat rib. Disc. 2013.

	$9,400	$7,750	$6,600	$5,000	$4,100	$3,350	$2,850	*$10,500*

Subtract 20% for receivers with "K-80" on side.

* ***K-80 Special Centennial Skeet*** – available in skeet configuration - special features as noted above on Centennial Model description listed under K-80 Trap. Mfg. 1986 only.

	$3,675	$3,150	$2,700	$2,425	$2,100	$1,800	$1,650	*$3,980*

GRADING - PPGS™	100%	98%	95%	90%	80%	70%	60%	LAST MSR

K-80 SPORTING CLAYS – 12 ga. only, 28 (disc.), 30 (new 1991), 32 (new 1993), or 34 (mfg. 2003-2009) in. barrels with 5 choke tubes, choice of 8mm VR skeet, tapered flat (broadway), or step rib (special order), sporting clay stock dimensions, satin finished receiver with sporting scroll engraving. New 1988.

MSR $12,395	$11,150	$9,750	$8,350	$7,600	$6,150	$5,000	$3,900	

Add $4,395 for extra set of O/U barrels with 5 choke tubes or $3,595 w/o choke tubes (disc.).
Subtract 10% for 28 in. barrels.

Many engraving and wood upgrades are available for this model. Please contact the importer direction for pricing.

K-80 TRAP – 12 ga. only, available in O/U, Unsingle, Top Single (single top barrel, disc. 2005 w/fixed rib), and Combo (O/U with extra trap barrel) configurations, standard model has silver finished receiver, adj. rib allowing variable points of impact (new 1993). In O/U configuration the barrels are separated, about 8 1/2 lbs. A wide variety of custom order options can be ordered on this model.

Add $400 for 3 screw-in chokes capability (single barrel guns only).
Add $3,495 (O/U) or $5,275 (Unsingle) per extra barrel(s), w/o choke tubes.
Add $595 for single release trigger or $995 for double release trigger.
Subtract 20% for old style receiver with "K-80" on side.

Additionally, Krieghoff offers many more custom engraving options. Please contact Krieghoff International Inc. for current engraving options and pricing on the K-80 Series.

* ***K-80 Trap Standard Unsingle*** – 32 (disc.) or 34 in. lower barrel with either fixed choke or choke tubes.

MSR $13,495	$12,150	$10,600	$9,100	$8,250	$6,700	$5,450	$4,250	

Add $500 for choke tubes.
Add $4,300-$5,000 for K-80 Trap Combo.

* ***K-80 Trap Standard O/U*** – 30 or 32 in. barrels with either fixed chokes or choke tubes.

MSR $11,795	$10,600	$9,300	$7,950	$7,200	$5,850	$4,800	$3,700	

Add $600 for choke tubes.
Add $6,200-$6,900 for K-80 Trap Combo.
Subtract 20% for top single variation (very limited mfg.).

* ***K-80 Trap Special*** – 12 ga., 3 in. chambers, 30 or 32 in. barrels with 5 choke tubes, 34 in. Unsingle or top single barrels with 3 choke tubes, fully adj. high post ventilated tapered rib, adj. single selective trigger, white pearl front bead and metal center bead sights, select Turkish walnut Monte Carlo stock with palm swell and adj. comb and satin epoxy finish, top tang push button safety, standard scroll engraving, includes fitted hard case, case hardened action, nickel plated steel receiver with satin grey finish, approx. 9 lbs. New 2007.

MSR $12,795	$10,900	$9,500	$8,150	$7,400	$6,000	$4,900	$3,800	

Add $1,200 for 34 in. unsingle or top single barrel with 3 choke tubes.
Add $5,900 for K-80 Trap Special Combo (O/U + Unsingle/Top Single, 8 choke tubes, adj. rib or Pro rib).

* ***K-80 Trap Centennial Model*** – 12 ga. only, available in combo configuration only, 100 only mfg. 1986 to commemorate Krieghoff's centennial year, ser. no. 14501-14600, H. Krieghoff's signature inlaid in gold on frame sides. Disc.

	$6,750	$5,500	$4,650	$3,900	$3,500	$3,000	$2,600	*$7,650*

K-80 2-BARREL LIGHTWEIGHT SKEET SET – 12 ga., includes one set of 28 in. barrels with Tula chokes and one set of carrier barrels allowing use of sub-gauge tubes (carrier barrels cannot be used for 12 ga.), 8mm rib, hard case standard. Mfg. 1988-99.

* ***K-80 2-Barrel Lightweight Skeet Set Standard Grade***

	$8,750	$7,000	$5,150	$4,300	$3,875	$3,300	$3,000	*$11,840*

Subtract $1,845 for heavy barrel variation, which does not include sub-gauge tubes.
Retail price for 2 barrel heavy set with choke tubes was $9,995.

* ***K-80 2-Barrel Lightweight Skeet Set Bavaria Model*** – game scene engraved silver receiver with light perimeter scroll work, select walnut. Imported 1988-99.

	$12,950	$10,000	$8,000	$7,200	$6,200	$5,250	$4,800	*$16,990*

Subtract $1,845 for heavy barrel variation, which does not include sub-gauge tubes.

Retail price for 2 barrel heavy set with choke tubes was $15,145.

* ***K-80 2-Barrel Lightweight Skeet Set Danube Model*** – fine English scroll work on receiver sides and floorplate. Imported 1988-1999.

	$22,945	$15,250	$17,750	$9,400	$7,750	$7,000	$6,650	*$28,090*

Subtract $1,845 for heavy barrel variation, which does not include sub-gauge tubes.

Retail price for two barrel heavy set with choke tubes was $26,245.

GRADING - PPGS™	100%	98%	95%	90%	80%	70%	60%	LAST MSR

* ***K-80 2-Barrel Lightweight Skeet Set Gold Target Model*** – deep chiseled scroll engraving with gold line accents, 100% coverage finest quality walnut. Importation disc. 1999.

	$25,975	$20,500	$15,950	$12,375	$9,950	$8,700	$7,500	*$31,635*

Subtract $1,845 for heavy barrel variation.

Retail price for heavy 2 barrel set with choke tubes was $29,790.

K-80 4-BARREL SKEET SET – 1 barrel each of 12, 20, 28 ga., and .410 bore, 12 ga. is Tula choked (even patterning), 8mm tapered flat or standard VR, includes hard case. Since most shooters prefer different gauge insert tubes (Briley, etc.) rather than barrel sets, values have gone down considerably recently for these 4 gauge sets.

* ***K-80 4-Barrel Skeet Set Standard Grade*** – satin finished receiver with skeet scroll engraving. Importation disc. 1999.

	$10,000	$8,000	$6,500	$5,350	$4,500	$4,000	$3,650	*$16,950*

* ***K-80 4-Barrel Skeet Set Bavaria Model*** – game scene engraved silver receiver with light perimeter scrollwork, select walnut. Importation disc. 1999.

	$14,000	$12,000	$9,500	$8,250	$6,900	$5,400	$4,350	*$22,100*

* ***K-80 4-Barrel Skeet Set Danube Model*** – fine English scroll work on receiver sides and floorplate. Importation disc. 1999.

	$22,500	$17,000	$13,000	$10,500	$8,700	$7,500	$6,250	*$33,200*

* ***K-80 4-Barrel Skeet Set Gold Target Model*** – deep chiseled scroll engraving with gold line accents, 100% coverage finest quality walnut. Importation disc. 1999.

	$29,650	$17,350	$13,000	$10,500	$8,700	$7,500	$6,250	*$36,745*

ULM-P LIVE PIGEON – 12 ga. only, live pigeon gun with hand detachable sidelocks, 28 or 30 in. VR barrels, standard grade has light scrollwork engraving.

	$17,500	$12,000	$9,175	$7,700	$6,000	$5,450	$4,995	*$22,500*

* ***ULM-P Live Pigeon Bavaria Grade*** – similar to Ulm-P, only with elaborate game scene engraving.

	$22,000	$16,000	$12,000	$9,000	$7,250	$6,000	$5,500	*$29,500*

KS-2 SERIES – any ga., full H&H type sidelocks, priced by individual special order. Prices started at $24,000. Disc. 1988.

SHOTGUNS: O/U OR COMBINATION GUNS

Add $1,150 for pivot mount system.

Add $695 for hand detachable sidelocks (Ulm only, disc.).

Add $1,290 for 4-claw scope mount system (disc.).

TECK MODEL – 12 and 16 ga., O/U shotgun or rifle/shotgun combo., various cals. (7x57R, 7x64mm, 7x65R, .30-06, or .308 Win.), boxlock action, Kersten double crossbolt, auto ejectors, 7 1/2 lbs. Importation disc. 2004.

	$6,650	$5,100	$4,400	$3,550	$3,000	$2,600	$2,295	*$7,750*

* ***Teck Model Dural*** – dural aluminum frame variation of the Teck, 6.8 lbs. Importation disc. 2004.

	$6,625	$5,100	$4,400	$3,550	$3,000	$2,600	$2,295	*$7,750*

ULM – similar to Teck, except sidelock and fully engraved with leaf Arabesques. Disc. 2013.

	$12,325	$9,250	$7,950	$6,350	$5,250	$4,400	$3,500	*$14,500*

* ***Ulm Dural*** – dural aluminum frame variation of the Ulm. Importation disc. 2004.

	$12,325	$9,250	$7,950	$6,350	$5,250	$4,400	$3,500	*$14,500*

ULM PRIMUS – similar to Ulm, except game scene engraved with English arabesques. Disc. 2011.

	$19,000	$13,750	$10,000	$8,750	$7,500	$6,250	$5,500	*$22,850*

* ***Ulm Primus Dural*** – dural aluminum frame variation of the Ulm Primus. Disc. 2011.

	$19,000	$13,750	$10,000	$8,750	$7,500	$6,250	$5,500	*$22,850*

ULTRA TS COMBINATION GUN – 12 (disc. 2007) or 20 ga., 3 in. chamber, combination O/U, various calibers (lower barrel), 25 in. barrels, "Kickspanner" mechanism allows manual cocking from thumb safety, satin finish receiver, VR, 6 lbs. New 1985.

MSR $8,895	$7,750	$6,300	$5,275	$4,500	$3,650	$2,950	$2,300	

* ***Ultra-B TS Combination Gun*** – similar to Ultra, except features a selector to switch the front set trigger to the top shotgun barrel. Disc. 1995.

	$6,750	$5,600	$4,500	$3,950	$3,400	$2,750	$2,100	*$4,990*

GRADING - PPGS™	100%	98%	95%	90%	80%	70%	60%	LAST MSR

SHOTGUNS: SxS

ESSENCIA BOXLOCK – 12, 16, 20, or 28 ga. 2 3/4 in. chambers, round body boxlock action, two frame sizes, 28 or 30 in. non-VR barrels choked IC/Mod., ejectors, DT or single non-selective trigger, Turkish walnut straight or Prince of Wales grip stock with semi-beavertail forearm, automatic sliding tang safety, fine English scroll engraving, gold plated cocking indicators and "Krieghoff" engraved in gold on receiver sides, leather case, color case hardened receiver, 6 1/4-7 lbs. New 2003.

MSR $28,550	$24,750	$21,000	$17,500	$13,500	$9,995	$8,500	$7,500	

Add $1,100 for 28 ga. Add $4,400 for 28 ga. with 30 in. barrels.
Add $1,595 for single non-selective trigger.
Add $2,200 for wood upgrade. Add $3,500 for Oak/leather case upgrade.
Add $7,150 for optional side-lever opening. Add $1,975 for initials on trigger guard or bottom of buttstock.
Add $1,925 for Briley thin wall choke tubes. Add $550 for custom non-standard choke tubes.

Krieghoff also manufactures special editions of this gun on a private label basis for LeArmes, featuring a North American Game Bird Series (including Woodland Grade, Upland Grade, and Sierra Nevada Grade).

ESSENCIA SIDELOCK – 12, 16, 20, 28 ga., or .410 bore, 2 3/4 or 3 (20 ga.) in. chambers, round body, back action sidelock (Purdey style), three frame sizes, 26 1/2 (disc.), 28, or 30 in. non-VR barrels choked IC/Mod., automatic selective ejectors (H&H style), DT or single non-selective gold wash trigger(s), trigger guard tang w/decorative tip, pearl bead sight, Turkish walnut straight grip or pistol grip stock with semi-beavertail forearm, automatic sliding tang safety, fine English scroll engraving, gold plated cocking indicators and "Krieghoff" engraved in gold on receiver sides, "Essencia" engraved in gold on bottom, Krieghoff leather case, color case hardened receiver, extra set of interchangable barrels, 6 3/4-7 lbs. New 2003.

MSR $34,895	$29,650	$25,945	$22,250	$20,175	$16,325	$13,350	$10,400	

Add $1,100 for 28 ga. or $4,955 for 28 ga. with 30 in. barrels.
Add $4,500 for 28 ga. on small frame (sidelock only) or $8,300 if with 30 in. barrels.
Add $5,055 for .410 bore on 28 ga. frame (sidelock only).
Add $1,925 for Briley thin wall choke tubes. Add $550 per fcustom choke (not standard).
Add $1,595 for single non-selective trigger. Add $2,200 for wood upgrade. Add $3,500 for oak and leather case.
Add $9,295-$16,995 for extra set of interchangable barrels, depending on ga./bore.
Add $8,695 for Hammer Gun variation.

Krieghoff also manufactures special editions of this gun on a private label basis for LeArmes, featuring a North American Game Bird Series (including Woodland Grade, Upland Grade, and Sierra Nevada Grade).

SHOTGUNS: SINGLE BARREL, TRAP

MODEL 32 – 12 ga., same action as Model 32 O/U, 32-34 in. barrel, VR, mod., imp. mod., or full choke.

	$2,500	$2,125	$1,800	$1,550	$1,425	$1,300	$1,200	

KS-5 – 12 ga. only, 32 or 34 in. barrel, adj. point of impact, innovative trigger configuration, optional choke tubes, redesigned streamlined receiver (new 1993). Mfg. 1985-99.

	$2,895	$2,450	$2,200	$2,000	$1,875	$1,625	$1,400	*$3,675*

Add $2,100 per additional barrel.
Add $200 for screw-in choke option.
Add $200 for factory adj. comb stock.
Subtract $250 if w/o factory aluminum case.
Subtract 20% for blued receiver.
Subtract 15% for receiver with "KS-5" engraved on sides.
Subtract 10% for 32 in. barrel.

Adj. point of impact on this model is achieved by means of different, optional front hangers.

* ***KS-5 Special*** – 12 ga. only, 32 or 34 in. barrel, features adj. rib and comb stock, cased. Mfg. 1990-99.

	$3,895	$3,500	$2,975	$2,575	$2,050	$1,750	$1,500	*$4,695*

Add $2,750 per additional barrel.
Add $200 for screw-in choke option.
Subtract 10% for 32 in. barrel.

KX-5 – 12 ga. only, 2 3/4 in. chamber, 32 (disc. 2005) or 34 in. barrel, adj. point of impact, innovative adj. trigger (pull or release type), adj. stock comb, light scroll engraving, includes choke tubes and aluminum case. Mfg. 2002-2011.

	$4,295	$3,650	$3,200	$2,700	$2,400	$2,100	$1,850	*$5,495*

Add $425 for factory release trigger.
Subtract 10% for 32 in. barrel.

GRADING - PPGS™	100%	98%	95%	90%	80%	70%	60%	LAST MSR

KX-6 – 12 ga. only, 3 in. chamber, 34 in. barrel with ventilated and fully adj. tapered high rib with three screw-in chokes, right or left-hand Krieghoff parallel off-set trap stock, matte black receiver finish, includes Krieghoff fitted case. Mfg. 2012-2015.

	$4,900	$4,175	$3,550	$3,000	$2,500	$2,100	$1,850	*$5,490*

Add $475 for adj. buttplate (new 2013).

KX-6 SPECIAL – 12 ga., 3 in. chamber, 34 in. barrel with screw-in chokes, ventilated and fully adj. tapered high rib, Krieghoff Parallel Offset Trap stock, with or w/o adj. buttplate, nickel receiver, includes Krieghoff fitted case with nylon cover. New 2016.

MSR $6,595	$5,600	$4,900	$4,200	$3,800	$3,100	$2,500	$1,950	

Add $495 for adjustable buttplate.

KRISS ARMS GROUP (KRISS SYSTEMS SA)

Current manufacturer of civilian and law enforcement firearms established in 2008 with factories located in Etoy, Switzerland, and Chesapeake, VA. Previously located in Nyon, Switzerland and Virginia Beach, VA. Distributor and dealer sales.

KRISS USA, Inc. is the North American extension of the Switzerland based KRISS Group, the pioneers of recoil mitigation technology and the world leaders in firearms innovation. KRISS USA manufactures, imports, and distributes KRISS Group firearms and accessories under KRISS, the brand dedicated to recoil mitigation and firearms technology; SPHINX, the brand dedicated to precision manufacturing and performance pistols; KRYTAC, the brand dedicated to training and firearms safety; and DEFIANCE, the brand dedicated to firearms enhancements designed to aid the shooter in overcoming asymmetric warfare conditions. The company's previous name was Transformational Defense Industries, Inc. In late 2010, the company acquired Swiss pistol maker Sphinx Sytems Ltd. In 2016, after Sphinx Systems Ltd. went out of business, Kriss USA assumed the manufacture of the Sphinx pistols under the Sphinx trademark.

PISTOLS: SEMI-AUTO

KRISS VECTOR SDP – 9mm Para. or .45 ACP cal., pistol variation of the KRISS Vector carbine, patented KRISS Super V Recoil Mitigation System, 5 1/2 or 6 1/2 (disc.) in. barrel with 1/2x28RH thread pitch, full-length Mil-Std 1913 Picatinny top receiver rail and Picatinny bottom accessory rail, compatible with Glock pistol magazines, flip sights, short throw safety lever, combat pivoting trigger, quick detach sling mount, 5.4 lbs. Mfg. 2011-2015.

	$1,225	$1,075	$925	$850	$675	$550	$450	*$1,349*

Add $100 for .45 ACP cal.

KRISS VECTOR GEN II SDP – 9mm Para., .357 SIG (disc. 2019), .40 S&W, 10mm, or .45 ACP cal., KRISS Super V Recoil Mitigation System, 5 1/2 in. barrel, 13 (.45 ACP), 15 (.357 SIG, .40 S&W, and 10mm), or 17 (9mm Para.) shot mag. Glock mag. compatible, smooth pivoting trigger with audible/tactile reset, low profile folding sights, stabilizing brace optional, ambidextrous short throw safety lever, full-length Mil-Std 1913 Picatinny rail and side accessory rail (optional), left side charging handle/brass check feature, quick detach sling swivel, available in black, FDE, ODG (mfg. 2019-2020), Combat Grey (mfg. 2019-2020), or Alpine finish, 5.9 lbs. New 2016.

MSR $1,425	$1,300	$1,100	$950	$850	$700	$600	$450	

Add $20 for .357 SIG (disc. 2019), .40 S&W, 10mm, or .45 ACP cal.

Add $80 for Alpine, OD Green (mfg. 2019-2020), Combat Grey (mfg. 2019-2020), or FDE finish.

KRISS VECTOR GEN II SDP-SB – 9mm Para., .357 SIG (disc. 2019), .40 S&W, 10mm, or .45 ACP cal., Super V recoil mitigation system, 5 1/2 in. barrel, 13 (.45 ACP), 15 (.357 SIG (disc. 2019), .40 S&W, and 10mm), or 17 (9mm) shot mag. Glock mag. compatible, smooth pivoting trigger with audible/tactile reset, low profile folding sights, stabilizing brace, ambidextrous short throw safety lever, Picatinny bottom rail and side accessory rail (optional), left side charging handle/brass check function, available in black, FDE, OD Green (disc.), Combat Grey (disc.), or Alpine finish, 6.7 lbs. New 2016.

MSR $1,575	$1,400	$1,250	$1,050	$950	$800	$650	$500	

Add $20 for .357 SIG (disc. 2019), .40 S&W, 10mm, or .45 ACP cal.

* ***Kriss Vector Gen II SDP-SB .22 LR*** – .22 LR cal., direct blowback action, 6 1/2 in. threaded barrel, 10 shot mag., 30 shot extended mag. available, low profile front and rear flip sights, SB Tactical stabilizing brace, ambidextrous safety, Picatinny top rail, last round bolt hold open feature, black, FDE, or Alpine White finish, 5.6 lbs. New 2020.

MSR $649	$550	$475	$425	$375	$300	$250	$200	

KRISS VECTOR GEN II SDP-SB ENHANCED – 9mm Para., .357 SIG (disc. 2019), .40 S&W (disc. 2020), 10mm, or .45 ACP cal., Super V recoil mitigation system, 6 1/2 in. barrel, 13 (.45 ACP), 15 (.357 SIG (disc. 2019), .40 S&W, and 10mm) or 17 (9mm Para.) shot mag. Glock mag. compatible, smooth pivoting trigger with audible/tactile reset, low profile folding sights, folding stabilizing brace, MK5

GRADING - PPGS™	100%	98%	95%	90%	80%	70%	60%	LAST MSR

Modular extended Picatinny rail handguard, hand stop (new 2019), ambidextrous shot throw safety lever, left side charging handle/brass check function, available in black, FDE, ODG (disc.), Combat Grey (disc.), or Alpine finish, 18 5/8 (folded) - 28 5/8 in. OAL, 7 1/2 lbs. New 2018.

MSR $1,625	$1,450	$1,300	$1,100	$1,000	$800	$650	$500	

Add $20 for .357 SIG (disc. 2019), .40 S&W (disc. 2020), 10mm, or .45 ACP cal.
Add $80 for Alpine, OD Green, Combat Grey, or FDE finish.

RIFLES: SEMI-AUTO

KRISS USA, Inc. also manufactures a select fire Vector submachine gun, chambered in .45 ACP and 9mm Para. cal. for military and law enforcement only, and the KRISS Vector SBR, a short barreled rifle variation of the KRISS Vector chambered in .45 ACP and 9mm Para. cal. Please contact the company directly for more information on these models.

KRISS VECTOR CRB – 9mm Para. or .45 ACP cal., carbine variation of the KRISS Vector, patented KRISS Super V Recoil Mitigation System, 16 in. barrel and barrel shroud, compatibe with Glock pistol magazines, flip-up front and rear sights, full-length Mil-Std 1913 Picatinny top receiver rail and Picatinny bottom accessory rail, short throw safety lever, combat pivoting trigger, adj. M4 stock, 5.8 lbs. Mfg. 2011-2017.

	$1,350	$1,175	$1,000	$900	$800	$675	$525	*$1,499*

Add $20 for .45 ACP cal.
Add $884 for TacPac option (includes tactical sling, bipod grip pod system, Surefire tactical light, and L-3 Eotech holographic sight system), mfg. 2012-disc.

KRISS VECTOR CRB ENHANCED – 9mm Para. or .45 ACP cal., carbine enhanced variation of the KRISS Vector, patented KRISS Super V Recoil Mitigation System, 16 in. barrel and enhanced barrel shroud, compatible with Glock pistol magazines, combat pivoting trigger, flip sights, adj. M4 stock, Magpul RVG vertical grip, short throw safety lever, KRISS hand stop, full-length Mil-Std 1913 Picatinny top receiver rail and Picatinny bottom accessory rail, Combat Grey Cerakote finish. Mfg. 2015-2017.

	$1,525	$1,350	$1,150	$1,050	$850	$700	$550	*$1,699*

Add $20 for .45 ACP cal.

KRISS VECTOR GEN II CRB – 9mm Para., .357 SIG (mfg. 2017-2019), .40 S&W (new 2017), 10mm (new 2018), or .45 ACP cal., delayed blowback KSV (KRISS Super V) recoil mitigation system, 16 in. Nitrided barrel with black anodized shroud, 13, 17, 25, or 33 shot mag., uses Glock mags., smooth pivoting trigger with audible and tactile reset, low profile folding sights, KRISS M4 stock adaptor with DEFIANCE M4 stock, ambidextrous short throw safety lever, bottom and full length top Picatinny rail, left side charging handle/brass check function, toolless caliber interchangeability, black, FDE, OD Green (disc.), Combat Grey (new 2018), or Alpine finish, 7.8 lbs. New 2016.

MSR $1,575	$1,400	$1,250	$1,050	$950	$800	$650	$500	

Add $20 for .357 SIG (mfg. 2017-2019), .40 S&W (new 2017), 10mm (new 2018), or .45 ACP cal.

KRISS VECTOR GEN II CRB ENHANCED – Disc. 2017.

	$1,525	$1,350	$1,150	$1,050	$850	$700	$550	*$1,699*

KRISS VECTOR GEN II CRB .22 LR – .22 LR cal., direct blowback action, 16 in. threaded barrel, 10 or 30 (proprietary extended) shot mag., low profile front and rear flip sights, 6-pos. Defiance M4 stock, Picatinny top rail, M-LOK modular handguard, last round bolt hold open, black, FDE, or Alpine White finish. New 2020.

MSR $675	$600	$550	$450	$425	$325	$275	$200	

KUFSTEINER WAFFENSTUBE

Current rifle manufacturer located in Kufstein, Austria.

RIFLES

Kufsteiner rifles are essentially built per individual order, and should be appraised by a knowledgeable person for an accurate price evaluation based on condition, quality of materials/construction, and special features. In addition to his unique bolt action, he also manufactures other bolt action designs and O/U rifles as well.

KAISERBUCHSE 3-S SYSTEM BOLT ACTION RIFLE – various cals. including Magnum calibers, unique short action allows for straight on cartridge loading, high strength alloy main parts, grip safety on lower pistol grip, unique uncocking device allowing manual cocking/decocking of the firing pin spring, 23.6 in. standard barrel, 3 shot detachable mag., iron sights, receiver drilled for scope mounts, best quality wood, available in either Schnabel forearm or Mannlicher configuration, many styles of engraving are optional, 7.14 lbs.

JAGERBUCHSE REPEATING RIFLE – various cals., bolt action, 3 front locking lugs, firing pin safety, ST, removable 5 shot mag., European walnut stock with Bavarian cheekpiece and Schnabel forearm, 5.8-10 lbs.

KUPEC, PAVEL

Previous longarm manufacturer located in the Czech Republic.

Pavel Kupec manufactured high quality hunting and sporting longarms made to custom order. These guns had little importation into the U.S.

L2D COMBAT

Current parts and accessories manufacturer located in Coral Springs, Florida.

L2D Combat manufactures a wide variety of pistol slides, barrels, triggers, and frame components for customizing pistols made by Glock, Smith and Wesson, and SIG. Please contact the company directly for more information including pricing, options, and availability.

L.A.R. MANUFACTURING, INC.

Previous rifle manufacturer established in 1968, located in West Jordan, UT until 2012. L.A.R. was acquired by the Freedom Group in late 2012 and closed its doors during 2013.

In addition to its .50 cal. bolt action rifles, L.A.R. also made upper receiver assemblies and associated parts/accessories for AR-15 style carbines/rifles.

GRADING - PPGS™	100%	98%	95%	90%	80%	70%	60%	LAST MSR

PISTOLS: SEMI-AUTO

GRIZZLY WIN. MAG. MARK I – .357 Mag., .357/.45 Grizzly Win. Mag. (new 1990), .45 ACP, 10mm, or .45 Win. Mag. cal., single action, based on the Colt 1911 design, 5.4 (new 1986), 6 1/2, 8 (new 1987), or 10 (new 1987) in. barrel, parkerized finish, 7 shot mag., ambidextrous safeties, checkered rubber grips, adj. sights, 48 oz. empty. Also can be converted to .45 ACP, 10mm (new 1988), .357 Mag., or .30 Mauser (disc.). Mfg. 1984-1999.

	100%	98%	95%	90%	80%	70%	60%	LAST MSR
	N/A	$2,500	$1,900	$1,700	$1,500	$1,300	$850	

* ***Grizzly Win. Mag. Mark I Short Barrel Lengths*** – 5.4 or 6 1/2 in. barrel.

	100%	98%	95%	90%	80%	70%	60%	LAST MSR
	N/A	$2,150	$1,850	$1,550	$1,400	$1,075	$950	*$1,000*

Add $375 for hard chrome or nickel frame.
Add $550 for full hard chrome or nickel.
Add $750 for .357 Mag., .45 ACP, or .45 Win. Mag. cal. conversion units.
Add $250 for muzzle compensator.

Conversion units include .357 Mag., 10mm, .40 S&W (1991-1993 only), and .45 ACP cals.

* ***Grizzly Win. Mag. Mark I Long Barrel Lengths*** – .357 Mag., .45 Win. Mag., or .357/.45 Grizzly Win. Mag. (new 1990) cal., 8 or 10 in. barrel, extended slides. Disc. 1995.

	100%	98%	95%	90%	80%	70%	60%	LAST MSR
	N/A	$4,500	$4,000	$3,500	$2,800	$2,300	$1,800	*$1,313*

Add $100 for 10 in. barrel.
Add $375 for hard chrome or nickel frame.
Add $550 for full hard chrome or nickel.
Add $750 for .357 Mag., .45 ACP, or .45 Win. Mag. cal. conversion units.
Add $250 for muzzle compensator.

* ***Grizzly Win. Mag. Mark I State Special Edition*** – .45 Grizzly Win. Mag., 50 mfg. beginning 1998 to commemorate each state (ser. numbers match the order each state was admitted to the union), features gold etchings on frame, gold small parts, faux mother-of-pearl grips, cased. Limited mfg. 1998-99.

Regional demand/interest preclude accurate pricing on this model.

GRIZZLY WIN. MAG. MARK II – .45 ACP, 10mm, or .45 Win. Mag. cal., similar to Mark I, except has fixed sights, standard safeties, and different metal finish. Mfg. 1986 only.

	100%	98%	95%	90%	80%	70%	60%	LAST MSR
	N/A	$1,750	$1,550	$1,350	$1,200	$975	$850	*$550*

Add $25 for .357 Mag.

GRIZZLY .44 MAG. MARK IV – .44 Mag. cal., 5.4, 6 1/2, 8, or 10 in. barrel, adj. sights, lusterless blue, parkerized, chrome, or nickel finish. Mfg. 1991-1999.

	100%	98%	95%	90%	80%	70%	60%	LAST MSR
	N/A	$3,500	$3,000	$2,750	$2,200	$1,825	$1,400	*$1,014*

Add $750 for .357 Mag. or .45 ACP cal. conversion units.
Add $500-$1,000 for 8 or 10 in. barrel.

GRIZZLY .50 MARK V – .50 Action Express cal., single action semi-auto, 5.4 or 6 1/2 in. barrel, 6 shot mag., checkered walnut grips, 56 oz. Mfg. 1993-99.

	100%	98%	95%	90%	80%	70%	60%	LAST MSR
	$3,800	$3,200	$3,000	$2,850	$2,500	$1,700	$1,350	*$1,152*

Add $895 per coversion unit (new 1996).

GRADING - PPGS™	100%	98%	95%	90%	80%	70%	60%	LAST MSR

RIFLES: BOLT ACTION

GRIZZLY BIG BOAR COMPETITOR RIFLE – .50 BMG cal., single shot, bolt action design in bullpup configuration, alloy steel receiver and bolt, 36 in. heavy barrel with compensator, thumb safety, match or field grade, includes bipod, scope mount, leather cheek pad and hard carry case, 30.4 lbs. Mfg. 1994-2011.

	$2,150	$1,725	$1,575	$1,375	$1,175	$1,050	$950	*$2,350*

Add $100 for parkerizing.
Add $250 for nickel trigger housing finish.
Add $350 for full nickel frame (disc. 2010).
Add $250 for stainless steel Lothar Walther barrel (disc. 2010).
Add $522 for redesigned (2002) tripod and pintle mount.
Last MSR was $4,841 for the Big Bore Hunter Rifle Package in 2011. This included: Nightforce scope and rings, cleaning kit, tripod with pintle mount, drag bag, and hard carry case.

GRIZZLY T-50 – .50 BMG cal., single shot, 32-36 in. barrel with muzzle brake, extended barrel shroud with top and bottom Picatinny rails, black parkerized finish, cheek saddle on frame, carry handle in front of trigger guard, extended bolt handle, 30 1/2 - 32 lbs. Mfg. 2009-2012.

	$3,000	$2,800	$2,600	$2,400	$2,200	$2,000	$1,800	*$3,200*

MSR on the A T-50 Tactical Package was $5,618. This package included: Nightforce scope and rings, cleaning kit, heavy duty bipod, carry handle, Accu-Shot monopod, drag bag, and hard carry case.

RIFLES: SEMI-AUTO

GRIZZLY 15 – .223 Rem. cal., GIO, patterned after the AR-15, available in either A2 or A3 configuration, limited mfg. 2004-2005.

	$675	$500	$425	$375	$335	$315	$295	*$795*

Add $85 for detachable carry handle.

GRIZZLY A2 SPEC CARBINE – 5.56 NATO cal., AR-15 style, GIO, 16 in. M4 chrome moly threaded barrel with A2 birdcage flash suppressor, 5-position collapsible carbine stock, Grizzly A2 aluminum upper receiver, Mil-Spec forged aluminum LAR Grizzly lower receiver, Mil-Spec or LAR split carbine quad rail handguard, A2 front sight, standard trigger group, A2 Mil-Spec pistol grip. Mfg. 2011-2012.

	$850	$550	$465	$395	$350	$325	$295	*$999*

GRIZZLY A3 SPEC CARBINE – 5.56 NATO cal., GIO, similar to Grizzly A2 Spec Carbine, except has Grizzly A3 aluminum flat-top upper receiver. Mfg. 2011-2012.

	$850	$550	$465	$395	$350	$325	$295	*$979*

OPS-4 GRIZZLY H-TACTICAL – 5.56 NATO cal., AR-15 style, GPO, 16 in. M4 chrome moly threaded barrel with A2 birdcage flash suppressor, 5-position collapsible carbine stock, LAR side charged forged aluminum flat-top upper receiver, Mil-Spec forged aluminum LAR Grizzly lower receiver, Mil-Spec or LAR split carbine quad rail handguard, hard anodized aluminum charging handle. Mfg. 2011-2012.

	$935	$575	$475	$415	$350	$325	$300	*$1,111*

OPS-4 GRIZZLY HUNTER – .223 Rem./5.56 NATO (.223 Wylde chamber) cal., AR-15 style, GIO, 18, 20, or 24 in. bull chrome moly (20 or 24 in.) or stainless steel (18 or 20 in.) barrel, standard A2 black stock, standard trigger or two-stage match trigger group, OPS-4 side charged forged aluminum flat-top upper receiver, Mil-Spec forged aluminum LAR Grizzly lower receiver, LAR free float tube rifle length handguard, LAR aluminum gas block, hard anodized aluminum charging handle. Mfg. 2011-2012.

	$850	$550	$465	$395	$350	$325	$295	*$989*

OPS-4 GRIZZLY OPERATOR – 5.56 NATO cal., AR-15 style, GIO, 16 in. chrome moly heavy threaded barrel with 5 port muzzle brake and compensator, Magpul CTR collapsible stock, Hogue rubber grip with finger grooves or Magpul MIAD pistol grip, standard trigger group, OPS-4 side charged forged aluminum flat-top upper receiver, Mil-Spec forged aluminum LAR Grizzly lower receiver, LAR mid-length quad rail handguard, LAR aluminum gas block with rail, hard anodized aluminum charging handle. Mfg. 2011-2012.

	$915	$575	$475	$415	$350	$325	$300	*$1,099*

OPS-4 GRIZZLY PRECISION OPERATOR – .223 Rem./5.56 NATO (.223 Wylde chamber) cal., AR-15 style, GIO, 18 or 20 in. bull stainless steel barrel, Magpul PRS stock, Magpul pistol grip and trigger guard or Magpul MIAD grip, standard trigger or two-stage match trigger group, LAR rifle length free floating quad rail handguard, LAR aluminum low profile gas block, otherwise similar to OPS-4 Grizzly Operator. Mfg. 2011-2012.

	$1,075	$675	$500	$450	$400	$350	$325	*$1,299*

GRADING - PPGS™	100%	98%	95%	90%	80%	70%	60%	LAST MSR

OPS-4 GRIZZLY SPEC CARBINE – 5.56 NATO cal., AR-15 style, GIO, 16 in. M4 chrome moly threaded barrel with A2 birdcage flash suppressor, standard trigger group, 5-position collapsible carbine stock, OPS-4 side charged forged aluminum flat-top upper receiver, Mil-Spec forged aluminum LAR Grizzly lower receiver, A2 front sight, Mil-Spec or LAR split carbine quad rail handguard, hard anodized aluminum charging handle. Mfg. 2011-2012.

	$825	$535	$450	$385	$340	$325	$295	*$959*

OPS-4 GRIZZLY SPEC RIFLE – 5.56 NATO cal., AR-15 style, GIO, 20 in. chrome moly heavy threaded barrel with A2 birdcage flash suppressor, standard trigger or two-stage match trigger group, standard A2 black stock, otherwise similar to OPS-4 Grizzly Spec Carbine. Mfg. 2011-2012.

	$850	$550	$465	$395	$350	$325	$295	*$999*

OPS-4 GRIZZLY STANDARD CARBINE – 5.56 NATO cal., AR-15 style, GIO, 16 in. M4 chrome moly threaded barrel with A2 birdcage flash suppressor, standard trigger group, 5-position collapsible carbine stock, LAR side charged forged aluminum flat-top upper receiver, Mil-Spec forged aluminum LAR Grizzly lower receiver, LAR aluminum gas block with rail, full chrome bolt carrier and gas key, hard anodized aluminum charging handle. Mfg. 2011-2012.

	$850	$550	$465	$395	$350	$325	$295	*$999*

OPS-4 GRIZZLY STANDARD RIFLE – 5.56 NATO cal., AR-15 style, GIO, 20 in. chrome moly heavy threaded barrel with A2 birdcage flash suppressor, standard trigger or two-stage match trigger group, standard A2 black stock, otherwise similar to OPS-4 Grizzly Standard Carbine. Mfg. 2011-2012.

	$915	$575	$475	$415	$350	$325	$300	*$1,099*

OPS-22 TERMINATOR – .22 LR cal., GIO, 16 in. carbon steel barrel, free float tube, 30 shot mag., collapsible buttstock. Mfg. 2011-2012.

	$575	$500	$425	$375	$325	$295	$275	*$649*

L E S INCORPORATED

Previous manufacturer located in Morton Grove, IL.

PISTOLS: SEMI-AUTO

P-18 ROGAK – 7.65mm Para. (limited mfg.) or 9mm Para. cal., DA/SA gas delayed blowback, 18 shot, 5 1/2 in. barrel, stainless steel, black plastic grips with partial thumb rest. Disc.

	$450	$395	$350	$325	$295	$275	$250
High Polish Finish	$525	$450	$395	$375	$325	$295	$275

Add 25% for 7.65mm Para. cal.

This pistol was patterned after the Steyr Model GB. Approx. 2,300 P-18s were mfg. before being disc.

LKCI LLC

Current distributor and importer of pistols, rifles, and shotguns, established in 1999, located in Newark, OH.

LKCI offers distribution of handguns, rifles, and shotguns for multiple worldwide manufacturers and is the exclusive importer for Tisas Trabzon Silah's line of Regent pistols and Omega Arms rifles and shotguns. For Tisas' Regent pistols, please refer to Regent in the R section. For Omega Arms rifles and shotguns, please refer to the O section.

LMT

Please refer to the Lewis Machine & Tool section.

LRB ARMS

Current manufacturer located in Floral Park, NY. Currently distributed by LRB of Long Island, NY.

For individual model listings, please go to BlueBookOfGunValues.com/overflow.

L.W. SEECAMP CO.

Current semi-auto pistol manufacturer located in Southwick, MA. Please refer to Seecamp listing in the S section.

LWRC INTERNATIONAL, INC.

Current manufacturer of AR-15 style rifles, pistols, and related AR-15 accessories established during 2006, located in Cambridge, MD. Dealer and distributor sales.

Please refer to BlueBookOfGunValues.com to order the *Blue Book of AR-15s & Variations*, available as a book or online subscription.

LA ARMERIA DE MADRID

Please refer to the LARM listing in this section.

GRADING - PPGS™	100%	98%	95%	90%	80%	70%	60%	LAST MSR

LABANU INCORPORATED

Labanu, Inc. SKSs were manufactured by Norinco in China, and imported exclusively until 1998 by Labanu, Inc., located in Ronkonkoma, NY.

RIFLES: SEMI-AUTO

MAK 90 SKS SPORTER RIFLE – 7.62x39mm cal., sporterized variation of the SKS with thumbhole stock, 16 1/2 in. barrel, includes accessories, 5 lbs. Importation began 1995, banned 1998.

	100%	98%	95%	90%	80%	70%	60%	LAST MSR
	$625	$550	$475	$425	$375	$325	$295	*$189*

LAHTI PISTOL

Previous manufacturer located in Husqvarna, Sweden. Also mfg. by Vkt (state rifle factory) in Jyvaskyla, Finland.

PISTOLS: SEMI-AUTO

SWEDISH MODEL 40 – 9mm Para. cal., 4 3/4 in. barrel, blue finish, fixed sights, plastic grips, mfg. 1940-44.

	100%	98%	95%	90%	80%	70%	60%	LAST MSR
	$950	$575	$425	$300	$260	$250	$240	

Add 10% for Holster-Rig.

It is important to note that there are diversely marked variations of this pistol, such as RPLT (Danish State Police); such police markings add value by about 10%.

FINNISH L-35 – 9mm Para., 4 basic variations - only the first 2 types have the more desirable shoulder stock lug. Military pistols are usually "SA" marked, approx. 9,100 mfg. 1938-1954.

- ***Finnish L-35 1st Variation*** – can be identified by "hump" for yoke locking piece and loaded indicator, ser. no. range 1001-3700.

	100%	98%	95%	90%	80%	70%	60%	LAST MSR
	$6,000	$4,500	$3,750	$3,000	$2,500	$2,000	$1,500	

- ***Finnish L-35 2nd Variation*** – does not have the "hump" for yoke locking piece, scarcer than 1st Variation, ser. no. 3701-4700.

	100%	98%	95%	90%	80%	70%	60%	LAST MSR
	$4,750	$4,000	$3,500	$3,000	$2,500	$2,000	$1,500	

- ***Finnish L-35 3rd Variation*** – can be identified by small changes in loaded indicator, most are marked "Valmet", ser. no. range 4701-6800.

	100%	98%	95%	90%	80%	70%	60%	LAST MSR
	$2,500	$2,000	$1,500	$1,000	$800	$700	$600	

- ***Finnish L-35 4th Variation*** – w/o loaded indicator, marked "Valmet," and sold commercially, ser. no. range 6801-9100.

	100%	98%	95%	90%	80%	70%	60%	LAST MSR
	$2,000	$1,750	$1,350	$1,000	$800	$700	$600	

- ***Finnish L-35 Shoulder Stocks*** – the shoulder stock for this model (w/o serial numbers) features a sheet metal compartment which contains a cleaning rod and extra magazine. Original stocks (only 50 mfg.) are currently selling in the $6,000 range, while more recently manufactured stocks utilizing original hardware are currently priced in the $2,500 range.

LAKE FIELD ARMS LTD.

Previous manufacturer located in Ontario, Canada. Lake Field Arms Ltd. was acquired by Savage Arms, Inc. during late 1994. Distributor sales only through most major U.S. distributors.

Lake Field rifles manufactured after the Savage acquisition are marked Savage - please refer to the Savage listing in the S section for current mfg.

RIFLES: .22 RIMFIRE

MARK I – .22 LR cal., single shot bolt action, 20 3/4 in. rifled or smoothbore barrel, adj. rear sight, thumb rotary safety, walnut finish hardwood stock, 5 1/2 lbs. Disc.

	100%	98%	95%	90%	80%	70%	60%	LAST MSR
	$110	$75	$65	$55	$50	$40	$30	*$135*

Add $14 for left-hand variation.

This model was also available in youth dimensions (19 in. barrel) at no extra charge (Model Mark I-Y).

MARK II – .22 LR cal., bolt action, 10 shot mag., 20 3/4 in. barrel, adj. rear sight, thumb operated rotary safety, walnut finish hardwood stock, 5 1/2 lbs. Disc.

	100%	98%	95%	90%	80%	70%	60%	LAST MSR
	$120	$80	$70	$60	$50	$40	$30	*$140*

Add $15 for left-hand variation (mfg. 1993-95).

This model was also available in youth dimensions (19 in. barrel) at no extra charge (Model Mark II-Y).

GRADING - PPGS™	100%	98%	95%	90%	80%	70%	60%	LAST MSR

MODEL 64B – .22 LR cal., semi-auto, side ejection, 10 shot mag., 20 1/4 in. barrel, adj. rear sight, thumb operated rotary safety, walnut finish hardwood stock, 5 1/2 lbs. Disc.

GRADING - PPGS™	100%	98%	95%	90%	80%	70%	60%	LAST MSR
	$120	$85	$75	$65	$55	$45	$40	*$143*

MODEL 90B (BIATHLON) – .22 LR cal., biathlon rifle, includes five 5 shot mags., 21 in. barrel, aperture sights, one-piece natural finish hardwood stock, 8 1/4 lbs. Mfg. 1991-95.

GRADING - PPGS™	100%	98%	95%	90%	80%	70%	60%	LAST MSR
	$430	$300	$225	$195	$170	$150	$130	*$570*

Add $55 for left-hand variation (new 1993).

MODEL 91T – .22 LR cal., target rifle, single shot, 25 in. barrel with aperture sights, dark hardwood finished stock, 8 lbs. Mfg. 1991-95.

GRADING - PPGS™	100%	98%	95%	90%	80%	70%	60%	LAST MSR
	$340	$255	$215	$175	$150	$135	$115	*$455*

Add $45 for left-hand variation (mfg. 1993-95).

* ***Model 91TR*** – repeater version of the Model 91T, 5 shot mag. Mfg. 1993-95.

GRADING - PPGS™	100%	98%	95%	90%	80%	70%	60%	LAST MSR
	$360	$265	$215	$175	$150	$135	$115	*$485*

Add $45 for left-hand variation (mfg. 1993-95).

MODEL 92S – .22 LR cal., 5 shot detachable mag., 21 in. barrel, hardwood stock with Monte Carlo cheekpiece, 8 lbs. Mfg. 1993-95.

GRADING - PPGS™	100%	98%	95%	90%	80%	70%	60%	LAST MSR
	$300	$240	$200	$175	$160	$150	$135	*$388*

Add $37 for left-hand variation.

MODEL 93M – .22 WMR cal., 5 shot mag., thumb operated rotary safety, 20 3/4 in. barrel, hardwood stock, 5 3/4 lbs. Mfg. 1995 only.

GRADING - PPGS™	100%	98%	95%	90%	80%	70%	60%	LAST MSR
	$140	$120	$100	$85	$75	$65	$55	*$168*

LAKELANDER

Previous trademark circa 1976-1999. Manufacture was by MIPRO AB (c. 1946-1999) in Sweden. Previously imported and distributed 1996-98 by Lakelander U.S.A., Inc. located in Gulfport, MS.

RIFLES: BOLT ACTION

LAKELANDER 389 – .270 Win., .30-06, or .308 Win. cal., unique design with many shooter enhancements, 4 shot integrated mag. with rotary swing plate, 3 configurations including Premium (22 in. barrel with skip-line checkering and Monte Carlo stock), Classic (22 in. barrel, standard stock with checkering), and Match-Maker (target model with 21.7 in. barrel and competition stock and adj. cheekpiece, .308 Win. only), 7.3-8.4 lbs. Mfg. 1996-98.

GRADING - PPGS™	100%	98%	95%	90%	80%	70%	60%	LAST MSR
	$1,425	$1,225	$995	$850	$700	$600	$500	*$1,599*

Add $500 for Match-Maker Model.

LAKESIDE MACHINE LLC

Previous manufacturer located in Horseshoe Bend, AR until late 2013. Previously located in Pound, WI.

RIFLES: SEMI-AUTO

Lakeside manufactured half-scale, semi-auto, belt fed replicas of many of America's famous machine guns, including the 1919 A4 ($3,995 last MSR), 1919 M37 ($3,895 last MSR, only 2 mfg.), 1917 A1 ($4,495 last MSR), M2 HB ($4,995 last MSR), M2 WC ($5,495 last MSR), and a dual mount M2 HB (was POR). Calibers included: .22 LR, .17 Mach 2 (optional), and .22 WMR. Additionally, Lakeside also manufactured a semi-auto, closed bolt, belt fed .22 LR cal. Model Vindicator BF1 with 16 1/4 in. shrouded barrel ($2,695 last MSR).

LAMBOY, S.R. & CO. INC.

Previous importer located in Victor, NY until 2003. S.R. Lamboy manufactured Ithaca Classic Doubles and imported Renato Caem and other high quality, low production long guns from Italy. Please check individual listings for more information.

LAMES

Previous manufacturer located in Italy.

SHOTGUNS: O/U

FIELD MODEL – 12 ga., 26, 28, or 30 in. barrels, various chokes, VR, engraving, SST, auto ejectors, checkered pistol grip stock with pad.

GRADING - PPGS™	100%	98%	95%	90%	80%	70%	60%	LAST MSR
	$400	$380	$365	$350	$325	$300	$275	

Add 25% for separated barrels.

GRADING - PPGS™	100%	98%	95%	90%	80%	70%	60%	LAST MSR

STANDARD TRAP – similar to Field, 30 or 32 in. various trap bore barrels, with wide VR, trap style Monte Carlo stock.

	$600	$575	$550	$525	$425	$400	$450	

CALIFORNIA TRAP – similar to Standard Trap, with separated barrels.

	$700	$675	$650	$625	$525	$500	$450	

SKEET MODEL – similar to Field, with 26 in. skeet bore barrels, skeet stock and separated barrels.

	$600	$575	$550	$525	$425	$400	$350	

LANBER

Previous shotgun (O/U and semi-auto only) trademark manufactured by ComLanber, S.A., located in Zaldibar, Spain 1973-2013. Previously imported beginning late 2006-late 2011 by Lanber USA, located in Westfield, MA. Previously located in Blakely, GA. Previously imported 1999-2006, O/U shotguns by Wingshooting Adventures, located in Coopersville, MI, 1996-99 by ITC International, Inc. located in Marietta, GA, until 1994, by Eagle Imports, Inc. located in Wanamassa, NJ, by Exel Arms of America, Inc., located in Gardener, MA, and by Lanber Arms of America located in Adrian, MI.

For individual model listings, please go to BlueBookOfGunValues.com/overflow.

LANCER SYSTEMS

Current AR-15 style rifle and accessories manufacturer located in Allentown, PA. Exclusive U.S. distributor/importer of the Alien Pistol for Laugo Arms, located in Czechoslovakia beginning 2019.

Please refer to BlueBookOfGunValues.com to order the *Blue Book of AR-15s & Variations*, available as a book or online subscription.

LANG, JOSEPH

Current trademark established in 1821 and manufactured by Atkin, Grant & Lang, located in Hertfordshire, England. No current U.S. importation.

For individual model listings, please go to BlueBookOfGunValues.com/overflow.

LANGDON TACTICAL

Current custom semi-auto pistol, shotgun, and parts manufacturer located in Gilbert, AZ.

PISTOLS: SEMI-AUTO

Langdon Tactical offers pistols with several trigger job options and finishes. Models below reflect base pricing only. Langdon also manufactures some pistols in partnership with Beretta and Springfield Armory. Please contact the company directly for more information regarding those models.

Most current 92 Series models will have the following available options:
Add $185 for trigger job.
Add $359 for trigger job and Spartan Sights.
Add $435 for trigger job and NP3 coating.
Add $574 for trigger job, Spartan Sights, and NP3 coating.
Add $770 for Carry Bevel.
Add $909 for Carry Bevel and Spartan Sights.

92 ELITE LTT – 9mm Para. cal., SA/DA, 4.7 in. barrel, three 10, 15 (disc. 2020), or 18 shot Mec-Gar mags., beveled magwell and oversized mag. release button, M9A1 frame w/radiused trigger guard, Vertec/M9A3 slide w/front cocking serrations and beveled rear, spurless hammer and D Model hammer spring, LTT trigger job, stainless steel trigger, dovetail fiber optic front and square notch serrated rear sight, ultra thin VZ/LTT G10 grips w/stainless steel Hex Head Grip screws, G-Model decock only function, solid steel guide rod, black Cerakote finish, 34.8 oz.

MSR $999	$900	$800	$700	$600	$500	$400	$325	

* ***92 Elite LTT RDO*** – 9mm Para. cal., similar to 92 Elite LTT, except has LTT RDO slide with front and rear cocking serrations and optics mounting plate, optic height iron sights, and includes Trijicon RMR and Holosun optics mounting screws.

MSR $1,515	$1,375	$1,200	$1,025	$925	$750	$625	$475	

GRADING - PPGS™	100%	98%	95%	90%	80%	70%	60%	LAST MSR

92 ELITE LTT CENTURION – 9mm Para. cal., SA/DA, 4.25 in. barrel, three 10 or 18 shot Mec-Gar mags., beveled magwell and oversized mag. release button, M9A1 frame w/radiused trigger guard, shortened 92G Vertec slide w/front cocking serrations and beveled rear, skeletonized Elite II hammer, stainless steel trigger, dovetail fiber optic front and square notch serrated rear sight, ultra thin VZ/LTT G10 grips w/stainless steel Hex Head Grip screws, G-Model decock only function, solid steel guide rod, black Cerakote finish, 31.6 oz.

MSR $1,164	$1,050	$925	$800	$725	$575	$475	$375

* ***92 Elite LTT Centurion RDO*** – 9mm Para. cal., similar to 92 Elite LTT Centurion, except has LTT RDO slide with front and rear cocking serrations and optics mounting plate, optic height iron sights, includes Trijicon RMR and Holosun optics mounting screws.

MSR $1,515	$1,375	$1,200	$1,025	$925	$750	$625	$475

92 ELITE LTT COMPACT – 9mm Para. cal., SA/DA, 4.25 in. barrel, three 10 or 15 shot Mec-Gar mags., beveled magwell and oversized mag. release button, M9A1 frame w/radiused trigger guard, shortened 92G Vertec slide w/front cocking serrations and beveled rear, spurless hammer and D Model hammer spring, stainless steel trigger, dovetail fiber optic front and square notch serrated rear sight, ultra thin VZ/LTT G10 grips w/stainless steel Hex Head Grip screws, G-Model decock only function, solid steel guide rod, black Cerakote finish, 28.5 oz.

MSR $1,164	$1,050	$925	$800	$725	$575	$475	$375

* ***92 Elite LTT Compact RDO*** – 9mm Para. cal., similar to 92 Elite LTT Compact, except has LTT RDO slide with front and rear cocking serrations and optics mounting plate, optic height iron sights, includes Trijicon RMR and Holosun optics mounting screws.

MSR $1,515	$1,375	$1,200	$1,025	$925	$750	$625	$475

PX4 CARRY – 9mm Para. cal., full size PX4 frame, 4 in. CHF barrel, two 17 shot and one 20 shot mag., optional bevel cut, competition trigger group, LTT trigger job, Ameriglo night sights, applied Talon grips, stealth decocking levers, black or Sniper Grey Cerakote finish, optional ROBAR NP3 finish.

MSR $795	$700	$600	$550	$475	$400	$325	$250

Add $80 for Sniper Grey Cerakote slide.
Add $260 for trigger job and ROBAR NP3 finish.

PX4 COMPACT CARRY (MOD 4/MOD 5) – 9mm Para. cal., SA/DA, compact size frame, 3.2 in. CHF barrel, 15 shot mag., LTT trigger job, accessory rail, low profile slide stop, integral retractable lanyard loop, FDE (disc.) or Sniper Grey Cerakote finish.

MSR $845	$750	$650	$550	$500	$425	$350	$275

Add $75 for trigger job and OP trigger bar.
Add $365 for trigger job, NP3 finishing, cut and crowned barrel, and spurless hammer (previously called the MOD 5).
Add $425 for trigger job, NP3 finishing, cut and crowned barrel, spurless hammer, and OP trigger bar.

SPRINGFIELD ARMORY XDE LANGDON TACTICAL EDITION – 9mm Para. or .45 ACP cal., SA/DA, single stack, 3.3 or 3.8 in. barrel, three 8 shot flush mags., additional mag. flush cap, low-profile hammer, LTT trigger job, Ameriglo CAP sights, LTT engraved slide, Sniper Gray Cerakote finish.

MSR $738	$650	$600	$500	$450	$375	$300	$225

Add $30 for .45 ACP cal.

SHOTGUNS: SEMI-AUTO

LTT 1301 TACTICAL – 12 ga., 18.5 in. barrel, 7 shot mag., Magpul tactical shotgun stock w/Aridus Industries stock adapter, Magpul Zhukov handguard with M-LOK rail mount options, QDC sling mounting point options, black finish.

MSR $1,599	$1,360	$1,190	$1,020	$925	$750	$600	$525

Add $125 for Aridus CROM Aimpoint Micro or RMR mount.
Add $151 for Aridus Universal QDC side saddle.

LANTAC USA, LLC

Current AR-15 style pistol, rifle, and parts manufacturer established in 2013, located in Ft. Worth, TX.

Please refer to BlueBookOfGunValues.com to order the *Blue Book of AR-15s & Variations*, available as a book or online subscription.

GRADING - PPGS™	100%	98%	95%	90%	80%	70%	60%	LAST MSR

LAPORTE HOLDING

Previous shotgun manufacturer located in Biot, France until circa 2005.

Laporte Holding manufactured a unique reduced recoil 12 ga. O/U shotgun called the SwingTrap/Pro II, reducing recoil by 50% and noise by 75%. This was accomplished by the barrels being surrounded by a round shroud, which dissipated most of the recoil and noise. These guns had little or no importation into the U.S.

The company continues to manufacture trap throwers and related equipment.

LARM (ARMERIA DE MADRID, LA)

Current long gun manufacturer established during 1995, and currently located in Madrid, Spain. No current U.S. importation.

La Armeria manufactures high quality bolt action rifles based on the Johannsen magnum action in .270 Win., .30-06, 7mm Wby. Mag., 9.3x62mm, .375 H&H, .338 Win. Mag., .300 Win. Mag., or .416 Rigby cal. Single shot rifles are POR. Express double rifles come in a variety of options and configurations. La Armeria also manufactures high quality SxS shotguns in 12, 16, 20, 28 ga. or .410 bore, with fine exhibition quality wood and hand engraving in a variety of styles. Please contact the company directly for a price quotation, available options, and delivery time.

LARUE TACTICAL

Current AR-15 style firearm manufacturer established in 1980, located in Leander, TX.

RIFLES: SEMI-AUTO

LaRue Tactical also offers a complete line of both parts and accessories, including scope mounts, trigger assemblies, and cases.

6.5 GRENDEL FDE RIFLE – 6.5 Grendel cal., 18 in. barrel, LaRue TranQuilo muzzle brake, 5 or 17 shot mag., LaRue MBT-2S trigger, 13 in. handguard, includes LT-104 30mm scope mount, FDE finish, 7 lbs. 13 oz.

	100%	98%	95%	90%	80%	70%	60%	LAST MSR
MSR $1,999	$1,775	$1,575	$1,450	$1,325	$1,100	$875	$675	

COSTA SIGNATURE EDITION – 5.56 NATO cal., GIO, 16.1 in. barrel, SureFire muzzle brake, FDE KG GunKote finish, "COSTA LUDUS" logo engraved on left side of receiver, black parts and rail covers, first 500 units are match numbered on the upper and lower. Mfg. 2013-2015.

	100%	98%	95%	90%	80%	70%	60%	LAST MSR
	$4,995	$4,500	$4,000	$3,500	$3,000	$2,500	$2,000	$2,895

FDE LIMITED EDITION PREDATAR – 7.62 NATO cal., AR-15 style, GIO w/PST (Port Selector Technology), 16 in. heavy barrel, LaRue M308 TranQuilo muzzle brake, 1/10 twist, three 20 round mags., FDE Cerakote finish w/select black parts and GAP rail covers. Approx. 125 mfg. Disc.

Rarity precludes accurate pricing on this model.

OBR (OPTIMIZED BATTLE RIFLE) – 5.56 NATO (new 2011) or .308 Win./7.62 NATO cal., AR-15 style, GIO, 16.1, 18, or 20 in. barrel, A2 flash hider or TranQuilo muzzle device (new 2020), 20 shot box mag., flared magwell, Troy front and optional BUIS rear sight, A2 fixed (20 in. barrel only) or Retract Action Trigger (R.A.T.) stock, A-PEG grip, adj. gas block, detachable side rails, Mil-Std 1913 one-piece upper rail, black anodized finish, approx. 10 lbs.

	100%	98%	95%	90%	80%	70%	60%	LAST MSR
5.56 MSR $2,245	$1,975	$1,775	$1,625	$1,475	$1,250	$975	$775	
7.62 MSR $3,370	$2,975	$2,650	$2,450	$2,225	$1,875	$1,450	$1,150	

A variety of accessories are available on this model for additional cost.

PREDATAR – 5.56 NATO or .308 Win./7.62 NATO (new 2013) cal., GIO, 16.1 or 18 in. contoured stainless steel barrel, A2 flash hider or LaRue TranQuilo muzzle device (new 2021), 30 shot mag., 6-position Magpul (disc.) or LaRue R.A.T. stock, A-PEG grip, skeletonized handguard, quad rail forend, charging lever, forward assist, Geissele two-stage trigger, black phosphate finish, approx. 6 1/2 lbs. New mid-2011.

	100%	98%	95%	90%	80%	70%	60%	LAST MSR
5.56 MSR $1,807	$1,600	$1,425	$1,300	$1,200	$1,000	$775	$625	
7.62 MSR $2,932	$2,575	$2,325	$2,125	$1,925	$1,625	$1,275	$1,000	

A variety of accessories are available on this model for additional cost.

PREDATOBR – 5.56 NATO, 7.62 NATO, 6.5 Creedmoor, or .260 Rem. cal., GIO, 16.1, 18, 20, or 22 (6.5 Creedmoor/.260 Rem) in. threaded free float barrel, LaRue TranQuilo muzzle device (new 2021), 20 (7.62) or 30 (5.56) shot mag., LaRue MBT trigger, 6-pos. Retract Action Trigger (R.A.T.) stock, adj. gas block, billet aluminum upper and lower receivers, 3 Mil-Std 1913 rail sections. New 2014.

	100%	98%	95%	90%	80%	70%	60%	LAST MSR
MSR $3,370	$2,975	$2,650	$2,450	$2,225	$1,875	$1,475	$1,150	

Subtract $1,125 for 5.56 NATO cal.

A variety of accessories are available on this model for additional cost.

GRADING - PPGS™	100%	98%	95%	90%	80%	70%	60%	LAST MSR

UDE LIMITED EDITION PREDATOBR – 5.56 NATO cal., AR-15 style, GIO w/PST (Port Selector Technology), 16 in. barrel, LaRue M556 TranQuilo muzzle brake, 1:8 twist, two 30 round mags., black LaRue MBT trigger, UDE LaRue R.A.T. stock and A-PEG pistol grip, UDE GAP rail covers and index clips, UDE finish w/select black part. Approx. 125 mfg. numbered 001-125. Disc.

	$2,950	$2,625	$2,250	$2,050	$1,650	$1,350	$1,050	

LASERAIM ARMS, INC.

Previous distributor located in Little Rock, AR. Previously manufactured until 1999 in Thermopolis, WY. Laseraim Arms, Inc. was a division of Emerging Technologies, Inc.

PISTOLS: SEMI-AUTO

SERIES I – .40 S&W, .400 Cor-Bon (new 1998), .45 ACP, or 10mm cal., SA, 3 3/8 (Compact Model), 5, or 6 in. barrel with compensator, ambidextrous safety, all stainless steel metal parts are Teflon coated, beveled magwell, integral accessory mounts, 7 (.45 ACP) or 8 (10mm or .40 S&W) shot mag., 46 or 52 oz. Mfg. 1993-99.

	$325	$295	$265	$215	$185	$150	$125	*$349*

Add $120 for wireless laser combo (new 1997).

* ***Series I Compact*** – .40 S&W or .45 ACP cal., 3 3/8 in. non-ported slide and fixed sights. Mfg. 1993-99.

	$325	$295	$265	$215	$185	$150	$125	*$349*

Series I Illusion and Dream Team variations were made during 1993-94. Retail prices respectively were $650 and $695.

SERIES II – .40 S&W (disc. 1994), .45 ACP, or 10mm cal., SA, similar technical specs. as the Series I, except has non-reflective stainless steel finish, fixed or adj. sights, and 3 3/8 (Compact Model, .45 ACP only), 5, or 7 (.45 ACP only) in. non-compensated barrel, 37 or 43 oz. Mfg. 1993-1996.

	$485	$385	$300	$240	$210	$180	$155	*$550*

Series II Illusion and Dream Team variations were made during 1993-94. Retail prices respectively were $500 and $545.

SERIES III – .45 ACP cal., 5 in. ported barrel, SA, serrated slide, Hogue grips. Mfg. 1994-disc.

	$595	$465	$415	$375	$345	$310	$275	*$675*

SERIES IV – .45 ACP cal., 3 3/8 (Compact Model) or 5 in. ported barrel, SA, serrated slide, diamond checkered wood grips. Mfg. 1994-disc.

	$550	$450	$400	$360	$330	$300	$265	*$625*

LASALLE

Previous manufacturer located in France.

SHOTGUNS

SLIDE ACTION SHOTGUN – 12 or 20 ga., 26, 28, or 30 in. barrels, various chokes, alloy frame, checkered pistol grip stock.

	$250	$225	$200	$175	$150	$125	$100	

SEMI-AUTO SHOTGUN – 12 ga., 26, 28, or 30 in. barrels, various chokes, gas operated, checkered pistol grip stock.

	$300	$275	$250	$225	$200	$175	$150	

LATEK LTD.

Current manufacturer established 1994, located in Kharkov, Ukraine. No current U.S. importation.

Latek's current brand names include: Altay, Churchill, and Safari. Please contact the manufacturer directly for more information.

LAUER CUSTOM WEAPONRY

Current manufacturer of DuraCoat® firearm finishes and custom AR-15 style rifles located in Chippewa Falls, WI.

Please refer to BlueBookOfGunValues.com to order the *Blue Book of AR-15s & Variations*, available as a book or online subscription.

LAUGO ARMS

Current semi-auto pistol manufacturer established in 2017, located in Prague, Czech Republic. Currently distributed/imported by Lancer Systems beginning 2019, located in Allentown, PA.

Laugo Arms manufactures a unique line of pistols called the Alien Pistol.

GRADING - PPGS™	100%	98%	95%	90%	80%	70%	60%	LAST MSR

PISTOLS: SEMI-AUTO

ALIEN PISTOL – gas piston delayed blowback, modular design, 4.8 in. fixed barrel, 17 shot mag., interchangeable top rail, 2.47 lbs. Importation began 2019.

Please contact the importer directly for pricing and U.S. availability on this model.

ALIEN PISTOL SIGNATURE EDITION – 9mm Para. cal., gas piston delayed blowback, modular design, 4.8 in. fixed barrel, three 17 shot mags., enhanced magwell, two interchangeable top rails, one with adj. competition sights, one with an included Laugo 6 MOA red dot sight, Elornis adj. Competition holster, cleaning kit, custom hard case, 2.2 lbs. Importation began 2019.

MSR $5,000	$4,500	$3,940	$3,375	N/A	N/A	N/A	N/A	

These pistols were the first 500 imported into the U.S. by Lancer Systems, and feature the signature of the designer, Jan Lucanksy, on the frame.

LAURONA ZABALA

Previous trademark from 2011-2013, and manufactured by Armas Eibar, S.A.L., located in Eibar, Spain. Previous trademark was Laurona from 1941-2011. During 2010, Laurona was absorbed by Norica, and the new company name was Norica Laurona. Previously imported until 1993 by Galaxy Imports located in Victoria, TX.

For individual model listings, please go to BlueBookOfGunValues.com/overflow.

LAW ENFORCEMENT ORDNANCE CORPORATION

Previous manufacturer located in Ridgway, PA until 1990.

SHOTGUNS: SEMI-AUTO

STRIKER-12 – 12 ga., 12 shot rotary mag., 18 1/4 in. alloy shrouded barrel with PG extension, folding or fixed tactical design stock, 9.2 lbs., limited mfg. 1986-1990.

	$1,000	$875	$750	$675	$600	$550	$500	*$725*

Add $200 for folding stock.

Add $100 for Marine variation ("Metal Life" finish).

Earlier variations were imported and available to law enforcement agencies only. In 1987, manufacture was started in PA and these firearms could be sold to individuals (18 in. barrel only). This design was originally developed in South Rhodesia.

LAYKE TACTICAL

Current manufacturer of AR-15 style rifles and pistols established in 2014, located in Phoenix, AZ.

Please refer to BlueBookOfGunValues.com to order the *Blue Book of AR-15s & Variations*, available as a book or online subscription.

HARRY LAWSON LLC

Current custom gunsmith established during 1965, located in Tucson, AZ. Consumer direct sales.

Harry Lawson is well-known for custom stock work. This company also customizes its own line of sporting rifles, most feature an innovative thumbhole stock design. Please contact the company directly for more information regarding customized models, pricing on stocking services, and related gunsmithing services.

RIFLES: BOLT ACTION

Harry Lawson manufactures the 650 Series in both Mountaineer and Ultralite configurations. These bolt action rifles are custom order, and can be built on a customer supplied Remington 700 barreled action or the action can be purchased separately from $650 - $850. With a customer supplied action, prices start at $3,115 for Grade II XX wood. Prices start at $2,665 for Grade II XX wood.

Current MSR is $4,730 for a Lawson 650 Series Weatherby Mark V factory barreled action in .300 Wby. Mag. cal. or smaller with Grade 5 EF French or claro walnut stock, or $4,080 for a similar gun with a Remington 700 action.

LAZZERONI ARMS COMPANY

Current manufacturer located in Tucson, AZ since 1995. Dealer and consumer direct sales through FFL.

RIFLES: BOLT ACTION

Lazzeroni ammunition is precision loaded in Lazzeroni's Tucson facility under rigid tolerances. All ammunition is sealed for absolute weatherproofing. Lazzeroni proprietary calibers are already established as being extremely effective at long distances.

GRADING - PPGS™	100%	98%	95%	90%	80%	70%	60%	LAST MSR

SAKO MODEL TRG-S – 7.21 Firebird (.284, new 2002) or 7.82 Warbird (.308) cal., Sako TRG action with free floating 26 in. barrel, 3 shot detachable mag., fully adj. trigger, and scope rings, 7.9 lbs. Mfg. 1999-2004.

	$825	$700	$600	$495	$430	$365	$315	*$900*

Add $400 for metal finish upgrade or $1,200 for metal finish upgrade with Burris 4-16x50mm mil-dot scope.

SAVAGE 16LZ – 7.21 Tomahawk (.284, disc. 2001) or 7.82 Patriot (.308) cal., stainless steel action with 2 locking lugs, 24 in. stainless barrel, detachable box mag., injection molded composite stock, 6.8 lbs. Mfg. 2001-2004.

	$475	$400	$350	$285	$250	$215	$185	*$550*

Add $100 for left-hand action.
Add $400 for Cabela's 4.5-14x42mm scope.

MODEL 700ST – various Lazzeroni cals., Rem. M-700 action, features remachined bolt face, squared recoil lug and receiver, mag. and follower are replaced with Lazzeroni style units, steel (disc.) or stainless steel (new 1999) action, blue steel or stainless steel 24 in. barrel. Mfg. 1998-99.

	$2,150	$1,750	$1,425	$1,255	$1,020	$885	$715	*$2,395*

MODEL 2000 SERIES – available in either Lazzeroni short magnum (6.17 Spitfire - .243 cal., 6.71 Phantom - .264 cal., 7.21 Tomahawk - .284 cal., 7.82 Patriot - .308 cal., 8.59 Galaxy - .338 cal., or 10.57 Maverick - .416 cal.) or Lazzeroni long magnums (6.53 Scramjet - .257 cal., 7.21 Firebird - .284 cal., 7.82 Warbird - .308 cal., 8.59 Titan - .338 cal., or 10.57 Meteor - .416 cal.), features precision machined steel (disc.) or stainless steel (new 1999) receiver, helically fluted bolt with heavy duty extractor, stainless steel match barrel with integral muzzle brake, adj. benchrest trigger, matte finish metal, 3-position firing pin safety on most models (new 1999), 2 or 3 (new 1999) shot internal mag., various stock configurations. Mfg. 1996-2005.

* ***Model L2000ST*** – features 27 in. barrel with conventional fiberglass stock, 8.1 lbs.

	$5,250	$4,100	$3,175	$2,650	$2,300	$1,950	$1,650	*$5,899*

* ***Model L2000ST-28*** – .308 Warbird cal., shoots 130 grain BarnesX boattail at 4,000 fps, 28 in. stainless steel fluted barrel, includes Schmidt & Bender 4-16x50mm scope, stainless action, black synthetic stock, approx. 8.3 lbs. Mfg. 1999-2001.

	$5,875	$5,250	$4,750	$4,250	$3,600	$3,100	$2,650	*$6,310*

This model was advertised as the flattest shooting hunting rifle at that time, and was at zero at 100, 200, and 300 yards.

* ***Model L2000ST-W*** – 27 in. barrel with conventional black wood laminate stock. Mfg. 1996 only.

	$4,400	$4,050	$3,600	$2,550	$2,200	$1,925	$1,625	*$4,795*

* ***Model L2000ST-WF Package*** – features 27 in. barrel with one conventional fiberglass and one black wood laminate stock. Disc. 1997.

	$4,875	$4,450	$4,050	$2,650	$2,400	$2,100	$1,750	*$5,295*

* ***Model L2000DG*** – .375 Saturn or .416 Meteor cal. only, features Fibergrain stock finish, removable muzzle brake, 3 shot mag., 24 in. barrel, includes sling swivels, 10.1 lbs. Mfg. 1998-2005.

	$5,575	$4,850	$4,350	$3,275	$2,800	$2,500	$2,000	*$6,199*

* ***Model L2000LLT*** – .257 Scramjet, .284 Firebird, .308 Warbird, or .338 Titan cal., lightweight variation with 26 in. barrel and detachable muzzle brake, 4 shot mag., right or left-hand action, 7.4 lbs. Mfg. 2004-2005.

	$5,400	$4,750	$4,250	$3,175	$2,750	$2,450	$1,950	*$5,899*

* ***Model L2000SA*** – .243 Spitfire, .264 Phantom, .284 Tomahawk, .308 Patriot, .338 Galaxy, .358 Eagle, .375 Hellcat, or .416 Maverick cal., short action cals. only, lightweight mountain configuration with 24 in. fluted barrel, 6.8 lbs. Mfg. 1998-2004.

	$4,750	$4,350	$3,800	$2,600	$2,350	$2,050	$1,750	*$5,499*

* ***Model L2000SLR*** – features 28 in. extra heavy fluted barrel and conventional fiberglass stock, not chambered in .338 Titan. Disc. 1999.

	$3,775	$3,400	$2,975	$2,600	$2,300	$2,000	$1,800	*$4,195*

* ***Model L2000SP*** – 25 in. fluted barrel, thumbhole fiberglass stock, 7.8 lbs. Disc. 2004.

	$4,750	$4,350	$3,800	$2,600	$2,350	$2,050	$1,750	*$5,499*

GRADING - PPGS™	100%	98%	95%	90%	80%	70%	60%	LAST MSR

* ***Model L2000SP-W*** – 23 in. barrel, thumbhole black wood laminate stock.

	$4,400	$4,050	$3,600	$2,550	$2,200	$1,925	$1,625	*$4,795*

* ***Model L2000SP-FW Package*** – features 23 in. barrel with one thumbhole fiberglass and one black wood laminate thumbhole stock. Disc. 1997.

	$4,875	$4,450	$4,050	$2,650	$2,400	$2,100	$1,750	*$5,295*

MODEL L2005 GLOBAL HUNTER SERIES – available in short magnum (7.21 Tomahawk - .284 cal., 7.82 Patriot - .308 cal., 8.59 Galaxy - .338 cal., 9.53 Hellcat - .375 cal., 10.57 Maverick - .416 cal., or 12.04 Lilmufu - .475 cal.) and long magnum (6.53 Scramjet - .257 cal., 7.21 Firebird - .284 cal., 7.82 Warbird - .308 cal., 8.59 Titan - .338 cal., 9.53 Saturn - .357 cal., 10.57 Meteor - .416 cal., or 12.04 Bibamufu - .475 cal.), right or left-hand action, 22-28 in. stainless steel receiver, match grade fluted or unfluted barrel with muzzle brake, 4 shot mag., Jewell competition trigger, slim line graphite composite stock, diamond fluted or helical cut bolt shaft, titanium firing pin, Limbsaver recoil pad (except Dangerous Game models), approx. 6.1-8.7 lbs. Mfg. 2005-disc.

* ***Model L2005SLT*** – 7.21 Tomahawk - .284 cal., 7.82 Patriot - .308 cal., or 8.59 Galaxy - .338 cal., right or left-hand Short Magnum Light, stainless steel receiver, match grade fluted or unfluted barrel with muzzle brake, 4 shot mag., Jewell competition trigger, slim line graphite composite stock, diamond fluted or helical cut bolt shaft, titanium firing pin, Limbsaver recoil pad, approx. 6.1 lbs. Mfg. 2005-circa 2013.

	$4,250	$3,700	$3,200	$2,900	$2,350	$1,900	$1,500	*$5,000*

* ***Model L2005LTH/L2005LLT/L2005LLR*** – 6.53 Scramjet - .257 cal., 7.21 Firebird - .284 cal., 7.82 Warbird - .308 cal., or 8.59 Titan - .338 long magnum cal., right or left-hand action available in Long Magnum Light, Long Magnum Thumbhole, or Special Long Range (Warbird cal. only) configuration, 25 (L2005LLT), 26 (L2005LTH), or 27-28 (L2005LLR) in. stainless steel receiver, match grade fluted or unfluted barrel with muzzle brake, 4 shot mag., Jewell competition trigger, slim line graphite composite stock with (L2005LTH) or w/o (L2005LLT) thumbhole, diamond fluted or helical cut bolt shaft, titanium firing pin, Limbsaver recoil pad, 7.4 - 7.7 lbs. Mfg. 2005-disc.

	$5,400	$4,750	$4,250	$3,175	$2,750	$2,450	$1,950	*$5,900*

* ***Model L2005SDG*** – 9.53 Hellcat - .375 cal., 10.57 Maverick - .416 cal., or 12.04 Lilmufu - .475 cal., right or left-hand, Short Magnum Dangerous Game, 22 in. stainless steel receiver, match grade fluted or unfluted barrel with muzzle brake, 4 shot mag., Jewell competition trigger, slim line graphite composite stock, diamond fluted or helical cut bolt shaft, titanium firing pin, 7.6 lbs. Mfg. 2005-circa 2013.

	$5,575	$4,850	$4,350	$3,275	$2,800	$2,500	$2,000	*$6,199*

* ***Model L2005LDG*** – 9.53 Saturn - .375 cal., 10.57 Meteor - .416 cal., or 12.04 Bibamufu - .475 cal., right or left-hand, Long Magnum Dangerous Game, 24 in. stainless steel receiver, match grade fluted or unfluted barrel with muzzle brake, 4 shot mag., Jewell competition trigger, slim line graphite composite stock, diamond fluted or helical cut bolt shaft, titanium firing pin, 8.7 lbs. Mfg. 2005-disc.

	$5,575	$4,850	$4,350	$3,275	$2,800	$2,500	$2,000	*$6,199*

MODEL L2012/M2012 SERIES – available in long magnum 6.53 Scramjet - .257 cal., 7.21 Firebird - .284 cal., 7.82 Warbird - .308 cal., 8.59 Titan - .338 cal., 9.53 Saturn - .357 cal., or 10.57 Meteor - .416 cal., right or left-hand action, stainless steel, match grade fluted or unfluted barrel with removable Vais muzzle brake, chrome moly receiver, heavy-duty extractor, Jewell competition trigger or Timney (new circa 2016), aluminum alloy trigger guard, slim line graphite composite stock, Limbsaver recoil pad, titanium 3-pos. firing pin safety w/bolt lock (except for Model 2012LTH), diamond fluted or helical cut bolt shaft, approx. 7.3-10.9 lbs. Mfg. 2010-disc.

* ***Model L2012LDG*** – 7.82 Warbird - .308 cal. or 8.59 Titan - .338 cal., right-hand only, Long Magnum Dangerous Game, stainless steel, match grade fluted or unfluted barrel with removable Vais muzzle brake, chrome moly receiver, heavy-duty extractor, Jewell competition trigger, aluminum alloy trigger guard, slim line graphite composite stock, Limbsaver recoil pad, titanium 3-pos. firing pin safety w/bolt lock, diamond fluted or helical cut bolt shaft. Mfg. 2011-disc.

	$6,800	$5,950	$5,100	$4,600	$3,750	$3,050	$2,400	*$8,000*

* ***Model L2012LLT*** – 6.53 Scramjet - .257 cal., 7.21 Firebird - .284 cal., 7.82 Warbird - .308 cal., or 8.59 Titan - .338 cal., right or left-hand action, Long Magnum Light, 26 in. stainless steel barrel with Vais muzzle brake, 4 shot mag., Jewell trigger, alum. alloy floorplate/trigger guard assembly, custom molded graphite/composite stock designs, Limbsaver recoil pad, 3-position safety, one-piece diamond fluted bolt shaft, black nitride or NP3 finish on all metal parts, 7.3 lbs. Mfg. 2011-disc.

	$5,100	$4,450	$3,800	$3,450	$2,800	$2,300	$1,800	*$6,000*

GRADING - PPGS™	100%	98%	95%	90%	80%	70%	60%	LAST MSR

* ***Model 2012 Mountain Lite Long Range (L2012LT/M2012LT-MTLR)*** – 6.53 Scramjet - .257 cal. (new 2016), 7.21 Firebird - .284 cal., 7.82 Warbird - .308 cal., right or left-hand (new circa 2016), Long Magnum Mountain Lite, 26 in. fluted barrel with muzzle brake, Vais muzzle brake, 4 shot mag., steel, Jewell or Timney trigger, no sights, textured black composite stock, 7.3 lbs. New 2015.

	100%	98%	95%	90%	80%	70%	60%	LAST MSR
MSR $6,000	$5,100	$4,465	$3,825	$3,470	$2,800	$2,300	$2,000	

* ***Model L2012LTH/M2012LTH-XTLR*** – 6.53 Scramjet - .257 cal. (disc.), 7.21 Firebird - .284 cal., 7.82 Warbird - .308 cal., 8.59 Titan - .338 cal., or 9.53 Saturn - .357 cal., right-hand only, extra long range, Long Magnum Thumbhole, 25 or 26 (M2012LTH) in. stainless steel barrel with muzzle brake, 4 shot mag., Jewell trigger, graphite/composite thumbhole stock, 20 MOA Picatinny style rail, 34mm or 30mm ring sets, 7.7-7.9 lbs. New 2011.

	100%	98%	95%	90%	80%	70%	60%	LAST MSR
MSR $7,000	$5,950	$5,200	$4,465	$4,050	$3,275	$2,680	$2,325	

* ***Model L2012SP/M2012SP-XTLR*** – 7.82 Warbird - .308 cal., 8.59 Titan - .338 cal., or 9.53 Saturn - .357 cal. (new 2016), right or left-hand action, extra long range (new 2016), Long Magnum Sporter, 28 in. heavy contour stainless steel barrel, 5 or 6 shot detachable mag., Jewell trigger, composite stock, Limbsaver recoil pad, 20 MOA Picatinny style rail, 34mm or 30mm rings, 8.8 lbs. New circa 2011.

	100%	98%	95%	90%	80%	70%	60%	LAST MSR
MSR $7,500	$6,400	$5,600	$4,800	$4,350	$3,500	$2,850	$2,250	

* ***Model L2012SP/M2012SP-XTLR DGHB*** – 10.57 Meteor - .416 cal., right or left-hand action, Sporter Dangerous Game, 24 in. heavy contour stainless steel, match grade barrel, Vais muzzle brake, 4 shot detachable mag. (extra long 3 shot internal mag. w/flooplate), Jewell trigger, composite stock, Limbsaver recoil pad, heavy duty Picatinny style rail, 34mm or 30mm rings, one-piece diamond fluted bolt shaft, 9.5 lbs. New circa 2011.

	100%	98%	95%	90%	80%	70%	60%	LAST MSR
MSR $7,500	$6,400	$5,600	$4,800	$4,350	$3,500	$2,850	$2,250	

* ***Model L2012TCT*** – 7.82 Warbird - .308 cal. or 8.59 Titan - .338 cal., right-hand only, Long Magnum Tactical, stainless steel, match grade fluted or unfluted barrel with removable Vais muzzle brake, chrome moly receiver, Jewell competition trigger, aluminum alloy trigger guard, slim line graphite composite stock, Limbsaver recoil pad, titanium 3-pos. firing pin safety w/bolt lock, diamond fluted or helical cut bolt shaft, Picatinny rail, black finish, 10.9 lbs. Mfg. 2011-2013.

	100%	98%	95%	90%	80%	70%	60%	LAST MSR
	$6,800	$5,950	$5,100	$4,600	$3,750	$3,050	$2,400	*$8,000*

LEAD STAR ARMS

Current AR-15 style pistol and rifle manufacturer located in West Columbia, SC.

Please refer to BlueBookOfGunValues.com to order the *Blue Book of AR-15s & Variations*, available as a book or online subscription.

LEADER ARMS TECHNOLOGY

Previous long arms manufacturer established in 1991, and located in Trabzon, Turkey, with offices located in Ankara, Turkey. No current U.S. importation.

SHOTGUNS

Leader Arms Technology manufactured single shot, O/U, slide action, semi-auto, and lever action shotguns under the Alpha Arms trademark.

LEBEAU-COURALLY

Current manufacturer established during 1865 and located in Liege, Belgium. Bespoke guns only - customers need to contact the factory directly for availability and pricing. Previously imported by Griffin & Howe, located in Bernardsville, NJ, and William Larkin Moore, located in Scottsdale, AZ until circa 2017. Previously imported by Heirloom Armes, located in Howard Lake, MN.

Lebeau-Courally manufactures only best quality rifles and shotguns. Approximately 30 are manufactured annually. Base prices listed do not include engraving on some models, and also do not include VAT (approx. 20%). Please contact the importer directly for a firm quotation on a Lebeau-Courally rifle or shotgun.

RIFLES: BOLT ACTION

Currently, Lebeau-Courally is building a bolt action rifle using a Mauser action, available in most calibers, and built to customer's specifications. Please contact the manufacturer directly for more information and pricing on this model, including engraving options.

RIFLES: O/U

VICOMTE – various plains game and dangerous game cals., top-of-the-line model.

Please contact the manufacturer directly for a current price quotation on this model.

RIFLES: SxS

AFRIQUE BOXLOCK EJECTOR - various cals., Anson & Deeley boxlock, ejectors, select French walnut stock, built per customer's specifications. Disc.

ARDENNES BOXLOCK EJECTOR - various cals., Anson & Deeley boxlock, ejectors, select French walnut stock, built per customer's specifications. Disc.

BIG FIVE SIDELOCK EJECTOR EXPRESS RIFLE - various dangerous game cals., top-of-the-line model.

Please contact the manufacturer directly for availability and pricing on this model.

DAUPHIN SIDELOCK EJECTOR EXPRESS RIFLE - various plains game cals., features light construction, chopper lump barrels, reinforced action, select French walnut stock, quarter rib with ramp front sight, engraving not included, approx. 8 lbs.

Please contact the manufacturer directly for availability and pricing on this model.

RIFLES: SINGLE SHOT

ARCHIDUC - various cals., best quality, top lever break open sidelock action with ejector, built per customer's specifications.

Please contact the manufacturer directly for availability and pricing on this model.

CHEVALIER - various cals., falling block takedown action.

Please contact the manufacturer directly for availability and pricing on this model.

SHOTGUNS: O/U

BARON - 12, 16, 20, 28, or .410 ga., several options available per individual custom order.

Please contact the manufacturer Moore directly for availability and pricing on this model.

BOSS VERREES - 12, 16, or 20 ga., top-of-the line sidelock ejector model.

Please contact the manufacturer directly for a current price quotation on this model.

BOXLOCK WITH SIDEPLATES - various gauges, black pewter or case colored frame and sideplates, gold inlays around perimeter of receiver. New 2000.

Please contact the manufacturer directly for availability and pricing on this model.

SIDELOCK - 12, 20, 28, or .410 ga., Greener locking system.

Currently, this model is POR.

VERSAILLES - 12, 16, or 20 ga., includes ornamental engraving, top-of-the line sidelock. Disc.

Last MSR was $30,000.

SHOTGUNS: SxS

Older mfg. Lebeau-Courally shotguns have a completely different action and locking system than the newer models.

PRINCE SIDELOCK EJECTOR - 12, 16, 20, 28 ga., or .410 bore, choice of classic or rounded action, 26, 28, or 30 in. chopper lump barrels, select French walnut stock, base price includes fine scroll full coverage engraving, choice of numerous engraving patterns (optional), double triggers.

Please contact the manufacturer directly for availability and pricing on this model.

SOLOGNE BOXLOCK EJECTOR - 12, 16, or 20 ga., choice of classic or rounded action, with or without sideplates, select French walnut stock, choice of numerous engraving patterns (optional), 26, 28, or 30 in. barrels, double trigger.

Please contact the manufacturer directly for availability and pricing on this model.

LECHNER & JUNGL GES.m.b.H.

Current manufacturer established circa 1821 and located in Graz, Austria.

Lechner & Jungl's history actually dates back to 1821, but the company started building guns circa 1874. In 1912, the demand for hunting and sporting guns grew and the company made a change of ownership to Hugo Kothe. Hugo's son, Gottlieb Kothe assumed ownership after his father in 1972 and continued to manufacture high-quality handmade firearms. All rifles and shotguns are high quality and are available in a wide variety of configurations, including Drillings, Vierlings, and Combination Guns. Since each gun is built per custom order, please contact the company directly for more information, including price, availability, options, and delivery time.

Lechner & Jungl also has a store in Graz stocked with a complete line of hunting, shooting, and sporting accessories.

LEE ARMS COMPANY

Previous rifle manufacturer with headquarters in New Haven, CT and manufacturing in Milwaukee, WI.

Please refer to the Remington Arms Company listing for those rifles (Models 1879, 1882, 1885, and 1899) produced by Lee Arms Company under contract to Remington.

100%	98%	95%	90%	80%	70%	60%	50%	40%	30%	20%	10%

LEFEVER ARMS COMPANY

Previous shotgun manufacturer located in Syracuse, NY circa 1885-1916. The company was purchased by Ithaca Gun Co. and moved to Ithaca, NY after 1916.

Lefever Arms Co. factory letters, information, and current factory letter pricing (for production between 1921-1939) may be obtained through the Cody Firearms Records Office at the Buffalo Bill Center of the West.

DOUBLE RIFLES

Lefever, along with some of his earlier partnerships, produced a limited number of high quality double rifles. These doubles are exceptionally rare and should be evaluated by an expert to determine price. Recent prices paid for steel barreled Lefever double rifles range from $30,000-$75,000.

SHOTGUNS: SxS

The Lefever was the first commercially successful hammerless double barrel shotgun made in America. They were made in Syracuse, NY from 1885-1916, at which time the company was acquired by Ithaca Gun Company. Ithaca made the Lefever after 1916. In 1921, the Box Lock Nitro Special was introduced and in 1934, the Lefever Grade A was introduced. Production of Lefever guns ceased in 1948.

The practice of assigning new serial numbers to guns returned to the factory for alterations absorbed approximately 5,000 numbers. Also, the serial number series started with 5,000, so approx. 62,000 guns were built.

The following is a percentage breakdown of gauges made between 1885-1916 (totaling 100%): 8 ga.-1/2%, 10 ga.-25%, 12 ga.-60%, 14 ga.-1/2%, 16 ga.-8%, 20 ga.-6%. Total serial numbers used was approx. 72,000 during this period. Damascus specimens of this trademark are worth approximately the same if in 10% or better original condition as their fluid steel barrel counterparts because of the rarity and desirability factors. Hammer guns are valued the same as Damascus hammerless guns (grade for grade). Subtract 10%-30% on values with respective condition factors 50%-10%. Prices shown for 90% and up condition are very difficult to evaluate and are meant as a guide only - any Lefever shotgun in over 95% is rare and hard to evaluate. Prices shown below are for factory original examples-guns with restoration of any kind will bring 10%-80% less. Lefever Arms Company guns with more modern stock dimensions (length of pull greater than 13-1/2 in. and drop at heel of 3 in. or less) will be more desirable and are reflected in the pricing below. Subtract 10%-40% for stock dimensions outside of those mentioned above. Add 30%-50% for auto ejectors on the following models, depending on original condition (designated with an "E" suffix).

SIDEPLATE MODELS – 10, 12, 16, or 20 ga., 26-32 in. barrels, any choke, boxlock action (even though model nomenclature referred to sidelock model), cocking indicators on all but DS and DSE grades, double triggers standard, checkered straight or pistol grip stock, auto ejectors designated by letter E after grade, most lower grades marked at water table near serial number. Mfg. 1885-1919.

Add 50% for 16 ga.
Add 100% for 20 ga.
Add 200-300% for 8 ga.
Add 20% for SST.
Prices for guns in top condition factors are extremely desirable and bring huge premiums.

*** *Model I Grade***

N/A	$2,350	$1,700	$1,050	$850	$680	$620	$550	$510	$340	$275	$220

Add 10% if the gun has a dolls head rib extension and cocking indicators.

*** *Model DS Grade***

N/A	$2,500	$1,775	$1,100	$925	$775	$680	$600	$425	$340	$275	$220

*** *Model H Grade***

N/A	$4,250	$2,125	$1,200	$800	$750	$550	$490	$340	$325	$300	$220

*** *Model G Grade***

N/A	$4,250	$2,550	$1,475	$1,050	$800	$600	$525	$375	$340	$300	$220

*** *Model F Grade***

N/A	$5,525	$3,400	$2,340	$1,785	$1,400	$1,200	$1,000	$850	$500	$475	$400

*** *Model E Grade***

N/A	$10,200	$7,650	$5,525	$5,100	$4,000	$2,750	$1,425	$1,150	$900	$750	$625

100%	98%	95%	90%	80%	70%	60%	50%	40%	30%	20%	10%
* ***Model D Grade***											
N/A	$14,250	$9,500	$8,075	$6,175	$4,950	$3,825	$1,800	$1,375	$1,075	$900	$675
* ***Model C Grade***											
N/A	$20,900	$14,725	$11,400	$7,125	$5,850	$5,175	$4,400	$3,600	$2,925	$2,525	$2,200
* ***Model B Grade***											
N/A	N/A	$30,875	$23,750	$16,625	$11,250	$9,300	$7,375	$6,250	$4,500	$3,375	$2,750
* ***Model A Grade*** – auto ejectors standard.											
N/A	N/A	$42,750	$35,150	$27,550	$20,700	$14,850	$12,600	$9,000	$7,200	$4,950	$4,050
* ***Model AA Grade*** – auto ejectors standard.											
N/A	N/A	$54,625	$39,900	$37,050	$24,750	$20,250	$15,750	$11,250	$9,000	$7,875	$7,200

* ***Model Optimus Grade*** – auto ejectors standard.

Prices typically range from $40,000-$85,000, depending on original condition. Later steel barreled examples tend to bring more than earlier Damascus barreled guns.

Buyers should be very cautious of upgraded versions of the Optimus Grade being sold as original, many more upgrades come to market than originals. Total production during all time periods likely around 25 original guns that are marked "Optimus" Grade Guns. More guns are of "Optimus Quality" but are not marked as to the grade. These guns should be evaluated individually and will bring similar prices to guns marked "Optimus".

* ***Model Thousand Dollar Grade*** – auto ejectors standard.

Only one known to exist - last paid price at approx. $250,000.

GRADING - PPGS™	100%	98%	95%	90%	80%	70%	60%	LAST MSR

NITRO SPECIAL – 12, 16, 20 ga., or .410 bore, 26-32 in. barrels, various chokes, boxlock, extractors, checkered pistol grip stock. Mfg. 1921-48.

12 ga.	$580	$520	$460	$360	$315	$280	$240
16 ga.	$710	$660	$580	$520	$460	$380	$320
20 ga.	$980	$880	$780	$700	$620	$540	$460
.410 bore	$2,800	$2,520	$2,240	$1,960	$1,720	$1,375	$1,120

Add 10% for ST.

GRADE A FIELD MODEL – 12, 16, 20 ga., or .410 bore, 26-32 in. barrels, various chokes, boxlock, checkered pistol grip stock. Mfg. 1934-42.

12 ga.	$880	$780	$700	$640	$580	$525	$460
16 ga.	$1,025	$900	$760	$700	$625	$540	$480
20 ga.	$1,320	$1,150	$1,000	$800	$700	$625	$540
.410 bore	$3,200	$2,850	$2,475	$2,200	$1,950	$1,725	$1,375

Add 33% for auto ejectors.

Add 10% for ST.

GRADE A SKEET MODEL – similar to Grade A, with 26 in. skeet bore barrels, auto ejector, single trigger and beavertail forearm standard.

12 ga.	$1,325	$1,160	$1,025	$860	$750	$650	$550
16 ga.	$1,600	$1,400	$1,175	$1,000	$860	$775	$640
20 ga.	$2,150	$1,850	$1,575	$1,350	$1,200	$1,000	$800
.410 bore (Very Rare)	$6,800	$6,400	$5,200	$3,200	$3,000	$2,600	$2,000

SHOTGUNS: SINGLE BARREL

TRAP GUN – 12 ga. only, 30 or 32 in. VR barrel, full choke, boxlock, auto ejector, checkered pistol grip stock. Disc. 1942.

$340	$280	$200	$175	$160	$140	$120

LONG RANGE FIELD – 12, 16, 20 ga., or .410 bore, 26-32 in. barrel, boxlock, extractor, checkered pistol grip stock. Disc. 1942.

$320	$280	$235	$210	$180	$135	$110

100%	98%	95%	90%	80%	70%	60%	50%	40%	30%	20%	10%

SPECIAL ORDER SHOTGUNS

Lefever provided clients with the option of having guns made by special request. In doing so, the only limit appears to have been budget and imagination. Special Order guns are extremely rare and hold no direct model designation due to the bespoke nature of each firearm. These guns are highly prized by collectors and prices vary widely with some of the more elaborate examples bringing up to $100,000. It is important for a buyer to have these guns assessed by an expert to determine value and authenticity.

LEFEVER, D.M.

Previous manufacturer circa 1901-1906. Company names and locations have been D.M. Lefever & Sons, Syracuse, NY (1901), D.M. Lefever, Sons & Co., Syracuse, NY (1901-1902), D.M. Lefever Gun Mfg., Defiance, OH (1903-1904), and D.M. Lefever Co., Bowling Green, OH (1905-1906).

"Uncle Dan Lefever" founded the Lefever Arms Co. in 1884. He left the company in 1901 to found the above listed companies. While all were short-lived, the last was dissolved in 1906 the year of his death. Lefever Arms Co. continued manufacturing shotguns until sold to Ithaca Gun Co. in 1916. Ithaca assembled the Lefever gun until circa 1921, when they started building the "Nitro Special".

SHOTGUNS

"Uncle Dan" Lefever, founder of Lefever Arms, designed and manufactured the first breech loading double hammerless shotgun made in the U.S. Production started in 1872 and continued in the Syracuse, NY plant until he sold his interest in the Lefever Arms Company during the early 1900s. He then moved to Ohio and started another factory under the name D.M. Lefever & Son. After his death a few years later the Ohio factory was closed, while his old company (Lefever Arms Co.) continued manufacturing Lefevers until being sold to Ithaca Gun Company in 1916. From that point, Lefever Arms Co. was a branch of Ithaca and continued to make shotguns until shortly after WWII.

Total production on D.M. Lefever shotguns between 1901-1904 totaled less than 1,200. Because of their inherent rarity, values listed show only 10%-80% condition specimens. D.M. Lefever specimens are so rare in 80%+ condition that prices cannot be accurately ascertained. Values jump dramatically at the high end.

On all Lefevers, the overall condition is so important to its value. Having a competent Lefever gunsmith check out the gun prior to purchasing is important. Also note that many times the barrels have been cut back to open up the shot pattern. And this affects the value of the gun considerably. The barrels should be exactly even lengths from 24-32 in. Cut barrels reduce a gun's value by 2/3. These guns seem to be heavily prone to shade tree gunsmiths and finding one with fine original condition screws is rare and hard to find. These specimens will bring a large premium to collectors.

Also a note to all Lefever buyers: there seems to be a supply of faked and upgraded Lefevers on the market from time to time. Research and caution is recommended when purchasing the higher grades.

The publisher would like to express his thanks to Mr. Josh Loewensteiner for his contributions in this section.

SHOTGUNS: SxS

Add 50% for 16 ga. (assuming original condition).
Add 100% for 20 ga. (assuming original condition).

NEW LEFEVER MODEL - 12, 16, or 20 ga., boxlock action, any length barrel and choke on order, auto ejectors standard on all grades except Model O Excelsior, double triggers standard on all except Uncle Dan grade, optional single triggers available, checkered walnut pistol grip or straight stock, grades differ as to engraving, wood, checkering, and overall quality. Mfg. 1901-1906.

100%	98%	95%	90%	80%	70%	60%	50%	40%	30%	20%	10%
**** New Lefever Model O Excelsior Grade***											
N/A	N/A	N/A	N/A	$1,650	$1,450	$1,150	$975	$800	$760	$550	$425
**** New Lefever Model F Grade, No. 9***											
N/A	N/A	$4,500	$2,900	$2,325	$1,900	$1,650	$1,425	$1,200	$1,075	$850	$675
**** New Lefever Model E Grade, No. 8***											
N/A	N/A	$7,225	$4,675	$2,975	$2,375	$2,150	$1,850	$1,625	$1,375	$1,125	$950
**** New Lefever Model D Grade, No. 7***											
N/A	N/A	$10,000	$7,000	$5,000	$3,500	$3,000	$2,500	$2,200	$1,750	$1,400	$1,300
**** New Lefever Model C Grade, No. 6***											
N/A	N/A	$13,000	$11,000	$9,250	$7,000	$5,600	$4,375	$3,925	$3,350	$3,000	$2,725

100%	98%	95%	90%	80%	70%	60%	50%	40%	30%	20%	10%
*** New Lefever Model B Grade, No. 5**											
N/A	N/A	N/A	$15,000	$12,500	$9,500	$7,550	$5,125	$4,100	$3,500	$3,150	$2,800
*** New Lefever Model AA Grade, No. 4**											
N/A	N/A	N/A	$25,000	$18,000	$14,000	$10,000	$8,325	$5,950	$5,400	$4,625	$3,850

UNCLE DAN GRADE – only two guns are known to exist. Original specimens are selling for $150,000+

Extreme rarity precludes accurate pricing on this model.

OPTIMUS

Extreme rarity precludes accurate pricing on this model.

It is highly recommended that this model be professionally evaluated by a competent Lefever gunsmith prior to selling or buying.

SHOTGUNS: SINGLE BARREL, TRAP

TRAP GUN – 12 ga., 26-32 in. full choke, auto ejector, boxlock, checkered pistol grip stock. Mfg. 1904-06. Extremely rare.

100%	98%	95%	90%	80%	70%	60%	50%	40%	30%	20%	10%
N/A	N/A	N/A	$4,500	$4,000	$2,750	$1,500	$1,200	$900	$700	$500	$350

LE FORGERON

Previous manufacturer located in Belgium. Previously imported and distributed by Midwest Gun Sport in Zebulon, NC.

RIFLES: SxS

GRADING - PPGS™	100%	98%	95%	90%	80%	70%	60%	LAST MSR
MODEL 6020 – 9.3x74R cal., boxlock action, beavertail forearm, pistol grip stock.	$4,450	$4,025	$3,750	$3,475	$3,100	$2,800	$2,550	*$4,900*
MODEL 6030 – sidelock action, engraved action with deluxe French walnut stock and forearm.	$8,475	$7,900	$7,100	$6,300	$5,500	$4,700	$4,000	*$8,950*

Add $700 for sideplates (Model 6040). (applies to Model 6020)

SHOTGUNS: SxS

Prices represent the importer's last available information (1989).

GRADING - PPGS™	100%	98%	95%	90%	80%	70%	60%	LAST MSR
BOXLOCK EJECTOR – 20 or 28 ga. only, with or without sideplates, select French walnut stock, choice of engraving patterns (optional), single trigger.	$3,975	$3,650	$3,325	$2,995	$2,600	$2,250	$1,900	*$4,400*
SIDELOCK EJECTOR – 20 or 28 ga. only, select French walnut stock, choice of engraving patterns (optional), rounded action, single trigger.	$10,200	$9,250	$8,500	$7,900	$7,100	$6,300	$5,500	*$11,600*

Add $1,000 for sideplates. (applies to Boxlock Ejector)

LE FRANCAIS PISTOLS

Previous trademark manufactured by Manufacture Francaise d'Armes et Cycles de Saint-Etienne, located in Saint Etienne, France. Trade name was MANUFRANCE.

PISTOLS: SEMI-AUTO

GRADING - PPGS™	100%	98%	95%	90%	80%	70%	60%
POCKET MODEL AUTOMATIC – .25 ACP cal., double action, 7 shot, 2 3/8 in. hinged barrel, blue, fixed sights, hard rubber grips. Mfg. 1914-1966.	$350	$300	$250	$200	$175	$150	$125
TYPE POLICEMAN MODEL AUTOMATIC – .25 ACP cal., similar to Pocket Model, except has 3 1/2 in. hinged barrel, some are marked "FRANCO". Mfg. 1922-1968.	$400	$300	$250	$210	$180	$150	$125
.32 AUTOMATIC MODEL – .32 ACP cal., double action, 8 shot, 3 1/4 in. hinged finned barrel, blue, fixed sights, rubber grips. 10,000 mfg. 1950-1969, very few imported into the U.S.	$1,500	$1,250	$1,000	$900	$800	$700	$600

Add 50%-100% for engraved models, depending on amount of coverage. (applies to Pocket Model Automatic and Type Policeman Model Automatic)

GRADING - PPGS™	100%	98%	95%	90%	80%	70%	60%	LAST MSR

TYPE ARMY MODEL AUTOMATIC - 9mm Browning Long cal., double action, 8 shot, 5 in. hinged barrel, blue, fixed sights, checkered walnut grips, some are marked "FRANCO". 4,000 mfg. 1928-1938. Early model with plain tapered barrel (1928), later model with finned barrel (1931).

$3,000	$2,500	$1,750	$1,250	$1,000	$750	$500	

Add 20% for later model with finned barrel (1931).

Add 50%-100% for engraved models, depending on amount of coverage.

LEGACY SPORTS INTERNATIONAL

Current importer located in Reno, NV. Previously located in Alexandria, VA.

Legacy Sports International imports a wide variety of firearms trademarks in various configurations, including pistols, rifles, and shotguns. Trademarks include: Citadel, Escort (disc. 2018), Hardy (new 2020), Howa, ISSC (disc. 2014), Lithgow Arms (disc. 2019), Pointer, Puma (disc. 2015), Verona (disc.), and Webley & Scott (disc. 2018). Please refer to these individual listings.

LEGEND

Previous rifle trademark manufactured circa 1996-2006 by D'Arcy Echols & Co., located in Millville, UT.

RIFLES: BOLT ACTION

Previous Legend rifles utilized an extensively modified and refined Winchester Model 70 claw extractor action. Synthetic stocks were built by special order. Current rifles may be found under the D'Arcy Echols & Co. listing in the D section.

LEGENDARY ARMS WORKS

Previous trademark established in 2014, located in Harrisburg, PA until 2020. Previously located in Elizabethtown, PA until 2015 and Reinholds, PA until 2017.

Legendary Arms Works was formed in 2014 after Trop Gun Shop Limited acquired Bansner's Ultimate Rifles L.L.C. and synthetic stock maker High-Tech Specialties Inc. The company also acquired the rights to the Ed Brown 704 rifle from Ed Brown Products, Inc.

RIFLES: BOLT ACTION

704 MAGPUL RIFLE - 6.5 Creedmoor or .308 Win. cal., LAW M704 action w/controlled round feed, triple-lapped, 20 or 24 in. match grade, stainless steel fluted, threaded barrel w/Wilson Arms removable thread cap, detachable box magazine, custom-tuned Timney trigger, Magpul Hunter 700 reinforced polymer stock w/anodized aluminum bedding block available in black, FDE, or OD Green, 2-pos. safety, one-piece Picatinny rail, Graphite Black Cerakote finish. Disc. 2020.

$1,800	$1,575	$1,350	$1,125	$950	$800	$650	*$1,999*

BIG FIVE - .375 H&H Mag., .416 Rem. Mag., or .458 Lott cal., LAW Model 704 action, 23 in. chrome moly barrel with banded swivel stud, slim line muzzle brake, Timney trigger, one-piece trigger guard, custom express sights, Legendary Arms Works fiberglass stock with Tri-Color Dark Brown speckle paint, aluminum bedding blocks, 1 in. Pachmayr Decelerator recoil pad, three position safety, spiral fluted bolt body, Graphic Black Cerakote finish, 9.3 lbs. Mfg. 2016-disc.

$2,475	$2,100	$1,825	$1,550	$1,350	$1,150	$950	*$2,743*

BOBCAT - .243 Win., .260 Rem., 6.5 Creedmoor, 7mm-08 Rem., .308 Win., or .338 Federal cal., LAW Model 704 action, 20 in. stainless steel fluted and threaded barrel with thread protector, Timney trigger, one-piece aluminum trigger guard, Legendary Arms Works fiberglass stock with Tri-Color Black speckle paint, aluminum bedding blocks, 1 in. Pachmayr Decelerator recoil pad, three position safety, Graphite Black Cerakote metal finish, 6.6-7 lbs. Mfg. 2016-disc.

$1,775	$1,550	$1,325	$1,100	$950	$800	$650	*$1,959*

CAPRA - 6.5 Creedmoor, .308 Win., .270 Win., .280 Rem., .30-06, 7mm Rem. Mag., or .300 Win. Mag. cal., LAW Model 704 action, 24 in. match grade stainless steel fluted barrel with removable muzzle brake and thread protector, controlled round feed, 3-pos. safety, Timney trigger, Tally scope bases, fiberglass stock, 1 in. Pachmayr Decelerator recoil pad, one-piece aluminum trigger guard, Cerakote metal finish, tri-color speckle paint stock in tan or brown, 6.6-7.4 lbs. Mfg. 2017-disc.

$2,795	$2,450	$2,100	$1,900	$1,550	$1,275	$1,000	*$3,099*

HELLCAT - .243 Win., 6.5 Creedmoor, .260 Rem., 7mm-08 Rem., .308 Win., or .338 Federal cal., 20 in. barrel, tan w/speckle stock finish, 3-position safety. Mfg. 2019-2020.

$2,100	$1,850	$1,600	$1,450	$1,150	$950	$750	*$2,499*

GRADING - PPGS™	100%	98%	95%	90%	80%	70%	60%	LAST MSR

PROFESSIONAL – available in .22-250 through .338 Win. Mag. cals., LAW Model 704 action, 24 or 26 in. stainless steel fluted barrel with removable muzzle brake and thread protector, Timney trigger, one-piece aluminum trigger guard, Legendary Arms Works fiberglass stock with Tri-Color OD Green speckle paint, aluminum bedding blocks, 1 in. Pachmayr Decelerator recoil pad, three position safety, Tactical Grey Cerakote metal finish, 6.6-7 lbs. Mfg. 2016-disc.

	100%	98%	95%	90%	80%	70%	60%	LAST MSR
	$1,800	$1,575	$1,350	$1,125	$950	$800	$650	*$2,000*

Add $50 for .28 Nosler, .26 Nosler, or .280 Ackley cal.

PROFESSIONAL II /PROFESSIONAL II CARBON – .243 Win., 6.5 Creedmoor, .260 Rem., 7mm-08, .308 Win., .25-06 Rem., .257 Wby. Mag., .270 Win., .280 Rem., .30-06, 7mm Rem. Mag., .300 Win. Mag., or .338 Win. Mag. cal., 24 or 26 (.25-06 and .257 Wby. Mag. only) in. stainless steel fluted or carbon fiber wrapped (Professional II Carbon) barrel w/removable muzzle brake, custom-tuned Timney trigger w/one-piece trigger guard, hand-laid fiberglass stock (available in black/black speckle, OD Green w/ speckle, or dark brown w/speckle finish), 2 or 3-position wing safety, 1 in. Pachmayr decelerator recoil pad, Weaver-style Mil-Spec 1913 bases, Tactical Grey Cerakote finish, 6.6.-7.1 lbs. Mfg. 2018-2020.

	100%	98%	95%	90%	80%	70%	60%	LAST MSR
	$2,250	$1,950	$1,700	$1,550	$1,250	$1,000	$800	*$2,499*

Add $1,000 for carbon fiber wrapped barrel.

PROFESSIONAL SLP – .22-250 through .338 Win. Mag. cal., LAW Model 704 action, 24 or 26 in. stainless steel fluted barrel with removable muzzle brake and thread protector, Timney trigger, one-piece aluminum trigger guard, Legendary Arms Works fiberglass stock with Tri-Color OD Green speckle paint, aluminum bedding blocks, 1 in. Pachmayr Decelerator recoil pad, three position safety, 12 1/2 in. LOP, Graphite Black metal finish, 6.6-7 lbs. Mfg. 2016-disc.

	100%	98%	95%	90%	80%	70%	60%	LAST MSR
	$1,800	$1,575	$1,350	$1,125	$950	$800	$650	*$2,000*

Add $50 for .26 Nosler, .28 Nosler, or .280 Ackley cal.

SENTINEL – .308 Win. cal. or 6.5 Creedmoor, M704 controlled round feed action, 20 in. triple lapped, air gauged, stainless steel, fluted barrel, fully adj. buttstock, CNC machined aluminum chassis, free floating handguard, 8 - 8.5 lbs. Disc.

	100%	98%	95%	90%	80%	70%	60%	LAST MSR
	$2,295	$2,010	$1,725	$1,560	$1,260	$1,050	$850	*$2,699*

TITAN LONG RANGE – 6.5 Creedmoor, .308 Win., 7mm Rem. Mag., or .300 Win. Mag. cal., 24 or 26 in. barrel, tan w/speckle stock, 3-position safety. Mfg. 2019-2020.

	100%	98%	95%	90%	80%	70%	60%	LAST MSR
	$2,300	$2,000	$1,700	$1,550	$1,250	$1,050	$800	*$2,699*

LEGION FIREARMS LLC

Previous AR-15 style firearm and 1911 style pistol manufacturer and importer located in Temple, TX until 2014.

Please refer to BlueBookOfGunValues.com to order the *Blue Book of AR-15s & Variations*, available as a book or online subscription.

LEGION USA INC.

Previous importer until 2011 of Saiga firearms manufactured by Izhmash, located in Izhevask, Russia.

Legion Ltd. was the custom shop of the Izhmash factory in Russia and Arsenal Inc. in Las Vegas, NV.

LEITNER-WISE DEFENSE, INC.

Previous AR-15 style parts/accessories manufacturer located in Alexandria, VA. The company discontinued its semi-auto line of rifles circa 2010 and fully dissolved in 2017.

Please refer to BlueBookOfGunValues.com to order the *Blue Book of AR-15s & Variations*, available as a book or online subscription.

LEITNER-WISE RIFLE CO. INC.

Previous manufacturer of AR-15 style rifles, located in Springfield, VA circa 2006. Previously located in Alexandria, VA 1999-2005.

Please refer to BlueBookOfGunValues.com to order the *Blue Book of AR-15s & Variations*, available as a book or online subscription.

LES BAER CUSTOM, INC.

Current manufacturer and customizer established in 1993, located in LeClaire, IA since 2008. Previously located in Hillsdale, IL until 2008. Dealer sales only.

PISTOLS: SEMI-AUTO, 1911 SERIES, SINGLE ACTION

For current models within this category, add $70 for Tactical Package (rounds the edges of the pistol).

AMERICAN HANDGUNNER SPECIAL EDITION 1911 – .45 ACP cal., NM steel frame, 5 in. Govt. barrel and custom fitted stainless steel bushing, two 8 shot mags., 5 in. Govt. slide with rear cocking serrations, lowered and flared ejection port, extended ejector, speed trigger, Baer low mount adj. Rolo rear sight

GRADING - PPGS™	100%	98%	95%	90%	80%	70%	60%	LAST MSR

and dovetail front sight, Tritium night sights, double diamond black and blue VZ grips, beavertail grip safety with pad, American Handgunner logo engraved on slide, special "AH" serial number prefix, brushed hard chrome lower with matte rounds, blue top end finish. New 2020.

MSR $2,995	$2,695	$2,360	$2,025	$1,835	$1,480	$1,215	$975	

BLACK BAER – 9mm Para. cal., SA, steel NM frame and slide, NM supported barrel with stainless bushing, two 9 shot mags., tuned extractor, extended ejector, deluxe hammer and sear, Baer deluxe fixed rear combat night sight, dovetail front sights, black recon grips, tactical extended combat safety, rear serrated slide, checkered slide stop, DuPont S coating on entire pistol. New 2016.

MSR $3,070	$2,765	$2,425	$2,075	$1,880	$1,525	$1,250	$1,000	

BOSS – .45 ACP cal., similar to the Premier II series, except features blued slide, extended combat safety, rear cocking serrations on the slide, fiber optic front sight, chromed complete lower, special tactical package.

MSR $2,715	$2,450	$2,150	$1,840	$1,665	$1,350	$1,100	$900	

BULLSEYE WADCUTTER PISTOL – .45 ACP cal., NM frame, slide, and barrel with stainless bushing, 7 shot mag., blued finish, checkered cocobolo grips, double serrated slide, high checkered front strap, Baer deluxe hammer and sear, beavertail grip safety with pad, Baer speed trigger, optical scope mount.

MSR $2,535	$2,285	$2,000	$1,715	$1,550	$1,255	$1,025	$825	

Add $94 for 6 in. slide with Lo-Mount LBC adj. sights and Baer optical mount.

CONCEPT I/CONCEPT II – .45 ACP cal., NM steel frame and slide, 5 in. barrel with stainless bushing, slide fitted to frame, double serrated slide, LBC adj. deluxe low mount rear sight with hidden leaf, dovetail front sight, or deluxe fixed combat sight (Concept II), checkered slide stop, fitted speed trigger with action job, deluxe Commander hammer, beavertail grip safety with pad, extended ambi safety, two 8 shot mags., checkered cocobolo grips, blued finish.

MSR $2,142	$1,925	$1,685	$1,450	$1,310	$1,060	$875	$700	

* ***Concept III/Concept IV*** – .45 ACP cal., similar to Concept I/Concept II, except has stainless steel frame and blued steel slide, and checkered front strap.

MSR $2,397	$2,150	$1,880	$1,615	$1,460	$1,185	$975	$750	

* ***Concept V*** – .45 ACP cal., similar to Concept I, except both frame and slide are stainless steel, available with 5 or 6 in. barrel, LBC adj. rear sight, checkered front strap.

MSR $2,376	$2,140	$1,875	$1,600	$1,450	$1,175	$975	$750	

Add $141 for 6 in. barrel.

* ***Concept VI*** – .45 ACP cal., similar to Concept V, except has 5 in. barrel, Baer deluxe fixed combat rear sight.

MSR $2,429	$2,185	$1,910	$1,640	$1,485	$1,200	$985	$775	

* ***Concept VII*** – .45 ACP cal., similar to Concept I, except has Commanche size 4 1/4 in. barrel, all blued steel, Baer deluxe fixed combat rear sight, and checkered front strap.

MSR $2,365	$2,125	$1,860	$1,595	$1,450	$1,175	$950	$775	

* ***Concept VIII*** – .45 ACP cal., similar to Concept I, except has Commanche size 4 1/4 in. barrel, all stainless steel, Baer deluxe fixed combat rear sight, and checkered front strap.

MSR $2,418	$2,175	$1,900	$1,625	$1,480	$1,195	$980	$800	

CUSTOM 25TH ANNIVERSARY SPECIAL COLLECTORS MODEL – .45 ACP cal., similar to Premier II, except also includes hand engraving on both sides of the slide and frame, Les Baer's actual signature and the legend "25th Anniversary" have been engraved, then inlaid with white gold on the top of the slide, rich charcoal blue finish, real ivory grips, also includes a special presentation box. Limited mfg. disc. 2015.

	$7,250	$6,400	$5,800	$5,000	$4,250	$3,500	$2,700	*$7,940*

CUSTOM CARRY – 9mm Para. (new 2017), .38 Super, or .45 ACP cal., NM steel frame, slide, and barrel with stainless bushing, 4 1/4 (Comanche length) or 5 in. throated barrel, blued or stainless steel finish, deluxe fixed combat sight, dovetail front sight, improved ramp style night sights, double serrated slide, checkered slide stop, Baer speed trigger, extended ambi safety, two 8 shot mags., checkered cocobolo grips.

MSR $2,323	$2,095	$1,835	$1,575	$1,425	$1,150	$950	$750	

Add $106 for stainless steel finish.

Add $381 for .38 Super or 9mm Para. (new 2017) cal.

Add $382 for 4 1/4 (Comanche length) in. throated barrel.

GRADING - PPGS™	100%	98%	95%	90%	80%	70%	60%	LAST MSR

CUSTOM CENTENNIAL MODEL 1911 PISTOL - .45 ACP cal., made to commemorate the 100th anniversary year of "Old Ironsides", similar to Premier II 5 in. model, except features rear serrated slide with the model name engraved on the slide, ivory grips, deluxe charcoal blue finish, extended tactical safety, three 8 shot mags., special presentation box. Disc. 2015.

	100%	98%	95%	90%	80%	70%	60%	LAST MSR
	$3,875	$3,450	$2,975	$2,450	$2,000	$1,675	$1,425	*$4,350*

GT MONOLITH STINGER - .45 ACP, 9mm Para. (new 2017), or .38 Super cal., Officer size frame, 4 1/4 in. slide (Comanche length), extra long dust cover matches length of slide, Rolo night sights, includes three mags., checkered cocobolo grips, blue (standard) or chrome (optional) finish. New 2015.

	100%	98%	95%	90%	80%	70%	60%
MSR $3,123	$2,800	$2,450	$2,100	$1,900	$1,540	$1,260	$1,000

Add $185 for .38 Super or 9mm Para. (new 2017) cal.
Add $300 for chrome finish.

* ***GT Monolith Stinger Heavyweight*** - .45 ACP, 9mm Para. (new 2017), or .38 Super cal., similar to GT Monolith Stinger, except has extra heavy dust cover with a flat bottom. New 2015.

	100%	98%	95%	90%	80%	70%	60%
MSR $3,414	$3,075	$2,690	$2,300	$2,090	$1,690	$1,385	$1,100

Add $185 for .38 Super or 9mm Para. (new 2017) cal.
Add $300 for chrome finish.

GUNSITE PISTOL - .45 ACP cal., 5 in. barrel with stainless match bushing, two 8 shot mags., steel NM frame and slide, lowered and flared ejection port, tuned extractor, deluxe hammer and sear, aluminum match trigger, LBC deluxe fixed combat rear sight with Tritium inserts, dovetail front sight with Tritium insert, deluxe special slim line grips, combat extended safety, checkered slide stop, blued finish, "GAI" serial number prefix, raven logo engraved on slide and grips. New 2019.

	100%	98%	95%	90%	80%	70%	60%
MSR $2,323	$2,095	$1,835	$1,575	$1,425	$1,150	$950	$750

HEMI 572 - .45 ACP cal., inspired by Chrysler's fast and fearsome 1970 Hemi Cuda, double serrated slide, fiber optic front sight with green insert, hex head grip screws, special tactical package with ambi safety, VZ black recon grips, complete hard chrome finish on all major components, DuPont S coating on slide stop, mag. catch and mag. catch lock, two 8 shot mags. New 2013.

	100%	98%	95%	90%	80%	70%	60%
MSR $2,853	$2,565	$2,250	$1,925	$1,750	$1,410	$1,150	$900

KENAI SPECIAL - 10mm cal., NM steel frame, 5 in. stainless steel supported barrel, two 9 shot mags., lowered and flared ejection port, extended ejector, deluxe Commander hammer and sear, low mount LBC adj. sight with hidden rear leaf, Baer fiber optic front sight, premium checkered grips, beavertail grip safety with pad, checkered slide stop, "KENAI XXX" serial number etched on top of slide and special bear paw logo with "KENAI SPECIAL" model name engraved on side of the slide, hard chrome finish. New 2019.

	100%	98%	95%	90%	80%	70%	60%
MSR $3,739	$3,350	$2,925	$2,515	$2,280	$1,850	$1,510	$1,250

LIMITED EDITION LES BAER PRESENTATION GRADE 1911 - .45 ACP cal., similar to Premier II, except also features detailed hand chiseled engraving, special charcoal blueing on all polished surfaces, rich nitre blue is used on pins, thumb safety, slide stop, grip screws, mag catch lock and hammer, real ivory grips, "LBC" engraving on top of the slide is inlaid with gold, optional to add name of the recipient engraved on the slide with the legend "To (name) by Les Baer", includes special presentation box.

	100%	98%	95%	90%	80%	70%	60%
MSR $7,575	$6,825	$5,975	$5,500	$4,750	$4,000	$3,250	$2,500

Add $232 for name engraving on slide.

MONOLITH - 9mm Para. (new 2017), .40 S&W (new 2017), .38 Super, or .45 ACP cal., NM steel Monolith frame, 5 in. barrel with stainless match bushing, two 8 shot mags., lowered and flared ejection port, tuned extractor, extended ejector, deluxe Commander hammer, speed trigger, low mount LBC adj. sight with hidden rear leaf, Baer dovetail front sight, beavertail grip safety with pad, checkered cocobolo grips, extended ambi safety, Monolith flat bottom double serrated slide, checkered slide stop, extra long dust cover, blued finish.

	100%	98%	95%	90%	80%	70%	60%
MSR $2,492	$2,240	$1,960	$1,680	$1,525	$1,225	$1,025	$825

Add $446 for supported chamber .38 Super, 9mm Para. (new 2017), or .40 S&W (new 2017).

* ***Monolith Heavyweight*** - 9mm Para. (new 2017), .40 S&W (new 2017), .38 Super, or .45 ACP cal., similar to Monolith, except has a heavier frame.

	100%	98%	95%	90%	80%	70%	60%
MSR $2,471	$2,150	$1,885	$1,615	$1,465	$1,185	$975	$750

Add $329 for supported chamber .38 Super, 9mm Para. (new 2017), or .40 S&W (new 2017).

MONOLITH COMANCHE - .45 ACP, 9mm Para. (new 2017), or .38 Super (new 2017) cal., NM steel Monolith frame, Monolith flat bottom double serrated slide, 4 1/4 in. barrel with stainless match bushing, Tritium night sights front and rear and deluxe fixed rear sight, checkered slide stop, speed trigger, deluxe Commander hammer, beavertail grip safety with pad, extended ambi safety, two 8

GRADING - PPGS™	100%	98%	95%	90%	80%	70%	60%	LAST MSR

shot mags., checkered cocobolo grips, blued finish, extra long dust cover, also includes front and rear Tritium night sights and deluxe fixed rear sight, edges are rounded for tactical carry.

MSR $2,555	$2,275	$1,990	$1,700	$1,550	$1,250	$1,025	$850	

Add $531 for 9mm Para. (new 2017) or .38 Super (new 2017) cal.

* ***Monolith Comanche Heavyweight*** – .45 ACP, 9mm Para. (new 2017), or .38 Super (new 2017) cal., similar to Monolith Comanche, except dust cover is slightly thicker to add weight and is flat on the bottom.

MSR $2,593	$2,325	$2,035	$1,750	$1,580	$1,280	$1,050	$850	

Add $530 for 9mm Para. (new 2017) or .38 Super (new 2017) cal.

NATIONAL MATCH HARDBALL PISTOL – .45 ACP cal., NM steel frame and slide, 5 in. barrel w/stainless bushing, 7 shot mag., lowered and flared ejection port, tuned extractor, Baer extended ejector, match trigger, mount LBC adj. sight with hidden rear leaf, dovetailed front sight, checkered cocobolo grips, checkered front strap, rear serrated slide, beveled magwell, blued finish.

MSR $2,450	$2,200	$1,925	$1,650	$1,500	$1,210	$1,000	$800	

PPC DISTINGUISHED MATCH PISTOL – 9mm Para. or .45 ACP cal., NM steel frame and slide, 5 in. barrel w/stainless bushing, 8 shot mag., lowered and flared ejection port, tuned and polished extractor, extended ejector, deluxe Commander hammer and sear, speed trigger, dovetail front sight, PPC sight, beavertail grip safety with pad, checkered cocobolo grips, extended ambi safety, double serrated slide, beveled magwell, blued finish.

MSR $2,641	$2,375	$2,080	$1,780	$1,615	$1,300	$1,075	$875	

Add $520 for 9mm Para. cal.

PPC OPEN CLASS – 9mm Para. or .45 ACP cal., similar to PPC Distinguished Match, except features 6 in. barrel.

MSR $2,888	$2,600	$2,275	$1,950	$1,775	$1,425	$1,175	$950	

Add $425 for 9mm Para. cal. with supported chamber.

PREMIER II 5 INCH MODEL – 9mm Para. (new 2017), .40 S&W (new 2017), .38 Super, .400 Cor-Bon (disc. 2016), 10mm supported (new 2019), or .45 ACP cal., NM steel frame, slide, and barrel with stainless bushing, 5 in. barrel, two 8 shot mags., extended ejector and lowered/flared ejection port, tuned and polished extractor, deluxe Commander hammer and sear, speed trigger, low mount LBC adj. sight with hidden rear leaf, dovetail front sight, Premium checkered grips, beavertail grip safety with pad, extended ambi safety, double serrated slide, high checkered front strap, beveled magwell, blued finish or stainless steel (disc. 2015).

MSR $2,312	$2,080	$1,825	$1,560	$1,415	$1,150	$935	$750	

Add $467 for .38 Super, 9mm Para. (new 2017), or .40 S&W (new 2017) cal.
Add $807 for 10mm supported cal. (new 2019).
Add $200 for .400 Cor-Bon cal. (disc. 2016).
Add $80 for stainless steel (disc. 2015).
Add $580 for .45 ACP/.400 Cor-Bon dual cylinder combo (disc. 2016).

* ***Premier II 5 Inch Model Heavyweight*** – .45 ACP cal., NM steel Monolith Heavyweight frame and slide, 5 in. barrel w/stainless bushing, two 8 shot mags., lowered and flared ejection port, tuned extractor, extended ejector, deluxe Commander hammer and sear, speed trigger, low mount LBC adj. sight with hidden rear leaf, dovetail front sight, beavertail grip safety with pad, checkered cocobolo grips, extended ambi safety, double serrated slide, high checkered front strap, beveled mag. well, chrome finish. New 2019.

MSR $2,977	$2,680	$2,350	$2,010	$1,825	$1,475	$1,200	$985	

PREMIER II 6 INCH MODEL – 9mm Para. (new 2017), .400 Cor-Bon (disc. 2016), .38 Super, or .45 ACP cal., similar to Premier II 5 Inch Model, except features 6 in. barrel, blued finish only.

MSR $2,565	$2,300	$2,015	$1,725	$1,565	$1,265	$1,035	$850	

Add $478 for .38 Super or 9mm Para. (new 2017) cal.
Add $100 for .400 Cor-Bon cal. (disc. 2016).

PREMIER II HUNTER – 10mm cal., NM steel frame, 5 (disc.) or 6 in. stainless steel barrel, two 9 shot mags., lowered and flared ejection port, extended ejector, deluxe Commander hammer and sear, low mount LBC adj. sight with hidden rear leaf, Baer fiber optic front sight, premium checkered grips, beavertail grip safety with pad, checkered slide stop, blued finish. New 2017.

MSR $3,149	$2,835	$2,480	$2,125	$1,925	$1,560	$1,275	$1,000	

GRADING - PPGS™	100%	98%	95%	90%	80%	70%	60%	LAST MSR

PREMIER II SUPER-TAC – 9mm Para. (new 2017), .38 Super, .400 Cor-Bon (disc. 2016), .45 ACP, or .45 ACP/.400 Cor-Bon combo (disc. 2016) cal., NM steel frame, barrel with stainless bushing, two 8 shot mags., NM steel frame, slide, and barrel with stainless bushing, Baer speed trigger, low mount LBC adj. rear sight and Baer dovetail front sight, both fitted with Tritium night sights, checkered cocobolo grips, extended ambi safety, beavertail grip safety with pad, deburred for tactical carry, DuPont S coating.

MSR $2,811	$2,525	$2,210	$1,895	$1,715	$1,390	$1,135	$925	

Add $297 for .38 Super or 9mm Para. (new 2017) cal.
Add $60 for .400 Cor-Bon cal. (disc. 2016).
Add $540 for .45 ACP/.400 Cor-Bon dual cylinder combo (disc. 2016).

PROWLER III – .45 ACP cal., NM steel frame (fitted to frame) and slide, 5 in. barrel with tapered cone stub weight, two 8 shot mags., lowered and flared ejection port, tuned extractor, deluxe Commander hammer, speed trigger, low mount BoMar sight with hidden leaf rear, dovetail front sight, beavertail grip safety with pad, checkered cocobolo grips, extended ambi safety, reverse plug, double serrated slide, checkered slide stop, blued finish. Disc. 2014.

	$2,400	$2,125	$1,800	$1,575	$1,300	$1,100	$925	*$2,710*

SHOOTING USA CUSTOM PISTOL – .45 ACP cal., 5 in. barrel, two 8 shot mags., NM steel frame, slide, and barrel with stainless bushing, lowered and flared ejection port, tuned extractor, extended ejector, Baer speed trigger, Baer dovetail front sight, checkered cocobolo grips, beavertail grip safety with pad, tactical extended safety, special serial number prefix with "S USA" and the number, the famous Shooting USA logo engraved on right side of the slide, beveled magwell, special DVD produced by Shooting USA, blued finish.

MSR $2,312	$2,080	$1,825	$1,560	$1,415	$1,150	$935	$750	

S.R.P. (SWIFT RESPONSE PISTOL) – .45 ACP cal., NM steel frame and slide with front and rear serrations, 4 1/4 (Comanche Model) or 5 in. barrel with stainless match bushing, deluxe fixed combat sight, dovetail front sight, checkered slide stop, speed trigger, deluxe Commander hammer, beavertail grip safety with pad, tactical style ambi safety, Tritium night sights installed front and rear, deburred for tactical carry, DuPont S coating on complete pistol, three 8 shot mags., checkered cocobolo grips, special wooden presentation box with glass lid.

MSR $3,013	$2,700	$2,365	$2,025	$1,835	$1,485	$1,215	$975	

STINGER MODEL – .45 ACP, 9mm Para. (new 2018), or .38 Super (new 2020) cal., NM Stinger frame, NM Commanche length slide with rear serrations, slide fitted to frame, 4 1/4 in. barrel with stainless bushing, two 7 shot mags., lowered and flared ejection port, tuned extractor, extended ejector, deluxe Commander hammer, speed trigger, low mount combat fixed rear sight, dovetail front sight, checkered cocobolo grips, extended ambi safety, checkered slide stop, beavertail grip safety with pad, blued finish.

MSR $2,376	$2,135	$1,875	$1,600	$1,450	$1,175	$960	$785	

Add $637 for 9mm Para. (new 2018) or .38 Super (new 2020) cal.

* ***Stinger Model Stainless*** – .45 ACP cal., similar to Stinger Model, except features stainless steel frame and slide.

MSR $2,450	$2,200	$1,925	$1,650	$1,495	$1,210	$1,000	$800	

.38 SUPER STINGER – .38 Super cal., NM Stinger frame, NM Commanche length slide with rear serrations only, 4 1/4 in. barrel with supported chamber and stainless steel bushing, deluxe fixed combat rear sight with night sight, dovetail ramp type with night sight, checkered slide stop, speed trigger, deluxe Commander hammer, beavertail grip safety with pad, tactical ambi safety, three 8 shot mags. with pads, checkered cocobolo grips, blue finish or optional chrome or DuPont S finish. Mfg. 2013-2018.

	$2,500	$2,175	$1,900	$1,625	$1,350	$1,100	$900	*$2,840*

SUPER COMANCHE – .38 Super cal., 4 1/4 in. throated barrel w/stainless steel bushing, two 9 shot mag. w/base pads, steel construction only, NM slide with rear serrations only, lowered and flared ejection port, deluxe hammer and sear, speed trigger, deluxe fixed combat rear sight with night sight, dovetail front sight ramp style with night sight, checkered cocobolo grips, extended ambi safety, checkered slide stop, high checkered front strap, blue finish or optional chrome or DuPont S finish. Mfg. 2013-2015.

	$2,275	$2,025	$1,775	$1,525	$1,275	$1,075	$875	*$2,550*

THUNDER RANCH 1911 25TH ANNIVERSARY SPECIAL EDITION – .45 ACP cal., steel NM frame, NM barrel with stainless match bushing, includes three stainless steel 7 shot mags., beveled magwell, steel NM slide with front and rear serrations, lowered and flared ejection port, extended and tuned ejector, deluxe Commander hammer and sear, aluminum match trigger, LBC deluxe fixed combat rear sight with Tritium insert, Baer dovetail front sight with Tritium insert, deluxe Thunder Ranch logo grips, extended tactical safety, beavertail grip safety with pad, checkered slide stop, high checkered front strap, Thunder Ranch logo engraved on slide, "TRXXV" serial numbers 001-0250, blued finish. Limited mfg. of 250 circa 2018.

	$2,225	$1,925	$1,550	$1,275	$1,050	$895	$795	*$2,520*

GRADING - PPGS™	100%	98%	95%	90%	80%	70%	60%	LAST MSR

THUNDER RANCH SPECIAL – .45 ACP cal., 5 in. barrel stainless barrel, three stainless steel 7 shot mags., steel slide with front and rear serrations, lowered and flared ejection port, extended ejector, deluxe Commander hammer and sear, aluminum match trigger, LBC deluxe fixed combat rear and dovetail front sights with Tritium inserts, beavertail grip safety with pad, deluxe special slim line grips with Thunder Ranch logo, combat extended safety, high checkered front strap, beveled magwell, Thunder Ranch logo engraved on slide, special serial numbers with "TR" prefix, blued finish. Mfg. 2018.

	$1,950	$1,625	$1,300	$1,075	$950	$800	$725	*$2,290*

THUNDER RANCH SPECIAL 2nd GENERATION – .45 ACP cal., NM frame, 5 in. barrel, lowered and flared ejection port, night sights, deluxe standard thickness Thunder Ranch logo grips, tactical ambi safety, chrome lower with blued top end, serial numbers with "TRS" prefix. Mfg. 2017-2018.

	$2,225	$1,925	$1,550	$1,275	$1,050	$895	$795	*$2,530*

ULTIMATE MASTER COMBAT SERIES – .38 Super, .400 Cor-Bon (disc. 2016), or .45 ACP cal., compensated 5 or 6 in. barrel, two 8 shot mags., lowered and flared ejection port, deluxe Commander hammer and sear, speed trigger, low mount LBC adj. sight with hidden rear leaf, dovetailed front sight, checkered cocobolo grips, extended ambi safety, double serrated slide, full-length recoil rod, steel frame and slide w/blued finish.

* ***Ultimate Master Combat Compensated Model*** – .38 Super or .45 ACP cal., compensated barrel. Disc. 2016.

	$2,700	$2,400	$2,075	$1,775	$1,575	$1,350	$995	*$3,240*

Add $150 for .38 Super cal.

* ***Ultimate Master Combat 5 Inch Model*** – 9mm Para. (new 2017), .38 Super, .400 Cor-Bon (disc. 2016), or .45 ACP cal., 5 in. barrel.

MSR $3,225	$2,900	$2,550	$2,175	$1,975	$1,600	$1,300	$1,075	

Add $106 for .38 Super or 9mm Para. (new 2017) cal.
Add $50 for .400 Cor-Bon cal. (disc. 2016).

* ***Ultimate Master Combat 6 Inch Model*** – 9mm Para. (new 2017), .38 Super, .400 Cor-Bon (disc. 2016), or .45 ACP cal., 6 in. barrel.

MSR $3,361	$3,025	$2,650	$2,275	$2,050	$1,665	$1,375	$1,100	

Add $84 for .38 Super or 9mm Para. (new 2017) cal.
Add $70 for .400 Cor-Bon cal. (disc. 2016).

ULTIMATE RECON PISTOL – .45 ACP cal., full size Caspian frame with integral Picatinny rail system for frame mounted light, comes standard with a Streamlight TLR-1, NM slide and 5 in. barrel with stainless bushing, deluxe fixed combat rear sight with night sights, dovetail front sight, double serrated slide, bead blast blue finish or optional bead blast chrome finish, deluxe hammer and sear, checkered slide stop, speed trigger, tactical style extended combat safety, checkered cocobolo grips, high checkered front strap, two 8 shot mags. Disc. 2018.

	$2,350	$2,075	$1,825	$1,575	$1,325	$1,100	$900	*$2,650*

Add $260 for bead blast chrome finish.

ULTIMATE TACTICAL CARRY – 9mm Para. (new 2017), .38 Super (new 2017), or .45 ACP cal., 5 in. barrel with stainless match bushing, three stainless steel 8 shot mags., steel NM frame and slide, lowered and flared ejection port, tuned extractor, deluxe hammer and sear, aluminum match trigger, LBC deluxe fixed combat rear sight with Tritium inserts, dovetail front sight with Tritium insert, deluxe special slim line grips, combat extended safety, checkered slide stop, blued finish.

MSR $2,349	$2,115	$1,850	$1,585	$1,440	$1,165	$950	$775	

Add $356 for 9mm Para. (new 2017) or .38 Super (new 2017) cal.

RIFLES: BOLT ACTION

CUSTOM TACTICAL VARMINT CLASSIC – .243 Win., .260 Rem., .300 Win. Mag. (new 2011) or .308 Win. cal., 24 in. match grade barrel, Still Tac 30 action and thick lug, Timney match trigger, front and back of action are glass bedded and lug is bedded into Bell & Carlson precision varmint stock, fitted Wyatts precision floorplate with box mag., Picatinny one-piece rail, DuPont S coated finish. Mfg. 2010-2011.

	$3,250	$2,850	$2,450	$2,000	$1,650	$1,375	$1,125	*$3,410*

Add $150 for .300 Win. Mag. cal. with Harris bipod and muzzle brake.

CUSTOM TACTICAL/TACTICAL RECON – .243 Win., .260 Rem., .308 Win., .338 LM, 6.5x284 Norma, or .300 Win. Mag. cal., 24, 26, or 27 in. match grade barrel with or w/o muzzle brake, Still Tac 30 action and thick lug, Timney match trigger, front and back of action are glass bedded and lug is bedded into Bell & Carlson adj. stock, fitted Wyatts precision floorplate with box mag., Picatinny one-piece rail, DuPont S coated finish, Harris bipod. Limited mfg. 2011 only.

	$3,300	$2,950	$2,500	$2,075	$1,695	$1,375	$1,125	*$3,560*

Add $200 for .300 Win. Mag. with enforcer muzzle brake or $330 for .338 LM with enforcer muzzle brake.

GRADING - PPGS™	100%	98%	95%	90%	80%	70%	60%	LAST MSR

RIFLES: SEMI-AUTO

CUSTOM ULTIMATE AR MODEL – .204 Ruger (new 2004), .223 Rem., or 6.5 Grendel (mfg. 2007-2009) cal., 18-24 in. stainless steel barrel, Picatinny flat-top rail, individual rifles are custom built with no expense spared, everything made in-house ensuring top quality and tolerances, all models are guaranteed to shoot 1/2-3/4 MOA groups, various configurations include Varmint Model (disc.), Super Varmint Model, Super Match Model (new 2002), M4 Flat-Top Model, Thunder Ranch (disc. 2010), CMP Competion (disc.) and IPSC Action Model. Mfg. 2001-2018.

$2,350 $2,050 $1,500 $1,000 $750 $650 $550 ***$2,590***

Add $50 for Super Varmint model in .223 Rem. or $280 in .204 Ruger cal. Add $950 with scope package.

Add $150 for Super Match model in .223 Rem. or $370 in .204 Ruger cal. Add $1,359 with scope package.

Add $300 for IPSC action model or $1,350 with scope package.

Add $349 for Thunder Ranch rifle (disc. 2010). Add $849 for CMP competition rifle (disc.).

Add $245 for Super Varmint model (.204 Ruger cal., disc.) or $210 for 6.5 Grendel cal. with M4 style barrel (disc.).

CUSTOM NRA MATCH RIFLE – .223 Rem. cal., 30 in. bench rest stainless steel barrel, 30 shot mag., forged upper and lower receivers, Picatinny flat-top rail, LBC chromed bolt, extractor, and National Match carrier, Geissele two-stage trigger, free float handguard with locking ring, custom grip with extra material under the trigger guard, Dupont S coating on upper, lower, and small parts, available with or without sights package. Disc. 2017.

$2,650 $2,300 $1,750 $1,250 $950 $800 $650 ***$2,950***

Add $1,040 for sights package.

CUSTOM SPECIAL TACTICAL RIFLE – .223 Rem., 16 in. stainless steel fluted bench rest barrel, two 20 shot mags., Geissele non-adj. two-stage trigger, free float handguard with mounted sling stud, forged upper and lower receivers, Picatinny style flat-top rail, extractor, unique sighting system, includes nylon weather proof sling and lockable front sling swivel, detachable carry handle, Dupont S coating, 7 lbs. 6 oz. Mfg. 2011-2018.

$2,450 $2,150 $1,625 $1,150 $875 $725 $600 ***$2,720***

.264 LBC-AR M4 FLATTOP – .264 LBC-AR cal., 16 in. medium weight barrel, two 14 shot mags., 9 in. four-way handguard with locking ring and integral Picatinny rail system, Versa-Pod installed, free float handguard, fixed stock, Dupont S coating, black finish, includes soft rifle case. Mfg. 2010-2018.

$2,475 $2,175 $1,635 $1,150 $875 $725 $600 ***$2,790***

.264 LBC-AR SUPER MATCH – .264 LBC-AR cal., stainless steel barrel, fixed stock, black finish, 14 shot mag., features similar to Super Match Model in .223 cal. Mfg. 2010-2018.

$2,550 $2,225 $1,685 $1,200 $915 $765 $625 ***$2,840***

.264 LBC-AR SUPER VARMINT – .264 LBC-AR cal., stainless steel bench rest barrel, two 14 shot mags., fixed stock, black finish, features similar to Super Varmint model in .223 cal. Mfg. 2010-2018.

$2,400 $2,100 $1,565 $1,075 $825 $685 $575 ***$2,640***

6x45 ULTIMATE AR – 6x45mm cal., 18-24 in. stainless steel barrel, available in Super Varmint, Super Match, and M4 Flat-top configurations, black finish, fixed stock, similar to Ultimate AR in .223 configuration. Mfg. 2010-2018.

$2,400 $2,100 $1,565 $1,075 $825 $685 $575 ***$2,640***

Add $100 for Super Match model.

POLICE SPECIAL – .223 Rem., .264 LBC-AR (disc.), or 6x45mm (disc.) cal., 16 in. precision button rifled steel barrel, 14 or 30 shot mag., removable carry handle with rear sight, Picatinny flat-top upper rail, National Match chromed carrier, flip-up front sight, six position ATI collapsible stock with adj. cheekpiece and grip, Picatinny four-way handguard, A2 flash hider, Timney match trigger group, lockable sling swivel mounted on stud on four-way handguard, includes two mags. Mfg. 2010-2014.

$1,600 $1,425 $1,050 $750 $575 $485 $395 ***$1,790***

.308 LBC ULTIMATE MATCH/SNIPER – .308 Win. cal., 18 or 20 in. stainless steel barrel with precision cut rifling, matte black finish, 20 shot mag., machined upper and lower, no forward assist, Picatinny flat-top rail, steel gas block, free float handguard with lock ring, two-stage trigger group, Dupont S coating on barrel, Harris bipod, fixed or adj. Magpul stock, with or w/o enforcer muzzle brake, available in Match or Sniper (disc.) configuration. Mfg. 2011-2018.

$3,350 $2,975 $2,350 $1,650 $1,275 $1,000 $800 ***$3,640***

Add $30 for Match model with PRS Magpul stock.

Add $300 for Sniper model with adj. stock and enforcer muzzle brake (disc.)

GRADING - PPGS™	100%	98%	95%	90%	80%	70%	60%	LAST MSR

.308 ULTIMATE MONOLITH SWAT MODEL – .308 Win. cal., 18 or 24 in. stainless steel barrel with precision cut rifling, matte black finish, 20 shot mag., similar to .308 Ultimate Match/Sniper, except has integrated Mil-Std 1913 Picatinny rail system, Magpul PRS adj. stock, Versa-Pod and adapter, integral trigger guard is bowed on bottom so shooter can wear gloves. Mfg. 2011-2018.

$4,100	$3,750	$3,250	$2,595	$1,950	$1,450	$1,000	*$4,390*

LEW HORTON DIST. CO.

Previous firearms distributor located in Westboro, MA until Dec. 31, 2019. While Lew Horton was not a manufacturer or an importer, this company was responsible for many special and limited editions which are listed with quantities but without prices, since they may vary greatly from region to region. Special/Limited Editions began in 1983.

For individual model listings, please go to BlueBookOfGunValues.com/overflow.

LEWIS MACHINE & TOOL COMPANY (LMT)

Current AR-15 style rifle, pistol, and accessories manufacturer established in 1980, located in Eldridge, IA. Previously located in Milan, IL.

Please refer to BlueBookOfGunValues.com to order the *Blue Book of AR-15s & Variations*, available as a book or online subscription.

LIBERATOR

Previously manufactured by the Guide Lamp Corporation (division of General Motors) circa 1942.

100%	98%	95%	90%	80%	70%	60%	50%	40%	30%	20%	10%

PISTOLS: SINGLE SHOT

LIBERATOR PISTOL (U.S. MODEL 42) – .45 ACP cal., 4 in. smoothbore barrel, action utilizing nonstrategic WWII materials, wood ejector rod, each gun was individually packaged in a paraffin-coated cardboard box with wood spacer, and a smaller box containing 10 rounds of .45 ACP ammo with a graphics only instruction sheet on top. Mfg. for European resistance movement during WWII, very limited number used in Europe, most used in Philippines and China. 1 million mfg. 1942 only.

N/A	$3,000	$2,750	$2,500	$2,250	$2,000	$1,750	$1,500	$1,250	$1,000	$850	$725

Add $650-$950 for original box, depending on condition.

Add $400-$600 for original B&W instruction sheet, depending on condition.

ADD $350-$550 for box of .45 ACP ammo, depending on condition.

An authentic instruction sheet will have a watermark reading "WHITING MUTUAL BOND RAG CONTENT", and all ammo will have a headstamp of "FA 42". This is the only pistol that could be mfg. (6.6 sec.) faster than it could be loaded (10 sec.). While the Liberator's appearance is crude, remember that the entire production run (1 million) was mfg. and ready for overseas shipment in 10-11 weeks.

Even though 1 million of these pistols were mfg., remaining specimens brought into the U.S. are rare. Complete pistols in original box are extremely rare.

LIBERTY

Previous trademark imported 1997-2003 by K.B.I., Inc. located in Harrisburg, PA.

For individual model listings, please go to BlueBookOfGunValues.com/overflow.

LIBERTY ARMS INTERNATIONAL LLC

Previous importer and manufacturer located in Victoria, TX until circa 2015. Previously located in Albion, NY until 2010.

RIFLES: SEMI-AUTO

Liberty Arms assembled an AK-47 design carbine manufactured from U.S. milled or stamped receivers, U.S. chrome lined barrels, and Bulgarian manufactured part kits. MSRs were $900 for the milled receiver, and $750 for the stamped receiver. Additionally, the company imported a variety of European firearms and ammunition.

LIBERTY ARMS WORKS, INC.

Previous manufacturer located in West Chester, PA circa 1991-1996.

GRADING - PPGS™	100%	98%	95%	90%	80%	70%	60%	LAST MSR

PISTOLS: SEMI-AUTO

L.A.W. ENFORCER – .22 LR, 9mm Para., 10mm, .40 S&W (new 1994), or .45 ACP cal., patterned after the Ingram MAC 10, SA, 6 1/4 in. threaded barrel, closed bolt operation, manual safety, 10 (C/B 1994) or 30* shot mag., 5 lbs. 1 oz. Mfg. 1991-96.

$575	$500	$450	$415	$385	$335	$295	*$545*

GRADING - PPGS™	100%	98%	95%	90%	80%	70%	60%	LAST MSR

LIEGEOISE D'ARMES

Previous manufacturer located in Belgium.

Small manufacturer that specialized in boxlock shotguns, normally engraved and with ejectors. Prices usually range from $600-$1,200, depending on condition and engraving.

LIGNOSE (BERGMAN)

Previous manufacturer located in Suhl, Germany.

PISTOLS: SEMI-AUTO

EINHAND MODEL 2A POCKET AUTOMATIC – 6.35mm/.25 ACP cal., 6 shot, 2 in. barrel, blue, rubber grips, can be cocked by rearward pressure on trigger guard.

$395	$325	$225	$185	$150	$120	$90	

MODEL 2 POCKET AUTOMATIC – similar to 2A, without one hand cocking trigger guard.

$325	$265	$215	$165	$90	$75	$55	

MODEL 3 POCKET AUTOMATIC – similar to 3A, except without one hand cocking trigger guard.

$300	$250	$200	$165	$140	$110	$85	

MODEL 3A POCKET AUTOMATIC – similar to 2A, except longer grip, 9 shot capacity.

$450	$350	$250	$200	$140	$110	$85	

LILIPUT

Previous trademark manufactured by August Menz, located in Suhl, Germany.

PISTOLS: SEMI-AUTO

4.25MM CAL. – 4.25mm centerfire Liliput cal. (shoots 12 grain bullet), blue or nickel finish, limited 1920s mfg.

$750	$700	$550	$425	$385	$340	$300	

Ammunition for this caliber is very rare, and is selling for approx. $20 per round.

6.35MM CAL. – .25 ACP cal., mfg. in large quantities pre-WWII.

$250	$200	$140	$110	$90	$75	$55	

LIND, AL

Current custom long gun maker established in 1972, and located in Lakewood, WA.

Al Lind is a member of the American Custom Gunmakers Guild and manufactures custom made gun stocks, shotguns and rifles, all built to customer specifications. Please contact Mr. Lind directly for more information, including pricing, delivery time, and availability.

LINDNER GUN COMPANY

Previous manufacturer located in Sandornville, NH circa 2007-2010.

While Lindner Gun Company advertised in many trade magazines, it appears that the company made no guns for consumers other than a few prototypes.

LINEBAUGH CUSTOM SIXGUNS

Current gunsmith located in Cody, WY.

Mr. John Linebaugh has made over 1,000 specialized, customized sixgun conversions since 1980. He is the inventor of the .475 Linebaugh cartridge (introduced 1988) and the .500 Linebaugh caliber (the first successful .50 caliber revolver and cartridge introduced in 1986). Current pricing on these conversions is $3,800 for blue, $4,200 for stainless steel, or $7,500 for LCS brass grip frame. For conversions using the customer provided Ruger SRM Maximum frame, the price is $3,500. Please contact him directly for more information.

LINGARD, MICHAEL

Current long arm manufacturer located in Angus, Scotland. Consumer direct sales through FFL.

Michael Lingard manufactures best quality shotguns and rifles in various configurations. Please contact him directly for more information, U.S. availability, a price quotation, and delivery time.

LINIE HABSBURG JAGDWAFFEN

Current custom riflemaker located in Ferlach, Austria.

Linie Habsburg manufactures high quality custom rifles built to customer specifications. Calibers range from .22 Hornet to .300 Win. Mag. Please contact the company directly for more information, including available options, pricing, and delivery time.

GRADING - PPGS™	100%	98%	95%	90%	80%	70%	60%	LAST MSR

LIONHEART INDUSTRIES USA

Current manufacturer of pistols and accessories, established in 2011 and located in Renton, WA. Previously located in Richmond, WA.

Lionheart Industries became strategic partners with S&T Motiv through an exclusive contract to co-design and manufacture a series of 9mm pistols.

PISTOLS: SEMI-AUTO

Lionheart Industries currently offers a custom built 1911-style Regulus pistol. Please contact the company directly for more information including options and availability on this model.

LH9 – 9mm Para. cal., SA/DA, milled aluminum frame in black or FDE finish, 4.1 in. barrel, 13 or 15 shot mag., 3-dot sights, manual safety, 28 oz. Mfg. 2013-2016.

	100%	98%	95%	90%	80%	70%	60%	LAST MSR
	$525	$450	$415	$375	$350	$325	$295	*$615*

LH9CN – 9mm Para. cal., DA, standard size, 3.6 in. chrome moly steel barrel, 6 groove rifling, 10 shot mag., Novak sights, polymer diamond grips, ambidextrous safety, firing pin block, forged aluminum frame and slide, ballistic field case, pistol lock, steel cleaning rod, Graphite Black, Patriot Brown, or Sniper Grey Cerakote finish, 23.8 oz.

	100%	98%	95%	90%	80%	70%	60%
MSR $799	$700	$650	$550	$500	$400	$325	$250

LH9N – 9mm Para. cal., DA, standard size, 4.1 in. chrome moly steel barrel, 6 groove rifling, 13 shot mag., Novak sights, polymer diamond grips, ambidextrous safety, firing pin block, forged aluminum frame and slide, ballistic field case, pistol lock, steel cleaning rod, Graphite Black, Patriot Brown, or Sniper Grey Cerakote finish, 25.9 oz.

	100%	98%	95%	90%	80%	70%	60%
MSR $799	$700	$650	$550	$500	$400	$325	$250

* ***LH9N-MKII*** – 9mm Para. cal., DA, standard size, 4.1 in. chrome moly steel barrel, 6 groove rifling, 13 shot mag., fiber optic sights, polymer diamond grips, ambidextrous safety, firing pin block, forged aluminum frame and slide, ballistic field case, pistol lock, steel cleaning rod, Burnt Bronze, Graphite Black, Patriot Brown, or Sniper Grey Cerakote finish, 26.4 oz. Disc.

	100%	98%	95%	90%	80%	70%	60%	LAST MSR
	$635	$555	$475	$435	$350	$285	$225	*$749*

LIPPARD, KARL

Current manufacturer and importer located in Colorado Springs, CO.

Karl Lippard is a well-known firearms designer, importer, shooter, and author of books on Perazzi and Fabbri. He invented the first interchangeable part sidelock O/U shotgun, and currently holds 11 firearm patents, in addition to 12 pistol patents. He also manufactures the only patented pistol and patented rifle in the firearms market today.

PISTOLS: SEMI-AUTO

NCO 1911A2 COMBAT T-1 (TACTICAL ONE) – .45 ACP cal., 5 in. barrel, includes two barrels, available in commercial production and close quarters battle pistol configurations. The only patented pistol in the USA. Accuracy 400 yards hand held. World record holder at 500, 600, and 1,000 yards.

	100%	98%	95%	90%	80%	70%	60%
MSR $3,650	$3,650	$3,350	$2,950	$2,750	$2,500	$2,250	$2,000

Add $1,400 for hand finish.

RIFLES: CUSTOM

BOXLOCK DOUBLE RIFLE – .375 H&H or .470 NE cal., boxlock action, SolidSolid barrels made from one-piece of steel, interchangeable parts, best quality wood. Disc.

Last MSR for this model was $14,750.

Add $4,500 for SolidSolid barrels.

SIDELOCK DOUBLE RIFLE – .375 H&H or .470 NE cal., similar to Boxlock Double rifle, except is sidelock action. Disc.

Last MSR on this model was $44,500.

BOLT ACTION RIFLE – SolidRifle model 300L action made from one solid piece of steel, composite stock.

Base MSR on this model starts at $1,999.

SolidRifle Model Daniel Morgan, various configurations, octagonal barrel and best wood stock starts at $4,500.

Add $11,000 for Signature SolidRifle, fully engraved. Only 20 to be made.

HSR (HOLCOMB SEMI-AUTO RIFLE) – gas operated, magazine fed, composite stock. Patented. Reserved for Indian Army for 2017.

Current MSR on this model is $3,250.

GRADING - PPGS™	100%	98%	95%	90%	80%	70%	60%	LAST MSR

SHOTGUNS: CUSTOM

CLASSIC O/U – 12 (disc.), 20, or 28 ga., sidelock action, interchangeable parts, one-piece MonoSolid barrel, all metal parts (except springs) are S7 vacuum arc remelt steel, classic English scroll engraving, best quality checkered wood. Disc.

Last MSR on this model was $42,950 - SolidSolid barrel models are additional.

Add $6,000 for 12 ga. (disc.).

SPECIAL O/U – similar to Classic, except has more engraving, better quality wood, other custom options. Limited mfg. Disc.

Last MSR on this model was $45,950.

BOXLOCK MODEL – best quality sculpted action boxlock, hidden third fastener, removable/replaceable hidden hinge pin, Joseph Brazier locking bolt, MonoSolid barrels, best quality wood. Disc.

Base price on this model was $10,500.

SIGNATURE SERIES – 12 (disc.), 20, or 28 ga., best quality wood, special engraving, wood treatment, acoutrements, interior engraving, personally designed by Karl Lippard, limited mfg. of 10 guns.

Base price on this model was $130,000.

WATCH MODEL – SolidSolid barrels, each gun is paired with a special wristwatch made exclusively to pair with the gun, watchmaker's design elements, each gun is individually unique, best quality wood. Disc.

Base price on this model was $65,000.

EXHIBITION MODEL – each gun engraved with unique historical subjects, SolidSolid barrels, best quality wood. Disc.

Base price on this model was $85,000.

PREMIER MODEL – 12 (disc. 2013), 20, or 28 ga., sidelock action, interchangeable parts, one-piece SolidSolid patended barrel, all metal parts (except springs) are S7 vacuum arc remelt steel, custom full engraving, best quality checkered wood.

Base price on this model is $130,000.

LITHGOW ARMS

Current civilian and military rifle manufacturer located in Lithgow, Australia. No current U.S. importer. Previously imported by Legacy Sports International, LLC, located in Reno, NV from 2016-2019.

RIFLES: BOLT ACTION

Lithgow Arms is still manufacturing the models listed below, however they are not being currently imported into the U.S. Please contact the manufacturer directly for pricing, options, and availability.

LA 101 CROSSOVER – .17 HMR, .22 LR, or .22 WMR cal., 21 in. cold hammer forged free floating barrel, 5 shot mag., integrated trigger guard, black polymer or walnut brown laminate stock, rubber recoil pad, adj. LOP, butt hook, Cerakote finished barrel, receiver, sight bases, and bolt handle, 6.6-7.2 lbs. Imported by Legacy Sports mid-2016-2019.

100%	98%	95%	90%	80%	70%	60%	LAST MSR
$1,050	$850	$775	$675	$575	$475	$400	*$1,199*

Add $100 for walnut brown laminate stock.

LA 102 CROSSOVER – .223 Rem., .243 Win., 6.5 Creedmoor (new 2019), or .308 Win. cal., 22 in. cold hammer forged free floating barrel, 4 or 5 shot mag., three lever style trigger module adjustable for weight, sear engagement, and over travel, black polymer or walnut brown laminate stock, rubber recoil pad, adj. LOP, integral Picatinny rail, Cerakote finished barrel, receiver, and bolt handle, 7.7-8.2 lbs. Imported by Legacy Sports mid-2016-2019.

100%	98%	95%	90%	80%	70%	60%	LAST MSR
$1,195	$1,050	$925	$775	$650	$550	$450	*$1,399*

Add $100 for walnut brown laminate stock.

LA 105 WOOMERA – .308 Win. or 6.5 Creedmoor cal., 24 in. threaded heavy barrel, 10 shot mag., 20 MOA Picatinny rail, KRG tactical stock, black finish, 11 lbs. Imported by Legacy Sports mid-2018-2019.

100%	98%	95%	90%	80%	70%	60%	LAST MSR
$1,875	$1,650	$1,400	$1,275	$1,025	$850	$675	*$2,199*

LITTLE SHARPS RIFLE MFG.

Previous rifle manufacturer established in 1996, and located in Big Sandy, MT. Consumer direct sales through FFL licensed dealers.

RIFLES: SINGLE SHOT

DELUXE SHARPS RIFLE – various rimmed cals. between .22 LR and .375 LSR, features scaled down frame for smaller cals. (20% smaller than original Sharps), octagon barrel, current mfg. features XXX Grade wood, gold inlays, and engraving, various barrel choices. Mfg. in U.S. 1998-disc.

100%	98%	95%	90%	80%	70%	60%	LAST MSR
$1,250	$1,100	$950	$850	$700	$550	$450	*$3,250*

Subtract approx. 40% if without engraving, gold inlays, and deluxe features XXX Grade wood stock and forearm.

GRADING - PPGS™	100%	98%	95%	90%	80%	70%	60%	LAST MSR

LIL RELIABLE – .17 HMR, .218 Bee, .22 LR (new 2008), .22 Hornet, .22 WMR (new 2009), .357 Mag., .30-30 Win., .38-55 WCF (new 2008), .44-40 WCF (new 2008), or .45 LC cal., 24 (rimfire only) or 26 in. tapered octagon barrel, case colored frame, mfg. by Armi Sport. Limited importation from Italy 2010-2011.

$1,125 $1,000 $900 $800 $725 $650 $575 *$1,229*

LJUNGMAN

Previously manufactured by Carl Gustaf, located in Eskilstuna, Sweden.

RIFLES: SEMI-AUTO

AG 42 – 6.5x55mm Swedish cal., 10 shot mag., wood stock, tangent rear and hooded front, bayonet lug, designed in 1941.

$850 $700 $600 $495 $450 $400 $365

This was the first mass produced, direct gas operated rifle. This weapon was also used by the Egyptian armed forces and was known as the Hakim, and chambered in 8x57mm Mauser.

LJUTIC LLC

Current shotgun manufacturer established circa 1955 and located in Yakima, WA. Dealer direct and retail sales.

Prior to 1960, Ljutic Industries, Inc. did business as Ljutic Gun Co. The name changed again in 2006 to Ljutic LLC.

SHOTGUNS: O/U

LM 6 – 12 ga. only, supplied with one set of O/U barrels, deluxe wood and checkering, separated barrels on O/U.

$17,500 $15,750 $11,000 $9,250 $8,400 $7,500 $6,600 *$19,995*

Add $7,000 for extra set of O/U barrels.
Add $9,000 for top single barrel (includes 2 full trigger groups, and 2 forearms).

DYNA BICENTENNIAL – 12 ga. only, includes one set of O/U barrels, steel or stainless steel frame, deluxe wood and checkered stock and forearm. Mfg. 2000-2007.

$16,500 $14,750 $10,000 $9,000 $8,000 $7,000 $6,000 *$18,995*

Subtract $2,000 for steel frame.

SHOTGUNS: SEMI-AUTO

BI MATIC AUTO LOADER – 12 ga., 2 shot, 26-32 in. barrels, low recoil, trap or skeet models available, stock and choking to customer specifications. Limited mfg. until 1999.

$5,995 $4,450 $2,500 $2,100 $1,750 $1,250 $900 *$5,995*

Add $2,000 for extra barrel.
Add $750 for extra release trigger.

SHOTGUNS: SINGLE BARREL, TRAP

To date approx. 15,000 target shotguns have been manufactured total (all models).

DYNATRAP MODEL – 12 ga., 33 in. barrel, full choke, push-button opening, extractor, trap stock.

$2,500 $2,150 $1,600 $1,475 $1,300 $1,200 $1,100

Add $300 for release trigger.
Add $400 for extra release trigger.
Add $250 for extra pull trigger.

MODEL X-73 MODEL – 12 ga., 33 in. barrel, full choke, push-button opening, high rib fancy Monte Carlo stock.

$2,500 $2,250 $2,000 $1,850 $1,700 $1,600 $1,500

Add $300 for extra pull trigger.
Add $500 for extra release trigger.

DYNOKIC MODEL – 12 ga., 32 (disc.) or 33 in. barrel with 2 choke tubes, patented recoil reduction system reduces felt recoil by 50%, checkered walnut stock, many options available. Mfg. 1997-2003.

$4,795 $4,000 $3,450 $2,900 $2,500 $2,000 $1,650 *$4,795*

Add $1,000 for stainless steel construction.

* ***Dynokic Model Supreme*** – similar to Dynokic Model, except has deluxe walnut stock with checkering. Mfg. 2000-2004.

$5,595 $4,250 $3,400 $3,000 $2,650 $2,300 $1,900 *$5,595*

GRADING - PPGS™	100%	98%	95%	90%	80%	70%	60%	LAST MSR

* ***Dynokic Model Centennial Pro Stainless*** – 12 ga., high grade walnut stock and forearm, 33 in. stainless steel barrel with 2 chokes, recoil reduction system reduces recoil by 50%.

	$7,995	$6,250	$4,875	N/A	N/A	N/A	N/A	*$7,995*

MONO GUN (STANDARD, MEDIUM, OR OLYMPIC RIB) – 12 ga., 34 in. barrel, fixed or screw-in chokes, pull (McCarthy trigger) or release trigger, 3A American or English walnut stock, built to customer specifications.

MSR $7,495	$7,495	$6,850	$6,200	$4,750	$4,250	$3,500	$2,500	

Add $400 for stainless choke tubes.
Add $1,000 for stainless steel construction.
Add $1,500 for stainless steel SLE Pro Model (disc.).
Add $1,000 for SLE Pro Package (includes Laib adj. comb, adj. alum. base plate with 2 pads, and Pro barrel with special bore). Disc.

* ***Mono Gun LTX (Deluxe Mono Trap)*** – similar to Mono Gun except has 33 (disc.) or 34 in. medium rib barrel and exhibition wood and checkering. Disc. 2006.

	$7,995	$6,800	$5,725	$4,750	$3,800	$2,900	$2,350	*$7,995*

Add $500 for extra pull trigger.
Add $650 if with release trigger.
Add $300 for choke tube barrel with 2 chokes.
Add $850 for extra release trigger.
Add $2,499 for extra barrel.
Add $1,200 for stainless steel package.

* ***Mono Gun Pro 3 (Deluxe Mono Trap)*** – 12 ga., similar to Mono Gun except is lighter weight, 34 in. medium rib ported barrel, exhibition wood and checkering, Briley Series 12 choke tubes, pull trigger. New 2000.

MSR $8,995	$8,995	$7,400	$6,100	$5,000	$4,000	$3,000	$2,500	

Add $1,000 for adj. comb.
Add $499 for "one touch" adj. rib.
Add $750 for extra pull trigger.
Add $650 if with release trigger.
Add $850 for extra release trigger assembly.
Add $2,599 for extra barrel with fixed chokes or $2,995 with SIC.
Add $1,000 for stainless steel Pro 3 Package.

PRO 3 – 12 ga. only, 34 in. barrel with three different rib variations and a choice of fixed or adj. chokes, features McCarthy trigger, upgraded 4A English or American walnut stock, screw-in hinge pint and internal flush mount or extended chokes, includes Americase, blued or stainless finish. New 2011.

MSR $8,995	$8,995	$7,400	$6,100	$5,000	$4,000	$3,000	$2,500	

SPACE GUN – 12 ga. only, single barrel, unusual design permits in-line round stock with recoil pad, circular forearm wraps around barrel, high post rib on muzzle half of barrel, patented recoil reduction system reduces recoil by 50%. Disc. 1999.

	$5,995	$4,150	$3,375	$2,825	$2,300	$2,000	$1,750	*$5,995*

LLAMA - Fabrinor S.A.L. (PREVIOUS MFG.)

Previous manufacturer established during 1904, and located in Alava, Spain from 1992-2005. Previously located in Vitoria, Spain until 1992. Previously distributed until 2005 by Import Sports, Inc. located in Wanamassa, NJ. Previously imported and distributed by Stoeger Industries, Inc. located in South Hackensack, NJ until 1993, and by R.S.A. Ent., Inc., located in Ocean, NJ. Previous company name was Llama - Gabilondo y Cia S.A.

During 1992, Llama Gabilondo/Vitoria went bankrupt. In January 2000, after arranging new financing, manufacture was taken over by approx. 60 employees of Gabilondo under the name Fabrinor S.A.L. - a cooperative which closed in 2006.

PISTOLS: SEMI-AUTO

Most of the pistols listed were imported by Stoeger, long time exclusive U.S. importer, and are so marked on the guns.

MODEL IIIA – .380 ACP cal., 7 shot, 3 in. barrel, adj. sights, blue, plastic grips., vent. rib slide. Mfg. 1951-disc.

	$350	$275	$200	$160	$140	$120	$110	

GRADING - PPGS™	100%	98%	95%	90%	80%	70%	60%	LAST MSR

MODEL XA – similar to Model IIIA, except .32 ACP.

	$325	$250	$180	$160	$140	$120	$110	

MODEL XV – similar to Model XA, except .22 LR.

	$365	$250	$180	$160	$140	$120	$110	

Add 50% for airweight.

MODEL XVII – .22 S cal.

	$325	$250	$200	$160	$140	$120	$110	

Add 100% for Deluxe Model if engraved and chromed. Add 200% if engraved and gold plated.
Add $3,000 if gold damascened in 95%+ condition.

MODEL XVIII – .25 ACP cal., blue finish standard, available with optional chrome or gold finish and stag grips.

	$300	$250	$200	$160	$140	$120	$110	

Add 100% for Deluxe Model if engraved and chromed. Add 200% if engraved and gold plated.
Add $2,500 if gold damascened in 95%+ condition.

MODELS C-IIIA, C-XA, C-XV – engraved chrome.

	$500	$400	$300	$275	$250	$225	$200	

MODELS BE-IIIA, BE-XA, BE-XV – similar to Model CE, except engraved, blue.

	$450	$375	$275	$225	$180	$155	$140	

Deluxe Models or chrome engraved with simulated pearl grips, add $20.

MODEL G-IIIA – similar to IIIA, except gold damascened, simulated pearl grips.

	$3,950	$3,500	$2,500	$2,000	$1,500	$1,250	$1,000	

MODEL VIII – .38 Super or 9mm Para. cal., 9 shot, 5 in. barrel, fixed sights, wood grips. Mfg. 1952-disc.

	$400	$295	$235	$195	$180	$165	$140	

Add 100% for 9mm Para. cal.

MODEL IXA – 9mm Para. or .45 ACP cal., vent. rib slide.

	$425	$375	$325	$280	$235	$190	$150	

MODEL XI – similar to Model IXA, except 9mm Para.

	$550	$295	$235	$195	$180	$165	$140	

Add 10% for NIB.
Add 100% for pistols mfg. 1946-1952.

MODELS C-VIII, C-IXA, C-XI – similar to Model VIII, except satin chrome.

	$375	$325	$285	$260	$220	$195	$165	

MODELS CE-VIII, CE-IXA, CE-XI

	$425	$350	$310	$285	$265	$220	$195	

MODELS BE-VIII, BE-IXA, BE-XI – similar to Model CE, except blue, engraving.

	$695	$600	$500	$400	$350	$300	$250	

Add $20 for Deluxe Models (simulated pearl grips).

OMNI – .45 ACP or 9mm Para. cal., double action, all steel construction, 2 sear bars, 3 safeties, 4 1/4 in. barrel, 7 shot mag. in .45 ACP, 13 shot mag. in 9mm Para., blue finish. Importation disc. 1986.

9mm Para.	$440	$380	$330	$295	$260	$225	$200	*$546*
.45 ACP	$395	$360	$320	$285	$250	$220	$195	*$500*

SMALL FRAME MODEL – .22 LR (disc. 1994), .32 ACP (disc. 1993), or .380 ACP cal., Colt 1911A1 design, single action, 3 11/16 in. barrel, 7 shot mag., 23 oz. Also available in satin chrome, optional engraving patterns. Disc. 1997.

	$325	$250	$200	$160	$140	$120	$110	*$259*

Add $75 for duo-tone finish (.380 ACP only, mfg. 1991-1993).
Add $50 for satin chrome finish (not avail. in .32 ACP cal.).

COMPACT FRAME MODEL (IX-B) – 9mm Para. (disc.) or .45 ACP cal., scaled down variation of the Large Frame Model, 4 1/4 in. barrel, 7 or 9 shot mag., 34 or 37 oz. Mfg. 1986-97.

	$325	$255	$200	$180	$160	$155	$150	*$409*

Add $16 for satin chrome finish.
Add $90 for duo-tone finish (mfg. 1990-1993).

GRADING - PPGS™	100%	98%	95%	90%	80%	70%	60%	LAST MSR

GOVERNMENT MODEL (IX-C) – 9mm Para. (disc.), .38 Super (mfg. 1988-1996), or .45 ACP cal., similar to Small Frame Model, 5 1/8 in. barrel, 36 oz., 9 shot mag. in 9mm Para., 7 shot mag. in .45 ACP. Engraved and deluxe models available also. Disc. 1997.

	$350	$255	$200	$180	$160	$150	$140	*$409*

Add $25 for satin chrome finish (.45 ACP only).
Add $100 for duo-tone finish (.45 ACP only, mfg. 1991-1993).

MAX I MODEL – 9mm Para. or .45 ACP cal., patterned after the Colt Govt. Model, 4 1/4 (Compact Model) or 5 1/2 in. barrel, SA, 3-dot combat sights, 7 (.45 ACP) or 9 (9mm Para.) shot mag., matte blue, satin chrome, or duo-tone finish, rubber grips, 34 or 36 oz. Mfg. 1995-99.

	$350	$265	$225	$200	$180	$160	$150	*$299*

Add $10 for duo-tone finish (.45 ACP cal. only).
Add $16 for satin chrome finish (new 1996).

* ***Max-I Model Compensated*** – .45 ACP only, 7 or 10 shot mag., features compensated barrel. Disc. 1997.

	$445	$385	$330	$250	$200	$180	$160	*$492*

Add $25 for 10 shot model.

MINI-MAX – 9mm Para. (disc. 1999), .40 S&W (disc. 2004), or .45 ACP cal., mini-compact variation featuring 6 or 8 shot mag., choice of matte, satin chrome, duo-tone (.45 ACP only), or stainless steel finish/construction, 34 oz. Mfg. 1996-2005.

	$300	$230	$190	$170	$150	$140	$130	*$309*

Add $25 for satin chrome finish.
Add $7 for duo-tone finish (.45 ACP only).
Add $66 for stainless steel construction (disc.).
Add 100% if with Jordain Crest (only 200 mfg., blue finish with numbered mags.).

* ***Mini-Max Sub Compact*** – 9mm Para. (disc. 2000), .40 S&W (disc. 2000), or .45 ACP cal., 3.14 in. barrel, all steel construction, 3-dot combat sights, 10 shot mag., polymer grips, choice of matte, satin chrome, or duo-tone finish, 31 oz. Mfg. 1999-2005.

	$270	$235	$195	$175	$150	$140	$130	*$316*

Add $26 for satin chrome finish.
Add $9 for duo-tone finish (.45 ACP cal. only).

MICRO-MAX – .32 ACP (mfg. 1999-2004, matte finish only) or .380 ACP cal., features standard or lightweight steel design, polymer grips, 7 or 8 shot mag., 3-dot combat sights, slimline slide and frame, non-glare matte or satin chrome finish, 23 oz. Mfg. 1998-2005.

	$375	$325	$275	$250	$200	$170	$130	*$282*

Subtract $15 for Ultra Lite Model (disc.).
Add $18 for satin chrome finish (.380 ACP cal. only, beginning 1999).

MAX II – 9mm Para. or .45 ACP cal., 4.25 (Compact) or 5 1/8 (Government) in. barrel, 3-dot combat sights, anatomically designed polymer grips, 13 (.45 ACP) or 17 (9mm Para.) shot mag., 39-41 oz. Limited mfg. 2005.

	$325	$240	$200	$180	$155	$140	$130	*$325*

MODEL 82 – 9mm Para. cal., double action, 4 1/4 in. barrel, blue finish, 3-dot sighting system, 15 shot mag., ambidextrous safety, loaded chamber indicator, black polymer grips, 39 oz. Imported 1988-93.

	$550	$500	$450	$400	$350	$300	$275	*$975*

MODEL 87 COMPETITION – 9mm Para. cal., competition variation of the Model 82, includes built in ported compensator, oversize magazine and safety release, fixed barrel bushing, beveled rapid load magwell, 14 shot mag., extended and serrated trigger guard, and adj. trigger. Imported 1989-93.

	$950	$800	$700	$600	$500	$450	$400	*$1,450*

REVOLVERS: DOUBLE ACTION

MARTIAL MODEL – .22 LR or .38 Spl. cal., 6 shot, 4 and 6 in. barrels, target sights, blue, checkered wood grips. Mfg. 1969-76.

	$220	$200	$180	$165	$140	$120	$100

DELUXE MARTIAL – similar to Martial, except finish as follows:

Satin chrome	$325	$295	$245	$195	$165	$140	$120
Chrome, engraved	$650	$550	$450	$400	$350	$300	$250
Blue, engraved	$750	$650	$500	$450	$375	$300	$250
Gold, damascened	$3,950	$3,500	$2,500	N/A	N/A	N/A	N/A

GRADING - PPGS™	100%	98%	95%	90%	80%	70%	60%	LAST MSR

COMANCHE I – .22 LR cal., similar to Martial DA, mfg. 1977-82.

	$400	$350	$300	$260	$220	$180	$140	

COMANCHE II – .38 Spl. cal., similar to Martial DA, mfg. 1977-82 and 1986 in .22 LR and .22 WMR cal. only.

	$425	$375	$325	$280	$235	$190	$150	*$272*

COMANCHE III – .22 LR (disc.) or .357 Mag. cal., 6 shot, 4, 6, or 8 1/2 (disc. 1986) in. barrel, blue, adj. sights, checkered walnut grips. Mfg. 1975-95. Before 1977, it was called "Comanche."

	$450	$400	$350	$300	$250	$205	$160	*$339*

*** *Comanche III Satin Chrome Finish***

	$500	$440	$375	$325	$275	$225	$175	*$395*

*** *Comanche III Gold Damascene Finish***

	$3,950	$3,500	$2,500	N/A	N/A	N/A	N/A	

SUPER COMANCHE IV – .44 Mag. cal., 6 or 8 1/2 in. VR barrel, adj. sights, blue only. Disc. 1998.

	$450	$350	$275	$250	$225	$200	$175	*$440*

SUPER COMANCHE V – .357 Mag. cal., 6 shot, 4, 6, or 8 1/2 in. VR barrel, adj. sights, blue only. Importation disc. 1988.

	$395	$350	$295	$250	$225	$200	$175	*$414*

LLAMA (NEW MFG.)

Current trademark established during 2016, manufactured in the Philippines by MetroArms Corp. Currently imported by Eagle Imports Inc., located in Wanamassa, NJ.

PISTOLS: SEMI-AUTO

MICROMAX – .380 ACP cal., SA, 3 3/4 in. forged steel barrel, 7 shot mag., steel slide and frame, skeletonized hammer, perforated trigger, fiber optic front sight, Novak style rear sight, choice of wood or black synthetic grips w/partial thumb rest, ambidextrous thumb and beavertail safety, double slide serrations, matte blue or hard chrome (new 2018) finish, 22.9 oz. New 2016.

MSR $468	$395	$350	$300	$275	$250	$225	$195	

Add $97 for hard chrome finish (new 2018).

MAX-1 – .38 Super (new 2017) or .45 ACP cal., SA, 5 in. barrel, 8 or 9 shot mag., spur hammer, Mil-Spec sights, lowered ejection port and Mil-Spec slide serrations, matte blue or hard chrome (.38 Super only) finish, 37 oz. New 2016.

MSR $565	$475	$400	$350	$300	$275	$250	$225	

Add $95 for hard chrome finish (.38 Super cal. only).

LOHMAN GUNSMITHING

Current custom manufacturer, gunsmith, and restoration specialist established in 2012, located in Houston, TX.

Brian Lohman MFG, manufactures bolt actions, pistols, and revolvers that are built to customer specifications. Lohman also specializes in period correct restorations and finishing. The finishes include period correct bone charcoal color case hardening, all types of bluing, custom stock making, custom part making, checkering wood and metal, Cerakote, and repairs and modifications of any type of firearm. Please contact Mr. Lohman directly for more information, including pricing, delivery time, and availability.

PISTOLS: SEMI-AUTO

YMIR 1911 – .45 ACP cal., Commander size, 4 1/4 in. Nowlin 416R stainless match grade barrel, Mec-Gar 7 and 8 shot mags., Novak 14 kt gold front and VU-notch rear sights, lace burl red wood grips, includes American Eagle seal and olive branch proof mark w/matching serial number to the pistol on 18 individual internal parts, case color frame w/two-tone polished finish and bluing on slide.

Current MSR on this model is $8,500, depending on configuration/options.

LOKI WEAPON SYSTEMS, INC.

Previous manufacturer and distributor circa 2009-2012 and located in Coalgate, OK.

Please refer to BlueBookOfGunValues.com to order the *Blue Book of AR-15s & Variations*, available as a book or online subscription.

LON PAUL CUSTOM GUNS

Current custom rifle manufacturer located in Mountain Center, CA.

Lon Paul builds high quality custom rifles with a variety of options. Please contact him directly for an individualized price quotation, including specifications and delivery time.

GRADING - PPGS™	100%	98%	95%	90%	80%	70%	60%	LAST MSR

LONE STAR ARMAMENT, INC.

Previous pistol manufacturer located in Stephenville, TX circa 1970-2004. During 2003, Lone Star Armament was absorbed by STI, located in Georgetown, TX.

PISTOLS: SEMI-AUTO

Lone Star Armament manufactured a lineup of M1911 style pistols. Models included: Ranger Match ($1,595 last MSR), Lawman Match ($1,595 last MSR), Lawman Series ($1,475 last MSR), Ranger Series ($1,475 last MSR), and the Guardian Series ($895 last MSR).

LONE STAR ARMORY

Current manufacturer of custom-built precision firearms established in 2004, located in Fort Worth, TX.

Please refer to BlueBookOfGunValues.com to order the *Blue Book of AR-15s & Variations*, available as a book or online subscription.

LONE STAR RIFLE CO., INC.

Previous rifle manufacturer circa 1992-2011 and located in Conroe, TX. The company specialized in Remington Rolling Block rifle reproductions.

RIFLES: REPRODUCTIONS

REMINGTON ROLLING BLOCK SERIES – various black powder cartridge cals., configurations, and options, case colored or nickel plated receiver, rust or nitre blue barrel, extra select checkered walnut, single or double set triggers.

* ***Remington Rolling Block Creedmoor*** – features competition long range 34 in. full octagon or half octagon/half round barrel with pistol grip and shotgun butt, single trigger set at 3 lbs., per Creedmoor rules, 10 lbs.

  $2,000 $1,650 $1,275 $995 $875 $725 $600 ***$2,195***

* ***Remington Rolling Block Silhouette (Target)*** – designed for silhouette competition, with 30, 32, or 34 in. full octagon or half octagon/half round barrel with pistol grip and shotgun butt. Disc. 2011.

  $2,250 $2,000 $1,650 $1,275 $995 $875 $725 ***$2,495***

* ***Remington Rolling Block Silhouette Standard Rifle*** – .40-65 or .45-70 Govt. cal., similar to #5 Sporting Standard Rifle, except has 32 or 34 in. barrel, steel shotgun buttplate, pistol grip stock, 11 lbs. Mfg. 1999-2006.

  $1,400 $1,150 $900 $750 $600 $550 $475 ***$1,595***

* ***Remington Rolling Block Cowboy Action Rifle*** – .32-40 WCF, .38-55 WCF, .40-65 WCF, .44-77, .45 LC (disc. 2002), .45-70 Govt., or .50-70 cal., heavy 28 in. barrel, 8 1/2 lbs. Mfg. 1999-2006.

  $1,400 $1,150 $900 $750 $600 $550 $475 ***$1,595***

* ***Remington Rolling Block #5 Sporting Standard Rifle*** – .25-35 WCF (new 2002), .30-30 Win. (new 2000) or .30-40 Krag cal., 26 in. round barrel, single trigger, case colored frame, standard American walnut stock and forearm, 6 lbs. Mfg. 1999-2006.

  $1,400 $1,150 $900 $750 $600 $550 $475 ***$1,595***

* ***Remington Rolling Block Classic #5*** – .22 Hornet, .25-35 WCF, .30-30 Win., .30-40 Krag, or .33 WCF cal., rapid taper octagon barrel, approx. 6 lbs. Mfg. 2007-2009.

  $3,250 $2,750 $2,375 $2,000 $1,750 $1,550 $1,250 ***$3,500***

* ***Remington Rolling Block #7 Sporting Rifle*** – .25-20 WCF, .32-20 WCF, or .22 Hornet cal. Mfg. 2002-2007.

  $3,000 $2,650 $2,350 $1,950 $1,725 $1,500 $1,200 ***$3,500***

* ***Remington Rolling Block Sporting Rifle*** – various cals., standard sporting rifle designed for accuracy, 28, 30, or 32 in. barrel, straight grip stock. Disc. 2011.

  $2,250 $2,000 $1,650 $1,275 $995 $875 $725 ***$2,495***

* ***Remington Rolling Block Deluxe Sporting Rifle*** – deluxe variation of the Sporting Rifle with 28, 30, or 32 in. full octagon or half octagon/half round barrel with pistol grip and shotgun butt, buckhorn rear sight and choice of front sight. Disc.

  $2,000 $1,650 $1,275 $995 $875 $725 $600 ***$2,195***

* ***Remington Rolling Block Custer Rifle*** – .50-70 cal., an exact reproduction of Gen. G.A. Custer's original Remington Rolling Block, 28 in. octagon barrel with SST, straight grip, crescent buttplate, and Schnabel forearm tip. Disc. 2011.

  $3,000 $2,650 $2,350 $1,950 $1,725 $1,500 $1,200 ***$3,500***

* ***Remington Rolling Block Buffalo Rifle*** – various cals., features relic finish enabling a new gun to appear somewhat worn, double set triggers, exact copy of the original, 16 lbs. Disc.

  $2,850 $2,400 $1,900 $1,625 $1,400 $1,200 $1,000 ***$3,200***

GRADING - PPGS™	100%	98%	95%	90%	80%	70%	60%	LAST MSR

* ***Remington Rolling Block Take Down Model*** – features take down action. Mfg. 2001-2002.

	$3,600	$3,150	$2,750	$2,300	$1,995	$1,700	$1,375	*$4,000*

GOVE ROLLING BLOCK – various cals., new rolling block with underlever design by Carlos Gove. Mfg. 1998-2002.

	$2,650	$2,250	$1,875	$1,625	$1,400	$1,200	$1,000	*$2,995*

LONE STAR TACTICAL SUPPLY

Previous AR-15 style firearms and current accessories manufacturer located in Tomball, TX.

For individual model listings, please go to BlueBookOfGunValues.com/overflow.

LONE WOLF DISTRIBUTORS

Current manufacturer of semi-auto pistols and accessories established in 1998, located in Priest River, ID.

PISTOLS: SEMI-AUTO

THE GUARDIAN – 9x19mm Para. cal., safe action, 4.02 in. black or gray barrel, 15 shot mag., square trigger guard, Taclock thumb safety, black or silver frame, 23.63 oz. New 2020.

MSR $779	$700	$600	$500	$475	$375	$325	$250

LONGTHORNE GUNMAKERS LTD

Current UK shotgun manufacturer established in mid-2010, located in Northampton, England. Previously located in Lancashire, England. Select models are currently being imported by Pacific Sporting Arms, located in Azusa, CA beginning 2020.

All of their guns incorporate their unique patented solid barrel construction (i.e. both barrels integrally constructed from one single block of high specification steel) assuring low felt recoil and muzzle flip. With 3 in. chambers can be London proofed for magnum steel shot, 3 in. chambers in 12, 20, or .410, 16 and 28 gauge models in 2 3/4 in. chambers London proofed for steel, either up to full (fixed) choke.

SHOTGUNS: O/U

Descriptions include base gun with standard options. A variety of options are available at the customer's request. Longthorne Gunmakers manufactures off-the-shelf models with matte black action, 30 or 32 in. Longthorne barrels w/right or left-hand opening, fixed chokes (standard), and stocks w/ skip-line checkering.

Prices do not include U.K. VAT of 20%.

BOXLOCK SPORTING MODEL – 12 ga., 3 in. chamber, boxlock, ultra low-profile action, 30 (flat rib) or 32 (ramped trap) in. sporting barrels, multi-chokes, adj. trigger, standard trigger guard, front bead sight, walnut stock, beavertail forend w/metalwork, plain underlever release catch, with or w/o engraving (Sporter Deluxe), satin finish. Importation began 2020.

MSR $16,775	$14,250	$12,500	$10,700	$9,700	$7,850	$6,400	$5,000

Add $6,420 for Sporter Deluxe.

BOXLOCK SPORTING SIDEPLATE – 12 ga., 3 in. chamber, sideplate boxlock action, 30 (flat rib) or 32 (ramped trap) in. style sporting barrels, multi-chokes, adj. trigger, medium grade walnut stock w/ checkered heel or recoil pad, rounded or beavertail forend, simple styled engraving work, leather trimmed case. Importation began 2020.

MSR $29,995	$25,500	$22,300	$19,100	$17,350	$14,000	$11,500	$8,900

CELTIC – 12, 16, 20, 28 ga., or .410 bore (mfg. 2016-2017), low profile action, (true) sidelock, game or sporting configuration, advanced patented barrel technology, assuring low recoil and low muzzle flip, fixed choke (standard), proofed for steel up to full choke (magnum steel in models with 3 in. chambers), bespoke Turkish walnut stock, fully bespoke, right or left-hand action, traditional celtic engraving with choice of thistle, shamrock, or welsh dragon on top lever, presented in an exemplary quality English bridle leather gun slip, approx. 7 lbs. New 2015.

Base price for this gun is £19,941.
Add £1,354 for 12 ga.
Add £3,386 for .410 bore (mfg. 2016-2017).

"HESKETH" – standard entry level, 12, 16, 20, 28 ga., or .410 bore (mfg. 2016-2017), low profile action, sidelock, right or left-hand action, gaming or sporting configuration, 26 to 34 in. solid barrels, fully bespoke, SST, English scroll engraving, bespoke Turkish walnut stock, includes green canvas case with hand sewn leather corners and Longthorne emblem (disc.) or presented in exemplary quality English bridle leather gun slip, approx. 7 lbs. with 30 in. bbls.

Base price for this gun is £14,500.
Add £1,744 for .410 bore (mfg. 2016-2017).

GRADING - PPGS™	100%	98%	95%	90%	80%	70%	60%	LAST MSR

"HESKETH" DELUXE – 12, 16, 20, 28 ga., or .410 bore (new 2016) 3 in. chambers, low profile action, sidelock, game or sporting configuration, 26-34 in. barrels, advanced patented barrel technology, fixed choke (standard), bespoke Turkish walnut stock, presented in an exemplary quality English bridle leather gun slip, proofed for steel up to full choke, fully bespoke, deep acanthus scroll engraving, right or left-hand action, approx. 7 lbs. with 30 in. bbls. New 2012.

Base price for this gun is £18,142.
Add £1,696 for .410 bore (new 2016).

NOUVEAU – 12, 16, 20, or 28 ga., game or sporting configuration, right or left-hand action, 26-34 in. barrels, low profile action, fixed choke (standard), gold plated SST, extended trigger tang w/grip cap, bespoke Turkish walnut stock, proofed for steel up to full choke, fully bespoke, very detailed engraving incorporating flora and insects and scrollwork, eight gold pins, presented in an exemplary quality English bridle leather gun slip, auto safe, approx. 7 lbs. with 30 in. bbls. New 2017.

Base price for this gun is £23,408.

This model is also available in a SxS and boxlock configuration (incorporating patented barrel technology).

RENAISSANCE – 12, 16, or 20 ga., gold plated trigger, extended full-length trigger guard, exhibition grade walnut stock cap, new style underlever forend release, Renaissance deep engraving w/gold inlaid game birds and flower, personalized gold stock oval, Malton bridle leather double gun slip and case. New 2019.

Base price range for a single gun is £39,950-£50,000. Base price for a pair is £79,000-£100,000 (including VAT of 20%).

RUTLAND – 12, 16, 20, 28 ga., or .410 bore (new 2016), low profile action, sidelock, game or sporting configuration, 28-30 in. barrels, advanced patented barrel technology, 8 Kt. gold plated single selective trigger, bespoke Turkish walnut stock, auto safety, fixed choke (standard), can be proofed for steel up to full choke (magnum steel in models with 3 in. chambers), right or left-hand action, elaborate and detailed engraving with gold inlay, presented in an exemplary leather case with the "Longthorne" emblem on the inside lid and an initialed brass plaque on outside of case, approx. 7 lbs. Mfg. 2012-2016.

Base price for this gun was £28,090.
Add £4,213 for .410 bore (new 2016).

SMALL ROSE & SCROLL – 12, 16, 20, 28 ga., or .410 bore (mfg. 2016-2017), O/U shotgun, (true) sidelock, game gun or sporting configuration, 26-34 in. barrels, fixed choke (as standard), bespoke Turkish walnut stock, proofed for steel up to full choke, fully bespoke, small scroll engraving, right or true left-hand action, presented in an exemplary quality English bridle leather gun slip, approx. 7 lbs. with 30 in. bbls. New 2015.

Base price for this gun is £15,625.
Add £1,466 for .410 bore (mfg. 2016-2017).

SPORTER (L1-SP) – 12 ga., 28 to 32 in. solid barrels, sidelock, SST, low profile action, English scroll engraving, semi-pistol grip or straight grip Turkish walnut stock, right or left-hand, includes green canvas case with hand sewn leather corners and Longthorne emblem, approx. 7 lbs., 8 oz.

Last base price in 2012 for this gun was £10,650.

SHOTGUNS: SXS

SIDE X SIDE – 12 or 20 ga., 3 in. chambers, sidelock, triple bite action, 28-32 in. barrels, ejector, non-selective inertia single trigger or double trigger, straight hand stock, available with "Acanthus Scroll", 6.5 lb. New 2017.

Base price for this gun is £23,500.

LORCIN ENGINEERING CO., INC.

Previous handgun manufacturer located in Mira Loma, CA, 1989-1999.

DERRINGERS: O/U

STAINLESS MODEL – .357 Mag. or .45 LC cal., 3 1/2 in. barrel, synthetic grips, tip-up action, rebounding hammer, fixed sights. Mfg. 1996-98.

	100%	98%	95%	90%	80%	70%	60%	LAST MSR
	$175	$155	$140	$125	$110	$100	$90	*$110*

PISTOLS: SEMI-AUTO

During the height of production in the mid-90s, Lorcin was making 40,000 semi-auto pistols a month. One year, its production totalled 400,000 units.

Before buying any Lorcin pistol, it is recommended that a competent gunsmith check it out.

GRADING - PPGS™	100%	98%	95%	90%	80%	70%	60%	LAST MSR

L-22 MODEL – .22 LR cal., similar to L-25 Model, except 2.55 in. barrel and 9 shot mag., black or chrome finish, 16 oz. Mfg. 1992-99.

	$75	$60	$50	$45	$40	$35	$35	*$89*

L-25 MODEL – .25 ACP cal., single action, 6 shot mag., 2.4 in. barrel, anatomically designed grips to fit hand better, choice of black and gold, chrome and pearl, satin chrome and pearl, Teflon camo finish (new 1992), or black and pearl finish, 13.5 oz. Mfg. 1989-99.

	$65	$50	$45	$40	$35	$35	$35	*$79*

Add $20 for lightweight frame (Model LT 25, new in 1990).

* ***L-25 Model Lady Lorcin*** – same specifications as the L-25 Model, except is available in chrome, satin chrome, or black exterior finish with pink grips. Mfg. 1990-99.

	$70	$60	$50	$45	$40	$35	$35	*$79*

L-32 – .32 ACP cal., single action, 7 shot mag., 3 1/2 in. barrel, available in black or chrome finish, 23 oz. Mfg. 1992-99.

	$80	$70	$60	$50	$45	$40	$35	*$89*

L-380 – .380 ACP cal., single action, 7 shot mag., 3 1/2 in. barrel, available in black or chrome finish, 23 oz. Mfg. 1992-99.

	$85	$75	$65	$55	$50	$45	$40	*$100*

LH-380 – .380 ACP cal., similar to L9MM, 36 oz. Mfg. 1995-99.

	$125	$115	$100	$90	$85	$80	$75	*$149*

L9MM – 9mm Para. cal., single action, 10 (C/B 1994) or 13* shot mag., 4 1/2 in. barrel, grip safety, black finish, 3-dot sights, 36 oz. Mfg. 1994-99.

	$125	$115	$100	$90	$85	$80	$75	*$149*

Add $20 for disc. 13 shot mag. variation.

LORENZO, CRESS

Previous rifle manufacturer located in Minersville, UT.

Custom gunmaker Cress Lorenzo specialized in custom express rifles built to customer specifications. Many options were available, in addition to general gunsmithing services.

LOSOK CUSTOM ARMS

Current semi-auto rifle manufacturer established in 2005, located in Delaware, OH.

Losok Custom Arms offers a limited manufacture of AR's in both 5.56 NATO and .308 Win. calibers.

RIFLES: SEMI-AUTO

VALKYR – various cals. between .30-06-.458 Win. Mag., various barrel configurations 18 to 28 in. sporter through heavy, choice of M1 Garand or M14 operating system, milled receiver, modified M1918 Browning BAR magazine, McMillan stock, Picatinny top rail, 16 1/2 lbs. Mfg. 2012-disc.

LUCCHINI, SANDRO

Current manufacturer located in Sarezzo (Brescia), Italy. No current U.S. importation.

Sandro Lucchini manufactures high quality, made to order, double rifles and SxS shotguns (approx. 10-20 guns annually). Starting prices for shotguns are as follows (not including engraving) - Purdey style rose and scroll is approx. €1,750, while elaborate work by a master engraver can exceed €18,000. Shotguns: €7,000 for Anson action without sideplates (add €1,200 for sideplates), €15,700 for standard sidelock, manual cocking extractor hammer guns start at €7,800, self cocking ejectors are €17,200. Add 10% for 28 ga. or .410 bore, and €450 for single trigger. All shotgun barrels are demi-bloc construction. New O/U scaled frame 20 and 28 ga. shotguns begin at €7,100, including fine line gold inlay and case colors. Double rifles start at €26,500 for calibers under .375 H&H, and are available up to .600 NE. All double rifles feature Ferlach barrels.

Please contact the importer directly for more information, including an individual price quotation and delivery time.

LUGERS WITH VARIATIONS

LUGER® REG. U.S. PAT. OFF.

Semi-auto pistol design originated by Georg Luger while at DWM, circa 1899. Several subsequent manufacturers - see main text for more information. Previous post-WWII manufacture (through 1997) was by Mauser-Werke Oberndorf Waffensysteme, located in Oberndorf, Germany.

Note: The Luger section in this book is arranged chronologically by year of manufacture under individual manufacturer/city arsenal headings.

Often times, year of production can be hard to nail down, especially on commercial models. An easier way to initially identify your Luger is to categorize by toggle marking first - then by chamber marking within groups (chronologically for dated chambers). Once you know period of manufacture, simply refer to the appropriate subheading in this section. While some rare variations will be excluded in this generalized overview, it will be very helpful to establish correct, basic knowledge about your particular Luger.

While many recently imported Lugers would make workable shooters, they have in no way lowered prices on 90%+ condition specimens with all matching original parts due to normal collector activity in original condition only pistols. Recently imported Lugers should have the importer's name visibly stamped on an exterior surface. Most of these recent imports are in the 9mm Para. - 4 in. barrel configuration. Recently imported Lugers with the importer's markings visible are typically priced in the $450-$700 range.

Every year more and more reblued, restrawed, regripped, reframed, and rebarreled Lugers are sold to unknowing military handgun collectors as rare variations. On any expensive contract variation, careful inspection for originality on all parts must be made before potentially purchasing. If in doubt, secure 2 or 3 additional appraisals/observations from qualified individuals. Lugers are a field in themselves and a specialized Winchester dealer would not be qualified to guesstimate the originality of these German handguns.

A final note on Lugers: Original pistols in 90%-100% condition have not been affected by the influx of recent imports as these newly imported guns are usually in 80% and lower condition or have been reblued.

It seems that every year the prices of top quality (98%+ condition) original Lugers get more expensive and less predictable. For this reason, the 100% values on many Lugers have been omitted intentionally, since rarity precludes accurate price evaluation in this condition factor. In many cases, the value for a mint original military Luger can double the 98% price listed.

For Borchardt models, please refer to Borchardt listing.

Values for all variations of Lugers assume a proper magazine and matching parts. All Lugers that were originally manufactured with numbered magazines should increase in value if that Luger has one or both original matching magazines.

REFERENCE GUIDE BY TOGGLE MARKING

DWM TOGGLE IDENTIFICATION

DWM stands for Deutsche Waffen-und Munitionsfabriken or Berlin.

DWM MODELS – mfg. from 1900 to 1930 in Berlin, Germany. All serial number ranges approximate.

* ***DWM Models 1900*** – original (i.e. old model) features dished toggles grips, leaf mainspring, spring steel extractor, grip safety, ser. nos. 1-24,999.
* ***DWM Models 1902*** – old model features, ser. nos. 21,001-25,000.
* ***DWM Transitional Models 1903-1904*** – mixture of old and new model features, ser. nos. listed with each model.
* ***DWM Models 1906*** – new model features fully checkered toggle grips, coil mainspring, loaded chamber indicating extractor, grip safety, many chamber markings, ser. nos. 25,051-71,000. All subsequent models have new model features.
* ***DWM Models 1908 Commercial*** – no grip safety, 9mm Para., ser. nos. range 39,000-74,000.
* ***DWM Model 1914 Commercial*** – stock lug, 9mm Para. cal., ser. nos. 70,000-74,000.
* ***DWM Models 1908 Military*** – no stock lug, undated or 1910-1913.
* ***DWM Models 1914 Military*** – stock lug, dated 1913-1918.
* ***DWM Models 1920 Commercial*** – usually w/o grip safety, 3 7/8 in. barrel - others available. Most common Luger, undated chamber, 7.65mm Para. or 9mm Para.

Note: Lugers with 4 inch barrels are most frequently encountered in military and commercial models. 6 in. barrels usually denote "Navy" models. 8 in. barrels usually denote "Artillery" models. Guns with barrels over 8 inches are rare and should be checked carefully for originality.

DWM COMMERCIAL LUGERS

DWM stands for Deutsche Waffen-und Munitionsfabriken. These are models manufactured from 1900-1923 found in the five digit serial range.

MODEL 1900 – ser. range 1-20,000. Configuration: 4 3/4 in. x 7.65mm Para., Commercial (blank chamber), American Eagle, Swiss.

MODEL 1900 – ser. range 20,001-21,000. Configuration: 4 3/4 in. x 7.65mm Para., Bulgarian contract.

MODEL 1902 – ser. range 21,001-25,000. Configuration: 9mm Para. x 4 in. "Fat Barrels" and 11 3/4 in. x 7.65mm Para. Carbine models, intermixed with 4 3/4 x 7.65mm Para. American Eagles and Commercials.

MODEL 1906 – ser. range 25,001-39,000. Configuration: Commercial, American Eagle, Navy Commercial and Swiss, both 4 3/4 in. x 7.65mm Para. and 9mm Para. x 4 in. grip safety models. Navy Commercial has 6 in. barrel.

MODEL 1908 – ser. range 39,001-71,000. Configuration: First 9mm Para. x 4 in. without grip safety, M1908 Commercials were interspersed with 7.65mm Para. and 9mm Para. Eagles, Commercials, Navy Commercials, and a few Carbines and Swiss. Carbines are Model 1902 in 50,000 serial range.

MODEL 1914 – ser. range 71,001-74,000. Configuration: Last pre-WWI Commercial Lugers, made with stock lug, with a few 9mm Para. Commercials mixed in.

MODEL 1920 – ser. range 2,000i-9,999u. Configuration: Post-WWI Commercials, mostly 3 7/8 in. x 7.65mm Para. cal.

MODEL 1923 – ser. range 89,001-91,000. Configuration: The last thousand or so made have "safe" on lever and "loaded" on the extractor, 3 7/8 in. x 7.65mm Para. barrels.

WWI DWM MILITARY SERIAL RANGES

CHAMBER DATE	OBSERVED LOW SERIAL	OBSERVED HIGH SERIAL	APPROXIMATE QTY. MADE
1908	(undated) 34	2636b	25,000
1910	5095b	5358d	20,000
1911	1524c	4825e	13,000
1912	599	9974	10,000
1913	2617	3850d	25,000
1914	282	6212c	40,000
1915	1398	5415d	100,000
1916	287	5438q	180,000
1917	587	3521m	60,000
1918	110	9018n	190,000

Production data appears courtesy of Jan C. Still.

ERFURT TOGGLE IDENTIFICATION

ERFURT MODELS – produced from 1911-1914 and 1916-1918 at the Royal Arms Factory in Erfurt, Germany. Military Model - Chamber dated 1911-1914 and 1916-1918. Erfurt models exhibit the most proof marks or individual parts numbering. Walnut grips.

WWI ERFURT MILITARY SERIAL RANGES

CHAMBER DATE	OBSERVED LOW SERIAL	OBSERVED HIGH SERIAL	APPROXIMATE QTY. MADE
1911	575	9548	10,000
1912	255	866b	22,000
1913	575	2563b	25,000
1914	2137	539A	25,000
1915	none observed		

CHAMBER DATE	OBSERVED LOW SERIAL	OBSERVED HIGH SERIAL	APPROXIMATE QTY. MADE
1916	13	5764b	80,000
1917	844	2854n	150,000
1918	304	5816s	180,000

Production data appears courtesy of Jan C. Still.

SIMSON & CO. TOGGLE IDENTIFICATION

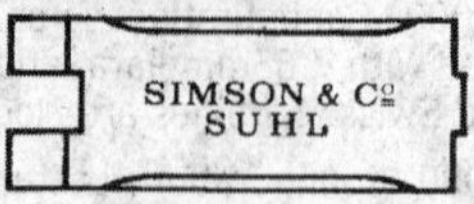

SIMSON & CO. – manufactured 1925 to 1934 in Suhl, Germany. During this period, Simson manufactured approx. 12,000 Lugers. Simson Lugers are military models (9mm - 4 in. barrels). During this 12 year period, Simson supplied the German Army with newly manufactured Lugers exclusively. Can be dated 1925 or 1926 or not dated at all. Many reworks of WWI DWM Military Lugers were refurbished by Simson, and can be detected by the Simson "Eagle-over-6" proof on repaired parts. Toggles are marked "Simson" or "S".

SWISS TOGGLE IDENTIFICATION

SWISS BERN MODELS – Manufactured 1918 to 1947 by WAFFENFABRIK Bern, Switzerland. Relatively rare - these Swiss models have "improved" changes (flat and curved front grip strap), 4 3/4 in. barrels, walnut or plastic grips, grip safety. 1929 model (flat front grip strap) has Swiss Cross in shield on front link.

MAUSER TOGGLE IDENTIFICATION

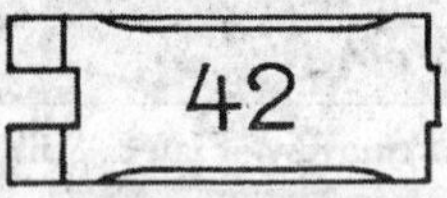

MAUSER VARIATIONS – Manufactured 1934-1942 in Oberndorf, Germany. Between 1930 and 1934 Mauser Werke was primarily engaged in reworking older Lugers, since transfer of machinery and personnel to the DWM plant in Berlin was completed in 1931. Mauser "Banner" models were made from 1934 to 1942, many are dated from 1936-1942 on the chamber. S/42 models are MOSTLY MILITARY contract guns manufactured between 1934 and 1940, usually chamber marked. "42" toggle marked guns (Mauser code) were mfg. 1939 and 1940 and are dated. "byf" marked toggles indicate guns made for German military use after 1940 and are more common than other military models. The Mauser Werke trademark also appears on those Lugers made in the 1970s.

KRIEGHOFF TOGGLE IDENTIFICATION

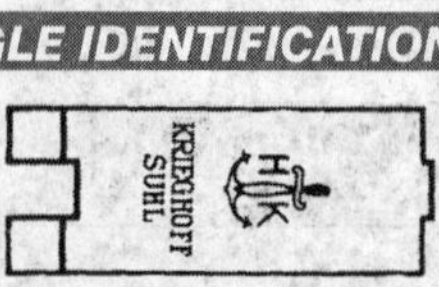

KRIEGHOFF MODELS – Manufactured between 1934-1946 in Suhl, Germany. Early Commercial Krieghoffs are side frame inscribed. The German Luftwaffe contracted with Krieghoff for military guns in 1935. Early military Krieghoffs have "G" (scarce) and then later "S" marked chambers, most are chamber dated between 1936 and 1945. Krieghoff Lugers are prized for their quality fit and finish and command higher prices because of their rarity factor. The vast majority of commercial Krieghoff Lugers have the letter P before the serial number. Estimated total Krieghoff produced between 13,000 and 14,000.

GRADING - PPGS™	100%	98%	95%	90%	80%	70%	60%	LAST MSR

VICKERS TOGGLE IDENTIFICATION

VICKERS – Manufactured by Vickers, Ltd., circa 1921 in England, possibly using some DWM parts for military contract sale to the Netherlands. Added barrel date is a date of arsenal refinish or refurbishing. Distinguishable by Vickers toggle and "Rust" marked safety. Serial range is 4,000-10,100. Grips can be finely checkered with shallow contour or very coarsely checkered. Configuration is 9mm Para., 4 in. barrel, and grip safety.

LUGERS: MATCHING MAGAZINE(S) & MILITARY HOLSTER ADD ONS

Values for all variations of Lugers listed assume a proper original magazine and matching parts.

Add approx. 50% for one original matching magazine on all Lugers listed below that were originally manufactured/issued with numbered magazines.

Add approx. 75%-100% for two original matching magazines on all Lugers listed in the following sections that were originally manufactured/issued with numbered magazines, depending on condition.

Add approx. $250-$400 for original military holster (4 in. barrel only), depending on condition.

PISTOLS: SEMI-AUTO, LUGERS & VARIATIONS

Lugers: Pre-1900 & 1900 DWM Mfg.

Values on most 100% Lugers have been omitted intentionally since rarity precludes accurate price evaluation in this condition factor.

1898/99 BORCHARDT LUGER TRANSITIONAL – 7.65mm Para. cal., 5 in. barrel, this is perhaps one of the most desirable Lugers, only few mfg. Examples scarce, no reported sales, an original example would command a price in the 6-figure range.

1899/1900 SWISS TEST MODEL – 7.65mm Para. cal., 4 3/4 in. barrel, 50 mfg., pre-production with wide border grips and thin frame rails, the very first true Luger. Hand engraved "Swiss Cross" chamber marking on first 35 pistols - stamped on later mfg.

	100%	98%	95%	90%	80%	70%	60%
	N/A	$75,000	$53,000	$40,000	$30,000	$25,000	$20,000

Approx. 50 pistols serial numbered in the 1-50 range.

Buyers should be very cautious when considering a purchase of this rare model, as good fakes do exist.

1900 COMMERCIAL DWM – 7.65mm Para. cal., 4 3/4 in. barrel, approx. 5,500 mfg.

	100%	98%	95%	90%	80%	70%	60%
	N/A	$5,500	$4,750	$4,250	$3,500	$2,750	$2,250

1900 SWISS COMMERCIAL DWM – 7.65mm Para. cal., 4 3/4 in. barrel, 2,000 commercially mfg.

	100%	98%	95%	90%	80%	70%	60%
	N/A	$5,000	$4,000	$3,000	$2,500	$2,000	$1,750
Unrelieved grip frame	N/A	$9,500	$8,250	$7,000	$5,500	$4,500	$3,500

1900 SWISS MILITARY DWM – 7.65mm Para. cal., 4 3/4 in. barrel, 5,000 military mfg.

	100%	98%	95%	90%	80%	70%	60%
	N/A	$5,500	$5,000	$4,500	$3,500	$2,860	$2,250
Unrelieved grip frame	N/A	$12,000	$9,500	$7,000	$5,500	$4,500	$3,500

1900 AMERICAN EAGLE DWM – 7.65mm Para. cal., 4 3/4 in. barrel, approx. 12,000 mfg.

	100%	98%	95%	90%	80%	70%	60%
	N/A	$5,500	$4,750	$4,250	$3,500	$2,750	$2,250

Add 40% for U.S. Test Model (approx. ser. no. range 6,009 - 7,500) - not marked Germany, has no proofmarks, take down lever numbered on axel, right side; some in 7,000 serial range have numbers on the left-side flat of the take down lever

1900 BULGARIAN DWM – 7.65mm Para. cal., 4 3/4 in. barrel, 1,000 mfg., very rare in U.S., most often seen in the 60% and lower condition.

	100%	98%	95%	90%	80%	70%	60%
	N/A	$8,500	$7,500	$6,250	$5,000	$4,000	$3,000

Subtract 30% if rebarreled.

Lugers: 1902-DWM Mfg.

1902 COMMERCIAL – 9mm Para. cal., 4 in. barrel, serial number range 22,300-22,400 and 22,900-23,500 (500-600 mfg.). Commonly called "Fat Barrel" model.

	100%	98%	95%	90%	80%	70%	60%
	N/A	$9,500	$8,250	$7,000	$6,000	$5,000	$4,000

GRADING - PPGS™	100%	98%	95%	90%	80%	70%	60%	LAST MSR

1902 AMERICAN EAGLE – 9mm Para. cal., 4 in. barrel, 600-700 mfg., commonly called the "Fat Barrel." Same ser. range as 1902 Commercial Model.

N/A	$13,500	$10,000	$7,500	$6,500	$5,500	$4,500	

1902 CARTRIDGE COUNTER AMERICAN EAGLE – 9mm Para. cal., only 50 mfg. with the Powell Indication Device; be extremely wary of fakes. Ser. no. range 22,401- 22,450.

N/A	$90,000	$75,000	$50,000	$35,000	$30,000	$20,000	

An excellent plus condition DWM Model 1902 Cartridge Counter American Eagle sold at auction in June, 2020 for $138,000.

1902 GERMAN TEST – 7.65mm Para. or 9mm Para. cal., blank toggle, 4 in. barrel, Crown D proofs.

N/A	$18,500	$15,000	$12,000	$9,000	$7,500	$6,000	

1902 CARBINE – 7.65mm Para. cal., 11 3/4 in. barrel, approx. 2500 mfg.

Gun w/matching stock	N/A	$18,500	$15,000	$12,500	$9,500	$7,500	$6,000	
Gun only	N/A	$11,000	$8,500	$7,000	$6,000	$5,000	$4,000	

Subtract 20% for non-matching stock.
Add 10% for early gun with single screw lug.

Lugers: 1903-1904 DWM Mfg.

1903 FRENCH TEST – 7.65mm Para. cal., 4 in. "fat" barrel, 50 mfg., extractor marked "charge," ser. range 25,000-25,050, with 90 degree toggle checkering and anti-bounce toggle lock. The first transitional Luger, several fakes reported - buyer beware.

N/A	$45,000	$37,500	$25,000	$20,000	$15,000	$12,500	

1904 NAVY DWM – 9mm Para. cal., 6 in. barrel, limited mfg., a Transitional Navy, "Fat Barrel" with 90 degree toggle checkering and toggle lock, should have 2-digit ser. no.

Extreme rarity precludes pricing for individual condition factors. The only verified example of this gun recently brought $120,000. Most of these pistols available for sale are fakes - buyer beware!

Lugers: 1906-DWM Mfg.

1906 COMMERCIAL 7.65mm Para. W/"GESICHERT" MARKED SAFETY – 7.65mm Para. cal., 4 3/4 in. barrel, "GESICHERT" marked safety, long frame. Approx. 750 mfg.

N/A	$5,500	$4,750	$4,250	$3,500	$2,750	$2,250	

1906 COMMERCIAL 9mm Para. – 9mm Para. cal., 4 in. barrel, 3,500-4,000 mfg. Scarcer than 7.65mm Para.

N/A	$3,500	$3,000	$2,500	$2,000	$1,450	$950	

1906 COMMERCIAL 7.65mm Para. – 7.65mm Para. cal., 4 3/4 in. barrel, area under safety polished bright, 5,000 mfg.

N/A	$2,750	$2,250	$1,900	$1,450	$1,000	$800	

1906 AMERICAN EAGLE 9mm PARA. CAL. – 9mm Para. cal., 4 in. barrel, American Eagle stamped in front of breech, approx. 3,000 mfg.

N/A	$3,950	$3,500	$3,000	$2,150	$1,600	$1,000	

1906 AMERICAN EAGLE 7.65mm PARA. CAL. – 7.65mm Para. cal., 4 3/4 in. barrel, 7,500-8,000 mfg.

N/A	$2,950	$2,500	$2,100	$1,675	$1,225	$800	

Add 20% for long frame.

1906 NAVY COMMERCIAL – 9mm Para. cal., 6 in. barrel, approx. 2,500 mfg.

N/A	$6,000	$5,000	$4,250	$3,750	$3,000	$2,500	

Add 100% for complete matching rig.
Add 50% for 7.65mm Para. cal. with 6 in. barrel.

1906 NAVY MILITARY FIRST ISSUE – 9mm Para. cal., 6 in. barrel, first issue, 19,000 mfg., mostly altered safety marking - "GESICHERT" in upper position. Ser. no. range 1-9,000a.

N/A	$6,000	$5,250	$4,500	$3,500	$2,750	$2,000	

Add 10% for Navy unit markings.
Add 25% for unaltered safety variation.

1906 NAVY MILITARY SECOND ISSUE – 9mm Para. cal., 6 in. barrel, second issue, 2,000 mfg. Ser. range 9,000a-1,000b.

N/A	$7,500	$6,000	$4,950	$3,750	$2,800	$1,850	

Add 10% for Navy unit markings.

GRADING - PPGS™	100%	98%	95%	90%	80%	70%	60%	LAST MSR

1906 SWISS COMMERCIAL – 7.65mm Para. or 9mm Para. cal., 4 3/4 in. barrel, less than 1,000 mfg., Swiss "Cross in Sunburst", short or long frame.

	N/A	$2,950	$2,350	$2,000	$1,500	$1,000	$800	

Add 10% for "Cross in Sunburst".

1906 SWISS MILITARY – 7.65mm Para. cal., 4 3/4 in. barrel, long frame, Swiss Police has either "Cross in Shield" or "Cross in Sunburst," serial range 5,000-15,215.

	N/A	$2,750	$2,150	$1,825	$1,550	$1,100	$875	

1906 DUTCH – 9mm Para. cal., 4 in. barrel, approx. 4,000 mfg., often seen as arsenal rework.

	N/A	$3,100	$2,800	$2,225	$1,850	$1,425	$1,000	
Original finish & bbl.	N/A	$5,250	$4,500	$3,750	$3,500	$2,750	$1,950	

1906 BRAZILIAN – 7.65mm Para. cal., 4 3/4 in. barrel, 5,000 mfg. from DWM and delivered in 1910, ser. no. 01-5000, grip safety, blued finish, w/strawed small parts, no coat of arms on the chamber, should have Brazilian inspector proof on right side of receiver (letter "B" inside of circle), and "CARREGADA" marked extractor (Portuguese), extremely rare in fine condition.

	N/A	$4,500	$3,500	$2,850	$2,200	$1,750	$1,400	

If pistol is chambered for 9mm Para. cal., it's probably an after market, non-original barrel.

1906 BULGARIAN – 7.65mm Para. cal., 4 3/4 in. barrel, 1,500 mfg., most rebarreled to 9mm Para.

	N/A	$7,500	$6,500	$5,500	$5,000	$4,000	$3,000	

Subtract 25% for versions rebarreled to 9mm Para. cal.

This is the rarest Bulgarian - most are fakes or have been restored.

1906 PORTUGUESE ARMY – 7.65mm Para. cal., 4 3/4 in. barrel, "Manuel II" crest on chamber. Approx. 5,000 mfg.

	N/A	$4,000	$3,400	$3,000	$2,500	$2,000	$1,600	

1906 ROYAL PORTUGUESE NAVY – 9mm Para. cal., 4 in. barrel, "Crown/Anchor" on chamber, very rare. Majority of high condition guns have been refinished. Buyer beware.

	N/A	$7,000	$6,000	$5,000	$3,750	$2,925	$2,100	

1906 REPUBLIC OF PORTUGAL NAVY – 9mm Para. cal., "R.P. Anchor" on chamber, very rare. Majority of high condition guns refinished. Buyer beware.

	N/A	$7,000	$5,850	$4,750	$3,750	$2,750	$1,750	

1906 RUSSIAN – 9mm Para. cal., 4 in. barrel, approx. 400 mfg., very few reported.

	N/A	$17,500	$15,500	$13,825	$11,025	$9,100	$7,000	

1906 FRENCH COMMERCIAL – 7.65mm Para. cal., 4 3/4 in. barrel marked "Manufacture Francaise d'Armes & Cycles de Saint-Etienne."

	N/A	$3,500	$2,750	$2,200	$1,750	$1,500	$1,250	
w/case & accessories	N/A	$5,000	$4,000	$3,500	$3,000	$2,500	$2,000	

Lugers: 1908 DWM & Erfurt Mfg.

1908 DWM COMMERCIAL AND MILITARY – 9mm Para. cal., 4 in. barrel, Test/Acceptance Model, approx. 500 mfg. Ser. no. range 69,000-71,200.

	N/A	$2,900	$2,600	$2,150	$1,775	$1,400	$1,000	

1908 BULGARIAN – 9mm Para. cal., 4 in. barrel, "DWM" on chamber, 10,000 mfg., extremely rare in mint condition.

	N/A	$4,500	$3,850	$3,400	$3,100	$2,500	$2,100	

1908 DWM COMMERCIAL – 9mm Para. cal., 4 in. barrel, no stock lug or hold open, blank chamber.

	N/A	$2,250	$1,900	$1,600	$1,375	$1,125	$900	

1908 NAVY COMMERCIAL – 9mm Para. cal., 6 in. barrel.

	N/A	$6,000	$5,500	$5,000	$4,500	$3,750	$3,000	

Add 25% for 7.65mm Para.

1908 NAVY – 9mm Para. cal., 6 in. barrel, scarce. Ser. no. range 1,000B-10,000B, 9,000 mfg.

	N/A	$8,000	$7,000	$6,000	$5,000	$4,000	$3,500	

1908 DWM UNDATED MILITARY – 9mm Para. cal., 4 in. barrel, undated 1st issue, w/o stock lug. Approx. 25,000 mfg. 1908-1909.

	N/A	$3,500	$3,000	$2,500	$2,000	$1,650	$1,275	

Add 20%+ for Imperial unit markings (depends on history of unit).

GRADING - PPGS™	100%	98%	95%	90%	80%	70%	60%	LAST MSR

1908 BOLIVIAN CONTRACT – 9mm Para. cal., 4 in. barrel.

N/A	$6,500	$5,500	$5,000	$4,500	$3,800	$2,750

Lugers: 1910-1918 Dated DWM & Erfurt Mfg.

1911-1914 DATED 1908 ERFURT MILITARY – 9mm Para. cal., 4 in. barrel (dated 1911-1914), 1911, 1912, and most 1913 chamber dates do not have stock lugs.

N/A	$2,250	$1,850	$1,500	$1,200	$995	$825

Add 20%+ for Imperial unit markings (depends on history of unit).
Add 50% for 1910 chamber date.
Add 20% for 1913 chamber date with stock lug.
Add 20% for 1914 date.
Add $250-$325 for original holster in average+ condition.

1913 COMMERCIAL DWM – 9mm Para. cal., 4 in. barrel, grip safety and stock lug, horizontal "N" proof mark, 71,000 ser. no. range, rare.

N/A	$3,500	$3,000	$2,500	$2,000	$1,650	$1,350

1914 COMMERCIAL DWM – 9mm Para. cal., 4 in. barrel, undated, stock lug, horizontal crown-N proofed.

N/A	$2,650	$2,200	$1,800	$1,500	$1,200	$900

1914 NAVY – 9mm Para. cal., 6 in. barrel, scarce. Dated 1916 and 1917.

N/A	$6,500	$5,500	$4,500	$3,750	$3,000	$2,400

Add 20% for 16 date.

Watch for fakes made from 1920 Commercials with new barrels and rear toggles added. Crown M proofs and date will look "fresh" (1917 date usually encountered).

1914-1918 DATED ERFURT MILITARY – 9mm Para. cal., 4 in. barrel, dated 1916-18, there are no known 1915 chamber dated Erfurts.

N/A	$1,995	$1,675	$1,450	$1,225	$1,000	$800

Add 20% for 1914 date.
Add 20%+ for Imperial unit markings (depends on history of unit).
Add $250-$325 for original holster in average+ condition.

Note: Date stamped on top frame is date of production; thus dates could be 1914, 1916, 1917, or 1918. All are military P.08s, however, 98%-100% Erfurts are rare.

1914 ERFURT ARTILLERY – 9mm Para. cal., 1914 date is only one seen, 8 in. barrel.

N/A	$4,250	$3,675	$3,125	$2,600	$2,150	$1,650

Add 20%+ for Imperial unit markings (depends on history of unit).

1910-1918 DATED WWI DWM MILITARY – 9mm Para. cal., 4 in. barrel. 1910-1918 dated. Most frequently encountered WWI military Luger, except for early production, most have stock lug, mfg. mid-1913-1918.

N/A	$1,995	$1,675	$1,450	$1,225	$1,000	$800

Add approx. 20% for 1910-1913 chamber dated mfg.
Add 20%+ for Imperial unit markings (depends on history of unit).
Add $250-$325 for original holster in average+ condition.

Note: Date stamped on top frame is date of production; thus, dates could be 1910 through 1918, but all are military P.08s. Approx. 20,000 dated 1910, 15,000 dated 1911, 10,000 dated 1912, 25,000 dated 1913.

1914-1918 DATED DWM ARTILLERY – 9mm Para. cal., 8 in. barrel. Dated 1914-18.

N/A	$3,500	$3,000	$2,500	$2,000	$1,850	$1,500

Add 100% for matching stock with complete holster rig, depending on condition.
Add $600 for proper non-matching stock.
Add $550 for original leather holster with shoulder strap.
Add 300% for rare 1914 chamber date.
Add 20% for 1915 chamber date.
Add 20%+ for Imperial unit markings (depends on history of unit).

Lugers: 1920-1930 DWM

Most common variations in good supply within this section in 50% or less condition will approximate the 60% value. This reflects its value as a representative shooter rather than a higher priced collector's gun.

1920 DWM OR ERFURT – 9mm Para. cal., 4 in. barrel, military and police, reworked and issued to police units, many thousand reworked, double date also, 1920 and 1921 dated.

N/A	$1,795	$1,450	$1,200	$950	$700	$500

GRADING - PPGS™	100%	98%	95%	90%	80%	70%	60%	LAST MSR

1920 COMMERCIAL – 7.65mm Para. or 9mm Para. cal., 3 7/8-4 in. barrel, available in many configurations, since these guns were assembled using the parts of previously manufactured Lugers, including 1900-06 mfg. with the grip safety on the frame.

	N/A	$1,795	$1,450	$1,200	$950	$700	$500	

Add 25% for 9mm Para. cal.

These prices reflect original condition, and are not to be confused with recent imports (with import markings).

1920 NAVY COMMERCIAL – 9mm Para. cal., 4 or 6 in. barrel, very rare rework, Navy rear sight.

	N/A	$3,600	$3,145	$2,425	$1,775	$1,185	$1,050	

Add 20% for 7.65mm Para.

1920 COMMERCIAL ARTILLERY – 9mm Para. cal., 8 in. barrel, very rare rework.

	N/A	$4,000	$3,400	$3,000	$2,500	$2,000	$1,600	

1920 "LONG BARREL" COMMERCIAL – 7.65mm Para. or 9mm Para. cal., 10-20 in. barrel, extremely rare.

	N/A	$3,950	$3,500	$2,875	$2,175	$1,500	$1,000	

Watch for fakes - these guns have to be evaluated one at a time.

1920 NAVY CARBINE – 7.65mm Para. cal., 11 3/4 in. barrel, long frame (if short frame, be wary of fakes, very few produced). Navy rear sight, no forearm under barrel.

	N/A	$4,500	$3,500	$2,500	$2,000	$1,500	$1,250	

1920 CARBINE – 7.65mm Para. cal., 11 3/4 in. barrel, very rare.

Gun only	N/A	$7,425	$6,100	$4,800	$3,800	$2,975	$2,250	
Gun with stock	N/A	$12,500	$10,500	$8,925	$6,775	$5,725	$4,850	

1920 SWISS REWORK – 7.65mm Para. cal., 3 5/8-6 in. barrel, several hundred produced.

	N/A	$2,325	$1,950	$1,525	$1,050	$925	$850	

1921 VICKERS DUTCH CONTRACT – 9mm Para. cal., 4 in. barrel, grip safety, safety marked "RUST". Approx. 6,100 procured from Vickers, Ltd, England.

	N/A	$4,350	$3,700	$3,275	$2,500	$2,000	$1,650	

ABERCROMBIE & FITCH COMMERCIAL – 7.65mm Para. or 9mm Para. cal., long frame, 4 3/4 in. barrel, 100 mfg., total for both cals.

	N/A	$9,500	$7,500	$6,000	$5,000	$4,250	$3,500	

Add 30% for 6 in. barrels (rare).

Inspect barrel legend very carefully (beware of fakes) - must have reinforced frame (look for rib in rear frame well).

1920/21-DWM – 9mm Para. cal., 4 in. barrel, dated, military issue, new manufacture.

	N/A	$1,800	$1,500	$1,100	$875	$650	$500	

Subtract 20% if arsenal reworked.

1920/23 STOEGER AMERICAN EAGLE – 7.65mm Para. or 9mm Para. cal., 3 5/8-24 in. barrels, less than 1,000 mfg., made by DWM for Stoeger, sold in USA, longer barrel models have higher value.

3 7/8 - 6 in. barrels	N/A	$5,000	$4,000	$3,150	$2,700	$2,100	$1,500	
8 in. barrel	N/A	$6,000	$5,000	$4,000	$3,250	$2,500	$2,300	

Add 50% for Mauser mfg., safe and loaded extractor, or V ser. no. suffix.

Be extremely careful when examining the frame markings on this variation as there are many fakes in the marketplace.

1923 DWM COMMERCIAL – 7.65mm Para. cal., 3 5/8 in. barrel, 14,000 mfg. ser. range 74,000-89,000.

	N/A	$2,000	$1,750	$1,500	$1,250	$1,050	$800	

1923 DWM "SAFE AND LOADED" COMMERCIAL – 7.65mm Para. cal., "safe and loaded" marked on frame and extractor, 7.65mm Para. cal., 3 7/8 in. barrel, safety and extractor marked in English, 2,000 mfg. ser. range 89,000-91,000.

	N/A	$2,600	$2,275	$2,050	$1,650	$1,350	$1,050	

1923 FINNISH LUGER – 7.65mm Para. cal., approx. 5,000-7,000 units made for Finnish military contract (Army and Navy), marked "SA" surrounded by a rectangle, most have been recently imported into the U.S.

	N/A	$1,950	$1,650	$1,200	$925	$750	$550	

1923 DWM DUTCH NAVY CONTRACT – 9mm Para. cal., 4 in. barrel, no grip safety, safety marked "RUST". Serial no. range 1-1484.

	N/A	$3,750	$3,250	$2,600	$2,200	$1,650	$1,350	

GRADING - PPGS™	100%	98%	95%	90%	80%	70%	60%	LAST MSR

Lugers: Krieghoff Mfg.

Please refer to the Krieghoff section for recently manufactured Krieghoff Lugers.

1923 DWM/KRIEGHOFF COMMERCIAL – 7.65mm Para. (3 7/8 in. barrel only) or 9mm Para. (4 in. barrel only), few mfg., reworked by Krieghoff, chamber dated 1921 or unmarked, most in "i" range, Krieghoff stamped on back of frame. Be wary of fakes.

	N/A	$3,000	$2,400	$1,800	$1,200	$1,050	$875	

DWM/KRIEGHOFF COMMERCIAL – 7.65mm Para. or 9mm Para. cal., 4 in. barrel, a few hundred made, side frame marked Krieghoff. Most are fake.

	N/A	$3,500	$3,000	$2,500	$2,000	$1,500	$1,000	

KRIEGHOFF COMMERCIAL – 7.65mm Para. or 9mm Para. cal., 4 or 6 in. barrel, approx. 1500 mfg., 1,000 with side frame marking, and 500 without side frame marking.

	N/A	$7,500	$6,500	$5,500	$4,500	$3,750	$3,000	

Add 30% for side frame marked 7.65mm Para.
Add approx. 30% if w/o side frame marking.

Almost all Krieghoff Commercial Lugers have the letter P before the serial number.

KRIEGHOFF S CODE EARLY – 9mm Para. cal., 4 in. barrel, approx. 1,800 mfg., German Luftwaffe. Has fat walnut grips, "H-K Suhl" toggle.

	N/A	$5,500	$4,500	$3,500	$3,000	$2,500	$2,000	

KRIEGHOFF S CODE MID SERIES – 9mm Para. cal., 4 in. barrel, approx. 500-700 mfg., Luftwaffe, ser. no. range 1600-2500, finely checkered plastic grips.

	N/A	$5,900	$5,250	$4,000	$3,000	$2,500	$2,000	

KRIEGHOFF S CODE LATE – 9mm Para. cal., 4 in. barrel, approx. 1,800 mfg., Luftwaffe, ser. no. range 2300-4200.

	N/A	$6,500	$5,500	$4,250	$3,550	$3,150	$1,675	

KRIEGHOFF 36 DATE – 9mm Para. cal., 4 in. barrel, approx. 500-700 made, Luftwaffe military, 2 digit date, coarsely checkered plastic grips.

	N/A	$6,500	$5,500	$4,250	$3,550	$3,150	$1,675	

KRIEGHOFF 1936-1945 DATED – 9mm Para. cal., 4 in. barrel, approx. 9,000 mfg., 4 digit chamber date, 1936, 1937, and 1940 most common.

1936-37 & 1940	N/A	$5,500	$4,750	$4,000	$3,250	$2,600	$1,850	
1938	N/A	$6,000	$5,000	$4,150	$3,350	$2,725	$1,900	
1941	N/A	$7,000	$6,000	$5,000	$4,100	$3,250	$2,650	
1942-43	N/A	$10,000	$8,000	$6,000	$4,150	$3,350	$2,750	
1944	N/A	$16,500	$12,500	$10,000	$8,250	$6,750	$5,000	
1945	N/A	$20,000	$15,000	$11,500	$9,000	$8,000	$7,000	

The 1941 "large date" is very rare - watch for fakes (re-dated frames) on this model in general.

POST-WAR KRIEGHOFF TYPE I – 9mm Para. cal., 4 in. barrel, approx. 150 mfg. for occupation forces, H-K marked toggle link.

	N/A	$6,500	$5,200	$4,000	$3,250	$2,500	$1,750	

POST-WAR KRIEGHOFF TYPE II – 9mm Para. cal., 4 in. barrel, approx. 150 mfg., unmarked toggle link, many parts proofed "Eagle-over-2".

	N/A	$6,000	$5,000	$4,000	$3,250	$2,500	$1,750	

POST-WAR KRIEGHOFF COMMERCIAL – 7.65mm Para. cal., 4 in. barrel, approx. 100-200 mfg., unmarked toggle, many parts proofed "Eagle-over-2".

	N/A	$5,500	$4,500	$3,500	$2,750	$2,000	$1,500	

Lugers: Mauser Mfg.

Most common variations in good supply within this section in 50% or less condition will approximate the 60% value. This reflects its value as a representative shooter rather than a higher priced collector's gun.

1935-06 PORTUGUESE GNR – 7.65mm Para. cal., 4 3/4 in. barrel, 564 mfg., "GNR" on chamber, Portuguese marked safety and extractor.

	N/A	$3,250	$2,700	$2,300	$2,000	$1,750	$1,350	

1934/06 MAUSER SWISS COMMERCIAL – 7.65mm Para. cal., 4 3/4 in. barrel, a few hundred produced, "Cross in Sunburst" or blank chamber, grip safety.

	N/A	$7,500	$6,000	$5,000	$4,250	$3,500	$2,750	

GRADING - PPGS™	100%	98%	95%	90%	80%	70%	60%	LAST MSR

1934 MAUSER BANNER COMMERCIAL – 7.65mm Para. or 9mm Para. cal., 4 in. barrel, hundreds produced, unmarked chamber, "v" suffix ser. no.

	N/A	$4,500	$4,000	$3,500	$3,000	$2,500	$2,050

Add 15% for "Kal. 7.65" barrel marking.

S/42 K DATE – 9mm Para. cal., 4 in. barrel, approx. 10,000 mfg. during 1934 only for military.

	N/A	$7,500	$6,500	$5,500	$4,500	$3,500	$3,000

Add 100% for "large eagle over M Navy" proofmark.

S/42 G DATE – 9mm Para. cal., 4 in. barrel, many thousand produced 1935 only.

	N/A	$3,000	$2,450	$2,100	$1,625	$1,350	$1,025

Add 50% for Navy markings.

S/42 DATED CHAMBER – 9mm Para. cal., 4 in. barrel, many thousands produced, "S/42" stamped rear toggle, chamber dated 1936-1940. One of the most frequently encountered WWII military Lugers.

w/o markings	N/A	$2,550	$2,100	$1,625	$1,300	$1,050	$950
w/Navy/Police markings	N/A	$4,500	$4,100	$3,240	$2,580	$2,100	$1,900

Add 20% for 1936 date.
Add 30% for "strawed" 1937 date.
Add $250 for original holster in average+ condition.

The last regular production S/42 Models were mfg. approx. April of 1939.

MAUSER PERSIAN (IRANIAN) CONTRACT – 9mm Para. cal., 4 and 8 in. barrels, approx. 1,000 mfg. with 8 in. barrel, and 2,000-3,000 mfg. in 4 in. barrel, Farsi numerals.

4 in. barrel	N/A	$6,000	$5,500	$4,500	$3,850	$3,250	$2,750
Artillery (8 in.)	N/A	$6,000	$5,500	$4,500	$3,850	$3,250	$2,750
Cutaway	N/A	$6,500	$5,800	$4,700	$4,000	$3,500	$3,000

Add 50% for Artillery with matching rig.

Mauser produced fifty 4 in. barrel cutaways with the Persian contract for training purposes, #1-50 in Farsi.

1936-1942 DATED MAUSER BANNER – 9mm Para. cal., 4 in. barrel, over 1,000 mfg., commercial and contract sales, wood grips, no sear safety, often have strawed small parts.

	N/A	$3,950	$3,250	$2,900	$2,075	$1,860	$1,430

MAUSER BANNER DUTCH CONTRACT – 9mm Para. cal., 4 in. barrel, 1,000 mfg., safety marked "Rust". Dated 1936-40.

	N/A	$3,950	$3,250	$2,825	$2,250	$1,860	$1,425

Add 25% for 1936, 1937, 1938, or 1939 chamber date.

MAUSER BANNER SWEDISH CONTRACT – 275 mfg. in 9mm Para. cal., 4 3/4 in. barrels, dated 1938, 25 mfg. in 9mm Para. cal., dated 1939, 30 mfg. in 7.65mm Para. cal., dated 1939, very rare in 7.65mm Para. dated 1940.

	N/A	$8,500	$7,100	$6,000	$5,000	$3,750	$2,750

Add 15% for 7.65mm Para. cal. (4 3/4 in. barrel).

MAUSER BANNER PORTUGUESE NAVY CONTRACTS – 9mm Para. cal., 4 in. barrel, grip safety, Portuguese marked safety and extractor. Approx. 200 mfg. in small groups between 1935-1941.

	N/A	$4,000	$3,600	$3,150	$2,600	$2,100	$1,500

CODE "S/42" COMMERCIAL CONTRACT – 9mm Para. cal., 4 in. barrel, a few hundred produced, dated 1938. Commercial proof marks only.

	N/A	$2,950	$2,580	$2,330	$1,860	$1,535	$1,180

CODE "42" – 9mm Para. cal., 4 in. barrels, dated 1939-1940, rear toggle marked "42." One of the most frequently encountered WWII military Lugers.

w/o markings	N/A	$2,500	$2,100	$1,675	$1,350	$1,200	$1,075
w/Navy markings	N/A	$3,950	$3,500	$2,950	$2,550	$2,000	$1,500

Add $350-$450 for original holster in average condition.

MAUSER BANNER POLICE – 9mm Para. cal., approx. 30,000 mfg., dated 1939-1942, police contract, have sear safeties, blue small parts. A few observed dated 1938.

	N/A	$3,500	$3,000	$2,750	$2,300	$1,825	$1,500

Add 30% with 1938 chamber date (rare).

GRADING - PPGS™	100%	98%	95%	90%	80%	70%	60%	LAST MSR

CODE "41-42" – 9mm Para. cal., 4 in. barrel, 2-digit date, approx. 7,000 mfg. in January of 1941, "41" dated chamber, "42" code, most 42 dates are reworks.

	N/A	$2,950	$2,500	$2,000	$1,750	$1,500	$1,250	

Add $250 for original holster in average condition.

CODE "byf" – 9mm Para. cal., 4 in. barrel, thousands made, chamber dated "41" and "42". Rear toggle is stamped "byf", standard magazine was "fxo" marked and had an un-numbered plastic bottom. One of the most frequently encountered WWII military Lugers.

	N/A	$2,750	$2,400	$2,150	$1,725	$1,400	$1,100	

Add 30% for original black bakelite grips.
Add $250 for original holster in average condition.

Code "byf" Lugers with black bakelite grips are referred to as the "Black Widow" variation.

AUSTRIAN BUNDES HEER – 9mm Para. cal., 4 in. barrel, several hundred produced, Austrian Federal Army, no serial letter suffix-same ser. placement as Mauser 42KU. Rarely encountered in mint condition.

	N/A	$2,900	$2,400	$2,095	$1,670	$1,380	$1,060	

MAUSER 1934 CODE BYF, S/42 AND 42 KU – 9mm Para. cal., 3,500 mfg. Post-1942 Luftwaffe subcontract.

	N/A	$3,250	$2,750	$2,350	$2,000	$1,850	$1,300	

Lugers: Reworks

DEATH'S HEAD REWORK – 9mm Para. cal., 4 in. barrel. The majority of Luger collectors consider this "variation" a fake. A great conversation piece.

	N/A	$2,250	$2,000	$1,950	$1,500	$1,250	$1,000	

SIMSON REWORK – 9mm Para. cal., 4 in. barrel, DWM toggles, Simpson Eagle proofs on reworked parts.

	N/A	$1,795	$1,550	$1,200	$900	700	$500	

DOUBLE DATED DWM/ERFURT – 9mm Para. cal., 4, 6, or 8 in. barrel, very scarce. 1920 over 1910-1918 chamber dates. Often with sear safety and mag. safety remnant.

w/o mag. safety	N/A	$1,500	$1,325	$1,100	$875	$750	$700	
w/intact mag. safety	N/A	$3,000	$2,650	$2,200	$1,750	$1,500	$1,400	

Add 40% for 8 in. barrel.

ARMY OFFICE REWORK – 9mm Para. cal., 4 in. barrel, 200-300 marked "KI 1933". These were pistols reworked by the Army equipment facility in Kassel, Germany in 1933. Some are fakes.

	N/A	$2,550	$2,050	$1,850	$1,215	$1,000	$770	

Lugers: Simson Mfg.

SIMSON & COMPANY – 7.65mm Para. or 9mm Para. cal., 3 7/8 or 4 in. barrel, military and possibly limited commercial sales, approx. 12,000 produced but rarely found.

	N/A	$4,500	$3,750	$3,250	$2,800	$2,350	$1,800	

SIMSON MILITARY DATED – 9mm Para. cal., 4 in. barrel, possibly 2,000 mfg., dated 1925.

	N/A	$7,000	$6,000	$5,500	$4,500	$3,500	$2,500	

This model is encountered with a 1925 or 1926 (rare) chamber date.

SIMSON S CODE/SIMSON MARKED TOGGLE – 9mm Para. cal., 4 in. barrel. Undated, scarce.

	N/A	$6,500	$5,650	$4,650	$3,550	$2,650	$2,350	

Lugers: Swiss Bern

1906/BERN (AKA 1906/24 BERN) – 7.65mm Para. cal., 4 3/4 in. barrel, "Waffenfabrik Bern" on toggle, Swiss military, bordered checkered walnut grips, exactly 17,874 mfg.

	$2,750	$2,400	$2,000	$1,850	$1,500	$1,250	$975	

1906/29 SWISS BERN – 7.65mm Para. or 9mm Para. (rare) cal., 4 3/4 in. barrel, 29,857 mfg., many machining changes to simplify production, straight front grip strap, P prefix designates commercial model, brown or black plastic grips.

	$2,000	$1,750	$1,400	$1,200	$1,000	$850	$700	

Add 20% for red plastic grips and mag. bottom.
Add 200% for 9mm Para. cal. (rare).

Lugers: KDF, Interarms, Stoeger, & Recent Import

Note: Post-WWII Lugers have been manufactured by Mauser Werke in Oberndorf, W. Germany during the 1970s, and by both Stoeger Industries and Mitchell Arms (see separate listing under Mitchell

GRADING - PPGS™	100%	98%	95%	90%	80%	70%	60%	LAST MSR

Arms) in recent years. Earlier Mauser importation was by Precision Imports, Inc. located in San Antonio, TX and Interarms of Alexandria, VA (and so marked on these guns).

Prices for 100% condition Lugers assume NIB status. If without box and accessories, deduct 15%.

INTERARMS MAUSER P.08 – 7.65mm Para. or 9mm Para. cal., 4 or 6 in. barrel, fully-contoured front grip strap.

	$2,100	$1,750	$1,500	$1,350	$1,100	$900	$700	

Add 10% for 6 in. barrel. in 9mm Para. cal.

INTERARMS "SWISS-STYLE" MAUSER EAGLE – 7.65mm Para. or 9mm Para. cal., "straight" front grip strap, American eagle logo on top of frame.

	$1,500	$1,250	$1,050	$925	$825	$675	$525	

Add 10% for 6 in. barrel in 9mm Para. cal.

NEW MODEL CARBINE WITH STOCK – 9mm Para. cal., authentic reproduction of the original Luger Carbine complete with matching stock, accessories, and case. Inventory was depleted during 1998.

	$7,500	$6,000	$5,000	N/A	N/A	N/A	N/A	*$7,431*

CARTRIDGE COUNTER – 9mm Para. cal., left grip is slotted and contains a numbered metal strip. Manufacture began 1983, and inventory was depleted during 1998.

	$5,500	$4,000	$3,000	N/A	N/A	N/A	N/A	*$3,865*

COMMEMORATIVE BULGARIAN – 7.65 Para. cal., 100 available on U.S. market.

	$3,000	$2,150	$1,500	N/A	N/A	N/A	N/A	

Add $200 for leather case.

COMMEMORATIVE RUSSIAN – 9mm Para. cal., 100 available on U.S. market.

	$3,200	$2,150	$1,500	N/A	N/A	N/A	N/A	

Add $200 for leather case.

* ***Commemorative Russian Matched pair of each***

	$5,000	$2,675	$1,950	N/A	N/A	N/A	N/A	

COMMEMORATIVE NAVY 75TH YEAR – 9mm Para. cal., complete with leather briefcase and accessories, 250 mfg., but Interarms only imported 10 pistols.

	$4,500	$3,250	$2,500	N/A	N/A	N/A	N/A	

MAUSER SPORT PARABELLUM – 7.65mm Para. or 9mm Para. cal., imported target barrel and adj. sights. Over 150 of the First Variation were mfg. (87 in 9mm Para. and 63 in 7.65mm Para. cal.). Second Variation had approx. 2 mfg. in 9mm Para. cal.

	$5,500	$2,750	$2,150	N/A	N/A	N/A	N/A	

STOEGER .22 CAL. LUGER – .22 LR cal., toggle action, all steel or aluminum construction, 4 1/2 or 5 1/2 in. barrel, right or left-hand safety, 10 shot mag., previously mfg. in the U.S. until 1985.

	$295	$265	$225	$190	$145	$120	$100	*$200*

* ***Stoeger .22 Cal. Luger "1 of 1,000"*** – .22 LR cal., 1,000 mfg. in 1984-85, includes wooden box and extra mag.

	$375	$325	$250	N/A	N/A	N/A	N/A	

STOEGER LUGER – 9mm Para. cal., choice of 4 or 6 (Navy) in. barrel, stainless steel construction, choice of polished stainless or matte black (new 1996) upper frame finish, American eagle engraved on top of frame, curved front grip strap, 7 shot mag., plastic mag. bottom, approx. 30 oz. Mfg. 1994-disc.

	$1,100	$950	$800	$650	$525	$450	$375	*$720*

Add $79 for matte black finish.

Lugers: Special Interest

SPANDAU LUGER – Assembled by the Spandau Arsenal near Berlin from surplus DWM and Erfurt parts. Approximately 200 produced, serial numbers all but one below 200, P 08 configuration, dated 1918, unique toggle and inspector marks. 10 known; beware of fakes.

MO4/05 G.L. BABY LUGER – 7.65mm Para. or 9mm Para. cal., 3 1/4 in. barrel, G.L. proofed, hand made under Georg Luger's supervision, four known to exist. Made with shortened barrel, mag., and grip frame.

BABY LUGER 1925/26 – .380 ACP/.32 ACP cal., prototype, probably 4 mfg., only one known is .380. Only Luger documented by the manufacturer.

VONO REWORK – 7.65mm Para. or 9mm Para. cal., 4 in. barrel, commercial, rework by W.P. Von Nordheim.

	$1,575	$1,350	$1,125	$950	$850	$725	$625	

GRADING - PPGS™	100%	98%	95%	90%	80%	70%	60%	LAST MSR

1900 DWM CARBINE – 7.65mm Para. cal., 11 3/4 in. barrel, very few manufactured, varying characteristics. Characterized by "Ski slope" sight on rear toggle.

Extreme rarity precludes accurate pricing on this model.

1902/06 TRANSITIONAL CARBINE – 9mm Para. cal., 11 3/4 in. barrel. Only 2 known, beware of fakes.

Extreme rarity precludes accurate pricing on this model.

1907 U.S. ARMY TEST TRIAL – .45 ACP cal., at least three originally mfg.

Extreme rarity precludes accurate pricing on this model. Undoubtedly, this is the most desirable semi-auto pistol ever manufactured, and would be priced accordingly. Mike Krause of San Mateo, CA has made a few .45 ACP Lugers done to exact measured specifications from one of the two surviving originals. Their values are in the $9,000 - $12,500 range.

CONVERSIONS: JOHN MARTZ – John Martz of Lincoln, CA has converted WWII P.38s (please refer to P.38 section) and WWI or WWII Lugers into various configurations since 1968. These conversions are known for their quality workmanship and functional accuracy. Below is a generalized listing of variations he has fabricated and their values to date with production totals.

* ***Conversions: John Martz .380 ACP Baby Luger*** – 6 fabricated, disc.

	$6,300	$3,375	$2,525	N/A	N/A	N/A	N/A

* ***Conversions: John Martz 7.65mm Para. Baby Luger (Grip Safety)*** – 213 mfg. total, includes 9mm Baby Luger also.

	$3,150	$2,625	$2,000	N/A	N/A	N/A	N/A

* ***Conversions: John Martz 9mm Para. Baby Luger*** – 2 1/4 (disc.), 2 1/2 (disc.), or 2 5/8 in. barrel.

	$3,150	$2,625	$2,100	N/A	N/A	N/A	N/A

* ***Conversions: John Martz Big-Bore .45 ACP Luger*** – 89 fabricated (5 are babies), .45 ACP cal., fixed sights, 2 3/4, 4, 6, or 8 in. barrel. Disc.

	$5,775	$3,525	$2,525	N/A	N/A	N/A	N/A

* ***Conversions: John Martz Navy Model*** – .45 ACP cal., 6 or 8 in. barrel, adj. rear Navy sight, estimated mfg. is 25 pistols, disc.

	$6,000	$4,675	$3,475	N/A	N/A	N/A	N/A

Add 10% for Navy Model with 100-200 meter rear sight.

* ***Conversions: John Martz Navy Model Ltd. Edition*** – .38 Super cal., 6 in. barrel, adj. rear Navy sight, 10 fabricated, disc.

	$5,250	$4,150	$3,250	N/A	N/A	N/A	N/A

Subtract 10% for fixed rear sight (standard model with 4 in. barrel).

* ***Conversions: John Martz Standard Model*** – .38 Super cal., 4 to 8 in. barrel, fixed sight, 3 fabricated.

	$4,500	$3,325	$2,525	N/A	N/A	N/A	N/A

* ***Conversions: John Martz Target Luger*** – .22 WMR cal., 6 or 9 in. barrel, fixed sight, 11 fabricated, disc.

	$7,875	$5,675	$3,575	N/A	N/A	N/A	N/A

* ***Conversions: John Martz Luger Carbines (with shoulder stock)*** – .22 WMR (disc.), 7.65mm Para., 9mm Para., or .38 Super cal., 11-18 in. barrel with adj. rear sights. Disc.

	$8,300	$5,950	$3,775	N/A	N/A	N/A	N/A

Add 20% for .22 WMR cal. (2 fabricated).

83 Luger carbines with 16 in. barrels were fabricated with shoulder stocks.

42 Luger carbines with 12 in. barrels were fabricated w/o shoulder stocks.

* ***Conversions: John Martz Experimental Lugers*** – experimental pistols have been made in .40 S&W (disc.), .41 AE (disc.), .357 SIG (11 mfg., 7, 8, or 9 in. barrel) and .357 Mag. Most have 8 in. barrels (except for .40 S&W cal., disc.). Extreme rarity (and not for sale status) precludes accurate price evaluation.

The .357 SIG model had a retail price of $3,500.

LUGERS: ACCESSORIES

WWI "SNAIL DRUM" CANVAS CARRIER/POUCH

	$2,000	$1,750	$1,500	$1,250	$1,000	$750	$500

WWI "RADIUM" FILLED REMOVABLE FRONT AND REAR SIGHT FOR ARTILLERY LUGER – "Radium" filled removable front and rear sight for the artillery Luger. Complete sets are very rare.

Front Sight Only	$1,000	$850	$725	$625	$525	$425	$350
Complete Set	$2,500	$2,250	$1,800	$1,550	$1,300	$1,100	$875

GRADING - PPGS™	100%	98%	95%	90%	80%	70%	60%	LAST MSR

LOADING TOOL – for drum magazines. Manufactured by BING and AEG.

	$2,200	$2,000	$1,850	$1,650	$1,375	$1,000	$850

Conversion Units - .22 cal.

ERMA – postwar, in green cardboard box.

	$950	$800	$725	$575	$475	$375	$325

ERMA-PREWAR IN WOODEN BOX

	$2,625	$2,325	$1,850	$1,500	$1,250	$1,050	$750

Add 50% for Nazi Navy property numbered.
Subtract 20% for mismatched.

Detachable Stocks

ARTILLERY TYPE FLAT BOARD

	$650	$575	$525	$420	$325	$275	$250

ARTILLERY HOLSTER RIG, COMPLETE

	$3,200	$2,850	$2,250	$1,925	$1,625	$1,350	$1,125

Subtract 20% if shoulder strap is missing.

NAVAL-TYPE FLAT BOARD

	$3,000	$2,600	$2,000	$1,700	$1,450	$1,200	$975

NAVAL HOLSTER RIG, COMPLETE

	$6,000	$4,950	$4,350	$3,700	$2,850	$1,975	$1,575

Subtract 20% if shoulder strap is missing.

CARBINE CONTOURED (ORIGINAL)

	$6,000	$4,950	$4,350	$3,700	$2,850	$1,975	$1,575

IDEAL TELESCOPING WITH GRIPS – mfg. in U.S. by Ideal Corp.

	$3,850	$3,200	$2,800	$2,300	$1,600	$1,200	$850

"Snail" Drum Magazines

1ST ISSUE – machined telescoping winder. Manufactured by BING and AEG.

	$2,500	$2,200	$1,850	$1,650	$1,250	$1,000	$750

2ND ISSUE TYPE I – stamped hinged winder with no drum reinforcement rings. Manufactured by BING.

	$2,250	$1,800	$1,500	$1,350	$1,200	$1,000	$800

2ND ISSUE TYPE II – stamped hinged winder with reinforcement rings.

	$2,000	$1,600	$1,350	$1,150	$1,000	$850	$700

SHOTGUNS: O/U

CLASSIC MODEL – see listing under Stoeger Industries, Inc. in the S section.

SHOTGUNS: SEMI-AUTO

ULTRA-LIGHT MODEL – see listing under Stoeger Industries, Inc. in the S section.

LU-MAR Srl

Previous shotgun manufacturer located in Gardone, Italy. Limited U.S. importation.

Lu-Mar made a wide variety of O/U shotguns. In addition to their fine O/U lineup, Lu- Mar also manufactured SxS shotguns. These guns had little or no importation into the U.S.

LUNA

Previous manufacturer located in Germany.

PISTOLS: SINGLE SHOT

MODEL 200 FREE PISTOL – .22 LR cal., 11 in. barrel, blue, target sights, checkered target grips, pre-WWII.

	$1,100	$990	$855	$770	$660	$605	$525

RIFLES: SINGLE SHOT

TARGET RIFLE – .22 LR or .22 Hornet cal., falling block action, 20 in. barrel, adj. sights, target type stocks, pre-WWII.

	$990	$880	$800	$690	$605	$550	$495

GRADING - PPGS™	100%	98%	95%	90%	80%	70%	60%	LAST MSR

LUSA USA

Previous manufacturer located in Hooksett, NH until circa 2008.

CARBINES: SEMI-AUTO

Lusa USA manufactured a 9mm Para. cal. carbine with a 16 in. barrel in three configurations - the 94 LE (last MSR $1,295), 94 SP89 Pistol (last MSR $999), 94 SA (A2 Standard, last MSR $999), the 94 PDW (side folding stock, last MSR $1,099), and the 94 AWB (fixed stock, last MSR $999-$1,099).

LUVO PRAGUE LTD.

Current pistol and rifle manufacturer located in Praha 2-Vinohrady, Czech Republic. No current U.S. importation.

For individual model listings, please go to BlueBookOfGunValues.com/overflow.

LUXUS ARMS LLC

Current manufacturer and importer located in Mt. Orab, OH. Previously located in Milford, OH until 2010.

Luxus Arms is well known for their premium Turkish walnut stocks. Luxus Products imports high quality double rifles, as well as SxS and O/U shotguns from Italy. Each gun is custom order and delivery time is approximately one year. Luxus Arms manufactures a single shot Model 11 in calibers from .22 Hornet to .375 H&H. Base price for Model 11 Custom LT is $4,995 and Model 11 Custom FQ is $5,995. Limited Edition rifles are also available. Prices range from $15,000-$26,995. Please contact the company directly for an individual price quotation.

LYMAN

Previous trademark of firearms manufactured by Lyman-Pachmayr-Trius Products, located in Middletown, CT. Lyman continues to make black powder reproductions, reloading supplies, and related accessories.

RIFLES: SHARPS REPRODUCTIONS

LITTLE SHARPS "IDEAL MODEL" – .17 HMR (disc. 2013), .22 LR (disc. 2013), .22 WMR (disc. 2013), .22 Hornet, .218 Bee (disc. 2013), .30-30 Win. (disc. 2013), .38-55 WCF, .44 Win. (disc. 2013), or .45 LC cal. (disc. 2013), 20% smaller version of the original Sharps rifle, 24, 26, or 32 in. octagon barrel, double set triggers, rear tang aperture sight, case colored frame, 5.9 lbs. Mfg. by Armi-Sport. Imported 2011-2015.

	100%	98%	95%	90%	80%	70%	60%	LAST MSR
	$1,575	$1,375	$1,175	$1,050	$875	$750	$575	*$1,750*

MODEL OF 1878 SHARPS – .45-70 Govt. cal., single shot, double set triggers, rear tang aperture sight, alloy frame, checkered pistol grip stock with shotgun style steel buttplate, period style laser engraving. Mfg. by Pedersoli. Importation began circa 2014.

	100%	98%	95%	90%	80%	70%	60%	LAST MSR
MSR $2,395	$2,185	$1,885	$1,585	$1,350	$1,195	$975	$795	

LYNX

Current trademark of bolt action rifles manufactured by Pirkan Ase Ltd., established in 1979, located in Orivesi, Finland. Previously located in Tampere, Finland. No current U.S. importation.

RIFLES: BOLT ACTION

Please contact the company directly for current U.S. availability and pricing on these models.

LYNX – available in standard or metric cals., features straight pull bolt system, variations include the Hunter with traditional checkered walnut stock, and the Target model with 10 shot mag. and thumbhole stock with adj. cheekpiece.

LYNX X.O./X.X.O. – various standard metric and Magnum (Model X.X.O.) cals., features 60 degree bolt, traditional styling, 3 shot mag.

M SECTION

M+M INDUSTRIES (M+M, INC.)

Current importer and manufacturer of semi-auto and bolt action firearms established in 2005, located in Northglenn, CO. Previously located in Eastlake, CO.

For individual model listings, please go to BlueBookOfGunValues.com/overflow.

MAB

Military MAB listings can be found under the French Military heading.

GRADING - PPGS™	100%	98%	95%	90%	80%	70%	60%	LAST MSR

PISTOLS: SEMI-AUTO

MODEL R – 9mm Para. cal., blowback action, blue finish, rotating barrel, commercial mfg., approx. 1,000 mfg., some imported by Western Arms Co.

	100%	98%	95%	90%	80%	70%	60%	LAST MSR
	$900	$595	$495	$400	$350	$300	$250	

Add 20% for NIB.
Add 25% for leather case.

MAC (METROARMS CORP.)

Current trademark of pistols imported and distributed by Eagle Imports, located in Wanamassa, NJ. Please refer to the MetroArms Corporation listing in this section.

MAC (MILITARY ARMAMENT CORP.)

Please refer to FMJ and Ingram sections in this text. MAC was located in Ducktown, TN.

MAG CUSTOM RIFLES

Current custom rifle manufacturer established in 1997, located in Brescia, Italy.

Vittorio Giani, the owner of Manifattura Armi Giani (MAG) specializes in a line of custom order (Brawo MAG) bolt action rifles, as well as SxS rifles and shotguns. All guns are built per customer specifications. Please contact him directly for more information, including an individualized price quotation and delivery time.

MAS

Previously manufactured by D'Armes St. Etienne (MAS) located in France.

Please refer to the French Military heading in this text.

MBA ASSOCIATES

Previous manufacturer circa 1966-1969 located in San Ramon, CA.

PISTOLS: SEMI-AUTO

MARK I GYROJET PISTOL (ROCKETEER AUTOMATIC ROCKET) – 12mm or 13mm cal., caseless, uses spin-stabilized rocket projectiles that accelerate to 1,250 FPS in .12 seconds, 2 in. (rare) or 5 in. barrel, 6 shot semi-auto action drives rocket projectile (primer activated) into fixed firing pin, smooth walnut grips, black, antique nickel, or gold-plated finish, 13 or 16 oz., "A" prefix until ser. no. 49, "B" prefixes followed, there are also other variations and experimental models in addition to the production models listed. Without rifling, this gun wasn't particularly accurate.

The rocket ammunition for this model is rare and typically sells in the $75-$100 round range per shell.

* ***Mark I Gyrojet Pistol Model A Cased*** – 13mm, black finish, smooth walnut grips, walnut cased with 10 rounds and medal.

	100%	98%	95%	90%	80%	70%	60%	LAST MSR
	$3,750	$3,250	$2,750	$2,250	$1,950	$1,750	$1,500	

Add 20% if gold plated and marked "experimental".

* ***Mark I Gyrojet Pistol Model B Cased*** – 13mm, black, nickel, satin, or green finish, many variations with different grips, casings, and barrel lengths, wood cased, includes 10 dummy rounds and bronze medal honoring rocket pioneers Robert H. Goddard and Joseph J. Stubbs.

	100%	98%	95%	90%	80%	70%	60%	LAST MSR
	$2,950	$2,450	$1,900	$1,550	$1,175	$1,050	$925	

Add approx. 25% for satin finish.

* ***Mark I Gyrojet Pistol Model B Uncased or Cardboard*** – either with cardboard case or no case, black finish.

	100%	98%	95%	90%	80%	70%	60%	LAST MSR
	$1,850	$1,350	$1,150	$950	$825	$700	$600	

* ***Mark II Gyrojet Pistol Model C Uncased or Cardboard*** – 12mm, black finish, walnut grips.

	100%	98%	95%	90%	80%	70%	60%	LAST MSR
	$1,850	$1,350	$1,150	$950	$825	$700	$600	

This variation was manufactured in 12mm to conform with the 1968 GCA, since any caliber over .50 was classified as a destructive device (i.e., 12mm = .49 cal. and 13mm =.51 cal.). In 1982, the 13mm guns were reclassified as curios and relics.

GRADING - PPGS™	100%	98%	95%	90%	80%	70%	60%	LAST MSR

RIFLES: SEMI-AUTO, CARBINES

MARK I MODEL A or B CARBINE – 13mm cal., same action as Mark I pistol, black (Model A, AR-15 type "space gun") or satin (Model B) finish, full stock with pistol grip extension, 18 in. barrel, nickel finish, 4 1/2 lbs. Limited mfg.

Model A	$4,250	$3,750	$3,250	$2,500	$2,000	$1,500	$1,250	
Model B	$3,250	$2,750	$2,000	$1,500	$1,250	$1,000	$800	

MGA (MACHINE GUN ARMORY)

Current pistol and rifle manufacturer established in the late 1990s, located in Sandy, UT. Previous company name was U.S. Machine Gun Armory LLC. Prior to that the company name was Practical Defense International.

For individual model listings, please go to BlueBookOfGunValues.com/overflow.

MG ARMS INCORPORATED

Current manufacturer of AR-15 style rifles and custom firearms established in 1980, located in Spring, TX. MG Arms Incorporated was previously named Match Grade Arms & Ammunition. Consumer direct sales.

PISTOLS: SEMI-AUTO

WRAITHE – 9mm Para. (new 2014) or .45 ACP cal., M1911 design, 4 1/4 in. match grade barrel, SA, aluminum alloy frame, choice of fixed or night sights, 3 1/2 lb. trigger, custom grip panels, high ride beavertail safety, choice of black, olive drab, desert tan, or titanium finish. New 2013.

MSR $2,895	$2,475	$2,150	$1,875	$1,450	$1,225	$1,175	$925	

REVOLVERS

CUSTOM BIG 5 – .45 LC+P, .454 Casull, .475 Linebaugh, .50 AE, or .500 Linebaugh cal., Ruger frame, stainless steel, 5 shot cylinder, custom barrels, standard finish or optional camo coverage. Mfg. 2000-2007.

	$1,175	$975	$875	$775	$700	$625	$525	*$1,295*

MG Arms also offered a conversion package for $795 (customer supplies Ruger revolver).

DRAGONSLAYER – .44 Mag., .45 Colt, .454 Casull, .50 AE (disc. 2011), .475 Linebaugh, .500 Linebaugh, .445 Super Mag. (disc. 2011), .450 Marlin (disc. 2011), .460 S&W Mag. (disc.), or .500 S&W Mag. (disc. 2011) cal., 5 shot, stainless steel construction, 2 1/2 lb. trigger, choice of grips, includes 20 rounds of custom loaded ammo. Mfg. 2008-2011, reintroduced 2013-2017. Limited production of 25 guns a year. Reintroduced 2018.

MSR $1,895	$1,675	$1,350	$1,100	$950	$825	$725	$625	

This model became special order only during 2014.

DRAGONFLY (RECENT MFG.) – .32 H&R Mag., .38 Spl., .44 Colt, or .44 Mag. cal., SA, finely tuned trigger, corrosion resistant PTFE metal finish (customer choice of color pattern), choice of cowboy (quick draw) or target (backpacking) configuration. Mfg. 2010-2011.

	$995	$875	$750	$625	$525	$450	$375	*$1,095*

DRAGONFLY (CURRENT MFG.) – .32 H&R Mag., .38+P Spl., or .44 Spl. cal., 6 shot cylinder, half cock loading, Titanium sleeved barrel, tuned trigger, adj. rear sight, many color and grip combinations available, PTFE or Cerakote metal finish, extra 20 rounds of custom loaded ammo, barrel porting optional, 21 oz. Limited mfg. of 25 revolvers per year.

MSR $1,295	$1,150	$1,000	$900	$800	$650	$500	$400	

RIFLES: BOLT ACTION

BANSHEE – various cals. from .223-.338 Lapua, blueprinted Rem. action, 16-26 in. National Match barrel, includes Picatinny scope base, 5 or 10 shot detachable mag., cryogenically treated stainless steel barrel, 2 1/2 lb. custom trigger, varmint weight fully adj., lightweight non-adj. (Banshee Lite and Banshee Classic), or fiberglass stock, custom bedded full-length aluminum pillar block, choice of PTFE or Cerakote finish. New 2012.

MSR $2,895	$2,450	$2,150	$1,850	$1,700	$1,350	$1,100	$850	

Add $150 for left-hand action.
Add $500 for Banshee w/fiberglass stock.
Subtract $200 for Banshee Lite (disc. 2018).

MGA SILVER EDITION – various cals., Model 7015 action, match grade #3 taper barrel, tuned trigger, 20 oz. fiberglass stock, PTFE metal finish. Mfg. 2009-2010.

	$2,500	$2,200	$1,925	$1,700	$1,500	$1,300	$1,050	*$2,635*

GRADING - PPGS™	100%	98%	95%	90%	80%	70%	60%	LAST MSR

SIGNATURE CLASSIC – various cals., Nesika Hunter (disc.) or Stiller action, chrome moly, PacNor (disc.), or Hart stainless steel match grade barrel with Super Eliminator muzzle brake, Jewell trigger, choice of Cascade fiberglass (disc.) or AAA fancy wood stock with satin oil finish, matte stainless steel, exhibition grade bluing, black PTFE, or Cerakote metal finish. Limited mfg. (approx. 10 guns per year) beginning 2000.

MSR $9,795	$9,495	$8,250	$7,000	$5,750	$4,500	$3,500	$3,000	

Subtract approx. 35% if with Cascade fiberlass stock (disc).

ULTRA-LIGHT MODEL – various cals., lightened and skeletonized Wby. Vanguard (disc. 2004), Rem. 700 (new 2005), or Win. Model 70 (disc.) action, stainless steel National Match barrel, Super Eliminator muzzle brake, bolt fluted and skeletonized, Sako style extractor, Jewell trigger, PTFE or Cerakote metal finish, textured epoxy stock with Pachmayr Decelerator pad, variety of camo finishes on stock (Zebra finish is standard), weight starts at 4 3/4 lbs.

MSR $3,995	$3,600	$3,250	$2,900	$2,450	$2,075	$1,750	$1,425	

Add $100 for ergonomic thumbhole stock.

Add $500 for Win. Model 70 action (disc.).

VARMINTER – various cals., squared and lapped Rem. M700 action, stainless steel National Match barrel with Super Eliminator muzzle brake, black Teflon metal finish, camo epoxy stock.

	$2,625	$2,300	$2,000	$1,650	$1,325	$1,050	$925	*$2,895*

RIFLES: SEMI-AUTO

BEHEMOTH – .50 BMG cal., 24 (new 2016), 29, or 31 in. stainless steel match grade skip line fluted barrel with Super Eliminator muzzle brake, 5 shot detachable mag., fully adjustable skeletonized custom buttstock, Picatinny style handrail with KeyMods, fully machined stainless steel lower receiver, PTFE or ceramic metal finish, Charcoal Camo finish. Mfg. 2015-2018.

	$11,000	$9,000	$7,250	$6,500	$5,500	$5,000	$4,500	*$12,200*

CK-4 – .223 Rem. or .300 Fireball cal., AR-15 style, GIO, 16 or 20 in. barrel with flash hider (16 in. only), 20 or 30 shot mag., MGA 3-piece lower receiver, A3 flat-top upper receiver, 6-position collapsible stock, free floating quad rail handguard, choice of PTFE resin finish, basic, or camo coverage. Mfg. 2011-2015.

	$1,750	$1,575	$1,450	$1,325	$1,100	$875	$675	*$1,995*

K-YOTE VARMINT SYSTEM – .17 Rem., .204 Ruger, .223 Rem., .243 Win., .260 Rem., 7mm-08 Rem., or .308 Win. cal., AR-15 style, GIO, choice of round fluted or 10-sided match grade fully free floating 20, 24, or 26 in. barrel, custom target trigger, fully adj. stock, 4 rail free floating handguard, machined lower receiver, integral Picatinny scope rail, standard or camo PTFE or Cerakote finish. New 2009.

MSR $3,695	$3,250	$2,925	$2,675	$2,425	$2,050	$1,600	$1,275	

TARANIS – 5.56 NATO or .300 AAC Blackout cal., AR-15 style, GIO, 16 in. lightweight match grade tapered barrel with titanium flash hider, 20 or 30 shot mag., custom trigger, CTR 6-position collapsible stock, upper receiver with flat-top Picatinny rail, carbon fiber handguard, skeletonized bolt, PTFE resin, basic, or Tan Zebra camo finish, approx. 4 1/2 lbs. Mfg. 2013-2016.

	$1,925	$1,725	$1,600	$1,450	$1,225	$950	$750	*$2,195*

TARANIS 2 – 5.56 NATO, .300 AAC Blackout, 6.5 Grendel, 6.8 SPC, .204 Ruger, or .50 Beowulf cal., 16 in. match grade ultralight barrel, Super Eliminator muzzle brake, 20 shot mag., 3 lb. match grade trigger, 6-way ultra light adj. stock, Tacti-Quik safety, carbon fiber handguard, ultralight skeletonized forged receivers, skeletonized bolt and bolt carrier, Picatinny top rail, choice of standard or camo PTFE or Cerakote finish, approx. 4 1/2 lbs. New 2017.

MSR $2,295	$2,025	$1,825	$1,650	$1,500	$1,275	$1,000	$775	

TARANIS X – 6.5 Creedmoor, .308 Win., or .338 Federal cal., 16 1/2 in. match grade ultralight barrel, MG Arms SE2 muzzle brake, 3 lb. match grade trigger, 6-way ultralight adj. stock, TactiQuick safety, ultralight skeletonized fully machined upper and forged lower receiver, Picatinny top rail, carbon fiber handguard, M-one/A-one charging handle, choice of standard or camo PTFE or Cerakote finish, 6 lbs. New 2019.

MSR $2,995	$2,650	$2,375	$2,175	$1,975	$1,650	$1,300	$1,025	

MGI

Current manufacturer of AR-15 style rifles and pistols located in Old Town, ME. Previously located in Bangor, ME until late 2010.

Please refer to BlueBookOfGunValues.com to order the *Blue Book of AR-15s & Variations*, available as a book or online subscription.

M-K SPECIALTIES INC.

Previous rifle manufacturer located in Grafton, WV circa 2000-2002.

GRADING - PPGS™	100%	98%	95%	90%	80%	70%	60%	LAST MSR

RIFLES: SEMI-AUTO

M-14 A1 - .308 Win. cal., forged M-14 steel receiver using CNC machinery to original government specifications, available as Rack Grade, Premier Match, or Tanker Model, variety of National Match upgrades were available at extra cost, base price is for Rack Grade. Mfg. 2000-2002.

$1,475	$1,275	$995	$875	$750	$625	$500	*$1,595*

Add $345-$955 for National Match upgrades.

MK ARMS INC.

Previous manufacturer located in Irvine, CA circa 1992.

CARBINES: SEMI-AUTO

MK 760 – 9mm Para. cal., steel frame, 16 in. shrouded barrel, fires from closed bolt, 14, 24, or 36 shot mag., parkerized finish, folding metal stock, fixed sights. Mfg. 1983-approx. 1992.

$725	$650	$575	$525	$475	$415	$375	*$575*

MKA ARMS

Previous manufacturer located in Konya, Turkey with headquarters in Istanbul.

MKA Arms manufactured an AR-15 style gas operated semi-automatic shotgun in 12 ga. Various configurations were available.

MKE

Current manufacturer located in Ankara, Turkey. MKE guns and ammunition are imported beginning 2021 by Century International Arms, located in Delray Beach, FL. Previously imported by Zenith Firearms, located in Afton, VA. Previously imported beginning 2011 by American Tactical Imports, located in Rochester, NY. Previously distributed by Mandall Shooting Supplies, Inc., located in Scottsdale, AZ.

MKE manufactures a wide variety of military and law enforcement models, in addition to a line of consumer semi-auto hunting rifles and semi-auto pistols.

PISTOLS: SEMI-AUTO

Add $80-$100 for customized covert carry case.

KIRIKKALE AUTOMATIC – 7.65mm Para. (disc.) or .380 ACP cal., double action, 7 shot, blue finish, fixed sights, checkered plastic grips. Disc. 1987.

$365	$295	$240	$215	$185	$170	$155	*$395*

This model is a close copy of Walther's PP and a former Turkish Army standard service pistol.

AT-94P/AT-94K – 9mm Para. cal., MP5 style, roller-delayed blowback system, 4.5 (AT-94K) or 16.4 (AT-94P) in. barrel, 30 shot mag., open sights (AT-94K only), matte black finish. Imported 2011-2012.

$1,395	$1,200	$1,000	$850	$700	$600	$525	*$1,596*

Z-5K CLASSIC AOW – 9mm Para. cal., roller-delayed blowback action, 4.6 in. CHF barrel, 30 shot mag., front post and rear drum sights, U.S.-made vertical "K" grip, includes customized covert carry case, boresnake and Slip 2000 cleaning oil, two extra takedown pins, Picatinny style optics rail, military style sling, and three mags., black finish, 12.79 in. OAL, 4.43 lbs. Mfg. in Turkey by MKE for Zenith Firearms. Disc. 2020.

$1,625	$1,425	$1,200	$1,075	$925	$795	$650	*$1,914*

Z-5K SB CLASSIC – 9mm Para. cal., roller-delayed blowback action, 4.6 in. CHF barrel, 30 shot mag., rear drum and front post sights, factory handguard, SB Tactical side folding pistol brace, Picatinny style optics rail, includes boresnake and Slip 2000 cleaning oil, two extra takedown pins, military style sling, and three mags., black finish, 12.79 in. OAL, 5 lbs. Mfg. in Turkey by MKE for Zenith Firearms. Disc. 2020.

$1,660	$1,450	$1,225	$1,085	$935	$800	$660	*$1,974*

Z-5K SB RAIL – 9mm Para. cal., roller-delayed blowback action, 4.6 in. CHF barrel, 30 shot mag., front post and rear drum sights, Midwest Industries M-LOK (new 2017) handguard, SB Tactical side folding pistol brace, Picatinny style optics rail, includes boresnake and Slip 2000 cleaning oil, two extra takedown pins, military style sling, and three mags., black finish, 12.79 in. OAL, 5 lbs. Mfg. in Turkey by MKE for Zenith Firearms. Disc. 2020.

$1,775	$1,525	$1,275	$1,125	$975	$850	$685	*$2,059*

GRADING - PPGS™	100%	98%	95%	90%	80%	70%	60%	LAST MSR

Z-5P SB CLASSIC – 9mm Para. cal., roller-delayed blowback action, 5.8 in. CHF barrel with 3-lug quick attachment and threaded muzzle, 30 shot mag., front post and rear drum sights, factory handguard, SB Tactical side folding pistol brace, Picatinny style optics rail, includes boresnake and Slip 2000 cleaning oil, two extra takedown pins, military style sling, and three mags., black finish, 13.7 in. OAL, 5.2 lbs. Mfg. in Turkey by MKE for Zenith Firearms. Disc. 2020.

$1,710	$1,500	$1,250	$1,100	$950	$825	$675	*$2,019*

Z-5RS SB CLASSIC – 9mm Para. cal., roller-delayed blowback action, 8.9 in. CHF barrel with 3-lug quick attachment and threaded muzzle, 30 shot mag., rear drum and front post sights, SB Tactical side folding pistol brace, Picatinny style optics rail, includes boresnake and Slip 2000 cleaning oil, two extra takedown pins, military style sling, three magazines, black finish, 26.75 in. OAL, 5.8 lbs. Mfg. in Turkey by MKE for Zenith Firearms. Disc. 2020.

1,725	$1,515	$1,250	$1,100	$950	$825	$675	*$2,039*

X-5RS SB RAIL – 9mm Para. cal., roller-delayed blowback, 8.9 in. CHF barrel with 3-lug quick attachment and threaded muzzle, 30 shot mag., front post and rear drum sights, Samson Picatinny tri-rail handguard, SB Tactical side folding pistol brace, Picatinny style optics rail, includes boresnake and Slip 2000 cleaning oil, two extra takedown pins, military style sling, and three mags., black finish, 26.75 in. OAL, 6.1 lbs. Mfg. in Turkey by MKE for Zenith Firearms. Disc. 2020.

$1,840	$1,600	$1,350	$1,175	$1,000	$860	$715	*$2,184*

Z-5RS WITH SB TACTICAL FIXED PISTOL BRACE – 9mm Para. cal., roller-delayed blowback action, 8.9 in. CHF barrel with 3-lug quick attachment and threaded muzzle, 30 shot mag., front post and rear drum sights, includes rugged plastic carry case, factory cleaning kit, two extra takedown pins, Picatinny style optics rail, military style sling, three mags., black finish, 25 3/4 in. OAL, 6.15 lbs. Mfg. in Turkey by MKE for Zenith Firearms. Disc. 2020.

$1,710	$1,500	$1,250	$1,100	$950	$825	$675	*$2,019*

Z-43P SB CLASSIC – 9mm Para. cal., roller-delayed blowback action, 12 in. CHF barrel w/muzzle brake, 30 shot mag., front post and rear drum sights, factory handguard, SB Tactical side folding pistol brace, includes boresnake and Slip 2000 cleaning oil, two extra takedown pins, Picatinny style optics rail, military style sling, and three mags., black finish, 23.3 in. OAL, 8.2 lbs. Mfg. in Turkey by MKE for Zenith Firearms. Disc. 2020.

$1,535	$1,350	$1,175	1,050	$900	$775	$625	*$1,824*

Z-43P SB RAIL – 5.56 NATO cal., roller-delayed blowback action, 12 in. CHF barrel w/muzzle brake, 30 shot mag., front post and rear drum sights, Midwest Industries M-LOK handguard, SB Tactical side folding pistol brace, Picatinny style optics rail, includes boresnake and Slip 2000 cleaning oil, two extra takedown pins, military style sling, and three mags., black finish, 23.3 in. OAL, 8.2 lbs. Mfg. in Turkey by MKE for Zenith Firearms. Disc. 2020.

$1,660	$1,450	$1,225	$1,085	$935	$800	$660	*$1,974*

RIFLES/CARBINES: SEMI-AUTO

AT-94R2 CARBINE – 9mm Para. cal., 16.4 in. barrel, patterned after H&K Model 94, roller delayed blowback action, A2 style MP5 stock, steel receiver, matte black finish, 10 shot detachable box mag. Imported 2011-2012.

$1,350	$1,125	$900	$800	$700	$600	$500	*$1,550*

AT-43 RIFLE – .223 Rem. cal., 17 in. barrel, patterned after H&K Model 93, roller-delayed blowback action, A2 style fixed stock, steel receiver, matte black finish, 30 shot detachable box mag. Imported 2011-2012.

$1,300	$1,075	$875	$775	$675	$575	$475	*$1,495*

Z-5 SPORT – 9mm Para. cal., roller-delayed blowback action, 16.15 in. CHF barrel, three 10 shot mags., front protected post sight and rear drum for elevation and windage, factory Picatinny style optics mount, black finish, includes factory sling and plastic carry case, 6.88 lbs. Mfg. in Turkey by MKE for Zenith Firearms. Mfg. 2015-2020.

$1,585	$1,385	$1,185	$1,065	$915	$785	$635	*$1,871*

MKS SUPPLY, INC.

Marketing company representing various companies including Hi-Point Firearms and Inland Manufacturing firearms. Previously represented Chiappa Firearms Ltd. MKS firearms were manufactured by Chiappa Firearms Ltd. located in Dayton, OH until 2014. Please refer to Hi-Point Firearms and Inland Manufacturing sections for individual model listings.

GRADING - PPGS™	100%	98%	95%	90%	80%	70%	60%	LAST MSR

SHOTGUNS

MKS Supply, Inc. offered the following shotguns until 2014: Aimpro Tactical 590 A1 with choice of 18 1/2 or 20 in. barrel with Hogue standard stock, and TacStar side saddle - MSRs were $897 and $945, Aimpro Tactical 590 A1 Breacher - last MSR was $868, and the Aimpro Tactical 590 A1 Elite with holographic sight and other accessories - last MSR was $1,495.

MMC ARMORY

Current AR-15 style firearm manufacturer established in 2008, located in Mark, IL.

Please refer to BlueBookOfGunValues.com to order the *Blue Book of AR-15s & Variations*, available as a book or online subscription.

MNR CUSTOM LLC

Current custom bolt action rifle manufacturer located in Springfield, VT.

MNR Custom manufactures high quality rifles built to customer specifications as well as offering gunsmithing services. Please contact the manufacturer directly for custom orders, pricing, availability, and services.

RIFLES: BOLT ACTION

All MSRs are considered base price. Many options and custom services are also available.

On the following models where applicable:
Add $300 for muzzle brake.
Add $600 for carbon fiber barrel.
Add $400 for 3-pos. safety.
Add $300 for drop box bottom metal.
Add $400 for custom scope bases for Talley rings.
Add $600 for custom one-piece bottom metal with trigger bow release.
Add $1,500 for integral barrel sight bases, sling swivel, and secondary recoil lug.
Add $600 - $2,500 for Richardson and Roberts, Stiller, or Granite Mountain Arms action.

CLASSIC – various cals., patterned after Winchester Model 70 or Remington 700 action, premium stainless steel barrel, pillar bedded premium fiberglass stock, Talley bases and rings, sling swivel studs, industrial grade speckle-tone paint, all-weather ceramic metal finish.

MSR $4,500	$3,800	$3,350	$2,850	$2,600	$2,100	$1,700	$1,350

HATARI – various cals., patterned after Winchester Model 70 or Mauser 98 action, premium barrel fitted, banded express sights and sling swivels fixed to barrel, customizable classic style stock and choice of select English walnut finish, wraparound point checkering pattern, custom scope bases for Talley QD rings, one-piece bottom metal w/straddle floorplate and trigger bow release, ebony tip, steel grip cap, inlaid rear swivel stud and steel crossbolts, hand-rubbed oil finish.

MSR $11,500	$9,800	$8,550	$7,350	$6,650	$5,400	$4,400	$3,400

LATALIS – various cals., Remington 700 action, fluted match grade barrel, Sako-style extractor, Jewell trigger, lightweight Talley scope mounts, pillar bedded lightweight custom fiberglass stock w/speckle tone finish, side bolt release, fluted bolt, All-Weather ceramic metal finish, available in BDL or ADL. New 2021.

MSR $4,500	$3,800	$3,350	$2,850	$2,600	$2,100	$1,700	$1,350

MCKINLEY – various cals., patterned after Winchester Model 70 or Mauser 98 action, premium barrel, express sights and barrel banded sling swivel, pillar bedded custom fiberglass stock shaped in classic style, custom scope bases for Talley QD rings, custom one-piece bottom metal w/straddle floorplate and trigger bow release, steel grip cap, inlaid rear swivel stud and steel crossbolts, industrial grade speckle tone finish, all-weather ceramic metal finish.

MSR $7,500	$6,400	$5,600	$4,800	$4,350	$3,500	$2,850	$2,250

M.O.A. CORPORATION

Previous trademark and manufacturer 2014-disc. by Pueblo Valley Firearms LLC, located in Fields, OR. Previously manufactured in Sundance, WY from 2005-2012. Previously located in Eaton, OH.

PISTOLS: SINGLE SHOT

Approx. 500-600 Maximum pistols were produced annually. Was a 4-6 month delivery rate.

GRADING - PPGS™	100%	98%	95%	90%	80%	70%	60%	LAST MSR

MAXIMUM – available in 30 standard chamberings between .22 Rimfire and .454 Casull cal., additional custom calibers are also available upon special order, single shot lever action pistol, falling block action, chrome moly receiver (disc. 1991), Armoloy coated Chromoly (disc. late 1992), or stainless steel (new 1991, standard 1992) receiver, 8 3/4 (new 1989), 10 1/2, or 14 in. interchangeable barrel, transfer bar safety, adj. open sights, walnut grips and forearm. Mfg. 1986-disc.

	$925	$825	$725	$625	$525	$425	$350	*$1,062*

Subtract 10% for older steel receiver.
Add $50-$60 for scope mounts.
Add $135 for muzzle brake.
Add $269 per extra steel barrel (disc.).
Add $389 per extra stainless steel barrel.

Barrels had to be fitted to individual receivers at the factory initially. Afterwards, they could be changed by the customer with the spanner wrench (included extra barrels).

* ***Maximum Carbine Model*** – cals. up to .250 Sav., stainless receiver, otherwise similar to Maximum, except has 18 in. blue barrel. Mfg. 1986-disc.

	$925	$850	$750	$650	$575	$525	$475	*$1,023*

MOA RIFLES, LLC

Current bolt action rifle manufacturer located in Redmond, OR.

RIFLES: BOLT ACTION

ASCENT/ASCENT CARBON – 6.5 PRC, .300 PRC, or .28 Nosler cal., Benchmark #2 fluted steel or carbon (Ascent Carbon, new 2021) barrel, Premium TriggerTech trigger, McMillan Hunter Stock, lightweight, black or tan carbon, KUIU Verde, or KUIU Vias finish. New 2019.

MSR $5,795	$4,900	$4,300	$3,700	$3,350	$2,700	$2,200	$1,700	

Add $500 for carbon barrel (Ascent Carbon, new 2021).

EVOLUTION/EVOLUTION CARBON – various cals., Evolution action, No. 4 non-fluted barrel, Radial-Barrel steel, match trigger, McMillan Game Scout fiberglass or carbon (Evolution Carbon, new 2019) stock, black, Barrett Brown, Burnt Bronze, or Tungsten Cerakote finish, approx. 7 lbs. Disc. 2020.

	$4,675	$4,100	$3,600	$3,150	$2,575	$2,100	$1,625	*$5,295*

Add $700 for carbon stock (Evolution Carbon, new 2019).

EVOLUTION SHORT ACTION – .22-250, .243 Win., .308 Win., .270 WSM, 7mm WSM, or .300 WSM cal., short action, 24 in. stainless steel barrel, multi-ported removable muzzle brake, Timney trigger, Mcmillan BDL stock, pillar bedded, black, white, or tan finish, 7 lbs. Disc.

	$3,325	$2,910	$2,495	$2,260	$1,825	$1,500	$1,175	*$3,700*

EVOLUTION LONG ACTION – 6.5-284 Norma, .26 Nosler, 7mm Rem. Mag., .28 Nosler, .300 Win. Mag., 7mm RUM, .300 RUM, or .338 RUM cal., long action, 26 in. stainless steel barrel, multi-ported removable muzzle brake, Timney trigger, McMillan BDL stock, pillar bedded, olive, black, or tan finish, 7 lbs. 8 oz. Disc.

	$3,325	$2,910	$2,495	$2,260	$1,825	$1,500	$1,175	*$3,700*

EVOLUTION LONG RANGE HUNTER – 6.5-284 Norma, .26 Nosler, 7mm Rem. Mag., .28 Nosler, .300 Win. Mag., .300 RUM, or .338 RUM cal., 26 in. Sendero contour match grade stainless steel barrel, multi-ported removable muzzle brake, plunger ejector, M16 Badger Ordnance extractor, Timney trigger, McMillan A3 stock, pillar bedded, tan, black, or white finish, 9 lbs. 12 oz. Mfg. 2015-disc.

	$3,595	$3,150	$2,695	$2,450	$1,975	$1,625	$1,275	*$3,995*

EVOLUTION EXTREME SUMMIT – 6.5-284 Norma, .26 Nosler, 7mm Rem. Mag., .28 Nosler, or .300 Win. Mag. cal., Evolution Extreme action, 26 in. stainless steel fluted barrel, radial multi-ported removable muzzle brake, plunger ejector, M16 Badger Ordnance extractor, Jewell trigger, McMillan Hunter Edge stock, 90 degree skeletal bolt handle, ultra lightweight billet aluminum bottom metal, pillar bedded, external bolt stop, black finish with tan and olive specs, 5 lbs. 6 oz. Mfg. 2016-disc.

	$5,175	$4,525	$3,875	$3,525	$2,850	$2,325	$1,825	*$5,745*

EVOLUTION EXTREME SPORTER – 6.5-284 Norma, .26 Nosler, .28 Nosler, 7mm RUM, .300 RUM, or .338 Lapua Mag. cal., Evolution Extreme action, 26 in. stainless steel match grade fluted barrel, multi-ported removable muzzle brake, plunger ejector, M16 Badger Ordnance extractor, Jewell trigger, McMillan Hunter Edge stock, 90 degree skeletal bolt handle, pillar bedded, external bolt stop, black finish with tan and olive specs, 7 lbs. 6 oz. Mfg. 2016-disc.

	$5,175	$4,525	$3,875	$3,525	$2,850	$2,325	$1,825	*$5,745*

GRADING - PPGS™	100%	98%	95%	90%	80%	70%	60%	LAST MSR

EVOLUTION EXTREME LONG RANGE HUNTER – 6.5-284 Norma, .26 Nosler, .28 Nosler, 7mm RUM, .300 RUM, or .338 Lapua cal., Evolution Extreme action, 26 in. match grade fluted stainless steel barrel, multi-ported removable muzzle brake, plunger ejector, M16 Badger Ordnance extractor, Jewell trigger, adj. McMillan A3-5 Edge stock, pillar bedded, 90 degree skeletal bolt handle, black finish with tan and olive specs, 8 lbs. Disc.

	$5,100	$4,450	$3,800	$3,450	$2,800	$2,300	$1,800	*$5,995*

EXTREME ALPINE/EXTREME CARBON ALPINE – various cals., Extreme action, 26 in. #5 fluted (Extreme Alpine) or #5 carbon (Extreme Carbon Alpine) barrel, side-port muzzle brake, McMillan Game Hunter carbon fiber stock, approx. 7 lbs. New 2019.

MSR $5,995	$5,100	$4,450	$3,800	$3,450	$2,800	$2,300	$1,800

Add $500 for carbon barrel (Extreme Carbon Alpine).

EXTREME BADLAND/EXTREME CARBON BADLAND – various cals., Extreme action, 26 in. steel (Extreme Badland) or carbon (Extreme Carbon Badland) barrel, side port muzzle brake, McMillan Game Scout carbon fiber stock, 7 lbs. 2 oz. New 2021.

MSR $5,995	$5,100	$4,450	$3,800	$3,450	$2,800	$2,300	$1,800

Add $500 for carbon barrel (Extreme Carbon Badland).

EXTREME SUMMIT/EXTREME CARBON SUMMIT – various cals., Extreme action, 25 in. #3 fluted (Extreme Summit) or #5 carbon (Extreme Carbon Summit) barrel, side-port muzzle brake, McMillan hunter carbon fiber barrel, approx. 6 lbs. New 2019.

MSR $5,995	$5,100	$4,450	$3,800	$3,450	$2,800	$2,300	$1,800

Add $500 for carbon barrel (Extreme Carbon Summit).

EXTREME SPORTER/EXTREME CARBON SPORTER – various cals., Extreme action, 26 in. #5 fluted (Extreme Sporter) or #5 carbon (Extreme Carbon Sporter) barrel, side-port muzzle brake, McMillan Rem. Hunter carbon fiber stock, 6-7 lbs. New 2019.

MSR $5,995	$5,100	$4,450	$3,800	$3,450	$2,800	$2,300	$1,800

Add $500 for carbon barrel (Extreme Carbon Sporter).

EXTREME LRH (LONG RANGE HUNTER)/EXTREME CARBON LRH – various cals., Extreme action, 27 in. #6 fluted (Extreme LRH) or Sendero carbon (Extreme Carbon LRH) barrel, side-port muzzle brake, McMillan A3-5 adj. stock, approx. 8 lbs. New 2019.

MSR $6,295	$5,350	$4,700	$4,000	$3,650	$2,950	$2,400	$1,900

Add $500 for Sendero carbon barrel (Extreme Carbon LRH).

M.R. NEW SYSTEM ARMS

Current designer and handgun manufacturer located in Cerrione, Italy. No current U.S. importation.

FIREARMS

Inventor and designer Marco Rigido manufactures a Mauser Model 92 carbine in both standard/Mag. cals. (€3,500), or a Safari Model in African calibers (€6,000). He also manufactures both SxS and O/U express rifles with either boxlock or sidelock action. Boxlocks start at €4,000, and the sidelock in Africa cals. is POR. Other products include both O/U and SxS shotguns with prices starting at €2,500 (O/U boxlock).

Perhaps his most famous guns are the 5 shot SA Model Cucciolo in .728 MR cal. (€30,000) and both a single shot pistol and rifle chambered for 1.000 caliber, the largest caliber ever offered for consumers. Please contact the company directly for more information, including U.S. availability and pricing.

MTs ARMS

Current trademark manufactured by Sporting and Hunting Guns Central Design and Research Bureau, a subsidiary of the State Unitary Enterprise, Instrument Design Bureau, (GUP "KBP" - "TsKIB SOO"), located in Tula, Russia. No current U.S. importation.

MTs Arms manufactures a variety of firearms, including SxS and O/U shotguns, combination guns, self-loading shotguns, slide action shotguns, bolt action rifles, Drillings, competition guns, and semi-auto rifles. TsKIB SOO is the only manufacturer of quality hunting guns in Russia and the countries of the CIS (Commonwealth of Independent States). Please contact the company directly for more information regarding this trademark and current domestic availability.

JAMES MacNAUGHTON & SONS

Current trademark owned and manufactured by John Dickson & Son located in Edinburgh, Scotland.

The business of James MacNaughton was founded in Edinburgh, Scotland in 1864 after MacNaughton had served an apprenticeship with John Dickson. The MacNaughton's established themselves as builders of fine guns and would go on to patent the "Edinburgh" gun in 1879 - a triggerplate action gun in the similar guise as

GRADING - PPGS™	100%	98%	95%	90%	80%	70%	60%	LAST MSR

the Dickson Round-Action. However, MacNaughton would introduce a variant, the bar-in-wood or "Skeleton" action. A reduction in the metal surface of the action instead of being covered with extending the stock over the action, showcases the beautiful wood, making for a very graceful and sleek looking action for which the gun has now become very sought after by enthusiasts and collectors. In 1947, the company was acquired by John Dickson and Son, who are the only manufacturers in the world with this action making it a truly unique Scottish, handmade side-by-side gun. The company also continues to provide a full repair, restoration, and record enquiry service for the vintage MacNaughton guns.

SHOTGUNS

SKELETON "ROUND-ACTIION" SHOTGUN – based on the 1879 triggerplate design. Bespoke specification and build.

Current base prices start at $75,000.

MAADI-GRIFFIN CO.

Previous rifle manufacturer located in Mesa, AZ until 2003. Consumer direct sales.

RIFLES: SEMI-AUTO

MODEL MG-6 – .50 BMG cal., gas operated, bullpup configuration, one-piece cast lower receiver, 5, 10, or 15 shot side mounted mag., 26-30 in. barrel, includes bipod, hard carrying case, and 3 mags., 23 lbs. Mfg. 2000-2003.

100%	98%	95%	90%	80%	70%	60%	LAST MSR
$5,500	$4,750	$3,850	$3,250	$2,600	$2,200	$1,800	*$5,950*

Add $450 for MK-IV tripod.

RIFLES: SINGLE SHOT

MODEL 89 – .50 BMG cal., one-piece cast lower receiver, 36 in. barrel, felt recoil is less than 12 ga., TIG welded interlocking assembly, no screws, tripod optional, 22 lbs. Mfg. 1990-2003.

100%	98%	95%	90%	80%	70%	60%	LAST MSR
$3,100	$2,750	$2,400	$2,050	$1,775	$1,500	$1,250	*$3,150*

Add $600 for stainless steel.

MODEL 92 CARBINE – .50 BMG cal., 20 in. barrel, 5 lb. trigger pull, 18 1/2 lbs. Mfg. 1990-2003.

100%	98%	95%	90%	80%	70%	60%	LAST MSR
$2,950	$2,550	$2,225	$1,875	$1,650	$1,400	$1,200	*$2,990*

Add $650 for stainless steel.

MODEL 99 – .50 BMG cal., similar to Model 89, except has 44 in. barrel, 28 lbs. Mfg. 1999-2003.

100%	98%	95%	90%	80%	70%	60%	LAST MSR
$3,150	$2,725	$2,450	$2,050	$1,775	$1,500	$1,250	*$3,350*

Add $650 for stainless steel.

MAGNUM RESEARCH, INC.

MAGNUM RESEARCH, INC.

Current trademark of pistols and rifles with company headquarters located in Greeley, PA (previously located in Blauvelt, NY 2010-2020), with manufacturing facilities located in Pillager, MN, and by I.W.I. (Baby and Desert Eagle Series), located in Israel. During June of 2010, Kahr Arms purchased the assets of Magnum Research, Inc. Desert Eagle Series was manufactured 1998-2008 by IMI, located in Israel. Previously manufactured by Saco Defense located in Saco, ME during 1995-1998, and by TAAS/IMI (Israeli Military Industries) 1986-1995. .22 Rimfire semi-auto pistols (Mountain Eagle) were previously manufactured by Ram-Line. Single shot pistols (Lone Eagle) were manufactured by Magnum Research sub-contractors. Distributed by Magnum Research, Inc., in Minneapolis, MN. Dealer and distributor sales.

MRI CUSTOM SHOP

In addition to the standard models listed, Magnum Research can also provide a variety of special order options through their custom shop, including many choices of Desert Eagle finishes, in addition to various sight systems and grips.

MRI's current custom shop Desert Eagle (not Baby Eagle) finish options with MSRs (vary slightly depending on caliber) are listed individually under each model listing.

PISTOLS: SEMI-AUTO

IMI SP-21 – 9mm Para., .40 S&W, or .45 ACP cal., DA/SA, traditional Browning operating system, SFO, polymer frame with ergonomic design, 3.9 in. barrel with polygonal rifling, 10 shot mag., finger groove grips, 3-dot adj. sights, reversible mag. release, multiple safeties, matte black finish, decocking feature, approx. 29 oz. Limited importation from IMI late 2002-2005.

100%	98%	95%	90%	80%	70%	60%	LAST MSR
$550	$395	$335	$300	$280	$260	$240	*$499*

The IMI SP-21 uses the same magazines as the Baby Eagle pistols. This model is referred to the Barak SP-21 in Israel.

GRADING - PPGS™	100%	98%	95%	90%	80%	70%	60%	LAST MSR

THE MOUNTAIN EAGLE – .22 LR cal., SA, 6 (new 1995) or 6 1/2 (disc. 1994) in. polymer and steel barrel, features alloy receiver and polymer technology, matte black finish, adj. rear sight, 15 or 20 shot mag. 21 oz. Mfg. 1992-96.

	$185	$155	$135	$115	$100	$85	$75	*$239*

* ***The Mountain Eagle Compact Edition*** – similar to Mountain Eagle, except has 4 1/2 in. barrel with shortened grips, adj. rear sight, 10 or 15 shot mag., plastic case, 19.3 oz. Mfg. 1996 only.

	$165	$135	$120	$105	$95	$80	$70	*$199*

* ***The Mountain Eagle Target Edition*** – .22 LR cal., Target variation of the Mountain Eagle, 8 in. accurized barrel, two-stage target trigger, jeweled bolt, adj. sights with interchangeable blades, 23 oz. Mfg. 1994-1996.

	$235	$185	$150	$135	$120	$105	$95	*$279*

PICUDA MLP-1722 – .17 Mach 2 or .22 LR cal., 10 in. graphite barrel, no sights, features MLR-22 frame, choice of laminated nutmeg, forest camo, or pepper colored Barracuda stock, integral scope base, target trigger, 10 shot mag., approx. 3 lbs. Mfg. 2007-2009.

	$595	$525	$450	$400	$350	$300	$250	*$699*

MLR-1722 – .22 LR cal., 10 in. ULTRA steel sleeved aluminum barrel with threaded muzzle, nutmeg laminate stock. New 2016.

MSR $592	$525	$450	$400	$365	$335	$300	$275	

PISTOLS: SEMI-AUTO, CENTERFIRE - EAGLE SERIES

Magnum Research offered a Collector's Edition Presentation Series. Special models included a Gold Edition (serial numbered 1-100), a Silver Edition (serial numbered 101-500), and a Bronze Edition (serial numbered 501-1,000). Each pistol from this series was supplied with a walnut presentation case, 2 sided medallion, and certificate of authenticity.

Alloy frames on the Desert Eagle Series of pistols were discontinued in 1992. However, if sufficient demand warrants, these models will once again be available to consumers at the same price as the steel frames.

Beginning late 1995, the Desert Eagle frame assembly for the .357 Mag., .44 Mag., and .50 AE cals. is based on the .50 caliber frame. Externally, all three pistols are now identical in size. This new platform, called the Desert Eagle Pistol Mark XIX Component System, enables .44 Mag. and .50 AE conversions to consist of simply a barrel and a magazine - conversions to or from the .357 Mag. also include a bolt.

The slide assembly on the Mark I and Mark VII is physically smaller than the one on a Mark XIX. Also, the barrel dovetail on top is 3/8 in. on a Mark I or Mark VII, while on a Mark XIX, it is 7/8 in., and includes cross slots for scopes.

Individual Desert Eagle Mark XIX 6 in. barrels are $408-$629, depending on finish, and 10 in. barrels were $509 (disc. 2016), depending on finish. Add $129 for Trijicon night sights (new 2006). Add $92 for Hogue Pau Ferro wooden grips (new 2007), $50 for Hogue soft rubber grips with finger grooves, $50 for Hogue rubber two-piece grips, or $130 for Hogue anodized black aluminum "Reaper" engraved or "The Bone Yard" engraved grips. During 2015, Magnum Research introduced 6 in. barrels in a variety of finishes that include the Clam Pack - a case, and two extra magazines. MSRs range from $495-$691, depending on metal finish.

MR9/MR40 EAGLE – 9mm Para. or .40 S&W cal., SA, SFO, fully adj. rear sight, 4 (9mm Para. cal., disc. 2013), 4.15 (.40 S&W cal., disc. 2013), or 4 1/2 (new 2014) in. barrel, interchangeable palm swells, 10, 11 (.40 S&W cal.), or 15 (9mm Para. cal.) shot mag., lower Picatinny rail, internal safeties, square trigger guard, cooperative manufacturing effort with Carl Walther supplying the black polymer frame with integral steel rails, while the stainless steel slide and barrel are manufactured and assembled in Pillager, MN, approx. 25 oz. Mfg. 2011-2016.

	$475	$425	$375	$325	$295	$275	$250	*$559*

MICRO DESERT EAGLE – .380 ACP cal., 2.2 in. barrel, DAO, blue or nickel Teflon finish, 6 shot mag., fixed sights, aluminum alloy frame, steel slide, oversized trigger guard, checkered black grips, 14 oz. Mfg. 2009-2013.

	$425	$375	$325	$275	$250	$225	$195	*$467*

Add $12 for nickel finish or nickel frame with blue slide and barrel (new 2010).

THE BABY EAGLE – 9mm Para., .40 S&W, .41 AE (disc.), or .45 ACP (3.7 in. barrel only, new 2000) cal., double action, all steel or polymer (3.5 or 3.7 in. barrel, 9mm Para. or .40 S&W only) frame construction, 3.5 (new 2000), 3.62 (mfg. 1993-99), 3.7 (new 2000), or 4.52 in. barrel, short recoil operation, polygonal rifling, combat styled trigger guard, decocking slide safety or frame mounted safety (Model 9mmF), blued (disc. 1995), standard black (new 1996), or chrome (disc. 1999) finish, 10 (C/B 1994), 13 (.40 S&W only, new 2005), 16* (9mm Para., disc.), 11* (.41 AE), or 15 (9mm Para. only, new 2005) shot mag., shipped with two magazines beginning 2006, 38 1/2 oz. Imported 1991-96. Reintroduced mid-1999-2007.

GRADING - PPGS™	100%	98%	95%	90%	80%	70%	60%	LAST MSR

* ***The Baby Eagle Full Size*** – 9mm Para. or .40 S&W cal., 4.52 in. barrel, steel frame only. Disc. 2007.

	$465	$385	$320	$275	$235	$210	$190	*$569*

Add $239 for conversion kit (9mm Para. to .41 AE or .41 AE to 9mm Para., includes barrel, spring, and mag.), disc. 1996.

This model was also available in various optional finishes, including brushed or polished chrome - MSR was $804, titanium gold - MSR was $1,069, or titanium carbon nitride - MSR was $1,069.

* ***The Baby Eagle Semi-Compact*** – 9mm Para., .40 S&W, or .45 ACP cal., same general specifications as Baby Eagle, except has 3.7 in. barrel, .45 ACP not available in polymer, 36 oz. (steel) or 29 oz. (polymer). Disc. 2007.

	$465	$385	$320	$275	$235	$210	$190	*$569*

This model was also available in brushed or polished chrome finish - MSR was $804, titanium gold or titanium nitride - MSR was $1,069.

* ***The Baby Eagle Compact*** – 9mm Para. or .40 S&W cal., same general specifications as Baby Eagle, except has 3 1/2 in. barrel, 10 or 12 (9mm Para. only) shot mag., 27 oz. (polymer) or 34 oz (steel). Disc. 2007.

	$465	$385	$320	$275	$235	$210	$190	*$569*

This model was also available in brushed chrome finish - MSR was $804.

THE BABY EAGLE II – 9mm Para., .40 S&W, or .45 ACP cal., DA/SA, choice of steel frame with black oxide finish, or polymer frame with black finish, 10, 12, or 15 shot mag., slide mounted decocking safety with dual levers and upgraded fixed combat sights with three white dots, well-designed snag free rear sight, tactical rail for optional lasers or flashlights (full size or semi-compact only), black, brushed chrome, or custom finishes. Mfg. by I.W.I. in Israel. Mfg. 2008-2014.

* ***The Baby Eagle II Full Size*** – 9mm Para. or .40 S&W cal., steel frame, 4 (mfg. 2010 only), 4.2 (mfg. 2010 only), or 4.52 in. barrel, lower Picatinny rail, black finish, 25 oz. Mfg. 2008-2014.

	$560	$475	$425	$375	$325	$275	$225	*$656*

Subtract $27 for polymer frame.
Add $235 for brushed or polished chrome (disc. 2009).
Add $500 for titanium gold (disc. 2009).

* ***The Baby Eagle II Semi-Compact*** – 9mm Para., .40 S&W (polymer frame only), or .45 ACP cal., similar to Baby Eagle II Full Size, except has 3.7 (disc.), or 3.93 (new 2011) in. barrel. Imported 2008-2014 by I.W.I.

	$560	$475	$425	$375	$325	$275	$225	*$656*

Subtract $27 for polymer frame.
Add $235 for brushed or polished chrome (disc. 2009).

* ***The Baby Eagle II Compact*** – 9mm Para. cal. only, 3.64 in. barrel w/o Picatinny rail, black finish. Imported 2008-2014 by I.W.I.

	$560	$475	$425	$375	$325	$275	$225	*$656*

Subtract $27 for polymer frame.
Add $235 for brushed chrome (disc. 2009).

BABY DESERT EAGLE III SERIES – 9mm Para., .40 S&W, or .45 ACP cal., DA/SA, this new series is sleeker and features an upgraded new design, precision land and groove match barrel, steel or polymer frame, full or semi-compact, fully interchangeable magazines with previous Baby Eagle models, reversible magazine catch, ambidextrous decocking mechanism on slide, white 3-dot sights, integral tactical rail, ergonomic grips, 28-37.9 oz. New spring 2015.

* ***Baby Desert Eagle III Full Size Polymer Frame*** – 9mm Para. or .40 S&W cal., 4.43 in. match barrel, includes two 10, 12 (.40 S&W only), or 15 (9mm only) shot mags., white 3-dot sights, integral accessory rail, black finish, 37.9 oz. New 2015.

MSR $646	$550	$480	$415	$375	$300	$250	$210	

* ***Baby Desert Eagle III Semi-Compact Polymer Frame*** – 9mm Para. or .40 S&W cal., DA/SA, black textured polymer frame with carbon steel slide, 3.85 in. match barrel, includes two 10, 12 (.40 S&W only), or 15 (9mm only) shot mags., combat type white 3-dot sights, ambi safety, integral accessory rail, black oxide finish, 25-26.3 oz. New 2015.

MSR $646	$550	$480	$415	$375	$300	$250	$210	

* ***Baby Desert Eagle III Full Size Steel Frame*** – 9mm Para., .40 S&W (disc. 2020), or .45 ACP cal., DA/SA, full size carbon steel frame, 4.43 in. match barrel, includes two 10, 12 (.40 S&W only, disc. 2020), or 15 (9mm only) shot mags., white 3-dot sights, ergonomic grip, slide mounted safety and decocker, black oxide finish, 38 oz. New 2015.

MSR $734	$625	$545	$475	$425	$345	$275	$225	

GRADING - PPGS™	100%	98%	95%	90%	80%	70%	60%	LAST MSR

* ***Baby Desert Eagle III Semi-Compact Steel Frame*** – 9mm Para., .40 S&W (disc. 2020), or .45 ACP cal., DA/SA, full size carbon steel frame and slide, 3.85 in. match barrel, includes two 10, 12 (.40 S&W only, disc. 2020), or 16 (9mm only) shot mags., combat type white 3-dot sights, ergonomic grip, ambi safety, integral accessory rail, black oxide finish, 37.9 oz. New 2015.

MSR $734	$625	$545	$475	$425	$345	$275	$225	

MARK I DESERT EAGLE .357 MAG – .357 Mag. cal., SA, similar to Mark VII, except has standard trigger and safety lever is teardrop shaped, and slide catch release has single serration, visible barrel welds, black/blue finish. Mfg. began in 1984 at ser. no. 3,001. Disc.

	$1,000	$925	$825	$725	$625	$525	$450	

MARK XIX .357 MAG. DESERT EAGLE – .357 Mag. cal., features .50 cal. frame and slide, SA, 6 or 10 (disc. 2011) in. barrel, full Picatinny top rail with fixed sights (U.S. mfg., late 2009-disc.) or Weaver style top accessory rail (current mfg.), standard black finish (other finishes additional), 4 lbs., 6 oz. Mfg. by Saco 1995-98, by IMI 1998-2009, and domestically beginning 2010.

MSR $1,668	$1,425	$1,250	$1,075	$975	$785	$650	$550	

Add $74 for integral muzzle brake (new 2015).
Add $293 for brushed chrome or polished chrome.
Add $540 for Titanium Gold finish.
Add $660 for Titanium Gold w/Tiger Stripe finish.
Add $87 for 10 in. barrel (disc. 2011).
Add $510 for 24K Gold finish (disc. 2016).
Add $276 for matte chrome, bright nickel, or satin nickel finish (disc. 2016).

* ***Mark XIX .357 Mag. Desert Eagle Aluminum Frame*** – .357 Mag. cal., black aluminum frame, 6 in. stainless steel slide and barrel with integral muzzle brake and black appointments, fixed combat sights, Picatinny bottom rail and Weaver style top accessory rail, 3 lbs. Mfg. 2017-2018.

	$1,825	$1,650	$1,425	$1,200	$1,025	$875	$750	*$2,137*

* ***Mark XIX .357 Mag. Desert Eagle Case Hardened*** – .357 Mag. cal., 6 in. carbon steel barrel, 9 shot, carbon steel frame and slide, gold plated trigger, combat style fixed sights, ships with walnut grip w/engraved Desert Eagle logo plus Hogue rubber grips with finger grooves, full Weaver style accessory rail, case hardened finish with clear protective coat, 4 lbs. 8 oz. New mid-2017.

MSR $2,415	$2,050	$1,800	$1,540	$1,395	$1,130	$925	$800	

* ***Mark XIX .357 Mag. Desert Eagle Stainless*** – .357 Mag. cal., carbon steel frame, 6 in. stainless steel barrel with integral muzzle brake and black appointments, fixed combat sights, Picatinny bottom rail, 4 lbs. 10 oz. New 2016.

MSR $2,186	$1,865	$1,650	$1,425	$1,275	$1,025	$875	$750	

MARK VII .357 MAG. DESERT EAGLE – .357 Mag. cal., SA, gas operated, 6 (standard barrel length), 10, or 14 in. barrel length with 3/8 in. dovetail rib, steel (58.3 oz.) or alloy (47.8 oz.) frame, adj. trigger, safety lever is hook shaped, slide catch/release lever has three steps, adaptable to .44 Mag. with optional kit, 9 shot mag. (8 for .44 Mag.). Mfg. 1983-95, limited quantities were made available again during 1998 and 2001.

	$1,100	$1,000	$875	$750	$650	$550	$475	*$929*

Add approx. $150 for 10 or 14 in. barrel (disc. 1995).
Add $495 for .357 Mag. to .41 Mag./.44 Mag. conversion kit (6 in. barrel). Disc. 1995.
Add approx. $685 for .357 Mag. to .44 Mag. conversion kit (10 or 14 in. barrel). Disc. 1995.

* ***Mark VII .357 Mag. Desert Eagle Whitetail Special*** – .357 Mag. cal., 14 in. barrel, includes scope mount, target walnut grips, and Desert Eagle premiums. Mfg. 1990-92.

	$1,175	$1,050	$900	$775	$650	$550	$475	*$1,088*

Add $50 for stainless steel frame.

* ***Mark VII .357 Mag. Desert Eagle Stainless Steel*** – similar to .357 Mag. Desert Eagle, except has stainless steel frame, 58.3 oz. Mfg. 1987-95.

	$1,100	$1,000	$875	$750	$650	$550	$475	*$839*

Add approx. $150 for 10 or 14 in. barrel.

MARK XIX .429 DE DESERT EAGLE – .429 DE cal., stainless steel frame with Picatinny bottom rail, 6 in. stainless steel barrel, ships with .50 AE 7 shot mag., stainless steel slide with integral muzzle brake and black appointments, black finish (new 2020), 71 oz. New 2019.

MSR $2,186	$1,865	$1,650	$1,425	$1,275	$1,025	$875	$750	

Subtract $483 if without integral muzzle brake and black appointments.

GRADING - PPGS™	100%	98%	95%	90%	80%	70%	60%	LAST MSR

DESERT EAGLE L5 SERIES - .357 Mag., .44 Mag. (new 2017), or .50 AE Mag. (new 2018) cal., black aluminum frame, 5 in. barrel, black carbon steel or brushed chrome (new 2020) slide/barrel with integral muzzle brake, fixed combat sights, Hogue finger groove rubber grips, includes high impact polymer case, 3 lbs. Mfg. in the U.S. beginning 2016.

MSR $1,900	$1,615	$1,415	$1,225	$1,100	$900	$725	$630	

Add $347 for brushed chome slide/barrel (new 2020).

DESERT EAGLE L6 SERIES - .50 AE, .44 Mag., or .357 Mag. cal., black aluminum frame with Picatinny bottom rail, 6 in. stainless steel slide and barrel with integral muzzle brake and black appointments or 6 in. carbon steel black slide and titanium gold barrel and appointments (new 2020), Hogue soft rubber grips with finger grooves, includes high impact polymer case. Mfg. in the U.S.

MSR $2,180	$1,865	$1,650	$1,425	$1,275	$1,025	$875	$750	

Add $32 for carbon steel black slide and titanium gold barrel and appointments (new 2020).

MARK VII .41 MAG. DESERT EAGLE - .41 Mag. cal., SA, similar to .357 Mag. Desert Eagle, except has 6 in. barrel only, 8 shot mag., steel (62.8 oz.) or alloy (52.3 oz.) frame. Mfg. 1988-1995, limited quantities available during 2001.

	$1,050	$975	$850	$725	$625	$525	$475	*$899*

Add $395 for .41 Mag. to .44 Mag. conversion kit (6 in. barrel only).

* ***Mark VII .41 Mag. Desert Eagle Stainless Steel*** - similar to .41 Mag. Desert Eagle, except has stainless steel frame, 58.3 oz. Mfg. 1988-95.

	$1,100	$1,000	$875	$750	$650	$550	$475	*$949*

MARK I DESERT EAGLE .44 MAG. - .44 Mag. cal., SA, similar to Mark VII, except has standard trigger and safety lever is teardrop shaped, and slide catch release has single serration, black/blue finish. Mfg. began in 1986 - disc.

	$1,200	$1,075	$925	$775	$675	$575	$495	

MARK XIX .44 MAG. DESERT EAGLE - .44 Mag. cal., features .50 cal. frame and slide, SA, 6 or 10 (disc. 2016) in. barrel, full Picatinny top rail with fixed sights became standard late 2009 (U.S. mfg.), standard Black finish (other finishes additional), walnut, G10, or Hogue rubber grips with finge grooves, 4 lbs. 6 oz. Mfg. by Saco 1995-98, by IMI 1998-2009, domestically by CCI beginning 2009, and by I.W.I. beginning 2012.

MSR $1,668	$1,425	$1,250	$1,075	$975	$785	$650	$550	

Add $74 for integral muzzle brake (new 2015).
Add $149 for Burnt Bronze Cerakote finish (new 2015).
Add $149 for Tungsten Cerakote (Dark Graphite Gray) with Black appointments (new 2016).
Add $333 for Brushed or polished chrome.
Add $343 for black with Tiger Stripes (new fall 2016) or White Matte Distressed Cerakote w/black appointments, G10 grips, (new fall 2016).
Add $583 for Titanium Gold finish or $704 for Titanium Gold w/Tiger Stripes finish.
Add $88 for 10 in. barrel (disc. 2016).
Add $552 for 24K Gold finish (disc. 2016).
Add $314 for matte chrome, satin nickel, or bright nickel finish (disc. 2016).
Add $221 for Kryptek Highlander pattern finish (mfg. 2015-2016).
Add $199 for black muzzle brake (limited mfg. 2010 only).
Add $238 for 6 in. barrel with muzzle brake, black finish (mfg. 2013-2014), or $615 for muzzle brake with brushed or polished chrome (mfg. 2013-2014).

* ***Mark XIX .44 Mag. Desert Eagle Case Hardened*** - .44 Mag. cal., 6 in. carbon steel barrel, 8 shot, carbon steel frame and slide, gold plated trigger, combat style fixed sights, ships with walnut grip w/engraved Desert Eagle logo plus Hogue rubber grips with finger grooves, full Weaver style accessory rail, case hardened finish with clear protective coat, 4 lbs. 6 oz. New mid-2017.

MSR $2,415	$2,050	$1,800	$1,540	$1,395	$1,130	$925	$800	

* ***Mark XIX .44 Mag. Desert Eagle Aluminum Frame*** - .44 Mag. cal., black aluminum frame, 6 in. stainless steel slide and barrel with integral muzzle brake and black appointments, fixed combat sights, Picatinny bottom rail and Weaver style top accessory rail. Mfg. 2017-2018.

	$1,825	$1,650	$1,425	$1,200	$1,025	$875	$750	*$2,137*

* ***Mark XIX .44 Mag. Desert Eagle Stainless*** - .44 Mag. cal., 6 in. stainless steel barrel with integral muzzle brake and black appointments, fixed combat sights, Picatinny bottom rail and Weaver style top accessory rail, 4 lbs. 10 oz. New 2016.

MSR $2,186	$1,865	$1,650	$1,425	$1,275	$1,025	$875	$750	

Add $114 for white tiger stripes and integral muzzle brake (new 2019).

GRADING - PPGS™	100%	98%	95%	90%	80%	70%	60%	LAST MSR

MARK VII .44 MAG. DESERT EAGLE – .44 Mag. cal., SA, similar to .357 Desert Eagle, 8 shot mag., steel (62.8 oz.) or alloy (52.3 oz.) frame. Originally mfg. 1986-1995, re-released 1998-2000.

	$1,100	$1,000	$875	$750	$650	$550	$475	*$1,049*

Add $100 for 10 (current) or 14 (disc. 1995) in. barrel.
Add $475 for .44 Mag. to .357 Mag. conversion kit (6 in. barrel). Disc. 1995.
Add $675 for .44 Mag. to .357 Mag. conversion kit (10 or 14 in. barrel). Disc. 1995.
Add $395 for .44 Mag. to .41 Mag. conversion kit (6 in. barrel). Disc. 1995.

* ***Mark VII .44 Mag. Desert Eagle Stainless Steel*** – similar to .44 Mag. Desert Eagle, except has stainless steel frame, 58.3 oz. Mfg. 1987-95.

	$1,175	$1,050	$900	$775	$675	$575	$475	*$949*

Add approx. $210 for 10 or 14 in. barrel.

HUNTER EDITION MARK VII – .357 or .44 Mag. cal., 6 in. barrel with extra 14 in. hunting barrel, includes Leupold 2X EER scope, scope mount. Mfg. late 1987-93.

	$1,200	$975	$825	$675	$550	$475	$425	*$1,350*

Add $110 for .44 Mag. cal.

MARK VII .50 AE DESERT EAGLE – .50 AE cal., SA, 6 in. barrel with 7/8 in. rib with cross slots for Weaver style rings, steel only, black standard finish, frame slightly taller than the Mark VII .357 Mag./.44 Mag., 7 shot mag., 72.4 oz. Mfg. 1991-1995 by IMI, limited quantities were made available again during 1998 only.

	$1,175	$950	$825	$700	$575	$500	$450	*$1,099*

This cartridge utilized the same rim dimensions as the .44 Mag. and was available with a 300 grain bullet. The .50 Action Express cal. has 20%-25% more stopping power than the .44 Mag., with a minimal increase in felt recoil.

MARK XIX CUSTOM 440 – .440 Cor-Bon cal., SA, similar to Mark XIX .44 Mag. Desert Eagle, 6 or 10 in. barrel, standard black finish, rechambered by MRI Custom Shop, limited mfg. 1999-2001.

	$1,175	$995	$850	$725	$575	$500	$450	*$1,389*

Add $40 for 10 in. barrel.

MARK XIX .50 AE DESERT EAGLE – .50 AE cal., SA, larger carbon steel frame, 6 or 10 (disc. 2016) in. barrel, full Picatinny top rail with fixed sights became standard late 2009 (U.S. mfg.), standard black finish, shipped in high impact polymer case, 4 lbs., 6 oz. Mfg. by Saco 1995-1998, by IMI (1998-2008 disc.), I.W.I. (new 2009), and CCI in the U.S. beginning 2010.

MSR $1,703	$1,450	$1,275	$1,095	$985	$800	$650	$550	

Add $73 for integral muzzle brake (new 2015).
Add $114 for Burnt Bronze Cerakote finish (new 2015).
Add $114 for Tungsten Cerakote (Dark Graphite Gray) with Black appointments (new 2016).
Add $337 for brushed chrome, polished chrome, or Black with Tiger stripes (new 2017).
Add $337 for White Matte Distressed Cerakote with Black appointments and G10 grips (new 2017).
Add $596 for Titanium Gold.
Add $712 for Titanium Gold w/Tiger Stripes finish.
Add $121 for 10 in. barrel (disc. 2016).
Add $595 for 24K Gold finish (disc. 2016).
Add $350 for matte chrome, bright nickel or satin nickel finish (disc. 2016).
Add $209 for muzzle brake (black finish, 6 in. barrel only, disc. 2014) or $592 for muzzle brake with brushed chrome (mfg. 2011-2014) or polished chrome (mfg. 2013-2014).

* ***Mark XIX .50 AE Desert Eagle Aluminum Frame*** – .50 AE cal., black aluminum frame, 6 in. stainless steel slide and barrel with integral muzzle brake and black appointments, fixed combat sights, Picatinny bottom rail and Weaver style top accessory rail, 3 lbs. 7 oz. Mfg. 2016-2018.

	$1,825	$1,650	$1,425	$1,200	$1,025	$875	$750	*$2,137*

* ***Mark XIX .50 AE Desert Eagle Case Hardened*** – .50 AE Mag. cal., 6 in. carbon steel barrel, 7 shot, carbon steel frame and slide, gold plated trigger, combat style fixed sights, ships with walnut grip w/engraved Desert Eagle logo plus Hogue rubber grips in the box, full Weaver style accessory rail, case hardened finish with clear protective coat, 4 lbs. 5 oz. New mid-2017.

MSR $2,415	$2,050	$1,800	$1,540	$1,395	$1,130	$925	$800	

* ***Mark XIX .50 AE Desert Eagle Stainless*** – .50 AE cal., stainless steel frame and slide with black appointments, 6 in. stainless steel barrel with or w/o integral muzzle brake, fixed combat sights, Picatinny bottom rail and Weaver style accessory top rail, 4 lbs. 8 oz. New 2015.

MSR $2,040	$1,735	$1,520	$1,300	$1,180	$955	$780	$680	

GRADING - PPGS™	100%	98%	95%	90%	80%	70%	60%	LAST MSR

Add $146 for integral muzzle brake and Black appointments.
Add $259 for white tiger stripes and integral muzzle brake (new 2019).

* ***Mark XIX .50 AE Desert Eagle Snakeskin*** – .50 AE cal., SA, carbon steel frame, 6 in. barrel, 7 shot, full Picatinny top rail, fiixed sights, Dark Snakeskin pattern finish, 4 lbs., 6 oz. Mfg. 2015-2016.

	$1,525	$1,335	$1,150	$1,035	$840	$685	$550	*$1,793*

* ***Mark XIX .50 AE Desert Eagle TIG Series*** - .50 AE cal., SA, larger frame, 6 in. barrel with or w/o muzzle brake, full Picatinny top rail with fixed sights, TIG logo, signature, and Beyond the Battlefield logo engraved on both sides of frame, Battle Worn Bronze Cerakote finish, 4 lbs., 6 oz. Limited mfg. of 250 mfg. 2018 only.

	$1,750	$1,550	$1,300	$1,200	$950	$800	$600	*$1,963*

The first 50 guns were sold as three gun sets (Auto Ordnance, Kahr ST9 Tig, and Magnum Research Desert Eagle TIG models). The set also included the book *13 Hours: The Inside Account of What Really Happened in Benghazi,* **signed by American Hero, John "TIG" Tiegen.**

* ***Mark XIX .50 AE Combo Caliber Kit*** – .50 AE/.44 Mag. or .50 AE/.429 DE (new 2020) cal., includes 6 in. black barrel and extra mag. New 2018.

MSR $2,060	$1,750	$1,530	$1,315	$1,190	$965	$790	$685	

MARK XIX 3 CAL. COMPONENT SYSTEM – includes Mark XIX .44 Mag. Desert Eagle and 5 barrels including .357 Mag. (6 and 10 in.), .44 Mag., and .50 AE (6 and 10 in.) cals., .357 bolt assembly and ICC aluminum carrying case. Also available in custom finishes at extra charge. Mfg. 1998-2011.

	$3,900	$3,450	$2,800	$2,400	$2,000	$1,750	$1,500	*$4,402*

* ***Mark XIX 3 Cal. Component System (6 or 10 in. Barrel)*** – includes component Mark XIX system in 6 or 10 in. barrel only. Mfg. 1998-2011.

	$2,550	$2,225	$1,775	$1,500	$1,250	$1,000	$850	*$2,910*

Add $262 for 10 in. barrel (disc. 2011).

* ***Mark XIX Component System (Current Mfg).*** – .357 Mag., .44 Mag., or .50 AE cal., 6 in. barrels only, available in Black or Burnt Bronze Cerakote finish, includes aluminum carrying case jacketed in black ballistic nylon. New 2017.

MSR $3,220	$2,750	$2,400	$2,050	$1,865	$1,500	$1,235	$1,075	

Add $113 for Burnt Bronze Cerakote finish.

MODEL 1911 DESERT EAGLE – 9mm Para. (mfg. 2015-2018) or .45 ACP cal., SA, 4.3 or 5 in. barrel, two 8 shot mags., skeletonized hammer, black oxide finish, double diamond checkered wood grips, fixed sights, grip safety, extended thumb safety and mag. release, aluminum checkered mainspring housing, stainless steel full-length guide rod, with (new 2014) or without tactical rail (5 in. barrel only, mfg. 2014-2017), 36.2 oz. Mfg. 2010-2020.

	$700	$615	$525	$475	$385	$315	$275	*$831*

Add $20 for 9mm Para. cal. (mfg. 2015-2018).
Add $260 for tactical rail (5 in. barrel only, mfg. 2014-2017).
Add $350 for .22 LR conversion kit (disc. 2011).

DESERT EAGLE 1911C/1911G – 9mm Para. (disc. 2018), .45 ACP, or 10mm (new 2020, 1911G only) cal., SA, 4.33 in. (1911C) bull or 5.01 in. (1911G) bushingless carbon steel barrel, includes two 8 or 9 shot mags., extended mag. release, beveled magwell, enlarged ejection port, skeletonized hammer, high profile sculptured rear sight, dovetailed front sight blade with horizontal serrations, Black/Grey G10 grips, high ride beavertail grip safety, extended thumb safety, stainless steel full length guide rod, matte black finish, 33.9-40.6 oz. Mfg. and imported by BUL Ltd. in Israel.

MSR $866	$740	$650	$550	$500	$400	$340	$285	

Subtract $15 for 10mm cal. (new 2020).
Add $44 for .45 ACP package (new 2017) or $67 for 10mm package (new 2020) which includes knife with Kydex sheath.
Add $20 for 9mm Para. cal. (disc. 2018) or $87 for 9mm Para. package including knife with Kydex sheath (mfg. 2017-2018).

* ***Desert Eagle 1911C Stainless/1911G Stainless*** – .45 ACP cal., similar to Desert Eagle 1911C and 1911G, except stainless steel. New 2015.

MSR $924	$790	$690	$595	$535	$435	$355	$300	

Add $43 for .45 ACP package including knife with Kydex sheath (new 2017).

MODEL 1911 DESERT EAGLE UNDERCOVER – 9mm Para. (mfg. 2015-2018) or .45 ACP cal., Series 70 design, aluminum frame, 3 in. bull barrel, 6 shot mag., adj. rear and blade front sights, ships with two magazines, G10 black/gray (discs.) or G10 blue grips, black finish, 25.8 oz. Mfg. and imported from BUL Ltd. in Israel. New 2014.

MSR $1,041	$885	$775	$665	$600	$495	$450	$395	

Add $45 for .45 ACP package including knife with Kydex sheath (new late 2017).
Add $70 for 9mm Para. package including knife with Kydex sheath (mfg. late 2017-2018).

GRADING - PPGS™	100%	98%	95%	90%	80%	70%	60%	LAST MSR

* ***Model 1911 Desert Eagle Undercover Stainless*** – .45 ACP cal., Series 70 design, anodized aluminum frame, 3 in. bull barrel, stainless steel slide, adj. rear sight, white dot front sight, G10 black/gray (disc.) or G10 blue grips, includes two magazines, high impact polymer case. Mfg. and imported from BUL Ltd. in Israel. New 2015.

MSR $1,019	$865	$750	$650	$595	$475	$400	$325	

Add $44 for package including knife with Kydex sheath (new late 2017).

CUSTOM DESERT EAGLE CRUSADER 1911 – .45 ACP cal., Magnum Research 1911GR series, 5 in. barrel, 8 shot mag., skeletonized trigger, front sight w/horizontal serrations, windage and elevation adj. rear dovetail sight, aluminum grips w/knights in armor design, extended beavertail grip safety, accessory rail, Crusader motto "Deus Vult" on right side of frame and crosses engraved on front and rear, Distressed Red and Black Cerakote finish by Outlaw Ordnance, 38.01 oz. Mfg. 2020 only.

	$1,075	$950	$800	$725	$600	$500	$415	*$1,250*

PISTOLS: SINGLE SHOT

LONE EAGLE (SSP-91) – .22 LR (disc. 1992), .22 WMR (disc. 1992), .22 Hornet, .22-250 Rem., .223 Rem., .243 Win., .260 Rem. (new 1997), .30-30 Win., .30-06, .300 Win. Mag. (Ltd. ed., mfg. 1997-99), .308 Win., 6mmBR (disc. 1992), 7mm-08 Rem., 7mmBR, .35 Rem., .357 Max. (disc. 1997, reintroduced 2001), .358 Win., .44 Mag., .440 Cor-Bon (new 1999), .444 Marlin, or 7.62x39mm (new 1996) cal., circular rear breech action, quick change 14 in. barrels (drilled and tapped), black or chrome (new 1997) finish, black synthetic Valox ambidextrous pistol grip, 4 lbs. 3 oz.-4 lbs. 7 oz. Mfg. 1991-2001.

	$450	$400	$350	$300	$250	$200	$175	*$438*

Add $40 for chrome finish.
Add $35 for adj. hunting sights.
Add $129 for adj. silhouette sights by RPM.
Add $319 for standard black finish barrel, $418 for standard barrel with muzzle brake, $359 for chrome barrel, and $469 for chrome barrel with muzzle brake.

The grip assembly ($119) and barreled actions were available individually on this model.

REVOLVERS

BFR LONG CYLINDER – .30-30 Win. (new 2004), .444 Marlin (disc. 2013, reintroduced 2017), .45 LC/.410 bore (Custom Shop only beginning 2013), .450 Marlin (mfg. 2002-2012, 10 in. barrel only, reintroduced 2017), .45-70 Govt., .460 S&W Mag. (new 2006), .500 S&W Mag. (new 2003), or .357 Mag. cal., SA, 5 shot, stainless steel, 7 1/2 or 10 in. barrel, checkered rubber (disc.), one-piece Hogue (new fall 2016), or Bisley (new 2017) grips, improved hammer (new fall 2016), factory black fixed front and rear adj. sights, brushed stainless steel finish, 4-4.36 lbs. New 1999.

MSR $1,255	$1,075	$940	$800	$725	$595	$485	$400	

Add $86 for Bisley grips (new 2017).
Add $91 for vent. rib on 7 1/2 in. stainless steel barrel (.45 LC/.410 only, new 2014).

This model was originally advertised as the BFR Maxine, then was changed to BFR (Biggest Finest Revolver).

BFR SHORT CYLINDER – .22 Hornet (disc. 2011), .44 Mag. (new 2010), .45 LC+P (disc. 2001), .454 Casull, .475 Linebaugh (disc. 2011), .480 Ruger (mfg. 2002, Custom Shop only 2013-disc.), .480/.475 Linebaugh (new 2017), .50 AE (disc. 2001, reintroduced 2004-2011, 2017-2020), .500 Linebaugh (new 2019), or .500 JRH (mfg. 2012, Custom Shop only in 2013, reintroduced 2017) cal., all stainless, 5, 5 1/2, 6 1/2, or 7 1/2 in. barrel, 5 shot, factory black fixed front and rear adj. sights, one-piece Hogue (new 2016) or Bisley (new 2017) grip, improved hammer (new 2016), brushed stainless steel finish, 3.6-4.86 lbs. New 1999.

MSR $1,255	$1,075	$940	$800	$725	$595	$485	$400	

Add $86 for Bisley grips (new 2017).
Add $185 for .500 Linebaugh cal.

This model was originally advertised as the BFR Little Max, then was changed to BFR (Biggest Finest Revolver).

RIFLES: BOLT ACTION

Magnum Research still offers Mountain Eagle centerfire rifles that can be custom ordered directly from the factory. Please contact Magnum Research customer service directly at 218-746-3459 for information on price and available configurations. Values listed below represent the last retail pricing available.

MOUNTAIN EAGLE RIFLE – .223 Rem. (new 2000), .270 Win., .280 Rem., .30-06, 7mm STW (mfg. 1998-99), .300 Win. Mag., .300 Wby. Mag., .338 Win. Mag., .340 Wby. Mag. (disc. 1997), 7mm Rem. Mag., .375 H&H, or .416 Rem. Mag. cal., Sako action, adj. trigger, 4 or 5 shot mag., match grade Krieger barrel with cut rifling, H-S Precision composite stock with aluminum bedding block, includes carrying case. Mfg. 1994-standard mfg. stopped 2000, currently special order.

	$1,325	$1,075	$900	$775	$625	$550	$495	*$1,499*

Add $200 for muzzle brake.

GRADING - PPGS™	100%	98%	95%	90%	80%	70%	60%	LAST MSR

Add $50 for left-hand action.
Add $300 for .375 H&H or .416 Rem. Mag. cal.

* ***Mountain Eagle Rifle Varmint*** – .222 Rem. or .223 Rem. cal., 26 in. stainless steel heavy fluted barrel, w/o sights, approx. 9 3/4 lbs. Mfg. 1996-standard production stopped 2000, currently special order.

	$1,425	$1,250	$1,075	$975	$795	$650	$500	*$1,629*

MOUNTAIN EAGLE MAGNUM LITE – .223 Rem. (varmint only), .22-250 Rem. (varmint only), .280 Rem., .30-06, .300 Win. Mag., .300 WSM (new 2003), 7mm WSM (new 2003), or 7mm Rem. Mag. cal., custom-built Rem. short action or Sako (disc.) action with one-piece forged bolt, adj. trigger, 24 in. sport tapered or 26 in. varmint bull graphite barrel with stainless steel liner, no sights, black swirl H-S Precision Kevlar graphite or Hogue overmolded (7mm WSM or .300 WSM only) stock, 4 or 5 shot mag, approx. 7 1/4 lbs. Mfg. 2001-standard production stopped 2011, currently special order.

	$1,925	$1,700	$1,400	$1,100	$825	$700	$575	*$2,173*

Magnum Lite graphite barrels are available in 3 configurations for $599 (disc. 2011).

MOUNTAIN EAGLE TACTICAL RIFLE – .223 Rem. (new 2002), .22-250 Rem. (new 2002), .308 Win., .300 Win. Mag., or .300 WSM (new 2002) cal., accurized Rem. M-700 action, 26 in. Magnum Lite barrel, H-S Precision tactical stock, adj. stock and trigger, 9 lbs., 4 oz. Mfg. 2001-standard production stopped 2011, currently special order.

	$2,150	$1,825	$1,475	$1,150	$850	$700	$575	*$2,475*

Add $96 for any cal. other than .300 WSM (disc. 2011).

MAGNUM LITE 77 – .17 HMR cal., features 22 in. graphite barrel mfg. 2006, standard production stopped 2008, currently special order.

	$875	$750	$625	$500	$400	$325	$250	*$999*

RIFLES: SEMI-AUTO

MAGNUM LITE RIFLE – .17 HMR (mfg. 2004-2009), .17 Mach 2 (mfg. 2005-2010), .22 LR or .22 WMR (new 2000) cal., features Ruger 10/22 WMR (.17 HMR or .22 WMR only beginning 2006) or one-piece Model 17/22 MLR receiver with large bolt handle machined from solid billet of aluminum (available in .22 LR or .17 Mach 2 cal.), with Acculite (disc.) or graphite (new 1999) barrel utilizing uni-directional graphite carbon fiber with stainless steel liner, barrel weighs 13 oz. New 1997.

* ***Magnum Lite Rifle Standard Stock*** – .17 HMR (disc.), .22 LR (disc. 2018), or .22 WMR cal., 17 (disc. 2018) or 19 in. graphite (disc.) or carbon barrel, walnut (mfg. 2006-2009), black Hogue Overmolded, or tactical black (disc. 2018) stock, 4.3-5.4 lbs. New 1997.

MSR $835	$700	$615	$525	$475	$385	$315	$275	

Add $13 for threaded muzzle (new 2020).
Add $125 for .17 HMR (disc. 2009) cal.
Add $159 for walnut stock (only available in .17 Mach 2 or .22 LR cal., Model 17/22, disc. 2009).

* ***Magnum Lite Rifle w/Fajen Thumbhole Stock*** – features choice of Fajen thumbhole sporter or thumbhole silhouette in midnight or coffee color. Mfg. 1997-99.

	$625	$525	$450	$395	$360	$330	$275	*$699*

Add $100 for thumbhole silhouette stock configuration.

* ***Magnum Lite Rifle w/Barracuda Stock*** – .22 LR (disc. 2018) or .22 WMR cal., 17 (disc. 2018) or 19 in. graphite (disc.) or carbon barrel, skeletonized sporter stock with thumbhole in Green (disc.), Nutmeg (mfg. 2006-2014, 2017), Forest Camo (mfg. 2006-2014, 2017), Pepper (mfg. 2006-2014, 2017), American Black walnut (new 2015), or Coffee (disc.) laminate, blued, red (disc. 2009), or blue (disc. 2009) anodized receiver, 4.4-5.4 lbs. New 1997.

MSR $975	$830	$725	$625	$565	$455	$395	$325	

Add $10 for American Black walnut stock (new 2015).
Add $117 for .17 HMR (disc. 2009) or .22 WMR cal. (Model 10/22 only, disc.).
Add $40 for red or blue anodized receiver (.17 Mach 2 or .22 LR cal. only, disc. 2009).

* ***Magnum Lite Rifle w/Graphite Ambidextrous Thumbhole Stock*** – .22 LR cal., 17 in. barrel, black synthetic ambidextrous thumbhole stock only. Mfg. 2012-2018.

	$535	$475	$400	$375	$330	$300	$275	*$625*

Add $194 for Forest Camo, Nutmeg, or Pepper Barracuda laminate stock (new 2017).

MAGNUM HEAVY VARMINT – .17 HMR (disc. 2009) or .22 WMR cal., blued steel (disc. 2010) or stainless steel 18 in. barrel, Hogue overmolded or Barracuda Forest camo (disc. 2010), Nutmeg (disc. 2010), or pepper colored laminate skeletonized sporter (disc. 2014) stock. New 2008.

MSR $803	$680	$600	$500	$450	$375	$325	$275	

Add $179 for Barracuda Forest Camo (disc. 2010), Nutmeg (disc. 2010), or pepper colored laminate (disc. 2014) skeletonized stock.

GRADING - PPGS™	100%	98%	95%	90%	80%	70%	60%	LAST MSR

MLR-1722 – .22 LR cal., 18 in. ULTRA patented modular barrel, with or w/o thread protector on threaded muzzle, 10 shot, integral scope base, black ambidextrous thumbhole stock, 4 lbs. 8 oz. Mfg. 2015-disc.

	$515	$450	$385	$350	$285	$230	$190	*$569*

Add $27 for thread protector on threaded muzzle.

MLR22ATTTS22 – .22 LR cal., 20 1/2 in. TTS22 barrel, 10 shot mag., integral scope base, ambidextrous thumbhole black stock, checkered semi-palm swell on both sides of pistol grip, hard rubber buttplate. Mfg. 2018 only.

	$725	$635	$550	$500	$400	$325	$250	*$860*

MLR .22 LR ALUMINUM TENSIONED RIFLE – .22 LR cal., 18 in. ULTRA aluminum tensioned barrel with threaded muzzle, black ambidextrous thumbhole stock, Switchbolt receiver. New 2019.

MSR $641	$540	$475	$400	$365	$300	$250	$210	

MLR SWITCHBOLT – .22 LR cal., 16 1/2 (with threaded muzzle, new 2020) or 17 in. carbon weave barrel, Hogue overmolded black, tactical black, ambidextrous thumbhole black, or ambidextrous Evolution laminate in Black Pepper, Blue, Forest Camo, or Red stock, forged aluminum Switchbolt receiver, integral Picatinny rail, ambi charging handle. New 2018.

MSR $684	$580	$510	$435	$395	$320	$265	$225	

Add $47 for black Hogue overmolded or tactical black stock.

Add $47 for 16 1/2 in. barrel with threaded muzzle and black Hogue overmolded stock (new 2020).

Add $209 for Black Pepper, Blue, Forest Camo, or Red ambidextrous Evolution laminate stock.

MAGTECH AMMUNITION CO., INC. (MAGTECH)

Current importer and distributor of CBC (Companhia Brasileria de Cartuchos) ammunition located in Lino Lakes, MN. Previously located in Centerville, MN, Madison, CT 1999-2001, and in Las Vegas, NV until 1999. Magtech previously imported firearms manufactured by CBC located in Brazil.

For individual model listings, please go to BlueBookOfGunValues.com/overflow.

MAJESTIC ARMS, LTD.

Previous firearms manufacturer established during 2000, located on Staten Island, NY. The company now produces firearms components, conversion kits, and accessories.

CARBINES: SEMI-AUTO

MA 2000 – .22 LR cal., Henry Repeating Arms Co. AR-7 takedown action, fiber optic sights, American walnut forearm, pistol grip, and buttplate, fixed tubular stock with butt bag, 16 1/4 in. Lothar Walther barrel with crown, black Teflon or silver bead blast finish, 4 lbs. Mfg. 2000-2008.

	$350	$295	$250	$225	$195	$175	$150	*$389*

MA 4 – .17 HMR, .17 Mach 2 (new 2005), .22 LR (new 2005), or .22 WMR cal., takedown action, traditional or wire frame stock, interchangeable barrel/bolt assembly.

While intially advertised during 2004 with an MSR of $399, this model did not go into production past the prototype stage.

SHOTGUNS: SLIDE ACTION

BASE-TAC – 12 or 20 ga., 3 in. chamber, based on M870 Remington action, approx. 18 in. barrel with ghost ring sights, black synthetic (12 ga.) or hardwood stock and forearm, extended 6 shot tube mag., 6-7 lbs. Mfg. 2004-2010.

	$675	$575	$500	$450	$400	$350	$300	*$759*

Add $30 for 20 ga.

MAKAROV

Pistol design originating from the former Soviet Union. Russian manufactured Makarovs may be found under the "Russian Service Pistol and Rifle" heading in this text. Pistols listed have recently been imported by various companies, including Century International Arms, Inc. located in St. Albans, VT.

PISTOLS: SEMI-AUTO

MAKAROV COPIES – 9mm Makarov cal., patterned after the Soviet PM pistol, mfg. in eastern Germany, Czechoslovakia, Bulgaria, and China, double action, blowback design, all steel, slide mounted safety that doubles as a decocking lever, 3.6 in. barrel, 8 shot mag., 25 oz.

No MSR	$295	$250	$235	$200	$150	$125	$100	

Add approx. $40 for silver matte finish (Bulgarian mfg. only).

GRADING - PPGS™	100%	98%	95%	90%	80%	70%	60%	LAST MSR

Add 30% if not import marked.
Add 100% if original Russian military configuration.

The importation of this type of pistol increased beginning 1992.

MAKURA HUNTING RIFLES

Current rifle manufacturer located in Schindellegi, Switzerland. Consumer direct sales through FFLs.

RIFLES: BOLT ACTION

Makura Hunting Rifles manufactures a high quality bolt action takedown rifle called the Takedown Ulrich. The action is based from a Blaser R93, but the takedown mechanism is completely proprietary. Since each model is essentially a custom order, please contact the factory directly for U.S. availability, pricing, features, engraving, and delivery time.

MALIN, F.E.

Previous manufacturer located in England. Previously imported by Saxon Arms, Inc. located in Clearwater, FL. Charles Boswell purchased Malin shortly before manufacture stopped.

SHOTGUNS: SxS, CUSTOM

BOXLOCK – made to individual order, choice of game scene engraving, Anson & Deeley boxlock actions, select European hybrid walnut, double triggers, leather cased.

Prices started at $3,750 and each shotgun was priced per individual special order.

SIDELOCK – made to individual order, choice of game scene engraving, H&H sidelock action, select European hybrid walnut, double triggers, leather cased.

Prices started at $5,000 and each shotgun was priced per individual special order.

MAMBA

Previously manufactured by Viper Mfg. Co. (a division of Sandock Austral Boksburg) located in South Africa.

PISTOLS: SEMI-AUTO

AUTO PISTOL – 9mm Para. cal., double action, 5 in. barrel, 14 shot mag., designed in Rhodesia, manufacture was not successful due to the non-hardened steel used in the investment cast construction process, poor exterior finish, less than 80 imported into the U.S., and 25 prototypes were built for Navy Arms.

	100%	98%	95%	90%	80%	70%	60%	LAST MSR
	$550	$475	$425	$375	$300	$250	$195	

Add 10% for box.
Add 50% for single digit ser. no.

Most of these models can be found in near new condition.

MANCHESTER ARMS INC.

Previous manufacturer located in Lenoir, TN.

PISTOLS: SEMI-AUTO

COMMANDO MARK 45 – .45 ACP cal., detachable mag., wood pistol grip, 5 in. barrel with muzzle brake. Disc.

	100%	98%	95%	90%	80%	70%	60%	LAST MSR
	$600	$525	$450	$395	$350	$300	$265	

MANDALL SHOOTING SUPPLIES, INC.

Previous importer, distributor, and retailer located in Scottsdale, AZ.

Mandall Shooting Supplies distributed and imported various firearms including pistols, revolvers, rifles, and shotguns, as well as other models.

MANIFATURRA ARMI ART

Current longarm manufacturer located in Gardone, Italy. Previously imported 2004-circa 2013 by William Larkin Moore & Co., located in Scottsdale, AZ.

Denis Fontana from Manifattura Armi Art manufactures high quality custom long guns, including rifles and shotguns. Guns may be marked "Art Armi" or "Denis Fontana". Please contact the importer directly for more information, including availability and pricing.

Currently imported models include a SxS Anson & Deeley boxlock action with rose and scroll engraving, a H&H type sidelock SxS shotgun with choice of H&H or Purdey style engraving, bolt action rifle in small and large calibers, and a SxS sidelock rifle in .375 H&H, .470 NE, or .500 NE cal., with rose and scroll engraving. All models are POR. Please contact the factory directly for more information, including pricing and delivery time.

GRADING - PPGS™	100%	98%	95%	90%	80%	70%	60%	LAST MSR

MÄNNEL SPORT SHOOTING GmbH

Previous rifle and airgun manufacturer located in Kronstorf, Austria.

Männel manufactured the ASB (advanced small bore) target rifle noted for its almost infinite amount of adjustments, including the forearm, stock, and trigger guard, in addition to a target air pistol.

MANNLICHER PISTOLS

Previously manufactured in Austria and Switzerland circa 1894-disc.

PISTOLS: SEMI-AUTO

MODEL 1894 – 6.5mm or 7.6mm cal., unique blow forward design, fewer than 100 mfg. by Fabrique d' Armes in Neuhausen Switzerland, and OWGS, Austria.

$19,500 $17,500 $15,000 $12,500 $10,000 $7,500 $6,000

Add 20% for 7.6mm cal.

MODEL 1897 – 7.63mm Mannlicher cal., first Mannlicher pistol with detachable mag. (matching), unique cocking lever on right frame, approx. 1,000 mfg.

$8,500 $7,000 $6,000 $5,500 $5,000 $4,500 $4,000

Add 150% for Model 1896 prototype in similar configuration, but with fixed mag.

Add 150% for pistol/carbine with extended barrel, adj. sight, and detachable shoulder stock.

Add 100% for true carbine. Only 5-10 known.

MODEL 1899 – 7.63 Mannlicher cal., rear sight mounted on barrel, large safety lever on left frame, approx. 300 mfg.

$9,500 $8,000 $6,500 $5,000 $4,000 $3,500 $3,000

MODEL 1901 – 7.63 Mannlicher cal., rear sight mounted on barrel, safety on rear of right slide, approx. 1,000 mfg.

$6,000 $4,500 $3,500 $2,750 $2,250 $1,750 $1,250

MODEL 1905 – 7.63 Mannlicher cal., final and most common variation.

$3,500 $2,500 $1,500 $1,000 $750 $650 $550

ARGENTINE MODEL 1905 – 7.65mm cal., Argentine crest on right panel is usually machined off. Values assume matching numbers but removed crest.

$900 $800 $700 $600 $500 $400 $300

* ***Argentine Model 1905*** – with Original Military Crest.

$4,500 $3,500 $3,000 $2,500 $2,000 $1,500 $1,000

MANNLICHER SCHOENAUER SPORTING RIFLES

Originally manufactured by Oesterreich Waffenfabrik-Gesellschaft in Steyr, Austria from 1900 until the occupation of Austria by Germany in 1938. The current manufacturer is Steyr-Mannlicher, also of Steyr, Austria. Products made from 1972 to date are listed under Steyr-Mannlicher current production. Please refer to the Steyr Arms (Steyr-Mannlicher) section.

Only a few sporting rifles were produced during the war period and were marked "Made in Germany". Production started again in 1950 with serial number 1 until 1973 with serial number 61154. The last rifle was manufactured in 7x64 cal.

RIFLES: BOLT ACTIONS, PRE-WWII

The M1924 is properly known as the "Sequoia Importing Co." model because of a San Francisco company that ordered 1,000 units in .30-06 cal. for sale in the U.S. Apparently, these rifles did not sell well, and several of them were returned to Steyr where they were re-stamped 7.62x63mm cal. on the receiver ring. By 1933, Sequoia listed the .30-06 as the M1925 indicating that the changeover must have taken place rapidly. Meanwhile, the Steyr Company began chambering the basic M1924 action in six assorted calibers (7x57, 7x64, .30-06, 8x60S, 9.3x62, and 10.75x68) and marketing the improved rifle as the M1925. This was in addition to their continued production of the M1903, M1905, M1908, and M1910, and other chamberings were available on special order.

Starting with the M1925, Steyr began to engrave the caliber on the receiver ring, as it is standard in all Post WWII models. A Mannlicher-Schoenauer with the caliber engraved upon the barrel has been rebarreled by a European gunsmith and reproved by the local proof authority.

A proper Mannlicher-Schoenauer will have either no caliber marking on the receiver, as caliber was assigned via model only, or that caliber will be engraved upon the receiver ring as the final line in the description. For example, KAL 7x64. If the caliber is engraved or stamped upon the barrel only, the rifle was rebarreled by a gunsmith.

Add approx. 25% for all takedown pre-war models.

GRADING - PPGS™	100%	98%	95%	90%	80%	70%	60%	LAST MSR

MODEL 1900 – 6.5x54mm Mannlicher Schoenauer cal., bolt handle with round knob, carbine, rifle, and takedown rifle configurations.

	100%	98%	95%	90%	80%	70%	60%
	N/A	$2,500	$2,100	$1,800	$1,600	$1,350	$1,100

MODEL 1903 CARBINE – 6.5x54mm Mannlicher Schoenauer cal., 5 shot, 17.7 in. barrel, rotary mag., flat "butterknife" bolt handle, two leaf rear sight, double set trigger, full-length stock.

	100%	98%	95%	90%	80%	70%	60%
	N/A	$2,500	$2,100	$1,800	$1,600	$1,350	$1,100

This caliber may also be referred to as 6.5x53mm. This model is normally encountered in poor condition.

The Greek government ordered over 100,000 M1903 rifles, and many of these have been modified to a sporting configuration. These converted guns can be difficult to differentiate from true commercial Model 1903s, and values above are for original sporting carbines.

MODEL 1903 RIFLE – 6.5x54mm Mannlicher Schoenauer cal., 5 shot, various barrel lengths up to 23 inches, flat "butterknife" bolt handle, otherwise similar to Carbine.

	100%	98%	95%	90%	80%	70%	60%
	N/A	$2,250	$1,995	$1,675	$1,475	$1,175	$975

Full stocked rifles may be encountered.

The Greek government ordered over 100,000 M1903 rifles, and many of these have been modified to a sporting configuration. These converted rifles can be difficult to differentiate from true commercial Model 1903s, and values above are for original sporting rifles.

MODEL 1905 CARBINE – similar to Model 1903, except 9x56mm Mannlicher Schoenauer cal., 19.7 in. barrel, flat "butterknife" bolt handle.

	100%	98%	95%	90%	80%	70%	60%
	N/A	$1,700	$1,495	$1,100	$850	$750	$650

This model is normally encountered in poor condition. It is perhaps the least desirable of pre-war models because of the wide variation in bore diameters.

MODEL 1905 RIFLE – similar to Model 1905 Carbine, except available in various barrel lengths up to 25 inches, flat "butterknife" bolt handle, also available in takedown configuration.

	100%	98%	95%	90%	80%	70%	60%
	N/A	$1,700	$1,495	$1,100	$850	$750	$650

MODEL 1908 CARBINE – 8x56mm Mannlicher Schoenauer cal., 5 shot rotary mag., 19.7 in. barrel, two leaf rear sight, double set or single trigger, full-length stock, flat "butterknife" bolt handle.

	100%	98%	95%	90%	80%	70%	60%
	N/A	$1,700	$1,495	$1,100	$850	$750	$650

This model is frequently noticed in better condition factors. Some exceptional takedown variations also exist within this model.

MODEL 1908 RIFLE – similar to Model 1908 Carbine, except available in various barrel lengths up to 24 inches, flat "butterknife" bolt handle, also available in takedown configuration.

	100%	98%	95%	90%	80%	70%	60%
	N/A	$1,400	$1,175	$900	$750	$625	$550

MODEL 1910 CARBINE – originally chambered for 9.5x57mm Mannlicher-Schoenauer (.375 Rimless Nitro Express or 9.5x57mm Mauser cal.) only, 19.7 in. barrel, 5 shot rotary magazine, flat "butterknife" bolt handle, two leaf rear sight, double set trigger, full-length stock.

	100%	98%	95%	90%	80%	70%	60%
	N/A	$1,600	$1,375	$975	$750	$650	$575

MODEL 1910 RIFLE – originally chambered for 9.5x57mm Mannlicher-Schoenauer cal. only, similar to 1910 Carbine, except available in various barrel lengths up to 26 inches.

	100%	98%	95%	90%	80%	70%	60%
	N/A	$1,400	$1,175	$900	$750	$625	$550

Fully stocked rifles may be encountered.

MODEL 1925 (HIGH VELOCITY SPORTING RIFLE) – .30-06, 7x64mm, 8x60mm, 9.3x62mm, or 10.75x68mm cal., 23.6 in. barrel, three leaf rear sight, half stock, double set or single trigger.

	100%	98%	95%	90%	80%	70%	60%
	N/A	$2,000	$1,675	$1,475	$1,200	$1,000	$875
10.75x68mm cal.	N/A	$4,000	$3,600	$3,200	$2,800	$2,500	$1,850

Fully stocked rifles may be encountered.

This model was referred to as the Model 1925 in Europe. The difference is that the Model 1925 has the caliber engraved on the receiver ring, and the Model 1924 does not.

RIFLES: BOLT ACTION, POST-WWII-1971 MFG.

Values represent standard models with no engraving. Original engraving will add at least $500-$1,500 to prices listed with some heavily engraved Premier & Alpine models selling for large premiums. A variation of the 1950-1952 Series is called the "GK" because of its swept back bolt handle (abbreviation for

GRADING - PPGS™	100%	98%	95%	90%	80%	70%	60%	LAST MSR

"gekroepfter Kammerstengel" in German). Of the calibers listed for post-WWII models, the 6.5x54mm is considered one of the most desirable, as well as the 9.3x62mm.

In 1951, Steyr (at Stoeger's request) made the following changes to the Model 1950 (named Improved Model 1950). These include: an ebony tip and fuller forend, left-side dummy plate cuts for side mount, left side of receiver was flattened to facilitate side scope mount, and flatter bolt handle requiring slot inside of stock.

In 1952, changes included a carved cheekpiece, change from 3/4 in. sling swivels to 1 in., swept back bolt handle, wood on left-side of stock over the dummy sideplate cutout thickened to strengthen the stock with a side mount in place, and removal of loading ears and clip guides, thereby streamlining the receiver and enabling lower scope mounting.

At one time Stoeger listed 18 versions of the M1950-52 family, defined as #S-1 through #S-18, with three major differences existing within each block of Model 1950, Improved Model 1950, and Model 1952. The differences were: single and double set triggers (DST), rifle or carbine style, 6.5mm Carbine, single trigger, or DST. The "GK" stock design was available as a special order variant after 1952 and is identical to the Model 1952.

From the M1950 through the improved M1952, these rifles were in continuous change and parallel production, thus rifles can be found with 1950 characteristics and proofmarks as late as 1954. Some examples are found with "nonstandard" markings such as "Model 1952" and no reference to the "Improved" standard. After mid-1965, U.S. market rifles were drilled and tapped for the Redfield scope mount. Some rifles were chambered for 8x57mm and 7x64mm.

During 1952-55, a small amount of Deluxe and Super Deluxe Mannlicher-Schoenauer were manufactured. These are typically encountered with better grade wood and model nomenclature is the same as the standard guns.

A method of differentiating Mannlichers made for the European market versus the U.S. market is by looking at the bolt. A blued bolt usually indicates a European market piece, while a polished bolt indicates a U.S. market piece. This is a usual identification; however, it is not always correct. A Stoeger logo on the floorplate is definite U.S. market proof.

Post World War II catalogs often list 6.5mm and 7mm as available calibers, but the actual calibers offered from the factory were 6.5x54mm, 6.5x55mm, 6.5x57mm, 7x57mm, and 7x64mm.

Add approx. 35% for 6.5x54mm, 9.3x62mm, .257 Roberts, or .244 Remington cal.

MANNLICHER-SCHOENAUER MAGNUM RIFLE – .257 Wby. Mag., 6.5x68mm, .264 Win. Mag., 8x68mm, 9.3x64mm, .338 Win. Mag., .458 Win. Mag. or 9.3x64mm cal., similar to Model 1956 MC, except has straight bolt handle, 5 shot rotary mag., 22 in. barrel with half stock, double set or single trigger.

100%	98%	95%	90%	80%	70%	60%
N/A	$3,600	$3,150	$2,450	$2,000	$1,625	$1,475

The only difference between rifles chambered for Magnum cartridges vs. non-Magnum cartridges, is that the bolt handle is straight and strengthened at the base to serve as a third safety locking lug. They are not marked Magnum Rifle anywhere on the barrel.

MODEL 1950 RIFLE – .270 Win., .30-06, 6.5x54mm, or 9.3x62mm Mauser, bolt action, 5 shot rotary mag., 24 in. barrel, straight style bolt handle, double or single set trigger, half stock.

100%	98%	95%	90%	80%	70%	60%
$1,995	$1,550	$1,175	$900	$750	$650	$550

MODEL 1950 CARBINE – 6.5x54mm cal., similar to Model 1950, except has 18 1/4 in. barrel and full-length stock.

100%	98%	95%	90%	80%	70%	60%
$2,200	$1,850	$1,625	$1,475	$1,175	$975	$750

IMPROVED MODEL 1952 RIFLE – .257 Roberts, .270 Win., .30-06, or 9.3x62mm cal., 24 in. barrel, 5 shot rotary mag., rear angled bolt handle, double set or single trigger, half stock.

100%	98%	95%	90%	80%	70%	60%
$1,800	$1,575	$1,175	$975	$800	$675	$550

IMPROVED MODEL 1952 CARBINE – .257 Roberts, 6.5x54mm, .270 Win., 7x57mm, .308 Win. (new 1953), or .30-06 cal., 18.25 (6.5x54mm cal. only) or 20 in. barrel, rear angled bolt handle, double or single trigger.

100%	98%	95%	90%	80%	70%	60%
$1,800	$1,575	$1,175	$975	$800	$675	$550

Add 20% for 6.5x54mm, .257 Roberts, or 7x57mm cal.

GRADING - PPGS™	100%	98%	95%	90%	80%	70%	60%	LAST MSR

MODEL 1956 MC RIFLE - .243 Win., 6.5x55mm, 6.5x57mm, 7x57mm, 7x64mm, 8x57mm, 8x60mm, 9.3x62mm, .244 Rem, .257 Rob, .270, .280, .308, .30-06, .358 WCF, or .30-06 cal., similar to Model 1952, high comb stock design, 5 shot rotary mag., 22 in. barrel, half length stock, double set or single trigger. Mfg. 1956-1961.

$1,800	$1,575	$1,175	$975	$800	$675	$550	

Add 20% for 6.5x54mm, .257 Roberts, or 7x57mm cal.

Add 20%-30% for advertised special order calibers such as 8x57mm, 7x64mm, and 9.3x64mm, depending on original condition.

MODEL 1956 MC CARBINE - .243 Win., 6.5x54mm, .257 Roberts, 6.5x55mm, 6.5x57mm, 7x64mm, 8x57mm, 8x60mm, .244 Rem, .280 Rem., 7x57mm, .270 Win., .30-06, .308 Win., or .358 Win. cal., similar to Model 1956 MC Rifle, except has 20 in. barrel with full stock, double set or single trigger. Mfg. 1956-1961.

$1,800	$1,575	$1,175	$975	$800	$675	$550	

Add 20%-30% for advertised special order calibers such as 8x57mm, 7x64mm, and 9.3x64mm, depending on original condition.

MODEL 1961 MCA RIFLE - .243 Win., .270 Win., or .30-06 cal., similar to Model 1956 Rifle, except has Monte Carlo stock, 5 shot rotary mag., 22 in. barrel with half stock, double set or single trigger. Mfg. 1961-1971.

$1,600	$1,300	$995	$825	$675	$575	$500	

Subtract $250 for models with plastic tang safety.

MODEL 1961 MCA CARBINE - .243 Win., 6.5x54mm, .270 Win., .30-06, 7x57mm, .308 Win., or .358 Win. (rare) cal., 20 in. barrel with full stock, similar to Model 1956 Carbine, except has Monte Carlo stock. Mfg. 1961-1971.

$1,800	$1,575	$1,175	$975	$800	$675	$550	

Add 20% for 6.5x54mm or 7x57mm cal.

Subtract $250 for models with plastic tang safety.

During production, the European market included the Model NO (Model MC/MCA) with GK stock and a straight pre-war bolt handle, produced in metric calibers such as 6.5x55mm Swedish, 7x64mm, and 8x57mm.

PREMIER/CUSTOM MODELS - 8x57mm or 7x64mm cal., these models were available from 1956 to 1968 and featured custom engraving of the metalwork and stock woodcarving. Some versions were also made for the market and such adornments were provided per the craftsmen at Steyr. These usually included individual engraved animal insets on the floorplate, receiver ring, and trigger guard, woodcarving in the oak leaf style, and wild animal figures on the buttstock. Gold inlays were available as well as monograms. All of these rifles offered single or double set triggers, and Steyr factory scope mounts, which were also engraved. Over a dozen standard engraving designs were offered for these rifles in any chambering.

$5,850	$5,400	$4,850	$4,350	$3,875	$3,400	$3,000	

ALPINE MODEL - .243 Win. or .30-06 cal., an MCA-1961 variant, offered between 1965 and 1968 as a version between the standard Mannlicher-Schoenauer and the Premier. It featured an engraved bolt handle and tasteful oak leaf carving on the pistol grip and forend. The Alpine was offered in carbine length only.

$3,650	$3,250	$2,950	$2,500	$2,250	$2,000	$1,800	

RIFLES: BOLT ACTION, CURRENT PRODUCTION 1972-PRESENT

Current production guns are now called Steyr Arms (Steyr-Mannlicher) models and can be located under this trademark in the S section.

MANU-ARM

Previous rifle and airgun manufacturer located in Veauche, France.

Manu-Arm manufactured good quality utilitarian .22 cal. bolt action and semi-auto rifles, in addition to an O/U in 9mm Para., .410 bore, and 32 ga.

MANUFRANCE

Current manufacturer established circa 1887, located in St. Etienne, France. No current U.S. importation.

Manufrance currently manufactures both SxS rifle and shotgun variations (the Robust Models being the most popular) that are not being currently imported into the U.S. Please contact the factory directly for more information, including model availability, parts, and domestic prices.

GRADING - PPGS™	100%	98%	95%	90%	80%	70%	60%	LAST MSR

SHOTGUNS: DISC.

SEMI-AUTO MODEL – 12 ga., 26, 28, or 30 in. imp. cyl., mod. and full, 2 3/4 or 3 in. chamber, gas operated, walnut stock, black matte receiver, VR.

$330 $305 $290 $275 $255 $240 $220

FALCOR O/U – 12 ga., VR, 26 in. imp. cyl. and mod., 28 in. mod. and full, SST, auto ejector, chrome-lined barrel, walnut checkered stock.

$715 $665 $635 $605 $550 $495 $470

MANURHIN

Current trademark manufactured by Manufacture d'Armes de tir Chapuis beginning in 1998, located in Saint Bonnet Le Chateau, France. Currently imported by Kebco LLC, located in Hanover, PA and J.J. Perodeau Gunmaker located in Sand Springs, OK. During 1998, Chapuis Armes purchased Manurhin, and new revolvers are currently being manufactured in the new Manufacture d. Armes de tir Chapuis facility located in Saint Bonnet Le Chateau, France, utilizing some of the original production machinery on the Model MR88 and all new machinery on the Model 73. Previously manufactured by Manurhin Equipment 1972-1998, located in Mulhouse, France. Previously owned by Matra Manurhin Defense. Previously imported and distributed by Sphinx U.S.A. located in Meriden, CT. Previously imported (1984-1986) directly by Matra-Manurhin International, Inc., located in Fort Lauderdale, FL.

Manurhin in France has been manufacturing models PP, PPK, and PPK/S since 1952. Previously, these guns were imported from 1953 by Tholson Co. of San Francisco, CA, and from 1956 by Interarms out of Alexandria, VA. In 1984, Manurhin imported their new models directly and they were marked Manurhin on the left front slide assembly. This differs from the previous Walther stamped guns. Also, no Interarms logo appears on the right side.

PISTOLS: SEMI-AUTO, DISC.

P-1 – 9mm Para. cal., similar to W. German P-38, double action, 5 in. barrel.

$600 $525 $450 $425 $325 $275 $200

MODEL P4 – 9mm Para. cal., P.38 variation issued to the French Police when in Berlin during post-WWII.

$650 $575 $500 $450 $375 $300 $225

MODEL PP – .22 LR, .32 ACP, or .380 ACP cal., 3 7/8 in. barrel, 10 shot mag.-.22 LR, 8 shot mag.-.32 ACP, 7 shot mag.-.380 ACP, blue only, all steel construction, double action with positive steel hammer block safety, 24 oz. Add $10 for .22 LR cal., $46 for Durgarde finish. Imported 1984-86.

$575 $500 $425 $400 $325 $275 $200 *$419*

* ***Model PP Collector Model*** – blue finish, special engraving. Imported 1986 only.

$750 $650 $575 $500 $425 $350 $275 *$529*

* ***Model PP Presentation Model*** – blue finish, special ornamentation. Imported 1986 only.

$1,150 $1,000 $850 $775 $625 $525 $400 *$819*

Also available with various engraving options in either blue, nickel, or gold finish - prices range from $222-$540.

MODEL PPK/S – .22 LR, .32 ACP, or .380 ACP cal., 3 1/4 in. barrel, 10 shot mag.-.22 LR, 8 shot mag.-.32 ACP, 7 shot mag.-.380 ACP, blue only, all steel construction, double action with positive steel hammer block safety, 23 oz. Imported 1984-86.

$575 $500 $425 $400 $325 $275 $200 *$419*

Add $75 for .22 LR cal.

* ***Model PPK/S Durgarde*** – similar to PPK/S, only with bonded brushed chrome finish.

$650 $575 $500 $440 $350 $300 $225 *$465*

Add $14 for .22 LR cal.

* ***Model PPK/S Collector Model*** – blue finish, special engraving. Imported 1986 only.

$750 $650 $575 $500 $425 $350 $275 *$529*

* ***Model PPK/S Presentation Model*** – blue finish, special ornamentation. Imported 1986 only.

$1,150 $1,000 $850 $775 $625 $525 $400 *$819*

Also available with various engraving options in either blue, nickel, or gold finish - prices range from $222-$540.

GRADING - PPGS™	100%	98%	95%	90%	80%	70%	60%	LAST MSR

PP SPORT – .22 LR cal. only, double action, 6.1 or 8.1 in. barrel, blue finish only, precision adj. sights, contoured plastic grips with thumbrest, 25 oz. New Manurhin design for 1985. Imported 1984-86.

	$1,275	$1,125	$950	$875	$700	$575	$450	*$635*

Add 10% for 8.1 in. barrel.

* ***PP Sport-C*** – .22 LR cal., similar to PP Sport, except has single action with lightened trigger pull.

	$1,200	$1,050	$900	$825	$675	$550	$425	*$635*

REVOLVERS

Approximately 400 Model MR 73's are currently manufactured annually.

MR32 MATCH – .32 S&W Long cal., 6 in. barrel, brilliant polished blue finish, 38 oz.

MSR $3,500	$2,975	$2,600	$2,230	$2,025	$1,630	$1,340	$1,165

MR38 MATCH – .38 Spl. cal., 5 3/4 in. barrel, brilliant polished blue finish, 38 oz.

MSR $3,500	$2,975	$2,600	$2,230	$2,025	$1,630	$1,340	$1,165

MR73 DEFENSE – .357 Mag./.38 Spl. or 9mm Para. cal., 6 shot, 2 1/2 (no longer importable), 3 (fixed sights only), or 4 in. barrel, checkered wood stocks, mfg. to precise tolerances, strawed hammer and trigger, bright high-polish blue finish, 31-33 1/2 oz. Imported 1988-disc.

Original Condition	$3,100	$2,600	$2,100	$1,500	$950	$700	$500
Refinished	$1,000	$850	$750	$625	$500	$400	$350

Add $1,000 for extra 9mm Para. cal. cylinder (rare).

Trausch branded models feature rubber or checkered wooden grips.

This model was also previously imported by Century International Arms, Inc. - this importation is usually encountered in poor condition.

MR73 GENDARMERIE – .357 Mag./.38 Spl. cal., 2 1/2, 2 3/4, 3, 4, 5 1/4, 6, or 8 (disc., reintroduced 2021) in. barrel, 6 shot, adj. sighting components, checkered wood grip, brilliant polished blue finish, 28.6-34.2 oz. Manufactured for police requirements. Importation began 1988.

MSR $3,200	$2,725	$2,385	$2,050	$1,850	$1,500	$1,225	$1,065

Add $300 for 8 in. barrel.
Add $1,000 for extra 9mm cylinder (rare, disc.).
Add $1,000 for .22 LR version (disc.).

MR73 MATCH – .32 S&W or .38 Spl. cal., SA/DA, extended sight, wood grips.

MSR $3,500	$2,975	$2,600	$2,230	$2,025	$1,630	$1,340	$1,165

MR73 SPORT – .22 LR (disc.), 9mm (rare, disc.), or .357 Mag./.38 Spl. cal., 4, 5 1/4, or 6 in. barrel, 6 shot, minimized hammer stroke, free release trigger, micrometer rear sight, Patridge front sight, wood or black rubber grips, brilliant polished blue finish. Importation began 1988.

MSR $3,000	$3,500	$3,000	$2,500	$2,000	$1,500	$1,000	$500

Add $1,000 for extra 9mm cylinder (rare, disc.).
Add $1,000 for .22 LR version (disc.).

MR73 SILHOUETTE – .22 LR or .357 Mag. cal., Silhouette variation with fully adj. rear sight and either 10 (.22 LR) or 10 3/4 (.357 Mag.) in. heavy barrel with full shroud, contoured wooden target grips, "Trausch" marked, approx. 4 lbs. Imported 1988-disc.

.357 Mag. cal.	$3,250	$2,800	$2,350	$1,850	$1,350	$700	$500
.22 LR cal.	$3,500	$3,000	$2,500	$2,000	$1,500	$1,000	$500

Add $1,000 for extra 9mm cylinder (rare).

MR88 – .38 Spl. or .357 Mag. cal., stainless steel, 3, 4, 5 1/4, or 6 in. barrel, fixed (.38 Spl. cal.) or adj. sights, rubber grips standard. Importation began 1996.

MSR $1,600	$1,700	$1,400	$1,100	$950	$800	$675	$550

MR96 – .357 Mag. cal., black finish, 3, 4, 5, or 6 in. VR barrel, adj. rear sight, ergonomic rubber grips. Imported 1996-disc.

	$750	$615	$425	$375	$350	$325	$295

This model allows the user to unlock, swing the cylinder out, and eject the cases with one movement of the hand.

MARATHON PRODUCTS, INC.

Previously manufactured by Santa Barbara Armaments exclusively for Marathon Products, Inc. Most of the models listed were also available in kit form, but are not shown in this book.

GRADING - PPGS™	100%	98%	95%	90%	80%	70%	60%	LAST MSR

PISTOLS: SINGLE SHOT

HOT SHOT MODEL – .22 LR cal., single shot, fixed sights, 14 3/4 in. barrel, hardwood stock with target grip configuration. Mfg. 1986-87.

$55	$45	$40	$35	$35	$30	$30	*$60*

RIFLES: BOLT ACTION

.22 FIRST SHOT – .22 LR cal., single shot, 16 1/2 in. barrel, hardwood stock, open sights, 31 in. total length, 3.8 lbs. Mfg. 1985-87.

$55	$45	$40	$35	$35	$30	$30	*$60*

* ***.22 First Shot Super*** – similar to First Shot, except with 24 in. barrel and regular dimension stock. Mfg. 1985-87.

$55	$45	$40	$35	$35	$30	$30	*$60*

CENTERFIRE MODEL – .243 Win., .270 Win., 7x57mm, 7mm Rem. Mag., .30-06, .300 Win. Mag., or .308 Win. cal., Mauser type action, 5 shot fixed box mag., 24 in. barrel, select walnut with recoil pad, adj. trigger, open sights, 7.9 lbs. Available 1985-86 only.

$295	$240	$215	$195	$180	$170	$160	*$320*

MARBLE ARMS & MFG. CO.

Previous firearms manufacturer established circa 1907, located in Gladstone, MI. Marble Gun Sights (current company name) currently manufactures sights, knives, and compasses.

In addition to axes and compasses, Marble Arms & Mfg. Co. also manufactured its Game Getter O/U combination gun from approx. 1907 to the early 1950s. During this period of production, the gun underwent quite a few changes including sights (an aperture sight mounted on the rear backstrap was optional in 1908), different configuration folding metal stock, and other changes.

During 2009, Marble Gun Sights announced plans to release the third generation of its Game Getter, but while a few prototypes were made, it never reached production.

COMBINATION GUNS

Marble Arms at one time had manufactured replacement parts for first and second generation 1908 and 1921 models. None known today. With the effect on collector values factory original configuration and condition have, determining originality has become very important. The original configuration can now be verified at www.marblearms.com.

GAME GETTER MODEL 1908 – starting manufacture in 1908, 2 variations of the Model 1908 Game Getter were offered, the 1908A featured a flexible rear sight mounted behind the hammer and the 1908B had a filler blank in that space. The 1908s featured a .22 cal. rifled top barrel, and in standard configuration, a smoothbored bottom barrel chambered for the .44 round ball or .44 shot. Very late in production, chambering for the 2 in. .410 could be ordered. Standard barrel lengths were 12, 15, and 18 in., but Marbles was ready to please their customers, and on special order 8, 10, 17, and 22 in. barrels were made, some were even shipped from the factory fitted with silencers, and very few guns were ordered without the milling for the round tubular folding stock. A pivoting striker on the hammer was used to select the barrel to be fired, and the tip-up barrels were opened by pressing the trigger guard to the rear. The top frame featured a folding leaf sight, and the front barrel band incorporated the front sight, the grips were checkered black hard rubber with fleur-de-lis design. On very early 1908 guns, the buttplate was a separate piece secured to the tubing with 2 screws and later stocks were all one-piece. A few guns were built with bottom barrels chambered for .25-20 & .32-20, but these are very rare. The gun was shipped in a dovetailed wooden box with sliding lid, and included a shoulder holster, cleaning rod, and directions for use. The first 1908 was shipped from the factory June 21, 1909, and serial letters A-M were used. Then, starting with serial number 1, they continued through 9981, and the last gun was shipped from the factory May 22, 1918.

$4,000	$3,800	$3,500	$3,000	$2,500	$2,000	$1,800

Add $500 for Model 1908A with original flexible tang sight.
Add $100-$200 for original holster, depending on condition of leather.
Add $1,200-$1,500 for correct original box, depending on condition.
Add $1,500-$2,000 for correct original box for 18 in. barrel variation, depending on condition.

Values assume legal 18 in. barrels or correct registration. If not legal configuration, the gun is basically a black market item subject to BATFE confiscation.

GRADING - PPGS™	100%	98%	95%	90%	80%	70%	60%	LAST MSR

GAME GETTER MODEL 1921 – the 1921 was an entirely new gun, with similar barrel lengths (12, 15, or 18 in.), not nearly as pleasing in appearance as the 1908. The same barrel lengths were standard, but the bottom barrel was chambered for the 2 in. .410. In 1924, the standard chamber was changed to 2 1/2 in. .410. It featured a bag style, oiled walnut grip, and a unique "Triple Combination Rear Sight," which was developed and made only for this model. A number of guns in the 14,000 to 16,000 serial number range can be found with brown plastic grips, conventional "v" notch rear sight adjustable for elevation. The 1921 featured a folding and hinged 3 piece stock with an improved lock which eliminated wobble, but had no adjustment for drop. It also had a shorter action than the 1908, which was a faster action, and the hammer rebounded to a safety notch after firing. As with the 1908 Model, Marbles would accomodate the wishes of the customer, and barrels as short as 8 in. can be found. Some guns were ordered choke bored, and some were chambered just for .44 Game Getter on the bottom barrel. A few had no provision for stock, at least 2 were shipped in .32-20, and as records are not complete, .38-40 cal. models are known to exist and calibers like the .25-20 are thought to exist. Supplied with a heavy cardboard box, shoulder holster, cleaning rod and instructions. First shipment was serial number 10,001 - shipped to William L. Marble, the west coast representative, on Oct. 4, 1921. Serial range 10,000-20,076.

	$3,000	$2,500	$2,200	$1,900	$1,600	$1,400	$1,300	

Add $150-$200 for original holster if in good condition.
Add $1,200-$1,500 for correct original box, depending on wood condition (very early 1921 only).
Add $300-$500 for cardboard box, depending on condition (just cardboard lift-off lid).

The first 200-300 of this model were shipped in 1908 boxes with 1921 yellow end label on the box.

Values assume legal 18 in. barrels or correct registration. If not legal configuration, the gun is basically a black market item subject to BATFE confiscation. The U.S. government and foreign countries continued to purchase 15 in. guns after the 1934 law was passed, and the last gun was shipped during the mid 1950s. 200 M1921 models with 15 in. barrels were assembled from parts and sold by Marbles as collector's items in 1960.

Not all, but many 1921s in this serial range approx. 14,000 - 16,000 had parkerized finish, no flip rear sight, one piece cardboard box with end flaps and no holster.

GAME GETTER MODEL 3RD GENERATION – .22 LR cal. over .410 bore, 18 1/2 in. barrels, patterned after the Game Getter Model 1921, folding sporting rear sight, aperture tang sight, original barrel band beaded front sight, includes replica leather holster and slide top pine wood box, assembled and finished by Doug Turnbull Restoration. Only prototypes were mfg.

While advertised at $1,995 circa 2011, this gun was never put into standard production.

MARCEL THYS & SONS

Previous SxS rifle and shotgun manufacturer circa 1960-2004 located in Crisnée, Belgium. The U.S. importer was JJ Perodeau Gunmaker, located in Sand Springs, OK.

Marcel Thys & Sons manufactured fine quality double rifles and shotguns, with many engraving options and special orders. Since these guns were custom made per individual order, each gun must be individually appraised.

MARCOLMAR FIREARMS

Current tactical rifle manufacturer located in Richmond, IN.

For individual model listings, please go to BlueBookOfGunValues.com/overflow.

MARGOLIN

Original pistol design by M.V. Margolin developed after WWII as a training firearm for members of the Russian shooting team. The Margolin is currently manufactured at the Izhevsk mechanical plant located in Izhevsk, Russia, and known as the "MTsN" sporting pistol. Limited importation.

PISTOLS: SEMI-AUTO

TARGET MODEL – .22 LR cal., originally developed from the TT (Tula Tokarev), manufactured to precise tolerances, many specimens are made to individual shooters' specifications, seldom encountered in the U.S., while rare, desirability to date has been limited, current mfg. - limited importation.

	$875	$825	$750	$675	$600	$525	$450	

While currently imported Chinese copies are considerably less expensive, they do not have the quality (or accuracy) of the Russian Margolins.

100%	98%	95%	90%	80%	70%	60%	50%	40%	30%	20%	10%

MARLIN FIREARMS COMPANY

Current trademark with headquarters located in Madison, NC beginning 2010. Currently manufactured by Remington in Ilion, NY beginning early 2011. Previous manufacturer located in North Haven, CT (1969-2010), and in New Haven, CT (1870-1969). The Marlin company manufactured firearms between 1870-2010.

On Nov. 10th, 2000, Marlin Firearms Company purchased H&R 1871, Inc. This includes the brand names Harrington & Richardson, New England Firearms, and Wesson & Harrington (please refer to individual sections in this text).

During 2005, Marlin Firearms Company once again started manufacturing an L.C. Smith line of both SxS and O/U shotguns.

Remington Arms Company, Inc. and The Freedom Group acquired Marlin Firearms Company, H&R 1871, LLC., New England Firearms (NEF), and L.C. Smith brand in January of 2008. The Freedom Group, Inc. announced the closure of its Marlin manufacturing facility, located in North Haven, Connecticut. During 2011, production was moved to Ilion, NY. Marlin Firearms Company had been a family-owned and operated business from 1921-2007.

Circa 2017, Marlin started a Custom Shop located in Sturgis, SD. This new Custom Shop service enables a customer to order a one-of-a-kind Marlin per individual specifications and requirements. In July 2020, Remington Outdoor Group filed for bankruptcy, ceased production of all firearms, and sold off all their trademarks. Sturm, Ruger, & Co. bought the Marlin trademark in September 2020 and said they have plans of reintroducing the Marlin brand during the second half of 2021.

PISTOLS: DERRINGERS AND REVOLVERS

For more information on Marlin antique pistols, derringers, and revolvers, please refer to the 2nd Edition of *Blue Book Antique American Firearms & Values.* Also available as an online subscription - please visit BlueBookOfGunValues.com for ordering information.

RIFLES: LEVER ACTION, ANTIQUE & OLDER MFG.

Factory information is available on the following models from the Cody Firearms Records Office at the Buffalo Bill Center of the West: serial numbers 4001-355504 of Models 1881, 1888, 1889, 1892, 1893, 1894, 1895, and 1897. As Marlin had only one series of serial numbers for all lever action repeating rifles from 1883-1906, they do not reflect sequence; a record may show two or three guns with the same serial number from the same time period.

Values are for standard models only without special order features. 98% and 100% prices have been intentionally noted with N/As (not applicable); these condition factors are seldom encountered and hard to accurately price as their values have dramatically increased during the past 3-5 years.

Add a premium for all mint condition guns with vibrant case coloring on receivers.

MODEL 1881 - .32-40 WCF, .38-55 WCF, .40-60 Marlin, .45-70 Govt., or .45-85 Marlin cal., tube mag., 28 in. octagonal barrel standard, top ejection, blued finish with case hardened hammer, lever, and buttplate. Approx. 20,000 mfg. 1881-1892.

100%	98%	95%	90%	80%	70%	60%	50%	40%	30%	20%	10%
N/A	N/A	$3,900	$3,100	$2,500	$2,100	$1,800	$1,600	$1,400	$1,250	$1,100	$900

Add approx. 15% for .45-70 or .45-85 cal.

Add 200-300% premium for rare First models (pre-ser. no. 600).

Add a premium for very early First models with hand engraved script barrel markings - approx. first 60 rifles mfg.

This model came in 3 frame styles for various calibers.

MODEL 1888 - .32-20 WCF, .38-40 WCF, or .44-40 WCF cal., 24 in. octagonal barrel most frequently encountered, top ejection, blued finish with case hardened hammer, lever, and buttplate, short throw lever action principle. Approx. 4,800 mfg. 1888-1889. Ser. range approx. 19,560-27,850.

100%	98%	95%	90%	80%	70%	60%	50%	40%	30%	20%	10%
N/A	N/A	$3,650	$2,750	$2,150	$1,850	$1,550	$1,400	$1,200	$975	$850	$750

Add 40% for half-round, half-octagon barrel (23 mfg.).

Add 20% for round barrel (266 mfg.).

Add 25% for half magazine (78 mfg.).

MODEL 1889 - .25-20 WCF (very rare), .32-20 WCF, .38-40 WCF, or .44-40 WCF cal., 24 (approx. 39,300 mfg.) or 28 (approx. 2,260 mfg.) in. octagonal barrel most frequently encountered, side ejection with solid top frame, blued finish with case hardened hammer, lever, and buttplate, short throw lever action principle. Approx. 55,000 mfg. 1889-1899. Ser. range approx. 25,000-100,000.

100%	98%	95%	90%	80%	70%	60%	50%	40%	30%	20%	10%
N/A	N/A	$1,950	$1,550	$1,250	$1,050	$925	$850	$775	$675	$550	$450

Add 300%-500% for Musket.

100%	98%	95%	90%	80%	70%	60%	50%	40%	30%	20%	10%

Add 25% for carbine.
Add 15% for .44-40 WCF cal.
Factory special orders/features will add premiums, depending on the desirability of each option and the gun's original condition factor.

Also available as Carbine with either a 15 in. (only 367 mfg.) or 20 in. (approx. 10,000 mfg.) barrel or Musket (30 in. barrel - very rare).

MODEL 1891 – .22 Rimfire and .32 Rimfire/Centerfire cal., 24 in. octagonal barrel most often encountered, choice of side loading (1st variation) or tube loading (2nd variation), blued finish with case hardened hammer, lever, and buttplate, sear safety system on lever action. Approx. 18,650 mfg. between 1891-1897. Ser. no. range is approx. 37,500-118,000.

100%	98%	95%	90%	80%	70%	60%	50%	40%	30%	20%	10%
N/A	N/A	$2,500	$2,150	$1,600	$1,300	$1,050	$975	$900	$825	$725	$650

Add 50% for deluxe, pistol grip checkered model.
Subtract 40% for tube loading model (.32 Centerfire).
Add $100 each for special sights (including correct Lyman, Marbles, Beeches combo, etc.).
Factory special orders/features will add premiums, depending on the desirability of each option and the gun's original condition factor.

MODEL 1892 – .22 S, L, or LR, .32 S or L cal., 16, 24, 26, or 28 in. barrel, tubular mag., open sight, plain straight stock. Mfg. 1892-1916.

100%	98%	95%	90%	80%	70%	60%	50%	40%	30%	20%	10%
N/A	N/A	$2,150	$1,650	$1,300	$1,125	$1,000	$925	$825	$750	$650	$550

Add 10% for .22 cal.
Subtract 10% for .32 cal.
Add $100 each for special sights (including correct Lyman, Marbles, Beeches combo, etc.).
Factory special orders/features will add premiums, depending on the desirability of each option and the gun's original condition factor.

MODEL 1893 RIFLE – .25-36 Marlin, .30-30 Win., .32 Spl., .32-40 WCF, or .38-55 WCF cal., 20-32 in. round or octagonal barrels, blue (Model B) or case colored receiver, 10 shot tube mag., straight grip stock. Mfg. 1893-1936.

100%	98%	95%	90%	80%	70%	60%	50%	40%	30%	20%	10%
N/A	N/A	$3,000	$2,400	$1,900	$1,350	$1,100	$900	$700	$600	$525	$450

Add 15%-20% for calibers other than .30-30 Win. or .32 Spl.
Add 15%-20% for takedown model, depending on condition.
Add approx. 20% for special Lightweight Model.
Subtract 10%-20% for the Model B with blue receiver.
Factory special orders/features will add premiums, depending on the desirability of each option and the gun's original condition factor.

Although incorrect, more than a few people refer to all 20 in. barrels as "Lightweight" models. Technically, the Lightweight variation has a 7 1/2 in. forearm rather than the standard 9 in.

Later production guns were marked "Model '93" and have less value. This model had two barrel variations - one was marked "special smokeless steel" while the other was marked "for Black Powder". The latter (also known as Model B) are 1st Models only and have blue receivers rather than case colored.

* ***Model 1893 Musket*** – similar to the Model 1893 Rifle, except has 30 in. barrel and military style forearm.

100%	98%	95%	90%	80%	70%	60%	50%	40%	30%	20%	10%
N/A	N/A	$6,000	$5,300	$4,750	$3,950	$3,400	$3,000	$2,650	$2,300	$1,950	$1,650

MODEL 1893 CARBINE – .30-30 Win., .32 Spl., .32-40 WCF cal., or .38-55 WCF cal., 15 (only 61 mfg.) or 20 in. round barrel, case colored receiver, 7 shot tube mag., straight or pistol grip stock. Mfg. 1893-1935.

Add 15%-20% for calibers other than .30-30 Win. or .32 Spl.
Factory special orders/features will add premiums, depending on the desirability of each option and the gun's original condition factor.

* ***Model 1893 Carbine 1st Model*** – with saddle ring. Mfg. 1893-1915.

100%	98%	95%	90%	80%	70%	60%	50%	40%	30%	20%	10%
N/A	N/A	$2,200	$1,625	$1,350	$1,200	$1,075	$975	$875	$775	$675	$550

Strong, original case colors over 95% condition can result in $2,500 asking prices.

* ***Model 1893 Carbine 2nd Model*** – .30-30 Win. or .32 HPS (High Power Special) cal., has "Bull's-eye" in stock, no saddle rings. Mfg. 1922-35.

100%	98%	95%	90%	80%	70%	60%	50%	40%	30%	20%	10%
N/A	N/A	$1,200	$1,050	$950	$875	$800	$775	$700	$625	$525	$425

* ***Model 1893 Carbine Sporting*** – .30-30 Win. or .32 Spl. cal., 20 in. round barrel, 2/3 mag., 5 shot, carbine style front sight, Rocky Mountain rear, straight stock, hard rubber buttplate, bull's-eye in stock. Mfg. 1923-35.

100%	98%	95%	90%	80%	70%	60%	50%	40%	30%	20%	10%
N/A	N/A	$1,800	$1,375	$1,125	$875	$775	$650	$550	$450	$375	$350

Subtract 40% for 2nd Model made in 1935 with "S" steel buttplate and ivory bead front sight.

100%	98%	95%	90%	80%	70%	60%	50%	40%	30%	20%	10%

MODEL 1894 – .25-20 WCF, .32-20 WCF, .38-40 WCF, or .44-40 WCF cal., case colored receiver, 10 shot tube mag., 24 in. round or octagon barrel, straight or pistol grip stock. Mfg. 1894-1934.

N/A	N/A	$3,650	$2,500	$2,000	$1,450	$1,000	$750	$650	$550	$450	$400

Add 25% for saddle ring carbine.
Add 10% for .44-40 WCF cal.
Add 40% for Baby Carbine with 18 in. barrel and 1/2 mag.
Add 15%-20% for takedown model, depending on condition.
Factory special orders/features will add premiums, depending on the desirability of each option and the gun's original condition factor.

Later production guns were marked "Model '94" and have less value. This model was also available in both a Carbine and Musket variation.

* ***Model 1894 Musket***

N/A	N/A	$5,500	$5,000	$4,500	$3,750	$3,250	$2,600	$2,000	$1,500	$1,250	$1,100

MODEL 1895 – .33 WCF, .38-56 WCF, .40-65 WCF, .40-70 WCF, .40-82 WCF, .45-70 Govt., or .45-90 cal., case colored receiver, 9 shot tube mag., 24 or 26 in. round or octagon barrel standard, other lengths were available, open sights, plain straight or pistol grip stock. Mfg. 1895-1915.

N/A	N/A	$4,650	$3,500	$3,000	$2,350	$1,750	$1,500	$1,200	$1,000	$850	$750

Premiums exist for .40-70 WCF (approx. 60 mfg.), .45-70 Govt., and .45-90 WCF cal.
Factory special orders/features will add premiums, depending on the desirability of each option and the gun's original condition factor.

In 1912, a lightweight variation was introduced with hard rubber buttplate and half-magazine, cals. were .33 WCF and .45-70 Govt. (commands a premium), and round barrels were either 22 or 24 in. A Carbine variation was also offered with approx. 200 mfg. - premiums may run as high as 150% over rifle values listed.

MODEL 1897 – .22 S, L, or LR cal., tube mag., 16, 24, 26, or 28 in. round or octagon barrel, case colored receiver, takedown, open sights, plain straight or pistol grip stock. Mfg. 1897-1922.

N/A	N/A	$3,000	$2,250	$1,675	$1,425	$1,150	$975	$750	$625	$525	$425

Add 100% for 16 in. barrel "Bicycle Rifle."
Add $100 each for special sights (including correct Lyman, Marbles, Beeches combo, etc.).
Factory special orders/features will add premiums, depending on the desirability of each option and the gun's original condition factor.

RIFLES: MODERN PRODUCTION INFORMATION

Year of manufacture can be determined from 1946-1968 by the following letter/numeral prefixes: 1946-C, 1947-D, 1948-E, 1949-F, 1950-G, 1951-H, 1952-J, 1953-K, 1954-L, 1955-M, 1956-N, 1957-P, 1958-R, 1959-S, 1960-T, 1961-U, 1962-V, 1963-W, 1964-Y,Z, 1965-AA, 1966-AB, 1967-AC, 1968-AD, 1969-69, 1970-70, 1971-71, 1972-72. Starting in 1973, the year can be determined by subtracting the first 2 numbers of the serial number from 100.

GRADING - PPGS™	100%	98%	95%	90%	80%	70%	60%	LAST MSR

RIFLES: CENTERFIRE

Rifles: Centerfire, Bolt Action

The models listed are in alphabetical sequence first, followed by numerical sequence for easy reference.

Machine cut checkering became standard on many Marlins beginning 1995. Safety locks have been shipped with every new rifle/shotgun beginning 1999.

All Marlin firearms manufactured before Jan. 2008 had "JM" on the barrel near the receiver.

MODEL MR-7 – .22-250 Rem. (advertised in 1998, but never mfg.), .243 Win. (advertised in 1998, but never mfg.), .25-06 Rem. (new 1997), .270 Win., .280 Rem. (new 1998), .30-06, or .308 Win. (advertised in 1998, but never mfg.) cal., 4 shot box mag. with removable hinged floorplate, 3-position safety, adj. 3-6 lb. trigger, 22 in. barrel, checkered American walnut stock, cocking indicator, forged receiver, damascened bolt, includes sling swivels, with or without sights, approx. 7 1/2 lbs. Mfg. 1996-99.

$550	$450	$375	$315	$275	$240	$215	*$603*

Add $40 for open sights (.270 Win., .280 Rem., or .30-06).

* ***Model MR-7B*** – .270 Win. or .30-06 only, similar to Model MR-7, except has birch stock and forearm with cut checkering. Mfg. 1998-99.

$475	$450	$350	$185	$165	$150	$130	*$483*

Add $40 for open sights (mfg. 1998 only).

GRADING - PPGS™	100%	98%	95%	90%	80%	70%	60%	LAST MSR

MODEL X7 SERIES – various cals., barrel joined to receiver by barrel nut, no sights, 4 shot internal mag., Pro-Fire adj. trigger system, two-position safety, recoil pad, fluted bolt, fully enclosed bolt shroud with cocking indicator, recessed target style muzzle crown, steel sling swivel studs. Mfg. 2008-2014.

* ***Model X7*** – .223 Rem. (new 2012), .243 Win., .25-06 Rem., .270 Win., .30-06, .308 Win. or 7mm-08 Rem. cal., short or long action, 22 in. barrel w/o sights, features black synthetic stock, blue metal finish, scope base included, approx. 6 1/2 lbs. Mfg. 2008-2014.

$400	$300	$260	$230	$210	$190	$170	*$403*

Add $54 for 3-9x40mm mounted scope and bore sighted (new 2012).

* ***Model X7S*** – similar to Model X7, except has stainless steel barrel. Mfg. 2009-2011.

$450	$345	$310	$265	$240	$215	$190	*$505*

* ***Model X7C*** – .243 Win., .25-06 Rem., .270 Win., .30-06, .308 Win., 7mm-08 Rem. cal., 22 in. barrel w/o sights, features Realtree APG HD camo stock. Mfg. 2008-2011.

$365	$310	$275	$240	$220	$195	$175	*$426*

* ***Model X7W*** – .270 Win. or .30-06 cal., similar to Model X7, except has walnut stock. Mfg. 2009-2011.

$475	$395	$360	$300	$260	$225	$200	*$580*

* ***Model X7L*** – similar to Model X7W, except has laminate stock. Mfg. 2009-2011.

$475	$395	$360	$300	$260	$225	$200	*$580*

* ***Model X7 Varmint Heavy Barrel*** – .22-250 Rem., .223 Rem. (new 2012) or .308 Win. cal., similar to Model X7, except has black synthetic stock, 24 (disc.) or 26 in. heavy barrel. 7 3/4 lbs. Mfg. 2011-2014.

$390	$300	$260	$230	$210	$190	$170	*$409*

* ***Model X7Y*** – .243 Win., .308 Win., or 7mm-08 Rem. cal., similar to Model X7, except has shortened black stock, 6 1/2 lbs. Mfg. 2008-2014.

$390	$300	$260	$230	$210	$190	$170	*$403*

Add $54 for 3-9x40mm mounted scope and bore sighted (new 2012).

MODEL 322 VARMINT – .222 Rem. cal., Sako Mauser type action, 3 shot mag., 24 in. medium weight barrel, 2 position aperture sight, checkered stock. Approx. 5,850 mfg. 1954-57.

$600	$500	$475	$400	$325	$300	$250

MODEL 455 SPORTER – .30-06, or .308 Win. cal., FN Mauser action with Sako trigger, 24 in. stainless steel barrel, Lyman aperture sight, checkered Monte Carlo pistol grip stock. 1,079 were mfg. in .30-06 cal., 59 in .308 Win. cal. Mfg. 1957-1959.

$690	$525	$375	$250	$220	$195	$165

Add 20% for .308 Win. cal.

Rifles: Centerfire, Lever Action

All Marlin firearms manufactured before Jan. 2008 had "JM" on the barrel near the receiver.

Circa 2017, Marlin started a Custom Shop located in Sturgis, SD. This new Custom Shop service enables a customer to order a one-of-a-kind Marlin per individual specifications and requirements. Marlin Custom Shop features and options include: checkering, Deburr and dehorn all metal, Cerakote, Nitre Blue small parts, case color receiver, high polish blue, engraving, hand-rubbed oil finish, porting barrels, one-piece ejector, action job, trigger job and upgrades, accurizing, shorten and recrown barrel, recoil pad upgrades, threaded barrel. Custom Shop models include: Custom 39A Fancy, Custom 39A Extra Fancy, Custom 39A Extra Fancy Plus, Modern Lever Hunter 336, Modern Lever Hunter 1894, Modern Lever Hunter 1895, Custom 336 Fancy, Custom 336 Extra Fancy, Custom 336 Extra Fancy Plus, Custom 1894 Fancy, Custom 1894 Extra Fancy, Custom 1894 Extra Fancy Plus, Custom 1895 Fancy, Custom 1895 Extra Fancy, Custom 1895 Extra Fancy Plus, and Custom Shop lever actions.

* ***Model 30TK*** – .30-30 Win. cal., 20 in. micro-grooved barrel, 6 shot, birch straight grip stock, sling swivels, sold through K-Mart.

$425	$325	$295	$275	$250	$225	$200

MODEL 30AS – please refer to Model 336A/336AS listing.

MODEL 36 - 1ST VARIATION – same as Model 1936 - called Model 36 in catalog only. Mfg. 1937-40.

$825	$700	$525	$400	$325	$275	$225

Add 10% for rifles and sporting carbines.

The Model 36 - 1st Variation has an upper tang inscription "Model 1936" and a case colored receiver. Also, the Model 36 - 1st variation did not have a letter prefix in the ser. no.

GRADING - PPGS™	100%	98%	95%	90%	80%	70%	60%	LAST MSR

MODEL 36 - 2ND VARIATION – similar to Model 1936, still has case colored receiver with "Model 1936" on upper tang, coiled main spring, buttstock is heavier style and no longer has fluted comb, buttplate is a thicker, slightly curved style - hard rubber, forearm is a heavier beaver-tailed style, "B" prefix in ser. no. Mfg. 1941.

	$890	$725	$550	$425	$350	$295	$250	

Add 10% for rifles and sporting carbines.

MODEL 36 ADL DELUXE RIFLE – similar to Model 1936, case colored receiver, checkered pistol grip buttstock and forearm, pistol grip cap, Winchester quick detachable swivels with 1 in. sling, "B" prefix in ser. no., has "Model 1936" on upper tang. Less than 50 mfg. in 1945 only.

	$1,425	$1,125	$875	$675	$475	$375	$300	

Both the rear and front swivel bases are attached with two wood screws and are not inletted into the wood.

MODEL 36 - 3RD VARIATION – .30-30 Win. or .32 SPEC cal., blued receiver, no upper tang markings, model no. and cal. marked on barrel, rifles have "A" suffix, Sporting Carbine has "SC" suffix, and regular carbine has "RC" suffix, small case "c" prefix in 1946, and large "D" prefix in 1947. Mfg. 1946-47.

	$700	$475	$400	$350	$315	$265	$225	

Add 10% for rifles and sporting carbines.

Some standard rifles may have the "ADL" barrel markings in 1946-47. 1946 mfg. has a lowercase "c" prefix and 1947 mfg. has a capital "D" prefix in ser. no.

* ***Model 36 3rd Variation ADL Deluxe*** – similar to Model 36 3rd Variation, has checkered pistol grip stock and forearm, forearm has checkering on sides and underneath, round swivel stud in buttstock and on forearm cap, deluxe quick detachable swivels and 1 in. leather sling, does not have model designation on upper tang or pistol grip cap, hooded front ramp screw on front sight, Rocky Mountain rear, letter prefix in ser. no. is "C" or "D."

	$975	$750	$600	$500	$425	$375	$350	

MODEL 36G/30/30A GLENFIELD – .30-30 Win. cal., 20 in. barrel, promotional Glenfield model with birch stock and pressed checkering. Mfg. 1964-83.

	$425	$325	$295	$275	$250	$225	$200	

This model was originally introduced as the Model 36G Glenfield in 1964. In 1966, it became the Model 30 Glenfield with no changes made to the gun. In 1971, it became the Model 30A with a full-length 6-shot magazine. In 1983, they introduced a cross-bolt safety and it became the Model 30AS. They also stopped using the Glenfield name in 1983 making it a Marlin Model 30AS.

MODEL 62 LEVERMATIC – .256 Mag. or .30 Carbine cal., 4 shot mag., 23 in. barrel, open sight, pistol grip Monte Carlo stock. Mfg. 1963-69.

.256 Mag.	$725	$500	$435	$375	$325	$265	$235	
.30 Carbine	$675	$400	$335	$275	$250	$225	$200	

MODEL 308MX – .308 Marlin Express cal., 22 in. barrel with blued finish, American black walnut pistol grip stock and forearm, cut checkering, rubber rifle buttpad, MarShield finish, swivel studs, 5 shot tube mag, 7 1/4 lbs. Mfg. 2007-2015.

	$675	$550	$450	$375	$315	$275	$250	*$686*

This model was developed to take advantage of the Hornady LEVERevolution ammunition, which greatly improves range, energy, and accuracy.

* ***Model 308MXLR*** – .308 Marlin Express cal., 24 in. stainless steel barrel, 5 shot tubular mag., Black/grey laminated pistol grip stock, deluxe recoil pad, nickel-plated swivel studs, fluted bolt, stainless steel metal components, 7 1/2 lbs. Mfg. 2007-2015.

	$850	$700	$525	$425	$375	$325	$275	*$905*

This model was developed to take advantage of the Hornady LEVERevolution ammunition, which greatly improves range, energy, and accuracy.

MODEL 336A (DISC.) – improved 36A, .30-30 Win., .35 Rem., or .32 Spl. cal., round breech bolt, 24 in. barrel with 2/3 mag. Mfg. 1948-1962, reintroduced 1973-1980.

	$625	$475	$400	$350	$315	$275	$230	

Add 20% for 1st Model mfg. 1948-52.
Add 10% for 1953-62 mfg.

The .35 Rem. cal. was added in 1950, .32 Spl. was disc. in 1962.

GRADING - PPGS™	100%	98%	95%	90%	80%	70%	60%	LAST MSR

* ***Model 336ADL*** – similar to Model 336A Rifle, except has deluxe checkered walnut stock and forearm, quick detachable swivels and 1 in. sling. Mfg. 1948-62.

	$750	$575	$550	$450	$375	$325	$275	

Add 20% for 2nd Model (1957-1962).
Add 20% for .32 Spl. or .35 Rem. cal.

The 336ADL 1st Model (mfg. 1948-56) did not have a raised comb or cheekpiece. The 2nd Model (mfg. 1957-62) is identifiable by a Monte Carlo buttstock with raised comb and cheekpiece. Wood was supplied by Bishop.

MODEL 336A/336AS (30AS) – .30-30 Win. cal. only, 20 in. barrel, 6 shot tube mag, walnut finished birch stock (pressed checkering became standard 1995, cut checkering became standard 1998), open sights (adj. rear sight became standard 1995), no frills version of the 336CS, 7 lbs. Mfg. 1983-2007.

	$575	$365	$335	$295	$265	$235	$200	*$423*

Add $50 for 4X scope (disc. 2006) or $41 for 3-9x32mm bore sighted scope.

Prior to 2000, this was designated the Model 30AS. The Model 30AS was formerly part of the Glenfield line. During 2001, this model's nomenclature was changed from 336AS to 336A.

MODEL 336W (30AW) – .30-30 Win. cal., 20 in. barrel, blued steel barrel band with swivel, gold trigger, satin blued finish, hammer block safety, 6 shot tubular mag., walnut finished cut checkered laminate pistol grip stock (laminate became standard 2012), rubber buttplate, padded nylon sling, adj. sights, with (new 2007) or without 3-9x32mm (disc. 2017, reintroduced 2019 only) bore sighted scope and mounts, 7 lbs. Disc. 2019.

	$440	$325	$300	$275	$250	$225	$200	*$518*

Add $53 for 4X scope (disc. 2006).
Add $100 for 3-9x32mm bore sighted scope and mounts.

This model was previously sold by Wal-Mart only. Model nomenclature was changed during 1998.

MODEL 336Y SPIKEHORN – similar to Model 336W, 5 shot tube mag, 16 1/2 in. barrel, shorter stock (12 1/2 in. LOP) with vent. recoil pad, 6 1/2 lbs. Mfg. 2003-2005.

	$475	$365	$335	$295	$265	$235	$200	*$566*

MODEL 336CC – similar to Model 336W, except has Mossy Oak Breakup camo stock and forearm, 7 lbs. Mfg. 2001-2004.

	$500	$375	$340	$300	$275	$250	$215	*$503*

MODEL 336BL – .30-30 Win. cal., lever action rifle, 18 1/2 in. blue barrel, 6 shot tube mag., adj. semi-buckhorn folding rear and ramp front with brass bead and wide-scan hood sights, cut checkered brown laminated hardwood stock with pistol grip, rubber buttpad, swivel studs, large loop lever, 7 1/2 lbs. New 2010.

MSR $728	$600	$525	$450	$375	$315	$260	$200	

MODEL 336C CARBINE (DISC.) – .30-30 Win., .32 Spl., or .35 Rem. cal., standard model carbine with 20 in. barrel. Mfg. 1969-83.

	$575	$450	$400	$350	$300	$265	$225	

Add 10% for .35 Rem. cal.

MODEL 336C LIMITED EDITION – .30-30 Win. or .35 Rem. cal., 20 in. barrel with blued finish, first of a multi-year series, Marlin horse & rider engraved on left side of receiver in 24Kt. gold, scroll work on right, "Limited Edition" stamped on barrel, gold plated trigger, B Grade walnut stock w/fleur de lis checkering. Limited mfg. 2014 only.

	$750	$650	$575	$510	$415	$350	$275	*$849*

MODEL 336SC SPORTING CARBINE – similar to Model 336C, with 20 in. barrel and 2/3 length mag. tube, raised comb buttstock (1957-63). Mfg. 1948-63.

	$700	$550	$475	$400	$350	$300	$250	

Add 10% for 1st Model mfg. 1948-52.

MODEL 336SC .219 ZIPPER – similar to Model 336SC, in .219 Zipper cal., 5 shot mag. 3,230 mfg. 1955-60.

	$875	$700	$600	$550	$500	$450	$400	

MODEL 336SD CARBINE (SPORTING DELUXE) – .30-30 Win., .32 Spl., or .35 Rem. cal., deluxe sporting carbine with 20 in. barrel, checkered stock and forearm, raised comb, no cheekpiece, quick detachable swivels and 1 in. sling. Mfg. 1954-62.

	$875	$700	$600	$425	$350	$300	$250	

GRADING - PPGS™	100%	98%	95%	90%	80%	70%	60%	LAST MSR

MODEL 336C (336CS) CARBINE – .30-30 Win. or .35 Rem. cal., 20 in. barrel, micro groove rifling (new 2019), blued steel barrel band with swivel stud, 6 shot tube mag., hammer block safety, gold-plated trigger, with (new 2020) or w/o scope, American black walnut or blond curly maple (new 2019) pistol grip stock (cut checkering became standard 1994), rubber rifle buttpad, hammer block safety, 7 lbs. Introduced 1984.

MSR $694 $575 $500 $425 $375 $315 $260 $200

Add $91 for scope (new 2020).

Add $259 for curly maple stock (new 2019).

During 2001, this model's nomenclature was changed from 336CS to 336C.

* ***Model 336C Compact*** – .30-30 Win. cal., 16 1/2 in. barrel w/Micro-Groove rifling, 5 shot tubular mag., ramp w/hooded front sight and semi-buckhorn rear adj. sight, hardwood pistol grip stock, blued finish, 6 1/2 lbs. New 2020.

MSR $694 $575 $500 $425 $375 $315 $260 $200

MODEL 336SS (336M) – .30-30 Win. cal. only, 20 in. barrel, 6 shot tube mag., stainless steel, adj. semi-buckhorn folding rear and ramp with brass bead and wide-scan hood front sights, cut checkered American black walnut pistol grip stock and forend with rubber buttpad and swivel studs, 38 1/2 in OAL, 7 lbs. New 2000.

MSR $842 $700 $600 $525 $450 $375 $325 $250

During 2001, this model's nomenclature was changed from 336M to 336SS.

MODEL 336XLR – .30-30 Win. or .35 Rem. (mfg. 2007-2011) cal., features stainless steel finish with 24 in. barrel, broached rifling, fluted bolt, 5 shot mag., black/grey laminate stock with deluxe recoil pad, adj. folding semi-buckhorn rear sight, hammer block safety, 7 1/2 lbs. New 2006.

MSR $1,027 $850 $725 $625 $550 $475 $385 $300

Add 30% for .35 Rem. cal.

This model was developed to take advantage of the Hornady LEVERevolution ammunition, which greatly improves range, energy, and accuracy.

MODEL 336Y – .30-30 Win. cal., 16 1/4 in. barrel, 5 shot tubular mag., gold plated trigger, adj. sights, checkered hardwood or laminate (2012-2015) PG stock and forearm, 12 1/2 in. LOP, rubber buttplate, blued steel barrel band with swivel, padded nylon sling, satin blued finish. Mfg. 2011-2019.

$520 $400 $350 $300 $250 $225 $200 *$564*

MODEL 336 COWBOY – .30-30 Win. (disc. 2001) or .38-55 WCF cal., 8 shot tube mag., squared off finger lever, 24 in. tapered octagon barrel with deep cut Ballard-type rifling (6 grooves), cut checkered (disc. 2001) straight grip walnut stock and forearm, adj. Marbles semi-buckhorn rear and carbine front sight, ser. no. is on left side of receiver, instead of on tang, 7 1/2 lbs. Mfg. 1999-2004.

$650 $575 $500 $425 $335 $295 $250 *$735*

Add 10% for .30-30 Win. cal.

MODEL 336ER (EXTRA RANGE) – .356 Win. cal., 5 shot tube mag., 20 in. barrel, walnut pistol grip stock, open sights, 7 lbs. 2,441 mfg. 1983-86.

$1,175 $1,025 $875 $800 $650 $525 $425 *$350*

Although advertised, this model was never manufactured in .307 cal.

MODEL 336DT CARBINE (DELUXE TEXAN) – .30-30 Win. or .35 Rem. cal., select stock version of 336T, longhorn and map of Texas carved on buttstock. Mfg. 1962-63.

$775 $675 $575 $510 $415 $350 $275

Add 10% for .35 Rem. cal.

MODEL 336 OCTAGON RIFLE – .30-30 Win. cal. only, with 22 in. octagon barrel, standard model. 2,414 mfg. 1973 only.

$575 $475 $385 $295 $250 $225 $200

MODEL 336LTS CARBINE – .30-30 Win. cal. only, 16 1/4 in. barrel, 5 shot tube mag., 6 1/2 lbs. 2,671 mfg. 1988-89 only.

$575 $475 $385 $295 $250 $225 $200 *$346*

MODEL 336 MAGNUM CARBINE – .44 Mag. cal., 20 in. standard carbine configuration, w/o saddle ring. 2,823 mfg. 1963-64 only.

$625 $475 $400 $350 $315 $275 $225

MODEL 336 MARAUDER CARBINE – .30-30 Win. or .35 Rem. cal., 16 1/4 in. barrel. 5,856 mfg. 1963-64.

$575 $475 $385 $295 $250 $225 $200

Add 10% for .35 cal.

Approx. 65% were mfg. in .30-30 Win. cal., and 35% were mfg. in .35 Rem. cal.

Be careful of re-barreled examples of this model.

GRADING - PPGS™ 100% 98% 95% 90% 80% 70% 60% LAST MSR

MODEL 336 PRESENTATION RIFLE – .30-30 Win. cal., one of the pair in the "Brace of 1,000," 22 in. octagon barrel, engraved receiver, sold with Model 39 Presentation. Mfg. 1970 only.

$1,000 $900 $775 $650 $525 $465 $350

Add a premium for serial numbers under 100.

MODEL 336RC CARBINE – .30-30 Win., .32 Spl., or .35 Rem. cal., standard model carbine. Mfg. 1948-68.

$625 $475 $400 $350 $315 $275 $225

Add 10% for 1st Model mfg. 1948-52.

MODEL 336T – .44 Mag. cal., with saddle ring, 13,895 mfg. 1965-67.

$750 $650 $575 $510 $415 $350 $275

MODEL 336T CARBINE "TEXAN" – .30-30 Win., .35 Rem., or .44 Mag. (1965-1967 only) cal., similar to 336C, with straight stock, 18 1/2 (1983 only) or 20 in. barrel, saddle ring (1965-1971 only). Mfg. 1954-83.

$750 $650 $565 $500 $450 $400 $325

MODEL 336TS TEXAN – similar to 336 CS, except is .30-30 Win. cal., 18 1/2 in. barrel, straight grip stock and squared finger lever, crossbolt safety. Mfg. 1984-87.

$700 $550 $475 $400 $350 $300 $250 *$314*

MODEL 336TDL TEXAN DELUXE – .30-30 Win. cal., light engraving with Marlin horse and rider inlaid in gold on receiver, 20 in. Micro-Groove barrel, 6 shot tube mag., hammer block safety, gold-plated trigger, Marble Arms semi-buckhorn adj. folding rear and ramp front with wide-scan hood sights, cut checkered B grade walnut straight grip stock, rubber buttpad, steel barrel band with swivel stud, 13 1/2 in. LOP, hammer block safety, blued finish, 38 1/2 in. OAL, 7 lbs. New 2018.

MSR $1,059 $900 $800 $750 $650 $550 $450 $350

MODEL 336 ZANE GREY CENTURY CARBINE – .30-30 Win. cal., similar to 336 Octagon, 22 in. octagon barrel, Zane Grey medallion inlaid in receiver, select walnut stock, pistol grip, brass buttplate and forearm cap. 7,871 mfg. in 1971.

$800 $700 $525 $425 $375 $325 $275

This model was mfg. to commemorate the 100th anniversary of the birth of Zane Grey.

MODEL 336 EXTRA FANCY – .30-30 Win. or .35 Rem. cal., action and trigger jobs, clocked screws, dehorned and deburred metal, accurized 20 in. barrel, steel barrel band with swivel stud, 6 shot tube mag., hammer block safety, ADJ. Skinner or Marble sights, hand fit and finished extra fancy grade American black walnut pistol grip stock, hand cut checkering, hand rubbed oil finish, rubber rifle buttpad, hammer block safety, function and range tested for accuracy, target included, high polish blued or color case hardened finish, 7 lbs.

MSR $3,495 $3,150 $2,750 $2,350 N/A N/A N/A N/A

Add $300 for color case hardened receiver.

Marlin Custom Shop mfg. available through Marlin Custom Dealers.

MODEL 336 DARK – .30-30 Win. cal., 16 1/4 in. barrel w/threaded muzzle, 5 shot mag. (full-length tubular mag.), XS lever rail w/ghost-ring rear sight, paracord-wrapped big loop lever and sling, Parkerized metal finish, black stock painted w/black webbing, 7.65 lbs. New 2019.

MSR $949 $825 $725 $625 $550 $450 $375 $300

CENTENNIAL MATCHED PAIR (MODELS 336 & 39) "BRACE OF 1,000" – Model 336 and Model 39 serial numbered the same, .30-30 Win. or .22 LR cal., engraved by Robert Kain and Winston Churchill, deluxe wood, inlaid medallions, cased. 1,000 mfg. sets in 1970.

$2,750 $2,500 $1,995 N/A N/A N/A N/A *$750*

MODEL 338MX – .338 Marlin Express cal., 22 in. barrel, 5 shot tube mag., American black walnut pistol grip stock, cut checkering, rubber rifle buttpad, blue finish, 7 1/2 lbs. Mfg. 2009-2011, reintroduced 2014-2015.

$625 $550 $450 $375 $315 $275 $250 *$683*

* ***Model 338MXLR*** – .338 Marlin Express cal., similar to Model 338MX, except has 24 in. stainless steel barrel and laminated stock, fluted bolt, 7 3/4 lbs. Mfg. 2009-2011, reintroduced 2014-2015.

$800 $700 $525 $425 $375 $325 $275 *$900*

MODEL 375 – similar to Model 336 CS, except is .375 Win. cal. 16,315 mfg. 1980-83.

$625 $475 $400 $350 $315 $275 $225

MODEL 444P OUTFITTER – .444 Marlin cal., 5 shot tube mag., 18 1/2 in. ported barrel with deep cut Ballard-type rifling (6 grooves), adj. semi-buckhorn folding rear sight with ramp front, checkered straight grip walnut stock and forearm, tapped for scope mount, approx. 7 lbs. Mfg. 1999-2002.

$550 $475 $400 $350 $315 $275 $230 *$631*

GRADING - PPGS™	100%	98%	95%	90%	80%	70%	60%	LAST MSR

MODEL 444 – .444 Marlin cal., 4 shot tube mag., 24 in. barrel, open sights, straight grip, Monte Carlo stock, recoil pad, swivels, sling, 1st Model. Mfg. 1965-71.

$500 $400 $335 $275 $250 $225 $200

MODEL 444 (CURRENT MFG) – .444 Marlin cal., 22 in. deep cut Ballard-type rifling, 6 grooves, side ejection, offset hammer spur, ramp front sight w/brass bead and wide-scanhood, adj. semi-buckhorn folding rear sight, American black walnut, checkered straight grip stock, hammer block safety, solid-top receiver tapped for scope mount, ventilated recoil pad, swivel studs, Marlin Shield finish, 7 lbs. New 2019.

MSR $815 $680 $575 $500 $450 $350 $300 $250

MODEL 444 DARK – .444 Marlin cal., 16 1/2 in. Ballard-style rifle, 4 shot mag., side ejection, XS sights lever rail w/ghost ring sight, black painted wood stock w/black webbing, hammer block safety, solid top receiver, polished steel, 8 lbs. New 2020.

Please contact the manufacturer directly for pricing and availability on this model.

MODEL 444 MARLIN 150TH ANNIVERSARY EDITION – .444 Marlin cal., 24 in. half-octagon/round barrel, 8 shot tubular mag., Skinner ladder sights, C-Grade American black walnut checkered stock w/pistol grip, hammer block safety, engraved receiver w/gold inlay, special serial no., comes in commemorative box, 7 lbs. New 2020.

MSR $1,899 $1,575 $1,375 $1,175 $1,075 $875 $700 $550

MODEL 444 (444SS) SPORTER – .444 Marlin cal., 22 in. barrel with deep cut Ballard-type rifling, blued finish metalwork, 5 shot tube mag., adj. semi-buckhorn folding rear sight and hooded front sight, American black walnut pistol grip stock with fluted comb (cut checkering became standard 1994), rubber rifle buttpad, 7-7 1/2 lbs. Mfg. 1984-2011, reintroduced 2014-2015.

$750 $650 $575 $510 $415 $350 $275 *$840*

During 2001, this model's nomenclature was changed from 444SS to 444.

* ***Model 444S*** – similar to Model 444SS, except has micro-groove rifling, barrel tapped for top-mounted scope, and a fluted comb stock. Mfg. 1972-1983.

$500 $400 $335 $275 $250 $225 $200

MODEL 444XLR – .444 Marlin cal., features stainless steel construction with 24 in. barrel, broached rifling, fluted bolt, 5 shot mag., black/grey laminate stock with deluxe recoil pad, adj. folding semi-buckhorn rear sight, hammer block safety, 7 1/2 lbs. Mfg. 2006-2010.

$750 $650 $575 $510 $415 $350 $275 *$861*

This model was developed to take advantage of the new Hornady LEVERevolution ammunition, which greatly improves range, energy, and accuracy.

MODEL 1894 (1969-1984 MFG.) – .44 Spl. or .44 Mag. cal., 20 in. bbl., 10 shot tube mag., adj. sights, straight grip walnut stock and forearm, 6 lbs. Mfg. 1969-84.

$625 $575 $500 $450 $400 $350 $295

MODEL 1894C CARBINE (1979-1984 MFG.) – .357 Mag. cal., 18 1/2 in. barrel, w/o hammer block safety, 6 lbs. Mfg. 1979-84.

$800 $700 $600 $425 $350 $300 $250

MODEL 1894 SPORTER – .44 Mag. cal. only, 6 shot half mag. tube, crescent shaped hard rubber buttplate, 1,398 mfg. 1973 only.

$800 $700 $600 $425 $350 $300 $250

MODEL 1894 (1894S) – .41 Mag. (disc. 1991), .44 Mag./.44 Spl., or .45 LC (mfg. 1988-91, reintroduced 2005 only) cal., Model 1894 with addition of crossbolt ("S" suffix) and hammer block safety, 20 in. barrel, 10 shot tube mag., adj. sights, finely checkered American black walnut straight grip stock and forearm (cut checkering became standard 1994), 6 lbs. Disc. 2002, reintroduced 2005.

MSR $835 $695 $600 $525 $425 $375 $335 $285

During 2001, this model's nomenclature was changed from 1894S to 1894.

MODEL 1894C SERIES CARBINE (1894CS) – .357 Mag./.38 Spl. cal., copy of original Model 1894, 9 shot mag., 18 1/2 in. round barrel, open sights (hooded front became standard 1999), straight grip stock (cut checkering became standard 1994), squared finger lever, 6 lbs. Mfg. 1984-2015.

$850 $700 $525 $425 $375 $325 $275 *$730*

During 2001, this model's nomenclature was changed from 1894CS to 1894C.

* ***Model 1894CP Carbine*** – similar to Model 1894C, except has 16 1/4 in. ported round barrel, 8 shot mag., approx. 5 3/4 lbs. Mfg. 2001-2002.

$1,175 $1,025 $875 $800 $650 $525 $425 *$566*

GRADING - PPGS™	100%	98%	95%	90%	80%	70%	60%	LAST MSR

* ***Model 1894CL Carbine*** – .32-20 Win. cal., 6 shot tube mag., 22 in. barrel with button rifling and barrel band, Marble sights, American walnut stock and forearm with cut checkering, 6 lbs. New 2005-2007.

	$695	$575	$525	$455	$385	$325	$250	*$755*

MODEL 1894C (CURRENT MFG.) – .357 Mag./.38 Spl. cal., 18 1/2 in. round barrel, 9 shot full-length tube mag., adj. semi-buckhorn folding rear and ramp front sight with brass bead and wide-scan hood, tapped for mount, cut checkered American black walnut straight grip stock, rubber buttpad, swivel studs, 13 3/8 in. LOP, squared finger lever, blue finish, 38 1/2 in. OAL, 6 lbs. New 2018.

MSR $836	$695	$600	$525	$425	$375	$335	$285	

MODEL 1894P CARBINE – .44 Mag./.44 Spl. cal., 16 1/4 in. ported barrel with deep-cut Ballard type 6 groove rifling, 8 shot tube mag., checkered straight grip walnut stock with vent. recoil pad, 5 3/4 lbs. Mfg. 2000-2002.

	$675	$595	$550	$460	$375	$300	$235	*$566*

* ***Model 1894S Carbine Limited*** – .44 Mag./.44 Spl. cal., features 16 1/4 in. barrel with "The Marlin Limited" roll stamped on barrel, approx. 1,500 mfg. 1996 only.

	$750	$650	$575	$510	$415	$350	$275	

MODEL 1894FG – .41 Mag. cal., similar to Model 1894, except has pistol grip stock with cut checkering and 10 shot mag., 6 1/2 lbs. Mfg. 2003-2007.

	$1,150	$1,000	$875	$750	$625	$495	$375	*$588*

MODEL 1894PG – .44 Mag. cal., similar to Model 1894FG. Mfg. 2003-2004.

	$675	$595	$550	$450	$395	$335	$285	*$622*

MODEL 1894SBL – .357 Mag./.38 Spl. or .44 Mag./.44 Spl. cal., stainless steel, 16 1/4 in. barrel, gray/black laminate stock and forearm, big loop lever, XS Ghost ring sights, includes scope mount. Limited mfg. 2011 only.

	$1,195	$1,075	$895	$800	$650	$525	$410	*$1,062*

MODEL 1894SBL (CURRENT MFG.) – .44 Mag./.44 Spl. cal., 16 1/2 in. barrel, 6 (disc. 2019) or 8 (new 2020) shot full-length tube mag., big loop lever, side ejection, hammer block safety, adj. XS receiver mounted ghost ring sights, checkered gray/black laminate stock and forearm, rubber buttpad, 13 3/8 in. LOP, swivel studs, stainless steel and nickel finish, 35 in. OAL, 6 1/2 lbs. New 2018.

MSR $1,215	$1,000	$875	$725	$650	$525	$450	$350	

MODEL 1894CSBL – .357 Mag./.38 Spl. cal., 16 1/2 in. barrel, 6 shot full-length tube mag., big loop lever, side ejection, hammer block safety, adj. XS receiver mounted ghost ring sights, checkered gray/black laminate stock and forearm, rubber buttpad, 13 3/8 in. LOP, swivel studs, stainless steel and nickel finish, 35 in. OAL, 6 1/2 lbs. New 2018.

MSR $1,215	$1,000	$875	$725	$650	$525	$450	$350	

MODEL 1894CST – .357 Mag./.38 Spl. cal., 16 1/2 in. threaded barrel, 6 shot full-length tube mag., big loop lever, side ejection, hammer block safety, adj. XS receiver mounted Ghost ring sights, black painted hardwood stock and forearm, rubber buttpad, 13 3/8 in. LOP, swivel studs, matte stainless steel finish, 35 in. OAL, 6 1/2 lbs. New 2018.

MSR $1,223	$1,025	$900	$725	$650	$525	$450	$350	

MODEL 1894SS/1894CSS – .357 Mag./.38 Spl. (new 2010), or .44 Mag./.44 Spl. cal., stainless steel, 20 in. barrel, 10 shot tube mag., straight grip, checkered black walnut stock and forearm, offset hammer spur, approx. 6 lbs. Mfg. 2002-2011.

	$1,175	$1,000	$875	$750	$625	$495	$375	*$829*

Add 30% for .357 Mag./.38 Spl. cal.

MODEL 1894 COWBOY (COWBOY II) – .32 H&R Mag. (mfg. mid-2004-2006), .357 Mag. (mfg. 1997-disc.), .44-40 WCF (mfg. 1997-99), .44 Mag. (mfg. 1997-disc.), or .45 LC cal., 10 shot tube mag., incorporates "cowboy action shooting" features, straight grip stock w/o or with checkering (disc. 2001), adj. Marbles-type rear sight, blued finish, 20 (new 2003, n/a in .45 LC cal.) or 24 (disc. 2009) in. tapered octagon barrel, 7 1/2 lbs. Mfg. 1996-2015.

	$975	$750	$600	$500	$425	$375	$350	*$1,041*

The Model 1894 Cowboy II refers to the three new cals. introduced in 1997. This model in .32 H&R Mag. cal. (new 2004) loads through a port in the front of the mag. tube, not a receiver port like the other cals.

* ***Model 1894 Cowboy Competition*** – .38 Spl. or .45 LC (new 2003) cal., 10 shot tube mag., 20 in. tapered octagon barrel with deep cut Ballard type rifling, hammer block safety, Marbles sights, case colored receiver, lever, and bolt, "factory tuned" to meet the demands of competitive shooters. 6 1/2 lbs. Mfg. 2002-2005.

	$1,025	$895	$775	$695	$535	$440	$340	*$986*

GRADING - PPGS™	100%	98%	95%	90%	80%	70%	60%	LAST MSR

MODEL 1894CB COWBOY – .38 Spl./357 Mag., (new 2018) .44 Mag. or .45 LC cal., 20 in. tapered octagon barrel with deep cut Ballard style rifling, 10 shot tube mag., adj. Marbles semi-buckhorn rear and blade front sights, American black walnut straight grip stock, 13 3/8 in. LOP, blued finish, 38 1/2 in. OAL, 6 1/2 lbs. New 2017.

MSR $1,158	$960	$775	$675	$600	$475	$375	$300	

Add $65 for .44 Mag.

MODEL 1894CL – .218 Bee (new 1990), .25-20 WCF or .32-20 WCF cal., 6 shot (two-thirds length) tube mag., 22 in. barrel, 6 1/4 lbs. Mfg. 1988-94.

	$695	$575	$525	$455	$385	$325	$250	*$502*

Add 20% for .218 Bee cal.

MODEL 1894 CENTURY LIMITED – .44-40 WCF cal., limited edition commemorative mfg. to celebrate the Model 1894's 100th Anniversary, 24 in. tapered octagon barrel with full 12 shot tube mag., Giovanelli engraved receiver, bolt, and lever, receiver is case colored using traditional methods, checkered straight grip stock and forearm, crescent buttplate, 6 1/2 lbs. 2,500 mfg. 1994 only.

	$1,500	$1,295	$1,100	N/A	N/A	N/A	N/A	*$1,088*

MODEL 1894 CENTURY LIMITED (EMPLOYEE SPECIAL EDITION) – employee special edition featuring gold inlaid Marlin horse and rider logo. 100 mfg. 1994-95 in ser. no. range 1-100.

	$4,150	$3,750	$3,250	N/A	N/A	N/A	N/A	

MODEL 1894C DARK – .357 Mag./.38 Spl. cal., 18 1/2 in. round barrel, 8 shot full-length tube mag., side ejection, adj. semi-buckhorn folding rear and ramp front sight with brass bead and wide-scan hood, tapped for mount, black painted wood straight grip stock, squared finger lever, deep blue finish, 38 1/2 in. OAL, 6 1/2 lbs. New 2020.

Please contact the manufacturer directly for pricing and availability on this model.

MODEL 1894 OCTAGON – similar to 1894 Carbine, with octagon barrel. Mfg. 1973.

	$825	$700	$525	$400	$325	$275	$225	

MODEL 1894 LIMITED EDITION – .45 LC cal., 20 in. barrel, 10 shot tubular mag., side ejection, gold trigger, adj. semi-buckhorn rear and brass bead ramp front sights, B Grade black walnut stock, hammer block safety, engraved receiver with 24K gold inlay, polished blue finish, 6 1/2 lbs. Limited mfg. of 1,500 during 2017.

	$1,175	$1,000	$875	$750	$625	$495	$375	*$1,349*

MODEL 1894 FANCY – .44 Rem. Mag./.44 Spl. cal., lever action rifle, action and trigger jobs, clocked screws, dehorned and deburred metal, accurized 20 in. barrel, steel barrel band with swivel stud, 10 shot tube mag., hammer block safety, ADJ. Skinner or Marble sights, hand fit and finished fancy grade American black walnut pistol grip stock, hand cut checkering, hand rubbed oil finish, rubber rifle buttpad, hammer block safety, function and range tested for accuracy, target included, high polish blued finish, 6 1/2 lbs.

MSR $3,795	$3,350	$2,950	$2,500	N/A	N/A	N/A	N/A	

Marlin Custom Shop mfg. available through Marlin Custom Dealers.

MODEL 1895 – .45-70 Govt. cal., 4 shot tube mag., 22 in. barrel, open sights, straight grip stock with curved buttplate, forearm cap, sling and swivels. Mfg. 1972-1984.

	$750	$650	$575	$510	$415	$350	$275	

Add 10% for guns mfg. 1972-1978.

Add 10% for pre-micro-groove.

Early new Model 1895 Marlins had cut rifling (8 grooves) suitable for cast bullets, while later mfg. was switched to Marlin's "Micro Groove" shallow rifling (12 grooves). Changes were also made from a straight stock to a pistol grip stock and from a traditional receiver to one with the newer hammer- block, push-button safety. Early guns with a straight grip stock, traditional receiver, and cut rifling command premiums over later mfg. Deep cut rifling (ser. no. to approx. 10,000) occurred during the first year of production only. More recently mfg. models have pistol grip, Micro Groove rifling, and hammer-block safety - these newer guns are the least desirable from a collector's standpoint.

* ***Model 1895S*** – similar to Model 1895, except has pistol grip stock and straight buttpad.

	$550	$475	$400	$350	$315	$275	$230	

MODEL 1895 (1895SS) – .45-70 Govt. cal., 22 in. barrel with micro groove (12 grooves) or deep cut Ballard-type (6 grooves new 1997) rifling, 4 shot 2/3 tube mag., adj. semi-buckhorn folding rear, ramp front with brass bead and wide-scan hood sights, tapped for scope mount, American black walnut pistol

GRADING - PPGS™	100%	98%	95%	90%	80%	70%	60%	LAST MSR

grip stock and forend with cut checkering, cut checkering became standard 1994, rubber rifle buttpad, MarShield finish, swivel studs 13 3/8 in. LOP, hammer block safety, deeply blued metal surfaces, 40 1/2 in. OAL, 7 lbs. New 1983.

MSR $806	$670	$575	$500	$425	$350	$275	$225	

During 2001, this model's nomenclature was changed from 1895SS to 1895. In 1997 Marlin released their new deep cut Ballard-type rifling with 6 grooves.

* ***Model 1895SS Cody Stampede 75th Anniversary*** – .45-70 cal., includes semi-fancy checkered walnut stock with medallion, serial numbered CS-001-CS-200, 200 mfg. 1994 only.

	$950	$795	$675	N/A	N/A	N/A	N/A	*$695*

* ***Model 1895 LTD V*** – .45-70 Gov't. cal., 24 in. half round/half octagon barrel, full-length 8 shot mag. tube, checkered walnut stock and forearm. Mfg. 2001.

	$900	$800	$700	$600	$495	$375	$295	

MODEL 1895 CENTURY LIMITED (CLTD) – .45-70 cal., commemorates Marlin's 125th Anniversary, engraving includes grizzly bear on left side, Marlin horse and rider logo on right, 24 in. half-round half-octagonal barrel, crescent buttplate, satin finished receiver, checkered walnut stock and forearm. Approx. 2,500 mfg. 1995 only.

	$1,550	$1,350	$1,150	N/A	N/A	N/A	N/A	*$1,104*

A Marlin Collector's Association Edition was also mfg. and was the same as the Model 1895 Century Limited.

* ***Model 1895 Century Limited (CLTD) Employee Edition*** – features 3 elk on left side and gold inlaid Marlin horse and rider logo on right. 100 mfg. 1995-96 in ser. no. range 1-100.

	$3,650	$3,150	$2,595	N/A	N/A	N/A	N/A	

MODEL 1895CB COWBOY – .45-70 Govt. cal., 26 in. tapered octagon barrel and 9 shot tube mag., uncheckered straight grip walnut stock and forearm, Marble front and rear (adj.) sights, 8 lbs. Mfg. 2001-2011, reintroduced 2014.

MSR $972	$810	$675	$575	$475	$400	$325	$250	

MODEL 1895CBA – .45-70 Govt. cal., 18 1/2 in. tapered octagon barrel, deep cut Ballard type rifling, 6 shot, full-length tube mag., Marbles semi-buckhorn rear and brass bead front sights, cut checkered American black walnut straight grip stock, swivel studs, 13 3/8 in. LOP, polished blued finish, 37 in. OAL, 7 lbs. Mfg. 2015-2016, reintroduced 2018.

MSR $972	$810	$675	$575	$475	$400	$325	$250	

MODEL 1895G GUIDE GUN – .45-70 Govt. cal., 18 1/2 in. ported barrel with Ballard-style cut rifling, cut checkered American black walnut straight grip stock and forearm, vent. recoil pad, MarShield finish, swivel studs, adj. folding buckhorn rear sight, 4 shot tube mag., porting was discontinued in 2002, hammer block safety, 7 lbs. 2,500 to be mfg. beginning 1998.

MSR $811	$675	$575	$500	$425	$350	$275	$225	

* ***Model 1895GBL*** – .45-70 Govt. cal., 18 1/2 in. barrel with Ballard-type rifling, 6 shot full-length tubular mag., large loop lever, hammer block safety,ramp front sight w/brass bead and wide scan hood, adj. semi-buckhorn folding rear sight, American pistol grip two-tone brown laminate stock with cut checkering and vent. recoil pad, Mar-Shield finish, swivel studs, 7 lbs. New 2010.

MSR $850	$700	$575	$500	$425	$350	$275	$225	

* ***Model 1895GS Guide Gun*** – .45-70 Govt. cal., similar to Model 1895G, except is stainless steel. New 2001.

MSR $969	$800	$650	$525	$450	$375	$300	$250	

MODEL 1895GSBL – .45-70 Govt. cal., 18 1/2 in. barrel, stainless steel with FNC plating, 6 shot tube mag., big loop lever, adj. Williams FireSights, green laminate pistol grip stock with black webbing, deluxe recoil pad, swivel studs, 8 lbs. Mfg. 2015-2019.

	$1,025	$900	$775	$675	$575	$495	$425	*$1,232*

MODEL 1895 LIMITED EDITION – .45-70 Govt. cal., 24 in. tapered octagon barrel with deep cut Ballard-type rifling, Marbles sights, 7 shot tube mag., American walnut straight grip stock, engraved with gold inlay, 8 lbs. Limited mfg. 2015 only.

	$1,150	$1,000	$865	N/A	N/A	N/A	N/A	*$1,349*

MODEL 1895M – .450 Marlin Mag. cal. (belted), 4 shot tube mag., 18 1/2 in. ported barrel, checkered straight grip walnut stock and forearm, vent. recoil pad, adj. folding buckhorn rear sight, 7 lbs. Mfg. 2000-2010.

	$650	$575	$525	$425	$375	$335	$285	*$715*

GRADING - PPGS™	100%	98%	95%	90%	80%	70%	60%	LAST MSR

MODEL 1895MR – similar to Model 1895M, except has 22 in. barrel, 7 1/2 lbs. Mfg. 2003-2004.

	$675	$595	$550	$425	$375	$335	$285	*$761*

MODEL 1895MXLR – .450 Marlin cal., features stainless steel construction with 24 in. barrel, broached rifling, fluted bolt, 4 shot mag., black/grey laminate stock with deluxe recoil pad, adj. folding semi-buckhorn rear sight, hammer block safety, 7 1/2 lbs. Mfg. 2006-2009.

	$675	$595	$550	$425	$375	$335	$285	*$806*

This model was developed to take advantage of the Hornady LEVERevolution ammunition, which greatly improves range, energy, and accuracy.

MODEL 1895RL – .480 Ruger/.475 Linebaugh cal., 6 (.480 Ruger) or 5 (.475 Linebaugh) shot tube mag., 18 1/2 in. barrel, walnut pistol grip stock, otherwise similar to Model 1895, 7 lbs. Limited mfg. 2004 only.

	$675	$595	$550	$425	$375	$335	$285	*$695*

MODEL 1895SBL – .45-70 Govt. cal., 18 1/2 in. stainless steel barrel with deep cut Ballard-type rifling, XS Ghost ring sights with HiViz front post, Scout scope mount, 6 shot full-length tube mag., big loop finger lever, side ejection, stainless steel metal components, Black/grey laminated hardwood pistol grip stock with fluted comb, cut checkering, deluxe recoil pad, nickel-plated swivel studs, Picatinny rail, 8 lbs. New 2009.

MSR $1,239	$1,030	$875	$725	$650	$525	$450	$350	

MODEL 1895TSBL TRAPPER – .45-70 Govt. cal., 16 1/2 in. stainless steel barrel with deep cut Ballard type rifling, 5 shot full-length tube mag., big loop finger lever, side ejection, XS Ghost ring sights with XS front post, black painted PG stock with fluted comb, black webbing, rubber recoil pad, swivel studs, 12 3/4 in. LOP, hammer block safety, 35 in. OAL, 7-8 lbs. New 2018.

MSR $1,215	$1,000	$875	$725	$650	$525	$450	$350	

MODEL 1895XLR – .45-70 Govt. cal., features stainless steel construction with 24 in. barrel, broached rifling, fluted bolt, 4 shot mag., black/grey laminate stock with deluxe recoil pad, adj. folding semi-buckhorn rear sight, hammer block safety, 7 1/2 lbs. Mfg. 2006-2011.

	$800	$700	$600	$550	$440	$360	$275	*$848*

This model was developed to take advantage of the Hornady LEVERevolution ammunition, which greatly improves range, energy, and accuracy.

MODEL 1895 MODERN HUNTER – .45-70 Govt. cal., Wild West Guns style big loop lever, action job and happy trigger, dehorned and deburred metal, accurized, 18 in. barrel, deep cut Ballard style rifling, 6 shot, full-length tube mag., stainless steel with Cerakote (choice of color) finish, adj. XS Ghost Ring Sights and scout scope mount, laminate painted stock with webbing (choice of color), rubber rifle buttpad, swivel studs, hammer block safety, function and range tested for accuracy, target included, 7 1/2 lbs.

MSR $1,995	$1,795	$1,575	$1,345	N/A	N/A	N/A	N/A	

Marlin Custom Shop mfg. available through Marlin Custom Dealers.

MODEL 1895 FANCY – .45-70 Govt. cal., action and trigger jobs, clocked screws, dehorned and deburred metal, accurized, 22 in. barrel, deep cut Ballard style rifling, 4 shot 2/3 tube mag., adj. Skinner or Marble sights, hand fit and finished fancy grade American black walnut pistol grip stock, hand cut checkering, hand rubbed oil finish, rubber rifle buttpad, swivel studs, hammer block safety, function and range tested for accuracy, target included, high polish blued finish, 7 1/2 lbs.

MSR $3,795	$3,350	$2,950	$2,500	N/A	N/A	N/A	N/A	

Marlin Custom Shop mfg. available through Marlin Custom Dealers.

MODEL 1895 DARK – .45-70 Govt. cal., 16 1/4 in. barrel w/threaded muzzle, 5 shot mag. (full-length tubular mag.), XS lever rail w/ghost-ring rear sight, paracord-wrapped big loop lever and sling, Parkerized metal finish, black stock painted w/black webbing, 7.65 lbs. New 2019.

MSR $949	$800	$650	$525	$450	$375	$300	$250	

MODEL 1936 – .30-30 Win. or .32 HPS (High Power Special) cal., similar to Model 36 1st variation, 6 shot, 20 or 24 in. barrel, tubular mag., open sights, pistol grip stock, barrel band, leaf mainspring, thinner "perch belly" forearm, case colored receiver, upper tang, buttstock has a fluted comb and flat hard rubber buttplate. Mfg. 1936-37.

	$900	$800	$700	$600	$495	$375	$295	

Add 10% for vivid case colors with strong greens, reds, and yellows.
Add 10% for rifles and sporting carbines.

Rifles have "A" suffix, sporting carbine has "SC" suffix, and regular and carbine has "RC" suffix.

The Model 1936 has an upper tang inscription "Model 1936" and a case colored receiver. Also, the Model 1936 did not have a letter prefix in the ser. no.

GRADING - PPGS™	100%	98%	95%	90%	80%	70%	60%	LAST MSR

Rifles: Centerfire, Miscellaneous

All Marlin firearms manufactured before Jan. 2008 had "JM" on the barrel near the receiver.

MODEL 9 CAMP CARBINE SEMI-AUTO – 9mm Para. cal. only, 16 1/2 in. barrel, 12 or 20 shot mag. (disc. 1989), 4 shot mag. became standard in 1990, sand blasted steel receiver, open sights, last shot automatic hold-open, 6 3/4 lbs. Mfg. 1985-99.

$675 $595 $495 $450 $350 $295 $225 *$443*

Add 10% for nickel plating (mfg. 1991-94, Model 9N).

A new high visibility orange front sight post with cutaway hood was added in 1989.

MODEL 27 SLIDE ACTION – .25-20 WCF, or .32-20 WCF cal., 2/3 tube mag., 7 shot, 24 in. octagon barrel, open sight, plain straight grip stock. Mfg. 1910-11.

$1,950 $1,700 $1,465 $1,325 $1,075 $875 $700

Subtract 15% for .25RF cal.

MODEL 27S SLIDE ACTION – .25RF, .25-20 WCF, or .32-20 WCF cal., similar to Model 27, except has safety button on right side of receiver, round or octagonal barrel added in 1913.

$1,675 $1,465 $1,250 $1,140 $925 $750 $600

MODEL 45 CARBINE SEMI-AUTO – .45 ACP cal. only, 7 shot mag., sandblasted steel receiver, 16 1/2 in. barrel, last shot hold open device, pressed checkering, adj. rear sight, 6 3/4 lbs. Mfg. 1986-99.

$725 $650 $575 $525 $395 $325 $250 *$443*

A new high visibility orange front sight post with cutaway hood was added in 1989.

RIFLES: RIMFIRE

From 1930 to date, Marlin has made a number of .22 cal. rimfire rifles, bolt action single shots, bolt action repeaters and auto loaders. These have normally been good quality, inexpensive weapons. In 1960, the name Glenfield was also used in connection with these guns. We will list these models for reference purposes with price ranges appearing at the end of each listing.

The models listed are in numerical sequence first, followed by alphabetical sequence, then end with promotional models for easy reference.

Machine cut checkering became standard on many Marlins beginning 1995. Safety locks have been shipped with every new rifle/shotgun beginning 1999. In 2004, the T-900 fire control system became standard on all Marlin 900 Series rifles, except the Papoose and the Model 717M2. This improved trigger has a pull of 3-5 lbs., features a new safety mechanism with positive click positions for fire and safe, and a crisp let-off.

In 2007, Marlin changed its bolt action rimfire synthetic stocks to a new classic design featuring a fluted comb, deep molded checkering, and sling swivel studs.

Rifles: Rimfire, Bolt Action

All Marlin firearms manufactured before Jan. 2008 had "JM" on the barrel near the receiver.

MODEL 15YN "LITTLE BUCKAROO" SINGLE SHOT – .22 S, L, or LR cal., single shot, 16 1/4 in. barrel, youth dimensions with 12 LOP, adj. rear sight, grooved receiver, pressed checkering, 4 1/4 lbs. Disc. 2003.

$175 $140 $105 $80 $75 $70 $65 *$209*

* ***Model 15YS "Little Buckaroo" Single Shot Stainless Steel*** – similar to Model 15YN, except is stainless steel and has Fire Sights. Mfg. 2002-2003.

$215 $175 $135 $85 $75 $70 $65 *$233*

MODEL 17V – .17 HMR cal., 7 shot detachable mag., 22 in. heavy barrel, walnut finished checkered hardwood Monte Carlo stock and forend, red cocking indicator, grooved receiver, includes scope mounts, 6 lbs. Mfg. 2002-2003.

$250 $200 $180 $170 $160 $145 $130 *$269*

* ***Model 17VS*** – similar to Model 17V, except has bead blasted stainless steel barrel and receiver, laminated black/grey hardwood Monte Carlo stock, 7 lbs. Mfg. 2002-2004.

$350 $275 $225 $175 $140 $125 $105 *$402*

MODEL 25MB – .22 WMR cal., 16 1/4 in. micro-groove barrel, 7 shot mag., hardwood stock, takedown action, 6 lbs. Mfg. 1987-88 only.

$145 $115 $95 $85 $75 $70 $65 *$173*

This model included both a scope and gun case.

MODEL 25MG GARDEN GUN – please refer to the Marlin bolt action shotgun section for information on this model.

GRADING - PPGS™	100%	98%	95%	90%	80%	70%	60%	LAST MSR

MODEL 25MN – .22 WMR cal., 7 shot mag., 22 in. barrel, choice of walnut finished hardwood or Mossy Oak Breakup camo (new 2001) stock (pressed checkering became standard 1994), grooved receiver, adj. rear sight (new 1995), 6 lbs. Mfg. 1989-2003.

$185	$140	$105	$85	$75	$70	$65	*$241*

Add $6 for 4X scope (disc. 2000).
Add $37 for Mossy Oak Breakup camo stock.

MODEL 25N – .22 LR cal., 7 shot mag., 22 in. barrel, press checkered Monte Carlo stock, 5 1/2 lbs. Disc. 2003.

$155	$135	$110	$80	$75	$70	$65	*$212*

Add $8 for 4X scope.

* ***Model 25NC*** – similar to Model 25N, except has Mossy Oak Breakup camo stock. Disc. 2003.

$190	$145	$105	$85	$75	$70	$65	*$248*

MODEL 81TS – .22 S, L, or LR cal., 22 in. barrel with 17-25 shot tube mag., black synthetic stock with molded checkering, adj. rear sight, 6 lbs. Disc. 2003.

$165	$130	$100	$80	$75	$65	$60	*$213*

MODEL 83TS – .22 WMR cal., 22 in. barrel, 12 shot mag., otherwise similar to Model 81TS, 6 lbs. Disc. 2003.

$195	$150	$125	$95	$85	$75	$70	*$259*

MODELS 780, 781, 782, and 783 – .22 LR or .22 WMR (Models 782 and 783) cal., tube or mag., 22 in. barrel. Disc. 1988.

$110	$85	$75	$70	$65	$55	$50	*$162*

Add $17-$25 for Models 782 and 783.

MODELS 880/881 – .22 LR or .22 WMR cal., replacement for Models 780, 781, Model 880 is .22 LR with 7 shot detachable mag. and 22 in. barrel, (cut checkering became standard 1994), Model 881 is .22 LR with 17 shot tube mag. and 22 in. barrel, 6 lbs. Mfg. 1989-97.

$185	$145	$100	$85	$75	$70	$65	*$251*

Add $10 for Model 881.

This model was also available in a Biathlon configuration - approx. 100 were mfg.

* ***Model 880SS*** – similar to Model 880, except is stainless steel, black fiberglass synthetic stock, approx. 6 lbs. Mfg. 1994-2003.

$240	$175	$115	$90	$75	$60	$40	*$316*

* ***Model 880SQ (Squirrel Rifle)*** – similar to Model 880, except has black fiberglass filled synthetic stock with checkering and heavy 22 in. barrel, without sights and grooved receiver, matte finish, 7 lbs. Mfg. 1996-2003.

$245	$190	$135	$100	$80	$70	$65	*$330*

MODELS 882/883 – .22 WMR cal., 7 shot detachable (Model 882) or 12 shot tube mag. (Model 883), 22 in. barrel, checkered (cut checkering became standard 1994), black walnut Monte Carlo stock with Mar-Shield finish, adj. semi-buckhorn rear sight and hooded front, thumb safety, 6 lbs. Mfg. 1989-2003.

$240	$185	$130	$95	$85	$75	$70	*$324*

Add $13 for Model 883.
Add $35 for nickel finish on Model 883N (disc. 1993).

The Models 882 and 883 are the replacements for Models 782 and 783.

* ***Model 882SS*** – .22 WMR cal., similar to Model 882, except is stainless steel and stock is black synthetic with molded-in checkering, fire sights (red fiber optic inserts with cutaway hood) became standard 1998, approx. 6 lbs. Mfg. 1995-2003.

$250	$190	$130	$100	$85	$70	$65	*$345*

* ***Model 882SSV*** – .22 WMR cal., features 22 in. bead blasted stainless barrel and receiver with black fiberglass reinforced synthetic stock, 7 shot mag., grooved receiver, w/o sights, ring mounts included, 7 lbs. Mfg. 1997-2003.

$245	$185	$125	$100	$85	$70	$65	*$338*

* ***Model 882L*** – similar to Model 882, except has two-tone brown laminated hardwood stock, 6 1/4 lbs. Mfg. 1992-2003.

$250	$200	$140	$100	$85	$75	$70	*$342*

* ***Model 883SS*** – .22 WMR cal., 12 shot tube mag., similar to Model 883, except barrel is stainless steel and stock is laminated two-tone brown birch with Monte Carlo cheekpiece. Mfg. 1993-2003.

$265	$205	$145	$115	$100	$85	$75	*$358*

GRADING - PPGS™	100%	98%	95%	90%	80%	70%	60%	LAST MSR

MODEL 915Y "LITTLE BUCKAROO" SINGLE SHOT – .22 S, L, or LR cal., 16 1/4 in. barrel, features T-900 fire control system, cocks on opening, youth dimensions, adj. rear sight, thumb safety, grooved receiver, walnut finished hardwood stock, 4 1/4 lbs. Mfg. 2004-2010.

	$175	$145	$115	$80	$75	$70	$65	*$219*

Add $26 for front fiber optic fire sight (Model 915YS, new 2004).

MODEL 917 – .17 HMR cal., black synthetic stock, 4 and 7 shot mags. supplied standard beginning 2007, T-900 fire control system, 22 in. barrel with sights, thumb safety, cocking indicator, adj. rear sight, 6 lbs. Mfg. 2006-2010.

	$200	$170	$150	$120	$110	$100	$90	*$253*

Add $49 for stainless steel finish (Model 917S, new 2007).

MODEL 917M2 – .17 Mach 2 cal., otherwise similar to Model 917V, 6 lbs. Mfg. 2005-2007.

	$185	$160	$145	$130	$100	$90	$80	*$232*

* ***Model 917M2S*** – similar to Model 917M2, except has laminated grey/black hardwood Monte Carlo stock and stainless steel barrel, 7 lbs. Mfg. 2005-2006.

	$300	$225	$175	$150	$125	$110	$100	*$410*

MODEL 917V SERIES – .17 HMR cal., 4 and 7 shot detachable mags. supplied standard beginning 2007, 22 in. heavy barrel, features T-900 fire control system, walnut finished checkered hardwood Monte Carlo stock, thumb safety, no sights, scope base included, 6 lbs. Mfg. 2004-2010.

	$225	$190	$160	$140	$120	$100	$90	*$279*

Add $41 for 3-9x32mm bore sighted scope (new 2007).

* ***Model 917VR*** – similar to Model 917, except has 22 in. heavy barrel, 7 lbs. Mfg. 2006-2010.

	$210	$175	$155	$135	$115	$100	$90	*$266*

* ***Model 917VS*** – similar to Model 917V, except has laminated grey/black hardwood Monte Carlo or synthetic carbon fiber pattern (mfg. 2007-2008) stock and stainless steel barrel. Mfg. 2004-2010.

	$315	$265	$210	$165	$135	$110	$100	*$396*

Add $24 for fluted barrel (Model 917VSF, new 2005).
Subtract $17 for synthetic stock (mfg. 2007-2008).

* ***Model 917VT*** – .17 HMR cal., features 22 in. heavy blue bull barrel, 4 or 7 shot mag., two-tone brown laminate stock with thumbhole pistol grip, swivel studs, rubber buttpad, no sights, drilled and tapped, 7 lbs. Mfg. 2008-2010.

	$325	$265	$200	$165	$135	$120	$110	*$402*

* ***Model 917VST*** – .17 HMR cal., similar to Model 917VT, except has stainless steel barrel, grey laminated thumbhole stock. Mfg. 2008-2010.

	$365	$275	$215	$175	$150	$125	$110	*$451*

MODEL 925 SERIES – .22 LR cal., 7 shot detachable mag., features T-900 fire control system, 22 in. barrel, thumb safety, adj. rear sight, grooved receiver, walnut finished hardwood stock with swivel studs, 5 1/2 lbs. Mfg. 2004-2010.

	$175	$140	$115	$80	$75	$70	$65	*$221*

Add $10 for 4x scope (disc. 2006).

* ***Model 925C*** – similar to Model 925, except has Mossy Oak Break Up camo stock. Mfg. 2004-2010.

	$200	$160	$130	$100	$80	$70	$65	*$258*

* ***Model 925R*** – similar to Model 925, except has Monte Carlo black synthetic stock, 5 1/2 lbs. Mfg. 2006-2010.

	$175	$145	$115	$80	$75	$70	$65	*$213*

Add $41 for 3-9x32mm bore sighted scope (Model 925R-W/S, new 2007).

MODEL 925M – .22 WMR cal., 4 and 7 shot detachable mags. supplied standard beginning 2007, features T-900 fire control system, 22 in. barrel, thumb safety, adj. rear sight, grooved receiver, walnut finished hardwood stock with swivel studs, 6 lbs. Mfg. 2004-2010.

	$200	$165	$135	$100	$90	$80	$75	*$252*

Add $40 for Model 925MC with Monte Carlo stock and Mossy Oak Break-Up camo finish (disc. 2006).

* ***Model 925RM*** – .22 WMR cal., similar to Model 925M, except has checkered black fiberglass synthetic stock with full pistol grip, 6 lbs. Mfg. 2009-2010.

	$190	$160	$130	$95	$85	$80	$75	*$239*

GRADING - PPGS™	100%	98%	95%	90%	80%	70%	60%	LAST MSR

MODEL 980S/980S-CF – .22 LR cal., 7 shot detachable mag., 22 in. stainless steel barrel, other metal parts stainless steel/nickel plated, T-900 fire control system, black fiberglass synthetic stock with molded checkering, thumb safety, adj. buckhorn rear sight, approx. 6 lbs. Mfg. 2004-2010.

	$250	$200	$165	$130	$110	$95	$85	*$315*

Add $30 for black synthetic stock with carbon fiber pattern (Model 980S-CF).

* ***Model 980V*** – similar to Model 980S, except has 22 in. heavy steel barrel with recessed muzzle, double bedding screws, swivel studs, no sights, grooved receiver with scope bases, drilled and tapped, 7 lbs. Mfg. 2004-2006.

	$265	$210	$170	$145	$120	$100	$80	*$349*

MODEL 981T – .22 S, L, or LR cal., 17-25 shot tube mag., 22 in. barrel, black fiberglass synthetic stock, features T-900 fire control system, thumb safety, adj. rear sight, approx. 6 lbs. Mfg. 2004-2010.

	$180	$145	$110	$90	$80	$70	$60	*$221*

Add $65 for stainless steel barrel (new 2010).

MODEL 982 – .22 WMR cal., 7 shot detachable mag., 22 in. regular barrel, T-900 fire control system, checkered American Monte Carlo stock, adj. buckhorn rear sight, thumb safety, rubber buttplate, 6 lbs. Mfg. 2004-2006.

	$255	$210	$170	$145	$120	$100	$80	*$341*

Add $20 for Model 982L with two-tone brown laminated stock (new 2004).

Add $23 for Model 982S with stainless steel barrel and nickel/stainless steel small parts (mfg. 2004-2005).

MODEL 982VS/982VS-CF – .22 LR cal., 22 in. heavy stainless barrel, 4 and 7 shot mags. supplied standard beginning 2007, adj. buckhorn rear sight, black synthetic stock or synthetic stock with carbon fiber pattern (Model 982-CF, mfg. 2007-2009), thumb safety, T-900 fire control system. Mfg. 2004-2010.

	$265	$210	$175	$150	$125	$110	$90	*$326*

Add $41 for synthetic stock with carbon fiber pattern (Model 982VS-CF, mfg. 2007-2009).

MODEL 983 SERIES – .22 WMR cal., 12 shot tube mag., 22 in. barrel, features T-900 fire control system, checkered walnut Monte Carlo stock, adj. folding buckhorn sight, 6 lbs. Mfg. 2004-2010.

	$265	$210	$175	$150	$125	$105	$85	*$325*

* ***Model 983T*** – .22 WMR cal., 12 shot tube mag., 22 in. barrel, features T-900 fire control system, black fiberglass synthetic stock with molded-in checkering, adj. rear sight, 6 lbs. Mfg. 2004-2010.

	$210	$175	$150	$130	$110	$90	$75	*$249*

* ***Model 983S*** – similar to Model 983T, except has stainless steel barrel and nickel plated/stainless steel parts, two-tone brown hardwood laminate stock, 6 lbs. Mfg. 2004-2010.

	$275	$225	$185	$145	$125	$105	$90	*$355*

MODEL 2000 TARGET – .22 LR cal., single shot (can be converted), 22 in. heavy barrel with match chamber and Lyman adj. sights, 2 stage target trigger, molded synthetic stock made from fiberglass and Kevlar with twice baked blue enamel, adj. buttplate, aluminum forearm rail, 8 lbs. Mfg. 1991-95.

	$600	$525	$450	$410	$325	$275	$225	*$602*

Add $34 for 5-shot conversion unit (for summer biathlon competition).

* ***Model 2000A Target*** – similar to Model 2000 Target, except has adj. comb, ambidextrous pistol grip, and molded-in logo. Mfg. 1994 only.

	$625	$550	$475	$425	$350	$275	$225	*$625*

* ***Model 2000L Target*** – .22 LR cal., updated version of the Model 2000, featuring grey/black laminated stock, adj. aperture rear and aperture insert front sight, double bedding screws, factory test target supplied with each gun, 8 lbs. Mfg. 1996-2002.

	$650	$575	$495	$440	$360	$295	$225	*$745*

MODEL XT SERIES – .17 HMR (XT-17 Series), .22 LR (XT-22 Series), or .22 WMR (XT-22M Series), 16 1/4 (Youth), or 22 in. barrel, features ProFire adj. trigger allowing 3-6 lb. trigger pull with zero creep, detachable or tubular mag., red cocking indicator, thumb and trigger safeties, black synthetic ergonomic stock with palm swell pistol grip, with or w/o (Varmint models) sights. New 2011.

* ***Model XT-17 Series*** – .17 HMR cal., 22 in. regular, varmint, or fluted varmint barrel, includes 4 and 7 shot mags., blue finish or stainless steel, 6-7 lbs. New 2011.

» **Model XT-17R** – .17 HMR cal., 22 in. sporter barrel, 4 or 7 shot mag., Pro Fire adj. trigger, adj. open rear and ramp front sight, black synthetic stock with palm swell, full pistol grip, molded in swivels, stippled grip areas, blue finish, 6 lbs.

MSR $274	$200	$175	$150	$135	$110	$90	$70	

GRADING - PPGS™	100%	98%	95%	90%	80%	70%	60%	LAST MSR

» **Model XT-17SR** – similar to Model XT-17R, except is stainless steel. Disc. 2013.

	$250	$220	$190	$165	$150	$135	$115	*$310*

» **Model XT-17V** – .17 HMR cal., 22 in. blued heavy varmint barrel, 4 or 7 shot mag., Pro-Fire adj. trigger, with sights, Monte Carlo walnut finished hardwood stock with swivel studs, full pistol grip, red cocking indicator, includes front and rear scope bases, Mar-Shield finish, 6 1/2 lbs.

MSR $305	$230	$195	$170	$150	$130	$120	$110	

Add $40 for 3x32mm mounted and bore sighted scope (Model XT-17VO, disc. 2014).

» **Model XT-17VR** – .17 HMR cal., 22 in. blued heavy varmint barrel, 4 or 7 shot mag., ProFire adj. trigger, no sights, black synthetic beavertail stock with palm swell, molded in swivels and stippled grip areas, full pistol grip, thumb and trigger safeties, red cocking indicator, includes front and rear scope bases, 6 1/2 lbs.

MSR $295	$230	$190	$165	$145	$130	$120	$110	

» **Model XT-17VSL** – .17 HMR cal., 22 in. stainless steel heavy varmint barrel, 4 or 7 shot nickel plated mags., stainless steel construction, Pro-Fire adj. trigger, Monte Carlo laminated gray/black hardwood stock with nickel plated sling swivel studs, full pistol grip, rubber buttpad, thumb safety, red cocking indicator, includes front and rear scope bases, Mar-Shield finish, 7 lbs.

MSR $438	$340	$285	$240	$210	$180	$150	$130	

Add $24 for 22 in. fluted varmint barrel w/o scope base blocks (Model XT-17VSFL). Disc. 2013.

» **Model XT-17VLB** – features brown laminate thumbhole stock, 22 in. varmint barrel, blue finish. Disc. 2013.

	$335	$285	$240	$210	$180	$150	$130	*$414*

» **Model XT-17VSLB** – features black/gray laminate thumbhole stock, stainless steel, 22 in. varmint barrel. Disc. 2013.

	$395	$325	$265	$230	$200	$175	$150	*$464*

* ***Model XT-22 Series*** – .22 S, L, or LR cal., 16 1/4 or 22 in. barrel, 7 shot detachable or tube (25 shot with .22 S, 19 shot with .22 L, or 17 shot with .22 LR) mag., blue finish or stainless steel, 6-7 lbs. New 2011.

» **Model XT-22** – .22 LR cal. only, 22 in. blued sporter barrel, 7 shot detachable mag., Pro-Fire adj. trigger, adj. rear and ramp front sights, Monte Carlo walnut finished hardwood stock with swivel studs, blue finish. New 2011.

MSR $244	$180	$145	$120	$100	$85	$70	$60	

» **Model XT-22R** – .22 LR cal. only, 22 in. blued sporter barrel, 7 shot detachable mag., adj. rear and ramp front sights, black synthetic pistol grip stock with palm swell and molded in swivel studs, blue finish, 6 lbs. New 2011.

MSR $234	$175	$145	$120	$100	$85	$70	$60	

Add $40 for 3-9x32mm mounted and bore sighted scope (Model XT-22RO, disc. 2014).

» **Model XT-22TR** – .22 S, L, or LR cal., 22 in. blued sporter barrel with Micro-Groove rifling, 17, 19, or 25 shot tubular mag., Pro-Fire adj. trigger, adj. sights, black synthetic stock with palm swell pistol grip and molded in swivel studs, blue finish, 6 lbs. New 2011.

MSR $240	$175	$145	$120	$100	$85	$70	$60	

» **Model XT-22TSR** – .22 S, L, or LR cal., 22 in. stainless steel sporter barrel with Micro-Groove rifling, 17, 19, or 25 shot tubular mag., Pro-Fire adj. trigger, semi-buckhorn folding rear/ramp with hood front sights, black synthetic pistol grip stock with palm swell and molded in swivel studs. New 2011.

MSR $305	$230	$195	$170	$150	$130	$120	$110	

» **Model XT-22Y1** – features compact hardwood stock, 16 1/4 in. barrel, single shot, blue finish. Mfg. 2011-2013.

	$175	$145	$120	$100	$85	$70	$60	*$219*

» **Model XT-22YS1** – features compact hardwood stock, 16 1/4 in. barrel, stainless steel, and fiber optic sights. Mfg. 2011-2014.

	$185	$150	$120	$100	$85	$70	$60	*$238*

» **Model XT-22YR** – .22 S, L, or LR cal., Youth Series,16 1/4 in. blued sporter barrel with Micro-Groove rifling, 7 shot detachable mag, single shot adaptor, adj. rear and ramp front sights, compact black synthetic stock with palm swell pistol grip and molded in swivel studs, front and rear scope bases included, blue finish, 4 1/2 lbs.

MSR $244	$180	$145	$120	$100	$85	$70	$60	

GRADING - PPGS™	100%	98%	95%	90%	80%	70%	60%	LAST MSR

» **Model XT-22YSR** – features compact black synthetic stock, stainless steel, 16 1/4 in. barrel, fiber optic sights. Mfg. 2011-2013.

	$195	$155	$125	$100	$85	$70	$60	*$247*

» **Model XT-22RC** – .22 LR cal., 22 in. blued barrel, 7 shot mag., Pro-Fire adj. trigger, synthetic camo stock, features Mossy Oak Break-Up Country. Mfg. 2011-2013.

	$200	$155	$125	$100	$85	$70	$60	*$258*

» **Model XT-22RO** – .22 LR cal., thumb safety, red cocking indicator, 22 in. threaded barrel, 7 shot detachable mag., Pro-Fire adj. trigger, 3-9x32 Scope and rings factory mounted and bore sighted, black synthetic stock with palm swell, full pistol grip, molded in swivels, stippled grip areas, 13 1/4 in. LOP, blue finish, 41 in. OAL, 6 1/2 lbs. New 2018.

MSR $274	$200	$175	$150	$135	$110	$90	$70	

» **Model XT-22RZ** – .22 LR cal., thumb safety, red cocking indicator, 22 in. threaded barrel, 7 shot detachable mag., Pro-Fire adj. trigger, receiver grooved for scope mount, also drilled and tapped for scope bases, black synthetic stock with palm swell, full pistol grip, molded in swivels, and stippled grip areas, 13 1/4 in. LOP, blue finish, 41 in. OAL, 6 lbs. Mfg. 2011-2014, reintroduced 2018.

MSR $274	$200	$175	$150	$135	$110	$90	$70	

» **Model XT-22SR** – .22 LR cal. only, black synthetic stock, stainless steel, 22 in. barrel with semi-buckhorn folding rear sight and hooded ramp front sight. Mfg. 2011-2014.

	$275	$225	$190	$165	$150	$135	$115	*$339*

» **Model XT-22VR** – .22 LR cal. only, 22 in. heavy varmint barrel, 7 shot detachable mag., Pro-Fire adj. trigger, black synthetic stock with palm swell pistol grip and molded in swivel studs, front and rear scope bases included, blue finish. New 2011.

MSR $244	$180	$145	$120	$100	$85	$70	$60	

* ***Model XT-22M Series*** – .22 WMR cal., 4 and 7 shot clip mag., or 12 shot tube mag., 22 in. barrel with or w/o sights, blue or stainless finish, 6 lbs. New 2011.

» **Model XT-22M** – .22 WMR cal., 22 in. blued sporter barrel, Pro-Fire adj. trigger, Monte Carlo walnut finished hardwood stock with swivel studs, adj. ramp sights. New 2011.

MSR $275	$200	$175	$150	$135	$110	$90	$70	

» **Model XT-22MR** – .22 WMR cal., 22 in. barrel, 4 and 7 shot clip or 12 shot tube mag., Pro-Fire adj. trigger, adj. ramp sight, black synthetic stock with swivel studs, blue finish, 6 lbs. New 2011.

MSR $264	$195	$150	$120	$100	$85	$70	$60	

» **Model XT-22MTR** – .22 WMR cal., 22 in. barrel, 12 shot tube mag., Pro-Fire adj. trigger, adj./ramp sights, black synthetic stock with swivel studs, blue finish, 6 lbs. New 2011.

MSR $274	$200	$175	$150	$135	$110	$90	$70	

» **Model XT-22MTSL** – .22 WMR cal., brown laminate stock, stainless steel, 12 shot tube mag., and semi-buckhorn folding rear sight with hooded ramp front sight. Mfg. 2011-2014, reintroduced 2018.

MSR $387	$295	$250	$220	$190	$170	$150	$130	

» **Model XT-22MTW** – .22 WMR cal., walnut stock, 12 shot tube mag., semi-buckhorn folding rear sight with hooded ramp front sight, blue finish. Mfg. 2011-2015.

	$275	$230	$190	$165	$150	$135	$115	*$345*

» **Model XT-22MVSR** – .22 WMR cal., 22 in. stainless steel heavy varmint barrel with Micro-Groove rifling, 4 or 7 shot mag., rear and front scope bases only, receiver grooved for scope mount, drilled and tapped for scope bases, black synthetic stock with palm swell, full pistol grip, molded in swivels, stippled grip areas, thumb safety, red cocking indicator, 6 lbs. Mfg. 2011-2014, reintroduced 2018.

MSR $352	$275	$230	$190	$165	$150	$135	$115	

MARLIN PROMOTIONAL MODELS – Models 15 (disc.), 15Y (disc.), 15N (mfg. 1998-99, last MSR $188), 15YN (refer to individual listing), 25 (disc.), 25M (disc.), 25N (refer to individual listing), 25NC (refer to individual listing), 70 (disc.), 70HC (mfg. 1989-95, last 1995 MSR was $167), 75C (disc.), 81TS (refer to individual listing), and 795 Semi-Auto (refer to individual listing), are inexpensive, utilitarian .22 LR or .22 WMR cal. (Model 25M only), rifles designed for inexpensive shooting.

Series 15 and 25 Models designate bolt action, Series 60 and 70 designate semi-auto design.

GRADING - PPGS™	100%	98%	95%	90%	80%	70%	60%	LAST MSR

REPEATING PROMOTIONAL MODELS

Model 80 - 1934-1939. Price Range $50 - $95.
Model 80E - 1934-1940. Price Range $55 - $100.
Model 80C - 1940-1970. Price Range $55 - $100.
Model 80DL - 1940-1965. Price Range $70 - $105.
Model 80G - 1960-1965, Marlin Glenfield. Price Range $45 - $80.
Model 20 - 1966-1981, Marlin Glenfield. Price Range $45 - $80.
Model 780 - 1971-1988. Price Range $50 - $85.
Model 781 - 1971-1988. Price Range $50 - $85.
Model 782 - 1971-1988, .22 WRM. Price Range $75 - $135.
Model 783 - 1971-1988, .22 WRM. Price Range $75 - $135.
Model 980 - 1962-1970, .22 WRM. Price Range $75 - $135.
Model 81 - 1937-1940. Price Range $50 - $95.
Model 81E - 1937-1940. Price Range $65 - $110.
Model 81C - 1940-1970. Price Range $65 - $110.
Model 81DL - 1940-1965. Price Range $65 - $100.
Model 81G - 1960-1965 Marlin Glenfield. Price Range $55 - $85.

SINGLE SHOT PROMOTIONAL MODELS

Model 65 - 1932-1938. Price Range $40- $75.
Model 65E - 1932-1938. Price Range $50 - $85.
Model 100 - 1936-1941. Price Range $50 - $85.
Model 100S Tom Mix Special - disc. Price Range $140 - $275.
Model 100SB - 1936-1941. Price Range $55 - $95.
Model 101 - 1941-1977. Price Range $50 - $85.
Model 101 DL - disc. Price Range $65 - $100.
Model 101 Crown Prince - 1959. Price Range $85 - $165.
Model 101G - 1960-1965, Marlin Glenfield. Price Range $45 - $80.
Model 10 - 1966-disc., Marlin Glenfield. Price Range $45 - $75.
Model 122 - 1966-disc. Price Range $45 - $70.

Rifles: .22 Cal., Lever Action

All Marlin firearms manufactured before Jan. 2008 had "JM" on the barrel near the receiver.

MODEL 39 – .22 S, L, or LR cal., 24 in. octagon barrel with tube mag., open sights, takedown, case hardened receiver and lever, S-shaped pistol grip stock, bluing on barrel, forend tip, mag. tube, bolt, hammer, and screws, various qualities of walnut (X, 2X, or 3X), hard rubber buttplate. Approx. 40-50,000 mfg. 1922-38.

N/A	$5,500	$5,000	$3,750	$2,950	$2,400	$1,750

Early models with fancy 2X-3X wood will bring a considerable premium.

Excellent original condition in this model is extremely hard to find since most specimens were well used due to the 16/25 shell mag. capacity, reliability, and the fact that the balance point of the gun (the receiver) normally wore first due to carrying wear. Earlier guns without a prefix or with an "S" prefix are noted for their superior workmanship and fine finish. Later "HS" prefix (High Speed) are not quite as valuable as these earlier guns, but offer practical shooting value.

MODEL 39A – similar to Model 39, with case hardened receiver (mfg. 1939-1945), includes 1st and 2nd Models with round barrel. 3rd Model 1st Variation was introduced in 1946 and has blue receiver, 3rd Model 2nd Variation has flutes in buttstock comb and was introduced in 1951, and 3rd Model 3rd Variation has Micro-Groove rifling, no pistol grip cap, and was introduced in 1954.

* ***Model 39A 1st Model*** – case colored frame, no prefix. Mfg. 1939 only.

$2,650	$2,350	$1,850	$1,350	$950	$775	$650

The first variation of the Model 39A mfg. in 1939 is distinguishable by a buttstock and lever similar to those on earlier Model 39s.

* ***Model 39A 2nd Model*** – case colored frame, "B" prefix. Mfg. 1941.

$2,150	$1,900	$1,425	$1,100	$900	$650	$550

The second variation had a rounded lever like current production and no "S" shape to bottom of pistol grip.

* ***Model 39A 3rd Model 1st Variation*** – features blued receiver, new ramp front sight, hard rubber buttplate, and Ballard rifling. Mfg. 1946-1950.

$1,350	$975	$775	$600	$500	$395	$350

GRADING - PPGS™	100%	98%	95%	90%	80%	70%	60%	LAST MSR

* ***Model 39A 3rd Model 2nd Variation*** – similar to 3rd Model 1st Variation, except has flutes in buttstock comb, white plastic spacer next to buttplate, and pistol grip cap with white spacer and brass insert. Mfg. 1951-53.

	$850	$725	$600	$500	$400	$300	$275	

* ***Model 39A 3rd Model 3rd Variation*** – similar to 3rd Model 2nd Variation, except has Micro-Groove rifling, and no pistol grip cap. Mfg. 1954-57.

	$825	$700	$575	$475	$375	$275	$250	

GOLDEN 39A (OLDER MFG.) – similar to Model 39A, with gold-plated trigger, sling swivels. Mfg. 1957-87.

	$775	$650	$475	$375	$325	$275	$225	

Add 30% to pre-1970 (oil finished stock) models.

MODEL 39A ANNIE OAKLEY – .22 S, L, or LR cal., takedown, 24 in. round barrel, tubular mag., gold trigger, open sights, American black walnut checkered pistol grip stock, one side of the receiver is scroll engraved w/portrait of Annie Oakley and "Annie Oakley" etched in gold, the other side of the receiver is scroll engraved and gold etched with "Little Sure Shot" and an Annie Oakley shooting scene including the Ace of Hearts, serial number series are 39A000x, 500 mfg., circa 1999.

	$1,200	$975	$775	$650	$525	$425	$325	

GOLDEN 39A (CURRENT/RECENT MFG.) – similar to Model 39A, with gold-plated trigger, sling swivels. Recently distributed by Davidson's Guns.

	$695	$575	$425	$350	$295	$250	$200	

Add 30% to pre-1970 (oil finished stock) models.

GOLDEN 39M – similar to Golden 39A, except is carbine variation. Mfg. 1972-1987.

	$695	$575	$425	$325	$275	$250	$200	

MODEL 39A "MOUNTIE" – straight grip stock, slim forearm, otherwise similar to 39A. Mfg. 1953-1957.

	$675	$575	$425	$325	$275	$250	$200	

* ***Model 39A "MOUNTIE" with K prefix*** – 24 in. barrel and slender forearm. 4,335 mfg. 1953 only.

	$950	$800	$650	$525	$425	$350	$300	

GOLDEN 39A MOUNTIE – mfg. 1957-1972.

	$695	$575	$425	$325	$275	$250	$200	

90TH ANNIVERSARY 39A RIFLE – 24 in. chrome barrel and action, select checkered walnut stock, carved squirrel on side of buttstock. 500 mfg. in 1960.

	$2,100	$1,750	$1,425	N/A	N/A	N/A	N/A	*$100*

90TH ANNIVERSARY MODEL 39M MOUNTIE CARBINE – similar to 90th Anniversary Model 39A, except 20 in. barrel, straight stock. 500 mfg. in 1960.

	$2,100	$1,750	$1,425	N/A	N/A	N/A	N/A	*$100*

Add $50-$75 for original box and papers.

MODEL 39AWL – special model made exclusively for Wal-Mart, supporting the Wildlife Management Institution and Wildlife Forever, features similar to Marlin 1897CL Classic, 24 in. half-round, half-octagon barrel, half mag., checkered black American walnut pistol grip stock, adj. semi-buckhorn rear sight, engraved receiver with scroll and "Wildlife for Tomorrow" and "Sportsmen Supporting Conservation". 2,000 mfg. 1997 only.

	$1,000	$825	$625	$550	$475	$375	$275	*$729*

MODEL 39A-DL – similar to 90th Anniversary, with blue barrel and action, regular production. Mfg. 1961-1963.

	$1,650	$1,300	$995	$850	$650	$525	$400	

This model is also known as the "Marlin 39A Squirrel Gun."

MODEL 39 PRESENTATION – .22 cal., one of the pair in the "Brace of 1,000," engraved receiver, 20 in. tapered octagon barrel, select fancy walnut straight grip stock and forend. Mfg. 1970 only.

	$1,995	$1,500	$1,150	N/A	N/A	N/A	N/A	

Add 10%-20% for extra fancy walnut.

MODEL 39A OCTAGON – similar to Golden 39A, with octagon barrel, no pistol grip cap, 2,551 rifles and 2,140 carbines were produced. Mfg. 1973.

	$975	$795	$650	$525	$450	$350	$265	

MODEL 39 CARBINE – similar to 39M, with light barrel, 3/4 tube mag. 9,695 mfg. 1963-67.

	$875	$700	$575	$450	$350	$275	$200	

MODEL 39D – similar to 39M, with pistol grip stock. Mfg. 1971-73.

	$595	$450	$375	$300	$225	$175	$150s	

GRADING - PPGS™	100%	98%	95%	90%	80%	70%	60%	LAST MSR

MODEL 39A/AS – .22 S, L, or LR cal., current production model, lever action, 19-26 shot tube mag., 24 in. barrel, American black walnut pistol grip stock (cut checkering became standard 1994) with fluted comb, rubber buttpad, grip cap, swivel studs, MarShield finish, open sights, gold trigger, takedown, 6 1/2 lbs. Disc. 2015.

$850 $675 $550 $425 $325 $250 $200 *$709*

This model was previously designated the Model 39A. In 1988, the Model 39AS became the standard production model and included a rebounding hammer and hammer block safety. In 2001, the model nomenclature was changed back to the Model 39A.

MODEL 39TDS – .22 S, L, or LR cal., tubular mag., carbine variation of the Model 39AS, 16 1/2 in. barrel with open sights, 5 1/4 lbs. Mfg. 1988-95.

$850 $725 $600 $500 $425 $350 $295 *$443*

MODEL 39M – carbine version of Model 39A, 20 in. lightweight barrel, 16 shot tube mag., squared finger lever, 6 lbs. Disc. 1987.

$675 $525 $425 $350 $275 $225 $175 *$304*

MODEL 39M OCTAGON – similar to Model 39M, with octagon barrel. 2,140 mfg. 1973.

$975 $800 $625 $525 $450 $375 $325

MODEL 39 CENTURY LTD – Marlin Centennial 1870-1970 Commemorative, 20 in. octagon barrel, select walnut straight stock, brass forearm cap and buttplate, name plate in butt. 35,388 mfg. 1970.

$1,100 $875 $675 N/A N/A N/A N/A

This model should have the original box for 100% values.

MODEL 39A ARTICLE II – NRA Centennial Commemorative 1871-1971, "Right to Bear Arms" medallion in receiver, 24 in. octagon barrel, fancy pistol grip stock, brass buttplate and forearm cap. 6,244 mfg. 1971.

$925 $750 $600 $500 $425 $350 $325

MODEL 39M ARTICLE II CARBINE – similar to 39A Article II, with 20 in. barrel, straight grip stock. Mfg. 3,824.

$925 $750 $600 $500 $425 $350 $325

MODEL 39A FANCY – .22 S, L, or LR cal., takedown, action and trigger jobs, clocked screws, dehorned and deburred all metal, accurized, 24 in. round barrel with Micro-Groove rifling, 19 (LR)-26 (S) shot tube mag., rebounding hammer, gold plated trigger, adj. semi-buckhorn folding rear and ramp front with brass bead and wide-scan hood, extra fancy American black walnut stock, hand cut checkering, hand fit and hand rubbed oil finish, hammer block safety, range tested, high polish blued finish, 6 1/2 lbs. Very limited quantities mfg. 2017.

$2,995 $2,650 $2,250 N/A N/A N/A N/A *$3,195*

Marlin Custom Shop mfg. available through Marlin Custom Dealers.

MODEL 56 – similar to Model 57 Levermatic, 22 or 24 in. barrel, with mag. Mfg. 1955-64.

$400 $350 $300 $250 $200 $150 $95

MODEL 57 LEVERMATIC – .22 S, L, or LR cal., tube mag., 22 in. barrel, open sight, Monte Carlo pistol grip stock. Mfg. 1959-65.

$550 $475 $400 $325 $275 $200 $150

MODEL 57M – .22 WMR cal., similar to Model 57 Levermatic, except has 24 in. barrel.

$600 $525 $425 $325 $275 $200 $150

MODEL 1894M (.22 WMR) – .22 WMR cal., with 20 in. barrel, 11 shot tube mag., straight grip walnut stock and forearm, 6 1/4 lbs. Mfg. 1983-1989.

$675 $575 $425 $325 $275 $250 $200 *$358*

MODEL 1897 COWBOY – .22 S, L, or LR cal., takedown action, 19 shot (.22 LR cal.), tube mag., rebounding hammer with block safety, 24 in. tapered octagon barrel with Micro-Groove (16 grooves) rifling, cut checkered walnut stock and forearm, adj. Marble semi-buckhorn rear and carbine front sight with brass bead, high polish blue, 6 1/2 lbs. Mfg. 1999-2001.

$875 $695 $575 $450 $350 $275 $200 *$708*

MODEL 1897T – .22 S, L, or LR cal., 14-21 shot mag., 20 in. tapered octagon barrel, hammer block safety, Marble front and rear sights, 6 lbs. Mfg. 2002-2003.

$875 $695 $575 $450 $350 $275 $200 *$748*

GRADING - PPGS™	100%	98%	95%	90%	80%	70%	60%	LAST MSR

MODEL 1897 CENTURY LIMITED LEVER ACTION – .22 LR cal., 100th anniversary of the Model 1897, features extensive receiver engraving and gold accenting, 24 in. half round/half octagon barrel with open sights, checkered fancy walnut stock and forearm. Limited mfg. 1997 only, limited quantities remained through 1999.

	$1,450	$1,100	$925	N/A	N/A	N/A	N/A	*$1,055*

* ***Model 1897 Century Limited Lever Action Employee Edition*** – .22 LR cal., features gold scroll work on lever, less than 100 mfg. 1997 only in ser. no. range 1-100.

	$2,100	$1,850	$1,550	N/A	N/A	N/A	N/A	

MODEL 1897 ANNIE OAKLEY – .22 LR cal., features 18 1/2 in. tapered octagon barrel with marble sights, blue receiver with rolled scroll engraving featuring gold Annie Oakley etched name on bolt, deluxe checkered walnut stock and forearm. Mfg. 1998 only.

	$1,325	$1,100	$925	$825	$700	$600	$500	*$1,054*

Add $300 for employee variation.

An employee variation of this model was made with gold inlays on finger lever, 100 mfg. total.

MODEL 1897T AO (ANNIE OAKLEY) – .22 S, L, or LR cal., 20 in. tapered octagon barrel, tubular mag., marble front and rear sights, semi-fancy wood, pistol grip or straight stock, hammer block safety. 117 mfg., circa 2003.

	$1,300	$1,150	$900	$800	$675	$575	$475	

Rifles: .22 Cal., Slide Action

All Marlin firearms manufactured before Jan. 2008 had "JM" on the barrel near the receiver.

MODEL 18 – .22 S, L, or LR cal., tube mag., 20 in. round or octagon barrel, open sight, exposed hammer, plain straight grip stock. Mfg. 1906-09.

	$1,500	$1,350	$1,200	$995	$850	$650	$550	

MODEL 20 – .22 S, L, or LR cal., 24 in. octagon barrel, open sight, exposed hammer, takedown, plain straight grip stock. Mfg. 1907-22.

	$1,500	$1,350	$1,200	$995	$850	$650	$550	

MODEL 25 – .22 Short cal. and CB cap., tube mag., 23 in. barrel, open sight, exposed hammer, takedown, plain straight grip stock. Mfg. 1909-10.

	$1,575	$1,375	$1,250	$1,050	$875	$700	$600	

MODEL 29 – similar to Model 20, with 23 in. round barrel, 1/2 tube mag. Mfg. 1913-16.

	$1,350	$1,175	$1,000	$850	$700	$600	$500	

MODEL 32 – .22 S, L, or LR cal., 2/3 tube mag., 24 in. octagon barrel, open sight, plain pistol grip stock, hammerless. Mfg. 1915 only.

	$1,850	$,650	$1,500	$1,250	$1,000	$800	$700	

MODEL 37 – similar to Model 29, with 24 in. barrel, full-length tube mag. Mfg. 1913-16.

	$1,325	$1,150	$950	$800	$650	$550	$475	

MODEL 38 – .22 S, L, or LR cal., 2/3 tube mag., 24 in. octagon barrel, open sights, hammerless, takedown, plain pistol grip stock. Mfg. 1920-30.

	$1,400	$1,200	$1,050	$900	$750	$650	$550	

Rifles: Rimfire, Semi-Auto

All Marlin firearms manufactured before Jan. 2008 had "JM" on the barrel near the receiver.

MODEL 60 – .22 LR cal., entry level rifle, 19 or 22 (disc. 2002) in. Micro-Groove barrel, 14 (new 1993) or 18 shot (LR) tube mag., aluminum receiver, adj. rear and front post sights, Monte Carlo plain hardwood or walnut finished laminated stock (laminated now standard) with pressed checkering, crossbolt safety, last shot hold open, blue finish, 4X scope (disc. 2006), approx. 5 1/2 lbs. New 1960.

MSR $213	$160	$125	$100	$85	$75	$65	$60	

Add 10% for Model 60 W/S with 4X scope (disc. 2006).

* ***Model 60C*** – .22 LR cal., 19 in. Micro-Groove barrel, 14 shot tube mag., aluminum receiver, adj. sights, Monte Carlo synthetic stock with full coverage Mossy Oak Breakup (disc.) or Realtree Hardwoods camo pattern finish, crossbolt safety, blue metal finish, 5 1/2 lbs. New 2000.

MSR $251	$180	$145	$115	$90	$80	$70	$60	

* ***Model 60DL*** – similar to Model 60, except has Walnutone walnut patterned finish. Mfg. 2004-2006.

	$175	$140	$110	$85	$75	$65	$60	*$236*

GRADING - PPGS™	100%	98%	95%	90%	80%	70%	60%	LAST MSR

* ***Model 60SN*** – .22 LR cal., 19 in. barrel, black synthetic stock, blue finish, includes sling swivel studs. New 2007.

MSR $205	$155	$125	$100	$80	$75	$65	$60	

Add $16 for 4x20mm bore sighted scope.

* ***Model 60DLX*** – .22 LR cal., 14 shot tube mag., checkered Monte Carlo walnut finished hardwood stock with full pistol grip, 19 in. barrel, engraved receiver with "50th Anniversary Edition" and gold barrel markings, swivel studs, semi-buckhorn folding rear sight, 5 1/2 lbs. Mfg. 2010-2013.

	$210	$175	$155	$135	$115	$100	$90	*$261*

MODEL 60SS STAINLESS – .22 LR cal., 19 or 22 (disc. 2002) in. stainless barrel, 14 shot tube mag., nickel plated aluminum receiver and other parts, laminated black/grey birch stock with Monte Carlo cheekpiece, Mar-Shield finish, most recent mfg. has adj. semi-buckhorn folding rear with high visibility post and removable cutaway Wide-scan hood front sight, 5 1/2 lbs. New 1993.

MSR $322	$255	$195	$165	$125	$110	$90	$80	

* ***Model 60SB Stainless*** – .22 LR cal., similar to Model 60SS, except has uncheckered (mfg. 1998 only) or press-checkered (new 1999) birch Monte Carlo stock, laminated hardwood became standard 2004, 5 1/2 lbs. New 1998.

MSR $270	$225	$180	$155	$125	$85	$70	$65	

Add $17 for 4X scope (disc. 2006).

This model was previously sold to Wal-Mart only.

* ***Model 60SS 150th Anniversary Edition*** – .22 LR cal., 19 in. stainless steel barrel w/Micro-Groove rifling, 14 shot tube mag. with patented closure system, autoloading, side ejection, manual and automatic "last-shot" bolt hold open, ramp front sight, adj. semi-buckhorn folding rear sight w/ high visibility post and removable cutaway wide-scan hood front sight, American Black walnut stock w/150th year anniversary medallion, special serial no., 5.5 lbs. New 2020.

MSR $399	$330	$270	$225	$190	$155	$130	$105	

* ***Model 60SSK Stainless*** – similar to Model 60SS, except has black fiberglass stock with Monte Carlo cheekpiece. Mfg. 1998-2006.

	$215	$180	$140	$110	$95	$80	$70	*$269*

Add $15 for 4X scope (disc. 2001).

* ***Model 60S-CF*** – .22 LR cal., similar to Model 60SN, except features synthetic stock with carbon fiber pattern, includes sling studs. Mfg. 2007-2009.

	$195	$160	$130	$100	$85	$75	$65	*$271*

MODEL 70P (PAPOOSE) – .22 LR cal. only, semi-auto, takedown carbine with 16 1/4 in. barrel, 7 shot mag., rustproof receiver, bolt hold open, is supplied with floating nylon carrying case. Mfg. 1986-94.

	$215	$180	$140	$110	$95	$80	$70	*$225*

Subtract $25 if without 4X scope (became standard 1993).

* ***Model 70PSS*** – .22 LR cal., 16 1/4 in. stainless steel barrel, nickel plated parts, 7 shot mag., black checkered synthetic stock with swing swivels, last shot hold-open became standard in 1996, includes blue nylon floatable case, adj. sights, 3 1/4 lbs. New 1995.

MSR $352	$275	$210	$170	$135	$110	$90	$80	

* ***Model 70HC*** – .22 LR cal., semi-auto, carbine with 18 in. barrel. Mfg. 1988-95.

	$185	$155	$130	$120	$110	$100	$90	

MODEL 75C – .22 LR cal., 14 shot tube mag., 18 in. Micro-Groove barrel, blue finish, aluminum receiver, Monte Carlo walnut finished hardwood stock, adj. rear sight, approx. 4 1/2 lbs. Mfg. 1967-1991.

	$200	$175	$150	$125	$100	$85	$65	

This rifle was offered as a Glenfield promotional Model 75 with a 9 shot tube mag. circa 1967-1982.

MODEL 717M2 – .17 Mach 2 cal., 7 shot detachable mag., 18 in. sporter barrel with open sights, walnut finished hardwood stock, last shot bolt hold open, crossbolt safety, 5 1/2 lbs. Mfg. 2005-2007.

	$180	$160	$140	$120	$110	$100	$90	*$222*

MODEL 795 – .22 LR cal., 18 in. blued steel barrel, 10 shot detachable nickel-plated mag., adj. sights, black synthetic Monte Carlo stock, grooved receiver, last shot bolt hold open, approx. 5 lbs.

MSR $192	$145	$110	$90	$80	$65	$60	$55	

Add $38 for 4x20mm mounted scope and bore sighted (mfg. 2012-2014).

* ***Model 795SS*** – .22 LR cal., similar to Model 795, except has stainless steel barrel and nickel plated parts, semi-buckhorn folding rear sight, hooded front sight. Mfg. 2002-2015.

	$200	$160	$130	$100	$85	$70	$65	*$262*

GRADING - PPGS™	100%	98%	95%	90%	80%	70%	60%	LAST MSR

MODEL 795 LTR – .22 LR cal., 18 in. barrel, 10 shot nickel-plated mag. (includes extra magazine), last shot bolt hold open, Tech sights, synthetic stock with M14 sling, 4 1/2 lbs. Mfg. 2015 only.

	$250	$220	$190	$170	$140	$115	$90	*$299*

MODEL 922M – .22 WMR cal., 7 shot detachable mag., 20 1/2 in. barrel, Garand style safety, alloy receiver, hold-open device, uncheckered or checkered (became standard 1994) walnut stock with solid pad, blue steel (hardcoated on receiver), 6 1/2 lbs. Mfg. 1993-2001.

	$360	$295	$240	$200	$185	$175	$165	*$454*

MODEL 990 – .22 LR cal. only, 18 shot tube mag., 22 in. barrel, last shot automatic bolt hold-open, Monte Carlo American black walnut stock with pistol grip, 5 1/2 lbs. Mfg. 1979-1988.

	$115	$90	$75	$65	$60	$55	$50	*$159*

MODEL 990L – .22 LR cal., 14 shot tube mag., 22 in. barrel, laminated two-tone brown Monte Carlo stock, gold trigger, adj. rear sight, grooved receiver, 5 3/4 lbs. Mfg. 1993-94.

	$180	$160	$145	$130	$120	$110	$100	*$223*

MODEL 995 – .22 LR cal., 7 shot mag., 18 in. barrel, Monte Carlo walnut stock, 5 lbs. Disc. 1994.

	$160	$125	$85	$70	$65	$60	$55	*$206*

* ***Model 995SS*** – .22 LR cal., stainless steel barrel and nickel-plated small parts, black fiberglass stock with molded-in checkering, adj. rear sight, last shot hold-open (new 1996), 5 lbs. Mfg. 1995-99.

	$195	$145	$110	$90	$75	$60	$50	*$255*

MODEL 7000 – .22 LR cal., 10 shot detachable mag., 18 in. heavy barrel without sights and recessed muzzle, black fiberglass synthetic stock with molded-in checkering, grooved receiver, no sights, last shot hold open, scope mounts provided, 5 1/2 lbs. Mfg. 1997-2006.

	$210	$190	$165	$140	$130	$120	$110	*$263*

* ***Model 7000T*** – .22 LR cal., target model with 18 in. heavy barrel, red, white and blue laminated hardwood stock with adj. pad, two-stage target trigger with stop, aluminum forend rail with adj. stop, grooved receiver w/o sights, 7 1/2 lbs. Mfg. 1999-2001.

	$365	$300	$240	$200	$185	$175	$165	*$465*

SEMI-AUTO PROMOTIONAL MODELS

Model 50 - 1931-1935. Price Range $85 - $150.
Model 50E - 1931-1934. Price Range $85 - $165.
Model A-1 - 1936-1940. Price Range $85 - $155.
Model A-1E - 1935-1946. Price Range $85 - $160.
Model A-1C - 1941-1946. Price Range $75 - $155.
Model A-1DL - 1941-1946. Price Range $75 - $155.
Model 88-C - 1948-1956. Price Range $75 - $150.
Model 88-DL - 1953-1956. Price Range $75 - $150.
Model 89-C - 1948-1961. Price Range $75 - $150.
Model 89-DL - 1950-1961. Price Range $75 - $150.
Model 98 - 1957-1959. Price Range $75 - $150.
Model 99 - 1959-1960. Price Range $75 - $150.
Model 99C - 1961-1978. Price Range $75 - $150.
Model 99G - 1960-1965, Marlin Glenfield. Price Range $75 - $150.
Model 60 - 1960-present, Marlin Glenfield (2000 MSR $200).
Model 99DL - 1960-1964. Price Range $75 - $150.
Model 49 - 1968-1970. Price Range $75 - $150
Model 49DL - 1971-1978. Price Range $75 - $150.
Model 99M1 - 1964-1978. Price Range $75 - $150.
Model 989M2 - 1966-disc. Price Range $75 - $150.
Model 989 - 1962-1965. Price Range $75 - $150.
Model 70 (HC) - 1966-1995, Marlin Glenfield. Price Range $85 - $160.
Model 75C - 1967-1991, Marlin Glenfield. Price Range $85 - $160.
Model 989G - 1962-1964, Marlin Glenfield. Price Range $75 - $150.
Model 990 - disc. Price Range $75 - $150.

SHOTGUNS: BOLT ACTION

All Marlin firearms manufactured before Jan. 2008 had "JM" on the barrel near the receiver.

MODEL 25MG GARDEN GUN – .22 WMR shot shell, features 22 in. smoothbore barrel with high visibility bead front sight only, 7 shot detachable mag., black synthetic stock, thumb safety, 6 lbs. Mfg. 1999-2002.

	$250	$195	$150	$125	$115	$100	$90	*$245*

GRADING - PPGS™	100%	98%	95%	90%	80%	70%	60%	LAST MSR

MODEL 50 DL – 12 ga. only, upland game model, 28 in. barrel bored M, black Rynite stock with molded-in checkering, 2 shot mag., 7 1/2 lbs. Mfg. 1997-99.

	$295	$220	$195	$175	$160	$145	$130	*$330*

MODEL 55 – 12, 16, or 20 ga., 2 shot detachable mag., 26 and 28 in. full choke barrel, plain pistol grip stock. Mfg. 1950-65.

	$125	$90	$65	$50	$35	$30	$25	
With adj. choke	$150	$95	$75	$65	$45	$40	$30	

MODEL 55 GOOSE GUN – similar to Model 55, except 12 ga. only, 36 in. full choke barrel, 3 in. chamber, 2 shot mag., leather carrying strap and detachable swivels, walnut stock with rubber recoil pad, 8 lbs. Mfg. 1962-96.

	$350	$185	$145	$125	$115	$100	$90	*$308*

* ***Model 55 Goose Gun GDL*** – similar to Model 55 Goose Gun, except has black Rynite synthetic stock. Mfg. 1997-2000.

	$425	$240	$200	$180	$160	$145	$130	*$396*

MODEL 55 SWAMP GUN – similar to Model 55, 12 ga., 20 in. adj. choke barrel, 3 in. mag. Mfg. 1963-65.

	$105	$90	$70	$55	$50	$45	$35	

MODEL 55S SLUG GUN – 24 in. barrel, cylinder bore, rifle sights. Mfg. 1974-83.

	$140	$120	$110	$95	$85	$55	$40	

MODEL 59 SINGLE SHOT – .410 bore, 2 1/2 or 3 in. chamber, 24 in. barrel bored F, walnut pistol grip stock and forearm, 48,447 mfg. 1956-1965.

	$150	$125	$110	$95	$85	$55	$40	

MODEL 512 SLUGMASTER – 12 ga., 3 in. chamber, bolt action, 2 shot box mag., 21 in. rifled barrel, adj. rear sight, receiver is drilled and tapped for scope mount (included), walnut finished birch stock with pressed checkering and vent. recoil pad, 8 lbs. Mfg. 1994-99.

	$295	$220	$195	$175	$160	$145	$130	*$361*

* ***Model 512DL Slugmaster*** – similar to Model 512 Slugmaster, except has black Rynite stock, Fire Sights (with red fiber optic inserts) became standard 1998. Disc. 1998.

	$310	$230	$200	$180	$160	$145	$130	*$372*

* ***Model 512P Slugmaster*** – 12 ga., 3 in. chamber, features 21 in. ported fully rifled barrel with front and rear Fire Sights (high visibility red and green fiber optic inserts), 2 shot detachable box mag., black fiberglass synthetic stock with molded-in checkering, receiver is drilled and tapped, 8 lbs. Mfg. 1999-2001.

	$315	$235	$200	$180	$165	$155	$145	*$388*

MODEL 5510 – 10 ga., 3 1/2 in. mag., 2 shot mag., 34 in. barrel, leather carrying strap and detachable swivels, rubber recoil pad, marked "The Original Super Goose 10", 10 1/2 lbs. Mfg. 1976-1985.

	$220	$170	$160	$150	$140	$130	$120	*$282*

SHOTGUNS: LEVER ACTION

All Marlin firearms manufactured before Jan. 2008 had "JM" on the barrel near the receiver.

MODEL .410 LEVER ACTION (1929-1932 MFG.) – .410 bore, 22 or 26 in. barrel, full choke, lever action, similar to 1893, exposed hammer, plain pistol grip stock. Mfg. 1929-32 as a stockholders' promotional firearm.

	$1,950	$1,650	$1,350	$950	$825	$675	$575	

Add 20% for 22 in. barrel.

* ***Model .410 Deluxe Lever Action*** – includes deluxe checkered walnut stock and forearm.

	$2,450	$1,950	$1,750	$1,450	$1,100	$900	$800	

Deluxe forearm does not have flute in it.

MODEL 1895 .410 – .410 bore, 2 1/2 in. chamber, 22 in. smooth barrel, choice of fixed open or flush choke tubes, 5 or 6 shot tube mag., side ejection, hammer block, fiber optic front sight and semi-buckhorn rear sight, American black walnut straight stock, polished blue finish, 8 lbs. New 2020.

MSR $847	$700	$615	$525	$475	$385	$315	$250	

NEW MODEL .410 – .410 bore, 2 1/2 in. chamber, 4-5 shot tube mag., 22 in. cylinder bore barrel, hammer block safety, checkered black American walnut stock and forend, folding rear with green fiber optic front sight, 9 1/2 lbs. Mfg. 2004-2005.

	$750	$550	$475	$400	$365	$335	$300	*$614*

GRADING - PPGS™	100%	98%	95%	90%	80%	70%	60%	LAST MSR

SHOTGUNS: O/U

Please refer to the L.C. Smith section for currently manufactured L.C. Smith O/U shotguns.

All Marlin firearms manufactured before Jan. 2008 had "JM" on the barrel near the receiver.

MODEL 90 SHOTGUN – 12, 16, 20 ga., or .410 bore shotgun or combination gun configuration (12 ga. over .30/30 barrels), 26, 28, or 30 in. barrels, boxlock, extractors, checkered pistol grip stock. Mfg. 1937-1958. Guns made from 1937-1949 had vent. separated barrels, after 1949 they had solid barrels.

* ***Model 90 Shotgun w/Double Triggers***

12, 16, or 20 ga.	$475	$425	$375	$330	$290	$265	$230
.410 bore	$1,995	$1,750	$1,550	$1,325	$1,175	$1,050	$975

Add 15% for 16 or 20 ga.

Add 20% for .410 Bore.

* ***Model 90 Shotgun w/Single Trigger***

12, 16, or 20 ga.	$625	$575	$525	$475	$440	$400	$375
.410 bore	$3,200	$2,950	$2,600	$2,300	$2,000	$1,700	$1,500

* ***Model 90 Shotgun Combination Gun*** – shotgun over .22 LR, .22 Hornet, .218 Bee, or .30-30 Win. cal., very rare, approx. 500 mfg. Mfg. 1937-1959.

$3,200	$2,750	$2,300	$2,000	$1,800	$1,600	$1,400

SHOTGUNS: SxS

Please refer to the L.C. Smith section for both older and newly manufactured L.C. Smith SxS shotguns.

SHOTGUNS: SINGLE SHOT

All Marlin firearms manufactured before Jan. 2008 had "JM" on the barrel near the receiver.

MODEL 60 – 12 ga., 30 or 32 in. barrel, full choke, top lever, break open, exposed hammer, pistol grip stock. Approx. 3,000 mfg. 1923.

$150	$135	$110	$90	$80	$70	$60

SHOTGUNS: SLIDE ACTION, 1898-1963 PRODUCTION

During 1998, Marlin issued a service bulletin recommending that the following slide action models should not be fired: exposed hammer Models 1898, 16, 17, 19, 19S, 19G, 19N, 21, 24, 24G, 26, 30, 42, 49, and 49N, and hammerless Models 28, 31, 43, 44, 53, and 63. Many of these guns are 70-100 years old and system failures can and do happen.

All Marlin firearms manufactured before Jan. 2008 had "JM" on the barrel near the receiver.

MODEL 1898 – 12 ga., 5 shot tube mag., 26-32 in. barrels, various chokes, exposed hammer, pistol grip stock, grades differ in quality of wood and engraving on C and D. Mfg. 1898-1905.

Grade A	$325	$275	$225	$200	$165	$150	$140
Grade B	$580	$495	$440	$415	$360	$305	$275
Grade C	$880	$715	$635	$580	$525	$495	$440
Grade D	$1,760	$1,540	$1,320	$1,210	$1,045	$965	$880

Factory information in the ser. range 19601-67000 may be obtained by contacting the Cody Firearms Records Office at the Buffalo Bill Center of the West.

MODEL 16 – 16 ga. only, 26 or 28 in. barrel, various chokes, takedown, pistol grip stock. Mfg. 1904-10.

Grade A	$325	$275	$225	$200	$165	$150	$140
Grade B	$495	$415	$360	$330	$305	$275	$250
Grade C	$635	$525	$495	$440	$415	$385	$330
Grade D	$1,320	$1,100	$990	$825	$715	$635	$550

MODEL 17 – 12 ga., 30 or 32 in. full choke barrel, solid frame, straight stock. Mfg. 1906-08.

$335	$275	$235	$200	$165	$150	$140

MODEL 17 BRUSH GUN – similar to Model 17, with 26 in. cylinder bore barrel. Mfg. 1906-08.

$400	$325	$275	$235	$200	$175	$150

MODEL 17 RIOT GUN – similar to Model 17, with 20 in. barrel. Mfg. 1906-08.

$400	$325	$275	$235	$200	$175	$150

MODEL 19 (19S, 19N, 19G, 19D) – improved lightened version of Model 1898, matte top surface on barrel. Mfg. 1906-07.

Grade A	$325	$275	$235	$200	$165	$150	$140
Grade B	$495	$415	$360	$330	$305	$275	$250
Grade C	$635	$525	$495	$440	$415	$385	$330
Grade D	$1,320	$1,100	$990	$825	$715	$635	$550

GRADING - PPGS™	100%	98%	95%	90%	80%	70%	60%	LAST MSR

MODEL 21 – straight grip version of Model 19.

Grade A	$325	$275	$235	$200	$165	$150	$140	
Grade B	$495	$415	$360	$330	$305	$275	$250	
Grade C	$635	$525	$495	$440	$415	$385	$330	
Grade D	$1,320	$1,100	$990	$825	$715	$635	$550	

MODEL 24 – improved 21, takedown, automatic recoil lock on slide, solid matte rib. Mfg. 1908-15.

Grade G	$295	$265	$225	$195	$165	$150	$140	
Grade A	$325	$275	$235	$200	$165	$150	$140	
Grade B	$525	$440	$385	$360	$330	$305	$275	
Grade C	$660	$550	$525	$470	$440	$415	$360	
Grade D	$1,375	$1,155	$1,045	$880	$770	$660	$580	

MODEL 26 – similar to Model 24 Grade A, with solid frame, 30 or 32 in. full choke barrel. Mfg. 1909-15.

	$275	$230	$210	$195	$165	$150	$140	

MODEL 26 BRUSH GUN – 26 in. cylinder bore barrel. Mfg. 1909-15.

	$350	$295	$250	$225	$195	$165	$150	

MODEL 26 RIOT GUN – 20 in. cylinder bore barrel. Mfg. 1909-15.

	$295	$250	$195	$180	$165	$150	$140	

MODEL 28 HAMMERLESS – 12 ga., 26-32 in. barrels, various chokes, takedown, matte top barrel, pistol grip stock. Mfg. 1913-22.

Grade A	$295	$265	$235	$200	$165	$150	$140	
Grade B	$495	$415	$360	$330	$305	$275	$250	
Grade C	$635	$525	$495	$440	$415	$385	$330	
Grade D	$1,320	$1,100	$990	$825	$715	$635	$550	

MODEL 28TS TRAP GUN – similar to Model 28, with 30 in. matte rib barrel, full choke, high comb straight grip stock. Mfg. 1915.

	$415	$330	$275	$250	$220	$195	$165	

MODEL 28T – similar to Model 28TS, with fancy wood, checkering, better finish. Mfg. 1915.

	$600	$525	$495	$470	$415	$360	$300	

MODEL 30 – similar to Model 16, with automatic recoil lock on slide, also mfg. in 20 ga. 1915-1917 (Model 30-20). Mfg. 1910-14.

Grade A	$325	$275	$235	$200	$165	$150	$140	
Grade B	$495	$415	$360	$330	$305	$275	$250	
Grade C	$635	$525	$495	$440	$415	$385	$330	
Grade D	$1,320	$1,100	$990	$825	$715	$635	$550	

MODEL 30 FIELD GRADE – similar to Model 30 Grade B, with 25 in. mod. barrel, straight stock. Mfg. 1913-17.

	$335	$275	$220	$180	$160	$130	$115	

MODEL 31 – scaled down small ga. (16 and 20 ga.) version of the Model 28, has 26 and 28 in. barrels, various chokes, Model 31-16 was mfg. 1914-17, Model 31-20 was mfg. 1911-23.

Grade A	$385	$305	$250	$220	$195	$165	$140	
Grade B	$495	$415	$360	$330	$305	$275	$250	
Grade C	$636	$525	$495	$440	$415	$385	$330	
Grade D	$1,320	$1,100	$990	$825	$715	$635	$550	

MODEL 31F FIELD GUN – 25 in. mod. barrel. Mfg. 1915-17.

	$395	$350	$325	$295	$265	$225	$200	

MODEL 42A – similar to Model 24, but lesser quality finishing. Mfg. 1922-34.

	$295	$250	$220	$195	$165	$140	$120	

MODEL 43 HAMMERLESS – similar to Model 28, with lesser quality finish. Mfg. 1923-30.

	$325	$275	$225	$200	$175	$150	$125	

MODEL 43TS – similar to Model 28T, lower quality.

	$525	$440	$415	$385	$360	$305	$275	

MODEL 44A – similar to Model 31 Grade A, 20 ga. only. Mfg. 1923-35.

	$350	$275	$250	$220	$195	$165	$140	

MODEL 44S – select checkered stock.

	$470	$385	$360	$330	$195	$165	$140	

MODEL 49 – lower priced version of Model 42A. They were given to purchasers of 4 shares of Marlin stock. 3,000 mfg. in 1925-28.

GRADING - PPGS™	100%	98%	95%	90%	80%	70%	60%	LAST MSR
	$440	$360	$305	$275	$220	$195	$165	

MODEL 53 – similar to Model 43 Hammerless. Mfg. 1929-30.

GRADING - PPGS™	100%	98%	95%	90%	80%	70%	60%	LAST MSR
	$330	$275	$250	$220	$195	$165	$140	

MODEL 63 – similar to Model 43 Hammerless, later model. Mfg. 1931-35.

GRADING - PPGS™	100%	98%	95%	90%	80%	70%	60%	LAST MSR
	$330	$250	$220	$195	$165	$140	$110	

MODEL 63TS – similar to Model 43TS, with trap style stock.

GRADING - PPGS™	100%	98%	95%	90%	80%	70%	60%	LAST MSR
	$385	$305	$250	$220	$195	$165	$140	

MODEL 120 MAGNUM – 12 ga., 3 in. chamber, 26-40 in. barrel, takedown, various chokes, checkered pistol grip stock. Mfg. 1971-1985.

GRADING - PPGS™	100%	98%	95%	90%	80%	70%	60%	LAST MSR
	$300	$250	$225	$200	$195	$180	$165	*$370*

Add 10%-15% for Model 120 MXR with 40 in. barrel (mfg. 1974-75).
Subtract $35 if without VR.

MODEL 778 – 12 ga. Mag. slide action, 20-38 in. barrels, 7 3/4 lbs. Disc. 1984.

GRADING - PPGS™	100%	98%	95%	90%	80%	70%	60%	LAST MSR
	$300	$250	$225	$200	$195	$180	$165	

PREMIER MARK I – 12 ga. only, aluminum receiver, takedown, manufactured in France for Marlin.

GRADING - PPGS™	100%	98%	95%	90%	80%	70%	60%	LAST MSR
	$225	$190	$180	$160	$150	$140	$120	

PREMIER MARK II – similar to Mark I, except with engraved receiver and checkering. Mfg. 1960-63 in France.

GRADING - PPGS™	100%	98%	95%	90%	80%	70%	60%	LAST MSR
	$275	$235	$200	$175	$150	$125	$100	

PREMIER MARK IV – similar to Mark II, only deluxe grade with better wood, more engraving. Mfg. 1960-63 in France.

GRADING - PPGS™	100%	98%	95%	90%	80%	70%	60%	LAST MSR
	$300	$250	$220	$195	$165	$140	$110	
With VR	$330	$275	$250	$220	$195	$165	$140	

MAROCCHI

Current trademark established in 1922, and currently manufactured by CD Europe SRL, located in Sarezzo, Italy. Currently imported by Whitworth Arms LLC, located in May, TX. Previously imported by Network Retailing LLC, located in Canby, OR, Glenn Rea Sport Guns located in Granbury, TX (2005-2007), by GSI, located in Trussville, AL. Previously distributed by Precision Sales International, Inc. located in Westfield, MA.

For individual model listings, please go to BlueBookOfGunValues.com/overflow.

MARTIN, ALEX

Current trademark managed and operated by John Dickson and Son, located in Edinburgh, Scotland.

The business of Alex Martin was established in Paisley, Scotland in 1837. The firm was most famous for its "ribless" shotgun and the regulation of .303 Lee Enfields. Alex Martin became part of John Dickson and Son in 1960. Currently, the business is managed and operated by John Dickson and Son. Although no new guns or rifles are currently produced under the Alex Martin name, a full repair, restoration, and recored enquiry service are offered for vintage Martin guns and rifles.

MARTINI

Please refer to the BSA Guns, Ltd. listing in the B section.

MARTINI GUNMAKERS

Current rifle manufacturer located in Creston, British Columbia, Canada since 2017. Previously located in Cranbrook, B.C., Canada 2000-2017.

Ralf Martini is a German-born Canadian who builds high-quality bolt action rifles based on the Mauser 98. From 2000 to 2007, Ralf teamed up with Martin Hagn building single shot falling block and bolt-action rifles as Martini & Hagn Gunmakers, Ltd. In 2008, Martini went back out on his own and continues to build rifles.

RIFLES

Current prices for Martini's bolt-action rifles range from $19,200-$26,300, depending on which company makes the action. A single shot rifle is also available built on a Hagn action. Variations include: Standard Grade - MSR is $17,500, Takedown Variation - MSR is $21,900, Mini Hagn - MSR is $14,500, and The Mini Max - MSR is $15,500.

GRADING - PPGS™	100%	98%	95%	90%	80%	70%	60%	LAST MSR

MASTERPIECE ARMS (MPA)

Current pistol and rifle manufacturer located in Comer, GA. Previously located in Carrollton, GA until 2013, also previously located in Braselton, GA.

For individual model listings, please go to BlueBookOfGunValues.com/overflow.

MASTERPIECE ARMS, INC.

Previous manufacturer of derringers located in Carrollton, GA from 2000-2004.

Masterpiece Arms manufactured derringers in both steel and stainless steel configuration.

MASQUELIER S.A.

Previous manufacturer located in Belgium. Previously distributed (until 1986) by Ambel Ltd., Inc. located in Sugarland, TX.

RIFLES: SxS

CARPATHE – .243 Win., .270 Win., .30-06, 7x57R, or 7x65R cal., single shot, hair trigger, push-down cocking system. Importation disc. 1986.

$3,500	$3,200	$2,900	$2,600	$2,300	$2,100	$1,850	*$3,850*

EXPRESS – .270 Win., .30-06, 8x57JRS, or 9.3x74R cal., O/U configuration, SST, ejectors. Add $800 for extra set of 20 ga. barrels. Importation disc. 1986.

$3,300	$3,000	$2,800	$2,600	$2,300	$2,100	$1,850	*$3,600*

ARDENNES MODEL – top-of-the-line model, custom order only. Importation disc. 1986.

$6,600	$6,000	$5,400	$4,800	$4,300	$3,900	$3,450	*$7,250*

SHOTGUNS: SxS

BOXLOCK – 12 ga. only, 2 3/4 in. chambers, Anson & Deeley boxlock action, ejectors, fine scroll engraving with French walnut stock. Importation disc. 1986.

$4,400	$4,000	$3,650	$3,300	$2,995	$2,600	$2,200	*$4,780*

SIDELOCK – 12 ga. only, 2 3/4 in. chambers, H&H style sidelocks, auto ejectors, English style fine scroll engraving with French walnut. Importation disc. 1986.

$12,500	$10,000	$8,750	$7,600	$6,700	$5,800	$5,000	*$15,850*

MATCHGUNS Srl

Current manufacturer established during 2001, located in Parma, Italy. No current U.S. importation. Distributed by Gehmann, located in Karlsruhe, Germany.

For individual model listings, please go to BlueBookOfGunValues.com/overflow.

MATCH GRADE ARMS & AMMUNITION

Please refer to MG Arms, Inc. listing in this section.

MATEBA

Previous manufacturer and trademark located in Pavia, Italy. Previously distributed by AWA USA, located in Hialeah, FL. Limited U.S. importation and distribution until 2004 by American Western Arms, located in Delray Beach, FL. Previously imported 2000-2001 by Keisler's Wholesale, located in Jeffersonville, IN, and by American Arms, Inc. until late 1999. Previously manufactured by Macchine Termo Balistiche located in Italy. Older mfg. has had little domestic importation.

PISTOLS: SEMI-AUTO

MATEBA M1911 – .45 ACP cal., choice of dual tone blue or hard chrome, 8 shot mag. Mfg. 2003-2008.

$1,375	$1,150	$895	$800	$675	$525	$450

REVOLVERS

MATEBA MTR-8 – offered in several calibers: .22, .32 S&W, .38 Spl., .357 Mag. Predecessor to 6 Unica. Production limited to about 500 revolvers, of which a few were carbines.

$5,500	$4,900	$4,350	$3,750	$3,000	$2,200	$1,900

MATEBA REVOLVER (6 UNICA AUTO REVOLVER) – various cals. (older mfg.), most recent mfg. is .357 Mag./.38 Spl., .44 Mag., or .454 Casull cal., combination semi-auto pistol and revolver, action allows cylinder and slide assembly to move back when fired, causing the cylinder to rotate, unique design permits barrel to fire lowest shell in cylinder (6 o'clock position), mechanism to rear of cylinder, single or double action, 6, 7 (older mfg.), or 8 (older mfg.) shot, 3, 4, 6, or 8 in. barrel, steel/alloy frame,

GRADING - PPGS™	100%	98%	95%	90%	80%	70%	60%	LAST MSR

blue finish, flared ergonomic walnut grips, interchangeable barrels, 2 3/4 lbs. Approx. 2,000 mfg. in all variations circa 1977-2005.

	$5,000	$4,300	$3,750	$3,400	$2,750	$2,250	$1,750	*$1,800*

Add $100 for frame mounted scope mount.
Add 25% for .454 Casull cal. or 20% for .44 Mag. cal.
Add $170 for polished nickel finish.

A carbine variation with 18 in. barrel is also available in this model. Price is the same for compatible caliber revolver.

MATEBA ITALIA Srl

Current manufacturer of semi-auto carbines, pistols, and rifles, located in Montebelluna, Italy. No current U.S. importation.

Please contact the company directly for more information, including pricing and U.S. availability.

MATHELON ARMES

Current SxS rifle and drilling manufacturer established in 2014, located in Rumilly, France. Previously imported by Kebco, LLC, located in Hanover, PA and by Rocky Mountain Armoury, located in Silverthorne, CO.

Mathelon Armes manufactures high quality drillings, double rifles, and stalking rifles. Models include the MX (disc.), and MX Express (disc.) double rifles, the MD Series, MXD Series, MXDL (disc.), and MXT drillings, Model MTL, MXD Series, and the MXDK Kipplauf stalking rifle (disc.). For more information, please contact the manufacturer directly.

MATRA MANURHIN DEFENSE

Please refer to the Manurhin heading in this section.

MATRIX ARMS

Current AR-15 style rifle/pistol manufacturer located in Claremont, NH.

Please refer to BlueBookOfGunValues.com to order the *Blue Book of AR-15s & Variations*, available as a book or online subscription.

MAUNZ MATCH RIFLES, LLC

Previous manufacturer located in Grand Rapids, OH 2011-2017.

For individual model listings, please go to BlueBookOfGunValues.com/overflow.

MAUNZ MFG., INC.

Previous firearms manufacturer located in Toledo, OH circa 1960s-1987.

For individual model listings, please go to BlueBookOfGunValues.com/overflow.

MAURITZ WIDFORSS AB

Current manufacturer, retailer, and auction house established in 1729, located in Stockholm, Sweden.

Widforss specializes in custom order long guns, hunting equipment and accessories, and holds several annual auctions. Please visit their website or contact the company directly for more information, including product availability and pricing.

MAUSER JAGDWAFFEN GmbH

Current trademark established during 1871, and currently owned by SIG Arms AG beginning late 2000. Mauser Model 98 Magnum bolt action rifles are currently manufactured by Mauser Jagdwaffen GmbH, located in Isny, Germany. Currently imported by Blaser Group (formerly known as Blaser USA), beginning circa 2012. Previously imported by Mauser USA, located in San Antonio, TX, 2009-2012.

In late 2000, SIG Arms AG, the firearms portion of SIG, was purchased by two Germans named Michael Lüke and Thomas Ortmeier, who have a background in textiles. Today the Lüke & Ortmeier group (L&O Group) includes independently operational companies such as Blaser Jadgwaffen GmbH, Mauser Jagdwaffen GmbH, J.P. Sauer & Sohn GmbH, SIG-Sauer Inc., SIG-Sauer GmbH and SAN Swiss Arms AG.

From late March, 2006-2009, Models 98 and 03 were distributed exclusively by Briley Manufacturing, located in Houston, TX. The former transition name was Mauser Jagd-und Sportwaffen GmbH. On January 1, 1999, Mauser transferred all production and distribution

GRADING - PPGS™	100%	98%	95%	90%	80%	70%	60%	LAST MSR

rights of both hunting and sporting weapons to SIG-Blaser. Mauser-Werke Oberndorf Waffensysteme GmbH continues to manufacture military defense contracts (including making small bore barrel liners for tanks), in addition to other industrial machinery.

Previously imported exclusively by Brolin Arms, located in Pomona, CA during 1997-98 only. During 1998, the company name was changed from Mauser-Werke Oberndorf Waffensysteme GmbH. During 1994, the name was changed from Mauser-Werke to Mauser-Werke Oberndorf Waffensysteme GmbH. Previously imported by GSI located in Trussville, AL, until 1997, Gibb's Rifle Co., Inc. until 1995, Precision Imports, Inc. located in San Antonio, TX until 1993, and KDF located in Seguin, TX (1987-89).

HANDGUNS: EARLY PRODUCTION

MODEL 1877 SINGLE SHOT - 9mm Para. cal., single shot, barrel release in usual hammer position and safety on left side. Examples are rare.

	N/A	$25,000	$20,000	$15,000	$10,000	$7,500	$5,000

MODEL 1878 "ZIG-ZAG" REVOLVER - 7.6mm, 9mm (most common) or 10.6mm cal., Zig-Zag refers to Z-pattern grooves cut into cylinder, earliest revolvers were solid frame, gate loaded, and chambered in 9mm, most were designed with a hinged frame, third and last version had an "improved" sliding release on the forward frame, most revolvers had a rust blue frame and barrel complementing a fire blue cylinder, grips were checkered or hard rubber with a floral pattern.

7.6mm cal.	N/A	$6,500	$5,000	$4,000	$3,000	$2,500	$2,000
9mm cal.	N/A	$7,000	$6,500	$6,000	$5,000	$4,000	$3,500
10.6mm cal.	N/A	$10,000	$8,500	$7,000	$5,500	$4,500	$3,500

Add 20% for earliest pistols with "midnight blue" finish. Premiums exist for solid frame, late improved model, and factory cased guns.

PISTOLS: SEMI-AUTO, DISC.

The Models 1906-08, 1912-14, and HSv are very rare and only infrequently encountered. A competent appraisal is advisable before buying or selling these models.

MODEL 1906-08 - 9mm Export (9x25mm) cal., detachable mag., incorporates features of both the pocket pistols and Model 1896 Broomhandle. Ser. range 1-100 (est.).

	N/A	$60,000	$52,500	$45,000	$37,500	$30,000	$25,000

MODEL 1912-14 - generally chambered for 9mm Para. cal., similar to pocket pistol configuration, but considerably larger, earliest specimens have inscribed slide legend. Those under serial number 100 (approx.) are not slotted for shoulder stock while those over 100 are generally slotted. Ser. range 1-175 (est.).

	N/A	$40,000	$35,000	$30,000	$25,000	$20,000	$15,000

Add 50% if slotted with matching shoulder stock.

This variation is very rare in .45 ACP cal. or with a tangent rear sight.

WTP MODEL I VEST POCKET AUTOMATIC - 6.35mm cal., 6 shot, 2 1/2 in. barrel, blue, rubber grips. Mfg. 1922-37.

	$750	$655	$565	$510	$415	$340	$265

WTP MODEL II - similar to Model I, but 2 in. barrel. Mfg. 1938-40.

	$1,350	$1,180	$1,015	$920	$745	$610	$475

Add 20% for brown grips or French contract.

POCKET MODEL 1910 - 6.35mm or 7.65mm cal., 9 shot, 3 in. barrel, blue fixed sights, checkered walnut or hard rubber grips. Mfg. 1910-34.

	$650	$570	$490	$440	$360	$295	$230

Add 30% for sidelatch variation.

POCKET MODEL 1914 - similar to Model 1910, but 7.65mm cal., 3.4 in. barrel. Mfg. 1914-1934.

	$650	$570	$490	$440	$360	$295	$230

Add 10% for military acceptance crown D proof by rear sight and/or Prussian eagle on trigger guard.

* ***Pocket Model 1914 Humpback Model***

	$6,500	$5,000	$4,000	$3,000	$2,500	$2,000	$1,500

Add 20% for long barrel version in the 200-400 serial number range.

POCKET MODEL 1934 - similar to Model 1914, but reshaped grip. Mfg. 1934-1939.

	$850	$700	$550	$475	$400	$325	$265
Waffenamt	$1,950	$1,650	$1,250	$1,100	$850	$675	$525
Nazi Police	$1,750	$1,600	$1,200	$1,100	$850	$675	$525
Nazi Navy marked	$2,350	$1,950	$1,650	$1,275	$1,030	$845	$655

GRADING - PPGS™	100%	98%	95%	90%	80%	70%	60%	LAST MSR

MODEL HSv – 9mm Para. cal., only 2 or 3 known, similar features to Model HSc, except has larger dimensions.

Extreme rarity precludes accurate pricing on this model.

Mauser Pistols: HSc Models

MODEL HSc DOUBLE ACTION – 7.65mm (8 shot) or .380 ACP (7 shot) cal., 3.4 in. barrel, blue or nickel, fixed sights, checkered walnut grips. Mfg. 1938-disc. (most recent mfg. was by R. Gamba in Italy circa 1996).

Mauser Pistols: HSc WWII Military Mfg.

* ***HSc WWII Military Mfg. Low Grip Screw*** – very rare, first variation with ser. numbers starting at 700,000, less than 2,000 mfg.

N/A	$8,500	$6,000	$5,000	$3,500	$2,000	$1,500	

Add 20% if Navy marked and matching. Beware of fakes!

* ***HSc WWII Military Mfg. Early Nazi Army*** – proofed 655 and 135.

N/A	$850	$600	$450	$300	$250	$200	

Add 100% for small 655 additionally test-proofed on left tang.

* ***HSc WWII Military Mfg. Early Nazi Navy*** – marked on front grip strap.

N/A	$1,950	$1,650	$1,250	$950	$750	$650	

* ***HSc WWII Military Mfg. Early Nazi Police*** – Eagle L proof only.

N/A	$950	$750	$500	$350	$300	$250	

* ***HSc WWII Military Mfg. Wartime Nazi Army*** – proof 135 and WaA 135. Eagle N proofed also.

N/A	$750	$575	$400	$325	$285	$245	

* ***HSc WWII Military Mfg. Wartime Nazi Navy*** – proofed on left side of trigger guard.

N/A	$1,650	$1,350	$1,000	$800	$600	$500	

* ***HSc WWII Military Mfg. Wartime Nazi Police*** – proofed Eagle L.

N/A	$700	$550	$375	$325	$285	$245	

Add 10% if Eagle F.

* ***HSc WWII Military Mfg. Wartime Commercial*** – standard WWII Commercial Model.

N/A	$550	$450	$325	$275	$250	$225	

* ***HSc WWII Military Mfg. Swiss Commercial*** – ser. range 800,000-900,000. Very rare.

N/A	$1,400	$1,250	$1,125	$995	$900	$850	

* ***HSc WWII Military Mfg. Cutaways*** – mfg. to visibly show mechanism. Should not be proofed.

N/A	$1,950	$1,500	$1,000	$900	$800	$750	

Mauser Pistols: HSc Post-WWII Mfg.

* ***HSc Post-WWII Mfg. French Manufacture*** – frequently encountered in poor condition - post-WWII production.

N/A	$400	$350	$300	$250	$200	$175	

* ***HSc Post-WWII Mfg. Mauser Production*** – .32 or .380 cal., 15 shot, mfg. 1968-1981.

$550	$450	$350	$300	$250	$200	$175	

Subtract 20% if not boxed or in .32 cal.

* ***HSc Post-WWII Mfg. Interarms Import*** – imported by Interarms from 1983-1985 (Mauser and Italian mfg. by Gamba).

$375	$300	$250	$220	$180	$150	$125	*$415*

* ***HSc Post-WWII Mfg. One of Five Thousand Edition*** – American Eagle edition (marked on gun), 5,000 total mfg. (serial numbered 1-5000).

$450	$400	$350	$300	$240	$210	$180	

* ***HSc Post-WWII Mfg. Armes De Chasse Import*** – previously imported by Armes De Chasse located in Chadds Ford, PA on a limited basis.

$475	$425	$330	$300	$260	$240	$220	*$695*

Add $195 for Limited Series.
Add $58 For G15 variation (9 shot).

* ***HSc Post-WWII Mfg. E.A.A. Import*** – imported by European American Armory, distributed by RSR Wholesale.

$265	$225	$195	$175	$150	$125	$110	

GRADING - PPGS™	100%	98%	95%	90%	80%	70%	60%	LAST MSR

* ***HSc Post-WWII Mfg. Recent Gamba Mfg.*** – .32 ACP or .380 ACP cal., steel construction, double action, double safety, stippled walnut grips, recently imported by Gamba, USA until approx. 1996, and reintroduced during 2005-circa 2006.

$395	$350	$295	$265	$240	$220	$200	

Mauser Pistols: Luger Mfg.

Both pre-war and post-war Mauser manufactured Lugers will be found in the Luger section of this book.

Mauser Pistols: P.38 Mfg.

Please refer to the P.38 entries in the P section.

PISTOLS: SEMI-AUTO, RECENT IMPORTATION

MODEL 80 SA – .380 ACP or 9mm Para. cal., semi-auto single action patterned after the Browning Hi-power, 4 2/3 in. barrel, blue finish with checkered walnut grips, round hammer, steel construction, 10 (C/B 1994) or 13* shot mag., 1.95 lbs. Mfg. by FEG in Hungary, imported 1992-96.

$450	$325	$275	$240	$215	$185	$165	*$520*

MODEL 90 DA – similar to Model 80 SA, except is double action, spur hammer, and has 10 (C/B 1994) or 14* shot mag., 2.15 lbs. Mfg. by FEG, imported 1992-96.

$445	$325	$275	$240	$215	$185	$165	*$516*

* ***Model 90 DAC*** – similar to Model 90 DA, except is compact model with 4 1/8 in. barrel, 2.05 lbs. Imported 1992-96.

$450	$325	$275	$240	$215	$185	$165	*$520*

M-2 – .357 SIG (disc. 2001), .40 S&W, or .45 ACP cal., short recoil operation, SFO, rotating 3.54 in. barrel lockup, manual safety, 8 (.45 ACP) or 10 shot, DAO, hammerless, aluminum alloy frame with nickel chromium steel slide, black finish, includes case and trigger lock, approx. 29 or 32 1/2 oz. Mfg. by SIG in Europe, limited importation 2000-04.

$450	$400	$350	$300	$275	$250	$225	

PISTOLS: SEMI-AUTO, MODEL 1896 BROOMHANDLES

Note: Manufactured in Oberndorf, Germany between 1897 & 1938.

While many variations of the famous 1896 Broomhandle exist, most common Broomhandles are pre-war Commercials, Model 1930 Commercials, Red 9s, and Bolos. They can be found in chronological order in this section. Holster stocks are a very popular accessory in this model. Commercial stocks may be matching or may not be serial numbered to gun (proper stock).

In 1984, Federal legislation once again allowed importation of non-domestic WWI and WWII military handguns. While many of these newer imports would make workable shooters, they have in no way lowered prices on 90%+ condition specimens due to normal collector activity in top quality only pistols. Recently imported Broomhandles should have the importer's name visibly stamped on an exterior surface.

Mauser Broomhandles: Conehammer Variations

STANDARD CONEHAMMER – 7.63 Mauser cal., distinguishable by circular machined upper hammer with concentric rings. 5 1/2 in. barrel, 23 groove wooden grips, rear adjustable sight available in 1-10, 50-500, 100-300, 50-300, 50-700 meter configurations, 10 shot mag.

N/A	$5,500	$3,500	$3,000	$2,500	$2,000	$1,500	

Add 100% for matching stock.

FIXED SIGHT CONEHAMMER – 7.63 Mauser cal., similar to Standard Conehammer, except has fixed rear sight.

N/A	$6,500	$5,000	$4,000	$3,000	$2,500	$2,000	

6 SHOT CONEHAMMER - FIXED SIGHT – 7.63 Mauser cal., 4 3/4 in. barrel, 6 shot mag., rare.

N/A	$9,500	$7,500	$5,500	$4,000	$3,000	$2,500	

* ***6 Shot Conehammer - Adjustable Sight*** – 7.63 Mauser cal., 5 1/2 in. barrel, very rare.

N/A	$15,000	$12,500	$10,000	$7,500	$5,000	$3,500	

Sales of this variation are extremely limited.

TURKISH CONEHAMMER – 7.63 Mauser cal., 5 1/2 in. barrel, 10 shot mag. Approx. 1,000 mfg. for Turkey in 1898, Farsi serial numbers.

N/A	$15,000	$12,500	$10,000	$9,500	$6,000	$4,500	

"SYSTEM MAUSER" CONEHAMMER – 7.63 Mauser cal., "SYSTEM MAUSER" marked on top of chamber, improved 5 1/2 in. tapered barrel, 10 shot mag.

N/A	$19,500	$15,000	$12,500	$9,000	$6,500	$4,500	

GRADING - PPGS™	100%	98%	95%	90%	80%	70%	60%	LAST MSR

* ***System Mauser Conehammer Stepped barrel variation*** – similar to System Mauser variation, except has older 5 1/2 in. stepped barrel with no taper.

N/A	$29,500	$23,500	$15,000	$10,000	$9,000	$8,000

Add 40% for "SYSTEM MAUSER" stock or 6 shot variation.

20 SHOT CONEHAMMER – 7.63 Mauser cal., 20 shot non-detachable mag., frame can either be flatside or have milled panels, 5 1/2 in. tapered barrel, extremely rare.

N/A	$50,000	$35,000	$28,500	$17,500	$12,000	$9,000

Add 20% for milled panel variation.

Add 40% for matching stock cut for 20 shot mag.

Many fake 20 shot pistols (especially flatsides with fake stocks) have surfaced over the last few years. Use extreme caution when considering purchase.

EARLY TRANSITIONAL LARGE RING HAMMER – 7.63 Mauser cal., distinguishable by large, open centered ring, 10 shot mag., 5 1/2 in. barrel.

N/A	$3,750	$3,000	$2,500	$2,000	$1,750	$1,500

This variation is normally found in the 12,000-15,000 serial range only.

Mauser Broomhandles: Flatside Variations

Add approx. $1,500-$2,000 for matching shoulder stock, $700-$1,000 for non-matching stock.

ITALIAN CONTRACT FLATSIDE – 7.63 Mauser cal., distinguishable by flatside frame and DV/AV proofmarks, 10 shot mag., 5 1/2 in. barrel.

N/A	$6,000	$4,000	$3,000	$2,250	$1,750	$1,250

This variation is found in the 1-5,000 serial range only.

FLATSIDE COMMERCIAL – 7.63 Mauser cal., 5 1/2 in. barrel, 23 groove walnut grips, adj. rear sight typically marked 1-10 or 50-1,000.

N/A	$4,500	$3,500	$2,500	$1,750	$1,250	$1,000

Add 20% for pinned sight.

Early specimens may have pinned rear sights. Found in serial range 20,000-30,000.

Mauser Broomhandles: Post-1900 Variations

Add approximately $2,000-$2,500 for a matching shoulder stock on the following models, $400-$550 for non-matching, depending on the original condition. Some exceptions are noted.

PRE-WAR LARGE RING BOLO – 7.63 Mauser cal., 3.9 in. barrel, floral grips, usually found in 29,000 and 40,000 serial range.

N/A	$4,500	$3,500	$2,500	$2,000	$1,550	$1,000

Add $1,250 for short pre-war bolo stock, $1,750 if stock matches pistol.

LARGE RING SHALLOW MILLING – 7.63 Mauser cal., 5 1/2 in. barrel, 23 groove walnut or hard rubber grips, normally found in the 30,000-33,000 ser. range.

N/A	$4,000	$3,250	$2,500	$2,000	$1,100	$850

Add $750 for pre-war stock, $1,500 if stock matches pistol.

LARGE RING DEEP MILLING – 7.63 Mauser cal., 5 1/2 in. barrel, 35 groove walnut or hard rubber grips, normally found in the 34,000 ser. range.

N/A	$4,000	$3,250	$2,500	$2,000	$1,100	$850

Add $750 for pre-war stock, $2,000 if stock matches pistol.

PRE-WAR SMALL RING BOLO – 7.63 Mauser cal., 3.9 in. barrel, floral/checkered rubber or 31-36 groove walnut grips, usually found in 40,000-44,000 serial range.

N/A	$3,500	$2,750	$1,800	$1,200	$750	$500

Add $1,000 for short pre-war bolo stock, $1,750 if stock matches pistol.

6-SHOT BOLO – 7.63 Mauser cal., distinctive 6 shot mag., 3.9 in. barrel, either fixed rear sight (more common) or adjustable, could have either large ring or small ring hammer.

N/A	$6,500	$5,000	$4,000	$3,000	$2,500	$2,000

Add $1,500 for short pre-war bolo stock, $2,000-$3,000 if stock matches pistol, depending on original condition.

STANDARD PRE-WAR COMMERCIAL – 7.63 Mauser cal., 5 1/2 in. barrel, 10 shot mag., 34 groove walnut or checkered black rubber grips, typically 50-1,000 meter adj. rear sight.

N/A	$2,250	$1,850	$1,500	$1,000	$775	$650

Original condition on this model is usually under 60% and prices usually start in the $400 range.

Add $1,000-$1,500 for matching stock, $400-$550 for non-matching, depending on original condition.

GRADING - PPGS™	100%	98%	95%	90%	80%	70%	60%	LAST MSR

This variation is the most commonly encountered of all M1896 broomhandles. It can be encountered in the 39,000-274,000 serial range. Early guns below serial no. 100,000 are often Von Lengerke and Detmold marked and can be encountered with hard rubber grips. Rifling changed from 4 groove to 6 groove at approx. serial no. 100,000.

Note: This model is once again being imported by domestic distributors/dealers. These specimens usually have been reblued in addition to other reworking because the original condition has generally been very poor.

MAUSER BANNER CHAMBER MARKED – 7.63 Mauser or 9mm Export/9mm Mauser (rare) cal., 5 1/2 in. barrel, distinguishable by Mauser banner trademark on top of chamber, 32 groove walnut grips. Approx. 10,000 mfg. in serial range 84,000-94,000.

N/A	$3,500	$2,250	$1,750	$1,250	$750	$500

This model is very similar in appearance to the Pre-War Commercial.

PERSIAN CONTRACT – 7.63 Mauser cal., 5 1/2 in. barrel, distinguished by Persian lion crest in left rear frame panel, must be in the 154,000 serial range, 50-1,000 meter adj. rear sight.

N/A	$5,000	$4,000	$3,000	$2,500	$2,000	$1,500

This variation is frequently faked - pay close attention to serial no. and Persian crest.

STANDARD WARTIME COMMERCIAL – 7.63 Mauser cal., 5 1/2 in. barrel, 10 shot mag., 30 groove walnut grips, adj. 50-1,000 meter rear sight.

N/A	$2,250	$1,750	$1,250	$900	$750	$600

Condition is somewhat poor, and prices usually start in the $250 range.

This variation is encountered almost as frequently as the Standard Pre-War Commercial. It is usually found in the 290,000-440,000 serial range. It was the first model to utilize the "new safety" design, and can be noticed by the "NS" marking on the back of hammer. Similar features as the Pre-War Commercial, except finish and polishing exhibit more machine and tooling marks.

Note: This model is once again being imported by domestic distributors/dealers. These specimens usually have been reblued in addition to other reworking because the original condition has generally been very poor.

RED-9 ADJ. SIGHT – 9mm Para. cal., 5 1/2 in. barrel, 10 shot mag., 24 groove walnut grips usually marked with large red no. 9, adj. 50-500 meter rear sight, standard WWI military contract model with separate serial range 1-150,000, generally poorly finished. Mfg. 1916-1918.

N/A	$3,500	$2,750	$2,250	$1,750	$1,250	$850

Add $700 for original leather.
Add 10% if Prussian Eagle proofed on front of magazine well.
Add $1,000-$1,500 for matching stock, $400-$550 for non-matching, depending on original condition.

The Red-9 may be the most popular Commercial Broomhandle whose value far outstrips its rarity.

Note: Be cautious for originality since metal refinishing is prevalent in this model. The last 10,000 guns of this German military contract are not military proofed, are better polished, and will command a slight premium.

RED-9 FIXED SIGHT – 9mm Para. cal., 3.9 in. barrel, this is a 1920 commercial rework of the Red-9 military, may be dated 1920 and/or have police markings on front grip strap.

N/A	$1,950	$1,750	$1,250	$1,000	$750	$500

Because of the Treaty of Versailles following WWI, barrels had to be shortened to less than 4 inches and the adj. rear sight removed.

FRENCH GENDARME – 7.63 Mauser cal., 3.9 in. barrel, distinguished by Bolo barrel length on large frame, hard rubber or walnut (rare) grips, found in the serial range 431,000-434,000, adj. 50-500 meter rear sight.

N/A	$3,000	$2,250	$1,750	$1,250	$750	$500

EARLY POST-WAR BOLO – 7.63 Mauser cal., 3.9 in. barrel, short extractor, small ring hammer, usually found in the 440,000-500,000 serial range. Fit with full size stock.

N/A	$2,250	$1,750	$1,100	$725	$600	$500

Add 50% for long barrel Bolos in approx. the 475,000 serial range.

LATE POST-WAR BOLO – 7.63 Mauser cal., 3.9 in. barrel, similar features of Early Post-War Bolo except has Mauser banner trademark on left rear frame panel, usually encountered in the 500,000-700,000+ serial range. Fit with full size stock.

N/A	$2,750	$2,000	$1,500	$1,000	$800	$600

Add 10% for late pistols with high polish salt blue finish.

GRADING - PPGS™	100%	98%	95%	90%	80%	70%	60%	LAST MSR

Mauser Broomhandles: Post-1930 Variations

EARLY MODEL 1930 COMMERCIAL – 7.63 Mauser cal., 5.2 (common) or 5 1/2 in. stepped barrel, 12 groove walnut grips, adj. 50-1,000 meter rear sight, usually found in the 800,000-890,000 serial range.

	N/A	$3,000	$2,300	$1,750	$1,450	$1,050	$850	

Add approximately $650-$1,500 for Mauser banner marked stock, depending on original condition.

This broomhandle variation had a high polish, salt blue finish. Small parts are still fire blue and milling grooves were machined in receiver rails.

LATE MODEL 1930 COMMERCIAL – 7.63 Mauser cal., 5 1/2 in. stepped barrel, similar appearance to early 1930 Commercial except has solid receiver rails and various small parts are salt blued. Ser. range 890,000-921,000 with production ending in late 1930s.

	N/A	$2,850	$2,300	$1,750	$1,450	$1,050	$850	

Add approximately $650-$1,500 for Mauser banner marked stock.

This model is serial numbered on rear top of barrel extension assembly.

MODEL 1930 REMOVABLE MAG. – 7.63 Mauser cal., 5 1/2 in. stepped barrel, 12 groove walnut grips, adj. 50-1,000 meter rear sight, very rare.

	N/A	$20,000	$15,000	$10,000	$8,500	$7,000	$5,500	

Original specimens of this variation have frames without the extra cuts required for the selector switch. Fakes are usually welded up Schnellfeuers made to look original. Only a very few are known in the 84,000-88,000 serial range.

SCHNELLFEUER (MODEL 712) – 7.63 Mauser cal., 5 1/2 in. stepped barrel, 12 groove walnut grips, adj. 50-1,000 meter rear sight, switchable full auto variation generally with selector switch, separate serial range 1-100,000, 10 or 20 shot detachable mag. 712 stock is internally grooved for selector switch.

	N/A	$15,000	$12,500	$10,000	$7,500	$6,000	$5,000	

Add $750-$1,500 for correct stock.

The Model 712 is classified as a machine gun and is subject to registration and payment of a $200 transfer tax.

Broomhandle Carbines

CONE HAMMER – 7.63mm cal., 11 3/4 in. barrel, experimental variation.

	N/A	$30,000	$25,000	$20,000	$15,000	$12,500	$10,000	

Deduct 30% for recent carbines with dealer import stamps prominent on receivers (from European collections).

LARGE RING HAMMER TRANSITIONAL – 7.63mm cal., 11 3/4 in. barrel.

	N/A	$23,500	$18,500	$13,500	$9,000	$8,000	$7,000	

Deduct 30% for recent carbines with dealer import stamps prominent on receivers (from European collections).

FLATSIDE TRANSITIONAL – 7.63mm cal., 11 3/4 in. barrel.

	N/A	$20,000	$16,000	$12,000	$8,500	$7,500	$6,500	

Deduct 30% for recent carbines with dealer import stamps prominent on receivers (from European collections).

LARGE RING HAMMER – 7.63mm cal., 14 1/2 in. barrel.

	N/A	$15,000	$12,500	$10,000	$8,500	$7,500	$6,500	

Deduct 30% for recent carbines with dealer import stamps prominent on receivers (from European collections).

SMALL RING HAMMER – 7.63mm cal., 14 1/2 in. barrel.

	N/A	$17,500	$13,500	$10,000	$8,500	$7,500	$6,500	

Deduct 30% for recent carbines with dealer import stamps prominent on receivers (from European collections).

Broomhandles: Copies from Other Countries

These pistols are Chinese manufactured copies of the original German design.

HAND-MADE MAUSER CHINESE MARKED AND OTHERS – 9mm Para. or .45 ACP cal., copies of the Mauser Broomhandle, many thousands made, fixed (.45 ACP cal.) or detachable (9mm Para.) mag., quality can vary significantly, recent imports will have import markings. IAR, Inc. imported these recently.

9mm Para. cal.	N/A	$1,300	$750	$600	$500	$400	$300	

Add $350 for reproduction shoulder stock holster (with or w/o leather) that holds 20 shot mag (if in excellent condition).

Add 20% for 10 and 20 shot matching numbered mags.

Subtract 25% for poor quality.

GRADING - PPGS™	100%	98%	95%	90%	80%	70%	60%	LAST MSR

HAND-MADE UNMARKED – poor quality.

	N/A	$800	$700	$600	$500	$450	$400	

ASIATIC FLATSIDE UNMARKED – better quality, not exceedingly rare.

	N/A	$2,500	$1,800	$1,550	$1,250	$750	$500	

TAKU-NAVAL DOCKYARD FLATSIDE – machine-made, better quality, approx. 6,000 mfg.

	N/A	$3,500	$3,000	$2,500	$2,000	$1,500	$1,000	

Add 30% if with correct stock.

SHANSEI ARSENAL .45 CAL. – .45 ACP cal., approx. 8,500 mfg., scarce and desirable in excellent condition, as most remaining original pistols are in rough condition, original stripper clips for this model are rare.

	N/A	$8,500	$7,500	$6,500	$5,500	$4,500	$3,500	

Newly made Shansei 45s are currently priced in the $2,000-2,500 range.

Recently, a small number of currently manufactured pistols have been marketed as "restorations." Buyer beware! Also, fake stocks have recently surfaced.

Broomhandles: Spanish Copies

VERY EARLY ASTRA-900 – Bolo grips, frame has single-line address, approx. 1,200 mfg.

	N/A	$4,500	$2,650	$2,250	$1,750	$1,500	$1,250	

EARLY ASTRA-900 – single-line address, approx. ser. range 1,200-12,000.

	N/A	$3,950	$3,000	$2,500	$2,000	$1,500	$850	

LATE ASTRA-900 – two and three-line address, two-line address ser. range is approx. 12,000-20,000, three-line address ser. range is approx. 20,000-34,400.

	$4,500	$3,500	$3,000	$2,500	$1,750	$1,500	$850	

Add 20% for Chinese character variation in the 27,000 serial range or 50% if in Nazi procurement range.

BEISTEGUI HERMANOS "ROYAL" SEMI-AUTO – early Royals are mostly seen in semi-auto with round bolts.

	N/A	$3,500	$2,700	$2,000	$1,500	$1,000	$750	

Add 100% if with detachable mag.

There were many variations of the Royals and values assume standard variation.

BEISTEGUI HERMANOS "ROYAL" SELECTIVE FIRE – 7.63mm cal., most of approx. 33,000 Royals manufactured were selective fire, several variations, Class III transferable only.

Class III	N/A	$7,500	$5,000	$3,500	$2,500	$2,000	$1,750	

Add 20% if detachable mag.

Add 100% if MM34 with pneumatic rate retarder (production under 1,000 pistols).

This model had either a fixed mag. or detachable mag. May have been fit with pneumatic rate retarder.

RIFLES: MILITARY PRODUCTION

As there were quite a few different manufacturers within Germany that produced the K98 military rifles and carbines, they have been listed by country in alphabetical order in this section. Most of the produced military contracts will be found under Mauser Mfg. - Oberndorf.

Add 20%-25% if with matching bayonet.

Subtract 50%-60% if bolt is not matching or contract crests have been removed, depending on remaining condition.

ARGENTINA

Model 1891 Rifle Argentine pattern	$800	$775	$750	$550	$500	$400	$275	
Model 1891 Carbine	$750	$725	$700	$550	$450	$300	$200	
Model 1909 Rifle	$900	$850	$750	$675	$550	$400	$300	
Model 1909 Sniper Rifle w/scope	$2,300	$2,100	$1,800	$1,600	$1,525	$1,200	$1,000	
Model 1909 Cavalry Carbine	$800	$700	$600	$550	$475	$400	$300	
Model 1909 Mountain Carbine	$800	$700	$600	$550	$475	$400	$300	
Model 1933 Mauser Banner	$700	$650	$550	$450	$400	$300	$250	
Model 1935 Mauser Banner	$700	$650	$550	$450	$400	$300	$250	

GRADING - PPGS™	100%	98%	95%	90%	80%	70%	60%	LAST MSR
AUSTRIA								
Model 1914 Rifle	N/A	N/A	$2,000	$1,750	$1,500	$1,000	$600	
BELGIUM								
Model 1889 Rifle FN mfg.	N/A	$2,400	$1,800	$1,450	$1,000	$750	$650	
Model 1889 Rifle Manufacture Armes Etat Arsenal mfg.	N/A	$2,700	$2,100	$1,650	$1,200	$850	$750	
Model 1889 Rifle Hopkins & Allen or Birmingham mfg.	$2,900	$2,600	$1,900	$1,250	$900	$750	$600	
Model 1889 Carbine (not modified pre-WWI)	$1,900	$1,800	$1,700	$1,500	$1,200	$900	$800	
Model 1916 Carbine (all WWI makes/modifications)	$700	$650	$600	$475	$400	$350	$300	
Model 1935 Short Rifle Manufacture Armes Etat mfg.	$1,200	$1,100	$950	$750	$650	$550	$450	
Model 1935 Short Rifle (FN receiver)	$1,500	$1,400	$1,250	$1,000	$850	$750	$650	
Model 1889/36 Short Rifle Manufacture Armes Etat mfg.	$900	$800	$750	$650	$500	$400	$300	
Model 1889/36 Short Rifle Pieper Herstal mfg.	N/A	$1,200	$950	$750	$650	$550	$450	
Post-War Model 30 "L" Crest	$800	$625	$475	$425	$350	$300	$225	
Post-War Model 30 "B" Crest	$700	$600	$450	$400	$325	$275	$200	
Post-War Model 30 Belgian Congo "FP" Crest	$2,200	$1,900	$1,600	$1,100	$875	$775	$600	
Model 30 .22 cal. Trainer "B" Crest	$1,900	$1,600	$1,400	$1,150	$800	$750	$550	
Model 30 .22 cal. Congo Trainer "FP" Crest	$2,400	$2,100	$1,900	$1,600	$1,500	$900	$700	

Add 25% for WWI German captured Belgian Model 1889 Mausers (rifles & carbines) converted by the Germans to 7.92mm cal. and marked with Imperial German proofs.

Add 50% for Belgian Civil Guard marked Model 1889 Mausers.

Add 50% for cyclist Model 1935 rifles with side swivels.

Post-war arsenal refinished rifles in grey paint do not command a premium.

GRADING - PPGS™	100%	98%	95%	90%	80%	70%	60%	LAST MSR
BOLIVIA								
Model 1895 Rifle(Argentine M1891 Rifle)	$600	$550	$450	$350	$250	$200	$125	
Model 1907 Rifle	$800	$750	$700	$600	$500	$400	$275	
Model 1907 Short Rifle	$800	$750	$700	$600	$500	$400	$275	
Czech marked Model VZ24 Short Rifle	$800	$750	$700	$600	$500	$400	$275	
Standard Model MauserBanner Short Rifle	$700	$650	$550	$425	$350	$275	$150	
Model 1950 Rifle Series B-50	$700	$650	$550	$425	$350	$275	$150	
BRAZIL								
Model 1894 Rifle, Loewe mfg.	$800	$650	$550	$450	$400	$300	$250	
Model 1894 Rifle, FN mfg.	$1,500	$1,150	$850	$650	$450	$400	$350	
Model 1894 Carbine Loewe mfg.	$1,000	$850	$650	$550	$450	$400	$350	
Model 1894 Carbine FN mfg.	$1,800	$1,500	$1,100	$950	$650	$500	$400	
Model 1904 Mauser Vergueiro Rifle	$600	$500	$400	$300	$225	$175	$100	
Model 1907 Rifle	$600	$500	$400	$300	$225	$175	$100	
Model 1907 Carbine	$600	$500	$400	$300	$200	$175	$100	

GRADING - PPGS™	100%	98%	95%	90%	80%	70%	60%	LAST MSR
Model 1908 Rifle	$1,500	$1,100	$900	$800	$600	$400	$200	
Model 1908 Short Rifle	$825	$775	$650	$500	$375	$250	$100	
FN Mle. 1922 Carbine	$750	$650	$550	$400	$300	$225	$125	
Model 1924 VZ 24 Carbine	$800	$675	$575	$450	$300	$225	$100	
Model 1924/34 Czech Carbine	$800	$675	$575	$450	$300	$225	$100	
Model 1908/34 Rifle .30-06 cal.	$800	$675	$575	$450	$300	$225	$100	
Model 1935 Mauser Banner Rifle	$1,500	$1,200	$900	$800	$600	$400	$200	
Model 1935 Mauser Banner Carbine	$1,100	$1,000	$900	$800	$600	$400	$200	
Model M954 Rifle .30-06 cal.	$800	$650	$500	$375	$200	$150	$100	
CHILE								
Model 1893 Rifle -Bent bolt handle	$700	$650	$575	$475	$375	$300	$175	
Model 1895 Rifle - Army	$700	$650	$590	$475	$325	$225	$100	
Model 1895 Rifle - Anchor crest	$700	$650	$590	$475	$325	$225	$100	
Model 1895 Short Rifle	$650	$600	$550	$425	$275	$175	$80	
Model 1895 Carbine	$600	$550	$450	$325	$250	$195	$100	
Model 1912 Rifle	$700	$650	$575	$495	$375	$250	$125	
Model 1912 Rifle (7.62 NATO)	$700	$650	$575	$495	$375	$250	$125	
Model 1912 Short Rifle	$700	$650	$575	$495	$375	$250	$125	
Model 1912 Short Rifle (7.62 NATO)	$700	$650	$575	$495	$375	$250	$125	
Model 1935 Carbine (7.62 NATO)	$650	$600	$550	$425	$275	$175	$80	
Mauser Banner	$900	$850	$775	$650	$550	$375	$250	
CHINA								
Gew 1871 Rifle - Chinese marked	$1,100	$1,050	$925	$850	$700	$550	$300	
Kar 1871 Rifle - Chinese marked	$1,100	$1,050	$925	$850	$700	$550	$300	
Kar 98a Carbine	$800	$750	$700	$550	$400	$275	$225	
Model 1907 Rifle - China contract	$1,000	$950	$900	$750	$500	$400	$300	
Model 1907 Carbine	$1,000	$950	$900	$750	$500	$400	$300	
Model 98/22 Rifle	$700	$650	$600	$475	$325	$250	$150	
FN Mle. 1924 or 1930 Short rifles	$700	$650	$600	$475	$325	$250	$150	
Model 21 Chinese-made VZ 24	$700	$650	$500	$400	$350	$250	$125	
Std. Model 1933 Mauser Banner Rifle	$900	$850	$800	$675	$550	$425	$300	
Std. Model 1933 Mauser Banner Carbine	$950	$875	$800	$675	$525	$350	$275	
Chiang Kai-Shek Rifle -Chinese copy	$800	$750	$675	$550	$400	$300	$175	
Chinese VZ 24 P prefix -"1937" SH. Rifle	$650	$550	$495	$350	$275	$175	$100	
Chinese copy VZ 24w/Jap. folding byt.	$1,000	$925	$800	$700	$550	$400	$300	

GRADING - PPGS™	100%	98%	95%	90%	80%	70%	60%	LAST MSR
COLOMBIA								
Model 1891 Rifle -Argentine pattern	$800	$750	$700	$600	$450	$300	$195	
Model 1912 Rifle - Steyr	$700	$600	$400	$250	$185	$150	$100	
Model 1912 Short Rifle - Steyr	$700	$600	$400	$250	$185	$150	$100	
Model VZ 24 Short Rifle	$700	$600	$400	$250	$185	$150	$100	
Model 29 Short Rifle - Steyr	$800	$700	$550	$425	$325	$225	$175	
FN Mle. 1930 Carbine	$850	$750	$700	$600	$500	$400	$350	
FN Mle. 1930 Short Rifle (1940, 7mm)	$600	$500	$400	$300	$275	$225	$175	
FN Mle. 1950 Short Rifle (Post War,.30-06 cal.)	$600	$500	$400	$300	$275	$225	$150	
COSTA RICA								
Model 1895 Rifle	$800	$700	$575	$425	$350	$250	$125	
Model 1910 Rifle	$700	$600	$495	$375	$295	$175	$100	
FN Mle. 1924/1930 Short Rifle	$750	$700	$600	$500	$450	$400	$375	
CZECHOSLOVAKIA								
Model 1919 Mauser - Jelen Rifle	N/A	N/A	$4,000	$3,500	$2,800	$1,900	$1,700	
Model 1921 Mauser - Jelen Rifle	N/A	N/A	$3,500	$3,000	$2,400	$1,800	$1,500	
Model 98/22 Rifle	$600	$500	$400	$295	$200	$150	$90	
Model VZ 23 Short Rifle	$600	$500	$400	$290	$200	$150	$100	
Model VZ 23A Short Rifle	$600	$500	$400	$290	$200	$150	$100	
Model VZ 24 Short Rifle	$600	$575	$500	$450	$325	$200	$100	
Model 98/29 Rifle	$600	$500	$400	$275	$200	$125	$90	
Model VZ 08/33 Carbine	$600	$550	$500	$450	$350	$250	$150	
Model VZ 12/33 Carbine - Light VZ 24	$700	$600	$500	$400	$290	$190	$125	
Model VZ 16/33	$800	$700	$550	$450	$325	$250	$175	
Model "JC" Short Rifle	$800	$700	$500	$400	$350	$300	$250	
Model "L" SH. Rifle cal., .303, Lithuania	N/A	$1,600	$1,300	$1,000	$800	$700	$600	
DOMINICAN REPUBLIC								
M1953 Rifle - Ex-Brazil M1908	$600	$475	$275	$175	$150	$100	$75	
M1953 SH. Rifle - Ex-Brazil M1908 SHR.	$600	$475	$275	$175	$150	$100	$75	
ECUADOR								
Model 71/84 Rifle	$600	$550	$350	$200	$150	$125	$900	
Model 1891 Rifle -Argentine pattern	$550	$495	$400	$275	$190	$125	$85	
Model 1907 Rifle	$600	$500	$400	$325	$250	$190	$150	
Model VZ 23 Short Rifle	$500	$425	$325	$275	$190	$150	$90	
Model VZ 24 Short Rifle	$500	$425	$325	$275	$190	$150	$90	
Model VZ 12/33 Short Rifle	$500	$425	$325	$275	$190	$150	$90	
FN Mle. 1930 Short Rifle	$750	$700	$600	$500	$450	$400	$375	

GRADING - PPGS™	100%	98%	95%	90%	80%	70%	60%	LAST MSR
EL SALVADOR								
Model 1895 Rifle - Chilean pattern	$600	$550	$500	$400	$300	$180	$90	
Model VZ 12/33 Carbine	$500	$450	$400	$300	$200	$125	$90	
Standard Model 1935 Export	$500	$450	$350	$290	$250	$150	$90	
FN M50 Israeli Short Rifle	$500	$450	$320	$260	$200	$125	$90	
ESTONIA								
Czech Model "L"Short Rifle - .303 cal.	N/A	N/A	$1,000	$825	$700	$595	$475	
ETHIOPIA								
FN Mle. 1930 Short Rifle	N/A	$3,500	$3,200	$2,800	$1,900	$1,400	$1,000	
FN Mle. 1930 Carbine	N/A	$3,600	$2,300	$2,900	$2,000	$1,500	$1,100	
Model 1933 Standard Model Rifle	N/A	$2,900	$2,500	$1,900	$1,600	$1,000	$900	

Values assume original configuration with original parts.

GRADING - PPGS™	100%	98%	95%	90%	80%	70%	60%	LAST MSR
svw MB | **FRANCE**								
Modified 98K Carbine - Hex. stacking rod	$600	$500	$400	$325	$250	$200	$150	
GERMANY								
Model 1871 Rifle - Gew 71	N/A	$1,500	$1,250	$1,000	$800	$600	$400	
Model 1871 Carbine - Kar 71	N/A	$1,200	$1,100	$1,000	$800	$600	$400	
Model 1871 Short Rifle - Jaeger 71	N/A	$1,400	$1,300	$1,200	$950	$700	$550	
Model 1871/84 Rifle	N/A	$1,500	$1,250	$1,000	$800	$600	$400	
Model 1888 Commission Rifle	N/A	$900	$850	$750	$600	$400	$275	
Model 1888/05 Commission Rifle	N/A	$900	$850	$750	$600	$400	$275	
Model 1888/14 Commission Rifle	N/A	$900	$850	$750	$600	$400	$275	
Model 1888 Commission Carbine	N/A	$900	$850	$750	$600	$400	$300	
Model 1891 Comm. Carbine w/stacking hook	N/A	$900	$850	$750	$600	$400	$300	
Model 1888/97 Rifle	N/A	N/A	N/A	$6,000	$5,000	$3,800	$3,000	
Model 1898 Rifle - Gew 98	N/A	$900	$800	$700	$600	$375	$250	
Model 1898 Carbine - Kar. 98, 16.9 in. bbl.	N/A	$6,000	$5,000	$4,200	$3,700	$3,200	$2,500	
Model 1898/17 Rifle Exp.	N/A	N/A	N/A	$5,000	$4,200	$3,200	$2,500	
Model 1898/18 Rifle Exp.	N/A	N/A	N/A	$5,000	$4,200	$3,200	$2,500	
Model 1909 Self Loading Carbine	N/A	$7,500	$5,500	$4,500	$4,000	$3,500	$2,800	
Model 1898A Carbine	N/A	$800	$725	$700	$600	$450	$250	
Model 1898AZ Carbine (also Model 98a)	N/A	$800	$725	$700	$600	$450	$250	
Model 1898b Carbine	N/A	$1,000	$950	$800	$600	$500	$350	
Model Gew. 98 (Transitional)	N/A	$700	$625	$550	$450	$325	$200	
Model 33/40 Carbine ("945" 1940)	N/A	$2,850	$2,150	$1,800	$1,500	$1,200	$800	

GRADING - PPGS™	100%	98%	95%	90%	80%	70%	60%	LAST MSR
Model 33/40 Carbine ("DOT" 1941-43)	N/A	$2,850	$2,150	$1,800	$1,500	$1,200	$800	
Model 24 (T) Rifle	N/A	$875	$800	$725	$600	$450	$300	
Model 98/40	N/A	$2,500	$2,000	$1,800	$1,500	$1,200	$800	
Model VG-1	N/A	N/A	N/A	$3,000	$2,500	$2,000	$1,800	
G 41M Semi-Auto Rifle	N/A	$25,000	$20,000	$17,500	$12,500	$9,000	$7,000	
G 41W Semi-Auto Rifle	N/A	$9,500	$8,250	$6,750	$5,250	$4,000	$2,750	
G/K 43 Sniper Rifle	N/A	$9,500	$8,250	$6,750	$5,250	$4,000	$2,750	
G/K 43 Semi-Auto Rifle	N/A	$3,500	$3,000	$2,500	$2,000	$1,500	$1,250	
Model 29/40 Rifle L/W issue	N/A	$2,250	$1,850	$1,500	$1,150	$875	$675	
Model 29/0 Rifle L/W Issue	N/A	N/A	N/A	$3,500	$3,000	$2,500	$2,150	
Model K98k "Para-troop Model"	N/A	$5,500	$4,900	$4,200	$3,800	$3,000	$2,700	

Many configurations and variants of the G/K 43 Sniper Rifle are serious fakes - consult a qualified expert before buying/selling/trading.

GREECE

FN Mle. 1930 Short Rifle	$1,150	$975	$850	$700	$600	$450	$350	

GUATEMALA

Czech VZ 24 Short Rifle	$700	$675	$600	$425	$350	$275	$75	
M1895 Rifle	$500	$450	$400	$275	$200	$125	$75	

HAITI

Post-War FN Mle. 1930 Short Rifle	$1,200	$1,000	$875	$750	$450	$350	$300	

IRAN (PERSIA)

Model 1895 Rifle	$600	$550	$500	$300	$200	$175	$125	
Model 98/29 Rifle	$900	$850	$800	$650	$500	$300	$195	
Model 98/29 Short Rifle	$875	$825	$775	$475	$360	$295	$175	
Model 49 Carbine	$800	$700	$550	$400	$300	$250	$195	
FN Mle. 1924 Short Rifle	$1,800	$1,700	$1,400	$900	$800	$700	$500	
VZ 24 Short Rifle	$900	$800	$700	$500	$375	$275	$200	

IRAQ

Model 1948 98k Carbine	$600	$500	$400	$300	$250	$195	$100	

ISRAEL

German 98k with Israeli marks	$600	$500	$400	$300	$200	$150	$90	
Czech 98k w/ large triggerguard	$600	$550	$450	$275	$200	$120	$80	
FN Mle. 1950 Short Rifle	$600	$550	$450	$425	$375	$325	$275	
FN Mle. 1950 .22 Single Shot Trainer	$1,100	$950	$750	$650	$550	$450	$400	
Model 1954 Short Rifle	$625	$575	$450	$350	$250	$180	$125	

LATVIA

Czech VZ 24 Short Rifle	$800	$750	$650	$500	$275	$225	$150	

LIBERIA

FN Mle. 1930 Short Rifle	N/A	N/A	$850	$750	$650	$500	$400	

GRADING - PPGS™	100%	98%	95%	90%	80%	70%	60%	LAST MSR
LITHUANIA								
Czech "L" Model Short Rifle (.303)	N/A	N/A	$900	$700	$600	$500	$425	
Model VZ 24 Short Rifle	N/A	N/A	$900	$800	$600	$450	$325	
FN Mle. 1930 Short Rifle	N/A	$3,500	$3,200	$2,700	$2,200	$1,500	$950	
Model 1900 Rifle	$800	$700	$600	$400	$325	$275	$190	
MANCHURIA								
Mukden Arsenal Rifle	$1,500	$1,400	$1,200	$950	$800	$650	$400	
MEXICO								
Model 1895 Rifle	$550	$475	$400	$250	$190	$125	$80	
Model 1895 Carbine	$550	$475	$400	$250	$190	$125	$80	
Model 1902 Rifle	$1,500	$1,400	$1,300	$1,050	$925	$800	$500	
Model 1907 Rifle	$600	$500	$450	$375	$300	$250	$125	
Model 1910 Rifle	$500	$400	$300	$200	$175	$125	$90	
Model 1910 Carbine	$500	$400	$300	$200	$175	$125	$90	
Model 1912 Rifle	$700	$600	$500	$325	$275	$225	$175	
Model 1912 Short Rifle	$700	$600	$500	$325	$275	$225	$175	
Model 1924 Short Rifle	$700	$650	$600	$475	$300	$250	$175	
Model 1924 Carbine	$700	$600	$500	$325	$275	$225	$175	
Model 1936 Short Rifle	$700	$675	$600	$475	$400	$275	$195	
Model 1954 Short Rifle	$675	$650	$600	$475	$425	$300	$225	
MOROCCO								
Post-War FN Mle. 1930 Carbine (7.62x51mm)	$650	$550	$475	$400	$350	$300	$250	
w/threaded barrel for grenade launcher	$700	$650	$600	$500	$450	$375	$300	
NETHERLANDS								
Post-War FN Mle. 1930 Carbine "W" crest	$900	$800	$700	$600	$500	$450	$375	
Post-War FN Mle. 1930 Carbine "J" crest	$850	$750	$650	$550	$450	$400	$350	
NICARAGUA								
Model VZ 12/33 Short Rifle	$700	$675	$625	$500	$400	$300	$195	
Model VZ 24 Short Rifle	$600	$550	$500	$400	$300	$195	$125	
ORANGE FREE STATE								
Model 1896 Rifle(OVS marked), DWM	$1,100	$1,000	$950	$825	$675	$525	$400	
Model 1896 Rifle (OVS marked), Loewe & Sons	$1,000	$900	$800	$650	$525	$400	$250	
Model 1896 Rifle, Chile overmark	$700	$625	$550	$425	$375	$300	$200	
Model 1895 Short Rifle	$700	$650	$550	$425	$350	$275	$195	
Model 1895 Carbine	$700	$650	$550	$425	$350	$275	$195	
PARAGUAY								
Model 1895 Rifle	$500	$425	$295	$200	$150	$110	$75	
Model 1907 Rifle (DWM)	$600	$425	$295	$200	$150	$110	$75	

GRADING - PPGS™	100%	98%	95%	90%	80%	70%	60%	LAST MSR
Model 1907 Carbine (Full-stocked)	$600	$425	$295	$200	$150	$110	$75	
Model 1927 Rifle (Oviedo)	$495	$400	$275	$200	$150	$100	$80	
Model 1927 Short Rifle	$495	$400	$275	$200	$150	$100	$80	
Model 1927 Carbine (Full-stocked)	$495	$400	$275	$200	$150	$125	$90	
FN Mle. 1930 Short Rifle	$850	$750	$650	$550	$450	$400	$350	
Model 1933 Standard Model Rifle	$550	$450	$380	$320	$260	$190	$120	
PERU								
Model 1891 Rifle (Lange sight)	$495	$450	$400	$300	$225	$150	$90	
Model 1891 Carbine (Lange sight)	$495	$450	$400	$300	$225	$150	$90	
Model 1909 Rifle	$1,750	$1,350	$1,000	$850	$725	$675	$500	
Model VZ 24 Short Rifle	$600	$550	$500	$395	$350	$295	$195	
Model VZ 32 Short Rifle(Model 32)	$700	$650	$600	$495	$375	$325	$225	
FN Short Rifle Modelo 1935	$700	$650	$600	$495	$375	$325	$225	
FN Carbine Modelo 1935	$900	$850	$775	$700	$550	$400	$295	
POLAND								
Model 1898 Rifle	$600	$550	$500	$395	$325	$275	$195	
Model 1898 Carbine (Kar 98a)	$600	$550	$500	$395	$325	$275	$195	
Model 1929 Short Rifle (Wz 29)	$800	$750	$700	$495	$425	$280	$175	
PORTUGAL								
Model 1904 Mauser-Verguiero Rifle	$700	$675	$600	$500	$425	$275	$180	
Model 1937 Short Rifle	$700	$675	$600	$475	$375	$250	$175	
Model 1937a Short Rifle	$700	$650	$600	$475	$375	$250	$180	
Model 1941 Short Rifle	$900	$850	$800	$650	$525	$300	$200	
ROMANIA								
Model VZ 24 Short Rifle, "M" or "C" Crest	$800	$750	$650	$550	$400	$250	$125	
SAUDI ARABIA								
Post-War FN Mle. 1930 Short Rifle or Carbine	N/A	$2,700	$2,400	$2,200	$1,800	$1,500	$1,000	
SERBIA/YUGOSLAVIA								
Model 1878/80 Rifle	$1,400	$1,300	$1,150	$900	$750	$600	$300	
Model 1885 Cavalry Carbine	$1,250	$1,175	$1,050	$900	$750	$600	$300	
Model 1886/6C and 1880/7C	$1,200	$1,100	$1,000	$850	$750	$600	$300	
Model 1899 Rifle	$650	$575	$500	$400	$275	$200	$110	
Model 1889/07 Rifle	$600	$525	$430	$325	$250	$125	$90	
Model 1899/08 Rifle	$600	$525	$430	$325	$250	$125	$90	
Model 1899C Short Rifle	$600	$525	$430	$325	$250	$125	$80	
Model 1899/08 Carbine	$900	$800	$700	$600	$400	$300	$195	

GRADING - PPGS™	100%	98%	95%	90%	80%	70%	60%	LAST MSR
Model 1910 Rifle	$525	$450	$390	$300	$225	$160	$125	
Model 1924 Short Rifle	$575	$500	$450	$400	$350	$300	$250	
Model 1924 Carbine	$850	$700	$650	$550	$450	$400	$350	
FN Mle 1924 Short Rifle	$600	$550	$450	$375	$295	$225	$160	
FN Mle 1924 Carbine	$700	$650	$600	$475	$395	$295	$195	
Czech VZ 24 Short Rifle	$600	$550	$450	$375	$250	$175	$115	
Model 1924 Short Rifle(Kragujevac)	$600	$550	$450	$375	$250	$175	$115	
M90T Short Rifle (ex-Turkish M1890)	N/A	$800	$700	$500	$400	$250	$150	
Model M24B Rifle (ex-Mexican M1912)	N/A	$800	$700	$500	$400	$250	$150	
Model 1948 Carbine (ex-German)	$900	$800	$750	$700	$600	$500	$300	
Model 1948 Carbine (Kragujevac)	$900	$800	$750	$700	$600	$500	$300	
SIAM (THAILAND)								
Model 1902 Rifle (Type 45)	$550	$450	$400	$390	$270	$195	$100	
Model 1923 Short Rifle (Type 66)	$550	$450	$400	$390	$270	$195	$100	
SLOVAK REPUBLIC								
Model VZ 24 Short Rifle	$800	$700	$600	$500	$375	$300	$180	
SOUTH AFRICAN REPUBLIC								
Model 1896 Rifle "ZAR" marked	$1,100	$1,025	$950	$775	$600	$400	$195	
SPAIN								
Model 1891 Rifle	$800	$750	$700	$550	$400	$300	$250	
Model 1892 Rifle	$1,300	$1,225	$1,100	$950	$800	$650	$500	
Model 1892 Carbine	$750	$700	$600	$500	$375	$295	$195	
Model 1893 Rifle	$750	$700	$600	$500	$375	$295	$195	
Model 1895 Carbine (Full-stocked)	$700	$625	$575	$495	$375	$295	$195	
Model 1916 Short Rifle	$600	$525	$475	$400	$325	$225	$180	
Model 1916 Experimental 8mm	$750	$700	$625	$450	$375	$295	$190	
Model 1943 Short Rifle	$500	$425	$350	$275	$195	$125	$75	
SWEDEN								
Model 1894 Carbine	$750	$700	$650	$600	$480	$390	$275	
Model 1896 Rifle	$600	$500	$400	$300	$220	$185	$120	
Model 1938 Short Rifle	$600	$500	$400	$300	$200	$125	$80	
Model 1940 Short Rifle (8mm)	$800	$700	$650	$500	$375	$295	$225	
Model 41 (1955) Sniper	$3,000	$2,500	$2,000	$1,750	$1,575	$1,325	$1,100	
SYRIA								
Model 1948 Carbine	$500	$400	$325	$275	$200	$120	$80	
TURKEY								
Model 1887 Rifle	$1,500	$1,400	$1,300	$1,100	$900	$700	$500	
Model 1887 Carbine	$1,500	$1,400	$1,300	$1,100	$900	$700	$500	
Model 1890 Rifle	$1,200	$1,150	$1,000	$900	$775	$625	$500	

GRADING - PPGS™	100%	98%	95%	90%	80%	70%	60%	LAST MSR
Model 1893 Rifle	$1,300	$1,225	$1,050	$900	$775	$675	$500	
Model 1903 Rifle 7.65mm	$1,200	$1,150	$1,000	$900	$700	$550	$400	
Model 1905 Carbine	$1,200	$1,150	$1,000	$900	$700	$500	$350	
Model VZ 98/22 Rifle	$600	$500	$400	$250	$190	$125	$90	
Model 1888 Rifle (Turkish marked)	$500	$400	$250	$200	$140	$90	$70	
Model 1888/38 Rifle (Improved)	$500	$400	$250	$200	$140	$90	$70	
Model 1938 Rifle 8mm	$500	$400	$250	$200	$140	$90	$60	
Model 1938 Short Rifle	$500	$400	$250	$200	$140	$90	$60	
URUGUAY								
FN Mle. 1893 Rifle	$1,200	$950	$775	$600	$400	$250	$125	
Model 1904 Rifle	$700	$625	$550	$400	$325	$260	$200	
Model 1908 Rifle	$800	$700	$600	$450	$400	$300	$200	
Model 1908 Short Rifle	$700	$600	$500	$450	$400	$300	$200	
Czech VZ 32 Short Rifle (Model 1934)	$800	$700	$600	$500	$290	$200	$120	
Czech VZ 24 Short Rifle (Model 1934)	$800	$700	$600	$500	$390	$275	$195	
FN Mle. 1930 Short Rifle	$675	$575	$500	$450	$400	$350	$300	
VENEZUELA								
Model 1910 Rifle	$500	$425	$350	$290	$240	$130	$90	
Czech VZ 24/26 Short Rifle	$600	$500	$450	$375	$300	$225	$160	
FN Mle. 1930 Short Rifle	$1,000	$800	$600	$500	$400	$300	$200	
FN Mle. 1930 Carbine	$975	$850	$600	$500	$400	$300	$225	
YEMEN								
FN Mle 1930 Short Rifle	N/A	N/A	$900	$800	$650	$550	$450	

YUGOSLAVIA – Please refer to listings under Serbia/Yugoslavia.

RIFLES: MILITARY PRODUCTION, K98k (KARBINE)

The following model listings represent the various manufacturers of K98k military carbines in Germany between 1934-1945. Codes following the year can be found on the guns, and will help in identification. *Backbone of the Wehrmacht: The German K98k Rifle* by Richard D. Law is an invaluable resource that lists all the codes and the placement.

The author wishes to express thanks to Wolf von Baumbach for making the following information available.

Add 15% for rifles marked M Marine (Navy) and L Luftwaffe (Air Force).

Add 100% for SS markings - beware of fakes and spurious markings.

MAUSER WERKE AG, OBERNDORF A/N

	100%	98%	95%	90%	80%	70%	60%	LAST MSR
1934 - Code S/42 K	N/A	$9,500	$7,500	$6,000	$4,500	$3,000	$2,000	
1935 - Code S/42 G	N/A	$8,500	$6,500	$4,500	$2,500	$1,800	$1,000	
1936 - Code S/42 1936	N/A	$6,000	$5,000	$4,000	$3,000	$1,800	$1,000	
1937 - Code S/42 1937	N/A	$5,000	$4,500	$3,500	$2,500	$1,800	$1,000	
1938 - E Code S/42 1938	N/A	$4,500	$3,950	$3,000	$2,250	$1,500	$850	
1938 - L Code 42 1938	N/A	$4,500	$3,950	$3,000	$2,250	$1,500	$850	
1939 - Code 42 1939	N/A	$4,500	$3,950	$3,000	$2,250	$1,500	$850	
1940 - Code 42 1940	N/A	$4,000	$3,450	$2,500	$1,750	$1,150	$650	
1941 - Code BYF 41	N/A	$4,100	$3,500	$2,500	$1,750	$1,150	$650	
1942 - Code BYF 42	N/A	$3,500	$3,150	$2,250	$1,500	$1,000	$550	
1943 - Code BYF 43	N/A	$3,500	$3,150	$2,250	$1,500	$1,000	$550	

GRADING - PPGS™	100%	98%	95%	90%	80%	70%	60%	LAST MSR
1944 - Code BYF 44	N/A	$3,000	$2,500	$1,950	$1,350	$850	$500	
1945 - Code Mod. 98 BYF 45	N/A	$3,000	$2,500	$1,950	$1,350	$850	$500	
1945 - Code Mod. 98 SVW	N/A	$3,000	$2,500	$1,950	$1,350	$850	$500	
1945 - Code Mod. 98 SVW MB	N/A	$4,500	$3,950	$3,000	$2,250	$1,500	$850	
J.P. SAUER UND SOHN GEWEHRFABRIK, SUHL								
1934 - Code S/147K	N/A	$9,000	$7,000	$5,500	$4,500	$2,500	$2,000	
1935 - Code S/147G	N/A	$8,000	$6,000	$4,000	$2,850	$1,800	$1,500	
1936 - Code S/147 1936	N/A	$6,000	$4,850	$3,750	$2,500	$1,350	$925	
1937 - Code S/147 1937	N/A	$5,000	$4,250	$3,250	$2,250	$1,150	$800	
1938 - E Code S/147	N/A	$4,500	$3,950	$3,000	$2,250	$1,500	$850	
1938 - L Code 147 1938	N/A	$4,500	$3,950	$3,000	$2,250	$1,500	$850	
1939 - Code 147 1939	N/A	$4,500	$3,950	$3,000	$2,250	$1,500	$850	
1940 - Code 147 1940	N/A	$4,000	$3,450	$2,500	$1,750	$1,150	$650	
1941 - Code CE 41	N/A	$3,500	$3,150	$2,250	$1,500	$1,000	$550	
1942 - Code CE 42	N/A	$3,500	$3,150	$2,250	$1,500	$1,000	$550	
1943 - Code CE 43	N/A	$3,000	$2,500	$1,950	$1,350	$850	$500	
1944 - Code CE 44	N/A	$3,000	$2,500	$1,950	$1,350	$850	$500	
ERMA (ERFURTER MASCHINENFABRIK), ERFURT								
1935 - Code S/27 G	N/A	$4,500	$3,950	$3,000	$2,250	$1,500	$850	
1936 - Code S/27 1936	N/A	$4,000	$3,450	$2,500	$1,750	$1,150	$650	
1937 - Code S/27 1937	N/A	$4,000	$3,450	$2,500	$1,750	$1,150	$650	
1938 - Code S/27 or 27 1938	N/A	$3,500	$3,150	$2,250	$1,500	$1,000	$550	
1939 - Code 27 1939	N/A	$3,000	$2,500	$1,950	$1,350	$850	$500	
1940 - E Code 27 1940	N/A	$3,000	$2,500	$1,950	$1,350	$850	$500	
1940 - L Code AX 1940	N/A	$3,000	$2,500	$1,950	$1,350	$850	$500	
1941 - Code AX 41	N/A	$3,000	$2,500	$1,950	$1,350	$850	$500	
MAUSER WERKE AG, BORSIGWALDE								
1935 - Code S/243 G	N/A	$4,500	$3,950	$3,000	$2,250	$1,500	$850	
1936 - Code S/243 1936	N/A	$4,000	$3,450	$2,500	$1,750	$1,150	$650	
1937 - Code S/243 1937	N/A	$4,000	$3,450	$2,500	$1,750	$1,150	$650	
1938 - E Code S/243 1937	N/A	$4,000	$3,450	$2,500	$1,750	$1,150	$650	
1938 L Code 243 1938	N/A	$4,000	$3,450	$2,500	$1,750	$1,150	$650	
1939 - Code 243 1939	N/A	$3,500	$3,150	$2,250	$1,500	$1,000	$550	
1940 - Code 243 1940	N/A	$3,500	$3,150	$2,250	$1,500	$1,000	$550	
1941 - Code AR 41	N/A	$3,000	$2,500	$1,950	$1,350	$850	$500	
1942 - Code AR 42	N/A	$3,000	$2,500	$1,950	$1,350	$850	$500	
1943 - Code AR 43	N/A	$3,000	$2,500	$1,950	$1,350	$850	$500	
1944 - Code AR 44	N/A	$2,500	$2,000	$1,600	$1,150	$850	$650	
BERLIN-LÜBECKER MASCHINENFABRIK, LÜBECK								
1936 - Code S/237 1936	N/A	$3,500	$3,150	$2,250	$1,500	$1,000	$550	
1937 - Code S/237 1937	N/A	$3,500	$3,150	$2,250	$1,500	$1,000	$550	
1938 - E Code S/237 1938	N/A	$3,000	$2,500	$1,950	$1,350	$850	$500	
1938 - L Code 237 1938	N/A	$3,000	$2,500	$1,950	$1,350	$850	$500	
1939 - Code 237 1938	N/A	$3,000	$2,500	$1,950	$1,350	$850	$500	
1940 - E Code 237 1940	N/A	$3,000	$2,500	$1,950	$1,350	$850	$500	

GRADING - PPGS™	100%	98%	95%	90%	80%	70%	60%	LAST MSR
1940 - L Code DUV 1940	N/A	$3,000	$2,500	$1,950	$1,350	$850	$500	
1941 - Code DUV 41	N/A	$2,500	$2,000	$1,600	$1,150	$850	$650	
1942 - Code DUV 42	N/A	$2,500	$2,000	$1,600	$1,150	$850	$650	
BERLIN-SUHLER-WAFFEN UND FAHRZEUGWERKE, (BSW)								
1937 - Code BSW 1937	N/A	$3,000	$2,600	$2,150	$1,600	$1,100	$750	
1938 - Code BSW 1938	N/A	$3,000	$2,500	$1,950	$1,350	$850	$500	
1939 - Code BSW 1939	N/A	$3,000	$2,500	$1,950	$1,350	$850	$500	
STEYR-DAIMLER-PUCH AG, STEYR								
1939 - Code 660 1939	N/A	$4,500	$3,950	$3,000	$2,250	$1,500	$850	
1940 - E Code 660 1940	N/A	$4,000	$3,450	$2,500	$1,750	$1,150	$650	
1940 - L Code BNZ 40	N/A	$4,000	$3,450	$2,500	$1,750	$1,150	$650	
1941 - Code BNZ 41	N/A	$3,500	$3,150	$2,250	$1,500	$1,000	$550	
1942 Code BNZ 42	N/A	$3,000	$2,500	$1,950	$1,350	$850	$500	
1943 - Code BNZ 43	N/A	$2,500	$2,000	$1,600	$1,150	$850	$650	
1943 - Code BNZ SS 43	N/A	$5,500	$4,750	$3,750	$2,750	$2,000	$1,250	
1944 - Code BNZ 44	N/A	$2,500	$2,000	$1,600	$1,150	$850	$650	
1944 - Code BNZ 4	N/A	$2,500	$2,000	$1,600	$1,150	$850	$650	
1944 - Code BNZ S 4	N/A	$5,500	$4,750	$3,750	$2,750	$2,000	$1,250	
1945 - Code Mod 98 BNZ 45	N/A	$3,000	$2,500	$1,950	$1,350	$850	$500	
1945 - Code SWJ XE 45	N/A	$7,000	$6,500	$5,500	$4,500	$3,500	$2,500	
GUSTLOFF WERKE, WEIMAR								
1940 - Code BSW 1940	N/A	$3,500	$3,150	$2,250	$1,500	$1,000	$550	
1940 - Code 337 1940	N/A	$3,500	$3,150	$2,250	$1,500	$1,000	$550	
1941 - Code BCD 41	N/A	$3,000	$2,500	$1,950	$1,350	$850	$500	
1942 - Code BCD 42	N/A	$3,000	$2,500	$1,950	$1,350	$850	$500	
1943 - Code BCD 43	N/A	$3,000	$2,500	$1,950	$1,350	$850	$500	
1944 - Code BCD 4	N/A	$2,500	$2,000	$1,600	$1,150	$850	$650	
1945 - Code BCD 45	N/A	$2,500	$2,000	$1,600	$1,150	$850	$650	
WAFFEN WERKE BRÜNN AG, BYSTRICA								
1942 - Code DOU 42	N/A	$3,000	$2,500	$1,950	$1,350	$850	$500	
1943 - Code DOU 43	N/A	$3,000	$2,500	$1,950	$1,350	$850	$500	
1944 - Code DOU 44	N/A	$2,500	$2,000	$1,600	$1,150	$850	$650	
1945 - Code Mod 98 DOU 45	N/A	$2,500	$2,000	$1,600	$1,150	$850	$650	
WAFFEN WERKE BRÜNN AG, BRÜNN								
1943 - Code DOT 43	N/A	$3,000	$2,500	$1,950	$1,350	$850	$500	
1944 - Code DOT 1944	N/A	$2,500	$2,000	$1,600	$1,150	$850	$650	
1945 - Code Mod 98 SWP 45	N/A	$2,500	$2,000	$1,600	$1,150	$850	$650	
DOUBLE CODES								
* ***Berlin Suhl/Gustloff Werke***								
1939 - Code 357/1939	N/A	$3,000	$2,500	$1,950	$1,350	$850	$500	
* ***Erma/Mauser Borsigwalde***								
1941 - Code AX/AR 41	N/A	$3,000	$2,500	$1,950	$1,350	$850	$500	
* ***Gustloff Werke/Mauser***								
1942 - Code BCD/AR 42	N/A	$3,000	$2,500	$1,950	$1,350	$850	$500	
1943 - Code BCD/AR 43	N/A	$3,000	$2,500	$1,950	$1,350	$850	$500	

GRADING - PPGS™	100%	98%	95%	90%	80%	70%	60%	LAST MSR
* ***Gustloff Werke/Steyr-Daimler Puch*** 1944- Code BCD/BNZ 4	N/A	$3,000	$2,500	$1,950	$1,350	$850	$500	

RIFLES: BOLT ACTION, 1898-1946 COMMERCIAL MFG.

Approx. 125,000 commercial sporting Mausers were built between 1898 and 1946. Three action lengths; overall measurements: Short (Kurz) 8 1/4 in., Standard 8 3/4 in., and Magnum 9 1/4 in. Optional squarebridge receiver rings for custom sight mounting. Innumerable variations of triggers, barrels, sights and checkering.

Add 50% for single square bridge action.
Add 100% for double square bridge action.
Add 100% for Short (Kurz) action, except on Type K below.
Add 100% for Magnum action, except on African Type below.

SPECIAL RIFLE, TYPE A – expressly made for English market, superior finish, with round tapered barrel, silver-bead front sight on sleeved-on block with matted surface, hinged floorplate, pear shaped bolt knob, horn forend tip and PG cap, sling eyes.

N/A	$7,000	$6,000	$5,000	$4,000	$3,000	$2,500

NORMAL RIFLE, TYPE B – 24 in. barrel, steel-capped PG, Schnabel forend, sling swivels, pear shaped bolt knob, hinged floorplate.

N/A	$5,000	$4,500	$3,750	$3,000	$2,250	$1,750

LIGHT SHORT RIFLE, TYPE K – 6.5x54 Mauser, 8x51mm, or .250-3000 Savage cal., short action, 22 in. barrel, steel PG cap, sling swivels, pear shaped bolt knob, hinged floorplate, hard rubber buttplate.

N/A	$8,000	$7,000	$6,000	$5,000	$4,250	$4,000

CARBINE, TYPE S – 20 or 24 in. barrel stocked to muzzle, steel PG cap, horn buttplate, sling swivels, pear shaped bolt knob, hinged floorplate.

N/A	$6,000	$5,000	$4,000	$3,500	$3,000	$2,000

CARBINE, TYPE M – 20 in. barrel stocked to muzzle with steel forend cap, steel PG cap, trapdoor steel buttplate holding sectional cleaning rod, butterknife bolt handle, hinged floorplate.

N/A	$6,000	$5,000	$4,000	$3,500	$3,000	$2,000

MILITARY SPORTING RIFLE, TYPE C – stepped round barrel, spherical bolt knob, half grip, banner Mauser imprint in side of buttstock.

N/A	$2,500	$2,000	$1,750	$1,500	$1,250	$1,000

AFRICAN TYPE – 28 in. round barrel, stocked to 4 in. from muzzle, Magnum action, pear shaped bolt knob.

N/A	$10,000	$8,000	$6,000	$4,500	$4,000	$4,000

EL-24 CONVERSION KIT – converts 8mm Mauser to .22 LR, includes subcaliber barrel insert, .22 cal. barrel was joined to a special bolt action breech mechanism, also available as repeating version with 5 shot mag., mfg. by Erma between the World Wars.

N/A	$1,375	$1,200	$1,050	$900	$750	$600

* ***EL Conversion Repeating*** – includes two matching mags., ser. numbered to unit, tool, and case.

N/A	$1,450	$1,250	$1,000	$850	$775	$695

RIFLES: BOLT ACTION, CURRENT/RECENT PRODUCTION

Values on currently manufactured models, except the M18, include rifle case, scope mount, and matching sling.

The following prices for accessories/wood upgrades were last published in 2017: Add $520 for left-hand action. Add $1,287 per interchangeable standard cal. barrel. Add $988 per bolt assembly, and/or $390 per bolt head. Add $996 for barrel fluting (standard cals. only). Beginning late 2006, Mauser began grading wood between grades 2-11. Grade 2 is standard wood, and the following additional charges apply to the additional wood upgrades (2016 MSRs): Grade 3 - $335, N/A domestically, Grade 4 - $555, Grade 5 - $1,120, Grade 6 - $2,235, Grade 7 - $3,353, Grade 8 - $4,688, Grade 9 - $6,030, Grade 10 - $7,815, Grade 11 - from $10,045.

MODEL 03 BASIC – various standard and Magnum cals., 22 or 24 in. barrel, Grade 2 classic walnut stock with black forend tip, fish scale checkering, cheekpiece, and recoil pad, 7 3/4 lbs. Disc. 2017

$4,195	$3,675	$3,150	$2,850	$2,325	$1,900	$1,500	*$4,660*

Add $538 for M03 Solid model with heavy barrel and adj. full steel open sights.

GRADING - PPGS™	100%	98%	95%	90%	80%	70%	60%	LAST MSR

* ***Model 03 Alpine*** – various cals., 23 or 25 in. barrel, Grade 2 (disc. 2011) or Grade 5 checkered walnut stock and forearm, slight pistol grip and Schnabel forend, steel sights, 7 3/4 lbs. Disc. 2017.

$5,895 $5,150 $4,425 $4,025 $3,250 $2,675 $2,100 ***$6,553***

Add $1,910 for Africa model. Add $538 for Solid model. Add $475 for Match model.

MODEL 03 EXPERT – various cals. between .222 Rem. - .375 H&H, Mauser square bridge action with safety/cocking lever on rear of breech bolt, interchangeable barrels, manual cocking, Combi-trigger can be used as single stage or set trigger, synthetic (Grey/PH Khaki) or wood stock (Grades 2-11, 2 is standard, 3 is standard in U.S.), 60 degree bolt lift, detachable mag., open sights standard (elevated rear sight at mid-barrel), Mauser double square bridge scope mount, approx. 7 3/4 lbs. Mfg. by Blaser in Isny, Germany beginning 2005. Importation disc.

$5,250 $4,600 $4,050 $3,575 $3,100 $2,500 $1,900 ***$5,887***

Add $553 for Grade 3 checkered walnut stock.

Add $1,460 (MSR is $5,936) for Arabesque model (features coin finished receiver, Arabesque engraving, Mauser logo on floorplate and Grade 4 wood).

Add $2,957 (MSR is $7,433) for De Luxe model (features coin finished receiver with game scene engraving and Grade 5 wood).

Add $4,325 (MSR is $8,801) for Old Classic Model (features case colored receiver with gold line accents and trigger and Grade 6 wood).

* ***Model 03 Extreme Trail*** – various standard and metric cals., features black synthetic stock with patterned elastomer inlays in both forend and pistol grip, open sights with mid-barrel rear sight, 23 in. barrel, approx. 7 3/4 lbs. Mfg. 2010-2015.

$4,875 $4,250 $3,650 $3,125 $2,550 $2,000 $1,650 ***$5,310***

* ***Model 03 Africa*** – various dangerous game cals., 23 or 25 in. barrel, Grey/Khaki (Extreme), Khaki colored synthetic (Africa PH, new 2012), or checkered Grade 4 Turkish walnut stock with installed kick stop, buckhorn rear sight, adj. front sight, sling swivels, approx. 9 3/4 lbs. Disc. 2017.

$5,500 $5,000 $4,500 $4,000 $3,500 $3,000 $2,350 ***$5,980***

Add $755 for checkered Grade 4 Turkish walnut stock.

Add $635 for Africa PH with Khaki colored synthetic stock.

Add $1,460 (MSR was $7,440) for Arabesque model (features coin finished receiver, Arabesque engraving, Mauser logo on floorplate and Grade 4 wood).

Add $2,959 (MSR was $8,939) for De Luxe model (features coin finished receiver with game scene engraving and Grade 5 wood).

Add $4,325 (MSR was $10,305) for Old Classic Model (features case colored receiver with gold line accents and trigger and Grade 6 wood).

* ***Model 03 Solid*** – various cals., 23 or 25 in. barrel (shorter lengths available upon request), thick barrel profile, adj. open sights, Grey/Khaki synthetic (Extreme) or checkered walnut stock and forearm, approx. 8 1/8 lbs. Disc. 2017.

$4,550 $4,000 $3,600 $3,200 $2,850 $2,350 $1,950 ***$4,960***

Add $553 for checkered walnut stock and forearm.

Add $1,460 (MSR was $6,420) for Arabesque model (features coin finished receiver, Arabesque engraving, Mauser logo on floorplate and Grade 4 wood).

Add $2,957 (MSR was $7,917) for De Luxe model (features coin finished receiver with game scene engraving and Grade 5 wood).

Add $4,325 (MSR was $9,285) for Old Classic Model (features case colored receiver with gold line accents and trigger and Grade 6 wood).

* ***Model 03 Jagdmatch*** – .222 Rem., .22-250 Rem., .308 Win., or .300 Win. Mag. cal., 23 or 25 in. barrel with or w/o fluting, Grey/Khaki synthetic (Extreme) or checkered Grade 3 walnut stock and forearm, approx. 8 1/2 lbs. Disc. 2015.

$4,500 $4,000 $3,600 $3,200 $2,850 $2,350 $1,950 ***$4,910***

Add $593 for checkered Grade 3 walnut stock and forearm.

Add $1,500 (MSR was $6,410) for Arabesque model. Add $2,997 (MSR was $7,907) for Deluxe model, and add $4,365 (MSR was $9,275) for the Old Classic model.

* ***Model 03 Stutzen*** – various cals., 23 or 25 in. barrel, full-length Grade 5 checkered walnut stock and forearm with pistol grip cap, double fold Bavarian cheekpiece, front sling swivel, approx. 7 1/4 lbs. Disc. 2015.

$7,100 $6,100 $5,200 $4,500 $3,875 $3,100 $2,550 ***$7,627***

Add $1,668 (MSR was $9,295) for De Luxe model (features coin finished receiver with game scene engraving and Grade 5 wood).

Add $3,035 (MSR was $10,662) for Old Classic Model (features case colored receiver with gold line accents and trigger and Grade 6 wood).

GRADING - PPGS™	100%	98%	95%	90%	80%	70%	60%	LAST MSR

MODEL 03 EXTREME – .243 Win., .270 Win., .308 Win., .30-06, 7mm Rem. Mag., .300 Win. Mag., .375 H&H Mag., 6.5x55SE, 7x64mm, 8x57IS, 9.3x62mm, or 8x68S cal., 22 in. barrel, 5 shot mag., "Mag-Safe" mag. lock, black trigger, universal open sights, Night Grey synthetic stock w/black buttpad, steel bolt ball, approx. 8 lbs. Mfg. 2018. Importation-disc.

	$3,400	$3,000	$2,650	$2,250	$1,850	$1,500	$1,250	*$3,745*

MODEL 03 PURE – .243 Win., .270 Win., .308 Win., .30-06, 7mm Rem. Mag., .300 Win. Mag., .375 H&H Mag., 6,5x55SE, 7x64mm, 8x57IS, 9mm Para., 3x62mm, 8x68S cal., 22 in. barrel, 5 shot steel mag. w/Mauser logo, (4 shot mag. in .375 H&H mag.), "Mag-Safe" mag. lock, black set trigger, universal sights, MO3 Classic Sporter Grade 2 walnut, matte oiled stock, forend w/ebony tip, steel bolt ball and receiver, matte black finish, 7.9 lbs. Mfg. 2018. Importation-disc.

	$4,400	$3,800	$3,250	$2,700	$2,150	$1,850	$1,650	*$4,941*

MODEL 03 TRAIL – .308 Win., .30-06, 8x57IS, 9.3x62mm cal., 18 1/2 in. barrel, 5 shot mag., "Mag-Safe" mag. lock, steel mag. w/Mauser logo, black trigger, 3-dot open sights, rotating muzzle sling swivel, steel bolt ball, matte black Nitride finish, 7.7 lbs. Mfg. 2018. Importation-disc.

	$3,995	$3,500	$3,000	$2,500	$2,000	$1,750	$1,500	*$4,410*

M-12 – .22-250 Rem., .243 Win., .270 Win., 6.5x55mm, 7x64, .30-06, .308 Win., 8x57IS, 9.3x62mm, 7mm Rem. Mag., .300 Win. Mag., or .338 Win. Mag. cal., available in standard or magnum action, 20 or 24 1/2 in. barrel with or without threading, 4 or 5 shot detachable magazine, small inset Remington-style extractor claw, Grade 2 high straight comb walnut stock with teardrop cheekpiece and open pistol grip, three position SRS (smooth-roll-safety), swing safety on the bolt shroud blocks the bolt, blocks the firing pin in the middle position and clears for firing when fully forward, 6 3/4 - 7 lbs. Mfg. 2013-2017.

	$1,625	$1,425	$1,225	$1,100	$895	$725	$575	*$1,799*

Add $200 for 20 in. solid heavy barrel.

Add $200 for M12 package including straight stock with Prince of Wales pistol grip, Minox 2-10x40 scope, and Talley lightweight rings (offered 2015 only).

M-12 MAX – various cals., 22 in. barrel, open sights, steel magazine floorplate with Mauser logo, steel bolt knob, laminated ambidextrous thumbhole stock. New 2016.

MSR $3,310	$2,700	$2,350	$2,025	$1,825	$1,475	$1,225	$950

* ***M-12 Big Max*** – similar to the M-12 Max, except has a 20 in. solid barrel. New 2021.

MSR $3,710	$3,000	$2,625	$2,250	$1,950	$1,650	$1,350	$1,050

M-12 EXTREME – .22-250 Rem., .243 Win., 6.5x55mm, .270 Win., 7x64mm, .308 Win., .30-06, 8x57IS, 9.3x62mm, 7mm Rem. Mag., .300 Win. Mag., or .338 Win. Mag. cal., 20 or 22 in. barrel, 5 shot mag., synthetic stock with soft touch coating, non-slip bolt handle, jeweled bolt, includes black removable synthetic zigzag magazine with embossed Mauser logo, 6 3/4 lbs.

MSR $2,460	$1,975	$1,725	$1,475	$1,325	$1,075	$900	$700

Add $300 for 20 in. heavy barrel (disc. 2017).

M-12 EXPERT – .22-250 Rem., .243 Win., .270 Win., .308 Win., 7mm Rem. Mag., .300 Win. Mag., .338 Win. Mag., 6.5x55SE, 7x64mm, 8x57IS, 9.3x62mm cal., 22 in. barrel, 5 shot mag., steel mag. floorplate w/Mauser logo, open sights, Classic Sporter Grade 5 walnut stock w/ebony noble forearm tip, steel bolt knob, 6.8 lbs. New 2018.

MSR $4,205	$3,400	$2,950	$2,550	$2,300	$1,875	$1,525	$1,200

M-12 IMPACT – .243 Rem. or .308 Win. cal., 20 in. fluted barrel, synthetic mag. with Mauser logo, only w/o open sights, Picatinny rail, synthetic stock, Ilaflon coating. New 2016.

MSR $2,790	$2,250	$1,975	$1,700	$1,525	$1,250	$1,025	$800

M-12 PRECISION – various cals., solid heavy barrel, black synthetic stock, black bolt, with or w/o Picatinny rail. Mfg. 2016-2017.

	$1,575	$1,375	$1,175	$1,075	$875	$750	$575	*$1,750*

Add $100 for Picatinny rail.

M-12 PURE – .22-250 Rem., .243 Win., .270 Win., .308 Win., .30-06, 7mm Rem. Mag., .300 Win. Mag., .338 Win. Mag., 6,5x55SE, 7x64mm, 8x57IS-mm, or 9.3x62mm cal., 22 in. barrel, 5 shot mag., steel mag. floorplate w/Mauser logo, open sights, Classic Sporter Grade 2 walnut stock w/ebony noble forearm tip, steel bolt knob, 6.8 lbs. New 2018.

MSR $3,195	$2,600	$2,275	$1,950	$1,750	$1,425	$1,175	$900

M-12 TRAIL – .308 Win., 8x57IS, 9.3x62mm cal., 18 1/2 in. barrel, 5 shot mag., rotating muzzle sling swivel, synthetic mag. w/Mauser logo, 3-dot open sights, signal orange-grey synthetic camo stock, large bolt ball, 6.6 lbs. New 2018.

MSR $2,825	$2,300	$2,025	$1,725	$1,575	$1,250	$1,000	$800

GRADING - PPGS™	100%	98%	95%	90%	80%	70%	60%	LAST MSR

M18 – .223 Rem. (new 2021), .243 Win., .308 Win., .270 Win., .30-06, 6.5 Creedmoor, 6.5 PRC (new 2019), 7mm Rem. Mag., or .300 Win. Mag. cal., 21 3/4 or 24 1/2 in. cold hammer forged barrel w/o sights, detachable 5 shot mag., adj. trigger, Polymer 2 stock with soft grip inlays, embedded Mauser logo, removable buttpad, 3-position safety, matte black metal finish, approx. 6 1/2 lbs. New 2018.

MSR $750	$700	$575	$500	$450	$400	$350	$300	

MODEL 66A – similar to Model 66S except has American configured laminate stock (wood grain), cals., action, and features are the same as the Model 66S. Imported 1988-89 only.

* ***Model 66A Standard Calibers***

	$1,900	$1,425	$1,150	$925	$800	$700	$650	*$2,100*

Add $630 per interchangeable barrel.

The "A" suffix on this model denotes American.

* ***Model 66A Magnum Calibers*** – includes Weatherby Mag. cals. also.

	$2,050	$1,500	$1,200	$975	$825	$700	$650	*$2,270*

Add $670 per interchangeable barrel.

* ***Model 66A Big Game Calibers*** – includes most popular Mag. cals. up to .458 Win. Mag.

	$2,350	$1,900	$1,425	$1,150	$950	$825	$750	*$2,700*

MODEL 66S STANDARD – telescoping short action, 5.6x57mm, 6.5x57mm, 7x57mm Mauser (disc. 1992), 7x64mm, 9.3x62mm, .243 Win., .270 Win., .30-06, or .308 Win. cal., 24 in. barrel, standard interchangeable barrels, single or double set triggers, adj. and detachable sights, Monte Carlo walnut stock with checkering, swivels, new safety, rosewood tipped forearm and pistol grip, rubber recoil pad, 7 1/2 lbs. Mfg. 1974-95.

	$2,350	$1,275	$995	$875	$775	$695	$625	*$2,722*

* ***Model 66 Standard Magnum*** – 28 in. barrel, 6.5x68mm, 8x68S, 9.3x64mm, 7mm Rem. Mag., .300 Win. Mag., or .300 Wby. Mag. cal., 7.9 lbs. Disc. 1995.

	$2,500	$1,325	$1,050	$900	$795	$695	$625	*$2,925*

* ***Model 66 Standard Carbine (Stutzen-Mannlicher)*** – .243 Win., .270 Win., .30-06, 7x64mm, or 9.3x62mm cal., 21 in. barrel, full-stock (Mannlicher only) and half-stock (disc. in 1989), double or single triggers, 7 1/2 lbs. Disc. 1995.

	$2,500	$1,325	$1,050	$900	$795	$695	$625	*$2,925*

This model was available in a half-stock "Ultra" variation until 1989. Values are similar to those listed.

* ***Model 66S Standard Diplomat*** – similar cals. as the Model 66S Standard, except not available in 5.6x57mm, similar features, except includes selected walnut and special engraving including deer and wild boar game scenes. Disc. 1995.

	$4,650	$3,850	$3,350	$2,750	$2,250	$1,850	$1,400	*$5,317*

Add $390 for Mag. cals. (similar to Model 66S Magnum).

* ***Model 66 Standard Safari/Big Game*** – .375 H&H or .458 Win. Mag. cal., single trigger, 9.3 lbs. Disc. 1995.

	$2,950	$1,850	$1,350	$1,025	$875	$775	$650	*$3,487*

MODEL 66SM – telescoping short action, .243 Win. (disc.), .270 Win., 7x57mm Mauser (disc.), 7x64mm, .308 Win., .30-06, or 6.5x57mm cal. (disc.), 24 in. barrel, standard interchangeable barrels, set trigger, adj. and detachable sights, Monte Carlo walnut stock with checkering, swivels, new safety, anatomical gripped select walnut stock with Mauser-nose, cocking lever on tang, rubber recoil pad, 7 1/4 lbs. Importation 1981-95.

	$2,875	$1,800	$1,325	$1,025	$875	$775	$650	*$3,398*

* ***Model 66SM Ultra*** – all standard cals., 21 in. barrel, 7 1/4 lbs.

	$1,625	$1,325	$1,140	$920	$760	$650	$550	*$1,903*

* ***Model 66SM Magnum*** – cals. similar to Model 66S Magnum, except not available in 9.3x64mm cal., 26 in. barrel, 8.4 lbs. Disc. 1995.

	$3,025	$1,925	$1,375	$1,025	$875	$775	$650	*$3,578*

* ***Model 66SM Diplomat*** – similar cals. as the Model 66SM Standard, similar features, except includes selected walnut and special engraving including deer and wild boar game scenes. Disc. 1995.

	$5,075	$3,975	$3,450	$2,775	$2,250	$1,850	$1,400	*$5,943*

Add $382 for Mag. cals. (similar to Model 66SM Magnum).

* ***Model 66SM Carbine (Mannlicher type full stock)*** – .30-06 cal., 21 in. barrel, 7 lbs. Disc. 1995.

	$3,025	$1,925	$1,375	$1,025	$875	$775	$650	*$3,578*

These models were previously available on a custom order only basis through KDF, Inc. located in Seguin, TX.

GRADING - PPGS™	100%	98%	95%	90%	80%	70%	60%	LAST MSR

MODEL 66SL – similar to Model 66SM, except features extra select walnut with special graining, 7 1/4 lbs. Disc. 1985.

	$1,370	$1,275	$890	$720	$580	$475	$420	*$1,470*

* ***Model 66SL Ultra*** – 7x64mm or .30-06 cal., 21 in. barrel, 7 1/4 lbs. Disc. 1985.

	$1,475	$1,325	$940	$750	$600	$450	$400	*$1,520*

* ***Model 66SL Magnum Calibers*** – similar to Model 66 S, 8.4 lbs. Disc. 1985.

	$1,475	$1,325	$940	$750	$600	$450	$400	*$1,520*

* ***Model 66SL Mannlicher Type Full Stock*** – 21 in. barrel, 7 lbs. Disc. 1985.

	$1,475	$1,325	$940	$750	$600	$450	$400	*$1,520*

MODEL 66SL DIPLOMAT – same specifications as Model 66SM, except includes selected walnut and special engraving including deer and wild boar game scenes.

Add $93 for Mannlicher full-stock (21 in. barrel). Add $387 for Mag. cals.

The last published retail price (1988) for a standard model without options was $3,167.

This model was available on an individual custom order basis only.

MODEL 660 – U.S. designation of 66S. Imported 1971-73.

	$925	$820	$720	$600	$500	$450	$400	

MODEL 66S DELUXE – special order engraved and inlaid, select wood. Priced per individual customer order. All guns are custom made only.

MODEL 66P – imported 1995 only.

	$4,250	$3,575	$3,075	$2,600	$2,075	$1,700	$1,375	*$4,888*

MODEL 66SP SUPER MATCH – .300 Win. Mag. or .308 Win. cal., telescoping short action, 27 1/2 in. heavy barrel with muzzle brake, no sights, match trigger, 3 shot mag., select European walnut stock with stippling and thumbhole, adj. cheekpiece and buttplate, includes premium scope, 12 lbs. Never imported domestically.

	$4,150	$3,500	$3,050	$2,600	$2,075	$1,700	$1,375	*$4,737*

MODEL 77 – .243 Win., .270 Win., 6.5x57mm, 7x64mm, .308 Win., or .30-06 cal., 24 in. barrel, set trigger on tang, adj. and detachable sights, walnut stock with European cheekpiece and hand checkering, swivels, new safety, steel detachable box mag., rubber recoil pad, 7 1/4 lbs. Disc.

	$1,130	$950	$875	$810	$750	$675	$595	*$1,331*

* ***Model 77 Ultra*** – 6.5x57mm, 7x64mm or .30-06 cal., 20 in. barrel, 7.7 lbs. Disc.

	$1,175	$975	$895	$835	$760	$675	$595	*$1,394*

* ***Model 77 Magnum Calibers*** – similar to Model 66S, 8 1/8 lbs. Disc.

	$1,175	$975	$895	$835	$760	$675	$595	*$1,394*

* ***Model 77 Mannlicher type full stock*** – 20 in. barrel, Mauser-set trigger, 7.7 lbs. Disc.

	$1,175	$975	$895	$835	$760	$675	$595	*$1,394*

* ***Model 77 Big Game Model*** – .375 H&H cal., 26 in. barrel, 8 1/8 lbs. Disc.

	$1,075	$1,000	$900	$795	$675	$575	$475	*$1,150*

MODEL 77 SPORTSMAN – .243 Win. or .308 Win. cal., sports version of the Model 77, set trigger on tang, no sights, 24 in. barrel, 9 lbs. Disc.

	$1,495	$1,230	$1,075	$985	$895	$820	$740	*$1,754*

Add $430 for Zeiss 2 1/2-10X scope and mounts.

MODEL 83 MATCH SINGLE SHOT – .308 Win. cal. only, cylinder locking action with 3 locking lugs in rear, match trigger, anatomical match stock with select walnut, adj. comb and buttplate. Disc.

	$2,170	$1,815	$1,660	$1,545	$1,400	$1,195	$925	*$2,594*

This model is a UIT standard rifle for 300-meter competition.

MODEL 83 MATCH UIT FREE RIFLE – .308 Win. cal. only, cylinder locking action with 3 locking lugs in rear, match trigger, anatomical match stock with select walnut, adj. comb and buttplate. Disc.

	$2,320	$1,940	$1,760	$1,600	$1,430	$1,195	$925	*$2,771*

MODEL 83 STANDARD RIFLE – similar to Model 83 Match, except has removable 10 shot steel mag., 26 in. barrel. Disc.

	$2,320	$1,950	$1,800	$1,625	$1,460	$1,250	$1,000	*$2,766*

MODEL 86 LAMINATED/FIBERGLASS (SR) – .308 Win. cal., updated version of the Model 83 action, 25.6 (disc.) or 28 3/4 (new 1997) in. fluted barrel with muzzle brake, black laminate wood (with thumbhole) or fiberglass (disc.) stock with rail in forearm, adj. trigger, 9 shot detachable mag., cased, 10.8 lbs. Imported 1989-1996, recent mfg. included a 2 1/2-10X power Zeiss tactical scope with detachable mount.

	$10,750	$8,900	$7,700	$6,500	$5,500	$4,500	$3,500	*$11,795*

GRADING - PPGS™	100%	98%	95%	90%	80%	70%	60%	LAST MSR

MODEL SR 93 – .300 Win. Mag. cal., precision rifle employing skeletonized cast magnesium/aluminum stock, combination right-hand/left-hand bolt, adj. ergonomics, 27 in. fluted barrel with muzzle brake, integrated bipod, 4 or 5 shot mag., approx. 13 lbs. without accessories. Disc. 1996.

	$20,000	$17,250	$14,750	$11,950	$8,700	$6,500	$5,000	*$21,995*

MODEL 94 – .243 Win., .270 Win., .30-06, .308 Win., .300 Win. Mag., 7x64mm, 7mm Rem. Mag., 8x68S (disc. 1996), or 9.3x62mm cal., 22 or 24 in. interchangeable barrel, aluminum block in stock bedding system, 60 degree bolt, 6 lug locking system, checkered walnut stock and forearm, 3 or 4 shot mag., lateral slide safety, approx. 7 1/4 lbs. Mfg. began 1994, U.S. importation was disc. 1995, resumed 1997 only.

	$1,925	$1,550	$1,325	$1,100	$925	$850	$775	*$2,295*

Add $799 per interchangeable barrel assembly.

MODEL 96 – .25-06 Rem. (new 1997), .270 Win., .30-06, .308 Win. (new 1997), 7x64mm (new 1997), .300 Win. Mag. (new 1997), or 7mm Rem. Mag. (new 1997) cal., 16 lug bolt slides straight back allowing for low scope mounts, 22 or 24 (Mag. cals., new 1997) in. barrel, safety mechanism in bolt in addition to rear 3-position tang safety, checkered walnut stock, 4 (Mag. cals., new 1997) or 5 shot top loading mag., w/o sights, 6 1/4 lbs. Imported 1996-97.

	$625	$550	$500	$450	$400	$360	$330	*$699*

MODEL 98 COMMERCIAL – various cals., features original breech mechanisms refurbished to new condition, barrel, trigger system, and stock are new from factory.

This model was mostly distributed in Europe with no domestic MSR.

MODEL 1898 COMMEMORATIVE – 8x57mm Mauser cal., special limited edition model mfg. to commemorate the 100th anniversary of the original M-98, bright royal blue on most major metal parts, bolt and receiver have silver satin finish, checkered select European walnut. 1,998 mfg. 1998 only.

	$2,175	$1,775	$1,500	N/A	N/A	N/A	N/A	*$2,300*

MODEL 98 1898-1998 CENTENARY RIFLE – .375 H&H Mag. or .416 Rigby cal., dangerous game sporting rifle with Model 98 Magnum action. 100 of each caliber were to be mfg. beginning 1998, observed serial no. ranges are H077-100 (.375 H&H cal.) and R016-100 and R077-100 (.416 Rigby cal.). Mfg. by Waffen Prechtl. Disc.

	$8,750	$7,750	$6,750	$5,750	$4,750	$4,000	$3,250	

This model chambered for .416 Rigby is actually marked ".416 Rygby" on the guns.

MODEL 98 STANDARD EXPERT – 7x57mm Mauser, 8x57IS, 9.3x62mm, .308 Win., or .30-06 cal., 22 in. cold hammered forged barrel, 5 shot mag., optimized trigger, front and rear sight on the barrel ring, Grade 5 walnut stock with dark stain and matte oil finish, front sling swivel, 3-pos. safety, black plasma Nitride steel parts, 8 lbs. New 2018.

MSR $12,478	$11,850	$10,375	$8,900	$7,800	$6,500	$5,250	$4,150	

MODEL 98 STANDARD DIPLOMAT – .308 Win., .30-06, 7x57mm Mauser, 8x57IS, or 9.3x62mm cal., 22 in. barrel, 5 shot mag., original hinged floorplate steel mag., crisp direct trigger, M98 open sights, M98 Classic Sporter Grade 2 walnut stock w/ebony forearm tip, steel bolt knob and pistol grip cap w/Mauser logo, black Nitride finish, 8 lbs. New 2018.

MSR $13,428	$12,700	$11,000	$9,500	$8,250	$7,000	$5,700	$4,500	

MODEL 98 STANDARD/MAGNUM SAFARI – various cals. from .22-250 Rem. to 9.3x62mm, Safari cals include .375 H&H (disc. 2002, reintroduced 2004), .338 Lapua Mag. (new 2004), .416 Rigby, .450 Dakota (new 2001), .458 Lott (new 2001), or .500 Jeffery (new 2001) cal., 3-5 shot mag., original M-98 Magnum square bridge action with 3 lugs, Model 70 style wing safety, folding express sights (Safari model only), 24 in. standard or heavy barrel, features custom workmanship, extra select checkered walnut stock, 8.8 lbs., delivery time is approx. 8-12 months. Limited mfg. 1998-2017.

	$10,750	$9,000	$7,750	$6,500	$5,500	$4,500	$4,000	*$12,495*

Add $2,400 for Magnum Safari in .500 Jeffery cal.
Add $949 for Grade 6 wood, $1,923 for Grade 7 wood.

MODEL 98 MAGNUM EXPERT – .308 Win., .30-06, 7x57mm Mauser, 8x57IS, 9.3x62mm cal., 24 in. barrel, 5 shot mag., original hinged floorplate steel mag., M98 express open sights, M98 Class Sporter Grade 5 walnut stock w/ebony forearm tip, steel bolt ball and pistol grip cap w/Mauser logo, black Nitride finish, 8 lbs. New 2018.

MSR $13,797	$13,050	$11,500	$9,750	$8,500	$7,250	$5,875	$4,600	

MODEL 98 MAGNUM DIPLOMAT – 24 in. barrel, 5 shot mag., original hinged floorplate steel mag., M98 express open sights, M98 Class Sporter Grade 7 walnut stock w/ebony forearm tip, steel bolt ball and pistol grip cap w/Mauser logo, black Nitride finish. New 2018.

MSR $14,772	$13,975	$12,000	$10,500	$9,000	$7,750	$6,250	$4,900	

GRADING - PPGS™	100%	98%	95%	90%	80%	70%	60%	LAST MSR

MODEL 99 – 5.6x57mm, 6.5x57mm, 7x57mm Mauser, 7x64mm, .243 Win., .25-06 Rem., .270 Win., .30-06 or .308 Win. cal., bolt action with 60 degree throw, 24 in. free floating barrel, jeweled bolt, available in either hand-rubbed oil or high-luster lacquer finish for stock, mini-claw extractor, adj. single stage trigger, 4 shot detachable mag., no sights, 8 lbs. Imported 1989-disc.

* ***Model 99 Classic Lacquer Finish*** – high-luster lacquer finish for stock. Disc.

$1,110	$925	$850	$775	$700	$625	$550	*$1,272*

This model was available with either a Schnabel forearm with regular stock or rosewood capped forearm with American Monte Carlo stock.

* ***Model 99 Classic Oil Finish*** – hand rubbed oil finish for stock. Disc.

$1,130	$995	$875	$775	$700	$625	$550	*$1,130*

This model was available with either a Schnabel forearm with regular stock or rosewood capped forearm with American Monte Carlo stock.

MODEL 99 MAGNUM – 8x68S, 9.3x62mm, 7mm Rem. Mag., .257 Wby. Mag., .270 Wby. Mag., .300 Wby. Mag., .300 Win. Mag., .338 Win. Mag., or .375 H&H cal., similar specifications as Model 99, except has 26 in. barrel and 3 shot mag. Imported 1989-disc.

* ***Model 99 Magnum Classic Lacquer Finish*** – high-luster lacquer finish for stock.

$1,135	$950	$875	$775	$700	$625	$550	*$1,322*

This model was available with either a Schnabel forearm with regular stock or rosewood capped forearm with American Monte Carlo stock.

* ***Model 99 Magnum Classic Oil Finish*** – hand-rubbed oil finish for stock. Disc.

$1,025	$895	$795	$725	$625	$550	$495	*$1,180*

This model is available with either a Schnabel forearm with regular stock or rosewood capped forearm with American Monte Carlo stock.

MODEL 225 – available in 13 cals. between .243 Win. and .300 Wby. Mag., bolt action, 60 degree bolt lift with 3 locking lugs, ultra fast lock time, adj. trigger, 24 or 26 (Mag. only) in. barrel, 3 or 5 shot mag., no sights, guaranteed 1/2 in. accuracy at 100 yards, many stock options available at an extra cost.

* ***Model 225 Deluxe Standard Sporter*** – standard model available in 6 regular cals. and 9 Mag. cals. Importation disc. 1989.

$1,275	$1,000	$875	$750	$625	$550	$495	*$1,400*

Add $90 for Mag. cals.

This model was formerly the KDF Model K-15.

MODEL 226 – left-handed variation of the Model 225 with slight changes. Disc. 1989.

$1,275	$1,000	$875	$750	$625	$550	$495	*$1,400*

MODEL 2000 (DISC.) – .270 Win., .308 Win., or .30-06 cal., 5 shot mag., 24 in. barrel, leaf rear sight, checkered walnut stock. Mfg. by F.W. Heym for Mauser, 1969-71.

$495	$475	$450	$400	$375	$350	$325	

MODEL 2000 CLASSIC – .270 Win., .30-06, .308 Win., .300 Win. Mag., or 7mm Rem. Mag. cal., features new design allowing interchangeable calibers from standard to standard and Magnum to Magnum models, bolt locks directly into barrel, detachable mag., deluxe walnut stock with checkering and rosewood forend, double function set trigger, high polish blue, includes studs. Limited importation 1998 only.

$1,595	$1,375	$1,125	$950	$825	$700	$575	*$1,800*

* ***Model 2000 Classic Varmint*** – .22-250 Rem. or .243 Win. cal., choice of black synthetic or special varmint wood stock with accessory rail, heavy fluted barrel. Limited importation 1998 only.

$1,900	$1,550	$1,350	$1,100	$900	$775	$650	*$2,200*

* ***Model 2000 Classic Sniper*** – .300 Win. Mag. or .308 Win. cal., features heavy fluted barrel, special set trigger system, bipod rail, and other special shooting performance features, satin blue metal finish, custom built with individual certificate. Limited importation 1998 only.

$1,900	$1,550	$1,350	$1,100	$900	$775	$650	*$2,200*

* ***Model 2000 Classic Professional*** – .300 Win. Mag. or .308 Win. cal., features recoil reduction compensator, camo all-weather special pistol grip stock, satin blue metal finish, custom built with individual certificate. Limited importation 1998 only.

$3,175	$2,725	$2,400	$2,100	$1,800	$1,500	$1,250	*$3,500*

GRADING - PPGS™	100%	98%	95%	90%	80%	70%	60%	LAST MSR

MODEL 3000 – .243 Win., .270 Win., .308 Win., or .30-06 cal., 5 shot mag., 22 in. barrel, no sights, walnut Monte Carlo style stock, rosewood forearm and pistol grip, skipline checkering, recoil pad and swivels. Mfg. 1971-74.

	$525	$475	$450	$425	$395	$335	$285	

MODEL 3000 MAGNUM – similar to 3000, except 7mm Rem. Mag., .300 Win. Mag., or .375 H&H cal., 3 shot mag., 26 in. barrel. Disc.

	$575	$525	$475	$450	$415	$350	$295	

This model was mfg. by Heym for Mauser.

MODEL 4000 VARMINT RIFLE – similar to 3000, except smaller action, .222 Rem. or .223 Rem. cal., folding leaf rear sight, rubber buttplate. Disc.

	$425	$400	$375	$350	$300	$260	$225	

This model was mfg. by Heym for Mauser.

LIGHTNING MODEL – .308 Win. or 7.62x39mm cal., slide-bolt action, locking bolt similar to M16 enabling locking directly onto free floating short barrel, fixed internal mag., specially bedded receiver, satin blue finish or stainless steel, open sights, synthetic stock available in black, light grey, blue, or NATO green. Limited importation 1998 only.

	$495	$425	$375	$325	$295	$275	$250	*$550*

LIGHTNING HUNTER MODEL – .243 Win., .270 Win., .30-06, .308 Win., .300 Win. Mag., or 7mm Rem. Mag. cal., slide-bolt mechanism, detachable mag., choice of satin blue or bright blue metal finish, checkered satin or high gloss walnut stock, with or w/o sights, free floating barrel, bedded receiver. Limited importation 1998 only.

	$650	$575	$500	$450	$400	$360	$330	*$730*

Add $50 for open sights.
Add $20 for bright blue metal finish with high gloss stock.

* ***Lightning Hunter Model Stainless Steel*** – similar to Lightning Hunter Model, except has satin finish stainless steel receiver and barrel, checkered satin finished walnut stock. Limited importation 1998 only.

	$665	$585	$500	$430	$375	$315	$270	*$750*

Add $50 for open sights.

LIGHTNING HUNTER ALL-WEATHER MODEL – similar to Lightning Hunter, except has black synthetic stock, satin blue metal finish, scope mounts included, with or w/o sights. Limited importation 1998 only.

	$625	$550	$475	$400	$350	$325	$295	*$700*

Add $50 for open sights.

* ***Lightning Hunter All-Weather Model Stainless Steel*** – similar to Lightning Hunter All-Weather Model, except is satin stainless steel. Limited importation 1998 only.

	$650	$575	$500	$425	$375	$325	$295	*$730*

Add $50 for open sights.

LIGHTNING VARMINT MODEL – .22-250 Rem. or .243 Win., features slide-bolt action, free floating heavy fluted barrel, satin blue metal finish, choice of special varmint wood or synthetic stock. Limited importation 1998 only.

	$895	$775	$675	$600	$525	$475	$425	*$1,000*

* ***Lightning Varmint Model Stainless*** – similar to Lightning Varmint Model, except is satin stainless steel. Limited importation 1998 only.

	$895	$775	$675	$600	$525	$475	$425	*$1,000*

LIGHTNING SNIPER MODEL – .300 Win. Mag. or .308 Win. cal., slide-bolt action, features free floating heavy fluted barrel w/o sights, special wood or synthetic stock with built-in bipod rail, detachable mag., satin blue metal finish. Limited importation 1998 only.

	$895	$775	$675	$600	$525	$475	$425	*$1,000*

* ***Lightning Sniper Model Stainless*** – similar to Lightning Sniper Model, except is satin stainless steel. Limited importation 1998 only.

	$895	$775	$675	$600	$525	$475	$425	*$1,000*

LIGHTNING PROFESSIONAL MODEL – .300 Win. Mag. or .308 Win. cal., slide-bolt action, features special black or camo synthetic adj. stock with pistol grip, special tuned trigger system, free floating heavy fluted barrel, recoil reduction compensator. Limited importation 1998 only.

	$1,595	$1,375	$1,125	$950	$825	$700	$575	*$1,800*

GRADING - PPGS™	100%	98%	95%	90%	80%	70%	60%	LAST MSR

RIFLES: BOLT ACTION, .22 CAL.

On pre-war Mauser .22 cal. Sport and Target rifles, an E prefix indicates single shot, M designates magazine loaded, and B refers to claw extractor.

MODEL EN310 - .22 LR cal., single shot, bolt action, 19 3/4 in. barrel, fixed sights, plain pistol grip stock, pre-1935.

N/A $365 $315 $280 $260 $225 $200

MODEL EL320 - .22 LR cal., single shot, bolt action, 23 1/2 in. barrel, fixed sights, checkered pistol grip stock.

N/A $395 $330 $295 $275 $250 $225

MODEL ES340 - .22 LR cal., single shot, bolt action, 25 1/2 in. barrel, adj. sights, checkered pistol grip, grooved forearm, pre-1935.

N/A $750 $625 $500 $425 $350 $295

MODEL ES350 - .22 LR cal., single shot, bolt action, 27 1/2 in. barrel, championship rifle, micrometer rear sight, ramp front sight, checkered full target stock, swivels, pre-1935.

N/A $850 $750 $625 $550 $475 $400

Add 15%-25% for double set triggers (rare).

MODEL MS 420 - .22 LR Sporter cal., bolt action, pre-war, 5 shot mag.

N/A $975 $850 $675 $575 $475 $425

Add 15%-25% for double set triggers (rare).

MODEL DSM34 (DEUTSCHES SPORTMODELL) - .22 LR cal., bolt action, 25.98 in. barrel. "Deutsches Sportmodell" lightweight trainer, side sling, no bayonet lug.

$3,000 $2,500 $1,750 $1,000 $750 $550 $475

MODEL MS350B - .22 LR cal., repeating action, 5 shot mag., 26 3/4 in. barrel, grooved receiver for scope or sight, micrometer rear sight, ramp front sight, target stock, checkered pistol grip and forearm, swivels.

$4,750 $3,850 $3,000 $2,200 $1,650 $1,350 $1,000

MODEL ES350B CHAMPIONSHIP RIFLE - .22 LR cal., single shot, 26 3/4 in. barrel, grooved receiver for scope or sight, micrometer rear sight, ramp front sight, target stock, checkered pistol grip and forearm, swivels.

$2,150 $1,850 $1,525 $1,300 $1,100 $900 $725

MODEL ES340B - .22 LR cal., bolt action, single shot, 26 3/4 in. barrel, adj. sight, plain pistol grip stock.

$2,000 $1,750 $1,500 $1,250 $900 $675 $475

MODEL MM410B - .22 LR cal., bolt action sporter, 5 shot mag., 23 1/2 in. barrel, adj. sights, lightweight stock, checkered pistol grip, swivels.

$4,000 $3,000 $2,250 $1,750 $1,350 $875 $675

MODEL MS420B - .22 LR cal., bolt action target, 5 shot mag., 26 3/4 in. barrel, adj. sights, target style stock, checkered pistol grip, swivels.

$3,000 $2,500 $2,000 $1,600 $1,250 $1,000 $750

MODEL KKW (KLEIN KALIBER WEHRSPORTGEWEHR) - .22 LR cal., single shot, bolt action, target, 26 in. barrel, tangent rear sight, military style stock with bayonet lug. This weapon was also produced by Walther, Gustloff, and Anschütz. It was used as a training rifle in addition to commercial sales.

$3,000 $2,500 $2,000 $1,000 $750 $575 $425

Deduct 15% for 4mm KKW Models.

MODEL 20/22 - .22 LR or .22 WMR cal., bolt action, features free floating barrel, precision trigger, standard or deluxe checkered walnut stock. Limited importation 1998 only.

$625 $550 $475 $400 $350 $325 $295 *$700*

Add $100 for Deluxe Model.

MODEL 107 STANDARD - .22 LR cal. only, bolt action, 19 1/2 in. barrel, 5 shot mag., adj. iron sights, 6 lbs. Imported 1988-89, reintroduced 1993 only.

$300 $260 $215 $185 $170 $155 $140 *$356*

This model is the same as KDF's previous Model 2107 mfg. by Voere.

- ***Model 107 Standard Deluxe*** - .22 LR or .22 WMR cal., similar to Model 107, except has deluxe checkered walnut. Imported 1988-89 only.

$290 $240 $210 $175 $150 $135 $120 *$320*

Add $90 for .22 WMR cal.

This model is the same as KDF's previous Model 2107 Deluxe mfg. by Voere.

GRADING - PPGS™	100%	98%	95%	90%	80%	70%	60%	LAST MSR

MODEL 201 – .22 LR or .22 WMR cal., bolt action, free floating 21 in. barrel, 5 shot mag., adj. trigger, scaled-down version of the K-15, unusual action incorporates two front-located locking lugs on bolt face that engage Stellite inserts on the front receiver portion, blue only, no sights, beechwood stock with cheekpiece, 6 1/2 lbs. Disc. 1997.

	$635	$515	$465	$415	$365	$315	$260	*$716*

Add $19 for sights (disc.).
Add $77 for .22 WMR cal. (Model 201-SM).

This model is the same as KDF's disc. Model K-22 mfg. by Voere. Before 1989, this model came standard with a walnut stock.

* ***Model 201 Luxus*** – similar to the Model 201 except has walnut stock with rosewood forend. Disc. 1997.

	$710	$650	$550	$475	$425	$375	$295	*$809*

Add $27 for sights (disc.).
Add $67 for .22 WMR cal.

This model is the same as KDF's previous Model K-22 Deluxe mfg. by Voere.

RIFLES: SEMI-AUTO, .22 LR

MODEL 105 STANDARD – .22 LR cal. only, 10 shot mag., approx. 5 lbs. Imported 1995-97.

	$285	$250	$205	$180	$170	$155	$140	*$330*

SHOTGUNS

Mauser shotguns were sub-contracted to various European firms and were made in various O/U (including field and target), SxS (both boxlock and sidelock), and single shot configurations. While they are relatively rare (these shotguns had limited importation into the U.S. by Bauer located in Michigan - models included the 496 single shot, 496 SxS, 580 SxS, 610 O/U, 620 O/U, 71E O/U, and others), collectability to date has been minimal. Values will depend on the grade, configuration, features, engraving, and overall desirability. Pricing guidelines are as follows: $95 - $175 for the Model 496 single shot, $300 - $650 for the Model 496, $995 - $3,500 for the 580 SxS (mfg. by R. Gamba - same as Ambassador model), and $475 - $1,350 for the boxlock O/U models, depending on configuration, features, and original condition.

MAVERICK ARMS, INC.

Current manufacturer located in Eagle Pass, TX, who completed a major expansion during 2014. Administrative offices are at O.F. Mossberg & Sons, located in North Haven, CT. Distributor sales only.

RIFLES: BOLT ACTION

ALL PURPOSE SHORT/LONG ACTION – .243 Win., .270 Win., .30-06, or .308 Win. cal., short or long action, 22 in. barrel, matte blue finish, synthetic stock, Weaver style base, top load magazine. Disc. 2011.

	$275	$250	$215	$195	$155	$130	$100	*$345*

SUPER BANTAM ALL PURPOSE SHORT ACTION – .243 Win. cal., 20 in. barrel, matte blue finish, synthetic stock, Weaver style base, top load magazine. Disc. 2011.

	$275	$250	$215	$195	$155	$130	$100	*$345*

SHOTGUNS

Beginning 1992, all Maverick slide action shotguns incorporate twin slide rails in the operating mechanism.

MODEL 60 SEMI-AUTO – while advertised, this model was never manufactured.

MODEL 88 CRUISER – 12 or 20 ga., 3 in. chamber, 18 1/2 or 20 in. barrel, cylinder bore choke, 6 or 8 shot, dual extractors, bead sight, black synthetic pistol grip stock, blue finish, 5.5-6.5 lbs. New 2020.

MSR $245	$200	$180	$155	$140	$115	$90	$80	

MODEL 88 FIELD SLIDE ACTION – 12 or 20 ga., 3 in. chamber, 24 (Deer Model with iron sights, disc. 1996), 26 (20 ga. only), 28 (12 ga. only), or 30 (disc.) in. plain (disc.) or VR barrel, wood (disc.) or black synthetic stock and forearm with recoil pad, fixed or Accu-chokes (disc. 1997, reintroduced 2002), 6 shot (w/two 3/4 in. shot shells), aluminum alloy receiver, crossbolt safety, 7 lbs. New 1989.

MSR $245	$200	$180	$155	$140	$115	$90	$80	

Add $20 for adj. sights (disc.).
Add $14 for Deer Model (24 in. cyl. bore barrel, disc. 1996).
Subtract 10% if w/o Accu-choke barrel.

Maverick 88 barrels are interchangeable with Mossberg Model 500 barrels within gauge and mag. capacity.

GRADING - PPGS™	100%	98%	95%	90%	80%	70%	60%	LAST MSR

* ***Model 88 Field Slide Action Camo*** – 12 or 20 ga., 3 in. chamber, 22 (youth) or 28 in. VR barrel, modified choke tubes, 5 shot, dual extractors, bead sights, synthetic stock with Mossy Oak Treestand camo, blue finish, 5.25 or 7 lbs. New 2020.

MSR $274	$230	$200	$175	$155	$125	$110	$90	

* ***Model 88 Field Slide Action Combat*** – 12 ga. only, combat design featuring pistol grip stock and forearm, black synthetic stock is extension of receiver, 18 1/2 in. cyl. bore barrel with vented shroud with built-in carrying handle, open sights. Mfg. 1990-92.

	$375	$330	$280	$255	$205	$170	$130	*$282*

* ***Model 88 Field Slide Action Deer Combos*** – includes various combinations of extra Deer barrels with rifle sights, 28 in. plain or VR barrel, or extra 18 1/2 in. cyl. bore barrel. Mfg. 1990-1995.

	$245	$215	$185	$165	$135	$110	$85	*$294*

Add $10 for VR barrel.
Add $17 for Accu-choke barrel.
Add $29 for wood stock and forearm (mfg. 1992 only).

* ***Model 88 Field Slide Action Security*** – 12 ga., 3 in. chamber, 18 1/2 (6 shot) or 20 (8 shot) in. barrel with cyl. bore fixed choke, bead sights, regular, pistol grip (disc. 1997), or ATI Shotforce top-folding (new 2018) synthetic stock with black or FDE (new 2018) finish, 6 or 8 shot, plain synthetic forearm, matte blue metal finish, 6 1/4-6 1/2 lbs. New 1993.

MSR $245	$200	$180	$155	$140	$115	$90	$80	

Add $14 for FDE finish (new 2018).
Add $29 for ATI Shotforce top-folding stock (new 2018).
Add $7 for 8 shot model with 20 in. barrel (disc. 2009).
Add $98 for bullpup configuration (6 or 9 shot, disc. 1994).
Add $47-$65 for combo package (disc.).

* ***Model 88 Field Slide Action Slug*** – 12 ga., 3 in. chamber, 6 shot, 24 in. fully rifled or cylinder bore barrel with adj. rifle sights, blue finish, black synthetic stock and forearm, 6 3/4 lbs.

MSR $244	$200	$180	$155	$140	$115	$90	$80	

Add $29 for fully rifled barrel.

* ***Model 88 Youth All Purpose*** – 20 ga., 3 in. chamber, 6 shot, 22 in. VR barrel, modified choke tubes, bead sights, 13 in. LOP, matte blue metal finish, Black synthetic stock, 5 1/4 lbs. New 2013.

MSR $245	$200	$180	$155	$140	$115	$90	$80	

MODEL 88 SECURITY/FIELD COMBO – 12 ga., 2 3/4 in. chamber, 18 1/2 in. cylinder bore barrel and 28 in. VR barrel with modified choke tubes, 6 shot mag., bead sights, black synthetic stock, blue metal finish, 6 1/4-7 lbs. New 2018.

MSR $274	$230	$200	$175	$155	$125	$110	$90	

MODEL 91 SLIDE ACTION – 12 ga. only, 3 1/2 in. chamber, 18 1/2 cyl. bore or 28 in. VR barrel with 1 choke tube, otherwise similar to Model 88. Mfg. 1991-95.

	$230	$200	$170	$155	$125	$105	$80	*$269*

Add $2 for VR barrel.

MODEL 95 BOLT ACTION – 12 ga. only, 3 in. chamber, synthetic stock with recoil pad, 25 in. barrel bored mod., crossbolt trigger guard safety. Mfg. 1995-1997.

	$155	$135	$115	$105	$85	$70	$55	*$184*

MODEL HS-12 TACTICAL O/U – 12 ga., 2 3/4 or 3 in. chambers, 18 1/2 in. barrels, cylinder bore or Imp. Mod chokes, matte black finish, synthetic stock, rear slot sight with fiber optic front sight, no under barrel mounted Picatinny rail beginning 2012. Mfg. 2011-2015.

	$475	$415	$355	$325	$260	$215	$165	*$564*

Add $18 for choke tubes.

MODEL HS-12 THUNDER RANCH – 12 ga., 3 in. chamber, 2 shot, 18 1/2 in. barrel, matte black finish, side mounted Picatinny rails, tang mounted safety and barrel selector, checkered black synthetic pistol grip stock and forearm with nylon shell holder, fiber optic front sight, engraved Thunder Ranch logo, 6 1/4 lbs. Mfg. 2013-2018.

	$485	$425	$365	$335	$300	$275	$250	*$594*

MODEL HUNTER FIELD O/U – 12 ga., 2 3/4 or 3 in. chambers, 28 in. VR barrels with Imp. Mod chokes, matte blue barrel finish, black synthetic stock, front bead sight, embellished receiver, 7 lbs. Mfg. 2010-2018.

	$425	$335	$275	$245	$200	$160	$125	*$528*

GRADING - PPGS™	100%	98%	95%	90%	80%	70%	60%	LAST MSR

MAWHINNEY, CHUCK

Previous trademark of sniper rifles manufactured by Riflecraft, Ltd. located in the United Kingdom. Imported by Chuck Mawhinney, located in Baker City, OR.

RIFLES: BOLT ACTION

M40 SNIPER – .308 Win. cal., based on the M700 Remington action, 24 in. matte black pillar bedded free floating barrel, walnut stock, engraved aluminum floorplate with Chuck Mawhinney's signature (former sniper for the Marines), includes 3-9x40mm Leupold scope. Serial numbered 1-103. Mfg. 2011-2012.

	100%	98%	95%	90%	80%	70%	60%	LAST MSR
	$5,000	$4,400	$3,750	$3,150	$2,500	$2,000	$1,650	*$5,000*

MAXIM DEFENSE

Current AR-15 style pistol and rifle manufacturer located in St. Cloud, MN.

Please refer to BlueBookOfGunValues.com to order the *Blue Book of AR-15s & Variations*, available as a book or online subscription.

MAXIM FIREARMS

Current AR-15 style firearm manufacturer located in the U.S.

Please refer to BlueBookOfGunValues.com to order the *Blue Book of AR-15s & Variations*, available as a book or online subscription.

MAXIMUS ARMS, LLC

Previous pistol manufacturer, gunsmith, and customizer located in Gallatin, TN from 1991-2016.

For individual model listings, please go to BlueBookOfGunValues.com/overflow.

MAYFAIR ENGINEERING

Current bolt action rifle and action manufacturer located in Suffolk, England.

RIFLES: BOLT ACTION

Mayfair Engineering manufactures high quality Magnum Mauser actions. Additionally, guns may be custom ordered featuring their actions. Please contact the company directly for more information and an individualized price quotation.

MAYZUS GUNSMITH COMPANY s.r.o.

Current manufacturer of hunting, sporting, and competition rifles established during 2015, located in Holice, Czech Republic. No current U.S. importation.

Please contact the factory directly for current U.S. availability and pricing.

McCANN INDUSTRIES

Previous rifle and current accessories manufacturer located in Spanaway, WA.

McCann Industries manufactured new Garand semi-auto rifles with design improvements that utilize a .338 or .458 Mag cal. cartridge (not Win. Mag.), in addition to a .300 Win. Mag. bolt action pistol. For more information, including pricing and availability, contact the company directly.

MCDUFFEE ARMS

Previous AR-15 style rifle manufacturer located in Westminster, CO 2010-2016.

Please refer to BlueBookOfGunValues.com to order the *Blue Book of AR-15s & Variations*, available as a book or online subscription.

McMILLAN BROS. RIFLE CO.

Previous division of McMillan Group International, located in Phoenix, AZ. Dealer and consumer direct sales. During 1998, the company name changed from McBros Rifles to McMillan Bros. Rifle Co. The company name changed again during 2007 to McMillan Firearms Manufacturing. Please refer to McMillan Firearms Manufacturing, LLC listing for recent models.

RIFLES: BOLT ACTION

AMERICAN HUNTER – available in 16 cals. between .22-250 Rem. and .416 Rem. Mag. (disc. 1997), camouflaged fiberglass stock, match grade stainless steel barrel, choice of MCRT (Rem. Model 700 custom type action mfg. to aerospace standards) or MCR (disc., Rem. Model 700 BDL action that has been trued). Mfg. 1993-2007.

	100%	98%	95%	90%	80%	70%	60%	LAST MSR
	$3,050	$2,550	$2,100	$1,825	$1,550	$1,375	$1,100	*$3,500*

* ***American Hunter Yukon Hunter*** – available in 6 Mag. cals. between .300 Wby. Mag. and .458 Win. Mag., built to aerospace tolerances for any hunting situation, barrel band sling swivel, folding leaf sight, black synthetic stock. Mfg. 1993-2005.

	100%	98%	95%	90%	80%	70%	60%	LAST MSR
	$3,350	$2,800	$2,400	$2,050	$1,775	$1,500	$1,350	*$3,700*

GRADING - PPGS™	100%	98%	95%	90%	80%	70%	60%	LAST MSR

* ***American Hunter Outdoorsman*** – .30-378 Wby. Mag., .338 Lapua (new 2004), or .338-378 Wby. Mag. (disc. 1997) cal., RT action only. Mfg. 1996-2008.

	$3,350	$2,800	$2,400	$2,050	$1,775	$1,500	$1,350	*$3,700*

MCR TACTICAL – .308 Win. or .300 Win. Mag. cal. Mfg. 1993-2007.

	$2,950	$2,400	$1,900	$1,500	$1,250	$1,050	$925	*$3,300*

This model was formerly designated the MCR Sniper Model.

* ***MCRT Tactical*** – .300 Win. Mag. or .338 Lapua (new 1998), similar to MCR Tactical. Mfg. 1993-2007.

	$3,050	$2,550	$2,100	$1,825	$1,550	$1,375	$1,100	*$3,500*

Add $500 for .338 Lapua Mag (muzzle brake is standard).

This model was formerly designated the MCRT Sniper Model.

BENCHREST COMPETITOR – .222 Rem., 6mm PPC, 6mm BR, 7mm BR, or .308 Win. cal., benchrest configuration. Mfg. 1993-99.

	$2,400	$1,925	$1,575	$1,275	$1,050	$900	$775	*$2,800*

1000 YARD BENCHREST (NATIONAL MATCH COMPETITOR) – .300 Win. Mag. (new 1996), .30-378 Wby. Mag. (new 1996), 7.82 Warbird (new 1996), .308 Win. (disc. 1995) or .338-378 Wby. Mag. (mfg. 1996-97) cal. Mfg. 1993-99.

	$2,450	$1,950	$1,575	$1,275	$1,050	$900	$775	*$2,875*

TUBB 2000 – .243 Win., .260 Rem., 7mm-08 Rem., 6mm, or .308 Win. cal., target rifle featuring metal 4 way adj. stock, Picatinny rail, hand lapped Schneider match barrel, Anschütz 2 stage trigger, state-of-the-art action, vent. handguard, 12 lbs. Mfg. 2000-2007.

	$2,875	$2,475	$2,000	$1,550	$1,250	$1,025	$875	*$3,150*

Add $400 for Tubb 2000 C (includes four 10 shot mags., cleaning rod guide, etc.).
Add $550 for Schneider custom stainless steel match barrel.

BIG MAC/BOOMER – .50 BMG cal., available as either single shot sporter, repeater sporter, light benchrest, or heavy benchrest variation. Mfg. 1993-2007.

	$4,450	$3,850	$3,250	$2,700	$2,225	$1,825	$1,525	*$4,900*

Add $300 for repeating action.
Add $500 for Tactical 50 variation.
Add $100 for Tactical single shot.
Add $100 for heavy benchrest variation.

McMILLAN FIREARMS MANUFACTURING, LLC

Current manufacturer located in Phoenix, AZ beginning 2007.

McMillan Group International is a group of McMillan family companies: McMillan Fiberglass Stocks, McMillan Firearms Manufacturing, and McMillan Machine Company. In 2013, the company was acquired by Strategic Armory Corps. This company also owns ArmaLite, Surgeon Rifles, AWC Silencers, and AWC Ammo.

RIFLES: BOLT ACTION, BENCH REST SERIES

50 LBR (LIGHT BENCH REST) – .50 BMG cal., single shot action, 32 in. match grade light target contoured barrel, matte black finish, BR muzzle brake with precision target crown, red/black competition stock, Jewell trigger, 28 lbs. Mfg. 2011-2014.

	$8,025	$7,025	$6,025	$5,450	$4,425	$3,615	$2,815	*$9,450*

TUBB 2000 – various cals., benchrest rifle featuring metal 4 way adj. stock, 10 or 20 box mag., Picatinny rail, hand lapped Schneider match barrel, Anschütz 2 stage trigger, state-of-the-art action, vent. handguard, 12 lbs. Mfg. 2009-2012.

	$4,750	$4,250	$3,750	$3,350	$2,950	$2,675	$2,400	*$5,000*

RIFLES: BOLT ACTION, HUNTING SERIES

McMillan's Custom Collection is a series of hunting rifles that is built to customer specification on the McMillan G31 action. Options include: triggers, match grade barrels, custom construction, and several accessories. Please contact the manufacturer directly for availability and pricing.

DYNASTY – .270 WSM, .300 WSM, 7mm Rem. Mag., .300 Win. Mag. or .338 Win. Mag. cal., 24 in. stainless steel match grade free floating barrel, target crown, drilled and tapped, McMillan G30 long action, black ultralight graphite Dynasty EDGE stock with pillar glass bedding and Pachmayr Decelerator pad, one-piece machined aluminum hinged floorplate, sling swivels, 6 lbs., 12 oz. - 7 lbs. Disc. 2018.

	$5,300	$4,650	$3,975	$3,600	$2,915	$2,385	$1,850	*$6,235*

GRADING - PPGS™	100%	98%	95%	90%	80%	70%	60%	LAST MSR

HERITAGE – 6.5 Grendel, .284 Norma, 7mm Rem. Mag., .284 Win., .30-06, .300 Win. Mag., .375 H&H (disc.) or .416 Rem. Mag. (disc.) cal., 24 (disc.) or 26 in. stainless steel match grade free floating barrel, target crown, drilled and tapped, McMillan G31 long action, black Heritage synthetic stock with pillar glass bedding and Pachmayr Decelerator pad (disc.) or McMillan Hunter stock, drop belly extended capacity one-piece hinged floorplate, tan, OD, black, green speckle, or tan speckle Cerakote finish, includes Talley bases, 7 1/4 lbs.

This model is part of McMillan's Custom Collection hunting rifles. Please contact the company for pricing and availability on this model.

LEGACY – .223 Rem., .270 Win. (disc.), .30-06 (disc.), .243 Win., 6.5 Creedmoor, .260 Rem., .300 WSM, .308 Win., or .300 Win. Mag. (disc.) cal., McMillan G31 or G32 short or long (disc.) action, 22 (.308 Win. cal. only) or 24 in. match grade stainless steel barrel, target crown muzzle, TriggerTech adj. trigger, McMillan Hunter stock, black ultralight graphite classic sporter stock with pillar glass bedding (disc.) and Pachmayr Decelerator pad, aluminum hinged floorplate, drilled and tapped, sling swivels, tan, OD, black, green speckle, or tan speckle Cerakote finish, one-piece or Talley base included, approx. 7 pounds.

This model is part of McMillan's Custom Collection hunting rifles. Please contact the company for pricing and availability on this model.

LONG RANGE HUNTER (LRH) – .243 Win., .308 Win., 7mm Rem. Mag., 7mm RUM, .300 Win. Mag., or .338 Lapua cal., G30 short or long action, 24, 26, or 27 in. stainless steel match grade medium heavy contour barrel with polygon rifling, McMillan A3 stock, fixed recoil pad, one-piece floorplate, optional box mag., matte black receiver or Duracoat metal finish in olive, gray, tan or Dark Earth, includes travel case, 9 1/2 - 10 lbs. Mfg. 2011-2018.

$5,750	$5,025	$4,325	$3,900	$3,175	$2,595	$2,000	*$6,775*

Subtract $200 if w/o muzzle brake.

OUTDOORSMAN – .300 RUM or .30-378 Wby. Mag. cal., 28 in. fluted stainless steel match grade free floating barrel, muzzle brake, target crown, drilled and tapped, McMillan G30 long action, black McMillan Hunter EDGE ultralight graphite synthetic stock with pillar glass bedding and Pachmayr Decelerator pad, machined one-piece aluminum hinged floorplate, sling swivels, 7 lbs., 11 oz. Disc. 2018.

$5,475	$4,795	$4,100	$3,725	$3,000	$2,475	$1,900	*$6,450*

PRESTIGE – .375 H&H or .416 Rem. Mag. cal., 24 in. match grade free floating chrome moly barrel, target crown, integral barrel band with one inch sling sloop, integral express quarter rib and front sight, McMillan G30 controlled round feed long action, black Prestige synthetic stock with pillar glass bedding and Pachmayr Decelerator pad, drop belly extended capacity one-piece stainless floorplate, express style iron sights, 8 lbs. 4 oz. Disc. 2018.

$6,375	$5,575	$4,775	$4,325	$3,500	$2,875	$2,225	*$7,495*

PRODIGY – .30-06, .270 WSM, .300 WSM, 7mm Rem. Mag., .308 Win., or .300 Win. Mag. cal., 22 (.308 Win. cal. only) or 24 in. stainless steel match grade free floating barrel, target crown, drilled and tapped, McMillan G30 long or short action, black ultralight graphite Hunters EDGE stock with pillar glass bedding and Pachmayr Decelerator pad, one-piece machined aluminum hinged floorplate, sling swivels, 6 lbs., 12 oz. - 7 lbs. Disc. 2018.

$5,300	$4,650	$3,975	$3,600	$2,915	$2,385	$1,850	*$6,235*

TACTICAL HUNTER – .243 Win., 7mm Rem. Mag., .308 Win. or .300 Win. Mag. cal., 22 or 24 in. fluted stainless steel match grade free floating barrel with #5 taper, target crown, drilled and tapped, McMillan G30 short or long action, black ultralight graphite Tactical Hunter EDGE stock with pillar glass bedding and Pachmayr Decelerator pad, one-piece machined aluminum hinged floorplate, sling swivels, approx. 7 lbs. Disc. 2018.

$5,450	$4,775	$4,095	$3,700	$3,000	$2,450	$1,915	*$6,415*

EOL SERIES – .300 EOL Mag., .30-378 EOL Mag., 7mm EOL Mag., or .338 Lapua Mag. cal., features McMillan G30 short or long action, 26 in. Schneider fluted match grade stainless steel barrel with polygon rifling, hinged floorplate or optional box mag., stock configurations include McMillan Hunter (EOL Outdoorsman), Tactical Hunter (EOL LRH-Light), or A-3LRH (EOL LRH), receiver is equipped with Picatinny rail, 8-9 1/2 lbs. Limited mfg. 2012.

$5,150	$4,375	$3,775	$3,200	$2,600	$2,000	$1,650	*$5,670*

Add $794 for EOL LRH configuration.
Add approx. $2,350 for night force scope.

* ***EOL Series Mountain Extreme*** – 6.5x284 Norma (Alpine model only), 7mm EOL Mag., 7mm RUM, .300 EOL Mag., .300 RUM, .338 EOL Mag., or .338 Lapua cal., 26, 27, or 28 in. match grade stainless steel fluted barrel, standard hinged floorplate, Edge Outdoorsman (Yukon), adj. A3-5

GRADING - PPGS™	100%	98%	95%	90%	80%	70%	60%	LAST MSR

(Denali), or McMillan Dynasty (Alpine) khaki stock with gray and brown specks, sling swivels, matte black barrel finish, NP3 muzzle brake bolt stop and cocking piece housing, includes hard case. Mfg. 2013-2018.

	$5,750	$5,025	$4,325	$3,900	$3,175	$2,595	$2,000	*$6,775*

Add $120 for Denali model.
Add $2,339-$2,405 for scope package.

RIFLES: BOLT ACTION, TACTICAL SERIES

ALIAS STAR – 6.5x47 Lapua, 6.5 Creedmoor, or .308 Win. cal., 18 to 24 in. stainless steel match grade barrel, threaded muzzle with thread cap, detachable 10 or 20 shot mag., tactical pistol grip, matte black finish, tube or quad rail forend, Anschutte trigger, includes case, 11.6 lbs. Mfg. 2013-2015, reintroduced late 2020.

MSR $5,590	$4,750	$4,150	$3,550	$3,250	$2,600	$2,150	$1,650	

Last MSR in 2015 was $8,300.

ALIAS TARGET – .260 Rem., 6.5x47 Lapua, 6.5 Creedmoor, .308 Win., .308 Palma, or 6XC cal., McMillan ALIAS action, 24 to 30 inch barrel, two detachable 10 shot mags, one single shot loading block, Anschutz trigger, competition buttstock and forend, competition pistol grip, matte black finish, 12 lbs. New 2013.

Please contact the manufacturer directly for availability and pricing on this model.

CS5 STANDARD – .308 Win cal., matte black finish, 18 1/2 in. stainless steel match grade barrel with threaded muzzle and thread cap., 10 or 20 shot detachable box magazine, Anschutz trigger, adj. buttstock, pistol grip, tactile safety button, upper Picatinny rail, optional suppressor and bipod, includes full size gun case. Mfg. 2012-2015.

Retail pricing was not available for this model.

TAC-300 – .300 Win. Mag. cal., McMillan G30 (disc.) or G31 long action, 26 in. medium heavy free floating contoured threaded barrel with cap and polygon rifling, detachable 5 shot box mag. or hinged floorplate, A5 composite stock w/adj. cheekpiece buttstock, 6 flush mount cups w/sling loops, hinged floorplate, drilled and tapped, adj. cheekpiece, two sling swivels, 20 MOA Mil-Std 1913 scope base, black, OD, gray (disc.), or tan Cerakote finish, includes locking hard case, 12 lbs.

MSR $6,000	$5,100	$4,450	$3,800	$3,450	$2,800	$2,300	$1,800	

TAC-308 – .308 Win. cal., McMillan G31 short action, 20 (disc., reintroduced 2021) or 24 (disc. 2020) in. match grade stainless steel medium heavy contoured threaded barrel with cap, drilled and tapped, detachable 5 shot box mag. or hinged floorplate, TriggerTech adj. trigger, A3 tactical buttstock with adjustable cheekpiece and LOP spacer system, two sling swivels, 20 MOA Mil-Std 1913 rail, black, OD green, gray (disc.), FDE (disc.), or tan Cerakote finish, includes locking hard case, 11 1/2 lbs. New 2016.

MSR $5,875	$5,000	$4,350	$3,750	$3,400	$2,750	$2,250	$1,750	

TAC-338 – .338 Lapua cal., McMillan G30 short (disc.) or TAC-338 action, 26 1/2 (disc. 2020) or 27 in. match grade stainless steel medium heavy contoured threaded barrel with muzzle brake, detachable 5 shot box mag. or hinged floorplate, Jewell adj. trigger, A-5 fiberglass buttstock with integral adjustable cheekpiece, drilled and tapped, six flushmount cups with sling loops, 20 MOA Mil-Std scope base, black, OD green, gray (disc.), FDE, or tan (disc. 2020) Cerakote finish, includes locking hard case, 13 lbs.

MSR $6,250	$5,300	$4,650	$4,000	$3,600	$2,900	$2,400	$1,850	

TAC-416 R/SS – .416 Barrett cal., single shot action, 29 in. match grade Navy contour or 30 in. light contour fluted threaded barrel with muzzle brake, drilled and tapped, McMillan synthetic stock with butthook and adj. saddle style cheekpiece, six flushmount cups with sling loops, bipod, decelerator pad, spacer system, adj. trigger, black, olive, gray, tan, or dark earth finish. Mfg. 2013-2017.

	$8,495	$7,425	$6,375	$5,775	$4,675	$3,825	$2,975	*$9,990*

TAC-50 A1 – .50 BMG cal., TAC-50 action, 29 in. match grade Navy contour fluted threaded barrel w/ muzzle brake, drilled and tapped, 5 shot detachable box mag., Jewell bottom safety trigger, McMillan synthetic stock and adj. saddle style cheekpiece, four flushmount cups w/sling loops, A1 bipod, decelerator pad, 30 MOA Picatinny rail, black, OD green, gray, tan, or FDE Cerakote finish, 26 lbs.

MSR $10,000	$8,500	$7,450	$6,400	$5,800	$4,700	$3,800	$3,000	

TAC-50 A1-R2 – .50 BMG cal., similar to Tac-50 A1, except has McMillan Tac-50 A1-R2 stock and R2 recoil mitigation system. Mfg. 2013-2017.

	$10,195	$8,925	$7,650	$6,925	$5,600	$4,595	$3,575	*$11,990*

GRADING - PPGS™	100%	98%	95%	90%	80%	70%	60%	LAST MSR

TAC-50C – .50 BMG cal., 29 in. match grade Navy contour fluted and threaded barrel with muzzle brake, 5 shot detachable box mag., folding Cadex Dual Strike chassis system with adj. cheekpiece and option for vertical adjustment, adj. LOP, decelerator pad, Jewell bottom safety trigger, black, OD green, tan, of FDE finish, 24 lbs. New 2016.

MSR $11,250	$9,550	$8,350	$7,150	$6,500	$5,250	$4,300	$3,350	

TAC-6.5 – 6.5 Creedmoor cal., detachable box mag., 24 in. match grade stainless steel, medium heavy contour barrel, Cadex Strike Nuke tactical stock, adj. cheekpiece, flush mount swivel cups, Stealth Shadow Vortex finish, 11 1/2 lbs. New 2020.

MSR $5,875	$5,000	$4,350	$3,750	$3,400	$2,750	$2,250	$1,750	

RIFLES: SEMI-AUTO

M1A – .308 Win. cal., 18 or 20 in. barrel, 10 shot mag., McMillan MFS-14 modular tactical system, SOCOM five position adj. buttstock, pistol grip with finger groove, M3A fiberglass stock with saddle type cheekpiece, Picatinny style side and bottom rails, four flushmount cups with sling swivels, two-stage military trigger, many other options available. Disc.

	$2,995	$2,750	$2,450	$2,125	$1,800	$1,525	$1,300	*$3,399*

Add $200 for compact model with 18 in. barrel.

M3A – .308 Win. cal., features McMillan M3A fiberglass stock with adj. cheekpiece, standard or full-length upper handguard tactical rail. Mfg. 2011-2012.

Retail pricing was not available for this model.

McMILLAN, G. & CO., INC.

Previous trademark established circa 1988, located in Phoenix, AZ.

G. McMillan & Co., Inc. had various barrel markings from 1988-1995 including G. McMillan, Harris - McMillan, and Harris Gunworks.

HANDGUNS

WOLVERINE – available in 9mm Para., 10mm, .38 Super, .38 Wad Cutter, .40 S&W, .45 ACP, or .45 Italian cal., interchangeable barrels, competition ready handgun patterned after the Colt 1911. Imported 1992-95.

* ***Wolverine Combat*** – combat features including 5 1/2 in. compensated barrel.

	$1,600	$1,350	$1,025	$875	$750	$625	$550	*$1,700*

* ***Wolverine Competition Match*** – competition features including 6 in. non-compensated barrel.

	$1,600	$1,350	$1,025	$875	$750	$625	$550	*$1,700*

SIGNATURE JR. BOLT ACTION – available in a variety of cals., utilizes Signature benchrest short action, choice of stainless steel barrel lengths, right or left-hand action, single shot or repeater, McMillan design fiberglass stock, choice of electroless nickel or Teflon finish, 5 lbs. Mfg. 1992-95.

	$2,175	$1,775	$1,350	$995	$895	$800	$700	*$2,400*

This model was also available in all titanium.

RIFLES: BOLT ACTION

The models listed were also available with custom wood stocks at varying prices. McMillan also manufactured a custom rifle from a supplied action. Features included new barreling, a fiberglass stock, matte black finish, and range testing to guarantee 3/4 M.O.A. Prices started at $1,400.

Add $150 for stainless steel receiver on most models.

TALON SPORTER – available in various cals. between .22-250 Rem. and .416 Rem. Mag., receiver available in either 4340 chrome molybdenum or 17-4 stainless steel, drilled and tapped, match grade barrel. Mfg. 1992-95.

	$2,375	$1,950	$1,650	$1,325	$1,000	$895	$800	*$2,600*

The Talon action was patterned after the Winchester pre-64 Model 70. It features a cone breech, controlled feed, claw extractor, and 3 position safety.

SIGNATURE CLASSIC SPORTER – various cals. available between .22-250 Rem. and .416 Rem., premium wood stock, matte metal finish, 22 or 24 in. stainless steel barrel with button rifling, McMillan action made from 4340 chrome moly steel (either left- or right-handed), 3 or 4 shot mag. supplied with 5 shot test target. Mfg. 1988-95.

	$2,250	$1,850	$1,350	$950	$850	$750	$675	*$2,400*

SIGNATURE VARMINTER – similar to Signature Model, except is available in 10 cals. between .22-250 Rem. and .350 Rem. Mag., hand bedded fiberglass stock, adj. trigger, 26 in. heavy contour barrel. Mfg. 1988-95.

	$2,250	$1,850	$1,350	$995	$895	$800	$700	*$2,400*

GRADING - PPGS™	100%	98%	95%	90%	80%	70%	60%	LAST MSR

SIGNATURE TITANIUM MOUNTAIN RIFLE – .270 Win., .280 Rem., .30-06, .300 Win. Mag., .338 Win. Mag., or 7mm Rem. Mag. cal., lighter weight variation with shorter barrel. Mfg. 1990-95.

$2,750 $2,195 $1,850 $1,450 $1,100 $925 $825 *$3,000*

Add $605 for titanium alloy light contour match grade barrel.

SIGNATURE ALASKAN – available in 11 cals. between .270 Win. and .416 Rem. Mag. Mfg. 1990-95.

$3,050 $2,475 $2,100 $1,575 $1,200 $1,000 $900 *$3,300*

TALON SAFARI – available in 15 cals. between .300 Win. Mag. and .460 Wby. Mag., hand-bedded fiberglass stock, 4 shot mag., 24 in. stainless steel barrel, matte black finish, 9 1/2 lbs. Mfg. 1988-95.

$3,275 $2,675 $2,300 $1,675 $1,300 $1,100 $950 *$3,600*

Add $600 for .300 Phoenix, .338 Lapua, .378 Wby. Mag., .416 Wby. Mag. or Rigby, or .460 Wby. Mag. cal.

The Talon action was patterned after the Winchester pre-64 Model 70. It featured a cone breech, controlled feed, claw extractor, and 3-position safety. Older Signature action rifles did not have this new Talon action.

M-40 SNIPER RIFLE – .308 Win. cal., Remington action with McMillan match grade heavy contour barrel, fiberglass stock with recoil pad, 4 shot mag., 9 lbs. Mfg. 1990-95.

$1,775 $1,475 $1,150 $925 $825 $725 $625 *$1,800*

M-86 SNIPER RIFLE – .300 Phoenix, .30-06 (new 1989), .300 Win. Mag. or .308 Win. cal., fiberglass stock, variety of optical sights. Mfg. 1988-95.

$1,825 $1,500 $1,150 $975 $85 $775 $675 *$1,900*

Add $550 for .300 Phoenix cal.
Add $200 for takedown feature (new 1993).

* ***M-86 Sniper Rifle System*** – includes Model 86 Sniper Rifle, bipod, Ultra scope, rings, and bases. Cased. Mfg. 1988-92.

$2,460 $2,050 $1,825 $1,600 $1,350 $1,100 $950 *$2,665*

M-87 LONG RANGE SNIPER RIFLE – .50 BMG cal., stainless steel bolt action, 29 in. barrel with muzzle brake, single shot, camo synthetic stock, accurate to 1,500 meters, 21 lbs. Mfg. 1988-95.

$3,650 $2,950 $2,500 $2,150 $1,900 $1,700 $1,575 *$3,735*

* ***M-87 Long Range Sniper Rifle System*** – includes Model 87 Sniper Rifle, bipod, 20X Ultra scope, rings, and bases. Cased. Mfg. 1988-92.

$4,200 $3,400 $2,875 $2,550 $2,250 $2,100 $1,800 *$4,200*

* ***M-87R Long Range Sniper Rifle*** – same specs. as Model 87, except has 5 shot fixed box mag. Mfg. 1990-95.

$3,995 $3,300 $2,700 $2,300 $2,000 $1,850 $1,700 *$4,000*

Add $300 for Combo option.

M-89 SNIPER RIFLE – .308 Win. cal., 28 in. barrel with suppressor (also available without), fiberglass stock adj. for length and recoil pad, 15 1/4 lbs. Mfg. 1990-95.

$2,200 $1,825 $1,575 $1,250 $1,050 $875 $750 *$2,300*

Add $425 for muzzle suppressor.

M-92 BULLPUP – .50 BMG cal., bullpup configuration with shorter barrel. Mfg. 1993-95.

$3,750 $2,950 $2,550 $2,200 $2,000 $1,850 $1,700 *$4,000*

M-93SN – .50 BMG cal., similar to M-87, except has folding stock and detachable 5 or 10 shot box mag. Mfg. 1993-95.

$3,950 $3,250 $2,750 $2,300 $2,000 $1,850 $1,700 *$4,300*

.300 PHOENIX LONG RANGE RIFLE – .300 Phoenix cal., special fiberglass stock featuring adj. cheekpieces to accommodate night vision optics, adj. buttplate, 29 in. barrel, conventional box mag., 12 1/2 lbs. Mfg. 1992 only.

$2,700 $2,195 $1,850 $1,450 $1,100 $925 $825 *$3,000*

.300 Phoenix was a cartridge developed to function at ranges in excess of 800 yards. It produced muzzle velocities of 3,100 ft. per second with a 250 grain bullet.

COMPETITION MODELS – available in Metallic Silhouette (.308 Win. or 7mm-08 Rem. cal. - disc. 1989), National Match (.308 Win. cal. only), Long Range (.300 Win. Mag. only), or Bench Rest (shooter's choice). Each model made specifically for individual competition events. Mfg. 1988-95.

$2,325 $1,775 $1,450 $1,100 $895 $800 $700 *$2,600*

Add $200 for Benchrest Model.
Subtract $300 for Metallic Silhouette model (disc. 1989).

GRADING - PPGS™	100%	98%	95%	90%	80%	70%	60%	LAST MSR

MCREES PRECISION

Previous fireams and current accessories manufacturer located in Lesterville, MO. McRees Precision is a division of McRees Multi Services. Consumer sales through FFL dealers.

RIFLES: BOLT ACTION

McRees Precision manufactured a bolt action rifle in various calibers with a 22 in. barrel. All rifles were guaranteed at least 1/2 MOA at 100 yards.

MEACHAM TOOL & HARDWARE, INC.

Current custom rifle manufacturer located Peck, ID. Consumer direct sales through FFL.

RIFLES: SINGLE SHOT

Meacham Tool & Hardware, Inc. manufactures a High Wall single shot rifle in a variety of calibers and options. Please contact the company directly for availability, options, and an individual price quotation.

MEDWELL & PERRETT LIMITED

Previous long gun manufacturer located in Suffolk, England.

For individual model listings, please go to BlueBookOfGunValues.com/overflow.

MELIOR - ROBAR & CO.

Previous trademark manufactured in Liege, Belgium.

For individual model listings, please go to BlueBookOfGunValues.com/overflow.

MENZ, AUGUST

Previous manufacturer located in Suhl, Germany.

Please refer to listings in the Liliput section of this text.

MERCURY (PISTOLS)

Previous manufacturer located in Belgium. Previously imported 1962-68 by Tradewinds, Inc. located in Tacoma, WA.

PISTOLS: SEMI-AUTO

MERCURY MODEL – .22 LR cal., 7 shot mag., steel frame, fixed sights.

	100%	98%	95%	90%	80%	70%	60%
	$400	$375	$325	$300	$275	$225	$200

MERCURY (SHOTGUNS)

Previous importer of Spanish manufactured shotguns.

SHOTGUNS: SxS

MAGNUM MODEL – 10, 12, or 20 ga. Mag., 28 and 32 in. barrels, full and mod., boxlock, extractors, double triggers, engraved frame, checkered pistol grip stock.

	100%	98%	95%	90%	80%	70%	60%
12 or 20 ga.	$300	$275	$250	$225	$200	$180	$150
10 ga.	$400	$375	$325	$300	$275	$225	$200

MERKEL

Current trademark manufactured by Suhler Jagd-und Sportwaffen GmbH in Suhl, Germany since 1898. Currently imported and distributed exclusively beginning 2010 by Steyr Arms, Inc., located in Bessemer, AL (previously located in Trussville, AL until 2013). Previously imported and distributed from 2005-2010 by Merkel USA, located in Trussville, AL. Previously imported during 2004 by Heckler & Koch, located in Sterling, VA, and by GSI located in Trussville, AL circa 1992-2003. Previously imported until 1992 by Armes De Chasse located in Chadds Ford, PA. Merkel USA was aquired by Steyr Arms during 2009.

MERKEL HISTORY

During the course of its existence, Merkel has been traded under a variety of names, including E.A. Merkel, Merco, Abesser & Merkel, B. Merkel, and Gebrüder Merkel. Most of these names were used by descendants of the family patriarch, Friedrich Ernst Ferdinand Merkel.

At the end of WWII, the Merkel company was initially taken over by American troops, but then after approx. 3 months, it was turned over to the Russians for the duration of their occupation. Once the communist German government was established, the factory was owned by the government until Germany was reunited. The East German economy, like that of most former Soviet bloc countries,

GRADING - PPGS™	100%	98%	95%	90%	80%	70%	60%	LAST MSR

suffered due to lack of capitalization and from very restrictive gun laws.

Merkel was first managed by the "Treuhand", the government trustee that tried to find new owners for all East German commerce and industry. Among the applicants who had an interest in taking over the remaining Suhl gun industry was Sturm, Ruger & Co., together with members of the Simson family, who owned the biggest gun factory in Suhl before the Nazis came to power. Their offer was rejected in favor of a group of investors who enriched themselves, and went out of business after only one year.

The "Treuhand" then turned the company over to a bank and the Austrian Steyr-Mannlicher Company circa 2001. A few years later, H&K took over the company and expanded it. They had 126 employees in 2003, and are now at 171 employees. Because of H&K's engineering and marketing, Merkel became profitable again and expanded into the Eastern Europe and US marketplaces. The company went back to the original name Merkel, and bought the business and facilities of GSI, located in Trussville, AL.

During 2007, Merkel was sold to Caracal International LLC, located in the United Arab Emirates.

For many years Merkel shotguns were unfairly disadvantaged in this country because of the politics of importing firearms from communist bloc countries (goods were subject to a 65% non-favored nation tax). With the reunification of Germany in 1991, this trademark became more competitive domestically. Merkel continues to manufacture high quality guns in Suhl, Germany.

Beginning in 1995, Merkel serialization employed an alphanumeric date code for year of manufacture, making it difficult to determine year of manufacture by serial number. Higher grade models (including the 300 Series) continue to be manufactured one at a time by hand, with less than 30 being mfg. annually.

Many Merkel collectors are now categorizing older production guns into three different categories. The first is guns made before 1962, when the Berlin Wall was created. The second is the GDR guns (German Democratic Republic). The last is after the Berlin wall came down (post-1991). Premiums are paid on pre-WWII manufacture and some GDR guns. All pre-war guns may have different actions such as square, half round, and square reinforced, etc. These older production models should be appraised by a knowledgeable person, since there are a lot of things to consider when evaluating these earlier Merkels. Some guns made up for the Nürnberg and Leipzig trade shows have top quality workmanship, especially the engraving.

The engraver's signature will appear on all factory engraved Merkels manufactured since 1992.

COMBINATION GUNS

O/U MODEL – 12, 16, or 20 ga. (2 3/4 in. chamber) over 5.6x50R, 5.6x52R, 6.5x55mm, 6.5x57R, 7x57R, 7x65R, 8x57JRS, 9.3x74R, .22 Hornet (disc. 1997), .222 Rem., .243 Win., .30-06, .308 Win., or .375 H&H (disc. 1994) cal., 25.6 in. barrels, various chokes. Disc. 1999.

* ***Model 210E***

	100%	98%	95%	90%	80%	70%	60%	LAST MSR
Model 210E	$5,700	$4,600	$3,700	$3,150	$2,600	$2,100	$1,800	*$6,195*

* ***Model 211E***

	100%	98%	95%	90%	80%	70%	60%	LAST MSR
Model 211E	$6,650	$4,750	$3,900	$3,300	$2,775	$2,275	$1,925	*$7,495*

* ***Model 213E*** – disc. 1997.

	100%	98%	95%	90%	80%	70%	60%	LAST MSR
Model 213E	$13,000	$10,750	$8,250	$6,975	$5,825	$4,600	$3,550	*$14,795*

* ***Model 240E-1*** – 20 ga. over .22 Rem., 7x57R, or .30-06 cal. Imported 2003-2005.

	100%	98%	95%	90%	80%	70%	60%	LAST MSR
Model 240E-1	$6,175	$5,150	$3,900	$3,400	$2,900	$2,400	$2,125	*$7,195*

* ***Model 313E*** – disc. 1997.

	100%	98%	95%	90%	80%	70%	60%	LAST MSR
Model 313E	$19,350	$14,950	$12,500	$9,950	$8,350	$7,100	$5,900	*$22,795*

MODEL 314 – 12 ga. over 7mm-.470 NE cal., detachable H&H sidelock system, elaborate scroll engraving. Disc. pre-WWII.

	100%	98%	95%	90%	80%	70%	60%	LAST MSR
Model 314	$21,250	$15,750	$13,000	$10,000	$8,500	$7,200	$6,200	

SxS MODEL – similar gauges and cals. to O/U Combination Gun, boxlock models included 8EI and 9EI, 10EI is a sidelock, boxlock models ranged in MSRs from $5,500-$7,000 and the Model 10EI MSR was $9,500. Importation disc. 1990.

Boxlock models ranged from an MSR of $5,500-$7,000.

The last MSR for Model 10EI was $9,500.

GRADING - PPGS™	100%	98%	95%	90%	80%	70%	60%	LAST MSR

DRILLINGS

Previously, the Drilling Models 90 (disc. 1994), 90S (disc. 1997), 90K (disc. 1997), 95 (disc. 1994), 95K (disc. 1998), and 95S (disc. 1997) were also imported. Models differ in the amount of engraving, cocking systems, and quality of wood.

MODEL 96K – choice of 12, 16 (disc. 2005), or 20 ga., with the rifle barrel being bored in most popular U.S. and metric cals. between .22 Hornet and 9.3x74R (current standard cals. are .30-06 or 9.3x74R), 23.6 in. barrels, extractors, DT, current models are boxlocks with Greener crossbolt and double under barrel locking lugs, tang mounted cocking for rifle, case hardened receiver with Arabesque scroll engraving, fitted leather case. Disc. 2016.

$7,950 $7,325 $5,900 $4,750 $3,650 $3,000 $2,500 *$8,495*

Add $1,300 for hunting scene engraving (Model 96K Engraved).

MERKEL ANSON – 12, 16, or 20 ga., calibers 7x57R, 8x57JR, and 9.3x74R cals. most common, others noted, usually 2 shotguns over rifle, although 2 rifles over shotgun have been noted, 25.6 in. or 21.6 in. barrels, boxlock, Anson & Deeley system, extractors, DT, checkered pistol grip stock, engraving, pre-WWII.

Engraved Model 142 $5,000 $4,000 $3,000 $2,750 $2,500 $2,200 $2,000

Less Engraved Model 142
$4,000 $3,500 $3,000 $2,500 $2,250 $2,100 $2,000

Model 145 (least engraving)
$3,000 $2,800 $2,700 $2,600 $2,500 $2,100 $1,900

MODEL 961L – 20 ga. only over .30-06 or 9.3x74R cal., drilling, similar to Model 96K, except does not have tang mounted cocking slide, 21.6 in. barrels, standard engraving is Arabesque scroll. Importation began 2008-2014.

$7,775 $6,500 $5,250 $4,500 $3,750 $3,000 $2,750 *$8,995*

Add $2,000 for silver finished receiver with fine hunting scenes.

* ***Model 961LS*** – similar to Model 961L, except has elaborately engraved sideplates. Disc. 2012.

$11,250 $9,000 $7,750 $6,750 $5,750 $5,000 $4,250 *$12,995*

RIFLES: BOLT ACTION

MHR 16 – .243 Win., 6.5 Creedmoor, .270 Win., .308 Win., .30-06, 9.3x62, .300 Win. Mag., or 7mm Rem. Mag. cal., repeater, steel action, hunting and target configuration, 22 or 24 (disc. 2019) in. barrel, 4 grooves, 2 or 3 shot detachable mag., polymer box, direct trigger, dripped and tapped for Savage style mounts, walnut or polymer stock, two-position trigger safety w/separate chamber lock, blued finish, approx. 7 lbs. Importation began 2017.

MSR $855 $700 $650 $550 $500 $400 $325 $250

Add $105 for walnut stock.

MODEL 190 – various cals., Mauser M-98 system, checkered walnut stock and extended forend, values depend on caliber and action size. Disc. pre-WWII.

$7,500 $6,500 $5,275 $4,200 $3,200 $2,350 $1,500

Premiums exist for Magnum or Kurz (short) action.

MODEL KR1 PREMIUM – .243 Win., .270 Win., .30-06, 7mm-08 Rem., .308 Win., 7mm Rem. Mag., .300 Win. Mag., .270 WSM, or .300 WSM cal., modular design allows changing a different cal. barrel, short lock and bolt movement, 3-position safety, 2 or 3 shot detachable mag., fine trigger with set feature, six locking lugs, quick release mount system, pistol grip stock with cheekpiece and swivels, approx. 6.4 lbs. Imported 2006-2012.

$1,750 $1,500 $1,300 $1,100 $900 $800 $700 *$1,995*

Add $500 for left-hand action.

Add $695 per interchangable barrel, $295 for scope mounts or $225 per individual bolt group.

Pricing may be higher on models ordered after 2012.

* ***Model KR1 Premium Stutzen Antique Carbine*** – .243 Win., .270 Win., .30-06, 7mm-08, .308 Win., or 9.3x62mm (new 2007) cal., similar to KR1 Premium, except has 20 1/4 in. barrel and full Mannlicher stock with fishscale carving. Imported 2006-2012.

$2,950 $2,600 $2,250 $1,850 $1,500 $1,250 $1,075 *$3,395*

Add $500 for left-hand action.

* ***Model KR1 Premium Weimar Luxury*** – .243 Win., .270 Win., .30-06, 7mm-08, .308 Win., 7mm Rem. Mag., .300 Win. Mag., .270 WSM, or .300 WSM cal., similar to KR1 Premium, except has deep relief hand engraved hunting scenes on silver-grey receiver, high grade stock with rosewood forearm tip, double fold Bavarian cheekpiece with modified Kaiser grip, gold plated trigger and bolt head. Limited importation 2006 only.

$8,850 $7,500 $6,250 $5,000 $4,000 $3,250 $2,500 *$9,995*

Add $200 for Mag. cals.

GRADING - PPGS™	100%	98%	95%	90%	80%	70%	60%	LAST MSR

MODEL RX HELIX – various cals. between .222 Rem.-.300 Win. Mag., takedown, straight pull bolt, 22 in. cold hammer forged carbon steel barrel, features a Helical breech with six locking lugs, detachable box mag., SST, fiber optic dot iron front and rear sights, two-piece checkered walnut pistol grip stock with cheekpiece, Picatinny rail, fixed bolt handle, includes hard case, black aluminum action (Helix Black model). Imported mid-2013-disc.

$3,500 $3,150 $2,850 $2,400 $2,000 $1,550 $1,250

Add $1,225 for Number 4 Grade walnut.
Last MSR for Helix Black Model was $3,870.

Other Helix models include: Arabesque Grade IV (last MSR was $5,095), Wild Boar (importation disc.), Spirit (importation disc.), Deluxe (importation disc.), Alpinist (in black or camo, importation disc.), Tracker (in black or camo, importation disc.), Sportster (thumbhole stock, importation disc.), Noblesse (premium rifle, importation disc.), and Helix Caron (last MSR was $5,495).

* ***Model Helix Explorer*** – various cals. between .222 Rem.-.300 Win. Mag., takedown, straight pull bolt, 22 in. cold hammer forged carbon steel barrel, features a Helical breech with six locking lugs, detachable box mag., SST, fiber optic dot iron front and rear sights, black or woodland camo synthetic stock with soft grip surface, straight buttstock with rubber recoil pad, universal forend, pistol grip with integrated grip element and thumb indent, Picatinny rail, includes hard case, fixed bolt handle, includes hard case. Imported mid-2013-disc.

$3,000 $2,650 $2,250 $1,900 $1,650 $1,450 $1,175 *$3,360*

RIFLES: DOUBLE

O/U MODEL – same cals. as the O/U Combination Gun, various actions, engraving options, and other special orders.

* ***Model 220E Boxlock*** – boxlock Blitz action, scroll engraved case hardened receiver, DTs, pistol grip with cheekpiece. Importation disc. 1994.

$9,575 $8,250 $7,150 $6,100 $5,100 $4,250 $3,500 *$10,795*

* ***Model 221E Boxlock*** – similar to 220E, except has silver-grey receiver with hunting scene engraving. Disc. 1998.

$12,500 $10,935 $9,375 $8,500 $6,875 $5,625 $4,375 *$10,895*

* ***Model 223E Sidelock*** – sidelock action with scroll or game scenes, removed without tools. Disc. 1997.

$22,500 $19,685 $16,875 $15,300 $12,375 $10,125 $7,875 *$17,895*

* ***Model 323E Sidelock*** – similar to 223E Sidelock, except has scrollwork or game scene engraving, top-of-the-line O/U double rifle. Disc. 1997.

$29,500 $26,750 $23,300 $20,000 $17,500 $13,500 $11,250 *$27,195*

MODEL 324 O/U – 6.5x55mm - .470 NE cal., premium quality pre-WWII double rifle, elaborate scroll engraving and best quality walnut. Disc. pre-WWII.

$26,500 $23,000 $20,000 $17,500 $13,500 $11,250 $9,750

B3 JAGD O/U BOXLOCK – .30-06 or 9.3x74R cal., boxlock action, 21.6 in. barrels, checkered walnut pistol grip stock and forearm, single trigger, standard Jagd configuration or deluxe with extra engraving. Imported 2007-2014.

$4,750 $4,155 $3,560 $3,230 $2,610 $2,135 $1,660 *$5,495*

Add $1,000 for B3 Deluxe with fishscale wood carving and better engraving.

SxS MODELS – same cals. as listed for the O/U Combination Gun.

* ***Model 128*** – various cals., scalloped Anson & Deeley action, deluxe checkered walnut stock and forearm, engine turned removable locks and hinged floorplate, elaborate scroll and game scene engraving (on barrels), pre-WWII mfg.

N/A $25,000 $21,250 $19,750 $15,750 $13,000 $10,000

* ***Model 132*** – various cals., boxlock action with triple Greener crossbolt system, barrels manufactured from Bohler steel, extractors (Model 132) or H&H system ejectors (Model 132E), DT, premium checkered walnut stock and forearm, triple Greener crossbolt system, elaborate engraving, pre-WWII mfg.

$12,000 $10,500 $9,000 $8,160 $6,600 $5,400 $4,200

Add 20% for ejectors (Model 132E).

* ***Model 140-1*** – Anson & Deeley boxlock action with cocking indicators, double triggers, engraved case hardened receiver. Imported 1994-2005.

$6,100 $5,335 $4,575 $4,150 $3,355 $2,745 $2,135 *$7,195*

Subtract approx. $400 if w/o H&H ejectors (pre-2002).
Add approx. $200 for set front trigger.
Add $1,100 for engraved hunting scenes on silver/grey receiver (Model 140-1.1).

GRADING - PPGS™	100%	98%	95%	90%	80%	70%	60%	LAST MSR

* ***Model 140-2*** – .375 H&H, .416 Rigby, .450-400 NE (new 2015), .470 NE, or .500 NE (new 2006) cal., Anson & Deeley boxlock action, 23.6 in. barrel, double triggers, pistol grip stock, scroll or game scene engraved silver grey receiver and positive ejectors, includes fitted leather luggage case. Importation began 2000.

MSR $13,920	$11,825	$10,250	$8,800	$8,000	$6,500	$5,350	$4,200	

» **Model 140-2.1** – .375 H&H, .416 Rigby, .470 NE, or .500 NE (new 2006) cal., similar configuration to Model 140-2, with or w/o ejectors, Africa game scene engraving. Importation began 2000.

MSR $14,990	$12,750	$11,150	$9,565	$8,675	$7,025	$5,750	$4,475	

» **Model 140-2.2** – .375 H&H, .470 NE or .500 NE cal., similar to Model 140 2.1, except has more engraving. Importation began 2007.

MSR $25,700	$21,850	$19,125	$16,395	$14,860	$12,025	$9,850	$7,650	

* ***Model 141-1*** – .30-06, .308 Win. (disc.), 7x57R (new 2007), or 9.3x74R cal., Greener crossbolt Anson & Deeley boxlock action with double underbarrel locking lugs, petite frame, 21.6 in. barrels, scroll engraved silver grey finish, ejectors, DT, deluxe checkered pistol grip walnut stock with cheekpiece and forearm, includes fitted leather case, 6.6 lbs. Importation began 2004.

MSR $12,415	$10,550	$9,230	$7,915	$7,175	$5,800	$4,750	$3,700	

» **Model 141-1.1 Engraved** – .30-06, .308 Win. (disc.), 7x57R (new 2007), or 9.3x74R cal., similar to Model 141-1, except has hunting scene engraving and single non-selective trigger. Importation began 2004.

MSR $13,920	$11,825	$10,250	$8,800	$8,000	$6,500	$5,350	$4,200	

Add $1,700 for Leupold scope combo (mfg. 2005-2007).

* ***Model 150-1*** – Anson & Deeley boxlock action with cocking indicators and sideplates, double triggers, silver grayed receiver with Arabesque engraving. Imported 1994-98.

	$6,500	$5,685	$4,875	$4,420	$3,575	$2,925	$2,275	*$7,495*

Add $385 for H&H ejectors.
Add approx. $200 for set front trigger.

» **Model 150-1.1** – similar to Model 150-1, except has elaborate hunting scene engraving. Importation disc. 2000.

	$7,750	$6,780	$5,810	$5,270	$4,260	$3,485	$2,710	*$8,995*

* ***Model 160S-1*** – sidelock action with Greener crossbolt featuring fine Arabesque engraving, H&H ejectors, DTs, pistol grip stock with cheekpiece. Disc. 1998.

	$11,400	$9,975	$8,550	$7,750	$6,270	$5,130	$3,990	*$13,295*

Add $415 for H&H ejectors.
Add approx. $500 for set front trigger.
Add approx. $1,000 for single non-selective trigger.

» **Model 160-1.1** – similar to Model 150-1, except has elaborate hunting scene engraving on silver-grey receiver. Importation disc. 2000.

	$13,250	$11,595	$9,935	$9,010	$7,285	$5,960	$4,635	*$14,995*

» **Model 160-2.1** – .375 H&H, .416 Rigby, .470 NE, or .500 NE (new 2006) cal., features octagon barrels, African game scene engraving on silver receiver, includes fitted leather luggage case, special order only. Imported 2002-2006.

	$20,400	$17,850	$15,300	$13,870	$11,220	$9,180	$7,140	*$23,995*

* ***Model 161-1.1*** – 7x57R, .30-06, or 9.3x74R cal., sidelock action built on 28 ga. frame, 21.6 in. barrels, Greener crossbolt with double barrel locking lugs, fine engraved hunting scenes with silver grey sidelocks, H&H ejectors, DT, high grade Turkish walnut pistol grip stock with cheekpiece and semi-beavertail forend, 6.6 lbs. Imported 2006, reintroduced 2017.

MSR $20,345	$17,300	$15,140	$12,975	$11,765	$9,525	$7,800	$6,450	

Last MSR in 2006 was $15,995.

RIFLES: SEMI-AUTO

SR1 – .223 Rem. (new 2013), .30-06, .308 Win., .300 Win. Mag., 9.3x62, 7x64 (European only), or 8x57 (European only) cal., 19.7 or 20.8 (.300 Win. Mag. cal. only) in. free floating precision barrel, gas operated, 2 or 5 shot mag., solid rotary bolt head with 2x3 locking lugs, trigger safety, checkered walnut stock and forearm, rubber recoil pad, Battue rib sight with contrast line, adj. front sight, approx. 7 lbs. Imported 2007-2011, reintroduced 2013-2014.

	$1,825	$1,600	$1,400	$1,200	$995	$800	$650	*$1,995*

GRADING - PPGS™	100%	98%	95%	90%	80%	70%	60%	LAST MSR

RIFLES: SINGLE SHOT

MODEL K3 JAGD (K1 JAGD) STALKING RIFLE – available in 11 cals. between .243 Win.-9.3x74R, Franz Jaeger break open action, cocking/uncocking slide type safety, matte silver receiver, adj. trigger pull, 23.6 or 25.6 (Wby. Mag. cals. only, disc. 2019) in. barrel, pistol grip w/cheekpiece and Hogback comb, rubber buttplate, includes 1 in. or 30mm quick detachable mounts, Z3 Swarovski 3x10-42 scope, silver border engraving is standard, 5-5 1/2 lbs. Importation began 2002.

MSR $4,495	$3,825	$3,250	$2,600	$2,000	$1,725	$1,450	$1,200	

Add $1,195 per extra barrel.
Add $300 for Premium Model with light arabesque scroll engraving (disc.).
Add $944 for Swarovski scope combo (mfg. 2005-2007).

During 2012, this model's nomenclature changed from K1 Jagd to K3 Jagd.

* ***Model K3 Jagd (K1 Jagd) Stalking Rifle Stutzen Carbine*** – .243 Win. (disc.), .270 Win., 7x57R (disc.), .308 Win., 7mm-08 Rem., or .30-06 cal., similar to K1 Jagd Stalking Rifle, except has 19.6 in. barrel with Mannlicher full stock, includes Z3 Swarovski 3x10-42 scope. Importation began 2006.

MSR $4,710	$4,000	$3,600	$2,875	$2,300	$1,900	$1,500	$1,275	

During 2012, this model's nomenclature changed from K1 Jagd to K3 Jagd.

* ***Model K3 Jagd (K1 Jagd) Elite Stutzen Rifle*** – .243 Win., 7x57R, 7x65R, .308 Win., 8x57IRS, 9.3x74R, .30R Blaser, or .30-06 cal., 19.7 in. barrel, Mannlicher full stock, includes Z3 Swarovski 3x10-42 scope, includes rifle case, 5.29 lbs.

MSR $5,250	$4,450	$3,900	$3,350	$3,050	$2,450	$2,000	$1,550	

During 2012, this model's nomenclature changed from K1 Jagd to K3 Jagd.

MODEL K-2/K-4 STALKING RIFLE – .243 Win., .270 Win., 7x57R, .308 Win., .30-06 cal., 7mm Rem. Mag., .300 Win. Mag., or 9.3x74R cal., Franz Jager single shot break open action, cocking/uncocking slide safety, octagon barrel, submodels vary in type and amount of engraving, includes best quality wood with stock carving. Importation began 2005.

* ***Model K-4 (K-2) Weimar Stalking Rifle*** – .30-06, .308 Win., .300 Win. Mag. or 7mm Rem. Mag. cal., features deep relief hand engraved hunting scenes. Disc. 2013.

	$13,750	$11,250	$9,000	$7,500	$6,250	$5,000	$4,150	*$15,995*

During 2012, this model's nomenclature changed from K-2 to K-4.

* ***Model K-2 Erfurt Stalking Rifle*** – features deep relief engraving on ornamental sideplates and silver pistol grip monogram. Limited importation 2005-2006.

	$18,350	$14,995	$12,500	$10,000	$8,250	$7,000	$5,750	*$20,995*

* ***Model K-2 Suhl Luxury Stalking Rifle*** – features deep relief engraving on ornamental sideplates, gold inlays, gold gilded trigger, and silver pistol grip monogram. Limited importation 2005-2006.

	$24,000	$20,000	$16,000	$13,000	$10,000	$8,500	$7,700	*$26,995*

MODEL 180 – various cals., with (Model 180E) or w/o ejector, double triggers, checkered walnut stock and extended forend, values depend on caliber and action size. Disc. pre-WWII.

	$8,500	$7,250	$5,775	$4,600	$3,750	$3,000	$2,500	

MODEL 183E – various cals., sidelock, top-of-the-line rifle with elaborate engraving. Disc. pre-WWII.

	$12,500	$10,750	$8,250	$6,975	$5,825	$4,600	$3,550	

SHOTGUNS: O/U, DISC.

MODEL 100 – 12, 16, or 20 ga., various barrel lengths and chokes, boxlock, Greener crossbolt, double triggers, extractors, checkered pistol grip or English style stock, pre-WWII.

Plain	$1,850	$1,675	$1,450	$1,250	$1,000	$925	$850	
Ribbed	$1,950	$1,775	$1,550	$1,300	$1,050	$950	$875	

MODEL 101 – similar to 100, except selective extractors, rib barrel, some English style scroll engraving, pre-WWII.

	$2,050	$1,850	$1,600	$1,325	$1,100	$1,000	$900	

MODEL 101E – similar to 100, except auto ejectors, pre-WWII.

	$2,200	$2,000	$1,750	$1,425	$1,250	$1,150	$1,000	

MODEL 400 – similar to 101, except Arabesque engraving and Kersten double crossbolt, pre-WWII.

	$2,075	$1,875	$1,650	$1,350	$1,200	$1,100	$975	

MODEL 400E – similar to 400, except auto ejector, pre-WWII.

	$2,250	$2,050	$1,800	$1,450	$1,325	$1,175	$1,025	

GRADING - PPGS™	100%	98%	95%	90%	80%	70%	60%	LAST MSR

MODEL 410 – similar to 400, except more engraving and fancier wood, pre-WWII.

$2,200 $2,000 $1,750 $1,425 $1,250 $1,150 $1,000

MODEL 410E – similar to 410, except auto ejectors, pre-WWII.

$2,325 $2,175 $1,900 $1,600 $1,450 $1,225 $1,100

MODEL 200 – 12, 16, 20, 24, 28, or 32 ga., ribbed barrels in various lengths, Kersten double crossbolt, scalloped frame, boxlock, double triggers, extractors, cocking indicators, either pistol grip or English style checkered stock.

$2,750 $2,475 $2,225 $2,000 $1,750 $1,400 $1,175

Add 10%-15% for 28 ga., depending on condition.

MODEL 210 – similar to 200, except engraved and better grade wood, pre-WWII.

$3,000 $2,750 $2,475 $2,250 $2,000 $1,650 $1,325

Add 10%-15% for 28 ga., depending on condition.

MODEL 201 – 12, 16, or 20 ga., Greener crossbolt, hunting engraving or fine Arabesque, dark walnut.

$3,250 $3,000 $2,625 $2,400 $2,200 $1,825 $1,500

MODEL 201E (PRE-WAR) – similar to 201, except with auto ejectors, pre-WWII.

$7,000 $6,250 $5,500 $4,950 $4,400 $3,750 $3,300

MODEL 202 (PRE-WAR) – similar to 201, except with false sideplates, higher quality wood, more profuse engraving, pre-WWII.

$8,000 $7,000 $6,250 $5,500 $4,950 $4,400 $3,750

MODEL 202E (PRE-WAR) – similar to 202, with auto ejectors, pre-WWII.

$8,000 $7,000 $6,250 $5,500 $4,950 $4,400 $3,750

MODEL 203E (PRE-WAR) – sidelock, similar to 202E, except better engraving and wood.

$8,000 $7,000 $6,250 $5,500 $4,950 $4,400 $3,750

MODEL 204E (PRE-WAR) – similar to 203E, but fine English scroll engraving and Merkel sidelocks, ejectors, scarce variation, pre-WWII.

$8,500 $7,750 $6,750 $5,750 $4,950 $4,400 $3,750

MODEL 300 – 12, 16, 20, 24, 28, 32 ga. or .410 bore, various lengths and choke ribbed barrels, Merkel-Anson boxlock, Kersten double crossbolt, two underlugs, scalloped frame, either English or pistol grip style stock, cocking indicators, pre-WWII.

$5,150 $4,600 $4,100 $3,600 $3,100 $2,650 $2,400

Add 10%-15% for 28 ga.

MODEL 300E – similar to Model 300, with auto ejectors, pre-WWII.

$5,750 $5,150 $4,600 $4,100 $3,600 $3,100 $2,650

This model is usually encountered without engraving and has standard wood.

MODEL 301 – similar to Model 300, but more profusely engraved and better grade wood, pre-WWII.

$6,750 $6,100 $5,250 $4,250 $3,995 $3,500 $3,000

MODEL 310E – similar to Model 300, with auto ejectors, pre-WWII.

$7,950 $7,200 $6,250 $5,300 $4,450 $3,900 $3,400

MODEL 302 – similar to Model 301, but has auto ejectors and more elaborate ornamentation, false sideplates and better grade wood.

$14,000 $12,000 $10,500 $8,500 $6,500 $5,750 $4,900

MODEL 304E – special order version of Model 303E, higher quality and more ornamentation, very fine scroll engraving similar to Model 303 EL Luxus, top of Merkel O/U line.

$22,500 $18,750 $15,750 $12,000 $10,500 $8,750 $7,500

SHOTGUNS: O/U, RECENT PRODUCTION

MODEL 200E BOXLOCK – 12, 16, or 20 ga., case hardened scalloped boxlock action with minor scroll engraving, 26 (disc.), 26 3/4, or 28 in. barrels, checkered European walnut stock and forearm, ejectors, SST or DT, pistol grip or English style stock, solid rib, 6-7 lbs. Importation disc. 1994, quantities remained until 1998.

$3,600 $3,150 $2,700 $2,450 $1,980 $1,620 $1,260 *$3,995*

* ***Model 200ES Boxlock Skeet*** – 12 ga. only, 26 3/4 in. VR barrels bored skeet/skeet. Imported 1993-94.

$4,550 $3,950 $3,500 $3,000 $2,500 $2,100 $1,625 *$4,995*

GRADING - PPGS™	100%	98%	95%	90%	80%	70%	60%	LAST MSR

* ***Model 200ET Boxlock Trap*** – 12 ga. only, 30 in. VR barrels bored full/full (other choke configurations available upon request). Importation disc. 1994.

	$4,400	$3,750	$3,300	$2,800	$2,300	$2,000	$1,550	*$5,195*

MODEL 2000CL – 12, 20, or 28 ga., 28 in. barrels with fixed IC/M chokes, Kersten double crossbolt lock, scroll engraved case hardened receiver, scalloped boxlock frame, modified Anson & Deely boxlock action, selectable ejectors, round knob, SST, high grade wood stock with semi-pistol grip or straight English style, three piece forearm, approx. 6.8 lbs. Importation began 2006.

MSR $13,850	$11,750	$9,900	$8,400	$6,950	$5,600	$4,600	$3,800	

* ***Model 2000CL Sporter*** – 12, 20, or 28 ga., similar to Model 2000CL, except chokes are SK/IC only. Limited importation 2006 only.

	$6,350	$5,400	$4,800	$4,200	$3,600	$3,000	$2,500	*$7,195*

MODEL 2000EL – 12, 20, 28 (new 1999) ga. or .410 bore (new 2004), Kersten double crossbolt lock, scroll engraved, silver receiver, modified Anson & Deeley boxlock action, 26 or 28 in. fixed choke barrels, ejectors, ST or DT, select checkered walnut with pistol grip or English style stock, three-piece forearm, 6.4-7 lbs. Imported 1998-2005.

	$5,700	$4,985	$4,275	$3,875	$3,135	$2,565	$1,995	*$6,495*

* ***Model 2000EL Sporter*** – 12, 20, or 28 ga., similar to Model 2000EL, except chokes are SK/IC only. Imported 1999-2005.

	$5,700	$4,985	$4,275	$3,875	$3,135	$2,565	$1,995	*$6,495*

MODEL 2001EL (201E) – 12, 16 (disc. 1997), 20, 28 (new 1995) ga. or .410 bore (mfg. 2004-2005), 26 3/4 (20 ga. only, disc. 2014), 28, or 30 (12 ga. only, disc. 2014) in. barrels, SK/IC or IC/M fixed chokes, coin finished action with light game scene engraving, three piece forearm, English or pistol grip stock, single trigger, current mfg. includes fitted luggage case, approx. 6.8 lbs.

MSR $13,920	$11,825	$10,250	$8,800	$8,000	$6,500	$5,350	$4,200	

This model's nomenclature was changed from 201E to 2001EL during 1998.

* ***Model 2001EL Sporter*** – 12, 20, or 28 (disc.) ga., 28 (disc.) or 30 in. barrels, SK/IC (disc.) or IC/M chokes, coin finished action with light game scene engraving. Importation began 1999.

MSR $16,020	$12,950	$11,250	$9,650	$8,650	$7,000	$5,750	$4,850	

* ***Model 201ES Skeet*** – 12 ga. only, 26 3/4 in. VR barrels bored skeet/skeet. Imported 1993-97.

	$7,850	$6,870	$5,885	$5,340	$4,315	$3,530	$2,745	*$8,495*

* ***Model 201ET Trap*** – 12 ga. only, 30 in. VR barrels bored full/full (other choke configurations available upon request). Importation disc. 1997.

	$7,850	$6,870	$5,885	$5,340	$4,315	$3,530	$2,745	*$8,495*

MODEL 2002EL (202E) – similar to Model 201E/2001EL, except has fine hunting scenes with Arabesque engraving on silver false sideplates, 3 piece forearm, choice of pistol grip or English straight grip stock, includes fitted luggage case. Imported 1993-2003.

	$10,625	$9,295	$7,970	$7,225	$5,845	$4,780	$3,720	*$12,395*

This model's nomenclature was changed from 202E to 2002EL during 1998.

MODEL 203E SIDELOCK – 12, 16 (disc. 1997), or 20 ga. (24, 28, and 32 gauges were once available but are now disc.), 26 (disc.), 26 3/4, or 28 in. barrels, VR, H&H ejectors, SST (current) or DT, elaborate scroll engraving on coin finished receiver, sidelock screws are H&H style but the removable sidelocks are not, choice of English or pistol grip stock, 6-7 lbs. Disc. 1998.

	$9,750	$8,530	$7,310	$6,630	$5,360	$4,385	$3,410	*$11,995*

* ***Model 203ES Sidelock Skeet*** – 12 ga. only, 26 3/4 in. VR barrels bored SK/SK. Imported 1993-1997.

	$12,050	$10,545	$9,035	$8,195	$6,625	$5,420	$4,215	*$14,595*

* ***Model 203ET Sidelock Trap*** – 12 ga. only, 30 in. VR barrels bored full/full (other choke configurations available upon request). Importation disc. 1997.

	$12,050	$10,545	$9,035	$8,195	$6,625	$5,420	$4,215	*$14,595*

MODEL 2016CL – similar to 2000CL, except is 16 ga., 28 in. barrels with fixed IC/Mod. chokes, approx. 6.8 lbs. Imported 2006-2012.

	$7,200	$6,300	$5,400	$4,900	$4,000	$3,250	$2,800	*$8,495*

Add $4,500 for two barrel set (16 and 20 ga., bored IC/Mod.).

MODEL 2016EL SIDELOCK – 16 ga., scroll engraved case hardened receiver, action similar to Model 2001EL, three piece forearm. Imported 2004-2005.

	$5,700	$4,985	$4,275	$3,875	$3,135	$2,565	$1,995	*$6,495*

Add $3,200 for 2 barrel set (16 and 20 ga. bored IC/Mod.).

GRADING - PPGS™	100%	98%	95%	90%	80%	70%	60%	LAST MSR

MODEL 2116EL SIDELOCK – 16 ga., 28 in. barrels with IC/M chokes, single trigger, English or pistol grip stock, upgraded wood and more engraving, approx. 6.8 lbs. Importation began 2004.

MSR $13,920	$11,825	$10,250	$8,800	$8,000	$6,500	$5,350	$4,200	

Add $4,280 for 2 barrel set (16 and 20 ga. bored IC/Mod.).

MODEL 303EL (LUXUS) – 12, 20, or 28 (new 1998) ga., 28 in. barrels, IC/M chokes, H&H type sidelock action with hidden thumbnail detachable sidelocks, double underlugs, more ornamentation and better wood, DT with articulated front. Importation disc. 2006, reintroduced 2015.

MSR $35,340	$31,000	$26,950	$22,750	$21,500	$16,800	$13,750	$11,000	

Last MSR in 2006 was $23,995.

Luxus variations are also encountered in the 201 and 203 series in addition to older pre-war models.

SHOTGUNS: SxS, PRE-WWII PRODUCTION

Merkel began manufacturing SxS shotguns during 1914.

MODEL 126E – 12, 16, or 20 ga., similar action as the Model 127, except features game scene and other engraving patterns, H&H style system ejectors, pre-WWII mfg.

N/A	$24,725	$21,500	$16,500	$12,500	$10,000	$8,800	

MODEL 127E – 12, 16, or 20 ga., various barrel lengths and chokes, H&H style hand detachable sidelocks, auto ejectors, double triggers, pistol or English style stock, elaborate scroll engraving only, this is a best grade gun, pre-WWII mfg.

N/A	$24,725	$21,500	$16,500	$12,500	$10,000	$8,800	

MODEL 128E – 12, 16, or 20 ga., scalloped Anson & Deeley action featuring engine turned removable locks and hinged floorplate, DT, H&H system ejectors, elaborate scroll and game scene engraving (including scroll work on barrels), deluxe checkered walnut stock and forearm, pre-WWII mfg.

N/A	$28,000	$24,000	$20,000	$16,500	$14,000	$12,000	

MODEL 130 – 12, 16, or 20 ga., various barrel lengths and chokes, Anson & Deeley action with false sideplates, boxlock, auto ejectors, English style or pistol grip stock, elaborate game scenes and Arabesque engraving, pre-WWII mfg.

N/A	$20,000	$16,500	$12,500	$9,500	$7,500	$6,350	

SHOTGUNS: SxS, RECENT PRODUCTION

Left-hand stocks are also available on some of the models in this category. Please contact Merkel USA directly for a price quotation.

MODEL 8 – 12, 16 (disc.), or 20 ga., case hardened scalloped boxlock action with light engraving, Greener crossbolt with chopper lump extension, extractors, SST (current) or DT, standard walnut with checkering, pistol grip or English style stock, sling swivels (disc. 1992). Disc. 1994.

$1,450	$1,250	$1,100	$1,000	$800	$650	$550	*$1,695*

MODEL 40E – 12, 16 (mfg. 2019 only), 20, or 28 ga., coin finished scalloped boxlock action with Anson & Deeley locks, 28 in. blue barrels, IC/MOD, 3 in chambers, ejectors, ST or DT, walnut checkered English or pistol grip buttstock w/cheekpiece, automatic safety, Arabesque scroll, coin finished, 5.5-6.8 lbs. Importation began 2015.

MSR $4,920	$4,200	$3,650	$3,150	$2,850	$2,300	$1,900	$1,450	

MODEL 47E – 12, 16 (disc. 2001), or 20 ga., case hardened scalloped boxlock action with chopper lump extension and Greener crossbolt, 26 (disc.), 26 3/4, or 28 in. barrels with fixed chokes, SST (current) or DT, ejectors, deluxe checkered walnut, pistol grip or English style stock, sling swivels (disc. 1992), 5.9-6.8 lbs. Importation disc. 2015.

$3,900	$3,400	$2,900	$2,650	$2,150	$1,750	$1,500	*$4,595*

* ***Model 47EL Custom Ltd. Ed.*** – 20 ga. only, 28 in. VR barrels with IC/Mod. fixed chokes, features luxury grade wood with English straight grip stock with medallion and DTs. Imported 2008-2012.

$4,900	$4,300	$3,700	$3,350	$2,700	$2,200	$1,900	*$5,795*

MODEL 47SL – 12, 16 (disc. 2001), 20, 28 (disc.) ga., or .410 (disc.) bore, coin finished sidelock action with scroll engraving, Greener crossbolt, ST (current) or DT, deluxe walnut stock (with cheekpiece) and forearm, sling swivels (disc. 1992). Importation disc. 2012.

$7,650	$6,700	$5,750	$5,200	$4,200	$3,450	$2,950	*$8,995*

Add approx. $600 for 28 ga. or .410 bore (mfg. 1992 only).

MODEL 76E – top-of-the-line boxlock shotgun. Importation disc. 1992.

$3,000	$2,600	$2,250	$2,000	$1,650	$1,350	$1,150	*$3,500*

GRADING - PPGS™	100%	98%	95%	90%	80%	70%	60%	LAST MSR

MODEL 122 – 12, 16, or 20 ga., Anson & Deeley boxlock action with silver greyed false sideplates, H&H ejectors, SST or DT, fine hunting scenes with Arabesque engraving, pistol grip or English style stock. Imported 1993-99.

	$3,800	$3,350	$2,850	$2,600	$2,100	$1,700	$1,400	*$4,495*

MODEL 122E – 12, 16, or 20 ga., coin finished boxlock action with Greener crossbolt and chopper lump extension, cocking indicators, ejectors, DTs, deluxe game scene engraving. Importation disc. 1991.

	$3,000	$2,600	$2,250	$2,000	$1,650	$1,350	$1,150	*$3,500*

MODEL 147 – 12, 16, 20, or 28 (new 1995, 147E only) ga., 26 3/4 or 28 in. barrels, Anson & Deeley boxlock, any choke, SST (current) or DT, extractors, straight or pistol grip stock, hunting scene engraved. Disc. 1998, some inventory remained until 1999.

	$2,550	$2,250	$1,900	$1,750	$1,400	$1,150	$900	*$2,995*

* ***Model 147E*** – 12 or 20 ga., similar to Model 147, except has ejectors, fixed choke barrels, 5.8-6.8 lbs. Importation disc. 2015.

	$7,050	$6,150	$5,300	$4,800	$3,900	$3,250	$2,700	*$8,295*

* ***Model 147EL*** – 12 or 20 ga., 26 3/4 (disc.) or 28 in. barrels, fixed choke, Anson & Deeley boxlock, IC/MOD choke, ejectors, ST or DT, straight or pistol grip stock, basic wood Class 6 or luxury wood upgrade, hand engraved game scene, approx. 6.1 lbs. Importation began 1999.

MSR $8,885	$7,550	$6,600	$5,650	$5,100	$4,125	$3,400	$2,700	

Add $500 for Model 147EL Custom Ltd. Ed. with English straight grip stock medallion and DTs (imported 2008-2012).

* ***Model 147EL Sporter*** – 12 or 20 ga., Anson & Deeley boxlock, 30 in. barrels with skeet chokes, SST or DT, ejectors, straight or pistol grip stock, luxury wood upgrade. Limited importation 2006, reintroduced 2008-2012.

	$6,500	$5,685	$4,875	$4,420	$3,575	$2,925	$2,275	*$7,195*

MODEL 147SL – 12, 16 (disc. 2001), 20, 28 ga. (disc. 2003), or .410 (mfg. 1992 only) bore, coin finished sidelock action with Greener crossbolt and chopper lump extension, 25 1/2 (disc.), 26 (disc.), 26 3/4, or 28 in. fixed choke barrels, ejectors, ST (current) or DT, pistol grip or English style sock, deluxe game scene engraving, 6-7 lbs.

MSR $13,920	$11,825	$10,250	$8,800	$8,000	$6,500	$5,350	$4,200	

Add $750 for .410 bore (mfg. 1992 only).

* ***Model 147SSL*** – similar to Model 147SL, except has luxury wood upgrade. Imported 1999-2003.

	$8,500	$7,450	$6,375	$5,780	$4,675	$3,825	$3,000	*$9,995*

28 ga. had limited availability during 2001.

MODEL 247SL – 12, 16 (disc. 2001), 20, or 28 ga., similar to Model 147SL, except has deluxe scroll engraving. Importation disc. 1991, resumed 1993-2003.

	$7,650	$6,700	$5,750	$5,200	$4,200	$3,450	$2,950	*$8,995*

MODEL 280 PETITE FRAME – 28 ga., Anson & Deeley boxlock action with Greener crossbolt and double under barrel locking lugs, 28 in. barrels bored IC/M, case hardened receiver, H&H ejectors, single or double trigger, English or pistol grip stock, scroll engraving, fitted luggage case, case hardened receiver. Imported 2002-2014.

	$4,250	$3,700	$3,200	$2,900	$2,350	$1,900	$1,600	*$4,995*

* ***Model 280/360 2 Barrel Set*** – includes 28 in. 28 ga. and .410 bore barrels bored IC/M. Imported 2002-2012.

	$6,550	$5,750	$4,900	$4,450	$3,600	$2,950	$2,500	*$7,695*

MODEL 280E PETITE FRAME – 28 ga., similar to Model 280 Petite Frame, except has fine hunting scenes engraved on silver receiver. Imported 2002-2015.

	$6,700	$5,850	$5,050	$4,550	$3,700	$3,000	$2,550	*$7,895*

MODEL 280EL PETITE FRAME – 28 ga. only, Anson & Deeley boxlock action with Greener crossbolt and double underbarrel locking lugs, 28 in. barrels bored IC/M, fine hunting scene engraving, ejectors, DT, pistol grip or English style stock, includes fitted luggage case, 5.2 lbs. Importation began 2000.

MSR $9,315	$7,925	$6,900	$5,950	$5,300	$4,375	$3,500	$2,825	

Add $700 for Model 280EL Custom Ltd. Ed. with luxury wood English style stock and DTs (imported 2008-2012).

* ***Model 280EL/360EL 2 Barrel Set*** – consists of both 28 ga. and .410 bore barrels, 28 in. barrels, fitted luggage case. Importation began 2000.

MSR $13,920	$11,825	$10,250	$8,800	$8,000	$6,500	$5,350	$4,200	

The Model 360EL was discontinued during 2005.

GRADING - PPGS™	100%	98%	95%	90%	80%	70%	60%	LAST MSR

MODEL 280SL PETITE FRAME – 28 ga. only, H&H style sidelock action with Greener crossbolt and double under barrel locking lugs, 28 in. barrels bored IC/M, English style Arabesque engraving featuring small scrolls, ejectors, DT, pistol grip or English style stock, includes fitted luggage case, 5.2 lbs. Importation began 2000.

MSR $13,920	$11,825	$10,250	$8,800	$8,000	$6,500	$5,350	$4,200	

* ***Model 280SSL Petite Frame*** – similar to Model 280SL Petite Frame, except has quick detachable sideplates. Imported 2002-2003.

	$8,900	$7,800	$6,700	$6,050	$4,900	$4,000	$3,200	*$10,495*

MODEL 347SL – 12, 16, or 20 ga., similar to Model 247S, except has more elaborate engraving and better walnut. Importation disc. 1991, resumed 1993-97.

	$6,700	$5,850	$5,050	$4,550	$3,700	$3,000	$2,550	*$7,895*

MODEL 360 PETITE FRAME – .410 bore, 28 in. barrels bored IC/F, otherwise similar to Model 280 Petite Frame. Imported 2002-2014.

	$4,250	$3,700	$3,200	$2,900	$2,350	$1,900	$1,600	*$4,995*

MODEL 360E PETITE FRAME – similar to Model 360 Petite Frame, except has fine hunting scenes engraved on silver receiver. Imported 2002-2006.

	$4,700	$4,100	$3,500	$3,200	$2,550	$2,100	$1,800	*$5,495*

MODEL 360EL PETITE FRAME – .410 bore, Anson & Deely boxlock action, 28 in. barrels with IC/M chokes, ejectors, single or double trigger, English style stock, Greener crossbolt, double under barrel locking lugs, fine hunting scene engraving, 5 1/2 lbs. Importation began 2000.

MSR $9,315	$7,925	$6,900	$5,950	$5,300	$4,375	$3,500	$2,825	

MODEL 360SL PETITE FRAME – .410 bore, sidelock action, 28 in. barrels with IC/M or MOD/full chokes, ejectors, single or double trigger, English style stock, Greener crossbolt, double under barrel locking lugs, fine hunting scene engraving, 5 1/2 lbs. Importation began 2000.

MSR $13,920	$11,825	$10,250	$8,800	$8,000	$6,500	$5,350	$4,200	

* ***Model 360SSL Petite Frame*** – .410 bore, similar to Model 360SL Petite Frame, except has quick detachable sideplates. Imported 2002-2003.

	$8,900	$7,800	$6,700	$6,050	$4,900	$4,000	$3,200	*$10,495*

MODEL 280SL/360SL 2 BARREL SET – consists of both 28 ga. and .410 bore barrels with fitted luggage case. Mfg. 2000-2012.

	$13,595	$11,900	$10,200	$9,250	$7,500	$6,100	$5,100	*$15,995*

The Model 360SL was discontinued during 2005.

MODEL 280SSL/360SSL 2 BARREL SET – 28 ga. and .410 bore, similar to 280SL/360SL 2 barrel set, except has quick detachable sideplates. Imported 2002-2003.

	$12,250	$10,700	$9,200	$8,300	$6,750	$5,500	$4,700	*$14,395*

MODEL 447SL – similar to Model 347S, except is also available in 28 ga. and has more delicate scroll engraving. Importation disc. 1991, resumed 1993-2003.

	$9,350	$8,200	$7,000	$6,350	$5,150	$4,200	$3,500	*$10,995*

MODEL 1620 – 16 ga., Anson & Deely boxlock action, 28 in. barrels with IC/M fixed chokes, Greener crossbolt with double underbarrel locking lugs, case hardened receiver with scroll engraving, H&H style ejectors, DT, English straight grip or pistol grip stock, includes fitted luggage case. Imported 2002-2014.

	$4,250	$3,700	$3,200	$2,900	$2,350	$1,900	$1,600	*$4,995*

* ***Model 1620 2 Barrel Set*** – includes 28 in. 16 and 20 ga. barrels bored IC/M. Imported 2002-2014.

	$6,550	$5,750	$4,900	$4,450	$3,600	$2,950	$2,500	*$7,695*

MODEL 1620E – 16 ga., Anson & Deeley boxlock action, 28 in. barrels with IC/M chokes, H&H style ejectors, English or pistol grip stock, fine engraved hunting scenes on silver receiver, includes fitted luggage case. Imported 2006-2015.

	$6,700	$5,850	$5,050	$4,550	$3,700	$3,000	$2,550	*$7,895*

MODEL 1620EL – 16 ga., Anson & Deeley boxlock action, 28 in. IC/M fixed chokes, single or double trigger, H&H style ejectors, English or pistol grip stock, finely engraved hunting scenes on silver receiver and luxury wood upgrade, approx. 6.1 lbs. Importation began 2002.

MSR $9,315	$7,925	$6,900	$5,950	$5,300	$4,375	$3,500	$2,825	

* ***Model 1620EL 2 Barrel Set*** – includes 28 in. 16 and 20 ga. barrels bored IC/M. Importation began 2002.

MSR $13,920	$11,825	$10,250	$8,800	$8,000	$6,500	$5,350	$4,200	

GRADING - PPGS™	100%	98%	95%	90%	80%	70%	60%	LAST MSR

MODEL 1620SL – 16 ga., similar to Model 1620EL, except has sidelock action. Importation began 2002.

MSR $13,920	$11,825	$10,250	$8,800	$8,000	$6,500	$5,350	$4,200	

* ***Model 1620SL 2 Barrel Set*** – includes 28 in. 16 and 20 ga. barrels bored IC/M. Imported 2002-2012.

	$13,595	$11,900	$10,200	$9,250	$7,500	$6,100	$5,100	*$15,995*

MODEL 1622 – 16 ga., 28 in. barrels, Greener crossbolt, double barrel under-barrel locking lugs, case hardened receiver with cocking indicators, Anson & Deely boxlock action with full sideplates, H&H ejectors, SST or DT, pistol grip or English style stock, 6.3 lbs. Imported 2006-2007.

	$4,700	$4,100	$3,500	$3,200	$2,550	$2,100	$1,800	*$5,495*

* ***Model 1622 2 Barrel Set*** – includes 28 in. 16 and 20 ga. barrels bored IC/M. Imported 2006-2007.

	$7,050	$6,150	$5,300	$4,800	$3,900	$3,250	$2,700	*$8,295*

* ***Model 1622E*** – 16 ga., similar to Model 1622, except had hand engraved game scenes on silver finished receiver. Imported 2006-2007.

	$5,850	$5,150	$4,400	$4,000	$3,200	$2,750	$2,300	*$6,895*

* ***Model 1622EL*** – 16 ga., similar to Model 1622E, except has luxury grade wood. Imported 2006-2007.

	$7,800	$6,850	$5,850	$5,300	$4,300	$3,600	$3,000	*$9,195*

* ***Model 1622EL 2 Barrel Set*** – includes 28 in. 16 and 20 ga. barrels bored IC/M. Imported 2006-2007.

	$10,200	$8,900	$7,650	$6,950	$5,600	$4,700	$3,850	*$11,995*

SHOTGUNS: SPORTING CLAYS

MODEL 47LSC SxS SPORTING CLAYS – 12 ga. only, features Anson & Deeley boxlock action with scroll engraved case hardened receiver, 28 in. barrels with Briley screw-in chokes, H&H style ejectors, SST adj. for length of pull, select grade checkered walnut stock with pistol grip and beavertail forearm, competition recoil pad. Disc. 1994.

	$2,725	$2,400	$2,050	$1,725	$1,450	$1,125	$925	*$2,995*

MODEL 200SC O/U SPORTING CLAYS – 12 ga. only, 3 in. chambers, 30 in. VR fixed choke barrels with lengthened forcing cones, Kersten double crossbolt lock, color case hardened receiver, Blitz action, SST, fitted luggage case. Imported 1995-96.

	$6,750	$4,600	$3,750	$3,200	$2,625	$2,175	$1,850	*$7,495*

Add $500 for Briley choke tubes (5 total).

MERRILL

Previous manufacturer located in Tucson, AZ. This original pistol design was by Rex Merrill.

A newer variation of the Sportsman, now designated the XL and Hunter Model XL was offered by R.P.M. Please refer to the R.P.M. listing for more information.

PISTOLS: SINGLE SHOT

SPORTSMAN MODEL – .17 Hornet, .22 S, L, or LR, .22 WMR, .22 Rem. Jet., .22 Hornet, .30 Herrett, .30 Merrill, .38 Spl., .357 Mag., .357 Herrett, 7mm Merrill, 7mm Rocket, .256 Win. Mag., .45 LC, .44 Mag., or .30-30 Win. cal., 9, 10 3/4, or 14 in. barrel, hinged break open action, smooth walnut grips.

	$650	$575	$525	$450	$395	$350	$300	

Add $70 for interchangeable barrels.
Add $25 for wrist support.

MERTMAK

Current shotgun manufacturer located in Turkey. Currently distributed and exported by Dorkas Foreign Trade, located in Konya, Turkey.

Mertmak currently manufactures a line of good quality semi-auto shotguns in a variety of configurations, including hunting and tactical. Many finishes and stock options are also available. Please contact the exporter directly for more information, including pricing and domestic availability.

MERWIN HULBERT & CO.

Previous company with headquarters located in New York, NY circa 1874-1891.

Merwin Hulbert offered very high quality revolvers which were serious competitors with the Colt, Smith & Wesson, and Remington large frame single actions during this era. Their guns are believed to have been manufactured in a separate section of the Hopkins & Allen plant. Most will have both Merwin Hulbert and Hopkins & Allen markings on the barrel.

Merwin revolvers have a unique twist-open mechanism. The latch on the bottom of the frame is pushed toward the rear, while barrel & cylinder are twisted clockwise and pulled forward. This design was intended to allow selective ejection of empty cases while leaving unfired cartridges in the cylinder.

100%	98%	95%	90%	80%	70%	60%	50%	40%	30%	20%	10%

A unique and highly desirable feature of Merwin revolvers is "suction". Due to the exceptionally tight machining tolerances of these revolvers, when the barrel and cylinder were twisted to the right, drawn forward, and let go of, they would return to an almost fully closed position on the frame due to the "suction" created by these tight tolerances. Merwins with extremely good "suction" will bring a 10%-20% premium.

Merwins will often be found with a distinctive and unusual "punch dot" style factory engraving, often with some sort of simple panel scene (animal, bird, flowers, etc.) on one or (rare) both sides of the frame. These will usually bring perhaps a 50% premium in lower grades, while in higher condition may bring double or triple what an undecorated gun will bring. The highest quality factory Exhibition/Presentation grade guns may bring four to five times what an undecorated gun will bring. These are exceptionally rare!

During 1868, Joseph Merwin merged with Hulbert Bros. to form an import/export company. In 1871, Merwin-Hulbert & Company of NY became the sole agent for Hopkins & Allen products. Joseph Merwin passed away in 1878. During 1880-1881, the company made some bad investments, and was forced into trusteeship. In 1887, Merwin, Hulbert & Co. claimed ownership of the Hopkins & Allen factory in Norwich. But by 1896, another chaotic financial situation brought about the demise of the company, as well as Hulbert Bros. Co.

REVOLVERS: LARGE FRAME

All chambered for either .44 Merwin Hulbert (usually no caliber markings), .44 Russian (usually marked "Russian Model"), or .44-40 (marked "Calibre Winchester 1873").

The Merwin Hulbert system was copied by various Spanish, Belgium, and possibly other makers. These foreign copies will bring significantly less than original Merwins.

Add 20%-25% for blue finish (rare, used on only about 5% of all Merwins). Add 10% for a rounded or "humpback" hammer that can be found on many of the earlier Merwins.

FIRST MODEL FRONTIER ARMY SA – .44 cal., square butt, open-top, scoop flutes on cylinder, 7 in. barrel, two screws above trigger guard.

100%	98%	95%	90%	80%	70%	60%	50%	40%	30%	20%	10%
$9,600	$7,200	$4,200	$3,300	$2,100	$1,850	$1,600	$1,400	$1,150	$1,050	$975	$825

SECOND MODEL FRONTIER ARMY SA – similar to First Model, except has only one screw above trigger guard.

100%	98%	95%	90%	80%	70%	60%	50%	40%	30%	20%	10%
$8,500	$7,000	$4,100	$2,800	$1,900	$1,700	$1,550	$1,400	$1,200	$1,000	$900	$800

SECOND MODEL POCKET ARMY SA – similar to Second Model Frontier Army, except has bird's head butt instead of square butt, 3 1/2 or 7 (scarce) in. barrel, may be marked "POCKET ARMY".

100%	98%	95%	90%	80%	70%	60%	50%	40%	30%	20%	10%
$7,500	$6,750	$4,000	$3,000	$2,500	$2,100	$1,750	$1,500	$1,250	$1,000	$800	$700

Add 10% for 7 in. barrel.

There are no First Model Pocket Army models.

THIRD MODEL FRONTIER ARMY SA – .44 cal., square butt, top strap, usually has conventional fluting on cylinder, but some have scoop flutes, 7 in. round barrel with no rib.

100%	98%	95%	90%	80%	70%	60%	50%	40%	30%	20%	10%
$7,000	$6,250	$3,750	$2,750	$2,250	$2,000	$1,500	$1,250	$1,000	$900	$750	$650

THIRD MODEL FRONTIER ARMY DA – .44 cal., similar to Third Model Frontier Army SA, except is double action.

100%	98%	95%	90%	80%	70%	60%	50%	40%	30%	20%	10%
$6,500	$3,500	$2,500	$2,000	$1,750	$1,500	$1,200	$1,000	$900	$825	$650	$550

There are no First or Second Model Army double action models.

THIRD MODEL POCKET ARMY SA – .44 cal., single action, bird's head butt, top strap, 3 1/2 in. or 7 in. round barrel with no rib., available with interchangeable 3 1/2 or 7 in. barrels.

100%	98%	95%	90%	80%	70%	60%	50%	40%	30%	20%	10%
$7,500	$4,750	$3,000	$2,500	$1,600	$1,400	$1,200	$1,000	$900	$750	$650	$550

Add 20% if barrels are numbered to the gun.

THIRD MODEL POCKET ARMY DA – .44 cal., similar to Third Model Pocket Army SA, except is double action, available with interchangeable 3 1/2 or 7 in. barrels.

100%	98%	95%	90%	80%	70%	60%	50%	40%	30%	20%	10%
$6,500	$5,000	$4,500	$3,000	$2,500	$2,000	$1,500	$1,200	$1,000	$900	$750	$600

Add 20% if barrels are numbered to the gun.

FOURTH MODEL FRONTIER ARMY SA – .44 cal., 3 1/2, 5 (most common), or 7 in. unique ribbed barrel, square butt, top strap, conventional flutes.

100%	98%	95%	90%	80%	70%	60%	50%	40%	30%	20%	10%
$9,000	$7,750	$6,000	$5,500	$4,500	$3,000	$2,500	$2,000	$1,550	$1,350	$1,150	$950

FOURTH MODEL FRONTIER ARMY DA – .44 cal., similar to Fourth Model Frontier Army SA, except is double action.

100%	98%	95%	90%	80%	70%	60%	50%	40%	30%	20%	10%
$8,000	$6,500	$5,500	$4,500	$3,750	$2,650	$2,250	$1,750	$1,500	$1,300	$1,100	$900

100%	98%	95%	90%	80%	70%	60%	50%	40%	30%	20%	10%

FOREIGN COPIES OF LARGE FRAME REVOLVERS - .44 cal.

These models may be based on any configuration, but 2nd & 3rd Frontier Army styles are probably the most commonly found. The words "Merwin Hulbert" (such as "Sistema Merwin Hulbert") may appear somewhere on the revolver, but are rarely, if ever, found with the Hopkins & Allen marking. These will usually bring half or less what a comparable genuine Merwin will bring.

REVOLVERS: MEDIUM & SMALL FRAME

Medium frame revolvers were usually 5 shot in .38 cal., or 7 shot in .32 cal. The .32 Long caliber 7 shot barrel and cylinder were adapted to fit the 5 shot .38 cal. medium frames. The small frame was a 5 shot in .32 cal. Models chambered for .38 MH or .32 MH cal. are very similar to the black powder loadings of the .38 S&W and .32 S&W cal. Folding hammer spurs may bring a 10-20% premium.

FIRST POCKET MODEL SA - .38 cal., 5 shot, spur-trigger, w/cyl. pin exposed at the front of the frame, distinguishing feature is round loading hole in recoil shield, with no loading gate.

100%	98%	95%	90%	80%	70%	60%	50%	40%	30%	20%	10%
$2,250	$2,000	$1,600	$1,225	$1,000	$900	$800	$700	$600	$500	$400	$350

SECOND POCKET MODEL SA - .38 cal., 5 shot, similar to First Model, except has sliding loading gate.

100%	98%	95%	90%	80%	70%	60%	50%	40%	30%	20%	10%
$1,800	$1,500	$1,250	$800	$700	$600	$500	$450	$400	$350	$300	$275

THIRD POCKET MODEL SA - .38 cal., 5 shot, similar to First Model, except has enclosed cylinder pin.

100%	98%	95%	90%	80%	70%	60%	50%	40%	30%	20%	10%
$1,600	$1,300	$900	$750	$675	$550	$475	$425	$375	$325	$275	$250

THIRD POCKET MODEL SA WITH TRIGGER GUARD - .38 cal., 5 shot, similar to Third Pocket Model, except has conventional trigger guard.

100%	98%	95%	90%	80%	70%	60%	50%	40%	30%	20%	10%
$1,500	$1,200	$900	$750	$600	$500	$450	$425	$375	$325	$275	$250

THIRD POCKET MODEL DA .38 - .38 cal., 5 shot, double action, may have folding hammer spur.

100%	98%	95%	90%	80%	70%	60%	50%	40%	30%	20%	10%
$1,350	$1,200	$1,000	$750	$600	$550	$500	$450	$400	$350	$325	$300

Add 10% for folding hammer spur.

THIRD POCKET MODEL DA .32 - .32 cal., 7 shot, double action.

100%	98%	95%	90%	80%	70%	60%	50%	40%	30%	20%	10%
$1,500	$1,200	$975	$825	$750	$650	$550	$450	$400	$300	$275	$250

SMALL FRAME DA POCKET MODEL - .32 cal., 5 shot, double action.

100%	98%	95%	90%	80%	70%	60%	50%	40%	30%	20%	10%
$1,200	$1,000	$750	$650	$575	$500	$450	$400	$350	$300	$275	$250

TIP-UP .22 MODEL - .22 rimfire cal., 7 shot, spur trigger, closely patterned after the S&W Model One. Very scarce.

100%	98%	95%	90%	80%	70%	60%	50%	40%	30%	20%	10%
$1,500	$1,250	$1,100	$950	$850	$750	$650	$550	$450	$400	$350	$300

RIFLES: SINGLE SHOT

These rimfire and centerfire rifles were generally patterned after the Hopkins & Allen single shots, and featured interchangeable barrels (including shotguns). Specimens are marked with either "MERWIN & HULBERT & Co." or the standard Hopkins & Allen barrel markings. Variations were made in limited quantities, including: Hunter's and Target Rifle (best quality), Gallery and Squirrel Rifle, and X.L. Shot Gun.

Values for Merwin & Hulbert single shot rifles can vary significantly depending on condition and the original quality/features of the models. Average condition plain Jane rifles and shotguns typically sell in the $125-$400 range. If with checkered stock and forearm, average condition specimens are usually in the $375-$750 range. Best quality guns in above average condition are rare and prices can top $1,500, depending on features and caliber.

MERWIN HULBERT & CO. (RECENT MFG.)

Previous trademark established in 2010. While the company secured a manufacturing facility located in Glenrock, WY, only a few prototypes were manufactured. Merwin Hulbert & Co. was a division of Sharps Rifle Co. located in Chamberlain, SD.

While Merwin Hulbert & Co. planned to begin the manufacture of the Merwin Hulbert revolvers based on the original specifications during 2010, only a few prototypes were produced. They included the 1878 Pocket Army, 1879 New Army, 1882 Pocket Army, and the 1883 New Army. During 2013, the Broadsword Group acquired the assets of Sharps Rifle Co. which also included Merwin Hulbert & Co.

GRADING - PPGS™	100%	98%	95%	90%	80%	70%	60%	LAST MSR

MESA PRECISION ARMS

Current manufacturer of bolt action rifles, established in 2017, located in Grand Junction, CO.

Mesa Precision Arms is owned and operated by U.S. Marine Corps. veteran, Chad Drayer. Chad provides custom made long range precision hunting rifles built to the customer's specification.

RIFLES: BOLT ACTION

Models listed below reflect base pricing. Custom made rifles come with options for Bartlein barrels, McMillan Stocks, TriggerTech triggers, and various finishes. Build time generally takes six to eight weeks. Please contact the manufacturer directly for pricing, options, and availability.

ASCENT – 6.5x284 Norma, .300 Win Mag., 7mm Rem. Mag., .28 Nosler, or 6.5 PRC cal., CRUX (disc. 2020) or Summit (new 2021) stainless steel action, 26 in. Bartlein #3 contour 5R cut rifle barrel, with or w/o threaded or index muzzle brake, TriggerTech trigger, glass-bedded fiberglass composite Altitude stock in Desert, Urban, or Woodland camo finish, choice of BDL hinged floorplate or HS Precision DBM, choice of bead blast, matte black, or FDE Cerakote finish, 7 1/2 lbs. New 2018.

MSR $3,700	$3,150	$2,750	$2,350	$2,150	$1,750	$1,400	$1,100	

Add $300 for HS Precision DBM.

CARBON HUNTER – 6.5x284 Norma, .300 Win. Mag., 7mm Rem. Mag., .28 Nosler, or 6.5 PRC cal., CRUX stainless or CRUX Titanium action, 24 or 26 in. Sendero Light carbon fiber barrel, with or w/o threaded cap or index muzzle brake, TriggerTech trigger, glass-bedded fiberglass composite Altitude stock in Desert, Urban, or Woodland camo finish, choice of BDL hinged floorplate or HS Precision DBM, includes case, choice of bead blast, matte black or FDE Cerakote finish, 6.1-6.7 lbs. New 2018.

MSR $4,500	$3,800	$3,350	$2,850	$2,600	$2,100	$1,700	$1,350	

Add $300 for HS Precision DBM.

Add $1,000 for CRUX titanium action or $1,300 for CRUX titanium action w/HS Precision DBM.

COMP – 6.5 Creedmoor, .308 Win., 6mm Creedmoor, 6mm Dasher, 6.5 PRC, or .22 Dasher cal., CRUX (disc. 2020) or Summit (new 2021) stainless steel action, 26 in. Bartlein #13 contour 5R stainless steel or MTU contour barrel, self-timing muzzle brake, 5 shot mag., TriggerTech Primary trigger, XLR JV Envy Heavy or XLR carbon stock and tactical buttstock, Ergo grip, XLR chassis w/side-folding adapter, with or w/o multicam or multicam black hydro-dip finish, 12 lbs. New 2018.

MSR $3,800	$3,250	$2,800	$2,400	$2,200	$1,800	$1,450	$1,150	

Add $200 for multicam finish.

METROARMS CORPORATION (MAC)

Current manufacturer of 1911 style semi-auto pistols located in the Philippines. Imported and distributed by Eagle Imports, located in Wanamassa, NJ.

MetroArms Corporation was established in 2005 under the expertise of former competitive shooter Hector Rodriguez. They also manufacture pistols under the American Classic trademark reintroduced Llama branded models in 2016.

PISTOLS: SEMI-AUTO

MAC 1911 BOBCUT – .45 ACP cal., SA, 4 1/4 in. barrel, steel frame, blue, hard chrome, or black chrome (new 2014) finish, 8 shot mag., hammer forged steel slide, fully adj. Novak style rear sight, dovetail fiber optic front sight, custom hardwood grips with MAC logo, approx. 35 oz. Mfg. 2013-2020.

	$765	$675	$575	$525	$425	$350	$275	*$902*

Add $76 for hard chrome finish.

Add $143 for black chrome finish (new 2014).

MAC 1911 BULLSEYE – .45 ACP cal., SA, 6 in. ramped match bull barrel, 8 shot mag., dovetail front and fully adj. Bomar-type rear sights, custom hardwood grips with MAC logo, ambidextrous thumb safety, flared and lowered ejection port, skeletal combat hammer and trigger, wide front and rear slide serrations, blue or hard chrome finish, approx. 47 oz. Mfg. 2013-2020.

	$1,040	$910	$780	$700	$575	$475	$365	*$1,219*

Add $75 for hard chrome finish.

MAC 1911 CLASSIC – .45 ACP cal., SA, 5 in. ramped match bull barrel, 8 shot mag., steel frame, hammer forged steel slide, fully adj. Bomar style rear sight, dovetail fiber optic front sight, flared and lowered ejection port, standard slide stop, enhanced beavertail grip safety, skeletal hammer, combat trigger, wide front and rear slide serrations, ambidextrous thumb safety, custom hardwood grips with MAC logo, wide magwell, blue, hard chrome, or black chrome (new 2015) finish, approx. 41 oz. Mfg. 2013-2020.

	$895	$795	$650	$595	$475	$395	$300	*$1,045*

Add $75 for hard chrome finish.

Add $159 for black chrome finish (new 2015).

GRADING - PPGS™	100%	98%	95%	90%	80%	70%	60%	LAST MSR

MAC RAPIDO – 9mm Para. or .38 Super cal., SA, double stack frame, 5 (9mm Para.) or 5 1/2 (.38 Super) in. threaded ramped barrel w/compensator, 17 shot mag., combat hammer, combat trigger, glass filled nylon polymer grip, ambidextrous thumb/enhanced beavertail grip safety, front and rear scope mounts, thumb rest, flared and lowered ejection port, forged steel slide, blue, hard chrome, or black chrome finish, 51.80 oz. Mfg. 2018-2020.

	$1,465	$1,285	$1,100	$995	$815	$665	$510	*$1,725*

MAC 3011 SLD (SSD) – .45 ACP, .40 S&W (new 2014), or 9mm Para. (new 2018) cal., SA, steel frame, 5 in. ramped match bull barrel, 14 (.45 ACP), 15 (.40 S&W), or 17 (9mm Para., new 2018) shot mag., hammer forged steel slide, flared and lowered ejection port, skeletal hammer, combat trigger, dovetail fiber optic front sight, fully adj. Bomar style rear sight, aluminum grips with MAC logo, ambidextrous thumb safety, enhanced beavertail grip safety, wide front and rear slide serrations, standard slide stop, hammer forged steel slide, wide magwell, blue or hard chrome (disc.) finish, approx. 46 oz. Mfg. 2013-2020.

	$1,100	$950	$800	$750	$600	$500	$375	*$1,289*

Add $76 for hard chrome (disc.) finish.

* ***MAC 3011 SSD Tactical*** – .45 ACP cal., similar to MAC 3011SSD, except features a tactical rail and matte black finish, 14 shot mag., 46 oz. Mfg. 2013-2017.

	$1,040	$895	$775	$695	$575	$450	$350	*$1,226*

MICHIGAN ARMS

Previous manufacturer located in Michigan until circa 1981.

PISTOLS: SEMI-AUTO

GUARDIAN - SS – .380 ACP cal., patterned after the Walther PPK, bears close resemblance to the Indian Arms .380 semi-auto, 3 1/4 in. barrel, checkered walnut grips with medallion, 6 shot finger extension mag., fixed sights. Limited mfg.

	$375	$295	$225	$210	$190	$170	$150	

This model was mfg. by using Indian Arms tooling.

M1911 A1 – .45 ACP cal., patterned after the Colt M1911 A1, fixed sights, 7 shot mag. Disc.

	$450	$395	$350	$275	$225	$210	$190	

MICOR DEFENSE, INC.

Previous firearms manufacturer located in Decatur, AL from 1999-circa 2013.

Micor manufactured a line of defense products that were available to the general public, as well as custom weapons and products for the defense and other related industries. Micor consisted of two companies - Micor Industries, Inc. and Micor Defense, Inc. While Micor Industries is still in operation and manufacturing parts and materials, Micor Defense has ceased firearm production.

RIFLES: SEMI-AUTO

Micor Defense manufactured the Leader 416 semi-auto bullpup rifle, Leader T2 semi-auto rifle, and the Leader 338 Bullpup rifle. Additionally, Micor offered the Gatekeeper 50 (Leader 50), a lightweight .50 BMG cal. rifle (last MSR was $9,995). All models were designed by Charles St. George, original designer of the Bushmaster M17 bullpup rifle.

MICROTECH SMALL ARMS RESEARCH, INC. (MSAR)

Previous rifle manufacturer located in Bradford, PA until 2015.

For individual model listings, please go to BlueBookOfGunValues.com/overflow.

MIDLAND ARMS

Current manufacturer/trademark of firearms located in Martinsburg, WV.

The Midland Arms trademark was purchased by the Navy Arms Company in 1991 and the brand was used sparingly until 2017.

SHOTGUNS: SINGLE SHOT

In 2020, Midland Arms introduced a U.S. Constitution stock finish, available in 12, 20 ga, or .410 bore with 18 1/2 or 26 in. barrels.

MIDLAND BACKPACK – 12, 20 ga., or .410 bore, 3 in. chamber, 18 1/2, 22 (new 2018), 24, or 26 in. barrel, threaded for interchangeable Beretta Mobil chokes (modified included), forged steel receiver, foldable synthetic stock checkered at wrist and forend, removable buttpad with recoil reducer, ambidextrous cheekpiece, positive trigger-block safety, cocking indicator.

MSR $150	$130	$110	$95	$85	$70	$60	$45	

Add $110 for interchangeable barrel.

GRADING - PPGS™	100%	98%	95%	90%	80%	70%	60%	LAST MSR

MIDLAND TURKEY – 20 ga., 3 in. chamber, 22 in. barrel, synthetic stock, 38 .5 in. OAL.

MSR $180	$155	$135	$125	$115	$85	$75	$55	

MIDLAND BEAGLE – .410 bore, 18 1/2 in. barrel, fixed-modified choke, 1 shot, synthetic stock, tan finish. New 2019.

MSR $189	$175	$150	$135	$125	$115	$95	$75	

MIDLAND RIFLES

Previous trademark of rifles manufactured by Gibbs Rifle Co. (please refer to the G section for previous models and pricing) and older models manufactured by Parker-Hale, Ltd. (please refer to the P section).

MIDWEST INDUSTRIES, INC.

Current manufacturer of AR-15 style pistols, rifles, and tactical accessories, located in Waukesha, WI.

Please refer to BlueBookOfGunValues.com to order the *Blue Book of AR-15s & Variations*, available as a book or online subscription.

MIIDA

Previously manufactured by Nikko Firearms, Ltd. in Tochigi, Japan. Previously imported by Marubeni America Corp. located in New York, NY circa 1972-1974.

SHOTGUNS: O/U

MODEL 612 FIELD – 12 ga., 26 or 28 in. barrels, VR, various chokes, boxlock, auto ejectors, single selective trigger, checkered pistol grip stock. Mfg. 1972-1974.

	$800	$725	$650	$575	$510	$440	$400	

MODEL 2100 SKEET GUN – similar to Model 612, with 27 in. VR, skeet bore barrels, more elaborate engraving. Mfg. 1972-1974.

	$875	$775	$700	$615	$550	$465	$425	

MODEL 2200T TRAP GUN – similar to Model 2100, except with 29 3/4 in. imp. mod. and full choke barrels, wide VR, 60% engraved coverage and select wood. Mfg. 1972-1974.

	$925	$825	$750	$665	$595	$500	$450	

MODEL 2200S SKEET GUN – similar to Model 2200T, except with 27 in. skeet bore barrels.

	$925	$825	$750	$665	$595	$500	$450	

MODEL 2300 SERIES TRAP OR SKEET – similar to Model 2200 Trap/Skeet but with more engraving. Mfg. 1972-1974.

	$975	$875	$800	$715	$630	$550	$500	

MODEL GRT GRANDEE TRAP GUN – 12 ga., 29 3/4 in. full choke barrels, single selective trigger, auto ejector, boxlock with sideplates, receiver fully engraved as well as breech ends of barrel, trigger guard and locking lever, gold inlaid, extensive silver line inlays, high grade select walnut stock. Mfg. 1972-1974.

	$2,500	$2,200	$1,900	$1,575	$1,250	$1,000	$850	

MODEL GRS GRANDEE SKEET GUN – similar to Model GRT, with 27 in. skeet bored barrels.

	$2,500	$2,200	$1,900	$1,575	$1,250	$1,000	$850	

MILLER ARMS

Previous trademark owned by Dakota Arms, located in Sturgis, SD, until June 5, 2009.

RIFLES: LEVER ACTION

SINGLE SHOT RIFLE – various cals. between .17 Dakota - .416 Rem. Mag., XXX English style checkered walnut stock and Schnabel forend, falling block action. Mfg. 2004-disc.

* ***Single Shot Classic*** – various centerfire cals. up to .375 H&H, 24 in. round barrel, Hi-Wall falling block action with curved Farquharson lever, plain matte receiver, 7 1/2 lbs. Disc. circa 2010.

	$4,950	$4,500	$3,900	$3,400	$2,925	$2,475	$1,950	*$5,590*

Add $100 for stainless steel action.

* ***Single Shot Low Boy*** – various centerfire cals., 24 in. half round, half octagon barrel, falling block action, case colored receiver with gold Miller banner, jeweled block, 7 lbs. Disc. circa-2010

	$4,950	$4,500	$3,900	$3,400	$2,925	$2,475	$1,950	*$5,590*

Add $100 for stainless steel action.

* ***Single Shot Model F*** – various centerfire cals. up to .45-110, 26 in. octagon barrel, lever style falling block action, perch belly buttstock, Queen Anne grip, cheekpiece, stainless steel receiver, tang sight with front globe, checkered steel buttplate or black recoil pad, 6 lbs.

	$5,650	$4,900	$4,100	$3,550	$3,100	$2,750	$2,250	*$6,095*

GRADING - PPGS™	100%	98%	95%	90%	80%	70%	60%	LAST MSR

MILLER CLASSIC – various cals., falling block action, 24 in. round barrel, includes XXX hand checkered walnut stock and forearm, English style buttstock, choice of matte, matte blue, or stainless steel metal, actions include choice of Classic or Low Boy, custom built per individual order, 7-7 1/2 lbs. Mfg. circa 2010-2011.

	$4,950	$4,500	$3,900	$3,400	$2,925	$2,475	$1,950	*$5,590*

MILLER, DAVID CO.

Please refer to the David Miller Co. listing in the D section.

MILLER PRECISION ARMS

Previous AR-15 manufacturer located in Columbia Falls, MT until 2017.

Please refer to BlueBookOfGunValues.com to order the *Blue Book of AR-15s & Variations*, available as a book or online subscription.

MIL-SPEC INDUSTRIES CORP.

Previous pistol manufacturer and current components supplier located in Roslyn Heights, NY since 1996.

PISTOLS: SEMI-AUTO

MIL-SPEC 1911 A1 - 9mm Para., 9x21mm, 9x22mm, .40 S&W, .45 HP, or .45 ACP cal., high tech polymer and stainless steel frame, beavertail grip safety, aluminum trigger, 10 shot mag., 3 15/16 (Compact), 5 5/16 (Combat with compensator), or 5 (Government) in. barrel, choice of wood, plastic, or rubber grips, 39 1/2-46 oz. Mfg. late 1996-2006.

	$625	$550	$500	$450	$400	$360	$330	*$690*

Add $5 for parkerized finish.
Add $45 for electroless nickel finish.
Add $50 for hard chrome finish.

MILTAC INDUSTRIES, LLC

Previous AR-15 style firearms manufacturer located in Boise, ID.

Please refer to BlueBookOfGunValues.com to order the *Blue Book of AR-15s & Variations*, available as a book or online subscription.

MILTEX, INC.

Previous handgun importer located in La Plata, MD. Miltex imported commercial Makarovs until approx. 2000.

MIROKU, B.C.

Current manufacturer established during 1893, located in Kochi, Japan. Miroku currently manufactures long arms for Browning and Winchester (please refer to individual sections), in addition to their own line of firearms mostly distributed in Europe.

Shotguns marked Miroku only without another trademark listing represent that period of manufacture before Miroku began manufacturing shotguns for other companies (i.e. Charles Daly, Browning, and others). Most guns marked Miroku were only made on a limited basis and although somewhat rare, collector desirability to date has been minimal. Since model notations were not specified in most instances (many shotguns were made to test market demand), a model rundown is virtually impossible. Values can be approximately ascertained by comparing a Miroku shotgun of similar gauge, features, engraving/wood, and condition to an equivalent Japanese Charles Daly model. Miroku also manufactured revolvers up until approximately 1964 which may be designated Liberty Chief - limited importation into the U.S.

MITCHELL ARMS, INC.

Previous manufacturer, importer, and distributor located in Fountain Valley, CA.

For individual model listings, please go to BlueBookOfGunValues.com/overflow.

MITCHELL'S MAUSERS

Current importer located in Fountain Valley, CA.

Please refer to the Escalade and Sabre sections for previously imported semi-auto and slide action shotguns.

PISTOLS: SEMI-AUTO

Mitchell's Mausers previously imported older Luger pistols in many variations. Last MSRs circa 2010 on the following models were: P08 WWI 4 in. $4,995, P08 WWII 4 in. $4,495, Navy Model 6 in. $6,495, Artillery Model 8 in. $7,900, P08 Treaty of Versailles $5,995, and $9,995 for Carbine w/stock. All were restored and were cased with accessories. Additionally, the company also imported a restored WWII P-38, cased with accessories, last MSR was $3,495.

GRADING - PPGS™	100%	98%	95%	90%	80%	70%	60%	LAST MSR

GOLD SERIES – 9mm Para., .40 S&W, or .45 ACP cal., M1911 design, blue finish or stainless steel construction, skeletonized fast hammer, lowered ejection port, front and rear slide serrations, extended thumb and beavertail grip safeties, adj. rear sight, checkered walnut grips. Disc.

Blue finish (disc. 2014)	$875	$725	$650	$550	$495	$450	$400	
Nickel finish	$2,500	$2,200	$1,800	$1,500	$1,200	$900	$600	

WHITE LIGHTNING – .17 Mach 2, .17 HMR, .22 LR, or .22 WMR cal., black synthetic frame with stainless steel barrel/slide, 8 1/2 in. barrel with Picatinny black synthetic rail and barrel rib, 9 shot mag. Mfg. 2006-2007.

	$535	$465	$435	$395	$360	$330	$295	*$595*

FALCON SERIES – 9mm Para., .40 S&W, or .45 ACP cal., DA/SA operation, Browning locking system operation, 3.9 (semi-compact) or 4 1/4 (compact) in. barrel, low profile sights, aluminum frame with steel frame and barrel, 12, 16, or 20 shot mag., loaded chamber indicator, approx. 32 oz. Mfg. in Serbia. Imported late 2011-disc.

	$725	$650	$575	$495	$425	$350	$295	*$795*

REVOLVERS

CENTURION – .357 Mag. cal., blue finish or stainless steel construction, 6 shot, target trigger, hammer and grips, adj. rear sight, laminated one-piece wood grip with medallion. Limited importation.

	$625	$550	$500	$450	$400	$350	$300	*$695*

VALKYRIE – .44 Mag. cal., red ramp front sight, laminated one-piece wood grip with medallion. Limited importation.

	$775	$650	$575	$500	$450	$400	$350	*$895*

RIFLES: BOLT ACTION

Beginning 1999, Mitchell's Mausers imported a sizeable quantity of WWII Mauser 98Ks manufactured in Yugoslavia during/after WWII. These guns are basically in new condition, having been only test fired over the past 50 years. They are supplied with bayonet and scabbard, military leather sling, original field cleaning kit, and leather ammo pouch. Caliber is 8mm Mauser (7.9x57mm), and all parts numbers match on these rifles.

BLACK ARROW – .50 BMG cal., Mauser action, 5 shot detachable box mag., fluted and compensated barrel, includes bipod and quick detachable scope mount, shock absorbing buttstock. Imported 2003-2006.

	$5,750	$4,950	$4,275	$3,600	$3,000	$2,400	$2,150	*$6,500*

G98 REPLICA – various standard and mag. cals., K98 design, configurations included hunting and sport tactical, 3 or 5 shot mag., approx. 7 lbs. Mfg. from Serbia late 2011-2020.

	$450	$400	$360	$330	$300	$275	$250	*$495*

MAUSER MAGNUM M98 – various big game cals. from .375 H&H - .500 Jeffery, double square bridge, magnum receiver, deluxe checkered walnut stock with forend cap, folding iron sights. Imported 2003-2010.

	$8,200	$7,400	$6,500	$5,500	$4,500	$3,500	$3,000	*$8,900*

Add $2,000 for .500 Jeffery cal.

MAUSER SPORTERS (K98/M98) – 8mm Mauser cal., sporterized military Mauser action with choice of black laminate, brown laminate or American walnut stock with rollover cheekpiece and recoil pad, adj. rear sight, adj. trigger, controlled round feeding. Importation began 2003.

	$440	$395	$375	$345	$295	$265	$235	*$495*

The above price was for the Premium rifle, with bayonet, scabbard, belt hanger and other accessories. Other grades included the Collector Grade - $295 last MSR (included bayonet and accessories), Service Grade - $175 last MSR, Trucker Grade - $149 last MSR.

* ***Model K98 Souvenir Grade*** – Disc. 2013.

	$360	$320	$285	$260	$240	$220	$200	*$399*

* ***Model K98 Collector Grade***

	$450	$395	$365	$335	$295	$260	$230	*$499*

* ***Model K98 Select Grade***

	$475	$400	$365	$335	$295	$260	$230	*$549*

* ***Model K98 Premium Grade***

	$525	$450	$400	$350	$325	$275	$250	*$599*

* ***Model K98 Premium Select***

	$595	$500	$450	$400	$350	$325	$295	*$699*

GRADING - PPGS™	100%	98%	95%	90%	80%	70%	60%	LAST MSR

* ***Model K98 Battle Anniversary Series*** – 8mm Mauser cal., various configurations and dates for important battles during WWII, plus the start and end of WWII. Disc. approx. circa 2010.

Retail pricing was not available for this model.

MODEL 98 NORTH AMERICAN – .270 Win., .270 WSM, .30-06, .308 Win., .300 RUM, .300 Win. Mag., or 7mm Rem. Mag. cal., Mauser 98 double square bridge receiver. Imported 2003-circa 2010.

	$7,400	$6,500	$5,500	$4,500	$3,500	$3,000	$2,500	*$7,900*

MODEL 98 VARMINTER – .220 Swift, .22-250 Rem., .223 Rem., or .223 WSM cal., features double square bridge receiver, varmint stock with Turkish walnut and fluted barrel, fully adj. trigger, 3-position side safety. Imported 2003-2006.

	$5,950	$5,250	$4,500	$3,750	$3,000	$2,250	$1,500	*$6,500*

MODEL M48 – 8mm Mauser cal., original Mauser 98K rifle manufactured with German technology in Serbia, various grades, matching serial numbers on all parts. Importation began 2006.

MSR $349	$325	$295	$275	$250	$240	$230	$220

The above price is for the Service grade rifle without accessories. Add $100 for Collector Grade, $150 for Custom Select Grade, $200 for BO (Stealth), $300 for Premium Grade, $350 for Premium Select Grade, and $400 for Premium Grade BO (Stealth).

A special Museum Grade with bayonet, scabbard, belt hanger, and other accessories was also available for $1,000 (disc.).

MODEL ZF-41 SNIPER RIFLE – 8mm Mauser cal., scope mount base permanently mounted to barrel, scope and mount not included. Disc.

	$900	$800	$700	$600	$500	$400	$300	*$999*

Add $100 for Select grade, $300 for Premium Grade, $400 for Premium Select Grade.

SOVIET MOSIN-NAGANT – various cals., original gun dated 1942 to commemorate the battle of Stalingrad. Limited importation 2009-disc.

U.S. pricing was not available on this model.

TANKER MAUSER M63 (MODEL M48) – .243 Win., .270 Win., .30-06, 8mm Mauser, or .308 Win. cal., similar to Model 48, except the barrel length is 17.4 in., 5 shot internal mag., 1400m adj. rear sight, hardwood stock with semi-gloss finish, 7.4 lbs. Imported 2006-circa 2010.

	$450	$395	$375	$345	$295	$265	$235	*$495*

RIFLES: SEMI-AUTO

BLACK LIGHTNING – .17 Mach 2 (disc.), .17 HMR (disc.), .22 LR (disc.), or .22 WMR cal., black polymer oversized thumbhole stock with full-length aluminum shroud and Picatinny rail, 18 in. stainless steel fluted heavy barrel, stainless steel action, 9 shot mag., detachable carry handle, detachable iron front sight, sling swivels, scope options. New 2006.

MSR $595	$500	$450	$375	$350	$300	$250	$200

PSH 41/22 / PPS50/22 – .22 LR cal., patterned after the Russian PPSh-41, 16.1 in. barrel, features stained hardwood stock, full-length perforated barrel heat shield, fixed sights, 10, 30, or 50 shot detachable drum magazine, with or w/o sling, 4.4 lbs. Importation began 2012.

MSR $495	$450	$400	$350	$300	$275	$250	$225

Add $150 for 50 shot, $50 for 30 shot, or $40 for 10 shot detachable drum mag.
Add $39 for reflex rear sight (mfg. 2014-disc.).
Add $23-$30 for sling.

MODULO MASTERPIECE

Previous manufacturer located in Torino, Italy.

Modulo Masterpiece manufactured high quality pistols and rifles. These models had very little importation into the U.S.

MOHAWK ARMORY

Current AR-15 style firearms manufacturer located in Midway, TN.

Mohawk Armory offers a line of AR-15 style semi-auto rifles and pistols. The company is also a Class III dealer and offers many products for law enforcement/military. Please contact the company directly for more information, including pricing and available options.

MOLL, M.F.

Previous custom rifle manufacturer and gunsmith located in Mönchengladbach, Germany.

M.F. Moll manufactured high quality reproductions of the Sharps Model 1874 rifle. He also provided many gunsmithing services, including his own proprietary color case hardening process.

GRADING - PPGS™	100%	98%	95%	90%	80%	70%	60%	LAST MSR

MOLOT ARMS

Current manufacturer established during 1941, and located in Vyatskie Polyany, Kirov region, Russia.

Currently manufactured trademarks include: Vepr rifles and shotguns, an SKS semi-auto rifle line, several models of bolt action rifles, including target models, in addition to Becas slide action and semi-auto shotguns. Please refer to these sections for more information.

MONTANA ARMORY, INC.

Current distributor of C. Sharps Arms Co., Inc. rifles located in Big Timber, MT. Please refer to the C. Sharps Arms Co., Inc. listing in the S section for more information.

MONTANA RIFLE COMPANY

Previous rifle manufacturer established circa 1999 and located in Kalispell, MT until March 2020.

RIFLES: BOLT ACTION

The Montana Rifle Company manufactured three different series of bolt action rifles, featuring its Model 1999 action, which is a hybrid between the Model 70 and the Mauser 98. This action utilized a clone Model 70 trigger and three position safety, but also incorporated the Mauser 98 breeching system with the C-ring and large claw extractor. It also has a five point gas venting system and a new style bolt release knob.

During 2011, a line of semi-custom production rifles were introduced in various standard and mag. cals. with either right or left-hand action.

ALR (AMERICAN LEGENDS RIFLE) – .270 WSM, .30-06, 7mm Rem. Mag., .300 Win. Mag., .338 Win. Mag., .243 Win., .25-06 Rem., 6.5 PRC, 6.5 Creedmoor, .270 WSM, .300 WSM, or .308 Win. cal., right or left-hand action, 24 in. button rifled barrel, blued chrome moly steel or stainless steel, fully adj. trigger, no sights, AA Grade American black walnut stock with black tip and grip wrap around checkered full forearm, 3-position wing safety, 7 lbs. 2 oz. Disc. 2020.

$1,525	**$1,300**	**$1,075**	**$975**	**$785**	**$650**	**$525**	***$1,699***

Add $50 for stainless steel.

ASR (AMERICAN STANDARD RIFLE) – available in 31 different cartridges, chrome moly steel or stainless steel MRC Model 1999 action, right or left-hand configuration, 22, 24, or 26 in. free floated button rifled chrome moly or stainless steel barrel, Mauser style ejector, adj. trigger, field grade American black walnut stock, sling swivel studs, 3-position safety. Mfg. 2011-2020.

$1,300	**$1,150**	**$1,000**	**$900**	**$700**	**$600**	**$450**	***$1,549***

Add $50 for stainless steel barrel/action.

AVR (AMERICAN VANTAGE RIFLE) – .35 Whelen, .375 Ruger, .375 H&H, .416 Ruger, .416 Rem. Mag., .458 Win. Mag., or .458 Lott cal., MRC Model 1999 action, 24 in. free floated button rifled chrome moly blued steel or 100% stainless steel barrel, glass bedded, Mauser style ejector, 3-position safety, Marble front and rear sights, adj. trigger, AA premium walnut stock, sling swivel studs, matte blue or stainless steel, right or left-hand configuration. Mfg. 2014-2019.

$1,575	**$1,365**	**$1,175**	**$1,050**	**$850**	**$700**	**$550**	***$1,776***

Add $49 for stainless steel barrel/action.

CBE (COLORADO BUCK EDITION) – .22-250 Rem. (disc.), 7mm Rem. Mag., .300 Win. Mag., .338 Norma, .338 Lapua mag., .22-250 Varmint (disc.), .375 H&H, or .505 Gibbs cal., right or left-hand, Model 1999 Action or "Double Square Bridge" PH action (right-hand only), 22, 24, or 26 in. match grade stainless steel barrel with Tungsten Grey Cerakote finish, Montana Rifle Flats muzzle brake, Mauser style extractor, fully adj. trigger, MRC synthetic stock, 3-pos. wing safety, sling swivel studs, carbon fiber Kevlar reinforced stock in Colorado Buck's signature color (caramel brown with black spider webbing), 6.6-6.9 lbs. Disc. 2020.

$2,175	**$1,900**	**$1,625**	**$1,475**	**$1,200**	**$1,000**	**$800**	***$2,547***

Add $1,272 for PH action.

CBSE (COLORADO BUCK SPECIAL EDITION) – 6.5 Creedmoor, .300 WSM, .22-250 Rem., 7mm Rem. Mag., .300 Win. Mag., .375 H&H, or .505 Gibbs cal., MRC Model 1999 action, right or left-hand configuration, 24 in. stainless steel free floated barrel with Tungsten Grey Cerakote finish, Montana Flats muzzle brake, Mauser style ejector, adj. trigger, MRC premium synthetic stock, sling swivel studs, 3-position safety, control round feed, HiViz Xcoil recoil pad, MDF logo on action and floorplate, Signature caramel brown color, includes Nikon Monarch 3 4-16x42mm Custom XR Turret scope. Mfg. 2017-2018.

$2,550	**$2,250**	**$1,900**	**$1,750**	**$1,400**	**$1,150**	**$900**	***$2,999***

GRADING - PPGS™	100%	98%	95%	90%	80%	70%	60%	LAST MSR

DGR/DGR SS (DANGEROUS GAME RIFLE) – .338 Lapua (no sights, includes threaded muzzle brake), .338 Norma Mag., .416 Rigby, .378 Wby. Mag., .460 Wby. Mag., or .505 Gibbs cal., MRC Model 1999 double square bridge PH action, 24 or 26 in. free floated button rifled chrome moly blued steel or stainless steel barrel, Marble iron sights, adj. trigger, Mauser style ejector, 3-position safety, American black walnut stock, dual steel crossbolts, sling swivel studs. Mfg. 2017 only.

	$1,675	**$1,575**	**$1,325**	**$1,200**	**$975**	**$800**	**$625**	***$1,849***

* ***DGR/DGR PH "The African"*** – .375 H&H Mag., .404 Jeffery, .416 Rigby, .378 Wby. Mag., .458 LOTT, .458 Win. Mag., .460 Wby. Mag., or .505 Gibbs cal., right or left-hand MRC Model 1999 or Model 1999 "Double Square Bridge" PH (right-hand only) action, 22 or 24 in. chrome moly steel, free floated, button rifled barrel, Mauser style ejector, fully adj. trigger, checkered American black walnut stock, sling swivel studs, 3-position wing safety, upgrades available, custom Cerakote finish, 6-9 lbs. Mfg. 2019-2020.

	$1,550	**$1,400**	**$1,200**	**$1,050**	**$850**	**$700**	**$550**	***$1,849***

Add $1,050 for PH action.

* ***DGR/DGR PH "The Alaskan"*** – .375 H&H Mag., .404 Jeffery, .416 Rigby, .378 Wby. Mag., .458 LOTT, .458 Win. Mag., .460 Wby. Mag., or .505 Gibbs cal., right or left-hand MRC Model 1999 or Model 1999 "Double Square Bridge" PH (right-hand only) action, 22 or 24 in. satin stainless steel, free floated, button rifled barrel, Mauser style ejector, fully adj. trigger, Marble iron sights, carbon fiber Kevlar synthetic stock, sling swivel studs, 3-position wing safety, upgrades available, custom Cerakote finish, 6-9 lbs. Mfg. 2019-2020.

	$1,650	**$1,450**	**$1,250**	**$1,100**	**$900**	**$750**	**$600**	***$1,949***

Add $1,039 for PH action.

MMR (MONTANA MARKSMAN RIFLE) – .308 Win., .300 WMS, .300 Win. Mag., 6.5x284 Norma, 6.5 Creedmoor, or 6.5x55 cal., MRC Model 1999 action, right or left-hand configuration, 24 in. free floated stainless steel barrel, heavy target contour, threaded muzzle with cap, tactical bolt knob, Timney trigger, Mauser style ejector, 3-position safety, T-11 stock, fully field adjustable for LOP and cheek height, dual front swivel studs, Sniper Grey Cerakote finish. Mfg. 2014-2017.

	$3,100	**$2,750**	**$2,300**	**$2,000**	**$1,600**	**$1,300**	**$1,025**	***$3,510***

MPR (MONTANA PREDATOR RIFLE) – .22-250 Rem., .243 Win., 6.5 Creedmoor, 6.5 PRC, .300 Win. Mag., or .300 WSM cal., Model 1999 action, stainless steel #5 heavy sporter/varmint barrel, threaded for muzzle brake/suppressor, thread cap included, T-H (Tactical Hunter) stock, adj. soft-pad cheekpiece and enhanced palm swell, dual front sling swivel studs, black with grey speckle finish. Mfg. 2018 only.

	$3,000	**$2,600**	**$2,250**	**$2,050**	**$1,650**	**$1,350**	**$1,050**	***$3,510***

MSR - MOUNTAIN SNOW RIFLE – .204 Ruger or .300 AAC Blackout cal., or .223/5.56 Wylde chamber, Model 1999 action, 18, 20, or 24 in. free floated stainless steel barrel, detachable box mag., adj. trigger, Mauser style ejector, synthetic stock hydrodipped with Kryptek Pontus camo pattern, HiViz XCoil recoil pad, 3-pos. safety, right or left-hand configuration. Mfg. 2017 only.

	$1,550	**$1,350**	**$1,175**	**$1,050**	**$850**	**$700**	**$550**	***$1,731***

MTR (MONTANA TACTICAL RIFLE) – .338 LM, 6.5 Creedmoor, 6.5x84 Norma, 6.5 PRC, .308 Win., .300 Win. Mag., .300 WSM, or .338 Norma Mag. cal., MRC Model PH (Professional Hunter) action, 26 in. free floated button rifled stainless steel barrel, muzzle brake, Mauser style ejector, Timney trigger, custom T-11 stock, fully adj. for LOP and cheek height, dual front swivel studs, 3-position safety, tactical bolt knob, Cerakote Sniper Grey finish. Disc.

	$3,275	**$2,850**	**$2,400**	**$2,165**	**$1,750**	**$1,450**	**$1,125**	***$3,625***

PRAIRIE RUNNER – .22-250 Rem., 100% stainless steel, right or left-hand configuration, 24 in. stainless steel barrel, muzzle brake, Boyds Varmint thumbhole Forest Camo laminate stock. Mfg. 2016-2017.

While advertised during 2016, retail pricing was not available for this model.

SCR (SEVEN CONTINENTS RIFLE) – .378 Wby., .416 Rigby, .460 Wby., .338 Norma Mag., or .505 Gibbs cal., MRC Model 1999 double square bridge PH (Professional Hunter) action, 24 or 26 in.free floated button rifled stainless steel barrel, Mauser style ejector, adj. trigger, steel Marble front and rear open sights, custom made carbon fiber Kevlar reinforced synthetic stock, sling swivel studs, 3-position safety. Mfg. 2018 only.

	$2,550	**$2,225**	**$1,925**	**$1,750**	**$1,400**	**$1,150**	**$950**	***$2,988***

V2 (EXTREME VANTAGE RIFLE) – .35 Whelen, .375 Ruger, .375 H&H, .416 Ruger, .416 Rem., .458 Win. Mag., or .458 Lott cal., MRC Model 1999 long action, right or left-hand configuration, bolt action rifle, 24 in. free floated button rifled blued steel (disc. 2015) or stainless steel barrel, Mauser style ejector, adj. trigger, Marble front and rear sights, MRC premium synthetic stock, sling swivel studs, HiViz recoil pad, glass bedding, 3-position safety. Disc.

	$1,575	**$1,365**	**$1,175**	**$1,050**	**$850**	**$700**	**$550**	***$1,775***

Subtract approx. $175 for blued steel barrel (disc. 2015).

GRADING - PPGS™	100%	98%	95%	90%	80%	70%	60%	LAST MSR

X2 (EXTREME RIFLE) – various cals., MRC Model 1999 long or short action, right or left-hand configuration, free floated button rifled blued steel (disc. 2015) or stainless steel barrel, adj. trigger, Mauser style ejector, 3-position safety, MRC premium synthetic stock, sling swivel studs, glass bedding, HiViz recoil pad, matte black hardened epoxy paint with grey highlights. Disc. 2017.

	$1,275	$1,115	$950	$865	$700	$575	$450	*$1,412*

Subtract approx. $125 if blued steel barrel.

X3 (XTREME RIFLE) – various cals., right or left-hand action, free floated button rifle barrel, satin finish stainless steel Model 1999 barreled action, MRC synthetic stock, HIVIZ XCoil recoil pad, aluminum pillar and glass bedded. Mfg. 2018-2020.

	$1,375	$1,150	$950	$850	$700	$600	$450	*$1,599*

Add $250 for XER (Xtreme Elite Rifle) variation, new 2019.

* ***Xtreme Elite*** – various short or long cals., right or left-hand action, free floated button rifle threaded barrel w/threaded cap, Montana Flats muzzle brake, satin finish stainless steel Model 1999 barreled action, MRC synthetic stock, HIVIZ XCoil recoil pad, aluminum pillar and glass bedded, 6-7 lbs. Mfg. 2019-2020.

	$1,500	$1,300	$1,100	$1,000	$800	$650	$500	*$1,749*

XAR (XTREME ASCENT RIFLE) – 6.5 Creedmoor, 6.5 PRC, .280 AI, .300 Win. Mag., .300 WSM, 7mm Rem. Mag., 7mm-08 Rem., or .308 Win. cal., MRC Model 1999 action, right or left-hand, 22 or 24 in. satin stainless steel fluted contour free float button rifled barrel, Montana Flats muzzle brake, Mauser style extractor, fully. adj. Pre-64 Win 70 trigger, MRC lightweight synthetic stock, 3-position wing safety, sling swivel studs, Cerakote finish. Mfg. 2020 only.

	$1,700	$1,450	$1,250	$1,150	$900	$750	$600	*$1,975*

XRR (XTREME RANCH RIFLE) – .243 Win., 6.5 Creedmoor, or .308 Win. cal., MRC Model 1999 action, right-hand only, 18 in. satin stainless steel featherweight, contour threaded free float barrel w/thread cap, button-rifled, Montana Flats muzzle brake, 5 shot detachable mag., Mauser style extractor, fully adj. trigger, MRC lightweight synthetic hydro-dipped stock, 3-pos. wing safety, drilled and tapped receiver, aluminum pillar and glass bedded, sling swivel studs, custom Cerakote finish, 6 lbs. 5 oz. Mfg. 2019-2020.

	$1,850	$1,650	$1,400	$1,250	$1,000	$850	$650	*$2,189*

XTH (XTREME TACTICAL HUNTER) – .243 Win., 6.5 Creedmoor, 6.5 PRC, .26 Nosler, .28 Nosler, 7mm Rem. Mag., .280 AI, .30 Nosler, .300 Win. Mag., .300 WSM, .300 RUM, or .308 Win. cal., Model 1999 action, right or left-hand, 22, 24, or 26 in. satin stainless, threaded free floated barrel w/thread cap, button-rifled, Montana Flats muzzle brake, Mauser style extractor, fully adj. Pre-65 Win 70 trigger, tactical synthetic stock, adj. cheekpiece, 3-pos. wing safety, enhanced palm swell, dual front and rear sling swivel studs, Cerakote finish. Mfg. 2019-2020.

	$1,700	$1,450	$1,250	$1,150	$900	$750	$600	*$1,975*

MONTGOMERY WARD

Catalog sales/retailer that has subcontracted various domestic and international manufacturers to private label various brand names under the Montgomery Ward conglomerate.

Montgomery Ward shotguns and rifles have appeared under various labels and endorsers, including Western Field and others. There have literally been hundreds of various models (shotguns and rifles) sold through the Montgomery Ward retail network. Most of these models were manufactured through subcontracts with both domestic and international firearms manufacturers. Typically, they were "spec." guns made to sell at a specific price to undersell the competition. Most of these models were derivatives of existing factory models with less expensive wood and perhaps missing the features found on those models from which they were derived. Please refer to the Store Brand Crossover Section in the back of this book under Western Field for converting Montgomery Ward models to the respective manufacturer.

To date, there has been very little interest in collecting Montgomery Ward guns, regardless of rarity. Rather than list Montgomery Ward models, a general guideline is that values generally are under those of their "1st generation relatives." As a result, prices are ascertained by the shooting value of the gun, rather than its collector value.

MORIARTI ARMAMENTS

Current AR-15 style firearm manufacturer established circa 2014, located in Miami, FL.

Please refer to BlueBookOfGunValues.com to order the *Blue Book of AR-15s & Variations*, available as a book or online subscription.

GRADING - PPGS™	100%	98%	95%	90%	80%	70%	60%	LAST MSR

MORINI COMPETITION ARM SA

Current target pistol manufacturer located in Bedano, Switzerland. Currently imported by Pilkington Competition Equipment, LLC, located in Monteagle, TN. Previously imported and distributed by Nygord Precision Products located in Prescott, AZ, and by Osborne's, located in Cheboygan, MI.

For more information and current pricing on both new and used Morini airguns, please refer to the *Blue Book of Airguns* - also available as an online subscription.

PISTOLS: TARGET

Morini was one of the first companies to develop a sophisticated anatomical grip for handgun target shooting, and continues to be a leader in grip design.

CM-22 SEMI-AUTO - .22 LR cal., design for NRA or ISSF "standard pistol" competition, split trigger guard, direct cartridge feed, fully adj. rear sight and trigger, 6 shot mag., 5.1 in. barrel, alloy and steel construction, adj. anatomical wood grips. New 2000.

No MSR	$1,840	$1,525	$1,325	$1,150	$925	$825	$725	

CM-32 SEMI-AUTO - .32 S&W Wadcutter cal., otherwise similar to CM-22. Mfg. 2000-2011.

	$1,875	$1,550	$1,395	$1,225	$995	$875	$775	

CM-80 STANDARD SINGLE SHOT - .22 LR cal. only, adj. grips, frame, and sights. Importation disc. 1989.

	$925	$825	$725	$650	$585	$520	$465	*$1,015*

Add $50 for left-hand model.

* ***CM-80 Standard Single Shot Super Competition*** - .22 LR cal., similar to CM-80 Standard, except has deluxe finish, and unique plexiglass front sighting system. Importation disc. 1989.

	$1,085	$920	$800	$690	$590	$520	$450	*$1,196*

Add $50 for left-hand model.

CM-84E FREE PISTOL - .22 LR cal., single shot, anatomical grips, unique electronic trigger features optic beam safety, cased.

No MSR	$1,925	$1,650	$1,325	$1,100	$925	$800	$675	

MODEL CM-102E SEMI-AUTO - .22 LR cal., advanced rapid fire competition pistol featuring updated ergonomic grips and flared trigger guard, first target pistol to utilize an electronic trigger. Mfg. 1992-97.

	$1,525	$1,250	$995	$895	$795	$695	$595	*$1,695*

MORTIMER, THOMAS

Current trademark managed and operated by John Dickson and Son, located in Edinburgh, Scotland.

Thomas Mortimer was the scion of a famed London gun-making family, H & T Mortimer, established in 1755 on Fleet Street. In 1835, Thomas came to Edinburgh to set up on Princess Street and the business merged with John Dickson and Son in 1938. Currently, the business is managed and operated by John Dickson and Son. Although no new guns or rifles are currently produced under the Mortimer name, a full repair, restoration, and record enquiry service are offered for classic Mortimer guns and rifles.

MOSIN-NAGANT

Please refer to the Russian Service Pistols and Rifles listing in the R section.

MOSSBERG, O.F. & SONS, INC.

Current manufacturer of rifles, shotguns, pistols, and AR-15 style firearms, located in North Haven, CT, 1962-present and New Haven, CT, 1919-1962.

Oscar Mossberg developed an early reputation as a designer and inventor for the Iver Johnson, Marlin-Rockwell, Stevens, and Shattuck Arms companies. In 1915, he began producing a 4-shot, .22 LR cal. palm pistol known as the "Novelty," with revolving firing pin. After producing approx. 600 of these pistols, he sold the patent to C.S. Shattuck, which continued to manufacture guns under the name "Unique." The first 600 had no markings except serial numbers, and were destined for export to South America. Very few of these original "Novelty" pistols survived in this country, and they are extremely rare specimens.

Mossberg acquired Advanced Ordnance Corp. during 1996, a high quality manufacturer utilizing state-of-the-art CNC machinery.

DERRINGERS

BROWNIE - .22 LR cal., top break action, rotating firing pin, 4-barrel, double action, 4 shot, approx. 32,000 mfg. 1919-1932.

	$800	$500	$400	$300	$250	$225	$200	

GRADING - PPGS™	100%	98%	95%	90%	80%	70%	60%	LAST MSR

PISTOLS: SEMI-AUTO

MC1sc – 9mm Para. cal., matte black or FDE (new 2020) polymer sub-compact frame, 3.4 in. button rifled barrel, 6 shot flush-fit or 7 shot extended mag., flat profile trigger, extended trigger guard, white 3-dot or TruGlo Tritium Pro sights, integrated trigger blade or crossbolt safety, DLC finish, 6.25 in. OAL, 19 oz. New 2019.

MSR $435	$365	$325	$275	$250	$200	$165	$145	

Add $7 for FDE polymer frame (new 2020).
Add $96 for Viridian E-Series red laser.
Add $108 for TruGlo Tritium Pro sights.

* ***MC1sc Centennial*** – 9mm Para. cal., sub-compact polymer frame with titanium Nitride and Cerakote small parts, 3.40 in. button rifled stainless steel titanium Nitride barrel with polished DLC finish and 24K plating, 6 shot flush-fit or 7 shot extended mag., stainless steel slide, flat profile trigger, extended trigger guard, white 3-dot sight, integrated trigger blade safety, 19 oz. Mfg. 2019 only.

	$585	$510	$440	$400	$325	$265	$200	*$686*

* ***MC1sc Stainless Two-Tone*** – 9mm Para. cal., bead-blasted stainless steel slide over matte black polymer sub-compact frame, 3.4 in. button rifled barrel, 6 groove, 6 shot flush-fit or 7 shot extended mag., flat profile trigger, extended trigger guard, white 3-dot sights, textured grips w/ palm swell and grip angle, integrated trigger blade or optional crossbolt safety (reversible for right or left-hand), Mossberg STS (Safe Takedown System), black DLC finish, 6.25 in. OAL, 19 oz. New mid-2019.

MSR $435	$365	$325	$275	$250	$200	$165	$145	

MC2c – 9mm Para. cal., matte black glass-reinforced polymer compact frame, 3.9 in. stainless steel barrel, 10 (flush, new 2021), 13 (flush) or 15 (extended) shot double stack mag., stainless steel slide with black DLC or matte stainless (two-tone) finish, flat profile trigger, oversized trigger guard, white 3-dot or TruGlo Tritium Pro sights, aggressive grip texturing and palm swell, integrated trigger blade or crossbolt safety, 21 oz. New 2020.

MSR $505	$425	$375	$325	$295	$235	$195	$165	

Add $108 for TruGlo Tritium Pro sights.

MODEL 715P – .22 LR cal., 6 in. blued barrel with A2 style muzzle brake, 10 (disc. 2015) or 25 shot mag., full-length top Picatinny rail with mounted adj. front/rear sights or 1x30mm red dot sight (715P Red Dot Combo), short vented quad rail forend, pistol grip synthetic stock, black finish, 3-3 1/2 lbs. Mfg. 2014-2017.

	$275	$250	$225	$200	$185	$175	$165	*$314*

Add $44 for 1x30mm red dot sight (715P Red Dot Combo).

MOSSBERG INTERNATIONAL 715P DUCK COMMANDER – .22 LR cal., 6 in. barrel with A2 muzzle brake, 25 shot mag., accessory loader, Picatinny rail mounted red dot sight, adj. front and rear sights, short quad rail forend, pistol grip stock, Realtree Max-5 camo finish, 3 1/2 lbs. Mfg. 2014-2015.

	$395	$365	$330	$300	$275	$250	$225	*$447*

RIFLES: DISC., 1919-1987 MFG.

The models listed appear alphabetically first, followed by numerical models in sequence. Mossberg also has made several .22 bolt action and semi-auto sporters that are in the $115-$130 price range. While they are good shooting models, they are not covered in this section, as they are not collectible.

MODEL K – .22 S, L, or LR cal., tube mag., hammerless, 22 in. bbl., takedown, open sights, plain straight stock. Mfg. 1922-31.

	$500	$350	$300	$200	$150	$100	$85	

MODEL M – similar to Model K, except has 24 in. octagonal bbl. Mfg. 1928-31.

	$500	$350	$300	$200	$150	$100	$85	

MODEL S – similar to Model K, except has shorter mag. tube and 19 3/4 in. bbl., very rare. Mfg. 1927-31.

	$1,500	$1,200	$1,000	$800	$700	$600	$500	

MODEL L – .22 S, L, or LR cal., falling block action, single shot, 24 in. takedown bbl., open sights, pistol grip stock. Mfg. 1929-32.

	$800	$600	$450	$400	$350	$300	$250	

MODEL L-1 – rare target version of Model L with Lyman 2A tang sight and factory sling.

Add $200 to Model L values.

MODEL R – .22 S, L, and LR cal., bolt action, 24 in. round bbl., first tube feed, ivory bead front sight, open sporting bbl. sight. Mfg. 1930-32.

	$350	$300	$250	$200	$150	$100	$85	

GRADING - PPGS™	100%	98%	95%	90%	80%	70%	60%	LAST MSR

MODEL RM-7 – .30-06 or 7mm Rem. Mag. cal., bolt action, 22 inch (.30-06) or 24 inch (7mm Rem. Mag.) round barrel, three-position safety, folding leaf rear sight, gold bead front sight, hand-checkered American walnut with grip cap, built on imported Swedish rotary magazine action, cartridge release lever for unloading magazine from top. 3 (7mm Rem. Mag.) or 4 (.30-06) shot mag. Mfg. approx. 1979-80.

$400 $325 $265 $245 $230 $215 $200

MODEL B – .22 S, L, or LR cal., single shot, bolt action, 22 in. round tapered bbl. Mfg. 1930-32.

$300 $200 $175 $150 $125 $100 $75

MODEL C – .22 S, L and LR cal., single shot, 24 in. bbl., ivory bead front sight, open sporting rear sight. Mfg. 1931-32.

$300 $200 $175 $150 $125 $100 $75

MODEL C-1 – target version of Model C, Lyman front and rear sights, leather sling and swivels, special walnut stock, rare.

Add $200 to Model C values.

MODELS 10, 14, 20, 21, 25, 25A, 125 – .22 S, L, or LR cal., single shot models. Mfg. 1933-38.

$300 $200 $150 $125 $100 $75 $50

Add 25% to prices for models equipped with aperture sights.

MODEL 26B – .22 S, L, or LR cal., entirely new design in single shot rifles, easily identified by bolt handle at extreme rear of bolt, 26 in. tapered barrel, hooded ramp front sight, No. 4 rear aperture and open bbl. sight, swivels. Mfg. 1938-1941.

$300 $200 $150 $125 $100 $75 $50

MODEL 26-C – similar to Model 26B with less expensive sights. Mfg. 1938-41.

$250 $200 $150 $125 $100 $75 $50

MODEL 26M (OR B26M) – rare version of 26 series model with two-piece Mannlicher-style stock. Mfg. 1938.

$600 $500 $400 $300 $250 $200 $150

MODEL 30 – .22 S, L, or LR cal., single shot, 24 in. bbl., rear peep and ramp front sights, swivels. Mfg. 1933-35.

$300 $250 $200 $150 $100 $75 $50

MODEL 34 – similar to Model 30, except with heavy stock, target style. Mfg. 1934-35.

$300 $225 $150 $100 $70 $55 $45

MODEL 35 – .22 S, L, or LR cal., single shot, first full target model, 26 in. heavy target bbl., walnut stock, hooded front ramp and No. 4 rear peep with adj. aperture sight, approx. 9 1/2 lbs. Mfg. 1935-1937.

$400 $300 $275 $225 $200 $150 $125

MODEL 35A – revised version of Model 35, with all-new "master action," approx. 8 1/4 lbs. Mfg. 1937.

$400 $300 $275 $225 $200 $150 $125

Add 50% for Model 35A-LS with Lyman sights.

MODEL 40 – .22 S, L, or LR cal., repeater with tube mag., 16 shot, 24 in. bbl., No. 3 Mossberg aperture rear sight, hooded ramp front sight, swivels, approx. 5 lbs. Mfg. 1933-1935.

$300 $200 $150 $90 $70 $65 $60

MODEL 44 – similar to Model 40, but with heavier target stock, approx. 6 lbs. Mfg. 1934-35.

$400 $300 $275 $225 $175 $135 $75

MODEL 42 – .22 S, L, or LR cal., first model with 7 rd. magazine, 24 in. bbl., front ramp, sporting bbl., and rear aperture sights, 42 in. overall length, approx. 5 lbs. Mfg. 1935-1937.

$250 $200 $125 $100 $70 $65 $60

MODEL 42A – .22 S, L, or LR cal., redesign of Model 42, new master action with shorter bolt and receiver. Mfg. 1937-38.

$250 $200 $125 $100 $70 $65 $60

MODEL 42B – .22 S, L, or LR cal., same basic specs. as Model 42A, approx. 6 lbs. Mfg. 1938-1941.

$250 $200 $125 $100 $70 $65 $60

MODEL 42C – .22 S, L, or LR cal., similar to Model 42B, with open bbl. and bead front sights. Mfg. 1938-1941.

$200 $150 $100 $90 $80 $70 $65

MODEL 42M – .22 S, L, or LR cal., 7 shot magazine, bolt action, two-piece Mannlicher-style stock, 23 in. barrel, 40 in. overall length, front ramp, open bbl., and receiver aperture sights, trapdoor buttplate for extra mag. in buttstock, 6 3/4 lbs. Mfg. 1940-1944.

$300 $250 $200 $150 $100 $75 $50

Add $40 for extra magazine in buttstock.

GRADING - PPGS™ 100% 98% 95% 90% 80% 70% 60% LAST MSR

MODELS 42M(a), 42M(b), 42M(c) – similar to Model 42M with minor changes in extractors and sights. Mfg. 1944-50.

$300 $250 $200 $150 $100 $75 $50

MODEL 42MB – military version of the Model 42M, approx. 50,000 mfg. for U.S. and British troops as a training rifle. "US Property" marked with serial number, usually found w/o bbl. sight. Mfg. 1942-43.

$350 $250 $200 $150 $110 $100 $75

Add $50 for Lend-Lease models with British proofs.

MODEL L42A – left-handed version of Model 42A with true left-handed aperture sight, walnut stock, 1 1/4 in. swivels. Mfg. 1937-1938.

$750 $600 $500 $400 $300 $200 $175

MODEL 43 – .22 S, L, or LR cal., target rifle, 7-round magazine, external trigger adjustment, 13/16 in. diameter barrel, 26 in. long walnut stock with four-position 1 1/4 in. swivels in front, Lyman 17A front sight, Lyman 57 MS receiver peep sight, rare. Mfg. 1937-38.

$350 $300 $250 $200 $175 $150 $135

Add $100 for 43S Model and $100 for 43SS Model.

MODEL L43 – left-handed version of Model 43 target rifle with left-handed Lyman 57 MS rear aperture sight, rare. Mfg. 1937-38.

$750 $600 $500 $400 $300 $225 $200

Add $100 for models with true left-handed Mossberg scope.

MODEL 43B – similar to Model 44B.

$350 $300 $250 $200 $175 $150 $135

MODEL 44B – .22 S, L, LR cal. target model, mag. fed, 26 in. heavy bbl., front ramp and No. 4 receiver aperture sights, four-position front swivels, walnut stock, 43 in. overall length, approx. 8 lbs. Mfg. 1938-41.

$350 $300 $250 $200 $185 $175 $150

MODEL 44US – .22 S, L, or LR cal. target model, 7 round magazine, bolt action, 26 in. heavy bbl., OAL 43 in., approx. 8 1/2 lbs., ramp front sight with hood, rear aperture sight, detachable swivels. Mfg. 1943-45.

$350 $275 $200 $165 $150 $135 $125

MODEL 44US (US PROPERTY MARKED) – used by all branches of military for target training, approx. 53,000 mfg. 1943-44.

$350 $300 $250 $175 $150 $125 $100

MODELS 44US(a), 44US(b), 44US(c), 44US(d) – same rifle as 44US with minor changes in sights and extractors. Mfg. 1944-49.

$300 $250 $200 $175 $150 $135 $125

MODEL 45 – .22 S, L, or LR cal., tube fed, bolt action, 24 in. heavy target bbl., hooded front, sporting barrel, and receiver aperture sights, OAL 42 1/2 in., approx. 6 3/4 lbs. Mfg. 1935-1937.

$250 $200 $150 $125 $100 $85 $65

MODEL 45-A – .22 S, L, or LR cal., similar to Model 45 with newer, master action. Mfg. 1937-38.

$250 $200 $150 $135 $125 $100 $85

MODEL L45-A – .22 S, L, or LR cal., similar to Model 45-A, true left-handed version. Mfg. 1937-1938.

$750 $500 $400 $300 $200 $150 $100

MODEL 46 – .22 S, L, or LR cal., tube fed, bolt action, 26 in. heavy bbl., overall 44 1/2 in., beavertail walnut stock, hooded ramp front, and rear aperture sight, 7 1/2 lbs. Mfg. 1935-1937.

$300 $250 $175 $135 $125 $100 $85

MODEL 46T – .22 S, L, or LR cal., similar to Model 46 with heavier bbl. and stock. Mfg. 1936-37.

$500 $400 $350 $250 $200 $150 $100

MODEL 46A – .22 S, L, or LR cal., similar to Model 46 with master action. Mfg. 1937-38.

$300 $200 $150 $135 $125 $100 $85

MODEL 46-ALS – .22 S, L, or LR cal., similar to Model 46-A with Lyman 17A front and 57 MS rear aperture sights, rare. Mfg. 1937-1938.

$350 $300 $250 $225 $200 $175 $150

MODEL L46-ALS – .22 S, L, or LR cal., similar to Model 46-ALS with true left-handed action and left-handed Lyman rear sight, very rare. Mfg. 1937-1938.

$750 $500 $400 $300 $225 $200 $175

GRADING - PPGS™	100%	98%	95%	90%	80%	70%	60%	LAST MSR

MODEL 46B – .22 S, L, or LR cal., tube fed, new streamlined design, 43 1/3 in. overall, walnut stock, 7 lbs. Mfg. 1938-45.

	$250	$200	$150	$110	$100	$85	$75	

MODEL 46B-T – .22 S, L, or LR cal., heavy barrel and stock, target version of Model 46-B, rare. Mfg. 1938.

	$450	$300	$250	$200	$150	$110	$95	

MODEL 46M – .22 S, L, or LR cal., bolt action, tube fed, with two-piece Mannlicher-style walnut stock, 23 in. bbl., overall 40 in., hooded front, sporting bbl., and rear aperture sights, 7 lbs. Mfg. 1940-1945.

	$350	$300	$250	$200	$150	$110	$95	

MODELS 46M(a), 46M(b) – .22 S, L, or LR cal., similar to Model 46M with minor changes in sights. Mfg. 1945-1952.

	$350	$300	$250	$200	$150	$110	$95	

MODEL 50 – .22 S, L, or LR cal., semi-auto, tube fed through buttstock, 24 in. bbl., overall 43 3/4 in., hooded front sight and open bbl. sights, no swivels, 6 3/4 lbs. Mfg. 1939-1942.

	$250	$200	$150	$135	$125	$110	$85	

MODEL 51 – .22 S, L, or LR cal., similar to Model 50 with receiver aperture sight, heavier, beavertail stock, QD swivels, 7 1/4 lbs. Mfg. 1939.

	$250	$200	$150	$125	$110	$85	$65	

MODEL 51M – .22 S, L, or LR cal., similar to Model 51 with two-piece Mannlicher style walnut stock, 20 in. bbl, 40 in. overall, front ramp, rear aperture, sporting bbl. sights, 7 lbs. Mfg. 1939-46.

	$300	$250	$175	$150	$125	$110	$95	

MODEL 140B – .22 S, L, or LR cal., bolt action, mag. fed, 24 1/2 in. bbl., 42 in. overall, walnut stock, front ramp, sporting bbl., and rear aperture sight, 5 3/4 lbs. Mfg. 1957-1958.

	$200	$150	$135	$125	$110	$85	$65	

MODEL 140K – .22 S, L, or LR cal., similar to Model 140B with post front and no rear aperture sight. Mfg. 1955-1958.

	$200	$150	$125	$80	$70	$60	$50	

MODEL 142A – .22 S, L, or LR cal., bolt action, 7 round mag., carbine model with fold down forearm, walnut stock with sling, 18 in. bbl., 27 in. overall length, rear aperture sight and military front sight, no bbl. sight, early models had "T" shaped bolt handles and wood forearms, later models had round knob bolt handle and black plastic forearm, 5 lbs. Mfg. 1949-1957.

	$300	$200	$150	$125	$110	$85	$65	

MODEL 142K – .22 S, L, or LR cal., similar to Model 142A with less expensive sporting barrel and post front type sights, no aperture sight. Mfg. 1953-1957.

	$300	$200	$150	$100	$80	$75	$55	

MODEL 144 – .22 S, L, or LR cal., full target rifle, heavy 26 in. bbl., 43 in. overall length, 8 lbs., QD swivels, four-position front swivels, rear aperture, front ramp sights, "T" shaped bolt handle. Mfg. 1949-1954.

	$350	$250	$200	$165	$150	$135	$125	

MODEL 144LS – .22 S, L, or LR cal., similar to Model 144, with round knob handle, Lyman 57 MS rear aperture and 17A front sight. Mfg. 1954-60.

	$350	$300	$275	$250	$200	$185	$165	

MODEL 144LS-A – .22 S, L, or LR cal., similar to Model 144LS, with Mossberg S 130 rear aperture in place of Lyman 57 MS sight. Mfg. 1960-1979.

	$350	$275	$250	$225	$185	$165	$150	

MODEL 144LS-B – .22 S, L, or LR cal., last generation of 144 series, 27 in. bbl., 15/16 in. diameter, 44 in. overall length, new Mossberg S 331 aperture, Lyman 17A front sight, 8 1/2 lbs. Mfg. 1979-85.

	$350	$275	$250	$210	$190	$175	$165	

MODEL 146-B – .22 S, L, or LR cal., bolt action, tube fed, capacity of 30S, 23L, 20LR, 26 in. bbl., OAL 43 1/4 in., ramp front, leaf bbl. and rear aperture sights, walnut Monte Carlo stock with cheekpiece, QD swivels, adj. trigger, Schnabel forend, 7 lbs. Mfg. 1949-1954.

	$300	$250	$175	$125	$100	$85	$65	

MODEL 146B-A – similar to Model 146-B, with different bbl. sight. Mfg. 1954-58.

	$300	$250	$175	$125	$100	$85	$65	

GRADING - PPGS™	100%	98%	95%	90%	80%	70%	60%	LAST MSR

MODEL 151-K – .22 S, L, or LR cal., semi-auto, butt fed, 24 in. bbl., overall 44 in., open sights, walnut Monte Carlo stock with cheekpiece and Schnabel forend, 6 lbs. Mfg. 1950-51.

$250 $175 $135 $100 $80 $70 $60

MODEL 151(M) – .22 S, L, or LR cal., semi-auto butt fed, capacity 15LR, 20 in. bbl., overall 40 in., two-piece Mannlicher-style walnut stock, QD swivels, steel buttplate, hooded ramp front, sporting rear, micro-click aperture sights, 7 lbs. Mfg. 1946-47.

$300 $250 $175 $135 $125 $100 $85

MODELS 151M(a), 151M(b), 151M(c) – similar to Model 151M with minor changes in buttplate and sights. Mfg. 1947-58.

$300 $250 $175 $135 $125 $100 $85

MODEL 152 – .22 S, L, or LR cal., 18 in. barrel, mag. fed with 7 round capacity, adj. receiver aperture and military post front sights, hinged, fold-down forend, walnut Monte Carlo stock with adj. sling, approx. 38 in. overall, 5 lbs. Mfg. 1948-1952.

$300 $200 $150 $125 $100 $85 $65

MODEL 152K – similar to Model 152 with open sights. Mfg. 1950-57.

$200 $150 $110 $100 $90 $75 $50

MODEL 320B – .22 S, L, or LR cal., single shot, junior target model, bolt action, new closed breech design, 24 in. bbl., overall 43 1/2 in., 5 3/4 lbs., walnut finish Monte Carlo stock with swivels and pistol grip, front ramp, rear aperture and sporting bbl. sights. Mfg. 1960-71.

$200 $150 $125 $110 $85 $75 $55

MODELS 320K, 320K-A – similar to Model 320B with open sights, no swivels, later models marked 321, 321K. Mfg. 1960-80.

$200 $150 $100 $70 $60 $55 $50

MODEL 333 – .22 LR cal., semi-auto, 20 in. barrel with full mag., checkered Monte Carlo pistol grip stock and forearm with sling swivels, blue finish, gold trigger, 6 1/4 lbs. Mfg. 1972 - disc.

$225 $175 $145 $125 $100 $85 $65

MODELS 340B, 340B-A – .22 S, L, or LR cal., bolt action, 7 round magazine, 24 in. sporting barrel, 43 1/2 in. overall length, walnut, Monte Carlo stock with cheekpiece and pistol grip, front ramp, rear aperture sights, 6 1/2 lbs. Mfg. 1958-1980.

$200 $150 $125 $110 $85 $75 $55

At least one example of a Model 340B smoothbore gun is known. This particular specimen was factory fitted with a stock that lacked a magazine cut-out, so the gun could only be fired as a single shot. The muzzle was not threaded to accept any sort of barrel adaptor.

MODELS 340K, 340K-A – similar to Model 340B with open sights, later models marked 341. Mfg. 1958-80.

$200 $150 $125 $100 $70 $60 $55

MODEL 340M – .22 S, L, or LR cal. bolt action, mag. fed, same operating design as other 340 series, with one-piece, walnut Mannlicher-style Monte Carlo stock with pistol grip and swivels, 18 1/2 in. bbl., 38 1/2 in. overall, open rear and bead front sights, rare, 5 1/4 lbs. Mfg. 1970-72.

$650 $500 $350 $250 $185 $175 $165

MODEL 342 – .22 S, L, or LR cal., bolt action, mag. fed, carbine model with hinged, black plastic, fold-down forend, walnut Monte Carlo stock with swivels and sling, 18 in. bbl., 38 in. overall length, military post front and rear aperture sights, 5 lbs. Mfg. 1957-1959.

$300 $200 $150 $110 $85 $75 $55

MODELS 342K, 342K-A – similar to Model 342 with open sights. Mfg. 1958-71.

$200 $175 $150 $100 $75 $55 $50

MODELS 344, 344K – .22 S, L, or LR cal., bolt action, mag. fed, walnut finish, checkered stock, 344K is carbine length. Mfg. 1985.

$300 $200 $150 $125 $85 $75 $55

MODEL 346B – .22 S, L, or LR cal., bolt action tube feed, closed-breech design, walnut Monte Carlo stock with cheekpiece, QD swivels, capacity 25S, 20L, 18LR, 24 in. bbl., 42 1/2 in. overall length, rear aperture, sporting bbl., hooded front ramp sights, 6 1/2 lbs. Mfg. 1958-1960.

$300 $250 $200 $150 $125 $85 $75

MODELS 346K, 346K-A – similar to Model 346B w/open sights. Mfg. 1958-68.

$200 $175 $150 $125 $80 $70 $55

GRADING - PPGS™	100%	98%	95%	90%	80%	70%	60%	LAST MSR

MODEL 350K – .22 LR cal., semi-auto, LR only, mag. fed, walnut Monte Carlo stock with pistol grip and cheekpiece, 23 1/2 in. bbl., OAL 43 1/2 in., open sights, 6 lbs. Mfg. 1958-1960.

$300	$200	$150	$125	$60	$50	$40	

MODEL 350 K-A – similar to Model 350K with dovetail bbl. sight. Mfg. 1960-1968.

$300	$200	$150	$100	$60	$50	$40	

MODEL 351K – .22 LR cal., semi-auto, tube fed through stock, walnut Monte Carlo stock with pistol grip, 24 in. bbl., 43 in. overall length, 6 lbs. Mfg. 1958-1960.

$300	$200	$150	$100	$60	$50	$40	

MODEL 351K-A – similar to Model 351K with dovetail bbl. sight. Mfg. 1960-1968.

$300	$200	$150	$100	$60	$50	$40	

MODEL 352 – .22 LR cal., mag. fed, carbine model with fold-down black plastic forend, walnut Monte Carlo stock, pistol grip, swivels, web strap, 18 in. bbl., OAL 38 in., rear peep, post front sights, 5 lbs. Mfg. 1957-1959.

$300	$200	$150	$100	$75	$65	$55	

MODELS 352K, 352 K-A, 352K-B – similar to Model 352 with open sights. Mfg. 1960-71.

$200	$175	$150	$100	$70	$65	$55	

MODEL 353 – similar to Model 352K-A, except has front ramp and open rear sights, w/o swivels, 5 lbs. Mfg. 1972-1985.

$300	$200	$150	$100	$70	$65	$55	

MODEL 354 – similar to Model 353, except stock configuration was altered. Mfg. 1985 - disc.

$250	$200	$150	$100	$70	$65	$55	

MODEL 377, "PLINKSTER" – .22 LR cal., semi-auto, tube fed, synthetic stock with thumbhole, capacity 15 rds., 20 in. bbl., OAL 40 in., 6 1/4 lbs., equipped with 4X scope. Mfg. 1977-1979.

$300	$250	$200	$150	$100	$85	$75	

MODELS 380, 380S – .22 LR cal., same basic design as Model 377, only with solid wood stock, open sights. Model 480 same in 1985. Mfg. 1980-85.

$250	$200	$150	$100	$75	$65	$55	

MODEL 400 "PALAMINO" – .22 S, L, and LR cal., lever action, tube fed, walnut, beavertail stock and forearm, crossbolt safety, 24 in. bbl., overall length, 41 in., bead front, open rear sights, 5 1/2 lbs. Mfg. 1959-64.

$350	$300	$250	$200	$150	$135	$100	

Model 400-A similar to in specs and value, dovetail.

MODEL 402 "PALAMINO" – carbine version of Model 400, 20 in. barrel. Mfg. 1961-71.

$350	$300	$250	$200	$150	$135	$100	

MODEL 430 – .22 LR cal., semi-auto, tubular mag. under bbl. with capacity of 18 LR, walnut checkered Monte Carlo stock and checkered forend, 24 in. bbl., OAL 43 1/2 in., open sights, 6 1/4 lbs. Mfg. 1970-1971.

$300	$250	$175	$100	$75	$65	$55	

MODEL 432 – similar to Model 430 with 20 in. bbl., straight grip, smooth stock and forend, walnut finish. Mfg. 1970-71.

$300	$250	$175	$100	$65	$60	$50	

MODEL 480 – .22 LR cal., similar to Models 380 and 380S.

$300	$250	$200	$150	$130	$120	$100	

MODEL 620K – .22 WMR cal., single shot, bolt action, walnut Monte Carlo stock, pistol grip, cheekpiece, sling swivels, 24 in. bbl., overall 44 3/4 in., open rear, post front sights, 6 lbs. Mfg. 1959-60.

$250	$200	$150	$115	$100	$85	$75	

MODEL 620K-A – similar to Model 620K with change in bbl. sight. Mfg. 1960-68.

$250	$200	$150	$115	$100	$85	$75	

MODELS 640K, 640K-S – similar to 620 series, but 5 shot mag. repeater. Mfg. 1959-84.

$300	$250	$200	$150	$125	$105	$90	

MODEL 640KS – .22 WMR cal., similar to Model 640K with deluxe checkered stock and gold trigger. Mfg. 1960-68.

$300	$250	$200	$150	$135	$120	$110	

GRADING - PPGS™	100%	98%	95%	90%	80%	70%	60%	LAST MSR

MODEL 640M – full-length, Mannlicher-styled stock, version of 640, checkered Monte Carlo cheekpiece, pistol grip, swivels and leather strap, heavy receiver, jeweled bolt, 20 in. bbl., overall 40 3/4 in., open rear and bead front sights, 6 lbs. Mfg. 1971.

	$650	$500	$400	$300	$200	$165	$150	

MODEL 642K - .22 WMR cal., carbine style, bolt action, 5 rd. mag., fold-down forend, walnut stock with web sling, 18 in. bbl., overall 38 1/4 in., open bbl. and bead front sights, 5 lbs. Mfg. 1960-1968.

	$400	$350	$300	$250	$200	$150	$125	

MODEL 800A/B/C/F - .222 Rem. (800F), .22-250 Rem. (800C), .243 Win. (800B), or .308 Win. (800A) cal., bolt action, 22 in. barrel, folding sight, checkered pistol grip stock. Mfg. 1967-disc.

	$500	$400	$325	$300	$275	$225	$150	

MODEL 800VT – similar to 800, except .222 Rem., .22-250 Rem., or .243 Win. cal., 24 in. heavy barrel, no sights. Mfg. 1968-disc.

	$500	$400	$325	$300	$275	$225	$150	

MODEL 800D – 6.5mm Mag., .22-250 Rem., .243 Rem., or .308 Win. cal., similar to 800, with roll-over combination and cheekpiece, checkered stock with rosewood forearm tip and pistol cap, no .222 Rem. available. Mfg. 1970 only.

	$500	$400	$325	$300	$275	$225	$150	

MODEL 800E - .350 Rem. Mag. cal., 4 shot mag., approx. 53 mfg. 1970 only.

	$850	$775	$700	$625	$550	$500	$450	

MODEL 800M - .22-250 Rem., .243 Win., or .308 Win. cal., similar to 800, except 20 in. barrel, full-length stock, spoon bolt handle. Mfg. 1969-1972.

	$750	$500	$400	$300	$200	$160	$145	

MODEL 810 - .270 Win., .30-06, 6.5mm Rem. Mag., or .338 Win. Mag. cal., bolt action, 22 or 24 in. barrel, rear leaf sight, checkered Monte Carlo stock. Mfg. 1970-disc.

	$500	$400	$325	$300	$275	$225	$150	

MODEL 1500 MOUNTAINEER GRADE I - .223 Rem., .243 Win., .270 Win., .30-06, or 7mm Rem. Mag. cal., bolt action, 22 or 24 (7mm Rem. Mag. only) in. barrel, 5 or 6 shot mag., available with or without sights, hardwood stock is satin finished, blued finish, about 7 lbs. 10 oz. Imported 1986-87 only.

	$325	$275	$240	$195	$180	$165	$150	*$335*

Add $15 for 7mm Rem. Mag. cal., $25 for iron sights.

In 1985, Mossberg purchased the parts inventory and importing rights for those Model 1500 rifles that Smith & Wesson imported from Howa of Japan. These models were identical to those models which S&W disc.

* ***Model 1500 Mountaineer Grade I Varmint*** – .22-250 Rem., .223 Rem., or .308 Win. cal., similar to Model 1500 Grade I, except has 24 in. heavy barrel only, Monte Carlo stock. Imported 1986-87 only.

	$385	$325	$300	$250	$205	$190	$175	*$457*

Add $10 for parkerized finish (oil finished stock with swivels - not available in .22-250 Rem. cal.).

Blue finish and high gloss wood finish available with .22-250 Rem. or .223 Rem. cal. only. Parkerized variation is available in .223 Rem. or .308 Win. cal. only (matte wood finish, includes swivels).

MODEL 1500 MOUNTAINEER GRADE II – .223 Rem., .243 Win., .270 Win., .30-06, .300 Win. Mag., .338 Win. Mag., or 7mm Rem. Mag. cal., similar to Grade I Mountaineer, except has select checkered American walnut stock. Imported 1986-87 only.

	$350	$295	$260	$205	$190	$175	$160	*$368*

Add $15 for Mag. cals.
Add $25 for iron sights.

MODEL 1550 – similar to Model 1500 Mountaineer Grade I, except has detachable mag. and available in standard cals. (.243 Win., .270 Win., or .30-06), with or without sights. Imported 1986-87 only.

	$365	$305	$275	$225	$190	$175	$160	*$391*

Add $24 for iron sights.

MODEL 1700 LS – .243 Win., .270 Win., or .30-06 cal., no sights, jeweled bolt body and knurled bolt handle, detachable mag., Schnabel forend, deluxe checkering, 7 lbs. Imported 1986-87 only.

	$450	$400	$350	$275	$225	$200	$190	*$492*

Mossberg "Targo" Smoothbore Models

These dual-purpose smoothbore rifles were designed to fire both .22 RF bullets and shotshell ammunition. Targo barrels are threaded either externally (Models 26T, 42TR, 42T, B42T) or internally (Models 320TR, 340TR) at the muzzle for attachment of rifled and smoothbore adapters which enable

GRADING - PPGS™	100%	98%	95%	90%	80%	70%	60%	LAST MSR

the shooter to use the gun as a standard rifle, or (with the smoothbore adapter installed) as a miniature shotgun. Mossberg produced a line of Targo accessories including a barrel-mounted miniature clay target launcher, a pistol grip hand trap frame, a hand thrower (three known variations), a target carrier, clay targets, hard rubber "practice" targets, and a target catching net. The presence of one or more of these accessories augments the value of any model Targo gun. Prices quoted are for guns with all listed features exclusive of Targo accessories.

MODEL 26-T SINGLE SHOT – .22 RF/shotshell cal., bolt action, thumb lever safety located at rear of bolt, black plastic buttplate and contoured black plastic trigger guard (#R413), rifle-style open rear sight with screw adjustments for windage and elevation, shotgun style elevated front bead sight with removable sight hood, smoothbore and rifled screw-on barrel adapters and spanner wrench for adapter removal and installation, stock generally provided with sling swivels, forend necks down toward muzzle, takedown screw has retaining bail to facilitate removal by hand. Mfg. 1940-42 (only 873 mfg.).

$600	$450	$375	$335	$280	$245	$220	

100% price is estimated since an example would be extremely rare.

MODEL 42T BOLT ACTION REPEATER – .22 RF/shotshell cal., box magazine (7- round) fitted with adapter screw to enable firing of .22 Short cartridges, same safety, buttplate, optional stock swivels, and shotgun style front sight as Model 26T, #R145 contoured black plastic trigger guard, supplied with the smoothbore barrel adapter only (rifled adapter, open rear sight, and front sight hood were not provided), produced 1940-42 (906 guns made), examples in 95% or better condition are uncommon.

$500	$325	$310	$295	$260	$235	$200	

MODEL 42TR BOLT ACTION REPEATER – .22 RF/shotshell cal., produced before and after WWII until roughly 1949. Pre-war (1940-42) guns identical to Model 42T except rifled adapter, open rear sight, and front sight hood were provided, and no stock swivels. The earliest pre-war 42TRs were marked using a 42T barrel stamp and a separate "R" (stamped to the right of the "T"). Post-war (1946-49) guns have slotted takedown screw, magazine plate, shorter unnecked forend, and (frequently) a blue bolt knob. The most common of all Targo guns. A total of 6,577 guns were produced during the period 1940-42 (post-war production figures are not available). Both early and late versions of this model are comparably priced.

$650	$400	$325	$280	$245	$190	$175	

Add $250 for cased gun with clay targets and Targo accessories.
Cased Targo guns with all accessories have been seen for $1,000+.

Note: A very small number of 42TRs were supplied with fitted cases and Targo accessories and may have been used as dealer displays. Several variations in the internal compartmentalization of these cases have been noted. The pre-war 42TR display guns came in a hard (plywood) luggage case. The post-war guns were supplied in a semi-hard (fiberboard) luggage case.

MODEL B42T BOLT ACTION REPEATER – .22 RF/shotshell cal., identical to the Model 42TR, except stock has sling swivels and metal buttplate with trapdoor for magazine storage. Gun was supplied with extended 15-round box magazine in addition to the standard 7-round mag. A comparatively scarce model marketed exclusively through mail order stores (e.g., Spiegel) in the early 1940s. According to factory records, only 250 guns were made, all in 1940.

$600	$465	$385	$350	$325	$285	$250	

The 15 round magazine originally supplied with this model is scarce - good specimens are currently selling for approx. $85-$120 (may exceed legal capacity limits, depending on state).

MODEL 320TR SINGLE SHOT BOLT ACTION – .22 RF/shotshell, automatic safety with thumb lever located on right side of receiver, black plastic buttplate and contoured black plastic trigger guard. Rifle-style ("U" notch) rear sight adjustable for elevation (via sliding wedge) and windage (by deflecting sight arm laterally by hand). Sporting type vertical blade front sight. Gun supplied with rifled and smoothbore screw-in barrel adapters. A wire target carrier and a hand thrower for launching miniature clay targets were included with each gun. Limited mfg. 1961-62.

$500	$300	$275	$190	$150	$135	$115	

Factory records indicate that only 962 guns were sold during the production period.

MODEL 340TR BOLT ACTION REPEATER – .22 RF/shotshell cal., 7-round box magazine featuring adjustable top bar to accommodate feeding of .22 S, L, or LR cartridges. Two known variations of thumb lever safety markings (words "OFF"/"ON" and red dot). Other features identical to Model 320TR. Limited mfg. 1961-62.

$500	$300	$275	$215	$165	$145	$125	

Factory records indicate that only 2,026 guns were sold during the production period.

GRADING - PPGS™	100%	98%	95%	90%	80%	70%	60%	*LAST MSR*

RIFLES: BOLT ACTION

4x4 RIFLE – .22-250 Rem. (new 2011), .25-06 Rem., .243 Win. (new 2011), .270 Win., .30-06, .270 WSM (mfg. 2010-2013), 7mm-08 Rem., 7mm WSM (mfg. 2010-2013), 7mm Rem. Mag., .300 Win. Mag., .300 WSM (mfg. 2010-2013), .308 Win. (new 2011), or .338 Win. Mag. cal., short or long action, 22 in. non-fluted or 24 in. fluted barrel with muzzle brake became standard in 2010, long action with 24 in. fluted barrel and no muzzle brake became available during mid-2011, 4 or 5 shot detachable box mag., matte blue or Marinecote finish, sculpted walnut, Monte Carlo grey or brown laminate (Marinecote only), black Classic (new 2010), skeletonized synthetic, or Classic (new 2009) stock, vent. forearm, Weaver style scope base, rifle sights (.30-06, .300 Win. Mag., or .338 Win. Mag. only), LBA adj. trigger became standard 2009, 6.7 - 7.8 lbs. Mfg. 2007-2014.

$415 $375 $325 $300 $250 $225 $195 *$485*

Add $49 for Marinecote finish.
Add $208 for laminate or $158 for walnut stock.
Add $158 for WSM cals. (disc. 2013).
Add $186 for 22 in. non-fluted barrel (select cals. only).
Add $49 for scope package (3-9x40mm, not available in .25-06 or .338 Win. mag. cal).

In 2009, a LBA (lightning bolt action) adjustable trigger became standard.

ATR (ALL TERRAIN RIFLE/MODEL 100) – .243 Win. (new 2006), .270 Win., .30-06, 7mm-08 Rem. (new 2011), or .308 Win. (new 2006) cal., 22 in. free floating non-fluted or fluted (new 2010) barrel, short or long action, matte blue or Marinecote (.270 Win. or .30-06, disc. 2011), walnut (new 2006), black synthetic, Dura-Wood synthetic (disc. 2009) or 100% Realtree AP (disc. 2012), Realtree Xtra (new 2013), Mossy Oak New Break-Up (disc.), Mossy Oak Brush, or Mossy Oak Break Up Infinity (new 2011) camo coverage stock with recoil pad, 3 shot top loading magazine, approx. 7 lbs. Mfg. 2005-2014.

$315 $275 $235 $210 $175 $140 $110 *$375*

Add $38 for 3-9x40mm scope (new 2006).
Add $38 for rifle sights and 22. in. non-fluted barrel (new 2007).
Add $50 for walnut or camo stock.
Add $47 for Marinecote (long action only, disc. 2011).
Add $38 for Dura-Wood synthetic stock (long action only, disc. 2009).

In 2009, a LBA (lightning bolt action) adjustable trigger became standard.

* ***ATR Bantam/Super Bantam (Model 100)*** – .243 Win., 7mm-08 Rem., or .308 Win. cal., short action, 20 in. fluted barrel, 5 shot, Weaver type base, matte blue metal finish, choice of black synthetic (Super Bantam) or walnut (Bantam) stock and forearm, Super Bantam has adj. 12-13 in. LOP, Bantam has fixed 12 in. LOP, 6 1/2 - 7 3/4 lbs. Mfg. 2007-2014.

$315 $275 $235 $210 $175 $140 $110 *$375*

Add $38 for 3-9x40mm scope (Super Bantam only).
Add $50 for walnut stock.

* ***ATR Deer Thugs Scoped Combo*** – .243 Win., .270 Win., .30-06, .308 Win., or 7mm-08 Rem. cal., 22 in. fluted barrel, matte blue finish, 5 shot, Weaver style base, LBA adj. trigger, synthetic stock with Deer Thugs engraving, Mossy Oak New Break-Up Infinity camo coverage, 3-9x40mm variable scope, sling, 6 3/4-7 lbs. Disc. 2014.

$415 $375 $325 $300 $250 $225 $195 *$485*

* ***ATR Night Train Special (Model 100)*** – .308 Win. cal., 22 in. fluted barrel, short action, 4 shot mag., adj. LBA trigger, Picatinny rail, top load magazine, matte blue finish, synthetic stock, includes 4-16x50mm variable scope w/sun shade and flip-open lens protector, bipod. Mfg. 2010-2014.

$525 $475 $400 $350 $300 $250 $200 *$615*

* ***ATR Night Train 2*** – .308 Win. cal., 22 in. fluted barrel, short action, 4 shot mag., matte blue or Digital Green camo (disc. 2011) finish, synthetic stock, Picatinny rail, top load magazine, adj. LBA trigger, Barska 6-24x60mm illuminated reticle scope and Harris bipod. Mfg. 2010-2014.

$775 $675 $575 $525 $425 $350 $275 *$891*

Add $39 for Digital Green camo finish (disc. 2011).

* ***ATR Night Train 3*** – .308 Win. cal., 22 in. fluted barrel, 5 shot, LBA trigger, matte blue finish, OD Green synthetic stock, Picatinny rail, includes 4-16x50mm variable scope with sun shade/lens protectors, and bipod. Mfg. 2012-2014.

$575 $509 $425 $400 $315 $275 $225 *$658*

* ***ATR Night Train 4*** – .308 Win. cal., 22 in. fluted barrel, 5 shot, LBA trigger, Picatinny rail, matte blue finish, Multi-Cam camo stock, includes 6-24x60mm variable scope with illuminated reticle/ sun shade/lens protectors, neoprene comb raising kit with foam inserts. Mfg. 2012-2014.

$775 $675 $575 $525 $425 $350 $275 *$891*

GRADING - PPGS™	100%	98%	95%	90%	80%	70%	60%	LAST MSR

MODEL 801 HALF-PINT PLINKSTER – .22 LR cal., 16 in. free floating tapered barrel, blue finish, 12 1/4 in. LOP, single shot, crossbolt safety, adj. rifle sights, pistol grip uncheckered hardwood stock, 4 lbs. Disc. 2018.

	$195	$170	$145	$135	$100	$90	$70	*$234*

MODEL 802 PLINKSTER – .22 LR cal., 18 or 21 (disc. 2014) in. barrel with adj. iron sights, aluminum alloy receiver, blue or brushed chrome (21 in. barrel only, mfg. 2007-2014) finish, wood (mfg. 2009-2019), black synthetic, black pink (mfg. 2009-2018), or pink marble (mfg. 2009-2018) synthetic stock with (disc. 2012) or w/o thumbhole, Sport Grip skeletonized stock became optional mid-2012-2018, 10 shot mag., 4-4.5 lbs. New 2006.

MSR $204	$175	$155	$130	$120	$95	$80	$65	

Add $12 for 4x scope (802 Plinkster Scoped Combo) in black sport grip stock (disc. 2018) or black synthetic stock (new 2019).
Add $45 for wood stock (mfg. 2009-2019).
Add $20 for brushed chrome finish (mfg. 2007-2014).
Add $44 for synthetic sport grip stock in Pink (disc. 2016) or Pink Marble finish (disc. 2018).

* ***Model 802 Bantam Plinkster*** – .22 LR cal., 18 in. barrel with adj. iron sights, aluminum alloy receiver, blue or brushed chrome (mfg. 2010-2012) finish, wood, black (disc. 2013) or pink marble (disc. 2013) synthetic stock with (mfg. 2010-2013) or w/o thumbhole, Sport Grip skeletonized stock became optional mid-2012, 10 shot mag., with or w/o Roadblocker muzzle brake (mfg. 2010-2012), scope became standard 2013, approx. 4 lbs. Disc. 2018.

	$195	$170	$145	$135	$100	$90	$70	*$234*

Add $10 for 4x scope.
Add $38 for pink or thumbhole stock (disc. 2012).
Add $19 for brushed chrome finish (thumbhole stock only, disc. 2012).
Add $124 for Roadblocker muzzle brake (mfg. 2010-2012).

* ***Model 802 Varmint Plinkster*** – .22 LR cal., 21 in. bull barrel with adj. iron sights, aluminum alloy receiver, blue or brushed chrome (mfg. 2007-2014) finish, classic wood, pink (disc.) or black synthetic stock with sport grip, or thumbhole stock with fold down forend (disc. 2012), Sport Grip skeletonized stock became optional mid-2012, 10 shot mag., 5-5 1/2 lbs. Mfg. 2006-2015.

	$195	$170	$145	$135	$100	$90	$70	*$230*

Add $42 for Classic wood stock.
Add $63 for brushed chrome finish (mfg. 2007-2014) with classic wood stock only.

MODEL 817 – .17 HMR cal., 21 in. barrel, 5 shot detachable mag., Weaver style scope bases, aluminum alloy receiver, blue or brushed chrome (disc. 2017) finish, black synthetic (new 2019), black synthetic sport grip (disc. 2018), wood (disc. 2019), or thumbhole (tip-down forend became standard with thumbhole during 2009, disc. 2012) stock, approx. 4 1/2-4 3/4 lbs. New 2007.

MSR $237	$200	$180	$155	$140	$115	$90	$80	

Add $44 for wood (disc. 2019) or thumbhole (disc. 2009) stock.
Add $16 for brushed chrome finish (disc. 2017).
Add $82 for Roadblocker muzzle brake (mfg. 2010-2012).
Add $14 for 3-9x40mm scope or $55 for 3-16x50mm scope with bipod (with Roadblocker muzzle brake only, mfg. 2010-2012).

* ***Model 817 Varmint*** – .17 HMR cal., 21 in. bull barrel, 6 shot, classic wood (disc. 2015) or black Sport Grip synthetic stock, blue or brushed chrome finish, 5-5 1/4 lbs. Disc. 2018.

	$225	$195	$170	$155	$125	$100	$80	*$274*

Add $10 for brushed chrome finish (disc. 2017).
Add $44 for classic wood/blue (disc. 2015) or $59 classic wood/chrome (disc. 2014).
Add $35 for thumbhole stock (disc. 2009).

MVP FLEX – 5.56mm or 7.62 NATO cal., 18 1/2 or 20 (disc. 2016) in. threaded or non-threaded sporter (disc. 2016) or medium bull barrel, matte blue finish, spiral fluted bolt, optional A2 flash suppressor, 10 shot mag., LBA trigger, Picatinny top rail, FLEX TLS-compatible 4-pos. adj./dual comb (new 2017) or 6-pos. adj. stock in black or tan (new 2014), 6 1/2-7 lbs. Mfg. 2013-2018.

	$650	$570	$490	$440	$360	$295	$260	*$764*

Add $15 for threaded barrel with A2 flash suppressor (disc. 2016).

* ***MVP Flex Scoped Combo*** – 5.56mm or 7.62 NATO (new 2014) cal., 18 1/2 in. medium bull fluted or 20 in. sporter fluted (disc. 2016) barrel, matte blue finish, 11 shot mag., LBA trigger, Picatinny top rail, FLEX TLS-compatible 6-pos. adj. stock in black, includes 3-9x32mm scope with lighted reticle and neoprene comb raising kit (disc. 2016) or Vortex Crossfire II 2-7x32mm scope with Dead-Hold BDC reticle (new 2017), 7 1/2-8 3/4 lbs. Mfg. 2013-2018.

	$765	$675	$575	$525	$425	$350	$275	*$897*

GRADING - PPGS™	100%	98%	95%	90%	80%	70%	60%	LAST MSR

* ***MVP Flex Youth*** – 5.56 NATO cal., 20 in. Sporter fluted barrel, 11 shot mag., LBA adj. trigger, matte blue finish, top Picatinny rail, standard black synthetic FLEX stock with 12 in. LOP, 6 lbs. Disc. 2016.

  $625 $545 $470 $425 $345 $285 $260 *$727*

MVP LC – 5.56 NATO, 7.62 NATO, or 6.5 Creedmoor cal., 16 1/4, 18 1/2, or 20 in. medium bull fluted and threaded barrel, SilencerCo ASR muzzle brake (thread cap included), LBA adj. trigger, MDT LSS light chassis aluminum stock, Mil-Spec Magpul CTR adj. LOP stock with A-frame profiile, oversized bolt handle, Picatinny rail, adj. bipod and optional Vortex Viper HS-T 4x zoom and MRAD reticle, matte blue metal finish, 7 1/2-7 3/4 lbs. New 2018.

MSR $1,082 $925 $800 $725 $625 $525 $425 $360

MVP LC (LIGHT CHASSIS) – 5.56 NATO, 7.62 NATO, or 6.5 Creedmoor (new 2017) cal., 16 1/4, 18 1/2, or 20 (new 2017) in. fluted and threaded medium bull barrel with muzzle brake, matte blue barrel finish, 10 shot mag., Picatinny rail, LBA adj. trigger, tactical bolt handle, no sights, lightweight Tan aluminum chassis, Magpul CTR adj. stock, MOE pistol grip, includes bipod, 8-8 1/2 lbs. Mfg. 2015-2017.

$1,200 $1,075 $950 $800 $700 $600 $495 *$1,407*

* ***MVP LC Scoped Combo*** – 5.56 NATO or 7.62 NATO cal., same features as the MVP LC, except includes a Vortex HS-T 4-16x44mm scope with rings, 10 1/8-10 5/8 lbs. Mfg. 2015-2017.

  $1,695 $1,485 $1,250 $1,100 $950 $825 $675 *$1,995*

MVP LR – 5.56 NATO (disc. 2018), 7.62 NATO, 6.5 Creedmoor (new 2017), or .224 Valkyrie (new 2019) cal., 20 or 22 (new 2017) in. fluted and threaded medium bull barrel, matte blue barrel finish, 10 shot Magpul PMAG, tactical bolt handle, dual front swivels, LBA adj. trigger, Picatinny rail, OD Green adj. comb benchrest style stock with integrated rubberized Mosscote finish cheek rest, 7 1/2-8 lbs. New 2015.

MSR $938 $800 $700 $600 $545 $440 $360 $310

MVP LR TACTICAL – 5.56 NATO or 7.62 NATO cal., 16 1/4 in. threaded medium bull barrel, matte blue barrel finish, 10 shot mag., Picatinny rail, oversized bolt handle, rifle sights, LBA adj. trigger, OD Green Patrol style adj. comb stock with integrated rubberized Mosscote finished cheek rest, 7-7 1/2 lbs. Mfg. 2015-2018.

$825 $720 $620 $560 $455 $375 $300 *$974*

MVP LR THUNDER RANCH – 5.56 NATO or 7.62 NATO cal., 20 in. fluted and threaded medium bull barrel, Magpul 10 shot PMAG, LBA trigger, MVP LR stock with KUIU camo finish and adjustable rubberized cheek rest, oversized tactical bolt handle, Picatinny rail, matte blue metal finish, 8 lbs. Mfg. 2019-2020.

$830 $725 $625 $565 $455 $375 $325 *$974*

MVP PATROL – 5.56mm, 7.62 NATO, or .300 ACC Blackout (mfg. 2014 only) cal., 16 1/4 in. medium bull threaded or non-threaded (disc. 2016) barrel, spiral fluted bolt, LBA adj. trigger, matte blue finish, textured stock in black or tan (mfg. 2014-2018) with checkered grip and forend, 10 shot mag., no sights or rifle sights, Picatinny rail, 6 3/4 - 7 1/2 lbs. New 2013.

MSR $613 $520 $455 $390 $355 $285 $235 $200

* ***MVP Patrol Scoped Combo*** – 5.56 NATO, 7.62 NATO (new 2014), or .300 AAC Blackout (disc. 2016) cal., 16 1/4 in. medium bull threaded or non-threaded (disc. 2016) barrel with A2 flash hider, similar to MVP Patrol, except features 3-9x32mm scope with lighted reticle and neoprene comb raising kit (disc. 2016) or 2-7x32mm Vortex Crossfire II variable scope and Vortex rings and neoprene comb raising kit (new 2017), textured black stock only, 8-8 1/2 lbs. Disc. 2018.

  $735 $645 $550 $500 $400 $330 $260 *$865*

MVP PATROL THUNDER RANCH – 5.56 NATO or 7.62 NATO (new 2015) cal., 18 1/2 in. threaded medium bull barrel with matte blue finish, 10 shot, OD Green textured stock with Thunder Ranch logo engraving, checkered grip and forend, 7-7 1/2 lbs. Mfg. 2013-2018.

$650 $570 $490 $440 $360 $295 $260 *$773*

MVP PRECISION – 7.62 NATO, 6.5 Creedmoor, or .224 Valkyrie (new 2019) cal., 20 or 24 in. medium bull threaded barrel, 10 shot PMAG, LBA adj. trigger, oversized trigger guard, Luth-AR MBA-3 adj. stock, Magpul MOE+ grip, features new Mossberg chassis design with stock takedown capability, scalloped bolt handle, Picatinny rail, anodized/matte blue finish, 9.2-10 lbs. New 2018.

MSR $1,450 $1,230 $1,075 $925 $835 $675 $550 $450

MVP PREDATOR – 5.56 NATO, 7.62 NATO (new 2013), 6.5 Creedmoor (new 2017, 20 in. only), or .224 Valkyrie (new 2019) cal., 18 1/2 or 20 in. button rifled fluted medium bull or sporter (mfg. 2013-2016, 20 in. only) barrel, with or without (disc. 2016) threading, matte blue finish, spiral fluted bolt, 10 shot Magpul PMAG (new 2017), compact sporter grey laminate stock forend/grip checkering, with ergonomic pistol grip and palm swell, sling swivels, Weaver style base, LBA trigger system, 7-7 1/2 lbs. Mfg. mid-2011-2020.

$600 $525 $450 $410 $325 $275 $225 *$700*

Add $140 for Vortex Crossfire II 3-9x40mm scope with Dead-Hold BDC reticle (mfg. 2017-2018).

Add $48 for MVP Predator Scoped Combo with 3-9x40mm scope w/rings (mfg. 2013-2016).

GRADING - PPGS™	100%	98%	95%	90%	80%	70%	60%	LAST MSR

MVP SCOUT – 7.62 NATO cal., 16 1/4 in. threaded barrel with A2 flash suppressor, 10 shot mag., matte blue finish, 11 in. forward mounted Picatinny rail, ghost ring rear sight, Picatinny rails on side of forend, LBA adj. trigger, tactical bolt handle, black synthetic stock, includes sling, 6 3/4 lbs. New 2015.

MSR $643	$540	$475	$400	$365	$300	$250	$210	

* ***MVP Scout Scoped Combo*** – 7.62 NATO cal., same features as MVP Scout, except includes a UTG Accushot 1-4x28mm variable scope with 30mm extended eye relief (mfg. 2015 only) or Vortex optics Scout 2-7x scope (new 2016), 8 3/4 lbs. New 2015.

MSR $804	$680	$600	$500	$450	$375	$300	$265	

MVP VARMINT – 5.56 NATO, .204 Ruger, or 7.62 NATO (new 2013) cal., 24 in. button rifled fluted medium bull barrel, with or without (disc. 2016) threading, matte blue finish, 5 or 10 shot mag., grey laminate benchrest stock with ergonomic pistol grip and palm swell, sling swivels, Weaver style base, LBA trigger system, 7 3/4-8 3/4 lbs. Mfg. mid-2011-2018.

	$640	$560	$480	$435	$350	$290	$225	*$753*

Add $182 for Vortex Crossfire II 4-12x44mm scope and bipod (new 2017).
Add $163 for MVP Varmint Scoped Combo with 4-16x50mm scope and bipod (disc. 2016).

PATRIOT – 6.5 Creedmoor (new 2017), .22-250 Rem., .243 Win., 7mm-08 Rem., .308 Win., .25-06 Rem., .270 Win., .30-06, 7mm Rem. Mag., .300 Win. Mag., .338 Win. Mag. (disc. 2020), .375 Ruger (disc. 2018), .450 Bushmaster (new 2019), or .350 Legend (new mid-2019) cal., 20 in. threaded (new 2019), 22 in. fluted, or 24 in. fluted/threaded (new 2020) barrel, 4 or 5 shot box mag., recessed crown, LBA adj. trigger, Weaver-style scope base or adj. fiber optic sights, matte blue or Marinecote (disc. 2018) barrel finish, classic walnut, classic laminate (disc. 2018), or synthetic stock in black finish, 6-1/2-7 1/4 lbs. New 2015.

MSR $421	$360	$315	$270	$245	$200	$160	$140	

Add $16 for .450 Bushmaster cal. (new 2019).
Add $150 for classic walnut stock.
Add $173-$188 for 24 in. threaded barrel, depending on caliber (new 2020).
Add $17 for .375 Ruger cal. (disc. 2018).
Add $66 for Marinecote finish (disc. 2018).
Add $165-$233 for Marinecote barrel finish and classic laminate stock, depending on caliber (disc. 2018).

* ***Patriot Scoped Combo*** – .22-250 Rem., .243 Win., .270 Win., .308 Win., .30-06, 6.5 Creedmoor (new 2018), or .300 Win. Mag. cal., similar to Patriot model, except includes 3-9x40mm variable scope, classic walnut or black synthetic stock, 7 1/2-8 lbs. Mfg. 2015-2018.

	$370	$325	$275	$250	$200	$165	$130	*$435*

Add $149 for classic walnut stock.

* ***Patriot Scoped Combo Mossy Oak Deer Thug*** – .243 Win., .270 Win., .30-06, .308 Win., or .300 Win. Mag. (new 2016) cal., 22 in. fluted barrel, similar to Patriot model, except includes 3-9x40mm variable scope, Deer Thugs engraved synthetic stock, Mossy Oak Break-Up Infinity (mfg. 2015 only), or Kryptek Highlander (new 2016) camo finish, sling, 7 1/2 lbs. Mfg. 2015-2018.

	$370	$325	$275	$250	$200	$165	$130	*$435*

* ***Patriot Vortex Scoped Combo*** – .22-250 Rem. (new 2019), .243 Win., .270 Win., .300 Win. Mag., .308 Win., 338 Win. Mag. (mfg. 2019-2020), 6.5 Creedmoor (new 2018), 7mm Rem. Mag. (new 2019), 7mm-08 Rem. (new 2019), .25-06 (new 2019), or .30-06 cal., 22 in. fluted or 24 in. fluted and threaded (new 2020) barrel, 5 shot box mag., LBA adj. trigger, Weaver-Style scope base, matte blue barrel finish, black synthetic or classic walnut (new mid-2015) stock, includes Vortex Crossfire II 3-9x40mm scope with Dead-Hold BDC reticle, fully multi-coated lenses, and resettable MOA turrets, 7 1/2 lbs. New 2015.

MSR $570	$485	$425	$365	$330	$265	$225	$190	

Add $15 for 24 in. fluted and threaded barrel (new 2020).
Add $182 for classic walnut stock (new mid-2015).

* ***Patriot Bantam*** – .243 Win., .308 Win., or 7mm-08 Rem. cal., 20 in. fluted barrel, 5 shot box mag., 12 in. LOP, adj. LBA trigger, Weaver style base, matte blue finish, walnut stock, 6 3/4 lbs. Mfg. 2015-2018.

	$455	$400	$340	$300	$250	$200	$160	*$542*

* ***Patriot Super Bantam*** – .243 Win., .308 Win., or 7mm-08 Rem. cal., 20 in. fluted barrel, 5 shot box mag., 12-13 in. LOP, adj. LBA trigger, Weaver style base, matte blue barrel finish, black or Kryptek Highlander (new 2016) synthetic stock, 6 1/2 lbs. Mfg. 2015-2018.

	$340	$300	$250	$225	$185	$150	$125	*$396*

Add $39 for Kryptek Highlander stock (new 2016).

GRADING - PPGS™	100%	98%	95%	90%	80%	70%	60%	LAST MSR

* ***Patriot Super Bantam Scoped Combo*** – .243 Win., .308 Win., .350 Legend (new mid-2019), 6.5 Creedmoor (new 2018), or 7mm-08 Rem. cal., 20 or 22 (new mid-2019) in. fluted barrel with matte blue finish, 5 shot mag., includes 3-9x40mm variable scope, synthetic stock with black, Muddy Girl (disc. 2017), Muddy Girl Serenity (new 2018), Muddy Girl Wild (new 2021), Mossy Oak Break-Up Infinity (disc. 2016), or True Timber Strata (new 2019) camo finish, 7 1/2 lbs. New 2015.

MSR $463	$390	$340	$295	$265	$215	$175	$150	

Add $56 for Muddy Girl Serenity (new 2018), Muddy Girl Wild (new 2021), or True Timber Strata (new 2019) camo stock.

Add $38 for Muddy Girl camo stock (disc. 2017).

Add $70 for Mossy Oak Break-Up Infinity camo finish with Deer Thugs engraved stock (disc. 2016).

* ***Patriot With Cerakote*** – 6.5 Creedmoor, .22-250 Rem. (new 2019), .243 Win., .25-06 Rem. (new 2019), 7mm Rem. Mag. (new 2019), 7mm-08 Rem., .300 Win. Mag. (new 2019), .308 Win., .270 Win., .338 Win. (new 2019), .30-06, or .375 Ruger (new 2019) cal., 22 in. fluted or 24 in. fluted/threaded (new 2020) barrel, 6 shot mag., black synthetic stock, Weaver style bases or adj. fiber optic sights, Cerakote finish, 6 1/2 lbs. New 2018.

MSR $483	$410	$360	$315	$285	$225	$185	$160	

Add $15 for 24 in. fluted and threaded barrel (new 2020).

Add $22 for .375 Ruger cal. (new 2019).

Add $36 for .338 Win. Mag. cal. with 24 in. fluted threaded barrel (new 2020).

PATRIOT LR HUNTER – .308 Win., 6.5 Creedmoor, 6.5 PRC, or .300 Win. Mag. cal., 22 or 24 in. fluted and threaded barrel, protective thread cap, 3, 4, or 5 shot drop box mag., LBA adj. trigger, Monte Carlo stock is polymer-coated in Spider Gray finish with light micro-texture, benchrest-style forend, dual swivel studs, top mounted Picatinny rail, spiral fluted bolt, oversized bolt handle, matte blue metal finish, 6.5-7.5 lbs. New 2021.

MSR $766	$655	$575	$490	$445	$360	$295	$250	

PATRIOT NIGHT TRAIN 1 – .308 Win. (disc. 2020) or 6.5 Creedmoor (new 2019) cal., 22 (disc. 2020) or 24 (new 2019) in. fluted standard or threaded barrel, 5 shot box mag., LBA adj. trigger, matte blue barrel finish, Picatinny rail, tactical bolt handle, synthetic stock, includes 4-16x50mm (.308 Win, disc. 2020.) or 6-24x50mm (new 2019, 6.5 Creedmoor) variable scope with lens caps and rings, adj. bipod, black (disc. 2020) or FDE (new 2019) finish, 8 3/4 lbs. New 2015.

MSR $871	$740	$650	$550	$500	$400	$340	$285	

Subtract approx. $180 for 4-16x50mm scope and black finish (disc. 2020).

PATRIOT NIGHT TRAIN 2 & 3 – .308 Win. (Night Train 2) or .300 Win. Mag. (Night Train 3) cal., 22 in. fluted suppressor-ready threaded barrel with removable SilencerCo Saker Trifecta muzzle brake, QD suppresor mounts, thread cap, includes neoprene comb-raising kit with interchangeable insert pads, 4 (Night Train 3) or 5 (Night Train 2) shot box mag., LBA adj. trigger, matte blue barrel finish, Picatinny rail, tactical bolt handle, OD Green synthetic stock, includes 6-24x50mm variable scope with lens caps and rings, adj. bipod, 9 lbs. New 2015.

MSR $871	$740	$650	$550	$500	$400	$340	$285	

PATRIOT PREDATOR – 6.5 Creedmoor, 6.5 PRC (new mid-2019), .243 Win., .308 Win., or .450 Bushmaster (new 2019) cal., 16 1/4 (new 2020), 22, or 24 (new 2019) in. fluted and threaded barrel, 3, 4, or 5 shot drop box mag., LBA adj. trigger, adj. rifle sights (new 2020, 16 1/4 in. barrel only), classic synthetic stock w/FDE finish, spiral fluted bolt, top mounted Picatinny rail, matte blue finish, 6 1/2 lbs. New 2017.

MSR $484	$410	$360	$310	$280	$225	$185	$160	

Add $30 for adj. rifle sights (16 1/4 in. barrel only, new 2020).

* ***Patriot Predator Camo*** – 6.5 Creedmoor, 6.5 PRC (new mid-2019), .22-250 Rem., .243 Win., or .308 Win. cal., 4 or 5 shot mag., 22 or 24 (new 2019) in. fluted and threaded barrel with Patriot Brown Cerakote finish, synthetic stock with True Timber Strata finish, top Picatinny rail, 6 1/2 lbs. New 2019.

MSR $574	$485	$425	$365	$330	$265	$225	$190	

PATRIOT REVERE – 6.5 Creedmoor, .243 Win., .308 Win., .270 Win., .30-06, or .300 Win. Mag. cal., 24 in. blued barrel, recessed match crown, 4 or 6 shot dropbox mag., LBA adj. trigger, highly figured Premier 2.0 Grade European walnut stock with oil finish, fine line checkering, rosewood forend tip and grip cap, maple spacer, Mossberg monogrammed "M" on cap, spiral fluted bolt, 7 lbs. Mfg. 2018-2020.

	$725	$635	$550	$500	$400	$325	$280	*$848*

RIFLES: LEVER ACTION

MODEL SSi-ONE INTERCHANGEABLE RIFLE/SHOTGUN – .22-250 Rem., .223 Rem., .243 Win., .270 Win., .30-06, or .308 Win. cal., also available in 12 ga., design allows interchangeable rifle/shotgun barrels, single shot, satin finished or Mossy Oak Breakup camo (new 2003, available in shotgun

GRADING - PPGS™	100%	98%	95%	90%	80%	70%	60%	LAST MSR

configuration only) checkered walnut stock and forearm, matte blue metal, 24 in. regular or heavy (.22-250 Rem. or .223 Rem. cal.) rifle barrel with ejector or 12 ga. (3 in. chamber with rifled bore for Slug, 3 1/2 in. chamber for Turkey) ported barrel, break open action, cocking indicator, drilled and tapped integral scope base, automatic safety, approx. 8 (regular) or 10 (heavy) lbs. Mfg. 2001-2004.

	$400	$350	$300	$270	$220	$180	$140	*$483*

Add $240 per interchangeable rifle barrel and $298 for SSi-One Slug Model barrel.
Add $55 for Mossy Oak Breakup stock and forearm (Turkey Model) or $77 for Mossy Oak Breakup stock and forearm (Slug Model).
Add $22 for heavy bull barrel or 12 ga. Slug (fully rifled bore) variation.

MODEL 464 – .22 LR (mfg. 2009-2013, reintroduced 2015-2019) or .30-30 Win. cal., 18 (.22 LR cal., disc. 2013, reintroduced 2015-2019) or 20 (.30-30 Win. cal.) in. blue barrel, 7 or 14 (disc. 2013) shot tube mag., top tang safety, uncheckered straight or pistol grip hardwood stock, drilled and tapped, side ejection, rubber buttpad, adj. fiber optic (disc. 2015) or bead front and adj. rear sights, blue or Marinecote metal (disc. 2014) finish, 6 3/4 lbs. New mid-2008.

MSR $568	$485	$425	$365	$330	$265	$225	$190	

Add $42 for pistol grip stock (.30-30 Win. cal. only).
Subtract approx. $33 for .22 LR cal. with 18 in. barrel (disc. 2019).

MODEL 464 SPX – .22 LR (disc. 2013, reintroduced 2015-2019) or .30-30 Win. cal., 16 1/4, 18 (.22 LR, mfg. 2015-2019), or 18 1/2 (disc. 2013) in. barrel with A2 style flash suppressor or muzzle brake (disc. 2019), 7 (.30-30 Win. cal.) or 14 (disc. 2013) shot mag., matte black finish, 6-position adj. tactical stock with elevated comb, tri-rail forearm with ladder rail covers, adj. fiber optic sights or dovetail receiver, drilled and tapped, 6-7 lbs. New 2012.

MSR $610	$520	$455	$390	$355	$285	$235	$200	

Subtract $49 for .22 LR cal. (disc. 2019).

MODEL 464 ZMB – .30-30 Win. cal., 6 (disc. 2013) or 7 (new 2014) shot mag., compact 16 1/4 in. barrel with removable A2 flash suppressor, matte blue finish, six position adj. tactical stock, tri-rail forend with rail covers, 3-dot adj. fiber optic or rifle sights, drilled and tapped, sling swivel studs, ZMB receiver engraving, 7 lbs. Mfg. 2012-2014.

	$480	$410	$350	$300	$250	$210	$175	*$581*

MODEL 472 CARBINE – .30-30 Win. or .35 Rem. cal., lever action carbine, 20 in. barrel, open sights, pistol grip or straight stock, saddle ring on straight model. Mfg. 1972-disc.

	$300	$250	$200	$150	$130	$120	$110	

MODEL 472 RIFLE – similar to Carbine, except 24 in. barrel, pistol grip stock. Mfg. 1974-76.

	$300	$250	$200	$155	$145	$130	$120	

MODEL 472 BRUSH GUN – similar to Carbine, except 18 in. barrel, straight stock only. Mfg. 1974-76.

	$300	$250	$200	$150	$130	$120	$100	

MODEL 472 ONE IN FIVE THOUSAND – .30-30 Win. or .35 Rem. cal., similar to Brush Gun, except Indian scene etched on receiver, brass buttplate, saddle ring and barrel bands, select stock, only 5,000 mfg., 1974.

	$700	$450	$300	$200	$165	$145	$120	

MODEL 479 PCA – .30-30 Win. cal., lever action, 20 in. barrel, 6 shot capacity.

	$300	$250	$200	$150	$130	$120	$100	

MODEL 479 RR – .30-30 Win. cal., limited edition "Roy Rogers" signature model, gold trigger, barrel bands, 5,000 total mfg. New 1983.

	$700	$450	$300	$200	$165	$145	$120	

MODEL 479 – .30-30 Win. cal. only, lever action, 6 shot tube mag., 20 in. barrel with adj. sights, 7 lbs. Mfg. 1985 only.

	$300	$250	$200	$160	$150	$145	$140	*$232*

RIFLES: SEMI-AUTO

BLAZE – .22 LR cal., 16 1/2 in. blued barrel, 10 (disc. 2020) or 25 shot mag., cantilever Picatinny rail (Kryptek Highlander only, disc. 2018), adj. rear rifle sights, polymer receiver, synthetic stock in Black, Kryptek Highlander (disc. 2018), Muddy Girl (disc. 2017), Muddy Girl Serenity (mfg. 2018-2019), or Wildfire Camo (disc. 2017) finish, 3 2/3 lbs. New 2015.

MSR $224	$190	$165	$145	$130	$105	$85	$70	

Add $59 for Muddy Girl Serenity camo finish (mfg. 2018-2019).
Add $57 for Muddy Girl or Wildfire camo finish (disc. 2017).
Add $90 for Kryptek Highlander finish (disc. 2018).

GRADING - PPGS™	100%	98%	95%	90%	80%	70%	60%	LAST MSR

* ***Blaze Bantam*** – .22 LR cal., 16 1/2 in. blued barrel, 10 shot mag., adj. sights, 12 in. LOP, black synthetic stock, 3 2/3 lbs. Mfg. 2015-2019.

	$175	$150	$130	$115	$95	$75	$60	*$210*

* ***Blaze Green Dot Combo*** – .22 LR cal., 16 1/2 in. blued barrel, 10 (disc. 2018) or 25 shot mag., Dead Ringer Holographic green dot sight w/base, adj. rear rifle sight, Picatinny top rail, black synthetic stock, 3 2/3 lbs. Mfg. 2015-2019.

	$235	$200	$175	$160	$130	$100	$80	*$281*

BLAZE 47 – .22 LR cal., AK-47 design, 16 /2 in. blued barrel, 10 or 25 shot mag., adj. fiber optic rear/raised front sights, fixed wood stock, fixed black synthetic (disc. 2016), or adj. synthetic stock in Black (disc. 2017) or FDE/Black (new 2020), 4 1/2-4 3/4 lbs. Mfg. 2015-2020.

	$300	$265	$225	$200	$165	$135	$115	*$357*

Add $63 for fixed wood stock.
Subtract approx. $50 for adj. black synthetic stock (disc. 2017).

MODEL 702 PLINKSTER – .22 LR cal., 18 or 21 (chrome finish only, disc. 2015) in. free floating barrel, 10 or 25 (mfg. 2013-2019) detachable shot mag., fully adj. rifle sights, blue or brushed chrome (disc. 2015) metal finish, wood (disc. 2018), black, pink (disc. 2015), Pink Marble (disc. 2019), walnut Dura-Wood synthetic (disc. 2007), tiger maple Dura-Wood (disc. 2010) synthetic, or carbon fiber (disc. 2011) stock, aluminum alloy receiver, crossbolt safety, approx. 4 lbs. New 2006.

MSR $143	$125	$100	$90	$80	$70	$65	$60	

Add $70 for 25 shot mag.
Add $103 for Pink Marble synthetic stock (disc. 2019).
Add $101 for wood (disc. 2018) or pink (disc. 2015) stock.
Add $22 for brushed chrome (21 in. barrel only, disc. 2015).
Add $109 for Roadblocker muzzle brake (mfg. 2010-2011).

* ***Model 702 Bantam Plinkster*** – .22 LR cal., 18 in. barrel with blue finish, 10 shot mag., 12 1/4 in. LOP, adj. rifle sights, black or pink (disc. 2016) synthetic stock, 4 lbs. New 2006.

MSR $204	$175	$155	$130	$120	$95	$80	$65	

Add $12 for scoped combo with 4x scope (disc. 2018).
Add $44 for pink synthetic stock (disc. 2016).

* ***Model 702 Plinkster Camo*** – .22 LR cal., 18 in. free floating barrel, 10 shot detachable mag., fully adj. rifle sights, blue metal finish, synthetic stock, Mossy Oak New Break-Up (disc. 2011) or Mossy Oak Break-Up Infinity (new 2012) camo finish, 4 lbs. Mfg. 2006-2015.

	$185	$160	$140	$125	$100	$85	$65	*$227*

* ***Model 702 Plinkster Scoped Combo*** – .22 LR cal., 10 shot, 18 in. barrel, blue finish, adj. rifle sights, includes 4x scope, black synthetic stock, 14 1/4 in. LOP, 4 1/2 lbs. Disc. 2019.

	$175	$150	$130	$115	$95	$75	$60	*$209*

* ***Model 702 Plinkster Thumbhole Tipdown*** – .22 LR cal., 18 or 21 (chrome finish only, disc. 2014) in. free floating barrel, 10 shot detachable mag., fully adj. rifle sights, blue or brushed chrome (disc. 2014) metal finish, Black synthetic thumbhole tipdown stock, 4 1/2 lbs. Mfg. 2009-2015.

	$195	$175	$150	$135	$100	$90	$75	*$230*

Add $20 for brushed chrome finish (21 in. barrel only, disc. 2014).

MOSSBERG INTERNATIONAL 702 PLINKSTER DUCK COMMANDER – .22 LR cal., 18 in. barrel, blue finish, 10 shot mag., adj. sights, Realtree Max-5 camo finish, logo engraved synthetic stock, 4 lbs. Mfg. 2014-2015.

	$240	$210	$185	$170	$160	$150	$140	*$282*

MOSSBERG INTERNATIONAL 715T FLAT-TOP DUCK COMMANDER – .22 LR cal., blowback action, 16 1/4 in. blued barrel with A2 style muzzle brake, quad rail forearm, Picatinny rail mounted adj. rifle sights, 25 shot mag., accessory loader, adj. tactical synthetic stock, Realtree Max-5 finish, includes American flag bandana, 5 1/2 lbs. Mfg. 2014-2015.

	$375	$300	$275	$250	$225	$200	$175	*$509*

MODEL 715T TACTICAL CARRY (TACTICAL 22) – .22 LR cal., AR-15 style, blowback action, 18 in. barrel, matte black finish, 10 or 25 shot mag., synthetic fixed or 6-position adj. stock, front post sight, adj. rifle sights, Picatinny quad rail forend, handle mounted top rail, mag. loading assist tool, integrated A2 style carry handle, 5 1/4 lbs. Mfg. 2011-2015.

	$225	$185	$175	$150	$125	$125	$125	*$308*

GRADING - PPGS™	100%	98%	95%	90%	80%	70%	60%	LAST MSR

MODEL 715T FLAT-TOP – .22 LR cal., blowback action, 16 1/4 in. barrel with A2 style muzzle brake, blue barrel finish, 10 or 25 shot mag., flat-top with full-length top rail, removable/adj. sights (disc. 2017) or 30mm red or green (new 2020) dot sights, fixed (disc. 2017) or adj. synthetic stock, black, Mossy Oak Brush (disc. 2015), Muddy Girl (mfg. 2014-2017), or Muddy Girl Serenity (mfg. 2018-2020) camo finish, 5.5-5.75 lbs. New 2012.

MSR $358	$300	$265	$225	$200	$165	$135	$115	

Add $51 for red or green (new 2020) dot combo model.
Add $66 for Muddy Girl camo finish (mfg. 2014-2017).
Add $69 for Mossy Oak Brush camo finish (disc. 2015).
Add $116 for Muddy Girl Serenity camo finish (mfg. 2018-2020).
Add $10 for removable A2 style Picatinny mounted front and rear sights (disc. 2017).

MMR CARBINE – 5.56 NATO cal., GIO, 16 1/4 in. barrel with A2 style muzzle brake, 10 (disc. 2018) or 30 shot mag., removable Picatinny mounted adj. front and rear sights, black fixed (disc. 2018) or synthetic 6-pos. adj. stock, Magpul MOE grip, 13 in. free float forend with M-LOK slots, black anodized finish, 6 3/4 lbs. New 2016.

MSR $997	$850	$750	$650	$575	$475	$385	$350	

MMR HUNTER – 5.56 NATO cal., GIO, 20 in. carbon steel barrel with black phosphate metal finish, 5 shot mag., SST, anodized aluminum receiver, Picatinny top rail, A2 black synthetic stock, SE-1 pistol grip with battery compartment, checkered aluminum tubular forend, black, Mossy Oak Treestand or Mossy Oak Brush camo finish, no sights, 7 1/2 lbs. Mfg. mid-2011-2015.

	$775	$600	$550	$475	$450	$425	$375	*$1,028*

Add $99 for camo finish.

MMR PRO – 5.56 NATO/.223 Rem. or .224 Valkyrie (new 2019) cal., GIO, 18 in. free floating stainless steel barrel, removable suppressor-ready SilencerCo muzzle brake with ASR mount, 28 (new 2019) or 30 shot Magpul PMAG, ejection port dust cover, JM Pro drop-in match trigger, black synthetic 6-pos. stock, adj. LOP, interchangeable FLEX pad, 15 in. slim profile forend with M-LOK, Magpul MOE grip and trigger guard, forward assist, full-length top Picatinny rail, AXTS Raptor ambidextrous charging handle, phosphate and hardcoat anodized metal finishes. New 2017.

MSR $1,478	$1,260	$1,100	$950	$850	$700	$575	$525	

MMR TACTICAL – 5.56 NATO cal., GIO, 16 1/4 in. carbon steel barrel with black phosphate metal finish, 10 or 30 shot mag., SST, anodized aluminum receiver, black synthetic fixed or 6-position collapsible stock, A2 style muzzle brake, no sights or removable Picatinny rail, Stark SE-1 deluxe pistol grip, quad rail forend, approx. 7-7 1/2 lbs. Mfg. mid-2011-2015.

	$1,050	$825	$750	$650	$600	$575	$525	*$987*

Add $41 for Picatinny rail.

MMR TACTICAL OPTICS READY – 5.56 NATO/.223 Rem. cal., GIO, 16 in. barrel, removable A2 style muzzle brake, 30 shot Magpul PMAG, JM Pro drop-in match trigger, black synthetic 6-pos. stock with FLEX pad, Magpul MOE grip and trigger guard, 13 in. slim profile forend with M-LOK handguard, full-length top Picatinny rail, phosphate and hardcoat anodized metal finishes, 7 lbs. Mfg. 2017-2019.

	$950	$750	$675	$600	$550	$500	$475	*$1,253*

Add $146 for Vortex StrikeFire II red/green dot sight with cantilever mount.

MOSSBERG INTERNATIONAL FLEX-22 – .22 LR cal., 16 1/4 in. free floating barrel with A2 style muzzle brake, adj. front and rear fiber optic sights, LOP adj. between 11 to 14 in. (controlled by integrated lever), removable Picatinny rail, dovetailed receiver, last shot hold open, adj. six position tactical style stock with stippled forend and pistol grip, 25 shot mag., magazine loading cap, matte black finish, blue metal finish, 5 1/2 lbs. Mfg. mid-2014-2017.

	$200	$175	$150	$125	$125	$125	$100	*$280*

Add $31 for takedown case (new 2015).

* ***Mossberg International Flex-22 Youth*** – .22 LR cal., similar to Flex-22, except features 18 in. barrel, fixed stock with stippled forend and pistol grip, 10 shot mag. Mfg. mid-2014-2015.

	$200	$150	$150	$125	$125	$100	$100	*$261*

SHOTGUNS: BOLT ACTION - DISC.

MODELS G-4, 70, 73, 73B – .410 bore, single shot, mfg. 1932-40.

	$150	$100	$85	$70	$60	$50	$40	

MODELS 80, 83, 83B, 83D – .410 bore, 3 or 4 shot, internal top-loading mag., mfg. 1933-46.

	$150	$110	$95	$75	$60	$50	$40	

GRADING - PPGS™	100%	98%	95%	90%	80%	70%	60%	LAST MSR

MODELS 75, 75A, 75B – 20 ga., bolt action, single shot, mfg. 1933-40.

	$150	$100	$85	$70	$60	$50	$40	

MODELS 85, 85A, 85B, 85D – 20 ga., 2 or 3 shot mag., mfg. 1934-40.

	$150	$100	$85	$70	$60	$50	$40	

MODELS 173, 173A, 173Y – .410 bore, single shot, "Y" designates youth model, mfg. 1957-73.

	$150	$100	$85	$70	$60	$50	$40	

MODELS 183, 183D, 283D(a), 183D-B, 183D-C, 183D-D, 183D-E, 183D-F, 183K, 183K-B, 183K-C, 183T, 184T, 184TY, 283T, 284T, 284TY – .410 bore, bolt action shotgun, 2 or 3 shot mag., various screw-on or C-Lect choke on some models, mfg. 1948-1985.

	$175	$150	$135	$110	$95	$85	$75	

MODELS 185, 185D, 185D-A, 185D-B, 185D-C, 185K, 185K-A, 185K-B – 20 ga., 2 shot 2 3/4 in. mag., various screw-on or C-Lect chokes, mfg. 1947-59.

	$175	$150	$135	$110	$95	$85	$75	

MODELS 190, 190D, 190D-A, 190K-A, 190K-B – 16 ga., bolt action, 2 shot 2 3/4 in. mag., various screw-on or C-Lect choke, mfg. 1955-58.

	$175	$150	$135	$110	$95	$85	$75	

MODELS 195, 195A, 195K-A, 195D – same as model 185 Series, only 12 ga. version, mfg. 1954-68.

	$175	$150	$135	$110	$95	$85	$75	

MODELS 385, 385K, 385KA, 385T, 485A, 485B – 20 ga., bolt action, 3 in. chamber, detachable box mag., mfg. 1960-86.

	$175	$150	$135	$110	$95	$85	$75	

MODELS 390, 390K-A, 390K-B, 490A – 16 ga., 3 in. chamber, detachable box mag., mfg. 1971-76.

	$175	$150	$135	$110	$95	$85	$75	

MODELS 395, 395K, 395KA, 395S, 395 SPL., 495A, 495B – 12 ga., 3 in. chamber, detachable box mag., mfg. 1963-83.

	$175	$150	$135	$110	$95	$85	$75	

Add $40 for slug barrel ("S" designation) or 38 in. barrel (Spl.).

MODELS 595, 595K – 12 ga., bolt action, special police stock, 4 shot mag., mfg. 1983-85.

	$175	$150	$135	$110	$95	$85	$75	

Add $40 for 38 in. barrel (Spl.).

MODEL 695 BOLT ACTION – 12 ga. only, with detachable 2 shot mag., 3 in. chamber, 22 in. barrel with fully rifled and ported (new 1999) or Accu-choke (disc. 1998) barrel, black synthetic or Woodlands camo (with bead sights, disc. 2001) on stock and forearm, rifle or TruGlo fiber optic sights, 7 1/2 lbs. Mfg. 1996-2002.

	$275	$220	$185	$150	$135	$120	$115	*$345*

Subtract approx. $50 for Accu-choke barrel.
Add $22 for TruGlo fiber optic sights (new 1998).
Add $52 for TruGlo fiber optic sights and Woodlands camo finish (disc. 2001).

SHOTGUNS: O/U

MOSSBERG INTERNATIONAL GOLD RESERVE BLACK LABEL – 12 ga., 3 in. chamber, Jeweled action, 30 in. VR chrome-lined barrels with 5 choke extended sport set, polished black receiver with scroll engraving and gold inlay, shell ejectors, Grade A black walnut stock with satin finish, polished blue barrel finish, 7.5 lbs. New 2021.

MSR $983	$840	$735	$630	$575	$460	$380	$325	

MOSSBERG INTERNATIONAL GOLD RESERVE SPORTING – 12, 20 ga., or .410 bore, 3 in. chamber, Jeweled action, 28 or 30 in. VR chrome-lined barrels with 5 choke extended sport set, Grade A black walnut stock with satin finish, tang mounted safety/barrel selector, polished silver receiver with scroll engraving and gold inlay, dual locking lugs, polished blue barrel finish, 6.5-7.5 lbs. New 2021.

MSR $983	$840	$735	$630	$575	$460	$380	$325	

MOSSBERG INTERNATIONAL GOLD RESERVE SUPER SPORT – 12 ga., 3 in. chamber, Jeweled action, 30 in. high profile vent rib chrome-lined barrels with 5 choke extended sport set, polished silver receiver with scroll engraving and gold inlay, shell ejectors, Grade A black walnut stock with satin finish, adj. LOP/comb, dual locking lugs, polished blue barrel finish, 7.5 lbs. New 2021.

MSR $1,221	$1,040	$910	$780	$700	$575	$475	$400	

GRADING - PPGS™	100%	98%	95%	90%	80%	70%	60%	LAST MSR

MOSSBERG INTERNATIONAL SILVER RESERVE – 12, 20, 28 ga., or .410 bore, 2 3/4 or 3 in. chamber, 26 or 28 (12 ga. only) in. VR barrels with 5 choke field set, satin silver finished receiver with engraved logo, shell extractors, bead sights, black walnut stock with satin silver finish, tang mounted safety/barrel selector, dual locking lugs, matte blue barrel finish, 6.5-7.5 lbs. New 2021.

MSR $692	$585	$510	$440	$400	$325	$275	$230	

* ***Mossberg International Silver Reserve Synthetic*** – 12 ga., 3 in. chamber, 28 in. VR barrels with 5 choke field set, matte blue finished receiver with engraved logo, shell extractors, fiber optic sights, black synthetic stock, tang mounted safety/barrel selector, dual locking lugs, matte blue barrel finish, 7 lbs. New 2021.

MSR $636	$540	$475	$400	$365	$300	$250	$210	

* ***Mossberg International Silver Reserve Youth Bantam*** – 20 ga., 3 in. chamber, 26 in. VR barrels with 5 choke field set, satin silver receiver with engraved logo, shell extractors, bead sights, black walnut stock with satin finish, 13.25 in. LOP, tang mounted safety/barrel selector, matte blue barrel finish, 7 lbs. New 2021.

MSR $692	$585	$510	$440	$400	$325	$275	$230	

ONYX RESERVE SPORTING – 12 ga. only, 2 3/4 or 3 in. chambers, 28 in. ported VR barrels with 10mm rib and front/mid bead sights, 5 chokes, blue receiver with scroll engraving, checkered walnut stock and forearm. Mfg. 2008-2012.

	$750	$675	$575	$500	$450	$400	$365	*$851*

SILVER RESERVE FIELD – 12, 20, 28 ga., or .410 bore, boxlock action with dual locking lugs, 26 or 28 in. barrels with extractors, features detailed gold inlaid game scenes engraved on silver receiver, ST, Sporting models (12 ga. only) have ported barrels with 10mm rib, wide rib, scroll engraving on silver or blue receiver, Bantam Model has 26 in. barrels and short LOP, mfg. by Khan in Turkey, 6 - 7.7 lbs. Mfg. 2005-2012.

	$595	$500	$450	$395	$360	$330	$295	*$693*

Add $349 for 12/20 ga. combo (new 2007).

SILVER RESERVE SPORTING – 12 ga. only, 3 in. chambers, 28 in. ported VR barrels with 10mm rib and front/mid bead sights, blue receiver with scroll engraving, checkered walnut stock and forearm, SST, extractors, five interchangeable choke tubes, 7.7 lbs. Disc. 2012.

	$750	$675	$575	$500	$450	$400	$365	*$851*

SILVER RESERVE II FIELD – 12, 20, 28 ga. or .410 bore, 2 3/4 or 3 in. chambers, 26 or 28 in. barrels with chokes, extractors or ejectors (disc. 2015), blue finish, front bead sight, silver receiver with scroll engraving, satin finished select black walnut stock, 6 1/2-7 1/2 lbs. New mid-2012.

MSR $822	$700	$615	$525	$475	$385	$315	$275	

Add $411 for 12/20 ga. or 20/28 ga. (disc. 2018) two-barrel set.
Add $89 for ejectors (disc. 2015).

* ***Silver Reserve II Bantam Field - Youth*** – 20 ga., 3 in. chambers, 26 in. VR blued barrel, 5 field chokes, front bead sights, chrome plated bores, dual locking lugs, 13 1/4 in. LOP, shell extractors, silver receiver with scroll engraving, satin select black walnut stock, 7 lbs.

MSR $822	$700	$615	$525	$475	$385	$315	$275	

SILVER RESERVE II SPORT – 12 ga., 3 in. chambers, 28 in. ported barrels, vent. rib, extended Skeet chokes, blue finish, front and mid-bead sights, silver receiver with scroll engraving, satin select black walnut stock and forearm, extractors (disc. 2015) or ejectors, dual locking lugs, 7 1/2 lbs. New mid-2012.

MSR $1,135	$975	$850	$725	$675	$550	$450	$375	

Subtract approx. $120 if with extractors.

SILVER RESERVE II SUPER SPORT – 12 ga., 3 in. chambers, 30 or 32 in. ported barrels with extra wide high rib and 5 extended Skeet chokes, blue finish, dual bead sights, silver receiver with scroll engraving, satin finished select black walnut stock with (disc. 2015) or w/o adj. comb, 6 1/2-7 1/2 lbs. New mid-2012.

MSR $1,235	$1,050	$920	$790	$715	$580	$475	$400	

Add $110 for adj. comb. (disc. 2015).

SHOTGUNS: SxS, RECENT PRODUCTION

SILVER RESERVE FIELD – 12, 20, 28 ga., or .410 bore (limited mfg.), 3 in. chambers, boxlock action, 26 or 28 in. VR barrels, SST, silver or blue receiver with scroll engraving, checkered black walnut stock and forearm with pistol grip, ambidextrous thumb safety, dual locking lugs, chrome plated chambers and bores, extractors, Sporting models (12 ga. only, disc. 2008) have ported barrels with 10mm rib, wide rib, Bantam model has 26 in. barrels and short LOP, 6 1/2 - 7.2 lbs. Mfg. 2008-2012.

	$850	$775	$635	$525	$425	$375	$325	*$1,005*

Add $140 for Sporting Model (disc. 2008). Add $311 for 12/20 or 20/28 ga. combo (disc. 2008).

GRADING - PPGS™	100%	98%	95%	90%	80%	70%	60%	LAST MSR

ONYX RESERVE SPORTING – 12 ga., similar to Silver Reserve Sporting Model, except has onyx colored metal finish. Disc. 2012.

	$850	$775	$635	$525	$425	$375	$325	*$1,005*

SILVER RESERVE II FIELD – 12, 20, or 28 ga., 26 or 28 in. barrels with standard 5 choke set, blue finish, silver receiver with scroll engraving, front bead sights, satin finished select black walnut stock and forearm, 6 1/2-7 1/2 lbs. Mfg. mid-2012-2015.

	$930	$800	$685	$625	$500	$410	$325	*$1,100*

SHOTGUNS: SEMI-AUTO

In 1985, Mossberg purchased the parts inventory and manufacturing rights for the shotguns that Smith & Wesson discontinued in 1984. These 1000 Series models (manufactured in Japan) are identical to those models which S&W discontinued. Parts and warranties are not interchangeable.

Beginning 1989, all Mossbergs sold in the U.S. and Canada have been provided with a Cablelock which goes through the ejection port, making the gun's action inoperable.

To celebrate its 75th anniversary, Mossberg released a new Crown Grade variation within most models during 1994, including the slide action 500 and 835 Series. These can be differentiated from previous manufacture by cut checkering, redesigned walnut or American hardwood stocks and forearms, screw-in choke tubes, and 4 different camo patterns. The Crown Grade was discontinued in 2000.

At the SHOT Show during 2014, Mossberg unveiled its new Duck Commander Series. Please refer to individual listings.

MODEL 712 SEMI-AUTO – 12 ga. only, gas operated, shoots 2 3/4 and 3 in. shells interchangeably, plain barrel or VR, top of receiver safety, checkered hardwood stock, rubber recoil pad, fixed or Accu-choke II choking. Mfg. 1986-88 only.

	$450	$395	$335	$305	$245	$200	$155	*$345*

Subtract $25 without Accu-II choking.
Add $90 for combo pack (includes 1 extra 24 in. slugster barrel).

* ***Model 712 Semi-Auto Steel Shot*** – similar to Model 712, except has Accu-steel choking system for steel shot, 28 in. VR barrel. Mfg. 1988 only.

	$450	$395	$335	$305	$245	$200	$155	*$349*

* ***Model 712 Semi-Auto Camo/Speedfeed*** – 12 ga. only, similar to Model 712, except has camo finished metal parts, stock, and forearm, 24 or 28 in. barrel. Mfg. 1986-87 only.

	$450	$395	$335	$305	$245	$200	$155	*$390*

Add $20 for Accu-II choke.

MODEL 712 REGAL SEMI-AUTO – 12 or 20 ga., action same as Model 712, special bright bluing, VR only, deluxe checkered walnut stock and forearm, gold trigger, inlaid medallion on receiver, top of receiver safety. Mfg. 1986-87 only.

	$310	$270	$230	$210	$170	$140	$110	*$366*

Add $20 for Accu-II choke.

MODEL 930 SEMI-AUTO – 12 ga. only, 3 in. chamber, various configurations, approx. 7 3/4 lbs. New 2005.

* ***Model 930 All Purpose Field*** – 12 ga. only, 26 (disc. 2018) or 28 in. ported VR barrel with Accu-set chokes, white bead or fiber optic (new 2017) front sight, walnut or black synthetic (new 2017) stock, blue metal finish. New 2005.

MSR $613	$520	$455	$390	$355	$285	$235	$200	

Add $153 for walnut stock.
Add $36 for Field/Security combo with 18 1/2 in. cylinder bore barrel (disc. 2009).

* ***Model 930 Hunting All Purpose Field Camo*** – 12 ga., 3 in. chamber, 26 in. VR barrel, Accu-set and X-Factor XX-Full turkey tube chokes, 5 shot mag., fiber optic front sights, synthetic stock, 14 in. LOP, 100% Mossy Oak New Bottomland camo finish, 7 3/4 lbs. New 2018.

MSR $701	$600	$525	$450	$410	$325	$275	$225	

* ***Model 930 Deer/Field Combo*** – 12 ga., 3 in. chamber, 5 shot, two barrel set includes 24 in. ported fully rifled Slugster barrel with adj. rifle sight and 26 in. VR ported Field barrel with Accu-Set chokes and fiber optic front sight, walnut stock, blue finish, 7 1/2-7 3/4 lbs. Mfg. 2006-2017.

	$665	$580	$500	$450	$365	$300	$235	*$781*

GRADING - PPGS™	100%	98%	95%	90%	80%	70%	60%	LAST MSR

* ***Model 930 Deer/Waterfowl Combo*** – 12 ga., 3 in. chamber, 5 shot, two barrel set includes 24 in. ported fully rifled Slugster barrel with adj. rifle sight and 28 in. VR ported waterfowl barrel with Accu-Set choke tubes and fiber optic front sight, black synthetic stock, matte blue finish, 7 1/2-7 3/4 lbs. New 2006.

MSR $759	$650	$570	$490	$440	$360	$295	$250	

* ***Model 930 Patrick Flanigan Rhythm Series*** – 12 ga., 28 in. matte blue ported barrel, blue/yellow marbled stock, extended 12 shot mag. tube, fiber optic front sight, engraved receiver, beveled loading gate, shorter forend, built to Flanigan's specifications. Mfg. 2012-2013.

	$700	$615	$525	$475	$385	$315	$245	*$833*

* ***Model 930 Slugster*** – 12 ga. only, 3 in. chamber, 24 in. ported fully rifled bore barrel, choice of walnut (disc. 2015), synthetic (disc. 2008), or Monte Carlo synthetic stock, rifle sights (disc. 2008) or integral scope base, matte blue metal, Realtree AP (mfg. 2007-2010), Mossy Oak New Break-Up (disc. 2010), or Mossy Oak Break-Up Country (mfg. 2016-2017) camo finish, 7 1/2 lbs. New 2005.

MSR $742	$625	$545	$475	$425	$345	$275	$225	

Add $64 for Mossy Oak Break-Up Country camo finish (mfg. 2016-2017).
Add $27 for walnut stock/forearm and rifle sights (disc. 2015).
Add $118 for 100% camo coverage (disc. 2010).

* ***Model 930 Turkey*** – 12 ga. only, 3 in. chamber, 24 in. VR ported barrel with XX-Full choke tube, vent. rib, adj. fiber optic sights, matte blue (disc. 2015), Mossy Oak New Break-Up (disc. 2008), Mossy Oak Obsession (mfg. 2007-2014, reintroduced 2016), Mossy Oak Break-Up Infinity (mfg. 2011-2015) or Realtree Hardwoods HD Green (disc. 2012) finish, synthetic (new 2016) stock, 7 1/2 lbs. New 2005.

MSR $690	$585	$510	$440	$400	$325	$275	$230	

Subtract approx. $140 for matte blue finish.

* ***Model 930 Turkey Pistol Grip*** – 12 ga., similar to Model 930 Turkey, except has 13 in. LOP, full-length pistol grip synthetic stock, matte blue (disc. 2014), 100% Mossy Oak Obsession (mfg. 2009-2010, 2016), or Mossy Oak Break-Up Infinity (mfg. 2011-2015) camo coverage, 7 1/2 lbs. New 2009.

MSR $805	$680	$600	$500	$450	$375	$300	$265	

Subtract approx. $135 for matte blue finish. Camo coverage became standard 2015.

* ***Model 930 Waterfowl*** – 12 ga., 3 in. chamber, 5 shot, 26 (disc. 2008) or 28 in. ported barrel with Accu-set choke, vent. rib, fiber optic front sights, walnut (disc. 2015) or synthetic stock, matte blue (wood stock only, disc. 2015), black (disc. 2017), Mossy Oak Duck Blind (mfg. 2007-2012), Mossy Oak New Break-Up (disc. 2008), Mossy Oak Shadow Grass Blades (new 2013), or Advantage Max-4 (disc. 2015) camo finish, 7 3/4 lbs. New 2005.

MSR $679	$580	$510	$435	$395	$320	$265	$225	

Subtract approx. $140 for black synthetic stock (disc. 2017).
Add $27 for walnut stock and foream with matte blue metal finish (disc. 2015).

MODEL 930 SEMI-AUTO TACTICAL/SPECIAL PURPOSE – 12 ga., 3 in. chamber, various configurations.

* ***Model 930 Special Purpose Home Security*** – 12 ga., 3 in. chamber, 5 shot, 18 1/2 in. cylinder bore barrel, bead sights, blue finish, black synthetic stock, 7 1/4 lbs. Mfg. 2007-2016.

	$550	$475	$400	$375	$300	$250	$200	*$662*

* ***Model 930 Field/Security Combo*** – 12 ga., 3 in. chamber, 5 shot, two barrel set includes 28 in. VR ported barrel with Accu-Set chokes and 18 1/2 in. cylinder bore barrel, bead sights, blue finish, black synthetic stock, 7 1/2-7 3/4 lbs. New 2010.

MSR $759	$650	$570	$490	$440	$360	$295	$250	

* ***Model 930 Special Purpose Roadblocker*** – 12 ga., 3 in. chamber, 18 1/2 in. barrel with large muzzle brake, 5 shot, matte blue finish, black synthetic stock, 7 3/4 lbs. Mfg. 2009-2011.

	$575	$495	$415	$375	$300	$245	$190	*$670*

* ***Model 930 Special Purpose SPX*** – 12 ga., 3 in. chamber, 8 shot mag., 18 1/2 in. cylinder bore barrel, Picatinny top rail, LPA ghost ring rear or XS ghost ring (mfg. 2015 only) sights, and winged fiber optic front sight, black synthetic stock with (new 2009) or w/o pistol grip, matte blue or Coyote Tan (new 2013) finish, 7 3/4 lbs. New 2008.

MSR $960	$815	$715	$610	$555	$450	$370	$320	

Add $118 for full length pistol grip stock (new 2009).
Add $185 for pistol grip stock with Coyote Tan finish (new 2013).
Add $47 for XS sights w/pistol grip (mfg. 2015 only).

GRADING - PPGS™	100%	98%	95%	90%	80%	70%	60%	LAST MSR

* ***Model 930 Special Purpose SPX Blackwater Series*** – 12 ga., 3 in. chamber, 8 shot, 18 1/2 in. cylinder bore barrel, receiver mounted sliding safety, matte black finish with Blackwater logo on right side of receiver, black composite pistol grip stock, Picatinny rail, XS sights: Ghost ring rear/AR-style Tritium stripe front, oversized cocking handle and bolt release, 7 3/4 lbs. Mfg. 2011-2014.

	$750	$650	$575	$510	$415	$350	$275	*$891*

* ***Model 930 SPX Typhon Camo*** – 12 ga., 3 in. chamber, 8 shot, 18 1/2 in. cylinder bore barrel, ghost ring/fiber optic sights, Picatinny rail, magazine extension, full-length synthetic stock with pistol grip, Kryptek Typhon camo, 7 3/4 lbs. Mfg. 2014-2017.

	$885	$775	$665	$600	$485	$400	$325	*$1,043*

* ***Model 930 Tactical*** – 12 ga., 3 in. chamber, 5 shot, 18 1/2 in. Standoff cylinder bore barrel, white dot sights, with or w/o heat shield, matte blue finish, black synthetic stock, 7 1/4 lbs. Mfg. mid-2008-2016.

	$585	$500	$425	$395	$315	$275	$225	*$714*

Add $25 for heat shield (new 2011).

* ***Model 930 Tactical 8 Shot*** – 12 ga., 3 in. chamber, 18 1/2 in. barrel, cylinder bore, 8 shot, bead sights, black synthetic stock, matte blue finish, 6.75 lbs. New 2017.

MSR $671	$575	$500	$430	$390	$315	$260	$220	

* ***Model 930 Tactical w/XS Express Sights*** – 12 ga., 3 in. chamber, 18 1/2 in. cylinder bore barrel with matte blue finish, 5 shot mag., XS Express sights, receiver mounted cantilever rail, black synthetic stock, 7 1/4 lbs. Mfg. 2015 only.

	$625	$550	$475	$425	$350	$285	$225	*$730*

* ***Model 930 Thunder Ranch*** – 12 ga., 3 in. chamber, 18 1/2 in. Standoff barrel, Breacher muzzle brake, cylinder bore, 5 shot mag., red fiber optic bead sights, synthetic stock with KUIU camo finsh, matte blue metal finish, 6 3/4 lbs. New 2019.

MSR $766	$650	$570	$490	$440	$360	$295	$250	

* ***Model 930 Watchdog*** – 12 ga., 3 in. chamber, 8 shot, 18 1/2 in. cylinder bore barrel, bead sights, synthetic stock, Proveil Watchdog camo finish, 6 3/4 lbs. Disc. 2017.

	$615	$550	$475	$425	$350	$275	$225	*$722*

This model could only be purchased through a Talo Group Distributor.

MODEL 930 SNOW GOOSE (HIGH PERFORMANCE) – 12 ga., 3 in. chamber, dual gas vent. system, 28 in. VR barrel, Accu-Set chokes, 13 shot extended mag. tube plus 5 shot conversion kit, beveled loading gate, stabilizing barrel clamp, extended knurled charging handle, fiber optic front sight, drilled and tapped receiver, matte blue (disc. 2018) or Kryptek Yeti camo finish on barrel, black (disc. 2018) or Kryptek Yeti camo synthetic stock, 7 3/4-8 1/4 lbs. New 2014.

MSR $920	$780	$685	$585	$530	$430	$350	$300	

Subtract approx. $60 for matte blue barrel and black synthetic stock (disc. 2018).

MODEL 930 PRO SERIES SPORTING – 12 ga., 28 in. VR ported barrel, Briley extended chokes, 5 shot, front green fiber optic sight, walnut target stock, Pro-Series enhanced internal parts kit, beveled loading gate, engraved receiver with Cerakote Tungsten finish, 7 3/4 lbs. New 2016.

MSR $1,162	$985	$850	$725	$675	$550	$450	$385	

MODEL 930 PRO SERIES WATERFOWL – 12 ga., 28 in. VR barrel, Accu-Set chokes, 5 shot mag., fiber optic front sight, synthetic stock with Mossy Oak Shadow Grass Blades coverage, Pro-Series enhanced internal parts kit with stainless steel recoil pad, Realtree Max-5 receiver finish, 7 3/4 lbs. New 2016.

MSR $844	$715	$625	$535	$485	$395	$320	$280	

MODEL 930 JM PRO SERIES – 12 ga., 3 in. chamber, 22 or 24 in. VR barrel, 9 or 10 shot, matte black or Kryptek Typhon camo (new 2014, 24 in. bbl. only) synthetic stock, fiber optic front sight, engraved receiver, beveled loading gate, shorter forend, extended magazine tube, adj. overtravel, built to Jerry Miculek's specifications. Mfg. 2012-2020.

	$715	$625	$535	$485	$395	$320	$280	*$839*

Add $32 for Kryptek Typhon camo finish (new 2014).

MODEL 930 DUCK COMMANDER SIGNATURE – 12 ga., 3 in. chamber, 26 in. VR barrel, Accu-Set chokes, 5 shot, Truglo Tru-Bead fiber optic sight, Realtree Max-5 synthetic tock and forend, OD Green metal finish with repeat duck-in-flight pattern and Duck Commander logo on front with "Faith. Family. Ducks." engraving on back, "Happy Happy Happy" magazine tube cap, 7 3/4 lbs. Mfg. 2014-2016.

	$825	$725	$625	$550	$495	$450	$395	*$928*

This model was available only through a Talo Group distributor.

GRADING - PPGS™	100%	98%	95%	90%	80%	70%	60%	LAST MSR

MODEL 930 DUCK COMMANDER WATERFOWL – 12 ga., 3 in. chamber, 26 in. VR barrel, Accu-Set chokes, 5 shot, TruGlo fiber optic sights, 100% Realtree Max-5 finish, Logo engraved synthetic stock, includes American Flag Bandana, 7 3/4 lbs. Mfg. 2014-2015.

	$765	$650	$550	$475	$425	$375	$325	*$890*

MODEL 930 DC PRO SERIES WATERFOWL – 12 ga., 3 in. chamber, 28 in. ported VR barrel, Accu-Set chokes, 5 shot mag., Truglo Tru-Bead fiber optic sights, DC PRO SERIES engraved receiver, synthetic stock, Realtree Max-5 camo finish, Pro Series premium coated parts, 7 3/4 lbs. Mfg. 2015 only.

	$785	$685	$590	$535	$430	$350	$275	*$919*

MODEL 935 MAGNUM PRO SERIES WATERFOWL – 12 ga., 28 in. overbored barrel, 5 shot mag., fiber optic front sight, synthetic stock, engraved receiver with Realtree Max-5 finish, Mossy Oak Shadow Grass Blades finish, 7 3/4 lbs. New 2016.

MSR $958	$815	$715	$610	$555	$450	$370	$320	

MODEL 935 MAGNUM SEMI-AUTO – 12 ga. only, 3 1/2 in. chamber, choice of turkey or waterfowl configuration, fiber optic sight, matte or camo metal finish, wood (disc.) or synthetic stock and forearm, choice of full coverage Mossy Oak New Break Up, Advantage Max-4, Mossy Oak Duck Blind (mfg. 2007-2012), Mossy Oak Shadow Grass (disc. 2007), Mossy Oak Obsession (mfg. 2007-disc.), Mossy Oak New Break-Up Infinity (new 2011), Realtree Xtra Green (new 2013), or Mossy Oak Shadow Grass Blades (new 2013), approx. 7 3/4 lbs. New 2004.

* ***Model 935 Magnum Slugster*** – 12 ga., 24 in. barrel, fully rifled bore, rifle sights (disc. 2008) or integral scope base, Synthetic (disc. 2008) or Monte Carlo synthetic stock with Realtree AP finish. Disc. 2010.

	$650	$575	$500	$450	$375	$300	$250	*$754*

* ***Model 935 Magnum Turkey*** – 12 ga., 3 1/2 in. chamber, 5 shot, 24 in. VR overbored barrel with Ulti-Full choke tubes, synthetic stock, matte blue (disc. 2007), Mossy Oak New Break-Up (disc. 2011), Mossy Oak Obsession (disc. 2010), Mossy Oak Break-Up Infinity (new 2011), Realtree Hardwoods HD Green (disc. 2012), or Realtree Extra Green (mfg. 2013-2014) camo coverage, 7 1/2 lbs. Disc. 2015.

	$740	$650	$550	$500	$400	$325	$250	*$866*

* ***Model 935 Magnum Turkey (Current Mfg.)*** – 12 ga., 3 1/2 in. chamber, 22 in. VR overbored barrel, X-Factor ported turkey tube chokes, 4 shot mag., fiber optic front sights, synthetic stock, 100% Mossy Oak Bottomland camo coverage, 7 1/2 lbs. New 2019.

MSR $829	$700	$615	$525	$475	$385	$315	$275	

* ***Model 935 Magnum Turkey Pistol Grip*** – 12 ga., 3 1/2 in. chamber, 5 shot, 22 in. VR overbored barrel with X-Factor ported choke tubes, adj. fiber optic sights, full-length synthetic pistol grip stock, Mossy Oak Obsession (disc. 2011, reintroduced 2016), Mossy Oak Break-Up Infinity (mfg. 2012-2015) camo coverage, 7 1/2 lbs. New 2009.

MSR $1,012	$860	$750	$650	$575	$475	$385	$325	

* ***Model 935 Magnum Turkey Grand Slam Series*** – 12 ga., 3 1/2 in. chamber, 5 shot, 22 in. VR overbored barrel with X-Factor ported tube, adj. fiber optic sights, synthetic stock, 100% Mossy Oak New Break-Up (disc. 2011), Mossy Oak Break-Up Infinity (mfg. 2012-2015), Mossy Oak Obsession (new 2016), Realtree Hardwoods HD Green (disc. 2012), or Realtree Extra Green (mfg. 2013-2014) camo coverage, sling, 7 1/2 lbs. Disc. 2018.

	$640	$560	$480	$435	$350	$300	$225	*$756*

* ***Model 935 Magnum Combo*** – 12 ga., 3 1/2 in. chamber, 5 shot, two barrel Turkey/Deer set includes 24 in. VR overbored barrel with Ulti-Full choke tube and adj. fiber optic sight and 24 in. fully rifled barrel with adj. rifle sight, two barrel Turkey/Waterfowl set includes 24 in. VR overbored barrel with Ulti-Full choke tubes and adj. fiber optic sight and 28 in. VR overbored barrel with Accu-Set chokes and fiber optic front sight, synthetic stock, 100% Mossy Oak New Break-Up (disc. 2011), or Mossy Oak Break-Up Infinity (disc. 2015), or Mossy Oak Break-Up Country (new 2016) camo coverage, 7 1/2 lbs. Mfg. 2005-2017.

	$850	$750	$640	$580	$470	$385	$300	*$1,004*

* ***Model 935 Magnum Waterfowl*** – 12 ga., 3 1/2 in. chamber, 5 shot, 26 (disc. 2015) or 28 in. VR overbored barrel with Accu-Mag Set chokes, fiber optic front sights, matte blue finish with black synthetic stock or synthetic stock with 100% Mossy Oak New Break-Up (disc. 2011), Mossy Oak Duck Blind (mfg. 2007-2012), Mossy Oak Shadow Grass (disc. 2007), Mossy Oak Shadow Grass Blades (mfg. 2013-2014, 2016), or Advantage Max-4 (disc. 2015) camo coverage, 7 3/4 lbs. New 2004.

MSR $729	$625	$545	$475	$425	$345	$275	$225	

Add $76 for 100% camo coverage.

GRADING - PPGS™	100%	98%	95%	90%	80%	70%	60%	LAST MSR

* ***Model 935 Magnum Waterfowl Flyway Series*** – 12 ga., 3 1/2 in. chamber, 5 shot, 28 in. VR overbored barrel with X-Factor ported choke tubes, camo sling, synthetic stock, Advantage Max-4 finish, 7 3/4 lbs. Disc. 2015.

	$790	$675	$575	$525	$425	$350	$275	*$924*

MODEL 935 MAGNUM DUCK COMMANDER WATERFOWL – 12 ga., 3 1/2 in. chamber, 28 in. barrel, Accu-Mag Set chokes, 6 shot, Realtree Max-5 finish on stock and forearm, OD Green metal finish, TruGlo Tru-Bead fiber optic sight, logo engraved synthetic stock, American Flag Bandana, 7 3/4 lbs. Mfg. 2014-2015.

	$850	$750	$650	$575	$500	$450	$395	*$966*

MODEL 935 DC PRO SERIES WATERFOWL – 12 ga., 3 1/2 in. chamber, 28 in. ported VR over-bored barrel, Accu Mag Set chokes, 5 shot mag., Truglo Tru-Bead fiber optic sights, DC PRO SERIES engraved receiver, synthetic stock, Realtree Max-5 camo finish, Pro Series premium coated parts, 7 3/4 lbs. Mfg. 2015 only.

	$860	$750	$650	$585	$475	$385	$300	*$1,009*

MODEL 940 JM PRO – 12 ga., 3 in. chamber, 24 in. matte blued VR barrel, Briley ext. set chokes, 5 (new 2021) or 10 shot mag., front fiber optic sight, black or multi-cam synthetic stock with adj. LOP, black or Tungsten Gray anodized receiver finish, 7.75 lbs. New 2020.

MSR $1,078	$915	$800	$685	$620	$500	$410	$360	

MODEL 1000 SEMI-AUTO – 12 or 20 ga., gas semi-auto, 2 3/4 in. chamber, scroll engraved aluminum alloy receiver, plain or VR barrel, also available in trap and skeet configuration, checkered walnut stock and forearm. Imported 1986-87 only. VR became standard in 1987.

	$410	$360	$305	$280	$225	$185	$145	*$472*

Add $28 for Multi-Choke II.
Deduct $50 if without VR.

Model 1000 barrels are not interchangeable with Model 1000 Super barrels.

Manufactured by Howa, Mossberg took over this series after Smith & Wesson decided to drop the line.

* ***Model 1000 Semi-Auto Junior*** – similar to Model 1000, except 20 ga. only, shortened stock, and 22 in. VR Multi-Choke barrel. Imported 1986-87 only.

	$425	$370	$320	$290	$235	$190	$150	*$499*

* ***Model 1000 Semi-Auto Slug*** – 12 or 20 ga., 22 in. barrel with rifle sights, recoil pad. Imported 1986-87 only.

	$405	$355	$305	$275	$225	$180	$140	*$464*

* ***Model 1000 Semi-Auto Skeet*** – 12 or 20 ga., steel receiver, 26 in. VR barrel bored skeet. Mfg. 1986 only.

	$395	$345	$295	$270	$215	$180	$140	*$439*

MODEL 1000 SUPER SEMI-AUTO – 12 or 20 (Super 20) ga., gas semi-auto, 3 in. chambers, shoots 2 3/4 and 3 in. shells interchangeably, steel receiver, vent. recoil pad, select checkered walnut stock and forearm, Multi-Choke II is standard (except on slug barrel). Slug models are approx. the same price as values listed directly below. Imported 1986-87 only.

	$495	$435	$370	$335	$270	$225	$175	*$577*

Model 1000 Super barrels are not interchangeable with Model 1000 barrels.

Manufactured by Howa, Mossberg took over this series after Smith & Wesson decided to drop the line.

* ***Model 1000 Super Semi-Auto Waterfowler*** – 12 ga. only, matte finished wood and metal, includes swivels and camouflaged sling, 28 in. Multi-Choke barrel. Imported 1986-87 only.

	$510	$445	$380	$345	$280	$230	$180	*$605*

* ***Model 1000 Super Semi-Auto Skeet*** – 12 or 20 ga., 25 in. barrel, jug choking. Imported 1986-87 only.

	$575	$505	$430	$390	$315	$260	$200	*$658*

* ***Model 1000 Super Semi-Auto Trap*** – 12 ga. only, 30 in. Multi-Choke II barrel with high VR, Monte Carlo stock, recoil pad. Mfg. 1986 only.

	$470	$410	$350	$320	$260	$210	$165	*$560*

MODEL 5500 SEMI-AUTO – 12 ga., 2 3/4 or 3 in. mag., gas operated, 18 1/2 - 30 in. barrels. Disc. 1985.

	$250	$220	$185	$170	$135	$110	$85	*$307*

Add $20 for VR.

* ***Model 5500 Semi-Auto Mag.*** – 12 ga. only, 3 in. chamber, 30 in. VR barrel. Disc. 1985.

	$275	$240	$205	$185	$150	$125	$95	*$325*

GRADING - PPGS™	100%	98%	95%	90%	80%	70%	60%	LAST MSR

MODEL 5500 MKII SEMI-AUTO – 12 ga. only, supplied with 2 VR barrels - 26 in. (2 3/4 in. chamber) and 28 in. (3 in. chamber) VR barrels, includes choice of Accu-II choke tubes (lead shot only) or Accu-Steel choke tubes, blue or camo finish (new 1990), checkered hardwood stock and forearm, top receiver safety, recoil pad, 7 1/2 lbs. Mfg. 1989-1992.

	$260	$225	$195	$175	$145	$115	$90	*$294*

Add $10 for 24 in. rifled slug barrel.

Add $43 for camo metal finish and synthetic stock.

Add $30 for Turkey Model (24 in. barrel, camo finish, and synthetic stock).

This model was also available with different Combo options. Prices varied between $463- $484, depending on configuration of barrel choking.

* ***Model 5500 Mk II Semi-Auto U.S. Shooting Team*** – 12 ga., 2 3/4 in. chamber, 26 in. non-Mag. barrel with VR and Accu-II chokes, blue finish, checkered walnut stock and forearm, 7 1/2 lbs. Mfg. 1991-92.

	$325	$285	$245	$220	$180	$145	$115	*$376*

* ***Model 5500 Mk II Semi-Auto NWTF Special Edition*** – 12 ga. only, 3 in. chamber, 24 in. VR barrel with 1 choke tube, Mossy Oak Camo finish with synthetic stock and forearm, 7.3 lbs. Mfg. 1991-92.

	$365	$320	$275	$250	$200	$165	$130	*$428*

MODEL 6000 SEMI-AUTO – 12 ga. only, 2 3/4 or 3 in. chamber, 28 in. VR barrel with Accu-choke, economical model with walnut finish stock, blue finish, 7.7 lbs. Mfg. 1993 only.

	$280	$245	$210	$190	$155	$125	$100	*$321*

MODEL 9200 CROWN SEMI-AUTO – 12 ga. only, 3 in. chamber, gas operated, shoots any shell interchangeably, 18 1/2 (SP only), 22 (Bantam only), 24 in. rifled, 24 (Turkey), 26 (U.S. Shooting Team variation, new 1993), or 28 in. VR barrel with 3 Accu-chokes, engraved aluminum receiver, synthetic (18 1/2 in. barrel only) or walnut stained hardwood stock (1 in. shorter on Bantam Model) and forearm, top receiver safety, approx. 7 1/2 lbs. Mfg. 1992-2001.

	$460	$400	$345	$310	$255	$205	$160	*$574*

Add approx. $73-$95 for combo package.

Add $33 for TruGlo fiber optic sights (mfg. 1998 only).

Add $23 for 24 in. rifled slug barrel with trophy scope base.

Subtract $90 for synthetic stock (Special Purpose with matte blue finish, 18 1/2 in. barrel).

* ***Model 9200 Crown Semi-Auto Viking*** – 12 ga. only, 28 in. VR barrel with one Accu-Choke and twin bead sights, matte finish with green synthetic stock and forearm, 7.7 lbs. Mfg. 1996-98.

	$365	$320	$275	$250	$200	$165	$130	*$429*

* ***Model 9200 Crown Semi-Auto Special Hunter*** – 12 ga. only, 28 in. VR barrel with Accu-II choke set, parkerized finish, black synthetic stock. Mfg. 1998-2001.

	$425	$370	$320	$290	$235	$190	$150	*$491*

* ***Model 9200 Crown Semi-Auto Camo*** – 12 ga. only, similar to Model 9200, except is supplied with OFM (disc. 1996), Mossy Oak (disc. 1999), Realtree (mfg. 1994-95), Realtree AP (mfg. 1996-99) or Woodlands (new 1995) camo finish, 24 (Turkey) or 28 in. VR barrel. Mfg. 1992-99.

	$445	$390	$335	$300	$245	$200	$155	*$556*

Subtract approx. $40 for Turkey Model with Woodlands camo and one choke tube.

» ***Model 9200 Crown Semi-Auto Camo New Turkey*** – 12 ga. only, 24 in. VR barrel with XX-full choke tube only and fiber optic sights, choice of 100% Woodlands or Mossy Oak Shadow Branch camo treatment. Mfg. 1999-2001.

	$415	$365	$310	$280	$230	$185	$145	*$517*

Add approx. $95 for Mossy Oak Shadow Branch camo coverage.

* ***Model 9200 Crown Semi-Auto Jungle Gun*** – 12 ga. only, 18 1/2 in. plain barrel with cyl. bore, parkerized metal, synthetic stock. Mfg. 1998-2001.

	$610	$535	$455	$415	$335	$275	$215	*$704*

MODEL SA-20 SEMI-AUTO – 20 ga., 3 in. chamber, 5 shot, 26 (new 2009) or 28 in. ported VR barrel with Sport Set choke tubes, gas operation, front bead sights, matte blue metal finish, black synthetic stock and forearm, 5 3/4 - 6 lbs., mfg. by Armsan in Turkey beginning 2008.

MSR $624	$525	$460	$395	$355	$290	$240	$200	

* ***Model SA-20 All Purpose Field*** – 20 ga., 2 3/4 chamber, 26 in. VR barrel with Sport set chokes, 5 shot mag., bead sights, walnut stock and forend, blue metal finish, 5 3/4 lbs. New 2016.

MSR $717	$615	$540	$460	$425	$345	$275	$225	

GRADING - PPGS™	100%	98%	95%	90%	80%	70%	60%	LAST MSR

* ***Model SA-20 Youth Bantam All Purpose Field*** – 20 ga., 3 in. chamber, 5 shot, 24 in. VR barrel with Sport Set chokes, 13 in. LOP, front bead sights, black synthetic or high gloss walnut (new 2018) stock, matte blue finish, 5 1/2 lbs. New 2009.

MSR $624	$525	$460	$395	$355	$290	$240	$200	

Add $93 for high gloss walnut stock (new 2018).

* ***Model SA-20 Muddy Girl All Purpose*** – 20 ga., 3 in. chamber, 26 in. VR barrel, Sport set chokes, matte blue metal finish, 5 shot, bead sight, synthetic stock with Muddy Girl finish, 5 3/4 lbs. Mfg. 2014-2018.

	$500	$440	$375	$340	$275	$225	$175	*$598*

* ***Model SA-20 Tactical/Railed*** – 20 ga., 3 in. chamber, 5 shot, 20 in. VR cylinder bore barrel, ghost ring/fiber optic front sights, matte blue metal finish, easy load elevator, mag tube cap with tri-rail, top rail, and black synthetic stock, with or without (disc. 2017) pistol grip, 5 3/4-6 lbs. New 2011.

MSR $630	$535	$475	$400	$365	$300	$250	$200	

* ***Model SA-20 Turkey*** – 20 ga., 22 in. VR barrel with extended turkey tube chokes, fiber optic 3-dot sights, Mossy Oak Obsession synthetic stock and forend, top rail, sling, matte blue metal finish, 6 1/4 lbs. New 2016.

MSR $706	$600	$525	$450	$410	$325	$275	$225	

* ***Model SA-20 Turkey Thugs Series*** – 20 ga., 3 in. chamber, 5 shot, 22 in. VR ported barrel with extended Turkey choke tube, top Picatinny rail, "Turkey Thugs" receiver engraving, fiber optic 3-dot sights, easy load elevator, matte blue metal finish, synthetic stock, Mossy Oak Obsession camo finish, sling, 6 1/4 lbs. Mfg. 2012-2015.

	$535	$450	$400	$350	$295	$250	$200	*$633*

MOSSBERG INTERNATIONAL SA-20 DUCK COMMANDER – 20 ga., 3 in. chamber, 28 in. VR barrel, Sport Set chokes, matte blued finish, 5 shot, TruGlo fiber optic sights, Realtree Max-5 finish on stock and forearm, logo engraved synthetic stock, includes American flag bandana, 6 lbs. Mfg. 2014-2015.

	$585	$500	$450	$425	$395	$375	$350	*$682*

MOSSBERG INTERNATIONAL SA-28 ALL PURPOSE FIELD – 28 ga., 3 in. chamber, 26 in. VR barrel with Sport set chokes, 5 shot mag., bead sights, walnut stock and forend, blue metal finish, 5 3/4 lbs. New 2017.

MSR $717	$615	$540	$460	$425	$345	$275	$225	

* ***Model SA-28 Youth Bantam All Purpose Field*** – 28 ga., 3 in. chamber, 5 shot, 24 in. VR barrel with 5 choke set, 12 1/2 in. LOP, front bead sights, black synthetic or high gloss walnut (mfg. 2018 only) stock, matte blue finish, 5 1/2-6 1/4 lbs. New 2018.

MSR $624	$525	$460	$395	$355	$290	$240	$200	

Add $84 for high gloss walnut stock (mfg. 2018 only).

SA-410 ALL PURPOSE FIELD – .410 bore, 3 in. chamber, 26 in. VR barrel, Sport Set chokes, 5 shot, front bead sight, black synthetic stock, matte blue finish, 6.5 lbs. New 2020.

MSR $655	$550	$480	$415	$375	$310	$260	$215	

SA-410 TURKEY – .410 bore, 3 in. chamber, 26 in. VR barrel, extended turkey chokes, fiber optic ghost ring sights, synthetic stock with Mossy Oak Original Bottomland camo coverage, matte blue metal finish, 6.5 lbs. New 2020.

MSR $781	$665	$580	$500	$450	$365	$300	$260	

SHOTGUNS: SLIDE ACTION

In 1985, Mossberg purchased the parts inventory and manufacturing rights for the shotguns that Smith & Wesson discontinued in 1984. These 3000 Series models (manufactured in Japan) are identical to those models which S&W discontinued. Parts and warranties are not interchangeable.

Beginning 1989, all Mossbergs sold in the U.S. and Canada have been provided with a Cablelock which goes through the ejection port, making the gun's action inoperable.

To celebrate its 75th anniversary, Mossberg released a new Crown Grade variation within most models during 1994, including the slide action 500 and 835 Series. These can be differentiated from previous manufacture by cut checkering, redesigned walnut or American hardwood stocks and forearms, screw-in choke tubes, and 4 different camo patterns. The Crown Grade was discontinued in 2000.

On April 30, 2013, Mossberg announced the manufacture of its 10 millionth Mossberg 500 model.

At the SHOT Show during 2014, Mossberg unveiled its new Duck Commander Series. Please refer to individual listings.

GRADING - PPGS™	100%	98%	95%	90%	80%	70%	60%	LAST MSR

MODEL 200K – slide action shotgun, 12 ga., 28 in., select choke, plain pistol grip stock, black nylon slide handle. Mfg. 1955-59.

	$275	$220	$185	$170	$135	$110	$85	

MODEL 200D – similar to 200K, except interchangeable choke tubes (2). Mfg. 1955-59.

	$275	$220	$185	$170	$135	$110	$85	

MODEL 500 SLIDE ACTION FIELD (1962-1998 MFG.) – 12, 20 ga., or .410 bore, slide action, 24 in. (with rifle sights) or 20-28 in. barrel (with various chokes), upper receiver slide safety, C-Lect (disc.) & Accu-choke (became standard 1994) choke system, checkered hardwood pistol grip stock after 1973. Mfg. 1962-98.

	$250	$220	$185	$170	$135	$110	$85	*$309*

Subtract 10% if without VR (disc.).

Subtract 10% for fixed choke barrel in 12 or 20 ga.

For recent Model 500 information and values, please refer to Model 500 Field - Current Mfg. later in this section.

* ***Model 500 Slide Action Field Slugster*** – 12, 16, or 20 (disc. 1997) ga., 24 in. cyl. (disc. 1997) or rifled bore (became standard 1998) barrel, barrel porting became standard in 1998, choice of sights, walnut finished hardwood stock and forearm. Disc. 1998.

	$270	$235	$200	$185	$150	$120	$95	*$336*

Subtract $75 if w/o barrel porting or rifled bore.

* ***Model 500 Slide Action Field Bantam*** – 20 ga. or .410 bore (new 1991) only, 22 in. (20 ga.), 24 in. fixed choke barrel (.410 bore), or 26 in. VR barrel with Accu-choke(s), blue or blue matte (disc.), Bantam Jake with Realtree Camo finish in 20 ga./22 in. VR barrel only (disc.), 20 ga. has walnut finish stock and .410 bore has synthetic stock (both stocks are tailored for youth dimensions), 6.9 lbs. Mfg. 1990-96, reintroduced 1998 only.

	$200	$175	$150	$135	$110	$90	$70	*$312*

Subtract $12 for .410 bore.

Add $45 for Bantam Jake configuration (disc. 1993).

* ***Model 500 Slide Action Field Turkey*** – 12 or 20 (new 1995) ga., 22 (20 ga. only), or 24 in. barrel, Woodlands metal/wood camo finish. Disc. 1997.

	$265	$230	$200	$180	$145	$120	$95	*$324*

Subtract $15 for 20 ga.

Add $60 for 24 in. VR barrel with Ghost Ring Sight (12 ga. only).

* ***Model 500 Slide Action Field Muzzleloader Combo*** – 12 ga. only, includes 24 in. (rifled bore only, new 1993) or 28 in. VR Accu-choke barrel and additional 24 in. .50 cal. muzzleloader conversion barrel with rifled bore and iron sights, walnut finished hardwood stock and forearm, 7.2 lbs. Mfg. 1991-96.

	$335	$295	$250	$225	$185	$150	$115	*$385*

* ***Model 500 Slide Action Field Quail Unlimited*** – 20 ga. only, 26 in. VR barrel with Accu-II chokes (3), engraved receiver and hand selected stock and forearm, 3,500 mfg. in 1991 to commemorate the 10th anniversary of Quail Unlimited.

	$350	$305	$260	$240	$190	$155	$120	*$359*

* ***Model 500 Slide Action Field Sporting Steel Shot*** – 12 ga. only, 3 in. chamber, 28 in. VR Accu-choke barrel with special Accu-steel tube for shooting steel shot. Mfg. 1987-90.

	$250	$220	$185	$170	$135	$110	$85	*$295*

Add $29 for camo stock (disc. 1989).

This model was phased out of production in 1990 since all Mossberg shotguns currently manufactured are capable of shooting steel shot safely.

MODEL 500 50TH ANNIVERSARY – 12 ga. only, 28 in. ported barrel with vent. rib., blue finish, high gloss walnut with classic style red buttpad, white Pachmayr spacer, gold trigger, jeweled bolt, 50th Anniversary logo engraved on receiver. Limited mfg. 2011.

	$360	$300	$250	$225	$185	$150	$115	*$448*

MODEL 500AA 50TH ANNIVERSARY – 12 ga., Pigeon grade, trap, field, and skeet configuration, hand checkered walnut stock, red bead front and middle sights, left side of receiver engraved with 50th Anniversary emblem in gold, 50th Anniversary on pistol grip cap. Limited mfg. 1969 only.

	$650	$500	$435	N/A	N/A	N/A	N/A	

GRADING - PPGS™	100%	98%	95%	90%	80%	70%	60%	LAST MSR

MODEL 500 REGAL SERIES – 12 or 20 ga., slide action, 26 or 28 in. barrel, select checkered walnut, VR. Disc. 1987.

	$240	$210	$180	$165	$130	$110	$85	*$286*

Add $39 for Combo pack (includes 1 extra 24 in. slugster barrel).
Add $19 for Accu-choke.

MODEL 500 HI-RIB TRAP – 12 ga. only, high post trap rib, 28 or 30 in. barrel. Disc. 1986.

	$375	$330	$280	$255	$205	$170	$130	*$334*

Add $20 for Accu-choke.

MODEL 500 SUPER GRADE – similar to Model 500 Field, except VR and checkered, no 16 ga. Mfg. 1965-76.

	$250	$220	$185	$170	$135	$110	$85	

MODEL 500 ATR SUPER GRADE – 12 ga., 30 in. full VR barrel, checkered Monte Carlo stock. Mfg. 1968-1971.

	$350	$305	$260	$240	$190	$155	$120	

MODEL 500 APR PIGEON GRADE – 12 or 20 ga., similar to 500 Super Grade, floating VR barrel, select checkered wood stock, etched and scroll engraving. Mfg. 1971-75.

	$385	$335	$290	$260	$210	$175	$135	

MODEL 500 APTR PIGEON GRADE TRAP – similar to 500 ATR, except trap style stock. Mfg. 1971-75.

	$440	$385	$330	$300	$240	$200	$155	

MODEL 500 DSPR DUCK STAMP COMMEMORATIVE – similar to Pigeon Grade, except wood duck etching. 1,000 mfg. 1975.

	$525	$460	$395	$355	$290	$235	$185	

MODEL 500L SERIES – similar to 500 Field Grade, except no 16 ga., etched receiver, new style stock and slide. Mfg. 1977-83.

	$250	$220	$185	$170	$135	$110	$85	

MODEL 500 SPECIAL HUNTER – 12 or 20 ga., 3 in. chamber, 26 or 28 in. VR barrel with or w/o porting and Accu-chokes set, parkerized metal finish, black synthetic stock and forearm. Mfg. 1999-2002.

	$260	$225	$195	$175	$145	$115	$90	*$327*

MODEL 500 VIKING – 12 or 20 ga., 24 (12 ga. only, with rifled barrel and sights, porting became standard in 1997), 26 (20 ga. only) or 28 (12 ga. only, porting became standard in 1997) in. ported (new 1997, 12 ga. only) or unported VR barrel with one Accu-choke and twin bead sights, matte finish with green synthetic stock and forearm, approx. 7 lbs. Mfg. 1996-98.

	$230	$200	$170	$155	$125	$105	$80	*$287*

Add $40 for 12 ga. rifled barrel.
Add $108 for Slug Shooting System with ported barrel.

* ***Model 500 Viking Turkey*** – 12 ga. only, 24 in. ported VR barrel, green synthetic stock, matte finish, Accu-choke. Mfg. 1997-98.

	$230	$200	$170	$155	$125	$105	$80	*$286*

MODEL 500 ATI SCORPION – 12 ga., 18 1/2 in. barrel, dual extractors, bead sight, ATI Akita (FDE/black) adj. Scorpion recoil stock and forend with heat shield and rails, ambidextrous safety, matte blue finish, 6 3/4 lbs. New 2016.

This model is available only through a Talo Group distributor. Visit taloinc.com for more information.

MODEL 500 ATI TACTICAL – 12 ga., 3 in. chamber, 18 1/2 in. barrel with heat shield and rails, 6 shot mag., winged post and bead sights, ATI 6-pos. adj. synthetic stock, Scorpion Recoil ATI Akita forend, Destroyer Gray/Black finish, 6 3/4 lbs. New 2019.

MSR $643	$540	$475	$400	$365	$300	$250	$210	

This model is available through a Talo Group Distributor.

MODEL 500 ATI TACTICAL CRUISER – 12 ga., 3 in. chamber, 18 1/2 in. barrel, 6 shot, winged post and bead sights, ATI T3 pistol grip (disc. 2018) or ATI 6-pos. adj. synthetic stock with FDE and black finish, Akita forend, Halo side saddle with top rail with 9 polymer add-a-shell holders, Halo heat shield and front rails, matte blue metal finish, 5.75-6.75 lbs. New 2017.

MSR $643	$540	$475	$400	$365	$300	$250	$210	

Subtract approx. $25 for ATI T3 pistol grip stock (disc. 2018).

This model is available through a Talo Group Distributor.

MODEL 500 BULLPUP – 12 ga., 18 1/2 (6 shot) or 20 (9 shot) in. barrel, bullpup configuration, 6 or 9 shot mag., includes shrouded barrel, carrying handle, ejection port in stock, employs high impact materials. Mfg. 1986-90.

	$650	$525	$450	$415	$325	$275	$215	*$425*

Add $15 for 8 shot mag. (disc.).

GRADING - PPGS™	100%	98%	95%	90%	80%	70%	60%	LAST MSR

MODEL 500 CAMPER – 12, 20 ga., or .410 bore only, 18 1/2 in. barrel, synthetic pistol grip (no stock), camo carrying case optional, blued finish. Mfg. 1986-90 only.

	$250	$220	$185	$170	$135	$110	$85	*$276*

Add $25 for .410 bore.
Add $30 for camo case.

MODEL 500 CAMO – 12 or 20 ga., 100% camo includes parkerized camo (disc.), OFM Camo (standard, mfg. 1991-96), Woodlands (mfg. 1995-2003), and various other camo finishes, metal and synthetic stock coverage, 24 (disc.), 26 (disc.), 28, or 30 (disc.) in. ported (standard 1997) or unported (disc. 2000) VR barrel (choice of cylinder bore with rifle sights or Accu-II chokes), front fiber optic sight, includes swivels, camo sling, and drilled and tapped receiver, older Speedfeed stock (disc. 1990) holds 4 extra shells, 7 1/2 lbs. New 1986.

Subtract 10% if without Accu-II choke system.
Add $30 for Speedfeed in synthetic stock (disc. 1990).

Accu-chokes became standard in 1991. Current models are supplied with 2 choke tubes.

* ***Model 500 Camo All Purpose*** – 12 or 20 ga. (disc. 2004), 26 in. barrel, fiber optic sights, 100% Mossy Oak New Break Up (12 ga. only) or Mossy Oak Shadow Grass (20 ga. only) camo coverage. Disc. 2010.

	$345	$300	$250	$225	$185	$150	$115	*$422*

* ***Model 500 Camo Combo*** – 12 or 20 ga., includes a wide variety of extra barrel combinations including slug barrel options, prices vary slightly depending on the configuration (gauge/barrel/choke set-up), rifled bores, VR barrels, and Accu-chokes became standard in the combo package late 1994. Disc. 1998.

	$375	$330	$280	$255	$205	$170	$130	*$434*

MODEL 500 CENTENNIAL LIMITED EDITION – 12 ga., 3 in. chamber, 28 in. VR barrel, interchangeable Accu-Set choke tubes, 5 shot mag., gold-plated trigger w/fixed LOP, dual bead sight, high polish walnut stock w/red rubber recoil pad and forend, fine checkered pistol grip, ambi top-mounted safety, jeweled bolt, "Mossberg 100th Anniversary" logo on right side and flushing grouse w/gold inlays on left side of frame, high polish blued barrel w/nickel finish receiver, 7 1/2 lbs. Limited 750 mfg. 2019 only.

	$800	$700	$600	$525	$425	$350	$300	*$910*

MODEL 500 CHAINSAW – 12 ga., 3 in. chamber, 18 1/2 in. stand-off barrel with cyl. bore choke, 6 shot mag., pistol grip synthetic stock, matte black finish, easily removable unique "chainsaw" forend grip provides muzzle control and stability, drilled and tapped, tri-rail forend, white dot sights, 6 lbs. Mfg. 2011-2019.

	$465	$400	$350	$315	$255	$210	$165	*$547*

MODEL 500 CHAINSAW ZMB – 12 ga., 3 in. chamber, 18 1/2 in. stand-off barrel with cyl. bore choke, 6 shot mag., matte black finish, easily removable unique "chainsaw" forend grip provides muzzle control and stability, drilled and tapped, tri-rail forend, white dot sights, includes light and laser combo, ZMB engraved logo on receiver, pistol grip black synthetic stock, 6 lbs. Mfg. 2012-2014.

	$550	$475	$425	$375	$300	$250	$200	*$650*

MODEL 500 CLASSIC – 12 ga., 28 in. ported barrel, vent. rib, Accu-Set choke, gold trigger, finely checkered high gloss walnut stock and forearm, jeweled bolt, red recoil pad with white Pachmayr spacer, 7 1/2 lbs.

MSR $526	$450	$400	$340	$300	$250	$200	$175	

MODEL 500 CRUISER – 12, 20 ga., or .410 (new 1993) bore, 3 in. chamber, 14 (12 ga. only, Law Enforcement Model, disc. 1995), 18 1/2, 20, or 21 (20 ga. only - mfg. 1995-2002) in. cylinder bore barrel, shroud is available in 12 ga. only, 6 or 8 (12 ga. only) shot mag., bead sights, black synthetic pistol grip stock, right or left (mfg. 2015-2018) hand configuration, 5 1/2-6 1/2 lbs. Mfg. 1989-2019.

	$395	$345	$295	$270	$215	$180	$140	*$466*

Add $18 for heat shield around barrel (12 ga. only).
Add $18 for 8 shot (20 in. barrel, 12 ga. only).
Add $32 for left-hand configuration (mfg. 2015-2018).
Add $96 for 14 in. barrel (disc.).
Add approx. $34 for camper case (1993-1996).

* ***Model 500 Crusier Blackwater Series*** – 12 ga., 3 in. chamber, 18 1/2 in. cylinder bore barrel, synthetic pistol grip, matte black finish, white dot front sight, ported stand off door breacher at muzzle, 6 shot, half-round ribbed forearm with nylon web strap, Blackwater logo on right side of receiver, approx. 6 lbs. Mfg. 2011-2014.

	$425	$375	$325	$295	$250	$200	$150	*$493*

GRADING - PPGS™	100%	98%	95%	90%	80%	70%	60%	LAST MSR

* ***Model 500 Cruiser Mil-Spec*** – 12 ga. only, 20 in. cylinder bored barrel with bead sights, built to Mil-Specs., parkerized finish. Mfg. 1997 only.

	$395	$345	$295	$270	$215	$180	$140	*$478*

* ***Model 500 Cruiser Road Blocker*** – 12 ga. only, 3 in. chamber, 6 shot, 18 1/2 in. heavy walled barrel with heat shield and large muzzle brake, bead sights, matte blue metal finish, black synthetic pistol grip (no stock), 5 3/4 lbs. Mfg. 2009-2014.

	$475	$415	$350	$325	$250	$200	$160	*$562*

* ***Model 500 Cruiser Rolling Thunder*** – 12 ga., 3 in. chamber, 6 shot, 23 in. heavy walled barrel with stabilizer, heat shield, Picatinny top rail, matte blue metal finish, Black synthetic pistol grip stock, 6 3/4 lbs. Mfg. 2009-2014.

	$475	$415	$350	$325	$250	$215	$175	*$553*

* ***Model 500 Cruiser Tactical Light Forend*** – 12 ga., 3 in. chamber, 6 shot, 18 1/2 in. cylinder bore barrel, white dot sights, matte blue metal finish, integrated Insight tactical light forend with 3-function ambidextrous touchpad, black synthetic pistol grip, 5 3/4 lbs. Mfg. 2008-2015.

	$560	$475	$415	$375	$300	$250	$200	*$670*

* ***Model 500 Cruiser Tactical Tri-Rail w/Center Mass Laser*** – 12 ga., 3 in. chamber, 6 shot, 18 1/2 in. cylinder bore barrel, bead sight, LaserLyte Center Mass laser with three modes (constant on, pulse, and auto off) mounted on tactical tri-rail forend, full-length bottom Picatinny rail, black synthetic pistol grip, matte blue metal finish, 5 3/4 lbs. Mfg. 2014-2015

	$585	$500	$425	$395	$315	$260	$200	*$695*

MODEL 500 DUCK COMMANDER – 12 ga., 3 in. chamber, 28 in. VR ported barrel, Accu-Set chokes, 100% Realtree Max-5 finish, TruGlo Tru-Bead fiber optic sight, logo engraved synthetic stock, American flag bandana, 7 1/2 lbs. Mfg. 2014-2016.

	$485	$425	$375	$335	$300	$275	$250	*$578*

MODEL 500 DUCK COMMANDER SIGNATURE – 12 ga., 3 in. chamber, 26 in. VR barrel, Accu-Set chokes, 6 shot, Truglo Tru-Bead fiber optic sight, Realtree Max-5 synthetic tock and forend, OD Green metal finish with repeat duck-in-flight pattern and Duck Commander logo on front with "Faith. Family. Ducks." engraving on back, "Happy Happy Happy" magazine tube cap, 7 1/4 lbs. Mfg. 2014-2016.

	$475	$425	$375	$335	$300	$275	$250	*$561*

This model was available through a Talo Group distributor only.

MODEL 500 FIELD - CURRENT MFG. – 12, 20 ga., or .410 bore, 2 3/4 (disc.) or 3 in. chamber, 24, 26, or 28 in. ported (new 1997, 12 ga. only, 26 (disc. 2013) or 28 in. barrel) or unported VR (unless with rifle sights) barrel, Slug model offers choice of 12 ga. with 24 in. ported barrel and rifle sights (mfg. 2001-2004) or .410 bore (new 2003) with adj. fiber optic sights and vent. rib, matte (12 or 20 ga. only, new 2005), Mossy Oak New Break-Up (disc. 2011) or Infinity (mfg. 2012-2013) camo, or blue finish, walnut finished or synthetic (.410 bore only) stock, safety on back of receiver top, Accu-chokes except for Slug Model and .410 bore, supplied with 1 Accu-choke, 6-7 1/2 lbs.

MSR $459	$390	$340	$295	$265	$215	$175	$150	

Add $65 for camo (disc. 2013).

Add $14 for Slug Model in .410 bore with adj. fiber optic sights and VR barrel (disc. 2004).

This model also includes the Crown Grade, manufactured 1994-2000.

* ***Model 500 Field Bantam*** – 12 (new 2001), 20 ga. or .410 bore (synthetic stock only), 3 in. chamber, similar to Model 500 Field, except has shortened, specially contoured stock and forearm (13 in. LOP), and 22 (20 ga. only) or 24 in. ported (12 ga. only, with VR) or unported barrel, 6 - 7 1/4 lbs.

MSR $459	$390	$340	$295	$265	$215	$175	$150	

Add $62 for Field combo w/22 or 24 in. fully rifled deer barrel (20 ga. only), wood stock.

* ***Model 500 Field Synthetic*** – 12, 20 ga. or .410 bore, 3 in. chamber, 24 (slug model with ported barrel with cylinder bore choke and adj. rifle sights, new 2001), 26 (20 ga. only), or 28 (12 ga. ported only) in. VR barrel, black parkerized metal finish, black synthetic stock and forearm, 7-7 1/2 lbs. Disc. 2004.

	$255	$225	$190	$175	$140	$115	$90	*$316*

Add $14 for .410 bore Bantam Slug Model.

* ***Model 500 Field/Deer Combo*** – 12 or 20 ga., 3 in. chamber, 6 shot, two barrel 12 ga. set includes 28 in. VR ported barrel with Accu-Set chokes and dual bead sight and 24 in. ported fully rifled slugster barrel with integral scope base (dual comb stock only), or 24 in. fluted fully rifled barrel with adj. rifle sights (wood stock only), 20 ga. two barrel set includes 26 in. VR ported barrel with

GRADING - PPGS™	100%	98%	95%	90%	80%	70%	60%	LAST MSR

Accu-Set chokes and dual bead sight and 24 in. ported fully rifled barrel with adj. rifle sights, blue finish, wood stock with or w/o dual comb (12 ga. only), 7-7 1/2 lbs.

MSR $521	$440	$385	$330	$300	$240	$200	$175	

Add $35 for dual comb wood stock.
Add $46 for left-hand configuration (mfg. 2015-2018).

* ***Model 500 Field/Deer Combo Camo*** – 12 or 20 ga., 3 in. chamber, 6 shot, two barrel 12 ga. set includes 28 in. VR ported Field barrel with Accu-Set choke and dual bead sight and 24 in. ported fully rifled Slugster barrel with adj. rifle sight, two barrel 20 ga. set includes 26 in. VR ported Field barrel with Accu-Set choke and dual bead sight and 24 in. ported fully rifled Slugster barrel with adj. rifle sight, synthetic stock with 100% Mossy Oak New Break-Up (disc. 2011), Mossy Oak Break-Up Infinity (mfg. 2012-2015), or Mossy Oak Break-Up Country (new 2016) camo coverage, 7 lbs.

MSR $591	$510	$450	$385	$350	$275	$225	$200	

* ***Model 500 Field/Deer Combo Recoil Reduction System*** – 12 ga., 3 in. chamber, 6 shot, two barrel set includes 24 in. ported barrel with adj. rifle sight and fully rifled bore and 28 in. VR ported barrel with dual bead sight and Accu-Set chokes, features Mathews Harmonic Damper Technology, dual comb synthetic stock, 100% Mossy Oak Break-Up Infinity camo coverage, 8 1/4 lbs. Mfg. 2013-2014.

	$500	$450	$375	$350	$275	$225	$175	*$586*

* ***Model 500 Field/Deer Scoped Combo*** – 12 or 20 ga., 3 in. chamber, 24 and 28 in. barrel (12 ga.) or 24 and 26 in. VR barrel (20 ga.), fully rifled bore with AccuSet chokes, 6 shot mag., dual bead sights, black synthetic dual comb stock, includes Dead Ringer 2.5x20mm scope, matte blue finish, 7 lbs. New 2019.

MSR $498	$425	$375	$325	$295	$235	$195	$165	

* ***Model 500 Field/Security Combo*** – 12 ga., 3 in. chamber, 6 shot, two barrel set includes 28 in. VR ported Field barrel with Accu-Set choke and dual bead sight and 18 1/2 in. cylinder bore barrel with bead sight, wood stock, blue finish, includes pistol grip kit, 6-3/4-7 1/2 lbs.

MSR $508	$425	$375	$325	$295	$235	$195	$165	

MODEL 500 FIELD SLUGSTER – 12 or 20 ga., 3 in. chamber, 24 in. ported (standard 1997) or unported (disc. 1996) barrel, choice of cyl. (disc. 2000) or rifled (standard 2001) bore, right or left-hand (mfg. 2015-2017) action, blue or Marinecote (mfg. 1995-97) finish, TruGlo fiber optic sights (12 ga. only, disc. 2004), or Trophy Slugster integral scope base, synthetic (disc.), press checkered hardwood stock and forearm, or dual comb stock with extra synthetic cheekpiece (new 2003), 6 3/4 -7 1/4 lbs. Disc. 2018.

	$355	$310	$265	$240	$195	$160	$125	*$419*

Add $33 for dual comb stock and integral scope base (new 2003, includes extra synthetic cheekpiece).
Add $47 for left-hand action with dual comb stock (mfg. 2015-2017).
Add $23 for TruGlo fiber optic sights (mfg. 1998-2004).
Add $125 for Marinecote finish (with synthetic stock, disc.).

This model also included the Crown Grade Slugster, manufactured 1994-2000.

* ***Model 500 Slugster Camo*** – 12 (disc. 2014) or 20 ga., 3 in. chamber, 24 in. ported barrel, fully rifled bore, 6 shot, integral scope base, synthetic (disc.) or hardwood dual comb stock, 100% Mossy Oak New Break-Up (disc. 2011), Mossy Oak Break-Up Infinity (mfg. 2012-2014), Realtree AP (disc. 2012), Realtree Extra (mfg. 2013-2015), or Mossy Oak Break-Up Country (new 2016) camo coverage, 6 3/4-7 1/4 lbs. Mfg. 2004-2017.

	$440	$385	$330	$300	$250	$200	$160	*$514*

* ***Model 500 LPA Slugster*** – 12 ga., 3 in. chamber, 24 in. fluted barrel, fully rifled bore, 6 shot, LPA adj. trigger, wood stock with rifle sights and blue finish or dual comb synthetic stock with integral scope base and Realtree AP (disc. 2012) or Realtree Extra camo finish (mfg. 2013-2014), 7 lbs. Mfg. 2011-2017.

	$395	$345	$295	$270	$215	$180	$140	*$461*

Add $96 for dual comb synthetic stock with camo finish (disc. 2014).

MODEL 500 FIELD SUPER BANTAM – 20 ga. only, 3 in. chamber, 22 in. VR barrel, Accu-Set chokes, 5 shot, dual bead sights, adj. 12-13 in. LOP, synthetic stock with spacers, matte blue, pink marble (mfg. 2009-2017), Muddy Girl Serenity (new 2018), or Muddy Girl Wild (new 2021) finish, right or left (new 2015) hand configuration, 5 1/4 lbs. New 2005.

MSR $459	$390	$340	$295	$265	$215	$175	$150	

Add $44 for Muddy Girl Serenity camo (new 2018) or pink marble (mfg. 2009-2017) stock.
Add $56 for Muddy Girl Wild camo stock (new 2021).
Add $14 for left-hand configuration (disc. 2019).

GRADING - PPGS™	100%	98%	95%	90%	80%	70%	60%	LAST MSR

* ***Model 500 Super Bantam Slugster*** – 20 ga., 3 in. chamber, 24 in. ported fully rifled Slugster barrel, 6 shot, adj. rifle sights or integral scope base, adj. synthetic stock with spacer, blue, 100% Mossy Oak New Break-Up (disc. 2008), Realtree AP (disc. 2012) or Realtree Extra (mfg. 2013-2014) camo finish, 5 1/4 lbs. Disc. 2017.

	$355	$310	$265	$240	$195	$160	$125	*$419*

Add $67 for 100% Realtree Extra camo coverage (disc. 2014).

* ***Model 500 Super Bantam Turkey*** – 20 ga. only, 3 in. chamber, 22 in. barrel, X-full chokes, adj. fiber optic sights, adj. 12-13 in. LOP, adj. synthetic stock and forearm, 100% Mossy Oak New Break-Up (disc. 2008, Slug model only), Mossy Oak Break Up Infinity (mfg. 2011-2015), Mossy Oak Obsession (mfg. 2009-2010, reintroduced 2013), or Realtree Hardwoods HD Green (disc. 2013) camo coverage. New 2005.

MSR $533	$460	$400	$350	$315	$250	$200	$175	

* ***Model 500 Super Bantam Waterfowl*** – 20 ga., 22 in. VR barrel, Accu-Set chokes, 6 shot, adj. fiber optic sight, adj. synthetic stock, 12-13 in. LOP, 100% Mossy Oak Shadow Grass Blades finish. New 2016.

MSR $533	$460	$400	$350	$315	$250	$200	$175	

* ***Model 500 Super Bantam Field/Deer Combo*** – 20 ga., 3 in. chamber, 6 shot, two barrel set includes 22 in. VR barrel with Accu-Set chokes and dual bead sights and 24 in. ported barrel with fully rifled bore and adj. rifle sights, 12-13 in. LOP, adj. synthetic stock with spacer, blue, Realtree AP (disc. 2012), Realtree Extra (mfg. 2013-2015), Mossy Oak New Break-Up (disc. 2011), Mossy Oak Break-Up Infinity (disc. 2015), or Mossy Oak Break-Up Country (new 2016) camo coverage, 5 1/4 lbs.

MSR $521	$440	$385	$330	$300	$240	$200	$175	

Add $70 for camo coverage.

MODEL 500 FLEX ALL PURPOSE – 12 ga., 3 in. chamber, 6 shot, 26 or 28 in. VR ported barrel, Accu-Set choke, twin bead sights, standard or LPA (disc. 2016) trigger, matte blue or Marinecote (26 in. only, disc. 2017) finish, black synthetic stock, TLS Tool-less locking system, right or left (mfg. 2015-2016) hand configuration, 7 1/2 lbs. New mid-2012.

MSR $536	$460	$400	$350	$315	$250	$200	$175	

Add $44 for Marinecote finish (disc. 2017).
Add $14 for left-hand configuration (mfg. 2015-2016).
Add $44 for LPA trigger (disc. 2016).

MODEL 500 FLEX DEER SECURITY COMBO – 12 ga., 24 in. ported barrel/cantilever mount with fully rifled bore and 18 1/2 in. security barrel with bead sights, 4-pos. adj. synthetic stock with dual comb in Mossy Oak Break-Up Infinity camo finish and a black synthetic pistol grip stock, railed forend, matte blue barrel finish, includes FLEX soft case, 5 3/4-7 3/4 lbs. Mfg. 2015-2018.

	$675	$590	$500	$460	$370	$300	$235	*$787*

MODEL 500 FLEX DUCK COMMANDER – 12 ga., 3 in. chamber, 28 in. barrel, Accu-Set chokes, 6 shot, TruGlo Tru-Bead fiber optic sight, FLEX TLS (Tool-less Locking System) Connectors, Realtree Max-5 finish on stock and forearm, OD Green metal finish, Logo engraved synthetic stock, includes American flag bandana, 7 1/2 lbs. Mfg. 2014-2015.

	$740	$655	$575	$525	$475	$425	$395	*$862*

MODEL 500 FLEX FIELD/SECURITY COMBO – 20 ga., 18 1/2 and 26 in. VR barrel, Accu-Set chokes, 6 shot, fiber optic front bead sight, black synthetic standard or pistol grip stock, standard or railed forend, matte blue finish, 5.75-7 lbs. Mfg. 2017-2018.

	$500	$440	$375	$340	$275	$225	$175	*$596*

MODEL 500 FLEX HUNTING – 12 ga., 3 in. chamber, 24 (disc. 2016) or 28 in. VR ported barrel, X-Factor ported, Accu-Set, XX full choke (disc.), or fully rifled bore (disc.), TLS Tool-less locking system, adj. fiber optic sight or integral scope base (adj. stock only, disc. 2016), standard or LPA (disc. 2016) trigger, standard synthetic or adj. synthetic (disc. 2016)stock with matte blue/Mossy Oak Break-Up Infinity (disc. 2014), Realtree Advantage Max-4 (disc. 2015), OD Green/Mossy Oak Break-Up Infinity (disc. 2016), or Tan/Realtree Advantage Max-4 finish, 7 1/4-7 3/4 lbs. Mfg. mid-2012-2018.

	$475	$415	$350	$325	$260	$215	$165	*$557*

Add $40 for LPA adj. trigger (disc. 2016). Add $122 for adj. stock (disc. 2016).

* ***Model 500 Flex Hunting 20 Ga.*** – 20 ga., 3 in. chamber, 24 (X Factor ported chokes) or 26 in. VR barrel, choice of matte blue (26 in.) or OD Green (24 in.) metal finish, 6 shot, TLS Tool-less Locking System, choice of black synthetic or 100% Mossy Oak Break Up Infinity camo stock and Field forend, twin bead or adj. fiber optic sights, 7 lbs. Mfg. 2014-2017.

	$415	$365	$310	$280	$230	$185	$150	*$489*

Add $109 for Mossy Oak Break Up Infinity camo stock and OD Green metal finish.

GRADING - PPGS™	100%	98%	95%	90%	80%	70%	60%	LAST MSR

MODEL 500 FLEX TACTICAL – 12 or 20 (new 2014) ga., 3 in. chamber, 6 shot, 20 in. cylinder bore barrel, matte blue, OD Green (disc. 2015), or tan barrel finish, XS ghost ring or plain bead sight, Picatinny top rail, tactical railed forend, standard or six position adj. black synthetic stock, TLS Tool-less locking system, 6 1/4-6 3/4 lbs. Mfg. mid-2012-2016.

	$535	$470	$400	$365	$295	$240	$185	*$630*

Add $29 for tan barrel finish.
Add $8 for XS ghost ring sight with OD Green barrel finish (disc. 2015).

MODEL 500 FLEX TACTICAL CRUISER – 12 or 20 (mfg. 2014-2016) ga., 3 in. chamber, 6 shot, 18 1/2 in. Standoff barrel with matte blue finish, cyl. bore, white dot sight, TLS Tool-Less Locking System, tactical tri-rail forend, black synthetic pistol grip stock, 5 3/4-6 3/4 lbs. New 2014.

MSR $640	$540	$475	$400	$365	$300	$275	$250	

MODEL 500 FLEX TURKEY SECURITY COMBO – 12 ga., 24 in. VR turkey and 18 1/2 in. security barrels, X-factor ported chokes, 6 shot, adj. fiber optic (24 in.) or bead (18 1/2 in.) sights, standard synthetic stock with Mossy Oak Break-Up Infinity or black pistol grip synthetic stock, includes Flex soft case, OD Green finish with two sets of stocks in Mossy Oak Break-Up Infinity and black synthetic pistol grip, 5 3/4-6 3/4 lbs. Mfg. 2015-2018.

	$580	$510	$435	$395	$320	$260	$200	*$683*

MODEL 500 FLEX WATERFOWL SECURITY COMBO – 12 ga., 28 in. VR waterfowl barrel with Accu-Set chokes and fiber optic front sights and 18 1/2 in. cylinder bore security barrel with bead sights, 6 shot, standard synthetic stock with Realtree Advantage Max-4 finish and black synthetic pistol grip stock, tan barrel finish, includes FLEX soft case, 5 3/4-7 1/2 lbs. Mfg. 2015-2018.

	$560	$490	$420	$380	$310	$250	$200	*$659*

MODEL 500 FLEX YOUTH – 20 ga., 2 3/4 in. chamber, 22 in. VR barrel, Accu-set chokes, dual bead sights, EZ-Reach forend/FLEX compact synthetic stock, 12 1/2 in. LOP, blue finish, 6 1/2 lbs. New 2019.

MSR $500	$425	$375	$325	$295	$235	$195	$165	

* ***Model 500 FLEX Youth Combo*** – 20 ga., 2 3/4 in. chamber, 22 and 24 in. VR barrel, Accu-set chokes, 5 shot mag., dual bead front and adj. rear sights, EZ-Reach forend/FLEX 4-pos. adj. stock, 12 3/4-14.625 in. LOP, blue finish, 6 1/2-6 3/4 lbs. New 2019.

MSR $582	$495	$435	$375	$335	$275	$225	$195	

MODEL 500 GHOST RING SIGHT – 12 ga. only, 3 in. chamber, 18 1/2 or 20 in. cyl. bore or Accu-choke (20 in. only - new 1995) barrel, 6 or 9 shot tube mag., blue or parkerized finish, synthetic field stock, includes ghost ring sighting device. Mfg. 1990-97.

	$270	$235	$200	$185	$150	$120	$95	*$332*

Add $53 for parkerized finish.
Add $49 for 9 shot mag. (20 in. barrel only).
Add $123 for Accu-choke barrel (parkerized finish only).
Add $134 for Speedfeed stock (new 1994 - 9 shot, 20 in. barrel only).

MODEL 500 HOME SECURITY HS410 – 20 (1996 only) ga. or .410 bore, 3 in. chamber, 18 1/2 in. barrel with spreader choke, Model 500 slide-action, 6 shot mag., blue metal finish, black or Muddy Girl (mfg. 2014-2016) synthetic field stock with pistol grip forearm, 5 1/2 lbs. Mfg. 1990-2019.

	$400	$350	$300	$275	$220	$180	$150	*$477*

Add $28 for Muddy Girl camo stock and forend (mfg. 2014-2016).

* ***Model 500 Home Security Laser .410*** – .410 bore, includes laser sighting device in right front of forearm. Mfg. 1990-1993.

	$400	$350	$300	$270	$220	$180	$140	*$451*

MODEL 500 20 GA. HOME DEFENSE – 20 ga., 2 3/4 or 3 in. chamber, 20 in. barrel, ghost ring sights, matte blue metal finish, 8 shot, matte black synthetic tactical 6-position adj. stock with pistol grip, ambidextrous safety, sling swivels, extended mag. tube, fixed cylinder bore choke, 6 lbs. 12 oz. Mfg. 2013-2019.

	$540	$475	$400	$365	$295	$250	$200	*$631*

MODEL 500 J.I.C. (JUST IN CASE) – 12 ga., 3 in. chamber, 18 1/2 or 20 (mfg. 2013-2015) in. cyl. bore barrel, 6 or 8 (2013-2015) shot, comes with pistol grip, impact resistant tube and strap, available in four configurations: 5.11 Pack (w/takedown 500 and tools), Cruiser (survival kit in a can, blue metal, OD Green tube), Mariner (multi-tool and knife, orange tube, Marinecote finish), Sandstorm (Desert camo tube and finish, disc. 2014), or black (8 shot only, mfg. 2013-2015), 5 1/2 lbs. New 2007.

MSR $549	$470	$410	$350	$325	$260	$215	$185	

Add $62 for Sandstorm model (disc. 2014) or $147 for Mariner model.

GRADING - PPGS™	100%	98%	95%	90%	80%	70%	60%	LAST MSR

* ***Model 500 J.I.C. Flex*** – 12 ga., 3 in. chamber, 18 1/2 in. cyl. bore barrel, 6 shot, matte blue finish, features Flex TLS Tool-less locking system, black pistol grip, neoprene soft carrying case, 5 1/2 lbs. New 2014.

MSR $556	$475	$410	$350	$325	$260	$215	$185	

* ***Model 500 J.I.C. Patriot*** – 12 ga., 3 in. chamber, 18 1/2 in. cyl. bore barrel, matte blue finish, 6 shot, bead sight, special commemorative edition with NRA logo receiver engraving, full color US Flag and 2nd Amendment graphics on water resistant tube with carrying strap, black pistol grip, 5 1/2 lbs. Mfg. 2014-2016.

	$475	$415	$355	$325	$260	$215	$165	*$550*

Mossberg donated a portion of the proceeds of every sale of this shotgun to NRA programs.

MODEL 500 MARINER – 12 ga. only, 3 in. chamber, 18 1/2 or 20 (disc.) in. cyl. bore barrel, 6 or 9 (disc. 2008) shot, bead, fixed (disc.), or ghost ring (mfg. 1995-99) sights, Marinecote finish on all metal parts (more rust-resistant than stainless steel), full-length black synthetic stock with pistol grip conversion kit, 5 3/4- 6 3/4 lbs. Disc. 2017.

	$540	$475	$400	$365	$295	$250	$200	*$636*

Add $51 for 9 shot model with 20 in. barrel (disc. 2008).
Add $68 for ghost ring rear sight (disc. 1999).
Add $23 for Speedfeed stock (mini-combo only - disc.).

MODEL 500 PERSUADER – 12, 20 (mfg. 1995-2016, reintroduced 2018) ga., or .410 (new 2017), 6 or 8 shot, 18 1/2 in. plain or Standoff barrel, cyl. bore or Accu-chokes (mfg. 1995-disc.), optional rifle (12 ga./20 in. cyl. bore barrel only), bead, white dot, or ghost ring (new 1999-2004, reintroduced 2013 only) sights, blue, matte (new 2006), or parkerized (12 ga. with ghost ring sights only, disc. 2004) finish, Speedfeed stock was disc. 1990, optional bayonet lug, plain pistol grip wood (disc. 2004), black synthetic stock with or w/o pistol grip, right or left (20 ga. only, mfg. 2015-2016) hand configuration, 5 1/2-7 1/2 lbs. Disc. 2019.

	$395	$345	$295	$270	$215	$180	$140	*$466*

Add $18 for pistol grip.
Add $48 for 20 ga. with Standoff barrel (new 2009).
Add $14 for left-hand configuration (20 ga. only, mfg. 2015-2016).
Add $18 for tri-rail Picatinny forend (mfg. 2011-2013).
Add $159 for ghost ring sights (mfg. 1999-2004, 2013 only).
Add $127 for parkerized finish and ghost ring sights (disc. 2004).
Add $40 for combo with pistol grip (disc.).
Add $23 for rifle sights (disc., 12 ga. only).

* ***Model 500 Persuader Bantam/Compact*** – 20 ga., 3 in. chamber, 20 in. cylinder bore barrel, matte blue finish, ghost ring sights, synthetic stock. Mfg. 2013-2019.

	$425	$375	$325	$295	$250	$200	$160	*$505*

* ***Model 500 Persuader Muddy Girl*** – 20 ga., 3 in. chamber, 20 in. barrel, matte blue metal finish, cyl. bore chokes, 8 shot mag., ghost ring sights, 6-position adj. synthetic stock, Muddy Girl camo finish, 6 3/4 lbs. Mfg. 2014-2016.

	$545	$475	$410	$370	$300	$250	$200	*$640*

* ***Model 500 Persuader Night Special Edition*** – 12 ga., includes synthetic stock and factory installed Mepro-Light night sight bead sight. Limited mfg. of 300 for Lew Horton Distributing in 1990 only.

	$350	$260	$225	$200	$160	$135	$115	*$296*

* ***Model 500 Persuader w/XS Express Sights*** – 12 ga., 3 in. chamber, 20 in. cylinder bore barrel with matte blue finish, 8 shot mag., XS Express sights, receiver mounted cantilever rail, black synthetic stock, 7 lbs. Mfg. 2015 only.

	$475	$415	$355	$325	$260	$215	$165	*$561*

MODEL 500 PERSUADER RETROGRADE – 12 ga., 3 in. chamber, 18 1/2 in. barrel, cylinder bore, 6 shot mag., bead sights, walnut stock, blue metal finish, 6 3/4 lbs. New 2019.

MSR $553	$470	$410	$350	$325	$260	$215	$185	

MODEL 500 PERSUADER ZMB – 12 ga., 3 in. chamber, 8 shot extended tube mag., 20 in. cylinder bore barrel, bead sight, matte blue finish, ZMB logo engraved on receiver, black synthetic stock with pistol grip, drilled and tapped, sling swivels, includes black padded sling. Mfg. 2012-2014.

	$400	$350	$300	$275	$225	$175	$150	*$475*

GRADING - PPGS™	100%	98%	95%	90%	80%	70%	60%	LAST MSR

MODEL 500 SPECIAL PURPOSE – 12 ga. only, 18 in. cylinder bored barrel, choice of blue or parkerized finish, synthetic stock with or without Speedfeed. Disc. 1996.

$350	$295	$250	$225	$200	$175	$160	*$378*

Add $21 for Speedfeed stock.
Add $76 for ghost ring sight (parkerized finish only).

MODEL 500 SPECIAL PURPOSE (RECENT MFG.) – 12 ga., 2 3/4 or 3 in. chamber, 18 1/2 in. cylinder bore barrel, 6 shot, matte blue finish, synthetic stock, plain bead sight, recoil reduction system. Mfg. 2013-2014.

$425	$375	$325	$295	$235	$195	$150	*$493*

MODEL 500 SPX SPECIAL PURPOSE – 12 ga. only, 3 in. chamber, 18 1/2 in. cylinder bore barrel with M16 style front sight, LPA ghost ring rear sight, Picatinny rail, matte blue metal finish, 6-pos. adj. tactical black synthetic stock with pistol grip, 6 3/4 lbs. Mfg. 2009-2016.

$625	$545	$470	$425	$345	$280	$220	*$732*

MODEL 500 SUPER BANTAM DUCK COMMANDER – 20 ga., 3 in. chamber, 22 in. VR barrel, Accu-Set chokes, 6 shot, TruGlo fiber optic sights, adj. 12-13 in. LOP stock with spacer, 100% Realtree Max-5 finish, logo engraved synthetic stock, includes American flag bandana, 5 1/4 lbs. Mfg. 2014-2015.

$485	$425	$375	$335	$300	$275	$250	*$574*

MODEL 500 TACTICAL8 SHOT (XS SECURITY) – 12 ga., 20 in. barrel with heat shield, ghost ring sights, synthetic black stock and forend, matte blue finish, 7 lbs. Mfg. 2016-2019.

$415	$365	$310	$280	$230	$185	$150	*$486*

MODEL 500 TACTICAL – 12 ga. only, 3 in. chamber, 18 1/2 in. cylinder bore barrel, 6 shot, 6-position adj. tactical black synthetic stock, choice of matte blue or Marinecoate (disc. 2015) finish, right or left (mfg. 2015-2016) hand configuration, 6 3/4 lbs. Mfg. 2006-2019.

$515	$450	$385	$350	$285	$230	$180	*$602*

Add $14 for left-hand configuration (mfg. 2015-2016).
Add $156 for Marinecote finish (disc. 2015).

* ***Model 500 Tactical Light Forend*** – 12 ga., 3 in. chamber, 6 shot, 18 1/2 in. cylinder bore barrel, 14 1/2 in. LOP, bead sight, integrated tactical light forend with 3-function ambidextrous touchpad, black synthetic stock, matte blue finish, 6 3/4 lbs. Mfg. 2011-2015.

$535	$450	$400	$350	$295	$235	$185	*$631*

MODEL 500 TACTICAL RECOIL REDUCTION SYSTEM – 12 ga., 3 in. chamber, 6 shot, 18 1/2 in. cylinder bore barrel, bead sight, features Mathews Harmonic Damper Technology, matte blue metal finish, dual comb black synthetic stock, 6 3/4 lbs. Mfg. 2013-2015.

$490	$425	$375	$325	$275	$225	$175	*$578*

MODEL 500 TACTICAL TRI-RAIL – 12 ga., 3 in. chamber, 6 (disc. 2015) or 8 shot, 18 1/2 (disc. 2015) or 20 in. cylinder bore barrel, bead (disc. 2015), ghost ring, or XS ghost ring (mfg. 2015) sights, blue (disc. 2015) or matte blue metal finish, tactical tri-rail forend, black synthetic fixed (disc. 2015) or 6-pos. adj. tactical stock, 6 3/4-7 lbs. Disc. 2019.

$565	$495	$425	$385	$310	$250	$200	*$657*

Subtract approx. $78 for XS ghost ring sights and 8 shot mag. (mfg. 2015 only).
Subtract approx. $135 for 6-pos. adj. stock, 6 shot mag., with bead sights. (disc. 2015).
Subtract approx. $196 for XS ghost ring sights and 6 shot mag., with adj. stock (mfg. 2015 only).

* ***Model 500 Tactical Tri-Rail w/Center Mass Laser*** – 12 ga., 3 in. chamber, 8 shot, 20 in. cylinder bore barrel, matte blue metal finish, bead sights, Laserlyte Center Mass laser with three modes (constant on, pulse, and auto off) mounted on tactical tri-rail forend, black synthetic stock, 7 lbs. Mfg. 2014-2016.

$595	$525	$450	$400	$325	$275	$210	*$695*

MODEL 500 THUNDER RANCH – 12 ga., 3 in. chamber, 18 1/2 in. cylinder bore barrel, 5 shot mag., matte black synthetic stock with 12 3/4 in. LOP, white dot sights, tri-rail Picatinny forend, non-glare matte blue metal finish, sling swivel studs, Thunder Ranch logo engraved on receiver, includes black padded sling. Mfg. mid-2011-2018.

$440	$385	$330	$300	$250	$200	$160	*$514*

MODEL 500 THUNDER RANCH 20TH ANNIVERSARY – 12 ga., 18 1/2 in. tactical barrel, 6 shot, Tri-Rail forend, white dot sight, receiver engraving with Thunder Ranch logo, sling, compact 13 in. LOP, matte blue barrel finish, black synthetic stock, 6 3/4 lbs. Mfg. 2013 only.

$425	$375	$325	$295	$235	$195	$150	*$493*

GRADING - PPGS™	100%	98%	95%	90%	80%	70%	60%	LAST MSR

MODEL 500 TURKEY – 12 or 20 ga., 3 in. chamber, 6 shot, 24 in. VR ported barrel, XX-Full chokes, adj. fiber optic sights, standard or LPA adj. trigger (12 ga. only), synthetic stock, 100% Mossy Oak Obsession (disc. 2010, reintroduced 2016), Mossy Oak New Break-Up (disc. 2011), or Mossy Oak Break-Up Infinity (mfg. 2012-2015) camo coverage, 7 1/4 lbs. Disc. 2017.

	$415	$365	$310	$280	$230	$185	$150	*$486*

Add $40 for LPA adj. trigger.
Add $105 for left-hand action (mfg. 2015 only).

* ***Model 500 Tactical Turkey*** – 12 or 20 (disc. 2017) ga., 20 in. VR barrel, X-Factor ported tube, 6 shot, adj. fiber optic sights, adj. tactical synthetic stock, with or w/o sling, 100% Mossy Oak Obsession coverage, 7 1/4 lbs. New 2016.

MSR $683	$580	$510	$435	$395	$320	$265	$225

Add $81 for 20 ga. with ported barrel (disc. 2017).

* ***Model 500 Turkey Grand Slam Series*** – 12, 20 ga., or .410 bore (new 2019), 3 in. chamber, 6 shot, 20, 22, or 26 (new 2019) in. VR barrel, X-Factor ported tube or fixed full chokes (new 2019, .410 bore), adj. fiber optic sights, synthetic stock, 100% Mossy Oak Obsession, Mossy Oak Bottomland (new 2019, .410 bore only), Mossy Oak New Break-Up (mfg. 2004-2011), Mossy Oak Break-Up Infinity (mfg. 2012-2015), Realtree Hardwoods HD Green (disc. 2012), or Realtree Extra Green (mfg. 2013-2014) camo coverage, sling, 6 3/4-7 lbs. New 2004.

MSR $549	$470	$410	$350	$325	$260	$215	$185

* ***Model 500 "Thug & Slug" Turkey Thugs Combo*** – 12 ga., 3 in. chamber, 24 in. Turkey barrel with adj. fiber optic sights and XX-Full choke and 24 in. fluted Slugster barrel with adj. rifle sights, 6 shot, LPA adj. trigger, 100% Mossy Oak Break-Up Infinity camo coverage, Turkey THUGS receiver engraving, synthetic stock, sling, 7 1/2 lbs. Mfg. 2012-2015.

	$535	$450	$400	$350	$295	$250	$185	*$631*

* ***Model 500 Turkey Bantam*** – 20 ga. only, 22 in. VR barrel with fiber optic sights and Accu-II X-full choke only, available in Woodlands (100% coverage), Mossy Oak Realtree Hardwoods HD Green (new 2004) or Mossy Oak Treestand camo (mfg. 2003 only) stock and forearm only, 6 1/2 lbs. Mfg. 1997-2004.

	$290	$255	$215	$195	$160	$130	$100	*$364*

* ***Model 500 Turkey Synthetic Thumbhole*** – 12 ga., 3 in. chamber, 6 shot, 20 in. VR barrel, X-Factor ported tube, adj. fiber optic sights, Black synthetic thumbhole stock with matte blue finish or synthetic thumbhole stock with 100% Mossy Oak New Break-Up (disc. 2011), Mossy Oak Break-Up Infinity (mfg. 2012-2013), Realtree Hardwoods HD Green (disc. 2012), or Realtree Extra Green (new 2013) camo coverage, 7 lbs. Mfg. 2007-2014.

	$415	$365	$310	$275	$225	$185	$150	*$484*

Add $59 for Realtree Extra Green camo coverage (new 2013).

* ***Model 500 Turkey Tactical*** – 12 ga., 3 in. chamber, 6 shot, 20 in. VR barrel, X-Factor ported tube, adj. fiber optic sights, adj. LOP, standard or LPA adj. (mfg. 2011-2014) trigger, 6-position adj. synthetic stock, 100% Realtree Hardwoods HD Green (disc. 2012), Mossy Oak New Break-Up (disc. 2011), Mossy Oak Break-Up Infinity (new 2012), or Mossy Oak Obsession (mfg. 2013-2014) camo coverage, sling, 7 1/4 lbs. Disc. 2015.

	$535	$450	$400	$350	$300	$250	$195	*$637*

Add $43 for LPA adj. trigger (disc. 2014).

* ***Model 500 Turkey Tactical Thugs*** – 12 or 20 ga., 3 in. chamber, 6 shot, 20 in. VR ported barrel, X-Factor ported tube (12 ga.) or XX-Full chokes (20 ga.), adj. fiber optic sights, adj. tactical synthetic stock, LPA adj. trigger (12 ga. only), "Turkey Thugs" engraved receiver, 100% Mossy Oak Obsession camo coverage, 7 1/4 lbs. Mfg. 2012-2015.

	$610	$525	$450	$410	$325	$275	$225	*$720*

* ***Model 500 Turkey Thug With LPA*** – 12 ga., 3 in. chamber, 6 shot, 24 in. VR ported barrel, XX-Full chokes, LPA adj. trigger, engraved receiver, adj. fiber optic sights, matte blue finish, black synthetic stock, 7 1/4 lbs. Mfg. 2011-2015.

	$395	$325	$295	$250	$210	$175	$125	*$466*

MODEL 500 TURKEY/DEER LPA COMBO – 12 ga., 3 in. chamber, 6 shot, two barrel set includes 24 in. VR barrel with adj. fiber optic sights and XX-Full chokes and 24 in. fluted barrel with adj. rifle sights and fully rifled bore, LPA adj. trigger, synthetic stock, Realtree Hardwoods HD Green (disc. 2012), Mossy Oak Obsession (mfg. 2013-2015), or Mossy Oak Break-Up Country (new 2016) camo coverage, 7 1/2 lbs.

MSR $637	$540	$475	$400	$365	$300	$275	$250

GRADING - PPGS™	100%	98%	95%	90%	80%	70%	60%	LAST MSR

MODEL 500 WATCHDOG – 12 ga., 3 in. chamber, 6 shot, 18 1/2 in. cylinder bore barrel, bead sights, synthetic stock with pistol grip conversion kit, Proveil Watchdog camo finish, 5 3/4-6 3/4 lbs. Disc. 2017.

	$395	$350	$300	$275	$215	$175	$150	*$460*

This model could only be purchased through a Talo Group Distributor.

MODEL 500 WATERFOWL – 12 ga. only, 3 in. chamber, 6 shot, 26 (disc. 2008) or 28 in. VR ported barrel with Accu-Set choke tubes, fiber optic front sight, right or left (mfg. 2015 only) hand action, synthetic stock and forearm, 100% Woodlands (disc.), Mossy Oak Duck Blind (mfg. 2007-2012), Advantage Max-4 (mfg. 2004-2015), Mossy Oak Shadow Grass Blades (new 2013), or Mossy Oak Shadow Grass (mfg. 2004-2007) camo coverage, 7 1/2 lbs. Disc. 2018.

	$415	$365	$310	$280	$230	$185	$150	*$486*

Add $105 for left-hand action (mfg. 2015 only).

* ***Model 500 Waterfowl Flyway Series*** – 12 ga. only, 3 in. chamber, 6 shot, 28 in. VR barrel with X-factor ported tube, fiber optic front sight, synthetic stock and forearm with Advantage Max-4 camo, includes padded sling and embossed logo, 7 1/2 lbs. Mfg. 2005-2015.

	$485	$425	$350	$325	$275	$225	$175	*$571*

MODEL 505 YOUTH ALL PURPOSE FIELD – 20 ga. or .410 bore, 3 in. chamber, 20 in. VR barrel with Accu-Set or fixed Mod. choke, 5 shot, brass mid-bead and white front bead sights, wood stock, blue metal finish, short 12 in. LOP, 5 1/4 lbs. New 2005.

MSR $459	$390	$340	$295	$265	$215	$175	$150	

Model 505 Youth barrels are not interchangeble with any Mossberg slide action shotgun.

MODEL 510 MINI SUPER BANTAM ALL PURPOSE – 20 ga. or .410 bore, 3 in. chamber, 18 1/2 in. VR barrel, Accu-Set or fixed choke, dual bead sights, adj. synthetic stock with spacer, Blue, Mossy Oak Break-Up Infinity (disc. 2015), Mossy Oak Break-Up Country (new 2016), Muddy Girl (mfg. 2014-2017), Muddy Girl Serenity (new 2018), or Muddy Girl Wild (new 2021) camo coverage, 10 1/2 or 11 1/2 in. LOP. New 2010.

MSR $459	$390	$340	$295	$265	$215	$175	$150	

Add $56 for Muddy Girl Wild camo (new 2021) or Muddy Girl Serenity camo (new 2018).
Add $58 for Mossy Oak Break-Up Country camo finish (new 2016).
Add $50 for Muddy Girl (mfg. 2014-2017) or $51 for Mossy Oak Break Up Infinity (disc. 2015) camo finish.

Model 510 barrels are not interchangeable with any Mossberg shotgun.

* ***Model 510 Mini Super Bantam Turkey Thug*** – 20 ga., 3 in. chamber, 4 shot, 18 1/2 in. VR barrel, Accu-Set chokes, dual bead sight, "Turkey Thug" engraved receiver, 10 1/2-11 1/2 in. LOP, adj. synthetic stock with spacer, 100% Mossy Oak Obsession camo coverage, 5 lbs. Mfg. 2012-2015.

	$435	$375	$325	$295	$250	$195	$150	*$515*

* ***Model 510 Mini Super Bantam Turkey*** – 20 ga., 18 1/2 in. VR barrel, Accu-Set chokes, 4 shot, dual bead sights, adj. synthetic stock with spacer, Mossy Oak Obsession finish, 5 lbs. Mfg. 2016-2017.

	$400	$350	$300	$270	$220	$180	$140	*$470*

MODEL 535 ATS (ALL TERRAIN SHOTGUN) – 12 ga. only, 3 or 3 1/2 in. chamber, features safety on rear of receiver, dual extractors, positive steel-to-steel lockup, twin action bars, anti-jam elevator for smooth operation, various configurations, 6 1/2 - 7 lbs. New 2005.

Model 535 barrels are not interchangeable with other Mossberg slide action shotgun models.

* ***Model 535 ATS All Purpose Field*** – 12 ga., 3 1/2 in. chamber, 6 shot, 28 in. VR barrel with Accu-set chokes, white bead front sight, blue metal finish, walnut stock, 6 3/4 lbs. Mfg. 2005-2018.

	$375	$330	$280	$255	$200	$165	$130	*$444*

* ***Model 535 ATS Field/Deer Combo*** – 12 ga., 3 1/2 in. chamber, 6 shot, 28 in. VR field barrel with Accu-Set chokes and dual bead sight and 24 in. fully rifled slugster barrel with adj. rifle sight, blue finish, wood stock, 6 3/4-7 lbs. Disc. 2018.

	$420	$370	$315	$285	$230	$190	$150	*$493*

* ***Model 535 ATS Slugster*** – 12 ga. only, 3 1/2 in. chamber, 6 shot, 24 in. fully rifled bore fluted or non-fluted barrel, adj. rifle sights or integral scope base, standard or LPA adj. trigger (new 2011), matte blue metal, Realtree AP (mfg. 2007-2012), Realtree Xtra (new 2013), or Mossy Oak New Break-Up (disc. 2007) camo finish, synthetic stock with or w/o dual comb, 7 lbs. Mfg. 2005-2014.

	$375	$325	$275	$250	$200	$175	$125	*$440*

Add $147 for integral scope base and LPA adj. trigger (new 2011).
Add $61 for 100% Realtree AP camo coverage w/o integral scope base (disc. 2012).

GRADING - PPGS™	100%	98%	95%	90%	80%	70%	60%	LAST MSR

* ***Model 535 ATS Turkey*** – 12 ga., 22 in. VR barrel with XX-full choke tubes, adj. fiber optic sights, standard or LPA adj. trigger (MO Break-Up Infinity only, mfg. 2011-2014), matte blue (disc. 2007), Mossy Oak New Break-Up (disc. 2011), Mossy Oak Obsession (disc. 2010, reintroduced 2013), Mossy Oak Break Up Infinity (mfg. 2011-2015), or Realtree Hardwoods HD Green (disc. 2012) finish, synthetic stock, 6 1/2 lbs. Mfg. 2005-2017.

$440	$385	$330	$300	$240	$200	$150	*$518*

Add $42 for LPA adj. trigger (mfg. 2011-2014).
Subtract approx. $60 for matte blue finish (disc. 2007).

* ***Model 535 ATS Turkey w/Marble Arms Bullseye Sights*** – 12 ga., 3 1/2 in. chamber, 22 in. VR barrel with XX-full choke tubes, Marble Arms Bullseye rear and front fiber optic sights, synthetic stock, Mossy Oak Obsession finish, 6 1/2 lbs. Mfg. 2015-2018.

$460	$400	$345	$315	$250	$200	$160	*$542*

* ***Model 535 ATS Tactical Turkey*** – 12 ga., 3 1/2 in. chamber, 6 shot, 20 in. VR barrel with X-Factor ported choke tube, adj. fiber optic sights, adj. synthetic tactical stock, 100% Mossy Oak New Break-Up (disc. 2011), Mossy Oak Break-Up Infinity (mfg. 2011-2015), Mossy Oak Obsession (new 2016), Realtree Hardwoods HD Green (disc. 2012), or Realtree Extra Green (mfg. 2013-2014) camo coverage, includes sling, 7 lbs. Mfg. 2006-2018.

$550	$480	$415	$375	$300	$250	$200	*$652*

* ***Model 535 ATS Turkey Thug With LPA*** – 12 ga., 3 1/2 in. chamber, 6 shot, 20 in. VR barrel with X-Factor ported tube, LPA adj. trigger, adj. fiber optic and TruGlo red dot sight, engraved receiver, top Picatinny rail, full-length pistol grip synthetic stock, Mossy Oak Break-Up Infinity (disc. 2015) or Mossy Oak Obsession (new 2016) camo coverage, 6 3/4-7 lbs. Mfg. 2011-2017.

$635	$550	$475	$430	$350	$285	$220	*$748*

Subtract approx. $70 if without TruGlo red dot sight (became standard 2015).

* ***Model 535 ATS Thumbhole Turkey*** – 12 ga., 3 1/2 in. chamber, 20 in. VR barrel with X-factor ported choke tube, 6 shot, adj. fiber optic sights, synthetic thumbhole stock, matte blue (black stock) or 100% Mossy Oak New Break-Up (disc. 2011), Mossy Oak Break-Up Infinity (new 2012), Realtree Hardwoods HD Green (disc. 2012), or Realtree Extra Green (new 2013) camo coverage, 7 lbs. Mfg. 2007-2014.

$425	$375	$325	$295	$250	$200	$150	*$503*

Add $74 for 100% camo coverage.

* ***Model 535 ATS Turkey Recoil Reduction System*** – 12 ga., 3 1/2 in. chamber, 6 shot, 22 in. VR barrel with XX-full choke tubes, adj. fiber optic sights, features Mathews Harmonic Damper technology, dual comb synthetic stock, advanced recoil pad, 100% Mossy Oak Break-Up Infinity camo coverage, 7 1/2 lbs. Mfg. 2013-2015.

$490	$425	$360	$325	$265	$215	$175	*$583*

* ***Model 535 ATS Turkey/Deer Combo*** – 12 ga., 3 1/2 in. chamber, 6 shot, two barrel set includes 22 in. VR barrel with XX-Full chokes and adj. fiber optic sight and 24 in. fully rifled slugster barrel with adj. rifle sight, synthetic stock, 100% Mossy Oak New Break-Up (disc. 2011), Mossy Oak Break-Up Infinity (disc. 2015), or Mossy Oak Break-Up Country (new 2016) camo coverage, 6 1/2-7 lbs. Disc. 2018.

$485	$425	$365	$330	$265	$220	$170	*$570*

* ***Model 535 ATS Turkey/Deer LPA Combo*** – 12 ga., 3 1/2 in. chamber, 6 shot, two barrel set includes 22 in. VR barrel with XX-full chokes and adj. fiber optic sight and 24 in. fluted fully rifled slugster barrel with adj. rifle sight, LPA adj. trigger, synthetic stock, 100% Mossy Oak Break-Up Infinity (disc. 2015) or Mossy Oak Break-Up Country (new 2016) camo coverage, 7 1/2 lbs. Mfg. 2012-2017.

$520	$450	$390	$355	$285	$235	$180	*$612*

* ***Model 535 ATS Waterfowl*** – 12 ga., 3 1/2 in. chamber, 6 shot, 26 (disc. 2008) or 28 in. VR barrel with Accu-Set choke, fiber optic front sight, synthetic stock, matte blue, Mossy Oak New Break-Up (disc. 2008), Mossy Oak Duck Blind (mfg. 2007-2012), Mossy Oak Shadow Grass Blades (new 2013), or Advantage Max-4 (disc. 2015) camo finish, 6 3/4 lbs. Mfg. 2005-2018.

$380	$335	$285	$260	$210	$170	$140	*$441*

Add $77 for 100% camo coverage.

* ***Model 535 ATS Waterfowl Recoil Reduction System*** – 12 ga., 3 1/2 in. chamber, 6 shot, 28 in. VR barrel with Accu-Set choke tubes, fiber optic front sights, features Mathews Harmonic Damper technology, dual comb synthetic stock, advanced recoil pad, 100% Advantage Max-4 camo coverage, 7 3/4 lbs. Mfg. 2013-2015.

$490	$425	$360	$325	$265	$215	$175	*$583*

GRADING - PPGS™	100%	98%	95%	90%	80%	70%	60%	LAST MSR

* ***Model 535 ATS Turkey/Waterfowl Combo*** – 12 ga., 3 1/2 in. chamber, 6 shot, two barrel set includes 22 in. VR barrel with XX-Full chokes and adj. fiber optic sight and 28 in. VR fully rifled barrel with fiber optic front sight, synthetic stock, 100% Mossy Oak New Break-Up (disc. 2011), Mossy Oak Break-Up Infinity (mfg. 2012-2015), or Mossy Oak Break-Up Country (new 2016) camo coverage, 6 1/2-6 3/4 lbs. Disc. 2018.

	$485	$425	$365	$330	$265	$220	$170	*$570*

MODEL 535 ATS DUCK COMMANDER WATERFOWL – 12 ga., 3 1/2 in. chamber, 6 shot, 28 in. VR barrel with Accu-Set choke tubes, TruGlo fiber optic sights, Realtree Max-5 finish, logo engraved synthetic stock, includes American flag bandana, 6 3/4 lbs. Mfg. 2014-2016.

	$525	$450	$400	$365	$335	$300	$275	*$617*

MODEL 500/590 INTIMIDATOR LASER – 12 ga. only, 3 in. chamber, 18 1/2 (Model 500) or 20 (Model 590) in. cyl. bore barrel, 6 (Model 500) or 9 (Model 590) shot tube mag., blue or parkerized finish, synthetic field stock, includes laser sighting device. Mfg. 1990-93.

* ***Model 500 Intimidator***

	$500	$385	$340	$300	$265	$230	$195	*$505*

Add $22 for parkerized finish.

* ***Model 590 Intimidator***

	$550	$495	$440	$375	$340	$295	$260	*$556*

Add $45 for parkerized finish.

MODEL 590 7 SHOT – 12 ga., 18 1/2 in. barrel with heat shield, 7 shot, bead sights, black synthetic stock with corncob forend, matte blue metal finish, 6.75 lbs. New 2016.

MSR $500	$425	$375	$325	$295	$235	$195	$165	

MODEL 590 9 SHOT – 20 ga., 3 in. chamber, 20 in. cylinder bore barrel, 9 shot, ghost ring sights, black compact synthetic stock, corncob forend, 13 in. LOP, matte blue finish, 7.25 lbs. New 2020.

MSR $539	$460	$400	$350	$315	$250	$200	$175	

MODEL 590 ADJUSTABLE CRUISER – 12 ga., 3 in. chamber, 18 1/2 or 20 in. cylinder bore barrel, 7 or 9 shot, bead, ghost ring, or rail mounted LPA ghost ring sights, black synthetic FLEX 6-pos. adj. stock and strapped forend, FLEX Connector-Equipped pistol grip, matte blue finish, 5.75-7.75 lbs. New 2020.

MSR $659	$560	$490	$420	$380	$310	$260	$215	

Add $143 for rail mounted LPA ghost ring sights.

MODEL 590 CHAINSAW – 12 ga., 3 in. chamber, 18 1/2 in. Stand-off barrel, cyl. bore, 6 shot, white dot sights, black synthetic stock with pistol grip, Tri-Rail forend, removable top grip, matte blue finish, 6 lbs. New 2020.

MSR $601	$510	$450	$385	$350	$275	$225	$200	

MODEL 590 CRUISER – 12 ga., 3 in. chamber, 18 1/2 in. Stand-off barrel, cyl. bore, white dot sights, black synthetic stock with pistol grip, corncob strapped forend, matte blue finish, 5.75 lbs. New 2020.

MSR $500	$425	$375	$325	$295	$235	$195	$165	

MODEL 590 FLEX TACTICAL – 12 ga., 3 in. chamber, 9 shot, 20 in. cylinder bore barrel, matte blue finish, bead sight, six position adj. black synthetic stock with rail, 7 lbs. New mid-2012.

MSR $736	$625	$545	$475	$425	$345	$275	$225	

MODEL 590 JIC SHOCKWAVE – 12 ga., 2 3/4 in. chamber, 14 in. heavy walled cylinder bore barrel, 6 shot mag. tube with screw-off cap, bead sights, strapped forend, International Orange water-resistant carrying tube/strap, Shockwave raptor bird's head-style grip, Cerakote stainless finish, 5.3 lbs. New 2018.

MSR $708	$600	$525	$450	$410	$325	$275	$225	

MODEL 590M – 12 ga., 2 3/4 in. chamber, 18 1/2 in. heavy-walled matte blue barrel, cylinder bore or Accu-chokes (Tri-Rail model), 10 shot mag., all steel mag. release button, removable floorplate, dual extractors, dual action bars, bead or ghost ring (Tri-Rail model) sights, black synthetic stock, ambidextrous top-mount safety, with or without tri-rail, 590M logo embellished receiver, drilled and tapped, black oxide finish on steel components, 7 3/4 lbs. New 2018.

MSR $599	$510	$450	$385	$350	$275	$225	$200	

Add $83 for Tri-Rail model with Accu-chokes and ghost ring sights.

MODEL 590M SHOCKWAVE – 12 ga., 2 3/4 in. chamber, 15 in. heavy walled barrel, cylinder bore, 10 shot detachable mag., dual extractors, bead sights, Shockwave Raptor grip/corncob forend with strap, top-mounted ambidextrous safety, drilled and tapped receiver, matte blue metal finish with logo embellished receiver, 7 3/4 lbs. New 2019.

MSR $599	$510	$450	$385	$350	$275	$225	$200	

GRADING - PPGS™	100%	98%	95%	90%	80%	70%	60%	LAST MSR

MODEL 590 NIGHTSTICK – 12 or 20 (new 2020) ga., compact, 14.375 in. heavy walled barrel, cylinder bore, 6 shot mag., bead sights, corncob forend with leather strap, bird's head wood grip, matte blue metal finish, 5 1/4 lbs. New 2019.

MSR $555	$475	$415	$350	$325	$260	$215	$185	

Add $18 for 20 ga. (new 2020).

MODEL 590 PERSUADER – 12 ga., 3 in. chamber, 20 in. cylinder bore barrel with or w/out heat shield, 9 shot, ghost ring sights, full length black synthetic stock, corncob or M-LOK forend, matte blue finish, 7.75 lbs. New 2020.

MSR $545	$460	$400	$350	$315	$250	$200	$175	

Add $58 for M-LOK forend.

* ***Model 590 Persuader w/Pistol Grip Conversion Kit*** – 12, 20 ga., or .410 bore, 3 in. chamber, 18 1/2 or 20 (with heat shield) in. cylinder bore barrel, 7 or 9 shot, bead sights, full length black synthetic stock, corncob forend, includes pistol grip conversion kit, matte blue finish, 7.75 lbs. New 2020.

MSR $500	$425	$375	$325	$295	$235	$195	$165	

Add $19 for 20 in. barrel with heat shield.

MODEL 590 RETROGRADE – 12 ga., 3 in. chamber, 18 1/2 or 20 in. cylinder bore barrel with heat shield, 7 or 9 shot, bead sights, walnut stock, corncob forend, matte blue finish, 7-7.25 lbs. New 2020.

MSR $594	$510	$450	$385	$350	$275	$225	$200	

Add $15 for 20 in. barrel.

MODEL 590 SHOCKWAVE – 12, 20 (new 2018) ga., or .410 bore (new mid-2018), 2 3/4 in. chamber, 14 in. heavy walled barrel, 6 shot, dual extractors, bead sights, black synthetic strapped forend, Shockwave Raptor bird's head pistol grip, matte blue or FDE Cerakote (new 2018) finish, 5.3 lbs. New 2017.

MSR $500	$425	$375	$325	$295	$235	$195	$165	

Add $53 for FDE Cerakote finish (new 2018).
Add $152 for Crimson Trace Lasersaddle (new 2019).

Important note: This model is fully BATFE compliant and requires no stamp for transfers.

* ***Model 590 Shockwave 7 Shot*** – 12 ga., 3 in. chamber, 18 1/2 in. heavy walled barrel, cylinder bore, 7 shot mag., bead sights, Shockwave Raptor bird's head grip stock, corncob forend with strap, matte blue metal finish, 5 1/2 lbs. New 2019.

MSR $500	$425	$375	$325	$295	$235	$195	$165	

MODEL 590 SHOCKWAVE SHOCK 'N SAW – 12 ga., 3 in. chamber, 14 3/4 in. heavy walled stand-off barrel, breacher muzzle, heat shield, 5 shot mag., bead sights, Shockwave Raptor bird's head pistol grip, aluminum railed forend, Chainsaw top handle, matte blue metal finish. New 2019.

MSR $613	$520	$455	$390	$355	$285	$235	$200	

MODEL 590 SHOCKWAVE SPX – 12 ga., 3 in. chamber, 14.375 in. heavy walled Standoff barrel, cylinder bore, Breacher muzzle, 6 shot mag., bead sights, Shockwave Raptor bird's head pistol grip, corncob forend with strap, heat shield, 5 shell holders, Picatinny rail, matte blue metal finish, 6.3 lbs. New 2019.

MSR $613	$520	$455	$390	$355	$285	$235	$200	

MODEL 590 SPECIAL PURPOSE SLIDE ACTION – 12 ga., 3 in. chamber, 9 shot mag., 20 in. cyl. bore barrel with or w/o (disc. 2015) heat shield and bayonet lug, bead or ghost ring sights, blue, matte blue (new 2016), or parkerized (disc. 2015) finish, black synthetic stock with or w/o (disc. 2015) Speedfeed, right or left (2015-2016) hand configuration, with (new 2016) or w/o tri-rail forend, 7 1/4 lbs. Mfg. 1987-2019.

	$475	$415	$355	$325	$260	$215	$165	*$559*

Add $54 for ghost ring sights, matte blue finish, and tri-rail forend (new 2016).
Add $14 for left-hand configuration (mfg. 2015-2016).
Add $41 for parkerized finish (disc. 2015).
Add $33 for Speedfeed (blue, disc. 1999) or $96 for Speedfeed (parkerized, disc. 2015) stock.
Add $75 for heavy barrel with ghost ring sights, metal trigger guard and safety (disc. 2011).

* ***Model 590 Special Purpose Bullpup*** – similar to Model 500 Bullpup except is 9 shot and has 20 in. barrel. Mfg. 1989-90 only.

	$650	$525	$450	$410	$325	$275	$210	*$497*

* ***Model 590 Special Purpose Double Action*** – 12 ga. only, 3 in. chamber, world's first double action shotgun (long trigger pull), 18 1/2 or 20 in. barrel, 6 or 9 shot, bead or ghost ring sights, black synthetic stock and forearm, top tang safety, parkerized metal finish, 7-7 1/4 lbs. Mfg. 2000-2003.

	$450	$395	$335	$305	$245	$200	$155	*$510*

Add $31 for 9 shot capacity.
Add $48 for ghost ring sights.
Add $124 for Speedfeed stock (20 in. barrel with ghost ring sights only).

GRADING - PPGS™	100%	98%	95%	90%	80%	70%	60%	LAST MSR

* ***Model 590 Special Purpose Line Launcher*** – special purpose Marine and rescue shotgun with blaze orange synthetic stock, line dispensing canister, floating and distance heads, nylon and spectra line refills, includes case and two boxes of launching loads. Disc.

	$850	$745	$635	$580	$465	$380	$295	*$927*

* ***Model 590 Special Purpose Mariner*** – 12 ga., 3 in. chamber, 9 shot, 20 in. cylinder bore barrel, bead sights, Marinecote finish, full-length black synthetic stock and pistol grip conversion kit, 6-7 lbs. Mfg. 1989-1993, reintroduced 2009.

MSR $764	$650	$570	$490	$440	$360	$295	$250	

Add 5% for Speedfeed stock (disc. 1990).
Subtract 10% if w/o pistol grip adapter (disc.)

* ***Model 590 Tactical Light Forend*** – 12 ga., 3 in. chamber, 9 shot, 20 in. cylinder bore barrel with heat shield, bead sight, matte blue metal finish, integrated Insight tactical light forend with 3-function ambidextrous touchpad, black synthetic stock, 7 1/4 lbs. Disc. 2015.

	$595	$525	$450	$400	$325	$275	$225	*$720*

* ***Model 590 Tactical Tri-Rail 9 Shot*** – 12 ga., 3 in. chamber, 9 shot, 20 in. cylinder bore barrel, Parkerized finish, heat shield, bead sight, tactical tri-rail forend, black synthetic stock with shell storage (Speedfeed), 7 1/4 lbs. Mfg. 2011-2015.

	$575	$500	$425	$385	$310	$250	$200	*$681*

* ***Model 590 Tactical w/XS Express Sights*** – 12 ga., 3 in. chamber, 20 in. cylinder bore barrel with matte blue finish, 9 shot mag., XS Express sights, receiver mounted cantilever rail, black synthetic stock, 7 1/4 lbs. Mfg. 2015 only.

	$625	$550	$475	$425	$350	$285	$225	*$740*

MODEL 590 THUNDER RANCH – 12 ga., 18 1/2 in. Standoff barrel, cylinder bore, 6 shot mag., red fiber optic bead sights, synthetic stock and tri-rail forend with KUIU camo finish, matte blue metal finish, 6 3/4 lbs. New 2019.

MSR $606	$515	$450	$385	$350	$285	$230	$200	

MODEL 590A1 RETROGRADE – 12 ga., 3 in. chamber, 20 in. heavy walled barrel, cylinder bore, 9 shot mag., ghost ring sights, walnut stock, top-mounted ambidextrous safety, anti-jam elevator, non-binding twin action bars, parkerized metal finish, 7 1/4 lbs. New 2019.

MSR $987	$840	$735	$630	$575	$460	$380	$325	

MODEL 590A1 SLIDE ACTION – 12 ga., 3 in. chamber, 6 (disc. 2015), 7 (new 2016), or 9 shot mag., 18 1/2 (disc. 2019) or 20 (new 2010) in. cylinder bore heavy barrel, parkerized finish, choice of 3-dot (disc. 2015), bead, ghost ring, or XS ghost ring (new 2020) sight, metal trigger guard and top safety, synthetic or Speedfeed (disc. 2015) stock, with or w/out Tri-rail (mfg. 2016-2019) or M-LOK (new 2020) forend, black finish, 7- 7 1/2 lbs. New 2009.

MSR $662	$560	$490	$420	$380	$310	$260	$215	

Add $49 for ghost ring sights with M-LOK forend (new 2020).
Add $80 for synthetic stock with 4-shell storage.
Add $80 for 9 shot/bead sights or $121 for 9 shot/ghost ring sights.
Add $56 for Speedfeed stock (disc. 2015).
Add $94 for choice of 3-dot or ghost rings sights with Speedfeed stock (disc. 2015).

* ***Model 590A1 Adj. Stock*** – 12 ga. only, 3 in. chamber, 20 in. heavy walled cylinder bore barrel, 6 or 9 shot, 3-dot (6 shot) or ghost ring (9 shot) sights, 6-position adj. aluminum stock with pistol grip, black finish, 6 3/4-7 lbs. Mfg. 2009-2015.

	$700	$610	$525	$475	$375	$315	$250	*$839*

Add $53 for 6 shot with 3-dot sights.

* ***Model 590A1 Adjustable*** – 12 ga., 3 in. chamber, 20 in. heavy walled cylinder bore barrel, 9 shot, ghost ring sights, black 6-pos. adj. stock, M-LOK forend, parkerized finish, 7.75 lbs. New 2020.

MSR $963	$815	$715	$610	$555	$450	$370	$320	

* ***Model 590A1 With LPA Adj. Trigger*** – 12 ga., 3 in. chamber, 6 shot, 18 1/2 in. fluted cylinder bore barrel, Parkerized finish, 3-dot sights, LPA adj. trigger, black synthetic stock, 6 3/4 lbs. Mfg. 2011-2014.

	$550	$475	$415	$375	$300	$250	$200	*$640*

* ***Model 590A1 Compact/Bantam*** – 12 ga., 3 in. chamber, 6 shot, 18 1/2 in. heavy walled cylinder bore barrel, parkerized finish, 13 in. LOP, ghost ring sights, black synthetic stock, 7 lbs. Mfg. 2009-2015.

	$595	$510	$450	$400	$325	$275	$225	*$712*

GRADING - PPGS™	100%	98%	95%	90%	80%	70%	60%	LAST MSR

* ***Model 590A1 Kryptek Typhon Camo*** – 12 ga., 3 in. chamber, 6 (disc. 2015) or 7 (new 2016) shot, 18 1/2 in. heavy walled barrel, ghost ring sight, synthetic stock, with (new 2016) or without (disc. 2015) tri-rail forend, Kryptek Typhon camo finish, 7 1/2 lbs. Mfg. 2014-2017.

	$600	**$525**	**$450**	**$410**	**$330**	**$270**	**$210**	*$704*

* ***Model 590A1 Mariner*** – 12 ga., 3 in. chamber, 18 1/2 in. heavy walled cyl. bore barrel, 6 (disc. 2015) or 7 (new 2015) shot, bead sights, black synthetic stock and forearm, with or without tri-rail (mfg. 2016-2019) or M-LOK (new 2020) forend, Marinecote finish, 6 3/4 lbs. New 2009.

MSR $829	**$700**	**$615**	**$525**	**$475**	**$385**	**$315**	**$275**	

* ***Model 590A1 Special Purpose (Disc.)*** – 12 ga., marked 590A1 on receiver, parkerized, ghost ring rear sight, synthetic stock and forend, ramp front sight. Disc. 1997.

	$550	**$480**	**$410**	**$375**	**$300**	**$245**	**$190**	

* ***Model 590A1 Special Purpose Blackwater Series*** – 12 ga., 3 in. chamber, 20 in. heavy wall cylinder bore barrel, 9 shot extended mag., military trigger guard, bayonet lug, parkerized metal finish, matte black furniture, Blackwater logo on right side of receiver, top Picatinny rail, integral adj. ghost ring rear sight, white post front sight, half-round ribbed forearm with three Picatinny rails, Speedfeed buttstock with two spare shell holders on each side, rubber buttpad, 7 1/4 lbs. Mfg. 2011-2014.

	$650	**$575**	**$500**	**$450**	**$375**	**$300**	**$250**	*$754*

* ***Model 590A1 SPX*** – 12 ga. only, 3 in. chamber, 9 shot, 20 in. heavy walled cyl. bore barrel, ghost ring rear and winged fiber optic front sights, parkerized finish, black synthetic stock and forearm, includes M9 bayonet and scabbard, receiver Picatinny rail, 7 lbs. New 2009.

MSR $987	**$840**	**$735**	**$630**	**$575**	**$460**	**$380**	**$325**	

* ***Model 590A1 Tactical Light Forend 6 Shot*** – 12 ga., 3 in. chamber, 6 shot, 18 1/2 in. heavy walled cylinder bore barrel, Parkerized metal finish, metal trigger guard and safety, clean out tube, bead sight, features Insight tactical light forend, black synthetic stock, 6 3/4 lbs. Disc. 2015.

	$635	**$550**	**$475**	**$425**	**$350**	**$275**	**$225**	*$764*

* ***Model 590A1 Tactical Tri-Rail Adjustable 9 Shot*** – 12 ga., 3 in. chamber, 20 in. Parkerized heavy walled barrel, 9 shot extended tube mag., ghost ring sights, tri-rail forend, 6-position adj. aluminum pistol grip stock, matte black finish, 7 3/4 lbs. Mfg. 2013-2019.

	$750	**$650**	**$580**	**$515**	**$450**	**$385**	**$340**	*$879*

* ***Model 590A1 Tactical Tri-Rail XS Ghost Ring Sights*** – 12 ga., 3 in. chamber, 20 in. parkerized heavy walled cylinder bore barrel, 9 shot mag., XS ghost ring sights, tri-rail forend, metal trigger guard and safety, black synthetic stock, right or left-hand configuration, 7 lbs. Mfg. 2015-2019.

	$575	**$500**	**$435**	**$365**	**$325**	**$280**	**$265**	*$678*

Add $14 for left-hand configuration.

* ***Model 590A1 U.S. Service Model*** – 12 ga., 3 in. chamber, 9 shot, 20 in. parkerized heavy walled barrel, bead sight, specially serialized, exclusive receiver engraving and "USSM" serial number prefx, black synthetic stock, matte blue finish, 7 1/4 lbs. Mfg. 2013-2015.

	$525	**$450**	**$400**	**$350**	**$300**	**$250**	**$200**	*$615*

NEW HAVEN BRAND – trademark used on previous models, plainer finish. Disc.

Values are 20% less per similar model.

SHOTGUNS: SLIDE ACTION, MODEL 835, 935, & 3000 SERIES

MODEL 835 SLUGSTER – 12 ga. only, 3 1/2 in. chamber, 6 shot mag., 24 in. ported rifled fluted (new 2011) or non-fluted (disc. 2010) slug barrel, integral scope base (disc. 2009) or rifle sights, choice of wood dual comb (disc. 2009) or synthetic stock, Realtree AP (disc. 2012) or Realtree Xtra (new 2013) camo coverage, LPA adj. trigger became standard 2011, 7 1/2 lbs. Mfg. 2007-2014.

	$535	**$460**	**$395**	**$350**	**$295**	**$235**	**$185**	*$639*

Add $31 for integral scope base and dual comb stock (disc. 2009).

MODEL 835 ULTI-MAG – 12 ga. with 3 1/2 in. chamber (new 1988), slide action, 24 (Turkey Model - new 1990) or 28 in. VR barrel with Accu-mag choke tubes, 6 shot mag., safety on top rear of receiver, choice of camo synthetic or checkered hardwood stock. Introduced late 1988, disc. 1991.

	$375	**$330**	**$280**	**$255**	**$205**	**$170**	**$130**	*$430*

Add $30 for synthetic camo field stock.

Various Combo packages were available in this model with prices ranging from $469-$534 depending on barrel chokings and scope base options.

This model was followed by the 835 Regal Series introduced in late 1991.

GRADING - PPGS™	100%	98%	95%	90%	80%	70%	60%	LAST MSR

MODEL 835 ULTI-MAG FIELD GRADE – 12 ga. only, 3 1/2 in. chamber, 24 in. cyl. bore (disc.), 24 in. VR (Turkey Special, disc. 1993), or 28 in. ported (new 1997) or unported VR barrel with 1 Accu-mag choke, walnut finish stock and forearm (pressed checkering became standard 1994), blue finish, approx. 7 1/2 lbs. Disc. 1998.

	$270	$235	$200	$185	$150	$120	$95	*$331*

Add $40 for combo package (disc. 1993).

MODEL 835 ULTI-MAG SYNTHETIC (SPECIAL HUNTER) – 12 ga. only, 3 1/2 in. chamber, 26 (disc. 1999, reintroduced 2004) or 28 in. VR ported barrel with mod. Accu-mag choke, parkerized finish, black synthetic stock, 7 3/4 lbs. Mfg. 1998-2005.

	$315	$275	$235	$215	$175	$140	$110	*$394*

MODEL 835 ULTI-MAG FIELD (CROWN GRADE) – similar to Field Grade, except has gold trigger and cut checkering on walnut finished hardwood stock, blue or OFM Woodland camo (24 in. Turkey only) finish, ported (standard 1997) or unported (disc.) VR barrel, 7 3/4 lbs. Mfg. 1994-2005.

	$315	$275	$235	$215	$175	$140	$110	*$394*

* ***Model 835 Ulti-Mag Field/Deer Combo*** – 12 ga., 3 1/2 in. chamber, 24 in. fully rifled bore barrel and 28 in. VR overbored barrel with Accu-Set chokes, 6 shot mag., bead or adj. sights, wood stock, blue finish, 6 /34 lbs. New 2019.

MSR $540	$460	$400	$350	$315	$250	$200	$175	

* ***Model 835 Ulti-Mag Field Turkey*** – 12 ga. only, 24 in. ported VR barrel, parkerized finish, walnut finished stock and forearm. Mfg. 1997-2000.

	$320	$280	$240	$215	$175	$145	$110	*$378*

* ***Model 835 Ulti-Mag Field New Turkey*** – 12 ga. only, 24 in. ported barrel with Ulti-full choke only, choice of Realtree Advantage Timber (new 2001), Realtree Hardwoods (mfg. 2000 only), Realtree Xtra brown (disc. 1999) or Woodlands (disc. 1999) 100% camo finish, fiber optic sights, 7 1/2 lbs. Mfg. 1999-2001.

	$450	$395	$335	$305	$245	$200	$155	*$525*

* ***Model 835 Ulti-Mag Field Crown Grade*** – 12 ga. only, 3 1/2 in. chamber, 28 in. VR ported (standard 1997) or unported barrel, walnut stock and forearm, Accu-mag choke. Disc. 1998.

	$365	$320	$275	$250	$200	$165	$130	*$421*

Add $7 for duo-comb stock.

MODEL 835 ULTI-MAG TURKEY – 12 ga., 3 1/2 in. chamber, 6 shot, 24 in. VR ported overbored barrel, Ulti-Full choke tubes, adj. fiber optic sights, synthetic stock with OFM Woodland Camo (all-purpose camo, combo. only with dual comb stock, mfg. 1997-99), Advantage Timber (mfg. 2001-2002), Brown Leaf (disc. 1999), Realtree (mfg. 1993-99), Realtree AP (all purpose grey, mfg. 1996-1999), Realtree Hardwoods (mfg. 2002-disc.), Realtree Xtra Brown (mfg. 2000-2002), Mossy Oak (mfg. 1994-99), Mossy Oak Forest Floor (mfg. 2003 only), Mossy Oak New Break-up (mfg. 2003-2011), Mossy Oak Break-Up Infinity (mfg. 2011-2015), Mossy Oak Obsession (mfg. 2004, reintroduced 2007-2010, 2016), Realtree Hardwoods HD Green (disc. 2012), or Woodlands (mfg. 2000-2011) finish, 7 1/2 lbs. Disc. 2017.

	$515	$450	$385	$350	$285	$230	$180	*$603*

* ***Model 835 Ulti-Mag All-Purpose*** – 12 ga., 2 3/4 in. chamber, 26 in. VR overbored barrel with Accu-Mag set chokes, 6 shot mag., bead sights, black synthetic stock, matte blue finish, 7 1/2 lbs. Mfg. 2018-2019.

	$385	$335	$295	$270	$215	$180	$140	*$444*

* ***Model 835 Ulti-Mag Turkey Grand Slam Series*** – 12 ga., 3 1/2 in. chamber, 6 shot, 20 in. VR overbored barrel with X-Factor ported tube, adj. fiber optic sights, synthetic stock with Realtree Hardwoods HD Green (disc. 2012), Realtree Xtra Green (mfg. 2013-2014), Mossy Oak New Break-Up (disc. 2011), Mossy Oak Break-Up Infinity (mfg. 2012-2015), or Mossy Oak Obsession (new 2016) camo coverage, padded sling, 7 1/4 lbs. Mfg. 2004-2017.

	$530	$465	$400	$360	$290	$240	$185	*$619*

* ***Model 835 Ulti-Mag Turkey Recoil Reduction System*** – 12 ga., 3 1/2 in. chamber, 6 shot, 24 in. VR ported overbored barrel with Ulti-Full tube choke, adj. fiber optic sight, features Mathews Harmonic Damper Technology, dual comb synthetic stock, Mossy Oak Break-Up Infinity (disc. 2015) or Mossy Oak Obsession (new 2016) camo finish, 8 1/2 lbs. Mfg. 2013-2017.

	$555	$485	$415	$375	$300	$250	$195	*$655*

* ***Model 835 Ulti-Mag Turkey Tactical*** – 12 ga., 3 1/2 in. chamber, 6 shot, 20 in. VR overbored barrel, X-Factor ported tube, adj. fiber optic sights, adj. tactical synthetic stock with Realtree Hardwoods HD Green (disc. 2012), Mossy Oak New Break-Up (disc. 2011), Mossy Oak Break-Up Infinity (new 2012), or Mossy Oak Obsession (mfg. 2013-2014) camo coverage, 7 1/4 lbs. Mfg. 2006-2015.

	$675	$590	$500	$450	$360	$300	$250	*$787*

GRADING - PPGS™	100%	98%	95%	90%	80%	70%	60%	LAST MSR

* ***Model 835 Ulti-Mag Turkey Thugs w/LPA Red Dot Combo*** – 12 ga., 3 1/2 in. chamber, 6 shot, 20 in. VR barrel, X-Factor ported tube, "Turkey Thugs" engraved receiver, Picatinny top rail, LPA adj. trigger, adj. fiber optic and TruGlo red dot sights, synthetic stock, Mossy Oak Break-Up Infinity camo coverage, 7 1/4 lbs. Mfg. 2011-2015.

	$610	$525	$450	$410	$325	$275	$225	*$730*

* ***Model 835 Ulti-Mag Turkey Thumbhole*** – 12 ga., 3 1/2 in. chamber, 6 shot, 20 in. VR overbored barrel with X-Factor ported tube, adj. fiber optic sight, standard trigger or LPA adj. trigger (mfg. 2011-2013), matte blue finish with black synthetic thumbhole stock (disc. 2013) or synthetic thumbhole stock with Mossy Oak New Break-Up (disc. 2011), Mossy Oak Break-Up Infinity (new 2012), Realtree Hardwoods HD Green (disc. 2012), or Realtree Extra Green (new 2013) camo coverage, 7 1/4 lbs. Mfg. 2007-2014.

	$575	$500	$425	$395	$325	$275	$215	*$667*

Subtract $87 for matte blue finish with black synthetic thumbhole stock (disc. 2013).
Add $41 for LPA adj. trigger (disc. 2013).

* ***Model 835 Ulti-Mag Laminate Turkey Thumbhole*** – 12 ga., 20 in. overbored VR barrel with X-Factor ported Turkey tube, adj. fiber optic sights, web sling, thumbhole laminated wood stock, Mossy Oak New Break-Up or Realtree Hardwoods HD Green camo finish. Disc. 2008.

	$550	$475	$415	$375	$300	$250	$200	*$648*

* ***Model 835 Ulti-Mag Turkey w/Marble Arms Bullseye Sights*** – 12 ga., 3 1/2 in. chamber, 24 in. ported VR barrel with Ulti-full chokes, 6 shot mag., Marble Bullseye rear sight and front fiber optic sight, ambidextrous safety, dual extractor, twin action bar, synthetic stock, Mossy Oak Obsession finish, includes shims, 7 1/2 lbs. New 2015.

MSR $594	$510	$450	$385	$350	$275	$225	$200	

MODEL 835 ULTI-MAG TACTICAL TURKEY – 12 ga., 3 1/2 in. chamber, 20 in. VR barrel, X-Factor ported turkey choke tubes, 6 shot mag., dual extractors, 6-pos. adj. synthetic stock, adj. fiber optic sights, top-mounted ambidextrous safety, 100% Mossy Oak Obsession camo coverage, 7 lbs. New 2019.

MSR $714	$610	$535	$460	$425	$345	$275	$225	

MODEL 835 ULTI-MAG TURKEY/DEER COMBO – 12 ga., 3 1/2 in. chamber, 6 shot, two barrel set includes 24 in. VR ported barrel with Ulti-Full tube choke and adj. fiber optic sight and 24 in. ported barrel with fully rifled bore and integral scope base, dual comb synthetic stock, Mossy Oak New Break-Up (disc. 2011), Mossy Oak Break-Up Infinity (mfg. 2012-2015), or Mossy Oak Break-Up Country (new 2016) camo coverage, 7 1/2 lbs.

MSR $624	$525	$460	$395	$355	$290	$240	$200	

MODEL 835 ULTI-MAG TURKEY/DEER LPA COMBO – 12 ga., 3 1/2 in. chamber, 6 shot, two barrel set includes 24 in. VR ported overbored turkey barrel with Ulti-Full tube choke and adj. fiber optic sight and 24 in. fluted Slugster barrel with fully rifled bore and integral scope base, LPA adj. trigger, dual comb synthetic stock, Mossy Oak New Break-Up (disc. 2011), Mossy Oak Break-Up Infinity (mfg. 2012-2015), or Mossy Oak Break-Up Country (new 2016) camo coverage, 7 1/2 lbs. Disc. 2017.

	$595	$520	$445	$400	$325	$270	$210	*$701*

MODEL 835 ULTI-MAG TURKEY/FIELD – 12 ga., 2 3/4 in. chamber, 26 in. VR overbored barrel, full Accu-Mag choke set, X-Factor ported turkey tube, 6 shot mag., fiber optic front sights, synthetic stock, Mossy Oak Bottomland camo finish, 7 1/2 lbs. New 2018.

MSR $568	$485	$425	$365	$330	$265	$225	$190	

MODEL 835 ULTI-MAG TURKEY/WATERFOWL COMBO – 12 ga., 3 1/2 in. chamber, 6 shot, two barrel set includes 24 in. VR ported barrel with Ulti-Full tube choke and adj. fiber optic sight and 28 in. VR ported barrel with fully rifled bore and fiber optic front sight, synthetic stock, Mossy Oak New Break-Up (disc. 2011), Mossy Oak Break-Up Infinity (mfg. 2012-2015), or Mossy Oak Break-Up Country (new 2016) camo coverage, 7 1/2-7 3/4 lbs.

MSR $624	$525	$460	$395	$355	$290	$240	$200	

MODEL 835 ULTI-MAG WATERFOWL – 12 ga., 3 1/2 in. chamber, 6 shot, 26 (mfg. 2004-2008) or 28 in. VR ported/overbored barrel, Modified tube or Accu-Mag Set chokes, Dual Bead or fiber optic front sights, blue finish with wood stock (disc. 2015), matte blue finish with black synthetic stock (disc. 2019), or synthetic stock with 100% Mossy Oak Shadow Grass (mfg. 2000-2007), Mossy Oak New Break-Up (disc. 2011), Mossy Oak Duck Blind (mfg. 2007-2012), Mossy Oak Shadowgrass Blades (new 2013), or Advantage Max-4 (mfg. 2004-2015) camo coverage, 7 3/4 lbs.

MSR $568	$485	$425	$365	$330	$265	$225	$190	

Add $85 for Advantage Max-4 (disc. 2015) camo coverage.

GRADING - PPGS™	100%	98%	95%	90%	80%	70%	60%	LAST MSR

* ***Model 835 Ulti-Mag Flyway Series Waterfowl*** – 12 ga. only, 3 1/2 in. chamber, 28 in. VR with X-factor porting barrel and choke tubes, 6 shot, fiber optic sights, synthetic stock and forearm with Advantage Max-4 camo, includes padded sling and embossed logo, 7 3/4 lbs. Mfg. 2005-2015.

$470 $400 $340 $300 $250 $200 $160 *$683*

* ***Model 835 Ulti-Mag Waterfowl Recoil Reduction System*** – 12 ga., 3 1/2 in. chamber, 6 shot, 28 in. VR ported overbored barrel with modified tube or Accu-Mag Set chokes, dual bead or fiber optic front sights, features Mathews Harmonic Damper Technology, dual comb synthetic stock, matte blue or Advantage Max-4 camo finish, 8 3/4 lbs. Mfg. 2013-2015.

$490 $425 $360 $325 $265 $215 $175 *$583*

Add $87 for Advantage Max-4 camo finish.

MODEL 835 ULTI-MAG DUCK COMMANDER WATERFOWL – 12 ga., 3 1/2 in. chamber, 28 in. ported VR barrel, 6 shot, TruGlo fiber optic sights, Accu-Mag set chokes, Realtree Max-5 finish, logo engraved synthetic stock, includes American flag bandana, 7 3/4 lbs. Mfg. 2014-2015.

$635 $550 $495 $450 $400 $365 $325 *$715*

* ***Model 835 Ulti-Mag Duck Commander Waterfowl Recoil Reduction System*** – 12 ga., 3 1/2 in. chamber, 28 in. ported VR barrel, 6 shot, Mathews Harmonic Damper Technology, TruGlo fiber optic sights, Accu-Mag set chokes, Realtree Max-5 finish, logo engraved receiver, Dual Comb synthetic stock, includes American flag bandana, 7 3/4 lbs. Mfg. 2014-2015.

$660 $575 $525 $475 $425 $395 $350 *$773*

MODEL 835 WATERFOWL LIMITED EDITION – 12 ga. with 3 1/2 in. chamber, 28 in. VR barrel with Accu-Mag chokes, camo finish, synthetic stock, camo sling. Mfg. 1990 only.

$425 $370 $320 $290 $235 $190 $150 *$480*

MODEL 835 WALNUT ULTI-MAG (REGAL) – 12 ga., 3 1/2 in. chamber, 28 in. VR barrel with Accu-Mag chokes (disc. 1996) or 24 in. rifled slug barrel, single (new 1993) or dual comb (2 comb inserts are provided for the stock affording different shooting positions), aluminum receiver, back-bored barrel, double slide bars, high gloss walnut stock with recoil pad, approx. 7 1/2 lbs. Mfg. 1991-96.

$350 $305 $260 $240 $190 $155 $120 *$404*

Add $8 for dual comb stock.

Add $30 for 24 in. slug barrel with trophy scope base and dual comb stock.

Add $72-$83 for combo package (includes extra slug barrel with choice of sights).

MODEL 835 WILD TURKEY FED. LIMITED EDITION – 12 ga. with 3 1/2 in. chamber, 24 in. VR barrel with Accu-Mag chokes, camo finish, includes camo sling, medallion in stock, and 10-pack of Federal Turkey loads. Mfg. 1989 only.

$425 $370 $320 $290 $235 $190 $150 *$477*

MODEL 835 NWTF SPECIAL EDITION – 12 ga. only, 24 in. VR barrel with Accu-Mag chokes, features Realtree camo finish, drilled and tapped receiver, 7 1/2 lbs. Mfg. 1991 only to commemorate the National Wild Turkey Federation.

$380 $330 $285 $260 $210 $170 $135 *$436*

MODEL 835 VIKING – 12 ga. only, 28 in. VR ported (standard 1997) or unported (1996 only) barrel with one Accu-Choke and twin bead sights, matte blue finish with green synthetic stock and forearm, 7.7 lbs. Mfg. 1996-98.

$260 $225 $195 $175 $145 $115 $90 *$316*

MODEL 935 MAGNUM SLUGSTER – 12 ga. only, 3 1/2 in. chamber, 24 in. fully rifled barrel, choice of Monte Carlo or regular synthetic stock and foream, choice of rifle sights (disc. 2008) or integral scope base, Realtree AP camo, 7 1/2 lbs. Mfg. 2007-2010.

$640 $550 $470 $425 $345 $280 $220 *$754*

MODEL 935 FLYWAY SERIES WATERFOWL – 12 ga. only, 3 1/2 in. chamber, 28 in. VR with X-factor ported barrel and choke tubes, fiber optic sights, synthetic stock and forearm with Advantage Max-4 camo, includes padded sling and embossed logo. Mfg. 2005-2014.

$735 $645 $550 $500 $400 $330 $250 *$870*

MODEL 3000 – 12 or 20 ga. only, 3 in. chamber, slide action, steel receiver, double action bars, various chokes and VR barrel lengths, checkered walnut stock and forearm, vent. recoil pad. This model was introduced in 1986 and the field version was disc. in 1987.

$325 $285 $245 $220 $180 $145 $115 *$360*

Add $25 for Multi-Choke II.

GRADING - PPGS™	100%	98%	95%	90%	80%	70%	60%	LAST MSR

* ***Model 3000 Waterfowler*** – 12 ga. only, similar to Model 3000, except has dull matte finish on wood and metal, includes swivels and camouflaged sling, VR only. Mfg. 1986 only.

	$340	$295	$265	$215	$185	$150	$120	*$386*

Add $30 for Multi-choke II option, $70 for camo/speedfeed stock.

* ***Model 3000 Law Enforcement*** – 12 or 20 ga. only, 18 1/2 or 20 in. cylinder bore only, rifle or bead sights. Mfg. 1986-87 only.

	$325	$285	$245	$220	$180	$145	$115	*$362*

Add $25 for rifle sights.
Add $33 for black Speedfeed stock.

SHOTGUNS: SLIDE ACTION MAGPUL SERIES

MODEL 500 MAGPUL – 12 ga., 3 in. chamber, 6 or 8 shot, 18 1/2 or 20 in. barrel, bead sights, parkerized finish, Magpul SGA adj. LOP stock with interchangeable cheek riser combs, MOE forend, Black finish, 7 lbs. Mfg. 2014-2015.

	$525	$450	$400	$375	$350	$325	$295	*$602*

Add $16 for 8 shot with receiver mounted sling plate.

* ***Model 500 Magpul Cruiser*** – 12 ga., similar to Model 500 Magpul, except features 18 1/2 in. Standoff barrel, white dot sights, 7 lbs. Mfg. 2014-2015.

	$575	$500	$450	$400	$350	$325	$295	*$655*

MODEL 590 MAGPUL – 12 ga., 3 in. chamber, 9 shot, 20 in. barrel, parkerized finish, ghost ring sights, black synthetic Magpul SGA stock with 4 LOP adj. spacers and 2 cheek rest combs, MOE forend, bayonet lug, 7 1/4 lbs. Mfg. 2014-2015.

	$675	$600	$525	$450	$425	$395	$375	*$773*

MODEL 590A1 MAGPUL – 12 ga., 3 in. chamber, 6 shot, 18 1/2 in. fluted barrel, bead sights, Magpul SGA adj. LOP stock with interchangeable cheek riser combs, MOE forend, metal trigger guard and safety button, black finish, 7 lbs. Mfg. 2014-2015.

	$650	$575	$495	$425	$395	$375	$350	*$758*

* ***Model 590A1 Magpul 9 Shot*** – 12 ga., 20 in. heavy walled barrel, XS Ghost ring rear/AR-style post front sights, top Picatinny rail, bayonet lug, receiver and barrel mounted sling plates, Magpul SGA adj. LOP stock with interchangeable cheek riser combs, MOE forend, sling plates, parkerized finish, 7 1/4 lbs. Mfg. 2014-2015, reintroduced 2017.

MSR $888	$750	$650	$550	$500	$400	$350	$285	

MOUNTAIN RIFLERY, LLC

Current custom rifle builder located in Pocatello, ID. Consumer direct sales.

John Bolliger has been producing top quality, custom made bolt action rifles for almost 35 years, in addition to being a noted Marlin fisherman. Currently, Mountain Riflery is concentrating on 3 series of rifles: the Signature Series, the Excalibur Series, and the Crown Series. The Signature Series has a price range of $14,500-$21,000. Please contact Mountain Riflery directly for more information, including pricing and options.

MOUNTAIN RIFLES INC.

Previous rifle manufacturer located in Palmer, AK 1995-98.

RIFLES: BOLT ACTION

MOUNTAINEER – various cals., choice of M-700 Rem. or M-70 Win. action, chrome moly barrel with ultra muzzle brake, Timney trigger, parkerized finish, fiberglass stock with decelerator pad, 5 1/2 lbs. Limited mfg. 1995-98.

	$1,825	$1,475	$1,100	$900	$750	$675	$550	*$1,995*

SUPER MOUNTAINEER – similar to the Mountaineer, except has Kevlar epoxy bedded stock with steel crossbolts on Mag. cals., 4 1/4 lbs. Limited mfg. 1995-98.

	$2,575	$2,025	$1,475	$1,100	$900	$750	$675	*$2,895*

PRO MOUNTAINEER K.S. – various cals., Winchester M-70 controlled feed action, choice of fiberglass pillar epoxy bedded, Kevlar, or KSDB (Kevlar Stock Drop Box mag.) stock with decelerator pad, parkerized finish. 6 lbs. Limited mfg. 1995-98.

	$2,395	$1,950	$1,425	$1,050	$875	$725	$650	*$2,695*

Add $500 for KSDB stock with drop mag.

PRO SAFARI – various cals., Winchester M-70 controlled feed action, high gloss bluing, exhibition grade English walnut with decelerator pad, 4 shot detachable mag. 7-9 lbs. Limited mfg. 1995-98.

	$3,795	$3,350	$2,875	$2,350	$1,775	$1,450	$1,200	*$3,995*

GRADING - PPGS™	100%	98%	95%	90%	80%	70%	60%	LAST MSR

ULTRA MOUNTAINEER – various cals., features stainless steel match grade barrel with black Kevlar/Graphite thumbhole stock, approx. 5 lbs. New 1997.

	$2,650	$2,075	$1,500	$1,100	$900	$750	$675	*$2,995*

Add $500 for Rigby length.

MUSGRAVE (PREVIOUS MFG.)

Previous manufacturer located in the Republic of South Africa.

Musgrave had very limited importation into the U.S. Newer models manufactured by Musgrave (imported into Austria and Switzerland) included the Model 90 (features Musgrave action) Standard Rifle, Model 90 Light Rifle, Mini-90, Model 90 Varmint, Model 90 De Luxe Rifle, and Magnum Rifle, in addition to the same series in the Mauser 98 action.

RIFLES: BOLT ACTION

VALIANT BOLT ACTION RIFLE – .243 Win., .270 Win., .30-06, .308 Win., or 7mm Rem. Mag. cal., 24 in. barrel, leaf sight, skipline checkered straight stock, pistol grip. Mfg. 1971-1976.

	$475	$425	$375	$325	$275	$250	$220	

PREMIER – similar to Valiant, with 26 in. barrel, select Monte Carlo stock, rosewood pistol grip cap and forearm tip. Disc.

	$525	$450	$375	$325	$275	$250	$225	

RSA SINGLE SHOT TARGET RIFLE – .308 Win. cal. only, 26 in. heavy barrel, target sights and stock. Mfg. 1971-1976.

	$600	$500	$425	$365	$315	$275	$250	

MUSGRAVE (NEW MFG.)

Current bolt action rifle manufacturer established circa 2009, located in South Africa.

South African Frikkie du Plooy bought the Musgrave patent and the remaining K98 actions from the previous factory. Together with gunsmith Gary Barnes he established a factory circa 2009 to build new Musgrave rifles.

RIFLES: BOLT ACTION

Musgrave rifles are available in four configurations: the Field (€1,395), Field Delux (€1,595), Sporter, Varminter (€1,595), and Exhibition (€2,500) with either walnut or laminated Black Pepper and Nutmeg stocks. For Mag. cals., add approx. €200. All rifles are manufactured using the VZ24 Mauser action, available in a variety of calibers. Currently, rifles are not imported into the U.S. Please contact the factory directly for more information, including U.S. availability and pricing.

MUSKETEER RIFLES

Previous trademark of rifles previously imported by Firearms International Company (FIC), located in Washington, D.C.

RIFLES: BOLT ACTION

CARBINE – 243 Win., .25-06 Rem., .270 Win., .264 Win. Mag., .308 Win., .30-06, 7mm Rem. Mag., or .300 Win. Mag. cal., FN Mauser action, 20 in. barrel, no sights, full-length stock.

	$450	$395	$350	$295	$250	$220	$195	

SPORTER – .243 Win., .25-06 Rem., .270 Win., .264 Win. Mag., .308 Win., .30-06, 7mm Rem. Mag., or .300 Win. Mag. cal., FN Mauser action, 24 in. barrel, no sights, checkered Monte Carlo stock. Mfg. 1963-1972.

	$450	$395	$350	$295	$250	$220	$195	

SPORTER DELUXE – .243 Win., .25-06 Rem., .270 Win., .264 Win. Mag., .308 Win., .30-06, 7mm Rem. Mag., or .300 Win. Mag. cal., FN Mauser action, 24 in. barrel, adj. trigger, no sights, select wood, tear drop pistol grip, skipline checkering.

	$525	$425	$375	$325	$275	$250	$225	

N SECTION

NS FIREARMS CORP.

Previous importer located in Atlanta, GA until 1994. NS Firearms was a division of KFS, Inc. located in Atlanta, GA. Previously manufactured in China.

GRADING - PPGS™	100%	98%	95%	90%	80%	70%	60%	LAST MSR

RIFLES: SEMI-AUTO

MODEL 522 SPORTER – .22 LR cal., 21 in. cold hammer forged barrel, 5 shot detachable mag., grooved receiver, checkered walnut stock, 7 3/4 lbs. Imported 1994 only.

	$250	$215	$185	$165	$145	$125	$110	*$299*

NAMBU PISTOLS

Previously manufactured in Japan for the Japanese military between 1902-1945.

PISTOLS: SEMI-AUTO

Please refer to Japanese Military Pistols for the Hamada variations and the Type 26 Revolver (1893 Revolver).

TYPE 14 – 8mm Nambu cal., recoil operated, 4.7 in. barrel, blue, wood grips, 8 shot mag., a simply designed pistol used by Japanese armed forces from 1925-45.

Add 25% for 3.X date Tokyo.
Add 50% for 2.X date Nagoya.
Add 400% for early Taisho era pistols dated 15.11 or 15.12 from Nagoya arsenal.
Add 10% for matching mag. on models listed.

Type 14 Nambus have a 3 or 4 digit number just forward of the lanyard ring on the right side of frame (on back of grip). Earliest Taisho era pistols are dated 15.11 or 15.12 from the Nagoya arsenal and can be identified by small trigger guard and other early features. Fewer than 100 mfg. To determine year and month of manufacture for most type 14 pistols, add "1925" to the first two digits and the last number will indicate the month (i.e. code 13.3 indicates a gun built in March of 1938).

- ***Type 14 1925-1930 Mfg.***

	$1,500	$1,300	$1,100	$975	$895	$715	$585

- ***Type 14 1930-1939 Mfg.*** – small trigger guard.

	$1,100	$965	$825	$750	$600	$495	$385

- ***Type 14 1939-1945 Mfg.*** – large trigger guard.

	$700	$615	$525	$475	$385	$315	$245

Add 10% for strawed trigger and safety.

TYPE 94 – 8mm Nambu cal., recoil operated, 3.8 in. barrel, blue, and bakelite wood grips, 6 shot mag. Mfg. 1935-1945.

	$525	$465	$395	$350	$295	$235	$185
10.X date	$2,625	$2,000	$1,750	$1,500	$1,250	$1,125	$1,000
11.X date	$1,575	$1,200	$1,050	$900	$750	$675	$600
12.X date	$1,050	$925	$795	$715	$575	$475	$375
pre-WWII	$695	$610	$525	$475	$375	$315	$245
Late square back	$950	$800	$700	$600	$500	$400	$300

Add 10% for matching magazine.

HAMADA NAMBU – Please refer to Japanese Military section.

BABY NAMBU – 7mm Nambu cal., 3 1/4 in. barrel, blue, wood grips, grip safety, one of the most desirable Japanese handguns.

	$4,500	$3,925	$3,375	$3,050	$2,475	$2,025	$1,575

Add 10% for matching mag. Add 50% for chamber marked "TGE" (Tokyo Gas & Electric).

PAPA NAMBU (MODEL 1904) – 8mm Nambu cal., 4.7 in. barrel, wood grips, grip safety, 8 shot mag., essentially the same action as the Baby, but a larger version. Mfg. 1904-25.

	$3,500	$3,000	$2,300	$2,250	$2,000	$1,750	$1,500

Add 10% for matching mag. Add 50% for chamber marked "TGE" (Tokyo Gas & Electric).

GRANDPA NAMBU – 8mm Nambu cal., similar to Papa Nambu, except has smaller trigger guard and fixed lanyard ring, cherry wood based mag., issued with 2 matching mags. Early Tokyo arsenal or later Thai issue, all Grandpa frames are slotted.

	$15,000	$12,500	$10,000	$8,000	$7,000	$6,000	$5,000
w/matching shoulder stock							
	$30,000	$25,000	$20,000	$17,500	$15,000	$12,500	$10,000

Add $8,000 for original stock. Add 20% for second matching mag.

Original stocks are rare and expensive, check for originality carefully.

GRADING - PPGS™	100%	98%	95%	90%	80%	70%	60%	LAST MSR

NAROH ARMS

Previous manufacturer of semi-auto pistols located in Rockledge, FL from 2013-2020.

PISTOLS: SEMI-AUTO

N1/N1 PRO – 9mm Para. cal., DAO, hammer fired, 3.125 in. stainless steel LiFe FNC coated barrel, two 7 shot mags., standard or Pro Trigger System (N1 Pro Model, new 2020), flush fit and extended floorplate, stainless steel slide, hardcoat anodized aluminum receiver, fixed polymer 3-dot sights with Glock-style dovetails, glass reinforced polymer grip frame, internal drop safety, Black FNC or Silver Stainless slide finish, 16 oz. Mfg. 2019-2020.

	$325	$275	$250	$225	$175	$150	$125	*$359*

Add $40 for N1 Pro Model (new 2020).

NATIONAL POSTAL METER

Previous WWII subcontractor of M1 carbines located in Rochester, NY.

Please refer to U.S. M1 Carbines/Rifles listings under U.S. Military Long Arms.

NATIONAL WILD TURKEY FEDERATION (NWTF)

Current national conservation organization located in Edgefield, SC.

For individual model listings, please go to BlueBookOfGunValues.com/overflow.

NAVY ARMS COMPANY

Current importer established during 1956, and located in Martinsburg, WV beginning 2014. Previously located in Ridgefield, NJ, 1962-2002. Navy Arms imports were fabricated by various manufacturers including the Italian companies Davide Pedersoli & Co., Pietta & Co., and A. Uberti & C. Navy Arms also owns Old Western Scrounger ammo, which markets obsolete and hard-to-find ammo. Distributor and dealer sales.

Navy Arms has also sold a wide variety of original military firearms classified as curios and relics. Handguns included the Mauser Broomhandle, Japanese Nambu, Colt 1911 Government Model, Tokarev, Browning Hi-Power, S&W Model 1917, and others. Rifles included Mauser contract models, Japanese Type 38s, Enfields, FNs, Nagants, M1 Carbines, M1 Garands, Chinese SKSs, Egyptian Rashids, French MAS Model 1936s, among others. Most of these firearms are priced in the $75-$500 price range depending on desirability of model and condition.

In 2014, Navy Arms made an agreement with Browning Arms Company, licensees of the Winchester brand name for firearms, to have Winchester-branded 1873 replica rifles made for Navy Arms with features and upgrades unique to Navy Arms guns. These improvements include a factory installed short-stroke kit, squared off shotgun style buttstock, and deluxe grade American walnut stocks fully checkered with an oil finish and full octagonal barrels. Navy Arms receives these guns from Winchester without finish on the metal. The receiver and all furniture are then bone color case-hardened and the barrels blued. These guns will be produced annually on a limited basis and are only available from Navy Arms. For information and up-to-date pricing regarding recent Navy Arms black powder models, please refer to the *Blue Book of Modern Black Powder Arms* (also available online).

PISTOLS

TU-711 MAUSER – 9mm Para. cal., patterned after Mauser 711 (semi-auto version of the Model 712 Schnellfeuer), 5 1/4 in. barrel, 712 upper receiver that has been converted to 9mm Para. and mounted on new lower receiver, supplied with 10 and 20 shot detachable mag., mfg. in China, 2 lbs. 11 oz. Imported 1992 only.

	$1,300	$925	$825	$725	$650	$600	$550	*$650*

Add 20% for 10 and 20 shot matching number mags.
Add $350 for stock with leather holster that holds 20 shot mag.

TT-OLYMPIA – .22 LR cal., patterned after the Walther Olympia that won 1936 Olympics, 4 5/8 in. barrel, checkered walnut grips, mfg. in China, 27 oz. Imported 1992-98.

	$295	$255	$225	$195	$175	$160	$150	*$290*

TU-90 PISTOL – .30 Tokarev or 9mm Para. cal., patterned after the rare Tokagypt variation (improved TT-33 Tokarev), 4 1/2 in. barrel, single action, wraparound synthetic grips, unique forward motion safety, mfg. in China, 30 oz. Imported 1992-98.

	$135	$100	$90	$80	$70	$60	$50	*$130*

Add $15 for 9mm Para. cal.
Add $40 for pistol combo (includes both cals.).

GRADING - PPGS™	100%	98%	95%	90%	80%	70%	60%	LAST MSR

LUGER MODEL - .22 LR cal. only, 10 shot mag., Luger toggle type action, available in blue or matte finish, 4, 6, or 8 in. barrel, checkered walnut stocks. Mfg. in U.S. 1986-87 only.

	$325	$285	$260	$225	$195	$175	$150	*$165*

GRAND PRIX SILHOUETTE - .30-30 Win., 7mm Spl., .44 Mag., or .45-70 Govt. cal., 13 3/4 in. barrel, non-glare matte blue finish, walnut forearm and grips, adj. heat dispersing aluminum rib, adj. target sights, 4 lbs. Mfg. 1985 only.

	$320	$280	$240	$220	$195	$175	$150	*$375*

REVOLVERS: REPRODUCTIONS

1872 OPEN TOP - .38 Spl. cal., 5 1/2 or 7 1/2 in. round barrel, case colored frame with blue cylinder and barrel, silver plated brass trigger guard and backstrap, 2 1/2-2 3/4 lbs. Limited importation 2000-2001 only.

	$335	$275	$220	$185	$165	$150	$135	*$400*

1873 SAA - GUNFIGHTER SERIES & VARIATIONS - .32-20 WCF (mfg. 2002, reintroduced 2007), .357 Mag. (new 1998), .44-40 WCF or .45 LC cal., reproduction of the Colt SAA, case hardened frame with blue or nickel (disc. 1998) finish, 3 (Sheriff's Model - mfg. 1992-98), 4 3/4, 5 1/2, or 7 1/2 in. barrel, the Gunfighter Series was introduced during 2003, approx. 36 oz. Disc. 2009.

	$415	$335	$295	$230	$180	$160	$145	*$511*

Add $65 for nickel finish (disc.).
Add $30 for Pinched Frame Model (7 1/2 in. barrel, .45 LC, disc. 2002).
Subtract $20 for brass trigger guard and backstrap (disc.).

The Gunfighter Series, introduced in 2003, was different than previous production in that it featured a U.S. mfg. Wolff spring kit, German silver plated backstrap and trigger guard, and black checkered gunfighter grips.

* ***1873 SAA Gunfighter Series Stainless Steel Model*** - .357 Mag. or .45 LC cal., 4 3/4, 5 1/2, or 7 1/2 in. barrel, stainless steel construction. Imported 2003-2009.

	$485	$375	$315	$250	$215	$185	$155	*$608*

* ***1873 SAA Gunfighter Series Deluxe Model*** - .32-20 WCF cal., deluxe model with color case hardened and charcoal blue finishes, high polish walnut grips, includes Wolff springs. Limited importation 2003.

	$365	$295	$230	$200	$180	$165	$140	*$435*

This model was sold exclusively through AcuSport.

* ***1873 SAA Gunfighter Series Economy Model*** - .44-40 WCF or .45 LC cal., 3, 4 3/4, 5 1/2, or 7 1/2 in. barrel, brass trigger guard and backstrap, 2-piece walnut grips. Imported 1993-96.

	$295	$230	$185	$160	$145	$130	$120	*$345*

* ***1873 SAA Gunfighter Series Deputy Model*** - .44-40 WCF or .45 LC cal., patterned after the Colt 1877 Thunderer double action, bird's head grips, 3, 3 1/2, 4, or 4 3/4 in. barrel, case colored frame. Imported 1997-1998 only.

	$350	$275	$210	$180	$160	$145	$130	*$405*

* ***1873 SAA Gunfighter Series Flat-top Target Model*** - .45 LC cal. only, flat-top frame, 7 1/2 in. barrel only, adj. spring loaded front sight and dovetailed rear sight, 30 oz. Imported 1999-2006.

	$425	$350	$285	$240	$205	$175	$150	*$514*

* ***1873 SAA Gunfighter Series Shootist Model*** - .357 Mag., .44-40 WCF, or .45 LC cal., interchangeable parts with original Colt 1st and 2nd Generation SAAs, designed for Cowboy Action Shooting, 4 3/4, 5 1/2, or 7 1/2 in. barrel, case colored frame and hammer, blue cylinder barrel, trigger guard and backstrap. Limited importation 2000 only.

	$350	$275	$210	$180	$160	$145	$130	*$385*

* ***1873 SAA Gunfighter Series Bisley Model*** - .44-40 WCF or .45 LC cal., patterned after the Colt Bisley, 4 3/4, 5 1/2, or 7 1/2 in. barrel, case colored frame, spur hammer, walnut grips. Imported 1997-2009.

	$415	$335	$295	$230	$180	$160	$145	*$511*

» **1873 SAA Gunfighter Series Bisley Model Flattop Target** - .44-40 WCF or .45 LC (disc. 2006) cal., flat-top frame, adj. front sight, and dovetailed rear sight, 40 oz. Imported 1999-2009.

	$485	$375	$315	$250	$215	$185	$155	*$608*

* ***1873 SAA Gunfighter Series Cavalry Model*** - .45 LC cal. only, exact replica of the original U.S. Government issue SAA, 7 1/2 in. barrel, arsenal stampings, inspector's cartouche on walnut stocks. Disc. 2009.

	$515	$385	$335	$280	$230	$200	$175	*$594*

GRADING - PPGS™	100%	98%	95%	90%	80%	70%	60%	LAST MSR

* ***1873 SAA Gunfighter Series Artillery Model*** – similar specifications to the Cavalry Model, except has 5 1/2 in. barrel. Disc.

$515 $385 $335 $280 $230 $200 $175 *$594*

* ***1873 SAA Gunfighter Series Scout Small Frame Model*** – .38 Spl. cal., scaled down variation of the SAA, 4 3/4 or 5 1/2 in. barrel only. Imported 2003-2009.

$415 $335 $295 $230 $180 $160 $145 *$511*

1875 REMINGTON REVOLVER – .44-40 WCF or .45 LC cal., reproduction of the 1875 Remington revolver, 7 1/2 in. barrel, case colored frame, 41 oz. Importation disc. 1991, resumed 1994-2000.

$360 $295 $260 $230 $200 $175 $150 *$435*

1890 REMINGTON REVOLVER – .44-40 WCF or .45 LC cal., reproduction of the 1890 Remington revolver, 5 1/2 in. barrel, brass trigger guard and lanyard loop, 39 oz. Importation disc. 1991, resumed 1994-2000.

$370 $295 $260 $230 $200 $175 $150 *$445*

1875 SCHOFIELD SERIES – various cals., patterned after the original S&W Schofield Model, blued finish, smooth wood grips, case colored hammer, trigger guard and opening lever. Imported 1994-2003.

.44-40 WCF or .45 LC cal., similar to Wells Fargo Model, except has 3 1/2 in. barrel, 34 oz. New 1999.
.45 LC cal., charcoal blue barrel and cylinder, case colored receiver, backstrap, trigger guard, and trigger, 7 1/2 in. barrel, white ivory tex grips. Importation began 2003.

.44-40 WCF or .45 LC cal., similar to Deluxe Schofield, except does not have gold inlays, extensive B or C coverage scroll engraving on both frame, cylinder, and barrel. Special order only beginning 1999.

.44-40 WCF or .45 LC cal., available in Cavalry, Wells Fargo, or Hideout configurations, with light scroll engraving on frame and cylinder with extensive frame, barrel, and cylinder gold line inlays and scroll motifs. Special order only 1999-2009.

$615 $535 $455 $375 $325 $250 $195 *$716*

* ***1875 Schofield Series Cavalry Model*** – .38 Spl. (new 2003), .44-40 WCF, or .45 LC cal., patterned after the original Schofield Cavalry Model, 7 1/2 in. barrel, 37 oz. Imported 1994-2009.

$715 $600 $485 $395 $335 $250 $195 *$849*

* ***1875 Schofield Series Wells Fargo Model*** – .38 Spl. (new 2003), .44-40 WCF, or .45 LC cal., 5 1/2 in. barrel, 35 oz. Mfg. 1994-2009, and 2011-2017.

$750 $625 $500 $400 $335 $250 $195 *$899*

* ***1875 Schofield Series Hideout Model*** – 3 1/2 in. barrel.

$715 $600 $485 $395 $335 $250 $195 *$849*

* ***1875 Schofield Series Founders Model*** – .38 Spl. or .45 LC cal., 7 in. barrel, features charcoal blue barrel and cylinder, case colored frame, backstrap, trigger and trigger guard, "VF" serial number prefix.

$800 $665 $515 $400 $350 $250 $195 *$946*

* ***1875 Schofield Series Engraved Model***

$1,425 $1,225 $1,000 $875 $750 $625 $525

Add $215 for C engraving.

* ***1875 Schofield Series Deluxe Model***

$1,675 $1,450 $1,250 $995 $875 $750 $625

NEW MODEL RUSSIAN – .44 Russian cal., patterned after the S&W Model 3 Russian Third Model Single Action, 6 1/2 in. barrel, blue metal with case colored trigger, trigger guard, and hammer, smooth walnut grips, 40 oz. Imported 1999-2009.

$765 $635 $500 $400 $350 $250 $195 *$908*

REVOLVERS: REPRODUCTIONS, COLT CARTRIDGE CONVERSIONS

1851 NAVY RICHARDS-TYPE CONVERSION – .38 Spl. or .38 LC cal., patterned after the Colt 1851 Navy Conversion, 5 1/2 or 7 1/2 in. barrel, case colored frame and hammer, blue cylinder and barrel, brass back strap and trigger guard, 40 or 44 oz. Imported 1999-2001.

$320 $255 $200 $175 $160 $145 $130 *$375*

1860 ARMY RICHARDS-TYPE CONVERSION – .38 Spl. or .38 LC cal., patterned after the Colt 1860 Army Conversion, other specifications similar to 1851 Navy Conversion. Imported 1999-2001.

$320 $255 $200 $175 $160 $145 $130 *$375*

1861 NAVY RICHARDS-TYPE CONVERSION – .38 Spl. or .38 LC cal., patterned after the Colt 1861 Navy Conversion, other specifications similar to 1851 Navy Conversion. Imported 1999-2001.

$320 $255 $200 $175 $160 $145 $130 *$375*

GRADING - PPGS™ 100% 98% 95% 90% 80% 70% 60% LAST MSR

REVOLVERS: PREMIUM BLUE REPRODUCTIONS, CARTRIDGE CONVERSIONS

During 2003, Navy Arms planned to introduce its line of Premium Blue custom guns. However, these guns were never manufactured, except for a few prototypes. Models included were: 1860 Army Richards Type I ($1,995 MSR), Richards-Mason Colt Pocket Navy Model ($2,995 MSR), Richards-Mason Colt Police Model ($2,695 MSR), 1842 Paterson Conversion Model ($2,100 MSR), Remington Navy .38 Colt Cartridge Conversion, Remington Army 5 Shot Cartridge Conversion ($1,295 MSR), and the Remington 6 Shot Cartridge Conversion ($1,495 MSR).

RIFLES: REPRODUCTIONS

REVOLVING CARBINE - .357 Mag., .44-40 WCF, or .45 LC cal., 6 shot cylinder, 20 in. barrel, case hardened frame, straight stock. Mfg. 1968-1984.

$575 $475 $425 $375 $325 $275 $225

REMINGTON ROLLING BLOCK BUFFALO RIFLE - .444 Marlin (disc.), .45-70 Govt., or .50-70 (disc.) cal., replica of Remington Rolling Block, 26 or 30 in. heavy octagon or 1/2 round/ 1/2 octagon barrel (disc. 2000), open sight, straight grip stock. Mfg. 1971-2003.

$655 $465 $350 $260 $195 $160 $140 *$850*

Brass fittings were disc. during 1998, and replaced with steel fittings.

* ***Remington Rolling Block Buffalo Carbine*** - similar to Rifle, with 18 in. barrel. Disc. 1985.

$385 $325 $280 $230 $180 $160 $140 *$375*

* ***Remington Rolling Block Buffalo Baby Rifle*** - .22 LR, .22 Hornet, .357 Mag., or .44-40 WCF cal., replica of small frame Remington, 20 in. octagon or 22 in. round barrel, open sight, straight stock. Mfg. 1968-84.

$215 $175 $140 $110 $90 $65 $55

REMINGTON ROLLING BLOCK BODINE RIFLE - single or double set triggers, 30 in. heavy matte finished octagon barrel, nickel or case colored finish, "Soule" target rear tang sight, and split level globe front sight, No. 2 configuration became available during 2003, 12 lbs. Disc.

$1,700 $1,425 $1,125 $950 $800 $650 $500 *$1,940*

REMINGTON ROLLING BLOCK #2 BODINE RIFLE - similar to Bodine model, except has double set triggers, nickel finished receiver and lightweight barrel. Mfg. 2010-2012.

$1,700 $1,425 $1,125 $950 $800 $650 $500 *$1,937*

ROLLING BLOCK PLAINS RIFLE - .45-70 Govt. cal., features 30 in. tapered octagon barrel with straight grip stock, bright polished receiver with steel furniture, 9 lbs. Imported 1997-98 only.

$650 $500 $400 $285 $195 $175 $150 *$800*

* ***Rolling Block Plains Rifle Deluxe*** - similar to Plains Rifle, except has hand engraved coin finished receiver and trigger guard, rust blue barrel with German silver forearm tip. Imported 1997-98.

$1,475 $1,250 $1,050 $850 $725 $600 $525 *$1,625*

ROLLING BLOCK NO. 2 CREEDMOOR TARGET - similar to Buffalo Rifle, in .45-70 Govt. or .50-70 (disc.) cal., with Creedmoor tang sight, color case hardened receiver, checkered walnut. Disc.

$1,450 $1,175 $975 $800 $650 $500 $400 *$1,754*

* ***Rolling Block No. 2 Creedmoor Target Deluxe*** - featured hand engraved coin finished receiver and trigger guard, rust blue barrel and German silver forearm tip. Imported 1997-98.

$1,625 $1,400 $1,200 $1,000 $850 $725 $600 *$1,875*

SHARPS NO. 2 SILHOUETTE - .45-70 Govt. cal., 30 in. octagon barrel, 10 3/4 lbs. Imported 2003-2009.

$1,450 $1,150 $995 $850 $750 $650 $575 *$1,739*

SHARPS NO. 2 HUNTER - limited importation 2003 only.

$750 $650 $575 $525 $475 $425 $375 *$815*

1874 SHARPS PLAINS RIFLE - .45-70 Govt. cal., 32 in. octagon barrel, case hardened receiver, checkered stock and forearm, double set triggers, 9 1/2 lbs. Mfg. 1996-2002.

$1,020 $900 $800 $725 $625 $575 $525 *$1,175*

Add $75 for vernier rear tang or $55 for globe sight.

* ***1874 Sharps Plains Rifle Engraved*** - .45-70 Govt. cal., features hand engraved coin finished receiver. Imported 1997-98.

$2,325 $2,000 $1,800 $1,600 $1,400 $1,200 $995 *$2,500*

Add $700 for gold inlays (Deluxe Model).

GRADING - PPGS™	100%	98%	95%	90%	80%	70%	60%	LAST MSR

1874 SHARPS BUFFALO RIFLE – .45-70 Govt. or .45-90 (disc. 2000) cal., 28 in. octagon heavy barrel, case colored receiver, checkered stock, 10 lbs. 10 oz. Mfg. 1996-2002.

$1,035	$925	$825	$725	$625	$575	$525	*$1,200*

Add $75 for vernier rear tang or $55 for globe sight.

* ***1874 Sharps Buffalo Rifle Engraved*** – .45-70 Govt. or .45-90 cal., features hand engraved coin finished receiver. Imported 1997-98.

$2,325	$2,000	$1,800	$1,600	$1,400	$1,200	$995	*$2,515*

Add $700 for gold inlays (Deluxe Model).

SHARPS SPORTING RIFLE – .45-70 Govt. cal., similar to Plains Rifle, except has pistol grip stock, No. 2 configuration became available during 2003. Imported 1997-2009.

$1,450	$1,150	$995	$850	$750	$650	$575	*$1,739*

1874 SHARPS QUIGLEY – .45-70 Govt. cal., 34 in. octagon barrel, exact reproduction of rifle used in the movie *Quigley Down Under*, with patchbox. Imported 2002-2012.

$1,625	$1,325	$1,075	$900	$725	$625	$550	*$1,981*

1874 SHARPS NO. 2 CREEDMOOR – .45-70 Govt. cal., 30 in. thin tapered round barrel, polished nickel frame and action, "Soule" rear tang sight with front globe, 9 lbs. Imported 2002-2012.

$1,525	$1,200	$1,025	$850	$750	$650	$575	*$1,844*

1874 SHARPS NO. 3 LONG RANGE – .45-70 Govt. cal., 34 in. medium weight octagon barrel with globe front target sight, shotgun buttplate, double set triggers, German silver forearm cap, 10 lbs. 14 oz. Imported 2000-2012.

$1,950	$1,575	$1,300	$1,100	$925	$725	$600	*$2,379*

1874 SHARPS SNIPER/INFANTRY RIFLE – .45-70 Govt. cal., patterned after the 3-band military sniper rifle, 30 in. barrel, color case hardened frame, hammer, and furniture, ST or DST (Sniper rifle, disc. 1995). Mfg. 1994-2000.

$895	$780	$650	$475	$395	$350	$325	*$1,060*

Add $55 for DST (Sniper).

1874 SHARPS SNIPER/INFANTRY CAVALRY CARBINE – .45-70 Govt. cal., patterned after Sharps Cavalry carbine, 22 in. barrel, color case hardened frame, hammer, patchbox, and furniture. Mfg. 1994-2009.

$975	$800	$665	$475	$395	$350	$325	*$1,246*

1873 SPRINGFIELD INFANTRY RIFLE – .45-70 Govt. cal., 32 1/2 in. barrel, 8 lbs, 4 oz. Imported 1997-2000.

$840	$750	$650	$475	$395	$350	$325	*$995*

1873 SPRINGFIELD INFANTRY CAVALRY CARBINE – similar to the 1873 Springfield Rifle, except has 22 in. barrel, 1 barrel band, 7 lbs. Imported 1997-2010.

$1,325	$1,050	$900	$775	$650	$550	$450	*$1,519*

Add $324 for Springfield Officer's Model.

KODIAK MARK IV DOUBLE RIFLE – .45-70 Govt. cal., patterned after the Colt Double rifle, semi-regulated 24 in. barrels, hammers, folding leaf rear sight, color cased hardened receiver, 10 lbs. 3 oz. Mfg. 1996-2000.

$2,450	$2,250	$2,000	$1,800	$1,600	$1,400	$1,200	*$2,815*

* ***Kodiak Mark IV Double Rifle Deluxe*** – similar to Kodiak Mark IV Double rifle, except has brown barrels and hand engraved satin finished receiver. Mfg. 1996-2000.

$3,300	$2,900	$2,600	$2,375	$2,000	$1,750	$1,500	*$3,690*

HENRY RIFLE – .44-40 WCF, .44 Rimfire (disc. 1989), or .45 LC (new 1998) cal., reproduction of Winchester's famous Henry Rifle, brass or iron frame. New 1985.

* ***Henry Rifle Military*** – 24 in. barrel, brass frame, blue barrel, walnut stock, original style sling swivels, 9 1/4 lbs. Mfg. 1985-2009.

$925	$725	$575	$450	$325	$250	$225	*$1,199*

* ***Henry Rifle Union Pacific Railroad Commemorative*** – .44-40 WCF cal., only 100 mfg.

$795	$575	$475	N/A	N/A	N/A	N/A	*$695*

* ***Henry Rifle Engraved*** – limited mfg., extensive engraving on brass frame. Disc. 1988.

$1,510	$1,275	$1,100	$900	$750	$650	$550	*$1,850*

Add $100 for steel frame.

* ***Henry Carbine*** – 24 in. barrel, limited edition of 1,000 units including 50 engraved specimens, no swivels, 8 1/4 lbs. Importation disc. 2002.

$685	$540	$450	$350	$275	$225	$195	*$875*

GRADING - PPGS™	100%	98%	95%	90%	80%	70%	60%	LAST MSR

* ***Henry Engraved Carbine*** – limited production, only 50 mfg. Disc. 1988.

	$1,450	$1,225	$1,075	$900	$750	$650	$550	*$1,750*

* ***Henry Rifle Trapper Model*** – 16 1/2 in. barrel, 7 1/4 lbs., 34 1/4 in. overall length. Disc. 2000.

	$685	$540	$450	$350	$275	$225	$195	*$875*

* ***Henry Rifle Iron Frame Model*** – with steel frame and buttplate, 24 in. blue barrel, select walnut, 9 1/4 lbs.

	$1,000	$825	$650	$550	$450	$375	$325	*$1,258*

Add $17 for color case hardened frame.

This model was available with either blue (.44-40 WCF cal. only) or color case hardened receiver.

MODEL 1866 YELLOWBOY CARBINE/RIFLE – .22 LR (disc.), .357 Mag. (disc.), .38 Spl. (new 1998), .44-40 WCF, or .45 LC (new 1998) cal., choice of rifle (24 1/4 in. octagon barrel, disc. 2009), short rifle (20 in. octagon barrel), or carbine (19 in. round barrel), brass (disc.) or case hardened receiver, replica of the Winchester Model 1866. Mfg. 1972-1984, reintroduced until 2010.

	$800	$625	$450	$350	$250	$225	$200	*$972*

Add $43 for rifle.

* ***Model 1866 Yellowboy 100th Anniversary Indian Victory in Little Big Horn***

	$725	$625	$525	$440	$385	$325	$280	

YELLOWBOY TRAPPER – .44-40 WCF cal., 16 1/2 in. barrel. Disc.

	$675	$575	$475	$425	$375	$325	$275	

MODEL 1873 CARBINE/RIFLE – .357 Mag. (new 1998), .44-40 WCF or .45 LC cal., choice of rifle (24 in. octagon barrel) or carbine (19 in. round barrel), replica of the Winchester Model 1873. Disc.

	$950	$750	$575	$450	$350	$295	$250	*$1,132*

Add $25 for rifle variation.

* ***Model 1873 Carbine Trapper*** – .44-40 WCF cal., similar to Carbine, with 16 1/2 in. barrel. Disc.

	$700	$600	$500	$425	$375	$325	$275	

* ***Model 1873 Border Model Rifle*** – .357 Mag., .44-40 WCF, or .45 LC cal., features 20 in. short octagon rifle barrel, case hardened receiver with blue barrel, 7 lbs. 6 oz. Imported 1999-2009.

	$915	$725	$685	$450	$350	$295	$250	*$1,079*

* ***Model 1873 Deluxe Border Model Rifle*** – similar to Model 1873 Deluxe Sporting Rifle, except has 20 in. barrel. Imported 2001-2017.

	$1,025	$825	$625	$500	$400	$300	$225	*$1,241*

* ***Model 1873 Deluxe Sporting Rifle*** – deluxe variation of the Model 1873 featuring case hardened receiver, lever, and hammer, checkered pistol grip stock, and choice of 24 1/4 or 30 (not available in .357 Mag. cal., disc. 2002) in. barrel, 8 lbs. 4 oz. or 8 lbs., 14 oz. Imported 1992-2009.

	$1,000	$825	$625	$500	$400	$300	$225	*$1,218*

Add $30 for 30 in. barrel (disc. 2002).

* ***Model 1873 Deluxe Sporting Rifle Long Range*** – .44-40 WCF cal., 30 in. barrel with rear tang sight. Imported 2003 only.

	$995	$800	$625	$475	$350	$300	$250	*$1,140*

* ***Model 1873 1 of 1,000*** – only 1,000 mfg., deluxe wood, special engraving. Disc.

	$1,000	$775	$550	$460	$395	$335	$285	

MODEL 1873 MFG. BY WINCHESTER – .357 Mag./.38 Spl. or .45 LC cal., choice of 20 or 24 1/4 in. octagon barrel, features bone charcoal case colored receiver, nitre blued accented screws, oil finished fully checkered stock and forearm, shotgun buttplate, includes installed short stroke kit. Mfg. by Miroku in Japan beginning 2014.

MSR $2,500	$2,250	$1,925	$1,700	$1,500	$1,250	$1,000	$850	

MODEL 1873 WINCHESTER RIFLE – .45 LC or .357 Mag. cal., 20 or 24 in. full octagon barrel, 10 or 14 shot, Marble's semi-buckhorn rear and gold bead front sight, Grade 1 American walnut stock with full checkering and "Winchester Red" finish, steel shotgun-style buttplate, French Grey finish (disc. 2016), bright blue, or bone charcoal color case hardened receiver and furniture, includes pre-installed Winchester short stroke kit, 7 lbs. 4 oz.-8 lbs. New 2016.

MSR $2,350	$2,075	$1,825	$1,550	$1,395	$1,150	$925	$750	

Add $150 for bone charcoal color case hardened finish.

GRADING - PPGS™	100%	98%	95%	90%	80%	70%	60%	LAST MSR

MODEL 1873 WINCHESTER CENTENNIAL PRESENTATION RIFLE – .44-40 WCF cal., 24 1/2 in. octagon barrel w/full mag. tube and nickel silver muzzle ring, Marbles semi-buckhorn rear and gold bead front sights, checkered Grade American walnut stock and forearm w/varnish finish, machine engraving by Baron Technology, bison engraved on left side plate and Buffalo Bill on horse back on right side, includes American walnut display case, color case hardened receiver and forearm cap. Only 1,000 mfg. by Miroku beginning 2017.

MSR $3,500	$3,500	$3,150	$2,750	$2,300	$2,000	$1,750	$1,500	

This model is sold exclusively by the Buffalo Bill Center of the West located in Cody, WY.

MODEL 1873 WINCHESTER CENTENNIAL EXHIBITION RIFLE – .44-40 WCF cal., 24 1/2 in. octagon barrel w/full mag. tube and nickel silver muzzle ring, Marbles semi-buckhorn rear and gold bead front sights, checkered Exhibition Grade American walnut stock and forearm w/varnish finish, hand engraving, bison engraved on left side plate and Buffalo Bill on horse back on right side, includes American walnut display case, included is the book "Top 100 Guns of the Cody Firearms Museum", color case hardened receiver and forearm cap w/bright blue barrel and mag. tube. Only 200 mfg. by Miroku beginning 2017.

MSR $7,995	$7,995	$7,000	$6,250	$5,500	$4,750	$4,000	$3,500	

This model is sold exclusively by the Buffalo Bill Center of the West located in Cody, WY.

MODEL 1885 HIGH WALL RIFLE – .45-70 Govt. cal., available with 30 in. medium heavy octagon barrel with crescent buttplate or 28 in. round barrel with shotgun style buttplate, standard or open target sights, case hardened frame and lever, uncheckered European walnut stock and forearm, 9 1/4 or 10 lbs. Imported 1999-2009.

	$975	$750	$625	$500	$400	$300	$275	*$1,169*

Add $117 for rear tang sight.

MODEL 1892 CARBINE/RIFLE – .357 Mag., .44-40 WCF, or .45 LC cal., features 20 (carbine, w/o forearm cap, disc. 2001) or 24 (rifle) in. octagon barrel, choice of brass (disc.), blue, or case hardened receiver and crescent buttplate, uncheckered straight grip walnut stock and forearm, 5 lbs. 14 oz. or 7 lbs. Imported 1999-2003.

	$465	$385	$335	$280	$240	$210	$185	*$561*

Subtract approx. $65 for carbine configuration (disc. 2001).

* ***Model 1892 Carbine/Rifle Stainless*** – similar to Standard Model 1892, except is stainless steel, not available in .44-40 WCF cal. Imported 2000-2003.

	$435	$360	$300	$240	$210	$180	$155	*$530*

Add $73 for rifle configuration.

* ***Model 1892 Short Rifle*** – also available in .32-20 WCF cal. (new 2002), similar to Model 1892 Standard Rifle, except has 20 in. short barrel, not available with brass frame, approx. 6 1/4 lbs. Imported 1999-2003.

	$465	$385	$335	$280	$240	$210	$185	*$561*

* ***Model 1892 Stainless Short Rifle*** – similar to Model 1892 Short Rifle, except is stainless steel. Imported 2000 only.

	$485	$360	$300	$240	$210	$180	$155	*$603*

MODEL 1892 WINCHESTER DELUXE SHORT RIFLE – .45 LC cal., 20 in. full octagon barrel, 10 shot, Marble's semi-buckhorn rear and gold bead dovetailed front sights, upper tang drilled and tapped for Marble's peep, Grade 1 American walnut stock, checkered at the wrist and forend, choice of bright blue (2016 only) or color case hardened receiver and furniture, nitre blued accented screws, 6 lbs. New 2016.

MSR $2,300	$2,050	$1,795	$1,550	$1,395	$1,125	$925	$725	

Subtract $300 for bright blue finish.

MODEL 1892 WINCHESTER "COYOTE KILLER" DELUXE SHORT RIFLE – .44 Rem. Mag. cal., 20 in. full octagon barrel, 10 shot, Marble's semi-buckhorn rear and gold bead dovetailed front sights, upper tang drilled and tapped for Marble's peep, Grade 1 American walnut pistol grip stock, checkered at the wrist and forend, choice of blue (2016 only) or color case hardened receiver and furniture, nitre blued accented screws, 6 lbs. New 2016.

MSR $2,300	$2,050	$1,795	$1,550	$1,395	$1,125	$925	$725	

Subtract $300 for bright blue finish.

LIGHTNING SLIDE ACTION – replica of original Colt Lightning, 24 in. octagon barrel, redesigned ejection system, checkered straight grip walnut stock, case colored finish, semi-buckhorn rear and gold bead front sights, mfg. by Pedersoli. Imported 2010-2012.

	$1,075	$850	$675	$550	$500	$450	$395	*$1,399*

GRADING - PPGS™	100%	98%	95%	90%	80%	70%	60%	LAST MSR

LIGHTNING DELUXE RIFLE/CARBINE – .45 LC or .357 Mag. cal., slide action, 20 (carbine) or 24 in. full octagon barrel with high polish blued finish, 10 or 13 shot, coil spring extractor, semi-buckhorn rear and gold bead dovetail front sights, hand selected Grade 1 American walnut stock, checkered at the wrist and forend, upper tang is drilled and tapped, blued (2016 only) or color case hardened receiver and furniture, accented with nitre blued screws, 6.39-6.83 lbs. Mfg. by Davide Pedersoli beginning 2016.

MSR $2,199	$1,975	$1,750	$1,475	$1,325	$1,075	$900	$725	

Add $80 for detachable pistol grip.
Add $80 for folding target front sights.
Subtract $300 for blue finish.

RIFLES: MODERN PRODUCTION

In addition to the models listed, Navy Arms in late 1990 purchased the manufacturing rights of the English firm Parker-Hale. In 1991, Navy Arms built a manufacturing facility, Gibbs Rifle Co., located in Martinsburg, WV and produced these rifles domestically 1991-1994 (see Gibbs Rifle Co. listing for more info on models the company currently imports).

TU-KKW TRAINING RIFLE – .22 LR cal., replica of the German "KKW" Gewehr training rifle, full sized Mauser 98K action with military sights, 26 in. barrel, detachable 5 shot mag., mfg. in China, 8 lbs. Imported 1992-94.

$240	$210	$180	$150	$135	$120	$105	*$310*

Add $125 for 2 3/4 power Type 89 quick mount scope (Sniper Trainer).

TU-33/40 CARBINE – .22 LR or 7.62x39mm cal., based on WWII Mauser G33/40 mountain carbine, 20 3/4 in. barrel, includes sling, adj. rear sight, mfg. in China, 7 lbs. 7 oz. Imported 1992-94.

$210	$180	$150	$135	$120	$105	$90	*$210*

JW-15 RIFLE – .22 LR cal., sporter bolt action based on Brno Model 5 action, 24 in. barrel, detachable 5 shot mag., receiver top is dovetailed, mfg. in China, 5 lbs. 12 oz. Imported 1992-94.

$85	$70	$60	$50	$40	$35	$30	*$100*

MARTINI TARGET RIFLE – .444 Marlin or .45-70 Govt. cal., single shot, 26 or 30 in. octagon barrel, tang sight, pistol grip stock. Mfg. 1972-84.

$480	$420	$350	$250	$195	$175	$150	

RPKS-74 – .223 Rem. or 7.62x39mm (new 1989) cal., semi-auto version of the Chinese RPK Squad Automatic Weapon, Kalashnikov action, 19 in. barrel, integral folding bipod, 9 1/2 lbs. Imported 1988-89 only.

$525	$445	$350	$250	$195	$175	$150	*$649*

MODEL 1 CARBINE/RIFLE – .45-70 Govt. cal., action is sporterized No. 1 MKIII Enfield, choice of 18 (carbine) or 22 (rifle) in. barrel with iron sights, black Zytel Monte Carlo (rifle) or straight grip walnut (carbine) stock, 7 (carbine) or 8 1/2 (rifle) lbs. Limited importation 1999 only.

$325	$255	$200	$175	$160	$145	$130	*$375*

MODEL 4 CARBINE/RIFLE – .45-70 Govt. cal., action is sporterized No. 4 MKI Enfield, choice of 18 (carbine) or 22 (rifle) in. barrel, blue metal, choice of checkered walnut Monte Carlo (rifle) or uncheckered straight grip (carbine, disc. 1999) stock, 7 or 8 lbs. Mfg. 1999-2001.

$325	$255	$200	$175	$160	$145	$130	*$375*

* ***Model No. 4 Carbine/Rifle Enfield Sporter Deluxe*** – .303 British cal., synthetic Zytel Monte Carlo stock, 25 in. barrel with original military sights, approx. 8 1/2 lbs. Mfg. 1999-2001.

$115	$95	$85	$75	$65	$55	$50	*$125*

2A HUNTER CARBINE/RIFLE – .308 Win. cal., action is sporterized 2A Enfield, 18 (carbine) or 22 (rifle) in. barrel with Parker-Hale style muzzle brake, includes scope mount, 12 shot mag., black enamel synthetic Zytel stock, 6 3/4 or 10 1/4 lbs. Mfg. 1999-2001.

$240	$210	$190	$175	$160	$145	$130	*$275*

Add $50 for rifle variation.

* ***2A Hunter Carbine/Rifle Enfield Sporter Deluxe*** – .308 Win. cal., 25 in. barrel, black Zytel Monte Carlo stock, original 2A Enfield military sights, approx. 8 1/2 lbs. Mfg. 1999-2001.

$130	$110	$95	$85	$75	$65	$55	*$150*

SHOTGUNS: O/U, RECENT IMPORTATION

Importation of the models listed was disc. in 1990.

MODEL 83 – 12 or 20 ga., manufactured in Italy by R. Luciano, 3 in. chambers, extractors, double triggers, engraved chrome receiver, vent. barrels (bored M/F or IC/M) and rib. Introduced 1985.

$280	$240	$215	$195	$170	$160	$150	*$320*

GRADING - PPGS™	100%	98%	95%	90%	80%	70%	60%	LAST MSR

MODEL 93 – 12 or 20 ga., manufactured in Italy by R. Luciano, 3 in. chambers, ejectors, double triggers, engraved chrome receiver, vent. barrels (bored M/F or IC/M) and rib. Introduced 1985.

	$325	$285	$250	$220	$200	$185	$160	*$380*

MODEL 95 – similar to Model 93, except with single trigger and multi-chokes (includes 5 tubes), extractors. Disc.

	$375	$330	$295	$265	$235	$210	$190	*$420*

MODEL 96 SPORTSMAN – 12 ga. only, 3 in. chambers, vent. barrels and rib, engraved chrome receiver, gold-plated receiver, multi-choked with 5 choke tubes, ejectors. Introduced 1985.

	$470	$425	$375	$330	$295	$260	$230	*$530*

MODEL 100 – 12, 20, 28 ga., or .410 bore, 3 in. chambers, 26 in. VR barrels, photo engraved hard chrome receiver, single trigger, extractors, checkered walnut stock and forearm, approx. 6 1/4 lbs. Introduced 1985.

	$225	$205	$190	$170	$160	$150	$140	*$250*

SHOTGUNS: SxS, RECENT IMPORTATION

MODEL 100 – 12 or 20 ga., 3 in. chambers, 27 1/2 in. barrels, checkered European walnut, double triggers, extractors, 6 1/2 or 7 lbs. Imported 1985-87 only.

	$380	$330	$290	$260	$230	$200	$170	*$475*

MODEL 150 – similar to Model 100, except with ejectors. Imported 1985-87 only.

	$455	$395	$350	$310	$280	$250	$220	*$574*

SHOTGUNS: SINGLE SHOT

MODEL 105 SINGLE BARREL – 12, 20 ga., or .410 bore, 26 or 28 in. full choke barrel only, folding action, engraved chrome receiver, checkered hardwood stock and forearm. Mfg. 1985-disc.

	$80	$70	$65	$60	$55	$50	$45	*$90*

This model was designated the Model 600 before 1988.

* ***Model 105 Single Barrel Deluxe*** – similar to Model 105, except has European walnut stock and VR.

	$95	$85	$75	$65	$60	$55	$50	*$105*

This model was designated the Model 600 Deluxe before 1988.

P.V. NELSON GUNMAKERS LTD.

Previous manufacturer located in Bucks, England.

P.V. Nelson manufactured best quality shotguns and double rifles per individual customer order. Double rifles featured back action locks, and bolsters for extra strength. Side-by-side and over/under shotguns were available in most gauges, with a choice of rounded or regular action. Guns should be appraised individually.

NEMESIS ARMS

Current rifle manufacturer located in Park City, KY since 2015. Previously located in Calimesa, CA.

For individual model listings, please go to BlueBookOfGunValues.com/overflow.

NEMO ARMS (NEW EVOLUTION MILITARY ORDNANCE)

Current AR-15 style rifle, pistol, and bolt action rifle manufacturer located in Nampa, ID beginning 2016. Previously located in Kalispell, MT.

Please refer to BlueBookOfGunValues.com to order the *Blue Book of AR-15s & Variations*, available as a book or online subscription.

NESIKA

Current trademark of actions and rifles (new 2014) manufactured by Nesika (formerly Nesika Bay Precision, Inc.), located in Sturgis, SD. Actions are currently distributed by Dakota Arms. Nesika also manufactured rifles circa 2004-2005. Previously located in Poulsbo, WA until 2003. Dealer and consumer sales.

On June 5, 2009, Remington Arms Company purchased Dakota Arms, Inc., including the rights to Nesika.

Nesika offers a complete line of custom made long-range, tactical, and hunting rifles built to customer specification. Please contact the manufacturer for availability and an individualized quotation.

RIFLES: BOLT ACTION

Nesika also sells its proprietary actions. Each action is available with the following options: right or left bolt, right or left port, micro-ejection port, single shot or repeater, double-pinned recoil lug, spiral, straight or non-fluted bolt, pinned trigger or trigger hanger, top safety cut on tang, plunger ejector,

aluminum or stainless bolt shroud, or Remington style tang.

Current model action MSRs are: Tactical Model (MSR $1,400-$1,700), Classic Model (MSR $1,275-$1,475), Hunter Model (MSR $1,055-$1,450), and Round Model (MSR $1,000-$1,350). A Model NXP bolt action single shot pistol model was also available. Last MSR was $1,100 circa 2008.

CLASSIC HUNTER – various cals., stainless Nesika action and barrel, adj. trigger, composite, laminated, or Turkish walnut stock, hinged floorplate, various options. Mfg. 2004-2005.

$3,450 $2,950 $2,650 $2,325 $2,000 $1,600 $1,250 *$3,710*

Add $60 for Model V or $450 for Model M.

CUSTOM HUNTER – various cals. in short or long action, right or left-hand action, 26 in. barrel with or w/o flutes and muzzle brake, Timney Calvin Elite or Jewell trigger, open sights, McMillan stock (choice of BDL, McClassic, Remington, or Hunter) w/Nesika Spatter finish in various colors, traditional vapor-honed smooth finish, bead blasted/matte finish. New late 2016.

MSR $4,695 $4,000 $3,500 $3,000 $2,700 $2,200 $1,800 $1,400

CUSTOM TACTICAL – various cals. in short or long action, left or right-hand action, 26 in. fluted premium heavy barrel w/o sights and target crown, detachable box mag., Timney, Calvin Elite, or Jewell trigger, black synthetic stock w/stippled pistol grip and forend, various finishes. New late 2016.

MSR $5,495 $4,650 $4,100 $3,500 $3,200 $2,550 $2,100 $1,650

CUSTOM VARMINT – various cals. in short or long action, right or left-hand action, 26 in. #3 contour barrel with or w/o flutes and muzzle brake, custom ADL style floorplate, choice of Timney, Calvin Elite, or Jewell trigger, open sights, McMillan choice of Nesika laminate, Remington Varmint, or Nesika Varmint stock with Nesika Splatter finish, fluted bolt (straight or spiral), traditional vapor-honed smooth finish or bead blasted matte finish. New late 2016.

MSR $3,795 $3,200 $2,800 $2,400 $2,200 $1,800 $1,450 $1,150

LONG RANGE – .300 Win. Mag., 7mm Rem. Mag., or 6.5x284 Norma (mfg. 2015, reintroduced 2021) cal., Nesika Hunter action, stainless steel receiver, 26 in. stainless steel Douglas air-gauged barrel with fluted Varmint/Tactical contour, Bell & Carlson Varmint/Tactical composite stock with aluminum bedding block, adj. Timney trigger, one-piece steel bolt, Cerakote finish, Leupold base, stainless steel Oberndorf-style hinged floorplate, 9 3/4 lbs. New 2014.

MSR $3,999 $3,400 $3,000 $2,550 $2,300 $1,850 $1,550 $1,200

SPORTER – .260 Rem. (mfg. 2015, reintroduced 2021), .280 Rem., .300 Win. Mag., .308 Win., .30-06, 7mm Rem. Mag., 7mm-08 Rem., or 6.5x284 Norma (mfg. 2015 only) cal., Nesika Hunter action, 24 or 26 in. stainless steel Douglas air-gauged barrel, stainless steel receiver, Bell & Carlson Medalist Sporter stock with aluminum bedding block, adj. Timney trigger, one-piece steel bolt, Cerakote finish, Leupold QRW base, stainless steel Oberndorf-style hinged floorplate, 8 lbs. New 2014.

MSR $3,499 $3,000 $2,600 $2,250 $2,000 $1,650 $1,350 $1,050

TACTICAL – .300 Win. Mag. or .338 Lapua Mag. cal., Nesika Tactical action, stainless steel receiver, 26 (.300 Win. Mag.) or 28 (.338 Lapua Mag. cal.) in. stainless steel Douglas air-gauged barrel with tactical contour, AAC Blackout muzzle brake and suppressor adapter, Cerakote black matte finish on all metalwork, 5 shot detachable steel box mag., one-piece stainless 1913-style rail, adj. Timney trigger, one-piece steel bolt, stainless steel Oberndorf-style hinged floorplate, Bell & Carlson tactical composite stock with aluminum bedding block, including spacer adj. LOP and adj. cheekpiece, 13 3/4 lbs. New 2014.

MSR $4,499 $3,800 $3,350 $2,850 $2,600 $2,100 $1,700 $1,350

URBAN TACTICAL – various tactical cals., heavy duty receiver with Picatinny rail and fluted 24 or 28 in. barrel, detachable box mag., black synthetic stock with adj. recoil pad. Mfg. 2004-2005.

$4,500 $4,000 $3,500 $3,000 $2,500 $2,000 $1,650 *$5,040*

Add $160 for heavy .308 Win. cal. or $520 for Lapua or Lazzeroni Warbird or Patriot cals.

VARMINT – various varmint cals., single shot or repeater, stainless Nesika action and helical fluted bolt, stainless barrel, composite or wood laminated stock, various options. Mfg. 2004-2005.

$3,050 $2,650 $2,375 $2,000 $1,750 $1,500 $1,250 *$3,440*

Add $60 for Model K.

NEW ADVANTAGE ARMS, INC.

Previous handgun manufacturer located in Tucson, AZ, circa mid-1990s.

DERRINGERS

4 BARREL DERRINGER – .22 LR or .22 WMR cal., double action, 2 1/2 in. barrel, 4 shot mag., high grade blue steel alloy or stainless steel, rotating hammer, fixed sights, walnut grips, 15 oz. Disc.

$175 $150 $120 $110 $100 $90 $80

GRADING - PPGS™	100%	98%	95%	90%	80%	70%	60%	LAST MSR

NEW DETONICS MANUFACTURING CORPORATION

Previous manufacturer located in Phoenix, AZ 1989-1992. Formerly named Detonics Firearms Industries (previous manufacturer located in Bellevue, WA 1976-1988). Detonics was sold in early 1988 to the New Detonics Manufacturing Corporation, a wholly owned subsidiary of "1045 Investors Group Limited."

PISTOLS: SEMI-AUTO, STAINLESS

MARK I - .45 ACP cal., matte blue. Disc. 1981.

$550 $450 $395 $335 $290 $245 $215

MARK II - .45 ACP cal., satin nickel finish. Disc. 1979.

$495 $375 $300 $240 $210 $180 $155

MARK III - .45 ACP cal., hard chrome finish. Disc. 1979.

$520 $390 $325 $265 $230 $195 $170

MARK IV - .45 ACP cal., polished blue. Disc. 1981.

$550 $425 $360 $295 $255 $220 $185

COMBATMASTER MC1 (FORMERLY MARK I) - .45 ACP, 9mm Para., or .38 Super cal., 3 1/2 in. barrel, two-tone (slide is non-glare blue and frame is matte stainless) finish, 6 shot mag., fixed sights, 28 oz. Disc. 1992.

$850 $650 $500 $400 $335 $280 $235 *$920*

Add $25 for OM-3 model (polished slide - disc. 1983).
Add $150 for 9mm Para. or .38 Super cal. (disc. 1990).

This model was originally the MC1, then changed to the Mark I, then changed back to the MC1.

COMBATMASTER MARK V - .45 ACP, 9mm Para., or .38 Super cal., 3 1/2 in. barrel, matte stainless finish, fixed sights, 6 (.45 ACP) or 7 (9mm Para. and .38 Super) shot mag., 29 oz. empty. Disc. 1985.

$750 $575 $475 $375 $300 $275 $225 *$689*

Add $150 for 9mm Para. or .38 Super cal.

COMBATMASTER MARK VI - .45 ACP, 9mm Para., or .38 Super cal., 3 1/2 in. barrel, 6 shot mag., adj. sights and polished stainless slide sides. Disc. 1989. - limited mfg. 1,000. Disc. 1985.

$850 $675 $575 $475 $375 $295 $250 *$795*

Add $125 for 9mm Para. or .38 Super cal.

**** Combatmaster Mark VI .451 Detonics Mag. Cal.***

$1,000 $900 $775 $665 $560 $465 $410 *$1,165*

COMBATMASTER MARK VII - similar to Mark VI, only no sights, special order only, 25 oz.

$850 $675 $575 $475 $375 $295 $250

Add $125 for 9mm Para. or .38 Super cal.
Add $350 for .451 Detonics Mag., (disc. 1982).

MILITARY COMBAT MC2 - .45 ACP, 9mm Para., or .38 Super cal., dull, non-glare combat finish, fixed sights. Comes with camouflaged pile-lined wallet, and Pachmayr grips. Disc. 1984.

$650 $550 $495 $435 $375 $315 $275

Add $75 for 9mm Para. or .38 Super.

O.S. MODEL - .45 ACP cal. only, emergency backup pistol, similar to Combatmaster, 6 shot mag., choice of satin stainless or all black finish. 2 mfg. 1991 only.

Extreme rarity precludes accurate price evaluation.

SCOREMASTER - .45 ACP or .451 Mag. cal., match gun with closer tolerances, 5 or 6 in. barrel. Millett adj. sights, grip safety, 7 or 8 shot mag., 42 oz. Disc. 1992.

$995 $850 $695 $585 $500 $415 $365 *$1,178*

Add $40 for 6 in. barrel.

COMPMASTER - .45 ACP cal. only, similar to Scoremaster, except is fully compensated. Mfg. 1988-92.

$1,995 $1,575 $1,250 $1,100 $895 $785 $630 *$1,550*

This model was called the Janus Competition Scoremaster in 1988-1989.

COMPETITION MASTER T.F. - .45 ACP cal., competition model with dual port compensator, rotational torque compensating vents, patented coned barrel system, hand tuned trigger, includes all competition modifications. Disc. 1992.

$1,995 $1,575 $1,250 $1,100 $895 $785 $630 *$1,550*

GRADING - PPGS™	100%	98%	95%	90%	80%	70%	60%	LAST MSR

SERVICEMASTER – .45 ACP cal. only, shortened version of the Scoremaster, non-glare combat finish, 4 1/4 in. barrel, coned barrel system, 8 shot mag., interchangeable front and adj. rear sights, 39 oz. Disc. 1986.

	$825	$675	$575	$480	$410	$350	$295	*$686*

* ***Servicemaster II*** – similar to Servicemaster, except has polished stainless steel finish. Mfg. 1986-92.

	$925	$750	$625	$515	$450	$375	$325	*$998*

POCKET 9 – 9mm Para. cal., double action, 3 in. barrel, 6 shot mag., soft matte sheen finish, 26 oz. Limited mfg. 1985-86 only.

	$495	$400	$335	$275	$235	$200	$175	*$458*

The entire Pocket 9 series was disc. 1986.

* ***Pocket 9 LS*** – similar to Pocket 9, except has 4 in. barrel. Limited mfg. 1986 only.

	$575	$450	$375	$315	$270	$230	$200	*$458*

* ***Pocket .380*** – similar to Pocket 9, except is .380 ACP cal., 23 oz. Limited mfg. 1986 only.

	$575	$450	$375	$315	$270	$230	$200	*$458*

POWER 9 – 9mm Para. cal., similar to Pocket 9, except has polished slide sides and is supplied with 2 mags. Disc. 1986.

	$575	$450	$375	$315	$270	$230	$200	*$509*

New Detonics Ladies Escort Series

This series was designed specifically to suit a woman's shooting requirements.

ROYAL ESCORT – .45 ACP cal., action similar to Combatmaster, 3 1/2 in. barrel, 6 shot mag., black frame, slide and grips are iridescent purple, hammer and trigger are 24Kt. gold-plated. Less than 25 were mfg. 1990-92.

	$1,000	$850	$650	$540	$465	$385	$335	*$990*

MIDNIGHT ESCORT – similar to Royal Escort, except is stainless with a black slide and smooth black grips. Less than 30 were mfg. 1990-92.

	$1,150	$925	$750	$640	$535	$450	$390	*$1,090*

JADE ESCORT – similar to Midnight Escort, except has stainless frame, jade colored slide and grips. Less than 10 were mfg. 1990 only.

	$1,200	$950	$600	$495	$430	$365	$315	*$918*

NEW ENGLAND ARMS CORP.

Previous importer, distributor, and retailer from 1975-2004, and located in Kittery Point, ME.

New England Arms Corp. imported, distributed, or retailed the following trademarks: Arrieta, P. Arrizabalaga, Bertuzzi, Luciano Bosis, Cosmi, Henri Dumoulin, Fair Techni-Mec (I. Rizzini), Antonio Gil, Lebeau-Courally, F.lli Rizzini, B. Rizzini, Luciano Rota, S.I.A.C.E., and Fabio Zanotti. These trademarks may be found under their own headings in this text.

New England Arms Corp. should not be confused with New England Firearms.

NEW ENGLAND CUSTOM GUN SERVICE, LTD. (NECG LTD.)

Current importer of various firearms manufacturers/trademarks, including AYA and Prechtl Mausers established during 1986 and currently located in Claremont, NH. The company previously represented custom-made guns from small makers in Germany, including Adamy-Jagdwaffen, Johannsen, and Max Ern.

NECG, Ltd. specializes in the design and production of open sights they supply to the gun trade. NECG gun services stock fitting/alterations, detachable rifle scope mounts including German Claw mounts, installation of open sights, and other gunsmithing services. NECG is licensed for both permanent and temporary exports through both the BATFE and DOS. Please contact the company directly regarding more information on their extensive line of products and services.

NEW ENGLAND FIREARMS

Current trademark established during 1987, located and previously manufactured in Gardner, MA until Nov. 1, 2007. Beginning Nov. 1, 2007, the NEF trademark applies to imported guns only. Distributor sales.

During late Jan. of 2008, Remington acquired the Marlin Firearms Company, which had purchased the H&R, New England Firearms (NEF), and L.C. Smith brands during 2000. On May 31st, 2007, Remington Arms Co. was acquired by Cerberus Capital.

GRADING - PPGS™	100%	98%	95%	90%	80%	70%	60%	LAST MSR

During 2000, Marlin Firearms Co. purchased the assets of H&R 1871, Inc., and the name was changed to H&R 1871, LLC. Brand names include Harrington & Richardson, New England Firearms, and Wesson & Harrington.

All NEF firearms utilize a transfer bar safety system and have a $10 service plan which guarantees lifetime warranty.

New England Firearms should not be confused with New England Arms Corp.

REVOLVERS: DOUBLE ACTION

Ultra Models listed were available in blue finish only. All Ultras were supplied with a lockable storage case beginning 1993.

STANDARD REVOLVER .22 (MODEL R92) - .22 S, L, and LR cal., 9 shot, swing out cylinder, 2 1/2 (disc. 1997), 3 (new 1998) or 4 in. barrel, blue or nickel finish, hardwood stocks, fixed rear sight, 25-28 oz. Mfg. 1988-99.

$125	$95	$85	$70	$60	$55	$40	*$144*

Add $10 for nickel finish.

* ***Standard Revolver .32 H&R Mag. (Model R73)*** - .32 H&R Mag. cal. similar to Standard Revolver .22, except has 5 shot cylinder, 2 1/2 (disc.), 3, or 4 in. barrel, choice of blue or nickel finish (not available with 4 in. barrel), 23-26 oz. Mfg. 1988-99.

$125	$95	$85	$70	$60	$55	$40	*$144*

Add $10 for nickel finish (2 1/2 or 3 in. barrel only).

ULTRA MODEL - .22 S, L, and LR cal., 9 shot, swing-out cylinder, 4 or 6 in. solid rib target-grade barrel with rebated muzzle and fully adj. rear sight, blue finish, smooth hardwood grips, 36 oz. Disc. 1999.

$150	$115	$95	$80	$70	$60	$55	*$180*

ULTRA MAG (MODEL R22) - .22 WMR cal., 6 shot, 4 (disc. 1997) or 6 in. solid rib barrel, adj. rear sight, swing-out cylinder, blue finish, 36 oz. Mfg. 1988-99.

$150	$115	$95	$80	$70	$60	$55	*$180*

LADY ULTRA - .32 H&R Mag. cal., swing-out cylinder, 5 shot, blue finish, 3 (disc. 1997, reintroduced 1999) or 4 (mfg. 1998 only) in. barrel with rib, adj. sights, thinner contoured grips, 31 oz. Mfg. 1991-99.

$150	$115	$95	$80	$70	$60	$55	*$180*

RIFLES: SEMI-AUTO

SPORTSTER SL - .22 LR cal., 19 in. barrel, 10 shot mag., uncheckered hardwood stock, grooved steel receiver, 5 1/2 lbs. Mfg. 2004 only.

$125	$100	$90	$80	$70	$60	$55	*$157*

RIFLES: SINGLE SHOT

Beginning Nov. 1, 2007, H&R 1871 decided that all products built in the USA will carry the H&R brand name, and all imported products will be sold under the NEF brand name. The Handi-Rifle, Super Light Handi-Rifle, Sportster, and Survivor are now under the H&R brand name.

HANDI-RIFLE - .204 Ruger (new 2005), .22 Hornet, .22-250 Rem. (mfg. 1992-94, reintroduced 2004), .223 Rem., .243 Win. (new 1992), .25-06 Rem. (new 2004), .270 Win. (new 1993), .280 Rem. (new 1996), .30-30 Win., .30-06 (new 1992), .308 Win. (new 1998), .35 Whelen (new 2006), .357 Mag. (mfg. 1999-2003), .44 Rem. Mag. (new 1996), .444 Marlin (new 2007), .45-70 Govt., 7mm-08 Rem. (new 2003), .500 S&W (new 2005), 7x57mm Mauser (mfg. 1998-2003), 7.62x39mm (new 2006), or 7x64mm Brenneke (mfg. 1998-2003) cal., break open single shot action, 22 or 26 (.280 Rem. only) in. regular or bull (.223 Rem., .243 Win., or .22-250 Rem.) barrel, blue receiver, regular or Monte Carlo walnut stained hardwood stock, scope mount rail or ramp front and adj. rear sights, sling swivels, 7 lbs. Mfg. 1989-2008.

$220	$180	$145	$110	$80	$70	$60	*$270*

Add $20 for Handi-Rifle .243 Win./Huntsman .50 cal. black powder muzzleloader rifle combo (disc. 2002).
Add $39 for 3-9x32mm mounted and bore sighted scope (.223 Rem. or .243 Win. cal. only).

This model in .22-250 Rem., .223 Rem., 7.62x39mm, or .243 Win. cal. was supplied with heavy barrel, scope mount, and no sights.

* ***Handi-Rifle Synthetic*** - .22 Hornet, .223 Rem., .243 Win., .270 Win., .280 Rem., .30-30 Win. (disc. 2003), .30-06, .357 Mag. (mfg. 2002-2003, reintroduced 2008), .44 Rem. Mag. (disc. 2003, reintroduced 2008), .444 Marlin (new 2008), or .45-70 Govt. cal., 22 or 26 (.280 Rem. only) in. barrel, blue finish, features black synthetic stock and forearm, adj. sights on some cals., scope base mount only on others, 7 lbs. Mfg. 1998-2008.

$220	$180	$140	$110	$80	$70	$60	*$278*

Add $23 for Handi-Rifle combo with 20 ga. Pardner barrel (not available in all cals., disc. 2006).
Subtract $42 for .357 Mag. or .44 Mag. cal.

GRADING - PPGS™	100%	98%	95%	90%	80%	70%	60%	LAST MSR

* ***Handi-Rifle Synthetic Stainless*** – .22-250 Rem. (new 2004), .223 Rem., .243 Win., .270 Win., or .30-06 (new 2004) cal., similar to Handi-Rifle Synthetic, features 22 in. matte stainless steel barrel with matte nickel finished receiver, 7 lbs. Mfg. 2003-2008.

	$255	$200	$160	$120	$80	$70	$60	*$319*

* ***Handi-Rifle Youth*** – .223 Rem., .243 Win., or 7mm-08 Rem. (new 2005) cal., features 22 in. barrel and shortened stock dimensions (13 1/2 in. LOP), blue finish, supplied with scope rail mount and hammer extension, no iron sights, approx. 7 lbs. Mfg. 1998-2006.

	$235	$185	$140	$110	$85	$70	$60	*$292*

* ***Handi-Rifle 10th Anniversary*** – same cals. as Handi-Rifle, limited edition features scroll engraving by Ken Hurst, deep bluing on receiver, steel trigger guard and forearm spacer, select hand checkered walnut, less than 100 mfg. 1997 only.

	$695	$475	$350	$285	$250	$215	$185	*$750*

* ***Handi-Rifle NTA Anniversary Edition*** – .223 Rem. only, 24 in. heavy barrel w/o sights, features checkered black/grey laminate stock and forearm with NTA (National Trapper's Association) medallion in stock. Limited production 1999 only.

	$225	$200	$175	$160	$145	$135	$125	*$272*

SUPER LIGHT HANDI-RIFLE – .22 Hornet, .223 Rem., or .243 Win. cal., break open single shot, black synthetic stock and forearm, recoil pad, 20 in. special contour barrel with rebated muzzle, .22 Hornet has sights (Model SB2-SL4), .223 Rem. has scope base and hammer extension (Model SB2-SL3), approx. 5 1/2 lbs. Mfg. 1997-2008.

	$220	$180	$140	$110	$80	$70	$60	*$278*

Add $23 for Handi-Rifle combo with 20 ga. Pardner barrel (not available in all cals., disc. 2006).
Add $31 for 3-9x32mm mounted and bore sighted scope (.243 Win. cal., Youth only, new 2007).

This model is also available as a Youth Model with shorter stock dimensions (11 3/4 in. LOP).

SPORTSTER – .17 HMR (new 2002), .17 Mach 2 (mfg. 2005-2007), .22 LR, or .22 WMR (new 2001) cal., 20 (mid-weight) or 22 (.17 HMR cal. only, heavy) in. barrel with Weaver style scope rail, no iron sights, available in either adult or youth (.22 LR cal. only) dimensions, black polymer stock and forearm. Mfg. 1999-2008.

	$120	$100	$85	$75	$65	$55	$50	*$148*

Add $13 for .17 Mach 2 (disc.) or $29 for .17 HMR cal.

SURVIVOR – .223 Rem., .308 Win. (new 1999), .357 Mag. (disc. 1998) or .410/45 LC (new 2007) cal., similar in design to the Survivor Series shotgun, removable forearm with ammo storage, thumbhole stock with storage compartment, no iron sights, 20 (.410/45 LC cal. only) or 22 in. barrel, blue or nickel finish, .357 Mag. cal. has open sights, .223 Rem. and .308 Win. cal. have heavy barrels and scope mount rail, 6 lbs. Mfg. 1996-2008.

	$230	$180	$145	$110	$80	$70	$60	*$281*

Add approx. $15 for nickel finish (disc. 1998, reintroduced 2007 for .410/45 LC cal. only).
Subtract $76 for .410/45 LC cal. (new 2007).

SHOTGUNS: SEMI-AUTO

EXCELL AUTO – 12 ga., 3 in. chamber, 28 in. VR barrel with screw-in choke tubes, 5 shot mag., black synthetic or walnut pistol grip stock with fluted comb, vent. recoil pad, bead front sight, approx. 7 lbs. Imported 2008-2010.

	$375	$315	$265	$225	$185	$160	$140	*$421*

Add $34 for walnut stock.

* ***Excell Auto Turkey*** – 12 ga., 3 in. chamber, 5 shot mag., 22 in. vent. rib barrel with choke tubes and fiber optic sights, Realtree Advantage Hardwoods camo covered pistol grip stock and barrel, 7 lbs. Imported 2008-2010.

	$450	$395	$345	$300	$265	$230	$195	*$513*

* ***Excell Auto Waterfowl*** – 12 ga., 28 in. VR barrel, 5 shot, 100% Advantage Wetlands camo coverage, 7 lbs. Imported 2008-2010.

	$450	$395	$345	$300	$265	$230	$195	*$513*

* ***Excell Auto Combo*** – includes 24 in. rifled slug barrel and 28 in. regular barrel, synthetic stock only. Imported 2008-2010.

	$495	$425	$380	$330	$290	$260	$230	*$576*

GRADING - PPGS™	100%	98%	95%	90%	80%	70%	60%	LAST MSR

SHOTGUNS: SINGLE SHOT

Beginning Nov. 1, 2007, H&R 1871 decided that all products built in the U.S.A. will carry the H&R brand name, and all imported products will be sold under the NEF brand name. The Pardner Series and Tracker Slug are now under the H&R brand name.

PARDNER – 10 (new 1988), 12, 16 (new 1989), 20, 28 (new 1991) ga. or .410 bore, 2 3/4, 3 in. (12, 20 ga., and .410 bore) or 3 1/2 in. (10 ga.) chamber, single shot, break open action, safety transfer bar mechanism on hammer, side lever release, color case hardened receiver, 14 in. LOP, 24 (disc.), 26, 28, or 32 in. barrel, fixed or mod. choke tube (12 or 20 ga. only, with black synthetic stock and forearm), extractor, walnut stained hardwood or black synthetic (12 or 20 ga. only) stock and forearm, 5-6 lbs. Mfg. 1987-2008.

$100	**$85**	**$75**	**$65**	**$55**	**$45**	**$40**	***$129***

Add $15 for 32 in. barrel (12 ga. only).
Add $22 for modified choke tube (12 or 20 ga. only).
Add $65 for Pardner 12 ga. Shotgun/Huntsman .50 cal. black powder muzzleloader combo (disc. 2002).

* ***Pardner Compact (Youth)*** – 12 (new 1998), 20, 28 ga., or .410 bore, similar to Pardner, except has 22 in. barrel and straight grip stock with recoil pad, 12 1/2 in. LOP. Disc. 2008.

$115	**$95**	**$75**	**$65**	**$55**	**$45**	**$40**	***$137***

Add $21 for Pardner Youth .22 cal. barrel/.410 bore Versa-Pack combo (disc. 2007).
Add $14 for modified choke tube (20 ga. only with black synthetic stock and forearm).

* ***Pardner Turkey Gun*** – 10 or 12 ga. only, 3 (disc.) or 3 1/2 in. chamber, 24 in. barrel with fixed or full choke tube, camo or matte black wood finish, 6 or 9 (10 ga.) lbs. Mfg. 1996-2008.

$135	**$115**	**$90**	**$80**	**$70**	**$60**	**$50**	***$176***

Add $10 for Mossy Oak Break-Up camo in 12 ga. with full choke bore.
Add $58 for 10 ga. in black matte wood finish (disc. 2007).
Add $88 for 10 ga. with camo wood finish.

* ***Pardner Youth Turkey*** – 20 ga. only, features 22 in. full choke barrel and camo painted wood. Mfg. 1996-2008.

$135	**$110**	**$90**	**$80**	**$70**	**$60**	**$50**	***$186***

* ***Pardner Waterfowl (Special Purpose)*** – 10 or 12 (mfg. 2002-2006) ga., 3 1/2 in. chamber, 28 or 32 (10 ga. only, new 1996) in. barrel, blue barrel and receiver, walnut or Mossy Oak Break Up camo (new 2002) finish on stock and forearm, recoil pad, 9 1/2 lbs. Mfg. 1988-2008.

$185	**$150**	**$125**	**$100**	**$85**	**$65**	**$55**	***$228***

Add $36 for camo.
Subtract 15% for 12 ga.

* ***Pardner NRA Foundation Youth*** – 20, 28 (disc. 2001) ga. or .410 bore, 22 in. barrel, high luster bluing, features "NRA Foundation Youth Endowment Edition" laser etched in black on stock, approx. 5 1/2 lbs. Mfg. 1996-2002.

$130	**$105**	**$90**	**$75**	**$65**	**$55**	**$45**	***$161***

* ***Pardner National Wild Turkey Federation (NWTF)*** – 10 or 20 (new 1993) ga., 22 (20 ga. only) or 24 in. barrel with full screw-in choke, full Mossy Oak camo treatment, includes swivels and sling. Mfg. 1992-96.

$190	**$160**	**$135**	**$110**	**$95**	**$80**	**$70**	***$230***

Subtract $80 for 20 ga.

This model was drilled and tapped for scope mounts.

SURVIVOR SERIES – 12 (disc. 2003), 20 (disc. 2003) ga. or .410/.45 LC (new 1995) bore, 3 in. chamber, 20 (.410/.45 LC) or 22 in. barrel with Mod. choke, blue or electroless nickel finish, synthetic thumbhole designed hollow stock with pistol grip, removable forend holds additional ammo, sling swivels, and black nylon sling, 13 1/4 in. LOP, 6 lbs. Mfg. 1992-93, reintroduced 1995-2006.

$175	**$150**	**$120**	**$100**	**$85**	**$75**	**$65**	***$219***

Add $18 for electroless nickel finish.
Subtract 20% for 12 or 20 ga.

TRACKER SLUG MODEL – 10 ga. (mfg. 1994 only), 12, or 20 ga., 3 (12 or 20 ga.) or 3 1/2 (10 ga. only) in. chamber, 24 in. cylinder bore barrel, case colored receiver, includes recoil pad and adj. sights, 6 lbs. Mfg. 1992-2001.

$120	**$90**	**$75**	**$60**	**$50**	**$45**	**$40**	***$143***

* ***Tracker Slug Model II*** – 12 or 20 ga., 3 in. chamber, similar to Tracker Slug Model except has 24 in. rifled slug barrel, 14 in. LOP, 5 1/4 lbs. Mfg. 1995-2008.

$150	**$120**	**$90**	**$75**	**$60**	**$50**	**$45**	***$194***

Add $44 for Tracker II 12 ga. Slug Gun/Huntsman .50 cal. black powder muzzleloader (disc. 2002).

GRADING - PPGS™	100%	98%	95%	90%	80%	70%	60%	LAST MSR

SHOTGUNS: SLIDE ACTION

Beginning Nov. 1, 2007, H&R 1871 decided that all products built in the U.S.A. will carry the H&R brand name, and all imported products will be sold under the NEF brand name. The Pardner Series is now under the H&R brand name.

PARDNER PUMP – 12 or 20 (new 2006) ga., 3 or 3 1/2 (mfg. 2006) in. chamber, steel receiver, crossbolt safety, double action bars, 28 in. VR barrel with choke tube, black synthetic (new 2005), synthetic with carbon fiber dip, or uncheckered walnut stock with or w/o camo (disc. 2010) coverage, recoil pad, matte black metal finish, 7 1/2 lbs. Mfg. 2004-2008.

$185	$165	$145	$115	$100	$85	$75	*$233*

Add $20 for walnut stock and forearm.
Add $20 for synthetic stock with carbon fiber dip (mfg. 2008-2009).
Add $57 for synthetic stock with 100% Realtree APG/HD camo coverage (disc. 2010).
Add $65 for 12 ga. with 3 1/2 in. chamber (disc. 2007).
Subtract $12 for 18 1/2 in. barrel with rifled cylinder bore choke.

* ***Pardner Pump Turkey*** – includes 100% Mossy Oak Breakup (disc.) or Realtree (new 2006) camo coverage, 22 in. barrel with TruGlo front and rear sights, one Turkey choke tube. Mfg. 2005-2010.

$265	$235	$200	$175	$150	$135	$120	*$332*

* ***Pardner Pump Combo*** – 12 ga. only, 3 in. chamber, includes 22 in. rifled slug and 28 in. barrel with modified choke tube. Mfg. 2005-2010.

$295	$250	$220	$185	$155	$125	$115	*$349*

* ***Pardner Pump Protector*** – .12 ga., black synthetic stock, 18 1/2 in. barrel, bead front sight, matte finished metal, swivel studs, vent. recoil pad, 5 shot tube mag., crossbolt safety. Mfg. 2006-2007.

$155	$135	$115	$100	$85	$75	$65	*$186*

* ***Pardner Pump Compact (Youth)*** – 20 ga., takedown action, 21 in. barrel, black American walnut (disc. 2010) or black synthetic pistol grip stock with or w/o camo (disc. 2010), fluted comb, vent. recoil pad, bead front sight, drilled and tapped, 5 shot mag., 13 in. LOP, approx. 6 1/2 lbs. Mfg. 2006-2010.

$185	$165	$145	$115	$100	$85	$75	*$233*

Add $20 for black walnut stock and forearm (disc. 2010).
Add $57 for 100% Realtree APG/HD camo coverage (mfg. 2008-2010).

* ***Pardner Pump Slug*** – 12 or 20 ga., takedown action, 21 (20 ga.) or 22 (12 ga.) in. rifled barrel, matte metal finish, black synthetic (12 ga.) or walnut (20 ga.) pistol grip stock with fluted comb, swivel studs, vent. recoil pad, ramp front sight, adj. rear sight, drilled and tapped, 5 shot mag., crossbolt safety, approx. 6 1/2 lbs. Mfg. 2006-2008.

$250	$215	$190	$160	$140	$115	$100	*$298*

Add $33 for full cantilever scope mount (new 2009).
Add $44 for walnut stock and forearm.

NEW FRONTIER ARMORY

Current dealer, distributor, and manufacturer of AR pistols and rifles established in 2009, located in North Las Vegas, NV.

Please refer to BlueBookOfGunValues.com to order the *Blue Book of AR-15s & Variations*, available as a book or online subscription.

NEW ULTRA LIGHT ARMS LLC

Current rifle manufacturer located in Granville, WV. Dealer sales.

RIFLES: BOLT ACTION

All New Ultra Light Arms rifles feature synthetic stocks in various color combinations and lightweight profile barrels w/o sights.

Add $100 for left-hand action.
Add $178 for Jewell HVR trigger or $68 for stainless steel barrel.
Add $29 for Remington ADL-style aluminum trigger guard.
Add $49 for patented two-position safety.

ULTRA LIGHT RIFLE – caliber to customer specs., various actions, 2-position 3-function safety in top of stock, Timney trigger, Douglas barrel, no sights, Kevlar stock reinforced with graphite, recoil pad, DuPont Imron epoxy finish, designed to customer specifications, includes hard case, 5 1/4-5 3/4 lbs. Disc. 2015.

Because this model was built to customer specifications, a retail price was not available.

GRADING - PPGS™	100%	98%	95%	90%	80%	70%	60%	LAST MSR

MODEL 20 (ULTIMATE MOUNTAIN RIFLE) – intermediate length action, available in .243 Win. - .308 Win. cals., 5 1/4 lbs.

MSR $3,500 $3,150 $2,650 $2,000 $1,450 $1,125 $975 $875

* ***Model 20 RF (Rimfire)*** – .22 LR cal., single shot or repeater, right or left-hand action, choice of synthetic sporter or bench rest style stock, 5 3/4 lbs.

MSR $1,800 $1,600 $1,375 $1,150 $1,025 $850 $700 $600

Add $50 for repeater action.
Add $58 for bench rest style stock.

* ***Model 20 Short*** – available in various short action cals., .17 Rem. - .30 Rem. AR, 20 oz. action, short barrel w/o sights, multi-color synthetic stock, 4 3/4 lbs.

MSR $3,500 $3,150 $2,650 $2,000 $1,450 $1,125 $975 $875

* ***Model 20 Varmint (Ultimate Varmint Rifle)*** – various short action centerfire cals. available between .17 Rem. and .358 Win., and various intermediate actions from .243 Win. to .308 Win., 2 1/2 in. wide classic varminter forend, 5 1/4 lbs.

MSR $3,500 $3,150 $2,650 $2,000 $1,450 $1,125 $975 $875

MODEL 24 (ULTIMATE PLAINS RIFLE) – various cals. between .25-06 Rem. - .338-06 cal., long action, includes scope, 5 3/4 lbs.

MSR $3,600 $3,200 $2,775 $2,350 $2,075 $1,650 $1,350 $1,050

MODEL 28 MAGNUM (ULTIMATE ALASKAN RIFLE) – various Mag. cals. between .264 Win. Mag. - .338 Win. Mag., 6 lbs.

MSR $3,900 $3,500 $3,100 $2,600 $2,250 $1,850 $1,525 $1,300

MODEL 28 SHORT – various cals. between 6.5mm and .350 Rem. Mag. cal., 5 3/4 lbs.

MSR $3,900 $3,500 $3,100 $2,600 $2,250 $1,850 $1,525 $1,300

MODEL 32 MAGNUM (PROFESSIONAL HUNTER) – 7mm STW, .375 H&H, .300 Wby. Mag., .340 Wby. Mag., or .404 Jeffery cal., other calibers available by request, dangerous game rifle. New 2005.

MSR $3,900 $3,500 $3,100 $2,600 $2,250 $1,850 $1,525 $1,300

MODEL 40 MAGNUM (ULTIMATE AFRICAN RIFLE) – .416 Rigby cal., other calibers available by request, otherwise similar to Model 28 Magnum.

MSR $3,900 $3,500 $3,100 $2,600 $2,250 $1,850 $1,525 $1,300

MELVIN FORBES SIGNATURE SERIES – built to commemorate 30 years of industry innovation and excellence, each Signature rifle will have its barrel personally hand signed by Melvin Forbes and will feature a custom pearl colored Timney trigger. Mfg. 2015-2020.

Retail pricing was not available for this model.

NEWTON ARMES

Current rifle manufacturer established in 2008, and located in Belgium.

While Newton Armes has advertised a "Leverbolt" straight pull/push bolt action rifle utilizing some features of the original Newton Arms Co. rifle combined with the styling of the older Mauser 98 Sporting rifles, only prototypes have been manufactured to date.

NEWTON ARMS CO.

Previous manufacturer located in Buffalo, NY and New Haven, CT 1914-1932.

RIFLES: BOLT ACTION

Rifles: Newton Arms Co. Inc. Buffalo, NY

MODEL 1914 RIFLE GROUP – .256 Newton, .30 Newton, .33 Newton, .35 Newton, and .40 Newton cal., three Grades (A, B and C) of Mauser and Sauer rifles converted to Adolph and Newton calibers, total production is unknown. Two Models (A & B) of Mauser rifles and one Model (C) full stocked carbine converted to .256 Newton comprising the only shipment of 24 rifles from Germany in 1914. Mauser rifles are of the Type B style with various patterns and features 24 in. barrels, checkered pistol grip, double set or single triggers, hunting or military rear sights and sling swivels. One Model (D) of a sporting Haenel rifle converted to .256 Newton with Marlin made barrels.

$6,500 $6,000 $5,500 $4,800 $3,800 $3,000 $2,000

NEWTON SPRINGFIELD – .256 Newton cal., Marlin made, square cut rifled barrels, marked "o-o-o" before and after the barrel address and Newton style stock were assembled on a Springfield action by Newton or sold separately to be assembled by the owner of the action, customer supplied the sights.

$1,800 $1,550 $1,200 $1,000 $900 $800 $700

Due to the low numbered receivers and the fact that many of these barrels were customer fitted, it is not advisable to fire these rifles until a competent gunsmith has performed an inspection.

GRADING - PPGS™ 100% 98% 95% 90% 80% 70% 60% LAST MSR

FIRST MODEL 1916 NEWTON RIFLE – .22 Newton (10-14 rifles), .256 Newton, .30-06, .30 Newton, .35 Newton, and .40 Newton (4 rifles) calibers, standard features are Mauser style action, 24 in. round barrel, pistol grip, checkered stock, steel buttplate and grip cap, double set triggers that both face forward, rear and front sights on barrel bands, all rifles are takedowns by unscrewing floorplate, options included bolt peep sight, Lyman 48 long tang sight, cheekpiece, serrated buttplate, long barrels, recoil pad, sling swivels and slings, barrels marked "Newton Arms Co. Inc. o-o Buffalo, N.Y. o-o." Total production about 4,000 rifles.

$4,000 $3,200 $2,800 $2,000 $1,500 $1,300 $1,100

Add $100 for optional bolt peep sight.

Add $100 for figured wood or cheekpiece.

Rifles: Chas. Newton Rifle Corp., Buffalo, NY

MODEL 1922 NEWTON MAUSER – .256 Newton cal., Mauser barreled action assembled into a sporting rifle by Sauer, checkered pistol grip, spoon bolt handle, double set triggers facing each other, three leaf rear sight and Schnabel forend, barrels converted to .256 Newton after they arrived in the U.S. A. Barrel markings vary, Chas. Newton Rifle Corporation, Krupp Steel or Rustless Steel. Made in Germany, 100 rifles imported.

$6,500 $5,000 $5,500 $5,000 $4,200 $3,800 $3,000

Rifles: Buffalo Newton Rifle Corp., New Haven, CT

MODEL 1924 BUFFALO NEWTON RIFLE – .256 Newton, .30 Newton, .35 Newton, and .30-06 cal., standard features are Mauser style action, 24 in. round barrel, pistol grip checkered stock, steel buttplate and grip cap, double set triggers facing each other, "dogleg" style bolt handle, crossbolt in the stock, rear sight dovetailed into the barrel, all rifles are takedowns by unscrewing the floorplate, barrels marked "Buffalo Newton Rifle Co New Haven Conn U.S.A.", some options include sling swivels and slings, Lyman 48 long or short tang sight. About 1,000 mfg.

* ***Meeker Rifles*** – similar to Model 1924 Buffalo Newton Rifle, except are marked "Meeker Arms Co, Model 1925, New Haven Conn." Total production is unknown although probably a low number.

$2,500 $2,000 $1,500 $1,200 $1,000 $850 $700

NEWTOWN FIREARMS

Previous AR-15 style firearm manufacturer located in Hangtown, CA until 2017.

Please refer to BlueBookOfGunValues.com to order the *Blue Book of AR-15s & Variations*, available as a book or online subscription.

NEXT GENERATION ARMS

Previous rifle manufacturer located in Hayden, ID until circa 2012.

Please refer to BlueBookOfGunValues.com to order the *Blue Book of AR-15s & Variations*, available as a book or online subscription.

NIGHTHAWK CUSTOM

Current manufacturer located in Berryville, AR, since 2004. Consumer custom order sales.

PISTOLS: SEMI-AUTO, SINGLE ACTION

Nighthawk Custom offers a complete line of high quality 1911 style semi-auto pistols. For more information on Nighthawk's custom pistols, please contact the company directly for more information on a wide variety of options, gunsmithing services and availability.

Add $50 for Barrel Crown upgrade. Add $75 for Fluted Barrel Hood upgrade. Add $225-$350 for Crimson Trace lasergrips on any applicable model (not bobtail). Add $120 for ambidextrous safety. Add $650 for Double Stack Upgrade (new 2019) on any Nighthawk Custom government model 9mm pistols.

10-8 – .45 ACP cal., SA, 5 in. barrel, 8 shot, long solid trigger with hidden fixed over travel stop, Hilton Yam/10-8 performance designed U-notched rear and serrated front sights with Tritium inserts, green or black linen Micarta grips, strong side only safety, low profile Dawson Light Speed Rail, front/rear cocking serrations, black Permakote finish, 42 oz. Mfg. 2009-2010.

$2,325 $2,025 $1,750 $1,575 $1,275 $1,050 $825 *$2,595*

AAC (ADVANCED ARMAMENT CORPORATION) – 9mm Para. or .45 ACP cal., 5 in. threaded barrel, SA, stainless steel thread protector, done in collaboration with Advanced Armament Corporation, lightening cuts on the top and sides of the slide, mainspring housing and front strap that match the Advanced Armament M4-2000 suppressor, tall Heinie Slant Pro Straight Eight front sights designed for use with suppressor, black Permakote finish in black, ultra thin Nighthawk Custom Alumagrips, solid, black aluminum trigger, 39 oz. Mfg. 2010-2016.

$3,150 $2,750 $2,375 $2,150 $1,725 $1,425 $1,100 *$3,495*

Add $100 for AAC Recon Model with integrated lower rail.

GRADING - PPGS™	100%	98%	95%	90%	80%	70%	60%	LAST MSR

AGENT 2 – 9mm Para. or .45 ACP cal., forged Government frame with lightened Recon rail, 5 in. match grade barrel, 10 shot mag., Nighthawk/Agency custom trigger, Heinie Black Ledge rear and fiber optic front sights, Railscales G10 grips, Agency front and rear cocking serrations, ultra hi-cut front strap, Nighthawk Smoke Cerakote finish, 40.1 oz. New 2018.

MSR $4,499	$4,050	$3,550	$3,000	$2,750	$2,225	$1,825	$1,500	

* ***Agent 2 Commander*** – 9mm Para. or .45 ACP cal., forged Commander frame with lightened Recon rail, 4.25 in. match grade barrel, 10 shot mag. (9mm Para.), Nighthawk/Agency custom trigger, Heinie Black Ledge rear and fiber optic front sights, Railscales G10 grips, Agency front and rear cocking serrations, ultra hi-cut front strap, faceted slide and side windows, one-piece mainspring housing/magwell, Nighthawk Smoke Cerakote finish, 38.6 oz. New 2020.

MSR $4,499	$4,050	$3,550	$3,000	$2,750	$2,225	$1,825	$1,500	

BOB MARVEL CUSTOM 1911 – 9mm Para. (new 2015) or .45 ACP cal., 4 1/4 in. barrel, proprietary bull barrel system, hand stippling on top of slide, bull nose front taper, fully adj. sights, one-piece mainspring housing and magwell, high cut front strap, lightweight aluminum medium solid match trigger, Nighthawk Custom/Marvel EVERLAST recoil system, black Melonite finish, 2 lbs. 6 oz. New 2012.

MSR $4,499	$4,050	$3,550	$3,000	$2,750	$2,225	$1,825	$1,500	

BORDER SPECIAL - .45 ACP cal., Concealed Carry Cut, Commander sized frame and slide, 4 1/4 in. match grade barrel, fluted barrel hood, 8 shot mag., custom trigger, Heinie black Slant Pro rear sight with solid gold bead front sight, cocobolo double diamond grips with Nighthawk logo, scalloped front strap, top slide serrations, completely dehorned, ultra hi-cut front strap, Cerakote Elite Midnight finish, 34.1 oz. New 2017.

MSR $3,799	$3,425	$3,000	$2,575	$2,325	$1,875	$1,550	$1,275	

BROWNING HI POWER - 9mm Para. cal., hand textured (stippled) frame and trigger guard, crowned barrel, two 13 shot mags., competition steel hammer, Heinie Slant Pro black rear and Nighthawk (14K) gold bead front sights, custom select cocobolo checkered grips with NH logo, custom extended beavertail, contoured magwell, French border, Cerakote satin rust resistant finish. Mfg. 2016-2018.

	$2,875	$2,525	$2,150	$1,950	$1,575	$1,300	$1,000	*$3,195*

THE BULL - .45 ACP or 9mm Para. (optional) cal., Government size frame, 5 in. match grade bull barrel, 8 shot mag., one-piece magwell/mainspring housing, Heinie Ledge Straight Eight Tritium rear and Nighthawk Tritium front sights, carbon fiber grips, Bow Tie plug, French border, Nighthawk curved slide stop, coarse rear cocking serrations, completely dehorned, ultra hi-cut front strap with Armstrong texture, Cerakote Elite Smoke finish, optional fluted hood, 38.8 oz. New 2017.

MSR $3,799	$3,425	$3,000	$2,575	$2,325	$1,875	$1,550	$1,275	

Add $75 for fluted barrel hood.

* ***The Bull Commander*** - .45 ACP or 9mm Para. (optional) cal., Commander size frame, 4 1/4 in. match grade crowed bull barrel, 8 shot mag., one-piece magwell/mainspring housing, Heinie Ledge Straight Eight Ledge Tritium rear and Nighthawk Tritium front sights, carbon fiber grips, Bow Tie plug, French border, Nighthawk curved slide stop, coarse rear cocking serrations, completely dehorned, ultra hi-cut front strap with texture, Cerakote Elite Smoke finish, 7.82 in. OAL, 36.7 oz. New 2019.

MSR $3,799	$3,425	$3,000	$2,575	$2,325	$1,875	$1,550	$1,275	

* ***The Bull Officer*** - .45 ACP or 9mm Para. cal., Officer size frame, 3.8 in. match grade bull barrel, 8 shot mag., one-piece magwell/mainspring housing, Heinie Ledge Straight Eight Tritium rear and Nighthawk Tritium front sights, carbon fiber grips, Bow tie plug, French border, Nighthawk curved slide stop, coarse rear cocking serrations, completely dehorned, ultra hi-cut front strap, Cerakote Elite Smoke finish, 32 oz.

MSR $3,799	$3,425	$3,000	$2,575	$2,325	$1,875	$1,550	$1,275	

CHAIRMAN - 9mm Para. or .45 ACP cal., forged Government sized frame, 6 in. match grade barrel with titanium gold Nitride finish, aluminum Nighthawk Custom tri-cavity trigger, gold bead front and fully adj. black rear sights, Railscales G10 grips, heavy angle lightning cuts on the slide, 25 LPI checkered front strap and mainspring housing, completely dehorned, DLC finish, 40.9 oz. New 2018.

MSR $4,199	$3,775	$3,300	$2,825	$2,575	$2,075	$1,700	$1,400	

CHRIS COSTA RECON - 9mm Para. (2012 only) or .45 ACP cal., 5 in. crowned barrel and beveled flush with the bushing, 8 (.45 ACP) or 10 (9mm Para.) shot mag., lightweight aluminum medium solid match trigger, red fiber optic or Tritium-dot front sights, Jardine Tactical Hook rear sights, EVERLAST recoil system, 10-8 Performance Hyena Brown grips, magwell with rounded butt, fully machined slide and one-piece mainspring housing, top serrations, extreme high cut checkered front strap, integrated recon light rail, multi-faceted slide top, COSTA logo engraved in silver, black Melonite finish, 2 lbs. 6 oz. Mfg. 2012-2015.

	$3,325	$2,900	$2,500	$2,275	$1,825	$1,500	$1,175	*$3,695*

GRADING - PPGS™ 100% 98% 95% 90% 80% 70% 60% LAST MSR

* ***Chris Costa Compact*** – .45 ACP cal. only, similar to Chris Costa Recon, except has smaller, officer-style frame, 4 1/4 in. barrel, black 10-8 Performance 5 LPI grips, 2 lbs. 4 oz. Mfg. 2012-2015.

$3,325 $2,900 $2,500 $2,275 $1,825 $1,500 $1,175 *$3,695*

COMPLETE CUSTOM STIPPLE (CCS) – .45 ACP or 9mm Para. cal., Government frame, 5 in. match grade barrel, custom trigger, Heinie 2-dot Slant Pro Tritium rear and Nighthawk Tritium front sight, cocobolo half smooth/half checkered grips with Nighthawk logo, aggressively stippled top and rear of slide, front strap, mainspring housing, hammer, slide stop, mag. release, thumb safety, and grip safety, heavy French border, front and rear cocking serrations, completely dehorned, ultra hi-cut front strap, bead blasted stainless steel finish with polished flats, 33.8 oz. New 2017.

MSR $4,399 $3,960 $3,465 $2,975 $2,690 $2,180 $1,780 $1,450

COUNSELOR – 9mm Para., Officer frame, 3 1/2 in. lightweight aluminum barrel, 8 shot mag., bobbed-concealment beavertail and hammer, Tritium front sight, Heinie Straight 8-Slant Pro rear sight, thin grips, grip safety, custom magwell, black anodized frame and Nitride slide finish, 27.9 oz. New 2019.

MSR $3,899 $3,500 $3,075 $2,625 $2,375 $1,925 $1,575 $1,300

CUSTOM COLT SERIES 70 – .45 ACP cal., Colt 1911 Classic, Government size frame, 5 in. crowned barrel w/bushing, 7 shot mag., polished extractor and ejector, match grade solid short trigger, solid gold bead front and retro rear sight, beavertail grip safety, hi-cut front strap, French border, fully machined disconnector, sear, hammer strut, and pin, custom engraving on dust cover, Smoked Nitride finish, 39 oz. New 2020.

MSR $2,699 $2,430 $2,125 $1,825 $1,650 $1,335 $1,095 $900

DOMINATOR – .45 ACP or 9mm Para. (optional) cal., 5 in. crowned match grade barrel, stainless steel frame with black Permakote slide, Nighthawk Custom fully adjustable rear sights, 8 shot, hand serrated rear og slide with serrated top slide, front and rear slide serrations, 25 LPI checkering on front strap, cocobolo double diamond grips with laser engraved Nighthawk Custom logo, two-tone finish, 40 oz.

MSR $3,799 $3,425 $3,000 $2,575 $2,325 $1,875 $1,550 $1,275

Add $100 for Recon Model with integrated lower rail (disc. 2014).

Add $350 for the FLX high capacity double stack frame (disc. 2011).

ENFORCER – .45 ACP or 9mm Para. cal., SA only, 5 in. barrel, Novak low mount Tritium or Heinie Slant Pro night sights, extended tactical mag. catch, aggressive no slip G10 Golf Ball grips or Mil-Tac G10 spiral logo grips in either black/gray or black/green (new 2012), unique frame with integrated plunger tube and magwell, hand serrations on rear of slide with serrated top slide, front and rear slide cocking serrations, lanyard loop mainspring housing, completely dehorned and ready for carry, black, green, Sniper Gray, Coyote Tan, or Titanium Blue Permakote finish, 39 oz.

MSR $3,799 $3,425 $3,000 $2,575 $2,325 $1,875 $1,550 $1,275

Add $100 for Recon Model with integrated lower rail (disc. 2014).

FALCON – 9mm Para., 10mm, .38 Super, or .45 ACP cal., 5 in. match grade stainless steel or carbon steel crowned barrel with chamfered bushing, one-piece fully machined mainspring/magwell combination, rear cocking serrations, golf ball dimple-pattern G10 grips in black, Coyote Tan, or OD Green finish with or without the Nighthawk logo, Heinie ledge rear sight, 38.8 oz. New 2011.

MSR $3,799 $3,425 $3,000 $2,575 $2,325 $1,875 $1,550 $1,275

Add $100 for 10mm or .38 Super cal.

* ***Falcon Commander*** – .45 ACP or 9mm Para. cal., similar to Falcon, except in Commander size. New 2013.

MSR $3,799 $3,425 $3,000 $2,575 $2,325 $1,875 $1,550 $1,275

FIRE HAWK – .45 ACP or 9mm Para. cal., full size Government frame, 5 in. single port compensator bull barrel and lightened slide, one-piece mainspring housing/magwell, 8 shot mag., solid aluminum curved trigger, coarse serrated rear slide, agent 1 grips, Heine Black Slant Pro rear sight and red gold bead front sight, black Nitride finish, 8.47 in. OAL, 39.6 oz. New 2019.

MSR $4,199 $3,775 $3,300 $2,825 $2,575 $2,075 $1,700 $1,400

GA PRECISION MODEL – .45 ACP cal., Nighthawk's Ever-last recoil system, Government frame, 5 in. barrel, 8 shot mag., Heinie Ledge night sights, thick tactical bushing and smooth recoil spring plug, serrated rear of slide, bevel and recess slide stop, custom one-piece MSH and magwell, black Nitride finish. Mfg. 2016-2020.

$3,325 $2,925 $2,500 $2,275 $1,825 $1,500 $1,175 *$3,699*

GRADING - PPGS™	100%	98%	95%	90%	80%	70%	60%	LAST MSR

GRP (GLOBAL RESPONSE PISTOL) – 9mm Para. (new 2012), 10mm (new 2012), .38 Super, or .45 ACP cal., SA only, 5 in. match grade barrel, 8 shot mag., match grade trigger, front and rear cocking serrations, Heinie or Novak Extreme Duty adj. night sights, Gator Back (disc.) or Golf Ball grips, black, Sniper Gray, green, Coyote Tan, or Titanium Blue Permakote ceramic based finish, tactical single side or ambi safety, 36.9 oz.

MSR $3,199	$2,880	$2,525	$2,160	$1,960	$1,585	$1,295	$1,065	

Add $100 for 10mm or .38 Super cal.
Add $100 for GRP II with 4 1/4 in. barrel (disc. 2011).
Add $200 Crimson Trace Lasergrips (disc. 2014).
Add $350 for the FLX high capacity double stack frame (disc. 2011).

* ***GRP Recon*** – 9mm Para., 10mm, .38 Super, or .45 ACP cal., similar to GRP, except includes frame with integrated lower rail for Surefire X300 weapon light, 39 oz.

MSR $3,299	$2,975	$2,600	$2,230	$2,025	$1,635	$1,340	$1,100	

Add $100 for .38 Super or 10mm cal.
Add $200 Crimson Trace Lasergrips (disc. 2014).

GRIFFON – 9mm Para. cal., Griffon Industries designed 1911, Government frame, 5 in. fitted threaded barrel, three Chip McCormick mags. laser engraved with the Griffon logo, 10-8 Performance flat trigger, VZ Super Scoop grips with magazine button relief scallop, recon rail, wide rear cocking serrations, Griffon Industries logo, with or w/o Trijicon RMR cut slide, includes Griffon Industries pistol pouch, carbon fiber holster and double mag. carrier, limited edition custom Griffon Industries morale patch. Limited mfg. 2016 only.

	$5,395	$4,725	$4,050	$3,675	$2,975	$2,450	$1,900	*$5,995*

HEINIE LONG SLIDE – 10mm or .45 ACP cal., 6 in. match grade barrel, black Permakote ceramic based finish, cocobolo wood grips with Heinie logo, Nighthawk Custom fully adjustable rear or fixed sights, 25 LPI checkering on front strap, contoured for carry, 44 oz.

MSR $3,999	$3,600	$3,150	$2,700	$2,450	$1,975	$1,625	$1,325	

Add $350 for unique Nighthawk Custom camouflage finish; available in Digital, Woodland or Desert Camo (disc. 2011).

HEINIE PDP – .45 ACP cal., 4 1/4 (Commander size) or 5 (Government size) in. Heinie match grade barrel, cocobolo wood grips with Heinie logo, fixed sights, scalloped front strap and mainspring housing, extended combat safety, contoured for carry magwell, Heinie match hammer, sear, and disconnector, serrated rear of slide & slide top, Heinie aluminum trigger, tactical mag. release, 38 oz. Disc. 2017.

	$3,225	$2,825	$2,425	$2,200	$1,775	$1,450	$1,125	*$3,595*

HEINIE SIGNATURE SERIES – 9mm Para. cal., available in Competition, Government Recon, and Officer Compact configurations, features silver Heinie Signature Series engraved logo on right of slide, features same thin frame as Lady Hawk model.

* ***Heinie Signature Series Compact*** – 9mm Para. cal., similar to the RECON and the Competition model, except has smaller officer-style frame designed for concealed carry, 4 1/2 in. barrel, and G10 grips. Mfg. 2012-2017.

	$3,325	$2,925	$2,500	$2,275	$1,825	$1,500	$1,175	*$3,695*

* ***Heinie Signature Series Competition*** – 9mm Para. cal., 5 in. barrel, hand signed thin grip panels, fully machined one-piece mainspring housing and magwell combination that has been thinned and scalloped, red fiber optic front sights, black Heinie Slant Pro rear sights, hand serrated rear of slide, slide top serrations, crowned and recessed match grade barrel, tool steel hammer and hammer strut, lightweight aluminum match grade trigger, recessed slide stop, chamfered frame, 40 oz. New 2012.

MSR $3,799	$3,425	$3,000	$2,575	$2,325	$1,875	$1,550	$1,275	

* ***Heinie Signature Series RECON*** – 9mm Para. cal., 5 in. match grade barrel, similar features as the Competition, except has integrated recon light rail X300 tactical light, and Heine Slant Pro Night Sights. New 2012.

MSR $3,899	$3,500	$3,075	$2,625	$2,375	$1,925	$1,575	$1,300	

HEINIE TACTICAL CARRY – .45 ACP cal., 5 in. Heinie match grade barrel, black Perma Kote ceramic based finish, double diamond cocobolo or aluminum grips with Heinie logo, Heinie Straight Eight Slant Pro night sights, Heinie trigger, complete carry dehorned, Heinie signature magwell, flat slide top with 40 LPI serrations, done in collaboration with renowned gunsmith Richard Heinie, 40 oz. Disc. 2013.

	$3,500	$3,075	$2,625	$2,375	$1,925	$1,575	$1,225	*$3,895*

GRADING - PPGS™	100%	98%	95%	90%	80%	70%	60%	LAST MSR

KESTREL – .45 ACP cal., forged frame, 4 1/4 in. Commander length slide, match grade crowned and recessed barrel, beveled magwell, tactical checkered extended mag. release, Heinie Slant Pro Straight Eight night sights, Nighthawk Custom ultra-thin alumagrips, hand serrated rear of slide, Heinie Signature scalloped front strap and contoured mainspring housing, black Nitride finish with stainless controls. New 2016.

MSR $3,799	$3,425	$3,000	$2,575	$2,325	$1,875	$1,550	$1,275	

LADY HAWK – 9mm Para., .38 Super, or .45 ACP cal., 4 1/4 in. crowned match grade barrel, ultra thin aluminum grips, Heinie Slant Pro Straight Eight sights, modified ultra thin chain link front strap and mainspring housing for reduced grip circumference, Titanium Blue Permakote finish with hard chromed controls, 36 oz.

MSR $3,799	$3,425	$3,000	$2,575	$2,325	$1,875	$1,550	$1,275	

Add $200 for anodized aluminum lightweight frame.
Add $200 for complete stainless steel model.
Add $100 for Recon Model with integrated lower rail (disc. 2014).

LADYHAWK 2.0 – 9mm Para. cal., forged Commander size frame, 4 1/4 in. match grade barrel, 10 shot mag., aluminum Nighthawk Custom tri-cavity trigger, Heinie Slant Pro Straight Eight Tritium night sights, custom Obsidian/Abalone/Zinc grips, serrated slide stop, scalloped front strap and mainspring housing, Heinie recoil spring plug, completely dehorned, DLC with rose gold TICN finish on controls and barrel, 36 oz. New 2018.

MSR $4,799	$4,325	$3,780	$3,240	$2,940	$2,375	$1,945	$1,600	

NHC CLASSIC – .45 ACP cal., Government frame, 5 in. match grade barrel, fluted barrel hood, 8 shot mag., stainless steel construction, med. solid aluminum Nighthawk custom trigger, Heinie Black Ledge rear and gold bead front sights, cocobolo half smooth/half checkered grips with Nighthawk logo, curved slide stop, round butt mainspring housing, flat-top with arrow serrations, script engraving, French border, 36.9 oz. New 2017.

MSR $3,999	$3,600	$3,150	$2,700	$2,450	$1,975	$1,625	$1,325	

NIGHTHAWK CARRY PLUS – 9mm Para. cal., Everlast Recoil System, Officer frame, 3.8 in. match grade bull barrel, fluted barrel hood, custom trigger, Heinie Slant Pro Straight Eight Tritium rear and Nighthawk Tritium front sights, G10 thin ETC Frag grips with thumb scoop, Bow Tie plug, Nighthawk tactical curved slide stop, coarse rear cocking serrations, completely dehorned, ultra hi-cut front strap, black Nitride/anodized finish, 28.5 oz. New 2017.

MSR $3,899	$3,500	$3,075	$2,625	$2,375	$1,925	$1,575	$1,300	

PREDATOR – 9mm Para., 10mm, or .45 ACP cal., SA only, 5 in. stainless steel barrel, black Permakote ceramic based finish with black slide, double diamond cocobolo, walnut, or black cristobal checkered grips, Heinie Slant Pro Straight Eight or Novak Lo-Mount night sights, hand checkering on rear of slide with serrated top slide, front and rear slide serrations, 25 LPI checkering on front strap, unique one-piece precision fit barrel designed to reduce muzzle flip and felt recoil, one inch at 25 yards guaranteed accuracy, top-of-the-line model, available in black, sniper gray, coyote tan, titanium blue, hard chrome, or stainless steel, 32-34 oz.

MSR $3,899	$3,500	$3,075	$2,625	$2,375	$1,925	$1,575	$1,300	

Add $100 for Recon Model with integrated lower rail.
Add $350 for the FLX high capacity double stack frame. (9mm & 10mm Government size only, disc. 2011)

* ***Predator II*** – 9mm Para., 10mm, or .45 ACP cal., similar to Predator, except has 4 1/4 in. barrel, checkered rear of slide, top serrations, 35.8 oz.

MSR $3,899	$3,500	$3,075	$2,625	$2,375	$1,925	$1,575	$1,300	

* ***Predator III*** – 9mm Para., 10mm, or .45 ACP cal., similar to Predator, except features Officer frame and 4 1/4 in. barrel, 2 lbs. 6 oz.

MSR $3,899	$3,500	$3,075	$2,625	$2,375	$1,925	$1,575	$1,300	

* ***Predator T5*** – 9mm Para. cal., 5 in. stainless steel bull barrel, stainless steel frame, Nighthawk two-piece magwell, single side safety, Heinie Ledge Straight Eight front and rear Tritium night sights, thinned cocobolo grips with diamond checkering, black Nitride finish, 40.3 oz. Mfg. 2015-2020.

	$3,500	$3,075	$2,625	$2,375	$1,925	$1,575	$1,225	*$3,899*

PRESIDENT – 9mm Para. cal., forged Government sized frame, 5 in. match grade crowned barrel with titanium gold Nitride finish, aluminum Nighthawk Custom tri-cavity trigger, gold bead front and Heinie Black Ledge rear sights, Railscales G10 grips, heavy angle lightning cuts on the slide, 25 LPI checkered front strap and mainspring housing, completely dehorned, DLC finish, 8.58 in. OAL, 38.2 oz. New 2019.

MSR $4,199	$3,775	$3,300	$2,825	$2,575	$2,075	$1,700	$1,400	

GRADING - PPGS™	100%	98%	95%	90%	80%	70%	60%	LAST MSR

SHADOW HAWK COMMANDER – 9mm Para. cal., 4 1/4 in. custom match carbon steel barrel, stainless steel frame, one-piece magwell, Heinie Ledge Straight Eight front and rear Tritium night sights, black and gray spiral cut custom grips, black Nitride finish, 36.7 oz. New 2015.

MSR $3,799 $3,425 $3,000 $2,575 $2,325 $1,875 $1,550 $1,275

SHADOW HAWK GOVERNMENT – 9mm Para. cal., 5 in. barrel, stainless steel frame, single side safety, Heinie Ledge Straight Eight front and rear Tritium night sights, aggressive cocking serrations, one-piece steel magwell/mainspring housing, black flat-faced trigger, front strap checkering, high beavertail, recessed and beveled slide stop, black and gray spiral cut G10 grips, black Nitride finish, 39 oz. New 2015.

MSR $3,799 $3,425 $3,000 $2,575 $2,325 $1,875 $1,550 $1,275

SHADOW HAWK LONG SLIDE – 10mm or .45 ACP cal., forged government size frame, 6 in. barrel, 9 shot mag., aggressive cocking serrations on the front and rear of slide, lightweight flat-faced aluminum trigger, adj. rear sight with dual Tritium lamps, Tritium front sight, G10 black and gray spiral cut grips with Nighthawk Custom logo, black Nitride finish, 42 oz. New 2020.

MSR $4,199 $3,775 $3,300 $2,825 $2,575 $2,075 $1,700 $1,400

* ***Shadow Hawk Government With Trijicon RMR*** – 9mm Para. cal., similar to Shadow Hawk Government, except features a mounted Trijicon RMR (Ruggedized Miniature Reflex) sight, front and rear Trijicon Tall Tritium night sights, 37.4 oz. New 2015.

MSR $4,899 $4,410 $3,860 $3,310 $3,000 $2,425 $1,985 $1,635

SILENT HAWK – 9mm Para. cal., Commander recon frame and Commander slide, 4 1/4 in. threaded barrel with protector, two Nighthawk Custom 8 shot stainless mags., Heinie Tritium tall suppressor night sights, G10 black and gray spiral cut grips with mag. release cutout and Nighthawk logo, custom checkering on front strap of frame, one-piece mainspring housing and magwell, custom NH/SilencerCo brand logos on slide, behind rear cocking serrations, hand serrated rear of slide, tri-cut top slide and custom cocking serrations to match Osprey silencer, built for SilencerCo., Nitride Black Out finish. New 2016.

MSR $4,299 $3,875 $3,385 $2,900 $2,630 $2,130 $1,740 $1,430

T3 – 9mm Para., .40 S&W (disc. 2011) or .45 ACP cal., 4 1/4 in. match grade stainless steel fully crowned barrel, Officer size frame, extended magwell, flush forged slide stop with chamfered frame, tactical mag. release, unique Nighthawk T3 magwell, horizontally serrated no-snag mainspring housing and rear of slide, skeletonized aluminum match trigger, Heinie straight 8 slant pro sights, Perma Kote finish, in black, Gun Metal Grey, Green, Coyote Tan, Titanium Blue, or hard chrome, 38 oz.

MSR $3,599 $3,240 $2,835 $2,430 $2,205 $1,780 $1,460 $1,200

Add $200 for anodized aluminum lightweight frame.

Add $495 for T3 Comp model (.45 ACP cal. only), with Schuemann AET hybrid comp. ported barrel (mfg. 2010-disc.).

* ***T3 Stainless*** – 9mm Para., .40 S&W (disc. 2011) or .45 ACP cal., similar to T3, except stainless steel.

MSR $3,799 $3,425 $3,000 $2,575 $2,325 $1,875 $1,550 $1,275

* ***T3 Thin*** – similar to the T3, except is smaller design for concealed carry. New 2012.

MSR $3,799 $3,425 $3,000 $2,575 $2,325 $1,875 $1,550 $1,275

T4 – 9mm Para. cal., 3.8 in. crowned barrel, Bob Marvel Everlast recoil system, steel, aluminum, or stainless steel (new 2015) proprietary thin frame, ultra-thin G10 grips. New 2013.

MSR $3,599 $3,240 $2,835 $2,430 $2,205 $1,780 $1,460 $1,200

Add $200 for aluminum or stainless steel (new 2015) frame.

TALON – 9mm Para., .40 S&W (disc. 2011), 10mm, or .45 ACP cal., 5 in. match grade barrel, lightweight aluminum match trigger, hand checkering on rear of slide with serrated top slide, front and rear slide serrations, 25 LPI checkering on front strap, Novak night sights, cocobolo, walnut, or black cristobal grips, tactical mag. release, Perma Kote ceramic based finish in black, Sniper Gray, Coyote Tan, Titanium Blue, hard chrome, or Diamond Black option available, 36-41 oz.

MSR $3,599 $3,240 $2,835 $2,430 $2,205 $1,780 $1,460 $1,200

Add $199 for Crimson Trace Lasergrips with Nighthawk logo.

Add $100 for Recon Model with integrated lower rail.

Add $200 for anodized aluminum lightweight frame.

Add $350 for the FLX high capacity double stack frame (disc. 2011).

* ***Talon II*** – 9mm Para., .40 S&W (disc. 2011), 10mm, or .45 ACP cal., similar to Talon, except features Commander size frame, 4 1/4 in. barrel, 2 lbs. 4 oz.

MSR $3,599 $3,240 $2,835 $2,430 $2,205 $1,780 $1,460 $1,200

GRADING - PPGS™	100%	98%	95%	90%	80%	70%	60%	LAST MSR

* ***Talon II CCC (Concealed Carry Curve)*** – .45 ACP cal., Commander size frame, CCC mainspring housing, 4 1/4 in. barrel, Heinie Slant Pro Straight Eight Tritium night sights, cocobolo double diamond grips, aluminum Nighthawk Custom tri-cavity trigger, 7.85 in. OAL, 2 lbs. 4 oz. New 2019.

MSR $3,749	$3,375	$2,950	$2,530	$2,295	$1,850	$1,525	$1,250	

* ***Talon II Bobtail*** – 9mm Para., .40 S&W (disc. 2011), 10mm, or .45 ACP cal., similar to Talon II, except features Ed Brown bobtail. Disc. 2017.

	$3,000	$2,625	$2,250	$2,050	$1,650	$1,350	$1,050	*$3,345*

* ***Talon IV*** – similar to Talon, except compact model with 3.6 in. barrel, gray frame and black slide, rear slide serrations, and black grips. Disc. 2010.

	$2,175	$1,900	$1,625	$1,475	$1,200	$975	$775	*$2,425*

THUNDER RANCH COMBAT SPECIAL – 9mm Para. or .45 ACP cal., 1911 style, 5 in. barrel, 8 shot mag., medium solid trigger, 18k gold bead front sight, Heinie black ledge rear sight, green Linen/Micarta scale grips, single GI "nub-style" thumb safety, "Thunder Ranch" logo behind rear cocking serrations, custom engraving, smoked Nitride finish, 41.3 oz. New 2019.

MSR $3,499	$3,150	$2,750	$2,365	$2,140	$1,735	$1,425	$1,165	

TRI-CUT CARRY – 9mm Para. cal., Commander frame, 4 1/4 in. match grade bull barrel, 10 shot mag., custom trigger, Heinie Ledge Straight Eight Tritium rear and Nighthawk Tritium front sight, black tri-cut aluminum grips, thinned tri-cut mainspring housing with center flat stippled, tri-cut slide with arrow serrations on top of slide, coarse rear cocking serrations, full-length guide rod with Bow Tie plug, completely dehorned, ultra hi-cut front strap, black Nitride finish, 34.7 oz. New 2017.

MSR $4,499	$4,050	$3,550	$3,000	$2,750	$2,225	$1,825	$1,500	

TROOPER – .45 ACP cal., full size Government frame, match grade 5 in. crowned barrel, lightweight aluminum Nighthawk Custom tri-cavity trigger, coarse serrated rear slide, G10 gator black grips with Nighthawk logo, Heinie Ledge Straight Eight Tritium night sights, black Nitride finish, 8.65 in. OAL, 37.1 oz. New 2019.

MSR $3,299	$2,975	$2,600	$2,230	$2,025	$1,635	$1,340	$1,100	

TRS COMMANDER – 9mm Para. cal., aluminum double stack grip frame, forged steel commander frame, 4 1/4 in. match grade stainless barrel, 17 shot mag., lightweight aluminum trigger, Heinie Ledge Straight Eight rear sight, Tritium front sight, full length dust rail, monolithic slide, dimpled cocking serrations to match grip, black Nitride finish, 36.7 oz. New 2020.

MSR $3,999	$3,600	$3,150	$2,700	$2,450	$1,975	$1,625	$1,325	

TRS COMP (TACTICAL READY SERIES) – 9mm Para. cal., aluminum double stack forged steel government frame, 5 in. match grade barrel, integrated compensator, 17 shot mag., lightweight aluminum trigger, Heinie Ledge black rear sight, 18K gold bead front sight, monolithic slide, full length dust cover, dimpled cocking serrations to match grip, black Nitride finish, 39.6 oz. New 2020.

MSR $4,599	$4,140	$3,625	$3,100	$2,810	$2,275	$1,865	$1,530	

TURNBULL VIP I – .45 ACP cal., collaboration between Nighthawk and Doug Turnbull, Turnbull polished case hardened frame finish, forged Government size frame and 5 in. match grade crowned barrel, 8 shot mag., 14K solid gold bead front sight, solid black Heinie Slant Pro rear sight, cross cut mastodon ivory grips, 3 vertical lines on ultra hi-cut front strap and mainspring housing, front and rear cocking serrations, completely dehorned, includes custom display box, high polished charcoal blued slide and controls finish. Limited mfg. beginning 2017.

MSR $7,999	$7,200	$6,300	$5,400	$4,895	N/A	N/A	N/A	

TURNBULL VIP 2 – .45 ACP cal., collaboration between Nighthawk and Doug Turnbull, forged Government size frame with Turnbull case hardened frame finish, 5 in. match grade crowned barrel, 8 shot mag., one-piece magwell, custom trigger, 14K gold bead front sight, solid black Heinie Slant Pro rear sight, cross cut mastodon ivory grips, heavy bevel on bottom of slide, 3 vertical lines on ultra hi-cut front strap and mainspring housing, front and rear cocking serrations, completely dehorned, includes custom display box, Turnbull Nitre blue on slide stop, mag. release, thumb safety, and pins, blued slide finish, 37.4 oz. Limited mfg. beginning 2017.

MSR $7,499	$6,750	$5,900	$5,060	$4,590	N/A	N/A	N/A	

VICE PRESIDENT – 9mm Para. or .45 ACP cal., forged Commander size frame, 4.25 in. match grade crowned barrel with titanium gold Nitride finish, 10 shot mag. (9mm Para. cal.), Nighthawk Tri-Cavity trigger, Heinie Black Ledge rear sight, gold bead front sight, Railscales G10 grips, 25 LPI checkering on front strap and mainspring housing, left side ext. thumb safety, slide features window cuts and heavy angled lightening cuts, DLC finish, 38.2 oz. New 2020.

MSR $4,199	$3,775	$3,300	$2,825	$2,575	$2,075	$1,700	$1,400	

GRADING - PPGS™	100%	98%	95%	90%	80%	70%	60%	LAST MSR

VIP (VERY IMPRESSIVE PISTOL) – .45 ACP cal., 5 in. crowned barrel, 14K gold-plated front bead sight, Heinie black rear sight, giraffe bone grips, deep hand engraving featured throughout, custom vertical front strap and mainspring serrations, hand serrated rear of slide and ejector, classic antique nickel finish, includes custom cocobolo hardwood presentation case. Limited mfg. 2016, reintroduced 2019.

MSR $7,999 $7,200 $6,300 $5,400 $4,895 N/A N/A N/A

VIP AGENT 2 – .45 ACP cal., forged Government frame with lightened Recon rail, 5 in. match grade barrel, 10 shot mag., drop-in trigger system, Nighthawk/Agency custom trigger, 18K solid gold bead front sight, solid black Heinie Ledge rear sight, mammoth ivory grips, Railscales G10 grips, Agency front and rear cocking serrations, ultra hi-cut front strap, matching texture on front strap, back strap, and controls, includes custom case, Turnbull color case hardened and polished frame, high polished charcoal blued slide stop, thumb safety, and mag. release, 39.6 oz. Limited mfg. in partnership between Nighthawk Custom, Turnbull Restoration, and Agency Arms beginning late 2020.

MSR $8,499 $7,650 $6,695 $5,740 $5,200 N/A N/A N/A

VIP BLACK – .45 ACP cal., 5 in. crowned barrel, 14K gold front bead sight, Heinie black Slant Pro rear sight, giraffe bone grips, deep hand engraving featured throughout, custom vertical front strap and mainspring serrations, hand serrated rear of slide and ejector, Black Diamond Like finish, includes custom walnut hardwood presentation case, 8.66 in. OAL. New 2019.

MSR $7,999 $7,200 $6,300 $5,400 $4,895 $3,960 $3,240 $2,665

WAR HAWK CCO (WAR HAWK COMPACT/OFFICER) – .45 ACP cal., 4 1/4 in. barrel, stainless steel Officer size frame, one-piece mainspring housing/magwell, Heinie Slant Pro night rear and Tritium front sights, Everlast Recoil System, solid aluminum match grade trigger, tri-cut slide with bold angles, heavy bevel on bottom of slide, thin G10 grips in Hyena Brown, War Hawk logo engraved on slide, black Nitride finish, 34.7 oz. Mfg. 2015-2016, reintroduced 2019 only.

MSR $3,999 $3,600 $3,150 $2,700 $2,450 $1,975 $1,625 $1,325 ***$3,895***

WAR HAWK GOVERNMENT – .45 ACP cal., full size Government frame, 5 in. barrel, one-piece mainspring housing/magwell, solid aluminum match grade trigger, Everlast Recoil System, multi-faceted slide, serrated arrow style slide top, heavy bevel on bottom of slide, War Hawk logo engraved on slide, aggressive G10 grips in Hyena Brown, tactical magazine catch, Jardine Hook rear sight and red fiber optic front sights, black Nitride finish, 39.6 oz. Mfg. 2015-2016, reintroduced 2019.

MSR $3,999 $3,600 $3,150 $2,700 $2,450 $1,975 $1,625 $1,325

* ***War Hawk Recon*** – .45 ACP cal., 5 in. barrel, one-piece mainspring housing/magwell, solid aluminum match grade trigger, multi-faceted slide, serrated arrow style slide top, War Hawk logo engraved on slide, Everlast Recoil System, aggressive G10 grips in Hyena Brown, Jardine black rear sight and red fiber optic front, integrated recon accessory rail, extended tactical mag catch, black Nitride finish, 39.6 oz. Mfg. 2015-2016, reintroduced 2019.

MSR $4,099 $3,690 $3,230 $2,775 $2,510 $2,030 $1,660 $1,365

REVOLVERS

In late 2016, Nighthawk Custom announced that it would be importing a line of Korth revolvers manufactured in Germany - please refer to listings in the Korth section.

RIFLES: BOLT ACTION

HUNTING RIFLE – various cals., bolt action, available in Hunting, Varmint, and Bench Rest configurations, Broughton barrel, synthetic stock. Mfg. 2011-2012.

$3,500 $3,100 $2,650 $2,250 $1,800 $1,375 $1,125 ***$3,895***

TACTICAL RIFLE – .308 Win., 7mm Rem. Mag., .300 Rem. Mag., or .338 Lapua cal., with or w/o Surgeon action, with or w/o bolt on Picatinny rail with choice of 0 or 20 MOA integral elevation, Jewell trigger, Perma Kote finish in choice of Desert Sand, OD Green, Sniper Gray, Desert camo, Woodland camo, or Urban camo finish, tactical synthetic stock with adj. comb. Mfg. 2009-2011.

$3,800 $3,350 $2,900 $2,500 $2,000 $1,500 $1,225 ***$4,250***

Add $550 for short Surgeon action.
Add $595 for 100% coverage Custom woodland or digital camouflage finish.
Add $625 for Magnum Surgeon action.
Add $650 for long Surgeon action.
Add $875 for XL action in .338 Lapua cal.

SHOTGUNS

OVERSEER MODEL 1 SLIDE ACTION SERIES – 12 ga., hand honed action and rails, 6 shot mag., two shot extension tube, Nighthawk's black custom tactical ghost ring rear sight and front red fiber optic sight, Hogue overmolded stock, receiver mounted Picatinny rail, 6 round side shell carrier, black Cerakote finish. New 2016.

MSR $1,499 $1,275 $1,115 $950 $865 $700 $600 $500

GRADING - PPGS™	100%	98%	95%	90%	80%	70%	60%	LAST MSR

* ***Overseer Model 2*** – 12 ga., similar to Overseer Model 1, except has SGA Magpul stock and forend upgrade with black finish and adaptor plates. New 2016.

MSR $1,699	$1,450	$1,275	$1,095	$985	$800	$650	$560	

* ***Overseer Model 2.5*** – 12 ga., similar to Overseer Model 1, except has Vang Comp System barrel port upgrade, SGA Magpul stock and forend with adapter plates, 39.25 in. OAL. New 2018.

MSR $1,899	$1,615	$1,415	$1,225	$1,100	$900	$725	$630	

* ***Overseer Model 3*** – 12 ga., similar to Overseer Model 1, except has SGA Magpul stock and forend upgrade with adaptor plates, custom Shadow Tan camo stock finish. New 2016.

MSR $1,999	$1,700	$1,490	$1,275	$1,155	$935	$775	$660	

* ***Overseer Model 4*** – 12 ga., similar to Overseer Model 1, except has SGA Magpul stock and forend upgrade with adaptor plates, Surefire Z2X combat light (320 Lumens, LED), barrel clamp with swivel and Picatinny rail, and custom Shadow Urban camo stock finish. New 2016.

MSR $2,199	$1,875	$1,640	$1,400	$1,275	$1,025	$850	$735	

* ***Overseer Model 5*** – 12 ga., similar to Overseer Model 1, except has SGA Magpul stock and forend upgrade with adaptor plates, custom Battle Worn Silver Patriot Complete finish. New 2016.

MSR $2,099	$1,785	$1,550	$1,325	$1,200	$950	$800	$700	

* ***Overseer Model 6*** – 12 ga., similar to Overseer Model 1, except has collapsible stock upgrade with Hogue pistol grip, Surefire forend (DSF870) light and forend for 870, includes ambidextrous momentary/constant on switches, isolated selector switch for high (600 lumens) and low (200 lumens) output modes, breeching device with 3-shot extension. New 2016.

MSR $2,199	$1,875	$1,640	$1,400	$1,275	$1,025	$850	$735	

TACTICAL SLIDE ACTION – 12 ga., reworked 3 in. chambered action for faster, smoother cycling, Hogue overmolded style stock with 12 or 14 in. LOP, Big Dome large safety, 2-shot extension, fully adjustable and protected ghost ring rear sight with red fiber optic front, 4 or 6 round shell carrier, Rust-Proof ceramic finish in a variety of colors including camo, (Hillbilly223 camo finish became standard in 2014). Disc. 2015.

	$1,250	$1,090	$940	$850	$690	$560	$490	*$1,450*

Add $35 for Tritium front sight upgrade.
Add $75 for Picatinny rail on top of receiver.
Add $85 for magazine clamp with rail & swing swivel.
Add $125 for breaching tool.
Add $125 for Surefire Tactical light with ring mount.
Add $165 for 5-position stock.

TACTICAL SEMI-AUTO – 12 ga., 2 3/4 in. chamber, 18 in. barrel, pistol grip synthetic stock, Surefire forend weapon light, hand tuned action, rust-proof ceramic finish in a variety of colors including camouflage patterns, tactical charging handle on the bolt, fully adjustable and protected ghost ring rear sight, red fiber optic front sight, 2-shot extension, 4 or 6 round shell carrier. Disc. 2011.

	$1,785	$1,550	$1,325	$1,200	$950	$800	$700	*$2,060*

Add $35 for Tritium front sight blade.
Add $75 for Picatinny rail on top of receiver.
Add $299 for Surefire forend tactical weapon light.

TOMAHAWK SLIDE ACTION – 12 ga., 16 in. barrel, Vang Comp barrel porting and backbore, 5 shot mag., front bead sight, Hogue overmolded pistol grip and forend, big button tactical safety, 4-round side saddle, solid billet extension tube to match barrel length, black Cerakote finish. Mfg. 2017-2018.

MSR $1,475	$1,250	$1,090	$940	$850	$690	$560	$490	*$1,395*

NIKKO FIREARMS CO., LTD.

Previous manufacturer located in Tochigi, Japan circa 1958-1989.

NIKKO HISTORY AND GENERAL INFORMATION

The publisher wishes to thank the Golden Eagle Collectors Association for providing this publication with the information listed. Please refer to the Golden Eagle heading in this text for information on Nikko manufactured Golden Eagle firearms.

Both Nikko Firearms Co., Ltd. and Nikko Arms Co., Ltd. were trade names used by the Kodensha Co., Ltd. of Tochigi, Japan on products they manufactured and distributed worldwide. Nikko is the name of the Prefecture, or district, in which Tochigi City is located, about 50 miles north of Tokyo. The word Nikko translates to English as "sunshine." Kodensha first manufactured or distributed under the Nikko name in April 1955, and exported out of Japan beginning in August 1958. Nothing is known of the origin of the Kodensha Co.

Kodensha first approached the American shotgun market in 1958 or 1959 using the Japanese export marketing firm of Kyowa-Boeki-Bussan. They contacted various U.S. distributors, and in about 1959 or 1960, Continental Arms Co. of New York City began importing the Nikko "Grade 5." Continental imported these Nikko over/unders, in various models and configurations, until about 1972.

In 1962, the Kodensha Co., Ltd. formed a joint venture with Olin/Winchester of New Haven, CT to produce the Winchester Model 101 over/under shotgun. This venture was known as the Olin- Kodensha Co. Ltd. Added a little later was the side-by-side Model 23, and the Model 96 Xpert (a budget priced 101). The "pre-Olin" Kodensha factory was considerably outdated, and the joint venture began a complete modernization process, with the financial and technical assistance of Olin. Millions of dollars of machinery and technology were brought in, and the entire manufacturing process was upgraded to the then current standards.

One of the conditions of the joint venture was that Kodensha restrict their own products (made in the same factory, but recorded separately from the joint venture) to sell in Japan only. At the outset of the 25 years that the joint venture existed, Kodensha was probably amenable to this, as they were reaping huge financial and technical benefits from Olin. But, by the mid 1960s, when the factory was in place and running smoothly, Kodensha essentially ignored that condition of the agreement, leaving Olin at somewhat of a disadvantage, not wanting to jeopardize their investment or production source. Additionally, Olin/Winchester was allowed only two permanent personnel, hardly enough to monitor the activities of a factory which employed up to 400 people. As an example, when walnut stock blanks arrived from France, Kodensha took first pick, and Olin got what was left over.

Kodensha converted an existing building near the manufacturing plant into an assembly area for Nikko, and other brands of guns. This building was probably the "true" Nikko Firearms Co., Ltd. Manufactured components from the Olin-Kodensha factory were carted to the Nikko plant for final assembly and fitting. This "dual-factory" arrangement continued until the mid 1980s. In 1981, for an unknown reason, the Olin-Kodensha name was changed to OK Firearms Co. Ltd. In October 1987, Olin/Winchester sold their interest in OK Firearms to Classic Doubles International, which continued making the 101 style shotgun under their own name. For reasons unknown, Classic Doubles went out of business in December 1988. Shortly thereafter, the entire factory was torn down.

During the "dual-factory" days, Nikko produced firearms for the following distributors or retailers: 1) Kanematsu Gosho of Arlington Heights, IL approx. 1974-1982 - distributed Nikko brand shotguns, Golden Eagle brand shotguns and rifles (1975 through March 1977 only); 2) Golden Eagle Firearms, Houston, TX March 1977 through early 1981 - Golden Eagle shotguns and rifles; 3) Tradewinds, Inc. of Tacoma, WA exported from Japan by Caspoll International, Tokyo January 1971 through December 1972 - Shadow Seven; Shadow Indy (Model 707); Gold, Silver, and Black Shadow over/ under shotguns; 4) Marubeni America, Inc. of New York City 1972-1974 - Miida brand over/under shotguns; 5) Winchester GMBH of West Germany, manufactured by Olin-Kodensha (dates unknown - early 1980s) - Winchester Model 777 rifle (Golden Eagle look-alike); 6) Parker Reproduction shotguns, distributed in the US by Reagent Chemical & Research, Inc. 1984-1988; 7) International Star Commerce Corp. (ISCC) of Salt Lake City, Utah approx. 1982 - distributor of Nikko brand shotguns; 8) Moore Supply Co. of Salt Lake City, UT beginning mid-1981 - distributor of Nikko brand shotguns; 9) USA Nikko, Inc. of Los Angeles, CA (factory reps and distributors of Nikko shotguns), initial date unknown, through December 1981; 10) Weatherby, Inc. of Los Angeles, CA May 1972 to 1981. Centurion semi-auto and Patrician pump shotguns, some Mark 22 rifles. Olympian O/U shotgun and possibly other O/Us from 1978-81. Model 82 semi-auto and Model 92 pump shotguns; 11) Savage Industries of Hamden, CT 1981-1982 - Savage/ Fox FA-1 and FP-1 shotguns; 12) Charles Daly. "Automatic" distributed by Sloans (Japanese made only) mid-1980s; 13) Sears, Roebuck Co. Ted Williams Model 400 and possibly others; 14) Churchill semi-auto, imported by Kassnar mid-1980s; 15) High Standard of Hamden, CT 1974-75 - Supermatic Shadow Indy (Model 707, an O/U), Supermatic Shadow Seven (also O/U), and Supermatic Shadow semi-auto.

NOTE: ALL of the semi-auto shotguns used essentially the same design. Each distributor may have made a few cosmetic or dimensional embellishments to differentiate their gun. Differences exist in barrel/breech fit, magazine caps, pistol grip caps, checkering pattern, piston size, ejector location, fluted bolt. Use caution if interchanging parts. Generally, the same statement can be made about the pump versions also.

GRADING - PPGS™	100%	98%	95%	90%	80%	70%	60%	LAST MSR

NOBLE MFG. CO.

Previous manufacturer and importer of Spanish SxS shotguns located in Haydenville, MA 1953-1971.

Noble manufactured semi-auto, lever, and slide action rifles and slide action shotguns, in addition to importing Spanish SxS shotguns. Shotgun models included the Model 420, 420 EK, and 450 E. While most models were relatively inexpensive, good working, utilitarian guns, there has been little collectibility to date and most rifles are seen priced in the $75-$295 price range while the shotguns are priced in the $125-$350 range, depending on gauge and features.

NOR-CAL PRECISION

Previous manufacturer and riflesmith circa 1989-2009 and located in American Canyon, CA.

Nor-Cal Precision manufactured custom rifles based on the Rem. M700 action, in addition to a variety of gunsmithing services.

NOREEN FIREARMS LLC

Current bolt action and AR-15 style rifle manufacturer located in Belgrade, MT.

RIFLES: BOLT ACTION

ELR (EXTREME LONG RANGE) – .50 BMG, .50 DTC, .416 Barrett, .408 CheyTac, .375 CheyTac, or .338 Lapua cal., based on the McMillan receiver inlet, 34 in. barrel, Noreen muzzle brake, 5 shot double stack mag., Timney Remington 700, adj. folding stock, 4140 hardened steel receiver and fluted one-piece bolt, Cadex or XLR chassis, black finish, 31 lbs. New 2019.

MSR $6,500	$5,500	$4,850	$4,150	$3,750	$3,050	$2,500	$1,950	

ULR (ULTRA LONG RANGE) – .338 Lapua (disc. 2020), .408 CheyTac (disc. 2020), .416 Barrett (disc. 2020), .50 DTC (disc. 2017), or .50 BMG cal., single shot, 32 (disc.) or 34 in. button rifled chrome moly barrel, Noreen muzzle brake, tactical black or desert camo finish, shell holder bolt, Timney adj. trigger, Picatinny top rail, folding rotating bipod, collapsible shoulder stock, A2 grip, 32 lbs.

MSR $2,175	$1,850	$1,625	$1,400	$1,275	$1,025	$850	$700	

Add $204 for .408 CheyTac, .338 Lapua, or .416 Barrett cal., all disc. 2020.

ULR EXTREME – .50 BMG, .50 DTC (disc. 2017), .416 Barrett, .408 CheyTac, or .338 Lapua Mag. cal., single shot, 34 in. barrel with muzzle brake, barrel shroud, Timney adj. trigger, fully adj. XLR folding stock, cheek rest, and recoil pad, Ergo grip, XLR chassis system, top Picatinny rail, black finish, 32 lbs. Disc. 2020.

	$3,400	$2,975	$2,550	$2,310	$1,875	$1,525	$1,200	*$4,000*

RIFLES: SEMI-AUTO

BAD NEWS GEN II (BAD NEWS ULTRA LONG RANGE - ULR) – .300 Win. Mag. (disc.), .338 Norma (mfg. 2014-2015), or .338 Lapua cal., side charging, one-piece bolt carrier, GPO, 26 in. barrel, custom muzzle brake, 5 or 10 shot detachable box mag., aluminum receiver, Mil-Spec (disc.) or match (new 2016) trigger, Magpul PRS adj. stock, A2 grip, Picatinny quad rail on handguard, matte black finish, 13 lbs.

MSR $6,255	$4,700	$3,725	$3,325	$2,925	$2,750	$2,550	$2,300	

In 2016, this model's nomenclature changed to Bad News Gen II because it received upgraded receivers, handguard, billet magazines, and a new adj. gas block.

BBN223 – 5.56x45mm cal., DI, 16 in. barrel, Noreen flash hider, 30 shot mag., Mil-Spec trigger, Magpul MBUS flip-up sights, 6-position collabsible stock, A2 pistol grip, sling mounts, matte black finish, 6 lbs. New 2016.

MSR $1,375	$1,025	$825	$725	$650	$600	$550	$500	

BN36 CARBINE ASSASSIN – .30-06 cal., GIO, 16 in. barrel with flash hider, 20 shot mag., Mil-Spec trigger, enlarged trigger guard, collapsible stock, A2 pistol grip, black finish, 7 lbs. Mfg. 2016-2017.

	$1,325	$1,050	$925	$825	$775	$700	$650	*$1,750*

BN36 CARBINE ASSASSIN-X – .30-06 cal., GIO, 16 in. barrel with flash hider, 20 shot mag., Mil-Spec trigger, Luth-AR stock, Tactical Dynamics pistol grip, black finish, 7 lbs. Mfg. 2016-2017.

	$1,550	$1,225	$1,100	$950	$900	$825	$750	*$2,050*

BN36X3 CARBINE – .30-06 cal., AR-10, DI, side charging, 16 in. barrel, flash hider, 20 shot mag., Mil-Spec trigger, optional sights, composite stock, A2 pistol grip, black finish, 7 lbs. New mid-2018.

MSR $1,895	$1,425	$1,125	$1,000	$900	$825	$775	$700	

GRADING - PPGS™	100%	98%	95%	90%	80%	70%	60%	LAST MSR

BN36X3 CARBINE X – .30-06 or .300 Win. Mag. (new 2019) cal., GIO, side charging, 16 in. barrel with flash hider, 5, 10, or 20 shot mag., Mil-Spec trigger, with or w/o sights, Luth-AR stock, Tactical Dynamics pistol grip, black finish, 7 lbs. New mid-2018.

MSR $2,255	$1,700	$1,350	$1,200	$1,050	$1,000	$925	$825	

Add $620 for .300 Win. Mag. cal.

BN36X3 CARBINE X FEATURELESS – .30-06 cal., GIO, side charging, 16 in. barrel with Noreen muzzle brake, 20 shot mag., match grade trigger, Thordsen barrel, black finish, 7 lbs. New 2018.

MSR $2,455	$1,850	$1,450	$1,300	$1,150	$1,075	$1,000	$900	

BN36X3 LONG RANGE (BN36 LONG RANGE ASSASSIN/BN36 SEMI-AUTO) – .25-06 Rem., .270 Win., .30-06, .300 Win. Mag., or 7mm Rem. Mag. (New 2016) cal., DI, side charging, 22 in. barrel, Noreen design muzzle brake, 5, 10, or 20 shot box mag., Mil-Spec or optional match trigger, fixed A2 (disc.) or Luth-AR stock with pistol grip, matte black finish, 9 lbs. New 2013.

MSR $2,254	$1,700	$1,350	$1,200	$1,050	$975	$925	$825	

Add $621 for .300 Win. Mag. or 7mm Rem. Mag. cal.

BN308 – .308 Win. cal., GIO, 16 in. barrel with flash hider, 20 shot mag., Mil-Spec trigger, Luth-AR stock, Tactical Dynamics pistol grip, updated forearm (new 2016) with Picatinny rail, Type III hardcoat anodized black finish, 8 lbs. Mfg. 2015-2020.

	$1,625	$1,275	$1,150	$1,000	$950	$875	$800	*$2,150*

BN408 - "THE BEAST" – .408 CheyTac cal., piston driven, side charging semi-auto, 28 in. barrel with black Nitride finish, Noreen muzzle brake, 10 shot double stack billet mag., match trigger, adj. AR-15 collapsible stock, A2 pistol grip, monolithic upper receiver, continuous Picatinny rail, ambidextrous controls, includes rear monopod and bipod, black oxide finish, 23 lbs. New 2016.

MSR $13,495	$12,150	$10,925	$9,850	$8,850	$7,550	$6,400	$5,400	

NORICA LAURONA

Previous firearms and current airgun manufacturer established in 1917 and located in Eibar, Spain. Norica changed its name to Norica Laurona in 2010. Norica started making airguns in 1917, and acquired the Laurona trademark in 2010.

For more information and current pricing on both new and used Norica airguns, please refer to the *Blue Book of Airguns* - also available as an online subscription.

NORINCO

Current division of China North Industries Corp. established in 1981, and located in Beijing, China. Norinco currently manufactures small arms and large military weapons for commercial, law enforcement, and military applications. No current U.S. importation. Distributed exclusiely throughout Europe by Norconia GmbH established during 1988, and located in Rottendorf, Germany. Previously imported and distributed exclusively by Interstate Arms Corp., located in Billerica, MA. Previous importers have included: Norinco Sports U.S.A., located in Diamond Bar, CA, Century International Arms, Inc. located in St. Albans, VT; China Sports, Inc. located in Ontario, CA; Interarms located in Alexandria, VA; KBI, Inc. located in Harrisburg, PA; and others.

Norinco pistols, rifles, and shotguns are manufactured in the People's Republic of China by China North Industries Corp. (Norinco has over 100 factories). Currently, due to government legislation, Norinco cannot legally sell weapons in the U.S.

PISTOLS: SEMI-AUTO

MODEL 213 – 9mm Para. cal., Tokarev style pistol, single action, left side thumb safety, satin blue finish, Imported 1988 only.

	$325	$225	$185	$150	$125	$115	$105	*$200*

Add 10% for NIB condition.

TYPE 54-1 TOKAREV STANDARD – 7.62x25mm Tokarev or .38 Super cal., Tokarev style pistol, single action, 4 1/2 in. barrel, 8 shot mag., fixed sights, blue finish, 29 oz., Imported 1989-95.

	$375	$325	$275	$250	$200	$175	$125	*$145*

Add 25% for .38 Super cal.

* ***Type 54-1 (213A Model) Tokarev Standard Double Column*** – 7.62x25mm Tokarev, .38 Super, or 9mm Para. cal., Tokarev style pistol, single action, 4 1/2 in. barrel, 10 (C/B 1994) or 13* shot mag., fixed sights, - similar to Standard Model, blue finish, 35 oz. Imported 1991-95.

	$400	$350	$300	$275	$225	$185	$140	*$185*

Add 10% for NIB condition.

GRADING - PPGS™	100%	98%	95%	90%	80%	70%	60%	LAST MSR

* ***Type 54-1 (213/201C/54T Model) Tokarev Standard Compact*** – .38 Super, 9mm Para., or 7.62x25mm Tokarev cal., Tokarev style pistol, single action, 3.8 in. barrel, 8 shot mag., 27 oz. Imported 1991-95.

$325	$275	$250	$225	$180	$150	$120	*$185*

Add 10% for NIB condition.

TYPE 59 MAKAROV – 9x18mm Makarov or .380 ACP cal., double action semi-auto, Makarov style pistol, 3 1/2 in. fixed barrel, 8 shot mag., heel mag release, steel frame and slide, fixed or adj. rear sight, checkered plastic grips, blued finish, 24 oz. Imported 1989-95.

$575	$500	$425	$400	$325	$275	$200	*$185*

Add 10% for Beta Arms import w/adj. sights.

TYPE 77B – 9mm Para. cal., single action, striker fired, gas-delayed blowback action, unique trigger guard similar to the older Chylewski/Bergmann/Lignose "Einhand" pistols permitting one handed operation of the slide by pulling the trigger guard rearward, 5 in. barrel, 8 shot single stack mag., adj. rear sight, black plastic grips, mag. disconnect safety, thumb safety, blued finish, 34 oz. Limited importation 1991-95.

$900	$575	$475	$400	$350	$300	$250	*$285*

MODEL 1911 A1 – .45 ACP cal. only, patterned after the Colt 1911 A1, 5 in. barrel, 7 shot mag., fixed sights, blue or parkerized finish, wood grips, 39 oz. Imported 1991-95.

$625	$550	$475	$425	$375	$325	$300	*$320*

RIFLES: SEMI-AUTO

TYPE 84S AKS RIFLE – .223 Rem. cal., semi-auto Kalashnikov action, 16.34 in. barrel, hardwood stock and pistol grip, 30 shot mag., 1,000 meter adj. rear sight, includes bayonet and sheath, 8.87 lbs. Imported 1988-89 only.

$1,450	$1,250	$1,150	$1,000	$925	$875	$795	*$350*

* ***Type 84S-1 AKS Rifle*** – similar to Type 84S AKS except has under-folding metal stock. Imported 1989 only.

$1,600	$1,500	$1,400	$1,250	$1,100	$1,000	$900	*$350*

* ***Type 84S-3 AKS Rifle*** – similar to Type 84S AKS except has fixed composite fiber stock (1 1/2 in. longer than wood stock). Imported 1989 only.

$1,295	$1,100	$1,000	$950	$900	$800	$750	*$365*

* ***Type 84S-5 AKS Rifle*** – similar to Type 84S AKS except has side-folding metal stock with plastic cheekpiece. Imported 1989 only.

$1,600	$1,500	$1,450	$1,350	$1,200	$1,100	$1,000	*$350*

NHM-90/91 (AK-47 THUMBHOLE) – .223 Rem. or 7.62x39mm cal., long stroke GPO, Kalashnikov style action, 16 or 20 in. Chrome-lined barrel, 5 shot mag., thumbhole stock for legalized import, Imported 1991-1993, configuration was restyled and renamed NHM-90/91 in 1994. Disc.

$750	$675	$575	$500	$450	$350	$300	*$375*

NHM-90/91 SPORT – 7.62x39mm cal., choice of 16.34 (NHM-90) or 23.27 (NHM-91) in. barrel, hardwood thumbhole stock, NHM-91 has bipod, 5 shot mag., 9-11 lbs. Imported 1994-95.

$550	$500	$450	$425	$385	$350	$325	

The .223 Rem. cal. was also available for the Model NHM-90. Each Model NHM-90/91 was supplied with three 5 shot mags., sling, and cleaning kit.

MODEL 320 THUMBHOLE – 9mm Para. cal., patterned after the Uzi, features sporterized thumbhole wood stock, 10 shot mag. Importation 1995 only.

$1,000	$925	$875	$840	$775	$725	$675	*$625*

Add $100 for original box and accessories.

R.P.K. RIFLE – 7.62x39mm cal., includes bipod. Importation disc. 1993.

$1,200	$1,000	$900	$800	$725	$650	$600	*$600*

TYPE 56 CARBINE (SKS) – .223 Rem. or 7.62x39mm cal., SKS action, 20.47 in. barrel, 10 (C/B 1994) or 30* shot mag., 1,000 meter adj. rear sight, hardwood stock, new design accepts standard AK mag., with or w/o folding bayonet, 8.8 lbs. Imported 1988-1989, reintroduced 1992-95 with Sporter configuration stock.

$475	$400	$350	$325	$300	$250	$225	*$150*

Add $100 for synthetic stock and bayonet.
Subtract 15% if refinished.

GRADING - PPGS™ 100% 98% 95% 90% 80% 70% 60% *LAST MSR*

TYPE 81S AKS RIFLE – 7.62x39mm cal., semi-auto Kalashnikov action, 17 1/2 in. barrel, 5, 30, or 40 shot mag., 500 meter adj. rear sight, fixed wood stock, hold open device after last shot, 8 lbs. Imported 1988-1989.

$1,200 $1,000 $900 $800 $725 $650 $600 *$385*

* ***Type 81S-1 AKS Rifle*** – similar to Type 81S AKS except has under-folding metal stock. Imported 1988-89.

$1,300 $1,075 $950 $850 $750 $625 $575 *$385*

TYPE 56S-2 – 7.62x39mm cal., older Kalashnikov design with side-folding metal stock. Importation disc. 1989.

$1,500 $1,350 $1,200 $1,100 $1,000 $900 $800 *$350*

TYPE 86S-7 RPK RIFLE – 7.62x39mm cal., AK action, 23.27 in. heavy barrel with built-in bipod, in-line buttstock, 11.02 lbs. Imported 1988-1989.

$1,500 $1,275 $1,075 $950 $850 $750 $650 *$425*

TYPE 86S BULLPUP RIFLE – 7.62x39mm cal., long stroke GPO, Kalashnikov action, bullpup configuration, 17.25 in. barrel, two 20 shot mags., stamped steel construction, carry handle with integral sights, stamped buttplate with cleaning kit carrier, folding foregrip, AK pattern pistol grip, right side safety lever above trigger, straight or curved ambidextrous charging handle, blued finish, box also comes with oil bottle, Chinese sling, and bayonet, 7 lbs. Imported 1989 only.

$2,850 $2,500 $2,200 $1,950 $1,750 $1,600 $1,300 *$400*

NDM-86 DRAGUNOV (MODEL 350) – 7.62x54mm Russian or .308 Win. cal., short stroke GPO, 24 in. barrel with flash hider, detachable 10 shot mag., milled steel receiver, rear tangent sight, hooded post front sight, gloss laminated skeletonized wood stock with vent. forearm, right side lever safety, 8 lbs. 9 oz., Importation disc. 1995.

$7,500 $6,575 $5,625 $5,100 $4,125 $3,375 $2,625 *$3,080*

This model was also imported by Gibbs Rifle Co. located in Martinsburg, WV.

* ***Dragunov Carbine*** – similar to Dragunov rifle, except shorter barrel, various accessories including a lighted scope were also offered, plastic furniture.

OFFICERS NINE – 9mm Para. cal., 16.1 in. barrel, action patterned after the IMI Uzi, 32 shot mag., black military finish, 8.4 lbs. Limited 1988-89.

$1,100 $995 $850 $725 $650 $575 $500 *$450*

RIFLES: .22 CAL.

MODEL EM-321 – .22 LR cal., slide action, 19 1/2 in. barrel, 10 shot tube mag., hardwood stock and forearm, fixed sights, 6 lbs. Importation began 1989-90, resumed 1994-disc.

$200 $175 $150 $135 $110 $90 $70

TYPE EM-332 – .22 LR cal., bolt action, 18 1/2 in. barrel with adj. rear sight, mag. holder on stock holds two extra 5 shot mags., Monte Carlo stock with cheekpiece and recoil pad, 4 1/2 lbs. Imported 1991-93.

$280 $250 $215 $190 $150 $125 $100

SHOTGUNS: O/U

TYPE HL12-203 – 12 ga. only, 2 3/4 in. chambers, boxlock action, ejectors, 30 in. vent. barrels and rib, single trigger, multi-chokes, checkered stock and forearm, 7 1/2 lbs. Imported 1989-1993.

$400 $350 $300 $265 $225 $200 $185

SHOTGUNS: SEMI-AUTO

MODEL 2000 FIELD – 12 ga. only, 2 3/4 in. chamber, steel receiver and aluminum alloy trigger guard, 26 or 28 in. VR barrel with M choke tube, choice of black synthetic or checkered hardwood stock and forearm, approx. 7 1/2 lbs. Limited importation 1999 only.

$260 $230 $200 $185 $170 $160 $150 *$299*

Add $8 for wood stock and forearm.

Choke tubes are interchangeable with the WinChoke system.

* ***Model 2000 Field Defense*** – 12 ga. only, 2 3/4 in. chamber, 18 1/2 in. barrel with cyl. choke tube and choice of bead, rifle, or ghost ring sights, matte black metal finish, black synthetic stock and forearm with recoil pad. Limited importation 1999 only.

$245 $225 $190 $175 $160 $155 $145 *$282*

Add $5 for rifle sights.

Add $17 for ghost ring sights.

GRADING - PPGS™	100%	98%	95%	90%	80%	70%	60%	LAST MSR

SHOTGUNS: SLIDE ACTION

TYPE HL12-102 – 12 ga. only, 2 3/4 in. chamber, 28.4 in. barrel, 3 shot mag., crossbolt safety on rear trigger guard, fixed chokes, 9.3 lbs. Imported 1989-93.

	$230	$200	$175	$165	$150	$135	$120	

MODEL 97 (M97) – 12 ga., 2 3/4 in. chamber, clone of Winchester M1897, 20 in. barrel, spur hammer, wooden stock and forearm, heat shield, M1917 pattern bayonet lug., blued finish. Disc.

	$550	$480	$425	$375	$300	$250	$180	

MODEL 98 FIELD – 12 ga. only, 3 in. chamber, 26 or 28 in. VR barrel with M choke tube, choice of black synthetic or uncheckered hardwood stock and forearm with recoil pad, approx. 7 lbs. Limited importation 1999 only.

	$185	$160	$140	$125	$110	$100	$90	*$205*

Add $8 for wood stock and forearm.

Add $55 for Field Combo (includes extra 18 1/2 in. barrel) or $82 for Field Combo with 22 in. slug or turkey barrel.

* ***Model 98 Field Turkey*** – similar to Model 98 Field, except has 22 in. VR barrel with extra full choke tube, black synthetic stock and forearm only. Limited importation 1999 only.

	$190	$165	$140	$125	$110	$100	$90	*$216*

* ***Model 98 Field Defense*** – 12 ga. only, 3 in. chamber, 18 1/2 in. barrel with cyl. choke tube and choice of bead, rifle, or ghost ring sights, matte black metal finish, black synthetic stock and forearm with recoil pad. Limited importation 1999 only.

	$170	$150	$130	$115	$100	$90	$80	*$190*

Add $15 for ghost ring sights.

MODEL 983 – 12 ga. only, 22 in. barrel with external rifled choke tube and adj. rifle sights, synthetic black stock. Limited importation 2002 only.

	$215	$170	$155	$135	$125	$105	$95	*$230*

MODEL 984/985/987 – 12 ga. only, 3 in. chamber, field series with 26 or 28 in. VR barrel and M choke tube, black synthetic or uncheckered hardwood stock and forearm, matte black metal finish. Limited importation 2001-2002.

	$200	$170	$155	$135	$125	$105	$95	*$235*

Add $10 for hardwood stock (Models 985 & 987).

NORINCO USA

Previous manufacturer located in Jefferson City, MO.

Retired Marine Jon Morgan applied for the Norinco trademark circa 2007 to be used for firearms manufactured in the U.S. However, no production firearms were manufactured using the Norinco name.

NORSMAN SPORTING ARMS & OUTFITTERS

Current rifle manufacturer/customizer located in Havre, MT since 1999. Previously located in Bismarck, ND until 1999. Consumer direct sales.

Norsman specializes in both wood and synthetic takedown rifles and multiple barrel/caliber configurations, in addition to a SxS double rifle and falling block rifle. Please contact the factory directly for additional information, prices, and delivery time.

RIFLES: BOLT ACTION

VIKING GRADE – most standard cals., unique NSA takedown action, many options, including left-hand models, custom orders also available.

MSR $8,000	$7,500	$6,750	$5,750	$5,250	$4,500	$3,750	$3,000	

Add $1,500 per interchangeable barrel.

VIKING GRADE MAGNUM – most standard Mag. cals., unique NSA takedown action, many options and custom orders available, including left-hand.

MSR $10,800	$10,250	$9,250	$8,000	$6,750	$5,500	$4,500	$3,500	

Add $2,000 per interchangeable barrel.

FIELD GRADE SYNTHETIC – most standard cals., unique NSA takedown action, many options and custom orders available.

MSR $4,250	$3,850	$3,350	$2,850	$2,500	$2,100	$1,850	$1,500	

Add $1,200 per interchangeable barrel.

GRADING - PPGS™	100%	98%	95%	90%	80%	70%	60%	LAST MSR

ODIN GRADE – .223 Rem. - .505 Gibbs cal., available in right or left-hand Mauser style action, presentation grade walnut stock, match grade barrel, competition trigger, three position wing safety, quarter rib with banded ramped front sights, barrel band swivel, gold monogram stock oval, metal pistol grip cap, leather covered recoil pad, hand cut checkering, quick detachable scope bases and rings, engraving with gold inlays. New 2003.

MSR $12,500	$11,500	$10,000	$8,500	$7,750	$6,500	$5,500	$4,150	

THOR GRADE – .223 Rem. - .416 Rem. cal., right or left-hand Mauser style action, extra fancy grade walnut stock, premium match grade barrel, competition trigger, three position wing safety, quarter rib with banded ramped front sights, barrel band swivel, metal pistol grip cap, rubber recoil pad, hand cut checkering, quick detachable scope bases and rings. New 2003.

MSR $10,200	$9,500	$8,500	$7,500	$6,500	$5,500	$4,500	$3,500	

TYR GRADE – .223 Rem. - .416 Rem. cal., right or left-hand Mauser style action, fiber core or Kevlar wrapped composite stock, premium match grade barrel, competition trigger, Teflon all-weather coating on metal and stock, adj. rear and banded ramped front sights, three position wing safety, swivel studs, rubber recoil pad, quick detachable scope bases and rings. New 2003.

MSR $7,900	$7,350	$6,450	$5,600	$4,750	$3,950	$3,250	$2,400	

VOYAGER GRADE – .223 Rem. - .416 Rem. cal., Mauser style titanium action, fiber core or Kevlar wrapped composite stock, premium match grade barrel, competition trigger, Teflon all-weather coating on metal and stock, adj. rear and banded ramped front sights, three position wing safety, swivel studs, rubber recoil pad, quick detachable scope bases and rings. New 2003.

MSR $12,500	$11,500	$10,000	$8,500	$7,750	$6,500	$5,500	$4,150	

RIFLES: SxS

VIKING GRADE – most standard cals. including .30-30 WCF, .30-40 Krag, .375 Win., .444 Marlin, .45-70 Govt., as well as traditional European NE cals. up to .600 NE, built per individual custom order. New 2000.

MSR $24,500	$22,550	$19,750	$16,400	$14,000	$12,000	$10,000	$8,500	

RIFLES: SINGLE SHOT

VIKING GRADE – standard cals. include .30-30 WCF, .30-40 Krag, .375 Win., .444 Marlin, or .45-70 Govt. cal., European cals. up to .600 NE also available, falling block Farquharson action, bespoke quality, built per individual custom order. New 2011.

MSR $24,500	$22,550	$19,750	$16,400	$14,000	$12,000	$10,000	$8,500	

NORTH AMERICAN ARMS, INC.

Current manufacturer established circa 1976, and currently located in Provo, UT. Distributor and dealer sales.

North American Arms was originally founded under the name Rocky Mountain Arms circa 1974-1975 by noted handgun entrepreneur Dick Casull. During 1976-1977, the company's name was changed to North American Arms, and it became part of the Tally Corp. of Newbury Park, CA. North American Arms was relocated from Salt Lake City to Provo, UT in 1978, and moved again in 1984 to Spanish Fork, UT. During 1986-1987, Teleflex Corp., an aerospace company, bought North American Arms' parent company, the Tally Corp. In 1992, Teleflex decided to sell off the gunmaking company, and North American Arms was purchased by Sandy Chisholm, a Teleflex employee. The company relocated again in 1994 to Provo, UT.

PISTOLS: SEMI-AUTO

All pistols are manufacturerd using stainless steel. In addition to many accessories being available for the Guardian Pistol Series, there is also a Guardian Custom Shop that offers consumers a customized Guardian model, with a wide variety of finish, slide, sight, grips, and serialization options. Please contact the company directly for more information on these custom shop special orders and options.

NAA .25 GUARDIAN – .25 NAA cal., DAO, 2.2 in. barrel, 6 shot, stainless steel construction, hammerless, Novak 3-dot night sights, dimpled black synthetic grips, 13 1/2 oz. New 2006.

MSR $409	$360	$315	$265	$240	$195	$160	$125	

NAA .32 GUARDIAN – .32 ACP cal., DAO, hammerless, smalll frame, stainless steel construction, 6 shot mag., 2 1/2 in. barrel, fixed low profile or XS Big Dot Tritium sights, dimpled black synthetic grips, 18.7 oz. New 1997.

MSR $409	$360	$315	$265	$240	$195	$160	$125	

Add $28 for ILS (integral locking system) option.
Add $129 for XS Big Dot Tritium sights (mfg. 2014-2019).

GRADING - PPGS™	100%	98%	95%	90%	80%	70%	60%	LAST MSR

NAA .32 NAA GUARDIAN – .32 NAA cal. (.380 ACP casing necked down to .32 cal.), DAO, larger version of the NAA .32 Guardian, 2.49 in. barrel, 6 shot mag., dimpled black grips, 18.7 oz. New 2002.

MSR $456	$390	$340	$290	$260	$210	$175	$135	

NAA .380 GUARDIAN – .380 ACP cal., DAO, larger version of the NAA .32 Guardian, 2.49 in. barrel, 6 shot mag., dimpled black grips, mfg. in partnership with Kahr Arms, 18.7 oz. New 2001.

MSR $456	$390	$340	$290	$260	$210	$175	$135	

Add $30 for ILS (integral locking system) option.

REVOLVERS: MINI SERIES

All NAA mini revolvers are manufactured from stainless steel to the highest quality control standards and have safety notches between chambers on the rear face of the cylinder allowing the hammer to lock up the cylinder between cartridges. This allows the gun to be carried fully loaded without the danger of accidental discharge.

MINI-MASTER BLACK WIDOW – .17 HMR (new 2003-disc.), 17 Mach 2 (new 2005-disc.), .22 LR or .22 WMR cal., 2 in. heavy VR barrel, fixed or adj. rear sight, full size black rubber grip, stainless or black PVD (True Black Widow, new 2019) finish, 8.8 oz. New 1991.

MSR $288	$245	$215	$185	$165	$135	$110	$85	

Add $24 for adj. rear sight (elevation only).
Add $30 for black PVD finish (new 2019).
Add $35 for extra combo cylinder.

This model was also available in hot fuschia colored oversized grips.

MINI-MASTER TARGET REVOLVER – .17 HMR (mfg. 2003-2009), .17 Mach 2 (mfg. 2005-2009), .22 LR, or .22 WMR cal., 4 in. heavy vent. barrel, unfluted bull cylinder, 5 shot, spur trigger, Marble Arms fixed or adj. white outline rear sight, oversized black rubber Mini-master grip, 10.7 oz. New 1990.

MSR $298	$250	$220	$190	$170	$140	$115	$90	

Add $34 for extra combo cylinder.
Add $30 for adj. rear sight (elevation only) and $65 for extra combo cylinder w/adj. rear sight.

This model was also available in hot fuschia colored oversized grips.

NAA .17 – .17 HMR or .17 Mach 2 cal., otherwise similar to NAA .22 Model. Mfg. 2005-2008.

	$155	$135	$115	$105	$85	$70	$55	*$193*

Add $22 for holster grip accessory.
Add $15 for .17 HMR cal.
Add $43 for .17 HMR cal. with extra .17 Mach 2 conversion cylinder.

NAA .22 S/LR – .22 Short (new 1994) or .22 LR cal., SA, 1 1/8, 1 5/8, or 2 1/2 (disc.) in. barrel with blade front and notched rear sight, 5 shot, stainless steel, spur trigger, blade front and notched rear sight, plastic (disc.) or laminated rosewood grips, approx. 4 1/2 oz. New 1975.

MSR $226	$195	$170	$145	$135	$100	$90	$70	

Add $15 for 2 1/2 in. barrel (disc.).
Add $30 for holster grip accessory.
Add $65 for quick-release belt buckle option (1 1/8 in. barrel only, disc.).

The optional holster grip allows the pistol to fold forward allowing concealability, safety, and has a clip which allows it to be attached to a belt.

NAA .22 MAGNUM – similar to .22 LR, except in .22 WMR cal., barrel porting became available during 2012, 6.5 oz.

MSR $236	$200	$175	$150	$135	$110	$90	$70	

Add $20 for ported barrel.
Add $35 for .22 LR/M conversion.
Add $30 for holster grip combination and $65 for holster grip combination conversion.
Add $18 for 2 1/2 in. barrel (disc.).

NAA .22 MAGNUM CONVERTIBLE – similar to NAA .22 WMR cal., except has extra LR cylinder in pouch. Disc. 2015.

	$215	$190	$165	$145	$115	$95	$75	*$261*

Add $18 for 2 1/2 in. barrel (disc.).
Add $30 for holster grip accessory.

NAA .22 MAGNUM SET – .22 Mag./.22 LR cal., SA, 5 shot, half-moon sight, rosewood bird's head grips, in walnut display case, high polish finish w/matte contours, 6.5 oz.

MSR $450	$380	$335	$285	$260	$210	$175	$150	

GRADING - PPGS™	100%	98%	95%	90%	80%	70%	60%	LAST MSR

CASED .22 MAG. – includes .22 WMR cal. model in walnut display case with high polish finish with matte contours. Disc.

	$335	$295	$250	$230	$185	$150	$125	*$392*

NAA DELUXE SET – 3 gun set (.22 Short, .22 LR, and .22 WMR cals.) in walnut display case with matching serial numbers, high polish finish on entire gun.

MSR $975	$830	$725	$625	$565	$455	$375	$325	

NAA PUG – .22 WMR cal., 1 in. standard or ported barrel, Tritium or white dot XS sight system, oversized pebble textured rubber grips, 6.4 oz. New mid-2007.

MSR $328	$280	$245	$210	$190	$155	$125	$100	

Add $19 for Tritium sights or $20 for ported barrel.
Add $32 for .22 LR/M conversion cylinder (new 2021).

NAA RANGER – .22 WMR cal., pivoting top-break action, 1 5/8 in. barrel, 5 shot, spur trigger, half-moon fixed sights, laminated grips, 7.2 oz. Limited mfg. 2011 only.

	$425	$365	$325	$285	$250	$225	$195	*$499*

NAA RANGER II – .22 WMR cal., pivoting top-break action, SA, 1 5/8, 2 1/2 (new 2021), or 4 (new 2021) in. standard (disc. 2020) or full-ribbed (new 2021) barrel, 5 shot, star ejector, spur trigger, fixed bead sights, rosewood bird's head grip, 6.9 oz. New late 2017.

MSR $479	$425	$365	$325	$285	$250	$225	$195	

Add $40 for 2 1/2 in. or $70 for 4 in. barrel.
Add $95 for extra .22 LR conversion cylinder.

NAA SINGLE ACTION REVOLVER – .45 Win. Mag. or .450 Mag. Express cal., polished stainless steel, transfer bar safety inside the hammer, 5 shot, 7 1/2 in. barrel, walnut grips, includes presentation case. Disc. 1984.

Matte finish	$1,200	$1,050	$900	$815	$660	$540	$420	
High polish finish	$1,400	$1,225	$1,050	$950	$770	$630	$490	
Both cylinders	$1,650	$1,445	$1,240	$1,120	$910	$745	$580	*$650*

This model was also available by special order with 10 1/2 in. barrel and optional scope. Extra cylinders were also available at $75-$100 and were fitted to the gun. A set including 2 cylinders could also be ordered. North American Arms cannot perform any repair work on .450 Mag. Express revolvers.

NAA STANDARD SET – 3 gun set (.22 Short, .22 LR, and .22 WMR cals.) in walnut display case with matching serial numbers, high polish finish with matte contours.

MSR $850	$725	$635	$550	$500	$400	$325	$280	

PORTED SNUB – .22 WMR cal., 5 shot, 1 1/8 in. ported barrel, bead front fixed sights, 6.2 oz. Mfg. 2012-2015.

	$210	$185	$160	$145	$120	$100	$80	*$246*

Add $35 for extra combo cylinder.

SIDEWINDER – .22 WMR cal., features a swing-out style cylinder assembly, 1 1/2, 2 1/2, or 4 in. barrel, stainless steel construction, 5 shot, stainless post sights, smooth walnut grips. New 2013.

MSR $350	$300	$265	$225	$200	$185	$170	$165	

Add $39 for 2 1/2 or 4 in. barrel.
Add $95 for .22 LR/M conversion cylinder assembly.
Add $158 for .22 Mag. conversion.

THE EARL – .22 WMR cal., 5 shot, SA, 2 1/2 (Sheriff Model, new 2012), 3, 4, or 6 (Hogleg Model, new 2012) in. heavy octagon barrel, stainless steel frame, wood grips, top strap channel, bead front sight, push-button latch (Sheriff Model only) or faux loading lever secures cylinder pin, available with or w/o .22 LR cal. conversion cylinder, approx. 9 oz. New 2009.

MSR $298	$255	$225	$190	$175	$140	$115	$100	

Add $24 for Cap & Ball configuration with 4 in. barrel.
Add $34 for .22 LR conversion cylinder.
Add $10 for Hogleg Model (new 2012) and $46 if w/extra .22 LR conversion cylinder.

THE WASP – .22 WMR cal., 1 1/8 (Wasp Snub) or 1 5/8 in. VR barrel, spur trigger, skeleton hammer, 5 shot, features black cylinder flutes and black lines on revolver, cylinder and lower shroud, stainless post front sight with notched rear, dimpled black synthetic grips, 6.4 oz. New 2011.

MSR $266	$230	$200	$175	$155	$125	$110	$90	

Add $35 for extra .22 LR conversion cylinder.

GRADING - PPGS™	100%	98%	95%	90%	80%	70%	60%	LAST MSR

NORTH AMERICAN SAFARI EXPRESS

Previous trademark for those rifles (SxS) assembled by A. Francotte of Belgium for exclusive importation by Armes de Chasse located in Chadds Ford, PA.

NORTHERN COMPETITION

Previous AR-15 style rifle manufacturer located in Racine, WI.

Please refer to BlueBookOfGunValues.com to order the *Blue Book of AR-15s & Variations*, available as a book or online subscription.

NORTHWEST ARMS

Please refer to Wilkinson Arms listing in the W section.

NOSLER, INC.

Current handgun, rifle, ammunition, and bullet manufacturer established during 1948, located in Bend, OR.

Founded in 1948, Nosler, Incorporated is a family owned company. Nosler is most known for revolutionizing the hunting bullet industry with bullets such as the Partition®, Ballistic Tip®, AccuBond®, E-Tip®, and most recently the AccuBond® LR. With the company motto of "Quality First", Nosler manufactures premium component bullets, reloading brass, ammunition, and semi-custom rifles, including AR-15 style rifles, for domestic and international customers making Nosler a comprehensive shooting products company.

Recent company caliber releases include the following: .26 Nosler - 2014, .28 Nosler - 2015, .30 Nosler - 2015, .33 Nosler - 2016, .22 Nosler - 2017, and .27 Nosler - 2020.

HANDGUNS: BOLT ACTION

M48 NCH (NOSLER CUSTOM HANDGUN) – .22 Nosler, .24 Nosler, 7mm-08 Rem., 6mm Creedmoor, 6.5 Creedmoor, or .308 Win. cal., single shot, 15 in. free floated Shilen stainless steel heavy barrel, threaded at the muzzle with thread protector, 12-18 in. barrels and fluting available upon request, solid bottom receiver, precision CNC machined single billet aluminum one-piece stock, black Hogue overmolded grips with finger grooves, Cerakote finish in variety of color options, 5.4 lbs. Mfg. 2019-2020.

	100%	98%	95%	90%	80%	70%	60%	LAST MSR
	$2,125	**$1,850**	**$1,600**	**$1,450**	**$1,175**	**$950**	**$825**	*$2,495*

M48 INDEPENDENCE HANDGUN – .22 Nosler, .24 Nosler, 6mm Creedmoor, 6.5 Creedmoor, 7mm-08 Rem., or .308 Win. cal., 15 in. stainless steel heavy contour barrel, threaded muzzle, one-piece billet aluminum stock, AR grips, NIC Industries Cerakote finish, 6 1/2 lbs. New 2019.

	100%	98%	95%	90%	80%	70%	60%
MSR $1,800	**$1,525**	**$1,335**	**$1,145**	**$1,035**	**$840**	**$700**	**$600**

RIFLES: BOLT ACTION

Nosler also has a Custom Firearm shop that enables customers to have individual guns built-to-order. Please contact the company directly for more information, availability, and pricing.

MODEL 48 SERIES – various cals., features NoslerCustom Model 48 push feed action, 3 or 4 shot mag., 24-26 in. barrel w/o sights, standard, 2, or 3-position safety, Rifle Basix or Timney trigger, various synthetic or wood stocks, Cerakote and Microslick metal coating. Guaranteed accuracy at 100 yards, available in production and Custom configurations, approx. 6 1/4-8 3/4 lbs. New 2005.

* ***Model 48 Custom*** – various cals. (.22 Nosler and .33 Nosler introduced 2017), 20-26 in. match grade stainless steel barrel, 3 or 4 shot mag., hand tuned trigger pull, no sights, Kevlar/carbon fiber stock in various colors or fancy walnut stock, glass and stainless steel pillar bedding, available in Long Range, Expedition, High Country, and Brush Country packages, Cerakote and Micro Slick metal finish, 6.5-7.5 lbs. Disc. 2020.

	100%	98%	95%	90%	80%	70%	60%	LAST MSR
	$2,200	**$1,925**	**$1,650**	**$1,500**	**$1,210**	**$1,000**	**$850**	*$2,595*

Add $700 for left-hand action (Kevlar/carbon fiber stock only).

* ***Model 48 Custom Varmint*** – .204 Ruger, .223 Rem., or .22-250 Rem. cal., 3 or 4 shot mag., Coyote tan Kevlar/carbon fiber stock, Graphite Black or Coyote Tan Cerakote finish, 7 1/4 lbs. Disc. 2011.

	100%	98%	95%	90%	80%	70%	60%	LAST MSR
	$2,650	**$2,200**	**$1,800**	**$1,450**	**$1,150**	**$1,000**	**$900**	*$2,995*

* ***Model 48 Custom Brush Country Package*** – recommended cals. include .30-06, .35 Whelen, 9.3x62mm, or .375 Ruger, NoslerCustom push feed action, 22 in. heavy contour barrel, hinged floorplate, adj. fiber optic sights, Onyx color Kevlar/carbon fiber stock with C2 finish, custom LOP, includes Leupold VX-6 1-6x24mm #4 dot scope, Leupold QR scope base and rings, two boxes of Nosler ammo, Pelican hard case, and Nosler leather sling. Limited mfg. 2015-2016.

	100%	98%	95%	90%	80%	70%	60%	LAST MSR
	$4,300	**$3,900**	**$3,500**	**$3,100**	**$2,675**	**$2,275**	**$1,675**	*$5,035*

GRADING - PPGS™	100%	98%	95%	90%	80%	70%	60%	LAST MSR

* ***Model 48 Custom Expedition Package*** – recommended cals. include .30-06, .300 Win., or .338 Win. cal., NoslerCustom push feed action, 24 in. Magnum contoured barrel with removable muzzle brake, hinged floorplate, Obsidian color Kevlar/carbon fiber stock with C2 finish, custom LOP, includes Talley steel scope base and steel quick detach scope rings, Swarovski Z5 3.5-18x44BT 4W scope, two boxes of Nosler ammo, Pelican hard case, and leather sling. Limited mfg. 2015-2016.

	$4,700	$4,250	$3,750	$3,225	$2,800	$2,400	$1,850	*$5,535*

* ***Model 48 Custom High Country Package*** – recommended cals. include .26 Nosler, .270 WSM, 7mm-08 Rem., or .308 Win., NoslerCustom push feed action, 24 or 26 in. Magnum contoured barrel with removable muzzle brake, hinged floorplate, Onyx color Kevlar/carbon fiber stock with C2 finish, custom LOP, includes Talley steel scope base and quick detach scope rings, Zeiss Conquest HD5 3-15x42 scope, two boxes of Nosler ammo, Pelican hard case, and Nosler leather sling. Limited mfg. 2015-2016.

	$4,325	$3,925	$3,500	$3,100	$2,675	$2,275	$1,675	*$5,075*

* ***Model 48 Custom Long Range Package*** – recommended cals. are .26 Nosler, .28 Nosler, and .300 WSM, NoslerCustom push feed action, 26 in. magnum contoured barrel with removable muzzle brake, 3 or 4 shot mag., Woodland color Kevlar/carbon fiber stock with C2 finish, custom LOP, Picatinny scope base, includes Nightforce lightweight rings, Nightforce SHV 4-14x56 scope, two boxes of Nosler ammo, Pelican hard case, and Nosler leather sling. Limited mfg. 2015-2016.

	$4,400	$3,975	$3,525	$3,100	$2,675	$2,275	$1,675	*$5,185*

* ***Model 48 Heritage*** – .22 Nosler (new 2017), 6mm Creedmoor, 6.5 Creedmoor, .26 Nosler, .270 Win., .27 Nosler, .280 Ackley Imp., 7mm Rem. Mag., .28 Nosler, .308 Win., .30-06, .300 WSM, .300 Win. Mag., .30 Nosler, or .33 Nosler (new 2017), 24 in. stainless steel match grade free floated barrel, target crown, hinged floorplate, hand oiled fancy walnut stock with 20 LPI checkering, Pachmayr Decelerator recoil pad, 2-position Rocker safety, Graphite Black Cerakote finish. New 2014.

MSR $2,095	$1,785	$1,550	$1,324	$1,200	$950	$800	$700	

* ***Model 48 Independence Day Rifle*** – .22 Nosler cal., Nosler Model 48 custom action, 24 in. stainless match grade barrel, threaded muzzle, Timney trigger, Kryptek Highlander dipped synthetic stock, 2-position Rocker safety, laser engraved hinged floorplate with the motto "We The People" above an American flag, glass and aluminum pillar bedding, Cerakote All-Weather finish. Limited mfg. of only 25. Mfg. mid-2017 only.

	$1,700	$1,475	$1,250	$1,100	$975	$825	$650	*$1,995*

* ***Model 48 Legacy*** – various cals., 24 in. standard or heavy barrel, no sights, deluxe checkered walnut stock, 3-position safety, special engraved floorplate bearing the signature of John A. Nosler, Midnight Blue Cerakote finish, 7 1/2-8 lbs. Disc. 2013.

	$2,295	$2,000	$1,725	$1,550	$1,250	$1,025	$800	*$2,695*

* ***Model 48 Liberty*** – various cals. from .22-250 Rem. to .35 Whelan cal. (.22 Nosler and .33 Nosler were introduced 2017), 24 in. stainless match grade barrel, hinged floorplate, lightweight Aramid fiber reinforced composite stock, 2-position Rocker safety, glass and aluminum pillar bedding, Cerakote All-Weather finish. Mfg. 2016-2020.

	$1,650	$1,450	$1,250	$1,125	$910	$750	$650	*$1,935*

» **Model 48 Liberty 26 Nosler SHV Package** – .26 Nosler cal., includes M48 Liberty or Custom rifle, Nightforce SHV 4-14x56 with illuminated MOAR reticle, Nightforce X-Treme Duty Ultralite scope rings and two-piece 20 MOA scope base. Mfg. 2016-2018.

	$3,150	$2,700	$2,300	$2,000	$1,750	$1,500	$1,225	*$3,695*

» **Model 48 28 Nosler VX-6 Package** – .28 Nosler cal., includes Model 48 Liberty rifle with custom engraved CDS turret, .28 Nosler logo is laser etched on the scope tube, Leupold VX-6 3-18x44 CDS-ZL with illuminated Wind-Plex Reticle, Leupold Dual-Dovetail rings and base. Mfg. 2016-disc.

	$3,225	$2,750	$2,325	$2,000	$1,750	$1,500	$1,225	*$3,795*

* ***Model 48 Long Range*** – 6.5 Creedmoor, .26 Nosler, .28 Nosler, .300 Win. Mag., .30 Nosler, or .33 Nosler cal., short or long action, 26 in. stainless match grade Shilen heavy barrel, Timney trigger, Manners MCS-T stock, two-position Rocker safety, hinge floorplate, graphite Cerakote finish. Mfg. 2017-2020.

	$2,275	$1,990	$1,700	$1,550	$1,250	$1,025	$875	*$2,675*

GRADING - PPGS™	100%	98%	95%	90%	80%	70%	60%	LAST MSR

* ***Model 48 Long Range Carbon*** – 6.5 Creedmoor, 6.5 PRC (new 2021), .26 Nosler, .27 Nosler (new 2020), .28 Nosler, .300 Win. Mag., .30 Nosler, or .33 Nosler cal., Model 48 custom action, 26 in. Proof Research light Sendero contour, carbon fiber-wrapped match grade barrel, threaded muzzle, hinged floorplate, Timney trigger, Manners MCS-T Elite Tac carbon fiber stock in Elite Midnight camo finish, 2-pos. safety, Cerakote Sniper Grey finish on action and bottom metal. New 2018.

MSR $3,285	$2,795	$2,450	$2,095	$1,900	$1,535	$1,260	$1,100	

* ***Model 48 Mountain Carbon*** – 6mm Creedmoor, 6.5 Creedmoor, 6.5 PRC (new 2021), .26 Nosler, .27 Nosler (new 2020), .280 Ackley Imp. (new 2021), .28 Nosler, .300 Win. Mag., .30 Nosler, or .33 Nosler cal., M48 action, 24 in. light Sendero contour carbon fiber wrapped barrel with threaded muzzle, hinged floorplate, Timney trigger, carbon fiiber reinforced Mountain Hunter stock in Granite Green or Shale Gray (new 2021), two-position safety, glass and aluminum pillar bedding, Tungsten Grey Cerakote finish on all steel surfaces, 6 lbs. New 2019.

MSR $3,235	$2,750	$2,400	$2,065	$1,875	$1,515	$1,275	$1,075	

* ***Model 48 Outfitter*** – .308 Win. (disc. 2016), .30-06, .338 Win. Mag., .35 Whelen, 9.3x62mm (disc. 2016), .375 Ruger (disc. 2016), or .458 Win. Mag. (disc. 2016) cal., 22 in. stainless match grade barrel, blind-bottom internal magazine, adj. open sights, black and spiderweb gray Bell & Carlson lightweight Aramid fiber reinforced composite stock, 1 in. recoil pad, 2-position Rocker safety, glass and aluminum pillar bedding, Cerakote All-Weather finish. Mfg. 2013-2017.

	$1,700	$1,475	$1,250	$1,100	$975	$825	$650	*$1,995*

* ***Model 48 Patriot*** – various cals., stainless match grade barrel, lightweight Aramid fiber reinforced composite stock, 2-position Rocker safety, glass and aluminum pillar bedding, hinged floorplate, Cerakote All-Weather finish. Mfg. 2014-2015.

	$1,525	$1,325	$1,125	$995	$800	$650	$525	*$1,795*

* ***Model 48 Professional*** – various cals., features black Bell & Carlson composite stock, matte black Cerakote finish, no sights, 6 1/2 -7 1/2 lbs. Mfg. 2012-2013.

	$2,295	$2,000	$1,725	$1,550	$1,250	$1,025	$800	*$2,695*

Add $100 for detachable magazine.
Add $200 for factory installed muzzle brake.

* ***Model 48 Trophy*** – various cals., 24 in. barrel, blind bottom magazine, Timney adj. trigger, no sights, black and spiderweb gray Bell & Carlson composite stock, magnesium color Cerakote finish, 6 1/2-7 lbs. Disc. 2013.

	$1,800	$1,575	$1,300	$1,050	$875	$750	$625	*$1,995*

Add $200 for factory installed muzzle brake.

* ***Model 48 Western*** – 6.5 Creedmoor, .26 Nosler, .280 Ackley Imp., 7mm Rem. Mag., .28 Nosler, .300 Win. Mag., .30 Nosler, or .33 Nosler cal., short or long action, 24 1/2 in. stainless match grade Helical fluted barrel w/removable muzzle brake, Timney trigger, synthetic sporter lightweight composite stock, two-position Rocker safety, hinge floorplate, graphite Cerakote all-weather finish. Mfg. 2017-2018.

	$1,700	$1,475	$1,250	$1,100	$975	$825	$650	*$1,995*

NCR - NOSLER CUSTOM RIFLE (CUSTOM LIMITED EDITION SERIES) – .280 Ackley Improved (Series 2), .300 WSM (Series 1, limited quantities), or .338 Win. Mag. (Series 3) cal., NoslerCustom barreled action, 24 in. match grade stainless steel barrel, one-piece steel hinged floorplate, no sights, fancy checkered American black walnut stock with forend and pistol grip caps, Pachmayr Decelerator recoil pad, subtle palm swell and shadow line cheekpiece, 3-position Rocker safety, integral Leupold QD scope mounts, shipped in Kalispel Aluminum (disc.) or Pelican hard case with leather sling, Cerakote and Micro Slick finishes, 9 lbs. Only 500 of each series mfg. (ser. no. range 001-500). Limited mfg. 2005-2016.

	$4,200	$3,800	$3,350	$2,875	$2,475	$2,150	$1,750	*$4,495*

Add $200 for Series 1 in .300 WSM cal. (limited quantities).

The Series 1 rifle comes with a Leupold VXIII 2.5-8x36 scope calibrated for the Nosler ammunition sold with the rifle.

The Series 2 rifles comes with a Leupold VXIII 2.5-8x36, VXIII 3.5-10x40, or VXIII 4.5-14x40 scope, calibrated for the Nosler ammunition sold with the rifle.

The Series 3 rifle comes with Leupold VXIII 2.5-8x36mm, VXIII 3.5-10x40, or VXIII 4.5-14x40 scope, calibrated for the Nosler ammunition sold with the rifle.

SANCTUARY EDITION SERIES – .270 WSM cal. only, 24 in. barrel, no sights, fancy grade checkered bubinga wood stock with forend and pistol grip caps, Pachmayr Decelerator recoil pad, integral Leupold QD scope mounts, only 25 mfg. (ser. no. range 001-025 w/SE prefix), shipped in Americase hard case with Leupold LPS or VX7 scope., matte black Cerakote finish. Mfg. 2012-2014.

	$5,100	$4,500	$4,000	$3,450	$2,950	$2,650	$2,250	*$5,495*

GRADING - PPGS™	100%	98%	95%	90%	80%	70%	60%	LAST MSR

RIFLES: SEMI-AUTO

VARMAGEDDON AR – .22 Nosler cal., 18 in. barrel with muzzle and thread protector, Precision Reflex 25 shot mag., Geissele SD-E trigger, MBUS Pro sights, Magpul PRS Gen 3 stock, Magpul MOE grip, STS ambi safety, Picatinny 9-slot rail, NSR 15 in. KeyMod handguard, Super Badass charging handle, quick detach sling swivels, KeyMod quick release swivel mount, KeyMod sling stud, includes NSR polymer accessory pack, soft case, and sling, FDE finish. Built by Noveske Rifleworks. Mfg. 2017-2018.

	100%	98%	95%	90%	80%	70%	60%	LAST MSR
	$2,525	$2,275	$2,075	$1,900	$1,575	$1,250	$975	*$2,870*

VARMAGEDDON 5.56 NATO – 5.56 NATO cal., AR-15 style, GIO, 18 in. stainless steel barrel, Geissele SD-E trigger, Magpul PRS stock, adj. LOP and comb, MOE grip, Noveske Gen III upper and lower receiver with Picatinny rail and integrated 13 1/2 in. NSR handguard with KeyMod system, extended feed ramp. Mfg. 2013-2016.

	100%	98%	95%	90%	80%	70%	60%	LAST MSR
	$2,650	$2,375	$2,175	$1,975	$1,650	$1,300	$1,025	*$2,995*

Add $900 for package with Leupold Varmageddon scope and CDS turret.

VARMEGEDDON .300 AAC BLACKOUT – .300 AAC Blackout cal., AR-15 style, GIO, 16 in. stainless steel barrel, Geissele SD-E trigger, Magpul STR stock features two storage compartments, adj. LOP, MOE grip, Noveske Gen. III upper and lower receiver with Picatinny rail and integrated 13 1/2 in. NSR handguard with KeyMod system, extended feed ramp. Mfg. 2013-2016.

	100%	98%	95%	90%	80%	70%	60%	LAST MSR
	$2,650	$2,375	$2,175	$1,975	$1,650	$1,300	$1,025	*$2,995*

Add $900 for package with Leupold Varmageddon scope and CDS turret.

NOVESKE RIFLEWORKS LLC

Current AR-15 style firearm manufacturer located in Grants Pass, OR.

Please refer to BlueBookOfGunValues.com to order the *Blue Book of AR-15s & Variations*, available as a book or online subscription.

NOWLIN MFG., INC.

Previous custom handgun manufacturer. Nowlin Guns continues to manufacture a wide variety of pistol components. The company was established in 1982, is currently located in Okmulgee, OK. Previously located in Claremore, OK.

PISTOLS: SEMI-AUTO

Nowlin discontinued all its pistols in late 2010. The following is a listing of its products with last MSRs. Nowlin Mfg., Inc. manufactured a complete line of high quality M1911 A1 styled competition and defense pistols, available in 9mm Para., 9x23mm, .38 Super, .40 S&W, or .45 ACP cal. Various frame types are available, including a variety of Nowlin choices. Recent models (available in blue or nickel finish) included the NRA Bianchi Cup (approx. 1997 retail was $2,750 - disc.), 007 Compact ($1,395 - disc.), Compact X2 ($1,436 - disc.), Match Classic ($1,695 - disc. 2010), Crusader ($1,999 - disc. 2010), Avenger w/STI frame ($2,279 - disc. 2010), Challenger ($2,049 - disc. 2010), World Cup PPC ($2,219 - disc. 2010), STI High Cap. Frame ($1,595 - disc. 1999), Mickey Fowler Signature Series ($2,187 - disc. 2010), Compact Carry ($1,695 - disc. 1999), Compact 4 1/4 in. ($1,750, .45 ACP, disc. 2002), Gladiator ($1,447 in .45 ACP cal., disc. 2002), Match Master ($2,795 - disc. 2010), Bianchi Cup Master Grade ($5,019, .38 Super cal., disc. 2010) and the Custom Shop Excaliber Series ($3,029 - disc. 2010).

NUOVA JAGER

Current AR-15 and AK-47 style rifle, carbine, and parts manufacturer located in Basaluzzo, Italy. No current U.S. importation.

Nuova Jager manufactures high quality AR-15 style rifles in various calibers and configurations. Please contact the factory directly for more information, including pricing and U.S. availability.

O SECTION

O'BRIEN RIFLE CO.

Previous bolt action rifle manufacturer located in Las Vegas, NV circa 1966-1971.

RIFLES: BOLT ACTION

Vern O'Brien manufactured high quality bolt action rifles, many of which were chambered for proprietary calibers, including the .17 Mach 4, .17 Javelina, .17-222, .17-222 Mag., and .17-223. There were basically two grades - a Field Grade with rosewood forend tip and pistol grip, and a Presentation Grade with basket weave checkering, Javelina inlaid in the stock opposite the cheekpiece, and a diamond inlaid below the action. All rifles were based on the Sako L-461 action. Circa 1971, Vern O'Brien sold his company to H&R, which produced a rifle similar to his called the 317 Ultra Wildcat. Values are hard to predict in today's marketplace because so few are encountered. A starting price range for the Standard Grade is $1,200-$1,600, and $2,500-$4,000+ for the Presentation Grade (Model 317P Grade).

O.D.I. (OMEGA DEFENSIVE INDUSTRIES)

Previous manufacturer located in Midland Park, NJ circa 1981-82.

Essex Arms, located in Island Pond, VT, acquired the remaining O.D.I. Viking inventory of parts for the Viking pistol, in addition to being a components supplier (slides and receivers) for M-1911 styled pistols. Previously, Randco Manufacturing, located in Monrovia, CA, was providing service (and had parts) for these older O.D.I. pistols.

GRADING - PPGS™	100%	98%	95%	90%	80%	70%	60%	LAST MSR

PISTOLS: SEMI-AUTO

VIKING & VIKING COMBAT – .45 ACP or 9mm Para. (advertised, but never mfg.) cal., design utilizes the Seecamp double action, Government size (Viking Model), Commander size (Viking Combat Model), 4 1/4 (Viking Combat Model) or 5 in. (Viking Model) barrel, 7 shot mag., all stainless steel construction, teakwood grips, 39 oz. Approx. 200-300 Viking Combat Models were made from kits.

	100%	98%	95%	90%	80%	70%	60%	LAST MSR
	$495	$385	$295	$240	$210	$180	$155	*$579*

Add $100 for slide with crossbolt safety.

OBERLAND ARMS

Current manufacturer located in Huglfing, Germany. Previously located in Habach, Germany. No current U.S. importation.

Oberland Arms manufactures a wide variety of high quality rifles, including an OA-10 and OA-15 series based on the AR-15 style carbine/rifle. Oberland Arms also used to manufacture pistols. Many rifle options and configurations are available. Please contact the company directly for more information, including pricing, options, and U.S. availability.

OBREGON

Previously manufactured by Fabrica de Armas Mexico located in Mexico City, Mexico.

PISTOLS: SEMI-AUTO

OBREGON – 11.43mm cal., Savage/Steyr type action, patterned after the Colt Model 1911A2, tubular slide marked "Sistema Obregon Cal 11.43mm". 1,000 pistols mfg. in Mexico for commercial sale during and after WWII.

	100%	98%	95%	90%	80%	70%	60%	LAST MSR
	$4,750	$4,250	$3,750	$3,250	$2,750	$2,250	$1,750	

OBSIDIAN ARMS

Current AR-15 style and bolt action rifle and parts manufacturer established in 2013, located in Little Canada, MN.

Please refer to BlueBookOfGunValues.com to order the *Blue Book of AR-15s & Variations*, available as a book or online subscription.

OHIO ORDNANCE WORKS, INC.

Current rifle and related components manufacturer established in 1981, and located in Chardon, OH.

Ohio Ordnance Works also manufactures machine guns, components, and accessories.

RIFLES: SEMI-AUTO

Many of Ohio Ordnance Works models are made-to-order and pricing can change based on a number of factors. Please contact the manufacturer directly for most recent pricing and availability.

GRADING - PPGS™	100%	98%	95%	90%	80%	70%	60%	LAST MSR

MODEL BAR 1918A3 SLR – .30-06 cal., patterned after the original Browning BAR (M1918A2) used during WWI, all steel construction utilizing original parts except for the receiver, 24 in. barrel, original folding type rear sight, matte metal and wood finish, Bakelite or American walnut stock and forearm, 20 lbs.

MSR $4,300 $3,650 $3,195 $2,750 $2,475 $2,000 $1,650 $1,275

Add $598 for 1918A3 SLR Bundle - includes two 20 shot mags., two 30 shot mags., carrying handle, web sling, bipod, flash hider, bolt open hold device, cleaning kit, and custom cut pelican case.

COLT 1918 SLR (MODEL BAR A1918 SLR) – .30-06 cal., 24 in. barrel, flash hider, two 20 shot mags., all steel construction utilizing original parts except for the receiver, two-stage trigger, front post and folding type rear sight, Bakelite (disc. 2007) or American walnut stock and forearm, includes web sling, cleaning kit, and deluxe case, royal blue metal finish, 16 lbs. Mfg. 2005-2007, reintroduced 2015-2018.

$8,250 $7,225 $6,200 $5,600 $4,550 $3,725 $2,300 *$8,799*

MODEL 1928 BROWNING – .30-06, 7.65mm, .308 Win., or 8mm (disc.) cal., semi-auto action patterned after the 1928 Browning watercooled machine gun, blue (disc.) or parkerized finish, includes tripod, water hose, ammo can, 3 belts, and belt loader. Limited production late 2001-2007.

$3,750 $3,400 $3,000 $2,650 $2,300 $2,100 $1,900 *$4,000*

Add $200 for .308 Win. or 8mm (disc.) cal.

Add approx. $2,000 for blue finish (limited mfg.).

MODEL M-240 SLR – 7.62 NATO cal., belt fed, gas operated, 20 in. barrel, adj. sights, air cooled, fires from closed bolt, sling, cleaning kit, ruptured case extractor, gas regulator cleaning tool, disassembly tools, 2500 M-13 links, custom fit hard case, 24.2 lbs. New 2007.

MSR $13,918 $11,850 $10,375 $8,895 $8,000 $6,800 $5,600 $4,500

MODEL VZ2000/VZ2000 SBR – 7.62x39mm cal., Czech VZ 58 copy, new milled receiver, original barrels, heat cured paint finish (matches original Czech finish), choice of wood-impregnated resin furniture with fixed or folding stock or pistol grip with quad Picatinny rail and vertical grip (VZ2000 Tactical), includes four 30 shot mags., pouch, sling, cleaning kit, original bayonet, 6 lbs. Disc. 2014.

$1,600 $1,400 $1,200 $1,100 $875 $725 $575 *$1,026*

MODEL 1917A1 WATERCOOLED – .30-06 or .308 Win. cal., semi-auto copy of the military 1917A1 machine gun, various packages are available. Mfg. 2011-2012.

$6,500 $5,750 $5,000 $4,650 $4,250 $3,850 $3,450 *$5,000*

Add $1,005 for deluxe package including 1917A1 tripod.

Add $1,500 for "The Works" package including 1917A1 tripod, water hose and can, wooden box, and linker.

MODEL 1919A4 SEMI-AUTO BELTFED – .308 Win. cal., copy of military 1919A4 machine gun, various packages available. Mfg. 2011-2012.

$4,000 $3,500 $3,000 $2,725 $2,200 $1,800 $1,400 *$2,000*

Add $550 for Deluxe Package including M2 tripod and pintle.

Add $945 for "The Whole Enchilada" package including M2 tripod with pintle, trunnion shield, 1919A4 linker, and .30-06 barrel.

H.C.A.R. (HEAVY COUNTER ASSAULT RIFLE) – .30-06 cal., 16 or 20 (disc. 2020) in. threaded barrel with Surefire muzzle brake, two 30 shot mags., newly designed trigger, Troy Industries front and rear flip-up sights, Magpul CTR buttstock, ergonomic pistol grip, newly designed handguard with four integrated Picatinny rails, ambi bolt release, hydraulic buffer system, includes custom hard case, black Nitride or FDE Cerakote finish. New 2015.

MSR $4,800 $4,325 $3,800 $3,300 $2,950 $2,375 $1,950 $1,550

Add $50 for 20 in. barrel (disc. 2020).

Add $299 for FDE Cerakote finish.

OLD-WEST GUN CO.

Previous importer and distributor that took over the inventory of Allen Firearms after they went out of business in early 1987.

Old-West Gun Co. changed their name to Cimarron Arms in late 1987. Please refer to Cimarron F.A. Co. in the C section for approximate prices on similar models from Old-West Gun Co.

OLLENDORFF, PHILIPP

Current manufacturer established during 1986, and located in Scharnitz, Austria.

FIREARMS

Philipp Ollendorff manufactures best quality double rifles, O/U shotguns, stalking rifles, and other long gun configurations. All guns are made to custom order, and there are many options available. Please contact the manufacturer directly for more information, including model availability and a price quotation.

GRADING - PPGS™	100%	98%	95%	90%	80%	70%	60%	LAST MSR

OLYMPIC ARMS, INC.

Previous manufacturer notable for making AR-15 style firearms, established in 1976. While the company announced its closing in Jan. 2017, Olympic Arms, Inc. remained open and was selling most of the semi-auto SKU's that it did prior to 2017 until late 2020. Company headquarters was located in Olympia, WA.

Olympic Arms, Inc. was founded by Robert C. Schuetz, and began as Schuetzen Gun Works (SGW) in 1956, manufacturing barrels in Colorado Springs, CO. Prior to that, Mr. Schuetz had been partnered in business with well-known gunsmith, P.O. Ackley. In 1975, the company moved to Olympia, WA. While its business in rifle barrels and barrel blanks thrived, it also began manufacturing complete custom bolt action rirfles. In 1982, Schuetzen Gun Works began to manufacture AR-15/M16 rifles and components under the trade name of Olympic Arms, Inc., while custom bolt action rifles continued to be produced under the SGW brand. In late 1987, Olympic Arms, Inc. acquired Safari Arms of Phoenix, AZ. As of Jan. 2004, the Safari Arms product name was discontinued and all 1911 style products were manufactured in the Olympic Arms facility in Olympia, WA. Schuetzen Pistol Works was the in-house custom shop of Olympic Arms. Olympic Arms was one of the few AR-15 style firearm manufacturers to make every major component part in-house.

PISTOLS: SEMI-AUTO

Please refer to the Safari Arms section for previously manufactured pistols made under the Safari Arms trademark.

On July 10, 2014, Olympic Arms announced the cancellation of all 1911 pistols, as well as 1911 frames and slides.

BIG DEUCE – .45 ACP cal., 6 in. longslide version of the MatchMaster, SA, matte black slide with satin stainless steel frame, smooth walnut (disc.) or cocobolo grips with double diamond checkering, double slide serrations, 44 oz. Mfg. 1995-2004, reintroduced 2006-2014.

$1,025 $900 $725 $600 $500 $400 $350 ***$1,164***

BLAK-TAC MATCHMASTER – .45 ACP cal., 5 in. National Match barrel, SA, 7 shot mag., widened and lowered ejection port, Blak-Tac treated frame and slide, low profile combat sights, adj. trigger, approx. 40 oz. Mfg. 2003-2008.

$875 $775 $675 $575 $500 $450 $400 ***$995***

COHORT – .45 ACP cal., Enforcer slide and MatchMaster frame, 4 in. stainless steel barrel, SA, beavertail grip safety, extended thumb safety and slide release, commander style hammer, smooth walnut grips with laser etched Black Widow logo (disc.) or checkered walnut grips, finger grooved front grip strap, fully adj. rear sight, 37 oz. Mfg. 1995-2014.

$850 $750 $650 $550 $450 $400 $350 ***$974***

ENFORCER – .45 ACP cal., 3.8 (disc.) or 4 in. bushingless stainless bull barrel, SA, 6 shot mag., shortened grip, available with max hard finish aluminum frame, parkerized, electroless nickel, or lightweight (disc.) anodized finishes, Triplex counterwound self-contained spring recoil system, flat or arched mainspring housing, adj. sights, ambidextrous safety, neoprene or checkered walnut grips, finger grooved front grip strap, 27 (lightweight model) or 35 oz. Disc. mid-2014.

$870 $740 $650 $585 $515 $450 $395 ***$1,034***

This model was originally called the Black Widow. After Safari Arms became Schuetzen Pistol Works, this model was changed extensively to include stainless construction, beavertail grip safety, and combat style hammer.

MATCHMASTER – .45 ACP cal., similar to the Enforcer, except has 5 or 6 in. barrel and 7 shot mag. rounded (R/S) or squared off trigger guard, finger grooved front grip strap, single or double (6 in. barrel) slide serrations, approx. 40 oz. Disc. mid-2014.

$870 $740 $650 $585 $515 $450 $395 ***$1,034***

Add $70 for 6 in. barrel.

STREET DEUCE – .45 ACP cal., M1911A1 styled frame, 5.2 in. stainless steel National Match bushingless barrel, stainless frame, steel slide, lowered and widened ejection port, 7 shot mag., diamond pattern checkered rosewood (disc.) or cocobolo grips, 38 oz. Mfg. by Custom Shop 2001-mid-2014.

$1,150 $1,000 $875 $775 $675 $575 $475 ***$1,294***

JOURNEYMAN – similar to Street Deuce, except has 4.2 in. bull barrel and 7 shot mag., 35 oz. Mfg. 2001-mid 2014.

$1,150 $1,000 $875 $775 $675 $575 $475 ***$1,294***

GRADING - PPGS™	100%	98%	95%	90%	80%	70%	60%	LAST MSR

WESTERNER – .45 ACP cal., 5 in. stainless steel barrel, 7 shot mag., 100% case colored finish on frame and slide, fitted barrel bushing, wide beavertail grip safety, shaped and tensioned extractor, fully adj. LPA rear sight, dovetail front blade sight, custom made laser etched smooth holly (disc.) or Westerner icon grips, 39 oz. Mfg. 2003-mid-2014.

	$1,025	$900	$725	$600	$500	$400	$350	*$1,164*

* ***Westerner Trail Boss*** – similar to Westerner, except has 6 in. barrel, dual slide serrations, 7 shot mag., laser etched Westerner icon grips, 43 oz. Mfg. 2005-mid-2014.

	$1,050	$925	$750	$625	$500	$400	$350	*$1,234*

* ***Westerner Constable*** – similar to Westerner, except has 4 in. barrel, compact frame, 35 oz. Mfg. 2005-mid-2014.

	$1,000	$875	$750	$650	$550	$450	$350	*$1,164*

WHITNEY WOLVERINE – .22 LR cal., patterned after original Whitney Wolverine, 4 5/8 in. barrel, lightweight polymer frame and vent. rib, marked "Olympic Arms" on side of frame, 10 shot mag., blade front and dovetail rear sights, matte black, pink (new 2011), desert tan (new 2011), or coyote brown (new 2011) finish, black checkered grips, bright pink polymer frame became an option during late 2010, 19.2 oz. Disc. 2018.

	$260	$230	$200	$185	$170	$165	$155	*$294*

K22 – .22 LR cal., SA, 6 1/2 in. button rifled stainless steel barrel, forged flat-top with Picatinny rails, gas block, free floating aluminum tube handguard with knurling, non-chromed bore, A2 flash suppressor, 4.3 lbs. Mfg. 2011-mid-2014.

	$775	$675	$575	$475	$425	$395	$375	*$896*

K23P SERIES – 5.56 NATO cal., GIO, SA, 6 1/2 in. chrome moly steel button rifled barrel with A2 flash suppressor, forged A2 upper with fully adj. rear sight, post front sight, no bayonet lug, free floating aluminum tube handguard with knurling, carbon recoil buffer in back of frame, with (K23P-FT) or w/o (K23P) flat-top receiver, 5.12 lbs. Mfg. 2007-2020.

	$775	$700	$600	$525	$475	$375	$300	*$876*

Add $65 for optics ready flat-top receiver and gas block (K23P-OR, new 2016).
Add $95 for A3 upper receiver (disc. 2011) or $91 for A3 upper w/Picatinny rail and Firsh handguard (K23P-A3TC, disc. 2011, reintroduced 2016).

K23PGL – 9mm Para. or .40 S&W cal., GIO, AR-15 style, 6 1/2 in. button rifled stainless steel barrel with black oxide finish, A1 style flash suppressor, AR-15 lower that is designed to accept Glock style magazines, forged A2 upper with fully adj. rear sight, elevated adj. post front sight, no bayonet lug, free floating aluminum tube with knurling, padded receiver extension tube, black finish, 5.12 lbs. Limited mfg. 2015 only.

	$925	$850	$725	$625	$550	$475	$425	*$1,091*

* ***K23PGL-OR*** – 9mm Para. or .40 S&W cal., GIO, AR-15 style, 6 1/2 in. button rifled stainless steel barrel with black oxide finish, A1 style flash suppressor, AR-15 lower that is designed to accept Glock style magazines, forged Picatinny flat-top upper, Picatinny gas block, no sights, free floating aluminum handguard, padded receiver extension tube, black finish, 5.12 lbs. Limited mfg. 2015 only.

	$885	$785	$685	$600	$535	$465	$415	*$1,037*

* ***K23P-9, K23P-10, K23P-40, K23P-45*** – 9mm Para., 10mm, .40 S&W, or .45 ACP cal., GIO, AR-15 style, 6 1/2 in. button rifled stainless steel barrel with black oxide finish, A1 style flash suppressor, 18 shot AR-15 magazines, forged A2 upper with fully adj. rear sight, elevated adj. post front sight, no bayonet lug, free floating aluminum tube with knurling, padded receiver extension tube, black finish, 5.12 lbs. Mfg. 2015-2020.

	$775	$685	$615	$550	$485	$415	$365	*$941*

Add $45 for OR (optics ready).

K24P – 5.56 NATO, .300 AAC Blackout, or 7.62x39mm cal., GIO, 11 1/2 in. button rifled barrel, choice of A2 fixed sights with carry handle or flat-top (K24P-FT), pistol grip with Fiberite ribbed handguard, extended recoil buffer in back of pistol grip, matte black finish, 6.77 lbs. Mfg. 2017-2020.

	$735	$665	$585	$515	$450	$385	$340	*$896*

K24P-OR – 5.56 NATO, .300 AAC Blackout, or 7.62x39mm cal., GIO, 11 1/2 in. button rifled barrel, no sights, pistol grip with Fiberite ribbed handguard, Picatinny flat-top with forward top rail on barrel, extended recoil buffer in back of pistol grip, matte black finish, 6.77 lbs. Mfg. 2015-2020.

	$815	$700	$625	$575	$500	$425	$375	*$973*

GRADING - PPGS™	100%	98%	95%	90%	80%	70%	60%	LAST MSR

K24P-9 – 9mm Para., 10mm, .40 S&W, or .45 ACP cal., GIO, 11 1/2 in. button rifled barrel, A2 sights, pistol grip with Fiberite ribbed handguard, extended recoil buffer in back of pistol grip, matte black finish, 6.77 lbs. Mfg. 2015-2020.

$775 $685 $615 $550 $485 $415 $365 *$928*

K24P-9-OR – 9mm Para., 10mm, .40 S&W, or .45 ACP cal., GIO, 11 1/2 in. button rifled barrel, A2 sights, pistol grip with Fiberite ribbed handguard, Picatinny flat-top w/forward top rail on barrel, extended recoil buffer in back of pistol grip, matte black finish, 6.77 lbs. Mfg. 2015-2020.

$815 $700 $625 $575 $500 $425 $375 *$974*

OA-93 PISTOL – .223 Rem. (older mfg.), 5.56 NATO, or 7.62x39mm (very limited mfg., disc.) cal., GIO, 6 (most common, disc.), 6 1/2 (new 2005), 9 (disc.), or 14 (disc.) in. button rifled stainless steel threaded barrel with Phantom flash suppressor, forged flat-top upper receiver utilizes integral scope mount base, 30 shot mag., free floating aluminum handguard tube with knurling, without buffer tube stock or charging handle, 4 lbs. 3 oz., approx. 500 mfg. 1993-94 before Crime Bill discontinued production, reintroduced late 2004-disc.

$1,065 $965 $835 $725 $625 $535 $450 *$1,277*

Add 100% for 7.62x39mm cal.

OA-96 AR PISTOL – .223 Rem. cal., GIO, 6 in. barrel only, similar to OA-93 Pistol, except has pinned (fixed) 30 shot mag. and rear takedown button for rapid reloading, 5 lbs. Mfg. 1996-2000.

$725 $650 $580 $515 $450 $385 $340 *$860*

OA-98 PISTOL – .223 Rem. cal., GIO, skeletonized, lightweight version of the OA-93/OA-96, 6 1/2 in. non-threaded barrel, 10 shot fixed (disc.) or detachable (new 2006) mag., denoted by perforated appearance, 3 lbs. Mfg. 1998-2003, reintroduced 2005-2007.

$895 $795 $685 $615 $545 $475 $415 *$1,080*

RIFLES: BOLT ACTION

In 1993, Olympic Arms purchased the rights, jigs, fixtures, and machining templates for the Bauska Big Bore Magnum Mauser action.

ULTRA MAG BBK-01 – various cals. between .300 Win. Mag.-.505 Gibbs, custom order rifle available with many barrel options and other special order features, price was on request from the factory.

This model was formerly the Bauska BBK-02.

BOLT ACTION SAKO – various cals. between .17 Rem.-.416 Rem. Mag., 26 in. fluted barrel, various stock configurations, values represent base price with no options. Disc. 2000.

$660 $575 $500 $450 $400 $360 $330 *$660*

ULTRA CSR TACTICAL RIFLE – .308 Win. cal., Sako action, 26 in. broach cut heavy barrel, Bell & Carlson black or synthetic stock with aluminum bedding, Harris bipod, carrying case. Mfg. 1996-2000.

$1,450 $1,250 $1,100 $1,000 $800 $700 $600 *$1,140*

COUNTER SNIPER RIFLE – .308 Win. cal., bolt action utilizing M-14 mags., 26 in. heavy barrel, camo-fiberglass stock, 10 1/2 lbs. Disc. 1987.

$1,300 $1,100 $975 $895 $750 $650 $600 *$1,225*

SURVIVOR I CONVERSION UNIT – .223 Rem. or .45 ACP cal., converts M1911 variations into carbine, bolt action, collapsible stock, 16 1/4 in. barrel, 5 lbs.

$275 $225 $195 $150 $125 $110 $95

This kit was also available for S&W and Browning Hi-Power models.

RIFLES: SEMI-AUTO

The PCR (Politically Correct Rifle) variations listed refer to those guns manufactured after the Crime Bill was implemented in September 1994 through 2004. PCR rifles have smooth barrels (no flash suppressor), a 10 shot mag., and fixed stocks. Named models refer to the original, pre-ban model nomenclature.

Olympic Arms also made some models exclusively for distributors. They included the K30R-16-SST (Sports South, LLC), K16-SST (Sports South, LLC), and the PP FT M4 SS (Lew Horton, disc.).

COMPETITOR RIFLE – .22 LR cal., Ruger 10/22 action with 20 in. fluted barrel with button rifling, Bell & Carlson thumbhole fiberglass stock, includes bipod, black finish and matte stainless barrel, 6.9 lbs. Mfg. 1996-1999.

$500 $450 $400 $360 $330 $300 $275 *$575*

GRADING - PPGS™	100%	98%	95%	90%	80%	70%	60%	LAST MSR

ULTRAMATCH/PCR-1 – .223 Rem. cal., GIO, AR-15 action with modifications, 20 or 24 in. match stainless steel barrel, Picatinny flat-top upper receiver, Williams set trigger optional, scope mounts, 10 lbs. 3 oz. Mfg. 1985-disc.

* ***Ultramatch PCR-1*** – disc. 2004.

$895	$575	$475	$395	$350	$325	$300	*$1,074*

* ***Ultramatch PCR-1P*** – .223 Rem. cal., GIO, premium grade Ultramatch rifle with many shooting enhancements, including Maxhard treated upper and lower receiver, 20 or 24 in. broach cut Ultramatch bull barrel, 1:10 in. or 1:8 in. rate of twist. Mfg. 2001-2004.

$1,075	$675	$500	$450	$400	$350	$325	*$1,299*

* ***Ultramatch UM-1*** – .223 Rem. cal., GIO, 20 in. stainless Ultramatch barrel with non-chromed bore, gas block, free floating aluminum tube with knurling, approx. 8 1/2 lbs. Disc. 1994, reintroduced late 2004-2012.

$1,125	$700	$525	$450	$400	$350	$325	

Last MSR in 1994 was $1,515, last MSR in 2012 was $1,329.

* ***Ultramatch UM-1P*** – .223 Rem. cal., GIO, similar to UM-1 Ultramatch, except has 20 (disc. 2006) or 24 in. Ultramatch bull stainless barrel, premium grade Ultramatch rifle with many shooting enhancements, 9 1/2 lbs. Mfg. 2005-2020.

$1,350	$875	$650	$525	$450	$385	$350	*$1,624*

INTERCONTINENTAL – .223 Rem. cal., GIO, synthetic wood-grained thumbhole buttstock and aluminum handguard, 20 in. Ultramatch barrel (free floating). Mfg. 1992-1993.

$1,135	$725	$525	$465	$415	$375	$350	*$1,371*

INTERNATIONAL MATCH – .223 Rem. cal., similar to Ultramatch, except has custom aperture sights. Mfg. 1991-93.

$1,050	$650	$495	$450	$395	$350	$325	*$1,240*

SERVICE MATCH/PCR SERVICE MATCH – .223 Rem. cal., AR-15 action with modifications, GIO, 20 in. SS Ultramatch barrel, carrying handle, standard trigger, choice of A1 or A2 flash suppressor (Service Match only), 8 3/4 lbs.

* ***Service Match SM-1*** – GIO, 9.7 lbs., disc. 1994, reintroduced late 2004-2012.

$1,065	$650	$500	$450	$395	$350	$325	

Last MSR in 1994 was $1,200, last MSR in 2012 was $1,273.

* ***Service Match SM-1P Premium Grade*** – .223 Rem. cal., GIO, Maxhard upper and lower receiver, 20 in. broach cut Ultramatch super heavy threaded barrel (1 turn in 8 in. is standard), flash suppressor, two-stage CMP trigger, Blak-Tak Armour bolt carrier assembly, Bob Jones NM interchangeable rear sight system, AC4 pneumatic recoil buffer, Turner Saddlery competition sling, GI-style pistol grip. Mfg. 2005-2012.

$1,425	$925	$700	$550	$475	$395	$350	*$1,728*

* ***Service Match PCR*** – disc. late 2004.

$895	$575	$475	$395	$350	$325	$300	*$1,062*

* ***Service Match PCR-SMP Premium Grade*** – .223 Rem. cal., GIO, 20 in. broach cut Ultramatch super heavy barrel (1 turn in 8 in. is standard), two-stage CMP trigger, Maxhard upper and lower receiver, Blak-Tak Armour bolt carrier assembly, Bob Jones NM interchangeable rear sight system, AC4 pneumatic recoil buffer, Turner Saddlery competition sling, GI-style pistol grip. Mfg. 2004 only.

$1,350	$875	$650	$525	$450	$385	$350	*$1,613*

MULTIMATCH ML-1/PCR-2 – .223 Rem. cal., GIO, tactical short range rifle, 16 in. Ultramatch barrel with A2 upper receiver, aluminum collapsible (Multimatch ML-1) or fixed (PCR-2) stock, carrying handle, A2 flash suppressor (Multimatch ML-1 only). Mfg. 1991-2012.

* ***Multimatch ML-1*** – 7.35 lbs. Disc. 2012.

$995	$625	$495	$450	$395	$350	$325	

Last MSR in 1994 was $1,200, last MSR in 2012 was $1,188.

* ***Multimatch PCR-2*** – disc. late 2004.

$825	$535	$450	$385	$340	$325	$295	*$958*

MULTIMATCH ML-2/PCR-3 – .223 Rem. cal., GIO, Picatinny flat-top upper receiver with stainless steel 16 in. Ultramatch bull (new 2005) barrel, carrying handle (disc.), approx. 7 1/2 lbs. Mfg. 1991-2015.

GRADING - PPGS™	100%	98%	95%	90%	80%	70%	60%	LAST MSR

* ***Multimatch ML-2*** – .223 Rem. cal., GIO, 16 in. Ultramatch stainless steel bull barrel, crowned muzzle, forged flat-top with Picatinny rails, gas block with Picatinny rails, free floating tubular aluminum handguard with knurling, A2 stock with trapdoor, 7 1/2 lbs. Disc. 1994, reintroduced late 2004-disc.

	$1,065	$650	$500	$450	$395	$350	$325	*$1,253*

* ***Multimatch PCR-3*** – disc. late 2004.

	$825	$535	$450	$385	$340	$325	$295	*$958*

AR-15 MATCH/PCR-4 – .223 Rem. cal., GIO, patterned after the AR-15 with 20 in. barrel and solid synthetic stock, 8 lbs. 5 oz. Mfg. 1975-2004.

* ***PCR-4***

	$695	$500	$425	$375	$335	$315	$295	*$803*

* ***AR-15 Match***

	$895	$575	$475	$395	$350	$325	$300	*$1,075*

CAR-15/PCR-5 – GIO, modified AR-15 with choice of 11 1/2 (disc. 1993) or 16 in. barrel, stow-away pistol grip and collapsible stock (CAR-15 only), 7 lbs. Mfg. 1975-1998, PCR-5 reintroduced 2000-2004.

* ***PCR-5*** – .223 Rem., 9mm Para. (new 1996), .40 S&W (new 1996), or .45 ACP (new 1996) cal., GIO. Disc. 1998, reintroduced 2000-2004.

	$665	$500	$415	$375	$335	$315	$295	*$755*

* ***CAR-15*** – .223 Rem., 9mm Para., .40 S&W, .45 ACP, or 7.62x39mm cal.

	$875	$550	$465	$395	$350	$325	$300	*$1,030*

CAR-97 – .223 Rem., 9mm Para., 10mm, .40 S&W, or .45 ACP cal., similar to PCR-5, except has 16 in. button rifled barrel, A2 sights, fixed CAR stock, post-ban muzzle brake, approx. 7 lbs. Mfg. 1997-2004.

	$675	$500	$425	$375	$335	$315	$295	*$780*

Add approx. 10% for 9mm Para., 10mm, .40 S&W, or .45 ACP cal.

* ***CAR-97 M4*** – .223 Rem. cal., GIO, M4 configuration with contoured barrel, fixed carbine tube stock, factory installed muzzle brake, oversized shortened handguard. Mfg. 2003-2004.

	$725	$500	$435	$375	$335	$315	$295	*$839*

Add $95 for detachable carrying handle (new 2004).

PCR-6 – 7.62x39mm cal., 16 in. barrel, post-ban only, GIO, A2 stowaway stock, carrying handle, 7 lbs. Mfg. 1995-2002.

	$745	$500	$435	$375	$335	$315	$295	*$870*

PCR-7 ELIMINATOR – .223 Rem. cal., GIO, similar to PCR-4, except has 16 in. barrel, 7 lbs. 10 oz. Mfg. 1999-2004.

	$725	$500	$435	$375	$335	$315	$295	*$844*

PCR-8 – .223 Rem. cal., GIO, same configuration as the PCR-1, except has standard 20 in. stainless steel heavy bull barrel with button rifling. Mfg. 2001-2004.

	$725	$500	$435	$375	$335	$315	$295	*$834*

* ***PCR-8 Mag.*** – .223 WSSM or .243 WSSM cal., GIO, otherwise similar to PCR-8. Mfg. 2004.

	$895	$575	$475	$395	$350	$325	$300	*$1,074*

This model was also scheduled to be available in .308 Olympic Mag. and 7mm Olympic Mag. cals.

PCR-9/10/40/45 – 9mm Para., 10mm, .40 S&W, or .45 ACP cal., similar to PCR-5 Carbine except for pistol cal., GIO, A2 upper standard, 16 in. barrel, A2 buttstock, Mil-Spec lower receiver. Mfg. 2001-2004.

	$725	$500	$435	$375	$335	$315	$295	*$835*

PCR-16 – .223 Rem. cal., GIO, 16 in. match grade bull barrel, two-piece aluminum free floating handguard, Picatinny receiver rail, 7 1/2 lbs. Mfg. 2003-2004.

	$615	$495	$415	$360	$325	$300	$275	*$714*

PCR-30 – .30 Carbine cal., GIO, forged aluminum receiver with matte black anodizing, parkerized steel parts, A2 adj. rear sight, accepts standard GI M1 .30 Carbine mags., 16 in. barrel with 1:12 in. twist, 7.15 lbs. Mfg. 2004.

	$765	$515	$440	$375	$335	$315	$295	*$899*

PLINKER – .223 Rem. cal., GIO, similar to PCR-5, except has 16 in. button rifled barrel standard, A1 sights, cast upper/lower receiver, 100% standard Mil-Spec parts, 7 lbs. Mfg. 2001-2004.

	$515	$450	$395	$350	$315	$295	$275	*$598*

GRADING - PPGS™	100%	98%	95%	90%	80%	70%	60%	LAST MSR

PLINKER PLUS – 5.56 NATO cal., GIO, IO, 16 in. button rifled threaded chrome moly steel barrel with A2 flash suppressor, standard A1 upper, cast upper/lower receiver, 100% standard Mil-Spec parts, A2 stock with trapdoor, 7-8.4 lbs. Mfg. 2005-2020.

$650	$500	$415	$370	$325	$300	$275	*$740*

* ***Plinker Plus Compact*** – 5.56 NATO cal., GIO, 16 in. button rifled chrome moly steel barrel with A2 flash suppressor, forged A1 upper with windage only adjustment, elevation adj. front sight post with bayonet lug, Fiberite carbine length handguard, A2 stock with trapdoor, pink handguard and stock, 7.37 lbs. Mfg. 2015-2020.

$595	$485	$415	$350	$315	$295	$275	*$688*

* ***Plinker Plus Flat-Top*** – 5.56 NATO cal., GIO, similar to Plinker Plus, except has flat-top with Picatinny rails, M4 six point collapsible stock. Mfg. 2012-2020.

$615	$495	$415	$360	$325	$300	$275	*$714*

* ***Plinker Plus 20*** – 5.56 NATO cal., GIO, 20 in. button rifled threaded chrome moly steel barrel with A2 flash suppressor, choice of forged A1 upper or flat-top upper with Picatinny rails, adj. post front sight with bayonet lug, 100% standard Mil-Spec parts, A2 stock with trapdoor, 7-8.4 lbs. Mfg. 2012-2020.

$645	$500	$415	$370	$325	$300	$275	*$740*

FAR-15 – .223 Rem. cal., GIO, featherweight model with A1 contour lightweight button rifled 16 in. barrel, fixed collapsible stock, 9.92 lbs. Mfg. 2001-2004.

$695	$500	$425	$375	$335	$315	$295	*$822*

GI-16 – 5.56 NATO cal., GIO, forged aluminum receiver with black matte finish, A1 type upper receiver, parkerized steel parts, A1 adj. rear sights, 16 in. button rifled match grade barrel, M4 collapsible stock, 6.6 lbs. Mfg. 2004, reintroduced 2006-2012.

$745	$500	$435	$375	$335	$315	$295	*$857*

GI-20 – .223 Rem. cal., similar to GI-16, except has 20 in. heavy barrel and A2 lower receiver, 8.4 lbs. Mfg. 2004.

$645	$500	$415	$370	$325	$300	$275	*$749*

OA-93 CARBINE – .223 Rem. cal., GIO, 16 in. threaded barrel, design based on OA-93 pistol, aluminum side folding stock, flat-top receiver, round aluminum handguard, Vortex flash suppressor, 7 1/2 lbs. Mfg. 1995, civilian sales disc. 1998, reintroduced 2004-2007.

$895	$575	$475	$395	$350	$325	$300	

Last MSR in 1998 was $1,550, last MSR in 2007 was $1,074.

* ***OA-93PT Carbine*** – .223 Rem. cal., GIO, aluminum forged receiver, black matte hard anodized finish, no sights, integral flat-top upper receiver rail system, match grade 16 in. chrome moly steel barrel with removable muzzle brake, push-button removable stock, vertical pistol grip, 7.6 lbs. Mfg. 2004 only, reintroduced 2006-2007.

$895	$575	$475	$395	$350	$325	$300	*$1,074*

LTF/LT-MIL4 LIGHTWEIGHT TACTICAL RIFLE – 5.56 NATO cal., GIO, available in LTF (fluted), LT-M4 (new 2011), or LT-MIL4 (disc. 2009) configuration, black matte anodized receiver, Firsh type forearms with Picatinny rails, parkerized steel parts, adj. flip-up sight system, 16 in. non-chromed fluted, M4 stainless steel (new 2011), or MIL4 threaded barrel with flash suppressor, tube style Ace FX buttstock, 6.4 lbs. Mfg. 2005-disc.

$1,050	$650	$495	$450	$395	$350	$325	*$1,240*

Subtract $97 for M4 style stainless steel barrel (new 2011).
Subtract approx. 10% if w/o fluted barrel.

LTF PREDATOR – .204 Ruger (new 2012), 5.56 NATO, 7.62 NATO (disc. 2015), or 6.8 SPC (new 2012) cal., GIO, 16 in. button rifled chrome moly barrel with A2 flash suppressor, forged flat-top with Picatinny rails, gas block with Picatinny rail, free floating aluminum tube handguard, Ergo grip, Ace FX skeleton stock, black or 100% camo coverage, 6.44 lbs. Mfg. 2011-disc.

$875	$550	$465	$395	$350	$325	$300	*$1,026*

Add $115 for 100% camo coverage.

MPR .308-15 – 7.62 NATO cal., GIO, 16, 18, or 24 in. stainless steel ultra match button rifled barrel w/o sights, 10 shot mag., billet aluminum upper and lower, rifle length Predator aluminum free float handguard (16 in. barrel with knurling), designed to accept all standard AR-15 upper receivers as well as Olympic Arms .308 style lowers, two-position front pivot pin, forward Picatinny rails, A2 buttstock, 9 lbs. Mfg. 2015-disc.

$1,065	$650	$500	$450	$395	$350	$325	*$1,267*

Add $291 for 18 in. barrel or $421 for 24 in. barrel.

GRADING - PPGS™	100%	98%	95%	90%	80%	70%	60%	LAST MSR

K3B CARBINE – 5.56 NATO, 6.8 SPC (new 2016), or .300 AAC Blackout (new 2016) cal., GIO, 16 in. match grade chrome moly steel threaded heavy barrel with A2 flash suppressor, adj. A2 rear sight, Fiberite carbine length handguard, A2 (disc.) or M4 collapsible (new 2012) buttstock, adj. front post sight, A3 flat-top receiver became standard 2011, 6 3/4 lbs. Mfg. 2005-2020.

$695	$500	$425	$375	$335	$315	$295	*$811*

* ***K3B-FAR Carbine*** – 5.56 NATO cal., GIO, 16 in. FAR button rifled stainless steel barrel with A2 flash suppressor, forged A2 upper with fully adj. rear sight or flat-top upper, post front sight with bayonet lug, Fiberite carbine length handguard, M4 6-pos. collapsible stock, 6 lbs. Mfg. 2005-2020.

$725	$500	$435	$375	$335	$315	$295	*$844*

* ***K3B-M4 Carbine*** – 5.56 NATO cal., GIO, 16 in. M4 button rifled stainless steel barrel with A2 flash suppressor, forged A2 upper with fully adj. rear sight or flat-top upper, post front sight with bayonet lug, Fiberite carbine length M4 handguard with heat shield, M4 6-pos. collapsible stock, 6.3 lbs. Mfg. 2005-2020.

$725	$500	$435	$375	$335	$315	$295	*$844*

Add $65 for detachable carry handle (K3BM4A3).

* ***K3B-M4-A3 Carbine*** – 5.56 NATO cal., GIO, similar to K3B-M4, except is tactical carbine version with Firsh handguard, flat-top upper receiver with Picatinny rail, and detachable carry handle, 6.7 lbs. Mfg. 2018-2020.

$785	$525	$450	$385	$340	$325	$295	*$909*

* ***K3B-M4-A3-TC Carbine*** – 5.56 NATO cal., GIO, similar to K3B-M4, except is tactical carbine version with Firsh handguard, flat-top upper receiver with Picatinny rail, and detachable carry handle, 6.7 lbs. Mfg. 2005-2020.

$850	$550	$465	$395	$350	$325	$295	*$993*

K4B/K4B68 – 5.56 NATO or 6.8 SPC (new 2010) cal., GIO, 20 in. match grade chrome moly steel button rifled threaded barrel with flash suppressor, adj. A2 rear sight, A2 buttstock, adj. front post sight, A2 upper receiver and handguard, 8 1/2 lbs. Disc. 2020.

$725	$500	$435	$375	$335	$315	$295	*$844*

Subtract $26 for flat-top upper with Picatinny rail (K4B-FT).
Add $254 for 6.8 SPC cal.

K4B-A4 – .223 Rem. cal., GIO, 20 in. barrel with A2 flash suppressor, elevation adj. post front sight, bayonet lug, Firsh rifle length handguard with Picatinny rails, flat-top receiver, 9 lbs. Mfg. 2006-2008.

$800	$525	$450	$385	$340	$325	$295	*$941*

K7 ELIMINATOR – 5.56 NATO cal., GIO, 16 in. stainless steel threaded barrel with flash suppressor, adj. A2 rear sight, A2 buttstock, adj. front post sight, 6.8 lbs. Mfg. 2005-2020.

$785	$525	$450	$385	$340	$325	$295	*$909*

Add $104 for K7-ORT (Optic Ready Tactical).

K8 – .204 Ruger (new 2012), 6.8 SPC (new 2012) or 5.56 NATO cal., GIO, 20 in stainless steel button rifled bull barrel, A2 buttstock, Picatinny flat-top upper receiver, gas block, free floating aluminum knurled tube, satin bead blast finish on barrel, 8 1/2 lbs. Mfg. 2005-2020.

$785	$525	$450	$385	$340	$325	$295	*$909*

This model is marked "Target Match" on mag. well.

* ***K8-MAG*** – similar to K8, GIO, except available in .223 WSSM, .243 WSSM, .25 WSSM, or .300 OSSM (new 2006) cals., and has 24 in. barrel, 5 shot mag., 9.4 lbs. Mfg. 2005-2020.

$1,135	$725	$525	$465	$415	$375	$350	*$1,364*

K9/K10/K40/K45 – 9mm Para. (K9), 10mm Norma (K10), .40 S&W (K40), or .45 ACP (K45) cal., GIO, 16 in. threaded stainless steel barrel with flash suppressor, adj. A2 rear sight, 10 shot converted Uzi (10mm, .40 S&W or .45 ACP cal.) or 32 (9mm Para.) shot converted Sten detachable mag., Fiberite carbine length handguard, M4 6-pos. collapsible buttstock, bayonet lug, 6.7 lbs. Mfg. 2005-early 2017.

$865	$550	$465	$395	$350	$325	$300	*$1,006*

* ***K9GL/K40GL*** – 9mm Para. or .40 S&W cal., GIO, 16 in. button rifled stainless steel barrel with flash suppressor, forged A2 upper with fully adj. rear sight, adj. post front sight with bayonet lug, lower receiver designed to accept Glock magazines, Fiberite carbine length handguard, M4 6-pos. collapsible stock, does not include magazine, 6.86 lbs. Mfg. 2005-early 2017.

$975	$595	$495	$425	$365	$335	$300	*$1,157*

GRADING - PPGS™	100%	98%	95%	90%	80%	70%	60%	LAST MSR

K16 – 5.56 NATO, 6.8 SPC (new 2012), 7.62x39mm (new 2012), or .300 AAC Blackout (new 2012) cal., GIO, 16 in. button rifled chrome moly bull barrel with crown muzzle, free floating aluminum tube handguard with knurling, forged flat-top upper receiver with Picatinny rails, gas block with Picatinny rails, A2 buttstock with trapdoor, 7 1/2 lbs. Mfg. 2005-2020.

$725	$500	$435	$375	$335	$315	$295	*$830*

Add $60 for .204 Ruger or .300 AAC Blackout cal.

K22 M4 – .22 LR cal., blowback action, 16 in. stainless steel barrel, A1 flash suppressor, M4 6-point collapsible stock, forged A2 upper, adj. rear sight, adj. post front sight with bayonet lug, Fiberite carbine length handguard with heat shield, 6.6 lbs. Mfg. 2011-2012.

$875	$550	$465	$395	$350	$325	$300	*$1,039*

K22 RIMFIRE TARGET MATCH – .22 LR cal., blowback action, 16 in. stainless steel bull barrel, A2 fixed trapdoor stock, flat-top with Picatinny rails, no sights, free floating aluminum handguard tube with knurling, muzzle crown, 8.6 lbs. Mfg. 2011-2015.

$725	$500	$435	$375	$335	$315	$295	*$831*

K22 SURVIVAL LIGHT – .22 LR cal., blowback action, 16 in. stainless steel featherweight barrel, side folding stock, flat-top with Picatinny rails, gas block, free floating slotted aluminum handguard, A1 flash suppressor, 6 lbs. Mfg. 2011-2012.

$725	$500	$435	$375	$335	$315	$295	*$883*

K30 – .30 Carbine cal., GIO, similar to K16, except has A2 upper receiver, collapsible stock, and threaded barrel with flash suppressor, 6.6 lbs. Mfg. 2005-2006.

$785	$525	$450	$385	$340	$325	$295	*$905*

Add $95 for A3 upper receiver.

K30R16 – 7.62x39mm cal., GIO, 16 or 20 (new 2016) in. stainless steel barrel, 6-point M4 collapsible stock, A2 flash suppressor, pistol grip, matte black anodized receiver, parkerized steel parts, A2 upper with adj. rear sight, 6 3/4 lbs. Mfg. 2007-2020.

$765	$515	$440	$375	$335	$315	$295	*$891*

Add $84 for K30R.

K68 – 6.8 SPC cal., GIO, 16 or 20 (optional) in. M4 button rifled stainless steel barrel with A2 flash suppressor, A2 upper with adj. rear sight, post front sight with bayonet lug, Fiberite M4 carbine length handguard, 6-position M4 collapsible stock, matte black anodized receiver, parkerized steel parts, pistol grip, 6.62 lbs. Mfg. 2017-2020.

$765	$500	$445	$375	$335	$315	$295	*$890*

K74 – 5.45x39mm cal., GIO, 16 in. button rifled stainless steel barrel with A2 flash suppressor, forged A2 upper with adj. rear sight and post front sight with bayonet lug, 6-position M4 collapsible stock, 6 3/4 lbs. Mfg. 2009-2020.

$895	$575	$475	$395	$350	$325	$300	*$1,058*

UMAR (ULTIMATE MAGNUM AR) – .22-250 Rem., .223 WSSM (disc.), .243 WSSM (disc.), .25 WSSM (disc.), .300 WSSM (disc.) or .300 OSSM (new 2019) cal., GIO, 20 (new 2019) or 24 in. heavy match grade stainless steel bull barrel, black matte anodized aluminum forged receiver, parkerized steel parts, flat-top/gas block with Picatinny rails, sling swivel mount, A2 stock w/trapdoor, Ergo tactical deluxe pistol grip, Predator Firsh free floating handguard, 9.4 lbs. Mfg. 2012-2020.

$1,065	$650	$500	$450	$395	$350	$325	*$1,299*

Add $98 for fluted bull barrel (new 2016).
Add $290 for .300 OSSM cal. (new 2019).

The upper receiver of this model will not work on standard AR-15 lowers.

GAMESTALKER CAMO – .204 Ruger (mfg. 2011 only), .243 WSSM, .25 WSSM, or .300 OSSM cal., GIO, 22 in. stainless steel barrel, flat-top upper receiver with Picatinny rail, ACE skeleton stock with Ergo SureGrip, 100% camo coverage, approx. 7 1/2 lbs. Mfg. 2010-early 2017, reintroduced 2019-2020.

$1,135	$725	$525	$465	$415	$375	$350	*$1,364*

GSG2 (GAMESTOCKER GEN 2) – 5.56 NATO, 6.8 SPC, or 7.62x39mm cal., GIO, 20 in. stainless steel barrel, flat-top upper receiver with Picatinny rail, free floating aluminum handguard, ACE FX skeleton stock with Ergo SureGrip, 100% camo coverage, approx. 7 1/2 lbs. Mfg. 2011-2020.

$1,050	$650	$495	$450	$395	$350	$325	*$1,234*

MPR GAMESTOCKER – .243 Win., .308 Win., .260 Rem., .300 WSM, or 7mm-08 cal., GIO, 22 in. stainless steel bull barrel, Ergo tactical deluxe (Fat Boy) rubberized pistol grip, billet aluminum upper and lower receiver, Picatinny rail, standard slotted aluminum free floating handguard, matte black finish. Mfg. 2016-disc.

$1,385	$895	$675	$525	$450	$385	$350	*$1,689*

GRADING - PPGS™	100%	98%	95%	90%	80%	70%	60%	LAST MSR

OMEGA

Previous trademark manufactured by Armero Specialistas Reunidas, located in Eibar, Spain, circa 1920s.

PISTOLS: SEMI-AUTO

SEMI AUTOMATIC PISTOL – 6.35mm or 7.65mm cal., "Eibar" type action, marked "Omega" on slide, 6 shot mag.

6.35 cal.	$275	$225	$150	$115	$70	$55	$40	
7.65 cal.	$295	$235	$160	$125	$80	$70	$55	

OMEGA ARMS

Current manufacturer of AR-15 style and semi-auto rifles and shotguns, established in 2012, located in Istanbul, Turkey. Distributed by Omega Arms USA LLC located in Heath, OH. Currently imported by LKCI LLC located in Newark, OH.

Please refer to BlueBookOfGunValues.com to order the *Blue Book of AR-15s & Variations*, available as a book or online subscription.

OMEGA FIREARMS

Previous manufacturer located in Flower Mound, TX circa 1965-1969.

RIFLES: BOLT ACTION

OMEGA III – various cals., 4 or 5 shot rotary mag., four cornered bolt locking system, premium walnut or laminated stock. Disc. late 1960s.

	$775	$650	$575	$495	$425	$360	$295	

OMEGA PISTOL

Previously manufactured and distributed by Springfield Armory located in Geneseo, IL. Omega conversion kits only were available until 1996 from Safari Arms located in Olympia, WA under license from Peters-Stahl in Germany.

PISTOLS: SEMI-AUTO

OMEGA – .38 Super, 10mm Norma, or .45 ACP cal., single action, ported slide, 5 or 6 in. interchangeable ported or unported barrel with polygon rifling, special lock-up system eliminates normal barrel link and bushing, Pachmayr grips, dual extractors, adj. rear sight. Mfg. 1987-90.

	$625	$560	$495	$425	$360	$295	$265	*$849*

Add $663 for interchangeable conversion units.
Add $336 for interchangeable 5 or 6 in. barrel (including factory installation).

Each conversion unit includes an entire slide assembly, one mag., 5 or 6 in barrel, recoil spring guide mechanism assembly, and factory fitting.

OMEGA RIFLES

Current bolt action and AR-15 style rifle manufacturer located in Meridian, TX.

RIFLES: BOLT ACTION

Omega Rifles offers customizations on the models listed below. Custom options include: additional calibers, custom barrel or action finishes, barrel fluting, muzzle threading, or muzzle brakes. Please contact the manufacturer directly for options and availability.

Add $200 for blended muzzle brake (radial or side port).
Add $200 for TriggerTech diamond trigger (adjustable).
Add $200+ for custom paint scheme.
Add $200 for HS Precision bottom metal.

BOSQUE – .28 Nosler, 6mm Creedmoor, .308 Win., .300 Win. Mag., .357 Raptor, 6.5 Creedmoor, or 7mm Rem. cal., Stiller (disc. 2020), Omega short (disc.), TL Custom (disc. 2020), or GRB (new 2021) short/long action, 20, 22 (.308 Win. only), 24, or 26 (.28 Nosler only, new 2019) in. Sendero (disc.) or Omega Hunter contour barrel, Switch Barrel System, Hawkins Precision 5 round (DBM Style) detachable mag., adj. trigger, carbon fiber aluminum pillar, glass bedded stock w/charcoal grey, additional stock colors available, Rachet, Spiral, Skip, Micro Straight, or Micro spiral fluting, Cerakote Elite Series in black or Smoke (disc.) finish.

MSR $2,999	$2,550	$2,250	$1,900	$1,750	$1,400	$1,150	$900	

GRADING - PPGS™ 100% 98% 95% 90% 80% 70% 60% *LAST MSR*

CARBON HUNTER - .28 Nosler (new 2019), 6mm Creedmoor (new 2019), .308 Win. (new 2019), .300 Win. Mag., .357 Raptor, 6.5 Creedmoor, or 7mm Rem. cal., Stiller (disc.), Omega short/long (disc.), GRB (new 2021), or TL Custom short/long (mfg. 2019-2020) action, 20, 22 (.308 Win.only), 24, or 26 (new 2019) in. Omega Hunter (new 2019) or Sporter (disc.) contour barrel, Switch Barrel System, HS Precision detachable mag. (disc.), three round BDL style (hinged floorplate), TriggerTech adj. trigger, carbon fiber aluminum pillar, glass bedded stock w/charcoal grey finish, other stock colors available, Cerakote Elite Series in black or Smoke (disc.) finish.

MSR $3,399 $2,900 $2,550 $2,150 $1,950 $1,600 $1,300 $1,100

ELEMENT - .308 Win., 6.5 Creedmoor, or .375 Raptor cal., Stiller or Omega Short Action, 20 or 22 in. Omega Sporter Contour barrel, Switch Barrel System, Magpul detached mag., TriggerTech adj. trigger, Magpul 700 polymer stock w/glass bedded recoil lug in black or FDE finish, stainless matte metal finish. Disc. 2020.

$2,200 $1,925 $1,650 $1,495 $1,210 $995 $775 ***$2,599***

GAME STALKER - .28 Nosler (new 2019), 6mm Creedmoor (new 2019), .308 Win., .300 Win. Mag., .357 Raptor, 6.5 Creedmoor, or 7mm Rem. cal., Stiller (disc.), Omega short/long (disc.), TL (disc. 2020), or GRB (new 2021) short/long action, 20, 22 (.308 Win. only, new 2019), 24, or 26 (.28 Nosler only, new 2019) in. Omega Hunter or Sporter (disc. 2019) contour barrel, Switch Barrel System, three round BDL style (hinged floorplate), TriggerTech adj. trigger, composite (disc.) or carbon fiber aluminum pillar glass bedded stock in Omega Green Camo, Omega Grey Stealth or stock colors of choice, Rachet, Spiral, Skip, Micro Straight, or Micro spiral fluting, Elite black Cerakote or stainless matte metal (disc. 2019) finish, available for upgrades.

MSR $2,999 $2,550 $2,250 $1,900 $1,750 $1,400 $1,150 $975

TAC-LITE - .308 Win., 6mm Creedmoor (new 2019), or 6.5 Creedmoor cal., Stiller (disc.), Omega short (disc.), or TL Custom short/long (new 2019)action, 22 or 24 in. stainless steel Omega Sendero contour threaded barrel, Switch Barrel System, three round BDL style bottom metal (hinged floorplate), TriggerTech adj. trigger, CNC machined aluminum (disc.) or MPA Hybrid chassis stock, Rachet, Spiral, Skip, Micro Straight, or Micro spiral fluting, Graphite Black or choice of single color Cerakote finish.

MSR $2,999 $2,550 $2,250 $1,900 $1,750 $1,400 $1,150 $975

OMEGA RIFLES/SHOTGUNS

Previous trademark of select rifles/shotguns imported by K.B.I., Inc. located in Harrisburg, PA, until 1994.

RIFLES

To date, there has been little collector interest for Omega rifles. Values are mostly determined by the shooting value rather than collector value. Current values typically range from $95-$150.

SHOTGUNS

STANDARD O/U - 12, 20 (disc.), 28 (disc.) ga., or .410 bore (disc.), boxlock action, folding design, SNT, 26 or 28 in. VR barrels, extractors, checkered walnut stock and forearm, 5 1/2-7 lbs. Disc. 1994.

$335 $290 $255 $220 $185 $160 $140

* ***Deluxe O/U*** - 12 ga. only, similar to Standard Model except has better walnut. Importation disc. 1990.

$425 $330 $295 $260 $230 $200 $180 ***$379***

STANDARD SxS - 20, 28 ga., or .410 bore, boxlock action, folding design, double triggers, hardwood stock and forearm, 26 in. barrels, extractors, 5 1/2 lbs. Disc. 1989.

$190 $165 $140 $120 $110 $100 $90 ***$229***

Add $40 for 28 ga. or .410 bore.

* ***Deluxe SxS*** - .410 bore only, similar to Standard Model except has better walnut. Disc. 1989.

$225 $200 $175 $155 $140 $130 $120 ***$249***

SINGLE BARREL - 12, 20 ga., or .410 bore, various barrel lengths, matte blue finish, extractor. Importation disc. 1987.

$85 $75 $65 $55 $45 $40 $35 ***$95***

STANDARD FOLDING SINGLE BARREL - 12, 16, 20, 28 ga., or .410 bore, 28 or 30 in. barrel, checkered hardwood stock, matte chrome receiver, approx. 5 1/2 lbs. Importation disc. 1987.

$160 $135 $115 $100 $85 $70 $65 ***$180***

DELUXE FOLDING SINGLE BARREL - 12, 16, 20, 28 ga., or .410 bore, similar to Standard Model, except has checkered walnut stock and forearm, blue receiver. Importation disc. 1987.

$195 $160 $135 $115 $100 $85 $70 ***$220***

GRADING - PPGS™	100%	98%	95%	90%	80%	70%	60%	LAST MSR

OMEGA WEAPONS SYSTEMS INC.

Previous shotgun manufacturer established circa 1998, and located in Tucson, AZ. Previously distributed by Defense Technology, Inc., located in Lake Forest, CA.

SHOTGUNS: SEMI-AUTO

OMEGA SPS-12 – 12 ga. only, 2 3/4 in. chamber, gas operation, 5 shot detachable mag., 20 in. barrel, protected ghost ring rear and front sight, synthetic stock (with or w/o pistol grip) and forearm, 9 lbs. Mfg. 1998-2005.

$195 $180 $165 $150 $135 $125 $115 *$225*

OMNI

Previous manufacturer located in Riverside, CA 1992-1998. During 1998, Omni changed its name to E.D.M. Arms. Previously distributed by First Defense International located in CA.

RIFLES: BOLT ACTION

LONG ACTION SINGLE SHOT – .50 BMG cal., competition single shot, chrome moly black finished receiver, 32-34 in. steel or stainless steel barrel with round muzzle brake, benchrest fiberglass stock, designed for FCSA competition shooting, 32 lbs. Mfg. 1996-98.

$3,600 $3,200 $2,800 $2,500 $2,150 $1,800 $1,500 *$3,500*

Add $400 for painted stock (disc. 1996).

SHELL HOLDER SINGLE SHOT – similar to Long Action Single Shot, except has fiberglass field stock with bipod, 28 lbs. Mfg. 1997-98.

$2,975 $2,750 $2,525 $2,150 $1,800 $1,500 $1,250 *$2,750*

MODEL WINDRUNNER – .50 BMG cal., long action, single shot or 3 shot mag., 1-piece I-beam, chrome moly black finished receiver, 36 in. barrel with round muzzle brake, fiberglass tactical stock, 35 lbs. Mfg. 1997-1998.

$6,950 $6,425 $5,875 $5,325 $4,750 $4,175 $3,500 *$7,500*

Add $750 for 3 shot repeater.

MODEL WARLOCK – .50 BMG or 20mm cal., single, 3 (20mm), or 5 (.50 BMG) shot fixed mag., fiberglass field stock, massive design chrome moly black finished receiver, muzzle brake, 50 lbs. Mfg. 1997-1998.

$10,750 $8,950 $7,750 $6,750 $5,500 $4,750 $3,950 *$12,000*

E.D.M. ARMS MODEL 97 – available in most cals. up to .308 Win., single shot or repeater (cals. .17 Rem. through .223 Rem. only), wire-cut one-piece receiver, black tactical stock with pillar-bedded chrome moly barrel, black finished receiver, unique trigger with safety, 9 lbs. Mfg. 1997-1998.

$2,525 $2,150 $1,800 $1,500 $1,250 $1,100 $925 *$2,750*

E.D.M. ARMS WINDRUNNER WR50 – .50 BMG cal., sniper rifle, 5 shot mag., removable tactical adj. stock, takedown action with removable barrel, wire-cut one-piece receiver, titanium muzzle brake, blackened chrome moly barrel, approx. 29 lbs. Mfg. 1998 only.

$11,750 $10,250 $9,500 $8,250 $7,000 $5,750 $4,500 *$12,900*

OMNI (CURRENT MFG.)

Please refer to the American Tactical Imports listing in the A section.

ONLY LONG RANGE

Please refer to Noreen Firearms LLC listing in the N section.

OPTIMA

Current trademark of O/U and single shot shotguns manufactured by Hatsan Arms Company, located in Izmir, Turkey. No current U.S. importation.

OPUS SPORTING ARMS, INC.

Previous manufacturer located in Long Beach, CA.

RIFLES: BOLT ACTION

OPUS ONE – .243 Win., .270 Win., or .30-06 cal., U.S.R.A. Co. Model 70 action, 24 in. barrel, deluxe checkered walnut stock with ebony forend cap, 6 3/4 lbs., Halliburton cased. Mfg. 1987-88 only.

$2,350 $1,995 $1,675 $1,250 $1,000 $875 $795 *$2,700*

OPUS TWO – similar to Opus One, except in 7mm Rem. Mag. or .300 Win. Mag. cal., 7 1/4 lbs., cased. Mfg. 1987-88 only.

$2,350 $1,995 $1,675 $1,250 $1,000 $875 $795 *$2,700*

OPUS THREE – similar to Opus Two, except in .375 H&H or .458 Win. Mag. cal., 10 1/4 lbs., cased. Mfg. 1987-88 only.

$2,600 $2,275 $1,800 $1,375 $1,050 $900 $825 *$2,850*

GRADING - PPGS™	100%	98%	95%	90%	80%	70%	60%	LAST MSR

OREGON ARMS

Please refer to the Chipmunk Rifles listing in the C section.

ORISKANY ARMS INC.

Current 1911-style pistol and gun components manufacturer established in 1947, and located in Oriskany, NY.

PISTOLS: SEMI-AUTO

In 2013, Oriskany Arms started manufacturing a line of full-size American made Series 1911 9mm and .45 ACP pistols. In 2015, they completed their 1911 series and introduced the Officer sized 350FP, followed by the Commander sized 425FP pistol.

MODEL 1911 TRADITIONAL 350 FP – 9mm Para., .38 Super (disc. 2019), or .45 ACP cal., 3 1/2 in. match grade steel barrel, heat-treated steel Officer style frame and slide, 7 (.45 ACP) or 9 (9mm Para.) shot mag., skeletonized hammer, 3-hole trigger with adj. screw, Novak 3-dot sights, black grips w/waffle patterning, high-rise extended beavertail safety, extended thumb safety, matte black oxide finish. New 2017.

MSR $915	$800	$700	$600	$550	$450	$375	$300	

Add $81 for .38 Super cal. (disc. 2019).

MODEL 1911 TRADITIONAL 425 FP – 9mm Para., .38 Super (disc. 2019), or .45 ACP cal., heat-treated steel Commander style frame and slide, 4 1/4 in. match grade steel barrel, 7 (.45 ACP) or 9 (9mm Para.) shot mag., skeletonized hammer, 3-hole trigger with adj. screw, Novak 3-dot sights, black grips w/waffle patterning, high-rise extended beavertail safety, extended thumb safety, front and rear slide serrations, matte black oxide finish. New 2017.

MSR $905	$800	$700	$600	$550	$450	$375	$300	

Add $81 for .38 Super cal. (disc. 2019).

MODEL 1911 TRADITIONAL 500 FP (TRADITIONAL FP) – 9mm Para., .38 Super (disc. 2019), 10mm (new 2020), or .45 ACP cal., heat-treated steel Government style frame and slide, 5 in. match grade steel barrel, 7 (.45 ACP) or 9 (9mm Para.) shot mag., skeletonized hammer, 3-hole trigger with adj. screw, Novak 3-dot sights, black grips w/waffle patterning, high-rise extended beavertail safety, extended thumb safety, front and rear slide serrations, matte black oxide finish. New 2014.

MSR $825	$750	$650	$550	$500	$400	$325	$250	

Add $76 for .38 Super cal. (disc. 2019).

MODEL 1911 CUSTOM 350 FP – 9mm Para., .38 Super (disc. 2019), or .45 ACP cal., 3 1/2 in. match grade steel barrel, 7 (.45 ACP) or 9 (9mm Para.) shot mag., heat-treated steel Officer style frame and slide, skeletonized hammer, 3-hole trigger with adj. screw, Novak sights, black grips w/waffle patterning, high-rise extended beavertail safety, extended thumb safety, metallic boron Nitride finish. New 2017.

MSR $1,015	$900	$800	$700	$600	$500	$400	$325	

Add $81 for .38 Super cal. (disc. 2019).

MODEL 1911 CUSTOM 425 FP – 9mm Para., .38 Super (disc. 2019), or .45 ACP cal., heat-treated steel Commander style frame and slide, 4 1/4 in. match grade steel barrel, 7 (.45 ACP) or 9 (9mm Para.) shot mag., skeletonized hammer, 3-hole trigger with adj. screw, Novak 3-dot sights, high-rise extended beavertail safety, extended thumb safety, front and rear slide serrations, metallic boron Nitride finish. New 2017.

MSR $1,005	$900	$800	$700	$600	$500	$400	$325	

Add $81 for .38 Super cal. (disc. 2019).

MODEL 1911 CUSTOM 500 FP (CUSTOM FP) – 9mm Para., .38 Super (mfg. 2017-2019), 10mm (new 2020), or .45 ACP cal., heat-treated steel Government style frame and slide, 5 in. match grade steel barrel, 7 (.45 ACP) or 9 (9mm Para.) shot mag., skeletonized hammer, 3-hole trigger with adj. screw, Novak 3-dot sights, black grips w/waffle patterning, high-rise extended beavertail safety, extended thumb safety, front and rear slide serrations, metallic boron Nitride finish. New 2014.

MSR $925	$850	$750	$600	$550	$450	$375	$300	

Add $76 for .38 Super cal. (mfg. 2017-2019).

MODEL 1911 SURVIVOR FP – 9mm Para., .38 Super, or .45 ACP cal., heat-treated steel Government style frame and slide, 5 in. match grade steel barrel, 7 shot mag., skeletonized hammer, three hole trigger with adj. screw, Novak tritium night sights, high-rise extended beavertail safety, extended thumb safety, front and rear slide serrations, lower Picatinny rail in front of squared off trigger guard, includes emergency survival kit inside of removable grip panel, OD Green Cerakote finish. Mfg. 2014-2016.

	$925	$775	$650	$550	$475	$400	$350	*$1,095*

GRADING - PPGS™ 100% 98% 95% 90% 80% 70% 60% LAST MSR

MODEL 1911 TACTICAL 350 FP – 9mm Para., .38 Super (disc. 2019), or .45 ACP cal., heat-treated steel Officer style frame and slide, 3 1/2 in. match grade steel barrel, 7 (.45 ACP) or 9 (9mm Para.) shot mag., skeletonized hammer, 3-hole trigger with adj. screw, Novak Tritium night sights, black grips w/waffle patterning, high-rise extended beavertail safety, extended thumb safety, FDE Cerakote finish. New 2017.

MSR $1,245 $1,100 $1,000 $850 $750 $600 $500 $400

Add $81 for .38 Super cal. (disc. 2019).

MODEL 1911 TACTICAL 425 FP – 9mm Para., .38 Super (disc. 2019), 10mm (new 2020), or .45 ACP cal., heat-treated steel Commander style frame and slide, 4 1/4 in. match grade steel barrel, 7 (.45 ACP) or 9 (9mm Para.) shot mag., skeletonized hammer, 3-hole trigger with adj. screw, Novak Tritium night sights, black grips w/waffle patterning, high-rise extended beavertail safety, extended thumb safety, front and rear slide serrations, lower Picatinny rail in front of squared off trigger guard, matte black oxide finish. New 2017.

MSR $1,140 $1,000 $900 $750 $700 $550 $450 $350

Add $81 for .38 Super cal. (disc. 2019).

MODEL 1911 TACTICAL 500 FP (TACTICAL FP) – 9mm Para. (new 2017), .38 Super (mfg. 2017-2019), 10mm (new 2020), or .45 ACP cal, heat-treated steel Government style frame and slide, 5 in. match grade steel barrel, 7 (.45 ACP) or 9 (9mm Para.) shot mag., skeletonized hammer, 3-hole trigger with adj. screw, Novak tritium night sights, black grips w/waffle patterning, high-rise extended beavertail safety, extended thumb safety, front and rear slide serrations, lower Picatinny rail in front of squared off trigger guard, matte black oxide finish. New 2014.

MSR $1,060 $950 $850 $700 $650 $500 $425 $325

Add $76 for .38 Super cal. (mfg. 2017-2019).

ORSI & ORSI

Current trademark of shotguns and rifles manufactured in Italy.

Massimo Orsi has manufactured approximately 75 shotguns and rifles for the past several decades. All Orsi guns must be appraised individually based on their desirability, features, and condition. Please contact Mr. Orsi directly for more information about his guns.

ORSIS

Current tactical rifle manufacturer located in Moscow, Russia. No current U.S. importation.

RIFLES

Orsis currently manufactures the following bolt action: Hunter Carbine Orsis 120, Orsis 140, Orsis 220, Orsis Hunter Deluxe, F-Class, SE T-5000 M sniper rifle, SE Hunter M, SE Alpine M, and SE Varmint M. Semi-auto models include: Orsis-K15 Brother and Orsis AR15J rifle. Previous models include: T-500, AR-10 National Match, and M-15 Carbine. Please contact the company directly for more information including pricing and U.S. availability.

SHOTGUNS

Orsis currently manufactures the following shotguns: Marocchi First, Marocchi First-E Deluxe, Marocchi Si-12/Walnut, and Marocchi Si-12/Plastic. Please contact the company directly for more information including pricing and U.S. availability.

ORTGIES PISTOLS

Previous trademark of pistols manufactured by Deutsche Werke A.G. located in Erfurt, Germany.

PISTOLS: SEMI-AUTO

VEST POCKET AUTOMATIC – .25 ACP cal., 6 shot, 2 3/4 in. barrel, blue or nickel finish, fixed sights, wood grips. Mfg. 1921-28.

$350 $250 $200 $175 $150 $125 $100

POCKET AUTOMATIC – .32 ACP cal. (8 shot) mfg. 1920-1928 or .380 ACP cal. (7 shot) mfg. 1922-1926, 3 1/4 in. barrel, blue or nickel finish, fixed sights, wood grips.

$400 $300 $200 $175 $150 $125 $100

Add 20% for .380 ACP cal. or double safety variation.

ORVIS

ORVIS

Current catalog retailer and importer of private label subcontracted shotguns located in Manchester, VT and many other locations.

Orvis imports various shotguns under subcontract with various international manufacturers, including Arrieta and Caesar Guerini. Typical custom order delivery time is 2-8 months. Most of these private label models will approximate the values of the equivalent model manufactured by the subcontractor unless there are additional features and/or options which will add to the value.

GRADING - PPGS™	100%	98%	95%	90%	80%	70%	60%	LAST MSR

SHOTGUNS: O/U

The MSR of currently manufactured models in this section also includes custom fitting to individual measurements - delivery is typically within 8 weeks.

SKB GREEN MOUNTAIN UPLANDER (MODEL 555) – 12, 20, 28 ga., or .410 bore, 25-27 in. barrels, blue frame, straight stock with leather covered recoil pad. Disc.

	100%	98%	95%	90%	80%	70%	60%	LAST MSR
	$750	$675	$600	$550	$500	$450	$400	*$995*

Add 15% for 28 ga. or .410 bore.

UPLANDER – 12, 20, 28 ga., or .410 bore, engraved coin finished boxlock action with sideplates, 26 (disc.) or 28 in. VR barrels with choke tubes (except 28 ga.), SST, straight (disc.) or pistol grip, select American black walnut with 26 LPI checkering, leather covered recoil pad since 1992, 6-7 lbs. Mfg. by P. Beretta of Italy. Importation disc.

	100%	98%	95%	90%	80%	70%	60%	LAST MSR
	$4,075	$3,575	$3,050	$2,775	$2,225	$1,825	$1,425	*$4,795*

Add $1,250 for 28/20 ga. combo with case.

WATERFOWLER – 12 ga. only, 3 in. chambers, matte metal finish, 28 in. barrels with choke tubes, steel shot compatible, 7 1/2 lbs. Mfg. by P. Beretta of Italy. Disc. 2011.

	100%	98%	95%	90%	80%	70%	60%	LAST MSR
	$3,150	$2,725	$2,150	$1,650	$1,250	$1,025	$900	

SPORTING CLAYS – 12 ga. only, 30 in. vented barrels with VR and choke tubes, adj. trigger, oil finished checkered walnut stock and forearm. Mfg. 1994-disc.

	100%	98%	95%	90%	80%	70%	60%	LAST MSR
	$3,750	$3,350	$2,875	$2,450	$2,100	$1,675	$1,350	*$4,100*

This model was also available in a women's configuration in 20 ga. with lightweight frame and included a carrying case.

ELOS – 12, 20, or 28 ga., 2 3/4 or 3 in. chambers, 28 in. VR barrels, 5 nickel plated chokes, brass bead sights, ELOS pistol grip stock with Triwood enhanced finish, standard checkering, interchangeable gel compound recoil pad, English walnut forend with semi-Schnabel design, receiver has Orvis logo and scroll engraving, color case hardened receiver with Invisalloy coating, 6 lbs. 8 oz., mfg. by FABARM of Italy. Imported 2018-2020.

	100%	98%	95%	90%	80%	70%	60%	LAST MSR
	$2,050	$1,795	$1,550	$1,395	$1,150	$925	$725	*$2,395*

ELOS D2 – 12, 20, or 28 ga., 28 in. chrome plated barrels w/VR rib, C/IC/M/IM/F, FABARM Hyperbolic screw-in chokes, ejectors, SST, brass bead front sight, oil-finished walnut stock, rubber buttpad, automatic safety, includes hard case, nickel finish receiver, mfg. by FABARM in Italy. Importation began 2018.

	100%	98%	95%	90%	80%	70%	60%	LAST MSR
MSR $2,850	$2,400	$2,100	$1,800	$1,650	$1,350	$1,100	$950	

FIELD – 12, 20, 28 ga., or .410 bore, case colored boxlock action with sideplates, ST, auto ejectors (12 and 20 ga. only), checkered Turkish walnut stock and forearm, 26 or 28 in. VR barrels with 5 choke tubes (except .410 bore), blue metal finish, mfg. in Turkey. Imported 2010-disc.

	100%	98%	95%	90%	80%	70%	60%	LAST MSR
	$1,825	$1,600	$1,300	$1,000	$850	$700	$550	*$1,995*

SUPER FIELD – 12 or 20 ga., 26 (Uplander 20 ga. only), 28 (All Rounder), or 30 (Sporting Clays) in. VR barrels, configurations include Uplander 20 ga. with straight grip stock, All Rounder 12 ga. with 28 in. barrels and pistol grip stock, and Sporting Clays 12 ga. with 30 in. barrels, wide rib, and pistol grip stock, blue receiver, choke tubes, mfg. in Italy. Limited importation 1995 only.

	100%	98%	95%	90%	80%	70%	60%	LAST MSR
	$1,495	$1,250	$1,000	$875	$750	$625	$500	*$2,150*

PREMIER GRADE – 12 or 20 ga., 3 in. chambers, 20 ga. features 28 in. barrels with straight grip stock, 12 ga. features pistol grip stock, select oil-finished European stock and forearm, choke tubes, blue frame with scrolled engraving, adj. trigger, cased, mfg. in Belgium 1995-98.

	100%	98%	95%	90%	80%	70%	60%	LAST MSR
	$6,450	$5,875	$5,250	$4,675	$4,000	$3,450	$2,675	*$6,450*

Add $100 for Premier Grade Sporting.

This model is also available as a 20 ga. Superlight with straight grip stock and 26 in. barrels.

ORVIS DELUXE GRADE – similar to Uplander and Waterfowler, except has engraved bird scenes and scroll work on antique coin-finished receiver, deluxe checkered walnut stock and forearm, case. Imported 1993-94 only.

	100%	98%	95%	90%	80%	70%	60%	LAST MSR
	$4,250	$3,575	$2,950	$2,300	$1,900	$1,500	$1,275	*$4,950*

RUGER/ORVIS MODEL – 12 or 20 ga., 3 in. chambers, Red Label Ruger action with customized Orvis features including blue receiver and straight grip English checkered stock. Disc. 1993.

	100%	98%	95%	90%	80%	70%	60%	LAST MSR
	$1,295	$975	$850	$725	$600	$495	$450	*$1,295*

KNOCKABOUT – 12, 20, 28 ga., or .410 bore, 28 in. barrel, checkered pistol grip walnut stock and forearm, rubber recoil pad, color case hardened frame, gold trigger. Disc.

	100%	98%	95%	90%	80%	70%	60%	LAST MSR
	$3,125	$2,725	$2,350	$2,125	$1,725	$1,400	$1,095	*$3,695*

This model was also available in a two and three barrel set, please contact Orvis directly for additional information.

GRADING - PPGS™	100%	98%	95%	90%	80%	70%	60%	LAST MSR

SHOTGUNS: SxS

WATERFOWLER – 12 ga. only, 3 in. chambers, matte metal finish, 28 in. barrels with choke tubes, 7 3/4 lbs. Mfg. by P. Beretta of Italy until 1993. Disc.

	$1,950	$1,725	$1,475	$1,125	$950	$825	$700	*$1,950*

CUSTOM UPLANDER – 12, 16, 20, 28 ga., or .410 bore, traditional frame, 25 or 27 in. barrels only, case colored or blue sidelock action with light engraving, DT, custom ordered gun, mfg. by Arrieta located in Spain.

	N/A	$2,525	$2,250	$1,950	$1,650	$1,450	$1,025	

Add $950 for SNT.
Add $1,200 for extra set of barrels (same ga.).

UPLAND CLASSIC – 12, 16, 20, 28 ga., or .410 bore, sidelock, Bellota steel chrome-lined barrels, ejectors, Anson-style forearm release, customer choice of stock and forearm design, barrel lengths, chokes, chamber size and rib design, hand made by Arrieta. Imported 2013-disc.

	$5,000	$4,375	$3,750	$3,400	$2,750	$2,250	$1,750	*$5,900*

FIELD GRADE – 12, 20, 28 ga., or .410 bore, case colored boxlock action with sideplates, ST, extractors, straight grip Turkish walnut stock and forearm, 26 or 28 in. VR barrels with 5 choke tubes (except .410 bore), blue metal finish, mfg. in Turkey. Imported 2010-disc.

	$1,825	$1,600	$1,300	$1,000	$850	$700	$550	*$1,995*

FINE GRADE – 12, 16, 20, 28 ga., or .410 bore, custom ordered gun, custom order barrel lengths, sidelock action, DT, mfg. by Arrieta located in Spain. Disc. 1999.

	$4,650	$3,775	$3,150	$2,500	$1,995	$1,500	$1,150	*$4,650*

Add $950 for SNT.
Add $1,950 for extra set of barrels (same ga.).

ORVIS ARTISAN – 12, 20, or 28 ga., 2 3/4 or 3 in. chambers, hand engraved rounded action, 28 in. barrels, fixed IC/M chokes, ejectors, single non-selective trigger, brass bead sights, AAA or AAAAA Grade walnut stock, Orvis logo with game scene/custom engraving, hand checkering, splinter forend, auto safety, parallel locking lugs, includes Chapuis Armes hard case, Old English coin finished receiver, 5 3/4-7 lbs. New 2018.

MSR $8,995	$7,650	$6,700	$5,750	$5,200	$4,225	$3,450	$3,000	

ORVIS CLASSIC – 12, 20, or 28 ga., 2 3/4 or 3 in. chambers, rounded action, 28 in. barrels, fixed IC/M chokes, ejectors, single non-selective trigger, brass bead sights, fancy walnut stock with hand rubbed oil finish, scroll engraving, auto safety, parallel locking lugs, includes Chapuis Armes hard case, Old English coin finished receiver, 5 3/4-7 lbs. New 2018.

MSR $4,595	$3,900	$3,425	$2,925	$2,650	$2,150	$1,750	$1,525	

Add $200 for 28 ga.

ROUNDED ACTION MODEL – sidelock, chopper lump Bellota steel chrome-lined barrels, hand oil finished checkered walnut stock and forearm, ejectors, 5-pin rounded action, DT, optional engraving, mfg. by Arrieta. New 2012.

MSR $10,495	$8,925	$7,800	$6,695	$6,075	$4,915	$4,000	$3,500	

* ***Rounded Action Uplander*** – similar to Rounded Action, except has less engraving, blue or case hardened frame. Mfg. 2000-disc.

	N/A	$4,450	$3,950	$3,500	$3,000	$2,500	$2,000	

FEATHERLIGHT – 20 or 28 ga., barrels up to 28 in., case colored round action, DT, accent engraving, 5 1/2 to 5 3/4 lbs. Mfg. 2013-disc.

	$5,350	$4,675	$4,000	$3,625	$2,950	$2,400	$2,050	*$6,300*

OSPREY ARMAMENT

Current M14 type and AR-15 style firearm manufacturer located in Hutto, TX. Previously located in Wilmington, NC.

Please refer to BlueBookOfGunValues.com to order the *Blue Book of AR-15s & Variations*, available as a book or online subscription.

OTTOMANGUNS

Current shotgun and airgun manufacturer located in Istanbul, Turkey. No current U.S. importation. Previously imported during 2011 by American Tactical Imports (ATI), located in Rochester, NY.

Ottomanguns manufactures a complete line of good quality shotguns in a variety of configurations, including O/U, SxS, semi-auto (including tactical models), slide action (including tactical models), and single barrel. Brand names include Bronco, Ottoman, Posh, Rigel, and TAC Series. The company also manufactures air rifles. For current U.S. availability and pricing, please contact the company directly.

GRADING - PPGS™	100%	98%	95%	90%	80%	70%	60%	LAST MSR

SHOTGUNS: SEMI-AUTO

SULTAN SERIES – 12 ga., 18 1/4 or 28 (walnut stock only) in. barrel, available with walnut stock and blue steel, or synthetic stock (camo, nickel or black pistol grip), 5 shot, black recoil pad. Importation disc. 2011.

	$240	$215	$185	$160	$140	$125	$110	*$279*

Add $29 for synthetic pistol grip stock.
Add $44 for Marine variation with nickel finish.
Add $29 for digital camo.
Add $117 for walnut stock.

SHOTGUNS: SLIDE ACTION

GRAND VAZIR SERIES – 12 ga., 5 shot, 18 1/2 in. barrel, synthetic stock with matte black, Marine nickel, or digital camo finish. Importation disc. 2011.

	$185	$160	$140	$120	$110	$100	$90	*$220*

Add $22 for Marine model with nickel finish.
Add $61 for digital camo.

OVERMATCH PRECISION ARMS

Current rifle and parts manufacturer located in Hutto, TX.

Overmatch Precision Arms manufactures the MK36 rifle that utilizes an AR-15 style lower receiver and M14/M1A style upper receiver.

RIFLES: SEMI-AUTO

MK36 H – .308 Win./7.62 NATO cal., GPO, 16, 18, or 20 in. match grade modified M1A contour barrel, 10 or 20 shot box-fed mag., Mil-Spec AR trigger, ambi controls, Mil-Spec Picatinny rail, 9, 11, or 13 in. M-LOK handguard, black, FDE, or black/FDE combo finish, 39 in. OAL, 8.8 lbs. New 2020.

MSR $2,995	$2,775	$1,825	$1,350	$750	$650	$595	$525	

Add $155 for 18 in. barrel.
Add $480 for 20 in. barrel.

OWEN, KEN

Current custom long gun manufacturer located in Moscow, TN.

RIFLES

Ken Owen specializes in building big bore double rifles and express boxlock rifles. All guns are built to customer order. Please contact Mr. Owen directly for more information, including a price quotation, available options, and delivery time.

ÖZKANLAR

Current shotgun manufacturer located in Turkey. Currently distributed and exported by Dorkas Foreign Trade, located in Konya, Turkey.

Özkanlar currently manufactures a line of good quality semi-auto shotguns under the Akrep, Kobra, Bavyer, and Lupus trademarks. Please contact the exporter directly for more information, including pricing and domestic availability.

P SECTION

P.38 MILITARY & COMMERCIAL PISTOLS

Previously manufactured P.38s from various German companies circa 1938-1946, including Mauser (byf & svw codes), Spreewerk (cyq code and cvq which was attributed to the use of a broken die), and Walther (480 & ac codes). See FRENCH MILITARY section for late war/post-war French mfg. (svw code with star proof). Also includes Walther post-war mfg. and recent conversions fabricated by John Martz.

Also See: CZ, Fabrique Nationale, Luger, Mauser, and Walther for other German military pistols.

GRADING - PPGS™	100%	98%	95%	90%	80%	70%	60%	LAST MSR

PISTOLS: SEMI-AUTO, CIRCA 1938-1946

A note on how values are affected by import marked P.38s: some of the earliest imported P.38s were discreetly marked by I.A.C. on the flat surface under the slide. A few were even marked under the grips. When lightly marked in those areas, there is little reduction in value. However, most recently imported P.38s are more visibly marked on the sides of the slide or the barrel. The more desirable the gun, the more gets subtracted for the visible markings (i.e., very few P.38 collectors are interested in an ac No Date or 480 Code if markings are visible). As a result, some P.38 values could be reduced as much as 50%, while hidden markings may lower the value only 10%-20%. It all depends on the variation and how visible the markings are.

Variation serial number ranges are to be used as a guide due to serial number overlapping during P.38 variation changes.

Subtract 40%-50% on most common P.38s if recently imported and/or refinished by importer.

Add 100% for two Walther matching magazines where applicable. Beware of fakes or post-war re-numbering.

AP "ARMEE PISTOLE" – 9mm Para. cal., 5 (most common) or 8 (first 10 guns) in. barrel, 8 shot (all examples came with 2 matching magazines), most examples have a steel frame, but the final examples had a dural aluminum frame, concealed hammer prototype from 1936, fixed rear (most common) or 2 position rear sight (first 10 guns only), walnut checkered grips., approx. 50 handmade examples in serial range 1-50, each one different in some details, first 10 guns were tang-slotted for a hollowed out shoulder stock with canvas carrier. Mfg. 1936.

* ***AP "Armee Pistole" Long Barrel*** – ser. no. range 1-10.

N/A	$75,000	$65,000	$55,000	$45,000	$35,000	$25,000	

Add 10% for matching magazine.
Add $15,000 for original stock/carrier.
Add $25,000 for matching stock/carrier.

* ***AP "Armee Pistole" Standard Barrel*** – approx. ser. no. range 11-50.

N/A	$35,000	$30,000	$25,000	$21,000	$18,000	$15,000	

Add 10% for matching magazine.
Add 15% for Dural aluminum frame (inspect carefully for cracks).

PROTOTYPE HP "HEERES PISTOLE" & FIRST MODEL P.38 – 7.65mm or 9mm Para. cal., first experimental production, ser. numbered 1010-1050, many different configurations, some have acid etched "Privat" markings on receiver, checkered takedown lever, thick safety lever, rectangular firing pin, thin rear sight.

It is recommended that early variations are evaluated and priced by an expert. Watch for fakes.

HP "HEERES PISTOLE" – 9mm Para. cal., early Walther commercial production begins at ser. no. 1050, high polish until approx. 13000, approx. 24,000 mfg. 1938-1944.

* ***HP "Heeres Pistole" Experimental "Concealed Extractor"*** – 7.65mm or 9mm Para., first experimental production ser. range 1050 - approx. 1080, handmade high polish finish, approx. 20 mfg. Rarely seen in U.S. market.

N/A	$13,000	$11,375	$10,275	$8,195	$6,750	$5,200	

Add 40% for 7.65mm Para. cal.
Add 30% for dural aluminum frame.

* ***HP "Heeres Pistole" "Swedish" HP*** – experimental first production HP for Swedish trials, serial range H1045-H2074, "H" prefix, rectangular firing pin and crown/N proofs, thin sight, thick safety lever, high polish, handmade craftsmanship.

N/A	$3,600	$3,225	$2,975	$2,425	$2,000	$1,550	

Add 30% for rare matching magazine.

GRADING - PPGS™	100%	98%	95%	90%	80%	70%	60%	LAST MSR

* ***HP "Heeres Pistole" Standard HP Production*** – ser. range 2080-approx. 24000, high polish finish until approx. ser. no. 13000 - then changed to military blue (1942).

N/A $2,850 $2,500 $2,225 $1,825 $1,450 $1,225

Add 20% for Nazi eagle over 359 (E/359) military proof.
Add 20% for high polish finish.
Add 200% for alloy frame, ser. range 6850-6950.
Add 30% for second "Swedish" contract (undelivered), found in approx. ser. range 2075-2838.

* ***HP "Heeres Pistole" 7.65mm Para HP Production*** – 7.65mm Para. cal., single or double action, very limited mfg., rarest collector category for standard production P.38s, most examples have checkered wood grips with thumb rest, can be found in ser. no. range 3000-3200.

N/A $15,000 $11,500 $9,000 $7,500 $6,500 $5,000

Add 100% for single action pistols, all having a long tang.

* ***HP "Heeres Pistole" Late War Mod. P.38 Production*** – marked "MOD P38" on left slide, rough military blue finish, some frames show heavy tool marks, ser. range 24150-25990.

N/A $3,200 $2,500 $2,025 $1,700 $1,450 $1,150

ZERO-SERIES – 9mm Para. cal., features Walther banner, high polish finish, black checkered grips, up to 5-digit number w/o suffix. Mfg. 1940, ser. no. range 01-013714.

* ***Zero Series - 1st Issue*** – internal extractor, square firing pin, ser. range 01-01000.

N/A $12,500 $10,850 $9,300 $7,500 $6,150 $4,900

Add 40% for matching mag.

* ***Zero Series - 2nd Issue*** – external extractor, thin slide, square firing pin, ser. range 02005-03478, more difficult to find than 1st Issue.

N/A $10,750 $9,275 $8,050 $6,425 $5,325 $4,075

Add 40% for matching mag.
Add 10% for mill cut on slide when used to remove 480 code.

* ***Zero Series - 3rd Issue*** – external extractor, round firing pin, ser. no. range 03520-013000, after ser. no. 010000, some models had brown military style grips, baseline for military P.38s to follow.

N/A $3,800 $3,000 $2,800 $2,200 $1,925 $1,425

Add 40% for matching mag.
Add 10% for military style grips.

P.38 – 9mm Para. cal., double action, 5 in. barrel, 8 shot mag., fixed sights, brown or black composite grips with primarily blue finishes. Many variations exhibiting a variety of metal finishes and codes, 34 oz. Over 1,000,000 manufactured during WWII.

Based on the prototype "Armee Pistol" from 1936, this model was adopted as the standard service pistol of the German Military in 1938 and refined in the "Zero Series". The P.38 was manufactured by Walther - code "480" and "ac" (mfg. April 1940-1945), Mauser - code "byf" and "svw" (mfg. late 1942-1945), and Spreewerk - "cyq" (mfg. 1942-1945). The finish on most WWII 1942 and Later P.38s is not of the same quality as the pre-war and early war Walther guns with the Spreewerk models being the poorest. Note: The cvq stamp is currently thought to be attributed to a broken die which was used intermittently, and not to a Spreewerk code change.

480 CODE FIRST MILITARY CONTRACT – 9mm Para. cal. "480" code replaces Walther banner on slide, approx. 7,200 mfg. with ser. range 1-7374, rare in any condition above 90%. Production started April 1940. "480" code changed to "ac" approx. October 1940.

N/A $8,000 $7,000 $6,000 $5,000 $4,000 $3,000

Add 40% for matching mag.
Add 5% for rectangular lanyard loop.

ac-NO DATE (UNDATED) – 9mm Para. cal., "ac" (Walther code) appears on slide without date, "ac" on left trigger guard, 2,620 mfg. with ser. range 7,384-9,912, rarest military coded P.38, rarely encountered in 90% or better original condition. Considerable ser. number overlap between ac-No Date and ac-40 Added.

N/A $9,600 $8,000 $6,875 $5,250 $3,850 $2,825

Add 40% for matching mag.

ac-40 ADDED (SURCHARGE) – 9mm Para. cal., hand pantographed or stamped "40" date added underneath "ac" code after the slide was blued, ser. range. 9988-5942a, 6,000 mfg., high polish, rare in any condition above 90%.

N/A $4,000 $3,500 $3,150 $2,525 $2,075 $1,625

Add 40% for matching mag.

GRADING - PPGS™	100%	98%	95%	90%	80%	70%	60%	LAST MSR

ac-40 STANDARD – 9mm Para. cal., machined stamped, "40" indicates 1940 mfg., approx. 14,000 mfg., ser. range 5942a-9965b.

	N/A	$3,000	$2,525	$2,250	$1,800	$1,400	$1,075	

Add 40% for matching mag.

ac-41 1ST AND 2ND VARIATION – 9mm Para. cal., last military high polish P.38s, only 1st var. has "ac" on left trigger guard (ser. range 1-4833b), 2nd var. continues to serial no. 4527i.

	N/A	$2,200	$1,800	$1,625	$1,400	$1,000	$800	

Add 40% for matching mag.
Add 25% for early variation with "ac" on trigger guard (until mid b-block).
Add 20% for mixed E/359 and E/WaA359 acceptance stamps. First variation approx. serial range 4892a-7109a.

* ***ac-41 3rd Variation*** – 9mm Para. cal., standard (dull) military blue finish over un-polished metal surface begins, ser. range. approx. 5015i-9973j.

	N/A	$1,950	$1,550	$1,350	$1,075	$925	$725	

Add 40% for matching mag.

ac-42 1ST AND 2ND VARIATIONS – 9mm Para. cal., dull military finish, serial range 1-9197k, ac-42 1st var. last P.38 to have E/359 stamped small parts to approx. 1000b. Serialized mag. stop at approx. 9500c.

	N/A	$1,200	$1,020	$870	$750	$630	$510	

Add 25% for 1st variation.
Add 40% for matching mag. (First variation only).

ac-43, ac-44 AND ac-45 STANDARD ISSUE – 9mm Para. cal., dull military finish, letters are followed by two digit code corresponding to year of mfg. 1943, 44 and 45. Early two-line "stacked" codes are more desirable than later single line models, except for ac-43 3rd var. Highest P.38 production occurred in 1943 and 1944.

	N/A	$925	$760	$650	$525	$460	$385	

Add 20% for ac-43 single line code.
Add 20% for fnh marked barrel.
Add 40% for FN frame (marked with "MI" or E/140).
Add 30% for ac-45 all matching "c" block.
Add 125% for */35 or 35/* on left side of frame. Considered very rare, the meaning of this stamp is currently unknown.
Subtract 20% for ac-45 "c" block mismatch (one E/359 slide stamp).
FN slide (ac-43 or ac-44). Extreme rarity precludes accurate pricing. Approx. 200-250 assembled by Walther.
Add 10% for stick eagle stamp on trigger guard and/or rear frame tang (ac-43 - ac-44). Considered rare, the meaning of this stamp is currently unknown.

ac-45 0-SERIES – 9mm Para. cal., late war 0-Series with rough milled finish, ser. range 025960-027659. Serialized in commercial manner.

	$3,350	$2,800	$2,350	$2,100	$1,650	$1,350	$1,050	

byf-42 STANDARD ISSUE – 9mm Para. cal., "byf" (Mauser code) appears on slide, dull military finish, ser. range 1-4783a. Some very early pistols have eagle 135 (E/135) stamped on up to six small parts (trigger, hammer, etc.)

	N/A	$2,500	$1,900	$1,675	$1,300	$1,075	$850	

Add 40% for early E/135 accepted parts.
Add 20% for "dusty" blue finished slides.

byf-43 & byf-44 STANDARD ISSUE – 9mm Para. cal., dull military finish, byf-43 ser. range 1-approx. 6500q, byf-44 9000p-10000z, and 1-approx. 5000e (overlap with svw-45).

	N/A	$925	$760	$700	$600	$525	$500	

Add 25% for mixed E/135 and E/WaA135 acceptance stamps on slide.
Add 100% for mixed blue and phosphate finish major components, also known as "Dual Tone".
Add 120% for all gray phosphate finish.
Add 250% for Mauser assembly with FN slide (marked ac-43 or ac-44 with E/WaA135 stamps) and mixed blue and phosphate finish major components.
Add 30% for byf-44 with all E/135 acceptance stamps on slide.
Add 40% for byf-43 with all E/WaA135 acceptance stamps on slide.

byf-43 & byf-44 POLICE ISSUE – 9mm Para. cal., dull military finish, eagle over "L" (E/L) or eagle over "F" (E/F) acceptance and commercial eagle over "N" (E/N) proof stamps, unique serial range 1-6000.

	N/A	$2,500	$2,050	$1,700	$1,625	$1,375	$975	

Add 20% for byf-43 E/L.
Add 75% for FN slide (ac-43 or ac44 marked).
Add 40% for byf-44 E/F.

GRADING - PPGS™	100%	98%	95%	90%	80%	70%	60%	LAST MSR

svw-45 STANDARD ISSUE – 9mm Para. cal., "svw" (Mauser code) appears on slide, Nazi proofed only, most with dual tone finish, few all blue (rare) or all gray.

	$3,200	$2,900	$2,425	$2,100	$1,700	$1,400	$1,100	

Add 10% for all gray phosphate finish.
Add 10% for "f" block suffix later.

Note: Late war/post-war svw code with star proof is located in the FRENCH MILITARY section.

* ***svw-45 Police Issue*** – 9mm Para. cal., dull military finish, E/F acceptance and E/N proof stamps.

Extreme rarity precludes accurate pricing. It is recommended that this variation is evaluated and priced by an expert. Watch for fakes.

cyq STANDARD ISSUE – 9mm Para. cal., "cyq" (Spreewerk code) appears on slide, the cvq stamp, which is attributed to a broken die, begins to appear during the later part of the production run, dull military finish, eagle over "88" (E/88) acceptance, variation typically exhibits rough machining with visible circular milling marks, ser. range 1-approx. 10,000z, no year dates were used by Spreewerk.

	N/A	$800	$650	$575	$475	$400	$325	

Add 225% for E/359 small parts (very few noted during initial production) approx. ser. range 1-500.
Add 15% for early features (early frame and secondary extractor cut), ser. range 1a - approx. 1000d.
Add 150% for FN frame (marked with "MI", "m", or E/140).
Add 100% for no suffix letter, approx. ser. range 501-10000.

cyq LATE PRODUCTION - SECOND ALPHABET SERIES – 9mm Para. cal., dull military finish, E/88 acceptance, approx. ser. range a1-b5000.

	N/A	$1,400	$1,160	$1,000	$800	$675	$490	

Add 40% for "b" prefix serial number.

cvq ZERO SERIES - NON-STANDARD PRODUCTION – 9mm Para. cal., dull military finish, E/88 acceptance, the use of the broken die (cvq) extends throughout the Zero Series production run, ser. range 01-approx. 08000.

	$2,100	$1,730	$1,360	$1,200	$1,050	$875	$650	

Add 50% for Spreewerk assembly with FN slide (marked ac-43 or ac-44 with E/88 stamps).

PISTOLS: SEMI-AUTO, WALTHER POST-WAR MFG.

MODEL P38 – post-war version of P38 Military, .22 LR, .7.65mm Luger, or 9mm Para. cal., 5 in. barrel, 8 shot, alloy frame, polished blue or matte black finish, 28 oz. W. German manufacture. Mfg. began 1956, currently imported into the U.S. by Earl's Repair Service. See German WWII Military Pistols for wartime listings.

	$850	$775	$560	$425	$375	$325	$275	

Add approx. $400 for .22 LR conversion kit.
Add 50% for high polish finish.

Note: Due to the release of large numbers of W. German Police and Army trade-ins of P.38 9mm Para. and PP .32 ACP cal. models, the actual value of original models in 90% or less condition has decreased somewhat. The two models most affected are the P-1 variation of the P.38, and the German PP in .32 ACP cal.

* ***Model P38 Long Barrel Special Edition*** – 9mm Para. cal., steel frame, 6, 7, or 8, in. barrel, wood grips, 60 mfg. 1988.

	$5,000	$4,000	$3,250	N/A	N/A	N/A	N/A	

* ***Model P38 Steel Frame*** – .22 LR, 7.65mm Luger or 9mm Para. cal., similar to regular P.38, except has steel frame, 34 oz. Imported 1987-89 only, and in limited quantities.

	$2,550	$2,050	$1,530	$1,025	$715	$615	$460	*$1,400*

Add 30% for 7.65mm Luger cal.

* ***Model P38 in .22 LR Cal.*** – disc. 1989.

	$1,500	$1,150	$850	$500	$350	$300	$275	*$1,050*

MODEL P38 II – similar to the Standard P.38, except has reinforced slide.

	$850	$635	$500	$425	$340	$325	$265	

MODEL P38K – 7.65mm Luger or 9mm Para. cal., shortened 2.8 in. barrel variation of P.38, front sight on slide, adj. rear sight, 27.9 oz. 3,000 mfg. Imported 1974-1980.

9mm Para.	$3,200	$2,400	$1,600	$1,075	$850	$640	$425	

Add 30% for 7.65mm Luger cal.

Beware of fakes!

GRADING - PPGS™	100%	98%	95%	90%	80%	70%	60%	LAST MSR

MODEL P38 SPECIAL EDITIONS/ENGRAVED

* ***Model P38 50th Year Commemorative*** – 9mm Para. cal., steel frame, carved grips, presentation engraved with deluxe walnut presentation case. Introduced 1987, inventory depleted 1992.

	$3,200	$2,350	$1,750	N/A	N/A	N/A	N/A	*$950*

* ***Model P38 HP 60th Year Commemorative*** – 9mm Para. or 7.65mm (.30 Luger) cal., special production, steel frame, high polish, wood grips, includes wood presentation case. Approx. 100 mfg. in each caliber. Mfg. 1998.

	$3,500	$2,600	$1,700	N/A	N/A	N/A	N/A	

Add 10% for 7.65mm cal.
Subtract 20% if w/o original factory walnut case and accessories.

* ***Model P38 100th Year Commemorative*** – 9mm Para. cal., alloy or steel frame with slide engraving "100 Jahre Walther 1886-1986." Imported by Interarms.

	$2,100	$1,675	$1,300	N/A	N/A	N/A	N/A	

Add 75% for steel frame.

* ***Model P38 Blue Engraved*** – .22 LR, 7.65mm Luger, or 9mm Para. cal.

9mm Para. cal.	$2,375	$1,850	$1,600	N/A	N/A	N/A	N/A	
7.65mm Luger cal.	$2,650	$2,125	$1,800	N/A	N/A	N/A	N/A	
.22 LR cal.	$2,650	$2,125	$1,600	N/A	N/A	N/A	N/A	*$1,850*

* ***Model P38 Chrome Engraved*** – .22 LR, 7.65mm Luger, or 9mm Para. cal.

	$3,000	$2,150	$1,450	N/A	N/A	N/A	N/A	*$2,125*

* ***Model P38 Silver Engraved*** – .22 LR, 7.65mm Luger, or 9mm Para. cal.

	$3,500	$2,575	$1,800	N/A	N/A	N/A	N/A	*$2,100*

* ***Model P38 Gold Engraved*** – .22 LR, 7.65mm Luger, or 9mm Para. cal.

	$4,000	$3,000	$2,100	N/A	N/A	N/A	N/A	*$2,050*

MODEL P1 – 9mm Para. and 7.65mm Luger cal., post-war commercial variation of the P.38 with steel slide and alloy frame, 5 in. barrel, 8 shot mag., blue or phosphate finish, black plastic grips. Disc.

As issued	$750	$600	$450	$350	$240	$215	$190	
Imp. Police Trade-Ins	$425	$375	$325	$250	$225	$200	$150	

Add 50% for 7.65mm Luger.

MODEL P1A1 – 9mm Para. cal., utilizes design elements from the P5 and P38, only 24 mfg. (all nearly new).

	$5,500	$5,000	$4,500	N/A	N/A	N/A	N/A	

MODEL P4 – 9mm Para. or 7.65mm Luger cal., modernized variation of the original P.38, 4 1/2 in. barrel, 8 shot mag., updates include reinforced steel slide and alloy frame, includes decocking lever and automatic safeties, rear sight, 29 oz. Mfg. 1975-81, importation disc. 1982.

	$950	$800	$650	$500	$400	$280	$250	

Add 30% for commercial variation.
Add 50% for 7.65mm Luger.

PISTOLS: SEMI-AUTO, JOHN MARTZ CONVERSIONS

P.38 - JOHN MARTZ CONVERSIONS BABY – 9mm Para. cal., shortened barrel (3 in.) grip, and two 7 shot mags., 70 fabricated.

	$3,900	$3,1200	$2,250	$2,000	$1,650	$1,425	$1,075	

P.38 - JOHN MARTZ CONVERSIONS – .38 Super (4 or 6 in. barrel, 9 fabricated) or .45 ACP (4 or 7 1/2 in. barrel, 24 fabricated) cal. Disc.

	$6,650	$4,300	$3,050	$2,575	$2,100	$1,775	$1,500	

P.38 - JOHN MARTZ CONVERSIONS CARBINE – 9mm Para. cal., 16 in. barrel, adj. rear sight, 30 fabricated w/shoulder stocks. Disc.

	$8,600	$6,775	$5,325	$4,250	$3,450	$2,850	$2,025	

P.A.F.

Previous manufacturer located in S. Africa. P.A.F. stands for Pretoria Arms Factory.

PISTOLS: SEMI-AUTO

.25 ACP PISTOL – .25 ACP cal., patterned after the Baby Browning, blue finish. Approx. 10,000 mfg.

	$300	$275	$250	$235	$225	$200	$180	

GRADING - PPGS™	100%	98%	95%	90%	80%	70%	60%	LAST MSR

P.A.W.S., INC.

Previous manufacturer located in Salem, OR. Distributor and dealer sales. Previously distributed by Sile Distributors, Inc. located in New York, NY.

CARBINES: SEMI-AUTO

ZX6/ZX8 CARBINE – 9mm Para. or .45 ACP cal., 16 in. barrel, 10 or 32* shot mag., folding metal stock, matte black finish, aperture rear sight, partial barrel shroud, 7 1/2 lbs. Mfg. 1989-2004.

	100%	98%	95%	90%	80%	70%	60%	LAST MSR
	$715	$635	$550	$475	$375	$300	$250	

The ZX6 is chambered for 9mm Para., while the ZX8 is chambered for .45 ACP.

PGW DEFENCE TECHNOLOGIES, INC.

Current manufacturer established in 1992, located in Winnipeg, Manitoba, Canada. Previous company name was Prairie Gun Works until 2003. Currently imported by Border View Services, located in Lynden, WA. Previously imported by Trigger Time Gun Club, located in Longmont, CO and by Leroy's Big Valley Gun Works, located in Glasgow, MT.

For individual model listings, please go to BlueBookOfGunValues.com/overflow.

PHSADC (PAKISTAN HUNTING & SPORTING ARMS DEVELOPMENT COMPANY)

Current manufacturer located in Peshawar, Pakistan. No current U.S. importation.

FIREARMS

PHSADC manufactures a complete line of shotguns, pistols, revolvers, rifles (disc.), and replicas of vintage guns. Currently, these guns are not imported into the U.S. Please contact the company directly for more information, including pricing and availability.

PHX PHOENIX AG

Current manufacturer of semi-auto pistols established in 2018, located in Interlocken, Switzerland. Currently imported by The Attic, Inc. located in Minot, ND.

PHX Phoenix AG current models include the Redback (Standard, Light, and Ultralight) and Fusion (Standard, Tactical, and Compact) models, available in 9mm Para. or 9x21mm cal., SA or SA/DA trigger, and carry optics. Please contact the company directly for more information, including options, availability, and pricing.

PKP, INC.

Previous manufacturer and distributor circa 1981-1993 located in Tempe, AZ.

PISTOLS

POWELL KNIFE PISTOL MR-38 – .38 Spl., unique knife-pistol design allows barrel to be incorporated into the upper rear portion of the break-action blade assembly, 2 in. barrel, stainless steel with wood handles, knife leather holster also included, 17 oz. Limited mfg. 1997-98.

	100%	98%	95%	90%	80%	70%	60%	LAST MSR
	$850	$725	$650	$550	$500	$450	$395	*$450*

POF USA

Please refer to the Patriot Ordnance Factory listing in this section.

PPK s.r.o.

Current manufacturer located in Holice, Czech Republic. No current U.S. importation.

Zbrojovka Holice is a registered trademark of PPK. The company currently makes Drulov pistols (see Drulov listings in the D section), a Model ZP SxS shotgun and a series of bolt action rifles based on the K98 Mauser - models include the Eco, Standard, and Lux, in addition to a Brno single shot, bolt action, and semi-auto rifle patterned after the ZKM-611. Please contact the company directly for more information, pricing and availability.

PSD MANUFACTURING (PALMETTO STATE DEFENSE, LLC)

Current AR-15 style rifle manufacturer established in 2008, located in Greer, SC.

Please refer to BlueBookOfGunValues.com to order the *Blue Book of AR-15s & Variations*, available as a book or online subscription.

P.S.M.G. GUN COMPANY

Previous manufacturer located in Arlington, MA.

PISTOLS: SEMI-AUTO

SIX IN ONE SUPREME – .22 LR, 7.65mm Luger, .38 Super, .38 Spl., 9mm Para., or .45 ACP cal., SA, 3 1/4, 5, or 7 1/2 in. barrel with solid cooling rib, adj. rear sight. Limited mfg. 1988-1989.

	100%	98%	95%	90%	80%	70%	60%	LAST MSR
	$700	$600	$500	$450	$400	$365	$330	*$895*

GRADING - PPGS™	100%	98%	95%	90%	80%	70%	60%	LAST MSR

Add $20-$55 for caliber options.
Add $25 for 7 1/2 in. barrel.
Add $35 for satin nickel plating.
Add $225 per extra barrel.
Add $450 per individual conversion unit.

PTK INTERNATIONAL, INC.

Previous distributor located in Atlanta, GA.

Please refer to listing under Poly-Technologies, Inc. in this section.

PTR

Current manufacturer located in Aynor, SC beginning circa 2016.

PTR was formed during 2016 and started manufacturing roller-delayed blowback firearms circa 2018. They manufacture virtually every component and completely assemble the firearms in their South Carolina plant.

PISTOLS: SEMI-AUTO

PTR 9C/9CT MODEL – 9mm Para. cal., roller delayed blowback action patterned after the MP5, 8.86 in. barrel with (PTR 9CT) or without (PTR 9C) threaded muzzle, two 30 shot mags., 4 1/2 in. welded top rail w/traditional iron sights, aluminum M-LOK handguard, polymer end cap w/swivel adapter, fitted range case, single point bungee sling and rear sight adjustment tool, Mil-Spec black anodized and Nitride finishes, 17.6 in. OAL, approx. 5 lbs. New 2018.

MSR $1,899	$1,750	$1,535	$1,300	$1,195	$965	$795	$650

PTR 9KT MODEL – 9mm Para. cal., roller delayed blowback action patterned after the MP5, 5.16 in. threaded barrel, two 30 shot mags., 2 1/2 in. welded top rail w/traditional iron sights, aluminum M-LOK handguard w/attached finger guard, aluminum end cap w/removable sling and attachable M1913 rail/stock adapter, fitted range case, single point bungee sling and rear sight adjustment tool, Mil-Spec black anodized and Nitride finishes, 13.38 in. OAL, 4.8 lbs. New 2018.

MSR $1,899	$1,750	$1,535	$1,300	$1,195	$965	$795	$650

PTR 32K PDWR MODEL – 7.62x39mm cal., roller delayed blowback action, 12.5 in. threaded bull barrel with flash hider, two 30 shot Magpul AK mags., welded top rail w/traditional iron sights, classic wide style polymer handguard, machined end cap w/swivel end adapter and M4 buffer tube compatibility, black finish, 28 in. OAL, 8 lbs. New 2018.

MSR $1,528	$1,325	$1,165	$995	$900	$735	$595	$465

PTR 32P PDWR MODEL – 7.62x39mm cal., roller delayed blowback action, 8 1/2 in. threaded bull barrel with flash hider, two 30 shot Magpul AK mags., welded top rail w/traditional iron sights, classic wide polymer handguard, machined end cap w/swivel end adapter and M4 buffer tube compatibility, black finish, 23 1/2 in. OAL, 8 lbs. New 2018.

MSR $1,418	$1,235	$1,085	$925	$845	$685	$550	$450

PTR 51P PDWR MODEL – .308 Win. or 7.62 NATO cal., roller delayed blowback action, 8 1/2 in. threaded bull barrel with flash hider, two 20 shot mags., welded top rail w/traditional iron sights, classic wide polymer handguard, machined end cap w/swivel end adapter and M4 buffer tube compatibility, black finish, 23 1/2 in. OAL, 7.9 lbs. New 2018.

MSR $1,355	$1,175	$1,035	$885	$800	$645	$535	$400

PTR PDWR MODEL – .308 Win. or 7.62 NATO cal., roller delayed blowback action, 8 1/2 in. threaded bull barrel with flash hider, two 20 shot mags., 7 1/2 in. welded top rail w/traditional iron sights, milled aluminum handguard, machined end cap w/swivel end adapter and M4 buffer tube compatibility, black finish, 23 1/2 in. OAL, 8.1 lbs. New 2018.

MSR $1,300	$1,125	$1,000	$865	$800	$645	$535	$400

PTR K3P PDWR MODEL – .308 Win. or 7.62 NATO cal., roller delayed blowback action, 12 1/2 in. threaded bull barrel with flash hider, two 20 shot mags., 7 1/2 in. welded top rail w/traditional iron sights, classic wide polymer handguard, machined end cap w/swivel end adapter and M4 buffer tube compatibility, black finish, 28 in. OAL, 8.7 lbs. New 2018.

MSR $1,391	$1,200	$1,050	$900	$815	$665	$545	$425

RIFLES: SEMI-AUTO

PTR A3S – .308 Win. or 7.62 NATO cal., roller delayed blowback action, polymer navy lower, paddle magazine release, 18 in. tapered barrel, 10 or 20 shot mag., 7 1/2 in. welded top rail w/traditional iron sights, black polymer fixed stock and pistol grip, slimline black polymer handguard, black powdercoat finish, 40 1/2 in. OAL, 9 1/2 lbs. New 2018.

MSR $1,213	$1,050	$925	$795	$715	$585	$475	$375

GRADING - PPGS™	100%	98%	95%	90%	80%	70%	60%	LAST MSR

* ***PTR A3SK*** – .308 Win. or 7.62 NATO cal., roller delayed blowback action, polymer navy lower, paddle magazine release, 16 in. tapered barrel, 10 or 20 shot mag., 7 1/2 in. welded top rail w/traditional iron sights, black polymer fixed stock and pistol grip, slimline black polymer handguard, black powdercoat finish, 40 1/2 in. OAL, 9 1/2 lbs. New 2018.

MSR $1,213	$1,050	$925	$795	$715	$585	$475	$375	

PTR FR MODEL – .308 Win. or 7.62 NATO cal., roller delayed blowback action, 18 in. threaded bull barrel, flash hider, 10 or 20 shot mag., Navy type polymer trigger group housing, 7 1/2 in. welded top rail w/traditional iron sights, fixed black polymer stock w/sling attachment, milled black aluminum handguard with 6 1/2 in. lower rail, paddle magazine release, black powdercoat finish, 40 1/2 in. OAL, 9 3/4 lbs. New 2018.

MSR $1,369	$1,195	$1,045	$895	$815	$650	$545	$425	

PTR GI MODEL – .308 Win. or 7.62 NATO cal., roller delayed blowback action, "SEF" steel lower, 18 in. threaded and tapered barrel with flash hider, 10 or 20 shot mag., traditional iron sights, green polymer fixed stock with sling attachment and green polymer slimline handguard, paddle magazine release, matte parkerized finish, 40 1/2 in. OAL, 9 1/2 lbs. New 2018.

MSR $1,067	$925	$800	$695	$635	$500	$425	$325	

* ***PTR GIR Model*** – .308 Win. or 7.62 NATO cal., roller delayed blowback action with "SEF" steel lower, 18 in. threaded bull barrel, flash hider, 10 or 20 shot mag., 7 1/2 in. welded top rail w/traditional iron sights, fixed green polymer stock with sling attachment, green slimline polymer handguard, paddle magazine release, matte parkerized finish, 40 1/2 in. OAL, 9 1/2 lbs. New 2018.

MSR $1,144	$995	$875	$745	$675	$545	$450	$350	

* ***PTR GIR FDE Model*** – .308 Win. or 7.62 NATO cal., roller delayed blowback action with "SEF" steel lower, 18 in. threaded bull barrel, flash hider, 10 or 20 shot mag., 7 1/2 in. welded top rail w/traditional iron sights, fixed Patriot brown polymer stock with sling attachment, Patriot brown slimline polymer handguard, paddle magazine release, FDE Cerakote finish, 40 1/2 in. OAL, 9 1/2 lbs. New 2018.

MSR $1,281	$1,125	$985	$845	$765	$625	$500	$395	

* ***PTR GIRK Model*** – .308 Win. or 7.62 NATO cal., roller delayed blowback action with "SEF" steel lower, 16 in. threaded bull barrel, flash hider, 10 or 20 shot mag., 7 1/2 in. welded top rail w/ traditional iron sights, fixed green polymer stock w/sling attachment, green slimline polymer handguard, paddle magazine release, matte parkerized finish, 9 1/2 lbs. New 2020.

MSR $1,144	$995	$875	$745	$675	$545	$450	$350	

PTR KFM4R MODEL – .308 Win. or 7.62 NATO cal., roller delayed blowback action, 16 in. threaded bull barrel with flash hider, 20 shot mag., Navy type polymer lower, 7 1/2 in. welded top rail w/traditional iron sights, Mil-Spec stock adaptor w/black polymer M4 6-position stock, milled aluminum handguard with 6 1/2 in. lower accessory rail, paddle magazine release, black finish, 41 1/2 in. OAL, 9.1 lbs. Mfg. 2018-2020.

	$1,300	$1,145	$975	$885	$715	$585	$450	*$1,506*

PTR MSG SHARPSHOOTER MODEL – .308 Win. or 7.62 NATO cal., roller delayed blowback action, Navy type polymer lower, 18 in. threaded free floating fluted barrel with flash hider, 10 or 20 shot mag., 7 1/2 in. welded top rail w/traditional iron sights, Magpul PRS-2 stock with adj. cheek weld and buttpad, black furniture, milled aluminum handguard with 6 1/2 in. lower accessory rail and adj. Harris bipod, paddle magazine release, black finish, 40 1/2 in. OAL, 11 lbs. Mfg. 2018-2020.

	$1,695	$1,485	$1,275	$1,150	$935	$765	$595	*$1,952*

PTR 9R MODEL – 9mm Para. cal., roller delayed blowback action, 16.2 in. crowned barrel, two 30 shot mags., 4 1/2 in. welded top rail with traditional iron sights, fixed polymer stock w/sling mount, aluminum M-LOK handguard, ships in plastic rifle case, Mil-Spec black anodized and Nitride finishes, 34 1/2 in. OAL, 6.32 lbs. New 2018.

MSR $1,770	$1,535	$1,345	$1,150	$1,045	$845	$695	$535	

PTR 32 KFM4R MODEL – 7.62x39mm cal., roller delayed blowback action, 16 in. threaded bull barrel with flash hider, 30 shot Magpul AK mag., Navy type polymer lower, 7 1/2 in. welded top rail w/ traditional iron sights, Mil-Spec stock adaptor w/black polymer M4 type 6-position stock, milled aluminum handguard with 6 1/2 in. lower accessory rail, paddle magazine release, black finish, 41 1/2 in. OAL, 9.1 lbs. Mfg. 2018-2020.

	$1,425	$1,245	$1,075	$975	$785	$645	$500	*$1,643*

PTR 32 KFR MODEL – 7.62x39mm cal., roller delayed blowback action, polymer navy lower, 16 in. threaded bull barrel with flash hider, 30 shot Magpul AK mag., 7 1/2 in. welded top rail w/traditional iron sights, black polymer fixed stock w/sling mount and pistol grip, slim line black polymer handguard, paddle magazine release, black finish, 38 1/2 in. OAL, 9.3 lbs. New 2018.

MSR $1,336	$1,150	$1,000	$865	$785	$635	$525	$400	

GRADING - PPGS™	100%	98%	95%	90%	80%	70%	60%	LAST MSR

PTR INDUSTRIES, INC. (PTR 91, INC)

Previous pistol and rifle manufacturer located in Aynor, SC circa 2014-2016. PTR Industries, Inc. was created in 2012 and was previously located in Bristol, CT and Farmington, CT until circa 2014. Represented by Vincent A. Pestilli & Associates, located in Brownfield, ME. Previous company names were PTR 91, Inc circa 2006-2012 and J.L.D. Enterprises circa 2002-2006.

PISTOLS: SEMI-AUTO

The following models utilized a delayed blowback roller-lock system action.

PTR PDW - .308 Win. cal., 8 1/2 in. barrel with flash hider, tactical handguard, black aluminum butt cap, H&K type polymer trigger group, includes one 20 shot mag., approx. 7 1/2 lbs. Mfg. 2012-2016.

$865 $725 $650 $585 $515 $450 $395 *$1,029*

PTR PDW R - .308 Win. or 7.62 NATO cal., 8 1/2 in. match grade bull barrel, removable flash hider, 20 shot mag., machined butt cap, paddle mag. release (new 2016), tactical aluminum handguard, sling mount end cap, welded scope mount, 7.8 lbs. Mfg. 2015-2016.

$1,025 $900 $775 $675 $575 $495 $425 *$1,229*

PTR-32 PDW - 7.62x39mm cal., otherwise similar to PTR-91 PDW, one 30 shot AK mag. Limited mfg. 2012 only.

$1,050 $950 $800 $700 $600 $500 $450 *$1,199*

This model was also available with a Picatinny rail (Model PTW-32 PDW-R), limited mfg. 2012 only.

PTR 32K PDW R GEN 2 - 7.62x39mm cal., 12.7 in. match grade bull barrel, flash hider, 30 shot Magpul AK PMAG, H&K Navy type polymer trigger group, wide polymer handguard, machined butt cap, welded scope rail, sling swivel, drilled and tapped for AR-15 "pig nose" buffer tube adapter, 8 lbs. Atlantic Firearms exclusive model. Disc. 2016.

$1,250 $1,050 $850 $725 $650 $550 $495 *$1,450*

PTR 32P PDW R GEN 2 - 7.62 NATO cal., 8 1/8 in. match grade bull barrel, flash hider, 30 shot Magpul AK PMAG, H&K Navy type polymer trigger group, MP5 wide polymer handguard, machined butt cap, welded scope rail, sling swivel, drilled and tapped for AR-15 "pig nose" buffer tube adapter, 7.8 lbs. Atlantic Firearms exclusive model. Disc. 2016.

$1,125 $975 $825 $725 $625 $525 $450 *$1,345*

PTR 51P PDW R - .308 Win. or 7.62 NATO cal., 8 1/8 in. match grade bull barrel, flash hider, 20 shot mag., machined butt cap, drilled and tapped for AR-15 buffer tube adapter, H&K Navy type polymer trigger group, MP5 wide polymer handguard, welded scope rail, sling swivel, 7.8 lbs. Atlantic Firearms exclusive model. Disc. 2016.

$1,075 $950 $825 $725 $625 $525 $450 *$1,279*

PTR K3P PDW R - .308 Win. or 7.62 NATO cal., 12.7 in. match grade bull barrel, flash hider, 20 shot mag., H&K Navy type polymer trigger group, HK 93 wide polymer handguard, machined butt cap, welded scope rail, sling swivel, drilled and tapped for AR-15 "pig nose" buffer tube adapter, 8 lbs. Atlantic Firearms exclusive model. Disc. 2016.

$1,100 $975 $825 $725 $625 $525 $450 *$1,320*

RIFLES: SEMI-AUTO

The following rifles utilize an H&K style roller-delayed blowback action. PTR Industries, Inc. (PTR 91, Inc.) also manufactured SBRs (Short Barrel Rifles) for military/law enforcement.

PTR-91 AI - .308 Win. cal., match grade rifle with polymer trigger group, match grade barrel with (PTR-91 AI C) or w/o (PTR-91 AI F) muzzle brake, pre-ban H&K flash hider, 20 shot mag., H&K style hooded front blade and four position diopter rear sight, steel bipod, steel handguard with bipod recesses. Mfg. 2005-2008.

$1,150 $925 $825 $725 $600 $500 $425 *$1,295*

PTR-91 CLASSIC - .308 Win. cal., 18 in. H&K type profile barrel with flash hider, 20 shot mag., black (Classic Black) or wood (Classic Wood) furniture with slimline handguard, black powdercoated finish, H&K navy type polymer trigger group. Limited mfg. 2012 only.

$875 $750 $625 $550 $500 $450 $395 *$969*

Add $30 for Classic Wood.

PTR-91F - .308 Win. cal., 18 in. barrel with pre-ban H&K flash hider, 20 shot mag., CNC machined scope mounts, H&K style hooded front blade and four position diopter rear sight, H&K Navy type polymer trigger group, one-piece forged cocking handle, parkerized finish, black tactical handguard, black polymer fixed stock, black powdercoat finish, 9 1/2 lbs. Disc. 2015.

$925 $850 $725 $625 $550 $475 $425 *$1,100*

Add $200 for tactical handguard, side folding stock, and pre-ban flash hider (PTR-91R, disc. 2008).
Add $200 for tactical handguard, side folding stock, and muzzle brake (PTR-91 RC, disc. 2008).

GRADING - PPGS™	100%	98%	95%	90%	80%	70%	60%	LAST MSR

PTR-91FR - .308 Win. cal., 18 in. match grade bull barrel, flash hider, 20 shot mag., black tactical aluminum handguard with 6 in. rail, welded scope mount, H&K Navy type polymer trigger group housing, paddle magazine release (new 2016), black polymer stock, black powdercoat finish, 9 3/4 lbs. Mfg. 2015-2016.

	$1,075	$950	$825	$700	$600	$500	$425	*$1,299*

PTR-91 G.I. - .308 Win. cal., 18 in. H&K type profile tapered match grade barrel, 20 shot mag., polymer trigger group, OD Green furniture, flash hider, paddle magazine release (new 2016), H&K OD Green polymer fixed stock and slimline handguard, matte parkerized finish, 9 1/2 lbs. Mfg. 2012-2016.

	$875	$750	$650	$575	$500	$425	$375	*$999*

* ***PTR-G.I. R*** - .308 Win. cal., 18 in. H&K profile match grade tapered barrel, flash hider, 20 shot mag., paddle magazine release (new 2016), OD Green polymer stock and slimline handguard, welded scope mount, classic fixed stock, matte parkerized finish, 9 3/4 lbs. Mfg. 2015-2016.

	$925	$800	$700	$600	$525	$450	$395	*$1,085*

* ***PTR-91 G.I. K*** - .308 Win. cal., similar to PTR-91 G.I., except has 16 in. barrel. Mfg. 2014 only.

	$950	$850	$725	$625	$500	$450	$425	*$1,049*

PTR-91 KC - .308 Win. cal., "Kurz" law enforcement carbine with 16 in. barrel, H&K style hooded front blade and four position diopter rear sight, 10 (compliant) or 20 (disc.) shot mag., tropical green (disc.) or black furniture, wide handguard with bipod recesses, pre-ban H&K flash hider or welded muzzle compensator (PTR-91KC). Mfg. 2005-2014.

	$1,150	$1,025	$900	$800	$700	$600	$550	*$1,245*

Add $100 for PTR-91 KFO with side folding stock and pre-ban flash hider (disc. 2006).

PTR-91 KF - .308 Win. cal., 16 in. match grade bull barrel, 20 shot mag., black furniture with tactical handguard, pre-ban H&K flash hider, standard fixed stock, H&K Navy polymer trigger group, black powdercoat finish, 9 lbs. Disc. 2015.

	$925	$850	$725	$625	$550	$475	$425	*$1,100*

PTR-91 KFM4 - .308 Win. cal., "Kurz" paratrooper carbine, 16 in. barrel, H&K style hooded front blade and four position diopter rear sight, 20 shot mag., tropical green (disc.) or black furniture, wide handguard with bipod recesses and three complete rails, H&K Navy type polymer trigger group, M4 type 6-pos. telescoping stock and flash hider, 10 lbs. Mfg. 2005-2014.

	$1,295	$1,100	$975	$850	$725	$625	$575	*$1,450*

* ***PTR-91 KFM4R*** - .308 Win. cal., 16 in. match grade bull barrel with flash hider, 20 shot mag., H&K Navy type polymer trigger group, H&K style hooded front blade and four position diopter rear sight, black polymer M4 stock with black polymer handguard, three complete rails, welded scope mount, paddle magazine release (new 2016), black powdercoat finish, 10 lbs. Mfg. 2011-2016.

	$1,200	$1,050	$900	$775	$675	$575	$475	*$1,429*

PTR-91 KPF GERMAN PARATROOPER - .308 Win. cal., 16 in. barrel, 20 shot mag., black furniture, three rails, pre-ban H&K flash hider, H&K Navy polymer trigger group, original German telescoping stock. Disc. 2014.

	$1,775	$1,575	$1,375	$1,150	$925	$800	$675	*$1,915*

Add $100 for welded scope mount (Model PTR-91 KPFR, mfg. 2011-2014).

PTR-MSG 91 SNIPER - .308 Win. cal., 18 in. fluted target barrel, paddle magazine release (new 2016), black furniture, tactical aluminum handguard, welded Picatinny accessory rail, Harris bipod, adj. Magpul stock with cheekpiece, pre-ban H&K flash hider, with (Model PTR-MSG 91 C) or w/o (PTR-MSG 91) welded muzzle compensator. Disc. 2016.

	$1,475	$1,325	$1,175	$1,025	$900	$750	$600	*$1,749*

PTR-MSG 91 SS SUPER SNIPER - .308 Win. or 7.62 NATO cal., roller-delayed blowback operation, 20 in. fluted free floating match grade crowned bull barrel, 10 shot mag., paddle magazine release (new 2016), no sights, Magpul PRS2 stock, adj. cheekpiece and LOP, tactical super sniper handguard, free floated black tactical super sniper handguard, welded Picatinny accessory rail, Harris bipod and adapter, welded scope mount, black powdercoat finish, 13 lbs. Disc. 2016.

	$2,450	$2,100	$1,800	$1,450	$1,175	$1,000	$875	*$2,875*

PTR-91 MSR - .308 Win. cal., 18 in. crown tapered target barrel, 5 shot mag., H&K Navy type polymer trigger group, sling swivel, earth tone furniture with free floating handguard, 8 in. welded scope mount, black synthetic stock with adj. cheekpiece. Mfg. 2012-2015.

	$925	$850	$725	$625	$550	$475	$425	*$1,099*

GRADING - PPGS™	100%	98%	95%	90%	80%	70%	60%	LAST MSR

PTR-91 SC SQUAD CARBINE – .308 Win. or 7.62 NATO cal., 16 in. match grade fluted bull barrel with welded scope mount, 20 shot mag., H&K style hooded front blade and four position diopter rear sight, standard fixed polymer stock, black furniture, tactical aluminum handguard with three rails, welded Picatinny accessory rail, with or w/o welded compensator (compliant model), paddle magazine release (new 2016), black powdercoat finish, 9 1/2 lbs. Disc. 2016.

$1,150	$1,025	$900	$775	$650	$550	$475	*$1,359*

PTR-91T – .308 Win. cal., similar to Model PTR-91, except has green furniture and original H&K flash hider. Limited mfg. 2005.

$895	$800	$700	$600	$500	$450	$400	*$995*

PTR-32 KF – 7.62x39mm cal., 16 in. barrel, H&K style hooded front blade and four position diopter rear sight, 30 shot AK mag., black furniture, tactical aluminum handguard, pre-ban H&K flash hider, H&K Navy type polymer trigger group, standard stock. Disc. 2013.

$1,050	$925	$825	$725	$600	$500	$450	*$1,175*

Add $50 for welded scope mount (Model PTR-32KFR, new 2011).

PTR-32 KFR GEN 2 – 7.62x39mm cal., roller-delayed blowback operation, 16 in. match grade tapered barrel, flash hider, 30 shot AK mag., H&K Navy type polymer trigger group housing, black polymer handguard, welded scope mount, paddle magazine release, black polymer fixed stock, black powdercoat finish, 9 1/2 lbs. Disc. 2016.

$1,075	$900	$775	$650	$550	$450	$395	*$1,265*

PTR-32 KC – 7.62x39mm cal., 16 in. barrel, H&K style hooded front blade and four position diopter rear sight, 10 shot mag., black furniture, tactical aluminum handguard, H&K Navy type polymer trigger group, welded muzzle compensator. Disc. 2013.

$1,050	$925	$825	$725	$600	$500	$450	*$1,175*

Add $50 for welded scope mount (Model PTR-32 KCR, new 2011).

PTR-32 KFM4 – 7.62x39mm cal., 16 in. barrel, H&K style hooded front blade and four position diopter rear sight, 30 shot AK mag., black furniture, tactical aluminum handguard with three rails, pre-ban H&K flash hider, H&K Navy type polymer trigger group, M4 6-pos. telescoping stock. Disc. 2013.

$1,325	$1,100	$975	$850	$725	$600	$500	*$1,485*

Add $100 for welded scope mount (model PTR-32 KFM4R, new 2011).

PTR-32 KFM4R GEN 2 – 7.62x39mm cal., roller-delayed blowback operation, 16 in. match grade tapered barrel, flash hider, 30 shot AK mag., H&K Navy type polymer trigger group housing, black polymer M4 6-pos. collapsible stock, black tactical HK 91 length handguard with 6 in. rail, welded scope mount, paddle magazine release, black powdercoat finish, 10 lbs. Disc. 2016.

$1,295	$1,125	$995	$825	$725	$625	$525	*$1,555*

PTR-32 KCM4 – 7.62x39mm cal., 16 in. barrel, H&K style hooded front blade and four position diopter rear sight, 10 shot mag., black furniture, tactical aluminum handguard with three rails, H&K Navy type polymer trigger group, M4 style fixed stock, welded compensator. Disc. 2013.

$1,325	$1,100	$975	$850	$725	$600	$500	*$1,485*

Add $100 for welded scope mount (Model PTR-32 KCM4R, new 2011).

PTR-32 KPF – 7.62x39mm cal., 16 in. barrel, 30 shot AK mag., black furniture, three rails, original German telescoping stock. Mfg. 2011-2013.

$1,825	$1,600	$1,400	$1,150	$925	$800	$675	*$1,980*

Add $100 for welded scope mount (Model PTR-32 KPF4).

PTR-32 SCCR – 7.62x39mm cal., 16 in. match grade tapered barrel with flash hider, H&K Navy type polymer trigger group housing, 30 shot AK mag., paddle magazine release, welded scope mount, black polymer fixed stock with HK 93 length black tactical handguard, custom engraving with gold inlay showing "We the People" and "Shall not be infringed...", custom receiver engraving showing Palmetto Tree and Crescent Moon, black powdercoat finish, 9 1/2 lbs. Limited mfg. for Ellet Bros. distribution. Disc. 2016.

$925	$850	$725	$625	$550	$475	$425	*$1,099*

PTR SCCR – .308 Win. cal., 18 in. match grade bull barrel with flash hider, H&K navy type polymer trigger group housing, supplied with three 20 shot mags., welded scope mount, black polymer fixed stock with slimline polymer handguard, custom barrel engraving showing "We the People" and "Shall not be infringed...", custom receiver engraving showing Palmetto Tree and Crescent Moon, nickel color powdercoat finish, 9 1/2 lbs. Mfg. 2014-2016.

$1,025	$925	$800	$685	$595	$515	$440	*$1,200*

GRADING - PPGS™	100%	98%	95%	90%	80%	70%	60%	LAST MSR

PTR SFR – .308 Win. cal., 18 in. match grade H&K profile tapered barrel, flash hider, 20 shot mag., H&K Navy type polymer trigger group housing, black Choate side folding stock with black polymer slimline handguard, black powdercoated finish, welded scope mount, 9 lbs. Disc. 2015.

	$1,100	$995	$875	$735	$650	$550	$465	*$1,300*

PTR TXR – .308 Win. cal., 16 in. match grade bull barrel, 20 shot mag., polymer trigger group housing, black 6-pos. collapsible M4 stock, black tactical handguard with 6 in. rail, welded scope mount, custom barrel engraving showing "Protect Our Border" and "Come And Take It", custom receiver engraving showing the outline of the state of Texas and star, FDE Cerakote finish, 11 lbs. Limited mfg. Disc. 2016.

	$1,100	$995	$875	$735	$650	$550	$465	*$1,300*

PTR A3R – .308 Win. cal., 18 in. match grade H&K profile tapered barrel, flash hider, 20 shot mag., paddle magazine release (new 2016), H&K Navy type polymer trigger group housing, black polymer fixed stock, black polymer H&K wide handguard, black powdercoated finish, welded scope mount, 10 lbs. Atlantic Firearms exclusive model. Disc. 2016.

	$885	$785	$685	$600	$535	$465	$415	*$1,045*

PTR A3S – .308 Win. cal., 18 in. match grade H&K profile tapered barrel, flash hider, 20 shot mag., paddle magazine release (new 2016), H&K Navy type polymer trigger group housing, black polymer slimline handguard, fixed stock, black powdercoat finish, welded scope mount, 10 lbs. Atlantic Firearms exclusive model. Disc. 2016.

	$975	$850	$750	$650	$550	$450	$395	*$1,149*

P.V. NELSON, (GUNMAKERS)

Please refer to the P.V. NELSON GUNMAKERS Ltd. listing in the N section.

PACIFIC INTERNATIONAL

Previous manufacturer located in Sacramento, CA circa mid-1970s-1980s.

PISTOLS: SEMI-AUTO

VEGA COMBAT MATCH – .45 ACP cal., stainless steel frame, 5 in. match grade barrel, 7 shot mag., rear slide serrations, checkered wood grips, extended speed safety.

	$475	$425	$350	$325	$300	$275	$250	

Add 15% for nickel finish.

MINI VEGA – .25 ACP cal., stainless steel frame, copy of the FN 1905 Browning Vest Pocket.

	$275	$235	$200	$180	$160	$140	$120	

M. PADRÓNE

Previous trademark manufactured by F.A.I.R. srl, located in Marcheno, Italy. Previously imported until 2011 by Padrone USA, located in San Antonio, TX.

M. Padróne guns were high quality round body boxlock O/U shotguns on a small action - 12 ga. was not available.

PALMETTO ARMS CO.

Previous manufacturer until 2007 and current retailer located in Brescia, Italy.

Palmetto Arms Co. manufactured black powder reproductions and replicas, but they produced only a small number of firearms, including the Outlaw SA revolver, Colt Root pistol, and the Lightning slide action rifle/carbine. Values are determined by each model's competitive shooting value, since there is almost no collectibility for this trademark.

PALMETTO STATE ARMORY

Current AR-15 style rifle, pistol, and related parts manufacturer with corporate offices located in Columbia, SC.

For individual model listings, please go to BlueBookOfGunValues.com/overflow.

PARAMOUNT

Previous trademark manufactured by Imperial Gun Co., Ltd., located in Surrey, England. Actions were previously imported by O.K. Weber, Inc. located in Eugene, OR and Olympic Arms, Inc. located in Olympia, WA.

RIFLES: SINGLE SHOT

THE IMPERIAL – .308 Win. cal., single shot target rifle featuring thumbhole stock and CPE aperture rear sight, fully adj. trigger, vent. forearm. Disc. 1994.

	$3,250	$2,700	$2,250	$1,850	$1,400	$1,000	$795	*$3,400*

GRADING - PPGS™	100%	98%	95%	90%	80%	70%	60%	LAST MSR

RANGEMASTER – various cals., single shot design, steel frame, contoured walnut grips, satin chrome finish, 8 1/2 lbs. Limited importation 1992-94.

	$1,600	$1,400	$1,200	$995	$895	$795	$695	*$1,800*

PALM PISTOL

Please refer to the Constitution Arms listing in the C section.

PAOLO PELI

Current manufacturer of high-quality O/U and SxS shotguns, bolt action rifles, and Safari SxS Express rifles located Marcheno, Italy. No current U.S. importation.

Paolo Peli also custom builds both Drillings, Vierlings, and Combination Guns. Since all firearms are custom ordered for individual requirements, please contact the company directly for a quotation.

PARA USA, LLC

Previous manufacturer specializing in 1911 style handguns and AR-15 style rifles. Trademark established in 1985 and discontinued in February of 2015. Previously located in Pineville, NC. Previous company names were Para-Ordnance Mfg. Inc. and Para USA Inc. Para-Ordnance Mfg. Inc was located in Scarborough, Ontario, Canada until June 2009. Previously located in Ft. Lauderdale, FL.

Para-Ordnance Mfg. was founded by Ted Szabo and Thanos Polyzos. Szabo was born in Hungary and his family fled the country when the Russians invaded during the Hungarian Revolution of 1956. Polyzos was born in Greece and later emigrated to Canada.

On Jan. 30, 2012, Freedom Group, Inc. purchased the assets of Para USA, Inc. Manufacturing continued in Pineville, NC until the trademark was retired in February 2015.

PISTOLS: SEMI-AUTO

From 1985-2009, pistols were marked "Made in Canada" with a Canadian maple leaf on the slide.

In 1999, Para-Ordnance introduced their LDA trigger system, originally standing for Lightning Double Action. During 2002, all alloy frame pistols were discontinued, and the abbreviation LDA became Light Double Action. Beginning 2003, all Para-Ordnance models were shipped with two magazines. Beginning Jan. 1, 2004, all Para-Ordnance models were replaced for the general market (except California) with the introduction of the new Power Extractor (PXT) models. The Griptor system, featuring front grip strap grasping grooves, became available during 2005, and the accessory mounting rail option became available during 2006.

Previous Para-Ordnance model nomenclature typically listed the alphabetical letter of the series, followed by a one or two digit number indicating magazine capacity, followed by the number(s) of the caliber. Hence, a Model P14.45 is a P Series model with a 14 shot mag. in .45 ACP cal., and a 7.45LDA indicates a .45 ACP cal. in Light Double Action with a 7 shot mag.

Previous Para nomenclature typically features the configuration type on the left side of the slide. The model designation is located on the right side of the slide and underneath it on the frame the product code (new 2006)/order number (changed to product code during 2006), which is alpha-numeric, may also appear.

Para offered the following finishes on its pistols: Regal (black slide, black frame w/stainless fire controls), Midnight Blue (blue slide, blue frame w/blue fire controls), Coyote Brown, Covert Black (black slide, black frame, and black fire controls), Black Watch (black slide, green frame, green (double stack) or black (single stack) fire controls), Spec Ops (green slide, green frame w/black fire controls), or Sterling (all stainless, black slide w/polished sides), in addition to stainless steel construction.

6.45 LDA/LLDA – Models 6.45 LDA (changed to Para-Companion, marked Para-Companion on left side of slide and C7.45LDA on right side of slide) and 6.45 LLDA were advertised in the 2001 Para-Ordnance catalog (became the Para-Carry, marked Para-Carry on left side of slide and 6.45 LLDA on right side of frame). Double action, bobbed hammer, rounded edges on compact stainless slide and frame, grips inlayed with Para emblem, Novak style sights. Limited Mfg. 2001-2003.

6.45 LDA "Para Carry"	$675	$600	$500	$450	$375	$300	$225	

C SERIES MODELS – .45 ACP cal., DAO, 3 (Carry), 3 1/2 (Companion or Companion Carry), 4 1/2 (CCW or Tac-Four), or 5 in. barrel, stainless steel only, single or double (Tac-Four only) stack mag., 6 (Carry), 7, or 10 (Tac-Four only) shot mag., approx. 30-34 oz. Mfg. 2003 only.

	$850	$750	$625	$575	$475	$375	$300	*$939*

Add $70 for Companion Carry Model.

GRADING - PPGS™	100%	98%	95%	90%	80%	70%	60%	LAST MSR

D SERIES MODELS – 9mm Para., .40 S&W, or .45 ACP cal., DAO, 3 1/2 or 5 in. barrel, 7 or 10 shot single stack mag., steel receiver, matte black finish or stainless steel. Mfg. 2003 only.

	$775	$675	$575	$525	$425	$350	$275	*$859*

Add $80 for stainless steel.

P SERIES MODELS – 9mm Para., .40 S&W, or .45 ACP cal., SA, 3 1/2, 4 1/4, or 5 in. barrel, 10 shot mag., matte black (5 in. barrel only) or stainless steel finish.

* ***P Series Model P10*** – 9mm Para. (new 1998), .40 S&W, .45 ACP, 10mm (mfg. 1998 only, stainless steel) cal., single action, super compact variation featuring 3 in. barrel and shortened grip, 10 shot double column mag., 3-dot sights, choice of alloy (matte black), steel (matte black), or stainless (duo-tone - disc. 2000, or bright finish) frame, 31 oz. with steel frame or 24 oz. with alloy frame. Mfg. 1997-2002.

	$675	$600	$525	$475	$375	$300	$250	*$740*

Add $10 for steel frame.
Add $49 for stainless steel.
Add $45 for stainless steel with duo-tone finish (disc. 2000).

* ***P Series Model P12*** – .40 S&W (disc. 2002) or .45 ACP cal., compact variation of the P14 featuring 10 (C/B 1994) or 12 shot mag. and 3 1/2 in. barrel, 33 oz. with steel frame (disc. 2002) or 24 oz. with alloy frame (disc. 2002) or stainless steel (standard beginning 2003, duo-tone stainless was disc. 2000). Mfg. 1990-2003.

	$975	$725	$625	$575	$450	$375	$275	*$899*

Subtract 10% for steel frame (disc. 2002).

* ***P Series Model P13*** – .40 S&W (disc. 2000) or .45 ACP cal., similar to P14, except has 10 (C/B 1994) or 13 shot mag., 4 1/4 in. barrel, 35 oz. with steel frame (disc. 2002) or 25 oz. with alloy frame (disc. 2002), stainless steel became standard 2003 (duo-tone stainless was disc. 2000). Mfg. 1993-2003.

	$825	$725	$625	$575	$450	$375	$275	*$899*

* ***P Series Model P14*** – .40 S&W (mfg. 1996-2000) or .45 ACP cal., patterned after the Colt Model 1911A1 except has choice of alloy (matte black, disc. 2002), steel (matte black), or stainless steel (stainless or duo-tone finish) frame that has been widened slightly for extra shot capacity (14 shot), 10 shot (C/B 1994) mag., single action, 3-dot sight system, rounded combat hammer, 5 in. ramped barrel, 38 oz. with steel frame or 28 oz. with alloy frame (disc. 2002), duo-tone stainless steel was disc. 2000. Mfg. 1990-2003.

	$750	$650	$575	$525	$425	$350	$275	*$829*

Add $70 for stainless steel.

* ***P Series Model P15*** – .40 S&W cal., otherwise similar to P13, 36 oz. with steel frame or 28 oz. with alloy frame. Mfg. 1996-99.

	$675	$600	$525	$475	$375	$300	$250	*$740*

Add $10 for steel frame.
Add $59 for stainless steel.
Add $45 for stainless steel with duo-tone finish.

* ***P Series Model P16*** – .40 S&W cal., otherwise similar to P14, steel or stainless steel (new 1997) frame only. Mfg. 1995-2002.

	$700	$625	$525	$475	$375	$325	$250	*$750*

Add $49 for stainless steel.
Add $35 for duo-tone stainless steel (disc. 2000).

* ***P Series Model P18*** – 9mm Para. cal., 5 in. ramped barrel, stainless steel, solid barrel bushing, flared ejection port, quadruple safety, adj. rear sight, 40 oz. Mfg. 1998-2003.

	$875	$775	$650	$600	$475	$400	$300	*$960*

PXT 1911 SINGLE STACK SERIES – .38 Super or .45 ACP cal., SA, features new power extractor design with larger claw (PXT), left slide is marked "Para 1911", right side marked with individual model names, various configurations, barrel lengths, and finishes, single stack mag., spurred or spurless (light rail models only) hammer. Mfg. 2004-disc.

* ***Slim Hawg*** – .45 ACP cal. only, 3 in. barrel, 6 shot mag., 3-dot sights, choice of stainless steel (disc. 2009) or Covert Black (new 2006) finish, 24 or 30 (stainless) oz. Disc. 2012.

	$925	$825	$725	$650	$525	$425	$350	*$949*

Add $140 for stainless steel (disc. 2009).

GRADING - PPGS™	100%	98%	95%	90%	80%	70%	60%	LAST MSR

* ***Super Hawg Single Stack*** – .45 ACP cal., similar to S14.45 Ltd., except has 6 in. barrel and stainless finish, 8 shot mag. Mfg. 2008-2010.

	$1,375	$1,225	$1,025	$925	$750	$625	$475	*$1,369*

* ***GI Expert*** – .45 ACP cal., 5 in. barrel, 8 shot mag., 3-dot sights, steel frame, black finish. Mfg. 2009-2012.

	$625	$550	$475	$425	$325	$275	$225	*$649*

» **GI Expert Stainless** – .45 ACP cal., 5 in. barrel, 8 shot mag., similar to GI Expert, except is weather resistant stainless steel. Mfg. 2010-2012.

	$675	$600	$525	$450	$375	$325	$275	*$699*

» **GI Expert ESP** – .45 ACP cal., 5 in. barrel, 8 shot mag., similar to GI Expert, except has beavertail grip safety with speed bump, lightweight match trigger with adj. overtravel, fiber optic front sight. Mfg. 2010 only.

	$675	$575	$500	$450	$375	$325	$275	*$699*

» **GI Expert LTC** – .45 ACP cal., 4 1/4 in. barrel, 8 shot mag., similar to GI Expert, except has compact frame, beavertail grip safety, competition trigger, fiber optic front sight, double diamond checkered wood grips, alloy receiver, black slide, black frame. Mfg. 2011-2012.

	$775	$675	$575	$475	$425	$350	$325	*$799*

* ***1911 Wild Bunch*** – .45 ACP cal., 7 shot mag., 5 in. barrel, black steel frame, 3-dot sights, traditional spur hammer, designed for SASS competition shooting, laser engraved SASS locking behind cocking serrations, checkered wood grips, stainless became standard during 2012. Mfg. 2011-2012.

	$875	$725	$575	$475	$375	$425	$300	*$949*

* ***1911 OPS*** – .45 ACP cal. only, 3 1/2 in. barrel, 7 shot mag., 3-dot sights, stainless steel construction, 32 oz. Disc. 2008.

	$1,075	$950	$800	$725	$575	$475	$375	*$1,099*

* ***1911 LTC*** – 9mm Para. (mfg. 2008-2010) or .45 ACP cal., 4 1/4 in. barrel, 8 or 9 (9mm Para.) shot mag., 3-dot sights, steel (disc.), alloy or stainless steel (disc. 2009) construction, Covert Black (9mm Para.) or Regal black finish, 28 (alloy) or 35 oz. Disc. 2012.

	$850	$750	$600	$475	$425	$375	$325	*$899*

Add $20 for steel (disc.), or $150 for stainless steel (disc. 2009).

* ***1911 SSP Series*** – .38 Super (disc. 2008) or .45 ACP cal., 5 in. barrel, SA, 8 or 9 (.38 Super cal. only) shot mag., fiber optic (new 2011) 3-dot or Novak adj. (Tactical Duty Model only, disc.) sights, carbon or stainless steel (mfg. 2006-2008) construction, Black Covert (new 2008) or Regal black (disc.) finish, steel frame (new 2011), stainless (disc. 2008), or bright stainless (.38 Super cal. only), premium cocobolo (new 2011), checkered wood (disc.) or pearl (.38 Super cal.) grips, 39 oz. Disc. 2008, reintroduced 2011-2012.

	$850	$750	$600	$475	$425	$375	$325	*$899*

Add $230 for stainless steel.
Add $250 for .38 Super cal., or $280 for .38 Super with pearl grips.
Add $250 for Tactical Duty SSP with Novak adj. sights (disc. 2008).

* ***1911 SSP Gun Rights*** – .45 ACP cal., 14 shot, 5 in. barrel, stainless steel construction, 40 oz. Mfg. mid-2009-2011.

	$1,125	$975	$850	$775	$625	$525	$425	*$1,149*

Para USA made a donation to the NRA-ILA fund for every pistol sold.

* ***1911 Black Ops*** – .45 ACP cal., 5 in. stainless steel match grade ramped barrel, two 8 shot mags., stainless steel frame and slide, beavertail grip safety, adj. skeletonized trigger, G10 grips, Tritium front and rear night sights, oversized and flared ejection port, EGW HD extractor, full-length one-piece guide rod, IonBond finish, 40 oz. Mfg. 2012-2015.

	$1,175	$1,050	$900	$800	$675	$575	$450	*$1,276*

* ***1911 Black Ops Ltd.*** – .45 ACP cal., 5 in. barrel, 8 shot mag., fiber optic front and adj. rear sight, stainless steel with black finish, gold Para. emblem on checkered wood grips, adj. trigger. Mfg. 2012-2013.

	$1,175	$1,050	$900	$800	$675	$575	$450	*$1,257*

* ***Black Ops 10.45*** – .45 ACP cal., 5 in. stainless steel barrel, two double stack 10 shot mags., stainless steel slide and frame, adj. skeletonized trigger, beavertail grip safety, G10 grips, IonBond finish, Tritium front and rear night sights, oversized and flared ejection port, EGW HD extractor, checkered front strap, 41 oz. Mfg. 2013-2015.

	$1,225	$1,075	$900	$800	$675	$575	$450	*$1,319*

GRADING - PPGS™	100%	98%	95%	90%	80%	70%	60%	LAST MSR

* ***Black Ops 14.45*** – .45 ACP cal., similar to Black Ops 10.45, except has two 14 shot double stack mags., 41 oz. Mfg. mid-2012-2015.

$1,200 $1,075 $900 $800 $675 $575 $450 ***$1,319***

* ***Black Ops Combat*** – .45 ACP cal., 5 1/2 in. stainless steel match grade threaded barrel, two double stack 14 shot mags., stainless steel slide and frame, beavertail grip safety, adj. skeletonized trigger, checkered front strap, G10 grips, EGW HD extractor, IonBond finish, high profile night sights, 41 oz. Mfg. 2013-2015.

$1,225 $1,075 $900 $800 $675 $575 $475 ***$1,345***

* ***Black Ops Recon*** – 9mm Para. (new 2014) or .45 ACP cal., 4 1/4 in. stainless steel barrel, two double stack 14 or 18 (9mm) shot mags., stainless steel slide and frame, beavertail grip safety, adj. skeletonized trigger, G10 grips, IonBond finish, Tritium front and rear night sights, checkered front strap, EGW HD extractor, 41 oz. Mfg. 2013-2015.

$1,200 $1,075 $900 $800 $675 $575 $450 ***$1,319***

* ***1911 Limited*** – .45 ACP cal., 5 in. barrel, 8 shot mag., fiber optic front and adj. rear sight, stainless steel with Sterling finish, gold Para emblem on checkered wood grips, adj. trigger, 39 oz. Disc. 2008, reintroduced 2011 only.

$1,275 $1,100 $925 $850 $675 $550 $450 ***$1,289***

* ***1911 100th Anniversary*** – .45 ACP cal., based on Browning's Government Model, includes 7 and 8 shot mag., 5 in. barrel, 3-dot sights, steel frame, black finish, smooth cocobolo grips, 100th Anniversary laser engraved on side of frame. Mfg. 2011 only.

$1,050 $900 $775 N/A N/A N/A N/A ***$1,079***

Add $1,320 for set of two pistols (1911 and 14.45 100th Anniversary) with carved walnut presentation box.

* ***1911 Nite-Tac*** – .45 ACP cal. only, 5 in. barrel, 8 shot mag., 3-dot sights, stainless steel construction, Covert Black finish or stainless, features light rail on frame, flush spurless hammer, 40 oz. Disc. 2008.

$1,125 $975 $825 $725 $600 $500 $425 ***$1,149***

* ***Todd Jarrett USPSA Limited Edition*** – .45 ACP cal., 5 in. barrel, 8 shot mag., features Novak adj. sights, steel construction, Covert Black/Sterling finish, 39 oz. Disc.

$1,700 $1,500 $1,275 $1,175 $925 $775 $600 ***$1,729***

EXPERT – 9mm Para. (new 2014) or .45 ACP cal., 5 in. stainless steel match grade barrel, two 8 (.45 ACP) or 9 (9mm Para.) shot mags., carbon steel frame and slide, beavertail grip safety, polymer grips, black Nitride finish, two-dot rear sights, fiber optic front sights, adj. skeletonized trigger, oversized flared ejection port (.45 ACP only), machined extractor (.45 ACP only), 39 oz. Mfg. 2013-2015.

$625 $550 $475 $425 $350 $275 $225 ***$673***

* ***Expert Stainless*** – .45 ACP cal., 5 in. stainless steel match grade barrel, two 8 shot mags., satin stainless steel finished frame and slide, beavertail grip safety, adj. skeletonized trigger, oversized flared ejection port, machined extractor, polymer grips, two-dot rear sights, fiber optic front sights, 39 oz. Mfg. 2013-2015.

$675 $575 $500 $450 $350 $300 $225 ***$724***

* ***Expert Carry*** – .45 ACP cal., 3 in. stainless steel match grade barrel, two 8 shot mags., stainless steel slide with black Nitride finish, aluminum frame w/black anodized finish, polymer grips, two-dot rear sights, fiber optic front sights, polymer grips, 26 oz. Mfg. 2013-2015.

$750 $650 $550 $500 $425 $325 $275 ***$811***

* ***Expert Commander*** – .45 ACP cal., 4 1/4 in. stainless match grade barrel, two 8 shot mags., steel slide, aluminum frame, polymer grips, Nitride/anodized finish, combat rear and fiber optic front sights, adj. skeletonized trigger, 28 oz. Mfg. 2013-2015.

$750 $650 $550 $500 $425 $325 $275 ***$811***

* ***Expert 10.45*** – .45 ACP cal., 5 in. stainless steel match barrel, two double stack 10 shot mags., steel or stainless steel slide and frame, polymer grips, Nitride finish, two-dot rear sights, fiber optic front sights, 40 oz. Mfg. 2013-2015.

$825 $725 $625 $575 $450 $375 $300 ***$898***

Add $35 for stainless steel.

* ***Expert 14.45*** – .45 ACP cal., 5 in. stainless steel match grade barrel, two double stack 14 shot mags., steel or stainless steel slide and frame, polymer grips, Nitride finish, two-dot rear sights, fiber optic front sights, 40 oz. Mfg. mid-2012-2015.

$825 $725 $625 $575 $450 $375 $300 ***$898***

Add $35 for stainless steel.

GRADING - PPGS™	100%	98%	95%	90%	80%	70%	60%	LAST MSR

PXT HIGH CAPACITY SERIES – 9mm Para., 40 S&W, or .45 ACP cal., SAO, 10 shot or higher capacity mag., various barrel lengths, construction, and finishes.

* ***Hawg 7*** – .45 ACP cal., similar to Hawg 9, except has 3 1/2 in. barrel, 7 shot mag., steel receiver, black finish, Griptor grasing grooves. Mfg. 2011-2013.

$850	$750	$625	$575	$475	$375	$325	*$899*

* ***Hawg 9*** – 9mm Para. cal., compact frame, 12 shot mag., 3 in. ramped barrel with guide rod, dovetailed low mount 3-dot fixed sights, alloy receiver, steel slide, spurred competition hammer, match grade trigger, black polymer grips, Regal black finish, three safeties, 24 oz. Mfg. 2005-2010.

$975	$850	$725	$675	$525	$425	$325	*$959*

* ***Lite Hawg 9*** – similar to Hawg 9, except is steel and has light rail, flush spurless hammer, Covert Black finish. Disc. 2008.

$1,075	$950	$825	$750	$600	$500	$375	*$1,099*

* ***Lite Hawg .45*** – .45 ACP cal., similar to Lite Hawg 9, except has 10 shot mag., flush spurless hammer, Covert Black finish. Disc. 2008.

$1,075	$950	$825	$750	$600	$500	$375	*$1,099*

* ***Warthog*** – .45 ACP cal., lightweight, compact design, 3 in. ramped stainless steel match grade barrel, steel or stainless steel frame, two double stack 10 shot mags., Tritium night (disc.) or 3-dot (upgraded fiber optic became standard during 2011) sights, spur competition hammer, match grade trigger, extended slide lock, beavertail grip and firing pin safeties, EGW HD extractor, black polymer grips, satin stainless steel or black Nitride (new 2011), Covert Black (Para-Kote, disc.), or Regal black (disc.) finish, 24 or 31 oz. Mfg. 2004-2015.

$825	$725	$625	$550	$450	$375	$300	*$898*

Add $35 for stainless steel.

* ***Nite Hawg*** – .45 ACP cal., 3 in. barrel, 10 shot mag., Tritium night sights, compact alloy frame, Covert Black finish, black plastic grips, 24 oz. Disc.

$1,100	$950	$825	$750	$600	$500	$375	*$1,099*

* ***Big Hawg*** – .45 ACP cal., 5 in. barrel, 14 shot mag., 3-dot sights, alloy frame, Regal black finish with chrome accents, black plastic grips, 28 oz. Disc.

$975	$850	$725	$650	$525	$425	$325	*$959*

* ***Super Hawg High Capacity*** – .45 ACP cal., similar to S14.45 Ltd., except has 6 in. barrel and stainless finish. Mfg. 2008-2010.

$1,375	$1,200	$1,025	$935	$750	$625	$475	*$1,369*

* ***P14.45*** – .45 ACP cal., 5 in. barrel, 14 shot mag., 3-dot (fiber optic became standard 2011) sights, Covert Black finish steel (new 2008) or brushed stainless steel (disc. 2009) construction, black synthetic grips, 40 oz. Disc.

$875	$800	$675	$625	$525	$425	$325	*$879*

Add $230 for stainless steel (disc .2009).

* ***P14.45 Stainless*** – .45 ACP cal., 5 in. barrel, 14 shot mag., similar to P14.45, except is all stainless steel, 40 oz. Mfg. 2012 only.

$825	$725	$575	$475	$425	$350	$325	*$899*

Add $30 for light rail.

* ***P14.45 Gun Rights*** – .38 Super or .45 ACP cal., 14 shot mag., 5 in. barrel, steel or stainless steel construction, Covert Black or bright stainless, 39 oz. Mfg. mid-2009-2011.

$1,125	$975	$850	$775	$625	$525	$425	*$1,159*

Para USA made a donation to the NRA-ILA fund for every pistol sold.

* ***P18.9*** – 9mm Para. cal., 5 in. barrel, 18 shot mag., adj. sights, stainless steel construction, black synthetic grips, brushed stainless steel, 40 oz. Disc.

$1,225	$1,075	$925	$850	$675	$550	$450	*$1,139*

* ***S14.45 Limited (PXT High Capacity Limited)*** – .45 ACP cal., single action, 10 (disc.) or 14 shot mag., adj. sights, 3 1/2 (stainless steel, disc. 2005), 4 1/4 (stainless steel, disc. 2005), or 5 (steel, disc. 2005, or stainless steel) in. barrel, Covert (disc. 2005) or Sterling finish, black synthetic grips, 40 oz. Disc.

$1,250	$1,100	$925	$850	$675	$550	$425	*$1,289*

Add $110 for Long Slide Limited Model (mfg. 2011).
Add $75 for 3 1/2 or 4 1/4 in. barrel or stainless steel (disc. 2006).

GRADING - PPGS™	100%	98%	95%	90%	80%	70%	60%	LAST MSR

* ***S16.40 Limited (PXT High Capacity Limited)*** – .40 S&W cal., single action, 10 (disc.) or 16 shot mag., adj. sights, 3 1/2 (stainless steel, disc. 2005), 4 1/4 (stainless steel, disc. 2005), or 5 (steel, disc. 2005, or stainless steel) in. barrel, Covert (disc. 2005) or Sterling finish, black synthetic grips, 40 oz. Disc.

	$1,250	$1,100	$925	$850	$675	$550	$425	*$1,289*

Add $75 for 3 1/2 or 4 1/4 in. barrel or stainless steel (disc. 2006).

* ***S12-45 Limited*** – .45 ACP cal., 3 1/2 in. ramped barrel, 10 or 12 shot mag., stainless steel frame with black slide, Novak adj. rear sight, spur competition hammer, checkered cocobolo grips with gold medallions, 34 oz. Mfg. 2005-2006.

	$1,100	$950	$825	$750	$600	$500	$375	*$1,105*

* ***18.9 Limited*** – 9mm Para. cal., 5 in. barrel, stainless steel frame, black Sterling finish, stainless slide, 10 or 18 shot mag., fiber optic front sights, adj. rear sights, includes two mags. Mfg. 2011-2012.

	$1,275	$1,100	$925	$850	$675	$550	$425	*$1,289*

* ***Todd Jarrett USPSA .40 Limited Edition*** – .40 S&W cal., SA, 16 shot mag., 5 in. barrel, Novak adj. sights, steel construction, Covert Black/Sterling finish, flared magwell, black synthetic grips, 40 oz. Disc. 2008.

	$1,650	$1,450	$1,225	$1,125	$900	$750	$575	*$1,729*

14.45 TACTICAL – .45 ACP cal., 4 1/4 (disc.) or 5 in. match grade barrel, SA, 14 shot mag., stainless steel frame, black finish, checkered front grip strap, Ed Brown National Match bushing and slide stop, Tactical II hammer, power extractor, flat checkered mainspring housing, alloy base pads, fiber optic sights. Mfg. 2011-2012.

	$1,500	$1,325	$1,125	$1,025	$825	$675	$525	*$1,599*

16.40 TT – .40 S&W cal., SA, 16 shot mag., 5 in. barrel, stainless steel frame, duo-tone finish, adj. sights, 42 oz. Mfg. 2012.

	$1,875	$1,600	$1,375	$1,150	$975	$825	$725	*$1,899*

PXT LDA SINGLE STACK (CARRY OPTION SERIES) – 9mm Para. (new mid-2006), .45 GAP (new mid-2006) or .45 ACP cal., DAO, single stack mag., various barrel lengths and finishes, Griptor grips (grooved front grip strap), spurless flush hammer and rounded grip safety.

* ***Carry Gap*** – .45 GAP cal., 3 in. barrel, 6 shot mag., 3-dot sights, steel frame, Covert Black finish, 30 oz. Disc. 2008.

	$1,050	$925	$800	$725	$575	$475	$375	*$1,079*

* ***CCO Gap*** – similar to Carry Gap, except has 7 shot mag. and 3 1/2 in. barrel, 31 oz. Mfg. 2006-2008.

	$1,050	$925	$800	$725	$575	$475	$375	*$1,079*

* ***Covert Black Carry*** – .45 ACP cal., 6 shot mag., 3 in. barrel, Novak adj. sights, stainless steel construction, Covert Black finish, 30 oz. Disc.

	$1,125	$975	$850	$775	$625	$500	$400	*$1,149*

* ***Carry*** – similar to Covert Black Carry, except has 3-dot sights and is brushed stainless steel. Disc.

	$1,125	$975	$850	$775	$625	$500	$400	*$1,149*

* ***Carry 9*** – 9mm Para. cal., 8 shot mag., 3 in. barrel, 3-dot sights, alloy frame, Covert Black finish, 24 oz. Mfg. mid-2006-2011.

	$975	$875	$750	$675	$550	$450	$350	*$999*

* ***Stealth*** – .45 ACP cal., 3 in. barrel, alloy frame, black anodized finish, night sights, 24 oz. Mfg. 2012-2013.

	$1,275	$1,125	$950	$875	$725	$575	$500	*$1,339*

* ***PDA*** – 9mm Para. cal., 3 in. barrel with fiber optic front and two-dot rear sights, alloy frame with Sterling/Covert Black finish. Mfg. 2008-2011.

	$1,225	$1,075	$900	$825	$675	$550	$425	*$1,249*

* ***PDA .45*** – .45 ACP cal., 3 in. barrel with 3-dot sights, 6 shot mag., alloy frame with stainless/Covert Black finish. Mfg. 2008-2011.

	$1,275	$1,100	$925	$850	$675	$550	$425	*$1,299*

* ***CCO*** – .45 ACP cal., 7 shot mag., 3 1/2 in. barrel, 3-dot sights, stainless steel construction, brushed stainless finish, 32 oz. Disc. 2008.

	$1,100	$975	$825	$750	$600	$500	$400	*$1,129*

GRADING - PPGS™	100%	98%	95%	90%	80%	70%	60%	LAST MSR

* **CCW** – similar to CCO model, except has 4 1/4 in. barrel, 34 oz. Disc. 2008.

	$1,100	$975	$825	$750	$600	$500	$375	*$1,129*

* **Companion** – .45 ACP cal., 3 1/2 in. barrel, 7 shot mag., stainless steel frame, LDA trigger system, black finish, fiber optic front sight, 2-dot rear sight. Mfg. 2011-2012.

	$975	$850	$725	$650	$525	$425	$325	*$999*

* **Companion II** – .45 ACP cal., 4 1/4 in. barrel, 8 shot mag., stainless steel frame, black finish, fiber optic sight, single stack, DA trigger system, gold trigger, checkered wood grips with gold Para logo, includes two mags. Mfg. 2011 only.

	$825	$725	$575	$475	$425	$375	$325	*$899*

LDA CARRY – 9mm Para. or .45 ACP cal., 3 in. stainless steel match grade ramped barrel, two 6 or 7 shot mags., stainless steel frame and slide, Tritium front and rear night sights, beavertail grip safety, IonBond finish, G10 grips, oversized and flared ejection port, EGW HD extractor, full-length one-piece guide rod, 30 oz. New 2013.

	$975	$850	$725	$650	$525	$425	$325	*$1,041*

LDA OFFICER – 9mm Para. or .45 ACP cal., 3 1/2 in. stainless steel match grade ramped barrel, two 7 shot mags., stainless steel frame and slide, Tritium front and rear night sights, IonBond finish, G10 grips, beavertail grip safety, oversized and flared ejection port, EGW HD extractor, full-length one-piece guide rod, 32 oz. New 2013.

	$975	$850	$725	$650	$525	$425	$325	*$1,041*

Add $203 for Crimson Trace Lasergrips (new 2014).

PXT LDA SINGLE STACK – .45 ACP cal., DAO, non-carry option models, spurless flush hammer, various configurations and barrel lengths.

* **CCO Companion Black Watch** – .45 ACP cal., 7 shot mag., 3 1/2 in. barrel, 3-dot sights, stainless steel construction, Black Watch finish, 32 oz. Disc.

	$1,075	$950	$800	$725	$575	$475	$375	*$1,099*

* **Covert Black Nite-Tac SS** – .45 ACP cal., 8 shot mag., 5 in. barrel, 3-dot sights, stainless steel construction, Covert Black finish, includes light rail, checkered wood grips, 40 oz. Mfg. 2006-2007.

	$1,100	$975	$825	$725	$600	$500	$425	*$1,125*

* **LDA SSP** – .45 ACP cal., 8 shot mag., 5 in. barrel, 3-dot sights, stainless steel construction, brushed stainless finish, 39 oz. Disc. 2009.

	$1,125	$975	$850	$775	$625	$500	$400	*$1,149*

* **Nite-Tac SS** – .45 ACP cal., 8 shot mag., 5 in. barrel, 3-dot sights, stainless steel construction, brushed stainless finish, includes light rail, checkered wood grips, 40 oz. Mfg. 2006-2007.

	$1,100	$975	$825	$725	$600	$500	$425	*$1,125*

* **PXT LDA Limited** – .45 ACP cal., DAO, single stack 7 shot mag., steel or stainless steel, 5 in. barrel. Disc.

	$1,025	$875	$775	$650	$550	$450	$375	*$1,035*

Add $75 for stainless steel.

* **Tac-S** – .45 ACP cal., 8 shot mag., 4 1/4 in. barrel, 3-dot sights, steel frame, Spec Ops finish, 35 oz. Disc.

	$950	$825	$725	$650	$525	$425	$325	*$999*

PXT LDA HIGH CAPACITY (CARRY OPTION SERIES) – 9mm Para., .40 S&W, or .45 ACP cal., DAO, spurless flush hammer, rounded grip safety, various options, barrel lengths and magazine capacity.

* **Carry 12** – .45 ACP cal., 12 shot mag., 3 1/2 in. barrel, low mount 3-dot Tritium night sights, stainless steel construction, black synthetic grips, brushed stainless finish, 34 oz. Disc.

	$1,150	$1,025	$875	$775	$625	$525	$400	*$1,199*

* **Tac-Four** – .45 ACP cal., 13 shot mag., 4 1/4 in. barrel, 3-dot sights, stainless steel construction, black synthetic grips, brushed stainless finish, 36 oz. Disc.

	$1,050	$925	$800	$675	$575	$475	$375	*$1,099*

* **Tac-Forty** – .40 S&W cal., 15 shot mag., 4 1/4 in. barrel, 3-dot sights, stainless steel construction, black synthetic grips, brushed stainless finish, 36 oz. Mfg. 2007 only.

	$1,025	$900	$800	$675	$575	$475	$375	*$1,049*

* **Tac-Five** – 9mm Para. cal., 18 shot mag., 5 in. barrel, Novak adj. sights, stainless steel construction, black synthetic grips, Covert Black finish, 37 1/2 oz. Mfg. 2007 only.

	$1,150	$1,000	$875	$775	$625	$525	$400	*$1,185*

This model was also available in a limited edition "Canadian Forces" model with a maple leaf on the slide.

GRADING - PPGS™	100%	98%	95%	90%	80%	70%	60%	LAST MSR

PXT LDA HIGH CAPACITY SERIES – .45 ACP cal., DAO, 14 shot mag., 5 in. barrel, 3-dot sights, steel or stainless steel construction, spurless flush hammer, Covert Black finish or stainless steel.

* ***Colonel*** – .45 ACP cal., 4 1/4 in. ramped barrel, low mount white 3-dot fixed sights, steel frame, 10 or 14 shot mag., spur competition hammer, LDA trigger, black polymer grips with medallions, green spec. ops. finish, 37 oz. Mfg. 2005-2006.

$875	$775	$650	$600	$475	$400	$300	*$899*

* ***Covert Black Hi-Cap .45*** – steel frame, Covert Black finish. Disc. 2008.

$1,050	$925	$775	$700	$575	$475	$375	*$1,099*

* ***Covert Black Nite-Tac .45*** – steel frame, Covert Black finish, includes light rail. Mfg. 2006-2008.

$1,050	$925	$800	$675	$575	$475	$375	*$1,099*

* ***Coyote Brown Nite-Tac .45*** – .45 ACP cal., similar to Covert Black Nite-Tac, except has adj. fiber optic sights and Coyote Brown finish. Disc.

$1,300	$1,125	$975	$875	$700	$575	$450	*$1,349*

* ***Hi-Cap .45*** – stainless steel construction, brushed stainless finish. Disc. 2008.

$1,050	$925	$800	$675	$575	$475	$375	*$1,099*

* ***Hi-Cap Limited .45*** – adj. sights, stainless steel construction, Sterling finish. Disc. 2009.

$1,175	$1,025	$875	$800	$650	$525	$425	*$1,279*

* ***Nite-Tac .45*** – stainless steel construction, brushed stainless finish, includes light rail. Mfg. 2006-2008.

$1,125	$1,000	$850	$725	$600	$500	$375	*$1,199*

PXT LDA HIGH CAPACITY LIMITED – 9mm Para., .40 S&W, or .45 ACP cal., DAO, 10, 14, 16, or 18 shot mag., steel or stainless steel, 5 in. barrel. Disc. 2006.

$1,025	$875	$775	$650	$550	$450	$375	*$1,035*

Add $75 for stainless steel.

PXT LTC HIGH CAPACITY – .45 ACP cal., 4 1/4 in. barrel, DAO, 10 or 14 shot mag., 3-dot fixed sights, stainless steel frame, match grade trigger, black polymer grips with medallions, green spec. ops. finish, three safeties, 37 oz. Mfg. 2005-2006.

$825	$725	$625	$575	$450	$375	$300	*$855*

S SERIES MODELS – .40 S&W or .45 ACP cal., SA, 3 1/2, 4 1/4, or 5 in. barrel, 10 shot mag., matte black (5 in. barrel only) or stainless steel finish.

* ***S Series Model S10 Limited*** – similar to P10, except has competition shooting features, including beavertail grip safety, competition hammer, tuned trigger, match grade barrel, front slide serrations, choice of steel or alloy frame with matte black finish or stainless steel, 40 oz. Mfg. 1999-2002.

$825	$725	$625	$575	$475	$375	$300	*$865*

Add $10 for steel receiver.
Add $24 for stainless steel.

* ***S Series Model S12 Limited*** – .40 S&W (disc. 2002) or .45 ACP cal., similar to P12, except has competition shooting features, including beavertail grip safety, competition hammer, tuned trigger, match grade barrel, front slide serrations, choice of steel or alloy (disc. 2002) frame, matte black (disc. 2002) or stainless steel finish, 40 oz. Mfg. 1999-2003.

$975	$875	$725	$675	$550	$450	$350	*$1,049*

Subtract 10% for steel frame (disc. 2002).

* ***S Series Model S13 Limited*** – .40 S&W (disc. 2002) or .45 ACP cal., similar to P13, except has competition shooting features, including beavertail grip safety, competition hammer, tuned trigger, match grade barrel, front slide serrations, choice of steel or alloy (disc. 2002) frame, matte black (disc. 2002) or stainless steel finish, 40 oz. Mfg. 1999-2003.

$975	$875	$725	$675	$550	$450	$350	*$1,049*

* ***S Series Model S14 Limited*** – .40 S&W (disc. 2002) or .45 ACP cal., similar to P14, except has competition shooting features, including beavertail grip safety, competition hammer, tuned trigger, match grade barrel, front slide serrations, matte black or stainless steel, 40 oz. Mfg. 1998-2003.

$925	$825	$700	$625	$525	$425	$325	*$989*

Add $60 for stainless steel.

GRADING - PPGS™	100%	98%	95%	90%	80%	70%	60%	LAST MSR

* ***S Series Model S16 Limited*** – .40 S&W cal., similar to P16, except has 5 in. barrel and competition shooting features, including beavertail grip safety, competition hammer, tuned trigger, match grade barrel, front slide serrations, matte black steel or stainless steel, 40 oz. Mfg. 1998-2003.

	$925	**$825**	**$700**	**$625**	**$525**	**$425**	**$325**	*$989*

Add $60 for stainless steel.

T SERIES MODELS – 9mm Para., .40 S&W (stainless steel only), or .45 ACP cal., DAO, 5 in. barrel, 7 (.45 ACP cal. only, single stack mag.) or 10 shot mag., steel or stainless steel, matte black finish or stainless steel. Mfg. 2003 only.

	$900	**$800**	**$675**	**$625**	**$500**	**$400**	**$325**	*$1,009*

Add $80 for stainless steel.

CUSTOM SERIES – 9mm Para., .40 S&W, or .45 ACP cal., 8, 10, 14, 16, or 18 shot mag., adj. target rear, fiber optic front or night sights, stainless steel or aluminum frame, stainless steel slide, IonBond finish, G10 grips. Mfg. 2013-2015.

* ***Executive Agent*** – .45 ACP cal., compact bobtail aluminum frame, 7 shot mag., 3 in. stainless steel match grade barrel, stainless steel slide, black IonBond finish, G10 grips, adj. skeletonized trigger, dovertail front and rear Trijicon sights, lowered and scalloped ejection port, beavertail grip safety. Mfg. 2013-2014.

	$1,300	**$1,125**	**$975**	**$875**	**$725**	**$575**	**$450**	*$1,399*

* ***Executive Carry*** – .45 ACP cal., 3 in. stainless steel match grade ramped bull barrel, stainless steel slide, aluminum frame, two 8 shot mags., beavertail grip safety, adj. skeletonized trigger, G10 grips, Tritium front and rear night sights, oversized and flared ejection port, EGW HD extractor, EGW fire control, Ed Brown bobtail mainspring housing, IonBond/anodized finish, 26 oz. Mfg. 2013-2015.

	$1,300	**$1,125**	**$975**	**$875**	**$725**	**$575**	**$450**	*$1,420*

* ***Pro Custom 10.45*** – .45 ACP cal., 5 in. stainless steel match grade ramped barrel, two 10 shot double stack magazines, stainless steel slide and frame, beavertail grip safety, skeletonized match grade trigger, adj. target rear and fiber optic front sights, oversized and flared ejection port, EGW fire control, HD extractor, and barrel bushing, full-length guide rod, Para oversized magwell, G10 grips, IonBond finish, 40 oz. Mfg. 2013-2015.

	$1,350	**$1,175**	**$1,025**	**$925**	**$750**	**$600**	**$475**	*$1,471*

* ***Pro Custom 14.45*** – .45 ACP cal., similar to Pro Custom 10.45, except has 14 shot mag. Mfg. 2013-2015.

	$1,350	**$1,175**	**$1,025**	**$925**	**$750**	**$600**	**$475**	*$1,471*

* ***Pro Custom 16.40*** – .40 S&W cal., similar to Pro Custom 10.45, except has 16 shot mag. Mfg. 2013-2015.

	$1,350	**$1,175**	**$1,025**	**$925**	**$750**	**$600**	**$475**	*$1,471*

* ***Pro Custom 18.9*** – 9mm Para. cal., similar to Pro Custom 10.45, except has 18 shot mag. Mfg. 2013-2015.

	$1,350	**$1,175**	**$1,025**	**$925**	**$750**	**$600**	**$475**	*$1,471*

* ***Pro Comp*** – 9mm Para. (mfg. 2014) or .40 S&W cal., two 8 or 9 (9mm Para.) shot mags., 5 in. stainless steel match grade ramped barrel, stainless steel slide and frame, beavertail grip safety, skeletonized match grade trigger, G10 grips, adj. target rear and fiber optic front sights, oversized and flared ejection port, EGW HD extractor, full-length guide rod, IonBond finish, 40 oz. Mfg. 2013-2015.

	$1,200	**$1,075**	**$900**	**$825**	**$650**	**$550**	**$425**	*$1,319*

* ***Tomasie Custom*** – .40 S&W cal., 5 in. stainless steel ramped Storm Lake bull barrel, stainless steel slide and frame with tri-top and lightening cuts, two double stack 16 shot magazines, beavertail grip safety, skeletonized match grade trigger, adj. target rear and fiber optic front sights, G10 grips, oversized and flared ejection port, EGW fire control and HD extractor, Para oversized magwell, IonBond finish, 40 oz. Mfg. 2013-2015.

	$1,875	**$1,650**	**$1,400**	**$1,275**	**$1,025**	**$850**	**$650**	*$2,029*

ELITE SERIES – 10mm or .45 ACP cal., 6, 7, 8, or 9 shot mag., 3, 3 1/2, 4 1/4, 5, or 6 in. barrel, two dot, fiber optic, adj. target, or night sights, stainless steel slide, stainless or aluminum frame, beavertail grip safety, adj. skeletonized trigger, oversized and flared ejection port, EGW HD extractor, IonBond or two-tone finish, cocobolo or G10 grips. Mfg. 2013-2015.

GRADING - PPGS™	100%	98%	95%	90%	80%	70%	60%	LAST MSR

* ***Elite*** – .45 ACP cal., 5 in. stainless steel match grade ramped barrel, two 8 shot mags., two-dot rear and fiber optic front sights, stainless steel slide and frame, IonBond finish, cocobolo grips, 39 oz. Mfg. 2013-2015.

$875	$775	$650	$600	$475	$400	$350	*$964*

Add $50 for Elite Stainless (all stainless).

* ***Elite Target*** – .45 ACP cal., 5 in. stainless steel match grade ramped barrel, two 8 shot mags., adj. rear and fiber optic front sights, stainless steel slide and frame, two-tone finish, cocobolo grips, 39 oz. Mfg. 2013-2015.

$925	$825	$700	$625	$525	$425	$350	*$1,014*

* ***Elite Pro*** – .45 ACP cal., 5 in. stainless steel ramped barrel, two 8 shot mags., Tritium front and rear night sights, stainless steel slide and frame, IonBond finish, G10 grips, 39 oz. Mfg. 2013-2015.

$1,150	$1,025	$875	$775	$625	$525	$425	*$1,268*

Add $51 for Elite Pro Stainless (all stainless).

* ***Elite LS Hunter*** – 10mm cal., 6 in. stainless steel match grade ramped barrel, two 9 shot mags., adj. rear and fiber optic front sights, stainless steel slide and frame, IonBond finish, G10 grips, 41 oz. Mfg. 2013-2015.

$1,150	$1,025	$875	$775	$625	$525	$425	*$1,268*

* ***Elite Commander*** – .45 ACP cal., 4 1/4 in. stainless steel ramped barrel, two 8 shot mags., two-dot rear and fiber optic front sights, stainless steel slide and frame, IonBond finish, cocobolo grips, 28 oz. Mfg. 2013-2015.

$875	$775	$650	$600	$475	$400	$350	*$964*

* ***Elite Officer*** – .45 ACP cal., 3 1/2 in. stainless steel ramped barrel, two 7 shot mags., two-dot rear and fiber optic front sights, stainless steel slide and frame, IonBond finish, cocobolo grips, 32 oz. Mfg. 2013-2015.

$875	$775	$650	$600	$475	$400	$350	*$964*

Add $203 for Crimson Trace Lasergrips (new 2014).

* ***Elite Carry*** – .45 ACP cal., 3 in. stainless steel match grade ramped barrel, two 6 shot mags., two-dot rear and fiber optic front sights, stainless steel slide, aluminum frame, IonBond/anodized finish, cocobolo grips, 24 oz. Mfg. 2013-2015.

$875	$775	$650	$600	$475	$400	$350	*$964*

RIFLES: SEMI-AUTO

TTR SERIES – .223 Rem. cal., DIGS (delayed impingement gas system) operation, 16 1/2 in. chrome-lined barrel, 30 shot mag., flat-top receiver with full length Picatinny rail, single stage trigger, flip-up front and adj. flip-up rear sight, various configurations available including, Short Rail with fixed stock (TTR-XASF mfg. 2009), or 5-pos. folding stock with Short Rail (TTR-XAS), Long Rail (TTR-XA), and Nylatron (TTR-XN, mfg. 2009) forearm configurations, black finish. Mfg. 2009-late 2011.

$1,800	$1,425	$1,275	$1,125	$1,050	$975	$875	*$2,397*

Add $100 for Nylatron forearm (mfg. 2009).

PARDINI, ARMI Srl

Current manufacturer located in Lido di Camaiore, Italy. Currently imported by Pardini USA, LLC beginning 2012 located in Tampa, FL. Previously imported until 2012 by Larry's Guns, located in Gray, ME. Previously imported until 2004 by Nygord Precision Products located in Prescott, AZ, and distributed until 1996 by Mo's Competitor Supplies & Range, Inc. located in Brookfield, CT, and until 1990 by Fiocchi of America, Inc., located in Ozark, MO.

For more information and current pricing on both new and used Pardini airguns, please refer to the *Blue Book of Airguns* - also available as an online subscription.

PISTOLS: SEMI-AUTO

PC45 – .40 S&W, .45 ACP, or 9x21mm cal., single action mechanism designed for stock competition category, adj. trigger pull. Limited importation by Nygord 2000-2004.

$1,400	$1,100	$875	$725	$600	$500	$450

Add $125 for 6 in. barrel and slide.

* ***PC45S*** – .40 S&W, .45 ACP, or 9x21mm cal., similar to PC, except has compensator and scope mount with optical sight.

$1,650	$1,350	$1,150	$950	$850	$725	$600

* ***PCS-Open*** – similar to PCS, except w/o scope and frame mount, top-of-the-line semi-auto.

$1,800	$1,500	$1,300	$1,100	$950	$850	$725

GRADING - PPGS™	100%	98%	95%	90%	80%	70%	60%	LAST MSR

GT9/PC40/GT45 DEFENSE/SPORT – 9mm Para., 9x21mm (disc. 2011), .40 S&W (disc, Model PC40), or .45 ACP cal., 5 or 6 in. barrel, SA, diamond wood grips, matte silver, 13 or 17 (9x21mm) shot mag., black, silver, bronze (disc. 2013), or two-tone (disc.) finish. Importation began late 2004.

MSR $2,650	$2,400	$2,100	$1,800	$1,600	$1,300	$1,100	$850	

Add $200 for 6 in. barrel.
Add $100-$350 for silver or bronze (disc. 2013) finish.
Add $50 for .45 ACP cal.
Add $95 for 6 in. barrel and slide (disc.).
Add $700 for titanium finish in 9mm Para. cal. with 6 in. barrel only (disc.)
Add $999 for 9mm Para. or .40 S&W cal. conversion kit for GT45 Model (disc. 2013).
Add $230 for GT45S Model with compensator in silver finish (disc. 2011).

* ***GT9/GT40 Defense Sport Inox*** – 9mm Para. or .40 S&W (IPSC) cal., features 5 or 6 in. stainless steel barrel, black or Ergal finish.

MSR $3,000	$2,650	$2,275	$1,925	$1,600	$1,300	$1,050	$875	

Add $100 for Ergal finish.
Add $200 for 6 in. barrel.
Add $800 for 5 in. barrel and 9mm Para. cal. or $1,100 for 9mm Para. cal. with 6 in. barrel (all disc. 2013).

PISTOLS: TARGET

Pardini pistols have always been known for their technological improvements developed from ongoing design research. During 1991, the entire Pardini pistol line was modified both internally and externally to improve function and reliability - these changes included the addition of grooves on the barrel shroud to accept scope mounts directly.

MODEL SP/MODEL SP NEW (STANDARD PISTOL) – .22 LR cal. only, semi-auto, target grips, adj. sights, 4.92 in. barrel, interchangeable grips, 5 shot detachable mag., SP features mechanical trigger, SP New features second generation electronic trigger, approx. 2.4 lbs. New 1991.

MSR $2,450	$2,100	$1,800	$1,550	$1,400	$1,150	$950	$750	

Add $100 for 5in. barrel or $250 for 6 in. Bullseye Edition w/gas compensator.
Add $330 for Bullseye Edition with MatchDot sights (disc.) or $350 for Bullseye Edition with MatchDot 2 sights
Add $350 for SP Rapid Fire.
Add $145 for SP Master Model (disc.).
Add $1,200 for .22 LR conversion kit.
Subtract approx. 10% for SP model with mechanical trigger.

MODEL SP1 – .22 LR cal., semi-auto, features electronic trigger, blue/silver two-tone finish, adj. anatomic target wood grips, includes six tungsten weights. Imported 2005-2013.

	$1,925	$1,750	$1,550	$1,350	$1,150	$1,000	$900	*$2,249*

MODEL SP1/SP1 NEW RAPID FIRE – .22 LR cal., semi-auto, similar to Model SP1, SP1 has second generation electronic trigger, SP1 New has mechanical trigger, developed for rapid fire discipline, includes six tungsten weights. Imported 2005-2013.

	$2,250	$1,925	$1,725	$1,500	$1,250	$1,000	$850	*$2,569*

LADIES PISTOL – .22 LR cal., similar to Model SP, except grips are suitable for smaller hands. Importation disc. 1999.

	$850	$700	$600	$520	$460	$410	$380	*$995*

MODEL GP/GP E (RAPID FIRE PISTOL) – .22 Short cal., semi-auto, features enclosed style grip assembly, adj. sights, choice of electronic (GP E, new 2004) or mechanical (GP) trigger, 5.12 in. barrel. Imported 1991-2004.

	$1,425	$1,250	$1,050	$875	$775	$675	$575	

Add $500 for "Schumann" Model (wraparound grip, special muzzle ports, sights, weights, etc.).

MODEL HP/HP E/HP NEW (CENTERFIRE PISTOL) – .32 S&W Wadcutter or .32 ACP (new 2012) cal., semi-auto, similar to Model SP Pistol, 4.92 in. barrel, beginning 2004, HP has second generation electronic trigger, HP E has electronic trigger, HP New has mechanical trigger, 5 shot mag., includes 4 (HP) or 6 (HP E (disc.) and HP New) weights. New 1991.

MSR $2,650	$2,250	$1,950	$1,700	$1,550	$1,250	$1,000	$800	

Add $350 for HP E model with electronic trigger (disc. 2013).
Add $1,100 for .22 LR cal. conversion kit (new 2012).

GRADING - PPGS™	100%	98%	95%	90%	80%	70%	60%	LAST MSR

MODEL K22 - .22 LR cal., top-of-the-line single shot target pistol, 11.8 in. barrel, mechanical trigger, toggle bolt pushes cartridge into chamber, unique ventilated front sight assembly that also supports counterweights, cocking lever action, 38 1/2 oz. Imported 2000-2008.

	$1,770	$1,475	$1,250	$1,050	$875	$775	$675	*$1,899*

MODEL K50 (FREE PISTOL) - .22 LR cal., single shot, sliding rotating bolt, 9.06 in. barrel, tilted anatomical grip, top-of-the-line match pistol. Mfg. 1991-99.

	$925	$750	$600	$500	$450	$420	$395	*$1,050*

PARDINI/NYGORD MASTER - .22 LR cal., designed for NRA bullseye shooting, micrometer rear sight and small Adco red dot sight, anatomical target grips. Imported 2000-2004.

	$1,325	$1,145	$875	$750	$650	$550	$450	

FPM/FPE FREE PISTOL - .22 LR cal., single shot, 11 in. barrel with elevated front sight designed by Buck Rogers, compensator, with (FPE) or w/o (FPM) electronic trigger, 2 1/2 lbs. Importation began 2009.

MSR $2,600	$2,200	$1,950	$1,650	$1,500	$1,200	$1,000	$850	

Add $280 for electronic trigger (FPE Model, disc. 2013).

PARDUS

Current firearms and airgun manufacturer established in 2007, located in Istanbul, Turkey. Previously distributed exclusively in the U.S. and Mexico by Neptune Arms.

SHOTGUNS

Pardus manufactures a complete line of good quality bolt action, lever action, O/U, SxS, semi-auto (including models with detachable box magazines), slide action (including tactical models), and single shot shotguns, in addition to air rifles. Currently these guns are not being imported into the U.S. Please contact the company directly for more information, including pricing and U.S. availability.

PARKER BROS. MAKERS

Current manufacturer established 1999, located in Meriden, CT and Ohio.

SHOTGUNS: O/U

Parker Bros. Makers manufactures an O/U shotgun in 12 and 28 ga. Grades are offered and MSRs are as follows: Invincible ($135,000), A-1 Special ($96,000), AA ($75,000), B ($40,000), C ($25,000), PA ($19,000), and V ($12,000). Lower volume manufacturer stressing quality and Made in the USA. Restorations & Parts: Full services to restore older Parker Bros. shotguns. Restored shotguns with new barrels.

PARKER BROTHERS

Previously manufactured in Meriden, CT from 1866-1934. Remington took over production in 1934, and in 1938, the plant was moved to Ilion, NY. Over 4,500 "Transition Guns" (exhibiting Meriden and Ilion characteristics) were produced in Meriden between 1934-1937 and about 1,600 Parkers were manufactured at the Ilion location before production stopped circa 1942. Total production reached approx. 242,487.

During 2006, Remington Arms Co. announced the release of a new AAHE 28 ga. Parker, manufactured in the U.S. by Connecticut Shotgun Co.

95% of the original Parkers bought and sold each year are in 30% or less condition (referring to original case colors). Percentages on following pages refer to the amount of original case colors remaining on frame.

Parker Gun Identification & Serialization was published in late 2002, and has been reprinted due to popular demand. Compiled by using records from *The Parker Story; Vols. I & II*, this title features more than 100 detailed images allowing easy visual identification on the grades, frame sizes, and other important information. Additionally, listings on over 155,000 serial numbers are provided, specifying the original configuration, including grade, action type, extra features, stock configuration, gauge, and barrel length - an invaluable asset when determining original configuration on most Parkers Brothers shotguns. The author wishes to especially thank Mr. William Mullins, in addition to Charles Price, Roy Gunther, Louis C. Parker III, and Daniel Cote for sharing the following Parker production statistics with this publication.

SHOTGUNS: MISC. FACTS

Values in the 95%-100% condition columns can vary a lot as there is very little supply and strong demand for these high condition "cream puffs."

Note: Values are for guns without ejectors, unless otherwise indicated. An "E" suffix indicates ejectors. Skeet models with ejectors, beavertail forearm, and single selective trigger are valued at approx. 50%-75% higher than values shown. Higher grade Parkers typically had ejectors, and ejectors typically add 25%-

30% value to a Parker in all grades. Also, lower condition, high grade models sometimes have their values established by the potential gain in refurbishing these specimens. Remember, it only costs a few hundred dollars more to refinish an A1 Special compared a VH Grade.

Due to the extremely high value of Parker Guns, extreme care should be taken in their purchase. There are many upgraded and refinished guns represented as original; expert advice should always be sought. Many collectors would rather own a specimen with 30% original case colors than a refinished gun that is 100% (regardless who did the work). Many advanced collectors will discount a refinished Parker's value 40%-60% off the price for an original gun. Misrepresentation of refinished or upgraded Parkers is rampant today - especially case colors. Also, beware of fake boxes and hanging tags - if the box and Parker shotgun are an original "pair," the value is enhanced tremendously. If the box/hanging tag is fake, you could pay as much as $1,500 to learn this lesson! In other words, do your homework, be careful, shop carefully, and above all, get a receipt for exactly what it is that you are purchasing.

Frame size on Parker shotguns is determined by the number on the bottom of the rear barrel lug on breech. Frame sizes (from largest to smallest) include 7, 6, 5, 4, 3, 2, 1 1/2, 1, 1/2, 0, 00, and 000. 8 ga. guns typically are framed 6 or 7. 10 ga. guns typically are 3 or 4. 12 ga. guns typically range from 2 through 1 (more desirable). "1/2" frame 12 ga. guns are very rare and desirable. 20 and 16 gauges range from 2 through 0 (more desirable, rare in 16 ga.). 28 ga. guns are either 0 or 00 (more desirable and approx. 50% more). .410 bore shotguns are 00 or 000 (most common and most desirable). 8 and 10 ga. steel barreled shotguns are very rare, and prices can equal .410 bore values if the original condition is there. Factory original 10 ga., 3 1/2 in. Mag. guns command premium prices, as very few were made and they are extremely rare. These guns are stamped "For 3 1/2 shells" on the barrel lug and are late serial numbered (240,000 range).

The grade on Parker shotguns is a number or initials located on the water table of the frame. An alphabetical designation would indicate the grade immediately. For numerals, a "2" would indicate a GH, while an "8" would specify an A-1 Special - interpolate for the others (numbers 3 through 7). Parker shotguns manufactured by Remington will have date codes stamped on left barrel flat that correspond to the month and the year (see Remington serialization in the Serialization Section). Also, if a Parker gun was returned to Remington for repair, alteration, or refinishing, it will usually have the date code stamped with a suffix of 3 (i.e., OK3 represents some type of rework completed in either July of 1941 or 1963). There is some ambiguity with the year as the year codes repeat.

Skeleton buttplates were furnished as standard on Parker guns starting with Grade 3 or on D and higher grades over most of the years of production. They were perhaps an option on the lower grades at times, and no doubt a customer could have ordered one as a special option on a lower grade for additional cost. Since skeleton buttplates were standard on the D Grades and above, they should not be considered an added value on these grades. And even if present on lower grades, if you cannot prove factory originality, a skeleton buttplate will not add any value.

A note about Parker condition: Percentages of condition indicate the amount of original case colors remaining on the frame, but sometimes these colors are faded and the rest of the gun is excellent - hence, all the separate condition factors must be considered when determining overall condition.

A Parker IS NOT 60% if the barrel bluing and stock/forearm varnish are 60% but case colors are only 10%. Typically, a 60% case color Parker shotgun will have 90%+ blue and varnish, yet this does not mean the gun is 90% overall. Similarly, a 20% case color Parker will probably have 90% barrel bluing remaining. Strong, original case colors are the key in determining Parker condition and subsequent values. However, for shotguns under 30% condition, the overall condition of the gun should determine value.

Collectors also place value on the screws on the receiver being aligned as they left the factory and not tampered with.

The Parker Story, Vol. I was published in late 1998. This book has production statistics derived from factory records, and the quantities manufactured listed in this text for steel-barreled hammerless Parker guns are taken from this book. This publication also has more detailed production statistics on Parker guns produced from 1869-1942, including a breakdown by action type (lifter, top lever, and hammerless), grade, barrel steel, gauge, and barrel length. Some grades, gauges, etc., are fewer in number than previously estimated. All the grades are pictured in color, including the Invincible. Parker Reproductions are also covered in detail, including production statistics.

Vol. II was published in late 2000.

The Parker Gun Collectors Association can also provide research letters on certain Parkers. Please refer to their listing under Firearms Organizations in the back of this text for contact information.

100%	98%	95%	90%	80%	70%	60%	50%	40%	30%	20%	10%

SHOTGUNS: SxS, DAMASCUS BARRELS & PRICING

Parker damascus barreled shotguns (hammer or hammerless) are very collectible if original condition is over 40%. Specimens in 80% or better condition with strong case colors can approximate values of the steel barrel models if the bores are in excellent condition (no pitting). Values for under 40% specimens fall off rapidly and are no longer comparable to steel barrel guns. As an example, a 12 ga. steel "D" Grade (without ejectors) has a price range from $2,500 to $9,000 (10%-100%) with a rather even downward progression of values in between the high and low ranges. A 100% damascus hammer "D" Grade could have a $15,000-$18,000 price tag hanging from the trigger guard, while a 5%-15% condition specimen is typically seen priced in the $2,000-$3,000 range. A truly 95%-100% original damascus barreled, hammer Parker is more rare and desirable than a similar grade damascus hammerless Parker or a steel barreled hammerless Parker. Remember, the guns are not rare but their condition is.

Due to articles in a national firearms quarterly publication discussing the "shootability" of damascus barreled guns (Parker and other major manufacturers), and the positive results obtained, there has been a renewed interest in these guns. Prices have increased accordingly, and in some instances values for high condition guns have exceeded their steel barreled counterparts.

SHOTGUNS: SxS, FLUID STEEL BARREL MODELS & PRICING

The desirability of older Parker shotguns in today's marketplace can be greatly enhanced if the stock dimensions fit today's potential owner (typically 13 1/2 in. - 14 1/2 in. LOP), adding value due to the shootability.

Add 20% for SST.
Add 20% for beavertail forearm.
Add 40%-50% for VR (rare on smaller gauges).
Add 20% for straight English stock.
Add 20% for original skeleton steel buttplate (standard on Grade D/3 and higher).
Add 20% for short barrels (26 in. with open chokes) on 12 ga.
Add 20% for 30 or 32 in. barrels on 16 and 20 ga.
Add 25% for 30 or 32 in. barrels on 28 ga.
Add 30% for 28 or 30 in. barrels on .410 ga.

TROJAN – Parker's lowest-priced gun, single or double triggers, but no auto ejectors available, very rarely found in mint condition because they were used a lot, a genuine utility gun, introduced 1912-13 with approx. 33,000 total mfg.

* ***Trojan 12 ga.***

N/A	N/A	N/A	$2,700	$2,300	$1,700	$1,400	$1,100	$1,000	$800	$700	$600

* ***Trojan 16 ga.***

N/A	N/A	N/A	$4,500	$3,100	$3,000	$2,600	$2,300	$2,000	$1,700	$1,400	$1,100

* ***Trojan 20 ga.***

N/A	N/A	N/A	$5,500	$5,000	$4,500	$4,000	$3,500	$3,000	$2,600	$2,000	$1,800

VH – Parker's biggest selling model, offered with all options, the most commonly found Parker. Approx. 79,000 mfg. 10 ga. is very rare in this model.

Add 25%-30% for ejectors, depending on original condition (VHE Model).

* ***VH 12 ga.***

N/A	N/A	N/A	$3,000	$2,500	$2,000	$1,700	$1,500	$1,400	$1,100	$900	$800

* ***VH 16 ga.***

N/A	N/A	N/A	$5,000	$4,500	$4,000	$3,600	$3,200	$2,900	$2,500	$2,200	$1,900

* ***VH 20 ga.***

N/A	N/A	N/A	$9,500	$8,500	$7,500	$6,000	$5,000	$4,500	$4,000	$3,500	$3,000

* ***VH 28 ga.***

N/A	N/A	N/A	$27,000	$21,000	$16,000	$13,000	$11,000	$10,000	$9,000	$8,000	$7,000

* ***VH .410 bore.***

N/A	N/A	N/A	$32,500	$28,000	$24,000	$20,000	$17,000	$15,000	$13,000	$11,000	$10,000

PH – offered for a very short time, most had twist barrels, prices here are for fluid steel barrels only. Approx. 1,400 mfg. A very few .410 bores were mfg. 10 ga. with fluid steel barrels is very rare in this model.

Add 25%-30% for ejectors, depending on original condition (PHE Model).

100%	98%	95%	90%	80%	70%	60%	50%	40%	30%	20%	10%
*** PH 12 ga.**											
N/A	N/A	N/A	$4,000	$3,400	$2,800	$2,500	$2,200	$1,900	$1,700	$1,400	$1,100
*** PH 16 ga.**											
N/A	N/A	N/A	$6,200	$5,700	$5,200	$4,800	$4,300	$3,800	$3,300	$2,800	$2,400
*** PH 20 ga.**											
N/A	N/A	N/A	$10,000	$9,000	$8,000	$7,000	$6,500	$6,000	$5,500	$5,000	$4,500

*** PH 28 ga. & .410 bore**

Extreme rarity precludes accurate price evaluation, but will be VERY expensive.

GH – very popular model, barrels marked "Parker Special Steel", engraved moderately with all options available. 10 ga. with fluid steel barrels is very rare in this model, approx. 4,300 mfg.

Add 25%-30% for ejectors, depending on original condition (GHE Model).

100%	98%	95%	90%	80%	70%	60%	50%	40%	30%	20%	10%
*** GH 12 ga.**											
N/A	N/A	N/A	$5,000	$3,800	$2,800	$2,500	$2,200	$1,900	$1,700	$1,400	$1,100
*** GH 16 ga.**											
N/A	N/A	N/A	$8,400	$7,000	$6,000	$5,000	$4,500	$4,000	$3,800	$2,300	$2,800
*** GH 20 ga.**											
N/A	N/A	N/A	$14,000	$11,000	$10,000	$9,000	$8,000	$7,500	$7,000	$6,000	$5,500
*** GH 28 ga.**											
N/A	N/A	N/A	$35,000	$29,000	$25,000	$21,000	$17,500	$15,000	$12,000	$10,000	$8,500
*** GH .410 bore**											
N/A	N/A	N/A	$70,000	$60,000	$50,000	$40,000	$30,000	$25,000	$20,000	$18,000	$16,000

DH – the most popular higher grade gun, very tastefully engraved and flawlessly finished, approx. 9,400 mfg.

Add 25%-30% for ejectors, depending on original condition (DHE Model).

100%	98%	95%	90%	80%	70%	60%	50%	40%	30%	20%	10%
*** DH 12 ga.**											
N/A	N/A	N/A	$6,000	$4,400	$3,400	$2,800	$2,500	$2,200	$1,900	$1,600	$1,400
*** DH 16 ga.**											
N/A	N/A	N/A	$9,000	$8,000	$7,000	$6,000	$5,700	$5,200	$4,700	$4,200	$3,800
*** DH 20 ga.**											
N/A	N/A	N/A	$15,000	$13,000	$12,000	$11,000	$10,000	$9,000	$8,000	$7,000	$6,000
*** DH 28 ga.**											
N/A	N/A	N/A	$44,000	$38,000	$32,000	$27,000	$23,000	$20,000	$18,000	$16,000	$14,000
*** DH .410 bore**											
N/A	N/A	N/A	$80,000	$70,000	$60,000	$55,000	$50,000	$45,000	$40,000	$35,000	$30,000

CH – scarce because they were only slightly more decorative than the DH, Acme steel barrels. Approx. 1,100 mfg. 10 ga. is very rare in this model.

Add 25%-30% for ejectors, depending on original condition (CHE Model).

100%	98%	95%	90%	80%	70%	60%	50%	40%	30%	20%	10%
*** CH 12 ga.**											
N/A	N/A	N/A	$9,400	$7,200	$5,800	$5,300	$4,700	$4,500	$4,200	$3,600	$3,300
*** CH 16 ga.**											
N/A	N/A	N/A	$16,000	$13,000	$10,500	$9,000	$8,500	$8,000	$7,500	$7,100	$6,500
*** CH 20 ga.**											
N/A	N/A	N/A	$28,000	$23,000	$20,000	$17,000	$15,000	$13,000	$11,000	$10,000	$9,000
*** CH 28 ga.**											
N/A	N/A	N/A	$80,000	$65,000	$55,000	$50,000	$45,000	$40,000	$35,000	$30,000	$25,000

*** CH .410 bore** – very rare, approx. 6 are known to exist.

This model/gauge is very rare, and prices typically start in the $60,000-$100,000 range, depending on original condition.

BH – quite popular and decorative, 4 styles of engraving available, Acme steel barrels. Approx. 700 mfg. 10 ga. is very rare in this model.

Add 25%-50% for ejectors, depending on original condition (BHE Model).

* ***BH 12 ga.***

100%	98%	95%	90%	80%	70%	60%	50%	40%	30%	20%	10%
N/A	N/A	N/A	$13,500	$10,500	$8,500	$7,300	$6,000	$5,600	$5,000	$4,500	$3,900

* ***BH 16 ga.***

100%	98%	95%	90%	80%	70%	60%	50%	40%	30%	20%	10%
N/A	N/A	N/A	$24,500	$21,000	$18,000	$15,000	$12,000	$10,500	$9,500	$8,500	$7,500

* ***BH 20 ga.***

100%	98%	95%	90%	80%	70%	60%	50%	40%	30%	20%	10%
N/A	N/A	N/A	$36,000	$31,000	$27,000	$23,000	$19,000	$16,000	$13,000	$11,000	$10,000

* ***BH 28 ga.***

100%	98%	95%	90%	80%	70%	60%	50%	40%	30%	20%	10%
N/A	N/A	N/A	$90,000	$75,000	$65,000	$55,000	$50,000	$45,000	$40,000	$35,000	$30,000

* ***BH .410 bore*** – only 4 guns are known in this grade.

Extreme rarity precludes accurate price evaluation, but will be VERY expensive.

AH – a scarce gun, extremely decorative and flawlessly executed, Acme steel barrels. Approx. 300 mfg. 10 ga. is very rare in this model.

Add 25%-50% for ejectors, depending on original condition (AHE Model).

* ***AH 12 ga.***

100%	98%	95%	90%	80%	70%	60%	50%	40%	30%	20%	10%
N/A	N/A	N/A	$27,000	$23,000	$18,000	$16,500	$15,000	$13,500	$11,500	$10,000	$8,500

* ***AH 16 ga.***

100%	98%	95%	90%	80%	70%	60%	50%	40%	30%	20%	10%
N/A	N/A	N/A	$47,500	$43,000	$38,000	$33,000	$30,500	$27,500	$25,000	$22,000	$19,000

* ***AH 20 ga.***

100%	98%	95%	90%	80%	70%	60%	50%	40%	30%	20%	10%
N/A	N/A	N/A	$65,000	$60,000	$55,000	$50,000	$45,000	$40,000	$35,000	$30,000	$25,000

* ***AH 28 ga.***

Extreme rarity (approx. 7 mfg.) precludes accurate price evaluation.

* ***AH .410 bore*** – it is believed that only one gun was manufactured.

Rarity precludes accurate pricing.

AAH – very elaborate model, early AAs have Whitworth barrels, late ones have Peerless. Approx. 240 mfg.

Add 25%-50% for ejectors, depending on original condition (AAHE Model).

* ***AAH 12 ga.***

100%	98%	95%	90%	80%	70%	60%	50%	40%	30%	20%	10%
N/A	N/A	N/A	$50,000	$37,500	$31,000	$25,000	$22,500	$20,000	$18,000	$15,500	$14,000

* ***AAH 16 ga.***

100%	98%	95%	90%	80%	70%	60%	50%	40%	30%	20%	10%
N/A	N/A	N/A	$80,500	$71,500	$62,000	$53,000	$47,500	$44,000	$40,000	$36,000	$33,000

* ***AAH 20 ga.***

100%	98%	95%	90%	80%	70%	60%	50%	40%	30%	20%	10%
N/A	N/A	N/A	$100,000	$90,000	$80,000	$75,000	$70,000	$65,000	$55,000	$50,000	$45,000

* ***AAH 28 ga.***

Extreme rarity (approx. 5 mfg.) precludes accurate price evaluation.

AAHE (RECENT MFG.) – 28 ga., available through Remington Arms Co., and made by Connecticut Shotgun, serialization continues from the last of the Parker Bros. production. Limited availability 2006-disc.

Last MSR was $49,995.

A-1 SPECIAL GRADE – 100% engraved, all were special ordered, each one inspected by the company president before being shipped. Approx. 80 mfg.

* ***A-1 Special Grade 12 ga.***

100%	98%	95%	90%	80%	70%	60%	50%	40%	30%	20%	10%
N/A	N/A	N/A	$80,000	$67,500	$48,000	$36,000	$28,000	$24,500	$22,500	$19,500	$16,500

* ***A-1 Special Grade 16 ga.***

100%	98%	95%	90%	80%	70%	60%	50%	40%	30%	20%	10%
N/A	N/A	N/A	$135,000	$110,000	$90,000	$85,000	$80,000	$75,000	$70,000	$65,000	$60,000

* ***A-1 Special Grade 20 ga.***

100%	98%	95%	90%	80%	70%	60%	50%	40%	30%	20%	10%
N/A	N/A	N/A	$200,000	$175,000	$150,000	$130,000	$110,000	$85,000	$80,000	$75,000	$70,000

* ***A-1 Special Grade 28 ga.***

Extreme rarity (approx. 7 mfg.) precludes accurate price evaluation.

100%	98%	95%	90%	80%	70%	60%	50%	40%	30%	20%	10%

INVINCIBLE GRADE – only 3 documented mfg. $1,250 MSR circa 1930, extreme rarity and desirability factors preclude accurate price evaluation on this model. Currently, all three guns are on loan to the National Firearms Museum in Fairfax, VA.

SHOTGUNS: SINGLE BARREL, TRAP

12 or 20 (rare) ga., 26 (20 ga. only, rare), 28 (very rare), 30 (rare), 32, or 34 (rare) in. barrels, any boring was available, as was stock configuration, boxlock, auto ejector. The grades differ only in engraving, checkering and wood finish.

It should be noted that single barrel trap guns cannot be compared to the SxS models, as they are not as desirable, even though they are more rare. Approximately 1,900 Parker single barrel trap guns were manufactured, mostly in SC Grade. Most SxS collectors are not that interested in single barrel trap models and very few collectors specialize in single barrels.

Add 15% for 30 or 34 in. barrel.

S.C. GRADE

100%	98%	95%	90%	80%	70%	60%	50%	40%	30%	20%	10%
N/A	N/A	N/A	$5,900	$5,000	$3,900	$3,400	$2,800	$2,200	$1,700	$1,400	$1,250

S.B. GRADE

100%	98%	95%	90%	80%	70%	60%	50%	40%	30%	20%	10%
N/A	N/A	N/A	$10,000	$9,000	$7,000	$6,500	$5,500	$4,500	$4,000	$3,500	$3,000

S.A. GRADE

100%	98%	95%	90%	80%	70%	60%	50%	40%	30%	20%	10%
N/A	N/A	N/A	$15,000	$13,000	$11,500	$10,500	$9,500	$8,500	$7,500	$7,000	$6,500

S.A.A. GRADE

Extreme rarity (research indicates only two manufactured) precludes accurate pricing.

S.A.-1 SPECIAL GRADE

Extreme rarity (research indicates only four manufactured) precludes accurate pricing.

PARKER GUNMAKERS

Previous division of Remington, established circa 2006-2011.

28 ga. AAHE Parker guns were manufactured by Connecticut Shotgun Manufacturing Company, located in New Britain, CT. Prices began at $49,000 and go up depending on customer specifications. Very few were manufactured.

PARKER PISTOLS

Please refer to the Wyoming Arms Mfg. Corp.listing in the W section.

PARKER REPRODUCTIONS

Previously imported by the Parker Reproduction Division of Reagent Chemical & Research, Inc., located in Middlesex, NJ. Previously distributed by Parker

Reproductions located in Webb City, MO. These shotguns were manufactured at the Olin-Kodensha plant in Tochigi, Japan to original Parker specifications by Winchester until the factory closed in January, 1989.

In 1984, Winchester was contracted by Reagent Chemical & Research, Inc. to manufacture a new Parker shotgun. The new SxS was a DHE model, available in 20 and 28 ga. initially. These models were fabricated in Japan to original Parker specifications, and the reproduction was so authentic that most parts are interchangeable with the late Parkers made by Remington in Ilion, NY. In 1993, a 16/20 ga. combo was introduced in some models. On Sept. 17, 1999, a flood destroyed all remaining inventory, including parts and most of the factory records.

During 2004, Connecticut Shotgun Manufacturing Company offered a limited quantity of A1 Specials in-the-white without metal finish and engraving in 12 or 20 ga. only, without cases or accessories. MSRs were $5,850 for one set of barrels and $6,750 for a 2 barrel set.

SHOTGUNS: SxS

12,268 Parker Reproductions shotguns were mfg. circa late 1983-1989. Because of the high quality and limited mfg. of these reproductions, they have become very collectible, as they offer the shooter the only realistic alternative to using an original Parker Bros. shotgun. Currently, higher grade Parker Reproductions in smaller gauges are very desirable, and 95%-100% values are getting harder to accurately determine.

GRADING - PPGS™	100%	98%	95%	90%	80%	70%	60%	LAST MSR

DHE GRADE – 12 (new 1986), 20, or 28 (new 1984) ga., 26 or 28 in. barrels, boxlock action, ejectors, single selective or double triggers, beavertail or splinter forend, straight or pistol grip stock, skeleton steel buttplate, Japanese engraving in original DH style, case hardened frame, rust blue barrels. Supplied with leather trunk case, canvas and leather cover, and snap caps. Disc.

	100%	98%	95%	90%	80%	70%	60%	LAST MSR
12 ga.	$4,500	$3,995	$3,450	$2,900	$2,500	$2,200	$2,000	
20 ga.	$5,000	$4,850	$3,950	$3,300	$2,850	$2,500	$2,250	
28 ga.	$6,500	$5,500	$4,500	$3,600	$3,200	$2,800	$2,500	

Add approx. 10% for DT.

Add $150 for beavertail forend.

Add $650 for Sporting Clays Model w/choke tubes (approx. 125 mfg. in 2 barrel sets).

Add $700-$1,150 per extra set of barrels, depending on gauge, configuration, and condition.

Quantities mfg. for this model are as follows: 12 ga. - 2,137 mfg., 20 ga. - 6,050 mfg., 28 ga. - 4,203 mfg.

* ***DHE Grade Steel Shot Special*** – similar to 12 ga. D Grade, except has strengthened chrome-lined 28 in. No. 1 1/2 barrels, 3 in. chambers, 7 1/4-7 1/2 lbs. Approx. 349 mfg. 1987-89.

	100%	98%	95%	90%	80%	70%	60%	LAST MSR
	$5,750	$4,650	$3,650	$3,150	$2,500	$2,000	$1,825	*$3,370*

Add $100 for beavertail forend.

* ***DHE Grade Small Gauge Combo*** – available in either 28 ga./.410 bore (disc.) or 16/20 ga. (mfg. 1993-97) combo with 2 barrels and 2 forends. Less than 160 mfg. of the 28 ga./.410 bore combo. Disc.

» **DHE Grade Small Gauge Combo 28 ga./.410 bore**

	100%	98%	95%	90%	80%	70%	60%	LAST MSR
	$16,500	$14,000	$12,000	$9,000	$7,500	$6,500	$5,500	*$4,970*

» **DHE Grade Small Gauge Combo 16/20 ga.** – new 1994 - disc.

	100%	98%	95%	90%	80%	70%	60%	LAST MSR
	$8,500	$7,500	$6,250	$5,150	$4,000	$3,250	$2,850	*$4,870*

* ***DHE Grade 3-Barrel Set*** – includes two 28 ga. and one .410 bore barrels, cased. Disc.

	100%	98%	95%	90%	80%	70%	60%	LAST MSR
	$20,000	$18,000	$16,000	$14,000	$12,000	$9,750	$8,500	*$5,630*

BHE GRADE LIMITED EDITION – 12, 20, 28 ga. or 410 bore, original Parker BH specifications, single selective or double trigger(s), 26 or 28 in. barrels, straight or pistol grip stock, engraved skeleton buttplate, Japanese bank note scroll engraving around game scenes, cased. Only 100 manufactured in 12 and 20 ga., seven in 28 ga., and nine in .410 bore during late 1987-1989. Disc.

	100%	98%	95%	90%	80%	70%	60%	LAST MSR
12 ga.	$9,000	$8,500	$7,250	$6,125	$5,000	$4,150	$3,250	
20 ga.	$11,000	$9,500	$8,000	$6,500	$5,500	$4,500	$3,750	
28 ga.	$20,000	$17,500	$15,000	$13,000	$10,500	$8,750	$7,000	
.410 bore	$22,000	$19,000	$17,000	$13,500	$11,250	$9,000	$7,250	
2 barrel set (28 ga. & .410 bore)	$32,500	$27,000	$23,000	$20,000	$17,500	$15,000	$12,500	

Last MSR was $3,970 (single ga.).

A 28 ga./.410 bore combo was also available with 2 forends, only two sets were made.

A-1 SPECIAL – 12, 16/20 ga. combo (introduced 1993), 20, or 28 ga., original Parker A-1 specifications, 26 or 28 in. barrels, single selective or double trigger(s), Japanese fine scroll engraving with game scenes, 32 lines/in. checkering, cased with accessories. Limited mfg. 1988-89.

	100%	98%	95%	90%	80%	70%	60%	LAST MSR
12 ga.	$16,000	$13,500	$11,750	$10,500	$7,475	$4,800	$4,350	
20 ga.	$20,000	$18,500	$14,500	$12,000	$10,000	$7,500	$5,750	
28 ga. 2 bbl combo w/410	$35,000	$30,000	$26,000	$20,000	$17,500	$15,500	$13,500	
2 barrel set (16 ga. & 20 ga)	$30,000	$28,000	$24,000	$20,000	$17,000	$15,000	$12,500	
3 barrel set (28 ga. & .410 bore)	$58,000	$48,000	$44,000	$35,000	$30,000	$27,000	$24,000	

Last MSR was $11,200 (single ga., one set of barrels).

Add $2,000 for 16 ga. barrel (splinter model only).

Approx. 350 sets were manufactured with factory engraving. Fourteen 3 barrel sets were mfg. in this grade, which included two 28 ga. barrels (26 and 28 in.) and one .410 bore barrel (26 in.).

* ***A-1 Special Custom Engraved*** – custom (per individual special order) engraving, available with two sets of barrels only, mostly coin finished, engraved and signed by Master Engraver Geoffrey Gournet, cased with accessories, approx. 80 sets mfg. during 1987-2002. Very few have changed hands among collectors in the $20,000 to $40,000 range with values and prices depending upon custom engraving gauge and extra barrels.

Prices started at $11,000 and went up according to individualized special features. This model needs to be appraised individually for ascertain current values.

GRADING - PPGS™	100%	98%	95%	90%	80%	70%	60%	LAST MSR

* ***A-1 Special Federal Duck Stamp Collector's Series*** – available in 12 or 20 ga., A-1 Special specifications, authorized by U.S. Department of Interior. Only 4 sets are known to exist in this model, two 12 ga. sets, and two 20 ga. sets (one is a cutaway gun).

12 ga. 2 barrel set	$49,500	$45,000	$41,000	$39,000	$36,500	$30,000	$27,500	*$14,000*

This model was also available as a 20 ga. 2 barrel set - extreme rarity factor precludes accurate pricing - last MSR was $14,000. This model included special case and 2 barrels per buyer's specifications.

PARKER-HALE LIMITED

Previous gun manufacturer located in Birmingham, England. Rifles were manufactured in England until 1991 when Navy Arms purchased the manufacturing rights and built a plant in West Virginia for fabrication. This new company was called Gibbs Rifle Company, Inc. and they manufactured models very similar to older Parker-Hale rifles during 1992-94. Shotguns were manufactured in Spain and imported by Precision Sports, a division of Cortland Line Company, Inc. located in Cortland, NY until 1993.

For individual model listings, please go to BlueBookOfGunValues.com/overflow.

PASTUSEK INDUSTRIES

Previous manufacturer located in Fort Worth, TX 1993-2000.

PISTOLS: SEMI-AUTO

HSK (SPORT KING) – .22 LR cal., 4 1/2 or 5 1/2 in. barrel. Mfg. 1995-2000.

$275	$250	$225	$195	$175	$150	$135	*$312*

HSS (SHARPSHOOTER) – .22 LR cal., 5 1/2 in. bull barrel. Mfg. 1995-2000.

$315	$275	$240	$210	$190	$165	$150	*$379*

HSC (SUPERMATIC CITATION) – .22 LR cal., 5 1/2 bull or 7 1/4 in. fluted barrel. Mfg. 1995-2000.

$340	$295	$265	$230	$210	$180	$165	*$388*

Add $22 for 7 1/4 in. fluted barrel.

This model was also available with an 8, 10, or 12 in. bull barrel.

HST (SUPERMATIC TROPHY) – .22 LR cal., 5 1/2 bull or 7 1/4 in. fluted barrel. Mfg. 1995-2000.

$400	$340	$275	$240	$220	$180	$165	*$494*

This model was also available with an 8, 10, or 12 in. bull barrel. Left-hand ejection is also an option on this model.

HSV (VICTOR) – .22 LR cal., 3 7/8, 4 1/2, 5 1/2, 8 (optional), or 10 (optional) in. VR barrel. Mfg. 1995-2000.

$475	$375	$300	$250	$230	$185	$165	*$569*

Add $30 for dovetail rib on 5 1/2 in. barrel only.
Add $79 for Weaver rib on 5 1/2 in. barrel only.

HSO (OLYMPIC) – .22 S or .22 LR cal., 6 3/4 in. barrel only. Mfg. 1995-2000.

$495	$395	$325	$265	$245	$195	$170	*$599*

PATRIOT ORDNANCE FACTORY (POF)

Current AR-15 style firearm manufacturer located in Phoenix, AZ. Previously located in Glendale, AZ.

Please refer to BlueBookOfGunValues.com to order the *Blue Book of AR-15s & Variations*, available as a book or online subscription.

PATRIOT PRECISION

Current manufacturer located in Show Low, AZ.

PISTOLS: SEMI-AUTO

Patriot Precision manufactured quality semi-auto pistols in various calibers and configurations. Previous pistols included: Conquer (Last MSR $2,200).

RIFLES: BOLT ACTION

All models can be built to customer's specifications with many options and upgrades available. Models listed below reflect base pricing. Please contact the company directly for more information including price quotes and availabilty.

46:12 DEFENDER – .223 Rem. to .338 Lapua cal., Operator model, long or short action, Rem. 700 Action, match grade stainless steel free floating barrel barrel, detachable box mag., choice of hunting rifle stock, glass bedded w/aluminum pillars, Teflon matte black coating, optional folding or detachable buttstock and titanium or carbon fiber components, Switch Barrel System available.

MSR $3,600	$3,050	$2,700	$2,300	$2,100	$1,700	$1,400	$1,050

Add $300 for Switch Barrel System.

GRADING - PPGS™	100%	98%	95%	90%	80%	70%	60%	LAST MSR

ARISTEROS - .17 Rem. to .458 Win. cal., Remington 700 left-hand action, match grade stainless steel barrel, glass bedded aluminum pillars, BDL bottom metal, Teflon matte black coating, optional Switch Barrel System (SBS), folding or detachable buttstock, or carbon fiber components.

MSR $3,900	$3,300	$2,900	$2,500	$2,250	$1,800	$1,500	$1,150	

Add $300 for Switch Barrel System.

CHECKMATE - .240 Wby. to .458 Win. cal., Winchester Model 70 CRF stainless steel action, adventurer model, match grade stainless steel free floating barrel, BDL bottom metal, glass bedded w/aluminum pillars, Teflon matte black coating, optional Switch Barrel System (SBS) and Titanium or carbon fiber components.

MSR $5,500	$4,675	$4,090	$3,505	$3,180	$2,570	$2,105	$1,635	

Add $300 for Switch Barrel System.

EMPRESS - .17 Rem. to .458 Win. cal., Remington 700 action, embellished model, match grade stainless steel, free floating barrel, factory tuned trigger, choice of hunting rifle stock, BDL bottom metal, glass bedded w/aluminum pillars, fluted and skeletonized bolt, Teflon matte black coating, optional Switch Barrel System (SBS), Titanium, and carbon fiber components.

MSR $4,150	$3,500	$3,100	$2,650	$2,400	$1,950	$1,600	$1,250	

Add $300 for Switch Barrel System.

KAIBAB - .17 Rem. to .458 Win. cal., Signature model, Long or Short actions available, recoil management system, fluted match grade stainless steel, free floating barrel, muzzle brake, fluted bolt body, BDL bottom metal, glass bedded aluminum pillars, Switch Barrel System available.

MSR $6,000	$5,100	$4,450	$3,800	$3,450	$2,800	$2,300	$1,800	

Add $300 for Switch Barrel System.
Add $100 for recoil management system.

PIONEER - .17 Rem. to .458 Win. cal., long or short action, match grade stainless steel free floating barrel, hunting rifle stock of choice, glass bedded w/aluminum pillars, Teflon matte black coating, Switch Barrel System available.

MSR $3,400	$2,900	$2,550	$2,150	$1,950	$1,600	$1,300	$1,000	

Add $300 for Switch Barrel System.

SKYLINE - .17 Rem. to .458 Win. cal., Extreme Mountain Rifle, compact model, Rem. 700 stainless steel long or short action, match grade stainless steel free floating barrel, glass bedded with aluminum pillars, ADL bottom metal, tuned 2 1/2 lb. factory trigger, hunting rifle stock of customer's choice, Teflon matte black coating, folding or detachable buttstock available.

MSR $3,800	$3,250	$2,800	$2,400	$2,200	$1,800	$1,450	$1,150	

SUNBEAM - .17 Rem. to .30-06 cal., Remington 700 action, match grade stainless steel, barrel, adj. buttplate and cheekpiece, pint sized model designed for children to be adjustable as they grow, long or short actions available optional Switch Barrrel System. Current Mfg.

MSR $3,500	$3,000	$2,600	$2,250	$2,000	$1,650	$1,350	$1,050	

Add $300 for Switch Barrel System.

RIFLES: SEMI-AUTO

Previous semi-auto rifles included: Adroit (last MSR was $2,200). Please contact the company directly for more information including pricing, options, and availability.

PATRIOT WEAPONRY

Current AR-15 style firearm manufacturer located in Waupaca, WI.

Please refer to BlueBookOfGunValues.com to order the *Blue Book of AR-15s & Variations*, available as a book or online subscription.

PAUZA SPECIALTIES

Previous manufacturer located in Baytown, TX circa 1991-96. Previously distributed by U.S. General Technologies, Inc., located in South San Francisco, CA.

Pauza previously manufactured the P50 semi-auto rifle for Firearms International, Inc. - please refer to that section for current information.

RIFLES: SEMI-AUTO

P50 SEMI-AUTO - .50 BMG cal., 24 (carbine) or 29 (rifle) in. match grade barrel, 5 shot detachable mag., one-piece receiver, 3-stage gas system, takedown action, all exterior parts Teflon coated, with aluminum bipod, 25 or 30 lbs. Mfg. 1992-96.

	$7,500	$6,750	$5,750	$5,000	$4,500	$4,000	$3,500	*$6,495*

GRADING - PPGS™	100%	98%	95%	90%	80%	70%	60%	LAST MSR

PAVONA

Current trademark of firearms manufactured by Tanfoglio and F.A.I.R. of Italy and Sarsilmaz of Turkey and imported by EAA Corp. Please refer to European American Armory listing for current information.

PEACE RIVER CLASSICS

Previous manufacturer of AR-15 style rifles located in Bartow, FL until 2001. Peace River Classics was a division of Tim's Guns.

RIFLES: SEMI-AUTO

PEACE RIVER CLASSICS SEMI-AUTO – .223 Rem. or .308 Win. (new 1998, possible prototypes only) cal., available in 3 configurations including the Shadowood, the Glenwood, and the Royale, GIO, hand-built utilizing Armalite action, patterned after the AR-15, match grade parts throughout, special serialization, laminate thumbhole stock. Very limited mfg. 1997-2001.

Last MSR on the .223 Rem. cal. in 2001 was $2,695, or $2,995 for .308 Win. cal.

Due to this model's rarity factor, accurate values are hard to ascertain.

PEDERSEN CUSTOM GUNS

Previously manufactured circa 1973-1975 by O.F. Mossberg located in North Haven, CT. Pedersen Custom Guns was a division of O.F. Mossberg.

For individual model listings, please go to BlueBookOfGunValues.com/overflow.

PEDERSEN DEVICE

Please refer to the Springfield Armory - Model 1903 Mark I listing in the S section.

PEDERSOLI, DAVIDE & C. Snc.

Current manufacturer of modern, black powder, and older historically significant firearms established in 1957, located in Brescia, Italy. Currently imported on a limited basis by IFG (Italian Firearms Group), located in Rockledge, FL, beginning 2011, Cabela's, located in Sidney, NE, Cimarron FA Co., located in Fredricksburg, TX, E.M.F., located in Santa Ana, CA, and Taylor's, located in Winchester, VA. Currently, full-line distributors include Cherry's Fine Guns, located in Greensboro, NC, Dixie Gun Works, Inc., located in Union City, TN, and Flintlocks, Etc., located in Richmond, MA.

For more information on Pedersoli models, please go to BlueBookOfGunValues.com/overflow.

PEERLESS RIFLE COMPANY

Current custom riflemaker and gunsmith established in 1988, located in Glendale, CA. Consumer direct sales.

Ray Riganian has been making quality custom bolt action rifles since 1988. Please contact him directly for current availability and more information.

RIFLES: BOLT ACTION

Values are for base rifle only. Please contact the company for a price quotation and available options.

PEERLESS I – various cals., various blueprinted actions, available in either a lightweight, long range hunting and varmint, tactical, or varmint configuration, McMillan fiberglass stock with Pachmayr Decelerator recoil pad, various barrel lengths, matte black metal finish, custom order only.

MSR	100%	98%	95%	90%	80%	70%	60%	LAST MSR
MSR $3,500	$3,500	$3,150	$2,750	$2,400	$2,100	$1,775	$1,500	

Add $1,000 for hunting configuration.

PEERLESS II – various cals., various blueprinted actions, features California English XXX walnut stock, various barrel lengths, matte black metal finish, custom order only.

	100%	98%	95%	90%	80%	70%	60%	LAST MSR
	$6,500	$5,750	$5,000	$4,300	$3,750	$3,150	$2,500	*$6,500*

Add $1,400 for .375 H&H cal.

Add $2,100 for .416 Rem., .458 Lott, or .470 Capstick.

Other calibers such as .416 Rigby, .505 Gibbs, and .500 Jeffery were quoted on an individual basis.

PEERLESS II SAFARI (CURRENT MFG.)/SPORTER – various cals., Win. Mod. 70 or Mauser 98 action, features California English XXX handcheckered walnut stock, ebony forend tip, steel grip cap, and cheekpiece, various match grade barrel lengths, matte black metal finish, custom order only.

MSR	100%	98%	95%	90%	80%	70%	60%	LAST MSR
MSR $8,500	$8,500	$7,995	$7,250	$6,500	$5,750	$4,950	$4,350	

Add $500 for Mag. cals.

Add $550 for Mauser 98 action.

Add $2,000 for Peerless II Safari in .375 H&H cal. or $3,000 for .416 Rem. or .458 Lott cal. (new 2011).

GRADING - PPGS™	100%	98%	95%	90%	80%	70%	60%	LAST MSR

PEERLESS ROYAL EXPRESS RIFLE – various cals., including .375 H&H, .416 Rem., or .458 Lott cals., similar features as the Sporter, extra deep Blackburn steel trigger guard and floorplate, 5 shot, custom made box mag. (.416 or .458 cal. only), quick detachable scope mount system, barrel band swivel base, front sight and bead, quarter rib with one standing leaf, custom order only.

MSR $12,500	$12,500	$10,500	$8,750	$7,500	$6,250	$5,000	$3,175	

Add $300 for Winchester MOD. 70 standard Mag.
Add $3,500-$5,000 for .375 H&H cal. and higher on Mauser 98 action.
Add $3,500-$5,000 for .375 H&H cal. and higher on Granite Mt. action.

PENTHENY de PENTHENY

Previous trademark owned by Wyoming Armory beginning 2009. Previous manufacturer and gunsmith 1987-2009, located in Santa Rosa, CA.

Currently, Wyoming Armory is not producing rifles. Please contact the company directly for more information.

RIFLES: BOLT ACTION

The rifles listed included ebony forend tips, old English style black recoil pads, steel skeleton grip caps, four panels of 22 LPI checkering, and other custom features. These models were built on a U.S.R.A. Model 70 action.

THE INVADER – small and medium bore cals., classic styled Claro walnut stock, blue finish.

	$5,400	$4,500	$3,850	$2,975	$2,400	$1,975	$1,500	*$5,400*

THE NORMAN – Mag. cals., classic styled English walnut stock, blue finish.

	$5,400	$4,500	$3,850	$2,975	$2,400	$1,975	$1,500	*$5,400*

THE CONQUEROR – large bore cals., classic styled English walnut stock, blue finish, rifle has secondary recoil lug, dual steel reinforcing bolts, and express sights including fixed and folding leaves.

	$6,300	$5,500	$4,750	$3,650	$3,000	$2,400	$1,975	*$6,300*

PERAZZI

Current manufacturer established in 1957, located in Brescia, Italy. Imported and distributed by Perazzi USA, Inc. located in Azusa, CA. Previously located in Monrovia, CA until 2002, and in Rome, NY during the 1980s.

Ivo Fabbri and Daniel Perazzi were partners in the shotgun manufacturing business beginning in 1960 - these guns are ser. no. 5001-5339.

Note: Perazzi shotguns were imported by both Winchester and Ithaca during the 1960s and 1970s. The company now has its own distribution network and its current model line-up is extensive. Perazzi shotguns are well known for their quality control standards and reliability in clay target championships and in-field conditions.

SHOTGUNS

Perazzi shotguns have incorporated many improvements during their manufacture, the most important being the forearm design/material and barrel lug attachment. There have been 4 Types: Type 1 is serial numbered 30000-33250, Type 2 is serial numbered 33251-35450, Type 3 is serial numbered 35451-51242, Type 4 started at serial no. 51243 and is still current. Due to the modifications, the desirability factor on a Type 4 forearm shotgun is much greater. If a Type 1 or 2 competition gun develops problems, they are automatically retrofitted to the Type 4 design - and these modifications are expensive. For these reasons, the serial number of a Perazzi competition gun will determine its type. Since Types 1 through 3 are discontinued, they will be less desirable (and less expensive) than the values listed for Type 4.

The most collectible models will be those specimens which exhibit the highest quality and are equally rare. Older SCO grades on small frames with older style "V" springs are at the top for desirability. Also, any older SPECIAL GUNS were all custom made - usually engraved by master engravers with Angelo Galeazzi being considered one of the best.

Perazzi Shotguns Information

Until 1988, most trap guns did not have a "Special" option package which includes an adjustable trigger group (designated P4). Models listed in the following sections assume a Type 4 forearm attachment design and are serial numbered 51243 and above. Models that are serial numbered below 51242 are an older design and will be priced less than the newer Type 4 models.

Rather than describe all the following models individually, descriptions will appear only once and are listed. The various grades have similar features and engraving (I.E., an SCO Grade Sideplate in American Skeet would appear similar to an American Trap SCO Grade Sideplate, except for stock dimensions).

Older SHO (Type 3s) and DHO models with rebounding hammers (disc.) are perhaps the most collectible Perazzi shotguns currently.

SC3 and other higher grade models have not been listed. The 14th Edition *Blue Book of Gun Values* did include all pertinent information, including 1993 pricing pertaining to the Perazzi higher grade models available at the time.

There have been some standard grade models modified by individual engraving or adding sideplates and other markings of higher grade models. These after market upgrades usually have the original markings polished off. Perazzi can verify any gun suspected of upgrading. These guns should be priced individually based on upgrading values. Perazzi discontinued "Mirage" model nomenclature during 1998.

Perazzi Grades and Descriptions

Because of relatively low manufacture, the higher grade Perazzis have been described but not individually priced. Please contact Perazzi, USA for more information and prices on these higher grades.

GRADES AND DESCRIPTIONS

* ***Special Model*** - introductory level model with high polished blue on barrels and receiver, normally with model name on lower frame sides in gold letters and numerals. Checkered walnut stock (interchangeable) and forearm, all have adjustable trigger assembly.
* ***Gold Outline Model*** - similar to Standard Model, except has gold line engraving around perimeter of frame, also features better grade of walnut. This configuration is very rare.
* ***SC3 Model*** - features coin finished receiver with different styles of scroll engraving and different patterns of game scene engraving (snipe, grouse, pointing bird dog, or woodcock). Better grade of walnut than the Gold Outline Model.
* ***SC3 100 Gold Model*** - pattern 100 SC3 scroll engraving with gold inlaid partridge, pheasant and duck on left, right and undersides respectively. Also available with gold inlaid accents dispersed amongst the pattern 100 scrolls (with no game animals). Optional case color hardened frame.
* ***SC3 Cesel Model*** - SC3 grade model with panels of deep relief chisel (cesello) engraved duck, pheasant, and partridge surrounded by more extensive pattern 100 scrolls.
* ***SCO Model*** - more elaborate than SC3 Model in that it features different styles of scroll engraving (deep relief "gargoyles" or fine English scroll) and different game scene engraving patterns. Again, a better grade of walnut (in addition to finer checkering) is utilized.
* ***SCO Gold Grade Model*** - differentiated from SCO Model in that it has engraving patterns featuring multiple gold inlays on receiver sides (including different duck scenes, separate grouse scenes, woodcock, and deep relief "gargoyle").
* ***SCO Grade Sideplate Model*** - includes coin finished receiver with game scene engraved sideplates (with trigger plate action). Game scene engraving choices include different duck scenes, grouse, "Chisel" relief scroll, and Diana Goddess of the Hunt pattern.
* ***SCO Gold Grade Sideplate Model*** - similar to SCO Grade Sideplate Model, except has game figures on sideplates in multiple gold inlays. Patterns include different grouse scenes, separate ducks patterns, and dogs flushing upland game. Earlier models had sideplates attached by screws to a different type of frame, and the detachment lever was an option.
* ***Extra Grade Model*** - with sideplates, denoted by top-of-the-line fine bank note style game scene engraving with elaborate scroll and relief work on metal perimeters. Game scene choices include different dog scenes, grouse, and duck. Top quality Circassian finely checkered walnut.
* ***Extra Gold Grade Model*** - top-of-the-line sideplate trigger plate model that differs from Extra Grade Model in that the scenes are gold inlaid. The sideplates detatchment lever has been discontinued on this model.
* ***Extra Super Grade Model*** - highest grade walnut stock offered by Perazzi, currently the highest grade sideplate model that has fine bulino engravings, also available in a 4 gun set.
* ***SHO Over & Under Model*** - features sidelock action with coin finished receiver and intricate bank note game scene engraving with choices including different duck patterns and pheasant. Top quality walnut and checkering. Type One SHOs have non-rebounding firing pins, while Type Two guns have rebounding firing pins (since 1985). Importation disc.

This model was individually handmade per customer's specifications. Currently, no orders are being taken for this series.

* ***SHO Gold Over & Under Model*** - similar to SHO Over & Under Model, except features game scene of wildlife in relief gold. This model was the best sidelock special order grade that Perazzi offered for sale. Importation disc.

GRADING - PPGS™	100%	98%	95%	90%	80%	70%	60%	LAST MSR

* ***DHO SxS Models*** – top-of-the-line sidelock model in 12 ga. only for DHO and DHO Gold grades. DHO Extra and DHO Gold Extra grades have similar engraving to Extra Grade and Extra Gold Grade models and were available in all gauges. The DHO Gold Extra was the most elaborate, highly finished SxS shotgun that an individual could special order from any company. The DHO model is exceedingly rare, and specimens should be appraised individually. Importation disc.

This model was entirely handmade per customer's specifications. Currently, no orders are being taken for this series.

RIFLES: O/U

Perazzi offered the following high grade O/U Express rifles from 2012-2019 with a total production of 30 units (inclusive of grade). All prices shown were the last MSR listed for 2019.

SCO Grade: Express SCO ($48,540 last MSR) or Express SCO w/sideplates ($62,250 last MSR).

SCO Gold Grade: Express SCO Gold ($55,600 last MSR) or Express SCO Gold w/sideplates ($69,580 last MSR).

Extra Grade: Express Extra ($113,700 last MSR), Express Extra Gold ($121,100 last MSR), or Express Extra Super ($131,300 last MSR).

EXPRESS SC2 – 9.3x74R or .375 flanged Magnum (disc. 2016) cal., boxlock action, 24 in. barrels, non-removable trigger group, fixed stock, barrel selector on trigger guard. Mfg. 2012-2019.

	100%	98%	95%	90%	80%	70%	60%	LAST MSR
	$18,650	$15,625	$12,750	$11,000	$8,850	$7,500	$6,500	*$26,340*

EXPRESS SC3 – 9.3x74R or .375 flanged Magnum (disc. 2016) cal., 24 in. barrels, non-removable trigger group, fixed stock, barrel selector on opening lever. Mfg. 2012-2019.

	100%	98%	95%	90%	80%	70%	60%	LAST MSR
	$25,250	$21,250	$17,750	$14,750	$12,000	$10,000	$8,000	*$35,670*

SHOTGUNS: AMERICAN TRAP, SINGLE BARREL & COMBINATIONS

All guns are 12 ga., equipped with Perazzi's removable trigger group (flat or coil springs), VR barrel lengths are currently 32, 34, or 35 inches, unless otherwise stated. Fixed chokes are standard.

Combo models typically include an extra set of O/U barrels without extra forearm - contact the importer for pricing.

Add $595 for four choke tubes on current models listed within this category.

DB81 – 12 ga., top single, features extra high fixed rib. Limited mfg. Disc.

	100%	98%	95%	90%	80%	70%	60%	LAST MSR
	$5,850	$5,175	$4,695	$3,795	$3,100	$2,425	$1,950	

MX-8 – 12 ga., top single configuration, features fixed rib chokes and stock, gold trigger, blue or nickel frame finish. Mfg. for U.S. market only.

	100%	98%	95%	90%	80%	70%	60%	LAST MSR
MSR $$11,300	$9,600	$8,400	$7,200	$6,530	$5,280	$4,325	$3,765	

Current MSR for MX-8 Combo Set is $16,900.

High Grade Combo Sets include: MX8 SC3 ($26,250 MSR), MX8 SCO ($42,530 MSR), MX8 SCO Gold ($47,160 MSR), MX8 SCO w/sideplates ($61,070 MSR), or MX8 SCO Gold w/sideplates ($67,760 MSR).

MX-10 – 12 ga., top single configuration, features adj. rib with 4 notches, adj. comb., blue or nickel frame finish, gold trigger. Mfg. for the U.S. marketplace only.

	100%	98%	95%	90%	80%	70%	60%	LAST MSR
MSR $13,000	$11,050	$9,670	$8,290	$7,515	$6,080	$4,975	$4,325	

Current MSR for MX-10 Combo Set is $19,900.

* ***MX-10 RS*** – 12 ga., unsingle configuration, features high profile adj. rib with 4 notches, adj. comb., blue or nickel frame finish. Mfg. for the U.S. marketplace only.

	100%	98%	95%	90%	80%	70%	60%	LAST MSR
MSR $13,000	$11,050	$9,670	$8,290	$7,515	$6,080	$4,975	$4,325	

Current MSR for MX-10 RS Combo set is $19,900.

MX-14/MX-14L TRAP COMBO – 12 ga., American Trap combo plus O/U unsingle, 32 or 34 in. fixed rib unsingle and 29 1/2 or 31 1/2 in. fixed rib O/U barrels, adj. comb, black trigger, blue or nickel frame finish, same plain side receiver as MX-15, squared monobloc, fixed stock, current production entry level model.

	100%	98%	95%	90%	80%	70%	60%	LAST MSR
MSR $16,400	$13,950	$12,200	$10,465	$9,485	$7,675	$6,280	$5,465	

Add $2,470 for MX-14L Model with light engraving (disc. 2018).
Subtract $2,000 for unsingle only.
Subtract $1,400 for O/U only.

MX-15 – 12 ga., unsingle configuration, with adj. rib, adj. comb, plain side receiver, black trigger, blue finish only, current production entry level model.

	100%	98%	95%	90%	80%	70%	60%	LAST MSR
MSR $10,290	$8,750	$7,650	$6,565	$5,950	$4,815	$3,950	$3,425	

GRADING - PPGS™	100%	98%	95%	90%	80%	70%	60%	LAST MSR

* ***MX-15L*** – 12 ga., unsingle configuration, nickel plated frame with light engraving, gold trigger, with adj. rib, adj. comb. Disc. 2018.

	$8,700	$7,300	$6,100	$5,400	$4,300	$3,300	$2,650	*$12,460*

MX-2000 – 12 ga. only, unsingle configuration with high tapered adj. rib with 5 notches, "Perazzi MX-2000" marked on receiver sides surrounded by engraving, gold trigger, blue or nickel frame finish. Mfg. for U.S. marketplace only. Disc. 2018.

	$9,325	$7,750	$6,500	$5,750	$4,600	$3,700	$2,750	*$13,290*

MX-2000/8 – 12 ga. only, top single configuration, fixed rib, chokes, and stock. Mfg. for U.S. marketplace only.

MSR $12,000	$10,200	$8,925	$7,650	$6,935	$5,610	$4,590	$4,000	

Current MSR for MX-2000/8 Combo Set is $18,500 (includes extra O/U barrel).

MX-2005 – 12 ga. only, 32, 34, or 35 in. barrel, unsingle configuration, removable trigger group, extra high tapered adj. rib with 5 notches, adj. comb, fixed chokes, gold trigger, blue or nickel frame finish, marked "Perazzi MX-2005" on both sides of receiver surrounded by light engraving. Mfg. for U.S. marketplace only.

MSR $13,700	$11,650	$10,200	$8,750	$7,925	$6,410	$5,245	$4,565	

Current MSR for MX-2005 Combo Set is $21,460 (includes extra O/U barrel).

TM1 – 12 ga., single barrel receiver, detachable trigger, disc.

	$3,500	$2,500	$2,100	$1,800	$1,500	$1,200	$1,100	

Add $150 for Special model with P4 adj. trigger.
Add $200 for TMS model with factory choke tubes.

TMX – 12 ga., American Trap model, newer production, similar to the TM1, except has high rib, disc.

	$3,600	$3,000	$2,500	$2,100	$1,800	$1,500	$1,200	

TM9 – 12 ga., top single configuration with non-adj. fixed VR, sculpted frame, blue or nickel frame finish, black trigger. Mfg. for U.S. marketplace only.

MSR $10,290	$8,750	$7,650	$6,565	$5,950	$4,815	$3,950	$3,425	

* ***TM9X*** – 12 ga., top single configuration, features adj. 4 notch rib, adj. comb, blue or nickel frame finish, black trigger. Mfg. for U.S. marketplace only.

MSR $11,980	$10,185	$8,910	$7,650	$6,925	$5,600	$4,585	$3,990	

SHOTGUNS: O/U, STANDARD MODELS (GAME, PIGEON, SKEET, SPORTING, & TRAP) & COMBINATIONS, RECENT MFG.

Perazzi manufactures approx. 1,500-2,400 O/U and single barrel shotguns annually, yet there are nearly 200 models and configurations! Because of this, only the Standard Grade models are listed and described individually and priced separately, with shooting discipline(s) listed also.

While many people refer to the standard configuration Perazzi shotgun as a boxlock mechanism, it actually is a trigger plate action, where the entire firing mechanism is attached to the trigger plate. On some of the larger competition models, this trigger mechanism is interchangeable.

Higher grade Perazzi models, including the SC3 Grade, SCO Grade, SCO Gold Grade, SCO Grade w/sideplates, and SCO Gold w/sideplates have current MSRs only and are listed under each individual model listing.

Combination models (available in Trap, Skeet, and Sporting configurations) include an extra single barrel available in 32, 34, or 35 in.

Throughout the years, Perazzi made many economical models: the MX-3, MX-3 Special, MX-5, MX-6, MX-7, MX-11, MX-14, MX-15, and the MX-16 models all have plain flat side, not sea shell sculpted receivers to save production costs. Among them, the MX-3, MX-5, MX-6, and the MX-7 models all have rounded monoblocs for further cost savings at the time. Another economical approach was the HG model, made for Perazzi by Franchi in low numbers, and sold into the USA, France, and UK in 1984/1985. HG was the only model built by another manufacturer under contract to Perazzi.

In the past when the dollar was strong, some grey market Perazzis were imported into the U.S. from the U.K. These guns may not have the same warranty as the shotguns imported by Perazzi USA.

Subtract 20% for O/U receiver but with only one single barrel, and non-adj. rib, unless originally priced as a single barrel trap gun.
Subtract 20% for fixed SK/SK chokes.

GRADING - PPGS™	100%	98%	95%	90%	80%	70%	60%	LAST MSR

GRANDITALIA – plain side receiver, fixed SST, squared monobloc, choke tubes in bottom barrel, fixed choke top. Mfg. 1980-1981.

	$4,900	$4,000	$3,400	$2,900	$2,400	$1,900	$1,700	

MIRAGE – similar features as the MX-8, in all configurations. The Mirage model nomenclature was discontinued in 1998.

	$6,800	$5,500	$4,700	$4,000	$3,500	$3,000	$2,700	

Subtract 15-20% for Type 3 guns.

DB81 – 12 ga., features extra high fixed rib. Limited mfg. Disc.

	$5,850	$5,175	$4,695	$3,795	$3,100	$2,425	$1,950	

This special model was manufactured to try and take advantage of the trap shooting fame achieved by Dan Bonillas (DB), even though Mr. Bonillas never used this model in competition. It was manufactured for only a few years.

MS 80 – named after the 1980 Moscow Olympics, sculpted receiver, fixed trigger group, squared monobloc, disc.

	$5,500	$4,300	$4,000	$3,500	$3,000	$2,500	$2,000	

MT-6 – named after the 1976 Montreal Olympics, early guns have silver strips on receiver, and different barrel under lug and forearm. Late production guns have blue receiver and type four forearm, fixed trigger group with barrel selector, squared monobloc. Disc.

Older mfg.	$4,750	$3,800	$3,200	$2,800	$2,300	$1,800	$1,600	

Add 20% for late production blue receiver with Type 4 forend.

MX-1/MX-2 – 12 ga., 29 1/2, 30 3/4, or 31 1/2 in. barrels, live pigeon and Olympic Trap gun, top firing first, choked tighter on bottom barrel, detachable trigger group, fixed stock. MX-2 disc. late 1996.

MSR $12,100	$10,285	$9,000	$7,715	$6,995	$5,655	$4,650	$4,025	

MX-3 – plain side receiver, detachable trigger group, top firing, choked tighter on bottom barrel, rounded monobloc, econo model. Disc.

	$4,000	$3,500	$3,000	$2,500	$2,100	$1,800	$1,600	

Add 10% for "MX-3 Special" model with adj. trigger group and square monobloc.

MX-4 – similar to the MX-3 Special, except without P4 trigger, European model, disc.

	$4,400	$3,900	$3,300	$2,800	$2,400	$2,000	$1,900	

MX-5 – plain side receiver, fixed trigger group, rounded monobloc, entry level model introduced in 1985, disc.

	$4,000	$3,400	$2,800	$2,400	$2,000	$1,700	$1,500	

MX-6 – plain side receiver, detachable trigger group, rounded monobloc, econo model, disc.

	$4,400	$3,900	$3,400	$2,800	$2,400	$2,000	$1,700	

MX-7 – plain side receiver, fixed trigger group, rounded monobloc, econo model introduced 1992, disc.

	$4,200	$3,500	$2,900	$2,500	$2,100	$1,800	$1,600	

MX-8 – 12 or 20 ga., named after the 1968 Olympics in Mexico City, this is the "standard" of all current Perazzi models, removable trigger group with flat or coil spring, available in all configurations.

Add $150 for P4 adj. trigger (MX-8 Special).

Subtract 15%-20% for older Type 3 guns.

Current MSRs for Combo Skeet/Sporting sets include: MX8 SC3 - $26,250, MX8 SC3 CESEL - $32,300, MX8 SC3 ORO - $34,600, MX8 SCO - $42,530, MX8 SCO Gold - $47,160, MX8 SCO sideplates - $61,070, or MX8 SCO Gold sideplates - last MSR in 2020 was $65,800.

Additional higher grade MSRs for Sporting, Trap, and Skeet are as follows: MX8 SC2 - $16,700, MX8 SC3 $20,970, MX8 SC3 CESEL - $27,500, MX8 SC3 Gold - $29,800, MX8 SCO - $35,500, MX8 SCO Gold - $39,500, MX8 SCO Sideplates - $53,630, or MX8 SCO Gold Sideplates - $60,520.

* ***MX-8 Sporting*** – 12 or 20 ga., 27 9/16, 28 3/8, 29 1/2, 31 1/2, or 34 in. barrels, removable trigger group, fixed rib, chokes, and sporting style stock, has barrel selector on safety lever.

MSR $12,100	$10,285	$9,000	$7,715	$6,995	$5,655	$4,650	$4,025	

Current MSR for Skeet/Sporting Combo set is $16,900 - includes extra set of barrels (29 1/2, 31 1/2, or 34 in., 12 ga. only).

* ***MX-8L Sporting*** – 12 ga. only, 27 9/16, 28 3/8, 29 1/2, 31 1/2, or 34 in. barrels, lightly engraved action, removable trigger group, fixed rib and chokes, fixed sporting style stock. Disc. 2018.

	$12,100	$10,590	$9,075	$8,230	$6,655	$5,450	$4,750	*$14,230*

Add $4,640 for Combo set.

GRADING - PPGS™	100%	98%	95%	90%	80%	70%	60%	LAST MSR

* ***MX-8C/MX-8 20C Sporting*** – 12 or 20 ga., 27 9/16, 28 3/8, 29 1/2, 3 1/2, or 34 in. barrels, 7 chokes, removable trigger group, fixed rib and stock, selector. Disc. 2016.

	$8,900	$7,600	$6,350	$5,550	$4,525	$3,625	$2,825	*$12,327*

* ***MX-8LC Sporting*** – 12 ga., 27 9/16, 28 3/8, 29 1/2, 31 1/2, or 34 in. barrels, removable trigger group, fixed rib and stock, 7 chokes, selector, engraving. Disc. 2016.

	$10,500	$9,100	$7,550	$6,675	$5,325	$4,300	$3,325	*$14,604*

* ***MX-8 Trap*** – 12 or 20 ga., 29 1/2, 30 3/4, or 31 1/2 in. barrels, removable trigger group, fixed rib and chokes, fixed trap style stock.

MSR $11,300	$9,600	$8,400	$7,200	$6,530	$5,280	$4,325	$3,765	

* ***MX-8L Trap*** – 12 ga. only, 29 1/2, 30 3/4, or 31 1/2 in. barrels, lightly engraved action, removable trigger group, fixed rib and chokes, fixed trap style stock. Disc. 2017.

	$11,750	$10,280	$8,815	$7,990	$6,465	$5,290	$4,600	*$13,820*

* ***MX-8 Vintage*** – 12, 20, 28 ga. or .410 bore, 29 1/2, 30 3/4, or 31 1/2 in. barrels, removable trigger group, fixed rib, chokes, and stock, features color case hardened frame. New 2015.

MSR $13,620	$11,575	$10,130	$8,680	$7,875	$6,365	$5,210	$4,550	

* ***MX-8 Skeet*** – 12 or 20 ga., 26 3/4, 27 9/16, 28 3/8, or 29 1/2 in. barrels, removable trigger group, fixed rib and chokes, fixed skeet style stock.

MSR $12,100	$10,285	$9,000	$7,715	$6,995	$5,655	$4,650	$4,025	

Current MSR for Combo set is $16,900 - includes extra set of barrels (28 3/8, 29 1/2, or 31 1/2 in., 12 ga. only).

* ***MX-8L Skeet*** – 12 ga. only, 26 3/4, 27 9/16, 28 3/8, or 29 1/2 in. barrels, lightly engraved action, removable trigger group, fixed rib and chokes, fixed skeet style stock. Disc. 2018.

	$12,100	$10,590	$9,075	$8,230	$6,655	$5,445	$4,745	*$14,230*

Add $4,520 for Combo set - includes extra set of barrels (28 3/8, 29 1/2, or 31 1/2 in.).

* ***MX-8 Special*** – similar to MX-8, except has ramped rib and adj. trigger. Disc. circa mid-1990s.

	$8,200	$6,200	$5,500	$5,000	$4,400	$3,800	$3,250	*$12,155*

* ***MX-8B*** – similar to the MX-8, except has a detachable coil spring trigger group, bottom barrel choke tubes, a promotional model at the time, limited configuration.

	$6,900	$6,000	$5,000	$4,000	$3,200	$2,900	$2,500	

MX-9 – with changeable mid sight and adj. comb for changing POI, disc.

	$7,000	$5,900	$4,900	$4,000	$3,200	$2,900	$2,500	

MX-10/MX-10RS – similar to the MX-8 Trap, except has adj. rib and stock, mostly in Trap configuration, RS model has higher adj. rib for American Trap. Importation disc.

	$8,350	$7,300	$6,265	$5,675	$4,595	$3,750	$2,925	*$11,914*

Add approx. $1,500 for combo model with top single barrel with adj. rib.

Add approx. $1,600 for RS combo model with unsingle barrel with adj. rib.

MX-11 – plain side receiver, square monobloc, detachable trigger group, newer entry level model.

	$5,800	$4,400	$3,600	$3,100	$2,800	$2,600	$2,200	

MX-12/MX-12C – 12 ga., available in Sporting or Game configuration, 27 9/16, 28 3/8, 29 1/2, 31 1/2, or 34 in. barrels, seashell sculpted receiver, non-detachable selective trigger, engravings on frame border, trigger guard, and forearm, fixed rib and chokes, fixed stock, selector.

MSR $13,100	$11,150	$9,755	$8,365	$7,580	$6,135	$5,020	$4,365	

Add $1,380 for 28 ga. or .410 bore barrels on 12 ga. frame.

Add $980 for factory choke tubes (Model MX-12C, Sporting configuration only). Disc.

Current MSR for Combo Set is: $18,300 - includes extra set of 12 ga. O/U barrels (Skeet and Sporting configuration, 29 1/2, 31 1/2, or 34 in.).

Additional higher grade MSRs are as follows: MX12 SC2 - $17,700, MX12 SC3 - $20,970, MX12 SC3 CESEL - $27,500, MX12 SC3 Gold - $29,800, MX12 SCO - $35,500, MX12 SCO Gold - $39,500, MX12 SCO Sideplates - $53,630, MX12 SCO Gold Sideplates - $60,520.

Additional higher grade MSRs for Skeet/Sporting Combo Sets are as follows: MX12 SC3 - $26,250, MX12 SCO - $42,530, MX12 SCO Gold - $47,160, MX12 SCO Sideplates - $61,070, MX12 SCO Gold Sidplates - $67,760.

GRADING - PPGS™	100%	98%	95%	90%	80%	70%	60%	LAST MSR

MX-12/3 & MX-12/3C – 12 ga., Sporting configuration only, 27 9/16, 28 3/8, 29 1/2, 31 1/2, or 34 in. barrels, non-detachable trigger group with coil springs, adj. VR with 3 notches, adj. comb, fixed (MX-12/3) or interchangeable (MX-12/3C) chokes, selector.

MSR $14,800 | $12,585 | $11,010 | $9,440 | $8,560 | $6,920 | $5,665 | $4,925

Add $1,010 for 7 interchangeable chokes (Model MX-12/3C).

MX-16 (OLDER MFG.) – 12 or 16 ga., limited production entry level model, plain side receiver, non-detachable, squared monobloc, selective trigger with flat spring.

$5,800 | $4,800 | $4,000 | $3,600 | $3,200 | $2,800 | $2,400

Add $1,000 for combo gun with extra top single barrel.

MX-16 (CURRENT MFG.) – 16 ga., built on a dedicated MX16 frame, scaled to size, non-removable trigger group.

MSR $16,680 | $14,185 | $12,400 | $10,630 | $9,640 | $7,795 | $6,380 | $5,550

Additional MSRs for higher grade models are as folows: MX16 SC2 - $21,280, MX16 SC3 - $25,550, MX16 SCO - $40,080, MX16 SCO Gold - $44,080, MX16 SCO Sideplates - $58,210, MX16 SCO Gold Sideplates - $65,100.

MX-20/MX-20C – 20 ga., available in Sporting or Game configuration, has a true 20 ga. frame, 27 9/16, 28 3/8, 29 1/2, 31 1/2, or 34 in. barrels, seashell sculpted receiver, non-detachable selective trigger, engravings on frame border, trigger guard, and forearm, fixed rib and chokes, fixed stock.

MSR $13,100 | $11,150 | $9,755 | $8,365 | $7,580 | $6,135 | $5,020 | $4,365

Add $1,380 for 28 ga. or .410 bore barrels on 20 ga. frame.
Add $980 for factory choke tubes (Model MX-20C, Sporting configuration only).

Additional higher grade MSRs are as follows: MX20 SC2 - $17,700, MX 20 SC3 - $20,970, MX20 SC3 CESEL - $27,500, MX20 SC3 Gold - $29,800, MX20 SCO - $35,500, MX20 SCO Gold - $39,500, MX20 SCO w/sideplates - $53,630, or MX20 SCO Gold sideplates - $60,520.

MX-28 GAME – 28 ga., scaled down frame with SC2 engraving, 26 3/4, 27 9/16, 28 3/8, or 29 1/2 in. barrels, non-removable trigger group, fixed rib and chokes, fixed stock, selector.

MSR $24,300 | $20,650 | $18,085 | $15,500 | $14,060 | $11,375 | $9,300 | $8,100

Additional higher grade MSRs are as follows: MX28 SC3 - $33,270, MX28 SCO - $47,180, MX28 SCO Gold - $51,600, MX28 SCO Sideplates - $65,900, MX28 SCO Gold Sideplates - $72,300.

MX-28B GAME – 28 ga., 26 3/4, 27 9/16, 28 3/8, or 29 1/2 in. barrels, non-detachable single selective trigger with coil springs, fixed rib and chokes, English or pistol grip fixed stock, Game or Schnabel forend.

MSR $16,680 | $14,185 | $12,400 | $10,630 | $9,640 | $7,795 | $6,380 | $5,550

MX-410 GAME – .410 bore frame, 26 3/4, 27 9/16, 28 3/8, or 29 1/2 in. barrels, non-removable trigger group, fixed rib and chokes, fixed stock, selector, with SC2 engraving.

MSR $24,300 | $20,650 | $18,085 | $15,500 | $14,060 | $11,375 | $9,300 | $8,100

Additional higher grade MSRs are as follows: MX410 SC3 - $33,270, MX410 SCO - $47,180, MX410 SCO Gold - $51,600, MX410 SCO Sideplates - $65,900, MX410 SCO Gold Sideplates - $72,300.

MX-410B GAME – .410 bore, Game configuration only, 26 3/4, 27 9/16, 28 3/8, or 29 1/2 in. barrels, non-detachable single selective trigger with coil springs, fixed rib and chokes, English or pistol grip fixed stock, Game or Schnabel forend.

MSR $16,680 | $14,185 | $12,400 | $10,630 | $9,640 | $7,795 | $6,380 | $5,550

MX-2000 SERIES – 12, 20, 28 ga., or .410 bore, choice of removable or non-removable trigger group, fixed or adj. VR, fixed or adj. comb stock, fixed chokes or choke tubes, MX-2000-style engraving and gold lettering on receiver, available in Trap (MX-2000/3 and MX-2000/8), Sporting (MX-2000 S/3), Skeet or Pigeon (MX-2000/8), or Game (MX-2000S).

Subtract 20% for top single barrel only.
Subtract 20% for fixed SK/SK choke Skeet models.
Subtract 15% for unsingle model with adj. rib.

* ***MX-2000S Game*** – 12, 20, 28 (on 20 ga. frame) ga. or .410 (on 20 ga. frame) bore, 26 3/4, 27 9/16, 28 3/8, or 29 1/2 in. barrels, non-removable trigger group, fixed rib and chokes, fixed sporting style stock, selector.

MSR $13,600 | $11,575 | $10,130 | $8,680 | $7,875 | $6,365 | $5,210 | $4,525

Current MSR for MX2000S Skeet and Sporting Combo or American Trap Combo is $18,500.

GRADING - PPGS™	100%	98%	95%	90%	80%	70%	60%	LAST MSR

» **MX-2000S Gold Game** – 12, 20, 28 (on 20 ga. frame) ga. or .410 (on 20 ga. frame) bore, 26 3/4, 27 9/16, 28 3/8, or 29 1/2 in. barrels, features gold inlays on receiver, non-removable trigger group, fixed rib, chokes, and sporting style stock. Disc. 2018.

	$16,250	$13,500	$11,000	$10,000	$7,800	$6,350	$4,850	*$23,500*

* ***MX-2000S/MX-2000SC Sporting*** – 12 or 20 ga., 27 9/16, 28 3/8, 29 1/2, 31 1/2, or 34 in. barrels, non-removable trigger group, fixed rib and chokes, fixed sporting style stock. Disc. 2017.

	$9,100	$7,650	$6,450	$5,600	$4,500	$3,600	$2,750	*$12,450*

Add $950 for seven choke tubes (Model MX-2000SC).
Add $5,000 for Combo Set - includes extra set of 12 ga. O/U barrels.

» **MX-2000S/MX-2000SC Gold Sporting** – 12 or 20 ga., features gold inlays on receiver, non-removable trigger group, fixed rib, chokes, and sporting style stock. Disc. 2017.

	$15,500	$13,000	$10,750	$9,750	$7,725	$6,250	$4,850	*$22,830*

Add $950 for seven interchangeable choke tubes (Model MX-2000SC Gold).

* ***MX-2000 S/3 and MX-2000 S/3C Sporting*** – 12 ga. only, 27 9/16, 28 3/8, 29 1/2, 31 1/2, or 34 in. barrels, non-removable trigger group with coil springs, adj. rib with 3 notches and adj. comb, fixed chokes, selector.

MSR $15,300	$13,000	$11,375	$9,750	$8,840	$7,150	$5,850	$5,100

Add $3,580 for 28 ga. or .410 bore barrels on 12 or 20 ga. frame.
Add $980 for seven interchangeable choke tubes (Model MX-2000 S/3C, disc.).

* ***MX-2000/3 (MX-2000/3 Pigeon/MX-2000/3 Trap)*** – 12 or 20 ga., 29 1/2, 30 3/4, or 31 1/2 in. barrels, removable (disc.) or non-removable trigger group, adj. rib with 3 notches, adj. comb, fixed chokes, available in pigeon, trap, sporting, skeet, trap, or game configurations.

MSR $15,300	$13,000	$11,375	$9,750	$8,840	$7,150	$5,850	$5,100

Add $10,300 for MX2000/3 Gold with adj. rib and comb (disc. 2020).

* ***MX-2000/8 Skeet*** – 12 or 20 ga., 26 3/4, 27 9/16, 28 3/8, or 29 1/2 in. barrels, removable trigger group, fixed rib and chokes, fixed sporting style stock.

MSR $13,600	$11,575	$10,130	$8,680	$7,875	$6,365	$5,210	$4,525

Current MSR for Combo Set is $18,500 (includes extra set of 12 ga. O/U barrels).

* ***MX-2000/8 Sporting*** – 12 or 20 ga., 27 9/16, 28 3/8, 29 1/2, 31 1/2, or 34 in. barrels, removable trigger group, fixed rib, chokes, and sporting style stock.

MSR $13,600	$11,575	$10,130	$8,680	$7,875	$6,365	$5,210	$4,525

Current MSR for Combo Set is $18,500 (includes extra set of 12 ga. O/U barrels).
Add $980 for seven choke tubes (Model MX-2000/8C, disc.).

* ***MX-2000/8 Pigeon / MX-2000/8 Trap*** – 12 ga. only, 29 1/2, 30 3/4, or 31 1/2 in. barrels, removable trigger group, fixed rib and chokes, fixed sporting (Pigeon model) or fixed trap (Trap model) style stock.

MSR $13,600	$11,575	$10,130	$8,680	$7,875	$6,365	$5,210	$4,525

Add $4,770 for Combo set.

* ***MX-2000/8 Gold*** – 12 or 20 ga., features gold inlays on receiver, removable trigger group, fixed rib and chokes, fixed stock, manufactured for Trap, Sporting, Skeet, Pigeon, and Game configurations. Disc. 2018.

	$16,000	$13,500	$11,000	$9,850	$7,825	$6,300	$4,850	*$23,500*

Add $1,638 for adj. rib with three notches and adj. comb (Model MX-2000/8 Gold Adj. Rib).

MX-2005 (MX-2005 PIGEON/MX-2005 TRAP) – 12 ga. only, 29 1/2 or 31 1/2 in. barrels, extra high (Trap model only) adj. rib with 5 notches, adj. comb., removable trigger group, fixed chokes, available in pigeon, trap, sporting, skeet, or game gun configurations.

MSR $15,300	$13,000	$11,375	$9,750	$8,840	$7,150	$5,850	$5,100

Current MSR for MX-2005 Combo Set is $21,460 (includes extra O/U barrel).

MX-2008 – 12 ga. only, 29 1/2 or 31 1/2 in. barrels, removable trigger group, adj. rib with 5 notches, adj. comb., fixed chokes, no single barrel available.

MSR $14,840	$10,350	$8,725	$7,275	$6,200	$4,800	$3,050	$2,925

MX-2000/10 TRAP COMBO – 12 ga., American Trap combo model includes adj. rib top single and adj. rib O/U barrels, adj. comb, gold trigger, blue or nickel frame finish, marked "Perazzi MX-2000" on side of receiver.

MSR $21,460	$18,250	$15,975	$13,690	$12,410	$10,040	$8,225	$7,150

This combo set is also available with a short rib.

GRADING - PPGS™	100%	98%	95%	90%	80%	70%	60%	LAST MSR

MX-2000/RS TRAP COMBO – 12 ga. only, similar to MX-2000/10 Trap, except has unsingle barrel with high profile adj. rib.

MSR $21,460	$18,250	$15,975	$13,690	$12,410	$10,040	$8,225	$7,150	

This combo set is also available with a short rib.

MXS SPORTING – 12 ga., 28 3/4, 30, or 32 in. barrels with fixed or removable choke tubes, non-detachable trigger group, checkered walnut stock and forearm, with or w/o adj. comb, blue or nickel finish, flat side receiver with beveled flat-sided monobloc. New 2013.

MSR $11,100	$9,450	$8,275	$7,090	$6,425	$5,200	$4,250	$3,700	

SHOTGUNS: O/U, HIGH GRADE COMBO SETS (TRAP, SKEET, AND SPORTING)

Perazzi offers a wide variety of combination sets in Trap, Skeet, and Sporting configurations. These combination sets include a choice of either 29 1/2 or 31 1/2 in. O/U VR barrels with or w/o choke tubes and one VR barrel (choice of top single or bottom single) with or w/o choke tubes. There are numerous configurations available, including many engraving, rib, and stock options. All shotguns, except the MX12, are equipped with a removable trigger group and flat springs.

Currently, Perazzi offers Trap, Skeet, and Sporting combination sets in the following high grades:SC3 Grade, SCO Grade, SCO Gold Grade, SCO Grade Models w/sideplates, or SCO Gold Grade Models w/sideplates.

Previous models included: MX-2005 ($20,964 last MSR), DB81 Trap ($16,023 last MSR), MX2000/8 Gold Trap ($26,467 last MSR), MX2000 Gold Trap ($24,400 last MSR), MX2000/8 Gold Skeet ($23,701 last MSR), and the MX2000S Gold Sporting ($21,296 last MSR).

MSRs for current high grade combo sets can be found under each individual model listing.

SHOTGUNS: O/U, TRAP, HIGHER GRADES

Perazzi offers the following high grade trap shotguns in 12 or 20 ga. Current barrel lengths include 29 1/2, 30 3/4, or 31 1/2 in.: SC2 Grade, SC3 Grade, SC3 CESEL, SC3 Gold, SCO Grade, SCO Gold Grade, SCO Grade w/sideplates, and SCO Gold Grade w/sideplates. Extra Grade: Extra ($102,000 MSR), Extra Gold ($109,700 MSR), and Extra Super ($120,200 MSR).

MSRs for current higher grade models can be found under each individual model listing.

SHOTGUNS: O/U, SKEET HIGHER GRADES

Perazzi offers a wide variety of competition style shotguns in 12 or 20 ga., 26 3/4, 27 9/16, 28 3/8, 29 1/2, or 34 in. barrels and various configurations. Special high grade options include: SC2 Grade, SC3 Grade, SC3 CESEL, SC3 Gold, SCO Grade, SCO Gold Grade, SCO Grade w/sideplates, and SCO Gold Grade w/sideplates. Extra Grade: Extra ($102,000 MSR), Extra Gold ($109,700 MSR), and Extra Super ($120,200 MSR).

MSRs for current higher grade models can be found under each individual model listing.

Subtract $250-$500 on older Mirage Models (without the "Special" designation) that do not have the adjustable 4 position trigger.

SHOTGUNS: O/U, 4-GAUGE SKEET SETS

STANDARD GRADE MODELS

* ***Standard Grade Model MX3 Special***

	$5,200	$4,875	$4,650	$4,500	$4,150	$3,650	$3,150	*$15,400*

* ***Standard Grade Model Mirage Special*** – disc. 1994.

	$5,850	$5,500	$4,850	$4,600	$4,200	$3,700	$3,200	*$17,500*

SHOTGUNS: O/U, SPORTING HIGHER GRADES

Perazzi offers a wide variety of competition style shotguns in 12 or 20 gauge in the following higher grades: SC2 Grade, SC3 Grade, SC3 CESEL, SC3 Gold, SCO Grade, SCO Gold Grade, SCO Grade w/sideplates, or SCO Gold Grade w/sideplates. Extra Grade: Extra ($102,000 MSR), Extra Gold ($109,700 MSR), and Extra Super ($120,200 MSR).

MSRs for current higher grade models can be found under each individual model listing.

SHOTGUNS: O/U, PIGEON-ELECTROCIBLES HIGHER GRADE

Perazzi offers a wide variety of Pigeon shotguns in the following higher grades: SC2 Grade, SC3 Grade, SC3 CESEL, SC3 Gold, SCO Grade, SCO Gold Grade, SCO Grade w/sideplates, or SCO Gold Grade w/sideplates. Extra Grade: Extra ($102,000 MSR), Extra Gold ($109,700 MSR), and Extra Super ($120,200 MSR).

MSRs for current higher grade models can be found under each individual model listing.

GRADING - PPGS™	100%	98%	95%	90%	80%	70%	60%	LAST MSR

SHOTGUNS: O/U, GAME/HUNTING - TRIGGER PLATE ACTION

Available in 12, 16, 20, 28 ga., or .410 bore, 26 (disc. on MX8/12 ga. and MX12 1994), 26 3/4, 27 9/16, 28 3/8, or 29 1/2 in. barrels. Perazzi offers a wide variety of game/hunting configurations. While many people generally refer to the standard Perazzi action as a boxlock, it is actually a trigger plate action because the firing mechanism is attached to the trigger plate.

Extra Grade: Extra ($102,000 MSR), Extra Gold ($109,700 MSR), and Extra Super ($120,200 MSR).

Four Game Shotgun Sets includes: 12, 20, 28 ga. and .410 bore shotguns: SC2 ($87,400 MSR), SC3 ($107,000 MSR), SCO ($181,000 MSR), SCO w/sideplates ($279,000 MSR), Extra ($408,000 MSR), Extra Gold ($439,000 MSR), or Extra Super ($481,000 MSR).

MSRs for current higher grade models will appear under each individual model listing.

SHOTGUNS: O/U, SIDELOCK MODELS

All Perazzi sidelock O/U models were discontinued in 1992. The most desirable configurations in this model are the Skeet, Pigeon, and Sporting variations (pricing follows new SHO Gold values).

O/U SIDELOCK TRAP MODELS – older models without rebounding hammers are not as desirable. The most desirable configurations in this model are the Skeet, Pigeon, and Sporting variations (pricing follows new SHO Gold values). All SHO sidelock models were disc. 1992.

* ***Sidelock Trap Model SHO Older Mfg.***

$12,000	$11,000	$10,000	$9,000	$8,500	$7,600	$6,800	

Add $6,000 for game scene engraving.

* ***Sidelock Trap Model SHO Newer Mfg.***

$28,500	$25,000	$21,500	$18,000	$16,500	$14,000	$12,000	*$43,000*

* ***Sidelock Trap Model SHO Gold Older Mfg.***

$17,000	$15,000	$13,000	$11,000	$9,950	$8,750	$7,000	

* ***Sidelock Trap Model SHO Gold Newer Mfg.***

$34,000	$29,500	$25,000	$21,250	$17,750	$14,000	$12,000	*$48,000*

* ***Sidelock Trap Model SHO Extra*** – while advertised, none were sold.

Last MSR was $80,000.

* ***Sidelock Trap Model SHO Gold Extra*** – while advertised, none were sold.

Last MSR was $86,000.

O/U SIDELOCK SKEET MODELS – older models without rebounding hammers are not as desirable.

* ***Sidelock Skeet Model SHO Older Mfg.***

$15,000	$12,000	$9,500	$8,500	$7,600	$6,800	$5,900	

* ***Sidelock Skeet Model SHO Newer Mfg.***

$35,850	$30,000	$25,000	$20,000	$17,000	$14,500	$12,750	*$43,000*

* ***Sidelock Skeet Model SHO Gold Older Mfg.***

$18,000	$15,750	$12,000	$9,500	$8,500	$7,600	$6,800	

* ***Sidelock Skeet Model SHO Gold Newer Mfg.***

$45,000	$34,500	$27,250	$22,000	$18,500	$15,950	$13,750	*$48,000*

* ***Sidelock Skeet Model SHO Extra*** – imported 1985-92.

$68,750	$54,700	$38,100	$32,000	$26,500	$21,250	$18,000	*$80,000*

* ***Sidelock Skeet Model SHO Gold Extra*** – similar to SHO Extra, except has gold inlays. Imported 1992 only.

$72,750	$56,500	$39,500	$33,000	$27,000	$22,000	$18,500	*$86,000*

Subtract $20,000 if not signed by a known engraver.

SHO HUNTING MODELS – all SHO Hunting models should be evaluated and possibly appraised by someone who has a great deal of knowledge of both newer and older higher grade Perazzi shotguns. There are many variables that can come into play for price consideration, therefore an expert opinion is encouraged before buying, selling or trading the following models.

* ***SHO Hunting Model Older Mfg.*** – older models without rebounding hammers are not as desirable.

$12,000	$9,500	$8,500	$7,600	$6,800	$5,950	$5,150	

* ***SHO Hunting Model Newer Mfg.*** – 12 ga. only, introductory sidelock O/U model with bank note game scene engraving on coin finished receiver.

$29,950	$25,000	$20,000	$17,000	$14,500	$12,750	$10,250	*$43,000*

GRADING - PPGS™	100%	98%	95%	90%	80%	70%	60%	LAST MSR

* ***SHO Hunting Model Gold Older Mfg.*** – older models without rebounding hammers are not as desirable.

	$18,000	$15,750	$12,000	$9,500	$8,500	$7,600	$6,800	

* ***SHO Hunting Model Gold Newer Mfg.*** – similar to SHO, except has game scenes in gold relief.

	$38,650	$31,500	$26,500	$21,250	$18,000	$15,500	$13,750	*$48,000*

* ***SHO Hunting Model Extra*** – importation began 1992.

	$68,750	$54,700	$38,100	$32,000	$26,500	$21,250	$18,000	*$80,000*

* ***SHO Hunting Model Gold Extra*** – similar to SHO Extra, except has gold inlays. Importation began 1992.

	$72,750	$56,500	$39,500	$33,000	$27,000	$22,000	$18,500	*$86,000*

SHOTGUNS: O/U, HIGH TECH SERIES

HIGH TECH – 12 or 20 ga., 27 9/16, 28 3/8, 29 1/2, 30 3/4, or 31 1/2 in. (or custom length) barrels, new interior barrel specification, reverse tapered rib, fixed chokes or choke tubes, removable or fixed trigger with coil or flat (removable only) springs, standard, custom, or adj. stock, stock and forearm engraved with High Tech logo (new contemporary logo became standard in 2020), large logo engraved on both sides of the receiver in various color options including gold or platinum inlays, black, nickel, or color case hardened frame, hinge pins engraved with a checkered design, rib, forearm, and stock have modern design motif, available in many configurations. New 2015.

MSR $12,850	$10,925	$9,560	$8,200	$7,425	$6,010	$4,915	$4,280

Current MSR listed above is for Olympic and Double Trap, Skeet, Sporting, Pigeon, Electrocibles, or Game Gun configuration.

Current MSR for American Trap single barrel model is $12,990.

* ***High Tech Combo*** – 12 ga., American trap combo model available in skeet or sporting configuration.

MSR $18,500	$15,725	$13,760	$11,800	$10,700	$8,650	$7,100	$6,175

* ***High Tech Platinum or Gold*** – 12 or 20 ga., removable trigger group, platinum logo with black frame or gold logo with case hardened frame.

MSR $18,780	$15,975	$13,980	$11,980	$10,865	$8,785	$7,200	$6,250

Current MSR for Combo Skeet and Sporting (12 ga. only) with extra O/U barrel is $24,900.

* ***High Tech SC3*** – 12 or 20 ga.

MSR $21,720	$18,475	$16,165	$13,855	$12,565	$10,160	$8,325	$7,250

Additional higher grades are available as follows: HT SC3 CESEL ($28,250 MSR) or HT SC3 Gold ($30,550 MSR).

Current MSR for High Tech SC3 Skeet/Sporting Combo (12 ga. only with extra O/U barrel) is $27,800.

Current MSR for High Tech SC3 CESEL Skeet/Sporting Combo (12 ga. only with extra O/U barrel) is $34,350.

Current MSR for High Tech SC3 Gold Skeet/Sporting Combo (12 ga. only with extra O/U barrel) is $36,600.

* ***High Tech SCO*** – 12 or 20 ga., removable trigger group.

MSR $36,250	$30,775	$26,930	$23,080	$20,925	$16,925	$13,850	$12,085

Current MSR for High Tech SCO Gold is $40,250.

HIGH TECH 3/HIGH TECH 5/HIGH TECH 8 – 12 or 20 ga., available in all configurations, adj. ventilated rib with three (HT 3 model) or five notches, adj. comb.

MSR $15,200	$12,925	$11,310	$9,695	$8,790	$7,110	$5,815	$5,065

Current MSRs for higher grade models are as follows: HT 3-5-8 Platinum or Gold ($21,130), HT 3-5 SC3 ($24,070), HT 3-5 SC3 CESEL ($30,600), HT 3-5 SC3 Gold ($32,900), HT 3-5 SCO ($38,600), HT 3-5 SCO Gold ($42,600).

HIGH TECH 10 (HT 10) – 12 ga., American trap single barrel, removable trigger group, adj. rib and comb.

MSR $15,340	$13,050	$11,420	$9,790	$8,875	$7,180	$5,875	$5,110

Current MSR for HT 10 American Trap Combo model with extra O/U barrel is $22,760, HTX 10 American Trap single barrel is $19,150, HTX 10 American Trap Combo with extra O/U barrel is $26,580.

HIGH TECH RS (HT RS) – 12 ga., American trap single barrel, removable trigger group, adj. rib and comb.

MSR $15,340	$13,050	$11,420	$9,790	$8,875	$7,180	$5,875	$5,110

Current MSR for HTX RS is $19,150, HTX RS American Trap Combo is $26,580, and HT RS American Trap Combo with extra O/U barrel is $22,760.

GRADING - PPGS™	100%	98%	95%	90%	80%	70%	60%	LAST MSR

HIGH TECH S (HT S) – 12 or 20 ga., available in skeet, sporting, pigeon, electrocibles, game, Olympic, and double trap configurations, fixed trigger with coil springs.

MSR $13,120	$11,150	$9,750	$8,365	$7,580	$6,135	$5,025	$4,375

Additional higher grades options include: HTS Platinum or Gold ($19,050 MSR), HTS SC3 ($21,720 MSR), HTS SC3 CESEL ($28,250), HTS SC3 Gold ($30,550 MSR), HTS SCO ($36,250 MSR), HTS SCO Gold ($40,250 MSR).

Current HTS Combo Skeet and Sporting with extra O/U barrel is $18,770. Additional Combo prices are as follows: HTS Platinum or Gold Combo ($25,130 MSR), HTS SC3 Combo ($27,800 MSR), HTS SC3 CESEL Combo ($34,350 MSR), HTS SC3 Gold Combo ($36,600 MSR), HTS SCO Combo ($42,350 MSR), HTS SCO Gold Combo ($46,330 MSR).

* ***High Tech S 3-5*** – 12 or 20 ga., available in Olympic and Double Trap, skeet, sporting, pigeon, electrocibles, or game gun configuration, non-removable trigger group.

MSR $15,470	$13,150	$11,500	$9,865	$8,940	$7,235	$5,925	$5,150

Current MSR for HTS 3-5 SC3 is $24,070, HTS 3-5 Platinum or Gold is $21,400, HTS 3-5 SC3 is $24,070, HTS 3-5 SC3 CESEL is $30,600, HTS 3-5 SC3 Gold is $32,900 MSR, HTS 3-5 SCO is $38,600, HTS 3-5 SCO Gold is $42,600.

HIGH TECH L (HT L) – 12 or 20 ga., available in skeet, sporting, pigeon, electrocibles, game, Olympic, and double trap configurations, removable trigger group. New 2020.

MSR $15,400	$13,100	$11,465	$9,825	$8,910	$7,200	$5,900	$5,125

Current MSR for Combo in Skeet or Sporting configuration is $21,050 (includes extra O/U barrel, 12 ga. only).

HIGH TECH X (HTX) – 12 or 20 ga., 27 9/16, 28 3/8, 29 1/2, 30 3/4, 31 1/2 in., or custom length barrels, choke tubes, removable trigger with coil or flat springs, HT pattern standard, custom, or adj. stock, deeply blued or nickel polished receiver, textural contrasts on the receiver sides with very fine checkering and High Tech polished embossed logo, polished letter "P" with checkered background on the top lever, double X with checkered background and polished outlines engraved on the underside of receiver. New 2017.

MSR $16,670	$14,175	$12,400	$10,630	$9,640	$7,795	$6,380	$5,550

Current MSR listed above is for Oympic and Double Trap, Skeet, Sporting, Pigeon, Electocibles, or Game Gun configuration.

Current MSR for American Trap single barrel configuration is $16,800, HTX 3-5 is $19,020. Current MSR for American Trap Combo with extra O/U barrel is $22,320.

Current MSR for HT X Combo Skeet/Sporting with extra O/U barrel is $22,320.

HIGH TECH S X (HTS X) – 12 or 20 ga., 27 9/16, 28 3/8, 29 1/2, 30 3/4, 31 1/2 in., or custom length barrels, fixed chokes, fixed trigger with coil springs, HT pattern standard, custom, or adj. stock, deeply blued or nickel polished receiver, textural contrasts on the receiver sides with very fine checkering and High Tech polished embossed logo, polished letter "P" with checkered background on the top lever, double X with checkered background and polished outlines engraved on the underside of receiver. New 2017.

MSR $16,940	$14,400	$12,600	$10,800	$9,790	$7,920	$6,480	$5,650

Current base MSR for HTS X 3-5 model is $19,290.

HIGH TECH 2020 (HT 2020) – 12 or 20 ga., 27 9/16, 28 3/8, 29 1/2, 30 3/4, 31 1/2 in. or custom length barrels, fixed chokes or choke tubes, removable trigger with coil or flat springs, HT pattern standard, custom, or adj. stock, deeply blued (Dec. 2018) or nickel finished receiver with brushed shine and matte contrasts, twenty deeply embossed contrasting "Perazzi" logos on each side, polished "2020" in circle on hinge pins and top lever, "P HIGH TECH 2020" within red circle on underside. New August 2018.

MSR $21,700	$18,475	$16,165	$13,855	$12,565	$10,160	$8,315	$7,240

Current MSR for HT 2020 3-5 model in all configurations is $24,050.

Combo models with extra O/U barrels include: HT 2020 American Trap Combo ($27,300 MSR), HT 2020 Combo Skeet/Sporting (12 ga. only) ($27,300 MSR), HT 2020 RS or HT 2020 10 American Trap Combo (12 ga. only) - ($31,560 MSR), HT 2020 3-5 Combo Skeet/Sporting ($31,560).

* ***High Tech 2020 Gold/High Tech 2020 Palladium*** – 12 or 20 ga., similar to High Tech 2020, except deeply blued receiver with the Perazzi logos selectively gold plated or plated with the precious metal palladium. New 2020.

MSR $23,200	$19,725	$17,260	$14,795	$13,415	$10,850	$8,875	$7,725

Current MSR for HT 2020 3-5 Palladium or Gold is $25,550.

HIGH TECH S 2020 (HT S 2020) – 12 or 20 ga., available in all configurations, non-removable trigger group.

MSR $21,970	$18,675	$16,350	$14,000	$12,700	$10,275	$8,400	$7,325

Current MSR for HTS 2020 3-5 is $24,320.

Current MSR for Combo Skeet and Sporting with extra O/U barrel is $27,570.

GRADING - PPGS™	100%	98%	95%	90%	80%	70%	60%	LAST MSR

* ***High Tech S 2020 Gold/High Tech 2020 Palladium*** – 12 or 20 ga., similar to High Tech S 2020, except has deeply blued receiver with the Perazzi logos selectively gold plated or plated with the precious metal palladium. New 2020.

MSR $24,320	$20,675	$18,095	$15,500	$14,060	$11,375	$9,300	$8,100	

Current MSR for HTS 2020 3-5 Gold or Palladium is $25,820.

* ***High Tech S 2020 Small Frame*** – 28 ga. or .410 bore built on a very small frame, 27 9/16, 28 3/8, 29 1/2, 30 3/4, 31 1/2 in. or custom length barrels, fixed chokes or choke tubes, fixed trigger with coil springs, HT pattern standard, custom, or adj. stock, deeply blued or nickel finished receiver with brushed shine and matte contrasts, twenty deeply embossed contrasting "Perazzi" logos on each side, polished "2020" in circle on hinge pins and top lever, "P HIGH TECH 2020" within red circle on underside. New 2019.

MSR $25,550	$21,725	$19,010	$16,300	$14,775	$11,950	$9,775	$8,510	

HIGH TECH 60TH ANNIVERSARY PLATINUM - LIMITED EDITION – 12 ga., 27 9/16, 28 3/8, 29 1/2, 30 3/4, 31 1/2 in., or custom length barrels, fixed chokes or choke tubes, removable trigger with coil or flat springs, HT pattern standard, custom, or adj. stock, high-polished black/bluing with all inlays in pure platinum, receiver sides inlaid with High Tech logo, underside inscription "Perazzi 60 Anniversary Platinum Limited Edition" and sequential numbering 00/60-60/60 (serial numbers 157900-157960, with the additional prototype gun being kept in the Perazzi display), commemorates the Perazzi firm's 60th Anniversary, 1957-2017. Limited mfg. beginning 2017.

Please contact the importer directly for pricing and availability on this model.

The prototype High Tech 28 (28 gauge) was unveiled in July 2018 and became gun No. 59/60 in the 60th Anniversary Platinum Series.

SHOTGUNS: SxS GAME SHOTGUNS

12 (DC12), 20 (DC20, disc. 2016) or 28 (DC28, although catalogued, only one DC28 model was ever built) ga. No DC410 (.410 bore) guns were ever manufactured.

Perazzi offers the following high grade SxS Game shotguns:

SC2 Grade: DC SC2 ($23,000 MSR)

SC3 Grade: DC SC3 ($27,270 MSR)

SCO Grade: DC SCO ($41,800 MSR), DC SCO w/sideplates ($59,900 MSR).

SCO Gold Grade: DC SCO Gold ($45,800 MSR), DC SCO Gold w/sideplates ($66,820 MSR).

DC Extra Grade: DC Extra ($108,000 MSR), DC Extra Gold ($116,000 MSR), and the DC Extra Super ($126,000 MSR).

DC (DOPPIETTA COMPETIZIONE) – 12 ga., first generation SxS with trigger plate action, flat-sided (not sculpted) receiver, circa 1966, serialization 40001-40276, approx. 205 examples were built, with a rare few having removable trigger mechanisms. DC1 Standard plain finish, DC2 English rose and scroll engraving, DC4 Extra Lusso, and DCO (Oro) Golden Series, discontinued 1974.

Retail pricing was not available for this model.

DC12 – 12 ga. only, trigger plate action, 26 3/4, 27 9/16, 28 3/8, 29 1/2, or 31 1/2 in. barrels, fixed chokes, flat tapered rib, English or pistol grip style sporting stock, game or beavertail forend, removable trigger group with flat springs, blued or nickel-plated frame, upon request additional customization is also available. New 2012.

MSR $18,400	$15,650	$13,695	$11,750	$10,650	$8,625	$7,050	$6,125	

DC20 – 20 ga., trigger plate action, 26 3/4, 27 9/16, 28 3/8, 29 1/2, or 31 1/2 in. barrels, fixed chokes, flat tapered rib, English or pistol grip style sporting stock, game or beavertail forend, removable trigger group with flat springs, upon request additional customization is also available. Mfg. 2012-2016.

	$11,350	$10,200	$8,650	$7,600	$6,250	$5,100	$4,250	*$16,780*

SHOTGUNS: SxS, HUNTING - SIDELOCK MODELS

DHO Models have not been included within the scope of this text due to the extreme rarity factor. Please contact Perazzi USA for more information on these models and current pricing.

Subtract 40% without rebounding hammers on older DHO models.

PEREGRINE INDUSTRIES, INC.

Previous company located in Huntington Beach, CA circa 1991.

While advertised, Peregrine Industries, Inc. never manufactured the Falcon Model.

GRADING - PPGS™	100%	98%	95%	90%	80%	70%	60%	LAST MSR

PERODEAU, J.J. GUNMAKER

Current custom long gun maker and importer located in Sand Springs, OK. Previously located in Enid, OK.

Jean-Jacques Perodeau makes high quality custom SxS rifles and shotguns. Please contact the company directly for more information, availability, and pricing. J.J. Perodeau is also an agent for George Granger, Chapuis Armes, Manurhin, and Marcel Thys & Sons (repair or service only).

PERUGINI-VISINI

Current manufacturer established during 1968, located in Mazzano, Brescia, Italy. Currently imported by P&V USA LLC, located in Lakeland, FL. Previously imported 2002-2004 by Old Friends Hunting & Shooting Co., located in Livingston, MT. Rifles were previously imported and distributed until 1992 by William Larkin Moore & Co., previously located in Westlake Village, CA. All other models listed were previously imported and distributed by Armes de Chasse located in Chadds Ford, PA until 1988.

For individual model listings, please go to BlueBookOfGunValues.com/overflow.

PETERS STAHL GmbH

Previous pistol manufacturer located in Paderborn, Germany until 2010. Previously imported until 2009 by Euro-Imports, located in Yoakum, TX. Previously distributed by Swiss Trading GmbH, located in Bozeman, MT. Previously imported 1998-1999 by Peters Stahl, U.S.A. located in Delta, UT, and by Franzen International Inc. located in Oakland, NJ until 1998.

PISTOLS: SEMI-AUTO

Peters Stahl manufactured high quality semi-auto pistols based on the Model 1911 design, but had limited U.S. importation. Models included the Multicaliber, 92-Sport, O7-Sport, HC-Champion and variations, 1911-Tactical/Classic, PLS, and a .22 LR. Peters Stahl also manufactures multicaliber conversion kits of the highest quality. Recent models previously imported (until 2000) included the Model Millennium (MSR was $2,195), Match 22 LR (MSR was $1,995), Trophy Master (MSR was $1,995), Omega Match (MSR was $1,995), High Capacity Trophy Master (MSR was $1,695), O7 Multicaliber (MSR was $1,995), and the 92 Multicaliber (MSR was $2,610-$2,720). In the past, Peters Stahl has manufactured guns for Federal Ordnance, Omega, Schuetzen Pistol Works, and Springfield Armory.

PFEIFER-WAFFEN

Current manufacturer located in Feldkirch, Austria. No current U.S. importation.

In 2003, Pfiefer-Waffen opened up their own shooting range near the Schattenburg.

FIREARMS

Pfeifer-Waffen manufactures the unique "safety-rifle". Current configurations include: SR2 and SR3 standard - base price begins at €2,835 and SR-Carbon base price begins at €4,997. Previous models included an SR-Sport (last MSR was €3,540), SR2 Magnum, SR2 Afrika, a Liliput youth rifle in .22 Hornet, a repeating rifle, and a Zeliska revolver in .458 Win. Mag. or .600 NE cal. Please contact the company directly for more information, including pricing and availability.

PHASE 5 TACTICAL

Current parts and components manufacturer and previous AR-15 style rifle and pistol manufacturer, located in Roseville, CA.

Please refer to BlueBookOfGunValues.com to order the *Blue Book of AR-15s & Variations*, available as a book or online subscription.

PHELPS MFG. CO.

Previous manufacturer located in Evansville, IN circa 1978-1996.

Phelps Manufacturing Company began shipping guns in early 1978. Phelps guns were investment cast in 4140 steel, with basic single action simplicity, and a transfer bar safety.

REVOLVERS

HERITAGE I – .45-70 cal., single action revolver, incorporates transfer bar hammer safety, blue finish (standard), nickel (optional), adj. rear sight, 8 in. barrel standard, other barrel lengths up to 20 in. available, 6 lbs. Disc. 1996.

	100%	98%	95%	90%	80%	70%	60%	LAST MSR
	$2,500	$2,000	$1,675	$1,425	$1,255	$1,020	$885	*$2,250*

Add $20 for each additional in. of barrel.

GRADING - PPGS™	100%	98%	95%	90%	80%	70%	60%	LAST MSR

EAGLE I – .444 Marlin cal., single action revolver, blue finish, adj. rear sight, barrel options same as Heritage I, 6 lbs. Disc. 1996.

	$2,050	$1,675	$1,425	$1,255	$1,020	$885	$715	*$2,250*

PATRIOT – .375 Win. cal., single action revolver, blue finish, adj. rear sight, barrel options are the same as Heritage I. Limited mfg. 1993-94.

	$1,925	$1,550	$1,350	$1,185	$965	$840	$670	*$2,225*

GRIZZLY .50-70 – .50-70 cal., otherwise similar to Heritage I. Mfg. 1992-96.

	$2,300	$1,875	$1,500	$1,325	$1,085	$930	$750	*$2,580*

Add $20 for each additional in. of barrel.

PHILLIPS & ROGERS, INC.

Previous manufacturer 1992-2003, located in Huntsville, TX since 1997. Previously located in Conroe, TX circa 1992-1997.

In addition to manufacturing the firearms listed, Phillips & Rogers also made a multi-caliber conversion cylinder for all Ruger .357 Mag., new model Blackhawk revolvers (disc. 1996) - the retail price was $145. Multi-caliber conversion cylinders were also available for the Ruger new Model Blackhawk (allows shooting .45 LC, .45 Win. Mag., or .45 ACP - retail price was $185) and the Ruger Super Blackhawk (converts .44 Mag. to .50 AE w/ barrel change - $550). A new version of the Ruger .50 AE conversion was also available for $995.

REVOLVERS

MEDUSA MODEL 47 REVOLVER – multi-caliber, over 25 cals. in the .355 - .380 diameter range (including .357 Mag., .38 Super, .38 Spl., 9mm Para., etc.), unique design does not utilize half-moon clips or cylinder/barrel changes, 2 1/2, 4, 5, 6, or 8 in. barrel, 6 shot, double action, matte blue finish, rubber or wood grips. Mfg. 1993-2003.

	$2,800	$1,900	$1,500	$1,100	$800	$550	$325	*$599*

Add $95 for 8 in. barrel.

RIFLES: BOLT ACTION

WILDERNESS EXPLORER – .218 Bee, .22 Hornet, .44 Mag., or .50 AE cal., bolt action, features 18 in. match grade barrel, quick change bolt face and barrel allowing interchangeable calibers, white speckled black synthetic stock, side safety, 5 1/2 lbs. Mfg. 1997 only.

	$925	$825	$725	$650	$575	$500	$425	*$995*

PHOENIX ARMS

Current manufacturer located in Ontario, CA since 1992. Distributor sales only.

PISTOLS: SEMI-AUTO

HP22A MODEL (HP MODEL) – .22 LR cal., SA, 3 in. VR barrel, 10 (C/B 1994) or 11* (disc.) shot staggered mag., alloy frame, external hammer, adj. rear sight, keyed mag. lock and safety cable lanyard, firing pin block safety, choice of polished blue (disc.), matte black, or satin nickel finish, laser sight and mount (mfg. 1998-disc.), 2-in-1 target barrel and magazine conversion kit (disc.), 20 oz. New 1994.

MSR $130	$125	$115	$100	$95	$85	$75	$50	

Add $99 for laser sight and mount (mfg. 1998-disc.).
Add $45 for 2-in-1 target barrel and magazine conversion kit (disc.).

* ***HP22A (HP) Model Range Kit*** – .22 LR cal., SA, 5 in. VR barrel, 10 shot extended mag., alloy frame, adj. rear sight, locking plastic storage case (compartmentalized during 2000), and cleaning kit, choice of polished blue (disc.), matte black, or satin nickel finish, 23 oz. New 1998.

MSR $150	$135	$125	$115	$100	$95	$65	$50	

* ***HP22A (HP) Model Deluxe Range Kit*** – .22 LR cal., SA, similar to HP Range Kit, 3 and 5 (target) in. barrels, extended mag., alloy frame, adj. rear sight, firing pin block safety, includes locking case and cleaning kit, choice of polished blue (disc.), matte black, or satin nickel finish. New 1999.

MSR $199	$175	$150	$135	$125	$100	$85	$75	

HP25A MODEL – .25 ACP cal., SA, 3 in. VR barrel, 9 or 10 (C/B 1994, disc.) shot mag., alloy frame, external hammer, serrated trigger, adj. rear sight, keyed mag. lock and safety cable lanyard, firing pin block safety, choice of blue (disc.), matte black, or satin nickel finish, laser sight and mount (mfg. 1998-disc.), 2-in-1 target barrel and magazine conversion kit., 20 oz. New 1994.

MSR $136	$125	$115	$100	$95	$85	$75	$50	

Add $99 for laser sight and mount (mfg. 1998-disc.).
Add $45 for 2-in-1 target barrel and magazine conversion kit (disc.).

GRADING - PPGS™	100%	98%	95%	90%	80%	70%	60%	LAST MSR

RAVEN - .25 ACP cal., SA, 2 7/16 in. barrel, 6 shot mag., alloy frame, choice of finishes and grips. Disc. 1998.

	$70	$50	$45	$40	$35	$30	$25	*$79*

This model was supplied with a magazine disconnect lock.

PHOENIX ARMS CO.

Previous importer located in Lowell, MA.

PISTOLS: SEMI-AUTO

PHOENIX - .25 ACP cal., Belgian semi-auto, previously manufactured by Robar et DeKerkhove located in Liege, Belgium.

	$495	$450	$400	$350	$300	$250	$200

This pistol bears slight resemblance to a FN Browning M1900 except for with forward slide serrations.

PHOENIX WEAPONRY

Current manufacturer of pistols and AR-15 style rifles established in 2014, located in Berthoud, CO.

For individual model listings, please go to BlueBookOfGunValues.com/overflow.

PICKERT (PICKERT ARMINIUS)

Previous trademark of revolvers manufactured in Germany beginning circa 1900 through circa 1940.

REVOLVERS

Pickert was known for making a series of small revolvers branded "Arminius", many of these revolvers at the time would categorically be considered "Velo-Dog" revolvers.

MODEL 3 - .25 ACP cal., folding trigger, hammerless.

	$175	$135	$125	$105	$100	$90	$80

MODEL 8 - .320 Revolver cal., folding trigger, hammerless.

	$175	$135	$125	$105	$100	$90	$80

MODEL 9 - .32 ACP cal.

	$185	$140	$130	$115	$105	$95	$85

MODEL 10 - .32 ACP cal., hammerless.

	$165	$125	$120	$100	$95	$85	$75

PIETTA, F.LLI

Current firearms, black powder, replica firearms and accessories manufacturer established in 1962 by Knight Giuseppe Pietta, located in Gussago, Italy. Pietta single action revolvers are currently imported and distributed by E.M.F., located in Santa Ana, CA, Cabela's, located in Sidney, NE, Cimarron F.A. Co., located in Fredericksburg, TX, Dixie Gun Works, located in Union City, TN, Heritage, located in Miami, FL, Navy Arms, located in Martinsburg, WV, Taylor's & Co, located in Winchester, VA, and Traditions, located in Old Saybrook, CT. Previously imported by Legacy Sports International (shotguns too), located in Reno, NV. Importers also stamp their own brand names on Pietta firearms, but all guns have Pietta listed as a manufacturer.

The company introduced a modern SAA revolver during 2003, in cals. .357 Mag., .44-40 WCF, and .45 LC, and it was awarded Best Gun of the Year from SASS twice. Semi-auto shotguns were previously imported under the Verona name into the U.S. by Legacy Sports International in 12 and 20 gauge until 2010. Please refer to the Verona section for these older models.

During 2010, Pietta introduced the PPS50 carbine in .22 LR cal. with shrouded barrel, in addition to the MK85 .22 LR cal. pistol with shrouded barrel and side mounted magazine.

Pietta firearms may be listed separately under the importers - please refer to the individual listings.

REVOLVERS: REPRODUCTIONS, SAA & VARIATIONS

Since Pietta importers establish their own MSR's, please contact them individually for current pricing and availability. Factory engraving and other embellishments or finishes (white steel, nickel, etc.) may be special ordered by contacting the importers directly.

Add $80 for antique patina finish. Add $125 for silver plating. Add $45 for white finish. Add $220 for Pietta S.A. photo engraving. Add $980 for Pietta S.A. full deep laser engraving. Add $105 for gold inlay initials. Add $60 for checkered grips. Add $22 for white plastic one-piece grips. Add $170 for nickel plating. Add $90 for action job.

GRADING - PPGS™	100%	98%	95%	90%	80%	70%	60%	LAST MSR

1873 PIETTA SAA & VARIATIONS – .22 LR, .357 Mag., .44-40 WCF, .44 Win. Mag., or .45 LC cal., 3 3/4, 4 3/4, 5 1/2, 7 1/2, 10, or 12 in. forged hammer barrel, brass or steel backstrap and trigger guard, 4140 steel or stainless steel, New Model cross pin frame (w/plunger), case colored frame or blue finish, beveled cylinder, original hammer design with transfer bar safety (.22 LR cal. only), one-piece European walnut, faux stag (new 2014), Patriot (American flag, new 2014), checkered walnut (new 2014), or black PVC Eagle (new 2014) grips.

* ***1873 Pietta SAA w/Steel Backstrap & Trigger Guard***

MSR N/A	$425	$375	$335	$300	$275	$250	$225

Add $260 for stainless steel.

* ***1873 Pietta SAA w/Brass Backstrap & Trigger Guard***

MSR N/A	$400	$350	$325	$300	$275	$250	$225

Add $260 for stainless steel.

* ***1873 Pietta Millenium SAA*** – .357 Mag. or .45 LC cal., 4 3/4 or 5 1/2 in. barrel, matte blue finish, brass backstrap and trigger guard.

MSR N/A	$325	$295	$265	$235	$200	$185	$160

* ***1873 Pietta Bird's Head SAA***

MSR N/A	$425	$375	$335	$300	$275	$250	$225

Add $260 for stainless steel.

* ***1873 Pietta SAA Model "T"***

MSR N/A	$450	$395	$350	$300	$275	$250	$225

Add $230 for stainless steel.

* ***1873 Pietta Buntline SAA*** – .45 LC cal., 12 in. barrel, blue finish, New Model frame with steel backstrap.

MSR N/A	$495	$450	$400	$365	$335	$300	$275

Add $125 for antique blue finish.
Add $225 for nickel plating.

* ***1873 Pietta .22 Cal. SAA***

MSR N/A	$325	$295	$265	$235	$200	$185	$160

GREAT WESTERN II ALCHIMISTA – .357 Mag., .44-40, or .45 LC cal., 4 3/4 (new 2016), 5 1/2 or 7 1/2 in. barrel, set-back trigger, brass backstrap and trigger guard, checkered walnut 1860 Army grips, case hardened/blue finish.

MSR $630	$535	$475	$400	$365	$300	$250	$200

Add $45 for .45 LC cal. or 5 1/2 in. barrel.

GREAT WESTERN II ALCHIMISTA II – .357 Mag. or .45 LC cal., factory action job, 4 3/4, 5 1/2, or 7 1/2 in. barrel, brass backstrap and trigger guard, Ruger hammer, checkered walnut 1860 Army grips, case hardened/blue finish.

MSR $675	$600	$550	$450	$425	$325	$275	$200

GREAT WESTERN II ALCHIMISTA III – .45 LC or .357 Mag. cal., 4 3/4 or 5 1/2 in. octagon barrel, steel backstrap and trigger guard, larger hammer, checkered walnut 1860 Army grips, case hardened/blue finish. Importation began 2016.

MSR $715	$650	$550	$475	$425	$350	$300	$225

GREAT WESTERN II DELUXE ALCHIMISTA III – .357 Mag. or .45 LC cal., 4 3/4, 5 1/2, or 7 1/2 in. octagon barrel, steel backstrap and trigger guard, large hammer, checkered walnut 1860 Army grip, laser engraving, Old Silver/blue finish. New 2017.

MSR $800	$700	$650	$550	$500	$400	$325	$250

* ***Great Western II Deluxe Alchimista III Junior*** – .357 Mag. or .45 LC cal., 3 1/2 in. round barrel, steel backstrap and trigger guard, lower wider hammer, checkered express grip, laser engraving, Old Silver/blue finish. Importation began 2018.

MSR $825	$750	$650	$550	$500	$400	$325	$275

GREAT WESTERN II BUNTLINE – .45 LC cal., 12 in. barrel, walnut or ultra ivory grips, case hardened/blue finish.

MSR $640	$600	$500	$425	$400	$325	$250	$210

Add $25 for ultra ivory grips.
Add $230 for ultra stag grip (disc. 2014).

GREAT WESTERN II CALIFORNIAN (TRADITIONAL) – .357 Mag., .44-40, or .45 LC cal., 4 3/4, 5 1/2, or 7 1/2 in. barrel, walnut grip, case hardened/blue finish.

MSR $565	$500	$450	$375	$350	$275	$225	$185

GRADING - PPGS™	100%	98%	95%	90%	80%	70%	60%	LAST MSR

GREAT WESTERN II CALIFORNIAN (TRANSFER BAR MODELS) – .22 LR or .44 Mag. cal., 4 3/4, 5 1/2, or 7 1/2 in. barrel, 6 or 10 shot, walnut grips, case hardened/blue or all blue finish. Mfg. by Pietta. Imported 2013-disc.

	$375	$335	$300	$275	$240	$210	$195	*$445*

Add $110 for .44 Mag. cal.

GREAT WESTERN II CALIFORNIAN DELUXE – .357 Mag. or .45 LC cal., 4 3/4 in. barrel, checkered walnut or ultra ivory (new 2016) grips, case hardened/blue finish.

MSR $565	$500	$450	$375	$350	$275	$225	$185	

Add $15 for ultra ivory grips (new 2016).

GREAT WESTERN II CALIFORNIAN DELUXE GRANDE – .357 Mag. or .45 LC cal., 4 3/4 in. barrel, one-piece checkered wood grip, Victorian scroll engraving w/sunbursts, casehardened finish. Importation began 2019.

MSR $665	$600	$500	$450	$400	$325	$275	$220	

GREAT WESTERN II CALIFORNIAN DELUXE STAINLESS STEEL – .357 Mag. (new 2016) or .45 LC cal., 4 3/4, 5 1/2 (mfg. 2016 only), or 7 1/2 (mfg. 2016 only) in. barrel, stainless steel, checkered walnut or ultra ivory grips. Imported 2013-disc.

	$660	$575	$475	$375	$300	$260	$235	*$785*

Add $5 for ultra ivory grips (new 2016).

GREAT WESTERN II CATTLEBRAND – .357 Mag. or .45 LC cal., nickel engraved frame, 4 3/4 or 5 1/2 in. barrel, ultra ivory (disc.), branded checkered, ultra black, or ultra stag (disc.) grips.

MSR $915	$800	$700	$600	$550	$450	$375	$300	

Add $25 for ultra stag grips (disc.).
Add $35 for ultra black grips.

GREAT WESTERN II CENTENNIAL – .45 LC cal., engraved frame, 7 1/2 or 12 in. barrel, two-piece black or white rubber Eagle grip, Old Silver or Old Silver/Blue finish. Imported 2017-2018.

	$600	$515	$425	$365	$310	$270	$230	*$725*

Add $65-$70 for 12 in. barrel.
Add $160 for Old Silver finish with white Eagle grip.

GREAT WESTERN II CUSTOM 1873 SA – .357 Mag., .44-40 WCF, or .45 LC cal., 4 3/4, 5 1/2, or 7 1/2 in. barrel, four metal finishes include all blue, blue w/case colored frame, bright nickel, or satin nickel, ultra ivory grips, mfg. by Pietta. Imported 2003-2009.

	$725	$625	$525	$425	$325	$285	$250	*$810*

Add $125 for ultra stag grips or $960-$1,300 for engraving options.
Add $25 for Express bird's head grips (4 3/4 in. barrel only).

* ***Great Western II Custom 1873 Stainless*** – .357 Mag. or .45 LC cal., 4 3/4 in. barrel, similar to Great Western II, except is stainless steel construction, choice of walnut or ultra-ivory grips. Imported 2006-disc.

	$675	$595	$500	$400	$325	$285	$250	*$800*

Add $40 for ultra-ivory or checkered walnut grips.
Add $10 for bird's head Express grips (4 3/4 in. barrel only, disc. 2013).

GREAT WESTERN II DELUXE PHOTO ENGRAVED MODEL – .357 Mag. or .45 LC cal., 4 3/4 in. barrel, all blue finish with photo engraving, ultra ivory grips. Mfg. 2008-2013, reimported 2016-2019.

	$575	$495	$425	$365	$310	$270	$230	

Last MSR in 2013 was $825.
Last MSR in 2019 was $660.

GREAT WESTERN II DELUXE STAINLESS STEEL – .357 Mag. or .45 LC Mag. cal., 4.75 in. barrel, stainless steel, checkered walnut or ultra ivory grips.

MSR $815	$700	$615	$525	$475	$385	$315	$275	

Add $5 for ultra ivory grips.

GREAT WESTERN II EXPRESS AGENT – .357 Mag. cal., 3 1/2 in. barrel, standard, express checkered, or ultra stag custom fitted walnut grips, case hardened/blue or stainless steel. Imported 2016-2020.

	$650	$550	$475	$425	$350	$275	$225	*$705*

Add $207 for express walnut grips.
Add $185 for stainless steel.
Add $250 for ultra stag express custom-fitted grips.

GREAT WESTERN II FREEDOM – .357 Mag. or .45 LC cal., 4 3/4 or 5 1/2 in. barrel, marked "Freedom" on barrel, eagle image on hammer, USA flag grips, laser engraved "United We Stand" on frame, "The Second Amendment" and "The Right of the People" on cylinder, black finish. Imported 2016-2020.

	$600	$500	$450	$400	$325	$275	$200	*$660*

GRADING - PPGS™	100%	98%	95%	90%	80%	70%	60%	LAST MSR

GREAT WESTERN II DELUXE FREEDOM - .357 Mag. or .45 LC cal., 4 3/4 in. barrel, brass trigger guard, Patriotic flag grip, Old Silver finish. Imported 2017-disc.

	$585	$500	$425	$365	$310	$270	$230	*$680*

GREAT WESTERN II FRONTIER AND U.S. MARSHAL - .357 Mag. or .45 LC cal., 4 3/4 in. barrel, one-piece walnut grips, brass backstrap and trigger guard, with or w/o laser engraved Old West U.S. Marshal's badge, casehardened finish. Importation began 2018.

MSR $525	$475	$425	$350	$325	$250	$225	$175	

Add $10 for laser engraving (U.S. Marshal model).

GREAT WESTERN II GAMBLER'S ROYALE - .357 Mag. or .45 LC cal., 4 3/4 in. black barrel, one-piece ultra black grips, Victorian scroll engraving, polished steel frame, Old Silver or blue engraved. Limited importation beginning 2019.

MSR $775	$700	$600	$500	$475	$375	$325	$250	

GREAT WESTERN II GENERAL PATTON STAINLESS ENGRAVED SHERIFF - .357 Mag. or .45 LC cal., 3 1/2, 4 3/4 (new 2017), 5 1/2 (new 2017), or 7 1/2 (new 2017) in. barrel, stainless steel, ultra ivory grips, engraved. Importation began 2016.

MSR $960	$850	$750	$650	$600	$475	$400	$320	

GREAT WESTERN II LIBERTY MODEL - .357 Mag. or .45 LC cal., 4 3/4 or 5 1/2 in. barrel, ultra ivory grips, laser engraving of Liberty Eagle on barrel, cylinder, and frame, all blue finish. Imported 2013-2020.

	$600	$500	$450	$400	$325	$275	$200	*$650*

GREAT WESTERN II LIMITED EDITION "BAT MASTERON" - .45 LC cal., 3 1/2 in. barrel, simulated Stag grips, nickel finish. Limited mfg. disc. 2020.

	$650	$550	$475	$425	$350	$275	$225	*$705*

GREAT WESTERN II PALADIN MODEL - .45 LC cal., 3 1/2 (Paladin III, disc.), 5 1/2 (Paladin Jr., disc.), or 7 1/2 in. barrel, ultra ivory grips, all blue finish. Mfg. by Pietta, importation began 2013.

MSR $610	$550	$475	$400	$375	$300	$250	$200	

Add $10 for 3 1/2 in. barrel (disc.).

GREAT WESTERN II PONY EXPRESS - .45 LC cal., 3 1/2 in. barrel, turned down hammer, standard, express checkered (disc.), or ultra stag custom fitted walnut grips, case hardened finish. Imported 2014-2020.

	$650	$550	$475	$425	$350	$275	$225	*$705*

Add $55 for express grips (disc.).
Add $250 for ultra stag express grips.

GREAT WESTERN II PONY EXPRESS STAINLESS - .357 Mag. (disc.) or .45 LC cal., 3 1/2 (disc., reintroduced) or 4 3/4 (mfg. 2017-2018) in. barrel, standard, express checkered, or ultra stag custom fitted walnut grips. Imported 2014-2020.

	$800	$700	$600	$550	$450	$350	$275	*$890*

Add $65 for 4 3/4 in. barrel (mfg. 2017-2018).
Add $55 for express walnut grips.
Add $250 for ultra stag express grips.

GREAT WESTERN II POSSE I - .357 Mag. cal., 3 1/2 in. round barrel, smooth walnut grip, casehardened and blued finish. Importation began 2018.

MSR $575	$500	$450	$400	$350	$275	$225	$175	

GREAT WESTERN II POSSE II - .357 Mag. cal., 3 1/2 in. octagon barrel, smooth walnut grip, casehardened and blued finish. Importation disc. 2020.

	$500	$450	$400	$350	$275	$225	$175	*$575*

GREAT WESTERN II R MODEL TRIBUTE - .45 LC cal., 4 3/4 in. barrel, caramel colored grip. Importation began 2021.

MSR $700	$600	$525	$450	$410	$325	$275	$225	

GREAT WESTERN II SHERIFF - .45 LC cal., case hardened frame, 3 1/2 in. barrel, no ejector housing, one-piece walnut grip, blued barrel and cylinder. New 2017.

MSR $545	$460	$400	$350	$315	$250	$200	$175	

GREAT WESTERN II DELUXE SHERIFF (OLDER MFG.) - .357 Mag. or .45 LC cal., stainless steel construction, 3 in. barrel, Ultra ivory grips, factory laser engraving. Mfg. late 2013-2016.

	$735	$650	$550	$475	$400	$325	$275	*$860*

GREAT WESTERN II DELUXE SHERIFF (RECENT MFG.) - .45 LC cal., 3 1/2 in. barrel, no ejector housing, two-piece rubber "Eagle" grip, all blue finish. Imported 2017-2018.

	$495	$450	$375	$325	$285	$250	$225	*$585*

GRADING - PPGS™	100%	98%	95%	90%	80%	70%	60%	LAST MSR

GREAT WESTERN II DELUXE SHERIFF STAINLESS – .357 Mag. or .45 LC cal., 3 1/2 in. barrel, ultra ivory grips, engraved stainless steel.

MSR $950	$850	$750	$650	$600	$475	$375	$300

GREAT WESTERN II THE SHOOTIST – .357 Mag. or .45 LC cal., 4 3/4 in. blued barrel and cylinder, ultra ivory grips, enhanced laser engraving. Importation began 2019.

MSR $690	$600	$550	$475	$425	$350	$275	$225

GREAT WESTERN II U.S. GRANT – .357 Mag. or .45 LC cal., 4 3/4 in., checkered walnut, ultra ivory, or ultra black grips, Victorian floral scroll work engraving, nickel-plated finish. New 2019.

MSR $800	$700	$650	$550	$500	$400	$325	$250

Add $15 for ultra ivory grips.
Add $40 for ultra black grips.

GUNFIGHTER – .357 Mag. or .45 LC cal., 4.75 in. barrel, checkered black rubber grip.

MSR $515	$440	$385	$330	$300	$240	$195	$170

SHOTGUNS

Pietta currently manufactures a Challenge semi-auto shotgun line including the Superior I, II, and III, the Ghibli, Gold Series, and Mistral models. The company also manufactures a slide action shotgun in both sporting and tactical configurations. Please refer to individual model listings under EMF in the E section.

PIONEER ARMS CORP.

Current manufacturer located in Radom, Poland. Currently imported by Pioneer Arms Corp. located in Port Orange, FL. Peviously located in North Bennington, VT and in Moline, IL. Previously imported by I.O., Inc. located in Palm Bay, FL.

Pioneer manufactures Sporter AKM-47 style rifles, Hellpup AKM-47 style pistols, PPS43-C pistols, a PM63-C model, and custom made SxS 12 ga. shotguns. Please contact the importer directly for more information, including options and availability.

PISTOLS: SEMI-AUTO

HELLPUP – 7.62x39mm cal., AK-47 type, approx. 11 3/4 in. barrel, 10, 20, 30, or 40 shot box mag., uses AK mags., front post and rear notch sight on sliding tangent, standard or side-folding stock, choice of classic wood, black, or brown synthetic handguard and pistol grip, Picatinny rail end-cup, matte parkerized finished. 6.32-7.38 lbs.

Please contact the importer for availability and pricing on this model.

PM63-C – 9x18mm Makarov cal., sporting pistol variant of PM63 RAK submachine gun, closed bolt blowback operation, 6 in. barrel with elongated muzzle brake, 15 or 25 shot box mag., fixed blade front and flip rear sights, stock and forearm grip are permanently fixed in their folded closed position to comply with NFA regulations, milled steel receiver and slide, black finish. 3.5-4.2 lbs.

Please contact the importer for availability and pricing on this model.

PPS43-C – 7.62x25mm Tokarev or 9x19mm cal., sporting, patterned after the 1943 Sudaev sub-machine gun, shoots from closed bolt position, approx. 10 in. barrel, muzzle brake, 35 shot detachable box mag., fixed blade front and L-shaped flip rear sights, stock is permanently fixed in the folded closed position to comply with NFA regulations, safety located on trigger guard, stamped steel receiver and barrel shroud, black finish, 6.7-8.1 lbs.

Please contact the importer for availability and pricing on this model.

RIFLES: SEMI-AUTO

SPORTER – 7.62x39mm cal., AK-47 type, approx. 16 in. barrel, 10, 20, 30, or 40 shot box mag., front post and rear notch sight on sliding tangent, standard fixed, underfolding, or side-folding stock, choice of classic wood, black, or brown synthetic handguard and pistol grip, matte parkerized finish, 7.49-8.59 lbs.

Please contact the importer for availability and pricing on this model.

SHOTGUNS: SXS

PIONEER – 12 ga., 3 in. Magnum chambers, Greener action, forged frame, 18 1/2 in. (18 1/2 and 24 in. combo) barrels, true hammered, solid steel trigger group, top rib large front sight, Turkish walnut or European hard wood finish, manual tang safety, 8.7-9.04 lbs. Limited mfg.

Please contact the importer for availability and pricing on this model.

PIOTTI

Current manufacturer established circa 1955, and located in Brescia, Italy. Currently imported and distributed exclusively by William Larkin Moore & Co. located in Scottsdale, AZ.

For individual model listings, please go to BlueBookOfGunValues.com/overflow.

PIRANHA

Previous trademark of a recoilless semi-auto 9mm Para. cal. pistol that was advertised circa 1996, but never manufactured by Recoilless Tech, Inc. located in Glendale and Phoenix, AZ. While advertised, Piranha pistols were never manufactured (except a few prototypes).

R.T.I. tried to develop its manufacturing capability for the semi-auto Piranha Recoilless Pistol, utilizing hesitation lock bi-angular springs to reduce 85% of the recoil, and which also allowed changing calibers by changing the barrel.

PISTOL DYNAMICS

Current semi-auto pistol and bolt action rifle manufacturer located in Palm Bay, FL.

PISTOLS: SEMI-AUTO

Pistol Dynamics manufactures high quality 1911-style semi-auto pistols. Current models include: Competition Pistol, Combat Special Evolution (base MSR $3,600). Previous models include: Signature (last base MSR $3,800, disc. 2020), Scout (last base MSR $2,900), Super Scout (last base MSR $3,695), 1911 Anniversary, STI/SVI Limited, and the X-O (last base MSR $2,400), and Combat Special Classic (last base MSR $4,600). Options and delivery times vary for each model. Please contact the company directly for availability and pricing.

RIFLES: BOLT ACTION

Pistol Dynamics produces a limited quantity of complete match rifles built exclusively on Kelbly actions. Please contact the manufacturer directly for pricing and availablity.

PLAINFIELD CARBINES

Please refer to the U.S. Military & Commercial Long Arms section.

PLAINS RIFLE

A Plains rifle is a modification of the Kentucky rifle. Its original purpose was for use on the western frontier.

The Plains rifle is often referred to as a half stock, and first appeared around the end of the first quarter of the 19th century, with production ending by 1880. There was a demand for shorter rifles to be carried on horseback and larger bores for bigger game. Bores ranged from .50 to .60 caliber, and barrel lengths were 36 to 40 inches. Plains rifles are generally found with percussion ignition systems.

Like the Kentucky rifle, Plains rifles were all handmade. Jacob and Samuel Hawken are considered the originators of the Plains rifle. They were the sons of Christian Hawken, Kentucky rifle maker of Hagerstown, MD. The popularity of Jacob's and Samuel's guns spread rapidly. Gunmakers from across the country began to copy the Plains style rifle. In addition to the Hawken brothers, other well-known makers were Horace Dimick, J.P. Gemmer, James Henry, and Henry Leman. Like Kentucky rifles, values for Plains rifles differ greatly, depending on the maker, condition, and style. Values can range anywhere from $500-$50,000! Flintlock Plains rifles are scarce.

The publisher would like to thank Mr. Jim Buelow for making the above information available to the *Blue Book of Gun Values*.

POINTER

Current trademark of shotguns manufactured in Turkey, imported until 2008, then resumed again in 2014 by Legacy Sports International, located in Reno, NV. Previously located in Alexandria, VA.

SHOTGUNS: O/U

ACRIUS – 12, 20, 28 ga., or .410 bore, 26 (20 ga. or .410 youth models only) or 28 in. chrome-lined barrel w/raised vented rib, 5 chokes, extractors, front fiber optic sight, Turkish walnut stock and forend, laser etched floral coin finished receiver. New 2021.

	100%	98%	95%	90%	80%	70%	60%
MSR $589	$500	$440	$375	$340	$275	$225	$195

GRADING - PPGS™	100%	98%	95%	90%	80%	70%	60%	LAST MSR

ARISTA – 12, 20, 28 ga., or .410 bore, 2 3/4 (28 ga. only) or 3 in. chambers, 28 in. chrome-lined black barrels, MC-5 chokes, raised VR, fiber optic front sight, Turkish walnut stock, floral coin finish receiver, 5-6.6 lbs. Imported 2019 only.

	$500	$450	$375	$350	$275	$225	$175	*$589*

* ***Arista Youth*** – 20 ga. or .410 bore, 3 in. chambers, 26 in. chrome-lined black barrels, MC-5 chokes, raised and ventilated rib, fiber optic front sight, Turkish walnut stock, 12 1/2 in. LOP, floral coin finish receiver. Imported 2019 only.

	$500	$450	$375	$350	$275	$225	$175	*$589*

POINTER 1000 FIELD (SPORTING SERIES) – 12, 20, 28 ga., or .410 bore, 3 in. chambers, 26 or 28 in. chrome-lined steel barrel, 5 interchangeable chokes (except .410), satin blued finish, high vent. sporting rib, silver receiver, brass bead front sight, single trigger, auto reset safety, ejectors (12 ga. only) or extractor, Turkish walnut stock. Imported 2014-disc.

	$525	$465	$425	$395	$350	$300	$275	*$619*

Add $30 for .410 bore.

A Youth model is also available in 20 ga. with 26 in. barrel. Disc.

POINTER CLAYS O/U – 12 ga., 3 in. chambers, 28 or 30 in. carbon steel chrome moly lined ported barrels, five interchangeable chokes, wide raised rib, fiber optic front and steel mid bead sights, Turkish walnut stock with fancy checkering and adj. comb, 8.9-9.2 lbs. Imported 2015-disc.

	$825	$725	$625	$550	$475	$400	$350	*$959*

POINTER FIELD OVER UNDER – 12, 20, 28 ga., or .410 bore, 2 2/4 (28 ga. only) or 3 in. chamber, 28 in. raised VR barrel, fiber optic front sight, Turkish walnut stock or synthetic stock w/black or Mossyoak Shadow Grass Blade finish (12 or 20 ga. only), floral engraving, coin finish receiver, 5-6.6 lbs. Importation began 2020.

MSR $589	$500	$450	$375	$350	$275	$225	$175	

This model is also available in Youth option with 26 in. barrel in 20 ga or .410 bore with walnut stock at no extra charge.

POINTER MXL – 12 or 20 ga., 3 in. chambers, 28 in. barrels, MC-5 chokes, raised VR, black synthetic stock, black barrel finish, 6.4-6.6 lbs. Importation began 2019.

MSR $589	$500	$450	$375	$350	$275	$225	$175	

* ***Pointer MXL Camo*** – 12 ga., 3 in. chambers, 28 in. barrels, MC-5 chokes, raised VR, synthetic stock with Realtree Max-5, Mossy Oak Bottomland, or Mossy Oak Shadow Grass Blades camo finish, Burnt Bronze Cerakote finish on barrel and receiver, 6.6 lbs. Importation began 2019.

MSR $729	$625	$550	$475	$425	$350	$280	$225	

POINTER SCT BASIC CLAY – 12 ga., 3 in. chambers, 30 in. black barrels, MC-5 EXT chokes, raised VR, fiber optic front sight, Turkish walnut stock with oil-rubbed finish, adj. cheekpiece, checkered walnut forend. Importation began 2019.

MSR $959	$825	$725	$625	$560	$450	$375	$300	

* ***Pointer SCT Basic Clay Youth*** – 12 ga., 3 in. chambers, 28 in. barrels, MC-5 EXT chokes, raised VR, fiber optic front sight, Turkish walnut stock with oil-rubbed finish, adj. cheekpiece, checkered walnut forend, 12 1/2 in. LOP. Importation began 2019.

MSR $959	$825	$725	$625	$560	$450	$375	$300	

POINTER SCT DELUXE CLAY – 12 ga., 3 in. chamber, 30 in. black barrel, MC-5 chokes, raised and ventilated rib, oil-rubbed walnut stock and forend, adj. cheekpiece, 7.9 lbs. Importation began 2019.

MSR $1,199	$1,025	$895	$775	$700	$575	$475	$375	

This model is also available as Youth with 28 in. barrel and 12 1/2 in. LOP at no extra charge.

POINTER SYNTHETIC – 12 or 20 (new 2018) ga., 3 in. chamber, 28 in. chrome moly carbon/steel barrels with five chokes, raised vent. rib, fiber optic front sight, black synthetic stock. Importation began 2016.

MSR $619	$525	$450	$400	$350	$315	$285	$250	

POINTER SYNTHETIC HOME DEFENSE – 12 ga., 3 in. chambers, 18 in. chrome moly barrels with five chokes, fiber optic front sight, black synthetic stock, Picatinny rail on top of receiver and lower barrel. Imported 2016-2017.

	$510	$445	$385	$345	$280	$230	$180	*$600*

POINTER TURKISH SPORTING/FIELD – 12 ga., 3 in. chambers, 28 in. barrels, blue (disc.) or electroless nickel finish with floral engraving, five multi-chokes, select walnut stock and forearm, KICK-EEZ buttpad, TruGlo sight, extractors, gold trigger, 7.7 lbs. Mfg. by Zafer Arms Co. in Turkey. Limited importation 2006-2007.

	$525	$460	$415	$350	$300	$260	$220	*$599*

GRADING - PPGS™	100%	98%	95%	90%	80%	70%	60%	LAST MSR

POINTER ITALIAN SPORTING/FIELD – 12, 20, 28 ga., or .410 bore, 3 in. chambers, 28 in. barrels, blue/nickel finish, fixed or multi-chokes, select walnut stock and forearm, ejectors, 6.1-7.4 lbs. Imported 2007-2008.

	$1,150	$995	$875	$750	$625	$525	$450	*$1,299*

Add $200 for 28 ga. or .410 bore.

POINTER ITALIAN SPORTING CLAYS – 12 ga., 3 in. chambers, 28 in. barrels, blue/nickel finish, multi-chokes, select walnut stock and forearm, ejectors, 7.6 lbs. Imported 2007-2008.

	$1,150	$995	$875	$750	$625	$525	$450	*$1,299*

POINTER LUX – 12 ga., 28 in. chrome-lined barrels w/raised vented rib, 5 chokes, extractors, front fiber optic sight, Turkish Grade 2 walnut stock and forend, white receiver w/raised gold mallards. New 2021.

MSR $699	$600	$525	$450	$410	$325	$275	$230

SPORT TEK/SPORT TEK 8 – 12 (Sport Tek) or 20 (Sport Tek 8) ga., 28 (youth barrel only) or 30 in. chrome-lined barrel w/raised vented rib, single shot is available, stock finishes in wood, colored finishes in blued. New 2021.

MSR $489	$415	$365	$315	$285	$230	$185	$160

SHOTGUNS: SEMI-AUTO

POINTER – 12, 20, or 28 ga., 3 in. chamber, gas operated, 28 in. barrel, five interchangeable chokes, 5 shot mag. with magazine cut-off, fiber optic front sights, Turkish walnut or gray laminate (12 ga. only) stock, 5.8-7 lbs. Imported 2015-2017.

	$595	$520	$445	$400	$325	$270	$210	*$700*

Add $15 for 28 ga. Add $96 for gray laminate stock.

POINTER STANDARD – 12 ga., 3 in. chamber, 28 in. chrome moly barrel with three chokes, raised VR, 5 shot mag., fiber optic front sight, black synthetic stock, includes hard black case, 6.2-6.8 lbs. Imported 2015-2017.

	$525	$460	$395	$355	$290	$235	$185	*$607*

POINTER DELUXE – 12 ga., 3 or 3 1/2 (new 2018) in. chamber, gas operated cycling system, 28 in. chrome moly lined barrel, five chokes, raised VR, single-round magazine cut-off, fiber optic sight, matte black or green (new 2018) synthetic stock or forearm, 3/8 in. dovetail accessory rail on top of receiver, includes black hard case, 7.2 lbs. Imported 2017-disc.

	$525	$450	$415	$365	$325	$295	$265	*$607*

Add $64 for 3 1/2 in. chamber.

POINTER DELUXE CAMO – 12 ga., 3 or 3 1/2 (new 2018) in. chamber, 28 in. chrome moly barrel with three chokes, raised VR, 5 shot mag., fiber optic front sight, synthetic stock and forearm with 100% Max-5, Bottomland (new 2018), or Obsession (new 2018) camo finish. Imported 2015-disc.

	$575	$500	$425	$390	$315	$260	$200	*$671*

Add $80 for 3 1/2 in. chamber.

POINTER FIELD TEK – 12, 20, 28 ga. or .410 bore, 28 in. chrome-lined barrel w/raised vented rib, front fiber optic sight, Turkish walnut or blue synthetic stock, Bronze, Gray, or Black Cerakote receiver and forend cap finish, Realtree Max 5 or Mossy Oak Bottomland camo patterns. New 2021.

MSR $409	$350	$300	$265	$240	$195	$160	$135

POINTER (PHENOMA) – 12, 20, 28 ga., or .410 bore, 3 or 3 1/2 in. chamber, gas operated, 28 in. chrome moly barrel, MC-5 chokes, single round magazine cut-off, fiber optic front sights, synthetic stock, 14 in. LOP, includes hard case, black or Realtree Original, 100% Realtree Max-5, Mossy Oak Bottomland, Mossy Oak Obsession, or Shadow Grass Blades camo finish, 5.9-7.2 lbs. Importation began 2019.

MSR $529	$450	$395	$350	$300	$250	$200	$160

POINTER (PHENOMA) CERAKOTE – 12, 20, 28 ga., or .410 bore, 3 or 3 1/2 in. chamber, gas operated system, 28 in. chrome moly barrel, MC-5 chokes, raised and ventilated rib, single round magazine cut-off, oil-rubbed Turkish walnut stock, includes hard case, bronze or gray Cerakote finish on barrel and receiver, 5.9-7.1 lbs. Importation began 2019.

MSR $669	$575	$500	$425	$390	$315	$260	$200

* ***Pointer Phenoma Cerakote Laser Etched*** – 12 ga., 3 in. chamber, 28 in. barrel, MC-5 chokes, raised and ventilated rib, fiber optic sights, synthetic stock with Mossy Oak Bottomland (new 2020), Realtree Max-5, or Realtree camo finish, camo patterns laser etched directly on Cerakote finished receiver in Burnt Bronze (disc. 2019), Midnight Bronze, or OD Green (disc.), 7.2 lbs. Importation began in 2019.

MSR $999	$750	$650	$550	$500	$400	$325	$250

POINTER SCT CLAY – 12 ga., 3 in. chamber, 30 in. barrel, sporting raised rib, MC-3 extended Beretta/Benelli Mobil chokes, 5 shot mag., fiber optic front and rear sights, Soft Touch synthetic stock, stock drop and LOP spacers, matte black finish, 7.3 lbs. Importation begin 2019.

MSR $639	$550	$480	$415	$375	$300	$250	$200

GRADING - PPGS™	100%	98%	95%	90%	80%	70%	60%	LAST MSR

POINTER SLUG COMBO – 12 or 20 ga., 3 in. chamber, 28 in. chrome-lined barrel with fiber optic sight and three chokes and a 24 in. rifled slug barrel with scope tang and rifle-style front sight with fiber optic insert, 5 shot mag., black synthetic stock, 6-6.8 lbs. Imported 2015-2016.

	$645	$565	$485	$440	$355	$290	$225	*$755*

POINTER SCT COMPETITION – 12 ga., 3 in. chamber, 24 in. barrel, sporting raised rib, MC-3 extended Beretta/Benelli Mobil chokes, 5 shot mag., fiber optic front and rear sights, Soft Touch black synthetic stock, stock drop and LOP spacers, oversize charging handle, black finish, 7 lbs. Importation begin 2019.

MSR $639	$550	$480	$415	$375	$300	$250	$200	

SHOTGUNS: SINGLE SHOT

POINTER BREAK ACTION – 12, 20, or .410 bore, single shot, 28 in. barrel, fixed modified choke, brass bead front sight, matte black metal parts, manual push-button safety, hammer safety, and a transfer bar safety, black synthetic stock, 4.8-5.4 lbs. Imported 2015-disc.

	$175	$150	$130	$120	$100	$85	$70	*$216*

* ***Pointer Break Action Youth*** – 20 ga. or .410 bore, 26 in. barrel, fixed mod. chokes, manual hammer, brass bead sight, black synthetic stock and forend, transfer bar safety, matte black finish, 4.8-5.2 lbs. Imported 2016-disc.

	$180	$155	$135	$120	$100	$85	$70	*$223*

POINTER KST-1230 – 12 ga., 2 3/4 in. chamber, 30 in. raised VR wide barrel, 5 extended chokes, ejector, fiber optic front sight, walnut stock w/adj. cheekpiece and beavertail forend. New 2020.

MSR $599	$500	$450	$375	$350	$275	$225	$175	

POINTER SINGLE BREAK ACTION ENTRY – 12 ga., single break action trap, 30 in. black VR barrel, checkered walnut stock and pistol grip. Importation began 2019.

MSR $459	$400	$350	$300	$275	$225	$175	$125	

POINTER SCT BASIC TRAP – 12 ga., 3 in. chamber, break action, 30 in. ported barrel with black finish, MC-5 chokes, raised and VR, fiber optic front sight, Turkish walnut stock, adj. cheekpiece. Importation began 2019.

MSR $989	$850	$750	$650	$580	$475	$385	$300	

* ***Pointer SCT Basic Trap Youth*** – 12 ga., 3 in. chamber, break action, 28 in. ported barrel with black finish, MC-5 chokes, raised VR, fiber optic front sight, Turkish walnut stock, adj. cheekpiece, 12 1/2 in. LOP. Importation began 2019.

MSR $989	$850	$750	$650	$580	$475	$385	$300	

POINTER SCT DELUXE TRAP – 12 ga., 3 in. chamber, break action, 30 in. black barrel, MC-5 chokes, fully adj. raised VR, fiber optic front sight, Turkish walnut stock with checkered grip, 7.9 lbs. Importation began 2019.

MSR $1,279	$1,085	$950	$815	$750	$600	$500	$400	

This model is also available for Youth with 28 in. barrel and 12 1/2 in. LOP at no extra charge.

SHOTGUNS: SLIDE ACTION

POINTER SLUG COMBO – 12 or 20 ga., 3 in. chamber, 28 in. chrome-lined barrel with fiber optic sight and three chokes and a 24 in. rifled slug barrel with scope tang and rifle-style front sight with fiber optic insert, 5 shot mag., black synthetic stock, 6-6.8 lbs. Imported 2015-2017.

	$525	$460	$395	$355	$290	$235	$185	*$620*

POINTER STANDARD SLIDE ACTION – 12 or 20 ga., 3 in. chamber, 28 in. chrome moly barrel with three chokes, 5 shot mag., fiber optic front sight, black synthetic stock, 6-6 1/2 lbs. Mfg. 2015 only.

	$350	$300	$265	$240	$195	$160	$125	*$404*

POLI, ARMI F.LLI

Current manufacturer established in 1966, located in Gardone, Italy. Currently imported by Deep River Sporting Clays, located in Sanford, NC. Previously imported by Cole Gunsmithing, located in Harpswell, ME, and by Anglo American Sporting Agency, located in Corona Del Mar, CA.

Armi F.lli Poli manufactures high quality, SxS and single barrel hammer shotguns in 12, 16, 20, 28 ga., or .410 bore. Current models include the Ivory (hammerless, boxlock action), Opal (hammerless, boxlock action with sideplates), Lapis (lightweight, scalloped boxlock action, hammerless), Onix (scalloped boxlock action, hammerless), Coral (sidelock back action w/hammers), Ruby (petite sidelock back action w/hammers), Emerald (sidelock back action w/hammers), Amethyst (sidelock, hammerless), Sapphire, Kristal, Zircon, and Zircon Deluxe. Please contact the importer for more information, including pricing and availability.

GRADING - PPGS™	100%	98%	95%	90%	80%	70%	60%	LAST MSR

POLI NICOLETTA & C. snc.

Current manufacturer established in 1975, and located in Brescia, Italy. No current U.S. importation.

Poli Nicoletta manufactures good quality lightweight hunting rifles and shotguns, in addition to choke tubes and scope mounts. Please contact the company directly for more information, including pricing (includes freight) and availability.

POLY TECHNOLOGIES, INC.

Previously distributed by PTK International, Inc. located in Atlanta, GA. Previously imported by Keng's Firearms Specialty, Inc., located in Riverdale, GA. Manufactured in China by Poly Technologies, Inc.

Poly Technologies commercial firearms are made to Chinese military specifications and have excellent quality control. These models were banned from domestic importation due to 1989 Federal legislation.

RIFLES: SEMI-AUTO

Add 10% for NIB.

AKS-762 - 7.62x39mm or .223 Rem. cal., 16 1/4 in. barrel, semi-auto version of the Chinese AKM (Type 56) rifle, 8.4 lbs., wood stock. Imported 1988-1989.

$1,495	$1,325	$1,100	$975	$875	$795	$750	*$400*

Add $100 for side-fold plastic stock.

This model was also available with a downward folding stock at no extra charge.

SKS - 7.62x39mm cal., 20 9/20 in. barrel, full wood stock, machined steel parts to Chinese military specifications, 7.9 lbs. Imported 1988-89.

$550	$475	$400	$350	$300	$275	$250	*$200*

AK-47/S (LEGEND) - 7.62x39mm cal., 16 3/8 in. barrel, semi-auto configuration of the original AK-47, fixed, side-folding, or under-folding stock, with or w/o spike bayonet, 8.2 lbs. Imported 1988-89.

$2,000	$1,800	$1,600	$1,350	$1,200	$1,000	$925	*$550*

Add 10% for folding stock.

The "S" suffix in this variation designates third model specifications.

* ***AK-47/S National Match Legend*** - utilizes match parts in fabrication.

$1,950	$1,750	$1,550	$1,275	$1,050	$975	$900	

RPK - 7.62x39mm cal. Disc.

$1,475	$1,300	$1,150	$1,025	$925	$850	$775	

M-14/S - .308 Win. cal., 22 in. barrel, forged receiver, patterned after the famous M-14, 9.2 lbs. Imported 1988-89.

$1,495	$1,325	$1,100	$975	$875	$795	$750	*$700*

POWELL & BROWN KNIFE PISTOL

Previously manufactured by Powell & Brown, circa 1993-1995, and located in Tucson, AZ.

PISTOLS: SINGLE SHOT

KNIFE PISTOL (PKP) - .22 LR cal., approx. 2 in. barrel integrated on top of a curved stainless steel knife, pivoting action, two-piece walnut grips, side lever opening, spur trigger, serrated hammer, OAL 10 3/4 in. All knife pistols were supplied with a letter from the ATF stating that it was a legal firearm to own. 150 mfg. 1993-1995.

$1,850	$1,650	$1,450	$1,275	$1,150	$1,000	$900	

Approx. original MSR was $550.

POWELL, WILLIAM & SON (GUNMAKERS) LTD.

Please refer to the William Powell & Son (Gunmakers) Ltd. listing in the W Section.

POWERS METAL WORKS, LLC

Current custom revolver/rifle manufacturer and gunsmith located in Duson, LA. Previously located in Magnolia, TX.

Powers Metal Works specializes in manufacturing custom ultra-precision long range rifles as well as a full line of gun services (gun repairs, firearm restoration, trigger/action jobs, barrel chambering, etc.). Please contact the company directly for more information on their firearms and gunsmithing services.

REVOLVERS / RIFLES

Powers Metal Works specializes in high quality custom ultra-precision long range rifles using Krieger, Bartlein, Proof, and Lilja barrels, Remington Actions (blueprinted), Surgeon Actions, Jewel and Trigger Tech triggers, and McMillan stocks. Custom revolvers are also available and include caliber conversions, making cylinders and barrels modifying frames, sights, etc. Please contact the company directly for pricing, options, and availability.

GRADING - PPGS™	100%	98%	95%	90%	80%	70%	60%	LAST MSR

PRAIRIE GUN WORKS

Please refer to PGW Defence Technologies, Inc. listing in this section.

PRANDELLI-GASPERINI

Previous manufacturer located in Brescia, Italy. Previously imported by Richland Arms located in Blissfield, MI.

Prandelli-Gasperini made both O/U and SxS shotguns in either sidelock or boxlock. Currently, values for the older boxlock models are in the $475-$725 range (assuming 80% or better original condition). Sidelock models in similar condition are usually valued in the $1,350-$2,100 range, depending on gauge, embellishments, and condition.

Approx. 250 specimens of this trademark were imported during Richland Arms importation.

PRECHTL JAGD & SPORTWAFFEN

Current rifle manufacturer specializing in Mauser actions located in Birkenau, Germany. Limited current importation. Previously imported by New England Custom Gun, located in Claremont, NH, and by Mitchell's Mausers, located in Fountain Valley, CA.

Prechtl Jagd & Sportwaffen specializes in manufacturing a Mauser 98 short, standard, or Magnum length bolt action rifle patterned after the Mauser drawings from the 1930s. Additionally, the company offers a line of GS 04 high precision target rifles. Prechtl also manufactures a new action based on Mauser patents, the model Prechtl Express 07. It features a closed receiver and fits a detachable mag. Magnum cals. are available from 8.68mm through .416 Rigby - it is designed for long range hunting. A limited edition is also available that features a match barrel and carbon fiber stock - it is a joint venture with German car tuner, Mansory. A wide variety of calibers and options are available. The company also has released a new single shot falling block action named the Katharina, in addition to offering a variety of rifle accessories. Please contact the importer for more information, including pricing and U.S. importation.

PRECISION FIREARMS

Current AR-15 style and bolt action firearm manufacturer located in Martinsburg, WV beginning in late 2013. Previously located in Hagerstown, MD. Dealer and consumer sales through FFL.

Please refer to BlueBookOfGunValues.com to order the *Blue Book of AR-15s & Variations*, available as a book or online subscription.

PRECISION REFLEX, INC.

Current AR-15 style firearm manufacturer located in New Bremen, OH.

Please refer to BlueBookOfGunValues.com to order the *Blue Book of AR-15s & Variations*, available as a book or online subscription.

PRECISION SMALL ARMS, INC. (PSA)

Current manufacturer established in 1983, and made under license from Fabrique Nationale, Herstal, Belgium in Minden, NV since 2017. Previously manufactured in Aspen, CO from 2007-2017, Montrose, CO during 2006 and in Charlottesville, VA until 1995.

PISTOLS: SEMI-AUTO

The PSP pistol was not in production from 1995-2006, but approx. 1,000 nickel plated units were sold to various dealers between 1995-2006 from inventory. The handgun business of Precision Small Parts Ltd (PSP) was put into a new entity called Precision Small Arms, Inc. (PSA) in 1997, although the pistol has been marketed as the PSA-25 since 1995. Beginning mid-2010, all pistols are machined from billet steel. All factory engraved variations are performed by Master Engraver Angelo Bee.

(PSP) PSA-25 STANDARD (TRADITIONAL)/NOUVEAU – .25 ACP (6.35mm), single action, striker fire, blowback mechanism, 2 1/8 in. barrel, 6 shot mag., checkered black polymer grips, all steel construction with choice of high polished blue (new 1990), black oxide (disc. 1998), brushed satin nickel (Nouveau Satin), high polished nickel finish (Nouveau Mirror), or "1911 Hot Blue" glass/zircon bead blasted finish (new 2008), triple safety system, 7 1/4-9 1/2 oz. Mfg. 1984-1995, reintroduced 2006.

MSR $850	$750	$650	$600	$500	$425	$350	$275

Add $50 for Standard Hybrid (hot blued) or Nouveau (nickel).
Add $100 for Standard Mirror and Nouveau Hybrid.
Add $150 for Nouveau Mirror.

GRADING - PPGS™	100%	98%	95%	90%	80%	70%	60%	LAST MSR

* ***PSA-25 Stainless Steel*** – features 303 stainless steel construction, satin, high polish, or vacuum deposition coated black finish. Introduced 2010.

MSR $850	$750	$650	$600	$500	$425	$350	$275	

Add $50 for Stainless Hybrid model.
Add $400 for Carbon Titanium Black finish.
Add $550 for Nitrate Blue finish on small parts (new 2019).
Add $15 for Nouveau Mirror finish (disc. 2011).
Add $35 for non-polished (disc. 2011).

* ***PSA-25 Bone & Charcoal*** – bone and charcoal color case hardening by Shiloh Sharps, 24Kt. gold-plated steel trigger, nickel plated mag., high polished exhibition grade Turkish walnut burl grip plates. Mfg. 2012-disc.

	$925	$800	$700	$550	$450	$375	$295	*$1,100*

* ***PSA-25 Featherweight*** – features 7075 T652 aircraft aluminum frame with high polish chrome over nickel steel slide and mag., gold-plated trigger, aluminum two tier serial numbered case and original 1931 FN style grips, Arctic Blue, Carbon Titanium Black, or Raspberry (new 2021) finish. 7.25 oz. Introduced 2010.

MSR $930	$850	$750	$650	$550	$450	$375	$300	

Add $40 for Arctic Blue or Raspberry (new 2021) frame.
Add $100 for black coated finish (CT-Black model).
Add $130 for stainless steel slide and Grade 5 titanium skeletonized trigger (T Model, disc.).

* ***PSA-25 HB/EN*** – 330 grit, bead blast, high polish hot blue or nickel finish. Disc. 2016.

	$600	$515	$425	$395	$325	$250	$200	*$725*

* ***PSA-25 Beauxart Stainless*** – high polish chrome over nickel plated finish, silver nickel grips with mother-of-pearl inlay, metal mag. catch and trigger. Introduced 2011.

MSR $1,149	$1,050	$900	$800	$700	$550	$475	$350	

* ***PSA-25 Case Colored*** – .25 cal., carbon steel frame and slide, stainless steel barel, 6 shot, Turkish walnut grips, 24Kt. gold plated trigger, two nickel plated magazines, ships with its own black or brown hand crafted Swedish leather zippered pouch, Sodium Cyanide or Ash Bone finish. Only 500 to be mfg. mid-2012.

MSR $1,250	$1,100	$1,000	$850	$750	$600	$500	$400	

* ***PSA-25 Montreux*** – engine turned barrel (current mfg.), polished sterling silver (new 2014, SP model), high polish 18Kt. (rose gold) or high polish 24Kt. (yellow gold) gold plated frame, slide, and external components, ivory (disc.) or carbon fiber (new 2014) grips. yellow gold introduced 1999, rose gold. Introduced 2010.

MSR $1,500	$1,350	$1,200	$1,000	$900	$750	$600	$475	

Add $300 for rose gold finish.

* ***PSA-25 Sterling*** – high polish sterling silver plated finish, 7 gram solid silver trigger, metal mag. catch, silver nickel grips with carbon fiber inlay. Mfg. 2010-2012.

	$1,095	$900	$825	$725	$625	$550	$495	*$1,250*

* ***PSA-25 Presidential*** – features high polished 24Kt. gold plated slide, frame, magazine, and trigger, Dendrite ivory grips. Disc. 1999.

	$600	$475	$375	$315	$270	$230	$200	*$725*

* ***PSA-25 Renaissance Series*** – available in High Polish (nickel plated, engraved, disc.), French Blue (330 grit, engraved, disc.), Charcoal Blue (600 grit, engraved), French Gray (600 grit/polished, engraved), Coin (glass/Zircon bead blasted nickel), and Gold (600 grit finish, bead blasted, engraved) finish, ivory (disc.) or Mother of Pearl grips, 24Kt. gold plated grip screw, nut, trigger, mag. catch and trigger, 9.5 oz.

MSR $3,800	$3,400	$3,000	$2,550	$2,300	$1,900	$1,550	$1,200	

* ***PSA-25 Signature Editions*** – similar to Imperiale, except has "Michael B. Kassnar" signature on left slide top in gold. Mfg. 1989-91.

	$325	$295	$260	$230	$200	$175	$160	*$385*

There were also two Limited Signature Editions (less than 10 mfg.) which retailed for $1,458 and approx. $2,150.

* ***PSA-25 Damascus Exhibition Series No. 1*** – etched random patterns Damascus slide and grip plates, polished 8620 Hot Blue, carbon steel frame, gold plated trigger and cocking indicator. Mfg. 2019-2020.

	$3,000	$2,500	$2,000	$1,750	$1,550	$1,150	$995	*$3,430*

GRADING - PPGS™	100%	98%	95%	90%	80%	70%	60%	LAST MSR

* ***PSA-25 Diplomat Exhibition Series*** – features blued, high polish frame and slide, 24Kt. gold plated external components, African ivory grips. New 1999.

MSR $1,650	$1,500	$1,300	$1,100	$1,000	$800	$650	$500

* ***PSA-25 Grand Exhibition Series No. 1*** – features hand inlaid 24Kt. orange, yellow and green gold scroll pattern with rosettes on frame and slide high polish hot blue finish, African ivory grip plates, 9.5 oz. Introduced 2009. Limited ediiton.

MSR $6,800	$6,100	$5,350	$4,600	$4,150	$3,350	$2,750	$2,150

* ***PSA-25 Imperiale Exhibition Series*** – features hand inlaid 24Kt. green, yellow, and orange gold scroll pattern on frame and slide by Angelo Bee, high polish black oxide finish, African ivory grips. Introduced 1997. Limited edition.

MSR $4,450	$4,000	$3,500	$3,000	$2,700	$2,200	$1,800	$1,400

PREDATOR CUSTOM SHOP

Previous custom AR-15 style firearm manufacturer located in Knoxville, TN until 2015.

PISTOLS

Predator Custom Shop built custom hand-fit 1911 pistols to customer specifications.

RIFLES: BOLT ACTION

Predator Custom Shop manufactured custom bolt action rifles built to customer specifications. Base rifles started at $2,050.

RIFLES: SEMI-AUTO

Predator Custom Shop manufactured custom AR-15 rifles built to customer specifications. Models included the 5.56 Carnivore and the 5.56 DMR.

PREDATOR TACTICAL LLC

Previous custom firearms and accessories manufacturer located at the Scottsdale Airpark in AZ 2010-2017. Predator Tactical LLC was founded by Champion Competition Shooter Matt Burkett.

For individual model listings, please go to BlueBookOfGunValues.com/overflow.

PREMIER

Previous trademark manufactured in Italy and Spain by various companies.

SHOTGUNS: SxS

Note: Premier is a trade name for guns that have been produced in both Spain and Italy for various importers.

REGENT MODEL – 12, 16, 20, 28 ga., or .410 bore, 26, 28, or 30 in. barrels, various chokes, checkered pistol grip stock and beavertail forearm. Mfg. 1955-disc.

$325	$275	$250	$220	$195	$140	$110

Add 33% for 28 ga. or .410 bore.

REGENT MAGNUM EXPRESS – 12 ga., 3 in. chambers only, 30 in. full barrels, recoil pad. Mfg. 1957-disc.

$375	$325	$275	$250	$220	$165	$140

REGENT 10 GAUGE MAGNUM – similar to 12 ga. Mag., but 10 ga., 3 1/2 in. chambers, 32 in. full and full barrels. Mfg. 1975-disc.

$550	$495	$450	$375	$325	$250	$195

BRUSH KING – 12 or 20 ga., 22 in. imp. cyl. and mod. barrels, straight grip stock. Mfg. 1959-disc.

$325	$275	$250	$220	$195	$140	$110

MONARCH SUPREME GRADE – 12 or 20 ga., 26 or 28 in. barrels, various chokes, boxlock, auto ejectors, select stock. Mfg. 1959-disc.

$575	$500	$450	$385	$360	$330	$275

PRESENTATION CUSTOM GRADE – custom-made, gold and silver game scene. Mfg. 1959-disc.

$1,350	$1,100	$990	$880	$825	$715	$600

AMBASSADOR MODEL – 12, 16, 20 ga., or .410 bore, 26 or 28 in. barrels, mod. and full choke, checkered pistol grip stock. Mfg. 1957-disc.

$440	$385	$360	$330	$305	$250	$220

Add 33% for .410 bore.

GRADING - PPGS™	100%	98%	95%	90%	80%	70%	60%	LAST MSR

PRENSES ARMS

Previous trademark of shotguns manufactured by Koc Arms, located in Konya, Turkey until circa mid-2015. No current U.S. importation.

Koc Arms manufactured a complete line of good quality semi-auto, slide action, and single barrel shotguns under the Prenses Arms trademark. A wide variety of configurations were available, including various receiver finishes, grip and stock options, as well as engraving.

PRIMARY WEAPONS SYSTEMS (PWS)

Current AR-15 style rifle and pistol manufacturer located in Boise, ID.

Please refer to BlueBookOfGunValues.com to order the *Blue Book of AR-15s & Variations*, available as a book or online subscription.

PRINZ

Previous manufacturer of bolt action rifles, single shot rifles, and combination guns. Previously imported and distributed by Helmut Hofmann Inc. located in Placitas, NM.

RIFLES

GRADE 1 BOLT ACTION – .243 Win., .30-06, .308 Win., .300 Win. Mag., or 7mm Rem. Mag. cal., single or double set trigger(s), oil finished walnut stock.

	100%	98%	95%	90%	80%	70%	60%
	$495	$440	$385	$360	$330	$275	$250

* ***Grade 1 Bolt Action Carbine*** – similar to Grade 1 except has carbine barrel.

	100%	98%	95%	90%	80%	70%	60%
	$570	$495	$435	$390	$360	$330	$275

GRADE 2 BOLT ACTION – similar to Grade 1 except has rosewood forend cap.

	100%	98%	95%	90%	80%	70%	60%
	$545	$485	$425	$385	$360	$330	$275

TIP-UP RIFLE – available in 8 cals. between .222 Rem. and .30-06, high quality and limited mfg. Importation began 1989.

	100%	98%	95%	90%	80%	70%	60%
	$2,175	$1,900	$1,675	$1,375	$1,100	$950	$775

PRINCESS MODEL 85 – combination gun available in 12 ga. (2 3/4 in. chamber) and choice of 8 cals. between .222 Rem. and .30-06.

	100%	98%	95%	90%	80%	70%	60%
	$1,450	$1,275	$1,100	$925	$800	$775	$650

This model came standard with a leather case.

PRINZ-WAFFEN

Current manufacturer of high-quality break-open single shot rifles, located in Maierhöfen, Germany. No current U.S. importation. Please contact the manufacturer directly for U.S. availability and pricing.

PROARMS ARMORY s.r.o.

Current AR-15 style rifle manufacturer located in Czech Republic. No U.S. importation.

Please refer to BlueBookOfGunValues.com to order the *Blue Book of AR-15s & Variations*, available as a book or online subscription.

PROCISION ARMS

Current manufacturer of custom bolt action rifles located in Avella, PA.

RIFLES: BOLT ACTION

ProCision Arms manufactures rifles in various calibers including: .22 Creedmoor, .22-250 Rem., .28 Nosler, .300 PRC, .300 RUM, .300 Win. Mag., .308 Win., .458 Win. Mag., 6.5-284 Norma, 6.5 Creedmoor, or 6.5 PRC and various Cerakote finishes including: Titanium, SIG Dark Grey, OD Green, Graphite, Desert Sand, Burnt Bronze, Barrett Brown, or Tungsten. Other calibers or finishes may be available upon request, please contact the manufacturer directly for current offerings and availability.

DEAD FIRE SERIES OH-600 – .458 Win. Mag. cal., ProCision Arms Receiver w/wire EDM cut raceways, 24 in. fluted match grade barrel w/optional muzzle brake, ext. mag. cut, upgraded Remington BDL style floorplate, TriggerTech adj. trigger, 20 MOA Picatinny rail, pillar bedded McMillan carbon fiber stock in various patterns and finishes, Picatinny rail on forearm and 5 flush mount QD sling sockets around stock, one-piece machined bolt w/removeable bolt knob, various Cerakote finishes available, approx. 8 lbs.

	100%	98%	95%	90%	80%	70%	60%
MSR $3,950	$3,550	$3,100	$2,675	$2,425	$1,950	$1,600	$1,250

Add $200 for 24 in. barrel w/muzzle brake.

GRADING - PPGS™	100%	98%	95%	90%	80%	70%	60%	LAST MSR

DEAD FIRE SERIES LONG RANGE HUNTER – various short or long action cals., ProCision Arms Receiver w/wire EDM cut raceways, 24 in. fluted match grade barrel w/optional muzzle brake, ext. mag. cut, upgraded Remington BDL style floorplate, TriggerTech adj. trigger, 20 MOA Picatinny rail, pillar bedded McMillan carbon fiber stock in various patterns and finishes, Picatinny rail on forearm and 5 flush mount QD sling sockets around stock, one-piece machined bolt w/removeable bolt knob, various Cerakote finishes available, approx. 8 lbs.

MSR $3,950	$3,550	$3,100	$2,675	$2,425	$1,950	$1,600	$1,250	

Add $200 for 24 in. barrel w/muzzle brake.

DEAD FIRE SERIES CARBON LONG RANGE HUNTER – various short or long action cals., ProCision Arms Receiver w/wire EDM cut raceways, 24 in. fluted match grade carbon fiber barrel w/optional muzzle brake, ext. mag. cut, upgraded Remington BDL style floorplate, TriggerTech adj. trigger, 20 MOA Picatinny rail, pillar bedded McMillan carbon fiber stock in various patterns and finishes, Picatinny rail on forearm and 5 flush mount QD sling sockets around stock, one-piece machined bolt w/removeable bolt knob, various Cerakote finishes available, approx. 7 lbs. 8 oz.

MSR $4,350	$3,925	$3,425	$2,950	$2,675	$2,175	$1,775	$1,375	

Add $200 for 24 in. barrel w/muzzle brake.

PROFESSIONAL ORDNANCE, INC.

Previous AR-15 style firearm manufacturer located in Lake Havasu City, AZ 1998-2003. Previously manufactured in Ontario, CA 1996-1997.

During 2003, Bushmaster bought Professional Ordnance and the Carbon 15 trademark. Please refer to the Bushmaster section for recently manufactured Carbon 15 rifles and pistols.

PISTOLS: SEMI-AUTO

CARBON-15 TYPE 20 – .223 Rem. cal., GIO, Stoner type operating system with recoil reducing buffer assembly, carbon fiber upper and lower receiver, hard chromed bolt carrier, 7 1/4 in. unfluted stainless steel barrel with ghost ring sights, 30 shot mag. (supplies were limited), also accepts AR-15 type mags., 40 oz. Mfg. 1999-2000.

	$1,275	$1,125	$1,025	$875	$750	$625	$525	*$1,500*

CARBON-15 TYPE 21 – .223 Rem cal., GIO, ultra lightweight carbon fiber upper and lower receivers, 7 1/4 in. "Profile" stainless steel barrel, quick detachable muzzle compensator, ghost ring sights, 10 shot mag., also accepts AR-15 type mags., Stoner type operating system, tool steel bolt, extractor and carrier, 40 oz. Mfg. 2001-2003.

	$775	$685	$615	$550	$485	$415	$370	*$899*

CARBON-15 TYPE 97 – .223 Rem. cal., similar to Carbon 15 Type 20, except has fluted barrel and quick detachable compensator, 46 oz. Mfg. 1996-2003.

	$815	$700	$630	$570	$500	$425	$380	*$964*

RIFLES: SEMI-AUTO

CARBON-15 TYPE 20 – .223 Rem. cal., GIO, same operating system as the Carbon-15 pistol, 16 in. unfluted stainless steel barrel, carbon fiber buttstock and forearm, includes Mil-Spec optics mounting base, 3.9 lbs. Mfg. 1998-2000.

	$1,275	$850	$600	$495	$425	$375	$350	*$1,550*

CARBON-15 TYPE 21 – .223 Rem. cal., GIO, ultra lightweight carbon fiber upper and lower receivers, 16 in. "Profile" stainless steel barrel, quick detachable muzzle compensator, Stoner type operating system, tool steel bolt, extractor and carrier, optics mounting base, quick detachable stock, 10 shot mag., also accepts AR-15 type mags., 3.9 lbs. Mfg. 2001-2003.

	$850	$550	$465	$395	$350	$325	$295	*$988*

CARBON-15 TYPE 97/97S – .223 Rem. cal., GIO, ultra lighweight carbon fiber upper and lower receivers, Stoner type operating system, hard chromed tool steel bolt, extractor and carrier, 16 in. fluted stainless steel barrel, quick detachable muzzle compensator, optics mounting base, quick detachable stock, 30 shot mag., also accepts AR-15 type mags., 3.9 lbs. Mfg. 2001-2003.

	$935	$575	$475	$415	$350	$325	$300	*$1,120*

Add $165 for Model 97S (includes Picatinny rail and "Scout" extension, double walled heat shield forearm, ambidextrous safety, and multi-point silent carry).

PROOF RESEARCH

Current manufacturer of semi-auto and bolt action rifles, located in Columbia Falls, MT. Consumer sales through FFL dealers.

For individual model listings, please go to BlueBookOfGunValues.com/overflow.

GRADING - PPGS™	100%	98%	95%	90%	80%	70%	60%	LAST MSR

PUMA

Previous trademark of firearms imported by Legacy Sports International LLC until 2014, located in Reno, NV. Previously located in Alexandria, VA.

HANDGUNS: LEVER ACTION

MODEL 92 BOUNTY HUNTER – .44-40 WCF, .44 Mag., .45 LC cal., 12 in. barrel with elevated post front and adj. rear sight, 6 shot full-length mag. tube with one barrel band on forearm, shortened Italian walnut stock with large loop lever, 24 in. overall length, case colored frame, hammer, and lever. Mfg. in Italy by Chiappa Firearms. Mfg. 2009-2013.

$1,025 $900 $800 $700 $625 $550 $425 ***$1,253***

PISTOLS: SEMI-AUTO

MODEL 1911-22 – .22 LR cal., 4 3/4 in. barrel, black finish, 10 shot mag., SA, checkered walnut grips, fixed sights, manual safety, 39 oz. Mfg. 2010-2011.

$275 $225 $200 $185 $170 $160 $150 ***$323***

REVOLVERS: SINGLE ACTION

Recent manufacture is by Pietta, except for the Model 1873.

WESTERNER – .357 Mag., .44-40 WCF, or .45 LC cal., 4 3/4, 5 1/2, or 7 1/2 in. barrel, case colored frame/ blue barrel or nickel finish, choice of all steel or brass trigger guard and gripstraps, choice of one-piece smooth walnut or synthetic ivory (nickel finish) grips, developed for cowboy action shooting, mfg. in Italy by Pietta. Mfg. 2009-2010.

$525 $465 $385 $335 $300 $275 $250 ***$589***

Add $70 for nickel finish with white synthetic ivory or walnut bird's head grips.
Add $10 for steel frame.
Add $100 for factory tuned model (not available in .44-40 WCF or 7 1/2 in. barrel).

* ***Westerner Stainless*** – .357 Mag. or .45 LC cal., otherwise similar to Westerner with white one-piece synthetic grips. Mfg. 2009-2010.

$750 $675 $600 $550 $495 $450 $395 ***$829***

MODEL 1873 – .22 LR cal., black oxide finish, 4 3/4, 5 1/2 (new 2011), or 7 1/2 (new 2011) in. barrel, 6 shot, black or antique finish, plain walnut or black synthetic (new 2011) grips with medallions, includes key operated hammer block safety on left recoil shield, fixed sights. Disc. 2014.

$165 $150 $130 $120 $110 $100 $90 ***$189***

Add $96 for 5 1/2 or 7 1/2 in. barrel (new 2011), includes extra cylinder.
Add $55 for .22 WMR cylinder only (new 2011).

BUNTLINE REVOLVER – .22 LR cal., 12 in. barrel, matte black finish, side loading gate, 6 shot, key operated safety, black or faux ivory polymer grips, 3 lbs. Disc. 2014.

$275 $240 $200 $185 $150 $125 $100 ***$310***

Add $40 for .22 LR/.22 Mag. extra cylinder.

RIFLES: LEVER ACTION

MODEL 1886 – .45-70 Govt. cal., patterned after the Winchester Model 1886, choice of 22 in. round or 26 in. octagon rifle barrel carbine with forearm barrel band, crescent buttplate, open sights, case colored frame with blued barrel and mag. tube, Italian walnut stock, standard loop lever, 7 or 8 shot mag., 8-9 lbs. Mfg. in Italy by Chiappa. Mfg. 2009-2014.

$1,250 $1,025 $875 $775 $700 $625 $550 ***$1,390***

MODEL 92 – .357 Mag./.38 Spl., .44 Mag., .45 LC, .454 Casull (new 2002, carbine only), or .480 Ruger (new 2004) cal., 9 (.454 Casull) or 10 shot tube mag., 20 in. round or 24 in. octagon barrel, choice of blue, brass (disc. 2008), case colored frame, or stainless steel (disc. 2008) receiver and barrel, regular or large loop (.357 Mag. or .45 LC cal. only, new 2005), uncheckered walnut stock and forearm. Mfg. by Rossi (2001-2008) and Chiappa Firearms (beginning 2009). Imported 2001-2014.

* ***Model 92 Round Barrel Carbine*** – .357 Mag./.38 Spl., 44-40 WCF (mfg. 2009-disc.), .44 Mag., .45 LC, .454 Casull (mfg. 2002-08), or .480 Ruger (mfg. 2004-08) cal., blue, brass (disc. 2008) case colored, or stainless steel (disc. 2008), 16, 18 (disc. 2010), or 20 in. ported (.44 Mag. or .454 Casull cal. only, new 2005) or unported barrel, 8 or 10 shot mag., with or w/o large loop lever (16 in. barrel only), high grade Italian walnut stock, 6.1 lbs. Disc. 2014.

$925 $800 $700 $600 $525 $450 $400 ***$1,055***

Add $87 for stainless steel construction (disc. 2008).
Add $30 for HiViz sights and ported barrel (not available on .357 Mag. or .45 LC cal., disc. 2008).

GRADING - PPGS™	100%	98%	95%	90%	80%	70%	60%	LAST MSR

Add $31 for .454 Casull (last MSR was $642) or $47 for .480 Ruger cal. (disc. 2008, last MSR was $660).
Subtract approx. 20% for Rossi mfg. (disc. 2008), except for .454 Casull or .480 Ruger cal.

* ***Model 92 Octagon Barrel Rifle*** – .357 Mag./.38 Spl., .44 Mag., or .45 LC cal., choice of blue/case colored, stainless steel (disc.) or stainless steel/brass (not available in .44 Mag. cal., disc.), 20 (new 2007) or 24 in. octagon barrel, 10 or 12 shot mag., 7.7 lbs. Disc. 2014.

$925	$800	$700	$600	$525	$450	$400	*$1,055*

Add $41 for brass (disc. 2008).
Add $93 for buckhorn sights and saddle ring (mfg. 2002-08).
Add $55 for stainless steel construction (disc. 2008).
Subtract approx. 40% for older Rossi mfg. (disc. 2008).

* ***Model 92 Chuck Connors Commemorative*** – .44-40 WCF cal., patterned after the rifle Chuck Connors used in "*The Rifleman*" TV Series, features include commemorative medallion in stock, signature engraved on left side of receiver, signature laser etched into right side of the stock, case colored frame, 1,000 to be mfg. sequentially. Mfg. 2009-2010.

$1,150	$975	$850	$775	$700	$625	$550	*$1,299*

RIFLES: SEMI-AUTO

PPS/22 – .22 LR cal., 16 in. shrouded barrel with open sights, choice of uncheckered wood or black, green, or sand colored synthetic or Wildcat tactical adj. stock, 10 (clip), 30 (clip or drum) or 50 shot drum mag., Wildcat stock includes optional Picatinny rail, pistol grip, and vertical forend grip, mfg. by Pietta. Mfg. 2009-2010.

$475	$425	$375	$325	$295	$275	$250	*$519*

Add $40 for 50 shot drum mag or wood stock.
Add $50 for black, green, or sand colored, or Wildcat synthetic stock.

SHOTGUNS: LEVER ACTION

MODEL 1887 – 12 ga., 2 3/4 in. chamber, patterned after the Winchester Model 1887, 22 or 28 in. barrel, case colored frame, blued barrel and mag tube, uncheckered pistol grip walnut stock and forearm, 5 shot mag. with FastLoad variation (22 in. barrel only) allows breech to accept 2 rounds, 7 1/2 lbs. Mfg. in Italy by Chiappa. Mfg. 2009-2015.

$975	$825	$775	$650	$550	$475	$375	*$1,179*

Add $45 for 28 in. barrel.

PURDEY, JAMES & SONS, LTD.

Current manufacturer established in 1814, located in London, England. Annual production is approximately 75 guns.

Purdey guns have long been regarded as among the finest in the world. They have typically been made to customer specifications, and as such, should be appraised individually for purposes of evaluation. Values vary with gauge, barrel length, chamber length and age. Listed are the modern models and approximate values for reference purposes.

Prices indicated for manufacturer's suggested retail and 100% condition factors are listed in English pounds. All MSRs on currently manufactured long arms do not include VAT (approx. 20%). Values for used guns in 98%-60% condition factors are priced in U.S. dollars.

JAMES PURDEY & SONS HISTORY

Founder James Purdey was born in 1784, and completed his first apprenticeship in 1805, working for both Joseph Manton and Reverend Alexander Forsyth before establishing his own business in 1814. In 1825, Purdey made its first gun for continental royalty, and the same year made a gun for the Duke of Gloucester, brother to King George IV. They have supplied guns to the royal family ever since. By the early 20th century, the firm could boast of being a gunmaker to all 9 crowned heads of Europe. They received their first Royal Warrant in 1868, and even today, Purdey are gunmakers by appointment to Her Majesty the Queen, the Duke of Edinburgh, and the Prince of Wales. Throughout its history, the firm was granted 17 patents, the most enduring being 1863's double bolt snap action - in essence, the famed Purdey bolts, which secures the barrels to the action of almost every SxS double gun made in the world today. There is also Frederick Beesley's self-opening action, which Purdey helped him patent and purchased from him in 1880, and has been the basis for the firm's best quality SxS ever since. During 1949, the company purchased James Woodward and Sons, and more than 650 best O/Us have since been made to a slightly modified Woodward design. During 1994, the company was sold to Vendome PLC (now Richemont), a Swiss luxury goods consortium, which launched another golden age of gunmaking at Audley House. The company celebrated its bicentenary in 2014 with the opening of a new factory, where it continues to combine traditional gunmaking skills with modern technology.

GRADING - PPGS™	100%	98%	95%	90%	80%	70%	60%	LAST MSR

RIFLES: CUSTOM ORDER & OLDER PRODUCTION

New rifle prices represent the base price with standard fine scroll and bouquet engraving.

BOLT ACTION STANDARD MODEL – .243-.300 Win. Mag. cal., 22-26 in. traditional London blacked threaded barrel with muzzle protector, quick detachable pivot scope mounts and scope rings (no iron sights), Exhibition Grade walnut stock with full pistol grip, palm swell, and satin finish, leather covered recoil pad, traditional Purdey rose and scroll engraving on magazine floorplate. New 2021.

Current MSR on this model is £29,500.

BOLT ACTION SAFARI MODEL – .375-.500 Jeffery cal., 22-26 in. traditional London blacked barrel, quick detachable pivot scope mounts and scope rings, iron sights (fixed with one folding leaf sight), Superior Grade walnut stock with full pistol grip, palm swell, and satin finish, ebony tip forend, leather covered recoil pad, traditional Purdey rose and scroll engraving on magazine floorplate. New 2021.

Current MSR on this model is £39,000.

PURDEY DOUBLE RIFLE (CURRENT MFG.) – various cals., 22-26 in. barrels, classic quarter rib available in stippled matte or plain finish, standard bead front and fixed rear with one folding leaf sight, double trigger with beaded trigger guard, Exhibition Grade walnut stock with cheekpiece, pistol grip, and metal grip cap, traditional checkered butt end stock, classic splinter forend, traditional Purdey rose and scroll engraving in silver or color hardened finish, includes leather case with cleaning accessories.

Current MSR for .375 H&H -.500 NE cal. is £168,000.
Current MSR for .577 NE and .600 NE cal. is £173,000.

Since each Purdey is basically a special order, new gun pricing is calculated per individual customer work order.

PURDEY DOUBLE RIFLE (OLDER MFG.)

.300 H&H cal. or less	N/A	$57,500	$52,250	$46,000	$42,000	$37,000	$32,000
Up to .375 H&H cal.	N/A	$70,000	$59,500	$51,000	$45,000	$40,000	$35,000
Up to .470 NE cal.	N/A	$92,500	$80,000	$72,500	$65,000	$57,500	$50,000
Up to .600 NE cal.	N/A	$100,000	$90,000	$80,000	$70,000	$60,000	$55,000

Add 30% for self-opening action. (If they are hammerless, they will always be self-opening)
Subtract 15% if w/o ejectors.

MAGAZINE RIFLE/MAGNUM MAGAZINE RIFLE – cals. below .375 H&H are built on modern Mauser style square bridge action, .375 H&H or larger cals. are built on modern Mauser style Magnum action, action is bedded into a titanium chassis, 22-26 in. free floated barrel, pivoting quickly-detachable scope mounts or leaf sights (Magnum Magazine Rifle only), 3-position safety, checkered best quality walnut pistol grip stock, individually built per customer specifications. Disc.

Last MSR for Magazine Rifle with .375 H&H or lower cal. was £29,950.
Last MSR for Magnum Magazine Rifle with .375 H&H or larger cal. was £39,000.

SHOTGUNS: CUSTOM ORDER & OLDER PRODUCTION

New shotgun prices represent the base price with standard fine scroll and bouquet engraving.

BEST QUALITY GAME GUN SxS – 10 (disc.), 12, 16, 20, 28 ga., or .410 bore, 2 3/4, 3, or 3 1/2 in. chamber, 26-32 in. barrels, solid concave or raised rib finished in stippled matted, cross hatched, or plain, fixed or Teague chokes, double trigger, beaded trigger guard, Exhibition Grade walnut stock with English straight hand or pistol grip (disc.), checkered butt end of stock, classic splinter forend, auto ejector, traditional Purday rose and scroll engraving available in silver or color hardened finish, includes leather case with cleaning accessories. Mfg. since 1880.

Current MSR on this model is £122,000.
Add £5,000 for 28 ga. or .410 bore.
Add £32,000 (same ga.) or £38,000 (different ga.) for extra set of barrels.

* ***Best Quality Game Gun SxS Damascus*** – both frame and barrels are made from 100% damascus steel. Mfg. since 2009.

Current MSR for this model is £154,500 (12/20 ga.) or £159,500 (28/.410).

* ***Best Quality Game Gun Older Mfg.***

$38,500	$32,500	$27,500	$21,500	$17,750	$15,250	$12,750

* ***Best Quality Heavy Duck Gun***

$20,500	$17,000	$14,000	$11,000	$9,500	$8,750	$7,500

Add 50% for 20 ga.
Add 100% for 28 ga. or .410 bore, depending on condition.
Subtract 10%-15% if not cased with accessories.
Add $1,000 for SST.

GRADING - PPGS™	100%	98%	95%	90%	80%	70%	60%	LAST MSR

BEST OVER-AND-UNDER SHOTGUN – 12, 16, 20, 28 ga., or .410 bore best quality sidelock action, 2 3/4, 3, or 3 1/2 in. chamber, 26-32 in. barrels, solid game rib, ventilated, or ribless finished in stippled matted, cross hatched, file cut, or plain, fixed or Teague chokes, auto ejectors, single or double trigger, beaded trigger guard, Exhibition Grade straight or pistol grip walnut stock, traditional checkered butt end stock, slim tapered forend, traditional rose and scroll engraving in silver or color hardened finish, includes leather case. Production started in 1923 with original Purdey design. In 1949, Purdey purchased James Woodward & Sons, and has manufactured the Woodward O/U action ever since. Very few early actions.

Current MSR on this model is £139,500.

Current MSR for 28 ga. or .410 bore is £145,500.

Add £39,000 (same ga.) or £45,000 (different ga.) for extra set of barrels.

* ***O/U Gun Damascus*** – both frame and barrels are made from 100% damascus steel. Mfg. since 2009.

Current MSR for this model is £166,000 (12/20 ga.) or £171,000 (28/.410).

* ***O/U Gun Older mfg.***

	100%	98%	95%	90%	80%	70%	60%	LAST MSR
	$47,500	$41,750	$37,500	$33,000	$29,950	$27,000	$25,000	
28 ga.	$107,500	$95,000	$85,000	$75,000	$68,750	$59,950	$55,000	

Add $3,000 for Woodward action.

Add 50% for 20 ga.

Add 10% for SST.

BEST SXS HAMMER SHOTGUN (HAMMER EJECTOR GAME GUN) – 12 or 20 ga., 2 3/4, 3, or 3 1/2 in. chamber, 26-32 in. barrels, fixed or Teague chokes, ejectors, top tang safety, double trigger, traditional Purdey rose and scroll engraving in silver or color hardened finish, Exhibition Grade checkered English straight grip stock and splinter forearm, includes leather case with cleaning accessories. First importation in U.S. during 2008. Mfg. since 2002.

Current MSR on this model is £129,000.

PURDEY SPORTER O/U – 12, 16, 20, or 28 ga., 26-34 in. barrels, trigger plate action, solid or vent. rib, single inertia or double (disc.) trigger, Exhibition grade walnut stock with a full pistol grip or straight hand grip, slim tapered forend, checkered butt or rubber recoil pad, silver oval including engraving of three initials, Sporter large scroll engraving in silver or color hardened finish, includes Purdey ABS travel case, major parts mfg. by Purdey and sent to Italy for assembly by Perugini-Visini. Mfg. since 2008.

Current MSR on this model is £39,500.

Add £6,000 for extra interchangeable barrels.

Add £8,000 for 28 ga. barrels (20 ga. frame only).

SINGLE BARREL TRAP GUN – 12 ga. Purdey action only, similar to O/U specifications. Mfg. 1923-1970s.

	100%	98%	95%	90%	80%	70%	60%	LAST MSR
	$11,250	$10,000	$8,750	$7,900	$7,200	$6,750	$5,950	

PUSKARSTVO SPENDAL d.o.o.

Current custom long arm manufacturer located in Slovenia, Slovakia.

Puskarstvo Spendal manufactures high quality shotguns and rifles in various configurations by custom order only. Please contact the company directly for more information including U.S. availability and pricing.

NOTES

Q SECTION

Q.S. ARMI

Previous pistol and ammunition manufacturer located in Lecco, Italy circa 2012. Previous company name was Q.S. Progetto Meccanica s.a.s.

Q.S. Armi manufactured a line of M1911-style semi-auto pistols. Previous models included the 2011 Tex, Hawk, 120 FS, 102 KP, 102 AM, 94CC, and the 94AM. The 120 FS, 102 KP, 94CC, and 94AM are available in Q.S. Armi's proprietary 7penna centerfire ammunition (7x23mm), as well as 9mm Para.

QFI (QUALITY FIREARMS INC.)

Previous manufacturer located in Opa-locka, FL circa December 1990-1992.

For individual model listings, please go to BlueBookOfGunValues.com/overflow.

QIQIHAR HAWK INDUSTRIES CO., LTD.

Current manufacturer established during 1956 located in Heilongjiang Province, China. No current U.S. importation.

Qiqihar manufactures good quality O/U, SxS, slide action, and semi-auto shotguns. Please contact the company directly for more information, including pricing and domestic availability.

QUACKENBUSH, H.M.

Previous manufacturer of rifles 1886-1922 and airguns 1871-1943, located in Herkimer, NY.

For more information on Quackenbush airguns, including the combination rimfire/airgun, please refer to the *Blue Book of Airguns* - also available as an online subscription.

GRADING - PPGS™	100%	98%	95%	90%	80%	70%	60%	LAST MSR

RIFLES: .22 CAL., RIMFIRE

Only one breech mechanism was used on all H.M. Quackenbush rimfire rifles, the company's only rifle configuration was a swinging breech single shot. The breech pivots to the right of the gun. All Quackenbush guns were .22 caliber rimfire because the action was not strong enough for more powerful cartridges. These models were supplied in several different boxes, and often came with a cleaning rod, catalog, and paper targets. These and other accessories will significantly add to the value of the firearms prices listed. No serial numbers were applied to Quackenbush guns. Many variations of these models are encountered, which can also add premiums to the values listed, and can be used to estimate date of manufacture. Quackenbush also manufactured heavy metal targets for these rifles 1884-1931. For more information on Quackenbush firearms, please refer to *Quackenbush Guns* by John Groenewold.

SAFETY RIFLE - .22 cal. rimfire, swinging breech, 18 (most common) or 22 in. barrel, walnut stock, nickel, brown, or blue finish. Mfg. 1886-1922.

	100%	98%	95%	90%	80%	70%	60%	LAST MSR
	$750	$650	$550	$300	$200	$125	$80	

Add 10% for each of the following: heavy cast iron buttplate, original factory blue finish, optional Town & Country combination rear and front sights, barrel and optional sights where rear sight is approx. 1 in. forward of the breech end of the barrel, and for factory walnut forearm.
Add 20% for a raised single line curved knurl ring around the barrel in front of the receiver.
Add 30% for original box.

JUNIOR SAFETY RIFLE - .22 cal. rimfire, 18 in. barrel only, wire stocked, swinging breech, tubular receiver, nickel or blue finish. Approx. 8,000 mfg. 1890-1920.

	100%	98%	95%	90%	80%	70%	60%	LAST MSR
	$750	$675	$600	$400	$300	$250	$150	

Add 10% for original factory blue finish.
Add 30% for original box.

BYCYCLE RIFLE - .22 cal. rimfire, 12 in. barrel, fixed rear sight, retractable wire stock and wire pistol grip, swinging breech, nickel or blue finish. Only 4,321 were sold during 1896-1919.

	100%	98%	95%	90%	80%	70%	60%	LAST MSR
	$1,250	$1,000	$800	$700	$600	$450	$300	

Add 10% for original factory blue finish.
Add 30% for original box.
Subtract 50% if retractable shoulder stock is missing.
Add 30% for original canvas and leather holster/case to be mounted to center bar on boy's bicycle.

QUAIL UNLIMITED, INC.

Previous national conservation organization with national headquarters located in Albany, GA until 2013. Previously located in Edgefield, SC.

For individual model listings, please go to BlueBookOfGunValues.com/overflow.

QUALITY ARMS

Previous AR-15 style rifle manufacturer located in Rigby, ID until 2018.

For individual model listings, please go to BlueBookOfGunValues.com/overflow.

QUALITY PARTS CO./BUSHMASTER

Quality Parts Co. was a division of Bushmaster Firearms, Inc. located in Windham, ME that manufactured AR-15 style rifles and various components and accessories for Bushmaster. Please refer to the Bushmaster Firearms International listing in the B section for current model listings and values.

NOTES

R SECTION

R GUNS

Current manufacturer, importer, and dealer located in Carpentersville, IL.

R Guns offers a line of AR-15 style rifles and carbines in various configurations, upper and lower receivers, accessories, and related components. Please contact the company directly for more information on models, availability, and pricing.

RAAC

Previous importer located in Scottsburg, IN until circa 2016.

Russian American Armory Company was an import company for Molot, located in Russia. Previous product/model lines included Vepr. rifles, in addition to a line of bolt action rifles that included the LOS/BAR Series, CM-2 Target rifle, Korshun, and Sobol hunting model.

GRADING - PPGS™	100%	98%	95%	90%	80%	70%	60%	LAST MSR

SHOTGUNS

MKA 1919 – 12 ga., 3 in. chamber, AR-15 style, self-adjusting GIO, 18 1/2 in. barrel with three choke tubes, 5 shot box mag., A2 configuration with carry handle and front sight, Picatinny rail, bolt hold open after last round, fixed or adj. synthetic stock, sling swivels, choice of matte black or 100% camo coverage. Mfg. in Turkey. Importation disc.

	$500	$450	$375	$350	$325	$300	$225	*$700*

Add $100 for 100% camo coverage.
Add $500 for flat-top receiver and adj. stock.

RAF

Previous manufacturer of shotguns and rifles located in St. Etienne, France circa 1994-96.

RAF manufactured superposed rifles, shotguns, combination guns, and semi-auto rimfire rifles.

RBA

Previous competition pistol manufacturer located in Granarolo dell'Emilia, Italy.

PISTOLS: SEMI-AUTO

Renzo Bonora Armi (RBA) manufactured high quality competition pistols in both .22 LR and .32 S&W Wadcutter. These pistols had little, if any, importation into the U.S.

R.F.M.

Current shotgun manufacturer established in 1956, and located in Sarezzo, Italy. No current U.S. importation.

SHOTGUNS

R.F.M. manufactures good quality shotguns. O/U shotguns include: the Model Twenty Five, SK Series (SKS, SK, SK One Trap, SK One Special), the Sm One, and Becassier Series. SxS models include: Zeus Series, Mythos, Forest (camo, divergent barrels), Becassier, Slug, Luparine (Luparino), Venus, Ares Express, and the Canard/Canard Plus. The Brta Brutto Anatroccolo sporting, and a combination SxS shotgun are also available. Semi-Auto models include: A Mystero (Mystery) semi-auto with left or right-ejection and KR 15 with fixed or telescopic or folding stock is also available. All models can be customized per customer's specifications. Please contact the company directly for more information, including pricing, options, and U.S. availability.

R.G. INDUSTRIES

Previous importer located in Miami, FL. Operations ceased in January of 1986.

HANDGUNS

R.G. Industries manufactured and imported plain utilitarian revolvers and semi-auto pistols. Unfortunately, because of a product liability situation, R.G. Industries was litigated out of business during 1986. Although their models represent good values, they are not collectible, and so a generalized listing is provided.

RG 14 S, RG 23, RG 31

	$95	$80	$70	$60	$55	$50	$45	

RG 40, RG 74, & HIGHNOON S.A.

	$125	$115	$95	$80	$70	$60	$55	

RG 26 SEMI-AUTO – .25 ACP cal., 6 shot mag., 2 1/4 in. barrel, plastic grips, single action, 12 oz.

	$65	$55	$50	$40	$35	$30	$25	*$66*

GRADING - PPGS™	100%	98%	95%	90%	80%	70%	60%	LAST MSR

RGS LLC

Current rifle manufacturer located in Casper, WY.

RGS LLC is owned and operated by Robert J. Stone, who studied for 16 years under Dale Storey of DGS, Inc. Stone is a master machinist and offers custom rifles in a variety of configurations, including tactical, long range, big game, and modern plains rifles. Many options are available. Please contact him directly for more information, including available options, pricing, and delivery time.

R.I.P. TACTICAL

Current custom AR-15 manufacturer located in Utah.

Please refer to BlueBookOfGunValues.com to order the *Blue Book of AR-15s & Variations*, available as a book or online subscription.

RND MANUFACTURING

Previous pistol and rifle manufacturer located in Longmont, CO 1978-circa 2017. Previously distributed by Mesa Sportsmen's Association, LLC located in Delta, CO.

PISTOLS: SEMI-AUTO

RND PISTOL – 5.56 NATO cal., AR-15 style, GIO, round shrouded handguard, 7 1/2 in. barrel with muzzle brake, pistol grip, full-length vent. Picatinny rail, titanium firing pin, 9 1/2 lbs. Mfg. 2010-circa 2017.

$1,775	1,575	$1,450	$1,325	$1,100	$875	$675	*$2,000*

RIFLES: SEMI-AUTO

RND EDGE SERIES – .223 Rem. (RND 400), .300 WSM (RND 1000, new 2003), .300 RUM (RND 2100, new 2003), .308 Win. (RND 800, new 2010), .338 Lapua Mag. (RND 2000, new 1999), .375 Super Mag. (RND 2600), .408 CheyTac (RND 2500) or 7.62x39mm (disc.) cal., patterned after the AR-15 style, GIO, 18, 20, 24, or 26 in. barrel, choice of synthetic (Grade I), built to individual custom order, handmade laminated thumbhole (Grade II, disc. 1998), or custom laminated thumbhole stock with fluted barrel (Grade III, disc. 1998), CNC machined, vented aluminum shroud, many options and accessories available, custom order only, approx. 11 1/2-16 lbs. Mfg. 1996-circa 2017.

Add $355 for Grade II (disc. 1998) or $605 for Grade III (disc.).

* ***RND 400*** – .223 Rem. cal., GIO, AR-15 style, 18-26 in. barrel, synthetic A2 style stock, CNC machined upper and lower receivers, integral Picatinny rail, titanium firing pin, free floating handguard, hard black anodized with grey or black finish, 9 1/2 lbs. Disc.

$2,025	$1,825	$1,650	$1,500	$1,275	$1,000	$775	*$2,295*

* ***RND 800*** – .308 Win./7.62 NATO cal., GPO, 20-26 in. super match free floating barrel, CNC machined matched upper and lower receivers, left side non-reciprocating charging handle, hard black anodized with black or gray gun coat, integral Picatinny rail, titanium firing pin, modular handguard, adj. stock, 11 lbs. Mfg. 2010-disc.

$3,350	$3,000	$2,750	$2,500	$2,100	$1,650	$1,300	*$3,795*

* ***RND 1000*** – .300 Win. Mag. cal., GPO, 20-26 in. Super match free floating barrel, CNC machined matched upper and lower receivers, left sided non-reciprocating charging handle, integral Picatinny rail, RND integrated buffer system, modular handguard, fully adj. stock, single feed double stack mag., hard black anodized with black or gray gun coat finish, 11 lbs. Mfg. 2003-disc.

$2,025	$1,825	$1,650	$1,500	$1,275	$1,000	$775	*$2,295*

* ***RND 2000*** – .338 LM cal., GPO, 20-26 in. Super match free floating barrel, CNC machined matched upper and lower receivers, left sided non-reciprocating charging handle, integral Picatinny rail, single feed double stack mag., RND integrated buffer system, modular handguard, fully adj. stock, hard black anodized with black or gray gun coat finish, 14 lbs. Mfg. 1999-disc.

$4,225	$3,800	$3,475	$3,150	$2,650	$2,075	$1,650	*$4,795*

* ***RND 2100*** – .300 RUM cal., GPO, otherwise similar to RND 2000. Mfg. 2003-disc.

$4,225	$3,800	$3,475	$3,150	$2,650	$2,075	$1,650	*$4,795*

* ***RND 2500*** – .408 CheyTac cal., GPO, similar to RND 2000, except features 26 in. Super match free floating barrel, 18 lbs. Mfg. 2004-disc.

$9,250	$8,300	$7,600	$6,900	$5,800	$4,550	$3,600	*$10,500*

* ***RND 2600*** – .375 CheyTac cal., GPO, 20-26 in. Super match free floating barrel, CNC machined matched upper and lower receivers, left sided non-reciprocating charging handle, integral Picatinny rail, single feed double stack mag., RND integrated buffer system, modular handguard, fully adj. stock, hard black anodized with black or gray gun coat finish, 18 lbs. Disc.

$9,250	$8,300	$7,600	$6,900	$5,800	$4,550	$3,600	*$10,500*

GRADING - PPGS™	100%	98%	95%	90%	80%	70%	60%	LAST MSR

* ***RND 3000*** – .50 BMG cal., GPO, 26 in. Super match barrel with muzzle brake, double stock mag., fully adj. stock, full-length integrated Picatinny rail, includes optics, scope, and bipod, black or various camo colors, 28 lbs. Disc.

	$10,350	$9,250	$8,250	$7,500	$6,750	$6,000	$5,250	*$11,500*

* ***RND 3100*** – .416 Rem. Mag. cal., GPO, otherwise similar to RND 3000. Mfg. 2012 only.

	$10,350	$9,250	$8,250	$7,500	$6,750	$6,000	$5,250	*$11,500*

RPA DEFENCE LTD. (RPA SYSTEMS LTD. / RANGEMASTER PRECISION ARMS / RPA INTERNATIONAL LTD.)

Current rifle manufacturer located in Warwickshire, England. Currently imported since 2014 by Accurate-Mag, located in Monroe, CT.

The company name changed in circa 2021 from RPA SYSTEMS LTD. to RPA DEFENCE LTD.; in mid-2019 from Rangemaster Precision Arms to RPA SYSTEMS LTD.; and in mid-2013, from RPA International Ltd. to Rangemaster Precision Arms.

RIFLES: BOLT ACTION LISTINGS

RPA DEFENCE LTD. manufactures high quality bolt action rifles, including a tactical long range sniper model, the Rangemaster ULTRA 7.62 Stubby (£4,330 MSR), Rangemaster ULTRA 7.62 (£4,330 MSR), Rangemaster ULTRA 338 (£4,655 MSR), and the Rangemaster ULTRA 50 (£5,690 MSR). The Rangemaster Series includes a folding stock, stainless steel barrel and muzzle brake, Picatinny rails and tactical bipod. The Interceptor is available in a single shot (£2,825 MSR) and a Repeater (£3,010 MSR) version. The Hunter rifle comes with or w/o a thumbhole stock (£2,915 base MSR), Highland Stalker (£3,045 MSR), Woodland Stalker (£2,915 MSR). The Target Rifle Series includes the Elite Single Shot (£2,940 MSR), and the Ranger (£2,655 MSR). Pricing does not include VAT. Additionally, the company makes custom rifles and actions. Please contact the company directly for complete pricing, U.S. availability and options.

RPB INDUSTRIES

Previous company located in Avondale, GA. RPB Industries' guns were made by Masterpiece Arms.

CARBINES: SEMI-AUTO

RPB CARBINE – .45 ACP cal., closed bolt blowback action, 16 1/4 in. barrel, fixed skeletonized stock and forearm pistol grip, accepts M-3 military submachine gun mags., black finish, 9 1/2 lbs. Mfg. 2000-2004.

	$450	$375	$325	$285	$260	$235	$210	

Add $75 for Deluxe Model with EZ cocker and installed scope mount.

RPM

Previous manufacturer located in Tucson, AZ until 2014. Previously located in Afton, MO 2002-2003.

During 2004, RPM changed the name of the company to Gateway Precision Arms. During 2008, the company name was changed back to RPM.

PISTOLS: SINGLE SHOT

XL PISTOL – many cals. available, tip-up action, 8, 10 3/4, 12, or 14 in. barrel, positive thumb safety, steel frame, cocking indicator, right or left-hand action. Disc.

	$785	$675	$600	$550	$500	$450	$395	*$858*

XL HUNTER – over 40 cals., tip-up action, stainless steel frame, 5 1/16 in. underlug, 12 or 14 in. Douglas chrome moly (new 2004) or stainless steel barrel, ISGW rear and Patridge or hooded front sights, with (became standard 2000) or w/o external positive extractor. Mfg. 1995-2015.

	$1,125	$975	$875	$725	$625	$525	$450	*$1,235*

Add $250 for stainless steel barrel.
Add $140 for integral muzzle brake.
Add $50 for left-hand action.
Add $380 or $424 per extra barrel, depending on length.

RWC (RUSSIAN WEAPON COMPANY)

Current importer located in Tullytown, PA.

RWC was an exclusive importer for Izhmash and Saiga rifles in addition to previously importing a line of tactical rifle accessories. RWC is the parent company of Kalashnikov USA, for current offerings please refer to that section, for previous offerings please refer to the Izhmash and Saiga sections, or contact the company for more information on model availability and pricing.

GRADING - PPGS™ 100% 98% 95% 90% 80% 70% 60% LAST MSR

RWS

Current trademark of airguns and ammunition manufactured by Dynamit Nobel GmbH which has been manufacturing firearms and airguns in Nuremberg, Stadeln, and Troisdorf, Germany since 1865. RWS became part of Dynamit Nobel in 1931. Dynamit Nobel is now a division of RUAG AmmoTec GmbH, located in Fürth, Germany. RWS firearms were imported until 1995 by Dynamit Nobel of America, Inc. located in Closter, NJ. Other trademarks (including Rottweil) by Dynamit Nobel can be located under individual heading names in this text.

For more information and current pricing on both new and used RWS airguns produced by Dianawerk, Mayer, and Grammelspacher, please refer to the *Blue Book of Airguns* - also available as an online subscription.

RIFLES: BOLT ACTION, TARGET

MODEL 820 L - .22 LR cal. only, 24 (disc.) or 26 in. barrel, no. 100 aperture sight, oil polished stock for 3-position match, stippled pistol grip and forearm, recoil pad, adj. trigger, 10.6 lbs. Disc. 1994.

$1,275 $1,000 $850 $700 $575 $475 $400 *$1,500*

Previous to 1986 this model was designated the 820 S and was supplied with a no. 75 aperture rear sight.

* ***Model 820 S*** - with Model 82 aperture sight. Disc.

$1,100 $895 $795 $650 $560 $480 $420 *$995*

MODEL 820 F MATCH - similar to Model 820 L, except has heavy match barrel, 15.4 lbs. Disc. 1994.

$1,750 $1,400 $1,275 $1,000 $850 $700 $575 *$2,000*

* ***Model 820 SF Match*** - with Model 820 L aperture sight. Disc.

$1,125 $900 $795 $650 $560 $480 $420 *$1,010*

MODEL 820 K - .22 LR cal. only, made for running boar competition, 24 in. barrel, stock similar to Model 820 SF, no sights, 9 1/2 lbs. without barrel weight or scope. Importation disc. 1986.

$900 $775 $695 $615 $540 $470 $420 *$870*

RADIAN WEAPONS

Current manufacturer of AR-15 pistols and rifles located in Redmond, OR.

Please refer to BlueBookOfGunValues.com to order the *Blue Book of AR-15s & Variations*, available as a book or online subscription.

RADICAL FIREARMS, LLC

Current manufacturer and retail operation located in Stafford, TX.

Please refer to BlueBookOfGunValues.com to order the *Blue Book of AR-15s & Variations*, available as a book or online subscription.

RADOM

Current trademark manufactured by Fabryka Broni, Lucznik - Radom Sp. z o.o., located in Radom, Poland. Previously imported on a limited basis by I.O., Inc., located in Monroe, NC. Previously manufactured 1925-1945 by the Polish Arsenal located in Radom, Poland & Steyr, Austria. Post WWII also manufactured by Z.M. Lucznik (Radom Factory) in Radom, Poland. Recent importation was by Dalvar of U.S.A., located in Seligman, AZ. Previously located in Richardson, TX and Henderson, NV.

Please also refer to FABRYKA BRONI LUCZNIK - RADOM SP.ZO.O section for more information on currently or recently imported models.

REVOLVERS

RADOM REVOLVER - Nagant design, dated 1931-36.

N/A $3,150 $2,625 $2,100 $1,575 $1,050 $775

PISTOLS: SEMI-AUTO, 1935-1939 PRODUCTION

Serial number ranges use #### for the non-alphabetical prefix series, 1/#### for the first alphabetical prefix series, and 2/#### for the second alphabetical prefix series. Mill marks became more prominent as the war progressed.

P-35 AUTOMATIC - 9mm Para. cal., 8 shot, blue finish, 4 3/4 in. barrel, fixed sights, black VIS/FB plastic grips. Mfg. 1935 through WWII.

* ***wz.35 VIS Polish Eagle*** - eagle logo, unblued barrel, rust blue, lanyard loop, ser. no. 01-49000, dated 1936, 1937 (rarest date), 1938, or 1939.

$7,500 $6,500 $5,000 $4,000 $2,900 $2,000 $1,350

Add 50% for 1937 mfg. if in 95%+ condition, otherwise, add 15%.
Add 25% for 1936 mfg. if in 95%+ condition, otherwise, add 10%.

GRADING - PPGS™	100%	98%	95%	90%	80%	70%	60%	LAST MSR

PISTOLS: SEMI-AUTO, LATE 1939-1945 PRODUCTION

Serial number ranges use #### for the non-alphabetical prefix series, 1/#### for the first alphabetical prefix series, and 2/#### for the second alphabetical prefix series. Mill marks became more prominent as the war progressed.

P.35 VIS POLISH EAGLE NAZI CAPTURE – 9mm Para. cal., eagle logo and WaA marks, rust blue, all 3 levers, lanyard loop, many small parts serial numbered, ser. no. range 47400-49500.

N/A	$4,225	$3,350	$2,675	$2,150	$1,600	$1,150	

Beware of fakes!

P.35 NAZI RADOM TYPE 1 - 3 LEVER & SLOT – 9mm Para. cal., rust blue, unblued barrel, lanyard loop, black VIS/FB plastic grips, many small parts ser. numbered, ser. nos. 01-12500 & 1/A0001-1/E8000 (1st Series) prefix.

$2,800	$2,200	$1,750	$1,200	$775	$675	$575	

Add 100% for Navy characteristics: Some Kreigsmarine Eagle/M marked, blued barrel, may/may not be "N"/"O" grip strap marked.

Add 50% for S/N Range 01-12500, early characteristics: blued barrel, early slide/logo position, no P.35(p), no lanyard loop.

Beware of fakes!

P.35 NAZI RADOM TYPE II - 3 LEVER & NO SLOT – 9mm Para. cal., salt blue, lanyard loop, early e/WaA77 on left frame and slide changes to later e/77, some brown VIS/FB plastic grips, a few with pressed VIS/FB wood grips, serial numbered 1/E8001-1/Z1000 (1st Series) prefix.

N/A	$1,350	$1,075	$800	$675	$475	$400	

Add 15% if P.35(p) marked if in 90%+ condition, otherwise add 10%.

P.35 NAZI RADOM TYPE III - 2 LEVER & NO SLOT – 9mm Para. cal., lanyard loop, salt blue, e/77 on left side of slide and frame, brown plastic VIS/FBN grips common, pressed VIS/FB wood grips rarely seen, serial numbered 1/Z1001-2/H8900.

N/A	$1,075	$900	$700	$575	$425	$375	

Certain Radoms w/German acceptance marks will bring a premium. Example: Add $50 for infrequently found left-hand Trigger Guard E/77 Inspection mark.

* ***P.35 Nazi Steyr Type III - 2 Lever & No Slot*** – 9mm Para. cal., salt blued or phosphate exterior with blued small parts also on phosphate models, serial numbered in late 2/A or 2/B with e/77 on left side of slide and frame and 2/H8901 through 2/K w/o e/77 on left side of slide and frame, e/623 on front left side of trigger guard, many with grooved wood grips, mostly all Steyr mfg.

$3,400	$2,800	$2,350	$2,000	$1,475	$1,200	$1,000	

* ***P.35 Nazi Steyr Type III - 2 Lever & No Slot "bnz" Slide*** – 9mm Para. cal., rough milled phosphate exterior, some "blank" slides noted, wood grips, serial numbered approx. 2/K1440-2/K2400, mostly all Steyr mfg.

N/A	$5,025	$4,025	$3,275	$2,800	$2,350	$2,000	

PISTOLS: SEMI-AUTO, RECENT PRODUCTION

VIS P-35 – 9mm Para. cal., patterned after the 1937 P-35, large Polish eagle stamped on left side of slide, with or w/o slotted rear grip strap for shoulder stock, 4 1/2 in. barrel, 36 oz. Limited mfg. 1997 only.

$2,600	$1,425	$1,215	$1,015	$925	$825	$750	*$2,999*

MODEL P-64 – 9x18mm Makarov cal., 6 shot mag., 3 1/4 in. barrel, fixed sights, blue finish, checkered composition grips, 6.1 in. OAL, 22.4 oz. Rare. Disc.

$250	$150	$125	$100	$95	$85	$80	

TOKAREV (PISTOLET TT) – Polish copy w/manual safety, well made. Disc.

$500	$400	$350	$325	$300	$250	$200	

* ***TT-33 (FB Radom)*** – 7.62x25 cal., includes two mags. and cleaning rod, mfg. FB Radom, Poland 1947-1950.

$275	$230	$200	$180	$165	$150	$140	

* ***TT-33 (Radom)*** – 7.62x25 cal., includes two mags. and cleaning rod, mfg. by Radom in Poland 1950-1954.

$275	$230	$200	$180	$165	$150	$140	

GRADING - PPGS™	100%	98%	95%	90%	80%	70%	60%	LAST MSR

VANAD P-83 – 9x18mm Makarov cal., 8 shot mag., available in Standard Military Issue or Special Eagle Limited Edition, loaded chamber indicator, firing pin block safety, steel receiver with external hammer, 3 1/2 in. barrel, drift adj. target sights, checkered composition grips, 26 oz. Imported 1994 (Standard Military Issue), 1997-circa 2008.

	$350	$290	$265	$235	$210	$190	$170	

Add $46 for Standard Military Issue.

* ***Vanad P-93 9mm*** – 9mm Makarov cal., similar to the Vanad P-83, except decocking lever is on the frame instead of the slide, black oxide finish, 3.9 in. barrel. Disc.

	$350	$250	$225	$200	$175	$150	$125	

MAG 95 – 9mm Para. cal., single or double action with firing pin block, external hammer, ambidextrous hammer drop safety, 4 1/2 in. barrel, two matching number mags., 37 oz. Limited importation 1997 only.

	$650	$550	$450	$400	$350	$300	$275	*$749*

MAG 98 – 9mm Para. cal., similar to Mag 95, except has two matching mags., holster, and cleaning rod. Most of these are police/military trade-ins. Disc.

	$550	$450	$400	$350	$300	$275	$250	

PISTOLS: CURRENT MFG.

VIS WZ.35 – 9mm Para. cal., patterned after the WWII Radom pistol, supplied with case. New 2011.

This model is currently not being imported into the U.S.

RIFLES: SEMI-AUTO

Fabryka Broni Lucznik currently manufactures a variety of semi-auto rifles and carbines designed after the Model 96 Beryl rifle. Please contact the manufacturer directly for U.S. availability and pricing.

RAINIER ARMS

Current firearms trademark (including a private label line of AR-15 style pistols, carbines, rifles, and bolt action rifles), accessories, and gunsmithing distributor, located in Auburn, WA.

Please refer to BlueBookOfGunValues.com to order the *Blue Book of AR-15s & Variations*, available as a book or online subscription.

RAM-LINE, INC.

Previous manufacturer located in Grand Junction, CO until 1995.

In addition to the Ram-Tech pistol, Ram-Line, Inc. also manufactured a complete line of synthetic and wood stocks for a variety of firearms. Ram-Line continues to manufacture a complete line of magazines for most popular pistols and rifles.

PISTOLS: SEMI-AUTO

EXACTOR PISTOL – .22 LR cal., single action, aircraft alloy receiver with 5 1/2 in. polymer VR barrel and steel liner, unique two-motion safety blocks hammer, trigger, and sear, 15 shot mag., matte finish, easy disassembly, injected molded grip, fixed sight, 20.3 oz., supplied with case. Mfg. 1990-93.

	$195	$165	$135	$110	$95	$75	$70	*$225*

* ***Exactor Pistol Target*** – similar to above, except has 7 1/2 in. barrel, 23 oz. Disc. 1993.

	$265	$230	$195	$150	$125	$110	$95	*$300*

RAM-TECH PISTOL – similar to Exactor pistol, except 4 1/2 in. barrel w/o VR. Mfg. 1994-95.

	$175	$145	$125	$100	$85	$70	$65	*$200*

RAMIREZ, TODD

Current custom rifle builder located in Alba, TX.

Todd Ramirez builds custom order bolt action rifles. Each gun is built per individual customer specifications, and a variety of options are available. Synthetic rifle Syn-Fle (starts at $12,500), and the Syn-Fle Classic (new 2015, starts at $12,500). Premium signature wood rifle starts at $30,000. Premium wood rifle starts at $32,000. New in 2013 was the Premium American Classic rifle starting at $30,000. New in 2017 is the Alchemist Warrior Rifle Series - Alchemist Avani rifle is a wood stock with a carbon fiber barrel available with optional stainless steel barrel (starts at $10,000). The Alchemist Ember uses a synthetic stock in a light sporter or tactical also with carbon fiber barrel (starts at $6,250) is available with custom paint. Alchemist Zephyr is a true tactical rifle using a chassis or a McMillan stock with a carbon fiber or stainless steel barrel, also custom paint (starts at $7,100). For complete details visit customgun.com.

He also offers gunsmithing, gun fitting, leather wrap pads, restoration, metal work, and other services. Please contact him directly for more information, including an individualized price quotation, available options, and delivery time.

GRADING - PPGS™	100%	98%	95%	90%	80%	70%	60%	LAST MSR

RAMO DEFENSE SYSTEMS

Previous rifle manufacturer located in Nashville, TN, 1999-2003.

RIFLES: BOLT ACTION

TACTICAL .308 - .308 Win. cal., Rem. M-700 long action, match grade stainless steel barrel, skeletonized black synthetic stock with cheekpad, matte black metal finish, 4 shot mag., 16 lbs. Mfg. 1999-2003.

	100%	98%	95%	90%	80%	70%	60%	LAST MSR
	$2,495	$2,100	$1,850	$1,600	$1,400	$1,200	$995	*$2,495*

M91/M91A2 - .308 Win. or .300 Win. Mag. cal., Rem. M-700 long action, black Kevlar and fiberglass stock, matte black metal finish, 4 shot mag., 14 lbs. Mfg. 1999-2003.

	100%	98%	95%	90%	80%	70%	60%	LAST MSR
	$2,695	$2,250	$1,950	$1,675	$1,475	$1,250	$995	*$2,695*

Add $200 for .300 Win. Mag. cal.

M600 SINGLE SHOT - .50 BMG cal., single shot, twin tube skeletonized stock with pistol grip and cheekpiece, 32 in. barrel with fins at breech and muzzle brake, 23 lbs. Mfg. 1999-2003.

	100%	98%	95%	90%	80%	70%	60%	LAST MSR
	$4,195	$3,700	$3,200	$2,750	$2,250	$1,950	$1,675	*$4,195*

M650 REPEATER - .50 BMG cal., repeater action with 6 shot detachable rotary mag., stock and barrel (30 in.) similar to M600, approx. 30 lbs. Mfg. 1999-2003.

	100%	98%	95%	90%	80%	70%	60%	LAST MSR
	$6,395	$5,750	$5,150	$4,500	$3,750	$3,000	$2,250	*$6,395*

RANDALL FIREARMS COMPANY

Previously manufactured in Sun Valley, CA. Manufactured between June 7, 1983 and December 15, 1984 - final plant closing was June 15, 1985.

Before manufacturing ceased in May of 1985, almost 10,000 pistols had been manufactured in 24 models, 12 variations, and 3 different calibers. In some instances, production on certain models was very limited and premiums for these low volume niches are starting to develop. Between June of 1983 and May of 1984, 9,968 handguns were manufactured with 75% of all 9mm Para. pistols being exported to Europe and 35% of 9mm Para. production employing a 10 groove barrel. Models manufactured after 1984 came equipped with an extended slide stop, long trigger, and beavertail grip safety. Production ser. nos. started at 02000 for right-hand models and 02100 for left-hand models. All but the first 200 (approx.) serial numbers started with "RF" and ended with "C" or "W." A few rare mis-marks are in circulation. Total mfg. for all models and variations was 9,968. Randall prototype serialization starts with a "T" - less than 45 were manufactured and these specimens command up to a 50% premium. In addition, 78 serial numbers under 2,000 were manufactured by special order.

Models listed are generally described with values per specific variations listed afterward.

PISTOLS: SEMI-AUTO

The following is a complete listing for Randall Firearms variations including production statistics. Values shown represent recent aftermarket prices, but it should be noted that regional interest can change these prices significantly. All original Randall pistols had no blue parts. Only the front and rear sights were finished in black oxide.

100% Randall prices assume NIB condition with paperwork.

Add 50% for prototypes with "T" serial numbers.

COMBAT MODEL - same size as Service Model, ribbed top fixed sight slide, Pachmayr grips on right-hand model only, left-hand models had Herrett walnut grips. While this model was advertised as having a flat mainspring housing, only few examples were manufactured.

Last MSR was $549.

RAIDER/SERVICE MODEL-C - 9mm Para. or .45 ACP cal., Colt Commander Model design, 4 1/4 in. barrel, 36 oz., total stainless steel construction, roll-marked Service Model-C in 1983 and Raider in 1984.

Last MSR was $460.

Add $130 for adj. sights/ribbed slide, available in either right-hand or left-hand (only 2 mfg.) model.

* ***Raider/Service Model-C Featherweight*** - .45 ACP cal. only, alloy receiver, stainless steel slide, roll-marked Service Model-C, T-type serial numbers, 29 oz. Disc. 1984, only 4 mfg.

SERVICE MODEL (FULL SIZE) - .38 Super, 9mm Para., or .45 ACP cal., Colt Model 1911 A1 design, 5 in. barrel, total stainless steel construction, 38 oz. Available in either right-hand or left-hand model.

Last MSR was $460.

GRADING - PPGS™	100%	98%	95%	90%	80%	70%	60%	LAST MSR

CURTIS E. LEMAY 4-STAR MODEL - 9mm Para. or .45 ACP cal., Gen. Curtis E. LeMay design, 4 1/4 in. barrel, 6 (.45 ACP) or 7 (9mm Para.) shot mag., total stainless steel construction, 35 oz. Available in either right-hand or left-hand model, left-hand models are a true mirror image with over 17 major parts changes.

Last MSR was $533.

This model was 1/2 in. shorter in magazine well and had a cast, squared-off trigger guard compared to the Colt 1911A1 design.

- ***Curtis E. LeMay 4-Star Model Featherweight*** - .45 ACP cal. only, alloy receiver, stainless steel slide, T-type serial numbers, 28 oz. Disc. 1984 (only one mfg.).

RANDALL MATCHED SETS - .45 ACP cal. only, each set consisted of a right-hand and a left-hand Service Model with matching serial numbers. Only 4 sets were mfg. on a special order basis. A111/B111 model configuration.

Last MSR was $1,250.

Randall Variations & Identification

Randall pistols are denoted by a four-character model notation, starting with an alphabetical prefix followed by three digits. The alphabetical prefix will be either A, B, or C. A designates right-hand configuration only, B designates left-hand configuration only, and C designates right-hand lightweight model. The first numerical digit will be 1, 2, or 3. 1 denotes Service Model, 2 denotes Service Model - C or Raider, and 3 represents the C.E. LeMay Model. The second numerical digit will be either 1, 2, or 3. 1 designates round top and fixed sight slide, 2 denotes flattop fixed sight slide, and 3 represents adj. sights, flattop frame. The third numerical digit will also be either 1, 2, or 3. 1 denotes .45 ACP cal., 2 designates 9mm Para., and 3 represents .38 Super. Hence, if you had a left-hand Randall in the service model size with a flattop adj. sight slide, and in .45 ACP cal., your model would be a B131. These model codes are not marked on the pistols.

A111 - 3,421 mfg.

$900	$775	$675	$575	$450	$375	$295

Five A111s were mfg. with Austrian proofmarks with premiums existing.

A112 - 301 mfg.

$1,000	$875	$750	$650	$525	$425	$350

A121 - 1,067 mfg.

$950	$825	$725	$575	$445	$385	$325

A122 - 19 mfg.

$1,650	$1,450	$1,250	$1,075	$865	$700	$550

A131 - 2,083 mfg.

$925	$825	$700	$595	$465	$385	$315

A211 - 992 mfg.

$950	$825	$725	$575	$445	$385	$325

A212 - 76 mfg.

$1,325	$1,150	$1,000	$850	$695	$565	$445

A231 - 574 mfg.

$1,050	$925	$800	$685	$550	$450	$350

A232 - 5 mfg.

Rarity precludes accurate price evalution.

A311 - 361 mfg.

$1,150	$1,000	$875	$750	$600	$495	$385

Most LeMay models (4 1/4 in. barrel) were shipped in gun rugs without a factory box. Original factory LeMay boxes are rare - add 10% premium. Beware of Randall LeMay and service model pistols made from parts kits. There were 226 LeMay receivers and 322 service model receivers (all right-hand) sold that could be parts guns.

A312 - 1 mfg.

Rarity precludes accurate price evalution.

A331 - 293 mfg.

$1,250	$1,100	$950	$815	$665	$545	$425

The note that appears for the Model A311 also applies to this variation.

GRADING - PPGS™	100%	98%	95%	90%	80%	70%	60%	LAST MSR
A332 - 9 mfg.								
	$1,700	$1,500	$1,275	$1,100	$895	$735	$575	
B111 - 297 mfg.								
	$2,375	$2,000	$1,775	$1,625	$1,300	$1,075	$825	
B121 - 110 mfg.								
	$2,500	$2,175	$1,875	$1,700	$1,375	$1,125	$875	

B122 - 2 mfg.

Rarity precludes accurate price evalution.

B123 - 2 mfg.

Rarity precludes accurate price evalution.

B131 - 225 mfg.								
	$2,750	$2,400	$2,075	$1,875	$1,525	$1,250	$975	
B311 - 52 mfg.								
	$3,000	$2,625	$2,250	$2,050	$1,650	$1,350	$1,050	

B312 w/.45 ACP FACTORY CONVERSION - 1 mfg.

Rarity precludes accurate price evalution.

B312 - 9 mfg.								
	$3,750	$3,275	$2,825	$2,550	$2,075	$1,700	$1,325	

B321 - 1 mfg.

Rarity precludes accurate price evalution.

The B321 was the only factory 3-slide set. It was fitted with the 3 different LH LeMay slides available (B311, B321, & B331). This model was mirror polished, engraved, and had ivory grips with the Randall logo.

B331 - 45 mfg.								
	$3,125	$2,725	$2,350	$2,125	$1,725	$1,400	$1,100	

B2/321 - 1 mfg.

Rarity precludes accurate price evalution.

This was the only factory model variation to leave Randall Firearms. This was a left-hand Raider with the C.E. LeMay slide.

C211 - 5 mfg.

Rarity precludes accurate price evalution.

C331 - 1 mfg.

Rarity precludes accurate price evalution.

C332 - 4 mfg.

Rarity precludes accurate price evalution.

* ***C332 Matched Sets*** - large premiums exist for different models with the same serial number if NIB condition. Only 4 were mfg.

RANGEMASTER PRECISION ARMS

Please refer to RPA SYSTEMS LTD located in this section.

RANGER ARMS INC.

Previous manufacturer located in Gainesville, TX until the early 1970s.

Ranger Arms Inc. manufactured good quality, bolt action rifles in various calibers and configurations, and were marked "Rangemaster Precision Arms". Although somewhat rare in that there were not a large number manufactured, collectibility to date has been limited with specimens in 90%+ condition, typically priced in the $375-$500 range.

RAPTOR ARMS CO., INC.

Previous rifle manufacturer located in Shelton, CT, approx. 1997-mid 1999. Previously distributed by Davidson's and Jerry's Sport Centers.

GRADING - PPGS™	100%	98%	95%	90%	80%	70%	60%	LAST MSR

RIFLES: BOLT ACTION

RAPTOR SPORTING RIFLE - .243 Win., .25-06 Rem., .270 Rem., .30-06, or .308 Win. cal., features "Taloncote" or blue (mfg. 1998 only) finished or stainless steel (new 1999) barreled action, black checkered fiberglass reinforced synthetic stock, adj. trigger, with or w/o sights. Mfg. 1997-99.

	$230	$195	$175	$160	$150	$140	$130	*$259*

Add $30 for sights (disc.).
Add $15 for blue finish (disc.).
Add $36 for heavy barrel.
Add $50 for stainless steel barreled action with sights (new 1999).

* ***Raptor Sporting Rifle Peregrine Deluxe*** - similar to Raptor Sporting Rifle, except has deluxe checkered or plain hardwood stock. Mfg. 1998 only.

	$265	$225	$195	$175	$160	$150	$140	*$309*

Subtract $10 for plain hardwood stock and no sights (blue finish only).

RASHEED (RASHID)

Previous Egyptian military rifle manufactured circa mid-1960s.

For individual model listings, please go to BlueBookOfGunValues.com/overflow.

RAVELL

Previous manufacturer located in Barcelona, Spain.

RIFLES: SxS

MAXIM DOUBLE RIFLE - .375 H&H or 9.3x74R cal., H&H type sidelock action with automatic ejectors, Purdey scroll engraving, 23 in. barrels, deluxe walnut with full pistol grip and rubber buttplate, double articulated triggers. Importation disc. circa 1998.

	$6,600	$6,100	$5,000	$4,000	$3,500	$2,950	$2,600	*$7,000*

Add 10% for .375 H&H cal.

RAVEN ARMS

Previous manufacturer located in Industry, CA circa 1970-1991. Approximately 2 million were mfg.

PISTOLS: SEMI-AUTO

P-25 - .25 ACP cal., single action, 2 7/16 in. barrel, 6 shot mag., walnut grips, available in nickel, blue, or chrome finish, 15 oz. Disc. 1984.

	$70	$60	$50	$40	$35	$30	$25	

MP-25 - similar to Model P-25, except die-cast slide serrations are slightly different. Disc. 1992.

	$60	$50	$45	$40	$35	$30	$25	*$70*

Walnut, slotted plastic, or ivory colored grips were available for this model. From 1987 on, a sear blocking safety was added to the MP-25.

REBEL ARMS CORP.

Previous AR-15 style parts and previous manufacturer of pistols and rifles located in East Stroudsburg, PA.

Please refer to BlueBookOfGunValues.com to order the *Blue Book of AR-15s & Variations*, available as a book or online subscription.

REC-ARMS

Current shotgun manufacturer established in 2009, located in Istanbul, Turkey. No current U.S. importation.

Please contact the company directly for more information including U.S. availability and pricing.

RECORD-MATCH

Previously manufactured by Anschütz, located in Zella-Mehlis, Germany circa pre-WWII.

PISTOLS: SINGLE SHOT, TARGET

MODEL 210 FREE PISTOL - .22 LR cal., Martini action, 11 in. barrel, single shot, blue, carved and checkered walnut grips and forearm, set trigger (button release), micrometer rear sight, deluxe target pistol, pre-WWII.

	$1,320	$1,265	$1,210	$1,100	$880	$745	$550	

MODEL 210A - similar to Model 210, except alloy frame.

	$1,265	$1,210	$1,155	$1,045	$825	$690	$495	

GRADING - PPGS™	100%	98%	95%	90%	80%	70%	60%	LAST MSR

MODEL 200 FREE PISTOL – similar to Model 210, except less deluxe features and spur trigger guard, pre-WWII.

	$990	$935	$770	$660	$525	$440	$360	

RED ARROW WEAPONS

Current AR-15 style rifle and parts manufacturer located in Fork Union, VA.

Please refer to BlueBookOfGunValues.com to order the *Blue Book of AR-15s & Variations*, available as a book or online subscription.

RED DESERT RIFLES

Current manufacturer of custom rifles located in Rock Springs, WY.

Red Desert Rifles specializes in hand selected Tiger (Curly) Maple. Other wood stocked rifles are available upon request.

RIFLES: BOLT ACTION

Red Desert Rifles manufactures a line of custom bolt action rifles. All rifles are built using: custom RDR action, match grade barrel, adj. trigger, muzzle brake, mercury tube, glass bedded custom stock, caliber of choice (standard or wildcats), and several finish options. Stock options include: custom fit thumb hole, engraving, wide forearm, finger grooves, fluted barrel, and satin or high gloss finish. Please contact the manufacturer directly for pricing and availability.

RED ROCK ARMS

Current manufacturer established April 2003 and located in Mesa, AZ. During late 2006, the company name was changed from Bobcat Weapons, Inc. to Red Rock Arms.

For individual model listings, please go to BlueBookOfGunValues.com/overflow.

RED ROCK PRECISION

Current manufacturer of precision rifles established during 2011, located in Morgan, UT.

All currently manufactured Red Rock Precision rifles are supplied with 40 rounds of match grade ammo custom loaded per individual rifle and also include a free shooting school.

RIFLES: BOLT ACTION

Red Rock Precision has a Build Your Own feature on their website which allows you to choose from several different options to select the custom gun of your choice. Each gun made by Red Rock Precision is built per individual custom order. The models listed below reflect base MSRs and information. Please contact the company directly for more information including options, a personal quotation, and delivery time

Beginning in 2018, the following options were also available:
Add $149 for radial muzzle brake.
Add $199 for directional muzzle brake.
Add $1,399 for Sig Sauer WHISKEY5 5-25x52mm scope.
Add $1,249 for Huskemaw Blue Diamond 4-16x32mm scope.
Add $1,449 for Huskemaw Blue Diamond 5-20x50 scope.
Add $1,863 for Nightforce NXS 3.5-15x50mm scope.
Add $2,028 for Nightforce NXS 5.5-22x50mm scope.

P2PX CARBON LITE – 7mm Rem. Mag., 6.5x284 Norma, .28 Nosler, .30 Nosler, or .300 RUM cal. (additional cals. available), stainless steel or titanium action, 26 in. carbon fiber barrel, Jewell trigger, McMillan A3 Sporter, McMillan Game Warden, or McMillan Game Hunter stock with Edge Technology and choice of finish, with (standard until 2018, became optional 2019) or w/out Huskemaw 5-20x50 Blue Diamond scope with two BDC turrets, 8.6 lbs. New 2016.

MSR $7,148	$6,100	$5,300	$4,550	$4,150	$3,350	$2,750	$2,385	

Add $599 for titanium action.

P2PX EXTREME RANGE MAGNUM – 7mm Rem. Mag., 6.5x284 Norma, .28 Nosler, .30 Nosler, or .300 RUM cal., stainless steel action, 26 in. match grade fluted barrel with muzzle brake, Jewell trigger, McMillan A3 Sporter stock with Edge Technology or McMillan HTG stock, choice of finish, with (standard until 2018, became optional 2019) or w/out Huskemaw 5-20x50 Blue Diamond scope with two BDC turrets, 9 lbs.

MSR $6,499	$5,500	$4,850	$4,150	$3,750	$3,050	$2,500	$2,165	

P2PXT (ULTRALITE) MOUNTAIN RIFLE – 7mm Rem. Mag., 6.5x284 Norma, .28 Nosler, .30 Nosler, or .300 RUM cal., titanium action, 24 in. match grade fluted barrel with muzzle brake, Jewell trigger, McMillan Game Hunter, Game Warden, or Game Scout stock with choice of finish, with (standard until 2018, became optional 2019) or w/out Huskemaw 4-16x42 scope with two BDC turrets, 8 lbs.

MSR $7,448	$6,325	$5,535	$4,750	$4,300	$3,480	$2,850	$2,485	

GRADING - PPGS™	100%	98%	95%	90%	80%	70%	60%	LAST MSR

P2PXT (ULTRALITE) SHEEP RIFLE – 6.5x284 Norma, 6mmx284, or 6XC cal., bolt action rifle, titanium action, 24 in. match grade fluted barrel, Jewell trigger, McMillan Hunter's Edge or McMillan Game Scout stock with choice of finish, with (standard until 2018, optional beginning 2019) Huskemaw 3-12x42 scope with two BDC turrets, 6 1/2 lbs. Disc. 2019.

	$6,000	$5,200	$4,500	$4,100	$3,300	$2,700	$2,100	*$7,049*

RED X ARMS

Current semi-auto rifle manufacturer located in central MN.

Please refer to BlueBookOfGunValues.com to order the *Blue Book of AR-15s & Variations*, available as a book or online subscription.

REDOLFI F.LLI S.N.C.

Current long gun manufacturer and retail gun shop located in Brescia, Italy. No current U.S. importation.

Redolfi F.lli manufactures good quality O/U rifles, in addition to boxlock O/U and SxS shotguns. Many custom options are available. Please contact the company directly for more information including pricing, U.S. availability, and delivery time.

GARY REEDER CUSTOM GUNS

Current custom handgun and rifle manufacturer located in Flagstaff, AZ. Consumer direct sales.

HANDGUNS / RIFLES

For over 35 years, Gary Reeder has specialized in customizing revolvers from various manufacturers, and is now building several series of custom revolvers on his own frames, in addition to customizing customer supplied handguns. Gary also manufactures several series of Model 1911 style pistols built to customers specifications in .45 ACP and 10mm. Reeder currently produces well over 80 different series of custom hunting handguns, cowboy guns, custom 1911s, and large caliber hunting rifles. For more information on his extensive range of custom guns, please contact the company directly.

REGENT

Current trademark of semi-auto pistols manufactured by Tisas Trabzon Gun Industry Corp., located in Turkey. Currently imported by LKCI LLC, located in Newark, OH (beginning 2018) and Brownells, located in Grinnell, IA. Currently distributed by Omega Arms located in Heath, OH. Previously imported by Umarex USA, Inc. 2011-2016.

Please refer to Tisas Trabzon Gun Industry Corp., located in the T section for listings.

REIMER JOHANNSEN GmbH (JOHANNSEN RIFLES)

Current rifle manufacturer by Reimer Johannsen GmbH, located in Neumünster, Germany. No current U.S. importation. Previously imported by New England Custom Gun Service, located in Plainfield, NH, and by Johannsen, Inc. until 2003.

RIFLES: BOLT ACTION

Johannsen rifles feature high quality Mini, short, medium, and Magnum Mauser actions in four sizes in many calibers. Actions are manufactured by Reimer Johannsen GmbH, using sophisticated CAD and CNC technology, in addition to Old World gunsmithing techniques.

Johannsen takedown express rifles are unique in that the bolt locks into the barrel with the same precision every time. This design ensures that point of impact remains identical after each assembly/disassembly. Please contact the company directly for more information, including domestic availability and current pricing.

PROFESSIONAL MODEL – .500 Jeffery or .505 Gibbs cal., double square bridge action, adj. trigger, flag safety, English stock, various options available. Importation disc.

Last MSR on this model was $14,450.

Add $1,350 for .505 Gibbs cal.

CLASSIC SAFARI – various cals. between .375 H&H to .458 Lott, single square bridge action with thumbcut, express sight with two leaves, safari English style stock, open sights, 8 lbs. 3 oz. Importation disc.

Last MSR on this model was $12,240.

SAFARI RIFLE – various cals. between .25-06 to .500 Jeffery, features medium or Magnum double square bridge action, adj. trigger, three position safety, express sight with two leaves, safari English stock with satin oil finish. Importation disc.

Last MSR on this model was $12,240.

Add $1,160 for .375 H&H, .404 Jeffery, .416 Rigby, .450 Rigby, .458 Lott, or .500 Jeffery cal.

Add $3,400 per extra takedown barrel.

GRADING - PPGS™	100%	98%	95%	90%	80%	70%	60%	LAST MSR

TRADITION RIFLE – various cals. between .17 Rem. to .458 Lott, available in mini, short, medium, or Magnum action, adj. trigger, three position safety, low bolt handle, pivot insert in front square bridge, express sight with one leaf, straight grip stock with satin oil finish. Importation disc.

Last MSR on this model was $12,780.
Add $2,400 for titanium action (new 2014).
Add $4,020 for mini-action, $1,850 for short action, or $1,220 for Magnum action.
Add $3,400 per extra takedown barrel.

MOUNTAIN RIFLE – various cals. between .243 Win. to 9.3x62mm, short or medium action, double square bridge action, adj. trigger, three-position safety, low bolt handle, integral scope mount in rear square bridge, express sight with one leaf, satin oil finished high gloss stock, lightweight. Imported 2007-disc.

Last MSR on this model was $12,780.
Add $1,850 for short action, $3,670 for mini action (disc.).

REISING ARMS COMPANY

Previous manufacturer originally located in Hartford, CT and later in New York, NY.

PISTOLS: SEMI-AUTO

TARGET AUTOMATIC PISTOL – .22 LR cal., 12 shot, 6 3/4 in. barrel, blue, brown hard rubber grips, hinged frame, outside hammer. Mfg. 1921-24.

	100%	98%	95%	90%	80%	70%	60%	LAST MSR
	$1,000	$900	$800	$675	$575	$475	$375	

This model was mfg. in Hartford, CT from serial number 1,001-4,000. The New York, NY address occurs in the serial range 10,000-12,000.

Warning: This pistol's slide may crack if modern high speed .22 LR ammo is used extensively.

RELLIM ARMS

Current AR-15 style pistol manufacturer established late 2014, located in Wichita, KS.

Please refer to BlueBookOfGunValues.com to order the *Blue Book of AR-15s & Variations*, available as a book or online subscription.

REMINGTON ARMS COMPANY, INC.

Current manufacturer and trademark established in 1816, with factories currently located in Ilion, NY, Lonoke, AR, Mayfield, KY, and Huntsville, AL.

Remington was founded by Eliphalet Remington II and originally located in Litchfield, Herkimer County, NY circa 1816-1828. Remington established a factory in Ilion, NY next to the Erie Canal in 1828, and together with his sons Philo, Samuel, and Eliphalet III pioneered many improvements in firearms manufacturing. Corporate offices were moved to Madison, NC in 1996. DuPont owned a controlling interest in Remington from 1933-1993, when the company was sold to Clayton, Dubilier & Rice, a New York City based finance company. The Mayfield, KY plant opened in 1997. On May 31st, 2007, a controlling interest in the company was sold to Cerberus Capital Management and Remington Arms along with Bushmaster, DPMS, and Cobb Manufacturing was renamed the Freedom Group. In December, 2007, Remington acquired Harrington & Richardson Firearms (H & R), and Marlin Firearms, and the company moved manufacturing to their Remington plant in Ilion, New York.

In 2013, Remington made significant improvements, including the expansion of its ammunition facility, growth of its firearms manufacturing capacity, secured competitive military and law enforcement contracts, and introduced a series of new products including the Ultimate Defense Handgun Ammunition and Model 783 bolt action rifle.

In February, 2014, Remington announced a major expansion with new manufacturing at the old Chrysler building in Huntsville, AL. In 2015, the Freedom Group holding company was renamed Remington Outdoor Company.

In March, 2018, Remington Arms Co., Inc. entered Chapter 11 bankruptcy protection in March, but emerged less than two months later with a creditor approved restructuring plan. However, Remington re-entered Chapter 11 bankruptcy protection less than two years later in July 2020 and halted all production of firearms. During a bankruptcy auction in September, 2020, Remington was sold to the Roundhill Group, LLC. Remington is planning to restart production of firearms at their Ilion factory as RemArms in the first quarter of 2021.

100%	98%	95%	90%	80%	70%	60%	50%	40%	30%	20%	10%

REMINGTON TRADEMARKS - 1816-PRESENT

1816-1847 - Remington (company manufactured and distributed rifle barrels to gunsmiths throughout America)
1847-1853 - E. Remington & Son
1854-1888 - E. Remington & Sons
1888-1914 - Remington Arms Company
1914-1916 - Remington Arms & Ammunition Company, Inc.
1916-1920 - Remington Arms - Union Metallic Cartridge Co., Inc.
1920 to date - Remington Arms Company, Inc.

HANDGUNS: 1857-1945 PRODUCTION

BEALS' FIRST MODEL POCKET REVOLVER - .31 cal. perc., 5 shot, smooth cylinder, 3 in. octagon barrel, blue finish, one-piece Gutta Percha grip, brass or iron trigger guard. Approx. 3,000 produced, 1857-58.

100%	98%	95%	90%	80%	70%	60%	50%	40%	30%	20%	10%
N/A	$4,000	$3,500	$3,000	$2,000	$1,700	$1,300	$900	$700	$500	$400	$300

Add $1,000 for original pasteboard box and accessories.

BEALS' SECOND MODEL POCKET REVOLVER - .31 cal. perc., 5 shot, smooth cylinder, 3 in. octagon barrel, blue finish, two-piece hard rubber grips, spur trigger. Less than 1,000 produced 1858-1859. Quite rare, but a large collection of these pistols came on the market in 2013, deflating the prices somewhat.

100%	98%	95%	90%	80%	70%	60%	50%	40%	30%	20%	10%
N/A	$5,000	$4,500	$4,000	$3,000	$2,200	$1,600	$1,300	$1,000	$700	$500	$400

Add $1,000 for original pasteboard box and accessories.

BEALS' THIRD MODEL POCKET REVOLVER - .31 cal. perc., 5 shot, smooth cylinder, 4 in. octagon barrel, blue finish, two-piece hard rubber grips, spur trigger, first Remington revolver with loading lever. Less than 1,000 mfg. 1859-1860.

100%	98%	95%	90%	80%	70%	60%	50%	40%	30%	20%	10%
N/A	$4,250	$4,000	$3,250	$3,000	$2,500	$2,000	$900	$800	$750	$600	$500

Add $1,000 for original pasteboard box and accessories.

BEALS' NAVY REVOLVER - .36 cal. perc., 6 shot, smooth cylinder, 7 1/2 in. octagon barrel, blue finish, two-piece walnut grips, some martially marked with inspector's initials and cartouche on grips. Approx. 15,000 produced, 1861-62. Barrel address is "Beals' Patent, Sept. 14, 1858 - Manufactured by Remingtons', Ilion, N.Y."

* ***Beals' Navy Revolver Martial/Commercial Model - not martially marked*** - single wing base pin (very rare), less than 400 mfg. Serial range under 400, very desirable.

100%	98%	95%	90%	80%	70%	60%	50%	40%	30%	20%	10%
N/A	$7,500	$6,500	$4,750	$3,000	$2,500	$2,000	$1,800	$1,500	$1,300	$1,100	$1,000

Add $1,250 for original pasteboard box and accessories.
Subtract 20% for rimfire cartridge conversion.

* ***Beals' Navy Revolver Martial/Commercial Model - not martially marked*** - several variations with approx. serialization 1-15,500, most were purchased by military but were not inspected.

100%	98%	95%	90%	80%	70%	60%	50%	40%	30%	20%	10%
N/A	$7,000	$6,000	$4,500	$3,000	$2,400	$2,000	$1,700	$1,400	$1,200	$1,000	$900

Add $1,250 for original pasteboard box and accessories.
Subtract 20% for rimfire cartridge conversion.

* ***Beals' Navy Revolver (clearly) Martially Marked*** - serial range 13,500 to approx. 16,000. Approx. 500 mfg.

100%	98%	95%	90%	80%	70%	60%	50%	40%	30%	20%	10%
N/A	$8,000	$6,500	$5,500	$3,500	$3,000	$2,500	$2,000	$1,750	$1,500	$1,200	$1,000

Subtract 20% for rimfire cartridge conversion.

BEALS' ARMY REVOLVER - .44 cal. perc., 6 shot, smooth cylinder, 8 in. octagon barrel, blue finish, two-piece walnut grips. Barrel address is "Beals' Patent, Sept. 14, 1858 - Manufactured by Remingtons', Ilion, N.Y."

* ***Beal's Army Revolver Martial/Commercial Model - not martially marked*** - .44 cal. perc., 6 shot, smooth cylinder, 8 in. octagon barrel, blue finish, two-piece walnut grips. Barrel address is "Beals' Patent, Sept. 14, 1858 - Manufactured by Remingtons', Ilion, N.Y."

100%	98%	95%	90%	80%	70%	60%	50%	40%	30%	20%	10%
N/A	$7,000	$6,500	$5,000	$3,500	$2,500	$2,000	$1,750	$1,500	$1,300	$1,000	$800

Add $1,250 for original pasteboard box and accessories.
Subtract 20% for conversion to metallic cartridge.

* ***Beals' Army Revolver (clearly) Martially marked*** - serial range is approx. 850-1,900 inspected by "WAT" or "CGC", very desirable. Approx. 1,000 mfg.

100%	98%	95%	90%	80%	70%	60%	50%	40%	30%	20%	10%
N/A	$9,000	$8,000	$7,000	$5,000	$4,000	$3,500	$3,000	$2,250	$2,000	$1,500	$1,250

Subtract 20% for converstion to metallic cartridge.

100%	98%	95%	90%	80%	70%	60%	50%	40%	30%	20%	10%

RIDER'S DOUBLE-ACTION POCKET REVOLVER – .31 cal. perc., 5 shot, unusual "mushroom-shaped" cylinder, 3 in. octagon barrel, blue finish, two-piece hard rubber grips, brass trigger guard, no loading lever. One of the earliest double action handguns produced. Approx. 20,000 produced, 1860-1870.

N/A	$2,250	$2,000	$1,800	$1,400	$1,000	$800	$700	$600	$500	$400	$300

Subtract 20% for conversion to metallic cartridge.
Add $800 for original pasteboard box and accessories.

RIDER'S SINGLE-SHOT BRASS PARLOR PISTOL – .17 cal. perc., all brass construction, grips included. Fewer than 1,000 produced, 1859-1860. MANY FAKES! Caveat emptor.

N/A	$9,000	$8,500	$7,500	$6,000	$4,000	$3,000	$2,500	$2,000	$1,750	$1,500	$1,250

MODEL 1861 (ELLIOT'S PATENT) NAVY REVOLVER – .36 cal. perc., 6 shot, unfluted cylinder, 7 1/2 in. octagon barrel, blue finish, two-piece walnut grips. Loading lever has slot allowing cylinder pin to be pulled forward without lowering lever. Approx. 6,000 produced 1862-63 in serial range approx. 15,000-21,000. Barrel address "Patented Dec. 17, 1861, 1858 - Manufactured by Remingtons', Ilion, N.Y."

* ***Model 1861 Navy Revolver Martial/Commercial Model - Not Martially Marked***

N/A	$5,500	$4,750	$4,000	$3,500	$3,000	$2,500	$2,000	$1,750	$1,500	$1,100	$900

Subtract 20% for conversion to metallic cartridge.

* ***Model 1861 Navy Revolver (clearly) Martially marked*** – over 4,000 martially inspected "CGC".

N/A	$8,000	$7,750	$6,500	$4,000	$2,750	$2,250	$2,000	$1,750	$1,500	$1,250	$900

MODEL 1861 (ELLIOT'S PATENT) ARMY REVOLVER (clearly) Martially Marked – .44 cal. perc., 6 shot, unfluted cylinder, 8 in. octagon barrel, blue finish, two-piece walnut grips. Majority are martially inspected "CGC". Loading lever has slot allowing cylinder pin to be pulled forward without lowering lever. Approx. 10,000 produced 1862-63 in approx. serial range 1,900-12,000. Barrel address "Patented Dec. 17, 1861, 1858 - Manufactured by Remingtons', Ilion, N.Y."

N/A	$8,500	$8,000	$7,000	$4,500	$3,000	$2,500	$2,250	$1,750	$1,500	$1,250	$900

Subtract 20% for conversion to metallic cartridge.

NEW MODEL ARMY REVOLVER – .44 cal. perc., 6 shot, unfluted cylinder, 8 in. octagon barrel, blue finish, two-piece walnut grips. Approx. 135,000 produced 1863-1888 in serial range 12,000-148,000. Barrel address "Patented Sept. 14, 1858 - Manufactured by Remingtons', Ilion, N.Y. - New Model." Early models lack "New Model" markings on barrel and have transition features from "1861" model. Erroneously called the "Remington Model 1858 Revolver."

N/A	$8,500	$8,000	$7,000	$4,500	$3,000	$2,500	$2,250	$1,750	$1,500	$1,250	$900

Subtract 20% for conversion to metallic cartridge (most are in .46 rimfire).
Subtract 25% if not martially inspected and cartouched.

NEW MODEL NAVY REVOLVER – .36 cal. perc., 6 shot, unfluted cylinder, 7 1/2 in. octagon barrel, blue finish, two-piece walnut grips. Approx. 18,000 produced in percussion from 1863-1878 with serial range 21,000-48,000. None were martially marked at time of mfg. Approx. 4,000 were purchased by U.S. Navy during 1863-65 in serial range 21,000-32,000. Barrel address "Patented Sept. 14, 1858 - Manufactured by Remingtons', Ilion, N.Y. - New Model." Early specimens lack "New Model" markings on barrel and have transition features from "1861" model.

N/A	$7,000	$6,750	$4,750	$3,750	$2,250	$1,800	$1,500	$1,400	$1,200	$900	$750

Subtract 20% for conversion to metallic cartridge (most are in .38 rimfire).
Subtract 25% if not martially inspected and cartouched.

NEW MODEL BELT REVOLVER, SINGLE ACTION – .36 cal. perc., 6 shot, unfluted or fluted cylinder, 6 1/2 in. octagon barrel, blue or nickel finish, two-piece walnut grips. Approx. 5,000 produced 1863-72.

N/A	$5,000	$4,500	$4,000	$3,000	$2,250	$1,900	$1,500	$1,300	$1,100	$900	$800

Add 30% for fluted cylinder (with cylinder numbered to the gun).
Add $1,000 for original pasteboard box with original label.
Subtract 20% for conversion to metallic cartridge (mfg. 1870-1886).

NEW MODEL BELT REVOLVER, DOUBLE ACTION – .36 cal. perc., 6 shot, smooth or fluted cylinder, 6 1/2 in. octagon barrel, blue or nickel finish, two-piece walnut grips. Approx. 2,500 produced 1863-72.

N/A	$5,000	$4,500	$4,000	$3,000	$2,250	$1,900	$1,500	$1,300	$1,100	$900	$800

Add 30% for fluted cylinder (most are not numbered to the gun).
Add $1,000 for original pasteboard box with original label.
Subtract 20% for conversion to metallic cartridge.

100%	98%	95%	90%	80%	70%	60%	50%	40%	30%	20%	10%

NEW MODEL POLICE REVOLVER – .36 cal. perc., 5 shot, smooth cylinder, 3 to 6 1/2 in. octagon barrels, blue or nickel finish, two-piece walnut grips. Approx. 18,000 produced 1863-1872.

N/A	$4,800	$4,400	$3,750	$2,750	$2,000	$1,750	$1,400	$1,200	$1,000	$850	$750

Add 10% for 6 1/2 in. barrel.
Add $1,000 for original pasteboard box with original label.
Subtract 20% for conversion to metallic cartridge.

NEW MODEL POCKET REVOLVER – .31 cal. perc., 5 shot, smooth cylinder, spur trigger, 3 to 4 1/2 in. octagon barrel, blue or nickel finish, two-piece walnut grips. Approx. 25,000 produced, 1863-1888.

N/A	$4,800	$4,400	$3,750	$2,750	$2,000	$1,750	$1,400	$1,200	$1,000	$850	$750

Add 25% for brass frame.
Add $1,000 for original pasteboard box with original label.
Subtract 20% for conversion to metallic cartridge.

ELLIOT'S "ZIG-ZAG" DERRINGER – .22 short rimfire cartridge, 6 shot, 6 barrel cluster (rotating), ring trigger, 3 in. barrel cluster, blue barrel finish/silver frame most commonly encountered, two-piece Gutta-Percha (hard rubber) grips. Less than 1,000 produced, long production from 1861 to early 1870s indicated by several nickel examples found in higher serial numbers, obsoleted nearly immediately with the introduction of the simpler design and cost of the Elliott 5 shot. Reputed to be Remington's first cartridge handgun. William Elliot's patent, desirable.

N/A	$6,000	$5,000	$4,000	$3,000	$2,400	$2,200	$2,000	$1,800	$1,500	$1,250	$1,000

Add $1,500 for original pasteboard box with original label.

ELLIOT'S SINGLE SHOT "MISSISSIPPI" DERRINGER – .41 RF cal., single shot, 2 1/2 in. round barrel, spur trigger, walnut two-piece grips, blue and/or nickel finish. Approx. 10,000 produced, 1867-1888. Also known as the "Mississippi Derringer."

N/A	$3,000	$2,750	$2,250	$2,000	$1,500	$1,250	$1,000	$900	$700	$600	$500

ELLIOT'S FIVE SHOT "RING TRIGGER" DERRINGER – .22 short rimfire cartridge, 5 shot, 5 barrel cluster (fixed), 3 in. barrel cluster, blue finish, two-piece Gutta-Purcha, walnut, ivory or pearl grips, ring trigger. Approx. 10,000 produced (combined production total with .32 cal.).

N/A	$5,000	$4,750	$3,500	$2,500	$2,250	$2,000	$1,750	$1,500	$1,400	$1,200	$950

Add $1,000 for original pasteboard box with original label.

ELLIOT'S FOUR SHOT "RING TRIGGER" DERRINGER – cartridge .32 RF cal., 4 shot, 4 barrel cluster (fixed), ring trigger, 3 3/8 in. barrel cluster, blue finish, two-piece Gutta-Purcha, walnut, ivory or pearl grips. Approx. 25,000 produced with 2 frame styles observed. Frame sides lowered similar to the .22 ring trigger pistols in serials after approximately 18,000.

N/A	$5,000	$4,750	$3,500	$2,500	$2,250	$2,000	$1,750	$1,500	$1,400	$1,200	$950

Add $1,000 for original pasteboard box with original label.

VEST POCKET PISTOL – RF .22, .30, .32, or .41 cal., single shot, various barrel lengths, blue or nickel (post 1870) finish, two-piece walnut grips, spur trigger. Rider's patent.

* ***Vest Pocket Pistol .22 Rimfire*** – approx. 20,000 produced, 1865-1888, early models are unmarked. Beware...many copied by European gunmakers.

N/A	$2,500	$2,000	$1,750	$1,400	$1,250	$1,000	$800	$600	$500	$400	$300

Subtract 25% for guns lacking company name.
Add $1,000 for original pasteboard box with original label.

* ***Vest Pocket Pistol .30 or .32 Rimfire*** – approx. 18,000 mfg. 1865-1888. Copied by European gunmakers.

N/A	$3,000	$2,750	$2,200	$1,700	$1,200	$1,000	$800	$700	$600	$500	$400

Early brass frame or .30 rimfire cal. will bring a premium.
Add $1,000 for original pasteboard box with original label.

* ***Vest Pocket Pistol .41 Rimfire*** – approx. 25,000 produced, 1865-1888. Copied by European gunmakers.

N/A	$3,100	$2,800	$2,100	$1,600	$1,100	$1,000	$900	$700	$600	$500	$400

Add $1,000 for original pasteboard box with original label.

ELLIOT'S O/U DERRINGER – .41 rimfire cal., 2 shot, 3 in. superimposed barrels, oscillating firing pin, spur trigger, many finishes, hard rubber, rosewood, walnut, ivory, pearl, or other two-piece grips. Approx. 112,000 produced between 1867 and 1935. William Elliot's patent.

Subtract 50% if barrel hinge is cracked.
Add 25% for original pasteboard box with original label.

The dates on the following sub-models are estimates calculated after examining original sales receipts found with guns in factory boxes which were then compared to the numbers of guns manufactured each year.

100%	98%	95%	90%	80%	70%	60%	50%	40%	30%	20%	10%

* ***E. Remington & Sons Production 1867-1888*** – first 100 made with side address: "MANUFACTURED BY E. REMINGTON & SONS ILION, NY", maker's name and patent data stamped between the barrels, no extractor, made for patent holder William H. Elliot, and sold independently from the manufacturer.

» **Manufactured by E. Remington & Sons Ilion NY Side Address** – first 100 made with side address for patent holder William H. Elliot, and sold independently from the manufacturer. Extremely hard to find in any condition. Maker's name and patent data stamped between the barrels, w/o extractor.

N/A	N/A	$8,000	$6,000	$5,000	$4,000	$3,500	$3,000	$2,750	$2,500	$2,250	$2,000

» **E. Remington & Sons. Ilion. N.Y. Side Address (1868-1869)** – maker's name and patent data stamped between the barrels, made without an extractor (about 1,600 produced).

N/A	N/A	$5,000	$3,000	$2,500	$2,000	$1,500	$1,250	$1,000	$900	$800	$700

» **E. Remington & Sons. Ilion. N.Y. Side Address (1868-1869)** – made with extractor (possibly more than 300 made).

N/A	N/A	$6,000	$4,500	$3,000	$2,500	$2,250	$2,000	$1,750	$1,500	$1,250	$1,000

» **Remingtons Ilion N.Y. U.S.A. Side Address (1868-1869)** – made without an extractor (around 130 mfg.), very rare.

N/A	N/A	$12,000	$10,000	$8,000	$6,000	$5,000	$4,250	$3,750	$3,000	$2,750	$2,500

» **Remingtons Ilion N.Y. U.S.A. Side Address (1868-1869)** – made with extractor (perhaps 20 made).

N/A	N/A	$9,000	$7,500	$6,000	$5,000	$4,000	$3,000	$2,500	$2,250	$1,750	$1,250

* ***E. Remington & Sons. Ilion. N.Y. Elliot's Patent Dec. 12th 1865 Two Line Address (Top of Barrel, 1870-1888)*** – made with extractor (12,000 to 18,000 produced between 1870 and 1888), sequential numbering ended within this address.

N/A	N/A	$4,000	$3,500	$3,000	$2,000	$1,750	$1,500	$1,250	$1,000	$800	$500

* ***Remington Arms Company Production (1889-1910)*** – there are six address variations during this production period. All are batch numbered.

Add 25% for slant-line gap (very scarce).

Add 25% for original cardboard box.

» **Remington Arms Co. Ilion. N.Y. Side Address (1889-1893)** – first address, short line, all are batch numbered, estimated production of 8,000.

N/A	N/A	$4,000	$3,500	$2,500	$1,750	$1,250	$1,000	$900	$600	$500	$300

» **Remington Arms Co. Ilion. N.Y. Side Address (1894-1898)** – second address, slant line, estimated production of 14,500.

N/A	N/A	$4,000	$3,500	$2,500	$1,750	$1,250	$1,000	$900	$600	$500	$300

» **Remington Arms C O. Ilion, N.Y. Side Address (1899)** – third address, slant line (C O gap), estimated production of 2,200.

N/A	N/A	$4,000	$3,500	$2,500	$1,750	$1,250	$1,000	$900	$600	$500	$300

» **Remington Arms Co. Ilion, N.Y. Side Address (1900-1903)** – fourth address, (big C, little o), estimated production of 12,000.

N/A	N/A	$4,000	$3,500	$2,500	$1,750	$1,250	$1,000	$900	$600	$500	$300

» **Remington Arms Co. Ilion. N.Y. Side Address (1904-1910)** – fifth address, (48mm long), estimated production of 8,000.

N/A	N/A	$4,000	$3,500	$2,500	$1,750	$1,250	$1,000	$900	$600	$500	$300

» **Remington Arms Co. Ilion, N. Y. Side Address (1904-1910)** – sixth address, (50mm gaps), estimated production is unknown.

N/A	N/A	$4,000	$3,500	$2,500	$1,750	$1,250	$1,000	$900	$600	$500	$300

* ***Remington Arms - U.M.C. CO. Ilion, N.Y. (1911-1935)*** – sequential numbering resumes.

Add 25% for original cardboard box.

» **Remington Arms - U.M.C.CO. Ilion, N.Y. First Variation (1911)** – no "L" serial number prefix, numbered 1-3000.

N/A	N/A	$4,750	$3,750	$3,000	$2,500	$2,000	$1,500	$1,000	$750	$400	$300

100%	98%	95%	90%	80%	70%	60%	50%	40%	30%	20%	10%

» **Remington Arms - U.M.C.CO. Ilion, N.Y. Second Variation 1911-1935** – "L" serial number prefix, numbered in two series from L90XXX-L99999 and the later group L75XXX-L76XXX, these are guns with the rib between the barrels, approx. 27,000 mfg.

100%	98%	95%	90%	80%	70%	60%	50%	40%	30%	20%	10%
N/A	N/A	$3,250	$2,500	$2,000	$1,500	$1,200	$900	$600	$500	$400	$300

» **Remington Arms - U.M.C.CO. Ilion, N.Y. Third Variation Monoblocks (1929-1935)** – these are among the last produced Remington Double Deringers and do NOT have ribs between the barrels, the rib area formerly now has been "fluted" with smooth contouring. Approx. 500 mfg.

100%	98%	95%	90%	80%	70%	60%	50%	40%	30%	20%	10%
N/A	N/A	$3,250	$2,500	$2,000	$1,500	$1,200	$900	$600	$500	$400	$300

MODEL 1866 NAVY ROLLING BLOCK PISTOL – .50 RF cal., single shot, 8 1/2 in. round barrel, spur trigger, walnut grip and forearm, blue finish. Approx. 6,500 produced, 1866-67. Erroneously designated as, "Model of 1865 Navy". Most of these pistols were later modified for the U.S. Navy (becoming the Model 1870 Navy), and as a result, the original Model 1866 Navy Pistols are quite rare!

* ***Model 1866 Navy Rolling Block Pistol Martially Marked***

100%	98%	95%	90%	80%	70%	60%	50%	40%	30%	20%	10%
N/A	N/A	$7,000	$6,000	$4,500	$4,000	$3,500	$3,000	$2,500	$2,000	$1,750	$1,500

Subtract 30% if not martially marked (A Commercial Model was mfg. 1866-1868).
Subtract 25% for pistols with a centerfire breech block.

Fewer than 150 remain in original condition. Martially marked specimens are very rarely encountered.

COMBINATION PISTOL-SHOTGUN – 20 ga., 11 3/4 in. single barrel with smoothbore, rolling block action, designed as a pistol or shotgun (with detachable shoulder stock). Mfg. circa mid-1920s by an unknown manufacturer (possibly Bannerman's). Rolling block receivers appear to have been from foreign made military rifles.

Extreme rarity factor precludes accurate pricing information.

In either configuration, this model is an NFA firearm that cannot be legally owned unless previously registered with the BATFE.

MODEL 1870 NAVY ROLLING BLOCK PISTOL – .50 CF cal., single shot, 7 in. round barrel, standard trigger with trigger guard, walnut grip and forearm, blue finish. Approx. 6,400 produced 1870-75. Modified by Remington from the Navy Model 1866 pistols.

100%	98%	95%	90%	80%	70%	60%	50%	40%	30%	20%	10%
N/A	N/A	$4,000	$3,000	$2,500	$1,800	$1,500	$1,300	$1,200	$1,100	$1,000	$900

Add approx. 20% for 8 in. commercial version (approx. 200-400 mfg.) without inspector's marks.

MODEL 1871 ARMY ROLLING BLOCK PISTOL – .50 centerfire cal., single shot, 8 in. round barrel, standard trigger with trigger guard, walnut grip and forearm, blue finish. Approx. 5,000 produced, 1871-72.

100%	98%	95%	90%	80%	70%	60%	50%	40%	30%	20%	10%
N/A	$4,000	$3,750	$3,000	$2,500	$2,000	$1,750	$1,500	$1,400	$1,100	$1,000	$900

Subtract 10% for Commercial Model w/o military markings and cartouche.

Smoothbored version was authorized by the U.S. Ordnance Department.

MODEL OF 1887 PLINKER ROLLING BLOCK PISTOL – .22, .25 RF and .32, .50 CF cals., single shot, utilizing surplus Model 1871 Army rolling block frames, 8 in. round barrel, standard trigger with trigger guard, walnut grip and forearm, blue finish. Approx. 800 mfg. 1887-91.

100%	98%	95%	90%	80%	70%	60%	50%	40%	30%	20%	10%
N/A	$3,000	$2,500	$2,000	$1,750	$1,500	$1,250	$1,000	$900	$800	$700	$600

Add 10% for Navy rolling block framed.

Navy framed 1887s are discernible by military proofs on right side of frame, Remington altered from original Navy Model 1870. Estimated mfg. of 100.

MODEL 1891 TARGET MODEL ROLLING BLOCK PISTOL – .22, .25 RF and .32 CF cals., single shot, 10 in. part octagon, part round barrel, standard trigger with trigger guard, smooth walnut grip and forearm, blue finish. Limited mfg. of 116 between 1891-1900.

100%	98%	95%	90%	80%	70%	60%	50%	40%	30%	20%	10%
N/A	$3,000	$2,750	$2,250	$1,750	$1,500	$1,250	$1,000	$800	$700	$600	$500

Removing the grips on this model may reveal a 4-digit number, indicating the refurbished military action.

MODEL 1901 TARGET ROLLING BLOCK PISTOL – .22 S and L, .25 RF, .32 CF, or .44 S&W Russian cal., single shot, 10 in. part octagon, part round barrel, standard trigger with trigger guard, checkered walnut grip and forearm, blue finish. Limited mfg. of only 734 sold between 1901-1909.

100%	98%	95%	90%	80%	70%	60%	50%	40%	30%	20%	10%
N/A	$3,500	$3,000	$2,500	$2,000	$1,500	$1,250	$1,000	$900	$800	$700	$600

Add $200 for .44 S&W Russian cal.

Removing the grips on this model may reveal a 4-digit number, indicating the refurbished military action.

100%	98%	95%	90%	80%	70%	60%	50%	40%	30%	20%	10%

REMINGTON-RIDER'S MAGAZINE PISTOL - .32 RF cal., 5 shot, 3 in. octagonal barrel, spur trigger, walnut, rosewood, ivory or pearl grips. Limited mfg. 1871-1888.

N/A	$3,000	$2,750	$2,500	$1,500	$1,400	$1,200	$1,000	$850	$750	$650	$500

Add 75% for original case hardened receiver and blued barrel.

Beware of faked blued finish. Most of this model were engraved, and a non-engraved specimen, while rare, is not necessarily more desirable.

NO. 1 (SMOOT'S PATENT) REVOLVER - .30 rimfire cal., 5 shot, 2 3/4 in. octagon barrel, spur trigger, walnut, hard rubber, pearl or ivory two-piece grips. Number produced debatable, 1873-1888.

N/A	$2,000	$1,800	$1,300	$900	$800	$600	$500	$400	$380	$350	$300

Add 30% on early No. 1s with revolving recoil shield.
Add 50% for original pasteboard box with label.

Nearly all were nickel plated. Beware of faked blue finish - a number have come on the market in the past few years.

On Number 1 through Number 4 Revolvers, ivory grips refer to Remington Celluloid, not genuine ivory. Only in rare instances does ivory appear.

NO. 2 (SMOOT'S PATENT) REVOLVER - .30 or .32 rimfire cal., 5 shot, 2 3/4 in. octagon barrel, spur trigger, hard rubber, pearl or ivory two-piece grips. Number produced debatable, 1873-1888.

N/A	$2,000	$1,800	$1,300	$900	$800	$600	$500	$400	$380	$350	$300

Add 50% for original pasteboard box with label.

Nearly all were nickel plated. Beware of fake blue finish. A number have come on the market in the past few years.

NO. 3 (SMOOT'S PATENT) REVOLVER - .38 rimfire or centerfire cal., 3 3/4 in. octagon barrel with or without barrel rib, spur trigger, hard rubber, ivory or pearl two-piece grips, "Bird-Head and Saw Handle" grip frame with Remington logo "R" on the "saw handle" hard rubber grips, Bird-Head referred to models with or without a barrel rib. Number produced debatable, 1875-1888.

N/A	$2,000	$1,800	$1,300	$900	$800	$600	$500	$400	$380	$350	$300

Add a small premium for centerfire calibers.
Add 50% for original pasteboard box with label.

Nearly all were nickel plated. Beware of fake blue finish. A number have come on the market in the past few years.

NO. 4 REVOLVER - .38 and .41 rimfire or centerfire cals., 5 shot, 2 1/2 in. round barrel, hard rubber, pearl or ivory two-piece grips. Number produced debatable, 1877-1888.

N/A	$2,000	$1,800	$1,300	$900	$800	$600	$500	$400	$380	$350	$300

Add a small premium for centerfire calibers.
Add 50% for original pasteboard box with label.

Nearly all were nickel plated. Beware of faked blue finish. A number have come on the market in the past few years.

IROQUOIS REVOLVER - .22 rimfire cal., 7 shot, 2 1/4 in. round barrel, spur trigger, hard rubber, pearl, or ivory two-piece grips, nickel finish, fluted or non-fluted cylinder. Approx. 10,000 produced 1878-1888.

N/A	$2,200	$2,000	$1,800	$1,500	$1,300	$1,000	$850	$750	$600	$450	$375

Subtract 25% if unmarked.
Add 25% for fluted cylinder.
Add 50% for original pasteboard box with label.
Add 50% for original factory engraving.

Nearly all were nickel plated. Beware of faked blue finish.

MODEL 1875 SINGLE ACTION "FRONTIER" REVOLVER - .44 Rem., .44-40 Win., or .45 Colt centerfire cal., 6 shot, 7 1/2 or 5 3/4 (scarce) in. round barrel, standard trigger with trigger guard, blue or nickel finish, walnut, ivory, or pearl two-piece grips, serial numbered in at least two batches. Approx. 30,000-40,000 produced, 1875-1888.

N/A	$10,000	$9,000	$6,000	$4,000	$3,000	$2,500	$2,250	$2,000	$1,500	$1,250	$1,000

Add 25% for blue finish.
Add 50% for U.S.I.D. "Indian Police" markings (beware of fakes).
Add 10% for .45 cal.
Add $1,500 for original passteboard box and label.

There is some debate over originality of the 5 3/4 in. barrel - some are known, but many were altered post-factory. Never cataloged.

100%	98%	95%	90%	80%	70%	60%	50%	40%	30%	20%	10%

MODEL 1888 SINGLE ACTION REVOLVER – .44 centerfire cal., resembles 1890 SA, has "E. Remington & Sons" barrel address, 5 3/4 in. barrel, nickel finish with walnut grips, very desirable and little known.

100%	98%	95%	90%	80%	70%	60%	50%	40%	30%	20%	10%
N/A	$10,000	$9,000	$6,000	$4,000	$3,000	$2,500	$2,250	$2,000	$1,500	$1,250	$1,000

This model was never listed in a Remington catalog nor price list. Rather, it first appeared in a Hartley & Graham ad in late 1888. This revolver was made from parts of Models 1875 & 1890 pistols. Model nomenclature was created by collectors, not the factory.

MODEL 1890 SINGLE ACTION REVOLVER – .44-40 WCF cal., 6 shot, 7 1/2 or 5 3/4 in. round barrel, standard trigger with trigger guard, hard rubber two-piece grips with Remington monogram, ivory or pearl grips on special order, blue or nickel finish. Approx. 2,000 produced, 1891-1894.

100%	98%	95%	90%	80%	70%	60%	50%	40%	30%	20%	10%
N/A	$10,000	$9,000	$6,000	$4,000	$3,000	$2,500	$2,250	$2,000	$1,500	$1,250	$1,000

Add 25% for blue finish.

Add $1,500 for original pasteboard box and label.

MODEL 51 SEMI-AUTO – .32 ACP or .380 ACP cal., 8 shot (7 in mag., 1 in chamber), hard rubber 2-piece grips with company's name, black finish. Approx. 65,000 mfg. 1918-1926.

100%	98%	95%	90%	80%	70%	60%	50%	40%	30%	20%	10%
$900	$800	$700	$600	$400	$350	$300	$250	$225	$200	$175	$160

Add $250 for original box, brochure, oiler, and cleaning rod.

Some fakes are now on the market.

Although the .380 ACP cal. is much more common than .32 ACP cal., it commands a slight premium.

MODEL 1911 REMINGTON - UMC – .45 ACP cal., WWI M1911 military contract, over 21,500 mfg. (ser. numbered 1-21,676) in 1918-19 only, blue finish.

100%	98%	95%	90%	80%	70%	60%	50%	40%	30%	20%	10%
N/A	$6,000	$5,000	$4,500	$3,000	$2,500	$2,000	$1,800	$1,600	$1,400	$1,200	$1,000

Many 98%-100% specimens encountered in this model have been professionally refinished - be careful.

MODEL 1911A1 REMINGTON RAND – approx. 1,086,624 mfg. between 1943-1945 in Syracuse, NY. Ser. no. ranges 916,405-1,041,404, 1,279,649-1,441,430, 1,471,431-1,609,528, 1,743,847-1,816,641, 1,890,504-2,075,103, 2,134,404-2,244,803, and 2,380,014-2,619,013, parkerized finish. Mfg. during WWII by Remington Rand Corp.

100%	98%	95%	90%	80%	70%	60%	50%	40%	30%	20%	10%
$2,500	$2,100	$1,900	$1,500	$1,200	$1,000	$900	$750	$650	$550	$450	$395

Add 20% with original cardboard shipping carton (watch for fakes).

These pistols were not made by Remington Arms Company during the war - Remington Rand was originally the Remington Standard Typewriter Company which was sold by E. Remington & Sons in 1884.

MARK III SIGNAL PISTOL – 10 ga., single shot, brass frame, 9 in. round steel barrel, spur trigger, walnut 2-piece grips. Approx. 25,000 produced, 1915-18.

100%	98%	95%	90%	80%	70%	60%	50%	40%	30%	20%	10%
$900	$850	$600	$400	$275	$250	$225	$200	$180	$160	$150	$125

Add $250 for original WWI canvas web belt, canvas holster, and canvas cartridge pouch.

GRADING - PPGS™	100%	98%	95%	90%	80%	70%	60%	LAST MSR

PISTOLS: BOLT ACTION

MODEL 700-CP – .300 AAC Blackout, .308 Win., 6.5 Creedmoor, or .223 Rem. cal., Rem. 700 action, aluminum frame, 10 1/2 or 12 1/2 in. light contour carbon steel threaded barrel with thread protector, 10 shot mag., X-Mark Pro adj. trigger, rear QD mount or SBA3 arm brace, QD sling plate adapter, Magpul MIAD pistol grip, forged aluminum Remington Precision chassis, M-LOK compatible free float aluminum handguard, full Picatinny rail for optics mounting, oversized bolt know, hardcoat anodized black finish, 6.3 oz. Mfg. 2019-2020.

100%	98%	95%	90%	80%	70%	60%	LAST MSR
$875	$765	$650	$600	$485	$400	$325	*$1,020*

PISTOLS: SEMI-AUTO, POST-WWII PRODUCTION

MODEL 1911 R1 – .45 ACP cal., SA, 5 in. satin stainless steel barrel, high polish blue slide and frame, checkered double diamond walnut grips, 7 shot mag., rear slide serrations, fixed sights, Remington logo on left side of slide, and 1911 R1 on right side of slide, 38 1/2 oz. Mfg. in USA mid-2010-2020.

100%	98%	95%	90%	80%	70%	60%	LAST MSR
$660	$580	$500	$450	$365	$300	$250	*$774*

* ***Model 1911 R1 Commander*** – .45 ACP cal., SA, 4 1/4 in. barrel, 7 shot mag., otherwise similar to Model 1911 R1. Mfg. 2014-2020.

100%	98%	95%	90%	80%	70%	60%	LAST MSR
$635	$550	$475	$430	$350	$285	$250	*$744*

* ***Model 1911 R1 Stainless*** – .45 ACP cal., SA, similar to Model 1911 R1, except features all stainless steel construction, 38 1/2 oz. Mfg. 2012-2020.

100%	98%	95%	90%	80%	70%	60%	LAST MSR
$715	$625	$535	$485	$395	$325	$275	*$837*

GRADING - PPGS™	100%	98%	95%	90%	80%	70%	60%	LAST MSR

MODEL 1911 R1 CARRY – .45 ACP cal., SA, 5 in. stainless steel match grade barrel and bushing, one 7 shot and one 8 shot mag., steel construction, bobbed hammer, skeletonized aluminum trigger, Novak low profile sights with Tritium front sight, partially checkered cocobolo grips, ambidextrous safety, beavertail grip safety, satin black oxide finish, 38 1/2 oz. Mfg. 2013-2017.

	$925	$800	$700	$600	$550	$495	$450	*$1,067*

MODEL 1911 R1 CARRY COMMANDER – .45 ACP cal., SA, de-horned forged carbon steel frame and slide, satin black oxide finish, 4 1/4 in. match grade stainless steel barrel with target crown, includes two 7 shot mags., lowered and flared ejection port, enhanced hammer, adj. machine skeletonized aluminum match trigger, Novak sights with Tritium front night sight, checkered front strap and mainspring housing, cocobolo grips, beavertail grip safety with checkered memory bump, ambidextrous safety. Mfg. mid-2013-2017.

	$925	$800	$700	$600	$550	$495	$450	*$1,067*

Add $283 for Crimson Trace laser sight (new 2014).

MODEL 1911 R1 ENHANCED – 9mm Para. (new 2014) or .45 ACP cal., SA, steel construction with blued finish, 5 in. barrel, 8 or 9 (9mm Para.) shot mag., front and rear slide serrations, skeletonized trigger, bobbed hammer, checkered black laminate grips, low profile rear sight and fiber optic front sight, 40 oz. Mfg. 2013-2020.

	$795	$700	$600	$550	$500	$450	$400	*$903*

Add $226 for Crimson Trace laser sight (.45 ACP cal. only), new 2014.

* ***Model 1911 R1 Enhanced Double Stack*** – .45 ACP cal., stainless steel frame and carbon steel slide, 5 in. stainless steel barrel, 15 shot, anodized aluminum match grade trigger, adj. rear and red fiber optic front sights, G10 grips, beavertail grip safety, front and rear slide serrations, 41 oz. Mfg. 2018-2020.

	$850	$750	$650	$595	$500	$450	$400	*$999*

* ***Model 1911 R1 Enhanced Stainless*** – .45 ACP cal., SA, 5 in. barrel, all stainless steel construction, features front and rear slide serrations, skeletonized trigger, bobbed hammer, checkered black laminate grips, 8 shot mag., low profile rear sight and fiber optic front sight, 40 oz. Mfg. 2013-2020.

	$850	$750	$650	$595	$475	$400	$325	*$990*

* ***Model 1911 R1 Enhanced Threaded Barrel*** – .45 ACP cal., SA, 5 3/4 in. threaded stainless steel barrel, all steel construction with blue finish, 8 shot mag., twin slide serrations, checkered black laminate grips, skeletonized trigger, bobbed hammer, 40 oz. Mfg. 2013-2020.

	$825	$725	$625	$550	$450	$375	$300	*$959*

MODEL 1911 R1 ENHANCED COMMANDER – .45 ACP cal., SA, carbon steel frame and slide, 4 1/4 in. match grade stainless steel barrel, two 8 shot mags., oversized and flared ejection port, adj. skeletonized trigger, red fiber optic front and Novak adj. rear sights, dark laminate grips, extended beavertail grip safety, black oxide finish, 38 oz. Mfg. 2015-2020.

	$795	$700	$600	$550	$500	$450	$400	*$903*

* ***Model 1911 R1 Enhanced Commander Stainless*** – .45 ACP cal., SA, similar to Model 1911 R1 Enhanced Commander, except has stainless steel frame and slide. Mfg. 2015-2020.

	$850	$750	$650	$595	$500	$450	$400	*$990*

MODEL 1911 R1 HUNTER – 10mm cal., SA, 6 in. stainless match grade barrel, two 8 shot stainless steel mags., stainless steel frame and slide, adj. skeletonized trigger, LPA fully adj. match sights, Operator II VZ G10 grips, extended beavertail grip safety, accessory rail, wide front and rear cocking serrations, black or FDE (new 2018) PVD finish. Mfg. mid-2016-2020.

	$1,195	$1,050	$925	$800	$700	$600	$500	*$1,310*

Add $30 for FDE finish (new 2018).

MODEL 1911 R1 LIMITED – 9mm Para. or .40 S&W cal., SA, stainless steel frame and slide, 5 in. match grade stainless steel barrel, 8 or 9 shot mag., G10 VZ operator grips, 38 oz. Mfg. 2017-2019.

	$1,095	$995	$875	$750	$650	$550	$450	*$1,250*

MODEL 1911 R1 LIMITED DOUBLE STACK – 9mm Para., .40 S&W, or .45 ACP cal., SA, stainless steel frame and slide, 5 in. ramped match grade stainless steel barrel, two double stack 16, 18, or 19 shot mags., oversized magwell, adj. match grade trigger, fiber optic front sight, fully adj. LPA target rear sight, G10 VZ operator grips, ambidextrous extended thumb safety, wide front and rear cocking serrations, full-length guide rod, checkered front strap and mainspring housing, 41 oz. Mfg. 2017-2020.

	$1,250	$1,075	$935	$800	$700	$600	$500	*$1,399*

GRADING - PPGS™	100%	98%	95%	90%	80%	70%	60%	LAST MSR

MODEL 1911 R1 RECON – 9mm Para. or .45 ACP cal., stainless steel frame, slide, and barrel, 4 1/4 in. ramped match grade barrel, 15 or 18 shot mag., adj. skeletonized trigger, Tritium night sights, G10 VZ Operator grips, ambidextrous extended thumb safety, wide front and rear cocking serrations, accessory rail, checkered mainspring housing, checkered front strap, PVD coating. Mfg. 2018-2020.

	$1,115	$1,000	$875	$750	$650	$550	$450	*$1,275*

MODEL 1911 R1 TACTICAL – .45 ACP cal., SA, stainless steel frame and slide, 5 in. match grade stainless steel barrel, 8 or 15 shot single or double stack mag., adj. match grade trigger, Trijicon front and rear night sights, G10 VZ operator grips, ambidextrous extended thumb safety, wide front and rear cocking serrations, checkered mainspring housing, railed frame, 38-41 oz. Mfg. 2017-2020.

	$1,095	$995	$875	$750	$650	$550	$450	*$1,250*

Add $25 for threaded barrel (Double Stack model only).
Add $49 for Double Stack model.

MODEL 1911 R1 TOMASIE – .40 S&W cal., SA, stainless steel frame and slide, 5 in. match grade stainless steel barrel, 18 shot mag., G10 VZ operator grips, 41 oz. Mfg. 2017-2020.

	$1,475	$1,250	$1,025	$875	$775	$675	$575	*$1,650*

MODEL 1911 R1 ULTRALITE COMMANDER – .45 ACP cal., aluminum frame, 4 1/4 in. stainless steel barrel, 8 shot mag., adj. trigger, fiber optic front and adj. rear sight, checkered laminate grips, PVD finished slide, Type III hardcoat anodized black finish, 31 oz. Mfg. mid-2017-2020.

	$750	$650	$550	$495	$465	$435	$395	*$849*

MODEL 1911 R1 ULTRALIGHT EXECUTIVE – .45 ACP cal., aluminum frame, 3 1/2 in. stainless steel barrel, 7 shot, G10 grips, 28 oz. Mfg. 2018-2020.

	$1,095	$995	$875	$750	$650	$550	$450	*$1,250*

REMINGTON-UMC COMMEMORATIVE 1911 – .45 ACP cal., SA, historically accurate reproduction of the original Model 1911-UMC mfg. 1918-1919, features US Property marks, carbona bluing, period metal markings, UMC-type grips with large diamonds, "E" on trigger guard or slide, 1,000 mfg. during 2014 only in serial no. range UMC21677-UMC22677.

	$2,400	$2,150	$1,850	$1,600	$1,350	$1,125	$900	*$2,665*

MODEL 1911 R1 CENTENNIAL LIMITED EDITION – .45 ACP cal., SA, 5 in. stainless barrel, 7 shot mag., 14K gold plated bead front sight, diamond checkered walnut grips, anniversary engraving with 24Kt. gold banner on slide, carbona blue finish, special serial no. range starting at JB1855001, includes walnut presentation case, 38 1/2 oz. Limited mfg. 2011-2015.

	$2,000	$1,700	$1,450	$1,225	$1,050	$825	$725	*$2,250*

MODEL 1911 R1 - 200TH YEAR ANNIVERSARY COMMEMORATIVE – .45 ACP cal., SA, 5 in. stainless steel match barrel, includes two 7 shot round mags., Commemorative engraved walnut grips, Classic GI-style thumb safety, grip safety, and hammer, satin black oxide finish. Limited mfg. 2016 only.

	$695	$600	$525	$475	$450	$425	$395	*$835*

MODEL 1911 R1 - 200TH YEAR ANNIVERSARY LIMITED EDITION – .45 ACP cal., SA, 5 in. stainless steel match barrel, includes two 7 shot round mags., high polished C-Grade walnut grips, classic American style engraving and gold inlay, special serial number, high polished forged slide and frame. Limited to quantity of 2,016. Limited mfg. 2016 only.

	$1,450	$1,275	$1,125	$1,000	$875	$775	$675	*$1,649*

MODEL R51 – 9mm Para. +P cal., SA, aluminum frame with black stainless slide, 3.4 in. stainless steel barrel, low profile fixed sights, 7 shot mag., ambidextrous grip safety, skeletonized trigger, lowered and flared ejection port, interchangeable grips, checkered front grip strap, 22 oz. Mfg. 2014-2015, reintroduced 2017-2019

	$385	$335	$295	$260	$210	$175	$135	*$448*

Add $200 for Crimson Trace laser sight mounted on front of trigger guard (non-Picatinny).

Early production R51s have been subject to a recall - please contact Remington at 1-800-243-9700 for the serial number range of this recall. R51 production restarted in late October 2014. All of the original production were recalled for safety retrofitting.

* ***Model R51 Smoke*** – 9mm Para. +P cal., aluminum frame with anodized gray (Smoke) finish, 3.4 in. match grade barrel, two flush 7 shot mags., slide has black FNC finish, single action trigger, 25% less muzzle flip, ergonomic design, checkered front strap. Mfg. 2018-2019.

	$395	$350	$300	$275	$215	$185	$150	*$460*

GRADING - PPGS™	100%	98%	95%	90%	80%	70%	60%	LAST MSR

MODEL RM380 MICRO – .380 ACP cal., SA, aluminum frame, 2.9 in. stainless steel barrel, 6 shot mag., fully ambidextrous mag. release, stainless steel slide, DAO trigger, snag-free sights, glass filled nylon grips, extended beavertail, checkered front strap, wide cocking serrations, fully functional slide stop, black, blue/silver (new 2018), or light blue/black Cerakote (new 2018) anodized finish, 12.2 oz. Mfg. 2016-2020.

	$285	$250	$215	$195	$155	$130	$100	*$328*

Add $20 for blue/silver (new 2018) or light blue/black (new 2018) frame finish.
Add $310 for Crimson Trace red touch button laser.

* ***Model RM380 Micro Executive*** – .380 ACP cal., DAO, stainless steel frame and slide, 2.9 in. ramped match grade stainless steel barrel, 6 shot mag., replaceable laminate grip panels, wide front and rear cocking serrations, accessory rail, low profile slide stop and ambi mag. release, anodized finish, 12.2 oz. Mfg. 2019-2020.

	$350	$300	$265	$250	$200	$175	$150	*$405*

* ***Model RM380 Micro Light Blue*** – .380 ACP cal., upgraded aluminum frame, 2.9 in. stainless steel barrel, 6 shot mag., magazine finger extension, replaceable grips, Light Blue/Stainless Cerakote finish, 12.2 oz. Mfg. 2019-2020.

	$355	$300	$265	$250	$200	$175	$150	*$415*

MODEL RP9 – 9mm Para. cal., SFO, black polymer frame, 4 1/2 in. stainless steel barrel with PVD finish, 10 (new 2017) or 18 shot double stack mag., reversible mag. release, dovetail front and rear sights or Tritium night sights (new 2020), black polymer grips, interchangeable back straps, Picatinny rail, loaded chamber indicator, 26.4 oz. Mfg. 2016-2020.

	$355	$300	$265	$250	$200	$175	$150	*$418*

Add $86 for Tritium night sights (new 2020).

MODEL RP45 – .45 ACP cal., SFO, black polymer frame, 4 1/2 in. stainless steel barrel with PVD finish, 10 (new 2018) or 15 shot double stack mag., reversible mag. release, flared and lowered ejection port, single action trigger, dovetail front and rear sights or Tritium night sights (new 2018), ambidextrous slide control, interchangeable back straps, Picatinny rail, loaded chamber indicator, 26.4 oz. Mfg. 2016-2020.

	$355	$300	$265	$250	$200	$175	$150	*$418*

Add $86 for Tritium night sights (new 2018).

PISTOLS: SINGLE SHOT, XP-100 & VARIATIONS

Manufacture stopped on the XP-100 at the end of 1994, and resumed briefly during 1998-99 (Model XP-100R).

MODEL XP-100 – .221 Rem. Fireball cal., bolt action, featuring the Model 40X short action, 10 1/2 in. VR barrel, one-piece brown DuPont Zytel (nylon) pistol grip stock with two diamond pattern inlays in forend, adj. sights, drilled and tapped for receiver sight and scope, dog leg bolt handle, 4-digit ser. no., 3 3/4 lbs. Mfg. 1963-1985.

	$900	$850	$800	$700	$500	$400	$300	

MODEL XP-100 CUSTOM – .22-250 Rem. (new 1992), .223 Rem., .250 Savage, 6mm BR Rem., 7mm BR Rem., .308 Win. (new 1992), .35 Rem., or 7mm-08 Rem. cal., choice of 14 1/2 in. standard or heavy barrel, choice of right or left-hand action, wood stock with contoured pistol grip, with or without sights. Mfg. by Custom Shop only 1986-94.

	$1,000	$950	$925	$800	$600	$500	$500	*$945*

MODEL XP-100 HUNTER – .223 Rem., 7mm BR Rem., 7mm-08 Rem., or .35 Rem. cal., 14 1/2 in. barrel, drilled and tapped for sights, laminated wood stock, 4 3/8 lbs. Mfg. 1993-1994.

	$900	$850	$800	$700	$500	$400	$300	*$548*

MODEL XP-100 VARMINT SPECIAL – .223 Rem. (new 1986) cal., single shot bolt action pistol, 14 1/2 in. barrel, drilled and tapped for receiver sights and scope, one-piece pistol grip nylon stock, 4 1/8 lbs. Mfg. 1986-1992.

	$900	$850	$800	$700	$500	$400	$300	*$419*

Add $100 for original hard zipper case.

MODEL XP-100 WALNUT – 7mm BR Rem. cal., 10 1/2 in. barrel, solid American walnut stock and target sights, 3 7/8 lbs. Mfg. 1993-94.

	$900	$850	$800	$700	$500	$400	$300	*$625*

MODEL XP-100R – .22-250 Rem., .223 Rem., .260 Rem., or .35 Rem. cal., 14 1/2 in. barrel, right-hand repeater with 4 or 5 shot blind mag., DuPont Kevlar stock, drilled and tapped receiver, approx. 4 1/2 lbs. Mfg. 1990-99.

	$900	$850	$800	$700	$500	$400	$300	*$665*

GRADING - PPGS™	100%	98%	95%	90%	80%	70%	60%	LAST MSR

MODEL XP-100R KS – .22-250 Rem. (new 1992), .223 Rem., .250 Savage (new 1991), 7mm-08 Rem., .308 Win. (new 1992), .35 Rem., or .350 Rem. Mag. (new 1991) cal., repeater variation, Kevlar synthetic stock, right-hand action only, open sights (except for .223 Rem. and .250 Savage) 4 1/8 lbs. Mfg. 1990-94.

	100%	98%	95%	90%	80%	70%	60%	LAST MSR
	$1,000	$950	$925	$800	$700	$600	$500	*$840*

This model was available through Remington's Custom Shop only.

MODEL XP-SILHOUETTE – .35 Rem. (mfg. 1987-92) or 7mm BR Rem. (mfg. 1980-92) cal., bench rest model, 14 1/2 in. barrel, drilled and tapped, nylon (disc. 1992) or walnut (new 1992) stock, 3 7/8 lbs. Disc. 1992.

	100%	98%	95%	90%	80%	70%	60%	LAST MSR
	$900	$850	$800	$750	$600	$400	$300	*$427*

Add $15 for .35 Rem. cal.

100%	98%	95%	90%	80%	70%	60%	50%	40%	30%	20%	10%

RIFLES: DISC.

REVOLVING PERCUSSION RIFLE – .36 or .44 (rare) cal., 6 shot unfluted cylinder, 24 or 28 in. octagon barrel, walnut stock with crescent butt, scroll trigger guard, blue with case hardened frame. Fewer than 1,000 mfg. 1866-1872.

100%	98%	95%	90%	80%	70%	60%	50%	40%	30%	20%	10%
N/A	N/A	$10,000	$9,000	$6,500	$5,000	$3,500	$3,000	$2,500	$2,000	$1,750	$1,500

Add 25% for factory engraved examples (only one known currently).

Frames were made especially for this model, and are not altered New Model revolvers. .38 R.F. factory conversions will be serial numbered on the recoil plate and cylinder. The ultimate in rarity in Remington Revolving Rifles is the .46 rimfire cal. Only five of this model are presently known.

MODEL 1862 "ZOUAVE RIFLE" – .58 cal., muzzle loading percussion, 33 in. round blue barrel, two barrel bands, case hardened lock, brass furniture. Mfg. 12,501, 1862-1865.

100%	98%	95%	90%	80%	70%	60%	50%	40%	30%	20%	10%
N/A	$4,500	$4,000	$3,500	$2,500	$1,750	$1,500	$1,250	$1,100	$1,000	$900	$800

Add $350 for correct sword type bayonet and scabbard in excellent condition.

Most models are in excellent condition, as few, if any, were distributed to the troops during the Civil War.

U.S. MILITARY MUSKET - PATTERN 1863 – .58 cal., muzzle loading percussion, 40 in. round barrel, three barrel bands, blue barrel, case hardened lock, iron furniture. 40,000 Mfg. in 1864.

100%	98%	95%	90%	80%	70%	60%	50%	40%	30%	20%	10%
N/A	$4,500	$4,000	$3,500	$2,500	$1,750	$1,500	$1,250	$1,000	$800	$700	$600

U.S. NAVY M1867 ROLLING BLOCK CARBINE – .50-45 CF cal., 23 1/4 in. barrel, open sight, blue with case hardened frame, bar and ring on frame, walnut straight grip stock. 5,000 mfg. 1868-1869 by Springfield Armory from receivers made by E. Remington & Sons in Ilion, NY.

100%	98%	95%	90%	80%	70%	60%	50%	40%	30%	20%	10%
N/A	N/A	$4,000	$3,750	$2,500	$2,000	$1,750	$1,500	$1,250	$1,000	$750	$500

U.S. NAVY "ANNAPOLIS CADET" MILITARY RIFLE – .50-45 CF cal., mfg. by Springfield Armory utilizing rolling block receivers supplied by E. Remington & Sons in Ilion, NY. Mfg. 1868.

100%	98%	95%	90%	80%	70%	60%	50%	40%	30%	20%	10%
N/A	N/A	$4,000	$3,750	$2,500	$2,000	$1,750	$1,500	$1,250	$1,000	$750	$500

Add $150 for correct angular bayonet in excellent condition.

U.S. ARMY MODEL 1870 "EXPERIMENTAL" TRIALS REMINGTON ROLLING BLOCK MILITARY CARBINE – .50-70 Govt. cal., single shot, rolling block action with sling ring on left side of receiver, mfg. by Springfield Armory under license from E. Remington & Sons. 331 mfg. 1870.

100%	98%	95%	90%	80%	70%	60%	50%	40%	30%	20%	10%
N/A	N/A	N/A	$14,000	$12,000	$10,000	$9,000	$8,000	$7,000	$6,000	$5,000	$4,000

This model is extremely rare, and fewer than six are known to be in private hands. Disposition after the military trials is not known.

U.S. ARMY MODEL 1870 "EXPERIMENTAL" TRIALS REMINGTON ROLLING BLOCK MILITARY RIFLE – .50-70 Govt. cal., single shot, rolling block action, mfg. by Springfield Armory under license from E. Remington & Sons. Mfg. 1870.

100%	98%	95%	90%	80%	70%	60%	50%	40%	30%	20%	10%
N/A	N/A	$6,000	$5,500	$5,000	$4,500	$4,000	$2,750	$2,250	$1,750	$1,250	$1,000

Approx. 1,041 were mfg. 1870 and issued to infantry troops on the frontier for trial. This is a rarely encountered Springfield firearm.

U.S. NAVY MODEL 1870 (TYPES 1 & 2) MILITARY RIFLE – mfg. by Springfield Armory under license from E. Remington & Sons. Mfg. 1870.

100%	98%	95%	90%	80%	70%	60%	50%	40%	30%	20%	10%
N/A	$5,000	$4,500	$4,000	$3,000	$2,000	$1,500	$1,250	$1,000	$800	$1,000	$600

Add $400 for correct Ames sword bayonet and scabbard. Beware of modern copies.

100%	98%	95%	90%	80%	70%	60%	50%	40%	30%	20%	10%

10,000 of these models were mfg. in 1870, but were not accepted by the U.S. Navy, reputedly because of the "unsafe" location of the rear sight (too close to the chamber). These "Type 1" Navy rifles were sold to Poultney & Trimble, who sold them to France. Springfield Armory subsequently manufactured 14,000 "Type 2" rifles with the rear sight moved up the barrel, and these models were accepted by the U.S. Navy. Values are the same for both types.

U.S. ARMY MODEL 1871 MILITARY RIFLE - .50-70 Govt. cal., single shot, rolling block action, mfg. by Springfield Armory under license from E. Remington & Sons. Mfg. 1872.

100%	98%	95%	90%	80%	70%	60%	50%	40%	30%	20%	10%
N/A	$3,000	$2,750	$2,500	$2,000	$1,750	$1,500	$1,200	$900	$700	$500	$400

10,101 of these models were mfg., but there is no evidence to suggest that they were ever issued to the troops. As a result, many of these models can be found in excellent or above average condition.

NO. 1 LONG RANGE "CREEDMOOR" TARGET RIFLE - .44-77, .44-90, or .44-100 cal., rolling block, 1/3 octagon barrel, case hardened receiver, long range tang sight, globe front sight, checkered pistol grip stock, blue. Approx. 500 mfg., 1873-1878.

100%	98%	95%	90%	80%	70%	60%	50%	40%	30%	20%	10%
N/A	$10,000	$9,500	$8,500	$7,000	$5,500	$3,000	$2,500	$2,000	$1,750	$1,500	$1,250

Add premiums for higher grade guns with select wood, additional checkering, and other deluxe features.
Add 25%+ for factory cased guns.
Subtract 25% for missing or incorrect tang "Long Range" sight.

Factory cased guns are rarely encountered. Buyers beware of post-factory cases.

NO. 1 SPORTING RIFLE - rolling block, .40-50, .40-70, .44-70, .44-77, .45-70, .50-45, or .50-70 CF, .38 or .46 RF cal., 28 or 30 in. octagon barrels, folding leaf sight, straight grip stock. Approx. 10,000 mfg., 1868-86.

100%	98%	95%	90%	80%	70%	60%	50%	40%	30%	20%	10%
N/A	$6,000	$5,500	$4,000	$3,000	$2,500	$2,000	$1,500	$1,000	$750	$500	$300

Subtract 25% for rimfire cals.
Add 20% for .44-77, .45-70, or .50-70 cal. (primary buffalo hunting cals.).

NO. 1 1/2 SPORTING RIFLE - .22, .25 Stevens, .25 Long, .32, and .38 Long & Extra Long RF cal., also in .32-20 WCF, .38-40 WCF, and .44-40 WCF, 24-28 in. octagon medium weight barrel, straight grip walnut stock, somewhat lighter than the No. 1 Sporting. Several thousand mfg., 1888-97.

100%	98%	95%	90%	80%	70%	60%	50%	40%	30%	20%	10%
N/A	$3,000	$2,500	$2,000	$1,750	$1,250	$900	$800	$650	$550	$450	$300

Add 20% for centerfire calibers.

NO. 2 SPORTING RIFLE - available in many rimfire cals. between .22 and .38 as well as several centerfire cals. between .22 and .38-40 WCF, blue barrel finish with case hardened frame, perch belly style walnut stock, many special orders available, smaller size action than the No. 1 and rear of frame is curved. Mfg. 1873-1909.

100%	98%	95%	90%	80%	70%	60%	50%	40%	30%	20%	10%
N/A	$2,500	$2,250	$1,750	$1,250	$750	$700	$600	$400	$300	$200	$150

LIGHT BABY CARBINE - .44-40 WCF cal., rolling block, 20 in. lightweight round blue barrel with band, straight stock, nickel or case colored receiver. Several thousand mfg., 1884-1902, a few early carbines are known to exist in .44 Long rimfire cal.

100%	98%	95%	90%	80%	70%	60%	50%	40%	30%	20%	10%
N/A	$6,000	$5,500	$4,000	$2,500	$2,000	$1,750	$1,500	$1,250	$900	$700	$600

Add 25% for blue barrel with color case hardened receiver.

Most made with nickel-plated receivers.

REMINGTON - HEPBURN NO. 3 SPORTING & TARGET RIFLES - falling block, single shot, side lever actuated, blued barrel, case hardened actions, patented 1879, first introduced 1880, many custom features were offered, variations as follows:

* ***Remington - Hepburn No. 3 Sporting & Target*** - various cals. from .22 RF to .50-90 Sharps, 26, 28, or 30 in. round or octagon barrel, open sight, semi-pistol grip stock. Mfg. 1880-1907.

100%	98%	95%	90%	80%	70%	60%	50%	40%	30%	20%	10%
N/A	$9,000	$8,500	$6,000	$4,000	$2,500	$2,250	$2,000	$1,500	$1,250	$1,000	$800

.22 rimfire caliber versions of this model are exceedingly rare.

* ***Remington - Hepburn No. 3 Match Rifle A Quality*** - various cals. from .22 rimfire to .50-90 Sharps, falling block, single shot, 26, 28, or 30 in. round or octagon blued barrel, case hardened actions, target match sights (tang), Schüetzen stock w/o cheekpiece, side lever actuated. Fewer than 1,000 mfg. 1883-1907.

100%	98%	95%	90%	80%	70%	60%	50%	40%	30%	20%	10%
N/A	$10,000	$9,000	$6,000	$4,000	$2,500	$2,250	$2,000	$1,500	$1,250	$1,000	$800

100%	98%	95%	90%	80%	70%	60%	50%	40%	30%	20%	10%

» **Remington - Hepburn No. 3 Match Rifle B Quality** – select grade wood and vernier rear tang sight, checkered at wrist and forearm, buttstock w/cheekpiece.

N/A	$9,500	$9,000	$6,000	$4,000	$2,500	$2,250	$2,000	$1,500	$1,250	$1,000	$800

* ***Remington - Hepburn No. 3 Long Range Creedmoor*** – .44-77, .44-90, or .44-105 CF cal., 32 or 34 in. barrel, target sight, often with heel sight, stock with shotgun butt. A few hundred mfg., 1880-1907.

N/A	$11,000	$10,000	$9,000	$6,250	$4,475	$3,875	$3,175	$2,700	$2,475	$2,150	$1,800

* ***Remington - Hepburn No. 3 Mid Range Creedmoor*** – similar to Long Range, in .40-65 WCF, rarely other cals., 28 in. barrel.

N/A	$11,000	$9,500	$7,000	$5,000	$3,500	$2,750	$2,500	$2,000	$1,750	$1,500	$1,000

* ***Remington - Hepburn No. 3 Long Range Military*** – similar to Creedmoor, with 34 in. full musket stock, in .44-75-520 Rem. cal., military sights, rarely encountered. Mfg. circa 1880s.

N/A	$10,000	$9,000	$8,000	$6,250	$4,475	$3,875	$3,175	$2,700	$2,475	$2,150	$1,800

* ***Remington - Hepburn No. 3 Walker-Hepburn Schuetzen Match*** – under-lever action, 30 or 32 in. barrel, tang sight, palm rest, special Schüetzen stock, approx. 23 mfg. in 1903-1904, perhaps the rarest single shot American rifle.

Extreme rarity factor precludes accurate price evaluation but a few have been observed with price tags in the $20,000-$50,000+ range, depending on condition.

* ***Remington - Hepburn No. 3 Walker-Hepburn Schuetzen Match With False Muzzle***

Add a premium according to condition - very rare.

NO. 4 ROLLING BLOCK RIFLE – .22 S-L-LR, .25 Stevens (barrels marked "25-10"), or .32 Short or Long cal. RF, 22 1/2 in. octagon barrel standard with round barrels available late in the series, smoothbore barrel was introduced approx. 1911, blue finish with case hardened frame, solid frame initially followed by takedown in 2 different types (lever release introduced approx. 1901, screw in approx. 1924), this model was Remington's smallest rolling block. Approx. 350,000 mfg. 1890-1933.

N/A	$1,400	$1,200	$900	$600	$500	$400	$300	$275	$225	$200	$175

Solid frame variations will command a slight premium, especially if over 90% original condition.

* ***No. 4 Rolling Block Rifle Cadet Model*** – similar to Boy Scout, 28 in. barrel, lever takedown, tapered forend, no handguard, no barrel band or bayonet lug, frame unmarked, pre-dates the Boy Scout Model. Mfg. 1911-1912, exceedingly rare.

N/A	N/A	$3,000	$2,000	$2,000	$1,750	$1,500	$1,200	$1,110	$1,000	$900	$800

The existence of this No. 4 variation has only recently been discovered. Almost unknown to even advanced collectors.

* ***No. 4-S Rolling Block Rifle "Boy Scout"***

N/A	$3,500	$3,000	$2,500	$2,000	$1,600	$1,300	$1,000	$900	$800	$700	$600

Original pot-metal bayonets for No. 4-S rifles are exceedingly rare and one in excellent condition may bring $1,250+. A correct leather scabbard can bring an additional $500+.

* ***No. 4-S Rolling Block Rifle Military*** – .22 S-L-LR cal., either marked "MILITARY MODEL" (most common) or "AMERICAN BOY SCOUT" (rare), 28 in. round barrel with musket type forend (1 barrel band), thought to have been used by military academies to train their young cadets.

N/A	$2,500	$2,250	$1,800	$1,700	$1,500	$1,200	$1,000	$900	$800	$700	$600

Original pot-metal bayonets for No. 4-S rifles are exceedingly rare and one in excellent condition may bring $1,250+. A correct leather scabbard can bring an additional $500.

NO. 5 HIGH-POWER, ROLLING BLOCK SPORTING & TARGET RIFLE – various CF calibers, including .30-40 Govt, .303 British, etc., round barrel. Manufactured in the early 20th century. Very few made - possibly only 300.

N/A	$6,000	$5,750	$5,000	$3,000	$2,000	$1,500	$1,250	$1,000	$900	$800	$700

NO. 6 FALLING BLOCK RIFLE – .22 S-L-LR or .32 short or long RF cal., 20 in. round barrel, boy's gun with small dimensions, takedown action, case hardened (early mfg.) or blue finish, also available in smoothbore, 497,000 mfg. 1901-33.

N/A	$600	$575	$500	$350	$300	$250	$225	$200	$180	$170	$150

Add 10% for smoothbore barrel.

Original case colors will bring a premium on this model.

Improved Model 6 became available circa 1905, and featured a blue frame in 24 in. barrel.

100%	98%	95%	90%	80%	70%	60%	50%	40%	30%	20%	10%

NO. 7 ROLLING BLOCK RIFLE – .22 S, .22 LR, or .25 Stev. RF cal., constructed on Rem. Model 1871 SS pistol action frame, 24, 26, or 28 in. 1/2 round, 1/2 octagon tapered barrels, marked "REMINGTON ARMS CO. ILION, NY USA" on barrel top flat, distinctive long tang pistol grip stock, checkered pistol grip and forearm, hard rubber buttplate, available in Target or Sporting configurations, with or w/o special Lyman tang mounted sight, ser. no. range 300,000. Last of the Rolling Block Rifles, very desirable. Approx. 350 mfg. 1903-1910.

N/A	$7,000	$6,750	$6,000	$4,500	$4,000	$3,000	$2,500	$2,000	$1,500	$1,250	$1,000

REMINGTON KEENE MAGAZINE BOLT ACTION RIFLE – .45-70 Govt., .40, or .43 cal. Approx. 5,000 mfg. 1880-1888.

* ***Remington Keene Magazine Bolt Action Rifle Frontier Model*** – those made for U.S. Dept. of Interior (Indian Police), marked U.S.I.D. will command a 50% premium.

N/A	N/A	$5,000	$4,000	$3,000	$2,225	$1,750	$1,500	$1,000	$900	$800	$700

* ***Remington Keene Magazine Bolt Action Rifle Full Stock Carbine Model*** – 22 in. barrel, full stock.

N/A	N/A	$5,500	$4,500	$3,000	$2,225	$1,750	$1,500	$1,000	$900	$800	$700

* ***Remington Keene Magazine Bolt Action Rifle Carbine Model*** – 20 in. barrel, half stock, very limited mfg.

Rarity precludes accurate pricing.

* ***Remington Keene Magazine Bolt Action Army Rifle*** – 32 1/2 in. barrel, full stock.

N/A	N/A	$5,000	$4,000	$3,000	$2,225	$1,750	$1,500	$1,000	$900	$800	$700

* ***Remington Keene Magazine Bolt Action Sporting Rifle*** – 1/2 oct. barrel, full or "BUTTON" mag. Add for pistol grip and select wood variations.

N/A	N/A	$5,000	$4,000	$3,000	$2,225	$1,750	$1,500	$1,000	$900	$800	$700

* ***Remington Keene Magazine Bolt Action Navy Rifle*** – 29 1/2 in. barrel, full stock.

N/A	N/A	$5,000	$4,000	$3,000	$2,225	$1,750	$1,500	$1,000	$900	$800	$700

REMINGTON-LEE MAGAZINE BOLT ACTION RIFLE (MODEL 1879) – marked "Lee Arms Co., Bridgeport, Conn, USA, patented Nov. 4th, 1879" on upper left flat of receiver but all rifles were made at E. Remington & Sons, Ilion, NY. Remington, on April 1, 1881, acquired all the materials, fixtures and tooling from Sharps to complete the US Navy contract, and used the Lee-Borchardt projected nose magazine or the Lee-Cook magazine with the sliding detent on the side.

* ***U.S. Navy First Contract*** – .45-70 Govt. cal., 29 in. barrel, one-piece bolt, bolt handle is forward and part of the right locking lug, serial numbers 1-300, US Navy Insp. WWK & HN, 300 delivered January 1882.

N/A	$4,000	$3,500	$3,000	$2,600	$2,200	$1,800	$1,400	$900	$400	$300	$200

* ***U.S. Navy Non-Contract*** – .45-70 Govt. cal., 29 in. barrel, Remington Rolling Block front and rear sights, bolt handle is forward and part of the right locking lug, serial number range 301-1300, U.S. Navy Insp. WMF, 700 delivered late 1884.

N/A	N/A	$3,400	$2,900	$2,400	$1,900	$1,400	$1,000	$700	$400	$300	$200

* ***Military Non-Contract*** – .43 Spanish cal., 29 or 32 in. barrel, one-piece bolt with the bolt handle moved to the classic Lee bent down position behind the right receiver wall, serial numbers 1301 - 7000, over 3,900 were sold to the Chinese Govt. in June 1884.

N/A	N/A	$3,400	$2,900	$2,400	$1,900	$1,400	$1,000	$700	$400	$300	$200

REMINGTON LEE MAGAZINE RIFLE (MODEL 1882) – marked "Lee Arms Co., Bridgeport, Conn, USA, Patented Nov. 4th, 1879" on upper left flat of receiver and "E. Remington & Sons, Ilion, NY, USA, Sole Manufacturers and Agents" on the left receiver side wall, uses the Lee-Diss box magazine with two grooves on the side, one-piece bolt with the bolt handle bent down and back of the right receiver wall.

* ***U.S. Army Trials*** – .45-70 Govt. cal., 32 1/2 in. barrel, serial number range 8800 - 9800, 750 were delivered September 1884 to the US Army, US Army Insp. DFC stamped on receiver, barrel and in a boxed script on the buttstock, field tested in 1885, withdrawn, declared surplus and about 400 were sold to a Boston arms dealer, these were later sold to the Massachusetts Naval Brigade and had stamped or painted unit markings applied to the buttstock. Front and rear sights are of the US Springfield pattern.

N/A	$4,000	$3,500	$3,000	$2,600	$2,200	$1,800	$1,400	$900	$500	$300	$200

100%	98%	95%	90%	80%	70%	60%	50%	40%	30%	20%	10%

* ***Chinese Contract*** - .45-70 Govt. or .43 Spanish cal., 20 1/2 (carbine), 28, 29, or 32 in. barrel, serial number range est. 11000 - 25000, over 14,000 produced starting in late 1884, around serial number 14000 the Lee Arms Co. markings were discontinued and the E. Remington & Sons markings moved to the upper left flat on the receiver, Chinese ideograms stamped on receiver ring. The Chinese defaulted on the contract in mid 1885, Remington resold the rifles after removing the Chinese markings, some rifles were fitted with a bayonet lug on the side of the barrel for a saber bayonet, front and rear sights are of the rolling block pattern.

N/A	N/A	$4,000	$3,500	$3,000	$2,500	$2,000	$1,600	$1,100	$700	$400	$250

Add 25% for carbine. Add 50% for conversion Model 1882 or 1885 (120 rifles and 100 carbines were inventoried with "altered bolts" in 1888).
Subtract 10% for .43 Spanish cal.

REMINGTON LEE MAGAZINE RIFLE (MODEL 1885) - 32 in. barrel, marked "E. Remington & Sons, Ilion, NY, USA, Sole Manufacturers and Agents, Patented Nov. 4th, 1879", serial number range 41000 - 47000, action revised to accept the new two-piece bolt with separate bolt head, uses the Lee-Diss box magazine with two grooves on the side. Mfg. after the 1886 bankruptcy and 1888 reorganization of E. Remington & Sons.

N/A	$3,800	$3,200	$2,700	$2,300	$1,900	$1,500	$1,100	$800	$500	$300	$250

Add 100% for New Zealand purchase, distinctively marked NZ with broad arrows over 87 on receiver ring. 500 sold to New Zealand in 1887.
Add 200% for British Trials rifle, 300 purchased January 1887, marked WD under broad arrow on buttstock and fitted with cutoff on right side of action.

* ***U.S. Navy Contract*** - .45-70 Govt. cal., 32 1/2 in. barrel, serial number range 50001 - 54000, front and rear sights are of the US Springfield pattern, over 3,400 were accepted by the US Navy from 1888 to 1894, marked on the receiver ring - USN over anchor over Navy serial number over US Navy inspector, the Naval serial numbers range from 1001 to over 4000, the Navy inspectors are: WWK, HHE, ACD, CEC, HE, and SWV, a few rifles were issued without being inspected.

N/A	$4,500	$4,000	$3,500	$3,000	$2,500	$2,000	$1,600	$1,100	$700	$400	$250

Add 50% for documented Hawaiian National Guard Purchase, NGH stamped on buttstock, no USN proofs. 350+ purchased in 1893 by Provisional Government of Hawaii.

REMINGTON LEE SMALL BORE MAGAZINE RIFLE (MODEL 1899) - marked "Remington Arms Company, Ilion, NY, USA, Patented Aug, 26th, 1884, Sept. 9th, 1884, March 17th, 1885, Jan. 18th 1887", two-piece bolt with two locking lugs on the bolt head, uses the Lee-Diss box magazine with three grooves on the side.

* ***Michigan National Guard Contract*** - .30-40 Govt. cal., 29 1/2 in. barrel, serial number range 100001 - 102200. 1,001 shipped in 1898 and 1,000 in 1899.

N/A	$3,800	$3,200	$2,700	$2,300	$1,900	$1,500	$1,100	$800	$500	$300	$250

* ***Cuban Contract*** - .30-40 Govt. cal., 20 (carbine) or 29 1/2 (rifle) in. barrel, serial number range 1 - 3000. 2,600 carbines and 400 rifles shipped to Cuba in 1905, the Cuban Coat of Arms and serial number are stamped on the receiver ring, in 1914 a number of the carbines and rifles were returned to Remington, the Cuban crest polished off, reblued and, in 1915, 1,153 carbines sold to the French Army for their Automobile Corps.

N/A	$3,800	$3,200	$2,700	$2,300	$1,900	$1,500	$1,100	$800	$500	$300	$250

Add 25% for carbine.

REMINGTON LEE SPORTING & TARGET RIFLES - The original 1879 Lee Arms catalog advertised a sporting rifle "to be made in the ensuing season". Only a few handmade, tool room model sporters were made at Sharps and at least one of these has the turned down bolt handle, a search of period E. Remington & Sons advertising from 1881 to 1888 has not turned up any mention of Remington Lee sporters, the Keene sporter apparently met the need for a bolt action sporter and any factory Remington Lee sporter from this period should be considered a tool room model.

* ***Remington Lee M1885*** - .43 Spanish, .44-77, .45-70 Govt., or .45-90 cal., 26 in. round barrel, the 1904-05 Remington Arms catalog advertised Remington Lee sporters, based on the US Navy M1885 action, checkered half pistol grip stock with rifle buttplate and two points facing the action, serial number range 54000.

N/A	N/A	$3,100	$2,500	$2,300	$1,900	$1,500	$1,100	$800	$500	$350	$300

* ***Remington Lee M1899*** - 6mm USN, 7mm Spanish Mauser, 7.65 Belgian Mauser, .30-30 Win., .30-40 Krag, .303 British, .32 Win. Spl., .32-40 B&W High Power, .35 Win., .38-55 High Power, .38-72 or .405 Win. cal., the Standard Grade sporter has 24, 26 (standard), or 28 in. round barrel,

100%	98%	95%	90%	80%	70%	60%	50%	40%	30%	20%	10%

checkered half pistol grip stock with rifle buttplate and two points facing the action, Standard Grade, Heavy Weight sporter has 24 and 26 in. heavy barrel, express sights, checkered half pistol grip stock with shotgun buttplate and three points facing the action, Special Remington Lee Sporter is high grade, 26 in. half round, half octagon barrel, select extra fine checkered English walnut stock, shotgun butt with center grain exposed and heel and toe steel tips and five points facing the action, wind gauge front Lyman sight and aperture rear sight, the standard three grooves on the side Lee-Diss magazine was used, to accommodate the shorter cartridges the .30-30, .32 Win. and .32-40 B&W magazines have a rear spacer while the .38-55 magazine has a front spacer. Serial number range 75001-76446. A total of 1,446 factory sporters were shipped from 1899 to 1909.

N/A	$3,500	$2,700	$2,100	$1,600	$1,100	$900	$750	$600	$450	$300	$250

Add 100% for Special Remington Lee Sporter.

Add 200-300% for documented Military or Sporting Target Rifle.

Original retail price for the Standard Grade Sporter was $25 in 1905. Original retail price for the Special Remington Lee Sporter was $60 in 1905.

MODEL 1903-A3 MAGAZINE BOLT RIFLE – please refer to listing under Springfield Armory.

MODEL 1917 U.S. RIFLE (ENFIELD) – Remington-UMC produced at its Ilion, NY plant and Remington of Delaware (separate company with connections to Rem.-UMC) produced in Eddystone, PA.

REMINGTON-BEALS SPORTING RIFLE – .32 Long Rimfire or .38 Long Rimfire cal., Fordyce Beals invented a single-shot, breechloading rifle that would bear his name--the Remington-Beals Single-Shot Rifle. The breech of this rifle is opened by lowering the under-lever, which slides the barrel forward. Two chamberings of this rifle were made between 1866 and 1872. Both iron (early production) and brass-framed receivers were made. The under-powered rifle was not very popular, as fewer than 900 were made in seven years of production.

N/A	N/A	$2,500	$2,000	$1,200	$1,000	$900	$800	$700	$600	$500	$400

RIFLES: CANE VARIATIONS

Patented by John F. Thomas on February 9, 1858. Manufactured by E. Remington & Sons from 1858 through 1886, in percussion (1858 - 1861), and later in rimfire (1866 to 1886).

REMINGTON RIFLE CANES - .31 PERCUSSION – different handle configurations include right angle, bulbous head, ball and claw (exceedingly rare), large dog's head, full curve with short and long upper shaft, other non-factory handle configurations (ivory, silver, gold) are known, cane coverings are black Gutta-Percha, black rifle cane coverings frequently turn brown with age and exposure to sunlight. Only about 300 percussion cane guns were made prior to the Civil War. Initially called Remington's New Patent Gun Cane.

N/A	$9,500	$8,500	$7,500	$7,000	$6,000	$5,500	$5,000	$4,500	$3,500	$3,000	$2,500

Add 20% for "dog's head".

Add 50% for "right angle", or "ball and claw", or "bulbous" handle.

Subtract 30% for after market or custom handles

Percussion rifle canes converted to .32 centerfire have been observed, but cannot be verified as factory conversions.

REMINGTON RIFLE CANES - .22 SHORT AND .32 LONG RIMFIRE – Remington No.1 Rifle Cane in .22 short RF - handle configurations include the small dog's head and two variations of curved handles (short shaft and long shaft). Remington No. 2 Rifle Cane in .32 short rimfire - handle configurations include the large dog's head and two variations of curved handles (short shaft and long shaft). Cane coverings are black Gutta-Percha, many different handle, barrel, shaft and overall lengths (33 1/2" to 36 1/2" known) were made. A number of after-market handles are known. Remington's rimfire cane guns were first made with internal hammers, but were improved with a rod driving the firing pin. At least 1,750 rimfire rifle canes were made after the Civil War and prior to 1886.

N/A	$8,000	$7,500	$7,000	$6,500	$6,000	$5,500	$4,000	$3,500	$3,000	$2,500	$2,000

Add 30% for "dog's head".

Subtract 30% for after market or non-factory custom handles.

Factory special order canes such as coral colored Gutta-Percha (.32 long rimfire cal.) or takedown canes are too rare to be priced. During 2010, a fourth example of a coral colored cane rifle in .32 cal. and standard curved handle was discovered.

GRADING - PPGS™	100%	98%	95%	90%	80%	70%	60%	LAST MSR

RIFLES: ROLLING BLOCK, MODERN MFG.

The following models are manufactured in limited quantities by the Remington Custom Shop.

NO. 1 ROLLING BLOCK CREEDMOOR MID-RANGE TARGET – .45-70 Govt. cal., rolling block action, patterned after the original Remington No. 1 mid-range Creedmoor-style configuration, 30 in. half-round half-octagon tapered barrel, includes rear tang aperture and front globe sight with four interchangeable inserts, checkered walnut stock and forearm, SST, case colored receiver, cased, 9 7/8 lbs. Mfg. 1997-98.

	$2,800	$2,500	$1,900	$1,665	$1,415	$1,140	$950	*$2,799*

Subtract $750 if w/o original case.

MODERN NO. 1 ROLLING BLOCK MID-RANGE SPORTING – .45-70 Govt. cal., 30 in. round barrel, checkered pistol grip sporter stock and forearm, blue barrel and receiver, adj. buckhorn rear sight, 8 3/4 lbs. Mfg. 1998-2011.

	$2,575	$2,275	$1,850	$1,600	$1,375	$1,100	$900	*$2,992*

MODERN NO. 1 ROLLING BLOCK SILHOUETTE – .45-70 Govt. cal., meets BPCR silhouette requirements, similar to No. 1 Rolling Block Mid-Range Sporter, except has 30 in. round heavy barrel w/o sights and single set or double triggers, blue or case colored receiver. Mfg. 2000-2011.

	$2,000	$1,750	$1,500	$1,200	$1,000	$800	$600	*$3,441*

Add $450 for case colored receiver.
Add $300 for single set trigger.

RIFLES: SEMI-AUTO, CENTERFIRE

The models have been listed in numerical sequence for quick reference.

Remington also manufactured models R4, R5, R10, R11, and ACR for military and law enforcement only. These models are not covered in this text.

MODEL FOUR – 6mm Rem., .243 Win., .270 Win., .280 Rem. (mfg. 1984-87), .30-06, .308 Win. (disc. 1984), or 7mm Express (mfg. 1981-83) cal., cartridge "head" imbedded in bottom of receiver, gas operation with metering system, 22 in. barrel, 4 shot detachable mag., deluxe Monte Carlo stock and forend, detachable sights. Mfg. 1981-87.

	N/A	$550	$375	$275	$225	$200	$175	*$475*

* ***Model Four Special Diamond Anniversary*** – .30-06 cal. only, commemorates the 75th anniversary of the Model 8, laser engraved with gold and premium checkered walnut stock and forearm. One grade only, approx. 1,400 shipped from 1982-1988, final 100 shipped in 1994 using Model 7400 stocks.

	$1,200	$1,000	$900	N/A	N/A	N/A	N/A	

* ***Model Four High Grades*** – only two mfg.

Extreme rarity precludes accurate pricing.

MODEL 5 – .30 Carbine cal., recoiling barrel, approx. 300 mfg.

	$1,750	$1,550	$1,350	$1,150	$950	$750	$600	

MODEL 8 – .25 Rem., .30 Rem., .32 Rem., or .35 Rem. cal., 22 in. barrel, open sights, 5 shot non-detachable box mag., plain stock. Approx. 60,000 mfg. 1906-1936.

	$1,500	$1,300	$1,100	$950	$750	$600	$500	

Add 35% for .25 Rem. cal.
Add 75% for C grades.
Add substantial premiums for higher grades D, E, and F.
Add substantial premiums for Military Trials Rifles and POE modified police extended detachable magazine models.

Early Model 8's that were modified by the Peace Officer Equipment Co. (POE RIFLES) are extremely rare. They were available in both .30 Rem. and .35 Rem. cals., but .35 Rem. is the most commonly encountered. Unlike most aftermarket modifications that detract from value, these modifications with their magazine greatly enhance the value. Prices generally grange from about $3,000 to $8,000 depending on originality and condition. Some rifles have no additional markings while some have had different markings added by the local police jurisditions, municipalities, prisons or owners, even if only an inventory or rack number.

MODEL 74 SPORTSMAN – .280 Rem. (European special order only) or .30-06 cal., 22 in. barrel, 4 shot mag., uncheckered hardwood stock and forearm, open sights, 7 1/2 lbs. Mfg. 1984-87.

	$300	$275	$250	$225	$200	$175	$150	*$353*

GRADING - PPGS™	100%	98%	95%	90%	80%	70%	60%	LAST MSR

MODEL 81 WOODSMASTER – .30 Rem., .32 Rem., .35 Rem., or .300 Savage cal., takedown action, 5 shot, non-detachable box mag., 22 in. round barrel, notched elevator rear sight. An improvement of the Model 8; was available in 5 grades. 56,091 mfg. 1936-1950.

	$1,350	$1,200	$1,000	$850	$700	$550	$425

Add 15% for early mfg. with beavertail forearm.
Add 75% for stamped B and C grades.
Add substantial premiums for higher grades D, E, and F.
Add substantial premiums for FBI "Special Police" rifle and "Special Police" rifle with extended detachable magazine.

The .32 Rem. cal. was dropped after WWII and the .300 Savage was added in 1940. A few specimens have been observed in .25 Rem. cal., which was advertised only the first year as a production model and were made as original factory models until remaining .25 Rem. barrels from Model 8 stock was depleted. Therefore, original factory production in .25 Rem. cal. would only be found in the first few years of model production.

MODEL 81 SPECIAL POLICE – .30 Rem. or .35 Rem. cal., 15 shot detachable mag. or standard 5 shot fixed mag., typically offered with 1-3 mags. serial numbered to the rifle, jurisdiction was typically factory machined engraved on the left side of the receiver.

Values on original condition rifles typically range from $3,000 - $10,000, based on amount of condition and the municipality.

MODEL 740 WOODSMASTER – .244 Rem. (mfg. 1957-59), .280 Rem. (mfg. 1957-59), .30-06 (first caliber, introduced 1955) or .308 Win. (introduced 1956) cal., 22 in. barrel, open sight, box mag., gas operated, plain pistol grip stock. Mfg. 1955-1959.

	N/A	$250	$200	$190	$175	$150	$125

MODEL 740ADL – similar to 740A, with checkered stock, grip cap and sling swivels. Mfg. 1955-1959.

.244 Rem./.30-06 cal.	N/A	$280	$250	$225	$200	$180	$150
.280 Rem./.308 Win. cal.	N/A	$280	$250	$225	$200	$180	$150

MODEL 740BDL – similar to 740ADL, with select wood. Mfg. 1955-1957.

.244 Rem./.30-06 cal.	N/A	$295	$260	$225	$200	$180	$150
.308 Win. cal.	N/A	$295	$260	$225	$200	$180	$150

BDLs were not listed in the 1958 or 1959 Remington price list.

MODEL 740D PEERLESS GRADE – similar to Model 740, with scroll engraving and fancy wood. Mfg. 1955-1960.

	$3,000	$2,000	$1,100	N/A	N/A	N/A	N/A

MODEL 740F PREMIER GRADE – similar to Model 740, with extensive hand engraved game scenes and scroll work, best grade wood.

	$6,500	$4,500	$3,750	N/A	N/A	N/A	N/A

* ***Model 740F Premier Grade w/Inlays*** – similar to Model 740F Premier Grade, except has game scenes inlaid with gold.

	$9,000	$7,500	$6,500	N/A	N/A	N/A	N/A

MODEL 742 (A) WOODSMASTER – 6mm Rem. (mfg. 1963), .243 Win. (mfg. 1968), .280 Rem. (marked 7mm Express 1979-1980), .30-06, or .308 Win. cal., 22 in. barrel, open sights, 4 shot box mag., gas operated, checkered pistol grip stock. Mfg. 1960-80.

	$325	$280	$250	$235	$200	$185	$160

Add 10% for .280 Rem. cal.

* ***Model 742ADL Deluxe*** – 6mm Rem., .243 Win., .280 Rem., .30-06, or .308 Win. cal., similar to the Model 742, except has fine checkering, sling swivels and roll engraved game scenes on receiver.

	$350	$275	$260	$235	$215	$195	$170

* ***Model 742BDL Deluxe*** – .30-06 or .308 Win. cal., 22 in. barrel, 4 shot box mag., step receiver, open sights, Monte Carlo basket weave checkered stock and forend, choice of right or left-hand cheekpiece, black pistol grip cap and forend tip. Mfg. 1966-1980.

	$350	$300	$260	$235	$215	$195	$170

MODEL 742C CARBINE – .280 Rem., .30-06, or .308 Win. cal., gas operated, 18 1/2 in. barrel, 4 shot box mag., open sights, checkered pistol grip stock. Mfg. 1961-1980.

	$400	$350	$300	$275	$250	$225	$195

GRADING - PPGS™	100%	98%	95%	90%	80%	70%	60%	LAST MSR

* ***Model 742CDL Deluxe Carbine*** – .280 Rem., .30-06, or .308 Win. cal., similar to Model 742C carbine, except has fine checkering, sling swivels and roll engraved game scenes on receiver. Mfg. 1961-1963.

$425 $375 $325 $300 $275 $250 $225

MODEL 742D PEERLESS GRADE – similar to Model 742ADL, with scroll engraving and fancy wood. Mfg. 1961-1980.

$3,000 $2,100 $1,100 N/A N/A N/A N/A

MODEL 742F PREMIER GRADE – similar to Model 742ADL, with extensive hand engraved game scenes and scroll work, best grade wood.

$6,500 $4,000 $2,750 N/A N/A N/A N/A

* ***Model 742F Premier Grade w/Inlays*** – similar to Model 742F Premier Grade, except has game scenes inlaid in gold.

$9,000 $7,000 $6,500 N/A N/A N/A N/A

MODEL 742 150TH YEAR ANNIVERSARY – .30-06 cal. only, 11,412 mfg. 1966 only.

$300 $250 $210 N/A N/A N/A N/A

MODEL 742 CANADIAN CENTENNIAL – 1,968 mfg. in 1967. Issue price was $200.

$475 $425 $375 N/A N/A N/A N/A

REMINGTON/RUGER CANADIAN CENTENNIAL SET – please refer to the Sturm Ruger section.

MODEL 742 BICENTENNIAL – similar to 742ADL, with inscription on receiver. 10,108 mfg. 1976 only.

$375 $325 $275 $250 $225Q $200 $175

MODEL 750 – .243 Win., .30-06, or .308 Win. cal., 18 1/2 (not avail. in .243 Win.) or 22 in. barrel with iron sights, replaces the wood stocked Model 7400, and features improved gas system, lower profile, rotary bolt lockup, redesigned black synthetic stock and forearm, sling swivels became standard 2007, R3 recoil pad, 7 1/2 lbs. Mfg. 2006-2016.

$735 $575 $475 $400 $350 $295 $265 *$902*

MODEL 750 WOODMASTER – .243 Win., .270 Win., .30-06, .308 Win., or .35 Whelen (disc.) cal., 18 1/2 (Woodsmaster Carbine) or 22 in. barrel with iron sights, replaces the wood stocked Model 7400, and features improved gas system, lower profile, rotary bolt lockup, checkered walnut stock and forearm, sling swivels became standard 2007, R3 recoil pad, 7 1/2 lbs. Mfg. 2006-2016.

$835 $700 $600 $500 $400 $350 $295 *$1,024*

Carbine variation is available in .30-06 or .308 Win. cal., and 18 1/2 in. barrel only.

MODEL 7400 – 6mm Rem. (disc. 1987), .243 Win., .270 Win., 7mm Express (mfg. 1981-83), .280 Rem. (introduced 1984, disc. 2000), .30-06, .308 Win., or .35 Whelen (mfg. 1993-95) cal., modified Model 742 action, gas operation, 22 in. barrel, 4 shot detachable mag., pressed checkered Monte Carlo walnut stock, 7 1/2 lbs. Mfg. 1981-2005.

N/A $410 $325 $260 $230 $210 $185 *$651*

Add 15% for .35 Whelen cal.

Beginning in 1991, a high gloss wood finish became available in cals. .270 Win. and .30-06 (Model 7400 High Gloss). From 1998-2003, receiver panels had fine line rolled game scene engraving.

* ***Model 7400 Carbine*** – .30-06 cal. only, similar to Model 7400 Rifle, except has 18 1/2 in. barrel, 7 1/4 lbs. Mfg. 1988-2005.

N/A $410 $325 $260 $230 $210 $185 *$651*

* ***Model 7400 SP (Special Purpose)*** – .270 Win. or .30-06 cal., similar to Model 7400, except has non-reflective matte finish on both wood and metalwork. Mfg. 1993-94.

N/A $370 $300 $255 $230 $210 $185 *$524*

* ***Model 7400 Weathermaster*** – .270 Win. or .30-06 cal., features matte nickel plated receiver, barrel, and magazine, black synthetic stock and forearm, 22 in. barrel with open sights, 7 1/2 lbs. Mfg. 2003-2004.

N/A $400 $315 $255 $230 $210 $185 *$624*

* ***Model 7400 Synthetic*** – same cals. as Model 7400, features black fiberglass reinforced synthetic stock and forend, matte black metal finish, 22 in. barrel only. Mfg. 1998-2006.

N/A $385 $330 $285 $265 $240 $220 *$589*

» ***Model 7400 Synthetic Carbine*** – .30-06 cal., similar to Model 7400 Synthetic, except has 18 1/2 in. barrel. 7 1/4 lbs. Mfg. 1998-2006.

N/A $385 $330 $285 $265 $240 $220 *$589*

GRADING - PPGS™	100%	98%	95%	90%	80%	70%	60%	LAST MSR

* ***Model 7400 175th Anniversary*** – .30-06 cal. only, Anniversary Model with roll engraving and high gloss finish. 5,000 mfg. in 1991 only.

	N/A	$450	$300	N/A	N/A	N/A	N/A	*$515*

A limited quantity of .270 Win. cal. were specially made in this 175th Anniversary Model for distributor Bill Hicks in MN. Pricing varies, since these rifles are a special edition.

* ***Model 7400 ADF Limited Edition*** – .30-06 cal. only, special edition 1997 only featuring Buckmaster's American Deer Foundation, special ADF engraving. Approx. 800 mfg. 1997 only.

	N/A	$500	$315	N/A	N/A	N/A	N/A	*$600*

MODEL 7400 ENGRAVED – the engraved Model 7400s were introduced 1988.

* ***Model 7400 D Grade (Peerless)*** – scroll engraving and fancy wood.

	N/A	$2,000	$1,100	N/A	N/A	N/A	N/A	*$4,532*

* ***Model 7400 F Grade (Premier)*** – extensive hand engraved game scenes and scroll work, best grade wood.

	N/A	$6,000	$3,750	N/A	N/A	N/A	N/A	*$8,799*

* ***Model 7400 F Grade with gold inlays (Premier Gold)*** – with game scenes inlaid in gold.

	N/A	$8,000	$7,000	N/A	N/A	N/A	N/A	*$11,999*

MODEL R-15 – .450 Bushmaster cal., GIO, 18 in. fluted barrel, 4 shot detachable mag., receiver length Picatinny rail, ergonomic pistol grip, fixed stock, Mossy Oak Break-up camo coverage, approx. 7 3/4 lbs. Mfg. 2010-2015.

	$1,250	$825	$575	$475	$425	$375	$350	*$1,499*

MODEL R-15 HUNTER – .30 Rem. AR cal., GIO, 22 in. fluted barrel, receiver length Picatinny rail, ergonomic pistol grip, 4 shot detachable mag., 100% Realtree AP HD camo coverage, approx. 7 3/4 lbs. Mfg. 2009-2015.

	$975	$775	$700	$600	$575	$525	$475	*$1,229*

MODEL R-15 VTR (VARMINT TARGET RIFLE) PREDATOR – .204 Ruger (disc. 2009) or .223 Rem. cal., GIO, 18 (carbine, .204 Ruger disc. 2009) or 22 in. free floating chrome moly fluted barrel, fixed or telestock (Carbine CS) with pistol grip, 5 shot fixed (new 2012, .223 Rem. cal. only) or detachable mag. (compatible with AR-15 style mags.), R-15 marked on magwell, single stage trigger, flat-top receiver with Picatinny rail, no sights, round vent. forearm, 100% Advantage Max-1 HD camo coverage except for barrel, includes lockable hard case, mfg. by Bushmaster in Windham, ME 2008-2011, and in Ilion, NY beginning 2011, 6.75-7.75 lbs. Mfg. 2008-2013.

	$1,000	$800	$700	$625	$575	$550	$500	*$1,327*

* ***Model R-15 VTR Stainless*** – .223 Rem. cal., GIO, AR-15 style, 24 in. free floated fluted button rifled stainless steel barrel with recessed hunting crown, 5 shot fixed (new 2012) or detachable mag. (compatible with AR-15 style mags.), single stage trigger, no sights, fixed stock and tubed forearm, pistol grip, receiver length Picatinny rail, OD Green (disc.) or Realtree Advantage Max-1 HDTM camo, 7 3/4 lbs. Mfg. 2009-2020.

	$975	$775	$700	$600	$575	$525	$475	*$1,299*

* ***Model R-15 VTR Thumbhole*** – .223 Rem. cal., similar to VTR Stainless, except has 24 in. fluted barrel, OD Green camo thumbhole stock. Mfg. 2009-2010.

	$1,100	$875	$775	$700	$650	$600	$550	*$1,470*

* ***Model R-15 VTR Byron South Signature Edition*** – .223 Rem. cal., GIO, 18 in. barrel, Advantage Max-1 HD camo pistol grip stock. Mfg. mid-2008-2011.

	$1,375	$1,100	$975	$875	$800	$750	$675	*$1,845*

* ***Model R-15 VTR Predator Carbine*** – .223 Rem. cal., GIO, AR-15 style, 18 (disc. 2013) or 22 in. free floating button rifled fluted barrel with recessed hunting crown, 5 shot mag., single stage trigger, fixed or collapsible (CS, disc. 2013) synthetic stock, forend tube drilled and tapped for accessory rails, ergonomic pistol grip, receiver length Picatinny rail, Reealtree Advantage Max-1 HDTM camo coverage on stock, receiver, and forearm, 6 3/4 (disc.) or 7 3/4 lbs. Disc. 2020.

	$900	$725	$650	$575	$525	$500	$450	*$1,199*

* ***Model R-15 VTR Predator Magpul MOE*** – .223 Rem. cal., GIO, 16 1/2, 18, or 22 in. fluted barrel with AAC 51 Tooth Blackout muzzle brake, 5 shot mag., polymer Magpul trigger guard, two-stage match trigger, Magpul MOE fixed or adj. stock, wraparound rubber overmolding on Magpul grip, Mossy Oak Brush camo coverage on stock, receiver, and forearm, 6 3/4-7 3/4 lbs. Disc. 2020.

	$900	$725	$650	$575	$525	$500	$450	*$1,199*

Add $100 for fixed stock.

GRADING - PPGS™	100%	98%	95%	90%	80%	70%	60%	LAST MSR

MODEL R-25 – .243 Win., 7mm-08 Rem., or .308 Win. cal., GIO, 20 in. free floating fluted chrome moly barrel, single stage trigger, ergonomic pistol grip fixed stock with 100% Mossy Oak Treestand camo coverage, front and rear sling swivels, 4 shot fixed (.308 Win. cal. only, new 2012) or detachable mag., R-25 marked on magwell, includes hard case, 7 3/4 lbs. Mfg. 2009-2014.

	$1,275	$1,000	$900	$800	$750	$700	$625	*$1,697*

MODEL R-25 GII – .243 Win. (disc. 2015), .260 Rem. (disc. 2015), .308 Win./7.62 NATO, or 7mm-08 Rem. (disc. 2015) cal., GIO, AR-15 style, 20 in. fluted stainless barrel, 4 shot mag., vented carbon fiber free float tube, forged anodized upper and lower receivers, improved extractor, steel feed ramp, dual ejectors, new Remington Hunter stock with SuperCell recoil pad, Hogue rubber pistol grip, single stage trigger, receiver length Picatinny rail, Mossy Oak Infinity camo finish, 7 5/8 lbs. Mfg. 2015-2020.

	$1,275	$1,000	$900	$800	$750	$700	$625	*$1,697*

RIFLES: SLIDE ACTION, CENTERFIRE

MODEL SIX – 6mm Rem. (disc. 1985), .243 Win., .270 Win., .30-06, or .308 Win. (disc. 1984) cal., cartridge "head" imbedded in bottom of receiver, 4 shot mag. Mfg. 1981-1987.

	$700	$600	$450	$375	$275	$225	$200	
6mm Rem. cal.	$1,750	$1,525	$1,250	$1,000	$750	$500	$350	*$439*

Add 50% for .243 and .308 cals.

* ***Model Six High Grades***

Extreme rarity precludes accurate pricing.

Only three high grade Model Sixes were manufactured.

MODEL 14/14A RIFLE – .25 Rem., .30 Rem., .32 Rem., or .35 Rem. cal., 22 in. barrel, 5 shot mag., open sights, plain pistol grip stock, 6 lbs. Mfg. 1912-1935.

	$900	$775	$700	$575	$400	$300	$250	

Add 10% for "thumbnail" safety on bolt (introduced in 1919).

Add 50% for .25 Rem.

Model 14 was used up to 1919 at which time Model 14A was stamped on new barrels. After 1924 "Model 14" was stamped on all receivers including those of the Model 14 1/2, and new barrels were no longer stamped with the Model. Exceptions will be found. This model was also manufactured in higher grades, including C, D, and F. Premiums vary according to originality and condition.

MODEL 14R CARBINE – .25 Rem., .30 Rem., .32 Rem., or .35 Rem. cal., 18 1/2 in. barrel, 5 shot mag., open sights, straight grip stock, with or w/o DCP inspection mark.

	$1,325	$1,150	$950	$750	$600	$400	$350	

Add 50% for .25 Rem. cal.

Add 10% for .35 Rem. cal.

Add 100% for DCP inspection marked examples.

The DCP inspection mark was done by Canadian inspectors on behalf of the British government. These models were purchased for the Royal Navy which assigned them to the Royal Naval Air Service to be placed in aircrafts for protection and air to air combat. DCP marked guns are very rare as only about 100 examples are known to exist.

MODEL 14 1/2 RIFLE – .38-40 WCF or .44-40 WCF cal., similar to 14A, with 10 shot mag., 22 1/2 in. barrel. Mfg. began Dec. 5, 1913-34.

	$1,950	$1,700	$1,350	$1,050	$860	$750	$700	

Add 10% for .44-40 WCF cal. with DCP proof mark.

Rifles and carbines made after 1924 are marked Model 14 on the receiver.

4,000 caliber .44-40 were contracted in 1914 by the British to be used in WWI, marked with a DCP proof mark.

MODEL 14 1/2 R CARBINE – .38-40 WCF or .44-40 WCF cal., 18 1/2 in. barrel, 8 shot mag., open sights, plain pistol grip stock.

	N/A	$2,300	$1,900	$1,800	$1,600	$1,200	$900	

MODEL 25/25A RIFLE – .25-20 WCF or .32-20 WCF cal., 24 in. barrel, open sights, tube mag., plain pistol grip stock. Mfg. 1923-35.

	N/A	$1,000	$900	$800	$700	$600	$475	

MODEL 25R CARBINE – .25-20 WCF or .32-20 WCF cal., 18 in. barrel (18 1/2 in. standard after 1934), tube mag., shielded rear sight, straight stock with sling eyes.

	N/A	$2,400	$2,200	$1,750	$1,500	$1,250	$995	

GRADING - PPGS™	100%	98%	95%	90%	80%	70%	60%	LAST MSR

MODEL 76 SPORTSMAN – .30-06 cal. only, 22 in. barrel, 4 shot mag., uncheckered hardwood stock and forearm, open sights, 7 1/2 lbs. Mfg. 1984-87.

	100%	98%	95%	90%	80%	70%	60%	LAST MSR
	$400	$350	$300	$260	$235	$215	$195	*$319*

MODEL 141/141A – .25 Rem. (very few mfg. during 1935 only), .30 Rem., .32 Rem., or .35 Rem. cal., 24 in. barrel, takedown, open sights, plain pistol grip stock. Mfg. 1935-1950. Approx. 2,000 model 141 rifles manufactured in 1935 with 22 in. barrels.

	100%	98%	95%	90%	80%	70%	60%
	$900	$725	$600	$500	$450	$300	$250
.25 Rem. cal.	$1,800	$1,550	$1,250	$950	$750	$550	$350

MODEL 141B/141C SPECIAL GRADE – .25 Rem. (very few mfg. during 1936 only), .30 Rem., .32 Rem., or .35 Rem. cal., takedown, 24 in. barrel, open sights, checkered fancy wood stock and forearm, early models were marked 141C.

	100%	98%	95%	90%	80%	70%	60%
	$1,500	$1,350	$1,100	$850	$650	$450	$300

Subtract 30% for plain forearm.

MODEL 141D PEERLESS GRADE – .25 Rem. (very few mfg. during 1936 only), .30 Rem., .32 Rem., or .35 Rem. cal., takedown, 24 in. barrel, open sights, checkered fancy wood stock and forearm, light engraving.

	100%	98%	95%	90%	80%	70%	60%
	$6,000	$5,250	$4,600	$4,000	$3,400	$2,650	$2,000

MODEL 141F PREMIER GRADE – .25 Rem. (very few mfg. during 1936 only), .30 Rem., .32 Rem., or .35 Rem. cal., takedown, 24 in. barrel, open sights, extra fancy wood stock and heavy engraving.

	100%	98%	95%	90%	80%	70%	60%
	$7,500	$6,500	$5,750	$5,250	$4,500	$3,750	$3,000

MODEL 141R CARBINE – plain stock and grooved forearm, 18 1/2 in. barrel. Mfg. 1935-1942.

	100%	98%	95%	90%	80%	70%	60%
	$1,600	$1,400	$1,200	$1,050	$950	$850	$700

Add 10% for .35 cal.
Add 30% for .25 cal.

MODEL 760 GAMEMASTER – .222 Rem. (mfg. 1958-61), .223 Rem. (limited mfg. 1964-69), 6mm Rem. (introduced 1969), .243 Win. (introduced 1968), .244 Rem. (mfg. 1956-59), .257 Roberts (mfg. 1955-58), .270 Win., .280 Rem. (mfg. 1958-1967), .30-06, .300 Sav. (disc. 1958), .308 Win., or .35 Rem. (mfg. 1952-67, and 1980) cal., 22 in. barrel, detachable mag., uncheckered or checkered (new 1964) pistol grip stock. Mfg. 1952-1980.

	100%	98%	95%	90%	80%	70%	60%
Standard calibers	$625	$500	$400	$300	$275	$250	$225
.222 Rem. cal.	$1,100	$925	$825	$725	$650	$575	$500
.223, & .280 Rem. cal.	$1,250	$1,000	$875	$775	$700	$625	$575
.244 Rem. & .257 Roberts. cal.	$850	$725	$575	$450	$400	$350	$300

MODEL 760C CARBINE – .270 Win., .280 Rem., .30-06, .308 Win., or .35 Rem. cal., 18 1/2 in. barrel.

	100%	98%	95%	90%	80%	70%	60%
.270 Win., .30-06, .308 Win.	$900	$800	$700	$550	$400	$275	$250
.280 Rem., .35 Rem.	$3,000	$2,500	$2,000	$1,500	$1,200	$800	$500

Subtract 10% for .30-06 cal.

MODEL 760 (CDL) CARBINE (FIVE DIAMOND) – .270 Win., .280 Rem., .30-06, or .308 Win. cal., 18 1/2 in. barrel, checkered stock, pistol grip cap and sling swivels. Mfg. 1961-1963.

	100%	98%	95%	90%	80%	70%	60%
	$900	$800	$700	$600	$500	$400	$300

Add 100% for .280 Rem. cal.

MODEL 760D PEERLESS GRADE – .270 Win., .280 Rem., .30-06, .308 Win. or .35 Rem. cal., 22 in. barrel, scroll engraving and fancy wood. Mfg. 1953-1980.

	100%	98%	95%	90%	80%	70%	60%
	$4,000	$3,000	$2,100	N/A	N/A	N/A	N/A

MODEL 760F PREMIER GRADE – .270 Win., .280 Rem., .30-06, .308 Win. or .35 Rem. cal., 22 in. barrel, extensive hand engraved game scenes and scroll work, best grade wood.

	100%	98%	95%	90%	80%	70%	60%
	$8,200	$6,500	$4,500	N/A	N/A	N/A	N/A

* ***Model 760F Premier w/Inlays*** – similar to Model 760F Premier Grade, except has game scenes inlaid in gold.

	100%	98%	95%	90%	80%	70%	60%
	$10,500	$9,000	$7,000	N/A	N/A	N/A	N/A

MODEL 760 150 YEAR ANNIVERSARY – .30-06 cal. only, 22 in. barrel, commemorative inscription roll engraved on receiver. 4,610 mfg. 1966 only.

	100%	98%	95%	90%	80%	70%	60%
	$1,000	$950	$850	N/A	N/A	N/A	N/A

MODEL 760 BICENTENNIAL – .30-06 cal. only, 22 in. barrel, commemorative inscription roll engraved on receiver. 3,804 mfg. 1976 only.

	100%	98%	95%	90%	80%	70%	60%
	$800	$700	$600	$450	$300	$250	$225

GRADING - PPGS™	100%	98%	95%	90%	80%	70%	60%	LAST MSR

MODEL 760ADL RIFLE (FIVE DIAMOND) – .222 Rem., .223 Rem., .244 Rem., .257 Roberts, .270 Win., .280 Rem., .30-06, .308 Win. or .35 Rem. cal., 22 in. barrel, checkered stock, grip cap, sling swivels. Mfg. 1953-1963.

	$800	**$700**	**$600**	**$450**	**$300**	**$250**	**$225**	
.222, .223, & .280 Rem. cal.								
	$1,750	**$1,550**	**$1,350**	**$1,050**	**$750**	**$550**	**$350**	

Add 30% for .244 Rem. and.257 Roberts cals.

MODEL 760BDL RIFLE (FIVE DIAMOND) – .222 Rem., .223 Rem., .244 Rem., .257 Roberts, .270 Win., .280 Rem., .30-06, .308 Win. or .35 Rem. cal., 22 in. barrel, checkered stock, grip cap, sling swivels, select grade wood. Mfg. 1953-1957.

	$900	**$800**	**$700**	**$525**	**$375**	**$295**	**$250**	
222, .223, & .280 Rem. cal.								
	$2,000	**$1,750**	**$1,500**	**$1,250**	**$950**	**$650**	**$450**	

Add 30% for .244 Rem. and.257 Roberts cals.

Only a few BDL grade rifles have been observed with the grade marked on the receiver. Flawed BDL grade stocks were downgraded and fitted to ADL grade rifles.

MODEL 760BDL DELUXE – similar to Model 760, except .270 Win., .30-06, or .308 Win. cal. only, step receiver, available with right or left-hand cheekpiece on Monte Carlo stock, basket weave checkering pattern, black pistol grip and forend tip. Mfg. 1966-1980.

	$600	**$450**	**$350**	**$300**	**$275**	**$250**	**$225**	

Add 20% for .308 Win. cal.

Add 10% for left-hand.

MODEL 7600 – 6mm Rem. (disc. 1984), .243 Win. (disc. 2015), .270 Win., .280 Rem. (mfg. 1988-2000), .30-06, .308 Win., or .35 Whelen (mfg. 1988-96) cal., modified 760 action, 22 in. barrel, 4 shot detachable mag., pressed checkered (disc.) or Monte Carlo pistol grip stock and forearm with satin or Hi-Gloss (disc. 2015) finish, 7 1/2 lbs. Mfg. 1981-2020.

	$710	**$550**	**$450**	**$375**	**$325**	**$275**	**$250**	***$918***

Add 30% for .35 Whelen and .280 Rem. cal. (disc.)

Depending on overall desirability, typical NIB asking prices for Grice Wholesale guns listed below will be 10%-15% higher than standard production.

In addition, walnut stocked rifles in .35 Whelen and carbines in .35 Rem. cal. were offered.

Beginning in 1990, a high gloss wood finish became available in cals. .270 Win. and .30-06 (Model 7600 High Gloss). From 1996-2003 receiver panels have fine line rolled game scene engraving.

A Pennsylvania distributor, Grice Wholesale, has offered a wide variety of special order, non-cataloged Model 7600s since 1990. The initial 1990 order was for 500 Model 7600s in 7mm-08 cal., followed by 1,000 7mm-08 cal. 175th Anniversary roll marked rifles in 1991. In 1992, the Deer Hunter Special, with a roll marked, gold filled deer scene was offered. This model was repeated in 1993 with a cabin and game scene engraving - 500 in .270 Win., 500 in .30-06, and 1,000 in 7mm-08 cal. were offered each year.

Over the years, Grice has also offered non-cataloged calibers such as 6mm Rem., .257 Roberts, .25-06 Rem., .260 Rem., .35 Rem. and .35 Whelen. Black and brown laminate stocks have also been offered.

The 2005 special orders were Model 7600s with maple stocks in 6mm Rem., .25-06 Rem., and 7mm-08 cal. 500 rifles were offered in .30-06 with a special roll marking commemorating the 100th anniversary of the .30-06, also with maple stocks.

In late 2006, Grice offered several Model 7600s with black laminated stocks - 7mm-08 cal., .30-06 cal. with a laser engraved "ONE OF 250 .30-06 100TH ANNIVERSARY 1906-2006" logo on the buttstock, and a Model 7615 in .223 Rem. cal. with a 22 in. barrel. Additionally, 300 walnut stocked Model 7600s in .300 Sav. cal. were also offered.

The 2007 Grice Special Run was in .280 Rem. with commemorative roll markings on the receiver and laser engraved "One of 500 280 Rem 50th Anniversary 1957 - 2007" on the high gloss finish walnut stock.

* ***Model 7600 Carbine*** – .30-06 cal., 18 1/2 in. barrel with polished blue finish, 4 shot detachable mag., Monte Carlo walnut stock and forearm with satin finish, 7 1/4 lbs. Disc. 2020.

	$710	**$550**	**$450**	**$375**	**$325**	**$275**	**$250**	***$918***

A total of 170 Larry Benoit Commemorative carbines were manufactured in 1999 and 2000 for Wilderness Trading and Supply Co. in VT. MSR was $995. Pricing varies on these models, since these guns were a limited special order.

* ***Model 7600P Patrol Rifle*** – .308 Win. cal., 16 1/2 in. barrel, synthetic stock, parkerized finish, Wilson Combat ghost ring sights, designed for police/law enforcement only.

Remington does not publish consumer retail pricing for this police/law enforcement model. Secondary prices for this model will be slightly higher than for current pricing on the Model 7600 Synthetic.

GRADING - PPGS™	100%	98%	95%	90%	80%	70%	60%	LAST MSR

* ***Model 7600 SP (Special Purpose)*** – .270 Win. or .30-06 cal., similar to Model 7600, except has non-reflective matte finish on wood and metalwork. Mfg. 1993-94.

	$425	$350	$300	$260	$235	$215	$195	*$496*

* ***Model 7600 Synthetic*** – .243 Win., .270 Win., .280 Rem. (mfg. 1998-2000), .30-06, or .308 Win. cal., 22 in. barrel only, features black fiberglass reinforced synthetic stock and forend, matte black metal finish, SuperCell recoil pad became standard 2011, 7 1/2 lbs. Mfg. 1998-2016.

	$610	$475	$385	$315	$265	$240	$225	*$771*

During 2007, Grice offered 500 Model 7600 QWAC (Quick Woods Action Carbine) in .308 Win. cal. with 18 1/2 in. barrels, Realtree AP camo synthetic stocks and fiber optic front and rear sights.

» ***Model 7600 Synthetic Carbine*** – .30-06 cal., similar to Model 7600 Synthetic, except has 18 1/2 in. barrel, SuperCell recoil pad became standard in 2011, 7 1/4 lbs. Mfg. 1998-2016.

	$610	$475	$385	$315	$265	$240	$225	*$771*

* ***Model 7600 175th Anniversary*** – also available in 7mm-08 Rem. cal., 1,000 mfg. 1991 only.

	$625	$525	$425	N/A	N/A	N/A	N/A	

* ***Model 7600 ADF Limited Edition*** – .30-06 cal. only, special edition 1997 only featuring Buckmaster's American Deer Foundation, special ADF engraving. Approx. 800 mfg. 1997 only.

	$600	$500	$325	N/A	N/A	N/A	N/A	*$567*

MODEL 7600 - 200TH YEAR ANNIVERSARY LIMITED EDITION – .30-06 cal., 22 in. barrel, C-Grade walnut stock with fleur-de-lis checkering, medallion in grip, Classic American style engraving and gold inlay, includes custom box, special serial number. Limited to quantity of 2,016. Limited mfg. 2016 only.

	$1,700	$1,500	$1,300	$995	$775	$650	$495	*$1,999*

MODEL 7600 ENGRAVED – hand engraved Model 7600s were mfg. 1988-2020.

* ***Model 7600 D Grade (Peerless)*** – features scroll engraving and fancy wood. Disc. 2020.

	N/A	$3,000	$2,100	N/A	N/A	N/A	N/A	

Last published MSR in 2007 was $4,532.

MSR for 2007-2020 was POR.

* ***Model 7600 F Grade (Premier)*** – features extensive hand engraved game scenes and scroll work and best grade wood. Disc. 2020.

	N/A	$6,500	$4,600	N/A	N/A	N/A	N/A	

Last published MSR in 2007 was $8,799.

MSR for 2007-2020 was POR.

* ***Model 7600 F Premier Grade w/Inlays*** – top-of-the-line custom shop model with game scenes inlaid in gold. Disc. 2020.

	N/A	$9,000	$7,000	N/A	N/A	N/A	N/A	

Last published MSR in 2007 was $11,999.

MSR for 2007-2020 was POR.

MODEL 7615 – .223 Rem., 10 shot AR-15 compatible detachable box mag., accepts AR-15 and M16 style magazines, 16 1/2 (tactical model with pistol grip and non-collapsible tube stock and Knoxx Special Ops NRS recoil suppressor), 18 1/2 (ranch rifle, walnut stock and forearm), or 22 (camo hunter, 100% Mossy Oak Brush camo coverage) in. barrel w/o sights, synthetic or walnut (ranch carbine) stock and forearm, drilled and tapped, approx. 7 lbs. Mfg. 2007-2008, mfg. in Ilion, NY.

	$790	$685	$575	$500	$450	$400	$350	*$955*

Add $54 for Camo Hunter with 100% camo coverage.

MODEL 7615P PATROL RIFLE – .223 Rem. cal., 16 1/2 in. barrel, 10 shot or extended mag., synthetic stock, parkerized finish, accepts AR-15 and M16 style magazines, Wilson Combat ghost ring sights, designed for police/law enforcement, 7 lbs.

Remington does not publish consumer retail pricing for this police/law enforcement model. Secondary prices for this model will be slightly higher than for current pricing on the Model 7600 Carbine.

MODEL 7615 SPS – .223 Rem. cal., 16 1/2 in. blue barrel, Picatinny rail, action, slide release and safety based on the Model 870, 10 shot mag, accepts AR-15 and M16 style mags., black pistol grip synthetic stock. Mfg. 2008.

	$695	$625	$550	$500	$450	$400	$350	*$805*

This model was available through Remington Premier dealers only.

GRADING - PPGS™	100%	98%	95%	90%	80%	70%	60%	LAST MSR

RIFLES: RIMFIRE, BOLT ACTION

From 1930-1960 Remington produced a number of bolt action .22 cal. Rimfire rifles, both single shot and repeaters. They were good quality, serviceable weapons with many slight variations upon a basic design. Whenever possible, models have been listed in numerical sequence.

On factory engraved E & F grade rifles, the ser. no. is usually engraved instead of stamped, and there is no standard factory engraving pattern on these grades.

Serialization began in 1968 on these models unless noted otherwise.

MODEL FIVE – .17 HMR (new 2008), .22 LR, or .22 WMR cal., 22 in. barrel with adj. flip-up rear sight, blued finish, 5 shot detachable mag., checkered satin finished brown laminated or European walnut (.22 LR only, mfg. 2008) stock and forend, grooved steel receiver, safety located next to bolt, includes sling swivels, 6 3/4 lbs., mfg. in Serbia. Mfg. 2006-2009.

$225 $195 $150 $130 $120 $90 $80 *$203*

Add 30% for walnut stock (disc. 2008, last MSR was $349).

* ***Model Five Youth*** – .22 LR cal., 16 1/2 in. barrel with open sights, shortened LOP, hardwood stock, 5 shot detachable mag. with single shot adapter. Mfg. 2008-2009.

$200 $175 $150 $125 $100 $65 $50 *$167*

MODEL 33 – .22 S, L, or LR cal.

$250 $225 $195 $175 $150 $115 $90

Approx. 263,557 of the Model 33 and variations were mfg. 1932-1936.

MODEL 33 NRA – .22 S, L, or LR cal.

$375 $350 $300 $275 $200 $175 $150

MODEL 33-P – .22 S, L, or LR cal.

$325 $300 $250 $210 $190 $140 $110

MODEL 33 SB – .22 LR Shot cal.

$400 $350 $325 $300 $250 $225 $175

MODEL 34 – .22 S, L, or LR cal.

$325 $300 $275 $250 $200 $175 $150

MODEL 34 NRA – .22 S, L, or LR cal.

$500 $475 $395 $350 $295 $235 $185

MODEL 34-P – .22 S, L, or LR cal.

$375 $325 $285 $260 $210 $185 $160

Approx. 162,941 of the Model 34 and variations were mfg. 1932-1936.

MODEL 37 "RANGEMASTER" TARGET RIFLE – .22 LR cal., 5 shot mag. with single shot adapter, 28 in. barrel, target sights and scope bases, target stock, 12 1/2 lbs. Mfg. 1937-1940.

$1,300 $1,200 $1,000 $850 $700 $550 $425

w/Orig. BBL Band on Stock

$2,200 $1,925 $1,650 $1,495 $1,210 $990 $770

Approx. 1,788 of the Model 37 and variations were mfg. 1936-1939.

MODEL 37 - 1940 – improved trigger and stock design. Mfg. 1939-1942.

$1,200 $1,100 $1,000 $850 $700 $550 $425

Approx. 2,032 of the Model 37-1940 variation were mfg. 1936-1939.

MODEL 341 A – .22 S, L, or LR cal.

$300 $275 $250 $195 $160 $135 $100

MODEL 341 P – .22 S, L, or LR cal.

$350 $300 $275 $250 $200 $160 $125

MODEL 341 SB – .22 LR Shot cal.

$500 $440 $375 $340 $275 $225 $175

131,604 of the Model 341 "Sportsmaster" and variations were mfg. 1936-1940.

MODEL 41 A – .22 S, L, or LR cal.

$250 $225 $190 $170 $140 $115 $90

306,880 of the Model 41 "Targetmaster" and variations were produced 1936-1939.

GRADING - PPGS™	100%	98%	95%	90%	80%	70%	60%	LAST MSR

MODEL 41 AS - .22 Rem. Spec. cal.

	$400	$350	$325	$300	$250	$200	$160	

MODEL 41 P - .22 S, L, or LR cal.

	$300	$260	$225	$200	$170	$140	$100	

MODEL 41 SB - .22 LR Shot cal.

	$400	$350	$300	$270	$200	$180	$140	

MODEL 411 - .22 CB Cap or Short cal.

	$600	$525	$450	$410	$330	$270	$210	

Add 50% premium for .22 Short.

The Model 411 is similar to the Model 41 single shot, but in CB Cap or .22 Short and without safety on rear of bolt. Eye screw for gallery use. 1,316 mfg. 1937-39 (although never cataloged).

MODEL 412 YOUTH BOLT ACTION - .22 LR cal., single shot with second shot holder, 19 3/4 in. barrel with adj. sights, automatic safety, uncheckered hardwood stock, blue finish, 4 1/2 lbs. Limited mfg. 2006.

While advertised with a MSR of $136, these rifles were mfg. in Mexico, but were not shipped to Remington.

MODEL 504 - .17 Mach 2 (new 2005) or .22 LR cal., bolt action, drilled and tapped solid steel receiver, 20 in. barrel w/o sights, matte metal finish, features 5-R button rifling (same as the Model 40-XR), dual bedding points, fully adj. trigger group, dual extractors, 6 shot detachable mag., checkered American walnut stock, cocking indicator, approx. 6 lbs. Mfg. 2004-2006 in Ilion, NY.

	$750	$700	$575	$450	$340	$275	$215	*$738*

* ***Model 504-T*** - .17 HMR or .22 LR cal., similar to Model 504, except has 20 in. heavy free floating barrel, Eley match chamber, 5 (.17 HMR) or 6 shot mag., brown laminate Monte Carlo stock with palm swell and beavertail forend, satin blue metal, approx. 6 1/2 lbs. Mfg. 2005-2006.

	$695	$610	$520	$475	$380	$315	$245	*$839*

Add $26 for .17 HMR cal.

MODEL 504 CUSTOM C GRADE - .22 LR cal., bolt action, 24 in. carbon steel blue barrel, "C" grade fancy semi-gloss American walnut stock with rosewood pistol grip and forend caps, 6 1/2 lbs., limited mfg. 2006-2008.

	$1,800	$1,600	$1,400	$1,250	$1,000	$750	$600	*$1,836*

MODEL 510 A "TARGETMASTER" - .22 S, L, or LR cal., single shot.

	$220	$195	$175	$150	$120	$110	$100	

Approx. 558,000 of the Model 510 and variations were mfg. 1939-1962.

MODEL 510 C (CARBINE) - .22 S, L, or LR cal.

	$375	$325	$275	$250	$200	$190	$175	

MODEL 510 P - .22 S, L, or LR cal.

	$300	$250	$225	$200	$165	$150	$130	

MODEL 510 ROUTLEDGE/SMOOTHBORE - .22 LR Shot cal.

	$400	$350	$325	$300	$250	$200	$175	

Add 25% for Mo-Skeet-O Bore.
Add 50% for Skeetrap.

MODEL 510-X - .22 S, L, or LR cal.

	$300	$275	$250	$200	$150	$125	$100	

Approx. 18,088 of the Model 510-X were mfg. 1964-1966.

MODEL 510-X SB - .22 LR Shot cal.

	$400	$375	$300	$250	$200	$125	$100	

Add $50 for grooved receiver.

Approx. 1,813 of the Model 510-X-SB were mfg.

MODEL 511 A "SCOREMASTER" - .22 S, L, or LR cal., 6 shot box mag.

	$250	$225	$195	$175	$150	$120	$110	
Smoothbore	$425	$390	$350	$250	$175	$160	$140	

Add $50 for grooved receiver.

Approx. 375,000 of the Models 511A and 511P were mfg. 1939-1962.

GRADING - PPGS™	100%	98%	95%	90%	80%	70%	60%	LAST MSR

MODEL 511 P – .22 S, L, or LR cal.

	$300	$275	$225	$195	$160	$150	$125	

These models were mfg. 1939-1962. Approx. 375,000 mfg.

Add $50 for grooved receiver.

MODEL 511-X – .22 S, L, or LR cal.

	$300	$275	$250	$200	$175	$125	$110	

Approx. 29,120 of the Model 511-X were mfg. 1964-1966.

MODEL 512 A "SPORTMASTER" – .22 S, L, or LR cal., 15 (.22 LR) shot tube mag.

	$250	$225	$195	$175	$150	$120	$100	
Smoothbore	$400	$350	$300	$225	$195	$160	$145	

Add $50 for grooved receiver.

Approx. 393,000 of the Model 512 and variations were mfg. 1940-1963.

MODEL 512 P – .22 S, L, or LR cal.

	$295	$255	$225	$195	$160	$150	$125	

Add $50 for grooved receiver.

MODEL 512-X – .22 S, L, or LR cal.

	$300	$275	$250	$200	$150	$125	$110	

Approx. 30,683 of the Model 512-X were mfg. 1964-1966.

MODEL 513S/513SA "MATCHMASTER" SPORTER – .22 LR cal., sporting variation of the Model 513T, with open sights and checkered sporter stock. 13,677 were mfg. 1940-1957 (including the Model 513SP).

	$900	$850	$750	$600	$470	$385	$300	

Add 15% for select figured or hand rubbed oil finished walnut stock.

The Model 513S Sporting Rifle designates either the 513SA or 513SP Model. Both guns were designated "Matchmaster", along with the Model 513T.

MODEL 513SP "MATCHMASTER" SPORTER – .22 LR cal., Remington Point-Crometer receiver aperture sight, checkered sporter, select figured, or hand rubbed oil finished walnut stock. Mfg. 1942-1950.

	$925	$775	$675	$600	$500	$400	$325	

Add 15% for select figured or hand rubbed oil finished walnut stock.

MODEL 513T "MATCHMASTER" (TARGET) – .22 S, L, or LR cal., 27 in. tapered barrel, raked bolt handle, Redfield aperture rear sight, target stock, 6 shot, sling swivels. Approx. 166,000 were mfg. 1940-1968.

	$500	$425	$375	$300	$250	$205	$160	

A "TR" suffix on this gun indicated with sights, a "TX" indicated w/o sights, a "TS" indicated sporter. Most 513s are marked either 513T (Target) or 513S (Sporter). Many are U.S. Property marked. Approx. 62,000 were made for military training for WWII and Korea.

MODEL 514 – .22 S, L, or LR cal.

	$200	$175	$150	$130	$100	$90	$85	

Approx. 757,000 of the Model 514 and variations were mfg. 1948-1970.

MODEL 514 P (1952-1971) – .22 S, L, or LR cal.

	$225	$200	$175	$155	$130	$120	$100	

MODEL 514 BC/BR (BOY'S CARBINE/BOY'S RIFLE) – .22 S, L, or LR cal.

	$225	$200	$170	$155	$120	$95	$80	

The suffixe of this model was changed to BR (Boy's Rifle) in 1965.

MODEL 514 ROUTLEDGE/SMOOTHBORE – .22 LR Shot cal.

	$350	$300	$275	$250	$200	$165	$150	

Approx. 5,557 of the Model 514 Routledge/Smoothbore were mfg. 1951-1969.

MODEL 521T/TL JR. – .22 LR cal., 25 in. barrel, Lyman target sights, takedown, 6 shot mag., target stock. Approx. 67,000 were mfg. 1947-1968.

	$425	$375	$300	$250	$200	$175	$150	

These models had no ser. no. until 1954. This model's nomenclature changed to 521T in 1959.

MODEL 540X RIMFIRE – .22 LR cal., single shot bolt action, 26 in. heavy barrel, no sights, target stock, adj. butt. Approx. 5,115 mfg. 1969-1974.

	$500	$450	$400	$325	$240	$190	$150	

GRADING - PPGS™	100%	98%	95%	90%	80%	70%	60%	LAST MSR

MODEL 540XR – .22 LR cal., single shot, 26 in. heavy barrel, large position style stock with adj. buttplate. Mfg. 1974-1983.

$650 $600 $500 $400 $325 $275 $200

Add 15% for original sights.

* ***Model 540XR JR*** – .22 LR cal., similar to Model 540X, except 1 1/2 in. shorter stock. Mfg. 1974-1983.

$575 $525 $450 $400 $300 $250 $200

MODEL 541S CUSTOM – .22 S, L, or LR cal., bolt action, 24 in. barrel, drilled and tapped, 5 shot mag., adj. match trigger, scroll engraved receiver and trigger guard, checkered walnut stock with rosewood pistol grip cap, buttplate, and forend tip. Mfg. 1972-1984.

$900 $850 $750 $700 $550 $375 $275

MODEL 541T – .22 LR cal. only, 5 shot mag., 24 in. standard or heavy (new 1993) barrel, checkered American walnut stock with satin finish, barrel is drilled and tapped, 5 7/8 lbs. Mfg. 1986-1999.

$600 $550 $450 $350 $300 $225 $175 *$465*

Add $50 for heavy barrel.
Add 50% for maple stock.

MODEL 541X – .22 LR cal. only, U.S. military training rifle, 27 in. barrel, 5 shot mag., ser. no. inscribed by hand on bolt, 9,077 mfg. 1984-1986.

$550 $500 $425 $400 $300 $250 $195

Add 15% for new in foil wrapper.

MODEL 547 CUSTOM CLASSIC – .17 HMR, .22 LR, or .22 WMR (new 2014) cal., Model 700 style action and bolt handle, high polished 22 in. Shilen custom barrel w/o sights, classic walnut stock with rosewood forend tip and grip cap, "CDL Style" checkering, 3 lbs. trigger pull, guaranteed 1/2 in. 5 shot groups at 50 yards. Mfg. by custom shop 2008-2015.

$1,125 $950 $825 $725 $625 $525 $450 *$1,350*

This model is also available in .17 Mach 2 or .22 WMR cal. on special request.

* ***Model 547-T Custom Classic*** – .17 HMR, .22 WMR (new 2014) or .22 LR cal., similar to Model 547 Classic, except has 18 1/4 in. stainless steel heavy target barrel, walnut target style stock. Mfg. by custom shop 2009-2015.

$1,350 $1,075 $925 $800 $700 $600 $550 *$1,600*

* ***Model 547-C Custom Classic*** – .17 HMR, .22 WMR, or .22 LR cal., similar to Model 547 Classic, except has 22 in. medium contour barrel, C Grade stock with rosewood forend tip and pistol grip cap. Mfg. by custom shop 2009-2015.

$1,800 $1,700 $1,500 $1,200 $900 $775 $650 *$1,999*

MODEL 580/MODEL 580SB SINGLE SHOT – .22 S, L, or LR cal., 24 in. barrel, open sights, Monte Carlo stock. Mfg. 1967-1978.

$225 $200 $180 $150 $100 $90 $70

Add 50% for smoothbore (Model 580SB).

MODEL 580BR – .22 S, L, or LR cal., Boy's Model, 1 in. shorter stock. Mfg. 1971-1978.

$225 $200 $175 $150 $110 $95 $75

MODEL 581 – .22 LR cal., 6 shot mag., converts to single shot. Mfg. 1967-1983.

$250 $225 $200 $160 $125 $100 $80

Add 25% for smoothbore.

MODEL 581 SPORTSMAN – .22 LR cal., 5 shot mag., 24 in. barrel, hardwood uncheckered stock, 4 3/4 lbs. Mfg. 1986-1999.

$225 $200 $180 $160 $125 $100 $80 *$239*

MODEL 582 – .22 LR cal., similar to 581, with tube mag. Mfg. 1967-1983.

$250 $225 $200 $160 $125 $100 $80

MODEL 591 – 5mm Rimfire Mag. cal., 24 in. barrel, open sight, 5 shot mag., Monte Carlo stock. Approx. 27,000 mfg. 1970-1974.

$400 $350 $300 $250 $200 $175 $120

MODEL 592 – 5mm Rimfire Mag. cal., similar to 591, with tube mag. Approx. 25,000 mfg. 1970-1974.

$400 $350 $300 $250 $200 $175 $120

MODEL 600 SERIES (MODELS 610, 611, & 613) – .267 rimfire cal., prototypes only, never offered commercially for sale. Mfg. circa late-1930s.

Extreme rarity factor precludes accurate values on these prototypes.

GRADING - PPGS™	100%	98%	95%	90%	80%	70%	60%	LAST MSR

RIFLES: RIMFIRE, "NYLON SERIES"

These models can be identified by the markings on the grip cap.

NYLON 10 SINGLE SHOT – .22 S, L, or LR cal., bolt action, automatic safety, 19 5/8 or 24 (mfg. 1964 only) in. barrel, Mohawk Brown nylon stock, approx. 4 lbs. 8,606 were mfg. 1962-1964.

19 5/8 in. bbl.	$800	$700	$550	$400	$300	$275	$250

Add 50% for 24 in. barrel.

* ***Nylon 10-SB Single Shot*** – .22 shot cal., similar to Nylon 10, except has 19 5/8 (2,064 mfg.) or 24 (rare, quantity unknown) in. smoothbore barrel used for .22 shot cartridges.

19 5/8 in. bbl.	$1,400	$1,250	$995	$850	$700	$600	$450

Add 50% for 24 in. barrel.

Nylon 10s with 24 in. smoothbore barrels are very rare, and accurate pricing is hard to ascertain. Some specimens have sold in the $2,000-$6,000 range, depending on original condition.

MOHAWK 10-C – .22 LR cal., similar to Model Nylon 77, renamed after changing to a 10 shot box mag, approx. 129,000 were mfg. 1971-1978.

	$325	$300	$250	$200	$175	$125	$110

MODEL 11 NYLON – .22 S, L, or LR cal., bolt action repeater, 6 or 10 shot detachable box mag., 19 5/8 or 24 (mfg. 1964 only) in. barrel, 4 1/2 lbs. 22,423 were mfg. 1962-1964.

19 5/8 in. barrel	$700	$650	$500	$350	$275	$250	$200

Add 50% for 24 in. barrel.

MODEL 12 NYLON – .22 S, L, or LR cal., 19 5/8 or 24 (mfg. 1964 only) in. barrel, 15 shot tube mag. 27,551 were mfg. 1962-1964.

19 5/8 in. bbl.	$700	$650	$500	$325	$275	$250	$200

Add 50% for 24 in. barrel.

NYLON 66 AUTOLOADER – .22 LR cal., 19 5/8 in. barrel, open sights, 14 shot buttstock tube mag., 4 lbs. Stock, receiver, and forearm made from Zytel plastic in black, brown, or green, metal receiver cover. 1,050,336 were mfg. 1959-90.

Mohawk Brown	$500	$400	$350	$300	$250	$200	$175
Black Diamond	$600	$500	$400	$350	$300	$260	$230
Apache Black/Chrome	$600	$525	$450	$400	$350	$300	$250
Seneca Green	$650	$600	$475	$425	$350	$300	$260
Gallery Special (.22 Short cal. only)	$1,000	$900	$800	$700	$525	$425	$325

Last MSR was $124.

Approx. 56,000 Black Diamond models were mfg., approx. 221,000 Apache Black/Chrome models were mfg., approx. 45,000 Seneca Green were mfg, approx. 675,052 Mohawk Brown were mfg., and approx. 16,474 Gallery Special were mfg.

NYLON 66 150TH ANNIVERSARY – 3,792 mfg. in 1966 only with 150th Anniversary Remington logo on receiver cover.

	$800	$700	$550	$425	$350	$275	$200

NYLON 66 BICENTENNIAL – .22 LR cal., inscription on receiver cover, Mohawk brown nylon stock only. 10,268 mfg. 1976 only.

	$700	$625	$550	$400	$300	$250	$175

NYLON 76 LEVER ACTION – .22 LR cal., short throw lever action, 19 5/8 in. barrel, open sights, 25,312 mfg. in standard with Apache Black/Chrome finish, 1,615 were mfg. in black chrome finish 1962-1964 only.

Mohawk Brown	$1,000	$900	$800	$700	$600	$450	$275
Apache Black/Chrome	$1,500	$1,325	$1,100	$850	$700	$575	$450

The Nylon 76 "Trail Rider" is the only lever action repeating rifle ever mfg. by Remington.

NYLON 77 – .22 LR cal., 19 5/8 in. barrel, open sights, 5 shot box mag., otherwise similar to Nylon 66. 15,327 were mfg. 1970-1971 only.

	$450	$350	$300	$225	$195	$175	$150

NYLON APACHE 77 – .22 LR cal., 19 5/8 in. barrel, 10 shot box mag., black painted external metal and dark olive green stock/receiver. Mfg. for K-Mart in 1987-1989.

	$400	$325	$250	$200	$150	$125	$75

GRADING - PPGS™	100%	98%	95%	90%	80%	70%	60%	LAST MSR

RIFLES: RIMFIRE, SEMI-AUTO

MODEL 16/16A AUTOLOADING RIFLE – .22 Rem. Autoloading cal., 22 in. barrel, open sights, tube mag. in buttstock, straight stock. 17,738 mfg. 1914-1928.

$1,400 $1,200 $900 $775 $575 $325 $275

* ***Model 16/16A Autoloading Rifle C Special Grade*** – .22 Rem. Autoloading cal., similar to Model 16/16A, except has select checkered walnut stock and forearm.

$1,600 $1375 $1,100 $875 $700 $525 $400

* ***Model 16/16A Autoloading Rifle D Peerless Grade*** – .22 Rem. Autoloading cal., similar to Model 16/16A C Special Grade, except has lightly scroll engraved receiver and barrel, hand honed internal parts.

$7,500 $7,000 $6,000 $5,000 $3,500 $3,000 $2,500

* ***Model 16/16A Autoloading Rifle F Premier Grade*** – .22 Rem. Autoloading cal., 22 in. barrel, top-of-the-line model with best quality checkered walnut stock, fully engraved receiver featuring rabbits or squirrels, gold nameplate on stock, open sights.

$12,000 $10,500 $9,000 $8,000 $6,000 $5,000 $3,750

MODEL 24/24A AUTOLOADING RIFLE – .22 S or LR cal., 19 in. barrel, open sights, Browning semi-auto design, bottom ejection, tube mag. through buttstock, takedown, plain pistol grip stock. Approx. 131,000 mfg. 1922-35.

$1,200 $1,000 $800 $600 $500 $400 $300

* ***Model 24/24A Autoloading Rifle C Special Grade*** – .22 S or LR cal., similar to Model 24/24A, except has select checkered walnut stock and forearm.

$1,750 $1,500 $1,250 $1,100 $1,000 $900 $600

* ***Model 24/24A Autoloading Rifle D Peerless Grade*** – .22 S or LR cal., similar to Model 24/24A C Special Grade, except has lightly scroll engraved receiver and barrel, hand honed internal parts.

$7,500 $6,500 $6,000 $5,500 $3,500 $3,000 $2,500

Add a 20% premium for .22 Short cal.

* ***Model 24/24A Autoloading Rifle E Expert Grade*** – .22 S or LR cal., similar to Model 24/24A D Peerless Grade, except has silver nameplate inlaid in stock.

$8,000 $7,000 $6,500 $6,000 $4,500 $4,000 $2,750

* ***Model 24/24A Autoloading Rifle F Premier Grade*** – top-of-the-line model with best quality checkered walnut stock, fully engraved receiver featuring rabbits or squirrels, gold nameplate on stock.

$11,000 $10,000 $9,000 $7,000 $6,000 $5,000 $3,750

MODEL 241A (LA/SA) SPEEDMASTER – .22 S (Model 241 SA) or LR (Model 241 LA) cal., 24 in. barrel, replaced the Browning designed Model 24, open sights, takedown (button located on left side of receiver), blue (most common) or chrome plated (either full plating or receiver and trigger plate only, scarce), 10 (.22 LR cal.) or 15 (.22 Short cal.) shot tube mag. in buttstock, non-checkered walnut stock and forearm, model name and ser. no. stamped on left side of receiver, "Speedmaster" and the Remington logo added during 1936, approx. 6 lbs. Approx. 107,000 mfg. 1935-1951, with serialization ending at approx. 132,000 (after 1946, serialization and dates became inaccurate).

$1,200 $1,000 $900 $775 $600 $450 $350

Add a 20% premium for .22 Short cal.
Add 50% for chrome finish.

The B Grade was introduced in early 1940.

* ***Model 241A Speedmaster C Special Grade*** – .22 S or LR cal., similar to Model 241A Speedmaster, except has select checkered walnut stock and forearm.

$1,700 $1,450 $1,275 $975 $800 $650 $500

* ***Model 241A Speedmaster D Peerless Grade*** – .22 S or LR cal., similar to Model 241A Speedmaster C Special Grade, except has lightly scroll engraved receiver and barrel, hand honed internal parts.

$6,750 $6,150 $5,600 $5,000 $4,000 $3,500 $2,000

* ***Model 241A Speedmaster E Expert Grade*** – .22 S or LR cal., similar to Model 241A Speedmaster D Peerless Grade, except has silver nameplate inlaid in stock.

$7,750 $6,650 $6,000 $5,000 $4,000 $3,500 $2,500

* ***Model 241A Speedmaster F Premier Grade*** – .22 S or LR cal., top-of-the-line model with best quality checkered walnut stock, fully engraved receiver featuring rabbits or squirrels, gold nameplate on stock.

$9,250 $8,150 $7,625 $6,500 $5,500 $4,500 $3,500

GRADING - PPGS™	100%	98%	95%	90%	80%	70%	60%	LAST MSR

MODEL 522 VIPER – .22 LR cal., semi-auto blowback action, 20 in. barrel, full-length black synthetic resin stock with beavertail forend, 10 shot mag., cocking indicator, adj. rear sight, grooved synthetic receiver, 4 5/8 lbs. Total production of 244,082. Mfg. 1993-1997.

$150 $125 $95 $85 $70 $60 $50 *$152*

MODEL 550A – .22 S, L, or LR cal., 24 in. barrel, open sights, shell deflector, dual extractors, tube mag., plain one-piece pistol stock. 34,577 mfg. 1941-1946.

$350 $300 $250 $210 $190 $125 $95

Add 100% if w/o shell deflector (not tapped).

MODEL 550-1 – .22 S, L, or LR cal., 24 in. barrel, tube mag., single extractor, open sights, plain one-piece pistol stock. Approx. 730,000 mfg. 1946-1970.

$300 $270 $250 $200 $170 $125 $90

MODEL 550P – .22 S, L, or LR cal., 24 in. barrel, tube mag., single extractor, aperture rear sight, plain one-piece walnut stock.

$400 $350 $325 $250 $200 $175 $125

MODEL 550-2G – .22 Short cal., 22 in. barrel, single extractor, open sights, plain one-piece pistol stock, eye screw for counter chain in shooting gallery.

$500 $450 $350 $300 $250 $200 $125

MODEL 552A SPEEDMASTER – .22 S, L, or LR cal., 23 in. barrel, open sights, tube mag., pistol grip stock. Mfg. 1957-disc.

$350 $300 $250 $200 $150 $125 $95

This model was also manufactured in a 150th Anniversary Model (1966 only, approx. 6,565 mfg.) and a 175th Anniversary (1991 only). Slight premiums are being asked if condition is 98% or better.

MODEL 552C – .22 S, L, or LR cal., 21 in. barrel, tube mag., open sights, pistol grip stock. Mfg. 1961-1977.

$350 $320 $300 $250 $200 $150 $110

MODEL 552 BDL DELUXE SPEEDMASTER – .22 S, L, or LR cal., 21 in. carbon steel barrel with polished blue finish, 15 shot mag., adj. iron sights, checkered gloss finished walnut Monte Carlo stock and forearm, 5 3/4 lbs. Mfg. 1966-2020.

$600 $525 $475 $350 $250 $200 $175 *$707*

* ***Model 552 BDL Deluxe Fieldmaster NRA Edition*** – features laser etched "NRA" on both sides of receiver. Limited mfg. 2006-2007.

$600 $550 $500 $350 $250 $180 $140 *$532*

MODEL 552 175th ANNIVERSARY – 1,000 mfg. 1991 only.

$600 $550 $450 $400 $275 $225 $175

MODEL 597 – .22 LR cal., 20 in. free floating carbon steel barrel, alloy receiver with nickel plated bolt, matte black metal finish, one-piece dark grey smooth synthetic stock, 10 shot staggered detachable mag., adj. iron sights, new trigger design, 5 1/2 lbs. Mfg. in Mayfield, KY. Mfg. 1997-2020.

$200 $175 $150 $125 $100 $75 $60 *$213*

Add $44 for 3-9x32mm scope combo (new 2007).

This model has also been available in several limited production runs. Prices are usually slightly higher than the standard pricing listed above.

* ***Model 597 Sporter*** – .22 LR cal., similar to Model 597, except has hardwood stock, includes sling swivel studs. Mfg. 1998-2000.

$200 $175 $150 $110 $90 $70 $55 *$199*

* ***Model 597 Stainless Sporter*** – .22 LR cal., similar to Model 597 Sporter, except has stainless steel barrel and hardwood stock. Mfg. 2000 only.

$225 $200 $175 $150 $105 $85 $65 *$239*

* ***Model 597 SS*** – .22 LR cal., similar to Model 597 Semi-Auto, except has stainless steel with satin finished receiver and barrel, and synthetic stock and beavertail style forend. Mfg. 1998-2007.

$250 $225 $200 $175 $150 $125 $100 *$283*

* ***Model 597 LSS*** – .22 LR cal., similar to Model 597 Semi-Auto, except has stainless steel barrel with matching finish alloy receiver, and satin finished brown wood laminate stock, 5 1/2 lbs. Mfg. 1997-2007.

$300 $250 $215 $195 $155 $130 $100 *$348*

GRADING - PPGS™ 100% 98% 95% 90% 80% 70% 60% LAST MSR

* ***Model 597 HB LS*** – .22 LR cal., 20 in. heavy steel barrel, 10 shot staggered detachable mag., stainless steel barrel with matching finish alloy receiver, adj. iron sights, satin finished brown wood laminate stock, matte black metal finish. Mfg. 2001-2007.

$300 $250 $210 $185 $150 $125 $95 *$337*

* ***Model 597 Heavy Barrel*** – .22 LR cal., 16 1/2 in. heavy barrel w/o sights, scope rail installed, OD Green or A-TACS digital camo (disc. 2015) synthetic stock, 5 3/4 lbs. Mfg. 2012-2020.

$225 $190 $160 $145 $120 $95 $75 *$254*

Add $102 for A-TACS Digital camo stock and threaded barrel (disc. 2015).

* ***Model 597 Camo*** – .22 LR cal., 20 in. free floating carbon steel barrel, 10 shot staggered detachable mag., TruGlo fiber optic sights, Mossy Oak Blaze Orange (disc. 2014) or Mossy Oak Pink camo stock, matte black metal finish, 5 1/2 lbs. Mfg. 2008-2020.

$260 $230 $195 $175 $145 $115 $100 *$306*

* ***Model 597 FLX*** – .22 LR cal., 20 in. carbon steel barrel, 10 shot mag., adj. iron sights, Next digital FLX camo synthetic stock, matte black metal finish. Mfg. 2009-2014.

$240 $195 $175 $145 $120 $95 $75 *$306*

* ***Model 597 AAC-SD*** – .22 LR cal., 16 1/2 in. threaded barrel with thread protector, accepts AAC and other flash hiders, muzzle brakes, or suppressors, black synthetic stock, includes scope rail, 10 shot mag., no sights, 5 1/2 lbs. Mfg. 2011-2014.

$225 $180 $130 $110 $100 $85 $75 *$257*

* ***Model 597 Threaded Barrel*** – .22 LR cal., 16 1/2 in. carbon steel threaded barrel, synthetic stock with Kryptek Mandrake camo finish, scope rail, matte blue finish, 5 1/2 lbs. Mfg. 2018-2020.

$250 $225 $195 $175 $150 $125 $100 *$289*

MODEL 597 TVP (TARGET VARMINT PLINKER) – .22 LR cal., stainless action and 20 in. heavy stainless barrel, bolt guidance system with twin steel guide rails, non-glare matte finish metal, ambidextrous laminated thumbhole stock with scalloped forend, 10 shot mag., includes scope mounting rail, 5 1/2 lbs. Mfg. 2008-2014.

$475 $380 $310 $260 $215 $200 $155 *$607*

MODEL 597 CUSTOM TARGET – .22 LR cal., 20 in. custom contoured satin finish heavy stainless free floating barrel w/o sights, match chamber, special green laminated stock with Monte Carlo profile and beavertail forend. Mfg. 1998-2000.

$500 $440 $375 $340 $275 $225 $175 *$599*

* ***Model 597 Custom Target .22 Mag.*** – .22 WMR cal., otherwise similar to Model 597 Custom Target. Disc. 2000.

$600 $525 $450 $410 $330 $270 $210 *$745*

MODEL 597 DALE EARNHARDT – First release 2000-2001. Limited Edition. No. 3 (Sr.) and No. 8 (Jr.).

$350 $325 $275 $200 $150 $140 $125

MODEL 597 MAGNUM SYNTHETIC – .17 HMR (mfg. 2003-2007) or .22 WMR cal., similar in appearance to Model 597, 8 shot mag., 20 in. barrel, black synthetic stock with sling swivel studs, 6 lbs. Mfg. 1997-2014.

$415 $330 $260 $220 $195 $175 $135 *$541*

* ***Model 597 Magnum Synthetic LS*** – .17 HMR (mfg. 2002-2003 only) or .22 WMR cal., similar to Model 597 Magnum Synthetic, except features brown laminate stock with sling swivel studs and steel barrel. Mfg. 1998-2003.

$315 $275 $235 $215 $175 $140 $110 *$377*

Remington issued a product safety recall notice on this model for .17 HMR cal. rifles during 2009.

* ***Model 597 Magnum LS Heavy Barrel*** – .17 HMR (disc. 2007) or .22 WMR cal., 20 in. satin finished blued carbon steel heavy barrel, drilled and tapped for scope rail, grooved receiver, 10 shot removable box magazine, brown hardwood laminated stock and sling swivel studs, 6 lbs. Mfg. 2001-2014.

$495 $410 $330 $285 $245 $210 $185 *$645*

Remington issued a product safety recall notice on this model for .17 HMR cal. rifles during 2009.

MODEL 597 TARGET RIFLE – .22 LR cal., heavy barrel, black, grey and yellow ShurShot target laminated skeletonized stock, scope rail, 10 shot detachable mag., last shot hold open, twin steel guide rails. Mfg. 2008 only.

$425 $370 $320 $290 $235 $190 $150 *$505*

This model was available through Remington Premier dealers only.

GRADING - PPGS™	100%	98%	95%	90%	80%	70%	60%	LAST MSR

MODEL 597 VTR (VARMINT TARGET RIFLE) – .22 LR or .22 WMR cal., 16 in. heavy barrel, 10 or 30 shot mag., Picatinny top rail, fixed A2 or Pardus collapsible stock with pistol grip, with (collapsible stock only) or w/o free floating quad rail, choice of matte black or A-TACS digital camo finish, nickel Teflon plating, 5 1/2 lbs. Mfg. 2010-2011.

$415	$375	$330	$300	$275	$250	$225	*$465*

Add $26 for .22 WMR cal. (fixed A2 stock only).
Add $153 for A-TACS overmolded stock or free-floating quad rail system.

RIFLES: RIMFIRE, SLIDE ACTION

MODEL 12A – .22 S, L, and LR cal., hammerless, 22 in. round or octagon barrel, open sights, tube mag., plain grip stock, approx. 840,000 (all variations) were mfg. 1909-1936.

$1,100	$900	$850	$725	$650	$500	$375

Originally this model was designated "The New .22 Repeater," and did not have a model number. In 1913, the model nomenclature changed from Grades 1-6 to Grades A-F.

MODEL 12B (GALLERY SPECIAL) – .22 Short cal., 24 in. octagon barrels, 15 shot mag., hammerless, open sights, half pistol grip (common) or straight grip (approx. 10%) stock.

$1,850	$1,775	$1,550	$1,250	$950	$725	$600

Add 15% for extended mag. tube.

MODEL 12C (NO. 3) – .22 S, L, and LR cal., 24 in. octagon barrel, half pistol grip (common) or straight grip (approx. 10%) stock, hammerless, open sights, tube mag.

$1,500	$1,350	$1,200	$980	$800	$700	$500

* ***Model 12C D Peerless Grade*** – 24 in. octagon barrel, fine scroll engraving on receiver with small game scenes, checkered English walnut stock with pistol grip, grooved forearm.

$7,750	$7,150	$6,150	$5,500	$4,500	$4,000	$2,500

* ***Model 12C E Expert Grade*** – .22 S, L, and LR cal., 24 in. octagon barrel, checkered English walnut stock with pistol grip, checkered forearm, upgraded wood, hand polished parts, fine scroll engraving on receiver with small game scenes.

$9,250	$8,150	$7,625	$7,000	$5,500	$4,500	$3,500

* ***Model 12C F Premier Grade*** – .22 S, L, or LR cal., top-of-the-line model with best quality checkered walnut stock, fully engraved receiver featuring rabbits and squirrels, very limited mfg.

$12,000	$11,000	$9,250	$7,400	$6,100	$5,000	$3,500

MODEL 12C NRA TARGET – .22 S, L, or LR cal., 24 in. octagon barrel and extended Lyman aperture rear sight and globe front sight, no barrel dovetails, designed for NRA sponsored smallbore rifle matches, limited manufacture beginning 1917.

$2,200	$1,950	$1,775	$1,550	$1,100	$1,000	$750

MODEL 12CS – chambered for .22 Rem. Spl. (.22 WRF) cal., 24 in. octagon barrel, hammerless, open sights, half pistol grip or straight grip stock.

$1,650	$1,425	$1,275	$1,100	$850	$700	$600

MODEL 121A – .22 S, L, or LR cal., 24 in. round barrel, hammerless, tube mag., plain pistol grip stock. 201,000 were mfg. 1936-1954.

$1,200	$995	$850	$725	$550	$450	$400

Add 50% for .22 Short cal. only.

Originally designated Model 121.

* ***Model 121A D Peerless Grade*** – .22 S, L, or LR cal., 24 in. round barrel, fine scroll engraving on receiver, checkered English walnut stock with pistol grip, grooved forearm.

$7,750	$7,200	$6,150	$5,600	$4,000	$3,150	$2,500

* ***Model 121A E Expert Grade*** – .22 S, L, or LR cal., checkered English walnut stock with pistol grip and checkered forearm, upgraded wood, hand polished parts, fine scroll engraving on receiver with small game scenes.

$9,250	$8,150	$7,650	$6,750	$5,500	$4,500	$3,000

* ***Model 121A F Premier Grade*** – .22 S, L, or LR cal., top-of-the-line model with best quality checkered walnut stock, fully engraved receiver featuring rabbits and squirrels, very limited mfg.

$11,500	$9,950	$8,250	$7,000	$6,000	$5,000	$3,500

MODEL 121S – .22 Rem. Spl. (rare) cal., 24 in. round barrel, tube mag., hammerless, plain pistol grip stock.

$1,550	$1,300	$950	$850	$700	$600	$500

GRADING - PPGS™	100%	98%	95%	90%	80%	70%	60%	LAST MSR

MODEL 121SB/ROUTLEDGE - .22 cal., 24 in. smoothbore barrel with at least 5 different chamberings and barrel markings, tube mag., hammerless, plain pistol grip stock. Approx. 3,000 were mfg. pre-WWII-1952.

	$1,875	$1,600	$1,325	$1,200	$900	$675	$550	

MODEL 572/572A LIGHTWEIGHT - .22 S, L, LR cal., slide action, anodized alloy receiver and barrel sleeve, steel barrel, checkered "Sun-Grain" stock and forend, 4 lbs. Offered in 3 colors. Approx. 34,785 mfg., 1958-62.

Buckskin Tan	$600	$500	$400	$325	$275	$225	$175	
Crow-Wing Black	$600	$500	$400	$350	$300	$250	$200	
Teal-Wing Blue	$1,200	$1,100	$900	$700	$600	$400	$300	

MODEL 572SB/ROUTLEDGE - .22 S, L, or LR cal., similar to Model 572A, except smoothbore.

	$900	$850	$700	$500	$400	$300	$250	

MODEL 572 FIELDMASTER - .22 S, L, or LR cal., 21 in. barrel, walnut stock and forearm, tube mag., 5 1/2 lbs. Mfg. 1955-1988.

	$450	$375	$350	$275	$225	$100	$125	*$176*

This model was also mfg. in a 150th Anniversary Model (1966 only). 20% premiums if condition is 98% or better.

MODEL 572 BDL DELUXE FIELDMASTER - .22 S, L, LR or .22 Smoothbore (mfg. 2007-2009) cal., 21 in. carbon steel barrel with polished blue finish, features smooth classic slide action, 15 shot tube mag., adj. iron sights, grooved receiver, checkered gloss finished walnut Monte Carlo stock and forearm, 5 3/4 lbs. Mfg. 1966-2020.

	$550	$450	$395	$275	$225	$200	$150	*$723*

Add 25% for .22 Smoothbore (Model 572SB, disc. 2009, last MSR was $659).

This model was also available in several limited production runs. Prices are usually slightly higher than the standard pricing listed above.

MODEL 572 175th ANNIVERSARY - 300 mfg. 1991 only.

	$600	$525	$375	$340	$275	$225	$175	

RIFLES: BOLT ACTION, CENTERFIRE

The models in this section have been listed in numerical sequence for quick reference.

Remington manufactured many limited production runs for various distributors and wholesalers over the years. These rifles are usually built to a specific configuration (caliber, stock, barrel length, finish, etc.), and are usually available until supplies run out. While these models are not included in this section, pricing in most cases will be similar to the base models from which they were derived.

Remington issued a recall on Model Seven's with the X-Mark Pro trigger manufactured between May 1, 2006-April 9, 2014.

MODEL SEVEN LIGHTWEIGHT - .17 Rem. (mfg. 1993-95), .222 Rem. (disc. 1984), .223 Rem. (new 1984), .243 Win., .260 Rem. (new 1997), 6mm Rem. (disc. 1994), 7mm-08 Rem., or .308 Win. cal., short action, 18 1/2 in. barrel, 4 or 5 shot mag., individually test fired, shortened LOP, oil finished American walnut stock, adj. rear and ramp front sight (w/o sights on .17 Rem.), 6 1/4 lbs. Mfg. 1983-1999.

	$625	$525	$395	$350	$250	$180	$165	*$585*

Add 5%-10% for .17 Rem. cal.

Add 10% for .222 Rem. cal.

All steel Model Sevens (including floorplate and trigger guard) are currently commanding a small premium.

* ***Model Seven Lightweight LS*** - .223 Rem., .243 Win., .260 Rem. (disc. 2001), .308 Win., or 7mm-08 Rem. cal., features brown laminated stock, 20 in. steel barrel, matte barrel and satin wood finish, 6 1/2 lbs. Mfg. 2000-2005.

	$650	$550	$410	$360	$225	$200	$180	*$735*

* ***Model Seven Lightweight LS Magnum*** - .300 Rem. SAUM or 7mm Rem. SAUM cal., short action, 22 in. barrel, blue action and barrel, 3 shot mag. with detachable floorplate, brown laminated stock, sling swivel studs, 7 1/8 lbs. Mfg. 2002-2005.

	$650	$550	$425	$375	$295	$250	$200	*$775*

* ***Model Seven Lightweight LSS*** - .22-250 Rem., .243 Win. (disc. 2001), or 7mm-08 Rem. cal., similar to Model Seven LS, except has stainless steel barrel w/o sights. Mfg. 2000-2003.

	$610	$445	$325	$265	$230	$195	$170	*$770*

GRADING - PPGS™	100%	98%	95%	90%	80%	70%	60%	LAST MSR

* ***Model Seven Lightweight SS*** – .223 Rem. (mfg. 1997-2002), .243 Win., .260 Rem. (new 1997), .308 Win., 6.8mm Rem. SPC (new 2006), or 7mm-08 Rem. cal., features stainless steel construction, 20 in. barrel w/o sights, and synthetic stock, 6 1/4 lbs. Mfg. 1994-2006.

$650	$475	$350	$260	$225	$195	$170	*$825*

* ***Model Seven Lightweight SS Magnum*** – .300 Rem. SAUM or 7mm Rem. SAUM cal., short action, satin finished stainless steel action and 22 in. barrel, 3 shot mag. with detachable floorplate, black synthetic stock, sling swivel studs, 7 1/8 lbs. Mfg. 2002-2006.

$675	$500	$375	$295	$255	$220	$185	*$852*

* ***Model Seven Lightweight Youth*** – .204 Ruger (limited mfg. 2004 only), .223 Rem. (new 2000), .243 Win., 6mm Rem. (disc. 1994), .260 Rem. (new 1998), .308 Win. (disc.), 6.8mm Rem. SPC (mfg. 2006), or 7mm-08 Rem. (new 1994) cal., also available in 20 in. barrel beginning 2000, uncheckered hardwood (.260 Rem. cal.) or synthetic (new 2004) stock shortened 1 in., 6 lbs. Mfg. 1993-2007.

$525	$425	$335	$275	$230	$200	$185	*$684*

Subtract $33 for limited edition synthetic stock model in .204 Ruger cal.

* ***Model Seven Lightweight FS*** – .243 Win., 7mm-08 Rem., or .308 Win. cal., 18 1/2 in. parkerized blue barrel, grey or grey camo Kevlar fiberglass stock, adj. rear sight, 5 1/4 lbs. Mfg. 1987-89 only.

$525	$455	$415	$375	$335	$310	$285	*$600*

* ***Model Seven Lightweight Threaded*** – .308 Win. or .300 AAC Blackout cal., Model 700 short action, 16 1/2 in. carbon steel barrel with threaded muzzle, 4 or 5 shot mag., X-Mark Pro externally adj. trigger, synthetic stock with KUIU Vias camo finish with hinged floorplate, matte blue finish, 6 lbs. Mfg. 2018-2019.

$675	$595	$500	$460	$375	$300	$250	*$795*

* ***Model Seven XCR Camo*** – .243 Rem., .270 WSM, .300 WSM, .308 Win., or 7mm-08 Rem. cal., 20 in. fluted stainless steel barrel, stainless steel action utilizing TriNyte corrosion protection, Realtree AP HD camo stock with R3 recoil pad, 3-4 shot non-detachable mag., approx. 7 lbs. Mfg. 2007 only.

$925	$825	$725	$625	$550	$475	$400	*$1,080*

Add 10% for WSM cals.

* ***Model Seven Synthetic*** – .223 Rem. (disc. 2015), .243 Win., .260 Win., .308 Win., or 7mm-08 Rem. cal., 18 1/2 (Youth only .243 Win. or 7mm-08 cal.) or 20 in. carbon steel barrel with matte blue finish, no sights, matte black synthetic stock with SuperCell recoil pad, X-Mark Pro externally adj. trigger, hinged floorplate, approx. 6 1/2 lbs. Mfg. 2011-2020.

$700	$600	$500	$425	$350	$285	$225	*$731*

* ***Model Seven Synthetic Stainless*** – .223 Rem., .243 Win., .260 Win., .308 Win., .300 WSM, 6mm Rem. (new 2016), or 7mm-08 cal., 20 in. stainless steel barrel, matte black synthetic stock with SuperCell recoil pad, X-Mark Pro externally adj. trigger, hinged floorplate, 6 1/2 lbs. Mfg. 2015-2020.

$750	$650	$535	$485	$395	$325	$250	*$838*

* ***Model Seven Stainless H-S*** – .308 Win., 6.5 Creedmoor, 7mm-08 Rem., or .243 Win. cal., 20 in. light contour stainless steel free floating barrel, 4 shot mag., X-Mark Pro externally adj. trigger, custom grade hand laminated H-S Precision composite stock with black/green webbing finish, aluminum bedding block, satin finish, 6 lbs. Mfg. 2019-2020.

$975	$850	$725	$665	$535	$450	$350	*$1,149*

* ***Model Seven Threaded Camo*** – .308 Win., .300 AAC Blackout, or 6.5 Creedmoor cal., 16 1/2 or 20 in. carbon steel barrel with threaded muzzle and thread protector, 4 or 5 shot mag., synthetic stock with Mossy Oak Bottomland Camo, 20 MOA Picatinny rail, matte blue barrel finish, 6 lbs. Mfg. 2020 only.

$675	$585	$500	$450	$375	$300	$250	*$795*

* ***Model Seven Laminate Stock*** – .223 Rem., .243 Win., .308 Win., 7mm-08 Rem. cal., 18 1/2 in. carbon steel barrel with satin blue finish, 4 or 5 shot mag., rifle sights, X-Mark Pro externally adj. trigger, hinged floorplate, brown laminate stock with satin finish, SuperCell recoil pad, 6 1/2 lbs. Mfg. 2015-2020.

$815	$650	$525	$425	$350	$300	$265	*$1,039*

* ***Model Seven Predator*** – .17 Rem. Fireball (disc. 2010), .204 Ruger (disc. 2010), .223 Rem., .22-250 Rem., or .243 Win. cal., Model 700 BDL action, 22 in. fluted barrel w/o sights, 100% Mossy Oak Brush camo coverage, 2 3/4 in. shorter than normal Model 700, SuperCell recoil pad became standard 2011, designed for smaller shooters, 7 lbs. Mfg. 2008-2015.

$800	$700	$575	$475	$400	$350	$295	*$895*

GRADING - PPGS™ 100% 98% 95% 90% 80% 70% 60% LAST MSR

* ***Model Seven Lightweight CDL (Classic Deluxe)*** – .17 Rem. Fireball (mfg. 2007-2010), .204 Ruger (disc. 2007), .223 Rem. (disc. 2007), .22-250 Rem. (disc. 2007), .243 Win., .260 Rem., 6.8mm Rem. SPC (mfg. 2006-disc.), 7mm-08 Rem., or .308 Win. cal., 20 or 22 (disc.) in. barrel, no sights, checkered deluxe American walnut stock and forearm with R3 (disc.) or SuperCell (new 2010) recoil pad, X-Mark Pro adj. trigger, satin blue barrel finish, 6 1/2 lbs. Mfg. 2006-2020.

$815 $650 $525 $425 $350 $300 $265 *$1,039*

* ***Model Seven Lightweight CDL Magnum*** – .270 WSM, 7mm RSAUM (disc. 2007), .300 RSAUM (disc. 2007), .300 WSM (disc. 2010), or .350 Rem. Mag. (disc. 2010) cal., 22 in. barrel, no sights except for .350 Rem. Mag., checkered deluxe walnut stock and forearm, R3 (disc. 2010) or SuperCell (new 2011) recoil pad, 7 3/8 lbs. Mfg. 2006-2011.

$865 $725 $600 $500 $400 $350 $300 *$1,054*

Subtract $28 for .350 Rem. Mag. cal. (disc. 2010).

* ***Model Seven Lightweight Custom MS (Mannlicher Stock)*** – .222 Rem., .22-250 Rem., .223 Rem., .243 Win., .250 Savage, .257 Roberts, .260 Rem. (new 1997), .308 Win., .35 Rem., .350 Rem. Mag., 6mm Rem., or 7mm-08 Rem. (disc. 2011) cal., 4 or 6 shot mag., 20 in. custom shop barrel with Model 7 action bedded to a Mannlicher style two-tone brown laminate full stock, hinged floorplate, 6 1/2 lbs. Mfg. 1993-2011, reintroduced 2015 only.

$2,575 $2,200 $1,900 $1,600 $1,300 $1,100 $900 *$2,999*

This model was available from the Custom Shop only (special order).

* ***Model Seven Lightweight Custom KS*** – .223 Rem. (new 1989), .260 Rem. (new 1998), 7mm BR Rem. (mfg. 1989-1990), 7mm-08 Rem. (new 1989), .308 Win. (new 1991), .35 Rem., or .350 Rem. Mag. cal., 20 in. barrel with (.35 Rem. or .350 Rem. Mag.) or w/o sights, Aramid/Kevlar fiberglass synthetic stock with solid recoil pad, 5 3/4 lbs. Mfg. 1987-2011.

$2,225 $1,900 $1,650 $1,400 $1,150 $925 $775 *$2,542*

This model was available from the Custom Shop only (special order).

* ***Model Seven Lightweight AWR (Alaskan Wilderness Rifle)*** – 6.8 Rem. SPC (mfg. 2005-2007), .300 Rem. SAUM, or 7mm Rem. SAUM cal., short action, stainless steel action and 22 in. barrel with matte black Teflon satin finish, 3 shot detachable mag., fiberglass matte black stock, sling swivel studs, 6 1/8 lbs. Mfg. 2002-2008.

$2,495 $2,150 $1,850 $1,550 $1,250 $1,000 $775 *$2,927*

This model was available from the Custom Shop only (special order).

* ***Model Seven Lightweight AWR II*** – .260 Rem. (disc. 2009), .270 WSM (disc. 2009), .300 WSM (disc. 2009), 7mm-08 Rem. (disc. 2009), .308 Win. (disc. 2009), 7mm RSAUM, .300 RSAUM, or .350 Rem. Mag. (disc. 2009) cal., 20 or 22 in. stainless steel black TriNyte coated barrel, Bell & Carlson reinforced olive green fiberglass stock, hinged floorplate, no sights, mfg. by custom shop, 6 1/8 lbs. Mfg. mid-2008-2011.

$2,575 $2,200 $1,900 $1,600 $1,300 $1,100 $900 *$2,992*

Additional calibers were available by request.

* ***Model Seven 25th Anniversary Ltd. Ed.*** – 7mm-08 Rem. cal., 20 in. barrel, Classic Deluxe style American walnut stock laser engraved with "Model Seven 25th Anniversary" 25th Anniversary medallion inletted in pistol grip cap, high lustre blue with jeweled bolt, X-Mark Pro trigger, 6 1/2 lbs. Mfg. 2008 only.

$800 $700 $575 $450 $395 $350 $295 *$969*

MODEL 30A RIFLE – .25 Rem., .30 Rem., .30-06 (original cal.), .32 Rem., .35 Rem., or 7x57mm Mauser (introduced 1931) cal., Enfield M/1917 type action, 22 in. barrel, checkered pistol grip stock. Mfg. 1921-1940.

$800 $700 $600 $500 $400 $325 $260

MODEL 30R CARBINE – .25 Rem., .30 Rem., .32 Rem., .35 Rem., or .30-06 cal., similar to Model 30A, with 20 in. barrel. Introduced 1927.

$850 $675 $600 $500 $400 $325 $275

MODEL 30 EXPRESS – .25 Rem., .30 Rem., .32 Rem., .35 Rem., or .30-06 cal. Introduced 1926.

$700 $640 $550 $500 $400 $325 $260

MODEL 30S (SPECIAL GRADE) – .25 Rem. Rimless (introduced 1931), .257 Roberts (new 1934), 7x57mm Mauser (introduced 1931), or .30-06 (original cal.) cal., deluxe version of Model 30A, 22 or 24 in. barrel, Lyman receiver sight, special stock, 7 1/2 lbs. Mfg. 1930-40.

$900 $800 $700 $600 $550 $375 $300

The Model 30S Express Rifle was introduced in 1934 in .257 Roberts cal.

GRADING - PPGS™	100%	98%	95%	90%	80%	70%	60%	LAST MSR

MODEL 78 SPORTSMAN – .223 Rem., .243 Win., .270 Win., .30-06, or .308 Win. cal., 22 in. barrel, 4 shot mag., uncheckered hardwood stock, open sights, 7 lbs. Mfg. 1984-89.

	$400	$365	$325	$295	$250	$225	$200	*$333*

MODEL XR-100 RANGEMASTER – .204 Ruger, .22-250 Rem., or .223 Rem. cal., features XP-100 single shot target pistol action with Model 40-XP target adj. trigger, 26 in. barrel, laminate thumbhole stock with vent. beavertail forend, 9 1/8 lbs. Mfg. 2005-2007.

	$875	$725	$625	$525	$450	$400	$375	*$1,057*

MODEL 600 – .222 Rem., .223 Rem. (very rare), 6mm Rem., .243 Win., .308 Win., or .35 Rem. cal., 18 1/2 in. VR barrel, dog leg bolt handle, checkered pistol grip stock. 94,086 were mfg. 1964-68.

6mm Rem., .243 Win., or .308 Win. cals.	$475	$365	$290	$220	$200	$180	$160
.35 Rem. cal.	$850	$700	$600	$450	$350	$300	$260
.222 Rem. cal.	$550	$500	$450	$400	$365	$340	$300
.223 Rem. cal.	$3,000	$2,500	$2,000	$1,400	$800	$550	$450

315 Model 600s in .223 Rem. cal. were mfg.

* ***Model 600 Montana Centennial*** – 6mm Rem. cal., 1,020 mfg. in 1964 only.

	$2,000	$1,500	$1,200	N/A	N/A	N/A	N/A	*$125*

MODEL 600 MAGNUM – 6.5mm Rem. Mag. or .350 Rem. Mag. cal., laminated walnut/beech stock with or without recoil pad (early mfg. walnut stocks did not have recoil pad). Mfg. 1965-1968.

	$1,200	$1,000	$825	$725	$600	$500	$425

MODEL 600 MOHAWK – .222 Rem., 6mm Rem., .243 Win., or .308 Win. cal., this variation was a promotional model, 18 1/2 in. barrel with no rib. 94,920 were mfg. 1971-79.

	$600	$475	$425	$350	$300	$275	$250

MODEL 660 STANDARD – .222 Rem., 6mm Rem., .243 Win., or .308 Win. cal., 20 in. barrel, open sights, dog leg bolt handle, checkered pistol grip stock, black pistol grip cap and forend tip. 50,536 were mfg. 1968-71.

	$550	$500	$450	$400	$365	$340	$310

Add 10% for .222 Rem. cal.

* ***Model 660 Standard .223 Rem. cal.*** – 227 total mfg. This cal. was never listed in a Remington catalog.

	$2,800	$2,200	$1,800	$1,200	$500	$400	$350

MODEL 660 MAGNUM – 6.5mm Rem. Mag. or .350 Rem. Mag. cal., VR is screwed on, laminated stock and recoil pad.

	$1,150	$950	$825	$725	$600	$500	$375

MODEL 673 GUIDE RIFLE – .350 Rem. Mag., .300 Short Action Ultra Mag (SAUM), 6.5mm Rem. Mag. (new 2004) or .308 Win. (new 2004) cal., patterned after the Model 600 Magnum and features the Model Seven action, 22 in. contoured barrel with VR and open sights, drilled and tapped receiver, two-tone tan wide striped checkered laminate stock with satin finish, sling studs and solid recoil pad, 3 shot internal box magazine with hinged floorplate, polished blue metal finish, 7 1/2 lbs. Mfg. 2003-2006.

	$800	$675	$600	$510	$450	$395	$365	*$893*

MODEL 710 SPORTSMAN – .270 Win., .243 Win. (new 2006), .30-06, 7mm Rem. Mag. (new 2004) or .300 Win. Mag. (new 2004) cal., unique bolt to barrel lockup design utilizing 3 locking lugs on bolt face that lock directly in an integrated rear barrel extension (as opposed to locking into the receiver), long action, steel (became standard 2005) or polymer receiver sleeve (disc. 2004), adj. trigger, detachable 4 shot box mag, 60 degree bolt throw, 22 in. ordnance grade steel barrel with matte finish, grey synthetic stock with solid pad, supplied with bore sighted 3-9x40mm Bushnell Sharpshooter scope and mounts, ISS (Integrated Security System) bolt locking safety, 7 1/8 lbs. Mfg. 2001-2006.

	$425	$375	$325	$295	$265	$250	$240	*$439*

Add $39 for limited edition Skyline Excel camo (mfg. 2004 only).

This model was also available in a Youth Model (.243 Win. cal. only, shortened LOP - includes scope, new 2006) at no extra charge.

MODEL 715 SPORTSMAN – .243 Win., .270 Win., .30-06, 7mm-08 Rem., 7mm Rem. Mag., or .300 Win. mag. cal., 22 or 24 in. blue ordnance grade barrel, black synthetic stock with molded sling swivel studs, 60 degree bolt lift, updated magazine latch, detachable 3-4 shot mag., no sights, Picatinny rail. Mfg. 2008 only.

	$400	$300	$250	$225	$200	$185	$170	*$349*

This model was available through Remington Premier dealers only.

GRADING - PPGS™	100%	98%	95%	90%	80%	70%	60%	LAST MSR

MODEL 720A – Enfield type action, .257 Roberts, .270 Win., or .30 - 06 cal., 22 in. barrel, open sights, 5 shot, checkered pistol grip stock, 2,500 mfg. 1941-44.

	$1,600	$1,400	$1,200	$1,000	$700	$550	$450	

Add 50%+ for .270 Win. cal.
Add 100%+ for .257 Roberts cal.

Most of this model was chambered for .30-06 cal.

MODEL 720 MILITARY – .257 Roberts, .270 Win., or .30-06 cal., purchased by the Dept. of Navy during 1942 and used for trophies, discernible by crossed cannon proofs on wood, approx. 100 were chambered for .270 Win. and 20 or less were chambered for the .257 Roberts. 920-1,000 mfg. 1942 only.

.30-06 cal.	$3,500	$3,150	$2,800	$1,575	$1,225	$1,000	$850	
.270 Win. cal. (scarce)	$3,800	$2,800	$2,300	$2,000	$1,575	$1,225	$1,000	
.257 Roberts cal. (rare)	$7,500	$6,500	$4,000	$3,200	$2,500	$1,800	$1,575	

MODEL 720R – similar to 720A, except with 20 in. barrel.

	$2,200	$1,700	$1,200	$1,000	$700	$575	$475	

This is the rarest variation in the Model 720 Series.

MODEL 720S – .257 Roberts, .270 Win., or .30-06 cal., Enfield type action, 24 in. barrel., 5 shot, open sights, checkered pistol grip stock.

	$1,750	$1,550	$1,325	$1,100	$775	$575	$475	

MODEL 721A – .264 Win. Mag., .270 Win., .280 Rem. (new 1960), or .30-06 cal., 24 in. barrel, open sights, 4 shot, plain pistol grip stock. Mfg. 1948-1962.

	$500	$450	$400	$325	$275	$250	$175	

Add 50% premium for .280 Rem. or .264 Win. Mag. cal.

.280 Rem. (688 mfg.) and .264 Win. Mag. (1,115 mfg.) are rare in this model.

MODEL 721ADL – similar to Model 721A, except has deluxe checkered stock.

	$625	$560	$500	$400	$350	$315	$220	

This model's suffix does not appear on the gun. ADL features will determine the model.

MODEL 721BDL – .264 Win. Mag., similar to Model 721ADL, except has extra select wood.

	$650	$500	$475	$425	$350	$315	$295	

This model's suffix does not appear on the gun. BDL features will determine the model.

MODEL 721A MAGNUM – .264 Win. Mag. or .300 H&H cal., 26 in. heavy barrel, recoil pad, 3 shot mag., 8 1/4 lbs.

	$900	$700	$600	$500	$450	$400	$350	

Add 15% for .264 Win. Mag. cal.

MODEL 721ADL MAGNUM – .264 Win. Mag. cal., similar to Model 721A Magnum, checkered. 1,115 mfg. 1961-1962, not cataloged.

	$975	$775	$675	$575	$500	$450	$400	

MODEL 721BDL MAGNUM – .264 Win. Mag. cal., similar to Model 721ADL Magnum, select wood.

	$850	$750	$700	$600	$500	$450	$400	

MODEL 722(A) – short action version of 721A, .222 Rem. (mfg. 1950-62), .222 Rem. Mag. (mfg. 1958-62), .243 Win. (mfg. 1960-62), .244 Rem. (mfg. 1957-62), .257 Roberts (disc. 1960), .300 Savage (disc. 1959), or .308 Win. (mfg. 1956-62) cal., 7 lbs. Mfg. 1948-1962.

	$625	$525	$450	$350	$300	$260	$200	

Subtract 10% for .300 Savage cal.
Add 20% for .257 Roberts or .308 Win. cal.

.222 Rem. Mag. (3,803 mfg.) and .243 Win. (2,186 mfg.) are rare in this model. Add approx. 25% to values for these cals.

MODEL 722ADL – similar to Model 722(A), except with deluxe checkered wood.

	$700	$600	$500	$400	$300	$275	$200	

This model's suffix does not appear on the gun. ADL features will determine the model.

MODEL 722BDL – similar to Model 722ADL, except features extra select wood.

	$850	$750	$700	$600	$500	$450	$400	

This model's suffix does not appear on the gun. BDL features will determine the model.

GRADING - PPGS™	100%	98%	95%	90%	80%	70%	60%	LAST MSR

MODEL 725ADL – .222 Rem., .243 Win., .244 Rem., .270 Win., .280 Rem., or .30-06 cal., 22 in. barrel, open sights, 4 shot mag., checkered Monte Carlo stock. 16,635 mfg. 1958-61.

.30-06 cal.	$650	$600	$550	$450	$400	$375	$350	
.270 Win. cal.	$750	$600	$550	$500	$375	$350	$325	
.280 Rem. cal.	$1,100	$950	$700	$550	$400	$350	$325	
.222 Rem. cal.	$1,100	$900	$700	$500	$400	$350	$325	
.244 Rem. cal.	$1,000	$800	$600	$500	$400	$350	$325	
.243 Win. cal.	$1,000	$800	$600	$500	$400	$350	$325	

Add 30-50% for NIB configuration.

Caliber mfg. breakdown is as follows: 7,657 in .30-06; 2,784 in .280 Rem.; 2,818 in .270 Win.; 840 in .244 Rem.; 1,478 in .222 Rem.; 998 in .243 Win.

MODEL 725 KODIAK – .375 H&H Mag. or .458 Win. Mag. cal., 26 in. barrel, 3 shot mag., recoil reducer in muzzle, deluxe checkered Monte Carlo stock, black pistol grip cap and forend tip. 52 mfg. 1961 only.

$7,000	$5,000	$3,800	$2,900	$2,200	$1,900	$1,650	

Only 24 rifles in .458 Win. Mag. were mfg. and 28 rifles in .375 H&H Mag.

MODEL 770 – .243 Win., .270 Win., .30-06, .308 Win., .300 Win. Mag., 7mm-08 Rem., or 7mm Rem. Mag. cal., matte black metal finish, Picatinny rail, 3 or 4 shot detachable mag., black synthetic stock with raised cheekpiece, includes factory mounted and bore sighted 3-9x40mm Bushnell scope, 20 (Youth Model only), 22 or 24 in. barrel, Model 700 based action with 60 degree bolt lift, "R" on pistol grip cap, also available in Youth model with short LOP (.243 Win. cal. only), 8 1/2 lbs. Mfg. in Mayfield, KY 2007-2014.

$330	$260	$230	$200	$185	$170	$165	*$383*

* ***Model 770 Stainless*** – .270 Win., .30-06, 7mm Rem. Mag., or .300 Win. Mag. cal., similar to Model 770, except has 22 or 24 in. stainless steel barrel and Realtree AP HD camo stock, 8 1/2 lbs. Mfg. 2008-2014.

$410	$375	$325	$295	$250	$225	$200	*$467*

MODEL 783 (WITH SCOPE) – 6.5 Creedmoor (new 2020), .22-250 Rem. (new 2015), .223 Rem. (new 2015), .243 Win. (new 2014), .270 Win., .30-06, .300 Win. Mag. (new 2014), .308 Win., 7mm-08 Rem., or 7mm Rem. Mag. cal., 22 or 24 in. button rifled free floating barrel w/o sights, 3 or 4 shot detachable mag., pillar bedded black synthetic stock with SuperCell recoil pad, CrossFire trigger system adj. from 2 1/2-5 lbs., matte blue finish, includes 3-9x40mm scope mounted and bore sighted (new 2015), approx. 7 1/4-8 1/2 lbs. Mfg. 2013-2020.

$340	$300	$250	$225	$185	$150	$125	*$399*

* ***Model 783 Camo (Recent Mfg.)*** – .270 Win., .30-06, .300 Win. Mag., .308 Win., or 7mm Rem. Mag. cal., similar to Model 783, except features Mossy Oak Break-Up Infinity camo finish. Mfg. 2014 only.

$450	$385	$350	$315	$285	$250	$215	*$503*

MODEL 783 CAMO (RECENT MFG.) – .223 Rem., .243 Win., 6.5 Creedmoor (new 2019), .270 Win., .30-06, .300 Win. Mag., 7mm Rem. Mag., or .308 Win. cal., 22 or 24 (7mm Rem. Mag. only) in. carbon steel button rifled free floating barrel, 3 or 4 shot steel detachable mag., Mossy Oak Break-Up Country camo finished pillar bedded stock and forearm, SuperCell recoil pad, includes 3-9x40mm scope (mounted and bore sighted), matte black finish on barrel and receiver. Mfg. 2016-2020.

$385	$335	$290	$260	$210	$175	$135	*$451*

MODEL 783 COMPACT – .243 Win. or .308 Win. cal., 20 or 22 in. (.243 only, mfg. 2014 only) barrel, 4 shot detachable mag., no sights, matte black synthetic stock with SuperCell recoil pad, 12 3/8 in. LOP, matte blue metal finish, 8 lbs. Mfg. 2014-2020.

$355	$300	$250	$225	$200	$175	$150	*$411*

MODEL 783 WALNUT – 6.5 Creedmoor (new 2018), .270 Win., .30-06, .308 Win., 7mm Rem. Mag., .243 Win., or .300 Win. Mag. cal., 22 or 24 in. barrel, 3 or 4 shot detachable mag., American black walnut stock with classic checkering, SuperCell recoil pad, matte blue metal finish, 7 1/2 lbs. Mfg. 2017-2020.

$450	$395	$335	$300	$275	$250	$225	*$514*

Add $181 for Vortex Crossfire II scope.

MODEL 783 SYNTHETIC (WITHOUT SCOPE) – .243 Win., .308 Win., .270 Win., .30-06, 7mm Rem. Mag., or .300 Win. Mag. cal., 22 or 24 in. carbon steel barrel with matte blue finish, 3 or 4 shot detachable box mag., matte black synthetic stock, SuperCell recoil pad, 7 1/2 lbs. Mfg. 2018-2020.

$300	$265	$225	$200	$170	$140	$115	*$354*

GRADING - PPGS™	100%	98%	95%	90%	80%	70%	60%	LAST MSR

MODEL 783 HBT - .223 Rem., .308 Win., .300 AAC Blackout, .450 Bushmaster (new 2020), or 6.5 Creedmoor cal., 16 1/2 or 24 (new 2019) in. carbon steel barrel with matte blue finish, 3, 4, or 5 shot mag., synthetic stock with FDE finish, 7-8 lbs. Mfg. 2018-2020.

$395	$350	$300	$275	$215	$185	$150	*$459*

Add $10 for 24 in. barrel (new 2019).

MODEL 783 VARMINT LAMINATE – .308 Win., .223 Rem., .22-250 Rem., .243 Win., or 6.5 Creedmoor cal., 26 in. heavy barrel, 4 or 5 shot steel detachable mag., adj. Crossfire trigger system, brown hardwood laminated stock with beavertail forend and satin finish, oversized bolt handle, Picatinny rail, black oxide finish, 8 1/2 lbs. Mfg. 2019-2020.

$525	$460	$395	$350	$295	$235	$185	*$625*

MODEL 788 – .222 Rem. (disc. 1979, reintroduced 1982-83), .22-250 Rem., .223 Rem. (new 1975), 6mm Rem. (mfg. 1969-1979), .243 Win. (new 1969), .308 Win. (new 1969), .30-30 Win. (disc. 1972), 7mm-08 Rem. (new 1980), or .44 Mag. (disc. 1970) cal., 18 1/2 (Carbine, .243 Win., .308 Win., or 7mm-08 Rem. cal.), 22 (6mm Rem., .243 Win., and .308 Win. cal.), or 24 (.222 Rem., .22-250 Rem., .223 Rem. cal. 1967-1979, .223 Rem. and .22-250 Rem. cal. 1980-83) in. barrel, short action, open sights, plain pistol grip Monte Carlo stock. Mfg. 1967-1983.

$650	$550	$425	$400	$350	$275	$250

Add 10% for .30-30 Win. cal.
Add 15% for 7mm-08 Rem. cal.
Add 50% for .44 Mag. cal.
Add 20% for left-hand action (6mm Rem. and .308 Win. cal. only, mfg. 1969-1979).

In 1970, this gun was also manufactured with a 4X scope as a promotion, but was a non-Remington catalog item.

MODEL 798 – various cals. between .243 Win. - .458 Win. Mag., features square bridge Mauser 98 long action, 22 or 24 in. steel or stainless steel (green laminate stock only) barrel w/o sights, polished blue finish, hinged floorplate, black synthetic (Model 798 SPS, new 2008), satin walnut, Realwood walnut (Safari Grade only, new 2008), or brown or green (mfg. 2007) laminate stock, controlled round feeding with claw extractor, sporter style two position safety, 7 lbs. Importation from Zastava 2006-2008.

$450	$415	$375	$350	$325	$300	$285	*$527*

Add $43 for .300 Win. Mag. or 7mm Rem. Mag. cal.
Add $443 for .375 H&H or $513 for .458 Win. Mag. cal. (26 in. barrel only).
Add $121 for satin walnut stock.

* ***Model 798 Safari Grade*** – .375 H&H or .458 Win. Mag. cal., 22 in. heavy barrel with adj. open sights, Realwood laminated stock, front barrel band with sling swivel, drilled and tapped, 8 1/4 lbs. Mfg. 2008.

$1,000	$900	$800	$700	$600	$500	$450	*$1,141*

Add $72 for .458 Win. Mag. cal.

MODEL 799 – .22 Hornet (detachable mag.), .22-250 Rem., .222 Rem., .223 Rem., or 7.62x39mm cal., features Mauser 98 short action, brown laminate stock, 20 in. barrel w/o sights, otherwise similar to Model 798. Imported 2006-2008.

$550	$475	$425	$375	$335	$295	$275	*$648*

Add 20% for .22 Hornet and 7.62x39mm cal.

R2MI – .50 BMG cal., R2Mi, right-port/left-bolt design, 30 in. Lothar Walther barrel, AAC Cyclops muzzle brake, two 10 shot mags., Magpul PRS Gen 3 adj. buttstock, Ergo deluxe tactical pistol grip, Mil-Std 1913 rail, vented handguard, steel bipod w/folding legs, custom Pelican Storm deployment case, Type III hardcoat anodized green finish. Mfg. 2020 only.

$3,900	$3,400	$2,950	$2,650	$2,150	$1,750	$1,350	*$4,599*

RIFLES: BOLT ACTION, MODEL 700 & VARIATIONS

Remington also manufactured Models M24, M24A2, M24A3, R700, XM2010, and MSR for military and law enforcement only. These models are not covered in this database.

Remington issued a recall on Model 700s with the X-Mark Pro trigger manufactured between May 1, 2006-April 9, 2014.

Model 700s manufactured up until the early 1980s featured a riveted extractor, scrolled bolt, and typically nicer wood. These Model 700s if above 95% original condition will command a small premium - the better the condition, the larger the premium (i.e., NIB specimens typically have up to a 10% premium, depending on the caliber and features).

GRADING - PPGS™	100%	98%	95%	90%	80%	70%	60%	LAST MSR

MODEL 700 - 200TH YEAR ANNIVERSARY LIMITED EDITION - 7mm Rem. Mag. cal., 24 in. barrel, rifle sights, C-Grade walnut stock with fleur-de-lis checkering, medallion in grip, Classic American style engraving and gold inlay, steel floorplate, includes custom box, special serial number, limited to quantity of 2,016. Limited mfg. 2016 only.

$2,250	$2,000	$1,800	$1,600	$1,400	$1,200	$1,000	*$2,399*

MODEL 700 2020 LONG RANGE - .30-06 cal., 26 in. heavy barrel w/o sights, Bell & Carlson M40 stock, features Remington's 2020 Digital Optic System. Mfg. 2014 only.

$4,950	$4,250	$3,800	$3,400	$3,000	$2,600	$2,200	*$5,575*

MODEL 700 2020 SPS TACTICAL - .308 Win. cal., Model 700 action, 26 in. (long range variation, .30-06 cal.) or 20 in. threaded (tactical variation, .308 Win.) barrel, Hogue overmolded green pillar bedded stock, 4 shot internal box magazine, features a TrackingPoint 3x-21x zoom scope with laser range finder, gyroscopes, and camera, programmable optics software adjusts for different ammunition, 10.3 lbs. Mfg. 2014-2015.

$4,950	$4,250	$3,800	$3,400	$3,000	$2,600	$2,200	*$5,575*

Remington claimed its 2020 system could make consistent accurate shots out to 500 yards.

MODEL 700 ABG (AFRICAN BIG GAME) - .375 H&H, .375 RUM, .416 Rem. Mag., or .458 Win. Mag. cal., 26 in. barrel with barrel band and safari sights, straight line 3 shot detachable box mag., checkered brown laminate stock with right-hand cheekpiece, open sights, matte blue finished steel receiver, custom shop special order only, 9 1/2 lbs. Mfg. 2001-2004, reintroduced 2006-2015.

$2,700	$2,325	$1,950	$1,800	$1,600	$1,350	$1,150	*$2,950*

MODEL 700 ADL DELUXE RIFLE/CARBINE - .22-250 Rem. (disc. 1991), .222 Rem. (disc.), .222 Rem. Mag. (disc.), .25-06 Rem. (disc. 1991), 6mm Rem. (disc.), .243 Win. (disc. 1997), .270 Win., .280 Rem. (disc. 1997 - marked 7mm Express 1979-82), .30-06, .308 Win. (disc. 2001), or 7mm Rem. Mag. (disc. 2002) cal., 20 (carbine mfg. 1962-1963), 22, or 24 in. barrel, open sights, 4 shot mag., checkered Monte Carlo stock or brown laminated stock (new 1988). Mfg. 1962-2005.

$475	$395	$360	$300	$260	$220	$195	*$580*

Add 5% for 7mm Rem. Mag. cal. (disc. 2002).
Add 60% for carbine with 20 in. barrel (mfg. 1962-63).
Add 50% for .222 Rem. Mag. or .280 Rem. cal. 20 in barrel.
Add 15% for 7mm Rem. Mag., .264 Win. Mag., or .300 Win. Mag. cal. with stainless steel barrel (mfg. 1962-1970).

During 1962-63, the 20 in. barrel was standard on .222 Rem., .222 Rem. Mag., .243 Win., .270 Win., .280 Rem., .30-06, or .308 Win. cal. In 1964, these cals. had a standard barrel length of 22 in.; 24 in. barrels were standard on 7mm Rem. Mag. and .264 Win. Mag. cal.

During 1984, Remington began stamping a safety warning on the barrel.

In 1987-89, Remington introduced a Model 700 Gun Kit that enabled the owner to assemble the stock to the barreled action. All metal work was completely finished and wood finishing was all that is required. This kit was available in most popular cals. - last MSR price was $333 (1989).

* ***Model 700 ADL Deluxe Rifle Synthetic*** - .22-250 Rem. (new 1999), .223 Rem., .243 Win., .270 Win., .30-06, .308 Win., .300 Win. Mag. (new 1999), or 7mm Rem. Mag., features fiberglass reinforced synthetic stock with positive checkering, black matte finish on metal, open sights, approx. 7 3/8 lbs. Mfg. 1996-2005.

$450	$395	$360	$300	$260	$220	$195	*$500*

Add $27 for .300 Win. Mag. or 7mm Rem. Mag. cal.

* ***Model 700 ADL Deluxe Rifle Synthetic Youth*** - .243 Win., .270 Win. (new 2004), .30-06 (new 2004), or .308 Win. cal., similar to Model 700ADL Synthetic, except has 20 in. barrel and 1 in. shorter LOP. Disc. 2005.

$450	$395	$360	$300	$260	$220	$195	*$500*

* ***Model 700 ADL/LS Deluxe Rifle*** - .243 Win. (mfg. 1989-1993), .270 Win. (new 1989), .30-06, or 7mm Rem. Mag. (mfg. 1988-1993) cal., brown laminate stock with checkering. Mfg. 1988-1993, reintroduced 2002-2004. This model was available through selected distributors only.

$475	$395	$360	$300	$260	$220	$195	*$580*

Add $27 for 7mm Rem. Mag. cal. (disc.).

MODEL 700 ADL WITH SCOPE - 6.5 Creedmoor (mfg. 2018-2020), .22-250 Rem., .223 Rem., .243 Win., .270 Win., .308 Win., .30-06, 7mm Rem. Mag., or .300 Win. Mag. cal., 20 (.243 Win. only), 24, or 26 in. carbon steel barrel, X-Mark Pro adj. trigger, matte black synthetic stock, includes scope, matte blue finish, 7 1/4 lbs. Mfg. 2016-2020.

$460	$400	$350	$315	$250	$200	$180	*$541*

GRADING - PPGS™	100%	98%	95%	90%	80%	70%	60%	LAST MSR

MODEL 700 ADL SS (WITH SCOPE) – .243 Win., .270 Win., .308 Win., or .30-06 cal., 24 in. stainless steel barrel, 4 shot mag., X-Mark Pro adj. trigger, matte black synthetic stock, satin finish, 7 3/4 lbs. Mfg. mid-2016-2020.

$550	$480	$415	$375	$300	$250	$200	*$641*

MODEL 700 ADL - 200TH YEAR ANNIVERSARY COMMEMORATIVE – .243 Win., .270 Win., .30-06, or .300 Win. Mag. cal., 24 or 26 (.300 Win. Mag. only) in. barrel, X-Mark Pro externally adj. trigger, walnut stock with fleur-de-lis checkering, Commemorative medallion in grip. Limited mfg. 2016 only.

$675	$600	$550	$495	$450	$395	$350	*$695*

MODEL 700 ALASKAN Ti – .25-06 Rem., .270 Win., .270 WSM, .280 Rem., 7mm-08 Rem., 7mm Rem. Mag., .30-06, .300 WSM, .300 Win. Mag., or .308 Win. (disc. 2007) cal., titanium receiver with spiral cut fluted bolt with skeletonized bolt handle, lightweight fluted stainless 24 in. barrel w/o sights, black pillar bedded Bell & Carlson synthetic stock with MaxxGuard finish and R3 recoil pad, X-Mark Pro adj. trigger, 3-4 shot mag., hinged floorplate, approx. 6 1/4 lbs. Mfg. 2007-2009.

$1,775	$1,500	$1,275	$1,075	$950	$825	$650	*$2,225*

Add $27 for 7mm Rem. Mag. and .300 Win. Mag., or $124 for WSM cals.

MODEL 700 APR (AFRICAN PLAINS RIFLE II) – .300 Win. Mag., .300 Wby. Mag., .300 RUM (new 1999), .338 Win. Mag., .338 RUM (new 2000), .375 H&H, 7mm Rem. Mag, 7mm STW (by request only, ltd. mfg.), 7mm RUM (new 2001), or .375 RUM (new 2001) cal., 26 in. custom shop barrel, 3 shot, machined steel trigger guard and floorplate, brown pressure laminted checkered wood stock with satin finish and buttpad, satin finish metal, 7 3/4 lbs., Mfg. 1994-2004, reintroduced 2006-2011.

$2,400	$2,075	$1,850	$1,650	$1,425	$1,225	$1,025	*$2,841*

MODEL 700 AS – .22-250 Rem., .243 Win., .270 Win., .280 Rem., .30-06, .308 Win., 7mm Rem. Mag., or .300 Wby. Mag. cal., synthetic stock is made from Arylon resin, matte black finished stock and metal, 22 or 24 in. barrel, 6 1/2 lbs. Mfg. 1989-91 only.

$550	$400	$360	$300	$260	$220	$195	*$528*

Add $21 for 7mm Rem. Mag. or .300 Wby. Mag. cal.

MODEL 700 AWR (ALASKAN WILDERNESS RIFLE) – .300 Win. Mag., .300 Wby. Mag., .300 RUM (new 1999), .338 Win. Mag., .338 RUM (new 2000), .375 H&H, 7mm STW (new 1998), 7mm Rem. Mag., 7mm RUM (new 2001), or .375 RUM (new 2001) cal., black synthetic fiberglass with Kevlar stock, black stainless steel action with Teflon coating, approx. 7 lbs. Mfg. 1994-2004, reintroduced 2006-2007.

$1,475	$1,250	$1,050	$925	$795	$685	$550	*$1,761*

Add $80 for left-hand action.

MODEL 700 AWR II (ALASKAN WILDERNESS RIFLE) – various cals., black TriNyte full-length stock with aluminum bedding block, adj. Model 40-X trigger, machined stainless steel trigger guard and floorplate, fluted barrel, 7 1/2 lbs. Mfg. 2008-2015.

$2,050	$1,750	$1,525	$1,275	$1,150	$975	$750	*$2,400*

This model is also available in left hand action at no extra charge.

MODEL 700 AWR (AMERICAN WILDERNESS RIFLE) – .270 Win., .30-06, .300 Win. Mag., .338 Win. Mag., 7mm Rem. Mag., .300 Rem. Mag., or .338 Rem. Ultra cal., 24 or 26 in. free floated stainless steel barrel with black Cerakote finish, 3 or 4 shot mag., X-Mark Pro externally adj. trigger, Grayboe fiberglass and epoxy stock, brown with black webbing finish, 7 3/8 lbs. Mfg. 2017-2020.

$995	$875	$775	$695	$575	$465	$375	*$1,150*

MODEL 700 BDL 50TH ANNIVERSARY EDITION – 7mm Rem. Mag. cal., 24 in. blued steel barreled action, X-Mark Pro trigger, open sights, B Grade walnut stock with cut fleur-de-lis checkering, black vent. recoil pad, white line spacers, hinged floorplate features commemorative laser engraving, satin finish, approx. 7 1/2 lbs. Mfg. 2012 only.

$1,175	$1,015	$875	$785	$675	$545	$435	*$1,399*

MODEL 700 BDL 200TH ANNIVERSARY SPECIAL EDITION – .30-06 cal., curly maple stock with ebony forend cap and pistol grip, 200th Anniversary and Remington cameo/caption laser etched on floorplate. Limited mfg. 1993 only.

$725	$625	$575	$500	$435	$395	$325

MODEL 700 BDL CUSTOM DELUXE – .17 Rem. (disc. 2007), .22-250 Rem. (disc. 2007), .222 Rem. (disc. 2007), .223 Rem. (disc. 2007), .243 Win., .25-06 Rem. (disc. 2007), .264 Win. Mag. (disc.), .270 Win., .280 Rem. (mfg. 1992-95, resumed 2000-2002), .300 Savage (mfg. 1992 only), .30-06, .308 Win. (disc. 1995), .35 Whelen (mfg. 1989-94), 6mm Rem. (disc. 1994), 7mm-08 Rem. (disc. 1994, reintroduced 2000-2002), 7mm Rem. Mag., 7mm-06 Rem. (designated 7mm-Exp Rem., approx. 200-300 mfg., disc.) .308 Win. (left-hand only, disc. 2004), .300 Win. Mag. (disc. 2007), .300 RUM

GRADING - PPGS™	100%	98%	95%	90%	80%	70%	60%	LAST MSR

(mfg. 1999-2015), .338 Win. Mag. (mfg. 1988-94, resumed 1997-2002), .338 RUM (mfg. 2000-2002, mfg. 2004 in left-hand only), .375 RUM (mfg. 2001-2002), 7mm RUM (mfg. 2001-2007), or 8mm Mag. (disc.) cal., right or left-hand (available in certain cals. only, short action .22-250 Rem. and .243 Win. cals. are scarce in left-hand, disc. 2004), 20 (in 1962 was standard on .222 Rem., .222 Rem. Mag., .243 Win., .270 Win., .280 Rem., .30-06, or .308 Win. cal.), 22, 24 (Magnum), or 26 (RSUM cals.) in. barrel, stainless steel barrel (7mm Rem. Mag., .264 Win. Mag., or .300 Win. Mag. call mfg. 1962-1970), X-Mark Pro adj. trigger became standard 2008, supplied with open sights the first year, hooded ramp front sight and adj. rear sight then became standard, American walnut stock with high gloss finish, distinctive black forend cap, white line spacers, Monte Carlo comb profile and finely cut checkering, R3 recoil pad supplied on Mag. cals., hinged floorplate, cut skipline checkering, receiver and floorplate fine line engraving was standard 1997-2001, non-embellished beginning 2002, sling swivel studs, metal work features deep, rich, high polished blue finish, approx. 7 1/4-7 5/8 lbs.

	$835	$745	$675	$615	$515	$425	$350
.222 Rem. Mag. cal.	$925	$850	$750	$675	$550	$475	$375
.350 Rem. Mag. cal.	$1,000	$900	$800	$725	$600	$485	$395
6.5mm Rem. Mag. cal.	$1,000	$900	$800	$725	$600	$485	$395

Last MSR was $994.

Add $30 for 24 in. barrel.

Add 15% for fine line engraving on receiver and floorplate (standard 1997-2001) if in 95% or better condition.

Add $27-$67 for left-hand model (available in certain cals. only, short action .22-250 Rem. and .243 Win. cals. are scarce in left-hand, disc. 2004).

Add 15% for 7mm Rem. Mag., .264 Win. Mag., or .300 Win. Mag. cal. with stainless steel barrel (mfg. 1962-1970).

In 1962, the 20 in. barrel was standard on .222 Rem., .222 Rem. Mag., .243 Win., .270 Win., .280 Rem., .30-06, or .308 Win. cal. In 1964, these cals. had a standard barrel length of 22 inches. 24 in. stainless steel barrels were standard on 7mm Rem. Mag., .264 Win. Mag., and .300 Win. Mag. (catalog 1962-1970) cals.

Remington mfg. the Model 700BDL in .350 Rem. Mag. and 6.5mm Rem. Mag. (1,584 mfg. between 1969-75). 1,558 were assembled in 1969, and sold through 1975. The .350 Rem. Mag. mfg. in 1969 is 3 times rarer than the 1985 Model 700 Classic chambered for .350 Rem. Mag.

During 1984, Remington began stamping a safety warning on the barrel.

MODEL 700 CLASSIC (LTD EDITION) – similar to 700BDL, except has classic straight stock, high polish bluing, has been offered in .17 Rem., .220 Swift, .221 Fireball (new 2002), .222 Rem., .22-250 Rem. (Classic only), .223 Rem., .250 Savage (250/3000), 6.5x55mm Swedish, 6mm Rem. (Classic only), 7x57mm Mauser, 8mm Rem. Mag., 8mm Mauser, .243 Win. (Classic only), .25-06 Rem., .257 Roberts, .264 Win. Mag., .270 Win. (Classic only), .280 Rem., .300 Savage (new 2003), .300 Win. Mag., .300 Wby. Mag., .30-06 (Classic only), .308 Win. (new 2005), 7mm-08 Rem., 7mm Wby. Mag., .338 Win. Mag., .350 Rem. Mag., .35 Whelen, .300 H&H, or .375 H&H cal. The original Model 700 Classic was mfg. 1978-1985. Limited edition calibers were introduced during 1981 (see listings), and continued to be produced annually until 2005.

$750	$650	$595	$525	$450	$395	$325	*$716*

Add 25% for 7x57mm Mauser, .220 Swift, .338 Win. Mag., .350 Rem. Mag., .250 Savage, .257 Roberts, .300 H&H, or .35 Whelen cal.

The Model 700 Classic was originally introduced in 1978 in .22-250 Rem., 6mm Rem., .243 Win., .270 Win., .30-06, and 7mm Rem. Mag., and was part of the standard Remington product lineup until 1985. Limited editions were introduced during 1981.

This model is produced in limited quantities of a different caliber each year. Add premiums for several calibers in NIB condition only (including 7x57mm Mauser, .257 Roberts, .300 H&H, and .375 H&H).

The following is a list of annual Limited Classic calibers offered previously with year of manufacture: 7x57mm Mauser (1981), .257 Roberts (1982), .300 H&H (1983), .250 Savage (1984), .350 Rem. Mag. (1985), .264 Win. Mag. (1986), .338 Win. Mag. (1987), .35 Whelen (1988), .300 Wby. Mag. (1989), .25-06 Rem. (1990), 7mm Wby. Mag. (1991), .220 Swift (1992), .222 Rem. (1993), 6.5x55mm Swedish (new 1994), .300 Win. Mag. (1995), .375 H&H Mag. (1996), .280 Rem. (1997), 8mm Rem. Mag. (1998), .17 Rem. (1999), .223 Rem. (2000), 7mm-08 Rem. (2001), .221 Fireball (2002), .300 Savage (2003), 8mm Mauser (2004), and .308 Win. (2005).

GRADING - PPGS™	100%	98%	95%	90%	80%	70%	60%	LAST MSR

MODEL 700 BDL DALE EARNHARDT JR. – .30-06 cal., 22 in. blue barrel, 4 shot mag., synthetic stock with Dale Earnhardt Jr. signature #8 logo, special ser. no. (DEJ8xxx), R3 recoil pad, no sights, drilled and tapped. Limited mfg. 2004 only.

$675	$525	$425	N/A	N/A	N/A	N/A	*$735*

MODEL 700 BDL DM (DETACHABLE MAG.) – .243 Win. (disc. 1999), .25-06 Rem. (disc. 1997), .260 Rem., .270 Win., .280 Rem. (disc. 1999), 6mm Rem. (disc. 1996), 7mm Rem. Mag., 7mm-08 Rem. (disc. 1999), .30-06, .308 Win. (disc. 1996), .300 Win. Mag. (disc. 2002), or .338 Win. Mag. (disc. 1996) cal., 22 or 24 in. barrel, Monte Carlo walnut stock with 20 LPI skip-line checkering, high polish bluing, black forend cap, receiver and floorplate fine line engraving was standard 1997-2001, open sights, 3-4 shot detachable mag. Mfg. 1995-2004.

$775	$675	$625	$550	$475	$395	$335	*$749*

Add $27 for .300 Win. Mag. and 7mm Rem. Mag. cals.

Left-hand actions on this model were disc. in 1999. Their last retail prices ranged from $665 - $692, depending on caliber.

MODEL 700 BDL EUROPEAN – .243 Win., .270 Win., .280 Rem., 7mm-08 Rem., 7mm Rem. Mag., .30-06, or .308 Win. cal., Monte Carlo stock with hand-rubbed oil finish, 22 or 24 (Mag. cals. only) in. barrel, hinged floorplate, iron sights, approx. 7 1/4 lbs. Disc. 1994.

$450	$395	$360	$300	$260	$220	$195	*$532*

Add $27 for 7mm Rem. Mag. cal.

MODEL 700 BDL LEW HORTON SPECIAL EDITION – .257 Roberts cal., 500 mfg. in 1990 only, first time the 700BDL has been offered in .257 Roberts cal.

$750	$650	$595	$525	$450	$395	$325	*$580*

MODEL 700 BDL MOUNTAIN RIFLE (FIXED MAG.) – .243 Win. (new 1988), .25-06 Rem. (new 1992), .257 Roberts (new 1991), .270 Win., 7mm-08 Rem. (new 1988), .280 Rem., .30-06, .308 Win. (new 1988), or 7x57mm Mauser (new 1990) cal., 22 in. tapered barrel, checkered satin finished American walnut stock with cheekpiece and ebony forend, 4 shot mag., without sights, 6 3/4 lbs. Mfg. 1986-94.

$450	$395	$360	$300	$260	$220	$195	*$532*

Add 20% for .257 Roberts or 7x57mm Mauser cal.

MODEL 700 BDL SS (STAINLESS SYNTHETIC) – .223 Rem. (mfg. 1993-94), .243 Win. (mfg. 1993-94), .25-06 Rem. (disc. 1994), .270 Win., .280 Rem. (disc. 1995), .30-06, .308 Win. (disc. 1994), 7mm Rem. (mfg. 1993-94), 7mm-08 Rem. (mfg. 1993-94), .300 Win. Mag. (new 1993), .300 RUM (new 1999), .300 RSUM (new 2003), .300 Wby. Mag. (mfg. 1993-94), .338 Win. Mag. (mfg. 1993-94, resumed 1997-2002), .338 RUM (new 2000), 7mm Rem. Mag., 7mm RUM (new 2001), 7mm RSUM (new 2003), 7mm Wby. Mag. (scarce, disc. 1994), .375 RUM (mfg. 2001-2002), or .375 H&H (mfg. 1997-2002) cal., features matte finished 416 stainless steel barrel, receiver, and bolt, black synthetic stock with checkering, R3 recoil pad became standard during 2004, drilled and tapped, hinged floorplate mag., 24 or 26 (RUM cals.) in. barrel, no sights, 6.25-7 lbs. Mfg. 1992-2004.

$775	$675	$625	$550	$475	$395	$335	*$735*

Add $26 for Mag. cals., except 7mm Rem. Mag.
Add $40 for RUM or RSUM cals.
Add approx. $100 for .223 Rem. cal., $150 for 7mm Wby. Mag. cal.

* ***Model 700 BDL LSS*** – .270 Win. (left-hand only, disc. 2000), .300 Win. Mag., .300 RUM (new 1999), .338 RUM (new 2000), .30-06 (left-hand only, disc. 2000), 7mm RUM, 7mm Rem. Mag., or .375 RUM cal., stainless steel barreled action, grey tinted laminate Monte Carlo wood stock, 24 or 26 (Rem. Ultra Mag. cals.) in. barrel, w/o sights, 7 1/2 lbs. Mfg. 1996-2004.

$800	$725	$650	$585	$485	$400	$335	*$827*

Add $13 for RUM cal.
Add $40 for Mag. cals. in left-hand action.

* ***Model 700 BDL SS DM (Detachable Mag.)*** – .243 Win. (disc. 1997), .25-06 Rem. (disc. 2002), .260 Rem. (mfg. 1997-2000), .270 Win., .280 Rem. (disc. 2002), 6mm Rem. (disc. 1995), 7mm Rem. Mag., 7mm-08 Rem. (disc. 1998, resumed 2000-2001), .30-06, .308 Win. (disc. 1999), .300 Win. Mag., .300 Wby. Mag. (disc. 2000), or .338 Win. Mag. (disc. 1996) cal., features 3-4 shot detachable mag., stainless steel, 24 in. barrel, satin finish metalwork, R3 recoil pad became standard during 2004, black non-reflective stock with checkering, receiver and floorplate fine line engraving was standard in 1997-2001, w/o sights, 7 3/8 lbs. Mfg. 1995-2004.

$800	$725	$650	$585	$485	$400	$335	*$801*

Add $27 for Mag. cals.
Add $89 for muzzle brake (Model 700BDL SS DM-B, mfg. 1996-2001, available in 7mm STW, 7mm Rem. Mag. [disc. 1999] or .300 Win. Mag. cals. only).

GRADING - PPGS™	100%	98%	95%	90%	80%	70%	60%	LAST MSR

MODEL 700 BDL SS CAMO RMEF – .300 RSUM (mfg. 2003), .300 RUM (mfg. 2001), .300 Win. Mag. (new 2004), or 7mm RUM (mfg. 2002) cal., Realtree Hardwoods camo stock treatment, satin finished receiver and round barrel, laser engraved floorplate including RMEF logo, limited special edition for the Rocky Mountain Elk Foundation, approx. 7 1/2 lbs. Mfg. 2001-2004.

	$680	$525	$405	N/A	N/A	N/A	N/A	*$835*

MODEL 700 BDL VARMINT SPECIAL – .22-250 Rem., .222 Rem., .223 Rem., .25-06 Rem., 6mm Rem., .243 Win., .308 Win., or 7mm-08 Rem. cal., 24 in. heavy barrel, checkered walnut stock, no sights. Mfg. 1967-1994.

	$1,100	$950	$850	$765	$650	$525	$425	*$565*

Add 50% for .223 Rem. cal.
Add 10% for .222 Rem. cal.

MODEL 700 CAMO SYNTHETIC – .22-250 Rem. (disc. 1993), .243 Win., .270 Win. (disc. 1993), .280 Rem. (disc. 1993), 7mm-08 Rem. (disc. 1993), 7mm Rem. Mag., .30-06, .308 Win. (disc. 1993), or .300 Wby. Mag. (disc. 1993) cal., 22 or 24 (Mag. only) in. barrel, features synthetic stock and is fully camouflaged in Mossy Oak Bottomland pattern, open sights, approx. 7 1/4 lbs. Mfg. 1992-94.

	$550	$400	$360	$300	$260	$220	$195	*$581*

Add $27 for Mag. cals.

MODEL 700 CDL 100TH ANNIVERSARY – .375 H&H cal., 22 in. barrel with open sights, satin checkered American walnut stock and forearm, SuperCell recoil pad and X-Mark Pro adj. trigger, approx. 7 1/2 lbs. Mfg. 2012 only.

	$1,200	$1,025	$885	$795	$685	$550	$435	*$1,450*

MODEL 700 CDL "BOONE & CROCKETT" SERIES – .243 Win., .270 Win., .270 WSM, .30-06, 7mm-08 Rem., 7mm Rem. Mag., .300 WSM, or .300 Win. Mag. cal., 24 or 26 in. fluted blue barrel, brown laminate stock, "Boone & Crockett" medallion insert on grip cap, "Boone & Crockett" laser engraved on barrel, X-Mark Pro adj. trigger. Mfg. 2008.

	$800	$725	$650	$585	$485	$400	$335	*$959*

Add 10% for regular Mag. cals. or 15% for WSM cals.

This model was offered through Remington Premier dealers only.

MODEL 700 CDL CLASSIC DELUXE – .223 Rem. (disc.), .243 Win., .270 Win., .25-06 (disc. 2016, reintroduced 2019), .30-06, .300 Win. Mag., .300 RUM (disc. 2015), .35 Whelen (disc.), 7mm-08 Rem., or 7mm Rem. Mag. cal., 24 or 26 (Mag. cals.) in. barrel w/o sights, classic style checkered walnut stock with satin finish, cheekpiece, black forend tip and pistol grip cap, satin blue or high polish (new 2008, select cals. only) metal finish, R3 recoil pad (disc. 2009), or SuperCell recoil pad became standard 2010, integral extractor, hinged floorplate, 3-5 shot mag., X-Mark Pro adj. trigger, approx. 7 1/2 lbs. Mfg. 2004-2020.

	$865	$775	$700	$635	$535	$435	$365	*$1,029*

Add $30 for Mag. cals.
Add $30 for left-hand action (select cals. only, mfg. 2005-2014).

This model was also manufactured in .204 Ruger cal. as part of a Friends of NRA limited edition - 1,050 were manufactured. Values can vary significantly depending on locality and perceived desirability.

* ***Model 700 CDL Classic Deluxe Detachable Mag*** – .243 Win. (disc.), .270 Win., .30-06, .300 Win. Mag., 7mm-08 Rem., or 7mm Rem. Mag. cal., features detachable box mag., 24 or 26 in. barrel, satin finished blued action and barrel, X-Mark Pro adj. trigger, straight comb walnut stock with cheekpiece. Mfg. 2011-2014.

	$885	$795	$725	$650	$550	$450	$365	*$1,041*

Add $29 for Mag. cals. (26 in. barrel only).

MODEL 700 CDL SF (STAINLESS FLUTED) – .17 Rem. Fireball (disc. 2009), .257 Wby. Mag. (new 2008), .270 Win., .270 WSM, 7mm-08 Rem., 7mm Rem. Mag., .30-06, or .300 WSM cal., 3-4 shot mag., 24 or 26 in. stainless fluted barrel, satin finished checkered walnut stock and forearm, R3 (disc. 2009) or SuperCell recoil pad became standard 2010, X-Mark Pro adj. trigger, approx. 7 1/2 lbs. Mfg. 2007-2020.

	$965	$850	$725	$650	$550	$450	$375	*$1,126*

Add $29 for Mag. cals. or $92 for WSM cals.

* ***Model 700 CDL SF Limited Edition*** – .300 Savage (new 2020), .25-06 Rem. (mfg. 2019), 6.5 Creedmoor (mfg. 2018), .17 Rem. Fireball (mfg. 2007), .22-250 (mfg. 2015), .223 Rem. (mfg. 2014), .257 Roberts (mfg. 2009), .260 Rem. (mfg. 2008), .280 Rem. (mfg. 2010), .30-06 (mfg. 2006), .35 Whelen (mfg. 2016), 6mm Rem. (mfg. 2011), 7mm Rem. Mag. (mfg. 2012), .300 Win. Mag. (mfg. 2013), or .300 Wby. Mag. (new 2017) cal., 24 in. stainless fluted barrel, checkered

GRADING - PPGS™	100%	98%	95%	90%	80%	70%	60%	LAST MSR

satin finished walnut stock, black forend tip and pistol grip cap, engraved floorplate, drilled and tapped, X-Mark Pro adj. trigger became standard 2007. Limited mfg. by caliber 2006-2020.

	$1,050	$925	$815	$725	$595	$475	$385	*$1,226*

The 7mm Rem. Mag. cal. released in 2012 features a 50th Anniversary commemorative floorplate.

MODEL 700 C GRADE (CUSTOM SHOP) – various standard and Mag. cals., from custom shop, 24 or 26 in. steel barrel, blued high polished action, no engraving, deluxe checkered Monte Carlo C grade wood stock with rosewood forearm cap and cheekpiece, BDL style trigger guard and hinged floorplate, 7 1/2 lbs. Mfg. 1964-1983, 2003-2004, reintroduced 2006-2015.

	$2,700	$2,325	$1,950	$1,800	$1,600	$1,350	$1,150	*$2,950*

MODEL 700 CUSTOM GRADE – special order only, grades differ in amount of engraving and type of walnut. Available as a custom order only through Remington. Values reflect 1991 information. The Remington Custom Shop should be contacted for a current price quotation and the availability of options.

Special order Model 700s mfg. between early '60s-1982 were designated C Grade, D Grade, or F Grade. Values will approximate Custom Grade Models I-III listed. In 1991, Remington discontinued Custom Grade Model designations.

* ***Model 700 Custom Grade Model I*** – mfg. 1983-1991.

	$1,400	$1,185	$1,000	$875	$750	$635	$500	*$1,314*

* ***Model 700 Custom Grade Model II*** – mfg. 1983-1991.

	$2,300	$2,000	$1,800	$1,600	$1,400	$1,200	$1,000	*$2,335*

* ***Model 700 Custom Grade Model III*** – mfg. 1983-1991.

	$2,900	$2,450	$2,050	$1,900	$1,675	$1,450	$1,175	*$3,650*

* ***Model 700 Custom Grade Model IV*** – mfg. 1983-1991.

	$4,875	$4,100	$2,950	N/A	N/A	N/A	N/A	*$5,695*

MODEL 700 CUSTOM KS MOUNTAIN RIFLE – .270 Win., .280 Rem., .300 Win. Mag., .300 Wby. Mag. (new 1989), .300 RUM (new 1999), .30-06, .338 Win. Mag. (new 1986), .338 RUM (new 2000), .35 Whelen (new 1989), 7mm STW (new 1999), 7mm Rem. Mag., 7mm RUM (new 2001), 8mm Rem. Mag. (new 1986), .375 RUM (new 2001), or .375 H&H cal., 22 (disc.), 24 or 26 (Ultra Mag. cals. only) in. carbon steel barrel, no sights, features extra lightweight Kevlar fiber-reinforced stock, available in either right or left-hand action, 6 3/8 - 7 lbs. Mfg. 1986-2004, reintroduced 2006-2008.

	$1,800	$1,525	$1,295	$1,100	$975	$850	$675	*$2,265*

Add $80 for left-hand action.

This model was available from the Custom Shop only (special order).

* ***Model 700 Custom KS Mountain Rifle Stainless*** – similar to Model 700 Custom KS Mountain Rifle, except has stainless steel action and barrel. Mfg. 1995-2004, reintroduced 2006.

	$1,950	$1,650	$1,425	$1,200	$1,075	$900	$725	*$2,465*

Add $80 for left-hand action.

* ***Model 700 Custom KS Mountain Rifle Wood Grained Kevlar*** – similar to Model 700 Custom KS Safari Grade, except has wood grained Kevlar stock. Mfg. 1992-1993.

	$1,000	$900	$800	$725	$600	$485	$395	*$1,109*

Add $63 for left-hand action.

MODEL 700 CUSTOM RIFLE – Mfg. 1992-2020.

	N/A	$3,000	$2,500	$1,500	$1,000	$850	$725	

Last published MSR in 2007 was $3,999.

MSR for 2007-2020 was POR.

Beginning 1992, Remington stopped Custom Grade Model designations in favor of individualized quotations per work order.

MODEL 700 CUSTOM SIXSITE – customer's choice of caliber, stainless steel button rifled barrel, threaded muzzle with thread protector, 700 stainless steel blue printed receiver, Remington Custom 40X trigger, carbon fiber stock by A.G. Composites with SIXSITE (Rana pattern) hand painted by Scalpel Arms, stainless steel BDL bottom metal with SIXSITE logo, skip fluting on bolt and barrel, custom bipod rail with QD cup, Badger Ordnance 20 MOA scope rail, available in right or left-hand configuration, Copper Cerakote finish on all metal parts. Mfg. by the Custom Shop 2019-2020.

	$2,800	$2,450	$2,100	$1,900	$1,550	$1,275	$1,000	*$3,295*

MODEL 700D PEERLESS GRADE (CUSTOM SHOP) – scroll engraving, best wood. Mfg. 1962-1983.

	$2,000	$1,695	$1,475	$1,250	$1,125	$950	$750	

GRADING - PPGS™	100%	98%	95%	90%	80%	70%	60%	LAST MSR

MODEL 700 ETRONX VS SF – .220 Swift (electronic primer), .22-250 Rem. (electronic primer), or .243 Win. (electronic primer) cal., features patented EtronX technology utilizing an electronic discharge for virtually instant cartridge ignition, CPU located in stock incorporates standard 9V battery, and allows electric signal to be passed through a ceramic coated firing pin, which in turn activates the specially designed electronic primer. There are no moving parts in this system, and therefore, nothing to delay ignition. Electronic trigger mechanism enables almost zero lock time. LED on top of grip indicates system status (fire or safe mode), chamber status (loaded or not loaded), low battery indicator, and any possible system malfunction. 26 in. heavy stainless steel barrel with black flutes, alumiunum bedding, Kevlar reinforced composite stock with matte black finish, 8 7/8 lbs. Mfg. late 1999-2003.

$1,150 $985 $865 $775 $665 $535 $435 *$1,332*

This model can fire only EtronX ammunition which used an electronic primer. Remington still manufactures EtronX ammunition in .22-250 Rem. and .220 Swift only.

Because the EtronX ignition system used an electronic primer the same size as a standard rifle primer, reloading was no different than using standard cases, powder, and bullets. The only thing that changed was the electronic primer. Ammunition is now scarce, but EtronX primers are still available from Remington.

MODEL 700 F PREMIER GRADE (CUSTOM SHOP) – elaborate engraving, best wood. Mfg. 1962-1983.

$3,450 $2,850 $2,450 $2,200 $1,950 $1,650 $1,350

MODEL 700 FS – .243 Win., .270 Win., .30-06, .308 Win., or 7mm Rem. Mag. cal., 22 in. polished blue barrel, grey or grey camo Kevlar fiberglass stock with solid recoil pad, open sights, 6 1/4 lbs. Mfg. 1987-88 only.

$600 $500 $415 $375 $335 $310 $285 *$613*

Add $20 for 7mm Rem. Mag. cal. (24 in. barrel).

MODEL 700 LONG RANGE – .25-06 Rem., .30-06, .300 Win. Mag., .300 RUM, or 7mm Rem. Mag. cal., 26 in. heavy varmint barrel, 4 shot mag., black with grey webbing Bell & Carlson M40 tactical stock, X-Mark Pro externally adj. trigger, drilled and tapped, 7 1/2 lbs. Mfg. 2014-2020.

$725 $615 $565 $495 $425 $375 $300 *$880*

* ***Model 700 Long Range Stainless*** – .300 Win. Mag., .300 RUM, 6.5 Creedmoor (new 2020), or 7mm Rem. Mag. cal., 26 in. stainless steel barrel, 3 shot mag., black with grey webbing Bell & Carlson M40 stock, 9 lbs. Mfg. 2018-2020.

$800 $700 $600 $550 $450 $375 $300 *$941*

MODEL 700 LSS – .257 Wby. Mag. or .300 Win. Mag. cal., 26 in. stainless steel barrel, black laminate stock, X-Mark Pro adj. trigger, SuperCell recoil pad. Mfg. 2008.

$850 $765 $685 $625 $525 $425 $350 *$972*

This model was available through Remington Premier dealers only.

MODEL 700 LV SF (LIGHT VARMINT STAINLESS FLUTED) – .204 Ruger (new 2005), .17 Rem., .221 Rem. Fireball, .223 Rem., or .22-250 Rem. cal., short action, 22 in. fluted barrel w/o sights, black composite stock with R3 recoil pad, stainless action and barrel, jeweled bolt, blind box mag., 6 3/4 lbs. Mfg. 2004-2007.

$835 $745 $675 $615 $515 $425 $350 *$1,040*

MODEL 700 MOUNTAIN RIFLE DM (DETACHABLE MAG.) – .243 Win. (disc. 1997), .260 Rem. (new 1998), .25-06 Rem. (disc. 2002), .270 Win., .280 Rem., 7mm-08 Rem., or .30-06 cal., detachable mag., 22 in. barrel, satin finished American walnut stock, R3 recoil pad became standard on Mag. cals. during 2004, satin bluing, without sights, approx. 6 1/2 lbs. Mfg. 1995-2006.

$695 $595 $545 $475 $415 $375 $315 *$841*

* ***Model 700 Mountain Rifle LSS (Laminated Stock Stainless)*** – .260 Rem. (disc. 2007), .270 Win., .280 Rem. (new 2007), .30-06, or 7mm-08 Rem. cal., features stainless action and 22 in. barrel w/o sights, brown laminate stock, X-Mark Pro adj. trigger became standard 2008, approx. 6 1/2 lbs. Mfg. 1999-2010.

$900 $825 $750 $675 $565 $465 $375 *$1,095*

MODEL 700 MAGPUL – .260 Rem., 6.5 Creedmoor (new mid-2017), .300 Win. Mag. (new 2018), or .308 Win. cal., 22 or 24 (new 2018, .300 Win. Mag. only) in. free floated carbon steel barrel with black Cerakote finish, threaded muzzle with thread protector, 5 shot detachable Magpul mag., X-Mark Pro externally adj. trigger, synthetic stock with Magpul Hunter finish, adj. LOP kit (13-15 in.), three comb-height inserts, 9 lbs. Mfg. 2017-2020.

$975 $875 $775 $695 $585 $465 $375 *$1,175*

GRADING - PPGS™	100%	98%	95%	90%	80%	70%	60%	LAST MSR

MODEL 700 MAGPUL ENHANCED – .308 Win., 6mm Creedmoor (new 2019), 6.5 Creedmoor, or .300 Win. Mag. (new 2019) cal., 20 or 24 (new 2019, .300 Win. Mag. only) in. heavy barrel with LTR flutes and black Cerakote finish, suppressor-ready threaded muzzle and protector, 10 shot Magpul mag., X-Mark Pro adj. trigger, Magpul Hunter stock with FDE finish, M-LOK bipod mount and folding bipod, 8 1/2 lbs. Mfg. 2018-2020.

	$1,060	$925	$815	$725	$600	$485	$400	*$1,249*

MODEL 700 MOUNTAIN RIFLE STAINLESS – .25-06 Rem., .270 Win., .280 Rem., or .30-06 cal., 22 in. barrel, black synthetic stock with pressed checkering, blind mag., 7 1/4 lbs. Mfg. 1993 only.

	$450	$395	$360	$300	$260	$220	$195	*$532*

MODEL 700 MOUNTAIN SS – .25-06 Rem., .270 Win., .280 Rem., .30-06, .308 Win., 6.5 Creedmoor (new 2019), or 7mm-08 Rem. cal., 22 in. stainless steel hammer forged light contour barrel with satin stainless finish, 4 shot mag., Bell & Carlson adj. synthetic stock, X-Mark Pro adj. trigger, 6 1/2 lbs. Mfg. 2012-2020.

	$975	$875	$775	$695	$585	$465	$375	*$1,152*

MODEL 700 NORTH AMERICAN CUSTOM – various cals., short or long action, blue steel or stainless steel fluted barrel, composite stock with full-length aluminum bedding block, Model 40-X adj. trigger, machined steel trigger guard and floorplate, 7 1/2 lbs. Mfg. 2008-2015.

	$1,800	$1,525	$1,295	$1,100	$975	$850	$675	*$1,999*

Add $151 for stainless steel action and barrel.

This model is also available in left-hand action at no extra charge.

MODEL 700 NRA AMERICAN HUNTER – 6.5 Creedmoor cal., 20 in. fluted carbon steel barrel with 5R rifling and threaded muzzle, 4 shot mag., adj. X Mark Pro trigger, Bell & Carlson stock with aluminum bedding block, upgraded Leupold Mark 4 scope bases, distinctly engraved floorplate, unique serial number dedicated to this limited edition offering, black Cerakote finish. Limited mfg. mid-2019-2020.

	$1,150	$1,000	$875	$785	$650	$525	$450	*$1,349*

This rifle was a collaboration between the NRA's American Hunter magazine and Remington.

MODEL 700P & VARIATIONS – various cals., long or short action, various barrel lengths, designed for police/law enforcement and military, current configurations include: 700P, 700P TWS (Tactical Weapons System, includes scope, bipod and case), 700P LTR (Light Tactical Rifle), 700P LTR TWS (Light Tactical Rifle/Tactical Weapons System, includes scope, bipod, and case), 700P USR (Urban Sniper Rifle), Model M24/M24A2/M24A3 Sniper Weapon System (combination of Model 700 and Model 40-XB design, with scope, case, and bipod), and from the Remington Custom Shop Model 40-XS Tactical Rifle System, Model 40-XB Tactical, and the Model 40-XS 338 Tactical. Disc. 2020.

Remington did not publish consumer retail pricing for these police/law enforcement models. Secondary prices for base models w/o scopes and other options will be slightly higher than for current pricing on the Model 700BDL Custom Deluxe. Prices for rifles with scopes and other features will be determined by how much the individual options and accessories add to the base value.

MODEL 700 PCR (PRECISION CHASSIS RIFLE) – .260 Rem. (disc. 2019), 6mm Creedmoor (new 2020), 6.5 Creedmoor, or .308 Win. cal., 24 in. carbon steel barrel with 5R rifling and black Cerakote finish, threaded muzzle with protector, 5 or 10 (new 2020) shot Magpul detachable mag., X-Mark Pro adj. trigger, black adj. Magpul PRS Gen 3 stock, Magpul pistol grip, Remington chassis, tactical bolt knob, aluminum handguard with SquareDrop, Picatinny rail, matte blue finish, 10 1/2 lbs. Mfg. 2018-2020.

	$1,025	$900	$800	$725	$600	$485	$400	*$1,199*

MODEL 700 RS – .270 Win., .280 Rem., or .30-06 cal., 22 in. matte finished barrel and action, grey or grey camo DuPont Rynite synthetic stock with smooth cheekpiece and solid recoil pad, open sights, 7 1/4 lbs. Mfg. 1987-1988 only.

	$650	$550	$495	$425	$375	$325	$275	*$547*

Add 30% for .280 Rem. cal.

In 1987 less than 500 rifles were dual barrel marked - 7mm EXP REM .280 REM. These specimens will command a 40% premium.

MODEL 700 SAFARI GRADE – .375 H&H, 8mm Rem. Mag. (new 1986), .416 Rem. Mag. (new 1989), or .458 Win. Mag. cal., heavier 700BDL barrel, 3 shot mag., 24 in. barrel, available with either Classic or Monte Carlo stock configuration, custom shop special order only, 9 lbs. Mfg. 1962-2000.

	$1,395	$1,185	$1,000	$875	$750	$635	$500	*$1,225*

Add $73 for left-hand model (Classic stock only).

GRADING - PPGS™	100%	98%	95%	90%	80%	70%	60%	LAST MSR

* ***Model 700 Safari Grade Custom KS*** – 8mm Rem. Mag., .375 H&H, .416 Rem. Mag., or .458 Win. Mag. cal., stock made from Aramid fiber or Kevlar (disc.) and fiberglass, 24 in. barrel with barrel band, including sling swivel, adj. safari sights, blind 3 shot mag., 9 lbs. Mfg. 1989-2004, reintroduced 2006-2011.

$2,400	**$2,075**	**$1,850**	**$1,650**	**$1,425**	**$1,225**	**$1,025**	***$2,841***

This model was also available in left-hand action at no extra charge.

* ***Model 700 Safari Grade Custom KS Stainless*** – .375 H&H, .416 Rem. Mag., or .458 Win. Mag. cal., features fiberglass and Aramid or Kevlar (disc.) stock and stainless steel action. Mfg. 1993-2004, reintroduced 2006-2011.

$2,575	**$2,225**	**$1,900**	**$1,750**	**$1,550**	**$1,300**	**$1,100**	***$3,067***

MODEL 700 SENDERO – .25-06 Rem., .270 Win. (disc. 2001), .300 Win. Mag., or 7mm Rem. Mag. cal., similar to Model 700 VS, except has long action for Mag. cals., 24 (non-cataloged) or 26 in. barrel, 9 lbs. Mfg. 1994-2002.

$635	**$510**	**$420**	**$335**	**$295**	**$265**	**$250**	***$788***

Add $27 for Mag. cals.
Add approx. $100 for fluted barrel (not cataloged).

* ***Model 700 Sendero Special SF (Stainless Fluted)*** – .25-06 Rem. (disc. 2002), .300 Win. Mag., .300 Wby. Mag. (mfg. 1997-2001), .300 RUM (new 1999), .300 RSUM (new 2003), .338 RUM (new 2000), 7mm STW (mfg. 1997-2002), 7mm Rem. Mag., 7mm RUM (new 2001), or 7mm RSUM (new 2003) cal., 26 in. varmint type fluted barrel, approx. 8 1/2 lbs. Mfg. 1996-2004.

$995	**$900**	**$800**	**$725**	**$600**	**$485**	**$395**	***$1,003***

* ***Model 700 Sendero Special SF-II*** – .25-06 (new 2016), .264 Win. Mag. (disc. 2011, reintroduced 2016), .300 Win. Mag., .300 RUM, .338 RUM (disc.), 7mm Rem. Mag., or 7mm RUM (disc. 2011) cal., 24 (disc.) or 26 in. fluted heavy barrel, 3-4 shot mag., stainless steel action, X-Mark Pro adj. trigger became standard 2007, black H-S Precision synthetic stock with grey webbing and full-length aluminum bedding, 8 1/2 lbs. Mfg. 2006-2020.

$1,245	**$1,045**	**$915**	**$815**	**$695**	**$565**	**$450**	***$1,502***

MODEL 700 SENDERO COMPOSITE – .25-06 Rem., .300 Win. Mag., or 7mm STW cal., features 26 in. composite barrel, matte black finished steel action, Kevlar reinforced black synthetic stock, 7 7/8 lbs. Mfg. 1999 only.

$1,395	**$1,185**	**$1,000**	**$875**	**$750**	**$635**	**$500**	***$1,665***

MODEL 700 SENDERO CUSTOM – various cals., 26 in. heavy barrel, features blue printed Model 700 stainless steel action, machined steel trigger guard with engraved floorplate, 40X (disc. 2012) or X-Mark Pro (new 2015) adj. trigger, composite stock with cheekpiece. Mfg. 2012 only, reintroduced 2015 only.

$2,250	**$2,000**	**$1,800**	**$1,600**	**$1,400**	**$1,200**	**$1,000**	

Last MSR in 2012 was $3,535.
Last MSR in 2015 was $2,500.

Add approx. $500 if mfg. in 2012 (with 40X trigger).

MODEL 700 SPS (SPECIAL PURPOSE SYNTHETIC) – .223 Rem., .243 Win., .260 Rem. (new 2014), 6.5 Creedmoor (new mid-2017), .270 Win., .270 WSM, .300 Win. Mag., .300 Rem. Ultra Mag., .300 WSM, 7mm-08 Rem., .308 Win., .30-06, or 7mm Rem. Mag. cal., 24 or 26 in. barrel, black synthetic stock with SuperCell (became standard 2010) or R3 (disc. 2009) recoil pad, X-Mark Pro adj. trigger standard, approx. 7 3/8 lbs. Mfg. in Ilion, NY 2005-2020.

$595	**$500**	**$445**	**$375**	**$325**	**$275**	**$225**	***$731***

This model was also available in left-hand action at no extra charge - calibers were .270 Win., .30-06, .300 Win. Mag., or 7mm Rem. Mag. (new 2009).

* ***Model 700 SPS Camo*** – .223 Rem. (disc. 2015), .243 Win. (disc. 2015), .270 Win., .300 Win., .30-06, 7mm-08 Rem. (disc. 2015), or 7mm Rem. Mag. cal., 20 (Compact model, disc. 2015), 22, or 24 in. barrel, matte blued finish, hinged floorplate, X-Mark Pro adj. trigger, Mossy Oak Break Up Infinity camo synthetic stock, 7- 7.5 lbs. Mfg. 2011-2020.

$675	**$575**	**$525**	**$450**	**$395**	**$350**	**$295**	***$809***

* ***Model 700 SPS DM*** – .243 Win., .270 Win., .30-06, 7mm-08 Rem., 7mm Rem. Mag. or .300 Win. Mag. cal., features detachable mag., X-Mark Pro trigger, otherwise similar to Model 700 SPS. Mfg. 2005-2010.

$575	**$495**	**$435**	**$375**	**$325**	**$275**	**$225**	***$717***

GRADING - PPGS™	100%	98%	95%	90%	80%	70%	60%	LAST MSR

* ***Model 700 SPS Stainless*** – .22-250 Rem., .223 Rem., .243 Win., 7mm-08 Rem., .308 Win., .25-06, .270 Win., .30-06, .270 WSM, .300 WSM, 7mm Rem. Mag., .300 Win. Mag., 7mm Rem. Ultra Mag. (disc.), or .300 Rem. Ultra Mag. cal., 24 or 26 in. stainless steel barrel, 3, 4, or 5 shot, no sights, matte black synthetic stock with rubberized overmold grip panels, R3 (disc. 2007) or SuperCell (new 2008) recoil pad, X-Mark Pro adj. trigger standard 2008, approx. 7 1/4 lbs. Mfg. 2005-2020.

$695 $595 $545 $475 $415 $375 $315 ***$838***

* ***Model 700 SPS Threaded Muzzle*** – .223 Rem., .243 Win., .30-06, or .308 Win. cal., 20 in. barrel, threaded muzzle with thread protector, matte blue barrel finish, 4 or 5 (.223 Rem. only) shot, hinged floorplate, X-Mark Pro externally adj. trigger, drilled and tapped for scope mounts, black synthetic stock with overmold grip panels, 7-7.25 lbs. Mfg. 2015-2020.

$635 $535 $485 $415 $365 $315 $265 ***$776***

* ***Model 700 SPS Varmint*** – .17 Rem. Fireball (disc. 2011) .204 Ruger, .22-250 Rem., .223 Rem., .243 Win. or .308 Win. cal., right or left (new 2008, not available in .204 Ruger) hand action, 26 in. heavy barrel, X-Mark Pro adj. trigger, matte black synthetic stock with vent. beavertail forend and overmold grip panels, SuperCell recoil pad, dual sling swivels, matte blue metal finish, approx. 8 1/2 lbs. Mfg. 2007-2020.

$625 $525 $475 $395 $350 $300 $250 ***$761***

* ***Model 700 SPS Wood Tech*** – .270 Win., .30-06, 7mm Rem. Mag., or .300 Win. Mag. cal., 22 or 24 in. barrel, walnut grained synthetic stock with Hogue Black overmolded grips, Supercell recoil pad and stippled pistol grip and forend, no sights, matte blue metal finish, X-Mark Pro externally adj. trigger, 7 3/8 lbs. Mfg. 2013-2015.

$675 $575 $525 $450 $395 $350 $295 ***$809***

* ***Model 700 SPS Youth/Compact*** – .243 Win., .270 Win. (disc.), 7mm-08 Rem., .30-06 (disc.) or .308 Win. (disc.) cal., 20 in. carbon steel barrel, matte black Youth synthetic stock, shorter LOP, approx. 7 3/8 lbs. Mfg. in Ilion, NY 2005-2020.

$595 $500 $445 $375 $325 $275 $225 ***$731***

This model is also available in left-hand action at no extra charge.

MODEL 700 SPS BUCKMASTERS EDITION – .243 Win., .270 Win., .30-06, .300 Win. Mag., 7mm-08 Rem., or 7mm Rem. Mag. cal., 3 or 4 shot mag., 20-26 in. barrel, engraved floorplate with Buckmasters logo, Realtree Hardwoods camo stock, also available in Youth (Youngbucks edition with 20 in. barrel), R3 recoil pad, approx. 7 1/8 lbs. Mfg. 2007-2010.

$595 $500 $445 $375 $325 $275 $225 ***$754***

MODEL 700 SPS LONG RANGE – .25-06 Rem., .300 Win. Mag., .300 RUM, or 7mm Rem. Mag. cal., 26 in. barrel w/o sights, black synthetic w/grey overmolded varmint stock, 8 3/4 lbs. Mfg. 2012-2013.

$625 $525 $475 $395 $350 $300 $250 ***$739***

MODEL 700 SPS TACTICAL – .223 Rem. or .308 Win. cal., 20 in. heavy contour barrel with black oxide finish, X-Mark Pro adj. trigger, black synthetic overmolded Hogue stock, matte black finish, 7 1/2 lbs. Mfg. 2008, reintroduced 2010-2020.

$650 $550 $495 $425 $375 $325 $275 ***$788***

This model was available through Remington Premier dealers only in 2008.

* ***Model 700 SPS Tactical AAC-SD*** – 6.5 Creedmoor (new 2018), .223 Rem., .300 AAC Blackout (new 2013), or .308 Win. cal., 16 1/2 (new 2013) or 20 (.308 only) in. heavy barrel with threaded muzzle, Hogue overmold Ghillie Green Pillar bedded stock, X-Mark Pro adj. trigger. Mfg. 2011-2020.

$695 $595 $545 $475 $415 $375 $315 ***$842***

* ***Model 700 SPS Tactical Blackhawk*** – .223 Rem. or .308 Win. cal., 20 in. triangular contoured barrel, Bell & Carlson Medalist adj. stock, pistol grip cap, steel floorplate and trigger guard, X-Mark Pro trigger, synthetic stock, tactical bolt handle, 8 1/2 lbs. Mfg. 2012 only.

$695 $595 $545 $475 $415 $375 $315 ***$850***

* ***Model 700 SPS Tactical Coyote Tan*** – 6.5 Creedmoor cal., 22 in. barrel, threaded muzzle, 4 shot mag., matte black Hogue overmolded stock, Coyote Tan Cerakote finish, 7 1/2 lbs. Mfg. 2018-2020.

$710 $600 $545 $475 $415 $375 $315 ***$875***

* ***Model 700 SPS Tactical Laser Engraved*** – .223 Rem. or .308 Win. cal., 16 1/2 in. barrel with threaded muzzle, laser engraved "Tactical" on barrel, carbon receiver and barrel with matte finish, Hogue Ghillie Green synthetic stock, X-Mark Pro externally adj. trigger, 7 1/2 lbs. Mfg. 2013-2014.

$675 $575 $525 $450 $395 $350 $295 ***$842***

GRADING - PPGS™	100%	98%	95%	90%	80%	70%	60%	LAST MSR

MODEL 700 STAINLESS 5R – .223 Rem., .308 Win., or .300 Win. Mag. cal., 20, 24, or 26 in. threaded (20 or 24 in. only) or non-threaded stainless steel barrel, 3, 4, or 5 shot mag., black with green web patterned H-S Precision stock, 8 1/2 lbs. Mfg. 2018-2020.

$925	$800	$675	$575	$475	$400	$350	*$1,100*

Add $50 for threaded barrel.

MODEL 700 STAINLESS 5R THREADED GEN 2 – .308 Win., .300 Win. Mag., or 6.5 Creedmoor cal., 20 or 24 in. stainless steel threaded barrel with black Cerakote finish, 3 or 4 shot mag., Sand with Black web patterned H-S Precision stock, 8 1/2 lbs. Mfg. 2018-2020.

$1,060	$925	$815	$725	$600	$485	$400	*$1,250*

MODEL 700 TACTICAL – 6.8 SPC cal., 20 in. parkerized barrel, synthetic stock, approx. 9 lbs. Limited availability 2005-2006.

$800	$725	$650	$585	$485	$400	$335	*$990*

MODEL 700 TACTICAL CHASSIS – .300 Win. Mag., .308 Win., or .338 Lapua Mag. cal., 24 or 26 in. free floating stainless steel barrel with black Cerakote finish, 5 shot mag., ratchet mount muzzle brake or AAC51-T muzzle brake (.338 Lapua only), X-Mark Pro externally adj. trigger, black Magpul MAG307 PRS fully adj. stock and pistol grip, target tactical bolt handle, ships in hard case, 11-1/4-12 1/2 lbs. Mfg. 2014-2020.

$2,425	$2,095	$1,875	$1,675	$1,475	$1,250	$1,025	*$2,900*

Add $200 for .300 Win. Mag. or $600 for .338 Lapua Mag. cal.

MODEL 700 TACTICAL TARGET – .308 Win. cal., 26 in. triangular contour barrel with 5-R tactical rifling, 4 shot mag., steel trigger guard and floorplate, X-Mark Pro adj. trigger, Bell & Carlson Medalist adj. stock, tactical bolt handle, OD Green finish, 11 3/4 lbs. Mfg. 2009-2014.

$1, 875	$1,600	$1,375	$1,150	$1,025	$900	$700	*$2,138*

MODEL 700 TITANIUM ULTIMATE LIGHTWEIGHT – .260 Rem., .270 Win., .30-06, .300 Rem. SAUM (new 2004), .308 Win. (new 2002), 7mm Rem. SAUM (new 2004), or 7mm-08 Rem cal., titanium receiver (drilled and tapped), spiral cut breech bolt with flutes and skeleton handle, 22 in. stainless steel barrel, satin stainless finish on receiver and barrel, ultra lightweight carbon fiber matte finished Kevlar reinforced stock, 3-4 shot fixed mag., sling swivel studs, 5 1/4 - 5 1/2 lbs. Mfg. 2001-2006.

$1,200	$1,025	$885	$795	$685	$550	$435	*$1,412*

Add $40 for Rem. SAUM cals.

MODEL 700 VARMINT SF – .17 Rem. Fireball (disc. 2010), .204 Ruger (disc. 2010), .220 Swift, .223 Rem., .22-250 Rem., or .308 Win. cal., 26 in. heavy stainless barrel, 4 or 5 shot mag., vent. forend, X-Mark Pro adj. trigger, matte black synthetic stock with Hogue overmolded grip panels, SuperCell recoil pad, approx. 8 1/2 lbs. Mfg. 2009-2020.

$825	$735	$665	$595	$495	$415	$345	*$991*

MODEL 700 VLS (VARMINT LAMINATED STOCK) – .204 Ruger (new 2005), .222 Rem. (mfg. 1995 only), .22-250 Rem., .223 Rem., .243 Win., 6mm Rem. (mfg. 1998-2007), .260 Rem. (disc. 1999), .308 Win., or 7mm-08 Rem. (mfg. 1997-99) cal., 26 in. heavy barrel w/o sights, blue metalwork, brown laminated stock with (disc. 2001) or w/o skipline checkering, beavertail shaped forend became standard 1998, X-Mark Pro adj. trigger became standard 2007, 9 3/8 lbs. Mfg. 1995-2020.

$875	$785	$715	$645	$545	$445	$365	*$1,056*

* ***Model 700 VL SS TH (Thumbhole)*** – .204 Ruger, .22-250 Rem., or .223 Rem. cal., stainless action with 26 in. heavy stainless barrel w/o sights, 4 or 5 shot mag., brown laminated thumbhole stock with vent. beavertail forend, X-Mark Pro adj. trigger became standard 2007, 9 1/4 lbs. Mfg. 2007-2011.

$950	$865	$775	$695	$585	$465	$375	*$1,130*

MODEL 700 VS COMPOSITE – .22-250 Rem., .223 Rem., or .308 Win. cal., 24 or 26 in. composite barrel, matte black finished steel action, Kevlar reinforced black synthetic stock. Mfg. by Custom Shop 1999-2000.

$1,550	$1,325	$1,100	$975	$850	$725	$575	*$1,912*

MODEL 700 VSF VARMINT SPECIAL – .17 Rem. Fireball (new 2007), .22-250 Rem., .223 Rem., or .308 Win. cal., updated Model 700VS with VS SFII stock design in desert tan with black webbing and R3 recoil pad, 26 in. fluted heavy blue barrel, blue receiver, available in right or left-hand action, 9 lbs. Mfg. 2005-2007.

$925	$835	$765	$685	$575	$465	$375	*$1,159*

Add $26 for left-hand action.

GRADING - PPGS™	100%	98%	95%	90%	80%	70%	60%	LAST MSR

MODEL 700 VS (VARMINT SYNTHETIC) – .220 Swift (disc. 1996), .22-250 Rem., .223 Rem., .243 Win. (mfg. 1997-98), or .308 Win. cal., short action, composite textured black and grey synthetic stock features Kevlar, fiberglass, and graphite, matte metal finish, 26 in. heavy barrel w/o sights, 9 1/8 lbs. Mfg. 1992-2004.

$650	$550	$495	$425	$375	$325	$275	*$811*

Add $26 for left-hand action.

The right-hand model was disc. 1998, but resumed in 2000.

* ***Model 700 VS SF/SF-P (Varmint Synthetic Stainless Fluted/Ported)*** – .220 Swift (ported barrel only until 2000), .22-250 Rem., .223 Rem. (w/o porting), .308 Win. (ported barrel only, disc. 1999) or .338 RUM (mfg. 2000 only) cal., stainless steel action with 26 in. barrel with flutes, 2 barrel ports became an option in some cals. during 1998-99 only (Model SF-P), 8 1/2 lbs. Mfg. 1994-2004.

$825	$735	$665	$595	$495	$415	$345	*$976*

Add 5% for ported barrel (Model 700VS SF-P, disc. 1999).

* ***Model 700 VS SF-II Varmint Special (Varmint Synthetic Stainless Fluted)*** – .17 Rem. Fireball (mfg. 2008-2010), .204 Ruger (disc. 2010), .220 Swift, .22-250 Rem., or .223 Rem. cal., updated Model 700 VS SF with reconfigured H-S Precision composite stock, palm swell and contoured beavertail forend, 26 in. heavy barrel with black fluting, black synthetic stock with spruce green webbing, X-Mark Pro adj. trigger became standard 2007, 8 1/2 lbs. Mfg. 2005-2011.

$1,150	$985	$865	$775	$665	$535	$435	*$1,387*

MODEL 700 VTR – .17 Rem. Fireball (mfg. 2009-2010), .204 Ruger (disc. 2010), .223 Rem., .22-250 Rem., .243 Win. (new 2009), or .308 Win. cal., 22 in. barrel, OD Green, desert camo (mfg. 2009), or A-TACS digital camo (new 2010) overmolded stock, integrated muzzle brake design, triangular shaped barrel contour, X-Mark Pro adj. trigger, approx. 7 1/2 lbs. Mfg. 2008-2013.

$725	$625	$575	$500	$435	$395	$325	*$908*

Add $51 for A-TACS stock (.223 Rem. or .308 Win. cal. only).

MODEL 700 VTR CARBON – .223 Rem., .22-250 Rem., .260 Rem., or .308 Win. cal., 22 in. carbon steel barrel with matte blue finish, integral muzzle brake, 4 or 5 shot mag., externally adj. trigger, FDE stock with black overmold, Super cell recoil pad, Picatinny rail, tactical bolt knob, includes bipod, 7 5/8 lbs. Mfg. 2014-2020.

$775	$675	$625	$550	$475	$315	$335	*$930*

MODEL 700 VTR SS (STAINLESS STEEL) – .223 Rem. or .308 Win. cal., 22 in. stainless steel barrel, X-Mark Pro externally adj. trigger, black stock with grey overmold, Picatinny rail, includes bipod, tactical bolt knob. Mfg. 2014-2020.

$825	$735	$665	$595	$495	$415	$345	*$980*

MODEL 700 XCR (XTREME CONDITIONS RIFLE) – 25-06 Rem. (new 2007), .270 Win., .270 WSM, .30-06, 7mm Rem. Mag., .300 WSM, .300 Win. Mag., 7mm RUM, 7mm-08 Rem. (new 2007), .300 RUM, .338 RUM, .338 Win. Mag., .375 H&H, or .375 RUM cal., bolt action rifle, right or left-hand action (available in .270 Win., .30-06, .300 Rem. Mag., or .300 Rem. Ultra Mag., mfg. 2008), 24 or 26 in. stainless steel barrel with TriNyte corrosion control, X-Mark Pro adj. trigger, patented black Hogue overmolded stock with R3 recoil pad, approx. 7 1/2 lbs. Mfg. 2005-2009.

$865	$775	$700	$635	$535	$435	$365	*$1,065*

Add $27 for Mag. cals. or $76 for WSM cals.

Add 10% for left-hand action (available in .270 Win., .30-06, .300 Rem. Mag., or .300 RUM, mfg. 2008).

* ***Model 700 XCR RMEF*** – .30-06 (mfg. 2009), 7mm Rem. Mag. (disc.), 7mm RUM (mfg. 2008), .300 RUM (mfg. 2007, again in 2010) or .300 WSM (mfg. 2006) cal., features RMEF camo Realtree Hardwood HD (disc. 2006) or AP (new 2007) camo overmolded stock with R3 recoil pad, X-Mark Pro adj. trigger became standard 2007. Mfg. 2005-2010.

$950	$865	$775	$695	$585	$465	$375	*$1,199*

Subtract approx. 10% for 7mm Rem. Mag. cal.

MODEL 700 XCR II (XTREME CONDITIONS RIFLE) – various cals., 24 or 26 in. barrel, stainless steel barrel and receiver with matte black TriNyte finish, Hogue OD green synthetic stock with overmolding in grip and forend areas, SuperCell recoil pad, X-Mark Pro adj. trigger, hinged floorplate, approx. 7 1/2 lbs. Mfg. 2010-2015.

$800	$725	$650	$585	$485	$400	$335	*$1,015*

Add $30 for standard Mag. cals.

Add $80 for .300 WSM cal.

GRADING - PPGS™	100%	98%	95%	90%	80%	70%	60%	LAST MSR

* ***Model 700 XCR II Camo Bone Collector Edition*** – .30-06 cal., 24 in. barrel, "Bone Collector" with logo engraved on floorplate, Realtree AP HD camo stock, TriNyte metal finish, X-Mark Pro adj. trigger, overmolded stock. Mfg. 2010-2011.

$875	$785	$715	$645	$545	$445	$365	*$1,063*

* ***Model 700 XCR II Camo RMEF Edition*** – .25-06 Rem. (new 2012) or .300 Win. Mag. cal., similar to Model 700 XCR II Camo Bone Collector, except does not have Bone Collector engraved floorplate, Realtree AP camo synthetic overmolded stock, 7 1/2 lbs. Limited edition mfg. 2011-2012.

$925	$835	$765	$685	$575	$465	$375	*$1,134*

MODEL 700 XCR TACTICAL – .223 Rem. (disc. 2015), .308 Win. or .300 Win. Mag. cal., 3-5 shot mag., 26 in. fluted stainless steel barrel with black TriNyte PVD coating, tactical Bell & Carlson Aramid fiber reinforced stock, full-length aluminum bedding, X-Mark Pro adj. trigger, OD Green with black web finish on stock, 9 1/8 lbs. Mfg. 2007-2020.

$1,275	$1,075	$950	$850	$725	$575	$450	*$1,540*

* ***Model 700 XCR Tactical .338 Lapua*** – .338 Lapua Mag. cal., 26 in. stainless steel barrel with black TriNyte PVD coating and AAC muzzle brake, 5 shot detachable box mag., steel trigger guard, X-Mark Pro adj. trigger, tactical Bell & Carlson OD Green stock with full-length aluminum bedding, 8 1/2 lbs. Mfg. 2011-2020.

$2,150	$1,825	$1,575	$1,325	$1,175	$1,000	$775	*$2,515*

* ***Model 700 XCR Compact Tactical*** – .223 Rem. (disc. 2015) or .308 Win. cal., compact frame, 20 in. fluted varmint contour stainless steel barrel with black TriNyte finish, 5 shot mag., X-Mark Pro adj. trigger, tactical Bell & Carlson stock with full-length aluminum bedding (disc.) or H-S Precision Aramid fiber reinforced stock, OD Green stock finish, 7 1/2 lbs. Mfg. 2008-2020.

$1,260	$1,065	$935	$835	$725	$585	$450	*$1,540*

MODEL 700 XHR (XTREME HUNTING RIFLE) – .243 Win., .25-06 Rem., .270 Win., 7mm-08 Rem., .30-06, 7mm Rem. Mag., .300 Win. Mag., 7mm RUM or .300 RUM cal., 24 or 26 (Mag. cals.) in. triangular barrel with satin black oxide metal finish, hinged floorplate, X-Mark Pro adj. adj. trigger, Hogue overmolded synthetic stock with Realtree AP HD camo, jeweled bolt, front and rear swivel studs, SuperCell recoil pad. Mfg. 2009-2010.

$750	$650	$595	$525	$450	$395	$325	*$915*

Add $28 for Mag. cals.

RIFLES: BOLT ACTION, MODEL 40X & VARIATIONS

MODEL 40X SPORTER – .22 LR cal. only, sporterized version of the Model 40X Target Rifle, 5 shot mag., custom 700 stock, a special order only gun from the factory. Rare, less than 700 mfg. 1969-77, parts clean-up to 1980.

$4,500	$3,750	$3,000	$2,600	$2,200	$1,800	$1,575

Add 20% if NIB.

This model was last listed in the 1977 Remington catalog - retail was $525.

MODEL 40X TARGET RIFLE (RANGEMASTER) – .22 LR cal., 28 in. heavy barrel, Redfield Olympic sights, scope bases, target stock, rubber butt, first production rifle with built in bedding device and adjustment screws, 12 3/4 lbs. Mfg. 1956-64.

W/ Sights	$1,500	$1,350	$1,150	$950	$825	$700	$600
No Sights	$1,375	$1,250	$1,050	$900	$800	$675	$575

MODEL 40X STANDARD BARREL (RANGEMASTER) – similar to Model 40X Target Rifle, with lighter barrel, 10 3/4 lbs.

W/ Sights	$1,375	$1,250	$1,050	$900	$800	$675	$575
No Sights	$1,275	$1,150	$975	$825	$750	$625	$525

MODEL 40X CENTERFIRE (RANGEMASTER) – similar to Model 40X Rimfire, except in .222 Rem., .222 Rem. Mag., .30-06, or .308 Win. cal. Mfg. 1961-64.

W/ Sights	$1,195	$1,050	$875	$750	$650	$550	$475
No Sights	$1,125	$1,025	$850	$725	$625	$525	$450

MODEL 40X INTERNATIONAL FREE RIFLE – .22 LR cal., top-of-the-line rimfire target rifle with heavy barrel, finished or unfinished laminated thumbhole stock with finger grooves, adj. palm rest, buttplate, and front sling swivel, choice of half-ounce set trigger, or 2 oz. target trigger, no sights, right or left-hand stock, 15 lbs. 123 mfg. 1960-1973.

$1,650	$1,450	$1,250	$1,050	$900	$750	$625

GRADING - PPGS™	100%	98%	95%	90%	80%	70%	60%	LAST MSR

MODEL 40-XB – .308 Win. cal., 27 1/4 in. stainless steel barrel, repeater action, Teflon coated synthetic H-S Precision stock, mfg. by the Custom Shop.

Remington does not publish consumer retail pricing for this police/law enforcement model. Secondary prices for base models w/o scopes and other options will be similar to the Model 40-XB Tactical listed above. Prices for rifles with scopes and other features will be determined by how much the individual options and accessories add to the base value.

MODEL 40-XB RANGEMASTER RIMFIRE – .22 LR cal., bolt action single shot, 28 in. light or heavy barrel, no sights, target stock with guide rail, rubber buttplate. Mfg. 1964-1974.

	100%	98%	95%	90%	80%	70%	60%	LAST MSR
	$1,375	$1,250	$1,050	$900	$800	$675	$575	

MODEL 40-XB RANGEMASTER CENTERFIRE – available in 18 cals. between .22 BR Rem. and .300 RSUM, custom made, 27 1/4 in. barrel (current production is stainless steel action and barrel), single shot or repeater (5 shot mag.), walnut stock, test fired, right or left-hand action, 10 1/2 -11 1/4 lbs. Mfg. by Custom Shop 1964-2018.

	100%	98%	95%	90%	80%	70%	60%	LAST MSR
	$2,140	$1,800	$1,525	$1,250	$995	$750	$600	*$2,595*

Add $152 for repeater model.
Add $302 for left-hand action.

An International Free Rifle was also offered - only 107 were mfg. with premiums being paid.

MODEL 40-XB KS (KEVLAR STOCK) – 18 short action cals. between .22 BR Rem.-.300 RSUM, 27 1/4 in. bright finished stainless steel barrel w/o sights, drilled and tapped, single shot or repeater, black finish Aramid fiber/Kevlar stock w/cheekpiece, right or left-hand action, no sights, 9 3/4 - 10 1/4 lbs. Mfg. by Custom Shop. Mfg. 1987-2005, reintroduced 2007-2019.

	100%	98%	95%	90%	80%	70%	60%	LAST MSR
	$2,425	$2,050	$1,725	$1,500	$1,200	$975	$775	*$2,863*

Add $151 for repeater model.
Add $300 for 2 oz. trigger.

MODEL 40-XBBR – similar to Model 40-XB Rangemaster Centerfire, except single shot only, 20 or 24 in. barrel.

	100%	98%	95%	90%	80%	70%	60%	LAST MSR
	$1,300	$1,150	$975	$800	$650	$500	$450	

Add $125 for 2 oz. trigger.

MODEL 40-XBBR BENCHREST – Rem. 40-X action, 27 1/4 in. stainless steel barrel, drilled and tapped, single shot or 5 shot repeater, uncolored stainless steel blued receiver (on left-hand models), adj. trigger, no sights, satin finished American walnut stock with front swivel block and forend guide rail, straight comb with cheekpiece, 1/2 in. black rubber pad, 13 1/2 in. LOP, 11 1/4 lbs. Mfg. by the Custom Shop. Disc. 2019.

	100%	98%	95%	90%	80%	70%	60%	LAST MSR
	$3,350	$2,950	$2,225	$1,800	$1,375	$1,075	$875	*$3,895*

MODEL 40-XBBR KS – .22 Rem. cal., similar to Model 40-XB KS, except is bench rest model and single shot, 10 1/2 lbs. Mfg. by Custom Shop 1987-2019.

	100%	98%	95%	90%	80%	70%	60%	LAST MSR
	$3,400	$2,975	$2,250	$1,825	$1,400	$1,100	$900	*$3,920*

MODEL 40-XC KS – .223 Rem. (mfg. 1995-99) or .308 Win. cal., 24 in. stainless steel barrel w/o sights, National Match Course 5 shot repeater rifle, adj. trigger pull, adj. comb, drilled and tapped, wood (disc. 1989) or fiberglass with Kevlar (standard 1990) stock, 11 lbs. Disc. 2004, reintroduced 2006-2014.

	100%	98%	95%	90%	80%	70%	60%	LAST MSR
	$2,625	$2,225	$1,800	$1,450	$1,200	$925	$800	*$3,067*

Subtract approx. $120 for wood stock.

MODEL 40-XB TACTICAL – .308 Win. cal., 27 1/4 in. button rifled fluted stainless barrel, repeater action with adj. 40-X trigger, aluminum bedding block, Teflon coated metal, matte black H-S Precision synthetic tactical stock with vertical pistol grip, 10 1/4 lbs. Mfg. 2004-2018.

	100%	98%	95%	90%	80%	70%	60%	LAST MSR
	$2,550	$2,200	$1,800	$1,450	$1,200	$925	$800	*$2,995*

MODEL 40-XB TDR (TARGET DEPLOYMENT RIFLE) – .308 Win. cal., super match stainless steel hand lapped barrel, BCS 1000, custom tuned match trigger, one-piece heavy duty steel trigger guard, heavy stainless recoil lug, integral mounting system with #8 screws, Picatinny rail, double pinned bolt handle, muzzle brake, MOA accuracy guaranteed to 600 yards, includes hard carrying case. Mfg. by the Custom Shop. Disc. 2020.

This model was POR.

MODEL 40-XB THUMBHOLE – .22-250 Rem., .260 Rem., or 7.62 NATO cal., 27 1/4 in. heavy stainless barrel w/o sights, single shot or repeater action, drilled and tapped, two-tone laminated satin finished thumbhole stock with rollover cheekpiece, 11 3/4 lbs. Mfg. 1999-2010, reintroduced 2015-2018.

	100%	98%	95%	90%	80%	70%	60%	LAST MSR
	$2,435	$2,050	$1,725	$1,500	$1,200	$975	$775	*$2,895*

Add $151 for repeater action (new 2000).

GRADING - PPGS™	100%	98%	95%	90%	80%	70%	60%	LAST MSR

MODEL 40-X TACTICAL MOD – .308 Win. cal., 20 in. barrel, barreled action colors include black, FDE, or OD Green. Limited mfg. 2011 only.

$4,300 $3,600 $3,000 $2,300 $1,875 $1,500 $1,325 *$4,850*

MODEL 40-X TARGET INTERDICTION RIFLE – Rem. 40-X short action, 24 in. match grade stainless steel hand lapped barrel, AAC 51T muzzle brake/adaptor, H-S PST25 tactical/vertical pistol grip stock, custom tuned match trigger, one-piece heavy duty steel trigger guard, heavy stainless recoil lug, integral mounting system with #8 screws, Picatinny rail, double pinned bolt handle, MOA accuracy guaranteed to 600 yards, includes hard carrying case. Mfg. by the Custom Shop. Disc. 2020.

$3,550 $3,050 $2,300 $1,850 $1,425 $1,125 $925 *$4,095*

MODEL 40-X TDR – .308 Win. cal., repeater action, 20 in. barrel, features various stock/receiver colors, including black, OD Green, tan, or FDE. Limited mfg. 2011 only.

$2,775 $2,275 $1,995 $1,675 $1,295 $1,150 $935 *$3,170*

MODEL 40-X TDR (TACTICAL DEPLOYMENT RIFLE) – various cals., Rem. 40X short action, 24 in. stainless steel barrel, ACC 51T muzzle brake/adaptor, tan with black web patterned Bell & Carlson stock, one-piece steel trigger guard, Picatinny rail, enhanced bolt knob. Mfg. by the Custom Shop. Disc.

$2,700 $2,300 $1,850 $1,475 $1,225 $950 $825 *$3,195*

MODEL 40-X TIR – .308 Win. cal., repeater action, 20 in. barrel, stock/slash receiver colors include black/black, black/OD Green, or black/tan. Limited mfg. 2011 only.

$3,600 $3,100 $2,400 $1,925 $1,500 $1,250 $1,000 *$4,087*

MODEL 40-XRBR KS RIMFIRE SINGLE SHOT – .22 LR cal., 24 in. heavy stainless barrel, no sights, adj. buttplate and palm stop, target wood (disc. 1989) or fiberglass with Kevlar (became standard 1990, and was available only in benchrest configuration) stock, Remington green stock became standard beginning 2007, approx. 9 3/4 lbs. Mfg. 1974-2004, reintroduced 2007-2011.

$2,550 $2,200 $1,800 $1,450 $1,200 $925 $800 *$2,992*

Subtract 20% for wood stock.

MODEL 40-XR KS SPORTER – .22 LR or .22 WMR cal., Model 40-XR action, match chambered, custom sporter contoured 24 in. barrel, fiberglass with Kevlar stock, drilled and tapped receiver, w/o sights, special order. Mfg. 1994-99.

$1,550 $1,375 $1,125 $950 $795 $690 $580 *$1,638*

MODEL 40-XR CUSTOM SPORTER – .22 LR or .22 WMR (new 2000) cal., repeater action, top-of-the-line sporter from the custom shop, individually made per customer's specifications. Disc. 2006, reintroduced 2008-2013.

$3,850 $3,150 $2,550 $2,000 $1,625 $1,325 $1,100 *$4,489*

MODEL 40-XR CUSTOM SPORTER HIGH GRADES – .22 LR cal. only, single shot, available on special order from Remington's Custom Shop only, Grades I-IV (disc. 1991) increase by amount of engraving, quality of wood, and other special order options and features. Mfg. 1986-1991.

Values for Custom Grades listed reflect 1991 (the year of discontinuance) price information. The Remington Custom Shop should be contacted directly regarding current values and options.

* ***Model 40-XR Custom Sporter High Grade Model I*** – mfg. 1986-91.

  $1,500 $1,350 $1,100 $925 $795 $690 $580 *$1,314*

* ***Model 40-XR Custom Sporter High Grade Model II*** – mfg. 1986-91.

  $2,750 $2,250 $1,995 $1,675 $1,295 $1,150 $935 *$2,335*

* ***Model 40-XR Custom Sporter High Grade Model III*** – mfg. 1986-91.

  $3,500 $2,900 $2,150 $1,750 $1,540 $1,265 $1,055 *$3,650*

* ***Model 40-XR Custom Sporter High Grade Model IV*** – mfg. 1986-91.

  $4,875 $4,100 $2,950 $2,650 $2,350 $2,000 $1,750 *$5,695*

MODEL 40-SSA SPECIAL LIMITED EDITION – .308 Win. cal., 24 in. barrel, re-creation of the 1966 Model 700 M40 to the U.S.M.C. specification of 1966, wood stock, endorsed and authenticated by the U.S. Marine Corps Scout/Sniper Association. 1,000 mfg. 2006-2007.

$2,500 $1,750 $1,500 N/A N/A N/A N/A

MODEL 40-XS TACTICAL – .308 Win. or .338 Lapua Mag. cal., stainless steel action and barrel, 24 or 26 in. heavy barrel, adj. trigger, non-reflective black polymer coating, titanium bedded McMillan A5 adj. stock, AR type extractor, detachable mag., muzzle brake (.338 Lapua cal.), steel trigger guard and floorplate. Mfg. by Custom Shop. Disc. 2020.

$3,675 $3,050 $2,500 $2,000 $1,650 $1,350 $1,175 *$4,395*

GRADING - PPGS™	100%	98%	95%	90%	80%	70%	60%	LAST MSR

Add $600 for .338 Lapua Mag. cal. (40-XS Tactical HB).

Add $3,300 for Model 40-XS Tactical Weapons System with Harris bipod, Picatinny rail, Leupold Mark IV 3.5-10x40mm long range M1 scope, Turner AWS tactical sling, and military grade hard case.

MODEL XM3 TACTICAL – .308 Win. cal., choice of steel or titanium action, match grade 18 1/2 in. stainless threaded barrel, Model 40-X action, custom bedded McMillan stock with adjustable LOP, Harris bipod, steel trigger guard, Nightfore NXS 3.5-15x50mm mil-dot scope, guaranteed MOA accuracy to 1,000 yards, Hardigg Storm case with all tools and maintenance equipment, mfg. by Custom Shop. Mfg. 2009-2011.

$9,250	$8,000	$7,000	$6,000	$5,000	$4,000	$3,500	*$10,281*

Add $2,128 for steel action.

SHOTGUNS: O/U

100% values listed for Model 3200s assume NIB condition - subtract 10%-15% if without box, warranty card, and original shipping container (with packing materials).

MODEL 32 – 12 ga., double lock action, DT (early mfg.) or SST (standard 1938), separated barrels, 26, 28, or 30 in. barrels without rib, SR, or VR. Approx. 6,050 mfg. (ser. range approx. 0001-5,053) 1931-1947. There is a discrepancy as to when serialization started on this model.

N/A	$2,000	$1,800	$1,500	$1,000	$800	$700

Add 10% for SST.

Add 10% for vent. or solid rib.

Add 20% for VR on 28 in. barrels.

Model 32 serialization is as follows: 1932 - 1-903; 1933 - 904-948; 1934 - 949-1,727; 1935 - 1,728-2,610; 1936 - 2,611-3,259; 1937 - 3,260 - 3,755; 1938 - 3,756-3,958; 1939 - 3,959-4,202; 1940 - 4,203-4,425; 1941 - 4,426-4,741; 1942 - 4,742 - 5,020; 1943 - 5,021-5,031; 1944 - 5,032-5,049; 1945 to 1947 - 5,050-5,053.

MODEL 32D TOURNAMENT

$3,750	$3,000	$2,500	$2,000	$1,750	$1,400	$1,175

MODEL 32E EXPERT – less than 35 mfg.

$4,500	$3,950	$3,500	$2,975	$2,650	$2,200	$1,875

MODEL 32F PREMIER

$6,500	$5,500	$5,000	$4,500	$3,520	$2,750	$2,300

Note: Grades differ in quality, grade of wood, and amount of engraving.

MODEL 32 SKEET – similar to 32A, with 26 or 28 (more desirable) in. skeet bored barrels, SST. Mfg. 1932-42.

N/A	$2,000	$1,800	$1,500	$1,000	$800	$700

Add 10% for VR.

Add 10%-15% for 28 in. barrels.

MODEL 32TC TARGET – similar to Model 32, with 30 or 32 in. VR full choke barrels, trap style stock. Mfg. 1932-42.

$3,000	$2,300	$1,800	$1,700	$1,600	$1,475	$1,300

Add 10% for 30 in. VR barrels.

MODEL 300 IDEAL – 12 ga. only, 3 in. chambers, boxlock action, features unique forearm latching system that incorporates barrel selector switch, 26, 28, or 30 in. 8mm VR barrels with twin beads and Rem Chokes (3), engraved receiver sides, gold SST, high polish blue, checkered satin finished American walnut stock and forearm with English style solid recoil pad, 7 3/8 - 7 7/8 lbs. Mfg. 2000-2001.

$1,150	$995	$875	$800	$750	$700	$650	*$1,332*

MODEL 332 – 12 ga. only, 3 in. chambers, new modified boxlock action with underlock, designed by custom shop, low profile receiver with Model 32 type styling, engraved frame panels, 26, 28, or 30 in. 8mm VR light contour monobloc barrels with Rem Chokes, glass-bead blasted black oxide metal finish which resembles Model 32 rust bluing, high gloss finished checkered walnut stock and slim forearm with solid rubber recoil pad, mechanical SST, ejectors, 7 1/2 - 8 lbs. Mfg. in Ilion late 2001-2006.

$1,425	$1,075	$925	$775	$625	$550	$475	*$1,759*

* ***Model 332 Engraved*** – introduced 2004.

» **Model 332 D Grade (Peerless)**

$3,150	$2,200	$1,500	N/A	N/A	N/A	N/A	*$4,184*

» **Model 332 F Grade (Premier)**

$6,300	$4,550	$2,975	N/A	N/A	N/A	N/A	*$7,706*

GRADING - PPGS™	100%	98%	95%	90%	80%	70%	60%	LAST MSR

» **Model 332 F Grade w/gold inlays (Premier Gold)** – top-of-the-line Custom Shop model. Disc.

	$9,375	$5,300	$3,575	N/A	N/A	N/A	N/A	*$11,122*

MODEL 396 SKEET/SPORTING CLAYS – 12 ga. only, satin finished boxlock action with engraved sideplates, 28 or 30 in. barrels with 10mm VR and Rem Chokes, select checkered walnut stock and target style forend, Sporting Clays Model has ported barrels, SST, ejectors, approx. 7 1/2 lbs. Mfg. 1996-1998.

* ***Model 396 Skeet***

	$1,750	$1,475	$1,250	$1,075	$925	$800	$700	*$1,993*

* ***Model 396 Sporting Clays***

	$1,875	$1,575	$1,300	$1,100	$950	$825	$725	*$2,126*

MODEL 3200 FIELD – 12 ga., 26, 28, or 30 in. barrels, VR, various chokes, boxlock, auto ejectors, single selective trigger, checkered pistol grip stock, separated barrels. Mfg. 1973-77.

	$1,500	$1,250	$1,100	$975	$825	$675	$525	

During 1998-2000, the custom shop once again manufactured a limited amount of the Model 3200 from existing parts (parts cleanup).

Model 3200s with shorter barrels (26 or 28 in.) and open choking are more desirable than 30 in. tubes bored F/M.

Model 3200 serialization is as follows: 1973 - 4,200-16,667; 1974 - 16,668-27,393; 1975 - 27,394-35,303; 1976 - 35,304-39,216; 1977 - 39,217-41,432; 1978 - 41,433-42,813; 1979 - 42,814-44,278; 1980 - 44,279-45,504; 1981 - 45,505-45,974; 1982 - 45,975-47,200; 1983 - 47,201-47,308.

MODEL 3200 MAGNUM – 12 ga., 3 in. chambers, 30 in. heavy wall barrels (steel shot compatible), less than 1,000 mfg. 1975-77.

	$1,800	$1,575	$1,350	$1,175	$1,000	$800	$625	

MODEL 3200 SKEET – similar to 3200 Field, with 26 or 28 in. skeet bored barrels, skeet style stock. Mfg. 1973-80.

	$1,650	$1,400	$1,250	$1,100	$900	$750	$575	

28 in. barrels will command a premium on this model.

This model was also mfg. in a 28 in. IM/F configuration with gold pigeon on bottom for live pigeon shooting. Since less than 300 were mfg., prices in the $2,700 range are being asked if NIB condition. This model generally had a trap style rib, but there have been some field ribs as well. Originally, it was called the "Competition Live Pigeon" and was mfg. with a competition receiver and trap grade style wood.

* ***Model 3200 Skeet Competition Four Ga. Set*** – includes 12, 20, 28 ga., or .410 bore, cased. Mfg. 1980-83.

	$5,500	$5,000	$4,600	$4,200	$4,000	$3,800	$3,500	

Add 10%-15% for 28 in. barrels.

MODEL 3200 COMPETITION SKEET – similar to 3200 Skeet, with scroll engraved frame and trigger guard, select wood. Mfg. 1976-83.

	$1,700	$1,450	$1,250	$995	$950	$850	$750	

Add 10%-15% for 28 in. VR barrels.

MODEL 3200 TRAP – similar to Model 3200 Field, with 30 or 32 in. barrels choked IM/F or F/F, stock and rib. Mfg. 1973-77.

	$1,650	$1,400	$1,250	$1,100	$900	$750	$575	

30 in. barrels are more desirable than 32 in.

MODEL 3200 SPECIAL TRAP – similar to 3200 Trap, except fancy wood. Mfg. 1973-80.

	$1,450	$1,300	$1,200	$1,000	$875	$800	$750	

MODEL 3200 COMPETITION TRAP – similar to 3200 Trap, with scroll engraving. Mfg. 1976-83.

	$1,950	$1,800	$1,675	$1,450	$1,200	$950	$875	
Pigeon Grade	$2,450	$2,150	$1,850	$1,500	$1,250	$995	$900	

The Pigeon Grade featured a gold pigeon on receiver bottom - approx. 250 mfg. 1979-83.

There was a special production of this model during 1991-92 which was limited to approx. 100 guns.

MODEL 3200 PREMIER – 12 ga., sold through Remington's International Division, 500 mfg. 1975 only, patterned after "One of 1000" series, regular or Monte Carlo stock.

	$2,900	$2,500	$2,150	$1,800	$1,500	$1,200	$1,025	

Add 125% for engraving (only 116 mfg., engraving was done in Belgium).

GRADING - PPGS™	100%	98%	95%	90%	80%	70%	60%	LAST MSR

MODEL 3200 "ONE OF 1000" – limited edition, elaborate engraving, fancy wood, supplied with hard case, made in both skeet and trap models. Mfg. 1,000 each model: 1973 (Trap) and 1974 (Skeet).

	100%	98%	95%	90%	80%	70%	60%	LAST MSR
Trap (30 IM/F or F/F)	$2,150	$1,750	$1,475	$1,325	$1,200	$1,075	$875	
Skeet (26 or 28 in. SK/SK)	$2,150	$1,750	$1,475	$1,325	$1,200	$1,075	$875	

Add 10% for 28 in. barrels on the Skeet Model.

PEERLESS FIELD GRADE – 12 ga. only, 3 in. chambers, 26, 28, or 30 in. VR barrels with Rem Chokes, boxlock with engraved sideplates, SST, ejectors, high-gloss checkered walnut stock and forearm with vent. recoil pad, 3.28 milliseconds lock time, blue metal, approx. 7 1/2 lbs. Mfg. 1993-98.

100%	98%	95%	90%	80%	70%	60%	LAST MSR
$1,050	$925	$800	$700	$575	$475	$375	*$1,172*

This model is an entirely new design not sharing any parts with either the Models 32 or 3200.

PREMIER FIELD MODEL – 12, 20, or 28 ga., 3 in. chambers, 26 or 28 in. 7mm VR barrels with Pro-Bore chokes, nickel finished receiver with game scene engraving, boxlock action, gold trigger, satin finished deluxe walnut stock with Schnabel forearm, solid recoil pad, SST, ejectors, includes hard case, 6 1/2 - 7 3/4 lbs. Previously imported 2006-2009 from Italy.

100%	98%	95%	90%	80%	70%	60%	LAST MSR
$1,850	$1,575	$1,325	$1,125	$975	$850	$725	*$2,086*

Add $42 for 28 ga.

* ***Premier Model Competition STS*** – 12 ga., similar to Premier Model, 28, 30, or 32 (new 2008) in. barrels, titanium PVD finished receiver, 10mm target type VR, five extended choke tubes, high gloss wood finish, barrel selector on tang safety, approx. 7 1/2 lbs. Mfg. 2006-2009.

100%	98%	95%	90%	80%	70%	60%	LAST MSR
$2,200	$1,925	$1,650	$1,450	$1,275	$1,050	$850	*$2,540*

Add $350 for adj. comb (new 2007).

* ***Premier Model Upland Special*** – similar to Premier Field Model, except has color case hardened receiver with gold game scene engraving and oil finished wood. Mfg. 2006-2010.

100%	98%	95%	90%	80%	70%	60%	LAST MSR
$1,950	$1,650	$1,375	$1,125	$975	$850	$725	*$2,226*

Add $42 for 28 ga.

* ***Premier Ruffed Grouse*** – 20 ga., 3 in. chambers, 26 in. vent. rib blue barrels, features two 14 Kt. ruffed grouse gold inlays on each side of frame, oil finished straight grip walnut stock, 6 3/4 lbs. Mfg. 2006-2009.

100%	98%	95%	90%	80%	70%	60%	LAST MSR
$2,050	$1,700	$1,400	$1,125	$975	$850	$725	*$2,380*

100%	98%	95%	90%	80%	70%	60%	50%	40%	30%	20%	10%

SHOTGUNS: SxS

Because E. Remington & Sons shotguns are classified as antique, it may be helpful to consult the "NRA Antique Condition Standards" section in the front of this text to convert to the Percentage Grading System listed.

For Remington serialization, please refer to the Serialization section.

MODEL 1873 "HAMMER LIFTER" – 10 or 12 ga., also known as Whitmore Hammer Lifter, 28 or 30 in. decarbonized, twist, or damascus barrels, top "thumb lever" action activated by pushing upward to open, rib top marked "E. REMINGTON & SONS, ILION, N.Y.", patented "AUG. 8, 1871, APRIL 16, 1872", steel buttplate, pistol grip was optional, grades above 3 were made to order. Approx. 5,000 mfg. from 1873-78, starting with ser. no. 1.

* ***Model 1873 "Hammer Lifter" Grade 1*** – decarbonized steel barrels, no checkering or engraving.

100%	98%	95%	90%	80%	70%	60%	50%	40%	30%	20%	10%
N/A	N/A	N/A	$1,400	$1,250	$750	$475	$400	$300	$225	$170	$150

* ***Model 1873 "Hammer Lifter" Grade 2*** – twist steel barrels, checkering, no engraving.

100%	98%	95%	90%	80%	70%	60%	50%	40%	30%	20%	10%
N/A	N/A	N/A	$1,900	$1,600	$1,000	$600	$500	$400	$300	$250	$180

* ***Model 1873 "Hammer Lifter" Grade 3*** – twist or Damascus steel barrels, checkering and engraving.

100%	98%	95%	90%	80%	70%	60%	50%	40%	30%	20%	10%
N/A	N/A	N/A	$3,500	$2,500	$1,500	$800	$700	$600	$450	$300	$225

Add 35% to Grade 3 prices for higher grades (extra fine engraving).

MODEL 1875 AND 1876 "LIFTER" (WHITMORE LIFTER) – 10 or 12 ga., 28 or 30 in. decarbonized, twist, or damascus barrels, top "thumb lever" action activated by pushing upward to open, rib top marked "E. REMINGTON & SONS, ILION, N.Y.", patented "AUG. 8, 1871, APRIL 16, 1872", steel buttplate, pistol grip was optional, the Model 1875 started with ser. no. 1, and went to approx. 3,350, the Model 1876 started with ser. no. 3,350 and went to approx. 5,900. Approx. 5,900 Model 1875s and 1876s were mfg. 1875-1882.

100%	98%	95%	90%	80%	70%	60%	50%	40%	30%	20%	10%

* ***Model 1875/1876 "Lifter" Grade 1*** – decarbonized steel barrels, no checkering or engraving.

N/A	N/A	N/A	$1,400	$1,200	$1,000	$700	$575	$425	$300	$250	$225

* ***Model 1875/1876 "Lifter" Grade 2*** – twist steel barrels, checkering, no engraving.

N/A	N/A	N/A	$1,600	$1,300	$1,100	$900	$750	$650	$500	$350	$250

* ***Model 1875/1876 "Lifter" Grade 3*** – twist or damascus steel barrels, checkered and engraving.

N/A	N/A	N/A	$3,200	$1,800	$1,400	$1,100	$1,000	$750	$600	$500	$400

* ***Model 1875/1876 "Lifter" Grade 4*** – twist or damascus steel barrels, checkered and extra fine engraving.

N/A	N/A	N/A	$4,000	$3,100	$2,400	$1,500	$1,200	$1,000	$700	$600	$350

* ***Model 1875/1876 "Lifter" Grade 5*** – damascus steel barrels, checkered and superior engraving.

N/A	N/A	N/A	$4,500	$3,500	$3,000	$2,500	$1,800	$1,200	$900	$700	$500

Add 50% to the few Model 1873s and 1875s that are rib marked "NEW YORK & LONDON" (approx. 16 known), and higher premiums if Birmingham proofed.

Add 75% for combination guns.

There were very few double rifles and combination guns made in Models 1873, 1875, and 1876 - they are very rare, and recent prices are in the $20,000 range.

MODEL 1878 HAMMER (HEAVY DUCK GUN) – 10 ga., called the Heavy Duck Gun, 30-32 in., 9 3/4 and 10 lbs., "thumb-lever" action, thick bolsters, top extension rib, no flash fences, steel buttplate. Approx. 2,500 mfg. from 1878-82, starting with ser. no. 1.

* ***Model 1878 Hammer Grade 1*** – decarbonized steel barrels, no checkering, no engraving.

N/A	N/A	N/A	$1,400	$1,200	$1,000	$700	$575	$425	$300	$250	$250

* ***Model 1878 Hammer Grade 2*** – twist steel barrels, checkered, no engraving.

N/A	N/A	N/A	$1,600	$1,300	$1,100	$900	$750	$650	$500	$375	$300

* ***Model 1878 Hammer Grade 3*** – laminated steel barrels, checkered, engraved.

N/A	N/A	N/A	$3,200	$1,800	$1,400	$1,100	$1,000	$750	$600	$500	$400

* ***Model 1878 Hammer Grade 4*** – damascus steel barrels, checkered, extra fine engraving.

N/A	N/A	N/A	$3,500	$2,700	$2,000	$1,500	$1,200	$1,000	$900	$650	$600

MODEL 1879 SxS HAMMER – some 10 ga., usually 12 ga., top extension rib, no flash fences, steel buttplate, only Whitmore model with Deeley & Edge forend catch, but there are some with wedge pin forends (look for extension rib). Ser. nos. within the Model 1878.

* ***Model 1879 SxS Hammer Grade 1*** – decarbonized steel barrels, no checkering, no engraving.

N/A	N/A	N/A	$1,700	$1,675	$1,250	$975	$875	$750	$425	$395	$350

* ***Model 1879 SxS Hammer Grade 2*** – twist steel barrels, checkered, no engraving.

N/A	N/A	N/A	$2,600	$1,825	$1,425	$1,250	$1,125	$875	$700	$550	$425

* ***Model 1879 SxS Hammer Grade 3*** – laminated steel barrels, checkered, engraved.

N/A	N/A	N/A	$3,300	$2,525	$2,000	$1,550	$1,200	$1,000	$850	$700	$550

* ***Model 1879 SxS Hammer Grade 4*** – damascus steel barrels, checkered, extra fine engraving.

N/A	N/A	N/A	$5,000	$4,500	$3,500	$2,525	$2,000	$1,500	$1,250	$1,000	$600

MODEL 1882 SxS HAMMER – (includes the unique Model 1883), 10 or 12 ga., 30 or 32 in. decarbonized, twist or damascus steel barrels, rib marked "E. REMINGTON & SONS, ILION, N.Y.", typical top lever, all grades have checkered pistol grip and forend with various designs according to grade. All contain Deeley & Edge forend catch. Approx. 16,000 Model 1882s, possibly 1,000 Model 1883s were mfg. from 1882-88. Started with ser. no. 1,000.

* ***Model 1882 SxS Hammer Grade 1*** – decarbonized steel barrels, no engraving, steel buttplate.

N/A	N/A	N/A	$1,200	$1,100	$900	$700	$600	$450	$300	$250	$200

* ***Model 1882 SxS Hammer Grade 2*** – twist steel barrels, no engraving, steel buttplate.

N/A	N/A	N/A	$1,300	$1,200	$1,000	$800	$675	$550	$375	$275	$225

* ***Model 1882 SxS Hammer Grade 3*** – laminated steel barrels, engraved, steel buttplate.

N/A	N/A	N/A	$1,600	$1,300	$1,200	$900	$750	$650	$450	$350	$250

100%	98%	95%	90%	80%	70%	60%	50%	40%	30%	20%	10%

* ***Model 1882 SxS Hammer Grade 4*** – damascus steel barrels, engraved, steel buttplate.

N/A	N/A	N/A	$2,300	$1,800	$1,400	$1,000	$850	$700	$550	$400	$300

* ***Model 1882 SxS Hammer Grade 5*** – fine damascus steel barrels, finely engraved, superior rubber or steel buttplate.

N/A	N/A	N/A	$3,300	$3,000	$2,600	$1,700	$1,400	$1,100	$900	$650	$500

* ***Model 1882 SxS Hammer Grade 6*** – extra fine damascus steel barrels, fine scroll engraved, superior rubber buttplate.

N/A	N/A	N/A	$5,000	$4,400	$3,800	$3,100	$2,700	$2,000	$1,300	$1,100	$900

Add 25% for optional auxiliary rifle barrel insert.

MODEL 1883 – identified by its hammer shape which is slightly different than the Model 1882, other than that, the guns are identical.

Add 25% to Model 1882 values for this model.

MODEL 1885/1887 SxS HAMMER – 10, 12, or 16 ga., different hammer style variation of the Model 1882, 28, 30, or 32 in. decarbonized, twist or damascus steel barrels, rib marked "E. REMINGTON & SONS, ILION, N.Y.", top lever, all grades are checkered pistol grip and forend with various designs according to grade, Deeley & Edge forend catch, rubber buttplate with ERS logo. Approx. 7,000 mfg. from 1885-88. Ser. nos. started at 16,700. Guns before ser. no. 20,200 are considered Model 1885s, ser. nos. after are considered Model 1887s.

* ***Model 1885/1887 SxS Hammer Grade 1*** – decarbonized steel barrels, no engraving.

N/A	N/A	N/A	$1,200	$1,100	$900	$700	$600	$450	$300	$250	$200

* ***Model 1885/1887 SxS Hammer Grade 2*** – twist steel barrels, no engraving.

N/A	N/A	N/A	$1,300	$1,200	$1,000	$800	$675	$550	$375	$300	$225

* ***Model 1885/1887 SxS Hammer Grade 3*** – damascus steel barrels, no engraving.

N/A	N/A	N/A	$1,600	$1,300	$1,200	$900	$750	$650	$450	$350	$250

* ***Model 1885/1887 SxS Hammer Grade 4*** – damascus steel barrels, engraved.

N/A	N/A	N/A	$2,100	$1,800	$1,400	$1,100	$900	$800	$675	$500	$400

* ***Model 1885/1887 SxS Hammer Grade 5*** – fine damascus steel barrels, finely engraved.

N/A	N/A	N/A	$3,300	$3,000	$2,600	$2,000	$1,500	$1,000	$700	$600	$500

* ***Model 1885/1887 SxS Hammer Grade 6*** – extra fine damascus steel barrels, fine scroll engraved.

N/A	N/A	N/A	$5,800	$5,000	$4,500	$3,500	$2,800	$2,000	$1,500	$1,200	$900

* ***Model 1885/1887 SxS Hammer Grade 7*** – superior damascus steel barrels, extra fine scroll engraved, game scene.

N/A	N/A	N/A	$9,000	$8,500	$7,800	$6,600	$4,800	$4,200	$3,400	$2,000	$1,000

Add 25% for optional auxiliary rifle barrel insert.
Add 33% for 16 ga.

MODEL 1889 SxS HAMMER – 10, 12, or 16 ga., 26 (a few known to exist), 28, 30, or 32 in. decarbonized, twist, or damascus barrels, exposed "circular" hammers, rib marked "REMINGTON ARMS CO. ILION, N.Y. U.S.A.", top lever, all grades have checkered pistol grip and forend with various designs according to grade, Deeley & Edge forend catch. Grade number is stamped on water table left of the ser. no. Rubber buttplate with RACo logo. 134,200 mfg. 1889-1908. Ser. range from 30,000 to 100,000. After the year 1900, ser. nos. are in the 200,000 range.

Add 25-35% for lightweight 12 gauge model, depending on condition.

* ***Model 1889 SxS Hammer Grade 1*** – decarbonized steel barrels, no engraving.

N/A	N/A	N/A	$1,800	$1,500	$1,200	$800	$675	$550	$375	$275	$225

* ***Model 1889 SxS Hammer Grade 2*** – twist steel barrels, no engraving.

N/A	N/A	N/A	$2,000	$1,750	$1,400	$1,000	$750	$650	$450	$350	$250

* ***Model 1889 SxS Hammer Grade 3*** – damascus steel barrels, no engraving.

N/A	N/A	N/A	$2,200	$1,800	$1,500	$1,200	$850	$750	$550	$400	$300

* ***Model 1889 SxS Hammer Grade 4*** – damascus steel barrels, engraved.

N/A	N/A	N/A	$4,000	$3,000	$2,500	$2,000	$1,600	$1,100	$900	$650	$500

* ***Model 1889 SxS Hammer Grade 5*** – damascus steel barrels, finely engraved.

100%	98%	95%	90%	80%	70%	60%	50%	40%	30%	20%	10%
N/A	N/A	N/A	$7,500	$6,000	$4,000	$3,500	$2,700	$2,000	$1,300	$1,100	$900

* ***Model 1889 SxS Hammer Grade 6*** – extra fine damascus steel barrels, fine scroll engraved.

100%	98%	95%	90%	80%	70%	60%	50%	40%	30%	20%	10%
N/A	N/A	N/A	$15,000	$12,000	$7,800	$6,500	$5,400	$4,200	$3,400	$2,200	$1,100

* ***Model 1889 SxS Hammer Grade 7*** – superior damascus steel barrels, extra fine scroll engraved, game scene.

100%	98%	95%	90%	80%	70%	60%	50%	40%	30%	20%	10%
N/A	N/A	N/A	$25,000	$20,000	$15,000	$12,000	$7,500	$5,000	$4,000	$3,000	$1,600

Add 33% for 16 ga.

Grades 4 through 7 may command higher values. To date, there are only 26 examples known of these engraved Model 1889 hammer guns - eleven Grade 4s, six Grade 5s, five Grade 6s, and four Grade 7s.

MODEL 1894 SxS HAMMERLESS – 10, 12, or 16 ga., 26 to 32 in. "Remington", "Ordnance", or damascus steel barrels, auto ejectors, boxlock, double triggers, checkered pistol grip or straight stock, Purdey forend snap. Grades A, B, C, and F have RACo hard rubber butt, Grade D, horn butt, Grade E, horn on heel and toe plates, push-button forearm release. Grade is usually stamped on water table. 16 and especially 10 ga., are considered scarce and will command a higher value. 41,194 mfg. between 1894-1910 in the 100000 block serial range.

* ***Model 1894 SxS Hammerless Grade AE*** – no engraving.

100%	98%	95%	90%	80%	70%	60%	50%	40%	30%	20%	10%
N/A	$3,000	$2,100	$1,750	$1,000	$900	$750	$600	$500	$350	$275	$175

* ***Model 1894 SxS Hammerless Grade BE*** – scroll and line engraving.

100%	98%	95%	90%	80%	70%	60%	50%	40%	30%	20%	10%
N/A	$4,000	$3,200	$2,900	$2,000	$1,650	$1,150	$1,000	$700	$550	$400	$250

* ***Model 1894 SxS Hammerless Grade FE Trap*** – scroll and line engraving.

100%	98%	95%	90%	80%	70%	60%	50%	40%	30%	20%	10%
N/A	N/A	$3,500	$3,000	$2,600	$2,200	$2,000	$1,500	$1,200	$1,000	$750	$500

* ***Model 1894 SxS Hammerless Grade CE*** – extra scroll engraving, silver name plate.

100%	98%	95%	90%	80%	70%	60%	50%	40%	30%	20%	10%
N/A	$8,500	$6,000	$4,800	$4,300	$3,800	$3,000	$2,400	$1,800	$1,100	$700	$600

* ***Model 1894 SxS Hammerless Grade DE*** – fine scroll and game engraving, silver name plate.

100%	98%	95%	90%	80%	70%	60%	50%	40%	30%	20%	10%
N/A	N/A	$18,000	$14,000	$8,500	$7,000	$5,000	$4,000	$3,000	$2,000	$1,500	$1,100

* ***Model 1894 SxS Hammerless Grade EE*** – finest quality scroll, bird and game engraving, gold name plate.

100%	98%	95%	90%	80%	70%	60%	50%	40%	30%	20%	10%
N/A	N/A	$35,000	$28,000	$20,000	$15,000	$10,000	$7,800	$6,000	$3,850	$2,750	$2,300

Add 33% for 10 or 16 ga.

Add 15% to CE and BE guns that are extractor only, which are called B and C grade.

Add 25% for "Ordnance" barrels.

Add 50% for small frame 12 ga. (12 ga. or 16 ga. frame) - usually later mfg.

A few Remington Model 1894 SPECIAL grade guns were produced; they are so rare, it is not practical to attempt a value. Recent sales have been in the $100,000+ range.

MODEL 1900 SxS HAMMERLESS – 12 or 16 ga., 28 or 30 in. "Remington" or Damascus steel barrels, lower priced gun to meet market competition, quality a cut below the Model 1894, but mechanically the same, snap forearm. No engraving was offered on this model. 98,475 mfg. between 1900-10 in the 300,000 block serial range.

* ***Model 1900 SxS Hammerless Grade K and KD*** – Remington or Damascus steel barrels, non-ejector.

100%	98%	95%	90%	80%	70%	60%	50%	40%	30%	20%	10%
N/A	N/A	$2,500	$2,200	$1,600	$1,200	$700	$500	$350	$300	$250	$200

* ***Model 1900 SxS Hammerless Grade KE and KED*** – Remington or damascus steel barrels, ejectors.

100%	98%	95%	90%	80%	70%	60%	50%	40%	30%	20%	10%
N/A	N/A	$3,700	$2,400	$1,800	$1,400	$1,200	$1,000	$650	$500	$350	$250

PARKER AHE – while advertised, the Remington re-issue of the original Parker AHE Model was never mfg. due to product liability considerations. Older Remington manufactured Parkers may be found in the Parker section.

PARKER AAHE – 28 ga., available through Remington Arms Co., and made by Connecticut Shotgun, serialization continues from the last of the Parker Bros. production. Limited availability 2006-disc.

Last MSR was $49,995.

PREMIER – 12, 20, 28 ga. or .410 bore, 2 3/4 (28 ga.) or 3 in. chambers, Anson & Deeley boxlock action, ejectors, gold SST, 27 (28 ga. or .410 bore) or 28 in. polished blue barrels with choke tubes, single bead sight, case colored receiver, oil finished walnut stock, semi beavertail forend, Remington "R" logo

GRADING - PPGS™	100%	98%	95%	90%	80%	70%	60%	LAST MSR

in gold on bottom of frame, gold woodcock inlaid on each side of receiver, three different frame sizes, 6 1/2-7 1/2 lbs. Limited mfg. 2007, imported from Spain.

	N/A	N/A	$1,325	$1,125	$975	$850	$725	*$2,086*

Subtract $56 for 12 or 20 ga.

* ***Premier Upland Special*** – 28 ga. or .410 bore, features 27 in. polished blue barrels with Rem Chokes, similar to Premier, except has straight grip English style stock, 6 1/2 lbs. Limited mfg. 2007.

	N/A	N/A	$2,000	$1,500	$1,200	$850	$725	*$2,086*

SHOTGUNS: SEMI-AUTO, MISC. MODELS

MODEL 878A "AUTOMASTER" – 12 ga. gas operated semi-auto, 26, 28, or 30 in. barrels, action similar to Model 58. Approx. 62,000 mfg., 1959-1962.

	$450	$395	$340	$300	$250	$205	$160	

Add 10% for VR.

Barrels on this model are interchangeable with those on the Model 58.

MODEL 11-96 EURO LIGHTWEIGHT – 12 ga. only, steel receiver with distinctive slight hump over chamber, 26 or 28 in. 6mm VR Rem Choke barrel, checkered walnut stock and forearm, receiver panel engraving, approx. 7 lbs. Mfg. 1996 only.

	$715	$615	$550	$475	$395	$335	$295	*$852*

MODEL 105 CTi – 12 ga. only, 3 in. chamber, skeletonized titanium receiver with carbon fiber shell, gas operated, 4 shot mag., TriNyte receiver coating, bottom feed and ejection, overbored 26 or 28 in. carbon fiber VR barrel with three ProBore chokes, rotary bolt lock-up, checkered walnut stock with bolt speed rate reducer (results in up to 50% recoil energy reduction), target grade roller sear trigger, R3 recoil pad, utilizing oil filled cylinder in stock, includes hardshell case, 7 lbs. Mfg. 2006-2008.

	$1,225	$1,000	$875	$775	$675	$600	$525	*$1,548*

MODEL 105 CTi-II – 12 ga. only, 26 or 28 in. barrel, improved variation of the original Model 105 CTi, with changes in the gas valve, bolt release/head, and other engineering improvements, including an adj. LOP kit. Limited mfg. 2009.

	$1,225	$1,000	$875	$775	$675	$600	$525	*$1,559*

Shotguns: Semi-Auto, Model 11 & Variations

REMINGTON AUTOLOADING SHOTGUN (PRE-MODEL 11) – 12 ga. only, 28 in. barrel, Full choke, Modified choke or Cylinder bore, chambered for cartridge up to 2 3/4 in., walnut stock with plain rounded pistol grip. Approx. 92,000 mfg.

	$1,000	$900	$800	$700	$600	$500	$450	

Also manufactured in: Special Grade; Trap Grade; Tournament Grade; Expert Grade; Premier Grade & Riot Gun. These higher grades command pricing premiums similar to Model 11 special grades.

MODEL 11/11A AUTOLOADER 5-SHOT – 12, 16 and 20 ga., walnut, American walnut (new 1925), or A Grade American walnut checkered (new 1940) stock. Number of Model 11s produced (to include the Sportsman) 837,328. Mfg. 1911-1949.

Plain barrel	$800	$700	$600	$500	$400	$300	$225	
Solid rib	$900	$800	$700	$600	$500	$400	$300	
Vent. rib	$1,000	$900	$800	$700	$550	$450	$350	

Add 35% for barrels marked "Long Range" - beware of fakes.

This model was mfg. under patent agreement with John Browning.

MODEL 11B SPECIAL – select figured walnut hand checkered stock and forearm.

Plain barrel	$1,500	$1,300	$1,100	$900	$700	$500	$400	

Solid and vent. rib models will bring additional premiums.

MODEL 11C TRAP GRADE – select figured walnut hand checkered straight grip stock and forearm.

Plain barrel	$1,700	$1,500	$1,300	$1,100	$850	$600	$500	

Solid and vent. rib models will bring additional premiums.

MODEL 11D TOURNAMENT – fine English or American Walnut stock and forearm with fine hand checkering, scroll engraving left and right side of receiver and barrel.

	$3,000	$2,500	$2,200	$1,700	$1,200	$1,000	$800	

Solid and vent. rib models will bring additional premiums.

GRADING - PPGS™	100%	98%	95%	90%	80%	70%	60%	LAST MSR

MODEL 11E EXPERT – best English or American Walnut hand checkered stock and forearm, scroll engraving on receiver and barrel with game panel scenes.

	$5,000	$4,500	$4,000	$3,500	$2,750	$2,000	$1,800	

Solid and vent. rib models will bring additional premiums.

MODEL 11F PREMIER – finest Circassian or figured American walnut elaborate hand checkered stock and forearm, extensive engraving of game scenes and fine scroll on receiver and barrel.

	$8,000	$7,000	$6,000	$5,000	$4,000	$3,000	$2,500	

Solid and vent. rib models will bring additional premiums.

Note: Grades differ in quality, grade of wood, and amount of engraving.

MODEL 11R – 12 ga. only, plain walnut stock.

	$1,200	$1,000	$800	$700	$500	$400	$275	

Shotguns: Semi-Auto, Model 48 & Variations

SPORTSMAN MODEL – 12, 16, or 20 ga., 26 (3 shot only) in. barrel, skeet choke, beavertail forend, manufactured in Field, Riot, and Skeet configurations. Mfg. 1931-1949.

Plain barrel	$500	$450	$400	$350	$300	$225	$200	
Solid rib	$600	$550	$500	$450	$375	$300	$250	
Vent. rib	$1,000	$900	$800	$700	$550	$450	$350	

Add a premium for Riot and Skeet configurations.

MODEL 48 MOHAWK (SPORTSMAN) – 12, 16, or 20 ga., 26, 28, or 32 in. barrels, 3 shot, mechanical (solid breech) ejection system, various chokes, rounded receiver, checkered pistol grip stock with cap. Approx. 275,000 mfg., 1949-60.

Plain barrel	$300	$225	$200	$185	$175	$165	$140	
VR barrel	$325	$275	$250	$200	$175	$165	$140	

MODEL 48B SELECT

	$420	$360	$310	$290	$245	$220	$195	

MODEL 48D TOURNAMENT

	$1,500	$1,300	$1,100	$950	$825	$700	$650	

MODEL 48F PREMIER

	$5,750	$5,250	$4,750	$3,500	$3,000	$2,500	$2,000	

MODEL 48A RIOT GUN – 12 ga. only, 20 in. plain barrel.

	$275	$220	$195	$165	$150	$140	$110	

MODEL 48SA SKEET – 26 in. barrel, skeet bore, ivory bead. Mfg. 1949-60.

Plain barrel	$305	$275	$255	$230	$210	$195	$165	
With VR barrel	$395	$350	$300	$260	$230	$210	$195	

MODEL 48SC SKEET – "C" suffix designates C-grade wood.

	$495	$450	$375	$325	$285	$250	$225	

MODEL 48SD TOURNAMENT – custom shop engraved.

	$1,500	$1,300	$1,100	$950	$825	$700	$650	

MODEL 48SF PREMIER – custom shop engraved.

	$5,750	$5,250	$4,750	$3,500	$3,000	$2,500	$2,000	

MODEL 11-48 – 12, 16, 20, 28 (introduced 1952) ga., or .410 (introduced 1954) bore, recoil operated action, walnut stock. Approx. 429,000 mfg., 1949-1968.

Plain barrel (12 or 16 ga.)	$300	$250	$225	$195	$175	$165	$140	
Plain barrel (20 ga.)	$350	$300	$265	$230	$200	$175	$150	
Plain barrel (28 ga.)	$675	$600	$525	$450	$375	$300	$250	
Plain barrel (.410 bore)	$725	$650	$550	$450	$375	$300	$250	

Add 10%-20% for VR barrel, depending on original condition.

Shotguns: Semi-Auto, Model 58 & Variations

MODEL 58ADL "SPORTSMAN - 58" – 12, 16, or 20 ga., 26, 28, or 30 in. barrel, gas operation, various chokes, 3 shot, checkered pistol grip stock, scroll game scene engraved. Approx. 271,000 mfg., 1956-63.

Plain Barrel	$350	$300	$265	$240	$195	$160	$125	
Vent. Rib	$400	$350	$300	$265	$220	$180	$140	

Add 5% for Magnum in 12 ga.

GRADING - PPGS™	100%	98%	95%	90%	80%	70%	60%	LAST MSR

MODEL 58 X-SERIES (SUNGRAIN) – similar to Model 58ADL semi-auto, except has blonde stock, available in Field (special order only), Skeet, or Trap configuration.

	$500	$440	$375	$325	$275	$225	$175	

MODEL 58BDL – similar to 58ADL, with select wood.

Plain Barrel	$400	$350	$300	$265	$220	$180	$140	
Vent. Rib	$450	$395	$340	$300	$250	$205	$160	

MODEL 58SA SKEET GUN – similar to 58ADL, with 26 in. skeet bore VR barrel, skeet stock.

	$750	$600	$500	$425	$350	$300	$265	

MODEL 58SC SKEET – "C" suffix designates C-grade wood.

	$1,000	$875	$750	$650	$550	$450	$350	

MODEL 58D TOURNAMENT – custom shop engraved.

	$1,500	$1,300	$1,100	$950	$825	$700	$650	

MODEL 58F PREMIER – custom shop engraved.

	$5,750	$5,250	$4,750	$3,500	$3,000	$2,500	$2,000	

Note: Models differ in grade of wood, amount of engraving, and gold inlays.

Shotguns: Semi-Auto, Model 1100 & Variations

3 in. shells (12 or 20 ga.) may be shot in Magnum receivers only, regardless of what the barrel markings may indicate (the ejection port is larger in these Magnum models with "M" suffix serialization).

Model 1100 serial numbers on the receiver started with the number 1001. All but the early guns also have a prefix letter. All Model 1100 Remington shotguns were serial numbered in blocks of numbers. Each serial number has a suffix and the following indicates the meaning: V = 12 ga. standard, M = 12 ga. Mag., W = 16 ga., X = 20 ga., N = 20 ga. Mag., K = 20 ga. lightweight, U = 20 ga. lightweight Mag., J = 28 ga., H = .410 bore.

Add $150-$250 per extra barrel, depending on configuration.

Add $877 for custom shop Etchen stock and forearm installed on new Model 1100s (mfg. 2000-circa 2010).

MODEL 1100 FIELD – 12 (disc. 1987), 16 (mfg. 1964-1980), or 20 (new 1964) ga., 26, 28, or 30 in. barrels, various chokes, gas operated, checkered pistol grip stock and forearm, "cut" checkering and receiver scroll markings became standard in 1979, Rem Chokes became standard 1987 (introduced 1986 as $40 option), VRs became standard in 1985 on this model, 20 ga. lightweight frame became standard 1972, prices assume VR and Rem Chokes. Mfg. 1963-1988.

	$500	$440	$375	$325	$275	$225	$175	*$545*

Add 75-100% for 16 ga.

Add 20% for 20 ga.

Add 75%-100% for left-hand ejection port in 20 ga. only, if in 95%+ original condition.

Subtract 10% if without VR.

Subtract 10% if without Rem. chokes.

The Model 1100 20 ga. Standard (12 ga. frame) was disc. in 1969 (mahogany wood stock and forearm - advertised as a Lightweight), except for Skeet A & B grades. This model was produced only in a Lightweight or Mag. 20 (3 in. chamber), 28 ga., or .410 bore, before the release of the Model 11-87.

The Model 1100 left-hand, with the ejection port on the left side of the receiver was introduced in 1972 in both 20 and 12 ga., with either VR or plain barrels. The 20 ga. left-hand model was disc. in 1977.

MODEL 1100 SPECIAL FIELD – 12, 20 ga., or .410 (limited mfg., disc.) bore, 21 (disc. 1993) or 23 (new 1994) in. VR barrel, various chokes, gas operated, checkered straight grip stock, VR standard, high gloss wood finish (1991 only) or satin wood finish. Rem Chokes became standard in 1987. Mfg. 1983-1999.

12 ga.	$550	$475	$400	$350	$300	$250	$195	
20 ga.	$700	$625	$550	$495	$450	$400	$350	
.410 bore	$850	$775	$700	$625	$550	$475	$400	

Last MSR was $665.

Subtract 10% if without Rem Chokes (12 or 20 ga. only).

Two hundred .410 bore models were mfg. for National Shooting Supplies in Houston, TX.

GRADING - PPGS™	100%	98%	95%	90%	80%	70%	60%	LAST MSR

MODEL 1100 SAM WALTON SPECIAL EDITION – 12 or 20 ga., manufactured for Wal-Mart stores at a lower price point with standard features and wood, 5,000 mfg. in both 12 and 20 ga., serialization was almost matching with the exception of the 12 or 20 after the prefix being different (an example being SMW12134 and SMW201234). Mfg. late 2001 only.

	$450	$395	$340	$300	$250	$205	$160	

MODEL 1100 CLASSIC FIELD – 12 (new 2006), 16, 20 (new 2004), 28 (new 2006) ga. or .410 bore (new 2006), 2 3/4 in. chamber, 25 (.410 bore or 28 ga. only), 26 or 28 in. VR light contoured barrel with Rem Choke, non-embellished receiver with blue finish, satin (disc.) or gloss finished American walnut stock and forearm, 7 lbs. Mfg. 2003-2006.

	$675	$550	$475	$400	$350	$300	$275	*$834*

Add 15% for 28 ga. or .410 bore (last MSR was $868).

MODEL 1100 "1 OF 3,000" FIELD – 12 ga. only, limited edition, serial numbered 1-3,000, deluxe walnut, gold washed etched hunting scenes on receiver, 28 in. modified VR barrel. Mfg. 1980 only.

	$1,100	$900	$600	$500	$425	$350	$300	

MODEL 1100 SMALL GAUGE – 28 ga. or .410 bore, 25 in. barrel, scaled down receiver, skeet and field fixed choke, VR standard. Mfg. 1969-94.

	$750	$650	$550	$475	$425	$365	$300	*$647*

MODEL 1100 LW-20 (LIGHTWEIGHT) – 20 ga. only, 2 3/4 in. chamber, lightweight scaled down receiver, mag. tube, and barrel, similar to 28 ga./.410 bore frame, standard length ejection port, with mahogany stock, 26 or 28 in. barrel, 6 1/2 lbs. Mfg. 1970-76.

	$750	$650	$575	$500	$425	$340	$265	

Subtract 10% if w/o VR.

Remington introduced a lightweight 20 ga. Model 1100 in 1961, with standard frame, mahogany stock and forearm. This model was disc. in Dec. 1969.

MODEL 1100 LT-20 – 20 ga. only, variation of Model 1100 LW-20, 2 3/4 in. chamber, has opened ejection port and barrel extension similar to 12 ga. (long), lightened receiver, 23, 26 (disc., gloss wood only) or 28 (disc., satin wood only) in. barrel, VR became standard 1985, hi-gloss (disc.) or satin finish walnut stock and forearm, 6 1/2 lbs. Mfg. 1977-95.

	$700	$600	$475	$375	$300	$250	$225	*$665*

Subtract 10% if without VR.
Subtract $34 for gloss walnut.

Rolled scroll receiver engraving became standard on 20 ga. in 1998.

MODEL 1100 LT-20 YOUTH – 20 ga. only, similar to Model 1100 Lightweight, except stock is 1 in. shorter and 21 in. barrel only. Disc. 1998.

	$575	$500	$425	$350	$275	$235	$210	*$659*

* ***Model 1100 LT-20 Youth Camo NWTG*** – 20 ga. only, features 100% Mossy Oak Break-up camo finish, TruGlo fiber optic sights, 6 1/2 lbs. Mfg. 1998 only.

	$550	$495	$415	$325	$265	$230	$210	*$652*

MODEL 1100 LT-20 MAG. (LIGHTWEIGHT MAGNUM) – chambered for 3 in. 20 ga. Mag., 20 (disc.), 26 (disc.), or 28 in. barrel, Rem Chokes became standard 1987. Introduced 1977, disc. 1998.

	$750	$650	$525	$450	$325	$275	$250	*$659*

Subtract 10% if without VR.

MODEL 1100 MAGNUM DUCK GUN – similar to Model 1100 Field, in 12 (disc. 1987) or 20 ga., 3 in. chamber, recoil pad, VR became standard 1984, Rem Chokes became standard 1987. Mfg. 1963-88.

	$450	$400	$325	$280	$260	$220	$200	*$533*

Add $80 for left-hand model (disc. 1986).
Subtract 10% if without VR.
Subtract 10% if without Rem Chokes.

* ***Model 1100 Magnum Duck Gun Special Purpose (SP)*** – 12 ga. only, low luster finish on stock and forearm, sand blasted metal parts. Mfg. 1985-86 only.

	$450	$395	$350	$295	$265	$235	$200	*$550*

Subtract 10% if without Rem. chokes.

MODEL 1100 DEER GUN – 12 (disc. 1987) or 20 ga., 20 (disc.), 21 in. (20 ga. only) or 22 (disc.) in. imp. cyl. barrel with rifle sights. Disc. 1996.

	$500	$440	$375	$325	$275	$225	$175	*$584*

Add 20% for left-hand model (disc. 1986).
Add 30% for 21 in. fully rifled cantilever deer barrel.

GRADING - PPGS™	100%	98%	95%	90%	80%	70%	60%	LAST MSR

* ***Model 1100 Deer Gun Special Purpose (SP)*** – similar to Model 1100 Deer Gun, except has low luster finish on stock and forearm, sandblasted metal parts. Mfg. 1986 only.

$400	$350	$300	$265	$220	$180	$140	*$495*

MODEL 1100 SYNTHETIC (INCLUDING LT-20) – 12, 16 (new 2003), or 20 (LT-20) ga., 2 3/4 in. chamber, 26 (20 ga. only) or 28 (12 ga. only) in. VR barrel with Rem Chokes, checkered black synthetic stock and forearm, matte metal finish, 7-7 1/2 lbs. Mfg. 1996-2004.

$500	$440	$375	$325	$275	$225	$175	*$549*

Add $157-$296 (factory MSR) per extra barrel (2 3/4 in. chamber only), depending on configuration.

* ***Model 1100 Synthetic Deer*** – 12 or 20 (LT-20) ga., 21 in. fully rifled barrel with choice of cantilever scope mount (12 ga. only, became standard 2004 in 12 ga.) or rifle sight (20 ga. only), 7 or 7 1/2 lbs. New 1997-2004.

$550	$475	$400	$350	$300	$250	$195	*$629*

Subtract approx. $50 for rifle sights.

* ***Model 1100 LT-20 Synthetic Youth*** – features 21 in. VR barrel, matte black synthetic stock and forearm. Mfg. 1999-2004.

$450	$395	$340	$300	$250	$205	$160	*$549*

Add 15% (Last MSR was $612) for Youth Turkey Camo - includes 3 in. chamber and 100% Realtree Advantage or Skyline Excel (mfg. 2003-04) camo on stock and forearm.

MODEL 1100 TACTICAL – 12 ga. only, 3 in. chamber, choice of Speedfeed IV pistol grip or black synthetic stock and forearm, 6 (Speedfeed IV) or 8 (22 in. barrel only) shot mag., 18 (Speedfeed IV with fixed IC choke) or 22 (synthetic with Rem Chokes and HiViz sights) in. VR barrel, OD Green metal finish, R3 recoil pad, approx. 7 1/2 lbs. Disc. 2006.

$640	$575	$515	$450	$400	$350	$295	*$759*

Add $40 for 22 in. barrel.

MODEL 1100 TAC-2/TAC-4 – 12 ga., 2 3/4 in. chamber, 18 (bead sight) or 22 in. VR barrel, Hi-Viz sights, bead blasted black oxide metal finish, black synthetic stock with (Tac-2 with SFIV stock) or w/o (Tac-4) pistol grip, fixed (18 in.) or Rem Chokes, 6 or 8 shot mag., sling swivels, R3 recoil pad, 7 1/2 - 7 3/4 lbs. Mfg. 2007-2015.

$795	$675	$575	$500	$450	$400	$350	*$943*

Add $72 for Tac-4 with 4 shot mag. and 22 in. VR barrel.

MODEL 1100 G3 – 12 or 20 ga., 3 in. chamber, steel receiver with titanium PVD coating, all internal operating parts feature a nickel/Teflon coating, pressure compensated overbored 26 or 28 in. VR barrel with five ProBore chokes, two-piece RealWood semi-fancy carbon fiber laminated wood stock and forearm with high gloss finish and machine cut checkering, "R" insignia on pistol grip cap, R3 recoil pad, satin finished receiver, includes high grade travel case, 6 3/4 - 7 5/8 lbs. Mfg. 2006-2008.

$1,045	$915	$775	$675	$575	$500	$450	*$1,239*

Add $90 for left-hand action (new 2008).

MODEL 1100 COMPETITION – 12 ga. only, 2 3/4 in. chamber with .735 bore diameter, 30 in. barrel with 10mm target style rib and five ProBore choke tubes, receiver and internal parts are nickel/Teflon finished, high gloss semi-fancy adj. or non-adj. American walnut (disc. 2011) or black synthetic (mfg. 2011-2020) stock and forearm, R3 recoil pad, 8 1/4 lbs. Mfg. 2006-2020.

$1,100	$965	$825	$750	$600	$500	$400	*$1,305*

Add approx. 15% for walnut stock and forearm (disc. 2011).

MODEL 1100 COMPETITION MASTER – 12 ga. only, 2 3/4 in. chamber, designed for 3 gun matches in practical shooting, 22 in. VR barrel with fiber optic front sight and Rem Chokes, 8 shot mag., grey synthetic stock and forearm, R3 recoil pad, matte black finish, 8 lbs. Mfg. 2003-2004.

$775	$600	$525	$465	$435	$395	$350	*$932*

MODEL 1100 TOURNAMENT SKEET – 12 or 20 (LT-20 variation disc. 1995) ga., 26 in. skeet bored or barrel with Rem Chokes, optional Cutts Compensator available from Jan. 1964 to Dec. 1976, 8 lbs. Mfg. 1963-1994, 1996-97, reintroduced 2003 in 12 ga. only. Disc. 2008.

$895	$675	$550	$475	$400	$350	$300	*$1,084*

Add 5% for left-hand model (disc. 1986).

MODEL 1100 SMALL GAUGE SKEET – 28 ga. or .410 bore, 25 or 26 (disc.) in. VR barrel, 6 1/2-7 1/4 lbs. Mfg. 1969-94.

$700	$600	$525	$450	$375	$315	$250	*$692*

2 1/2 in. chamber is standard on the .410 bore (Skeet only).

GRADING - PPGS™	100%	98%	95%	90%	80%	70%	60%	LAST MSR

MODEL 1100 SKEET MATCHED PAIR – 28 ga. and .410 bore, walnut stock and forearm. 5,067 cased Skeet sets were mfg. 1969 and 1970 only.

	$1,250	$995	$875	$765	$635	$530	$455	

MODEL 1100 SPORTING – 12 (mfg. 2000-2020), 20 (mfg. 1998-2020, LT variation mfg. 2006-2020), 28 ga., or .410 bore (mfg. 2004-2020), 25 (28 ga. only, disc. 2003), 27 (small gauge only, mfg. 2004-2020) or 28 (20 ga. only) in. VR Rem Chokes barrel with 4 extended Briley choke tubes, 12 ga. has lightweight 28 in. VR target barrel, high gloss checkered deluxe walnut stock and forearm, 6 1/2-8 lbs. Mfg. 1996-2020.

	$1,065	$925	$800	$725	$585	$480	$400	*$1,254*

Add 10-20% for 28 ga. or .410 bore.

MODEL 1100 PREMIER SPORTING – 12, 20, 28 ga., or .410 bore, 2 3/4 in. chamber, 27 or 28 in. VR barrel with 4 Briley extended choke tubes, nickel finished receiver with gold trigger and receiver inlays, high gloss finish select walnut stock and forearm, includes travel case, 6 1/2 - 8 lbs. Mfg. 2008-2011.

	$1,195	$1,000	$825	$725	$625	$525	$475	*$1,415*

Add $56 for 28 ga. or .410 bore.

MODEL 1100 TA TRAP – 12 ga., 30 in. barrel, recoil pad on regular stock, available in left or right-hand. Mfg. 1979-86.

	$450	$395	$340	$300	$250	$205	$160	*$570*

Add 5% for Monte Carlo stock.
Add 10% for left-hand model.

MODEL 1100 TB TRAP – 12 ga., 30 in. VR full choke barrel, special trap stock, select wood, right or left side ejection port. Mfg. 1963-1981.

	$500	$440	$375	$325	$275	$225	$175	
Monte Carlo Stock	$550	$475	$415	$350	$300	$250	$195	

Some left-handed trap shooters may pay a premium for the left side ejection port.

MODEL 1100 TD TOURNAMENT TRAP – 12 ga., 30 in. VR full choke barrel, special trap stock, extra select wood. Mfg. 1979-86.

	$550	$495	$425	$365	$325	$285	$250	*$675*

Add 5% for Monte Carlo stock.

MODEL 1100 CLASSIC TRAP – 12 ga. only, features 30 in. VR light contour target barrel, high gloss checkered walnut Monte Carlo stock and forearm, high polish blue, receiver features fine line engraving and gold inlays, 8 1/4 lbs. Mfg. 2000-2020.

	$1,125	$985	$850	$775	$625	$525	$425	*$1,334*

MODEL 1100 AMERICAN CLASSIC – 12, 20, or 28 ga., 25, 26, or 28 in. VR barrel with Rem choke tubes, features fleur-de-lis checkering on "B" Grade American walnut stock and forearm, machine cut engraved receiver with gold filled "American Classic" banner on right side, white diamond forearm grip cap, vent. recoil pad and white line spacer, high polished blued finish, 6 1/2-8 lbs. Mfg. 2014-2016.

	$1,495	$1,275	$1,050	$925	$800	$675	$550	*$1,682*

MODEL 1100 50TH ANNIVERSARY LIMITED EDITION – 12 ga., 3 in. chamber, 28 in. VR barrel, features machine cut and engraved receiver with gold fill (patterned after the 2 millionth Model 1100 in the Remington Museum in Ilion, NY), gold trigger, B Grade walnut stock with press checkering, solid rubber recoil pad with white line spacers, high polish bluing, 8 1/4 lbs. Limited mfg. 2013 only.

	$1,775	$1,575	$1,375	$1,100	$900	$700	$525	*$1,999*

MODEL 1100 150TH ANNIVERSARY – limited mfg. in 1966 only.

	$495	$450	$400	$340	$290	N/A	N/A	

MODEL 1100 - 200TH YEAR ANNIVERSARY LIMITED EDITION – 12 ga., 28 in. barrel, C-Grade walnut stock with fleur-de-lis checkering, medallion in grip, Classic American style engraving and gold inlay, special serial number, limited to quantity of 2,016. Limited mfg. 2016 only.

	$1,850	$1,650	$1,450	$1,250	$1,050	$900	$800	*$1,999*

MODEL 1100 BICENTENNIAL – 12 ga. only, configurations include Trap, Skeet, and Trade, mfg. to commemorate U.S. Bicentennial (1776-1976).

Trap or Skeet	$500	$425	$350	N/A	N/A	N/A	N/A	
Trade	$400	$325	$250	N/A	N/A	N/A	N/A	

In 1976, the 1100 Bicentennial Trap retailed for $320 ($330 w/Monte Carlo stock), the Skeet retailed for $285, and the Trade retailed for $270.

GRADING - PPGS™	100%	98%	95%	90%	80%	70%	60%	LAST MSR

MODEL 1100 DUCKS UNLIMITED – for individual listings, including chapter dinner guns and special/limited editions, please refer to Ducks Unlimited section, available online at BlueBookofGunValues.com/overflow.

There are two main variations of Model 1100 DU shotguns. The most desirable are those guns specifically manufactured for DU individual chapters, which are auctioned off at each chapter's annual banquet. These shotguns are referred to as "dinner guns", and since they are individually auctioned off at each chapter, prices can vary considerably from one chapter location to another. Please refer to individual listings in the Ducks Unlimited section for Model 1100 DU dinner guns and current values.

The second Model 1100 DU variation is a special/limited edition which is typically not auctioned off at the individual DU chapters. These limited/special editions are usually sold through normal firearms distribution, which includes both distributors and dealers. Values for these Model 1100 DU special/limited editions generally command a small premium above normal Model 1100 prices, if condition is NIB.

MODEL 1100 D-GRADE (TOURNAMENT) – custom order only, any gauge. Mfg. 1963-2020.

N/A	$2,900	$2,075	N/A	N/A	N/A	N/A	*$4,532 (2007)*

MODEL 1100 F-GRADE (PREMIER) – custom order only, any gauge. Mfg. 1963-2020.

N/A	$7,500	$5,500	N/A	N/A	N/A	N/A	*$8,799 (2007)*

MODEL 1100 F-GRADE W/GOLD (GOLD PREMIER) – with gold inlay, custom order only. Mfg. 1963-2020.

N/A	$9,000	$7,250	N/A	N/A	N/A	N/A	*$11,999 (2007)*

SPORTSMAN 12 AUTO – 12 ga. only, 2 3/4 in. chamber, 28 or 30 in. VR barrel, similar to Model 1100 action, hardwood stock and forearm, 7 3/4 lbs. Mfg. 1985-86 only.

$300	$260	$220	$195	$170	$160	$150	*$405*

Add 10% for Rem. chokes (mfg. 1986 only).

This model was a plain version of the Model 1100 sold by many popular retailers including Target, Kmart, and Wal-Mart.

Shotguns: Semi-Auto, Model 11-87 & Variations

Model 11-87 barrels will not fit the Model 1100 or Model 11-87 Super Magnum models.

Remington MSRs on extra barrels (3 in. chamber standard) for the following currently manufactured models range from $280-$358 per barrel, depending on configuration.

Many options are available from the Custom Shop, and are POR.

MODEL 11-87 SPORTSMAN SYNTHETIC/CAMO – 12 or 20 ga., 3 in. chamber, gas operated, 20 (fully rifled with cantilever scope rail, 20 ga. only, mfg. 2005-2017), 21 (fully rifled with cantilever, 12 ga. only, mfg. 2005-2017), 26, or 28 in. VR barrel with Rem Chokes, choice of black synthetic stock and forearm or 100% Mossy Oak New Break-Up camo (mfg. 2005-2017) finish, 7 1/4-8 1/4 lbs. Mfg. 2005-2017, 2019-2020.

$550	$480	$415	$375	$300	$250	$200	*$649*

Add $195 for 20 or 21 in. fully rifled barrel with cantilever scope mount (mfg. 2005-2017).
Add $181 for 100% Mossy Oak New Break-Up camo (mfg. 2005-2017).
Add $13 for NRA Edition with Mossy Oak New Break-Up on stock and forearm (12 ga. only, disc. 2006).

* ***Model 11-87 Sportsman Synthetic ShurShot*** – 12 ga., synthetic ShurShot Realtree Hardwoods HD camo stock, 21 in. fully rifled barrel, thumbhole stock, otherwise similar to Model 11-87 Sportsman Synthetic/Camo. Mfg. 2008-2012.

$875	$775	$675	$575	$500	$425	$350	*$1,012*

* ***Model 11-87 Sportsman Field*** – 12 or 20 ga., 3 in. chamber, 26 or 28 in. VR barrel with Rem chokes, 4 shot mag., dual bead sights, American walnut stock and forearm with Fleur-De-Lis checkering, matte metal finish, satin finish on stock, 7 1/4 or 8 1/4 lbs. Mfg. 2010-2020.

$695	$610	$525	$475	$380	$315	$250	*$816*

* ***Model 11-87 Sportsman Youth*** – 20 ga., 3 in. chamber, 21 in. VR barrel with Rem Chokes, 13 in. LOP, Mossy Oak New Break-Up 100% camo coverage. Mfg. 2008 only.

$650	$550	$475	$400	$350	$295	$250	*$818*

This model was available through Remington Premier dealers only.

* ***Model 11-87 Compact Sportsman*** – 20 ga., 3 in. chamber, 21 in. VR barrel with Rem Choke, black synthetic or 100% Mossy Oak Break-Up camo (mfg. 2009-2017) stock, adj. LOP allows up to 1 in. of adjustment with three spacers, SuperCell recoil pad, compact features, 6 1/2 lbs. Mfg. 2009-2017.

$550	$480	$415	$375	$300	$250	$200	*$649*

Add 30% (Last MSR was $830) for 100% camo finish (mfg. 2009-2017).

GRADING - PPGS™	100%	98%	95%	90%	80%	70%	60%	LAST MSR

MODEL 11-87 PREMIER – 12 or 20 (new 1999, LT-20) ga. (3 in. chamber), 26, 28, 30 (12 ga. only, new 2000) or 32 (disc. 1996) in. VR barrel with Rem Chokes, successor to Model 1100, gas compensating action adaptable to all loads, stainless steel magazine tube, polished blue finish, high gloss or satin (current mfg. is in 12 ga./28 in. barrel only) finished and checkered walnut stock and forearm, a high gloss wood finish option became available in 1991 at N/C, and is now standard, fine line receiver engraving (referred to as embellished receiver) became standard during 1999, solid recoil pad, 8 1/8-8 3/8 lbs. Mfg. 1987-2006.

$685	$525	$435	$375	$315	$275	$250	*$860*

Add $84 for 21 in. fully rifled cantilever deer barrel.
Add $67 for left-hand action (12 ga. only).

Note: Model 11-87 Premier barrels are not interchangeable with Model 1100 barrels.

* ***Model 11-87 Premier Upland Special*** – 12 or 20 ga., 3 in. chamber, 23 in. (light contour barrel on 12 ga.) VR barrel, straight grip satin finished checkered walnut stock and forearm, high polish metal with engraving, 6 1/2 or 7 1/4 lbs. Mfg. 2000-2006.

$685	$525	$435	$375	$315	$275	$250	*$860*

MODEL 11-87 PREMIER 3 1/2 IN. SUPER MAGNUM – 12 ga. only, 3 1/2 in. chamber, 28 in. VR barrel with Rem Chokes, blue high polish non-embellished receiver and barrel, checkered high gloss walnut stock and forearm or 100% Mossy Oak Break-Up camo (disc. 2004) coverage, 8 1/4 lbs. Mfg. 2001-2006.

$750	$600	$525	$450	$375	$325	$275	*$932*

Add approx. 10% for camo (disc. 2004).

MODEL 11-87 SP (SPECIAL PURPOSE) – 12 ga. only, 3 in. chamber, 26, 28, or 30 (disc.) in. VR barrel with Rem Chokes, parkerized metal with satin finish wood stock and forearm, vent. recoil pad, camouflaged nylon sling, 8 1/4 lbs. Mfg. 1987-2003.

$590	$465	$395	$350	$315	$275	$250	*$765*

MODEL 11-87 SP (SPECIAL PURPOSE) 3 1/2 IN. SUPER MAGNUM – 12 ga. only, 3 1/2 in. chamber, non-reflective black matte finish on barrel and receiver, 26 or 28 in. VR barrel with Rem Chokes, satin finished stock and forearm, approx. 8 1/8 lbs. Mfg. 2000-2005.

$725	$525	$450	$375	$325	$300	$280	*$912*

MODEL 11-87 P (POLICE) – 12 ga. only, 18 in. barrel, improved cylinder choke, synthetic stock, parkerized finish, choice of bead or rifle sights, 7 shot extended mag., designed for police/law enforcement.

Remington does not publish consumer retail pricing for this police/law enforcement model. Secondary prices for this model will be slightly higher than for current pricing on the Model 11-87 SPS.

MODEL 11-87 SPS (SPECIAL PURPOSE SYNTHETIC) – see individual sub-models listed below.

* ***Model 11-87 SPS 3 in. Magnum*** – similar to Model 11-87 SP 3 in. Mag., except is supplied with black synthetic stock and forearm. Disc. 2004.

$610	$475	$400	$360	$315	$275	$250	*$791*

* ***Model 11-87 SPS Camo (Special Purpose Synthetic Camo)*** – 12 ga. only, 3 in. chamber, 21 (mfg. 1999-2005), 26 or 28 (disc. 1998) in. VR barrel with Rem Chokes, available in Mossy Oak Bottomland (disc. 1996), Mossy Oak Obsession (new 2006) or Mossy Oak Break-Up (mfg. 1997-2005) finish. Mfg. 1994-2006.

$765	$575	$450	$375	$325	$300	$280	*$963*

* ***Model 11-87 SPS Waterfowl*** – 12 ga., 3 in. chamber, 100% Mossy Oak New Shadow Grass camo coverage, 28 in. VR barrel with HiViz front sight (interchangeable), includes sling and swivels, 8 1/4 lbs. Mfg. 2004-2006.

$825	$625	$525	$450	$400	$350	$300	*$999*

* ***Model 11-87 SPS-BG Camo (Special Purpose Synthetic Big Game)*** – 12 ga. only, 21 in. plain barrel with rifle sights and Rem Choke. Mfg. 1994 only.

$555	$425	$350	$290	$250	$225	$200	*$692*

* ***Model 11-87 SP/SPS (Special Purpose Deer Gun)*** – 12 ga. only, 3 in. chamber, 21 in. IC or Rem Chokes (Model SP, mfg. 1989-2003) or fully rifled (new 1993, became standard 2004) barrel with rifle sights, parkerized metal with matte finished wood or black synthetic (Model SPS, new 1993) stock and forearm, vent. recoil pad, includes camouflaged nylon sling, 7 1/4 lbs. Mfg. 1987-2005.

$695	$525	$450	$395	$350	$300	$250	*$908*

Subtract 10% for fixed choke barrel or if w/o cantilever (became standard 2005) scope mount.

Rem Chokes were standard on this model between 1989-1992.

GRADING - PPGS™	100%	98%	95%	90%	80%	70%	60%	LAST MSR

* ***Model 11-87 SP Thumbhole Deer Gun*** – 12 ga., features grey laminate thumbhole wood stock and forearm, 21 in. rifled barrel with cantilever scope mount, 8 lbs. Mfg. 2006-2007.

$925	$825	$725	$625	$550	$500	$425	$1,135

* ***Model 11-87 SPS-T (Special Purpose Turkey)*** – 12 ga. only, 3 in. chamber, 21 in. VR barrel with Rem Choke, available in flat black (disc. 2000) or 100% camo treatment in Mossy Oak (disc. 1996), Mossy Oak Break Up (new 1999), Realtree X-tra Brown (mfg. 1997 only), or Greenleaf (disc. 1996), TruGlo rifle sights became standard in 2002 (Model SPS-T Turkey Gun RS/TG). Disc. 2003.

$765	$550	$460	$385	$335	$300	$280	$963

Add $324 for Leupold Gilmore red dot sights, Monte Carlo stock and superfull choke tube (mfg. 2000 only).

Subtract approx. $20 if w/o TruGlo rifle sights.

» ***Model 11-87 SPS Turkey Camo NWTF*** – 20 ga. only, features 100% Mossy Oak Break-Up camo finish, TruGlo fiber optic sights, 6 1/2 lbs. Mfg. 1998 only.

$675	$575	$450	$395	$325	$290	$265	$832

MODEL 11-87 SPS 3 1/2 IN. SUPER MAGNUM – choice of 26 or 28 in. VR barrel with Rem Chokes, black synthetic or 100% Mossy Oak Break-Up (disc. 2005) or Mossy Oak Obsession (new 2006) camo covered stock and forearm, approx. 8 1/8 lbs. Mfg. 2000-2007.

$950	$825	$725	$575	$475	$400	$350	$1,076

Add $99 for camo coverage.

* ***Model 11-87 SPS-T 3 1/2 in. Super Magnum Turkey Camo*** – 12 ga. only, 3 1/2 in. chamber, full coverage Mossy Oak Break-Up (disc. 2003) or Obsession (new 2005) camo treatment, 23 in. barrel with TruGlo rifle sights and Rem Choke tubes, thumbhole stock became optional 2006, 8 1/8 lbs. Mfg. 2001-2007.

$1,000	$875	$775	$675	$600	$525	$450	$1,175

Add $66 for thumbhole stock (new 2006).

* ***Model 11-87 SPS 3 1/2 in. Waterfowl*** – 12 ga., 30 in. barrel with HiViz sight system and Rem Chokes, 100% Mossy Oak Duck Blind camo coverage, Speedfeed synthetic stock, 8 1/4 lbs. Mfg. 2007.

$1,025	$875	$775	$675	$600	$525	$450	$1,199

MODEL 11-87 3 1/2 IN. SPORTSMAN SUPER MAG – 12 ga. only, 28 in. VR barrel with Rem Chokes and HiViz sights, 3 lbs. trigger pull, black synthetic stock and forearm with SuperCell recoil pad, overmolded grips became standard 2010, 8 1/4 lbs. Mfg. 2008-2012.

$750	$675	$575	$500	$450	$400	$375	$859

Subtract 5% if w/o overmolded grips.

* ***Model 11-87 3 1/2 in. Sportsman ShurShot Turkey*** – 12 ga., 100% RealTree AP Green HD camo coverage with skeletonized ShurShot stock, elevated HiViz sights, extended choke tubes, SuperCell recoil pad, overmolded grips became standard 2010, 7 5/8 lbs. Mfg. 2008-2012.

$885	$750	$650	$575	$500	$450	$395	$998

* ***Model 11-87 3 1/2 In. Sportsman Super Mag Waterfowl*** – 12 ga., features 100% Mossy Oak Duck Blind camo coverage, Speedfeed stock with SuperCell recoil pad, HiViz sights, overmolded grips became standard 2010, 8 1/4 lbs. Mfg. 2008-2012.

$885	$750	$650	$575	$500	$450	$395	$998

MODEL 11-87 3 1/2 IN. SUPER MAGNUM XCS (XTREME CONDITIONS) – 12 ga., 28 in. VR barrel with Rem Chokes, features choice of black synthetic Speedfeed stock and forearm, or Mossy Oak Duck Blind camo coverage, grey TriNyte PVD coating on receiver and barrel, nickel plated internal components. Mfg. 2008 only.

$1,000	$875	$775	$675	$600	$525	$450	$1,188

Add $40 for Mossy Oak Duck Blind stock and forearm camo coverage.

This model was available from Remington Premier dealers only.

MODEL 11-87 SPORTING CLAYS – 12 ga. only, 26 (disc. 1996) or 28 in. VR barrel with extended Rem Choke (knurled extension chokes allow for no-wrench field changes), specially balanced, satin finished walnut, top metal surfaces have fine matte finish, radiused recoil pad, twin bead sights on 5/16 wide VR, 7 1/2 lbs. Mfg. 1992-1999.

$675	$575	$450	$395	$325	$290	$265	$833

* ***Model 11-87 Sporting Clays NP*** – 12 ga. only, features matte nickel plated receiver with engraving, satin finished checkered stock and forearm, 28 (new 1998) or 30 in. VR ported barrel with extended choke tubes, 7 3/4 lbs. Mfg. 1997-2001.

$775	$650	$525	$450	$375	$325	$295	$948

GRADING - PPGS™	100%	98%	95%	90%	80%	70%	60%	LAST MSR

MODEL 11-87 PREMIER SKEET – 12 ga. only, 26 in. VR barrel with Rem Chokes, deluxe walnut with quality cut checkering, 7 3/4 lbs. Mfg. 1987-1999.

$650	$550	$475	$425	$375	$325	$275	*$799*

Add approx. $70 for left-hand action.
Subtract 10% if without Rem Chokes.

MODEL 11-87 PREMIER TRAP – 12 ga. only, 30 in. raised VR barrel with Rem Chokes, deluxe walnut stock (Monte Carlo became standard in 1996) with quality cut checkering, 8 1/4 lbs. Mfg. 1987-1999.

$725	$625	$525	$425	$325	$295	$260	*$833*

Subtract $30 if without Monte Carlo stock.
Add approx. $40 for left-hand action (disc. 1994).
Subtract 10% if without Rem Chokes.

MODEL 11-87 175TH ANNIVERSARY – 12 ga. only, 28 in. barrel with Rem Choke, 175th Anniversary Model (1816-1991) with light engraving and high gloss wood finish. 4,606 mfg. 1991 only.

$515	$425	$335	N/A	N/A	N/A	N/A	*$618*

MODEL 11-87 DALE EARNHARDT COMMEMORATIVE – 12 or 20 ga., features "7 Time Winston Cup Champion" tributary banner on right side with gold letters, 28 in. light contoured VR barrel, select checkered American walnut stock and forearm, serialization starts with DE, 7 3/4 lbs. Mfg. 2003-2004.

$800	$650	$575	N/A	N/A	N/A	N/A	*$972*

MODEL 11-87 D-GRADE (TOURNAMENT) – custom order only, any gauge. Mfg. 1987-2020.

N/A	$2,900	$2,075	N/A	N/A	N/A	N/A	*$4,532 (2007)*

MODEL 11-87 F-GRADE (PREMIER) – custom order only, any gauge. Mfg. 1987-2020.

N/A	$7,500	$5,500	N/A	N/A	N/A	N/A	*$8,799 (2007)*

MODEL 11-87 F-GRADE W/GOLD (GOLD PREMIER) – with gold inlay, custom order only. Mfg. 1987-2020.

N/A	$9,000	$7,250	N/A	N/A	N/A	N/A	*$11,999 (2007)*

Shotguns: Semi-Auto, SP-10 Models

MODEL SP-10 – 10 ga., 3 1/2 in. chamber, semi-auto stainless steel gas system operation, lighter recoil than most 12 ga. mags., 30 in. barrel with 3/8 in. VR and Rem chokes (2), checkered stock and forearm with low gloss satin finish, matte metal finish, crossbolt safety, R3 recoil pad became standard 2004, supplied with camo sling, approx. 11 lbs. Mfg. 1989-2010.

$1,475	$1,200	$1,050	$925	$825	$725	$625	*$1,845*

The first 5,000 SP-10s were assigned special serialization (LE89 prefix) - no premiums exist at this time, however. This model is NOT a re-designed Ithaca Mag-10 and the parts are NOT interchangeable. The SP-10 is a newer design.

* ***Model SP-10 Magnum Camo*** – 10 ga., 23 (Turkey Model, mfg. 1999-2000, reintroduced 2007 with Williams Firesights), or 26 in. VR barrel, choice of Mossy Oak (disc. 1996), full coverage Mossy Oak Break-Up (mfg. 1997-2004), full coverage Mossy Oak Obsession or Duck Blind (new 2007), regular or thumbhole (Turkey only) stock, R3 recoil pad (became standard 2005), or Bottomland (mfg. 1994-96) camo finish. Mfg. 1993-2010.

$1,550	$1,200	$1,000	$900	$800	$700	$625	*$2,012*

Add $14 for Magnum Waterfowl with 100% Mossy Oak Duck Blind camo and special waterfowl choke tubes (new 2007).
Add $125 for Turkey Magnum with 100% Mossy Oak Obsession camo and thumbhole stock (new 2007).
Subtract 10% for disc. camo finishes.

* ***Model SP-10 Magnum Synthetic*** – 10 ga., features lightweight black synthetic stock and forearm, matte non-reflective metal finish, 26 in. barrel only, 10 3/4 lbs. Mfg. 2000-2004.

$995	$875	$785	$675	$575	$550	$475	*$1,331*

* ***Model SP-10 Turkey Camo NWTF 25th Anniversary*** – 10 ga., limited mfg. to commemorate the 25th Anniversary of the NWTF during 1998, TruGlo fiber optic sights. Mfg. 1998 only.

$1,050	$925	$775	N/A	N/A	N/A	N/A	*$1,225*

* ***Model SP-10 Turkey Combo*** – includes choice of either 26 or 30 in. VR regular barrel and extra 22 in. deer barrel with rifle sights. Mfg. 1991-94.

$1,295	$1,125	$925	$775	$700	$650	$625	*$1,132*

GRADING - PPGS™	100%	98%	95%	90%	80%	70%	60%	LAST MSR

Shotguns: Semi-Auto, V3 & Versa Models

V3 FIELD SPORT – 12 ga., 3 in. chamber, Versaport Gas System, 26 or 28 in. VR barrel, adj. shim system, low recoil, black synthetic or American walnut stock, 7 1/4 lbs. Mfg. 2015-2020.

$775	$680	$580	$525	$425	$350	$275	*$895*

Add $100 for American walnut stock with satin finish.

V3 FIELD SPORT CAMO – 12 ga., 3 in. chamber, 26 or 28 in. VR barrel, twin bead sights, synthetic stock with Mossy Oak Blades, Mossy Oak Break-Up Country (disc. 2019), or Realtree Timber (mfg. 2019-2020) camo finish, 7 3/4 lbs. Mfg. 2015-2020.

$875	$750	$650	$585	$475	$385	$325	*$995*

V3 FIELD SPORT COMPACT – 12 ga., 2 3/4 or 3 in. chamber, VersaPort gas piston system, 22 in. light contour barrel, 3 shot mag., black synthetic stock, black oxide finish, 7 1/4 lbs. Mfg. mid-2018-2020.

$785	$680	$580	$525	$425	$350	$275	*$915*

V3 TAC-13 COMPACT – 12 ga., 2 3/4 or 3 in. chamber, 13 in. lightweight cylinder bore contour barrel, Versaport gas system, 5 shot mag., bead sights, bird's head pistol grip, adj. hand strap, lightweight aluminum receiver, black oxide finish, 26 1/2 in. OAL. Mfg. 2018-2020.

$785	$680	$580	$525	$425	$350	$275	*$915*

V3 TURKEY PRO – 12 ga., 2 3/4 or 3 in. chamber, VersaPort gas system, 22 in. light contour VR barrel, TruGlo Headbanger choke tube, TruGlo fiber optic sights, synthetic stock with SuperCell recoil pad, 100% Realtree Timber finish. Mfg. 2019-2020.

$1,025	$895	$775	$700	$575	$475	$375	*$1,195*

V3 WATERFOWL PRO – 12 ga., 2 3/4 or 3 in. chamber, VersaPort gas system, 28 in. light contour VR barrel, three extended black chokes, Hi-Viz fiber optic front sight and steel mid-bead, synthetic stock with Mossy Oak Shadow Grass Blades, Realtree Max-5, or Realtree Timber (new 2020) camo finish, oversized bolt handle, widened loading port, sling included, Cerakote finish on receiver and barrel, 7 1/2 lbs. Mfg. 2019-2020.

$1,025	$895	$775	$700	$575	$475	$375	*$1,195*

VERSA MAX – 12 ga., 3 1/2 in. chamber, self-cleaning Versaport gas system regulates cycling pressure based on shell length (2 3/4-3 1/2 in.), 26 or 28 in. VR barrel with 5 Pro Bore flush choke tubes, overmolded black synthetic stock/forearm with grey checkered insert panels, Soft-Touch matte black finish, adj. stock with SuperCell recoil pad, HiViz interchangeable sights, right or left (new 2014) hand action, 7 3/4 lbs. Mfg. late 2010-2020.

$1,225	$1,050	$900	$775	$650	$525	$425	*$1,456*

Remington has found that a limited number of its Versa Max shotguns may have hammers out of specification. This condition may result in inconsistent firearm performance. Inconsistent firearm performance may result in property damage, serious personal injury or death.

If you have a Remington Versa Max shotgun, immediately discontinue use of the shotgun and contact Remington at 1-800-243-9700, Prompt #4. Remington will arrange for the return shipment of your Versa Max shotgun and upon receipt will immediately inspect and retrofit your Versa Max shotgun and return it at no cost to you. All Versa Max shotguns that have the hammer enhancement will contain a "V" stamp that can be seen by looking in the ejection port or through the carrier.

* ***Versa Max Waterfowl Camo*** – 12 ga., similar to Versa Max, except features 4 extended Pro Bore choke tubes, overmolded camo synthetic stock/forearm with black checkered insert panels, Mossy Oak Duck Blind or Realtree AP HD 100% camo finish, right or left (mfg. 2014-2020) hand action, 7 3/4 lbs. Mfg. late 2010-2020.

$1,475	$1,295	$1,095	$995	$800	$650	$525	*$1,664*

* ***Versa Max Waterfowl Pro*** – 12 ga., 3 1/2 in. chamber, 28 in. barrel with ProBore 14 choke tubes, Mossy Oak Shadow Grass Blades camo stock and forend, tactical bolt handle, enlarged feeding port, flat-faced carrier, includes sling, 7 3/4 lbs. Mfg. 2014-2020.

$1,575	$1,365	$1,175	$1,050	$850	$700	$550	*$1,765*

* ***Versa Max WoodTech*** – 12 ga., 3 1/2 in. chamber, 28 in. VR barrel with ProBore choke tubes, complete set comb inserts (low/med/high), synthetic stock and forend with overmolded grips and Wood Tech Finish, 7 3/4 lbs. Mfg. 2014-2015.

$1,450	$1,275	$1,095	$995	$800	$650	$525	*$1,630*

VERSA MAX COMPETITION TACTICAL – 12 ga., 3 1/2 in. chamber, 22 in. barrel with ProBore choke tubes, 8 shot with extension, anodized aluminum receiver with green Cerakote finish, black synthetic stock with overmolded grips, QD sling swivel cups on stock and forend, 8 lbs. Mfg. 2014-2020.

$1,485	$1,300	$1,115	$1,000	$800	$675	$550	*$1,733*

GRADING - PPGS™	100%	98%	95%	90%	80%	70%	60%	LAST MSR

VERSA MAX TACTICAL – 12 ga., 3 1/2 in. chamber, 22 in. VR barrel with HiViz sights, extended mag tube, anodized aluminum receiver, includes Picatinny rail (except for Zombie finishes), black, Zombie Gargoyle Green (mfg. 2013 only), or Zombie Pink Explosion (mfg. 2013 only) synthetic stock with overmolded grips, SuperCell recoil pad, 7 3/4 lbs. Mfg. 2012-2020.

	$1,240	$1,085	$925	$825	$675	$550	$450	*$1,456*

Add $200 for Zombie Gargoyle Green or Zombie Pink Explosion finish (mfg. 2013 only).

VERSA MAX SPORTSMAN – 12 ga., 3 1/2 in. chamber, Versaport operating system, 26 or 28 in. VR barrel, includes one modified pro bore choke tube, HiVIz interchangeable sights, black synthetic stock with matte blue metal finish, textured grip panels, SuperCell recoil pad. Mfg. 2013-2020.

	$910	$775	$700	$625	$550	$495	$425	*$1,066*

* ***Versa Max Sportsman Camo*** – 12 ga., similar to Versa Max Sportsman, except features 100% Realtree Edge (mfg. 2020 only), Mossy Oak Bottomland (mfg. 2020 only), Mossy Oak Duck Blind (disc. 2019), Mossy Oak Shadow Grass Blades (disc. 2014), or Realtree AP (disc. 2019) camo finish. Mfg. 2013-2020.

	$1,025	$825	$725	$625	$550	$495	$425	*$1,222*

* ***Versa Max Sportsman Turkey Model*** – 12 ga., 3 1/2 in. chamber, 22 in. barrel with vent. rib and fixed sights, one TXF choke tube, synthetic stock with 100% Mossy Oak Obsession camo coverage, 7 3/4 lbs. Mfg. 2013-2020.

	$1,025	$825	$725	$625	$550	$495	$425	*$1,222*

100%	98%	95%	90%	80%	70%	60%	50%	40%	30%	20%	10%

SHOTGUNS: SINGLE SHOT

MODEL NO. 3 RIDER SINGLE BARREL – 12 ga., single barrel, 30 or 32 in. barrels, top lever break open, button release forend, plain pistol grip stock. Approx. 87,850 mfg. 1893-1903.

N/A	$450	$400	$300	$260	$200	$150	$130	$110	$90	$75	$65

MODEL NO. 9 RIDER SINGLE BARREL – 12 ga., similar to No. 3, screw release forend, auto ejector. 65,698 mfg. 1902-1910.

N/A	$450	$400	$300	$260	$200	$150	$130	$110	$90	$75	$65

GRADING - PPGS™	100%	98%	95%	90%	80%	70%	60%	LAST MSR

MODEL 90-T (TRAP) – 12 ga., 32 (disc. 1993) or 34 in. VR barrel with fixed full choke, matte black receiver and wood around tang area, deluxe checkered stock and forearm, short throw top-lever release, elongated forcing cone, approx. 8 3/4 lbs. Mfg. 1992-1997.

	$1,850	$1,550	$1,375	$1,175	$1,025	$925	$850	*$3,199*

Add $50 for factory porting.

* ***Model 90-T HPAR (High Post w/adj. Rib)*** – high post, adj. rib. Mfg. 1994-1997.

	$2,300	$1,875	$1,700	$1,550	$1,450	$1,325	$1,075	*$3,992*

MODEL 310 SKEET – .32 Rimfire case loaded with No. 12 leadshot, break open single shot, .310 bore shotgun, used in conjunction with a self-operated trap set which threw half-size clay targets, entire set-up included gun, shooting booth, ammunition, and trap thrower, 5 1/2 lbs., mfg. circa late 1960s.

Gun only	$425	$350	$300	$250	$195	$175	$150	

Add 25%-75% depending on the amount of original accessories included.

This model was mfg. by CBC in Brazil, and imported into the U.S. as the .310 Skeet. This model was never mass produced, but test marketed for approx. 5 years in CT, NJ, PA, and TX, primarily at amusement parks. It failed commercially due to lack of sales.

SHOTGUNS: SLIDE ACTION, MODELS 10, 17, & 29 & VARIATIONS

REMINGTON REPEATING SHOTGUN – 12 ga., hammerless, bottom ejection, takedown, plain barrel only, blue finish, sight notch on receiver top, marked "REMINGTON ARMS CO." with February 3rd, 1903 and May 18th, 1905 patent dates, walnut pistol grip stock and short forearm, hard rubber buttplate, 7 1/2 lbs. Approx. 10,000 mfg. 1908-1910.

	$395	$350	$295	$225	$200	$175	$150	

Add 10% for 32 in. barrel.

There were 7 grades of this model (Numbers 0-6) that were originally priced from $27 to approx. $140. This model was renamed the Model 10 in 1911.

100% 98% 95% 90% 80% 70% 60% 50% 40% 30% 20% 10%

MODEL 10A – 12 ga., 26-32 in. barrels, various chokes, takedown, plain pistol grip stock. Mfg. 1911-29.

$395 $350 $300 $275 $200 $175 $150

Add 10% for 32 in. full choke barrel.

Add 35% for guns marked "Long Range" - beware of fakes.

MODEL 17A – 20 ga., 26-32 in. barrel, various chokes, takedown, bottom ejection, 4 shot mag., plain grip stock. Approx. 48,000 mfg. 1917-1933.

Plain barrel	$350	$275	$220	$195	$165	$140	$110
Solid. rib	$450	$375	$325	$290	$270	$250	$210

Grades range from "A" - "F" in suffix form, "F" being the highest. Large premiums are paid for mint condition, higher grade models.

MODEL 17R – 20 ga. only, security configuration, 20 in. cylinder bore barrel, 4 shot mag. Mfg. circa 1920s.

$325 $265 $235 $200 $150 $120 $100

MODEL 29A – 12 ga., 26-32 in. barrel, bottom ejection, various chokes, takedown, 5 shot mag., checkered pistol grip stock. Approx. 24,000 mfg. 1929-1933.

$375 $325 $265 $235 $200 $150 $120

Add 15% for solid rib, 25% for VR.

* ***Model 29A 32 in. Long Range barrel*** – should be marked "Long Range" - beware of fakes.

$525 $475 $425 $350 $250 $200 $180

Grades range from A - C and TA - TF, lowest to highest. Premiums exist for finer condition upper grades. The Model 29 was similar in appearance to the Model 10.

MODEL 29R – 12 ga. only, security configuration, 20 in. cylinder bore barrel, 5 shot mag. Mfg. circa 1920s.

$375 $325 $265 $235 $200 $150 $120

MODEL 29S – "Trap Special" with trap style straight grip stock, matted or VR rib.

$500 $450 $425 $375 $350 $325 $300

Add 20% for VR rib.

SHOTGUNS: SLIDE ACTION, MODEL 31 & VARIATIONS

In January 1930, Crawford C. Loomis began working on a pump-action shotgun to replace both the Remington Model 17 and Model 29. Receiving assistance from Charles H. Barnes and Oliver H. Loomis, a new 12 gauge shotgun was introduced by Remington in August 1931, selling for $48.95. The Model 31 was Remington's first side-ejecting, single-loading, repeating shotgun. Remington began offering Model 31 shotguns in 16 and 20 gauge in 1933.

Remington produced the Model 31 shotgun in thirty-five variations and grades, including: the Model 31A Standard Grade (1931); Model 31AC and Model 31AP (both 1937, replacing the Model 31A); Model 31B Special Grade (1932); Model 31D Tournament Grade (1932); Model 31E Expert Grade (1932); M31F Premier Grade (1932); M31H Hunter's Special; Model 31 Police Gun with 18 1/2" barrel (1931); Model 31R Riot Gun with 20" barrel (1932); Model 31 Skeet Gun (1935); Model 31D Skeet Tournament; Model 31E Skeet Expert; Model 31F Skeet Premier; Model 31 Trap Special Grade (1932); Model 31S-D Trap Tournament; Model 31S-E Trap Expert; Model 31 S-F Trap Premier; Model 31 TC Trap (or Target) Grade (1932); Model 31 T-D Target Tournament; Model 31 T-E Target Expert; and the Model 31T-F Target Premier.

Remington began offering this gun with a Cutts Compensator in April 1939, and the Remington Special Long Range "Aero-dyne" Polychoke the following year.

In 1941, Remington expanded their Model 31 shotgun line by also offering:

New Improved standard weight guns - the Model 31 New Improved Skeet Gun (in 12, 16 and 20 ga.); M31 New Improved TC Target Grade (in 12 gauge only); M31 New Improved Police Special (in 12 gauge only); and the Model 31R New Improved Riot Gun (in 12, 16 and 20 ga.);

New Improved Lightweight 12 gauge shotguns with aluminum receivers - Model 31 New Improved Lightweights: Model 31LA Standard Grade; Model 31LB Lightweight Special Grade; Model 31LD Tournament Grade; Model 31LE Expert Grade; Model 31LF Premier Grade; Model 31L Skeet Gun; and the M31LR Riot Grade; and

Long Range guns advertising "greater killing range, closer patterns and no greater recoil - the Model 31 XA Standard Grade; New Improved Model 31 XA Standard Grade; New Improved Model 31 XS Trap

GRADING - PPGS™	100%	98%	95%	90%	80%	70%	60%	LAST MSR

Special Grade; New Improved Model 31 XH Hunter's Special Grade; and the New Improved Model 31 XTC Trap Grade shotguns, and were sold only in 1941 and 1942.

During World War II, Remington supplied 8,992 Model 31 shotguns to the U.S. Armed Forces, primarily for aerial gunnery training.

Remington Model 31 shotguns were popular selling sporting arms for the company and were manufactured from 1931 to 1949. In those eighteen years a grand total of 189,243 Model 31 shotguns were made, including 117, 739 in 12 gauge, 40,312 in 16 gauge, and 31,192 in 20 gauge.

MODEL 31A – 12, 16, or 20 ga., side ejection, 2 or 4 shot mag., 26-32 in. barrels, various chokes, takedown, pistol grip stock. 189,243 mfg., 1931-1949.

Plain barrel	$395	$345	$300	$265	$225	$185	$150	
Solid rib	$455	$385	$345	$300	$270	$230	$190	
Vent. rib	$475	$415	$375	$320	$290	$250	$210	

Add 15% for 20 ga.

Grades range from A - F suffixes. Higher grades will bring considerable premiums in excellent condition.

Early models will command a small premium in this model.

TC suffix is Target Model. During WWII, Remington supplied 8,992 Model 31 shotguns to the U.S. Armed Forces, primarily for aeriel gunnery training. During the course of production, there were over 35 variations and grades offered for sale.

MODEL 31B "SPECIAL" – higher grade wood and hand checkered pistol grip stock and forearm.

	$650	$550	$440	$385	$360	$300	$275	

MODEL 31R "RIOT" GRADE – features shortened barrel.

	$500	$440	$375	$325	$275	$225	$175	

MODEL 31D TOURNAMENT – features scroll engraving.

	$1,600	$1,350	$1,100	$880	$715	$580	$525	

MODEL 31E EXPERT – features scroll engraving with game scene on left side of receiver.

	$1,750	$1,500	$1,325	$1,100	$935	$880	$770	

MODEL 31F PREMIER – features scroll engraving and game scenes on both sides of receiver. Introduced 1942.

	$2,950	$2,550	$2,200	$1,875	$1,600	$1,500	$1,300	

Add 20% for 20 ga.

Note: Grades differ in quality, grade of wood, and amount of engraving.

This model was also available with a Cutts compensator 1940-49, or a Poly Choke on special order from 1941-49.

MODEL 31TC TRAP – similar to 31A, with 12 ga. only, 30 or 32 in. VR barrel milled out of one-piece of steel, full choke, trap stock and beavertail forend, pad.

	$875	$795	$675	$575	$450	$375	$300	

Subtract 10% for lightweight receiver.

TC stands for Trap with C Grade wood.

MODEL 31S TRAP SPECIAL – solid rib barrel, plainer wood.

	$550	$500	$450	$400	$365	$345	$325	

MODEL 31H HUNTER – similar to 31S, with sporter stock. Mfg. 1941-disc.

	$395	$350	$300	$275	$250	$220	$195	

MODEL 31L LIGHTWEIGHT – features an alloy receiver, available in both field and skeet. Mfg. 1941-1950.

	$350	$325	$300	$275	$250	$225	$200	

MODEL 31 SKEET – similar to 31A, with 26 in. skeet bored barrel, standard solid rib, beavertail forend.

Plain barrel	$495	$450	$395	$365	$335	$265	$220	
Vent. rib	$650	$550	$495	$425	$375	$340	$295	

Subtract 10% for lightweight receiver.

Add 20% for 20 ga. with VR barrel.

SHOTGUNS: SLIDE ACTION, MODEL 870 & VARIATIONS

3 in. shells (12 or 20 ga.) may be shot in Magnum receivers only regardless of what the barrel markings may indicate (the ejection port is larger in these Magnum models with M suffix serialization).

GRADING - PPGS™	100%	98%	95%	90%	80%	70%	60%	LAST MSR

Remington has manufactured many limited production runs for various distributors and wholesalers over the years. These shotguns are usually built to a specific configuration (gauge, stock, barrel length, finish, etc.), and are usually available until supplies run out. While these models are not included in this section, pricing in most cases will be similar to the base models from which they were derived.

In April 2009, Remington made its 10 millionth Model 870 slide action shotgun, making it the most manufactured shotgun in firearms history.

Remington also manufactures the Models R870 and MCS for military and law enforcement only. These models are not covered in this text.

Add 25%-35% for 16 ga. on older mfg., if original condition is 95%+.

Add $100-$200 per extra barrel, depending on configuration.

MODEL 870AP – "Wingmaster," 12, 16, or 20 ga., 26, 28, or 30 in. barrel, 5 shot, various chokes, plain pistol grip stock. Mfg. 1950-63.

Plain Barrel	$350	$300	$265	$240	$195	$160	$125	
Vent. Rib	$400	$350	$300	$265	$220	$180	$140	

Add 15% for "Sungrain" blonde maple wood (mfg. 1959-1961).

MODEL 870ADL – deluxe checkered version of 870AP. Mfg. 1950-63.

Plain Barrel	$400	$350	$300	$265	$220	$180	$140	
Matted Top Barrel	$425	$370	$320	$280	$235	$190	$150	
Vent. Rib	$450	$395	$340	$300	$250	$205	$160	

MODEL 870BDL – select walnut stock.

Plain Barrel	$450	$395	$340	$300	$250	$205	$160	
Vent. Rib	$500	$440	$375	$325	$275	$225	$175	

SPORTSMAN 12 PUMP – 12 ga. only (3 in. chamber), 28 or 30 in. barrel, recoil pad, VR standard, hardwood stock and forearm, Model 870 type action, 7 1/2 lbs. Mfg. 1984-86.

	$350	$300	$265	$240	$195	$160	$125	*$270*

Add 10% for Rem. chokes.

MODEL 870 DM – 12 ga., 18 1/2 in. barrel, fixed cylinder choke, 6 shot mag., bead sight, matte black synthetic or tactical hardwood stock, corn cobb forend, SuperCell recoil pad, matte blue finish, 7 1/2 lbs. Mfg. 2018-2020.

	$450	$395	$340	$300	$250	$200	$160	*$529*

* ***Model 870 DM Magpul*** – 12 ga., 18 1/2 in. barrel, Rem choke, 6 shot mag., XS ghost ring sights, matte black Magpul SGA stock and forend, tactical rail, matte blue finish, 7 1/2 lbs. Mfg. 2018-2020.

	$685	$600	$515	$465	$375	$310	$250	*$799*

* ***Model 870 DM Predator*** – 12 ga., 18 1/2 in. Rem choke barrel with two Trulock chokes, 3 or 6 shot mag., XS ghost ring sights, ShurShot overmolded stock, corn cob forend, Kryptek Highlander finish, 7 1/2 lbs. Mfg. 2018-2020.

	$685	$600	$515	$465	$375	$310	$250	*$799*

* ***Model 870 DM Tactical*** – 12 ga., 18 1/2 in. Rem choke barrel, ported tactical choke, 6 shot mag., XS ghost ring sights, matte black synthetic pistol grip stock, tactical corn cob forend, tactical rail, matte blue finish, 7 1/2 lbs. Mfg. 2018-2020.

	$685	$600	$515	$465	$375	$310	$250	*$799*

MODEL 870 EXPRESS – 12, 16 (mfg. 2002-06), 20 (mfg. 1991-2020), 28 ga. (disc., reintroduced 2002-04), or .410 bore (mfg. 1987-disc., reintroduced 2002-04, 2019), 2 3/4 or 3 in. chamber, 25 (28 ga. or .410 bore only), 26, or 28 in. VR Rem Chokes (12 or 20 ga., supplied with Mod. Rem Choke) barrel, parkerized metal, matte finished hardwood stock and forearm, solid recoil pad, 6-7 1/4 lbs. Mfg. 1987-2020.

	$355	$310	$265	$240	$195	$160	$125	*$417*

Add $128 for fully rifled cantilever in 12 (23 in.) or 20 (18 1/2 in., disc. 2015) ga.

Add $134 for .410 bore.

Add 15% for 28 ga. (disc.).

Add 10% (Last MSR was $447) for left-hand action (12 ga., 28 in. barrel only, mfg. 1998-2020).

Various combination packages (includes regular and deer barrels) are available in both 12 and 20 ga. Last MSR prices ranged from $550-$627.

* ***Model 870 Express Youth*** – 20 ga., 3 in. chamber, similar to Model 870 Express, except features 21 in. VR barrel, laminate stock, youth dimensions. Mfg. 1987-2020.

	$355	$310	$265	$240	$195	$160	$125	*$417*

GRADING - PPGS™	100%	98%	95%	90%	80%	70%	60%	LAST MSR

* ***Model 870 Express Synthetic*** – 12 or 16 ga. (disc. 2005), 26 or 28 in. VR barrel with one Rem Choke, black synthetic stock and forearm. Mfg. 1994-2020.

$355	$310	$265	$240	$195	$160	$125	*$417*

» **Model 870 Express Synthetic Youth Combo** – 20 ga., 3 in. chamber, 21 in. VR barrrel and 20 in. fully rifled deer barrel, Rem Chokes, rifle sights, 13 in. LOP, black finish, 6 lbs. Mfg. 1994-2020.

$525	$475	$400	$350	$300	$250	$200	*$627*

» **Model 870 Express Synthetic Deer** – 12 or 20 (disc. 2010) ga., 20 in. fully rifled barrel, 4 shot mag., rifle sights, black synthetic Monte Carlo stock, matte blue finish, 7 lbs. Mfg. 2002-2020.

$400	$350	$300	$275	$225	$185	$150	*$477*

* ***Model 870 Express Deer Gun*** – 12 or 20 (disc.) ga., 20 in. IC choked barrel or fully rifled barrel with rifle sights, Monte Carlo stock. Mfg. 1991-2020.

$355	$310	$265	$240	$195	$160	$125	*$417*

Add $46 for fully rifled barrel with rifle sights (Model 870 Express Fully Rifled Deer).
Add $126 for fully rifled barrel with cantilever scope mount in 12 (23 in. barrel) or 20 (18 1/2 in. barrel) ga. (disc. 2011).
Add $87 for fully rifled barrel with cantilever scope mount and Bushnell scope (12 or 20 ga., mfg. 2005).
Add $78 for cantilever scope mount and IC Rem Choke (disc. 1991).

* ***Model 870 Express Magnum ShurShot Deer*** – 12 or 20 ga., 23 in. fully rifled barrel with cantilever scope mount, black thumbhole ShurShot synthetic stock and forearm. Mfg. 2008-2014.

$475	$415	$350	$325	$275	$215	$180	*$536*

* ***Model 870 Express Turkey*** – 12 ga. only, 21 in. plain or VR barrel with Rem. turkey choke, choice of wood with flat finish (disc. 2008), Realtree Advantage (mfg. 1998-2005), Skyline Excel (mfg. 2003-05), or Mossy Oak New Break-Up (mfg. 2006-2020) camo stock and forearm, 7 1/4 lbs. Mfg. 1990-2020.

$425	$375	$325	$295	$235	$185	$160	*$492*

Subtract approx. 10% for wood stock and forearm.

* ***Model 870 Express Magnum Shurshot Turkey Camo*** – 12 ga., 21 in. VR barrel, Rem Chokes, 4 shot mag., with sights, Shurshot skeletonized Mossy Oak Obsession camo stock and forend, drilled and tapped for use with Weaver rail. Disc. 2020.

$460	$400	$350	$315	$255	$200	$160	*$536*

MODEL 870 EXPRESS COMBO – 12 ga., includes 23 in. cantilever fully rifled barrel and 28 in. VR barrel with Rem Chokes, matte finished hardwood stock and forearm, matte blue finish, 6 lbs. Mfg. 2008-2020.

$520	$450	$390	$350	$285	$240	$195	*$606*

This model was available through Remington Premier dealers only.

MODEL 870 EXPRESS COMPACT LAMINATE – 20 ga., 21 in. VR barrel with mod. Rem Chokes, matte black receiver and barrel finish, 13 in. LOP, laminate stock, 6 1/2 lbs. Disc. 2014.

$335	$270	$220	$190	$170	$155	$135	*$411*

* ***Model 870 Express Compact Synthetic*** – 20 ga., 21 in. VR barrel with Rem Chokes, 13 in. LOP and adj. LOP kit, SuperCell recoil pad, black synthetic stock and forearm, matte blue finish, 6 lbs. Mfg. 2009-2020.

$355	$310	$265	$240	$195	$160	$125	*$417*

* ***Model 870 Express Compact Camo*** – 20 ga., 21 in. barrel with Rem Chokes, 13 in. LOP and adj. LOP kit, SuperCell recoil pad, synthetic stock and forearm with RealTree Hardwoods or Mossy Oak Pink Blaze camo coverage, 6 lbs. Mfg. 2009-2020.

$400	$350	$300	$275	$225	$185	$150	*$468*

* ***Model 870 Express Compact (Youth)*** – 16 (mfg. 2004-2005) or 20 ga. only, 21 in. VR barrel with Rem Chokes, 13 in. LOP with recoil pad, choice of RealTree Advantage (mfg. 1998-2005), Mossy Oak Break-Up (mfg. 2006-2012), or Skyline Excel (mfg. 2003-05) camo or regular wood finish on stock and forearm, 6 lbs. Disc. 2012.

$335	$270	$220	$190	$170	$155	$135	*$411*

Add $43 for Youth Deer Gun (fully rifled 20 in. barrel, mfg. 1994-2008).
Add $87 for Youth Turkey with choice of NWTF Jake's Skyline Excel camo (disc. 2005).
Add $72 for Youth Turkey with camo (disc. 2006, reintroduced 2008-2009).

GRADING - PPGS™	100%	98%	95%	90%	80%	70%	60%	LAST MSR

MODEL 870 EXPRESS JUNIOR – 20 ga., 18 3/4 in. VR barrel, features Mossy Oak Break-Up camo finish on stock and forearm, matte metal finish, 6 lbs. Mfg. 2006-2008.

$360	$310	$270	$235	$200	$180	$160	*$445*

* ***Model 870 Express Jr. Compact*** – 20 ga., 18 3/4 in. barrel with Rem Choke, black synthetic stock and forearm, SuperCell recoil pad, 12 in. LOP and adj. LOP kit, matte blue finish, 5 3/4 lbs. Mfg. 2009-2020.

$355	$310	$265	$240	$195	$160	$125	*$417*

MODEL 870 EXPRESS HARDWOOD HOME DEFENSE – 12 ga., 18 1/2 in. barrel, fixed cylinder choke, 4 or 6 shot mag., single bead sights, traditional dark stain hardwood stock with satin finish, matte blue receiver finish, 7 1/2 lbs. Mfg. 2016-2020.

$355	$310	$265	$240	$195	$160	$125	*$420*

Add 5% (Last MSR was $444) for 6 shot mag.

MODEL 870 EXPRESS SYNTHETIC TACTICAL (HD, HOME DEFENSE) – 12 or 20 (mfg. 2007-2020, 7 shot mag. only) ga., 18 1/2 in. with fixed cyl. choked barrel with bead front sight, black synthetic stock and forend, black oxide metal finish, 7 1/2 lbs. Mfg. 1991-2020.

$375	$330	$280	$255	$200	$175	$135	*$443*

Add 5% (Last MSR was $467) for 12 ga. 6 shot tube mag.
Add 10% for 20 ga. 7 shot tube mag. (disc. 2015).
Add $187 for ghost ring sights with Rem Chokes.

* ***Model 870 Express Tactical*** – 12 ga., 18 1/2 in. barrel, fixed cylinder choke, 6 shot mag., single bead sights, matte black 6-pos. synthetic stock, Hogue pistol grip, matte blue finish. Mfg. 2018-2020.

$560	$475	$415	$375	$300	$250	$200	*$619*

* ***Model 870 Express Tactical Knoxx 20 Ga.*** – 20 ga., 18 1/2 in. barrel with fixed cyl. choke, 7 shot mag., Knoxx Spec-Ops stock, matte black finish, drilled and tapped, 6 lbs. Mfg. 2009-2015.

$450	$375	$320	$280	$240	$210	$180	*$555*

* ***Model 870 Express Tactical Camo*** – 12 ga., 18 1/2 in. barrel with Rem choke, 6 shot mag. with 2 shot mag. extension, XS Ghost Ring Sight Rail and XSR Ghost Ring sights, Speedfeed IV pistol grip synthetic stock with A-TACS camo coverage, SuperCell recoil pad, 7 1/2 lbs. Mfg. 2010-2015.

$585	$485	$435	$380	$325	$275	$225	*$720*

* ***Model 870 Express Tactical Magpul (2013-15 Mfg.)*** – 12 ga., 3 in. chamber, 18 1/2 in. barrel with tactical extended Rem choke, one-piece magazine tube, 6 shot, receiver Picatinny rail with fully adj. XS Ghost Ring rear sight with removable white bead front sight, features Magpul SGA stock, MOE forend, black or FDE (new 2014 only) Cerakote finish, includes "The Art of the Dynamic Shotgun" DVD, 7 1/2 lbs. Mfg. 2013-2015.

$775	$700	$600	$550	$450	$350	$275	*$898*

* ***Model 870 Express Tactical Magpul (2018-2020 Mfg.)*** – 12 ga., 18 1/2 in. barrel, fixed cylinder choke, 6 shot mag., single bead sights, matte black Magpul stock, tactical-style forend, 7 1/2 lbs. Mfg. 2018-2020.

$495	$435	$375	$335	$275	$225	$180	*$582*

* ***Model 870 Express Tactical Pachmayr*** – 12 ga., 18 1/2 in. barrel with cyl. choke, Pachmayr pistol grip, one-piece high strength magazine tube, black synthetic stock. Mfg. 2014-2015.

$425	$375	$335	$300	$250	$225	$195	*$497*

* ***Model 870 Express Tactical Side Folder*** – 12 or 20 ga., 18 1/2 in. barrel, Rem choke threaded muzzle, 6 shot mag., single bead sights, black synthetic right-hand folding stock, Versa Max soft touch adj. cheekpiece insert, QD cup attachment points, SuperCell recoil pad, adj. LOP kit, Tapko AK pattern SAW grip, MOE M-LOK compatible forend, drilled and tapped receiver, 8 lbs. Mfg. 2019-2020.

$925	$810	$695	$630	$510	$425	$325	*$1,095*

* ***Model 870 Express Specialty*** – 12 or 20 ga., 18 in. cylinder bore or Rem Choke barrel, folding or Knoxx Spec-Ops pistol grip stock, 2 or 7 shot mag extension. Mfg. 2008 only.

$365	$315	$270	$235	$200	$180	$160	*$452*

Add $27 for 2 shot mag. extension with Knoxx Spec-Ops stock.
Add $53 for synthetic folding stock with 7 shot mag extension.

This model was available through Remington Premier dealers only.

GRADING - PPGS™	100%	98%	95%	90%	80%	70%	60%	LAST MSR

MODEL 870 EXPRESS SUPER MAGNUM – 12 ga., 3 1/2 in. chamber, 23 (disc.), 26 (synthetic only), 28 or 30 (2007-disc) in. VR barrel, Rem Chokes, choice of checkered natural hardwood, black synthetic, or 100% camo stock and forearm (disc.), recoil pad, approx. 7 1/2 lbs. Mfg. 1998-2020.

$400 $350 $300 $275 $225 $185 $150 *$483*

Add $15 for synthetic non-camo Turkey Model with 23 in. barrel (mfg. 1999-2007).
Add $124 for 100% Skyline Fall Flight camo coverage (mfg. 2005).
Add $165 for combo package (hardwood only, includes 26 in. regular and 20 in. fully rifled deer barrel).

* ***Model 870 Express Super Magnum Camo*** – 12 ga., 26 in. vent. rib. barrel, Rem Chokes, 100% Mossy Oak Break-Up camo coverage, sling swivels, HiViz sights, camo sling. Mfg. 2008 only.

$430 $340 $275 $225 $185 $160 $145 *$545*

This model was available through Remington Premier dealers only.

* ***Model 870 Express Super Magnum Synthetic Camo*** – 12 ga., 3 1/2 in. chamber, 23 or 26 in. VR barrel with Rem Chokes, 100% Mossy Oak Break-Up camo coverage, wood or synthetic stock and forearm. Mfg. 1999 only.

$385 $320 $265 $240 $220 $200 $180 *$532*

* ***Model 870 Express Super Magnum Turkey Camo (1998-2010 Mfg.)*** – features Mossy Oak Break-Up (mfg. 2006-2010), 100% RealTree Advantage (disc. 2005) or Skyline Excel (mfg. 2003-05) camo on metal and stock/forearm, 23 in. VR barrel only with Turkey extra full Rem Choke, 7 1/4 lbs. Mfg. 1998-2010.

$475 $415 $360 $325 $280 $250 $225 *$587*

* ***Model 870 Express Super Magnum Turkey Camo (2010-2020 Mfg.)*** – 12 ga., 3 1/2 in. chamber, 26 in. barrel with one modified ProBore choke tubes and Hi-Viz sights, 100% Mossy Oak Bottom Land camo coverage, includes sling, 8 1/4 lbs. Mfg. 2010-2020.

$535 $470 $400 $365 $300 $250 $200 *$629*

* ***Model 870 Express Super Magnum Waterfowl Camo*** – 12 ga., 3 1/2 in. chamber, 28 in. barrel with extended waterfowl over decoys choke and Hi-Viz sights, 100% Mossy Oak Duck Blind or Mossy Oak Shadow Grass Blades (mfg. 2018-19) camo coverage, includes sling, 7 1/2 lbs. Disc. 2020.

$535 $470 $400 $365 $300 $250 $200 *$629*

MODEL 870 EXPRESS TRAP – 12 ga., 2 3/4 or 3 in. chamber, 30 in. VR barrel, Rem chokes, 4 shot, steel receiver with matte black finish, twin action bars, gold trigger, mid-bead and ivory front sights, black hardwood Monte Carlo stock and forend with satin finish, 7 1/2 lbs. Mfg. 2020 only.

$525 $460 $395 $350 $290 $235 $185 *$609*

MODEL 870 SPS SUPER MAG TURKEY/PREDATOR W/SCOPE – 12 ga., 3 1/2 in. chamber, 20 in. barrel, Rem Chokes, TruGlo red dot sights, 100% Mossy Oak Obsession camo coverage, includes scope and overmolded grips, 7 1/8 lbs. Mfg. 2010-2020.

$625 $550 $475 $425 $350 $300 $250 *$732*

MODEL 870 SPS SUPER MAG TURKEY – 12 ga., 3 1/2 in. chamber, 23 in. rifle sighted barrel, 100% RealTree AP HD camo coverage with ShurShot thumbhole stock and SuperCell recoil pad, Wingmaster HD extended Rem Choke, black sling, sling swivels, TruGlo fiber optic sights, 7 1/2 lbs. Mfg. 2008-2015.

$565 $470 $420 $365 $325 $295 $260 *$681*

MODEL 870 SPS SUPER MAG. MAX GOBBLER – 12 ga., 23 in. rifle sighted barrel, 100% RealTree APG HD camo Knoxx Spec-Ops stock, drilled and tapped, Williams Fire Sight fiber optic sights, R3 recoil pad, sling, Rem Chokes. Mfg. 2008 only.

$675 $550 $450 $350 $315 $275 $250 *$819*

MODEL 870 SPS SUPER SLUG – 12 ga., 3 in. chamber, 25 1/2 in. extra heavy fully rifled fluted barrel, ShurShot pistol grip stock with Mossy Oak Treestand camo coverage, drilled and tapped, Weaver rail, sling swivels, SuperCell recoil pad, 7 7/8 lbs. Mfg. 2009-2020.

$725 $625 $550 $495 $400 $325 $250 *$854*

MODEL 870 SPECIAL PURPOSE MARINE MAGNUM – 12 ga. only, 3 in. chamber, 18 in. plain barrel bored cyl., electroless nickel plated metal finish, 6 or 7 (disc.) shot mag., R3 recoil pad became standard during 2004, sling swivels and Cordura sling, 7 1/2 lbs. Disc. 2020.

$715 $625 $535 $485 $395 $320 $250 *$841*

Add $117 for XCS Marine Model with black TriNyte metal coating (mfg. 2007-08).

MODEL 870 SPORTSMAN FIELD – 12 or 20 ga., 3 in. chambers, 26 or 28 in. VR barrel, Rem Chokes, twin bead sights with HiViz sight kit, gold-plated trigger, satin finished Mahogany laminate stock and forend with fleur-de-lis checkering. Disc. 2015.

$425 $375 $325 $300 $225 $195 $150 *$477*

GRADING - PPGS™	100%	98%	95%	90%	80%	70%	60%	LAST MSR

MODEL 870 WINGMASTER – 12 or 20 ga., 26 or 28 in. vent. rib. barrel, Rem Chokes, high gloss semi-fancy Claro walnut stock, engraved receiver with pheasant and duck scenes, gold trigger, silver grip cap with raised Remington "R" logo. Mfg. 2008 only.

	$795	$725	$650	$575	$500	$450	$395	*$955*

This model was available through Remington Premier dealers only.

* ***Model 870 Wingmaster Claro*** – 12 ga., 28 in. VR barrel with Rem choke, 4 shot mag., twin bead sights, gloss finished Claro walnut stock, high polish blue finish, 7 lbs. Mfg. 2018-2020.

	$815	$715	$610	$550	$450	$365	$285	*$959*

MODEL 870 FIELD WINGMASTER – 12, 16 (disc. 1980, reintroduced late 2001), 20 (LW-20), 28 (disc. late 1994, reintroduced 1999) ga., or .410 (disc. late 1994, reintroduced 1999) bore, various barrel lengths (26, 28, and 30 are current mfg.), incorporates twin slide rails, 3 in. chamber in 12 ga. became standard in 1985, Rem Chokes became standard in 1987, lightweight frame on 20 ga. was introduced 1972, checkered walnut stock and forearm, a choice of high gloss or satin (28 in. barrel only) wood finish became available in 1991, approx. 6 1/2-7 1/4 lbs. Mfg. 1964-1984.

	$500	$425	$375	$325	$275	$225	$175	

* ***Model 870 Field Wingmaster With Vent. Rib*** – 12, 16 (disc.), or 20 (LW-20) ga., right or left-hand model (12 ga. only, disc. 1994), 26 or 28 in. VR barrel with Rem Choke, twin bead sights, satin or high gloss American walnut stock, high polish blued finish, 6 3/4-7 lbs. Mfg. 1985-2020.

	$725	$635	$545	$495	$400	$325	$255	*$847*

Subtract 10% without Rem Chokes.
Add $48 for left-hand model (12 ga. only, disc. 1994).
Add $80 for 20 in. fully rifled deer barrel with cantilever scope mount (12 ga. - mfg. 1992-99 or 20 ga. - mfg. 1992-95).

Beginning 1998, rolled scroll engraving started to appear on 20 ga. guns only. During 2005, a Wingmaster Jr. was released in a LW-20 in 20 ga. with 12 in. LOP and 18 3/4 in. barrel at no extra charge.

* ***Model 870 Field Wingmaster Small Gauge*** – 28 ga. or .410 bore, scaled down 870 on lightweight smaller frame, 25 in. fixed (F or M, .410 bore only) or Rem Choke (28 ga. only, mfg. 1999-2020) barrel, VR became standard 1984, satin finished American walnut stock, 6-6 1/2 lbs. Mfg. 1969-94, reintroduced 1999-2020.

	$765	$675	$575	$525	$425	$350	$300	*$904*

Add $58 for 28 ga.
Subtract 15% if w/o VR.

* ***Model 870 Field Wingmaster 50th Anniversary Classic Trap*** – 12 ga. only, 2 3/4 in. chamber, high polish blue fine line embellished receiver with gold inlays, 30 in. low profile light contour barrel, checkered high gloss semi-fancy American walnut stock and forearm with cut checkering, 8 lbs. Mfg. 2000-2020.

	$975	$850	$725	$665	$535	$450	$350	*$1,153*

* ***Model 870 Field Wingmaster 100th Anniversary*** – 12 ga., features "100th Anniversary of Pump Action Shotguns" embellished on left side of receiver with gold banners, fleur-de-lis laser engraved checkering on high gloss walnut stock and forearm. Mfg. 2008 only.

	$830	$665	$500	$400	$350	$300	$285	*$1,035*

This model was available through Remington Premier dealers only.

* ***Model 870 Field Wingmaster Dale Earnhardt Tribute*** – 12 (mfg. 2005 only) or 20 (mfg. 2006 only) ga., 28 in. VR barrel with Rem Chokes, special embellishments featuring Dale Earnhardt. Mfg. 2005-06.

	$710	$575	$475	$400	$345	$300	$265	*$820*

* ***Model 870 Field Wingmaster NRA Edition*** – 12 ga., 28 in. VR barrel, features NRA Heritage logo on receiver. Mfg. 2006 only.

	$495	$395	$325	$275	$220	$195	$175	*$685*

MODEL 870 WINGMASTER - 200TH YEAR ANNIVERSARY LIMITED EDITION – 12 ga., 26 in. barrel, C-Grade walnut stock with fleur-de-lis checkering, medallion in grip, Classic American style engraving and gold inlay, includes special serial number, limited to quantity of 2,016. Limited mfg. 2016 only.

	$1,375	$1,150	$975	$850	$725	$600	$500	*$1,499*

MODEL 870 WINGMASTER 3 1/2 IN. SUPER MAGNUM – 12 ga. only, 28 in. VR barrel with choke tubes, high polish blue with receiver engraving, high gloss walnut stock and forearm with cut checkering, 7 1/2 lbs. Mfg. 2000-2006.

	$610	$500	$410	$355	$300	$265	$250	*$732*

GRADING - PPGS™ 100% 98% 95% 90% 80% 70% 60% LAST MSR

MODEL 870 WINGMASTER AMERICAN CLASSIC – 12, 20, or 28 (mfg. 2014 only) ga., 25 (mfg. 2014 only), 26, or 28 in. VR barrel with Rem choke tubes, features fleur-de-lis checkering on "B" Grade American walnut stock and forearm, machine cut engraved receiver with gold filled "American Classic" banner on right side, white diamond forearm grip cap, vent. recoil pad, white line spacer, high polished blued finish, 6 1/2-8 lbs. Mfg. 2014-2016.

$1,075 $950 $775 $650 $525 $425 $375 *$1,249*

MODEL 870 MAGNUM DUCK GUN – 3 in. chamber, 12 or 20 ga., 26, 28, or 30 in. full or mod. barrel, recoil pad, 3 in. chambers became standard on all Model 870s starting in 1985. Rem Chokes became standard 1987 (introduced 1986 as $40 option). Mfg. 1964-disc.

$500 $425 $375 $325 $275 $225 $175

MODEL 870 SPECIAL PURPOSE – 12 ga. only, differs only in that metal parts are sand blasted, choice of Mossy Oak Camo (new 1992), black synthetic, or checkered wood stock with low luster finish, 21 (Turkey barrel), 26, or 28 in. VR barrel. Rem Chokes were introduced 1986.

Add $75 for wood stock and forearm (disc. 1992).
Subtract 10% without Rem Chokes.

* ***Model 870 Special Purpose Super Magnum Synthetic Camo*** – 12 ga. only, 3 1/2 in. chamber, 26 or 28 in. VR barrel with Rem Chokes, available in either Mossy Oak (disc. 1995), Bottomland (disc. 1996), full coverage Mossy Oak Break-Up (mfg. 1997-2005) or Mossy Oak Obsession (mfg. 2006-07) finish. Mfg. 1994-2007.

$575 $475 $375 $300 $265 $225 $190 *$741*

* ***Model 870 Special Purpose SPS-T (Turkey) Super Magnum*** – 12 ga. only, features 3 1/2 in. chamber, choice of 23, 26 (disc. 2004), or 28 (mfg. 2001-2004) in. VR barrel with Rem Chokes, fully camouflaged in Mossy Oak Break-Up (disc. 2005) or Obsession (new 2005) pattern, choice of standard wood, thumbhole (new 2005), or synthetic (26 in. barrel only) stock. Mfg. 2000-2007.

$575 $475 $375 $300 $265 $225 $190 *$741*

Add $58 for TruGlo rifle sights thumbhole stock and with 100% Mossy Oak Obsession coverage (new 2005).
Add $18 for cantilever scope mount (mfg. 2001-2005) with Turkey super full choke tube.
Add approx. $330 if with Leupold Gilmore red dot sights and Turkey super full choke tube - 23 in. barrel only (mfg. 2000 only).
Add $58 for Maxx Gobbler model with 100% RealTree APG HD camo coverage, Knoxx Special Ops stock, and Williams Fire Sights (new 2007).

* ***Model 870 Special Purpose SPS-BG Camo (Special Purpose Synthetic Big Game)*** – 12 ga. only, 20 in. plain barrel with rifle sights and Rem Chokes. Mfg. 1994 only.

$350 $285 $235 $200 $170 $150 $130 *$442*

* ***Model 870 Special Purpose Deer*** – 12 ga., 3 in. chamber, grey laminate thumbhole stock and forearm with R3 recoil pad, 23 in. fully rifled barrel with cantilever scope mount, 8 1/8 lbs. Mfg. 2006-2007.

$650 $575 $525 $450 $400 $365 $335 *$799*

* ***Model 870 Special Purpose Synthetic ShurShot*** – 12 ga., features 23 in. fully rifled barrel with cantilever scope mount, 3 lbs. trigger pull, ShurShot thumbhole stock with SuperCell recoil pad and extended forearm grip, RealTree Hardwoods HD camo on stock and forend. Mfg. 2008-2009.

$525 $475 $425 $365 $325 $275 $235 *$652*

* ***Model 870 Special Purpose Turkey (SPS-T)*** – 12 (disc. 2004) or 20 ga., 20 (new 2002) or 21 in. VR barrel, Rem Chokes, available in flat black, Mossy Oak (disc. 1996, reintroduced 2002), Greenleaf (disc. 1996), or Realtree X-tra Brown (full SPS-T-camo, mfg. 1997 only) finish. Disc. 1999, reintroduced 2002-2005.

$460 $365 $285 $250 $215 $180 $170 *$621*

This model was also available 2002-2003 in a Youth Model with 1 in. shorter LOP.

* ***Model 870 Special Purpose Deer Gun (SPS-Deer)*** – 12 ga. only, 3 in. chamber, 20 in. Rem Chokes barrel (disc. 1992) or fully rifled barrel with rifle sights (new 1993), satin finished (disc. 1992) or black synthetic (new 1993) stock and forearm, matte black metal, 7 1/4 lbs. Mfg. 1989-1999.

$350 $300 $265 $240 $195 $160 $125 *$436*

Add $28 for deer barrel with Rem Chokes and cantilever scope mount (disc. 1996).
Add $60 for fully rifled deer barrel with cantilever scope mount.
Add $65 for cantilever scope mount system (disc. 1992).

GRADING - PPGS™	100%	98%	95%	90%	80%	70%	60%	LAST MSR

* ***Model 870 Special Purpose Super Slug Deer (SPS Super Slug Deer)*** – 12 or 20 (new 2004) ga., 3 in. chamber, 23 in. fully rifled barrel with cantilever scope mount, matte black metal finish, black synthetic Monte Carlo stock and forearm, approx. 8 lbs. Mfg. 1999-2004.

$470	$375	$310	$255	$225	$195	$175	*$580*

MODEL 870 XCR (XTREME CONDITIONS) – 12 ga., 28 in. VR barrel, Rem Chokes, black synthetic or Mossy Oak Duck Blind (Waterfowl) camo coverage, TriNyte PVD coating, Speedfeed stock, nickel plated internal parts. Mfg. 2008 only.

$675	$550	$425	$350	$315	$275	$250	*$899*

Add $56 for Waterfowl model with camo.

This model was available through Remington Premier dealers only.

MODEL 870 LIGHTWEIGHT – 20 ga. only, lighter and shorter mahogany stock than magnum model, 23 in. barrel. Mfg. 1972-83.

$350	$300	$265	$240	$195	$160	$125	

Add 10% for VR.

MODEL 870 LIGHTWEIGHT (MAGNUM) – 20 ga., 3 in. chamber, 26 or 28 in. barrel, Rem Chokes became standard 1987, 6 lbs. Mfg. 1972-1994.

$400	$350	$300	$265	$220	$180	$140	*$460*

Subtract 10% without Rem Chokes.
Subtract $40 without VR.

MODEL 870 SPECIAL FIELD – 12 or 20 (LW-20) ga., lighter straight grip stock with solid recoil pad, 21 (disc. 1993) or 23 (new 1994) in. VR barrel, Rem Chokes became standard 1987 (introduced 1986 as $40 option), 6 1/4 or 7 lbs. Mfg. 1984-1995.

$400	$350	$300	$265	$220	$180	$140	*$473*

Subtract 10% without Rem Chokes.

MODEL 870 BRUSHMASTER – 12 or 20 (disc.) ga., 20 in. barrel with imp. cyl. (disc.) or Rem Chokes and rifle sights, 3 in. chamber standard for 1985, normal bluing with satin finished wood. Disc. 1994.

$400	$350	$300	$265	$220	$180	$140	*$452*

Add $43 for left-hand model.

MODEL 870 POLICE – 12 ga. only, 18 or 20 in. plain barrel, choice of blue or parkerized finish, bead or rifle (disc. 1995, 20 in. barrel only) sights, Police cylinder (disc.) or IC choke. Mfg. 1994-2006 (last year of civilian sales).

$450	$395	$340	$300	$250	$205	$160	*$492*

Add $13 for parkerized finish.
Add $44 for rifle sights (disc. 1995).

Remington also offers a Model 870P, 870P MAX, 870MCS, and 870P Synthetic for police/law enforcement, featuring extended capacity magazines, improved cylinder chokes, collapsible stocks, with some models having shorter than 18 in. barrels. While Remington does not publish consumer retail pricing for these police/law enforcement models, secondary prices for these guns will be slightly higher than for current pricing on the Model 870 Police.

MODEL 870 TACTICAL – 12 ga. only, 3 in. chamber, 18 or 20 in. fixed IC choke barrel, 6 or 7 (20 in. barrel only) shot mag., OD Green metal finish, black synthetic tactical or Knoxx Spec-Ops adj. recoil absorbing stock with pistol grip, open sights, approx. 7 1/2 lbs. Mfg. 2006 only.

$515	$465	$425	$385	$350	$320	$290	*$599*

Add $26 for Spec-Ops adj. stock.

MODEL 870 TAC-2/TAC-3 – 12 ga., 3 in. chamber, 18 or 20 (disc) in. cyl. bore barrel, black oxide metal finish, black synthetic stock and forearm, pistol grip with choice of Knoxx Spec-Ops folding stock (Tac-2 FS), Knoxx Spec-Ops tube stock or regular synthetic (disc. 2008) stock, 6 (Tac-2 w/18 in. barrel) or 8 (Tac-3 w/20 in. barrel, disc. 2008) shot mag., bead sights, R3 recoil pad on fixed stock, approx. 7 lbs. Mfg. 2007-2016.

$615	$535	$470	$415	$380	$340	$300	*$750*

MODEL 870 TAC-14 SERIES – 12 or 20 ga., 2 3/4 in. chamber, 14 in. barrel w/raised front bead sight, features short Shockwave Raptor pistol grip stock, various configurations. Mfg. 2018-2020.

* ***Model 870 Tac-14*** – 12 or 20 ga., 2 3/4 in. chamber, 14 in. cyl. bore barrel w/raised front bead sight, 4 shot tube mag., choice of hardwood shortened buttstock and grooved forearm or black synthetic shortened buttstock and Magpul M-LOK forearm, matte blue frame and barrel, approx. 5 1/2 lbs. Mfg. 2018-2020.

$400	$365	$335	$310	$285	$265	$250	*$456*

Add $22 for 20 ga.
Add $295 for arm brace.
Add $58 for hardwood stock and grooved forearm.

GRADING - PPGS™	100%	98%	95%	90%	80%	70%	60%	LAST MSR

* ***Model 870 DM Tac-14*** – 12 ga., 2 3/4 in. chamber, 14 in. barrel w/raised front bead sight, 6 shot detachable mag., black synthetic shortened buttstock and Magpul M-LOK forearm, 6 lbs. Mfg. 2018-2020.

	$500	$450	$400	$365	$335	$310	$285	*$576*

* ***Model 870 Tac-14 Marine Magnum*** – 12 ga., 2 3/4 in. chamber, 14 in. barrel w/raised front bead sight, 4 shot tube mag., black synthetic shortened buttstock and Magpul M-LOK forearm, Electroless nickel plated frame and barrel, approx. 5 1/2 lbs. Mfg. 2018-2020.

	$750	$650	$575	$500	$425	$375	$325	*$866*

MODEL 870 TACTICAL BLACKHAWK – 12 ga. only, 3 in. chamber, 18 in. barrel with fixed cyl. choke, grooved pistol grip with Blackhawk Spec Ops II adj. stock, 6 shot mag., blasted black oxide finish, 7 lbs. Mfg. 2012-2016.

	$550	$465	$415	$365	$325	$295	$260	*$638*

MODEL 870 TACTICAL DESERT RECON – 12 ga., 18 or 20 in. barrel, Digital Tiger TSP Desert Camo stock and forend, special ported tactical extended Rem Choke tubes, Speedfeed stock with 2 or 3 shot carrier. Mfg. 2008-2009.

	$575	$500	$450	$400	$365	$335	$295	*$692*

Add $67 for 20 in. barrel.

MODEL 870 RIOT – 12 ga. only, 18 or 20 in. barrel, choice of blue or parkerized metal finish. Disc. 1991.

	$400	$350	$300	$265	$220	$180	$140	*$355*

Add $40 for police rifle sights (20 in. barrel only).

MODEL 870 D-GRADE (TOURNAMENT) – custom order only, any gauge. Mfg. 1950-2020.

	N/A	$2,900	$2,075	N/A	N/A	N/A	N/A	*$4,532 (2007)*

MODEL 870 F-GRADE (PREMIER) – custom order only, any gauge. Mfg. 1950-2020.

	N/A	$6,500	$4,500	N/A	N/A	N/A	N/A	*$8,799 (2007)*

MODEL 870 F-GRADE W/GOLD (GOLD PREMIER) – with gold inlays, custom order only. Mfg. 1950-2020.

	N/A	$8,000	$6,000	N/A	N/A	N/A	N/A	*$11,999 (2007)*

MODEL 870 DUCKS UNLIMITED – for DU individual chapter dinner guns, please refer to listings in the Ducks Unlimited section, "DU" in serial number, disc., available online at BlueBookofGunValues.com/overflow.

There are two main variations of Model 870 DU shotguns. The most desirable are those guns specifically manufactured for DU individual chapters, which are auctioned off at each chapter's annual banquet. These shotguns are referred to as "dinner guns", and since they are individually auctioned off at each chapter, prices can vary considerably from one chapter location to another. Please refer to individual listings in the Ducks Unlimited section for Model 870 DU dinner guns and current values.

The second Model 870 DU variation is a special/limited edition which is typically not auctioned off at the individual DU chapters. These limited/special editions are usually sold through normal firearms distribution, which includes both distributors and dealers. Values for these Model 870 DU special/limited editions generally command a small premium above normal Model 870 prices, if condition is NIB.

MODEL 870 "WILDLIFE FOR TOMORROW" – 12 ga. only, side panels fine line laser etched with gold engraving, special wood, 2,000 mfg. for Wildlife Forever fundraiser 1996.

	$325	$250	$175	N/A	N/A	N/A	N/A

MODEL 870 150TH ANNIVERSARY – 12 ga. only, 2,534 mfg. 1966 only.

	$400	$325	$275	N/A	N/A	N/A	N/A

MODEL 870 - 200TH YEAR ANNIVERSARY COMMEMORATIVE – 12 ga., 28 in. barrel, A-Grade walnut stock with fleur-de-lis checkering, medallion in grip, matte black finish. Limited mfg. 2016 only.

	$550	$475	$425	$375	$325	$275	$225	*$599*

MODEL 870 BICENTENNIAL – 12 ga. only, configurations include Trap, Skeet, and Trade, mfg. to commemorate U.S. Bicentennial (1776-1976).

Trap or Skeet	$450	$375	$300	N/A	N/A	N/A	N/A
Trade	$400	$325	$250	N/A	N/A	N/A	N/A

In 1976, the 870 Bicentennial Trap retailed for $255 ($265 w/Monte Carlo stock), and the Skeet retailed for $220.

GRADING - PPGS™	100%	98%	95%	90%	80%	70%	60%	LAST MSR

MODEL 870 SC SKEET – 12, 16 (disc. 1960), or 20 ga., 26 in. VR skeet bore barrel, C grade hand checkered wood stock. Mfg. 1950-79.

	$600	$445	$365	$280	$245	$210	$185	

MODEL 870 SKEET MATCHED PAIR – includes .410 bore and 28 ga., 1,503 cased sets mfg. 1969 only.

	$1,150	$995	$895	$785	$655	$550	$465	

MODEL 870 TA TRAP – 12 ga. trap model, deluxe walnut, VR. Mfg. 1978-86.

	$425	$375	$325	$275	$250	$225	$200	*$430*

Add $15 for Monte Carlo stock.

MODEL 870 TB TRAP – similar to 870, with 28 or 30 in. VR full choke barrel, trap stock, recoil pad. Mfg. 1950-81.

	$425	$375	$325	$275	$250	$225	$200	

MODEL 870 TC TRAP – higher grade walnut and special VR, Rem Chokes became standard 1987. Mfg. 1950-1979, reintroduced 1996-1999.

	$600	$475	$400	$350	$275	$240	$220	*$680*

Subtract 5% if w/o Monte Carlo stock.
Add 20% for early Model 870 TC Trap guns with hand cut checkering.

MODEL 870 COMPETITION TRAP – 12 ga. single shot competition model, reduced recoil, competition walnut stock with cut checkering, VR. 5,300 mfg. 1980-86.

	$550	$475	$395	$350	$315	$275	$250	*$680*

MODEL 870 ALL AMERICAN TRAP – 30 in. full choke barrel, engraved receiver, trigger guard and barrel, deluxe trap stock. Approx. 1,000 mfg. 1972-76.

	$795	$700	$650	$605	$495	$440	$385	

MODEL 887 NITRO MAG SPS – 12 ga., 3 1/2 in. chamber, action design based on Model 870, 26 or 28 in. VR threaded barrel, Rem Chokes, steel liner encased in thick polymer jacket, SuperCell recoil system, HiViz front sight, synthetic stock and forearm with specially contoured grip panels, push-button trigger guard safety, sling swivels, features Armorlokt coating on all exterior metal surfaces which eliminates rust, matte black finish, approx. 7 1/2 lbs. Mfg. 2009-2015.

	$375	$315	$280	$250	$225	$200	$180	*$445*

* ***Model 887 Nitro Mag Waterfowl Camo*** – 12 ga., 3 1/2 in. chamber, similar to Model 887 Nitro Mag SPS, except has 28 in. barrel, 100% RealTree Advantage Max-4 HD camo coverage. Mfg. 2009-2015.

	$480	$430	$365	$325	$295	$265	$240	*$594*

Add $145 for combo package with Mossy Oak Break Up camo and extra 22 in. turkey barrel (disc. 2012).

* ***Model 887 SPS Bone Collector*** – 12 ga., 3 in. chamber, 26 in. VR barrel, Rem Chokes, 100% AP HD camo coverage, features "Bone Collector" logo, otherwise similar to Model 887 Nitro Mag SPS, 7 1/4 lbs. Mfg. 2010-2011.

	$525	$475	$425	$365	$325	$285	$240	*$642*

MODEL 887 NITRO MAG TACTICAL – 12 ga., 3 in. chamber, 18 1/2 in. threaded barrel with Rem Chokes, Hi-Viz front sight, black synthetic stock and forearm, 4 shot mag. and 2 shot extension with mag. tube hanger bracket, Picatinny rail, SuperCell recoil pad, ArmorLokt coated metal finish, 6 7/8 lbs. Mfg. 2010-2015.

	$425	$380	$335	$295	$260	$230	$195	*$534*

RENATO GAMBA

Please refer to the Gamba listing in the G section.

RENETTE, GASTINNE

Please refer to the Gastinne Renette listing in the G section.

REPUBLIC ARMS, INC.

Previous manufacturer 1997-2001, and located in Chino, CA.

PISTOLS: SEMI-AUTO

THE PATRIOT – .45 ACP cal., DAO, ultra compact with 3 in. barrel, 6 shot mag., ultra compact black polymer frame and stainless steel slide (either brushed or with black Melonite coating, new 2000), locked breech action, checkered grips, 20 oz. Mfg. 1997-2001.

	$265	$230	$210	$185	$175	$165	$155	

Last MSR $299.

GRADING - PPGS™	100%	98%	95%	90%	80%	70%	60%	LAST MSR

REPUBLIC ARMS OF SOUTH AFRICA

Previous manufacturer located in Jeppestown, Union of South Africa. Previously imported until 2002 by TSF Ltd., located in Fairfax, VA.

PISTOLS: SEMI-AUTO

RAP 401 - 9mm Para. cal., 8 shot mag., otherwise similar to Rap-440. Importation 1999-circa 2002.

$550	$450	$400	$350	$325	$300	$275	

RAP-440 - .40 S&W cal., compact DA/SA, 3 1/2 in. barrel with high contrast 3-dot sights, last shot hold open, hammer drop safety/decocking lever, firing pin block safety, 7 shot mag., all steel construction, 31 1/2 oz., includes case, spare magazine, and lock. Imported 1998-circa 2002.

$545	$475	$425	$395	$375	$330	$300	

Add $50 for Trilux Tritium night sights.

SHOTGUNS: SLIDE ACTION

MUSLER MODEL - 12 ga., lightweight shotgun, polymer reinforced stock and forearm, action opening release lever, action locks open after the last round. Imported 1998-circa 2002.

$625	$550	$475	$425	$375	$330	$300	

REPUBLIC FORGE

Current pistol manufacturer established in 2014, located in Friona, TX and Albuquerque, NM. Previously located in Perryton, TX.

Republic Forge builds world-class 1911 pistols by hand, with American-made parts, one gun at a time, in the USA.

PISTOLS: SEMI-AUTO

Republic Forge has a Build Your Own feature on their website which allows you to choose from several different options to select the custom gun of your choice. Each gun made by Republic Forge is built per individual custom order. The models listed below reflect base MSRs and information. Please contact the company directly for more information including options, a personal quotation, and delivery time.

REPUBLIC FORGE CUSTOM MODEL - built per customer specifications with the following standard options for the Defiant, General, Long Slide, Patriot, Raider, Republic, or Stryker models: .45 ACP cal., Officer, Commander, or Government slide and frame, loop hammer, Texas star hammer, or National Match Zia hammer, standard or ambi safety, front sights include red or green fiber optic or gold bead, rear sights include Novak night or Novak adj. sights, standard grip options include Black Desert Sand, Black Grey, Desert Camo, Dirty Olive, Green Canvas, Hyena Brown, Recon Black, Republic Forge, Tiger Stripe, or walnut, standard frame or slide finish options include Burnt Bronze, Barret Bronze, Blue Titanium, Graphite Black, OD Green, Multicam, Sniper Grey, Socom Blue, Texas Tan, or Tungsten Grey, other options include magwell, carry cut, contrasting controls, lightweight frame, RMR, or front serrations.

Add $135 for 9mm Para., 10mm, .38 Super, or .40 S&W cal.
Add $300 for Bison Bone grips.
Add $425 for blued, hard chrome, or color case finish.
Add $900 for Mammoth Ivory, $1,050 for Mammoth Ivory Exotic, or $1,200 for Mammoth Tooth Ivory grips.
Add $1,700 for Damasteel slide finish.

* ***Defiant*** - 3.5 in. Officer slide on Commander frame.

Current base MSR is $3,120.

* ***General*** - 3.5 in. Officer slide and frame.

Current base MSR is $3,120.

* ***Long Slide*** - 6 in. long slide on Government frame.

Current base MSR is $3,720.

* ***Patriot*** - 4.25 in. Commander slide and frame.

Current base MSR is $3,120.

* ***Raider*** - 5 in. Government Recon model with light rail.

Current base MSR is $3,270.

* ***Republic*** - 5 in. Government slide and frame.

Current base MSR is $3,120.

* ***Stryker*** - 4.25 in. Commander Recon model with light rail.

Current base MSR is $3,270.

GRADING - PPGS™	100%	98%	95%	90%	80%	70%	60%	LAST MSR

TEXAN – .45 ACP, 9mm Para., 10mm, .38 Super, or .40 S&W cal., Commander frame, Double Stack slide, 4 1/4 in. barrel, 25 LPI checkering on front strap, serrations on top of slide, color coordinated VZ grips, choice of finish. Disc.

	$2,975	$2,600	$2,225	$2,025	$1,650	$1,350	$1,050	*$3,295*

Add $125 for 9mm Para., 10mm, .38 Super, or .40 S&W cal.

VALIANT – .45 ACP, 9mm Para., 10mm, .38 Super, or .40 S&W cal., Officer frame/Commander slide (.40 S&W and .45 ACP cal. only), 4 1/4 in. barrel, 25 LPI checkering on front strap, serrations on top of slide, color coordinated VZ grips (Standard or Magwell only), choice of finish. Disc. 2020.

Last base MSR was $3,120.

Add $135 for 9mm Para., 10mm, .38 Super, or .40 S&W cal.

WAR HAMMER – .45 ACP, 9mm Para., 10mm, .38 Super, or .40 S&W cal., Government frame, double stack slide, 5 in. barrel, color coordinated VZ grips, 25 LPI checkering on front strap, serrations on top of slide, choice of finish. Disc.

	$2,975	$2,600	$2,225	$2,025	$1,650	$1,350	$1,050	*$3,295*

Add $125 for 9mm Para., 10mm, .38 Super, or .40 S&W cal.

RETAY ARMS CORP.

Current manufacturer located in Konya, Turkey. Currently imported by Retay USA, located in Easton, MD. Previously located in Darnestown, MD.

Retay Arms Corp. manufactures a line of good quality semi-auto shotguns using an inertia action and removable trigger assembly. The company also manufactures a complete lineup of blank pistols, air rifles, and spear guns. Please contact the importer directly for a listing of current dealers that will provide model information, availability, and pricing.

SHOTGUNS: SEMI-AUTO

MASAI MARA SERIES – 12 ga., 3 or 3 1/2 in. chamber, Inertia System w/Inertia Plus Rotating Bolt, 24-30 in. drilled Bohler barrel, removable Marapro chokes, 3 or 4 shot mag, RTS (Removable Trigger System), TruGlo or AR-style w/Picatinny rail mounted adj. ghost ring (Tactical) fiber optic sights, walnut (Upland model only) or molded ABS stock w/adj. fit plate and shim system, crossbolt push-button safety, steel upper and aluminum, anodized, hydrographic, or Cerakote lower receiver, black finish, additional Cerakote finishes are available, 6-7 lbs. Importation began circa 2017.

MSRs on this model and variations can range from $1,099-$2,100.

REVOLUTIONARY ROLLER LOCKS

Current manufacturer of firearms and accessories, located in Frisco, TX.

Revolutionary Roller Locks offers H&K style roller-delayed blowback firearms, custom builds, and additional gunsmithing services. Please contact the manufacturer directly for pricing and availability on their models.

REX

Current trademark of pistols and rifles manufactured by AREX, located in Slovenia and imported by the FIME Group, LLC located in Las Vegas, NV. Please see AREX in the A section for individual model listings.

REXIO

Previous trademark of guns manufactured in Argentina beginning late 1999. Previously imported and distributed until 2002 by VAM Distribution Company, LLC, located in Wooster, OH.

For individual model listings, please go to BlueBookOfGunValues.com/overflow.

RHINO RIFLES (RHINO ARMS)

Previous rifle manufacturer located in St. Louis, MO until 2017. Previously located in Washington, MO.

For individual model listings, please go to BlueBookOfGunValues.com/overflow.

RHODE ISLAND ARMS COMPANY

Previous manufacturer located in Hope Valley, RI.

SHOTGUNS: O/U

MORRONE MODEL – 12 or 20 ga., 26 or 28 in. plain barrels, boxlock, extractors, single trigger, checkered straight or pistol grip stock. Mfg. 1949-1953, only 500 of these guns were mfg., 450 in 12 ga., and 50 in 20 ga., very few with VR, they are quite rare although collector interest is not overwhelming.

	$1,100	$880	$770	$660	$550	$495	$440	

Add 20% for 20 gauge. Add 20% for VR.

GRADING - PPGS™	100%	98%	95%	90%	80%	70%	60%	LAST MSR

RIB MOUNTAIN ARMS, INC.

Previous rifle manufacturer circa 1992-2000, and located in Beresford and Sturgis, SD.

RIFLES: BOLT ACTION

MODEL 92 – .50 BMG cal., match grade barrel with muzzle brake, long action, walnut thumbhole stock, Timney trigger, approx. 28 lbs. Mfg. 1997-2000.

	$3,175	$2,725	$2,275	$2,000	$1,750	$1,575	$1,300	*$3,475*

MODEL 93 – similar to Model 92, except has short action with removable shell holder bolt, approx. 25 lbs. Mfg. 1997-2000.

	$3,175	$2,725	$2,275	$2,000	$1,750	$1,575	$1,300	*$3,475*

RICHLAND ARMS COMPANY

Previous importer (until 1986) located in Blissfield, MI. The models listed were made by various manufacturers located in either Italy or Spain.

SHOTGUNS

MODEL 80 LS SINGLE SHOT – 12, 20 ga., or .410 bore, 26 or 28 in. full choke barrel. Mfg. 1986 only.

	$140	$120	$110	$100	$90	$80	$70	*$162*

MODEL 711 MAGNUM SxS – 10 ga., 3 1/2 in. chamber, 12 ga., 3 in. chamber, 32 in. full and full, 30 in. full and full, 20, 28 ga., and .410 bore also available on special order, hammerless, boxlock, extractors, checkered walnut stock, recoil pad. Mfg. 1963-1985 in Spain.

10 gauge	$400	$325	$275	$250	$230	$210	$190	
12 gauge	$340	$295	$265	$250	$230	$210	$190	
20 gauge	$450	$340	$295	$260	$230	$210	$195	

MODEL 707 DELUXE SxS – 12 or 20 ga., 3 in. chambers, 26, 28, or 30 in. barrels, various chokes, boxlock, extractors, double triggers, checkered stock and forend. Mfg. 1963-1972 in Spain.

	$330	$300	$275	$250	$230	$210	$190	

MODEL 200 FIELD GRADE SxS – 12, 16, 20, 28 ga., or .410 bore, 22, 26, and 28 in. barrels, various chokes, Anson & Deeley boxlock, extractors, double triggers, checkered stock, 6 lbs. 2 oz. - 7 lbs. 4 oz. Mfg. 1963-85 in Spain.

	$330	$300	$275	$250	$230	$210	$190	*$379*

Add 20% for 20 ga., or 50% for 28 ga. or .410 bore.

MODEL 202 ALL PURPOSE SxS – similar to Field, except 2 sets of barrels, 12 and 20 ga. only. Mfg. 1963-disc. in Spain.

	$450	$400	$350	$300	$275	$250	$225	

Add 20% for 20 ga., or 50% for 28 ga. or .410 bore.

MODEL 41 ULTRA O/U – 20, 28 ga., or .410 bore, 3 in. chambers (.410 bore only), single non-selective trigger, 26 or 28 in. barrels, extractors, VR, engraved silver finished receiver, select checkered walnut stock and forearm, 6 lbs. 2 oz. Importation disc. 1986.

	$395	$350	$300	$260	$230	$200	$180	*$298*

MODEL 747 O/U – 12 or 20 ga. only, 3 in. chambers, Greener crossbolt, boxlock action, VR and barrels, SST, extractors. Importation disc. 1986.

	$475	$425	$350	$325	$310	$295	$280	*$464*

MODEL 757 O/U – 12 ga., 3 in. chambers, boxlock action with Greener crossbolt, vent. barrels and rib, double triggers, extractors, walnut stock and forearm, 7 lbs. 4 oz. New 1986. Importation disc. 1986.

	$325	$275	$225	$200	$185	$170	$155	*$325*

Add 20% for multi-chokes (Model 7570).

MODEL 787 O/U – 12 ga. only, 3 in. chambers, boxlock action with silver finish, single trigger, vent. barrels and rib, extractors, walnut stock with recoil pad, is supplied with 5 interchangeable choke tubes, 7 1/4 lbs. Made 1986 only.

	$495	$440	$380	$340	$310	$280	$250	*$471*

MODEL 808 O/U – 12 ga., 26, 28, or 30 in. barrels, various chokes, boxlock, extractors, checkered stock. Mfg. 1963-1968 in Italy.

	$425	$375	$330	$315	$290	$270	$230	

MODEL 810 O/U – 10 ga., 3 1/2 in. chambers, ST, extractors. Disc.

	$600	$550	$500	$460	$430	$395	$360	

MODEL 828 O/U – 28 ga., single non-selective trigger, extractors, engraved, only 250 imported. Disc.

	$650	$550	$500	$450	$400	$350	$325	

GRADING - PPGS™	100%	98%	95%	90%	80%	70%	60%	LAST MSR

RIEDL RIFLE COMPANY

Previous single shot rifle manufacturer.

RIFLES: SINGLE SHOT

SINGLE SHOT RIFLE – many cals., 22-30 in. barrel, rack and pinion action, operated by trigger guard/lever, fully adj. trigger, select walnut stock, basically custom made.

	100%	98%	95%	90%	80%	70%	60%	LAST MSR
	$495	$470	$440	$415	$385	$330	$300	

* ***Single Shot Rifle Stainless Barrel***

	100%	98%	95%	90%	80%	70%	60%	LAST MSR
	$560	$535	$500	$480	$450	$395	$370	

RIFLE CRAFT, LTD.

Please refer to Mawhinney, Chuck listing in the M section.

RIFLES, INC.

Current custom rifle manufacturer located in Pleasanton, TX. Previously located in Cedar City, UT. Dealer or direct consumer sales.

Riflemaker and custom gunsmith Lex Webernick has been manufacturing lightweight sporting rifles for more than 20 years.

RIFLES: BOLT ACTION

On the following models, the customer must provide a Remington or Winchester action. Standard metal finishes in black, dark grey, or black w/grey. Cerakote finishes in black, brown, or green camo.

Add $200 for muzzlebrake (stainless quiet Slimbrake II) on Classic and Master Series.

Add $350 for Cerakote finish.

CANYON – various cals., designed for long range shooting, synthetic stock with adj. cheekpiece available in 6 colors, stainless steel action/barrel with muzzle brake, blind or hinged floorplate, McMillan HTG stock, adj. cheekpiece, 10 lbs. New 2011.

	100%	98%	95%	90%	80%	70%	60%	LAST MSR
MSR $3,500	$3,150	$2,650	$2,100	$1,775	$1,500	$1,215	$1,000	

CLASSIC – various cals. up to and including .375 H&H, varmint, target, or hunter specifications, match grade stainless steel barrel, matte stainless finish, laminated fiberglass stock with pillar glass bedding, approx. 6 1/2 lbs. New 1996.

	100%	98%	95%	90%	80%	70%	60%	LAST MSR
MSR $2,900	$2,650	$2,375	$2,125	$1,650	$1,225	$1,085	$875	

Add $100 for left-hand action (disc.).

LIGHTWEIGHT STRATA STAINLESS – various cals. up to and including .375 H&H, lightened stainless Remington action, match grade stainless steel barrel with Slimbrake, blind or aluminum hinged floorplate, hand laminated Kevlar/Graphite and boron stock, matte stainless finish, 5 lbs. New 1996.

	100%	98%	95%	90%	80%	70%	60%	LAST MSR
MSR $3,200	$2,875	$2,575	$2,225	$1,800	$1,450	$1,175	$1,000	

Add $150 for left-hand action (disc.).

LIGHTWEIGHT 70 – most cals. up to .375 H&H, features Winchester Model 70 stainless controlled round feeding blue printed action, match grade stainless steel barrel with muzzle brake, matte stainless finish, laminated Kevlar/boron/graphite stock with glass bedding, approx. 5 1/2-5 3/4 lbs. New 1997.

	100%	98%	95%	90%	80%	70%	60%	LAST MSR
MSR $3,100	$2,775	$2,500	$2,100	$1,725	$1,475	$1,150	$995	

Add $150 for left-hand action (disc.).

MASTER'S SERIES – various cals. up to and including .300 RUM, designed for long range accuracy, blue printed Rem. Model 700 action, fiberglass stock, guaranteed 1/2 MOA accuracy, 7 1/2-7 3/4 lbs. New 1998.

	100%	98%	95%	90%	80%	70%	60%	LAST MSR
MSR $3,200	$2,875	$2,575	$2,225	$1,800	$1,450	$1,175	$1,000	

PEAR FLAT LTD. ED. – 6.5-.284 cal., features distinctive skip fluting pattern on barrel, bolt, and shroud, barb wire camo synthetic stock, pear flat engraved on floorplate. Only 100 to be mfg. beginning 2009. Disc. 2010.

	100%	98%	95%	90%	80%	70%	60%	LAST MSR
	$2,950	$2,550	$2,000	$1,740	$1,495	$1,215	$1,000	*$3,250*

SAFARI – .375 H&H, .416 Rem., or .458 Lott cal., Win. Model 70 action, features match grade barrel with Slimbrake, matte stainless or black Teflon finish, various options are available, 8 1/2 lbs. New 1996.

	100%	98%	95%	90%	80%	70%	60%	LAST MSR
MSR $3,500	$2,975	$2,625	$2,225	$2,000	$1,600	$1,350	$1,050	

SIGNATURE SERIES – .300 RUM cal., blue printed, Rem. M-700 stainless receiver, honed trigger assembly, 27 in. fluted match grade stainless steel barrel with matte finish, w/o sights, synthetic McMillan sporter stock, each gun is signed by Lex Webernick on the floorplate, guaranteed 1/2 MOA accuracy. Limited mfg. 2000-2006.

	100%	98%	95%	90%	80%	70%	60%	LAST MSR
	$2,600	$2,050	$1,700	$1,500	$1,235	$1,030	$855	*$2,800*

Add $175 for Slimbrake.

Add $150 for left-hand action.

GRADING - PPGS™	100%	98%	95%	90%	80%	70%	60%	LAST MSR

TITANIUM STRATA – various cals., based on lightened and blue printed Rem. 700 action, titanium receiver, 4 1/2 lbs. Mfg. 2002-2014.

	$3,150	$2,650	$2,100	$1,775	$1,500	$1,215	$1,000	*$3,500*

VARMINT/TARGET – similar to Classic, except has different stock design and dimensions, different barrel contour. Mfg. 1998-99.

	$1,800	$1,375	$1,075	$960	$775	$655	$550	*$1,900*

Add $250 for Varmint brake.

RIGANIAN, RAY (RIFLEMAKER)

Please refer to the Peerless Rifle Company listing in the P section.

RIGBY, JOHN & CO. (GUNMAKERS), INC.

Current manufacturer established in 1775 and located in Dublin, Ireland. Rigby guns have been manufactured in Dublin from 1775-1897, and in London, England 1865-2020, including a 13 year period in California 1997-2010. Rigby is currently owned by the German based L and O group and operates from its London based premises on Pensbury Place. Managing Director Marc Newton who was apprenticed under the last UK owner Paul Roberts, overseas production of Rigby's current firearms. Rigby has built a variety of different types of firearms over the past 245 years, including duelling pistols, shotguns, fowling pieces, magazine rifles and double rifles. The company is most notable for its association with dangerous game cartridges and rifles, including the design of the world famous .416 Rigby.

Details of Rigby's dealers from around the world can be found at www.johnrigbyandco.com. Rigby also offers a historical research service for details of guns made by the company in the past.

RIFLES: BOLT ACTION, CURRENT MFG.

Prices on new guns do not include VAT.

BIG GAME (CURRENT MFG.) – .375 H&H (double square bridge only), .416 Rigby, or .450 Rigby (single square bridge only) cal., built on a barreled Mauser action, 22 (single square bridge only) or 24 in. lightweight barrel, heat-blued extractor, Rigby express sights with a single fixed V and two folding leaves dovetailed into the quarter rib, Turkish walnut stock, red rubber recoil pad, horizontal Winchester-style safety catch, original pattern engraving, case hardened recoil bars, plasma nitriding on all exposed metal surfaces, approximate weights are from 10 lbs.

Current MSR on this model is $15,995 for single square bridge, or $16,995 for double square bridge. Prices do not include VAT.

BIG GAME PH (CURRENT MFG.) – .375 H&H (double square bridge only), .416 Rigby, or .450 Rigby (single square bridge only) cal., built on a barreled Mauser action, 22 in. (single square bridge only) or 24 in. lightweight barrel, heat-blued extractor, Rigby express sights with a single fixed V and two folding leaves dovetailed into the quarter rib, Turkish walnut stock, red rubber recoil pad, horizontal Winchester-style safety catch, original pattern engraving, case hardened recoil bars, boasts classic lines and rock-solid engineering of the original Big Game rifle, plasma nitriding on all exposed metal surfaces, 10 lbs.

Current MSR on this model is $12,995 for single square bridge, or $13,995 for double square bridge. Prices do not include VAT.

BIG GAME VINTAGE (CURRENT MFG.) – .416 Rigby cal., built on a barreled Mauser action (single square bridge), 24 in. lightweight barrel, heat-blued extractor, Rigby express sights, traditional Turkish walnut stock, red rubber recoil pad, 14 1/2 in. LOP, 3-position flag safety, original pattern engraving, case hardened recoil bars, plasma nitriding on all exposed metal surfaces, 10 lbs. 8 oz.

Current MSR on this model is $18,995. Prices do not include VAT.

HIGHLAND STALKER (CURRENT MFG.) – .275 Rigby, .30-06, .308, 8x57, or 9.3x62 cal., Mauser 98 bolt action built to original specifications, 22 in. barrel, 4 or 5 shot mag., traditional Rigby pattern iron sights, Grade 5 walnut round pistol grip ambidextrous stock, rounded grip shape, drilled and tapped for scope mounts, hand-finished checkering and original style engraving, available in both mens (14.25 in. LOP) and ladies (13.875 in. LOP) versions, approximate weights are from 7.8 lbs.

Current MSR on this model is $10,995. Prices do not include VAT.

THE LONDON BEST (CURRENT MFG.) – choice of any caliber, choice of Mauser action in right or left-hand configuration, single or double square bridge, choice of barrel length and profile featuring premium quality barrels, custom fitted stock made from minimum Grade 7 Turkish walnut, shaped to customer specifications, leather covered recoil pad, all models feature maker's name on the barrel, checkered bolt handle, stippled rib and front sight, engraved pins and recoil bar and gold inlaid details, choice of exquisite engraving from some of the world's best renowned engravers, London Best barrel black and oil finish.

Current MSR on this model is £22,950 (not including VAT) for standard lengh action or £23,950 (not including VAT) for magnum length action.

THE LONDON BEST VINTAGE (CURRENT MFG.) – .275 Rigby, .350 Rigby, or .416 Rigby cal., choice of Mauser action in right or left-hand configuration, single or double square bridge, choice of barrel length and profile featuring premium quality barrels, optional takedown system, custom fitted stock made from minimum Grade 7 Turkish walnut, shaped to customer specifications, leather covered recoil pad, all models feature maker's name on the barrel, checkered bolt handle, stippled rib and front sight, engraved pins and recoil bar and gold inlaid details, choice of exquisite engraving from some of the world's best renowned engravers, built from a historic pattern and bears a number of features that evoke the Rigby's of the past, London Best barrel black and oil finish.

Current MSR on this model is £19,500 (not including VAT) for .275 Rigby cal. or £20,500 (not including VAT) for .350 and .416 Rigby cals.

RIFLES: SxS, CURRENT MFG.

RISING BITE DOUBLE RIFLE (CURRENT MFG.) – .350 Rigby -.600 Nitro Express cal., mirror-bored chopper lump barrels, best sidelock ejector with dipped edge lock plates, Grade 7 custom fitted Turkish walnut stock, vertical-bolt locking system, lever forend release catch and ejector regulating switch inside forend, features traditional Rigby pattern full scroll engraving, carved folding leaves on fences, and gold inlaid details, color case hardened action, forend iron, and furniture, plus "London Best" barrel black and oil finish.

Current MSR on this model is £98,500 (not including VAT) for .350 Rigby, .375, .416, .450/400 3 in., .470 NE and .500 NE cal., or £110,000 (not including VAT) for .577 NE and .600 NE cal.

RIFLES: OLDER MFG.

Over the decades, John Rigby has manufactured a wide variety of bolt action, SxS, and single shot rifles in many calibers and configurations, some with special order features including various levels of engraving, cases, and accessories. These Rigby rifles have long been regarded as among the finest in the world, and many (especially SxS) were made per customer specifications. As such, these guns need to be valued individually by a competent appraiser who is well-versed in fine English long arms.

SHOTGUNS: SxS, CURRENT MFG.

RISING BITE SHOTGUN – 12, 28, or 32 ga. or .410 bore, 2 3/4 in. chambers, chopper lump barrels in choice of lengths, concave game rib, fixed chokes, best sidelock ejector with signature Rigby dipped edge lock plates, double triggers, Grade 7 custom walnut stock, traditional lever forend release catch, traditional English straight hand grip with hand checkered butt, silver oval, traditional "Rigby Scroll" pattern with carved folding leaves on fences, gold inlaid "J. Rigby & Co." on sidelocks and barrels, available with either case color hardened or brush bright finish on action, "London Best" barrel black and finishing.

Current MSR on this model is £79,000 (not including VAT) for 12 ga., £87,000 (not including VAT) for 28 ga. and .410 bore, or £89,000 (not including VAT) for 32 ga.

SHOTGUNS: SxS, OLDER MFG.

Over the decades, John Rigby & Co. has manufactured a wide variety of shotguns, including both boxlock and sidelock models and hammer variations in many gauges and barrel lengths. Many SxS's were special ordered with optional features such as various levels of engraving, cases, and accessories. These Rigby shotguns have long been regarded as among the finest in the world, and many, especially the sidelock models, were made per customer specifications. As such, these guns need to be valued individually by a competent appraiser who is well-versed in fine English long arms.

RISE ARMAMENT

Current AR-15 style carbine/rifle manufacturer located in Broken Arrow, OK. Distributed exclusively by RSR Group, Inc. located in several regions of the country.

Please refer to BlueBookOfGunValues.com to order the *Blue Book of AR-15s & Variations*, available as a book or online subscription.

RITTER & STARK

Previous manufacturer located in Feistritz, Austria from 2015-2018. Previously imported and distributed by Euro Optic, located in Montoursville, PA.

For individual model listings, please go to BlueBookOfGunValues.com/overflow.

RIVERMAN GUN WORKS

Current rifle manufacturer located in Dalton Gardens, ID. Previously located in Coeur d'Alene/Dalton Gardens, ID.

Please refer to BlueBookOfGunValues.com to order the *Blue Book of AR-15s & Variations*, available as a book or online subscription.

GRADING - PPGS™	100%	98%	95%	90%	80%	70%	60%	LAST MSR

RIZZINI & TANFOGLIO Srl

Previous longarm manufacturer established 2005-early 2010, located in Gardone, Italy.

Rizzini & Tanfoglio combined two great names of Italian gunmaking into one company. Rizzini & Tanfoglio manufactured best quality shotguns and rifles, utilizing some of Europe's top engravers. Prices varied depending on custom order features. For current models, please refer to Battista Rizzini listing.

RIFLES

Calibers .375 H&H, .470 NE, .500 NE, and .600 NE were POR on the following models.

BOXLOCK SxS – various cals., choice of traditional or round body action, express sights, engraving quoted separately, custom order only.

Base price on this model was €26,240, including IVT tax.
Add €1,830 for round body action.

SIDELOCK SxS – various cals., traditional action only, express sights, engraving quoted separately, custom order only.

Base price on this model was €36,612, including IVT tax.

SHOTGUNS

Add 10% for 28 ga. or .410 bore.

HAMMER SxS – various gauges, choice of round or RT style round body action, rose and scroll engraving, custom order only.

Base price on this model was €21,967, including IVT tax.
Add €1,221 for RT style round body action.

BOXLOCK SxS – various gauges, choice of traditional English style or round body action, rose and scroll engraving, custom order only.

Base price on this model was €12,814, including IVT tax.
Add €4,882 for round body action.

401 SIDELOCK O/U – various gauges, Boss type locking system, chopper lump barrels, ST, best quality wood, engraving quoted separately, custom order only.

Base price on this model was €35,736, including IVT tax.

SIDELOCK SxS – various gauges, choice of English, special RT style, or round body action, engraving quoted separately, custom order only.

Base price on this model ranged approx. €29,900, including IVT tax.
Add €3,662 for special RT style action.
Add €4,882 for round body action.

RIZZINI, BATTISTA

Current manufacturer established during 1966, and located in Marcheno, Italy. Currently imported exclusively and distributed by Rizzini USA (owned and operated by Fierce Products beginning 2012), Redmond, UT. Previously located in Gunnison, UT (2012-2019), New Britain, CT (2008-2011) and West Chester, PA. Also distributed by William Larkin Moore, located in Scottsdale, AZ. Previously imported in the U.S. 2002-2003 by SIG Arms, located in Exeter, NH, and by New England Arms Corp. located in Kittery Point, ME. Dealer direct sales

COMBINATION GUNS

Currently manufactured models are available in the following standard calibers: 7x65R, 8x57 JRS, 9.3x74R, .270 Win., .30-06, .30R Blaser, .308 Win. (disc.), .444 Marlin, or .45-70 Govt. cal.

KOMBO MODEL – various cals., 12 or 20 ga., boxlock action, 22 or 24 in. barrels (rifle barrel has rifling), extractors, double triggers. Imported late 2014-2017.

	100%	98%	95%	90%	80%	70%	60%	LAST MSR
	$2,750	$2,300	$1,950	$1,750	$1,550	$1,325	$1,100	*$2,973*

CUSTOM SHOP

Battista Rizzini and Ivano Tanfoglio established a Custom Shop in late 2014. All guns are built on a custom order only basis and include the following configurations: Competition and Hunting O/U models, SxS Hunting models, Express O/U and SxS boxlock rifles, H & H style O/U and SxS shotguns, Anson & Deeley boxlock SxS shotguns, hammer SxS shotguns, sidelock SxS Express rifles, and large caliber sidelock rifles. Please contact the importer directly for custom order quotation, including delivery time and pricing.

GRADING - PPGS™	100%	98%	95%	90%	80%	70%	60%	LAST MSR

RIFLES: O/U

Currently manufactured models are available in the following standard calibers: 7x65R, 8x57 JRS, 9.3x74R, .270 Win., .30-06, .30R Blaser, .308 Win. (disc.), .444 Marlin, or .45-70 Govt. cal.

Add $708 for scope mount w/built-in rings on currently manufactured models.

EXPRESS 90L – various cals., 20 ga. frame, Express O/U rifle, standard dimensions, 24 in. barrels, ejectors, ST, Bavarian style stock, deluxe wood features, includes case, 7 3/4 lbs. Importation disc. 2015.

	$3,750	$3,300	$2,950	$2,600	$2,300	$1,750	$1,500	*$4,495*

EXPRESS 92EL – similar to Express 90L, except has sideplates, elaborate engraving, custom dimensions available, includes Nizzoli case, 7 3/4 lbs. Importation disc.

	$11,500	$9,950	$9,000	$8,100	$7,200	$6,300	$5,400	*$12,548*

92 S – 24 in. barrels on 28 ga. frame, ejectors, single trigger, Bavarian style stock, sideplates, hand-finished engraving, select woods, includes case, 6.6 lbs. Importation began 2014.

MSR $7,026	$6,300	$5,550	$4,750	$4,300	$3,500	$2,850	$2,200	

PYRRUM – 24 in. barrels on 20 ga. frame, ejectors, ST, Bavarian style stock, cased. Importation began 2014.

MSR $4,053	$3,650	$3,200	$2,750	$2,500	$2,000	$1,650	$1,350	

WILD EXPRESS – various cals., low profile boxlock action express, ejectors, ST, oil finished hand checkered pistol grip select walnut stock with cheekpiece and Schnabel forend, pistol grip select walnut stock, coin finished receiver with relief game scene engraving. Imported 2004-2012.

	$5,250	$4,500	$3,950	$3,250	$2,750	$2,300	$1,950	*$5,754*

SMALL ACTION – various cals., 28 ga. frame, approx. 23 1/2 (disc.) or 24 in. barrels, ejectors, ST, high-grade Bavarian style stock and forearm, hand-finished relief engraving, includes case. Current importation.

MSR $6,249	$5,650	$4,900	$4,200	$3,850	$3,100	$2,550	$2,000	

ROUND BODY – 28 ga. frame, approx. 23 1/2 in. barrels, ejectors, ST, high-grade Bavarian style stock and forearm, hand-finished engraving, includes case. Current importation.

MSR $8,005	$7,200	$6,300	$5,400	$4,900	$3,950	$3,250	$2,625	

RIFLES: SxS

BR 550 EXPRESS – various cals. upon request, scalloped boxlock action, 22 in. barrels, extractors or ejectors, ST, open sights, select checkered walnut stock w/cheekpiece and forearm, floral scroll engraving standard, includes case, coin finish. Current importation.

MSR $6,995	$6,300	$5,500	$4,700	$4,300	$3,450	$2,850	$2,275	

BR 550 RHINO EXPRESS – .416 Rigby, .470 or .500 NE cal., scalloped boxlock action, 23 in. barrel, extractors or ejectors, DT, orange fiber optic front sight, folding leaf rear sight, No. 3 checkered Turkish walnut stock w/cheekpiece and forearm, solid rubber buttplate, manual safety, includes "Big Five" game scene engraving by Bottega Giovanelli, coin or color case hardened finish. Importation began 2016.

MSR $10,250	$9,250	$8,100	$6,900	$6,300	$5,100	$4,150	$3,325	

SHOTGUNS: O/U

During 2012, Rizzini upgraded the wood and the engraving on its currently manufactured models.

COMP 16 – 16 ga., boxlock action, steel sporting frame w/sideplates, 30 or 32 in. chrome-lined barrels w/fixed ramp or adj. vent. rib, interchangeable chokes, automatic ejectors, SST, select grade Turkish Walnut stock (adj. comb optional) and rounded forearm w/checkering, 5 nickel plated chokes, Rizzini ABS hardcase, minimal engraving with "Competition 16" logo, coin finish, 8 lbs.

MSR $3,875	$3,500	$3,075	$2,625	$2,380	$1,925	$1,575	$1,225	

SPORTING EL – includes multi chokes, case. Importation disc. 2000.

	$2,975	$2,850	$2,500	$2,225	$1,950	$1,675	$1,500	*$3,750*

UPLAND EL – all gauges, 27 1/2 in. VR barrels with choke tubes (except .410 bore), deluxe walnut stock and forearm, hard case, case hardened receiver. Imported 1994-2003.

	$2,625	$2,400	$2,100	$1,800	$1,500	$1,200	$995	*$2,800*

INVERNESS ROUND BODY DELUXE (ROUND BODY EL) – all gauges, two frame sizes, 26, 28, 29, or 30 in. solid rib barrels, five screw-in flush chokes, ejectors, SST, fancy Turkish checkered walnut stock and forearm, scroll engraving, coin finished or case colored steel frame, approx. 6 lbs. Importation disc. 2012.

	$5,500	$4,950	$4,400	$3,850	$3,300	$2,600	$2,150	*$6,078*

Add $607 for 28 ga. or .410 bore (small frame).

GRADING - PPGS™	100%	98%	95%	90%	80%	70%	60%	LAST MSR

INVERNESS ROUND BODY DELUXE (ROUND BODY EM) – all gauges, two frame sizes, 26, 28, 29, or 30 in. VR barrels, five screw-in flush chokes, ejectors, SST, fancy Turkish checkered walnut stock and forearm, scroll engraving, coin finished or case colored steel receiver, approx. 6 lbs. Imported 2007-2012.

$4,500 $3,750 $3,300 $2,850 $2,400 $2,000 $1,650 *$4,985*

Add $644 for 28 ga. or .410 bore (small frame).

OMNIUM (EM) FIELD – all gauges, two frame sizes, 24 1/2 (disc.), 26, 28, or 30 in. VR barrels with choke tubes, ejectors, SST, scroll engraving, includes case, blued frame, approx. 6 3/4 lbs. Imported 2004-2016.

$1,925 $1,650 $1,425 $1,200 $1,000 $875 $750 *$2,175*

Add $20 for alloy frame with coin finish and gold birds (Ominum Light).
Add $1,575 for 20/28 ga. or 28 ga./.410 bore barrel sets.

AURUM (CLASSIC) FIELD SERIES – 12, 16 (disc., reintroduced 2019), 20, 28 ga. or .410 bore, boxlock action, three frame sizes, 24 1/2(disc.) or 26 - 30 in. VR barrels with choke tubes (except 16 ga.), ejectors, SST, hand checkered, oil finished, select pistol grip walnut stock and Schnabel forend, case hardened receiver with light engraving. Importation began 1996.

MSR $3,435 $3,100 $2,700 $2,300 $2,100 $1,700 $1,400 $1,100

Add $100 for Aurum small frame 28 ga. and .410 bore.
Add $1,654 for Aurum small action combo (28 ga. and .410 bore).
Available as Aurum (Classic) 20/28 ga. combo ($1,702 MSR).
Available as triple barrel set 20, 28 ga., and .410 bore ($3,043 MSR).

* ***Aurum (Classic) Light Field*** – 12, 16, 20, 28 (new 2014) ga., or .410 bore (new 2014), scroll engraving with gold inlays, includes case, nickel plated alloy frame, approx. 6 1/4 lbs. Imported 2000-2004, reintroduced 2007.

MSR $3,640 $3,300 $2,850 $2,450 $2,250 $1,800 $1,500 $1,150

* ***Aurum (Classic) Teutonic Field*** – all gauges, boxlock action, 24 1/2 - 30 in. VR barrels with five screw-in flush choke tubes, oil finished checkered pistol grip stock and Schnabel forend, hand-finished relief game scene engraving, includes case. Imported 2004-2011.

$2,825 $2,350 $1,850 $1,525 $1,250 $1,025 $950 *$3,194*

ARTEMIS (CLASSIC) FIELD SERIES – 12, 16, 20 ga., or .410 bore, case hardened or coin boxlock action with three frame sizes, 24 1/2 (disc.), 26 - 30 in. VR barrels with 5 flush choke tubes, ejectors, SST, oil finished checkered select walnut pistol grip stock and Schnabel forend, hand-finished game scene engraved sideplates w/gold inlays, approx. 6 - 6 3/4 lbs. Imported 1996-2013, re-importation began 2015.

MSR $4,077 $3,650 $3,200 $2,750 $2,500 $2,000 $1,650 $1,300

Add $100 for small frame in 28 ga. or .410 bore.
Double Combo set available in 20/28 ga., 28ga./.410 bore (disc.), or 20ga/.410 bore for MSR $1,777.
Triple Combo set available in 20/28 ga./.410 bore for MSR $3,319.

ARTEMIS DELUXE FIELD – all gauges, boxlock action in three frame sizes, 24 1/2 (disc. 2013), 26-30 in. chrome-lined VR barrels with fixed or interchangeable chokes, ejectors, SST, oil finished hand checkered pistol grip, select walnut stock w/Schnabel forend, game scene engraved, coin finished frame w/sideplates, approx. 6 3/4 lbs. Disc. 2015.

MSR $6,975 $6,300 $5,500 $4,700 $4,250 $3,450 $2,800 $2,200

Add $200 for Artemis small action in 28 ga. or .410 bore.

* ***Artemis Deluxe Field Small Action*** – 28 ga. or .410 bore, small action, 26-30 in. VR barrels w/o choke tubes, Prince of Wales grip, choice of coin or color case hardened finish w/gold bird inlays. Current importation.

MSR $4,661 $4,250 $3,750 $3,325 $2,825 $2,375 $2,100 $1,825

Add $1,845 for 28 ga./.410 bore combo.

ARTEMIS DELUXE SPORTING – 12 ga., coin finished action, sideplates with hand finished game scenes, SST, ejectors, extra select walnut stock, 28, 29 1/2, 30, or 32 in. barrels, 10mm rib, 5 extended chokes, cased. Imported 2004-2013.

$6,950 $5,750 $4,500 $3,650 $3,150 $2,750 $2,450 *$7,679*

ARTEMIS EL FIELD – top-of-the-line gun with hand engraving, three frame sizes. Importation disc. 2000, reintroduced 2004-2012.

$16,500 $14,250 $11,250 $9,500 $8,350 $7,100 $6,250 *$18,750*

Add $3,750 for small action in 28 ga. or .410 bore.

GRADING - PPGS™	100%	98%	95%	90%	80%	70%	60%	LAST MSR

ARTEMIS SPECIAL FIELD - 12, 16, or 20 ga., boxlock action, regular or small frame, 26-30 in. VR barrels with 5 interchangeable chokes, ejectors, SST, pistol grip or English style stock, scroll engraved sideplates with color case frame and gold birds, coin finish or color case hardened finish, 6-6 3/4 lbs. Mfg. 2014-2017.

	$3,850	$3,400	$3,000	$2,600	$2,200	$1,875	$1,500	*$4,186*

Add $475 for Artemis small action in 28 ga. or .410 bore.

ARTEMIS LIGHT FIELD - 12, 16, 20, 28 ga., or .410 bore, boxlock action, 26 (disc.) or 28-30 in. VR barrels with 5 interchangeable chokes (except 16 ga.), ejectors, SST, pistol grip or English style stock, light scroll engraved sideplates w/gold inlays, available in right or left-hand, 5.2-6.4 lbs. Importation began 2014.

MSR $4,206	$3,800	$3,300	$2,850	$2,600	$2,100	$1,700	$1,300

Add $200 for small action in 28 ga. or .410 bore.

ROUND BODY EM/DELUXE - 12, 16, 20, 28 ga., or .410 bore, boxlock action, round body steel frame, 26-30 in. chrome-lined barrel, 5 chokes, auto ejectors, SST, extended trigger tang, Grade 3 Turkish walnut stock, rounded forend, pistol grip, scroll engraving on frame (Round Body EM) or engraving on frame/extended trigger guard and grip end cap (Round Body Deluxe), coin or case-hardened finish, includes Rizzini ABS case, 6.2-7 lbs. New 2020.

MSR $4,424	$4,000	$3,500	$3,000	$2,700	$2,200	$1,800	$1,400

Add $3,932 for Round Body Deluxe model.

ROUND BODY EL GAME - 12, 16, 20, 28 ga., or .410 bore, 2 3/4 or 3 in. chambers, round body game gun, 26-30 in. barrels with interchangeable chokes and vent. top rib or optional solid rib, (barrels longer than 30 in. are also available by special order), ejectors, SST, deluxe oil finished checkered Prince of Wales pistol grip walnut stock and forearm, includes case, case hardened or coin finished receiver with full hand-engraved coverage foliate scroll, 6.2-7 lbs. Importation began 2014.

MSR $6,975	$6,300	$5,500	$4,700	$4,250	$3,450	$2,800	$2,200

Add $922 for small action (28 ga. or .410 bore), $1,885 for small ga. combo w/small action, or $3,439 for triple combo (20 ga., 28 ga., and .410 bore barrels).

Add $1,885 for 12/28 ga. or 20/28 ga. combo set.

ROUND BODY FIELD - 12, 16, 20, 28 ga., or .410 bore, 2 3/4 or 3 in. chambers, round body game gun, 26-30 in. barrels with interchangeable chokes and vent. top rib or optional solid rib, (barrels longer than 30 in. are also available by special order), ejectors, SST, oil finished select checkered Prince of Wales pistol grip walnut stock and forearm, includes case, case hardened or coin finished receiver with full coverage foliate scroll, 6.2-7 lbs. New 2014.

MSR $4,424	$4,000	$3,500	$3,000	$2,700	$2,200	$1,800	$1,400

Add $852 for small action (28 ga. or .410 bore), $1,885 for small ga. combo w/small action, or $3,439 for triple combo (20 ga., 28 ga., and .410 bore barrels).

Add $1,885 for 12/28 ga. or 20/28 ga. combo set.

ROUND BODY SPORTING SERIES - 12 or 20 ga., rounded large frame, 30 or 32 in. VR back bored barrels w/5 choke tubes and extended forcing cones, SST, scroll engraved, gloss blued barrels w/matte black frame. Importation began 2017.

MSR $2,625	$2,375	$1,975	$1,775	$1,550	$1,375	$1,125	$875

Add $893 for Sporting Model, $549 for Sporting II, or $1,625 for Premium Sporting Model.

FIERCE 1 (COMPETITION) - 12, 20 (Sporting only), 28 (Sporting only) ga., 26 (disc.) 28 (disc.) 30, or 32 in. vent. rib back bored barrels with fixed or interchangeable chokes and extended forcing cones, gold (disc.) SST, hand oil finished select checkered walnut stock and forearm, available in Skeet (disc. 2015), Trap, Double Trap (disc. 2015), and Sporting configurations, includes case, color case hardened frame with light scroll engraving and gold Rizzini name. New 2014.

MSR $3,875	$3,300	$2,900	$2,450	$2,250	$1,800	$1,500	$1,150

Add $319 for Trap model w/ramp rib/raised comb or $1,483 for adj. rib and comb. (disc.)

Add $2,270 for Trap combo set w/top single barrel w/ramped rib or $3,633 for combo set w/top single barrel w/adj. rib and comb. (disc.)

FIERCE 1 BABY SPORTING - 28 ga. or .410 bore, 30 in. VR barrels with 5 choke tubes, SST, checkered walnut stock and forearm, solid rubber recoil pad, includes case, choice of black receiver finish w/light engraving and gold inlay, 6.6 lbs. New 2016.

MSR $4,186	$3,600	$3,200	$2,750	$2,500	$2,200	$1,875	$1,400

GRADING - PPGS™	100%	98%	95%	90%	80%	70%	60%	LAST MSR

GRAND REGAL (EL)/DELUXE/EXTRA – 12, 16, 20, 28, 32 ga., or .410 bore, 2 3/4 or 3 in. chamber, low profile case hardened or coin finished round boxlock acanthus leaf engraved round body action, frame with sideplates, 26-30 in. chrome moly steel barrel with glossy blued finish, ventilated (disc.) or solid (on EL model only) rib, interchangeable chokes, automatic ejectors, SST, Prince of Wales pistol grip stock and Boss-style forend in select Grade 4 Turkish walnut, 26 LPI checkering, polished oil finish, hand engraved scolling (Grand Regal) or game scene (Grand Regal Extra) by master engraver Bottega Incisioni di Cesare Giovanelli, 6.2-7 lbs. Importation began 2020.

MSR $12,500	$11,250	$9,850	$8,450	$7,650	$6,200	$5,050	$3,950	

Add $200 for 28 ga. or .410 bore.

Please contact importer directly for pricing on Grand Regal Deluxe model.

MODEL BR 110 FIELD – 12, 16, 20, 28 ga., or .410 bore, two frame sizes (small frame 28 ga. and .410 bore), 26-30 in. VR barrels w/choke tubes, SST, front bead sight, checkered walnut stock and Schnabel forearm w/solid black rubber recoil pad, includes case, choice of matte black or coin finish frame, 5.2-6.6 lbs. New 2017.

MSR $2,150	$1,835	$1,600	$1,375	$1,250	$1,000	$825	$650	

Available in 20/28 ga. or 28ga./.410 bore combo set w/two barrels and choke tubes (MSR $1,675).

* ***Model BR 110 Field Light*** – 12, 16, 20, 28 ga., or .410 bore, two alloy frame sizes (small frame 28 ga. and .410 bore), 26-30 in. VR barrels w/choke tubes, SST, front bead sight, checkered walnut stock and Schnabel forearm w/solid black rubber recoil pad, includes case, coin finish frame w/ gold birds inlaid, 5-6.75 lbs. Importation began 2017.

MSR $2,407	$2,150	$1,900	$1,600	$1,500	$1,200	$1,000	$750	

Available in 20/28 ga. or 28ga./.410 bore combo set w/two barrels and choke tubes (MSR $1,675).

MODEL BR110/BR110X SPORTER (SPORTING) – 12, 20, 28 ga., or .410 bore (.28 and .410 ga. on small frame), 28, 30, or 32 in. VR or V mid-rib (BR110 X model) barrel, 5 extended chokes, XL bore 18.6, SST, with or w/o adj. comb (BR110 X model), cased, matte grey Cerakote finish. New 2020.

MSR $2,505	$2,125	$1,850	$1,600	$1,450	$1,175	$950	$825	

Add $270 for BR110 X model w/ventilated mid-rib and adj. comb.

MODEL BR 320 COMPETITION – 12 or 20 ga., 2 3/4 or 3 in. chambers, boxlock action, 28-34 in. chrome-lined bore barrels, fixed chokes, solid or VR side rib and VR 10 mm rib, automatic ejectors, SST, pistol grip stock with palm swell and round forend, light scroll engraving with Rizzini name in gold, available in Skeet, Trap, Double Trap, and Sporting configurations, color case hardened, adj. comb (optional). Mfg. 2007-2016.

	$3,000	$2,700	$2,300	$1,950	$1,725	$1,500	$1,250	*$3,495*

MODEL BR 440 COMPETITION – 12 or 20 (disc. 2016) ga., 28-32 in. VR barrels with fixed (Skeet or Trap) or interchangeable chokes (Sporting), removable trigger group, SST, checkered pistol grip walnut stock and forearm, available in Skeet, Sporting, Trap, and Double Trap configurations, blue finish, 8.3 lbs. Mfg. 2007-2017.

	$6,500	$5,750	$5,000	$4,250	$3,500	$3,000	$2,550	*$7,733*

MODEL BR 440 EL COMPETITION – 12 or 20 ga. (disc. 2016), 28-32 in. VR barrels with fixed (Skeet or Trap) or interchangeable chokes (Sporting), removable trigger group, SST, deluxe checkered pistol grip, walnut stock and forearm, hand-finished and hand engraved, available in Skeet, Sporting, Trap, and Double Trap configurations, blue finish, 8.3 lbs. Mfg. 2007-disc.

	$10,250	$8,750	$7,150	$6,150	$5,150	$4,350	$3,700	*$12,203*

MODEL BR 460/460EL COMPETITION (SPORTING/SPORTING EL) – 12 ga., Boss style locking system, 28, 30, or 32 in. VR barrels, 5 flush type chokes, long forcing cones, SST (Sporting model), removable trigger groups, scroll engraving (BR460EL model), matte black Cerakote (BR460 model) or coin finish (BR460EL model). New 2020.

MSR $7,667	$6,500	$5,700	$4,875	$4,425	$3,575	$2,925	$2,550	

Add $2,224 for BR460EL model.

780 FIELD SERIES – 10, 12, or 16 ga., boxlock action, DTs, extractors, checkered walnut stock and forearm. Importation disc. 1998.

	$1,075	$875	$750	$675	$595	$525	$450	*$1,225*

Add $550 for 10 ga.

Add $150 for ejectors (Model S780 E).

Add $200 for SST with ejectors (Model S780 EM).

Add $350 for SST, ejectors, and upgraded wood (Model S780 EML).

A Model S780 EMEL was also available that is entirely hand-finished and engraved for $5,995.

GRADING - PPGS™	100%	98%	95%	90%	80%	70%	60%	LAST MSR

* ***780 Field Series Competition*** – includes Skeet, Trap, and Sporting Clays configuration. Importation disc. 1998.

	$1,375	$1,050	$925	$825	$725	$625	$525	*$1,600*

* ***780 Field Series Small Gauge*** – includes 20, 28, or 36 (.410 bore) ga., DTs, ejectors. Importation disc. 1998.

	$1,275	$975	$875	$800	$725	$625	$525	*$1,500*

Add $50 for SST (Model 780 EM).

S 780 EMEL FIELD – 12, 16, 20, 28 ga. or .410 bore, highly polished coin finish, 28 or 29 1/2 in. barrels, hand engraved ornamental motifs and game scenes, SST, ejectors, extra select hand checkered and polished walnut stock, includes Nizzoli case. Disc. 2012.

	$13,000	$11,000	$9,250	$7,800	$6,800	$5,350	$4,850	*$14,470*

Add $2,896 for small frame in 28 ga. or .410 bore.

782 EM FIELD SERIES – 12 or 16 ga., boxlock action with sideplates, SST, ejectors or extractors, checkered walnut stock and forearm. Importation disc. 1998.

	$1,450	$1,150	$995	$875	$750	$675	$550	*$1,700*

Add $450 for Slug variation (Model 782 EM Slug).
Add $350 for better engraving and wood (Model 782 EML).
A Model S7820 EMEL was also available that was entirely hand-finished and engraved for $12,000.

* ***S 782 EMEL Field Series Deluxe*** – all gauges, individually made per customer specifications, 27 1/2 in. VR barrels with choke tubes (except .410 bore), coin finished receiver with sideplates featuring elaborate Bulino game scene engraving with gold inlays and fine scroll borders, deluxe English walnut, Nizzoli best leather case. Imported 1994-2012.

	$13,995	$11,850	$10,350	$8,900	$7,500	$6,250	$5,200	*$15,565*

Add $3,110 for small action in 28 ga. or .410 bore.

790 SERIES COMPETITION – 12 or 20 ga., choice of Trap, Skeet, or Sporting Clays configuration, features black frame outlined with gold line engraving. Importation disc. 1999.

	$1,725	$1,475	$1,300	$1,050	$925	$825	$695	*$2,275*

Subtract $150 for 20 ga. Trap.
Subtract $50 for 20 ga. Skeet.
Add $1,050 for 20 ga. Sporting (includes sideplates and quick detachable stock).
A Model 790 Trap EL was also available that was entirely hand-finished with 18Kt. gold and hand engraving - prices began at $5,650 in 12 ga., $5,200 in 20 ga.

* ***790 Series Competition Small Gauge*** – similar to 790 Competition Series, except in 20, 28, or 36 (.410 bore) ga., SST and ejectors standard. Importation disc. 2000.

	$1,375	$1,150	$995	$875	$750	$675	$550	*$1,750*

A Model 790 EMEL was also available that was entirely hand-finished with 18Kt. gold and hand engraving - prices began at $9,600.

S 790 EL SERIES COMPETITION – 12 ga., hand polished frame, 28-32 in. VR flared barrels w/choice of fixed (Skeet or Trap) or 5 flush choke tubes (Sporting only), deluxe checkered walnut stock and forearm, hand engraving w/gold inlays, cased. Disc.

	$8,450	$7,350	$6,200	$5,450	$4,600	$3,700	$2,800	*$9,720*

S 790 EMEL SERIES FIELD – all gauges, individually made per customer specifications, 27 1/2 in. VR barrels with choke tubes (except .410 bore), color case hardened or coin finished receiver with ornate ornamental engraving and Rizzini crest, deluxe English walnut, Nizzoli best leather case. Imported 1994-2012.

	$10,000	$8,500	$7,000	$6,000	$5,000	$4,250	$3,625	*$11,875*

Add $2,375 for small action in 28 ga. or .410 bore.

792 SMALL GAUGE MAG. SERIES – 20, 28, or 36 (.410 bore) ga., Mag. chambers, SST, ejectors, includes engraved sideplates. Importation disc. 1998.

	$1,675	$1,325	$1,100	$895	$750	$675	$595	*$2,000*

A Model 792 EMEL was also available that was entirely hand finished with 18Kt. gold and hand engraving - prices began at $8,250.

S 792 EMEL FIELD – all gauges, individually made per customer specifications, 27 1/2 in. VR barrels with choke tubes (except .410 bore), coin finished receiver with sideplates featuring upgraded bulino game scene engraving and fine scroll borders, deluxe English walnut, Nizzoli leather case. Imported 1994-2012.

	$10,650	$9,500	$8,250	$7,000	$6,000	$5,000	$4,150	*$12,485*

Add $2,496 for small action in 28 ga. or .410 bore.

GRADING - PPGS™	100%	98%	95%	90%	80%	70%	60%	LAST MSR

MODEL 2000 TRAP – 12 ga. only, VR barrels and rib., gold trigger, includes nickel finished receiver with sideplates, A Model 2000 Trap EL was also available that was entirely hand finished with 18Kt. gold and hand engraving. Importation disc. 1998.

	$1,675	$1,375	$1,275	$1,025	$925	$825	$695	*$2,200*

A Model 2000 Trap EL was also available that was entirely hand finished with 18Kt. gold and hand engraving - prices began at $5,290.

MODEL 2000-SP – 12 ga. only, 26, 28, 30, or 32 in. overbored barrels with choke tubes, includes engraved sideplates, semi-fancy select walnut with quick detachable stock, cased. Imported 1994-98.

	$3,000	$2,700	$2,400	$1,975	$1,600	$1,300	$1,000	*$3,650*

S 1000 COMPETITION – 12, 20, or 28 (disc.) ga., 28 - 32 in. VR barrels w/5 extended choke tubes, 10mm rib, long forcing cones, ejectors, SST, standard walnut checkered pistol grip stock w/palm swell, machine engraving, available in Skeet(disc. 2015), Sporting, Trap, or Double Trap (disc. 2015) configuration, cased, chromium finished action. Disc. 2017.

	$4,250	$3,750	$3,325	$2,825	$2,375	$2,100	$1,825	*$4,647*

Add $312 for Trap model w/ramp and rib/raised comb or $1,483 for adj. rib and comb.

Add $2,519 for Trap combo set w/top single barrel w/ramped rib or $3,491 for combo set w/top single barrel w/adj. rib and comb.

S 1000 BABY SPORTING – 28 ga. or .410 bore, 30 in. VR barrels w/5 choke tubes, SST, checkered walnut stock and forearm, solid rubber recoil pad, includes case, choice of black receiver finish w/light engraving and gold inlay, cased, 6.6 lbs. Mfg. 2016-disc.

	$4,250	$3,750	$3,325	$2,825	$2,375	$2,100	$1,825	*$4,647*

S 2000 COMPETITION – 12 ga., 20 ga., 28 ga. or .410 bore, 28 (disc.) 30, or 32 in. VR barrels, 10mm rib, long forcing cones, 5 extended chokes, ejectors, SST, extra select walnut checkered pistol grip stock with palm swell, sideplates with English scroll and border engraving, available in Skeet (disc. 2015), Sporting (new 2004), Trap, or Double Trap (disc. 2015) configuration, includes case, chromium finished action. Imported 2004-2017, reintroduced 2019.

MSR $4,610	$3,900	$3,425	$2,925	$2,675	$2,200	$1,780	$1,550	

Add $331 for Trap model w/ramped rib. (disc.)

Add $2,368 for Trap combo set w/top single barrel w/top single barrel w/adj. rib and comb. (disc.)

S 2000 BABY SPORTING – 28 ga. or .410 bore, chromium finished action, 30 VR barrels, ejectors, SST, 10mm rib, long forcing cones, 5 extended chokes, sideplates with English scroll and border engraving, extra select walnut checkered pistol grip stock with palm swell, available in Sporting configuration only, cased. Mfg. 2015-disc.

	$5,375	$4,625	$3,970	$3,600	$2,910	$2,385	$1,855	*$5,770*

PREMIER SPORTING – 12 or 20 ga., 28, 29 1/2, 30, 32 or 34 in. multi-choke (5 extended chokes) barrels, includes hard case, custom dimensions upon application. Imported 1994-2006.

	$2,600	$2,050	$1,650	$1,375	$1,100	$900	$750	*$2,995*

PREMIER II – similar to Premier Sporting configuration, European target style stock and beavertail forearm, extra select walnut, blued receiver. Limited importation-2004 only.

	$2,950	$2,800	$2,275	$1,775	$1,450	$1,300	$1,075	*$4,050*

VENUS FIELD – 20, 28 ga., or .410 bore, boxlock action, steel round body receiver, 26 or 28 in. chrome-lined solid barrel, 5 flush mount chokes, steel round body receiver, auto ejectors, SST, Turkish walnut checkered stock, rounded forend, floral scroll engraving on frame and trigger guard, includes Rizzini case, coin finish, 6.2-6.5 lbs. Importation began 2021.

MSR $5,690	$5,100	$4,500	$3,850	$3,500	$2,800	$2,300	$1,800	

VENUS SPORT – 12, 20, or 28 ga., boxlock action, steel roundbody frame, 28, 30, or 32 in. chrome-lined solid VR barrels, interchangeable choke tubes, automatic ejectors, SST, select grade Turkish Walnut stock and rounded forearm w/checkering, 5 nickel plated extended chokes, Rizzini ladies ABS hardcase, floral scroll engraving w/venus logo, coin finish, 6.2-6.8 lbs. New 2021.

MSR $5,369	$4,575	$4,000	$3,430	$3,110	$2,515	$2,075	$1,800	

VERTEX COMPETITION – 12, 20, or 28 ga (disc.), chromium finished (disc.), or matte black finished action, light border and scroll engraving (disc.), ejectors, ST or SST, hand checkered oil finished select walnut pistol grip stock and forend, 28 - 32 in. barrels, long forcing cones, 5 extended chokes, available in Sporting (new 2004), Skeet (disc. 2016), Trap, or Double Trap (disc.) cased. Imported 2004-2017.

	$2,150	$1,725	$1,575	$1,375	$1,100	$950	$800	*$2,410*

Add $1,448 for adj. rib and stock comb on Trap or $1,200 for Double Trap Model (disc.).

Add $265 for adj. comb (disc.) or $392 for raised rib/adj. comb on Trap Model.

GRADING - PPGS™	100%	98%	95%	90%	80%	70%	60%	LAST MSR

VERTEX BABY SPORTING – 28 ga. or .410 bore, 30 in. VR barrels w/5 choke tubes, SST, checkered walnut stock and forearm, solid rubber recoil pad, includes case, choice of blue or coin finish receiver, 6.6 lbs. Mfg. 2016-2019.

	$2,150	$1,725	$1,575	$1,375	$1,100	$950	$800	*$2,410*

VERTEX 3 LADIES/YOUTH COMPETITION – 12 or 20 ga., 28 - 32 in. barrels, long forcing cones on Sporting Model, 5 extended chokes, ejectors, ST or SST, hand checkered oil finished select walnut pistol grip stock and forend, pistol grip stock, available in Sporting or Trap, light border and scroll engraving, includes case, matte black finish. Mfg. 2016-2019.

	$2,300	$1,850	$1,675	$1,425	$1,150	$995	$850	*$2,625*

Add $1,767 for adj. rib and stock comb on Trap.
Add $319 for adj. high comb and ramped rib on Trap Model.

VERTEX 3 LADIES/YOUTH BABY SPORTING – 28 ga. or .410 bore, 30 in. VR barrels with 5 choke tubes, SST, checkered walnut stock and forearm, solid rubber recoil pad, includes case, choice of black receiver, 6.6 lbs. Mfg. 2016-2019.

	$2,300	$1,850	$1,675	$1,425	$1,150	$995	$850	*$2,625*

REGAL EL/DELUXE/EXTRA – 12, 16, 20, 28 ga., .410 bore, boxlock action, steel round body low-profile frame and sideplates, 26-30 in. chrome lined barrels, auto ejectors, SST, Grade 3 Turkish walnut stock and forearm, Prince of Wales pistol grip, choice of scroll engraving on frame and trigger guard (RB Regal EL), round body frame/sideplates/trigger guard (Regal Deluxe), or scroll engraved game scene on frame/sideplates/tang and grip cap (Regal Extra), coin or case hardened finish, Rizzini ABS case, 6.2-7 lbs. New 2020.

MSR $7,418	$6,700	$5,850	$5,000	$4,550	$3,650	$3,000	$2,350	

* ***Regal EM*** – 12, 16, 20, 28 ga., .410 bore, boxlock action, steel round body low-profile frame and sideplates, 26-30 in. chrome lined VR barrels, 5 nickel colored chokes, auto ejectors, SST, select Turkish walnut stock, Prince of Wales pistol grip, ornamental scroll frame/sideplates and trigger guard, coin or case hardened finish, Rizzini ABS case, 6.2-7 lbs. Importation began 2020.

MSR $4,887	$4,400	$3,850	$3,300	$3,000	$2,400	$2,000	$1,550	

SHOTGUNS: SxS

BR 550 FIELD – 12 (disc. 2013), 20, 28 ga., or .410 bore, scalloped boxlock action, 26 1/2, 28, or 29 1/8 in. barrels w/multi chokes, ejectors, DT or SST, English style walnut stock, checkered straight grip, floral scroll engraving, coin or case colored finish. Importation began 2006-disc.

	$4,450	$3,725	$3,175	$2,875	$2,300	$1,900	$1,550	*$4,895*

Add $200 for small action in 28 ga. or .410 bore.

BR 550 (ROUND BODY FIELD) – 20, 28 ga., or .410 bore, SxS shotgun, scalloped boxlock action, multi chokes, 26-30 in. barrels, ejectors, DT or SST, English style walnut stock, checkered straight grip, floral scroll engraving, coin or case colored finish. New circa 2015.

MSR $4,535	$3,850	$3,350	$2,900	$2,600	$2,100	$1,750	$1,350	

Add $240 for 28 ga. or .410 bore (Round Body small frame).

BR 552 FIELD – 20, 28 ga., or .410 bore, engraved boxlock action w/sideplates, 26-30 in. barrels, multi chokes, ejectors, DT or SST, checkered walnut pistol grip stock, extensive floral scroll engraving. Imported 2006.

MSR $5,047	$4,330	$3,800	$3,250	$2,945	$2,380	$1,950	$1,700	

Add $220 for small action in 28 ga. or .410 bore (small frame).

UPLAND EL – various gauges, standard dimensions only, deluxe engraving with premium grade checkered walnut straight grip stock and forearm. Disc. 2012.

	$4,350	$3,950	$3,500	$2,950	$2,400	$1,850	$1,500	*$4,700*

SHOTGUNS: SEMI-AUTO

LEONESSA – 12 ga., 3 in. chamber, gas operation, 28 in. VR barrel with 3 choke tubes, chrome-plated trigger, fiber optic front sight, choice of black synthetic, wood, or 100% camo stock with Micro-Core recoil pad, carry case. Limited importation 2016 only.

	$975	$825	$725	$625	$525	$450	$375	*$1,135*

Add $30 for black synthetic stock.
Add $100 for 100% camo finish.

GRADING - PPGS™	100%	98%	95%	90%	80%	70%	60%	LAST MSR

RIZZINI, EMILIO

Current trademark owned by Fausti Stefano srl. since 1999. Previous shotgun manufacturer established circa 1974-1999, and located in Brescia, Italy. No current U.S. importation. Previously imported by Tristar Sporting Arms, Ltd., located in N. Kansas City, MO, and by Traditions, located in Old Saybrook, CT (see Traditions section for listings). Some models were also previously imported by Armsport, Inc, located in Miami, FL.

Fausti Stefano srl acquired Emilio Rizzini in 1999. All Emilio Rizzini shotguns were equipped with a patented Four Locks locking system. Models listed were introduced during 1999. Most Emilio Rizzini field shotguns were available with fixed or interchangeable choke tubes.

SHOTGUNS: O/U

CLASS MODEL – 12, 16, 20, 28 ga., or 410 bore, boxlock action with reinforced frame, hand engraving, select wood, ejectors, SST. Importation disc. 2000.

$1,625	$1,400	$1,125	$975	$875	$750	$675	*$1,870*

Add $70 for sideplates and case (Class SL Model).

CLASS DE LUXE MODEL – 12, 16, 20, 28 ga., or 410 bore, boxlock action with reinforced frame, hand finished game scene engraving with gold inlays, ejectors, SST, cased. Importation disc. 2000.

$3,675	$3,325	$2,975	$2,625	$2,300	$1,950	$1,675	*$4,185*

Add $170 for sideplates (Class SL De Luxe Model).

BRIXIAN DE LUXE – all gauges, top-of-the-line model, boxlock action with reinforced frame, master fine scroll engraving, ejectors, SST, deluxe English wood, individually made per customer's specifications, leather cased. Importation disc. 2000.

$8,350	$7,600	$6,950	$5,700	$4,500	$3,650	$2,950	*$8,975*

Add $1,986 for sideplates and best leather case (Brixian SL DE Luxe).

TR-I FIELD (NOVA I) – 12 or 20 ga., blue boxlock action, SST, extractors, 26 or 28 in. vent. barrels with 7mm VR and fixed chokes, checkered standard grade walnut stock and forearm, gold trigger, approx. 7 1/4 lbs. Imported 1998-2001.

$585	$485	$430	$375	$330	$300	$275	*$687*

* ***TR-I Field Plus*** – 12 or 20 (disc. 2004) ga., 3 in. chambers, includes choke tubes, 7mm vent. rib, Imported 2000-disc.

$650	$575	$485	$435	$375	$330	$300	*$779*

TR-II FIELD (NOVA II) – 12, 16 (fixed chokes, disc. 2004), 20 (disc. 2004), 28 (disc. 2004) ga., or .410 bore (fixed chokes, disc. 2004), similar to Nova I, except has choke tubes and ejectors. Mfg. 1998-2005.

$795	$675	$575	$475	$415	$355	$300	*$919*

Add $50 for 20, 28 ga., or .410 bore (disc. 2004).

TR-MAG. (NOVA MAG.) – 10 (mfg. 2000-2002) or 12 ga. only, 3 1/2 in. chambers, SST, ejectors or extractors (10 ga. only), 24 or 28 in. vent. barrels with 7mm VR and choke tubes, matte finished wood and metal or Mossy Oak/Shadowgrass camo wood finish (new 2000), 7 1/4 - 9 1/4 lbs. Imported 1998-2004.

$665	$585	$475	$435	$375	$330	$300	*$799*

Add $170 for camo (new 2000).
Add $368 for 10 ga. with camo (mfg. 2000-2002).

SHOTGUNS: O/U, COMPETITION SERIES

The following models were available in either Trap, Skeet, or Sporting Clays configuration. Sporting Clays models have 5 interchangeable multi-chokes.

COMPACT MODEL – 12, 16, or 20 ga., boxlock action with reinforced frame, ejectors, SST, model and company name inlaid on black finished action, select checkered walnut stock and forearm, cased. Importation disc. 2000.

$1,725	$1,650	$1,450	$1,100	$900	$775	$700	*$2,135*

GARA MODEL – similar to Compact, except has hand engraving and wood upgrade. Importation disc. 2000.

$3,100	$2,850	$2,600	$2,200	$1,800	$1,400	$1,250	*$3,765*

Add $351 for Gara Cup Model (company logo inlaid in gold).
Add $1,022 for Gara SL Model (includes engraved sideplates).

GRADING - PPGS™	100%	98%	95%	90%	80%	70%	60%	LAST MSR

GARA DE LUXE – top-of-the-line competition model, ornamental pattern engraved by master engraving, deluxe wood, best leather case. Importation disc. 2000.

	$6,100	$5,750	$5,250	$4,400	$3,500	$2,750	$2,450	*$7,375*

SHOTGUNS: O/U, PREMIER SERIES

Last MSRs for the models listed are as follows: Premier - $1,599, Premier Deluxe - $2,199, Premier SL - $1,899, Premier SL Deluxe - $2,399, Premier EL - $1,999, Premier EL Gold - $2,699, Premier ELX Gold - $3,199.

PREMIER SERIES – 12 or 20 ga., various configurations, oil finished stock and forearm, ST or DT, includes 3 choke tubes. Limited importation by Traditions 2003 only.

The Premier Series had limited importation during 2003 only, and MSRs ranged from $1,599-$3,199. Current values for these models range from 35%-75% of the values listed above, depending on condition.

SHOTGUNS: O/U, SPORTING CLAYS

TR-SC (NOVA SC) – 12 or 20 (mfg. 1999-2003) ga. only, 3 in. chambers, sporting clays model, silver finished boxlock action, gold SST, 28 or 30 in. vent. barrels with 10mm VR and mid-rib sight beads, fancy checkered walnut stock and forearm, approx. 7 1/2 lbs. Imported 1998-2005.

	$885	$775	$675	$575	$475	$395	$350	*$1,047*

Add $80 for 20 ga. (mfg. 1999-2003).

TR-L – similar to Nova SC, except has stock dimensions for female shooter (13 1/2 LOP), was also available in 20 ga. until 2004, approx. 7 3/4 lbs. Imported 1999-2004.

	$890	$780	$680	$575	$450	$395	$350	*$1,063*

TR-ROYAL – 12, 20 (disc. 2004), or 28 (disc. 2004) ga., 3 in. chambers, similar to the TR-SC, except has special dimension stock designed to reduce recoil, 28 or 30 in. VR barrels with 7mm-10mm tapered rib and rhino ported extended choke tubes, ejectors, silver finished boxlock action, deluxe checkered walnut stock and forearm, silver frame with gold accents, approx. 7 1/2 lbs. Imported 1999-2005.

	$1,075	$935	$825	$700	$600	$500	$400	*$1,319*

TR-CLASS SL – 12 ga. only, 2 3/4 in. chambers, features select materials, silver finished boxlock action with engraved sideplates, ejectors, SST, 28 or 30 VR barrels with choke tubes, 7 3/4 lbs. Imported 1999-2002.

	$1,525	$1,275	$1,025	$900	$800	$700	$575	*$1,775*

RIZZINI, F.LLI

Current manufacturer located in Magno V.T., Italy. Currently imported in the U.S. by William Larkin Moore or consumer direct sales through FFL dealer. Some models were previously imported by New England Arms Corp. located in Kittery Point, ME, and by L. Michael Weatherby, located in Laguna Niguel, CA. Please contact the company directly for more information, including an individualized quotation and delivery time.

F.lli Rizzini manufactures some of the most technologically advanced rifles and shotguns in the world, approx. 11 guns per year.

RIFLES: SxS, CUSTOM

R1-E SAFARI SIDELOCK EJECTOR – 8x57 JRS, 9.3x74R, .375 H&H or .470 NE cal., every possible refinement, best quality double rifle, includes Purdey English scroll engraving and case. New 2005.

Current MSR is $128,400 for .444 Marlin, 9.3x74R, or 8x57JRS cals. Current MSR is $165,600 for .375 H&H or .470 NE cal.

Delivery time on this model is approx. 2-4 years, depending on the engraver and amount of engraving.

R3-E SAFARI BOXLOCK – 8x57 JRS, 9.3x74R, or .444 Marlin cal. only, best quality boxlock double rifle, includes Purdey English scroll engraving and case. New 2005.

Currently, this model needs to be quoted indiviually. The last published MSR of €95,250.

Delivery time on this model is approx. 2-4 years, depending on the engraver and amount of engraving.

SHOTGUNS: O/U, OLDER MFG.

In the past the Rizzini brothers collaborated with Rinaldo Zoli to make boxlock shotguns that were usually imported by Abercrombie & Fitch. These guns are normally marked on the water table "Zoli Rizzini". The Zoli Rizzini gun factory closed in 1971.

Zoli Rizzini manufactured an O/U boxlock with sideplates in most gauges, including 28 ga. and .410 bore. They were available with or w/o ejectors, and single or double triggers. Current values range from $1,250 - $3,750, depending on gauge and configuration, with the smaller gauges being worth more than the 12 or 20.

GRADING - PPGS™	100%	98%	95%	90%	80%	70%	60%	LAST MSR

SHOTGUNS: SxS, CUSTOM, OLDER MFG.

Zoli Rizzini guns are not to be confused with the quality of current Rizzini F.lli mfg. Normally these older Field Grade models (non-ejector, boxlock action in 12, 16, 20, 28 ga. or .410 bore) sell in the $500-$1,200 range, with a 25% premium for 28 ga. or .410 bore. Deluxe Field Models with scalloped boxlock action ad ejectors are currently valued in the $1,500-$2,500 range with a 30% premium for 28 ga. or .410 bore. The Extra Lusso Model (top-of-the-line) currently sells in the $3,500 range in 12 ga., $4,750 in 28 ga., and $4,250 in .410 bore.

SHOTGUNS: SxS, CUSTOM, RECENT MFG.

Today's F.lli Rizzini shotguns are made to individual custom order only. Prices do not include engraving and will be substantially more for famous name engravers such as Pedersoli, Fracassi and Torcoli. F.lli Rizzini makes their own barrels in-house, and use their patented mechanisms.

Please contact the manufacturer directly for a quotation on special engraving options.

R1-E SIDELOCK EJECTOR – 12, 16, 20, 28 ga., or .410 bore, F.lli Rizzini patented sidelocks, select Circassian walnut, various barrel lengths, without engraving.

Currently MSR on this model is $122,800 for 12, 16, or 20 ga., $132,000 for 28 ga. or .410 bore.
Add 20% for matched pair.

Engraving on this model is quoted on a special order basis. Estimates may only be given at time of order. Only the best quality engravers are used for this model.

R2-E BOXLOCK EJECTOR – 12, 16, 20, 28 ga. or .410 bore, select walnut, detachable bottom inspection plate, various barrel lengths, without engraving. Disc. 1995.

100%	98%	95%	90%	80%	70%	60%	LAST MSR
$10,500	$9,000	$8,000	$7,000	$6,200	$5,500	$4,750	*$25,000*

Add 25% for 28 ga. or .410 bore.

R3-E BOXLOCK EJECTOR – best quality patented boxlock ejector model w/o engraving, Importation began 2000.

Currently MSR on this model is $91,100 for 12, 16, or 20 ga., $100,500 for 28 ga. or .410 bore. Add 20% for matched pair.

Delivery time on this model is approx. 2-4 years, depending on engraver and amount of engraving.

RIZZINI, I. (ISIDORA)

Please refer to the F.A.I.R. srl (Fair Tecni-Mec) listing in the F section.

ROAM

Current AR-15 style rifle and accessories manufacturer established in 2018, located in Grand Forks, ND.

Please refer to BlueBookOfGunValues.com to order the *Blue Book of AR-15s & Variations*, available as a book or online subscription.

THE ROBAR COMPANIES, INC.

Previous semi-auto firearms manufacturer and customizer located in Phoenix, AZ from 1986-2019.

For individual model listings, please go to BlueBookOfGunValues.com/overflow.

ROBERT HISSERICH COMPANY

Previous gunsmith and previous custom rifle manufacturer located in Mesa, AZ. Previous company name was Stockworks.

RIFLES: BOLT ACTION

ROBERT HISSERICH BOLT GUN – various cals., features Weatherby Vanguard action, Pac-Nor stainless steel barrel, Pachmayr Decelerator pad, hinged floorplate, black synthetic stock. Mfg. 2003-disc.

100%	98%	95%	90%	80%	70%	60%	LAST MSR
$1,795	$1,500	$1,250	$1,050	$875	$750	$625	

LIGHTWEIGHT RIFLES SLR – various cals., Rem. long or short action, Kevlar/fiberglass MPI stock, match grade Pac-Nor barrel, straight flutes in bolt body, Timney trigger, straight line muzzle brake, pillar bedded action, free floating barrel, "window" cuts in action for lightening, black oxide finish on carbon or stainless steel, English or Claro walnut deluxe checkered stock, custom order only. Approx. 4 3/4-5 lbs.

100%	98%	95%	90%	80%	70%	60%	LAST MSR
$2,600	$2,300	$2,000	$1,800	$1,600	$1,400	$1,200	

Add $200 for stainless steel.

SHARPSHOOTER – various cals., Win. Model 70 action with controlled feeding, precision long range hunting rifle with Schnieder stainless steel fluted barrel, laminated stock with ebony forend tip, titanium firing pin, pillar glass bedded with free floating barrel, includes Leupold 6.5-20x40mm scope, custom order only.

100%	98%	95%	90%	80%	70%	60%	LAST MSR
$5,950	$5,100	$4,500	$3,900	$3,400	$2,850	$2,150	

GRADING - PPGS™	100%	98%	95%	90%	80%	70%	60%	LAST MSR

ROBERTS DEFENSE

Previous semi-auto pistol manufacturer located in Oshkosh, WI from 2011-2019.

PISTOLS: SEMI-AUTO

EDGE PRO – .45 ACP cal., forged stainless steel frame and slide, 5 in. barrel, 8 shot mag., Bomar adj. rear sight, fiber optic front, single sided thumb safety, GI guide rod, black Nitride finish, 36.6 oz. Disc. 2016.

$1,775	$1,575	$1,375	$1,175	$975	$825	$675	*$1,950*

RECON SERIES – 9mm Para. or .45 ACP cal., Government or Commander style aircraft aluminum alloy frame, available in Recon Carry (3 1/2 in. bull barrel), Recon Custom (4 1/4 in. barrel), or Recon Pro (5 in. barrel), 8 shot, forged stainless steel slide, black combat rear sights, fiber optic front sights, single sided thumb safety, black Teflon (disc.) or black Cerakote frame coating, black nitride slide, 27.6-31.3 oz. Disc. 2019.

$2,025	$1,775	$1,525	$1,375	$1,125	$925	$725	*$2,370*

Add $200 for 9mm Para. cal.

* ***Recon Robin Egg*** – 9mm Para. or .45 ACP cal., forged alloy frame with Robin Egg Cerakote finish, 3 1/2, 4 1/4, or 5 in. barrel, 8 or 9 shot mag., forged stainless steel slide with satin stainless finish, Heinie black rear with red fiber optic front sights, single-sided thumb safety, one-piece full-length recoil system, 28.3-32.3 oz. Disc. 2019.

$2,185	$1,925	$1,650	$1,485	$1,200	$985	$775	*$2,570*

Add $200 for 9mm Para. cal.

OPERATOR SERIES – 9mm Para. or .45 ACP cal., Government or Commander style frame, forged stainless steel frame and slide, satin stainless Cerakote (Urban Ops), black Cerakote (Dark Ops), or black Cerakote slide and FDE Cerakote frame (Desert Ops) finish, available in 4 1/2 (Custom) or 5 (Pro) in. barrel, 8 shot mag., black serrated front and black combat rear sights (disc.) or Heinie Ledge Pro Tritium sights, ambi thumb safety, GI guide rod, universal rail, K-trigger, 36.6-41.4 oz. Disc. 2019

$2,000	$1,750	$1,500	$1,375	$1,125	$925	$725	*$2,350*

Add $200 for 9mm Para. cal.
Add $140 for black Cerakote finish (Dark Ops) or black Cerakote slide and FDE frame (Desert Ops) finish.

* ***Operator SRO*** – .45 ACP cal., 1911 style, suppressor and optic ready, 5 in. threaded barrel, 10 shot mag., Trijicon RMR sight, ambi thumb safety, forged stainless steel w/slide cuts, universal rail, black finish, 42 oz. Mfg. 2019 only.

$2,950	$2,600	$2,200	$2,000	$1,650	$1,350	$1,050	*$3,489*

SUPERGRADE STAINLESS – 9mm Para. or .45 ACP cal., forged stainless steel frame and slide, 3 1/2, 4 1/4, or 5 in. barrel, 8 or 9 shot mag., Heinie Slant Pro Tritium sights, GI guide rod, satin stainless steel finish, 33-39 oz. Disc. 2019.

$1,925	$1,685	$1,450	$1,325	$1,075	$875	$700	*$2,270*

Add $200 for 9mm Para. cal.

* ***Supergrade Edge*** – 9mm Para. or .45 ACP cal., forged stainless steel frame and slide, 5 in. barrel, 8 or 9 shot mag., adj. rear with green fiber optic front sight, GI guide rod, black Cerakote slide and frame finish, black hardware, 33-39 oz. Disc. 2019.

$2,285	$2,000	$1,725	$1,550	$1,250	$1,050	$900	*$2,690*

Add $200 for 9mm Para. cal.

* ***Supergrade Two-Tone*** – 9mm Para. or .45 ACP cal., forged stainless steel frame and slide, 3 1/2, 4 1/4, or 5 in. barrel, 8 or 9 shot mag., Heinie Slant Pro Tritium sights, GI guide rod, black Cerakote slide finish, satin stainless frame finish, black hardware, 33-39 oz. Disc. 2019.

$2,035	$1,775	$1,525	$1,375	$1,125	$925	$725	*$2,390*

Add $200 for 9mm Para. cal.

ROBERTS, J & SON (GUNMAKERS) LTD.

Please refer to the J. Roberts & Son (Gunmakers) Ltd. listing in the J section.

ROBERTSON

Current trademark manufactured by Boss & Co., Ltd. in Birmingham, England.

Please refer to the individual listings in the Boss section for this trademark.

ROBINSON ARMAMENT CO.

Current pistol and rifle manufacturer located in Salt Lake City, UT. Previously distributed by ZDF Import/Export, Inc., located in Salt Lake City, UT. Dealer and consumer direct sales.

For individual model listings, please go to BlueBookOfGunValues.com/overflow.

GRADING - PPGS™	100%	98%	95%	90%	80%	70%	60%	LAST MSR

ROBINSON CUSTOM GUNS LLC

Current custom rifle manufacturer located in Waynesburg, PA. Direct sales through FFLs.

Robinson Custom also offers rifles and shotgun restocking services in several wood grades and three designs: Classic, Monte Carlo, and Rollover. For more information, please contact the manufacturer directly.

RIFLES: BOLT ACTION

Additionally, Robinson Custom Guns also restocks guns and offers metal finishing services. For more information on these models and services, please contact the company directly.

GRIZZLY GRADE – .378-.460 Wby. cals., Weatherby Mark V action or Montana Magnum action Safari Grade, precision fit Douglas air gauged lapped chrome moly barrel, metal work is either polished or bead blasted blue finish, XXX Grade Bastogne walnut classic or Monte Carlo stock, checkered with a beautiful point pattern and finished in Satin, Medium, or High Gloss, includes recoil brake, inletted classic swivel studs, and a choice of recoil pads along with a choice of exotic wood tip and cap or steel fixtures.

Base MSR for this model is $5,100.

MOUNTAINEER – various cals., Howa or Weatherby Vanguard barreled action, Claro AAA Grade walnut stock in customer's choice of either Classic or Monte Carlo design, checkered with a beautiful point pattern and finished in Satin, Medium, or High Gloss, glass bedded, includes recoil pad, swivel studs, and the proper tip and cap of exotic wood.

Base MSR for this model is $3,100.

ROYAL STAG GRADE – .222-.340 Wby. cals., Douglas Montana action, precision fit air gauged lapped chrome moly barrel in customer's choice of caliber, taper, and length, either polished or bead blasted finish, XXXX Grade Bastogne walnut classic Monte Carlo stock, checkered with a beautiful point pattern and finished in Satin, Medium, or High Gloss, includes inletted classic swivels, recoil pad, and exotic wood tip and cap.

Base MSR for this model is $4,500.

WHITETAIL – .222-.340 Wby. cals., Weatherby Vanguard or Howa 1500 action, precision fit air gauged Douglas lapped chrome moly barrel in customer's choice of caliber, taper, and length, polished or bead blasted finish, American or Claro AAA Grade walnut Monte Carlo stock, checkered with a beautiful point pattern and finished in Satin, Medium, or High Gloss, includes recoil pad, swivel studs, and exotic wood cap.

Base MSR for this model is $3,700.

ROCHE, CHRISTIAN

Previous manufacturer located in Veauche, France.

Christian Roche manufactured quality SxS shotguns and double rifles built to individual specifications.

ROCK ISLAND ARMORY

Previous WWII Springfield Model 1903 rifle subcontractor located in Rock Island, IL. Please refer to the Springfield Armory listing in the S section.

ROCK ISLAND ARMORY (CURRENT MFG.)

Current trademark manufactured by Armscor (Arms Corp. of the Philippines) and Armscor USA beginning in 2016 and located in Pahrump, NV. Philippines manufactured firearms are currently imported by Armscor USA, located in Pahrump, NV.

PISTOLS: SEMI-AUTO

M1911-A1 CSP – .45 ACP cal., officer's configuration with 3 1/2 in. barrel, checkered hardwood grips, 2.16 lbs. Imported 2002-2014.

	100%	98%	95%	90%	80%	70%	60%	LAST MSR
	$425	$375	$335	$300	$275	$245	$225	

Add $52 for two-tone finish (disc. 2011).
Add $105 for stainless steel (disc. 2011).
Add $58 for Model 1911-A1 CS RIA Tactical.

M1911-A1 FSP – 9mm Para. (new 2011), .38 Super or .45 ACP cal., patterned after the Colt Govt. Model, SA, 7 shot mag. (2 provided), 5 in. barrel, parkerized (disc. 2001), nickel, blue (new 2002), two-tone (new 2002), or stainless steel (new 2002), skeletonized combat hammer and trigger, front and rear slide serrations, hard rubber grips, 38 oz. Imported 1996-97, reintroduced 2001-disc.

	100%	98%	95%	90%	80%	70%	60%	LAST MSR
	$425	$375	$340	$310	$285	$265	$245	*$538*

Add $10 for MSP Model or for .38 Super cal.
Add $48 for Duracoat finish.

GRADING - PPGS™	100%	98%	95%	90%	80%	70%	60%	LAST MSR

Add $34 for two-tone finish.
Add $100 for stainless steel (disc. 2011)
Add $60 for a high capacity configuration (Model 1911-A2 HC, 13 shot mag., disc. 2009).
Add $60 for Model 1911-A1 FS RIA Tactical (.45 ACP cal. only) or $84 for FS RIA Tactical with Duracoat (new 2012).
Add $205 for Model 1911-A2 FS RIA Match Model (.45 ACP cal. only).
Add $55 for nickel finish (Model 1911-A1 FSNP).
Add $100 for night sights (new 2012).

M1911-A1 MICRO MAG – .22 TCM and 9mm Para. cals., supplied with 2 barrels and 2 mags., 22 shot mag., features an appearance similar to M1911-A1 FS Tactical. Mfg. 2011-2014.

	$575	$500	$425	$375	$325	$300	$275	

Add $45 for Micro Mag Target Model (new 2012).

M1911-A2 MS TACTICAL – .22 TCM cal., SA, 5 in. barrel, parkerized finish, 17 shot mag., fiber optic front sight, adj. rear sight, combat hammer, skeletonized trigger and magwell. Imported 2013-2017.

No MSR	$845	$745	$635	$575	$465	$375	$295	

BBR STANDARD CS (M1911-A380 "BABY ROCK")/BBR 3.10 – .380 ACP or .45 ACP (disc. 2019) cal., single action, blowback operation, 3 3/4 in. barrel, 7 shot mag., all steel construction, pivoting external extractor, Commander style hammer, front sight mounted on dovetail cut, snag free style rear sight, checkered black rubber grips, beavertail grip and thumb safety, parkerized finish, 23.5 oz. New 2016.

MSR $460	$400	$350	$300	$275	$225	$175	$150	

* ***BBR 3.10*** – .45 ACP cal., compact size, 3.10 in. barrel, 10 shot mag., pivoting external extractor, dovetail front fiber optic and MPS2 adj. rear snag free style rear sights, G10 grips, beavertail grip safety, parkerized finish. New 2020.

MSR $699	$600	$500	$450	$400	$325	$275	$200	

GI STANDARD FS – 9mm Para., .45 ACP, or .38 Super cal., full size 1911 style, 5 in. barrel with (new 2018, .45 ACP only) or without threading, 8 or 9 shot, fixed sights, smooth wood grips, parkerized, nickel, matte nickel (new 2020), or Duracoat (disc. 2018) finish, 2.47 lbs.

MSR $522	$450	$400	$325	$300	$250	$200	$150	

Add $30 for threaded barrel (.45 ACP cal., new 2018).
Add $7 for .45 ACP or $23 for .38 Super cal.
Add $38 for Duracoat finish (disc. 2018).
Add $292 for nickel finish.

* ***GI Standard FS High Capacity*** – .45 ACP cal., 5 in. barrel, 10 shot double stack mag., fixed low profile sights, black checkered polymer grips, black parkerized finish, 2.56 lbs.

MSR $608	$525	$475	$425	$385	$325	$285	$250	

GI STANDARD MS – .45 ACP cal., mid-size 1911 style, 4 1/4 in. barrel, 8 shot, fixed sights, smooth wood grips, black parkerized finish, 2.36 lbs.

MSR $537	$450	$400	$350	$300	$250	$200	$150	

GI STANDARD CS – .45 ACP cal., compact size 1911 style, 3 1/2 in. barrel, 7 shot, fixed sights, smooth wood grips, parkerized finish, 2.16 lbs.

MSR $545	$425	$375	$340	$310	$285	$265	$245	

MAP FS – 9mm Para. cal., full size metal frame, 4 in. barrel, 15 shot, integrated front and snag free rear sights, black finish, 2.53 lbs. Disc. 2018.

	$425	$375	$335	$285	$250	$225	$200	*$492*

MAP MS – 9mm Para. cal., mid-size metal frame, 4 in. barrel, 15 shot, integrated front and snag free rear sights, black finish, 2.35 lbs. Disc. 2018.

	$425	$375	$335	$285	$250	$225	$200	*$492*

MAPP FS – 9mm Para. cal., full size polymer frame, 3 1/2 in. barrel, 10 shot, integrated front and snag free rear sights, lower Picatinny rail, black finish, 2.13 lbs.

MSR $492	$425	$375	$335	$285	$250	$225	$200	

MAPP MS – 9mm Para. cal., mid-size polymer frame, 3 1/2 in. barrel, 10 shot, integrated front and snag free rear sights, lower Picatinny rail, black finish, 1.83 lbs.

MSR $492	$425	$375	$335	$285	$250	$225	$200	

MAPP TCM9R – TCM9R cal., 3.8 in. barrel, 16 shot mag., MPS2 adj. sights, black polymer grips, Picatinny rail, parkerized finish, 2.22 lbs. Mfg. 2017-2020.

	$425	$375	$335	$285	$250	$225	$200	*$492*

GRADING - PPGS™	100%	98%	95%	90%	80%	70%	60%	LAST MSR

MAPP FS TCM9R – 22TCM9R cal., 4.64 in. barrel, 16 shot mag., MPS2 adj. sights, black polymer grips, Picatinny rail, parkerized finish, 2.22 lbs. Mfg. 2017-2018.

	$385	$345	$315	$265	$235	$210	$185	$492

PRO MATCH (TAC) ULTRA – .45 ACP cal., 6 in. barrel, 8 shot mag., Picatinny rail, skeletonized trigger, extended beavertail, adj. rear and fiber optic front sights, parkerized finish, 2 1/2 lbs. New 2015.

MSR $1,126	$965	$875	$775	$650	$575	$485	$435

PRO MATCH ULTRA (M1911-A1 FS MATCH) – .45 ACP cal., 5 or 6 (disc.) in. barrel, 8 shot mag., fiber optic front sight and adj. LPA rear sight, extended beavertail, skeletonized trigger and bobbed hammer, double diamond checkered walnut (5 in. model) or black plastic (6 in, disc.) grips, parkerized finish, 2 1/2 lbs. New 2011.

MSR $862	$735	$650	$575	$475	$400	$350	$300

Add $104 for 6 in. barrel (disc. 2016).

* ***Pro Match Ultra HC*** – .40 S&W cal., 5 in. barrel, 16 shot mag., black grips, otherwise similar to Pro Match Ultra model. New 2015.

MSR $1,077	$925	$815	$750	$625	$550	$450	$400

PRO MATCH ULTRA 6 IN./ULTRA HC 6 IN. – 10mm cal., SAO, 6 in. barrel, 8 or 16 (HC model) shot mag., skeletonized hammer, adj. LPA rear sight and high visibility fiber optic front sight, rubber or G10 (HC model) grips, full-length Picatinny rail, extended beavertail, black parkerized finish, 2.49-2.9 lbs. New 2015.

MSR $1,168	$975	$875	$800	$675	$600	$515	$465

Add $154 for double stack frame, 16 shot mag., and G10 grips (high capacity model).

ROCK STANDARD CS – .45 ACP cal., SAO, compact size, 3 1/2 in. button rifled barrel, 7 shot, skeletonized hammer and trigger, dovetail mounted front and fixed rear sight, checkered rubber grips, ambi safety, full-length guide rod, parkerized matte or stainless (new 2020) finish, 2.16 lbs.

MSR $618	$535	$485	$435	$395	$335	$295	$265

ROCK STANDARD FS – 9mm Para. or .45 ACP cal., SAO, full size 1911 style, parkerized or nickel frame and slide, 5 in. button rifled barrel, 8 shot, skeletonized hammer and trigger, low profile angled rear sight, checkered rubber grips, ambi safety, full-length guide rod, matte nickel, Duo-tone, or parkerized finish, 2.49 lbs.

MSR $592	$515	$465	$415	$375	$315	$275	$250

Add $2 for 9mm Para. cal.
Add $68 for Duo-tone or $137 for nickel finish.

ROCK STANDARD MS – .45 ACP cal., 4 1/4 in. button rifled barrel, 8 shot mag., skeletonized hammer and trigger, dovetail-mounted standard front sight, fixed rear sight, rubber grips, ambi safety, parkerized matte finish. Mfg. 2016-2018.

	$515	$465	$415	$375	$315	$275	$250	$592

ROCK ULTRA CCO – .45 ACP or 9mm/22TCM9R combo (new 2020) cal., SAO, aluminum frame, 4.25 in. button rifled barrel, Commander length slide, 8 shot, skeletonized hammer and trigger, fiber optic front sight and LPA MPS1 type adj. rear sight, G10 tactical grips, black hardcoat anodized/parkerized finish. New 2016.

MSR $760	$645	$565	$515	$475	$415	$365	$345

ROCK ULTRA CS/CS-L – .45 ACP or 9mm/22TCM9R combo (mfg. 2020 only) cal., 3 1/2 or 3.62 in. button rifled barrel, 7 or 8 (combo, mfg. 2020 only) shot mag., dovetail fiber optic front sight, LPA MPS1 type adj. rear sight, G10 grips, ambi safety (CS model only), skeletonized hammer and trigger w/adjustable over travel stop, black oxide frame and parkerized finish, 2.35 lbs. New 2016.

MSR $731	$600	$550	$475	$425	$350	$275	$225

Add $14 for Rock Ultra CS-L (Lightweight, new 2017).

ROCK ULTRA CS WARRIOR – .45 ACP cal., 3.15 in. barrel, dovetail mounted front and fixed rear sights, G10 grips, parkerized finish. Mfg. 2016-2017.

	$695	$615	$565	$525	$445	$400	$375	$814

ROCK ULTRA FS (M1911-A1 FS TACTICAL II) – 9mm Para., 9mm/22TCM9R combo (mfg. 2020 only), 10mm, .40 S&W, or .45 ACP cal., SA, full size frame, 5 in. button rifled barrel, 8 or 9 (9mm Para. only) shot mag., combat hammer, skeletonized trigger, adj. rear sight, fiber optic front sight, VZ (disc.) or G10 tactical grips, ambi safety, full-length guide rod, parkerized finish, 2.49 lbs. New 2013.

MSR $722	$615	$535	$485	$435	$385	$335	$315

Add $23 for 10mm cal.

GRADING - PPGS™	100%	98%	95%	90%	80%	70%	60%	LAST MSR

* ***Rock Ultra FS High Capacity (M1911-A2 FS Tactical/Tactical II)*** – 22 TCM (disc.), 9mm Para. (disc.), .40 S&W (disc.), 10mm, or .45 ACP (disc. 2016) cal., SA, 5 in. barrel, 14 (disc.), 16, or 17 (disc.) shot mag., combat hammer, skeletonized trigger, orange fiber optic front and adj. rear sight, ambi safety, ext. beavertail grip safety, full-length guide rod, Parkerized finish, 2.9 lbs. Mfg. 2013-2018, reintroduced 2020 only.

	$675	$595	$545	$515	$435	$385	$365	*$802*

Subtract approx. $25 for 9mm Para., .40 S&W, .22 TCM, or .45 ACP cal. (disc. 2016).
Add $40 for rail (disc. 2016).

ROCK ULTRA MS – .45 ACP, 10mm (disc. 2018), or .40 S&W (disc. 2016) cal., 4.25 in. button rifled barrel, 8 shot, skeletonized hammer, low profile rear and fiber optic front sights, G10 grips, ambi safety, full-length guide rod, parkerized matte finish, 2.36 lbs.

MSR $731	$625	$545	$495	$450	$395	$350	$325	

Add $21 for 10mm cal. (disc. 2018).

TAC STANDARD FS (M1911-A1 FS TACTICAL) – .45 ACP cal., SA, 5 in. barrel, 8 shot mag., skeletonized trigger, rear slide serrations, bobbed hammer, lower Picatinny rail, diamond checkered walnut grips, parkerized finish, standard or night sights (disc.), full dust cover rail, single stack. New 2011.

MSR $685	$575	$500	$450	$415	$365	$325	$300	

Add $121 for night sights (disc.).

TAC ULTRA CS – 9mm Para. or .45 ACP cal., compact model, 3 1/2 in. barrel, 7 or 8 shot mag., combat hammer, skeletonized trigger, extended beavertail, G10 grip, tactical rail, ambi safety and slide, full dust cover rail, 2-dot tactical adj. rear and fiber optic front sights, front and back wide-angled slide serrations. New 2014.

MSR $786	$665	$585	$535	$500	$425	$365	$350	

TAC ULTRA FS – .45 ACP, 10mm, .or 40 S&W (mfg. 2015-2016) cal., 5 in. barrel, 8 shot, full dust cover rail, combat trigger, extended beavertail, 2-dot tactical adj. rear and orange fiber optic front sights, front and back wide-angled slide serrations, ambi safety, tactical rail, single stack (.40 S&W only), G10 or VZ grip, 2 1/2 lbs.

MSR $775	$650	$575	$525	$495	$415	$350	$345	

Add $31 for 10mm cal.

* ***Tac Ultra FS HC (High Capacity)*** – 9mm Para., 9mm/22TCM9R combo (mfg. 2020 only), .45 ACP, or .40 S&W (mfg. 2015-2016) cal., similar to Tac Ultra FS, except has 10 (combo, mfg. 2020 only), 14 (.45 ACP), 16 (.40 S&W), or 17 (9mm) shot, 3 lbs.

MSR $906	$775	$695	$645	$585	$500	$450	$395	

TAC ULTRA MS – 9mm Para. (disc. 2016), 9mm/22TCM9R combo (mfg. 2020 only), 10mm, .40 S&W (disc. 2016), or .45 ACP (disc. 2016) cal., mid-size model, 8, 9 (9mm only), or 17 (combo, mfg. 2020 only) shot, combat hammer, skeletonized trigger, extended beavertail, tactical rail, ambi safety and slide, full dust cover rail, 2-dot tactical adj. rear and fiber optic front sights, front and back wide-angled slide serrations, G10 grip. Mfg. 2015-2018, reintroduced 2020.

MSR $814	$700	$600	$500	$475	$375	$300	$250	

Subtract approx. $25 for 9mm Para., .40 S&W, or .45 ACP cal. (all disc. 2016).

TAC FS TITANIUM – .45 ACP cal., full size, 8 shot, titanium construction. Mfg. 2015-2016.

	$1,000	$900	$775	$650	$575	$485	$435	*$1,156*

TCM PREMIUM FS – .22 TCM cal., 5 in. barrel, 17 shot, ordnance steel, skeletonized hammer and trigger, fiber optic front and 2-dot LPA rear sight, G10 tactical grips, parkerized finish. New 2020.

Please contact the manufacturer directly for pricing and availability on this model.

TCM ROCK STANDARD FS HIGH CAP – .22 TCM or .22 TCM9R cal., full size frame, 5 in. barrel, 7 shot, outfitted with an original Armscor cartridge, combat trigger, fiber optic front and adj. rear sights, extended beavertail, slide serrations, black checkered synthetic grips, Parkerized finish, standard or target configuration, Micro Mag. also comes with a 9mm barrel for practice, 2.6 lbs. Mfg. 2013-2019.

	$715	$635	$585	$535	$450	$400	$375	*$837*

Add $31 for Target configuraton.

* ***TCM Rock Standard MS High Cap*** – .22 TCM or .22 TCM9R cal., 4.2 in. barrel, similar to TCM Rock Standard FS High Cap, except has mid-size frame. Mfg. 2013-2019.

	$715	$635	$585	$535	$450	$400	$375	*$837*

TCM ROCK ULTRA CCO – .22 TCM or .22 TCM9R cal., 4 1/4 in. barrel, 8 shot mag., aluminum frame, dovetail fiber optic front sight, LPA MPS 1 Type adj. rear sight, G10 grips, skeletonized hammer and trigger, parkerized/anodized coated finish. Mfg. 2016 only.

	$725	$650	$600	$550	$465	$415	$385	*$845*

GRADING - PPGS™	100%	98%	95%	90%	80%	70%	60%	LAST MSR

TCM ROCK ULTRA CS-L – .22 TCM or .22 TCM9R cal., aluminum frame, 3.62 in. barrel, 8 shot, single stack beveled magwell, skeletonized hammer, fiber optic front and adj. rear sight, G10 grips, includes 9mm accessory barrel, black parkerized finish, 2.91 lbs. Mfg. 2016-2019.

$715 $635 $585 $535 $450 $400 $375 *$837*

TCM ROCK ULTRA FS – .22 TCM or .22 TCM9R cal., full size, 5 in. barrel, 10 shot mag., combat trigger, fiber optic front and adj. rear sights, G10 grips, ambi safety, full-length guide rod, tactical rail, extended beavertail, Parkerized finish. Mfg. 2015-2017, reintroduced 2019 only.

$685 $600 $500 $515 $435 $385 $365 *$806*

* ***TCM Rock Ultra MS*** – .22 TCM or .22 TCM9R cal., similar to TCM Rock Ultra FS, except has mid-size frame. Mfg. 2015-2017.

$715 $635 $585 $535 $450 $400 $375 *$835*

TCM STANDARD FS – .22 TCM cal., 5 in. barrel, 17 shot, ordnance steel, skeletonized hammer and trigger, low profile anti-snag front and rear sights, checkered polymer grips, parkerized finish. New 2020.

Please contact the manufacturer directly for pricing and availability on this model.

TCM STANDARD MS – .22 TCM cal., 4.25 in. barrel, 17 shot, ordnance steel, skeletonized hammer and trigger, low profile anti-snag front and rear sights, checkered polymer grips, parkerized finish. New 2020.

Please contact the manufacturer directly for pricing and availability on this model.

TCM TAC ULTRA FS – .22 TCM or .22 TCM9R cal., full size, 10 shot mag., combat trigger, 2-dot adj. rear LPA and TruGlo high visibility front sights, front and back wide angled slide serrations, full dust cover rail, ambi safety, tactical rail, extended beavertail, G10 grips, Parkerized finish, includes 9mm conversion barrel, 3 lbs. Mfg. 2015-2017, reintroduced 2019 only.

$765 $685 $635 $585 $500 $450 $400 *$891*

* ***TCM Tac Ultra MS*** – .22 TCM or .22 TCM9R cal., similar to TCM Tac Ultra FS except has mid-size frame. Mfg. 2015-2017.

$765 $685 $635 $585 $500 $450 $400 *$882*

TCM TAC ULTRA FS HIGH CAP COMBO – .22 TCM or .22 TCM9R cal., full size, 5 in. barrel, 17 shot mag., outfitted with an original Armscor cartridge, combat trigger, fiber optic front and adj. rear sights, tactical rail, extended beavertail, G10 grips, Parkerized finish, 3 lbs. Mfg. 2015-2019.

$825 $745 $685 $635 $550 $495 $435 *$960*

* ***TCM Tac Ultra MS High Cap Combo*** – .22 TCM or .22 TCM9R cal., 4.2 in. barrel, similar to TCM Tac Ultra FS, except has mid-size frame, 2 1/2 lbs. Mfg. 2015-2019.

$825 $745 $685 $635 $550 $495 $435 *$960*

XT 22 STANDARD – .22 LR cal., delayed blowback action, steel construction, 5 in. modular barrel, 10 or 15 shot mag., skeletonized trigger, bobbed hammer, integral rail mount, checkered synthetic grips, parkerized finish, 38 oz. Mfg. 2011-2018.

$515 $465 $415 $375 $315 $275 $250 *$595*

* ***XT 22 Standard Combo*** – .22 LR/.45 ACP cal., steel construction, 5 in. modular barrel, 8 or 10 shot mag., delayed blowback action with integral rail mount, low profile snag free sights, checkered synthetic grips, parkerized finish, 2.22 lbs.

MSR $885 $765 $685 $635 $585 $500 $450 $400

* ***XT 22 Magnum/Magnum Target/Magnum Pro*** – .22 Mag. cal., steel construction, 5 in. modular (disc.), solid state (new 2020, Magnum or Target models), or exposed bull (Magnum Pro, new 2020) barrel, 14 (new 2020) or 15 shot mag., delayed blowback action with integral rail mount, fixed dovetail front sights and MPS2 adj. rear (Target) or low profile snag free sights, checkered synthetic grips, parkerized finish, 2.22 lbs. Mfg. late 2014-2018, reintroduced 2020.

MSR $614 $515 $465 $415 $375 $315 $275 $250

* ***XT 22 TAC*** – .22 LR cal., steel construction, modular barrel, 10 shot mag., top Picatinny rail, skeletonized trigger, bobbed hammer, checkered synthetic grips, parkerized finish, 2.22 lbs. Mfg. 2014-2016.

$535 $450 $400 $365 $335 $300 $275 *$712*

REVOLVERS

MODEL 200 – .38 Spl. cal., 6 shot, double action, 4 in. barrel with shroud, transfer bar safety, combat style rubber grips, blue finish only, fixed rear sight, 26 oz. Importation began 2015.

MSR $275 $225 $200 $175 $150 $125 $100 $75

GRADING - PPGS™	100%	98%	95%	90%	80%	70%	60%	LAST MSR

MODEL 206 – .38 Spl. cal., SA/DA, 2 in. barrel, 6 shot, checkered wood grips, parkerized finish, 24 oz. Importation began 2015.

MSR $283	$250	$200	$175	$175	$125	$100	$75	

* ***Model 206 Spurless*** – .38 Spl. cal., 2 in. fully shrouded barrel, 6 shot, fixed sights, spurless hammer, checkered wood grip, parkerized or matte nickel finish, 1.59 lbs. New 2015.

MSR $492	$425	$375	$325	$275	$225	$200	$150	

RIFLES: BOLT ACTION

M22 TCM BA – .22 TCM cal., 22 3/4 in. grooved barrel with contoured rear end, 5 shot mag., solid wood stock with classic checkering, ebony forearm tip, and dark wood grip cap, includes receiver rail mount for scope attachment. New 2016.

MSR $454	$375	$325	$300	$250	$200	$175	$125	

* ***M22 TCM Tactical*** – .22 TCM cal., 22 in. ordinance steel barrel, 5 shot mag., polymer stock, includes receiver rail mount for scope attachment, parkerized/anodized finish, 7 lbs. New 2019.

MSR $449	$375	$325	$300	$250	$200	$175	$125	

M14Y YOUTH RIFLE – .22 LR cal., 18 3/4 in. contoured threaded (new mid-2020) or unthreaded barrel, 6 shot (disc.), 10 shot, or optional 15 (new mid-2020) shot mag., hooded bead ramp front sight and leaf type rear sight, natural finish Philippine wood junior size stock, Monte Carlo style with plastic buttpad, Parkerized finish, 5 lbs.

MSR $146	$120	$110	$100	$85	$75	$65	$50	

RIFLES: SEMI-AUTO

M20P SA – .22 LR cal., 21 in. straight tapered barrel, 6 shot, hooded bead ramp front and leaf type rear sights, natural finish Philippine wood Monte Carlo style stock with plastic buttpad, parkerized finish, 6 1/2 lbs.

MSR $152	$130	$110	$100	$85	$75	$70	$65	

M1600 SA – .22 LR cal., 18 1/2 in. barrel, 10 or 15 (high capacity mag.) shot, carry handle, A2 front sight post, fixed stock, black finish.

MSR $202	$185	$160	$140	$125	$115	$100	$90	

MAK22 SA AL (MAK22 SA) – .22 LR cal., AK-47 design, 18 1/4 in. barrel, 10 shot mag., post front and open U-notch rear sights, wood stock pistol grip, blue finish, 7 lbs.

MSR $206	$185	$160	$140	$125	$115	$100	$90	

MIG 22 STANDARD – .22 LR cal., 16 1/4 in. free floated match grade barrel, 15 shot, fixed stock, one-piece billet aluminum receiver with integral accessory rail, parkerized finish. New 2017.

MSR $399	$350	$295	$260	$230	$210	$190	$175	

MIG 22 TACTICAL – .22 LR cal., 16 1/4 in. free floated match grade barrel, 15 shot, fixed pistol grip stock, one-piece billet aluminum receiver with integral accessory on top and bottom, black parkerized finish. New 2017.

MSR $549	$475	$400	$350	$300	$265	$235	$200	

MIG 22 TARGET – .22 LR cal., 18 in. free floated match grade barrel, 15 shot mag., fixed stock, billet aluminum receiver with integral accessory rail, parkerized/anodized finish. Mfg. 2017-2019.

	$435	$370	$315	$275	$240	$215	$185	*$499*

SHOTGUNS: O/U

OVER/UNDER COMPETITION – 12 ga. 2 3/4 or 3 in. chambers, 28 in. VR barrels w/vent. mid rib, threaded for chokes, 2 shots, automatic ejectors, fiber optic front sight, fixed walnut stock w/adj. cheekpiece, walnut forearm, high gloss blued finish, 7 lbs. New 2019.

MSR $1,045	$885	$775	$665	$600	$485	$400	$325	

OVER UNDER PLUS 1 – 12 ga., 2 3/4 or 3 in. chambers, 28 in. contour barrels, bead front sight, fixed deluxe walnut stock, blued or silver anodized finish, 7.2. lbs. Mfg. 2019 only.

	$1,550	$1,350	$1,165	$1,050	$850	$700	$600	*$1,832*

OVER/UNDER STANDARD – 12 ga. 2 3/4 or 3 in. chambers, 28 in. VR barrels w/vent. mid rib, threaded for chokes, 2 shots, front bead sight, walnut stock and forearm, parkerized black or matte blued finish, 7 lbs. New 2019.

MSR $615	$525	$460	$395	$350	$300	$250	$200	

S40 O/U – 12 ga., 28 in. VR barrels, includes F/M/IC choke tubes, automatic ejectors, fine checkering, vented recoil pad, high gloss finish, 7.71 lbs. Mfg. 2016-2017.

	$465	$415	$365	$335	$300	$275	$250	*$537*

GRADING - PPGS™	100%	98%	95%	90%	80%	70%	60%	LAST MSR

SHOTGUNS: SEMI-AUTO

LION PRINCIPAL SA – 12 ga., 28 in. threaded VR barrel, 4 or 5 (new 2020) shot mag., fiber optic front sight, adj. open rear sight, fixed polymer stock, black anodized, Real Tree Max-5 (new 2020) or Timber (new 2020) finish, 7.4 lbs. Mfg. 2019-2020.

	$335	$285	$250	$210	$190	$180	$155	*$382*

LION TACTICAL SA – 12 ga., 18 in. threaded VR barrel, 4 shot mag., fiber optic front sight, adj. open rear sight, fixed polymer stock, black anodized finish, 7 lbs. New 2019.

MSR $399	$350	$300	$250	$225	$175	$150	$125	

S605 TAC SA SHOTGUN – 12 ga., 20 in. steel barrel, white/black chrome receiver, 5 shot, fixed pistol grip stock, black finish. Mfg. 2015-2017.

	$365	$315	$265	$225	$200	$185	$160	*$415*

SA SHOTGUN LONG STANDARD – 12 ga., 2 3/4 or 3 in. chamber, inertia action, 18 1/2 in. VR barrel with F/M/IC choke tubes, 4 shot, bead front sight, lightweight aluminum receiver, lightweight polymer furniture. Mfg. 2017-2019.

	$345	$295	$255	$215	$190	$180	$155	*$399*

SA SHOTGUN TACT – 12 ga., 2 3/4 or 3 in. chamber, inertia action, 18 1/2 in. VR barrel with three choke tubes, 4 shot, black chrome receiver, polymer stock. Mfg. 2017-2019.

	$345	$295	$255	$215	$190	$180	$155	*$399*

LION CONCEAL C/ LION CONCEAL P – 12 ga., 28 in. contoured barrel, 4 shot mag., bead front sight, polymer stock, camo or Muddy Girl camo finish, 7.6 lbs. Mfg. 2019 only.

	$450	$400	$350	$300	$275	$250	$225	*$533*

LION SPORT/LION WANDERER/LION ELEGANCE – 12 ga., 28 in. threaded contour barrel, 5 shot mag., bead front sight, top rail rear sight (Elegance), fixed polymer or walnut (Wanderer) stock, black/red or silver (Wanderer and Elegance) anodized finish, 7.6 lbs. Mfg. 2019 only.

	$350	$300	$260	$215	$195	$180	$155	*$407*

Add $126 for top rail rear sight w/silver anodized finish.

VR60 SHOTGUN STANDARD – 12 ga., 2 3/4 or 3 in. chamber, semi-auto, AR-15 style, gas operated, 20 in. barrel with F/M/IC choke tubes, 5 shot, bead front sights, enlarged polymer handguard, aluminum alloy upper receiver, removable A2 carry handle, integral Picatinny rail, manual safety, polymer pistol grip stock, red chrome (disc. 2019) or gray chrome (disc. 2019) finish. New 2017.

MSR $499	$450	$400	$360	$330	$295	$265	$240	

Add $16 for gray chrome finish (disc. 2019).

VR60 PLUS 1 – 12 ga., 2 3/4 or 3 in. chamber, semi-auto AR-15 style, gas operated, 20 in. barrel with three choke tubes, 5 shot, bead front sight, polymer stock, raised cheekpiece, rubber buttpad, enlarged polymer handguard, aluminum alloy upper receiver, removable A2 carry handle, integral Picatinny rail, black (disc. 2018), FDE, or red (disc. 2018) finish. Mfg. 2017-2019.

	$475	$425	$375	$335	$300	$275	$250	*$562*

Subtract approx. $20 for black finish (disc. 2018).

VR80 – 12 ga., 2 3/4 or 3 in. chamber, gas operated, AR-15 style ergonomics and controls, 20 in. contoured barrel, fluted barrel shroud, 5 shot mag., thumbhole stock, 7075 T6 aluminum receiver, flip-up front and rear sights, reciprocating charging handle, black anodized or Realtree Timber (Mfg. 2020 only) finish, 8.27-9.03 lbs. New 2019.

MSR $699	$595	$525	$450	$395	$350	$300	$275	

VR82 – 20 ga., 2 3/4 or 3 in. chamber, gas operated, AR-15 ergonomics and controls, 18 in. contoured barrel w/fluted barrel shroud, 5 shot mag., thumb hole stock, 7075 T6 aluminum receiver, black anodized finish, 8.5 lbs., New 2020.

MSR $729	$625	$540	$450	$395	$350	$300	$275	

VRBP100 – 12 ga., bullpup design, 20 in. contour barrel, 5 shot, polymer w/rubber spacers, left side charging handle, matte black, 7.94 lbs. New 2019.

MSR $774	$655	$575	$495	$445	$360	$295	$230	

SHOTGUNS: SINGLE SHOT

TRADITIONAL SINGLE SHOT – 12 (disc.), 20 ga., or .410 bore, 3 in. chamber, 20 in. contoured VR chrome-lined barrel, bead front sight, woodgrain polymer forearm and stock w/extra LOP buttpad spacers, black parkerized finish, 5 lbs. New 2019.

MSR $139	$120	$100	$90	$80	$70	$60	$50	

Add $560 for .410 bore.

GRADING - PPGS™	100%	98%	95%	90%	80%	70%	60%	LAST MSR

SHOTGUNS: SLIDE ACTION

AG "ALL GENERATIONS" PUMP ACTION - 12, 20 ga., or .410 bore, 2 3/4 or 3 in. chamber, 18 1/2 in. VR contoured barrel w/cylinder bore or 26 (.410 bore or 20 ga. only) or 28 in. VR barrel w/ interchangeable chokes, 5 shot mag., aluminum recveiver, bead front sight, polymer forearm and stock w/adj. cheekpiece and LOP, 7.1-8.82 lbs. New 2020.

MSR $299	$275	$225	$175	$175	$125	$100	$75	

M30 M5 SLIDE ACTION - 12 ga., 2 3/4 in. chamber, 20 in. barrel with vented heat guard, 4 shot, bead front sight, black polymer stock and forend with rubber buttpad, matte nickel finish, 7 1/2 lbs. Disc.

	$200	$170	$155	$140	$130	$120	$110	*$231*

MERIVA 3-IN-1 SHOTGUN - 12 ga., 18 1/2 in. cylinder bore barrel and 28 in. VR barrel, Slug, F/M/IC choke tubes, 4 shot, bead front sight, chrome receiver, synthetic rear removable stock, optional pistol grip. New 2017.

MSR $375	$325	$275	$250	$225	$175	$150	$100	

MERIVA STANDARD PUMP - 12 ga., 18 1/2 in. contoured barrel, 5 shot, fixed front sights, polymer stock, black anodized finish, 5.9 lbs. New 2019.

MSR $232	$200	$175	$150	$125	$100	$100	$75	

VRPA40 - 12 ga., 2 3/4 or 3 in. chamber, 20 in. contour barrel, 5 shot detachable mag., aluminum construction, Marine black anodized finish, 6.9 lbs. New 2019.

Please contact the manufacturer directly for pricing and availability on this model.

ROCK-OLA MANUFACTURING CO.

Previous WWII M1 carbine subcontractor located in Chicago, IL. Please refer to the U.S. Military Long Arms listing US M1 carbines/rifles in the U section.

ROCK RIVER ARMS, INC.

Current handgun and rifle manufacturer established in 1996 and located in Colona, IL beginning 2004. Previously located in Cleveland, IL until 2003. Dealer and consumer direct sales.

PISTOLS: SEMI-AUTO

Rock River Arms made a variety of high quality M-1911 based semi-autos through 2011. They specialized in manufacturing their own National Match frames and slides. Previous models included: the Standard Match (disc. 2003, last MSR was $1,150), Ultimate Match Achiever (disc. 2003, last MSR was $2,255), Matchmaster Steel (disc. 2001, last MSR was $2,355), Elite Commando (disc. 2005, last MSR was $1,725), Hi-Cap Basic Limited (disc. 2003, last MSR was $1,895), and the Doug Koenig Signature Series (disc. 2003, last MSR was $5,000, .38 Super cal.). Rock River Arms still offers parts, and reintroduced a 1911 model in 2013. In 2015, Rock River Arms reintroduced several of their renowned steel frame 1911-A1 models.

Add $200 for 1911-A1 Cerakote finish options in Barrett Bronze, Graphite Black, Gunmetal Gray, SOCOM Blue, Magpul Flat Dark Earth, Burnt Bronze (disc.), or Tan (disc.).

1911 POLY - .45 ACP cal., SA, 1911 style polymer frame, 5 in. chrome moly barrel, steel slide, two 7 shot mag., overmolded pistol grips, beavertail grip safety, Commander hammer, parkerized finish, aluminum speed trigger, dovetail front and rear sight, includes two mags., polymer holster, mag. loader, lock, and fitted case, 36 oz. Advertised 2013. Became available 2015.

MSR $1,025	$900	$795	$675	$615	$495	$400	$315	

1911-A1 BASIC LIMITED (BASIC LIMITED MATCH) - 9mm Para. (disc. 2010, reintroduced 2020), .38 Super (disc. 2010), .40 S&W (disc. 2010), or .45 ACP cal., SA, 4 1/4 (disc. 2010), 5, or 6 (disc. 2010) in. throated barrel, slide with double serrations, includes one mag., National Match frame with beveled magwell, low mount Bo-Mar hidden leaf rear and RRA dovetail front sights, Match Commander hammer and match sear, extractor and extended ejector, lowered and flared ejection port, beavertail grip safety, aluminum speed trigger, two-piece recoil guide rod and polished feed ramp, serrated slide stop and ambidextrous safety, deluxe checkered rosewood grips, blue, hard chrome (disc. 2010), black "T" (disc. 2010), or black/green "T" duotone (disc. 2010) finish. Disc. 2010, reintroduced 2015.

MSR $1,950	$1,750	$1,550	$1,300	$1,200	$950	$800	$600	

Last MSR in 2010 was $1,840.

GRADING - PPGS™	100%	98%	95%	90%	80%	70%	60%	LAST MSR

1911-A1 BULLSEYE WADCUTTER – 9mm Para. (disc. 2011, reintroduced 2020), .38 Super (disc. 2011), .40 S&W (disc. 2011), or .45 ACP cal., SA, 4 1/4 (disc. 2011), 5, or 6 (disc. 2011) in. barrel, throated NM KART barrel w/NM bushing (new 2015), 7 shot mag., forged National Match frame with choice of RRA Slide mount, Bo-Mar rib (disc. 2011), Bullseye rib (new 2015), Caspian frame mount sights (disc. 2011), or Weigand 3rd Gen. frame mount (disc.), double slide serrations, beavertail grip safety with raised pad, serrated slide stop and two-piece recoil guide rod, polished feed ramp, ext. ejector, lowered and flared ejection port, Commander hammer and match sear, aluminum speed trigger, checkered rosewood grips, blue, hard chrome (disc. 2011), black "T" (disc. 2011), or black/green "T" duotone (disc. 2011) finish. Disc. 2011, reintroduced 2015.

MSR $2,500	$2,250	$1,970	$1,690	$1,530	$1,250	$1,025	$800	

Last MSR in 2011 was $1,715.

Add $100 for Bullseye rib (new 2015).
Add $300 for 9mm or $400 for 9mm w/Bullseye rib.
Add $100 for Weigand frame mount (disc.).
Add $35 for Caspian frame mount or Bo-Mar rib (disc. 2011).

1911-A1 CARRY PISTOL (BASIC CARRY) – .45 ACP or 9mm Para. (mfg. 2020 only) cal., SA, 5 in. National Match throated barrel, double slide serrations, parkerized finish, checkered rosewood grips, RRA forged National Match frame, extended ejector, lowered and flared ejection port, RRA dovetail front sight with Tritium inserts, Heinie or Novak (new 2015) rear sight, Match Commander hammer and match sear, aluminum speed trigger, beavertail grip safety, standard (disc.) or tactical (new 2015) mag. catch, safety, and standard recoil system. Disc. 2010, reintroduced 2015.

MSR $1,650	$1,485	$1,300	$1,115	$1,010	$815	$675	$525	

1911-A1 LIMITED MATCH – 9mm Para. (disc. 2010, reintroduced 2020), .38 Super (disc. 2010), .40 S&W (disc. 2010), or .45 ACP cal., SA, 4 1/4 (disc. 2010), 5, or 6 (disc. 2010) in. barrel with double slide serrations and RRA borders, National Match frame with beveled magwell, checkered front and rear strap, low mount hidden leaf rear sight, RRA dovetail front sight, Match Commander hammer, aluminum speed trigger, lowered and flared ejection port, extended mag. release button, beavertail grip safety with raised pad, ambi thumb safety, deluxe checkered (disc. 2010) or G10 black laminate (new 2015) grips, two-piece recoil guide rod, blue (disc. 2010), brushed hard chrome, black "T" (disc. 2010), or black/green duo-tone (disc. 2010) finish, includes one mag. Disc. 2010, reintroduced 2015.

MSR $3,600	$3,240	$2,835	$2,430	$2,200	$1,780	$1,475	$1,150	

Last MSR in 2010 was $2,185.

1911-A1 NM HARDBALL (NATIONAL MATCH HARDBALL) – 9mm Para. (disc. 2011, reintroduced 2020), .38 Super (disc. 2011), .40 S&W (disc. 2011), or .45 ACP cal., SA, 4 1/4 (disc. 2011), 5, or 6 (disc. 2011) in throated KART. barrel, forged NM frame with beveled magwell, choice of rear or double (disc. 2011) slide serrations, aluminum speed trigger, checkered front strap, hidden leaf rear and dovetail front sights, lowered and flared ejection port, tuned and polished extractor and extended ejector, checkered rosewood (disc. 2011) or deluxe walnut grips, beavertail grip safety w/raised pad, blue, hard chrome (disc. 2011), black "T" (disc. 2011), or black/green "T" duotone (disc. 2011) finish, includes one mag. Disc. 2011, reintroduced 2015.

MSR $2,600	$2,350	$2,050	$1,765	$1,600	$1,295	$1,050	$825	

Last MSR in 2010 was $1,550.

Add $300 for 9mm. Para.

1911-A1 TACTICAL PISTOL – 9mm Para. (disc. 2011, reintroduced 2020 only), .38 Super (disc. 2011), .40 S&W (disc. 2011), or .45 ACP cal., SA, 5 in. barrel with double slide serrations, checkered front strap, RRA bar stock frame with integral light rail, lowered and flared ejection port, RRA dovetail front sight with Tritium inserts, Heinie (disc.) or Novak (mfg. 2015-disc.) RRA hidden leaf rear sight with Tritium inserts, aluminum speed trigger, tuned and polished extractor, extended ejector, Commander and match sear, beavertail grip safety with raised pad, tactical mag. catch and safety, standard recoil system, completely dehorned for carry, checkered rosewood grips, blue, hard chrome (disc. 2011), black "T" (disc. 2011), black ROCkote (new 2020), or black/green "T" duotone (disc. 2011) finish. Disc. 2011, reintroduced 2015.

MSR $2,200	$1,980	$1,735	$1,485	$1,350	$1,095	$895	$720	

RRA PRO CARRY – 9mm Para., .38 Super, .40 S&W, or .45 ACP cal., SA, 4 1/4, 5, or 6 in. barrel with slide serrations, RRA National Match frame, checkered front strap, lowered and flared ejection port, RRA dovetail front sight with Tritium inserts, Match Commander hammer, aluminum speed trigger, tuned and polished extractor, extended ejector, deluxe rosewood grips, choice of Heinie or Novak rear sight with Tritium inserts, beavertail grip safety. Disc. 2010.

	$1,675	$1,465	$1,255	$1,140	$920	$755	$585	*$1,920*

RRA SERVICE AUTO – 9mm Para. cal., similar to RRA Pro Carry, except with 5 in. barrel and double slide serrations. Mfg. 2009-2010.

	$1,575	$1,380	$1,180	$1,070	$865	$710	$550	*$1,790*

GRADING - PPGS™ 100% 98% 95% 90% 80% 70% 60% LAST MSR

LIMITED POLICE COMPETITION – 9mm Para. cal., 5 in. National Match barrel, SA, blue, hard chrome, black "T", or black/green "T" duotone finish, RRA forged National Match frame with beveled magwell with choice of 20, 25, or 30 LPI checkered front strap, double slide serrations, 3-position rear sight, choice of wide or narrow blade, RRA dovetail front sight (tall, thinned, and relieved for PPC), Smith & Alexander flared magwell, lowered and flared ejection port, Match Commander hammer and match sear, tuned and polished extractor and extended ejector, beavertail grip safety and flat checkered mainspring housing, deluxe checkered grips, ambidextrous safety, tuned and polished feed ramp, two-piece recoil spring guide rod. Disc. 2010.

$2,095 $1,825 $1,600 $1,375 $1,250 $1,000 $775 *$2,375*

UNLIMITED POLICE COMPETITION – 9mm Para. cal., forged 6 in. KKM (National Match) barrel, SA, RRA forged National Match frame with beveled magwell, choice of 20, 25, or 30 LPI checkered front strap, Aristocrat 3-position rear sight, double slide serrations, rosewood grips, includes two mags., similar configuration as Limited Police Competition. Disc. 2010, reintroduced 2020.

MSR $3,000 $2,700 $2,350 $2,000 $1,850 $1,500 $1,200 $950

Last MSR in 2010 was $2,375.

LAR-BT9G (BT-9) PISTOL – 9x19mm cal., 7 or 10 1/2 in. chrome moly or chrome-lined (10 1/2 in. only) barrel, A2 flash hider, SST (mfg. 2020 only) or two-stage trigger, SB Tactical SBA3 5-position adj. stabilizing arm brace, BT-9 billet aluminum lower with Glock compatible flared magwell and integral winter trigger guard, extruded aluminum A4 upper, 6, 7 1/4 (disc. 2020), or 9 1/4 in. lightweight free floating handguard (M-LOK compatible), RRA NSP Hogue overmolded pistol grip, 26 in. OAL, 5.4-6 lbs. New 2019.

MSR $1,315 $1,175 $1,050 $900 $800 $700 $575 $450

* ***LAR-BT9G RUK-9BT Pistol w/SBA3Brace*** – 9mm Para. cal., BT-9 billet aluminum lower with Glock compatible flared magwell with Glock compatible flared magwell, integral winter trigger guard, and extruded aluminum A4 upper receiver, extruded aluminum A4 upper, 4 1/2 chrome-lined barrel, Smith Vortex Flash Suppressor, RRA two stage trigger, flip-up front and rear sight, SB Tactical SBA3 5-position adj. stabilizing arm brace, Hogue rubber grips, extruded aluminum A4 upper and billet aluminum LAR-BT9G lower receiver, 4 1/4 in. lightweight aluminum free float rail (M-LOK compatible), pistol length, black finish, 23 in. OAL, 5.4 lbs. New 2021.

MSR $1,420 $1,275 $1,125 $975 $875 $750 $600 $500

LAR-9M (LAR-9) A4 PISTOL – 9mm Para. cal., 7 or 10 1/2 in. chrome moly or chrome-lined barrel, A2 flash hider, SST, receiver height sight base (10 1/2 in. barrel only), with or w/o SBA3 arm brace (new 2019), Hogue rubber grip, forged RRA LAR-9 lower receiver with integral magwell, extruded aluminum A4 upper receiver with port door, Picatinny rail, 6 or 9 1/4 in. RRA TRO free float handguard or R4 (10 1/2 in only) handguard, approx. 5-6 lbs.

MSR $920 $825 $725 $650 $575 $500 $400 $325

Add $105 for SBA3 arm brace.

* ***LAR-9M RUK-9 A4 Pistol w/SBA3 Brace*** – 9mm Para. cal., 4 1/2 chrome-lined barrel, Smith Vortex flash suppressor, one 9mm Colt SMG compatible mag., SST, flip-up front and rear sight, SB Tactical SBA3 arm brace, Hogue rubber grip, extruded aluminum A4 w/port door and forged LAR9M lower receiver, 4 1/4 in. lightweight aluminum free float rail (M-LOK compatible), black finish. New 2021.

MSR $1,160 $1,050 $925 $800 $700 $625 $500 $400

* ***LAR-9 A4 Pistol With SBX-K Arm Brace*** – 9mm Para. cal., 7 or 10 1/2 in. chrome moly barrel, A2 flash hider, single stage trigger, SB Tactical SBX-K stabilizing arm brace, Hogue rubber pistol grip, forged LAR-9 lower receiver and extruded aluminum A4 upper receiver with port door, 6 or 9 1/4 in. extended length RRA lightweight aluminum free float handguard (M-LOK compatible), 5.6-6.3 lbs. Disc. 2019

$875 $775 $675 $600 $525 $425 $350 *$980*

LAR-15M (LAR-15) A4 PISTOL – .223 Rem. cal., GIO, 7 (chrome moly) or 10 1/2 (chrome-lined) in. barrel, A2 flash hider, SST, forged LAR-15M (LAR-15) lower and A4 upper receivers, R-4 handguard with receiver height sight base (10 1/2 in. barrel) or low profile gas block, Picatinny rail, 6 in. RRA TRO free floating aluminum (M-LOK compatible) or R-4 (10 1/2 in. only) handguard, Hogue rubber pistol grip, includes one mag., 5.2 lbs.

MSR $920 $825 $725 $650 $575 $500 $400 $325

* ***LAR-15M (LAR-15) A4 Pistol w/SBA3 Arm Brace*** – 5.56 NATO cal., 7 (chrome moly) or 10 1/2 (chrome-lined) in. barrel, A2 flash hider, SST, 5-pos. stock, SB Tactical SBA3 stabilizing arm brace, Hogue rubber grip, low profile gas block, forged A4 upper and LAR-15 lower, 6 or 9 1/4 in. lightweight aluminum free float rail, M-LOK compatible, 5.6-6.3 lbs. New 2019.

MSR $975 $875 $775 $675 $600 $525 $425 $350

Add $25 for 10 1/2 in. barrel.

GRADING - PPGS™	100%	98%	95%	90%	80%	70%	60%	LAST MSR

* ***LAR-15M RUK-15 Pistol w/SBA3 Brace*** – 5.56 NATO cal., 4 1/2 in. chrome-lined barrel, Smith Vortex flash suppressor, SST, flip-up front and rear sight, SB Tactical SBA3 adj. stabilizing arm brace, Hogue rubber grip, low profile gas block, forged A4 upper and LAR-15M lower receiver, 4 1/4 in. lightweight aluminum free float rail (M-LOK compatible), black finish, includes one mag. New 2021.

MSR $975	$875	$775	$750	$675	$575	$475	$375	

LAR-15M (LAR-15) MOUNTAIN PISTOL – 5.56 NATO chambered for 5.56mm and .223 Rem. cal., 10 1/2 in. chrome-lined barrel, A2 flash hider, SST, winter trigger guard, Hogue rubber pistol grip, forged A4 upper and RRA LAR-15M (LAR-15) lower receiver, low profile gas block, 9 1/2 in. RRA aluminum Mountain Pistol handguard with full length top rail (includes two 1 3/4 in. accessory rails), 5.3 lbs. New 2019.

MSR $1,260	$1,125	$1,000	$875	$775	$675	$550	$425	

LAR-15M (LAR-15) RRAGE PISTOL – 5.56 NATO chambered for 5.56mm and .223 Rem. cal., GIO, 7 or 10 1/2 (new 2020) in. chrome moly barrel with long A2 flash hider, SST, SB Tactical SBX-K (disc.) or SBA3 stabilizing arm brace, A2 pistol grip, low profile gas block, forged LAR-15M lower receiver and extruded aluminum A4 upper with port door, RRAGE lightweight aluminum 7 1/4 in. free floating handguard (M-LOK compatible), includes one mag., 4.8-5.7 lbs. New 2019.

MSR $940	$850	$750	$650	$575	$500	$400	$325	

Add $10 for 10 1/2 in. barrel (new 2020).

LAR-15LH PISTOL – 5.56mm NATO or .223 Rem. cal., left handed, 10 1/2 in. chrome moly threaded barrel with A2 flash hider, ambi mag. release, SST, 9.25 in. lightweight aluminum free floating M-LOK compatible handguard, Hogue rubber grip, low profile gas block, SBA3 adj. stabilizing arm brace, forged LAR-15LH lower and A4 LEF-T upper receivers, left handed charging handle, right side bolt catch, includes one mag., 6.3 lbs. New 2020.

MSR $1,075	$975	$850	$750	$650	$575	$450	$375	

LAR-40 PISTOL – .40 S&W cal., GIO, 7 or 10 1/2 in. barrel, forged lower receiver with integral magwell, A2 or A4 upper, single stage trigger, Hogue rubber pistol grip, approx. 5 lbs. Mfg. 2010-2011.

	$1,000	$900	$775	$675	$600	$475	$400	*$1,120*

Add $45 for 7 in. barrel and free float tube handguard.
Add $10-$15 for gas block sight base.

LAR-PDS PISTOL (PISTON DRIVEN SYSTEM) – 5.56 NATO, .223 Rem. or .300 AAC Blackout (mfg. 2015-2019) cal., GPO, 8 (disc. 2019) or 9 (new 2013) in. chrome moly barrel, A2 flash hider, single (disc. 2012) or two-stage (new 2013) trigger, ribbed forend, Hogue rubber pistol grip, full-length upper and LAR-15 partial lower Picatinny rails, injection molded ribbed or aluminum tri-rail handguard, folding ambidextrous non-reciprocating charging handles, two-position regulator, includes one mag., approx. 5 lbs. New 2010.

MSR $1,260	$1,125	$1,000	$875	$775	$675	$550	$425	

Add $65 for .300 AAC Blackout cal. (disc. 2019).
Add $55 for aluminum tri-rail handguard.

LAR-22 PISTOL – .22 LR cal., 7 (disc. 2020) or 9 (new 2021) in. chrome moly barrel with A2 flash hider, two-stage trigger, SB Tactical SBX-K (disc.) or SB Tactical stabilizing arm brace with short or long receiver extention, A2 pistol grip, forged aluminum LAR-15M or poly LAR-22 lower and forged aluminum or poly A4 upper receiver, RRA 6 or 7 1/4 in. extended lightweight free floating handguard (M-LOK compatible), 3.8 lbs. New 2019.

MSR $605	$550	$475	$425	$375	$325	$250	$200	

Add $90 for forged aluminum lower and A4 upper receivers.

RIFLES: BOLT ACTION

RBG BOLT GUN SERIES – 6.5 Creedmoor or .308 Win. cal., short action, 20, 22, or 24 in. Wilson, fluted stainless steel barrel, detachable box mag., AICS compatible, TriggerTech trigger, KRG or McMillan A-6 fiberglass tactical (mfg. 2020 only) chassis, knurled oversized bolt handle, 20 MOA bases, Picatinny rail, black, green, or tan finish, approx. 10.2 lbs. New 2020.

MSR $4,235	$3,600	$3,150	$2,700	$2,450	$2,000	$1,600	$1,250	

McMillan A-6 fiberglass tactical chassis models are POR (mfg. 2020 only).

RIFLES/CARBINES: SEMI-AUTO

Rock River Arms makes a variety of AR-15 style rifles/carbines in .223 Rem. cal. Previous models included the CAR UTE (disc. 2004, last MSR was $850), Tactical Carbine A2, M4 Entry (disc. 2003, last MSR was $875), and NM A2-DCM Legal (disc. 2005, last MSR was $1,265).

Beginning 2006, Rock River Arms released a series of rifles in 9mm Para. cal. Also during 2006, the company released a series of rifles in .308 Win. cal. A wide variety of options are available for each rifle. Base model assumes black furniture.

GRADING - PPGS™	100%	98%	95%	90%	80%	70%	60%	LAST MSR

BT-3 ENHANCED MID-LENGTH A4 – .308 Win./7.62 NATO cal., mid-length gas system, 16 in. fluted stainless steel heavy barrel, A2 flash hider, two-stage trigger, 6-position Operator CAR stock, Hogue rubber grip, low profile gas block, LAR BT-3 billet lower and A4 upper receiver, 13 in. extended lightweight free float rail, M-LOK compatible, black finish, 8.2 lbs. New 2020.

MSR $1,575	$1,425	$1,250	$1,100	$975	$825	$675	$550	

BT-3 PRECISION RIFLE – .308 Win./7.62 NATO cal., mid-length gas system, 18 in. fluted stainless steel heavy barrel, two-stage trigger, 6-position Operator CAR stock, ERGO ambi Suregrip (mfg. 2020 only) or Hogue rubber grip, low profile gas block, LAR BT-3 billet A4 upper and lower receiver, 17 in. extended lightweight free float rail, M-LOK compatible, includes one mag., black finish, 8.2 lbs. New 2020.

MSR $1,635	$1,475	$1,300	$1,125	$1,000	$875	$700	$575	

BT-3 SELECT TARGET RIFLE – .308 Win./7.62 NATO cal., rifle length gas system, 16 (mfg. 2020 only) or 20 (new 2021) in. fluted stainless steel heavy barrel, A2 flash hider, two-stage trigger, Magpul Gen 3 Precision rifle stock, Hogue rubber grip, low profile gas block, BT-3 billet A4 upper and lower receiver, 17 in. extended lightweight free float rail, M-LOK compatible, black finish, includes one mag., 8.6 lbs. New 2020.

MSR $1,895	$1,700	$1,500	$1,325	$1,150	$1,000	$800	$650	

BT-3 VARMINT RIFLE – .308 Win./7.62 NATO cal., rifle length gas system, 20 in. stainless steel bull barrel, two-stage trigger, 6-position NSP-2 Operator CAR stock, Hogue rubber grip, low profile gas block, LAR BT-3 billet A4 upper and lower receiver, 17 in. extended lightweight free float rail, M-LOK compatible, includes case, black finish, includes one mag., 9.8 lbs. New 2020.

MSR $1,575	$1,425	$1,250	$1,100	$975	$825	$675	$550	

BT-6 – .338 Lapua Mag. cal., quick takedown design, 24 in. black Nitride stainless steel barrel, four port muzzle brake, two 10 shot mags., Ultra Match two-stage trigger, Magpul PRS stock, A2 overmolded grips, ambi-selector safety, adj. low profile gas block, billet aluminum upper and lower receiver, 17 in. quick detach lightweight free float rail, M-LOK compatible, includes case, black finish, 13.5 lbs. New 2020.

MSR $5,310	$4,775	$4,225	$3,675	$3,250	$2,825	$2,275	$1,850	

BT-9G (BT-9) CAR A4 – 9mm Para. cal., gas block w/receiver height sight base, 16 in. chrome moly barrel, A2 flash hider, SST, integral winter trigger guard, tactical CAR stock, 6-pos., Hogue rubber grip, extruded aluminum A4 upper and LAR BT9G billet aluminum lower w/Glock compatible flared magwell, R4 handguard, black finish, includes one Glock mag., 7.1 lbs. New 2021.

MSR $1,000	$900	$800	$700	$600	$525	$425	$350	

BT-9G (BT-9) MID-LENGTH A4 – 9mm Para. cal., gas block w/receiver height sight base, 16 in. chrome moly barrel, A2 flash hider, SST, integral winter trigger guard, tactical CAR stock, 6-pos., Hogue rubber grip, extruded aluminum A4 upper and LAR BT9G billet aluminum lower w/Glock compatible flared magwell, mid-length handguard, black finish, includes one Glock mag., 7.1 lbs. New 2021.

MSR $970	$875	$775	$675	$600	$525	$424	$325	

BT-9G (BT-9) R9 COMPETITION – 9mm Para. cal., 16 in. chrome moly barrel, 9mm mini muzzle brake, Glock compatible flared magwell, two-stage trigger, integral winter trigger guard, 6-pos. Operator CAR stock, overmolded A2 pistol grip, Star safety, BT-9 billet aluminum lower receiver, extruded aluminum A4 upper receiver, 15 in. extended RRA lightweight free float rail (M-LOK compatible), 6.8 lbs. New 2019.

MSR $1,315	$1,175	$1,025	$900	$800	$650	$525	$425	

LAR-15M 6.8 (LAR-6.8) CAR A2/A4 – 6.8 SPC cal., GIO, 16 in. Wilson chrome moly barrel, A2 flash hider, two-stage match trigger, A2 pistol grip, 6-pos. tactical CAR stock, choice of CAR length or mid-length handguard, forged A2 (disc. 2012) or A4 upper receiver and LAR-15M lower receiver, black finish, includes one mag. and case, 7.1-7.5 lbs. Disc. circa 2019, reintroduced 2021.

MSR $1,000	$900	$800	$700	$600	$525	$425	$350	*$1,055*

LAR-15M 6.8 (LAR-6.8) COYOTE CARBINE – 6.8 SPC cal., GIO, 16 in. Wilson chrome moly HBAR barrel, Smith Vortex flash hider, Weaver style light varmint gas block with sight rail, two-stage match trigger, winter trigger guard, A2 stock, Hogue rubber pistol grip, forged A4 upper and LAR-15M lower receiver, Hogue overmolded free float tube handguard (disc.) or CAR length deluxe extended free float handguard with 3 short accessory rails (disc. 2019), 12 1/2 in. lightweight free float rail (M-LOK compatible), black finish, includes one mag. and case, 7 lbs. Disc. 2019, reintroduced 2021.

MSR $1,290	$1,150	$1,025	$900	$800	$675	$550	$450	*$1,310*

LAR-15M 6.8 (LAR-6.8) MID-LENGTH A4 – 6.8 SPC cal., 16 in. chrome moly barrel, A2 flash hider, two-stage trigger, gas block with receiver height sight base, 6-pos. tactical CAR stock, A2 pistol grip, mid-length gas system, forged A4 upper and LAR-6.8 or LAR-15M lower receiver, mid-length handguard, 7.1 lbs. Disc. 2019, reintroduced 2021.

MSR $1,000	$900	$800	$700	$600	$525	$425	$350	*$1,055*

GRADING - PPGS™	100%	98%	95%	90%	80%	70%	60%	LAST MSR

LAR-15M 6.8 (LAR-6.8) X-1 RIFLE – 6.8 SPC II cal., GIO, 18 in. fluted stainless steel HBAR barrel, RRA Beast or Hunter muzzle brake, low profile gas block, forged A4 upper and LAR15M lower receiver, two-stage trigger, winter trigger guard, RRA TRO-XL extended length free float rail, RRA Operator A2 or Operator CAR stock, Hogue rubber pistol grip, black or tan finish, includes one 9 in. XL accessory rail and two 2 in. short accessory rails for handguard, 7.9 lbs. Mfg. 2014-2019, reintroduced 2021.

MSR $1,490 | $1,350 | $1,175 | $1,025 | $900 | $800 | $650 | $525 | *$1,595*

Add $40 for RRA Hunter muzzle brake and tan finish.

LAR-8 ELITE OPERATOR – .308 Win. cal., GIO, 16 in. barrel with Smith Vortex flash hider, two-stage match trigger, flip front sight gas block assembly, Operator CAR stock, Hogue rubber grip, advanced half quad free float mid-length handguard with three ladder rail covers, forged A4 upper receiver, forged LAR-8 lower receiver, black finish, 9.1 lbs. Mfg. 2010-2020.

$1,350 | $1,200 | $1,050 | $925 | $800 | $650 | $525 | *$1,500*

LAR-8 MID LENGTH A2/A4 – .308 Win. cal., GIO, 16 in. chrome moly barrel with A2 flash hider, two-stage trigger, gas block with receiver height sight base, 6-pos. tactical CAR stock, Hogue rubber grip, forged A2 (disc. 2012) or A4 upper receiver and forged LAR-8 lower receiver, mid-length handguard, black finish, includes one mag. and case, 8.1 lbs. New 2010.

MSR $1,260 | $1,125 | $1,000 | $875 | $775 | $675 | $550 | $425

LAR-8M PREDATOR HP – .243 Win or 6.5 Creedmoor cal., GIO, 20 or 24 (6.5mm Creedmoor only) in. fluted stainless steel barrel, with or without muzzle brake, two-stage trigger, winter trigger guard, Operator A2 or CAR stock, Hogue rubber grip, forged LAR-8M lower and A4 upper receiver, low profile gas block, 17 in. RRA LAR-8 DLX free float handguard (M-LocK compatible), accessory rails, black finish, includes one mag., 9.2 lbs. New 2017.

MSR $1,575 | $1,425 | $1,250 | $1,100 | $975 | $825 | $675 | $550

Add $30 for 20 in. 6.5mm Creedmoor.

LAR-8 PREDATOR HP – .308 Win./7.62 NATO cal., GIO, 20 in. bead blasted lightweight stainless steel fluted barrel, with or w/o muzzle brake, two-stage trigger, winter trigger guard, Operator A2 or CAR stock, Hogue rubber pistol grip, forged LAR-8 lower and A4 upper receiver, low profile gas block, free float tube handguard (disc.) or 17 in. LAR-8 DLX free float rifle length handguard with three short accessory rails (new 2017), black finish, 9.2-9.5 lbs. New 2010.

MSR $1,660 | $1,500 | $1,325 | $1,150 | $1,025 | $875 | $700 | $575

LAR-8 PREDATOR HP MID LENGTH – .308 Win./7.62 NATO cal., 16 in. fluted stainless steel barrel, with or w/o muzzle brake, two-stage trigger, winter trigger guard, Operator A2 or CAR stock, Hogue rubber grip, low profile gas block, forged LAR-8 lower and A4 upper receiver, LAR-8 DLX free float rail, rifle length handguard with three short accessory rails, black finish, 8.9-9.2 lbs. New 2017.

MSR $1,605 | $1,450 | $1,275 | $1,125 | $975 | $850 | $700 | $550

LAR-8 STANDARD A2/A4 – .308 Win./7.62 NATO cal., GIO, gas block w/receiver height sight rail, 20 in. chrome moly barrel with A2 flash hider, two-stage trigger, gas block sight base, A2 buttstock, Hogue rubber pistol grip, forged LAR-8 lower and A2 (disc. 2012) or A4 upper receiver, A2 handguard, includes one mag., 9 lbs. New 2010.

MSR $1,260 | $1,125 | $1,000 | $875 | $775 | $675 | $550 | $425

LAR-8 STANDARD OPERATOR – .308 Win./7.62 NATO cal., GIO, 16 (disc.) or 20 in. barrel, Smith Vortex flash hider, two-stage trigger, flip front sight gas block assembly, Operator A2 stock, Hogue rubber grip, forged LAR-8 lower and forged A4 upper receiver, rifle length advanced half quad free float handguard with three ladder rail covers, black finish, 10.2 lbs. Mfg. 2010-2020.

$1,350 | $1,200 | $1,050 | $925 | $800 | $650 | $525 | *$1,790*

LAR-8 VARMINT A4 – .308 Win./7.62 NATO cal., GIO, 20 or 26 in. cryo treated stainless steel bull barrel, two-stage varmint trigger, winter trigger guard, A2 buttstock, Hogue rubber pistol grip, forged A4 upper receiver with forward assist and port door, forged LAR-8 lower, varmint gas block with sight rail (disc.) or low profile gas block, rifle length LAR-8 free float tube handguard with one standard and two short TRO accessory rails, black finish, includes one mag., 10.4-11.6 lbs. New 2011.

MSR $1,525 | $1,375 | $1,225 | $1,050 | $925 | $800 | $650 | $525

Add $50 for 26 in. barrel.

LAR-8 X-1 RIFLE – .308 Win./7.62 NATO cal., GIO, 18 in. fluted bead blasted stainless steel barrel, RRA Beast or Hunter muzzle brake, two-stage trigger, winter trigger guard, RRA Operator A2 or Operator CAR stock, black or tan Hogue rubber pistol grip, Star safety, RRA custom low profile gas block, rifle length free float rail with one 8 1/2 in. accessory rail and two 2 in. accessory rails, forged LAR-8 lower and A4 upper with forward assist and port door, 13 in. lightweight extended handguard (M-LOK compatible), black or tan finish, includes one mag., 9 1/2 lbs. New 2014.

MSR $1,685 | $1,525 | $1,350 | $1,175 | $1,025 | $900 | $725 | $575

Add $30 for RRA Hunter muzzle brake and tan finish.

GRADING - PPGS™	100%	98%	95%	90%	80%	70%	60%	LAST MSR

LAR-9M (LAR-9) CAR A2/A4 – 9mm Para. cal., GIO, 16 in. chrome moly heavy barrel, A1 (disc.) or A2 flash hider, SST, gas block with front sight base, 6-pos. tactical CAR stock, A2 (disc.) or Hogue rubber grip, forged LAR-9 lower with integral magwell, forged A2 (disc. 2012) or A4 upper receiver w/port door, R4 handguard, black finish, includes one mag., 7.1 lbs.

MSR $920	$825	$725	$650	$575	$500	$400	$325	

Add $50 for Operator stock.

LAR-9M (LAR-9) R9 COMPETITION RIFLE – 9mm Para. cal., GIO, 16 in. stainless steel, chain link fluted and cryogenically treated barrel w/ 9mm mini muzzle brake, two-stage match trigger, Operator CAR stock, Hogue rubber pistol grip, Star safety, forged LAR-9M (LAR-9) lower with integral magwell and forged A4 upper receiver w/forward assist, mid-length handguard w/upper Picatinny rail (disc. 2017) or 15 in. lightweight free float M-LOK rail (new 2018), matte black finish, includes one mag., 7.4 lbs. New 2017.

MSR $1,235	$1,100	$975	$850	$750	$650	$525	$425	

LAR-9 MID-LENGTH A4 – 9mm Para. cal., GIO, 16 in. chrome moly heavy barrel, A2 flash hider, SST, gas block front sight base, 6-pos. tactical CAR stock, Hogue rubber pistol grip, mid-length handguard, forged extruded A4 upper receiver w/port door, forged LAR-9M (LAR-9) lower with integral magwell, black finish, includes one mag. and case, 7.1 lbs.

MSR $920	$825	$725	$650	$575	$500	$400	$325	

Add $50 for Operator stock.

LAR-10 MID-LENGTH A2/A4 – .308 Win. cal., GIO, forged A2 or A4 upper receiver with forward assist and ejection port door, 16 in. Wilson chrome moly barrel, A2 flash hider, A2 front sight or A4 gas block with sight base, two-stage match trigger, mid-length handguard, Hogue rubber pistol grip, 6-position tactical CAR stock, approx. 8 lbs. Disc. 2009.

	$1,000	$875	$775	$675	$575	$475	$375	*$1,100*

Add $50 for A2 sights.

LAR-10 STANDARD A2/A4 – .308 Win. cal., GIO, forged A2 or A4 upper receiver, with forward assist and ejection port door, 20 in. Wilson chrome moly barrel, A2 flash hider, A2 front sight or A4 gas block sight base, two-stage match trigger, A2 handguard, Hogue rubber pistol grip, A2 buttstock, 9.3 lbs. Disc. 2009.

	$1,000	$875	$775	$675	$575	$475	$375	*$1,100*

Add $45 for A2 sights.

LAR-10 VARMINT A4 – .308 Win. cal., GIO, forged A4 upper receiver with forward assist and port door, 26 in. Wilson stainless steel bull barrel, Weaver type sight base gas block, two-stage match trigger, knurled and fluted free floating aluminum tube handguard, Hogue pistol grip, A2 buttstock, 11.6 lbs. Disc. 2010.

	$1,200	$1,075	$925	$825	$725	$575	$475	*$1,350*

LAR-15 9.11 COMMEMORATIVE – .5.56 NATO or .223 Rem. cal., GIO, 16 in. lightweight chrome moly barrel, forged A4 upper receiver, low profile gas block, chromed bolt carrier group, RRA tactical muzzle brake, two-stage chrome trigger group, winter trigger guard, Star safety, overmolded pistol grip, Hogue free float tube handguard, non-collapsible or 6-position tactical CAR stock, flat black finish with American flag, and "9*11 Tenth Year Commemoration" engraved on receiver. Limited mfg. mid-2011.

	$995	$850	$725	N/A	N/A	N/A	N/A	*$1,011*

Add $25 for non-collapsible stock, pinned/welded tactical muzzle brake, and 10 shot mag.

LAR-15M ATH V2 (LAR-15 ATH ADVANCED TACTICAL HUNTER) CARBINE – .223 Wylde chambered for 5.56mm and .223 Rem. cal., GIO, 18 in. heavy match cryo treated stainless steel barrel, muzzle brake, two-stage trigger, winter trigger guard, fixed (mfg. 2018 only) or Operator CAR stock, Ergo SureGrip (disc. 2020) or Hogue rubber (new 2021) pistol grip, Star safety, mid-length gas system, forged A4 upper and LAR-15 lower receiver, low profile gas block, half-quad free float handguard with three ladder rail covers (disc. 2019) or 11 in. lightweight free float rail (M-LOK compatible, new 2020), matte black finish, includes one mag. and case, 7.6 lbs. New 2011.

MSR $1,210	$1,075	$975	$850	$750	$650	$525	$425	

Subtract $25 for fixed stock (mfg. 2018 only).

LAR -15 BTB CARBINE – 5.56 NATO cal., 16 in. chrome moly HBAR barrel, A2 flash hider, SST, NSP flip-up front and rear sights, NSP2 6-pos. CAR stock, NSP overmolded pistol grip, low profile gas block, forged A4 upper receiver and forged LAR-15 lower receiver, NSP CAR length drop-in rail, includes carrying case and two mags., black or tan finish, 7 lbs. Mfg. 2017-2019.

	$750	$650	$575	$500	$450	$350	$275	*$825*

LAR-15M (LAR-15) CAR A2 – 5.56 NATO chambered for 5.56mm and .223 Rem. cal., GIO, 16 in. Wilson chrome moly barrel (disc.) or 16 in. chrome moly HBAR (new 2018), A2 flash hider, two-stage match trigger, A2 front sight base (new 2018), fixed (disc. 2012) or 6-position tactical CAR stock, overmolded A2 pistol grip, forged A2 upper and forged LAR-15M lower receiver, CAR length handguard, black finish, includes one mag. and case, 7 1/2 lbs. Disc. 2012, reintroduced 2018.

MSR $975	$875	$775	$675	$600	$525	$425	$350	

GRADING - PPGS™	100%	98%	95%	90%	80%	70%	60%	LAST MSR

LAR-15M (LAR-15) CAR A4 – 5.56 NATO chambered for 5.56mm and .223 Rem. cal., 16 in. chrome moly HBAR barrel, A2 flash hider, two-stage trigger, A2 front sight base or gas block with receiver height sight base, 6-pos. tactical CAR stock, overmolded A2 grip, forged A4 upper and forged LAR-15M (LAR-15) lower receiver, mid-length CAR handguard, black finish, available in left-hand configuration, 7.1 lbs.

MSR $920	$825	$725	$650	$575	$500	$400	$325	

Add $130 for left-hand (LAR-15LH Lef-T CAR A4, new 2013).

LAR-15M CAR A4 .350 LEGEND – .350 Legend cal., 16 in. chrome moly or stainless steel barrel, Operator (military style) muzzle brake, two-stage trigger, winter trigger guard, Operator CAR stock, A2 overmolded grip, standard safety selector, low profile gas system, forged A4 upper and LAR15M multi-caliber marked lower, 13 in. lightweight free float rail (M-LOK compatible), includes one 10 shot mag. and case, black finish, 6.8 lbs. New 2020.

MSR $1,160	$1,050	$925	$800	$700	$625	$500	$400	

Add $50 for stainless steel barrel.

LAR-15M (LAR-15) COYOTE CARBINE – 5.56 NATO chambered for 5.56mm and .223 Rem. cal., GIO, 16 in. chrome moly HBAR barrel with Smith Vortex flash hider, two-stage varmint trigger, winter trigger guard, ACE ARFX skeleton (disc. 2013) or Operator CAR (new 2014) stock, Hogue rubber pistol grip, Star safety, forged LAR-15M (LAR-15) lower and A4 upper receiver, Weaver style light varmint gas block with sight rail (disc. 2013) or low profile gas block (new 2014), Hogue overmolded free float tube handguard (disc. 2013) or 12 in.RRA deluxe extended free float rail (M-LOK compatible, new 2014), includes one mag. and case, available in left-hand configuration, 7.2 lbs.

MSR $1,210	$1,075	$975	$850	$750	$650	$525	$425	

Add $80 for left-hand (LAR-15LH, Lef-T, new 2013).

LAR-15M (LAR-15) COYOTE RIFLE – .223 Wylde chambered for 5.56mm and .223 Rem. cal., GIO, 20 in. chrome moly HBAR barrel with Smith Vortex flash hider, two-stage match varmint trigger, winter trigger guard, ACE ARFX skeleton (disc. 2013) or RRA Operator A2 (new 2014) stock, Hogue rubber pistol grip, Star safety, forged A4 upper receiver and LAR-15M (LAR-15) lower receiver, Weaver style light varmint gas block with sight rail (disc. 2013) or low profile gas block (new 2014), Hogue overmolded free float tube handguard (disc. 2013) or 15 in. RRA deluxe extended free float rail with three short accessory rails (new 2014), black finish, includes one mag. and case, available in left-hand configuration, 8.4 lbs.

MSR $1,210	$1,075	$975	$850	$750	$650	$525	$425	

Add $80 for left-hand (LAR-15LH, Lef-T, new 2013).

LAR-15 DELTA CAR – .223 Rem. cal., GIO, forged upper and lower, 16 in. chrome moly HBAR barrel, A2 flash hider, low profile gas block, two-stage trigger, winter trigger guard, Delta CAR stock, Ergo SureGrip, Delta quad rail CAR two-piece drop-in handguard or mid-length (disc. 2018) handguard, 7-7.3 lbs. Mfg. 2013-2019.

	$975	$875	$750	$675	$575	$475	$375	*$1,085*

Add $15 for mid-length handguard (Delta Car Mid-Length), disc. 2018.

LAR-15M (LAR-15) ELITE CAR A4 – 5.56 NATO chambered for 5.56mm and .223 cal., GIO, 16 in. chrome-lined or chrome moly barrel with A2 flash hider, two-stage trigger, Star safety, forged LAR-15M lower and A4 upper receivers, mid-length handguard, 6-pos. tactical CAR stock, Hogue rubber pistol grip, slide mount sling swivel, includes one mag. and case, 6.8-7.7 lbs.

MSR $950	$850	$750	$650	$575	$500	$400	$325	

Add $25 for chrome-lined barrel.

LAR-15 ELITE CAR UTE2 – .223 Rem. cal., GIO, 16 in. Wilson chrome moly barrel, A2 flash hider, two-stage match trigger, mid-length handguard, forged Universal Tactical Entry 2 upper receiver, 6-pos. tactical CAR stock, Hogue rubber pistol grip, 7.7 lbs. Disc. 2012.

	$950	$850	$725	$650	$500	$450	$375	*$1,060*

LAR-15 ELITE COMP – 5.56 NATO chambered for 5.56mm and .223 Rem. cal., GIO, 16 in. chrome-lined barrel with tactical muzzle brake, forged receivers, flip front sight gas block assembly, two-stage trigger, winter trigger guard, Star safety, A.R.M.S. low profile flip-up rear sight, Magpul CTR (disc.) or Operator CAR stock, Ergo Suregrip pistol grip, free floating half-round, half-quad handguard, 8.4 lbs. Mfg. 2008-2017.

	$1,350	$1,200	$1,050	$925	$800	$650	$525	*$1,515*

LAR-15M (LAR-15) ENTRY TACTICAL – 5.56 NATO or .223 Rem. cal., GIO, 16 in. chrome-lined or chrome moly. oR-4 heavy barrel with A2 flash hider, two-stage trigger, forged LAR-15M lower and A4 upper receiver, Star safety, Hogue rubber pistol grip, R-4 handguard with double heat shields, 6-position tactical CAR stock, black finish, includes one mag., 7.5 lbs.

MSR $950	$850	$750	$650	$575	$500	$400	$325	

Add $25 for chrome-lined barrel.

GRADING - PPGS™	100%	98%	95%	90%	80%	70%	60%	LAST MSR

LAR-15M (LAR-15) FRED EICHLER SERIES PREDATOR – .223 Wylde chambered for 5.56mm and .223 Rem. cal., GIO, mid-length gas system, 16 in. bead blasted stainless steel cryogenically treated barrel, custom muzzle brake, 20 shot mag., low profile hidden gas block, chrome RRA National Match two-stage varmint trigger with parkerized finish on trigger shoe, winter trigger guard, RRA Fred Eichler Series free floating handguard with full-length Picatinny top rail and 2 1/2 in. rails, tan Hogue rubber grips, Operator A2, or CAR stock, Star safety, forged A4 upper flat-top and LAR-15M lower receivers, BCMGunfighter charging handle, two-tone black/tan finish, includes one mag. and hard case, 7.6 lbs. New 2012.

MSR $1,475	$1,325	$1,175	$1,025	$900	$775	$625	$500	

LAR-15M (LAR-15) FRED EICHLER SERIES PREDATOR 2 – .223 Wylde chambered for 5.56mm and .223 Rem. cal., GIO, 16 in. fluted stainless steel barrel with directionally tuned and ported muzzle brake, two-stage chrome varmint trigger, winter trigger guard, Operator A2 or CAR buttstock, Hogue rubber pistol grip, Star safety, forged A4 upper and LAR-15M lower receivers, low profile gas block, Fred Eichler Series free float extended length handguard with two rail covers and full top Picatinny rail, BCMGunfighter charging handle, receivers and handguard in tan, Gunmetal Gray, or Ghost Camo (new 2017) ROCKote finish, includes one mag. and case, 7.6 lbs. New 2015.

MSR $1,685	$1,525	$1,350	$1,175	$1,025	$900	$725	$575	

Add $500 for Ghost camo (new 2017).

LAR-15M (LAR-15) FRED EICHLER SERIES LIGHT PREDATOR2L – .223 Wylde chambered for 5.56mm and .223 Rem. cal., 16 in. cryo treated bead blasted lightweight stainless steel fluted barrel, Fred Eichler Series (FES) muzzle brake, chrome two-stage trigger, winter trigger guard, Operator CAR stock, Hogue rubber grip, Star safety, low profile gas block, mid-length gas system, forged A4 upper and LAR-15M lower receivers, BCM Gunfighter charging handle, FES extended carbon fiber free float rail, black or Gunmetal Gray finish, includes one mag. and case, 6.9 lbs. New 2018.

MSR $1,945	$1,750	$1,550	$1,350	$1,200	$1,025	$825	$675	

Add $65 for Gunmetal Gray finish.

LAR-15 HUNTER – .223 Rem. cal., GIO, 16 in. chrome moly barrel with RRA tactical muzzle brake, forged A4 upper receiver, low profile gas block, two-stage trigger, winter trigger guard, half-quad free float mid-length handguard with three rail covers, Operator CAR stock, Hogue rubber pistol grip, WYL-Ehide or PRK-Ehide (disc.) anodized camo finish, 7.6 lbs. New 2012.

	$1,400	$1,225	$1,075	$950	$825	$675	$550	*$1,550*

LAR-15 IRS – 5.56 NATO chambered for 5.56mm and .223 cal., GIO, 16 or 18 (XL model only) in. fluted chrome moly barrel with RRA Helical brake, low profile gas block, forged upper and lower receivers, two-stage trigger, winter trigger guard, IRS CAR, MID, STD, or XL length handguard with integral folding sights, Operator CAR stock, Hogue pistol grip, 7.8-8 lbs. Mfg. 2015-2019.

	$1,375	$1,225	$1,075	$950	$825	$650	$525	*$1,540*

Add $25 for Mid-length handguard (LAR-15 MID).
Add $50 for STD length handguard (LAR-15 STD).
Add $80 for XL length handguard (LAR-15 XL).

LAR-15 LIGHTWEIGHT – 5.56 NATO chambered for 5.56mm and .223 cal., GIO, 16 in. chrome moly lightweight barrel with A2 flash hider, low profile gas block, two-stage trigger, winter trigger guard, forged A4 upper and LAR-15 lower receiver, carbon fiber free float extended handguard in CAR (disc. 2018), Mid, STD, or XL lengths, 6-pos. tactical CAR stock, Hogue rubber pistol grips, 5.6-6.1 lbs. Mfg. 2015-2019.

	$1,200	$1,075	$925	$825	$725	$575	$475	*$1,350*

Add $25 for STD length handguard (Lightweight STD model).
Add $50 for XL length handguard (Lightweight XL model).

LAR-15M (LAR-15) LIGHTWEIGHT MOUNTAIN RIFLE – 5.56 NATO chambered for 5.56mm and .223 Rem. cal., GIO, 16 in. chrome moly lightweight barrel with A2 flash hider, lightweight low profile gas block, Star safety, two-stage trigger, winter trigger guard, forged A4 upper and LAR-15M lower receivers, RRA lightweight aluminum Mountain Rifle handguard w/full length top rail, 6-pos. tactical CAR stock, Hogue rubber pistol grip, black finish, includes one mag. and case, 6.2 lbs. New 2015.

MSR $1,135	$1,025	$900	$800	$700	$600	$475	$400	

LAR-15M LONG RANGE RIFLE – .224 Valkyrie, 24 in. stainless steel cryo treated barrel, tactical muzzle brake, 10 shot. mag., two-stage trigger, winter trigger guard, Operator A2 stock, Hogue rubber grip, Star safety, forged A4 upper and LAR-15M lower receivers, 17 in. extended lightweight free float rail (M-LOK compatible), black finish, 9.2 lbs. New 2021.

MSR $1,235	$1,100	$975	$850	$750	$650	$525	$425	

GRADING - PPGS™	100%	98%	95%	90%	80%	70%	60%	LAST MSR

LAR-15M (LAR-15) MID-LENGTH A2 – 5.56 NATO chambered for 5.56mm and .223 Rem. cal., GIO, 16 in. chrome moly lightweight barrel, A2 flash hider, two-stage trigger, A2 buttstock (disc. 2012) or 6-pos. tactical CAR stock (new 2018), overmolded A2 pistol grip, mid-length handguard, forged LAR-15M (LAR-15) lower and A2 upper receiver, A2 front sight base (new 2018), black finish, includes one mag. and case, 6.2-7 lbs. Disc. 2012, reintroduced 2018.

MSR $975	$875	$775	$675	$600	$525	$425	$350	

LAR-15M (LAR-15) MID-LENGTH A4 – 5.56 NATO chambered for 5.56mm and .223 Rem. cal., GIO, 16 in. chrome moly barrel with A2 flash hider, two-stage trigger, forged LAR-15M (LAR-15) lower and forged A4 upper receiver, available with gas block sight base or A2 front sight base, mid-length handguard, 6-pos. tactical CAR stock, overmolded A2 pistol grip, includes one mag. and case, black finish, right or left-hand configuration, 7.1 lbs.

MSR $920	$825	$725	$650	$575	$500	$400	$325	

Add $130 for left-hand configuration (LAR-15 LEF-T Mid-Length A4).

LAR-15M MID-LENGTH A4 .450 BUSHMASTER – .450 Bushmaster cal., GIO, mid-length gas system, 16 in. stainless steel cryo treated barrel with low profile gas block, RRA Operator brake, two-stage trigger, winter trigger guard, RRA Operator CAR stock, forged RRA LAR-15M multi-caliber marked lower receiver, forged A4 upper, forward assist, ejection port door, RRA 13 in. lightweight free floating handguard (M-LOK compatible), RRA overmolded A2 pistol grip, includes one mag. and case, 37 1/2 in. OAL, 6.8 lbs. New 2019.

MSR $1,160	$1,050	$925	$800	$700	$625	$500	$400	

LAR-15M (LAR-15) NATIONAL MATCH A2 – .223 Wylde chambered for 5.56mm and .223 Rem. cal., GIO, 20 in. heavy match stainless barrel with A2 flash hider, 20 shot mag., two-stage match trigger, match front and rear sights, A2 buttstock, A2 pistol grip, forged LAR-15M (LAR-15) lower and forged A2 upper receiver, free float thermo mold handguard, black finish, 9.7 lbs.

MSR $1,315	$1,175	$1,050	$900	$800	$700	$575	$450	

LAR-15M (LAR-15) NATIONAL MATCH A4 – .223 Wylde chambered for 5.56mm and .223 Rem. cal., GIO, 20 shot mag., 20 in. heavy match stainless steel cryo treated barrel, A2 flash hider, two-stage match trigger, A2 buttstock, A2 pistol grip, match A2 front and rear sights, with or w/o gas block sight base, chrome BCG, free float thermo mold handguard with NM barrel sleeve, forged LAR-15M (LAR-15) lower and forged A4 upper with detachable NM carry handle, black finish, includes case, 9.7 lbs.

MSR $1,235	$1,100	$975	$850	$750	$650	$525	$425	

Add $160 if w/o gas sight base.

LAR-15M (LAR-15) NATIONAL MATCH A4 CMP RIFLE – .223 Wylde chambered for 5.56mm and .223 Rem. cal., 16 or 20 in. cryo treated and air gauged heavy match stainless steel barrel, A2 flash hider, 20 shot mag., two-stage match chrome trigger group, gas block with receiver height sight base, Operator CAR stock, A2 pistol grip, forged LAR-15M lower and A4 upper receiver, NM CMP TRO 7 1/4 (carbine length) or 12 1/2 (rifle length) in. free float handguard with three TRO modular rails and NM sling swivel, black finish, includes case, 7.3 lbs. New 2016.

MSR $1,235	$1,100	$975	$850	$750	$650	$525	$425	

Add $55 for 20 in. barrel.

LAR-15 NSP CAR – 5.56 NATO chambered for 5.56mm and .223 cal., GIO, 16 in. fluted R4 profile chrome moly barrel with RRA Operator brake, forged upper and lower receivers, gas block with front sight base, RRA NSP flip front and rear sights, NSP two-piece drop-in CAR length rail, two-stage trigger, NSP CAR stock, NSP overmolded pistol grips, black, tan, or pink NSP handguard, stock, grip, sights, and magazine, 7 lbs. Mfg. 2015-2019.

	$1,000	$900	$775	$675	$600	$475	$400	*$1,120*

LAR-15 OPERATOR III – 5.56 NATO cal., GIO, similar to Operator Series, except has low profile mid-length gas system, Operator muzzle brake, TRO free float mid-length handguard, Mil-Spec top rail, includes two 30 shot mags. and case, Hogue grip, 8 lbs. Mfg. 2014-2017.

	$950	$850	$750	$650	$575	$450	$375	*$1,065*

LAR-15 OPERATOR SERIES – .223 Rem. cal., GIO, 16 in. chrome moly barrel, tactical muzzle brake, forged LAR-15 lower, forged A4 upper receiver, upper Picatinny rail, Operator CAR stock, matte black finish, two-stage trigger, winter trigger guard, Ergo SureGrip, configurations include the Entry (R-4 handguard and barrel profile), the Tactical (R-4 handguard), and the Elite (half-quad free float handguard with mid-length gas system), designed for left-handed shooters, 7.2-8 lbs. Mfg. 2011-disc.

	$1,225	$1,075	$950	$825	$725	$575	$475	*$1,360*

Beginning 2013, this model became available in left-hand only (LAR-15LH, Lef-T).

GRADING - PPGS™ 100% 98% 95% 90% 80% 70% 60% LAST MSR

LAR-15M (LAR-15) PREDATOR PURSUIT RIFLE/MID-LENGTH – .223 Wylde chamber for 5.56mm and .223 Rem. cal., GIO, 16 (mid-length model only) or 20 (rifle length model only) in. air gauged heavy match stainless steel barrel, forged A4 upper and LAR-15M lower receiver, low profile gas block, two-stage match varmint trigger, winter trigger guard, 12 1/2 or 15 in. deluxe extended free float rail (M-LOK compatible) with rifle or mid-length handguard, A2 buttstock, Hogue rubber pistol grip, black finish, includes one mag., available in left-hand configuration, 7-7.9 lbs.

MSR $1,210 $1,075 $975 $850 $750 $650 $525 $425

Add $80 for left-hand (LAR-15LH, Lef-T Predator Pursuit, new 2013).

LAR-15 PRO-SERIES ELITE – .223 Rem. cal., GIO, forged A4 upper receiver, chrome-lined 16 in. Wilson chrome moly barrel, RRA tactical muzzle brake, flip front sight and gas block assembly, two-stage match trigger, winter trigger guard, Badger tactical charging handle latch, A.R.M.S. #40L low profile flip-up rear sight, Ergo SureGrip pistol grip, 6-position tactical CAR stock, MWI front sling adapter, MWI CAR stock endplate adapter loop rear sling mount, Daniel Defense 12.0 FSPM quad rail handguard, SureFire M910A-WH vertical foregrip weaponlight, Aimpoint Comp M2 red dot optical sight and QRP mount with spacer, 9 1/2 lbs. Disc. 2012.

$2,475 $2,200 $1,900 $1,675 $1,450 $1,175 $950 *$2,750*

LAR-15 PRO-SERIES GOVERNMENT – .223 Rem. cal., GIO, 16 in. chrome-lined Wilson chrome moly barrel, A2 flash hider, two-stage match trigger, flip-up rear sight, EOTech 552 Holosight red-dot optical sight, 6-position tactical CAR stock, Hogue rubber pistol grip, forged A4 upper receiver, SureFire M73 quad rail handguard, SureFire M951 WeaponLight system, side mount sling swivel, 8.2 lbs. Disc. 2012.

$2,125 $1,900 $1,650 $1,450 $1,250 $1,025 $825 *$2,375*

LAR-15 QMC (QUICK MAGAZINE CHANGE) – 5.56 NATO cal., 16 in. barrel with RRA Beast muzzle brake, two-stage trigger, winter trigger guard, MAG-CAR stock with removable spare magazine holder, Hogue rubber pistol grip, RRA Star safety, 14 1/2 in. rifle length free float aluminum rail handguard with 2 short accessory rails, forged lower and A4 upper receiver, BCM Gunfighter charging handle, matte black (disc. 2018) or tan finish, 7.9 lbs. Mfg. 2017-2019.

$1,050 $925 $800 $725 $625 $500 $400 *$1,165*

Subtract approx. $50 for matte black finish (disc. 2018).

LAR-15M (LAR-15) R3 COMPETITION – .223 Wylde chambered for 5.56mm and .223 cal., GIO, 18 in. fluted stainless steel barrel with directionally-tuned and ported muzzle brake, 30 shot mag., low profile gas block, mid-length gas system, forged LAR-15M (LAR-15) lower and forged A4 upper receiver, two-stage match trigger, winter trigger guard, Star safety, 17 in. RRA TRO-XL free float handguard (M-LOK compatible), RRA adj. Operator A2 or CAR stock, Hogue rubber pistol grips, matte black finish, 7.6 lbs. New 2013.

MSR $1,315 $1,175 $1,025 $900 $800 $650 $525 $425

LAR-15M (LAR-15) RRAGE CARBINE – 5.56 NATO cal., 16 in. lightweight chrome moly barrel, A2 flash hider, 30 shot polymer mag., SST, 6-pos. tactical CAR buttstock, A2 pistol grip, CAR length free floated aluminum handguard with MS1913 top rail (M-LOK compatible), CAR length gas system with low profile gas block, forged LAR-15M (LAR-15) lower and extruded aluminum A4 upper receiver with port door and no forward assist, black, Veil Tac-Black camo, Veil Alpine camo, or Patriotic finish, 5.7-6.5 lbs. New 2018.

MSR $800 $725 $625 $550 $500 $425 $350 $275

Add $165 for Veil Tac-Black camo, Veil Alpine camo, or Patriotic finish.

LAR-15M (LAR-15) RRAGE 3G RIFLE – 5.56 NATO cal., 16 in. chrome moly barrel, A2 flash hider, 30 shot polymer mag., SST, 6-pos. tactical CAR stock, A2 grip, CAR length gas system with low profile gas block, 15 in. RRAGE 3G handguard (M-LOK compatible), extruded aluminum A4 upper receiver with port door, forged LAR-15M (LAR-15) lower receiver, 6.5 lbs. New 2019.

MSR $860 $775 $675 $600 $525 $450 $375 $300

LAR-15M (LAR-15) STANDARD A2 – .223 Rem. (disc. 2012) or .223 Wylde chambered for 5.56 NATO and .223 Rem. cal., GIO, 20 in. Wilson chrome moly (disc. 2012) or chrome moly HBAR barrel, A2 flash hider, two-stage trigger, A2 buttstock, overmolded A2 grip, A2 handguard, forged LAR-15M (LAR-15) lower and A2 upper receiver, A2 front sight base (new 2018), black finish, includes one mag. and case, 8.6 lbs. Disc. 2012, reintroduced 2018.

MSR $970 $875 $775 $675 $600 $525 $424 $325

LAR-15M (LAR-15) STANDARD A4 – .223 Wylde chambered for 5.56mm and .223 Rem. cal., GIO, 20 in. chrome moly HBAR barrel with A2 flash hider, A2 front sight base, rifle length gas system, forged LAR-15M (LAR-15) lower and A4 upper receivers, two-stage trigger, A2 handguard, A2 buttstock, overmolded A2 pistol grip, black finish, includes one mag. and case, available in left-hand configuration, 8.2 lbs.

MSR $920 $825 $725 $650 $575 $500 $400 $325

Add $130 for left-hand (LAR-15LH, Lef-T Standard A4, new 2013).

GRADING - PPGS™	100%	98%	95%	90%	80%	70%	60%	LAST MSR

LAR-15 TACTICAL CAR UTE2 – .223 Rem. cal., GIO, forged Universal Tactical Entry 2 upper receiver, 16 in. Wilson chrome moly barrel, A2 flash hider, two-stage match trigger, Hogue rubber pistol grip, R-4 handguard, 6-position tactical CAR stock, 7 1/2 lbs. Disc. 2012.

	$950	$850	$725	$650	$550	$450	$375	*$1,060*

LAR-15M (LAR-15) TACTICAL CAR A4 – .223 Rem. cal., GIO, 16 in. chrome-lined chrome moly or chrome moly barrel, A2 flash hider, forged A4 upper and LAR-15M lower receiver, two-stage trigger, Hogue rubber pistol grip, Star safety, R-4 handguard, 6-position tactical CAR stock, 7.5 lbs.

MSR $950	$850	$750	$650	$575	$500	$400	$325	

Add $25 for chrome-lined barrel.
Add $115 for left-hand (LAR-15LH, Lef-T, mfg. 2013-2014).

LAR-15 LEF-T TACTICAL OPERATOR-L – 5.56 NATO chambered for 5.56mm and .223 Rem. cal., left-hand specific, 16 in. chrome moly barrel, tactical muzzle brake, two-stage trigger, winter trigger guard, flip front sight gas block assembly, Operator CAR stock and buttstock, Ergo SureGrip (disc. 2019) or Hogue rubber grips (new 2021), CAR length gas system, CAR length quad rail free float handguard with three ladder rail covers, left-handed charging handle, forged A4 LEF-T upper and LAR-15LH lower receiver, includes one mag. and case, black finish, 8 lbs. Disc. 2019, reintroduced 2021.

MSR $1,160	$1,050	$925	$800	$700	$625	$500	$400	*$1,360*

LAR-15 TEXAS RIFLE – .223 Wylde chambered for 5.56mm or .223 Rem. cal., GIO, 16 in. fluted stainless steel barrel with black Cerakote finish, tuned and ported muzzle brake, low profile gas block, two-stage chrome trigger, winter trigger guard, forged A4 upper, Star safety, RRA Texas XL free float handguard with two rail covers, A2 or CAR buttstock, Hogue rubber pistol grip, BCM Gunfighter charging handle, receivers and handguard finished in Cerakote Magpul FDE, Burnt Bronze, or Barrett Bronze, 7.6 lbs. Mfg. 2015-2017.

	$1,525	$1,350	$1,175	$1,050	$900	$725	$600	*$1,700*

Add $10 for Operator A2 stock.

LAR-15M (LAR-15) VARMINT A4 – .223 Wylde chambered for 5.56mm and .223 Rem. or .308 Win. (mfg. 2010-2011) cal., GIO, 16, 18, 20, or 24 in. Wilson (disc.) air gauged, cryo treated stainless steel bull barrel, two-stage match trigger, winter trigger guard, A2 buttstock, Hogue rubber pistol grip, forged LAR-15M (LAR-15) lower and forged A4 upper receiver, Weaver style light varmint gas block with sight rail (disc.) or low profile gas block, knurled and fluted free floating aluminum tube handguard (disc.) or 11 in. TRO free float handguard with octagonal top rail and three TRO accessory rails (M-LOK compatible), black finish, includes one mag. and case, available in left-hand configuration, 7.9-11.6 lbs.

MSR $1,210	$1,075	$975	$850	$750	$650	$525	$425	

Add $25 for 18 in., $50 for 20 in., or $105 for 24 in. barrel.
Add $80 for 16 in., $105 for 18 in., $135 for 20 in., or $150 for 24 in. (disc. 2020) barrel w/left-hand (LAR-15LH, Lef-T Varmint A4, new 2013).
Add $395 for .308 Win. cal. (mfg. 2010-2011).

* ***LAR-15M Varmint A4 .204 Ruger*** – .204 Ruger cal., GIO, 20 in. fluted stainless steel bull barrel w/ cryogenic treatment, two-stage varmint trigger, winter trigger guard, A2 buttstock, Hogue rubber pistol grip, Star safety, rifle length free floating octagon Picatinny rail, LAR-15M forged lower and A4 upper receiver, matte black finish, includes one mag. and case, 9 lbs. New 2017.

MSR $1,260	$1,125	$1,000	$875	$775	$675	$550	$425	

LAR-15M (LAR-15) VARMINT EOP (ELEVATED OPTICAL PLATFORM) – .223 Wylde chambered for 5.56mm or .223 Rem. cal., GIO, 16, 18, 20, or 24 in. Wilson air gauged stainless steel bull barrel, forged EOP upper and LAR-15M receiver, low profile gas block, Weaver style light varmint gas block with sight rail, two-stage match trigger, winter trigger guard, knurled and fluted free floating aluminum tube (disc.) or TRO free float handguard, Hogue rubber pistol grip, A2 buttstock, 8.2-10 lbs. Disc. 2019, reintroduced 2021.

MSR $1,210	$1,075	$975	$850	$750	$650	$525	$425	*$1,300*

Add $25 for 18, $50 for 20, or $105 for 24 in. barrel.

LAR-15M (LAR-15) X-1 RIFLE – .223 Wylde chambered for 5.56 NATO or .223 cal., GIO, 18 in. fluted stainless steel barrel, RRA Beast or Hunter muzzle brake, forged A4 upper and LAR-15M lower receivers, low profile gas block, two-stage varmint trigger, Star safety, winter trigger guard, RRA TRO-XL 15 in. extended length lightweight free float rail, Operator A2 or Operator CAR stock, Hogue rubber pistol grip, includes 9 in. XL accessory rail and two 2 in. short accessory rails, black or tan finish, includes one mag.and case, 7.7 lbs. New 2014.

MSR $1,370	$1,225	$1,100	$950	$850	$725	$575	$475	

Add $30 for tan finish with Hunter muzzle brake and Operator A2 or CAR stock.

GRADING - PPGS™	100%	98%	95%	90%	80%	70%	60%	LAST MSR

LAR-22 MID (MID-LENGTH) A4 – .22 LR cal., 16 in. chrome moly barrel, A2 flash hider, single stage trigger, gas block sight base, 6-pos. adj. tactical CAR stock, A2 pistol grip, RRA forged aluminum or poly LAR-22 lower and A4 upper receiver, mid-length handguard with heat shields, black finish, 36 in. OAL, 5.4 lbs. New 2019.

MSR $465 $425 $375 $325 $275 $250 $200 $150

Add $95 for forged aluminum receivers.

LAR-22 NM AR A4 RIFLE – .22 LR cal., 20 in. stainless steel heavy HBAR barrel, A2 flash hider, two-stage match chrome trigger group, A2 buttstock, A2 pistol grip, forged aluminum A4 upper and forged aluminum LAR15M lower receiver, high temp thermo mold free float handguard, 8.9 lbs. New 2020.

MSR $875 $775 $700 $600 $525 $475 $375 $300

LAR-22 NM A4 CMP TRAINER – .22 LR cal., 20 in. stainless steel heavy barrel, A2 flash hider, two-stage match chrome trigger group, 6-pos. Operator CAR stock, A2 pistol grip, forged aluminum A4 upper and forged aluminum LAR-22 lower receiver, rifle length NM CMP TRO free float handguard with three TRO modular rails and an NM sling swivel, black finish, includes one mag., 8.8 lbs. New 2019.

MSR $930 $825 $750 $650 $575 $500 $400 $325

LAR-22 TACTICAL CARBINE – .22 LR cal., 16 in. chrome moly barrel, A2 flash hider, two-stage trigger, winter trigger guard, 6-pos. adj. NSP CAR stock, Hogue rubber pistol grip, RRA forged aluminum or poly LAR-22 lower and A4 upper receivers, RRA 11 (disc. 2019) or 15 (new 2020) in. extended lightweight 3G free floating handguard (M-LOK compatible), black finish, includes one mag., 37 1/4 in. OAL, approx. 5.4 lbs. New 2019.

MSR $580 $525 $450 $400 $350 $300 $250 $200

Add $85 for forged aluminum receivers.

LAR-40 CAR A2/A4 – .40 S&W cal., GIO, forged A2 (disc. 2011) or A4 upper receiver, 16 in. chrome moly barrel, A2 flash hider, single stage trigger, R-4 handguard, 6-position tactical CAR stock with Hogue pistol grip, approx. 7 lbs. Disc. 2011, reintroduced 2013-2017.

$1,125 $1,000 $875 $775 $675 $550 $425 *$1,260*

Add $145 for quad rail.

Add $50 for Operator stock.

LAR-40 MID-LENGTH A2/A4 – .40 S&W cal., GIO, forged A2 (disc. 2011) or A4 (new 2013) upper, 16 in. chrome moly barrel, A2 flash hider, two-stage match trigger, mid-length handguard, Hogue rubber pistol grip, 6-position tactical CAR stock, approx. 7 lbs. Mfg. 2010-2011, reintroduced 2013-2017.

$1,125 $1,000 $875 $775 $675 $550 $425 *$1,260*

LAR-47 CAR A4 – 7.62x39mm cal., GIO, 16 in. chrome-lined HBAR barrel with A2 flash hider, gas block front sight base, forged LAR-47 lower and A4 upper receiver, two-stage trigger, CAR handguard, 6-pos. CAR tactical stock, A2 pistol grip, ambidextrous mag. release, 6.4 lbs. New 2013.

MSR $1,080 $975 $850 $750 $650 $575 $475 $375

LAR-47 COYOTE CARBINE – 7.62x39mm cal., GIO, 16 in. chrome-lined HBAR barrel with Smith Vortex flash hider, ambi mag. release, two-stage trigger, NSP CAR stock, Hogue rubber pistol grip, forged LAR-47 lower and A4 upper receiver, low profile gas block, deluxe extended free float rifle length handguard with three 2 in. accessory rails, 7.8 lbs. New 2015.

MSR $1,420 $1,275 $1,125 $975 $875 $750 $600 $500

LAR-47 DELTA CARBINE – 7.62x39mm cal., GIO, 16 in. chrome-lined HBAR barrel with A2 flash hider, 10 shot mag., ambi mag. release, two-stage trigger, winter trigger guard, gas block front sight base, 6-position Delta CAR stock, Ergo SureGrip, forged lower and A4 upper receiver, two-piece quad rail handguard, 7 3/4 lbs. Mfg. 2013-2020.

$1,000 $900 $775 $700 $600 $475 $400 *$1,125*

LAR-47 TACTICAL COMP – 7.62x39mm cal., GIO, 16 in. chrome-lined HBAR barrel with Operator muzzle brake, flip front sight gas block assembly, forged A4 upper and LAR-47 lower receivers, two-stage trigger, ambidextrous mag. release, CAR length free float quad rail, Operator CAR stock, overmolded pistol grips, black finish, includes one AK mag. and case, 7.8 lbs. New 2015.

MSR $1,290 $1,150 $1,025 $900 $800 $675 $550 $450

LAR-47 X-1 RIFLE – 7.62x39mm cal., GIO, 18 in. fluted stainless steel bull barrel, RRA Beast or Hunter muzzle brake, forged A4 upper and LAR-47 lower receivers, low profile gas block, two-stage varmint trigger, 15 in. RRA TRO-XL extended length free float rail (M-LOK compatible), Operator A2 or Operator CAR stock, Hogue rubber pistol grip, 9 in. XL accessory rail and two 2 in. short accessory rails for handguard (disc. 2019), black or tan finish, includes one AK mag. and case, 8.2 lbs. Mfg. 2015-2019, reintroduced 2021.

MSR $1,490 $1,350 $1,175 $1,025 $900 $800 $650 $525 *$1,600*

Add $30 for RRA Hunter muzzle brake and tan finish.

GRADING - PPGS™	100%	98%	95%	90%	80%	70%	60%	LAST MSR

LAR-300 CAR A4 – .300 ACC Blackout cal., GIO, pistol length gas system, 16 in. chrome moly HBAR barrel with A2 flash hider, forged A4 upper and LAR-15M lower receiver, two-stage trigger, gas block w/receiver height sight base or A2 front sight base (new 2020), CAR length handguard, 6-pos. tactical CAR stock, overmolded A2 grip, 7.1 lbs. New 2015.

MSR $975	$875	$775	$675	$600	$525	$425	$350	

LAR-300 COYOTE CARBINE – .300 ACC Blackout cal., GIO, 16 in. chrome moly HBAR barrel with Smith Vortex flash hider, two-stage trigger, winter trigger guard, Operator CAR stock, Hogue rubber pistol grip, low profile gas block, forged A4 upper and LAR-300 lower, deluxe extended CAR handguard with three accessory rails, black finish, 7.2 lbs. New 2015.

MSR $1,235	$1,100	$975	$850	$750	$650	$525	$425	

LAR-300 DELTA CARBINE – .300 ACC Blackout cal., GIO, 16 in. chrome moly barrel with A2 flash hider, low profile gas block, two-stage trigger, winter trigger guard, Delta CAR stock, Ergo SureGrip pistol grip, Delta quad rail CAR length two-piece drop-in handguard, 7 lbs. Mfg. 2015-2019.

	$1,000	$900	$775	$675	$600	$475	$400	*$1,120*

LAR-300 TACTICAL CAR A4 – .300 ACC Blackout cal., GIO, 16 in. chrome moly HBAR barrel with A2 flash hider, A2 front sight base with side mount sling swivel, two-stage trigger, forged A4 upper and LAR-15M lower receiver, R-4 handguard, 6-pos. tactical CAR stock, Hogue rubber grip, 7.5 lbs. Mfg. 2015-2019, reintroduced 2021.

MSR $1,000	$900	$800	$700	$600	$525	$425	$350	*$1,100*

LAR-300 X-1 RIFLE – .300 ACC Blackout cal., GIO, 18 in. fluted stainless steel HBAR barrel, RRA Beast or Hunter muzzle brake, forged A4 upper and LAR-15M lower receivers, low profile gas block, two-stage varmint trigger, winter trigger guard, RRA TRO-XL extended length free float rail, Operator A2 or Operator CAR stock, Hogue rubber pistol grip, Star safety, black or tan finish, includes 9 in. XL accessory rail and two 2 in. short accessory rails (disc. 2019), 7.9 lbs. Mfg. 2015-2019, reintroduced 2021.

MSR $1,490	$1,350	$1,175	$1,025	$900	$800	$650	$525	*$1,585*

Add $30 for RRA Hunter muzzle brake and tan finish.

LAR-458 DEVASTATOR (BEAST) – .458 SOCOM cal., GIO, 14 1/2 in. chrome moly bull barrel with pinned and welded Beast brake (for 16 in. barrel length), two-stage trigger, Delta 6-pos. CAR stock, Hogue rubber pistol grip, forged LAR-458 lower and A4 upper receiver, low profile gas block, TRO-STD (disc. 2019) or lightweight 13 in. extended (new 2020) free float handguard, rifle length with one STD and two short accessory rails, black finish, 7.6 lbs. New 2018.

MSR $1,370	$1,225	$1,100	$950	$850	$725	$575	$475	

LAR-458 CAR A4 – .458 SOCOM cal., GIO, 16 in. Wilson chrome moly bull barrel, A2 flash hider, two-stage trigger, Weaver style varmint gas block with sight rail (disc.), A2 buttstock (disc.) or Operator CAR (new 2010) stock, overmolded A2 pistol grip, forged A4 upper and LAR-458 lower receiver, low profile gas block, knurled and fluted free floating aluminum tube handguard (disc.) or lightweight free float rail handguard, M-LOK compatible, black finish, 7.6 lbs.

MSR $1,160	$1,050	$925	$800	$700	$625	$500	$400	

LAR-458 MID-LENGTH A4 – .458 SOCOM cal., GIO, forged A4 upper receiver, 16 in. chrome moly bull barrel, A2 flash hider, gas block with sight rail, two-stage match trigger, knurled and fluted free floating aluminum tube handguard, A2 buttstock and pistol grip, 7.8 lbs. Mfg. 2010-2017.

	$1,100	$975	$850	$750	$650	$525	$425	*$1,220*

Add $290 for Operator model with half quad free float with full length top rail, Vortex flash hider, and CAR stock (new 2010).

LAR-458 TACTICAL CARBINE – .458 SOCOM cal., 16 in. chrome moly bull barrel with Operator muzzle brake, two-stage trigger, winter trigger guard, NSP 6-pos. CAR stock, Hogue rubber pistol grip, Star safety, forged A4 upper and LAR-458 lower receiver, low profile gas block, deluxe extended free float rail, rifle length with 3 short accessory rails, black finish, includes one mag. and case, 7.8 lbs. New 2015.

MSR $1,235	$1,100	$975	$850	$750	$650	$525	$425	

LAR-458 X-1 RIFLE – .458 SOCOM cal., GIO, 18 in. fluted stainless steel bull barrel, RRA Beast or Hunter muzzle brake, low profile gas block, forged RRA LAR-458 lower and A4 upper receiver, two-stage trigger, winter trigger guard, RRA TRO-XL extended length free float rail, RRA Operator A2 or Operator CAR stock, Hogue rubber pistol grip, black or tan finish, includes one 9 in. XL accessory rail and two 2 in. short accessory rails for handguard, 8.7 lbs. Mfg. 2014-2019.

	$1,425	$1,275	$1,100	$975	$850	$675	$550	*$1,595*

Add $10 for Operator A2 stock.
Add $50 for RRA Hunter muzzle brake and tan finish.

GRADING - PPGS™	100%	98%	95%	90%	80%	70%	60%	LAST MSR

LAR-PDS CARBINE (PISTON DRIVEN SYSTEM) – 5.56 NATO (new 2020) or .223 Rem. cal., GPO, 16 in. chrome moly barrel, A2 flash hider, two-stage trigger, ribbed forend, side folding 6-position tactical stock with receiver extension storage compartment, Hogue rubber pistol grip, full-length forged A4 upper and LAR-15 forged lower w/partial Picatinny rails, injection molded ribbed or tri-rail handguard, folding ambidextrous non-reciprocating charging handles, two-position regulator, black finish, includes one mag. and case, approx. 7.4 lbs. New 2011.

MSR $1,420	$1,275	$1,125	$975	$875	$750	$600	$500	

Add $80 for tri-rail handguard.

PRO-SERIES TASC – .223 Rem. cal., GIO, chrome-lined 16 in. Wilson chrome moly barrel with Smith Vortex flash hider, two-stage match trigger, oversize winter trigger guard, A2 rear sight with lockable windage and elevation, Midwest Industries A2 adj. cantilever sight mount, 6-position tactical CAR stock, Hogue rubber pistol grip, graphite foregrip, forged A2 upper receiver, SureFire M85 mid-length quad rail, EOTech 511 Holosight, Midwest Industries A2 adj. cantilever sight mount, 8.7 lbs. Disc. 2009.

	$1,800	$1,600	$1,400	$1,225	$1,050	$850	$700	*$2,000*

TASC RIFLE – .223 Rem. cal., GIO, 16 in. Wilson chrome moly barrel, A2 flash hider, forged A2 upper receiver with lockable windage and elevation adj. rear sight, two-stage match trigger, Hogue rubber pistol grip, A2 buttstock or 6-position CAR tactical buttstock, choice of R-4 or mid-length handguard, approx. 7 1/2 lbs. Disc. 2009.

	$850	$750	$650	$575	$500	$400	$325	*$950*

Add $15 for six-position collapsible stock.

ROCKY MOUNTAIN ARMS CORP.

Previous manufacturer of mini revolvers circa mid-1960s, and located in Salt Lake City, UT.

For individual model listings, please go to BlueBookOfGunValues.com/overflow.

ROCKY MOUNTAIN ARMS, INC.

Previous firearms manufacturer located in Longmont, CO 1991-circa 2017.

Rocky Mountain Arms was a quality specialty manufacturer of rifles and pistols. All firearms were finished in a DuPont Teflon-S industrial coating called "Bear Coat".

PISTOLS: BOLT ACTION

BAP (BOLT ACTION PISTOL) – .308 Win., 7.62x39mm, or 10mm Rocky Mountain Thunderer (10x51mm) cal., 14 in. heavy fluted Douglas Match barrel, Kevlar/graphite pistol grip stock, supplied with Harris bipod and black nylon case. Mfg. 1993 only.

	$1,425	$1,275	$1,100	$950	$825	$700	$575	*$1,595*

PISTOLS: SEMI-AUTO

1911A1-LH – .40 S&W or .45 ACP cal., specifically designed for left-handed shooters, featuring left side ejection port and right side controls, gold cup size, stainless steel construction, hand fitted parts, Match barrel, adj. Novak style night sights (new 2015), integral ramp barrel, Millett adj. sights, includes test target, case, and five magazines. Mfg. 1991-93, reintroduced circa 2014-2017.

	$3,250	$3,000	$2,850	$2,700	$2,600	$2,500	$2,400	*$3,500*

Add $100 for Bo-Mar sights.

BACKUP PLUS – .45 ACP cal., hand tuned AMT Backup pistol, black DuPont Teflon-S finish, Tritium front night sight. Mfg. 1995-97.

	$575	$515	$450	$400	$360	$330	$300	*$650*

22K PISTOLS – .22 LR cal., AR style pistol, blowback action, 7 in. barrel, choice of matte black or NATO Green Teflon-S finish, will use Colt conversion kit, choice of carrying handle or flat-top upper receiver, 10 or 30 shot mag., includes black nylon case. Mfg. 1993 only.

	$450	$385	$335	$285	$250	$230	$215	*$525*

Add $50 for flat-top receiver with Weaver style bases.

KOMRADE – 7.62x39mm cal., floating 7 in. barrel, 5 shot mag., includes carrying handle upper receiver with fixed sights, red finish only, 5 lbs. Very limited mfg. was pre-ban 1994 only.

Last MSR was $1,995.

Rarity precludes accurate pricing on this model. Recent sales with case is in the $3,500 range.

PATRIOT PISTOL – .223 Rem. cal., AR-15 style, GIO, 7 in. match barrel with integral Max Dynamic muzzle brake, available with either carrying handle upper receiver and fixed sights or flat-top receiver with Weaver style bases, fluted upper receiver became an option in 1994, accepts standard AR-15 mags, 21 in. OAL, 5 lbs. Mfg. 1993-94 (per C/B), reintroduced 2005-2017.

	$2,550	$2,225	$1,825	$1,575	$1,300	$1,100	$950	*$3,000*

GRADING - PPGS™	100%	98%	95%	90%	80%	70%	60%	LAST MSR

RIFLES: BOLT ACTION

NINJA SCOUT RIFLE – .22 WMR cal., takedown rifle based on Marlin action, 16 1/2 in. match grade crowned barrel, 7 shot mag., black stock, forward mounted Weaver style scope base, adj. rear sight. Mfg. 1991-1995.

$640 $575 $525 $460 $430 $390 $360 *$695*

Add $200 for illuminated dot scope (1.5-4X) w/extended eye relief.

PRAIRIE STALKER – .223 Rem., .22-250 Rem., .30-06, .308 Win., or .300 Win. Mag. cal., choice of Remington, Savage, or Winchester barreled action, includes Choate ultimate sniper stock, lapped bolt and match crown, "Bear Coat" all-weather finish, includes factory test target. Limited mfg. 1998 only.

$1,595 $1,350 $1,150 $950 $875 $775 $675 *$1,795*

* ***Prairie Stalker Ultimate*** – similar to Prairie Stalker, except custom barrel and caliber specifications are customer's choice. Limited mfg. 1998 only.

$2,200 $1,875 $1,625 $1,400 $1,200 $1,000 $895 *$2,495*

PROFESSIONAL SERIES – .223 Rem., .30-06, .308 Win., or .300 Win. Mag. cal., bolt action rifle utilizing modified Mauser action, fluted 26 in. Douglas premium heavy match barrel with integral muzzle brake, custom Kevlar-Graphite stock with off-set thumbhole, test target. Mfg. 1991-95.

$2,050 $1,650 $1,275 $995 $850 $725 $600 *$2,200*

Add $100 for .300 Win. Mag. cal.
Add $300 for left-hand action.

PRO-GUIDE – .280 Rem., .35 Whelen, .308 Win., 7x57mm Mauser, or 7mm-08 Rem. cal., Scout Rifle design with 17 in. Shilen barrel, "Bear Coat" finish, approx. 7 lbs. Mfg. 1999-2002.

$2,025 $1,800 $1,600 $1,425 $1,200 $1,000 $825 *$2,295*

PRO-VARMINT – .22-250 Rem. or .223 Rem. cal., RMA action, 22 in. heavy match barrel with recessed crown, "Bear Coat" metal finish, Choate stock with aluminum bedding. Mfg. 1999-2002.

$995 $875 $800 $725 $650 $575 $450 *$1,095*

POLICE MARKSMAN – .308 Win. or .300 Win. Mag. cal., bolt action rifle utilizing modified Mauser action, 26 in. fluted Douglas premium heavy match barrel with integral muzzle brake, 40X-C stock featuring adj. cheekpiece and buttplate, target rail, Buehler micro-dial scope mounting system. Mfg. 1991-95.

$2,325 $1,995 $1,650 $1,325 $1,100 $900 $700 *$2,500*

Add $100 for .300 Win. Mag. cal.
Add $400 for left-hand action.
Add $400 for illuminated dot scope (4-12x56mm).

* ***Police Marksman II*** – .308 Win. cal., RMA action, 22 in. heavy match barrel with recessed crown, "Bear Coat" metal finish, Choate stock with aluminum bedding. Mfg. 1999-2002.

$995 $875 $800 $725 $650 $575 $450 *$1,095*

SCOUT SEMI-AUTO – .22 WMR cal., patterned after Marlin action. Mfg. 1993-95.

$650 $575 $495 $395 $350 $295 $260 *$725*

Add $200 for illuminated dot scope (1.5-4X) w/extended eye relief.

RIFLES: SEMI-AUTO

M-SHORTEEN – .308 Win. cal., compact highly modified M1-A featuring 17" match crowned barrel, custom front sight, mod. gas system, hand honed action and trigger, custom muzzle brake. Mfg. 1991-94.

$1,650 $1,425 $1,175 $995 $850 $725 $600 *$1,895*

Add $200 for Woodland/Desert camo.

VARMINTER – .223 Rem. cal. only, AR-15 style, GIO, 20 in. fluted heavy match barrel, flat-top receiver with Weaver style bases, round metal National Match handguard, free float barrel, choice of NATO green or matte black Teflon-S finish, supplied with case and factory test target (sub-MOA accuracy). Mfg. 1993-94.

$1,975 $1,150 $925 $650 $575 $495 $425 *$2,495*

PATRIOT MATCH RIFLE – .223 Rem. cal., AR-15 style, GIO, 20 in. bull match barrel, regular or milled upper and lower receivers, two-piece machined aluminum handguard, choice of DuPont Teflon finish in black or NATO green, 1/2 MOA accuracy, hard case. Mfg. 1995-97, reintroduced 2005-2017.

$2,050 $1,250 $950 $650 $575 $495 $475 *$2,500*

SHOTGUNS: SLIDE ACTION

870 COMPETITOR – 12 ga., 3 in. chamber, security configuration with synthetic stock, hand-honed action, ghost ring adj. sights, "Bear Coat" finish, high visibility follower. Mfg. 1996-97.

$695 $625 $550 $500 $450 $400 $360 *$795*

GRADING - PPGS™	100%	98%	95%	90%	80%	70%	60%	LAST MSR

ROCKY MOUNTAIN ELK FOUNDATION

Current national conservation organization with national headquarters located in Missoula, MT.

RIFLES: BOLT ACTION

RUGER NO. 1-A LIGHT SPORTER – .35 Whelen cal., features gold inlaid elk on right side of receiver and mountain scene with gold accents on left side, engraved by Adams & Son, blue finish, deluxe wood, 50 mfg. 1995 only.

$2,395	$1,850	$1,475	N/A	N/A	N/A	N/A	*$2,395*

SAUER MODEL 90 – .270 Win. or .30-06 cal., banquet offering only, total mfg. unknown.

$1,375	$1,100	$925	N/A	N/A	N/A	N/A	

ROEDALE PRECISION

Current custom rifle manufacturer located in Hasbergen, Germany. No current U.S. importation.

Pete Lincoln makes a custom precision Viper series of bolt action rifles, in addition to related components. Please contact the company directly for more information, pricing, and current availability.

ROGAK

Please refer to the L E S Incorporated listing in the L section.

ROGER'S GUN WORKS, INC.

Current custom rifle manufacturer established in 1991, located in Fayetteville, GA.

Roger Ferrell manufactures custom made to order rifles. Many options and configurations are available. Please contact the company directly for more information.

ROGUE RIVER RIFLEWORKS

Previous manufacturer located in Paso Robles, CA. Rogue River Rifleworks also manufactured the John Rigby line of rifle and shotguns until circa 2011.

RIFLES

BOLT ACTION MODEL – 7mm STW, .300 Win. Mag., .30-378 Wby. Mag., 8mm Rem. Mag., .375 H&H, .416 Rem. Mag., or .458 Win. Mag. cal., choice of Remington M-700 or Winchester M-70 action, Pac-Nor match grade barrel (with cryogenic treatment), engraved receiver, floorplate, and grip cap, jewelled bolt, exhibition grade checkered walnut stock with ebony forend cap. Limited mfg. 1998-2004.

$7,250	$6,250	$5,400	$4,500	$3,500	$2,750	$1,925	*$10,500*

LEVER ACTION MODEL – .243 Win., .260 Rem., 7mm-08 Rem., .308 Win., or .358 Win. cal., features rebuilt Winchester Model 88 action, match grade chrome moly barrel, exhibition grade walnut, choice of American classic or Mannlicher stock design. Limited mfg. 1998-2004.

$3,500	$3,100	$2,600	$2,000	$1,400	$950	$600	*$5,100*

SxS MODEL – .470 NE, .500 NE, or .577 NE cal., Anson & Deeley action, Purdey double locking lugs, Greener crossbolt, Southgate selective ejectors, quarter rib with rear sights, exhibition grade wood, case colored or coin finished receiver. Limited mfg. 1998-2000.

Prices started at $12,500 for .470 NE cal. A 12, 16, or 20 ga. shotgun barrel conversion kit was also available for $3,800.

RÖHM

Previous firearms manufacturer located in Sontheim an der Brenz, Germany. Limited importation into the U.S. Röhm still manufactures gas alarm pistols, mostly for European sales.

Röhm produced inexpensive revolvers for the U.S. marketplace during the late 1960s-1970s. Most of these guns were built as sub-contracts for U.S. companies and/or distributors (i.e., Hy-Score, a previous distributor located in Brooklyn, NY). Some of the models included are RG-7 through RG-88 (21 variations), Romo, Thalco, Valor, Vestpocket, Western Style, Zephyr, and others. Röhm also manufactured a few semi-auto pistols (RG-25 and RG-26) at approx. the same time. Currently, these guns are seen priced in the $35-$125 range, as the shooting value determines the price tag, not collector interest.

DERRINGERS

DERRINGER – .22 LR cal., blue, copy of Remington O/U derringer. Excellently made, but half-cock safety is old design and could fail if dropped.

$150	$115	$95	$85	$75	$65	$55	

GRADING - PPGS™	100%	98%	95%	90%	80%	70%	60%	LAST MSR

ROHRBAUGH FIREARMS CORP.

Previous manufacturer located in Bayport, NY until 2014. Previously located in Deer Park, NY.

PISTOLS: SEMI-AUTO

R-9 – 9mm Para. or .380 ACP (new 2007) cal., DAO, 2.9 in. barrel, free bored to reduce felt recoil, frame is 7075-T651 aluminum, stainless steel or black Stealth slide, 6 shot mag., parts cut from solid billets, all internal parts are stainless, short recoil locked breech with cam operated tilting barrel locking system, recessed hammer, carbon fiber (disc.) or G10 grips, no sights, 12.8 (carbon fiber grips) or 13 1/2 (G10 grips) oz. Mfg. 2003-disc.

$1,000	$875	$750	$680	$550	$450	$350	*$1,150*

Add $45 for black Stealth slide.

* ***R9S Model*** – similar to Model R-9, except has fixed open sights, 9mm Para. cal. variations include Tribute (silver gun with black/blue CF grips, new 2012), Coyote (Coyote Tan metal finish, new 2012), and Covert (black with sights, new 2012). Mfg. 2004-disc.

$1,000	$875	$750	$680	$550	$450	$350	*$1,150*

Add $45 for black Stealth slide.
Add $200 R9S Tribute (new 2012). Add $600 for R9S Coyote or Covert (new 2012).
Add $45 for Elite Custom Model (Model R9SE, disc.).

ROHRBAUGH ROBAR R9 SERIES – similar to original R9, except frame, barrel, slide and trigger are treated with Robar Industries NP3 coating (corrosion resistant and self lubricating), polished stainless steel, limited lifetime warranty. Mfg. 2010 only.

$1,500	$1,315	$1,125	$1,020	$825	$675	$525	*$1,795*

ROPER

Previously manufactured revolving rifles and shotguns made circa 1866-1876 in Amherst, MA and Hartford, CT.

Sylvester Roper manufactured revolving rifles and shotguns in Amherst, MA beginning circa 1866 under the name Roper Repeating Rifle Company. Production was later moved to Hartford, CT circa 1869, and the company name was changed to Roper Sporting Arms Company.

Guns should be evaluated individually to determine value.

ROSS RIFLE COMPANY

Previous manufacturer located in Quebec City, Canada, circa 1900-1917.

The Ross rifle was the design of Sir Charles Henry Augustus Frederick Lockhart Ross (1872-1942), 9th Baronet of Balnagown, born in Scotland. He came to Canada in 1897, and left in 1917, following government expropriation of his plant.

While still a student at England's Eton College in 1893, Ross patented his first rifle design, which never left the drawing board. His patent of 1897 was more practical, and reached limited production first in Hartford, CT, then shortly after by the Chas. Lancaster firm in England. Ross worked with J.A. Bennett in Hartford until 1905, and apparently supplied components to Charles Lancaster in London, England until just before WWI began in 1914. By 1903, the new Ross Plant in Quebec City had begun production of early commercial rifles.

Ross was responsible for developing the first commercially available high velocity round in 1906, the .280 Ross, which developed a muzzle velocity in excess of 3,000 FPS, supplied initially as the 1907 Scotch Deerstalker Model. Patterns were sent to Eley in England, who produced the early ammunition for Ross.

While early Ross Commercial Sporting Rifles could almost be considered to be "custom" rifles with many available variations, it would appear the military rifle production was considered to be the "bread and butter" for the Ross Plant in Canada.

It must be recognized that while Ross provided the basic military designs for the MK I, MK II, and MK III variations, on-going military production was entirely at the mercy of a multitude of Canadian government inspectors, insisting upon almost daily alterations at several points. Overall lengths, weights, and even sights were decided by others. Politically, it was found expedient to lay all the blame for any and all faults real or imagined squarely upon Sir Charles himself.

Unfortunately, the Ross MK III was saddled with a Crown of Thorns similar to low-numbered Springfield 1903 receivers. The reality was (and still is) that with considerable difficulty, a MK III bolt can be reversed 180 degrees in its sleeve, then with added brute force and ignorance, can be partially inserted in its receiver and fired, with highly unpleasant results. A complete mechanical inspection by a competent gunsmith who is familiar with Ross rifles is urged before firing one of these guns, but verifying that the gas escape port in the bolt-head is visible with the bolt pulled back provides confirmation that all is as it should be.

GRADING - PPGS™	100%	98%	95%	90%	80%	70%	60%	LAST MSR

The author wishes to express his thanks to Mr. Barry DeLong, Mr. Steve Engleson, and Mr. Gordon Hanlan for making the following information available.

Further information on Ross Rifle Co. products can now be found on the Internet at RossRifle.com. All new and/or unusual findings can be offered for review and discussion, and any questions regarding Ross can likely be intelligently answered.

RIFLES: BOLT ACTION

The values listed are for specimens that have been unaltered except where noted.

MODEL 1897 SPORTER – .303 Brit. cal., 26 in. barrel, 5 round magazine, known as the "hammer model" because the bolt cocked the hammer as it traveled over it, clip loaded Mannlicher type magazine, bolt head design of solid opposing locking lugs with vertical travel and horizontal locking. Hartford, CT version has checkered walnut straight stock and a two leaf rear sight, Lancaster version has checkered walnut pistol grip stock, V notch rear sight and tang mounted peep sight. Mfg. 1897-1900.

This variation is encountered with such low frequency that consistent market pricing cannot be established.

MODEL 1900 SPORTER – similar to the Model 1897, except has no hammer and a coil mainspring and internal bolt striker. Mfg. 1900-01.

This variation is encountered with such low frequency that consistent market pricing cannot be established.

RIFLES: BOLT ACTION, CANADIAN PRODUCTION

Canadian production of Ross Rifles consisted of three basic centerfire actions and one rimfire. All four were produced in sporting and military configurations. Commerical rifles typically have a serial number on the left side of the barrel immediately ahead of the receiver. Military rifles are numbered on the right side of the stock - a three digit number from 1-999 over the year manufactured/accepted, followed initially by one letter, then two letters. The Military Contract Cadets are numbered similarly, but the letter is ahead of the number over the date.

MARK I (MILITARY)/MODEL 1903 (SPORTING) – a modification of the Model 1900, "Patented 1903" on left side of receiver, slide button safety, slimmed and completely knurled bolt cocking-piece and thumbpiece mag. lifter, enclosed mag.

* ***Mark I*** – .303 Brit. cal., 28 in. barrel, walnut stock, OAL 45 5/8th inches, H-type hinged rear sight adjustable to 2,200 yards with adjustments for windage and elevation. These will normally be found with a modified Ross MkI sight, referred to as the MkI* sight. The original sights are extremely scarce.

$2,500	$2,000	$1,750	$1,500	$1,200	$900	$800

Those models with the original Mk I or Mk I* sight and original nosecap would bring a premium with values up to $3,500 for a top condition specimen.

In 1905, the first 1,000 rifles were delivered to the Royal Northwest Mounted Police in Regina, Saskatchewan. The early Mk Is used the Ross Mk I and Mk I* rear sight. Most were retrofitted with the Ross Mk II sight. The early nosecaps were formed from sheet metal.

* ***Model 1903 Sporter*** – .303 British (most common), .256 Mannlicher, or .370 Express cal., 26 or 28 in. barrel, walnut checkered stock, two leaf English style rear sight, 5 round mag. Long thought to be mfg. in Hartford, CT USA and Quebec City, Canada. Recent information that has come to light indicate mfg. by Lancaster in England (under Ross patents).

$3,000	$2,500	$2,000	$1,500	$1,200	$900	$600

Add 50% for .256 Mannlicher cal.
Add 50% for .370 Express cal.

MARK II (MILITARY)/MODEL 1905 (SPORTING) – "1905 Patented" on left side of receiver, action is cocked on opening, bolt action camming to initiate cartridge extraction, did not have bolt knurled thumbpiece, improved extractor added to later Model 1905 variations. Mfg. beginning 1906.

* ***Mark II Original (No Star and slightly modified MkII*)*** – .303 Brit. cal., Ross MKII or MKIII sight, early model with flat buttplate and "stepped" nosecap (similar to MKI rifles), fitted with the Ross MkII sight (aka "ski-jump" sight). Mfg. 1906.

$2,000	$1,750	$1,500	$1,000	$750	$550	$500

The seldom-found "MkII with the MkIII rear sight" (flat-top" and fragile sight) produced in 1907 variant is at least as scarce as this one, and can be considered to be of comparable value.

* ***Mark II 2**** – .303 Brit. cal., 30 1/2 in. heavy barrel, military issue, but primarily a target rifle. Hindsight determined that this was likely the best Military rifle that Ross had ever produced. Scarce variation and seldom seen today. There are four basic variants: (1) Sutherland sight on barrel, no receiver base or sight, and extended sword bar to fit the MkII bayo (2) Sutherland sight on barrel, stamped receiver base and full-length wood so the new MkII bayonet now fits (3) Sutherland sight on barrel, milled base on

GRADING - PPGS™	100%	98%	95%	90%	80%	70%	60%	LAST MSR

receiver with MkIII Battlesight and (4) One-piece top wood (no barrel sight) and milled base on receiver with MkIII Battlesight.

	$2,600	$2,200	$1,900	$1,600	$1,200	$900	$800	

NOTE: This variant really shares very little with the other MkII rifles. When it was first introduced in 1908, both Ross and the Canadian Government referred to it as the "Rifle, Ross MkIII". This continued until what is now known as the MkIII was later introduced in 1910, and at that time, it was decided to call it the MkII.**

* ***Mark II 3**** – .303 Brit. cal., 28 in. barrel, most commonly encountered example, includes 20,000 sold to U.S. with flaming bomb proofmark added, found with the Canada Tool barrel sight, U.S. contract rifles were fitted with a "Kerr NOBUCKL" sling in the U.S.

	$1,500	$1,250	$975	$800	$675	$550	$475	

The scarce U.S. sub-variation was shortened by approx. 7/8 in. and has a rechambered barrel. This model is seldom seen and commands a premium, particularly if still fitted with the unique MkI bayonet with the "cranked" crossguard. Suspicions are that a small run was modified and then used by rifle teams.

* ***Mark II 4**** – .303 Brit. cal., 28 in. barrel, similar to MKII 3*, except that reportedly, it was initially fitted with the earlier Ross MKIII sight (flat-top) then later were converted to MkII 3* condition, using the Canada Tool ladder sight.

	$1,500	$1,250	$900	$800	$700	$600	$550	

* ***Mark II 5**** – .303 Brit. cal., 28 in. barrel. A relatively seldom encountered variant that has the Sutherland "H" type sight variation fitted. Several of these, as well as MkII 4*'s converted back to MkII 3* status have surfaced with US acceptance marks.

	$1,500	$1,250	$900	$800	$700	$600	$550	

* ***Model 1905 M Sporter*** – .303 Brit. cal., 28 in. barrel, illustrated in 1906 catalog only, Enfield barrel sight. Very few known.

	$1,450	$1,175	$900	$750	$675	$550	$475	

Note: this model is basically a sporterized military rifle done by the factory. Rifles have been altered after leaving the factory and can appear similar to an original specimen. There were reportedly three different variations. Factory specimens should not have military markings.

* ***Model 1905 R Sporter*** – .303 Brit. cal., 26 or 28 in. barrel, no checkering on stock, originally fitted with Winchester semi-buckhorn sight. The Military short MkII barrel with the coarse LH threads were used.

	$1,050	$800	$700	$650	$600	$550	$500	

* ***Model 1905 E Sporter*** – .303 Brit. or .35 WCF cal., 22, 24, 26 or 28 in. barrel, built up on MKII** receiver, fine-thread heavy barrel, checkered pistol grip wood, found with or without the Harris lever, several different multi-leaf "express" sights found on this model. Can almost be considered a "Factory Custom" model.

	$1,900	$1,400	$1,100	$900	$800	$725	$600	

Add 25% for .35 WCF cal.
Add $500 if fitted with a Lyman 50 sight (catalog option).

* ***Mark II** Commercial Target Model*** – .303 Brit. cal., 30 1/2 in. barrel, identical to the Military 2* rifle but typically found with commercial finish on wood and no sling swivels, target sight on bridge over receiver and serial number on barrel.

	$2,600	$2,350	$2,000	$1,800	$1,500	$1,250	$1,000	

Add $500 for Presentation Target Rifle w/o inscription.
Values increase for a model with an engraved inscription, depending on documentation.
With the multitude of commercially available sights that were acceptable for official Matches in Canada, Britain and the USA, the prices above reflect no sights, and sight values should be added.

This model won almost all rifle matches from 1908 to 1913. A Presentation Target Rifle with deluxe wood and finish, and with a sterling silver medallion in stock was offered in several catalogs, but is seldom encountered.

MODEL 1907 & 1905/1910 MATCH TARGET RIFLE – between the MkII (1905) and the MkIII (1910), two important and scarce rifles were built and sold on a modified MkII action with threaded, not solid, locking lugs.

* ***Model 1907 "Scotch Deer Rifle Stalking Pattern"*** – .280 Ross cal., 26 or 28 in. barrel, 4 shot mag., walnut pistol grip checkered stock, finely finished for Canadian/U.S. market, usually fitted with steel buttplate. For the British and Colonial market, it appears that major components were supplied by Ross "in the white" to British gunmakers for completion, usually found U.K. proofed, finer finish on steel and wood with checkered walnut butt.

	$3,000	$2,800	$2,500	$2,000	$1,750	$1,500	$1,250	

Add $500+ if English customized and cased.
These variants are definitely considered to be Custom Rifles, and should be priced based upon the

GRADING - PPGS™	100%	98%	95%	90%	80%	70%	60%	LAST MSR

Maker's reputation along with the individual rifle's features and overall current condition.

This model was a favorite in England circa 1908-1912 for use in both India and Africa. English gunmakers such as Cogswell & Harrison, Gibbs, Westley Richards and others offered this model and the Model 1910 in their catalogs. The majority of British Makers catalogues show both the Standard Factory Ross Sporters as well as "custom" rifles available.

* ***Model 1905/Model 1910 Match Target Model*** - .280 Ross cal., single-shot with 30 1/2 in. barrel, tangent rear sight on heel of butt and optical hooded front sight, free floated barrel, can be found in early (tapered forend) and later (deep forend with finger grooves) versions. Very scarce and none found blued (left in the white). If found with barrel-weight marked in grains on the barrel, this is usually an indication of Bisley use. Prices below assume no target sights.

$4,500 $4,000 $3,500 $2,500 $2,250 $2,000 $1,800

Add $1,000 to $2,000 for heel-mounted rear sight and hooded front sight. Sights were provided by several manufacturers.

MKIII (MILITARY)/MODEL 1910 (SPORTER) RIFLE - replaced the previously used solid lugs which traveled vertically, has the "triple thread, interrupted-screw, double-bearing cam bolt" with the bolt head traveling horizontally.

It must be noted here that ALL rifles Military and Commercial that Ross built on the basic 1910 receiver have either M-10 or M-1910 roll-engraved on the receiver ring. This being the case ONLY the .280 Commercial Sporter is correctly referred to as an M-10. All other variants have their own designation, and are clearly not M-10's. This has increasingly been used, usually deliberately to the seller's advantage, on Internet Auctions over the last few years, and amounts to deliberate misrepresentation. The newly-designed bolt replaced the previously used solid lugs which traveled vertically, and has the "triple thread, interrupted-screw, double-bearing cam bolt-head" with the bolt head traveling with its lugs horizontal, rather than vertically, as with the two previous designs. It is these models where the report of "bolt blowbacks" have occurred. The bolt on these models, could, with some difficulty be rotated 180 degrees and hence not close completely. If fired in this situation, the bolt could blow back and potentially injure the shooter. Sporters were produced in three grades: R (economy), E (military box magazine and checkered wood) and the top of the line - the M-10.

* ***MKIII/MKIII B Military*** - .303 Brit. cal., 30 1/2 in. barrel, slight changes only through the production run, early models had stamped sheet metal nosecaps, later ones were forged. Models found with British proofs were likely in the trenches in France and later used by WWII British Homeguard. For the MkIII B, the only change from Canadian issue is the front and rear sights, plus the lack of expected identification and acceptance marks stamped in the buttstock.

$2,000 $1,850 $1,500 $1,250 $1,000 $750 $650

* ***Military Match Target Model*** - .280 Ross cal., 26 in. barrel, box mag. (same as M-10 Sporter with flat floorplate), light walnut stocks with a commercial finish and a Ross MkIII battle sight, recalibrated for .280 Ross cal. Mfg. circa 1913. Extremely scarce.

$10,000 $7,500 $6,500 $5,000 $3,500 $2,500 $2,000

While originally thought to have been produced in 1912, recent information points to a manufacture date in late 1913. Ross considered this model to be the perfect military rifle. A suspected total of 25 rifles were built on the commercial line and all known examples are serial numbered in the 10,200 range. The large majority of these were reported as destroyed in Quebec post-WWII.

* ***Model R-10*** - .303 Brit. cal., 26 or 28 in. barrel, no checkering, Winchester semi-buckhorn rear sight, military five shot box mag., plain steel uncheckered rifle buttplate.

$1,300 $1,050 $875 $700 $600 $550 $500

There is the possibility that Ross used previously rejected military components in these rifles. This is a fairly plain rifle, but seldom encountered.

* ***Model E-10*** - .303 Brit. or .35 WCF cal., 26 or 28 in. barrel, checkered straight grain walnut stock, M-10 pattern checkering on bottom of pistol grip, military box mag, several different express sights can be found on this model. Scarce.

$1,500 $1,200 $950 $800 $700 $600 $550

Add 25% for .35 WCF cal.
Add $200-$300 for Lyman "long-staff" 48 rear sight (catalog option).

* ***Model M-10*** - .280 Ross cal., 24, 26 or 28 in. barrel, enclosed four shot double row mag., beautifully finished, checkered walnut pistol grip stock, grip cap screwed to pistol grip, flat floorplate, 0 to 500 yard sight on barrel, some are equipped with Porter "pop up" sight on the rear receiver bridge.

$1,800 $1,300 $1,000 $875 $700 $600 $500

Add $200-$250 for rifles with Porter aperture sight or factory Catalog option Lyman 48S sight.
Factory-custom features like a cheekpiece also add at least 25%.

GRADING - PPGS™	100%	98%	95%	90%	80%	70%	60%	LAST MSR

* ***Mark III Homeguard Model*** – .303 Brit. cal., identical to the Canadian issued Mk III Military Model but appears to have superior finish and fit on wood and metal, serial number will be found on the barrel just ahead of the receiver, issue stamps may (or may not) be stamped in the stock, considered to be commercial, not military. Less than 1,000 mfg. The serial number always shows a prefix of "HG".

  $2,500 $2,200 $2,000 $1,700 $1,400 $1,200 $950

MODEL 1912 CADET

* ***Model 1912 Cadet Commercial*** – serial number on the left side of the barrel, ahead of the receiver, usually found stocked with fine-grain light walnut, with a semi-gloss finish very similar to the commercial centerfire Sporters, as opposed to the open-grain dark walnut of the Military Cadets.

  $800 $750 $550 $450 $375 $350 $300

* ***Model 1912 Cadet Military*** – serial number stamped in stock over year of acceptance, preceeded by a letter, usually multiple "CC" (Cadet Corps) stamps also.

  $850 $775 $600 $475 $375 $350 $300

The Canadian government through the Dept. of Militia and Defence (M&D) ordered 10,000 Cadets, of which only approx. 6,000 were delivered beginning in 1913 and ending in 1916. The majority of these military Cadets were destroyed by the Canadian government. Any military accepted Cadets from the four contract years are scarce. When the Ross Plant was expropriated in 1917 by the Canadian Government, a large quantity of unfinished Ross Cadet components remained. These were later assembled and sold on the Commercial Market in Canada, and are now referred to as "Clean-Up Run" Cadets. These Cadets appear to be the same as the Military version, with open-grain walnut stocks, rather than the much better-finished light walnut Commercial stocks. No serials or proof-stamps in either wood or steel are usually found, but occasionally, light inspectors stamps have been noted stamped on the bottom of the wrist. Also, it appears that Canada's authorities have stamped their own identification numbers and/or letters on some. This has likely only been done relatively recently.

* ***Model 1912 Cadet Carbine*** – This unique Cadet Model first appeared in the commercial catalog issued in early 1913. The same catalog, destined for the U.S. market, serviced by Post & Floto in New York City was essentially the same catalog, but all prices were manually over-stamped with red ink. The page illustrating and describing this new half-stock Cadet addition shows "For Canada Trade Only". For many years, it was considered that this Model wasn't produced, but was only "floated" in the catalogs to gauge the potential market. Over the last few years, extensive searches and correspondence with other collectors found that currently, at least four identical specimens survived in advanced Ross Collections. For whatever reason, Ross offered it with a unique forged buttplate, rather than the early MkIII Military buttplate with the brass trap-door used for all the other Cadets. The stocks on all four examples seen to date appear to have used the same grade of light straight-grain walnut used for the Commercial MkII** Target rifles and finished similarly as well.

  $1,500 $1,200 $1,000 $850 $600 $550 $500

ROSSI

Current trademark manufactured by Amadeo Rossi S.A., established in 1889, located in Sao Leopoldo, Brazil. Currently imported exclusively by BrazTech, International since 1997. BrazTech is located in Bainbridge, GA beginning late 1997. Previously located in Miami, FL 1997-mid-2019. Previously imported by Interarms, located in Alexandria, VA.

PISTOLS: LEVER ACTION

RANCH HAND – .38 Spl./.357 Mag., .44 Mag., or .45 LC cal., 12 in. barrel, "mare's leg" style with large loop lever, blue steel or case colored (.45 LC cal. only) receiver, adj. buckhorn rear sights, milled front post sights, uncheckered Brazilian hardwood stock and forearm, single stage trigger, 6 shot shortened mag. tube, saddle ring with leather strap, steel buttplate, includes Taurus Security System safety, 4.9 lbs. Mfg. mid-2010-2016.

$750 $650 $575 $500 $425 $350 $275 *$597*

Add $64 for case colored receiver (.45 LC cal. only).

PISTOLS: SINGLE SHOT

ROCKET SINGLE SHOT – .22 LR, .22 Hornet, .22-250 Rem., .220 Swift, .223 Rem., .30-30 Win., .357 Mag., .44 Mag., or .45 LC cal., break open single shot action. Limited importation 2000 only.

$135 $120 $110 $100 $90 $80 $75 *$149*

Add $36 for stainless steel.

Add 25% for Centerfire calibers.

MATCHED PAIR PISTOL – includes .22 LR barrel and extra .45 LC/.410 bore (2 1/2 in. chamber) barrels with fiber optic sights, 11 in. barrels, blue finish only, combat style wrap-around rubber grips with red insert, Taurus security system. Mfg. 2012-disc.

$325 $285 $250 $225 $180 $145 $115 *$383*

GRADING - PPGS™	100%	98%	95%	90%	80%	70%	60%	LAST MSR

REVOLVERS: DOUBLE ACTION

All discontinued models in this section were imported by Interarms only, not BrazTech. BrazTech is the exclusive North American importer for Rossi firearms starting late 1997. Taurus manufactures three models of .38 Special revolvers and four models of .357 Magnum revolvers under contract with Rossi. Revolvers sold by BrazTech with the Rossi name are manufactured in a facility owned by Taurus in SaoLeopoldo, Brazil. Much of the tooling and many of the machines were acquired from Rossi during negotiations between the companies.

All currently manufactured Rossi firearms incorporate the Taurus Security System safety. As of 2018, Rossi issued a Safety Warning covering .38 Special and .357 Mag. revolver models manufactured between 2005 and 2017. The models include: R351, R352, R461, R462, R851, R971, and R972 with serial numbers beginning with the letter Y, Z, or A through K. Please go to www.rossisafetynotice.com for further assistance.

MODEL 31 – .38 Spl. cal., 5 shot, 4 in. medium barrel, target trigger and hammer, 22 oz. Disc. 1985.

$200 $175 $150 $135 $110 $90 $70 *$139*

Add $5 for nickel.

MODEL 51 – .22 LR cal., 6 shot, 6 in. barrel, blue only, adj. sights. Disc. 1985.

$225 $200 $175 $150 $125 $100 $80 *$149*

* ***Model 51 Sportsman 511 Stainless*** – .22 LR cal. only, stainless steel, 4 in. barrel with matted rib, adj. rear sight, 6 shot, hardwood stocks, 30 oz. Imported 1986-90 only.

$225 $200 $175 $150 $125 $100 $80 *$235*

MODEL 68 – .38 Spl. cal., 5 shot, 2 or 3 in. barrel, blue or nickel (3 in. barrel only), choice of wood or rubber grips with 2 in. barrel. Disc. 1998.

$240 $210 $180 $165 $130 $110 $85 *$225*

MODEL 69 – .32 S&W cal., 6 shot, 3 in. barrel, walnut grips. Disc. 1985.

$200 $175 $150 $135 $110 $90 $70 *$139*

Add $5 for nickel finish.

MODEL 70 – .22 LR cal., 6 shot, 3 in. barrel. Disc. 1985.

$225 $200 $175 $150 $125 $100 $80 *$139*

Add $5 for nickel finish.

MODEL 84 STAINLESS – .38 Spl. cal., 6 shot, 3 or 4 in. solid raised rib barrel, standard service sights, checkered hardwood grips, 27 1/2 oz. Imported 1985-86 only.

$260 $225 $200 $175 $150 $120 $100 *$205*

MODEL 85 STAINLESS – please refer to Model 851 Stainless.

MODEL 88 STAINLESS – .38 Spl. cal., 5 shot, stainless steel construction, 2 or 3 in. barrel, hardwood or rubber (2 in. barrel only) grips, 21 oz. Disc. 1998.

$260 $225 $200 $175 $150 $120 $100 *$255*

* ***Model 88 Stainless Lady Rossi*** – .38 Spl. cal., 2 in. barrel, stainless steel, slim round grips. Imported 1995-1998.

$260 $225 $200 $175 $150 $120 $100 *$285*

MODEL 89 STAINLESS – .32 S&W cal. only, 6 shot, 3 in. barrel. Imported 1985-86. Reintroduced 1989-90.

$200 $175 $150 $135 $110 $90 $70 *$215*

MODEL 94 – .38 Spl. cal., 6 shot, 3 or 4 in. barrel, blue finish only, 27 1/2 oz. Imported 1985-1988.

$260 $225 $200 $175 $150 $120 $100 *$185*

MODEL 95 – please refer to Model 951.

MODEL R351 – .38 Spl. +P cal., steel construction, 2 in. barrel, 5 shot, combat rubber grips, supplied with key lock, Taurus Security System, blue finish, 24 oz. Imported 1999-2018.

$295 $250 $215 $185 $170 $160 $150 *$349*

MODEL R352 – .38 Spl. +P cal., 2 in. barrel, 5 shot, rubber grip, Taurus Security System, stainless steel, 24 oz. Imported 1999-2018.

$300 $250 $215 $185 $170 $160 $150 *$359*

MODEL R461 – .357 Mag. +P cal., steel construction, 2 in. barrel, 6 shot, combat rubber grips, supplied with key lock, blue finish, 26 oz. Imported 1999-2018.

$295 $250 $215 $185 $170 $160 $150 *$349*

MODEL R462 – .357 Mag. cal., 2 in. barrel, 6 shot, rubber grip, Taurus Security System, stainless steel, 26 oz. Imported 1999-2018.

$300 $250 $215 $185 $170 $160 $150 *$359*

GRADING - PPGS™	100%	98%	95%	90%	80%	70%	60%	LAST MSR

MODEL 515(M) STAINLESS – .22 LR or .22 WMR (Model 515M) cal., double action, 6 shot, classic kit gun design, stainless steel with shrouded ejector rod, adj. rear sight, checkered custom wood grips, 4 in. barrel, 30 oz. Imported 1992 only.

$250	$220	$180	$160	$140	$100	$80	*$248*

MODEL 515 STAINLESS – .22 WMR cal., similar to 515(M), supplied with 2 pairs of grips (checkered wood and rubber wraparound). Imported 1994-98.

$260	$225	$200	$175	$150	$120	$100	*$270*

MODEL 518 STAINLESS – .22 LR cal., otherwise similar to Model 515 Stainless. Disc. 1998.

$260	$225	$200	$175	$150	$120	$100	*$255*

MODEL 677 FS – .357 Mag. cal., 6 shot, 2 in. heavy barrel, enclosed ejector rod, rubber combat grips, matte blue finish, 26 oz. Imported 1997-98.

$260	$225	$200	$175	$150	$120	$100	*$260*

MODEL 720 STAINLESS – .44 Spl. cal., choice of hammer or hammerless (new 1994) design, 3 in. ribbed barrel, double action, 5 shot with fluted or unfluted cylinder, full ejector rod shroud, adj. rear sight, rubber combat grips, stainless, 27 1/2 oz. Imported 1992-98.

$500	$440	$375	$340	$275	$225	$175	*$290*

* ***Model 720C Stainless*** – similar to Model 720 Stainless, except hammerless.

$520	$450	$400	$350	$280	$240	$180	*$290*

MODEL 851 – .38 Spl. +P cal., 4 in. VR barrel, 6 shot, integral key lock, adj. rear sight, elevated front sight w/red insert, checkered combat rubber grips, blue finish, 32 oz. Imported 2001-2018.

$285	$250	$220	$200	$150	$130	$100	*$333*

MODEL 851 STAINLESS – .38 Spl. cal., 3 (disc. 1994) or 4 in. VR barrel, 6 shot, walnut grips, adj. rear sight, 27 1/2 oz. Mfg. 1985-98.

$260	$225	$200	$175	$150	$120	$100	*$255*

MODEL 877 FS STAINLESS – .357 Mag. cal., 6 shot, small frame, 2 in. barrel with full ejector rod housing, rubber combat grips, 26 oz. Mfg. 1996-98.

$300	$260	$225	$200	$160	$140	$100	*$290*

MODEL 951 – .38 Spl. cal., 6 shot, 3 or 4 in. VR barrel, blue finish only, 27 1/2 oz. Imported 1985-90.

$260	$225	$200	$175	$150	$120	$100	*$233*

MODEL 971 – .357 Mag. cal., 4 in. solid rib barrel with ejector rod, 6 shot, adj. rear sight, blue only, hardwood grips, 36 oz. Imported 1988-98.

$350	$300	$260	$240	$200	$160	$125	*$255*

* ***Model 971 Stainless*** – .357 Mag. cal., 2 1/2 (new 1992), 4, or 6 in. solid rib barrel with full ejector rod shroud, 6 shot, combat style rubber grips, adj. rear sight, 35.4 - 40 1/2 oz. Imported 1989-98.

$360	$320	$275	$250	$200	$160	$125	*$290*

* ***Model 971 Compensated*** – .357 Mag. cal., stainless steel, 3 1/4 in. compensated barrel, 32 oz. Imported 1993-98.

$380	$340	$280	$260	$210	$170	$140	*$290*

MODEL 971 VRC STAINLESS – .357 Mag. cal., stainless steel, 6 shot, choice of 2 1/2, 4, or 6 in. barrel with 8-port compensator and full-length ejector shroud, combat rubber grips, adj. rear sight, 30-39 oz. Mfg. 1996-98.

$400	$350	$300	$275	$225	$180	$140	*$340*

MODEL 971 (RECENT MFG.) – .357 Mag. cal., 4 in. barrel with solid rib and full ejector shroud, 6 shot, checkered combat rubber grips, adj. rear sight, elevated front sight with red inserts, integral key lock, blue finish, 32 oz. Imported 2001-2017.

$350	$300	$275	$250	$200	$160	$125	*$399*

MODEL 972 – .357 Mag. cal., 6 in. barrel, 6 shot, adj. rear sight, elevated front sight with red inserts, rubber grip, Taurus Security System, stainless steel finish, 35 oz. Imported 2001-2018.

$360	$300	$250	$215	$195	$175	$155	*$429*

CYCLOPS (MODEL 988 STAINLESS) – .357 Mag. cal., 6 or 8 shot, 8 or 10 3/4 (ported or unported, new 1998) in. full shroud slab-side barrel with 8 compensation ports, squared-off trigger guard, black rubber grips, 51 oz. Imported 1997-98.

$950	$825	$725	$650	$525	$425	$350	*$429*

Add $50 for unported 10 3/4 in. barrel.
Add $60 for ported 10 3/4 in. barrel.

GRADING - PPGS™	100%	98%	95%	90%	80%	70%	60%	LAST MSR

PLINKER (MODEL R981) - .22 LR cal., 2, 4 (new 2015), or 6 (new 2015) in. vent. rib barrel, 8 shot, fiber optic front sight, adj. rear sight, swing out alloy cylinder, Ribber grips, polished black or polished stainless (new 2016) finish, 29 oz. Mfg. 2013-2016.

	$285	$215	$150	$125	$115	$100	$85	*$326*

* ***.22 Mag. Plinker (R99)*** - .22 Mag. cal., double action, 2, 4, or 6 in. barrel, 8 shot, solid steel construction, hammer block, fiber optic front and fully adj. rear sights, Ribber grip, Taurus Security System, blue or matte stainless steel finish, 35 oz. New 2015.

MSR $341	$295	$215	$150	$125	$115	$100	$85	

RIFLES

For previous information on Rossi manufactured Puma rifles imported by Legacy, please refer to the Puma section.

CIRCUIT JUDGE .22 REVOLVING CYLINDER - .22 LR/.22 WMR cal., includes interchangeable cylinders, SA/DA, 9 shot, 18 1/2 in. barrel, adj. rear and fiber optic front sight, black synthetic thumbhole stock, lower Picatinny rail on forearm, includes scope mount base and hammer extension, blue finish, Taurus Security System, 5 1/2 lbs. Mfg. mid-2012-2016.

	$625	$550	$475	$425	$350	$275	$225	*$716*

CIRCUIT JUDGE .44 MAG. REVOLVING CYLINDER - .44 Mag. cal., 5 shot revolving cylinder, SA/DA operation, 18 1/2 in. barrel with cushioned recoil pad with spacer, fiber optic front, uncheckered Monte Carlo wood stock with recoil pad and forearm, includes scope mount base and hammer extention, Taurus Security System, blue finish, 5.2-5.6 lbs. Mfg. 2011-2015.

	$575	$500	$425	$395	$315	$260	$200	*$669*

FIELD GRADE SINGLE SHOT RIMFIRE - .17 HMR (new 2003), .22 LR (disc. 2003), or .22 WMR (disc. 2003) cal., 23 in. matte finished blue or stainless steel barrel, natural (matte blue) or black (stainless steel) finished wood, adj. sights, ejector, 4 3/4-6 1/4 lbs. Disc. 2006.

	$140	$115	$95	$80	$70	$60	$60	*$175*

Add $47 for stainless steel.

FIELD GRADE FULL SIZE SINGLE SHOT CENTERFIRE - .22-250 (mfg. 2005-disc.), .223 Rem. (new 2002), .243 Win. (new 2002), .270 Win. (mfg. 2004-disc.), .30-06 (mfg. 2004-disc.), .308 Win. (new 2004-disc.), .357 Mag./.38 Spl. (disc. 2003), .44 Mag., 7.62x39mm (mfg. 2005-disc.), or .410/45 LC (disc. 2003) cal., 23 in. standard or heavy (new 2005, w/o sights) barrel, choice of matte blue or matte stainless steel (disc. 2004), Monte Carlo stock became an option in 2002 (disc.), black synthetic stock with recoil pad, removable cheekpiece, blue finish, extra wide extractor, ejector, adj. rear sight, Taurus Security System safety, includes scope mount base, 6 1/4 lbs. Imported 2001-2014.

	$265	$225	$200	$180	$145	$120	$95	*$307*

Add $7 for heavy barrel.

FIELD GRADE YOUTH SIZE SINGLE SHOT CENTERFIRE - .223 Rem. or .243 Win. cal., 22 in. button rifled barrel, black synthetic stock with recoil pad, removable cheekpiece, blue finish, fiber optic front sight, scope mount base and hammer extension, Taurus Security System safety, 6 1/4 lbs., includes carrying case. Imported 2001-2014.

	$265	$225	$200	$180	$145	$120	$95	*$307*

MODEL 59 SLIDE ACTION - .22 WMR cal. version of Model 62 SA, 10 shot mag., 5 1/2 lbs. Importation disc. 1998.

	$425	$375	$325	$300	$240	$200	$150	*$280*

MODEL 62 SA SLIDE ACTION - .22 LR cal., copy of Win. 1890 "Gallery" model, rifle (23 in. barrel) or carbine (16 1/2 in. barrel) available, takedown action, blue or nickel finish, round or octagon barrel, 12 or 13 shot tube mag. Importation disc. 1998.

	$450	$400	$340	$300	$250	$200	$160	*$240*

Add $10 for nickel finish.
Add $10 for octagon barrel.

* ***Model 62 SA Slide Action Stainless*** - similar to regular model, except is stainless steel. Imported 1986 only.

	$475	$420	$360	$325	$260	$220	$175	*$192*

MODEL 62 SAC CARBINE LEVER ACTION - similar to Model 62 SA, except has 16 1/2 in. carbine barrel with full-length mag. tube (12 shot), 4 1/4 lbs. Imported 1988-98.

	$450	$400	$340	$300	$250	$200	$160	*$240*

Add $10 for nickel finish.

* ***Model 62 SAC Carbine Stainless Lever Action*** - similar to Model 62 SAC Carbine, except is stainless steel. Imported 1998 only.

	$475	$420	$360	$325	$260	$220	$175	*$280*

GRADING - PPGS™	100%	98%	95%	90%	80%	70%	60%	LAST MSR

MODEL 65/92 SRC LEVER ACTION – .38 Spl./.357 Mag., .44 Spl./.44 Mag., .44-40 WCF (mfg. 1995-98), or .45 LC (mfg. 1995-98) cal., patterned after Win. Model 92, 16 (.38 Spl./.357 Mag. only), 20 (blue or stainless) or 24 (new 1997, half round/half octagon) in. barrel, 5-5 3/4 lbs. Importation disc. 1998.

	$500	$450	$375	$350	$275	$225	$175	*$360*

Add approx. $70 for 24 in. half-round, half-octagon barrel.

This model in .44 Spl./.44 Mag., .44-40 WCF, or .45 LC cal. is sometimes known as the Model 65. This model was also available in matte blue finish at no extra charge.

MODEL 92 EL JEFE OCTAGON BARREL LEVER ACTION – .357 Mag./.38 Spl., .44 Mag., or .45 LC cal., 20 or 24 in. octagon barrel, blued barrel with choice of blue, blue/case colored, stainless, and blue/brass finish, 10 or 12 shot tube mag., open sights, uncheckered walnut stock with curved buttplate and forearm, regular lever loop, includes Taurus security system, 7 lbs. Mfg. 2009-2018.

	$650	$575	$500	$450	$360	$300	$230	*$629*

Add $62 for stainless steel frame and barrel.
Add $100 for brass frame with 24 in. barrel (.45 LC cal. only, disc.).

MODEL 92 ROUND BARREL LEVER ACTION (EL JEFE) – .357 Mag./.38 Spl., .44 Mag., .45 LC, or .454 Casull (disc. 2014) cal., 8 or 10 shot tube mag., 16 or 20 in. round barrel, blue or stainless steel finish, uncheckered walnut stock with crescent buttplates, open sights, Taurus Security System safety, regular or large loop (disc.) lever, 4.8-5 lbs. Mfg. 2009-2018.

	$650	$575	$500	$450	$360	$300	$230	*$629*

Add $11 for large loop lever (.357 Mag., or .45 LC cal. only, disc. 2009, introduced 2011).
Add $30 for stainless steel.
Add $36 for scope mount, base and rings (disc. 2015).
Add $118 for .454 Casull cal. (disc. 2014).

PICK 4 YOUTH GUN – includes .22 LR barrel with fiber optic adj. sight, .243 Win. with fixed fiber optic sight, 20 ga. and .410 barrel with brass bead front sights, blue finish, barrels change w/o screw, removable cheekpiece, Taurus security system, break-open design, black synthetic or hi-def green (disc. 2011) stock, includes softside custom carry case, approx. 7 lbs. Mfg. 2011-2013.

	$465	$400	$350	$315	$250	$210	$165	*$547*

RB22 BOLT ACTION – .17 HMR, .22 LR, or .22 WMR cal., 18 (.22 LR) or 21 (.17 HMR and .22 WMR) in. button rifled barrel, blued finish, 5 or 10 shot mag., choice of fiber optic or scope base, ergonomic black synthetic stock, manual safety, dovetail scope base (.22 LR only), black finish, approx. 4.3 lbs. New 2019.

MSR $172	$145	$125	$110	$100	$80	$65	$55	

Add $29 for .22 WMR or .17 HMR cal.

Also in 2019, Rossi began offering Special Editions of this model with various stock finishes. Current MSR is $216.

RS22 SEMI-AUTO – .22 LR or .22 WMR cal., semi-auto, blowback action, 18 or 21 in. free float threaded (18 in. barrel .22 LR cal.) or non-threaded barrel, 10 shot detachable mag., fully adj. fiber optic sights (.22 LR only) or Weaver scope base (.22 WMR only), black synthetic Monte Carlo stock, crossbolt safety, dovetail scope base, matte black finish, 4.1 lbs. New 2019.

MSR $145	$125	$110	$95	$85	$70	$55	$50	

Add $12 for threaded barrel.
Add $167 for .22 WMR cal.

Also in 2019, Rossi began offering Special Editions of this model with various stock finishes. MSRs currently range from $147-$262.

R92 CARBINE – .357 Mag./.38 Spl+P, .44 Mag., or .45 LC cal., SAO, lever action, 16 or 20 (disc. 2018, reintroduced 2021) in. round barrel, 8 or 10 shot mag., fixed front and adj. Buckhorn rear sights, Brazillian hardwood stock and forend, crescent buttplate, polished black or polished stainless steel, 4.8-5.6 lbs. New 2017.

MSR $725	$625	$545	$475	$425	$345	$275	$225	

Add $5 for 20 in. barrel length.
Add $10 for large loop lever (disc. 2018).
Add $46 for polished stainless steel.

R92 GOLD – .357 Mag. or .44 Mag. cal., lever action, 20 in. barrel, 10 shot mag., Buckhorn sights, Brazilian hardwood stock, thumb safety, gold barrel bands and lever, polished black finish, 5.6-6 lbs. New 2020.

MSR $811	$700	$615	$525	$475	$385	$315	$275	

R92 OCTAGONAL BARRELS – .357 Mag. /.38 Spl.+P or .44 Mag. cal., lever action, 24 in. octagonal barrel, Buckhorn sights, 12 shot mag., Brazilian hardwood stock, thumb safety, polished black finish or stainless steel, 7.5 lbs. New 2020.

MSR $831	$700	$615	$525	$475	$385	$315	$275	

Add $45 for stainless steel.

GRADING - PPGS™	100%	98%	95%	90%	80%	70%	60%	LAST MSR

R92 TRIPLE BLACK – .357 Mag. /.38 Spl+P or .44 Mag. cal., lever action, 16 1/2 in. threaded barrel, 8 shot, peep sights, scope base, black wood stock, thumb safety, black Cerakote finish, 5.9-6.1 lbs. New 2020.

MSR $927	$790	$690	$595	$535	$435	$355	$300	

RIO BRAVO LEVER ACTION – .22 LR cal., 18 in., 15 shot mag., fiber optic or Buckhorn sights, German beechwood or black polymer stock and forearm w/polished metal finish, crossbolt safety, matte black finish, 5.2 lbs. New 2020.

MSR $324	$275	$240	$200	$185	$150	$125	$100	

Add $43 for German beechwood furniture.

RIO GRANDE LEVER ACTION (2010-14 MFG.) – .30-30 Win. or .45-70 Govt. (new 2012) cal., 20 in. barrel, blue or stainless, 6 shot, adj. buckhorn rear sight, post front, Brazilian hardwood stock or Realtree APG camo (disc. 2013) with recoil pad, regular or large loop lever, 7 lbs. Mfg. mid-2010-2014.

	$550	$475	$415	$375	$300	$250	$225	*$643*

Add $30 for stainless steel or camo (disc. 2013).

RIO GRANDE LEVER ACTION (2017-18 MFG.) – .30-30 Win. or .45-70 Govt. cal., 20 in. barrel, 6 shot, adj. buckhorn rear and post front sights, Brazilian hardwood stock with recoil pad, blue or stainless, 7 lbs. Mfg. 2017-2018.

	$325	$285	$250	$225	$200	$185	$175	*$379*

Add $40 for stainless steel.

ROCKET SINGLE SHOT – .22 LR, .22 Hornet, .22-250 Rem., .220 Swift, .223 Rem., .30-30 Win., .357 Mag., .44 Mag., or .45 LC cal., action and other specifications similar to Model S12 shotgun. Limited importation 2000 only.

	$160	$145	$130	$115	$100	$90	$80	*$179*

Add $30 for stainless steel.
Add 15% for Centerfire cals.

ROSSI GALLERY – .22 LR cal., slide action, 18 in. barrel, 15 shot, Buckhorn sights, black synthetic or German beechwood stock, crossbolt safety, polished black finish, 5.5 lbs. New 2020.

MSR $315	$275	$240	$200	$185	$150	$125	$100	

Add $44 for German beechwood stock.

SINGLE SHOT RIFLE – .243 Win. or .270 Win. cal., 22 or 23 in. button rifled barrel without sights, ejector, spur hammer, black synthetic stock and forearm with removable cheekpiece, scope mount base, blue finish, 6 1/4 lbs. Mfg. 2017-2018.

	$230	$195	$175	$160	$145	$135	$125	*$269*

TRIFECTA YOUTH GUN – includes .22 LR barrel with fiber optic adj. sight, choice of .243 Win. or .44 Mag. barrel with fixed fiber optic sight, 20 ga. barrel with brass bead front sights, blue finish, barrels change w/o screw, removable cheekpiece, Taurus security system, break-open design, black synthetic, colored laminate (disc.), or hi-def green (with scope mount, disc. 2013) stock, includes softside custom carry case, 6.3 lbs. Mfg. 2007-2014.

	$395	$350	$295	$275	$215	$180	$140	*$455*

Add $86 for pink/black, black, or green/brown laminate stock (disc.).

WIZARD SINGLE SHOT – .22-250, .223 Rem., .243 Win., .270 Win., .30-06, or .308 Win. cal., 23 in. carbon steel button rifled barrel with fiber optic front sight and adj. rear sight, break open single shot, blue or nickel (.243 cal. only, disc. 2012) finish, Brazilian hardwood Monte Carlo stock, Realtree APG (disc.), or Green camo (disc. 2012) with vent. recoil pad, includes Weaver scope base, single stage trigger, transfer bar, manual safety and Taurus Security System, interchangeable barrels, approx. 7 lbs. Mfg. 2010-2013.

	$315	$275	$235	$215	$175	$140	$110	*$378*

Add $10 for nickel finish (.243 Win. cal. only, disc. 2012).
Add $50 for Realtree APG (disc.), or Green (disc. 2012) camo.

* ***Wizard Single Shot Youth Model*** – .223 Rem., .243 Win., or .308 Win. cal., 22 in. carbon steel button rifled barrel with fiber optic front sight and adj. rear sight, break open single shot, blue finish, Brazilian hardwood Monte Carlo stock, Realtree APG (disc.), or Green (disc. 2012) camo with vent. recoil pad, includes Weaver scope base, single stage trigger, transfer bar, manual safety and Taurus Security System, interchangeable barrels, 13 1/4 in. LOP stock, 6 1/4 lbs. Mfg. 2010-2013.

	$315	$275	$235	$215	$175	$140	$110	*$378*

Add $55 for camo (disc.).

R92 454 CASULL – .454 Casull cal., lever action, 20 in. stainless steel barrel, 9 shot, Buckhorn sights, Brazilian hardwood stock, thumb safety, 6.4 lbs. New 2020.

MSR $948	$800	$700	$600	$545	$440	$360	$310	

GRADING - PPGS™	100%	98%	95%	90%	80%	70%	60%	LAST MSR

SHOTGUNS: LEVER ACTION

RIO GRANDE – .410 bore (2 1/2 in. chamber), 20 in. smoothbore barrel, blue finish or stainless steel, uncheckered hardwood stock with vent. recoil pad and forearm, side ejection, adj. buckhorn sights, includes scope mount base, Taurus Security System, 5.8 lbs. Mfg. 2012-2014.

	$500	$425	$375	$325	$275	$225	$175	*$597*

Add $46 for stainless steel.

SHOTGUNS: REVOLVING

Add approx. $60 for .22 LR/.22 Mag. convertible cylinder (disc).

CIRCUIT JUDGE – .45 LC/.410 bore or 28 ga. (prototypes only), 5 shot revolving cylinder, SA/DA operation, 18 1/2 in. barrel with fiber optic sights (.410 bore only) or bead front sight only (28 ga.), uncheckered Monte Carlo wood stock with recoil pad with spacer, polished black, blue finish, or stainless steel, includes scope mount base and hammer extention, Taurus Security System (manual safety), 5.2-5.6 lbs. New 2011.

MSR $730	$630	$525	$440	$400	$320	$260	$200	

Add $52 for stainless steel.

CIRCUIT JUDGE TUFFY – .45 LC/.410 bore (3 in. chamber), SA/DA, 18 1/2 in. barrel with fiber optic sights, 5 shot, matte black finish, black synthetic thumbhole stock with buttstock indicator and lower Picatinny rail on forearm, includes scope mount base, hammer extension, threadguard, straight rifled choke and choke tube wrench, Taurus Security System, 4.6 lbs. Mfg. mid-2012-2019.

	$635	$525	$440	$400	$315	$260	$200	*$738*

CIRCUIT JUDGE LEVER ACTION – .410 bore/.45 LC cal., shoots .410 bore (3 in. chamber), or .45 LC cal. ammunition, 5 shot revolving cylinder, lever action operation, 18 1/2 in. barrel with iron sights, Monte Carlo wood stock and forearm with recoil pad, stainless steel (mfg. 2011 only) or blue finish, shrouded low profile hammer, SA trigger, includes scope mount base, thread guard, straight rifled choke, and choke tube wrench, 5.2 lbs. Mfg. 2011-2013.

	$575	$500	$425	$395	$315	$260	$200	*$684*

SHOTGUNS: SxS

OVERLAND – 12, 20 ga., or .410 bore, exposed hammers, 20 (Coach Model), 26, or 28 in. barrels, double triggers. Importation disc. 1988.

	$725	$625	$550	$500	$400	$325	$250	*$332*

SQUIRE – 12, 20 ga., or .410 bore, hammerless, 20, 26 or 28 in. barrels, double triggers, raised matted rib, beavertail forearm, pistol grip, hardwood stock, 3 in. chambers. Imported 1985-90.

	$300	$245	$195	$160	$150	$140	$130	*$350*

SHOTGUNS: SINGLE SHOT

410/22 MATCHED PAIR – .22 LR, .22 WMR (disc. 2020), or .410 bore, 2 1/2 and 3 in. chambers, break action, 18 1/2 or 22 in. barrel, fixed modified choke, fiber optic (.22 LR and .22 WMR) or bead (.410) sights, Black, Tan, Olive Drab, or Gray synthetic ergonomic stock, includes cartridge storage for both .22 and .410, manual safety, matte black finish, 5.6 lbs. New 2019.

MSR $220	$185	$160	$140	$125	$100	$85	$65	

Add $38 for .22 WMR /.410 pair. (disc. 2020).

MATCHED PAIR RIMFIRE RIFLE/SHOTGUN – includes choice of .17 HMR, .22 LR (disc. 2013), or .22 WMR (disc. 2013) cal. rifle 23 in. barrel and interchangeable 12 or 20 ga. shotgun 28 in. barrel, rifle barrel has standard (disc.) or fiber optic front sights, black synthetic stock and forearm, blue finish, Taurus Security System, recent mfg. included scope mount base on rifle barrel, and matched pair carrying case, 5 1/4 or 6 1/4 lbs. Imported 2000-2014.

	$250	$225	$195	$175	$140	$115	$90	*$298*

Add $65 for 23 in. barrel.
Add $83 for stainless steel (.410 bore and .22 LR or .17 HMR cal. only, disc. 2009).
Add approx. $95 for pink, black, or green/brown laminate stock (20 ga. or .410 bore only, disc. 2012).
Add $20 for nickel.

* ***Matched Pair Rimfire Rifle/Shotgun Youth*** – similar to Matched Pair Rimfire Rifle/Shotgun, except is Youth model with same 13 1/4 in. LOP, choice of .17 HMR or .22 LR rifle barrel (18 1/2 in.) or 20 ga. or .410 bore shotgun barrel (22 in.), fiber optic sights on rifle barrel, blue or nickel finish, black synthetic stock and forearm, Taurus Security System, recent mfg. included matched pair carrying case, 3 1/4-5 3/4 lbs. Imported 2000-2014.

	$200	$175	$145	$135	$100	$90	$70	*$245*

Add $27 for .17 HMR cal.
Add $83 for stainless steel (.410 bore and .22 LR or .17 HMR cal. only, disc. 2009).
Add $9 for fiber optic sights (20 ga./.22 LR only).
Add approx. $95 for pink, black, or green/brown laminate stock (20 ga. or .410 bore only).
Add $72 for .410 bore and .17 HMR rifle barrel.
Add $18 for nickel.

GRADING - PPGS™	100%	98%	95%	90%	80%	70%	60%	LAST MSR

MATCHED PAIR CENTERFIRE RIFLE/SHOTGUN - includes 12 or 20 ga. barrel and choice of .223 Rem., .243 Win., .270 Win. (disc.), .30-06 (disc.), or .308 Win. (disc.) cal., 28 in. shotgun barrel, or 23 in. rifle barrel with fiber optic sights, Taurus Security System, recent mfg. included matched pair carrying case, 5-6 1/4 lbs. Imported 2000-2014.

$300	$265	$225	$200	$165	$135	$100	*$345*

Add $7 for .243 Win. cal.

* ***Matched Pair Centerfire Rifle/Shotgun Youth*** - includes 20 ga. barrel and choice of .22-250 Rem. (mfg. 2005-disc.), .223 Rem., .243 Win., .270 Win. (disc.), .30-06 (disc.), .308 Win. (disc.), .44 Mag. cal., 22 in. shotgun and rifle barrel, 5 1/4 lbs. Disc. 2014.

$300	$265	$225	$200	$165	$135	$100	*$345*

Add $7 for .243 Win. cal.

SINGLE SHOT SHOTGUN - 12, 20, or .410 bore, 2 1/2 or 3 in. chambers, single shot, break action, 18 1/2, 22 (Youth Model), or 28 in. barrel, spurred hammer, bead sights, Black synthetic thumbhole stock, matte black or nickel finish, 3.8 -5.25 lbs. Mfg. 2017-2018.

$125	$110	$95	$85	$70	$55	$45	*$139*

MODEL S12/S20/S41 - 12, 20 ga., or .410 bore, 3 in. chamber, 22 (Youth) or 28 (Standard) in. barrel, lightweight break open action with external hammer, ejector, uncheckered hardwood (disc. 2011), or black synthetic (new 2012) stock and forearm with sling swivels, blue finish, supplied with trigger lock, approx. 5 lbs. Imported 1999-2014.

$150	$125	$115	$100	$85	$70	$55	*$171*

Add $151 for 12 or 20 ga. Slug gun with 23 in. fully rifled barrel with adj. TruGlo sights (new 2004).
Add $57 for 12 ga. Turkey Model w/3 1/2 in. chamber, fiber optic sights and removable choke (mfg. 2007-2011).

This model is also available as a Youth Model in 20 ga. or .410 bore (.410 bore weighs approx. 4 lbs.) - prices are the same as listed.

TRIFECTA YOUTH GUN - Please refer to listing in the Rifle section.

TUFFY (2009-2014 MFG.) - .410 bore, break open single shot with safety mounted on left side of receiver, 18 1/2 in. barrel with brass bead front sight, black synthetic sculpted thumbhole stock with 4 shell storage capacity, ejector, matte black, blue, or nickel finish, transfer bar safety, 3 lbs. Mfg. 2009-2014.

$135	$100	$90	$80	$70	$60	$55	*$205*

Add $7 for nickel finish.

TUFFY (CURRENT MFG.) - .410 bore, 3 in. chamber, break action, carbon steel frame, 18 1/2 in. barrel, fixed modified choke, ejectors, brass bead front sight, Black, Gray, Tan, or Olive Drab synthetic thumbhole/pistol grip stock includes stock checkering and 8 cartridge capacity (4 on each side), matte black finish, 4.5 lbs. New 2019.

MSR $170	$150	$130	$115	$100	$85	$70	$55

TUFFY TURKEY - .410 bore, single shot, break action, 26 in. barrel, choke tube, bead sights, Olive Drab synthetic extended thumbhole stock with 4 shell holders, crossbolt safety, Picatinny rail, matte black finish, 4 lbs. New 2020.

MSR $221	$190	$165	$145	$130	$105	$85	$70

YOUTH MATCHED PAIR - .410 bore/.22 LR cal., break action, 18 1/2 in. (rifle) and 22 in. (shotgun) interchangeable barrels, carbon steel action, spurred hammer, brass bead front and fiber optic adj. rear sights, black synthetic stock with contoured buttplate, four safety features including a manual safety and the exclusive Taurus Security System, includes carry case, matte black finish, 5-5.6 lbs. Disc. 2018.

$165	$145	$125	$110	$90	$75	$60	*$189*

ROESSLER (ROBLER) WAFFEN GmbH

Current bolt action rifle manufacturer located in Kufstein, Austria. The Titan Series of bolt action rifles are currently imported by TR Imports beginning 2013, located in Keller, TX.

RIFLES: BOLT ACTION

TITAN 3/TITAN 6 - .22-250 Rem., .223 Rem., .243 Win., .270 Win., .30-06, .300 Win. Mag., 6.5x55SE, or 7x57 cal., right or left-hand action, 16 (disc.), 22, or 24 in. deep blued barrel, various configurations include the Standard, Luxury, Exclusive, All-Around (synthetic stock only), Stutzen (Mannlicher full stock) with or w/o checkering, or thumbhole stock, also available as Carbon, Hunter, Hybrid, or Target configuration (Titan 3 and Titan 6 models only, new 2019), 60 degree cocking angle with 3 or 6 locking lugs, top tang safety, approx. 6.6 lbs. Mfg. in Austria by Roessler beginning 2016.

MSR $1,287	$1,095	$960	$825	$750	$600	$500	$425

Base MSR listed above reflects All-Around configuration.
Base MSR for Standard model is $1,382.
Base MSR for Luxus model is $1,647.
Base MSR for standard thumbhole configuration is $1,695.

GRADING - PPGS™	100%	98%	95%	90%	80%	70%	60%	LAST MSR

TITAN 16 – .243 Rem., .270 Win., 6.5x55 Creedmoor, .30-06, .308 Win., 7mm Rem. Mag., or 7x57mm cal., straight-pull bolt w/16 locking lugs, 22 or 24 in. Carbonitride barrel, black synthetic (All-Around model) or Italian walnut stock w/Bavarian (Luxus model) or Monte Carlo (Standard model) cheekpiece.

MSR $1,557	$1,325	$1,155	$990	$900	$725	$600	$515	

Add $97 for Monte Carlo stock (Standard).
Add $362 for Bavarian stock (Luxus).

TITAN ALPHA – .25-06 Rem., .270 Win., 6.5x55SE, 7x64, .30-06, 8x57IS, or 7mm Rem. Mag. cal., 22 or 24 in. deep blued barrel, various configurations include the Standard, Luxury, Exclusive, All-Around (synthetic stock only), or Stutzen (Mannlicher full stock) with or w/o checkering, top tang safety. Mfg. in Austria by Roessler beginning 2012. Imported by TR Imports beginning 2013.

MSR $1,190	$1,020	$895	$765	$695	$560	$460	$395	

ROTA, LUCIANO

Previous manufacturer located in Brescia, Italy until 2009. Previously imported and distributed 2002-2005 by Tristar, located in N. Kansas City, MO, and by New England Arms Corp., located in Kittery Point, ME.

For individual model listings, please go to BlueBookOfGunValues.com/overflow.

ROTH PERFORMANCE

Current shotgun and accessories manufacturer established in 2006, located in Kaukauna, WI.

SHOTGUNS: SEMI-AUTO

XB3G COMPETITION 3-GUN – 21, 24, or 26 in. Benelli M2 Field VR barrel, factory chokes, XM2BE 10 shot monotube mag. tube w/captured follower, XB3G quad vacuum port receiver with or w/o Picatinny rail, Mark Roth signature laser receiver, choke wrench and stock shims, two QD sling inserts, XTRA shell port caddy, reduced recoil spring, black finish.

MSR $2,700	$2,250	$1,950	$1,700	$1,500	$1,200	$1,000	$800	

This is a custom order product, please contact the manufacturer directly for pricing, additional options, and availability on this model.

ROTTWEIL

Previous firearms manufacturer located in Rottweil, Germany. Previously imported on a limited basis by RUAG Ammotec, USA located in Closter, NJ, and by Rottweil Competition, located in Orange, CA.

For individual model listings, please go to BlueBookOfGunValues.com/overflow.

ROYAL AMERICAN SHOTGUNS

Previously imported by Royal Arms International, located in Woodland Hills, CA circa 1985-87.

SHOTGUNS

MODEL 100 O/U – 12 or 20 ga., 2 3/4 in. chambers, double triggers, extractors, vent. rib and barrels. Imported 1985-87 only.

	$325	$265	$240	$220	$200	$180	$170	*$390*

Add $40 for 3 in. chambers, single trigger, and auto ejectors.

MODEL 600 BOXLOCK SxS – 12, 20, 28 ga., or .410 bore, sideplates, silver finished receiver, 3 in. chambers, single trigger, auto ejectors. Imported 1985-87 only.

	$365	$295	$265	$235	$210	$195	$180	*$420*

Subtract 25% for double triggers and 2 3/4 in. chambers.

MODEL 800 SIDELOCK SxS – 12, 20, 28 ga., or .410 bore, sidelock with sideplates, silver finished receiver, 3 in. chambers, single trigger, checkered select walnut straight grip stock, auto ejectors. Imported 1985-87 only.

	$775	$650	$595	$550	$500	$460	$435	*$899*

ROYAL ARMS INTERNATIONAL

Current firearms and component manufacturer/distributor established in 1984, located in Lewisburg, CA. Previously located in Oxnard, CA.

SHOTGUNS: SLIDE ACTION

Royal Arms International customizes Remington Model 870 actions into several models of breaching shotguns. Current models include: Royal 870 Express Breaching Shotgun (MSR $599) and the Royal 870 Police Parkerized Shotgun (MSR $799). The company also offered shotgun kits that included ammunition and a case. Previous model kits included: Express Breaching Shotgun Kit (last MSR $1,996) and the Police Breaching Shotgun Kit (last MSR $2,150).

GRADING - PPGS™	100%	98%	95%	90%	80%	70%	60%	LAST MSR

RUBY

Previous trademark manufactured by Gabilondo, located in Eibar, Spain.

RUGER

Please refer to the Sturm, Ruger, & Co. listing in the S section.

RUKO SPORTING GOODS, INC.

Previous importer (non-exclusive) located in Buffalo, NY that imported Arms Corp. of the Philippines firearms circa 1990-95. Ruko Sporting Goods, Inc. (previously Ruko Products) firearms were manufactured by the Arms Corporation of the Philippines. In 1991, Ruko Products, Inc. became the exclusive domestic importer for arms manufactured by Arms Corp. of the Philippines. These firearms were marked "Ruko-Armscor" on the barrels.

Please refer to the Armscor section for current importation, as well as previous importation by Armscorp Precision, Inc. and Ruko Products, Inc.

RUSSIAN AMERICAN ARMORY COMPANY

Please refer to the RAAC listing in this section.

RUSSIAN SERVICE PISTOLS AND RIFLES

Previously manufactured at various Russian military arsenals (including Tula).

HANDGUNS

MODEL TT30 & TT33 TOKAREV AUTOMATIC - 7.62mm Tokarev cal., modified Colt 1911 design, Petter-type unitized trigger/hammer assembly, 8 shot, 4 1/2 in. barrel, blue finish. Mfg. 1930-1954.

	100%	98%	95%	90%	80%	70%	60%
1930-1945 Mfg.	$1,200	$1,050	$900	$815	$660	$540	$420
TT30 Model	$2,400	$2,100	$1,800	$1,630	$1,320	$1,080	$840

Add 20% for matching mag.

Subtract 30% for post-war version mfg. 1946-1954.

Values listed assume original condition - no recent imports with importer markings.

* ***Model TT Tokarev Automatic Recent Import*** - 7.62x25mm Tokarev cal., must be stamped by importer, most modified by addition of a thumb safety, Russian Arsenal mfg., previously imported by Century Arms International, Inc. and others. Disc.

100%	98%	95%	90%	80%	70%	60%
$275	$225	$175	$155	$125	$100	$80

Add 50% if w/o thumb safety.

NAGANT REVOLVER - 7 shot, cylinder comes forward to seal barrel. Disc.

100%	98%	95%	90%	80%	70%	60%
$450	$350	$250	$200	$175	$150	$125

Add 10% for pre-communist Imperial marked.

Add 400% for "GRU" gun (Armed Forces Intelligence) with shorter barrel and grip frame.

MAKAROV MD - 9mm Makarov (9x18mm) cal., 8 shot mag. double action, 3.7 in. barrel, mfg. circa 1952, standard Russian Service pistol 1957-2003.

100%	98%	95%	90%	80%	70%	60%
$750	$600	$450	$350	$300	$250	$200

Add approx. 50% for one matching mag., or 100% for two matching mags.

Add 100% for pistols without import markings.

Recent commercial models with adj. rear sight are currently selling in the $150-$175 range.

MODEL PSM - 5.45x18mm Soviet cal., based on the Walther PPK design, with steel penetrator cored bullet designed to defeat Kevlar body armor, usually found with thin brown holster and extra mag., configurations include: military with black anodized aluminum grips, and the commercial with grey ribbed plastic grips.

	100%	98%	95%	90%	80%	70%	60%
Military	$8,500	$7,000	$5,500	$4,000	$3,000	$2,000	$1,500
Commercial	$7,000	$6,000	$5,000	$4,000	$3,000	$2,000	$1,500

Add 100% for factory engraved/wood display case Commercial pistols.

These models are usually encountered in high condition.

RIFLES

Original Soviet Mosin-Nagant bolt action rifles/carbines include: M1891 rifle, M1891 Dragoon, M1891/30 Rifle, M1891/30 Sniper Model, M1910 Carbine, M1938 Carbine, and the M1944 Carbine. Values for these older original military configurations will approximate values listed for the original mfg. Mosin-Nagant.

The Editor and Publisher would like to thank Matthew DiRisio and Luke Mercaldo for providing much of the information in this section.

GRADING - PPGS™	100%	98%	95%	90%	80%	70%	60%	LAST MSR

TOKAREV M1938 & M1940 (SVT) SEMI-AUTO - 7.62x54R cal., SVT M40 is the more common variation, while the SVT M38 sniper is very rare, 10 shot mag., first Russian military semi-auto, large quantities manufactured beginning 1938, but original surviving specimens in excellent condition are now very scarce.

SVT M38	$4,500	$4,000	$3,500	$3,000	$2,500	$2,000	$1,500	
SVT M40	$1,800	$1,500	$1,200	$1,000	$800	$700	$600	

MOSIN-NAGANT M1891 - 7.62x54R, 5 round non-detachable mag., loaded individually or with 5 round stripper clips, 51 1/2 in. OAL. Manufactured by Chatellerault (1892-1895), Tula (1891-1926), Izhevsk (1891-1920), Sestroryetsk (1892-1919), Remington (1916-1918), and New England Westinghouse (1916-1918). In Russian service it was referred to as the "3-line rifle M1891". The M1891 was used widely in WWI and can be found with marks from many different countries (purchased or captured). By the outbreak of WWII, the M1891 was relegated to second-line status, with the Finnish Army being a notable exception. All M1891 rifles were built on hexagonal receivers.

Non-Import	$1,500	$1,250	$1,000	$850	$700	$600	$500	
Recent Import	$500	$450	$375	$325	$275	$250	$225	

Add 100% for New England Westinghouse or Remington production.
Add 50% for Chatellerault production.
Add 25% for Sestroryetsk production.
Add 10% for Finnish produced barrel.
Add 10% if marked with Imperial Eagle on both barrel and receiver.

MOSIN-NAGANT M1891/30 - 7.62x54R, 5 round non-detachable mag., loaded individually or with 5 round striper clips, 48 1/2 in. OAL. Manufactured by Tula (1930-1944) and Izhevsk (1930-1947). In 1926, production of the 1891 rifle ceased, production was consolidated on the shorter Dragoon variant. In 1930, further changes to the Dragoon were implemented and resulted in the "7.62mm rifle, Model of the Year 1891-30" rifle, ordinarily known in the U.S. as the M1891/30 or M91/30. Notable changes included a globe and post front sight design, and the tangent rear sight pattern. The hexagonal receiver was phased out and replaced with the simplified round receivers at Izhevsk and Tula (1935-1936). Many rifles dated prior to 1930 are found in M91/30 configuration but retain the original markings on the barrel shank with dates prior to 1930. These were upgraded in Soviet arsenals and are known among collectors as "ex-dragoons". The end of WWII would see the curtailment of M91/30 production in the Soviet Union. Notable outliers include small postwar Hungarian, Romanian, and Albanian production. Additionally, the Finns rebuilt approximately 20,000 M91/30s with domestic stocks and barrels made by Tikkakoski. The M91/30 is common and is generally the least expensive of all Mosin-Nagant variations. Disc.

Non-Import	$1,000	$850	$750	$600	$500	$475	$350	
Recent Import	$350	$325	$300	$275	$250	$225	$200	

Add 300% for Albanian production.
Add 100% for Hungarian or Romanian production.
Add 50% for Finnish production.
Add 25% for an Ex-Dragoon rifle (pre-1930).
Add 10% for a laminate stock.

RPD SEMI-AUTO - 7.62x39mm cal., converted from belt fed to semi-auto only, fired from closed bolt, milled receiver, includes 50 shot mag., recent importation. Disc.

$3,795	$3,495	$2,950	$2,600	$2,300	$2,000	$1,750	

RUTTEN HERSTAL

Previous firearms manufacturer of O/U shotguns located in Herstal, Belgium. Previously imported by Labanu, Inc. located in Ronkonkoma, NY.

For more information and current pricing on both new and used Rutten airguns, please refer to the *Blue Book of Airguns* - also available as an online subscription.

SHOTGUNS: O/U

MODEL RM 100 - 12 ga., 3 in. chambers, VR multi-choke barrels, ejectors, checkered walnut stock and forearm, hard case. Imported 1995-98.

$875	$775	$675	$575	$500	$450	$400	*$1,095*

MODEL RM 285 - similar to Model RM 100, except has engraved sideplates and silver engraved receiver, select walnut with Schnabel forearm, hard case. Imported 1995-98.

$1,025	$850	$725	$600	$500	$450	$400	*$1,295*

S.A.C.M.

Previous company located in Cholet, France. S.A.C.M. stands for Societe Alsacienne de Construction Mechanique.

GRADING - PPGS™	100%	98%	95%	90%	80%	70%	60%	LAST MSR

PISTOLS: SEMI-AUTO

FRENCH MODEL 1935A – 7.65mm Long cal., 8 shot, 4.3 in. barrel, blue, fixed sights, checkered stocks, used by French troops in WWII and Indochina 1945-1954. Mfg. 1935-45.

	100%	98%	95%	90%	80%	70%	60%
	$500	$400	$350	$300	$250	$200	$150

Add 50% for Nazi WWII mfg. (Waffenamt proofed).

S.A.M.

Please refer to Shooter Arms Manufacturing Incorporated listing in this section.

S.I.A.C.E.

Current shotgun and rifle manufacturer located in Gardone V.T., Italy. S.I.A.C.E. also offers an extensive variety of gunsmithing services. Limited importation only on a custom order basis. Previously imported on a private label basis by Dakota Arms, located in Sturgis, SD, Luxus Arms, located in Millford, OH, and by New England Arms Corp., located in Kittery Point, ME.

For individual model listings, please go to BlueBookOfGunValues.com/overflow.

S.P.S.

Current handgun manufacturer established in 1997, located in Ripollet, Spain. Currently imported by Eagle Imports Inc., located in Wanamassa, NJ.

S.P.S. manufactures a variety of semi-auto pistols based on the M1911 design, primarily used for competition. Many configurations are available, including standard and compact models in 9mm Para., .38 Super, .40 S&W, and .45 ACP cal.

PISTOLS: SEMI-AUTO

SPS Series pistols are manufactured by S.P.S. in Spain, then assembled in the U.S.

SPS PANTERA – 9mm Para. (new 2016), .45 ACP, or .40 S&W (new 2014) cal., SA, 5 in. ramped match bull barrel, 12 (.45 ACP), 16 (.40 S&W, new 2014), or 18 shot mag., steel frame, hammer forged steel slide, fully adj. Bomar style rear sight, dovetail fiber optic front sight, flared and lowered ejection port, standard slide stop, enhanced beavertail grip safety, skeletal hammer, lightweight polymer trigger, wide front and rear slide serrations, ambidextrous thumb safety, glass filled nylon polymer grips with S.P.S. logo, wide magwell, blue, hard chrome, or black chrome (.40 S&W and .45 ACP only) finish, approx. 37 oz. New 2013.

	100%	98%	95%	90%	80%	70%	60%
MSR $1,730	$1,475	$1,295	$1,100	$1,000	$810	$675	$525

Add $75 for hard chrome finish.
Add $165 for black chrome finish.

SPS PANTERA STAR – 9mm Para., steel frame, 5 in. match grade bull barrel, 18 shot mag., hammer forged steel slide with wide front and rear serrations, flared and lowered ejection port, skeletal hammer, dovetail fiber optic front and fully adj. Bomar-type rear sight, textured polymer grips, ambi thumb safety and beavertail safety, checkered front strap serration, wide front and rear, hard chrome finish, 40 oz. New 2021.

	100%	98%	95%	90%	80%	70%	60%
MSR $3,075	$2,625	$2,300	$1,975	$1,785	$1,450	$1,200	$1,025

SPS VISTA – 9mm Para. (Vista Short) or .38 Super (Vista Long) cal., SA, 5 1/2 in. ramped match threaded barrel, steel frame, 21 shot mag., hammer forged steel slide, scope mount, flared and lowered ejection port, standard slide stop, enhanced beavertail grip safety, skeletal hammer, lightweight polymer trigger, wide front and rear slide serrations, ambidextrous thumb safety, glass filled nylon polymer grips with S.P.S. logo, wide magwell, black chrome finish, approx. 42-43 oz. New 2013.

	100%	98%	95%	90%	80%	70%	60%
MSR $2,450	$2,175	$1,900	$1,625	$1,475	$1,195	$975	$750

S.W.A.T. FIREARMS

Previous manufacturer of AR-15 style pistols and rifles located in Campbell, TX 1999-2017.

Please refer to BlueBookOfGunValues.com to order the *Blue Book of AR-15s & Variations*, available as a book or online subscription.

S.W.D., INC.

Previous manufacturer located in Atlanta, GA.

Similar models have previously been manufactured by R.P.B. Industries, Inc. (1979-82), and met with BATF disapproval because of convertibility into fully automatic operation. "Cobray" is a trademark for the M11/9 semi-automatic pistol.

CARBINES

SEMI-AUTO CARBINE – 9mm Para. cal., same mechanism as M11, 16 1/4 in. shrouded barrel, telescoping stock.

	100%	98%	95%	90%	80%	70%	60%
	$550	$495	$450	$400	$325	$275	$235

GRADING - PPGS™	100%	98%	95%	90%	80%	70%	60%	LAST MSR

PISTOLS: SEMI-AUTO

COBRAY M-11/NINE MM – 9mm Para. cal., fires from closed bolt, SA, 3rd generation design, stamped steel frame, 32 shot mag., parkerized finish, similar in appearance to Ingram Mac 10. Disc.

	$475	$395	$350	$300	$295	$275	$250	

This model was also available in a fully-auto variation, Class III transferable only.

REVOLVERS

LADIES HOME COMPANION – .45-70 Govt. cal., double action design utilizing spring wound 12 shot rotary mag., 12 in. barrel, steel barrel and frame, 9 lbs. 6 oz. Mfg. 1990-94.

	$650	$525	$400	$360	$335	$310	$290	

SHOTGUNS: SINGLE SHOT

TERMINATOR – 12 or 20 ga., tactical design shotgun with 18 in. cylinder bore barrel, parkerized finish, ejector. Mfg. 1986-88 only.

	$150	$125	$95	$80	$70	$60	$55	*$110*

SAE

Previous importer located in Miami, FL. SAE stands for Spain America Enterprises Inc. SAE imported Felix Sarasqueta shotguns from Spain until circa 1988.

For individual model listings, please go to BlueBookOfGunValues.com/overflow.

SBR (SOUTHERN BALLISTIC RESEARCH)

Current manufacturer of semi-auto rifles, parts, and accessories located in Brunswick, GA.

Please contact the company directly for more information including pricing, options, and availability.

SCCY INDUSTRIES

Current pistol manufacturer established in 2003, located in Daytona Beach, FL. Previously located in South Daytona, FL.

PISTOLS: SEMI-AUTO

SCCY offers a lifetime guarantee on all its pistols. Beginning 2016, the entire CPX-1 and CPX-2 lines are now available in the following frame colors: black, crimson, FDE, orange, pink, purple, SCCY Blue, Sniper Gray, or white.

CPX-1/CPX-1RD – 9mm Para. cal., DAO, lightweight compact polymer frame with stainless steel slide, 3.1 in. stainless steel barrel, includes two 10 shot double stack mags. with flat bases, 3-dot sights, Zytel polymer grips, ambi manual safety, black Nitride or natural stainless steel finish in two-tone black, crimson, FDE, orange, pink, purple (new 2015), SCCY Blue, Sniper Gray, white, Kryptek Highlander (mfg. 2018 only), Kryptek Pontus (mfg. 2018 only), or Kryptek Inferno (mfg. 2018 only), 15 oz.

MSR $284	$250	$215	$185	$165	$135	$110	$85	

Add $65 for Crimson Trace CTS-1500 red dot sight (CPX-1RD, new 2020).

CPX-2/CPX-2RD – 9mm Para. cal., similar to CPX-1, except has no manual safety, optional Crimson Trace CTS-1500 red dot sight (CPX-2RD, new 2020). New 2011.

MSR $270	$225	$195	$175	$165	$135	$110	$85	

Add $69 for Crimson Trace CTS-1500 red dot sight (CPX-2RD, new 2020).

CPX-3/CPX-3RD – .380 ACP cal., DAO, features the Roebuck Quad Lock system (locks the barrel to the slide in four distinct areas), 2.96 in. barrel, includes two 10 shot mags. with two base plates, 3-dot sights or optional Crimson Trace CTS-1500 red dot sight (CPX-3RD, new 2021), laser etched slide, all steel recoil spring system (including steel guide rod), black Nitride or matte stainless steel finish, 15 oz. New 2016.

MSR $305	$265	$225	$200	$185	$150	$120	$95	

Add $34 for Crimson Trace CTS-1500 red dot sight (CPX-3RD, new 2021).

CPX-4/CPX-4RD – .380 ACP cal., DA, Roebuck quad-lock, 2.96 in. barrel, machined from bar stock, seven lands and grooves, three double stack 10 shot mags. (one w/finger extension base installed, two w/flat bases), internal hammer w/inertial firing pin, custom trigger guard lock, 3-dot rear sight (adj. for windage w/locking screw) or optional Crimson Trace CTS-1500 red dot sight (CPX-4RD, new 2021), finger grooved ergonomic Zytel black polymer grips, ambi manual safety, black Nitride or natural stainless slide finish, 15 oz. New late 2019.

MSR $305	$265	$225	$200	$185	$150	$120	$95	

Add $44 for Crimson Trace CTS-1500 red dot sight (CPX-3RD, new 2021).

GRADING - PPGS™	100%	98%	95%	90%	80%	70%	60%	LAST MSR

DVG-1/DVG-1RD – 9mm Para. cal., SFO, 3.1 in. barrel, Quadlock Barrel System, 10 shot mag., with or w/o CTS-1500 red dot optic (DVG-1RD), H&M black Nitride finish, 15.5 oz. New 2020.

MSR $299	$250	$225	$200	$175	$150	$125	$100	

Add $100 for Crimson Trace CTS-1500 red dot sight (DVG-1RD).

SD TACTICAL ARMS

Current rifle manufacturer located in Prescott, AZ. Previously located in Menomonie, WI.

RIFLES/CARBINES: SEMI-AUTO

SD Tactical Arms manufactures a line of AR style semi-auto carbines and rifles built per individual customer specifications. The company also offers a complete line of tactical gear and accessories, including rails and magazines. Since each rifle is built per custom order, please contact the company directly for pricing, available options, and delivery time.

SI DEFENSE, INC.

Previous AR-15 style carbine/rifle manufacturer located in Kalispell, MT until 2015.

Please refer to BlueBookOfGunValues.com to order the *Blue Book of AR-15s & Variations*, available as a book or online subscription.

SKB SHOTGUNS

Current trademark established in 2013. The SKB Shotgun line is manufactured in Turkey by Akus and Akdas Makina. These companies are licensed to produce the SKB brand by the U.S. owners, SKB Shotguns, USA located in Omaha, NE. Previously manufactured by the SKB Arms Company located near Tokyo, Japan from 1855-until December, 2009. Dealer and distributor sales.

SKB Arms Company exported its first shotguns into the U.S. during 1966. SKB also manufactured shotguns for Browning, Weatherby, and Birmingham Small Arms (BSA). In 1986, SKB had produced its one millionth shotgun. SKB also manufactured many other models and variations of O/Us, SxS, and semi-auto shotguns that were not imported into the U.S. Most of these shotgun variations were brought back from Japan directly by US military service members. In 1987, importation resumed on most SKB models. While the model numbers have changed, quality is similar to those models imported previously by Ithaca. In most cases, the newer models are derived closely from their previous counterparts. Listings in this section will differentiate older, disc. models from more recently imported models. Ithaca imported from 1968 to 1978, Mitsui and Co. Chicago, IL from 1980 to 1983, and G.U. Inc from 1987 to 2010.

Early in 2010, the owners made the difficult decision to close the SKB Shotguns factory and negotiated the sale of the brand name, mechanical drawings and all of the remaining parts to G.U. Inc.

SHOTGUNS: O/U

MODEL 85 TARGET SUPER SPORT (TSS) – 12, 20, 28 ga., or .410 bore, monobloc barrel construction, 2 different frame sizes, Greener crossbolt, non-detachable trigger assembly, silver nitride receiver finish, polished blue barrels, available in Sporting Clays, Skeet, or Trap configuration (including sets), Mag-na-ported barrels, Hi-Viz competition front sight, available with or w/o adj. comb stock (Graco CTS systems), matte wood finish. Mfg. 2002-2008.

* ***Model 85 TSS Sporting Clays*** – choice of fixed or adj. comb stock, 28, 30, or 32 in. VR barrels, 8.5mm (28 ga. or .410 bore) or 12mm (12 or 20 ga.) stepped VR, 7 1/2-8 1/2 lbs. Mfg. 2002-2008.

$1,850	$1,525	$1,225	$950	$875	$800	$725	*$2,199*

Add $90 for .410 bore and 28 ga.
Add $230 for adj. comb on stock.
Add $190 for pigeon porting by Mag-na-port.
Add $400 for high grade wood (limited availability, new 2003).

» ***Model 85 TSS Sporting Clays 2 Gauge Set*** – includes 2 sets of barrels in different gauges. Mfg. 2002-2008.

$3,000	$2,525	$2,050	$1,800	$1,600	$1,400	$1,200	*$3,549*

Add $230 for adj. comb on stock.
Add $380 for pigeon porting by Mag-na-port.
Add $470 for high grade wood (limited availability).

» ***Model 85 TSS Sporting Clays 3 Gauge Set*** – includes 20 ga., 28 ga. and .410 bore and 30 in. barrels, includes aluminum case. Mfg. 2002-2008.

$4,800	$4,200	$3,600	$3,265	$2,640	$2,160	$1,680	*$5,349*

Add $230 for adj. comb on stock.
Add $550 for high grade wood (limited availability, new 2004).

GRADING - PPGS™	100%	98%	95%	90%	80%	70%	60%	LAST MSR

* ***Model 85 TSS Skeet*** – choice of fixed or adj. comb stock, 28, 30, or 32 in. VR barrels, 8.5mm (28 ga. or .410 bore) or 9.5mm (12 ga.) sloped VR, 7 lbs. 6 oz.-8 lbs. 6 oz. Mfg. 2002-2008.

$1,850 $1,525 $1,225 $950 $875 $800 $725 ***$2,199***

Add $90 for .410 bore and 28 ga.
Add $230 for adj. comb on stock.
Add $400 for high grade wood (limited availability, new 2003).

» **Model 85 TSS Skeet 3 Gauge Set** – includes 20 ga., 28 ga. and .410 bore and 28 in. barrels, includes aluminum case. Mfg. 2002-2008.

$4,800 $4,200 $3,600 $3,265 $2,640 $2,160 $1,680 ***$5,349***

Add $230 for adj. comb on stock.
Add $550 for high grade wood (limited availability, new 2004).

* ***Model 85 TSS Trap*** – choice of 30 or 32 in. barrels, fixed or adj. comb standard or Monte Carlo stock, 8 3/4 lbs. Mfg. 2002-2008.

$1,850 $1,525 $1,225 $950 $875 $800 $725 ***$2,199***

Add $230 for adj. comb.
Add $190 for pigeon porting by Mag-na-port.

* ***Model 85 TSS Trap Un-Single*** – 12 ga. only, bottom un-single, 32 or 34 in. barrel with adj. rib, fixed or adj. comb stock, standard or Monte Carlo stock, 8 3/4 lbs. Mfg. 2002-2008.

$2,100 $1,750 $1,375 $1,050 $975 $850 $750 ***$2,499***

Add $230 for adj. comb on stock.
Add $400 for high grade wood (limited availability, new 2003).
Add $114 for pigeon porting by Mag-na-port.

» **Model 85 TSS Un-Single Combo** – includes bottom un-single barrel and extra 30 or 32 in. VR O/U barrels. Mfg. 2002-2008.

$2,975 $2,450 $2,000 $1,750 $1,500 $1,250 $1,000 ***$3,489***

Add $230 for adj. comb on stock.
Add $400 for high grade wood (limited availability, new 2003).
Add $300 for pigeon porting by Mag-na-port.
Add $210 for combo with 13 1/2 in. LOP stock (adj. comb only).

MODEL 85TTR TRAP SERIES – 12 ga., 3 in. chambers, 30, 32, or 34 in. barrels, low profile boxlock action, ejectors, Greener crossbolt, silver nitride finish receiver with scroll engraving, fixed or adj. Grade II/III American black walnut checkered stock with matte finish, 9mm tapered top rib, competition choke tubes, HiViz comp. sight, SST, Pachmayr XLT recoil pad. Mfg. 2009-2010.

$2,050 $1,750 $1,425 $1,100 $875 $775 $650 ***$2,329***

Add $230 for adj. comb.
Add $570 for high grade deluxe wood.

* ***Model 85TTR Un-Single*** – 32 or 34 in. barrels, fixed or adj. comb stock. Disc. 2010.

$2,400 $2,150 $1,825 $1,600 $1,350 $1,100 $895 ***$2,799***

Add $230 for adj. comb.
Add $400 for high grade deluxe wood.

* ***Model 85TTR Combo*** – includes choice of 30, 32, or 34 in. barrels, adj. comb stock, also available in short (13 1/2 in.) LOP. Disc. 2010.

$3,625 $3,250 $2,825 $2,400 $2,000 $1,650 $1,350 ***$4,049***

Add $400 for high grade deluxe wood.

MODEL 90TSS TARGET – 12 or 20 ga., skeet, sporting, and trap configurations, right or left-hand, sculpted boxlock action with laser engraving and bright blue highlights, 28, 30, or 32 in. barrels, mechanical SST powered by coil springs, fully adj. Pachmayr buttpad, Grade II checkered oil finished walnut stock and forearm with fixed (skeet) or adj. comb. Importation began 2014.

* ***Model 90TSS Skeet*** – 12 or 20 ga., 2 3/4 in. chambers, choice of 28, 30, or 32 in. VR barrels with SKB choke system, fixed comb, target sights, right or left-hand action, oil finished Grade II walnut stock, adj. comb and buttplate, Pachmayr buttpad, blued finish, 7 lbs. 10 oz.-8 lbs. 8 oz. Disc. 2018.

$1,250 $1,095 $940 $850 $690 $575 $500 ***$1,470***

* ***Model 90TSS Sporting*** – 12 or 20 ga., right or left-hand action, 28, 30, or 32 in. VR barrels with SKB choke tubes, adj. comb and buttplate, blue (disc. 2017) or white chrome frame finish, 7 lbs. 12 oz.-8 lbs. 12 oz. New 2015.

MSR $2,019 $1,715 $1,500 $1,285 $1,165 $950 $775 $675

Subtract $100 for blue frame finish (disc. 2017).

* ***Model 90TSS Trap*** – 12 ga., 30 or 32 in. VR barrels with SKB choke tubes, right or left-hand action, adj. comb and buttpad, blue (disc. 2017) or white chrome frame finish. New 2015.

MSR $2,019 $1,715 $1,500 $1,285 $1,165 $950 $775 $675

Add $850 for Trap Combo with 30 and 32 or 32 and 34 in. barrels (new 2016).
Subtract $100 for blue frame finish (disc. 2017).

MODEL 500 – 12, 20, 28 ga., or .410 bore, field grade, selective ejectors, VR, SST, 26 in. imp. cyl. and mod., 28 in. full and mod., and 30 in. full and mod. barrels, checkered stock. Prices below assume 50% engraving coverage and gold SST. Mfg. in Japan by SKB 1966-1979, imported by Ithaca.

$1,000 $875 $750 $680 $550 $450 $350

Add 10% for 28 ga. or .410 bore.
Add 10%-15% for fully engraved frame with pheasant, or duck/quail and dog game scene if in 98%+ condition.

The Model 500 varied quite a bit during the course of production in the amount of factory engraving (engraved animals or not), the quality of wood, style of checkering, and also had either silver or gold trigger. This model should also be checked carefully for hairline cracks in the buttstock, where it joins the receiver. Also, beware of bluing wear on frame bottom, and on the front and back of the trigger guard.

* ***Model 500 Magnum*** – 12 ga., 3 in. Mag., field grade, similar to Model 500, except 3 in. Mag. chambers. Disc.

$1,000 $875 $750 $680 $550 $450 $350

MODEL 505 FIELD – 12, 20, 28 ga., or .410 bore, blue (new 1998) or silver Nitride engraved frame (disc. 1997), 3 in. chambers, 26 or 28 in. barrels (supplied with choke tubes), single selective trigger, ejectors, matte finished (new 2006) or high gloss (disc. 2005) checkered walnut stock and forearm, recoil pad, 6 3/4-7 3/4 lbs.

$1,225 $975 $800 $700 $550 $500 $450 ***$1,429***

Add $500 for combo package.
Add 10% for 28 ga. or .410 bore.

The combo package included either 12/20 ga. barrels with Inter-chokes or 28 ga./.410 bore barrels.

* ***Model 505 Sporting Clays*** – 28 or 30 in. multi-choke barrels, blue frame with light engraving, dimensioned for Sporting Clays competition, 1997 importation features Schnabel forearm, semi-wide channeled rib, and lengthened forcing cones, approx. 8 1/4 lbs. Older importation, in addition to new model imported 1997-2002.

$1,100 $975 $825 $750 $600 $495 $385 ***$1,299***

* ***Model 505 Trap*** – 12 ga., 30 or 32 in. choke tube barrels with or without Monte Carlo stock, high rib. Disc.

$1,100 $975 $825 $750 $600 $495 $385 ***$995***

Add $400 for O/U Trap Combo.

The above Combo includes one set of O/U Trap barrels and a top single Trap barrel.

* ***Model 505 Skeet*** – 12, 20, 28 ga., or .410 bore, 28 in. barrels with multi-chokes. Disc.

$1,100 $975 $825 $750 $600 $495 $385 ***$995***

Add 10% for 28 ga. or .410 bore.

* ***Model 505 3-Ga. Skeet Set*** – includes 20, 28 ga., and .410 bore fitted 28 in. barrel sets with individual forends, aluminum case. Disc.

$2,800 $2,450 $2,100 $1,900 $1,525 $1,250 $975 ***$2,195***

MODEL 585 FIELD – 12, 20, 28 ga., or .410 (new 1995) bore, silver nitride engraved receiver, 3 in. chambers, 26 or 28 in. barrels (supplied with choke tubes), similar to 505 Series, except has .735 in. diameter bore on 12 ga. models and includes lengthened forcing cones with extended length "Competition Series" Inter-Choke System designed to improve shot patterns and reduce recoil, SST, ejectors, high gloss (disc. 2005), matte finished (new 2006), or checkered walnut stock with recoil pad and forearm (Youth/Ladies model is also available with 13 1/2 LOP), 6 lbs. 10 oz.-7 lbs. 11 oz. Imported 1992-2008.

$1,425 $1,200 $1,000 $850 $725 $600 $550 ***$1,699***

Add 10% for 28 ga. or .410 bore.
Add $200 for Gold Package featuring choice of silver or blue receiver, gold plated trigger, and 2 gold game scenes with Schnabel forearm - new 1998.

GRADING - PPGS™	100%	98%	95%	90%	80%	70%	60%	LAST MSR

* ***Model 585 Field Set*** – includes 12/20 ga., 20/28 ga., 28 ga./.410 bore, 26 or 28 (new 1994) in. VR barrels with SKB Inter-choke system, silver nitride receiver with finely engraved scroll game scenes, low profile receiver, crossbolt locking system, SST, ejectors, manual safety, checkered high gloss (disc. 2005) or matte finish (new 2006) American walnut stock and forearm. Disc. 2008.

$2,375	$2,000	$1,700	$1,350	$1,100	$975	$850	*$2,749*

Add $80 for 20/28 ga. set or 28 ga./.410 bore set.
Add approx. $340 for Gold Package featuring choice of silver or blue (disc. 2004) receiver, gold plated trigger, and 2 gold game scenes with Schnabel forearm - new 1998.

* ***Model 585 Medallion*** – 12 or 20 ga., 3 in. chambers, features two inlaid medallions in gold or bronze finish (medallion artwork by Ron Van Gilder and Rocky Capece), very limited production. Mfg. 2000-2005.

$1,610	$1,275	$1,025	$900	$800	$700	$600	*$1,819*

* ***Model 585 Upland*** – 12, 20, or 28 ga., 3 in. chambers for 12 and 20 ga., features straight grip stock with recoil pad and 26 in. VR barrels, Schnabel forearm, 6 lbs. 10 oz.-7 lbs. 10 oz. Mfg. 1997-2005.

$1,425	$1,250	$1,075	$975	$785	$640	$500	*$1,549*

Add 10% for 28 ga.
Add $200 for Gold Package featuring choice of silver or blue receiver, gold plated trigger, and 2 gold game scenes with Schnabel forearm - mfg. 1998-2005.

* ***Model 585 Trap*** – 12 ga., 30 or 32 in. choke tube barrels with or w/o Monte Carlo stock, high rib. Disc. 2002.

$1,425	$1,250	$1,075	$975	$785	$640	$500	*$1,619*

Add $200 for Gold Package featuring choice of silver or blue receiver, gold plated trigger, and 2 gold game scenes with Schnabel forearm - mfg. 1998-2002.
Add $800 for O/U Trap Combo or $1,100 for O/U Trap Combo with Gold Package.

The above Combo included one set of O/U Trap barrels and a top single Trap barrel.

* ***Model 585 Skeet*** – 12, 20, 28 ga., or .410 bore, 28 or 30 (12 ga. only - new 1994) in. barrels with multi-chokes. Disc. 2002.

$1,425	$1,250	$1,075	$975	$785	$640	$500	*$1,619*

Add 10% for 28 ga. or .410 bore.
Add $200 for Gold Package featuring choice of silver or blue receiver, gold plated trigger, and 2 gold game scenes with Schnabel forearm - mfg. 1998-2002.

* ***Model 585 3-Ga. Skeet Set*** – includes 20, 28 ga., and .410 bore fitted 28 in. barrel sets with individual forend, aluminum case. Disc. 2002.

$3,175	$2,550	$2,000	$1,700	$1,525	$1,400	$1,300	*$3,779*

Add $450 for Gold Package featuring choice of silver or blue receiver, gold plated trigger, and 2 gold game scenes with Schnabel forearm - mfg. 1998-2002.

* ***Model 585 Sporting Clays*** – 12, 20, 28 ga., or .410 bore, 3 in. chambers (12 and 20 ga.), 28 or 30 in. multi-choke barrels, dimensioned for Sporting Clays competition, narrow rib (3/8 in.) became available 1994. Disc. 2002.

$1,425	$1,250	$1,075	$975	$785	$640	$500	*$1,679*

Add 10% for 28 ga. or .410 bore.
Add $200 for Gold Package featuring choice of silver or blue receiver, gold plated trigger, and 2 gold game scenes with Schnabel forearm - mfg. 1998-2002.

» ***Model 585 Sporting Clays Set*** – includes 2 sets of barrels (12 ga. - 30 in., 20 ga. - 28 in.). Mfg. 1996-2002.

$2,135	$1,775	$1,495	$1,200	$1,050	$925	$825	*$2,419*

Add $300 for Gold Package featuring choice of silver or blue receiver, gold plated trigger, and 2 gold game scenes with Schnabel forearm - mfg. 1998-2002.

* ***Model 585 Waterfowler*** – 12 ga. only, 3 in. chambers, oil finished stock and forearm, matte finished barrel and receiver. Imported 1995-2000, reintroduced 2005.

$1,425	$1,250	$1,075	$975	$785	$640	$500	*$1,549*

* ***Model 585 Youth/Ladies*** – 12 or 20 ga., 26 or 28 (12 ga. only) in. VR barrels, features 13 1/2 in. LOP, barrels have .735 in. bores with lengthened forcing cones. Imported 1994-2008.

$1,425	$1,200	$975	$850	$725	$600	$550	*$1,699*

Add $200 for Gold Package featuring choice of silver or blue receiver, gold plated trigger, and 2 gold game scenes with Schnabel forearm - new 1998.

GRADING - PPGS™	100%	98%	95%	90%	80%	70%	60%	LAST MSR

MODEL 585 150th ANNIVERSARY – 12 or 20 ga., 3 in. chambers, silver nitride engraved receiver with gold game scenes, matte finished metal, 26 or 28 in. barrels, matte finish high grade black American walnut stock with finger groove forend, 6 lbs. 12 oz.-7 lbs. 14 oz. 150 mfg. 2005 only.

$2,100 $1,825 $1,575 N/A N/A N/A N/A *$1,999*

A total of 150 of this model was manufactured - 70 in 12 ga. w/28 in. barrels, 25 in 12 ga. w/26 in. barrels, 30 in 20 ga. w/28 in. barrels, and 25 in 20 ga. w/26 in. barrels.

MODEL 590 FIELD – 12 or 20 ga., chrome-lined 3 in. chambers, sculpted steel boxlock action with laser engraving, 26, 28, or 30 in. VR backbored barrels with SKB choke tube system, SST, ejectors, jeweled monobloc, oil finished pistol grip checkered walnut stock and forearm with Pachmayr pad, Youth Model also available with smaller stock dimensions, matte finished receiver, approx. 7 1/2 lbs. Imported 2014-2016.

$1,175 $1,000 $900 $800 $700 $575 $475 *$1,300*

MODEL 600 FIELD GRADE – similar to Model 500, except silver-plated frame and select wood and fully engraved. Disc.

$1,200 $1,050 $900 $815 $650 $550 $425

Add 10% for 28 ga. or .410 bore.

An unknown quantity of Model 600s were mfg. with hand engraved blue receivers - a small premium may be asked.

MODEL 600 MAGNUM – similar to Model 600 Field, except chambered for 3 in. Mag., 12 ga. Mfg. 1969-72 by SKB.

$1,200 $1,050 $900 $815 $650 $550 $425

MODEL 600 TRAP GRADE – similar to Model 600 Field Grade, except 12 ga. only, trap stock, recoil pad, select wood. Disc.

$1,200 $1,050 $900 $815 $650 $550 $425

MODEL 600 DOUBLES GUN – similar to Model 600 Trap, except choked for 21 yd. and 30 yd. targets. Mfg. 1973-75.

$1,200 $1,050 $900 $815 $650 $550 $425

MODEL 600 SKEET GRADE – 12, 20, 28 ga., or .410 bore, 26 or 28 in. barrels, bored S&S, otherwise similar to Model 600 Trap. Disc.

$1,200 $1,050 $900 $815 $650 $550 $425

Add 10% for 28 ga. or .410 bore.

MODEL 600 SKEET GRADE COMBO SET – similar to Model 600 Skeet, except fitted with matched set of 20, 28 ga., and .410 bore barrels, in fitted case. Disc.

$2,650 $2,250 $1,875 $1,550 $1,325 $1,175 $1,025

MODEL 605 FIELD – similar to Model 505 Deluxe Field except has silver finished engraved receiver with better walnut. Importation disc. 1992.

$1,275 $1,125 $950 $875 $700 $575 $450 *$1,195*

Add $500 for extra set of barrels (Combo).
Add 10% for 28 ga. or .410 bore.

* ***Model 605 Trap*** – 12 ga., 30 or 32 in. choke tube barrel with or without Monte Carlo stock, high rib. Disc.

$1,275 $1,125 $950 $875 $700 $575 $450 *$1,195*

Add $400 for O/U Trap Combo.

The above Combo included one set of O/U Trap barrels and a top single Trap barrel.

* ***Model 605 Skeet*** – 12, 20, 28 ga., or .410 bore, 28 in. barrels with multi-chokes. Disc.

$1,275 $1,125 $950 $875 $700 $575 $450 *$1,195*

Add 10% for 28 ga. or .410 bore.

* ***Model 605 3-Ga. Skeet Set*** – includes 20, 28 ga., and .410 bore fitted 28 in. barrel sets with individual forends, aluminum case. Disc.

$2,900 $2,550 $2,175 $1,975 $1,595 $1,300 $1,000 *$2,395*

* ***Model 605 Sporting Clay*** – 28 or 30 in. multi-choke barrels, dimensioned for Sporting Clay competition. Disc.

$1,275 $1,125 $950 $875 $700 $575 $450 *$1,245*

GRADING - PPGS™	100%	98%	95%	90%	80%	70%	60%	LAST MSR

* ***Model 605 DU Sponsor Gun*** – mfg. for DU chapters - dinner auction gun, 850 mfg. in 12 ga. (1990) and 850 mfg. in 20 ga. (1991). Features gold inlays and presentation case. Mfg. 1990-91.

Currently, prices seem to range between $1,200-$1,400.

MODEL 680 ENGLISH – similar to Model 600 Field, except English style stock, select walnut and fine scroll engraving. Mfg. 1973-76.

	100%	98%	95%	90%	80%	70%	60%	LAST MSR
	$1,300	$1,150	$975	$850	$725	$650	$600	

Add 10% for 20 ga.

MODEL 685 FIELD – similar to Model 585 Deluxe Field, except has silver finished engraved receiver with gold inlays and better walnut, engine turned monobloc. Imported 1992-1995.

	100%	98%	95%	90%	80%	70%	60%	LAST MSR
	$1,525	$1,325	$1,150	$1,025	$850	$675	$525	*$1,549*

Add 10% for 28 ga. or .410 bore.

* ***Model 685 Field Set*** – includes 12/20, 20/28 ga., 28 ga./.410 bore, 26 or 28 (new 1994) in. VR barrels with SKB Inter-choke system (on 12, 20, and 28 ga.), silver nitride receiver with finely engraved scroll game scenes, low profile receiver, crossbolt locking system, SST, ejectors, manual safety, checkered high gloss American walnut stock and forearm. Disc.

	100%	98%	95%	90%	80%	70%	60%	LAST MSR
	$2,225	$1,950	$1,675	$1,500	$1,225	$1,000	$775	*$2,149*

* ***Model 685 Trap*** – 12 ga., 30 or 32 in. choke tube barrels with or w/o Monte Carlo stock, high rib. Disc.

	100%	98%	95%	90%	80%	70%	60%	LAST MSR
	$1,525	$1,325	$1,150	$1,025	$850	$675	$525	*$1,595*

Add $600 for O/U Trap Combo.

The above Combo included one set of O/U Trap barrels and a top single Trap barrel.

* ***Model 685 Skeet*** – 12, 20, 28 ga., or .410 bore, 28 or 30 (12 ga. only - new 1994) in. barrels with multi-chokes. Disc.

	100%	98%	95%	90%	80%	70%	60%	LAST MSR
	$1,525	$1,325	$1,150	$1,025	$850	$675	$525	*$1,595*

Add 10% for 28 ga. or .410 bore.

* ***Model 685 3-Ga. Skeet Set*** – includes 20, 28 ga., and .410 bore fitted 28 in. barrels sets with individual forends, aluminum case. Disc.

	100%	98%	95%	90%	80%	70%	60%	LAST MSR
	$3,300	$2,895	$2,475	$2,250	$1,800	$1,475	$1,150	*$2,949*

* ***Model 685 Sporting Clays*** – 28 (all gauges), 30 (12 ga. only), or 32 (12 ga. only) in. multi-choke barrels, dimensioned for Sporting Clays competition, 3/8 in. narrow rib became available 1994. Importation disc. 1995.

	100%	98%	95%	90%	80%	70%	60%	LAST MSR
	$1,525	$1,325	$1,150	$1,025	$850	$675	$525	*$1,595*

Add 10% for 28 ga.

* ***Model 685 Sporting Clays Set*** – includes one set of 12 ga. (28, 30, or 32 in. VR barrels) and 20 ga. (28 in. only) or one set of 32 and 28 in. barrels in 12 ga only. Imported 1994-95.

	100%	98%	95%	90%	80%	70%	60%	LAST MSR
	$2,225	$1,950	$1,675	$1,500	$1,225	$1,000	$775	*$2,295*

MODEL 690 FIELD – 12, 20, 28 ga., or .410 bore, 3 in. chambers, boxlock action, 26 or 28 in. VR barrels with 5 choke tubes, auto ejectors, mechanical single trigger, checkered Grade 2 Turkish walnut pistol grip stock and Schnabel forearm with high gloss polyurethane finish, white chrome frame finish with scroll motif engraving pattern, 6 lbs. 10 oz.-7 lbs. 14 oz. New 2017.

	100%	98%	95%	90%	80%	70%	60%	LAST MSR
MSR $1,329	$1,130	$990	$850	$775	$625	$510	$445	

Add $40 for 28 ga. or .410 bore.
Add $800 for 28 ga. and .410 bore combo.

Youth model 12 or 20 ga., 26 in. barrel is available at no extra charge.

MODEL 700 TRAP GRADE – 12 ga., similar to Model 600 Trap, except more engraving, better grade wood, wide rib. Mfg. 1969-75.

	100%	98%	95%	90%	80%	70%	60%	LAST MSR
	$1,300	$1,125	$975	$875	$715	$585	$450	

MODEL 700 DOUBLES GUN – 12 ga., similar to Model 700 Trap, except choked for 21 yd. and 30 yd. targets. Mfg. 1973-75.

	100%	98%	95%	90%	80%	70%	60%	LAST MSR
	$1,300	$1,125	$975	$875	$715	$585	$450	

MODEL 700 SKEET GRADE – similar to Model 700 Doubles, only bored S&S, available in 12 or 20 ga. Disc.

	100%	98%	95%	90%	80%	70%	60%	LAST MSR
	$1,300	$1,125	$975	$875	$715	$585	$450	

GRADING - PPGS™	100%	98%	95%	90%	80%	70%	60%	LAST MSR

MODEL 720 FIELD – 12, 20, 28 ga., .410 bore, or 28 ga./.410 bore set (28 in. barrel only), 2 3/4 (set) or 3 in. chamber, chrome moly steel boxlock receiver, 26, 28, or 30 (12 ga. only) in. VR high polished blued barrels, auto ejector, Turkish walnut, polyurethane finish stock and forend, integral safety, white chrome finish w/laser engraved waterfowl game scenes, accented with gold and scroll, 6 lbs. 8 oz.-7 lbs. New 2021.

MSR $1,530	$1,300	$1,140	$975	$885	$700	$600	$510	

Add $800 for 28 ga./.410 bore set.

20 ga., 26 in. youth model available at no extra cost.

MODEL 785 FIELD – 12, 20, 28 ga., or .410 bore, silver Nitride engraved receiver, 3 in. chambers, 26 or 28 in. barrels (supplied with choke tubes), similar to 585 Series, except has chrome-lined bores on all models and also includes lengthened forcing cones with extended length "Competition Series" Inter-Choke System designed to improve shot patterns and reduce recoil, SST, ejectors, checkered walnut stock with recoil pad and forearm, 6 lbs. 10 oz.-7 lbs. 11 oz. Imported 1995-2002.

	$1,900	$1,650	$1,400	$1,150	$1,000	$900	$800	*$2,119*

Add 10% for 28 ga. or .410 bore.

* ***Model 785 Field Set*** – includes 12/20, 20/28 ga., 28 ga./.410 bore, 26 or 28 in. VR barrels with SKB Inter-Choke system (on 12 and 20 ga.), silver nitride receiver with finely engraved scroll game scenes, low profile receiver, crossbolt locking system, SST, ejectors, manual safety, checkered high gloss American walnut stock and forearm. Importation disc. 2002.

	$2,680	$2,300	$1,925	$1,600	$1,500	$1,375	$1,275	*$3,019*

Add $100 for 20/28 ga. set or 28 ga./.410 bore set.

* ***Model 785 Medallion*** – 12, 20, or 28 ga., 3 in. chambers, features inlaid medallions in gold or bronze finish (medallion artwork by Ron Van Gilder and Rocky Capece), very limited production. Mfg. 2000-2005.

	$2,075	$1,750	$1,450	$1,175	$1,050	$925	$825	*$2,389*

Add 10% for 28 ga.

* ***Model 785 Trap*** – 12 ga., 30 or 32 in. choke tube barrels with or w/o Monte Carlo stock, high rib. Importation disc. 2002.

	$1,940	$1,625	$1,365	$1,125	$995	$895	$800	*$2,199*

Add $880 for O/U Trap Combo.

The above Combo includes one set of O/U Trap barrels and a top single Trap barrel.

* ***Model 785 Skeet*** – 12, 20, 28 ga., or .410 bore, 28 or 30 (12 ga. only) in. barrels with multi-chokes. Importation disc. 2002.

	$1,940	$1,625	$1,365	$1,125	$995	$895	$800	*$2,199*

Add 10% for 28 ga. or .410 bore.

* ***Model 785 3-Ga. Skeet Set*** – includes 20, 28 ga., and .410 bore fitted 28 in. barrel sets with individual forends, aluminum case. Importation disc. 2002.

	$3,835	$2,975	$2,350	$2,000	$1,600	$1,400	$1,295	*$4,439*

* ***Model 785 Sporting Clays*** – 12, 20, or 28 ga., 28 in. (all gauges), 30 in. (12 ga. only), or 32 in. (12 ga. only) multi-choke barrels, dimensioned for Sporting Clays competition with 12mm narrow rib. Importation disc. 2002.

	$2,000	$1,675	$1,375	$1,150	$995	$895	$800	*$2,269*

Add 10% for 28 ga.

» ***Model 785 Sporting Clays Set*** – includes 2 sets of barrels (12 ga. - 30 in., 20 ga. - 28 in.). Imported 1996-2002.

	$2,775	$2,450	$2,125	$1,825	$1,625	$1,400	$1,200	*$3,149*

MODEL 800 TRAP GRADE – 12 ga., similar to Model 700 Trap, except more engraving, better grade wood, wide rib. Limited mfg. 1969-1975.

	$1,500	$1,300	$1,125	$1,025	$825	$675	$525	

MODEL 800 SKEET GRADE – 12 or 20 ga., skeet chokes. Mfg. 1969-1975.

	$1,500	$1,300	$1,125	$1,025	$825	$675	$525	

MODEL 880 CROWN GRADE – 12, 20, 28 ga., or .410 bore, coin finished receiver, extensively engraved sideplates, SST, ejectors, select walnut with fleur-de-lis scroll style checkering, double crossbolt action. Limited mfg. Disc. 1980.

	$2,000	$1,825	$1,625	$1,300	$1,150	$975	$890	

Add 25% for 28 ga. or .410 bore (extremely rare).

GRADING - PPGS™	100%	98%	95%	90%	80%	70%	60%	LAST MSR

MODEL 885 – available in Field, Skeet, or Trap configuration, coin finished boxlock action with sideplates, fine scroll engraving with game scenes, beginning 1992 the 885 Series in 12 ga. featured lengthened forcing cones, .735 in. bore, and a competition series of extended length multi-choke tubes. Imported 1988-94.

* ***Model 885 Field*** – 12, 20, 28 ga., or .410 bore, field dimensions, 26 or 28 in. barrels include choke tubes. Imported 1989-94.

$2,100	$1,825	$1,575	$1,425	$1,150	$950	$725	*$1,895*

Add 10% for 28 ga. or .410 bore.

* ***Model 885 Trap*** – 12 ga., 30 or 32 in. barrels with multi-chokes, standard or Monte Carlo stock. Disc.

$2,100	$1,825	$1,575	$1,425	$1,150	$950	$725	*$1,949*

Add $700 for O/U Trap Combo.

The above Combo included one set of O/U Trap barrels and a top single Trap barrel.

* ***Model 885 Skeet*** – 12, 20, 28 ga., or .410 bore, 28 or 30 (12 ga. only - new 1994) in. barrels with multi-chokes. Disc.

$2,100	$1,825	$1,575	$1,425	$1,150	$950	$725	*$1,949*

Add 10% for 28 ga. or .410 bore.

* ***Model 885 Field Set*** – includes 12/20, 20/28 ga., 28 ga./.410 bore 26 or 28 (new 1994) in. VR barrels with SKB Inter-Choke system (on 12 and 20 ga.), silver nitride receiver with finely engraved scroll game scenes, low profile receiver, crossbolt locking system, SST, ejectors, manual safety, checkered high gloss American walnut stock and forearm. Disc.

$2,800	$2,450	$2,100	$1,900	$1,525	$1,250	$975

* ***Model 885 3-Ga. Skeet Set*** – includes 20, 28 ga., and .410 bore fitted 28 in. barrel sets with individual forends, aluminum case. Disc.

$4,000	$3,500	$3,000	$2,725	$2,200	$1,800	$1,400	*$3,595*

* ***Model 885 Sporting Clays*** – 28 (all gauges), 30 (12 ga. only), or 32 (12 ga. only) in. multi-choke barrels, dimensioned for Sporting Clays competition, 3/8 in. narrow rib became available 1994.

$2,100	$1,825	$1,575	$1,425	$1,150	$950	$725	*$1,949*

MODEL 5600 – 12 ga. only, 26, 28 and 30 in. barrels available as Trap or Skeet only, boxlock action, VR and ventilated barrels, ejectors, mechanical trigger, no barrel selector, blued receiver no engraving select walnut. Imported 1980-1981.

$1,200	$1,050	$900	$815	$650	$550	$425

MODEL 5700 – 12 ga. only, 26, 28, or 30 in. barrels available as Trap or Skeet only, boxlock action, VR and ventilated barrels, ejectors, mechanical trigger, no barrel selector, receiver has a nitride case hardened finish with hand engraved game scene and scroll pattern, select walnut. Imported 1980-1981.

$1,600	$1,400	$1,200	$1,095	$875	$725	$550

MODEL 5800 – 12 ga. only 26, 28 and 30 inch barrels available as Trap or Skeet only, boxlock action, VR and ventilated barrels, ejectors, mechanical trigger, no barrel selector, receiver has a nitride case hardened finish with a lavish hand engraved scroll pattern, select walnut with ivory grip cap. Imported 1980-1981.

$2,500	$2,195	$1,875	$1,700	$1,375	$1,125	$875

* ***Model 5800 Custom Deluxe*** – 12 ga. only, 26, 28 and 30 inch barrels available as Trap or Skeet only, boxlock action, VR, and ventilated barrels, ejectors, mechanical trigger, no barrel selector, receiver has a nitride case hardened or blue finish with a lavish hand engraved scroll and 24kt gold game scene inlays pattern, select walnut with ivory. Very limited importation 1984.

$5,000	$4,375	$3,750	$3,400	$2,750	$2,250	$1,750

GC 7 GAME BIRD SERIES – 12, 20, 28 ga., or .410 bore, 3 in. chambers (except 28 ga.), low profile boxlock action, Greener crossbolt, silver nitride finished receiver with scroll engraving, 26 or 28 in. monobloc barrels, lengthened forcing cones, Briley F2 choke tubes, top vent. rib, SST, inertia (12 or 20 ga.), or mechanical (28 ga. or .410 bore) trigger, Grade I, II, or III checkered American black walnut stock and forearm, black Pachmayr or plastic recoil pad. Mfg. 2009-2010.

$1,395	$1,200	$995	$850	$700	$600	$525	*$1,569*

Add $90 for 28 ga. or .410 bore.
Add $250 for Grade II.
Add $630 for Grade III.

GRADING - PPGS™	100%	98%	95%	90%	80%	70%	60%	LAST MSR

* ***GC 7 Game Bird Youth & Ladies*** – 12 or 20 ga., 3 in. chambers, low profile boxlock action, Greener crossbolt, silver nitride finished receiver with scroll engraving, 26 or 28 in. monobloc barrels, lengthened forcing cones, Briley F2 choke tubes, top vent. rib, SST, inertia (12 or 20 ga.) trigger, standard or deluxe checkered American black walnut stock and forearm, black Pachmayr or plastic recoil pad. Mfg. 2009-2010.

	100%	98%	95%	90%	80%	70%	60%	LAST MSR
	$1,395	$1,200	$995	$850	$700	$600	$525	*$1,569*

Add $250 for Grade II.
Add $630 for Grade III.

* ***GC 7 Game Bird Multi-Gauge Set*** – includes 12 and 20 ga., 20 and 28 ga., or 28 ga. and .410 bore 28 in. barrel sets. Disc. 2010.

	100%	98%	95%	90%	80%	70%	60%	LAST MSR
	$2,375	$2,100	$1,800	$1,500	$1,250	$1,000	$850	*$2,629*

Add $300 for Grade II.
Add $820 for Grade III.
Add $90 for 28 ga. or .410 bore.

GC 7 CLAYS SERIES – 12, 20, 28 ga., or .410 bore, 3 in. chambers (except 28 ga.), low profile boxlock action, ejectors, Greener crossbolt, silver nitride finished receiver with game scene engraving, 28, 30, or 32 in. monobloc barrels, lengthened forcing cones, Briley F2 choke tubes, top vent. rib, SST, inertia (12 or 20 ga.), or mechanical (28 ga. or .410 bore) trigger, fixed or adj. comb Grade I, II, or III checkered American black walnut stock and forearm, black Pachmayr recoil pad. Mfg. 2009-2010.

	100%	98%	95%	90%	80%	70%	60%	LAST MSR
	$1,495	$1,275	$1,050	$850	$725	$600	$550	*$1,679*

Add $100 for 28 ga.
Add $420 for adj. comb.
Add $600 for Grade II.
Add $870 for Grade III.

* ***GC 7 Clays 2 Barrel Set*** – includes 12 and 20 ga., 20 and 28 ga., or 28 ga. and .410 bore 30 in. barrel sets. Disc. 2010.

	100%	98%	95%	90%	80%	70%	60%	LAST MSR
	$3,150	$2,800	$2,475	$2,150	$1,800	$1,500	$1,250	*$3,449*

Add $100 for 20 and 28 ga. or 28 ga. and .410 bore.
Add $450 for Grade II.
Add $600 for Grade III.

* ***GC 7 Clays 3 Barrel Set*** – includes 20, 28 ga. and .410 bore with choice of 28 or 30 in. barrel sets. Disc. 2010.

	100%	98%	95%	90%	80%	70%	60%	LAST MSR
	$4,800	$4,200	$3,600	$3,265	$2,625	$2,150	$1,675	*$4,999*

Add $200 for adj. comb.
Add $400 for Grade III.

GC 7 TRAP SERIES – 12 ga., 30, 32, or 34 in. barrels, Briley X2 extended choke tubes, top vent. rib, fixed or adj. comb Grade II or III checkered American black walnut stock and forearm, black Pachmayr XLT recoil pad. Mfg. 2009-2010.

* ***GC 7 Trap Top Single*** – 32 in. barrels, 13 1/2 in. LOP, adj. comb Grade I stock. Disc. 2010.

	100%	98%	95%	90%	80%	70%	60%	LAST MSR
	$1,425	$1,200	$1,000	$825	$700	$575	$475	*$1,599*

* ***GC 7 Trap Un-Single*** – 32 or 34 in. barrels, fixed or adj. comb Grade II/III stock. Disc. 2010.

	100%	98%	95%	90%	80%	70%	60%	LAST MSR
	$2,450	$2,125	$1,800	$1,500	$1,250	$995	$850	*$2,799*

Add $200 for adj. comb.
Add $400 for Grade III.

* ***GC 7 Trap Un-Single Combo*** – includes 30, 32, or 34 in. barrels, adj. comb Grade II/III stock. Disc. 2010.

	100%	98%	95%	90%	80%	70%	60%	LAST MSR
	$3,650	$3,300	$2,950	$2,600	$2,200	$1,800	$1,475	*$4,049*

Add $400 for Grade III.

SHOTGUNS: O/U, DETACHABLE TRIGGER MODELS

SKB began producing the detachable trigger models in 1984 with very limited importation into the U.S. market These Models included the 4000, 5100, 5500, 5700D, 5800D 5900D 5000, 6000, 8000 and the Medalist. These models and the MJ series were primarily exported to Europe.

MEDALIST – 12 ga. only, 30 and 32 in. barrels, choke tube barrels available as Sporting Clays only, boxlock action, VR, ejectors, and ventilated barrels, mechanical trigger, no barrel selector, silver nitride finished frame, hand engraved scroll, detachable trigger, select walnut. Only eight pieces imported in 2009.

	100%	98%	95%	90%	80%	70%	60%	LAST MSR
	$4,000	$3,500	$3,000	$2,725	$2,200	$1,800	$1,400	*$4,200*

Add $300 for additional trigger group.

GRADING - PPGS™	100%	98%	95%	90%	80%	70%	60%	LAST MSR

MODEL 4000 – 12 ga. only, boxlock action, 26, 28 and 30 inch barrels, fixed choke, available as Trap or Skeet only, VR, ejectors, and ventilated barrels, mechanical trigger, no barrel selector, silver nitride finished frame, hand engraved scroll, detachable trigger select walnut. Very limited importation.

$3,200 $2,800 $2,400 $2,175 $1,750 $1,425 $1,125 ***$3,500***

Add $300 for additional trigger group.
Add $200 for choke tube barrels.

MODEL 5000 – 12 ga. only, boxlock action w/sideplates, 26, 28 and 30 in. barrels available as Trap, Skeet and Sporting Clays, VR and ventilated barrels, mechanical trigger, no barrel selector, silver nitride finished frame, hand engraved scroll, detachable trigger, select walnut. Very limited importation.

$5,000 $4,375 $3,750 $3,400 $2,750 $2,250 $1,750 ***$5,500***

Add $300 for additional trigger group.
Add $200 for choke tube barrels.

MODEL 5100 – 12 ga. only, boxlock action, 26, 28 and 30 in. ventilated barrels available as Trap or Skeet only, VR, ejectors, detachable mechanical trigger, no barrel selector, silver nitride finished frame, hand engraved scroll, select walnut. Very limited importation.

$3,200 $2,800 $2,400 $2,175 $1,750 $1,425 $1,125 ***$3,500***

Add $300 for additional trigger group.
Add $200 for choke tube barrels.

SHOTGUNS: SxS

Ithaca Gun Company imported the Models 100, 150, 200E, and 280 from 1967 to 1977. These SxS were available in 12 and 20 ga. only and featured 25 to 30 in. barrels with fixed chokes, and all were boxlock actions. The more expensive models differ in the amount of engraving, grade of walnut, style of checkering.

Mitsui Trading Company imported the Models 100, 200, 280, 300, 400 and 480 from 1979 to 1981.

G. U. Inc. imported the Model 200, 200E, 400, 400E, 385 and 485 from 1989 to 2004. These SxS models all had silver nitride (coin) finished receiver and choke tube barrels. The Model 200, 200E, 400 and 400E were produced in 1989 only. The 385 and 485 were produced from 1996 -2004.

Add approx. 10% for NIB condition on the following models.

ROYAL DELUXE – 12 ga., 2 3/4 in. chambers, 26, 28 or 30 in. barrels with fixed chokes and swamped rib, the base model was fitted with ejectors, double triggers, beavertail forend and pistol grip stock, receiver was hand engraved with a game scene. Special Order models included: Trap and Skeet and Heavy Duck with 3 in. chamber. Imported by Stoeger Arms Corporation 1960-1961.

$1,400 $1,225 $1,050 $950 $775 $625 $495

Add 15% for ejectors.
Add 15% for SST.
Add 15% for solid VR.
Add 15% for floating VR.
Add 10% for custom engraving.

MODEL 100 – 12 or 20 ga, SST, extractors, chrome barrels, splinter forend, pistol grip stock, light scroll engraving. The Mitsui imports had a game scene engraving pattern and beavertail forends.

$1,050 $925 $795 $715 $575 $475 $375

Add 20% for 20 ga.
Add 10% for NIB condition.
Add 10% for fully engraved receiver with pheasant, or duck/quail and dog game scene if in 98%+ condition.

MODEL 150 – 12 or 20 ga, SST, extractors, chrome barrels, beavertail forend, pistol grip stock, and scroll engraving. Mfg. from 1972-1974.

$1,050 $925 $795 $715 $575 $475 $375

Add 20% for 20 ga.
Add 10% for NIB condition.

MODEL 200/200E – 12 or 20 ga, gold SST, ejectors, chrome-lined barrels, beavertail forend, pistol grip stock, early models had a blued frame with hand cut scroll engraving, the later models were acid etched engraved with German silver plating. The Mitsui models were similar to the later Ithaca models.

$1,400 $1,225 $1,050 $950 $775 $625 $495

Add 20% for 20 ga.
Add 10% for NIB condition.

GRADING - PPGS™	100%	98%	95%	90%	80%	70%	60%	LAST MSR

MODEL 200/200E (RECENT MFG.) – 12 or 20 ga., scalloped boxlock action with silver nitride (coin) finished with a game scene engraving pattern, gold SST, ejectors, and beavertail forend. Model 200 featured a pistol grip stock, the Model 200E had an English straight stock, choke tube barrels. Very limited production, imported by G.U. Inc. in 1989.

$1,750 $1,525 $1,300 $1,195 $950 $795 $600 *$895*

Add 10% for NIB condition.

Add 20% for 20 ga models.

MODEL 200 FIELD (RECENT MFG.) – 12, 20, 28 ga. or .410 bore, boxlock, 26, 28, or 30 in. chrome-lined barrels with high luster deep blue finish, thin wall Teague style choke tubes (20 and 28 ga. only), auto ejectors, non-selectable single trigger, Grade II Turkish walnut Prince of Wales stock with checkered butt, oil finished beavertail forend, manual safety, bison bone charcoal color casing on receiver, forend metal piece, and trigger guard, 5 lbs. 8 oz.-7 lbs. 9 oz. Imported 2014-2019.

$1,875 $1,650 $1,450 $1,250 $1,050 $900 $700 *$2,100*

Add $150 for 28 ga. or .410 bore.

Add $1,100 for 28 ga. and .410 bore Combo (new 2016).

MODEL 200 HR TARGET (SPORTING) – 12, 20, 28 ga., or .410 bore, 28, 30, or 32 in. target barrels with raised VR, Teague style thin wall chokes (20 and 28 ga. only), ejectors, SST, target sights, select checkered and oil finished Turkish walnut pistol grip stock, Schnabel forend, Pachmayr SC100 sporting pad, V springs, right or left-hand configuration, scalloped bone charcoal case hardened colored hand engraved receiver. Imported 2014-2019.

$2,250 $1,950 $1,725 $1,500 $1,250 $995 $850 *$2,500*

Add $125 for 28 ga. or .410 bore.

Add $1,100 for 28 ga. and .410 bore Combo (new 2016).

MODEL 250 FIELD – 20, 28 ga., or .410 bore, similar to Model 200 Field, except has bison bone charcoal case hardening and hand engraved sculpted sideplate receiver. Imported 2014-2019.

$2,325 $2,000 $1,750 $1,500 $1,250 $995 $850 *$2,600*

Add $125 for 28 ga. or .410 bore.

Add $1,100 for 28 ga. and .410 bore combo (new 2016).

MODEL 280 – 12 or 20 ga, gold SST, ejectors, chrome barrels, beavertail forend, English straight grip stock, blued receiver with hand cut game scene with scroll engraving wrapping around receiver. The Mitsui models were similar to the later Ithaca models.

$1,400 $1,225 $1,050 $950 $775 $625 $495

Add 20% for 20 ga.

Add 10% for NIB condition.

MODEL 300 – 12 or 20 ga, gold SST, ejectors, chrome-lined barrels, beavertail forend, and pistol grip stock, frames are etched with a Florentine scroll pattern plated with German silver, barrel monobloc is engraved with scroll.

$1,450 $1,275 $1,095 $975 $800 $650 $500

Add 20% for 20 ga.

Add 10% for NIB condition.

MODEL 385 FIELD – 12 (new 1998), 20, or 28 ga., scalloped boxlock action with silver nitride receiver, engraved scroll and game scene designs, SST, ejectors, automatic safety, semi-fancy gloss or matte finished American walnut, English or pistol grip stock, beavertail or satin finished splinter forearm. Imported 1992-2004.

$2,200 $1,925 $1,650 $1,495 $1,200 $995 $775 *$2,049*

* ***Model 385 Field Set*** – includes a pair of 20 and 28 ga., 26 or 28 in. barrels, choice of pistol grip or English straight stock with high gloss or matte finish, beavertail or splinter forearm. Imported 1992-2004.

$3,200 $2,800 $2,400 $2,175 $1,750 $1,425 $1,125 *$2,929*

* ***Model 385 Field DU Commemorative*** – features gold inlaid mallards on both receiver sides and gold inlaid DU duck head on receiver bottom, includes hard shell case, and signed letter from SKB president, DU serial number, includes pair of 20 and 28 ga. 26 in. barrels, pistol grip stock, beavertail forearm, high gloss finish. Imported 1992.

$4,200 $3,675 $3,150 N/A N/A N/A N/A *$5,000*

This model was a DU "Collectors Series" gun.

* ***Model 385 Field Sporting Clays*** – 12, 20 (new 2000), or 28 (new 2000) ga., 3 in. chambers (12 ga.), 28 or 30 (new 2003) in. barrels with raised VR and double bead sights, pistol grip stock, beavertail forearm, approx. 7 1/2 lbs. Imported 1998-2004.

$2,300 $2,000 $1,725 $1,550 $1,250 $1,025 $800 *$2,159*

GRADING - PPGS™	100%	98%	95%	90%	80%	70%	60%	LAST MSR

» **Model 385 Field Sporting Clays Set** – includes a pair of 20 and 28 ga., 28 or 30 (new 2003) in. barrels. pistol grip stock, beavertail forearm, high gloss or matte finish. Imported 1992-2004.

	$3,200	$2,800	$2,400	$2,175	$1,750	$1,425	$1,125	*$3,059*

MODEL 400 – 12 or 20 ga, gold SST, ejectors, chrome barrels, beavertail forend, pistol grip stock, receivers are etched with a Florentine scroll pattern plated with German silver, barrel monobloc is extensively engraved with matching scroll, presentation grade walnut with 24 line checkering.

	$1,800	$1,575	$1,350	$1,225	$995	$800	$625	

Add 20% for 20 ga.
Add 10% for NIB condition.

MODEL 400/400E (RECENT MFG.) – 12 or 20 ga, boxlock action with sideplates, silver nitride (coin) finished with game scene engraving patterns, gold SST, ejectors, and beavertail forend, choke tube barrels. Model 400 featured a pistol grip stock, the Model 400E had an English straight stock. Very limited production, imported by G.U. Inc. in 1989.

	$2,000	$1,750	$1,500	$1,350	$1,100	$900	$700	*$1,195*

Add 10% for NIB condition.
Add 20% for 20 ga. models.

MODEL 480 (ENGLISH) – 12 or 20 ga, moderately engraved coin finished receiver, gold SST, ejectors, English straight stock, floorplate, trigger guard and top lever were a black chrome finish.

	$1,800	$1,575	$1,350	$1,225	$995	$800	$625	

Add 20% for 20 ga.
Add 10% for NIB condition.

MODEL 485 FIELD – 12 (new 1998), 20 or 28 ga., sideplate boxlock action with silver nitride finish, engraved upland game scene designs, 26 or 28" barrels with raised VR rib SST, ejectors, automatic safety, semi-fancy American walnut in either high gloss or matte finish (new 2002), English or pistol grip stock, beavertail or splinter forearm. Imported 1997-2004.

	$2,900	$2,525	$2,175	$1,975	$1,595	$1,300	$1,000	*$2,769*

* ***Model 485 Field Set*** – includes a pair of 20 and 28 ga., 26 or 28 in. barrels, choice of pistol grip or English straight stock, beavertail or splinter forearm, high gloss or matte finish, very limited production. Imported 1998-2004.

	$4,200	$3,675	$3,150	$2,850	$2,300	$1,895	$1,475	*$3,949*

MODEL 7000 SL SIDELOCK – 12 or 20 ga., H&H style action with 7 pin removable sidelocks with safety sears, 28 or 30 in. bright blue chrome-lined barrels, thin wall Teague style choke tubes, single trigger, Grade III Turkish walnut Prince of Wales stock, grip areas and butt end are hand checkered and finished with hand rubbed oil, beavertail forearm, pistol grip, hand engraved sculpted sidelock receiver with bone charcoal color case hardened finish, 6 lbs. 12 oz.-7 lbs. 6 oz. Importation began mid-2014.

MSR $6,500	$5,525	$4,850	$4,150	$3,750	$3,050	$2,495	$1,950	

SHOTGUNS: SEMI-AUTO

HS300 FIELD – 12 or 20 ga., 3 in. chamber, inertia bolt w/gas operation, 26 or 28 in. VR barrel with choke tubes, choice of checkered walnut or 100% field camo finish stock and forearm, right or left-hand ejection port, approx. 7 lbs. New 2017.

MSR $799	$680	$600	$500	$450	$375	$300	$265	

Add $40 for 100% field camo coverage.

IS300 FIELD/IS300 TARGET – 12 ga. only, 3 in. chamber, inertia system with rotating bolt, 26, 28 (disc.), or 30 in. VR barrel with competition choke tube system, choice of black synthetic, 100% camo, or walnut stock and forearm, includes shims for stock adjustments, 6 lbs. 15 oz. Imported 2014-2017.

	$525	$475	$425	$400	$375	$325	$300	*$625*

Add $90 for 100% camo finish or checkered walnut stock and forearm.
Add $245 for Target Model w/adj. comb.

MODEL 300 STANDARD – 12 or 20 ga., 3 in. chamber, recoil operated, 26 in. imp. cyl., 28 in. mod., or 30 in. full plain barrel, checkered pistol grip stock. Mfg. 1968-72.

	$350	$300	$265	$240	$195	$160	$125	

MODEL 900 STANDARD – 12 or 20 ga., 3 in. chamber, recoil operated, similar to Model 300 standard, except has vent. rib. barrel. Mfg. 1968-1972.

	$350	$300	$265	$240	$195	$160	$125	

GRADING - PPGS™	100%	98%	95%	90%	80%	70%	60%	LAST MSR

MODEL 1300 UPLAND – 12 or 20 ga., 3 in. chamber, gas operated, 22, 26, or 28 in. VR barrel with multi-chokes, matte black receiver, checkered walnut stock and forearm. Importation resumed 1988-96.

	$550	$475	$415	$375	$300	$250	$195	*$495*

This model was previously designated the Model XL-300. The new Model 1300 was available in Slug configuration with 22 in. barrel/iron sights at no extra charge. Recent Model 1300s have a magazine cutoff system on front left side of frame.

MODEL 1900 – 12 or 20 ga., 3 in. chamber, gas operated, 22, 26, or 28 in. VR barrel with multi-chokes, deluxe outdoor field scene etched on receiver, gold trigger, approx. 1,000-2,000 mfg. per year. Importation disc. 1996.

	$585	$510	$440	$400	$325	$265	$200	*$545*

This model was previously designated the Model XL 900. The Model 1900 was available in Slug configuration with 22 in. barrel and iron sights or Trap Model at no extra charge. Recent Model 1900s have a magazine cutoff system on front left side of frame.

MODEL 3000 – 12 or 20 ga., 3 in. chamber, gas operated, (shoots both 2 3/4 and 3 in. shells interchangeably) with semi-squareback styling, elaborate game scenes etched on both sides of receiver, deluxe checkered walnut stock and forearm. Imported 1988-90.

	$650	$575	$495	$440	$360	$295	$225	*$597*

Add $50 for Trap model (2 3/4 in. chamber).

This model has not previously been imported in this configuration.

RS300 TARGET – 12 ga., 3 in. chamber, 28 or 30 in. VR barrel, competition chokes, checkered walnut stock and forearm with adj. comb, buttplate, drop, and gas assisted Hybrid Recoil System (RS), right or left hand configuration, 7 lbs. 12 oz. Importation began 2014.

MSR $1,139	$975	$850	$725	$675	$550	$450	$375

Available as youth model, 12 (26 or 28 in. bbl.) or 20 (28 in. bbl. only) ga., at no additional cost.

RS400T – 12 ga., 3 in. chamber, 28 or 30 in. VR barrels, competition chokes, checkered walnut stock and forend with adjustable comb and buttplate system, parallel comb stock, and gas assisted Hybrid Recoil System (RS), also available in youth model, with 13 in. LOP and left eject models. Importation began in 2019.

MSR $1,139	$975	$850	$725	$675	$550	$450	$375

XL 300 – 12 or 20 ga., 2 3/4 (12 ga.) or 3 (20 ga.) in. chamber, gas operated, white alloy receiver with light game scene etching, 4 shot mag., 26-30 in. plain barrel. Disc.

	$375	$325	$275	$250	$200	$175	$125

XL 900 – similar to XL 300, except has vent. rib barrel and no recoil pad, 6 1/4 lbs. Disc.

	$400	$350	$300	$275	$225	$180	$140

XL 900 MR – 12 ga. only, gas operated, 26-30 in. barrel, 5 shot, alloy receiver, engraved game bird scroll work on receiver, shoots both 2 3/4 and 3 in. shells by interchanging barrels. Disc. 1980.

	$400	$350	$300	$275	$225	$180	$140

XL 900 TRAP GRADE – similar to XL 900 MR, 12 ga. only, scroll engraved black chrome receiver, 30 in. imp. mod. or full barrel, trap style stock, straight or Monte Carlo, recoil pad. Mfg. 1980-disc.

	$400	$350	$300	$275	$225	$180	$140

XL 900 SKEET GRADE – similar to XL 900 MR, except scroll engraved black chrome receiver, 26 in. barrel, skeet stock. Mfg. 1972-disc.

	$400	$350	$300	$275	$225	$180	$140

XL 900 SLUG GUN – similar to XL 900 MR, except 24 in. slug barrel, rifle sights, no rib. Mfg. 1972-disc.

	$400	$350	$300	$275	$225	$180	$140

SHOTGUNS: SINGLE BARREL, TRAP

95ATR TRAP COMBO – 12 ga., 3 in. chamber, 30/32 (youth model), 30/34, or 32/34 in. VR barrel/unsingle barrel combination w/adj. rib, Hi Viz comp. sight, checkered walnut stock with right or left hand configuration, adj. comb stock and 5-way buttplate, Pachmayr XLT recoil pad, Negrini Hard Case., brushed white chrome finish with laser engraving, approx. 8 lbs. 12 oz. Importation began 2019.

MSR $3,670	$3,125	$2,730	$2,340	$2,125	$1,710	$1,400	$1,225

MODEL 505 TRAP – 12 ga., 32 or 34 in. barrel with multi-chokes, regular or Monte Carlo stock. Disc.

	$875	$725	$650	$525	$475	$430	$395	*$995*

MODEL 605 TRAP – 12 ga., 32 or 34 in. barrel with multi-chokes. Disc.

	$1,075	$850	$750	$675	$575	$500	$450	*$1,195*

GRADING - PPGS™	100%	98%	95%	90%	80%	70%	60%	LAST MSR

CENTURY TRAP – 12 ga., 32 or 34 in. VR barrel, engraved, auto ejector, full choke, checkered walnut stock. Mfg. 1973 and 1976.

	$750	$650	$550	$500	$425	$350	$275	

This model was imported by Ithaca.

CENTURY II TRAP – improved trap stock version of Century, Monte Carlo stock. Disc.

	$600	$550	$495	$470	$415	$385	$350	

This model was imported by Ithaca.

CENTURY III TRAP – 12 ga., 2 3/4 in. chamber, boxlock action, jeweled monobloc, right or left-hand action, 30 or 32 in. VR barrel with competition choke tube, shell extractor, gold trigger, target sights, fixed comb (disc. 2015), adj. comb, or adj. comb and buttplate, standard or Monte Carlo oil finished Grade II checkered walnut stock and forearm with Pachmayr XLT buttpad, manual top tang safety, available in youth configuration with 13 in. LOP, bright blue or white chrome finish. Imported 2014-2016.

	$1,295	$1,050	$900	$750	$600	$550	$495	*$1,470*

Add $70 for white chrome finish.

Subtract $170 if without adj. comb and buttplate.

CENTURY III TRAP (CURRENT MFG.) – 12 ga., 2 3/4 in. chamber, boxlock action, jeweled monobloc, right or left-hand action, 30, 32, or 34 in. VR barrel with matte black chrome exterior, competition choke tubes, lengthened forcing cone, steel receiver, shell extractor, gold trigger, target sights, standard or adj. comb and buttplate, checkered walnut stock and forearm with Pachmayr XLT buttpad, manual top tang safety, available in youth configuration with 13 1/2 in. LOP, white chrome finish, 8 lbs. 4 oz. Importation began 2018.

MSR $1,640	$1,395	$1,225	$1,050	$950	$775	$625	$550	

SHOTGUNS: SLIDE ACTION

MODEL 7300 – 12 or 20 ga., 2 3/4 or 3 in. chambers, blue only, hand checkered French walnut stock, twin action slide bars. Disc. 1980.

	$350	$300	$265	$240	$195	$160	$125	

MODEL 7900 – trap or skeet variation of the Model 7300. Disc.

	$350	$300	$265	$240	$195	$160	$125	

SKS

SKS designates a semi-auto rifle design originally developed by the Russian military, and manufactured in Russia by both Tula Arsenal (1949-1956) and by Izhevsk Arsenal from 1953-1954. Currently manufactured in Russia, China, and many other countries. Previously manufactured in Russia, China (largest quantity), N. Korea, East Germany, Romania, Albania, Yugoslavia, and North Vietnam.

SKS DEVELOPMENT & HISTORY

SKS (Samozaryadnyi Karabin Simonova) - developed by Sergei Gavrilovich Simonov in the late 1940s to use the 7.62 cartridge of 1943 (7.62x39mm). The SKS is actually based on an earlier design developed by Simonov in 1936 as a prototype self-loading military rifle. The SKS was adopted by the Soviet military in 1949, two years after the AK-47, and was originally intended as a complement to the AK-47s select-fire capability. It served in this role until the mid-to-late 1950s, when it was withdrawn from active issue and sent to reserve units and Soviet Youth "Pioneer" programs. It was also released for use in military assistance programs to Soviet Bloc countries and other "friendly" governments. Much of the original SKS manufacturing equipment was shipped to Communist China prior to 1960. Since then, most of the SKS carbines produced, including those used by the Viet Cong in Vietnam, have come from China.

Like the AK-47, the Simonov carbine is a robust military rifle. It, too, was designed to be used by troops with very little formal education or training. It will operate reliably in the harshest climatic conditions, from the Russian arctic to the steamy jungles of Southeast Asia. Its chrome-lined bore is impervious to the corrosive effects of fulminate of mercury primers and the action is easily disassembled for cleaning and maintenance.

The SKS and a modified sporter called the OP-SKS (OP stands for Okhotnichnyi Patron) are the standard hunting rifles for a majority of Russian hunters. It is routinely used to take everything from the Russian saiga antelope up to and including moose, boar, and brown bear. The main difference between the regular SKS and the OP variant is in the chamber dimensions and the rate of rifling. The OP starts as a regular SKS, then has the barrel removed and replaced with one designed to specifically handle a slightly longer and heavier bullet.

Prior to the "assault weapons" ban, hundreds of thousands of SKS carbines were imported into the U.S.

GRADING - PPGS™	100%	98%	95%	90%	80%	70%	60%	LAST MSR

The SKS was rapidly becoming one of the favorites of American hunters and shooters. Its low cost and durability made it a popular "truck gun" for those shooters who spend a lot of time in the woods, whether they are ranchers, farmers, or plinkers. While the Russian made SKS is a bonafide curio and relic firearm and legal for importation, the Clinton administration suspended all import permits for firearms having a rifled bore and ammunition from the former Soviet Union in early 1994. In order to get the ban lifted, the Russian government signed a trade agreement, wherein they agreed to deny export licenses to any American company seeking SKS rifles and a variety of other firearms and ammunition deemed politically incorrect by Clinton & Gore. The BATF then used this agreement as a reason to deny import licenses for any SKS from any country.

Most of the SKS carbines imported into the U.S. came from the Peoples Republic of China. They were a mix of refurbished military issue, straight military surplus, and even some new manufacture. Quality was rather poor. Compared to the SKS Chinese carbines, only a few Russian made SKSs ever made it into the U.S. All are from military stockpiles and were refurbished at the Tula Arms Works, probably the oldest continuously operating armory in the world. Recently, more SKS carbines have been imported from the former Yugoslavia by Century International Arms. These carbines carry the former Soviet Bloc designation of "Type 58" and feature milled receivers. Quality is generally good, and values are comparable to other Russian/European SKS imports. Values for unmodified Russian and Eastern European made SKS carbines (those with the original magazines and stock) are higher than the Chinese copies.

The most collectible SKS is East German mfg., and SKS rifles mfg. in N. Korea and N. Vietnam are also quite rare in the U.S.

Over 600 million SKS carbines have been manufactured in China alone, by over 45 different manufacturers, in addition to the millions manufactured in other former Soviet Bloc countries. The Simonov carbine was the best selling semi-auto rifle in America (and other countries) during 1993-94, and remains a popular choice for plinking, hunting, and protection in the new millennium.

RIFLES: SEMI-AUTO

SKS – 7.62x39mm Russian cal., Soviet designed, original Soviet mfg. as well as copies mfg. in China, Russia, Yugoslavia, and many other countries, gas operated weapon, 10 shot fixed mag., wood stock (thumbhole design on newer mfg.), with or w/o (newer mfg.) permanently attached folding bayonet, tangent rear and hooded front sight, no current importation from China, Russia, or the former Yugoslavia.

Please refer to individual importers for other SKS listings, including Norinco, Poly-Technologies, and Mitchell Arms.

	100%	98%	95%	90%	80%	70%	60%	LAST MSR
* ***SKS Mfg. in Russia, Yugoslavia, Romania***								
	$495	$450	$375	$325	$275	$235	$195	
* ***SKS Chinese Recent Mfg. w/Thumbhole Stock***								
	$375	$325	$275	$250	$225	$200	$175	

SMI ARMS

Previous pistol and rifle manufacturer located in Merriam, KS until 2017.

For individual model listings, please go to BlueBookOfGunValues.com/overflow.

SRM ARMS

Current shotgun manufacturer located in Meridan, ID. Available through several national firearm distributors.

SHOTGUNS: SEMI-AUTO

MODEL 1216 – 12 ga., 2 3/4 or 3 in. chamber, semi-auto roller-locked delayed blowback system, 18 1/2 in. hammer forged threaded barrel with fixed choke, features a rotating detachable 16 shot mag. with four separate tubes, ambidextrous receiver with tip up action, full-length top Picatinny rail and three handguard rails, pistol grip configuration, matte black or FDE finish, 32 1/2 in. OAL, 7 1/4 lbs. New late 2011.

	100%	98%	95%	90%	80%	70%	60%	LAST MSR
MSR $1,800	$1,525	$1,350	$1,175	$1,050	$900	$775	$625	

The concept of the SRM shotgun began in the early 2000s when special forces personnel described their dream shotgun to the SRM developers. The first model was previewed in 2008, with final versions arriving late 2011.

MODEL 1228 – 12 ga., Aguila minishells (new 2018), 2 in. chamber, roller-locked delayed blowback system, pistol grip configuration, 18 1/2 in. barrel with fixed choke, rotating detachable 28 shot mag. with four separate tubes, ambidextrous receiver with tip-up action, full length top Picatinny rail and three handguard rails, matte black or FDE finish, 32.5 in. OAL, 7 1/4 lbs. New 2019.

	100%	98%	95%	90%	80%	70%	60%	LAST MSR
MSR $2,150	$1,825	$1,595	$1,375	$1,250	$1,000	$825	$650	

GRADING - PPGS™	100%	98%	95%	90%	80%	70%	60%	LAST MSR

SSK FIREARMS (SSK INDUSTRIES)

Current customizer and Class II manufacturer located in Wintersville, OH since 1977.

SSK Industries manufactures complete guns, and furnishes a wide variety of gunsmithing services.

SSK Industries manufactures complete rifles and suppressors for police, military, and civilian use (where legal in accord with BATFE regulations). Their custom shop works on virtually anything 20mm or smaller.

SSK Industries used Thompson Center flatside frames and applied an industrial hard chrome finish prior to the introduction of stainless steel receivers. Most SSK handguns and rifles are extensively customized in exotic calibers, finishes, and various engraving options. Receivers and barrels could be purchased separately - values below are for complete assembled pistols.

SSK has also manufactured various limited editions including the Handgun Hunters International (HHI) Models 1, 2, and 3. Issue prices on these guns were $1,100 (Model 3), $1,200 (Model 2), and $1,300 (Model 1). Only 50 were mfg. total in 1987. SSK also customized a Ruger Super Redhawk (.44 Mag. or .45 LC cal.). This variation came with either a scoped 7 1/2 in. octagon barrel (Beauty Model) or a 6 in. bull barrel with muzzle brake (Beast Model). Prices started at $1,430 - add $245 extra for .45 LC cal.

PISTOLS: SINGLE SHOT

Values listed are for basic models with no options or special features.

SSK-CONTENDER – over 150 cals. available from .17 Bee to .50-70, various custom barrels available, basically, this is a custom order only gun and the pricing info reflects the costs of the indiviual components.

Contender G2 actions in either stainless or blue finish are not available.

Individual barrels range in price from $537-615.

SSK ENCORE – over 400 calibers available with plain, fluted, and heavy barrels. This is a custom order only gun and the pricing info reflects the costs of the indiviual components.

Encore actions are currently available in either stainless steel w/Flex-Tech hardwood stock ($650 MSR), or Encore Stainless Pro Hunter w/grips ($495 MSR).

Individual barrels range in price from $395-$505.

SSK-XP100 – various cals. between .17 and .50, includes TSOB mount and rings.

	100%	98%	95%	90%	80%	70%	60%	LAST MSR
	$1,700	$1,500	$1,300	$1,150	$1,025	$925	$850	*$1,700*

The .50 cal. XP100 (12.9 X 50.8 JDJ) came with SSK muzzle brake, scope, dies, and new reinforced fiberglass stock.

RIFLES

Values listed are for basic models with no options or special features. In addition, SSK custom manufactures a bolt action rifle available in almost any caliber and configuration - prices start at approx. $2,000 and can go as high as $6,000, depending on the customer's individual special orders. SSK also has developed a 6.5mm, 7mm, or .30 cal. upper unit conversion for AR-15s and M-16s utilizing heavy sub-sonic "whisper" ammunition. SSK also manufactures a line of .50 cal. rifles, and a complete AR-15 starts at $1,500.

SSK TCR 87 – .14 through .500 cals., Nitro Express cals. are also available, features Thompson Center TRC 87 receiver, and SSK custom barrels, muzzle brakes, and exotic finishes were available at extra cost.

	100%	98%	95%	90%	80%	70%	60%	LAST MSR
	$1,700	$1,500	$1,300	$1,150	$1,025	$925	$850	

SSK RUGER NO. 1 – many cals. including .577 NE (optional), custom order rifle based on a Ruger No. 1 frame.

	100%	98%	95%	90%	80%	70%	60%	LAST MSR
	$2,000	$1,800	$1,600	$1,400	$1,250	$1,100	$1,000	

SSK BOLT ACTION – various cals., ground up custom order rifle.

	100%	98%	95%	90%	80%	70%	60%	LAST MSR
	$2,500	$2,250	$1,800	$1,600	$1,400	$1,250	$1,100	

STI INTERNATIONAL

Please refer to Staccato in this section.

ST. GEORGE ARMS

Current trademark of semi-auto rifles manufactured by K&M Arms with company headquarters located in Murfreesboro, TN.

For individual model listings, please go to BlueBookOfGunValues.com/overflow.

STL

Current bolt action rifle manufacturer located in Marienberg, Germany. Previously located in Heiligkreuzsteinach, Germany.

STL manufactures both hunting and match rifles in calibers from .222 Rem.-.50 BMG. Many configurations and options are available. Please contact the manufacturer directly for more information, including U.S. availability and pricing.

GRADING - PPGS™	100%	98%	95%	90%	80%	70%	60%	LAST MSR

STP (MFG. BY PROMMERSBERGER)

Current trade name manufactured by Karl Prommersberger established in 2006, located in Kühbach, Germany. No current U.S. importation.

Karl Prommersberger manufactures a line of sport target pistols under the trade name STP. Current model series include: Black Major, Dag (new 2019), Duty, Igel, Lodur (new 2019), Loki, Max Open, Monocomp, P 19 Striker Fire (new 2019), Perfect Classic, RM Series, Sentry, Sparta, Speed, Swat, TM Bomar, Walhall Polygon, Thor Fieldshooting, and Wotan. They also manufacture a line of custom made pistols built to customer specification. Please contact the company directly for more information, including U.S. availability and pricing.

SWS 2000

Previous rifle manufacturer located in Krefeld, Germany until 2010. Previously imported until 2009 by Euro-Imports, located in Yoakum, TX.

RIFLES

SWS 2000 manufactured a variety of sporting and tactical style rifles in a variety of configurations.

Prices ranged from €2,600-€3,759 for sporting and hunting models, and €6,162-€7,910 for tactical rifles.

SABATTI s.p.a.

Current manufacturer located in Gardone, Italy with history tracing back to 1674. Select rifles, shotguns, and combination guns are currently imported by the Italian Firearms Group (IFG), located in Rockledge, FL. SxS double rifles were previously imported by EAA, located in Rockledge, FL. Sabatti sub-contracts some of its models for private label sales.

In 1960, the sons of Antonio Sabatti formed the current company, and manufacture currently includes good quality O/U and SxS shotguns, O/U combination and double rifles, bolt action and semi-auto rifles, and slide action and single shot shotguns. The importers should be contacted directly regarding more information and domestic availability on their extensive firearms lineup.

COMBINATION GUNS

FOREST/FOREST STE COMBO – 12 or 20 ga. over various cals including but not limited to .223 Rem., .30-06, .308 Win., 9.3x74R, or .45-70 Govt. cal., combination gun, 24 or 25.6 in. chrome moly barrels, shotgun barrel with Fixed/Mod. chokes, CHF rifle barrel, standard triggers (Forest) or set trigger (rifle barrel only, Forest STE), oil polished pistol grip stock, checkered forearm, 7.8 lbs. Imported 2013-2016.

$1,295 $1,125 $965 $875 $700 $575 $450 *$1,514*

RIFLES: BOLT ACTION

BLIZZARD – .243, 25-06, .270 Win., 30-06, .308 Win. .300 Win. Mag., 7mm Rem. Mag., .223 Rem., or .223 Win. cal., wood or synthetic stock, with or w/o thumbhole. Imported 2018-2020.

$575 $500 $425 $395 $325 $275 $225 *$680*

Add $40 for thumbhole.

Add $75 for synthetic stock.

ROVER – various short and long action cals. from .222 Rem. to .458 Win. Mag., right or left hand action, 22-25.5 in. CHF chrome moly barrel, 3, 4, or 5 shot mag., fixed blade front sight, adj. rear sight, oil-polished walnut, synthetic wood, synthetic, or synthetic thumbhole stock, right side thumb safety, front and rear sling swivels, blued finish, 7.1-7.3 lbs.

Please contact the importer for pricing and availability on this model.

ROVER BATTUE – various short and long action cals. from .308 Win. to .300 Win. Mag., right hand action, 22-24 in. CHF chrome moly barrel, 2, 3, 4, or 5 shot mag., fixed fiber optic front sight blade, "Battue" style rear ramp rib sight, synthetic thumbhole stock, right side thumb safety, front and rear sling swivels, blued finish, 7.3 lbs.

Please contact the importer for pricing and availability on this model.

ROVER COMPACT SCOUT – .308 Win. or .30-06 cal., right hand action, 19.68 in. CHF chrome moly barrel, detachable muzzle brake (barrel threaded 1/2x20 UNF), 5 or 7 shot detachable AICS pattern mag., fixed fiber optic front sight blade, adj. rear sight, synthetic thumbhole stock w/adj. cheekpiece, right side thumb safety, front, mid, and rear sling swivels, blued finish, 7.3 lbs.

Please contact the importer for pricing and availability on this model.

ROVER CUSTOM – .243 Win., .308 Win., 6.5 Creedmoor, or .300 Win. Mag. cal. Imported 2017-2018.

$1,325 $1,150 $975 $850 $725 $600 $500 *$1,556*

GRADING - PPGS™	100%	98%	95%	90%	80%	70%	60%	LAST MSR

ROVER TRAQUER – various short and long action cals. from .308 Win. to .300 Win. Mag., right hand action, 19.68 in. CHF chrome moly barrel, 2, 3, 4, or 5 shot mag., fiber optic sights, sling swivel integrated into front sight, synthetic stock with blaze orange camouflage finish or black finish, right side thumb safety, front and rear sling swivels, blued finish, 7.3 lbs.

Please contact the importer for pricing and availability on this model.

ST17-US – 6.5 Creedmoor or .308 Win. cal., tactical configuration w/pistol grip and AR-15 adj. buttstock, black finish. Imported 2017 only.

	100%	98%	95%	90%	80%	70%	60%	LAST MSR
	$925	$825	$725	$625	$525	$425	$350	*$1,057*

ST-18 – .260 Rem. (mfg. 2019 only), .223 Rem. (new 2020), 6mm Creedmoor (new 2020), 6.5x47 Lapua, 6.5 Creedmoor, or .308 Win. cal., 20 or 24 in. CHF chrome moly threaded barrel w/muzzle brake, detachable 5 shot AICS pattern mags., no sights, Picatinny optics rail, ST-18 modular aluminum alloy chassis w/AR-15 style stock attachment, folding stock w/adj. cheekpiece and LOP, free floating KeyMod handguard, AR-15 style ergonomic grip, black finish. New 2019.

Please contact the importer for pricing and availability on this model.

STR-US – 6.5 Creedmoor, 6.5x47 Lapua, or .308 Win. cal., Sabatti signature short action, 26 in. CHF chrome moly barrel with or w/o muzzle brake, no sights, features modular folding AR-15 style stock w/adj. cheekpiece and LOP, vent. tubular forearm w/removable Picatinny rails, AR-15 style ergonomic grip, black Cerakote or Desert (mfg. 2018-2020) finish, 13.6 lbs. Importation began 2017.

	100%	98%	95%	90%	80%	70%	60%	LAST MSR
MSR $2,470	$2,100	$1,850	$1,575	$1,425	$1,150	$950	$800	

Add $635 for Desert finish (mfg. 2018-2020).

STR SPORT – 6.5 Creedmoor, 6.5x47 Lapua, .284 Shehane, .308 Win. or .300 Win. Mag. cal., Sabatti signature short or long action, 28 in. CHF chrome moly heavy profile (1.1 in. diameter) barrel, no sights, features modular AR-15 style stock w/Anschutz style bag rider rail and adj. cheekpiece and LOP, free float open-top forearm, AR-15 style ergonomic pistol grip, right side thumb safety, black or red finished chassis, 14.0 lbs. 46.9 in. OAL. Importation began 2018.

	100%	98%	95%	90%	80%	70%	60%	LAST MSR
MSR $2,535	$2,150	$1,875	$1,625	$1,475	$1,200	$975	$825	

SAPHIRE – .243 Win., 6.5 Creedmoor, 6.5x55 Swedish (SE), 308 Win., 7x57, 7x64, 7mm-08 Rem., .270 Win., 7mm Rem. SAUM, 7mm Rem. Mag., 8x57, .30-06, or .300 Win. Mag. cal., Saphire short or long action, 24 or 25.5 in. CHF chrome moly threaded barrel, 3 shot mag., with or w/o open sights, integrated Picatinny action rails, walnut, black synthetic, or synthetic thumbhole (new 2018) stock, sling swivels, 7.3-7.4 lbs. Importation began 2017.

	100%	98%	95%	90%	80%	70%	60%	LAST MSR
MSR $1,230	$1,050	$910	$780	$700	$575	$475	$400	

Add $250 for walnut stock.
Add $95 for thumbhole stock.

SAPHIRE E.R. (EXTENDED RANGE) – .243 Win., 6.5 Creedmoor, 6.5x55 Swedish (SE), 308 Win., 7x57, 7x64, 7mm-08 Rem., .270 Win., 7mm Rem. SAUM, 7mm Rem. Mag., 8x57, .30-06 Springfield, or .300 Win. Mag. cal., Saphire short or long action, 24 or 25.5 in. CHF chrome moly heavy threaded barrel, 3 shot mag., no sights, integrated Picatinny action rails, synthetic thumbhole stock w/adj. cheek riser, Picatinny bipod rail under forearm, sling swivels, 7.3-7.4 lbs.

Please contact the importer for pricing and availability on this model.

SAPHIRE TACTICAL CARBON – 6.5 Creedmoor, .308 Win., or .300 Win. Mag. cal., Saphire short or long action, 26 in. carbon fiber and Kevlar wrapped CHF chrome moly threaded barrel, 3 shot mag., no sights, integrated Picatinny action rails, synthetic fiberglass reinforced stock w/adj. cheek riser, oversized interchangeable bolt handle, 7.3-7.4 lbs.

Please contact the importer for pricing and availability on this model.

SAPHIRE VARMINT CARBON – 6.5 Creedmoor, .308 Win., or .300 Win. Mag. cal., Saphire short or long action, 26 in. carbon fiber and Kevlar wrapped CHF chrome moly threaded barrel, 3 shot mag., no sights, integrated Picatinny action rails, synthetic thumbhole stock w/adj. cheek riser, oversized interchangeable bolt handle, front, mid, and rear sling swivels, 7.3-7.4 lbs.

Please contact the importer for pricing and availability on this model.

TACTICAL-US (ROVER TACTICAL) – .223 Rem. (disc.), .308 Win., .300 Win. Mag. (disc.), 6.5x55mm (disc.), 6.5x47mm Lapua (disc.), or 6.5 Creedmoor cal., 24 or 25 1/2 (.300 Win. Mag. cal. only) in. heavy fluted barrel, checkered laminated pistol grip stock and forearm, recoil pad, match grade trigger, Desert (new 2018) finish, 11.7 lbs. Importation began 2013.

	100%	98%	95%	90%	80%	70%	60%	LAST MSR
MSR $1,295	$1,100	$965	$825	$750	$600	$500	$400	

Add $110 for Konus scope.
Add $550 for Desert finish (new 2018).

GRADING - PPGS™	100%	98%	95%	90%	80%	70%	60%	LAST MSR

TACTICAL EVO US - .308 Win., 6mm Creedmoor (new 2020), 6.5 Creedmoor (new 2020), 6.5x47 Lapua, 6.5x55 Swedish (SE), .284 Shehane (new 2020), or .300 Win. Mag. cal., 22 or 26 in. barrel, 7 shot mag., lightweight polymer stock w/adj. cheekpiece, Picatinny bipod rail, QD sling sockets, black, chrome, or Desert finish, 11.4-12.3 lbs. Importation began 2020.

Please contact the importer for pricing and availability on this model.

URBAN SNIPER - .223 Rem. (new 2020), 6.5 Creedmoor (new 2020), 6.5x47 Lapua, 7mm Rem. SAUM, or .308 Win. cal., 20 in. CHF chrome moly barrel w/muzzle brake, 10 shot mag. w/extended mag. release lever outside trigger guard, standard trigger, no sights, Picatinny optics rail, synthetic thumbhole stock w/adj. cheekpiece and LOP, Picatinny bipod rail, interchangeable tactical bolt handle, matte blued finish, 10.22 lbs. Importation began 2018.

MSR $1,220	$1,040	$910	$780	$700	$575	$475	$400	

TLD - 6.5x47 Lapua, 6.5 Creedmoor, .284 Shehane, or .308 Win. cal., 26 or 28 in. CHF chrome moly heavy barrel w/optional threading, 3 shot mag., no sights, "F-Class" benchrest style laminate stock w/adj. cheekpiece, traditional varnish laminate (TLD Gold model) or red skull hydrodip pattern finish (TLD Red model), 14.3 lbs.

Please contact the importer for pricing and availability on this model.

RIFLES: O/U

MODEL 190/195 EXPRESS (EUROPA/EUROPA EDL) - various cals. including but not limited to 9.3x74Rmm through .45-70 Govt. cal., boxlock action, 24 in. chrome moly barrels, extractors, single non selective trigger, fiber optic open sights, checkered oil polished walnut pistol grip stock and standard forearm or Schnabel style forearm and Bavarian cheekrest stock (Model 195/Europa DL), sling swivels, partial or full (Model 195/Europa DL) coverage engraving on receiver. Importation began 2017.

MSR $1,900	$1,700	$1,500	$1,300	$1,150	$950	$750	$600	

MODEL 230 EXPRESS - 9.3x74Rmm or .45-70 Govt. cal., boxlock action, extractors, single non selective trigger, Batue rib w/open sights, checkered walnut stock and forearm, sling swivels. Imported 2017-disc.

	$1,950	$1,700	$1,450	$1,300	$1,050	$850	$700	*$2,125*

MODEL 345 EXPRESS - 9.3x74Rmm or .45-70 Govt. cal., boxlock action w/engraved sideplates, extractors, single non selective trigger, open sights, checkered walnut stock and forearm, sling swivels. Imported 2017-disc.

	$2,350	$2,050	$1,750	$1,600	$1,300	$1,050	$800	*$2,595*

RIFLES: SxS

SAB92SF - .45-70 Govt. or 9.3x74Rmm (new 2010) cal., 24 in. barrels, scalloped boxlock action, extractors, drilled and tapped, walnut stock, nickel (disc.) or case colored receiver. This model was sold exclusively by Cabela's. Imported 2009-2011.

	$3,200	$2,800	$2,500	$2,100	$1,875	$1,650	$1,500	*$3,432*

* ***SAB92SF Deluxe*** - .375 H&H (disc. 2011), .416 Rigby, .450 NE, .458 Win. Mag. (disc. 2011), .45-70 Govt., .470 NE, .500 NE, or .600 NE (limited mfg. only) cal., 24 in. barrels, scalloped engraved boxlock action, ejectors or extractors, drilled and tapped, deluxe checkered walnut stock, nickel receiver, beavertail forend, this model was sold exclusively by Cabela's. Imported 2009-2012.

	$5,975	$5,300	$4,700	$4,150	$3,600	$3,050	$2,500	*$6,482*

Add $492 for ejectors.
Subtract $1,282 for .45-70 Govt. cal.

CLASSIC 92 - 7x65R, 30R Blaser, 8x57, 9.3x74Rmm, .444 Marlin, or .45-70 Govt. cal., solid steel action, 24 in. chrome moly barrels, extractors or ejectors, double triggers standard, single trigger available by request, beavertail forearm, fine hand checkered and oil finished walnut stock with cheekpiece, deluxe engraving with sideplates, 7 1/2 lbs. Importation began 2013.

MSR $2,895	$2,675	$2,350	$2,000	$1,800	$1,600	$1,400	$1,200	

Add $510 for ejectors.

CLASSIC SAFARI SERIES - 9.3x74Rmm or .45-70 Govt. cal., 24 in. chrome moly barrels, double triggers standard, single trigger available by request, solid steel action, beavertail forearm, fine hand checkered and oil finished walnut stock with cheekpiece, extractors or ejectors, deluxe engraving with sideplates optional, 7 1/2 lbs. Importation began 2013.

MSR $4,010	$3,650	$3,200	$2,800	$2,400	$2,000	$1,800	$1,600	

Add $510 for ejectors.
Add $1,580 for sideplates and ejectors.

GRADING - PPGS™	100%	98%	95%	90%	80%	70%	60%	LAST MSR

CLASSIC SAFARI BIG 5 – .375 Flanged, .416 Rigby, .450/400 NE, .450 NE, .470 NE or .500 NE cal., solid block steel action, 24 in. chrome moly barrels, extractors (.416 Rigby only) or auto ejectors, open sights, beavertail forearm, fine hand checkered and oil finished walnut stock with cheekpiece, deluxe engraving w/sideplates, case color (disc.) or nickel plated receiver, 9.9 lbs. Importation began 2013.

MSR $7,925	$6,750	$5,900	$5,075	$4,600	$3,725	$3,050	$2,400	

RIFLES: SINGLE SHOT

SKL 98 EDL DELUXE – .223 Rem., .243 Win., .270 Win., .30-06, 9.3x74Rmm, .45-70 Govt., or .308 Win. cal., 23.6 in. CHF barrel, single shot takedown stalking rifle, solid block steel action, select walnut with checkered forearm and pistol grip, deluxe engraving with sideplates, 6.1 lbs. Imported 2013-2016.

	$1,860	$1,630	$1,395	$1,265	$1,025	$835	$650	*$2,191*

SABRE

Previous trademark of shotguns imported by Mitchell's Mausers, located in Fountain Valley, CA.

For individual model listings, please go to BlueBookOfGunValues.com/overflow.

SABRE DEFENCE INDUSTRIES LLC

Previous manufacturer from 2002-2010, with production headquarters located in Nashville, TN, and sales offices located in Middlesex, U.K. This company was previously known as Ramo Mfg., Inc., which was founded in 1977. Sabre Defence was also the U.S. distributor for Sphinx pistols until 2009.

Please refer to BlueBookOfGunValues.com to order the *Blue Book of AR-15s & Variations*, available as a book or online subscription.

SACO DEFENSE INC.

Previous firearms manufacturer located in Saco, ME. Saco Defense was purchased by General Dynamics in July of 2000, and continues to produce guns for military defense contracts. This company was previously owned by Colt's Manufacturing Company, Inc. during late 1998-2000.

In the past, Saco Defense utilized their high-tech manufacturing facility to produce guns for Magnum Research, Weatherby (contract ended Sept., 2001), and others.

SAFARI ARMS

Previous trademark manufactured in Olympia, WA. M-S Safari Arms, located in Phoenix, AZ, was started in 1978 as a division of M-S Safari Outfitters. In 1987, Safari Arms was absorbed by Olympic Arms. Safari Arms manufactured 1911 style pistols since the acquisition of M-S Safari Arms in 1987. In Jan. 2004, the Safari Arms name was discontinued and all 1911 style pistols are now being manufactured by Olympic Arms. Please refer to the Olympic Arms section for previously manufactured models.

Safari Arms previously made the Phoenix, Special Forces, Camp Perry, and Royal Order of Jesters commemoratives in various configurations and quantities. Prices average in the $1,500 range except for the Royal Order of Jesters ($2,000).

SCHUETZEN PISTOL WORKS

Schuetzen Pistol Works was the custom shop of Olympic Arms. Some of the pistols made by Safari Arms had the "Schuetzen Pistol Works" name on them (c. 1994-96). Until Jan. 2004, all pistols were marked with the Safari Arms slide marking. All pistols, however, have been marked "Safari Arms" on the frame. The pistols formerly in this section have been moved to the PISTOLS: SEMI-AUTO category.

PISTOLS: SEMI-AUTO, SINGLE ACTION

Safari Arms manufactured mostly single action, semi-auto pistols derived from the Browning M1911 design with modifications. Please refer to Olympic Arms listing for previously manufactured pistols.

GI SAFARI – .45 ACP cal., patterned after the Colt Model 1911, Safari frame, beavertail grip safety and commander hammer, parkerized matte black finish, 39.9 oz. Mfg. 1991-2000.

	$500	$455	$395	$350	$295	$275	$250	*$550*

CARRYCOMP – .45 ACP cal., 5 in. barrel, utilizes W. Schuemann designed hybrid compensator system, 7 shot mag., rounded or squared off trigger guard, single slide serrations, finger grooved front grip strap, available in stainless steel or steel, 38 oz. Mfg. 1993-99.

	$1,030	$875	$750	$600	$500	$425	$375	*$1,160*

* ***CarryComp Enforcer*** – similar to Safari Arms Enforcer, except utilizes W. Schuemann designed hybrid compensator system, available in stainless steel or steel, 36 oz. Mfg. 1993-96.

	$1,175	$1,025	$875	$750	$600	$500	$425	*$1,300*

GRADING - PPGS™	100%	98%	95%	90%	80%	70%	60%	LAST MSR

CARRIER – .45 ACP cal. only, reproduction of the original Detonics ScoreMaster, except has upgraded sights, custom made by Richard Niemer from the Custom Shop. New 1999-2001.

	$750	$625	$575	$500	$450	$400	$350	*$750*

RENEGADE – .45 ACP cal., left-hand action (port on left side), 4 1/2 (4-star, disc. 1996) or 5 (new 1994) in. barrel, 6 shot mag., adj. sights, stainless steel construction, 36-39 oz. Mfg. 1993-98.

	$955	$800	$700	$600	$525	$450	$395	*$1,085*

Add $50 for 4-star (4 1/2 in. barrel, disc.).

RELIABLE – similar to Renegade, except has right-hand action. Mfg. 1993-98.

	$730	$620	$525	$450	$425	$400	$375	*$825*

Add $60 for 4-star (4 1/2 in. barrel, disc.).

GRIFFON PISTOL – .45 ACP cal., 5 in. stainless steel barrel, 10 shot mag., standard govt. size with beavertail grip safety, full-length recoil spring guide, commander style hammer, smooth walnut grips, 40 1/2 oz. Disc. 1998.

	$855	$725	$650	$575	$500	$450	$395	*$920*

BLACK WIDOW – .45 ACP cal., 3.9 in. barrel, hand contoured front gripstrap, schrimshawed ivory Micarta grips with Black Widow emblem, 6 shot mag., 27 oz. Inventory was depleted 1988.

	$565	$510	$460	$430	$400	$375	$350	*$595*

BILL OF RIGHTS BICENTENNIAL MATCHED SET – includes the MatchMaster Pistol and ServiceMatch Rifle, features beryllium receivers and special engraving. Disc.

	$8,950	$6,500	$4,750	N/A	N/A	N/A	N/A	*$7,400*

PARTNER – .22 LR cal., formerly the Whitney Wolverine, 8 shot mag., black plastic grips, non-adj. sights. Advertised beginning late 1997.

While advertised in 1997, this gun was not manufactured commercially.

MODEL 81 TARGET PISTOL – .38 Spl. or .45 ACP cal., 5 in. barrel, hand contoured front gripstrap, 2 lbs. 10 oz. Disc. 1987.

	$775	$695	$550	$440	$410	$375	$350	*$875*

Add $50 for Deluxe Model (with Herrett adj. grips).

* ***Model 81L Target Pistol*** – .38 Spl. or .45 ACP cal., 6 in. barrel, 2 lbs. 13 oz. Disc. 1987.

	$850	$775	$695	$550	$440	$410	$375	*$975*

Add $50 for Deluxe Model (with Herrett adj. grips).

* ***Model 81 NM Target Pistol*** – .38 Spl. or .45 ACP cal., similar frame as Model 81, except has flat front gripstrap, 5 in. barrel, 2 lbs. 5 oz. Disc. 1987.

	$775	$695	$550	$440	$410	$375	$350	*$875*

* ***Model 81BP Target Pistol*** – .38 Spl. or .45 ACP cal., 6 in barrel, contoured front gripstrap, faster cycle time, 2 lbs. 9 oz. Disc. 1987.

	$875	$775	$695	$550	$440	$410	$375	*$995*

* ***Model 81 Target Pistol Silueta*** – .45 ACP or .38/.45 Wildcat cal., 10 in. extended barrel, designed for silhouette shooting, 2 lbs. 14 oz. Disc. 1987.

	$875	$775	$695	$550	$440	$410	$375	*$1,050*

PISTOLS: SINGLE SHOT

ULTIMATE/UNLIMITED – various cals., bolt action target pistol, 14 15/16 in. barrel, black finished metal, laminated stock. Disc. 1987.

	$850	$775	$695	$550	$440	$410	$375	*$975*

SAFARI CLUB INTERNATIONAL

SCI is an international hunting and conservation organization with headquarters located in Tucson, AZ.

Although Safari Club International (SCI) is not a manufacturer or importer, this organization is responsible for special and limited editions similar to the one listed. Additionally, SCI also has one custom-built rifle manufactured for each annual SCI convention with an auction determining the price of the rifle.

Manufacturer/Model	Quantity	Year	Issue Price
SPECIAL/LIMITED EDITIONS			
Winchester Super Grade 25th Anniversary	200	1997	$1,395

GRADING - PPGS™	100%	98%	95%	90%	80%	70%	60%	LAST MSR

SAFETY HARBOR FIREARMS, INC.

Previous fireams manufacturer and current accessories manufacturer located in Safety Harbor, FL.

Safety Harbor Firearms manufactured a line of KEG (Kompact Entry Gun) slide action shotguns (12 and 20 ga.), in short barrel lengths that were classified as NFA weapons.

RIFLES: BOLT ACTION

SHF R50 - .50 BMG cal., 18, 22, or 29 in. barrel, side mounted 3 (disc. 2009) or 5 shot mag., black reinforced fixed tube stock with vent. recoil pad, partially shrouded barrel with muzzle brake, Picatinny rails, 16 1/2-20 lbs. Disc. 2020.

$1,915	$1,685	$1,425	$1,225	$1,035	$885	$735	*$2,250*

Add $150 for 29 in. barrel.

SHF S50 - .50 BMG cal., single shot, 18, 22, or 29 in. barrel, similar stock and handguard as the SHF R50, but in lightweight configuration. Mfg. mid-2009-2020.

$1,575	$1,385	$1,185	$1,065	$915	$785	$635	*$1,850*

Add $100 for 29 in. barrel.

SHF R/S ZOMBIE - .50 BMG cal., choice of repeater or single shot action, 18 or 22 in. barrel. Mfg. 2014-2015.

$1,995	$1,750	$1,500	$1,350	$1,095	$900	$800	*$2,199*

Add $500 for Mag. fed repeater action.

SAIGA

Current trademark manufactured by Izhmash, located in Izhevsk, Russia since 1807. Previously imported exclusively beginning 2012 by RWC Group LLC, located in Tullytown, PA. Previously imported by US Sporting Goods, Inc., located in Rockledge, FL, RAAC (Russian American Armory Company), located in Scottsburg, IN, Arsenal Inc., located in Las Vegas, NV, K-VAR Corp., located in Las Vegas, NV, and European American Armory Corp., located in Sharpes, FL.

On July 16, 2014, economic sanctions were placed against Russian firearms imports, and they are currently no longer allowed to be imported into the U.S. As a result, quantities of Saiga firearms may be in short supply.

RIFLES: BOLT ACTION

BI-7-2KO - .22 LR cal., straight pull action, 5 shot mag., screw adjustable for pull, travel, and release, oversized trigger guard, iron sights, birch hardwood hunting stock or birch contoured pistol grip stock w/cutout for 4 extra mags., integral rail on barrel, 7.7 lbs. Disc.

$1,050	$900	$800	$700	$600	$500	$425	*$1,299*

RIFLES/CARBINES: SEMI-AUTO

SAIGA RIFLE - .223 Rem. (Model IZ-114), 5.45x39mm (Model IZ-240), or .308 Win. (Model IZ-139) cal., Kalashnikov type action, black synthetic or hardwood (new 2003, only available in .308 Win. cal.) stock and forearm, 16, 20, or 21 (.308 Win. cal. only) in. barrel length, matte black metal, 7-8 1/2 lbs. Imported 2002-2004 and 2006-2014.

$850	$750	$650	$575	$475	$375	$300	*$649*

Add $200 for .308 Win. cal.

Prices above are for unconverted Saiga rifles in original factory condition.

SAIGA 100 - .223 Rem., .30-06, .308 Win., or 7.62x39mm cal., hunting configuration, 22 in. barrel, 3 or 10 shot detachable mag., black plastic reinforced housing around receiver, open sights, black synthetic stock and forearm, crossbolt safety, bolt hold open button in front of of trigger guard, 7.7 lbs. Imported 2006-disc.

$650	$595	$550	$495	$450	$400	$350	

Add 15% for .308 Win. cal.

SAIGA CARBINE CONVERSION - 7.62x39mm cal., AK-style carbine, polymer furniture. Mfg. 2012-disc.

$775	$675	$575	$525	$425	$350	$275	*$900*

Add $20 for Tuning B Model (CBS collapsible stock, RS47SET polymer forward handguard, four rails and G47 pistol grip).

Add $525 for Tuning C Model (ARSNL fully adj. stock, XRS47 aluminum 5 rails handguard, UPG47 pistol grip w/interchangeable finger grooves and backstraps).

GRADING - PPGS™	100%	98%	95%	90%	80%	70%	60%	LAST MSR

SGL21/26 SERIES – 7.62x39mm cal., Russian made, long stroke GPO, 16.3 in. original Russian chrome-lined hammer forged barrel, gas block with accessory lug, front sight block with bayonet lug, AK-74 style muzzle brake, 5 shot mag. accepts AK mags., stamped receiver, U.S. made double stage trigger group, 1000 meter rear sight leaf, original fixed Warsaw length stock, fixed NATO length stock, or black polymer side folding buttstock with trapdoor for cleaning kit, left side scope rail, black, OD Green, Plum, or Desert Sand (new 2012) finish. Mfg. by Izhmash, imported by Arsenal, Inc. 2011-disc.

$1,800	$1,575	$1,350	$1,225	$975	$825	$625	*$959*

Add $10 for NATO buttstock.
Add $10 for 40 shot mag.
Add $105 for forend rails (new 2012).
Add $422 for black polymer side folding buttstock.

SGL31/34 SERIES – 5.45x39mm cal., Russian made, long stroke GPO, 16.3 in. original Russian chrome-lined hammer forged barrel, gas block with accessory lug, front sight block with bayonet lug, bare muzzle or AK-74 style muzzle brake, 10 shot mag., accepts AK-74 mags., stamped receiver, US made double stage trigger group, 1000 meter rear sight leaf, original Warsaw-length fixed polymer stock (SGL31-68) or black polymer side folding buttstock with trapdoor for cleaning kit (SGL31-94), left side scope rail, black, OD Green, plum or Desert Sand (new 2012) finish. Mfg. by Izhmash, imported by Arsenal Inc. 2011-disc.

$2,100	$1,850	$1,575	$1,425	$1,150	$950	$725	*$1,499*

Add $10 for 30 shot mag.
Add $50 for plum, green, or Desert Sand (new 2012) finish.
Add $105 for forend rails (new 2012).
Add $150 for black polymer side folding buttstock.

SHOTGUNS: SEMI-AUTO

SAIGA-12 – 12 or 20 ga., 3 in. chamber, 5 shot detachable box mag., Kalashnikov type action, black synthetic stock and forearm, 19-22 in. barrel length, matte black metal, with or w/o side rail, optional adj. leaf sight or notch rear sight, 6.7-10 lbs. Imported 2002-2004, reintroduced 2006, importation ceased 2014.

$800	$700	$600	$550	$450	$375	$275	*$900*

Add $25 for adj. leaf sight or $13 for notch rear sights.
Add $50 for 20 ga.
Add $40 for RPK handguard (disc.).
Add 10% for choke tubes (12 ga. only, disc.).

Prices above are for unconverted Saiga shotguns in original factory condition.

* ***Saiga-12, LE Variation (SGL12-94)*** – 12 ga., 3 in. chamber, Kalashnikov type action, 19 in. barrel length, 8 shot detachable box mag., front bead sight located on gas block with rear notch sight, black synthetic side folding stock, RPK handguard with tactical forward tri-rail, AK style pistol grip, right side safety lever, 6.85 lbs. Importation ceased 2014.

$1,800	$1,575	$1,350	$1,225	$1,000	$825	$625	

* ***Saiga .410 Bore (SGL-41)*** – .410 bore, 19 or 21 in barrel, 4 or 10 (disc.) shot detachable box mag., NATO or Warsaw Pact buttstock, with or w/o side scope rail, otherwise similar to Saiga Shotgun, approx. 6.6 lbs. Imported 2002-2004, reintroduced 2006, importation ceased 2014.

$725	$625	$525	$450	$400	$350	$295	*$800*

* ***Saiga Skeletonized Stock*** – 12 ga. only, 19 in. barrel, plastic or laminated skeletonized stock, Picatinny rail, with or w/o magwell, 4 or 5 shot mag., AK sights. Imported 2012-2014.

$850	$750	$650	$575	$475	$375	$300	*$994*

Add $81 for laminated stock.

* ***Saiga Hunting Model*** – 12 ga. only, 19 in. barrel, wooden or plastic Monte Carlo or hunting style stock, with or w/o magwell, Picatinny rail, optional leaf or AK sights, 4 or 5 shot mag. Imported 2012-2014.

$750	$650	$575	$500	$415	$350	$275	*$885*

Add $45 for wooden stock.
Add $144 for optional leaf sight.
Add $80 for hunting stock.

SAKO, LTD.

Current rifle manufacturer established circa 1921, located in Riihimäki, Finland. Current models are being imported by Beretta USA, located in Accokeek, MD. Previously imported by Stoeger Industries, Inc. located in Wayne, NJ, Garcia, and Rymac.

During 2000, Sako, Ltd. was purchased by Beretta Holding of Italy. All currently produced Sakos are imported by Beretta USA Corp. located in Accokeek, MD.

GRADING - PPGS™	100%	98%	95%	90%	80%	70%	60%	LAST MSR

Beginning 2000, most Sako rifles (except the Action I in .223 Rem. cal.) are shipped with a Key Concept locking device. This patented system uses a separate key to activate an almost invisible lock which totally blocks the firing pin and prevents bolt movement.

PISTOLS: SEMI-AUTO

Less than 200 Triace pistols were imported into the United States.

TRIACE – .22 Short, .22 LR, or .32 S&W Wadcutter cal., target pistol incorporating unique action, competition walnut grips with thumbrest and adj. heel, blue finish with chrome accents. Imported 1985-86 only.

$1,450	$1,225	$1,000	$825	$700	$600	$500	*$1,395*

* ***Triace Pistol Kit*** – consists of Triace frame, .22 Short, .22 LR, and .32 S&W barrels. Cased with accessories. Imported 1985-86 only.

$2,500	$2,200	$2,000	$1,500	$1,300	$1,175	$1,025	*$2,385*

RIFLES: BOLT ACTION, DISC.

Sako used FN Mauser-style long actions under the Sako name circa 1951-1960. Serial numbers started with 100,001. During 1962, Sako introduced its L61R action, but older FN long actions remained at the factory. Sako also manufactured commercial Mauser actioned rifles for Weatherby and others. Previous importation for these FN actioned Sakos included Firearms International. Note: Prices are for pre-1972 Sako rifles, unless stated otherwise. Pre-1972 Sakos utilize the L-46, L-461, L-469, L-579, L-591, L-57, and L-61 R actions.

Model names on previous imported Sako rifles from Garcia are located on the bottom of the barrel in front of the forend.

Add 10%-15% for popular Mag. cals. on rifles listed.
Subtract approx. 25% for post-1972 models.

DELUXE – various cals., Monte Carlo stock, skipline checkering, long, medium, or short actions, contrasting pistol grip cap and forend tip, engraved floorplate. Disc.

$1,250	$1,075	$950	$800	$700	$600	$500

STANDARD SPORTER – long, medium, and short actions. Disc.

$850	$725	$625	$500	$450	$410	$375

HEAVY BARREL MODEL – long, medium, and short actions. Disc.

$725	$625	$500	$450	$410	$375	$300

FINNBEAR MODEL SPORTER – .25-06 Rem., .264 Win., .270 Win., .30-06, .300 Win. Mag., .338 Win. Mag., 7mm Rem. Mag., .300 H&H, or .375 H&H cal., long L-61 R action, 24 in. barrel, half stock. Disc.

$1,100	$975	$800	$725	$550	$475	$425

FINNBEAR MODEL MANNLICHER CARBINE – .25-06 Rem., .264 Win., .270 Win., .30-06, .300 Win. Mag., .338 Win. Mag., 7mm Rem. Mag., or .375 H&H cal., similar to Finnbear Sporter, except has 20 in. barrel and Mannlicher stock. Disc.

$1,300	$1,100	$975	$800	$725	$550	$475

FINNBEAR DELUXE – .25-06 Rem., .264 Win., .270 Win., .30-06, .300 H&H, .300 Win. Mag., .338 Win. Mag., 7mm Rem. Mag., or .375 H&H cal., select French walnut stock and forearm with rosewood forearm and pistol grip caps, skipline checkering, engraved floorplate.

$1,650	$1,400	$1,200	$995	$850	$725	$600

FORESTER MODEL SPORTER – .22-250 Rem., .243 Win., .244 Rem., or .308 Win. cal., 23 in. barrel, medium L-579 action, sporter half stock. Disc.

$1,050	$925	$775	$700	$525	$450	$400

FORESTER MODEL MANNLICHER CARBINE – .22-250 Rem., .243 Win., or .308 Win. cal., 20 in. barrel, medium L-579 action, Mannlicher stock. Disc.

$1,300	$1,100	$975	$800	$725	$550	$475

VIXEN MODEL SPORTER – .222 Rem., .222 Rem. Mag., or .223 Rem. cal., short L-461 action, 23 1/2 in. barrel, sported half stock. Disc.

$1,050	$925	$775	$700	$525	$450	$400

L-46 action pre-Vixen Sakos had detachable mags.

VIXEN MODEL HEAVY BARREL SPORTER – .222 Rem., .222 Rem. Mag., .223 Rem., or 7x33 Sako cal., short L-461 action, similar to the Vixen Model Sporter, except has 23 1/2 in. heavy barrel. Disc.

$1,050	$925	$775	$700	$525	$450	$400

L-46 action pre-Vixen Sakos had detachable mags.

GRADING - PPGS™	100%	98%	95%	90%	80%	70%	60%	LAST MSR

VIXEN MODEL MANNLICHER CARBINE – .222 Rem., .222 Rem. Mag., .223 Rem., or .243 Win. cal., short action, 20 in. barrel, Mannlicher stock. Disc.

$1,300	$1,100	$975	$800	$725	$550	$475	

MAUSER ACTION (FN) – .270 Win. or .30-06 cal., long action. Mfg. 1950-57.

$725	$550	$475	$400	$325	$280	$260	

MAGNUM MAUSER (FN) – 8x60S, 8.2x57mm, .300 H&H, or .375 H&H cal. Disc.

$745	$635	$580	$495	$450	$410	$375	

MODEL 74 – various cals.

$725	$625	$550	$500	$400	$325	$275	

MODEL 78 – .22 LR, .22 WMR, or .22 Hornet cal., detachable mag., same size as short action Standard Model. Importation disc. 1986.

$1,250	$1,100	$975	$850	$700	$600	$500	*$647*

Add 15% for .22 WMR. or Hornet cal., if original condition is 90%+.

FINNSPORT MODEL 2700 – available in long (AIII) action only, .270 Win., .300 Win. Mag. cals., select checkered walnut. Disc. 1985.

$800	$700	$625	$575	$525	$475	$425	*$910*

ANNIVERSARY MODEL – 7mm Rem. Mag. cal. only, 1,000 mfg. Disc.

$2,750	$1,625	$975	N/A	N/A	N/A	N/A	

The 100% value on this model refers to NIB unfired condition with factory papers.

RIFLES: BOLT ACTION, CURRENT/RECENT PRODUCTION

Beginning late 2001, Sako established a custom shop, which allows the consumer to select from a wide variety of finishes, options, and special orders, including individual stock dimensions. Please contact Beretta USA for more information regarding the Sako custom shop.

All Sako left-handed models are available in medium or long action only.

Some older model TRG rifles (Models TRG-S, TRG-22, and TRG-42) have experienced firing pin breakage. Ser. no. ranges on these U.S. distributed rifles are 202238 - 275255 and 973815 - 998594. Please contact Beretta USA directly (str@berettausa.com or 800-803-8869) for a replacement firing pin assembly if you have a rifle within these serial number ranges.

A7 BIG GAME ROUGHTECH – .270 Win., .30-06, 7mm Rem. Mag., .300 Win. Mag., .308 Win., or 6.5 Creedmoor (new 2017) cal., cold hammer forged 24.4 in. heavy or medium contour fluted barrel, checkered synthetic Roughtech pistol grip stock with fully integrated aluminum bedding, Hi-Viz rubber recoil pad, two-position safety, adj. trigger, wide forend, drilled and tapped, bolt has 3 locking lugs, stainless finish, approx. 7-8 lbs. Mfg. mid-2014-2017.

$1,100	$950	$825	$725	$600	$500	$425	*$1,275*

A7 COYOTE ROUGHTECH – .22-250 Rem. .243 Win., or .25-06 Rem. cal., cold hammer forged 24.4 in. barrel, checkered synthetic Roughtech pistol grip stock with wide forend, drilled and tapped, bolt has 3 locking lugs, matte black finish, approx. 7-8 lbs. Mfg. 2016-2017.

$1,050	$925	$800	$700	$600	$500	$400	*$1,225*

A7 LONG RANGE ROUGHTECH – .25-06 Rem. (mfg. 2016 only), .308 Win., .300 Win. Mag., 7mm Rem. Mag., or 6.5 Creedmoor (new 2017) cal., cold hammer forged 24.4 (new 2017) or 26 in. barrel, checkered synthetic Roughtech pistol grip stock with wide forend, drilled and tapped, bolt has 3 locking lugs, matte black finish, approx. 7-8 lbs. Mfg. 2016-2017.

$1,275	$1,050	$925	$800	$700	$600	$500	*$1,425*

CLASSIC GRADE – .243 Win., .270 Win., .30-06, or 7mm Rem. Mag. cal., short (AI disc. 1992), medium (AII), or long (AIII) action, classic styled stock, finely checkered French walnut with matte lacquer finish. Disc. 1985, reintroduced 1992-1997.

$895	$745	$600	$545	$475	$430	$400	*$1,050*

Add $50 for Mag. cal.
Add $35 for long action.
Add $120-$135 for left-hand action (disc. 1994) (.270 Win. or 7mm Rem. Mag cal. only).

In 1992, the Classic Grade was once again imported into the U.S. in .243 Win., .270 Win., .30-06, or 7mm Rem. Mag. cal.

GRADING - PPGS™	100%	98%	95%	90%	80%	70%	60%	LAST MSR

DELUXE LIGHTWEIGHT RIFLE – available in short action (AI) in .17 Rem., .222 Rem., or .223 Rem. cal., medium action (AII) in .22-250 Rem., .243 Win., .308 Win., or 7mm-08 Rem. cal., or long action (AIII) in .25-06 Rem., .270 Win., .280 Rem., .30 - 06, 7mm Rem. Mag., .300 Win. Mag., .300 Wby. Mag., .338 Win. Mag., .375 H&H, or .416 Rem. Mag. (new 1991) cal., 21 1/4, 21 3/4, or 22 in. barrel, deluxe quality skipline checkered walnut stock with rosewood forend tip. Disc. 1997.

$1,185 $965 $750 $650 $595 $540 $500 *$1,475*

Add $35 for long action.
Add $50-$70 for Mag. cals.
Add $150-$175 for left-hand action (disc. 1994, available in long action only).

FIBERCLASS MODEL – available in medium action (disc. 1992) in .22-250 Rem., .243 Win., .308 Win., or 7mm-08 Rem. cal., or long action in .25-06 Rem., .270 Win., .280 Rem., .30-06, 7mm Rem. Mag., .300 Win. Mag., .338 Win. Mag., .375 H&H, or .416 Rem. Mag. (new 1991) cal., has black fiberglass stock. Disc. 1996.

$1,170 $930 $785 $725 $630 $560 $510 *$1,388*

Add $17-$37 for Mag. cals.
Subtract $40 for medium action cals. (disc. 1992).
Add $80 for left-hand action (disc. 1989).

* ***FiberClass Model Carbine (Handy)*** – available in medium action in .243 Win. or .308 Win. cal. and long action in .25-06 Rem. (disc.), .270 Win. (disc.), .30-06, 7mm Rem. Mag. (disc.), .300 Win. Mag. (disc.), .338 Win. Mag., or .375 H&H (new 1991) cal., 18 1/2 in. barrel with fiberglass stock. Mfg. 1986-1991.

$995 $895 $775 $725 $630 $560 $510 *$1,239*

Add $50-$65 for Mag. cals.

FINNFIRE – .22 LR cal., 22 in. regular or heavy (new 1996) or 23 (Sporter/Varmint and Target) in. cold hammer forged free floating barrel, M-P94S action, single stage adj. trigger, 50 degree bolt lift, 2 position safety, European walnut pistol grip or adj. Target competition (new 2003) stock, cocking indicator, available in Hunter, Target (new 2003)/Sporter (new 1999), or Varmint configuration, 5 or 10 shot mag., integral 11mm dovetail (for scope mounting), with (new 1996) or w/o open sights, 5 3/4 (Target/Sporter) lbs. Imported 1994-2005.

$850 $725 $625 $525 $450 $400 $350 *$1,044*

Add $45 for Varmint Model with heavy barrel.
Add $125 for Target/Sporter Model with 10 shot mag. and adj. competition stock.

FINNFIRE II – .17 HMR or .22 LR cal., Finnfire full metallic bolt handle, 22 in. barrel, 6 shot detachable mag., single stage trigger, open sights are optional, oil finished checkered pistol grip walnut stock with cheekpiece, rubber recoil pad, sling swivels, blued receiver and barrel finish, 6.3 lbs. Mfg. mid-2014-2017.

$950 $825 $725 $650 $525 $450 $350 *$1,100*

HUNTER LIGHTWEIGHT RIFLE – available in short action (AI) in .17 Rem., .222 Rem., or .223 Rem. cal., medium action (AII) in .22-250 Rem., .243 Win., .308 Win., or 7mm-08 Rem. cal., or long action (AIII) in .25-06 Rem., .270 Win., .280 Rem., .30 - 06, .270 Wby. Mag. (disc. 1996), 7mm Wby. Mag. (disc. 1996), 7mm Rem. Mag., .300 Win. Mag., .300 Wby. Mag., .338 Win. Mag., .340 Wby. Mag. (disc. 1996), .375 H&H, or .416 Rem. Mag. (new 1991) cal., 21 1/4, 21 3/4, or 22 in. barrel, classic styled stock with choice of oil (disc. 1996) or matte lacquer finish, finely checkered French walnut. Disc. 1997.

$850 $685 $550 $490 $460 $430 $410 *$1,050*

Add $35 for long action.
Add $50-$70 for Mag. cals.
Add approx. $80 for left-hand action (available in all Mag. cals. - mfg. 1994-96).

* ***Hunter Lightweight Rifle Carbine (Handy)*** – available in medium action in .22-250 Rem. (disc. 1990), .243 Win. (new 1991), .308 Win. (new 1991) cal. or long action in .25-06 Rem. (disc. 1990), 7mm Rem. Mag. (disc. 1990), .338 Win. Mag. cal., or .375 H&H (new 1990) cal., 18 1/2 in. barrel with iron sights, oil or lacquer finished deluxe walnut stock with checkering, approx. 7 lbs. Mfg. 1986-91.

$725 $650 $600 $490 $460 $430 $410 *$945*

Add $50-$65 for long action (Mag. cals.).

LAMINATED RIFLE – available in short action (disc. 1989), medium action in .22-250 Rem., .243 Win., .308 Win., or 7mm-08 Rem. cal., or long action in .25-06 Rem., .270 Win., .280 Rem., .30-06, 7mm Rem. Mag., .300 Win. Mag., .338 Win. Mag., .375 H&H, or .416 Rem. Mag. (new 1991) cal., features laminated wood stock. Mfg. 1988-95.

$985 $790 $635 $550 $495 $460 $430 *$1,200*

Add $35 for short action.
Add $55 for long action.

GRADING - PPGS™	100%	98%	95%	90%	80%	70%	60%	LAST MSR

Add $75-$95 for Mag. cals.
Add approx. $100 for left-hand action (disc.).

The left-hand action was available in .270 Win., .280 Rem., .30-06, 7mm Rem. Mag., .300 Win. Mag., .338 Win. Mag., .375 H&H, or .416 Rem. Mag. cal.

LONG RANGE HUNTING MODEL – available in long action in .25-06 Rem., .270 Win., .300 Win. Mag., or 7mm Rem. Mag. cal., 26 in. heavy barrel only w/o sights. Mfg. 1996-97.

$1,030	$785	$625	$545	$495	$465	$440	*$1,275*

Add $15 for Mag. cals.

MANNLICHER CARBINE – available in short action (disc. 1989), medium action in .243 Win. or .308 Win. cal., or long action in .25-06 Rem. (disc. 1991), .270 Win., .30 - 06, 7mm Rem. Mag. (disc. 1991), .300 Win. Mag. (disc. 1991), .338 Win. Mag., or .375 H&H cal., 18 1/2 in. barrel, two-piece full Mannlicher style stock, open sights. Disc. 1996.

$1,050	$825	$650	$550	$500	$465	$440	*$1,275*

Add approx. 5% for long action.
Add $60-$75 for Mag. cals.

PPC MODEL – .22 PPC or 6mm PPC cal., 21 3/4 or 23 3/4 (Benchrest Model) in. barrel, single shot in Benchrest Model, 4 shot mag. in Hunter or Deluxe Model, checkered walnut stock, Deluxe Model has rosewood pistol grip and forearm caps plus skip line checkering, matte lacquer finish on Hunter and Deluxe, oiled finish on Benchrest, 6 1/4 or 8 3/4 (Benchrest Model with heavy barrel) lbs. Imported 1989-97.

$1,250	$950	$750	$650	$600	$540	$500	*$1,535*

Add $320 for Deluxe Hunter Model (disc. 1993).
Add $85 for Benchrest Model (disc. 1993).

QUAD – .17 HMR, .17 Mach 2, .22 LR, or .22 WMR cal., 22 in. barrel, black synthetic stock with ambidextrous palm swell and adj. buttpad, interchangeable rimfire barrels, 50 degree bolt lift, blued finish, 5 shot mag., no sights, 5 3/4 lbs. Mfg. 2005-2007.

$760	$650	$575	$500	$425	$375	$325	*$925*

* ***Quad 2-Barrel Combo*** – .17 HMR and .22 LR cal., includes two interchangeable barrels, fitted aluminum case. Limited importation 2008.

$1,500	$1,250	$1,000	$875	$775	$700	$625	*$1,750*

* ***Quad 4-Barrel Combo*** – includes four interchangeable 22 in. rimfire barrels in cals. .17 HMR, .17 Mach 2, .22 LR, and .22 WMR, barrels are color coded to indicate caliber and change quickly with barrel tool, choice of oil finished walnut or black synthetic (new 2008) stock, single stage trigger, detachable 5 shot mag., approx. 6.1-7.7 lbs. Mfg. 2005-circa 2010.

$1,475	$1,275	$1,050	$900	$800	$700	$650	*$1,700*

Add $275 for wood stock.

SAFARI GRADE – available in long (AIII) action only, .300 Win. Mag. (disc. 1989), .338 Win. Mag., .375 H&H, or .416 Rem. Mag. (new 1991) cal., deluxe walnut with sculptured cheekpiece, 22 in. barrel, 4 shot mag., open sights, sling swivels. Disc. 1996.

$2,235	$1,785	$1,475	$1,250	$1,050	$900	$795	*$2,765*

SAKO 75 80TH ANNIVERSARY – .375 H&H cal., limited edition rifle featuring Mauser style claw extractor, premium grade checkered walnut with ebony forend tip, cold hammer forged match grade barrel has 1/4 rib with open sights, 5 shot internal mag. with hinged floorplate, includes Swarovski PV-1 scope and case, only 80 rifles (serial numbered 200101-200180) mfg. 2001-2007.

$16,500	$14,000	$11,000	$9,000	N/A	N/A	N/A	*$19,550*

SAKO 75 CUSTOM DELUXE – .270 Win. or .30-06 cal., extra grade deluxe oil finished walnut stock with rosewood forend tip and pistol grip cap, 7 3/4 lbs. Imported late 2003-2007.

$3,750	$3,250	$2,575	$2,175	$1,850	$1,550	$1,350	*$4,325*

This model was available through Sako showcase dealers only.

SAKO 75 HUNTER – available in 5 action sizes, .17 Rem. (mfg. 1998-2002), .222 Rem. (mfg. 1998-2002), .223 Rem. (new 1998), .22-250 Rem., .243 Win., .308 Win., 7mm-08 Rem., .25-06 Rem., .260 Rem. (new 2005), .270 Win., .270 WSM (new 2004), .280 Rem. (disc. 2004), .30-06, .270 Wby. Mag. (disc. 2001), 6.5x55mm (new 2005), 7mm RUM (mfg. 2002-2003), 7mm Wby. Mag. (disc. 2003), 7mm STW (disc. 2003), 7mm WSM (new 2005), 7mm Rem. Mag., .300 WSM (new 2004), .300 Win. Mag., .300 Wby. Mag. (disc. 2003), .300 RUM (mfg. 2000-2003), .338 Win. Mag., .340 Wby. Mag. (disc. 2003), .375 H&H, or .416 Rem. Mag. (disc. 2001) cal., hammer forged 22-24 3/8 in. barrel,

GRADING - PPGS™	100%	98%	95%	90%	80%	70%	60%	LAST MSR

utilizes 3 locking lugs, mechanical ejector, 5 bolt sliding guides with 70 degree bolt lift, 3-position rear tang safety, available with top loading fixed mag. (hinged floorplate, .300 Rem. Ultra Mag., .416 Rem. Mag., and 7mm Rem. Ultra mag. cals. only), or detachable staggered 4-6 shot mag., checkered walnut stock, no sights, approx. 7 3/4 lbs. Mfg. 1997-2007.

	$1,125	$900	$725	$625	$550	$500	$450	$1,375

Add $100 for .375 H&H cal.

This model was also available in left-hand action in .270 Win. or .30-06 cal. at no extra charge.

* ***Sako 75 Deluxe*** – similar cals. as Sako 75 Hunter, features hinged floorplate and deluxe walnut stock with gloss finish, skipline checkering, and rosewood forend and pistol grip caps, custom stock bedding and iron sights available on .375 H&H or .416 Rem. Mag. cals., approx. 7 3/4 lbs. Mfg. 1997-2007.

	$1,700	$1,450	$1,200	$925	$750	$625	$550	$2,050

Add $125 for .416 Rem. Mag.

SAKO 75 GREY WOLF – .22-250 Rem., .223 Rem., .243 Win., .25-06 Rem., .260 Rem., .270 Win., .30-06, .308 Win., .270 WSM, .300 WSM, 7mm WSM, or 7mm-08 Rem. cal., available in 4 frame sizes and 3 barrel lengths. Mfg. 2005-2007.

	$1,225	$925	$800	$700	$600	$525	$450	$1,550

SAKO 75 KING RANCH – .270 Win., .30-06, or .300 WSM cal., 22 7/8 or 24 3/8 (.300 WSM cal. only) in. barrel, similar to Sako 75 Deluxe, except has King Ranch "W" stock checkering and gold-filled "W" emblem on floorplate. Mfg. 2006-2007.

	$2,050	$1,650	$1,325	$1,050	$875	$750	$625	$2,475

SAKO 75 SINGLE SHOT – .22-250 Rem. (disc. 2005), .243 Win. (disc. 2005), 7mm-08 Rem. (disc. 2005), 6mm PPC (disc. 2005), or .308 Win. cal., medium III action, stainless steel action and barrel, heavy free floating fluted barrel w/o sights, 9 lbs. Mfg. 2004-2007.

	$2,850	$2,375	$2,125	$1,850	$1,550	$1,350	$1,150	$3,450

SAKO 75 STAINLESS SYNTHETIC – available in .22-250 Rem., .243 Win., .25-06 Rem., .260 Rem. (new 2005), .270 Win., .270 WSM (new 2004), .30-06, .308 Win., .300 Win. Mag., .300 Wby. Mag. (mfg. 1999-2003), .300 WSM (new 2004), .300 RUM (mfg. 2000-2003), 7mm-08 Rem. (new 1998), 7mm STW (mfg. 1998-2003), 7mm WSM (new 2006), 7mm Rem. Mag., 7mm RUM (mfg. 2002-2003), .338 Win. Mag., or .375 H&H cal., 3-4 shot detachable mag. (except for floorplate with Rem. Ultra Mag. cals.), features black composite stock with soft rubber grip inserts in pistol grip and forearm area, matte stainless steel metal, 7 3/4 lbs. Mfg. 1997-2007.

	$1,150	$900	$750	$640	$535	$450	$390	$1,425

SAKO 75 STAINLESS WALNUT – .270 Win., .30-06, .300 Win. Mag., .300 Wby. Mag., .338 Win. Mag., 7mm STW, or 7mm Rem. Mag. cal., features checkered walnut stock and forearm. Imported 1999-2002.

	$1,050	$840	$685	$575	$485	$400	$350	$1,239

Add $35 for Mag. cals.

SAKO 75 VARMINT – .17 Rem. (disc. 2003), .22-250 Rem., .222 Rem. (disc. 2002), .223 Rem., .22 PPC (mfg. 1999-2003), or 6mm PPC (mfg. 1999-2003) cal., 23 5/8 in. heavy barrel w/o sights and beavertail forend, 5 or 6 shot detachable mag., 8 5/8 lbs. Mfg. 1998-2005.

	$1,400	$1,000	$850	$725	$650	$575	$500	$1,628

SAKO 75 VARMINT W/SET TRIGGER – similar to Sako 75 Varmint, except is also available in .204 Ruger, .243 Win., .260 Rem., or .308 Win. cal., set trigger. Mfg. 2005-2007.

	$1,575	$1,275	$975	$800	$700	$600	$500	$1,850

SAKO 75 STAINLESS VARMINT LAMINATED – .22-250 Rem., .222 Rem. (disc. 2002), .223 Rem., .22 PPC (disc. 2003), 6mm PPC (disc. 2003), or 7mm-08 Rem. (new 2002) cal., similar to Sako 75 Varmint, features stainless steel action and barrel, brown laminated wood stock, 9 lbs. Mfg. 1999-2005.

	$1,475	$1,175	$875	$765	$635	$530	$455	$1,794

SAKO 75 STAINLESS VARMINT LAMINATED W/SET TRIGGER – similar to Sako 75 Stainless Varmint Laminated, except is also available in .204 Ruger, .243 Win., .260 Rem., or .308 Win. cal., set trigger. Mfg. 2005-2007.

	$1,675	$1,375	$1,025	$850	$725	$600	$500	$1,950

SAKO 75 SUPER DELUXE – a limited edition rifle available special order only, presentation grade walnut with both checkering and carving, rosewood forend tip.

Limited availability precludes accurate pricing on this model.

GRADING - PPGS™	100%	98%	95%	90%	80%	70%	60%	LAST MSR

SAKO 85 BAVARIAN – .270 Win., .270 WSM (disc. 2016), .30-06, .300 Win. Mag., .300 WSM (disc. 2016), .308 Win., 6.5x55mm Swedish, 6.5 Creedmoor (new 2020), 7mm-08 Rem. (disc. 2016), or 7mm Rem. Mag. (disc. 2016) cal., four action sizes, 22 7/16 or 24 3/8 in. barrel, features high grade checkered European walnut stock with Bavarian cheekpiece and rosewood pistol grip cap, open sights, set trigger, 4-6 shot detachable mag., left-hand action became available in 2014, 7-7 3/4 lbs. New 2009.

MSR $2,199	$1,850	$1,650	$1,400	$1,250	$1,050	$850	$650	

Subtract $75 for 6.5 Creedmoor cal. (new 2020).
Add $50 for WSM cals. (disc. 2016).

SAKO 85 BLACK WOLF – .308 Win., .30-06, .300 Win. Mag., 7mm Rem. Mag., or 6.5 Creedmoor cal., 24 in. barrel, rear wood stock with adj. LOP and cheekpiece, double sling studs, top ergonomic pistol grip. Mfg. 2018-2019.

	$2,025	$1,775	$1,525	$1,375	$1,115	$910	$710	*$2,375*

SAKO 85 CARBONLIGHT STAINLESS – .22-250 Rem. (disc. 2016), .243 Win. (disc. 2016), .260 Rem., .308 Win., 7mm-08 Rem., or 6.5 Creedmoor (new 2018) cal., 20 1/4 or 24.3 (new 2018, 6.5 Creedmoor only) in. stainless steel fluted barrel, 5 shot mag., adj. trigger, two-position safety, carbon fiber stock, rubber recoil pad. New 2015.

MSR $3,099	$2,650	$2,300	$2,000	$1,800	$1,450	$1,200	$900	

SAKO 85 CARBON WOLF – .308 Win., .30-06, .300 Win. Mag. (disc. 2020), 7mm Rem. Mag., or 6.5 Creedmoor cal., 24 in. barrel, lightweight synthetic carbon fiber stock with adj. LOP and cheekpiece, features soft touch coating. New 2018.

MSR $3,499	$3,000	$2,600	$2,250	$2,000	$1,650	$1,350	$1,050	

SAKO 85 CLASSIC – .25-06 Rem., .270 Win., .30-06, .308 Win. (new 2010), .300 Win. Mag., .338 Win. Mag., .370 Sako Mag. (limited mfg., disc.), .375 H&H, .270 WSM, .300 WSM, 7mm-08 Rem. (new 2020), 7mm Rem. Mag., or 6.5 Creedmoor (new 2020) cal., available in four action sizes, 22 7/16, 24 (new 2020), or 24 3/8 in. barrel, 5 or 6 shot detachable mag., single stage trigger, pistol grip checkered walnut stock with rosewood forend and pistol grip cap, open sights, approx. 7 lbs. New 2009.

MSR $2,299	$1,950	$1,700	$1,450	$1,350	$1,100	$900	$700	

Subtract $75 for 7mm-08 Rem. cal. (new 2020).

SAKO 85 FINN BEAR – .270 Win., .30-06, .300 Win. Mag., or 7mm Rem. Mag. cal., 24 in. barrel, 4 shot mag., two-position safety, adj. trigger, integral tapered scopemount dovetails, square style walnut stock with raised cheekpiece, bear silhouette grip cap and rosewood-tipped forend, rubber recoil pad. Mfg. 2015 only.

	$2,035	$1,675	$1,350	$1,000	$875	$800	$700	*$2,325*

SAKO 85 FINNLIGHT STAINLESS (FINNLIGHT) – .22-250 Rem. (new 2010), .243 Win, .25-06 Rem., .260 Rem. (mfg. 2006-2008, reintroduced 2015), .270 Win., .270 WSM (new 2004), .280 Rem. (disc. 2007), .30-06, .308 Win., .300 Win. Mag., .300 WSM (new 2003), .338 Win. Mag. (disc. 2008), 6.5x55mm, 7mm-08 Rem., 7mm WSM (mfg. 2005-2007), or 7mm Rem. Mag. cal., stainless steel action with four sizes, 20 1/4 (disc., reintroduced 2015 in .260 Rem. cal. only), 20 7/8, 22 7/16, or 24 3/8 in. stainless steel free floating fluted barrel, alloy trigger guard/mag. bottom, black synthetic stock with soft gray overmolded grips, rubber recoil pad, adj. trigger, 4 or 5 shot detachable mag., no sights, 6 1/2 lbs. Importation began 2001.

MSR $1,849	$1,550	$1,400	$1,200	$1,050	$850	$700	$550	

SAKO 85 FINNLIGHT II STAINLESS – .22-250 Rem., .243 Win., .308 Win., .25-06 Rem., .270 Win., .30-06, .260 Rem., .300 Win. Mag. (disc. 2020), .270 WSM, .300 WSM, 6.5x55, 7mm-08 Rem., 7mm Rem. Mag., or 6.5 Creedmoor cal., 20 1/4, 22.7, or 24.2 in. barrel, Cerakote treated stainless steel action, composite stock with carbon fiber bedding, adj. cheekpiece. New 2018.

MSR $2,499	$2,100	$1,850	$1,600	$1,450	$1,150	$950	$750	

SAKO 85 GREY WOLF – .270 Win., .270 WSM, .30-06, .300 Win. Mag., .300 WSM, 7mm Rem. Mag., or 6.5 Creedmoor (new 2018) cal., 22 7/16 or 24 3/8 in. stainless barrel, 5 shot detachable mag., integral tapered scopemount dovetails, single stage trigger, checkered grey laminate stock, rubber recoil pad. Importation began 2007.

MSR $1,799	$1,525	$1,350	$1,150	$1,050	$850	$685	$550	

SAKO 85 HUNTER – various cals. between .22-250 - .375 H&H, 3 lug bolt, available in 5 action sizes, checkered walnut stock and forearm, 22 1/2 or 24 3/8 in. blue barrel, blue action, 4-5 shot detachable mag., short claw extractor on bolt, two-position safety, adj. trigger, guaranteed 1 MOA 5 shot groups, approx. 7 1/2 lbs., mfg. to celebrate Sako's 85th anniversary during 2006. Importation 2006-2008.

	$1,400	$1,100	$875	$775	$675	$575	$525	*$1,700*

Add $50 for .370 Sako Mag., .375 H&H, or WSM cals.

GRADING - PPGS™	100%	98%	95%	90%	80%	70%	60%	LAST MSR

SAKO 85 KODIAK – .338 Win. Mag. (disc. 2013) or .375 H&H cal., stainless steel action and barrel with special matte coating, long action, 21 1/4 in. barrel with band, 4 shot detachable mag., grey laminated reinforced hardwood stock with two crossbolts and checkering, adj. open sights, 8 lbs. New 2009.

MSR $1,999	$1,700	$1,500	$1,300	$1,150	$950	$750	$600	

SAKO 85 LONG RANGE – .300 Win. Mag. (disc. 2020), or .338 Lapua Mag. cal., 26 in. barrel with muzzle brake, 4 shot detachable mag., single stage trigger, no sights, checkered laminated stock with rubber buttpad, approx. 9 1/2 lbs. New 2016.

MSR $2,799	$2,400	$2,100	$1,800	$1,600	$1,300	$1,050	$850	

SAKO 85 STAINLESS SYNTHETIC – similar to Sako 85 Hunter, except has black synthetic stock with overmolded grips and matte stainless steel barrel/action, FinSoft recoil reduction system. Imported 2007-2008.

	$1,275	$975	$775	$675	$575	$525	$475	*$1,575*

Add $50 for WSM cals.

SAKO 85 SYNTHETIC – .270 Win., .30-06, 6.5x55mm, or .308 Win. cal., 22 7/16 in. black fluted barrel, 6 shot mag., matte black metal parts, soft touch coated checkered black synthetic pistol grip stock and forearm with rubber recoil pad, sling swivels, 6 3/8 lbs. Mfg. mid-2014-2015.

	$1,485	$1,175	$900	$800	$700	$625	$550	*$1,750*

SAKO 85 VARMINT – .204 Ruger, .22-250 Rem., .223 Rem., .243 Win., .308 Win., or 6.5 Creedmoor (new 2020) cal., two action sizes, 23 5/8 or 24 3/8 (new 2020) in. heavy blue (walnut stock, disc.) or stainless barrel w/o sights, 5 or 6 shot mag., set trigger, uncheckered walnut (disc.) or laminate brown stock (standard w/stainless barrel beginning 2009), rubber recoil pad. Importation began 2008.

MSR $1,999	$1,700	$1,500	$1,300	$1,150	$950	$750	$600	

Add $50 for 6.5 Creedmoor cal. (new 2020).
Subtract approx. 10% for uncheckered walnut stock (disc. 2008).

SAKO A-7 – various short and medium action cals. between .22-250 Rem. - .300 Win. Mag., 22 7/16 or 24 3/8 in. hammer forged match grade barrel, adj. trigger, lightweight synthetic stock with recoil lugs, detachable top loading magazine, Weaver style scope base, two position safety. Mfg. 2009-2011.

	$825	$700	$600	$550	$500	$450	$400	*$935*

Add $45 for WSM cals.

* ***Sako A-7 Stainless*** – current cals. are .270 WSM, and .300 WSM, previously avail. in various cals. between .22-250 Rem. and .300 Win. Mag., similar to A-7, except has 24 3/8 in. stainless steel action and barrel. Mfg. 2009-2013.

	$1,200	$1,050	$875	$750	$625	$500	$400	*$1,375*

Subtract approx. $350 if without Tecomate finish.
Subtract approx. $50 for non-WSM cals.

SAKO S20 – .243 Win., .270 Win., 7mm Rem. Mag., .308 Win., .30-06, .300 Win. Mag., 6.5 Creedmoor, or 6.5 PRC cal., 20 (.308 Win. only) or 24 in. fluted cold hammer forged barrel, muzzle brake, blackened steel or tungsten construction, Precision or Hunter Cerakote stock, black finish. New 2021.

MSR $1,699	$1,450	$1,250	$1,100	$1,000	$800	$650	$550	

Add $100 for Precision Cerakote stock.

SUPER DELUXE – a limited edition rifle available on special order only, various cals. are available in the short (AI), medium (AII), and long (AIII) actions, presentation grade walnut with both checkering and carving, rosewood forend tip. Disc. 1997.

	$2,400	$1,825	$1,475	$1,250	$1,050	$900	$795	*$3,100*

TRG M10 – .308 Win., .338 Lapua Mag., or .300 Win. Mag. cal., 20 or 27 in. fluted barrel, detachable mag., fully adj. right folding pistol grip stock with interchangeable backstrap, ambidextrous controls, black or Coyote Brown finish. Mfg. mid-2017-2019, reintroduced 2021.

MSR $11,999	$10,200	$8,900	$7,650	$6,950	$5,600	$4,600	$3,550	*$11,899*

TRG-21 – .308 Win. cal., 25 3/4 in. stainless steel barrel, new design features modular synthetic stock construction with adj. cheekpiece and buttplate, cold hammer forged receiver, and resistance free bolt, 10 shot detachable mag., 10 1/2 lbs. Imported 1993-99.

	$2,300	$2,000	$1,800	$1,600	$1,400	$1,200	$975	*$2,699*

TRG 22 – .308 Win. or 6.5 Creedmoor (new 2017) cal., 20 or 26 in. stainless steel barrel, updated TRG-21 design featuring adj. modular synthetic stock in tan (new 2020), green (disc. 2016), desert tan (disc.), or all black construction with adj. cheekpiece and buttplate, competition trigger, Picatinny rail became standard circa 2011, choice of blue (disc. 2002) or phosphate (new 2002) metal finish, cold hammer forged receiver, and resistance free bolt, 10 shot detachable mag., approx. 10 1/4 lbs. Importation began 2000.

MSR $3,479	$2,950	$2,600	$2,200	$2,000	$1,600	$1,350	$1,150	

Add $2,575 for folding stock in green finish (disc. 2016).
Subtract approx. 10% if without Picatinny rail.

GRADING - PPGS™	100%	98%	95%	90%	80%	70%	60%	LAST MSR

TRG 22A1 - .308 Win., .260 Rem., or 6.5 Creedmoor cal., 26 in. barrel, folding stock with 2-point attachment, M-LOK forend, full aluminum middle chassis. New 2018.

MSR $6,499	$5,500	$4,850	$4,150	$3,750	$3,050	$2,500	$1,950	

TRG-41 - .338 Lapua Mag. cal., similar to Model TRG-21, except has long action and 27 1/8 in. barrel, 7 3/4 lbs. Imported 1994-99.

	$2,700	$2,425	$2,150	$1,850	$1,625	$1,400	$1,200	*$3,099*

TRG 42 - .300 Win. Mag. (disc. 2012) or .338 Lapua Mag. cal., updated TRG-41 design featuring long action and 27 1/8 in. barrel, Picatinny rail became standard during 2011, choice of black composite/blue finish, desert tan (disc. 2013), or green composite/phosphate (new 2002) finish, 5 shot mag., 11 1/4 lbs. Importation began 2000.

MSR $4,479	$3,800	$3,350	$2,850	$2,600	$2,100	$1,700	$1,350	

Add $2,550 for folding stock with Picatinny rail (green finish only, disc. 2016).

Subtract approx. $775 if without Picatinny rail (desert tan stock only, disc. 2013).

TRG 42A1 - .300 Win. Mag. or .338 Lapua Mag. cal., 27 in. barrel, folding stock with 2-point attachment, M-LOK forend, full aluminum middle chassis, black or Coyote Tan (new 2021) finish. New 2018.

MSR $7,499	$6,400	$5,600	$4,800	$4,350	$3,500	$2,850	$2,250	

TRG-S - available in medium action (disc. 1993) in .243 Win. or 7mm-08 cal., or long action in .25-06 Rem. (Mfg. 1994-98), .270 Win. (disc. 2000), 6.5x55mm Swedish (disc. 1998), .30-06 (disc.), .308 Win. (disc. 1995), .270 Wby. Mag. (disc. 1998), 7mm Wby. Mag. (Mfg. 1998), 7mm Rem. Mag. (disc.), .300 Win. Mag. (disc.), .300 Wby. Mag. (mfg. 1994-99), .30-378 Wby. Mag. (new 1998, 26 in. barrel only), .338 Win. Mag. (disc. 1999), .338 Lapua Mag. (new 1994), .340 Wby. Mag. (disc. 1998), 7mm STW (26 in. barrel only, disc. 1999), .375 H&H (disc. 1998), or .416 Rem. Mag. (disc. 1998) cal., black synthetic stock, Sporter variation derived from the Model TRG-21, 22 (disc.), 24 (Mag. cals. only, disc.), or 26 in. barrel, 3 or 5 shot detachable mag., fully adj. trigger, 60 degree bolt lift, matte finish, 8 1/8 lbs. Imported 1993-2004.

	$775	$650	$525	$475	$440	$415	$380	*$896*

VARMINT RIFLE - available in short action (AI) in .17 Rem., .222 Rem., or .223 Rem., and medium action (AII) .22-250 Rem., .243 Win., .308 Win., or 7mm-08 cal., 22 3/4 in. heavy barrel, no sights. Disc. 1997.

	$1,025	$795	$615	$545	$475	$430	$400	*$1,240*

RIFLES: LEVER ACTION

FINNWOLF - .243 Win. or .308 Win. cal., lever action, LV63 action, 4 shot mag. early model, 3 shot mag. later model. Mfg. 1962-1974.

	N/A	$1,750	$1,500	$1,300	$1,100	$875	$650	

Add 20% for .243 Win. cal.

Add 15% for early model with 4 shot mag.

* ***Finnwolf Sako Collectors Association*** - .243 Win. or .308 Win. cal., gold lettering on left side of breech, approx. 175 (in each caliber) mfg. in 1982.

	N/A	$2,250	$1,750	$1,400	$1,175	$925	$700	

The 100% value on this model refers to NIB unfired condition with factory papers.

SALERI, W.R. di SALERI WILLIAM & C. snc

Current long gun manufacturer established in 1998, located in Gardone, Italy. No current U.S. importation. Previously imported by Kevin's Fine Outdoor Gear & Apparel, located in Thomasville, GA, by MacGregor Wing and Clay, located in Cary, NC, and by S.R. Lamboy, located in Victor, NY.

RIFLES AND SHOTGUNS

W.R. Saleri manufactures high quality boxlock O/U and SxS shotguns, Express SxS rifles, and single barrel shotguns and rifles. Saleri offers square frame and round body models. Please contact the company directly for more information, including pricing, delivery time, and availability.

SALIENT ARMS INTERNATIONAL

Current manufacturer of pistols, rifles, shotguns, and related parts and components, located in Las Vegas, NV.

For individual model listings, please go to BlueBookOfGunValues.com/overflow.

SAMCO GLOBAL ARMS, INC.

Previous importer and distributor located in Miami, FL until late 2015.

Samco Global Arms purchased the Charles Daly trademark in late 2012, and was importing a variety of Charles Daly shotgun configurations (see Charles Daly in the C section). Samco also imported Akkar shotguns from Turkey, as well as a variety of foreign and domestic surplus military rifles, including various contract Mausers, Loewe, Steyr, Czech, Lee Enfield, Mosin-Nagant, etc. Samco also imported European surplus pistols. Most of these guns offered excellent values to both shooters and collectors.

SAN JUAN ENTERPRISE

Current manufacturer of knife pistols located in Colorado Springs, CO.

PISTOLS: SINGLE SHOT

PKP KNIFE PISTOL - .22 LR or .22 Mag. cal., (interchangeable barrel inserts), tip-up action, patterned after the Powell Knife Pistol (PKP), aircraft aluminum w/steel components, exposed hammer, most recent variations include the Sierra Madre (original MSR was $1,249) and the Kiowa edition (only 10 mfg. - last MSR was $3,800), carved wood grips with blade etching (early mfg.). Limited mfg. beginning circa 2016.

Please contact the company directly for more information, availability, and current pricing.

SAN SWISS ARMS AG

Current company established during late 2000, with headquarters located in Neuhausen, Switzerland. Imported exclusively by JDI Firearms, Inc. since 2015, located in Frisco, TX.

In late 2000, SIG Arms AG, the firearms portion of SIG, was purchased by two Germans named Michael Lüke and Thomas Ortmeier, who have a background in textiles. Today the Lüke & Ortmeier Group (L&O Group) includes independently operational companies such as Blaser Jadgwaffen GmbH, Mauser Jagdwaffen GmbH, John Rigby, J.P. Sauer & Sohn GmbH, SIG-Sauer Inc., SIG-Sauer GmbH and SAN Swiss Arms AG. Please refer to individual listings.

RIFLES

In 2010, San Swiss Arms purchased the rights to the A.M.S.D. Model OM 50 Nemesis. Model nomenclature has been changed to the San 511. Please contact the company directly for more information on this model including options, pricing, and U.S. availability.

SAN TAN TACTICAL

Current custom AR-15 style rifle and accessories manufacturer located in Chandler, AZ.

Please refer to BlueBookOfGunValues.com to order the *Blue Book of AR-15s & Variations*, available as a book or online subscription.

SAR ARMS

Sar Arms is a member of the Sar Arms International (Sarsilmaz) Firearms Group, which is one of the largest firearms manufacturers in the world. Please refer to the Sarsilmaz listing in this section.

SARASQUETA, FELIX

Previous manufacturer located in Eibar, Spain. Previously imported and distributed by SAE (Spain America Enterprises), Inc. located in Miami, FL.

For individual model listings, please go to BlueBookOfGunValues.com/overflow.

SARASQUETA, J.J.

Previous manufacturer located in Eibar, Spain. Imported until 1984 by American Arms, Inc. located in Overland Park, KS.

For individual model listings, please go to BlueBookOfGunValues.com/overflow.

SARASQUETA, VICTOR

Previous manufacturer established in 1883 located in Eibar, Spain. Trademark was sold to Diarm S.A. circa 1986.

For individual model listings, please visit the Online Only/Removed Manufacturer's List at BlueBookOfGunValues.com.

SARCO, INC.

Current importer and wholesaler located in Stirling, NJ.

Sarco Inc. imports a wide variety of foreign and domestic surplus military style rifles and shotguns that offer excellent values for the shooter. Please contact the company directly, as inventory changes constantly.

SARDIUS

Please refer to the Sirkis Industries, LTD listing in this section.

GRADING - PPGS™ 100% 98% 95% 90% 80% 70% 60% LAST MSR

SARRIUGARTE, FRANCISO S.A.

Previous manufacturer located in Elgoibar, Spain. Previously part of the Diarm S.A. Group which was imported and distributed by American Arms, Inc. located in North Kansas City, MO.

SARSILMAZ (SAR ARMS)

Current manufacturer established during 1880, located in Istanbul, Turkey. Currently imported (pistols only) by SAR USA beginning 2018, located in Des Plaines, IL. Previously imported by European American Armory, located in Rockledge, FL until circa 2018 and TR Imports located in Fort Worth, TX. Recently imported by Armalite, Inc., located in Geneseo, IL (refer to listings in Armalite section). Select slide action shotguns are imported by U.S. Sporting Goods Inc. located in Rockledge, FL. Previously distributed 2000-2003 by PMC, located in Boulder City, NV. Previously imported and distributed until 2000 by Armsport, Inc. located in Miami, FL.

For individual model listings, please go to BlueBookOfGunValues.com/overflow.

SATTERLEE ARMS, LLC

Current custom rifle manufacturer located 12 miles south of Deadwood, SD.

RIFLES: BOLT ACTION, CUSTOM

Stuart Satterlee builds a series of bolt action custom rifles utilizing a Mauser style action. Current series include: Alpine, Legacy Classic, North American, British Express Rifle, and the SPR (Satterlee Professional Rifle). Previous series include: Ultimate Mountain Rifle and the African. Please contact him directly for more information, including available options, pricing, and delivery time.

SAUER, J.P., & SOHN

Current manufacturer located in Eckernförde, Germany since 1751 (originally Prussia). Currently imported by Blaser Group (formerly Blaser USA Inc. until late 2019), located in San Antonio, TX. Previously manufactured in Suhl pre-WWII. Previously imported and warehoused 1995-2007 by SIG Arms, located in Exeter, NH. Rifles were previously imported until 1995 by the Paul Company Inc. located in Wellsville, KS and until 1994 by G.U., Inc. located in Omaha, NE.

In 1972, J.P. Sauer & Sohn entered into a cooperative agreement with SIG. During 2000, SAN Swiss Arms AG purchased SIG Arms AG, including the J.P. Sauer & Sohn trademark. The L&O Group, an international industrial holding company, currently has controlling interest of J.P. Sauer and Sohns. Production remains in Eckernförde, Germany.

DRILLINGS & COMBINATION GUNS

COMBO BBF 54 O/U – standard grade combination gun, 16 ga./.222 Rem., .243 Win., 6.5x57Rmm, 7x57Rmm, 7x65Rmm, or .30-06 cals., ejectors, double triggers with front set trigger, moderate engraving on coin finished receiver, Greener crossbolt with double barrel lugs, 6 lbs. Importation disc. 1986.

$2,200 $2,060 $1,760 $1,565 $1,380 $1,250 $1,125 *$2,495*

* ***Combo BBF 54 O/U Luxury Grade*** – similar to Combo BBF 54, except game scene engraved and deluxe crotch walnut.

$2,450 $2,200 $2,000 $1,785 $1,600 $1,475 $1,300 *$2,745*

SAUER COMBINATION GUN O/U – 20 ga. over 7x57Rmm, 7x65Rmm, 8x57mmJS, or 9.3x74Rmm cal., double underlug, Greener crossbolt, 23.6 in. barrels, express sight, brass foresight bead, gold DT, silver Nitride receiver with game scene and fine Arabesque scroll engraving, best quality checkered walnut stock and forearm with German cheekpiece, silver pistol grip cap. Mfg. 2012-disc.

Last MSR was $67,461.

This model is also available with larger sideplates and interchangeable barrels, please contact the importer for information and pricing.

SAUER MODEL 3000 DRILLING – available in either 16 ga./.30-06, 6.5x57Rmm, 7x57Rmm, 7x65Rmm, or 12 ga./.222 Rem. (disc.), .243 Win., .30-06, 6.5x57Rmm, 7x57Rmm, 7x65Rmm, or 9.3x74Rmm cal., Greener crossbolt and double barrel lug locking, cocking indicators, front set trigger, automatic safety, walnut pistol grip stock with hog-back and cheekpiece, Grade III scroll engraving, 7 1/4 lbs. Importation disc. 1999.

$4,500 $3,750 $3,200 $2,725 $2,250 $1,800 $1,400 *$4,600*

This model was also previously imported by Weatherby and Colt - please refer to separate listings for more information.

GRADING - PPGS™	100%	98%	95%	90%	80%	70%	60%	LAST MSR

* ***Sauer Model 3000 Drilling Luxury Grade*** – similar to Model 3000 standard, except select root timber and extensive engraving featuring two animals. Importation disc. 1999.

	$5,550	$4,875	$4,400	$3,875	$3,475	$3,000	$2,575	*$6,100*

LUFTWAFFE M30 SURVIVAL DRILLING – 12 or 16 ga. (65mm) SxS over 9.3x74Rmm, 28 in. barrels, large eagle and swastika on stock and breech end of right barrel. Originally mfg. for Luftwaffe pilots during WWII. approx. 2,450 mfg. 1941-1942.

	$20,000	$17,500	$15,000	$13,000	$11,000	$8,000	$7,000	

Subtract 40% if w/o original aluminum case or accessories.

SAUER MODEL 3000E DRILLING – see listing under Colt Sauer Drilling.

PISTOLS: SEMI-AUTO

MODEL 1913 POCKET AUTOMATIC – .32 ACP cal., 7 shot, 3 in. barrel, fixed sights, black rubber grips, blue finish. Mfg. 1913-1930.

	$550	$450	$350	$250	$200	$150	$135	

MODEL 1913 25 AUTOMATIC – .25 ACP cal., 7 shot, 2 1/2 in. barrel, fixed sights, black rubber grips, blue finish. Mfg. 1913-1930.

	$450	$400	$350	$250	$200	$150	$135	

MODEL 28 – .25 ACP cal., 7 shot, 3 in. barrel, fixed sights, black rubber grips, blue finish. Mfg. 1930-1938.

	$375	$325	$275	$225	$175	$150	$135	

BEHÖRDEN "AUTHORITY" M1930 MODEL – .32 ACP cal., 3 in. barrel, blue, black lacquer, or white, black plastic grips.

	$550	$450	$300	$250	$200	$150	$135	

Very rare alloy frame and slide examples can sell for $4,500-$6,500.

MODEL 38 H DOUBLE ACTION AUTOMATIC – .22 LR (extremely rare), .32 ACP, or .380 ACP (rare) cal., 3 1/4 in. barrel, fixed sights, blue, plastic grips. Mfg. 1938-1945.

.32 ACP cal.	$850	$650	$550	$450	$400	$350	$300	

Add 100% for early high polish guns.
Add 20% for Waffenamt proofing.
Add 25%-50% for police markings.
Rarity precludes accurate pricing on the .22 LR and .380 ACP cal. models, but it is estimated these can sell in the $7,500-$12,500 range.

REVOLVERS: SA/DA

Sauer manufactured .38 cal. double action revolvers circa 1960-1985, and also licensed other manufacturers, including Armi San Paolo. Most had blue finish and walnut grips. Current values range from $200-$400, depending on condition.

RIFLES: BOLT ACTION

SAUER PRE-WWII BOLT ACTION RIFLE – most popular European cals. and .30 - 06, 22 or 24 in. barrel, raised solid rib, Krupp steel, double-set triggers, folding 3 leaf express sight, checkered sporter stock. Mfg. pre-WWII.

	$1,500	$1,300	$1,100	$1,000	$800	$700	$550	

MODEL 90 STANDARD – .22-250 Rem., .222 Rem. (only 3 mfg.), .243 Win., .25-06 Rem., 6.5x55mm, .270 Win., .30-06, .308 Win. (late mfg.), .300 Win. Mag., .300 Wby. Mag., 7mm Rem. Mag., .375 H&H, or .458 Win. Mag. cal., 24 in. barrel, 3 or 4 shot detachable mag., satin, oil finished checkered walnut stock with Monte Carlo cheekpiece and rosewood forend cap, 2 stage set trigger, free floated barrel, approx. 7 1/2 lbs. Importation disc.

	$1,200	$1,050	$900	$800	$650	$550	$425	*$1,175*

Early importation rifles came standard with a half stock and barrel band, and also had European sling swivels with milled stops. In 1989, this model's design changed to look more like the Colt Sauer rifle (w/o sights, gloss finished stock and set trigger was removed). During 1985-1989, Sauer exported to Sigarms 2,300 Model 90 rifles, 1,100 of these were in Mag. cals.

* ***Model 90 Standard Stutzen*** – .22-250 Rem., .222 Rem. (3 mfg.), or .243 Win., Mannlicher style full stock, not available in European or Mag. cals. Importation disc. 1989.

	$1,350	$1,175	$1,025	$925	$750	$600	$475	*$1,225*

* ***Model 90 Standard Safari*** – .458 Win. Mag cal., 23.62 in. barrel, 10 1/2 lbs. Imported 1986-88 only.

	$1,500	$1,300	$1,100	$1,000	$800	$700	$550	*$1,675*

GRADING - PPGS™	100%	98%	95%	90%	80%	70%	60%	LAST MSR

MODEL 90 SUPREME (LUX) - .243 Win., .25-06 Rem., 6.5x55mm Swedish, .270 Win., .30 - 06, .300 Win. Mag., .300 Wby. Mag., 7mm Rem. Mag., .338 Win. Mag., or .375 H&H cal., similar to Model 90, satin finished deluxe stock with Monte Carlo cheekpiece and rosewood forearm and pistol grip caps, gold trigger, no sights, 7.1-7.7 lbs. Importation 1987-98.

	$2,250	$1,950	$1,700	$1,550	$1,250	$1,000	$800	*$1,350*

Add approx. 60% for Grade I engraving, 100% for Grade II, 125% for Grade III, and 160% for Grade IV.

*** *Model 90 Supreme (Lux) Safari***

While advertised, this model had limited importation. MSR was set at $1,795.

*** *Model 90 Supreme (Lux) Stutzen***

While advertised, this model had little importation. MSR was set at $1,200.

MODEL 100 CERATECH - .223 Rem., .243 Win., .270 Win., .300 Win. Mag., .30-06, .308 Win., 6.5 Creedmoor, 6.5x55mm, 6.5 PRC, 7mm Rem. Mag. 7mm-08, 8x57mm IS, or 9.3x62mm, cal., right or left-hand action, EVER REST action bedding, 22 or 24 in. cold hammer forged original Sauer barrel, detachable 4 or 5 shot double stack mag., forged steel receiver, adj. single stage trigger, Ergo Max black synthetic stock with symmetrical palm swells, rubber recoil pad, three position safety, three-lug bolt head, 60 degree bolt lift, Cerakote coating on barrel, action and knob. New 2019.

MSR $950	$900	$775	$675	$575	$500	$400	$325	

MODEL 100 CHEROKEE - .270 Win., .300 Win. Mag., .308 Win., 6.5 Creedmoor, 6.5 PRC, 7mm Rem. Mag. or 7mm-08 cal., right or left-hand action, EVER REST action bedding, 22 or 24 in. cold hammer forged original Sauer barrel, detachable 4 or 5 shot double stack mag., forged steel receiver, adj. single stage trigger, Ergo Max synthetic stock with symmetrical palm swells, rubber recoil pad, three position safety, three-lug bolt head, 60 degree bolt lift, Cerakote "Tundra Green" coating on barrel, action and knob, Woodland Digi Camo stock. New late 2018.

MSR $1,100	$990	$875	$750	$650	$550	$450	$350	

MODEL 100 CLASSIC - .222 Rem. (disc.), .223 Rem., .243 Win., .270 Win., .308 Win., .30-06, 6.5 Creedmoor, 6.5x55mm, 8x57mmIS, 9.3x62mm, 7mm Rem. Mag., .300 Win. Mag., 7mm-08 (new 2018), or 6.5 PRC (new 2018) cal., right or left-hand action, EVER REST action bedding, 22 or 24 1/2 in. cold hammer forged original Sauer barrel, detachable 4 or 5 shot double stack mag., forged steel receiver, adj. single stage trigger, dark stained beechwood ambidextrous stock with symmetrical palm swells, rubber recoil pad, three position safety, three-lug bolt head, 60 degree bolt lift, suitable for all Remington scope bases, matte black surface finish, 6 lbs. 9 oz. New 2016.

MSR $1,000	$900	$790	$675	$610	$495	$400	$330	

MODEL 100 CLASSIC XT - .222 Rem. (disc.), .223 Rem., .243 Win., .270 Win., .308 Win., .30-06, 6.5 Creedmoor, 6.5x55mm, 8x57mmJS, 7mm-08 (new 2018), 9.3x62mm, 7mm Rem. Mag., 6.5 PRC (new 2018), or .300 Win. Mag. cal., right or left-hand action, EVER REST action bedding, 22 or 24 1/2 in. cold hammer forged original Sauer barrel, detachable 4 or 5 shot double stack mag., forged steel receiver, adj. single stage trigger, Ergo Max polymer stock with symmetrical palm swells, rubber recoil pad, three position safety, three-lug bolt head, 60 degree bolt lift, suitable for all Remington scope bases, matte black surface finish, 6 lbs. 9 oz. New 2016.

MSR $850	$765	$675	$575	$525	$425	$350	$280	

MODEL S100 PANTERA - .223 Rem., .243 Win., .300 Win. Mag., .30-06, .308 Win., 6.5 Creedmoor, or 6.5 PRC cal., 20 or 22 in. heavy fluted barrel, threaded muzzle, 4 or 5 shot double stack mag., adj. trigger, adj. cheekpiece, sculpted palm swell, recoil pad, bipod adapter, EVER REST action bedding, Cerakote Black Recon finish on barrel and action. New late 2018.

MSR $1,650	$1,485	$1,300	$1,110	$1,015	$815	$675	$550	

MODEL S100 FIELDSHOOT - .223 Rem., .243 Win., .308 Win., 6.5 Creedmoor, 6.5 PRC, or 6.5x55 SE cal., 24 in. heavy fluted barrel, threaded muzzle, 4 or 5 shot double stack mag., adj. trigger, adj. cheekpiece, sculpted palm swell, recoil pad, bipod adapter, EVER REST action bedding, matt blue barrel and action, wooden laminate stock with dark oil finish. New 2019.

MSR $1,650	$1,485	$1,300	$1,110	$1,015	$815	$675	$550	

MODEL S101 ALASKA - .22-250 Rem., .243 Win., .270 Win., .308 Win., .30-06, 6.5x55mm SE, 7x64mm, 8x57mmJS, 9.3x62mm, 7mm Rem. Mag., .300 Win. Mag., or .338 Win. Mag. cal., 22 or 24 (Mag. cals. only) in. barrel, silver revolver bolt knob, M15x1 muzzle thread, DURA SAFE firing pin safety, silver Ilaflon coating on barrel and receiver, Grey laminated ERGO MAX stock with adj. comb and quick detachable sling swivels, 7 1/4 lbs. Imported 2015-2020.

	$1,850	$1,625	$1,395	$1,250	$1,025	$850	$725	*$2,052*

GRADING - PPGS™	100%	98%	95%	90%	80%	70%	60%	LAST MSR

MODEL S101 ARTEMIS – .243 Win., .270 Win., .308 Win., .30-06, 7x64mm, 8x57mmJS, or 9.3x62mm cal., 20 in. barrel, DURA SAFE firing pin safety, jeweled bolt, walnut bolt knob, fully adj. iron sights, walnut ERGO compact stock, "Laserline" stock grain, special stock and barrel length created for the lady hunter, 6 1/4 lbs. Importation began 2015.

MSR $2,995	$2,700	$2,350	$2,025	$1,825	$1,475	$1,200	$950	

MODEL S101 CLASSIC – .22-250 Rem., .243 Win., .270 Win., .308 Win., .30-06, 6.5x55mm, 7x64mm, 8x57mmJS, 9.3x62mm, 7mm Rem. Mag., .300 Win. Mag., or .338 Win. Mag. cal., machined steel receiver, matte black finish, 22 or 24 (Mag. cals. only) in. steel rifled barrel, 6-lug bolt locks directly into the barrel, removable double stack 4 or 5 shot detachable box magazine, optional adjustable open sights, ambidextrous ERGO Max oiled Grade I walnut stock, soft rubber recoil pad, direct firing pin safety, ergonomic slide located right on the bolt shroud, 60° bolt rotation, accepts Remington 700 long action scope base mounts, approx. 7 lbs. New mid-2013.

MSR $2,630	$2,350	$2,050	$1,750	$1,600	$1,300	$1,050	$800	

* ***Model S101 Classic XT*** – .22-250 Rem., .243 Win., .270 Win., .308 Win., .30-06, 6.5x55mm, 7x64mm, 8x57mmJS, 9.3x62mm, 7mm Rem. Mag., .300 Win. Mag., or .338 Win. Mag. cal., similar to Model S101 Classic, except features ERGO MAX polymer stock with soft touch coating, approx. 7 lbs. New mid-2013.

MSR $2,330	$2,100	$1,850	$1,600	$1,450	$1,150	$950	$750	

» **Model S101 Classic XTA** – similar to the Model S101 Classic XT, except has an adj. comb. New 2020.

MSR $2,550	$2,300	$2,000	$1,700	$1,550	$1,250	$1,050	$800	

MODEL S101 FOREST – .308 Win., .30-06, 8x57mmJS, or 9.3x62mm cal., 20 in. heavy medium barrel, double stack magazine, machined steel receiver, EVER REST action bedding, DURA Safe firing pin safety, ambidextrous Grade 1 oiled walnut ERGO MAX stock with symmetrical palm swells, matte black finish, 7 lbs. Imported 2015-2020.

	$1,875	$1,650	$1,400	$1,275	$1,025	$850	$725	*$2,083*

* ***Model S101 Forest XT*** – .308 Win., .30-06, 8x57mmJS, or 9.3x62 cal., similar to Model S101 Forest, except features ERGO MAX polymer stock with Soft Touch coating, 7 lbs. Imported 2015-2020.

	$1,685	$1,475	$1,265	$1,150	$925	$775	$650	*$1,875*

MODEL S101 GTI – .22-250 Rem., .243 Win., 6.5x55mmSE, .270 Win., 7x64mm, .308 Win., .30-06, 8x57IS, 9.3x62, 7mm Rem. Mag., .300 Win. Mag., or .338 Win. Mag. cal., right or left-hand action, 22 or 24 in. barrel, EVER REST action bedding, single stage trigger, Ergo Max laminated thumbhole stock, adj. comb, removable sling swivels. Importation began 2018.

MSR $3,210	$2,900	$2,550	$2,200	$1,950	$1,600	$1,300	$1,000	

MODEL S101 HIGHLAND XTC – .243 Win., .270 Win., 6.5x55 SE, 7x64, .308 Win., .30-06, 8x57, .308 Win., .300 Win. Mag., or 7mm Rem. Mag. cal., 20 or 22 in. fluted barrel with DLC finish, 4 or 5 shot mag., match grade trigger, hand-laid carbon fiber stock w/advanced recoil, Dura Safe direct firing pin safety, fluted bolt, 5.4 lbs. New 2020.

MSR $3,000	$2,700	$2,375	$1,975	$1,825	$1,475	$1,225	$950	

MODEL S101 SCANDIC – .243 Win., .270 Win., .30-06, .308 Win., 7x64mm, 8x57mmJS, or 9.3x62 cal., 20 in. barrel, DURA SAFE firing pin safety, forend has factory bipod adapter, fully adj. high contrast sights, laminated ERGO MAX stock with quick detachable sling swivel, Tundra Green finish, bolt knob made from laminated wood, includes additional sling swivel port on side of buttstock, 6 1/2 lbs. Imported 2015-2020.

	$1,750	$1,525	$1,315	$1,185	$965	$785	$650	*$1,958*

MODEL S101 SELECT – .22-250 Rem., .243 Win., .270 Win., .30-06, .308 Win., 6.5x55mm SE, 7x64mm, 8x57mmJS, 9.3x62mm, 7mm Rem. Mag., .300 Win. Mag., or .338 Win. Mag. cal., 22 or 24 (Mag. cals. only) in. barrel, DURA SAFE firing pin safety, fully adj. iron sights, jeweled bolt, aluminum bolt knob, walnut ERGO MAX stock with "Laserline" stock grain, 7 lbs. Importation began 2015.

MSR $2,995	$2,700	$2,375	$1,975	$1,825	$1,475	$1,225	$950	

MODEL 200 BOLT ACTION – available in 15 cals. between .243 Win. and .375 H&H, short and medium actions only, 23.62 in. unique interchangeable barrels, 6 lug bolt, easily detachable stock and forearm, optional set trigger, detachable mag. with hidden release button, 7.7 lbs. Production disc. 1993.

	$1,225	$925	$800	$700	$600	$525	$450	*$1,395*

Add $100 for 7mm Rem. Mag. or .300 Win. Mag. cal.
Add $300 for extra interchangeable barrel (standard or takedown action).
Add approx. 35% for takedown action.

During 1986-89, Sauer exported to Sigarms 4,170 Model 200 rifles, 1,370 of these were in Mag. cals.

GRADING - PPGS™	100%	98%	95%	90%	80%	70%	60%	LAST MSR

* ***Model 200 Bolt Action Lightweight*** – similar to Model 200, only with alloy receiver, 6.6 lbs. Disc.

	$1,225	$925	$800	$700	$600	$525	$450	*$1,395*

Add $150 for left-hand version.

* ***Model 200 Bolt Action Lux*** – similar to Model 200, except has deluxe walnut, rosewood forend tip and pistol grip cap, marmorized bolt and gold trigger. Disc.

	$1,395	$1,175	$925	$800	$700	$600	$525	*$1,595*

* ***Model 200 Bolt Action Lux American*** – similar to Model 200 Lux, except has high gloss Monte Carlo stock, 24 in. barrel, jeweled bolt, and gold trigger. Disc.

	$1,395	$1,175	$925	$800	$700	$600	$525	*$1,595*

Add $150 for left-hand version.

* ***Model 200 Bolt Action Lux European*** – similar to Model 200 Lux, except has European configured stock with Schnabel forearm, 26 in. barrel. Disc.

	$1,395	$1,175	$925	$800	$700	$600	$525	*$1,595*

Add $95 for left-hand version.

* ***Model 200 Bolt Action Carbon Fiber*** – similar to Model 200, except has carbon fiber stock. Imported 1987-88 only.

	$1,500	$1,300	$1,100	$1,000	$800	$700	$500	*$1,200*

MODEL 202 SUPREME (LUX) – .22-250 Rem. (new 2001), .243 Win. (disc. 1998, resumed 2000), .25-06 Rem., .270 Win., .30-06, .308 Win., 6.5x55mm Swedish (disc. 2000), or 7x64mm (disc. 1997) cal., steel receiver, modular design allowing barrel change within 2 minutes, dual safety, two-piece figured walnut stock, cocking indicator, detachable 3-5 shot mag., takedown with interchangeable barrels, right or left-hand action, 7 1/2 lbs. Imported 1994-2004.

	$2,500	$2,250	$2,000	$1,750	$1,500	$1,300	$1,050	*$3,400*

Add $300 for left-hand action (.30-06 cal. only).
Add $900 per extra barrel in non-Mag. cals.

Also available in left-hand action in .270 Win. (disc. 2000) or .30-06 cal.

* ***Model 202 Supreme (Lux) Magnum*** – .300 Win. Mag., .300 Wby. Mag., .338 Win. Mag. (disc. 1997), .375 H&H, 7mm Rem. Mag., 6.5x68mm (importation disc. 1997), or 8x68mm (importation disc. 1997) cal., converts to 7 cals., 7.7 lbs. Imported 1994-2004.

	$2,750	$2,350	$2,100	$1,800	$1,550	$1,350	$1,150	*$3,600*

Add $200 for .375 H&H cal.

Was also available until 2000 in left-hand action in .300 Win. Mag. or 7mm Rem. Mag. cal.

MODEL 202 ALASKA

While advertised in 1994, this model was never imported. MSR was set at $1,335.

MODEL 202 CLASSIC – various cals., choice of aluminum or steel receiver, Classic styling with Monte Carlo walnut checkered Grade 2 stock and forearm with ebony forend tip, iron sights on barrel, includes sling swivels, round bolt handle, right or left-hand action, 2-3 shot mag., black Ilaflon metal finish. Limited importation 2012-2014.

	$3,200	$2,850	$2,400	$2,000	$1,750	$1,500	$1,250	*$3,509*

MODEL 202 CLASSIC XT (STANDARD) – similar to Model 202 Synthetic, except has checkered walnut stock and forearm, 7.7 lbs. Imported 2001-2014.

	$2,695	$2,350	$2,100	$1,450	$1,050	$900	$775	*$2,995*

MODEL 202 ELEGANCE – various cals., features Grade 4 walnut Monte Carlo stock with ebony forend tip and pistol grip cap, jeweled bolt, swept back bolt handle, detachable mag., 23 1/2 or 25 1/2 in. barrel with iron sights. Importation disc. 2014.

	$4,050	$3,500	$3,050	$2,600	$2,400	$2,000	$1,500	*$4,495*

MODEL 202 FOREST – .270 Win., 7x64, .308 Win., .30-06, 8x57mm, or 9.3x62mm cal., 20 in. black Ilaflon barrel, 4 shot mag., aluminum receiver, round bolt handle, set trigger, forest sights, Grade 3 walnut stock and forend with cheekpiece, synthetic mag. floorplate, drilled and tapped. Imported 2009-2014.

	$3,625	$3,225	$2,675	$2,250	$1,825	$1,500	$1,250	*$3,979*

MODEL 202 HARDWOOD – 9.3x62mm, 8x57mmJS, or .308 Win. cal., similar to Model 202 Outback, except has shorter 18.1 in. barrel, 5 shot detachable box mag., sling swivels, black or Realtree AP HD Blaze camo synthetic stock, not available in left-hand. Imported late 2011-2014.

	$3,600	$3,175	$2,675	$2,100	$1,750	$1,495	$1,325	*$4,029*

GRADING - PPGS™	100%	98%	95%	90%	80%	70%	60%	LAST MSR

MODEL 202 HIGHLAND – various cals., 20 in. black Ilaflon fluted barrel, 3 shot mag., aluminum receiver, round bolt handle, set trigger, steel front sight, Grade 3 Monte Carlo walnut stock and Schnabel forend with cheekpiece, synthetic mag. floorplate, drilled and tapped. Imported 2009-2014.

	$3,625	$3,225	$2,675	$2,250	$1,825	$1,500	$1,250	*$3,979*

MODEL 202 HUNTER MATCH

While advertised in 1994, this model was never imported. MSR was set at $1,495.

MODEL 202 LIGHTWEIGHT – .22-250 Rem., .243 Win., .25-06 Rem., .270 Win., .30-06, .308 Win., and various metric cals., 24 in. fluted barrel w/o sights, aluminum alloy receiver with integral Weaver rail, Ilaflon (disc.) or Teflon coated metal, black synthetic stock, 6 1/2 lbs. Imported 2001-2008.

	$2,600	$1,500	$1,225	$975	$800	$700	$600	*$2,999*

MODEL 202 OUTBACK – various cals., 22 in. black Ilaflon fluted barrel, 3 shot mag., aluminum receiver, flat bolt handle, set trigger, steel front sight, synthetic Monte Carlo stock with Soft Touch, synthetic mag. floorplate, drilled and tapped, 6.4 lbs. Imported 2009-2014.

	$3,325	$2,850	$2,100	$1,825	$1,600	$1,400	$1,225	*$3,719*

MODEL 202 POLAR – various cals., 20 or 22 in. silver Ilaflon fluted barrel, 3 shot mag., steel receiver, round bolt handle, set trigger, synthetic Realtree AP HD Snow camo Monte Carlo stock with Soft Touch, drilled and tapped. Imported 2009-2014.

	$3,325	$2,850	$2,325	$1,825	$1,600	$1,400	$1,225	*$3,772*

MODEL 202 SYNTHETIC – .22-250 Rem. (new 2001), .243 Win. (new 2001), .25-06 Rem., .270 Win., .30-06, .308 Win., .300 Win. Mag., 7mm Rem. Mag. (new 2000), .300 Wby. Mag., .375 H&H (disc. 2005), or 6.5x55mm Swedish (disc. 2000) cal., features black synthetic stock, 24 or 26 in. barrel w/o sights, 7.7 lbs. Imported 1999-2008.

	$1,750	$1,200	$995	$875	$750	$675	$600	*$1,999*

Add $200 for Mag. cals., $400 for .375 H&H cal.

Add $900 for interchangeable standard cal. barrel, or $1,000 for Mag. cal. barrel.

MODEL 202 STUTZEN – various cals., steel or lightweight alloy receiver, full-length Grade III checkered walnut Mannlicher stock and forearm, swept back bolt handle. Limited importation 2012-2014.

	$4,100	$3,600	$3,150	$2,650	$2,150	$1,850	$1,550	*$4,641*

MODEL 202 SUPER GRADE

While advertised in 1994, this model was never imported. MSR was set at $1,020.

MODEL 202 TAKEDOWN SERIES – available in many standard and Mag. cals., 2 or 4 shot mag., takedown action allows disassembly within seconds, point of impact remains constant, open sights on .375 H&H Mag. cal., 6 bolts connect forend with action, and can be detached by pressing a button, deluxe checkered walnut (Grade 4 standard beginning 2010), round or flat bolt handle, approx. 8.8 lbs. Imported 2003-2014.

	$5,850	$5,100	$4,450	$3,750	$3,150	$2,775	$2,125	*$6,333*

Add $380 for Forest model with Grade III walnut.

Add $1,258 for Elegance model with Grade IV walnut.

* ***Model 202 Takedown Hatari*** – .375 H&H, .416 Rem. Mag., or .458 Lott cal., 23.6 in. barrel with express sights with H&H style fold down front sight, blued steel receiver, Ilaflon coated metal parts, large forend, four different wood choices (Grades 3-6), 3 shot mag. Importation disc. 2014.

	$7,825	$7,100	$6,500	$5,700	$4,900	$4,000	$3,000	*$8,488*

Add $268 for Grade 4 wood, $705 for Grade 5, and $1,436 for Grade 6 wood.

MODEL 202 YUKON – various cals., 20 or 22 in. black Ilaflon fluted barrel, 3 shot mag., steel receiver, round bolt handle, set trigger, synthetic Realtree AP HD camo Monte Carlo stock with Soft Touch, drilled and tapped. Imported 2009-2014.

	$3,325	$2,850	$2,325	$1,825	$1,600	$1,400	$1,225	*$3,772*

MODEL 202 VARMINTER – .22-250 Rem., .243 Win., or .25-06 Rem. cal., 24 in. match grade fluted bull barrel with no sights, 3 shot mag., matte black finish, adj. cheekpiece on checkered Turkish walnut stock, 9 1/2 lbs. Imported 2001-2005.

	$2,950	$1,500	$1,225	$975	$800	$700	$600	*$3,400*

MODEL 205 TR TARGET – 6.5x55mm or .308 Win. cal., true left-hand variation, 200 meter diopter sights, modular design allows changing single components including caliber, free floating barrel with vent. forearm, 5 shot mag., interchangeable barrel systems, 12.1 lbs. Imported 1994-97.

	$1,775	$1,575	$1,400	$1,250	$1,100	$950	$825	*$1,900*

GRADING - PPGS™	100%	98%	95%	90%	80%	70%	60%	LAST MSR

MODEL S404 ARTEMIS – various cals., right or left-hand action, 22 in. barrel, black anodized receiver, twin ejectors, Quattro trigger, ErgoLux compact stock in Grade 2 figured walnut, cheekpiece with well-defined palm swell, slender pistol grip, MagLock magazine safety, Sauer Universal mount. Importation began 2018.

MSR $5,229	$4,650	$4,000	$3,500	$3,150	$2,500	$2,100	$1,625	

MODEL S404 AVANTGARDE GRANDE LUXE – various cals., 22 in. barrel, 2 or 3 shot mag., engraved nitrated aluminum or steel receiver, open sights, checkered Grade 7 walnut stock with removable forend, safety includes manual cocking system, quatro trigger system on left side of frame allows 4 different trigger pull weights, interchangeable jeweled bolt assemblies, approx. 7 lbs. New 2016.

MSR $18,635	$16,800	$14,700	$12,600	$11,425	$9,250	$7,550	$5,875	

Add $900 for left-handed stock and receiver.
Add $413 for standard Mag. cals. or $688 for .375 H&H cal.
Add $710 for steel receiver.

MODEL S404 CLASSIC – various cals., 22 in. barrel, 2 or 3 shot mag., black anodized aluminum or steel receiver, open sights, checkered Grade 2 walnut stock with removable forend, safety includes manual cocking system, quatro trigger system on left side of frame allows 4 different trigger pull weights, interchangeable jeweled bolt assemblies, approx. 7 lbs. New 2016.

MSR $5,229	$4,650	$4,000	$3,500	$3,150	$2,500	$2,100	$1,625	

Add $900 for left-handed stock and receiver.
Add $413 for standard Mag. cals. or $688 for .375 H&H cal.
Add $710 for steel receiver.

MODEL S404 CLASSIC XT – various cals., 22 in. barrel, 2 or 3 shot mag., aluminum alloy receiver, open sights, Ergo Max polymer flat green stock with removable forend, safety includes manual cocking system, quatro trigger system on left side of frame allows 4 different trigger pull weights, interchangeable jeweled bolt assemblies, approx. 7 lbs. New 2016.

MSR $4,345	$3,900	$3,400	$2,925	$2,650	$2,150	$1,750	$1,375	

Add $900 for left-handed stock and receiver.
Add $413 for standard Mag. cals. or $688 for .375 H&H cal.
Add $710 for steel receiver.

MODEL S404 ELEGANCE – various cals., 22 in. barrel, 2 or 3 shot mag., black anodized aluminum or steel receiver, open sights, checkered Grade 5 walnut stock with removable forend, safety includes manual cocking system, quatro trigger system on left side of frame allows 4 different trigger pull weights, interchangeable jeweled bolt assemblies, approx. 7 lbs. New 2016.

MSR $6,253	$5,650	$4,950	$4,250	$3,8450	$3,100	$2,550	$1,975	

Add $900 for left-handed stock and receiver.
Add $413 for standard Mag. cals. or $688 for .375 H&H cal.
Add $710 for steel receiver.

MODEL S404 SELECT – various cals., 22, 24, or 27 in. cold hammer forged barrel, black anodized receiver, adj. trigger blade, Ergo Lux laser grained walnut stock, adj. trigger pull, MagLock magazine safety, integral scope mount bases, front sling swivel, hard anodized matte black finish. Imported 2018-2020.

	$4,685	$4,100	$3,515	$3,185	$2,575	$2,100	$1,650	*$5,207*

MODEL S404 STUTZEN SELECT – various cals., 22, 24, or 27 in. cold hammer forged barrel, continuous Stutzen front stock with integrated carbon rail and laser line shaft texturing, black anodized receiver, adj. trigger blade, Ergo Lux laser grained walnut stock, adj. Sauer Quattro trigger, MagLock magazine safety, integral scope mount bases, front sling swivel, hard anodized matte black finish. New 2020.

MSR $7,465	$6,750	$5,900	$5,075	$4,600	$3,725	$3,050	$2,375	

MODEL S404 SYNCHRO XT – various cals., 22 in. barrel, 2 or 3 shot mag., aluminum alloy receiver, open sights, thumbhole Ergo Max polymer flat green stock with adj. cheekpiece with removable forend, safety includes manual cocking system, quatro trigger system on left side of frame allows 4 different trigger pull weights, interchangeable jeweled bolt assemblies, approx. 7 lbs. New 2016.

MSR $5,193	$4,650	$4,000	$3,500	$3,150	$2,500	$2,100	$1,625	

Add $900 for left-handed stock and receiver.
Add $413 for standard Mag. cals. or $688 for .375 H&H cal.
Add $710 for steel receiver.

* ***Model S404 Synchro XTC*** – similar to the Model S404 Synchro XT, except has a carbon fiber stock, 6.1 lbs. New 2020.

MSR $8,691	$7,800	$6,825	$5,850	$5,300	$4,300	$3,500	$2,750	

GRADING - PPGS™	100%	98%	95%	90%	80%	70%	60%	LAST MSR

» **Model S404 Synchro XTC Camo** – similar to the Model S404 Synchro XTC, except has a camo carbon fiber stock, 6.1 lbs. New 2020.

MSR $8,595	$7,700	$6,750	$5,775	$5,235	$4,235	$3,450	$2,700	

SSE 3000 PRECISION RIFLE – .308 Win. cal., very accurate, law enforcement counter Sniper Rifle, built to customer specifications. Disc.

	$4,845	$3,655	$3,200	$2,850	$2,500	$2,275	$2,000	

SSG 2000 – available in .223 Rem., 7.5mm Swiss, .300 Wby. Mag., or .308 Win. (standard) cal., bolt action, 4 shot mag., no sights, deluxe sniper rifle featuring thumbhole style walnut stock with stippling and thumbwheel adj. cheekpiece, 13 lbs. Importation disc. 1986.

	$2,480	$2,260	$1,950	$1,700	$1,500	$1,300	$1,100	*$2,850*

This model was available in .223 Rem., .300 Wby. Mag., or 7.5mm cal. by special order only.

SSG 3000 – .223 Rem., 22 1/2 in. barrel, Parker-Hale bipod, two-stage match trigger, includes 2 1/2-10x52mm Zeiss scope, 200 mfg. for Swiss police. Disc.

	$12,000	$10,000	$8,500	$7,000	$6,750	$5,500	$4,250	

SSG 3000 (RECENT MFG.) – See listing under Sig-Sauer.

RIFLES: SxS

SAUER DOUBLE RIFLE – 7x57Rmm or 9.3x74mm cal., best quality walnut stock and forearm, forged steel receiver with game animals, hunting scenes and Arabesque scroll engraving. Mfg. 2012-disc.

Last MSR was $67,461.

RIFLES: SEMI-AUTO

MODEL 303 – .30-06, .300 Win. Mag., 7x64mm, 8x57mm, or 9.3x62mm cal., gas operated, 2 shot mag., 20 or 22 in. interchangeable barrel, Classic XT black synthetic stock standard with various walnut stock upgrades including thumbhole (GTI Classic or GTI Elegance), noiseless cocking and decocking lever on back of receiver, Nitrobond metal finish, open sights with HiViz front and rear Battue rib optional, Elegance model has polished jewelled bolt, approx. 7 1/8 lbs. Imported 2010-2017.

	$3,000	$2,600	$2,200	$1,850	$1,575	$1,275	$1,100	*$3,352*

Add $483 for Classic Grade II walnut or $1,400 for Elegance Grade IV walnut stock and forearm.
Add $1,700 for Grade II walnut on GTI Classic with thumbhole stock (new 2012), or $2,988 for Grade IV walnut on GTI Elegance model with thumbhole stock (new 2012).

SHOTGUNS

J. P. Sauer and Sohn restarted shotgun production in Eckernforde, West Germany in 1951. Stoeger Arms Corporation imported, distributed, and marketed Sauer Shotguns from 1953 to 1964.

MEISTERWERK SxS – sidelock, best quality checkered walnut stock and forearm, DT, alloy receiver with traditional pre-war English Arabesque engraving standard, other engraving options available. New 2011.

The model has a current MSR of $84,327.

MODEL IX SxS – 20 ga., boxlock, 28 in. barrels with quarter and half choke, forged steel color case hardened or silver nitride receiver with light Arabesque scroll engraving and scalloped borders, double underlug, Greener action, H&H style ejectors, gold DT, straight grip English style Grade 7 hand checkered walnut stock and forearm, recoil pad. New 2011.

This model has a current MSR of $45,536.

MODEL 60 SxS – 12, 16, and 20 ga., 26, 28, or 30 in. barrels, various fixed chokes, Anson Deeley boxlock action with underlocking lugs, case hardened finish with game scene engraving, DT, extractors, splinter forend and cheekpiece pistol grip stock hand carved from European walnut, this model was the standard model of its period. Disc.

	$1,050	$925	$800	$715	$575	$475	$375	

Add 20% for 20 ga.
Add 10% for NIB condition.
Add 25% for beavertail forend.

MODEL 60 DELUXE – 12, 16, and 20 ga., 26, 28, or 30 in. barrels, various fixed chokes, Anson Deeley boxlock action with double underlocking lugs, case hardened finish with game scene engraving, non-selective single trigger, automatic ejectors, beavertail forend and cheekpiece pistol grip stock, hand carved from European walnut. Disc.

	$1,400	$1,225	$1,050	$950	$775	$625	$500	

Add 20% for 20 ga.
Add 10% for NIB condition.

GRADING - PPGS™	100%	98%	95%	90%	80%	70%	60%	LAST MSR

ROYAL MODEL SxS – 12, 16 or 20 ga., 26, 28, or 30 in. barrels, various fixed chokes, Anson Deeley boxlock action with double under locking lugs, Greener crossbolt through rib extension, side clips, cocking indicators, scalloped engraved frame, SST, auto ejectors, Krupp steel barrel, case hardened finish with hand engraved Sauer motif and Arabesque scroll, splinter forend and cheekpiece pistol grip stock hand carved from European walnut. Mfg. 1955-1977.

	100%	98%	95%	90%	80%	70%	60%	LAST MSR
	$1,650	$1,375	$1,210	$1,100	$880	$770	$660	

Add 20% for 20 ga.
Add 10% for NIB condition.
Add 25% for beavertail forend.
Add 25% for single selective trigger.

APOLLON O/U – 12 or 20 ga., 3 in. chamber, O/U, Anson action, engraved black steel frame, 28 or 30 in. barrels, 5 interchangeable choke tubes, brass bead sight, laser line grained dark walnut stock, golden SAUER logo on hinge pin, 7.26 lbs. Importation began 2018.

	100%	98%	95%	90%	80%	70%	60%	LAST MSR
MSR $2,195	$1,850	$1,650	$1,450	$1,250	$1,050	$850	$725	

Add $200 for 20 ga.

ARTEMIS O/U – 12 or 20 ga., 3 in. chamber, O/U, Anson action, engraved black frame, 28 or 30 in. barrels, 5 interchangeable chokes, brass bead sight, laser line grained dark walnut Monte Carlo stock, red rubber recoil pad, 13.6 in. LOP, 7.26 lbs. Importation began 2018.

	100%	98%	95%	90%	80%	70%	60%	LAST MSR
MSR $2,195	$1,850	$1,650	$1,450	$1,250	$1,050	$850	$725	

Add $200 for 20 ga.

ARTEMIS SxS – 12 ga., 28 in. barrels, mod. and full choke, H&H type sidelock, SST, auto ejector, Krupp steel, checkered pistol grip stock. Mfg. 1966-77.

* ***Artemis SxS Grade I*** – fine line engraved. Disc.

	100%	98%	95%	90%	80%	70%	60%	LAST MSR
	$5,500	$4,620	$3,850	$3,520	$3,080	$2,640	$2,200	

* ***Artemis SxS Grade II*** – extensive engraving. Disc.

	100%	98%	95%	90%	80%	70%	60%	LAST MSR
	$6,600	$5,500	$4,840	$4,235	$3,850	$3,300	$3,080	

GRADE 380 SxS

	100%	98%	95%	90%	80%	70%	60%	LAST MSR
	$4,500	$4,000	$3,500	$3,000	$2,500	$2,200	$1,500	

GRADE F-40 SxS

Rarity factor precludes accurate price evaluation.

MODEL F-45 SxS

	100%	98%	95%	90%	80%	70%	60%	LAST MSR
	$12,000	$10,500	$9,000	$8,000	$6,500	$5,000	$3,200	

MODEL F-60 SxS

	100%	98%	95%	90%	80%	70%	60%	LAST MSR
	$23,000	$20,000	$17,000	$14,000	$12,000	$9,000	$5,000	

MODEL 66 O/U FIELD GUN – 12 ga., 28 in. mod. and full, Krupp steel barrels, H&H type sidelocks, SST, auto ejectors, checkered pistol grip stock, available in three grades of engraving. Mfg. 1966-75.

	100%	98%	95%	90%	80%	70%	60%	LAST MSR
Grade I	$2,200	$1,760	$1,540	$1,320	$1,100	$880	$770	
Grade II	$3,080	$2,420	$1,980	$1,650	$1,430	$1,210	$990	
Grade III	$3,850	$3,300	$2,860	$2,420	$1,980	$1,650	$1,320	

MODEL 66 O/U SKEET GUN – similar to Field Gun, with 26 in. VR skeet bored barrel and vent. forearm. Mfg. 1966-1975.

	100%	98%	95%	90%	80%	70%	60%	LAST MSR
	$2,300	$1,800	$1,600	$1,400	$1,150	$925	$775	

MODEL 66 O/U TRAP GUN – similar to 66 Skeet, with 30 in. barrels, full and full, or mod. and full choke, trap style stock.

	100%	98%	95%	90%	80%	70%	60%	LAST MSR
Grade I	$2,090	$1,760	$1,540	$1,320	$1,100	$880	$770	
Grade II	$3,080	$2,420	$1,980	$1,650	$1,430	$1,210	$880	
Grade III	$3,850	$3,300	$2,860	$2,420	$1,980	$1,650	$1,320	

SAUER/FRANCHI STANDARD GRADE O/U – 12 ga. only, double triggers, checkered walnut stock and forearm, SST, blue finish only, sling swivels, VR. Importation disc. 1986.

	100%	98%	95%	90%	80%	70%	60%	LAST MSR
	$450	$375	$340	$315	$290	$275	$260	*$785*

* ***Sauer/Franchi Standard Regent Grade O/U*** – similar to Standard grade, except has single trigger and lightly engraved silver finished receiver. Importation disc. 1986.

	100%	98%	95%	90%	80%	70%	60%	LAST MSR
	$550	$475	$395	$350	$310	$290	$275	*$825*

GRADING - PPGS™	100%	98%	95%	90%	80%	70%	60%	LAST MSR

* ***Sauer/Franchi Standard Favorit Grade O/U*** – similar to Regent Grade, except has elaborate scroll engraving on coin finished receiver, gold-plated trigger. Importation disc. 1986.

	$675	$550	$495	$450	$420	$385	$350	*$875*

* ***Sauer/Franchi Standard Diplomat Grade O/U*** – similar to Favorit Grade, except has more elaborate scroll engraving and with model name gold filled on receiver sides and barrel, extra grain French walnut, cased.

	$875	$750	$625	$550	$495	$460	$435	*$1,520*

SAUER/FRANCHI SPORTING S O/U – 12 ga. only, 28 in. barrels, ejectors, SST, select European walnut with checkered stock and forearm, 10mm VR, plain silver finished receiver with model name gold filled on both sides. Importation disc. 1986.

	$800	$700	$600	$500	$450	$420	$395	*$1,375*

SAUER/FRANCHI MODEL TRAP O/U – similar to Sporting S, except has 29 in. barrels, trap chokes and stock dimensions. Importation disc. 1986.

	$875	$750	$625	$550	$495	$460	$435	*$1,375*

SAUER/FRANCHI MODEL SKEET O/U – similar to Sporting S, except has skeet chokes. Importation disc. 1986.

	$875	$750	$625	$550	$495	$460	$435	*$1,375*

STANDARD MODEL V – 12, 16, or 20 (introduced 1957) ga., 26, 28, or 30 in. barrels, various fixed chokes, Anson & Deeley boxlock action with double under locking lugs, case hardened finish with scroll or game scene engraving, DT, extractor, splinter forend and cheekpiece pistol grip stock hand carved from European walnut. Imported 1953-1959.

	$1,050	$925	$800	$715	$575	$475	$375	

Add 20% for 20 ga.
Add 10% for NIB condition.
Add 25% for beavertail forend.

MODEL VIII – 12, 16, or 20 (introduced 1957) ga., 26, 28, or 30 in. barrels, various fixed chokes, Anson & Deeley boxlock action with double underlocking lugs, Greener crossbolt through rib extension, side clips, cocking indicators, case hardened finish with hand engraved Sauer motif and Arabesque scroll, DT, extractor, splinter forend and cheekpiece pistol grip stock hand carved from walnut. Imported 1953-1959.

	$1,250	$1,100	$950	$850	$700	$575	$450	

Add 20% for 20 ga.
Add 10% for NIB condition.
Add 25% for beavertail forend.

MODEL VIII E – 12, 16, and 20 (introduced 1957) ga., 26, 28, or 30 in. barrel, various fixed chokes, Anson & Deeley boxlock action with double under locking lugs, Greener crossbolt through rib extension, side clips, cocking indicators, scalloped receiver, case hardened finish with hand engraved Sauer motif and Arabesque scroll, DT, automatic ejectors, splinter forend and cheekpiece pistol grip stock hand carved from European walnut. Imported 1953-1959.

	$1,400	$1,225	$1,050	$950	$775	$625	$500	

Add 20% for 20 ga.
Add 10% for NIB condition.
Add 25% for beavertail forend.
Add 50% for special order custom hand engraved pattern.
Add 200% for Deluxe Model with sideplates, custom hand engraved pattern.

MODEL 8 DES – 12 and 16 ga., 26, 28, or 30 in. barrels, various fixed chokes, Anson & Deeley boxlock action with double under locking lugs, Greener crossbolt through rib extension, side clips, cocking indicators, scalloped receiver, case hardened finish with hand engraved Sauer motif and Arabesque scroll, SST, automatic ejectors, beavertail forend with black horn inlay, non-cheekpiece pistol grip stock, hand carved from European walnut, with silver monogram plate and black diamond horn inlays. Imported 1953-1959.

SL5 SEMI-AUTO – 12 ga., 3 in. chamber, inertia driven semi-auto, aluminum frame, 28 or 30 in. barrel, 5 interchangeable choke tubes, 4 shot mag., laser grained walnut stock, rubber recoil pad, includes ABS case, satin finish, 6.61-6.83 lbs. Importation began 2018.

MSR $1,699	$1,530	$1,340	$1,150	$1,040	$840	$700	$550	

GRADING - PPGS™	100%	98%	95%	90%	80%	70%	60%	LAST MSR

SAVAGE ARMS, INC.

Current manufacturer located in Westfield, MA since 1959, with sales offices located in Suffield, CT. Previously manufactured in Utica, NY - later manufacture was in Chicopee Falls, MA. Dealer and distributor sales.

This company originally started in Utica, NY in 1894. The Model 1895 was initially manufactured by Marlin between 1895-1899. After WWI, the name was again changed to the Savage Arms Corporation. Savage moved to Chicopee Falls, MA circa 1946 (to its Stevens Arms Co. plants). In the mid-1960s the company became The Savage Arms Division of American Hardware Corp., which later became The Emhart Corporation. This division was sold in September 1981, and became Savage Industries, Inc. located in Westfield, MA (since the move in 1960). On November 1, 1989, Savage Arms Inc. acquired the majority of assets of Savage Industries, Inc. On June 24, 2013, ATK acquired Caliber Company, the parent company of Savage Sports Corporation. During 2013, Savage Arms became a division of the Vista Outdoor Group. On July 1, 2019, Vista announced that it sold Savage's (and its subsidiaries Stevens and Fox) firearms to Long Range Acquisition, LLC.

Savage Arms, Inc. will offer service and parts on their current line of firearms only (those manufactured after Nov. 1, 1995). Warranty and repair claims for products not acquired by Savage Arms, Inc. will remain the responsibility of Savage Industries, Inc. Parts for pre-1989 Savage Industries, Inc. firearms may be obtained by contacting the Numrich Gun Parts Corporation located in West Hurley, NY.

Savage Arms pre-December 1968 serial number records can be researched from the original company ledgers for rifles, pistols, and shotguns that were serialized. Information on Savage post-December 1968 guns (non-serialized firearms) is not available. Factory letters may be obtained through the Cody Firearms Records office at the Buffalo Bill Center of the West. For more Savage model information, please refer to the Serialization section in the back of this text.

Please refer to the *Blue Book of Modern Black Powder Arms* (also available online) for more information and prices on Savage's lineup of modern black powder models. For more information and current pricing on both new and used Savage airguns, please refer to the *Blue Book of Airguns* - also available as an online subscription.

COMBINATION GUNS

All Model 24s are under the domain of Savage Arms, Inc.

Add 20% for .22 Mag. cal. on models listed below, where applicable.

MODEL 24 O/U - .22 LR over .410 bore, open rifle sight, visible hammer, break open, plain pistol grip stock. Mfg. 1950-65.

$700 $600 $525 $450 $400 $325 $250

This model featured top lever opening, except on the Models 24S and 24MS.

MODEL 24B-DL - .22 LR or .22 WMR cal. over .410 bore.

$750 $650 $575 $500 $425 $340 $265

MODEL 24P - .22 LR over 20 ga. or .410 bore.

$750 $650 $575 $500 $425 $340 $265

MODEL 24S - .22 LR cal. over 20 ga. or .410 bore barrel, similar to Model 24, side lever, dovetail for scope. Mfg. 1964-1971.

$750 $650 $575 $500 $425 $340 $265

MODEL 24MS - similar to Model 24S, with .22 WMR cal. barrel. Mfg. 1964-71.

$900 $775 $675 $575 $475 $400 $325

MODEL 24DL - .22 LR cal. over 20 ga. or .410 bore barrel, similar to Model 24S, with top lever, satin chrome frame and checkered stock. Mfg. 1962-69.

$750 $650 $575 $500 $425 $340 $265

MODEL 24MDL - similar to Model 24DL, with .22 WMR cal. barrel and chrome frame. Mfg. 1962-69.

$900 $775 $675 $575 $475 $400 $325

MODEL 24FG - similar to Model 24DL, w/o Monte Carlo stock, with top lever. Mfg. 1972-disc.

$700 $600 $525 $450 $400 $325 $250

Action was changed to under lever opening in front of trigger guard circa 1980.

MODEL 24 FIELD - .22 LR or .22 WMR over 20 ga. or .410 bore, under lever opening in front of trigger guard introduced circa 1980, lightweight field version, 24 in. separated barrels, 3 in. chambers, 6 3/4 lbs. Disc. 1989.

$600 $525 $450 $375 $325 $265 $215 *$209*

GRADING - PPGS™	100%	98%	95%	90%	80%	70%	60%	LAST MSR

MODEL 24F (PREDATOR) – .17 HMR (new 2004), .22 Hornet, .222 Rem. (disc. 1989), .223 Rem., or .30-30 Win. (12 ga. only) cal., over 12, 20 ga., or .410 bore (mfg. 1998-2000), 3 in. chamber, 24 in. barrels, 12 ga. barrel is available either with fixed choke or choke tube, wood (disc.) or matte black DuPont Rynite synthetic stock, hammer block safety, DTs, approx. 8 lbs. Mfg. 1989-2007.

	$700	$600	$525	$450	$375	$325	$265	*$698*

Add $31 for 12 ga.
Add $55 for .410 bore adaptor (12 ga. only, disc. 2000).
Add $14 for Camo Rynite stock (disc., Model 24F-T, Turkey Model-12 ga./.22 Hornet or .223 Rem. cal. only).

MODEL 24V – similar to Model 24, in .22 Hornet (disc. 1984), .222 Rem. (new 1967), .223 Rem., .30-30 Win., .357 Max., or .357 Mag. (disc.), 20 ga., 3 in. chamber, 24 in. barrels, single trigger, 7 lbs. Mfg. 1967-1989.

	$1,000	$850	$750	$650	$550	$450	$350	

Action was changed to under lever opening in front of trigger guard circa 1980.

MODEL 24D – .22 LR or .22 WMR over .410 bore or 20 ga., black or case hardened frame, game scene decoration was eliminated in 1974, forearm not checkered after 1976. Introduced 1971.

	$750	$650	$575	$500	$425	$340	$265	

Action was changed to under lever opening in front of trigger guard circa 1980.

MODEL 24E – .22 LR cal. over .410 bore, case colored frame, wood stock and forearm. Disc.

	$750	$650	$575	$500	$425	$340	$265	

MODEL 24C CAMPER'S COMPANION – .22 LR over 20 ga., 20 in. barrel cylinder bore, buttplate opens to store ten .22 LR cartridges and one 20 ga. shell in buttstock, nickel finish, carrying case, 5 3/4 lbs. Mfg. 1972-88.

	$800	$675	$600	$525	$450	$375	$300	*$239*

Add 10% for nickel finish (Model 24CS - shipped with pistol grip stock also).
Action was changed to under lever opening in front of trigger guard circa 1980.

MODEL 24 VS – similar to Model 24CS, only .357 Mag. over 20 ga., nickel finish, accessory pistol grip stock is included.

	$750	$650	$575	$500	$425	$340	$265	

MODEL 389 – 12 ga. with 3 in. chamber over choice of .308 Win. or .222 Rem., choke tubes standard, hammerless, double triggers, checkered walnut stock and forearm with recoil pad. Mfg. 1988-90 only.

	$850	$750	$650	$550	$450	$375	$315	*$919*

MODEL 42 TAKEDOWN – .22 LR or .22 WMR cal. over .410 bore, 3 in. chamber, takedown (breaks down with push of one button), 20 in. separated barrels with open sights, black synthetic stock with recoil pad and forearm with red accents, sling swivels, opening lever in front of trigger guard, includes Uncle Mike's Go Bag for easy transport (new 2016), 6.1 lbs. New 2013.

MSR $529	$450	$400	$340	$300	$275	$250	$225	

* ***Model 42 Compact (Youth)*** – .22 LR over .410 bore, break-action hammer gun, 20 in. barrel, adj. sights, black synthetic stock with red accents, 6 lbs. New 2015.

MSR $529	$450	$400	$340	$300	$275	$250	$225	

MODEL 2400 O/U – 12 ga. full choke barrel over .222 Rem. or .308 Win. rifle barrel, 23 1/2 in. barrels, folding leaf sight, solid rib, dovetailed for scope mount, checkered Monte Carlo stock. Mfg. by Valmet 1975-1980.

	$900	$775	$675	$575	$475	$400	$325	

PISTOLS: BOLT ACTION

MODEL 501F SPORT STRIKER – .22 LR cal., left-hand bolt, right side ejection, 10 in. button rifled barrel with scope blocks, 10 shot mag., grey fiberglass/graphite composite stock, 4 lbs. Mfg. 2000-05.

	$250	$220	$190	$170	$140	$115	$90	*$245*

Add $46 for XP package (Model 501FXP, includes scope and mounts).

MODEL 502F SPORT STRIKER – similar to Model 501F Sport Striker, except is .22 WMR cal., and 5 shot mag. Mfg. 2000-05.

	$325	$285	$245	$220	$180	$145	$115	*$269*

MODEL 503F SPORT STRIKER – similar to Model 501F Sport Striker, except available in .17 HMR cal., 4 lbs. Mfg. 2003-05.

	$350	$300	$265	$230	$195	$160	$125	*$295*

* ***Model 503FSS Sport Striker*** – similar to Model 503F Sport Striker, except is stainless steel. Mfg. 2003-04.

	$400	$350	$300	$260	$220	$180	$140	*$335*

GRADING - PPGS™	100%	98%	95%	90%	80%	70%	60%	LAST MSR

MODEL 510F STRIKER CENTERFIRE – .22-250 Rem. (disc. 2002), .223 Rem. (new 1999), .243 Win., .260 Rem. (mfg. 1999-2000), .308 Win., or 7mm-08 Rem. cal., left-hand short bolt action with right-hand ejection, 14 in. free floating unported barrel, 2 shot internal box mag., blue barrel action, black composite stock with grooved forend and wide bottom swell, drilled and tapped, 5 lbs. Mfg. 1998-2003.

	$500	$425	$360	$325	$295	$275	$250	*$469*

MODEL 516FSS STRIKER – similar to 510F Striker, except has stainless steel barreled action. Mfg. 1998-2000.

	$525	$450	$375	$335	$300	$280	$260	*$462*

* ***Model 516FSAK Striker*** – .243 Win., .270 WSM (mfg. 2003-2004), .300 WSM (new 2003), .308 Win., 7mm WSM (disc. 2004), or 7mm-08 Rem. cal., similar to 516FSS Striker, except has adj. muzzle brake (AMB), 14 in. ported barrel. Mfg. 1998-2005.

	$650	$575	$500	$450	$400	$350	$300	*$621*

* ***Model 516FSAK Striker Camo*** – .300 WSM cal., similar to 516FSAK Striker, except has camo treatment stock. Mfg. 2002 only.

	$650	$575	$500	$450	$400	$350	$300	*$538*

MODEL 516BSAK/BSS SUPER STRIKER – similar cals. to Model 510F Striker, features dual pillar bedded short action and custom designed thumbhole laminate grey stock, stainless steel frame and fluted 14 in. barrel with adj. muzzle brake (AMB), new ESP (Engineered Step Performance) adj. two-stage trigger, approx. 5 lbs. Mfg. 1999-2001.

	$725	$650	$575	$500	$450	$400	$350	*$618*

Subtract approx. $50 if w/o muzzle brake (Model 516BSS, disc. 2000).

PISTOLS: SEMI-AUTO

.25 CALIBER SAVAGE AUTOMATIC – .25 ACP cal., blowback operation, striker fired, fixed barrel, 6 shot mag., steel frame and slide, black hard rubber grips, grip safety, left side thumb safety, early models have wide/heavy slide serrations, late models have thin slide serrations, blued finish, limited production beginning circa 1912 and ending circa 1917, approximately 40 guns were made.

Extreme rarity precludes acurrate pricing on this model.

MODEL 1907 AUTO PISTOL – .32 ACP or .380 ACP cal., 9 (.380 ACP) or 10 (.32 ACP) shot mag., 3 13/16 (.32 ACP) or 4 5/16 (.380 ACP) in. barrel, blue, fixed sights, metal (early mfg. in .32 ACP only until ser. no. 10,980) or hard rubber grips, exposed cocking piece. Approx. 259,000 .32 ACP cal. and approx. 27,500 .380 ACP cal. mfg. 1910-17.

.32 ACP cal.	N/A	$700	$650	$475	$325	$200	$150
.380 ACP cal.	N/A	$1,000	$825	$750	$550	$425	$300

Add 40% for original box with instructions (beware of recent reproductions).

Add large premiums for factory nickel, silver (approx. 4 mfg.), or gold (approx. 12 mfg.) finish (rare).

There were four different types of pearl grips: the early variation was a snap-on with an S/A logo, screw-on with an indian head logo, flared 1917 with no logo, and the pearl inlay type with rivets holding two pearl inlays on each side of standard rubber grips. Asking prices for the grips alone are in the $250-$1,000 range (this also applied to the Model 1915 Hammerless and Model 1917 Automatic).

MODEL 1915 HAMMERLESS – similar to Model 1907, with grip safety and no visible cocking piece. Mfg. 1915-17.

.32 ACP cal.	N/A	$1,400	$1,150	$900	$650	$450	$300
.380 ACP cal.	N/A	$1,800	$1,600	$1,400	$1,100	$850	$500

Add 40% with original box and instruction manual.

MODEL 1917 AUTOMATIC – similar to Model 1907, with spur cocking piece and trapezoidal grips. Mfg. 1920-28.

.32 ACP cal.	N/A	$700	$625	$550	$450	$375	$300
.380 ACP cal.	N/A	$900	$750	$650	$525	$425	$350

Add 40% with original box and instruction manual.

M1907 U.S. ARMY TEST TRIAL .45 ACP – .45 ACP cal., large version of Model 1907, exposed hammer. Approx. 288 mfg. 1907-11 for military trials.

Original	$35,000	$30,000	$27,500	$22,500	$17,500	$12,500	$10,000
Reworked	$16,000	$14,500	$13,000	$11,750	$10,500	$9,250	$8,000

Add 10% for matching magazine.

Experimental M1910 and M1911s are too rare to accurately value.

Original legend on top test pistols rib was in two line "MANUFACTURED BY SAVAGE ARMS CO." over "UTICA N.Y. U.S.A. PAT. NOV. 21.1905." followed in larger stamps by "CAL. 45.". Most pistols were repurchased from the government, reconditioned, and resold to the public as commercial models. The only marking, which appears on the rib of the Pre WWI reconditioned pistols "CAL. 45". On Post WWI reconditioned pistols resold to the public as commercial models were marked on the barrel below the rib "SAVAGE ARMS CORP. UTICA N.Y. U.S.A." with "CAL. 45" on the rib.

GRADING - PPGS™	100%	98%	95%	90%	80%	70%	60%	LAST MSR

MSR 15 BLACKOUT – .300 AAC Blackout cal., 10 1/2 in. Melonite QPQ coated carbon steel barrel, Savage helical flash hider, detachable box mag., Magpul MBUS flip-up front and rear sights, black synthetic stock, KAK Shockwave brace, Hogue pistol grip, fixed pistol length gas system, aluminum receiver, free float handguard with M-LOK, matte black finish. Mfg. mid-2018-2019.

	$975	$875	$775	$675	$575	$475	$375	*$1,099*

PISTOLS: SINGLE SHOT

MODEL 101 – .22 LR cal., 5 1/2 in. barrel, single action, adj. sight, swing out barrel, blue, wood grips. Mfg. 1960-68.

	$300	$250	$215	$175	$145	$115	$85	

RIFLES: LEVER ACTION, DISC.

Whenever Savage made an engineering change on a model, it was usually designated with a letter suffix after the model number. These letters were added to the basic model numbers as the changes were made. The engineering changes could be dimensional on any part, cosmetic, or a total component redesign. The letter suffixes indicated to the company what changes were incorporated into that variation. Most model suffixes are preceeded with a dash. These alphabetical suffix variations are not listed separately in this section, but values will be similar to the base model, unless denoted otherwise.

MODEL 1895 – .303 Savage cal. only, lever action, mfg. in either carbine (22 in.), rifle (26 in.), or musket (30 in.) variations, round (scarce) or octagon barrel that has Marlin proofmark under the forend, open top, solid breech, side ejecting, 6 shot rotary mag., some had unfired shots indicator. Originally mfg. by Marlin, marked "Savage Repeating Arms Co. Utica, N.Y. U.S.A. Pat. Feb. 7, 1893", approx. 6,000 mfg. 1895-99, early models had hole in top of bolt - later ones were smooth.

	N/A	$6,500	$4,800	$3,900	$3,200	$2,600	$2,200	

Values assume rifle configuration - add a 150%+ premium for the carbine (rare) and musket (rare) and for unfired shots indicator.

MODEL 1895 ANNIVERSARY – a replica of the original M1895, .308 Win. cal., 24 in. octagon barrel, engraved receiver, brass-plated lever, straight stock, Schnabel forend, medallion in stock, brass crescent buttplate. Mfg. 9,999 in 1970 only, to commemorate Savage's 75th year. Mfg. by Savage Arms, Division of Emhart.

	$600	$550	$500	$450	$375	$300	$250	*$195*

MODEL 1899 – improvement of Model 1895 with squared-off front end of breech bolt and cocking indicator as opposed to viewing hole indicator. Early Model 1899s have oblong cocking indicator located on the top of the breech bolt. In approx. 1908, this was changed to a pin on the upper tang. A wide variety of special order features were available including special length barrels (up to 30 in.), pistol grip stocks, checkering, woods, plating, grades of engraving, sights, etc., all of which can command a moderate to sizeable premium.

Add 20% for .25-35 WCF, .32-40 WCF, or .38-55 WCF cal.

Add approx. 100% for fancy checkered deluxe grade wood or 30% for checkered plain grain wood on models below that apply.

Any factory engraved Savage 99 is rare (less than 1,000 mfg. to date) with values having to be computed one gun at a time. Engraved Model 1899s range from $2,500-$75,000+, depending on the level of engraving and original condition. Values assume standard rifle with no engraving options (Grades A through G).

In 1905 Savage broadened the variety of this model and added the 1899A2, CD, BC, AB, Excelsior, Leader, Crescent, Victor, Rival, Premier, and Monarch (top-of-the-line model). Prices at the time ranged from $21 to $250 - quite a range.

All Model 1899s and 99s fall within the domain of Savage Arms, Inc.

Rifles under ser. no. 90,000 should be inspected before firing for possible receiver cracking at rear left corner.

From 1899-circa 1950, Model 1899s had serial numbers stamped on buttplate, buttstock, and forearm. A factory drilled and tapped Model 1899 has the model nomenclature moved to the left side.

* ***Model 1899A Rifle*** – .303 Savage, .30-30 Win., .25-35 WCF, .32-40 WCF, .38-55 WCF, or .300 Sav. cal., 26 in. round barrel, straight grip stock, crescent or shotgun butt with steel buttplate, takedown added 1909. Mfg. 1899-1927, Short rifle (22 in.) mfg. 1899-1922.

	$1,300	$1,050	$850	$750	$675	$625	$550	

* ***Model 1899B Rifle*** – .303 Savage, .30-30 Win., .25-35 WCF, .32-40 WCF, or .38-55 WCF cal., 26 in. octagon barrel, straight grip stock, crescent or shotgun butt with steel buttplate. Mfg. 1899-1915.

	$1,400	$1,200	$950	$775	$700	$575	$525	

Add 35% for .25-35 WCF, .32-40 WCF. and .38-55 WCF.

GRADING - PPGS™	100%	98%	95%	90%	80%	70%	60%	LAST MSR

* ***Model 1899C Rifle*** – .303 Savage, .30-30 Win., .25-35 WCF, .32-40 WCF, or .38-55 WCF cal., 26 in. half octagon barrel, straight grip, crescent or shotgun butt with steel buttplate. Mfg. 1899-1915.

$1,700	$1,550	$1,200	$1,075	$900	$725	$625	

Add 35% for .25-35 WCF, .32-40 WCF, or .38-55 WCF.

* ***Model 1899-D Military Rifle (Musket)*** – .30-30 Win. or .303 Savage cal., 28 or 30 in. round barrel with two barrel bands, straight grip stock with bayonet lug.

$8,000	$7,000	$6,000	$5,000	$4,000	$3,500	$3,000	

Substantial premium for presence of bayonet and bayonet sheath.

* ***Model 1899-F Carbine*** – various cals., three cataloged variations, first variation w/small barrel band is controversial as to whether or not it exists, all variations have sling ring and carbine butt.

$2,700	$2,250	$2,000	$1,600	$1,300	$1,000	$850	

Add approx. 25% for Winchester calibers.
Add 10% for .30-30 Win. cal.

* ***Model 1899H Rifle*** – .22 Hi-Power, .25-35 WCF, .30-30 Win., or .303 Savage cal., 20 in. featherweight barrel, straight grip, shotgun butt with steel or hard rubber buttplate, takedown added in 1909. Mfg. 1905-1915.

$1,350	$1,150	$950	$725	$625	$575	$525	

Add 10% for .22 Hi-Power.
Add 20% for .25-35 WCF.

* ***Model 1899 .250-3000 Rifle*** – takedown frame only, pistol grip checkered stocks with corrugated steel buttplate, fine cross-checkered trigger (unique to this model). Mfg. 1914-1921.

$1,500	$1,275	$900	$850	$690	$565	$440	

MODEL 99A – .30-30 Win., .300 Sav., or .303 Sav. cal., 24 in. barrel, open sight, hammerless, straight grip stock, crescent butt. Mfg. 1920-1936.

$1,000	$850	$700	$625	$525	$450	$375	

MODEL 99A RECENT PRODUCTION – similar to original, with .243 Win., .250 Sav., .300 Sav., .308 Win., or .375 Win. (1981 only, approx. 1,500 mfg.) cal., 20 or 22 in. barrel, tang safety, conventional butt. Mfg. 1971-81.

$600	$500	$400	$325	$275	$225	$165	

Add 100% for .375 Win. or 50% for .250 Sav. cal.

MODEL 99B – takedown version of original Model 99A, 24 (introduced 1926-27) or 26 (initial standard barrel length) in. barrel. Mfg. 1920-34.

$1,100	$1,000	$850	$775	$650	$540	$420	

MODEL 99H CARBINE – .250-3000 Sav., .30-30 Win., .300 Sav. (scarce) or .303 Sav. cal., solid frame, carbine type stock. Mfg. 1923-40.

$1,300	$1,125	$850	$750	$625	$500	$450	

Add 30% for .250 Sav. and .300 Sav. cal.

There were four variations of this model - the latter three had barrel bands. The first variation did not have a barrel band or side panels on the buttstock.

MODEL 99E – .22 Hi Power, .250-3000 Sav., .30-30 Win., .300 Sav., or .303 Sav. cal., 20, 22, or 24 in. barrel, solid frame, straight stock. Mfg. 1922-1934.

$1,300	$1,050	$875	$650	$500	$450	$400	

Add 35% for .22 Hi Power or .250 Sav. cal.

MODEL 99E CARBINE – .243 Win., .250 Sav., .300 Sav., or .308 Win. cal., 22 in. barrel, checkered pistol grip stock, 5 shot rotary mag. Mfg. 1960-82.

$600	$550	$500	$450	$375	$300	$250	*$343*

Add 25% for early Schnabel forearm.

MODEL 99F FEATHERWEIGHT – similar to pre-war Model 99E, except takedown and 1/2 pound lighter, also mfg. with .410 bore shotgun barrel. Mfg. 1920-40.

$1,375	$1,175	$900	$825	$725	$625	$600	

Add 35% for .410 bore shotgun barrel.
Add 10% for cut checkering.
Add 10% for .22 HP or .250 Sav. cal.

GRADING - PPGS™	100%	98%	95%	90%	80%	70%	60%	LAST MSR

MODEL 99F – .243 Win., .250-3000 Sav., .284 Win., .300 Sav., .308 Win., or .358 Win. cal., solid frame, checkered pistol grip stock. Mfg. 1955-73.

	$750	$655	$565	$510	$415	$340	$265	

Add 35% for .250-3000 Sav.
Add 15% for .243 Win. or .308 Win. cal.
Add 75% for .284 Win. or .358 Win. cal.

This model, in many cases, had the receiver marked "99M".

MODEL 99G – similar to Model 99E pre-war, with checkered pistol grip stock and takedown. Mfg. 1922-41.

	$1,400	$1,175	$875	$725	$675	$575	$500	

Add 35% for .250 Sav. cal.

MODEL 99EG – similar to Model 99G, with solid frame and no checkering. Mfg. 1935-41.

	$795	$685	$600	$525	$400	$350	$300	

Add 35% for .250-3000 Sav. cal.
Add 40% for .22 HP cal.

MODEL 99EG POST-WAR – .243 Win., .250 Sav., .300 Sav., .308 Win., or .358 Win. cal., checkered stock. Mfg. 1946-60.

	$575	$525	$450	$395	$340	$295	$260	

Add 255 for .243 Win. cal.
Add 50% for .358 Win. or .250 Sav. cal.

MODEL 99R PRE-WAR – .250-3000 Sav., .303 Sav., or .300 Sav. cal., 22 or 24 in. barrel, large pistol grip stock and forearm. Mfg. 1932-42.

	$800	$625	$525	$425	$380	$325	$300	

Add 35% for .250-3000 Sav. cal.

MODEL 99R POST-WAR – .250-3000 Sav., .300 Sav., .308 Win., .358 Win., or .243 Win. cal., similar to Pre-War, 24 in. barrel only, swivel studs. Mfg. 1946-60.

	$600	$525	$450	$400	$350	$325	$300	

Add 35% for .250-3000 Sav. or .358 Win. cal.

MODEL 99RS PRE-WAR – similar to Model 99R Pre-War, with Lyman aperture sight, swivels and sling. Mfg. 1932-42.

	$950	$800	$640	$580	$470	$385	$300	

MODEL 99RS POST-WAR – similar to Model 99R Post-War, with Redfield receiver sight. Mfg. 1946-58.

	$700	$615	$525	$475	$385	$325	$300	

MODEL 99T – 20 or 22 in. barrel, solid frame, lightweight, checkered pistol grip stock. Mfg. 1935-40.

	$1,600	$1,400	$1,100	$1,000	$900	$750	$600	

Add 50% for .22 HP cal.

MODEL 99K – engraved receiver and fancy wood stock, Lyman aperture sight and folding middle sight. Mfg. 1926-40.

	$3,750	$3,500	$3,000	$2,750	$2,500	$2,200	$1,875	

MODEL 99DL – .243 Win., .250-3000 Sav., .284 Win., .300 Sav., .308 Win., or .358 Win. cal., Monte Carlo stock and sling swivels. Post-war mfg. 1960-73.

	$700	$615	$525	$475	$385	$325	$300	

Add 10% for cut checkering.
Add 35% for .250-3000 Sav. cal.
Add 35% for .284 Win. or .358 Win. cal.

MODEL 99C – available in .22-250 Rem. (rare), .243 Win., .284 Win. (disc.), 7mm-08 (disc.), or .308 Win. cal., similar to Model 99F Post-War, 22 in. barrel, Monte Carlo stock with cut checkering and recoil pad, top tang safety, cocking indicator, open sights, detachable 4 shot box mag., high gloss bluing, drilled and tapped, 7 3/4 lbs. Mfg. 1965, reintroduced 1995-1997 in cals. .243 Win. or .308 Win. only.

	$575	$495	$425	$375	$300	$250	$200	*$629*

Add 50% for .22-250 cal.
Add 75% for .284 Win. or 7mm-08 cal.

MODEL 99CD – similar to Model 99C, with Monte Carlo cheekpiece stock. Mfg. 1975-81.

	$625	$550	$475	$425	$350	$300	$250	

GRADING - PPGS™	100%	98%	95%	90%	80%	70%	60%	LAST MSR

MODEL 99-CE (CENTENNIAL EDITION) - .300 Sav. cal. only, limited edition featuring fully engraved nickel receiver and lever, 24Kt. gold-plated receiver figures, trigger, and safety, deluxe hand checkered walnut stock and forearm, 1,000 mfg. 1996-97 only, serial numbered AS0001-AS1000.

$1,500	$1,100	$750	N/A	N/A	N/A	N/A	*$1,660*

MODEL 99-358 (BRUSH GUN) - .358 Win. cal., recoil pad. Mfg. 1977-80.

$1,300	$1,100	$900	$800	$700	$600	$550

MODEL 99-375 (BRUSH GUN) - .375 Win. cal., recoil pad, fluted forearm. Mfg. 1980 only.

$1,500	$1,300	$1,050	$950	$875	$800	$725

MODEL 99PE - elaborately engraved and plated receiver, tang, and lever, fancy wood with hand cut checkering. Mfg. 1966-70.

$1,800	$1,600	$1,400	$1,200	$1,000	$850	$700

This model had the receiver marked "99M".

MODEL 99DE CITATION - similar to Model 99PE, except with less engraving and pressed checkering. Mfg. 1968-70.

$1,200	$1,050	$900	$800	$700	$600	$500

This model had the receiver marked "99M".

MODEL 99M - while the receivers on Models 99F, 99PE, and 99DE were marked "99M" this is not a model designation. Rather, the "M" barrel designation indicated Monte Carlo stock.

RIFLES: DISC., CENTERFIRE & RIMFIRE

Savage made a wide variety of inexpensive, utilitarian rifles that, to date, have attracted mostly shooting interest, but little collector interest. A listing of these models may be found in the back of this text under "Serialization."

Whenever Savage made an engineering change on a model, it was usually designated with a letter suffix after the model number. These letters were added to the basic model numbers as the changes were made. The engineering changes could be dimensional on any part, cosmetic, or a total component redesign. The letter suffixes indicated to the company what changes were incorporated into that variation. Most model suffixes are preceeded with a dash. These alphabetical suffix variations are not listed separately in this section, but values will be similar to the base model, unless denoted otherwise.

MODEL 1903 STANDARD SLIDE ACTION - .22 S, L, or LR cal., 24 in. barrel, open sights, box mag., pistol grip stock. Mfg. 1903-1922.

$675	$590	$505	$460	$370	$305	$235

* ***Model 1903 Standard Slide Action Grade EF*** - features "B" grade checkering on fancy English walnut stock, Savage #22B front sight, and #21B micrometer open rear sight.

$950	$875	$655	$595	$480	$395	$305

* ***Model 1903 Standard Slide Action Expert Grade*** - features "A" grade engraving on receiver, "B" grade checkering on fancy American walnut stock, standard sights.

$1,950	$1,705	$1,465	$1,325	$1,075	$880	$685

* ***Model 1903 Standard Slide Action Grade GH*** - features "A" grade checkering on plain American walnut stock, no engraving, #22B front sight, and #21B micrometer open rear sight.

$900	$800	$600	$545	$440	$360	$280

* ***Model 1903 Standard Slide Action Gold Medal*** - features animal ornamentation on receiver, less elaborate checkering on plain American walnut stock, standard sights.

$1,050	$920	$790	$715	$580	$475	$370

MODEL 1909 SLIDE ACTION - similar to Model 1903, with 20 in. round barrel. Mfg. 1909-1915.

$750	$655	$565	$510	$415	$340	$265

MODEL 1904 SINGLE SHOT - .22 S, L, or LR cal., bolt action, 18 in. barrel, straight stock. Mfg. 1904-17.

$175	$155	$130	$120	$95	$80	$60

MODEL 1905 SINGLE SHOT - similar to Model 1904, except 24 in. barrel, takedown. Mfg. 1905-19.

$200	$155	$130	$120	$95	$80	$60

MODEL 1911 BOLT ACTION - .22 S cal. only, bolt action, 20 shot tubular mag. in buttstock, 20 in. barrel. Limited mfg. 1911-12.

$500	$350	$300	$270	$220	$180	$140

GRADING - PPGS™	100%	98%	95%	90%	80%	70%	60%	LAST MSR

MODEL 1912 AUTOLOADER – .22 LR cal., semi-auto, 20 in. barrel, takedown, straight stock. Mfg. 1912-16.

	$850	$655	$565	$510	$415	$340	$265	

MODEL 1914 SLIDE ACTION – .22 S, L, and LR cal., 24 in. octagon barrel, plain pistol grip stock. Mfg. 1914-26.

	$450	$395	$340	$305	$250	$205	$160	

MODEL 19 NRA BOLT ACTION – .22 LR cal., 25 in. barrel, adj. aperture sight, 5 shot, military stock. Approx. 50,000 mfg. 1919-32.

	$400	$350	$300	$270	$220	$180	$140	

Between 1943-45 approx. 6,000 Model 19s were made under military contract - add 15%.

MODEL 19 BOLT ACTION TARGET – .22 LR cal., 25 in. barrel, speed lock, adj. aperture sight, target stock. Mfg. 1933-46.

	$325	$285	$245	$220	$180	$145	$115	

MODEL 19L – similar to Model 19, with Lyman receiver sight. Mfg. 1933-42.

	$350	$305	$265	$240	$195	$160	$125	

MODEL 19M – similar to Model 19, with 28 in. heavy barrel and scope bases. Mfg. 1933-42.

	$350	$305	$265	$240	$195	$160	$125	

MODEL 19H – similar to Model 19, except .22 Hornet cal. Mfg. 1933-42.

	$600	$525	$450	$410	$330	$270	$210	

MODEL 1920 BOLT ACTION – Mauser type action, .250-3000 Sav. or .300 Sav. cal., 22 or 24 in. barrel, open sights, 5 shot stripper clip, checkered pistol grip, Schnabel forend. Mfg. 1920-31.

	$900	$775	$675	$575	$500	$450	$400	

Add 10% for .250-3000 Sav. cal.

MODEL 1920-1926 – similar to Model 1920, with 24 in. barrel, Lyman aperture sight, Mfg. 1926-31.

	$900	$775	$675	$575	$500	$450	$400	

Add 10% for .250-3000 cal.

MODEL 1922 – .22 LR cal., predecessor of the Model 23A, mfg. 1922 only.

	$250	$220	$190	$170	$140	$115	$90	

MODEL 23A BOLT ACTION RIFLE – .22 LR cal., 23 in. barrel, open sights, plain pistol grip stock, Schnabel forend. Mfg. 1923-33.

	$250	$220	$190	$170	$140	$115	$90	

MODEL 23AA – improved version of Model 23A, with speedlock and checkered stock. Mfg. 1933-42.

	$300	$265	$225	$205	$165	$135	$105	

MODEL 23B – .25-20 WCF cal., same configuration as Model 23A, 25 in. barrel, full forearm. Mfg. 1923-42.

	$300	$265	$225	$205	$165	$135	$105	

MODEL 23C – .32-20 WCF cal., similar to Model 23B. Mfg. 1923-42.

	$350	$305	$265	$240	$195	$160	$125	

MODEL 23D – .22 Hornet cal., similar to Model 23B. Mfg. 1933-47.

	$375	$325	$275	$240	$225	$185	$140	

MODEL 25 SLIDE ACTION – .22 S, L, or LR cal., 24 in. octagon barrel, open sights, takedown, hammerless, tube mag., plain pistol grip stock. Mfg. 1925-29.

	$350	$305	$265	$240	$195	$160	$125	

MODEL 40 SPORTER – .250-3000 Sav., .300 Sav., .30-30 Win., or .30-06 cal., bolt action, 22 or 24 in. barrel, open sights, 4 shot mag., plain pistol grip stock, Schnabel forend. Mfg. 1928-1940.

	$350	$305	$265	$240	$195	$160	$125	

Add 10% for .250-3000 Sav. cal.

MODEL 45 SUPER SPORTER – similar to Model 40, with Lyman receiver sight and checkered stock. Mfg. 1928-1940.

	$400	$350	$300	$270	$220	$180	$140	

MODEL 29 SLIDE ACTION – .22 S, L, or LR cal., 22 in. barrel, octagon until 1940, round on post-WWII, open sights, checkered pistol grip stock on pre-war, plain on late model. Mfg. 1929-67.

Pre-war	$350	$305	$265	$240	$195	$160	$125	
Late model	$300	$265	$225	$205	$165	$135	$105	

GRADING - PPGS™	100%	98%	95%	90%	80%	70%	60%	LAST MSR

MODEL 3 SINGLE SHOT – .22 S, L, or LR cal., bolt action, 26 in. barrel, 24 in. barrel on post-war, open sights, plain grip stock. Mfg. 1930-47.

	$125	$110	$95	$85	$70	$55	$45	

MODEL 3S – similar to Model 3, with aperture sight. Mfg. 1930-47.

	$150	$130	$115	$100	$85	$70	$55	

MODEL 3ST – similar to Model 3S, with swivels and sling. Mfg. 1930-47.

	$175	$155	$130	$120	$95	$80	$60	

MODEL 4 BOLT ACTION REPEATER – .22 S, L, or LR cal., 24 in. barrel, open sights, takedown, 5 shot, checkered pistol grip stock on pre-war, plain stock on post-war. Mfg. 1933-65.

Pre-war	$150	$130	$115	$100	$85	$70	$55	
Post-war	$135	$120	$100	$90	$75	$60	$45	

MODEL 4S – similar to Model 4, with aperture sight. Mfg. 1933-42.

	$175	$155	$130	$120	$95	$80	$60	

MODEL 4M – similar to Model 4, except .22 WMR cal. Mfg. 1961-65.

	$175	$155	$130	$120	$95	$80	$60	

MODEL 5 – similar to Model 4, with tubular mag. Mfg. 1938-64.

	$175	$155	$130	$120	$95	$80	$60	

MODEL 5S – similar to Model 5, with aperture sight. Mfg. 1936-42.

	$200	$175	$150	$135	$110	$90	$70	

MODEL 6 AUTOLOADER – .22 S, L, or LR cal., 24 in. barrel, tubular mag., takedown, checkered pistol grip stock on pre-war, plain stock on post-war. Mfg. 1938-68.

Pre-war	$200	$175	$150	$135	$110	$90	$70	
Post-war	$175	$155	$130	$120	$95	$80	$60	

MODEL 6S – similar to Model 6, with aperture sight. Mfg. 1938-42.

	$200	$175	$150	$135	$110	$90	$70	

MODEL 7 AUTOLOADER – similar to Model 6, with box mag. Mfg. 1939-51.

Pre-war	$200	$175	$150	$135	$110	$90	$70	
Post-war	$175	$155	$130	$120	$95	$80	$60	

MODEL 7S – similar to Model 7, with aperture sight. Mfg. 1938-42.

	$175	$155	$130	$120	$95	$80	$60	

MODEL 60 AUTOLOADER – .22 LR cal., 20 in. barrel, leaf sight, tubular mag., checkered Monte Carlo walnut stock. Mfg. 1969-72.

	$150	$130	$115	$100	$85	$70	$55	

MODEL 90 AUTOLOADING CARBINE – similar to Model 60, with 16 1/2 in. barrel, plain carbine stock, with barrel band.

	$150	$130	$115	$100	$85	$70	$55	

MODEL 88 AUTOLOADER – similar to Model 60, except has walnut finished hardwood stock. Mfg. 1969-72.

	$150	$130	$115	$100	$85	$70	$55	

MODEL 63/63K SINGLE SHOT – .22 S, L, or LR cal., bolt action, 18 in. barrel, open sights, trigger locks with key (only on Model 63K), full-length pistol grip walnut finished hardwood stock, Model 63s were mfg. 1964-69, Model 63Ks were mfg. 1970-72.

	$275	$240	$205	$185	$150	$125	$95	

MODEL 63KM – .22 WMR cal., similar to Model 63K.

	$300	$265	$225	$205	$165	$135	$105	

MODEL 219 SINGLE SHOT – .22 Hornet, .25-20 WCF, .32-20 WCF, or .30-30 Win. cal., 26 in. barrel, open sights, hammerless, break open, top lever, plain pistol grip stock. Mfg. 1938-65.

.30-30 Win. cal.	$195	$170	$145	$135	$105	$90	$70	

Add 15% for all other cals.

MODEL 219L – similar to Model 219, with side lever. Mfg. 1965-67.

	$200	$175	$150	$135	$110	$90	$70	

MODELS 221, 222, 223, 227, 228, AND 229 – single shot, similar to Model 219, only supplied with additional interchangeable shotgun barrel, different model numbers are for different cals., gauges, and barrel lengths, all have been disc.

	$200	$175	$150	$135	$110	$90	$70	

GRADING - PPGS™	100%	98%	95%	90%	80%	70%	60%	LAST MSR

MODEL 34 – .22 S, L, or LR cal., 20 in. barrel, grooved receiver, open sights, 5 shot, checkered hardwood pistol grip stock, approx. 5 lbs. Mfg. 1969-1973.

$150 $130 $115 $100 $85 $70 $55

MODEL 34M – similar to Model 34, chambered for .22 WMR cal. Mfg. 1969-73.

$175 $155 $130 $120 $95 $80 $60

MODEL 35 – .22 LR cal., bolt action, 22 in. barrel, 5 shot detachable mag., open sights, hardwood Monte Carlo stock. Disc. 1985.

$150 $130 $115 $100 $85 $70 $55 *$100*

MODEL 36 – .22 LR cal., single shot, otherwise similar to Model 35. Mfg. 1983-84.

$150 $130 $115 $100 $85 $70 $55

MODEL 46 – .22 S, L, or LR cal., similar to Model 34, with tubular mag. Mfg. 1969-1973.

$150 $130 $115 $100 $85 $70 $55

MODEL 65 – .22 S, L, or LR cal., bolt action, 20 in. barrel, 5 or 10 shot mag., open sights, checkered walnut stock, blue finish. Mfg. 1969-1973.

$150 $130 $115 $100 $85 $70 $55

MODEL 65M – .22 WMR cal., bolt action, 20 or 22 (new 1976) in. barrel, 5 or 6-shot mag., adj. rear and ramp front sights, checkered Monte Carlo walnut stock. Mfg. 1969-1979.

$200 $175 $150 $135 $110 $90 $70

SAVAGE/FOX MODEL FB-1 – .22 LR cal., bolt action, 24 in. barrel, hooded front sight, Williams adj. rear sight, premium walnut stock with rollover cheekpiece, rosewood tip and forend cap, fancy cut checkering. Mfg. 1981 only.

$225 $195 $170 $155 $125 $100 $80

SAVAGE/STEVENS MODEL 72 "CRACKSHOT" – please refer to listing under Stevens section.

SAVAGE/STEVENS MODEL 73 – similar to Model 63, w/o Monte Carlo stock. Mfg. 1964-69.

$125 $110 $95 $85 $70 $55 $45

SAVAGE/STEVENS MODEL 89 SINGLE SHOT – please refer to listing under Stevens section.

MODEL 340 BOLT ACTION – .22 Hornet, .222 Rem., .223 Rem., or .30-30 Win. cal., 22 and 24 in. barrel, open sights, 4 or 5 shot mag., 7 1/2 lbs., plain pistol grip stock. Mfg. 1950-85.

$225 $195 $170 $155 $125 $100 $80 *$257*

EL 340C – similar to Model 340, with aperture sight, checkered stock, and sling swivels. Mfg. 1952-60.

$235 $205 $175 $160 $130 $105 $80

MODEL 340V – .225 Win. cal., varmint configuration, 24 in. barrel. Limited mfg. in late 1960s.

$295 $260 $220 $200 $160 $135 $105

MODEL 340S DELUXE – similar to Model 340, with aperture sight, checkered stock, sling swivels. Mfg. 1952-60.

$300 $265 $225 $205 $165 $135 $105

MODEL 342 AND 342S – .22 Hornet cal., similar to Model 340. Mfg. 1950-55.

$300 $265 $225 $205 $165 $135 $105

MODEL 982DL/MDI – .22 LR (DL) or .22 WMR (MDI) cal., bolt action, 22 in. barrel, ramp front sight, folding leaf rear sight, checkered American walnut stock with Monte Carlo comb, matte receiver finish. Mfg. 1981 only.

$195 $175 $150 $125 $100 $85 $65

Add 20% for .22 WMR cal.

RIFLES: RIMFIRE, CURRENT/RECENT PRODUCTION

Savage introduced a new line of rimfire rifles during 1996. Recent Savage nomenclature usually involves alphabetical suffixes which mean the following: B - wood laminate stock, BT - wood-laminate thumbhole stock, C - Clip, EV - Evolution Stock, F - composite/synthetic stock, G - hardwood stock, H - hinged floorplate, K - Muzzlebrake, L - left-hand, NS - No Sights, P - Police, RD - Red Dot Sight, RJ - Royal Jacaranda Stock, SR - Suppressor Ready, S/SS - stainless steel, T - (Rimfire) peep sights, TR - Tactical Style Rimfire, TRR - Tactical Style Rimfire w/Picatinny Rail, V - heavy barrel (previously Long Range/Varmint w/heavy barrel), XP - scoped rifle package, Y - Compact/Youth/Ladies Model (shortened dimensions). Hence, the Model Mark II-GLY designates a Mark II model with hardwood stock, left-hand action in a Youth configuration. A Model 93 Series with BTVSS suffix indicates a laminated thumbole stock with heavy barrel in stainless steel.

Subtract 10% if w/o AccuTrigger (became standard on most rimfire rifles 2006, except Model 64 and Model 200).

GRADING - PPGS™	100%	98%	95%	90%	80%	70%	60%	LAST MSR

A17 HM2 – .17 Mach 2 cal., bolt action, delayed blowback action, 20 in. free floating button rifled carbon steel Sporter barrel, 10 shot rotary mag., steel receiver, AccuTrigger, black synthetic stock, two-piece Weaver style bases, matte black finish, 5.55 lbs. New 2019.

MSR $389	$325	$285	$250	$225	$180	$150	$125	

A17 OVERWATCH – .17 HMR cal., semi-auto, delayed blowback action, 22 in. carbon steel black barrel with high luster finish, 10 shot rotary mag., lightweight aluminum receiver, AccuTrigger, synthetic stock with Mossy Oak Overwatch camo, two sling swivels, drilled and tapped with two-piece bases, 5.8 lbs. New 2019.

MSR $559	$475	$415	$350	$325	$260	$215	$185	

A17 PRO VARMINT – .17 HMR cal., delayed blowback action, 22 in. fluted heavy barrel, 10 shot rotary mag., AccuTrigger, Pro Varmint black hardwood stock, one-piece rail, 7.1 lbs. New 2018.

MSR $695	$585	$510	$440	$400	$325	$275	$230	

A17 SEMI-AUTO – .17 HMR cal., delayed blowback action, carbon steel barrel with high luster finish, 10 shot detachable rotary mag., case hardened receiver, drilled and tapped, hard chromed bolt with dual controlled round feed, AccuTrigger, synthetic stock, 5.41 lbs. New 2015.

MSR $505	$425	$375	$325	$295	$235	$195	$165	

Add $20 for heavy fluted barrel (A17 heavy barrel, disc. 2017, reintroduced 2019).

A17 SPORTER – .17 HMR cal., semi-auto, 22 in. blued sporter barrel, 10 shot rotary mag., AccuTrigger, gray laminate sporter stock, 5.6 lbs. New 2016.

MSR $585	$500	$440	$375	$340	$275	$225	$195	

A17 TARGET SPORTER LAMINATE – .17 HMR cal., semi-auto, delayed blowback action, 22 in. blued heavy barrel, 10 shot rotary mag., AccuTrigger, gray laminate sporter stock, oversized bolt handle, 5.6-6.8 lbs. New 2016.

MSR $605	$515	$450	$385	$350	$285	$230	$200	

A17/A22 MAGNUM – .17 HMR (new late 2019) or .22 WMR cal., semi-auto, delayed blowback action, 20 (.17 HMR, new late 2019) or 22 in. barrel, 10 shot rotary mag., AccuTrigger, black synthetic stock, oversized bolt, 5.6 lbs. New 2016.

MSR $505	$425	$375	$325	$295	$235	$195	$165	

A17/A22/A22 TARGET THUMBHOLE – .17 HMR, .22 WMR, or .22 LR (new 2018) cal., semi-auto, straight (.22 LR) or delayed blowback action, 22 in. blued heavy fluted barrel, 10 shot rotary mag., AccuTrigger, gray laminate thumbhole stock, oversized bolt handle, 5.6-7.08 lbs. New 2016.

MSR $469	$395	$340	$295	$265	$215	$175	$150	

Add $200 for .17 HMR or .22 WMR cal.

A17 XP – .17 HMR cal., delayed blowback action, 22 in. button rifled carbon steel Sporter barrel, 10 shot rotary mag., AccuTrigger, matte black synthetic stock, black satin finish. Mfg. 2016-2020.

	$500	$440	$375	$340	$275	$225	$195	*$589*

A22 .22 LR – .22 LR cal., delayed blowback action, 22 in. button rifled carbon steel barrel, 10 shot rotary mag., AccuTrigger, adj. open steel sights, black synthetic lightweight stock, oversized bolt, drilled and tapped for optional optic, 5.6 lbs. New 2016.

MSR $295	$250	$220	$190	$170	$140	$115	$95	

A22 BNS-SR – .22 LR cal., straight blowback action, 18 in. matte black carbon steel sporter barrel, threaded w/cap, 10 shot rotary mag., adj. AccuTrigger, Timber hardwood laminate stock w/ergonomic design, two-piece weaver style bases, Forest Green finish, 6.5 lbs. New 2020.

MSR $495	$415	$365	$315	$285	$230	$185	$160	

A22 FSS – .22 LR cal., 22 in. Sporter stainless steel barrel, 10 shot rotary mag., AccuTrigger, black synthetic stock, 5 lbs. New 2018.

MSR $365	$310	$275	$235	$210	$175	$140	$120	

A22 FV-SR – .22 LR cal., semi-auto, straight blowback action, 16 1/2 in. matte black carbon steel heavy barrel, threaded muzzle, target crown, 10 shot rotary mag., user adj. AccuTrigger, composite stock, two QD studs, drilled and tapped with one-piece Picatinny rail, matte black finish, 5.6 lbs. New 2020.

MSR $365	$310	$275	$235	$210	$175	$140	$120	

A22 FV-SR OVERWATCH – .22 LR cal., semi-auto, straight blowback action, 16 1/2 in. carbon steel heavy barrel with matte black finish, threaded muzzle, 10 shot rotary mag., user adj. AccuTrigger, synthetic stock with Mossy Oak Overwatch camo, two sling swivels, drilled and tapped with one-piece Picatinny rail, 5.26 lbs. New 2020

MSR $399	$340	$300	$255	$230	$185	$155	$130	

GRADING - PPGS™	100%	98%	95%	90%	80%	70%	60%	LAST MSR

A22 PRECISION – .22 LR cal., 18 in. carbon steel heavy threaded barrel w/flush cap, 10 shot detachable rotary mag., adj. AccuTrigger, billet aluminum one-piece MDT chassis, one-piece rail, oversized charging handle, matte black finish, approx. 7.3 lbs. New 2020.

MSR $619	$525	$460	$395	$355	$290	$240	$200	

A22 PRO VARMINT – .22 LR or .22 WMR cal., straight (.22 LR) or delayed (.22 WMR) blowback action, 22 in. fluted heavy barrel, 10 shot rotary mag., AccuTrigger, Pro Varmint black hardwood stock, 7.1 lbs. New 2018.

MSR $529	$450	$400	$340	$300	$250	$200	$175	

Add $166 for .22 WMR cal. (A22 Magnum Pro Varmint).

B17/B22 PRECISION – .17 HMR, .22 LR, or .22 WMR cal., 18 in. carbon steel heavy threaded barrel w/ flush cap, 10 shot detachable rotary mag., adj. AccuTrigger, aluminum one-piece MDT chassis, one-piece Picatinny rail, matte black finish, 7.38 lbs. New 2020.

MSR $619	$525	$460	$395	$355	$290	$240	$200	

B17 F/B22 MAGNUM F – .17 HMR, .22 LR (new mid-2020), or .22 WMR cal., right or left (new 2018) hand action, 21 in. blued carbon steel barrel, 10 shot rotary mag., AccuTrigger, black synthetic stock, target style vertical pistol grip, top tang safety, 5 1/2 lbs. New 2017.

MSR $299	$255	$225	$190	$175	$140	$115	$100	

Add $20 for .17 HMR or .22 WMR cal.

* ***B17 F Compact/B22 F Compact/B22 Magnum F Compact*** – .17 HMR, .22 LR, or .22 WMR cal., bolt action, 18 in. carbon steel Sporter barrel, 10 shot rotary mag., AccuTrigger, black synthetic stock, 5 lbs. New 2018.

MSR $299	$255	$225	$190	$175	$140	$115	$100	

Add $20 for .17 HMR or .22 WMR cal.

B17 FV/B22 FV/B22 MAGNUM FV – .17 HMR, .22 LR, or .22 WMR cal., bolt action, 21 in. blued heavy carbon steel heavy barrel, 10 shot rotary mag., AccuTrigger, black synthetic stock, target style vertical pistol grip, top tang safety, 6 lbs. New 2017.

MSR $329	$275	$240	$200	$185	$150	$125	$100	

Add $20 for .17 HMR (B17 FV) or .22 WMR (B22 Magnum FV) cal.

B17 FVSS/B22 FVSS/B22 MAGNUM FVSS – .17 HMR, .22 LR, or .22 WMR cal., 21 in. heavy stainless steel barrel, 10 shot rotary mag., AccuTrigger, black synthetic stock, 13.5 in. LOP, target style vertical pistol grip, top tang safety, 6 lbs. New 2017.

MSR $409	$350	$300	$265	$240	$195	$160	$135	

Add $10 for .17 HMR (B17 FVSS) or .22 WMR (B22 Magnum FVSS) cal.

B17 FV-SR/B22 FV-SR/B22 MAGNUM FV-SR – .17 HMR, .22 LR, or .22 WMR cal., 16 1/4 in. threaded heavy barrel, 10 shot rotary mag., AccuTrigger, black synthetic stock, target style vertical pistol grip, top tang safety, top Picatinny rail, 6 lbs. New 2017.

MSR $339	$290	$255	$220	$195	$160	$130	$110	

Add $20 for .17 HMR (B17 FV-SR) or .22 WMR (B22 Magnum FV-SR) cal.

B17 FV-SR OVERWATCH/B22 FV-SR OVERWATCH – .17 HMR or .22 LR cal., bolt action, 16 1/2 in. carbon steel heavy barrel with threaded muzzle, target crown, 10 shot rotary mag., AccuTrigger, synthetic stock with Mossy Oak Overwatch camo, vertical pistol grip, top tang safety, drilled and tapped with one-piece Picatinny rail, matte black finish, 5.6 lbs. New 2019.

MSR $369	$310	$270	$235	$210	$170	$140	$120	

Add $50 for .17 HMR cal.

B17 G/B22 G/B22 MAGNUM G – .17 HMR, .22 LR, or .22 WMR cal., bolt action, 21 in. carbon steel barrel with matte black finish, 10 shot rotary mag., adj. AccuTrigger, adj. iron sights, ergonomic walnut-stained hardwood stock with modern checkering, top tang safety, drilled and tapped scope mounts, 5 1/2 lbs. New 2017.

MSR $469	$395	$340	$295	$265	$215	$175	$150	

Add $20 for .17 HMR (B17 G) and .22 WMR (B22 Magnum G) cal.

B17 BSN-SR/B22 BNS-SR – .17 HMR, .22 LR, or .22 WMR cal., bolt action, 18 in. carbon steel threaded sporter barrel, 10 shot rotary mag., AccuTrigger, two-piece Weaver style bases, Timber Hardwood laminate stock, top tang safety, matte black finish, 6.6 lbs. New 2020.

MSR $499	$425	$375	$325	$295	$235	$195	$165	

Add $20 for .17 HMR or .22 WMR cal.

GRADING - PPGS™	100%	98%	95%	90%	80%	70%	60%	LAST MSR

B.MAG 17 SERIES BOLT ACTION – .17 WSM cal., 22 in. carbon steel sporter barrel, 8 shot detachable rotary mag., AccuTrigger, matte black finish, black synthetic stock, drilled and tapped, 4 1/2 lbs. New 2013.

MSR $399	$340	$300	$255	$230	$185	$155	$130	

In August 2015, Savage Arms issued a recall notice due to the discovery that some B.MAG rifles may inadvertently catch the safety button and slide it forward into the "fire" position. While Savage has received no reports of accidents due to this condition, they are offering free retrofits of all B.MAG rifle bolts out of an abundance of caution. Do not use your B.MAG rifle until your bolt has been retrofitted with a new bolt handle and cap. Please contact Savage for more information by calling 844-784-3301, or check their website at savagearms.com/recall/bmagbolt/.

* ***B.MAG Blued Heavy Barrel*** – .17 WSM cal., bolt action, 22 in. blued heavy barrel, 8 shot rotary mag., AccuTrigger, black synthetic stock, 6 lbs. New 2016.

MSR $425	$360	$315	$270	$245	$200	$160	$140	

* ***B.MAG Beavertail (Heavy Barrel Laminate Stock)*** – .17 WSM cal., bolt action, 22 in. stainless steel (disc. 2019) or carbon steel (new 2020) heavy barrel, 8 shot rotary mag., AccuTrigger, gray laminate stock, 6 lbs. New 2016.

MSR $579	$495	$435	$375	$335	$275	$225	$195	

* ***B.MAG Sporter*** – .17 WSM cal., bolt action, 22 in. stainless steel (disc. 2019) or carbon steel (new 2020) heavy barrel, 8 shot rotary mag., AccuTrigger, gray laminate thumbhole stock, 6 lbs. New 2016.

MSR $535	$455	$400	$340	$310	$250	$200	$175	

* ***B.MAG Stainless Heavy Barrel*** – .17 WSM cal., 22 in. heavy stainless steel barrel, 8 shot detachable rotary mag., AccuTrigger, matte black finish, black synthetic stock, drilled and tapped, 5 lbs. New 2015.

MSR $459	$390	$340	$295	$265	$215	$175	$150	

* ***B.MAG Target*** – .17 WSM cal., bolt action, 22 in. heavy stainless steel barrel, 8 shot detachable rotary mag., AccuTrigger, gray laminate thumbhole stock. New 2015.

MSR $615	$520	$455	$390	$355	$285	$235	$200	

B22 F – .22 LR cal., bolt action, right or left (new 2018) hand action, 21 in. barrel, 10 shot rotary mag., AccuTrigger, adj. sights, black synthetic stock, target style vertical pistol grip, top tang safety, 5 1/2 lbs. Mfg. 2017-2019.

	$250	$225	$200	$175	$150	$125	$100	*$305*

CUB (G) – .17 Mach 2 (mfg. 2005 only), or .22 LR cal., single shot Youth Model with 16 1/8 in. barrel and shortened hardwood stock in regular or pink (new 2009) finish, traditional safety, aperture rear sight, AccuTrigger became standard 2006, 4 1/2 lbs. Mfg. 2003-2011.

	$175	$155	$130	$120	$95	$80	$60	*$227*

Add 10% for .17 Mach 2 cal. (mfg. 2005).
Add $14 for pink stock.

* ***Cub Target*** – .22 LR cal., similar to Cub Model, except has ergonomic thumbhole stock. Mfg. 2007-2011.

	$225	$195	$170	$155	$125	$100	$80	*$282*

Add $14 for pink stock (new 2008).

RASCAL SERIES – .22 S, L, or LR cal., single shot, 16 in. barrel, AccuTrigger, manual safety, cocks by lifting bolt, fixed front and aperture rear sights, feed ramp, walnut hardwood or black, pink, blue, red, yellow, orange, green, or purple (new mid-2016) synthetic stock, right or left (hardwood, black, or pink stock only) hand configuration, 2.66 lbs. New 2012.

MSR $195	$175	$155	$130	$120	$95	$80	$65	

Add $45 for hardwood stock.

* ***Landry Rascal*** – .22 S, L, or LR cal., single shot, 16 in. barrel, AccuTrigger, peep sight, Gator Camo synthetic stock, endorsed by famous TV Gator Hunter Troy Landry, 2.66 lbs. New 2015.

MSR $235	$200	$170	$150	$135	$110	$90	$75	

* ***Rascal FV-SR/Rascal FLV-SR*** – .22 S, L, or LR cal., single shot, heavy carbon steel barrel with threaded muzzle, AccuTrigger, black or pink synthetic stock, tactical bolt handle, right or left (FLV-SR) hand configuration, blued finish. New mid-2018.

MSR $230	$195	$170	$150	$135	$110	$90	$75	

* ***Rascal Minimalist*** – .22 S, L, or LR cal., single shot, 16.1 in. carbon steel threaded matte black barrel, Boyd's laminate stock, 11.25 in. LOP, 3.3 lbs. New 2021.

MSR $285	$240	$210	$180	$165	$130	$110	$90	

GRADING - PPGS™	100%	98%	95%	90%	80%	70%	60%	LAST MSR

* ***Rascal Red, White, & Blue*** – .22 LR cal., bolt action, single shot, 16.1 in. carbon steel sporter blued barrel, adj. AccuTrigger, adj. peep sights, synthetic stock with American flag camo pattern finish, 11.5 in. LOP, manual safety, blued receiver, feed ramp, cocks by lifting bolt, unloads w/o pulling trigger, 2.71 lbs. New 2020.

MSR $235	$200	$170	$150	$135	$110	$90	$75

* ***Rascal Target*** – .22 LR cal., bolt action, 16 1/8 in. heavy contour carbon steel barrel, threaded muzzle, adj. AccuTrigger, precision hardwood stock, one-piece Picatinny rail, straight bolt w/ oversize knob, matte blue finish, 4.42-4.8 lbs. New mid-2018.

MSR $330	$280	$245	$210	$190	$155	$125	$110

* ***Rascal Target XP*** – .22 LR cal., single shot, 16 1/8 in. carbon steel heavy barrel, threaded muzzle, AccuTrigger, compact black hardwood stock, one-piece Picatinny rail, oversized bolt handle, includes mounted and boresighted 4x32mm scope, bipod sling swivel stud mount, right or left-hand configuration, matte blue finish, 5.95 lbs. New mid-2018.

MSR $420	$360	$315	$270	$245	$200	$160	$140

MARK I-G SERIES BOLT ACTION – .22 S-L-LR or LR shot (Mark I - GSB) cal., single shot, self-cocking, 19 (Mark I-GY, Youth Model), 20 3/4 (disc.), or 21 in. barrel, checkered hardwood stock, AccuTrigger became standard 2006, open sights, satin blued finish, approx. 5 lbs. New 1996.

MSR $295	$250	$220	$190	$170	$140	$115	$95

Subtract $36 for Mark I-GY (Youth Model).
Add $35 for Youth Color (mfg. 2002-2005) or $31 for Camo Youth (mfg. 2002-2004).
Add $7 for scope (Model Mark I-GYXP only, mfg. 2002-2004).

This Model was also available with left-hand action (Mark I-GL, disc. 2003), Youth Model (Mark I-GY), Youth Color (Mark I-GLY, features blue/green/grey laminate stock, mfg. 2002-2009), Camo Youth (Mark I-Y Camo, mfg. 2002-2004), or with smoothbore barrel (Mark I-GSB, disc. 2009).

* ***Mark I-FVT Series Bolt Action*** – .22 S, L, or LR cal., 21 in. matte blued heavy barrel, aperture target sights, AccuTrigger, black synthetic stock, 13.75 in. LOP, right or left (new 2019) hand configuration, 5 1/4 lbs. New 2005.

MSR $505	$425	$375	$325	$295	$235	$195	$165

MARK II-F SERIES BOLT ACTION – .17 HM2 (mfg. 2004-2017, reintroduced 2019) or .22 LR cal., 21 in. blued carbon steel sporter barrel, 10 shot detachable box mag., AccuTrigger became standard 2006, open sights, checkered black synthetic stock, 5 lbs. New 1998.

MSR $245	$200	$180	$155	$140	$115	$90	$80

Add $90 for .17 Mach 2 cal. (mfg. 2004-2017, reintroduced 2019).
Add $7 for Mark II-FXP package (includes 4x15mm scope, disc. 2005).

* ***Mark II BRJ*** – .22 LR cal., bolt action, 21 in. carbon steel heavy barrel with spiral fluting and blued finish, 5 shot detachable box mag., AccuTrigger, tri-color/Royal Jacaranda wood laminate stock, 7 lbs. New 2010.

MSR $550	$470	$410	$350	$325	$260	$215	$185

* ***Mark II BSEV*** – .22 LR cal., bolt action, 21 in. stainless steel heavy barrel with spiral fluting, 5 shot detachable box mag., AccuTrigger, tri-color wood laminate thumbhole (disc.) or Royal Jacaranda laminate Evolution (new 2018) stock, no sights, 6.9 lbs. New 2010.

MSR $655	$550	$480	$415	$375	$310	$260	$215

* ***Mark II BTV*** – .22 LR cal., bolt action, 21 in. heavy barrel, AccuTrigger, 5 shot detachable box mag., laminate thumbhole stock, no sights, blued finish, 6 1/2 lbs. New 2009.

MSR $415	$350	$300	$265	$240	$195	$160	$135

* ***Mark II BTVS/BTVLS*** – .22 LR cal., bolt action, right or left (new 2009) hand configuration, 21 in. heavy stainless barrel w/o sights, 5 shot detachable box mag., AccuTrigger, brown laminated thumbhole stock with vent. forend, stainless steel action, 7 1/2 lbs. New 2007.

MSR $499	$425	$375	$325	$295	$235	$195	$165

Add $49 for left-hand configuration (new 2009).

* ***Mark II BV/LV*** – .17 Mach 2 (mfg. 2005) or .22 LR cal., bolt action, 21 in. heavy blued barrel, 5 shot mag., no sights, grey (disc.) or brown laminated hardwood stock with (Mark II LV, disc. 2004) or w/o (Mark II BV) cut checkering, 6 1/2 lbs. New 1997.

MSR $365	$310	$270	$235	$210	$170	$140	$120

Add 10% for Mark II BVSS (stainless) in .17 Mach 2 cal. - grey finish only, mfg. 2005.

GRADING - PPGS™	100%	98%	95%	90%	80%	70%	60%	LAST MSR

* ***Mark II Camo*** – .22 LR cal. only, bolt action, 21 in. blued satin carbon steel sporter barrel, 10 shot detachable box mag., open sights, AccuTrigger, synthetic stock with Next G1 camo finish, 5 1/2 lbs. New 2002.

MSR $270	$230	$200	$175	$155	$125	$110	$90	

Add $183 for Mark II XP Camo package with 3-9x32mm scope (mfg. 2008-disc.).

* ***Mark II Classic*** – .22 LR cal., bolt action, 21 (disc.) or 24 in. matte blue barrel, 5 shot detachable box mag., hinged floorplate, checkered pistol grip walnut stock, no sights. Mfg. 2007-2010.

	$485	$425	$365	$330	$265	$220	$170	*$575*

Add $33 for MK Classic T with target sights (mfg. 2008).

* ***Mark II FSS*** – .17 Mach 2 (mfg. 2004-2005) or .22 LR cal., bolt action, 21 in. stainless steel barrel with fiber optic sights, 10 shot detachable box mag., AccuTrigger, black graphite/polymer stock with checkering, dovetailed receiver, 5 lbs. New 1997.

MSR $315	$265	$230	$195	$180	$145	$120	$100	

Add 10% for .17 Mach 2 cal.

* ***Mark II FV*** – .17 Mach 2 (mfg. 2004, reintroduced 2019) or .22 LR cal., bolt action, 21 in. carbon steel heavy barrel, no sights, AccuTrigger, black synthetic stock, 5 shot detachable mag., blued satin finish, Weaver style bases included, 5 1/2-6 lbs. New 1998.

MSR $265	$225	$195	$165	$150	$120	$100	$85	

Add $105 for .17 Mach 2 cal.
Add $60 for Mark II-FVSS (stainless) in .17 Mach 2 cal. (mfg. 2005, reintroduced 2019).
Add $63 for Mark II-FVXP package (includes 4x32mm scope, disc. 2004, reintroduced 2006 with 3-9x40 scope).

* ***Mark II FVT*** – .22 LR cal., bolt action, 21 in. carbon steel heavy barrel with target sights, AccuTrigger, 5 shot detachable mag., black synthetic stock, blued finish, 6 lbs. New mid-2005.

MSR $499	$425	$375	$325	$295	$235	$195	$165	

* ***Mark II FV-SR*** – .22 LR cal., bolt action, 16 1/2 in. fluted heavy barrel with threaded muzzle, AccuTrigger, no sights, black synthetic stock, 5 shot detachable box mag., one-piece scope rail, 5 1/2 lbs. New 2011.

MSR $275	$230	$200	$175	$155	$125	$110	$90	

* ***Mark II FV-SR Gator Camo (Landry)*** – .22 LR cal., bolt action, 16 1/2 in. heavy fluted barrel with threaded muzzle, AccuTrigger, no sights, 5 shot detachable box mag., one-piece scope rail, Gator Camo stock, endorsed by famous TV Gator Hunter Troy Landry, 5 1/2 lbs. New 2015.

MSR $320	$275	$240	$200	$185	$150	$125	$100	

* ***Mark II FVXP*** – .22 LR cal., bolt action, 21 in. blued heavy barrel, 5 shot detachable box mag., AccuTrigger, black synthetic stock, includes 3-9x40 Bushnell scope, 6 lbs.

MSR $329	$280	$245	$210	$190	$155	$125	$110	

* ***Mark II FXP*** – .22 LR cal., bolt action, 21 in. carbon steel Sporter barrel with satin blued finish, AccuTrigger, 10 shot detachable box mag., no sights, OD Green synthetic stock, includes 3-9x40 Bushnell scope, 6 lbs. New 2014.

MSR $309	$265	$230	$195	$180	$145	$120	$100	

* ***Mark II G*** – .17 Mach 2 (mfg. 2004-2005) or .22 LR cal., bolt action, 21 in. barrel with satin blued finish, 10 shot detachable box mag., AccuTrigger, open sights, checkered hardwood walnut stock, right or left (GL) hand configuration, 5 1/2 lbs. New 1996.

MSR $255	$220	$190	$160	$145	$120	$95	$80	

Add $64 for Mark II-GV (mfg. 2005).
Add $7 for Mark II-GXP package (includes 4x15mm scope, disc. 2004).
Add $7 for Mark II-GLXP package (left-hand, includes 4x15mm scope, disc. 2004).

This Model was also available with Varmint Left Hand (Mark II GLV, disc. 2005) at no additional charge.

* ***Mark II G Compact (GY Youth)*** – .22 LR cal., bolt action, 19 in. barrel with satin blued finish, 10 shot detachable box mag., AccuTrigger, open sights, checkered hardwood walnut stock, right or left (GLY) hand configuration, 5 1/2 lbs. New 1996.

MSR $255	$220	$190	$160	$145	$120	$95	$80	

* ***Mark II Minimalist*** – .22 WMR cal., bolt action rifle, 18 in. carbon steel threaded and button rifled Sporter barrel with matte black finish, 10 shot detachable box mag., adj. AccuTrigger, Boyds green or brown laminate stock w/natural finish, two-piece Weaver bases, 5.68 lbs. New late 2019.

MSR $350	$300	$265	$225	$200	$165	$135	$115	

GRADING - PPGS™	100%	98%	95%	90%	80%	70%	60%	LAST MSR

* ***Mark II TR*** – .22 LR cal., bolt action, 22 in. fluted carbon steel heavy barrel, 5 shot detachable box mag., black hardwood tactical (disc.) or Boyds black hardwood ProVarmint stock, AccuTrigger, matte black finish, 7 1/2 lbs. New 2010.

MSR $565	$475	$415	$350	$325	$260	$215	$185	

» **Mark II TRR/TRR-SR** – .22 LR cal., bolt action, similar to Mark II TR Model, except has top Picatinny rail, Model TRR-SR with threaded barrel became standard 2011, 7.8 lbs. New 2010.

MSR $645	$550	$480	$410	$375	$300	$250	$210	

MODEL 64 SERIES SEMI-AUTO – .22 LR cal., 20 1/4 or 21 in. barrel with adj. rear sight, 10 shot detachable mag., choice of black synthetic (Model 64F), checkered hardwood (Model 64G), or camo stock, thumb operated rotary safety, Accu-Trigger not available, 5 1/2 lbs. New 1996.

* ***Model 64BTV*** – .22 LR cal., semi-auto, 10 shot detachable box mag., 21 in. heavy barrel, laminated walnut thumbhole stock, AccuTrigger not available, rear aperture sight, 7 1/2 lbs. Mfg. 2008-2012.

	$325	$285	$250	$225	$175	$150	$115	*$381*

* ***Model 64 Camo*** – .22 LR cal., semi-auto, 21 in. blued barrel, open sights, 10 shot detachable box mag., synthetic stock with Realtree Hardwoods HD (disc.) or Next G1 camo finish, 5 lbs. New 2003.

MSR $205	$175	$155	$130	$120	$95	$80	$65	

* ***Model 64F/64FL/64FV*** – .22 LR cal., semi-auto, 20 1/4 regular (disc. 2012) or 21 (Model 64FV, mfg. 1998-2004, in 2013 21 in. became standard) in. heavy barrel, black graphite/polymer checkered stock, not available w/AccuTrigger, right or left (64 FL, new 2015) hand configuration, 5 or 6 lbs. New 1997.

MSR $149	$125	$110	$95	$85	$70	$55	$50	

Add $3 for left-hand (Model 64FL).
Add $48 for Model 64FV with heavy barrel (disc. 2004).
Add $61 for Model 64-FRD (Red Dot sight, mfg. 2009-2011).

* ***Model 64FSS*** – .22 LR cal., semi-auto, 21 in. stainless steel barrel, 10 shot detachable box mag., open sights, checkered black synthetic stock, 5 lbs. New 2002.

MSR $220	$190	$165	$145	$130	$105	$85	$70	

» **Model 64FVSS** – semi-auto, similar to Model 64FSS, except has 21 in. heavy barrel, 6 lbs. Mfg. 2002-2004.

	$190	$165	$145	$130	$105	$85	$65	*$240*

* ***Model 64 F Takedown*** – .22 LR cal., blowback action, semi-takedown, 16 1/2 in. matte black carbon steel barrel, 10 shot detachable box mag., matte black synthetic stock, drilled and tapped receiver for scope mounts, right or left-hand configuration, includes Uncle Mike's Bug-Out bag. New 2019.

MSR $249	$215	$190	$160	$145	$120	$95	$80	

* ***Model 64 FV-SR*** – .22 LR cal., semi-auto, 16 1/2 in. fluted and threaded heavy barrel with matte black finish, one-piece rail, AccuTrigger not available, 10 shot detachable box mag., black synthetic stock, 5 lbs. New 2014.

MSR $180	$155	$135	$115	$100	$85	$75	$60	

* ***Model 64 FVXP Package*** – .22 LR cal., semi-auto, 21 in. heavy barrel with satin blued finish, 10 shot detachable box mag., black synthetic stock, includes 4x32mm scope (mfg. 2006-2013) or 3-9x40 Bushnell scope (new 2014), 5 1/2 lbs.

MSR $260	$220	$195	$165	$150	$120	$100	$85	

* ***Model 64 FXP Package*** – .22 LR cal., semi-auto, 21 in. barrel with satin blued finish, 10 shot detachable box mag., open sights, black synthetic stock, includes unmounted 4x15mm scope, right or left (64 FLXP, new 2015) hand configuration.

MSR $199	$175	$155	$130	$120	$95	$80	$65	

* ***Model 64G*** – .22 LR cal., semi-auto, 21 in. carbon steel Sporter barrel, AccuTrigger not available, 10 shot detachable box mag, checkered hardwood (disc.) or Boyds hardwood walnut stock, open sights, blued finish, 5 1/2 lbs.

MSR $245	$200	$180	$155	$140	$115	$90	$80	

Add $9 for Model 64-GXP package (includes 4x15mm scope, disc. 2005).

* ***Model 64TR-SR*** – .22 LR cal., semi-auto, 16 1/2 in. threaded heavy fluted barrel, 10 shot detachable box mag., no sights, matte finish, AccuTrigger is not available, scope rail, black hardwood tactical stock, 6.6 lbs. New 2011.

MSR $380	$325	$285	$245	$220	$180	$150	$125	

GRADING - PPGS™	100%	98%	95%	90%	80%	70%	60%	LAST MSR

MODEL 93 SERIES MAGNUM BOLT ACTION – .22 WMR cal., 21 in. barrel with adj. rear sight, 5 shot detachable mag., checkered right or left-hand (Model 93 GL) hardwood Monte Carlo stock, AccuTrigger became standard 2006, 5 3/4 lbs. New 1996.

* ***Model 93 G/GL*** – .22 WMR cal., bolt action, 21 in. barrel, AccuTrigger, 5 shot detachable box mag., checkered hardwood walnut stock, open sights, blued finish, right or left (Model 93GL) hand action, 5 3/4 lbs.

MSR $290	$250	$220	$190	$170	$140	$115	$95	

* ***Model 93F/FV*** – .22 WMR cal., bolt action, 21 in. blue regular (F) or heavy (FV) barrel with checkered black synthetic graphite polymer stock, 5 shot detachable box mag., open (93F) or no (93FV) sights, AccuTrigger, 5 1/2-6 lbs. New 1998.

MSR $299	$255	$225	$190	$175	$140	$115	$100	

Add $21 for Model 93FV with heavy barrel (new 2006).
Add $66 for 3-9x40 Bushnell scope package (Model 93 FXP), new 2014.

* ***Model 93FSS*** – .22 WMR cal., bolt action, 21 in. stainless steel sporter barrel and action with checkered black synthetic graphite/polymer stock, AccuTrigger, 5 shot detachable box mag., fiber optic (new 2013) open sights, 5 lbs. New 1997.

MSR $365	$310	$270	$235	$210	$170	$140	$120	

* ***Model 93FVSS*** – .22 WMR cal., bolt action, 21 in. heavy stainless steel barrel with recessed crown and button rifling, drilled and tapped, 5 shot detachable box mag., black synthetic stock, Weaver bases included, 6 lbs. New 1998.

MSR $375	$320	$285	$245	$220	$180	$150	$125	

Add $74 for Model 93FVSSXP package (includes 3-9x40mm scope and mounts).

* ***Model 93F Camo*** – bolt action, similar to Model 93G, except has Realtree Hardwoods HD camo finish. Mfg. 2003-2004.

	$180	$160	$135	$120	$100	$80	$65	*$211*

* ***Model 93 FV-SR*** – .22 WMR cal., 16 1/2 in. heavy threaded barrel with matte black finish, one-piece rail, AccuTrigger, 5 shot detachable box mag., black synthetic stock, 5 1/2 lbs. New 2014.

MSR $335	$285	$245	$210	$190	$155	$125	$110	

* ***Model 93 FV-SR Gator Camo (Landry Series)*** – .22 WMR cal., 16 1/2 in. heavy barrel, suppressor ready, 5 shot detachable box mag., AccuTrigger, Gator Camo stock, endorsed by famous TV Gator Hunter Troy Landry, 5 1/2 lbs. New 2015.

MSR $365	$310	$270	$235	$210	$170	$140	$120	

* ***Model 93 FXP Package*** – .22 WMR cal., bolt action, 21 in. carbon steel heavy barrel, 5 shot detachable box mag., black synthetic stock, includes 3-9x40mm Bushnell scope, 6 lbs.

MSR $349	$300	$265	$225	$200	$165	$135	$115	

* ***Model 93XP Camo*** – .22 WMR cal., bolt action, 22 in. barrel, 5 shot detachable box mag., AccuTrigger, 100% Mossy Oak Brush camo finish, includes 3-9x40 Bushnell scope and mounts, 5 1/4 lbs.

MSR $560	$475	$415	$350	$325	$260	$215	$185	

* ***Model 93 BRJ*** – .22 WMR cal., bolt action, 21 in. heavy blued barrel with spiral fluting, 5 shot detachable box mag., AccuTrigger, tri-color/Royal Jacarnada wood laminate stock, no sights, 7 lbs. New 2010.

MSR $575	$485	$425	$365	$330	$265	$225	$190	

* ***Model 93 BSEV*** – .22 WMR cal., bolt action, 21 in. heavy stainless steel barrel with spiral fluting, 5 shot detachable box mag., AccuTrigger, oversized thumbhole laminate Evolution stock, 6.8 lbs. New 2010.

MSR $685	$585	$510	$435	$395	$320	$265	$225	

* ***Model 93 BTVSS*** – .22 WMR cal., bolt action, stainless steel action, 21 in. heavy stainless steel barrel, no sights, AccuTrigger, 5 shot detachable box mag., Boyds brown laminated thumbhole stock, 7 1/2 lbs. New 2007.

MSR $555	$475	$410	$350	$325	$260	$215	$185	

* ***Model 93 Classic*** – .22 WMR, bolt action, 24 in. regular or heavy high luster blue barrel with or w/o aperture rear sight, 5 shot detachable box mag., with (Model 93 Classic-T) or w/o sights. Mfg. 2008-2010.

	$485	$425	$365	$330	$265	$220	$170	*$582*

Add $35 for heavy barrel with aperture rear sight (Model 93 Classic-T, disc. 2008).

GRADING - PPGS™	100%	98%	95%	90%	80%	70%	60%	LAST MSR

* ***Model 93 Minimalist*** – .22 WMR cal., 18 in. carbon steel button rifled threaded Sporter matte black barrel w/cap, 10 shot detachable mag., adj. AccuTrigger, Boyds brown or green laminate Minimalist stock w/natural finish, two-piece Weaver bases, 5.48 lbs. New 2020.

MSR $350	$300	$265	$225	$200	$165	$135	$115	

MODEL 93R17 SERIES BOLT ACTION – .17 HMR cal., black synthetic, camo, or hardwood stock and forearm, 16 1/2, 20 3/4, 21, or 22 in. barrel, otherwise similar to Model 93 Series, AccuTrigger became standard 2006, 5 lbs. New 2003.

* ***Model 93R17 BRJ*** – .17 HMR cal., bolt action, 21 in. spiral fluted carbon steel heavy barrel, 5 shot detachable box mag., AccuTrigger, tri-color/Royal Jacaranda wood laminate stock, 7 lbs. New 2010.

MSR $575	$485	$425	$365	$330	$265	$225	$190	

* ***Model 93R17 BSEV*** – .17 HMR cal., bolt action, 21 in. spiral fluted heavy stainless steel barrel, 5 shot detachable box mag., oversized thumbhole laminate Evolution stock, 6.8 lbs. New 2010.

MSR $685	$585	$510	$435	$395	$320	$265	$225	

* ***Model 93R17 BTV*** – .17 HMR cal., bolt action, 21 in. heavy carbon steel barrel, laminated hardwood thumbhole stock, no sights, 5 shot detachable mag., AccuTrigger, 7 1/2 lbs. New 2009.

MSR $479	$410	$360	$310	$280	$225	$185	$160	

* ***Model 93R17 BTVSS*** – .17 HMR cal., bolt action, right or left-hand configuration, 21 in. stainless steel heavy barrel, 5 shot detachable box mag., AccuTrigger, laminated hardwood thumbhole stock, target sights, 7 1/2 lbs. New 2003.

MSR $499	$425	$375	$325	$295	$235	$195	$165	

Add $51 for left-hand configuration (new 2009).

* ***Model 93R17 BV*** – .17 HMR cal., bolt action, 21 in. blued barrel, steel action, 5 shot detachable mag., AccuTrigger, no sights, walnut lacquer hardwood stock, 7 lbs. New 2003.

MSR $435	$370	$320	$275	$250	$200	$165	$145	

* ***Model 93R17 BVSS*** – .17 HMR cal., bolt action, 21 in. stainless steel heavy barrel, stainless steel action, no sights, 5 shot detachable box mag., AccuTrigger, grey laminated hardwood stock, 6 lbs. New 2003.

MSR $459	$390	$340	$295	$265	$215	$175	$150	

* ***Model 93R17 Camo*** – .17 HMR cal., bolt action, 21 in. blued barrel, 5 shot detachable box mag., AccuTrigger, synthetic stock, Realtree Hardwoods HD (disc.) or Next G1 camo finish, 5 lbs. New 2003.

MSR $325	$275	$240	$200	$185	$150	$125	$100	

* ***Model 93R17 XP Camo Package*** – .17 HMR cal., 22 in. barrel, 5 shot detachable box mag., AccuTrigger, synthetic stock, 100% Realtree Hardwoods Snow camo (disc. 2019) or Mossy Oak Brush camo coverage, includes 3-9x40mm Bushnell scope, 5 1/4 lbs. New 2008.

MSR $550	$470	$410	$350	$325	$260	$215	$185	

* ***Model 93R17 F*** – .17 HMR cal., bolt action, 21 in. blued barrel, 5 shot detachable box mag., AccuTrigger, checkered black synthetic stock, no sights, 5 lbs.

MSR $285	$240	$210	$180	$165	$130	$110	$90	

* ***Model 93R17 FXP Package*** – .17 HMR cal., bolt action, 21 in. blued barrel, 5 shot detachable box mag., black synthetic stock, includes 3-9x40mm Bushnell scope, 6 lbs. New 2006.

MSR $359	$310	$270	$235	$210	$170	$140	$120	

* ***Model 93R17 FSS*** – .17 HMR cal., bolt action, 21 in. stainless steel sporter barrel, 5 shot detachable box mag., checkered black synthetic graphite/polymer stock, 5 1/2 lbs. New 2003.

MSR $355	$300	$265	$225	$200	$165	$135	$115	

* ***Model 93R17 FVSS*** – .17 HMR cal., bolt action, 21 in. heavy stainless steel barrel with recessed crown and button rifling, 5 shot detachable box mag., AccuTrigger, drilled and tapped, black synthetic stock, Weaver bases included, 5 1/2 lbs. New 2003.

MSR $380	$325	$285	$245	$220	$180	$150	$125	

* ***Model 93R17 FV*** – .17 HMR cal., bolt action, 21 in. heavy carbon steel barrel, 5 shot detachable box mag., AccuTrigger, black synthetic stock, 5 1/2 lbs. New 2003.

MSR $305	$255	$225	$190	$175	$140	$115	$100	

* ***Model 93R17 FV SR*** – .17 HMR cal., 16 1/2 in. heavy threaded barrel with matte black finish, one-piece scope rail, 5 shot detachable box mag., AccuTrigger, matte black synthetic stock, 5 1/2 lbs. New 2014.

MSR $345	$295	$255	$220	$195	$160	$130	$110	

GRADING - PPGS™	100%	98%	95%	90%	80%	70%	60%	LAST MSR

* ***Model 93R17 GV/GLV*** – .17 HMR cal., bolt action, 21 in. heavy blued varmint barrel, 5 shot detachable box mag., AccuTrigger, checkered hardwood stock, right or left-hand (GLV) action, 5 lbs. New 2003.

MSR $315	$270	$230	$195	$180	$145	$120	$100	

* ***Model 93R17 GVXP Package*** – .17 HMR cal., bolt action, 21 in. blued heavy barrel, 5 shot detachable box mag., Boyds hardwood stock, AccuTrigger, includes 3-9x40mm Bushnell scope, 6 lbs. New 2006.

MSR $399	$340	$300	$255	$230	$185	$155	$130	

* ***Model 93R17 Minimalist*** – .17 HMR cal., 18 in. carbon steel button rifled threaded Sporter matte black barrel w/cap, 10 shot detachable mag., adj. AccuTrigger, brown or green wood laminate Minimalist thumbhole stock w/natural finish, two-piece Weaver base, 5.48 lbs. New 2020.

MSR $350	$300	$265	$225	$200	$165	$135	$115	

* ***Model 93R17 TR*** – .17 HMR cal., bolt action, 22 in. threaded heavy barrel, 5 shot detachable box mag., black hardwood tactical stock, AccuTrigger, 7 1/2 lbs. Mfg. 2010-2020.

	$485	$425	$365	$330	$265	$225	$190	*$569*

» **Model 93R17 TRR/TRR-SR** – .17 HMR cal., bolt action, similar to Mark 93R17 TR Model, except has top Picatinny rail, TRR-SR Model with threaded barrel became standard 2011, 7.8 lbs. New 2010.

MSR $605	$515	$450	$385	$350	$285	$230	$200	

* ***Model 93R17/93R17T Classic*** – .17 HMR cal., bolt action, 24 in. high luster blue barrel, 5 shot detachable box mag., walnut stock, no sights, Model 93R17T Classic with target barrel and aperture rear sight (new 2008) became standard during 2011, 6 1/2 lbs. Mfg. 2007-2012.

	$540	$475	$405	$365	$295	$245	$190	*$659*

MODEL 900 SERIES – .22 LR cal., single (Target/Silhouette Model) or 5 shot (Biathlon Model), 21 or 25 (Target Model) in. free floated barrel, uncheckered hardwood stock, right or left-hand action, approx. 8 lbs. Mfg. 1996-2001.

* ***Model 900B Series Biathlon*** – blonde stock, supplied with five 5 shot mags., includes shooting rail and barrel snow cover, aperture rear sight. Mfg. 1996-97.

	$445	$390	$335	$305	$245	$200	$155	*$498*

This model was also available with left-hand action (Model 900B-LH, new 1997).

* ***Model 900S Series Silhouette*** – brown hardwood stock, heavy 21 in. barrel with muzzle crown, scope bases installed, w/o sights. Mfg. 1996-97.

	$300	$265	$225	$205	$165	$135	$105	*$346*

This model was also available with left-hand action (Model 900S-LH, mfg. 1997).

* ***Model 900TR Series Target*** – 25 in. barrel, aperture sights, shooting rail with handstop. Disc. 2001.

	$395	$345	$295	$270	$215	$180	$140	*$448*

This model was also available with left-hand action (Model 900TR-LH, new 1997).

RIFLES: CENTERFIRE, CURRENT/RECENT PRODUCTION

The 110 Series was first produced in 1958. Beginning in 1992, Savage Arms, Inc. began supplying this model with a master trigger lock, earmuffs, shooting glasses (disc. 1992), and test target.

Beginning 1994, all Savage rifles employ a laser etched bolt featuring the Savage logo. During 1996, Savage began using pillar bedded stocks for many of their rifles.

Recent Savage nomenclature usually involves alphabetical suffixes which mean the following: B - laminated wood stock, BT - laminated thumbhole stock, C - detachable box mag., EV - Evolution stock, F - composite/synthetic stock, G - hardwood stock, H - hinged floorplate, K - AccuStock or standard muzzle brake, AK - adj. muzzle brake with fluted barrel, L - left-hand, LE - Law Enforcement, NS - no sights, P - police (tactical) rifle, SB - smooth bore, SE - safari express, SR - suppressor ready, SS - stainless steel, SS-S - stainless steel single shot, T - Target (aperture rear sight), TR - tactical style rimfire, TRR - tactical style rimfire w/rail, U - high luster blue, blue metal finish and/or stock finish, V - Long Range (Varmint w/heavy barrel), XP - package gun (scope, sling, and rings/base), Y - Youth/Ladies Model. A 2 digit model number (10) designates new short action. A 3 digit model number (110) indicates long action.

Hence, the Model 111FCNS designates a 111 Series firearm with synthetic stock, detachable magazine, and no sights. Likewise, a Model 11FYCXP3 indicates a Model 11 Series with synthetic stock, youth

GRADING - PPGS™	100%	98%	95%	90%	80%	70%	60%	LAST MSR

dimensions, detachable magazine, is a packaged gun which includes scope. The Model 116FHSAK indicates a long action rifle with hinged floorplate, synthetic stock, stainless steel action/barrel with adj. muzzlebrake.

During 2003, Savage released its new patented AccuTrigger, which allows the consumer to adjust the trigger pull from the outside of the rifle from 1 1/2 lbs. - 6 lbs. using a proprietary tool. The AccuTrigger also has almost no trigger creep and is infinitely adjustable. Initially, it was released in all Varmint, LE, and heavy barrel long range rifles, and during 2004, the AccuTrigger became standard on nearly all Savage centerfire rifles, except the Model 11 and 11FCXP3 and 10/110G Package guns. During 2007, Savage began offering target actions with AccuTrigger, right bolt, and choice of left or right port ejection with .223 Rem. bolt head - MSR is $725-$769.

During 2008, Savage Arms introduced a new personal anti-recoil device (P.A.D.), which is installed in many Savage bolt action centerfire rifles. The P.A.D. reduces recoil by 45% from OEM solid and vented pads.

In 2009, Savage Arms introduced its Accustock, which incorporates a rigid aluminum rail and 3D bedding cradle that is firmly imbedded in the stock throughout the length of the rifles forend. Many Savage Centerfire rifles now incorporate the Accustock bedding system.

Also during 2009/2010, Savage introduced varmint short actions, along with both long and short sporter actions. Sporter actions had an MSR of $481, while the varmint short actions' MSR was $505. A dual port receiver, allowing left loading and right ejection was also released in 2009 - MSR was $595.

During 2010, Target actions became available in stainless steel only (in either single or dual port configuration) - MSR on the single port is $613, and $651 for the dual port.

During 2012, Savage introduced its new AXIS Series.

In 2018, Savage introduced the AccuFit system - the new synthetic stock design allows shooters to quickly adjust comb height and length of pull for a customized fit and consistent, more comfortable shooting.

Subtract approx. 10% on models listed below w/o AccuTrigger (became standard on all centerfire rifles in 2004).

MODEL 10BA/BAS-K – .308 Win. cal., 24 in. fluted heavy barrel with muzzle brake, short action, 10 shot detachable box mag., all aluminum AccuStock, AccuTrigger, Magpul PRS-G3 buttstock, Picatinny rail, no sights, matte blued finish, oversized bolt handle, 13.4 lbs. Mfg. 2009-2016.

$2,000	$1,750	$1,500	$1,360	$1,100	$900	$700	*$2,446*

* ***Model 10BAT/S-K*** – .308 Win. cal., 24 in. barrel with muzzle brake, short action, 10 shot detachable box mag., similar to Model 10BAS-K, except has tactical stock with adj. buttpad. Mfg. 2009-2010.

$1,750	$1,450	$1,125	$925	$800	$700	$600	*$2,071*

MODEL 10 BA STEALTH – 6.5 Creedmoor, .223 Rem. (new 2017), or .308 Win. cal., right or left-hand action, 16 1/2 (new 2017), 20, or 24 in. carbon steel matte black fluted heavy barrel, threaded muzzle with protector, 10 shot detachable box mag., adj. AccuTrigger, M-LOK forend, Fab Defense GLR-16 buttstock with adj. cheekpiece, one-piece EGW scope rail, 9.2 lbs. Mfg. late 2016-2019.

$1,050	$925	$795	$715	$580	$475	$375	*$1,229*

MODEL 10 BA STEALTH EVOLUTION – .223 Rem., .308 Win., 6.5 Creedmoor or 6mm Creedmoor cal., right or left-hand configuration, 20, 24, or 26 in. fluted heavy barrel with 5R rifling, muzzle brake, 10 shot detachable box mag., AccuTrigger, Fab Defense buttstock, adj. LOP, factory blue printed action, oversized bolt handle, monolithic aluminum chassis, FDE receiver finish, 10.8 lbs. Mfg. 2018-2020.

$1,550	$1,350	$1,175	$1,050	$900	$775	$625	*$1,819*

MODEL 10FCM SCOUT – 7.62x39mm (new 2011), .308 Win. or 7mm-08 Rem. (disc. 2002) cal., 20 in. barrel with removable ghost ring rear sight, one-piece barrel mount (allows long scope eye relief), 4 shot detachable mag., satin blue action with large ball bolt handle, black synthetic dual pillar bedded stock, AccuStock became standard 2009, includes swivel set and sling, tripod became standard 2007, 6 1/8 lbs. Mfg. 1999-2003, reintroduced 2007-2013.

$725	$575	$450	$365	$295	$260	$230	*$865*

Subtract 15% if w/o AccuStock.

MODEL 10FM (SIERRA) – .243 Win., .308 Win., .270 WSM (new 2003), .300 WSM (new 2002), or 7mm-08 Rem. (new 1999) cal., short action, lightweight, features black synthetic stock with dual pillar bedding, button rifling and recessed crown, 20 (Sierra, standard weight, new 1999) or 24 (heavy only, disc. 1998) in. barrel, w/o sights, 6 lbs. Mfg. 1998-2004.

$450	$395	$340	$305	$250	$205	$160	*$511*

This model was also available in left-hand action (disc.).

GRADING - PPGS™	100%	98%	95%	90%	80%	70%	60%	LAST MSR

MODEL 10FCM (SIERRA) – .243 Win., .270 WSM, .300 WSM, .308 Win., or 7mm-08 Rem. cal., 20 in. barrel, synthetic stock, short action, detachable box mag., no sights, 6 1/4 lbs. Mfg. 2005-06.

	$475	$400	$350	$325	$260	$215	$165	*$540*

MODEL 10 50TH ANNIVERSARY – .300 Savage cal., short action, hinged floorplate with Indian chief engraving and 50th Anniversary markings, 4 shot mag., 22 in. barrel, drilled and tapped, semi-fancy American walnut Monte Carlo stock with shadowline cheekpiece and fleur-de-lis checkering, 24kt. gold plated double barrel bands, 24kt. gold plated AccuTrigger, embossed recoil pad, ltd. ed. of 1,000 rifles, approx. 7 lbs. Mfg. 2008 only.

	$1,475	$1,250	$1,050	$875	$750	$650	$595	*$1,724*

MODEL 10 LAW ENFORCEMENT SERIES – .223 Rem., .260 Rem. (mfg. 1999-2001), .308 Win., or 7mm-08 (mfg. 1999-2001) cal., short action, tactical/law enforcement model, checkered black synthetic stock, features 20 (new 2006) or 24 in. heavy barrel w/o sights, AccuTrigger became standard 2003, 8 lbs. Mfg. 1998-2007.

	$505	$440	$380	$345	$280	$225	$175	*$621*

* ***Model 10FP/10FLP*** – .223 Rem. or .308 Win. cal., short action, 20 or 24 in. heavy free floating and button rifled barrel, 4 shot box mag., black McMillan synthetic sporter style stock, drilled and tapped, swivel stud, oversized bolt handle, 6 1/4 lbs. Mfg. 1998-2010.

	$625	$500	$425	$365	$335	$295	$275	*$775*

This model was also available in left-hand action (Model 10FLP, 24 in. barrel only, disc. 2009).

* ***Model 10FP-SR*** – .223 Rem. or .308 Win. cal., short action, 22 in. threaded barrel, 4 shot box mag., AccuTrigger, black McMillan synthetic sporter style stock, matte blued finish, no sights, oversized bolt handle. Mfg. 2011-2013.

	$625	$500	$425	$365	$335	$295	$275	*$775*

* ***Model 10FP Duty*** – similar to Model 10FP, except has open iron sights. Mfg. 2002 only.

	$435	$355	$290	$250	$215	$180	$165	*$525*

* ***Model 10FP 20 In. (LE1/LE1A)*** – .223 Rem. (LE1A only, disc. 2007) or .308 Win. cal., similar to Model 10FP, except has 20 in. heavy barrel with no sights, choice of standard (LE1, disc. 2005) or Choate (LE1A) stock (folding only, new 2006). Mfg. 2002-2010.

	$865	$695	$565	$475	$425	$350	$300	*$1,034*

Subtract 20% for standard stock (LE1).

* ***Model 10FP 26 In. (LE2/LE2A)*** – .223 Rem. (LE2A only) or .308 Win. cal., similar to Model 10FP-LE1/LE1A, except has 26 in. heavy barrel and choice of standard (LE2, disc. 2005) or Choate stock (LE2A). Mfg. 2002-2006.

	$625	$500	$400	$360	$330	$300	$275	*$754*

Subtract 20% for standard stock.

* ***Model 10FP McMillan (LE2B)*** – .308 Win. cal., short action, features McMillan tactical fiberglass stock with stippled grip areas, 4 shot mag., 26 in. heavy barrel. Mfg. 2003-2006.

	$860	$725	$625	$525	$425	$325	$265	*$1,033*

* ***Model 10FP H-S Precision*** – .308 Win. cal., 24 in. barrel, features H-S Precision stock. Mfg. 2006 only.

	$720	$585	$475	$425	$350	$300	$275	*$864*

* ***Model 10FPCPXP/10FPXP (LE/LEA)*** – .308 Win. cal. only, short action, features skeletonized synthetic stock, 24 (new 2006) or 26 (disc. 2005) in. barrel w/o sights, H-S Precision stock became standard 2006, LEA has Choate stock, LE has standard stock (disc. 2005), includes Burris (disc.) or Leupold (new 2004) 3.5-10x50mm scope with flip covers and sling, 4 shot internal (FPXP, disc. 2006) or detachable (FPCPXP, new 2007) mag., Harris bipod, aluminum case, 10 1/2 lbs. Mfg. 2002-2009.

	$2,275	$1,850	$1,550	$1,300	$1,100	$900	$750	*$2,715*

Subtract 20% for LE standard stock or 10% for Choate stock (Model 10FPXP-LEA package).

* ***Model 10FCP HS Precision*** – .308 Win. cal., short action, 24 in. barrel, 4 shot detachable box mag., oversized bolt handle, no sights, H-S Precision stock, matte blued finish, 9.6 lbs. Mfg. 2007-2020.

	$1,140	$1,000	$855	$775	$625	$525	$445	*$1,339*

» **Model 10FCPXP H-S Precision Package** – .308 Win. cal., 24 in. barrel, includes top Picatinny rail, 3-9x40mm scope, and bipod, 9.6 lbs. Mfg. 2010-2011.

	$2,550	$2,250	$1,900	$1,625	$1,275	$1,000	$875	*$2,908*

GRADING - PPGS™	100%	98%	95%	90%	80%	70%	60%	LAST MSR

* ***Model 10FCP Choate*** – .308 Win. cal., 24 in. barrel, features Choate stock, detachable box mag. Mfg. 2007 only.

	$700	$575	$475	$425	$350	$300	$275	*$833*

* ***Model 10FCP McMillan*** – .308 Win. cal., 24 in. heavy barrel, 4 shot detachable box mag., no sights, matte blued finish, oversized bolt handle, AccuTrigger, McMillan fiberglass stock, 10 lbs. Mfg. 2007-2016.

	$1,325	$1,025	$895	$750	$650	$550	$475	*$1,591*

* ***Model 10 FCP-K/Model 10 FLCP-K*** – .223 Rem. or .308 Win. cal., short action, 24 in. heavy blue barrel with muzzle brake, 4 shot detachable box mag., drilled and tapped, black synthetic AccuStock with aluminum spine and 3-D bedding cradle, swivel stud for bipod, oversized bolt handle, 8.9 lbs. Mfg. 2009-2013.

	$850	$725	$595	$475	$425	$350	$300	*$975*

This model was also available in left-hand action at no extra charge (Model 10 FLCP-K).

MODEL 10 FCP-SR – .308 Win. cal., short action, 20 or 24 in. fluted heavy barrel with threaded muzzle, 10 shot detachable box mag., AccuTrigger, one-piece scope rail, black synthetic AccuStock, right or left (10FLCP-SR) hand action, matte finish, 8.9 lbs. Mfg. 2015-2016.

	$660	$575	$495	$425	$375	$300	$250	*$785*

MODEL 10 PRECISION CARBINE – .223 Rem., .308 Win., or .300 AAC Blackout (mfg. 2012 only) cal., 20 in. matte blue free floating button rifled threaded (new 2012) or un-threaded (disc. 2011) barrel, 4 shot detachable box mag., swivel stud, oversized bolt handle, green camo AccuStock with aluminum spine and 3-D bedding cradle, 7 lbs. Mfg. 2009-2014.

	$810	$675	$550	$425	$375	$350	$300	*$952*

* ***Model 10FCP-SR*** – .308 Win. cal., short action, 24 in. heavy fluted threaded barrel, 10 shot detachable box mag., matte black metal finish, synthetic tan digital camo stock, AccuTrigger, AccuStock, one-piece scope rail, 8 3/4 lbs. Mfg. 2012-2013.

	$1,100	$950	$825	$725	$625	$525	$425	*$1,250*

MODEL 10 PREDATOR HUNTER – .204 Ruger, .22-250 Rem., .223 Rem., .243 Win. (new 2008), .260 Rem. (new 2011), 6.5 Creedmoor (new 2011), or 6.5x.284 Norma (left-hand action only, mfg. 2012 only) cal., 22 or 24 in. matte blued fluted medium contour barrel, 4 shot detachable box mag., AccuTrigger, oversized bolt handle, Accustock became standard during 2010, 100% Mossy Oak Brush (disc. 2014), Snow (mfg. 2009-2011), or RealTree Max 1 (new 2010) patterned camo synthetic stock, no sights, includes scope blocks, right or left (mfg. 2012-2014) hand action, 7 1/4 lbs. Mfg. 2007-2018.

	$825	$675	$525	$450	$395	$350	$300	*$999*

Add $35 for Model 10XP Predator package, which includes scope (right-hand action only, mfg. 2008-2013).

MODEL 10 GRS – 6mm Creedmoor, 6.5 Creedmoor, 6.5 PRC (new 2019), or .308 Win. cal., bolt action, 20, 24, or 26 in. fluted heavy threaded barrel, 10 shot AI style detachable box mag., adj. AccuTrigger, GRS adj. stock w/fiberglass-reinforced Durethan, slim grip and forend with textured rubber grip surfaces, one-piece rail, flush cup sling loops included, sling mount for bipod, 8.9-9.2 lbs. New 2017.

MSR $1,539	$1,310	$1,150	$985	$890	$725	$590	$510	

MODEL 10GY – .223 Rem., .243 Win., or .308 Win. cal., ladies/youth model with shorter checkered hardwood stock and 22 in. barrel with open sights. Disc. 2007.

	$455	$360	$295	$240	$200	$175	$160	*$541*

* ***Model 10GYXP3 Package*** – .223 Rem., .243 Win., or .308 Win. (disc. 2009) cal., ladies/youth model with shorter checkered hardwood stock and 22 in. barrel with open sights, includes scope, bipod, and case. Disc.

	$515	$410	$315	$250	$200	$175	$160	*$691*

MODEL 10GXP3 PACKAGE – various short action cals., 22 or 24 in. blue free floating and button rifled barrel, 2 or 4 shot mag., checkered Monte Carlo walnut stock, includes 3-9x40mm scope, approx. 7 1/2 lbs. Disc. 2011.

	$525	$415	$325	$250	$200	$175	$160	*$712*

Add $28 for .270 WSM or .300 WSM cal.

This model is also available in left-hand at no charge (Model 10GLXP3, not available in WSM cals., disc. 2011).

GRADING - PPGS™	100%	98%	95%	90%	80%	70%	60%	LAST MSR

* ***Model 10GXP3/110-GXP3 Package*** – .22-250 Rem., .223 Rem., .243 Win., .250 Savage (disc. 1995), .25-06 Rem., .270 Win., .270 WSM (new 2003), .300 Sav. (disc. 1995), .30-06, .300 RSUM (mfg. 2002-2003), .308 Win., 7mm-08 Rem. (disc. 1995, reintroduced 1999), 7mm WSM (mfg. 2003-2007), 7mm Rem. Mag., 7mm RSUM (mfg. 2003), .300 WSM (new 2005), .300 RUM (mfg. 2002-2006), or .300 Win. Mag. cal., short (10GXP3) or long (110-GXP3) action, similar to Model 110-G, except has no sights, includes 3-9x32 scope, rings, bases, QD swivels, and deluxe rifle sling, includes integral Weaver type scope bases. Mfg. 1989-2011.

	$525	$415	$325	$250	$200	$175	$160	*$712*

Add $29 for WSM cals. (Model 10GXP3 only).

Was also available in left-hand action at no additional charge (Model 10GLXP3/110-GLXP3).

MODEL 10 SAVAGE ASHBURY PRECISION – .308 Win. or 6.5 Creedmoor cal., 24 in. barrel, Magpul PMAG AICS 5 shot detachable box mag., AccuTrigger, Saber modular rifle chassis system with double-locking side folding stock, Magpul MOE pistol grip and buttstock, adj. LOP, octagonal aluminum handguard with M-LOK attachment system, factory blue printed short action, 10 1/2 lbs. Mfg. 2017-2018.

	$1,525	$1,350	$1,175	$1,050	$900	$775	$625	*$1,799*

MODEL 10 TROPHY HUNTER XP PACKAGE – .22-250 Rem., .223 Rem., .243 Win., or .308 Win. cal., short action, 4 shot detachable box mag., 22 in. barrel, matte black metal finish, satin finished wood stock, Accutrigger, includes 3-9x40 Nikon BDC scope, 8.3 lbs. New 2012.

MSR $729	$625	$545	$475	$425	$345	$275	$225	

MODEL 11 DOA HUNTER XP – .243 Win., 6.5 Creedmoor, 7mm-08 Rem., .260 Rem., .308 Win., .270 WSM, or .300 WSM cal., 22 or 24 in. barrel, 2 or 4 shot detachable box mag., AccuTrigger, black synthetic stock, 13.8 in. LOP, includes 3-9x40 Bushnell Trophy scope, Weaver Steel Grand Slam rings and bases, 7.25 lbs. Mfg. 2017-2018.

	$575	$500	$450	$415	$375	$335	$295	*$684*

Add $28 for WSM cals.

MODEL 11 HUNTER XP PACKAGE – .22-250 Rem., .223 Rem., .243 Win., or .308 Win. cal., short action, 4 shot detachable box mag., 22 in. barrel, matte black metal finish, black synthetic stock, includes 3-9x40 Bushnell scope, AccuTrigger not available on this model, 7 1/4 lbs. Mfg. 2012-2014.

	$450	$400	$360	$330	$300	$275	$250	*$525*

MODEL 11 LADY HUNTER – .223 Rem. (disc. 2018), .22-250 Rem. (disc. 2013), .243 Win., .308 Win., 6.5 Creedmoor, or 7mm-08 Rem. cal., short action, 20 in. barrel without sights, black matte metal finish, 4 shot detachable box mag., AccuTrigger, drilled and tapped, satin finished walnut with pressed checkering and forward angled Monte Carlo stock with recoil pad, stock features include shorter LOP, higher front angled comb, slimmer forend and pistol grip, three-position safety, sling swivels, 6 lbs. New mid-2012.

MSR $949	$810	$710	$610	$550	$445	$365	$315	

MODEL 11 LIGHTWEIGHT HUNTER – .223 Rem. (disc. 2018), .243 Win., 6.5 Creedmoor, 7mm-08 Rem. (disc. 2018), .260 Rem. (disc. 2018), or .308 Win. cal., short action, 20 in. barrel without sights, AccuTrigger, 4 shot detachable box mag., hinged floorplate, blue finish, uncheckered walnut stock, spiral fluted bolt, 5 1/2 lbs. New 2011.

MSR $1,039	$885	$775	$665	$600	$485	$415	$350	

MODEL 11 HOG HUNTER – .223 Rem., .308 Win., or .338 Federal (new 2015) cal., short action, 20 in. threaded barrel, matte black metal finish, 4 shot internal box mag., AccuTrigger, oversized bolt handle, iron sights, OD Green synthetic stock, 7 1/4 lbs. Mfg. 2012-2017.

	$485	$425	$375	$335	$295	$265	$235	*$595*

MODEL 11 LONG RANGE HUNTER – .260 Rem. (new 2011), 6.5 Creedmoor (new 2011), .308 Win., .300 WSM, or .338 Federal (new 2015) cal., short action, 26 in. fluted carbon steel matte blued barrel with fixed muzzle brake, drilled and tapped, Karsten adj. and detachable cheekpiece, matte black synthetic AccuStock and forearm, 2 or 3 shot detachable box mag., AccuTrigger, 8.4 lbs. Mfg. 2010-2017.

	$975	$765	$625	$525	$425	$365	$325	*$1,171*

Add $46 for .338 Federal cal. (new 2015).

MODEL 11 SCOUT – .308 Win. cal., short action, 18 in. barrel with fixed muzzle brake, 10 shot detachable box mag., AccuTrigger, adj. LOP, adj. iron sights, Scout style scope mount, FDE AccuStock, adj. cheekpiece, 7.8 lbs. Mfg. 2015-2017.

	$685	$600	$500	$460	$375	$300	$250	*$818*

GRADING - PPGS™	100%	98%	95%	90%	80%	70%	60%	LAST MSR

MODEL 11 TROPHY HUNTER XP PACKAGE – .204 Ruger, .22-250 Rem., .223 Rem., .243 Win., .260 Rem., .270 WSM, .300 WSM, .308 Win., 6.5 Creedmoor, 7mm-08 Rem., or .338 Federal (mfg. 2015-2018) cal., short action, 4 shot detachable box mag., 22 or 24 (WSM cals. only) in. barrel, matte black metal finish, synthetic black stock, AccuTrigger, includes 3-9x40 Nikon scope, right or left-hand action. 7 1/4 lbs. Mfg. 2012-2020.

	$550	$500	$450	$415	$375	$335	$295	*$639*

Add $30 for WSM cals.

MODEL 11 TROPHY HUNTER XP YOUTH PACKAGE – .223 Rem., .243 Win., .308 Win., or 7mm-08 Rem. cal., right or left-hand configuration, short action, 20 in. barrel, 4 shot detachable box mag., matte black metal finish, synthetic black stock, AccuTrigger, includes 3-9x40 Nikon scope, right or left-hand action, 7 lbs. Mfg. 2012-2020.

	$550	$500	$450	$415	$375	$335	$295	*$639*

* ***Model 11 Trophy Hunter XP Youth Package Camo*** – .223 Rem., .243 Win., .308 Win., or 7mm-08 Rem. cal., short action, 20 in. matte blued barrel, AccuTrigger, 4 shot detachable box mag., no sights, Muddy Girl camo stock, includes 3-9x40 Nikon BDC scope, 7 lbs. Mfg. 2014-2020.

	$595	$525	$450	$415	$375	$335	$295	*$699*

MODEL 11 TROPHY PREDATOR HUNTER XP – .223 Rem., .22-250 Rem., .243 Win., or 6.5 Creedmoor cal., short action, 22 in. medium contour barrel, matte blue barrel finish, 4 shot detachable box mag., AccuTrigger, Snow Camo or Mossy Oak Brush camo stock, includes 3-9x40 Nikon scope, 9 lbs. Disc. 2018.

	$600	$525	$450	$410	$330	$275	$225	*$714*

MODEL 11BTH HUNTER – .204 Ruger (disc. 2011), .22-250 Rem., .223 Rem., .243 Win., or .308 Win. cal., short action, 22 in. barrel with no sights, drilled and tapped, hinged floorplate, 4 shot mag, ventilated forend, pillar bedding, AccuTrigger, brown laminated thumbhole stock, matte blue barrel finish, 6 3/4 lbs. Mfg. 2008-2018.

	$815	$675	$550	$450	$400	$350	$300	*$979*

MODEL 11FNS (11F) HUNTER – .22-250 Rem., .223 Rem., .243 Win., .260 Rem. (mfg. 1999-2000), .270 WSM (mfg. 2003-2008), .308 Win., .300 RSUM (mfg. 2003), .300 WSM (mfg. 2002-2008), 7mm RSUM (mfg. 2003), 7mm WSM (mfg. 2003-2005, reintroduced 2007-2008 in left-hand only), or 7mm-08 Rem. (new 1999) cal., short action, dual pillar bedding, checkered black synthetic stock, 22 or 24 (WSM cals. only) in. blue barrel with open sights (disc. 2008) or no sights (standard beginning 2009), 6 3/4 lbs. Mfg. 1998-2011.

	$475	$400	$340	$285	$230	$200	$175	*$609*

Add $23 for WSM cals. (left-hand only, disc. 2008).

This model is also available in left-hand action (Model 11FL).

MODEL 11FCNS/FHNS (11FC) – .204 Ruger (new 2008), .22-250 Rem., .223 Rem. (new 2008), .243 Win., .260 Rem. (disc. 2000, reintroduced 2011-2014), 7.62x39mm (mfg. 2011 only), .270 WSM (mfg. 2005-2013), .308 Win., .300 WSM (mfg. 2005-2013), 7mm WSM (mfg. 2005-2008, FHNS only 2008-2009), or 7mm-08 Rem. cal., 22 or 24 (disc.) in. barrel without sights, blue finish, short action, fixed (disc. 2004), detachable box mag. (new 2005, Model FCNS), or hinged floorplate (mfg. 2006-disc., Model FHNS), AccuTrigger, dual pillar bedded black synthetic stock, AccuStock became standard 2009, 6 3/8 lbs. Mfg. 1999-2001, reintroduced 2003-2017.

	$625	$475	$375	$325	$295	$260	$230	*$792*

Add $30 for WSM cals. (disc. 2013).

This model was also available in left-hand action (Model 11FLC, disc. 2001).

The Model FHNS is not available in WSM cals.

MODEL 11/111-FCXP3 PACKAGE – .243 Win. (Model 11FCXP3), .270 Win., .30-06, .300 Win. Mag. (disc. 2001, reintroduced 2005), 7mm-08 Rem. (mfg. 2009), or 7mm Rem. Mag. (disc. 2001, reintroduced 2005) cal., 4 shot detachable box mag., checkered black synthetic stock, 22 or 24 in. barrel, package includes bore sighted 3-9x32mm scope, rings, bases, QD swivels, and deluxe rifle sling, not available w/AccuTrigger, 6 1/2 lbs. Mfg. 1994-2011.

	$425	$350	$300	$275	$225	$200	$175	*$525*

This model was also available with left-hand action (Model 111-FLCXP3 - disc. 2000).

MODEL 11FCXP3 PACKAGE – .243 Win. or .308 Win. cal., detachable box mag., 22 in. barrel, AccuTrigger not available, black synthetic stock, includes scope. Disc. 2011.

	$425	$350	$300	$275	$225	$200	$175	*$525*

GRADING - PPGS™	100%	98%	95%	90%	80%	70%	60%	LAST MSR

MODEL 11FYXP3 PACKAGE – .223 Rem. (new 2003), .243 Win., 7mm-08 Rem. (new 2003) or .308 Win. (new 2009) cal., similar to 11F Hunter, except is Youth Model with 12 1/2 LOP, 22 in. barrel, AccuTrigger, includes 3-9x40mm scope, 6 1/2 lbs. Mfg. 2002-2011.

	$525	$450	$380	$310	$240	$210	$185	*$678*

This model is also available in left-hand action in all calibers beginning 2009.

MODEL 11FYCXP3 YOUTH PACKAGE – .243 Win. cal., short action, detachable 4 shot box mag., Youth model w/shorter dimensions, 22 in. barrel, AccuTrigger not available, includes scope, 6 1/2 lbs. Mfg. 2006-2011.

	$425	$350	$300	$275	$225	$200	$175	*$525*

MODEL 11FYCAK – .243 Win., 7mm-08 Rem., or .308 Win. cal., 22 in. barrel, detachable box mag., Youth Model with shortened LOP. Mfg. 2006-2010.

	$585	$435	$355	$300	$270	$235	$200	*$712*

MODEL 11FXP3 – see listing later in this category, combined with Model 111FXP3 package.

MODELS 11FXP3 & 111-FXP3 PACKAGES – .204 Ruger (new 2005), .22-250 Rem., .223 Rem., .243 Win., .250 Savage (disc. 1996), .25-06 Rem., .270 WSM (new 2003), .270 Win., .300 Sav. (disc. 1996), .30-06, .308 Win., .300 RUM (mfg. 2003-2004), .300 Win. Mag., .300 WSM (new 2002), .338 Win. Mag., 7mm WSM (mfg. 2003-2007), 7mm RSUM (mfg. 2003), 7mm Rem. Mag., 7mm RUM (mfg. 2002-2003), or 7mm-08 Rem. (disc. 1996, reintroduced 1999-2001, again in 2009) cal., short (11FXP3) or long (111-FXP3) action, 22 or 24 in. barrel, black graphite/fiberglass composite stock, non-glare finish, package consists of bore sighted 3-9x32 scope, rings, bases, QD swivels, and deluxe rifle sling, approx. 7 1/4 lbs. Mfg. 1994-2011.

	$525	$450	$380	$310	$240	$210	$185	*$678*

Add $27 for WSM cals. (Model 11FXP3 only).

This model was also available with left-hand action (Model 11FLXP3/111-FLXP3, disc. 2002).

MODEL 11GNS/GCNS (11G) HUNTER – similar to 11F Hunter, except has wood stock with pressed fleur-de-lis checkering, 22 in. barrel, AccuTrigger, no sights (Model 11GNS), also available with detachable box mag (new 2005, Model 11GCNS, standard beginning 2011). Mfg. 1998-2011.

	$500	$415	$325	$250	$200	$175	$160	*$699*

Add $25 for .270 WSM or .300 WSM cals. (11GCNS Model only, disc.).
Subtract $10 if w/o sights (Model 11GNS, disc. 2004).

This model was also available in left-hand action (Model 11GL or Model 11GLNS). This model's nomenclature changed from 11G to 11GNS during 2009 (no sights).

MODEL 11GC – .22-250 Rem., .243 Win., .260 Rem. (disc. 2000), .308 Win. or 7mm-08 Rem. cal., detachable mag., hardwood stock, open sights, 22 in. barrel, blue finish, 6 3/8 lbs. Mfg. 1999-2001.

	$375	$310	$270	$230	$200	$175	$160	*$441*

This model is also available in left-hand action (Model 11GLC).

MODEL 12 LONG RANGE PRECISION – .243 Win., .260 Rem., or 6.5 Creedmoor cal., short action, 26 in. fluted carbon steel full profile barrel, Target AccuTrigger, H-S Precision fiberglass stock, 4 shot detachable box mag., no sights, oversized bolt handle, matte blued finish, 11 lbs. New 2011.

MSR $1,365	$1,175	$1,025	$875	$800	$650	$550	$450

MODEL 12 VARMINTER LOW PROFILE – .204 Ruger (new 2005), .22-250 Rem., .223 Rem., .243 Win. (new 2007), .300 WSM (new 2007), or .308 Win. (new 2007) cal., choice of repeater or single shot (.204 Ruger, .22-250 Rem., or .223 Rem. cals. only, disc. 2009), short action, 26 in. fluted stainless heavy barrel and action, right-hand bolt, smaller ejection port on left side of receiver, 2 or 4 shot detachable box mag., AccuTrigger standard, low profile brown laminated stock with extra wide beavertail forend, no sights, oversized bolt handle, 10 lbs. New 2004.

MSR $1,249	$1,065	$930	$800	$725	$585	$480	$415

Add $55 for .300 WSM cal.
Subtract $40 for single shot (disc. 2009).

During 2005, this model became available in left-hand action at no extra charge in select cals.

MODEL 12 LRPV (LONG RANGE PRECISION VARMINTER) – .204 Ruger, .22-250 Rem., .223 Rem., or 6mm Norma BR (new 2008) cal., single shot, right-hand bolt, left port ejection or dual port with left load and right eject (became standard 2011), stainless short action, 26 in. X-Tra heavy fluted free floating stainless steel barrel, black synthetic H-S Precision varmint stock with molded alloy bedding system, no sights, drilled and tapped, target AccuTrigger, oversized bolt handle, swivel studs, 12 lbs. New 2005.

MSR $1,649	$1,400	$1,225	$1,050	$950	$775	$625	$550

During 2005-2006, this model was available in left-hand action at no extra charge.

GRADING - PPGS™	100%	98%	95%	90%	80%	70%	60%	LAST MSR

MODEL 12 LONG RANGE PRECISION VARMINTER REPEATER – .204 Ruger, .22-250 Rem., .223 Rem., or 6mm Norma BR cal., 26 in. barrel, short action, detachable box mag., target AccuTrigger. Mfg. 2008-2010.

	$1,085	$925	$825	$725	$625	$525	$450	*$1,319*

MODEL 12BTCSS VARMINTER THUMBHOLE – .204 Ruger, .22-250 Rem., or .223 Rem. cal., 26 in. heavy fluted stainless steel barrel, stainless short action, 4 shot detachable box mag., pillar bedding, laminated thumbhole stock, AccuTrigger, no sights, drilled and tapped, oversized bolt handle, 10 lbs. New 2008.

MSR $1,369	$1,175	$1,025	$875	$800	$650	$550	$450	

MODEL 12BVSS – .204 Ruger (mfg. 2009-2010), .22-250 Rem., .223 Rem., .243 Win. (mfg. 2002-2006), .300 WSM (mfg. 2003-2006), or .308 Win. (disc. 1999, reintroduced 2001-2006, again in 2009) cal., short action, right bolt, left port ejection, 26 in. heavy fluted stainless barrel w/o sights, dual pillar bedding, brown laminated wood stock with flat beavertail forend, AccuTrigger became standard 2003, 9 lbs. New 1998.

MSR $1,215	$1,035	$910	$780	$700	$575	$475	$400	

This model was also available in left-hand action in cals. .22-250 Rem. and .223 Rem. at no extra charge (mfg. 2004, Model 12BLVSS).

* ***Model 12BVSS-S*** – .220 Swift (new 2004), .22-250 Rem., .223 Rem., or .308 Win. cal., similar to Model 12BVSS, except is single shot, AccuTrigger became standard 2003. Mfg. 1998-2001, mfg. 2002-2005.

	$600	$490	$395	$335	$290	$245	$215	*$721*

* ***Model 12BVSS-SXP*** – similar to Model 12BVSS, except not available in .243 Win. cal., target style heavy prone laminate stock with Wundhammer palm swell and black forend cap, 26 in. fluted stainless barrel w/o sights, includes 6-18x37mm scope and black aluminum hard case, 12 lbs. Mfg. 2002-2004.

	$1,050	$895	$775	$665	$560	$465	$410	*$1,225*

MODEL 12FVSS – .22-250 Rem., .223 Rem., .270 WSM (mfg. 2003-2008), .300 WSM (mfg. 2003-2008), or .308 Win. cal., short action, right-hand bolt, left ejection port, features 26 in. fluted heavy stainless free floating barrel w/o sights, black checkered synthetic stock with dual pillar bedding, drilled and tapped, AccuTrigger became standard 2003, 9 lbs. Mfg. 1998-2012.

	$800	$700	$600	$525	$450	$375	$300	*$895*

Add $30 for WSM cals. (disc. 2009).

This model was also available in left-hand action (Model 12FLVSS, not available in WSM cals., disc. 2004).

* ***Model 12FVSS-S*** – similar to Model 12FVSS, except is single shot and not available in .308 Win. cal. Mfg. 1998-2001.

	$480	$405	$335	$275	$235	$200	$175	*$549*

* ***Model 12VSS/12VSS-S*** – .22-250 Rem., .223 Rem., or .308 Win. cal., available in long (12VSS) or short (12VSS-S, mfg. 2003-2004, not available in .308 Win. cal.) action, semi-skeletonized Choate adj. black synthetic stock with cheekpiece, 24 (disc. 2004) or 26 in. fluted stainless barrel, blue stainless steel receiver, 4 shot mag., drilled and tapped receiver, AccuTrigger became standard 2003, 11 1/4 lbs. Mfg. 2000-2006.

	$700	$595	$495	$425	$375	$315	$270	*$865*

MODEL 12FV/FVY – .204 Ruger (new 2005), .22-250 Rem., .223 Rem., .243 Win. (mfg. 2002-2009), or .308 Win. (mfg. 1999-2008) cal., short action, right bolt, left ejection port, features 26 in. regular barrel with low luster bluing, black synthetic stock with dual pillar bedding, 5 shot top loading mag., drilled and tapped, AccuTrigger became standard 2003, right or left-hand action, 9 lbs. Mfg. 1998-2014.

	$610	$475	$415	$365	$335	$300	$275	*$732*

This model was also available as a Youth Model (Model 12FVY, available in .22-250 Rem. and .223 Rem. cal. only, mfg. 2003-2004). This model is also available in left-hand action (Model 12FLV, disc. 2001, reintroduced during 2004, not available in .243 Win. or .308 Win. cal.).

MODEL 12 F/TR TARGET – .223 Rem. (new 2010) or .308 Win. cal., short action, single shot, 30 in. stainless steel barrel, target features, target AccuTrigger, oversized bolt handle, no sights, pillar bedding, grey laminate stock, 12 1/2 lbs. New 2007.

MSR $1,629	$1,385	$1,210	$1,050	$950	$760	$625	$545	

GRADING - PPGS™	100%	98%	95%	90%	80%	70%	60%	LAST MSR

MODEL 12FCV – .204 Ruger, .22-250 Rem., or .223 Rem. cal., 4 shot detachable box mag., 26 in. heavy blued barrel, AccuTrigger, checkered pistol grip matte black AccuStock, no sights, 9 lbs. Mfg. 2010-2018.

	$665	$580	$500	$450	$365	$300	$235	*$781*

MODEL 12 F CLASS – 6.5x284 Norma or 6mm Norma BR (new 2008) cal., short action, single shot, 30 in. stainless steel barrel, target features, target AccuTrigger, ergonomic grey laminate stock, oversized bolt handle, no sights, 13 lbs. New 2007.

MSR $1,745	$1,475	$1,295	$1,100	$1,000	$810	$675	$575	

MODEL 12 BENCHREST – 6.5x284 Norma (disc. 2019), 6mm Norma BR, or .308 Win. cal., short dual port action featuring left load with right eject, 29 in. heavy barrel, stainless steel action and barrel, target AccuTrigger, heavy laminate stock with vented wide forend, 12 3/4 lbs. New 2009.

MSR $1,775	$1,515	$1,325	$1,135	$1,025	$835	$685	$575	

MODEL 12 PALMA – .308 Win. cal., short action, single shot, 30 in. heavy stainless steel barrel, gray laminated stock with adj. comb and buttplate, vent. forend, target AccuTrigger, oversized bolt handle, 11 1/2 lbs. New 2009.

MSR $2,275	$1,930	$1,685	$1,450	$1,310	$1,060	$875	$750	

MODEL 14 CLASSIC/AMERICAN CLASSIC – .204 Ruger (mfg. 2008-2011), .22-250 Rem. (disc. 2012), .223 Rem. (mfg. 2008-2012), .243 Win. (also avail. w/stainless steel barrel), .250 Savage (mfg. 2009-2013), 7mm-08 Rem. (new 2011), .270 WSM (left-hand only, disc. 2012), .300 WSM (left-hand only, disc. 2012), .300 Savage (mfg. 2009-2011), .325 WSM (mfg. 2007-2008), or .308 Win. (also avail. w/ stainless steel barrel) cal., 22 or 24 (Mag. cals. only, disc.) in. steel or stainless steel (new 2011) barrel, detachable box mag. (American Classic, right or left (new 2008) hand action) or hinged floorplate (Classic, mfg. 2006-2011), no sights, checkered walnut stock and black forend tip, high polish blue, AccuTrigger standard, 7 or 7 1/2 lbs. Mfg. 2005-2018.

	$810	$675	$550	$475	$400	$350	$300	*$979*

Add $34 for WSM cals. (disc. 2012).

Subtract $72 for stainless steel in .243 Win. or .308 Win. (mfg. 2011-2013) cal. only.

MODEL 14 EURO CLASSIC – .22-250 Rem. (disc. 2009), .243 Win., or .308 Win. cal., 22 in. barrel, detachable box mag., AccuTrigger standard, open sights with adj. rear sight on barrel, checkered walnut stock with cheekpiece, 7 1/2 lbs. Mfg. 2006-2010.

	$750	$595	$525	$445	$375	$325	$275	*$909*

MODEL 16 BEAR HUNTER – .300 WSM, .338 Federal (new 2015), or .325 WSM (disc. 2013) cal., short action, 23 in. stainless steel fluted barrel with adj. muzzle brake, 2 shot mag., hinged floorplate, AccuStock, AccuTrigger, checkered synthetic (disc.) or Mossy Oak Break-Up Infinity camo stock, 7 1/2 lbs. Mfg. 2011-2018.

	$940	$750	$650	$550	$500	$400	$325	*$1,098*

Add $37 for .338 Federal cal. (new 2015).

MODEL 16FXP3 PACKAGE – .204 Ruger (new 2005), .22-250 Rem. (new 2003), .223 Rem., .243 Win., .270 WSM (new 2003), .300 RSUM (mfg. 2003), .308 Win., .300 WSM, .325 WSM (mfg. 2007-2008), 7mm-08 Rem. (new 2010), 7mm WSM (mfg. 2003-2008), or 7mm RSUM (mfg. 2003) cal., short action, stainless action and 22 or 24 in. stainless barrel w/o sights, checkered black synthetic stock, includes nickel finished 3-9x40mm scope and mounts, supplied with sling, approx. 6 1/2 lbs. Mfg. 2002-2011.

	$625	$495	$425	$360	$315	$270	$225	*$782*

Add $31 for WSM cals.

MODEL 16 TROPHY HUNTER XP PACKAGE – .204 Ruger, .22-250 Rem., .223 Rem., .243 Win., .260 Rem., .270 WSM, .300 WSM, .308 Win., 6.5 Creedmoor, .338 Federal (mfg. 2015-2018), or 7mm-08 Rem. cal., short action, 22 or 24 (WSM cals. only) in. stainless barrel, 4 shot detachable box mag., black synthetic stock, Accutrigger, includes 3-9x40 Nikon BDC scope, 7 1/4 lbs. Mfg. 2012-2020.

	$650	$575	$500	$450	$350	$300	$250	*$775*

Add $34 for WSM cals.

MODEL 16BSS WEATHER WARRIOR – .270 WSM (new 2003), .300 WSM, .300 RSUM (disc. 2002), 7mm WSM (new 2003), or 7mm RSUM (disc. 2002) cal., 24 in. barrel w/o sights, 2 or 3 shot mag., brown laminated stock with cut checkering, stainless action and barrel, 7 3/4 lbs. Mfg. 2002-2003.

	$560	$460	$355	$290	$250	$215	$185	*$668*

MODEL 16FCSS WEATHER WARRIOR – .243 Win., .260 Rem. (disc. 2000), .308 Win., or 7mm-08 Rem. cal., stainless steel barreled action with 22 in. barrel, detachable mag., dual pillar bedded black synthetic stock, 6 3/4 lbs. Mfg. 1999-2001.

	$460	$395	$325	$265	$230	$195	$170	*$532*

This model was also available in left-hand action at no additional charge (Model 16FLCSS).

GRADING - PPGS™	100%	98%	95%	90%	80%	70%	60%	LAST MSR

MODEL 16FCSAK WEATHER WARRIOR – .243 Win., .270 WSM, .300 WSM, .308 Win., 7mm-08 Rem., or 7mm WSM cal., short action, 22 or 24 in. fluted barrel with adj. muzzle brake, detachable box mag., no sights. Mfg. 2005 only.

	$560	$495	$415	$350	$315	$275	$245	*$661*

MODEL 16FSS – .204 Ruger (new 2005), .22-250 Rem. (new 2003), .223 Rem., .243 Win., .260 Rem. (mfg. 1999-2000), .270 WSM (disc. 2009), .308 Win., .300 WSM (mfg. 2002-2009), .300 RSUM (mfg. 2002-2003), 7mm WSM (mfg. 2003-2007), 7mm RSUM (mfg. 2002-2003), or 7mm-08 Rem. (mfg. 1999-2009) cal., short action, stainless steel 22 or 24 (WSM and RSUM cals only) in. barreled action w/o sights, checkered black synthetic stock with dual pillar bedding, 6 3/4 lbs. Mfg. 1998-2011.

	$575	$475	$415	$330	$285	$240	$210	*$720*

Add $27 for WSM cals.

Was also available in left-hand action at no additional charge (Model 16FLSS, not available in WSM or .204 Ruger cals.).

* ***Model 16FCSS*** – .204 Ruger (disc. 2014), .22-250 Rem., .223 Rem., .243 Win., .260 Rem. (mfg. 2011-2014), .270 WSM, .300 WSM, .308 Win., .338 Federal (new 2015), 6.5 Creedmoor (new 2011), or 7mm-08 Rem. cal., short action, stainless steel, 22 or 24 in. barrel, AccuTrigger, 2 or 4 shot detachable box mag., AccuStock standard beginning 2009, no sights, 7 lbs. Mfg. 2005-2018.

	$750	$625	$525	$450	$400	$350	$275	*$939*

Add $40 for WSM cals.

* ***Model 16FLCSS*** – .22-250 Rem., .223 Rem., .243 Win., .308 Win., or 7mm-08 Rem. cal., short action, left-hand, 22 in. stainless steel barrel, AccuTrigger, 4 shot detachable box mag., black synthetic AccuStock, no sights, 7 lbs. Mfg. 2014-2018.

	$750	$625	$525	$450	$400	$350	$275	*$939*

* ***Model 16FHSS*** – .22-250 Rem., .223 Rem., .243 Win., .250 Savage, .270 WSM, .300 WSM, .308 Win., 7mm-08 Rem. (left-hand only) cal., short action, stainless steel, 22 or 24 in. barrel, AccuTrigger, 2 or 4 shot mag., hinged floorplate, AccuStock became standard 2009, right or left-hand action, no sights. Mfg. 2006-2013.

	$725	$625	$525	$450	$400	$350	$275	*$850*

Add $35 for WSM cals.

This model was also available in left-hand action at no additional charge (Model 16FLHSS, new 2007, not available in Savage cals.).

* ***Model 16FHSAK*** – .243 Win. (disc. 2009), .270 WSM, .300 WSM, or .308 Win. cal., 22 or 24 in. barrel, similar to Model 16FHSS, except has adj. muzzle brake, AccuStock became standard 2009. Mfg. 2006-2010.

	$715	$540	$465	$410	$350	$300	$250	*$864*

MODEL 16 LIGHTWEIGHT HUNTER – .223 Rem., .243 Rem., .308 Win., or 7mm-08 Rem. cal., 20 in. stainless steel barrel, 4 shot detachable box mag., AccuTrigger, black synthetic stock, 5 1/2 lbs. Mfg. 2016-2018.

	$640	$560	$480	$435	$350	$290	$225	*$752*

MODEL 25 LIGHTWEIGHT VARMINTER – .17 Hornet (new 2012), .22 Hornet, .204 Ruger or .223 Rem. cal., 22 (Classic, disc. 2010) or 24 in. barrel, short action, 4 shot detachable box mag., AccuTrigger, brown laminated stock or Classic walnut stock with checkering and black forend tip (disc. 2010), 3 lug bolt with 60 degree throw, Weaver style base, triple pillar bedding, 7 lbs. New 2008.

MSR $819	$700	$615	$525	$475	$385	$315	$275

Add $25 for 22 in. barrel (Model 25 Classic, disc. 2010).

* ***Model 25 Lightweight Varminter-T*** – .17 Hornet (new 2012), .22 Hornet (new 2011), .222 Rem. (new 2011), .223 Rem., .204 Ruger, or 5.7x28mm (mfg. 2011 only) cal., 24 in. barrel, short action, 4 shot detachable box mag., satin finished laminated thumbhole stock and vent. forend, AccuTrigger, includes Weaver scope bases, 8 1/4 lbs. New 2008.

MSR $869	$740	$650	$550	$500	$400	$340	$285

MODEL 25 WALKING VARMINTER – .17 Hornet (new 2012), .22 Hornet, .204 Ruger, .222 Rem., .223 Rem., or 5.7x28mm (mfg. 2011 only) cal., short action, 22 in. barrel, black synthetic stock, AccuTrigger, 4 shot detachable box mag., 7.1 lbs. New 2011.

MSR $659	$560	$490	$420	$380	$310	$260	$215

* ***Model 25 Walking Varminter Camo*** – .17 Hornet, .22 Hornet, or .223 Rem. cal., short action, 22 in. barrel, synthetic stock, Realtree Extra (mfg. 2013 only) or Realtree Max-1 (new 2014) camo finish, AccuTrigger, 4 shot detachable box mag., 7 lbs. New 2013.

MSR $715	$615	$540	$460	$425	$345	$275	$225

GRADING - PPGS™	100%	98%	95%	90%	80%	70%	60%	LAST MSR

MODEL 40 VARMINT HUNTER SINGLE SHOT – .22 Hornet or .223 Rem. (disc. 2004) cal., single shot action, varmint configuration featuring 24 in. heavy contour barrel and brown laminate stock with full beavertail forend, AccuTrigger became standard 2003, 7 3/4 lbs. Disc.

	$465	$360	$310	$265	$220	$190	$170	*$582*

MODEL 110 125TH ANNIVERSARY – various cals., detachable box mag. w/engraved 125th anniversary detail bottom, adj. AccuTrigger, American black walnut Monte Carlo stock w/cheekpiece and gloss finish, drilled and tapped receiver, engraved receiver and grip cap, high-gloss finish, built to customer's order, 7.46 lbs. Limited mfg. of 1,849. Mfg. 2019 only.

	$1,215	$1,050	$900	$815	$660	$550	$425	*$1,449*

All 125th Anniversary models are built in Savage's Special Order Shop quarterly throughout 2019.

MODEL 110-B – similar to Model 110E, except available in .243 Win., .270 Win. or .30-06 cal., select stock and pistol grip cap, features blind mag., walnut Monte Carlo stock. Reintroduced 1989 with laminate stock (Model 110-B Laminate). Mfg. 1978-1979.

	$400	$350	$300	$270	$220	$180	$140	

This model was also available in left-hand action (Model 110-BL).

MODEL 110-B LAMINATE – similar to Model 110-B, except is available in .300 Win. Mag. or .338 Win. Mag. cal. also, has brown laminate hardwood stock with iron sights, approx. 7 1/2 lbs. Mfg. 1989-91.

	$425	$370	$320	$290	$235	$190	$150	*$477*

MODEL 110BA/BAS – .300 Win. Mag. or .338 Lapua cal., right or left (110BA LH, new 2013) hand action, 26 in. fluted carbon steel barrel with muzzle brake, 5 or 6 shot detachable box mag., drilled and tapped, open sights, includes Picatinny top rail, matte black aluminum tactical AccuStock with handguard, AccuTrigger, 15 3/4 lbs. Mfg. 2010-2017.

	$2,175	$1,900	$1,625	$1,450	$1,150	$925	$775	*$2,638*

MODEL 110 BA STEALTH – .300 Win. or .338 Lapua cal., bolt action, right or left (new 2017) hand configuration, 24 in. carbon steel matte black barrel, threaded muzzle with protector, 5 shot detachable box mag., adj. AccuTrigger, M-LOK forend, Fab Defense GLR-SHOCK buttstock, one-piece Picatinny rail, 11.15 lbs. Mfg. late 2016-2019.

	$1,550	$1,350	$1,150	$1,050	$850	$700	$550	*$1,819*

Add $140 for .338 Lapua cal.

MODEL 110 BA STEALTH EVOLUTION – .300 Win. Mag. or .338 Lapua Mag. cal., bolt action, right or left-hand configuration, 24 in. fluted heavy barrel with 5R rifling, muzzle brake, 10 shot detachable box mag., AccuTrigger, Fab Defense buttstock, adj. LOP, factory blue printed action, oversized bolt handle, monolithic aluminum chassis, FDE receiver finish, 11.3 lbs. Mfg. 2018-2019.

MSR $2,099	$1,785	$1,550	$1,325	$1,200	$950	$800	$700	

Add $100 for .338 Lapua Mag. cal.

MODEL 110 SPORTER BOLT ACTION – .243 Win., .270 Win., .308 Win., or .30 - 06 cal., 22 in. barrel, open sight, 4 shot, checkered pistol grip stock. Mfg. 1958-63.

	$400	$350	$300	$270	$220	$180	$140	

MODEL 110-MC – similar to Model 110, with Monte Carlo stock. Mfg. 1959-69.

	$425	$370	$320	$290	$235	$190	$150	

MODEL 110-M – similar to Model 110MC, except 7mm Rem. Mag., .264 Win. Mag., .300 Win. Mag., or .338 Win. Mag. cal., recoil pad. Mfg. 1963-69.

	$400	$350	$300	$270	$220	$180	$140	

MODEL 110-C/CL – various cals., push-button detachable mag., walnut stock. Mfg. 1966-85.

	$450	$395	$340	$305	$250	$205	$160	

MODEL 110-D – .22-250 Rem. (disc.), .223 Rem., .243 Win., .25-06 Rem. (disc.), .270 Win., .308 Win. (disc.), .30-06, 7mm Rem. Mag., .300 Win. Mag. (disc.), or .338 Win. Mag. cal., similar to Model 110B, hinged floorplate (1972-75 only), checkered walnut stock, removable and adj. rear sight, 7 1/2 lbs. Mfg. 1966-88.

	$350	$305	$265	$240	$195	$160	$125	*$409*

Add $80 for left-hand version.

MODEL 110-E – .22-250 Rem., .223 Rem., .243 Win., .270 Win., 7mm Rem. Mag., .308 Win., or .30-06 cal., 22 or 24 (Mag. only) in. barrel, open sights, unchecked hardwood Monte Carlo stock, blind internal magazine with floorplate, 7 lbs. Mfg. 1963-1988.

	$350	$305	$265	$240	$195	$160	$125	*$325*

Subtract $16 without sights.

GRADING - PPGS™	100%	98%	95%	90%	80%	70%	60%	LAST MSR

MODEL 110-F – .22-250 Rem., .223 Rem., .243 Win., .250 Sav. (new 1993), .25-06 Rem. (new 1993), .308 Win., .30-06, .270 Win., 7mm-08 Rem. (new 1993), 7mm Rem. Mag., .300 Sav. (new 1993), .300 Win. Mag., or .338 Win. Mag. (new 1991) cal., 22 or 24 (Magnum) in. barrel, black DuPont Rynite stock with swivel studs and recoil pad, adj. rear sight, drilled and tapped for scope mounts, 4 or 5 shot mag., 6 3/4 lbs. Mfg. 1989-1993.

$350 $305 $265 $240 $195 $160 $125

* ***Model 110-FNS*** – similar to Model 110-F, except has no sights. Mfg. 1991-93.

$350 $305 $265 $240 $195 $160 $125

* ***Model 110-FXP3*** – .22-250 Rem. (new 1992), .223 Rem. (new 1992), .243 Win., .270 Win., .30-06, .308 Win. (new 1992), 7mm Rem. Mag., or .300 Win. Mag. cal., similar to Model 110-F except is without sights and has integral Weaver type scope bases. Mfg. 1989-93.

$425 $370 $320 $290 $235 $190 $150

MODEL 110-GY – .223 Rem. (Mfg. 1993-99), .243 Win. (disc. 1999), .270 Win. (new 1994), .300 Sav. (disc. 1995), or .308 Win. (mfg. 1994-99) cal., 22 in. barrel, youth/ladies variation with shortened classic stock, open sights, 6 1/2 lbs. Mfg. 1991-2000.

$400 $350 $300 $270 $220 $180 $140 *$395*

MODEL 110-WLE – .250-3000 Sav., .300 Sav., or 7x57mm Mauser cal. Mfg. 1991-93.

$450 $395 $340 $305 $250 $205 $160

Approx. 1,000 of each cal. were mfg. in this model.

* ***Model 110-WLE 1 of 1,000*** – 7x57mm Mauser cal., features select walnut stock with Monte Carlo cheekpiece, high luster blue finish with laser etched Savage logo on bolt body, drilled and tapped, 1,000 mfg. beginning 1992, 7 3/4 lbs. Mfg. 1992-93 only.

$475 $415 $355 $325 $260 $215 $165

MODEL 110-FM SIERRA ULTRA LIGHT – .243 Win. (disc. 1998), .270 Win., .30 - 06, or .308 Win. (disc. 1998) cal., features 20 in. high gloss barrel w/o sights, black graphite/fiberglass-filled stock with non-glare finish, drilled and tapped, 6 1/4 lbs. Mfg. 1996-2000.

$425 $370 $320 $290 $235 $190 $150 *$449*

MODEL 110-FP LAW ENFORCEMENT (TACTICAL POLICE) – .223 Rem. (disc. 1998), .25-06 Rem. (new 1995), .300 Win. Mag. (new 1995), .30-06 (mfg. 1996-2006), .308 Win. (disc. 1998), or 7mm Rem. Mag. (mfg. 1995-2007) cal., long action, 24 in. heavy barrel pillar bedded tactical rifle, all metal parts are non-reflective, 4 shot internal mag., black DuPont Rynite stock, right or left-hand (mfg. 1996-2001) action, drilled and tapped for scope mounts, AccuTrigger became standard 2003, 8 1/2 lbs. Mfg. 1990-2001, reintroduced 2003-2008.

$575 $465 $360 $310 $265 $240 $210 *$678*

Was also available in left-hand action at no additional charge (mfg. 1996-2001, Model 110-FLP).

* ***Model 110FCP*** – .25-06 Rem. or .300 Win. Mag. cal., 24 in. heavy barrel with Savage muzzle brake, 4 shot detachable box mag., black synthetic AccuStock with aluminum spine and 3-D bedding cradle, drilled and tapped, swivel stud for bipod, oversized bolt handle, 9 lbs. Mfg. 2009 only.

$725 $600 $500 $425 $375 $350 $300 *$866*

MODEL 110-G – .22-250 Rem., .223 Rem., .243 Win., .250 Sav. (new 1992), .25-06 Rem. (new 1992), .300 Sav. (new 1993), .308 Win., .30-06, .270 Win., 7mm-08 Rem. (new 1992), 7mm Rem. Mag., or .300 Win. Mag. cal., top loading internal box mag., 22 or 24 in. barrel, adj. iron sights, checkered hardwood stock, approx. 7 lbs. Mfg. 1989-93.

$350 $305 $265 $240 $195 $160 $125

Subtract $10-$20 if without sights (Model 110-GNS).

* ***Model 110-GC*** – .270 Win., .30-06, 7mm Rem. Mag., or .300 Win. Mag. cal., features detachable 3 or 4 shot mag., 22 or 24 in. barrel, checkered hardwood stock, adj. sights, 6 3/4 lbs. Mfg. 1992-93.

$425 $370 $320 $290 $235 $190 $150

Add $20 for Mag. cals.

* ***Model 110-GCXP3 Package*** – .270 Win., .30-06, .300 Win. Mag., or 7mm Rem. Mag. cal., 22 or 24 in. barrel, checkered hardwood stock, detachable box mag., package includes 3-9x32 scope, rings, bases, QD swivels, and deluxe rifle sling, 7 1/4 lbs. Disc. 2001.

$450 $395 $340 $305 $250 $205 $160 *$524*

Was also available in left-hand action at no additional charge (Model 110-GLCXP3 - disc. 2000).

GRADING - PPGS™	100%	98%	95%	90%	80%	70%	60%	LAST MSR

MODEL 110 TROPHY HUNTER XP PACKAGE – .270 Win., .30-06, .300 Win. Mag. (new 2013), or 7mm Rem. Mag. (new 2013) cal., long action, 4 shot detachable box mag., 22 or 24 (new 2014) in. barrel, matte black metal finish, satin finished wood stock, AccuTrigger, includes 3-9x40 Nikon BDC scope, 8.3 lbs. Mfg. 2012-2019.

	$625	$545	$475	$425	$345	$275	$225	*$729*

* ***Model 110-GL*** – .30-06, .270 Win., or 7mm Rem. Mag. cal., left-hand variation of the Model 110-G. Mfg. 1989-93.

	$350	$305	$265	$240	$195	$160	$125	

* ***Model 110-GLNS*** – similar to Model 110-GL, except has no sights. Mfg. 1991-1993.

	$325	$285	$245	$220	$180	$145	$115	

MODEL 110-K – .243 Win., .270 Win., or .30-06 cal., laminated camouflage stock. Mfg. 1986-88.

	$350	$305	$265	$240	$195	$160	$125	*$399*

MODEL 110-S – .308 Win., 7mm-08 Rem. (mfg. 1981-1983) cals., silhouette model, 22 in. heavy barrel, Wundhammer swell pistol grip with stippling, no sights, 4 shot mag., 8 lbs. 10 oz. Disc. 1985.

	$375	$330	$280	$255	$205	$170	$130	*$385*

Add 50-75% for 7mm-08 Rem. cal.

MODEL 110-V – .22-250 Rem. or .223 Rem. cal. only, varmint model, 26 in. heavy barrel, no sights, 5 shot mag., stippled walnut Wundhammer pistol grip stock, 9 1/4 lbs. Disc. 1989.

	$400	$350	$300	$270	$220	$180	$140	*$439*

MODEL 110-GV – .22-250 Rem. or .223 Rem. cal., varmint variation, 24 in. medium barrel, no sights, checkered hardwood stock with rubber recoil pad, drilled and tapped for scope, 8 1/4 lbs. Mfg. 1989-1993.

	$400	$350	$300	$270	$220	$180	$140	

MODEL 110FCP HS PRECISION – .300 Win. Mag. or .338 Lapua cal., long action, 24 or 26 in. carbon steel heavy barrel, matte black metal finish, 4 shot detachable box mag., black HS Precision fiberglass stock with V-Block, drilled and tapped, AccuTrigger, oversized bolt handle, 9 lbs. Mfg. 2012-2019.

	$1,140	$1,000	$855	$775	$625	$515	$445	*$1,339*

Add $420 for .338 Lapua cal.

MODEL 110 APEX HUNTER XP – .223 Rem., .204 Ruger, .22-250 Rem., .243 Win., 6.5 Creedmoor, 7mm-08 Rem., .260 Rem., .308 Win., .270 WSM, .300 WSM, .350 Legend (new 2020), 6.5 PRC, .450 Bushmaster, .25-06 Rem., 6.5x284 Norma, .270 Win., .30-06, 7mm Rem. Mag., .300 Win. Mag., or .338 Win. Mag. cal., 20, 22, or 24 in. carbon steel sporter barrel, 2, 3, or 4 shot detachable box mag., AccuTrigger, black synthetic stock with adj. LOP, one-piece rail, includes Vortex Crossfire II 3-9x40 mounted and bore-sighted scope, right or left-hand configuration, 7.67-8.12 lbs. New 2019.

MSR $665	$565	$500	$450	$415	$375	$335	$295	

Add $94 for .450 Bushmaster cal.

* ***Model 110 Apex Hunter XP Muddy Girl*** – .243 Win., 6.5 Creedmoor, 7mm-08 Rem., or .308 Win. cal., 20, 22, or 24 in. carbon steel sporter barrel, 4 shot detachable box mag., AccuTrigger, Muddy Girl camo synthetic stock with adj. LOP, one-piece rail, includes Vortex Crossfire II 3-9x40 mounted and bore-sighted scope, 7.67-7.73 lbs. New 2019.

MSR $725	$615	$540	$460	$425	$375	$335	$295	

MODEL 110 APEX PREDATOR XP – .223 Rem., .22-250 Rem., .204 Ruger, .243 Win., 6.5 Creedmoor, or .308 Win. cal., bolt action, 20 or 24 in. threaded carbon steel heavy barrel, 4 shot detachable box mag., AccuTrigger, synthetic stock with Mossy Oak Mountain Terra camo finish, adj. LOP, one-piece rail, includes Vortex Crossfire II 4-12x44 mounted and boresighted scope, matte black finish, 8.41-9.91 lbs. New 2019.

MSR $785	$650	$575	$500	$450	$350	$300	$250	

MODEL 110 APEX STORM XP – .223 Rem., .204 Ruger, .22-250 Rem., .243 Win., 6.5 Creedmoor, 7mm-08 Rem., .260 Rem., .308 Win., .350 Legend (new 2020), .270 WSM, .300 WSM, 6.5 PRC, .25-06 Rem., .270 Win., .30-06, 7mm Rem. Mag., .300 Win. Mag., or .338 Win. Mag. cal., bolt action, 20, 22, or 24 in. stainless steel sporter barrel, 3 or 4 shot detachable box mag., AccuTrigger, black synthetic stock with adj. LOP, one-piece rail, includes Vortex Crossfire II 3-9x40 mounted and boresighted scope, approx. 8 lbs. New 2019.

MSR $769	$655	$575	$490	$445	$360	$295	$250	

GRADING - PPGS™	100%	98%	95%	90%	80%	70%	60%	LAST MSR

MODEL 110 BEAR HUNTER – .300 WSM, .338 Federal (disc. 2020), .338 Win. Mag., .300 Win. Mag., or .375 Ruger cal., short or long action, 23 in. stainless steel barrel with muzzle brake, 2 or 4 shot mag., hinged floorplate, Mossy Oak Break-Up Country Camo AccuStock, soft grip forend and pistol grip surfaces, AccuFit system, new Model 110 design and ergonomics, 7 1/2 lbs. New 2018.

MSR $1,055	$900	$785	$675	$600	$495	$425	$350	

MODEL 110 BRUSH HUNTER – .338 Win. Mag. or .375 Ruger cal., long action, 20 in. stainless steel barrel, 3 shot detachable box mag., AccuTrigger, open sights, gray synthetic stock, adj. LOP inserts, new Model 110 design and ergonomics, 7.38 lbs. New 2018.

MSR $699	$600	$525	$450	$410	$325	$275	$225	

MODEL 110 CLASSIC – .243 Win., .270 Win., .30-06, .300 Win. Mag., .308 Win., 6.5 Creedmoor, 7mm Rem. Mag., or 7mm-08 Rem. cal., bolt action, 22 or 24 (7mm Rem. or .300 Win.) in. carbon steel matte black barrel with threaded muzzle, 4 shot detachable box mag., adj. AccuTrigger, drilled and tapped receiver for scope mounts, classic brown walnut stock with modern ergonomics and oil finish, fully adj. LOP and comb, two sling swivel studs, 3-pos. safety, 8.06 lbs. New 2020.

MSR $1,035	$875	$765	$650	$595	$475	$400	$325	

MODEL 110 ELITE PRECISION – .223 Rem., .308 Win., 6.5 Creedmoor, 6mm Creedmoor, .300 Win. Mag., .300 Norma (mfg. 2020 only), .300 PRC (new 2021), or .338 Lapua Mag. cal., 26 or 30 in. stainless steel barrel, self-timing taper aligned muzzle brake, 5 or 10 shot AICS detachable box mag., adj. AccuTrigger, aluminum stock w/grey Cerakote finish, adj. Core Competition chassis, MDT Vertical grip, titanium Nitride bolt, full-length ARCA rail, matte black stainless steel receiver, 12.6-14.95 lbs. New 2020.

MSR $1,999	$1,700	$1,500	$1,300	$1,150	$950	$775	$660	

Add $200 for .300 Win. Mag., .300 PRC (new 2021), or .338 Lapua Mag. cal.
Add $150 for .300 Norma cal. (mfg. 2020 only).

MODEL 110 ENGAGE HUNTER XP – .243 Win., .260 Rem., .270 WSM (disc. 2020), .300 WSM, .308 Win., .338 Federal (disc. 2020), .30-06, 6.5 Creedmoor, 6.5 PRC (new late 2019), 7mm-08 Rem., .25-06 Rem., .270 Win., .300 Win. Mag., 6.5x284 Norma (disc. 2020), 7mm Rem. Mag., .280 Ack. Imp., .338 Win. Mag. (disc. 2020), .450 Bushmaster (new 2019), or .350 Legend (new 2020) cal., short or long action, 22 or 24 in. stainless steel barrel, 2 or 4 shot detachable box mag., AccuTrigger, gray synthetic stock, adj. LOP inserts, new Model 110 design and ergonomics, includes Bushnell Engage 3-9x40 scope, 7 1/4-8 1/4 lbs. New 2018.

MSR $625	$525	$460	$395	$355	$290	$240	$200	

MODEL 110 HAYMAKER (WOLVERINE) – .450 Bushmaster cal., short action, 18 in. heavy threaded barrel with muzzle brake, 4 shot AICS mag., AccuTrigger, AccuStock, soft grip forend and pistol grip surfaces, AccuFit system, matte black finish, 7.9 lbs. New 2018.

MSR $945	$800	$700	$600	$545	$440	$360	$310	

MODEL 110 HIGH COUNTRY – .308 Win., .243 Win., 6.5 Creedmoor, 7mm-08 Rem., .300 WSM, 6.5 PRC, .270 Win., .30-06, .280 Ackley Improved, 7mm Rem. Mag., .300 Win. Mag., or .28 Nosler (new 2021) cal., 22 or 24 in. medium contour threaded and fluted barrel, muzzle brake on Mag. cals. only, 3 or 4 shot detachable box mag., AccuTrigger, True Timber Strata camo AccuStock with AccuFit, fluted bolt, PVD finish, 8.1-8.5 lbs. New 2019.

MSR $1,165	$985	$850	$725	$675	$550	$450	$385	

MODEL 110 HOG HUNTER – .223 Rem., .308 Win., .350 Legend (new 2020), or .338 Federal (disc. 2019) cal., short action, 18 (.350 Legend only, new 2020) or 20 in. black threaded barrel, 4 shot detachable box mag., AccuTrigger, open sights, OD Green synthetic stock, adj. LOP, new Model 110 design and ergonomics, 7.3 lbs. New 2018.

MSR $630	$535	$475	$400	$365	$300	$250	$200	

MODEL 110 HUNTER – .204 Ruger, .22-250 Rem., .223 Rem., .243 Win., .308 Win., 7mm-08 Rem., 6.5 Creedmoor, .25-06 Rem., .270 Win., .30-06, .280 Ack. Imp., 7mm Rem. Mag., or .300 Win. Mag. cal., short or long action, 22 or 24 in. black barrel, 3 or 4 shot detachable box mag., AccuTrigger, gray synthetic AccuStock, soft grip forend and pistol grip surfaces, AccuFit system, new Model 110 design and ergonomics, 7 1/4 lbs. New 2018.

MSR $795	$675	$600	$500	$450	$375	$300	$265	

MODEL 110 LIGHTWEIGHT STORM – .223 Rem., .243 Win., .308 Win., 6.5 Creedmoor, 7mm-08 Rem., or .270 Win. cal., short or long action, 20 in. stainless steel barrel, fluted bolt, 4 shot detachable box mag., AccuTrigger, black synthetic stock, adj. LOP inserts, skeletonized receiver, new Model 110 design and ergonomics, 6 1/2 lbs. New 2018.

MSR $795	$675	$600	$500	$450	$375	$300	$265	

GRADING - PPGS™	100%	98%	95%	90%	80%	70%	60%	LAST MSR

MODEL 110 LONG RANGE HUNTER – .260 Rem. (disc. 2020), 6.5 Creedmoor, .308 Win., .300 WSM, 6.5x284 Norma, .280 Ack. Imp., 7mm Rem. Mag., .300 Win. Mag., .300 PRC (new 2021), .28 Nosler (new 2021), .338 Federal (disc. 2020), or .338 Lapua Mag. cal., short or long action, 26 in. black barrel with muzzle brake, 2, 3, 4, or 5 shot detachable box mag., AccuTrigger, gray synthetic AccuStock, soft grip forend and pistol grip surfaces, AccuFit system, new Model 110 design and ergonomics, 8-8.85 lbs. New 2018.

MSR $1,169	$995	$870	$745	$675	$545	$450	$390	

Add $210 for .338 Lapua Mag. cal.

MODEL 110 MAGPUL HUNTER – .308 Win. or 6.5 Creedmoor cal., bolt action, 18 in. carbon steel heavy threaded barrel, 5 shot AICS Magpul mag., AccuTrigger, Magpul Hunter stock with aluminum bedding block, tactical knurled bolt handle, one-piece 20 MOA rail, M-LOK slots on forend, Tungsten Cerakote finish on barrel, receiver, and bolt handle, 8.9 lbs. New 2021.

MSR $1,049	$895	$785	$675	$600	$495	$425	$350	

MODEL 110 PRAIRE HUNTER – .224 Valkyrie cal., bolt action, 22 in. carbon steel button rifled threaded barrel, target crown, detachable box mag., AccuTrigger, ergonomic gray synthetic stock with adj. LOP and comb height, beavertail forend, three QD studs, drilled and tapped with one-piece 20 MOA rail. Mfg. 2019 only.

	$650	$575	$500	$450	$350	$300	$250	*$759*

MODEL 110-P PREMIER GRADE – similar to Model 110B, with select French walnut stock, skip checkered, rosewood forend and pistol grip cap, sling swivels, 7mm Mag. has recoil pad. Mfg. 1964-70.

	$450	$395	$340	$305	$250	$205	$160	
7mm Mag. cal.	$500	$440	$375	$340	$275	$225	$175	

MODEL 110-PE PRESENTATION GRADE – similar to Model 110P, with engraved receiver, floorplate and trigger guard. Mfg. 1968-70.

	$700	$600	$525	$450	$400	$325	$250	
7mm Mag. cal.	$750	$650	$575	$500	$425	$340	$265	

MODEL 110 PRECISION – .308 Win., .300 Win. Mag., .300 PRC (new 2021), .338 Lapua, or 6.5 Creedmoor cal., right or left (new 2021) hand blueprinted action, 20 or 24 in. heavy carbon steel, matte black threaded barrel, BA muzzle brake, 5 or 8 shot detachable AICS mag., adj. AccuTrigger, exclusive skeletonized stock w/fully adj. comb, MDT LSS XL chassis, one-piece EGW rail, FDE Cerakote finish, 8.9-9.5 lbs. New 2020.

MSR $1,549	$1,320	$1,155	$990	$900	$725	$600	$515	

MODEL 110 PREDATOR – .22-250 Rem., .223 Rem., .204 Ruger, .243 Win., 6.5 Creedmoor, .308 Win., or .260 Rem. cal., short action, 22 or 24 in. threaded heavy black barrel, 4 shot detachable box mag., AccuTrigger, Realtree Max-1 camo AccuStock, soft grip forend and pistol grip surfaces, adj. LOP, AccuFit system, new Model 110 design and ergonomics, 8.5-8.69 lbs. New 2018.

MSR $945	$800	$700	$600	$545	$440	$360	$310	

MODEL 110 PREDATOR HUNTER – 6.5x284 Norma cal., right or left (new 2012) hand action, 24 in. barrel, RealTree Max 1 patterned camo AccuStock, AccuTrigger, no sights, includes scope blocks, 4 shot detachable box mag., 7 1/4 lbs. Mfg. 2011-2014.

	$815	$700	$575	$475	$425	$375	$325	*$915*

MODEL 110 RIDGE WARRIOR – .308 Win. or 6.5 Creedmoor cal., Model 110 stainless steel action with AccuFit system, 24 in. fluted heavy stainless steel barrel with threaded muzzle, 10 shot detachable box mag., AccuTrigger, Mossy Oak Overwatch camo synthetic stock with beavertail forend, 12.75 in. LOP, 3-pos. safety, drilled and tapped receiver, Picatinny rail, Gunsmoke Gray PVD coating on barrel, receiver, knurled bolt handle, trigger guard, and magwell, 8.87 lbs. New 2019.

MSR $980	$835	$725	$625	$565	$455	$375	$325	

MODEL 110 SCOUT – .308 Win., .223 Rem., .338 Federal (disc. 2019), or .450 Bushmaster cal., short action, 18 in. black barrel with muzzle brake, 10 shot detachable box mag., AccuTrigger, FDE synthetic AccuStock, soft grip forend and pistol grip surfaces, AccuFit system, new Model 110 design and ergonomics, 7.72 lbs. New 2018.

MSR $865	$740	$650	$550	$500	$400	$340	$285	

MODEL 110 STORM – .223 Rem., 6.5 Creedmoor, .308 Win., .270 WSM, .338 Federal (disc. 2020), .243 Win., 7mm-08 Rem., .300 WSM, .338 Win. Mag. (new 2019), .25-06 Rem. (new 2019), 6.5x284 Norma, .270 Win., .30-06, .280 Ackley Imp., 7mm Rem. Mag., 6.5 PRC (mfg. 2019-2020), .22-250 Rem. (disc. 2020), or .300 Win. Mag. cal., short or long action, 22 or 24 in. stainless steel barrel, 2 or 4 shot detachable box mag., AccuTrigger, gray synthetic AccuStock, soft grip forend and pistol grip surfaces, right or left-hand configuration, AccuFit system, new Model 110 design and ergonomics, 7 1/4 lbs. New 2018.

MSR $900	$765	$670	$575	$520	$420	$350	$300	

GRADING - PPGS™	100%	98%	95%	90%	80%	70%	60%	LAST MSR

MODEL 110 TACTICAL – .308 Win., 6mm ARC (new 2021), 6.5 PRC (new late 2019), .300 Win. Mag., or 6.5 Creedmoor (new 2019) cal., short action, 18 (new 2021), 20, or 24 in. heavy fluted threaded black barrel, 10 shot detachable box mag., AccuTrigger, gray synthetic AccuStock, soft grip forend and pistol grip surfaces, AccuFit system, new Model 110 design and ergonomics, top Picatinny rail, right or left (24 in. only) hand configuration, 6.7-9.1 lbs. New 2018.

MSR $830	$700	$615	$525	$475	$385	$315	$275	

* ***Model 110 Tactical Desert*** – 6.5 Creedmoor, 6mm Creedmoor, .300 Win. Mag., or 6.5 PRC (new late 2019) cal., right or left (6.5 Creedmoor only)-hand configuration, short action, 24 or 26 in. threaded heavy black barrel, 10 shot AICS detachable box mag., AccuTrigger, FDE synthetic AccuStock, soft grip forend and pistol grip surfaces, AccuFit system, new Model 110 design and ergonomics, top Picatinny rail, 8.87 lbs. New 2018.

MSR $815	$695	$610	$520	$475	$380	$315	$270	

MODEL 110 TIMBERLINE – 6.5 Creedmoor, .308 Win., .300 WSM, .243 Win., 7mm-08 Rem., 6.5 PRC, .300 Win. Mag., .30-06, .270 Win., .28 Nosler, .280 Ackley Imp. (new 2021), or 7mm Rem. Mag. cal., bolt action, right or left-hand factory blueprinted action, 22 or 24 in. carbon steel threaded medium profile contour barrel with straight fluting, omni-port muzzle brake, target crown, 4 shot detachable box mag., drilled and tapped receiver, AccuTrigger, Realtree Excape Camo AccuFit stock with adj. LOP, comb height, and overmold surfaces, drilled and tapped receiver, target crown, OD Green Cerakote finish on barrel and receiver, 8.1 lbs. New 2020.

MSR $1,165	$990	$850	$725	$675	$550	$450	$385	

MODEL 110 ULTRALITE – .308 Win., 6.5 Creedmoor, .300 WSM, 6.5 PRC, .280 Ackley Imp., .270 Win., .30-06, or .28 Nosler cal., bolt action, 22 or 24 in. black carbon fiber wrapped PROOF Research stainless steel barrel, threaded muzzle w/flush fit cap, 2 or 4 shot detachable box mag., stainless steel receiver with Melonite finish, adj. AccuTrigger, AccuFit Sporter stock w/adj. comb, drilled and tapped receiver, spiral fluted bolt, grey finish, 5.8-6 lbs. New 2020.

MSR $1,545	$1,315	$1,150	$985	$890	$725	$590	$510	

* ***Model 110 Ultralite Camo*** – .308 Win., .28 Nosler, .30-06, 6.5 Creedmoor, or 6.5 PRC cal., right-hand action, 22 or 24 in. PROOF carbon fiber stainless barrel, threaded muzzle w/flush fit cap, 4 shot detachable box mag., adj. AccuTrigger, KUIU Verde 2.0 Camo AccuFit stock w/adj. comb, spiral fluted bolt, lightweight stainless steel receiver w/Melonite finish, 5.8 lbs. New late 2020.

MSR $1,589	$1,350	$1,180	$1,000	$910	$735	$600	$525	

MODEL 110 VARMINT – .223 Rem., .22-250 Rem., or .204 Ruger cal., short action, 26 in. black barrel, 4 shot detachable box mag., AccuTrigger, gray synthetic AccuStock, soft grip beavertail forend and pistol grip surfaces, AccuFit system, new Model 110 design and ergonomics, 9.88 lbs. New 2018.

MSR $795	$675	$600	$500	$450	$375	$300	$265	

MODEL 111B HUNTER – .25-06 Rem., .270 Win. or .30-06 cal., long action, 22 in. barrel with no sights, hinged floorplate. Ltd. mfg. 2008.

	$625	$525	$460	$400	$350	$300	$250	*$735*

MODEL 111BTH HUNTER – .25-06 Rem., .270 Win., or .30-06 cal., 4 shot mag., 22 in. barrel with no sights, drilled and tapped, hinged floorplate, ventilated forend, AccuTrigger, brown laminated thumbhole stock, 7 lbs. Mfg. 2010-2018.

	$815	$675	$550	$450	$400	$350	$300	*$979*

MODEL 111 CHIEFTAIN ACTION – .243 Win., .270 Win., 7x57mm, 7mm Rem. Mag., or .30-06 cal., 22 or 24 (Mag. cals.) in. barrel, leaf sight, 4 shot detachable mag., checkered walnut Monte Carlo stock, pistol grip cap, sling swivels. Mfg. 1974-1978.

	$400	$350	$300	$270	$220	$180	$140	
Mag. cals.	$450	$395	$340	$305	$250	$205	$160	

MODEL 111 DOA HUNTER XP – .25-06 Rem., .270 Win., 6.5x284 Norma, .30-06, .300 Win. Mag., .338 Win. Mag., or 7mm Rem. Mag. cal., 22 or 24 in. barrel, 3 or 4 shot detachable box mag., AccuTrigger, black synthetic stock, 13.8 in. LOP, includes 3-9x40 Bushnell Trophy scope, Weaver Steel Grand Slam rings and bases, 8-8 1/4 lbs. Mfg. 2017 only.

	$575	$500	$425	$395	$325	$250	$200	*$684*

MODEL 111 HUNTER XP PACKAGE – .270 Win., .300 Win. Mag., .30-06, or 7mm Rem. Mag. cal., long action, 4 shot detachable box mag., 22 or 24 in. barrel, matte black metal finish, black synthetic stock, includes 3-9x40 Bushnell scope, AccuTrigger is not available on this model, 7 1/4 lbs. Mfg. 2012-2014.

	$465	$400	$360	$330	$300	$275	$250	*$525*

GRADING - PPGS™	100%	98%	95%	90%	80%	70%	60%	LAST MSR

MODEL 111 LADY HUNTER – .270 Win. or .30-06 cal., long action, 20 in. barrel without sights, black matte metal finish, 4 shot mag., drilled and tapped, satin finished walnut with pressed checkering and forward angled Monte Carlo stock with recoil pad, stock features include shorter LOP, higher front angled comb, slimmer forend and pistol grip, three-position safety, sling swivels, 6 lbs. New mid-2012.

MSR $949	$810	$710	$610	$550	$445	$365	$315	

MODEL 111 HOG HUNTER – .338 Win. Mag. cal., long action, 4 shot internal box mag., 20 in. threaded barrel with iron sights, matte black metal finish, AccuTrigger, OD Green synthetic stock, 8 lbs. Mfg. 2012-2016.

	$475	$425	$365	$335	$295	$265	$235	*$560*

MODEL 111 LIGHTWEIGHT HUNTER – .270 Win., .30-06, or 6.5x284 Norma (disc. 2013) cal., long action, 20 in. barrel, AccuTrigger, 4 shot detachable box mag., hinged floorplate, no sights, blued finish, walnut stained stock, 6 lbs. New 2011.

MSR $1,039	$885	$775	$665	$600	$485	$415	$350	

MODEL 111 LONG RANGE HUNTER – .25-06 Rem. (disc. 2014), 6.5x284 Norma, 7mm Rem. Mag., or .300 Win. Mag. cal., 3 shot mag., 26 in. fluted carbon steel barrel with adj. muzzle brake, drilled and tapped, AccuTrigger, Karsten adj. and detachable cheekpiece, matte black synthetic AccuStock and forearm, no sights, hinged floorplate, 8.65 lbs. Mfg. 2010-2017.

	$975	$765	$625	$525	$425	$365	$325	*$1,171*

* ***Model 111 Long Range Hunter .338 Lapua*** – .338 Lapua cal., 26 in. matte blued barrel, fixed muzzle brake, 5 shot detachable box mag., AccuTrigger, no sights, black synthetic AccuStock, adj. cheekpiece, oversized bolt handle, one-piece rail, 9.25 lbs. Mfg. 2012-2017.

	$1,200	$1,050	$900	$815	$660	$550	$425	*$1,421*

MODEL 111 TROPHY HUNTER XP PACKAGE – .25-06 Rem., .270 Win., .30-06, .300 Win. Mag., .338 Win. Mag. (new 2014), 6.5x284 Norma (right hand only, disc. 2013, reintroduced 2019), or 7mm Rem. Mag. cal., long action, 4 shot detachable box mag., 22 or 24 in. barrel, matte black metal finish, synthetic black stock, AccuTrigger, includes 3-9x40 Nikon scope, right or left-hand action, 7 1/4 lbs. Mfg. 2012-2020.

	$550	$500	$450	$415	$375	$335	$295	*$639*

MODEL 111FNS (111-F) – similar to Model 111-G, except has black graphite/fiberglass stock (with non-glare finish) and was also available in .338 Win. Mag. (disc. 2005) cal., long action, 22, 24, or 26 (disc. 2003) in. barrel, solid recoil pad, no sights (reintroduced 2009 as the Model 111FNS), 6 1/2 lbs. Mfg. 1994-2011.

	$475	$400	$340	$285	$230	$200	$175	*$609*

This model's nomenclature changed during 2009 to the Model 111FNS. This model was previously discontinued in 2002, and was not available in .300 Rem. Ultra Mag. or 7mm Rem. Ultra Mag. cals.

This model was also available in left-hand (Model 111-FL. disc. 2008, or Model 111FLNS (no sights, mfg. 2009-2013).

* ***Model 111-FC*** – .270 Win., .30-06, .300 Win. Mag., or 7mm Rem. Mag. cal., 22 or 24 in. barrel, detachable box mag., black graphite/fiberglass stock, 6 1/2 lbs. Mfg. 1994-2003.

	$450	$395	$340	$305	$250	$205	$160	*$468*

This model was also available with left-hand action (Model 111-FLC).

* ***Model 111-FCNS Hunter*** – .25-06 Rem., .270 Win., .30-06, .300 Win. Mag., .338 Win. Mag. (disc.), .375 Ruger (mfg. 2012-2013), or 7mm Rem. Mag. cal., 22 or 24 in. barrel, no sights, 4 shot detachable box mag., AccuStock became standard 2009, AccuTrigger, black synthetic stock, approx. 7 lbs. Mfg. 2005-2017.

	$625	$500	$425	$365	$325	$275	$225	*$792*

* ***Model 111-FHNS*** – .25-06 Rem., .270 Win., or .30-06 cal., long action, 4 shot mag., 22 in. barrel, AccuTrigger, no sights, hinged floorplate, synthetic AccuStock (became standard 2009), blued finish, 7 1/4 lbs. Mfg. 2006-2012.

	$575	$495	$425	$365	$325	$275	$225	*$696*

MODEL 111FYCAK – .270 Win.or .30-06 cal., 22 in. barrel with adj. muzzle brake, detachable box mag., long action, Youth Model with shortened LOP. Mfg. 2006-2009.

	$525	$400	$340	$300	$270	$235	$200	*$652*

MODEL 111-FAK EXPRESS – .270 Win., .30-06, .300 Win. Mag., .338 Win. Mag., or 7mm Rem. Mag. cal., 22 in. barrel with adj. muzzle brake, black or black matte graphite/fiberglass-filled stock, w/o sights, 6 3/4 lbs. Mfg. 1996-98.

	$425	$370	$320	$290	$235	$190	$150	*$450*

GRADING - PPGS™	100%	98%	95%	90%	80%	70%	60%	LAST MSR

MODEL 111GNS (111-G) – .22-250 Rem. (disc. 1998), .223 Rem. (disc. 1998), .243 Win. (disc. 1998), .250 Savage (disc. 1996), .25-06 Rem., .270 Win., .300 Sav. (disc. 1996), .30-06, .308 Win. (disc. 1998), .300 Win. Mag. (disc. 2007), .300 RUM (mfg. 2002-2003), .338 Win. Mag. (disc. 1993 - not available with wood stock), 7mm-08 Rem. (disc. 1996), 7mm RUM (mfg. 2002-2003), or 7mm Rem. Mag. (disc. 2007) cal., long action, walnut finished hardwood stock with cut checkering and vent. recoil pad, open sights, top tang safety with red dot indicator, 22, 24, or 26 (disc. 2005) in. barrel, drilled and tapped, no sights, 6 3/8 or 7 lbs. Mfg. 1994-2010.

$515 $465 $410 $350 $300 $250 $200 *$635*

This model's nomenclature changed in 2009 to the Model 111-GNS, which was originally disc. in 2004 and not available in .300 RUM or 7mm RUM cals.

This model was also available in left-hand (Model 111-GL, not available in 7mm Rem. Ultra Mag.).

* ***Model 111-GC*** – .270 Win., .30-06, .300 Win. Mag., or 7mm Rem. Mag. cal., 22 or 24 in. barrel, detachable box mag., walnut finished hardwood stock with cut checkering and vent. recoil pad. Mfg. 1994-2001.

$425 $370 $320 $290 $235 $190 $150 *$441*

This model was also available with left-hand action (Model 111-GLC - disc. 2000).

* ***Model 111-GCNS*** – .25-06 Rem., .270 Win., .30-06, .300 Win. Mag. (disc. 2008), or 7mm Rem. Mag. (disc. 2008) cal., features detachable box mag., no sights, 22 or 24 in. barrel, approx. 7 lbs. Mfg. 2005-2012.

$500 $415 $325 $250 $200 $175 $160 *$699*

MODEL 112V VARMINT RIFLE – .220 Swift, .222 Rem., .223 Rem. (new 1976), .22-250 Rem., .243 Win., or .25-06 Rem. cal., single shot, bolt action, 26 in. heavy barrel, no sights, heavy select walnut stock, checkered, swivels. Mfg. 1975-78.

$400 $350 $300 $270 $220 $180 $140

MODEL 112 VARMINTER LOW PROFILE – .25-06 Rem. or .300 Win. Mag. cal., stainless long action, right-hand bolt, smaller ejection port on left side of receiver, 26 in. heavy fluted free floating barrel, low profile laminated stock with extra-wide beavertail forend, drilled and tapped, AccuTrigger, oversized bolt handle, 4 shot internal box mag., swivel studs, 10 lbs. Mfg. 2006 only.

$665 $545 $435 $370 $325 $260 $225 *$806*

MODEL 112 R – .22-250 Rem., .25-06 Rem., or .243 Win. cal., similar to Model 112V, except has 4 shot mag. Disc. 1980.

$400 $350 $300 $270 $220 $180 $140

MODEL 112-BV – .22-250 Rem. or .223 Rem. cal., alloy steel construction, 26 in. barrel with recessed muzzle, 4 shot mag., brown laminate stock with ambidextrous Wundhammer style pistol grip, 9 1/2 lbs. Mfg. 1993 only.

$500 $440 $375 $340 $275 $225 $175

MODEL 112-BVSS LONG RANGE – .22-250 Rem. (disc. 1998), .223 Rem. (disc. 1998), .25-06 Rem. (new 1996), .30-06 (new 1996), .308 Win. (mfg. 1996-98), .300 Win. Mag. (new 1996), or 7mm Rem. Mag. (new 1996) cal., 4 shot, pillar bedded laminate wood stock with Wundhammer palm swell, right-hand bolt, smaller ejection port on left side of receiver, 26 in. stainless steel fluted barrel, bolt handle and trigger guard, recessed muzzle, AccuTrigger became standard 2003, 10 1/2 lbs. Mfg. 1994-2005.

$600 $525 $450 $410 $330 $270 $210 *$721*

* ***Model 112-BVSS-S Long Range*** – .220 Swift, .223 Rem. (disc. 1998), .22-250 Rem. (disc. 1998), or .300 Win. Mag. (new 1996) cal., single shot, 26 in. stainless steel fluted barrel, with target features, 10 1/2 lbs. Mfg. 1994-2001.

$550 $480 $415 $375 $305 $250 $195 *$595*

MODEL 112-BT COMPETITION GRADE – .223 Rem. or .308 Win. cal., laminated pillar bedded wood stock with adj. cheek rest and Wundhammer palm swell, vent. forend, 5 shot internal mag., alloy steel receiver with 26 in. matte black finished heavy stainless steel barrel w/o sights, drilled and tapped receiver, approx. 10 7/8 lbs. Mfg. 1994-2001.

$950 $825 $725 $650 $525 $425 $325 *$1,049*

* ***Model 112-BT-S Competition Grade*** – .300 Win. Mag. cal., single shot, otherwise similar to Model 112 - BT Competition Grade. Mfg. 1995-2001.

$900 $775 $675 $600 $500 $425 $325 *$1,049*

MODEL 112-FV – .22-250 Rem. or .223 Rem. cal., varmint variation with 26 in. heavy barrel, with or w/o iron sights, 4 shot mag., black Rynite synthetic stock with recoil pad, 8 7/8 lbs. Mfg. 1991-98.

$400 $350 $300 $270 $220 $180 $140 *$410*

GRADING - PPGS™	100%	98%	95%	90%	80%	70%	60%	LAST MSR

* ***Model 112-FVS*** – similar to Model 112-FV, except is single shot with solid bottom receiver and is available in .220 Swift (new 1993) cal. Mfg. 1992-93 only.

	$375	$330	$280	$255	$205	$170	$130	

* ***Model 112-FVSS (Long Range)*** – .22-250 Rem. (disc. 1998), .223 Rem. (disc. 1998), .25-06 Rem. (new 1995), .30-06 (new 1996), .308 Win. (mfg. 1996-98), .300 Win. Mag. (new 1995), or 7mm Rem. Mag. (new 1995) cal., alloy receiver with 26 in. fluted stainless steel barrel, 4 shot mag., black synthetic pillar bedded sporter stock w/o sights, 8 7/8 lbs. Mfg. 1993-2002.

	$500	$440	$375	$340	$275	$225	$175	*$569*

This model was also available with left-hand action (Model 112-FLVSS, mfg. 1996-2002, not available in .30-06 cal.).

* ***Model 112-FVSS-S*** – .220 Swift, .22-250 Rem. (disc. 1998), .223 Rem. (disc. 1998), or .300 Win. Mag. (new 1996) cal., single shot variation, pillar bedded stock, 8 7/8 lbs. Mfg. 1994-2001.

	$475	$415	$355	$325	$260	$215	$165	*$549*

MODEL 112 MAGNUM TARGET – .338 Lapua cal., long action, single shot, 26 in. heavy barrel with muzzle brake, target AccuTrigger, oversized bolt handle, pillar bedding, gray laminate stock, matte finish, 12 lbs. New 2015.

MSR $1,039	$885	$775	$665	$600	$485	$415	$350	

MODEL 114 AMERICAN CLASSIC/CLASSIC – .270 Win., .30-06, .300 Win. Mag., or 7mm Rem. Mag. cal., features detachable box mag. (American Classic) or hinged floorplate (Classic, mfg. 2006-2011), 22 or 24 in. steel barrel, AccuTrigger, long action, drilled and tapped, satin lacquer American walnut with ebony forend and wraparound checkering, right or left (mfg. 2008-disc.) action, no sights, 7 or 7 1/2 lbs. Mfg. 2005-2018.

	$810	$675	$550	$475	$400	$350	$300	*$979*

Add $50 for Classic Model (disc. 2011).

* ***Model 114 American Classic Stainless*** – .270 Win., .30-06, .300 Win. Mag., or 7mm Rem. Mag. cal., 22 or 24 in. stainless steel barrel, oil finished American walnut stock, right hand action, otherwise similar to American Classic model, 7 1/2 lbs. Mfg. 2011-2014.

	$875	$750	$650	$575	$500	$425	$350	*$995*

MODEL 114 EURO CLASSIC – .270 Win. or .30-06 cal., 22 in. barrel, detachable box mag., AccuTrigger standard, checkered oil finished Monte Carlo walnut stock with cheekpiece, high polished blued action/ barrel, open sights, 7 3/4 lbs. Mfg. 2006-2010.

	$750	$595	$525	$445	$375	$325	$275	*$909*

MODEL 114-C (CLASSIC) 114-CU (CLASSIC ULTRA) – .270 Win., .30-06, .300 Win. Mag., or 7mm Rem. Mag. cal., 22 or 24 in. barrel, features high gloss classic American black walnut stock with cut checkering, fitted grip cap, and recoil pad, removable 3 or 4 shot staggered box mag., available with deluxe adj. sights (Model 114-CU, disc. 1995) or w/o sights (Model 114-C, new 1996), approx. 7 1/8 lbs. Mfg. 1991-2000.

	$500	$440	$375	$340	$275	$225	$175	*$556*

MODEL 114-U – similar to Model 114-C, except is also available in 7mm STW (disc. 2002) cal., 3 shot internal mag, no sights, approx. 7 lbs. Mfg. 1999-2004.

	$500	$440	$375	$340	$275	$225	$175	*$569*

MODEL 114-CE (CLASSIC EUROPEAN) – same cals. as the Model 114-C, except also available in 7x64mm Brenneke cal., features oil finished stock with Schnabel forend and skip-line checkering, high luster bluing, 22 or 24 in. barrel with adj. rear sight, 7 1/8 lbs. Mfg. 1996-2001.

	$500	$440	$375	$340	$275	$225	$175	*$554*

MODEL 116 ALASKAN BRUSH HUNTER – .338 Win. Mag. or .375 Ruger cal., satin stainless steel action with 20 in. barrel with iron sights, large bolt handle knob, AccuTrigger, black synthetic stock, blind magazine, 7.6 lbs. Mfg. 2012-2018.

	$635	$500	$450	$395	$325	$300	$275	*$785*

MODEL 116 BEAR HUNTER – .300 Win Mag., .338 Win. Mag., or .375 Ruger (new 2012) cal., long action, 23 in. stainless steel fluted barrel with adj. muzzle brake, hinged floorplate, 3 shot mag., AccuTrigger, checkered synthetic AccuStock (disc.) or Mossy Oak Break-Up Infinity camo finish, 7 3/4 lbs. Mfg. 2011-2016.

	$940	$750	$650	$550	$500	$400	$325	*$1,098*

GRADING - PPGS™	100%	98%	95%	90%	80%	70%	60%	LAST MSR

MODEL 116-BSS WEATHER WARRIOR – .270 Win., .30-06, .300 Win. Mag., .300 RUM or 7mm Rem. Mag. cal., long action, brown wood laminate stock with cut checkering, stainless steel action and tapered barrel, 2-4 shot internal mag., 24 or 26 in. barrel, 7-7 3/4 lbs. Mfg. 2001-2002.

$560	$480	$410	$345	$295	$250	$220	*$644*

MODEL 116 FSS – .22-250 Rem. (mfg. 1992 only), .223 Rem. (mfg. 1992-98), .243 Win. (mfg. 1993-98), .270 Win., .30-06, .308 Win. (disc. 1998), 7mm Rem. Mag., 7mm STW (mfg. 2001-2002), 7mm RUM (mfg. 2002-2003), .300 Win. Mag., .300 RUM (mfg. 2001-2006), .338 Win. Mag., or .375 H&H (mfg. 2002, reintroduced 2007-2008) cal., short (disc.) or long (new 2001) action, features black DuPont Rynite synthetic stock, stainless steel metal parts, drilled and tapped for scope mounting, 22, 24, or 26 (disc. 2005) in. barrel, 3 or 4 shot mag., 6 3/4 lbs. Mfg. 1991-2011.

$575	$475	$415	$330	$285	$240	$210	*$720*

Add $145 for .375 H&H cal. (iron sights only).

This model is also available with left-hand action (Model 116-FLSS, not available in .375 H&H).

* ***Model 116 FCSS*** – .25-06 Rem. (new 2009), .270 Win., .30-06, 6.5x284 Norma (new 2011), 7mm Rem. Mag., .300 Win. Mag., .338 Win. Mag. (new 2005), or .375 Ruger (mfg. 2012-2013) cal., 22 or 24 in. stainless steel barrel, detachable 3 or 4 shot box mag. with recessed push-button release, AccuStock became standard 2009, AccuTrigger, black synthetic stock, 7 1/4 lbs. Mfg. 1992-2001, reintroduced 2005-2017.

$750	$625	$525	$450	$400	$350	$275	*$939*

* ***Model 116 FLCSS*** – .270 Win., .30-06, .300 Win. Mag., or 7mm-08 Rem. cal., long action, 24 in. stainless steel barrel, left-hand, AccuTrigger, 4 shot detachable box mag., black synthetic AccuStock, no sights, 7 1/2 lbs. Mfg. 2014-2017.

$750	$625	$525	$450	$400	$350	$275	*$939*

* ***Model 116 FHSS/116 FHSAK*** – .270 Win., .30-06, .300 Win. Mag., .338 Win. Mag., or 7mm Rem. Mag. cal., 22 or 24 in. free floating barrel with muzzle brake (Model FHSAK only), drilled and tapped stainless action, hinged floorplate, AccuTrigger, 3 or 4 shot mag., black synthetic stock, AccuStock became standard 2009, 6 1/2 - 7 1/2 lbs. Mfg. 2006-2013.

$725	$625	$525	$450	$400	$350	$275	*$850*

Add $86 for Model FHSAK with muzzle brake (disc. 2010).

This model was also available in left-hand action (Model 116-FLHSS, new 2007).

* ***Model 116-FSK (Kodiak)*** – similar cals. as Model 116-FCSS, except also available in .338 Win Mag. cal., stainless steel construction, 22 in. barrel with recoil arrester, cocking indicator, 3 shot mag., black synthetic sporter stock, no sights, 6 1/2 lbs. Mfg. 1993-2000.

$495	$430	$370	$325	$290	$260	$230	*$569*

This model was also available with left-hand action (Model 116-FLSK).

MODEL 116-US (ULTRA STAINLESS) – .270 Win., .30-06, 7mm Rem. Mag., or .300 Win. Mag. cal., 24 in. stainless steel barrel, checkered walnut stock and forearm with ebony tip, no sights, 7 1/8 lbs. Mfg. 1995-98.

$625	$550	$500	$450	$400	$360	$330	*$700*

MODEL 116-SE (SAFARI EXPRESS) – .300 Win. Mag. (disc. 2002), .300 RUM (mfg. 2002), .338 Win. Mag. (disc. 2001), .375 H&H (mfg. 2000-2002), .425 Express (mfg. 1995 only), or .458 Win. Mag. cal., stainless steel receiver and 24 in. barrel with adj. muzzle brake, controlled round feeding, select grade checkered walnut stock with solid recoil pad and ebony forend, 3-leaf express sights, 8 1/2 lbs. Mfg. 1994-2004.

$895	$775	$685	$625	$575	$535	$475	*$1,045*

MODEL 116-FSAK – .270 Win., .30-06, .300 Win. Mag., .300 RUM (new 2001), .338 Win. Mag., .375 H&H (mfg. 2002 only), 7mm STW (mfg. 2001-2002), 7mm RUM (mfg. 2002 only), or 7mm Rem. Mag. cal., short (disc.) or long (new 2001) action, features 22 in. fluted stainless steel barrel with adj. muzzle brake, 6 1/2 lbs. Mfg. 1994-2004.

$530	$465	$390	$340	$295	$265	$235	*$619*

This model was also available with left-hand action (Model 116-FLSAK, not available in 7mm STW, 7mm RUM or .375 H&H cals.).

MODEL 116-FCSAK – .270 Win., .30-06, .300 Win. Mag., .338 Win. Mag. (new 2005), or 7mm Rem. Mag. cal., features push-button activated detachable box mag., 22 or 24 (new 2005) in. fluted barrel with adj. muzzle brake, 6 1/2 lbs. Mfg. 1994-2000, reintroduced 2005.

$560	$495	$415	$350	$315	$275	$245	*$661*

This model was also available with left-hand action (Model 116-FLCSAK).

GRADING - PPGS™	100%	98%	95%	90%	80%	70%	60%	LAST MSR

MODEL 116FXP3 PACKAGE – .270 Win., .30-06, .300 RUM (disc. 2003), .300 Win. Mag., .338 Win. Mag. (disc. 2010), 7mm STW (disc. 2002), 7mm Rem. Mag., or 7mm RUM (disc. 2003) cal., stainless long action, 22, 24, or 26 (disc. 2010) in. stainless barrel w/o sights, checkered black synthetic stock, includes nickel finished 3-9x40 scope and mounts, supplied with sling, AccuTrigger, approx. 6 1/2 - 7 lbs. Mfg. 2002-2011.

	$625	$495	$425	$360	$315	$270	$225	*$782*

MODEL 116 LIGHTWEIGHT HUNTER – .270 Win. cal., bolt action, 20 in. stainless steel barrel, 4 shot detachable box mag., AccuTrigger, black synthetic stock, 6 lbs. Mfg. 2016 only.

	$650	$575	$500	$450	$350	$300	$250	*$752*

MODEL 116 TROPHY HUNTER XP PACKAGE – .25-06 Rem., .270 Win., .30-06, .300 Win Mag., .338 Win., .375 Ruger (disc. 2014), 6.5x284 Norma (disc. 2014), or 7mm Rem. Mag. cal., long action, stainless action with 22 or 24 in. stainless barrel, 4 shot detachable box mag., black synthetic stock, AccuTrigger, includes 3-9x40 Nikon BDC scope, 7 1/4 lbs. New 2012.

MSR $775	$650	$575	$500	$450	$350	$300	$250

MODEL 170C – .30-30 Win. cal. only, similar to 170, 18 1/2 in. barrel. Mfg. 1974-81.

	$300	$265	$225	$205	$165	$135	$105

MODEL 170 PUMP RIFLE – .30-30 Win. or .35 Rem. (rare) cal., 22 in. barrel, folding leaf sight, 3 shot tube mag., checkered pistol grip stock. Mfg. 1970-81.

	$325	$285	$245	$220	$180	$145	$115

Add 20% for .35 Rem. cal.

This model was mfg. by Emhart.

EDGE BOLT ACTION – .223 Rem., .22-250 Rem., .243 Win., 7mm-08 Rem., .308 Win., .25-06 Rem., .270 Win., or .30-06 cal., 22 in. barrel, drilled and tapped, carbine steel construction, synthetic stock, 4 shot detachable box mag., matte black or camo finish, not available with AccuTrigger, approx. 6 1/2 lbs. Mfg. mid-2010-2011.

	$285	$265	$245	$225	$200	$185	$170	*$329*

Add $50 for camo.

* ***Edge XP Bolt Action*** – .223 Rem., .22-250 Rem., .243 WIn., 7mm-08 Rem., .308 Win., .25-06 Rem., .270 Win., or .30-06 cal., similar to Edge, except has matte blued 3-9x40 scope, mounted and bore sighted, matte black or camo finish, approx. 6 1/2 lbs. Mfg. mid-2010-2011.

	$335	$295	$265	$245	$215	$195	$180	*$379*

IMPULSE BIG GAME – 6.5 Creedmoor, .243 Win., .308 Win., .300 WSM., .30-06, or .300 Win. Mag. cal., straight pull bolt action, 22 in. carbon steel fluted and threaded barrel, 2, 3, 4 shot detachable box mag., aluminum receiver, user adj. AccuTrigger, adj. synthetic AccuStock with AccuFit and KUIU Verde 2.0 matte camo finish, AccuFit adj. length of pull and comb height, 20 MOA rail, Hazel Green Cerakote finish, 8.8-8.9 lbs. New 2021.

MSR $1,449	$1,230	$1,075	$925	$835	$675	$550	$450

IMPULSE HOG HUNTER – .308 Win., 6.5 Creedmoor, .30-06, or .300 Win. Mag. cal., straight pull rifle, 18, 20, or 24 in. carbon steel fluted and threaded heavy barrel, 3 or 4 shot detachable box mag., aluminum receiver, user adj. AccuTrigger, synthetic matte OD green AccuStock, AccuFit adj. length of pull and comb height, integral 20 MOA rail, matte black finish, 8.4-9.1 lbs. New 2021.

MSR $1,379	$1,175	$1,025	$875	$800	$650	$550	$460

IMPULSE PREDATOR – .22-250 Rem., .243 Win., .308 Win., or 6.5 Creedmoor cal., straight pull rifle, 20 in. carbon steel threaded barrel, 10 shot AICS ambi release detachable box mag., aluminum receiver, user adj. AccuTrigger, synthetic matte Mossy Oak Terra Gila Camo AccuStock, AccuFit adj. length of pull and comb height, integral 20 MOA rail, matte black finish, 8.7 lbs. New 2021.

MSR $1,379	$1,175	$1,025	$875	$800	$650	$550	$460

RIFLES: BOLT ACTION - AXIS SERIES

During 2012, Savage introduced its new AXIS Series. Whenever possible, the models within this category have been listed in numerical sequence.

AXIS – .223 Rem., .22-250 Rem., .243 Win., .25-06 Rem., .270 Win., .30-06, .308 Win., 6.5 Creedmoor (new 2017), .350 Legend (new 2020), or 7mm-08 Rem. cal., short or long action, 18 (new 2020, .350 Legend only) or 22 in. carbon steel matte black barrel with button rifling and floating bolt head (new 2019), no sights, 4 shot detachable box mag., right or left (new 2012, not avail. on camo) hand action, synthetic stock (updated with new ergonomic design in 2019) in matte black or Mossy Oak Breakup Camo (disc. 2014), recoil pad, drilled and tapped for scope mounts, AccuTrigger not available, thread-in headspacing (new 2019), 6 1/2 lbs. New 2011.

MSR $389	$325	$285	$245	$220	$180	$150	$125

Add $63 for Mossy Oak Breakup camo stock (disc. 2014).

GRADING - PPGS™	100%	98%	95%	90%	80%	70%	60%	LAST MSR

* ***AXIS Heavy Barrel*** – .223 Rem., .22-250 Rem., .243 Win., or .308 Win. cal., short action, 22 in. heavy varmint taper barrel, pillar bedding, 4 shot detachable box mag., black synthetic stock, 8 lbs. Disc. 2016.

	$350	$300	$265	$245	$225	$200	$185	*$392*

* ***AXIS Stainless*** – .223 Rem., .22-250 Rem., .243 Win., .25-06 Rem., .270 Win., .30-06, .308 Win., or 7mm-08 Rem. cal., stainless action with 22 in. stainless steel barrel, right hand action, matte black synthetic stock, no sights, AccuTrigger not available on this model, otherwise similar to AXIS model, 6 1/2 lbs. Mfg. 2011-2013.

	$360	$325	$295	$275	$250	$225	$200	*$425*

* ***AXIS Youth Model*** – .223 Rem. (new 2012), .243 Win., 6.5 Creedmoor (new 2019), or 7mm-08 Rem. cal., 20 in. carbon steel sporter barrel, right or left-hand (.243 Win. and 7mm-08 Rem. only) action, 4 shot detachable mag., matte black synthetic stock, redesigned in 2019 with fresh look and improved ergonomics, 12.5 in. LOP, 6.2 lbs. New 2011.

MSR $389	$325	$285	$245	$220	$180	$150	$125	

AXIS SR – .223 Rem. or .308 Win. cal., short action, 20 in. carbon steel threaded barrel, matte black finish, 4 shot detachable box mag., matte black synthetic stock, no sights, pillar bedding, drilled and tapped for scope mounts, AccuTrigger not available on this model, 6 1/2 lbs. Mfg. 2012-2018.

	$350	$300	$265	$245	$225	$200	$185	*$394*

AXIS XP PACKAGE – .223 Rem., .22-250 Rem., .243 Win., .25-06 Rem., .270 Win., .30-06, .308 Win., .350 Legend (new 2020), 6.5 Creedmoor, or 7mm-08 Rem. cal., 18 (new 2020, .350 Legend only) or 22 in. carbon steel Sporter barrel with matte black finish, 4 shot detachable box mag., matte black synthetic stock, AccuTrigger not available, includes mounted and boresighted 3-9x40 Bushnell scope, 6 1/2 lbs. New 2011.

MSR $430	$365	$320	$275	$250	$200	$165	$145	

* ***AXIS XP Stainless Package*** – .223 Rem., .22-250 Rem., .243 Win., .25-06 Rem., .270 Win., .30-06, .350 Legend (new 2020), .308 Win., 6.5 Creedmoor, or 7mm-08 Rem. cal., 18 (new 2020, .350 Legend) or 22 in. stainless steel barrel, includes mounted and bore sighted 3-9x40 Weaver scope, redesigned look and ergonomics in 2019, 7 lbs. New 2011.

MSR $539	$460	$400	$350	$315	$250	$200	$175	

* ***AXIS XP Compact/Youth Package*** – .223 Rem. (new 2012), .243 Win., 6.5 Creemoor, or 7mm-08 Rem. cal., short action, 20 in. carbon steel barrel, 4 shot detachable box mag., 3-9x40 Bushnell scope, matte black synthetic stock, 6.8 lbs. New 2011.

MSR $430	$365	$320	$275	$250	$200	$165	$145	

* ***Axis XP Camo/Camo Compact/Camo Youth*** – .223 Rem.,.22-250 Rem., .243 Win., 6.5 Creedmoor, 7mm-08 Rem., .308 Win., .25-06 Rem., .270 Win., .30-06, or .350 Legend cal., 18 (.350 Legend only), 20 (Compact model), or 22 in. barrel, 4 shot detachable box mag., AccuTrigger not available on this model, includes mounted and bore sighted 3-9x40 Weaver scope, Realtree Extra (disc. 2013), Mossy Oak Break-Up (mfg. 2014-2018), Mossy Oak New Break-Up Country Camo (new 2019), or Muddy Girl camo stock, redesigned in 2019 with a fresh look and improved ergonomics, 6.2 lbs. New 2013.

MSR $515	$440	$385	$330	$300	$240	$195	$170	

AXIS II – .223 Rem., .22-250 Rem., .243 Win., 6.5 Creedmoor, 7mm-08 Rem., .308 Win., .25-06 Rem., .270 Win., .30-06, .280 Ackley Improved, or .350 Legend (new 2020) cal., right or left-hand action, 18 (new 2020, .350 Legend only) or 22 in. carbon steel sporter barrel, 4 shot detachable box mag., AccuTrigger, black synthetic stock, 13.5 in. LOP, matte black finish, 5.83-6.3 lbs. New 2019.

MSR $449	$380	$335	$285	$260	$210	$175	$145	

* ***Axis II Blackout*** – .300 AAC Blackout cal., 16 1/8 in. heavy carbon steel barrel with threaded muzzle, 1:8 twist, 4 shot detachable box mag., AccuTrigger, black synthetic stock, 13.5 in. LOP, two sling swivels, drilled and tapped with one-piece Picatinny rail, matte black finish, 6.62 lbs. New 2019.

MSR $445	$380	$335	$285	$260	$210	$175	$145	

* ***AXIS II Compact/Youth*** – .223 Rem., .243 Win., 6.5 Creedmoor, or 7mm-08 Rem. cal., 20 in. carbon steel sporter barrel, 4 shot detachable box mag., AccuTrigger, black synthetic stock, 12.5 in. LOP, matte black finish, 6.25 lbs. New 2019.

MSR $449	$380	$335	$285	$260	$210	$175	$145	

* ***Axis II Overwatch*** – .223 Rem., .22-250 Rem., .243 Win., 6.5 Creedmoor, 7mm-08 Rem., .308 Win., .25-06 Rem., .270 Win., .280 Ackley Improved, or .30-06 cal., 20 in. Sport barrel, 4 shot detachable box mag., stainless steel barreled action, AccuTrigger, Mossy Oak Overwatch camo synthetic stock, Gunsmoke Gray PVD coating, 6.5 lbs. New 2020.

MSR $549	$470	$410	$350	$325	$260	$215	$185	

GRADING - PPGS™	100%	98%	95%	90%	80%	70%	60%	LAST MSR

AXIS II PRECISION – .243 Win., .223 Rem., .270 Win., .30-06 Springfield, .308 Win., or 6.5 Creedmoor cal., 22 in. carbon steel heavy button-rifled and threaded barrel w/cap, 5 or 10 shot detachable AICS mag., adj. AccuTrigger, one-piece 20 MOA rail, exclusive black aluminum MDT chassis w/adj. comb, black/OD Green finish, 9.8 lbs. New 2020.

MSR $980	$835	$725	$625	$565	$455	$375	$325

AXIS II XP – .223 Rem., .22-250 Rem., .243 Win., .25-06 Rem., .270 Win., .308 Win., .30-06, 6.5 Creedmoor, .350 Legend (new 2020), or 7mm-08 Rem. cal., short or long action, 18 (new 2020, .350 Legend only) or 22 in. barrel with matte blued finish, 4 shot detachable box mag., no sights, built on Axis platform, AccuTrigger, black or FDE (new 2020) synthetic stock, includes factory mounted bore sighted Weaver KASPA (disc. 2017) or 3-9x40 Bushnell (new 2018) scope, 6 1/2 lbs. New 2014.

MSR $499	$425	$375	$325	$295	$235	$195	$165

* ***AXIS II XP Hardwood*** – .223 Rem., .22-250 Rem., .243 Win., 7mm-08 Rem., .308 Win., .30-06, .25-06 Rem., .270 Win., or 6.5 Creedmoor (new 2017) cal., 22 in. carbon steel sporter matte blued barrel, 4 shot detachable box mag., AccuTrigger, hardwood stock, pillar bedding, includes 3-9x40 Weaver (disc.) or Bushnell Banner scope, 6 1/2 lbs. New 2016.

MSR $619	$525	$460	$395	$355	$290	$240	$200

* ***AXIS II XP Stainless*** – .223 Rem., .22-250 Rem., .243 Win., 7mm-08 Rem., .308 Win., .30-06, .25-06 Rem., .270 Win., 6.5 Creedmoor (new 2019), .350 Legend (new 2020), or .280 Ackley Improved (mfg. 2019-2020) cal., 18 (new 2020, .350 Legend only) or 22 in. stainless steel barrel, 4 shot detachable box mag., AccuTrigger, black synthetic stock, pillar bedding, includes 3-9x40 Weaver (disc. 2017) or 3-9x40 Bushnell (new 2018) scope, 6 1/2 lbs. New 2016.

MSR $589	$500	$440	$375	$340	$275	$225	$195

* ***AXIS II XP Youth*** – .243 Win., 6.5 Creedmoor, or .350 Legend (new 2020) cal., short action, 18 (new 2020, .350 Legend only) or 20 in. barrel, AccuTrigger, no sights, 4 shot detachable box mag., black synthetic or Muddy Girl camo stock, pillar bedding, includes factory mounted, bore sighted Weaver KASPA (disc. 2017) or 3-9x40 Bushnell (new 2018) scope, 6.2 lbs. New 2014.

MSR $499	$425	$375	$325	$295	$235	$195	$165

Add $56 for Muddy Girl camo stock.

RIFLES: SEMI-AUTO - MSR SERIES

MSR 10 COMPETITION HD – .308 Win. cal., 18 in. Proof Research carbon fiber wrapped stainless steel barrel, ported muzzle brake, 20 shot mag., two-stage trigger, Magpul CTR stock, Hogue pistol grip, nickel boron bolt carrier, custom forged upper and lower receiver with side charging handle, free float handguard with M-LOK, matte black finish, 9.05 lbs. New mid-2018.

MSR $3,735	$3,350	$2,975	$2,600	$2,275	$1,975	$1,600	$1,300

MSR 10 HUNTER – .308 Win., .338 Federal (disc. 2019), or 6.5 Creedmoor cal., GIO, AR-10 design, 16 (disc. 2018) or 18 in. Melonite QPQ treated medium barrel, muzzle brake, 20 shot mag., Blackhawk Blaze two-stage target trigger, Blackhawk Knox buttstock and pistol grip, adj. LOP, custom forged upper and lower receiver, free float handguard, adj. gas block, 8 lbs. New 2017.

MSR $1,615	$1,450	$1,275	$1,125	$1,000	$850	$700	$550

MSR 10 HUNTER OVERWATCH – .308 Win. or 6.5 Creedmoor cal., 16 1/4 in. carbon steel Melonite QPQ barrel with 5R button rifling, 20 shot detachable box mag., two-stage trigger, black Magpul MOE buttstock and pistol grip, Mossy Oak Overwatch camo on forend and custom forged aluminum upper and lower receivers, free float M-LOK handguard, matte black finish, 7.8 lbs. New 2019.

MSR $1,715	$1,550	$1,375	$1,200	$1,050	$900	$725	$600

MSR 10 LONG RANGE – .308 Win., 6mm Creedmoor (new 2018), or 6.5 Creedmoor cal., compact AR-10 design, 20, 22 (disc. 2019), or 22 1/2 in. Melonite QPQ treated medium heavy barrel, muzzle brake, 10 shot mag., Blackhawk Blaze two-stage target trigger, adj. gas block, Magpul PRS Gen3 buttstock, pistol grip, custom forged upper and lower receiver, non-reciprocating charging handle, free float M-LOK rail, 9 1/2 lbs. New 2017.

MSR $2,490	$2,225	$1,975	$1,725	$1,525	$1,325	$1,075	$875

MSR 10 PRECISION – .308 Win., 6.5 Creedmoor, or 6mm Creedmoor cal., GIO, adj. gas system, 22 1/2 in. stainless steel heavy barrel, 20 shot detachable box mag., two-stage trigger, Magpul PRS stock, red QD front sling mount, TangoDown Battlegrip Flip grip, ambi safety, 18 in. free float handguard with Arca rail and M-LOK, non-reciprocating side charging upper receiver, matte black finish, 11.4 lbs. New 2019.

MSR $2,655	$2,375	$2,125	$1,850	$1,625	$1,400	$1,150	$925

GRADING - PPGS™	100%	98%	95%	90%	80%	70%	60%	LAST MSR

MSR 15 COMPETITION – .223 Rem. or .224 Valkyrie cal., 18 in. Proof Research carbon fiber wrapped stainless steel heavy barrel, ported muzzle brake, 30 shot detachable box mag., ambi mag. release, two-stage trigger, Magpul CTR stock, Hogue pistol grip, integral Picatinny rail, adj. gas block, custom forged upper and lower receiver, nickel boron bolt carrier, non-reciprocating side charging handle, free float handguard with M-LOK, anti-glare grooves and red QD sling mount, red ambi selector, receiver endplate with QD mount, and removable custom magwell flare, matte black finish, 5.8 lbs. New mid-2018.

MSR $3,115 $2,800 $2,475 $2,150 $1,900 $1,650 $1,325 $1,075

MSR 15 LONG RANGE – .224 Valkyrie cal., 22 in. stainless steel barrel, two-port muzzle brake with taper-lock interface, detachable box mag., two-stage trigger, black synthetic stock, Hogue pistol grip, non-reciprocating side charging handle, low profile adj. gas block, custom forged upper and lower receivers, custom-length gas system, free float handguard with M-LOK. New mid-2018.

MSR $1,859 $1,675 $1,475 $1,300 $1,150 $975 $800 $650

MSR 15 PATROL – .223 Rem./5.56 Wylde chamber, 16.13 in. Melonite QPQ treated barrel with 5R rifling, flash hider, 30 shot mag., Mil-Spec trigger, A-frame gas block front sight with Blackhawk rear, Blackhawk furniture, adj. LOP, Mil-Spec upper and lower receiver, mid-length gas system, 6 1/2 lbs. New 2017.

MSR $910 $825 $725 $625 $550 $475 $400 $325

MSR 15 RECON – .223 Rem./5.56 Wylde chamber, 16.13 in. Melonite QPQ treated barrel with 5R rifling, flash hider, 30 shot mag., Blackhawk Blaze trigger, Blackhawk flip-up sights, Blackhawk buttstock and grip, mid-length gas system, free float rail, 7 lbs. Mfg. 2017-2019.

$900 $800 $700 $625 $525 $425 $350 *$1,009*

MSR 15 RECON 2.0 – .223 Rem./5.56 NATO cal., 16 1/2 in. carbon steel barrel, 30 shot detachable box mag., aluminum receiver, synthetic pistol grip stock, matte black finish, 7.3 lbs. New 2019.

MSR $1,085 $975 $875 $750 $675 $575 $475 $375

MSR 15 RECON 2.0 OVERWATCH – .223 Rem./5.56 NATO cal., .223 Wylde target chamber, gas block with Savage gas block nut and straight gas tube, 16 1/4 in. carbon steel 5R button rifled barrel with A2 muzzle brake, 30 shot detachable box mag., two-stage trigger, integrated trigger guard, Magpul MOE pistol grip and buttstock, forend, upper receiver, and custom forged lower receiver finished in Mossy Oak Overwatch camo, 7.3 lbs. New 2019.

MSR $1,179 $1,050 $950 $825 $725 $625 $500 $400

MSR 15 RECON LRP – .224 Valkyrie, .22 Nosler, 6.8 SPC, or .223 Rem. (mfg. 2018 only) cal., 18 in. Melonite QPQ barrel with 5R rifling, muzzle brake, 25 shot mag., two-stage target trigger, Magpul CTR stock, black Hogue pistol grip, custom forged lower, mid-length gas system, adj. gas block, free float M-LOK handguard, 7.42 lbs. New 2018.

MSR $1,355 $1,225 $1,075 $950 $825 $725 $575 $475

MSR 15 VALKYRIE – .224 Valkyrie cal., adj. mid-length gas system, 18 in. Melonite QPQ heavy barrel, Savage MSR tunable muzzle brake, 25 shot PRI mag., two-stage target trigger, Hogue pistol grip, Magpul UBR buttstock, custom forged lower, free float M-LOK handguard, adj. gas block, Elite Series FDE Cerakote finish, 7.88 lbs. New 2018.

MSR $1,625 $1,450 $1,300 $1,125 $1,000 $850 $700 $575

SHOTGUNS: DISC.

Most Savage shotguns (except the Model 312 Series) fall under the domain of Savage Industries, Inc. Savage made a wide variety of inexpensive, utilitarian shotguns that, to date, have attracted mostly shooting interest, but little collector interest. A listing of these models may be found in the back of this text under "Serialization."

The models listed are grouped by configuration, and are not in numerical sequence.

MODEL 220 SINGLE BARREL – 12, 16, 20, 28 ga., or .410 bore, 26-32 in. barrel, various chokes, hammerless, plain pistol grip stock. Mfg. 1938-65.

$200 $175 $150 $135 $110 $90 $70

MODEL 220P – similar to Model 220, with poly choke, not made in .410 bore.

$175 $155 $130 $120 $95 $80 $60

MODEL 220 AC – similar to Model 220, with Savage adj. choke.

$200 $175 $150 $135 $110 $90 $70

MODEL 220L – similar to Model 220, with sidelever. Mfg. 1965-72.

$175 $155 $130 $120 $95 $80 $60

GRADING - PPGS™	100%	98%	95%	90%	80%	70%	60%	LAST MSR

MODEL 420 O/U – 12, 16, or 20 ga., 26-30 in. barrel, various chokes, boxlock, single or double trigger, extractors, plain pistol grip stock. Mfg. 1937-43.

Double Trigger	$425	$370	$320	$290	$235	$190	$150
Single Trigger	$500	$440	$375	$340	$275	$225	$175

MODEL 430 O/U – similar to Model 420, with checkered stock and solid rib, recoil pad.

Double Trigger	$475	$415	$355	$325	$260	$215	$165
Single Trigger	$550	$480	$415	$375	$305	$250	$195

MODEL 720 AUTOLOADER STANDARD – 12 or 16 ga., Browning A-5 style semi-auto action, 26-32 in. barrels, various chokes, checkered pistol grip stock. Mfg. 1930-49.

$400 $350 $300 $270 $220 $180 $140

MODEL 720 RIOT – see the "Trench/Riot Shotgun" category in the T section for more information and prices.

MODEL 726 SEMI-AUTO UPLAND SPORTER – similar to Model 720, except 2 shell mag. Mfg. 1931-49.

$350 $305 $265 $240 $195 $160 $125

MODEL 740C SKEET GUN – similar to Model 726, with Cutts Compensator and skeet stock, 24 1/2 in. barrel. Mfg. 1936-49.

$375 $330 $280 $255 $205 $170 $130

MODEL 745 LIGHTWEIGHT – similar to Model 720, with alloy receiver, 12 ga. only, 28 in. barrel. Mfg. 1940-49.

$400 $350 $300 $270 $220 $180 $140

MODEL 750 SEMI-AUTO – 12 ga., Browning patterned semi-auto, 26 or 28 in. barrels, various chokes, checkered pistol grip stock. Mfg. 1960-69.

$350 $305 $265 $240 $195 $160 $125

MODEL 750AC – similar to Model 750, with poly choke.

$350 $305 $265 $240 $195 $160 $125

MODEL 750SC – similar to Model 750, with Savage Super Choke.

$350 $305 $265 $240 $195 $160 $125

MODEL 755 STANDARD SEMI-AUTO – 12 or 16 ga., 26, 28, or 30 in. barrel, various chokes, rounded-off receiver, checkered pistol grip stock. Mfg. 1949-58.

$350 $305 $265 $240 $195 $160 $125

MODEL 755SC – similar to Model 755, with Savage Super Choke.

$350 $305 $265 $240 $195 $160 $125

MODEL 775 LIGHTWEIGHT SEMI-AUTO – similar to Model 755, with alloy receiver. Mfg. 1950-65.

$350 $305 $265 $240 $195 $160 $125

MODEL 775SC – similar to Model 775, with Savage Super Choke.

$350 $305 $265 $240 $195 $160 $125

MODEL 21 SLIDE ACTION – similar to Model 28, except stock has no checkering. Mfg. 1920-28.

$350 $305 $265 $240 $195 $160 $125

MODEL 28 SLIDE ACTION – 12, 16, or 20 ga., patterned after the Winchester Model 12. Mfg. 1927-34.

$375 $330 $280 $255 $205 $170 $130

This model was available in either standard configuration (Models 28A and 28B), Riot (28C), Trap (28D), or Special (28S).

MODEL 30 SLIDE ACTION – 12, 16, 20 ga., or .410 bore, 26, 28, or 30 in. barrels, various chokes, VR, plain pistol grip stock. Mfg. 1958-70.

	$250	$220	$190	$170	$140	$115	$90
Checkered Late model	$300	$265	$225	$205	$165	$135	$105

MODEL 30AC – similar to Model 30, with adj. choke, checkered wood, 12 ga. only. Mfg. 1959-70.

$300 $265 $225 $205 $165 $135 $105

MODEL 30T TRAP AND DUCK GUN – similar to Model 30, with 30 in. full barrel, 12 ga. only, Monte Carlo stock and pad. Mfg. 1963-70.

$350 $305 $265 $240 $195 $160 $125

MODEL 30FG TAKEDOWN ACTION – 12, 20 ga., or .410 bore, 26, 28, or 30 in. barrel, various chokes, checkered pistol grip stock. Mfg. 1970-75.

$250 $220 $190 $170 $140 $115 $90

GRADING - PPGS™	100%	98%	95%	90%	80%	70%	60%	LAST MSR

MODEL 30T TAKEDOWN TRAP – 12 ga. only, 30 in. full barrel, Monte Carlo stock with pad. Mfg. 1970-73.

	$275	$240	$205	$185	$150	$125	$95	

MODEL 30AC TAKEDOWN – similar to Model 30FG, with adj. choke, 12 or 20 ga., 26 in. barrel. Mfg. 1971-72.

	$275	$240	$205	$185	$150	$125	$95	

MODEL 30 TAKEDOWN SLUG GUN – similar to Model 30FG, with 32 in. cylinder bore barrel, rifle sights. Mfg. 1971-disc.

	$275	$240	$205	$185	$150	$125	$95	

MODEL 30D TAKEDOWN – similar to Model 30FG, with VR, engraved receiver and pad. Mfg. 1971-disc.

	$275	$240	$205	$185	$150	$125	$95	

MODEL 67 SLIDE ACTION – see listing under the Stevens, J.,Arms Company Section.

FOX MODELS B, B-SE – see listings under Fox, A.H. in the F section.

SAVAGE/FOX MODEL FA-1 – 12 ga., 2 3/4 in. chamber, semi-auto, gas operated, walnut stock and forend, cut checkering, 28 or 30 in. vent. rib barrel. Mfg. 1981-82 in Japan.

	$400	$350	$300	$270	$220	$180	$140	

SAVAGE/FOX MODEL FP-1 – 12 ga., similar to Model FA-1, except is slide action. Mfg. 1981-82 in Japan.

	$325	$285	$245	$220	$180	$145	$115	

MODEL 242 O/U – .410 bore, single exposed hammer, single trigger, barrel selector lever, full chokes. Mfg. 1977-1981.

	$750	$650	$575	$500	$425	$340	$265	

MODEL 440/440B O/U – 12 or 20 ga., 26, 28, or 30 in. barrels, various chokes, boxlock, ST (Model 440) or SST (Model 440B), extractors, checkered pistol grip stock, VR. Imported from Italy 1968-72.

	$550	$475	$415	$375	$305	$250	$195	

MODEL 440T – similar to Model 440, 12 ga., 30 in. barrel only, imp. mod. or full choke, wide VR, trap style stock, pad. Mfg. 1969-72.

	$600	$525	$450	$400	$325	$275	$210	

MODEL 444 DELUXE – similar to Model 440, with auto ejectors, select walnut. Mfg. 1969-72.

	$600	$525	$450	$400	$325	$275	$210	

MODEL 550 SxS – 12 or 20 ga., 26, 28, or 30 in. barrels (made by Valmet - rare), various chokes, boxlock, auto ejectors, single trigger, checkered pistol grip stock. Mfg. 1971-73.

	$400	$350	$300	$270	$220	$180	$140	

KIMEL KAMPER SINGLE SHOT – 20 ga. or .410 bore, 3 in. chamber, 18 1/2 in. barrel, pistol grip hardwood stock and forearm, butt trap holds 3 shells, bottom opening, exposed hammer. Mfg. 1979-c.1981

	$250	$220	$190	$170	$140	$115	$90	

MODEL STEVENS 311 – see listing under the Stevens, J., Arms Company Section.

MODEL 312 SERIES O/U – 12 ga. only, boxlock action, 3 in. chambers, vent. barrels, satin chrome finished receiver, checkered walnut stock and forearm, SST, choke tubes, approx. 7 lbs. Mfg. 1990-93.

The Model 312 Series falls under the domain of Savage Arms, Inc.

* ***Model 312 Series O/U Field*** – 26 or 28 in. VR barrels with choke tubes.

	$500	$440	$375	$340	$275	$225	$175	

* ***Model 312 Series O/U Trap*** – 30 in. barrels only, Monte Carlo stock with recoil pad.

	$550	$475	$415	$375	$305	$250	$195	

* ***Model 312 Series O/U Sporting Clays*** – 28 in. barrels only with 7 choke tubes provided, recoil pad.

	$525	$460	$395	$355	$290	$235	$185	

MODEL 330 O/U – 12 or 20 ga., 26, 28, or 30 in. barrels, various chokes, boxlock, SST, extractors, checkered pistol grip stock. Mfg. by Valmet 1969-1980.

	$450	$395	$340	$305	$250	$205	$160	

Add 25% for extra set of barrels.

MODEL 333T – similar to Model 330, with 30 in. VR barrels bored imp. mod. and full choke, trap stock with pad. Mfg. by Valmet 1972-1980.

	$500	$440	$375	$340	$275	$225	$175	

GRADING - PPGS™	100%	98%	95%	90%	80%	70%	60%	LAST MSR

MODEL 333 O/U – 12 or 20 (rare) ga., 26, 28, or 30 in. VR barrels, various chokes, boxlock, SST, auto ejectors, checkered pistol grip stock. Mfg. by Valmet 1973-1980.

	$600	$525	$450	$400	$325	$275	$210	

Add 25% for extra set of barrels.
Add 30% for 20 ga.

SHOTGUNS: CURRENT/RECENT MFG.

Currently manufactured Stevens shotguns can be found in the Stevens section.

FOX A-GRADE SHOTGUN – 12 or 20 ga., 3 in. chambers, SxS shotgun, Anson Deeley style boxlock action, 26 or 28 in. barrels with solid game rib, includes interchangeable improved cylinder, modified, and full chokes, 2 shot, Holland & Holland style ejectors, double triggers, front brass bead sight, American black walnut stock with oil finish and precision cut checkering, straight buttstock grip and splinter forend, automatic safety, bone and charcoal case color finished receiver, polymer carrying case, 6.5-7.2 lbs. Mfg. 2018-2020.

	$3,500	$3,050	$2,600	$2,400	$1,900	$1,550	$1,200	*$4,105*

MILANO O/U – 12, 20, 28 ga., or .410 bore, ejectors, 28 in. chrome-lined vent. rib barrels, satin nickel finished boxlock action, satin finished Turkish walnut stock and forearm with laser engraved checkering, rubber recoil pad, Schnabel forend, SST, fiber optic front sight, includes three choke tubes (except for .410 bore), elongated forcing cones, 6 1/4 - 7 1/2 lbs., imported from Italy. Mfg. mid-2006-2008.

	$1,350	$1,175	$1,025	$925	$750	$600	$475	*$1,714*

MODEL 210F SLUG WARRIOR BOLT ACTION (MASTER SHOT) – 12 ga. only, 3 in. chamber, built on Model 100 action with controlled round feeding, 24 in. rifled barrel (1:35 twist), 2 shot detachable mag., 60 degree bolt lift, Realtree camo finished (new 2003) or black synthetic stock with checkering and recoil pad, top tang safety, no sights, 7 1/2 lbs. Mfg. 1997-2009.

	$500	$400	$350	$300	$260	$230	$200	*$634*

Add $42 for camo finish (Model 210F Camo).
Add $41 for Turkey configuration with 24 in. barrel and camo coverage (Model 210FT Camo, mfg. 2005-2006).

* ***Model 210FT Slug Warrior Bolt Action*** – similar to Model 210F, except has Advantage camo stock and mag., 24 in. smoothbore barrel accepts Win. style choke tubes. Mfg. 1997-2000.

	$410	$350	$305	$265	$235	$215	$195	*$466*

MODEL 212 SLUG GUN – 12 ga., 22 in. barrel, 2 shot detachable box mag., black or grey (new late 2019) synthetic, 100% Realtree Hardwoods (mfg. 2011 only), Mossy Oak Breakup Infinity (disc. 2019), or Mossy Oak Breakup Country (new 2020) camo coverage stock, AccuStock system (new late 2019), approx. 7 1/2 lbs. New 2011.

MSR $745	$625	$545	$475	$425	$345	$275	$225	

Add $70 for Mossy Oak Breakup Country camo (new 2020).

MODEL 212/220 TURKEY – 12 or 20 ga., 2 in. chamber, bolt action, 22 in. carbon steel free floating blued barrel, EF choke, 2 shot detachable box mag., AccuTrigger, Mossy Oak Obsession camo synthetic AccuStock with AccuFit, 13.8 in. LOP, one-piece rail, matte black metal finish, 7 lbs. New 2019.

MSR $725	$620	$540	$460	$425	$345	$275	$225	

Add $90 for 12 ga.

MODEL 220 SLUG GUN – 20 ga., bolt action, available in right or left (new 2012) hand action, 22 in. carbon steel barrel, 2 shot detachable box mag., AccuTrigger, matte black, grey (new 2020), Mossy Oak Breakup Infinity (disc. 2019), or Mossy Oak Country (new 2020) camo synthetic stock, AccuStock (new late 2019), drilled and tapped, cut checkering, oversized bolt handle, matte blue finish, 7 lbs. New 2010.

MSR $655	$550	$480	$415	$375	$310	$260	$215	

Add $70 for blued barrel with camo finish and AccuStock (new 2020).

* ***Model 220 Slug Gun Stainless*** – 20 ga., 22 in. stainless steel barrel, 2 shot detachable box mag., AccuTrigger, oversized bolt handle, Mossy Oak Break-Up Infinity camo stock, AccuStock (new late 2019), no sights, 7 lbs. New 2012.

MSR $835	$700	$615	$525	$475	$385	$315	$275	

* ***Model 220 Slug Gun Youth*** – 20 ga., 22 in. barrel, similar to Model 220 Slug Gun, except has youth dimensions, black synthetic stock only, 7 lbs. Mfg. 2010-2019.

	$535	$475	$400	$365	$295	$240	$200	*$629*

MODEL 220 THUMBHOLE – 20 ga., 22 in. barrel, 2 shot detachable mag., AccuTrigger, featherweight thumbhole stock, one-piece Picatinny rail, stainless steel option available, Pepper Laminate finish, 7.75 lbs. New 2020.

MSR $825	$700	$615	$525	$475	$385	$315	$275	

Add $144 for stainless steel model.

GRADING - PPGS™	100%	98%	95%	90%	80%	70%	60%	LAST MSR

MODEL 320 – 12 or 20 ga., 3 in. chamber, 18 1/2 in. chrome alloy steel barrel, 5 shot bottom-loading tube mag., ghost-ring sight or front bead sight, matte black synthetic thumbhole stock and forend, adj. cheek riser, rugged textured grips, recoil pad, swivel stud on stock and mag. cap. New 2020.

MSR $275	$225	$200	$175	$150	$125	$100	$75	

Add $30 for ghost-ring sights.

RENEGAUGE COMPETITION – 12 ga., semi-auto, D.R.I.V gas system, 24 in. fluted VR carbon steel barrel with black Melonite finish, extended Skeet2 light modified flush chokes, 9 shot extended mag. tube, aluminum receiver with red Cerakote finish, red Hi-Viz Tri-Comp front sight, matte black fully adj. Monte Carlo synthetic stock and forend, oversized controls, lightweight bolt carrier, 8.2 lbs. New 2021.

MSR $1,959	$1,665	$1,455	$1,250	$1,125	$910	$750	$625	

RENEGAUGE FIELD – 12 ga., 3 in. chamber, semi-auto, D.R.I.V. gas system, 26 or 28 in. fluted carbon steel VR barrel w/Melonite finish, 4 interchangeable choke tubes, 4 shot tube mag., competition-ready loading mag. port, aluminum receiver, red fiber optic sight, matte grey Monte Carlo adj. synthetic stock, oversized controls, includes hard carrying case, 8 lbs. New 2020.

MSR $1,489	$1,265	$1,100	$950	$850	$700	$560	$490	

RENEGAUGE PRAIRIE – 12 ga., semi-auto, D.R.I.V. gas system, 28 in. fluted VR barrel with Cerakote Sand finish, F/IC/M flush chokes included, 4 shot tube mag., aluminum receiver, red fiber optic front sight, fully adj. synthetic stock and forend with True Timber Prairie camo finish, oversized controls, includes hard carrying case, 7.9 lbs. New 2021.

MSR $1,599	$1,360	$1,190	$1,020	$925	$750	$625	$530	

RENEGAUGE TURKEY – 12 ga., 3 in. chamber, D.R.I.V. gas system, 24 in. carbon steel fluted barrel with Melonite finish, extended full chokes (F/IC/M), 4 shot tube mag., aluminum receiver, VR with red fiber optic sight, Monte Carlo style synthetic stock and forend, adj. LOP, comb height, drop and cast, one-piece chrome plated action bar assembly, oversized controls, includes hard carrying case, 100% Mossy Oak Obsession or Mossy Oak Bottomland camo finish, 7.8 lbs. New 2020.

MSR $1,599	$1,360	$1,190	$1,020	$925	$750	$625	$530	

RENEGAUGE WATERFOWL – 12 ga., 3 in. chamber, D.R.I.V. gas system, 26 or 28 in. carbon steel fluted barrel with Melonite finish, includes F/IC/M chokes, 4 shot tube mag., competition-ready loading mag. port, aluminum receiver, VR rib with red fiber optic sight, Monte Carlo style synthetic stock, adj. for LOP, comb height, and drop & cast, one-piece chrome plated action bar assembly, oversized controls, 100% Mossy Oak Shadow Grass Blades camo finish, 8 lbs. New 2020.

MSR $1,599	$1,360	$1,190	$1,020	$925	$750	$625	$530	

SAVIN, J.C.

Previous manufacturer located in St. Etienne, France. J.C. Savin manufactured only best quality shotguns and rifles per custom order. Annual production was approx. 25 long guns. Each gun should be individually appraised and evaluated based on configuration and options.

RIFLES: DOUBLE, CUSTOM

Guns were available in either O/U or SxS sidelock or Anson & Deeley boxlock, in various cals. (.30 - .577 NE), 24 or 26 in. barrels.

SHOTGUNS: DOUBLE, CUSTOM

Guns were available in either O/U or SxS sidelock configuration, 12 or 20 ga., DT or ST, premier quality. A SxS round action Dixon model with trigger plate was also available in 12 or 20 ga.

SAXONIA

Previous manufacturer located in Schwarzenberg, Germany.

Saxonia manufactured good quality semi-auto pistols, security/combat shotguns, and bolt action sniper rifles in various configurations. These guns had very little or no importation in the U.S.

SCATTERGUN TECHNOLOGIES INC. (S.G.T.)

Current manufacturer located in Berryville, AR since 1999. Previously located in Nashville, TN 1991-1999. Distributor, dealer, and consumer sales.

During 1999, Wilson Combat purchased Scattergun Technologies. S.G.T. manufactures practical defense, tactical, and hunting shotguns in 12 ga. only, utilizing Remington Models 870 and 11-87 (disc.) actions in various configurations as listed. All shotguns feature 3 in. chamber capacity and parkerized finish.

SHOTGUNS: SEMI-AUTO

Add $15 for short stock on models listed.
Add $125 for Armor-Tuff finish on models listed.

GRADING - PPGS™	100%	98%	95%	90%	80%	70%	60%	LAST MSR

K-9 MODEL – 12 ga., 18 in. barrel, adj. ghost ring sight, 7 shot mag., side saddle, synthetic buttstock and forearm. Disc. 2003.

$1,100	$875	$775	$665	$560	$465	$410	*$1,325*

URBAN SNIPER MODEL – 12 ga., 18 in. rifled barrel, scout optics, 7 shot mag., side saddle, synthetic buttstock, forearm and bipod. Disc. 1999.

$1,225	$1,075	$950	$835	$685	$585	$485	*$1,390*

SHOTGUNS: SLIDE ACTION

Add $15 for short stock on models listed.

Subtract approx. $100 if w/o Armor-Tuff finish. (Armor-Tuff finish became standard in 2003).

BORDER PATROL (MODEL 20) – 12 or 20 (disc. 2011) ga., 18 1/2 or 20 (disc. 2011) in. barrel, similar to Patrol Model, except has 7 shot mag., synthetic stock and forearm, black, FDE, OD Green, Green Base Camo, Gray Base Camo, or FDE Base Camo finish, 7.7 lbs. Disc. 2020.

$975	$885	$765	$655	$575	$495	$435	*$1,135*

Add $400 for Green, Gray, or FDE Base Camo.

Add $35 for 20 ga. (disc. 2011).

CQB SHOTGUN – 12 ga., 18.4 in. cylinder bore barrel with 3 in. Magnum chamber, 6 shot mag., Super-Stoc carbine buttstock, aluminum collapsible stock adaptor, quick detach swivel sling mounts, jumbo head safety, Mil-Spec buffer tube, heavy-duty stainless mag. tube spring, high-visibility non-binding follower, black Armor-Tuff finish, 8 lbs. 8 oz. Disc. 2020.

$1,450	$1,285	$1,100	$950	$800	$700	$600	*$1,695*

EXPERT MODEL – 12 ga., 18 in. barrel with mod. choke, nickel/Teflon finished receiver, adj. ghost ring sight, forearm incorporates 11,000 CP flashlight. Mfg. 1997-2000.

$1,200	$995	$775	$665	$560	$465	$410	*$1,350*

F.B.I. MODEL – 12 or 20 ga., 3 in. chamber, 18 1/2 in. barrel, 5 shot mag., adj. ghost ring sight, side saddle, synthetic buttstock and forearm with 11,000 CP flashlight, parkerized finish. Disc. 1999.

$715	$625	$490	$420	$370	$305	$265	*$770*

LESS LETHAL – 12 ga., 3 in. chamber, 18 in. cylinder bore barrel, 6 shot extended mag. tube, adj. Trak-Lock ghost ring rear sight, ramp-type front sight with fiber optic insert, Hogue Less Lethal stock and forend, Jumbo Head safety, aluminum shell carrier by Mesa Tactical, Armor-Tuff finish, 7 lbs. 4 oz. Mfg. 2017-2020.

$1,000	$875	$750	$680	$550	$450	$350	*$1,185*

* ***Less Lethal CQB*** – 12 ga., 3 in. chamber, 18 in. cylinder bore barrel, 6 shot extended mag. tube, adj. Trak-Lock ghost ring rear sight, ramp-type front sight with fiber optic insert, Hogue Less Lethal forend, Mil-Spec buffer tube and Super-Stoc carbine buttstock, Wilson Combat/BCM Starburst Gunfighter grip, Jumbo Head safety, aluminum collapsible stock adaptor with quick detach swivel sling mounts, Armor-Tuff finish, 7 lbs. 6 oz. Mfg. 2017-2020.

$1,125	$985	$850	$775	$625	$500	$400	*$1,320*

LOUIS AWERBUCK SIGNATURE MODEL – 12 ga., 3 in. chamber, 18 in. barrel with fixed choke, 5 shot mag., adj. ghost ring sight, wood buttstock with recoil reducer and forearm, parkerized finish. Mfg. 1994-1999.

$625	$490	$385	$325	$275	$230	$200	*$705*

MILITARY MODEL – 12 ga., 3 in. chamber, 18 in. barrel with vent. handguard and M-9 bayonet lug, 7 shot mag., adj. ghost ring rear sight, synthetic stock and grooved corncob forearm, parkerized finish. Mfg. 1997-1998.

$625	$490	$385	$325	$275	$230	$200	*$690*

PATROL MODEL – 12 ga., 3 in. chamber, 18 in. barrel, 5 shot mag., adj. ghost ring sight, synthetic buttstock and forearm, parkerized finish. Disc. 1999.

$545	$500	$465	$405	$350	$290	$250	*$595*

PRACTICAL TURKEY MODEL – 12 ga., 3 in. chamber, 20 in. barrel with extra full choke, adj. ghost ring sight, 5 shot mag. for 3 in. shells, synthetic buttstock and forearm, parkerized finish. Mfg. 1995-99.

$545	$500	$465	$405	$350	$290	$250	*$595*

ROB HAUGHT SPECIAL SHOTGUN – 12 ga., 3 in. chamber, 18 in. cylinder bore barrel, 5 shot mag., extended mag. tube, Magpul SGA stock, MOE M-LOK forend, aluminum shell carrier by Mesa Tactical, adjustable Trak-Lock "U" Notch rear sight, ramp-type front sight with fiber optic insert, rigid magazine tube sling mount, Blue Force gear, Vickers Combat Applications sling, black Armor-Tuff finish. Disc. 2020.

$1,085	$950	$800	$750	$600	$500	$375	*$1,275*

GRADING - PPGS™	100%	98%	95%	90%	80%	70%	60%	LAST MSR

STANDARD MODEL – 12 or 20 (disc. 2011) ga., 18 1/2 in. barrel, adj. ghost ring sight, 7 shot mag., side saddle, synthetic buttstock and forearm with 11,000 CP flashlight, black, green, gray, Federal Brown, FDE, or Green Base Camo finish. Disc. 2020.

	$1,315	$1,165	$1,050	$915	$785	$665	$550	*$1,540*

Add $400 for Green Base Camo.

SCHALL & CO. (SCHALL)

Previous manufacturer located in New Haven, CT.

Schall provided parts and repair service for Fiala pistols and produced additional repeating pistols with the Schall name between 1930-1936.

PISTOLS

REPEATING HANDGUN – .22 LR cal., frame marked "Schall & Co. New Haven, Conn. USA", 10 round mag., manual repeating action, 4 1/2 or 7 1/2 in. fixed tapered barrel with fixed sights and blue finish, ribbed vertical striation walnut grips, Schalls appear to fall at the end of the serial number range for Fialas/Schalls between ser. no. 5567 and 7398 with those between 5638 and 5794 having no rolls with markings.

4 1/2 in. barrel	$700	$575	$525	$475	$425	$375	$325
7 1/2 in. barrel	$650	$525	$500	$450	$400	$350	$300

SCHEIRING GmbH

Current custom rifle manufacturer located in Ferlach, Austria.

H. Scheiring manufactures best quality rifles (including O/U, SxS, and Stalking variations) per individual customer special order. Scheiring was a member of the Ferlach Guild until it was dissolved in 2004. Please contact the company directly for more information on current models and domestic availability.

SCHELLER SPEZIALWAFFEN

Previous manufacturer located in Suhl, Germany that specialized in bolt action rifles.

SCHERZ, MICHAEL

Please refer to Gila River Gun Works in the G section.

SCHILLER BUCHSENMACHER

Current custom rifle manufacturer located in Leutershausen, Germany.

All Schiller rifles are custom made per individual special order. Please contact the company directly for information, including U.S. availablity and pricing.

SCHILLING, FA. ALFRED

Current rifle manufacturer and gunsmith established in 1898, located in Zella-Mehlis, Germany. Special order guns were previously imported exclusively by Sundog Firearms, located in Kimberly, OR.

RIFLES: CUSTOM

Current owner Jorg Schilling manufactures high quality hunting and target rifles in many configurations, in addition to providing gunsmithing services, including traditional case color hardening, bluing, restoration of damascus barrels and engravings, plus a line of unique accessories. All guns are custom order and include the standard Schilling bolt action rifle ($17,245-$22,995), the single shot rifle ($20,125), the Hagn falling block rifle now in 4 different sized actions ($11,997-$21,297), the breech block rifle ($22,425), the varmint rifle ($10,920), and the Aydt target model ($17,245). Please contact the manufacturer for more information, including an individual price quotation, delivery time and availability.

SCHMEISSER GmbH

Current manufacturer located in Krefeld, Germany. Previously distributed (select models only) by American Tactical Imports, located in Summerville, SC, and previously Rochester, NY. No current U.S. importation.

PISTOLS: SEMI-AUTO

Schmeisser GmbH currently manufactures pistols. Current models include the 1911 Hugo, 1911ER Hugo (disc.), and SLP-9 (disc.). Please contact the company directly for more information including options, pricing, and U.S. availability.

GRADING - PPGS™	100%	98%	95%	90%	80%	70%	60%	LAST MSR

RIFLES: SEMI-AUTO

Schmeisser GmbH currently manufactures AR-15 style rifles in several calibers and configurations. Current models include AR15 M4, AR15 M4F, AR15 M5, AR15 M5F, AR15 M4FL, AR15 M5FL, AR15 A4 (16 and 20 in.), AR15 DMR, AR15 Dynamic, AR15 Dynamic L, AR15 LMR, AR15 Ultramatch (20 and 24 in.), AR15 Ultramatch STS, AR15 S4F, AR15 M4-Solid (disc.), and AR15 M5-Solid (disc.), or V22 (disc). Please contact the company directly for more information including options, pricing, and U.S. availability.

SCHMIDT-RUBIN RIFLES

Please refer to the Swiss Military listing in this section.

SCHMITT FRERES

Previous manufacturer located in Saint Etienne, France.

This manufacturer produced copies of 1894 patent Darne R model guns until 1956. While higher grades do exist, they do not command the prices given for the later patent (1909) Darne-produced guns. Lower grade guns will be priced in the same range as Soleihac and lower grade Darne R models.

SCHROEDER BAUMAN

Previous semi-auto pistol manufacturer located in Fort Wayne, IN until circa 2015.

PISTOLS: SEMI-AUTO

Prices reflected base price only. Additional options were available.

AMERICAN DEFENDER – .45 ACP cal., 1911 style full size stainless steel frame machined from solid block billet, 5 in. barrel, 3 available slide serrations, beavertail grip safety, slide stop and thumb safety machined from billet with Electron beam welded pins, fully adj. Novak sights, includes two Chip McCormack 8 shot Power Mags, wire EDM magwell, 20 LPI checkered finger grip or straight grip strap, 37-46 oz. Disc. circa 2015.

100%	98%	95%	90%	80%	70%	60%	Last MSR
$1,700	$1,495	$1,275	$1,150	$950	$775	$595	*$2,000*

AMERICAN LIBERTY – .45 ACP cal., similar to American Defender, except has Officer size aluminum frame with 3.6 in. barrel and Actmag 7 shot mag., 25-32 oz. Disc. circa 2015.

100%	98%	95%	90%	80%	70%	60%	Last MSR
$1,100	$975	$825	$750	$600	$495	$395	*$1,295*

AMERICAN PATRIOT – .45 ACP cal., similar to American Defender, except has 4 1/4 in. barrel, 35-43 oz. Disc. circa 2015.

100%	98%	95%	90%	80%	70%	60%	Last MSR
$1,100	$975	$825	$750	$600	$495	$395	*$1,295*

SCHUERMAN ARMS, LTD.

Previous bolt action rifle manufacturer located in Desert Hills, AZ until 2013. Previously located in Scottsdale, AZ.

RIFLES: BOLT ACTION

MODEL SA40 – various cals., including WSMs (disc.), WSSMs (disc.), and Rem. Ultra Mags., right or left-hand action (four sizes) features three rotating locking lugs in short throw bolt, 70 degree bolt lift, 20-26 in. matte stainless steel barrel and ultra smooth action, trigger safety, controlled round feeding, fully enclosed case head, three-position safety, choice of detachable mag., hinged floorplate, or blind box mag., laminated fiberglass sporter style stock made in-house, integral scope base and muzzle brake became standard 2008. Mfg. 2001-2013.

100%	98%	95%	90%	80%	70%	60%	Last MSR
$5,750	$5,100	$4,250	$3,600	$3,000	$2,225	$2,000	*$6,850*

SCHUETZEN PISTOL WORKS

Schuetzen Pistol Works was the in-house custom shop of Olympic Arms. Schuetzen Pistol Works customized Safari Arms and Olympic Arms 1911 style pistols beginning 1997. For previously manufactured pistols, please refer to the Olympic Arms listing. For discontinued models, please refer to the Safari Arms listing.

SCHUETZEN RIFLES

A Schuetzen Rifle is a special single-shot target rifle. During the time span 1875-1945 this target configuration rifle was very popular with competition shooters, especially in Europe. Many of these guns had elaborate locking systems, top quality sights, double-set triggers, heavy barrels, palm and thumbrests, sculptured cheekpiece, Swiss style buttplate, etc. Rather than list all the various domestic and European makers (there are hundreds), it should be noted that, since there are so many combinations of options for this configuration, most guns have to be examined and appraised individually. Most non-major trademarks sell in the $900 - $6,500 range, depending on features and condition. A famous trademark specimen (Ballard, Stevens, Winchester, etc.) in a rare model with elaborate factory engraving, and superior original condition can bring over $25,000. Schuetzen Rifles are a field in themselves and a knowledgeable dealer/collector should be consulted before buying or selling one of these guns.

GRADING - PPGS™	100%	98%	95%	90%	80%	70%	60%	LAST MSR

SCHULTZ & LARSEN

Current rifle manufacturer located in Hoerning, Denmark. Previously located in Rask Molle, Denmark 1994-circa 2016. Previously manufactured in Otterup, Denmark circa 1889-1994. The company also manufactures barrels, scope mounts, and other components, in addition to having a custom shop. No current U.S. importation.

RIFLES: BOLT ACTION

Schultz & Larsen currently manufactures the following models: Legacy, Classic DL, Victory, Ambassador, and Tactical. Please contact the manufacturer directly for U.S. availability and pricing.

NO. 47 MATCH RIFLE - .22 LR cal., single shot, 28 in. heavy barrel, target sights, set trigger, free rifle stock.

$660	$550	$495	$440	$385	$360	$330	

M61 MATCH RIFLE - .22 LR cal., single shot, 28 in. heavy barrel, target sights, set trigger, free rifle stock, palm rest.

$895	$825	$740	$680	$600	$550	$500	

M62 MATCH RIFLE - various cals., single shot, 28 in. heavy barrel, target sights, set trigger, free rifle stock, palm rest.

$995	$875	$780	$700	$620	$550	$500	

MODEL 54 FREE RIFLE - any American centerfire standard caliber, plus 6.5x55mm, 27 in. heavy barrel, target sights, free rifle stock.

$825	$745	$690	$605	$550	$495	$440	

MODEL 54J SPORTING RIFLE - .244 Rem., .270 Win., .30-06, 6.5x55mm, or 7x61 Sharpe and Hart cal., 3 shot, 24 in. barrel, checkered Monte Carlo stock, no sights. Mfg. 1954-1957.

$650	$550	$470	$415	$360	$330	$300	

MODEL 60 - 7x61 S&H cal. only, improved Model 54J, mfg. 1957-1960.

$675	$575	$475	$425	$375	$330	$300	

MODEL 65 - .308 Norma Mag., .358 Win. Mag., or 7x61 S&H cal., improved Model 60, replaced by the Model 68DL, mfg. 1960-1967.

$675	$575	$475	$425	$375	$330	$300	

MODEL 68 DL - .22-250 Rem., .243 Win., 6mm Rem., .264 Win. Mag., .270 Win., .30-06, .308 Win., 7x61 S&H, 7mm Rem. Mag., 8x57JS, .300 Win. Mag., .308 Norma Mag., .338 Win. Mag., .358 Norma Mag., or .458 Win. Mag. cal., 24 in. barrel, Bofors Steel receiver, bolt has 4 rear locking lugs, select French walnut stock, adj. trigger, no sights except for .458 Mag. Mfg. 1967-mid-1980s.

$725	$650	$575	$525	$495	$460	$430	

MODEL 97-DL - various cals., configurations include Target, Takedown, and Sporter variations. No current U.S. importation.

Please contact the company directly for more information regarding pricing and availability on this model.

SHOTGUNS: O/U

Schultz & Larsen also manufactured a very limited quantity of O/U shotguns, including a 20 ga. boxlock. Values reflect shooting value more than collectibility.

SCHWABEN ARMS GMBH

Current manufacturer located in Rottweil, Germany. No current U.S. importation.

Schwaben Arms GmbH manufactures 600-800 guns annually. Production includes an extensive lineup of quality tactical rifles and carbines, primarily patterned after H&K models and other historically significant military rifles/carbines, including a .308 Win. cal. semi-auto MP5. Both commercial and military/law enforcement models are available. Please contact the factory directly for U.S. availability and pricing.

SCORPION

Current trademark of shotguns manufactured by the Hedef Arms Company, located in Konya, Turkey. No current U.S. importation.

A wide variety of semi-auto, slide action, and O/U shotguns are manufactured. Many configurations are available, including wood, synthetic, and carbon fiber stocks, various finishes, engraving, and gold inlays. Please contact the manufacturer for more information, including domestic availability and pricing.

GRADING - PPGS™	100%	98%	95%	90%	80%	70%	60%	LAST MSR

SCORPION TACTICAL

Previous AR-15 rifle manufacturer and current AR-15 parts and accessories manufacturer, located in Leander, TX.

Please refer to BlueBookOfGunValues.com to order the *Blue Book of AR-15s & Variations*, available as a book or online subscription.

SCOTT, W.C., LTD.

Previous manufacturer established during 1834, located in Birmingham, England. All operations ceased during 1991.

Established in 1834 by William Scott, located in Birmingham, England, and remained in the family until 1897. Scott then merged with P. Webley & Son to form Webley & Scott Revolver and Arms Co., Ltd. (later changed to Webley & Scott Ltd.). Even though Scott family members were no longer associated with this new company, the Scott product line was continued with the trademark intact until 1935. Thereafter, only a few guns were marked Scott. In 1979, Webley & Scott ceased manufacture of all firearms. A new company, W. & C. Scott, was formed in 1980 utilizing mostly employees of Webley & Scott. W. & C. Scott remained part of its parent company, Harris & Sheldon (also had controlling interest in Hardy and Churchill trademarks), until 1985 when Scott was purchased by Holland & Holland. Manufacture of Scott guns decreased substantially after the merger, and in September 1991, W. & C. Scott ceased operation altogether. During its 157 years of production, Scott and Webley & Scott produced approximately, 150,000 double guns, 10,000 rifles (either double or bolt-action) and thousands of single guns and single rifles.

SHOTGUNS: SxS

All W.C. Scott Shotguns were discontinued in 1990. W.C. Scott also manufactured many hammer guns that vary in price from $250-$2,500, depending on grade and original condition.

KINMOUNT - 12, 16, 20, or 28 ga., boxlock action, ejectors, deluxe checkered walnut, scroll engraving.

$6,500	**$5,750**	**$5,000**	**$4,500**	**$4,000**	**$3,000**	**$2,500**	***$11,000***

Add 20% for 28 ga. or .410 bore.
Add 10% for SNT.

BOWOOD - 12, 16, 20, or 28 ga., boxlock action, ejectors, deluxe checkered walnut, extensive scroll engraving.

$7,500	**$6,500**	**$5,750**	**$5,000**	**$4,500**	**$4,000**	**$3,500**	***$12,500***

Add 20% for 28 ga. or .410 bore.
Add 10% for SNT.

CHATSWORTH - 12, 16, 20, or 28 ga., top-of-the-line boxlock action, ejectors, deluxe checkered walnut, extensive scroll engraving.

$8,750	**$7,500**	**$6,500**	**$5,750**	**$5,000**	**$4,500**	**$4,000**	***$14,000***

Add 20% for 28 ga. or .410 bore.
Add 10% for SNT.

BLENHEIM - 12 bore only, upgraded models, custom-made to individual specifications, originally priced per individual order.

Specimen rarity precludes percentage grading pricing.

Individual appraisals have to be secured on this model.

SEARCY, B. & CO.

Current custom rifle manufacturer established in 1975, located in Boron, CA.

RIFLES: CUSTOM

B. Searcy & Co. manufactures a unique stainless steel double rifle in a variety of calibers. Current models include: PH Boxlock Model w/ejectors ($15,500 MSR), Classic ($20,000 MSR), Deluxe Grade (last MSR was $25,500), Back Action Sidelock ($30,000 MSR), .600 NE Sidelock ($50,000 MSR), .577 NE Boxlock ($25,000 MSR), .577 NE Sidelock ($35,000 MSR), .600 NE Boxlock ($45,000 MSR), .700 NE Boxlock (last MSR was $85,000), Under Lever Model (last MSR was $25,000), and the .700 NE Sidelock (last MRS was $100,000).

Beginning in 2010, B. Searcy & Co. makes a Rigby Bisell patterned rising bite sidelock in .450 NE cal., followed by a .577 and .500 NE cal. Each gun is built per order and prices begin at $45,000-$55,000.

B. Searcy also manufactures a bolt action rifle - starting price is $15,000, and many options are available. Additionally, a Stalking Rifle is available in cals. .22-250 Centerfire-.506 Gibbs with a base price of $8,500 or $14,500 for Takedown Rifle. Please contact the company directly for current model information, availability, pricing for options, and delivery time.

GRADING - PPGS™	100%	98%	95%	90%	80%	70%	60%	LAST MSR

SEARS, ROEBUCK AND CO.

Catalog merchandiser that, in addition to selling major trademark firearms, also private labeled many configurations of firearms (mostly longarms) under a variety of trademarks and logos (i.e., J.C. Higgins, Ted Williams, Ranger, etc.). Sears discontinued the sale of all firearms circa 1980, and the Ted Williams trademark was stopped circa 1978.

A general guideline for Sears Roebuck and related labels (most are marked "Sears, Roebuck and Co." on left side of barrel) is that values are generally lower than those of the major factory models from which they were derived. Remember, 99% of Sears Roebuck and related label guns get priced by their shootability factor in today's competitive marketplace, not collectibility. An extensive crossover listing (see Storebrand Cross-Over List) has been provided in the back of this text for linking up the various Sears Roebuck models to the original manufacturer with respective "crossover" model numbers.

SECURITY INDUSTRIES

Previous manufacturer located in Little Ferry, NJ.

REVOLVERS

MODEL PSS 38 DOUBLE ACTION – .38 Spl. cal., 5 shot cylinder, 2 in. barrel, stainless steel, fixed sights, wood grips. Mfg. 1973-78.

$175	$150	$140	$130	$125	$110	$100	

MODEL PM357 – .357 Mag. cal., similar to Model PSS 38, 2 1/2 in. barrel. Mfg. 1975-disc.

$225	$175	$165	$150	$140	$125	$110	

MODEL PPM 357 – .357 Mag. cal., 5 shot, 2 in. barrel, spurless hammer until 1977, new models have spur. Mfg. 1965-disc.

$225	$175	$165	$150	$140	$125	$110	

SEDCO INDUSTRIES, INC.

Previous manufacturer located in Lake Elsinore, CA until 1991.

PISTOLS: SEMI-AUTO

MODEL SP-22 – .22 LR cal., single action, 2 1/2 in. barrel, rotary safety, serrated slide, nickel, satin nickel (new 1990), or black metal finish, simulated pearl grips in white, blue, grey, or pink, 11 oz. Mfg. 1989-90 only.

$60	$55	$50	$45	$40	$35	$35	*$69*

SEDGLEY, R.F., INC.

Previous manufacturer located in Philadelphia, PA.

RIFLES: BOLT ACTION

SPRINGFIELD SPORTING RIFLE – .218 Bee, .220 Swift, .22-3000, .22-4000, .22 Hornet, .25-35 WCF, .250-3000 Sav., .257 Roberts, .270 Win., 7x57mm Mauser, or .30-06 cal., '03 Springfield bolt action, 24 in. barrel, Lyman receiver sight, checkered pistol grip stock, pre-WWII.

$1,250	$1,125	$995	$875	$750	$625	$495	

SPRINGFIELD CARBINE SPORTER – similar to Rifle, with 20 in. barrel, and full-length stock.

$1,450	$1,250	$1,125	$995	$875	$750	$625	

SEECAMP, L.W. CO., INC.

Current handgun manufacturer located in Southwick, MA. Previously located in Milford, CT. Dealer direct sales only.

Ludwig (Louis) Wilhelm Seecamp (1901-1989), after whom the company was named, was trained as a master gunsmith in the technical academy system of pre-WW II Germany. Having survived the Eastern Front in an elite Gebirgsjaeger (Mountain Troops) unit, he brought his family to the United States in 1959 by way of Canada. From 1959 until his retirement in 1971, he was the gun designer for O.F. Mossberg.

L.W. Seecamp Co, Inc. was founded in 1973 as a family business specializing in Ludwig's patented double action conversion of the venerable 1911 semi-auto pistol (Colt .45). This conversion, done during a period when the single-action versus double-action controversy was at its peak, resulted in the first commercially available DA .45 autoloaders anywhere in the world. Nearly 2000 such DA conversions were done from the early 70s to the early 80s.

PISTOLS: SEMI-AUTO

All Seecamp pistols are hand machined and fitted from stainless steel. Manufacture has always emphasized quality over quantity - this explains why values can exceed the company's retail pricing.

GRADING - PPGS™	100%	98%	95%	90%	80%	70%	60%	LAST MSR

LWS .25 ACP MODEL – .25 ACP cal., DAO, 2 in. barrel, 7 shot mag., stainless steel, matte finish, no sights, 12 oz. Approx. 4,000 mfg. 1981-85, reintroduced 2019.

MSR $510	$450	$350	$300	$250	$195	$165	$140

Add $55 for flat black finish (new 2019).

LWS .32 MODEL – .32 ACP cal., (mfg. recommends .32 ACP Win. Silvertip ammo only), DAO-delayed blowback, 2.06 in. barrel, stainless steel, 6 shot mag., no sights, 11 1/2 oz. Mfg. began Jan. 1985.

MSR $510	$450	$350	$300	$250	$195	$165	$140

Add $25 for California edition (with trigger mounted safety, disc. 2019, reintroduced 2021).
Add $55 for flat black finish (new 2019).

This model is available in either a matte or polished finish. The polished finish carries a slight premium.

MATCHED PAIR – includes both .25 ACP and .32 ACP pistols with the same serial number, approx. 200 sets were mfg. before the BATFE stopped this practice. Disc.

	$1,200	$1,000	$850	$740	$620	$515	$440

This set contained a matte finished .25 ACP and a polished .32 ACP.

LWS .380 MODEL – .380 ACP cal. (mfg. recommends .380 ACP Win. Silvertip ammo only), identical in appearance to the LWS 32 Model, DAO-delayed blowback, 2.06 in. barrel, delayed blowback mechanism, polished stainless steel, 6 shot, checkered black glass filled nylon grips, no sights, 11 1/2 oz. Very limited production beginning 2000.

MSR $595	$525	$400	$350	$300	$250	$200	$175

Add $55 for flat black finish (new 2019).

SEEKINS PRECISION

Current AR-15 style and bolt action firearms manufacturer located in Lewiston, ID.

Please refer to BlueBookOfGunValues.com to order the *Blue Book of AR-15s & Variations*, available as a book or online subscription.

SEITZ

Previous manufacturer located in Portland, OR circa mid-1980s-1993.

SHOTGUNS: SINGLE BARREL, TRAP

SINGLE BARREL TRAP GUN – 12 ga. only, single barrel, various barrel lengths, pull or release trigger, only 45 guns mfg.

	$18,500	$16,000	$13,000	$10,000	$8,500	$7,700	$6,950

SEMMERLING

Current trademark owned by American Derringer Corp., located in Waco, TX. Previously manufactured by Semmerling Corporation, located in Boston, MA from 1977-1982.

Less than 600 LM-4 pistols were originally mfg. by the Semmerling Corporation.

PISTOLS: SLIDE ACTION

LM-4 PISTOL – .45 ACP cal., 2 in. barrel, blue, smallest .45 ACP repeater available, 4 shot mag., slide is worked manually with thumb on serrated slide-top, extremely high quality, hand fitted and choice of finishes include chrome, electroless nickel, or high polish blue.

Chrome	$2,950	$2,600	$2,300	$2,100	$1,950	$1,725	$1,600
Electroless nickel	$3,200	$2,950	$2,600	$2,300	$2,100	$1,950	$1,725
High polish blue	$4,950	$4,500	$4,000	$3,600	$3,200	$2,800	$2,500

The original U.S. Army contract pistol mfg. by Semmerling in Boston had an MSR for $5,000. Earlier mfg. by Lichtman will also command a premium over values listed.

* ***LM-4 Pistol (Current Mfg.)***

Please refer to the American Derringer in the A section.

SENNI ARMS CO.

Previous manufacturer located in Queensland, Australia until circa 2016. No current U.S. importation.

Senni Arms manufactured a complete line of 1911-style semi-auto pistols that included the Stinger, 2010, Black Snake, Lawson, Silhouette, Razorback, and the Trooper. Senni Arms also manufactured the Siege semi-auto tactical shotgun and the Elysium M4 semi-auto tactical carbine.

SENTINEL ARMS

Previous importer of Arsenal Bulgaria pistols and rifles.

GRADING - PPGS™	100%	98%	95%	90%	80%	70%	60%	LAST MSR

SERBU FIREARMS, INC.

Current manufacturer located in Tampa, FL.

Serbu Firearms also manufactures a Super-Shorty short barreled slide action shotgun based on the Remington 870 or Mossberg 500. These shotguns are classified NFA only.

RIFLES: BOLT ACTION

BFG-50 RIFLE/CARBINE - .50 BMG cal., single shot bolt action, 22 (carbine), 29 1/2 (rifle), or 36 (alloy or stainless, new 2011) in. match grade barrel with muzzle brake, AR-15 style trigger and safety, screwed-on Picatinny rail, parkerized finish, 17-22 lbs. New 1999.

MSR $2,520	$2,150	$1,900	$1,600	$1,450	$1,200	$950	$750

Add $185 for bi-pod.
Add $400 for 36 in. heavy barrel (alloy or stainless, new 2011).

BFG-50A - .50 BMG cal., gas operated, 26 in. alloy steel barrel with 8 port Shark Brake muzzle brake, 10 shot mag., 3-lug bolt, sliding plate extractor, dual plunger ejectors, removable barrel extension and handguard, includes Serbu Picatinny bipod and Plano case with cut foam, black PQP Nitride and manganese phosphate finish, 23 lbs. New 2008.

MSR $7,720	$6,550	$5,750	$4,900	$4,450	$3,600	$2,950	$2,300

RN-50 - .50 BMG or .50 DTC (many cals. available) cal., unique takedown action, 18, 22, 29, or 36 in. barrel, tubular stock, pistol grip, approx. 13-25 lbs. New 2018.

MSR $1,259	$1,050	$950	$800	$750	$600	$475	$375

Add $400 for 36 in. heavy barrel or $125 for 18 in. barrel.

SERENGETI RIFLES, INC.

Previous custom rifle manufacturer and stock maker located in Kalispell, MT until 2010.

Serengeti was famous for its stealth lamination stocks, originally called the Acra-Bond laminate. Stealth lamination technology provides greater stock stability, while preserving the full beauty, figure, and feel of a traditional walnut stock.

Please refer to the Kilimanjaro Rifles listings in the K section for more information on the new Serengeti rifle.

RIFLES: BOLT ACTION, CUSTOM

Serengeti Rifles Inc. manufactured a complete line of high-quality, custom-order bolt action rifles, including the Standard African ($7,369 last MSR), Dangerous Game African ($8,249 last MSR), Montanan ($6,269 last MSR), Red Mist ($6,269 last MSR), TigerCat ($6,869 last MSR), and the Walkabout ($6,269 last MSR). A number of options were available. Additionally, Serengeti Rifles manufactured its own line of proprietary actions and high quality walnut stocks.

SERO LTD.

Current rifle manufacturer located in Budapest, Hungary. No U.S. importation.

RIFLES: SEMI-AUTO

GEPARD GM6 LYNX - 14.5x114mm Soviet or .50 BMG cal., bullpup configuration, 28 3/4 in. barrel with muzzle brake, 100% desert camo coverage, 5 shot mag. is located in back of the pistol grip, full Picatinny rail, 25.3 lbs. New 2012.

Please contact the company directly for U.S. availability and pricing.

SHADOW SYSTEMS LLC

Current manufacturer of semi-auto pistols established in 2016, located in Plano, TX.

PISTOLS: SEMI-AUTO

DR920 COMBAT - 9x19mm cal., striker fire, compact or full size, textured polymer frame, 4 or 4 1/2 in. match grade, unthreaded, spiral fluted, stainless steel barrel, 10, 15, or 17 shot mag., optional magwell, stainless steel construction, flat-faced aluminum trigger, green Tritium night front sight and black serrated rear sight, aggressive textured grips, beavertail safety, front and rear directional serrations, interchangeable backstraps, recoil control ledge, black Nitride or Bronze TiCN finish, 23 oz. New 2021.

MSR $799	$700	$650	$550	$500	$400	$325	$250

Add $100 for full size frame.

DR920 ELITE - 9x19mm cal., striker fire, compact, or full size, textured polymer frame, 4 or 4 1/2 in. match grade, unthreaded, spiral fluted, stainless steel barrel, 10, 15, or 17 shot mag., optional magwell, stainless steel construction, flat-faced aluminum trigger, green Tritium night front sight and black serrated rear sight, standard optic cut, aggressive textured grips, beavertail safety, front, rear, and top side directional serrations, interchangeable backstraps, recoil control ledge, black Nitride or

GRADING - PPGS™	100%	98%	95%	90%	80%	70%	60%	LAST MSR

Bronze TiCN finish, available as compact frame long slide, 23 oz. New 2021.

MSR $969	$850	$750	$650	$600	$475	$400	$300	

Add $20 for full size frame.

Add $30 for compact long slide variation.

MR918 COMBAT – 9mm Para. cal., polymer frame, 4 in. 416R stainless steel spiral fluted barrel, 17-4 stainless steel slide with DLC finish, forward and rear slide serrations, two 15 shot Magpul mags., flat-faced polymer trigger, TTI Ultimate connector, 4-4.5 lb. trigger pull, solid black metal rear sight with high visibility green outlined Tritium front post, 3 interchangeable grip backstraps, 1 lb. 5.3 oz. Disc. 2020.

	$750	$650	$575	$525	$425	$350	$290	*$879*

Add $50 for RMR cut.

MR918 ELITE – 9mm Para. cal., polymer frame, 4 or 4 1/2 (threaded) in. 416R stainless steel spiral fluted barrel, 17-4 stainless steel slide with DLC finish, forward and rear slide serrations with window cuts, two 15 shot Magpul mags., flat-faced trigger, TTI Ultimate connector, solid black metal rear sight with high visibility green outlined Tritium front post, slide cut for RMR, 3 interchangeable grip backstraps, 1 lb. 4.5 oz. Disc. 2020.

	$850	$750	$650	$585	$475	$385	$325	*$989*

Add $50 for RMR cut or $60 for RMR cut with threaded barrel.

C. SHARPS ARMS, INC.

Current manufacturer located in Big Timber, MT.

C. Sharps Arms Co. Inc. currently distributes smokeless powder replicas of C. Sharps rifles/carbines and the Winchester Model 1885 single shot. They are able to shoot both smokeless and black powder loads. Most models are available in the following cals.: .38-55, .40-50, .40-65, .40-70, .40-90, .45-70, .45-90, .45-100, .45-110, .45-120, .50-70, .50-90, .50-100, and .50-140. All models are authentically reproduced and high quality.

RIFLES: REPRODUCTIONS, SHARPS BLACK POWDER

Because each rifle is a special order, there are many options available which would be added to the base price shown. Please contact the company directly for more information including upgrades, serial numbers, and delivery time.

NEW MODEL 1874 BRIDGEPORT SPORTING RIFLE – various cals., 26, 28, or 30 in. tapered octagon barrel, DT, drilled and tapped, straight grip walnut stock with Schnabel forend, checkered steel buttplate, color case hardened receiver, approx. 10 1/2 lbs.

MSR $1,995	$1,695	$1,485	$1,270	$1,150	$925	$775	$625	

In addition to the 1874 Sporting Model, a custom long range target rifle or Schuetzen short range target rifle is available in this model.

NEW MODEL 1874 HARTFORD SPORTING RIFLE – various cals., 26, 28, or 30 in. tapered octagon barrel, DT, drilled and tapped, Hartford semi-crescent military and sporting smooth steel buttplate and silver nose cap, straight grain American walnut stock with oil finish, color case hardened receiver, approx. 10 1/2 lbs.

MSR $2,195	$1,875	$1,650	$1,400	$1,275	$1,050	$850	$675	

1874 SEMI-CUSTOM CLASSIC HARTFORD SPORTING RIFLE – .38-55, .40-65, .40-70, .45-70, or .50-70 cal., 26, 28, or 30 in. tapered octagon barrel, single trigger with small lever or double set trigger, drilled and tapped, Hartford style crescent butt with toe plate (in steel or brass), cheek rest with accent line and silver nose cap, straight grain American walnut with oil finish, 14 in. LOP, metal finish, color case hardened receiver group and buttplate, 10 1/2 lbs.

MSR $2,595	$2,200	$1,925	$1,650	$1,500	$1,225	$1,000	$800	

NEW MODEL 1874 CARBINE HUNTER – .38-55, .40-65, .40-70, .45-70, or .50-70 cal., 22, 24, or 26 in. tapered round barrel with buckhorn and silver blade front sights, semi-crescent military style buttstock, slender forend, color case hardened receiver, DT, drilled and tapped.

MSR $1,925	$1,640	$1,450	$1,250	$1,125	$900	$750	$600	

CUSTOM NEW MODEL 1874 BOSS GUN – various cals., 30, 32, or 34 in. Standard or No. 1 heavy tapered octagon barrel, deluxe long range tang sight, Buckhorn and globe with post front sight, Hartford nose cap, double set trigger, straight grip smooth steel shotgun butt, Hartford style heavy buttstock, cheek rest with accent line, Hartford forend with cast German silver nose cap, Grade I hand engraving, right side with S-Banner with BOSS GUN on raised receiver flat, left side with oval for customer initials, plus accent engraving on lockplate and receiver, French Grey metal finish on rec. group and buttplate, 9 3/4-10 3/4 (standard) or 12-13 1/2 (heavy) lbs.

MSR $4,995	$4,250	$3,725	$3,200	$2,900	$2,350	$1,925	$1,500	

Add $750 for Grade II engraving (includes additional engraving on all receiver group parts). Disc. 2020.

GRADING - PPGS™	100%	98%	95%	90%	80%	70%	60%	LAST MSR

NEW MODEL 1874 CUSTOM GRADE III ENGRAVED BOSS GUN – .45-70 cal., 34 in. heavy tapered part octagon barrel with Hartford collar, cut rifling and lapped, hand-polished to high gloss finish, presentation Fiddleback American walnut stock, full pattern checkering, silver nose cap, French grey receiver group and smooth steel buttplate, globe with post and ball front sight, buckhorn rear and deluxe L-R tang sight, includes Grade III engraving. Mfg. 2014-2020.

	$5,900	$5,175	$4,425	$4,025	$3,250	$2,675	$2,100	*$6,950*

NEW MODEL 1874 HARTFORD SPORTING RIFLE (CUSTOM MODEL) – various cals., 34 in. No. 1 heavy tapered octagon barrel, deluxe long range tang sight, Buckhorn and globe with post front sight, Hartford nose cap, double set trigger, straight grip smooth steel shotgun butt, X fancy Hartford style heavy buttstock, cheek rest with accent line, Hartford forend with cast German silver nose cap, French Grey metal finish on rec. group and buttplate, 9 3/4-10 3/4 lbs. Mfg. 2014-disc.

	$3,400	$2,975	$2,550	$2,325	$1,875	$1,550	$1,200	*$3,995*

1874 HEAVY HARTFORD LONG RANGE SPORTING & TARGET RIFLE (CUSTOM MODEL) – various cals., 34 in. No. 1 heavy part octagon barrel with Hartford collar, front globe sight, deluxe long range tang sight, 14 in. LOP, double set triggers, ebony inlay, full pattern hand checkering, forend ebony nose cap, Presentation American walnut stock, hand polished to high luster then back to satin finish, 12 1/2 lbs. New 2014.

MSR $7,950	$6,750	$5,900	$5,075	$4,595	$3,725	$3,050	$2,375	

NEW MODEL 1875 CARBINE – various cals., 24 in. tapered round barrel. Mfg. 1996-1998.

	$1,350	$1,100	$875	$750	$675	$600	$500	*$810*

1875 SHARPS CLASSIC RIFLE – various cals., 26, 28, or 30 in. tapered full octagon blued barrel, single trigger, drilled and tapped, receiver with octagon top, 14 in. LOP, Hartford style forend with cast German steel nosecap, premium straight grain oil finished Amercan walnut straight grip buttstock with crescent butt and toeplate, metal finish, color case hardened receiver group and buttplate, 9 lbs. 8 oz.

MSR $1,775	$1,500	$1,325	$1,125	$1,025	$825	$700	$550	

NEW MODEL 1875 BUSINESS RIFLE – various cals., receiver with round top, 28 in. heavy tapered round barrel. Disc. 1998.

	$1,350	$1,100	$875	$750	$675	$600	$500	*$810*

Add $50 for barrel sights.

NEW MODEL 1875 CLASSIC HARTFORD – receiver with octagon top, 26, 28, or 30 in. tapered full octagon barrel, straight grip stock with steel toe plate, 9 1/2 lbs. Mfg. 1992-2014.

	$2,125	$1,860	$1,595	$1,450	$1,175	$975	$750	*$2,495*

NEW MODEL 1875 SPORTING RIFLE – various cals., 28 or 30 in. tapered octagon blued barrel, receiver with round crown, single trigger, drilled and tapped, Bridgeport checkered steel buttplate, 14 in. LOP, premium straight grain oil finished American walnut straight grip buttstock, Schnabel style forend, metal finish, case hardened receiver group and buttplate, 9 lbs. 4 oz.

MSR $1,475	$1,250	$1,095	$950	$850	$700	$575	$450	

NEW MODEL 1875 TARGET SPORTING RIFLE – .38-55, .40-65, .40-70 Sharps Straight, .45-70 Govt., or .45-90 cal., 30 in. heavy tapered round barrel American walnut stock with pistol grip, black buttplate, color case receiver, drilled and tapped, single trigger, 11 lbs. Limited mfg. 2004 only, reintroduced 2011.

MSR $1,425	$1,215	$1,065	$910	$825	$675	$550	$450	

NEW MODEL 1875 SADDLE RIFLE – various cals., receiver with octagon top, 26 in. barrel only. Disc. 1998.

	$1,475	$1,200	$950	$800	$700	$600	$500	*$910*

CUSTOM NEW MODEL 1877 – .44-90, .45-70 Govt., .45-90, or .45-100 cal., 32 or 34 in. tapered round barrel, presentation grade American or English walnut stock, checkered pistol grip and forend, ebony forend tip, classic long range sights, 10 lbs. Limited production 2004 only.

	$5,250	$4,750	$4,450	$4,100	$3,750	$3,450	$3,100	*$5,500*

CUSTOM 1877 LONG RANGE TARGET RIFLE – various cals. including .44-90, .45-70, .45-90, or .45-100 Sharps or Rem. cal., single shot, 32 or 34 in. tapered round barrel with the Rigby flat, classic long range target sights with windage, Presentation American or English walnut stock, checkered pistol grip and forend, ebony forend tip and inlay in grip, engraving and presentation cases available for additional charge, approx. 10 lbs. Limited to custom production only beginning 2014.

MSR $6,000	$5,100	$4,465	$3,825	$3,475	$2,800	$2,925	$1,795	

MSR reflects base price only. Please contact the company directly for more information including options, upgrades, serial numbers, and delivery time.

GRADING - PPGS™	100%	98%	95%	90%	80%	70%	60%	LAST MSR

* ***Model 1877 Standard Long Range Target Rifle*** – various cals. including .44-90, .45-70, .45-90, or .45-100 Sharps or Rem. cal., single shot, 30 in. tapered oct. barrel, classic long range target sights with windage, American walnut stock, checkered pistol grip and forend, ebony forend tip, engraving and presentation cases available for additional charge, approx. 10 lbs.

MSR $2,590	$2,250	$1,975	$1,695	$1,535	$1,245	$1,015	$850	

* ***Model 1877 J.P. Lower Style Rifle*** – various cals. including .44-90, .45-70, .45-90, or .45-100 Sharps or Rem. cal., single shot, 26, 28, or 30 in. tapered oct. barrel, classic long range target sights with windage, American walnut stock with checkered steel buttplate, schnable forend, engraving and presentation cases available for additional charge, approx. 10 lbs.

MSR $2,440	$2,075	$1,815	$1,550	$1,410	$935	$810	$700	

MODEL 1877 PRESENTATION GRADE CASED LONG RANGE RIFLE – long range cals., 32 or 34 in. cut rifled and hand lapped tapered round barrel with Rigby flat, high grade satin finish, engraved and accented with gold inlay and wire, globe sight with apertures and spirit level, French grey receiver, Presentation grade black and English walnut stock with full fill satin finish, engraved brass plate, includes two custom turnscrews, cleaning rod, dust mop, and oil bottle, custom and individually built one rifle at a time by master craftsmen and artists, reserved serial numbers 77-001 to 77-025. Limited mfg. beginning 2014.

This model is is POR.

1879 HEPBURN MID-RANGE TARGET & SPORTING RIFLE – .22 RF cal., 30 in. tapered octagon barrel, Soule mid-range vernier tang and globe sights, semi-fancy walnut pistol grip stock, cheek rest with accent line, forend with ebony nose cap, accent panels at receiver, double set trigger, color cased receiver and smooth or checkered steel buttplate. New 2014.

MSR $3,100	$2,675	$2,275	$1,950	$1,725	$1,400	$1,125	$900	

Subtract $500 if without sight package.

1885 CUSTOM ENGRAVED GRADE II HIGHWALL SPORTING RIFLE – various cals., 30 in. tapered part octagon barrel with high luster or satin finish, single set trigger, French Grey receiver and buttplate, fancy American walnut pistol grip stock with silver inlay, cheek rest with accent line, forend with silver inlay in tip and hand checkered, satin oil finish, Grade II traditional Highwall pattern engraving. New 2014.

MSR $4,800	$4,075	$3,575	$3,050	$2,775	$2,250	$1,850	$1,450	

1885 CUSTOM ENGRAVED GRADE III CLASSIC SPORTING RIFLE – various cals., 28 in. tapered part octagon satin finished barrel, C.S.A. New Ideal tang and silver blade front sights, single set trigger, oil finished XXX fancy American walnut stock, crescent buttplate, pistol grip with ebony inlay, cheek rest with accent line, forend with ebony inlay and hand checkered, Grade III traditional Highwall pattern engraving, French Grey action group. New 2014.

MSR $6,250	$5,325	$4,675	$4,000	$3,625	$2,950	$2,400	$1,875	

NEW MODEL 1885 HIGHWALL & LOWWALL CLASSIC RIFLE – various cals., 18, 20, 22, 24, 26, 28, or 30 in. tapered full octagon blued barrel, receiver with octagon top, single trigger, drilled and tapped, Bridgeport checkered steel buttplate, 14 in. LOP, straight grip American walnut stock, crescent butt with cheek rest and silver inlay in forend tip, metal finish, color case hardened or French Grey receiver and buttplate, 9 lbs. 4 oz.

MSR $1,975	$1,675	$1,475	$1,250	$1,150	$925	$775	$625	

NEW MODEL 1885 HIGHWALL & LOWWALL SPORTING RIFLE – various cals. including .22 LR, .22 Hornet, .219 Zipper, .30-40 Krag, .32-40, .348 Win., .38-55 WCF, .40-65, .405 Win., .444 Marlin, or .45-70 cal., patterned after the Winchester Model 1885 single shot, falling block action, 26, 28, or 30 in. tapered full octagon barrel, receiver with octagon top, drilled and tapped, Bridgeport checkered steel buttplate, 14 in. LOP, Schnabel style forend, premium straight grain oil finished American walnut straight grip buttstock, metal finish, color case hardened receiver group and buttplate (French Grey receiver also available), 9 lbs. 4 oz. Mfg. 1992-2008, reintroduced 2011.

MSR $1,875	$1,595	$1,395	$1,195	$1,085	$875	$725	$575	

1885 HIGHWALL SCHUETZEN RIFLE – various cals. including .30-30, .32-40, .38-55, or .40-50 SS cal., 24, 26, 28, or 30 in. full tapered octagon blued barrel with matte finish, adj. palm rest, octagon or round rec. top, 14 in. LOP, globe front sights, single set trigger, straight grain American walnut stock, pistol grip and cheek rest on left side, color case hardened receiver group and Schuetzen buttplate with bottom tang. Mfg. 2014-disc.

	$2,450	$2,150	$1,850	$1,675	$1,350	$1,100	$875	*$2,875*

GRADING - PPGS™	100%	98%	95%	90%	80%	70%	60%	LAST MSR

1885 LOWWALL SCHUETZEN RIFLE – various cals. including .22 LR, .22 Hornet, .38-40 WCF, or .40-55 SS cal., 24, 26, 28, or 30 in. full tapered octagon barrel, single set trigger, octagon or round receiver top, color cased receiver group and Schuetzen buttplate with bottom tang, blued barrel with matte finish adj. palm rest, 14 in. LOP, globe front sights, straight grain American walnut stock, pistol grip and cheek rest on left side. Mfg. 2014-disc.

	$2,450	$2,150	$1,850	$1,675	$1,350	$1,100	$875	*$2,875*

HOPKINS & ALLEN RIFLE – .22 LR, .22 Mag., or .17 HMR cal., rifles, 16-22 in. tapered octagon barrel, gold bead blade front sight and marble semi-buckhorn barrel sight, American walnut stock and forend, hard rubber checkered buttplate. New 2019.

MSR $830	$700	$600	$550	$475	$400	$325	$250

SHARPS, CHRISTIAN

Previously manufactured by Sharps Rifle Manufacturing Company circa 1851-1855 and located in Windsor, VT. Also manufactured in Hartford, CT under same name between 1855-1874. Reorganized as Sharps Rifle Company in 1876 with production resuming in Hartford (1876 only) and Bridgeport, CT from 1877-1881.

100%	98%	95%	90%	80%	70%	60%	50%	40%	30%	20%	10%

HANDGUNS

SHARPS BREECH-LOADING SINGLE SHOT PISTOL – 5 in. round barrel, dropping block, lever action single shot percussion, patent 1848 style carbine action of reduced size, all iron mountings, walnut grips. Made mid-1850s in Philadelphia, about 850 total of two types produced.

* ***Type I*** – .31-.34 cal., "SHARPS PATENT/ARMS MFrd FAIRMOUNT/PHILA. PA" stamped within an oval panel on left side of frame, serial numbered from 1 to approx. 500.

N/A	N/A	$10,000	$8,000	$7,500	$6,500	$6,000	$5,000	$4,500	$4,000	$3,500	$2,500

* ***Type 2*** – .36 cal., 6 1/2 in. round barrel, "C. SHARPS & CO./PHILA.PA." or "C. SHARPS & CO'S RIFLE WORKS/PHILA. PA." stamped on right frame, "C. SHARPS/PATENT/1848" stamped on left side of frame. Approx. 350 mfg., serial numbers between 470-950.

N/A	N/A	$11,000	$8,500	$8,000	$7,500	$6,500	$6,000	$5,000	$4,500	$4,000	$3,500

SHARPS PISTOL RIFLE – .31 and .38 cal., lever action single shot percussion, using the single shot pistol action with the additions of a longer barrel and a rifle pistol grip buttstock, various barrel lengths with 28 in. being most common, early rifles have German silver buttplate, forend cap and escutcheon plates on forend which is held on by a wedge, standard production uses iron mountings, dropping block. Made mid-1850s in Philadelphia. About 650 total of two types produced.

* ***Type I*** – pistol action, ramrod mounted under barrel, German silver mountings, "C. SHARPS PATENT 1848-52" marked on left side of frame. Approx. 50 mfg.

N/A	N/A	$15,000	$10,000	$9,000	$8,500	$7,500	$7,000	$6,500	$6,000	$4,500	$3,500

* ***Type 2*** – standard model, iron mountings, no ramrod, "C. SHARPS & CO. PHILADA. PA" marked on left side of frame. Approx. 600 made.

N/A	N/A	$10,000	$9,000	$8,000	$7,500	$7,000	$6,500	$6,000	$5,500	$4,500	$3,500

REVOLVER, PERCUSSION – .25 cal., 3 in. octagonal tip-up barrel with rib, 6 shot. Mfg. circa 1850s in Philadelphia, approx. 2000 produced.

N/A	N/A	$6,000	$4,500	$4,000	$3,700	$3,500	$3,200	$2,800	$2,500	$2,300	$1,750

PEPPERBOX PISTOL – also marked Sharps and Hankins, breech-loading, .22, .30, or .32 rimfire cal., rotating firing pin, brass frame with silver plating or case-hardening on iron frame.

* ***Pepperbox Pistol First Model*** – 5 variations, 2 1/2 in. barrel. Scarcer variations can be worth up to 150% more.

N/A	N/A	$1,200	$1,000	$900	$750	$700	$650	$550	$500	$450	$400

* ***Pepperbox Pistol Second Model*** – 5 variations, 3 in. barrel. Scarcer variations can be worth up to 150% more.

N/A	N/A	$1,200	$1,000	$950	$800	$750	$600	$550	$500	$450	$400

* ***Pepperbox Pistol Third Model*** – Sharps and Hankins markings, .32 rimfire short, 4 variations, 3 1/2 in. barrel. Premium for scarcer variations.

N/A	N/A	$1,250	$1,100	$950	$800	$750	$600	$550	$500	$450	$400

100%	98%	95%	90%	80%	70%	60%	50%	40%	30%	20%	10%

* ***Pepperbox Pistol Fourth Model*** - 4 variations, 2 1/2, 3, or 3 1/2 in. barrel, bird's head grip, .32 rimfire long. Premium for scarcer variations.

N/A	N/A	$1,800	$1,500	$1,200	$1,000	$900	$800	$700	$600	$500	$400

RIFLES: BREECH LOADING

The earliest Sharps rifles and carbines were made for Christian Sharps by A.S. Nippes, in Mill Creek, PA circa 1850, and a year later by Robbins and Lawrence Co. of Windsor, VT. Not until 1856 did the Sharps Rifle Co. of Hartford, CT begin to manufacture its own guns.

MODEL 1849 RIFLE - .36 or .44 cal., percussion breech loader, 30 in. barrels and brass patchboxes were standard, very few examples exist, less than 100 mfg, serial numbered. These are the first of all Sharps long guns, there is no fixed value range.

Depending on condition, values could range from $5,000 to $50,000+.

MODEL 1850 RIFLE - .36 or .44 cal., incorporated the Maynard tape primer on right side of breech, features similar to Model 1849, approx. 150 mfg. by A.S. Nippes, very rare.

Depending on condition, values could range from $5,000 to $40,000.

MODEL 1851 CARBINE - .52 cal. percussion, 21 5/8 barrel, hammer mounted inside frame, Maynard tape primer. Approx. 1,800 mfg. by Robbins and Lawrence, 200 went to U.S. Government - these will bring a premium.

N/A	N/A	$12,000	$10,000	$9,500	$8,500	$8,000	$7,500	$6,500	$5,500	$4,500	$3,500

MODEL 1852 CARBINE - this design became standard for all the Sharps for the next two decades, first to be called "slant breech," established Christian Sharps as a major gun manufacturer. Approx. 5,000 mfg. by Robbins and Lawrence, U.S. military markings will command a premium.

N/A	N/A	$8,000	$7,500	$6,500	$6,000	$5,500	$5,000	$4,500	$4,000	$3,500	$3,000

MODEL 1853 CARBINE - .52 cal., very similar to Model 1852, with walnut stock and brass patchbox, Sharps patented pellet primer feed, ser. no. range 9000-19000.

N/A	N/A	$9,000	$8,500	$7,500	$6,500	$6,000	$5,500	$5,000	$4,000	$3,500	$2,500

Approx. 10,000 mfg. by Robbins and Lawrence 1854-1858, an additional 3,000 rifles mfg. - subtract 25%.

MODEL 1855 CARBINE - .52 cal., U.S. military model, all with Maynard tape primer, this was the period during which Robbins and Lawrence failed, and Sharps Rifle Co. took over production. 800 mfg.

N/A	N/A	$12,000	$11,000	$10,000	$9,000	$8,500	$8,000	$7,000	$6,500	$5,500	$5,000

Sharps "New Model"

Manufactured in Hartford, CT by Sharps Rifle Manufacturing Co. circa 1859-1866. Visibly different from earlier models because of straight breech and pellet priming feature built into lock plate. Approx. 115,000 were built, all in .52 cal. breechloading paper cartridge. Carbines had 22 in. barrels, rifles came standard with 30 in. round barrels. After ser. nos. reached 100,000, a "C" prefix was used in the number - i.e. C500 represents ser. no. 100,500.

MODEL 1859 CARBINE - standard with all-iron furniture and patchbox, first 3,000 had brass instead of iron, ser. no. range 30000-75000. Approx. 33,000 mfg.

N/A	N/A	$8,000	$7,000	$6,000	$5,500	$5,000	$4,500	$4,000	$3,500	$3,000	$2,500

MODEL 1863 CARBINE - made with and w/o iron patchbox, ser. no. range 75,000 - 140,000. Approx. 65,000 mfg. - those with patchbox will bring a premium.

N/A	N/A	$9,000	$7,000	$6,000	$5,500	$4,800	$4,500	$4,000	$3,500	$3,000	$2,500

MODEL 1865 CARBINE - made w/o patchbox, ser. no. range 140000-145000. Only 5,000 mfg.

N/A	N/A	$7,000	$6,500	$5,000	$4,500	$4,000	$3,750	$3,500	$3,250	$3,000	$2,500

MODEL 1859 RIFLE - iron patchbox only, long forearm fastened with three barrel bands, approx. 4,300 mfg. in carbine ser. range with lug on barrel for attachment of saber bayonet. Approx. 600 were mfg. with 36 in. long barrel - these will command a premium.

N/A	N/A	$8,000	$7,500	$6,500	$5,500	$5,000	$4,500	$4,000	$3,500	$3,000	$2,500

COFFEE MILL MODEL - experimental variation buttstock with a grinding device and detachable handle that was fitted to several Model 1859 & 1863 Carbines. Designed to provide a quick and easy method for cavalry troops in the field to process coffee beans or corn for meals. Field trials are believed to have been in Trenton, NJ circa 1863. Very few originals known - no official records indicating government acceptance. Original condition carbines are extremely rare and values could range from $15,000-$65,000.

Buyer beware! Many fakes exist.

100%	98%	95%	90%	80%	70%	60%	50%	40%	30%	20%	10%

MODEL 1863 RIFLE – adapted for socket bayonet, shared ser. range with carbine. Approx. 6,000 mfg.

N/A N/A $7,500 $6,500 $5,000 $4,500 $4,250 $4,000 $3,500 $3,350 $2,750 $2,250

MODEL 1865 RIFLE – only 1,000 mfg. in carbine ser. range.

N/A N/A $8,000 $7,500 $7,000 $6,500 $6,000 $5,500 $5,000 $4,500 $4,000 $3,500

Sharps Cartridge Conversions

In 1867, the U.S. government decided to convert their percussion Sharps carbines and rifles to the new .50/70 metallic cartridge. Approx. 31,000 carbines and 1,000 rifles were converted by the Sharps Co. Any original, six groove barrels that were worn beyond specification had a groove liner installed. Those barrels meeting specs. remained unaltered. All buttstocks were stamped on the left side with "D.F.C." in a ribbon cartouche, the initials for the principal sub-inspector, David F. Clark. Damaged buttstocks were all replaced with the plain (no patchbox) Model 1865 buttstock, regardless of the model of the carbine; however, many of the old style buttplates with notches for patchboxes were retained.

.50/70 CARBINES – most had relined three groove barrels, approx. 31,000 remodeled. Those found with original six groove barrels will command a slight premium, as will those Model 1859s & Model 1863s with original patchbox buttstocks.

N/A N/A $5,500 $5,000 $4,500 $4,250 $4,000 $3,500 $3,000 $2,750 $2,500 $2,000

.50/70 RIFLES – all had three groove relined barrels, approx. 1,000 converted in 1867. More rare, but do not command any higher prices than their carbine counterparts.

SPRINGFIELD/SHARPS MODEL 1870-1871 – approx. 1,000 rifles and 300 carbines altered by Springfield Armory to fire .50/70 metallic cartridge, in addition to those done by Sharps Co., rifle barrels 35 1/2 in., carbine barrels 22 in., receivers color case hardened, all other metal parts bright finish, own ser. range, and numbered on receiver tang and left side of barrel.

* ***Springfield/Sharps Model 1870-1871 Rifles***

N/A N/A $5,500 $5,250 $5,000 $4,500 $4,000 $3,500 $2,500 $2,000 $1,500 $1,200

* ***Springfield/Sharps Model 1870-1871 Carbines***

N/A N/A $8,000 $7,850 $7,500 $7,250 $7,000 $6,500 $6,250 $6,000 $5,500 $5,000

Sharps Metallic Cartridge Models

MODEL 1874 – mfg. in several configurations and a variety of calibers, designed to fire metallic cartridges and was not a conversion from percussion parts, made famous for its deadly accuracy at long distances and became known as the "Buffalo Rifle" of its day. Mfg. in Hartford, CT circa 1874-76, and in Bridgeport, CT circa 1881.

* ***Model 1874 Sporting Model*** – .40, .44, .45, or .50 cal., variety of barrel lengths and weights, many special order features. Approx. 6,500 mfg.

N/A N/A $8,000 $7,500 $6,500 $6,000 $5,500 $5,000 $4,500 $4,000 $3,500 $3,000

* ***Model 1874 Business Rifle*** – no frills version of the 1874 Sporting, with shorter, round barrel and open sights.

N/A N/A $6,000 $5,500 $5,000 $4,500 $4,000 $3,500 $3,250 $3,000 $2,750 $2,500

* ***Model 1874 Military Rifle*** – .45/70 or .50/70 cal., long forearm and three barrel bands. Approx. 1,700 mfg.

N/A N/A $7,000 $6,500 $6,000 $5,000 $4,000 $3,750 $3,500 $3,250 $3,000 $2,500

* ***Model 1874 Military Carbine*** – most in .50/70 cal., very similar to previous Sharps carbines. Less than 500 mfg.

N/A N/A $9,000 $8,500 $8,000 $7,750 $7,500 $7,000 $6,000 $5,500 $5,000 $4,500

* ***Model 1874 Meachan Type Conversion*** – most in .45/70 cal., very similar to Business Rifle, with both round and octagon barrels, mfg. from Civil War Sharps carbine actions and surplus, as well as new parts by several commercial firms in the 1880s after Sharps Rifle Co. closed. Sharps Co. assembled several hundred of these from 1879-1881 from existing parts on hand.

N/A N/A $6,000 $5,000 $4,500 $4,000 $3,500 $3,250 $3,000 $2,500 $2,250 $2,000

While of lesser quality than the Model 1874, these rifles were widely used on the Western frontier and have become very desirable to today's firearms collectors.

100%	98%	95%	90%	80%	70%	60%	50%	40%	30%	20%	10%

MODEL 1878 SHARPS-BORCHARDT – many cals. and barrel lengths, single trigger, hammerless action designed by Hugo Borchardt, carbines, military, sporting, and target rifles were all mfg., but sales suffered from a bolt and lever action market glut. Less than 9,000 mfg. by Sharps Rifle Co. in Bridgeport, CT c. 1878-81.

N/A	N/A	$6,000	$5,000	$4,500	$4,250	$4,000	$3,750	$3,500	$3,250	$3,000	$2,500

Special order or deluxe models with other than standard features will command a premium.

SHARPS-LEE – material for 1,300 rifles was purchased in 1879 but little work was done on the U.S. Navy order for 300 rifles before Sharps ceased operations Oct. 18, 1880. Only a few hand-made tool room models for demonstration purposes were completed.

N/A	N/A	$8,000	$7,850	$7,500	$7,250	$7,000	$6,500	$6,250	$6,000	$5,500	$5,000

Add 50% for carbine or factory sporting rifle.

SHARPS MILSPEC

Previous trademark and division of Sharps Rifle Company, located in Chamberlain, SD 2011 only.

For individual model listings, please go to BlueBookOfGunValues.com/overflow.

SHARPS RIFLE COMPANY

Current manufacturer of AR-15 rifles and trademark of ammunition owned by the Broadsword Group, established in 2013, located in Glenrock, WY. Previous parent company of A-Square Rifles & Ammunition, Hermann H. Heiser Manufacturing and Co., Merwin Hulbert & Co., and Sharps MilSpec, and manufacturing facility was located in Glenrock, WY. Previous corporate headquarters located in Chamberlain, SD until 2011. Please check individual listings for recent information and pricing.

GRADING - PPGS™	100%	98%	95%	90%	80%	70%	60%	LAST MSR

RIFLES: SEMI-AUTO

The model listed below reflects base pricing only. Additional rifle options for barrels, handguard, and mags. exist. Please contact the manufacturer directly for pricing, options, and availability.

SHARPS 25-45 FIELD MASTER RIFLE – .25-45 Sharps cal., 16, 18, or 20 in. HBAR, stainless steel HBAR or light profile shot peen precision barrel, thread protector, 10, 20, or 30 shot PMAG, laser engraved ejection port door cover, CMC trigger group, M4 feed ramps, Sharps Relia-Bolt and XPB BCG, 13 1/2 in. free floating Diamond handguard, black finish, includes 5 boxes of HotCore cartridges and SRC logo case. New late 2020.

MSR $1,399	$1,250	$1,125	$975	$850	$750	$600	$475

SHAW PRECISION GUNS

Please refer to the E.R. Shaw, Inc. listing in the E section.

SHERIDAN PRODUCTS INCORPORATED

Previous manufacturer located in Racine, WI.

PISTOLS: SINGLE SHOT

KNOCABOUT – .22 S, L, or LR cal., 5 in. barrel, checkered plastic grips, fixed sights. Mfg. 1953-1960.

$275	$225	$200	$150	$110	$100	$85

SHILEN RIFLES, INCORPORATED

Current rifle, barrel, action, and trigger manufacturer established in 1955, located in Ennis, TX.

RIFLES: BOLT ACTION

Older Shilen rifles have become very desirable for target shooters and other accuracy enthusiasts. Because of their small quantities of manufacture (approx. 3,350 mfg.) and new-found demand, prices have gone up considerably on this trademark.Originally, the Sporters retailed in the $600-$700 range, but at the end, prices were in the $3,200-$3,600 range. Shilen Rifles offers custom actions for $950 and barreled custom actions for $1,500. Models listed below reflect base prices. Please contact the company directly for more information, pricing, and availability.

CUSTOM DGV/DGR RIFLE (CURRENT MFG.) – various cals., DGV or DGR action , 26 in. select /match, glass peened barrel. This model is custom order only and includes a wide variety of stock, barrel, trigger, and finish options.

Current MSR for DGV model ranges from $3,200-$3,500.
Current MSR for DGR model ranges from $3,300-$3,600.

Complete rifle packages include: Shilen table mat, gun case, jag, bore guide and brush, cleaning cloths, and a cleaning rod.

GRADING - PPGS™	100%	98%	95%	90%	80%	70%	60%	LAST MSR

DGA SPORTER – .17 Rem., .223 Rem., .22-250 Rem., .220 Swift, 6mm Rem., .243 Win., .250 Savage, .257 Roberts, .284 Win., .308 Win., or .358 Win. cal., 3 shot mag., 24 in. barrel, no sights, Claro walnut stock.

$1,475	$1,175	$950	$800	$675	$575	$495	

DGA VARMINTER – similar to Sporter, except 25 in. medium heavy barrel.

$1,395	$1,100	$900	$775	$650	$575	$495	

DGA SILHOUETTE RIFLE – similar to Varminter, .308 Win. cal. only.

$1,395	$1,100	$900	$775	$650	$575	$495	

DGA BENCHREST RIFLE – single shot, choice of cals., 26 in. heavy or medium barrel, no sights, choice of fiberglass or walnut stock, thumbhole available.

$1,450	$1,200	$950	$800	$650	$575	$495	

Actions for this model are currently selling in the $450 - $550 range.

SHILOH SHARPS RIFLE MANUFACTURING COMPANY

Current firearms and accessories manufacturer located in Big Timber, MT since 1976. Previously manufactured by Shiloh Products, a division of Drovel Tool Company of Farmingdale, NY, 1976-1983. Dealer or consumer direct sales.

For individual model listings, please go to BlueBookOfGunValues.com/overflow.

SHOOTERS ARMS MANUFACTURING INCORPORATED

Current manufacturer established in 1992, and located in Cebu, the Philippines. Currently imported by Century International Arms, located in Delray Beach, FL. Previously imported by Pacific Arms Corp. in Modesto, CA.

Shooters Arms Manufacturing Inc. makes semi-auto pistols, including the Elite, Commodore, Military, GI, Desert Storm, Seahawk, 1911A1, Eagle, Hawk, and the Trojan. Previous models have included the React, React-2, Military Enhanced, GI Enhanced, Elite Sport, Chief, Scout, Falcon, Raven, Omega, and Alpha. Shooters Arms Manufacuring Inc. also manufactures a revolver, the Protector, and a 12 ga. shotgun called the SAS 12. Please contact the importer directly for more information, including pricing and U.S. availability.

SIBERGUN

Current trademark of shotguns and airguns manufactured by Yazicilarav, located in Trabzon, Turkey. No current U.S. importation.

Please refer to Yazicilarav in the Y section.

SIDEWINDER

Previous trademark manufactured by D-Max, Inc. located in Bagley, MN circa 1993-96. Dealer or consumer sales.

REVOLVERS

SIDEWINDER – .45 LC or 2 1/2/3 in. .410 bore shotshells/slugs, 6 shot, stainless steel construction, 6 1/2 or 7 1/2 in. bull barrel (muzzle end bored for removable choke), Pachmayr grips, transfer bar safety, adj. rear sight, unique design permits one cylinder to shoot above listed loads, cased with choke tube, 3.8 lbs. Mfg. 1993-1996.

$695	$575	$475	$415	$360	$300	$255	*$775*

SIG ARMS AG

Current Swiss company (SIG) established during 1860 in Neuhausen, Switzerland. P 210 pistols are currently imported and distributed by SIG Sauer (formerly SIG Arms, Inc.), established in 1985, located in Exeter, NH. Previously located in Herndon, VA and Tysons Corner, VA.

In late 2000, SIG Arms AG, the firearms portion of SIG, was purchased by two Germans named Michael Lüke and Thomas Ortmeier, who have a background in textiles. Today the Lüke & Ortmeier group includes independently operational companies such as Blaser Jadgwaffen GmbH, Mauser Jagdwaffen GmbH, J.P. Sauer & Sohn GmbH, SIG-Sauer Inc., SIG-Sauer GmbH and SAN Swiss Arms AG. Please refer to individual listings.

PISTOLS: SEMI-AUTO

SIG Custom Shop variations of the P 210 were also available in three configurations - United We Stand ($8,990 last MSR) and two variations of the 50 Year Jubilee ($4,995 or $5,999 last MSR).

Add approx. $1,500 for .22 LR cal. conversion kit (most are numbered to guns) on the following models (not available on the P 210-8).

GRADING - PPGS™	100%	98%	95%	90%	80%	70%	60%	LAST MSR

TRAILSIDE/TRAILSIDE COMPETITION – please refer to the Hämmerli AG section for more information and current pricing on these models.

P 210 & VARIATIONS – 9mm Para. or 7.65mm Para. (disc.) cal., single action, 4 3/4 in. barrel, 8 shot mag., standard weapon of the Swiss Army, 2 lbs.

Originally mfg. in 1947, this pistol was first designated the SP 47/8 and became the standard military pistol of the Swiss Army in 1949. Later designated the P 210, this handgun has been mfg. continuously for over 55 years.

* ***P 210 Danish Army*** – 1-16,607 marked HTK, high polish blue and wood grips, 16,608-25,513 marked FKF, parkerized and black plastic grips, 35025-36441 marked HTK, black grips. Many refinished when surplused. Mfg. 1948-1962.

	100%	98%	95%	90%	80%	70%	60%	LAST MSR
	$3,500	$3,000	$2,500	$2,000	$1,500	$950	$800	

Add 20% for early, high polish pistols.

* ***P 210-1*** – 9mm Para. or 7.65mm Para. cal., polished finish, walnut grips, fixed sights. Introduced 1949 with SN P50,001.

	100%	98%	95%	90%	80%	70%	60%	LAST MSR
	$2,500	$2,000	$1,500	$1,250	$1,000	$900	$750	*$1,861*

Add 20% for 9mm Para. cal.

Add 20% for police markings.

* ***P 210-2*** – 9mm Para. or 7.65mm Para. cal., similar to P 210-1, except has matte finish, checkered black plastic grips.

	100%	98%	95%	90%	80%	70%	60%	LAST MSR
	$2,500	$2,000	$1,500	$1,250	$1,000	$900	$750	

* ***Swiss Army P49*** – 9mm Para. cal., high polish finish with serrated wood grips (approx. S/N range A100001-A109xxx) or matte finish with checkered black plastic grips (approx. S/N range A109xxx-A200xxx), fixed sights.

	100%	98%	95%	90%	80%	70%	60%	LAST MSR
High polish finish	$3,500	$3,000	$2,500	$2,000	$1,500	$1,200	$850	
Matte finish	$2,500	$2,150	$1,800	$1,500	$1,200	$900	$750	*$1,680*

Add 10% for early pistols whose hammer group does not have a half cock notch.

Add $250-$350 for holster and spare magazine in excellent condition.

* ***P 210-3*** – 9mm Para. or 7.65mm Para. cal., mostly encountered with high polish finish, loaded chamber indicator, fixed sights, wood grips, scarce pistol. Mostly sold to Swiss Police.

	100%	98%	95%	90%	80%	70%	60%	LAST MSR
	$4,500	$3,750	$3,250	$2,750	$2,250	$1,750	$1,500	

* ***P 210-4*** – 9mm Para. cal., modified version of the P210-2 that omits the lanyard loop and includes loaded chamber indicator. Serial number range D0001-D5000.

	100%	98%	95%	90%	80%	70%	60%	LAST MSR
	$3,500	$3,000	$2,500	$2,000	$1,500	$1,250	$1,000	

Add $250-$350 for holster and spare magazine in excellent condition.

Mfg. for the German border guards Bundesgrenzschutz. Early pistols have wood grips, later variations have checkered black plastic grips.

* ***P 210-5*** – 9mm Para. or 7.65mm Para. cal., heavier frame, micrometer target sights, 150mm or 180mm (disc.) extended barrel, hard rubber (disc.) or wood (current mfg.) grips, bottom (EU) or push-button side mounted (U.S.) mag. release, very limited mfg. Introduced late 1950s.

	100%	98%	95%	90%	80%	70%	60%	LAST MSR
	$3,500	$3,000	$2,500	$2,000	$1,500	$1,250	$1,000	

Add 10% for early "SP 47/8" pistols, or high polish finish.

Deduct 10% for 7.65mm Para. cal.

* ***P 210-6*** – 9mm Para. or 7.65mm Para. cal., matte blue finish, fixed or micrometer sights, standard length 120mm barrel, trigger adjustment screw under tang, several minor variations.

	100%	98%	95%	90%	80%	70%	60%	LAST MSR
	$3,000	$2,500	$2,000	$1,500	$1,125	$925	$775	

* ***P 210-7*** – limited to .22 LR cal., high polish blue, wood grips. Very few mfg.

	100%	98%	95%	90%	80%	70%	60%	LAST MSR
	$5,500	$4,500	$3,500	$3,000	$2,500	$2,150	$1,850	
.22 Conv. Kit only	$1,750	$1,550	$1,350	$1,150	$950	$750	$675	

.22 conversion kits sold separately. NIB start at $1,750.

* ***P 210-8*** – 9mm Para. cal., features heavy frame, target sights, and wood grips. Special order only. Limited importation 2001-2003.

	100%	98%	95%	90%	80%	70%	60%	LAST MSR
	$7,500	$6,000	$5,000	$4,000	$3,000	$2,000	$1,000	*$4,289*

* ***P 210 Deluxe Models*** – various models differ in the amount of engraving, gold inlays, carved wood grips, presentation cases, and other special order features available from the factory.

These models were available by special order only, and should be appraised individually. Values generally fall in the $5,000-$7,000 range.

* ***P 210 Legend*** – please refer to listing in the Sig Sauer section, new mfg.

GRADING - PPGS™	100%	98%	95%	90%	80%	70%	60%	LAST MSR

RIFLES: BOLT ACTION

SHR 970 – .25-06 Rem., .270 Win., .280 Rem., .30-06, .308 Win., .300 Win. Mag., or 7mm Rem. Mag. cal., steel receiver, standard model featuring easy takedown (requires single tool) and quick change 22 or 24 (Mag. cals. only) in. barrel, detachable 3 or 4 shot mag., 65 degree short throw bolt, 3-position safety, standard medium gloss walnut stock with checkering, ultra-fast lock time, Nitride bore, no sights, includes hard carry case, approx. 7.3 lbs. Mfg. 1998-2002.

$600	$525	$475	$400	$350	$300	$250	*$550*

Add $395 for extra barrel.

* ***SHR 970 Synthetic*** – similar to SHR 970, except has checkered black synthetic stock with stippled grip. Mfg. 1999-2002.

$550	$475	$425	$350	$300	$275	$225	*$499*

STR 970 LONG RANGE – .308 Win. or .300 Win. Mag. cal., includes stippled black McMillan composite stock with precision bedding blocks, 24 in. fluted heavy barrel with integral muzzle brake and non-reflective Ilaflon metal coating, cased, 11.6 lbs. Mfg. 2000-2002.

$875	$795	$675	$575	$525	$475	$425	*$899*

RIFLES: SEMI-AUTO

MODEL 1908 MONDRAGON – 7.5mm cal. and others, serial number is stamped externally in four locations, unique operating mechanism, first semi-auto military contract rifle, approx. 500 rifles Mexican contract.

$30,000	$25,000	$20,000	$16,000	$13,000	$10,000	$7,000	

PE-57 – 7.5mm Swiss cal. only, semi-auto version of the Swiss military rifle, 24 in. barrel, includes 24 shot mag., leather sling, bipod and maintenance kit. Importation disc. 1988.

$15,000	$12,500	$10,000	$8,000	$7,000	$6,000	$5,000	*$1,745*

The PE-57 was previously distributed in limited quantities by Osborne's located in Cheboygan, MI.

SIG-AMT RIFLE – .308 Win. cal., semi-auto version of SG510-4 auto rifle, roller delayed blowback action, 5, 10, or 20 shot mag., 18 3/4 in. barrel, wood stock, folding bipod. Mfg. 1960-1988.

$8,500	$7,500	$6,500	$5,500	$4,500	$3,500	$2,500	*$1,795*

SG 550/551 – .223 Rem. cal. with heavier bullet, Swiss Army's semi-auto version of a tactical design rifle (SIG 90), 20.8 (SG 550) or 16 in. (SG 551 Carbine) barrel, some synthetics used to save weight, 20 shot mag., diopter night sights, built-in folding bipod, 7.7 or 9 lbs.

SG 550 (Rifle)	$10,000	$8,500	$7,000	$6,250	$5,500	$4,950	$4,500	
SG 551 (Carbine)	$11,000	$9,500	$8,500	$8,000	$7,250	$6,500	$5,600	*$1,950*

This model had very limited domestic importation before 1989 Federal legislation banned its configuration.

SIG 556 – Please refer to the Sig Sauer section.

SIG-HÄMMERLI

Previously manufactured by Hämmerli Ltd. in Lenzburg, Switzerland.

PISTOLS: SEMI-AUTO

P240 TARGET PISTOL – .32 S&W Long Wadcutter or .38 Mid-range (disc.) cal., single action, 5 shot mag., 5.9 in. barrel, blue finish, thumbrest walnut grips, adj. sights and trigger, 3 lbs. Importation mostly disc. 1986.

$1,850	$1,350	$1,000	$875	$775	$700	$660	*$1,350*

Add $100 for Morini adj. grips.

.38 Mid-range cal. is very desirable in this model - healthy (and inconsistent) premiums are being asked.

* ***P240 Target Pistol .22 Conversion Unit***

$550	$495	$400	$335	$290	$245	$215	*$595*

SIGNAL 9 DEFENSE

Previous pistol manufacturer located in Gallatin, TN from late 2015-circa 2017. Previous company name was Edge Arms until 2015 (see separate listing in E section).

PISTOLS

RELIANT – .32 ACP, .32 HR Mag., .380 ACP, or .38 Spl. cal., break action, steel and aluminum construction, 2.63 in. barrel, 4 shot with 4-round speedloader in the grip (.380 and .32 ACP speedloader w/moonclip), shielded trigger, grip-activated integral red or green laser kit by LaserMax is optional, various hardcoat anodized and black phosphate finishes, approx. 16 oz. Mfg. 2015-circa 2017.

$395	$350	$295	$265	$235	$200	$175	*$449*

Add $175 per additional barrel.
Add $149 for red laser kit.
Add $299 for green laser kit.

GRADING - PPGS™	100%	98%	95%	90%	80%	70%	60%	LAST MSR

SIG SAUER

Current firearms trademark manufactured by SIG Arms AG (Schweizerische Industrie-Gesellschaft) located in Neuhausen, Switzerland. Most models are currently manufactured in the U.S., and some models continue to be imported from Switzerland. SIG SAUER, Inc. was established in 2007, and is located in Newington, NH. Previously imported and distributed from 1985-2006 by Sigarms, Inc. located in Exeter, NH. Previously located in Herndon, VA and Tysons Corner, VA.

In late 2000, SIG Arms AG, the firearms portion of SIG, was purchased by two Germans named Michael Lüke and Thomas Ortmeier (L&O Group), who have a background in textiles. Headquarters for L&O are in Emsdetten, Switzerland. Today the Lüke & Ortmeier group includes independently operational companies such as Blaser Jadgwaffen GmbH, Mauser Jagdwaffen GmbH, John Rigby, J.P. Sauer & Sohn GmbH, SIG-Sauer Inc., SIG-Sauer GmbH and SAN Swiss Arms AG. Please refer to individual listings.

On Oct. 1, 2007, SIG Arms changed its corporate name to SIG SAUER.

PISTOLS: SEMI-AUTO

Beginning 2001, SIG started manufacturing variations which are compliant by state. They include CA (10 shot mag. max only), MA (requires a loaded chamber indicator), and NY (must include empty shell casing) are priced slightly higher than the standard models available for the rest of the states.

The Sigarms Custom Shop, located in Exeter, NH, has recently been established and offers a wide variety of custom shop services, including action enhancement, full servicing, DA/SA conversions, trigger and hammer modifications, barrel replacement, and many refinishing options. Please contact Sigarms Custom Shop directly for more information and current pricing on these services.

During 2005, the Sigarms Custom Shop produced 12 limited editions, including the P229 Rail (January), P245 w/nickel accents and Meprolight night sights (February), P220 .45 ACP Rail (March), P239 Satin Nickel w/Hogue rubber grips (April), GSR 1911 Reverse Two-Tone (May), P229 Satin Nickel Reverse Two-Tone (June), P232 Rainbow Titanium (July), P226 Rail (August), P220 Sport Stock (September), P239 w/extra .357 SIG cal. barrel (October), P228 Two-Tone (November), and the P226 package w/Oakley glasses (December).

Early SIG SAUER pistols can be marked either with the Herndon or Tysons Corner, VA barrel address, and can also be marked "W. Germany" or "Germany". Earlier mfg. had three proofmarks on the bottom front of the slide, with a fourth on the frame in front of the serial number. Early guns with these barrel markings will command a slight premium over prices listed below, if condition is 98%+.

Add $399 for caliber X-Change kit on current models.

MOSQUITO – .22 LR cal., compact design similar to P226, 3.98 in. barrel, polymer frame, 10 shot mag., DA/SA, decocker, ambidextrous manual safety, Picatinny rail on bottom of frame, internal locking device, adj. rear sight, molded composite grips, black, nickel (mfg. 2007-2008), blue (disc. 2012), two-tone, Desert Digital camo (mfg. 2009-2012), pink (new 2009), reverse two-tone (new 2007), carbon fiber (mfg. 2012 only), FDE (new 2012), multi-cam (mfg. 2012 only), OD (new 2012), or deep purple (new 2012) frame finish, 24.6 oz. Mfg. 2005-2014.

	100%	98%	95%	90%	80%	70%	60%	LAST MSR
	$350	$300	$260	$230	$210	$190	$170	*$408*

Add $18 for hot pink, FDE (new 2012), OD, or deep purple frame finish.
Add $34 for threaded barrel.
Add $15 for nickel (disc. 2008) finish. Add $79 for carbon fiber or multi-cam (mfg. 2012 only).
Add $112 for Desert Digital camo frame with threaded barrel, disc. 2012.
Add $142 for camo finish, threaded barrel, and tactical trainer package (disc. 2009).
Add $75 for long slide with barrel weight (black finish only, new 2007, Sporter model). Disc. 2012.

SIG M400 ELITE PSB – 5.56 NATO cal., GIO, 11 1/2 in. barrel, 30 shot mag., SIG enhanced trigger, SIG PSB, free float M-LOK handguard, Microlight gas block, black or titanium finish. Mfg. 2018 only.

	100%	98%	95%	90%	80%	70%	60%	LAST MSR
	$1,175	$1,025	$900	$800	$700	$550	$450	*$1,303*

Add $71 for titanum finish.

SIG M400 TREAD PISTOL – 5.56 NATO cal., GIO, aluminum frame, 11 1/2 in. Nitride coated, carbon steel barrel, polished/hardcoat flat blade SST, flip-up front and rear iron sights, Magpul SL-K 6-pos. telescoping stock, multi-configuration M-LOK grip kits, aluminum receiver, free floating M-LOK handguard, ambi charge handle and controls, dual roll pin design, Shockwave Blade multi-position pistol brace, hardcoat anodized black finish, 6 lbs. New mid-2019.

	100%	98%	95%	90%	80%	70%	60%
MSR $880	$750	$650	$550	$500	$400	$350	$285

GRADING - PPGS™	100%	98%	95%	90%	80%	70%	60%	LAST MSR

SIG MCX 9 IN. – 5.56 NATO (mfg. 2015 only), 7.62x39mm (mfg. 2015 only), or .300 ACC Blackout cal., GPO, 9 in. barrel, 30 shot mag., aluminum KeyMod handguard, folding sights (disc. 2016), black or FDE (new 2016) finish, includes SBX stabilizing device and polymer hard case. Mfg. 2015-2017.

$1,975 $1,750 $1,525 $1,350 $1,175 $950 $775 *$2,199*

Add $136 for FDE finish.
Add $475 for 5.56 NATO conversion kit (disc. 2016).

SIG MCX 11 1/2 IN. – 5.56 NATO cal., 11 1/2 in. barrel, 30 shot aluminum mag., folding sights, aluminum KeyMod handguard, pistol stabilizing brace, black or FDE finish. Mfg. 2016-2017.

$1,975 $1,750 $1,525 $1,350 $1,175 $950 $775 *$2,199*

Add $136 for FDE finish.

SIG MCX RATTLER CANEBRAKE – .300 AAC Blackout cal., GPO, 5 1/2 in. cold hammer forged barrel, SIG Matchlite Duo Coyote Tan flat-blade trigger, folding fixed PCB brace, PDW M-LOK SD handguard, 7.62 inert trainer, Cerakote finish, 6 1/2 lbs. New 2019.

MSR $2,700 $2,425 $2,150 $1,875 $1,650 $1,425 $1,150 $925

SIG MCX RATTLER PCB – 5.56 NATO or .300 AAC Blackout cal., 5 1/2 in. cold hammer forged barrel, 30 shot polymer mag., SIG Matchlite Duo trigger, folding fixed PCB brace, M-LOK handguard, ambi controls, steel reinforced cam path, feed ramp, and steel charging handle latch points, 5.1 lbs. New 2018.

MSR $2,530 $2,275 $2,025 $1,750 $1,550 $1,350 $1,075 $875

SIG MCX RATTLER PSB – .300 AAC Blackout cal., GPO, 5 in. cold hammer forged barrel, 30 shot aluminum mag., SIG enhanced trigger, telescoping 3-pos. pistol brace, PDW grip, aluminum M-LOK handguard, 5.1 lbs. Mfg. 2018 only.

$2,450 $2,175 $1,875 $1,675 $1,450 $1,175 $950 *$2,719*

SIG MCX VIRTUS PCB/PSB – 5.56 NATO or .300 AAC Blackout cal., GPO, 9 or 11 1/2 in. interchangeable cold hammer forged barrel, 30 shot polymer mag., Matchlite Duo trigger, 3-pos. collapsible pistol stabilizing brace (mfg. 2018) or folding fixed PCB brace (new 2019), polymer grips, ambi controls, aluminum M-LOK free floating handguard, Elite Concrete (Gray) or FDE (disc. 2019) finish, 7-7.4 lbs. New 2018.

MSR $2,200 $1,980 $1,735 $1,525 $1,325 $1,150 $925 $750

SIG MPX-P – 9mm Para. cal., AR-15 style pistol, GPO, 8 in. barrel, aluminum handguard, reflex sights, 30 shot mag., with or without pistol stablizing brace. Mfg. 2014-2015.

$1,425 $1,250 $1,100 $975 $825 $675 $550 *$1,576*

Add $309 for pistol stabilizing brace (PSB).

SIG MPX – 9mm Para. cal., GPO, 4 1/2 (new 2018) or 8 (disc. 2017) in. barrel, 30 shot mag., folding sights (disc. 2017), no stock, short aluminum KeyMod handguard with handstop, ambidextrous AR-style controls, hardcoat anodized black or FDE (new 2018) finish, 4.6 lbs. Mfg. 2016-2018.

$1,800 $1,600 $1,400 $1,225 $1,075 $875 $700 *$2,016*

Add $136 for FDE finish (new 2018).

SIG MPX COPPERHEAD – 9mm Para. cal., GPO, 3 1/2, or 4 1/2 (new 2020) in. barrel with integrated brake, 20 shot polymer mag., Rapid Deploy PCB brace, monolithic upper, Coyote Tan E190 or Black (new 2020) Cerakote finish, 4 1/2 lbs. New 2019.

MSR $1,780 $1,600 $1,400 $1,225 $1,075 $925 $750 $600

Add $150 for 4 1/2 in. barrel (new 2020).

SIG MPX K (SIG MPX PCB) – 9mm Para. cal., 4 1/2 in. cold hammer forged carbon steel barrel, Timney single stage trigger, folding fixed PCB brace, polymer grip, free floating M-LOK (mfg. 2018 only) or KeyMod handguard, hardcoat anodized black or Cerakote E190 Coyote finish, 5 lbs. New mid-2018.

MSR $2,100 $1,885 $1,650 $1,425 $1,285 $1,050 $850 $700

SIG MPX WITH PISTOL STABILIZING BRACE – 9mm Para. cal., GPO, 4 1/2 (new 2018) or 8 (disc. 2017) in. barrel, 30 shot mag., folding sights (disc. 2017), aluminum KeyMod handguard with handstop, pistol stabilizing brace, black or FDE (new 2017) finish. Mfg. 2016-2018.

$1,950 $1,725 $1,500 $1,325 $1,150 $925 $750 *$2,162*

Add $136 for FDE finish (new 2017).

SIG PRO SP2009 – 9mm Para. cal., otherwise identical to SP2340, 28 oz. Mfg. 1999-2005.

$510 $450 $355 $290 $260 $220 $195 *$640*

Add $60 for Siglite night sights.
Add $31 for two-tone finish.

GRADING - PPGS™	100%	98%	95%	90%	80%	70%	60%	LAST MSR

SIG PRO SP2022 – 9mm Para., .357 SIG, or .40 S&W cal., 10, 12 or 15 (9mm Para. cal. only) shot mag., 3.85 in. barrel, DA/SA, polymer frame, Picatinny rail, Nitron, blue, or two-tone (disc. 2005) stainless steel slide, black Nitron finish, convertible to DAO, optional interchangeable grips, 26.8 (9mm Para.) or 30 oz. Mfg. 2004-2007.

	$495	$440	$355	$290	$260	$220	$195	*$613*

Subtract 10% if w/o Siglite night sights (became standard 2007).

SIG PRO SP2340 – .357 SIG, or .40 S&W cal., features polymer frame and one-piece Nitron finished stainless steel or two-tone (new 2001) finished slide, 3.86 in. barrel, DA/SA, includes two interchangeable grips, 10 shot mag., approx. 30.2 oz. Mfg. 1999-2005.

	$510	$450	$355	$290	$260	$220	$195	*$640*

Add $60 for Siglite night sights.
Add $31 for two-tone finish.

SP2022 – 9mm Para., .357 SIG (mfg. 2015 only), or .40 S&W (disc. 2020) cal., DA/SA, 3.9 in. carbon steel barrel, polymer frame with integrated lower Picatinny rail, stainless steel slide with black Nitron or natural stainless (disc.) finish, modular fire control unit, interchangeable grip assemblies, 10 (disc.) 12, or 15 (9mm Para. only) shot mag., contrast or Siglite night sights, two-tone (disc.), black Nitron, or FDE (mfg. 2014-disc.) finish, 29 oz. New 2011.

MSR $680	$580	$510	$435	$395	$320	$265	$225	

Add $70 for FDE or two-tone finish (disc.).
Add $141 for threaded barrel (9mm Para. only, disc. 2016).
Add $92 for .357 SIG cal. with Siglite Night sights (mfg. 2015 only).

* ***SP2022 Diamond*** – 9mm Para. cal., similar to Model SP2022, except has two-tone or black Nitron finish with "Diamond Plate" engraving, and Siglite night sights. Mfg. 2012 only.

	$550	$475	$400	$350	$300	$250	$225	*$626*

* ***SP2022 TacPac*** – 9mm Para. or .40 S&W cal., 12 or 15 shot mag., Siglite sights, one-piece enhanced E2 grip, black Nitron finish, STL 900L, includes holster. Mfg. 2013-2015.

	$615	$550	$495	$450	$395	$325	$295	*$719*

PISTOLS: SEMI-AUTO, P210, P220, P224, & P225 SERIES

P 210 LEGEND – 9mm Para. cal., SAO, 4 3/4 in. barrel with fixed 2-dot or adj. target sights, black Nitron finish, side release 8 shot mag., checkered wood grips, improved and extended beavertail, grooved grip straps, nickel plated safety, hammer, trigger, and slide release. Imported 2011-2014.

	$2,175	$1,925	$1,700	$1,475	$1,250	$1,050	$875	*$2,428*

Add $214 for adj. target sights.

For pre-2011 manufacture, please refer to listings in the Sig Arms AG section.

P 210 SUPER TARGET – 9mm Para. cal., SAO, 6 in. barrel, Nitron stainless steel slide and frame, 8 shot, redesigned 1911-style safety lever and extended slide catch lever, adj. target sights, enhanced controls, beavertail, stippled ergonomic wood grips with integral magwell, black Nitron finish. Mfg. 2014 only.

	$3,500	$3,150	$2,750	$2,500	$2,250	$2,000	$1,750	*$3,993*

P210 TARGET – 9mm Para. cal., SAO, full size stainless steel frame and slide, 5 in. stainless steel barrel, 8 shot steel mag., Target grade trigger, adj. sights, walnut grips, Nitron finish, 36.9 oz. New 2018.

MSR $1,650	$1,400	$1,225	$1,050	$950	$775	$630	$550	

P220 – .22 LR (disc.), .38 Super (disc.), 7.65mm (disc.), 9mm Para. (disc 1991), or .45 ACP cal., 4.4 in. barrel, 7 (.45 ACP, disc.) or 8 shot mag., full size, DA/SA, SAO, or DAO (.45 ACP cal. only), decocking lever, choice of matte blue (disc. 2006), black nitron (new 2007), stainless steel (mfg. 2001-2007), K-Kote (disc. 1999), electroless nickel (disc. 1991), two-tone with nickel finished slide (disc. 2011), or Ilaflon (mfg. 2000 only) finish, lightweight alloy frame, black plastic grips, optional DAK trigger system (DAO with 6 1/2 lb. trigger pull) available during 2005 only, tactical rail became standard 2004 at no extra charge (blue or stainless only), contrast (disc. 2015) or Siglite night sights became standard 2016, approx. 30.4 or 41.8 (stainless steel) oz. Mfg. 1976-2019.

	$950	$735	$625	$525	$450	$400	$350	*$1,087*

Add $339 for .22 LR conversion kit or $680 for older mfg. .22 LR conversion kit.
Subtract $114 for contrast sights (disc. 2015).
Add $149 for black stainless with Hogue rubber grips and Siglite night sights (mfg. 2012-2013).
Add $40 for DAK trigger system (limited mfg. 2005).
Add $103 for two-tone (nickel slide) finish (disc. 2011).

continued on following page

GRADING - PPGS™	100%	98%	95%	90%	80%	70%	60%	LAST MSR

Add $100 for P220 SAO Model (single action only, disc. 2009).
Add $306 for Crimson Trace Lasergrips w/night sights (disc. 2009).
Add $95 for stainless steel frame & slide (mfg. 2001-2007).
Add $40 for Ilaflon finish (disc. 2000).
Add $45 for factory K-Kote finish (disc. 1999).
Add $70 for electroless nickel finish (disc. 1991).
Subtract 10% for "European" Model (bottom mag. release - includes 9mm Para. and .38 Super cals.).

Values are for .45 ACP cal. and assume American side mag. release (standard 1986).

This model was also available as a Custom Shop Limited Edition during July, 2004 (MSR was $800) and November, 2004 (MSR was $861).

* ***P220 Combat*** – .45 ACP cal., 4.4 in. non-threaded barrel, FDE finish, alloy frame, Nitron stainless slide, corrosion resistant parts, 8 shot mag., M1913 Picatinny rail, Siglite night sights, 30.4 oz. Mfg. 2007-2012, reintroduced 2014-2015.

$1,125	$950	$825	$725	$625	$525	$425	*$1,290*

» ***P220 Combat Threaded*** – .45 ACP cal., DA/SA, 4.4 in. threaded barrel, FDE anodized alloy frame, Nitron stainless slide, corrosion resistant parts, 8 or 10 shot steel mag., M1913 Picatinny rail, Siglite night sights, polymer grip, 30.4 oz. Mfg. 2007-2012, reintroduced 2014-2016.

$1,075	$915	$800	$725	$625	$525	$425	*$1,282*

* ***P220 Elite*** – .45 ACP cal., DA/SA, 4.4 in. barrel, two 8 shot steel mags., SRT, Siglite night sights, E2 grip, black finish. New 2021.

MSR $1,100	$935	$825	$700	$635	$515	$425	$365

* ***P220 Elite/Dark Elite*** – .45 ACP cal., similar to P220, except has short reset trigger, DA/SA or SAO, two-tone (limited mfg.), or black Nitron finish, 8 shot mag., ergonomic beavertail, Picatinny rail, front cocking serrations, Custom Shop wood or black aluminum (Dark Elite) grips. Mfg. 2007-2014.

$1,095	$950	$850	$725	$625	$525	$425	*$1,253*

Add $61 for Elite Dark with threaded barrel (disc. 2012).

* ***P220 Elite Stainless*** – .45 ACP cal., DA/SA, 4.4. in. barrel, stainless steel frame and slide, 8 shot, Picatinny rail, short reset trigger, ergonomic beavertail grip, Siglite night sights, custom rosewood grips or checkered aluminum (Platinum Elite, disc. 2011) grips, 39.1 oz. Mfg. 2007-2018.

$1,325	$1,125	$1,000	$875	$750	$625	$500	*$1,495*

Add $72 for platinum Elite with aluminum grips (stainless only), disc. 2011.

* ***P220 Equinox*** – .45 ACP cal., DA/SA, 4.4 in. barrel, lightweight hard anodized alloy frame, two-tone accented slide with Nitron finish, 8 shot, Picatinny rail, TruGlo TFO front sight, Siglite rear sight, black or gray laminated wood grips w/Custom Shop logo, 30.4 oz. Mfg. 2007-2015.

$1,125	$950	$850	$725	$625	$525	$425	*$1,290*

* ***P220 Extreme*** – .45 ACP cal., DA/SA, 4 in. barrel, 8 shot mag., forward slide serrations, SRT trigger system, Siglite night sights, Hogue black and gray G10 Extreme grips, black Nitron finish, approx. 30 oz. Mfg. 2012-2015.

$1,095	$935	$825	$700	$600	$500	$400	*$1,256*

* ***P220 Match*** – .45 ACP cal., similar to P220, except has 5 in. cold hammer forged barrel, DA/SA or SAO, ambidextrous safety, two-tone or stainless (Match Elite) finish, adj. sights, black polymer or custom shop wood (Super Match) grips, Elite Match became standard during 2010. Mfg. 2007-2012.

$1,175	$975	$850	$725	$625	$550	$450	*$1,368*

Add $7 for Super Match model.
Subtract approx. $200 for Match (disc. 2009, last MSR was $1,170).

* ***P220 Match Elite (Recent Mfg.)*** – .45 ACP cal., DA/SA, full size frame, 5 in. barrel, 8 shot mag., beavertail frame, front strap checkering, SRT, Siglite night sights, adj. target sights, Picatinny rail, black anodize aluminum grips, stainless finish, 39.1 oz. Disc. 2015.

$1,450	$1,275	$1,100	$985	$800	$650	$525	*$1,713*

* ***P220 Super Match (Recent Mfg.)*** – .45 ACP cal., SAO, 5 in. barrel, 8 shot mag., lightweight alloy beavertail frame with hardcoat anodized finish, front strap checkering, front cocking serrations, adj. target sights, Picatinny rail, rosewood grips, Sig Sauer Custom Shop logo engraved on slide, natural stainless slide finish, 33.6 oz. Limited production Custom Shop model. Disc. 2016.

$1,275	$1,150	$1,000	$900	$750	$600	$475	*$1,467*

GRADING - PPGS™	100%	98%	95%	90%	80%	70%	60%	LAST MSR

* ***P220 Nightmare*** – .45 ACP cal., SAO, full size alloy frame with Nitron finish, 4.4 in. carbon steel barrel, two 8 shot steel mags., X-RAY3 day/night sights, black Hogue Classic Contour SL G10 grip, SIG rail, blacked out Custom Works engraved stainless steel slide and blacked out frame with nickel-plated contrasting controls giving the distinct Nightmare look, comes in premium Custom Works Negrini pistol case with SIG Custom Works challenge coin and certified custom certificate, 30.4 oz. New late 2020.

Please contact the company directly for price and availability.

* ***P220 NRALE*** – .45 ACP cal., features NRA Law Enforcement logo and the words "NRA Law Enforcement" engraved in 24Kt. gold, cocobolo grips with NRA medallions, gold trigger and appointments. Limited production of 1,000, including P226 NRALE 2002-2003.

	$850	**$650**	**$495**	**N/A**	**N/A**	**N/A**	**N/A**	***$911***

* ***P220 Scorpion Elite*** – .45 ACP cal., 4.4 in. threaded or non-threaded barrel, 8 shot mag., front cocking serrations, short reset trigger, FDE metal finish, beavertail, Siglite night sights and Hogue G10 Parana grips, 30.4 oz. Mfg. 2012-2015.

	$1,195	**$1,025**	**$875**	**$750**	**$650**	**$550**	**$450**	***$1,348***

Add $57 for threaded barrel.

* ***P220 Sport*** – .45 ACP cal., features 4.8 in. heavy compensated barrel, stainless steel frame and slide, 10 shot mag., target sights, improved trigger pull, single or double action, 46.1 oz. Imported 1999-2000, reintroduced 2003-2005.

	$1,375	**$975**	**$800**	**$695**	**$585**	**$485**	**$415**	***$1,600***

* ***P220 Stainless Nitron*** – .45 ACP cal., DA/SA, 4.4 in. barrel, 8 shot mag., Siglite night sights, Hogue rubber grips, all stainless Nitron finish, 39.1 oz. Disc. 2015.

	$975	**$800**	**$665**	**$535**	**$465**	**$415**	**$365**	***$1,199***

* ***P220 Stainless Reverse Two-Tone*** – .45 ACP cal., DA/SA, 4.4 in. barrel, 8 shot mag., Siglite night sights, Hogue rubber grips, all stainless reverse two-tone finish, Nitron coated slide, 39.1 oz. Disc. 2015.

	$975	**$800**	**$665**	**$535**	**$465**	**$415**	**$365**	***$1,199***

* ***P220R*** – .22 LR cal., 4.4 in. barrel, 10 shot mag., DA/SA, matte black anodized finish, adj. sights, otherwise similar to standard P220. Mfg. 2009-2012.

	$565	**$500**	**$450**	**$395**	**$350**	**$300**	**$275**	***$642***

* ***P220 TacPac*** – .45 ACP cal., features black Nitron finish, Siglite sights, one-piece enhanced E2 grip, STL 900L, includes holster. Mfg. 2013-2014.

	$1,075	**$925**	**$825**	**$725**	**$625**	**$525**	**$425**	***$1,238***

P220 .22 LR – .22 LR cal., full size, 4.4 in. barrel, DA/SA trigger, black anodized alloy slide, 10 shot mag., adj. sights, black anodized finish. Mfg. 2014-2015.

	$695	**$595**	**$495**	**$425**	**$365**	**$335**	**$295**	***$685***

Add 30% for early production with "H" prefix.

P220 CARRY – .45 ACP cal., compact model w/full size frame, 3.9 in. barrel, 8 shot single stack mag., DA/SA, DAK, or SAO, black Nitron finish, Picatinny rail, black polymer factory grips, contrast (disc. 2015) or Siglite night sights. Mfg. 2007-2016.

	$885	**$750**	**$635**	**$525**	**$450**	**$400**	**$350**	***$1,087***

Subtract $114 for contrast sights (disc. 2015).
Add $100 for SAO trigger (disc. 2008).

* ***P220 Carry Elite*** – .45 ACP cal., DA/SA, 3.9 in. barrel, front cocking serrations, ergonomic beavertail grip, Picatinny rail, stainless or black Nitron (mfg. 2009-2012) finish, Siglite adj. combat night sights, wood (disc.) or Hogue aluminum grips, 30.4 oz. Mfg. 2007-2014.

	$1,250	**$1,025**	**$895**	**$750**	**$650**	**$550**	**$450**	***$1,396***

Subtract $140 for black nitron finish (disc. 2012).

* ***P220 Carry Stainless Elite*** – .45 ACP cal., DA/SA, 3.9 in. barrel, 8 shot mag., front cocking serrations, SRT, Siglite night sights, natural stainless steel slide, Elite stainless steel beavertail frame, Hogue rubber (mfg. 2012-2013) or custom rosewood grips (new 2013), 39.1 oz. Mfg. 2012-2017.

	$1,325	**$1,075**	**$950**	**$825**	**$725**	**$600**	**$500**	***$1,495***

* ***P220 Carry Equinox*** – .45 ACP cal., DA/SA, 3.9 in. barrel, accessory rail, two-tone accented Nitron stainless steel slide with lightweight black hard-anodized frame, TruGlo TFO front sight, Siglite rear sight, black or grey laminated wood grips w/custom shop logo, 30.4 oz. Mfg. 2007-2015.

	$1,095	**$935**	**$825**	**$700**	**$600**	**$500**	**$400**	***$1,256***

GRADING - PPGS™	100%	98%	95%	90%	80%	70%	60%	LAST MSR

* ***P220 Carry SAS*** - .45 ACP cal., DA/SA or SAO (disc. 2014), 3.9 in. barrel, SRT, Nitron or two-tone finish with black frame and stainless steel slide, Dehorning, SIG Anti-Snag treatment on slide/frame, custom shop brown wood grips (disc.) or one-piece black polymer grips, contrast (disc. 2013) or Siglite night sights (became standard 2014), Gen. 2 features became standard 2008, 30.4 oz. Mfg. 2010-2017.

	$915	$775	$650	$525	$465	$415	$365	*$1,119*

P220 COMPACT - .45 ACP cal., DA/SA or SAO (disc.), 3.9 in. barrel, compact beavertail frame, 6 shot mag., black Nitron or two-tone (disc. 2010) finish, contrast (disc.) or Siglite night sights, lower Picatinny rail, black polymer grips. Mfg. 2007-2013, reintroduced 2015 only.

	$925	$775	$650	$525	$450	$400	$350	*$1,142*

Add $75 for two-tone finish (disc. 2010).

* ***P220 Compact SAS*** - .45 ACP cal., DA/SA or SAO (disc.), 3.9 in. barrel, 6 shot mag., SRT, contrast (disc.) or Siglite night sights (became standard 2014), dehorned, black polymer or custom shop wood (disc.) grips, Gen. 2 features became standard 2012, Nitron stainless steel slide, SIG Anti-Snag treatment on slide/frame, 29.6 oz. Mfg. 2007-2015.

	$975	$800	$665	$535	$465	$415	$365	*$1,199*

P220 HUNTER - 10mm cal., SAO, stainless steel slide and frame coated in a custom Kryptek camo pattern, 5 in. match grade barrel, 8 shot steel mag., adj. rear and fiber optic front sights, Hogue black and gray G10 grips, ambi safety, 39.4 oz. Mfg. 2016-2018.

	$1,400	$1,225	$1,075	$950	$775	$625	$525	*$1,629*

P220 LEGION - .45 ACP or 10mm (new 2018) cal., DA/SA or SAO, full size alloy frame, 4.4 or 5 (new 2018) in. barrel, 8 shot steel mag., Nitron stainless steel slide, Grayguns Inc. designed P-SAIT trigger or Master Shop flat trigger (SAO variant only), X RAY3 day/night sights, black G10 grips with Legion medallion, aggressive checkering, SIG accessory rail, Legion Gray finish, 30.4 oz. New 2017.

MSR $1,330	$1,135	$995	$850	$775	$625	$525	$445	

Add $450 for 10mm cal. (new 2018).

* ***P220 Legion Carry SAO*** - .45 ACP cal., SAO, carry-size alloy frame, 3.9 in. barrel, three 8 shot steel mags., Nitron stainless steel slide, Custom Works flat trigger, X RAY3 day/night sights, black G10 grips with Legion medallion, aggressive checkering, SIG accessory rail, Cerakote Elite Legion Gray finish, 30.4 oz. Limited mfg. beginning late 2020.

Please contact the manufacturer directly for price and availability.

P224 - 9mm Para., 357 SIG, or .40 S&W cal., 3 1/2 in. barrel, DA/SA or DAK trigger, alloy frame with stainless steel slide, 10 or 12 (9mm Para. only) shot mag., satin nickel slide and controls (P224 Nickel), Siglite night sights, wood (disc.) or one-piece enhanced E2 (new 2013) grips, 25.4 oz. Mfg. 2012-2015.

	$925	$775	$650	$525	$450	$400	$350	*$1,142*

Add $57 for satin nickel slide and controls (Model P224 Nickel).

* ***P224 SAS Gen. 2*** - 9mm Para., .40 S&W, or .357 Sig cal., DA/SA or DAK (9mm only), similar to P224, except has Sig Anti-Snag (SAS) treatment on slide and frame, black Nitron finish, dehorned metal parts, SRT, Siglite night sights, and one-piece enhanced E2 grip, 29 oz. Mfg. 2012-2015.

	$950	$795	$665	$535	$465	$415	$365	*$1,176*

* ***P224 Extreme*** - 9mm Para. or .40 S&W cal., DA/SA, 3 1/2 in. barrel, 10 or 12 shot mag., short reset trigger, Siglite night sights, Hogue black and grey Extreme G10 grips, black Nitron finish, Nitron stainless steel slide, 29 oz. Mfg. 2012-2015.

	$975	$800	$665	$535	$465	$415	$365	*$1,199*

* ***P224 Equinox*** - .40 S&W cal. only, DA/SA, 3 1/2 in. barrel, 10 shot mag., two-tone polished Nitron slide finish, black hard anodized frame finish, TruGlo TFO front sight with Siglite rear night sight, Hogue black G10 grips, 29 oz. Mfg. 2012-2015.

	$1,095	$935	$825	$700	$600	$500	$400	*$1,256*

P225 - 9mm Para. cal., DA/SA or DAO, similar to P220, shorter dimensions, 3.85 in. barrel, 8 shot single stack mag., thumb actuated mag. release, fully adj. sights, 28.8 oz. Disc. 1998.

	$595	$525	$450	$425	$395	$350	$310	*$725*

Add $45 for factory K-Kote finish.
Add $105 for Siglite night sights.
Add $45 for nickel finished slide (new 1992).
Add $70 for electroless nickel finish (disc. 1991).
Add up to 100% for special Swiss police markings.

This model was also available as a Custom Shop Limited Edition during March, 2004. MSR was $803.

GRADING - PPGS™	100%	98%	95%	90%	80%	70%	60%	LAST MSR

P225-A1 – 9mm Para. cal., DA/SA, black hardcoat alloy frame, 3.6 in. barrel, 8 shot single stack mag., Nitron or two-tone (natural) stainless steel slide, short reset trigger, Siglite night sights, black checkered G10 grips with medallion or custom checkered wood grips (disc.), 30.5 oz. Mfg. 2016-2019.

$875	$775	$650	$535	$465	$425	$350	*$1,032*

PISTOLS: SEMI-AUTO, P226, P227 & P228 SERIES

P226 – .357 SIG (mfg. 1995-2016), 9mm Para. (disc. 1997, reintroduced 1999), or .40 S&W (mfg. 1998-disc.) cal., full size, choice of DA/SA or DAO (new 1992) operation, 10 (C/B 1994), 12 (new mid-2005, .357 SIG or .40 S&W cal.) or 15* (9mm Para. cal. only) shot mag., 4.4 in. barrel, alloy frame, currently available in blackened stainless steel (Nitron finish became standard 2000), two-tone (disc. 2011), reverse two-tone (.40 S&W cal. only - mfg. 2012 only), or nickel (disc. 2002) finish (stainless slide only), tactical rail became standard 2004, choice of traditional DA or DAK (disc.) trigger system (DAO with 6 1/2 lb. trigger pull, not available in all stainless) available beginning 2005, E2 grips became standard 2011, high contrast sights (9mm & .40 S&W, disc. 2015) or Siglite night sights became standard 2016, automatic firing pin block safety, 31.7 or 34 oz. New 1983.

MSR $1,100	$935	$825	$700	$635	$515	$425	$365

Subtract $114 if with contrast sights (disc. 2015).
Add $339 for .22 LR cal. conversion kit (disc.).
Add $149 for reverse two-tone finish - all stainless with Siglite night sights and Hogue rubber grips (mfg. 2012 only).
Add $306 for Crimson Trace Lasergrips w/Siglite night sights (mfg. 2007).
Add $95 for stainless steel frame and slide (mfg. 2004-2005).
Add $103 for two-tone finish (nickel finished stainless steel slide) w/night sights, (disc. 2011).
Add $45 for K-Kote (Polymer) finish (mfg. 1992-97, 9mm Para. only).
Add $70 for electroless nickel finish (disc. 1991).
Add up to 100% for special Swiss police markings.

This model is also available in double action only (all finishes) at no extra charge.

This model was also available as a Custom Shop Limited Edition during Feb., 2004 (MSR was $1,085). A limited edition P226 America with blue titanium and gold finishes was also available from SIG's Custom Shop (MSR was $7,995).

This model is also available as the P226R Tactical, sold exclusively by Ellett Bros. distributors - no pricing information is available.

* ***P226 ASE Full Size*** – 9mm Para. or .40 S&W cal., DA/SA, full size alloy frame, 4.4 in. carbon steel barrel, 10, 12, or 15 shot steel mag., Siglite night sights, walnut grips, front cocking serrations, stainless steel PVD frame and slide finish, 34.4 oz. Disc.

$875	$775	$650	$535	$465	$425	$350	*$1,030*

* ***P226 Combat*** – 9mm Para. cal., DA/SA, 4.4 in. threaded or non-threaded barrel, 10 or 15 shot mag., Siglite night sights, FDE frame and grips, black Nitron slide, Picatinny rail, 34 oz. Mfg. 2008-2012, reintroduced 2015 only.

$1,095	$935	$825	$700	$600	$500	$400	*$1,256*

» **P226 Combat Threaded Barrel** – 9mm Para. cal., DA/SA, 4.4 in. threaded barrel, 10 or 15 shot mag., Siglite night sights, FDE frame and grips, black Nitron slide, Picatinny rail, 34 oz. Mfg. 2008-2012, reintroduced 2015-2016.

$1,075	$915	$800	$725	$625	$525	$425	*$1,282*

* ***P226 Elite*** – 9mm Para., .357 SIG, or .40 S&W, or .45 ACP cal., DA/SA (disc.), 4.4 in. barrel, Beavertail Elite frame, 15 shot mag., forward cocking serrations, Siglite night sights, two-tone (disc.), or black Nitron finish, black polymer grips, 34.4 oz. Mfg. 2007-2015.

$1,095	$935	$825	$700	$600	$500	$400	*$1,256*

Add $72 for platinum Elite with aluminum grips (disc. 2011).
Add $71 for TB Model with threaded barrel (9mm Para. only), disc. 2012.

* ***P226 Elite (Recent Mfg.)*** – 9mm Para. cal., SAO, 4.4 in. barrel, two 15 shot steel mags., Reflex/tall Siglite night sights, polymer grip, black finish. Mfg. 2017 only.

$1,250	$1,025	$900	$800	$700	$600	$500	*$1,481*

* ***P226 Elite SAO*** – .22 LR cal., SAO, 4.6 in. barrel, 10 shot mag., adj. sights, checkered wood grips, ambidextrous manual safety, integral accessory rail, black hardcoat anodized slide. Mfg. 2018 only.

$595	$550	$475	$425	$385	$325	$285	*$679*

* ***P226 Dark Elite*** – 9mm Para., .357 SIG, or .40 S&W (new 2011), DA/SA, similar to P226, except has Black Nitron finish, 12 or 15 shot mag., aluminum checkered grips. Mfg. 2007-2014.

$1,050	$925	$825	$725	$625	$525	$425	*$1,243*

GRADING - PPGS™	100%	98%	95%	90%	80%	70%	60%	LAST MSR

* ***P226 Elite Stainless*** – 9mm Para., .357 SIG (disc. 2012), .40 S&W (new 2011), or .45 ACP (disc. 2011) cal., DA/SA, 4.4 in. barrel, 10, 12, or 15 shot mag., SRT, ergonomic beavertail grip, front cocking serrations, front strap checkering, lower Picatinny rail, stainless steel, custom shop wood grips (disc.) or checkered rosewood grips, Siglite night sights, 42.2 oz. Mfg. 2007-2018.

	$1,300	$1,065	$925	$800	$700	$600	$500	*$1,413*

* ***P226 Emperor Scorpion*** – 9mm Para. or 40 S&W (disc. 2018) cal., DA/SA, full size alloy frame, 4.4 in. barrel, two 15 shot steel mags., stainless steel slide, SRT, black G10 grips, Siglite night sights, SIG accessory rail, front cocking serrations, FDE finish, 34.4 oz. Mfg. 2017-2019.

	$1,025	$825	$700	$575	$500	$450	$400	*$1,282*

* ***P226 Enhanced Elite*** – 9mm Para., .357 SIG (disc. 2015), or .40 S&W (disc. 2015) cal., DA/SA, 4.4 in. barrel, 12 (.357 Sig) or 15 shot mag., includes lower Picatinny rail in front of trigger guard, SRT, beavertail, Siglite night sights, E2 polymer grips, black Nitron finish, 34.4 oz. Mfg. 2011-2012, reintroduced 2015-2018.

	$950	$785	$650	$535	$465	$415	$365	*$1,174*

Add $34 for .40 S&W or $35 for 9mm Para. cal. (disc. 2015).

* ***P226 Engraved*** – 9mm Para. cal., DA/SA, full size frame, 4.4 in. barrel, 15 shot mag., polished Nitron stainless steel slide with custom engraving, black hardcoat anodized (mfg. 2015 only) or stainless steel frame and slide, Siglite night sights, custom wood grips with SIG medallion, 34 oz. Mfg. 2015-2016.

	$1,350	$1,075	$895	$750	$625	$525	$425	*$1,631*

Subtract $365 for black hardcoat anodized frame and slide (mfg. 2015 only).

* ***P226 Equinox*** – 9mm Para. (new 2015) or .40 S&W cal., DA/SA, 4.4 in. barrel, two-tone Nitron stainless steel slide, lightweight black anodized alloy frame, nickel accents, 12 shot mag., TruGlo TFO front sight, rear Siglite night sight, Picatinny rail, grey laminated wood grips, 34 oz., mfg. by the Custom Shop. Mfg. 2006-2012, reintroduced 2015 only.

	$1,095	$935	$825	$700	$600	$500	$400	*$1,256*

» **P226 Equinox Full-Size** – 9mm Para. cal., alloy frame with a hard coat anodized finish, 4.4 in. carbon steel barrel, two 15 shot steel mag., DA/SA, XRAY3 day/night sights, black Hogue SL G-10 grip, stainless steel slide with Nitron finish, 34 oz. New 2020.

Limited edition comes in Custom Works Negrini case with a SIG Custom Works challenge coin and a certified custom certificate.

* ***P226 Extreme*** – 9mm Para. or .40 S&W cal., DA/SA, 4.4 in. barrel, 12 or 15 shot mag., SRT, front cocking serrations, Siglite night sights, lower Picatinny rail, Hogue Black and Grey Extreme Series G10 grips, black Nitron finish, 34 oz. Mfg. 2011-2015, reintroduced 2018 only.

	$1,095	$935	$825	$700	$600	$500	$400	*$1,255*

* ***P226 E2*** – 9mm Para. cal., 15 shot mag., black Nitron finish, ergonomic slim profile one-piece grips, Siglite night sights, short reset trigger, integral accessory rail, includes three mags. New 2010 only.

	$1,000	$895	$775	$675	$575	$525	$450	*$1,149*

* ***P226 Jubilee*** – 9mm Para. cal., limited edition commemorating SIG's 125th anniversary, features gold-plated small parts, carved select walnut grips, special slide markings, cased. Mfg. 1985 only.

	$1,500	$1,250	$1,000	$800	$700	$600	$500	*$2,000*

* ***P226 MK25 Navy Version*** – 9mm Para. cal., DA/SA, 4.4 in. non-threaded or 4.9 in. threaded (disc. 2017) barrel, three 15 shot mags., black Nitron or FDE (mfg. 2014-2017) finish with phosphated small components, features anchor engraving, Picatinny rail, UID label on right side of slide, Siglite night sights, black polymer grips, 34.4 oz. New 2012.

MSR $1,100	$935	$825	$700	$635	$515	$425	$365	

Add $57 for FDE finish (mfg. 2014-2017), or $68 for threaded barrel (disc. 2017).

* ***P226 Nightmare*** – 9mm Para. cal., DA/SA, full size alloy frame, 4.4 in. carbon steel barrel, two 15 shot steel mags., stainless steel slide with Nitron finish, X-RAY3 day/night sights, classic contour SL G10 black grip, SIG rail, 34 oz. Custom Works limited edition. New 2021.

Please contact the company directly for price and availability.

* ***P226 NRALE*** – .40 S&W cal., features NRA Law Enforcement logo and the words "NRA Law Enforcement" engraved in 24Kt. gold, cocobolo grips with NRA medallions, gold trigger and appointments. Limited production of 1,000, including P220 NRALE, 2002-2003.

	$850	$650	$495	N/A	N/A	N/A	N/A	*$911*

GRADING - PPGS™	100%	98%	95%	90%	80%	70%	60%	LAST MSR

* **P226R** – .22 LR cal., Nitron finish, adj. sights, DA/SA or SAO, 10 shot mag., with or w/o beavertail grips and stainless reverse two-tone. Mfg. 2009-2012.

	$585	$515	$465	$400	$350	$300	$275	*$656*

Add $33 for beavertail and stainless reverse two-tone.

* **P226 RX** – 9mm Para. cal., DA/SA, full size alloy frame, 4.4 in. barrel, 15 shot mag., Nitron coated stainless steel slide and frame, contrast sights or Siglite night sights with ROMEO1 reflex sight, one-piece ergonomic grip, SIG rail, 34.4 oz. Mfg. 2017-2019.

	$975	$800	$675	$550	$475	$425	$375	*$1,201*

Add $109 for Siglite night sights.

* **P226 Scorpion Elite** – 9mm Para. cal. only, DA/SA, 4.4 in. threaded or non-threaded barrel, 10 or 15 shot mag., SRT, beavertail, Siglite night sights, Picatinny rail, FDE finish, Hogue Extreme G10 grips, 34 oz. Mfg. 2012 only, reintroduced 2015 only.

	$1,125	$950	$825	$725	$625	$525	$425	*$1,348*

Add $57 for threaded barrel.

* **P226 Select** – 9mm Para. cal., lightweight alloy frame, 4.4 in. barrel, 15 shot mag., Nitron stainless steel slide, Siglite night sights, SELECT G10 grips, front cocking serrations, SIG accessory rail. Mfg. 2018-2019.

	$975	$800	$675	$550	$475	$425	$375	*$1,195*

* **P226 Special Editions** – 9mm Para. or .40 S&W (Cops Commemorative only, disc. 2008) cal., engraved, variations include Navy (black Nitron finish, phosphate components and anchor engraving), Cops Commemorative (Siglite night sights and wood grips, disc. 2008). Series disc. 2011.

	$895	$775	$675	$575	$475	$400	$350	*$1,020*

* **P226 Sport** – 9mm Para. cal., DA/SA or DAO, features 5.6 in. match or heavy compensated barrel, stainless steel frame and slide, 10 shot mag., target sights, improved trigger pull, rubber grips, 48.8 oz. Mfg. 2003-2005.

	$1,600	$975	$800	$695	$585	$485	$415	*$1,600*

* **P226 ST** – 9mm Para., .40 S&W, or .357 Mag. cal., 4.4 in. barrel, white stainless slide and frame, blue barrel, Picatinny rail, 10 shot mag., 38.8 oz.

While advertised during 2006, this model never went into production - prototypes only.

* **P226 Super Cap Tactical** – .40 S&W cal., similar to P226 Tactical, black Nitron finish, TruGlo front sight, Siglite rear sight, includes four 15 shot mags. Mfg. 2009-2010.

	$1,025	$925	$825	$725	$625	$525	$425	*$1,156*

* **P226 TACOPS** – 9mm Para., .357 SIG (disc. 2016), or .40 S&W (disc. 2016) cal., DA/SA, 4.4 in. barrel, 15 or 20 shot mag., Picatinny rail, SRT, TruGlo TFO front sight and Siglite rear night sight, Elite beavertail frame, front cocking serrations, polymer Magwell grips, black Nitron or FDE coated (mfg. 2015 only) finish, 34 oz. Mfg. 2011-2017.

	$1,095	$935	$825	$725	$625	$525	$425	*$1,304*

Add $22 for .357 Sig (disc. 2016).
Add $80 for FDE finish (mfg. 2015 only).

* ***P226 TACOPS TB (Threaded Barrel)*** – 9mm Para. cal., DA/SA, Elite Beavertail frame, 4.9 in. threaded barrel, 15 shot mag., short reset trigger, TruGlo front and Siglite rear night sights, Picatinny rail, front cocking serrations, polymer Magwell grips, black Nitron finish, 34 oz. Disc. 2019.

	$1,150	$1,000	$865	$775	$650	$525	$425	*$1,359*

* **P226 TacPac** – 9mm Para. or .40 S&W cal., black Nitron finish, Siglite sights, one-piece enhanced E2 grip, STL 900L, includes holster. Mfg. 2013-2014.

	$1,075	$950	$825	$725	$625	$525	$425	*$1,238*

* **P226 Tactical/Blackwater Tactical** – similar to P226, black Nitron finish, Picatinny rail, threaded barrel, post and dot contrast Siglite night sights, available in standard (disc. 2009) and Blackwater configuration (black Nitron finish, Siglite night sights, and wood grips). Mfg. 2007-2010.

	$1,150	$975	$850	$750	$650	$550	$450	*$1,300*

Subtract approx. $50 for standard tactical - (disc. 2009, last MSR was $1,245).

* **P226 Tribal Nitron** – 9mm Para. cal., black hardcoat frame, polished tribal pattern Nitron slide, custom engraved tribal aluminum grips. Mfg. 2015 only.

	$1,125	$950	$825	$725	$625	$525	$425	*$1,348*

GRADING - PPGS™	100%	98%	95%	90%	80%	70%	60%	LAST MSR

* ***P226 Tribal Two-Tone*** – 9mm Para. cal., black hardcoat frame, polished tribal pattern stainless steel slide, custom tribal engraved aluminum grips. Mfg. 2015 only.

	$950	$795	$665	$535	$465	$415	$365	*$1,176*

* ***P226 USPSA*** – 9mm Para. cal., short reset trigger, 4.4 in. barrel, 15 shot mag., Dawson fiber optic front sight, Warren rear sight, polymer grips, aluminum frame with stainless steel slide, black Nitron finish, USPSA engraving, includes three mags. Mfg. 2009-2010.

	$1,095	$950	$825	$725	$625	$525	$400	*$1,246*

P226 .22 LR – .22 LR cal., DA/SA, full size alloy frame, 4.4 in. barrel, 10 shot mag., adj. sights, E2 grip, black anodized finish. Mfg. 2014 only, reintroduced 2017-2018.

	$525	$475	$425	$375	$325	$300	$275	*$630*

Add $23 for beavertail and short reset trigger (SRT, disc. 2014).
Add 100% for early guns in "H" prefix serial range.

P226 LEGION – 9mm Para., .40 S&W (disc. 2019), or .357 SIG (disc. 2019) cal., DA/SA, or SAO, 4.4 in. barrel, X-Ray3 day/night sights, 12 (.40 S&W or .357, disc. 2019) or 15 shot mag., short reset trigger, black G10 grips, X-RAY, gray finish. New 2016.

MSR $1,330	$1,135	$995	$850	$775	$625	$525	$445	

* ***P226 Legion RX*** – 9mm Para. cal., DA/SA or SAO, full size alloy frame, 4.4 in. barrel, 12 or 15 shot mag., Nitron stainless steel slide, Grayguns Inc. designed P-SAIT trigger or Master Shop Super Flat match trigger (SAO variant only), X RAY3 day/night sights with SIG ROMEO1 Reflex sight, black G10 grips with Legion medallion, checkered front strap and under trigger guard, SIG accessory rail, Legion Gray finish, 34 oz. New 2018.

MSR $1,550	$1,325	$1,160	$995	$900	$725	$600	$515	

P226 X-FIVE – 9mm Para. or .40 S&W cal., SAO, adj. trigger, 5 in. stainless steel barrel and slide, ambidextrous thumb safety, all stainless construction with magwell, low profile adj. sights, 14 (.40 S&W) or 19 (9mm Para.) shot mag., available in blue, two-tone, stainless or black Nitron finish, checkered walnut grips, includes 25 meter test target, checkered front grip strap, 47.2 oz. Mfg. mid-2005-2012.

	$2,400	$2,050	$1,700	$1,400	$1,225	$1,000	$850	*$2,747*

* ***P226 X-Five Competition*** – 9mm Para. or .40 S&W cal., similar to X-Five, except has black polymer grips. Mfg. 2007-2012.

	$1,725	$1,475	$1,250	$1,050	$875	$700	$650	*$1,976*

* ***P226 X-Five All Around*** – 9mm Para. or .40 S&W cal., adj. sights, ergonomic beavertail grip, DA/SA, stainless slide and frame, black polymer grips. Mfg. 2007-2012.

	$1,425	$1,200	$975	$850	$750	$650	$550	*$1,696*

* ***P226 X-Five Tactical*** – 9mm Para. cal., SAO, black Nitron finish, contrast sights, lightweight alloy frame, Picatinny rail, ergonomic beavertail grips. Mfg. 2007-2012.

	$1,425	$1,200	$975	$850	$750	$650	$550	*$1,696*

P226 X SERIES – 9mm Para. or .40 S&W cal., individual models are marked on left side of slide between slide serrations. New series mfg. 2014 only.

* ***P226 X All Around*** – 9mm Para. or .40 S&W cal., DA/SA, natural stainless steel slide and frame extended for 5 in. barrel, adj. rear sight, front cocking serrations, integral Picatinny accessory rail, standard magazine and mag. catch, black laminated grips. Mfg. 2014 only.

	$1,900	$1,750	$1,525	$1,325	$1,125	$950	$750	*$2,245*

* ***P226 X Classic*** – 9mm Para. or .40 S&W cal., SAO, 5 in. barrel, natural stainless steel slide and frame, user adj. SAO trigger, fully adj. target sights, M1913 Picatinny accessory rail, custom walnut grips. Mfg. 2014 only.

	$2,275	$2,000	$1,750	$1,500	$1,300	$1,100	$900	*$2,679*

* ***P226 X Entry*** – 9mm Para. or .40 S&W cal., SAO, 5 in. barrel, natural stainless steel slide and frame, fixed rear sight, M1913 Picatinny accessory rail, standard magazine catch, black polymer grips. Mfg. 2014 only.

	$1,495	$1,300	$1,125	$995	$850	$700	$575	*$1,763*

* ***P226 X Match*** – 9mm Para. or .40 S&W cal., SAO, natural stainless steel slide and frame extended for a 5 in. barrel, front cocking serrations, skeletonized hammer, fully adj. target sights, M1913 Picatinny accessory rail, extended magazine catch, black laminate grips. Mfg. 2014 only.

	$1,450	$1,250	$1,075	$950	$800	$650	$550	*$1,728*

Add $1,192 for .40 S&W cal.
Add $1,078 for shorter barrel (XFive Match Short model).

GRADING - PPGS™	100%	98%	95%	90%	80%	70%	60%	LAST MSR

* ***P226 X Open*** – 9mm Para. cal., SAO, natural stainless steel slide and frame, 5 in. barrel with compensator, user adj. SAO straight match trigger, Sport takedown lever, M1913 Picatinny accessory rail, black G10 grips, bridge mount, ambidextrous slide racker, extended magazine catch. Mfg. 2014 only.

	$4,200	**$3,800**	**$3,350**	**$2,800**	**$2,300**	**$1,900**	**$1,625**	***$4,852***

* ***P226 X Super Match*** – 9mm Para. or .40 S&W cal., 5 or 6 (XSix Super Match) in. barrel, sport takedown lever, natural stainless steel slide and frame, fully adj. target sights, M1913 Picatinny accessory rail, extended magazine catch, black G10 grips, straight trigger. Mfg. 2014 only.

	$2,600	**$2,300**	**$2,000**	**$1,750**	**$1,500**	**$1,250**	**$1,000**	***$3,042***

Add $241 for 6 in. barrel (XSix Super Match model).

* ***P226 X Tactical*** – 9mm Para. or .40 S&W cal., SAO, Nitron slide, black alloy frame, black polymer grips. Mfg. 2014 only.

	$1,450	**$1,250**	**$1,050**	**$875**	**$750**	**$625**	**$550**	***$1,678***

P227 – .45 ACP cal., DA/SA, 4.4 in. stainless steel barrel, 10 shot mag., contrast sights (disc. 2015) or Siglite night sights, lower Picatinny rail, one-piece enhanced E2 grip, black Nitron or FDE (mfg. 2015-2016) finish, 32 oz. Mfg. 2013-2018.

	$925	**$750**	**$635**	**$525**	**$450**	**$400**	**$350**	***$1,087***

Add $54 for FDE slide and frame finish with Siglite night sights (disc. 2016).
Subtract $114 for contrast sights (disc. 2015).

* ***P227 Carry*** – .45 ACP cal., DA/SA, 3.9 in. stainless steel barrel, 10 shot mag., Siglite night sights, lower Picatinny rail, one-piece polymer grips, black Nitron finish, 30 1/2 oz. Mfg. 2013-2016.

	$885	**$750**	**$650**	**$525**	**$450**	**$400**	**$350**	***$1,087***

* ***P227 Carry SAS*** – .45 ACP cal., Gen. 2, 3.9 in. stainless steel barrel, black Nitron finish, dehorning, SRT, contrast (disc.) or Siglite night sights, Sig anti-snag treatment on slide and frame with no rail, one-piece ergonomic grips, 30 1/2 oz. Mfg. 2013-2018.

	$915	**$765**	**$650**	**$535**	**$465**	**$415**	**$365**	***$1,119***

* ***P227 Enhanced Elite*** – .45 ACP cal., DA/SA, 4.4 in. barrel, 10 shot mag., beavertail, SRT, Siglite night sights, one-piece enhanced E2 grip, black Nitron finish. Mfg. 2015-2018.

	$950	**$795**	**$650**	**$545**	**$475**	**$420**	**$365**	***$1,174***

* ***P227 Equinox*** – .45 ACP cal., DA/SA, 3.9 (Carry Equinox, new 2016) or 4.4 in. barrel, 10 shot mag., two-tone polished Nitron finish, TruGlo TFO front sight, Siglite night sights, wood grips. Mfg. 2014-2016.

	$1,050	**$915**	**$815**	**$725**	**$625**	**$525**	**$425**	***$1,228***

* ***P227 Nitron RX*** – .45 ACP cal., DA/SA, full size lightweight alloy frame, 4.4 in. barrel, 10 shot mag., Nitron stainless steel slide, Siglite night sights with ROMEO1 Reflex Sight, E2 grips, SIG accessory rail, 32 oz. Mfg. 2018 only.

	$1,275	**$1,065**	**$935**	**$825**	**$675**	**$575**	**$475**	***$1,440***

* ***P227 Tactical*** – .45 ACP cal., DA/SA, 4.9 in. threaded barrel, 10 or 14 shot mag., SRT, Siglite sights, E2 grip, black Nitron finish. Mfg. 2014-2016.

	$1,050	**$915**	**$815**	**$725**	**$625**	**$525**	**$425**	***$1,228***

* ***P227 TACOPS*** – .45 ACP cal., DA/SA, 4.4 in. barrel, four 14 shot mags., Elite beavertail frame, SRT, TFO/Siglite night sight combo, G10 Magwell grips, black Nitron finish, 35 oz. Mfg. 2015-2018.

	$1,250	**$1,050**	**$925**	**$825**	**$700**	**$600**	**$500**	***$1,413***

* ***P227R TacPac*** – .45 ACP cal., DA/SA, 45 Nitron, Siglite sights, STL-900L, 10 shot mag., includes holster. Mfg. 2014 only.

	$1,050	**$950**	**$825**	**$725**	**$625**	**$525**	**$425**	***$1,238***

P228 (OLD MFG.) – 9mm Para., DA/SA or SAO (new 1992) operation, compact design, 3.86 in. (compact) barrel, 10 (C/B 1994) or 13* (reintroduced 2004) shot mag., automatic firing pin block safety, high contrast sights, alloy frame, choice of blue, Nitron (new 2004), nickel (mfg. 1991-97), or stainless steel (new 2004) slide, or K-Kote (disc. 1997) finish, 29.3 oz. Mfg. 1990-97, reintroduced 2004-2006.

	$700	**$600**	**$500**	**$450**	**$400**	**$350**	**$310**	***$840***

Add $50 for Siglite night sights.
Add $376 for .22 LR cal. conversion kit.
Add $45 for K-Kote (Polymer) finish (disc. 1997).
Add $45 for nickel finished slide (1991-97).
Add $70 for electroless nickel finish (disc. 1991).
Add up to 100% for special Swiss police markings.

This model was also available in double action only (all finishes) at no extra charge.
This model was also available as a Custom Shop Limited Edition during April, 2004 (MSR was $800).

GRADING - PPGS™	100%	98%	95%	90%	80%	70%	60%	LAST MSR

PISTOLS: SEMI-AUTO, P229, P230, & P232 SERIES

P229 – .357 SIG (mfg. 1995-2016), 9mm Para. (mfg. 1994-96, reintroduced 1999), or .40 S&W cal., compact size, 3.9 in. barrel, choice of DA/SA or DAK trigger system (DAO with 6 1/2 lb. trigger pull) available beginning 2005, blackened Nitron or satin nickel (disc.) finished stainless steel slide with aluminum alloy frame, 10 (C/B 1994), 12* (.357 SIG or .40 S&W cal. only), or 13 (9mm Para. cal. only, new 2005) shot mag., E2 (enhanced ergonomics) grips became standard 2011, tactical rail became standard in 2004 (Nitron finish only), contrast (9mm or .40 S&W only, disc. 2015) or Siglite night sights became standard in 2016, includes lockable carrying case, 31.1 or 32.4 oz. New 1991.

MSR $1,000	$850	$750	$650	$580	$475	$385	$325	

Subtract $114 for contrast sights (disc. 2015).
Add $306 for Crimson Trace Lasergrips w/Siglite night sights (mfg. 2007-2008).
Add $180 for black Nitron finish with TruGlo TFO front and Siglite rear sights with four hi-cap mags. (Super Cap Tactical model, not available in .357 SIG cal.), disc. 2010.
Add $103 for two-tone finish (nickel finished stainless steel slide) with night sights (disc. 2011).
Add $349 for .22 LR cal. conversion kit (disc.).

This model was also available in double action only at no extra charge.

This model was also available as a Custom Shop Limited Edition during June, 2004 (MSR was $873), during August, 2004 (MSR was $916) and during Dec. 2004 (MSR was $844).

* ***P229 ASE Compact*** – 9mm Para. or .40 S&W cal., DA/SA, compact alloy frame, 3.9 in. barrel, 10, 12, or 15 shot mag., SRT, Siglite night sights, walnut grips, front cocking serrations, SIG accessory rail, stainless steel PVD finish on frame and slide, 34.4 oz. Mfg. 2018 only.

	$950	$785	$650	$535	$465	$415	$365	*$1,174*

* ***P229 Combat*** – 9mm Para. cal., DA/SA, 3.9 in. barrel, 15 shot mag., Siglite night sights, FDE finished alloy frame, stainless steel slide with Nitron finish, Picatinny rail, vertical front strap serrations, FDE polymer grips, 32 oz. Mfg. 2015-2017.

	$1,035	$895	$800	$700	$600	$500	$400	*$1,195*

* ***P229 Elite*** – 9mm Para., .40 S&W, or .357 SIG cal., DA/SA or SAO, 3.9 in. barrel, 10, 12, or 13 shot mag., SRT, two-tone (disc.), or black Nitron finish, ergonomic beavertail, Picatinny rail, front cocking serrations, Siglite night sights, custom rosewood or aluminum grips (Platinum Elite, disc. 2011), 33.5 oz. Mfg. 2007-2012.

	$1,050	$925	$825	$725	$625	$525	$425	*$1,218*

Add $71 for TB model with threaded barrel.
Add $72 for platinum Elite with aluminum grips (disc. 2011).

* ***P229 Elite (Current Mfg.)*** – 9mm Para. cal., DA/SA, 3.9 in. barrel, two 15 shot mags., SRT, Siglite night sights, E2 grip, black finish. New 2021.

MSR $1,100	$935	$825	$700	$635	$515	$425	$365	

* ***P229 Elite Stainless*** – 9mm Para. or .40 S&W cal., DA/SA, 3.9 in. barrel, stainless steel slide and frame, 10, 12 (.40 S&W only), or 15 (9mm Para.) shot mag., SRT, ergonomic beavertail, Picatinny rail, front cocking serrations, Siglite night sights, Custom Shop rosewood grips, natural stainless finish, 40.2 oz. Mfg. 2007-2016.

	$1,225	$1,015	$900	$800	$700	$600	$500	*$1,359*

* ***P229 Elite Dark*** – 9mm Para., .357 SIG (disc. 2012), or .40 S&W cal., DA/SA, 3.9 in. barrel, SRT (short reset trigger), Black Nitron finish, 12 or 15 shot mag., ergonomic beavertail, Picatinny rail, front cocking serrations, front strap checkering, Siglite night sights, custom aluminum grips. Mfg. 2009-2014.

	$1,050	$925	$825	$725	$625	$525	$425	*$1,243*

Add $71 for TB model with threaded barrel (disc. 2013).

* ***P229 Enhanced Elite*** – 9mm Para., .40 S&W (disc. 2015), or .357 SIG (disc. 2015) cal., DA/SA, 3.9 in. barrel, 10 (disc. 2015), 12 (disc. 2015), or 15 shot mag., beavertail frame with front strap checkering and accessory rail, SRT, E2 polymer grips, Siglite night sights, black Nitron finish, 32 oz. Mfg. 2011-2013, reintroduced 2015-2017.

	$950	$795	$650	$545	$475	$420	$365	*$1,174*

* ***P229 Scorpion Elite*** – 9mm Para. or .40 S&W cal., 3.9 in. threaded (9mm only) or non-threaded barrel, beavertail, SRT, Siglite night sights, Hogue Extreme G10 grips, FDE finish. Mfg. 2012-2015.

	$1,125	$950	$825	$725	$625	$525	$425	*$1,348*

Add $57 for threaded barrel (9mm Para. only).

GRADING - PPGS™	100%	98%	95%	90%	80%	70%	60%	LAST MSR

* **P229 Emperor Scorpion** – 9mm Para. cal., DA/SA, full size alloy frame, 3.9 in. barrel, 15 shot mag., stainless steel slide, SRT trigger, Siglite night sights, G10 Piranha grips, front cocking serrations, SIG accessory rail, FDE PVD coated slide and frame, 34.4 oz. Mfg. 2018-2019.

$1,025	$825	$700	$575	$500	$450	$400	*$1,282*

* **P229 Equinox** – .40 S&W cal., 3.9 or 4.4 (disc.) in. barrel, two-tone Nitron stainless steel slide, lightweight black anodized alloy frame, nickel accents, 10 or 12 shot mag., TruGlo TFO front sight, rear Siglite night sight, Picatinny rail, grey laminated wood grips, 34 oz. Mfg. by the Custom Shop 2007-2012, reintroduced 2015-2016.

$1,050	$900	$800	$700	$600	$500	$400	*$1,195*

» **P229 Equinox Compact** – 9mm Para. cal., alloy frame with hard coat anodized finish, 3.9 in. carbon steel barrel, two 15 shot steel mags., stainless steel slide with Nitron finish, DA/SA, X-Ray3 day/night sights, black Hogue SL G-10 grips, 34 oz. New 2020.

Limited edition comes in Custom Works Negrini case with a SIG Custom Works challenge coin and a certified custom certificate.

* **P229 Extreme** – 9mm Para. cal., DA/SA, 3.9 in. barrel, 10 or 15 shot mag., front slide serrations, SRT, Siglite night sights, Picatinny rail, Hogue Extreme Series G10 grips, black Nitron finish, 32 oz. Mfg. 2012-2013, reintroduced 2015 only.

$1,095	$935	$825	$700	$600	$500	$400	*$1,256*

* **P229 E2** – 9mm Para. cal., 15 shot mag., black Nitron finish, ergonomic slim profile one-piece grips, Siglite night sights, short reset trigger, integral accessory rail, includes three mags. Mfg. 2010 only.

$1,000	$895	$775	$675	$575	$525	$450	*$1,149*

* **P229 M11-A1** – 9mm Para. cal., DA/SA, 3.9 in. threaded (disc. 2016) or non-threaded barrel, includes three 15 shot double stack mags., SRT, Siglite night sights, black polymer factory grips, black hard anodized frame finish with one-piece stainless steel slide, corrosion protection on internal components, controls, and barrel, black nitron or FDE (mfg. 2014-2016) finish, 32 oz. New 2013.

MSR $1,100	$935	$825	$700	$635	$515	$425	$365

Add $55 for FDE finish or threaded barrel (mfg. 2014-2016).

This model was previously incorrectly identified as a Model P228 M11-A1 (new mfg.).

* **P229 Nightmare Compact** – 9mm Para. cal., DA/SA, compact alloy frame, 3.9 in. barrel, two 15 shot steel mags., Custom Works engraved stainless steel slide with Nitron finish, X-RAY3 day/night sights, Hogue Classic Contour SL G10 black grips, SIG rail, comes packaged in Custom Works Negrini pistol case with SIG Custom Works challenge coin and certified custom certificate, 34 oz. Custom Works Limited Edition. New 2021.

Please contact the company directly for price and availability.

* **P229 RX** – 9mm Para. cal., DA/SA, compact frame, 3.9 in. barrel, stainless steel slide, two 15 shot mags., black G10 grips, Siglite night sights, M1913 accessory rail, slide-mounted reflex optic ROMEO1 reflex sight, 34.4 oz. Mfg. 2018-2019.

$1,095	$935	$825	$725	$625	$525	$425	*$1,310*

* **P229 SAS** – 9mm Para., .357 SIG, or .40 S&W cal., DA/SA, 3.9 in. barrel, 12 or 13 shot mag., DAK (disc.) or SRT, smooth dehorned stainless steel slide with engraved Custom Shop logo, contrast (disc.) or Siglite night sights, lightweight black hard anodized frame, rounded trigger guard, checkered wood (disc.) or one-piece E2 grips, designed for snag-free profile for concealed carry, Generation II features became standard 2009, two-tone (disc.) or black Nitron (new 2009) finish, 32 oz. Mfg. by Custom Shop. Mfg. 2005-2012, reintroduced 2015 only.

$950	$795	$665	$535	$465	$415	$365	*$1,176*

Add $30 for two-tone finish (disc. 2010).

* **P229 Select Compact** – 9mm Para. cal., DA/SA, compact alloy frame, 3.9 in. barrel, 15 shot mag., Nitron stainless slide, Siglite night sights, SELECT G10 grips, front cocking serrations, low profile controls, SIG accessory rail, 34.4 oz. Mfg. 2018-2019.

$975	$800	$650	$535	$465	$415	$365	*$1,195*

* **P229 Sport** – .357 SIG or .40 S&W (new 2003) cal., DA/SA or SAO, 4.8 in. match or heavy (disc. 2000) compensated barrel, stainless steel frame and slide, target sights, improved trigger pull, 43.6 oz. Mfg. 1998-2000, reintroduced 2003-2005.

$1,375	$975	$800	$695	$585	$485	$415	*$1,600*

GRADING - PPGS™	100%	98%	95%	90%	80%	70%	60%	LAST MSR

* ***P229 TacPac*** – 9mm Para. or .40 S&W cal., features black nitron finish, Siglite sights, one-piece enhanced E2 grip, STL 900L, includes holster. Mfg. 2013-2014.

	$1,075	$950	$825	$725	$625	$525	$425	*$1,238*

* ***P229 HF (Heritage Fund)*** – .40 S&W cal., 10 shot, 3.9 in. barrel, slide marked "10th Anniversary P229", frame marked "1992-2002", gold engraving and accents, brushed stainless steel, gold trigger, cocobolo Hogue grips with NSSF Heritage Fund medallion, includes wood display case. Limited mfg. late 2001-2004.

	$1,195	$750	$600	N/A	N/A	N/A	N/A	*$1,299*

* ***P229R .22 LR*** – .22 LR cal., DA/SA, 4.4 in. barrel, 10 shot mag., matte black anodized finish, adj. sights, E2 polymer grip, otherwise similar to standard P229. Mfg. 2009-2012, reintroduced 2015 only.

	$725	$625	$550	$475	$400	$350	$275	*$858*

P229 LEGION COMPACT – 9mm Para., .40 S&W (disc. 2020), or .357 Mag. (disc. 2020) cal., DA/SA, compact alloy frame, 3.9 in. barrel, 12 (.40 S&W or .357, disc. 2020) or 15 shot mag., stainless steel slide, GraygunsInc. P-SAIT trigger, X-Ray day/night sights, black G10 grips with Legion medallion, SIG accessory rail, Legion Gray frame finish, 34.4 oz. New 2016.

MSR $1,330	$1,135	$995	$850	$775	$625	$525	$445	

* ***P229 Legion RX Compact*** – 9mm Para. cal., DA/SA, compact alloy frame, 3.9 in. barrel, three 15 shot steel mags., stainless steel slide, P-SAIT trigger, X-RAY3 day/night sights with ROMEO1 Reflex Sight, black G10 grips, SIG accessory rail, Legion Gray frame finish, 32 oz. New 2018.

MSR $1,550	$1,325	$1,160	$995	$900	$725	$600	$515	

* ***P229 Legion Compact SAO*** – 9mm Para. cal., SAO, compact alloy frame, 3.9 in. barrel, three 15 shot mags., stainless steel slide, Master Shop flat trigger, X-RAY3 day/night sights, black G10 grips with Legion medallion, SIG accessory rail, contoured elite beavertail, front strap checkering, front cocking serrations, Legion Gray PVD coating, 32 oz. New mid-2018.

MSR $1,330	$1,135	$995	$850	$775	$625	$525	$445	

P230 – .22 LR (disc.), .32 ACP, .380 ACP, or 9mm Ultra (disc.) cal., DA/SA or DAO, 7, 8, or 10 shot mag., 3.6 in. barrel, blue, composite grips, 17.6 oz. Mfg. 1976-1996.

	$475	$450	$325	$275	$250	$215	$190	*$510*

Add $35 for stainless slide (.380 ACP only).
Add 20% for Police marked pistols in 9mm Ultra.

* ***P230 SL Stainless*** – similar to Model P230, except stainless steel construction, 22.4 oz. Disc. 1996.

	$525	$450	$375	$315	$270	$230	$200	*$595*

P232 – .380 ACP cal., DA/SA or DAO, 3.6 in. barrel, 7 shot mag., aluminum alloy frame, compact personal size, blue (disc.), black nitron or two-tone stainless (disc. 2012) slide, automatic firing pin block safety, composite (disc.) or Hogue rubber grips, Siglite night sights (became standard 2010), 17.6 oz. Mfg. 1997-2014.

	$725	$650	$550	$475	$425	$350	$295	*$809*

Add $29 for two-tone finish (mfg. 2007-2012).
Subtract $71 if w/o Siglite night sights (became standard 2010).

* ***P232 Stainless*** – .380 ACP cal., similar to Model P232, except stainless steel construction, natural finish, 22.4 oz. Mfg. 1997-2014.

	$795	$650	$525	$450	$375	$325	$295	*$889*

Subtract approx. $75 if w/o Siglite night sights and Hogue grips (standard beginning 2007).

PISTOLS: SEMI-AUTO, P238, P239, P245, P250, & P290 SERIES

P238 – 9mm Para. (mfg. 2012 only), or .380 ACP cal., lightweight aluminum frame, 2.7 in. barrel, 6 shot mag., stainless steel slide, SAO trigger, thumb safety, black Nitron or two-tone finish, fixed or Siglite night sights, fluted grips (new 2012), 15.2 oz. Mfg. 2009-2013.

	$550	$475	$450	$375	$340	$300	$275	*$679*

Add $14 for two-tone finish.
Subtract $40 if w/o Siglite night sights (standard beginning 2010).

This model with specific features was disc. in 2013, and replacement model is the P238 Two-Tone Tribal (features black tribal engraving pattern on slide).

GRADING - PPGS™	100%	98%	95%	90%	80%	70%	60%	LAST MSR

* ***P238 Army*** – .380 ACP cal., SAO, micro-compact Army Green alloy frame, 2.7 in. barrel, 6 shot steel mag., Nitron stainless steel slide, Hogue rubber finger groove grips, Siglite sights, 15.2 oz. Special Edition version available exclusively through Talo Distributors. Disc. 2020.

	$595	$525	$485	$450	$395	$325	$295	*$692*

* ***P238 ASE*** – .380 ACP cal., micro-compact alloy frame, stainless PVD frame and slide, walnut grips, Siglite sights, front cocking serrations, 5.5 in. OAL, 15.2 oz. Disc. 2019.

	$615	$565	$485	$435	$395	$335	$295	*$740*

* ***P238 Blackwood*** – .380 ACP cal., SAO, 2.7 in. barrel, 6 shot, Siglite night sights, anodized alloy beavertail style frame, stainless steel slide, two-tone finish, blackwood grips, 15.2 oz. Mfg. 2010-2019.

	$615	$565	$475	$425	$385	$325	$285	*$715*

Add $28 for ambi safety (mfg. 2012 only).

* ***P238 BRG*** – .380 ACP cal., SAO, micro-compact alloy frame, 2.7 in. barrel, 7 shot mag., stainless steel slide with Nitron finish, Siglite night sights, black Hogue rubber grips, hardcoat anodized finish, 15.2 oz. Disc. 2019.

	$610	$550	$475	$425	$385	$325	$285	*$706*

* ***P238 Desert*** – .380 ACP cal., SAO, 2.7 in. barrel, X-Grip 7 shot mag., Siglite night sights, Hogue one-piece FDE rubber grips, ambi safety (mfg. 2012 only), Desert tan (two-tone FDE) finish. Mfg. 2012-2020.

	$595	$525	$450	$400	$325	$275	$225	*$700*

Add $28 for ambi safety (mfg. 2012 only).

* ***P238 Diamond Plate*** – .380 ACP cal., lightweight aluminum frame, 2.7 in. barrel, 6 shot mag., stainless steel slide, SAO trigger, Siglite night sights, two-tone or black Nitron (mfg. 2012 only) finish, "Diamond Plate" engraving, and black G10 grips. Mfg. 2011-2013.

	$650	$575	$475	$425	$375	$325	$275	*$752*

Add $28 for ambi safety (mfg. 2012 only).

* ***P238 Edge*** – .380 ACP cal., SAO, alloy beavertail style frame, 2.7 in. barrel, 6 shot steel mag., stainless steel slide with serrations, Siglite night sights, checkered black G10 grips, custom Edge PVD coated slide and controls, 20.1 oz. Mfg. 2015-2017.

	$665	$595	$495	$435	$395	$335	$295	*$738*

* ***P238 Emperor Scorpion*** – .380 ACP cal., SAO, micro-compact alloy frame, 2.7 in. barrel, Nitron stainless steel slide, skeletonized trigger, Siglite night sights, Hogue G10 Piranha grips, front cocking serrations, FDE PVD coated slide and frame, 16 oz. Mfg. 2018-2019.

	$650	$595	$500	$450	$400	$340	$300	*$801*

* ***P238 Engraved*** – .380 ACP cal., SAO, 2.7 in. barrel, 6 shot steel mag., polished Nitron engraved slide, Siglite night sights, rosewood grips with SIG medallion, black hardcoat anodized frame, 15.2 oz. Mfg. 2015-2017.

	$700	$625	$525	$450	$400	$340	$300	*$798*

* ***P238 Equinox*** – .380 ACP cal., SAO, beavertail style frame, 2.7 in. barrel, 6 shot mag., Siglite rear sight, TruGlo TFO front sight, custom black wood grips, ambi safety, two-tone Nitron finish, approx. 16 oz. Mfg. 2010-2017.

	$635	$575	$485	$435	$395	$335	$295	*$738*

Add $28 for ambi safety (mfg. 2012 only).

* ***P238 Extreme*** – .380 ACP cal., SAO, 2.7 in. barrel, X-Grip 7 shot mag., Siglite night sights, black/gray Hogue Extreme G10 grips, black Nitron finish. Mfg. 2012-2017.

	$645	$585	$495	$435	$395	$335	$295	*$738*

* ***P238 HD*** – .380 ACP cal., SAO, 2.7 in. barrel, 6 shot mag., stainless beavertail style frame with black accents, stainless steel slide with slide serrations, Siglite night sights, black G10 polymer grips, includes lockable hard case, 20.1 oz. Mfg. 2015 only.

	$680	$615	$515	$450	$400	$340	$300	*$799*

* ***P238 HDW*** – .380 ACP cal., SAO, 2.7 in. barrel, 6 shot mag., stainless steel frame and slide, Siglite night sights, locked breech mechanism, frame mounted thumb safety, rosewood grips, natural stainless finish, 20.1 oz. Mfg. 2015 only.

	$680	$615	$515	$450	$400	$340	$300	*$799*

GRADING - PPGS™	100%	98%	95%	90%	80%	70%	60%	LAST MSR

* **P238 HD Nickel** – .380 ACP cal., SAO, beavertail style stainless steel frame with nickel coating, 2.7 in. barrel, 6 shot mag., stainless steel slide with serrations, Siglite night sights, custom Blackwood grips with SIG medallion, 20.1 oz. Mfg. 2015-2016.

	$710	$625	$535	$485	$415	$350	$300	*$793*

* **P238 Lady** – .380 ACP cal., 2.7 in. barrel, 6 shot mag., Siglite night sights, red Cerakote alloy frame with "rose and scroll" 24K gold engraving, rosewood grips. Mfg. 2011-2013.

	$650	$575	$475	$425	$375	$325	$275	*$752*

* **P238 Legion Micro-Compact** – .380 ACP cal., 2.7 in. carbon steel barrel, alloy frame, three 7 shot steel mags., flat SAO aluminum trigger, X-RAY3 day/night sights, Legion Black G-10 grips w/ Legion medallion, ambidextrous thumb safety, front cocking serrations, extended magwell, Legion Gray finish in Cerakote Elite, 5 1/2 in. OAL, 15.2 oz. Mfg. 2018-2019.

	$700	$650	$550	$500	$400	$325	$250	*$850*

* **P238 Nightmare** – .380 ACP cal., SAO, anodized alloy beavertail style frame, 2.7 in. barrel, 6 shot mag., stainless steel slide with serrations, Siglite night sights, Hogue black G10 grips, black Nitron finished frame and slide. Mfg. 2015-2018.

	$615	$565	$485	$435	$395	$335	$295	*$738*

* **P238 Nitron** – .380 ACP cal., SAO, 2.7 in. barrel, 6 shot mag., beavertail style frame, contrast (new 2017) or Siglite night (disc. 2016) sights, fluted polymer grips, black Nitron finish, 15.2 oz.

MSR $650	$550	$480	$415	$375	$300	$250	$215	

Subtract approx. $25 if without Siglite night sights.

* **P238 Polished/Pearl** – .380 ACP cal., SAO, 2.7 in. barrel, 6 shot, polished frame and engraved stainless steel slide, Siglite night sights, Hogue Pink Rubber (disc.), Pink Pearlite (disc. 2016), Black Pearlite, or White Pearlite (disc. 2017) grips, 15.2 oz. Mfg. 2014-2019.

	$650	$595	$500	$450	$400	$340	$300	*$798*

* **P238 Rainbow** – .380 ACP cal., SAO, beavertail frame, 2.7 in. barrel, 6 shot mag., Siglite night sights, rosewood grips, Rainbow titanium slide and accents, 15.2 oz. Mfg. 2010-2020.

	$595	$525	$450	$400	$325	$275	$225	*$700*

* **P238 Rose Gold** – .380 ACP cal., SAO, micro-compact hard anodized frame, 2.7 in. barrel, 6 shot mag., polished and engraved rose gold stainless steel slide, skeletonized hammer, Siglite night sights, black G10 grips with rose gold medallion, rose gold controls, 15.2 oz. Mfg. 2018-2019.

	$795	$675	$550	$475	$415	$360	$315	*$932*

* **P238 Rosewood** – .380 ACP cal., 2.7 in. barrel, 6 shot mag., beavertail style frame, Siglite night sights, rosewood grips, black Nitron finish, 15.2 oz. Mfg. 2010-2019.

	$615	$565	$475	$425	$385	$325	$285	*$715*

Add $29 for ambi safety (mfg. 2012 only).

* **P238 SAS** – .380 ACP cal., SAO, 2.7 in. barrel, 6 shot mag., dehorned frame and slide, Siglite night sights, Custom Shop (disc.) or brown Goncalo checkered wood grips, ambi safety (mfg. 2012 only), logo engraved on slide, two-tone finish. Mfg. 2011-2019.

	$635	$575	$485	$435	$395	$335	$295	*$738*

Add $29 for ambi safety (mfg. 2012 only).

* **P238 Scorpion** – .380 ACP cal., 2.7 in. barrel, 7 shot mag., Siglite night sights, black/hreen Hogue G10 grips, ambi safety, FDE finish. Mfg. 2012-2016.

	$650	$595	$500	$450	$400	$340	$300	*$760*

* **P238 Select** – .380 ACP cal., SAO, micro-compact alloy frame, 2.7 in. carbon steel barrel, 6 shot mag., Nitron stainless steel slide, skeletonized hammer, Siglite night sights, SELECT G10 grips, front cocking serrations, 15.2 oz. Mfg. 2018-2019.

	$635	$575	$485	$435	$395	$335	$295	*$738*

* **P238 Spartan** – .380 ACP cal., SAO, 2.7 in. barrel, stainless steel frame and slide, X-Grip 7 shot mag., slide is engraved with the Greek phrase "MOLON LABE", custom grips feature the inlaid Spartan helmet, Siglite night sights, oil-rubbed bronze PVD finish, 20.1 oz. Mfg. 2015-2018.

	$850	$725	$600	$525	$450	$365	$300	*$1,013*

* **P238 Spartan II** – .380 ACP cal., SAO, micro-compact alloy frame, 2.7 in. carbon steel barrel, 7 shot mag., custom Spartan grips with inlaid Spartan helmet, stainless steel slide engraved with the Greek phrase "MOLON LABE", Distressed Coyote finish, 15.2 oz. Mfg. 2019-2020.

	$595	$525	$450	$400	$325	$275	$225	*$700*

GRADING - PPGS™	100%	98%	95%	90%	80%	70%	60%	LAST MSR

* ***P238 Stainless*** – .380 ACP cal., similar to P238, except has stainless steel frame and slide, Siglite night sights, G10 or rosewood (disc. 2012) grips, approx. 20 oz. Mfg. 2010-2013.

$680	$615	$515	$450	$400	$340	$300	*$786*

* ***P238 Tactical Laser*** – .380 ACP cal., SAO, lightweight aluminum frame, 2.7 in. barrel, 6 shot mag., stainless steel slide, two-tone finish, Siglite night sights, black checkered aluminum grips, ambi safety (new 2012), ambi laser module. Mfg. 2010-2012.

$725	$625	$525	$475	$425	$375	$325	*$829*

* ***P238 Texas Flag*** – .380 ACP cal., SAO, micro-compact alloy frame, 2.7 in. barrel, 6 shot mag., stainless steel slide with two-tone FDE finish and Texas flag, Siglite night sights, custom black grips with Lone Star medallion, 5.5 in. OAL,15.2 oz. Disc. 2019.

$650	$575	$485	$435	$395	$335	$295	*$760*

* ***P238 Trigger Guard Laser*** – .380 ACP cal., 6 shot mag., contrast sights, removable trigger guard laser, polymer grips, black Nitron finish. Mfg. 2015 only.

$680	$615	$515	$450	$400	$340	$300	*$799*

* ***P238 Two-Tone Tribal*** – .380 ACP cal., SAO, 2.7 in. barrel, 6 shot, two-tone finish with Nitron tribal pattern engraving on slide, Siglite night sights, custom tribal engraved aluminum grips, 15.2 oz. Mfg. 2014-2015.

$665	$595	$495	$435	$395	$335	$295	*$776*

* ***P238 Rosewood Tribal*** – .380 ACP cal., SAO, 2.7 in. barrel, 6 shot, two-tone nickel plated stainless slide with Rainbow titanium tribal pattern engraving, Siglite night sights, custom rosewood grips, 15.2 oz. Mfg. 2014-2015.

$665	$595	$495	$435	$395	$335	$295	*$776*

* ***P238 We The People*** – .380 ACP cal., SAO, micro-compact alloy frame, 2.7 in. carbon steel barrel, stainless steel slide, contrast sights, custom aluminum grips with 25 stars engraved on each side, 13 stars and "WE THE PEOPLE" engraved on top of slide, "1776" engraved on slide flats, custom distressed finish, 15.2 oz. Mfg. 2018-2019.

$625	$565	$475	$425	$385	$325	$285	*$728*

P238 LEGION – .380 ACP cal., micro compact frame, 2.7 in. barrel, 7 shot mag., extended magwell, skeletonized hammer, flat trigger, X-RAY3 day/night sights, Legion Gray finished SAS slide and frame. Mfg. 2019 only.

$700	$650	$550	$500	$400	$325	$250	*$850*

P239 – .357 SIG, 9mm Para., or .40 S&W (new 1998) cal., compact personal size, DA/SA or DAO, 3.6 in. barrel, stainless steel slide and aluminum alloy frame, DAK trigger, firing pin block safety, 7 or 8 (9mm Para. only) shot mag., contrast or Siglite night sights, black polymer or one-piece enhanced E2 grip, black Nitron or two-tone (disc. 2009) finish, approx. 29 oz. Mfg. 1996-2015.

$925	$775	$650	$525	$450	$400	$350	*$1,142*

Subtract $114 if without Siglite night sights.
Add $305 for Crimson Trace Lasergrips and night sights (mfg. 2007).
Add $135 for two-tone stainless slide with night sights (disc. 2009).

This model was also available as a Custom Shop Limited Edition during May, 2004 (MSR was $673).

* ***P239 Rainbow*** – .40 S&W cal., otherwise similar to P239, Rainbow titanium finish, Siglite night sights. Mfg. 2012 only.

$925	$825	$725	$625	$525	$450	$350	*$1,000*

* ***P239 SAS*** – 9mm Para. (new 2008), .357 SIG (disc. 2012, reintroduced 2015), or .40 S&W cal., 3.6 in. barrel, 7 or 8 shot mag., DAK (disc.) or short reset trigger, smooth dehorned stainless steel slide, contrast (disc.) or Siglite night sights, lightweight black hard anodized frame, black Nitron or two-tone (disc. 2013) finish, rounded trigger guard, checkered/carved wood grips, designed for snag-free profile for concealed carry, Generation II features became standard 2009, 29 1/2 oz. Mfg. by Custom Shop June 2005-2017.

$835	$725	$625	$525	$450	$400	$350	*$1,032*

Add $14 for two-tone finish (disc. 2013).

* ***P239 Scorpion Elite*** – 9mm Para., .357 SIG, or .40 S&W cal., DA/SA, 3.6 in. barrel, 7 or 8 shot mag., SRT, Siglite night sights, FDE finish, Hogue G10 Piranha grips, 29.5 oz. Mfg. 2014-2015.

$1,095	$935	$825	$700	$600	$500	$400	*$1,256*

GRADING - PPGS™	100%	98%	95%	90%	80%	70%	60%	LAST MSR

* ***P239 Tactical*** – 9mm Para. cal., DA/SA, 4 in. threaded barrel, 8 shot mag., front cocking serrations, SRT, Siglite night sights, black polymer grips, black Nitron finish, 29.5 oz. Mfg. 2010-2012, reintroduced 2015 only.

	$1,095	$935	$825	$700	$600	$500	$400	*$1,256*

P245 – .45 ACP cal., DA/SA, compact model featuring 3.9 in. barrel, includes 6 and 8 shot mag., blue, two-tone (disc. 2005), Ilaflon (mfg. 2000 only), or K-Kote (disc. 1999) finish, approx. 30 oz. Mfg. 1999-2006.

	$695	$585	$495	$440	$400	$350	$310	*$840*

Add $75 for Siglite night sights.
Add $56 for two-tone or K-Kote finish (disc.).
Add $50 for Ilaflon finish (mfg. 2000 only).

P250 FULL SIZE – 9mm Para., .357 SIG (disc. 2010, reintroduced 2015 only), .40 S&W, or .45 ACP cal., DAO, full size frame, 4.7 in. barrel, steel frame with black polymer grip shell, features modular synthetic frame with removable fire control assembly, 10 (.45 ACP), 14 (.40 S&W and .357 SIG), or 17 (9mm Para.) shot mag., ambidextrous slide release lever, black Nitron or two-tone (disc. 2010) finish, contrast or Siglite night (disc. 2015) sights, integrated Picatinny rail, converts into various calibers by changing slides, grip modules, and magazine, 27.6 oz. Mfg. mid-2008-2013, reintroduced 2015-2016.

	$415	$395	$365	$325	$285	$260	$230	*$480*

Add $58 for Siglite night sights (disc. 2015).
Add $15 for two-tone finish (not available in .45 ACP cal.), disc. 2010.
Add $243 for 2 SUM package, includes sub-compact caliber exchange kit (not available in .357 SIG or .45 ACP cal.), disc.

* ***P250 Compact*** – 9mm Para., .357 SIG (disc. 2015), .380 ACP (new 2015), .40 S&W or .45 ACP cal., 3.9 in. threaded (9mm, 2015 only) or non-threaded barrel, 9 (.45 ACP), 10 (.22 LR), 13 (.357 SIG or .40 S&W) or 15 (9mm or .380 ACP) shot mag., contrast or Siglite night (disc. 2015) sights, interchangeable polymer grips, Picatinny rail, black Nitron or two-tone (disc. 2010) finish, 24.6 oz. Mfg. mid-2008-2016.

	$425	$395	$365	$325	$285	$260	$230	*$480*

Add $58 for Siglite night sights (disc. 2015).
Add $195 for threaded barrel (9mm Para. cal. with Siglite night sights), (mfg. 2015 only).
Add $94 for ambidextrous manual safety (9mm Para. cal. only), mfg. 2012 only.
Add $141 for threaded barrel and Siglite night sights (9mm Para. cal. only), mfg. 2012 only.
Add $15 for two-tone finish (disc. 2010).
Add $215 for desert digital camo finish (9mm Para. cal. only), includes Siglite night sights, medium grips, and DAO (mfg. 2009-2010).

* ***P250 Compact .22 LR*** – .22 LR cal., DAO, 3.9 in. barrel, two 10 shot mags., adj. contrast sights, modular black polymer grips, M1913 accessory rail, black hardcoat anodized slide, 21.2 oz. Mfg. 2015-2017.

	$335	$285	$250	$225	$200	$185	$170	*$379*

* ***P250 Compact Diamond*** – similar to P250 Compact, except has black nitron or two-tone finish with "Diamond Plate" engraving, Siglite night sights. Mfg. 2012 only.

	$495	$425	$375	$325	$275	$250	$225	*$582*

Add $15 for two-tone finish (disc. 2010).
Add $215 for desert digital camo finish (9mm Para. cal. only), includes Siglite night sights, medium grips, and DAO (mfg. 2009-2010).

* ***P250 Subcompact*** – 9mm Para., .357 SIG (disc. 2015), .380 ACP (mfg. 2012-2015), .40 S&W, or .45 ACP cal., DAO, 3.6 in. barrel, 6 (.45 ACP), 10 (.357 SIG or .40 S&W), or 12 (9mm Para. or .380 ACP) shot mag., contrast or Siglite night (disc. 2015) sights, interchangeable polymer grips, black Nitron finish, 24.9 oz. Mfg. mid-2008-2016.

	$425	$395	$365	$325	$285	$260	$230	*$480*

Add $58 for Siglite night sights (disc. 2015).
Add $80 for integrated accessory rail (disc. 2015).
Add $172 for .380 ACP or .45 ACP with Siglite night sights (disc. 2015).
Add $15 for two-tone finish (9mm Para. or .40 S&W cal.), disc. 2010.
Add $375 for Desert Digital camo finish (9mm Para. cal. only), includes Siglite night sights, medium grips, and DAO (mfg. 2009-2010).

* ***P250 TacPac*** – 9mm Para. or .40 S&W cal., full size frame, Siglite sights, 14 or 17 shot mag., black Nitron finish, Picatinny rail, includes STL-900 compatible holster. Mfg. 2014-2015.

	$575	$525	$450	$395	$350	$300	$265	*$662*

GRADING - PPGS™	100%	98%	95%	90%	80%	70%	60%	LAST MSR

P290RS (P290) – 9mm Para. or .380 ACP (mfg. 2015-2016) cal., DAO, sub-compact design utilizing light polymer black or pink (mfg. 2015 only) frame, 2.9 in. barrel, 6 or 8 (new 2012) shot mag., Re-strike firing pin (became standard in 2012), black polymer grips, contrast (new 2015) or Siglite night sights, options include integrated laser module and personalized grip inserts, black Nitron finish, 20 oz. Mfg. 2011-2017.

	$425	$385	$365	$325	$285	$260	$230	*$492*

Add $92 for integrated laser module (disc. 2015).
Subtract $57 if without Siglite night sights.

In 2014, the model nomenclature changed to P290RS.

* ***P290RS Black Diamond Plate*** – 9mm Para. cal., similar to Model P290RS, except has 6 shot mag., Nitron slide with diamond plate engraving, black polymer grips. Mfg. 2012 only.

	$510	$450	$385	$350	$285	$230	$185	*$595*

* ***P290RS Enhanced*** – 9mm Para. (disc. 2015) or .380 ACP (new 2015) cal., DAO, Re-strike firing pin, black polymer frame, 2.9 in. barrel, 6 or 8 (.380 ACP only) shot mag., Siglite night sights, black and green (disc. 2015) or black and pink (new 2015) Enhanced G10 grips, black Nitron/natural stainless steel slide, 20.5 oz. Mfg. 2014-2016.

	$465	$415	$375	$340	$300	$280	$250	*$543*

Subtract approx. $35 for 9mm Para. cal. (disc. 2015).

* ***P290RS ORB*** – 9mm Para. cal., DAO, sub-compact, 2.9 in. barrel, 6 or 8 shot mag., Siglite night sights, removable enhanced G10 grip plates, oil rubbed bronze nitron coated slide, black polymer frame, 20.5 oz. Mfg. 2014-2016.

	$465	$415	$375	$340	$300	$280	$250	*$543*

* ***P290RS Rainbow*** – 9mm Para. cal., sub-compact frame, 2.9 in. barrel, 6 shot mag., Siglite night sights, black polymer grips, Rainbow Titanium finish, 20.5 oz. Mfg. 2015 only.

	$485	$425	$375	$340	$300	$280	$250	*$570*

* ***P290RS Two-Tone*** – 9mm Para. or .380 ACP (new 2015) cal., similar to P290RS, except has stainless steel slide, black polymer frame and grips, and optional integrated laser module (new 2014), 20.5 oz. Disc. 2016.

	$425	$375	$325	$300	$250	$200	$150	*$488*

Add $92 for integrated laser module (mfg. 2014-2015).
Add $149 for .380 ACP cal. with integrated laser module (mfg. 2015 only).

PISTOLS: SEMI-AUTO, P320, P365, PM400, P516, P522, P553, P556, & P716 SERIES

P320 AXG SCORPION – 9mm Para. cal., striker fired, stainless steel frame with FDE Cerakote Elite coating, 3.9 in. carbon steel barrel, three 10 or 17 shot steel mags., stainless steel engraved slide with FDE finish, skeletonized flat trigger, SIG Pro Series removable optics plate with dovetail X-RAY3 day/night sights, Scorpion G10 grips from Hogue, extended beavertail, M1913 accessory rail, delivered in Negrini Custom Works case with Custom Works challenge coin and certified custom certificate, 31.3 oz. Custom Works Limited Edition beginning 2021.

Please contact the company directly for price and availability.

P320-M17 MILITARY RETURN – 9mm Para. cal., striker fired, full size stainless steel frame and slide, 4.7 in. carbon steel barrel, two 17 shot mags., SIGLITE front night sight and removable night sight rear plate, polymer grip, M1913 accessory rail, Coyote-Tan PVD finish, 29.6 oz. Mfg. 2017 only.

	$2,500	$2,250	$2,000	$1,750	$1,375	$1,125	$875	

The M17 in Desert Tan finish were initially distributed to the U.S. military. Later, they switched to black models and the tan versions were returned to Sig Sauer that were reworked as necessary and then distributed. These should have an "FTO" prefix and there were about 5,000 of these returned.

P320-M17 COMMERCIAL/CIVILIAN MODEL – 9mm Para. cal., striker fired, full size stainless steel frame and slide, 4.7 in. carbon steel barrel, two 17 shot mags., SIGLITE front night sight and removable night sight rear plate, polymer grip, M1913 accessory rail, Coyote-Tan PVD finish, 29.6 oz. New 2018.

MSR $680	$580	$510	$435	$395	$320	$265	$225	

P320-M18 – 9mm Para. cal., patterned after the U.S. Military (MHS) M18, stainless steel carry size frame, 3.9 in. carbon steel barrel, one 17 shot and two 21 shot mags., standard striker trigger, SIGLITE sights w/removable night sight rear plate, modular polymer grips, ambi manual safety, optic ready slide, M1913 Picatinny rail, Coyote Tan PVD finish, 28.1 oz. New late 2019.

MSR $680	$580	$510	$435	$395	$320	$265	$225	

GRADING - PPGS™	100%	98%	95%	90%	80%	70%	60%	LAST MSR

P320 NITRON – 9mm Para., .357 SIG (mfg. 2015-2016), .40 S&W (disc. 2020), or .45 ACP (mfg. 2015-2019) cal., SFO, DAO, full size frame, 4.7 in. barrel, 10 (.45 ACP), 14 (.357 SIG or .40 S&W, disc. 2020) or 17 (9mm Para.) shot mag., contrast or Siglite night sights, interchangeable fire control assembly and grip panels, reversible mag. release, lower Picatinny rail, front and rear slide serrations, black Nitron finish, 29.4 oz. New 2014.

MSR $550 $475 $415 $350 $325 $260 $225 $185

Subtract $82 if without Siglite night sights.

On January 19, 2017, the U.S. Army announced it had selected the P320 to replace the Beretta M9 service pistol. The P320 is the first modular pistol with interchangeable grip modules that can also be adjusted in frame size by the operator. Both full size and compact 320s will be delivered to the Army over a period of 10 years.

* ***P320 Carry Nitron*** – 9mm Para., .357 SIG, .40 S&W, or .45 ACP (new 2016) cal., 3.9 in. threaded (2015-2016, 9mm only) or non-threaded barrel, 10 (.45 ACP), 14 (.357 SIG or .40 S&W) or 17 (9mm Para.) shot mag., contrast (disc. 2016) or Siglite night sights, interchangeable grip panels, lower Picatinny rail, front and rear slide serrations, black Nitron finish, 26 oz. Mfg. 2014-2020.

$490 $425 $375 $340 $300 $280 $250 *$600*

Add $68 for threaded barrel (9mm Para. only, mfg. 2015-2016).

Subtract $82 if without Siglite night sights.

P320 COMPACT – 9mm Para., .357 SIG (disc. 2020), .40 S&W (disc. 2020), or .45 ACP cal., SFO, DAO, compact frame, 3.9 in. barrel, 9 (.45 ACP), 13 (.40 S&W or .357 SIG, disc. 2020), or 15 (9mm) shot mag., Picatinny rail, contrast or Siglite night sights, modular polymer or small (.45 ACP, FDE, mfg. 2016 only) grips, manual safety (9mm or .45 ACP, new 2017), black Nitron or FDE Nitron (disc. 2019) finish. New 2015.

MSR $550 $475 $415 $350 $325 $260 $225 $185

Add $68 for threaded barrel (9mm Para. cal. only).

Subtract $82 if without Siglite night sights.

* ***P320 Compact Lima*** – 9mm Para. cal., striker fired, compact frame, 3.9 in. barrel, 15 shot mag., Nitron stainless steel slide. Mfg. 2019 only.

$750 $650 $565 $510 $415 $350 $275 *$884*

Add $68 for integrated red or green laser.

* ***P320 Subcompact*** – 9mm Para. or .40 S&W (new 2016) cal., DAO, 3.6 in. barrel, 12 shot mag., contrast (disc. 2016) or Siglite night sights, modular polymer or medium (.40 S&W only, new 2016) grips, with or without accessory rail, black Nitron finish. Mfg. 2015-2019.

$595 $535 $485 $450 $395 $325 $295 *$679*

Subtract $82 if without Siglite night sights.

P320 MAX – 9mm Para. cal., striker fired, 1911 style recoil spring, stainless steel frame and slide, 5 in. carbon steel match grade bull barrel, 21 shot steel mag., flat skeletonized trigger, SIG SAUER Electro-Optics 6MOA ROMEO3MAX, gray TXG full size grips (TXG XGRIP module), Custom Works P320Max slide w/wraparound serrations, one-piece stainless steel guide rod, Nitron slide finish, 43.5 oz. New 2021.

MSR $1,600 $1,360 $1,190 $1,020 $925 $750 $625 $530

P320 RX FULL SIZE – 9mm Para. cal., striker fire, full size frame, 4.7 in. barrel, two 17 shot steel mags., stainless steel slide and frame, contrast or Siglite night sights with ROMEO1 Reflex sight, black polymer grips, 1913 accessory rail, 29.5 oz. Mfg. 2017-2019.

$750 $650 $565 $510 $415 $350 $275 *$887*

Add $81 for Siglite night sights.

* ***P320 RX Compact*** – 9mm Para. cal., striker fire, compact frame, 3.9 in. barrel, two 15 shot steel mags., stainless steel slide and frame, contrast or Siglite night sights with ROMEO1 Reflex sight, black polymer grips, 1913 accessory rail, 25.8 oz. Mfg. 2017-2019.

$740 $650 $565 $510 $415 $350 $275 *$867*

Add $101 for Siglite night sights.

P320 RXP FULL SIZE – 9mm Para. cal., striker fired, full size frame, 4.7 in. carbon steel barrel, two 17 shot steel mags., stainless steel slide with Nitron finish, ROMEO1PRO with suppressor contrast 3-dot sights, black polymer grips, M1913 accessory rail, 30 oz. New 2020.

MSR $880 $750 $650 $550 $500 $400 $350 $285

* ***P320 RXP Compact*** – 9mm Para. cal., striker fired, compact frame, 3.9 in. carbon steel barrel, two 15 shot steel mags., stainless steel slide with Nitron finish, ROMEO1PRO with suppressor contrast 3-dot sights, black polymer grips, M1913 accessory rail, 26.3 oz. New 2020.

MSR $880 $750 $650 $550 $500 $400 $350 $285

GRADING - PPGS™	100%	98%	95%	90%	80%	70%	60%	LAST MSR

P320 RXP XFULL SIZE – 9mm Para. cal., striker fired, full size stainless steel frame, 4.7 in. carbon steel barrel, two 17 shot steel mags., stainless steel slide with Nitron finish, XSeries straight trigger, ROMEO1PRO with XRAY3 suppressor sights, black XCarry polymer grips, M1913 accessory rail, 30 oz. New 2020.

MSR $1,000	$850	$750	$650	$580	$475	$385	$325	

* ***P320 RXP XCompact*** – 9mm Para. cal., striker fired, stainless steel compact frame, 3.6 in. carbon steel barrel, two 15 shot steel mags., stainless steel slide with Nitron finish, XSeries straight trigger, ROMEO1PRO with XRAY3 suppressor sights, black XCompact polymer grips, M1913 accessory rail, 25.8 oz. New 2020.

MSR $1,000	$850	$750	$650	$580	$475	$385	$325	

P320 SPECIAL EDITION TEXAS RANGER – 9mm Para. cal., striker fired, 4.7 in. barrel, 17 shot mag., SIGLITE night sights, Nitron slide with Texas badge and "One Riot, One Ranger" engraved, polymer modular grip, special features of commemorate includes a Texas Ranger TXR serial number, two 17 shot mags, and a commemorative challenge coin, 29.6 oz. New 2020.

P320 SPECIAL EDITION THIN BLUE LINE – 9mm Para. cal., striker fired, serialized trigger group, SIGLITE night sights, interchangeable polymer group module, slide is adorned with imagery of a Thin Blue Line flag and black background. Mfg. in partnership with NAPED to honor the fallen and the sacrifices being made every day by the men and women in blue. Available to law enforcement only. Limited mfg. beginning mid-2018.

Retail pricing is not available for this model.

P320 TACOPS – 9mm Para. cal., striker fire, full size frame, 4.7 in. barrel, four 21 shot mags., stainless steel frame and slide, fiber optic front and Siglite rear night sights, black polymer grips, M1913 accessory rail, Nitron slide finish. 29.5 oz. Disc. 2017.

	$675	$595	$525	$475	$415	$340	$315	*$762*

* ***P320 Tacops Carry*** – 9mm Para. cal., striker fire, 3.9 in. threaded barrel, four 21 shot mags., stainless steel frame and slide, fiber optic front and Siglite rear night sights, black polymer grips, M1913 accessory rail, Nitron slide finish, 29.5 oz. Disc. 2019.

	$725	$625	$550	$500	$435	$350	$325	*$830*

P320 XCARRY – 9mm Para. cal., striker fired, carry size polymer frame, 3.9 in. barrel, two or three (disc. 2018) 17 shot mags., Nitron stainless steel slide with lightening cuts, Straight X-Series trigger, X RAY3 day/night sights, ROMEO1 compatability, modular polymer X-Series grip, reduced slide catch lever, 1913 rail, LCI flag (new 2019), black or Coyote Tan (new 2019) finish, 27 oz. Mfg. 2017-2019.

	$750	$625	$550	$500	$450	$400	$350	*$862*

P320 XCOMPACT – 9mm Para. cal., compact frame, 3.6 in. carbon steel barrel, 15 shot mag., 4-sided beveled magwell, stainless steel slide, flat-face trigger, deep trigger guard undercut, X-RAY3 day/night sights, night sight rear plate, optic ready, XCompact grip module, extended beavertail, 25.3 oz. New 2019.

MSR $680	$580	$510	$435	$395	$320	$265	$225	

P320 XFIVE – 9mm Para. or .40 S&W cal., striker fired, full size polymer frame, 5 in. bull barrel, four 21 shot steel mags., 4-sided beveled magwell, Nitron stainless slide, enhanced flat trigger, Dawson adj. rear sight plate, Dawson fiber optic front sight, ROMEO1 optic compatible, X Grip module, 1913 rail, improved slide serrations, extended beavertail, extended slide catch lever, black or Coyote Tan (new 2019) finish, 35.6 oz. New 2017.

MSR $1,005	$895	$775	$675	$575	$475	$375	$340	

P320 XFIVE LEGION – 9mm Para. cal., striker fired, stainless steel frame and slide, 5 in. carbon steel bull barrel, three 10 (disc. 2020) or 17 shot mags. with Henning Group aluminum basepads, removable magwell and grip weight, skeletonized trigger, Dawson Precison fiber optic adj. sights, TXG Tungsten infused heavy XGrip module, M1913 rail, Legion Gray PVD slide with rear optic plate and lightening cuts, Romeo1PRO optic ready slide, Legion Gray finish, 43.5 oz. New mid-2019.

MSR $1,000	$850	$750	$650	$580	$475	$385	$325	

P320 XFULL – 9mm Para. cal., 4.7 in. barrel, 17 shot mag., X-RAY3 day/night sights, night sight rear optic plate, optic ready, XCarry grip module, black finish. New 2019.

MSR $680	$580	$510	$435	$395	$325	$260	$225	

P320 X-VTAC – 9mm Para. cal., striker fired, full size stainless steel frame, 4.7 in. barrel, three 18 shot mags., stainless steel slide with front serrations and FDE finish, X-Series straight trigger, high undercut trigger guard, VTAC day/night sights, modular polymer X-Series grips, extended beavertail, M1913 accessory rail, fiber optic pipes on top of tritium inserts (new 2019), 29.5 oz. New 2018.

MSR $780	$665	$580	$500	$450	$365	$300	$260	

GRADING - PPGS™	100%	98%	95%	90%	80%	70%	60%	LAST MSR

P365 NITRON MICRO COMPACT – 9mm Para. cal., striker fired, micro-compact stainless steel frame, 3.1 in. barrel, 10, 12, or 15 shot double stack mag., Nitron stainless steel slide, XRAY3 day/night sights, fully textured polymer grip, with or w/o manual safety, SIG rail, front and rear slide serrations, 17.8 oz. New 2018.

MSR $600	$510	$450	$385	$350	$275	$225	$200	

* ***P365 SAS*** – 9mm Para. cal., striker fired, micro-compact stainless steel frame, 3.1 in. carbon steel ported barrel, one 10 shot flush/one 10 shot extended mag., Nitron stainless steel slide, standard trigger, FT Bullseye sight, fully textured polymer grip, flat controls, front and rear slide serrations, anti-snag-free slide treatment for concealed carry, black finish, 17.8 oz. New late 2019.

MSR $680	$580	$510	$435	$395	$320	$265	$225	

* ***P365 XL*** – 9mm Para. cal., striker fired, micro-compact stainless steel frame, 3.7 in. carbon steel barrel, two 12 shot steel mags., stainless steel slide with Nitron finish, "X" signature flat trigger, XRAY3 day/night sights w/rear sight plate or ROMEO ZERO with XRAY3 front sight (new 2020), black 365 XSeries fully textured polymer grip, with or w/o manual safety, extended beavertail and integrated magwell, SIG rail, front and rear slide serrations, 20.7 oz. New 2019.

MSR $680	$580	$510	$435	$395	$320	$265	$225	

Add $150 for ROMEO ZERO with XRAY3 front sight (new 2020).

PM400 – 5.56 NATO cal., pistol equivalent of the M400 carbine/rifle, GIO, 11 1/2 in. barrel, 30 shot mag., flip-up rear sights, Picatinny flat-top upper, integral ambi QD sling, B5 Systems pistol grip, KeyMod handguard, FDE finish, with or w/o pistol stabilizing brace, 7 lbs. Mfg. 2014-2015.

	$1,295	$1,150	$995	$900	$750	$600	$475	*$1,519*

Subtract approx. $125 if without pistol stabilizing brace.

* ***PM400 SWAT PSB*** – 5.56 NATO cal., GIO, 11 1/2 in. barrel, 10 shot mag., aluminum handguard, pistol stabilizing brace, flip-up rear sight, integral ambi QD sling mounts, black fnish, 6 lbs. Mfg. 2015-2016.

	$1,275	$1,150	$1,000	$900	$750	$600	$475	*$1,467*

* ***PM400 Elite*** – 5.56 NATO (new 2016) or .300 AAC Blackout cal., GIO, 9 in. barrel, 30 shot mag., flip-up front and rear sights, rotating locking bolt, integral ambi QD sling mounts, aluminum KeyMod handguard, pistol stabilizing brace, black finish, 6 lbs. Mfg. 2015-2017.

	$1,400	$1,235	$1,100	$975	$830	$720	$585	*$1,650*

P516 – 5.56 NATO cal., short stroke pushrod GPO with adj. gas valve, 7 or 10 (new 2012) in. barrel with muzzle brake, Magpul MOE grip, flip-up adj. iron sights, 10 or 30 (disc.) shot mag., aluminum quad rail, black finish, with (new 2014) or without pistol stabilizing brace (PSB, became standard 2015). Mfg. 2011-2012, reintroduced 2014-2015.

	$975	$800	$665	$535	$465	$415	$365	*$1,199*

Subtract approx. $175 if without pistol stabilizing brace (PSB).

P516G2 – 5.56 NATO cal., 11 1/2 in. barrel, 30 shot mag., aluminum handguard, pistol stabilizing brace, black finish. Mfg. 2017 only.

	$1,750	$1,550	$1,350	$1,150	$975	$825	$675	*$1,990*

P522 – .22 LR cal., blowback action, 10.6 in. barrel, aluminum flat-top upper receiver, choice of polymer or quad rail (P522 SWAT) forend, flash suppressor, 10 or 25 shot polymer mag., ambidextrous safety selector, sling attachments, with (new 2014) or without pistol stabilizing brace (PSB, became standard 2015), approx. 6 1/2 lbs. Mfg. 2010 only, reintroduced 2014-2015.

	$525	$450	$400	$360	$315	$290	$260	*$628*

Subtract approx. $125 if without pistol stabilizing brace (PSB).
Add $71 for P522 SWAT model with quad rail forend (mfg. 2010 only).

Last MSR for P522 SWAT model (disc. 2010) was $643.

553 – 5.56 NATO cal., gas operated, 9 in. cold hammer forged barrel, 30 shot mag., adj. diopter rear sight, flip-up front sight, M1913 accessory rail, includes plastic hard case, black finish. New 2009. Limited imporaton into the U.S. 2014-2019.

	$3,250	$2,850	$2,450	$2,200	$1,795	$1,450	$1,145	*$3,772*

P556 – 5.56 NATO cal., GPO similar to SIG 556 carbine, 10 in. cold hammer forged barrel with A2 type flash suppressor, Picatinny top rail, pistol grip only, ribbed and vented black polymer forearm, black Nitron finish, mini red dot front sight, aluminum alloy two-stage trigger, ambidextrous safety, 30 shot mag. (accepts standard AR-15 style mags.), 6.3 lbs. Mfg. 2009-2010.

	$1,825	$1,650	$1,450	$1,300	$1,200	$1,100	$1,000	*$1,876*

Add $147 for P556 SWAT model with quad rail forend.

GRADING - PPGS™	100%	98%	95%	90%	80%	70%	60%	LAST MSR

* ***P556 Lightweight*** – 5.56 NATO cal., similar to Model P556, except has lightweight polymer lower unit and forend. Mfg. 2010-2013.

	$1,075	$950	$825	$725	$625	$525	$425	*$1,207*

Add $133 for quad rail forend (SWAT Model).

P556xi – 5.56 NATO or 7.62x39mm cal., GPO, 10 in. barrel, polymer handguard, flip-up sights, 30 shot mag., with (became standard 2015) or without pistol stabilizing brace. Mfg. 2014-2016.

	$1,415	$1,250	$1,075	$965	$835	$695	$550	*$1,663*

Add $131 for 7.62x39mm cal.
Subtract approx. $120 if without pistol stabilizing brace (became standard 2015).

P556xi SWAT – 5.56 NATO or 7.62x39mm cal., GPO, 10 in. barrel, aluminum handguard, flip-up sights, 30 shot mag., pistol stabilizing brace. Mfg. 2015-2016.

	$1,525	$1,350	$1,175	$1,050	$875	$725	$575	*$1,794*

Add $141 for 7.62x39mm cal.

P716 – 7.62 NATO cal., short stroke GPO with 4-position gas valve, 12 in. barrel, 20 shot mag., locking flip-up front and rear sights, integral ambi QD sling mounts, includes pistol stabilizing brace (PSB), 8.6 lbs. Mfg. 2015 only.

	$2,085	$1,800	$1,575	$1,350	$1,100	$950	$825	*$2,456*

PISTOLS: SEMI-AUTO, P938 SERIES

P938 – 9mm Para. cal., SAO, micro-compact alloy frame, 3 in. carbon steel barrel, stainless steel slide with Nitron finish, Siglite night sights (disc. 2019) or 3-dot contrast sights (new 2020), black polymer grips, ambi safety, thumb safety, hardcoat anodized frame finish, 16 oz. Mfg. 2012-2020.

	$600	$525	$450	$410	$325	$275	$225	*$700*

* ***P938 Aluminum*** – 9mm Para. cal., 3 in. barrel, 6 shot mag., Siglite night sights, ambi safety, black aluminum grips, black Nitron finish. Mfg. 2013-2015.

	$725	$575	$475	$425	$395	$350	$295	*$856*

* ***P938 ASE*** – 9mm Para. cal., SAO, micro-compact alloy frame, 3 in. barrel, stainless steel slide, 6 shot, Siglite night sights, walnut grips, ambi safety, front cocking serrations, PVD finish, 16 oz. Disc. 2019.

	$725	$625	$550	$500	$435	$350	$325	*$820*

* ***P938 Black Rubber Grips (BRG)*** – 9mm Para. cal., 3 in. barrel, 6 shot mag., black Nitron finish, Siglite night sights, ambi safety, black rubber grips. New 2013.

MSR $700	$600	$525	$450	$410	$325	$275	$225	

* ***P938 Blackwood*** – 9mm Para. cal., 3 in. barrel, 6 shot mag., black Nitron finish, Siglite night sights, ambi safety, Hogue blackwood grips, two-tone black Nitron frame/stainless slide finish. Mfg. 2012-2019.

	$685	$615	$535	$485	$415	$350	$300	*$793*

* ***P938 Combat*** – 9mm Para. cal., SAO, micro-compact sized alloy frame, 3 in. barrel, extended 7 shot mag., Nitron stainless steel slide, Siglite night sights, FDE rubber grips, front cocking serrations, FDE frame finish, 16 oz. Mfg. 2016-2019.

	$695	$550	$465	$425	$395	$350	$295	*$815*

* ***P938 Edge*** – 9mm Para. cal., 3 in. barrel, 6 shot, stainless steel slide with serrations and Edge finish (custom PVD coating), Siglite night sights, ambi safety, checkered black G10 grips, shipped in lockable hard case with one 6 shot mag., 16 oz. Mfg. mid-2015-2017.

	$695	$550	$465	$425	$395	$350	$295	*$815*

* ***P938 Emperor Scorpion/TB (Threaded Barrel)*** – 9mm Para. cal., SAO, micro-compact alloy frame, 3 or 3 1/2 (threaded) in. barrel, 7 shot steel mag., stainless steel slide, Siglite sights, G10 Piranha grips, front cocking serrations, FDE PVD coated slide and frame, 16 oz. Mfg. 2018-2019.

	$740	$650	$565	$510	$415	$350	$275	*$869*

Add $109 for threaded barrel (Emperor Scorpion TB).

* ***P938 Equinox*** – 9mm Para. cal., 3 in. barrel, two-tone polished Nitron finish, TruGlo front and Siglite rear sights, ambi safety, Hogue black diamondwood grips. Mfg. 2012-2017.

	$695	$550	$465	$425	$395	$350	$295	*$815*

* ***P938 Extreme*** – 9mm Para. cal., black anodized beavertail style frame, 3 in. barrel, X-Grip 7 shot mag., Nitron coated stainless slide, Siglite night sights, Hogue G10 Piranha grips in black and gray, ambi safety, black Nitron finish, 16 oz. Mfg. 2012-2018.

	$695	$550	$465	$425	$395	$350	$295	*$815*

GRADING - PPGS™	100%	98%	95%	90%	80%	70%	60%	LAST MSR

* ***P938 Navy*** – 9mm Para. cal., SAO, micro-compact frame, 3 in. barrel, 7 shot mag., stainless steel slide, Siglite night sights, black Hogue rubber grips, ambi safety, 17 oz. Mfg. 2019 only.

	$615	$565	$485	$435	$395	$335	$295	*$747*

* ***P938 Nightmare*** – 9mm Para. cal., 3 in. barrel, 7 shot mag., black Nitron finish, Siglite night sights, ambi safety, Hogue black G10 grips. Mfg. 2013-2018.

	$685	$550	$465	$425	$395	$350	$295	*$815*

* ***P938 Polished*** – 9mm Para. cal., 3 in. barrel, engraved slide, Siglite night sights, 6 shot mag., rosewood medallion grips, ambi safety, polished Nitron coated finish. Mfg. 2015-2017.

	$725	$575	$475	$425	$395	$350	$295	*$855*

* ***P938 Rose Gold*** – 9mm Para. cal., SAO, micro-compact alloy frame, 3 in. barrel, 7 shot mag., polished and engraved rose gold slide, skeletonized hammer, Siglite night sights, custom black G10 grips with rose gold medallion, rose gold controls, hardcoat anodized black finish, 16 oz. Mfg. 2018-2019.

	$835	$700	$600	$535	$465	$415	$350	*$986*

* ***P938 Rosewood*** – 9mm Para. cal., 3 in. barrel, 6 shot mag., black Nitron finish, Siglite night sights, ambi safety, rosewood grips. Mfg. 2012-2017.

	$685	$615	$535	$485	$415	$350	$300	*$793*

* ***P938 Rosewood .22 LR*** – .22 LR cal., lightweight micro-compact frame, 3.3 in. barrel, 10 shot mag., adj. contrast or Siglite night sights, rosewood or black rubber grips, ambi safety, black hard anodized finish, 16 oz. Mfg. 2015 only.

	$565	$475	$425	$375	$325	$290	$260	*$685*

Add $34 for threaded barrel.

* ***P938 Rosewood .22 LR Target*** – .22 LR cal., 4.1 in. barrel, 10 shot mag., adj. contrast sights, rosewood grips, ambi safety, black finish. Mfg. 2015-2019.

	$575	$525	$485	$450	$395	$325	$295	*$651*

* ***P938 SAS*** – 9mm Para. cal., 3 in. barrel, Siglite night sights, brown Goncalo checkered wood grips, ambi safety, dehorning, two-tone finish. Mfg. 2012-2013, reintroduced 2015-2019.

	$695	$550	$465	$425	$395	$350	$295	*$815*

* ***P938 SAS Micro-Compact*** – 9mm Para. cal., SAO, micro-compact alloy frame, 3 in. carbon steel barrel, 7 shot extended mag., stainless steel slide with Nitron finish, single action trigger, FT Bullseye sight, black rubber grip, ambi safety, SIG Anti-Snag Treatment, hard coat anodized finish, 16 oz. New mid-2020.

MSR $780	$665	$580	$500	$450	$365	$300	$260	

* ***P938 Scorpion*** – 9mm Para. cal., 3 in. threaded (new 2015) or non-threaded barrel, 6 shot mag., Siglite night sights, ambi safety, Hogue G10 grips, FDE finish, 16 oz. Mfg. 2014-2015.

	$775	$600	$500	$450	$425	$365	$315	*$913*

Add $115 for threaded barrel (new 2015).

* ***P938 Select*** – 9mm Para. cal., SAO, micro-compact alloy frame, 3 in. barrel, 7 shot mag., Nitron stainless steel slide, skeletonized hammer, Siglite night sights, SELECT G10 grips, front cocking serrations. Mfg. 2018-2019.

	$995	$875	$775	$675	$575	$475	$375	*$1,195*

* ***P938 Spartan II*** – 9mm Para. cal., SAO, micro-compact alloy frame, 3 in. carbon steel barrel, 7 shot mag., custom Spartan grips with inlaid Spartan helmet, stainless steel slide engraved with the Greek phrase "MOLON LABE", Distressed Coyote finish, 16 oz. Mfg. 2019-2020.

	$665	$580	$500	$450	$365	$300	$260	*$780*

* ***P938 Stand*** – 9mm Para. cal., SAO, micro-compact stainless steel frame, 3 in. barrel, 7 shot mag., Nitron stainless steel slide, skeletonized hammer, Siglite night sights, black custom grips with flag medallion, ambi safety, stars and strips slide with "STAND" engraving, 16 oz. Mfg. 2018-2019.

	$695	$550	$465	$425	$395	$350	$295	*$815*

* ***P938 We The People*** – 9mm Para. cal., SAO, micro-compact alloy frame, 3 in. carbon steel barrel, 7 shot steel mag., stainless steel slide, contrast sights, custom aluminum grips with 25 stars engraved on each side, 13 stars and "WE THE PEOPLE" engraved on top of slide, "1776" engraved on slide flats, custom distressed finish, 16 oz. Mfg. 2018-2019.

	$655	$595	$500	$450	$400	$340	$300	*$772*

GRADING - PPGS™	100%	98%	95%	90%	80%	70%	60%	LAST MSR

P938 LEGION MICRO COMPACT – 9mm Para. cal., micro compact alloy frame, 3 in. carbon steel barrel, three 7 shot steel mags., extended magwell, stainless steel slide, skeletonized hammer, flat SAO aluminum trigger and checkered trigger guard, X-RAY3 day/night sights, custom Legion black G10 grips with Legion medallion, ambi thumb safety, front cocking serrations, Legion Gray finish in Cerakote Elite, 17 oz. New 2019.

MSR $780	$665	$580	$500	$450	$365	$300	$260	

PISTOLS: SEMI-AUTO 1911 TYPE

1911 FULL SIZE (GSR REVOLUTION) – .40 S&W (new 2014) or .45 ACP cal., SA, 5 in. match grade barrel, choice of white (disc.), standard blue (disc.), two-tone, reverse two-tone (mfg. 2007-2010), or black Nitron finish, includes two 8 shot mags., with or w/o under frame Picatinny rail, firing pin safety, front and rear strap checkering, Novak (disc.) or low profile sights, checkered wood (all stainless), rosewood, aluminum, or synthetic (blued stainless) grips, approx. 41 oz. Mfg. in Exeter, NH. Mfg. 2004-2015.

	$925	$775	$650	$525	$450	$400	$350	*$1,142*

Add $34 for M-1913 Picatinny rail.
Add $57 for Fastback rounded frame (with black Nitron finish and rosewood grips), new 2015.
Add $100 for platinum Elite with two-tone finish, adj. combat night sights and aluminum grips (mfg. 2008-2011).
Add $120 for Blackwater model (mfg. 2009-2010).
Subtract $40 for reverse two-tone finish (disc. 2010).

The abbreviation GSR on this model stands for Granite Series Revolution.

* ***1911 Desert*** – .45 ACP cal., Desert Tan finish, contrast sights, Ergo XT OD Green grips, otherwise similar to the 1911. Mfg. 2012 only.

	$950	$825	$725	$625	$525	$450	$375	*$1,070*

* ***1911 Engraved Texas*** – .45 ACP cal., 5 in. barrel, 8 shot mag., Siglite night sights, custom Texas grips, polished slide with gold or silver engraving. Mfg. 2015-2017.

	$1,350	$1,195	$1,000	$900	$775	$650	$525	*$1,553*

Add $347 for gold engraving.

* ***1911 Extreme*** – .45 ACP cal., full size frame, 5 in. barrel, Magwell housing, two 8 shot mags., flat trigger, Siglite night sights, black/gray Hogue Extreme G10 grips, ambi safety, integral accessory rail, black Nitron finish. Mfg. 2012 only, reintroduced 2015-2017.

	$985	$825	$715	$575	$475	$415	$375	*$1,234*

* ***1911 Fastback*** – .45 ACP cal., Fastback rounded frame, two 8 shot mags., black Nitron finish, low profile night sights, rosewood grips, otherwise similar to the 1911. Mfg. 2012 only.

	$1,025	$875	$750	$625	$525	$450	$375	*$1,170*

* ***1911 Max*** – 9mm Para. (new 2017), .40 S&W (new 2014), or .45 ACP cal., Custom Competition, 5 in. barrel, 8 shot mag., forward cocking serrations, external extractor, flat trigger, Koenig speed hammer, fiber optic front and adj. rear sights, ICE Magwell, Wilson Mag., custom Hogue chainlink G10 grips, Max logo, reverse two-tone finish, 41.6 oz. Mfg. 2012-disc.

	$1,425	$1,275	$1,100	$965	$835	$695	$550	*$1,663*

* ***1911 Nickel Rail*** – .45 ACP cal., full size stainless steel side and frame, 5 in. barrel, 8 shot mag., Siglite night sights, integral 1913 accessory rail, custom brown Vector grips, stainless steel magwell, nickel PVD finish, 41.6 oz. Mfg. 2015-2018.

	$975	$800	$675	$550	$475	$415	$365	*$1,221*

* ***1911 Nightmare*** – .45 ACP or .357 SIG (new 2016) cal., Fastback rounded frame, 4.2 (new 2018) or 5 (disc. 2017) in. barrel, two 8 shot mags., stainless controls, Siglite night sights, black G10 grips, black Nitron finish. Mfg. 2012-disc.

	$1,075	$950	$835	$750	$650	$550	$425	*$1,244*

* ***1911 POW-MIA*** – .45 ACP cal., 5 in. barrel, two 8 shot steel mags., Siglite night sights, custom Hogue grips with POW-MIA seal, slide is engraved with barbed wire and there are dog tags and an American flag engraved with an inscription on the top of the slide, black Nitron finish. Mfg. 2012 only, reintroduced 2015-2016.

	$1,175	$1,025	$875	$750	$650	$550	$450	*$1,304*

Add $143 for custom engraved stainless, engraved KaBar knife, and Pelican case (mfg. 2012 only).

GRADING - PPGS™	100%	98%	95%	90%	80%	70%	60%	LAST MSR

* ***1911 Scorpion*** – .45 ACP cal., 5 in. barrel, 8 shot mag., front cocking serrations, low profile night sights, ambi safety, Hogue Extreme Series G10 grips, FDE finish, 41.6 oz. Mfg. 2011-2015.

$1,000 $825 $700 $575 $475 $415 $375 *$1,233*

Add $80 for threaded barrel.

* ***1911 Emperor Scorpion*** – .45 ACP cal., full size frame, 5 in. barrel, 8 shot mag., stainless steel frame and slide, skeletonized combat hammer and trigger, Siglite night sights, Hogue G10 Piranha grips and mainspring housing, M1913 accessory rail, front cocking serrations, FDE PVD finish, 41.6 oz. New 2015.

MSR $1,280 $1,085 $950 $810 $725 $595 $485 $425

* ***1911 Spartan (Molon Labe)*** – .45 ACP cal., 5 in. barrel, features custom oil rubbed bronze Nitron finish with 24Kt. gold inlay Molon Labe engraving on slide (Ancient Greek meaning "Come and Take Them"), Hogue grips with Spartan helmet, and low profile sights, otherwise similar to the 1911. Mfg. late 2012-2018.

$1,250 $1,075 $900 $750 $650 $550 $450 *$1,397*

* ***1911 Spartan II*** – .45 ACP cal., stainless steel slide and frame, 5 in. barrel, two 8 shot mag., SIGLITE sights, custom Spartan grips, ambi safety, MOLON LABE engraved slide, Distressed Coyote Tan finish. Mfg. 2019-2020.

$1,085 $950 $815 $750 $600 $500 $425 *$1,280*

* ***1911 Stainless*** – .45 ACP cal., features stainless finish and blackwood grips, otherwise similar to the 1911. Disc. 2013.

$995 $875 $750 $650 $550 $450 $425 *$1,156*

Subtract $43 if without M-1913 Picatinny rail (disc. 2012).

* ***1911 STX*** – .45 ACP cal., full size frame, 5 in. barrel, 8 shot mag., adj. combat night sights, burled maple grips, ambi safety, beavertail grip safety, flat-top, reverse two-tone finish, 41.6 oz.

MSR $1,200 $1,025 $900 $775 $700 $575 $475 $400

* ***1911 Super Target*** – .45 ACP cal., 5 in. barrel, 8 shot mag., adj. target rear and fiber optic front sights, beavertail grip safety, black Nitron (disc. 2016) or stainless steel finish, custom walnut (disc. 2016) or birch (stainless model) grips with SIG medallion, 41.6 oz. Mfg. 2015-2018.

$1,425 $1,250 $1,075 $950 $825 $675 $550 *$1,609*

* ***1911 TTT*** – .45 ACP cal., features two-tone finish, black controls, adj. combat night sights and wood grips, otherwise similar to the 1911. Disc. 2012.

$1,025 $875 $750 $650 $550 $450 $375 *$1,170*

* ***1911 Tacops*** – 10mm (new 2019), .45 ACP (disc.) or .357 SIG (mfg. 2016-2019) cal., 5 in. threaded (disc. 2018) or non-threaded barrel, four 8 shot mags., Siglite night sights, Magwell Ergo XT grips, ambi thumb safety, integral accessory rail, black Nitron finish. New 2011.

MSR $1,280 $1,085 $950 $810 $725 $595 $485 $425

Add $70 for threaded barrel (disc. 2018).

* ***1911 Tacpac*** – .45 ACP cal., features 1911 XO, holster with attached mag. pouch, magazine loader, and 3 magazines, otherwise similar to the 1911. Mfg. 2012-2013.

$950 $825 $725 $625 $525 $450 $375 *$1,070*

* ***1911 Railed Tacpac*** – .45 ACP cal., features 1911 XO with lower Picatinny rail, includes holster with attached mag. pouch and two magazines, laser module. Mfg. 2013-2015.

$925 $775 $650 $525 $450 $400 $350 *$1,142*

* ***1911 Target*** – .45 ACP cal., features black Nitron or stainless finish, adj. target sights, and rosewood or blackwood grips. Mfg. 2011-2012.

$975 $850 $725 $625 $525 4450 $400 *$1,113*

Add $29 for stainless finish with blackwood grips.

* ***1911 XO*** – .45 ACP or .357 SIG (mfg. 2016 only) cal., 5 in. match grade barrel, stainless steel slide and frame, beavertail grip safety, 8 shot mag., low profile contrast sights, Ergo XT grips, black Nitron or stainless (disc. 2012) finish, with (mfg. 2016, .357 SIG only) or without accessory rail, 41.6 oz. Mfg. 2007-2019.

$865 $725 $635 $535 $450 $400 $350 *$1,010*

Add $56 for .357 SIG cal. and accessory rail (mfg. 2016 only).

Add $28 for stainless finish (disc. 2012).

GRADING - PPGS™	100%	98%	95%	90%	80%	70%	60%	LAST MSR

1911 TRADITIONAL FULL SIZE – .45 ACP cal., SA, 5 in. barrel, rounded top slide, front cocking serrations, stainless frame with matte black Nitron slide and small parts, 3 hole speed trigger, Hogue custom black wood grips, low profile Siglite night sights, two 8 shot mags., reverse two-tone finish, approx. 41 oz. Mfg. 2011-2012, reintroduced 2015 only.

	$950	$795	$665	$535	$465	$415	$365	*$1,176*

* ***1911 Traditional Compact*** – .45 ACP or .357 SIG (new 2015) cal., compact slide with 3.9 in. barrel, rounded top slide, stainless frame, 3 hole speed trigger, Hogue custom black wood grips, low profile Siglite night sights, two 7 shot mags., stainless finish, approx. 35 oz. Mfg. 2011-2012, reintroduced 2015 only.

	$950	$795	$665	$535	$465	$415	$365	*$1,176*

* ***Model 1911 Traditional Tacops*** – .45 ACP or .357 SIG (new 2015) cal., stainless frame, 5 in. barrel, 8 shot mag., low profile Siglite night sights, black Ergo XT grips, stainless magwell, ambi safety, M1913 rail, black Nitron finish, 41.6 oz. Mfg. 2012-2015.

	$985	$815	$665	$550	$475	$420	$365	*$1,221*

1911 TRADITIONAL STAINLESS STEEL – 9mm Para., .38 Super (disc. 2015), .40 S&W, or .45 ACP cal., SA, stainless steel. New 2014.

* ***1911 Traditional Stainless Match Elite*** – 9mm Para., .38 Super (disc. 2015), .40 S&W, or .45 ACP (mfg. 2015 only) cal., stainless frame, 5 in. barrel, 8 or 9 shot mag., adj. sights, blackwood grips. Mfg. 2014-disc.

	$965	$785	$660	$535	$465	$415	$365	*$1,164*

* ***1911 Traditional Stainless Nightmare*** – .45 ACP cal., Fastback frame, Siglite sights, Nitron finish. Mfg. 2014-2015.

	$1,095	$935	$825	$700	$600	$500	$400	*$1,256*

* ***1911 Traditional Stainless Scorpion*** – .45 ACP cal., stainless steel frame, Siglite sights, FDE finish. Mfg. 2014-2015.

	$995	$825	$675	$545	$475	$420	$365	*$1,233*

1911 CARRY (REVOLUTION) – .45 ACP cal., SA, carry configuration with short stainless slide, 4 in. barrel, stainless steel frame (disc. 2012) or black Nitron finish, Novak (disc. 2010) or low profile night sights, 8 shot mag., rosewood grips became standard with black Nitron finish during 2011, black wood grips became standard on stainless finish during 2011. Mfg. 2007-2012, reintroduced 2015 only.

	$925	$775	$650	$525	$450	$400	$350	*$1,142*

* ***1911 Carry Fastback*** – .45 ACP cal., Fastback rounded frame, black Nitron finish, low profile night sights, two 8 shot mags., and rosewood grips, otherwise similar to the 1911 Carry. Mfg. 2012 only, reintroduced 2015 only.

	$975	$800	$665	$535	$465	$415	$365	*$1,199*

* ***1911 Fastback Emperor Scorpion Carry (Stainless Emperor Scorpion)*** – .45 ACP cal., Carry size Fastback frame, 4.2 in. barrel, two 8 shot mags., stainless steel frame and slide (with traditional contour), Siglite night sights, Hogue G10 Piranha grips and mainspring housing, ambi safety, FDE PVD coated finish, 35 oz. New 2015.

MSR $1,280	$1,085	$950	$810	$725	$595	$485	$425	

* ***1911 Carry Nightmare*** – .45 ACP or .357 SIG (mfg. 2015 only) cal., Fastback rounded frame, 4.2 in. barrel, two 8 shot mags., stainless controls, Siglite night sights, black G10 grips, black Nitron finish. New 2012.

MSR $1,280	$1,085	$950	$810	$725	$595	$485	$425	

* ***1911 Carry Scorpion*** – .45 ACP cal., features FDE finish, low profile night sights, ambi safety, magwell housing, and Hogue Extreme Series G10 grips, otherwise similar to 1911 Carry. Mfg. 2012-2015.

	$995	$825	$675	$545	$475	$420	$365	*$1,233*

Add $80 for threaded barrel.

* ***1911 Carry Spartan*** – .45 ACP cal., 4.2 in. barrel, 8 shot mag., Siglite sights, Molon Labe engraved slide, oil-rubbed bronze Nitron finish with 24Kt. gold inlay engraving, Hogue custom Spartan grips, 38.8 oz. Mfg. 2014-2018.

	$1,275	$1,075	$900	$775	$650	$550	$450	*$1,397*

* ***1911 Carry Spartan II*** – .45 ACP cal., stainless steel slide and frame, 4.2 in. carbon steel barrel, two 8 shot mag., skeletonized SAO trigger, SIGLITE sights, custom Spartan grips, ambi safety, "MOLON LABE" engraved slide, M1913 Picatinny rail, Distressed Coyote Tan finish, 35 oz. Mfg. 2019-2020.

	$1,085	$950	$815	$750	$600	$500	$425	*$1,280*

GRADING - PPGS™	100%	98%	95%	90%	80%	70%	60%	LAST MSR

* ***1911 Carry Tacops*** – .45 ACP cal., 4.2 or 4.9 in. threaded or non-threaded barrel, four 8 shot mags., Siglite night sights, Magwell Ergo XT grips, ambi thumb safety, M1913 rail, black Nitron finish. Mfg. 2012 only, reintroduced 2015-2018.

	$985	$825	$685	$550	$475	$420	$365	*$1,221*

Add $70 for threaded barrel.

1911 COMPACT (REVOLUTION) – .45 ACP cal., SA, short slide and compact frame, 6 shot, stainless or black Nitron finish, 4 in. barrel, night sights. Mfg. 2007-2009.

	$975	$850	$725	$625	$525	$450	$400	*$1,170*

* ***1911 Compact C3*** – .45 ACP cal., 4.2 in. barrel, 7 shot mag., black hardcoat anodized alloy frame, stainless slide, low profile contrast sights, slim profile rosewood grips, two-tone finish. Mfg. 2011-disc.

	$865	$725	$640	$535	$450	$400	$350	*$1,010*

Add $214 for magwell and black CTC laser grips (mfg. 2012 only) or add $243 for magwell and wood grain CTC laser grips (mfg. 2012 only).

* ***1911 Compact RCS*** – .45 ACP cal., dehorning and anti-snag treatment, black Nitron or two-tone finish, 7 shot, low profile night sights, custom wood grips, otherwise similar to 1911 Compact. Disc. 2012.

	$975	$850	$725	$625	$525	$450	$400	*$1,170*

Add $15 for two-tone finish.

* ***1911 Compact Nickel*** – .45 ACP cal., 4.2 in. barrel, 7 shot mag., low profile night sights, custom Vector grips, Magwell, checkered front strap, nickel Nitron coated finish, 38.8 oz. Mfg. 2015-2017.

	$965	$800	$675	$550	$475	$425	$375	*$1,198*

1911 ULTRA COMPACT – 9mm Para. (new 2015) or .45 ACP cal., SA, 3.3 in. barrel, 3 hole trigger, aluminum frame, slim profile custom wood rosewood or blackwood grips, low profile night sights, two 7 or 8 (new 2016, 9mm only) shot mags., Nitron or two-tone finish, 28 oz. Mfg. 2011-disc.

	$900	$775	$650	$535	$465	$415	$365	*$1,119*

1911-22 – .22 LR cal., black frame and slide finish, 5 in. barrel, low profile 3-dot contrast sights, 3 hole trigger, bobbed hammer, beavertail, Hogue custom rosewood grips, one 10 shot mag., black, camo (new 2013), FDE (new 2012), or OD Green (new 2012) finish, 34 oz. Mfg. 2011-2014.

	$395	$350	$315	$275	$260	$240	$200	*$460*

Add $58 for FDE, OD Green (new 2012), or camo (new 2013) finish.

1911 MATCH ELITE – 9mm Para., .40 S&W, or .45 ACP cal., round top, 5 in. barrel, double slide serrations on frame, adj. target sights, 3 hole trigger, Hogue custom wood grips, choice of stainless or two-tone (.45 ACP cal. only) finish. Mfg. 2011-2012.

	$925	$875	$750	$650	$550	$450	$400	*$1,170*

1911 SELECT – .45 Auto cal., SAO, Nitron stainless steel slide and frame, 5 in. match grade barrel, 8 shot mag., low profile night sights, SELECT G10 grips, beavertail grip safety, extended thumb safety, front strap checkering, front cocking serrations, tactical accessory rail. Mfg. 2018-2019.

	$1,000	$825	$700	$575	$475	$415	$375	*$1,234*

1911 STAND – .45 ACP cal., full size stainless steel frame and slide, 5 in. stainless steel match grade barrel, two 7 shot steel mags., SAO skeletonized trigger, low profile SIGLITE night sights, custom grips with embedded flag medallion, beavertail grip safety, extended thumb safety, M1913 accessory rail, stars and stripes engraved slide, 25 LPI checkering on front strap, Nitron finish on frame and slide, 41.6 oz. Special commemorative edition mfg. mid-2018-2019.

	$1,325	$1,100	$900	$775	$650	$550	$500	*$1,481*

1911 WE THE PEOPLE – .45 Auto cal., SAO, full size stainless steel frame and slide, 5 in. carbon steel barrel, skeletonized trigger, low profile night sights, custom aluminum grips with 25 stars engraved on each side, 13 stars and "WE THE PEOPLE" engraved on top of slide, "1776" engraved on slide flats, custom distressed finish, 41.6 oz. Mfg. 2018-2019.

	$1,325	$1,100	$900	$775	$650	$550	$500	*$1,481*

RIFLES: BOLT ACTION

CROSS RIFLE – 6.5 Creedmoor, .308 Win., or .277 FURY cal., 16 or 18 in. stainless steel barrel, 5 shot polymer mag., AICS type, two-stage match trigger, folding SIG Precision stock, alloy forend, black polymer grips, one-piece aluminum receiver, M-LOK accessory rail, black anodized or First Lite Cipher Armakote finish, 6.5 lbs. Mfg. in USA beginning 2020.

MSR $1,650	$1,400	$1,225	$1,050	$950	$775	$630	$550	

Add $230 for First Lite Cipher Armakote finish.

GRADING - PPGS™	100%	98%	95%	90%	80%	70%	60%	LAST MSR

TACTICAL 2 – .223 Rem. (mfg. 2010-2012), .308 Win., .300 Win. Mag. (disc. 2013), or .338 Lapua Mag. cal., left or right-hand straight pull action, 24.7 (.308 Win. cal. only), 25.6 (.300 Win. cal. only, disc. 2013), or 27 (.338 Lapua cal. only) in. fluted barrel with muzzle brake, aluminum receiver, black hardcoat anodized finish, adj. single stage trigger, 4 or 5 shot polymer box mag., ambidextrous Blaser adj. composite pistol grip stock with adj. buttplate and cheekpiece, Picatinny rail, optional Harris bipod, 12-12 1/2 lbs. Mfg. 2007-2014.

	$3,700	$3,300	$2,900	$2,400	$1,900	$1,750	$1,500	*$4,171*

Add $303 for .338 Lapua Mag. cal.
Add $299-$565 per individual bolt head depending on caliber.
Add $1,689 per interchangeable barrel.

SIG 50 – .50 BMG cal., 29 in. fluted barrel with muzzle brake, 5 shot detachable mag., helical bolt, Desert Tan finish, detachable buttstock or McMillan tactical stock, includes bipod, 23.4 lbs. Mfg. 2011-2012, reintroduced 2014-2015.

	$9,100	$7,750	$6,350	$5,100	$4,850	$3,900	$3,200	*$9,825*

SSG 3000 PRECISION TACTICAL RIFLE – .308 Win. cal., modular design, ambidextrous McMillan tactical stock with adj. comb, 23.4 in. barrel with muzzle brake, folding aluminum chassis (new 2012), 5 shot detachable mag., supplied in 3 different levels, Level I does not have bipod or scope, cased, 12 lbs. Mfg. 2000-2012.

	$2,400	$2,100	$1,700	$1,500	$1,250	$1,000	$875	*$2,799*

Add $933 for folding aluminum chassis (new 2012).
Add $1,500 for Level II (includes Leupold Vari-X III 3.5-10x40mm duplex reticle scope and Harris bipod, disc.).
Add $2,300 for Level III (includes Leupold Mark 4 M1 10x40mm Mil-Dot reticle scope and Harris bipod, disc.).
Add $1,500 for .22 LR cal. conversion kit (disc.).

* ***SSG 3000 Patrol*** – .308 Win. cal., 18 or 23 1/2 in. barrel with (new 2014) or w/o threading, black or FDE (new 2014) finish, Patrol stock with integral aluminum bedding. Mfg. 2012-2015.

	$1,295	$1,100	$950	$825	$700	$575	$495	*$1,499*

S404 SYNCHRO XTC – .243 Win., 30-06, 6.5 Creedmoor, or .308 Win. cal., cold hammer forged barrel, adj. trigger blade, carbon fiber Synchro XTC stock w/adj. comb, Maglock mag. safety, aluminum receiver, SUS combination tool fixed to front sling, universal tool integrated to rear sling swivel, matte black or Camo green carbon fiber finish, 6.1 lbs. New 2020.

MSR $8,199	$6,950	$6,100	$5,200	$4,750	$3,850	$3,150	$2,450

RIFLES: SEMI-AUTO

State compliant rifles on some of the currently manufactured models listed within this section include CA, CO, HA, IL, MA, MD, NJ, and NY. Compliance features will vary from state to state, and typically, these compliant state MSRs are slightly higher than the standard models available from the rest of the states.

SIG M400 – 5.56 NATO cal., GIO, 16 in. barrel, A2 grip, M4 buttstock, 600 meter adj. and removable rear sight, 30 shot mag., includes hard case. Mfg. 2012-2015.

	$1,100	$975	$850	$750	$650	$525	$425	*$1,233*

Add $93 for aluminum quad rails (disc. 2014).
Add $40 for lightweight steady ready platform (mfg. 2012 only).

* ***SIG M400 B5 Series*** – 5.56 NATO cal., GIO, 16 in. barrel, 30 shot mag., rear flip-up sights, B5 Systems SOPMOD 6-pos. telescoping stock, pistol grip, KeyMod carbine handguards, Picatinny rail, Gray or Foliage finish, 6.7 lbs. Mfg. 2015 only.

	$1,200	$1,075	$925	$825	$725	$575	$475	*$1,348*

* ***SIG M400 Carbon Fiber*** – 5.56 NATO cal., GIO, 16 in. barrel, carbon fiber forend or choice of SIG or carbon fiber rifle stock, 30 shot Lancer mag. Mfg. 2014-2015.

	$1,950	$1,725	$1,500	$1,325	$1,150	$925	$750	*$2,170*

Add $172 for carbon fiber forend and carbon fiber rifle stock.

* ***SIG M400 Classic*** – 5.56 NATO cal., GIO, M4 style polymer handguard, SIG grips, fixed front and rear flip-up sights, 30 shot mag., telestock, black finish. Mfg. 2014-2016.

	$1,125	$1,000	$875	$775	$675	$525	$425	*$1,250*

* ***Sig M400 Elite*** – 5.56 NATO cal., GIO, 16 in. barrel, 30 shot mag., SIG enhanced trigger, with or without red dot sights, 6-pos. telescoping stock, aluminum free floating M-LOK handguard, black or titanium finish, 6 1/2 lbs. Mfg. 2017-2018.

	$1,075	$950	$825	$725	$625	$525	$425	*$1,201*

Add $135 for titanium finish.
Add $158 for Romeo5 red dot sights.

GRADING - PPGS™	100%	98%	95%	90%	80%	70%	60%	LAST MSR

* ***SIG M400 Elite Vanish*** – .223 Rem. cal., DI, AR-15 style, 20 in. carbon steel heavy contour precision barrel, 10 shot mag., SIG Matchlite Duo trigger, Magpul MOE stock, alloy forend, MOE grip, free floating 15 in. handguard with M-LOK accessory rail, Microlight gas block, Kuiu Vias camo finish, 7 lbs. Mfg. 2018-2019.

$1,200	**$1,075**	**$925**	**$825**	**$700**	**$575**	**$475**	***$1,336***

* ***SIG M400 Enhanced Carbine*** – 5.56 NATO cal., GIO, 16 in. barrel, MOE handguard, MOE grip, MOE stock, flip-up rear sights, black, OD Green, or FDE finish, otherwise similar to SIG M400. Mfg. 2012-2014.

$1,100	**$975**	**$850**	**$750**	**$650**	**$525**	**$425**	***$1,234***

Add $66 for FDE finish.

* ***SIG M400 Enhanced Patrol*** – 5.56 NATO or .300 AAC Blackout cal., GIO, 16 in. barrel, flip-up sights, 30 shot mag., polymer handguard, black, FDE, OD Green (new 2015), or Muddy Girl (disc. 2015) finish. Mfg. 2014-2016.

$1,275	**$1,125**	**$975**	**$875**	**$750**	**$600**	**$500**	***$1,413***

Add $34 for Muddy Girl finish (disc. 2015).

* ***SIG M400 Hunting*** – 5.56 NATO cal., GIO, 20 in. barrel, 1:8 twist, MOE handguard and grip, optic ready, black or Mix Pine2 finish, otherwise similar to SIG M400. Mfg. 2012 only.

$975	**$875**	**$775**	**$675**	**$575**	**$475**	**$375**	***$1,099***

Add $90 for Mix Pine2 finish.

* ***SIG M400 Magpul*** – 5.56 NATO cal., GIO, 20 in. barrel, black finish, Magpul rifle stock, MOE grip and forend. Mfg. 2014-2015.

$1,150	**$1,025**	**$900**	**$800**	**$675**	**$550**	**$450**	***$1,287***

* ***SIG M400 Predator*** – 5.56 NATO or .300 AAC Blackout (new 2016) cal., GIO, 18 in. heavy match grade threaded and capped stainless steel barrel, 5 shot mag., Geissele two-stage match trigger, Hogue synthetic rubber grip stock with free float forend, flat-top upper, extended charging handle, no sights, aluminum handguard, black finish, 7.6 lbs. Mfg. 2013-2017.

$1,425	**$1,250**	**$1,100**	**$975**	**$850**	**$675**	**$550**	***$1,582***

* ***SIG M400 SDI Competition*** – .223 Wylde chambered, GIO, adj. gas block with mid-length gas system, 16 in. lightweight fluted stainless steel barrel, 3-chamber compensator, flared magwell, SIG Matchlite Duo Coyote Tan flat blade trigger, adj. Precision stock, ambi controls including bolt catch and release. Mfg. 2019 only.

$1,475	**$950**	**$725**	**$550**	**$475**	**$395**	**$350**	***$1,768***

* ***SIG M400 SDI V-TAC*** – 5.56 NATO cal., Microlite gas block with mid-length gas system, 16 in. 5R fluted barrel, Hybrid compensating flash hider, 30 shot mag., flared magwell, SIG Matchlite Duo flat blade trigger, Magpul SL stock, ambi controls including bolt catch and release, Coyote Tan finish. Mfg. 2019 only.

$1,600	**$1,400**	**$1,225**	**$1,075**	**$950**	**$750**	**$625**	***$1,768***

* ***SIG M400 SWAT*** – 5.56 NATO cal., GIO, 16 in. barrel, quad rail, SIG grip, M4 style buttstock, rear flip sight, 20 shot mag., black finish. Mfg. 2012 only, reintroduced 2014-2017.

$1,175	**$1,050**	**$925**	**$800**	**$700**	**$575**	**$450**	***$1,319***

* ***SIG M400 Varmint*** – 5.56 NATO cal., GIO, 22 in. heavy stainless steel barrel, 5 shot mag., match trigger. Mfg. 2014 only.

$1,250	**$1,100**	**$975**	**$850**	**$750**	**$600**	**$475**	***$1,395***

* ***SIG M400 Varminter*** – 5.56 NATO cal., GIO, 22 in. heavy match grade stainless steel threaded and capped barrel, 5 shot mag., Geissele two-stage match trigger, Hogue rubber grip synthetic stock with free float forend, flat-top upper, extended charging handle, 8.1 lbs. Mfg. 2013-2014.

$1,250	**$1,100**	**$975**	**$850**	**$750**	**$600**	**$475**	***$1,395***

SIG M400 TREAD – 5.56 NATO cal., Microlite gas block with mid-length gas system, aluminum frame, 16 in. stainless steel barrel, 3-prong flash hider, single stage polished/hardcoat trigger, Magpul SL-K 6-pos. telescoping stock, free floating M-LOK handguard, ambi controls, 7 lbs. New late 2018.

MSR $880	**$800**	**$700**	**$600**	**$550**	**$475**	**$375**	**$300**

* ***SIG M400 TREAD Coil*** – 5.56 NATO cal., AR-15 style, DI, 16 in. stainless steel barrel, 30 shot polymer mag., two-stage match trigger, ROMEO5 red dot sight, 6-pos. Magpul SL stock, alloy forend, polymer grip, M-LOK accessory rail, 13 in. lightweight handguard, ambi controls, 7 lbs. New 2021.

MSR $1,330	**$1,200**	**$1,050**	**$925**	**$825**	**$700**	**$575**	**$450**

GRADING - PPGS™	100%	98%	95%	90%	80%	70%	60%	LAST MSR

SIG 516 – 5.56 NATO cal., short stroke GPO, 3 or 4 position gas valve, various configurations. New 2011.

* ***SIG 516 Basic Patrol*** – 5.56 NATO cal., GPO, polymer handguard and 2 Picatinny rails - one on top of receiver and the other in front of handguard, 16 in. free floating barrel with muzzle brake, Magpul stock and pistol grip, 30 shot mag. Mfg. 2011 only.

$1,065	**$650**	**$500**	**$450**	**$395**	**$350**	**$325**	*$1,252*

* ***SIG 516 Patrol*** – 5.56 NATO or 7.62x39mm (mfg. 2012 only) cal., GPO, 16 in. cold hammer forged barrel with muzzle brake, Magpul MOE adj. stock and MOE grip (disc.) or B5 Systems Bravo SOPMOD stock, rear charging handle, free floating quad Picatinny rail, 3-position gas valve, 30 shot mag., ladder rail covers (new 2012), PMAG (new 2012), aluminum KeyMod handguard (new 2016), black, FDE (new 2012) or OD Green (mfg. 2012-2015) finish. Mfg. 2011-2019.

$1,700	**$1,500**	**$1,300**	**$1,150**	**$1,000**	**$800**	**$650**	*$1,888*

Add $136 for FDE finish (new 2012).

* ***SIG 516 Carbon Fiber*** – 5.56 NATO cal., GPO, 16 in. barrel, flip-up sights, carbon fiber forend, carbon fiber SIG or rifle stock, 30 shot Lancer mag. Mfg. 2014-2015.

$1,800	**$1,600**	**$1,400**	**$1,225**	**$1,075**	**$850**	**$700**	*$2,004*

Add $192 for carbon fiber rifle stock and forend.

* ***SIG 516 Precision Marksman*** – 5.56 NATO cal., GPO, 18 in. free floating match barrel w/o muzzle brake, 30 shot mag., free floating quad Picatinny rail, two-stage trigger, Magpul PRS stock, MIAD grip. Mfg. 2011-2013.

$2,150	**$1,900**	**$1,675**	**$1,475**	**$1,275**	**$1,025**	**$825**	*$2,399*

* ***SIG 516 SRP (Sight Ready Platform)*** – 5.56 NATO cal., GPO, 16 in. barrel, 30 shot mag., aluminum handguard, black or OD Green finish. Mfg. 2015 only.

$1,550	**$1,325**	**$1,200**	**$1,050**	**$900**	**$725**	**$600**	*$1,713*

* ***SIG 516 Sport Configuration Model (SCM)*** – 5.56 NATO, GPO, fixed stock, A2 pistol grip, 10 shot mag. Mfg. 2011-2012.

$1,315	**$850**	**$625**	**$500**	**$435**	**$375**	**$350**	*$1,599*

SIG 522 – .22 LR cal., 16 in. barrel, blowback action, 10 or 25 shot mag., black polymer lower receiver, folding/telescopic or non-folding Swiss style (disc.) stock, polymer (w/rail kit) or aluminum forend, flash suppressor, ambi safety and mag. release, approx. 6 1/2 lbs. Mfg. 2009-2015.

Add $199 for mini red dot sight (disc. 2012).
Add $53 for non-folding stock (disc.).
Add $222 for rotary rear sight (disc. 2009).
Add $210 for Harris bipod (disc. 2010).
Add $66 (Variable Power) or $106 (Prismatic Scope) with polymer handguards and telescopic stock (mfg. 2011 only).

* ***SIG 522 Classic*** – .22 LR cal., 16 in. barrel, features folding/telescopic stock, polymer handguards, rail kit, 10 or 25 shot mag. Disc. 2015.

$495	**$435**	**$365**	**$315**	**$275**	**$250**	**$230**	*$570*

* ***SIG 522 Classic SWAT*** – .22 LR cal., 16.6 in. barrel, features folding/telescopic stock, aluminum quad rail, 10 or 25 shot mag. Disc. 2015.

$665	**$585**	**$510**	**$440**	**$385**	**$340**	**$325**	*$776*

* ***SIG 522 Commando*** – .22 LR cal., 16 in. barrel, polymer handguard, folding/telescopic stock, tactical training suppressor, rail kit. Mfg. 2011-2015.

$575	**$500**	**$435**	**$365**	**$325**	**$280**	**$265**	*$662*

* ***SIG 522 Commando SWAT*** – .22 LR cal., quad rail handguard, folding/telescopic stock, tactical training suppressor. Mfg. 2012 only.

$615	**$540**	**$470**	**$400**	**$350**	**$310**	**$295**	*$707*

* ***SIG 522 Field*** – .22 LR cal., 20 in. barrel, folding/telescopic stock, polymer handguard, rail kit, 10 shot mag. Mfg. 2012-2014.

$465	**$410**	**$330**	**$285**	**$250**	**$230**	**$220**	*$534*

* ***SIG 522 Target*** – .22 LR cal., 20 in. barrel, Hogue free floating forend, folding/telescopic stock, variable power scope, 10 shot mag. Mfg. 2012-2015.

$725	**$650**	**$580**	**$515**	**$450**	**$385**	**$340**	*$856*

GRADING - PPGS™	100%	98%	95%	90%	80%	70%	60%	LAST MSR

SIG 551A1 – 5.56 NATO cal., GPO, 16 in. barrel, rotary bolt, utilizes original Swiss 550-style 20 or 30 shot translucent mags., black polymer folding skeletonized stock and forearm that surrounds barrel, gray finish, post front sight, adj. rotary diopter drum rear sight, two-stage trigger, top accessory rail, 7 lbs. Mfg. 2012-2014.

$1,315 $1,150 $985 $895 $725 $595 $465 *$1,599*

SIG 556 CLASSIC – 5.56 NATO cal., GPO, rotary bolt, 16 in. barrel with muzzle brake, alloy trigger housing, polymer forearm or choice of SIG quad rail (SWAT Model) or tri-rail, integrated Picatinny rails, two-stage trigger, collapsible or collapsible/folding tube stock, Magpul CTR Carbine stock type (SWAT) or M4 style stock (556ER or 556 Holo), 30 shot AR-15 type mag., 7.8-8.7 lbs. Mfg. 2007-2013.

$1,065 $935 $800 $725 $585 $485 $375 *$1,266*

Add $133 for quad-rail system (Classic SWAT Model).
Add $45 for Holo model with holographic sight (disc. 2009).
Add $150 for collapsible stock with GLR and Stoplite (disc. 2009).
Add $306 for Classic 16 with adj. folding stock and red dot sight (disc. 2009).
Add $456 for Classic 17 with adj. folding stock and rotary sight (disc. 2009).
Add $300 for 16 in. barrel with GLR and Stoplite (disc. 2009).
Subtract $200 if w/o iron sights (became standard 2008).

* ***SIG 556R*** – 7.62x39mm cal., GPO, 16 in. barrel, polymer handguards or aluminum quad rail (mfg. 2012 only) forend, folding/telescopic (mfg. 2011 only), or Swiss style (new 2012) stock, mini red dot sight, 5 (Hunting Model, mfg. 2012 only) or 30 shot AK type mag. Mfg. 2011-2013.

$1,125 $985 $845 $765 $625 $500 $395 *$1,332*

Add $34 for Hunting Model (mfg. 2012 only).
Add $133 for aluminum quad rail (mfg. 2012 only).

* ***SIG 556 DMR*** – 5.56 NATO cal., GPO, similar to Model 556, except has 18 in. heavy barrel w/o sights, adj. Magpul PRS stock, vented synthetic forearm, Picatinny rail on bottom of forearm and top of receiver, includes tactical bipod, 12 lbs. Mfg. 2008-2013.

$1,425 $1,245 $1,075 $975 $785 $645 $500 *$1,732*

* ***SIG 556 Patrol*** – 5.56 NATO cal., GPO, similar to SIG 556, 16 in. barrel, 30 shot mag., steel upper receiver, choice of polymer (Patrol) or alloy quad rail (Patrol SWAT) forend, black anodized finish, A2 flash suppressor, folding collapsible Swiss style stock, rotary diopter sight, 7 1/2 lbs. Mfg. 2010-2013.

$1,065 $935 $800 $725 $585 $485 $375 *$1,266*

Add $133 for SWAT model with quad rail forend.

* ***SIG 556 xi Patrol Swat*** – 5.56mm NATO cal., GPO, 16 in. barrel, steel receiver with M1913 rail, flip-up front and rear sights, M1913 quad rail forend, removable barrel, ambi safety, ambi mag. release, Swiss style stock. Mfg. 2012 only.

$1,175 $1,035 $885 $800 $645 $530 $425 *$1,424*

SIG 556xi – 5.56 NATO, 7.62x39mm, or .300 AAC Blackout (mfg. 2014 only) cal., GPO, 16 in. barrel, flip-up sights, 30 shot mag., polymer handguard, folding stock, black finish. Mfg. 2014-2016.

$1,275 $1,115 $950 $865 $700 $575 $445 *$1,522*

Add $141 for 7.62x39mm cal.
Add $133 for .300 AAC Blackout cal. (mfg. 2014 only).

SIG 556xi SWAT – 5.56 NATO or 7.62x39mm cal., GPO, 16 in. barrel, 30 shot mag., lock sights, folding stock, aluminum handguard, black finish. Mfg. 2015-2016.

$1,385 $1,225 $1,045 $945 $765 $625 $485 *$1,663*

Add $131 for 7.62x39mm cal.

SIG 556/P226 MATCHED PAIR – 5.56 NATO/9mm Para. cals., GPO, includes matched set of Desert Digital Special Editions of SIG 556 ER folding stock and P226 pistol. Both rifle and pistol have unique matching serial numbers, includes Pelican hard carry case in FDE, certificate of authenticity. Limited production run of 1,500 sets. Mfg. 2012.

Retail pricing was not available for this set.

SIG 716G2 DMR (DESIGNATED MARKSMAN) – 7.62 NATO (disc. 2019) or 6.5 Creedmoor (new 2018) cal., short stroke pushrod operating system with 4 position gas valve, 16 or 18 (new 2018, 6.5 Creedmoor only) in. free floating barrel with enhanced muzzle brake, two-stage match trigger, Magpul PMAG, aluminum KeyMod handguard with Picatinny rail, Magpul UBR stock and MIAD grip, ambi controls, black (disc. 2019) or FDE (new 2016) furniture, 12.3 lbs. Mfg. 2015-2020.

$2,575 $2,250 $1,925 $1,750 $1,425 $1,175 $1,000 *$3,030*

Add $136 for FDE furniture.
Add $136 for 6.5 Creedmoor cal. and 18 in. barrel (new 2018).

GRADING - PPGS™	100%	98%	95%	90%	80%	70%	60%	LAST MSR

SIG 716 PATROL – 7.62 NATO cal., GPO, 16 in. barrel, 20 shot mag., Magpul ACS stock and MIAD grip, quad rail, black, FDE, or OD Green (disc. 2015) finish. Mfg. 2011-2016.

	$1,795	$1,050	$875	$625	$550	$475	$425	*$2,283*

Add $55 for FDE finish (new 2012).

SIG 716G2 PATROL – 7.62 NATO cal., GPO, 16 in. stainless steel free floating barrel with enhanced muzzle brake, 20 shot mag., 6-pos. telescoping stock, polymer grip, aluminum KeyMod handguard, black or FDE (disc. 2019) hardcoat anodized finish, 9.5 lbs. Mfg. 2017-2019.

	$2,100	$1,900	$1,650	$1,450	$1,250	$1,000	$825	*$2,385*

Add $136 for FDE finish (disc. 2019).

SIG 716 PRECISION MARKSMAN – 7.62 NATO cal., short stroke GPO, 18 in. barrel, 20 shot PMAG, four position gas valve, threaded muzzle, upper and lower rails, two-stage Geissele match trigger, MIAD grip, Magpul UBR stock, folding backup iron sights, matte black finish, 11 lbs. Mfg. 2013 only.

	$2,125	$1,325	$995	$675	$595	$525	$475	*$2,666*

716i TREAD – .308 Win./7.62 NATO cal., AR-10 platform, DI, 16 in. stainless steel barrel, micro gas block, 3-prong flash hider, 20 shot polymer mag., two-stage Matchlite Duo trigger, Magpul SL-K 6-pos. stock, ambi controls, free floating M-LOK aluminum handguard, top Picatinny rail, hardcoat anodized black finish, 8.5 lbs. New 2020.

MSR $1,430	$1,275	$1,150	$1,000	$875	$750	$625	$500

SIG SCM – 5.56 NATO cal., GIO, 16 in. barrel, 10 shot mag., steel upper receiver, polymer forend with lower accessory rail, Holo sight, aluminum lower, target crowned muzzle, A2 fixed stock, Picatinny top rail, approx. 8 lbs. Mfg. 2010-2011.

	$995	$875	$745	$675	$545	$450	$350	*$1,191*

SIG SCM 22 – .22 LR cal., 18 in. barrel, choice of polymer handguard, or aluminum quad rail, blowback operating system, adj. iron sights, fixed stock, 10 shot mag. Mfg. 2011 only.

	$525	$450	$375	$325	$275	$250	$230	*$587*

Add $103 for aluminum quad rail.

SIG MCX – 5.56 NATO or .300 AAC Blackout cal., 16 in. barrel, 30 shot mag., KeyMod aluminum handguard, folding iron sights, thin folding stock, black anodized or FDE (new 2016) finish, 5.6 lbs. Mfg. 2015-2016.

	$1,600	$1,400	$1,200	$1,095	$885	$725	$565	*$1,903*

SIG MCX PATROL – 5.56 NATO or .300 AAC Blackout cal., GPO, 16 in. barrel, 30 shot mag., folding/telescoping 3-pos. stock, aluminum KeyMod handguard, ambi charging handle, black or FDE finish, 6.9 lbs. New 2017.

	$1,725	$1,525	$1,295	$1,175	$950	$775	$600	*$2,131*

Add $136 for FDE finish.

SIG MCX VIRTUS PATROL – 5.56 NATO or .300 AAC Blackout (disc. 2019) cal., GPO, 16 in. cold hammer forged carbon steel barrel, 30 shot polymer mag., Matchlite Duo trigger, 5-pos. telescoping folding stock, polymer grips, aluminum M-LOK free float handguard, ambi controls, Elite Concrete or FDE (disc. 2019) finish, 7.9 lbs. New 2018.

MSR $2,200	$1,975	$1,750	$1,525	$1,350	$1,175	$950	$775

Add $231 for red dot sights (disc. 2019).

SIG MPX – 9mm Para. cal., converts to .357 SIG or .40 S&W cal., closed, fully locked short stroke pushrod gas system, 16 in. free float barrel with permanently attached muzzle brake, 30 shot mag., ambidextrous magazine release, MPX Reflex sight, telescoping or folding stock, pistol grip, ambidextrous safety selector, extended carbon fiber rail adaptable handguard (disc. 2015) or aluminum KeyMod handguard (new 2016), monolithic upper receiver with integral M1913 rail, AR-style controls, rear charging handle, matte black or FDE (mfg. 2017 only) finish. Mfg. mid-2013-2018.

	$1,675	$1,465	$1,250	$1,145	$925	$750	$585	*$2,016*

Add $136 for FDE finish (mfg. 2017 only).

SIG MPX PCC – 9mm Para. cal., 16 in. threaded barrel, 3 chamber compensator, 30 shot mag., Timney single stage trigger, 5-pos. telefolding stock, narrow M-LOK free floating handguard, hardcoat anodized black finish, 6.63 lbs. New 2019.

MSR $2,100	$1,875	$1,675	$1,450	$1,275	$1,125	$900	$725

SHOTGUNS: O/U

The following Aurora shotguns were mfg. by Battista Rizzini, located in Marcheno, Italy.

L.L. BEAN NEW ENGLANDER SERIES – 12, 20, 28 ga., or .410 bore. Imported 2001-2004.

	$1,895	$1,575	$1,325	$1,100	$950	$800	$675

GRADING - PPGS™	100%	98%	95%	90%	80%	70%	60%	LAST MSR

AURORA TR20 FIELD (APOLLO) – 12, 20, 28 ga., or .410 bore, 3 in. chambers except for 28 ga., 26 or 28 in. VR barrels with choke tubes, satin finished low profile boxlock receiver, monobloc construction, removable hinge pins, gold SST, ejectors, deluxe checkered round pistol grip walnut stock and forearm, 6-7 lbs. Mfg. 2000-2005.

$1,995 $1,750 $1,475 $1,265 $1,050 $925 $800 ***$2,250***

* ***Aurora TR20U Field (Apollo)*** – similar to Apollo/Aurora TR20 Field, except has straight English stock (Upland Model) and color case hardened receiver. Mfg. 2000-2005.

$1,995 $1,750 $1,475 $1,265 $1,050 $925 $800 ***$2,250***

AURORA TR30 FIELD (APOLLO) – similar to Apollo/Aurora TR20 Field, except has color case hardened receiver with sideplates. Mfg. 2000-2005.

$2,275 $1,900 $1,675 $1,375 $1,150 $975 $850 ***$2,650***

AURORA TR40 GOLD/SILVER (APOLLO) – similar to Apollo/Aurora TR30 Field, except receiver and sideplates are engraved and have multiple gold bird inlays, choice of color case hardened (Gold Series) or silver receiver (Silver Series) finish, deluxe checkered walnut stock and forearm. Mfg. 2000-2005.

$2,575 $2,125 $1,850 $1,575 $1,350 $1,100 $950 ***$3,050***

* ***Aurora TR40U Gold/Silver (Apollo)*** – similar to Apollo/Aurora TR40 Gold/Silver, except has straight English grip stock and silver finished receiver only. Imported 2000 only.

$2,250 $1,950 $1,725 $1,500 $1,300 $1,000 $825 ***$2,595***

AURORA TT25 COMPETITION (APOLLO) – 12 or 20 ga., 3 in. chambers, features include polished 5 in. forcing cones and American stock dimensions with palm swell and Schnabel forearm, oil finished checkered walnut stock and forearm, matte finished 28, 30, or 32 (12 ga. only) in. VR barrels, 6 3/4 or 7 1/4 lbs. Mfg. 2000-2005.

$2,475 $2,000 $1,750 $1,500 $1,300 $1,075 $950 ***$2,950***

AURORA TT45 COMPETITION – 12 or 20 ga., 28, 30, or 32 (12 ga. only) in. VR barrels. Imported 2001-2005.

$2,745 $2,250 $1,925 $1,700 $1,500 $1,300 $1,100 ***$3,350***

SA 3 – 12 or 20 (new 1998) ga., 3 in. chambers, scalloped coin finished monobloc boxlock action with game scene engraving, field or Sporting Clays (new 1998) configuration, 26, 28, or 30 (Sporting Clays only) in. separated barrels with VR and choke tubes, ejectors, SST, checkered walnut stock and forearm, approx. 7 lbs. Mfg. 1997-98 only.

$1,175 $925 $775 $650 $550 $475 $400 ***$1,335***

SA 5 – 12 or 20 ga., 3 in. chambers, features coin finished boxlock action with hand engraved detachable sideplates, ejectors, SST, select checkered walnut stock and forearm, field or Sporting Clays (new 1998) configuration, 26 1/2, 28, or 30 (Sporting Clays only) in. barrels with VR and choke tubes, supplied with lockable case, 6 or 7 lbs. Mfg. 1997-99.

$2,175 $1,775 $1,450 $1,225 $1,075 $900 $775 ***$2,670***

Add $130 for Sporting Clays Model (12 ga. only, 28 or 30 in. barrels).

SILE DISTRIBUTORS

Previous distributor, importer, and previous manufacturer located in New York, NY.

In addition to distributing a wide variety of firearms and related accessories (including the mfg. of stocks and grips), Sile Distributors also had some firearms "private labeled" to their specifications.

SILMA SPORTING GUNS

Current manufacturer established during 1949 and located in Brescia, Italy. No current U.S. importation. Previously distributed and imported beginning 2000 on a limited basis by Legacy Sports, International, LLC, located in Alexandria, VA (Model 70 EJ variations only). All Silma shotguns, double rifles, and combination models are high quality and utilize premium materials in their manufacture.

For individual model listings, please go to BlueBookOfGunValues.com/overflow.

SILVA ARMS

Current shotgun and airgun manufacturer located in Istanbul, Turkey. No current U.S. importation.

Silva Arms manufactures good quality semi-auto and slide action shotguns, in addition to air rifles. Please contact the company directly for more information, including U.S availability and pricing.

GRADING - PPGS™	100%	98%	95%	90%	80%	70%	60%	LAST MSR

SILVER EAGLE

Current trademark of shotguns manufactured in Huglu, Turkey and imported by TR Imports, located in Keller, TX.

Please refer to the TR Imports listing in the T section.

SILVER SEITZ

Current trademark of high grade shotguns manufactured by AIM, Inc., located in Parkton, MD. Consumer direct sales.

SHOTGUNS: CUSTOM, TRAP

Silver Seitz builds guns to customer specification. Models listed below reflect base prices only. Please contact the company directly for a list of available options.

SILVER SEITZ – stainless steel receiver, choice of 33, 34, or 35 in. adj. rib barrels, top of the line, made to order, custom trap shotgun per customer's specifications, large number of options available, including choke tubes, quality of wood, and custom fit.

Base price for this model starts at $12,800 for adj. comb and goes up accordingly, depending on options.

SILVER SEITZ DOUBLE GUN – double release triggers, exhibition English wood and adj. comb., optional upgrade to Turkish wood, adj. rib, choice of Titanium, gold, or black Titanium Nitride receiver, additional choke tubes, optional gun case.

Base price for this model starts at $20,000 for Exhibition English wood and adj. comb and goes up accordingly, depending on options.

SILVER SHADOW ADVANCED SECURITY SYSTEMS LTD.

Current AR-15 style and bolt action firearms manufacturer established in 1995, located in Israel. Currently imported by Gilboa USA, located in Dayton, OH.

Silver Shadow manufactures the Gilboa Series, SBR, and DMR rifles. For more information on Gilboa rifles, please refer to Gilboa on our website at BlueBookOfGunValues.com/overflow.

SIMILLION, GENE

Current custom rifle maker located in Gunnison, CO. Consumer direct sales.

RIFLES: BOLT ACTION, CUSTOM

CLASSIC HUNTER RIFLE – various cals., new Winchester Model 70 Classic action, options include LOP, caliber, and barrel length, deluxe walnut, custom made to individual customer specifications. Disc. 2004.

	100%	98%	95%	90%	80%	70%	60%	LAST MSR
	$7,250	$6,000	$5,300	$4,650	$3,825	$3,100	$2,500	*$7,500*

Add $1,000 for Mag. cals. up to .375 H&H.
Add $1,500 for heavy Mag. cals. .375 H&H. and larger.

EXTREME HUNTER RIFLE – various cals., customer supplied Winchester Model 70 Classic action, match grade barrel, McMillan fiberglass stock, 8 1/2-10 lbs. New 2003.

	100%	98%	95%	90%	80%	70%	60%
MSR $9,300	$8,650	$7,450	$6,150	$5,150	$4,150	$3,500	$3,000

Add $800 for Mag. cals through .338.
Add $1,100 for heavy Mags. cals. .375 H&H and greater.

PREMIER MODEL 70 RIFLE – various cals., mostly Winchester new Model 70 action (others available), custom made to individual customer specifications, finest materials and workmanship, individually tested.

	100%	98%	95%	90%	80%	70%	60%
MSR $15,500	$14,800	$12,500	$9,995	$8,650	$7,600	$6,550	$5,500

Add $1,000 for Mag. cals. up to .375 H&H.
Add $1,700 for heavy Mag. cals. .375 H&H and larger.

PREMIER MODEL 98 RIFLE – various cals., Granite Mountain Arms Model 98 short or long action, custom made to individual customer specifications, exhibition grade walnut, ebony forend tip, swivel bases, solid steel grip cap, wide variety of custom options. New 2005.

	100%	98%	95%	90%	80%	70%	60%
MSR $16,300	$15,000	$13,000	$10,500	$9,150	$7,950	$6,850	$5,850

Add $300 for standard length action, or $2,000 for long Magnum action.
Add $4,900 for scope sighted rifle with long Mag. action.

SIMSEK

Previous shotgun manufacturer located in Turkey.

Simsek manufactured shotguns in O/U, SxS, and semi-auto configurations. They had very limited importation into the U.S.

GRADING - PPGS™	100%	98%	95%	90%	80%	70%	60%	LAST MSR

SIMSON

Previous firearms and airgun manufacturer established in 1856 and located in Suhl, Germany. Simson & Co. began building guns and gun barrels circa 1856, and continued its enterprise until 1936, when Hitler's dictatorship forced the Simson family to flee the country. The factory continued to build firearms, bicycles, and cars until 1945, when the Soviets took over and the factory was integrated into a Russian state motorcycle company. In 1952, the USSR returned the control of the factory to the GDR. Production of sporting arms, prams, and bicycles slowly resumed, with the main focus on motorcycle manufacture. The company struggled during the 1980s to modernize the production and the facility, but the company finally ceased operations in late 2002, and bankruptcy was declared in Feb. 2003.

Simson made a wide variety of handguns, rifles and shotguns, including some private labels. A comprehensive listing of everything Simson made would be nearly impossible, as most of its guns were not imported in the U.S. on a regular basis, and much of the company's history was destroyed after the Russians occupied Suhl after WWII. A general rule for evaluating Simson firearms is to determine the overall desirability of the configuration which takes into consideration the following - action type (boxlock or sidelock), caliber/gauge, ejectors or extractors, plain or engraved frame, special features, cocking indicators, overall eye appeal, and of course, original condition. Each Simson's unique mix of these factors determines the value, and as a result, each gun must be appraised individually. A good pricing guideline is to compare a Simson with other major European trademarks such as Heym, Krieghoff, Merkel, or Sauer determine the value on those, and use them as a comparison.

SINO DEFENSE MANUFACTURING (SDM)

Previous manufacturer of carbines and rifles. Distributed by Prima Armi located in Pinerolo, Italy.

SDM manufactured AR-15 style and AK-47 design rifles and carbines. The company also made a Dragunov and Mauser 98 style carbine, including a sniper variation.

SIONICS WEAPON SYSTEMS

Current AR-15 style pistol and rifle manufacturer located in Tucson, AZ.

Please refer to BlueBookOfGunValues.com to order the *Blue Book of AR-15s & Variations*, available as a book or online subscription.

SIPAHILER

Current manufacturer of shotguns located in Konya, Turkey, with offices in Istanbul, Turkey. Previously imported by U.S. agent located in Piscataway, NJ. No current U.S. importation.

Sipahiler manufactures a complete line of semi-auto shotguns in hunting, sporting, and tactical configurations. Many options are available, including receiver finishes, stocks, and engraving. The company also offers O/U high quality shotguns based on the Browning Superposed design. Please contact the manufacturer directly for more information, including U.S. domestic availability and pricing.

SIRKIS INDUSTRIES, LTD.

Previous manufacturer located in Ramat-Gan, Israel. Previously imported and distributed by Armscorp of America, Inc. located in Baltimore, MD.

PISTOLS: SEMI-AUTO

S.D. 9 - 9mm Para. cal., double action mechanism, frame is constructed mostly of heavy gauge sheet metal stampings, 3.07 in. barrel, parkerized finish, loaded chamber indicator, 7 shot mag., plastic grips, 24 1/2 oz. Imported under the Sirkis and Sardius trademarks between 1986-90.

100%	98%	95%	90%	80%	70%	60%	LAST MSR
$375	$295	$250	$200	$190	$180	$170	*$350*

RIFLES

MODEL 35 MATCH RIFLE - .22 LR cal. only, single shot bolt action, 26 in. full floating barrel, select walnut, match trigger, micrometer sights. Disc. 1985.

100%	98%	95%	90%	80%	70%	60%	LAST MSR
$650	$625	$595	$550	$510	$460	$420	*$690*

MODEL 36 SNIPER RIFLE - .308 Win. cal. only, gas operated action, carbon fiber stock, 22 in. barrel, flash suppressor, free range sights. Disc. 1985.

100%	98%	95%	90%	80%	70%	60%	LAST MSR
$670	$580	$520	$475	$430	$390	$350	*$760*

SISK RIFLES LLC

Current rifle manufacturer located in Hawesville, KY.

GRADING - PPGS™	100%	98%	95%	90%	80%	70%	60%	LAST MSR

RIFLES: BOLT ACTION

Charlie Sisk builds high quality bolt action rifles per individual customer specifications. The STAR (Sisk Tactical Adaptive Rifle) has a base price of $5,600. Hunting models start at $5,600. A wide variety of options and accessories are available. Please contact the company directly for more information, including availability, delivery time, pricing and options.

SJOGREN

Previous trademark of semi-auto shotguns invented by Carl Axel Theodor Sjögren in Sweden, and manufactured in Copenhagen, Denmark circa early 1900s.

SHOTGUNS: SEMI-AUTO

SJOGREN – 12 ga., unusual inertia operating system features fixed barrel and fully locked breech block, marked "AUTOMAT SYSTEM SJÖGREN PATENT" on three lines on frame above trigger guard. Approx. 5,000 mfg. 1907-1909.

100%	98%	95%	90%	80%	70%	60%	LAST MSR
N/A	$1,750	$1,450	$1,100	$800	$675	$525	

SKELI, LLC

Current manufacturer of semi-auto rifles established during 2012, located in Scottsdale, AZ.

RIFLES: SEMI-AUTO

X11 – 5.56 NATO cal., GPO, modular carbine, aluminum frame, 16 in. threaded barrel, Stanag M16 mag., aluminum frame, enlarged trigger guard, folding sights, folding stock with 13 in. LOP, polymer grip, safety selector, Picatinny rail with M-LOK mounts, 3-position adj. gas setting, ambi non-reciprocating charging handle, AR-15 Mil-Spec fire control group, black finish, 6.8 lbs.

MSR	100%	98%	95%	90%	80%	70%	60%
MSR $1,450	$1,225	$1,075	$925	$835	$675	$550	$450

SKORPION

Current semi-auto or select-fire pistol model manufactured in the Czech Republic. Currently imported by Czechpoint, Inc. located in Knoxville, TN beginning 2010. CZ USA purchased the VZ 61 Skorpions from Czechpoint between 2009-2010.

Please refer to the Czechpoint in the C section for models.

SMITH-CORONA

Previous WWII subcontractor of 1903 Springfield rifles located in Syracuse, NY.

Please refer to the Springfield Armory listing for more information.

SMITH, L.C.

L.C. Smith shotguns were manufactured by W.H. Baker & Company and L.C. Smith Maker, Syracuse, NY (1878-1889); Hunter Arms Company, Fulton, NY (1890-1950); L.C. Smith Gun Company, Fulton, NY (1946-1950); Marlin Firearms Company, North Haven, CT (1968-1971). L.C. Smith trademarked shotguns were also manufactured in Italy and Spain and imported by Marlin Firearms Company, North Haven, CT (2004-2009).

The L.C. Smith sidelock shotgun with its famous rotary locking bolt is considered an "American Best" and is recognized as one of America's most prestigious and collectible shotguns. The *Blue Book of Gun Values* strongly recommends an expert appraisal when contemplating a purchase of a higher grade L.C. Smith, particularly in 90%+ original condition. L.C. Smith shotguns with a second set of barrels (usually marked "2") and forend serial numbered to the gun (1 and 2) with matching serial numbers and forends are valued at 50% more if they were made at the factory when the shotgun was built. A second set of barrels will add 33% to the value if the shotgun was sent back to the factory to be fitted with the second set. Guns that are mechanically factory original, but have been professionally restored (barrels, receivers, and wood) are of less interest to collectors. Therefore, these expertly restored guns should be valued at about 50% of the highest value listed for a particular grade in this section, assuming the restored gun exhibits little, if any wear. Values are dependent upon grade and craftsmanship and are not included in these suggested values.

Factory records are available for the following: Hunter Arms Company shotguns 1890-1918, production and shipping records 1918-1946 (Ranger, Fulton, Gladiator, and Hunter Special), L.C. Smith Gun Co. records 1946-1950 ("FWS" prefix), and Marlin records 1968-1971 ("FWM" prefix). Information in these letters includes configuration, complete manufacture and shipping dates, numbers in each grade, barrel length, description of engraving and special features, retail price, and current worth. A letter of authentication increases the value of any grade from any era by a minimum of $100.

L.C. Smith factory letters may also be obtained through the Cody Firearms Records Office at the Buffalo Bill Center of the West.

The L.C. Smith Collectors Association offers a variety of services as well as a quarterly collector's journal. Readers may reach the organization at lcsca.clubexpress.com. Price of factory letters are $50 for members and $75 for non-members.

The price guide in this book is based on the remaining percentage of original case color finish. Original bold, vivid case colors will command a substantial premium on most grades.

SHOTGUN-RIFLES: BAKER 3-BARREL, HAMMER-DAMASCUS, SYRACUSE MFG. 1878-1888

Shotgun barrels were 12 or 10 ga. Rifle barrels were .44-.40, .45-.70, .38-55, and others. The ser. no. range is 1-1,600, and estimated total shotguns produced is 1,186.

	100%	98%	95%	90%	80%	70%	60%	50%	40%	30%	20%	10%
QUALITY NO. 1	N/A	N/A	N/A	N/A	$3,500	$3,000	$2,500	$2,000	$1,500	$1,200	$1,000	$800
QUALITY NO. 2	N/A	N/A	N/A	N/A	$4,200	$3,800	$3,400	$2,500	$2,000	$2,000	$1,500	$1,100
QUALITY NO. 3	N/A	N/A	N/A	N/A	$4,900	$4,500	$4,250	$4,000	$3,750	$3,500	$3,000	$2,500
QUALITY NO. 4	N/A	N/A	N/A	N/A	$7,500	$7,000	$6,500	$6,000	$5,500	$4,500	$3,500	$3,000
QUALITY NO. 5	N/A	N/A	N/A	N/A	$9,000	$7,750	$7,000	$5,200	$4,500	$4,100	$3,500	$3,000

SHOTGUNS: SXS, BAKER HAMMER-DAMASCUS, SYRACUSE MFG. 1878-1884

The ser. no. range is 50-10,000, and estimated total shotguns produced is 8,305.

	100%	98%	95%	90%	80%	70%	60%	50%	40%	30%	20%	10%
QUALITY F	N/A	N/A	N/A	N/A	$850	$700	$550	$475	$350	$300	$250	$200
QUALITY E	N/A	N/A	N/A	N/A	$1,000	$800	$700	$600	$450	$375	$300	$225
QUALITY D	N/A	N/A	N/A	N/A	$1,200	$1,000	$850	$750	$600	$450	$325	$250
QUALITY C	N/A	N/A	N/A	N/A	$1,400	$1,200	$1,000	$800	$650	$500	$400	$300
QUALITY B	N/A	N/A	N/A	N/A	$1,600	$1,400	$1,100	$900	$800	$550	$475	$400
QUALITY A	N/A	N/A	N/A	N/A	$2,100	$1,800	$1,500	$1,200	$900	$700	$600	$500

QUALITY AA

Extreme rarity precludes accurate pricing on this model.

SHOTGUNS: SxS GLADIATOR HAMMER GUNS, MFG. 1917-1919

Gladiator hammer guns were made by the Hunter Arms Company for Sears Roebuck & Company.

GLADIATOR FIELD GRADE – Gladiator Field Grades were made in 12 ga. (5) and 16 ga. (114).

GLADIATOR IDEAL GRADE – Gladiator Ideal grades were made in 12 ga. (100)

	100%	98%	95%	90%	80%	70%	60%	50%	40%	30%	20%	10%
GLADIATOR FIELD GRADE	N/A	N/A	N/A	N/A	$550	$475	$375	$300	$275	$250	$200	$175
GLADIATOR IDEAL GRADE	N/A	N/A	N/A	N/A	$700	$650	$600	$550	$475	$425	$375	$350

SHOTGUNS: SxS, L.C. SMITH SIDELOCK, HAMMER-DAMASCUS & FLUID STEEL, MFG. 1884-1934

L.C. Smith hammer guns are popular with collectors and shooters, and this popularity coincided with the availability of commercially manufactured black powder loads and smokeless low pressure loads. The vast majority of these shotguns had best English stub twist or damascus barrels. Collectors' interest in damascus barrels has increased in recent years. The values shown are based on damascus-barreled shotguns with 90% original finish, without pitting, reboring or polishing out. Royal fluid steel was available 1898-1934. All

100%	98%	95%	90%	80%	70%	60%	50%	40%	30%	20%	10%

damascus barreled guns should be examined by an expert gunsmith before being shot.

Serial number ranges for bar action (mainspring before tumbler) Syracuse-made guns: 10,000-25,600 (approximately) and Fulton-made bar action guns: 27,766-29,999.

Serial numbers from 50,000-72,999 are Fulton-made guns with bar action lock.

Serial numbers from 73,000-89,999 are Fulton-made hammer guns, now with a back action lock (mainspring is behind tumbler)

No guns found in the 70,000-78,999 OR THE 86,000-86,999 serial number range.

Serial numbers 79,000-89,999 are hammer gun serial numbers.

Hammer gun serial numbers started again at 125,000 in 1902, and ended in 1918 at 180,925

Sometime in 1918 the serial numbers for hammer and hammerless were mixed and hammer guns from then on will have an "H" prefix before the serial numbers. Production continued until 1934 to about serial number 140,000.

Add 33% for 10 ga. in all grades.
Add 50% for 16 ga. in all grades.
Deduct 33% for shortened (cut) barrels.

QUALITY F – Three different Quality/Grade F shotgun barrel steels were used, (Damascus, Best English Stub Twist, and Royal fluid steel).

N/A	N/A	N/A	$1,700	$1,375	$1,100	$900	$700	$550	$400	$300	$250

QUALITY E

N/A	N/A	N/A	$2,300	$2,000	$1,700	$1,500	$1,200	$900	$700	$600	$500

QUALITY D

N/A	N/A	N/A	$3,600	$3,000	$2,600	$2,200	$1,800	$1,500	$1,200	$1,000	$900

QUALITY C

N/A	N/A	N/A	$4,250	$3,900	$3,400	$3,000	$2,600	$2,100	$1,600	$1,100	$900

QUALITY B

N/A	N/A	N/A	$5,100	$4,600	$4,200	$3,800	$3,200	$2,500	$1,800	$1,200	$1,000

QUALITY A – approx. 104 mfg.

N/A	N/A	N/A	$10,000	$7,700	$6,000	$5,000	$4,500	$3,500	$3,000	$2,000	$1,500

QUALITY AA – approx. 50 mfg., 1888 and earlier.

N/A	N/A	N/A	$19,000	$16,000	$13,000	$10,000	$8,000	$6,000	$4,000	$3,000	$2,500

SHOTGUNS: SxS, L.C. SMITH SIDELOCK, HAMMERLESS-DAMASCUS, MFG. 1886-1890

The L.C. Smith Syracuse-made hammerless guns in 8, 10, and 12 gauge have become extremely popular with serious collectors. All of the shotguns manufactured in Syracuse had Damascus barrels. The values shown are based on Damascus barrels with 90% original finish, without pitting, reboring, or polishing out.

Serial number range for Syracuse-made guns: 16,000-16,999, 18,000-20,999, 22,000-23,500.

Add 50% for a factory second set of barrels on all grades.
Add $500 for a gold dog inlay on the trigger guard.
Add $1,000 for gold dog inlays on the lock plates.
Add 800% for 8 ga.
Deduct 33% for shortened (cut) barrels.
Syracuse made shotguns did not have single triggers or automatic ejectors.

QUALITY 2

N/A	N/A	N/A	N/A	$2,000	$1,700	$1,300	$1,000	$750	$600	$450	$400

QUALITY 3

N/A	N/A	N/A	N/A	$2,400	$1,900	$1,500	$1,100	$825	$650	$500	$425

QUALITY 4 – approx. 330 mfg.

N/A	N/A	N/A	N/A	$3,800	$3,000	$2,200	$1,700	$1,300	$1,000	$700	$500

QUALITY 5 – approx. 138 mfg.

N/A	N/A	N/A	N/A	$5,500	$4,300	$3,400	$2,500	$2,000	$21,500	$1,000	$700

100%	98%	95%	90%	80%	70%	60%	50%	40%	30%	20%	10%
QUALITY 6 – approx. 47 mfg., disc. 1892.											
N/A	N/A	N/A	N/A	$13,000	$10,000	$8,500	$6,800	$5,100	$4,300	$3,500	$2,800
QUALITY 7 – approx. 35 mfg.											
N/A	N/A	N/A	N/A	$19,000	$15,000	$12,000	$9,500	$8,000	$6,500	$5,000	$4,500

SHOTGUNS: SxS, L.C. SMITH/HUNTER ARMS, SIDELOCK, HAMMERLESS, FLUID STEEL OR DAMASCUS BARRELS, MFG. 1890-1913

Pre-1913 guns - Individual grades were designated as Quality from 1892 to 1895 and as Grade from 1896 to about 1913. Values for Qualities and Grades are equal in the prices presented below. All values listed are for hammerless 12 ga. guns with fluid steel barrels (except the A-1 Grade). Guns were manufactured on regular weight frames in 8 ga. and 10 ga., and regular and light frames in 12, 16, and 20 ga. Guns with Damascus barrels are nearly equal in value if the Damascus barrels have 90% original finish, without pitting, reboring or polished out. L.C. Smith shotguns are uncommon and were all made to exacting standards. Collector interest is high, and guns in 90%+ original condition are difficult to evaluate. The values shown are meant as a guide only.

Add 25% for 10 ga. in all grades.
Add 100% for 20 ga. on all grades.
Add 60% for 16 ga. on all grades.
Add 1,000% for 8 ga. on all grades (approx. 53 mfg.)
Add $400 for auto ejectors on all grades with values of $1,500+, or 33% for values less than $1,500.
Add $400 for a Hunter One-Trigger on all grades with values of $1,500+, or 33% for values less than $1,500.
Add 25% for fluid steel barrels on the A-1.
Add 25% for Krupp Steel barrels.
Add 33% for uncommon barrel lengths (24, 25, 27, 29, 31, and 33 in.)
Add 10% for straight grip (English) stocks.
Add 25% for Monte Carlo stocks.
Deduct 20%-40% for Damascus barrels, if condition is under 80%.
Deduct 33% for shortened (cut) barrels.
Deduct 25% for shortened stocks.
Deduct $100-$500 for missing or incorrect butt pad, depending on condition and grade.
Deduct $50 for missing brass or $100 for missing ivory sighting beads.

100%	98%	95%	90%	80%	70%	60%	50%	40%	30%	20%	10%
NO. 00 – 57,096 mfg. 1898-1914.											
N/A	N/A	N/A	$1,900	$1,350	$950	$750	$650	$550	$500	$450	$400
NO. 0 – 29,061 mfg. 1894-1914.											
N/A	N/A	N/A	$2,000	$1,450	$1,050	$850	$750	$650	$600	$550	$450
NO. 1 – 9,211 mfg. 1890-1913.											
N/A	N/A	N/A	$2,200	$1,600	$1,200	$1,000	$900	$800	$700	$650	$550
NO. 2 – 12,483 mfg. 1890-1914.											
N/A	N/A	N/A	$2,400	$1,800	$1,400	$1,200	$1,000	$900	$800	$700	$650
NO. 3 – 3,042 mfg. 1894-1913.											
N/A	N/A	N/A	$3,600	$3,100	$2,600	$2,100	$1,700	$1,400	$1,200	$1,100	$1,000
PIGEON GUN – 1,397 mfg. 1893-1913.											
N/A	N/A	N/A	$6,500	$5,800	$4,000	$3,000	$2,500	$2,000	$1,500	$1,200	$900
NO. 4 – 495 mfg. 1894-1914.											
N/A	N/A	N/A	$7,000	$6,000	$5,000	$4,000	$3,500	$3,000	$2,500	$2,250	$2,000
NO. 5 – 523 mfg. 1894-1912.											
N/A	N/A	N/A	$10,000	$8,000	$7,000	$6,000	$5,000	$4,000	$3,750	$3,500	$3,000
MONOGRAM – 107 mfg. 1892-1912, with an additional 199 mfg. 1913-1945.											
N/A	N/A	N/A	$16,000	$13,000	$10,000	$8,000	$7,000	$6,000	$5,500	$5,250	$5,000
A-1 – Syracuse-style frames, 752 mfg. 1891-1901.											
N/A	N/A	N/A	$6,400	$5,100	$4,300	$3,400	$3,000	$2,600	$2,300	$2,000	$1,800
A-2 – 213 mfg. 1891-1916.											
N/A	N/A	N/A	$18,500	$15,500	$14,000	$13,000	$12,000	$9,000	$8,000	$7,000	$6,000
A-3 – 19 mfg. 1894-1909.											
N/A	N/A	N/A	$90,000	$80,000	$70,000	$60,000	$50,000	$40,000	$35,000	$32,000	$29,000

100%	98%	95%	90%	80%	70%	60%	50%	40%	30%	20%	10%

SHOTGUNS: SxS, L.C. SMITH/HUNTER ARMS, SIDELOCK, HAMMERLESS, FLUID STEEL BARRELS, MFG. 1913-1950

Post 1913 guns - Values shown are for hammerless 12 ga. guns with fluid steel barrels. Guns were manufactured in 12, 16, 20 ga. and .410 bore on either regular-weight or feather-weight frames. Shotguns with Damascus barrels are nearly equal in value if the Damascus barrels have 90%+ original finish, without pitting, reboring, or polished out. L.C. Smith shotguns were all made to exacting standards. Collector interest can be high, and guns in 90%+ original condition are very difficult to evaluate and the values shown are meant as a guide only.

Add 33% for 10 ga. Field and Ideal Grades; 50% for Trap and Specialty Grades; and 100% for Eagle, Crown, and Monogram Grades.
Add 75% for 20 ga. in all grades.
Add 100% for 20 ga. with 32 in. barrels.
Add 60% for 16 ga. in all grades.
Add 75% for 16 ga. with 32 in. barrels.
Add 400% for .410 bore in Field and Ideal Grades.
Add 600% for .410 bore in Specialty and higher grades.
Add 33% for Long Range and Wild Fowl models.
Add $400 for automatic ejectors in all grades with values of $1,500+ (except Premier Skeet, Premier, and De Luxe Grades), or 33% for values less than $1,500.
Add $400 for selective or nonselective Hunter One-Trigger on all grades with values of $1,500+, or 33% for values less than $1,500.
Add $500 for ventilated rib on all grades with values of $1,500+, or 33% for values less than $1,500.
Add 25% for Krupp Steel barrels in any grade.
Add $200 for a Curtis forend release.
Add 33% for uncommon barrel lengths (22, 24, 25, 27, 29, 31, and 34 in.)
Add 10% for straight grip (English) stocks.
Add 25% for Monte Carlo stocks.
Deduct 15% for FWS serial number prefix (Marlin mfg. 1946-1950).
Deduct 33% for shortened (cut) barrels.
Deduct 25% for shortened stocks.
Deduct $100-$500 for missing or incorrect butt pad, depending on condition and grade.
Deduct $50 for missing brass or $100 for missing ivory sighting beads.

FIELD – 199,384 mfg. 1912-1950.

N/A	N/A	$2,300	$1,700	$1,100	$900	$750	$600	$550	$500	$450	$400

IDEAL – 26,686 mfg. 1912-1950.

N/A	N/A	$3,100	$2,500	$1,900	$1,400	$1,250	$1,000	$700	$600	$500	$450

SKEET SPECIAL – standard with automatic ejectors, Hunter One-Trigger, and beavertail forend. 778 mfg. 1926-1948.

N/A	N/A	$4,000	$3,500	$3,000	$2,500	$2,100	$1,900	$1,800	$1,700	$1,600	$1,500

OLYMPIC – 26 mfg. 1931-1937.

N/A	N/A	$18,000	$15,000	$12,000	$11,000	$10,000	$9,000	$8,000	$7,000	$6,000	$5,500

PREMIER SKEET – standard with automatic ejectors, Hunter One-Trigger, and beavertail forend. 515 mfg. 1949-1950.

N/A	N/A	$5,500	$4,000	$3,000	$2,000	$1,800	$1,600	$1,400	$1,200	$1,000	$900

TRAP – 3,346 mfg. 1912-1940.

N/A	N/A	$4,000	$3,200	$2,500	$2,000	$1,500	$1,100	$900	$700	$600	$500

SPECIALTY – 6,911 mfg. 1912-1950.

N/A	N/A	$4,700	$3,700	$3,000	$2,500	$2,100	$1,800	$1,500	$1,300	$1,200	$1,100

EAGLE – 562 mfg. 1912-1939.

N/A	N/A	$8,500	$7,500	$6,500	$5,500	$4,800	$4,100	$3,400	$2,700	$2,200	$1,800

CROWN – 862 mfg. 1912-1950.

N/A	N/A	$11,000	$9,500	$8,000	$6,000	$5,000	$4,000	$3,600	$3,300	$3,100	$3,000

MONOGRAM – 199 mfg. 1913-1945, with an additional 107 mfg. 1892-1912.

N/A	N/A	$17,000	$15,000	$12,500	$9,500	$7,500	$6,500	$5,800	$5,400	$5,200	$5,000

100%	98%	95%	90%	80%	70%	60%	50%	40%	30%	20%	10%

PREMIER – 27 mfg. 1919-1940.

N/A	N/A	$65,000	$50,000	$40,000	$35,000	$30,000	$25,000	$20,000	$17,500	$15,000	$12,500

DELUXE – 30 mfg. 1908-1946.

N/A	N/A	$105,000	$90,000	$75,000	$60,000	$50,000	$40,000	$30,000	$25,000	$20,000	$17,500

SHOTGUNS: SINGLE BARREL TRAP, BOXLOCK, HAMMERLESS, MFG. 1917-1950

The L.C. Smith Single Barrel Trap (SBT) is considered one of America's best made guns, and awards for both the guns and shooters are legendary, including Olympic medals and world titles. Collector interest can be high, and an expert appraisal is recommended on guns in 80%+ condition. Single barrel trap models were made in 12 ga. only, with 30, 32, or 34 in. ventilated rib barrel, boxlock, auto ejector, checkered pistol grip stock, recoil pad, and beavertail forend. A total of 2,281 were mfg. between 1917 and 1951. In addition to the grades listed, SBTs were made in the following grades and quantities: Ideal (6), Field (2), and Whippet (12). Extreme rarity excludes accurate pricing on these grades.

OLYMPIC – 596 mfg. 1927-1950.

N/A	$3,500	$2,900	$2,400	$2,000	$1,500	$1,200	$1,000	$900	$800	$700	$600

SPECIALITY – 1,470 mfg. 1917-1948.

N/A	$4,600	$3,600	$3,100	$1,900	$1,500	$1,250	$1,000	$900	$800	$700	$600

EAGLE – 90 mfg. 1918-1940.

N/A	$7,200	$5,800	$4,800	$4,000	$3,200	$2,400	$1,900	$1,400	$1,300	$1,200	$1,100

CROWN – 86 mfg. 1918-1940.

N/A	$12,000	$10,500	$9,000	$7,000	$6,000	$4,000	$3,200	$2,700	$2,300	$2,100	$2,000

MONOGRAM – 15 mfg. 1920-1940.

N/A	$18,000	$14,000	$10,000	$9,000	$8,000	$7,000	$6,000	$5,000	$4,000	$3,200	$2,700

PREMIER – 2 mfg. 1920 and 1936.

Extreme rarity precludes accurate pricing on this model.

DELUXE – 3 mfg. 1925, 1929, and 1937.

Extreme rarity precludes accurate pricing on this model.

SHOTGUNS: SxS, HUNTER ARMS, FULTON BOXLOCK, HAMMERLESS, FLUID STEEL, MFG. 1915-1945

These models should not be confused with actual L.C. Smith sidelock shotguns. In reality, these models are high quality, less expensive boxlocks built with quality similar to Field Grade L.C. Smiths. The receiver, forend iron, trigger guard and triggers were all machined (not stamped) from forgings. These models have excellent durability and collector interest is increasing.

Manufactured in 12, 16, 20 ga. and .410 bore.

Add 75% for 20 ga.
Add 50% for 16 ga.
Add 500% for .410 bore.
Add $200 for a non-selective Hunter One-Trigger.
Add $150 for beavertail forend.

FULTON – all have plain checkered stock with half pistol grip. 35,881 mfg. 1918-1946.

N/A	N/A	$900	$850	$625	$500	$400	$350	$300	$275	$250	$225

An additional 38,754 early (1904-1918) boxlocks are in the records, but they are not further identified and little is known about them.

FULTON SPECIAL – all have a checkered stock with full pistol grip, engraved (roll-marked) frame. 3,475 mfg. 1918-1941.

N/A	N/A	$1,100	$900	$750	$600	$500	$450	$400	$350	$325	$300

HUNTER SPECIAL – similar to Fulton Special, except has L.C. Smith rotary locking bolt system and a different roll-mark. 5,971 mfg. 1937-1945.

N/A	N/A	$1,300	$1,000	$750	$600	$525	$475	$425	$375	$350	$325

RANGER – made for Sears Roebuck, similar to the Fulton. 8,237 mfg. 1937-1939.

N/A	N/A	$650	$600	$525	$425	$350	$325	$300	$275	$250	$225

100%	98%	95%	90%	80%	70%	60%	50%	40%	30%	20%	10%

GLADIATOR FIELD – made for Sears Roebuck, similar to the Fulton. 166 mfg. 1918-1919.

100%	98%	95%	90%	80%	70%	60%	50%	40%	30%	20%	10%
N/A	N/A	N/A	N/A	$550	$500	$450	$350	$275	$250	$225	$200

GLADIATOR TOURNAMENT – made for Sears Roebuck, similar to the Fulton. 61 mfg. 1918-1919.

100%	98%	95%	90%	80%	70%	60%	50%	40%	30%	20%	10%
N/A	N/A	N/A	N/A	$650	$600	$550	$450	$375	$350	$325	$300

GLADIATOR DIAMOND – made for Sears Roebuck, similar to the Fulton. 53 mfg. 1918 only.

100%	98%	95%	90%	80%	70%	60%	50%	40%	30%	20%	10%
N/A	N/A	N/A	N/A	$650	$600	$550	$450	$375	$350	$325	$300

SHOTGUNS: SxS, L.C. SMITH/MARLIN, SIDELOCK, HAMMERLESS, FLUID STEEL, MFG. 1968-1971

The Marlin Firearms Company reintroduced the L.C. Smith trademark in 1968. These models are considered real L.C. Smiths, not copies, and collector interest is increasing. The following Marlin-manufactured shotguns with an "FWM" prefix.

FIELD GRADE MODEL – 12 ga., 28 in. barrels, aluminum ventilated rib, F/M chokes, extractors, double triggers, checkered pistol grip stock. 2,038 mfg. 1968-1971.

100%	98%	95%	90%	80%	70%	60%	50%	40%	30%	20%	10%
N/A	$1,700	$1,200	$1,000	$900	$850	$800	$750	$700	$675	$650	$600

DELUXE MODEL – 12 ga., 28 in. barrels, Simmons floating ventilated rib, F/M chokes, extractors, double triggers, checkered select walnut pistol grip stock, beavertail forearm. 189 mfg. 1971 only.

100%	98%	95%	90%	80%	70%	60%	50%	40%	30%	20%	10%
N/A	$2,200	$1,750	$1,500	$1,250	$1,150	$1,100	$1,050	$1,000	$975	$950	$925

GRADING - PPGS™	100%	98%	95%	90%	80%	70%	60%	LAST MSR

SHOTGUNS: O/U, L.C. SMITH/MARLIN, MFG. 2005-2009

MODEL LC12 – 12 ga., 28 in. vent. rib barrels with choke tubes, SST, ejectors, fleur-de-lis checkered walnut pistol grip stock with fluted comb, recoil pad, bead front sight, approx. 7 1/4 lbs. Mfg. for Marlin in Italy and Spain 2005-2009.

100%	98%	95%	90%	80%	70%	60%	LAST MSR
N/A	$500	$400	$300	$275	$250	$225	*$1,385*

MODEL LC20 – 20 ga., 26 in. vent. rib barrels with choke tubes, otherwise similar to LC12, approx. 6 3/4 lbs. Mfg. for Marlin in Italy and Spain 2005-2009.

100%	98%	95%	90%	80%	70%	60%	LAST MSR
N/A	$700	$550	$450	$350	$325	$300	*$1,385*

SHOTGUNS: SxS, L.C. SMITH/MARLIN, MFG. 2005-2009

MODEL LC12-DB – 12 ga., boxlock action, 28 in. vent. rib barrels with choke tubes, single trigger, ejectors, detachable sideplates, semi-beavertail forearm, fleur-de-lis checkered walnut pistol grip stock with fluted comb, recoil pad, bead front sight, approx. 7 1/2 lbs. Mfg. for Marlin in Italy and Spain 2005-2009.

100%	98%	95%	90%	80%	70%	60%	LAST MSR
N/A	$850	$750	$650	$600	$550	$500	*$2,167*

MODEL LC20-DB – 20 ga., 26 in. vent. rib barrels with choke tubes, otherwise similar to Model LC12-DB, approx. 6 1/2 lbs. Mfg. for Marlin in Italy and Spain 2005-2009.

100%	98%	95%	90%	80%	70%	60%	LAST MSR
N/A	$1,000	$900	$800	$700	$600	$550	*$2,167*

MODEL LC28-DB/LC410-DB – 28 ga. or .410 bore, 26 in. vent. rib barrels with three choke tubes, scaled down version of the Model LC20-DB, gold game scenes on sides and bottom of receiver, approx. 6 1/4 - 6 1/2 lbs. Mfg. for Marlin in Italy and Spain 2007-2009.

100%	98%	95%	90%	80%	70%	60%	LAST MSR
N/A	$1,400	$1,300	$1,100	$900	$850	$800	*$2,167*

SMITH & WESSON

Smith&Wesson

Current manufacturer located in Springfield, MA, 1857 to date. Partnership with Horace Smith & Daniel B. Wesson 1856-1874. Family owned by Wesson 1874-1965. S&W became a subsidiary of Bangor-Punta from 1965-1983. Between 1983-1987, Smith & Wesson was owned by the Lear Siegler Co. On May 22, 1987, Smith & Wesson was sold to R.L. Tomkins, an English holding company. During 2001, Tomkins sold Smith & Wesson to Saf-T-Hammer, an Arizona-based safety and security company. Smith & Wesson was the primary distributor for most Walther firearms and accessories in the United States from 2002-2012. During 2012, Carl Walther GmbH Sportwaffen and Umarex announced the formation of Walther Arms, Inc. to import, sell, and market all Walther products in the U.S. beginning Jan. 1, 2013.

	Above Average	Average	Below Average

Smith & Wessons have been classified under the following category names - PISTOLS: LEVER ACTION, ANTIQUE, TIP-UPS, TOP-BREAKS, SINGLE SHOTS, EARLY HAND EJECTORS (Named Models), NUMBERED MODEL REVOLVERS (Modern Hand Ejectors), SEMI-AUTOS, RIFLES, and SHOTGUNS.

Each category is fairly self-explanatory. Among the early revolvers, Tip-ups have barrels that tip up so the cylinder can be removed for loading or unloading, whereas Top-breaks have barrels & cylinders that tip down with automatic ejection.

Hand Ejectors are the modern type revolvers with swing out cylinders. In 1957, S&W began a system of numbering all models they made. Accordingly, the Hand Ejectors have been divided into two sections - the Early Hand Ejectors include the named models introduced prior to 1958. The Numbered Model Revolvers are the models introduced or continued after that date, and are easily identified by the model number stamped on the side of the frame, visible when the cylinder is open. The author wishes to express his thanks to Mr. Sal Raimondi, Jim Supica, Rick Nahas, and Roy Jinks, the S&W Historian, for their updates and valuable contributions.

Factory special orders, such as ivory or pearl grips, special finishes, engraving, and other production rarities will add premiums to the values listed. After 1893, all ivory and pearl grips had the metal S&W logo medallions inserted on top.

FACTORY LETTER OF AUTHENTICITY - S&W charges $50 for a formal letter of authenticity. A form is available for downloading on their website: www.smith-wesson.com for this service. Turnaround time is usually 8-12 weeks.

For more information and current pricing on both new and used Smith & Wesson airguns, please refer to the *Blue Book of Airguns* - also available as an online subscription.

PISTOLS: LEVER ACTION, ANTIQUE

Pistols were produced in Norwich, CT from 1853-1855 using the 1854 patent of Horace Smith and Daniel B. Wesson. The pistol fired a projectile that was chambered in the pistol using a newly designed lever action mechanism. The pistol was loaded by inserting the ammunition into a integral tube located below the barrel when the follower was moved forward and rotated, exposing the loading tube. The barrel assembly contained a steel spring and follower that aided in the loading of the ammunition into the receiver. This design was later perfected in the Henry rifle. The pistol was produced in two different models.

NO. 1 (SMALL FRAME) – .31 cal., 4 in. half-round barrel, steel frame, moderate rose and scroll engraving, varnished walnut (bag style shape standard), or ivory grips, blue frame with brown barrel assembly, approx. 1,200-1,300 mfg.

	Above Average	Average	Below Average
	$12,000-$16,000	**$10,000-$12,000**	**$7,000-$10,000**

Add 20% for ivory grips.

Barrels are marked: "SMITH WESSON, NORWICH, CT, CAST STEEL" and "FEB. 14, 1854 PATENT" marked on the barrel flats. Stamping variations are common as to placement, depth, off-center to barrel flats, and even slight double stamps have been observed. "CAST STEEL" is even observed upside down on some guns. Serial numbered from 1-100 initially and then 1-100 again for each letter prefix A-F on the frame and inside the grips for a total of 700 guns. The last 500-600 guns were assembled by the New Haven Arms company using letter prefixes G,H,I. Specimens usually exhibit pitting and or lack of finish.

NO. 2 (LARGE FRAME) – .41 cal., 6 or 8 in. half-round barrel, steel frame, moderate rose and scroll engraving, flared type flat bottom design varnished walnut grips, blue frame with brown barrel assembly, approx. 500 mfg.

	Above Average	Average	Below Average
	$15,000-$25,000	**$10,000-$15,000**	**$8,000-$10,000**

Add 30% for 6 in. barrel.

Barrels are marked: "SMITH WESSON, NORWICH, CT, CAST STEEL" and "FEB. 14, 1854 PATENT" marked on the barrel flats. Stamping variations are common as to placement, depth, off-center to barrel flats, and even slight double stamps have been observed. Serial numbered from 1-500 (est.) on the inside of the grips and on small parts such as the rear sight. Specimens usually exhibit pitting and or lack of finish.

TIP-UPS

Spur-trigger rimfires, these include the earliest S&W revolvers, made 1857-1881. A latch at the bottom front of the frame allows the hinged barrel to be tipped up and the cylinder removed for loading and unloading. These pistols are listed in order of model number (1, 1 1/2, 2).

MODEL NO. 1 FIRST ISSUE TIP-UP – .22 Short cal., single action, 7 shot non-fluted cylinder, 3-3/16 in. octagon barrel, bottom break, spur trigger, silver-plated brass frame, blue barrel and cylinder, square rosewood grips, circular sideplate, cross-section of frame is oval with rounded frame sides. Approx. 11,671 mfg. 1857-1860.

100%	98%	95%	90%	80%	70%	60%	50%	40%	30%	20%	10%

* ***Model No. 1 First Issue Tip-Up First Type*** – serial range approx. 1-213.

Extreme rarity factor of this model precludes accurate pricing - a nice condition model can easily exceed $10,000.

Advanced S&W collector said he only knows of 1.

* ***Model No. 1 First Issue Tip-Up Second Type*** – serial range approx. 214-1130.

Extreme rarity factor of this model precludes accurate pricing - a nice condition model can easily exceed $10,000.

* ***Model No. 1 First Issue Tip-Up Third Type*** – has spring loaded barrel catch, serial range approx. 1131-3000.

N/A	N/A	$8,000	$7,000	$5,500	$5,000	$4,500	$3,000	$2,500	$2,000	$1,500	$1,000

* ***Model No. 1 First Issue Tip-Up Fourth Type*** – diameter of recoil plates is reduced, serial range approx. 3000-4200.

N/A	$6,500	$5,500	$4,500	$3,500	$3,000	$2,500	$2,150	$1,750	$1,500	$1,150	$900

* ***Model No. 1 First Issue Tip-Up Fifth Type*** – rifling changed from three left-hand to five right-hand, serial range approx. 4200-5500.

N/A	$6,000	$5,000	$4,000	$3,250	$2,750	$2,250	$1,950	$1,500	$1,250	$1,000	$800

* ***Model No. 1 First Issue Tip-Up Sixth Type*** – eliminate rotating plate, serial range approx. 5500-11500.

N/A	$2,000	$1,900	$1,800	$1,600	$1,500	$1,400	$1,300	$1,100	$900	$800	$750

MODEL NO. 1 SECOND ISSUE TIP-UP – similar to First Issue, except flat-sided frame and irregular-shaped sideplate. 114,900 mfg. 1860-1868. Serial range approx. 11500 - approx. 126000.

$2,500	$2,250	$1,950	$1,750	$1,500	$1,250	$1,000	$900	$750	$500	$450	$300

An early sideplate variation with 2 patent dates on cylinder occurred in the serial range 11500-12100. The second sideplate variation with 2 patent dates occurred in the serial range 12100-20000.

* ***Model No. 1 Second Issue Tip-Up Second Quality***

Extreme rarity precludes accurate pricing on this model. May bring double or triple values over the Model No. 1 Second Issue Tip-Up. Beware of fakes!

MODEL NO. 1 THIRD ISSUE TIP-UP – similar to Second Issue, except fluted cylinder, round barrel, and bird's head grip. This model has its own serial range no. 1-131163. Mfg. 1868-1882.

* ***Model No. 1 Third Issue Tip-Up 3 3/16 in. Barrel Model.*** – will have markings on top of barrel.

$1,500	$1,150	$950	$800	$725	$675	$550	$500	$450	$395	$325	$295

* ***Model No. 1 Third Issue Tip-Up Short Barrels 2 11/16 - 2 3/4 in.*** – will have markings on side of barrel.

$1,900	$1,650	$1,350	$1,150	$925	$875	$750	$600	$550	$425	$400	$275

MODEL NO. 1 1/2 OLD MODEL (MODEL 1 1/2 FIRST ISSUE) – .32 rimfire, single action, 3 1/2 or 4 (rare) in. octagon barrel, 5 shot non-fluted cylinder, spur trigger, blue or nickel, rosewood grips, square butt. 26,300 mfg. 1865-1868. Serial range 1-approx. 26300.

$1,200	$950	$750	$600	$525	$475	$450	$400	$350	$325	$300	$275

Early production had 2 patent dates with the barrel markings (approx. serial range 1-15500). Later production had 3 patent dates (approx. serial range 15501-26300).

* ***Model No. 1 1/2 Old Model 4 in. Barrel*** – S&W collector estimate approx. 200 mfg.

Extreme rarity precludes accurate pricing on this model

May bring double values over the Model No. 1 1/2 Old Model. Watch for fakes (i.e. stretched barrels).

* ***Model 1 1/2 Old Model Transitional*** – octagon barrel with bird's head grips, serial range 27200-28800, rare.

$3,000	$2,500	$1,800	$1,500	$1,350	$1,275	$1,200	$1,125	$1,075	$1,000	$950	$900

MODEL NO. 1 1/2 NEW MODEL (MODEL 1 1/2 SECOND ISSUE) – similar to First Issue, with bird's head grips and round barrel, fluted cylinder. 100,800 mfg. 1868-1875. Serial range 26301-127100.

* ***Model No. 1 1/2 New Model Short Barrel Model*** – barrel markings on side, length varies from 2 1/2-2 3/4 in. (scarce).

Extreme rarity precludes accurate pricing on this model. May bring double or triple values over the Model No. 1 1/2 New Model. Beware of fakes!

100%	98%	95%	90%	80%	70%	60%	50%	40%	30%	20%	10%

* ***Model No. 1 1/2 New Model 3 1/2 in. Barrel Model***

$1,200	$950	$750	$600	$525	$475	$450	$400	$350	$325	$300	$275

MODEL NO. 2 ARMY TIP-UP – .32 rimfire long, similar in appearance to No. 1 1/2 First Issue, except 6 shot cylinder, different barrel lengths, used as a sidearm during Civil War. 77,155 mfg. 1861-1874. Serial number range 1-77155.

* ***Model No. 2 Army Tip-Up 5 or 6 in. Standard Model***

$3,000	$2,500	$1,500	$1,000	$900	$800	$700	$625	$525	$450	$400	$375

Premiums exist for early 2 pin models under ser. no. 3000. Large premiums will be asked for 4 in. barrel - beware of fakes!

TOP-BREAKS

These revolvers have a latch just in front of the hammer, which locks the barrel to the frame. When the action is opened, the barrel & cylinder tip down, with an automatic extractor ejecting the shells. Mfg. 1870-1940, they include single action (spur-trigger or trigger guard), double action, and safety hammerless designs. They are listed in order of frame size. Model 1 1/2 is the smallest or .32 cal. pocket sized frame; Model 2 is the medium or .38 cal. belt sized frame; Model 3 is the large holster or .44 cal. frame. Within each frame size, they are listed by action type - SA, DA, or Hammerless, as applicable.

Changes from one Top-Break model type to another are not necessarily definitive at a specific serial number. Therefore, an overlap of serial numbers from one model to another may be observed.

.32 SINGLE ACTION (MODEL 1 1/2 CENTERFIRE) – .32 S&W cal., spur trigger, top break, rebounding hammer, auto extraction, 3, 3 1/2, 6 (rare), 8 (rare) or 10 (rare) in. barrel, w/o external strain screw. 97,599 mfg. 1878-1892. Serial range 1-97599.

$1,250 $995 $875 $700 $625 $575 $515

* ***.32 Single Action Later Model*** – with external strain screw, remainder of serial range.

$1,000	$925	$850	$675	$600	$525	$500	$425	$365	$325	$225	$150

Add 10%-15% for early models under ser. no. 6000 w/o strain screw.

Add 50%-100% for factory original 6, 8, or 10 in. barrel, depending on the original condition factor.

.32 DOUBLE ACTION FIRST MODEL – .32 S&W cal., 5 shot fluted cylinder, 3 in. round barrel, square edged side plate, blue or nickel finish, black rubber grips, one of the rarest of all S&Ws. Only 30 mfg. 1880. Serial range 1-30.

Extreme rarity precludes accurate pricing on this model, a nice condition model can easily exceed $10,000.

.32 DOUBLE ACTION SECOND MODEL – .32 S&W cal., 3, 3 1/4, 4, 5, or 6 in. barrel, 5 shot fluted cylinder, black rubber grips, irregular shaped sideplate, serial range 31-22172, blue or nickel finish, 22,142 mfg. 1880-1882.

$600	$465	$425	$375	$325	$285	$250	$225	$200	$180	$150	$125

.32 DOUBLE ACTION THIRD MODEL – .32 S&W cal., 3, 3 1/2, or 6 in. barrel, 5 shot, no groove around fluted cylinder, black rubber grips, irregular shaped sideplate, serial range 22173-43405, blue or nickel finish, 22,232 mfg. 1882-1883.

$600	$465	$425	$375	$325	$285	$250	$225	$200	$180	$150	$125

.32 DOUBLE ACTION FOURTH MODEL – .32 S&W cal., 3, 3 1/2, 6 (scarce), 8 (rare) or 10 (rare) in. barrel, 5 shot, no groove around fluted cylinder, rounded trigger guard, pinned front sight, black rubber grips, irregular shaped sideplate, serial range 43406-approx. 282999, blue or nickel finish. Approx. 239,600 mfg. 1883-1909.

$500	$425	$400	$350	$300	$265	$225	$200	$175	$165	$145	$135

An 8 or 10 in. barrel on this model will command a premium.

.32 DOUBLE ACTION FIFTH MODEL – .32 S&W cal., 3, 3 1/2, or 6 (scarce) in. barrel, 5 shot, no groove around fluted cylinder, rounded trigger guard, integral front sight, black rubber grips, irregular shaped sideplate, serial range approx. 282300-327641, blue or nickel finish. 44,641 mfg. 1909-1919.

$400	$375	$350	$325	$275	$250	$215	$185	$165	$145	$135	$115

.32 SAFETY HAMMERLESS FIRST MODEL (LEMON SQUEEZER) – .32 S&W cal., double action only, 5 shot fluted cylinder, 2 (rare), 3 (most common), 3 1/2, or 6 (rare) in. round barrel, blue or nickel, black rubber grips. This model was officially called the New Departure. 91,417 mfg. 1888-1902. Serial range 1-91417.

Short 2 in. barrel versions known as "Bicycle model" will bring 25% to 50% premium on all Safety Hammerless models. Six inch barrels will bring a premium as well.

100% 98% 95% 90% 80% 70% 60% 50% 40% 30% 20% 10%

* ***.32 Safety Hammerless First Model Standard*** – 2, 3, 3 1/4, or 3 1/2 in. barrel.

$750 $650 $550 $450 $400 $375 $350 $325 $275 $235 $185 $150

.32 SAFETY HAMMERLESS SECOND MODEL – .32 S&W cal., 2 (rare), 3, 3 1/2, or 6 (rare) in. barrel, similar to First Model with pinned front sight and T-shaped latch. 78,500 mfg. 1902-1909. Serial range 91418-170000.

$600 $465 $425 $375 $325 $285 $250 $225 $200 $180 $150 $125

.32 SAFETY HAMMERLESS THIRD MODEL – .32 S&W cal., 2 (rare), 3, 3 1/2, or 6 (rare) in. barrel, usually has forged front sight, discernible feature is push down catch in top strap. 73,000 mfg. 1909-1937. Serial range 163082-242981 (with some overlap from the Second Model).

$500 $425 $400 $350 $300 $265 $225 $200 $175 $165 $145 $135

.38 SINGLE ACTION FIRST MODEL (BABY RUSSIAN) WITH SPUR TRIGGER – .38 S&W cal., 5 shot fluted cylinder, 3 1/4 or 4 in. barrel, blue with wood grips, nickel with "S&W" monogram hard black or red rubber grips. 25,548 mfg. 1876-1877. Serial range 1-25548.

$2,200 $2,000 $1,650 $1,350 $1,050 $875 $750 $650 $575 $500 $425 $375

Substantial premiums will be asked for "Aldritch" safety models (first 50-100 guns). Add a slight premium for ser. nos. under 1500 with filler screws on right side of frame.

.38 SINGLE ACTION SECOND MODEL – .38 S&W cal., similar to .38 Single Action First Model, except very short ejector housing under barrel, 3 1/4, 4, 5 (scarce), 6 (scarce), 8 (rare), or 10 (rare) in. barrel, 108,225 mfg. 1877-1891. Serial range 1-108255.

$1,250 $995 $875 $700 $625 $575 $515 $465 $415 $375 $250 $195

* ***.38 Single Action Second Model 8 or 10 in. Barrel***

Extreme rarity precludes accurate pricing on this barrel length variation.

.38 SINGLE ACTION THIRD MODEL (MODEL OF 1891) – .38 S&W cal., similar to .38 Single Action Second Model, except has trigger guard, cal. and cylinder same as above, 3 1/4, 4, 5 (scarce), or 6 (scarce) in. barrel (also accepts the single shot barrel), blue or nickel finish with "S&W" monogram, hard black rubber grips. 26,850 mfg. 1891-1911. Serial range 1-28107 which also includes the serial number range of the Single Action First Model in .22 LR, .32 S&W, or .38 S&W cal. and the .38 S.A. Mexican Model described below. Barrel marked "Model of 1891".

$3,250 $2,750 $2,450 $2,125 $1,900 $1,700 $1,500 $1,250 $995 $800 $700 $600

Add 50%-75% for single shot barrel with matching serial number.

.38 SINGLE ACTION MEXICAN MODEL – .38 S&W cal., essentially same as above, except has inserted spur trigger, .38 S&W cal., 5 shot fluted cylinder, 3 1/4, 4, 5, or 6 in. barrel, blue or nickel finish, "S&W" monogram checkered hard rubber or walnut grips. Features unique to this model are flat sided hammer, half cock notch, and "inserted" spur trigger assembly (not integral with frame). This model would also accept the single shot barrel, limited mfg. 1891-1911. Approx. 2,000 mfg. in ser. no. range 1-28107. Watch out for fakes (and conversions)!

N/A $4,000 $3,500 $2,750 $2,000 $1,650 $1,400 $1,250 $1,150 $1,050 $975 $950

Add 50%-75% for single shot barrel with matching serial number.

Mint example recently sold at auction for $11,000.

.38 DOUBLE ACTION FIRST MODEL – .38 S&W cal., 5 shot fluted cylinder, 3 1/4 or 4 in. barrel, blue or nickel finish, "S&W" monogram checkered hard rubber grips. 4,000 mfg. 1880. Serial range 1-4000.

$1,250 $995 $875 $700 $625 $575 $515 $465 $415 $375 $250 $195

.38 DOUBLE ACTION SECOND MODEL – .38 S&W cal., cylinder same as above, 3 1/4, 4, 5, or 6 in. barrel, blue or nickel finish, "S&W" monogram checkered hard rubber grips in black or red. 115,000 mfg. 1880-1884. Serial range approx. 4001-approx. 119000.

$850 $550 $475 $425 $360 $315 $275 $250 $225 $200 $170 $150

.38 DOUBLE ACTION THIRD MODEL – .38 S&W cal., cylinder same as above, 2 (rare), 3 1/4, 4, 5, 6, 8, or 10 in. barrel, blue or nickel finish, "S&W" monogram hard rubber grips. 203,700 mfg. 1884-1895. Serial range approx. 119001-322700.

$850 $550 $475 $425 $360 $315 $275 $250 $225 $200 $170 $150

Add 175%-300% for 2 in. barrel depending on condition.

* ***.38 Double Action Third Model 8 or 10 in. Barrel*** – target variation, rare.

Extreme rarity precludes accurate pricing on this barrel length variation.

100%	98%	95%	90%	80%	70%	60%	50%	40%	30%	20%	10%

.38 DOUBLE ACTION FOURTH MODEL - .38 S&W cal., cylinder same as above, 2 (rare), 3 1/4, 4, 5, or 6 in. barrel, blue or nickel finish, "S&W" monogram checkered hard rubber grips, also offered in an extended square butt target style. 216,300 mfg. 1895-1909. Serial range 322701-539000.

$650	$485	$435	$385	$335	$295	$265	$235	$200	$185	$165	$135

Add 175%-300% for 2 in. barrel depending on condition.

.38 DOUBLE ACTION FIFTH MODEL - .38 S&W cal., 3 1/4, 4, 5, or 6 in. barrel, cylinder and grip specifications same as above with the additional availability of an extended square butt target style walnut grip as an accessory. 15,000 mfg. 1909-1911. Serial range approx. 539001-554077.

$650	$485	$435	$385	$335	$295	$265	$235	$200	$185	$165	$135

Add 175%-300% for 2 in. barrel depending on condition.

.38 DOUBLE ACTION PERFECTED MODEL - .38 S&W cal., 3 1/4, 4, 5, or 6 in. barrel, trigger guard is integral part of frame, and side plate is on right side, not left side. The last of the S&W break open revolvers. 59,400 mfg. 1909-1920. Serial range 1-59400. Identified by having both top latch and side latch.

$1,250	$995	$875	$700	$625	$575	$515	$465	$415	$375	$250	$195

* ***.38 Double Action Perfected Model Top Latch Only*** – as above, except no side latch thumbpiece - rare.

Add a substantial premium for trigger guard with integral frame.

Extreme rarity precludes accurate pricing on this model.

.38 SAFETY HAMMERLESS FIRST MODEL (.38 NEW DEPARTURE) - .38 S&W cal., 5 shot fluted cylinder, 3 1/4, 4, or 5 in. barrel, blue or nickel finish, "S&W" monogram checkered hard rubber grips, features side operated catch in top latch ("Z-Bar" latch). Approx. 5,000 mfg. in 1887. Serial range 1-5250.

$1,575	$1,325	$875	$775	$600	$525	$475	$415	$360	$315	$275	$250

Add 25% for blue finish.

* ***.38 Safety Hammerless First Model 5 or 6 in. Barrel***

Extreme rarity factor precludes accurate pricing on this model. Beware of fakes.

.38 SAFETY HAMMERLESS SECOND MODEL - .38 S&W cal., cylinder same as above, 3 1/4, 4, or 5 in. barrel, finish and grips same as above, discernible feature is push down catch in top of frame. 37,350 mfg. 1887-1890. Serial range approx. 5251-42483.

$900	$600	$525	$475	$425	$365	$325	$295	$250	$225	$195	$175

U.S. MARTIALLY MARKED – 100 purchased by Govt. in 1890, serial range 41333 - 41470, serial numbers in Second Model range, but are true Third Models.

Extreme rarity precludes accurate pricing on this model. Beware of fakes!

.38 SAFETY HAMMERLESS THIRD MODEL - .38 S&W cal., cylinder same as above, 3 1/4, 4, 5, or 6 in. barrel, finish and grips same as above, discernible feature is push down catch in top strap. 73,500 mfg. 1890-1898. Serial range 42484-116002.

$750	$650	$550	$450	$400	$375	$350	$325	$275	$235	$185	$150

.38 SAFETY HAMMERLESS FOURTH MODEL - .38 S&W cal., cylinder, barrel lengths, finishes and grips same as above, discernible feature is lift up T catch in top strap. 104,000 mfg. 1898-1907. Serial range 116003 to approx. 220000.

$650	$485	$435	$385	$335	$295	$265	$235	$200	$185	$165	$135

.38 SAFETY HAMMERLESS FIFTH MODEL - .38 S&W cal., cylinder same as above, 2 (rare), 3 1/4, 4, 5, or 6 in. barrel, blue or nickel finish, "S&W" monogram checkered hard rubber or checkered walnut grips. Similar features to Fourth Model, except has integral front sight. 41,500 mfg. 1907-1940. Serial range 220000-261493.

$750	$650	$550	$450	$400	$375	$350	$325	$275	$235	$185	$150

.38 SAFETY HAMMERLESS BICYCLE MODEL W/2 IN. BARREL – Manufactured in both the Fourth and Fifth Models.

Extreme rarity factor precludes accurate pricing on this model. Beware of fakes.

MODEL 3 AMERICAN FIRST MODEL (SINGLE ACTION) - .44 S&W American or .44 rimfire Henry cal., single action, 6 shot fluted cylinder, 6, 7, or 8 in. round barrel, blue or nickel finish, walnut grips. 8,000 mfg. 1870-1872. Serial range 1-approx. 8000. Serial number overlaps on the variations below are known to exist.

Slight premiums will be asked for models with vent. hole (oil hole) in rear extractor housing under barrel (approx. first 1,500).

Original barrel lengths other than 8 in. are worth a premium - beware of cut barrels.

100%	98%	95%	90%	80%	70%	60%	50%	40%	30%	20%	10%

* ***Model 3 American First Model Standard*** – without hole in extractor.

100%	98%	95%	90%	80%	70%	60%	50%	40%	30%	20%	10%
N/A	$8,000	$6,250	$5,750	$4,250	$3,750	$3,550	$3,150	$2,750	$2,250	$1,850	$1,350

* ***Model 3 American First Model Transitional*** – includes locking notch on hammer, with small trigger pin, serial range 6700-8000.

100%	98%	95%	90%	80%	70%	60%	50%	40%	30%	20%	10%
N/A	$8,000	$6,250	$5,750	$4,250	$3,750	$3,550	$3,150	$2,750	$2,250	$1,850	$1,350

* ***Model 3 American First Model .44 Rimfire Henry*** – limited mfg. Watch for fakes!

100%	98%	95%	90%	80%	70%	60%	50%	40%	30%	20%	10%
N/A	$8,250	$7,000	$6,000	$5,000	$4,000	$3,750	$3,500	$3,250	$2,650	$2,250	$1,650

* ***Model 3 American First Model U.S. Marked*** – approx. 1,000 mfg., 800 in blue, and 200 in nickel finish, most nickel plated revolvers are serial numbered above 1,950 - watch for fakes. Serial range 125 - 2199.

100%	98%	95%	90%	80%	70%	60%	50%	40%	30%	20%	10%
N/A	$15,000	$10,750	$9,100	$8,100	$7,250	$6,500	$5,900	$5,375	$4,850	$4,450	$4,000

* ***Model 3 American First Model Nashville Police*** – very rare, only 32 manufactured, marked "Nashville Police" on backstrap.

Scarcity precludes accurate pricing - beware of fakes.

MODEL 3 AMERICAN SECOND MODEL – .44 S&W American or .44 rimfire Henry cal., single action, 6 shot fluted cylinder, mechanism allows the hammer to lock the barrel latch in place, larger trigger pin, 5, 5 1/2, 6, 6 1/2, 7, or 8 in. barrel, blue or nickel, walnut grips. 19,635 mfg. 1872-1874, serial range approx. 8000-32800 which includes commercial version of Model 3 Russian First Model.

* ***Model 3 American Second Model Standard*** – .44 S&W American cal., 8 in. barrel standard length.

100%	98%	95%	90%	80%	70%	60%	50%	40%	30%	20%	10%
N/A	$7,000	$5,750	$4,250	$3,750	$3,250	$2,850	$2,550	$2,250	$1,750	$1,500	$1,100

Add 35% for 5, 5 1/2, 6, 6 1/2, or 7 in. barrel.

Add 50% if factory cut for stock or 100% if accompanied with original factory shoulder stock.

Smith & Wesson Historian Verification of Factory Cut for Stock required for premium value.

Add 20% if professionally retrofitted with NON-Factory stock if accompanied with stock.

608 were factory cut for shoulder stock.

Mint example recently sold at auction for $22,000.

* ***Model 3 American Second Model Standard .44 Rimfire Henry*** – 6, 7, or 8 in. barrel, non-locking hammer below approx. serial number 25000. 3,014 mfg.

100%	98%	95%	90%	80%	70%	60%	50%	40%	30%	20%	10%
N/A	$8,000	$6,250	$5,750	$4,250	$3,750	$3,550	$3,150	$2,750	$2,250	$1,850	$1,350

MODEL 3 FIRST MODEL RUSSIAN (OLD OLD MODEL RUSSIAN) – .44 S&W Russian, 6, 7, or 8 in. barrel, Russian contract revolvers had 8 in. barrels, blue finish, and Cyrillic barrel markings, commercial mfg. had blue or nickel finish, walnut grips, looks similar to First and Second Model American. 5,165 mfg. 1871-1874 for commercial sale and 20,014 for Russian Contract (separate ser. no. range). Serial range 6000-32800, see Model 3 Second Model American.

* ***Model 3 First Model Russian Commercial Version*** – 4,665 mfg.

100%	98%	95%	90%	80%	70%	60%	50%	40%	30%	20%	10%
N/A	$8,500	$7,500	$6,500	$5,500	$4,500	$3,995	$3,850	$3,450	$2,850	$2,450	$1,850

* ***Model 3 First Model Russian Reject (Russian Contract)*** – approx. 500 mfg., can be determined by the barrel, latch, and cylinder having a full serial number, rather than assembly numbers.

100%	98%	95%	90%	80%	70%	60%	50%	40%	30%	20%	10%
N/A	$5,000	$4,000	$3,250	$2,750	$2,250	$2,150	$1,850	$1,650	$1,450	$1,250	$1,100

* ***Model 3 First Model Russian (Russian Contract)*** – 20,014 mfg., rare, most sent to Russia, Cyrillic marked. Serial range 1-approx. 20,014.

100%	98%	95%	90%	80%	70%	60%	50%	40%	30%	20%	10%
N/A	N/A	$6,750	$5,975	$5,125	$4,450	$3,800	$3,350	$2,950	$2,600	$2,250	$2,000

MODEL 3 SECOND MODEL RUSSIAN (OLD MODEL RUSSIAN) – 2nd and 3rd Model Russians have an extreme knuckle at the top of backstrap and trigger guard spur, 85,200 mfg. in all variations between 1873-1878, 7 in. barrel, small screw in top-strap of frame, features longer ejector housing and "Russian Model" marking on top of barrel. Ser. nos. started at 32800.

* ***Model 3 Second Model Russian Commercial Version*** – 6,200 mfg.

100%	98%	95%	90%	80%	70%	60%	50%	40%	30%	20%	10%
N/A	$6,750	$5,500	$4,125	$3,450	$3,000	$2,650	$2,250	$2,000	$1,500	$1,250	$950

* ***Model 3 Second Model Russian .44 Rimfire Henry*** – approx. 500 mfg.

100%	98%	95%	90%	80%	70%	60%	50%	40%	30%	20%	10%
N/A	$5,500	$5,000	$4,500	$4,000	$3,525	$3,050	$2,650	$2,250	$2,150	$1,850	$1,650

* ***Model 3 Second Model Russian Contract*** – approx. 70,000 mfg. for Russian Military contract, Cyrillic marked, rare in U.S.

100%	98%	95%	90%	80%	70%	60%	50%	40%	30%	20%	10%
N/A	N/A	$6,250	$5,750	$4,250	$3,750	$3,550	$3,150	$2,750	$2,250	$1,850	$1,350

100%	98%	95%	90%	80%	70%	60%	50%	40%	30%	20%	10%

* ***Model 3 Second Model Turkish Model*** – 1,000 mfg. in their own serial number range in .44 Rimfire, features rimfire hammer, but the cylinder is chambered for .44 Russian. This is probably the rarest and most valuable variation.

N/A N/A $10,000 $8,000 $7,000 $5,500 $4,500 $3,600 $3,200 $2,825 $2,500 $2,275

This model was converted to rimfire from .44 S&W Russian cal.

* ***Model 3 Second Model Japanese Contract*** – may be marked with an anchor.

N/A N/A $3,200 $2,600 $2,300 $2,050 $1,825 $1,650 $1,500 $1,375 $1,250 $1,175

MODEL 3 THIRD MODEL RUSSIAN – commonly called the "New Model Russian" and is similar to old model, except has shorter extractor housing, 6 1/2 in. barrel, front sight is forged as an integral part of barrel instead of an interchangeable part, large knurled screw in top-strap of frame, shorter ejector housing, butt is usually marked with "1874" in a square, approx. 60,600 mfg. 1874-1878. Values are similar to old model for comparable variations. In addition, the Tula Arsenal in Russia also mfg. 300,000-400,000 pistols for domestic use and Ludwig & Loewe in Germany mfg. 100,000.

* ***Model 3 Third Model Russian Commercial Version*** – approx. 13,500 mfg.

N/A $8,500 $7,500 $6,500 $5,500 $4,500 $3,995 $3,850 $3,450 $2,850 $2,450 $1,850

* ***Model 3 Third Model Russian .44 Rimfire Henry***

N/A $9,750 $7,750 $6,750 $5,250 $4,250 $3,350 $3,000 $2,625 $2,250 $2,075 $1,750

* ***Model 3 Third Model Russian Contract*** – 41,138 mfg. Cyrillic markings.

N/A $9,650 $7,650 $6,650 $5,150 $4,150 $3,150 $2,800 $2,525 $2,150 $1,875 $1,650

* ***Model 3 Third Model Russian Ludwig & Loewe, & Tula Copies*** – these copies were manufactured by private Foreign Arsenals, as contracted by the Russian Government to circumvent paying contractual obligations to Smith & Wesson. These are not Smith & Wesson manufacture; however, the quality is impeccable and in some aspects, not only meets but exceeds the quality and craftsmanship of those manufactured by Smith & Wesson.

N/A $2,800 $2,500 $2,250 $2,000 $1,800 $1,625 $1,475 $1,350 $1,225 $1,100 $950

Add 40% for Tula copies.

* ***Model 3 Third Model Turkish Contract*** – 5,000 mfg., utilizes .44 Russian cylinder - chambered for .44 Rimfire.

N/A $6,500 $5,250 $4,100 $3,250 $2,750 $2,450 $2,200 $1,750 $1,350 $1,150 $995

* ***Model 3 Third Model Japanese Contract*** – 1,000 made.

N/A $6,200 $5,000 $4,000 $3,000 $2,500 $2,250 $2,000 $1,500 $1,150 $1,000 $795

MODEL 3 SCHOFIELD FIRST MODEL – .45 S&W cal., single action, 7 in. barrel, 6 shot fluted cylinder, blue finish only, walnut grips, serial no. range 1-3035. 3,035 mfg. 1875.

* ***Model 3 Schofield First U.S. Issue*** – 3,000 mfg., "U.S." marked on the butt.

N/A $18,000 $11,500 $8,500 $6,500 $5,500 $4,850 $4,200 $3,950 $3,500 $2,995 $2,950

* ***Model 3 Schofield First Commercial Model (not U.S. marked)*** – 35 were produced without U.S. markings, very rare - beware of fakes - there could be more phony ones than real ones.

Extreme rarity factor of this model precludes accurate pricing.

* ***Model 3 Schofield First Wells Fargo and Company*** – barrel cut to approx. 5 in. with Wells Fargo markings.

N/A N/A N/A N/A $7,000 $5,100 $4,550 $4,175 $3,750 $3,350 $3,050 $2,750

Warning - Beware of fakes! There may be more fake Wells Fargo Schofields than authentic ones. While most fakes are usually poor quality, others may be quite impressive.

Many Schofields are found with cut 5 in. barrels and no Wells Fargo marking - these will bring approx. 66% of uncut values, or if they have fake WF markings, then their value is 1/2 of the uncut values.

MODEL 3 SCHOFIELD SECOND MODEL – serial no. range 3036-8969. 5,934 mfg. 1876-1877.

The most apparent difference between 1st and 2nd Models is the shape of the latch and serial range.

* ***Model 3 Schofield Second Standard Model*** – "U.S." on butt.

N/A $14,000 $8,000 $5,500 $4,500 $4,000 $3,600 $3,400 $3,200 $3,000 $2,600 $2,250

* ***Model 3 Schofield Second Commercial Model*** – blue or nickel finish, 650 mfg.

N/A $9,500 $7,000 $5,000 $4,500 $4,000 $3,600 $3,400 $3,200 $3,000 $2,600 $2,250

100%	98%	95%	90%	80%	70%	60%	50%	40%	30%	20%	10%

* ***Model 3 Schofield Second Wells Fargo and Company*** – barrel cut to 5 in. with Wells Fargo markings.

N/A	N/A	N/A	N/A	$7,000	$5,100	$4,550	$4,175	$3,750	$3,350	$3,050	$2,750

Warning - Beware of fakes! There may be more fake Wells Fargo Schofields than authentic ones. While most fakes are usually poor quality, others may be quite impressive. Many Schofields are found with cut 5 in. barrels and no Wells Fargo marking - these will bring approx. 66% of uncut values, or if they have fake WF markings, then their value is 1/2 of the uncut values.

NEW MODEL NO. 3 – features very short extractor housing under the barrel, barrel lengths are from 3 1/2 to 8 in., with 6 1/2 in. standard, knuckle on backstrap is less pronounced than Russian Models, single action, round butt. 35,796 mfg. between 1878-1912.

Slight premiums will be asked for cut shoulder stock ($750-$1,250), target sights (standard non-target models only).

Add a premium for barrel lengths other than 6 1/2 in. (beware of .44 DA barrels!), and for calibers other than .44 Russian, .32-44, or .38-44.

Add a premium for .44 Target variations if all numbers match (usually found in the 25000 - 35796 ser. no. range).

Substantial Premium for Factory Verified Target Models in calibers other than .44 Russian, .32-44 and .38-44 , if all numbers match.

NOTE: Numbers on frame, cylinder, barrel, and latch must match. There are also numbers on the ejector star/rod and the front sight (when removed). As the front Target sights were easily damaged and often replaced, deduct slightly if front sight replaced with correct, original sight.

Early production had rack and gear extractor (serial number range 1-13,500), and will bring a slight premium over the later mfg. Also, premiums do exist for all but 6 and 6 1/2 in. barrel lengths; premiums for unusual chambering's.

* ***New Model No. 3 Commercial Version***

$8,500	$5,000	$2,850	$2,000	$1,800	$1,625	$1,475	$1,325	$1,175	$995	$795	$695

* ***New Model No. 3 Japanese Navy Model*** – Japan purchased approx. 1/3 of total production.

Add 50% over the Commercial Version for Japanese characters on ejector housing. Japanese anchor brings only a small premium, if any.

* ***New Model No. 3 Australian Model*** – 7 in. barrel, detachable stock, for Australian Colonial Police, broad arrow marking on both pistol and stock, stocks were originally numbered to the matching pistol, but are seldom seen with matching numbers today, approx. 250 mfg., usually found in the low 12,000-low 13,000 ser. no. range.

Add a substantial premium over the Commercial Version if with shoulder stock.

Original holsters for this model are extremely scarce. Holster is a double flap type which will holster the gun with or w/o shoulder stock attached. There is also a separate holster for shoulder stock when it is not attached to the gun. All types are scarce, and have Broad Arrow stamp.

* ***New Model No. 3 Argentine Model*** – unknown total production, marked "Ejercito Argentina" (very rare).

Add a premium over the Commercial Version.

* ***New Model No. 3 State of Maryland Model*** – "U.S." marked, serial number range 7126-7405.

Add a premium over the Commercial Version.

Add a premium over the Commercial Version for Revenue Cutter Service (Coast Guard) model, identifiable only by ser. no.

* ***New Model No. 3 Frontier Japanese Purchase*** – 786 converted to .44 Russian cal., cylinder should measure 1 9/16 in., in the Frontier serial range of 1-2072.

N/A	$5,000	$3,000	$2,250	$1,800	$1,625	$1,475	$1,325	$1,175	$995	$795	$695

* ***New Model No. 3 Frontier*** – .44-40 WCF cal., single action, 4, 5, or 6 1/2 in. barrel, blue or nickel finish, walnut or hard rubber grips, ser. no. range 1-2072. 2,072 mfg. 1885-1908.

$9,000	$6,000	$3,500	$3,000	$2,500	$2,250	$2,000	$1,850	$1,600	$1,400	$1,250	$1,100

* ***New Model No. 3 - .38-40 WCF*** – separate ser. range, only 74 mfg., ser. no. 1-74. Mfg. 1900-1907.

Extreme rarity factor of this model precludes accurate pricing.

* ***New Model No. 3 Target Model*** – .32-44 S&W or .38-44 S&W cal., target sights, ser. no. range 1-4333. 4,333 mfg. between 1887-1910.

$6,500	$3,250	$2,500	$2,250	$1,925	$1,700	$1,500	$1,350	$1,100	$950	$800	$700

100%	98%	95%	90%	80%	70%	60%	50%	40%	30%	20%	10%

* ***New Model No. 3 Turkish*** – .44 rimfire cal., 5,461 mfg. 1879-1888, in separate serial number series, 1 - 5461.

N/A	$7,000	$4,675	$4,350	$4,050	$3,750	$3,450	$3,150	$2,850	$2,550	$2,275	$1,950

.44 CAL. DOUBLE ACTION FIRST MODEL – .32-44 (rare), .38-44 (rare), .38 Military (rare), .44 S&W Russian (most common), and .455 (rare) cal., caliber markings on later production for .44 S&W Russian is ".44 Smith & Wesson", 6 shot fluted cylinder, 4, 5, 6, or 6 1/2 in. barrel, blue or nickel finish, "S&W" monogram checkered hard rubber or walnut grips. Walnut grips with "S&W" inlays will be found after 1900. 53,590 mfg. 1881-1913. Serial range 1-54668.

Add 100% for cals. other than .44 S&W Russian with target sights on sub-models listed.

* ***.44 Cal. Double Action First Model Standard***

$4,500	$1,900	$1,500	$1,275	$1,000	$925	$825	$695	$650	$575	$475	$375

* ***.44 Cal. Double Action First Model Wesson Favorite*** – similar to Standard Model, but in 5 in. barrel only with special front sight, blue or nickel finish, patent markings are on the cylinder rather than on the barrel, grooved barrel rib, external and internal lightening cuts to reduce weight. Approx. 1,000 mfg. 1882-1883. Serial numbers within the .44 Double Action First Model range, approx. 8900 - 10100.

N/A	$10,000	$8,000	$7,000	$5,500	$4,500	$3,600	$3,200	$2,825	$2,500	$2,275	$2,000

Add 30%-40% for blue finish.

.38 WIN. DOUBLE ACTION – .38-40 WCF cal., 4, 5, 6, or 6 1/2 in. barrel, only 276 mfg. in separate ser. range 1-276. Mfg. 1900-1910.

N/A	$6,000	$5,000	$4,000	$3,000	$2,500	$2,000	$1,750	$1,500	$1,300	$1,225	$1,125

.44 DOUBLE ACTION FRONTIER – .44-40 WCF cal., 4, 5, 6, or 6 1/2 in. barrel, only 15,340 mfg. in separate ser. range 1-15340. Mfg. 1886-1913.

$4,500	$1,900	$1,500	$1,275	$1,000	$925	$825	$695	$650	$575	$475	$375

Add 100% for factory target sights.

.44 DOUBLE ACTION WESSON FAVORITE – .44 S&W Russian cal., ser. no. range 8900-10100. Approx. 1,000 mfg. 1882-1883.

N/A	N/A	$10,000	$8,200	$7,500	$6,500	$6,000	$5,000	$4,000	$2,500	$2,000	$1,500

SINGLE SHOTS

FIRST MODEL (SINGLE SHOT MODEL OF 1891) – .22 LR (862 mfg.), .32 S&W (229 mfg.), or .38 S&W (160 mfg.) cal., 6, 8, or 10 in. barrel marked "Model of 1891", blue or nickel, hard rubber extension grips, single action trigger. 1,251 mfg. 1893-1905, ser. range (same as Third Model 38 Single Action) 1-28107. Serial number is located on the front strap.

* ***First Model .22 LR*** – approx. 862 mfg.

N/A	$2,700	$2,475	$2,100	$1,900	$1,575	$1,325	$1,075	$875	$625	$500	$375

Add a premium for .32 S&W or .38 S&W cals.

SECOND MODEL .22 LR – similar to First Model, but will not accommodate a revolver cylinder, flatsided frame (does not have recoil shield) 6 (rare), 8, or 10 in. barrel, single action trigger, black hard rubber extension grips, 4,617 mfg. 1905-1909. Ser. range 1-4617 (ser. no. located on front gripstrap).

N/A	$2,200	$2,000	$1,825	$1,575	$1,375	$1,200	$975	$775	$550	$450	$350

Add 20% for 6 or 8 inch barrels.

THIRD MODEL .22 (PERFECTED MODEL) – similar to Second Model, except is built on "I" solid frame with integral trigger guard, side plate on right side, will fire in both single or double action, checkered walnut extension grips. 6,949 mfg. 1909-1923. Serial range 4,618-11,641 (ser. no. located on front gripstrap).

N/A	$2,200	$2,000	$1,825	$1,575	$1,375	$1,200	$975	$775	$550	$450	$350

Add 30% for Olympic Model with shorter .22 LR rifle chamber (bullet nose engages rifling).

FOURTH MODEL STRAIGHT LINE TARGET SINGLE SHOT – .22 LR cal., single shot, 10 in. barrel, sideswing barrel, blue, target sights, smooth walnut grips, shaped like an autoloader. 1,870 mfg. 1925-36. Ser. range 1-1,870. Values below assume steel case and accessories.

N/A	$3,500	$2,950	$2,200	$1,975	$1,675	$1,400	$1,125	$900	$650	$525	$400

Subtract 30% w/o case and accessories.

EARLY HAND EJECTORS (NAMED MODELS)

Named Models. 1896-1957. *Listed in order by caliber*, **except where newer mfg. might also include model number. These will NOT have any model number stamped on the frame. Many were continued after 1957 as Numbered Models, so be sure to check that section as well.**

100%	98%	95%	90%	80%	70%	60%	50%	40%	30%	20%	10%

MODEL .22 HAND EJECTOR (LADYSMITH) – originally chambered for .22 S&W (same as .22 Long) cal., 7 shot fluted cylinder, small frame, available in blue or nickel finish, nicknamed "Ladysmith" due to its small size, Tiny "M" frame. Over 26,000 mfg. between 1902-1921.

* ***Model .22 Hand Ejector First Model*** – .22 L cal., 2 1/4, 3, or 3 1/2 in. barrel, serial numbered 1-4,575, checkered hard rubber grips, round butt. 4,575 mfg. 1902-1906. Serial range 1-4575. Identifiable by small frame mounted cylinder release button.

100%	98%	95%	90%	80%	70%	60%	50%	40%	30%	20%	10%
N/A	$2,500	$2,000	$1,500	$1,250	$975	$800	$650	$550	$475	$435	$390

* ***Model .22 Hand Ejector Second Model*** – .22 L cal., 3, or 3 1/2 in. barrel, distinguishable from first model in that cylinder locking device was placed on barrel bottom, locking both ends. 9,400 mfg. 1906-1910. Serial range 4576-13950.

100%	98%	95%	90%	80%	70%	60%	50%	40%	30%	20%	10%
N/A	$2,500	$2,000	$1,500	$1,250	$975	$800	$650	$550	$475	$435	$390

* ***Model .22 Hand Ejector Third Model*** – .22 L cal., 2 1/4 (rare), 3, 3 1/2, or 6 in. barrel, smooth walnut grips with "S&W" medallion inlays, square butt. 12,200 mfg. 1910-1921. Serial range 13951-26154.

100%	98%	95%	90%	80%	70%	60%	50%	40%	30%	20%	10%
N/A	$2,500	$2,000	$1,500	$1,250	$975	$800	$650	$550	$475	$435	$390

Add 200% for 6 in. barrel with target sights.

Add 95% for 6 in. barrel with plain sights.

.22/.32 HAND EJECTOR (ALSO KNOWN AS .22/32 BEKEART MODEL) – .22 LR cal., 6 shot fluted cylinder, 6 in. barrel, blue, checkered walnut grips with "S&W" medallions, extension style square butt, there were several hundred thousand of the standard .22/.32 Hand Ejector mfg. The first 3,000 mfg. will be found with a separate ser. no. (1-3000) stamped into the bottom of the wood grips. This model was cataloged as the .22/.32 Heavy Frame Target Model in 1931. Mfg. 1911-1941.

* ***.22/.32 Hand Ejector Bekeart Model*** – will be found with separate identification number on bottom of its wooden grip. Serial numbers for early Bekeart models start at 138226-139275.

100%	98%	95%	90%	80%	70%	60%	50%	40%	30%	20%	10%
N/A	$1,850	$1,500	$1,200	$875	$750	$650	$550	$450	$350	$275	$200

Add 100% premium for revolvers that were shipped to Philip Bekeart (one of the 292).

Add 50% premium for ser. no. 1-1044 stamped in the wood grip ("True Bekearts").

Add 20% over the values listed for early production in lower ser. no. range 1045-3000 also stamped in the wood grip.

This model was specifically mfg. for a San Francisco retailer, Philip Bekeart. Originally, Mr. Bekeart ordered 1,000 guns to his specifications, S&W mfg. 5,000. While the first 1,000 revolvers in ser. no. range 138226 to 139275 with grip numbered 1-1000 are accepted as "True Bekearts", only 292 were actually delivered to Philip Bekeart.

* ***.22/.32 Hand Ejector Standard Model*** – Prewar guns are found from serial number 139276 - approx. 551000 mixed within the .32 Hand Ejector.

100%	98%	95%	90%	80%	70%	60%	50%	40%	30%	20%	10%
N/A	$1,375	$1,275	$875	$675	$550	$450	$400	$350	$300	$250	$200

* ***Model of 1953 .22/.32 Target*** – mfg. approx. 1913-1953, in a serial range of 101 to 135465, with 6 inch barrel, circa 1953-1969, continued as the Model 35.

100%	98%	95%	90%	80%	70%	60%	50%	40%	30%	20%	10%
$1,500	$1,150	$900	$675	$495	$400	$275	$225	$175	$135	$115	$100

.22/.32 KIT GUN PRE-WAR – similar to Standard .22/32 Hand Ejector Model, 4 in. barrels, round or square butt. Mfg. 1935-1941, serial number overlaps occur within .32 Hand Ejector Series.

Blue Finish

100%	98%	95%	90%	80%	70%	60%	50%	40%	30%	20%	10%
$3,500	$3,000	$2,650	$2,000	$1,650	$1,250	$950	$750	$575	$450	$385	$275

Nickel Finish (3 known)

100%	98%	95%	90%	80%	70%	60%	50%	40%	30%	20%	10%
$7,500	$6,500	$5,000	$3,500	$2,000	$1,500	$1,400	$1,300	$1,250	$1,200	$1,000	$900

Add 10% for original box.

Pre-war kit guns in ser. no. range approx. 525670 to 536684 will bring a 400%-500% premium over above values, if in 95%+ condition. Mfg. 1935-1941.

Early post-war kit guns in ser. no. range approx. 536685 to 590000 similar values in like condition. Mfg. 1946-1952.

* ***Model of 1953 .22/.32 Kit Gun "Pre-Model 34" Production*** – Improved I or J frame, continued in 1957 as the Model 34.

100%	98%	95%	90%	80%	70%	60%	50%	40%	30%	20%	10%
$1,450	$1,200	$900	$550	$400	$300	$250	$200	$175	$160	$140	$120

Add 50% for original box and tools.

100%	98%	95%	90%	80%	70%	60%	50%	40%	30%	20%	10%

* ***Model of 1953 .22/.32 Kit Gun Airweight*** – Early alloy frame "Airweight" (not "Airweight" marked) kit guns (pre-Model 43), ser. no. range 5000-135465 in the 1953 Kit Gun series.

100%	98%	95%	90%	80%	70%	60%	50%	40%	30%	20%	10%
$2,000	$1,850	$1,500	$1,175	$850	$700	$550	$450	$385	$315	$250	$180

2 in. barrel

100%	98%	95%	90%	80%	70%	60%	50%	40%	30%	20%	10%
$4,200	$3,375	$3,000	$2,650	$2,300	$1,950	$1,550	$1,050	$750	$575	$450	$325

Add 200% for nickel.

K-22 OUTDOORSMAN - K-22 1st MODEL – .22 LR cal., 6 shot, 6 in. round barrel, K-frame, blue, pre-micrometer adj. sights, walnut grips, serial numbers in the 600,000 range with the .38 M&P 1905 4th change. Approx. 19,500 mfg. 1931-1940.

100%	98%	95%	90%	80%	70%	60%	50%	40%	30%	20%	10%
N/A	$2,400	$2,100	$1,850	$1,600	$1,400	$1,200	$1,000	$850	$750	$675	$550

Add $100 for original box and $700 for original tools.

Add 100% for Coast Guard issue (25 w/service sights were shipped to the Coast Guard at Curtis Bay, MD in 1935 - ser. no. range is 650929 to 650953).

A small quantity were shipped to the U.S. Army for use in the 1932 Olympics - needs to be verified by factory letter.

Ser. no. 657624 was shipped to Col. Rex Applegate on June 25, 1946 with a 2 in. barrel and fixed sights - this is the only example known in this configuration.

K-22 MASTERPIECE (PRE WAR K-22 2nd MODEL) – .22 LR cal., 6 shot, 6 in. round barrel, K-frame, first early micrometer click target sights, walnut grips, serial numbers in the 682404-696952 range, with the .38 M&P 1905 4th change. Scarce - approx. 1,067 mfg. 1940-1941.

100%	98%	95%	90%	80%	70%	60%	50%	40%	30%	20%	10%
$6,500	$4,950	$4,500	$3,950	$3,300	$2,750	$2,150	$1,550	$1,200	$850	$575	$395

Add 20% for original box and tools.

The nomenclature used by collectors to identify this model is in question so both are listed.

K-22 MASTERPIECE (POST WAR K-22 3rd MODEL) – similar to K-22 Outdoorsman, has micro click rear sight, short action, ribbed round barrel, has 1st "K" serial prefix and number K101 - end of series. Generally made from 1946-1957 until guns are numbered.

100%	98%	95%	90%	80%	70%	60%	50%	40%	30%	20%	10%
$1,600	$1,200	$950	$750	$700	$600	$550	$500	$400	$300	$275	$250

Add 10% for early serial numbers with large ejector rod.

Add 50% for factory nickel finish.

This model is also known as the "PRE-MODEL 17".

.224 HARVEY K-CHUCK – ammunition made from .22 Hornet case shortened 5 thousandths inch, then fire formed, 6 in. blue barrel, relocated firing pin and chamber bored from the .224 K-Chuck cartridge, reloading dies available, model made from Pre-Model 17 revolvers by Jim Harvey circa 1957, some found on Pre-Model 48 or Pre-Model 18 revolvers. Approx. 35 mfg. by Jim Harvey with only 2 caliber marked, rest are unmarked. Another approx. 300 mfg. by Lakeland Gun Works with added barrel markings.

100%	98%	95%	90%	80%	70%	60%	50%	40%	30%	20%	10%
N/A	$2,400	$1,850	$1,400	$1,150	$875	$700	$550	$450	$375	$335	$290

Add 10% for NIB condition.

THE K-22 COMBAT MASTERPIECE "PRE-MODEL 18" – .22 LR cal., double action revolver built on the square butt K Target frame with 5 screws, similar to K-22 masterpiece except with 4 inch pinned barrel, blue finish, (nickel scarce) combat style 1/8 in. Baughman Quick Draw on plain ramp base front sight, micrometer click adjustable rear sight, short action. Mfg. circa 1949-1957, continued thereafter as the Model 18.

100%	98%	95%	90%	80%	70%	60%	50%	40%	30%	20%	10%
$1,500	$1,085	$850	$675	$500	$450	$400	$350	$300	$275	$250	$225

Add 100% for nickel guns that letter as factory.

THE .22 MILITARY AND POLICE (POST OFFICE MODEL) – .22 LR cal., double action revolver built on the square butt K frame with 5 screws, designated as a training gun for the U.S. Postal Service, the only K frame produced in .22 LR with fixed sights, blue finish, 6 shot with 4 inch round barrel, not cataloged by S&W. Mfg. circa 1948-1957 and continued as the Model 45.

100%	98%	95%	90%	80%	70%	60%	50%	40%	30%	20%	10%
$4,500	$3,675	$3,300	$2,950	$2,600	$2,200	$1,750	$1,250	$850	$575	$450	$300

Add 50% for 25 six inch models made for the Boston PD and a small run made after the Boston guns.

MODEL K-.256 WINCHESTER TEST REVOLVER – .256 Win. cal., DA, K target (and also N target) frame, made as a test gun in the trials between the .22 Centerfire Magnum (Jet) cartridge and the standard .256 Winchester cartridge, essentially a K-22 frame with a cylinder chambered for this cartridge, built on a 4 screw K frame, 6 were built as prototypes circa 1960. No K frame sales have been reported.

Extreme rarity precludes accurate pricing.

100%	98%	95%	90%	80%	70%	60%	50%	40%	30%	20%	10%

.22 HORNET CALIBER EXPERIMENTAL REVOLVER – .22 Hornet cal., DA, aluminum alloy N target frame, barrel marked "S&W .22 Magnum" and fitted with target hammer and trigger, pinned Patridge front sight, micrometer click rear sight. Also see the 38/44 Alloy N frame.

Extreme rarity precludes accurate pricing - Last known selling price was $30,000.

2 known with "X" serial prefix.

9MM CALIBER TEST REVOLVER – 9mm cal., double action revolver built on the N frame. A small number of test revolvers were built on a prewar N frame. Serial #3 and possibly serials #6 and #9 were made on a test basis for the Chinese government in June of 1945. Originally requested to be in 8mm Nambu, S&W did not have an 8mm reamer, but instead supplied a sample chambered in 9mm. This rare 1940s vintage prototype should not be confused with the production 9mm revolvers which were regular cataloged items in later decades. You will find those listed in the Numbered Model Revolver section at Models 547 and 940. No sales reported.

Extreme rarity precludes accurate pricing.

.30 CALIBER CARBINE TEST REVOLVER – .30 M1 Carbine cal., double action revolver built on N target frame. S&W produced several revolvers with fixed and target sights, chambered in .30 Carbine, which were built on a five screw N frame on a test basis. Some of these were submitted to the Army for evaluation and tested on Jan. 17, 1944 at APG . These revolvers passed an endurance test with no breakages, but shooters objected to the severe muzzle blast, and the Army did not see a military requirement for further purchase. The military report also states that the shooters did not wear hearing protection. In this case it is apparent that muzzle blast would be excessive. At least three examples are known to still exist in private collections. Serial number 4 is of a prewar target configuration with a cylinder length of 1.6 in. using half moon clips when needed. It has a 5 in. barrel with a Patridge front sight and prewar features with post war grips on a frame with a 6 groove backstrap and forestrap. In October 2003, serial number 2 was auctioned by James D. Julia and is the revolver in the 1944 test by APG as tracked by the assembly number used in that test report. Reports are that this and two others were ordered by General "Hap" Arnold, further accurate details are unknown. Records in the National Archives about this revolver are scarce, but research is still on-going by Charles Pate.

Any of these revolvers are extremely rare among collectors, and would probably bring in the low five figures.

.32 HAND EJECTOR FIRST MODEL (MODEL OF 1896) – .32 S&W Long cal., 6 shot fluted cylinder, 3 1/4, 4 1/4, or 6 in. barrel, blue or nickel, black rubber grips, round butt, cylinder stop is mounted in frame top-strap, patent markings are on cylinder, rather than on barrel. 19,712 mfg. 1896-1903. Serial range 1-19712.

$1,000	$775	$650	$600	$550	$525	$475	$425	$400	$375	$335	$300

Add 10% for short hammer variation.

This is S&W's first production Hand Ejector.

.32 HAND EJECTOR SECOND MODEL (MODEL OF 1903) – .32 S&W Long cal., 6 shot fluted cylinder, 3 1/4, 4 1/4, or 6 in. barrel, blue or nickel, black rubber grips. 19,425 mfg. 1903-1904. Serial range 1-19425.

N/A	$1,175	$1,000	$800	$675	$550	$500	$400	$350	$250	$225	$200

* ***.32 Hand Ejector Second Model (Model of 1903 - 1st Change)*** – .32 S&W Long cal., 6 shot fluted cylinder, rubber grips, 3 1/2, 4 1/4, or 6 in. barrel, blue or nickel. 31,700 mfg. 1904-1906. Serial range 19426-51126.

N/A	$1,850	$1,625	$1,375	$1,100	$875	$625	$425	$300	$250	$200	$175

* ***.32 Hand Ejector Second Model (Model of 1903 - 2nd Change)*** – .32 S&W Long cal., 6 shot fluted cylinder, rubber grips, 3 1/2, 4 1/4, or 6 in. barrel, blue or nickel. 44,373 mfg. 1906-1910. Serial range 51127-95500.

N/A	$650	$575	$475	$375	$300	$275	$250	$225	$200	$175	$150

* ***.32 Hand Ejector Second Model (Model of 1903 - 3rd Change)*** – .32 S&W Long cal., 6 shot fluted cylinder, rubber grips, 3 1/2, 4 1/4, or 6 in. barrel, blue or nickel. 624 mfg. 1909-1910. Serial range 95501-96125.

N/A	$650	$575	$475	$375	$300	$275	$250	$225	$200	$175	$150

* ***.32 Hand Ejector Second Model (Model of 1903 - 4th Change)*** – .32 S&W Long cal., 6 shot fluted cylinder, rubber grips, 3 1/2, 4 1/4, or 6 in. barrel, blue or nickel. 6,374 mfg. 1910. Serial range 96126-102500.

N/A	$650	$575	$475	$375	$300	$275	$250	$225	$200	$175	$150

100%	98%	95%	90%	80%	70%	60%	50%	40%	30%	20%	10%

* ***.32 Hand Ejector Second Model (Model of 1903 - 5th Change)*** – .32 S&W Long cal., 6 shot fluted cylinder, rubber grips, 3 1/2, 4 1/4, or 6 in. barrel, blue or nickel. Serial range 102501-to approx. 263000. Approx. 160,499 mfg. 1910-1917.

N/A	$650	$575	$475	$375	$300	$275	$250	$225	$200	$175	$150

.32 HAND EJECTOR THIRD MODEL – .32 S&W Long cal., 6 shot fluted cylinder, 3 1/4, 4 1/4, or 6 in. barrel, blue or nickel finish, grips of checked hard rubber with "S&W" monogram, round butt. 271,531 mfg. 1917-1942. Serial range approx. 263001-534532.

$1,000	$750	$575	$475	$375	$300	$275	$250	$225	$200	$175	$150

Add 300% for Target model (6 in. barrel only, blue finish).

.32 HAND EJECTOR POST WAR (PRE-MODEL 30) – .32 S&W Long cal., 6 shot, 2 (rare), 3 1/4, 4 1/4, or 6 in. barrel, blue or nickel, fixed sights, walnut or rubber grips. Serial range 536685 -712953 as an "I" frame mfg. 1946-1960.

$800	$600	$500	$400	$300	$275	$250	$225	$200	$175	$150	$125

This model was designated Model 30 after 1958.

.32 REGULATION POLICE (PRE-WAR) – .32 S&W cal., 6 shot, 3 1/4, 4 1/4, or 6 in. barrel, square butt, walnut grips, fixed sights, blue or nickel, wide serial range of 260000 to 536000 s/n on front tang. Mfg. 1917-1942.

$1,200	$1,000	$850	$625	$525	$475	$325	$300	$275	$250	$225	$150

Add 300% for Regulation Police Target (6 in. barrel only, blue).

.32 REGULATION POLICE POST WAR (PRE-MODEL 31) – .32 S&W cal., double action revolver, 2, 3, 4, or 6 in. barrel, 6 shot, fixed sights, square butt, walnut grips, wide serial range of 536000 to 712953 s/n on front tang, blue or nickel finish, Mfg. 1946-1957.

$750	$650	$575	$475	$375	$300	$275	$250	$225	$200	$175	$150

Add 300% for Regulation Police Target (6 in. barrel only, blue).

K-32 HAND EJECTOR FIRST MODEL (K-32 TARGET) – .32 S&W Long cal., double action revolver built on the square butt K target 5 screw frame, 6 in. round and pinned barrel, 6 shot fluted cylinder with a nominal length of 1.56 in., blue finish, 1/8 or 1/10 in. Patridge front sights were cataloged, with gold bead available, adjustable rear sight for windage and elevation, both magna and standard walnut grips with a diamond around the screw escutcheon were available, 34oz. Built on the Model 1905 .38 M&P 4th Change frame in serial number range 653388 to 682207. About 94 mfg. circa 1936-1941.

N/A	$18,500	$15,000	$12,500	$10,500	$9,000	$7,000	$5,000	$3,750	$2,500	$1,250	$800

K-32 HAND EJECTOR (POST WAR) K-32 MASTERPIECE "PRE-MODEL 16" – .32 S&W Long cal., double action revolver built on the square butt K target 5 screw frame, short cocking action, anti-backlash trigger, 6 groove tangs and serrated trigger, 1/8 or 1/10 in. Patridge front sights were cataloged, micrometer click rear sight, narrow ribbed 6 in. barrel, checkered walnut stocks with S&W monograms, large S&W trademark on sideplate, 38.5 oz. Mfg. circa 1946-1957, then continued as the Model 16.

N/A	N/A	N/A	$4,425	$4,100	$3,600	$3,200	$2,750	$2,150	$1,650	$1,300	$1,000

A scarce gun, with serial number ranges hard to pin down. Known serial numbers include: all of K-58921 through K-58970 and K-67601 through K-67670, ranges in K-68470 to K-68530and ranges in K-767574 to K-767599. All have the narrow rib. In 1950, the wide rib was introduced, and some K-32s from 1956 will be found in the K-271792 to K-271836 serial number range. Additional known serial number ranges listed under Model 16.

.32 MILITARY & POLICE – .32 S&W Long cal., double action revolver built on the square butt K 5 screw frame, 2 and 4 in. barrel lengths are found and approximately 910 with a 5 in. barrel are reported, a small group of revolvers were chambered for .32 Long rather than the .38 and built on the larger .38 M&P K frame., fixed sights with round blade front and square notch rear. 6 shot cylinder with a nominal length of 1.56 in. "Smith & Wesson 32 Long CTG" on the barrel's left side, with the right side blank. "Made in U.S.A." on the frame next to the trigger guard. Large S&W Monogram on the sideplate. .240 in. serrated trigger and checkered hammer spur. Serial prefixes of S and C are found mixed in the 38 M&P series with 4,813 mfg. circa 1948-1950.

N/A	$3,250	$2,800	$2,500	$2,000	$1,500	$1,250	$1,050	$850	$650	$450	$250

.32-20 WCF HAND EJECTOR FIRST MODEL – .32-20 WCF cal., 6 shot fluted cylinder, 4, 5, 6, or 6 1/2 in. barrel, blue or nickel, case hardened trigger and hammer, hard rubber with "S&W" monogram or non-monogrammed walnut grips, round butt style, serial range 1-5311. Mfg. 1899-1902.

N/A	$2,800	$2,450	$2,100	$1,850	$1,500	$1,200	$950	$750	$550	$350	$250

Add 50%-100% for Target Model.

100%	98%	95%	90%	80%	70%	60%	50%	40%	30%	20%	10%

.32-20 WCF HAND EJECTOR SECOND MODEL (MODEL OF 1902) – .32-20 WCF cal., 6 shot fluted cylinder, 4, 5, or 6 1/2 in. barrel, blue or nickel, hard rubber with "S&W" monogram or walnut round butt style grips. 4,499 mfg. 1902-1905. Serial number range 5312-9811.

N/A	$1,850	$1,625	$1,375	$1,100	$875	$625	$425	$300	$250	$200	$175

Add 50%-100% for Target Model.

* ***.32-20 WCF Hand Ejector Second Model (Model of 1902 - 1st Change)*** – .32-20 WCF cal., 6 shot fluted cylinder, 4, 5, or 6 1/2 in. barrel, blue or nickel, hard rubber grip, also available in checkered walnut. 8,313 mfg. 1903-1905. Serial number range 9812-18125.

N/A	$1,850	$1,625	$1,375	$1,100	$875	$625	$425	$300	$250	$200	$175

Add 50%-100% for Target Model.

.32-20 WCF HAND EJECTOR (MODEL OF 1905) – .32-20 WCF cal., 4, 5, or 6 1/2 in. barrel, blue or nickel, hard rubber grip also available in checkered walnut, (revolvers manufactured until approx. 1916 were marked .32 Winchester, .32 WCF between 1916-1928, and late production was marked .32/20), cylinder and barrel specifications same as above, with round or square butt grip. 4,300 mfg. 1905-1906. Serial number range 18126-22426.

N/A	$1,850	$1,625	$1,375	$1,100	$875	$625	$425	$300	$250	$200	$175

Add 50%-75% for Target Models.

* ***.32-20 WCF Hand Ejector (Model of 1905 - 1st Change)*** – .32-20 WCF cal., 4, 5, 6, or 6 1/2 barrel, blue or nickel, grips same as above, round or square butt. 11,073 mfg. 1906-1909. Serial number range 22427 to approx. 33500.

N/A	$1,850	$1,625	$1,375	$1,100	$875	$625	$425	$300	$250	$200	$175

Add 50%-100% for Target Model.

* ***.32-20 WCF Hand Ejector (Model of 1905 - 2nd Change)*** – .32-20 WCF cal., 4, 5, 6, or 6 1/2 in. barrel, cylinder and grip specifications same as above, serial number range 33501-45200. 11,699 mfg. 1906-1909 with overlap to the 1905 1st change.

N/A	$1,850	$1,625	$1,375	$1,100	$875	$625	$425	$300	$250	$200	$175

Add 50%-100% for Target Model.

* ***.32-20 WCF Hand Ejector (Model of 1905 - 3rd Change)*** – .32-20 WCF cal., cylinder same as above, 4 or 6 in. barrel, finish and grips same as above. 20,499 mfg. 1909-1915. Serial number range approx. 45201-65700.

N/A	$1,850	$1,625	$1,375	$1,100	$875	$625	$425	$300	$250	$200	$175

Add 50%-100% for Target Model.

* ***.32-20 WCF Hand Ejector (Model of 1905 - 4th Change)*** – .32-20 WCF cal., cylinder same as above, heat treated cylinders began at serial number 81287, 4, 5, or 6 in. barrel, finish and grips same as above, serial number range 65701-144684. 78,983 mfg. 1915-1940.

N/A	$1,850	$1,625	$1,375	$1,100	$875	$625	$425	$300	$250	$200	$175

Add 50%-100% for Target Model.

.38 MILITARY & POLICE FIRST MODEL (MODEL OF 1899) – .38 S&W Special cal., early Army & Navy models were marked "S&W .38 MIL.", civilian guns and standard models are 2-line barrel marked ".38 S&W SPECIAL & U.S. SERVICE CTG'S" with the "Maltese Cross" emblem stamped both before and after the caliber, these models are also referred to as .38 Hand Ejectors, 6 shot fluted cylinder, 4, 5, or 6 1/2 in. barrel, blue or nickel finish, "S&W" monogram checkered hard rubber or checkered walnut grips with walnut grips exhibiting an impressed circle at top, left plain for civilian issue, marked with inspector's initials for military issue. 20,975 mfg. 1899-1902. Serial number range 1-20975.

On these models, barrel markings are somewhat confusing, generally marked .38 S&W Spl. & U.S. Service cartridge, Military Issue is typically marked .38 Military. Fixed sights are referred to as Military & Police Models while target sights are referred to as .38 Hand Ejectors.

* ***.38 Military & Police First Model Standard*** – Civilian Issue

N/A	$1,850	$1,625	$1,375	$1,100	$875	$625	$425	$300	$250	$200	$175

Add 100%-200% for target sights, depending on condition.

* ***.38 Military & Police First Model U.S. Navy*** – 1,000 revolvers in .38 S&W Spl. cal. with 6 in. barrel, blue, checkered walnut grips, delivered in 1900. Stamped on butt "U.S.N." with an anchor and inspector's initials. All in S&W serial range 5001-6000. U.S. Navy serial number range 1-1000.

N/A	$3,600	$3,300	$2,875	$2,500	$1,975	$1,550	$1,100	$825	$685	$550	$425

100%	98%	95%	90%	80%	70%	60%	50%	40%	30%	20%	10%

* ***.38 Military & Police First Model U.S. Army*** – 1,000 revolvers in .38 Military cal. with 6 in. barrel, blue, checkered walnut grips, inspector's initials "K.S.M." on right grip panel with "J.T.T.1901" on left grip panel. Stamped on butt "U.S. ARMY/MODEL 1899", lanyard ring. S&W serial number range 13001-14000.

N/A	$3,600	$3,300	$2,875	$2,500	$1,975	$1,550	$1,100	$825	$685	$550	$425

.38 MILITARY & POLICE SECOND MODEL (MODEL OF 1902) – .38 S&W Special and .38 Military cal., civilian and standard models barrels have a 2-line marking ".38 S&W SPECIAL & U.S. SERVICE CTG'S" with the "Maltese Cross" emblem stamped both before and after the caliber, 6 shot, fluted cylinder, 4, 5, 6, and 6 1/2 in. barrels, blue or nickel, "S&W" monogram checkered hard rubber or checkered walnut grips. 12,827 mfg. 1902-1903. Serial number range 20976-33803.

* ***.38 Military & Police Second Model Standard*** – civilian issue, all in .38 S&W Special cal.

N/A	$1,475	$1,275	$1,150	$900	$775	$650	$525	$400	$300	$250	$200

Add 100%-200% for target sights, depending on condition.

* ***.38 Military & Police Second Model U.S. Navy*** – 1,000 revolvers in .38 United States Service caliber with 6 in. barrel, delivered in 1902, "U.S.N." with "J.A.B.", anchor, and arrow through horizontal "S" and "No." (Naval Ser. No. designation) stamped on butt, Navy ser. no. range is 1001 - 2000. S&W serial range 25001 to 26000 on the front tang.

N/A	$4,425	$4,100	$3,600	$3,200	$2,750	$2,150	$1,650	$1,300	$1,000	$800	$600

.38 MILITARY & POLICE SECOND MODEL OF 1902 - 1ST CHANGE – .38 S&W Special cal., 6 shot fluted cylinder, 4, 5, or 6 1/2 in. barrel, blue or nickel, "S&W" monogram checkered hard rubber or checkered walnut grips, rounded butt style. 28,645 mfg. 1903-1904. Serial number range 33804-62449.

Add 100%-200% for target sights, depending on condition.

* ***.38 Military & Police Second Model 1st Change Standard Round Butt*** – hard rubber or checkered walnut grips, round butt.

N/A	$1,475	$1,275	$1,150	$900	$775	$650	$525	$400	$300	$250	$200

* ***.38 Military & Police Second Model 1st Change Standard Square Butt*** – checkered walnut or hard rubber grips or square butt to frame style. All will have serial numbers above the 58000 range.

N/A	$1,275	$1,150	$900	$775	$650	$525	$400	$300	$250	$200	$175

.38 MILITARY & POLICE (MODEL OF 1905) – .38 S&W Special cal., 6 shot fluted cylinder, 4, 5, or 6 1/2 in. barrel, blue or nickel finish, "S&W" monogram checkered hard rubber (round butt) or checkered walnut (square butt) grips. 10,800 mfg. 1905-1906. Serial number range 62450-73250.

N/A	$1,400	$1,225	$1,050	$850	$775	$650	$525	$400	$300	$250	$200

Add 50% for Target Model.

* ***.38 Military & Police (Model of 1905 - 1st Change)*** – .38 S&W Special cal., 6 shot fluted cylinder, 4, 5, 6, or 6 1/2 in. barrel, blue or nickel finish, grips same as above. 73,648 mfg. (including Model 1905 2nd change), exact quantity of both models has not been determined. The first change mfg. in 1906-1909. Serial number range 73251 - 146899 overlapping with the 1904 2nd model change.

N/A	$1,400	$1,225	$1,050	$850	$775	$650	$525	$400	$300	$250	$200

Add 50% for Target Model.

* ***.38 Military & Police (Model of 1905 - 2nd Change)*** – .38 S&W Special cal., cylinder barrel lengths, finishes and grip styles same as above. 73,648 (including Model 1905 1st change) mfg. Exact quantity unknown. The second change mfg. in 1906-1909 overlapping the 1905 1st change in a serial number range 73251 to 146899.

N/A	$1,400	$1,225	$1,050	$850	$775	$650	$525	$400	$300	$250	$200

Add 50% for Target Model.

* ***.38 Military & Police (Model of 1905 - 3rd Change)*** – .38 S&W Special cal., 6 shot fluted cylinder, 4, 5, or 6 in. barrel, finishes and grip styles same as above. 94,803 mfg. 1909-1915. Serial number range 146900-241703.

N/A	$1,400	$1,225	$1,050	$850	$775	$650	$525	$400	$300	$250	$200

Add 50% for Target Model.

* ***.38 Military & Police (Model of 1905 - 4th Change)*** – .38 S&W Special cal., 6 shot fluted cylinder, 2, 4, 5, or 6 in. barrel, finishes and grip styles same as above. 758,296 mfg. 1915-1942. Serial number range 241704-approx. 1000000.

N/A	$1,125	$900	$850	$700	$600	$500	$400	$325	$250	$225	$175

Add 50% for Target Model.
Add a premium for 2 in. variation with factory letter.

100%	98%	95%	90%	80%	70%	60%	50%	40%	30%	20%	10%

.38/200 BRITISH SERVICE REVOLVER – .38 S&W cal., 200 grain bullet, 4, 5, or 6 in. barrel, approx. 110,379 sold to British with black Magic finish at around serial number 680000 and continues in the 1905 4th model series in a wide range from 700000 to 1000000. And also numbered within the Victory Model series from V1-V769000. Ser. nos. start with an SV prefix (to indicate a new hammer block) from SV769000 to SV811119. Serials are mixed with guns in .38 Spl. cal.

100%	98%	95%	90%	80%	70%	60%	50%	40%	30%	20%	10%
N/A	$750	$625	$500	$425	$375	$340	$300	$265	$225	$160	$90

GRADING - PPGS™	100%	98%	95%	90%	80%	70%	60%	LAST MSR

VICTORY MODEL – .38 Spl. (post-WWII commercial sales), .38 S&W Spl. (U.S. government sales), or .38 S&W (Lend-Lease arms to Allied Forces) cal., 2 (rare) or 4 in. barrel, mfg. in accordance with British/American Lend-Lease agreement of WWII, parkerized finish, most with "V" prefix, approx. 240,000 mfg. 1942-1945.

GRADING - PPGS™	100%	98%	95%	90%	80%	70%	60%	LAST MSR
U.S. Govt. Models	$750	$655	$565	$510	$415	$340	$265	
Lend-lease mfg.	$700	$615	$525	$475	$385	$315	$245	
Post WWII Commercial	$700	$615	$525	$475	$385	$315	$245	

Add 200% for factory lettered 2 in. variation.

Post-WWII Victory models sold commercially went through the Defense Supply Commission, and had no U.S. markings. These models will bring a premium. Be careful of fake markings.

100%	98%	95%	90%	80%	70%	60%	50%	40%	30%	20%	10%

.38 MILITARY & POLICE (POST WAR) "PRE-MODEL 10" – .38 S&W Special cal., double action revolver built on the square butt K 5 screw frame. Mfg. circa 1946-1957

100%	98%	95%	90%	80%	70%	60%	50%	40%	30%	20%	10%
$1,250	$1,050	$895	$650	$550	$475	$325	$300	$275	$250	$225	$150

This model is a continuation of the previous model without the V serial prefix or the lanyard ring. S serial prefix postwar guns began as early as Dec. 27, 1944 at around s/n S769000. Postwar production frames will also have the four address lines of "Made In U.S.A., Marcas Registradas, Smith & Wesson Springfield, Mass." on the right side. C serial prefix began on March 22, 1948 starting over at C-1, and was also numbered concurrently with the M&P Airweights and the M&P .22 or pre-Model 45. Available in 2, 4, 5, or 6 in. round pinned barrel lengths with a 1/10 inch fixed round blade front sight and a square notch rear sight (later changed to 1/8 in.). Available in blue or nickel finish. Serial numbers are found on the butt, cylinder face, barrel flat, yoke face (viewed through a charge hole), the rear of the star extractor, and on the right grip panel. The round butt frame variation became available in late 1947. The 2 in. variation will have "Smith & Wesson" and the caliber marking on the left side of the barrel. Weight is 29.5 oz for a 4 in. version. Became the Model 10 in 1957.

.38 MILITARY AND POLICE AIRWEIGHT "PRE-MODEL 12" – .38 S&W Special cal., double action revolver built on the round or square butt KA 5 screw aluminum alloy service frame, similar to the Model 10 but made with an alloy frame and originally an alloy cylinder, which was later changed to steel due to problems with cylinders cracking, numbered with the Model 10, 11, 45, and Aircrewman revolvers with a C serial prefix in production. Alloy frame is slightly thinner than a standard K frame by .080 in. and has a smooth backstrap and forestrap. Mfg. 1951-1957, then continued as the Model 12.

100%	98%	95%	90%	80%	70%	60%	50%	40%	30%	20%	10%
$1,650	$1,250	$975	$775	$700	$600	$550	$500	$400	$300	$275	$250

Add 20% for matching numbered alloy cylinder.

USAF M-13 (THE AIRCREWMAN) – .38 Special cal., double action revolver originally built on the round butt alloy K frame, blue anodized finish, 2 in. pinned barrel, diamond insert walnut grips, 1/10 in. serrated ramp front sight w/square notch rear, similar to the Model 12, has "Revolver, Lightweight, M13" stamped on the topstrap, "Property of U.S. Air Force" stamped on the backstrap, most were destroyed by the government, C serial prefix in a range of C247000 to C405363. Numbered concurrently with Model 10, 11, 12, and 45.

Extreme rarity precludes accurate pricing.

THE AIRCREWMAN 6 SHOT – A production run of 605 early versions (6 shot) were serial numbered with an "A.F.NO" serial prefix (serial Range A.F.NO.1190 to A.F.NO.1794). These are a 5 screw variation with "Aircrewman" on the barrel, but with no topstrap markings and will have Air Force medallions in the grip circles with a smooth backstrap. A "P" inspectors stamp is found on the left side of the frame above the trigger guard. These early Genuine Aircrewman's have all matching serial numbers on the frame, cylinder face, grips, and barrel. Many were repaired by military armorers who interchanged parts, especially cylinders with non-matching numbers.

100%	98%	95%	90%	80%	70%	60%	50%	40%	30%	20%	10%
N/A	$22,400	$17,350	$6,750	$3,250	$2,500	$1,750	$1,400	$1,300	$1,250	$1,200	$1,000

100%	98%	95%	90%	80%	70%	60%	50%	40%	30%	20%	10%

THE AIRCREWMAN 5 SHOT (BABY AIRCREWMAN) – .38 S&W Special cal., double action revolver built on the alloy J-frame with 4 screws, 5 shot alloy cylinder, fixed sight, 605 Aircrewman versions (serial no.s "A.F.NO. 1795" to "A.F.NO. 2399") were shipped to the U.S. Air Force 1951-1952, four others went to The Springfield Amory. Marked with "AIRCREWMAN" on barrel and "PROPERTY OF U.S. AIR FORCE" on smooth backstrap, P proof mark over trigger guard with air force medallions in grip circles, 10.5 oz. Mfg. 1951-1952.

100%	98%	95%	90%	80%	70%	60%	50%	40%	30%	20%	10%
N/A	$17,400	$10,350	$6,750	$3,250	$2,500	$1,750	$1,400	$1,300	$1,250	$1,200	$1,000

Most of these guns were destroyed and very few authentic examples exist. It is estimated that 10 to 15 have survived, so beware of many counterfeit examples.

GRADING - PPGS™	100%	98%	95%	90%	80%	70%	60%	LAST MSR

.38 REGULATION POLICE (PRE-WAR) – .38 S&W cal., 5 screw I-frame, 4 in. barrel, fixed sights, round butt frame enclosed by a square butt walnut wood grip, built on .32 cal. frame, serial number range 1-54474, blue finish. Mfg. 1917-1940.

	100%	98%	95%	90%	80%	70%	60%	LAST MSR
	$450	$375	$275	$175	$150	$135	$125	

Add $100 for 5 screw frame.

.38 REGULATION POLICE (PRE-WAR) "PRE MODEL 33" – .38 S&W cal., 5 screw I-frame, improved I-frame with 4 screws and 3 screws (1956), and later the J-frame, 4 in. barrel, 5 shot, built on a .32 cal. round or square butt frame, serial range 54474-122678, blue or nickel finish. Mfg. 1949-1957.

	100%	98%	95%	90%	80%	70%	60%	LAST MSR
	$450	$375	$275	$175	$150	$135	$125	

Add $100 for 5 screw frame.

.38/32 TERRIER (PRE-WAR) – .38 S&W cal., round butt I-frame with 5 screws, 2 in. barrel, 5 shot, fixed sights, walnut (scarce) or hard rubber grips, built on .32 cal. frame, serial range 38976-54474 within the Regulation Police series, blue or nickel finish. Mfg. 1936-1940.

	100%	98%	95%	90%	80%	70%	60%	LAST MSR
	$450	$375	$275	$175	$150	$135	$125	

Add $100 for 5 screw frame.

.38/32 TERRIER (POSTWAR) "PRE MODEL 32" – .38 S&W cal., 5 screw I-frame, Improved I-frame with 4 screws and 3 screws (1956), and later the J-frame, 2 in. barrel, 5 shot, fixed sights, walnut grips, built on .32 cal. frame, serial range 54474-122678 within the Regulation Police series, blue or nickel finish. Mfg. 1948-1957.

	100%	98%	95%	90%	80%	70%	60%	LAST MSR
	$450	$375	$275	$175	$150	$135	$125	

100%	98%	95%	90%	80%	70%	60%	50%	40%	30%	20%	10%

THE K-38 TARGET MASTERPIECE "PRE-MODEL 14" – .38 S&W Special cal., double action revolver built on the square butt K target 5 screw frame, original postwar Model has 6 in. barrel with narrow barrel rib, 1/8 or 1/10 in. Patridge front sight with micrometer click rear sight, blue finish. 38.5 oz. Introduced at s/n K1661. Mfg. 1946-1957.

100%	98%	95%	90%	80%	70%	60%	50%	40%	30%	20%	10%
$1,425	$1,225	$1,125	$900	$775	$650	$525	$400	$300	$250	$200	$175

The major distinction between the K-38 Target Masterpiece and the K-38 Combat Masterpiece is the barrel length and front sight.

This is the companion gun to the K-32 and K-17 and became the Model 14 in 1957.

THE K-38 COMBAT MASTERPIECE "PRE-MODEL 15" – .38 S&W Special cal., double action revolver built on the square butt K Target 5 screw frame, 4 in. pinned and ribbed barrel with markings "38 S&W Special CTG" on right side, blue or nickel finish, 1/8 in. Baughman Quick Draw plain ramp base front sight with Micrometer click adjustable rear sight, diamond walnut grips, original K serial prefix. Mfg. 1949-1957, K-38 Combat Masterpiece continued as the Model 15.

100%	98%	95%	90%	80%	70%	60%	50%	40%	30%	20%	10%
$1,525	$1,100	$875	$675	$500	$450	$400	$350	$300	$275	$250	$225

.38 CHIEFS SPECIAL "PRE-MODEL 36" – .38 Spl. cal., round or square butt steel J frame, coiled mainspring, 5 shot, fluted cylinder, 2 in. round pinned or 3 in. barrel, blue or nickel finish, early production had round blade front sight on five screw round butt frame with standard thumbpiece, smooth backstrap and rounded trigger guard, can be found with five, four, or three screw frames with ramp front sight, checkered walnut grips, later production had longer trigger guard with serrated ramped front sight, ser. no. range 1-786544. Mfg. began in 1950, by 1957 this model became known as the Model 36.

100%	98%	95%	90%	80%	70%	60%	50%	40%	30%	20%	10%
$900	$715	$600	$475	$360	$325	$250	$225	$200	$175	$150	$125

100%	98%	95%	90%	80%	70%	60%	50%	40%	30%	20%	10%

THE .38 CHIEFS SPECIAL AIRWEIGHT " PRE- MODEL 37" - .38 S&W Special cal., double action revolver built on the round or square butt alloy J 4 screw frame, 5 shot, later built with a steel cylinder due to cracks in the alloy cylinders, 2 in. barrel with round or square butt or 3 in. barrel with square butt only, available in blue or nickel finish, earliest production frames were a 5 screw alloy frame with a rounded trigger guard and a shorter grip and grip frame, examples of this frame are extremely rare. Continued as the Model 37.

$1,000	$850	$625	$525	$475	$325	$300	$275	$250	$225	$150	$90

Add 20% for numbered alloy cylinder.

About 3,777 were manufactured with an alloy cylinder. Original serial number range approximately 13000 to 786544 numbered in the Chiefs Special series.

THE BODYGUARD AIRWEIGHT "PRE-MODEL 38" - .38 S&W Special cal., double action revolver built on the round butt alloy 4 screw J frame, with the obvious distinguishing characteristic of having the frame built up at the top rear to form an integral shroud for the hammer, 2 in. pinned barrel with some production of 3 in. barrels (very rare), blued or nickel aluminum finish, walnut diamond grips, Airweight stamped on the barrel, also found in combinations of nickel cylinder with blue frame and barrel (scarce), serrated ramp front sight, .240 in. shrouded service hammer, .312 in. smooth trigger. Serial range 66000 to 786544 in the Chiefs Special series. 14oz. Mfg. circa 1955-1957.

$1,250	$1,050	$875	$650	$550	$475	$325	$300	$275	$250	$225	$150

THE CENTENNIAL "PRE-MODEL 40" - .38 S&W Special cal., double-action-only revolver built on the round butt steel J 4 screw frame, distinctive features of "hammerless" design (actually concealed hammer), and lemon-squeezer style grip safety on grip frame backstrap, 5 shot, blue or nickel finish, 2 in. pinned barrel, fully concealed hammer, numbered concurrently with the Model 42. 19 oz. Serial number range in an original series 1 to 30160 mfg. circa 1952-1957.

$1,300	$1,200	$900	$550	$400	$300	$250	$200	$175	$160	$140	$120

Add 200% for three digit serial numbers. Add 300% for three digit serial numbers with nickel finish.

THE CENTENNIAL AIRWEIGHT "PRE-MODEL 42" - .38 S&W Special cal., double-action-only revolver built on the round butt alloy J 4 screw frame, a lightweight version of the Centennial Model, 5 shot, steel cylinder (37 manufactured with an alloy cylinder), blue or nickel finish, 2 in. pinned barrel, numbered concurrently with Model 40. Very early production may have a small lock screw on the upper sideplate screw. Ramped front sight with serrations and notch cut rear sight. Serial range of 1 to 30160 in an original series. Mfg. circa 1952-1957.

$1,300	$1,200	$900	$550	$400	$300	$250	$200	$175	$160	$140	$120

Add 20% for factory nickel finish.

Add 70% for factory alloy cylinder.

THE .38/44 HEAVY DUTY (PRE-WAR) - .38 S&W Special or .38/44 S&W Special cal., double action revolver built on the larger square butt N 5 screw frame, 6 shot, 5 in. round pinned barrel w/limited production of 4 or 6 1/2 in. barrels, blue or nickel finish. Guns mfg. 1930-1935 shipped in maroon boxes, guns mfg. 1935-1940 shipped in Blue Picture Boxes. 41 oz., 11,111 mfg. April 1930-1941.

N/A	$2,100	$1,900	$1,650	$950	$725	$600	$475	$350	$300	$250	$200

Add 20% for original box.

Add 30% for 4 or 6 in. barrel.

Add a premium for .45 Colt cal. (5-6 known).

12 are documented to be chambered in .45 Colt, some of which were shipped in 1937, 1938, and 1939 to law enforcement.

Originally intended for a high powered .38 Special round, at times called the .38 Super Police (predecessor of the .357 Magnum). Serial number range 35037 to 62335 in the .44 Hand Ejector 3rd Model series.

THE .38/44 HEAVY DUTY TRANSITION (POSTWAR TRANSITIONAL) - .38 S&W Special cal., reintroduced in June of 1946, double action revolver built on the square butt N 5 screw frame, 4 or 5 in. barrels (6-1/2 in. rare). Reintroduced postwar with an S serial prefix beginning at approximately S62496, incorporating a new slide action hammer block. A short throw hammer was introduced in 1948 at approximately serial number S72300. This postwar model has the "Made in U.S.A." marking in early models and will be found with the Four Line address as it is produced closer to 1950. Serial number range is approximately S62496 to S75206 with about 2500 mfg. circa 1946-1950. Guns were shipped in either maroon or gold boxes.

$2,300	$1,850	$1,500	$1,175	$850	$700	$550	$450	$385	$315	$250	$180

Add 20% for original box.

THE .38/44 HEAVY DUTY MODEL OF 1950 "PRE-MODEL 20" – .38 S&W Special cal., introduced in September of 1950, double action revolver built on the square butt N 5 screw frame, having 4 or 5 in. barrels (6-1/2 in. rare), the 1950 Model became the Model 20 in 1957. Serial number range is spread over a wide range from approximately S75000 to S256133 with 9,493 mfg. circa 1950-1966.

100%	98%	95%	90%	80%	70%	60%	50%	40%	30%	20%	10%
$1,800	$1,500	$1,175	$850	$750	$650	$475	$375	$295	$245	$195	$135

Add 20% for original box.

THE .38/44 OUTDOORSMAN (PRE-WAR) – .38 S&W Special or .38/44 S&W Special cal., double action revolver built on the square butt N target 5 screw frame as target version of the Heavy Duty, Patridge front sight, adjustable rear sight leaf rounded and contoured to the frame, approx. 4,761 mfg. November 1931-1941.

100%	98%	95%	90%	80%	70%	60%	50%	40%	30%	20%	10%
N/A	$2,800	$2,350	$1,700	$1,425	$1,150	$750	$550	$475	$350	$275	$195

Add 20% for original box.

Serial number range 38939 to 62077 in the .44 Hand Ejector 3rd Model series. Another source reports the last pre-war Outdoorsman as s/n 62023 on 1/3/1941.

THE .38/44 OUTDOORSMAN TRANSITION (POSTWAR-TRANSITIONAL) – .38 S&W special cal., double action revolver built on the square butt N 5 screw Target frame, reintroduced with new sliding hammer block and S serial prefix (beginning at approx. S62940), 6 1/2 in. pinned barrel w/shrouded extractor, (4 and 5 in. rare, estimated 50-100 mfg.), 1/10 in. front sight blade, early postwar guns known with Pre-war Magnum barrels with checked ribs. Serrated backstrap and forestrap with 6 grooves. Approximate serial number range S62940 to S75000. Approx. 2,326 mfg. Reintroduced August 1946-1949.

100%	98%	95%	90%	80%	70%	60%	50%	40%	30%	20%	10%
N/A	$2,100	$1,900	$1,650	$950	$725	$600	$475	$350	$300	$250	$200

Add 20% for original box.

THE .38/44 OUTDOORSMAN MODEL OF 1950 "PRE-MODEL 23" – .38 S&W Special cal., reintroduced September 1950, double action revolver built on the square butt N 5 screw Target frame, introduced with a raised ribbed barrel and a micrometer click rear sight and short throw hammer and trigger, blue finish is now a polished blue or nickel finish, the S&W trademark is now found on the sideplate, checkered Magna diamond walnut grips. Approximate serial number range S75000 to S261999 in the N frame S series with a total of 6,039 mfg. circa 1950-1957.

100%	98%	95%	90%	80%	70%	60%	50%	40%	30%	20%	10%
$2,100	$1,900	$1,650	$950	$725	$600	$475	$350	$300	$250	$200	$150

THE .38/44 HEAVY DUTY/OUTDOORSMAN ALLOY FRAME – .38 S&W Special cal., DA revolver built on square butt alloy N 5 screw frame, approx. 12 aluminum alloy N frame handguns were made in various cals. and configurations as specials in 1955, several were 38/44 configuration with a steel cylinder, both 4 and 5 in. barrels made, "S" serial prefixes and "X" serial prefixes have been observed. It was verified that both target and fixed sight models were made in blue and nickel finish, alloy frames are 6 ounces lighter than their steel counterparts. Two are known in a private collection. See also .22 Hornet caliber.

Last known traded price was $20,000.

.38 CHIEFS SPECIAL TARGET "PRE-MODEL 50" – .38 S&W Special cal., satin blue original finish (military post-war type), early production (1955-1956), found sporadically in the 55000 - 57000 ser. no. range, polished blue finish from 1957-1959 (in approx. 149000 - 150000 ser. no. range).

GRADING - PPGS™	100%	98%	95%	90%	80%	70%	60%	LAST MSR
	$1,250	$950	$850	$675	$475	$385	$300	

Add 20% for early guns.

.38 REGULATION POLICE – .38 S&W cal., 5 shot, 4 in. barrel, square butt, walnut grips, fixed sights, blue or nickel, serial range 1-54474. Mfg. 1917-1940.

GRADING - PPGS™	100%	98%	95%	90%	80%	70%	60%	LAST MSR
Pre-war	$750	$655	$565	$510	$415	$340	$265	
Post-war Pre-Model 33	$600	$525	$450	$325	$260	$215	$165	

Add 300% for Regulation Police Target (6 in. barrel only, blue).

Add 200% for Post office variation with 2 in. barrel marked "RMS PO DEPT" on backstrap - 500 mfg.

.357 REGISTERED MAGNUM – .357 Mag. cal., this model could be custom ordered with any barrel length from 3 1/2 - 8 3/4 inches in 1/4 in. increments (23 barrel lengths in all), adj. sights, blue (most common), or nickel (only 174 mfg.) finish, two hammer styles, checkered walnut grips, hand fitted and registered to the buyer by a number found on the inside of the yoke, ser. no. with "REG" prefix (approx. 5,500 were mfg.). This practice was disc. 1939 due to the tremendous demand for the .357 Mag. revolver. Mfg. 1935-1939.

Values for this model range between $7,000 and $20,000 depending on original condition and desirability factors.

GRADING - PPGS™	100%	98%	95%	90%	80%	70%	60%	LAST MSR

Common barrel lengths were 3 1/2, 4, 5, 6 1/2, and 8 3/4 in. Production totals by barrel length are as follows: 4 1/2 in. (108 mfg.), 5 1/2 in. (140 mfg.), 5 in. (869 mfg.), 6 1/2 in. (1,518 mfg.), 6 in. (839), 7 1/2 in. (79 mfg.), and 8 3/4 in. (735 mfg.). Rest of production was divided between the other barrel lengths.

Be wary of fakes - it is highly recommended to get a factory letter when buying, selling, or trading this model. This is perhaps S&W most collectible revolver currently, and prices have risen significantly in the past several years.

.357 MAGNUM PRE-WAR NON-REGISTERED – similar to above, but not registered. 1,142 mfg. 1938-1941.

	100%	98%	95%	90%	80%	70%	60%
	N/A	$6,800	$4,875	$4,425	$3,575	$2,925	$2,275

Add $1,000 for correct box.

.357 MAGNUM POST-WAR "PRE-MODEL 27" – ser. no. had "S" prefix, 3 1/2, 5, 6, 6 1/2, or 8 3/8 in. barrel. Mfg. 1947-1957.

	100%	98%	95%	90%	80%	70%	60%
	N/A	$1,730	$1,480	$1,345	$1,085	$890	$690

Add 10% for 8 3/8 in. barrel.

THE .357 COMBAT MAGNUM "PRE-MODEL 19" – .357 Magnum cal., double action revolver built on the square butt K target 4 screw frame that is slightly larger than a standard K frame in the yoke area. Available in bright blue or nickel (scarce) finish and originally available in 4 in. barrel length only with a 1/8 in. Baughman Quick Draw on plain ramp base front sight with an adjustable micrometer click rear sight. 6 shot fluted and counter-bored cylinder with a nominal length of 1.67 in. Mfg. circa 1955-1957, the .357 Combat Magnum continued as the Model 19 until 1999. K serial prefix.

	100%	98%	95%	90%	80%	70%	60%
Blue	$2,500	$2,150	$1,850	$1,500	$1,100	$750	$550
Nickel	N/A	$2,400	$2,000	$1,600	$1,200	$850	$625

THE HIGHWAY PATROLMAN "PRE-MODEL 28" – .357 Magnum/.38 Special cal., introduced in April 15, 1954, double action revolver built on the square butt N target frame with 5 screws, pinned barrel and recessed cylinder. A utility version of the pre-Model 27 with a satin blue finish, this model is the only "N" frame with an adj. rear sight leaf that is not serrated as well as no serrations on the barrel, available with 4 or 6 in. barrel, Magna style or target walnut grips with S&W medallions and diamond around the screw escutcheon. This model has a 6 groove serrated backstrap and forestrap. Has "Highway Patrol" stamped on the barrel, 1/8 in. Baughman Quick Draw front sight with adj. micrometer click rear sight, shrouded extractor rod, .400 in. semi target hammer, .265 in. serrated or .400 in. smooth trigger, original test production marked "PATROLMAN", 8,427 manufactured in the first year of production. Frame change in 1956 to 4 screw at about SN S171584. Mfg. circa 1954-1957, continued as the Model 28. "S" serial prefix.

	100%	98%	95%	90%	80%	70%	60%
	N/A	$1,000	$875	$790	$630	$520	$400

100%	98%	95%	90%	80%	70%	60%	50%	40%	30%	20%	10%

.44 HAND EJECTOR FIRST MODEL (.44 HAND EJECTOR NEW CENTURY OR .44 TRIPLE LOCK) – .38-40 WCF, .44 S&W Special (standard), .44-40 WCF, .44 S&W Russian, .45 LC, or .455 Mark II cal., 4, 5, 6 1/2, or 7 1/2 in. barrel, non-monogrammed checkered walnut grips and square butt on early production, gold monogram inlay on later production. 15,375 mfg. 1908-1917. Serial range 1-15375 (overlapping occurs between the 1st and 2nd models, and there is some ser. no. duplication with the .455 Mark II). Revolver named "Triple Lock" for the third lock at the yoke.

* ***.44 Hand Ejector First Model Special Caliber*** – .38-40 WCF, .44 Russian, .44-40 WCF, .45 LC (marking, only 21 mfg.), or .455 Mark II (commercial) cal.

100%	98%	95%	90%	80%	70%	60%	50%	40%	30%	20%	10%
$12,500	$10,500	$9,000	$7,500	$6,000	$4,750	$4,000	$3,250	$2,500	$1,750	$1,450	$1,000

* ***.44 Hand Ejector First Model Conversion*** – .455 Mark II cal.

100%	98%	95%	90%	80%	70%	60%	50%	40%	30%	20%	10%
$5,500	$4,650	$4,250	$3,700	$3,250	$2,750	$2,350	$1,850	$1,325	$950	$650	$525

Only 808 factory conversions of .44 Special to .455 cal. were mfg. and sold to the British government.

* ***.44 Hand Ejector First Model Standard*** – .44 S&W Special cal.

	100%	98%	95%	90%	80%	70%	60%	50%	40%	30%	20%	10%
Fixed Sights	N/A	$1,525	$1,325	$1,100	$1,000	$900	$800	$715	$630	$545	$460	$400
w/Factory Target Sights	$6,500	$5,000	$4,500	$3,750	$3,300	$2,975	$2,650	$2,300	$1,850	$1,450	$1,200	$995

* ***.44 Hand Ejector First Model British Target Triple Lock*** – .455 cal., 6 1/2 or 7 1/2 in. barrel, with drift adj. sights (not screw operated) for shooting at Bisley, England, typically unmarked for cal., very few mfg.

100%	98%	95%	90%	80%	70%	60%	50%	40%	30%	20%	10%
N/A	$4,950	$2,675	$2,350	$1,875	$1,650	$1,450	$1,275	$1,130	$985	$840	$695

100%	98%	95%	90%	80%	70%	60%	50%	40%	30%	20%	10%

.44 HAND EJECTOR 2ND MODEL – .44 S&W Special cal. as standard, .38-40 WCF, .44-40 WCF, or .45 LC cal., 4, 5, 6, or 6 1/2 in. barrel, blue or nickel finish, checkered walnut square butt grips, with or w/o "S&W" monogram inlays. 17,510 mfg. circa 1915-1940. Ser. range 15376-approx. 60000.

* ***.44 Hand Ejector 2nd Model Standard Caliber*** – .44 S&W Special cal., mfg. 1915-1940

100%	98%	95%	90%	80%	70%	60%	50%	40%	30%	20%	10%
N/A	$2,375	$2,050	$1,850	$1,500	$1,200	$900	$625	$475	$350	$250	$200

Add 50% for factory target sights.

* ***.44 Hand Ejector 2nd Model Special Calibers*** – .38-40 WCF, .44-40 WCF, or .45 LC cal.

Due to the rarity of these calibers, prices could be 200% or more above Standard Model values.

.44 HAND EJECTOR THIRD MODEL (MODEL 1926 HAND EJECTOR THIRD MODEL) – .44 S&W Special cal., very rare in .44-40 WCF or .45 LC cal., 6 shot fluted cylinder, 4, 5, or 6 1/2 in. barrel, finishes and grips same as above, same ser. range as the Second Model .44 Hand Ejectors, approx. 4,976 mfg. pre-war. Ser. range 28358-61412. Mfg. 1926-1941.

* ***.44 Hand Ejector Third Model Standard*** – .44 S&W Special cal.

100%	98%	95%	90%	80%	70%	60%	50%	40%	30%	20%	10%
$4,500	$3,675	$3,300	$2,950	$2,600	$2,200	$1,750	$1,250	$850	$575	$450	$300

There is also a post-war variation of this model mfg. 1946-49 in ser. range S62490-S74000 (approx. 1,432 mfg. 1946-1949). These transitional guns have hammer block safeties but long actions. The values are about 2/3 of the pre-war models.

* ***.44 Hand Ejector Third Model 1926 Target*** – pre-war, target sights, blue only, otherwise same as above. Mfg. 1926-1941.

100%	98%	95%	90%	80%	70%	60%	50%	40%	30%	20%	10%
N/A	$9,500	$8,550	$7,250	$6,500	$5,500	$4,500	$3,500	$3,000	$2,200	$1,500	$1,100

There is also a post-war variation of this model mfg. 1946-49 in ser. range S62,490-S74,000. These transitional guns have hammer block safeties but long actions. The post-war Target Model has a barrel rib and 1950s style micrometer rear sight. The values are similar to those listed.

GRADING - PPGS™	100%	98%	95%	90%	80%	70%	60%	LAST MSR

.44 MAGNUM PRE-MODEL 29 (5 SCREW) – .44 Mag. cal., 5 screw, can be discerned by 3 visible screws on right sideplate, 1 hidden under the grip, and 1 in front of the trigger guard, 4 (scarce), 5 (only 2 mfg.), or 6 1/2 in. barrel. Approx. 6,500 mfg. during 1956-1958, mfg. began with ser. no. S130927.

GRADING - PPGS™	100%	98%	95%	90%	80%	70%	60%	LAST MSR
Bright blue finish	$6,000	$4,250	$3,250	$2,500	$1,900	$1,500	$1,050	
Nickel (approx. 11 mfg.)	$15,000	$12,000	$9,500	$8,000	$6,000	$5,000	$4,000	

.44 MAGNUM PRE-MODEL 29 (4 SCREW) – similar to 5 screw model, except has four screws total, the top sideplate screw was eliminated, serialization began at approx. S167600. Mfg. 1957-1958.

GRADING - PPGS™	100%	98%	95%	90%	80%	70%	60%	LAST MSR
	$3,000	$2,600	$2,100	$1,600	$1,200	$900	$875	
5 in. barrel, blue	$8,500	$6,500	$5,000	$4,000	$2,500	$2,000	$1,500	
5 in. bbl., nickel, 10 mfg.	$10,000	$8,550	$7,250	$6,500	$5,500	$4,500	$3,500	

Add 40% for nickel finish.

Add $500 for correct blue/black case with tools.

Approx. 300-400 .44 Magnums with a 5 in. barrel were manufactured between the Pre-Model 29 with a 4 screw frame, and the Model 29-2 with a 3 screw frame. Most models were primarily shipped from 1958-1963.

.45 HAND EJECTOR (MODEL OF 1917) – .45 Auto Rim, or .45 ACP (in half moon clip) cal., 6 shot, 5 1/2 in. barrel, fixed sights, satin blue on military - high gloss blue on commercial, smooth walnut on military, checkered walnut on commercial models. Early military revolvers have concentric groove cut on the sides of the hammer (approx. serial range 1-15000), 210,866 mfg. 1917-1948, ser. no. range 1-210866.

* ***.45 Hand Ejector Military*** – approx. 175,000 mfg., 1917-1919.

GRADING - PPGS™	100%	98%	95%	90%	80%	70%	60%	LAST MSR
	$2,500	$2,195	$1,875	$1,685	$1,375	$1,125	$875	

Add 25% for early military mfg. with concentric groove cut on the sides of the hammer.

Military overruns (unissued guns) were sold to the civilian market. Be sure to properly identify.

* ***.45 Hand Ejector Commercial*** – mfg. 1920-1948.

GRADING - PPGS™	100%	98%	95%	90%	80%	70%	60%	LAST MSR
	$2,450	$2,145	$1,845	$1,665	$1,350	$1,100	$865	

Add $500 for original box.

There was also a "1917 Army" commercial mfg. May 14, 1946-July 25, 1947 (approx. 991 mfg.). At approx. ser. no. 210321, from October 1947, guns were mfg. with a hammer block safety and ser. nos. had an "S" prefix.

GRADING - PPGS™	100%	98%	95%	90%	80%	70%	60%	LAST MSR

* ***.45 Hand Ejector Brazilian Contract of 1937*** – Brazilian National Coat of Arms and 1937 contract date stamped on sideplate.

$1,600	$1,300	$1,150	$1,000	$850	$700	$550	

37,000 originally sold to Brazil, serial numbers scattered throughout the 1-210,000 range. First delivery of 25,000 circa 1937-1938 in the 181983 - 207043 S/N range (with checkered S&W silver medallion wood grips and "square" rear sight notch), second delivery of 12,000 guns circa 1946 in the 1-210,000 S/N range (with plain wood grips and "U" rear sight notch) assembled from old factory stockpiled parts. Approx. 14,000 with heavy use were imported back to the U.S. circa late 1980s.

100%	98%	95%	90%	80%	70%	60%	50%	40%	30%	20%	10%

.455 HAND EJECTOR FIRST MODEL – .455 Mark II cal., ser. range 1-5000 in its own range, English or Canadian proof marks.

N/A	$1,750	$1,550	$1,325	$1,150	$975	$885	$765	$675	$600	$540	$480

Add 25% for commercially sold revolvers.
Subtract 20%-40% for conversion to American caliber.

.455 HAND EJECTOR SECOND MODEL – ser. range 5001-74755, generally British or Canadian proof marks.

N/A	$1,350	$1,175	$1,000	$875	$750	$650	$550	$450	$350	$250	$200

Add 25% for commercially sold revolvers.
Subtract 20%-40% for conversion to American caliber.

THE .45 HAND EJECTOR MODEL OF 1950, MILITARY (1950 ARMY) "PRE-MODEL 22" – .45 ACP cal., introduced November 1951, double action revolver built on the square butt N 5 screw frame, similar to the 1917 Model with a new shorter throw hammer and trigger with a new slide action hammer block as indicated with an S serial prefix, 5 1/2 inch round barrel, the lanyard ring was now discontinued, 6 shot fluted cylinder with a nominal length of 1.53 in. Magna style walnut grips, 1/10 in. forged round blade front sight with square notch rear sights, 203 were reported chambered in .45 Colt at serial S103000, but only one has been found. This model can be marked "45 CAL MODEL 1950" or "S&W D.A. 45" on the barrels right side. Became the Model 22 in 1957. The four standard address lines now appear on the frame's right side, with a large S&W trademark on the sideplate. Serial number range S85000 to S236000 in the N frame series and possibly as high as S263000. One collector reports a serial number in the S2558xx serial area. 3,976 reported mfg. circa 1951-1966.

$4,200	$3,375	$3,000	$2,650	$2,300	$1,950	$1,550	$1,050	$750	$575	$450	$325

Only three known to be made in .45 Colt - last sale was $15,000. Must letter to determine if factory.

THE 1950 .45 TARGET MODEL (LIGHT BARREL) "PRE-MODEL 26" – .45 ACP (standard) or .45 Colt (scarce) cal., double action revolver built on the square butt N Target 5 screw frame with 6-1/2 in. ribbed and pinned barrel, 6 shot, 1.55 (.45 ACP) or 1.67 (.45 Colt) in. fluted cylinder, blue finish, Patridge front sight with micrometer click rear sight, .400 in. semi-target hammer, .265 in. grooved trigger standard with .500 in. target trigger optional, shrouded extractor rod with uniform diameter, barrel marked ".45 CAL MODEL 1950", checkered magna-type diamond walnut stocks or smooth rosewood target stocks, S serial prefix with s/n range S76212-S211000 with 2,768 reportedly mfg. February 1950-1961.

$7,200	$4,500	$4,150	$3,500	$3,150	$2,550	$2,150	$1,650	$1,125	$850	$650	$525

Add 300% for .45 Colt cal. Must letter to determine if factory.
Eight original 5 inch models made. Must letter to determine if factory.

200 were chambered in .45 Colt over several years of production.

.45 ACP cal. with tapered barrel became the Model 26. Earliest production may lack caliber marking on the side of barrel.

GRADING - PPGS™	100%	98%	95%	90%	80%	70%	60%	LAST MSR

THE 1955 .45 TARGET MODEL (HEAVY BARREL) "PRE-MODEL 25" – .45 ACP cal., introduced March 1955, double action revolver built on the square butt N target frame with 5 screws having a 6 1/2 in. pinned barrel. Heavy barrel version of the 1950 Target Model with .500 in. target hammer and .500 in. target trigger, target stocks, shrouded barrel marked "45 CAL. MODEL 1955", supplied with half-moon clips, Patridge front sight with Micrometer click rear sight, S serial prefix, designated the Model 25 in 1957. Serial number range is S143XXX to S333454, and continued with the N serial prefix in 1969. Approximately 1000 units with barrels marked ".45 Caliber Model of 1950" during 1976. Mfg. circa 1955-1992.

$3,000	$2,650	$2,250	$1,800	$1,500	$1,195	$850	

Nine original 5 inch models made - must letter to determine if factory.

GRADING - PPGS™	100%	98%	95%	90%	80%	70%	60%	LAST MSR

REVOLVERS: NUMBERED MODEL/RECENT MFG. (MODERN HAND EJECTORS)

Smith & Wesson handguns manufactured after 1957 are stamped with a model number on the frame under the cylinder yoke. The number is visible when the cylinder is open. All revolvers manufactured by S&W from 1946-1956 were produced without model numbers.

To locate a particular revolver in the following section, simply swing the cylinder out to the loading position and read the model number inside the yoke. The designation Mod. and a two- or three-digit number followed by a dash and another number designates which engineering change was underway when the gun was manufactured. Hence, a Mod. 15-7 is a Model 15 in its 7th engineering change (and should be indicated as such when ordering parts). Usually, earlier variations are the most desirable to collectors unless a particular improvement is rare.

Some models might have a few engineering changes listed, and that's because their values are different. However, if engineering changes are not listed individually, it means that the values are the same as for those without. Hence a Model 19-6 (.357 Combat Magnum) that's not listed simply means that its value is the same as an earlier variation, in this case, the Model 19-3.

Beginning 1994, S&W started providing synthetic grips and a drilled/tapped receiver for scope mounting on certain models.

S&W revolvers are generally categorized by frame size. Frame sizes are as follows: J-frame (small), K-frame (medium), L-frame (medium), N-frame (large), and X-frame (extra large). All currently manufactured S&W revolvers chambered for .38 S&W Spl. cal. will also accept +P rated ammunition.

Current S&W abbreviations for revolver feature codes used on its price sheets and literature are as follows: Grips: CTG - Crimson Trace laser grips, RG - rubber grips, WG - wood grips. Sights: R/ADJ - adjustable, R/ADJV - adjustable V-notch, R/BB - black blade, R/FIXED - fixed, R/FO - fiber optic, R/NS - night sight, R/SN -square notch, R/WO - white outline, F/DWD - dovetail white dot, F/INTCH - interchangeable front, FIX - fixed, F/FO - fiber optic, F/GB - gold bead front, F/BB - black blade, F/INTEG - integral front, F/PAT - Patridge front, F/NS - night sight, F/RR - red ramp front, SN - square notch, F/WB - white bead, and WO - white outline. Frame Material: AL - alloy, SS - stainless, CS - carbon steel. Frame Sizes: SM - Small/Compact, MD - Medium, LG - Large, XL - Extra Large. Older finish abbreviations include: ZB - Blue/Black, ZC - Clear Cote, ZG - Grey, ZM - Matte, ZS - Satin. Cylinder: CA - alloy, CC - carbon, CS - stainless, CT - titanium. Barrel: BF - full lug, BO - one piece, BP - PowerPort, BT - traditional, B2 - two piece. Action: DAO - double action only, SA/DA - single action/double action. Older finish abbreviations include: ZB - Blue/Black, ZC - Clear Cote, ZG - Grey, ZM - Matte, ZS - Satin. Cylinder: CA - alloy, CC - carbon, CS - stainless, CT - titanium.

Pre-2010 S&W abbreviations for revolver feature codes used on its price sheets and literature are as follows: Grips: GC - Crimson Trace laser grips, GR - rubber grips, GW - wood grips, GF - finger groove grips. Sights: SA - adj., SB - black blade front, SC - interchangeable front, SF - fixed, SG - gold bead front, SH - Hi-Viz, SI - integral front, SP - Patridge front, SN - front night, SR - red ramp front, SW - white outline adj. rear. Frame Material: FA - alloy, FS - stainless, FC - carbon.

During 2009, S&W started manufacture of the Classic Firearms series of revolvers. These guns incorporate many features of S&W's older and most famous/collectible revolvers, but have also been enhanced with modern engineering changes. This series is referred to as Classic or Classics in the model nomenclature, as opposed to Classic which indicates standard production S&W models and nomenclature.

Add 15%-20% for those models listed that are pinned and recessed (pre-1981 mfg.), if in 90% or better condition, or 10%-15% if condition is 60%-80%.

Add 20%-35% for no-dash models if in 95% or better original condition. Earlier mfg. on the following models with lower engineering change numbered suffixes are more desirable than later mfg. (i.e., a Model 10-1 is more desirable than a Model 10-14).

Factory error stamped revolvers generally bring a small premium (5%-10%, if in 95%+ original condition) over a non-error gun, if the right collector is found.

N/As listed instead of values in this section indicate the value in that condition factor is not available. Since asking prices do fluctuate greatly in these higher condition factors, it is impossible to accurately ascertain a single value.

M&P BODYGUARD 38 (MODEL BG38) – .38 Spl. + P cal., DAO, small J-frame, 1.9 in. stainless steel barrel, 5 shot, steel reinforced polymer lower frame, aluminum alloy upper frame, stainless steel cylinder, internal hammer, fixed sights, with or w/o (new 2019) Crimson Trace Integrated red laser module next to cylinder latch behind the recoil shield and activated with thumb, round butt, integrated black or gray polymer grips, matte black finish, 14.3 oz. New late 2010.

MSR $414	$350	$300	$265	$240	$195	$160	$135

Add $125 for Crimson Trace integrated red laser.

GRADING - PPGS™	100%	98%	95%	90%	80%	70%	60%	LAST MSR

GOVERNOR – .45 LC/.410 shotshell or .45 ACP/.410 shotshell, 2 1/2 in. shotshell, SA/DA, new Z-frame, 2 3/4 in. stainless steel barrel, 6 shot, black blade or Tritium front night sight, fixed rear sight, Scandium alloy frame with stainless steel PVD cylinder, matte black finish, black synthetic finger groove or Crimson Trace Lasergrips (disc. 2020), 29.6-30.3 oz. New 2011.

MSR $885	$760	$700	$625	$550	$475	$395	$325	

Add $250 for Crimson Trace Lasergrips (disc. 2020).

* ***Governor Stainless*** – .45 Colt, .45 ACP, or .410 shotshell, SA/DA, Scandium Alloy frame, 2.75 in. stainless steel barrel, stainless steel cylinder, black ramp front and fixed rear sights, black synthetic grips, matte silver frame finish, 30.3 oz. New 2014.

MSR $825	$710	$650	$575	$495	$425	$350	$275	

MOUNTAIN GUN VARIATIONS – .357 Mag., .41 Mag., .44 Mag., .45 ACP, .45 LC cal., DA, N-frame, 4 in. tapered barrel with or w/o porting, blued steel or stainless steel, smooth combat trigger, fixed front with adj. rear sight, with or w/o finger groove wood or rubber grips, the Mountain Gun commonly refers to a 4 in. barrel configuration (various models), approx. 35-40 oz. Circa 1989-2005.

Model 25	$900	$750	$650	$575	$475	$375	$300	
Model 29	$1,100	$900	$750	$650	$525	$425	$325	
Model 57	$950	$850	$725	$650	$525	$425	$325	
Model 625 (.45 ACP)	$1,100	$950	$825	$750	$625	$495	$395	
Model 625 (.45 LC)	$950	$850	$725	$650	$525	$425	$325	
Model 629	$1,000	$875	$750	$675	$550	$450	$350	
Model 657	$1,000	$875	$750	$675	$550	$450	$350	
Model 686	$850	$750	$575	$425	$350	$300	$275	
Model 686 Plus (ported)	$1,100	$950	$825	$750	$625	$495	$395	

S&W started offering the Mountain Gun configuration in 1989. These various Mountain Gun models were never included in the annual master price lists, but were usually introduced as mid-year releases. These variations were typically limited production, and quantities for each model are unknown.

MODEL 10 (.38 M&P POST-WWII) – .38 Spl. +P cal., 6 shot, K-frame, round or square butt (4 in. barrel only starting 1992), fixed sights, 2 (disc. 1996), 3 (disc.), 4 (standard - disc. or heavy), 5 (disc.), or 6 (disc.) in. barrels, utilizes Uncle Mike's combat grips, 36 oz. Dozens of variations. Disc. 2010.

	$695	$550	$450	$375	$335	$295	$250	*$814*

Add $12 for nickel finish (disc. 1991, 4 in. barrel only).

The Model 10 is currently available in 4 in. heavy barrel only (a 4 in. heavy barrel nickel square butt variation was disc. in 1992).

To date, there have been 14 engineering changes in this model.

MODEL 10 CLASSIC – .38 S&W Spl. +P cal., K-frame, 4 in. barrel, 6 shot, carbon steel frame/cylinder, checkered wood grips, fixed sights, blue finish, internal lock, approx. 36 oz. New 2010.

MSR $772	$660	$575	$495	$445	$365	$295	$235	

MODEL 11 (.38/200 M&P) – .38 S&W cal. only, similar to Model 10, limited production, as most were made for British Commonwealth countries. Mfg. 1938-1965.

	$2,125	$1,275	$1,075	$925	$650	$525	$475	

Add 100% for 6 in. barrel.

There were 4 engineering changes in this model.

MODEL 12 (.38 M&P AIRWEIGHT) – similar to Model 10, except alloy frame, steel cylinder, 2 or 4 in. barrel. Disc. 1986.

	$950	$850	$725	$650	$525	$425	$325	*$320*

Add $40 for nickel finish (disc.).
Add 50% for version 12-4.

There were 4 engineering changes in this model.

One known in 6 in. with factory letter.

MODEL 13 (.357 MAG. M&P) – .357 Mag. cal., K-frame, 6 shot, fixed sights, 3 (round butt, disc. 1996) or 4 (square butt) in. heavy barrel. Mfg. 1974-1998.

	$725	$675	$600	$525	$475	$385	$285	*$411*

Add $20 for nickel finish (disc. 1986).

There were 5 engineering changes in this model.

GRADING - PPGS™	100%	98%	95%	90%	80%	70%	60%	LAST MSR

* ***Model 13 M & P - N.Y. State Police*** - .357 Mag. cal., K-frame, 4 in. barrel, blue, fixed sights, 1,200 were mfg. for the N.Y. State Police and are marked 10-6. All 1,200 were recalled by S&W and exchanged for Model 28s.

$925	$850	$725	$625	$500	$400	$300	

MODEL 14 (K-38 TARGET MASTERPIECE) - .38 Spl. cal., K-frame, 6 or 8 3/8 (new 1959) in. barrel, target model, blue only. Mfg. 1947-1981.

$1,250	$1,050	$925	$750	$575	$450	$350	

Add $100 for single action.
There were 4 engineering changes on this model.

MODEL 14 K-38 FULL-LUG - .38 Spl. cal., 6 in. full lug barrel, K-frame, adj. rear sight, combat style Morado wood square butt grips, blue finish, 47 oz. Mfg. 1991-1999. Scarce.

$1,800	$800	$625	$500	$400	$350	$300	*$498*

There were 3 engineering changes on this model.

MODEL 14 CLASSIC (RECENT MFG.) - .38 S&W Spl. +P cal., blue or nickel (disc. 2010) finish, 6 in. barrel, 6 shot, SA/DA, medium frame, wood grips, adj. rear sight, Patridge front sight, internal lock. Mfg. 2009-2011.

$695	$550	$450	$375	$335	$295	$250	*$909*

Add $79 for nickel finish (disc. 2010).

MODEL 15 (K-38 COMBAT MASTERPIECE) - .38 Spl. cal., adj. sights, K-frame, 6 shot, square butt, 2 (disc.), 4, 6 (mfg. 1986-91), or 8 3/8 (new 1986, disc.) in. barrel. Disc. 1999.

$725	$675	$600	$525	$475	$385	$285	*$450*

Add $31 for TT or TH (disc. 1991).
Add $11 for 8 3/8 in. barrel (disc.).
Add $20 for nickel finish (disc. 1987).
Add 300% for USAF marked (mfg. 1965).
There were 9 engineering changes on this model.

MODEL 15 CLASSIC (RECENT MFG.) - .38 S&W Spl. +P cal., blue finish, 4 in. barrel, 6 shot, SA/DA, medium carbon frame, wood grips, adj. rear sight, Patridge front sight, internal lock. Mfg. 2010-2011.

$780	$560	$350	$300	$265	$240	$220	*$919*

MODEL 16 (K-32 MASTERPIECE) - .32 S&W Long cal., K-frame, 6 shot, 6 in. barrel, adj. sights, checkered walnut grips, blue finish. Only 3,630 mfg. 1947-1974.

N/A	$3,125	$2,750	$1,825	$1,525	$1,250	$1,000	

There were 3 engineering changes to this model.

MODEL 16-4 MASTERPIECE (FULL LUG) - .32 H&R Mag. cal., K-frame, 6 shot, 4 (mfg. 1990-91 only), 6, or 8 3/8 (disc. 1991) in. full lug barrel, square butt, blue finish only, TH, TT. Mfg. 1990-1992.

$2,500	$1,850	$1,650	$1,200	$950	$850	$750	*$419*

Add 5%-10% for 8 3/8 in. barrel.

MODEL 17 (K-22 MASTERPIECE) - .22 LR cal., K-frame, blue only, 6 shot, 4 (mfg. 1986-1993), 6, or 8 3/8 (disc. 1992) in. barrel. Disc. 1993, reintroduced 1996-1998.

$925	$850	$725	$625	$500	$400	$300	*$508*

Add 25% for 17-1 variation.
Add 25% for 8 3/8 in. barrel.
Add 50% for factory nickel finish.
There were 5 engineering changes to this model.

MODEL 17 FULL LUG - .22 LR cal., 6 (mfg. 1990-95) or 10 (mfg. 1996-99) shot, 4, 6, or 8 3/8 in. full lug barrel, steel (6 shot) or alloy (10 shot) cylinder.

$1,200	$800	$650	$500	$375	$400	$280	

Add $39 for full lug 6 in. barrel (w/TT & TH, disc.).
Add $100 for full lug 4 in. and 8 3/8 in. barrel (w/TT & TH, disc. 1992).
There were 3 engineering changes to this model.

MODEL 17-2 PROTOTYPE MERCOX DART PROJECTILE GUN - .530 Dart Projectile, .22 Ramset blank gas generator, 12 in. barrel, blue finish only, 25 prototype units mfg. 1966 only.

$5,000	$4,500	$3,500	N/A	N/A	N/A	N/A	

Add $500 for handmade Safariland holster.
Add $100-$500 depending on variation of projectile (six known).

GRADING - PPGS™	100%	98%	95%	90%	80%	70%	60%	LAST MSR

MODEL 17 CLASSIC (CURRENT MFG.) - .22 LR cal., SA/DA, K-frame (medium), 6 in. carbon steel barrel, 6 shot, adj. rear sight, wood grips, part of S&W's Classic Firearms Series, blue finish, 40 oz. New 2009.

MSR $1,017	$865	$750	$650	$590	$500	$425	$350	

MODEL 18 (.22 COMBAT MASTERPIECE) - .22 LR cal., adj. rear sight, Baughman front sight, 4 in. barrel, blue only. Disc. 1985.

	$1,250	$1,050	$925	$750	$575	$450	$350	*$352*

Add $30 for TT and TH. Add $100 for 5 screw frame.

There were 4 engineering changes to this model. One model in nickel finish is known.

MODEL 18 CLASSIC (RECENT MFG.) - .22 LR cal., blue finish, 4 in. barrel, otherwise similar to Model 18, part of S&W's Classic Firearms Series, includes key lock, 37.6 oz. Mfg. 2009-2011.

	$695	$550	$450	$375	$335	$295	$250	*$919*

MODEL 19 - .357 Mag. cal., 4 in. barrel, 4 screw frame, bright blue or nickel finish.

Bright blue finish	N/A	$1,100	$950	$825	$700	$575	$450	
Nickel finish	N/A	$1,600	$1,375	$1,050	$875	$675	$550	

MODEL 19-1 - .357 Mag. cal., 4 in. barrel, 4 screw frame, stamped "MOD. 19-1" in the yoke cut, bright blue or nickel finish.

	N/A	$1,600	$1,375	$1,050	$875	$675	$550	

MODEL 19-2 - .357 Mag. cal., 2 1/2, 4, or 6 in. barrel, bright blue or nickel finish.

2 1/2, 4, or 6 in. barrel	N/A	$595	$425	$375	$245	$220	$195	
3 or 5 in. barrel (rare)	N/A	$4,000	$3,400	$2,800	$2,200	$1,600	$1,000	

MODEL 19-3 & LATER VARIATIONS (.357 COMBAT MAGNUM) - .357 Mag. cal., (some variations found in .38 Spl. cal.), K-frame, 2 1/2 in. (round butt, disc. 1998), 4 in. (square butt), or 6 in. (square butt, disc. 1996) barrel, adj. rear sight, synthetic grips became standard 1994, drilled/tapped receiver became standard 1994, bright blue or nickel (disc. 1992) finish. Disc. 1999.

	$725	$675	$600	$525	$475	$385	$285	*$457*

Add $9 for 4 in. or $14 for 6 in. (disc. 1996) barrel.
Add $35 for white outline rear sight (disc. 1994).
Add $20 for nickel finish - disc. 1991.
Add $60 for TS, TT, TH, RR, and WO - disc. 1991 (6 in. barrel only).

This model was supplied with a round butt on 2 1/2 in. barrel. The 2 1/2 and 6 in. barrels (blue finish) were disc. in 1991 along with the 4 and 6 in. nickel variations.

There were 8 engineering changes to this model.

MODEL 19 CLASSIC (CURRENT MFG.) - .357 Mag./.38 S&W Spl. +P cal., SA/DA, carbon steel medium frame, 4 1/4 in. stainless steel barrel, 6 shot, case colored hardened trigger and hammer, red ramp front sights, black blade adj. rear sights, custom wood grips, blue finish, classic style thumbpiece, 37.2 oz. New 2019.

MSR $863	$745	$685	$625	$550	$475	$395	$325	

MODEL 20 HEAVY DUTY (.38/44 HEAVY DUTY) - .38 Spl. cal., 6 shot, 4, 5, or 6 1/2 in. barrel lengths, N frame, fixed sights, walnut grips, blue or nickel, walnut grips. Mfg. 1930-1941 and reintroduced 1946 (with "S" prefix starting at serial 62930), became the Model 20 in 1957. (Model marked 20 is very scarce.)

.38/44 H.D. Pre-war	$1,950	$1,750	$1,500	$1,300	$1,075	$875	$700	
Pre-Model 20 (1950-57 mfg.)	$1,125	$975	$825	$700	$575	$500	$425	
Post-war (1958-1966 mfg.)	$2,250	$1,875	$1,600	$1,350	$1,100	$900	$750	

Add 40% for 6 1/2 in. barrel.

Early post-war models had pre-war long action (ser. range S62489-approx. S74000).

There were two engineering changes in this model.

MODEL 21 (.44 HAND EJECTOR FOURTH MODEL - MODEL OF 1950 MILITARY) - .44 S&W cal., 6 shot, 4, 5, or 6 1/2 in. (scarce) barrel, N frame, blue or nickel finish, features short action and redesigned hammer block, walnut grips, fixed sights, 1,200 mfg. scattered throughout serial range S75000-S263000. Mfg. 1950-1966.

	$2,950	$2,500	$2,000	$1,200	$950	$750	$600	

Add 50% for 6 1/2 in. (scarce to rare).
There were 3 engineering changes for this model.

GRADING - PPGS™	100%	98%	95%	90%	80%	70%	60%	LAST MSR

MODEL 21-4 "THUNDER RANCH SPECIAL" - .44 Spl. cal., 4 in. barrel, 24Kt. gold plated Thunder Ranch insignia, blue or nickel finish, round butt and key lock. Mfg. 2004-2006.

	$750	$675	$600	$525	$450	$375	$300	*$958*

MODEL 22 (.45 HAND EJECTOR MODEL OF 1950 MILITARY) - .45 Auto Rim (disc. 1966) or .45 ACP cal., same specifications as 1917 Army, 5 1/2 in. barrel with redesigned hammer block, short action, fixed sights. Approx. 1,200 mfg. 1950-1966. Model marked 22 is scarce.

	$2,800	$2,150	$1,850	$1,500	$1,250	$995	$750	

There were 2 engineering changes for this model from 1950-1966.

MODEL 22 CLASSIC - .45 ACP cal., 6 shot, N-frame, 4 or 5 1/2 in. barrel, case colored frame, blue or nickel finish, pinned half-moon service front sight, Altamont wood grips, lanyard ring, carbon steel frame and cylinder, key lock, 37.2 oz. Mfg. 2007-2010.

	$850	$750	$575	$425	$350	$300	$275	*$1,090*

Add $87 for nickel finish.
Add $182 for case colored frame.

MODEL 22 CLASSIC, MODEL OF 1917 - .45 ACP cal., large frame, 6 shot, 5 1/2 in. barrel, blue finish only, Altamont checkered wood grips, lanyard ring, key lock, 37.2 oz. Mfg. 2008-2012.

	$775	$650	$525	$465	$415	$375	$325	*$999*

MODEL 22-4 "THUNDER RANCH SPECIAL" - .45 ACP cal., 6 shot, 4 in. barrel, blue finish only, Altamont checkered wood grips, lanyard ring, square butt, key lock, 37.2 oz. Mfg. 2005-circa 2014.

	$875	$750	$625	$550	$450	$395	$350	*$999*

PRE-MODEL 23 - please refer to .38/44 Outdoorsman Model of 1950 in the Early Hand Ejectors section.

MODEL 23 (.38-44 OUTDOORSMAN) - .38 Spl. cal., similar to Model 20 in .38 Spl., except with rear adj. sight, blue only, featured ribbed 6 1/2 in. barrel standard (4 and 5 in. variations are rare). Mfg. 1946-1967.

Post-war (1946-49)	N/A	$1,550	$1,350	$1,150	$950	$775	$625	
Numbered Mod. 23	N/A	$2,250	$1,950	$1,700	$1,500	$1,250	$1,000	

Early post-war models had long action with barrel rib and micrometer sights (ser. range S62489-approx. S74000). There were 4,761 pre-war revolvers, 2,036 post-war transitional, and 6,039 styled after the 1950 model.

The "44" in this model's name refers to the size frame, not the caliber. This variation was designated the Model 23 after 1958.

There were 2 engineering changes for this model.

MODEL 24 (.44 HAND EJECTOR FOURTH MODEL - 1950 TARGET) - .44 Spl. cal., redesigned hammer, short action, 6 1/2 in. ribbed barrel standard, satin blue (standard), bright blue (optional), or nickel (optional) finish, micrometer rear sight, ser. no. range S75000 - S263000. 5,050 mfg. 1950-1966.

	$4,200	$2,850	$2,450	$2,000	$1,750	$1,350	$1,100	

Add 20% for bright blue.
Add 50% for 4 in. barrel.
Add 200% for 5 in. barrel.

There were 6 engineering changes for this model.

The "44" in this model's nomenclature refers to the frame size, not the caliber.

MODEL 24-3 REINTRODUCTION - .44 Spl. cal., 4 (2,625 mfg.), 5 (rare), 5 1/2 (rare), or 6 1/2 in. (4,875 mfg.) barrel, bright blue only, checkered Goncalo Alves target grips (without speedloader cutout), barrel and frame not pinned, 7,500 mfg. 1983-1984 only.

	$925	$850	$725	$625	$500	$400	$300	*$359*

This model's serialization is triple alpha - 4 numeric (i.e. ABC0123).

* ***Model 24 Lew Horton Special*** - .44 Spl. cal., 3 in. barrel, round butt, adj. rear sight, blue finish, includes special fitted holster. Mfg. 1983 only.

	$925	$850	$725	$625	$475	$375	$300	

Subtract 10% without holster.

MODEL 24-6 CLASSIC (RECENT MFG.) - .44 Spl. cal., N-frame, 3 (Lew Horton only) or 6 1/2 in. barrel, choice of blue or nickel (disc. 2009) finish, carbon steel frame and cylinder, square butt wood grips, key lock, 43 oz. Mfg. 2006-2012.

	$765	$640	$525	$465	$415	$375	$325	*$979*

Add $56 for nickel finish (6 1/2 in. barrel only, disc. 2009).

There have been three additional engineering changes in this model.

GRADING - PPGS™	100%	98%	95%	90%	80%	70%	60%	LAST MSR

MODEL 25 & VARIATIONS (1955 TARGET MODEL) - .45 ACP, .45 Auto Rim, or .45 LC (earlier mfg.) cal., N-frame, blue finish only, target grips, 4, 6 (later mfg.), 6 1/2 (earlier mfg.), or 8 3/8 (later mfg.) in. barrel, pinned and recessed variation was disc. in the middle of 25-5 mfg. (circa 1988). Disc. 1999.

.45 ACP or .45 Auto Rim	$1,250	$1,050	$925	$750	$575	$450	$350	
.45 LC cal.	N/A	$3,675	$3,150	$2,855	$2,310	$1,890	$1,470	*$347.*

Last MSR for Model 25-5 was $429 (disc. 1991).

Add $150 for 6 1/2 in. barrel (with pinned barrel, mfg. until 1982).
Add 5%-10% for 8 3/8 in. barrel.
Add 50% for early 4 screw.

After 1961, the Model 25 in .45 ACP cal. was designated Model 25-2, with trigger guard screw eliminated. Generally odd numbered dash numbers are chambered in .45 LC (3-5-7-9-11-13), while even numbers (2-4-6-8-10-12) are chambered in .45 ACP. There were 13 engineering changes in two calibers to this model.

MODEL 25-5 - .45 LC cal., N-frame, 4, 6, or 8 3/8 in. barrel, blue or nickel (no extra charge - disc. 1987) finish, target grips, pinned and recessed variation was disc. in the middle of 25-5 mfg. (circa 1988). Mfg. 1978-1991.

.45 LC cal.	$1,250	$1,050	$925	$750	$575	$450	$350	*$429*

Add 5%-10% for 8 3/8 in. barrel.

Generally odd numbered dash numbers are chambered in .45 LC (3-5-7-9-11-13), while even numbers (2-4-6-8-10-12) are chambered in .45 ACP. There were 13 engineering changes in two calibers to this model.

MODEL 25 CLASSIC (CURRENT MFG.) - .45 ACP or .45 LC cal., 6 shot, N-frame, 3 (Lew Horton) or 6 1/2 in. barrel, blue or nickel (disc. 2010) finish, square butt wood grips, carbon steel frame and cylinder, red ramp front sight, 45 oz. New 2008.

MSR $1,038	$885	$775	$675	$600	$525	$450	$375

Add $55 for nickel finish (6 1/2 in. barrel only), disc. 2010.

MODEL 26 (MODEL 1950 45 TARGET LIGHT BARREL) - .45 ACP cal., adj. rear sight, 4 (rare), 5 (rare) or 6 1/2 in. thin ribbed barrel, Patridge front sight, 2,768 mfg. 1950-1960.

	N/A	$4,000	$3,500	$2,750	$2,000	$1,500	$1,000

Model marked "Model 26" is very rare - extreme rarity factor precludes accurate pricing.

Model 26-1 mfg. for Georgia Highway Patrol.

MODEL 27 - .357 Mag. cal., N-frame, 3 1/2 (disc. 1977), 4 (disc. 1991), 5 (disc. 1977), 6, 6 1/2, or 8 3/8 (disc. 1991) in. barrel, blue or nickel (disc. 1987) finish. Disc. 1994.

4 screw	$1,400	$1,150	$995	$775	$595	$450	$350
3 screw	$850	$750	$575	$425	$350	$300	$275

Last MSR was $486.

Add 50% for 3 1/2 or 5 in. barrel.
Add $28 for white outline rear sight - (disc. 1991).
Add 10% for 8 3/8 in. barrel - (disc. 1991).

There were 7 engineering changes to this model.

* ***Model 27 3 1/2 and 5 in. barrel*** - mfg. 1991.

$1,200	$1,050	$900	$815	$650	$540	$425

MODEL 27 CLASSIC (CURRENT MFG.) - .357 Mag. or .38 Special +P cal., N-frame, 4 or 6 1/2 in. barrel, wood grips, blue or nickel (disc. 2010) finish. New 2008.

MSR $1,053	$895	$785	$675	$600	$525	$450	$375

Add $38 for 6 1/2 in. barrel.
Add approx. $65 for nickel finish (disc. 2010).

MODEL 28 HIGHWAY PATROLMAN - .357 Mag. cal., "Highway Patrol" utility model, dull blue or brushed nickel (very rare) finish, adj. rear sight, standard grips, blue only, 4 or 6 in. barrel, delete diamond grip in 1968. Change to "N" serial prefix in 1969. Mfg. 1957-1986.

1956-1961 mfg. 4 screw frames	$975	$875	$775	$675	$575	$475	$400
1961-1986 mfg. 3 screw frames	$700	$600	$500	$400	$295	$275	$250

Last MSR was $306.

Add $20 for Target stocks.
Add 30% for 5 screw variation (pre-Model 28).
Add 300% for brushed nickel finish (beware of fakes).

There were 3 engineering changes to this model. 28-1 change extractor rod. 28-2 eliminate trigger guard screw. 28-3 eliminate pinned barrel and recessed cylinder.

GRADING - PPGS™	100%	98%	95%	90%	80%	70%	60%	LAST MSR

MODEL 29 .44 MAGNUM (5 SCREW) – please refer to listing under Early Hand Ejectors, Named Models.

MODEL 29 .44 MAGNUM (4 SCREW) – .44 Mag. cal., 4 screw, can be discerned by 2 exposed screws on lower right sideplate (one is concealed by the right grip, and one in front of the trigger guard). Mfg. began 1957 after approx. ser. no. S172250 and was disc. 1961.

	100%	98%	95%	90%	80%	70%	60%	LAST MSR
	$3,000	$2,650	$2,000	$1,500	$1,000	$875	$775	
5 in. barrel (scarce, must letter)	$9,000	$6,500	$5,000	$3,500	$3,000	$2,500	$1,750	
5 in. barrel/nickel (14 known, must letter)	N/A	$9,500	$8,500	$6,500	$5,500	$4,500	$3,500	
5 1/2 in. (13 known, must letter)	$15,000	$12,000	$9,000	$7,500	$5,000	$4,000	$3,000	

Add 100% for nickel finish.

Approx. 300-400 .44 Magnums with a 5 in. barrel were manufactured between the Pre-Model 29 with a 4 screw frame, and the Model 29-2 with a 3 screw frame. Most models were primarily shipped from 1958-1963. Only one 5 in. barrel variation stamped MOD-29 has been documented.

It is recommended that all non-standard barrel lengths be documented by a factory letter when buying or selling.

There are 10 engineering changes to this model.

MODEL 29-1 & LATER VARIATIONS (3 & 4 SCREW) – .44 Mag. cal., 4, 6, 6 1/2, or 8 3/8 in. barrel, eliminated top screw on sideplate and screw in front of trigger guard. Disc. 1999.

Older .44 Magnum Pre-Model 29 mfg. (4 & 5 screw variations) will appear under the previous subheading: "EARLY HAND EJECTORS (NAMED MODELS)."

* ***Model 29-1*** – .44 Mag. cal., DA revolver, 4, 6 1/2, or 8 3/8 in. barrel, stamped "MOD. 29-1" in the yoke cut. Mfg. 1960-1962.

	100%	98%	95%	90%	80%	70%	60%	LAST MSR
	$5,500	$4,250	$3,500	$2,500	$2,000	$1,600	$1,200	

Rare variations of this model include a 4 screw frame, nickel finish (2 known to exist), and a 5 in. barrel (3 known to exist). Values range from $7,500-$12,000, if original condition is better than 95%.

Add $300 for correct box and tools.

* ***Model 29-2*** – .44 Mag. cal., DA revolver, 3 screw frame, 4, 6 (new 1979), 6 1/2, or 8 3/8 in. barrel, bright blue or nickel finish. Mfg. 1962-1982.

	100%	98%	95%	90%	80%	70%	60%	LAST MSR
S prefix ser. no. (1962-1969)	$2,200	$1,750	$1,325	$1,195	$975	$795	$625	
N prefix ser. no. (1970-1983)	$1,550	$1,250	$1,000	$825	$725	$625	$525	
5 in. barrel	N/A	$3,950	$3,400	$3,050	$2,500	$2,000	$1,575	

Add 10%-20% premium for 4 in. barrel.

The "S" serial number prefix was used on this model until 1969, at which time the law required a new numbering system, and the serial number prefix was changed to "N". The "S" prefix originally designated the additional hammer block safety.

Approx. 300-400 .44 Magnums with a 5 in. barrel were manufactured between the Pre-Model 29 with a 4 screw frame, and the Model 29-2 with a 3 screw frame. Most models were primarily shipped from 1958-1963.

One 5 1/2 in. variation in nickel finish is known.

* ***Model 29-3 & Higher Dash Numbers***

	100%	98%	95%	90%	80%	70%	60%	LAST MSR
	$900	$800	$650	$500	$465	$435	$400	*$574*

Add $25-$50 for 4 in. barrel.
Add 50% for 3 in. barrel.
Add $25 for nickel finish (disc. 1991).
Add $500 for combat grips with scope mount - disc. 1991 (8 3/8 in. barrel only - must have rings).

The Model 29 has had 10 engineering changes.

* ***Model 29-4 With Scope Mount*** – .44 Mag. cal., 8 3/8 in. barrel with factory broaching to accommodate S&W scope mounting system, .500" target hammer, .400" serrated target trigger, red ramp front sight with white outline rear sight, two scope rings and two mounting bases included, blue finish, 54.5 oz. 1,000 reported. Mfg. 1989 only.

Last MSR in 1989 was $504.

Current value range is $1,200-$2,200 if NIB.

GRADING - PPGS™	100%	98%	95%	90%	80%	70%	60%	LAST MSR

MODEL 29 CLASSIC SERIES (MFG. 1990-1994) – .44 Mag. cal., 5, 6 1/2, or 8 3/8 in. full lug barrel, blue only, round butt with Hogue conversion square butt grips, interchangeable front sight with only one included, white outline rear sight, frame is drilled and tapped to accept scope mounts, blue finish only. Mfg. 1991-1994.

	$1,250	$975	$850	$650	$500	$450	$400	*$591*

Add $25 for 8 3/8 in. barrel.
Add $100 for 5 in. barrel.

* ***Model 29 Classic DX (Mfg. 1991-1992)*** – similar to Model 29 Classic, except supplied with 2 sets of grips, 5, 6 1/2 or 8 3/8 in. barrel, 5 interchangeable front sights included, numbered test target, 51-54 oz. Mfg. 1991-1992.

	$1,500	$1,200	$850	$650	$550	$475	$425

Add $250 for 5 in. barrel.

MODEL 29 CLASSIC (CURRENT MFG.) – .44 Mag. or .44 Spl. cal., N-frame, 6 shot, 3 (Lew Horton), 4 (Talo exclusive first year, blue finish only), or 6 1/2 in. barrel, Altamont walnut (6 1/2 in. only), square butt wood (3 in. only), or custom Hogue Monogrip (4 in. only), adj. white outline rear sight, black or red ramp front sight, blue or nickel (disc. 2012) finish, key lock, 39.3-48 1/2 oz. New 2008.

MSR $1,031	$875	$775	$675	$595	$525	$450	$375

Add $169 for 6 1/2 in. barrel.
Add $158 for machine engraving and wooden mahogany presentation case (4 in. barrel only, new 2010).

MODEL 29 SILHOUETTE – .44 Mag. cal., 10 5/8 in. barrel, adj. front and rear sights, bright blue only, Goncalo Alves target stocks. Mfg. 1983-1991.

	$1,650	$1,300	$1,000	$750	$600	$500	$400	*$536*

Add $100 for N prefix serial number.
Add $250 for original presentation case.
Rarely seen with frame stamped 29-2 - add 50%.

MODEL 29 MAGNA CLASSIC – .44 Mag. cal., 7 1/2 in. full lug barrel, high polish bright bluing, round butt, interchangeable front sight, supplied with cherry wood display case mfg. in England, 1,200 mfg. in 1990 only.

	$1,500	$900	$800	$625	$500	$450	$395	*$999*

MODEL 29 CLASSIC HUNTER – .44 Mag. cal., 6 in. barrel with full-length barrel lug, non-fluted cylinder, Hogue grips, four position adj. front sight. Mfg. 1987 only.

	$1,250	$750	$550	$450	$400	$350	$300

5,000 of these were manufactured especially for Lew Horton.

MODEL 29 50TH ANNIVERSARY – .44 Mag. cal., N-frame, blue finish, 6 1/2 in. barrel, 6 shot, 24Kt. gold anniversary logo medallion on rear frame signifying 50th anniversary, checkered African cocobolo grips, red ramp front sight, adj. white outline rear sight, includes mahogany presentation case. Limited mfg. 2006.

	$1,450	$950	$825	N/A	N/A	N/A	N/A
Factory Engraved	$5,800	$3,800	$3,300	N/A	N/A	N/A	N/A

Last MSR was $1,129 (non-engraved).

There were only 50 factory engraved revolvers in this model.

MODEL 29 STATE QUARTER LIMITED EDITION COLLECTORS SERIES – .44 Mag. cal., N-frame, 6 1/2 in. barrel, gold bead front sight, Altamont bonded ivory grips, Class "A" engraving, 24Kt. gold cylinder bands and barrel bands, image of state quarter inlaid in 24Kt. gold on side plate, includes black walnut glass top presentation case, state coin collector's quarter, a roll of uncirculated state quarters and letter of authenticity.

S&W released these guns through Ellett Brothers circa 2006. While a series of 100 revolvers (2 per state) were planned, only 14 were actually completed. Each gun should be evaluated individually when determining value.

MODEL 30 (THE 32 HAND EJECTOR) – .32 S&W Long cal., improved I-frame and J-frame, 6 shot, 2, 3, 3 1/4, 4, 4 1/4, or 6 in. barrel, round or square butt, walnut grips, fixed sights, blue or nickel finish. H serial prefix starts in 1969. Mfg. 1948-1976.

	$695	$550	$450	$375	$335	$295	$250

There was one engineering change to this model.

GRADING - PPGS™	100%	98%	95%	90%	80%	70%	60%	LAST MSR

MODEL 31 (THE 32 REGULATION POLICE) - .32 S&W Long cal., improved I-frame and J-frame, fixed sights, 2, 3, 3 1/4, 4, or 4 1/4 in. barrel, square butt, blue or nickel only. H serial prefix starts in 1969. Mfg. 1948-1991.

$695 $550 $450 $375 $335 $295 $250 *$365*

Add 25% for early flatlatch models.

There were 3 engineering changes to this model.

MODEL 32 (.38/32 TERRIER) - .38 S&W cal., 5 shot, 2 in. barrel, improved I-frame and J-frame, walnut or rubber grips, blue or nickel, round butt, fixed sights, built on .32 cal. frame. R serial prefix starts in 1969. Mfg. 1948-1974.

$750 $695 $625 $550 $475 $395 $325

Add $300 for 5 screw frame.

There was one engineering change to this model.

MODEL 032 - .32 Mag. cal., 6 shot, alloy J-frame, 2 in. barrel, blue, scarce, mfg. 1992 only.

$1,250 $1,050 $925 $750 $575 $450 $350

MODEL 33 (.38 REGULATION POLICE) - .38 S&W cal., 5 shot, 4 in. barrel, square butt, walnut grips, fixed sights, blue or nickel finish, I-frame, improved I-frame and J-frame. R serial prefix starts in 1969. Mfg. 1953-1974.

$725 $675 $600 $525 $475 $385 $285

There was one engineering change to this model.

MODEL 34 (MODEL OF 1953 22/32 KIT GUN) - .22 LR cal., adj. sights in J-frame, improved I-frame and J-frame, 6 shot, 2 or 4 in. barrel, round or square butt, blue or nickel (disc. 1986) finish, "M" serial prefix starts in 1969. Mfg. 1953-1991.

$900 $750 $600 $500 $350 $300 $275 *$366*

Add $100 for nickel finish.

Add 25% for early flatlatch models.

There were 2 engineering changes to this model.

MODEL 35 (.22/32 TARGET MODEL OF 1953) - .22 LR cal., micrometer rear sight, 6 shot, 6 in. barrel, improved I and J-frame, target grips on square butt frame, M serial prefix starts 1969. Mfg. 1953-1973.

$1,500 $1,100 $850 $700 $500 $450 $400

There was one engineering change to this model.

MODEL 36 CHIEFS SPECIAL CLASSIC (.38 CHIEFS SPECIAL) - .38 Spl. cal., 5 shot, J-frame, round or square (disc. 1991) butt, 1 7/8 in. regular or 3 in. (heavy only, disc. 1994, reintroduced 2008-2009) barrel, case colored frame (mfg. 2008-2009), blue or nickel (disc. 1992, reintroduced 2008-2012) finish, 19 1/2 oz. Disc. 1999, reintroduced 2008 as part of S&W's Classic Firearms series. Later production rated for +P when built on J Magnum frame in 1996.

MSR $789 $675 $585 $500 $450 $365 $300 $260

Add $20 for nickel finish (disc. 2012).

Add $20 for 3 in. barrel (disc. 2010).

Add $158 for case colored frame (mfg. 2008-2009).

Add 100% for early small trigger guard and grips (below ser. no. 2,500).

Add 400% for half moon front sight.

Note: 1st models with high polish blue and diamond grips will bring premiums when mint in original box.

There were 10 engineering changes to this model through 2007.

MODEL 36 TARGET - .38 Spl. cal., 5 shot, J-frame, 2 in. barrel, square butt, usually marked 36-1 with target sights, mfg. started 1955. Also see Model 50.

$1,375 $1,000 $875 $600 $500 $400 $350

MODEL 36-6 TARGET - .38 Spl. cal., 5 shot, J-frame, 3 in. full lug barrel, square butt, target sights, blue finish. Approx. 615 were mfg. in 1989.

$925 $850 $575 $500 $400 $350 $300

MODEL 36 LADYSMITH (36LS) - .38 Spl. +P cal., 5 shot, J-frame, 1 7/8 in. standard or 3 (disc. 1991) in. standard or heavy barrel, blue finish only, Combat Dymondwood grips are anatomically designed for women (round butt on 1 7/8 in., wood combat grips on 3 in.), fixed sights, redesigned double action, 20-23 oz., Morocco grained (disc. 1991) or soft side jewelry case. Rated for +P in 1997 on J Magnum frame. Mfg. 1990-2008.

$675 $550 $485 $350 $185 $180 $175 *$672*

GRADING - PPGS™	100%	98%	95%	90%	80%	70%	60%	LAST MSR

MODEL 37 CHIEFS SPECIAL AIRWEIGHT – .38 Spl. cal., 5 shot, J-frame, similar to Model 36 Chiefs Special, except alloy frame and 1 7/8 or 3 (disc. 1988) in. barrel, J-frame, blue or nickel (disc. 1995) finish, barrels are marked "Airweight", no internal lock, 15 oz. Rated for +P in 1997 on J Magnum frame.

	100%	98%	95%	90%	80%	70%	60%	LAST MSR
	$725	$675	$600	$525	$475	$385	$285	*$602*

Add $16 for nickel finish (disc.).

There were 3 engineering changes to this model.

MODEL 38 BODYGUARD AIRWEIGHT – .38 S&W Spl. cal., 5 shot, alloy frame, round butt, shrouded hammer, 2 or 3 (very rare) in. barrel, blue or nickel (disc. 1996) finish. Mfg. 1955-1999. Rated for +P in 1997 on J Magnum frame.

	100%	98%	95%	90%	80%	70%	60%	LAST MSR
	$625	$500	$425	$350	$325	$295	$250	*$462*

Add $15 for nickel finish (disc. 1996).

There were 3 engineering changes for this model.

MODEL 40 CENTENNIAL/CENTENNIAL CLASSIC – .38 S&W Spl. cal., 1 7/8 (new 2008) or 2 (disc. 1974) in. barrel, double action only, fully concealed hammer, grip safety, smooth walnut grips, case colored frame, blue or nickel finish. Mfg. 1952-1974 (non-Classic), reintroduced 2007-2012 as the 40-1 Classic in .38 Spl. +P with a case colored frame or blue or nickel finish.

	100%	98%	95%	90%	80%	70%	60%	LAST MSR
	$645	$535	$425	$350	$315	$275	$235	*$877*

Add $32 for nickel finish.
Add $174 for case colored frame (disc. 2009).

This model commands a premium for the first series with no letter prefix. After 1968, "L" prefix series began. One engineering change.

MODEL 42 CENTENNIAL AIRWEIGHT – .38 S&W Spl. cal., aluminum variation of Model 40 Centennial, mfg. 1953-1974. Reintroduced 2009-2012 as the 42-1 Classic in .38 Spl. +P.

	100%	98%	95%	90%	80%	70%	60%	LAST MSR
Blue	$825	$725	$550	$400	$325	$285	$265	
Nickel	$1,250	$1,100	$950	$875	$775	$675	$550	

This model commands a premium for the first series with no letter prefix. After 1968, "L" prefix series began.

37 were mfg. with alloy cylinder. One engineering change.

MODEL 42 CLASSIC (RECENT MFG.) – .38 Spl. +P cal., 5 shot, aluminum alloy J Magna frame, 1 7/8 in. barrel, blue finish, grip safety lever, DAO, integral black ramp front sight, fixed rear sight, walnut grips, 14.4 oz. Mfg. mid-2009-2010. Model 42-1.

	100%	98%	95%	90%	80%	70%	60%	LAST MSR
	$635	$500	$425	$350	$325	$295	$250	*$861*

MODEL 042 – .38 Spl. cal., 5 shot, blue finish, alloy frame. Approx. 4,400 mfg. 1992 only.

	100%	98%	95%	90%	80%	70%	60%	LAST MSR
	$825	$725	$550	$400	$325	$285	$265	

MODEL 43 (.22/32 KIT GUN AIRWEIGHT) – .22 LR cal., 3 1/2 in. barrel, round or square butt, adj. sights, aluminum frame and cylinder, not Airweight marked. Mfg. 1955-1974.

	100%	98%	95%	90%	80%	70%	60%	LAST MSR
	$1,200	$950	$700	$500	$400	$300	$250	

Add 100% for factory nickel finish (rare).
Add 200% for factory 2 in. barrel.

MODEL 43C CENTENNIAL – .22 LR cal., 1 7/8 in. barrel, alloy J-frame, blue finish, 8 shot, internal hammer, DAO, rubber grips, fixed rear sight, white bead front sight, no internal key lock, 11 oz. New 2010.

	100%	98%	95%	90%	80%	70%	60%	LAST MSR
MSR $709	$600	$525	$450	$410	$325	$275	$225	

MODEL 45 (.22 MILITARY & POLICE) – .22 LR cal. only, originally mfg. as training gun, 4 or 6 (scarce) in. barrel, fixed sights, not cataloged. Mfg. 1948-1978.

	100%	98%	95%	90%	80%	70%	60%	LAST MSR
	$3,200	$2,850	$2,150	$1,750	$1,250	$975	$775	

Add 50% for 6 in. barrel.

There were 3 engineering changes to this model.

MODEL 48 (K-22 MRF MASTERPIECE) – .22 MRF (.22 WMR) cal., 4, 6 or 8 3/8 in. barrel, blue only, auxilary .22 LR cylinder optional, Patridge front sight. Mfg. 1959-1986.

	100%	98%	95%	90%	80%	70%	60%	LAST MSR
	$1,500	$1,200	$850	$650	$550	$475	$425	*$320*

Add $100 for 8 3/8 in. barrel.
Add $50 for TT, TH, and TS (disc.).
Add $200 for 4 screw frame.

There were 5 engineering changes to this model.

GRADING - PPGS™	100%	98%	95%	90%	80%	70%	60%	LAST MSR

MODEL 48 CLASSIC (CURRENT MFG.) – .22 MRF (.22 WMR) cal., K frame, 4 or 6 in. barrel, blue finish, wood grips, adj. rear sight, Patridge front sight, carbon steel frame/cylinder, key lock, approx. 38 oz. New 2010.

MSR $976	$830	$725	$625	$565	$455	$375	$325	

Add $41 for 6 in. barrel.

MODEL 49 BODYGUARD – similar to Model 38, only steel frame, 2 in. barrel, blue or nickel (disc.) finish. Mfg. 1959-1996.

	$450	$350	$300	$250	$225	$200	$175	*$409*

Add $25 for nickel finish (disc.).
There were 3 engineering changes to this model.

MODEL 50 (.38 CHIEFS SPECIAL TARGET) – .38 S&W Spl. cal., Chiefs Special Target, mfg. from 1955 in 2 in. (see Model 36 Target listing and .38 Chiefs Special Target under Early Hand Ejectors) or 3 (211 mfg. beginning 1973) in. barrels, target sights, most were unmarked for model number, approx. 1,100 mfg. The other variation was designated Model 36 Target. Mfg. 1955-1975.

	$1,500	$1,200	$850	$650	$550	$475	$425	

The Model 50 designation was not used until 1970.

MODEL 51 – .22 MRF cal. only, variant of the .22/32 kit gun, 3 1/2 in. barrel, 6 shot, adj. rear sight, blue or nickel, square or round (rare) butt, walnut stocks. Mfg. 1960-1974.

	$1,250	$750	$550	$450	$400	$350	$300	

Add 100% for nickel.
Add 200%-300% for round butt.
Add $150 for extra .22 LR cylinder.

MODEL 53 .22 REM. JET – .22 Jet cal. with .22 S, L, or LR rimfire inserts, 6 shot, 4, 6, or 8 3/8 in. barrel, blue, walnut grips, adj. rear sight. Mfg. 1960-1974.

4 screw	$1,950	$1,650	$1,350	$950	$675	$575	$500	
3 screw (53-2)	$1,450	$1,050	$900	$700	$500	$450	$375	

Add 10% for 8 3/8 in. barrel.
Add 15% for 4 in. barrel.
Add $300 for extra matching .22 LR cylinder.
There was one engineering change to this model.

MODEL 56 "USAF" – .38 Spl. cal., 2 in. barrel marked "U.S." on smooth backstrap, non-serrated top strap or rear sight leaf. 15,205 mfg. 1963 only.

	N/A	$5,750	$5,000	$4,500	$3,500	$2,900	$2,200	

MODEL 57 – .41 Mag. cal., N-Target frame, 6 shot, 4 (disc. 1991), 5 (1 known, nickel finish), 6, or 8 3/8 (disc. 1991) in. barrel, blue or nickel finish, micrometer rear sight, special oversize Goncalo Alves grips, shrouded extractor rod, "S" ser. no. prefix 1964-1969, changed to "N" prefix during 1969, 44-52 oz. Mfg. 1964-1993.

N prefix ser. no.	$1,500	$1,200	$850	$650	$550	$475	$425	
S prefix ser. no.	N/A	$1,600	$1,375	$1,100	$800	$600	$450	

Last MSR was $466.

Add 25% for nickel finish.
Add 5% for 8 3/8 in. barrel.
Current value for the 5 in. barrel model is approx. $12,000.

There were 6 engineering changes to this model.

MODEL 57 CLASSIC (CURRENT MFG.) – .41 Mag. cal., N-frame, 4 (disc. 2010) or 6 in. barrel, blue or nickel (disc. 2010) finish, 6 shot, single action/double action, wood grips, adj. target sights, key lock, 48.1 oz. New 2009.

MSR $1,038	$885	$775	$675	$600	$525	$450	$375	

Add approx. $55 for nickel finish (disc. 2010).

MODEL 58 – .41 Mag cal., M&P, fixed sights, 4 in. barrel, blue or nickel finish. Mfg. 1964-1977.

	$1,100	$900	$875	$750	$575	$500	$400	

Add 10% for nickel finish or "S" serial number prefix.

MODEL 58 CLASSIC (RECENT MFG.) – .41 Mag. cal., 6 shot, SA/DA, bright blue or nickel (disc. 2010) finish, integral ramp front sight, fixed rear sight, wood grips, carbon steel frame/cylinder, key lock, 40.8 oz. Mfg. mid-2009-2011.

	$775	$650	$525	$465	$415	$375	$325	*$969*

Add $56 for nickel finish (disc. 2010).

GRADING - PPGS™	100%	98%	95%	90%	80%	70%	60%	LAST MSR

MODEL 60 .38 SPL. CHIEFS SPECIAL – .38 S&W Spl. cal., stainless version of Chiefs Special, 2 or 3 in. standard or full lug barrel, first stainless steel revolver mfg. by S&W. Mfg. 1965-1996.

	N/A	$500	$425	$375	$250	$150	$125	*$458*

Subtract $25 for 2 in. barrel.

Add 50% for early Model 60s without letter prefix and bright satin finish.

The full lug barrel option began in 1990 with limited mfg. It had been tested for +P ammo and features an adj. rear sight - 24 1/2 oz.

There were 18 engineering changes to the base model in two calibers.

MODEL 60 .357 MAG. CHIEFS SPECIAL – .357 Mag. or .38 Spl. +P cal., DA/SA, J-frame, 2 1/8, 3 (new 1997), or 5 (mfg. 2005-2008) in. barrel, 5 shot, stainless steel frame, barrel, and cylinder, exposed hammer, blade front and fixed rear sight, black blade front and adj. rear sight (3 in. full lug barrel, new 1997), or Hi-Viz (3 in. full lug only, disc.), round butt synthetic, Uncle Mike's Combat (disc.) or wood (5 in. barrel only, mfg. 2005-2008) grips, satin stainless finish, 21.4-23.2 oz. New 1996.

MSR $755	$635	$550	$475	$425	$350	$285	$250	

Add $31 for 3 in. full lug barrel with adj. rear sight - new 1997, choice of Hi-Viz (disc.) or black blade front sight.

Add $71 for 5 in. barrel (mfg. 2005-2008).

MODEL 60LS (LADYSMITH) – .38 S&W Spl. +P or .357 Mag. cal. (rated for +P in 2000), J-frame, DA/SA, stainless steel frame, barrel, and cylinder, 2 in. regular (disc. 1996), 2 1/8 (new 1997), or 3 in. heavy (disc. 1991) barrel, 5 shot, Combat Dymondwood grips are anatomically designed for women (round butt on 2 in., wood combat grips on 3 in.), fixed sights, Morocco grained (disc. 1991) or soft side jewelry case, matte stainless finish. New 1990.

MSR $786	$665	$580	$500	$450	$365	$300	$260	

MODEL 63 .22/32 KIT GUN – .22 LR cal., J-frame, stainless steel kit gun, 2 or 4 in. barrel, 19 oz. Disc. 1998.

	$1,000	$850	$750	$600	$500	$450	$400	*$476*

Add 50% for 2 in. barrel.

Add 10% for R prefix serial number.

There were 4 engineering changes to this model.

MODEL 63 (CURRENT MFG.) – .22 LR cal., SA/DA, J-frame, 3 or 5 (disc. 2009) in. stainless steel barrel, 8 shot, stainless steel frame and cylinder, adj. black blade rear sight, black ramp (disc. 2009) or HI-VIZ fiber optic red front sight (new 2010), black rubber grips with finger grooves, 24.8 oz. New 2008.

MSR $800	$680	$600	$500	$450	$375	$300	$265	

Add 10% for 5 in. barrel.

MODEL 64 – .38 Spl. +P cal., K-frame, satin stainless version of the Model 10, 6 shot, 2 (disc. 2005), 3 (square butt, disc. 1992) or 4 in. (square butt only) heavy barrels, Uncle Mike's combat grips, 30 1/2-36 oz. Disc. 2020.

	$585	$515	$445	$400	$350	$275	$225	*$693*

There have been 8 engineering changes to this model.

MODEL 65 – .357 Mag. cal., stainless version of Model 13, K-frame, has 3 (round butt, disc. 2000) or 4 (square butt) in. heavy barrels, satin stainless steel, recent production uses Uncle Mike's grips, fixed sights, 35 oz. Disc. 2004.

	N/A	$450	$400	$250	$200	$175	$150	*$563*

There have been 7 engineering changes to this model.

MODEL 65 LADYSMITH – .357 Mag. cal., K-frame, 3 in. barrel with round butt, glass beaded stainless finish, soft side jewelry case, smooth Dymondwood combat grips, 32 oz. Mfg. 1992-2004.

	$500	$400	$350	$275	$225	$200	$180	*$618*

MODEL 66 COMBAT MAGNUM – .357 Mag. cal., K-frame, satin stainless steel version of Model 19, has 2 1/2, 3 (disc., only 2,500 mfg.), 4, or 6 (disc.) in. barrel, recent production used Uncle Mike's Combat grips, 32-39 oz. Disc. 2004.

	N/A	$650	$525	$425	$375	$300	$235	*$614*

Add 10% for 2 1/2 in. barrel.

Add $29 for 6 in. barrel (disc.).

Add $48 for TH (target hammer) and TT (target trigger) with 4 (disc. 1991) or 6 in. barrel only (disc. 1999).

Note: Several variations of the Model 66 were made - such features as an all-stainless steel rear sight and a recessed cylinder will bring a slight premium if NIB. There were 6 engineering changes to this model.

GRADING - PPGS™	100%	98%	95%	90%	80%	70%	60%	LAST MSR

MODEL 66 COMBAT MAGNUM (CURRENT MFG.) – .357 Mag. or .38 Special+P cal., SA/DA, K-frame, 2 3/4 (new 2017) or 4 1/4 in. stainless steel two-piece barrel, 6 shot, stainless steel frame and cylinder, full length extractor rod, red ramp front and adj. black blade rear sight, black synthetic grips, matte stainless finish, 36.6 oz. New 2014.

MSR $874	$745	$685	$625	$550	$475	$395	$325	

MODEL 67 COMBAT MASTERPIECE – .38 S&W Spl. +P cal. (rated for +P in 2000), K-frame, satin stainless version of Model 15, has 4 in. barrel, current production uses Uncle Mike's Combat grips, 36 oz. Disc. 1988, reintroduced 1991-2020.

	$650	$575	$495	$445	$365	$295	$235	*$752*

1991 mfg. included square butt and red ramp front sight insert.

There have been 6 engineering changes to this model.

MODEL 68 – .38 S&W Spl. cal., similar in appearance to the Model 66, except is in .38 Spl. cal., 6 in. barrel, approx. 7,500 mfg.

	$1,250	$750	$550	$450	$400	$350	$300	

Add 30% for CHP markings.

This model was originally ordered by CA Highway Patrol (usually has "OHB" overstamp).

MODEL 69 COMBAT MAGNUM – .44 Mag. or .44 S&W Special cal., L-frame, 2 3/4 (new 2017) or 4 1/4 in. barrel, 5 shot, rubber grips, white outline rear and red ramp front sights, matte stainless steel. New 2014.

MSR $874	$745	$685	$625	$550	$475	$395	$325	

MODEL 73 – .38 Spl. cal., built on C-frame, 6 shot. 5,000 mfg.

A general price range for this model is $5,000-$10,000.

Most copies of this model were destroyed by S&W in 1973. S&W collectors believe approx. 4 examples have survived.

MODEL 242 AIRLITE Ti CENTENNIAL – .38 Spl. +P cal., L-frame, 7 shot, similar to Model 296, alloy frame, titanium cylinder, Uncle Mike's Boot grips. Mfg. 1990 only.

	$1,250	$1,050	$925	$750	$575	$450	$350	

MODEL 296 AIRLITE Ti CENTENNIAL – .44 S&W Spl. cal., L-frame, 5 shot, 2 1/2 in. barrel, similar to Model 242 in construction materials, alloy frame and titanium cylinder, Uncle Mike's Boot grips, 18.9 oz. Mfg. 1999-2002.

	$1,300	$1,100	$950	$775	$575	$450	$350	*$754*

MODEL 310 NIGHTGUARD – 10mm or .40 S&W cal., 2 1/2 in. barrel, matte black finish, Scandium alloy N-frame with stainless steel cylinder, 6 shot, SA/DA, XS 24/7 standard dot Tritium night front sight, fixed rear sight, Pachmayr grips, 28 oz. Mfg. 2009-2010.

	$1,350	$1,175	$975	$800	$600	$475	$375	*$1,185*

MODEL 315 NIGHTGUARD – .38 Spl. +P cal., 2 1/2 in. barrel, K-frame, blue/black finish, 6 shot, rubber grips, front night sight, fixed rear sight, alloy frame with stainless cylinder. Mfg. 2009 only. Scarce.

	$2,000	$1,750	$1,550	$1,100	$850	$650	$550	*$995*

MODEL 317 AIRLITE (KIT GUN) – .22 LR cal., DA/SA, J-frame, 1 7/8 or 3 (new 1998, Hi-Viz sights became standard in 2001, Model 317 Kit Gun) in. stainless steel barrel, 8 shot, aluminum alloy frame and cylinder, current mfg. has HI-VIZ fiber optic green front sight, adj. rear sight, round (Kit gun) or square butt, round butt black synthetic or Dymondwood Boot (disc. 1998) grips, brushed aluminum (disc.), clear coat (1 7/8 in., disc. 2012) or matte silver (3 in., new 1998) finish, 11.7 oz. New 1997.

MSR $786	$665	$580	$500	$450	$365	$300	$260	

Add $33 for Dymondwood Boot grips (disc.).

Add 25% for "ULT" serial prefix (first run).

There have been three engineering changes to this model.

* ***Model 317 Airlite LadySmith*** – .22 LR cal., 1 7/8 in. barrel only, includes Dymondwood Boot grips, 9.9 oz. Mfg. 1998-2002.

	$500	$440	$375	$340	$275	$225	$175	*$596*

MODEL 325 PD-AIRLITE Sc – .45 ACP cal., 2 1/2 (disc. 2006) or 4 in. barrel, otherwise similar to Model 329 PD, approx. 21 1/2 - 25 oz. Mfg. 2004-2007.

	$1,100	$950	$825	$750	$625	$495	$395	*$1,067*

GRADING - PPGS™	100%	98%	95%	90%	80%	70%	60%	LAST MSR

MODEL 325 NIGHTGUARD - .45 ACP cal., two-piece 2 1/2 in. barrel, alloy frame with stainless steel cylinder, black alloy finish, 6 shot, N-frame, SA/DA, rubber grips, fixed rear sight with front night sight, 28 oz. Mfg. 2008-2012.

	$1,100	$950	$825	$750	$625	$495	$395	*$1,049*

MODEL 327 PD-AIRLITE Sc - .357 Mag. cal., 8 shot, N-frame, 4 in. two-piece barrel, wood grips, Scandium frame with titanium cylinder, matte black finish, 26 1/2 oz. Mfg. 2008-2009.

	$950	$725	$550	$450	$350	$315	$285	*$1,264*

MODEL 327 NIGHTGUARD - .357 Mag. cal., two-piece 2 1/2 in. barrel, alloy frame with stainless steel cylinder, black alloy finish, 8 shot, N-frame, SA/DA, rubber grips, fixed rear sight with front night sight, 27.6 oz. Mfg. 2008-2012.

	$1,100	$950	$825	$750	$625	$495	$395	*$1,049*

MODEL 329 PD-AIRLITE Sc - .44 Mag./.44 Spl. cal., 4 in. barrel, N-frame, 6 shot, Scandium frame and titanium cylinder with matte black metal finish, wood Ahrends grips with finger grooves, and Hogue rubber Monogrip, Hi-Viz front sight, approx. 26 oz. New 2003.

MSR $1,179	$1,000	$875	$750	$680	$550	$455	$390

MODEL 329 XL HUNTER AIRLITE Sc - .44 Mag. or .44 Spl. cal., N-frame, SA/DA, 6 1/2 in. barrel, blue finish, rubber grips, fixed rear sight, fiber optic front sight. Mfg. 2010 only.

While cataloged with an MSR of $1,138, this model only made it to the prototype stage - only 5 mfg.

MODEL 329 NIGHTGUARD - .44 Mag. cal., two-piece 2 1/2 in. barrel, alloy frame with stainless steel cylinder, black alloy finish, 6 shot, N-frame, SA/DA, rubber grips, fixed rear sight with front night sight, 29.3 oz. Mfg. 2008-2012.

	$825	$650	$525	$425	$350	$300	$275	*$1,049*

MODEL 331 AIRLITE Ti CHIEFS SPECIAL - .32 H&R Mag. cal., J-frame, 6 shot, 1 7/8 in. barrel with stainless steel liner, features titanium cylinder and aluminum alloy frame, barrel shroud, and yoke, fixed sights, Uncle Mike's or Dymondwood Boot (disc.) wood grips, two-tone matte stainless/grey finish approx. 12 oz. Mfg. 1999-2003.

	$1,200	$1,000	$900	$725	$550	$425	$325	*$716*

Add $24 for Dymondwood Boot grips (mfg. 1999 only).

MODEL 332 AIRLITE Ti CENTENNIAL - .32 H&R Mag. cal., J-frame, similar to Model 331 Airlite Ti, except is hammerless and double action only, recent production used Uncle Mike's Boot grips, 12 oz. Mfg. 1999-2003.

	$1,200	$1,000	$900	$725	$550	$425	$325	*$734*

Add $24 for Dymondwood Boot grips (mfg. 1999 only).

MODEL 332 AIRWEIGHT CENTENNIAL - .32 H&R Mag. cal., J-frame, 6 shot, blue finish. Approx. 380 mfg., most exported during 1994 only.

	$2,000	$1,750	$1,550	$1,100	$850	$650	$550

MODEL 337 AIRLITE Ti CHIEFS SPECIAL - .38 S&W Spl. +P cal. (rated for +P in 2000), J-frame, 5 shot, 1 7/8 in. barrel, similar design as the Model 331, 11.9 oz. Mfg. 1999-2003.

	$675	$595	$500	$460	$370	$300	$235	*$716*

Add $24 for Dymondwood Boot grips (mfg. 1999 only).

MODEL 337 AIRLITE Ti KIT GUN - .38 S&W Spl. +P cal. (rated for +P in 2001), J-frame, 5 shot, 3 1/8 in. barrel with Hi-Viz front sight (new 2001), choice of Dymondwood or Uncle Mike's combat grips, approx. 13 oz. Mfg. 2000-2003.

	$850	$725	$650	$500	$465	$435	$400	*$779*

MODEL 337 PD AIRLITE Ti - .38 S&W Spl. +P cal., J-frame, 5 shot, 1 7/8 in. barrel, black/grey finish, black Hogue Bantam grips, "PD" marked, 10.7 oz. Mfg. 2000-2003.

	$700	$650	$575	$500	$450	$365	$265	*$740*

MODEL 340 AIRLITE Sc CENTENNIAL - .357 Mag. cal., J-frame, 5 shot, 1 7/8 in. barrel only, Scandium alloy frame, barrel shroud, and yoke, titanium cylinder, two-tone matte stainless/grey finish, hammerless, Hogue Bantam grips, 12 oz. Mfg. 2001-2008.

	$775	$575	$475	$400	$340	$295	$250	*$1,019*

MODEL 340 PD AIRLITE Sc (CENTENNIAL) - .357 Mag. or .38 Spl.+P cal., revolver, DAO, J-frame, 1 7/8 in. stainless steel barrel, 5 shot, Scandium alloy frame, titanium alloy cylinder, snag-free enclosed hammer, HI-VIZ fiber optic green or red ramp front sight, fixed rear sight, (Hi-Viz sight became standard 2009), synthetic grips, available with no internal lock (new 2011), black/grey finish, "PD" marked, 11.8 oz. New 2000.

MSR $1,055	$895	$785	$675	$600	$525	$450	$375

GRADING - PPGS™	100%	98%	95%	90%	80%	70%	60%	LAST MSR

MODEL 340 M & P (CENTENNIAL) – .357 Mag./.38 Spl.+P cal., 5 shot, J-frame, DAO, concealed hammer, 1 7/8 in. stainless steel barrel, XS Sights 24/7 Tritium night front and integral U-notch rear sights, Scandium alloy frame with stainless steel cylinder, also available with no internal lock (new 2011), matte black frame finish, synthetic or Crimson Trace Lasergrips (disc. 2020), "M&P" marked, 13.3 oz. New 2007.

MSR $896	$765	$695	$625	$550	$475	$395	$325	

Add $260 for Crimson Trace Red Lasergrips (disc. 2020).

MODEL 342 AIRLITE Ti CENTENNIAL – .38 S&W Spl. +P cal. (rated for +P in 2000), similar to Model 337, except is hammerless and double action only, matte stainless/grey finish, Uncle Mike's Boot grips, 12 oz. Mfg. 1999-2003.

	$625	$500	$425	$350	$325	$295	$250	*$734*

Add $24 for Dymondwood Boot grips (mfg. 1999 only).

MODEL 342 PD AIRLITE Ti CENTENNIAL – .38 S&W Spl. +P cal., J-frame, 5 shot, double action only, aluminum alloy frame with titanium cylinder and stainless steel 1 7/8 in. barrel, hammerless, black/grey finish, "PD" marked, Hogue Bantam grips, 10.8 oz. Mfg. 2000-2003.

	$595	$460	$390	$340	$310	$280	$250	*$758*

MODEL 351 PD AIRLITE Sc (CHIEFS SPECIAL) – .22 MRF (.22 WMR) cal., DA/SA, J-frame, 1 7/8 in. stainless steel barrel, 7 shot, aluminum (new 2007) or Scandium (disc. 2006) alloy frame and cylinder, external hammer, Hi VIZ fiber optic orange front and fixed U-Notch rear sight, wood grips, matte black finish, 10.6-11.2 oz. New 2004.

MSR $786	$700	$585	$500	$450	$365	$300	$260	

MODEL 351C AIRLITE (CENTENNIAL) – .22 MRF (.22 WMR) cal., DAO, Centennial style, J-frame, 1 7/8 in. stainless steel barrel, 7 shot, aluminum alloy frame and cylinder, internal hammer, XS Sights white dot front sight and fixed U-notch rear sight, synthetic grips, matte black metal finish, 11.5 oz. New 2010.

MSR $709	$600	$525	$450	$410	$350	$275	$225	

MODEL 357 PD – .41 Rem. Mag. cal., N frame, Scandium alloy frame with titanium cylinder, 4 in. two-piece barrel, 6 shot, Ahrends wood grips with finger grooves, Hi-Viz front sight, adj. V-notch rear sight, matte black finish, 27 1/2 oz. Mfg. mid-2005-2007.

	$1,200	$1,000	$900	$725	$550	$425	$325	*$1,067*

MODEL 357 NIGHTGUARD – .41 Mag. cal., 2 1/2 in. barrel, N-frame, matte black metal finish, 6 shot, black synthetic grips, alloy frame with stainless steel cylinder, fixed rear sight, front night sight, 29.7 oz. Mfg. 2010 only.

	$1,300	$1,100	$950	$775	$575	$450	$350	*$1,185*

MODEL 360 AIRLITE Sc CHIEFS SPECIAL – .357 Mag. cal., J-frame, Scandium alloy frame with titanium cylinder, 1 7/8 in. two-piece barrel, 5 shot, Hogue Bantam grips, fixed sights, matte stainless/grey finish, 12 oz. Mfg. 2001-2007.

	$775	$575	$475	$400	$340	$295	$250	*$1,019*

MODEL 360 AIRLITE Sc KIT GUN – .357 Mag. cal., J-frame, 5 shot, 3 1/8 in. barrel with adj. rear and Hi-Viz front sight, Scandium alloy frame with titanium cylinder, matte stainless/grey finish, Uncle Mike's Combat grips, 14 1/2 oz. Mfg. 2001-2007.

	$775	$650	$525	$435	$365	$325	$280	*$940*

MODEL 386 AIRLITE Sc MOUNTAIN LITE – .357 Mag. cal., L-frame, Scandium alloy frame with titanium cylinder, 2 1/2 (new 2007) or 3 1/8 (disc. 2006) in. two-piece stainless steel barrel, 7 shot, adj. rear and Hi-Viz front sight, Hogue Bantam grips, two-tone matte stainless/grey finish, 18 1/2 oz. Mfg. 2001-2007.

	$1,100	$900	$750	$650	$525	$425	$325	*$869*

MODEL 360 (MODEL 360 SCANDIUM) – .357 Mag. / 38 S&W Spl. + P cal., DA/SA, J-frame, 1.88 in. stainless steel barrel, 5 shot, Scandium alloy frame, stainless steel unfluted cylinder, external hammer, red ramp front sight, integral U-notch rear sight, FDE synthetic grips, stainless steel unfluted cylinder, PVD black finish, 14.9 oz. Mfg. late 2017-2020.

	$675	$590	$500	$460	$370	$300	$235	*$790*

MODEL 360 PD AIRLITE Sc (CHIEFS SPECIAL) – .357 Mag. or .38 Spl.+ P cal., SA/DA, variation of the Model 360 Chief Special AirLite, J-frame, 1 7/8 in. stainless steel barrel, 5 shot, Scandium alloy frame with titanium alloy cylinder, external hammer, Hi-Viz fiber optic orange front (became standard 2009) and fixed rear sight, Hogue Bantam grips, "PD" marked, matte black frame finish, 11.7 oz. New 2002.

MSR $1,055	$895	$785	$675	$600	$525	$450	$375	

GRADING - PPGS™	100%	98%	95%	90%	80%	70%	60%	LAST MSR

MODEL 360 M & P (CHIEFS SPECIAL) – .357 Mag. cal., 5 shot, J-frame, SA/DA, 1 7/8 in. barrel, includes XS sights (24/7 Tritium night and integral U-notch), Scandium alloy frame with stainless steel cylinder, matte black finish, synthetic grips, M&P marked, 13.3 oz. Mfg. 2007-2012.

	$725	$600	$475	$350	$300	$250	$225	*$869*

MODEL 386 PD AIRLITE Sc – .357 Mag. cal., L-frame, 7 shot, 2 1/2 in. stainless barrel with adj. black rear sight, Scandium alloy frame with titanium cylinder, black/grey finish, Hogue Bantam grips, 17 1/2 oz. Mfg. 2001-2005.

	$665	$500	$415	$355	$315	$285	$250	*$872*

Add $22 for Hi-Viz front sight (disc. 2005).

MODEL 386 Sc/S – .357 Mag. cal., L-frame, 7 shot, 2 1/2 in. barrel, synthetic finger groove grips, matte black finish, Scandium alloy frame with stainless steel cylinder, red ramp front sight, adj. rear sight, 21.2 oz. Mfg. mid-2007-2008.

	$775	$600	$475	$385	$335	$295	$265	*$948*

MODEL 386 NIGHTGUARD – .357 Mag. cal., two-piece 2 1/2 in. barrel, alloy frame with stainless cylinder, black alloy finish, 7 shot, L-frame, SA/DA, rubber grips, fixed rear sight with front night sight, 24 1/2 oz. Mfg. 2008-2012.

	$950	$850	$725	$650	$525	$425	$325	*$979*

MODEL 386 XL HUNTER (AIRLITE Sc) – .357 Mag. or .38 Spl. +P cal., 7 shot, L-frame, SA/DA, 6 in. barrel, black synthetic grips, adj. rear sight, Hi-Viz fiber optic front sight, alloy frame with stainless steel cylinder, matte black finish, 30 oz. Mfg. 2010-2012.

	$1,800	$1,100	$950	$775	$575	$450	$350	*$899*

MODEL 396 AIRLITE Ti MOUNTAIN LITE – .44 S&W Spl. cal., L-frame, aluminum alloy frame with titanium cylinder, 3 1/8 in. two-piece barrel, 5 shot, adj. rear and Hi-Viz front sight, Hogue Bantam grips, matte stainless/grey finish, 18 oz. Mfg. 2001-2004.

	$825	$725	$550	$400	$325	$285	$265	*$812*

There has been one engineering change to this model.

MODEL 396 NIGHTGUARD – .44 Spl. cal., two-piece 2 1/2 in. barrel, alloy frame with stainless steel cylinder, black alloy finish, 5 shot, L-frame, SA/DA, rubber grips, fixed rear sight with front night sight, 24.2 oz. Mfg. 2008-2009.

	$825	$650	$550	$475	$425	$375	$335	*$1,074*

MODEL 430 AIRWEIGHT – .32 H&R Mag. cal., J-frame, 6 shot, 2 in. barrel, Chief Special style, blue finish. Mfg. export only.

	$1,825	$1,725	$950	$800	$325	$285	$265	

MODEL 431 AIRWEIGHT – .32 H&R Mag. cal., J-frame, 6 shot, 2 in. barrel, Chief Special style, blue finish. Mfg. mid-2004-2005.

	$825	$725	$550	$400	$325	$285	$265	*$450*

MODEL 432 CENTENNIAL AIRWEIGHT – .32 H&R Mag. cal., J-frame, DAO, 6 shot, 2 in. barrel, blue finish. New mid-2004-2005.

	$625	$500	$425	$350	$325	$295	$250	*$469*

Add $263 for Crimson Trace Lasergrips (new 2005).

MODEL 437 CHIEFS SPECIAL AIRWEIGHT – .38 Spl. +P cal., blue finish with stainless cylinder, barrel and small parts, special edition - not cataloged. Limited mfg. 2010.

	$495	$450	$375	$325	$250	$215	$185	

MODEL 438 AIRWEIGHT (BODYGUARD) – .38 Spl. +P cal., 1 7/8 in. barrel, shrouded hammer, matte black metal finish, J-frame, 5 shot, black synthetic grips, SA/DA, fixed rear sight, black blade front sight, alloy frame with stainless steel cylinder, approx. 15 oz. Mfg. 2009-2011.

	$450	$395	$340	$300	$250	$200	$160	*$449*

MODEL 442 AIRWEIGHT (CENTENNIAL) – .38 S&W Spl.+P cal. (rated for +P in 1997), DAO, J-frame, 1 7/8 in. stainless steel barrel, 5 shot, aluminum alloy frame, carbon steel cylinder, hammerless, integral front and rear fixed sights, round butt black synthetic, Uncle Mike's Boot (disc.) or pink (mfg. 2012-2020) grips, no internal lock became an option during 2011, blue (disc.), matte black (current mfg.), or nickel (disc. 1995) finish, 15 oz. New 1993.

MSR $497	$425	$375	$325	$295	$235	$195	$165	

Add $275 for machine engraving and wooden mahogany presentation case (new 2010).
Add $15 for nickel finish (disc.).
Add $16 for pink grips (mfg. 2012-2020).
Add $50 for red LaserMax (mfg. 2016-2017).

There have been two engineering changes to this model.

GRADING - PPGS™	100%	98%	95%	90%	80%	70%	60%	LAST MSR

MODEL 460V – .460 S&W Mag., .454 Casull, or .45 Colt cal., SA/DA, X-frame, 5 in. stainless steel barrel, 5 shot, stainless steel frame, red ramp front and adj. rear sights, black synthetic grip, satin stainless finish, 60.7 oz. Mfg. 2005-2010. Reintroduced 2013.

MSR $1,389	$1,175	$1,025	$875	$800	$650	$550	$460	

MODEL 460 XVR (X-TREME VELOCITY REVOLVER) – .460 S&W Mag., .454 Casull, or .45 Colt cal., SA/DA, X-frame, 8 1/2 in. stainless steel barrel, removable interchangeable compensator, 5 shot, stainless steel frame, Hi-Viz (disc.) or interchangeable front and adj. white outline rear sights, black synthetic grips, matte finish (disc., approx. 16 mfg. in blue/black finish) or satin stainless finish, 72.2 oz. New 2005.

MSR $1,389	$1,175	$1,025	$875	$800	$650	$550	$460	

* ***Model 460 XVR Limited Edition Bone Collector*** – .460 S&W Mag. cal., SA/DA, PC tuned action, similar design to Model 460 V/XVR, 7 1/2 in. XVR barrel w/muzzle brake, 5 shot, stainless steel construction, chrome teardrop hammer and trigger, fiber optic front sight and adj. white outline rear sight, black synthetic grips, internal lock safety, includes gun rug and sling, two-tone finish, 77.8 oz. Limited mfg. of 1,500 in 2015 only.

	$2,400	$2,200	$2,000	$1,800	$1,700	$1,600	$1,500	*$1,680*

MODEL 500 – .500 S&W Mag. cal., many variations and barrel lengths, X-frame, 5 shot, DA, two-piece 4 (new 2004), 6 1/2 (mfg. 2009-2020), or 8 3/8 in. ported barrel with full shroud, stainless steel, recoil compensator, new Sorbothane Hogue wraparound rubber finger groove grips, micrometer click adj. rear sight, red ramp (4 in. barrel) or interchangeable front sight blades (8 3/8 in. barrel only), frame is drilled and tapped, 56 or 72 1/2 oz., satin stainless finish. New 2003.

MSR $1,319	$1,125	$985	$850	$765	$625	$500	$440	

Add $70 for 4 in. barrel.
Add $70 for Hi-Viz sights (8 3/8 in. barrel only, new 2005).

* ***Model 500 SCI "Big 5" Master's Edition*** – features hand engraving by S&W master engraver Wayne D'Angelo, with 24Kt. gold inlays of the African Big 5 animals, ivory grips, includes presentation case, serial numbered SCI001-SCI005. Limited mfg. of 5 during 2004.

	$10,000	$8,000	$6,000	N/A	N/A	N/A	N/A	*$10,000*

* ***Model 500 SCI "Big 5" Limited Edition*** – features roll engraving, with 24Kt. gold inlays of the African Big 5 animals, ivory grips, includes presentation case, serial numbered SCI0006-SCI0300. Limited mfg. of 300 during 2004.

	$3,000	$2,250	$1,500	N/A	N/A	N/A	N/A	*$3,000*

* ***Model 500 Bone Collector Limited Edition*** – .500 S&W Mag. cal., SA/DA, X-frame, 10 1/2 in. barrel with "X of 1000" engraved on side, 5 shot, stainless steel construction, dovetail red ramp, adj. white outline sight, synthetic grips, frame is drilled and tapped, many variations, satin finish. Limited mfg. of 1,000 in 2003 only.

	$2,700	$2,500	$2,200	$1,900	$1,700	$1,500	$1,200	

MODEL 520 (1980 MFG.) – .357 Mag. cal., 4 in. barrel, fixed sights, N-frame, originally ordered for N.Y. State Police but never purchased. Approx. 3,000 mfg. with box during 1980 only.

	$1,125	$975	$825	$700	$575	$500	$425	

MODEL 520 (RECENT MFG.) – .357 Mag. cal., L-frame, two-piece, semi-lug 4 in. barrel, 7 shot, adj. rear sight, wood grips with finger grooves, matte black finish, carbon steel frame with titanium cylinder, Hi-Viz front sight, 37.9 oz. Mfg. mid-2005-2006.

	$650	$575	$495	$445	$365	$295	$235	*$731*

MODEL 544 – please refer to the Commemorative section.

MODEL 547 M & P – 9mm Para. cal., 3 or 4 in. heavy barrel, 6 shot, round (3 in. barrel) or square (4 in. barrel) butt, blue only, special extractor, fixed sights, 32 oz. Disc. 1985.

	$1,350	$1,175	$975	$800	$600	$475	$375	*$317*

Add 10% for 3 in. model.

MODEL 581 DISTINGUISHED SERVICE MAGNUM – .357 Mag. cal., L-Frame, fixed sights, 4 in. full lug barrel, 6 shot, blue or nickel finish, 38 oz. Disc. 1992.

	$750	$650	$565	$510	$415	$340	$265	*$335*

Add $20 for nickel (mfg. 1980-88).

MODEL 586 DISTINGUISHED COMBAT MAGNUM – .357 Mag. cal., L-Frame, 4, 6, or 8 3/8 (disc. 1991) in. barrel, adj. rear sight, blue or nickel (disc. 1991) finish. Disc. 1999.

	$825	$725	$550	$400	$325	$285	$265	*$494*

Add 5%-10% for nickel finish (disc.).

GRADING - PPGS™	100%	98%	95%	90%	80%	70%	60%	*LAST MSR*

Add $4 for white outline rear sight (disc. 1994).
Add $5 for 6 in. barrel.
Add $22 for 8 3/8 in. barrel (disc. 1991).
Add $35 for adj. front sight - disc. 1991 (6 in. barrel only, new 1986).

There have been 7 engineering changes to this model.

MODEL 586 CLASSIC DISTINGUISHED COMBAT MAGNUM – .357 Mag. or .38 S&W Spl. +P cal., L-frame, 6 shot, 4 or 6 in. barrel, carbon steel frame, barrel, and cylinder, blue finish, red ramp front, adj. white outline rear sights, key lock, wood grips, 46.3 oz. New 2012.

MSR $871	$750	$695	$615	$545	$465	$385	$315	

MODEL 586-3 WITH SCOPE MOUNT – .357 Mag. cal., 8 3/8 in. factory barrel broaching for scope mount, blue finish, Goncalo Alves Combat stocks. 1,000 reported. Mfg. 1989 only.

Current value range is $1,200-$2,200 if NIB.

MODEL 610 CLASSIC – 10mm or .40 S&W cal., N-frame, 6 shot, 4 (new 2001), 5 (disc. 2000), or 6 1/2 (disc. 2000) in. full lug barrel, stainless steel construction, fluted or unfluted (4 or 6 1/2 in. barrel only) cylinder, round butt, adj. rear sight, recent production uses Hogue rubber grips, target hammer optional, 50 oz., approx. 5,000 mfg. 1990 only, reintroduced 1998-2004.

	$1,200	$1,050	$900	$815	$650	$540	$425	*$833*

There have been three engineering changes to this model.

MODEL 610 (CURRENT MFG.) – 10mm Auto or .40 S&W cal., SA/DA, large N-frame, 4 or 6 1/2 in. stainless steel barrel, 6 shot, stainless steel frame and cylinder, black blade interchangeable front and adj. white outline rear sight, black synthetic grips, includes 3 moon clips, 42.6-50 oz. New 2019.

MSR $1,007	$860	$750	$650	$575	$500	$425	$350	

MODEL 610 (RECENT MFG.) – 10mm Auto or .40 S&W cal., 3 7/8 or 6 in. barrel, stainless N-frame, satin finish, 6 shot, SA/DA, rubber grips, black blade front sight, adj. rear sight. Mfg. 2009.

	$1,000	$900	$750	$675	$600	$525	$450	*$1,043*

MODEL 617 K-22 MASTERPIECE STAINLESS – .22 LR cal., K-frame, stainless steel variation of the Model 17 (K-22 Masterpiece), 4, 6, or 8 3/8 (disc. 2002) in. full lug barrel, 6 (6 in. full lug barrel only mfg. 1999-2009) or 10 (new 1997, current mfg.) shot, satin stainless finish, combat trigger and Hogue rubber grips are standard on current production, semi-target, 41-52 1/2 oz. New 1990.

MSR $853	$745	$685	$615	$545	$465	$385	$315	

Add $100 for 8 3/8 in. barrel (disc. 2002).
Add 10% for 10 shot aluminum cylinder.
Add 100% for special limited production variations.
Subtract 5% for 6 shot cylinder.

In 2000, this model included target hammer with 8 3/8 in. barrel. 4 and 6 in. barrels were standard during a limited production period in 1991.

MODEL 619 – .357 Mag. cal., L-frame, 7 shot, two-piece 5 in. barrel, stainless steel with satin finish, rubber grips, fixed sights, 37 1/2 oz. Mfg. 2005-2006.

	$450	$375	$275	$225	$185	$150	$125	*$646*

MODEL 620 – .357 Mag. cal., 4 in. barrel, similar to Model 619, except has white outline rear sight and red ramp front sight, 38 oz. Mfg. 2005-2009.

	$585	$465	$385	$325	$270	$225	$195	*$893*

MODEL 624 .44 TARGET – .44 S&W Spl. cal., 6 shot, 4 or 6 1/2 in. barrel, 42 oz. Mfg. 1986-1987 only.

	$1,000	$900	$750	$675	$600	$525	$450	*$449*

Add $14 for 6 1/2 in. barrel.

MODEL 625 (MODEL OF 1988/MODEL OF 1989) – .45 ACP or .45 LC cal., DA, round butt N target frame with three screws, 6 shot, fluted cylinder, 3, 4, or 5 in. full lug barrel, Pachmayr or Hogue grips, non-glare glass bedded matte finish, smooth combat trigger, adj. rear sight, first introduction of this model is actually Model 625-2, early variations can be marked "Model of 1988" or "Model of 1989". Mfg. 1989-disc.

	$1,200	$1,050	$900	$815	$650	$540	$425	

MODEL 625 JM – .45 ACP or .45 Colt (disc.) cal., N-frame, stainless variation of the Model 25-2, 6 shot, 3 (disc. 1991), 4 (disc. 1991, reintroduced 2002), or 5 (disc. 2010) in. barrel, round butt, choice of matte (mfg. 2005-2007) or satin stainless finish, ramp front (3 or 4 in. barrel) or Patridge front (5 in. barrel) sight, full lug barrel, Pachmayr (disc.), Jerry Miculek wood or Hogue rubber combat (disc. 2008) grips, 45 oz. Mfg. 1988-2020.

	$850	$750	$650	$575	$500	$425	$350	*$979*

Subtract approx. 5% if w/o Jerry Miculek initialed wood grips, which became standard during 2009

GRADING - PPGS™	100%	98%	95%	90%	80%	70%	60%	LAST MSR

(originally introduced during 2007).

Approx. 1,500 of the 5 in. barrel models had the frame stamped "625-2", roll engraved barrel with "45 Cal Model of 1989" barrel inscription, and a ramp front sight. Laser engraving replaced roll stamping in 1989.

There have been 10 engineering changes for this model.

MODEL 627 (OLDER MFG.) – .357 Mag. cal., 6 shot, originally marked "357 Magnum Model of 1989" (stamped on barrel), N-frame, smooth combat grips, S&W medallion logo, round butt, unfluted cylinder, full underlug 5 1/2 in. barrel. Mfg. 1989-1997

	100%	98%	95%	90%	80%	70%	60%	LAST MSR
	$1,750	$1,550	$1,300	$1,050	$875	$750	$625	

This model evolved into a Performance Center model.

MODEL 627 (RECENT MFG.) – .357 Mag. cal., 8 shot, SA/DA, 4 in. barrel, N-frame, adj. rear sight, red ramp front sight, stainless steel frame, rubber finger groove grips, 42 oz. Mfg. 2008-2009.

	100%	98%	95%	90%	80%	70%	60%	LAST MSR
	N/A	$600	$425	$350	$300	$275	$250	*$1,003*

MODEL 629 PINNED BARREL – .44 Mag. cal., 4, 6, or 8 3/8 in. barrel, adj. rear sight, features pinned barrel and counter bored (recessed) charge holes in cylinder. Mfg. 1979-1982.

	100%	98%	95%	90%	80%	70%	60%	LAST MSR
6 or 8 3/8 in. barrel	$1,000	$900	$750	$675	$600	$525	$450	
4 in. barrel	$1,500	$1,250	$900	$750	$650	$550	$500	
Pre-production	N/A	$3,050	$2,625	$2,375	$1,925	$1,575	$1,225	

During 1978, 100 pre-production revolvers were made with pinned barrels and recessed cylinders, serial range is N629062-N629200, includes wood box. Values for these prototype Model 629 revolvers range from $1,500-$3,000 depending on original condition.

MODEL 629 – .44 Mag./.44 S&W Spl. cal., N-frame, 6 shot, similar to Model 29, available with 4, 5 (disc.), 6, or 8 3/8 (disc. 2002) in. stainless steel barrel, red ramp front and adj. white outline rear sights, satin stainless finish, current production uses Hogue rubber combat grips, most varied production of any S&W handgun, 41 1/2-49 1/2 oz. New 1982.

	100%	98%	95%	90%	80%	70%	60%	LAST MSR
MSR $969	$825	$720	$620	$560	$455	$400	$350	

Add $47 for fully shrouded 5 in. barrel (disc.) or $39 for 8 3/8 in. barrel (disc.).

Add $100 for combat grips and barrel scope mount (cut across barrel rib) - disc. 1991 (8 3/8 in. barrel only).

Add $198 for Model 629 ES (Emergency Survival) kit with blankets, knife, compass, whistle, signal mirror, fire starter, tinder, chain saw, "Bear Attacks of the Century" book and waterproof storm case (disc.).

* ***Model 629 Backpacker*** – .44 Mag./.44 S&W Spl. cal., similar to Model 629, except 3 in. barrel, Hogue rubber grips, red ramp front sight, white outline rear sight, 40 oz. Mfg. 1994-Disc.

	100%	98%	95%	90%	80%	70%	60%	LAST MSR
	N/A	$700	$650	$600	$525	$475	$375	

MODEL 629 CLASSIC – .44 Mag./.44 S&W Spl. cal., satin stainless steel variation of the Model 29 Classic, 5, 6 1/2 (with or w/o PowerPort), or 8 3/8 (disc. 2010) in. barrel, current production uses Hogue rubber combat grips, 49.5-53.5 oz. New 1990.

	100%	98%	95%	90%	80%	70%	60%	LAST MSR
MSR $1,009	$900	$750	$650	$575	$500	$425	$350	

Add $16 for PowerPort (disc. 2008).

Add $27 for 6 1/2 in. barrel with white outline rear sight (disc.).

Add $54 for Hi-Viz front sight, 6 1/2 in. barrel only (disc.).

Add $245 for Crimson Trace Lasergrips (Model 629CT, mfg. 2006).

* ***Model 629 Classic DX*** – similar to Classic, except is supplied with 2 sets of grips (Hogue combat square and Morado wood round buttstocks), 6 1/2 or 8 3/8 in. barrel, satin stainless finish, 5 interchangeable front sights, numbered test target, 51-54 oz. Mfg. 1992-2002.

	100%	98%	95%	90%	80%	70%	60%	LAST MSR
	$1,250	$1,050	$925	$750	$575	$450	$350	*$986*

Add 10% for 5 in. barrel.

Add $32 for 8 3/8 in. barrel.

* ***Model 629 Magna Classic*** – .44 Mag. cal., similar to Model 29 Magna Classic, 1,800 mfg. during 1990 only.

	100%	98%	95%	90%	80%	70%	60%	LAST MSR
	$1,350	$1,100	$950	$775	$650	$550	$450	*$999*

MODEL 629 DELUXE – .44 Mag./.44 S&W Spl. cal., DA/SA, N-frame (large), 3 or 6 1/2 in. barrel, 6 shot, Scandium alloy frame, Hi-Viz fiber optic front sight, textured combat (3 in. barrel) or standard (6 1/2 in. barrel) checkered grips, satin finish. New 2017.

	100%	98%	95%	90%	80%	70%	60%	LAST MSR
MSR $999	$850	$750	$650	$575	$500	$425	$350	

Add $30 for 6 1/2 in. barrel.

GRADING - PPGS™	100%	98%	95%	90%	80%	70%	60%	LAST MSR

MODEL 629-3 WITH SCOPE MOUNT – .44 Mag. cal., 8 3/8 in. barrel with factory barrel broaching to accommodate S&W scope mounting system, .500" target hammer, .400" serrated target trigger, red ramp front sight with white outline rear sight, two scope rings and two mounting bases included, Goncalo Alves Combat stocks, satin stainless finish, 54.5 oz. 4,810 reported. Mfg. 1989 only.

Last MSR in 1989 was $537.

Current value range is $1,200-$2,200 if NIB.

MODEL 631 – .32 H&R Mag. cal., 6 shot, 2 (fixed sight) or 4 (adj. sight) in. barrel, combat stocks, round butt only, stainless steel J-frame, approx. 5,500 mfg. 1990-1992.

	$1,100	$900	$750	$650	$525	$425	$325	*$386*

MODEL 631 LADYSMITH – .32 H&R Mag. cal., 2 in. barrel only, rosewood stocks, "LadySmith" marked, stainless steel J-frame construction, scarce.

	$1,200	$1,050	$900	$815	$650	$540	$425	*$400*

MODEL 632 CENTENNIAL - .32 H&R Mag. cal., 2 or 3 (mfg. 1991 only) in. barrel, stainless/alloy construction, fully concealed hammer, J-frame, Santoprene combat grips, fixed sights, 15 1/2 oz. Mfg. 1991-1992.

	$600	$550	$350	$250	$195	$165	$140	*$410*

Add 20% for 3 in. barrel.

MODEL 632 PRO SERIES - .327 Federal Mag. cal., 2 1/8 (new 2010) or 3 (disc.) in. black PowerPort barrel, blue/black finish, 6 shot, stainless steel small J frame and cylinder, rubber grips, SA/DA, adj. sight, night sights (new 2010), approx. 23 oz. Mfg. 2009-2012.

	$600	$575	$550	$450	$375	$350	$300	*$809*

Add $90 for 3 in. PowerPort barrel and blue/black metal finish with SA/DA action (marked MOD 632-1).

MODEL 637 AIRWEIGHT (CHIEFS SPECIAL) – .38 S&W Spl.+P cal. (rated in 1997 for +P cal.), DA/SA, J-frame, 1 7/8 (current mfg.), 2 1/8 (PowerPort only, disc.), or 2 1/2 (mfg. 2010 only) in. stainless steel barrel and cylinder, 5 shot, alumunim alloy frame, external hammer, integral front and fixed rear sights, black synthetic, Uncle Mike's Boot (disc.), Crimson Trace Laser (new 2005), or pink (mfg. 2012-2020) grips, matte silver finish, 15 oz. 560 mfg. during 1991, reintroduced 1996.

MSR $497	$425	$375	$325	$295	$235	$195	$165	

Add $16 for pink grips (mfg. 2012-2020).
Add $16 for Carry Combo configuration (mfg. 2004-2008).
Add $227 for Crimson Trace Lasergrips (new 2005).
Add $70 for Red LaserMax (mfg. 2016-disc.).
Add $150 for 2 1/2 in. full lug barrel (mfg. 2010 only).
Add $142 for 2 1/8 in. barrel with PowerPort (Pro Series, mfg. 2009-2010).

MODEL 638 AIRWEIGHT (BODYGUARD) – .38 S&W Spl.+P cal. (rated for +P in 1998), DA/SA, J-frame, 1 7/8 or 2 1/2 (mfg. 2010 only) in. stainless steel barrel and cylinder, 5 shot, alloy frame, shrouded hammer, integral front and fixed rear sights, round butt black synthetic, Uncle Mike's Boot (disc.), Crimson Trace Laser, or pink (mfg. 2012-2020) grips, 15 oz. 1,200 mfg. during 1990 only, reintroduced 1998.

MSR $497	$425	$375	$325	$295	$235	$195	$165	

Add $16 for pink grips (mfg. 2012-2020).
Add $227 for Crimson Trace Lasergrips (Model 638 CT, mfg. 2010-2020).
Add $70 for Red LaserMax (mfg. 2016 only).
Add $150 for 2 1/2 in. full lug barrel (disc. 2010).

MODEL 640 (CENTENNIAL) - .357 Mag./.38 Spl.+P or .38 S&W Spl. (disc.) cal., DAO, J-frame, 1 7/8 (mfg. 1998-2001), 2 1/8 (new 1991), or 3 (disc. 1992) in. stainless steel barrel, 5 shot, stainless steel frame and cylinder, hammerless, black blade front and fixed rear sights, round butt, black synthetic or Uncle Mike's Combat (disc.) grips, satin stainless finish, 23 oz. New 1991.

MSR $755	$635	$565	$495	$445	$365	$295	$250	

Add $214 for machine engraving and wooden mahogany presentation case (new 2009).

The .38 Spl. was rated for +P in 1997 and the .357 Mag. calilber was rated for +P in 2000.

MODEL 642 AIRWEIGHT (CENTENNIAL) – .38 S&W Spl. +P cal. (rated for +P in 1997), J-frame, DAO, 1 7/8, 2 (disc. 1997), 2 1/8 (PowerPort, mfg. 2009-2010), 2 1/2 full lug (mfg. 2010 only), or 3 (disc. 1991) in. stainless steel barrel, aluminum alloy frame, stainless steel cylinder, combat or pink (new 2012) grips, hammerless, satin stainless finish, fixed rear sight, no internal lock became an option during 2011, 15 oz. Mfg. 1990-1992, reintroduced 1996.

MSR $497	$425	$375	$325	$295	$235	$195	$165	

Add $16 for pink grips (new 2012).
Add $142 for 2 1/8 in. barrel with PowerPort (mfg. 2009-2010).
Add $150 for 2 1/2 in. full lug barrel (mfg. 2010 only).

GRADING - PPGS™	100%	98%	95%	90%	80%	70%	60%	LAST MSR

* ***Model 642 CT Airweight (Centennial)*** – .38 S&W cal., similar to Model 642 Centennial Airweight, except has Crimson Trace Lasergrips in black or Robin's Egg Blue (disc. 2020), no internal lock became an option during 2011. New 2004.

MSR $724	$615	$540	$460	$425	$345	$275	$225	

MODEL 642 LASERMAX LASER – .38 S&W Spl. +P cal., J-frame, DAO, 5 shot, 1 8/7 in. barrel, aluminum alloy/stainless steel frame, features LaserMax laser module built in in front of trigger guard and underneath barrel, small internal hammer, integral fixed sights, black synthetic grip with finger grooves, matte silver finish, 15 oz. Mfg. 2015-2016.

	$525	$375	$315	$265	$225	$190	$170	*$539*

MODEL 642 LADYSMITH (AIRWEIGHT) – .38 Spl. +P cal. (rated for +P in 1997), J-frame, 5 shot, 1 7/8 in. barrel, stainless steel/alloy construction, smooth wood grips, satin stainless finish, includes soft side carry or jewelry case, "Ladysmith" marked, 14 1/2 oz. New 1996.

MSR $528	$450	$400	$340	$300	$250	$200	$175	

MODEL 646 – .40 S&W cal., 4 in. barrel, stainless steel, L-frame, 6 shot, titanium cylinder. Limited mfg. during 2000 and 2003.

	$1,200	$1,050	$900	$815	$650	$540	$425	

MODEL 647 – .17 HMR cal., K-frame, 6 shot, stainless steel, 8 3/8 in. barrel with full lug, Hogue rubber grips with finger grooves, Patridge front and adj. rear sight, 52 oz. Mfg. 2003-2004.

	$950	$850	$725	$650	$525	$425	$325	*$697*

MODEL 648 – .22 MRF (.22 WMR) cal., SA/DA, medium K-frame, 6 in. full underlug barrel, 8 shot, stainless steel construction, semi-target hammer, combat trigger, patridge front and adj. rear sight (new 2019), black synthetic finger groove combat grips, square butt, 46.2 oz. Mfg. 1989-1996, reintroduced 2019.

MSR $772	$1,250	$900	$650	$445	$365	$295	$250	

* ***Model 648-2*** – .22 WMR cal., DA revolver, K-frame with internal key lock system, 6 in. barrel with full lug, 6 or 8 (new 2020) shot cylinder, stainless steel, Patridge front and adj. rear sight, Hogue rubber grips with finger grooves, 45 oz. Mfg. 2003-2005, reintroduced 2020 only.

	$850	$750	$575	$425	$350	$300	$275	*$703*

MODEL 649 (BODYGUARD) – .357 Mag./.38 S&W Spl. +P or .38 S&W Spl. (disc.) cal. (rated for +P in 1997), J-frame, otherwise similar to Model 49 Bodyguard, except has stainless steel frame, barrel, and cylinder with satin stainless finish, 1 7/8 (mfg. 1998 only), 2 (disc. 1997), or 2 1/8 (new 1998) in. barrel, shrouded hammer, current production uses Uncle Mike's Combat grips, 23 oz. Mfg. 1986-2020.

	$635	$565	$495	$445	$365	$295	$235	*$735*

There have been five engineering changes to this model.

MODEL 650 KIT GUN – .22 MRF (.22 WMR) cal., service kit gun, stainless steel, 3 in. heavy barrel, J-frame, fixed sights. Mfg. 1983-1987.

	$1,500	$1,250	$1,000	$775	$575	$450	$350	*$305*

Add $150 for extra .22 LR cylinder.

MODEL 651 KIT GUN – .22 MRF (.22 WMR) cal., target kit gun, stainless steel, 4 in. barrel, J-frame, adj. rear sight. Mfg. 1983-87, re-released in late 1990, disc. 1998.

	$1,300	$1,100	$950	$775	$575	$450	$350	*$478*

Add 50% for 2 in. barrel.

This model could be ordered with a factory fitted optional .22 LR cylinder until 1987 (last mfg. sug. retail was $295 for the cylinder alone). This variation with the extra cylinder is very desirable.

MODEL 657 – .41 Mag. cal., N-frame, 4 (disc.), 6 (disc. 2000), 7 1/2 (new 2001), or 8 3/8 (disc. 1992) in. barrel, satin stainless steel, recent production uses Hogue rubber combat grips, approx. 53 oz. Mfg. 1986-2008.

	$825	$725	$550	$400	$325	$285	$265	*$869*

There have been 5 engineering changes to this model.

MODEL 681 DISTINGUISHED SERVICE MAGNUM – .357 Mag. cal., stainless steel, 4 in. barrel, fixed sights, L-Frame. Mfg. 1980-1992.

	$625	$550	$495	$435	$350	$285	$225	*$412*

1991 mfg. includes square butt. There were 5 engineering changes to this model.

MODEL 686 – .357 Mag./.38 Spl. + P cal., SA/DA, L-frame, 4.13 or 6 in. stainless steel barrel, 6 shot, stainless steel frame and cylinder, red ramp front and adj. white outline rear sights, black synthetic grips, Bossed mainspring, satin stainless finish, 39.7-44.8 oz. New 2010.

MSR $853	$745	$685	$615	$545	$465	$385	$315	

GRADING - PPGS™	100%	98%	95%	90%	80%	70%	60%	LAST MSR

MODEL 686 DISTINGUISHED COMBAT MAGNUM – .357 Mag./.38 Spl. +P cal., L-Frame, stainless steel construction, 6 shot, 2 1/2 (new 1990), 4, 6 with (disc.) or w/o PowerPort, or 8 3/8 (disc. 2002) in. barrel, fixed (disc.) or adj. sights, blue (disc.), stainless, or midnight black (mfg. 1989 only) finish, current production uses Hogue rubber grips, 35-51 oz. New 1980.

MSR $853	$840	$725	$550	$500	$400	$325	$280	

Midnight Black finish was offered in 1989 only as a limited edition with 1,559 being mfg. in a 4 in. barrel, and 2,876 being mfg. in a 6 in. barrel.

* ***Model 686 Plus (Distinguished Combat Magnum Plus)*** – .357 Mag./.38 Spl. +P cal., L-frame, 7 shot, 2 1/2, 3 (new 2007), 4, or 6 in. barrel, synthetic or Hogue rubber (disc.) grips, stainless steel construction, round (2 1/2 in. barrel only) or square butt, red ramp front or adj. white outline rear sight, satin stainless finish, 34 1/2-43 oz. New 1996.

MSR $874	$835	$725	$625	$565	$450	$375	$295	

MODEL 686 PLUS "3-5-7" MAGNUM SERIES – .357 Mag./.38 Spl. cal., L frame, 3, 5, or 7 in. full lug barrel, 7 shot, adj. white outline rear and red ramp front sights, wood grips marked ".357", unfluted cylinder, satin finished stainless steel. New 2017.

MSR $899	$825	$725	$625	$565	$450	$375	$300	

MODEL 686 PLUS DELUXE – .357 Mag./.38 Spl. cal., L frame, 3 or 6 in. full lug barrel, 7 shot, adj. white outline rear and red ramp front sights, combat (3 in. barrel only) or squared (6 in. barrel only) textured wood grips, fluted cylinder, satin finished stainless steel. New 2017.

MSR $899	$825	$725	$625	$565	$450	$375	$300	

MODEL 686-3 WITH SCOPE MOUNT – .357 Mag. cal., 8 3/8 in. factory barrel broaching for scope mount, glass bead finish, Goncalo Alves Combat stock. 1,100 reported. Mfg. 1989 only.

Current value range is $1,200-$2,200 if NIB.

MODEL 696 – .44 S&W Spl. cal., L-frame, 5 shot, 3 in. barrel with full shroud, Hogue rubber (disc. 2000) or Uncle Mike's Combat grips, satin stainless steel, adj. rear sight, 36 oz. Mfg. 1997-2002.

	$950	$825	$750	$650	$600	$550	$500	*$620*

MODEL 940 CENTENNIAL – 9mm Para. cal., fully concealed hammer, 2 or 3 (disc. 1992) in. barrel, fixed rear sight, Santoprene combat grips, 23-25 oz. Mfg. 1991-1998.

	$1,025	$925	$775	$685	$600	$525	$450	*$493*

Add 20% for 3 in. barrel.

MODEL 986 PRO SERIES – 9mm Para. cal., L-frame, 7 shot, 5 in. barrel w/full shroud, Hogue rubber, satin stainless steel, adj. rear sight, 36 oz. Mfg. 2014-disc.

	$950	$825	$750	$650	$600	$550	$500	

PISTOLS: SEMI-AUTO, CENTERFIRE

Listed in order of model number (except .32 and .35 Automatic Pistols). Alphabetical models will appear at the end of this section.

To understand S&W 3rd generation model nomenclature, the following rules apply. The first two digits (of the four-digit model number) specify caliber. Numbers 39, 59, and 69 refer to 9mm Para. cal. The third digit refers to the model type. 0 means standard model, 1 is for compact, 2 is for standard model with decocking lever, 3 is for compact variation with decocking lever, 4 is for standard with double action only, 5 designates a compact model in double action only, 6 indicates a non-standard barrel length, 7 is a non-standard barrel length with decocking lever, and 8 refers to non-standard barrel length in double action only. The fourth digit refers to the material(s) used in the fabrication of the pistol. 3 refers to an aluminum alloy frame with stainless steel slide, 4 designates an aluminum alloy frame with carbon steel slide, 5 is for carbon steel frame and slide, 6 is a stainless steel frame and slide, and 7 refers to a stainless steel frame and carbon steel slide. Hence, a Model 4053 refers to a pistol in .40 S&W cal. configured in compact version with double action only and fabricated with an aluminum alloy frame and stainless steel slide.

A few semi-auto models have had engineering changes during their manufacture. These will be denoted by a dash followed by another number after the main model number. Unless there is an additional price line, models with engineering changes will have the same value as those without. This model nomenclature does not apply to 2 or 3 digit model numbers (i.e., Rimfire Models and the Model 52).

This book does not include compliant configurations such as those variations made for California and Massachusetts. These guns may have different features than those that are not compliant restricted.

Current S&W abbreviations for pistol feature codes used on its price sheets and literature are as follows:

GRADING - PPGS™	100%	98%	95%	90%	80%	70%	60%	LAST MSR

Grips: CTG - Crimson Trace laser grips, PG - plastic grips, RG - rubber grips, WG - wood grips. Sights: R/ADJ - adjustable, R/ADJFO - adj. fiber optic R/ADJFO- adjustable fiber optic, R/FIXEDB - fixed black,R/NS - night sight, R/WD - white dot, F/LMC - low mount carry, F/BB - black blade, F/BP - black post,F/FO - fiber optic, F/GB - gold bead - F/INTCH - interchangeable, F/NS - night sights, F/PAT - Patridge, F/RR - red ramp, F/WB - white bead, F/WD - white dot. Frames: AL - alloy, SS - stainless steel, CS - carbon frame, MCR - maximum corrosion resistant, (SM - stainless melonite), POLY - polymer. Safeties: AMBI - ambidextrous, MS - magazine safety, NMS - no magazine safety, IL - internal lock, TS - thumb safety, TLCI - tactile loaded chamber indicator. Action: DA - double action only, SA - single action only, SA/DA - single action/double action, SF - striker fire.

Pre-2010 S&W abbreviations are as follows: Grips: GC - Crimson Trace laser grips, GR - rubber grips, GW - wood grips, GF - finger groove grips, GP - plastic grips. Sights: SA - adj., SB - black blade front, SC - interchangeable front, SD - dot front, SF - fixed, SG - gold bead front, SH - Hi-Viz, SL - Lo Mount Carry, SP - Patridge front, SR - red ramp front, SV - black post, S1 - front night. Frame Material: FA - alloy, FS - stainless, CF - carbon, FM - stainless Melonite, FP - polymer. Frame Sizes: SM - Small/Compact, MD - Medium, LG - Large, XL - Extra Large. Finishes: ZB - Blue/Black, ZC - Clear Cote, FDE- Flat Dark Earth, ZG - Grey, ZL - Melonite, ZM - Matte, ZS - Satin Stainless, ZT - Two-Tone, ZW - Camo. Barrel: BC - carbon, BL - light, BO - one piece, BS - stainless, BT - traditional, BX - heavy, B2 - two piece. Action: AD - double action only, AF - striker fire, AS - single action only, AT - traditional double action. Slide: DS - stainless steel, DC- carbon, DM - stainless Melonite.

When applicable, early variations of some of the older semi-auto models listed in this category will be more desirable than later mfg.

.32 AUTOMATIC PISTOL – .32 ACP cal., 7 shot mag., 3 1/2 in. barrel, blue with "S&W" monogram inlaid plain walnut grip. 957 mfg. 1924-1936. Serial range starting with S/N 1.

	100%	98%	95%	90%	80%	70%	60%
2 in. barrel	$3,500	$2,950	$2,350	$1,850	$1,500	$1,250	$1,000

.35 AUTOMATIC PISTOL (MODEL 1913) – .35 S&W Auto cal., 7 shot mag., 3 1/2 in. barrel, blue or nickel w/"S&W" monogram inlaid in plain walnut grips. 8,350 mfg. 1913-1921. Serial range starting with no. 1.

	100%	98%	95%	90%	80%	70%	60%
	$1,500	$1,150	$850	$700	$600	$500	$400

A slight premium might exist for the first model (up to ser. no. 3,125).

MODEL 39 ALLOY FRAME EARLY MFG. (PRE-39) – 9mm Para. cal., short safety, short tang, approx. ser. no. range 1001-2600. Mfg. 1954-1957.

	100%	98%	95%	90%	80%	70%	60%
	$1,950	$1,675	$1,425	$1,000	$800	$700	$600

Add 200% for early manufacture original military trial guns. Factory letter/military documentation.
Add 10% for NIB condition.

The distinguishing features of the Pre-39 compared to the Model 39 are as follows: short safety, short tang, a unique frame back strap insert and hammer stirrup, a unique left grip (no safety relief), no trigger play spring, no model number on frame, no patent pending on early slides (Late Pre-39 slides have the patent pending; however, slides were fitted without regard for serial numbers. For example, serial number 1069, which was shipped from the factory on Oct. 4, 1955, has the patent pending marking, while 1,150 that shipped on July 7, 1955 does not), two types of early flat magazine followers were used before standardizing on a third type, supplied with an instruction booklet (only the Pre-39s and early Model 39s to about serial number 7,000 were supplied with the instruction booklet).

MODEL 39 ALLOY FRAME – 9mm Para. cal., alloy frame, model nomenclature marking on pistol started after ser. no. approx. 2,600, long safety lever and extractor, checkered walnut grips, blue or nickel finish. Mfg. started 1957.

	100%	98%	95%	90%	80%	70%	60%
	$1,000	$800	$600	$500	$400	$395	$350

Add 15% for NIB.
Large premiums exists for nickel finish.

S&W completed one lot of 200 guns for commercial sales with nickel finish, in addition to guns that were produced with nickel finish for special orders. The model change from the Model 39 to the Model 39-2 took place with the change from the long extractor to the new short type. Collectors report an approx. ser. no. range 1001-120000 with long extractor. This model was the first commercially mfg. 9mm Para. double action semi-auto in the U.S.

Models 39 Alloy Frame & Model 39 Alloy Frame Early Mfg. (Pre-39) are intermixed, as is the production of the two variations. There is no positive serial number that can be established when the Model number was

GRADING - PPGS™	100%	98%	95%	90%	80%	70%	60%	LAST MSR

added, however it occurred between serial number 2500 and 5000, with the production changes taking place somewhat randomly over the same serial range. It must be remembered that Smith & Wesson did not make pistols in order of serial number. Also the serial numbers are intermixed with the Model 41 pistols and the Model 52. The guns that were submitted for military testing went to the Springfield Armory, and had X prefix serial numbers. The first shipments of Model 39s was in Dec. 1954, the model numbers were assigned in 1957.

MODEL 39 STEEL FRAME - 9mm Para. cal., 8 shot, 4 in. barrel, long ejector, walnut stocks, adj. rear windage only sight, double action, short tang, walnut grips, blue finish, 927 mfg. during 1966 only in 3 ser. no. ranges.

	100%	98%	95%	90%	80%	70%	60%	LAST MSR
	$2,250	$1,950	$1,600	$1,400	$1,000	$850	$735	

MODEL 39-2 ALLOY FRAME (LATER PRODUCTION) - 7.65mm (.30 Luger) or 9mm Para. cal., double action, 8 shot mag., 4 in. barrel, checkered walnut grips, adj. sight, alloy frame, approx. 1971, the 39-2 was introduced as an improved version. Mfg. 1970-82.

	100%	98%	95%	90%	80%	70%	60%	LAST MSR
9mm Para. cal.	$750	$600	$450	$300	$250	$225	$200	
7.65mm cal.	$2,450	$2,100	$1,850	$1,550	$1,150	$950	$850	

Add 15% for nickel finish.
Add 20% if NIB.

The .30 Luger cal. (7.65mm) was mfg. for the European marketplace only. Very hard to find in the U.S.

In 1971 approximately 500 Model 39-2s were shipped to West Germany without barrels. The pistols were fitted with 7.65mm barrels in West Germany and were then proofed and shipped to an Italian distributor for commercial sales in that country. The slides, barrels, and frames of these guns all have the West German 1971 Ulm Proof House Marks. Three of these guns were imported by Sarco in 1995, serial numbers A129,214,A129,498, and one with an unknown serial number. There is one other 7.65mm Model 39 known. The gun (serial number A166,311) had smooth grips with a nickel finish and is without the German Proof Marks.

MODEL 44 - 9mm Para. cal., single action design, S&W's rarest cataloged semi-auto pistol, 10 mfg. Identified by no model number, single action trigger, and unique walnut grips. Serialized in the 1200 range of the Pre-39 serial numbers.

Original examples are typically seen in the $20K-$25K range, depending on condition.

MODEL 52-A (39-1) - The Model 39-1 was developed to handle the .38 AMU cartridge using same action as Model 39. 87 pistols were mfg, 10 of which were supplied to U.S. Army Marksman Training Unit. The remaining 77 guns were sold on the commercial market in 1977. To avoid confusion with the 9mm Model 39, all the guns sold commercially were marked Model 52-A. The guns supplied to the military were left unmarked.

	100%	98%	95%	90%	80%	70%	60%	LAST MSR
	$3,750	$3,250	$2,750	$2,250	$1,950	$1,600	$1,300	

MODEL 52 - .38 S&W Spl. Wadcutter cal. only, similar action to Model 39, except incorporates a set screw locking out the double action, 5 in. barrel, 5 shot mag., and an adj. barrel bushing. Approx. 3,500 mfg. 1961-1963.

	100%	98%	95%	90%	80%	70%	60%	LAST MSR
	$1,800	$1,600	$1,400	$1,000	$800	$700	$600	

MODELS 52-1 & 52-2 - the Model 52-1 is the same as the Model 52 except SA only, and the frame was grooved for a counterweight. The Model 52-2 is the same as the 52-1, except has a new extractor. The original extractor was overly complex, expensive to make and prone to breakage. The new extractor was a relatively simple hook tensioned by a coil spring.

	100%	98%	95%	90%	80%	70%	60%	LAST MSR
	$1,200	$1,000	$850	$725	$625	$525	$450	*$908*

The Model 52-1 was mfg. 1963-1971, and the Model 52-2 was mfg. 1971-1993.

MODEL 59 - 9mm Para. cal., similar to Model 39, except has 14 shot mag., black nylon grips, DA/SA, total production approx. 231,841. Mfg. 1972-1981.

	100%	98%	95%	90%	80%	70%	60%	LAST MSR
	$750	$625	$400	$335	$285	$235	$215	

Add $50 for nickel finish.
Add $150 for smooth front (ungrooved) grip frame.
Add 200% for smooth front and rear grip straps (20 mfg.).

MODEL 147-A - 9mm Para. cal., 14 shot, steel frame, 4 in. barrel, black plastic grips, adj. sights for windage only, similar to Model 59, except has steel frame, 130 mfg. serial numbered between A490000 to A4901291. A total of 112 guns were released for commercial sales in November 1979.

	100%	98%	95%	90%	80%	70%	60%	LAST MSR
	$3,000	$2,500	$2,200	$1,800	$1,400	$1,200	$975	

This model was originally marked Model 47, prefix (1) and suffix (-A) were hand stamped before the guns were sold.

GRADING - PPGS™	100%	98%	95%	90%	80%	70%	60%	LAST MSR

MODEL 410 – .40 S&W cal., Value Series, DA/SA, steel slide with alloy frame, blue finish, 4 in. barrel, 10 or 11 shot mag., single side safety, 3-dot sights, straight backstrap with synthetic grips, 28 1/2 oz. Mfg. 1996-2007.

$525	$375	$275	$225	$195	$175	$165	*$687*

Add $25 for Hi-Viz front sight (mfg. 2002-2003).

* ***Model 410S*** – .40 S&W cal., Value Series, similar to Model 410, except has stainless steel slide with alloy frame, 28 1/2 oz. Mfg. 2005-2006.

$545	$375	$275	$245	$205	$175	$165	*$711*

Add $100 for Crimson Trace Lasergrips.

MODEL 411 – .40 S&W cal., Value Series, 4 in. barrel, DA/SA, 11 shot mag., fixed sights, blue finish, aluminum alloy frame, manual safety. Mfg. 1992-1996.

$475	$400	$350	$325	$295	$280	$265	*$525*

MODEL 439 – 9mm Para. cal., DA/SA, 4 in. barrel, blue or nickel finish, alloy frame, 8 shot mag., checkered walnut grips, 30 oz. Mfg. 1981-1988.

$750	$415	$350	$325	$260	$215	$165	*$472*

Add $50 for nickel finish (disc. 1986).
Add $26 for adj. sights.

Production began on February 26, 1981 with serial number A669101. The first few thousand were supplied with a short wide extractor before reverting back to the Model 39-2 style extractor. The gun was discontinued in the fall of 1988 and replaced by the third-generation Model 3904.

MODEL 457 COMPACT – .45 ACP cal., Value Series, DA/SA, alloy frame and steel slide, 3 3/4 in. barrel, single side safety, 3-dot sights, 7 shot mag., straight backstrap, blue finish only, black synthetic grips, 29 oz. Mfg. 1996-2006.

$525	$365	$270	$225	$195	$175	$165	*$681*

* ***Model 457S Compact*** – similar to Model 457, Value Series, except has stainless steel slide with alloy frame, 29 oz. Mfg. 2003-2006.

$545	$390	$280	$245	$200	$175	$165	*$710*

MODEL 459 – 9mm Para. cal., 14 shot version of Model 439, checkered nylon stocks, limited mfg. with squared-off trigger guard with serrations. Mfg. 1981-1988.

$550	$400	$350	$300	$275	$255	$240	*$501*

Add $25 for adj. sights.
Add $50 for nickel finish (disc. 1986).
Add 30% for Model 4590 (Transitional 5903).

Production started in 1981, at approximately serial number A668439, and was discontinued in 1988. It is estimated that the first 10,000 guns were produced with the short wide extractor.

* ***Model 459 Brushed Finish*** – 9mm Para. cal., 14 shot, 4 in. barrel, dull finish, fixed sights, special grips made to F.B.I. or police specs., 803 mfg. in 1984.

$1,100	$625	$550	$440	$385	$330	$300

Add 100%-200% for F.B.I. guns, very few released. Values assume proper F.B.I. documentation (be wary).

There are several variations of interest in the Model 459: the so called "FBI Model", which were never delivered to the FBI, the Federal Bureau of Investigation pistols which were delivered to the FBI, the XM9 military test of 30 guns with there unique rear sight, the XM10 military test guns, and the U.S. marked United States Customs guns. All of the these variations have a special dull finish and matching dull nylon grips.

MODEL 469 "MINI" – 9mm Para. cal., DA/SA, alloy frame, 12 shot finger extension mag., short frame, bobbed hammer, 3 1/2 in. barrel, sandblast blue or satin nickel finish, ambidextrous safety standard (1986), molded Delrin black grips, 26 oz. Mfg. 1983-1988.

$600	$525	$450	$375	$275	$250	$225	*$478*

The first eleven guns were completed in 1982 (serial numbers starting at A796437) and were used for test and evaluation samples. Full production began in August of 1983 with serial number A840000. 25 of the first 100 guns were nickel finish, class "A" engraved and shipped with a presentation case, marked "First 100". However while they were marked "First 100" they were not necessarily the first hundred serial numbers.

MODEL 539 – 9mm Para. cal., double action, steel frame, steel slide, 8 shot, 4 in. barrel, blue or nickel. Approx. 8,300 mfg. 1981-1983.

$850	$475	$415	$375	$350	$325	$300

Add $50 for nickel finish.
Add $30 for fixed rear sight.

GRADING - PPGS™	100%	98%	95%	90%	80%	70%	60%	LAST MSR

MODEL 559 – The Model 559 is the carbon steel version of the 14 round double stack magazine second-generation pistol, DA/SA. The gun was introduced in 1980 with shipments starting in 1981, at approximately serial number A672725. The majority of the guns were produced with the short wide extractor. Only 200 to 250 were supplied with the Model 39-2 type extractor. After production of 10,609 units, 8,973 in blue finish and 1,636 in nickel, the gun was discontinued October 1982.

$850	$525	$450	$375	$275	$250	$225	

Add $50 for nickel finish.
Add $30 for fixed rear sight.

MODEL 639 STAINLESS – 9mm Para. cal., DA/SA, similar to Model 439, only stainless steel, 8 shot mag., ambidextrous safety became standard 1986, 36 oz. Mfg. 1982-1988.

$750	$400	$350	$300	$250	$200	$165	*$523*

Add $27 for adj. sights.

The pistol was introduced on May 24, 1982, with serial number A769806. The gun was first available with the short wide extractor but that was changed to the Model 39-2 type on September 15, 1982 after approximately 600 had been produced.

MODEL 645 STAINLESS - .45 ACP cal. only, 5 in. barrel, SA, 8 shot mag., squared-off trigger guard, black molded nylon grips, ambidextrous safety, fixed sights, 37 1/2 oz. Mfg. 1985-1988.

$750	$625	$550	$440	$385	$330	$300	*$622*

Add approx. 25% for the approx. 479 Model 6450 "Interim" pistols were mfg. in 1988 only.
Add $27 for adj. sight.

The first 28 prototype pistols were produced in October 1984 and were serial numbered from A883222 to A883249. Production started in November 1985 with shipments starting in December of 1985 at serial number TAK0001.

MODEL 659 STAINLESS - 9mm Para. cal., DA/SA, similar to Model 459, only stainless steel, 14 shot mag., ambidextrous safety became standard 1986, 39 1/2 oz. Disc. 1988.

$700	$400	$350	$300	$250	$215	$180	*$553*

Add approx. 30% for the approx. 150 Model 6590 "Interim" or "transitional" pistols were mfg. in 1988 only.
Add $27 for adj. sights.

The gun was introduced in 1982 beginning with serial number A782700 and was discontinued in 1988. It was replaced by the Model 5906. A limited number of this model were supplied with the short wide extractor and are considered scarce.

MODEL 669 STAINLESS - 9mm Para. cal., smaller version of Model 659 with 12 shot finger extension mag., 3 1/2 in. barrel, fixed sights, molded Delrin grips, ambidextrous safety standard, 26 oz. Mfg. 1986-88 only.

$600	$375	$275	$225	$195	$175	$165	*$522*

Add approx. 30% for the approx. 150 Model 6690 "Interim" or "transitional" pistols were mfg. in 1988 only.

The Model 669 was introduced in 1985 beginning with serial number TAE 0001. The gun had a stainless steel slide and barrel with aluminum alloy frame. The first 100 guns were set aside for special orders; 25 of these were class "A" engraved by an outside contractor and marked "1 of 25." It took ten years for all of these engraved guns to be sold. In 1988 the Model 669 was discontinued and replaced by the Model 6906. Total production of the Model 669 was 54,074 pistols.

MODEL 745 – .45 ACP cal., single action, 5 in. barrel, stainless steel frame with steel slide, hammer, and trigger, checkered walnut stocks, Novak adj. competition rear sight, 38 3/4 oz. Mfg. 1987-1990.

$895	$725	$595	$450	$350	$265	$225	*$699*

Introduced in 1987 as a target model for use in IPSC style events. The first 5,000 pistols were commemorative guns for the 10th Anniversary of IPSC and were so marked. After the completion of the IPSC pistol run a standard production model was introduced without the commemorative markings. A total of approx. 9,704 units were produced through 1990. In 1990, a special limited production run of approx. 100 pistols fitted with adj. sights was mfg.

MODEL 908 COMPACT – 9mm Para. cal., Value Series, compact variation of the Model 909/910, DA/SA, 3 1/2 in. barrel, 3-dot sights, 8 shot mag., straight backstrap, 24 oz. Mfg. 1996-2007.

$495	$355	$275	$230	$195	$175	$165	*$648*

GRADING - PPGS™	100%	98%	95%	90%	80%	70%	60%	LAST MSR

* ***Model 908S Compact*** – Value Series, similar to Model 908, except has stainless steel slide with alloy frame, 24 oz. Mfg. 2003-2007.

	$495	$355	$275	$230	$195	$175	$165	*$648*

Add $24 for carry combo variation (includes Kydex carry holster, new 2004).

MODEL 909 FULL SIZE – 9mm Para. cal., Value Series, 4 in. barrel, traditional double action, large frame, 9 shot mag., fixed sights, single side safety, alloy frame and steel slide, curved backstrap with black synthetic grips, 27 oz. Mfg. 1994-1996.

	$450	$375	$300	$250	$210	$190	$175	*$443*

MODEL 910 FULL SIZE – Value Series, similar to Model 909, except has 10 or 15 shot mag., 28 oz. Mfg. 1994-2007.

	$450	$375	$300	$250	$210	$190	$175	*$616*

Add $22 for Hi-Viz front sight (disc. 2003).

* ***Model 910S*** – Value Series, similar to Model 910, except has stainless steel slide with alloy frame, 28 oz. Mfg. 2003-2007.

	$450	$375	$300	$250	$210	$190	$175	*$624*

MODEL 915 – 9mm Para. cal., Value Series, 4 in. barrel, fixed sights, 10 (C/B 1994) or 15* shot mag., manual safety, aluminum alloy frame, blue finish. Mfg. 1993-1994.

	$450	$350	$275	$225	$200	$190	$175	*$467*

MODEL 1006 STAINLESS – 10mm cal., stainless steel construction, 5 in. barrel, DA/SA, exposed hammer, 9 shot mag., fixed or adj. sights, ambi safety, 26,979 units produced 1990-1993.

	$850	$675	$550	$425	$325	$245	$215	*$769*

Add $27 for adj. rear sight.

MODEL 1026 STAINLESS – 10mm cal., 5 in. barrel, DA/SA, features frame mounted decocking lever, 9 shot mag., straight backstrap, 3,135 units produced 1990-1991 only.

	$875	$685	$565	$435	$335	$265	$235	*$755*

MODEL 1046 STAINLESS – 10mm cal., 5 in. barrel, DAO, fixed sights, 9 shot mag., straight backstrap, 151 units produced 1991 only.

	$1,500	$1,200	$875	$550	$400	$300	$250	*$747*

MODEL 1066 STAINLESS – 10mm cal., 4 1/4 in. barrel, DA/SA, 9 shot mag., straight backstrap, ambidextrous safety, traditional double action, fixed sights, 5,067 units produced 1990-1992.

	$750	$625	$500	$400	$325	$250	$225	*$730*

Add $75 for Tritium night sights - disc. 1991 (Model 1066-NS).

Only 1,000 Model 1066-NSs were manufactured.

MODEL 1076 STAINLESS – 10mm cal., similar to Model 1026 Stainless, except has 4 1/4 in. barrel, 13,805 units produced 1990-93.

	$1,200	$1,000	$850	$725	$625	$525	$450	*$778*

* ***Model 1076 Stainless FBI Contract Gun*** – needs to be verified by S&W semi-auto pistol expert.

	$2,800	$2,500	$2,200	$1,800	$1,400	$1,200	$975	

MODEL 1086 STAINLESS – 10mm cal., similar to Model 1066 Stainless, except is double action only, 1,660 units produced 1990-1992.

	$900	$700	$525	$400	$325	$250	$210	*$730*

MODEL 1911 ENGRAVED – .45 ACP cal, 5 in. stainless steel barrel, 8 shot mag., white dot front and adj. rear sights, engraved wood grips, features machine engraving, manual thumb safety, Glass bead finish, includes wooden mahogany presentation case, 39.1 oz. New 2017.

MSR $1,239	$1,060	$950	$850	$750	$650	$550	$450	

SW1911 – .45 ACP cal., patterned after the Colt M1911, large frame, SA, 5 in. barrel, 8 shot single stack mag., alloy (disc. 2006), steel or stainless steel frame, steel slide, matte, blue/black (new 2005) or Clear Coat finish, patented S&W firing pin safety release activated by the grip safety, pinned-in external extractor, Wolff springs throughout, Texas Armament match trigger, Hogue rubber (standard) or wood (new 2004) grips, McCormick hammer and thumb safety, Briley barrel bushing, two Wilson magazines, full-length heavy guide rod, high profile Wilson beavertail safety, adj. rear black blade, or Novak Lo-Mount Carry sights, 39 oz. Mfg. 2003-2011.

	$875	$685	$565	$435	$335	$265	$235	*$1,039*

Add $60 for rear adj. sight.

Add $270 or Doug Koenig Model w/two-tone finish and adj. rear sight.

GRADING - PPGS™	100%	98%	95%	90%	80%	70%	60%	LAST MSR

* ***SW1911 Stainless*** – features stainless steel frame and slide, checkered wood or black synthetic grips, 39.4 oz. Disc. 2016.

	$925	$725	$550	$425	$395	$350	$325	*$1,079*

Add $120 for wood grips and adj. rear sight.
Add $93 for matte finish with black blade front sight (disc. 2006).
Add $72 for tactical lower frame rail w/wood grips (mfg. 2006-2010).
Add $301 for Crimson Trace Lasergrips (mfg. 2005-2010).

* ***SW1911 w/no firing pin block*** – similar to SW1911, except does not have firing pin block, Melonite finish. Mfg. 2009-2011.

	$925	$750	$525	$450	$400	$375	$350	*$1,099*

SW1911 PD (Sc) – similar to Model SW1911, except has 4 1/4 or 5 (new 2007) in. barrel with small Scandium alloy frame, 8 shot, black finish, and wood grips. Mfg. 2004-2011.

	$1,150	$975	$825	$725	$625	$525	$475	*$1,109*

Add $240 for Crimson Trace Lasergrips.
Add $120 for Gunsite model with gold bead front sight.
Add $30 for tactical lower rail.

SW1911 E SERIES – .45 ACP cal., SA, stainless steel frame and slide, 5 (new 2011) in. stainless steel barrel, 8 shot, white dot (disc. 2018) or Tritium night sights, wooden laminate E-Series grips or Crimson Trace Laser grips (disc. 2017), grip and thumb safety, fish scale slide serrations, with or w/o lower tactical rail (new 2018), satin stainless, matte silver, or matte black (disc. 2020) frame finish, 39.6-41 oz. New 2009.

MSR $997	$850	$750	$650	$575	$475	$385	$325	

Add $420 for lower tactical rail (new 2018).
Add $240 for machine engraving (new 2018).
Add $170 for Crimson Trace Lasergrips (disc. 2017).

* ***SW1911 SC (E Series Scandium Alloy Frame)*** – .45 ACP cal., SA, round butt Scandium alloy frame, 4 1/4 in. stainless steel barrel, 7 or 8 shot mag., stainless steel slide, Tritium night sights, wooden laminate E-Series grips, grip and thumb safety, choice of two-tone (satin stainless) or Melonite (black) frame finish, 28.8-29.6 oz. New 2011.

MSR $1,469	$1,250	$1,095	$940	$850	$685	$575	$490	

SW1911 PRO SERIES – .45 ACP (disc. 2016) or 9mm Para. (new 2009) cal., SA, 5 in. barrel, 8 (.45 ACP) or 10 (9mm Para.) shot mag., 3-dot (9mm Para. cal. only), Novak fiber optic front and rear or Black Dovetail rear adj. sights, checkered wood grips, stainless steel frame and slide, choice of GIs bead or satin stainless finish (disc. 2016), Pro Series features include 300 LPI front strap checkering, hand polished barrel feed ramp, crisp 4 1/2 lb. trigger pull, full-length guide rod, oversized external extractor, ambidextrous frame safety, precision crowned muzzle, 41 oz. New mid-2007.

MSR $1,579	$1,275	$1,025	$850	$725	$625	$525	$450	

Subtract $120 for .45 ACP cal. (disc. 2016).
Add $130 for adj. Black Dovetail rear sight (new late 2011).

* ***SW1911 SC Pro Series Sub-Compact*** – similar to SW1911 Pro Series, except has 3 in. barrel, 7 shot mag., and subcompact frame, black metal finish, 26 1/2 oz. Mfg. 2009-disc.

	$950	$795	$675	$550	$450	$400	$350	*$1,229*

Add $101 for black metal finish.

MODEL 3904 – 9mm Para. cal., DA/SA, aluminum alloy frame, 4 in. barrel with fixed bushing, 8 shot mag., Delrin one-piece wraparound grips, exposed hammer, ambidextrous safety, beveled magwell, extended squared-off trigger guard, adj. or fixed rear sight, 3-dot sighting system, 28 oz. Mfg. 1989-1991.

	$650	$375	$275	$225	$195	$175	$165	*$541*

Add $25 for adj. rear sight.

MODEL 3906 STAINLESS – stainless steel variation of the Model 3904, 35 1/2 oz. Mfg. 1989-91.

	$675	$525	$450	$375	$275	$250	$225	*$604*

Add $28 for adj. rear sight.

MODEL 3913 COMPACT STAINLESS – stainless steel variation of the Model 3914, 25 oz. Mfg. 1990-99.

	$550	$440	$365	$305	$260	$220	$190	*$662*

* ***Model 3913NL Compact Stainless*** – similar to Model 3913 Ladysmith, except does not have Ladysmith on the slide. Disc. 1994.

	$575	$475	$395	$350	$295	$250	$220	*$622*

GRADING - PPGS™	100%	98%	95%	90%	80%	70%	60%	LAST MSR

* ***Model 3913 LS Compact Stainless (Ladysmith)*** – similar to Model 3913 Stainless, except is matte stainless with white Delrin grips and mag. does not have finger extension, includes case, 25 oz. Mfg. 1990-2006.

$710	$525	$400	$335	$290	$245	$215	*$901*

MODEL 3913TSW TACTICAL – 9mm Para. cal., DA/SA, compact frame, 3 1/2 in. barrel, 8 shot mag., Novak Lo-Mount 2-dot sights, stainless steel slide, aluminum alloy frame, matte stainless finish, straight black backstrap synthetic grips, 24.8 oz. Mfg. 1998-2006.

$750	$520	$400	$335	$290	$245	$215	*$876*

MODEL 3914 COMPACT – 9mm Para. cal., DA/SA, aluminum alloy frame, 3 1/2 in. barrel, hammerless, 8 shot finger extension mag., fixed sights only, ambidextrous safety, blue finish, straight backstrap grip, 25 oz. Mfg. 1990-1995.

$525	$425	$350	$325	$295	$280	$265	*$562*

This model was also available with a single side manual safety at no extra charge - disc. 1991 (Model 3914NL).

* ***Model 3914 Compact LadySmith*** – similar to Model 3914, except has Delrin grips, 25 oz. Mfg. 1990-91 only.

$650	$525	$400	$335	$290	$245	$215	*$568*

* ***Model 3914 TSW*** – similar to Model 3914, except slide is marked "9 Tactical", blue finish, 8 shot mag. 1,060 mfg. 1990 only.

$900	$650	$475	$395	$345	$280	$235	

MODEL 3953 COMPACT STAINLESS – 9mm Para. cal., DAO, aluminum alloy frame with stainless steel slide, compact model with 3 1/2 in. barrel, 8 shot mag. Mfg. 1990-1999.

$575	$440	$365	$305	$260	$220	$190	*$662*

MODEL 3953TSW – similar to Model 3913TSW, except is DAO, 24.8 oz. Mfg. 1998-2002.

$600	$475	$380	$320	$275	$230	$200	*$760*

MODEL 3954 – similar to Model 3953, except has blue steel slide. Mfg. 1990-92.

$550	$395	$350	$325	$295	$280	$265	*$528*

MODEL 4003 STAINLESS – .40 S&W cal., DA/SA, 4 in. barrel, 11 shot mag., white dot fixed sights, ambidextrous safety, aluminum alloy frame with stainless steel slide, one-piece Xenoy wraparound grips, straight gripstrap, 28 oz. Mfg. 1991-1993.

$575	$495	$395	$330	$285	$240	$215	*$698*

* ***Model 4003TSW Stainless*** – similar to Model 4003 Stainless, but has aluminum alloy frame, 10 shot mag., stainless steel slide, S&W tactical features, including equipment rail and Novak Lo-Mount Carry sights, traditional double action only, satin stainless finish, 28 1/2 oz. Mfg. 2000-2004.

$700	$600	$500	$450	$400	$360	$330	*$940*

MODEL 4004 – .40 S&W cal., similar to Model 4003, except has aluminum alloy frame with blue carbon steel slide. Mfg. 1991-92.

$540	$460	$375	$325	$295	$280	$265	*$643*

MODEL 4006 STAINLESS – .40 S&W cal., 3 1/2 (Shorty Forty) or 4 in. barrel, DA/SA, 10 (C/B 1994) or 11* shot mag., satin stainless finish, exposed hammer, Delrin one-piece wraparound grips, 3-dot sights, 38 1/2 oz. Mfg. 1990-1999.

$655	$545	$400	$335	$290	$245	$215	*$791*

Add $31 for adj. rear sight.
Add $115 for fixed Tritium night sights (new 1992).

The bobbed hammer option on this model was disc. in 1991.

* ***Model 4006TSW Stainless*** – similar to Model 4006 Stainless, except has stainless steel frame and slide, S&W tactical features, including equipment rail, traditional double action only, 37.8 oz. Mfg. 2000-2004.

$700	$600	$500	$450	$400	$360	$330	*$963*

Add $38 if w/o Novak Lo-Mount Carry (NLC) sights.
Add $133 for night sights (disc.).

MODEL 4013 COMPACT STAINLESS – .40 S&W cal., DA/SA, 3 1/2 in. barrel, 8 shot mag., fixed sights, ambidextrous safety, alloy frame. Mfg. 1991-1996.

$595	$485	$385	$300	$250	$225	$200	*$722*

GRADING - PPGS™	100%	98%	95%	90%	80%	70%	60%	LAST MSR

MODEL 4013TSW TACTICAL – .40 S&W cal., DA/SA, 3 1/2 in. barrel, 9 shot mag. with reversible mag. catch, aluminum alloy frame with stainless steel slide, satin stainless finish, black synthetic grips, fixed 3-dot Novak Lo-Mount Carry sights, ambidextrous safety, 26.8 oz. Mfg. 1997-2006.

	$825	$635	$465	$395	$350	$295	$250	*$1,021*

MODEL 4014 COMPACT – similar to Model 4013, except is steel with blue finish. Mfg. 1991-93.

	$1,000	$800	$600	$500	$400	$395	$350	*$635*

MODEL 4026 STAINLESS – .40 S&W cal., traditional double action with frame mounted decocking lever, 10 (C/B 1994) or 11* shot mag., fixed sights, curved backstrap, 36 oz. Mfg. 1991-93.

	$625	$525	$400	$335	$290	$245	$215	*$731*

MODEL 4040 PD – .40 S&W cal., compact frame using Scandium, 3 1/2 in. barrel, DA/SA, Hogue rubber grips, Novak Lo-Mount Carry 3-dot sights, matte black finish, 25.6 oz. Mfg. 2003-2005.

	$625	$525	$400	$335	$290	$245	$215	*$840*

MODEL 4043 STAINLESS – .40 S&W cal., DAO, aluminum alloy frame with stainless steel slide, 4 in. barrel, 10 (C/B 1994) or 11* shot mag., one-piece Xenoy wraparound grips, straight backstrap, white dot fixed sights, 30 oz. Mfg. 1991-1999.

	$635	$510	$390	$325	$280	$240	$210	*$772*

* ***Model 4043TSW Stainless*** – .40 S&W cal., DAO, similar to Model 4043 Stainless, but has S&W tactical features, including equipment rail, 28 1/2 oz. Mfg. 2000-2002.

	$650	$550	$425	$350	$290	$245	$215	*$886*

MODEL 4044 – .40 S&W cal., similar to Model 4043, except has carbon steel slide. Mfg. 1991-92.

	$540	$460	$375	$325	$295	$280	$265	*$643*

MODEL 4046 STAINLESS – similar to Model 4006 Stainless, except is DAO, 4 in. barrel only. Mfg. 1991-1999.

	$655	$540	$400	$335	$290	$245	$215	*$791*

Add $115 for Tritium night sights (new 1992).

* ***Model 4046TSW Stainless*** – DAO, similar to Model 4046 Stainless, but has S&W tactical features, including equipment rail, 37.8 oz. Mfg. 2000-2002.

	$700	$625	$500	$455	$400	$360	$330	*$907*

Add $133 for night sights.

MODEL 4053 COMPACT STAINLESS – .40 S&W cal., DAO variation of the Model 4013. Mfg. 1991-1997.

	$625	$525	$400	$335	$290	$245	$215	*$734*

MODEL 4053TSW (TACTICAL) – .40 S&W cal., DAO, 3 1/2 in. barrel, 9 shot mag. with reversible mag. catch, alloy frame with stainless steel slide, satin stainless finish, black synthetic grips, fixed sights, ambidextrous safety, 26.8 oz. Mfg. 1997-2002.

	$730	$580	$425	$360	$315	$260	$225	*$886*

MODEL 4054 – .40 S&W cal., DAO variation of the Model 4014. Mfg. 1991-1992.

	$650	$550	$425	$350	$290	$245	$215	*$629*

MODEL 4056TSW (TACTICAL) – .40 S&W cal., DAO, 3 1/2 in. barrel, 9 shot mag. with reversible mag. catch, stainless steel frame and slide, satin stainless finish, black synthetic grips, fixed sights, ambidextrous safety, 37 1/2 oz. Mfg. 1997 only.

	$675	$575	$450	$350	$290	$245	$215	*$844*

MODEL 4505 – .45 ACP cal., carbon steel variation of the Model 4506, fixed or adj. rear sight. 1,200 mfg. 1991 only.

	$750	$625	$550	$440	$385	$330	$300	*$660*

Add $27 for adj. rear sight.

MODEL 4506 STAINLESS – .45 ACP cal., 5 in. barrel, DA/SA, 8 shot mag., combat trigger guard, exposed hammer, fixed or adj. rear sight, straight backstrap (curved is optional), Delrin one-piece grips, 40 1/2 oz. Mfg. 1990-1999.

	$725	$625	$400	$335	$285	$235	$215	*$822*

Add $33 for adj. rear sight.

Approx. 100 Model 4506s left the factory mismarked Model 645 on the frame. In NIB condition they are worth $700.

MODEL 4513TSW – .45 ACP cal., DAO, compact frame, 3 3/4 in. barrel, 7 shot mag., 3-dot Novak Lo-Mount Carry sights, stainless steel slide, aluminum alloy frame, satin stainless finish, 28.6 oz. Mfg. 1998-2004.

	$725	$625	$475	$395	$340	$285	$240	*$980*

GRADING - PPGS™	100%	98%	95%	90%	80%	70%	60%	LAST MSR

MODEL 4516 COMPACT STAINLESS – .45 ACP cal., bobbed hammer, compact variation of the Model 4506, 3 3/4 in. barrel, DA/SA, 7 shot mag., ambidextrous safety, fixed rear sight only, 34 oz. Mfg. 1990-1997.

	$650	$525	$400	$335	$290	$245	$215	$787

Original model is marked 4516 while later mfg. changed slide legend to read 4516-1. Original mfg. is more collectible and slight premiums are being asked.

MODEL 4526 STAINLESS – similar to Model 4506 Stainless, except has frame mounted decocking lever. Mfg. 1990-91 only.

	$825	$635	$465	$395	$350	$295	$250	$762

MODEL 4536 STAINLESS – .45 ACP cal., similar to Model 4516 Compact, except has frame mounted decocking lever only. Mfg. 1990-91 only.

	$825	$635	$465	$395	$350	$295	$250	$762

MODEL 4546 STAINLESS – .45 ACP cal., similar to Model 4506 Stainless, except is double action only. Mfg. 1990-91 only.

	$825	$635	$465	$395	$350	$295	$250	$735

MODEL 4553TSW – .45 ACP cal., similar to Model 4513TSW, except is double action only. Mfg. 1998-2002.

	$755	$595	$450	$385	$335	$280	$235	$924

MODEL 4556 STAINLESS – .45 ACP cal., DAO, 3 3/4 in. barrel, 7 shot mag., fixed sights. Mfg. 1991 only.

	$750	$625	$450	$390	$340	$280	$235	$735

MODEL 4563TSW – .45 ACP cal., DA/SA, 4 1/4 in. barrel, 8 shot mag., aluminum alloy frame with stainless steel slide, satin stainless finish, includes S&W tactical features, including equipment rail and Novak 3-dot sights, synthetic black straight backstrap grips, 30.6 oz. Mfg. 2000-2004.

	$750	$625	$450	$390	$340	$280	$235	$977

MODEL 4566 STAINLESS – .45 ACP cal., DA/SA, ambidextrous safety, 4 1/4 in. barrel, 8 shot mag. Mfg. 1990-1999.

	$650	$550	$410	$345	$300	$250	$220	$822

* ***Model 4566TSW Stainless*** – similar to Model 4566, except has ambidextrous safety, 39.1 oz. Disc. 2004.

	$725	$600	$450	$390	$340	$280	$235	$1,000

MODEL 4567-NS STAINLESS – similar to Model 4566 Stainless, except has Tritium night sights, stainless steel frame and carbon steel slide. 2,500 mfg. in 1991 only.

	$875	$685	$565	$435	$335	$265	$235	$735

MODEL 4576 STAINLESS – .45 ACP cal., features 4 1/4 in. barrel, DA/SA, frame mounted decocking lever, fixed sights. Mfg. 1990-1992.

	$635	$535	$410	$345	$300	$250	$220	$762

MODEL 4583TSW – similar to Model 4563TSW, except is DAO, 30.6 oz. Mfg. 2000-2002.

	$700	$575	$450	$380	$330	$275	$230	$921

MODEL 4586 STAINLESS – .45 ACP cal., full size 4 1/4 in. barrel, DAO, 8 shot mag. Mfg. 1990-1999.

	$695	$575	$425	$345	$300	$250	$220	$822

* ***Model 4586TSW Stainless*** – similar to Model 4566TSW, except is DAO, 39.1 oz. Mfg. 2000-2002.

	$700	$600	$445	$380	$330	$275	$230	$942

MODEL 5903 – 9mm Para. cal., DA/SA, 4 in. barrel, stainless steel slide and alloy frame, exposed hammer, 10 (C/B 1994) or 15* shot mag., adj. (disc. 1993) or fixed rear sight, ambidextrous safety. Mfg. 1990-1997.

	$650	$575	$475	$395	$365	$325	$300	$701

Add $30 for adj. rear sight (disc).

* ***Model 5903TSW*** – 9mm Para. cal., DA/SA, aluminum alloy frame with stainless slide, satin stainless finish, includes S&W tactical features, such as equipment rail and Novak Lo-Mount Carry sights, black synthetic grips with curved backstrap, 28.9 oz. Mfg. 2000-2004.

	$875	$580	$430	$385	$330	$275	$250	$892

* ***Model 5903-SSV*** – 9mm Para. cal., similar to Model 5903, except has 3 1/2 in. barrel, bobbed blue hammer, Novak Lo-Mount fixed two-dot rear sight, two-tone finish, straight backstrap with Delrin wraparound grip, 15 shot mag. 1,500 mfg. during 1990 only.

	$750	$595	$430	$385	$330	$275	$250	

GRADING - PPGS™	100%	98%	95%	90%	80%	70%	60%	LAST MSR

MODEL 5904 – 9mm Para. cal., similar to Model 5903, except has blue steel slide and blue alloy frame, 26 1/2 oz. Mfg. 1989-1998.

$650	$525	$400	$335	$290	$245	$215	*$663*

Add $30 for adj. rear sight (disc. 1993).

MODEL 5905 – 9mm Para. cal., similar to Model 5904, except has blue carbon steel frame and slide. Approx. 5,000 mfg. 1990-1991 only.

$925	$725	$550	$425	$395	$350	$325	

MODEL 5906 STAINLESS – 9mm Para. cal., stainless steel variation of the Model 5904, 37 1/2 oz. Mfg. 1989-1999.

$750	$500	$400	$335	$290	$245	$215	*$751*

Add $37 for adj. rear sight.
Add $115 for Tritium night sights.
Add 100% for Model 5906M (South American military model with Melonite finish).

* ***Model 5906TSW Stainless*** – 9mm Para. cal., DA/SA, similar to Model 5906 Stainless, but has S&W tactical features, including equipment rail, 38.3 oz. Mfg. 2000-2004.

$925	$575	$475	$350	$300	$265	$235	*$915*

Add $44 if w/o Novak Lo Mount Carry sight.
Add $132 for night sights (disc.).

MODEL 5924 – 9mm Para. cal., blue steel version of the 5903, 4 in. barrel, features frame mounted decocking lever, 15 shot mag., 37 1/2 oz. Mfg. 1990-91 only.

$650	$550	$475	$375	$335	$300	$280	*$635*

MODEL 5926 STAINLESS – 9mm Para. cal., stainless variation of the Model 5924. Disc. 1992.

$625	$525	$425	$350	$295	$250	$210	*$697*

MODEL 5943 STAINLESS – 9mm Para. cal., DAO, 4 in. barrel, aluminum alloy frame with stainless steel slide, straight backstrap, 15 shot mag. Mfg. 1990-1991 only.

$625	$525	$400	$335	$290	$245	$215	*$655*

* ***Model 5943-SSV Stainless*** – 9mm Para. cal., similar to Model 5943 Stainless, except has 3 1/2 in. barrel, Tritium night sights. Mfg. 1990-91 only.

$800	$550	$475	$395	$330	$285	$240	*$690*

* ***Model 5943TSW Stainless*** – 9mm Para. cal., DAO, aluminum alloy frame with stainless steel slide, includes S&W tactical features, equipment rail, and Novak Lo-Mount Carry sights, 28.9 oz. Mfg. 2000-2002.

$750	$575	$450	$375	$325	$280	$265	*$844*

MODEL 5944 – 9mm Para. cal., similar to Model 5943 Stainless, except has blue finish slide and frame. Mfg. 1990-1991 only.

$625	$550	$475	$400	$350	$300	$280	*$610*

MODEL 5946 STAINLESS – 9mm Para. cal., DAO, one-piece Xenoy wraparound grips, all stainless steel variation of the Model 5943, 39 1/2 oz. Mfg. 1990-1999.

$650	$500	$400	$335	$290	$245	$215	*$751*

* ***Model 5946TSW Stainless*** – 9mm Para. cal., DAO, includes S&W tactical features, equipment rail, and Novak Lo-Mount Carry sights, 38.3 oz. Mfg. 2000-2002.

$725	$600	$450	$375	$315	$260	$225	*$863*

MODEL 6904 COMPACT – 9mm Para. cal., compact variation of the Model 5904, 3 1/2 in. barrel, DA/SA, 10 (C/ B 1994) or 12* shot finger extension mag., fixed rear sight, 26 1/2 oz. Mfg. 1989-1997.

$600	$475	$400	$350	$325	$300	$280	*$625*

MODEL 6906 COMPACT STAINLESS – 9mm Para. cal., stainless steel variation of the Model 6904, 26 1/2 oz. Mfg. 1989-1999.

$675	$470	$380	$320	$275	$235	$200	*$720*

Add $116 for Tritium night sights (new 1992).

MODEL 6926 STAINLESS – 9mm Para. cal., 3 1/2 in. barrel, DA/SA, features frame mounted decocking lever, aluminum alloy frame with stainless slide, 12 shot mag. Mfg. 1990-1991 only.

$650	$575	$450	$375	$315	$270	$230	*$663*

MODEL 6944 – 9mm Para. cal., DAO, 3 1/2 in. barrel, 12 shot mag., aluminum alloy frame with blue steel slide. Mfg. 1990-1991 only.

$700	$600	$500	$450	$400	$360	$330	*$578*

GRADING - PPGS™	100%	98%	95%	90%	80%	70%	60%	LAST MSR

MODEL 6946 STAINLESS – 9mm Para. cal., similar to Model 6944, except has stainless steel slide, semi-bobbed hammer, 26 1/2 oz. Mfg. 1990-1999.

$600	$525	$425	$350	$295	$250	$210	*$720*

MODEL CS9 CHIEFS SPECIAL – 9mm Para. cal., compact design with traditional double action, 3 in. barrel, 7 shot mag., alloy frame/stainless slide, matte blue or stainless steel (disc. 2000), Hogue wraparound rubber grips, 3-dot Novak Lo-Mount sights, 20.8 oz. Mfg. 1999-2006.

$600	$460	$380	$325	$270	$230	$195	*$777*

MODEL CS40 CHIEFS SPECIAL – .40 S&W cal., similar to Model CS9, except has 3 1/4 in. barrel, 24.2 oz. Mfg. 1999-2002.

$575	$435	$375	$315	$275	$230	$195	*$717*

MODEL CS45 CHIEFS SPECIAL – .45 ACP cal., similar to Model CS40, except has 6 shot mag., matte finished stainless steel slide, 23.9 oz. Mfg. 1999-2006.

$660	$485	$410	$335	$285	$230	$195	*$826*

A Model CS45D was produced similar to the CS45, except is double action only.

SIGMA MODEL SW9F SERIES – 9mm Para. cal., DAO, SFO, 4 1/2 in. barrel, fixed sights, polymer frame and steel slide, blue finish only, 10 (C/B 1994) or 17* shot mag., 26 oz. Mfg. 1994-1996.

$475	$400	$350	$325	$295	$280	$265	*$593*

Add $104 for Tritium night sights.

* ***Sigma Model SW9C Series Compact*** – 9mm Para. cal., similar to Sigma Model SW9F, except has 4 in. barrel, 25 oz. Mfg. 1996-1998.

$450	$355	$325	$295	$280	$265	$240	*$541*

* ***Sigma Model SW9M Series Compact*** – 9mm Para. cal., SFO, features 3 1/4 in. barrel, 7 shot mag., fixed channel rear sight, grips integral with frame, satin black finish, 18 oz. Mfg. 1996-1998.

$375	$270	$240	$220	$195	$175	$160	*$366*

SIGMA MODEL SW9VE/GVE (SW9E/SW9P/SW9G/SW9V) – 9mm Para. cal., DAO, SFO, features 4 in. standard or ported (SW9P, mfg. 2001-2003) barrel, 10 or 16 (new late 2004) shot mag., 3-dot sighting system, grips integral with grey (disc. 2000), NATO Green (SW9G, disc. 2003), or black polymer frame, black (SW9E, mfg. 1999-2002) or satin stainless steel (SW9VE) slide, 24.7 oz. Mfg. 1997-2012.

$325	$275	$235	$200	$175	$150	$135	*$379*

Add $8 for Allied Forces model w/Melonite slide (mfg. 2007-2009).
Add $380 for SW9VE/SW40VE Allied Forces model w/emergency kit, including space blankets, emergency food, first aid kit, crank radio/flashlight, multi-tool, and pocket survival pack, cased (mfg. 2007-2009).
Add $48 for SW9P or SW9G with night sights (disc. 2003).
Add $210 for Tritium night sights (disc. 2000).

The Enhanced Sigma Series Model SW9VE was introduced during 1999, after the SW9V was discontinued.

SIGMA MODEL SW40F SERIES – .40 S&W cal., DAO, SFO, 4 1/2 in. barrel, fixed sights, polymer frame, blue finish only, 10 (C/B 1994) or 15* shot mag., 26 oz. Mfg. 1994-1998.

$450	$355	$325	$295	$280	$265	$240	*$541*

Add $104 for Tritium night sights (disc. 1997).

* ***Sigma Model SW40C Series Compact*** – .40 S&W cal., similar to Sigma Model SW40F, except has 4 in. barrel, 26 oz. Mfg. 1996-1998.

$450	$355	$325	$295	$280	$265	$240	*$541*

SIGMA MODEL SW40VE/SW40P/SW40G/SW40GVE (SW40E/SW40V) – .40 S&W cal., SFO, features 4 in. standard or ported (SW40P, mfg. 2001-2005) barrel, 10 or 14 (new mid-2004) shot mag., 3-dot sighting system, grips integral with grey (disc. 2000), NATO green (SW40G) or black polymer frame, black slide with Melonite finish (SW40E, mfg. 1999-2002) or satin stainless steel slide, 24.4 oz. Mfg. 1997-2012.

$320	$275	$230	$200	$175	$150	$140	*$379*

Add $8 for Allied Forces model w/Melonite slide, (mfg. 2007-2009).
Add $210 for Tritium night sights (disc.).
Add $145 for Model SW40P or SW40G (includes night sights, disc. 2005).
Add $380 for SW9VE/SW40VE Allied Forces model w/emergency kit, including space blankets, emergency food, first aid kit, crank radio/flashlight, multi-tool, and pocket survival pack, cased (mfg. 2007-2009).

The Enhanced Sigma Series Model SW40VE was introduced during 1999, after the SW40V was discontinued.

GRADING - PPGS™	100%	98%	95%	90%	80%	70%	60%	LAST MSR

MODEL SW99 – 9mm Para., .40 S&W, or .45 ACP (new 2003) cal., traditional DA, SFO, 9 (.45 ACP cal.) or 10 shot mag., similar to the Walther P99, black polymer frame with black stainless slide and barrel, 4, 4 1/8 (.40 S&W cal. only), or 4.25 (.45 ACP cal. only, new 2003) in. barrel, black finish, ambidextrous mag. release, frame equipment groove, interchangeable backstraps, decocking lever, cocking indicator, adj. 3-dot or night sights, 25.4 (9mm Para. cal.) or 28 1/2 oz. Mfg. 2000-2004.

$600 $485 $430 $380 $340 $300 $275 *$667*

Add $123 for night sights.
Add $41 for .45 ACP cal. (new 2003).

* ***Model SW99 Compact*** – similar to SW99, except is compact version, not available in .45 ACP cal., 3 1/2 in. barrel, 8 (.40 S&W cal.) or 10 (9mm Para. cal.) shot mag. with finger extension, approx. 23 oz. Mfg. 2003-2004.

$565 $485 $430 $380 $340 $300 $275 *$667*

MODEL SW990L – 9mm Para., .40 S&W, or .45 ACP cal., DAO, SFO, 9 (.45 ACP cal. only), 10 (all cals. except .45 ACP), 12 (.40 S&W cal.) or 16 (9mm Para.) shot mag., similar to the Walther P99, black polymer frame with black stainless Melonite slide and barrel, 4 (9mm Para. cal. only), 4 1/8 (.40 S&W cal. only), or 4.25 (.45 ACP cal. only) in. barrel, black finish, approx. 25 oz. Mfg. 2005-2006.

$615 $515 $450 $400 $350 $300 $275 *$729*

Add $44 for .45 ACP cal.

* ***Model SW990L Compact*** – 9mm Para. or .40 S&W cal., similar to SW990L, except is compact version with small polymer frame, not available in .45 ACP cal., 3 1/2 in. barrel, 8 (.40 S&W cal.) or 10 (9mm Para. cal.) shot mag. with finger extension, approx. 23 oz. Mfg. 2005-2006.

$610 $515 $450 $400 $350 $300 $275 *$729*

SIGMA MODEL SW357 – .357 SIG cal., SFO, 4 in. barrel, 10 shot mag., black finish, stainless steel. Mfg. 1998 only.

$525 $450 $375 $325 $250 $195 $165

SIGMA MODEL SW380 – .380 ACP cal., DAO, SFO, 3 in. barrel, fixed sights, polymer frame and steel slide, striker firing system, blue finish only, 6 shot mag., shortened grip, 14 oz. Mfg. 1996-2000.

$285 $245 $210 $190 $180 $170 $160 *$358*

MODEL SW SD9 – 9mm Para. cal., DAO, SFO, w/o hammer, 4 in. barrel, 10 or 16 shot mag., stainless steel slide/barrel, black polymer frame with Picatinny rail, front and rear slide serrations, Tritium night front sight, two-dot fixed rear sight, black Melonite finish, 22.7 oz. Mfg. 2010-2011.

$425 $325 $295 $275 $250 $225 $200 *$459*

Add $40 for home defense kit that includes NanoVault lockable case and S&W Micro90 compact pistol light (disc. 2011).

MODEL SD9 – 9mm Para. cal., striker fire action, polymer frame, 4 in. stainless steel barrel and slide, 16 shot, white dot front and white two-dot rear sight, textured polymer grip, gray or FDE (new 2018) frame finish, 22.3 oz. New 2015.

MSR $389 $375 $285 $245 $220 $180 $150 $125

MODEL SD9 VE – 9mm Para. cal., large frame, striker fired action, 4 in. barrel, 10 or 16 shot, polymer/stainless steel frame, black plastic grip, white dot front and fixed 2-dot rear or Hi-Viz (new 2018) sights, two-tone finish, 22.7 oz.

MSR $389 $375 $285 $245 $220 $180 $150 $125

Add $20 for tactile loaded chamber indicator (TLCI, new 2015).
Add $40 for Hi-Viz sights (new 2018).

MODEL SW SD40 – .40 S&W cal., DAO, striker fire action, w/o hammer, 4 in. barrel, 10 or 14 shot mag., stainless steel slide/barrel, black polymer frame with Picatinny rail, front and rear slide serrations, Tritium night front sight, two-dot fixed rear sight, black Melonite finish, 22.7 oz. Mfg. 2010-2011.

$375 $325 $295 $275 $250 $225 $200 *$459*

Add $40 for home defense kit that includes NanoVault lockable case and S&W Micro90 compact pistol light (disc. 2011).

MODEL SD40 – .40 S&W cal., striker fire action, polymer frame, 4 in. stainless steel barrel and slide, 14 shot, white dot front and white two-dot rear sight, no thumb safety, gray or FDE frame finish, 22.3 oz. New 2017.

MSR $389 $375 $285 $245 $220 $180 $150 $125

MODEL SD40 VE – .40 S&W cal., large frame, striker fire action, 4 in. barrel, 10 or 14 shot, black plastic grip, white dot or Hi-Viz (new 2018) sights, polymer/stainless frame and slide, two-tone finish, optional loaded chamber indicator, 22.7 oz.

MSR $389 $375 $285 $245 $220 $180 $150 $125

Add $20 for Tactile Loaded Chamber Indicator (TLCI).
Add $40 for Hi-Viz sights (new 2018).

GRADING - PPGS™	100%	98%	95%	90%	80%	70%	60%	LAST MSR

PISTOLS: SEMI-AUTO, M&P/M&P M2.0 SERIES

Smith & Wesson began manufacturing the M&P pistol in 2006 with several variations in each caliber.

In 2017, Smith & Wesson introduced the M&P M2.0 featuring upgrades to nearly every aspect of the original M&P. Built on the great M&P platform in three calibers, this next generation model includes an extended stainless steel chassis, high grip to barrel bore axis ratio for reduced muzzle rise and faster aim recovery, fine-tuned crisper M&P M2.0 trigger, tactile audible reset, and an aggressively textured grip and four interchangeable palm swell inserts. The striker-fire, polymer pistol is available in matte black or FDE finish, includes two magazines, a limited lifetime warranty, and a lifetime service policy.

M&P SERIES – 9mm Para., .40 S&W, .357 SIG (disc. 2010), .380 (new 2014), or .45 ACP (new 2007) cal., DAO, SFO, black Melonite finished stainless steel barrel and slide with twin scalloped slide serrations, black Zytel polymer frame reinforced with stainless steel, matte black or FDE (Dark Earth brown, new 2007) finish, 6 (new 2014), 8, 10, 12, 15, or 17 shot mag., ramp front sights, Novak Lo-Mount Carry rear sight, ambidextrous manual safety became an option during 2009, 6 1/2 lbs. trigger pull, 18 degree grip angle, Picatinny rail in front of trigger guard, three interchangeable grip sizes, 24 1/4-29 1/2 oz. Approx. 25 variations in each caliber. New 2006.

Add $50 for ambidextrous manual safety with lanyard loop on non-compact models.

M&P 9 – 9mm Para. cal., SFO, 10 or 17 shot mag., 4 1/4 in. standard or threaded (new 2015) barrel, full size polymer frame, white dot or steel ramp dovetail front sight, steel low profile or Novak Lo-Mount carry rear sight, stainless steel slide and barrel, black Melonite, carbon fiber (mfg. 2015 only) or FDE (new 2015) finish, with or w/o thumb safety, black grips with three interchangeable palm swell grip sizes or Crimson Trace Lasergrips (new 2008), lower accessory rail, includes two magazines, 24 oz. Disc. 2020.

$395 $350 $295 $270 $220 $200 $180 *$462*

Add $119 for carry and range kit - includes Blade Tech Kydex holster, double magazine pouch, Maglula Uplula speed loader, ear plugs, and extra magazine.

Add $260 for Crimson Trace Lasergrips (mfg. 2008-disc.) or add $130 Crimson Trace green Laserguard (mfg. 2016-disc.).

Add $120 for threaded barrel kit (disc.).

* ***M&P 9c (Compact)*** – 9mm Para. cal., SFO, 10 or 12 shot mag., 3 1/2 in. barrel, steel ramp dovetail mount front sight, Novak Lo-Mount carry rear sight, compact Zytel polymer frame with stainless steel slide and barrel, black Melonite, carbon fiber (new 2015) or FDE (new 2015) finish, with or w/o thumb safety, ambidextrous safety, with or w/o three interchangeable palm swell or Crimson Trace Lasergrips (disc. 2017), 22 oz. Mfg. 2007-2020.

$395 $350 $295 $270 $220 $200 $180 *$462*

Add $30 for carbon fiber (mfg. 2015 only) or FDE finish (new 2015).

Add $260 for Crimson Trace Red Lasergrips (disc. 2019) or $130 for Crimson Trace Green Laserguard (mfg. 2016-2019).

Add $150 if w/o thumb safety and interchangeable grips (disc. 2011).

* ***M&P 9 JG*** – 9mm Para. cal., SFO, 17 shot mag., similar to M&P 9, except has fiber optic front sight, Warren tactical rear sight, five interchangeable palm swell grip sizes (three black and two pink), breast cancer awareness ribbon engraved on slide, designed in collaboration with champion Julie Goloski-Golob. Disc. 2012.

$465 $375 $325 $300 $280 $250 $215 *$619*

* ***M&P 9 L*** – 9mm Para. cal., SFO, 17 shot mag., 5 in. barrel, full size polymer frame, white dot or steel ramp dovetail front sight, steel low profile carry rear sight, stainless steel slide and barrel, black Melonite finish, three interchangeable palm swell grip sizes, includes two magazines, 25 oz. Disc. 2011.

$575 $475 $395 $350 4325 4295 $250 *$758*

M&P 9 PRO SERIES – 9mm Para. cal., striker fire action, 4 1/4 or 5 in. barrel, black polymer frame, 17 shot, lower Picatinny rail, blue/black or satin stainless steel, plastic grips, Lo-Mount Carry, night sights, Fiber optic Green Novak reduced glare sights (disc. 2013), or optics ready, 26 oz. Mfg. 2012-2018.

$575 $475 $400 $350 $300 $265 $235 *$699*

Add $140 for optic ready threaded barrel (new 2016).

Add $70 for optic ready barrel (new 2017).

Subtract $10 if satin finish stainless steel w/o night sights (5 in. barrel only).

M&P 9 SHIELD – 9mm Para. cal., striker fire DAO, black or FDE (mfg. 2018 only) polymer frame, 3.1 in. barrel, 7 or 8 shot mag., choice of 3-dot sights or Tritium night sights (mfg. 2016-2017), with or w/o thumb safety, textured grip surfaces, stainless steel slide w/black Armornite finish, approx. 18 oz. New mid-2012.

MSR $385 $325 $285 $245 $225 $200 $180 $160

Add $98 for loaded chamber indicator.

Add $100 for Tritium night sights (mfg. 2016-2017).

Add $140 for Crimson Trace green Laserguard (mfg. 2015-2017).

GRADING - PPGS™	100%	98%	95%	90%	80%	70%	60%	LAST MSR

M&P 9 VTAC (VIKING TACTICS) – 9mm Para. cal., SFO, 17 shot mag., 4 1/4 in. barrel, full size polymer frame, VTAC Warrior front and rear sights, durable PVD coated stainless steel slide, FDE finish, 24 oz. Disc. 2019.

	$640	$535	$425	$375	$325	$295	$250	*$799*

M&P 9 M2.0 – 9mm Para. cal., 4 1/4, 4.625 (threaded with suppressor height sights, new 2018), or 5 in. stainless steel barrel, 10 (new 2018), 15, or 17 shot mag., tactile and audible trigger reset, choice of low profile red or TruGlo TFX (4 1/4 in., FDE only, new 2018) sights, textured grips w/4 interchangeable palm swell grip inserts, with or w/o thumb safety, extended rigid embedded stainless steel chassis, lower Picatinny rail, 18 degree grip angle, front and rear slide serrations, includes 2 magazines, Armornite black or FDE Cerakote finish, 24.7 oz. New 2017.

MSR $599	$510	$450	$395	$365	$335	$295	$275

Add $140 for TruGlo TFX sights (new 2018, FDE model only).
Add $40 for M&P9 M2.0 Carry & Range Kit (new 2018).

* ***M&P 9 M2.0 Compact*** – 9mm Para. cal., black polymer frame, 3.6 (new 2019) or 4 in. stainless steel barrel, 15 shot mag., tactile and audible trigger reset, white dot front and low profile carry rear sight, with or w/o thumb safety, lower Picatinny rail, includes four interchangeable grip inserts, stainless steel slide w/black Armornite or FDE (new mid-2019) finish, approx. 24.7 oz. New 2018.

MSR $569	$485	$425	$385	$360	$335	$295	$275

Add $60 for Crimson Trace Rail Master universal tactical light (new 2019).
Add $150 for Crimson Trace Green Laserguard (new mid-2018).

» **M&P 9 M2.0 Compact Threaded** – 9mm Para. cal., striker fire, black polymer frame, 4.625 in. stainless steel threaded barrel, 10 or 15 shot mag., tactile and audible trigger reset, suppressor height white dot sights, aggressive textured polymer grip, lower Picatinny rail, includes four interchangeable palm swell grip inserts, Armornite finish, 27.2 oz. New 2019.

MSR $569	$485	$425	$385	$360	$335	$295	$275

* ***M&P 9 M2.0 Sub-Compact*** – 9mm Para. cal., SFO, black polymer sub-compact frame, 3.6 in. stainless steel barrel, 12 or 15 shot mag., tactile and audible trigger reset, white dot front and white two-dot rear sight, polymer grip with four interchangeable palm swell grip inserts, with or w/o thumb safety, lower Picatinny rail, stainless steel slide w/black Armornite finish, 25 oz. New mid-2019.

MSR $569	$485	$425	$385	$360	$335	$295	$275

M&P 9 SHIELD M2.0 – 9mm Para. cal., striker fire DAO, 3.1 in. barrel, 7 or 8 shot mag., choice of white 3-dot or Tritium night sights, black polymer frame with textured grip surfaces, with or w/o thumb safety, includes two mags. (one flush fit and one extended w/finger grooves), stainless steel slide w/ black Amornite finish, approx. 18 oz. New 2018.

MSR $490	$415	$365	$315	$285	$230	$210	$190

Add $34 for Crimson Trace integrated red laser.
Add $89 for Tritium night sights.
Add $98 for Crimson Trace integrated green laser.
Add $200 for Crimson Trace Laserguard Pro with green laser/light combo.

M&P 9 SHIELD EZ M2.0 – 9mm Para. cal., hammer fired, polymer frame, 3.675 in. stainless steel barrel, two 8 shot mags., reversible mag. release, white dot sights, with or w/out Crimson Trace Red Laserguard, black polymer grip, with or w/o manual thumb safety, Picatinny-style equipment rail, Tactile Loaded Chamber Indicator (TLCI), Armornite finish, 23.2 oz. New 2020.

MSR $490	$415	$365	$315	$285	$230	$185	$160

Add $101 for Crimson Trace Red Laserguard.

M&P 15 PISTOL – 5.56 NATO cal., gas operated, 7 1/2 in. threaded barrel with blast diverter, 30 shot PMAG, forged integral trigger guard, Palmswell grip with 4 interchangeable grip inserts, M&P free float handguard with M-LOK slots, adj. arm brace with closure strap, full length Picatinny rail, QD sling swivel attachment, black finish, 88 oz. New 2020.

MSR $896	$675	$525	$475	$425	$400	$375	$325

M&P15-22P – .22 LR cal., 6 in. threaded carbon steel barrel with A1 style compensator, 25 shot detachable mag., blowback action similar to M&P 15-22 rifle, quad rail handguard, adj. sights on top Picatinny rail, polymer lower receiver, matte black finish, black pistol grip, 51 oz. Mfg. mid-2010-2011.

	$725	$635	$550	$450	$350	$295	$250	*$519*

M&P 15-22 PISTOL – .22 LR cal., blowback operated, 8 in. threaded carbon steel barrel with flash suppressor, 25 shot mag., SB Tactical SBA3 adj. arm brace with closure strap, 2-pos. receiver-mounted safety lever, M&P handguard with M-LOK slots, functioning charging handle and shell deflector, full length Picatinny rail, QD sling swivel attachment point in arm brace, black finish, 53.6 oz. New mid-2020.

MSR $504	$375	$300	$275	$250	$225	$200	$175

GRADING - PPGS™	100%	98%	95%	90%	80%	70%	60%	LAST MSR

M&P 22 - .22 LR cal., SFO, 4.1 in. threaded barrel, single action hammerless, 10 or 12 shot mag., plastic grips, fixed backstrap, aluminum alloy slide, adj. rear sight, black blade front sight, blue/black finish, ambidextrous manual safety and slide stop, reversible mag release, lower Picatinny rail, approx. 24 oz. Mfg. 2011-2020.

	$350	$315	$285	$260	$240	$220	$195	*$419*

* ***M&P 22 Compact*** - .22 LR cal., compact frame, 3.6 in. threaded barrel, 10 shot mag, polymer frame with aluminum alloy slide, articulated trigger, drop safety, adj. 3-dot sights, textured polymer grips, ambidextrous safety, features Picatinny rail in front of trigger guard, reversible mag. release, FDE finish (new 2017), 15.3 oz. New 2015.

MSR $389	$335	$285	$245	$220	$180	$150	$125

Add $20 for suppressor ready barrel (new 2016) or $40 for FDE finish suppressor ready.

M&P 40 - .40 S&W cal., 10 or 15 shot mag., SFO, 4 1/4 in. barrel, similar to Model M&P9, with or w/o thumb safety, 24 1/4 oz. Disc. 2020.

	$395	$350	$295	$270	$220	$200	$180	*$462*

Add $30 for carbon fiber (mfg. 2015 only).
Add $120 for carry and range kit - includes Blade Tech Kydex holster, double magazine pouch, Maglula Uplula loading tool, ear plugs, and extra magazine. (Disc.)
Add $130 for Crimson Trace green Laserguard (new 2016).
Add $260 for Crimson Trace red Lasergrips.

* ***M&P 40c (Compact)*** - .40 S&W cal., SFO, 10 shot mag., 3 1/2 in. barrel, steel ramp dovetail mount front sight, Novak Lo-Mount carry rear sight, compact Zytel polymer frame with stainless steel slide and barrel, black Melonite, carbon fiber (mfg. 2015 only), or FDE (mfg. 2015-2018) finish, with or w/o thumb safety, with or w/o three interchangeable palm swell or Crimson Trace Lasergrips (mfg. 2016-2019), 22 oz. Mfg. 2007-2020.

	$395	$350	$295	$270	$220	$200	$180	*$462*

Add $30 for carbon fiber (mfg. 2015 only) or FDE finish (mfg. 2015-2018).
Add $247 for Crimson Trace Lasergrips (mfg. 2016-2019) or $154 for Crimson Trace Green Laserguard (mfg. 2016-2017).

M&P 40 PRO SERIES - .40 S&W cal., striker fire action, 4 1/4 or 5 in. barrel, 15 shot, black polymer frame with black stainless steel slide, lower Picatinny rail, night or fiber optic sights, or optics ready (new 2013), 26 oz. Mfg. 2012-disc.

	$575	$475	$400	$350	$300	$265	$235	*$699*

Add $70 for optic ready variation (new 2013).
Subtract $10 for fiber optic sights (5 in. barrel only).

M&P 40 SHIELD - .40 S&W cal., striker fire DAO, black or FDE (mfg. 2018 only) polymer frame, 3.1 in. barrel, 6, 7, or 8 shot mag., white dot front and rear sights or Tritium night sights (mfg. 2016-2017), with or w/o thumb safety, textured front and back straps, black Melonite finish, 19 oz. New mid-2012.

MSR $385	$325	$285	$245	$225	$200	$180	$160

Add $100 for Tritium night sights (mfg. 2016-2017).
Add $140 for Crimson Trace green Laserguard (mfg. 2015-disc.).

M&P 40 VTAC (VIKING TACTICS) - .40 S&W cal., SFO, 15 shot mag., 4 1/4 in. barrel, full size polymer frame, VTAC Warrior front and rear sights, durable PVD coated stainless steel slide, FDE finish, 27.9 oz. Disc. 2018.

	$640	$535	$425	$375	$325	$295	$250	*$799*

M&P 40 M2.0 - .40 S&W cal., 4 1/4 or 5 in. stainless steel barrel and slide, 10 (new 2018) or 15 shot mag., tactile and audible trigger reset, low profile 3-dot sights or TruGlo TFX sights (4 1/2 in., FDE only, mfg. 2018-2020), textured grips w/4 interchangeable palm swell grip inserts, with or w/o thumb safety, lower Picatinny rail, 18 degree grip angle, with or w/o loaded chamber indicator, front and rear slide serrations, includes 2 magazines, Armornite black or FDE Cerakote (disc. 2020) finish, approx. 25.9 oz. New 2017.

MSR $599	$510	$450	$395	$365	$335	$295	$275

Add $40 for M&P 40 M2.0 Carry & Range Kit (new 2018).
Add $120 for TruGlo TFX sights (FDE model only, mfg. 2018-2020).

* ***M&P 40 M2.0 Compact*** - .40 S&W cal., black polymer frame, 3.6 (new 2019) or 4 in. stainless steel barrel and slide w/Armornite finish, 13 shot mag., tactile and audible trigger reset, white dot front and low profile carry rear sight, with or w/o thumb safety, lower Picatinny rail, includes four interchangeable grip inserts, approx. 24.7 oz. New 2018.

MSR $569	$475	$425	$385	$360	$335	$295	$275

Add $150 for Crimson Trace Green Laserguard (mfg. mid-2018-2020).

GRADING - PPGS™	100%	98%	95%	90%	80%	70%	60%	LAST MSR

* ***M&P 40 M2.0 Sub-Compact*** – .40 S&W cal., SFO, black polymer frame, 3.6 in. stainless steel barrel, two 10 shot mags., tactile and audible trigger reset, white dot front and white two-dot rear sight, with or w/o thumb safety, lower Picatinny rail, includes four interchangeable grip inserts, stainless steel slide w/black Armornite finish, approx. 26 oz. Mfg. mid-2019-2020.

	$480	$425	$385	$360	$335	$295	$275	*$569*

M&P 40 SHIELD M2.0 – .40 S&W cal., striker fire DAO, 3.1 in. barrel, 6 or 7 shot mag., choice of white 3-dot or Tritium night sights, black polymer frame with textured grip surfaces, with or w/o thumb safety, includes two mags. (one flush fit and one extended w/finger grooves), stainless steel slide w/ black Armornite finish, approx. 18 oz. New 2018.

MSR $490	$415	$365	$315	$285	$230	$210	$190	

Add $90 for Crimson Trace integrated green laser.
Add $89 for Tritium night sights.
Add $29 for Crimson Trace integrated red laser (disc. 2020).
Add $190 for Crimson Trace Laserguard Pro with green laser/light combo (disc. 2020).

M&P 45/M&P 45 MID – .45 ACP cal., SFO, 10 shot mag., 4 (mid-size) or 4 1/2 in. standard or threaded (new 2015) barrel, full size black polymer frame, Melonite or FDE brown finish, otherwise similar to M&P9, 29.6 oz. Disc. 2020.

	$440	$385	$330	$300	$240	$210	$190	*$519*

Add $29 for manual safety.
Add $120 for threaded barrel kit (new 2015).
Add $28 for ambidextrous safety with black or FDE finish.
Add $90 for night sights (disc. 2012).
Add $230 for Crimson Trace Lasergrips (disc. 2012).

* ***M&P 45c (Compact)*** – .45 ACP cal., SFO, compact polymer frame, 4 in. stainless steel barrel, 8 shot mag., steel ramp dovetail mount front sight, Novak Lo-Mount carry rear sight, with or without three interchangeable palm swell grips, with or without thumb safety, black melonite or FDE finish, 27 oz. Mfg. 2007-2020.

	$415	$365	$310	$280	$230	$210	$190	*$490*

Add $29 for ambidextrous safety with either Melonite (disc. 2015) or FDE finish.

M&P 45 M2.0 – .45 ACP cal., 4.6 or 5 (threaded with suppressor height sights, new 2019) in. stainless steel barrel and slide, 10 shot mag., tactile and audible trigger reset, low profile 3-dot sights or TruGlo TFX sights (new 2019), textured grips with 4 interchangeable palm swell grip inserts, with or w/o thumb safety, lower Picatinny rail, 18 degree grip angle, front and rear slide serrations, includes 2 magazines, Armornite finish on barrel and slide, matte black or Cerakote FDE finish over Armornite, approx. 27 oz. New 2017.

MSR $599	$510	$450	$395	$365	$335	$295	$275	

Add $140 for TruGlo TFX sights (new 2019, FDE model only).

* ***M&P 45 M2.0 Compact*** – .45 ACP cal., striker fire, compact polymer frame, 4 in. stainless steel barrel, 10 shot mag., tactile and audible trigger reset, white dot sights, black polymer textured grips, includes four interchangeable palm swell grip inserts, with or w/o manual thumb safety, Armornite finish. New 2018.

MSR $569	$485	$425	$385	$360	$335	$295	$275	

* ***M&P 45 M2.0 Sub-Compact*** – .45 ACP cal., SFO, black polymer frame, 4 in. stainless steel barrel, two 8 shot mags., tactile and audible trigger reset, white dot front and white two-dot rear sight, with or w/o thumb safety, lower Picatinny rail, includes four interchangeable grip inserts, stainless steel slide w/black Armornite finish, approx. 27.5 oz. Mfg. 2019-2020

	$485	$425	$385	$360	$335	$295	$275	*$569*

M&P 45 SHIELD M2.0 – .45 ACP cal., striker fire DAO, 3.3 in. stainless steel barrel, 6 (disc.) or 7 shot mag., choice of white 3-dot or Tritium night sights, black polymer frame with textured grip surfaces, with or w/o thumb safety, includes two mags. (one flush fit and one extended w/finger grooves), stainless steel slide with black Armornite finish, approx. 20.5 oz. New 2019.

MSR $490	$415	$365	$315	$285	$230	$210	$190	

Add $89 for Tritium night sights.
Add $110 for Crimson Trace Green Laserguard (mfg. 2019 only)
Add $34 for red integrated Crimson Trace laser or $90 for Green integrated Crimson Trace laser (disc. 2020).

M&P357 – .357 SIG cal., SFO, 4 1/4 in. barrel, 10 or 15 shot mag., similar to M&P9. Disc. 2010.

	$625	$525	$400	$335	$290	$245	$215	*$727*

GRADING - PPGS™	100%	98%	95%	90%	80%	70%	60%	LAST MSR

* ***M&P357 Compact*** – .357 SIG cal., 10 shot mag., 3 1/2 in. barrel, similar to M&P9 Compact, 22 oz. Mfg. 2007-2010.

$575 $475 $375 $335 $285 $260 $230 ***$727***

M&P 380 SHIELD EZ – .380 Auto cal., internal hammer fired action, polymer frame, 3 5/8 in. stainless steel barrel, 8 shot mag., white dot front and adj. white dot rear sights, grip safety standard, polymer grips, with or w/o thumb safety, Crimson Trace Green Laserguard (disc. 2020), lower Picatinny rail, Armornite finish, 18.5-19.1 oz. New 2019.

MSR $428 $365 $320 $275 $250 $200 $165 $145

Add $180 for Crimson Trace Green Laserguard (disc. 2020).

M&P BODYGUARD 380 (MODEL BG380) – .380 ACP cal., DAO (hammer fired), sub-compact polymer frame with matte black or FDE (mfg. 2017-2020) finish, 2 3/4 in. stainless steel barrel, 6 shot, stainless steel drift adj. sights, black synthetic finger groove grips, with or w/o (mfg. 2016-2020) thumb safety, stainless steel slide with black melonite, FDE (mfg. 2017-2020), or two-tone finish, 12 oz. New 2014.

MSR $379 $325 $285 $245 $220 $180 $160 $140

Add $26 machine engraved slide (two-tone finish).
Add $70 for Crimson Trace integrated red laser.
Add $140 for Crimson Trace green Laserguard (mfg. 2016-2020).

M&P C.O.R.E. (COMPETITION OPTICS READY EQUIPMENT) – 9mm Para. or .40 S&W cal., SFO, 4 1/4 or 5 in. barrel, 10 or 17 shot mag., polymer frame, stainless steel slide, striker fire action, ambidextrous controls, black Melonite finish, lower Picatinny rail, fixed two dot rear sight, white dot dovetail front sight, accepts six different popular styles of optics, also available in Pro Series configuration, 24 oz. Mfg. 2013-2017.

$650 $575 $495 $450 $360 $295 $230 ***$769***

PISTOLS: SEMI-AUTO, RIMFIRE

MODEL 22A SPORT SERIES – .22 LR cal., single action, 10 shot mag., aluminum alloy frame, stainless steel slide, choice of 4 (disc. 2012) in. standard, 5 1/2 in. standard or bull, or 7 in. standard barrel with raised solid rib, adj. rear and Hi-Viz (5 1/2 in. bull barrel only, new 2001) sights, 2-piece black polymer hard (disc.) or Soft Touch and Dymondwood (5 1/2 bull barrel only) grips, blue/black, two-tone (new 2006, 5 1/2 in. barrel only), or Realtree APG HD camo (new 2004, 5 1/2 in. barrel only) finish, 28-39 oz. Mfg. 1997-2015.

$325 $255 $210 $170 $140 $125 $110 ***$329***

Add $10 for 4 (disc. 2012), 5 1/2 or 7 in. barrel with blue/black finish. Add $40 for 5 1/2 in. bull barrel with Hi-Viz green dot front sight. Add $40 for wood target grips and adj. rear sight (5 1/2 in. barrel only), disc. 2012. Add $40 for two-tone frame/slide finish with Hi-Viz green dot front sight. Add $40 for 100% Real Tree APG HD camo finish. Add $127 for 5 1/2 in. bull barrel with camo finish (disc. 2007). Add $114 for 5 1/2 in. bull barrel with Dymondwood target grips (disc. 2005). Add $71 for 5 1/2 in. bull barrel with 2 piece target grips and thumbrest (disc. 2000).

The standard Model 22A has a two-tone finish with Patridge front and adj. rear sights.

MODEL 22S SPORT SERIES – .22 LR cal., single action, 10 shot mag., aluminum alloy frame, stainless steel slide, choice of 5 1/2 standard or bull (disc. 2005) or 7 (disc. 2004) in. standard barrel with raised solid rib, adj. rear and Hi-Viz (5 1/2 in. bull barrel only, new 2001) sights, 2-piece black polymer (hard or soft) or Dymondwood (5 1/2 in. bull barrel only) grips, satin stainless finish, 41-48 oz. Mfg. 1997-2007.

$325 $255 $210 $170 $140 $125 $110 ***$419***

Add $40 for 7 in. standard barrel with thumb rest soft-touch grips (disc. 2004).
Add $83 for 5 1/2 in. bull barrel with Dymondwood target grips (disc. 2004).
Add $102 for 5 1/2 in. bull barrel with Hi-Viz sights (mfg. 2001-2004).
Add $44 for 5 1/2 in. bull barrel with 2 piece target grips and thumb rest (disc. 2000).

SW22 VICTORY – 22 LR cal., blowback action, 5 1/2 in. barrel with or w/o threading, brushed stainless steel or Kryptek Highlander camo finish, adj. trigger stop, fiber optic front and rear sights, black polymer grips, includes top Picatinny rail, 36 oz. New 2016.

MSR $428 $375 $325 $275 $250 $225 $200 $185

Add $14 for threaded barrel.
Add $31 for 100% Kryptek Highlander camo finish.

SW22 VICTORY TARGET – .22 LR cal., SA, stainless steel frame and slide, 5 1/2 in. stainless steel bull barrel, 10 shot, beveled magwell, target trigger, target sights, black polymer grip with target thumb rest, Picatinny style rail, 9.2 in. OAL, 36 oz. New mid-2018.

MSR $442 $380 $335 $285 $260 $240 $220 $195

GRADING - PPGS™	100%	98%	95%	90%	80%	70%	60%	LAST MSR

MODEL 41/41-1 – .22 S (disc., Model 41-1) or LR cal., match target pistol, single action, 10 shot mag., adj. rear and Patridge front sights, checkered walnut grips with thumbrest, 5 (disc.), 5 1/2 (heavy, new 1963), 7 (standard), or 7 3/8 (disc. 2004) in. barrel, blue finish only, 41 oz. New 1957.

MSR $1,389	$1,175	$1,025	$875	$800	$650	$550	$460	

Add $250 for 5 1/2 in. barrel with extended sight (mfg. 1965-1976) or add $35 for 7 3/8 in. barrel with muzzle brake (disc.).

Add 150% for .22 Short cal. with counterweight and muzzle brake (disc.).

Add 15%-40% for early variations with cocking indicator (disc. 1978).

Add $475 for full counterweight set.

Factory engraving Model 41s with cocking indicator in NIB condition are currently selling in the $5,500 range.

The Model 41 was introduced in 1957 with a 7 3/8 in. barrel, starting with serial number 1401. At approximately serial number 16000, relief cuts at rear of trigger guard were added. At approximately serial number 27500, the model number stamping moved to the right side of frame. The 5 in. barrel was introduced in 1959. The .22 Short Model 41-1 was introduced September 29, 1960, total production under 1,000 units. In 1976, 28 Model 41-1s were assembled from leftover parts. The 5 1/2 in. heavy barrel was introduced in 1963. In 1965, the 5 1/2 in. barrel extended front sight was introduced, then discontinued in 1976. In 1978, the revised Model 41 was introduced at approximately serial number A494000 with the following changes: (A) The 7 3/8 in. barrel replaced with the new 7 inch barrel. (B) The cocking indicator was discontinued. In 1984, S&W introduced the three letter prefix serial numbers, Model 41s start at "TAA". In 1992, the 12 shot magazine was introduced, and discontinued in 1994. In 1994, Millett rear sights replaced S&W rear sights, and the slide was drilled and tapped for scope mount. In 1996, the 5 in. barrel "optics only" version was available with Weaver base. In 1997, laminated hardwood stocks were introduced. In 1998, ten Model 41s were produced in the Performance Center called "Classic 41". In 2011, the Model 41 Performance Center Super Target Special was introduced.

* ***Model 41 50th Anniversary*** – similar to Model 41 with 5 1/2 in. barrel, except has blue finish with gold line engraving, 500 mfg. to commemorate the 50th year of the Model 41, ser. no. range FYA001-FYA500, 41 oz. Mfg. 2007-2009.

	$1,795	$1,575	$1,350	$1,150	$925	$800	$675	*$2,150*

MODEL 46 – .22 LR cal., 5 (1,000 mfg.), 5 1/2 (500 mfg.), or 7 (2,500 mfg.) in. barrel, blue, nylon grips, adj. sights. Mfg. 4,000, 1957-1966.

	$1,800	$1,600	$1,350	$1,150	$925	$800	$650	

Add 50% for 5 1/2 in. heavy barrel.

Add 25% for 5 in. field barrel.

Add 100% for Military Issue.

This model is similar to the Model 41, but does not have high polish bluing, has brown plastic grips, and machined with straight cut lines rather than radiused.

MODEL 61 ESCORT – .22 LR cal., 5 shot, blue or nickel, 2 1/2 in. barrel, plastic grips. Mfg. 1970-1974.

Blue finish	$450	$350	$225	$175	$150	$140	$110	
Nickel finish	$500	$400	$235	$185	$155	$140	$110	

Total production of 64,938 units of which approximately 6,600 were in nickel. During this period the pistol underwent 3 model changes. The first was the addition of a magazine safety, which resulted in the Model 61-1. Next was the addition of the barrel nut which locked the barrel in place. Finally, the original die cast frame and side plate were replaced with forged machined aluminum parts resulting in the 61-3.

MODEL 422 FIELD – .22 LR cal., single action, 4 1/2 or 6 in. barrel, aluminum frame with steel slide, 10 shot mag., fixed sights, black plastic or wood grips, matte blue finish, 22 oz. Mfg. 1987-1996.

	$335	$275	$200	$150	$125	$90	$65	*$235*

* ***Model 422 Target*** – .22 LR cal., single action, 4 1/2 or 6 in. barrel, aluminum frame with steel slide, 10 shot mag., adj. rear sight, checkered walnut grips, matte blue finish, 22 oz. Mfg. 1987-1996.

	$450	$400	$350	$300	$275	$225	$200	*$290*

MODEL 622 (FIELD) – .22 LR cal., single action, 4 1/2 or 6 in. barrel, stainless/alloy construction, 10 shot mag., fixed sights, black plastic grips, 21 1/2 or 23 1/2 oz. Mfg. 1990-96.

	$325	$200	$175	$150	$120	$100	$75	*$284*

* ***Model 622 Target*** – .22 LR cal., single action, 4 1/2 or 6 in. barrel (VR was an option in 1996 only), stainless steel/alloy construction, 10 shot mag., adj. rear sight, black plastic or checkered walnut grips, 21 1/2 or 23 1/2 oz. Mfg. 1990-1996.

	$475	$400	$375	$325	$300	$250	$200	*$337*

Add 20% for vent. rib variation.

GRADING - PPGS™	100%	98%	95%	90%	80%	70%	60%	LAST MSR

MODEL 2206 STAINLESS (FIELD) – .22 LR cal., similar to Model 622 Field, except stainless steel slide, black plastic grips, 6 in. barrel with standard (disc. 1995) or adj. rear sight, 35 or 39 oz. Mfg. 1990-96.

	$350	$300	$175	$135	$115	$100	$85	*$385*

Subtract $58 if w/o adj. sights.

* ***Model 2206 Stainless Target*** – similar to Model 2206 Stainless, except has adj. target sight, black plastic or wood stocks, and is drilled and tapped. Mfg. 1994-1996.

	$400	$325	$225	$175	$140	$125	$105	*$433*

MODEL 2213 STAINLESS "SPORTSMAN" – .22 LR cal., single action, 3 in. barrel, alloy frame with stainless steel slide, 8 shot mag., 2 dot fixed rear sight, black plastic molded grips, 18 oz., includes holster/carry case. Mfg. 1992-99.

	$300	$300	$200	$130	$115	$100	$85	*$340*

MODEL 2214 "SPORTSMAN" – .22 LR cal., similar to Model 2213, except has alloy frame with blue carbon steel slide with matte black finish, and no case. Mfg. 1991-1999.

	$400	$325	$200	$150	$140	$130	$120	*$292*

PRE-2009 ENGRAVING OPTIONS FOR HANDGUNS

The prices listed were for original factory finished guns with no extra engraving.

CLASS "C" ENGRAVING - 1/3 METAL COVERAGE

Pistols - add $1,108.
For J Frame - add $876.
10 5/8 in. N Frame - add $1,343.
2-5 in. K, L, or N Frame - add $1,130.
6-8 3/8 in. K, L, or N Frame - add $1,285.

CLASS "B" ENGRAVING - 2/3 METAL COVERAGE

Pistols - add $1,448.
For J Frame - add $1,430.
10 5/8 in. N Frame - add $1,672.
2-5 in. K, L, or N Frame - add $1,477.
6-8 3/8 in. K, L, or N Frame - add $1,599.

CLASS "A" ENGRAVING - FULL COVERAGE

Pistols - add $1,761.
For J Frame - add $1,501.
10 5/8 in. N Frame - add $2,006.
2-5 in. K, L, or N Frame - add $1,814.
6-8 3/8 in. K, L, or N Frame - add $1,919.

LASERSMITH ENGRAVING – laser etching was available 1989-90 only. This process involved a digitally-controlled laser producing a variety of designs, logos, commemorative messages, or autograph on the metal surface(s). Some of these designs were made exclusively for major firearms distributors. Others were custom designed for clubs or organizations. Retail prices started at just under $18 and went as high as $150+, depending on the amount and complexity of the laser etching. To date, premiums are not being paid for these "rarer" variations.

CURRENT ENGRAVING OPTIONS FOR HANDGUNS

SPECIAL ENGRAVING – Also available with custom artwork: inlays, seals, scenes, lettering - prices quoted on request. Please call 1-800-331-0852, ext. 216 - a free color brochure on custom engraving services is available.

MASTER ENGRAVING – 100% coverage.

J-frame - $3,325
K, L, and N frame (2-5 in. barrel) - $4,015, $4,245 for 6 or 8 3/8 in. barrel, or $4,445 for over 8 3/8 in. barrel.
X-frame (4 in. barrel) - $8,290, $8,450 for over 8 in. barrel.
Pistols - $4,015.

CLASS A ENGRAVING – 75% coverage.

J-frame - $2,310
K, L, and N frame (2-5 in. barrel) - $2,790, $2,950 for 6 or 8 3/8 in. barrel, or $3,090 for over 8 3/8 in. barrel.
X-frame (4 in. barrel) - $5,710, $5,865 for over 8 in. barrel.
Pistols - $2,790.

GRADING - PPGS™	100%	Issue Price	Qty. Made

CLASS B ENGRAVING – 50% coverage.

J-frame - $1,840
K, L, and N frame (2-5 in. barrel) - $1,895, $2,060 for 6 or 8 3/8 in. barrel, or $2,155 for over 8 3/8 in. barrel.
X-frame (4 in. barrel) - $4,285, $4,445 for over 8 in. barrel.
Pistols - $1,895

CLASS C ENGRAVING – 25% coverage.

J-frame - $1,085
K, L, and N frame (2-5 in. barrel) - $1,385, $1,585 for 6 or 8 3/8 in. barrel, or $1,650 for over 8 3/8 in. barrel.
X-frame (4 in. barrel) - $2,865, $3,025 for over 8 in. barrel.
Pistols - $1,425

DIFFERENTIAL FINISHES

J-frame
100% - $325, 75% - $240, 50% - $210, 25% - $185
K, L, N-frame
100% - $470, 75% - $415, 50% - 385, 25% - $350
X-frame
100% - $645, 75% - $585, 50% - $525, 25% - $470

S&W SPECIAL/LIMITED EDITIONS

During the course of a year, I receive many phone calls and letters on special editions and limited editions that do not appear in this section. Many of these are listed separately under the Davidson's or Lew Horton sections. It should be noted that a commemorative issue is a gun that has been manufactured, marketed, and sold through the auspices of the specific trademark (in this case S&W). During the past several decades, hundreds of limited editions have been ordered through various police agencies, state highway patrol units, and other law enforcement organizations. Many of these variations do not have the special suffix serialization (and may not have had a retail price when issued). Since most of these special editions/commemoratives were made for a specific organization, regional demand has a lot to do with determining values (a Model 27 special edition mfg. for a sheriff's dept. in Arkansas will not bring a premium in California). For this reason, most of these guns will not appear in this section and you should contact the factory to learn more about the provenance of these special editions. Remember - values on these models can vary A LOT from one region to another and an averaged "national" single price is almost impossible. While these guns do have special interest, they do not have the collectability or desirability of many of the standard models listed. As one anonymous contributing editor states, "Hard to price, no real guidelines, generally seem to be dogs to sell, always cost more but bring less."

S&W FACTORY COMMEMORATIVES

These variations listed represent only factory S&W Commemoratives manufactured to date. Anything else will be a special or limited edition made for a organization, company, or special event.

MODEL 19 TEXAS RANGER – .357 Mag., with or without knife, approx. 8,000 with knife, approx. 2,000 without, cased. Mfg. 1973 only.

	100%	Issue Price	Qty. Made
	$900	$250	10,000

Subtract 15% if without knife.

* ***Model 19 Texas Ranger Deluxe*** – approx. 50 mfg. with a serial numbers divisible by 10, class A engraved, cased.

	100%	Issue Price	Qty. Made
	$3,500	N/A	50

MODEL 25 125TH ANNIVERSARY COMMEMORATIVE – .45 LC cal., plain variation was called Model 25-3, 10,000 mfg. total in 1977, cased with nickel silver medallion, and Roy Jinks's book, *125th Anniversary of Smith & Wesson.*

	100%	Issue Price	Qty. Made
	$1,395	$350	10,000

* ***Model 25 125th Anniversary Commemorative Deluxe*** – Model 25-4, approx. 50 mfg. with S&W prefix serial numbers divisible by 10, cased, sterling silver medallion, and a leather-bound *History of Smith & Wesson* book by Roy Jinks.

	100%	Issue Price	Qty. Made
	$3,500	N/A	50

MODEL 26-1 GEORGIA STATE PATROL COMMEMORATIVE – .45 LC cal. Mfg. 1988 only.

	100%	Issue Price	Qty. Made
Overrun of 40 unmarked	$2,000	N/A	800

GRADING - PPGS™	100%	Issue Price	Qty. Made

MODEL 29 ELMER KEITH COMMEMORATIVE – .44 Mag. cal., 4 in. barrel, standard and deluxe editions, approx. 2,500 total mfg.

Standard	$975	N/A	2,500
Deluxe	$2,000	N/A	100

50TH ANNIVERSARY OF THE .357 MAGNUM – Model 27, both standard and deluxe editions. Mfg. 1985 only.

Standard	$1,025	N/A	2,500
Deluxe	$1,900	N/A	N/A

MODEL 544 TEXAS WAGON TRAIN COMMEMORATIVE – .44-40 WCF cal. only, 6 shot, 5 in. barrel, bright blue finish, adj. sights, 4,782 mfg. 1986 to commemorate the Texas Sesquicentennial (1836-1986). Special markings on frame and barrel, smooth Goncalo commemorative grips, ser. no. TWT0001-TWT7800 (estimated). Made 1986 only.

	$600	N/A	7,800

S&W PERFORMANCE CENTER FIREARMS

The Performance Center (PC) of Smith & Wesson got its start in 1990 from the efforts of two Master Gunsmiths, Paul Liebenburg and John French. The Performance Center is today managed by Tom Kelly and has grown to about 26 employees, all of which are engaged in the handgun shooting sports, a condition of being in the Center. The Performance Center generally does not take production guns and improve them. These handguns are built from scratch. Using two CNC machines, the Performance Center turns out about 400+ guns a month. There is no inventory of PC products. They are pre-sold before they are made. Once a new design is made and prototyped, it is shown to distributors of specialty guns. The distributor is given an exclusive on a particular model and those handguns are sold through the distributor's network of retailers. Currently, the major distributors ordering PC products include: Lew Horton (disc.), RSR Group, Camfour, and Talo Dist. The Performance Center delivers limited production runs, unique design and special feature firearms, and also provides gunsmithing services to existing S&W standard products. Please refer to individual Performance Center categories for current information and values.

While we have tried to list all the Performance Center guns in this section, it is possible that you may find some models listed with their corresponding numbered model in the Semi-Auto Pistols and Numbered Model Revolvers section in this text. Models are listed in the general order of the model number upon which they are based, with descriptions of each gun. At the end of the model descriptions, you may find a collected listing of variations, changes, and/or product codes for PC guns based on a particular model. In the Serialization section in the back of this text, a listing of all Performance Center guns in order of Product Code number has been provided.

During the past 10 years, all PC guns have been marked with the Performance Center trademark on the frame. The product codes are only on the shipping container or box. The 170XXX Performance Center product code indicates a handgun that has been designed and made from scratch by the Performance Center, while the 178XXX code indicates an existing product/SKU that has been improved/changed.

Pricing of Performance Center Firearms

Whenever possible, original PC model MSRs have been provided. In some cases, the distributor never posted an MSR on a particular PC model. N/As designate that more research is under way to find out more about the original MSRs, if they exist, and will be included in future editions and our online services.

As a general rule, the easiest way to determine values for Performance Center handguns is to look at the current pricing of the models from which they are derived. In other words, on a PC Model 442 Ultralight, check the standard Model 442 pricing in this text, and use the MSR - 100% price range to establish a base price, assuming the condition is NIB. Depending on the desirability of the PC configuration, such as finishes, barrel lengths, styling, special orders/features (i.e., laser or hand engraving, precious metal inlays, ivory or exotic wood grips, etc.), special sights, and other production variances from the standard model, premiums may exist over the 100% or current MSR values listed for the standard model. If a particular PC model has an original MSR that's significantly higher than the standard model, the buyer and seller are going to have to interpolate a possible premium which both feel comfortable with.

It is important to note that PC models are essentially limited runs of custom guns, which sell out in a relatively short period of time, and only resurface sporadically in the secondary marketplace. Many can be found in NIB or Excellent condition. Also, dealer or retail pricing is very rarely published on these models, making values difficult to determine for the secondary marketplace. Semi-auto pistols generally sell for more than revolvers. Elaborate engraving, custom shop options, and the desirability of the configuration make all the difference when determining the value of an S&W Performance Center handgun.

GRADING - PPGS™	100%	98%	95%	90%	80%	70%	60%	LAST MSR

Heritage Series From Lew Horton & Performance Center Handguns

Beginning in 2001, Lew Horton Distributors and the Performance Center manufactured a series of specials from Smith & Wesson called "The Heritage Series." These were produced over a period of 2 years and included case color Models (10 & 24) and other models no longer manufactured but were very popular over the last century. This series included Models 10, 15, 17, 19, 24, 25, 29, and the Model of 1917 in various finishes. Each had a gold color antique style box unique to the Heritage series, with a picture of Horace Smith and Daniel Wesson on the top with blue metal corners and a modern end label. All guns were shipped with a fired case from the gun in a small sealed envelope signed by the shooter, along with a trigger lock or cable lock. Mfg. 2001-2003.

Pistols: Semi-Auto, Performance Center Variations

Some more standardized Performance Center variations will be found under their respective categories.

MODEL 41 OPTIC READY – .22 LR cal., Model 41 action, SA, 5 1/2 in. carbon steel button rifled barrel, 10 shot mag., removable front and adj. rear sights, checkered custom wood target grips, thumb safety, features full-length Picatinny rail on top of slide, blue frame and slide finish, 41 oz. New 2013.

MSR	100%	98%	95%	90%	80%	70%	60%
MSR $1,639	$1,395	$1,225	$1,050	$950	$775	$650	$550

MODEL 686 – .38 Spl./.357 Mag. cal., SA/DA action, 4 in. stainless steel VR barrel, 6 shot mag., custom teardrop hammer, chrome trigger with trigger stop, interchangeable front sight, adj. rear sight, synthetic grip, unfluted cylinder, PC tuned action, speed release thumbpiece, 37.9 oz. New late 2017.

MSR	100%	98%	95%	90%	80%	70%	60%
MSR $1,006	$850	$750	$650	$575	$475	$385	$325

MODEL 845 LIMITED – .45 ACP cal., full target version of the Model 745, Bo-Mar low profile sights, extended beavertail, checkered front strap, fitted barrel bushing, Hi-Impact plastic grips, 8-round magazine, extra recoil spring, S/N prefix "MPC" (1995) "SDN" (1998). Distributed by Lew Horton.

Last MSR was $1,496.

The gun was produced in two lots, the first run of 427 pistols were not model marked. The second lot of 159 guns, is marked on the slide "845 Model of 1998".

MODEL 945 SPECIAL PERFORMANCE CENTER .45 MATCH PISTOL – .45 ACP cal., 5 in. barrel, SA, titanium coated spherical barrel bushing, 8 round mag., Performance Center markings, post front sight, adj. Bo-Mar rear sight, checkered two-piece laminated wood grips, bead blast stainless steel finish, ambidextrous frame mounted thumb safety, grip safety as part of the short beavertail, Master trigger lock, "Performance Center" marked foam-filled aluminum case starting in 1999, ser. nos. LEW0001-LEW1368, 43.5 oz. (1998) 42 oz. (1999 and later mfg.) Mfg. 1998-2000.

* ***Model 945 Special Performance Center .45 Match Pistol 170104*** – 5 in. barrel, stainless steel, 8 shot, 43.5 oz. Mfg. 1998 only.

Last MSR was $1,618.

* ***Model 945 Special Performance Center .45 Match Pistol 170147*** – 5 in. barrel, two-tone or blue finish, lightened trigger, grip safety, Bo-Mar rear sight, post front sight, stainless steel, ambidextrous frame mounted safety, 42 oz. Distributed by RSR. Mfg. 1998-2000.

Last MSR was N/A.

* ***Model 945 Special Performance Center .45 Match Pistol 170152*** – 4 in. barrel, black finish, 8 shot mag., post front and Novak 2 Dot Lo-Mount Carry rear sight, frame mounted safety, titanium coated spherical bushing, 20 LPI checkering front and back strap, extended magazine catch, checkered two-piece wood grips, stainless steel, grip safety, S/N prefix "PCZ", 36 oz. Distributed by Camfour, 2000.

Last MSR was N/A.

* ***Model 945 Special Performance Center .45 Match Pistol 170153*** – 4 in. barrel, post front and Novak 2 Dot Lo-Mount carry rear sight, grip safety, checkered two-piece wood grips, lightened trigger, bead blast stainless steel finish, frame mounted safety, S/N prefix "PCZ", 36 oz. Distributed by RSR, 2000.

Last MSR was N/A.

* ***Model 945 Special Performance Center .45 Match Pistol 170169*** – 3 3/4 in. barrel, white dot dovetail front and Novak 2 Dot Lo-Mount Carry rear sight, grip and single side frame mounted safety, 7 round mag., checkered laminate wood grips, lightened trigger, black finish alloy frame and stainless steel slide, S/N Prefix "CMF", 28 oz. Distributed by Camfour, 2000.

Last MSR was N/A.

GRADING - PPGS™	100%	98%	95%	90%	80%	70%	60%	LAST MSR

* ***Model 945 Special Performance Center .45 Match Pistol 170177*** – 3 1/4 in. barrel, white dot dovetail front and Novak 2 Dot Lo-Mount Carry rear sight, beavertail grip and single-side frame mounted safety, 6 round mag., checkered Hogue laminated wood grips, alloy frame with clear glass bead stainless steel slide, Performance Center carry case, 2 mags., 24.5 oz. Distributed by Camfour, 2001.

Last MSR was N/A.

* ***Model 945 Special Performance Center Match Pistol 170180*** – .40 S&W cal., 3 3/4 in. barrel, white dot dovetail front and Novak 2 Dot Lo-Mount Carry rear sight, beavertail grip and single-side frame mounted safety, 7 round mag., checkered Hogue laminated wood grips, alloy frame w/glass bead finish stainless steel slide, titanium coated barrel bushing, Performance Center carry case, 2 mags., 25.7 oz. 158 mfg. and distributed by Sports South in 2001.

Last MSR was N/A.

* ***Model 945 Special Performance Center .45 Match Pistol 170184*** – 3 1/4 in. glass bead black barrel, white dovetail front and Novak 2 Dot Lo-Mount Carry rear sight, grip and single side frame mounted safety, 6 round mag., checkered Hogue laminated wood grips, alloy frame with stainless steel slide, lightened trigger, S/N prefix "PCZ", 24 oz. Distributed by RSR, 2001.

Last MSR was N/A.

MODEL 945-1 – .45 ACP cal., 8 shot mag., SA, 5 in. barrel, features scalloped slide serrations, all stainless (disc.) or two-tone finish, checkered front and rear gripstrap, checkered wood panel grips, stainless steel construction, adj. rear sight, target trigger and bobbed hammer, 40 1/2 oz., released during 2003, reintroduced 2005-2010.

	$1,925	$1,650	$1,425	$1,225	$1,000	$900	$800	*$2,410*

MODEL 952 – 9mm Para. cal., 5 in. match grade black finish stainless steel barrel, titanium coated spherical barrel bushing, 9 round mag., loaded chamber indicator, dovetail post front and adj. Wilson rear sight, carbon steel frame and slide, two-piece wood grip panels w/alloy backstrap, slide mounted decocking lever, marked "Performance Center 952" with small "mm" in the curl of the 9, Performance Center case, 200 mfg., 41 oz. Distributed by Bangers, 2000.

Last MSR was N/A.

After completing the 400 guns for Bangers, the Performance Center introduced the Model 952 as a standard production handgun with the product code 170220, serial number range KAZ0404 TO KAZ0459 . The dash one was added to the model number at serial number KAZ0461 and continued to KAZ1734 until 2003 for a total production of 1735 blue Model 952s of all variations.

MODEL 952-1 – 9mm Para. cal., 5 in. barrel, 9 shot mag., SA, checkered wood panel grips, black finish, steel frame with stainless steel barrel, released during 2003.

Last MSR was $1,515.

MODEL 952-2 STAINLESS – 9mm Para. cal., 5 or 6 (mfg. 2004, reintroduced 2007) in. barrel, large frame, 9 shot mag., checkered wood grips, stainless steel frame, wide spur hammer, firing pin block safety, wide smooth trigger with overtravel stop, adj. dovetailed black post front sight and Wilson adj. black rear sight, 39.2 oz., released during 2004. Disc. 2012.

	$1,825	$1,625	$1,400	$1,150	$1,000	$875	$750	*$2,129*

Add $480 for 6 in. barrel.

MODEL 1911 PRO SERIES – .45 ACP cal., SA, large frame, 4 1/4, or 5 in. barrel, choice of satin stainless steel frame and slide (5 in. bbl.), or blue scandium alloy frame/stainless steel slide with round butt (4 1/4 in. bbl.), 8 shot mag., two-tone G10 brown (4 1/4 in. bbl.) or custom wood (5 in. bbl.) grips, 6 diagonally cut ported slide cuts, skeletonized trigger, bobbed hammer, adj. rear sight, 29.6 oz (4 1/4) or 40 1/2 (5 in.). New 2013.

MSR $1,609	$1,365	$1,195	$1,020	$925	$750	$650	$550

SW1911 PRO SERIES – 9mm Para. or .45 ACP cal., SA, Scandium alloy sub-compact frame with square or round butt (new 2018), 3 in. stainless steel barrel, 7 or 8 shot mag., stainless steel slide, oversized external extractor, 3-hole curved trigger with overtravel stop, white dovetail front and fixed 2-dot rear sights, fully stippled synthetic grip, grip and ambi thumb safety, full length guide rod, black frame finish, 25 oz.

MSR $1,249	$1,065	$930	$800	$725	$585	$480	$415

Add $121 for 9mm Para. cal. with round butt frame (new 2018).

* ***SW1911 Pro Series Stainless*** – 9mm Para. or .45 ACP cal., SA, stainless steel frame, 5 in. stainless steel barrel, precision crowned muzzle, 8 (.45 ACP) or 10 (9mm Para.) shot, extended magwell, with or w/o oversized external extractor, stoned hammer and sear, Novak dovetail fiber optic front and adj. fiber optic rear, black dovetail front and adj. rear sights, or white dovetail front and fixed

GRADING - PPGS™	100%	98%	95%	90%	80%	70%	60%	LAST MSR

white 2-dot rear sights, wood grips, grip and ambi thumb safety, double sided frame safety, full length guide rod, with or w/o 30 LPI front strap checkering, matte silver slide and matte silver or two-tone frame finish, 38.2-41.1 oz.

MSR $1,479	$1,260	$1,100	$950	$850	$700	$560	$490	

Add $120 for 9mm Para. cal. with white dovetail front and fixed white 2-dot rear sights.
Add $150 for 9mm Para. cal. with black dovetail front and adj. rear sights.

MODEL 1911 (2004-2012) – .38 Super (mfg. 2005-2010) or .45 ACP cal., 5 in. barrel, SA, 8 or 10 (.38 Super cal.) shot mag., dovetailed black front sight with adj. micro-click black rear sight, checkered laminate wood grips, stainless steel or stainless Melonite (new 2005) frame/barrel, glass bead finish, full-length guide rod, ambidextrous frame mounted safety, 30 LPI front strap checkering, hand lapped and polished fitted barrel, frame and slide, unique front and rear serrations, includes two magazines, black finish, 41 oz., released during 2004.

	$1,795	$1,575	$1,325	$1,150	$1,000	$875	$750	*$2,209*

Add $160 for Melonite finish.

* ***Model 1911 (2005)*** – .45 ACP cal., two additional variations of this model were produced during 2005, stainless steel with glass bead satin finish, 8 shot mag., 5 in. barrel, SA, Doug Koenig speed hammer, lightweight match trigger with over travel stop, black dovetail front sight with black micro adj. rear sight, laminate fully checkered grips, oversized external extractor, full-length guide rod and oversized magwell extension, custom front and rear slide serrations, ambidextrous frame mounted safety, shipped with two 8 shot mags, other variation had high polished flats on the slide and barrel.

Last MSR was N/A.

* ***Model 1911 .38 Super cal. (2005)*** – .38 Super cal., another variation of the original 2004 model, part of Doug Koenig Professional Series, 5 in. barrel, SA, satin stainless steel finish, 10 shot mag., Doug Koenig speed hammer, competition match trigger with overtravel stop, black dovetail front sight, Doug Koenig logo on smooth black Micarta grips, oversized external extractor, full-length guide rod, competition magwell, 30 LPI front strap checkering. Mfg. 2005 only.

Last MSR was N/A.

MODEL 3566 – .356 TSW (9x21.5 mm) cal., 3 1/2 (approx. 200 mfg. Compact), 4 1/4 (Tactical), or 5 in. (approx. 545 mfg., .356 TSW Limited) match grade barrel, titanium barrel bushing, stainless frame, matte blue and hand rubbed stainless finish, oversize frame rails, 12 shot (Compact) or 15 shot (Limited) mag., adj. trigger, fitted slide and barrel, adj. Bo-Mar sights, checkered front strap, extended magwell, Hogue rubber grips w/S&W logo or plastic panel grips, Performance Center trademark on the right side of the slide, S/N prefix "TSW". Distributed by Lew Horton, 1993.

Last MSR was $1,000-$1,350

THE SHORTY 9 & SHORTY 9 MKIII – 9mm cal., match grade 3 /12 in. barrel w/hand fitted titanium bushing, DA/SA, alloy frame, blue steel slide, over-size slide rails, ambidextrous safety, Performance Center action tuning job, adj. Novak Lo-Mount sights, wraparound plastic grips, the MKIII included Zippo lighter with Performance Center logo. 611 were mfg. and distributed by Lew Horton with ser. nos. PCV0001 - PCV0611 in 1993.

Last MSR was $1,024.

9 RECON – 9mm Para. cal., 3 1/2 in. match grade barrel, DA/SA, titanium coated spherical barrel bushing, double stack 12 + 1 mag., white dot front and Novak 2 Dot Lo-Mount rear sight, traditional DA trigger, hand lapped oversize rails, ambidextrous spring loaded decocker, 20 LPI checkering on the front strap, Hogue wraparound rubber grips, compact frame, two-tone finish with a clear anodized alloy frame and a carbon steel blue slide, aluminum carry case, 27.2 oz. Distributed by RSR, 1999-2000.

Last MSR was N/A.

The 9mm Recon is similar to the Shorty 40 except the 9 Recon was a RSR exclusive while the Shorty 8 was a Lew Horton exclusive. The Recon does have forward slide serrations, ambidextrous safety, Hogue grips and the slide is marked RECON.

S&W 4006 SHORTY FORTY – .40 S&W cal., 3 1/2 in. barrel, DA/SA, spherical bushing, bobbed hammer, Novak Lo-Mount carry sights, 9-round single stack magazine, alloy frame, grips and frame may be stamped with Performance Center logo, beveled trigger, adj. front dovetail sight, oversize slide rails, 500 mfg., 27 oz. Distributed by Lew Horton, 1992, 1993, and 1995.

Last MSR was $1,500.

A total of 1,583 guns were produced with serial numbers PCS0001 to PCS1583, The initial order was for 500 guns when first released, however they sold so well that the run was extended of the first generation pistols. There were some minor changes within the first group, to the blued hammer and trigger on the later guns. There are subtle differences between the first and second production runs (e.g.: grip tang extended, horizontal

checkering added to the front strap, color variations on some parts) product code 170060. The 3rd generation pistols were the ones with the higher production numbers some of which were marked "MK III". These were released in blue, product Code 170061 and stainless steel, Product code 170076. The fourth variation was Model 4006 Shorty Forty PC Y2000 was made for Camfour Dist. product #170164 in blue finish.

* ***S&W 4006 Shorty Forty Tactical*** - .40 S&W cal., full size companion to Shorty Forty, 5 in. barrel. Distributed by Lew Horton & RSR, limited production 1993-1997.

Last MSR was $1,500.

* ***S&W 4006 Shorty Forty Compensated*** - .40 S&W cal., compensator mounted on 5 1/4 in. ported Bar-Sto barrel. 500 mfg. and distributed by Lew Horton.

Last MSR was $1,700.

* ***S&W 4006 Shorty Forty MK III*** - third variation S/N prefix "PCW". Mfg. 1995.

Last MSR was $949.

* ***S&W 4006 Shorty Forty MKIII 1997*** - ambidextrous safety, low mount adj. sights, hand fitted titanium barrel bushing, precision checkered front strap, hand honed double action, S/N prefix "KPC". Distributed by Lew Horton.

Last MSR was $1,025.

* ***S&W 4006 Shorty Forty .40 S&W Tactical*** - .40 S&W cal., 5 in. match grade barrel, fixed Tritium night front and Novak 2-dot rear sight, stainless steel frame w/carbon steel slide materials, tactical black matte slide w/satin stainless frame finish, 10 round mag., box cut frame and slide rails for 100% contact, balanced slide, ambidextrous decocker, 41.6 oz. Distributed by RSR, 1997.

Last MSR was $1,146.

* ***S&W 4006 Shorty Forty TSW Stocking Dealer*** - .40 S&W cal., 4 1/4 in. barrel. Mfg. August, 1994.

Last MSR was N/A.

MODEL 4006 SHORTY FORTY Y2000 - .40 S&W cal., 3 1/2 in. barrel, DA/SA, white dot dovetail front sight, Novak Lo-Mount Carry 2 Dot rear sight, aluminum frame with stainless slide, 9 round mag., two-tone black finish, Performance Center aluminum case. Distributed by Camfour 2000.

Last MSR was N/A.

PERFORMANCE CENTER 40 RECON - .40 S&W cal., 4 1/4 in. match grade barrel w/compensator, DA/SA, titanium coated spherical barrel bushing, white dot post front and all black Novak Lo-Mount rear sight, 7 round magazine, ambidextrous spring loaded decocker, Hogue wraparound rubber grip, stainless steel material with matte black finish, laser etched with "40 RECON Performance Center" on the left side. Distributed by RSR, 1998.

Last MSR was N/A.

PERFORMANCE CENTER 45 RECON - .45 ACP cal., 4 1/4 in. match grade ported barrel, DA/SA, titanium coated spherical barrel bushing, white dot post front and black Novak Lo-Mount rear sight, ambidextrous spring loaded decocker, Hogue wraparound rubber grip, 7 round magazine, stainless steel construction, stainless or matte black finish, laser etched "45 RECON Performance Center" on the left side, aluminum carry case, S/N prefix "SFF", 27.8 oz. Distributed by RSR, 1998.

Last MSR was $1,022.

PERFORMANCE CENTER 45 CQB PISTOLS (CLOSE QUARTERS BATTLE) - .45 ACP cal., 4 in. match grade barrel, SA, two variations offered in 1998, Novak Lo-Mount Dot front and Novak Lo-Mount 2 Dot rear sight, 7 round mag., straight backstrap grip, stainless steel slide, titanium coated spherical barrel bushing, alloy frame with a matte black finish (Model CQB-AL) or stainless steel frame with a matte stainless (Model CQB-SS) finish, ".45 C.Q.B. Performance Center" laser etched on the slide's left side. Distributed by Lew Horton, 1998-1999.

Last MSR was $1,235.

THE SHORTY .45 - .45 ACP cal., match grade barrel, ambidextrous safety, adj. sights, hand fitted titanium barrel bushing, oversize frame and slide rails, precision checkered front strap, hand honed double action. Mfg. 1997.

Last MSR was $1,146.

This model was the first of the Performance Center compact .45s. Shipped on June 3, 1996. Total production was 660 units with serial numbers starting at SFF0001-SFF0660.

THE .45 LIMITED - 45 ACP cal., match grade barrel, SA, oversize precision cut frame and slide rails, hand fitted titanium barrel bushing and slide lock, adj. sights, oversized magwell, tuned action, Zippo lighter with Perf. Center logo. Distributed by Lew Horton, 1997.

Last MSR was $1,470.

MODEL 5906 PC-9 - 9mm cal., 3 1/2 in. barrel with spherical titanium bushing, DA/SA, 15 shot mag., blue slide with satin stainless frame, smooth trigger, bobbed hammer, dovetail front and Novak Lo-Mount fixed rear sight, 27 oz. Distributed by Lew Horton in 1993.

Retail pricing was not available for this model.

GRADING - PPGS™	100%	98%	95%	90%	80%	70%	60%	LAST MSR

M&P 9 – 9mm Para. cal., striker fire action, black polymer frame, 4 1/4 in. stainless steel ported barrel (with or w/o threading), 17 shot mag., stainless steel slide, adj. trigger stop, white dot sights or HI VIZ fiber optic sights (new 2017), 17.9 oz. New 2016.

MSR $519	$450	$415	$385	$350	$325	$300	$275	

Add $400 for 4 1/4 in. threaded barrel.
Add $181 for center ported barrel or $293 for center ported barrel w/white dot sights (new 2017).
Subtract $9 for everyday carry kit including folding knife, flashlight, carrying case, and two mags (new 2018).

* ***M&P 9L*** – 9mm Para. cal., striker fire action, 5 in. ported barrel and slide, 17 shot mag., adj. trigger stop, white dot Dovetail front and drift adj. rear sights or HI VIZ fiber optic front and adj. rear sights (new 2017). New 2016.

PC M&P 9L PORTED – 9mm Para. cal., SFO, PC tuned action, polymer frame, 5 in. ported stainless steel barrel and slide, 17 shot, adj. trigger stop, C.O.R.E. (Competition Optics Ready - includes optics mounting kit), SHIELD sights SMS-4MOA MiniSight, white dot dovetail front, fixed 2-dot rear, 3 interchangeable textured palm swell grips, black Armornite finish, 24.1 oz. Mfg. 2018 only.

	$450	$415	$385	$350	$325	$300	$275	*$519*

PC M&P 9 M2.0 C.O.R.E. PRO SERIES – 9mm Para. cal., striker fire, PC tuned action, matte black frame, 4 1/4 or 5 in. stainless steel barrel, 17 shot mag., audible trigger reset, 3-dot white sights, C.O.R.E. (Competition Optics Ready Equipment) slide, black synthetic textured grips, four interchangeable palm swell grip inserts, no thumb safety, front cocking serrations, Picatinny-style rail, includes PC cleaning kit, Armornite finish, 27.2 oz. New 2020.

MSR $720	$615	$540	$460	$425	$345	$275	$225	

Add $21 for 5 in. barrel.

PC M&P 9 M2.0 PORTED/C.O.R.E. – 9mm Para. cal., striker fire, PC tuned action, matte black polymer frame, 4 1/4 or 5 in. stainless steel ported barrel and slide, 17 shot mag., audible trigger reset, white dot sights, C.O.R.E. (Competition Optics Ready Equipment), black synthetic textured grips, four interchangeable palm swell grip inserts, no thumb safety, Picatinny-style rail, front cocking serrations, Armornite finish, 26.9 oz. New 2020.

MSR $734	$625	$550	$475	$425	$350	$275	$225	

Add $21 for 5 in. barrel.
Add $140 for Crimson Trace red dot (new 2021).

PC M&P 9 M2.0 PRO SERIES – 9mm Para. cal., striker fire, PC tuned action, full size frame, 4.25 or 5 in. stainless steel standard or ported barrel, 17 shot mag., stainless steel slide with Armornite finish, audible trigger reset, green fiber optic front and red adj. fiber optic rear sights, synthetic grips with aggressive texturing, front cocking serrations, extended rigid embedded stainless steel chassis system, matte black frame finish, 28-30 oz. New 2021.

MSR $662	$560	$490	$420	$380	$310	$260	$215	

Add $21 for 5 in. barrel.
Add $58-$79 for ported barrel.

PC M&P 9/M&P 9L PRO SERIES – 9mm Para. cal., black polymer frame, 4 1/4 or 5 (M&P 9L) in. stainless steel barrel and slide, 10 or 17 shot, Tritium night sights (M&P 9) or fiber optic front and Novak reduced glare rear sights (M&P 9L), three interchangeable textured palm swell grips, 27.7-28.5 oz. Disc. 2018.

	$595	$525	$450	$400	$325	$275	$225	*$689*

PC M&P 9 PRO SERIES C.O.R.E. – 9mm Para. cal., black polymer frame, 4 1/4 in. standard barrel or 4 1/4 and 4.7 in. threaded barrel, stainless steel slide and barrel, 10 or 17 shot, enhanced trigger, white dot dovetail front and fixed 2-dot rear sights, C.O.R.E. (Competition Optics Ready Equipment), three interchangeable textured palm swell grips, Performance Center plunger and sear, 27-29.6 oz. Disc. 2018.

	$650	$550	$500	$450	$350	$300	$225	*$769*

Add $70 for threaded barrel.

PC M&P 9L PRO SERIES C.O.R.E. – 9mm Para. cal., black polymer frame, 5 in. stainless steel barrel, 10 or 17 shot, enhanced trigger, white dot dovetail front and fixed 2-dot rear sights, increased sight radius, C.O.R.E. (Competition Optics Ready Equipment), three interchangeable textured palm swell grips, Performance Center sear and plunger, 27.9-30.7 oz.

	$650	$550	$500	$450	$350	$300	$225	*769*

PC M&P 9 SHIELD – 9mm Para. cal., striker fire action, black polymer frame, 3.1 in. stainless steel ported barrel and slide, 8 shot mag., Hi Viz fiber optic sights or Tritium night sights (new 2017), 18.1 oz. Mfg. 2016-2018.

	$450	$415	$385	$350	$325	$300	$275	*$519*

Add $81 for Tritium night sights (new 2017).

GRADING - PPGS™	100%	98%	95%	90%	80%	70%	60%	LAST MSR

* ***PC M&P 9 Shield Ported*** – 9mm Para. cal., striker fire action, black polymer frame, 3.1 in. ported stainless steel barrel and slide, 8 shot, HIVIZ fiber optic or Tritium night sights, front cocking serrations, 18.1 oz. Disc. 2018.

	$450	$415	$385	$350	$325	$300	$275	*$519*

Add $81 for Tritium night sights.

PC M&P 9 SHIELD EZ – 9mm Para. cal., internal hammer fired action, polymer frame, 3.83 in. stainless steel ported barrel and slide with Armornite finish, 8 shot mag., PC flat face black, silver, or gold anodized aluminum trigger and grip safety, HI-VIZ Litewave H3 Tritium/Litepipe sights, available with manual or no thumb safety, Picatinny style rail, tactile loaded chamber indicator, includes Performance Center cleaning kit, matte black finish, 23.2 oz. New mid-2020.

MSR $606	$515	$450	$385	$350	$285	$230	$200	

PC M&P 9 SHIELD M2.0 – 9mm Para. cal., striker fire, PC tuned action, polymer frame with matte black finish, 4 in. stainless steel standard or ported barrel, 7 or 8 shot mag., stainless steel slide with Armornite finish, tactile and audible trigger reset, green fiber optic front and red fiber optic rear sights, black synthetic grip with aggressive grip texture, front cocking serrations, includes Performance Center branded cleaning kit (collapsible cleaning rod with rotating T-handle, 10 cotton cleaning patches, nylon cleaning brush, bronze bore brushes and nylon jags, nylon slotted tips), 19.7-20.9 oz. New 2019.

MSR $560	$475	$415	$385	$350	$325	$300	$275	

Add $303 for optics ready slide and 4 MOA red dot sight.
Add $331 for ported barrel and optics ready slide with 4 MOA red dot sight.

* ***PC M&P 9 Shield M2.0 Ported*** – 9mm Para. cal., PC tuned action, striker fired, matte black polymer frame, 3.1 in. stainless steel ported barrel and slide, 7 or 8 shot mag. (one flush-fit, one extended finger groove), HI VIZ fiber optic red sights or Tritium night sights, manual thumb safety, front cocking serrations, includes PC brand cleaning kit, Armornite slide finish, 20.4 oz. New 2019.

MSR $567	$485	$425	$385	$350	$325	$300	$275	

Add $88 for Tritium night sights.
Add $14 for Every Day Carry Kit (includes one 7 and one 8 shot mag., M&P Oasis liner lock folding knife, M&P Delta Force CS LED flashlight, and PC branded discreet gun portfolio).

PC M&P 40/M&P 40L PRO SERIES – .40 S&W cal., black polymer frame, 4 1/4 or 5 (M&P 40L) in. stainless steel barrel and slide, 15 shot, enhanced trigger, Tritium night sights (M&P 40) or fiber optic front and Novak reduced glare rear sights (M&P 40L), three interchangeable textured palm swell grips, Performance Center sear and plunger, 27.9-29.2 oz. Disc. 2018.

	$595	$525	$450	$400	$325	$275	$225	

Last MSR was $689.

PC M&P 40/M&P 40L PRO SERIES C.O.R.E. – .40 S&W cal., black polymer frame, 4 1/4 or 5 (M&P 40L) in. stainless steel barrel and slide, 15 shot, enhanced trigger, white dot dovetail front and fixed 2-dot rear sights, C.O.R.E. (Competition Optics Ready Equipment), three interchangeable textured palm swell grips, 27-28.3 oz.

	$650	$550	$500	$450	$350	$300	$225	*$769*

PC M&P 40 M2.0 C.O.R.E. PRO SERIES – .40 S&W cal., striker fire, PC tuned action, matte black frame, 4 1/4 or 5 in. stainless steel barrel, 15 shot mag., audible trigger reset, 3-dot white sights, C.O.R.E. (Competition Optics Ready Equipment) slide, black synthetic textured grips, four interchangeable palm swell grip inserts, no thumb safety, front cocking serrations, Picatinny-style rail, includes PC cleaning kit, Armornite finish, 27.2 oz. New 2020.

MSR $720	$615	$540	$460	$425	$345	$275	$225	

Add $21 for 5 in. barrel.

PC M&P 40 M2.0 PORTED/C.O.R.E. – .40 S&W cal., striker fire, PC tuned action, matte black polymer frame, 4 1/4 or 5 in. stainless steel ported barrel and slide, 15 shot mag., audible trigger reset, white dot sights, C.O.R.E. (Competition Optics Ready Equipment), black synthetic textured grips, four interchangeable palm swell grip inserts, no thumb safety, Picatinny-style rail, front cocking serrations, Armornite finish, 27.8 oz. New 2020.

MSR $734	$625	$550	$475	$425	$350	$275	$225	

Add $21 for 5 in. barrel.

PC M&P 40 M2.0 PRO SERIES – .40 S&W cal., striker fire, PC tuned action, full size frame, 4.25 or 5 in. stainless steel standard or ported barrel, 15 shot mag., stainless steel slide with Armornite finish, audible trigger reset, green fiber optic front and red adj. fiber optic rear sights, synthetic grips with aggressive texturing, front cocking serrations, extended rigid embedded stainless steel chassis system, matte black frame finish, 29.1-30.4 oz. New 2021.

MSR $662	$560	$490	$420	$380	$310	$260	$215	

Add $21 for 5 in. barrel.
Add $58-$79 for ported barrel.

GRADING - PPGS™	100%	98%	95%	90%	80%	70%	60%	LAST MSR

PC M&P 40 SHIELD PORTED – .40 S&W cal., striker fired, black polymer frame, 3.1 in. stainless steel ported barrel and slide, 6 or 7 shot mag., enhanced trigger, Tritium night sights, black polymer grip, thumb safety, Armornite slide finish. Mfg. 2017-2018.

	$450	$415	$385	$350	$325	$300	$275	*$519*

Add $81 for Tritium night sights.

PC M&P 45 SHIELD PORTED – .45 ACP cal., striker fire action, 3.3 in. stainless steel ported barrel and slide, 7 shot mag., polymer frame, enhanced trigger, front and rear HI VIZ fiber optic sights or choice of front or rear Tritium night sights, plastic grip, front cocking serrations, Armornite black finish, 22.6 oz. Mfg. 2017-2018.

	$525	$465	$425	$380	$350	$325	$295	*$609*

Add $133 for Tritium night sights.

PC M&P 40 SHIELD M2.0 – .40 S&W cal., striker fire, PC tuned action, polymer frame with matte black finish, 4 in. stainless steel standard or ported barrel, 6 or 7 shot mag., stainless steel slide with Armornite finish, tactile and audible trigger reset, green fiber optic front and red fiber optic rear sights, black synthetic grip with aggressive grip texture, front cocking serrations, includes Performance Center branded cleaning kit (collapsible cleaning rod with rotating T-handle, 10 cotton cleaning patches, nylon cleaning brush, bronze bore brushes and nylon jags, nylon slotted tips, 19.7-20.9 oz. New 2019.

MSR $560	$475	$415	$385	$350	$325	$300	$275

Add $303 for optics ready slide and 4 MOA red dot sight.
Add $331 for ported barrel and optics ready slide with 4 MOA red dot sight.

* ***PC M&P 40 Shield M2.0 Ported*** – .40 S&W cal., striker fire, PC tuned action, matte black polymer frame, 3.1 in. stainless steel ported barrel and slide, 6 or 7 shot mag., Hi-Viz fiber optic green front or red rear sights or Tritium night sights, manual thumb safety, front cocking serrations, includes PC branded cleaning kit, Armornite finish, 20.1 oz. New 2019.

MSR $567	$485	$425	$385	$350	$325	$300	$275

Add $88 for Tritium night sights.

PC M&P 45 SHIELD M2.0 – .45 ACP cal., striker fire, PC tuned action, matte black polymer frame, 4 in. stainless steel barrel, stainless steel slide with Armornite finish, tactile and audible trigger reset, fiber optic green front and fiber optic red rear sights, black synthetic textured grips, front cocking serrations, includes PC branded cleaning kit, 24.8 oz. New 2019.

MSR $560	$475	$415	$385	$350	$325	$300	$275

Add $303 for optics ready slide and 4 MOA red dot sight.
Add $331 for ported barrel and slide, ptics ready, and 4 MOA red dot sight.

* ***PC M&P 45 Shield M2.0 Ported*** – .45 Auto cal., striker fired, matte black polymer frame with embedded stainless steel chassis system, 3.3 in. stainless steel ported barrel and slide, 6 and 7 shot mag. (one standard flush-fit and one extended finger groove), HiViz or Tritium night sights, black synthetic grip, front cocking serrations, includes Performance Center branded cleaning kit, Armornite finish, 22.6 oz. New 2019.

MSR $567	$485	$425	$385	$350	$325	$300	$275

Add $88 for Tritium night sights.

PC M&P 380 SHIELD EZ M2.0 – .380 ACP cal., PC action, 3.8 in. ported stainless steel barrel with black Armornite, gold TiN coated, or silver high bright finish, two 8 shot mags., PC flat face black anodized aluminum trigger, HIVIZ Litewave H3 Tritium/Litepipe sights, polymer grips, PC enhanced black anodized aluminum grip safety, lightning cuts in slide, tactile loaded chamber indicator, Picatinny-style rail, includes Performance Center branded cleaning kit (collapsible cleaning rod, 10 cotton cleaning patches, nylon cleaning brush, bronze bore brushes and nylon jags, nylon slotted tips), black frame finish, 18.5 oz. New 2019.

MSR $532	$450	$415	$385	$350	$325	$300	$275

PC SW22 VICTORY TARGET MODEL – .22 LR cal., SA, stainless steel frame, 6 in. fluted target stainless steel or carbon fiber barrel, custom muzzle brake, two 10 shot mags., extended mag. release button, beveled magwell, flat face target trigger with adj. trigger stop, fiber optic front and adj. fiber optic rear sight or Red Dot sight, Tandemkross "hiveGrips" with Target thumbrest, steel reinforced polymer thumb safety, Picatinny-style rail, 37.6 oz. New 2019.

MSR $706	$600	$525	$450	$400	$325	$300	$275

Add $199 for red dot sight.

Revolvers: Performance Center Variations

SCHOFIELD MODEL OF 2000 – .45 (.45 Schofield) cal., 6 shot, 7 in. barrel, SA, this 3rd Model Schofield is a modern top break, features the design concepts of the original Model 3 Schofield and incorporates the technical and engineering advantages of the last 125 years, modern hammer block safety, case colored hammer, smooth case colored trigger, 1st edition latches, fixed notch rear and pinned half moon post front sights, walnut grips, carbon steel frame w/polished blue finish, 40 oz., 12 1/2 in. overall, Serial prefix of "GWS" for Col. George W. Schofield. Mfg. began in Jan. 2000.

Last MSR was $1,800.

* ***Schofield Model of 2000 w/Nickel Finish*** – .45 S&W (.45 Schofield) cal., 7 in. barrel, nickel finish, "US" stamped on the butt with ser. no., black pinned round blade front sight with Mod 3 Schofield 1875" on the right side, case colored hammer, latch and trigger guard, shipped in the Heritage Series box. Mfg. began in Nov. 2001.

Last MSR was $1,520.

* ***Schofield Model of 2000 Wells Fargo Editions*** – .45 S&W (.45 Schofield) cal., 5 in. barrel, blue or nickel finish, black pinned round blade front sight, case colored hammer, latch and trigger guard, similar to other editions with "US" on butt with ser. no., marked ".45 S&W" on left side of barrel, and "Schofield Pat. Apr. 22nd 1873" on right side, shipped in Heritage Series box. Mfg. beginning Nov. 2001.

Last MSR was $1,500.

LEW HORTON MODEL 10 – .38 S&W Spl. cal., DA, case colored square butt or round butt frame and yoke, blue 4 1/4 in. tapered barrel, blue cylinder and thumb piece, brown laminated magna style wood grips with silver medallions, limited production from Lew Horton Dist. "Heritage Series", serial prefix of CRS0001-CRS0080, model stampings of 10-7 and 10-9 have been observed.

Last MSR was $790.

MODEL PC-13 – .357 Mag. cal., DA, 6 shot, 3 in. Magna ported barrel, fixed rear w/ramp front sight, Eagle Secret Service boot or Uncle Mike's grips on a K-frame, matte blue finish with beveled cylinder latch, trigger, and charge holes, shrouded extractor rod, trigger has an overtravel stop, 400 mfg., distributed by Lew Horton during 1995.

Last MSR was $760.

MODEL 14 PPC – .38 Spl. cal., DA, 4 in. full lug barrel, precision crowned muzzle, custom duty action, polished forcing cone, shipped to a law enforcement distributor in Mississippi for the National Police Shooting Championships, received by the MS Highway Patrol and L.A.P.D. pistol teams, accurized by the Performance Center, not for retail trade. Limited production of less than 100 units 1995-96.

Last MSR was N/A.

LEW HORTON HERITAGE SERIES MODEL 15-8 – .38 Spl. cal., special case colored frame and yoke, 4 in. blue barrel, blue cylinder, ramp on ramp base front sight with micrometer click rear sight, drilled and tapped, smooth trigger with checked hammer spur, round butt frame with wood laminated checkered grips, Performance Center logo under the thumbpiece, ser. no. prefix CSC0164 (example), shipped in a Heritage Series box with metal corners. Mfg. Aug. 2001.

Last MSR was $922.

LEW HORTON HERITAGE SERIES MODEL 15-8 NICKEL – .38 Spl. cal., similar to previous model, except has bright nickel finish, wood laminate grips on round butt 3 screw frame, ser. prefix NSC0170 (example). Mfg. Sept. 2001.

Last MSR was $922.

LEW HORTON HERITAGE SERIES MCGIVERN MODEL 15-9 – .38 Spl. cal., 6 in. barrel, new Model 15-9 round butt frame with integral frame lug, commemorates Ed McGivern's world speed records in 1934, 6 shot with Patridge front sight and McGivern gold bead, micrometer click rear sight, Altamont fancy checkered service grips, color case hardened, nickel or blue finish, McGivern speed record sideplate attached. Mfg. 2001.

Last MSR was $1,059.

LEW HORTON HERITAGE SERIES MODEL 17-8 – .22 LR cal., DA, 6 shot, all blue or case colored frame with blue barrel and cylinder, 4 screw sideplate, blue finish, serial numbers w/LRM prefix on the butt and in two places on the frame under the grips, Performance Center logo under the thumbpiece, shipped in "Heritage Series" box. Distributed by Lew Horton in 2003.

Last MSR was $1,040.

MODEL 19 PERFORMANCE CENTER K COMP – .38 Spl./.357 Mag. cal., DA, blue matte finish, Target K-frame w/round butt, 6 shot fluted cylinder with counterbores, 3 in. full lug ported barrel, blue matte finish, smooth combat trigger, set back Tritium night front sight on post, black blade adjustable rear sight, contoured thumbpiece, rubber combat grips, 36 oz. Mfg. 1994 and 2000.

Last MSR was $800.

GRADING - PPGS™	100%	98%	95%	90%	80%	70%	60%	LAST MSR

MODEL 19 CARRY COMP – .357 Mag./.38 Spl. + P cal., DA/SA, PC tuned action, medium K-frame, 3 in. PowerPort vented stainless steel barrel, 6 shot, carbon steel frame and cylinder, trigger overtravel stop, Tritium front night sight and black blade adj. rear sight, black synthetic stock, custom wood and synthetic boot grips, 34.2 oz. New 2019.

MSR $1,132	$975	$850	$725	$675	$550	$450	$375	

LEW HORTON HERITAGE SERIES MODEL 24-5 – .44 Spl. cal., case colored frame, blue 6 1/2 in. barrel, blue cylinder, 4 screw sideplate, round butt frame, ball detent lockup at yoke, traditional thumpiece, diamond checkered walnut grips with S&W monogram, PC trademark under thumbpiece, ser. prefix "CSH". 150 mfg. May 2001.

	$765	$650	$525	$465	$415	$375	$325	*$1,110*

* ***Lew Horton Heritage Series Model 24-5 Blue Finish*** – similar to previous model except has all blue finish, ser. prefix of BCBxx66. Mfg. Sept. 2001.

	$765	$650	$525	$465	$415	$375	$325	*$1,050*

MODEL 25-10 "HAND EJECTOR" 2001 – .45 Colt cal., 6 in. tapered barrel with shrouded extractor, pinned gold bead Patridge front sight with black blade micrometer click rear sight, 1955 Hand Ejector features built on the most modern N-frame design, yoke has a ball detent front lockup with the normal extractor rod lock, 4 screw sideplates, chamfered charge holes, wood grips with S&W medallions, bright blue finish, supplied with Certificate signed by the Performance Center manager, shipped with aluminum PC locking gun case, 42 oz., approx. 150 mfg. Distributed by Sports South, Inc. in 2001.

Last MSR was N/A.

MODEL 25-11 CASE COLORED – .45 Colt cal., 6 1/2 in. blue barrel, case colored frame, adj. rear sight, 6 shot fluted cylinder, 4 screw frame stamped Model 25-11, ser. prefix "GBP", marked "45 Colt CTG" on right side of barrel, shipped in Heritage Series gold box. 150 mfg. July 2001.

Last MSR was $1,150.

MODEL 25-11 BLUE FINISH – .45 LC cal., 6 1/2 in. barrel, all blue finish, adj. rear sight, 6 shot fluted cylinder, 4 screw frame stamped Model 25-11, ser. prefix "BAK", marked "45 Colt CTG" on right side of barrel, shipped in Heritage Series gold box. Mfg. July 2001.

Last MSR was $1,150.

LEW HORTON HERITAGE SERIES MODEL OF 1917 – .45 ACP cal., 5 1/2 in. barrel, blue finish, fixed rear sight, lanyard ring and half moon clips, 4 screw frame, marked Model 25-12, 6 shot fluted cylinder, marked ".45 ACP" on right side of barrel and "S&W D.A. 45" on left, PC logo under thumbpiece, ser. no. prefix "NCS", shipped in Heritage Series gold box. 150 mfg. Aug. 2001.

Last MSR was $1,050.

* ***Lew Horton Heritage Series Model of 1917 Case Colored*** – similar to Lew Horton Heritage Series Model of 1917, except has case colored finish. 150 mfg. Sept. 2001.

Last MSR was $1,050.

* ***Lew Horton Heritage Series Model of 1917 Military*** – similar to Lew Horton Heritage Series Model of 1917, except has dull military-style finish.

Last MSR was $1,050.

MODEL 27-7 – .357 Mag. cal., 8 shot, 100 with 4 in. barrel with black ramp front sight, 100 with 6 1/2 in. barrel with black Patridge front sight, Magna combat grips, 42-45 oz. Distributed by Bangers.

Last MSR was N/A.

"CLASSIC SERIES" MODEL 27 – .357 Mag. cal., the last 6 shot Model 27s were mfg. with frame and barrels from 50th Anniversary Commemoratives, and frames recessed cylinders from the "Outnumbered" series, "AVU" ser. prefix. 14 were mfg. and sold through Lew Horton in June 1999.

Last MSR was N/A.

MODEL 27-8 "THE REGISTERED MAGNUM" – .357 Mag. cal., 3 1/2 or 5 in. barrel, bright blue or nickel, 8 shot, modern CNC square butt frame with four screws and serrated tangs, two variations were designed with machining which characterizes the famous revolver with top strap checkering and checkering along the barrel rib, shipped containing a Registered Magnum Certificate of a design made in 2007. Introduced during SHOT Show 2007-Disc.

	$875	$675	$625	$525	$495	$475	$450	*$1,000*

MODEL 28 – .357 Mag., red ramp front sight with white outline rear sight, 4 in. barrel with recessed cylinder, during 2000 approx. five Model 28s were stamped with the Performance Center trademark, ser. no. N951647 Model 28-2 is one example.

Extreme rarity precludes accurate pricing on this model.

GRADING - PPGS™	100%	98%	95%	90%	80%	70%	60%	LAST MSR

MODEL 29 "AMERICAN PRIDE" – .44 Mag. cal., first ever carbon steel Performance Center Hunter model, Hi-Viz interchangeable front sight, high polish blue finish, unique barrel design with removable scope base, 4 screw sideplate, unfluted cylinder, checkered wood grips with American Pride logo, internal key lock. 200 mfg. 2005.

Last MSR was N/A.

MODEL 29-9 HERITAGE SERIES – .44 Mag. cal., 6 1/2 in. barrel, blue finish, adj. rear sight, 6 shot fluted cylinder, 4 screw frame stamped "Model 29-9", extractor shroud, PC logo under thumbpiece, target grips, shipped in Heritage Series gold box. Mfg. 2002.

Last MSR was $1,045.

* ***Heritage Series Model 29-9 Lew Horton*** – similar to Model 29-9 Heritage Series, except has nickel finish, serial prefix is BBR. Mfg. 2002-disc.

Last MSR was $1,045.

MODEL 29 CLASSIC SERIES – 7 1/2 in. full lug barrel, frame molded, Pres. case. 200 mfg. Disc.

	100%	98%	95%	90%	80%	70%	60%	LAST MSR
	$2,500	$2,000	$1,000	N/A	N/A	N/A	N/A	

MODEL 41 – "Classic 41", approx. 10 mfg.

Last MSR was N/A.

MODEL 60 ET COMP – .38 Spl. +P cal., 3 in. ported full lug barrel, dovetail front and adj. rear sight, round butt frame, contoured thumbpiece, rosewood laminate or pearl inlaid synthetic grips, blue hard case, approx. 300 mfg. Distributed by Lew Horton, 1993.

Last MSR was $795.

MODEL 60 PRO SERIES – .357 Mag. or .38 S&W Spl.+P cal., SA/DA, J-frame, 3 in. stainless steel barrel, 5 shot, stainless steel frame and cylinder, adj. rear sight, front pinned ramp night sight, ergonomic high-hand hold oversized laminate wood grip, chamfered charge holes, matte stainless finish, 22.9 oz. New mid-2007.

	100%	98%	95%	90%	80%	70%	60%	LAST MSR
MSR $839	$715	$650	$575	$495	$425	$350	$280	

MODEL 66 F COMP (1993) – .357 Mag. cal., 3 in. full lug ported barrel, dovetailed tritium front night sight, tuned action, round butt w/rubber grips, counterbored cylinder, contoured cylinder latch, "LHF" serial number prefix, approx. 300 mfg. Distributed by Lew Horton, 1993.

Last MSR was N/A.

MODEL 66 THE SUPER K – .357 Mag. cal., 3 in. specially contoured barrel with 2 port magna porting, white synthetic grip with S&W medallions, Performance Center Tuned action and overtravel trigger stop. Distributed by Lew Horton, 1997.

Last MSR was N/A.

MODEL 66 F-COMP – .357 Mag. cal., 3 in. full lug ported barrel with drift adj. dovetailed ramp front sight and micrometer click rear sight, 6 shot cylinder with chamfered charge holes, front sight set behind barrel port, glass bead finish, shipped with walnut combat grips and an additional Hogue Bantam monogrip.

Last MSR was $798.

MODEL 67 F-COMP – .38 Spl. cal., 6 shot, 3 in. full lug Power Port barrel, adj. white outline rear and tritium front sights, stainless steel frame, matte black finish, synthetic finger groove grips, 35 oz. Mfg. mid-2007-2009.

	100%	98%	95%	90%	80%	70%	60%	LAST MSR
	$1,025	$875	$750	$625	$525	$450	$400	*$1,311*

MODEL 325 THUNDER RANCH – .45 ACP cal., 4 in. barrel, 6 shot, interchangeable front sight, adj. rear sight, Scandium alloy N-frame with stainless steel cylinder, matte black finish, rubber finger groove grips, 31 oz. Mfg. 2008-2020.

	100%	98%	95%	90%	80%	70%	60%	LAST MSR
	$1,085	$895	$750	$625	$525	$425	$350	*$1,329*

MODEL 327 Sc – .357 Mag. cal., 8 shot, 2 in. barrel with titanium shroud, black finish with natural grey titanium cylinder, Scandium alloy N-frame, teardrop color case hammer and trigger with overtravel stop, Ahrends cocobolo round butt grips with finger grooves, small lanyard pin, PC logo under thumbpiece, fixed or adj. sights, shipped with black PC marked gun rug made by Allen with internal pouch, 2 full moon clips, special ser. no. range. New 2006.

	100%	98%	95%	90%	80%	70%	60%	LAST MSR
MSR $1,344	$1,140	$1,000	$855	$775	$625	$515	$445	

Add $16 for 5 in. barrel with adj. sights (disc.).

MODEL 327 Sc JERRY MICULEK – similar to Model 327 Sc, 5 in. barrel, 8 shot, unfluted titanium cylinder, adj. rear sights, orange Hi-Viz fiber optic front sight, unique new two-piece barrel design, Jerry Miculek signature grip and extra Hogue rubber grips. Mfg. 2005 only.

Last MSR was $1,149.

GRADING - PPGS™	100%	98%	95%	90%	80%	70%	60%	LAST MSR

MODEL 327 TRR8 - .357 Mag. /.38 Spl.+ P cal., SA/DA, PC tuned action, large Scandium alloy frame, 5 in. stainless steel barrel, 8 shot, titanium alloy (disc.) or stainless steel cylinder, teardrop hammer, PC trigger with trigger stop, adj. V-notch rear sight, interchangeable front sight, synthetic finger groove grips, Picatinny-style rail, removable equipment rail, cylinder cut for moon clips (moon clips included), matte black frame finish, 34.7 oz. New mid-2007.

MSR $1,360	$1,160	$1,010	$865	$785	$635	$525	$450	

MODEL 329-1 AIRLITE PD - .44 Mag. cal., serrated and ported 3 in. barrel, round butt Scandium alloy N-frame, 6 shot titanium cylinder, painted red ramp front sight, adj. black blade front sight, Ahrends cocobolo finger groove wood grips. Mfg. 2003.

Last MSR was $1,100.

All Model 329-1 Airlites were recalled by S&W during July, 2004 due to frame cracks. DO NOT FIRE THIS GUN!

MODEL 442 CRIMSON TRACE - .38 Spl.+P cal., DAO, PC tuned action, J-frame, 1 7/8 in. stainless steel barrel, 5 shot, aluminum alloy frame, stainless steel cylinder with matte finish and high polished cylinder flutes, Crimson Trace L6-105 Lasergrips with red laser, no internal lock, two-tone finish, 15 oz. New 2021.

MSR $782	$665	$580	$500	$450	$365	$300	$260	

MODEL 442 PRO SERIES - .38 Spl.+P cal., DAO, small J-frame, 1.8 in. stainless steel barrel, 5 shot, aluminum alloy frame/carbon steel cylinder, snag-free enclosed hammer, integral fixed sights, black synthetic grips, no internal lock, full moon clips, matte black finish, 14.6 oz. New 2010.

MSR $531	$450	$395	$340	$300	$250	$200	$175	

MODEL 442 THE ULTRALIGHT - .38 S&W Spl. cal., similar to Model 442 Centennial, it has been reported (and photographed) that a few (approx. 10) with an alloy cylinder were made for the U.S. Secret Service as prototypes but were never sold or released to the general public. These prototypes have no markings on the sideplate, and have a matte blue finish. One observed Ser. no. prefix is "BSS". Mfg. 1997.

Last MSR was N/A.

This model was never offered for commercial sale.

MODEL 460 AIRWEIGHT - .38 S&W Spl. cal., DA only, alloy J-frame w/round butt, 5 shot fluted steel cylinder, fully concealed hammer, 2 in. steel Magna Ported barrel, fixed sight, blue matte finish, Eagle Secret Service grips, smooth trigger, ser. no. prefix "SDE", 15.8 oz. approx. 450 mfg. 1994.

Last MSR was $595.

MODEL 460 HUNTER - .460 S&W Mag. cal., 14 in. fluted barrel with Patridge front sight in back of integral muzzle brake, adj. rear sight, upper and lower Picatinny rails on rear of barrel, unfluted cylinder, rubber grips, satin stainless steel, 88 oz. Mfg. 2011-disc.

	$1,250	$1,050	$925	$800	$700	$600	$525	*$1,559*

MODEL 460XVR SERIES - .460 S&W Mag. cal., capable of shooting both the .45 Colt and .454 Casull cartridges, PC tuned action, X-frame, 3 1/2 (disc.), 6 1/2 (disc. 2008), 7 1/2 (disc. 2008), 10 1/2, 12 (fluted, mfg. 2008-2020), or 14 in. stainless steel barrel with mounted recoil reducer/muzzle brake, 5 shot, stainless frame and cylinder, chromed custom teardrop hammer, chromed trigger, interchangeable green Hi-Viz front sight (disc.), fiber optic sights, or black ramp front and adj. rear sights, Hogue dual density monogrip with S&W monogram, integral Weaver style scope mount, Uncle Mike's detachable sling and swivels, with or w/o bipod, glass bead or satin stainless finish, 82 1/2 oz. New 2006.

MSR $1,598	$1,360	$1,190	$1,020	$925	$750	$625	$530	

Add $67 for fiber optic sights and satin stainless finish.
Add $60 for 12 in. barrel (disc. 2020).

Lew Horton ordered a number of 3 1/2 in. models.

The 6 1/2 in. barrel does not have sling mounts.

In late summer 2005, a 7 1/2 in. barrel version was manufactured for Ellett Bros. distributors with black finish, stainless steel cylinder, muzzle brake, and shoulder sling. This model included a Lothar-Walther custom rifled barrel and a special ser. no. (EBD0001-EBD0500).

* ***Model 460XVR 3 1/2 In. (New Mfg.)*** - .460 S&W Mag. cal., 3 1/2 in. barrel, unfluted cylinder, chrome teardrop hammer, 5 shot, Hi-Viz fiber optic Green front sight, adj. rear sight, black synthetic grip, stainless steel frame/cylinder, chrome trigger with stop, glass bead finish. 59.5 oz. New 2014.

MSR $1,649	$1,400	$1,225	$1,050	$950	$775	$630	$550	

GRADING - PPGS™	100%	98%	95%	90%	80%	70%	60%	LAST MSR

* ***Model 460XVR 7 1/2 in. (New Mfg.)*** – .460 S&W cal., PC tuned action, 7 1/2 in. stainless steel barrel with muzzle brake, unfluted cylinder, 5 shot, chromed custom teardrop hammer, chrome trigger, HI VIZ fiber optic green front sight, adj. white outline rear sight, integral scope base, includes gun rug and sling, 72.8 oz. New 2017.

MSR $1,799	$1,525	$1,335	$1,145	$1,035	$840	$695	$600	

MODEL 500 (MAGNUM HUNTER) – .500 S&W Mag. cal., X-frame, 5 shot, fluted cylinder, 3 1/2 (new 2017), 6 1/2 (Compensated Hunter, mfg. 2004 only), 7 1/2, or 10 1/2 in. tapered lug barrel, with recoil compensator and integral Weaver base, Hogue mono-grip, stainless steel, glass bead finish with flash chromed hammer and trigger, adj. white outline rear sight, includes black nylon sling, swivels, and soft case, 82 oz. New 2004.

MSR $1,619	$1,370	$1,195	$1,020	$925	$750	$650	$550	

Add $17 for 10 1/2 in. barrel.
Add $30 for 3 1/2 in. barrel (new 2017).

MODEL 500 MAGNUM BONE COLLECTOR – .500 S&W Mag. cal., 10 1/2 in. barrel with Picatinny rail on rear, adj. white outline rear and red ramp front sight, two-tone finish, stainless steel, features animal rack graphics on rear of frame and marked "Bone Collector", barrel engraved "X of 1,000", 82 oz., 1,000 mfg. 2011 only.

	$1,150	$1,025	$900	$800	$700	$600	$500	*$1,389*

MODEL 586 L-COMP – .357 Mag./.38 Spl.+P (new 2017) cal., PC tuned action, 3 in. full lug ported barrel with Tritium dot front and micrometer click rear sight, Altamont Rosewood grips, 7 shot cylinder rebated for moon clips, black or blue finish, shipped with locking aluminum case & Master Gun Lock, first blue finish revolver in 7 shot offered by S&W, 37 1/2 oz. Distributed by Camfour, 2000 and 2004. Reintroduced 2017.

MSR $1,248	$1,075	$940	$800	$775	$650	$525	$415	

MODEL 610 – 10mm cal., 6 1/2 in. barrel.

Last MSR was N/A.

MODEL 617 – .22 LR cal., new profile barrel for export, only 327 mfg. 1995 and 1999.

Last MSR was N/A.

MODEL 625/MODEL 625-8 – .45 ACP cal., PC tuned action, N-frame (large), 4 in. stainless steel barrel with full shroud, deep cut broached rifling, 6 shot fluted cylinder with chamfered charge holes, cylinder cut for moon clips, PC Custom tear drop hammer, black trigger with stop and black thumbpiece, adj. rear sight, interchangeable Patridge front sight with gold bead, round butt with smooth Hogue Combat red, white, and blue laminated wood grips, satin stainless finish, 42 oz. Mfg. 2010-2020.

	$925	$725	$575	$475	$400	$350	$300	*$1,079*

MODEL 625-5 JERRY MICULEK DESIGN – .45 ACP cal., 5 1/4 in. barrel, Patridge front w/gold bead and adj. black blade rear sight, reduced cylinder freebore, 6 shot fluted cylinder w/chamfered charge holes, deep cut broached rifling, hand honed bore, satin stainless finish, "Jerry Miculek" Hogue Laminate combat grips, lockable aluminum case, 42 oz. Distributed by Camfour, 2001.

Last MSR was $899

MODEL 625-6 FLUTED HUNTER – .45 Colt cal., 6 in. ported barrel, 6 shot cylinder w/chamfered charge holes, red ramp dovetailed front sight, round butt frame, serrated backstrap & forestrap, will accept Weaver style scope mount on the integral rail system, removable weights and spacers attach to the barrel with a small allen wrench, ser. no. prefix "LHD", most were sent to Germany with about 50 remaining in the U.S. Distributed by Lew Horton, 1997.

Last MSR was N/A.

MODEL 625-6 HUNTER – .45 Colt cal., 6 in. ported slabside barrel, non-fluted cylinder, marked "45 Colt CTG". Mfg. 1997 only.

Last MSR was N/A.

MODEL 625-6 "V COMP" – .45 ACP cal., 4 in. slabside barrel with a removable compensator or a replacement muzzle to protect the crown, 6 shot non-fluted cylinder has a ball-detent lockup in the yoke, Millett dovetailed red ramp front and micrometer click rear sight, Hogue Combat wood grips, semi-target hammer, smooth combat trigger w/overtravel stop, shipped w/double combo lock aluminum carry case, 43 oz. Distributed by RSR, 1999.

Last MSR was $925.

GRADING - PPGS™	100%	98%	95%	90%	80%	70%	60%	LAST MSR

MODEL 625-7 LIGHT HUNTER – .45 Colt cal., 6 in. ported match grade barrel with integral Weaver style base rail, ball detent lockup, fluted cylinder w/chamfered charge holes, Millett dovetail front sight, forged and flash chromed trigger and hammer, satin stainless finish, Hogue wood combat grips, shipped with aluminum PC carry case, 43 oz. Distributed by RSR, 1999.

Last MSR was N/A.

MODEL 625-10 – .45 ACP cal., 6 shot, 2 in. barrel, Scandium N-frame, fixed V-notch rear sight with serrated and dovetailed ramp front sight, Eagle wood and Hogue rubber grips, stainless steel cylinder, glass bead finish, barrel marked ".45 ACP", includes PC locking case, 24 oz. Distributed by Lew Horton Sept. 2003.

Last MSR was $925.

MODEL 625-11 – .45 Colt cal., 1 1/8 in. barrel, 6 shot, aluminum/Scandium N frame, fixed sight, V-notch rear sight, serrated and dovetailed black ramp front sight with white dot, Eagle wood grip, includes extra Hogue rubber grip, stainless steel cylinder, chamfered charge holes, smooth trigger and checkered teardrop hammer, Performance Center locking case, 25 oz. 103 mfg. for Lew Horton 2005.

Last MSR was $1025.

MODEL 627-2 STAINLESS – .357 Mag./.38 Spl. cal., stainless steel version of the Model 27, 8 shot cylinder, 5 in. tapered barrel, interchangeable front sights, drilled & tapped for scope mount, chamfered charge holes, flash chrome teardrop hammer, Hogue hardwood combat grips, new thumbpiece, engraved ".357 Magnum 8 Times" on barrel, floating firing pin, RJM serial prefix, 44 oz. Distributed by Lew Horton, 1997-1998.

Last MSR was $1,000.

MODEL 627 1998 LEW HORTON SPECIAL "HUNTER STYLE" – .357 Mag. cal., 6 1/2 in. Magna ported slabside barrel, fluted cylinder w/beveled edges, contoured thumb latch, integral scope mount and weight system, adj. sights, rosewood grips.

Last MSR was $1,025.

MODEL 627PC 1998 LEW HORTON SPECIAL – .357 Mag. cal., 8 shot, 6 in. barrel. ser. no. prefix "LHV", unfluted cylinder, engraved ".357 Magnum 8 Times" with floating firing pin.

Last MSR was N/A.

MODEL 627-3 "V-COMP JERRY MICULEK SPECIAL" – 8 shot cylinder, 5 in. barrel, removable compensator, removable/interchangeable cap to protect the rifling, smooth combat trigger w/overtravel stop, TH, drift adj. red ramp front sight, micrometer click rear sight. "Jerry Miculek" design Hogue wooden grips, locking aluminum case, 47 oz. Distributed by RSR in 2000.

Last MSR was N/A.

On July 24th 1999, Jerry Miculek set a world record for firing a S&W 8 shot revolver. The results were: 8 Shots on 1 target in 1.00 seconds and 8 Shots on 2 targets in 1.06 seconds. Both records were set using a Model 627 from the Performance Center.

MODEL 627-PC – .357 Mag. cal., 8 shot, 2 5/8 in. barrel, Millett red ramp drift adj. front sight with micrometer click white outline rear sight, Eagle wood boot grips, flash chromed custom teardrop hammer, smooth combat trigger, full-length extractor, stainless steel with glass bead finish, shipped with aluminum double lock carrying case, 37.6 oz. Approx. 302 mfg. 1999-2000.

Last MSR was $1,025.

MODEL 627-4 – .38 Super cal., 8 shot, black non-fluted cylinder, 5 1/2 in. barrel, angled cut removable compensator and cap, red/white/blue Jerry Miculek designed grip, Patridge front sight with adj. black outline rear sight, chrome teardrop hammer and chrome trigger with overtravel stop, stainless steel, glass bead finish, drilled and tapped. Mfg. for Banger's 2002.

Last MSR was N/A.

MODEL 627 (627-5) – .357 Mag. or .38 Spl.+ P cal., SA/DA, N-frame, 2 5/8 (new 2010) or 5 in. tapered and countoured stainless steel barrel with fluted or unfluted cylinder, 8 shot, chrome flashed custom teardrop hammer, trigger overtravel stop, orange ramp front (2 in.) or gold bead interchangeable front (5 in.) sight with black blade adj. rear sight, wood grips (second synthetic grip included with 5 in. model), internal lock system, cylinder cut for moon clips (moon clips included), shipped with black PC marked gun rug (disc.), matte silver finish, 37.8-43.2 oz.

MSR $1,113	$945	$825	$700	$635	$515	$425	$365

Add $209 for 5 in. barrel.

GRADING - PPGS™	100%	98%	95%	90%	80%	70%	60%	LAST MSR

* ***Model 627-5 (Disc.)*** – .357 Mag. cal., 8 shot, 5 in. full lug barrel, removable cap and crown, wood grips with extra Hogue grip, fluted cylinder, black drift adj. front sight, black rear sight, marked ".357 Magnum-V8" on left side of barrel and "Performance Center" on right, floating firing pin, internal lock system, new frame design, ser. no. prefix "VCM". Limited mfg. 2004.

	100%	98%	95%	90%	80%	70%	60%	LAST MSR
	$875	$600	$525	$475	$425	$375	$335	*$1,106*

MODEL 627 PRO SERIES – .357 Mag. or .38 Spl.+P cal., SA/DA, N-frame, 4 in. custom barrel with recessed precision crown, 8 shot mag., stainless steel frame, barrel, and cylinder, teardrop hammer, adj. rear sight, red ramp front sight, rubber finger groove (disc.) or synthetic grips, chamfered charge holes, bossed main spring, titanium cylinder, cylinder cut for moon clips, matte silver finish, 41.4 oz. New 2008.

	100%	98%	95%	90%	80%	70%	60%	LAST MSR
MSR $1,024	$865	$750	$650	$575	$500	$425	$350	

MODEL 627 V-COMP – .357 Mag./.38 Spl.+P cal., SA/DA, PC tuned action, N-frame, 5 in. stainless steel barrel, removable barrel compensator, 8 shot, chromed custom teardrop hammer, chromed trigger with trigger stop, adj. orange dovetail front and adj. rear sights, synthetic rubber or wood laminate (disc. 2011) finger groove grips, cylinder cut for moon clips (moon clips included), two-tone matte or satin stainless (disc. 2011) finish, 46.7 oz. New 2008.

	100%	98%	95%	90%	80%	70%	60%	LAST MSR
MSR $1,598	$1,360	$1,190	$1,020	$925	$750	$625	$530	

MODEL 629 (S&W #170277) – .44 Mag. cal., 7 1/2 in. flat sided compensated barrel, unfluted cylinder, adj. sights, integral 11 slot Weaver style base on top of barrel, chamfered charge holes, beveled cylinder edges, over travel stop installed on trigger, hand tuned action, 250 units mfg. between April 2006 and June 2007 (26 embellished with gold Performance Center logo on cylinder), 25 (embellished with a silver Performance Center logo on cylinder), 199 (no embellishment). Mfg. 2006-2007.

	100%	98%	95%	90%	80%	70%	60%	LAST MSR
	$1,375	$1,175	$995	$875	$750	$625	$550	*$1,490*

MODEL 629 CARRY COMP – .44 Mag. cal., 6 shot, 3 in. barrel, adj. orange dovetail front sight, stainless steel frame and cylinder, matte stainless finish, fixed notch rear sight, large frame, wood combat grips with finger grooves, 38 oz. Mfg. mid-2007-2009.

	100%	98%	95%	90%	80%	70%	60%	LAST MSR
	$1,025	$875	$750	$625	$525	$450	$400	*$1,311*

MODEL 629 COMPETITOR – .44 Mag. cal., PC tuned action, N-frame, 6 in. stainless steel barrel with removable adj. barrel weights, 6 shot, glass beaded stainless steel frame and cylinder, chrome hammer, chrome trigger with trigger stop, Patridge dovetail front and adj. rear sights, black Hogue synthetic grips with finger grooves, vented lower shroud contains up to five barrel weights, Picatinny rail on top of barrel, matte silver finish, 57.2 oz. New 2013.

	100%	98%	95%	90%	80%	70%	60%	LAST MSR
MSR $1,582	$1,340	$1,175	$1,000	$910	$735	$600	$525	

MODEL 629 FLUTED BARREL – .44 Mag. or .44 S&W Special cal., N-frame, stainless steel frame and cylinder, 8 3/8 in. fluted barrel, chrome teardrop hammer, 6 shot, adj. rear and orange glow blade front sights, checkered custom wood grips, chrome trigger with stop, top Picatinny sight rail, glass bead finish, 59 oz. Mfg. mid-2013-2020.

	100%	98%	95%	90%	80%	70%	60%	LAST MSR
	$1,150	$950	$800	$675	$575	$475	$400	*$1,399*

MODEL 629 STEALTH HUNTER – .44 Mag. cal., N-frame, 6 shot, 7 1/2 in. barrel, stainless steel frame and cylinder, matte black finish, adj. front and rear sight, synthetic finger groove grips, 56 oz. New mid-2007.

	100%	98%	95%	90%	80%	70%	60%	LAST MSR
MSR $1,658	$1,410	$1,235	$1,060	$960	$775	$650	$550	

MODEL 629-3 CARRY COMP STAINLESS – .44 Mag. cal., 3 in. barrel, integral compensator, dovetailed interchangeable red ramp front sight, fixed rear sight, beveled cylinder, semi-target hammer, smooth combat trigger, N-frame, round butt, Goncalo Alves grips w/finger grooves, contoured thumbpiece, 42 oz. Distributed by Lew Horton, 1992.

Last MSR was $1,000.

MODEL 629-3 THE CLASSIC HUNTER I – .44 Mag. cal., fluted cyl. Distributed by Lew Horton, 1992.

Last MSR was $1,234.

MODEL 629-3 CARRY COMP II – .44 Mag. cal., 3 in. barrel, adj. rear sight, compensator system, unfluted Classic Hunter style cylinder, hard case, approx. 100 mfg. Distributed by Lew Horton, 1993.

Last MSR was $1,000.

MODEL 629-4 .44 MAGNUM LIGHT HUNTER – .44 Mag. cal., 6 in. Magna ported slabside barrel, non-fluted cylinder, round butt frame, scope broaching, recessed crown, radiused smooth trigger w/ overtravel stop, serial number range RSR3500-RSR4000, 500 mfg. Distributed by RSR.

Last MSR was N/A.

May 1995. Two additional variations were also made for Lew Horton Dist.

GRADING - PPGS™	100%	98%	95%	90%	80%	70%	60%	LAST MSR

MODEL 629-4 THE CLASSIC HUNTER II – .44 Mag. cal., 6 in. slab side barrel, integral variable weight system, Weaver scope mount rail system, Magna ported, non fluted chamfered cylinder, red ramp dovetail front sight, ser. no. prefix "LHK". Distributed by Lew Horton, 1996.

Last MSR was $1,234.

MODEL 629 "THE AVENGER" – .44 Mag. cal., 3 in. Dual Magna-port barrel, unfluted cylinder, 26 Mfg.

Last MSR was N/A.

MODEL 629 MAGNUM HUNTER PLUS – .44 Mag. cal., 7 1/2 in. slabside barrel, Magna ported, integral Weaver Scope Rail, unfluted cylinder. Distributed by RSR, 1996.

Last MSR was N/A.

MODEL 629-4 TROPHY WHITE TAIL – .44 Mag. cal., 6 1/2 in. ported barrel, dovetailed front sight, adj. rear sight, target hammer, smooth trigger with stop, chamfered cylinder, contoured thumbpiece, Hogue Grips with S&W trademark, two deer scene laser etched on the sideplate, with "Trophy Whitetail" etched on the barrel's right side, drilled and tapped for scope mount, Performance Center logo on the frame, ser. no. range is ZAN0001-ZAN0200. 200 mfg. Distributed by Zanders Sports, 1997.

Last MSR was N/A.

MODEL 629-4 "SCOPE ONLY" MASTER HUNTER – .44 Mag. cal., 7 1/2 in. barrel, non-fluted cylinder, drilled and tapped for scope mount only w/rear cutout for a standard rear sight, smooth barrel without a rib, satin stainless finish, Performance Center logo, ser. no. prefix "MHS". Mfg. 1997.

Retail pricing wasn't available for this model.

MODEL 629-4 "COMPED HUNTER" – .44 Mag. cal., 6 in. barrel, Weaver integral base, adj. micrometer click rear sight, dovetailed Millett red ramp front sight, removable 4 port compensator, w/replacement muzzle, glass bead finish, stainless steel, N-frame, round butt, Altamont wood grips, unfluted cylinder with chamfered charge holes, ball detent lock up, flash chromed and radiused hammer, smooth combat trigger with overtravel stop, "CMH" ser. no. prefix, 58.9 oz. Distributed by RSR, 1998.

Last MSR was $1,080.

MODEL 629-4 COMP & CAP – .44 Mag. cal., 6 1/2 in. barrel, removable muzzle brake with replaceable end cap, rosewood grips. Distributed by Lew Horton, 1998.

Last MSR was N/A.

MODEL 629-5 V-COMP – .44 Mag. cal., N-frame, 4 in. slabside barrel with removable compensator, muzzle cap, non-fluted cylinder, ball-detent lockup in the yoke, flash chromed semi-target hammer, smooth combat trigger w/overtravel stop, dovetail red ramp front sight, micrometer click rear sight, Hogue wood combat grips w/S&W Monogram, aluminum carry case, 43 oz. Distributed by RSR in 1999, reintroduced 2009-2020.

	100%	98%	95%	90%	80%	70%	60%	LAST MSR
	$1,250	$1,100	$975	$850	$725	$600	$525	*$1,559*

MODEL 629-5 DEFENSIVE REVOLVER – .44 Mag. cal., 2 5/8 in. barrel, ball detent lockup system in the yoke, 6 shot non-fluted cylinder, flash chromed teardrop hammer and smooth combat trigger, Millett dovetailed red ramp front sight, micrometer click rear sight, Hogue wood combat grips, glass bead stainless steel finish, aluminum carry case with the Performance Center logo, 39.6 oz. Distributed by Lew Horton, 1999-2000.

Last MSR was $1,026.

MODEL 629-5 "THE EXTREME HUNTER" – .44 Mag./.44 S&W Special cal., 12 in. barrel, 6 shot fluted cylinder, Wilson rubber combat grips, round butt N-frame, Uncle Mike's swivels and sling, long under extension to support the long barrel and front swivel mount, dovetailed Patridge front sight, Wilson Silhouette rear sight, glass bead stainless steel finish, modern frame with floating firing pin and MIM hammer and trigger, Waller 21 in. gun rug, ser. no. prefix "AMH", 65 oz. Distributed by Lew Horton, 2000.

Last MSR was $1,201.

MODEL 629-5 "STEALTH HUNTER" – .44 Mag. cal., 7 1/2 in. Magna ported Hunter style barrel, 6 shot unfluted flat black cylinder with ball detent lockup and chamfered charge holes, integral Weaver style rib and counterbored muzzle, drift adj. Millett red ramp front sight, white outline micrometer adj. rear sight, Hogue black rubber monogrip with the S&W trademark, black smooth trigger with overtravel stop, black tapered hammer spur, NATO green stainless steel frame and barrel, black contrasting screws, grip, cylinder, thumbpiece, hammer, and trigger, Performance Center aluminum case, ser. no. prefix "FBS", approx. 50 oz. Distributed by Camfour, 2000-2001.

Last MSR was $1,200.

GRADING - PPGS™	100%	98%	95%	90%	80%	70%	60%	LAST MSR

MODEL 629-5 "COMPENSATED HUNTER" - .44 Mag. cal., 7 1/2 in. ported barrel, glass bead finish, stainless steel, fixed compensator, 6 shot fluted cylinder w/chamfered charge holes, ball detent lock-up, adj. front sight w/orange ramp insert, adj. micrometer black blade rear sight, removable stainless steel scope mount, rosewood laminate grips, extra Hogue monogrip, round butt frame, lockable Performance Center aluminum case, 52.2 oz. Distributed by Talo, 2001.

Last MSR was $1,104.

MODEL 629-5 "LIGHT HUNTER PLUS" - .44 Mag. cal., 7 1/2 in. barrel, all black Birdsong finish, barrel is cut for scope mount with Weaver rail, unfluted cylinder, gold bead front sight, Hogue monogrip, ser. no. prefix "DEL". Mfg. 2002.

Last MSR was N/A.

MODEL 629 (LIGHT HUNTER) - .44 Mag. cal., N-frame, 6 shot, 2 5/8 (new 2010) or 7 1/2 (disc. 2020) in. barrel with integral muzzle brake, stainless steel, tapered ejector rod housing, wood combat grips, includes scope rail, 49.7 oz. New 2003.

MSR $1,113	$950	$825	$700	$635	$515	$425	$350

Add $240 for 7 1/2 in. barrel (disc. 2020).

MODEL 629 HUNTER – .44 Mag. cal., N-frame, 7 1/2 in. barrel with extended muzzle brake, 6 shot, two-tone finish with black frame and satin finished cylinder and barrel sides, Picatinny rail, red ramp adj. rear sight, black synthetic grips with finger grooves, 57 1/2 oz. New 2011.

MSR $1,398	$1,190	$1,050	$900	$815	$675	$550	$475

MODEL 629-7 "HUNTER PLUS" - .44 Mag. cal., black finish, 7-1/2 in. polished slabside barrel with compensator, 6 shot unfluted polished cylinder, ".44 MAGNUM HUNTER PLUS" on the barrels right side. Mfg. 2007.

Last MSR was N/A.

MODEL 632-1 – .327 Federal Mag. cal., 3 in. ported barrel, ramp front sight with adjustable rear sight, black overall finish with Uncle Mike's combat grips, stainless steel frame and cylinder and steel internal parts. Mfg. 2009.

Last MSR was N/A.

This model was the first production handgun in this caliber made by S&W.

MODEL 637 ENHANCED ACTION – .38 Spl.+P cal., SA/DA, J-frame, 1 7/8 in. stainless steel barrel and cylinder, 5 shot, aluminum alloy frame, rear fixed sights, front integral sights, custom wood grips, matte silver finish, 14.6 oz. New 2017.

MSR $565	$490	$430	$365	$330	$295	$275	$250

MODEL 637 GUNSMOKE – .38 S&W Spl. +P cal., DAO, J-frame, aluminum alloy construction, stainless steel cylinder and barrel, 1.87 in. barrel, 5 shot, hammerless, integral front sight, fixed notch rear sight, polymer clip grip, built for Rich Wyatt's Gunsmoke gun shop in CO, has Gunsmoke logo on barrel and "WYATT DEEP COVER" on side of frame, 14 oz. Mfg. mid-2013-disc.

$495	$425	$365	$335	$300	$275	$250	*$559*

MODEL 637-2 POWER PORT - .38 Spl. cal., 2 1/8 in. ported barrel, black finish, Uncle Mike's combat grips, white dot front sight, U notch cut rear sight, does not have the Performance Center trademark, with internal lock. Mfg. 2008 only.

Last MSR was N/A.

MODEL 640 CARRY COMP - .38 Spl. +P cal., 2 in. ported barrel, adj. front sight, fixed rear sight, radiused hammer and trigger, 150 mfg. w/rosewood grips, 150 mfg. w/Bader mother-of-pearl inlaid finger groove grips, blue plastic case w/Performance Center logo, 23 oz. Distributed by Lew Horton. Mfg. 1993.

Last MSR was $750.

MODEL 640 LEW HORTON - .357 Mag. cal., 5 shot, 2 1/8 in. ported barrel, dovetail front sight with tritium insert on black post, matte stainless finish, Performance Center tuned action, Pachmayr Decelerator grips, chrome smooth combat trigger. Mfg. 1996.

Last MSR was $839.

At least one Model 640 is known to have been chambered in .38 Super caliber for test purposes by the Performance Center.

MODEL 640 "LEW HORTON .357 MAGNUM" - .357 Mag. cal., 2 1/8 in. Quad Port barrel, glass bead finish. Mfg. 1999.

Last MSR was $851.

GRADING - PPGS™	100%	98%	95%	90%	80%	70%	60%	LAST MSR

MODEL 640 "PAXTON QUIGLEY" – .38 Spl. cal., 2 5/8 in. barrel, integral compensator, dovetailed adj. front sight, tuned by the S&W Performance Center, laminated wood grips w/mother-of-pearl inlaid heart, Boyt tapestry case and letter of authenticity from Paxton Quigley, author of *Armed & Female.* Distributed by Lew Horton, 1994. Limited production of 250.

Last MSR was $725.

MODEL 640 PRO SERIES – .357 Mag./.38 Spl. +P cal., DAO, J-frame, 2.13 in. fluted barrel, 5 shot, stainless steel frame, barrel, and cylinder, concealed hammer, front and rear dovetail Tritium night sights, black synthetic grips, full moon clips, no internal lock, satin stainless finish, 23 oz. New 2010.

MSR $879 $760 $700 $650 $545 $465 $385 $315

MODEL 640 RSR SPECIAL – .357 Mag. cal., 2 1/8 in. Magna-Ported barrel, 5 shot non-fluted cylinder, glass bead stainless steel finish, concealed hammer, J-frame, round butt, Heritage walnut grips, chrome smooth combat trigger, pinned black ramp front sight, square notch rear sight, 25 oz. Mfg. 1996 only.

Last MSR was N/A.

MODEL 642 – 38 Spl.+P cal., DAO, aluminum alloy frame, 1.88 in. stainless steel barrel, 5 shot, integral front and rear fixed sights, synthetic grip with wood inserts, matte silver two-tone finish, 14.4 oz. New 2017.

MSR $576 $500 $440 $375 $335 $300 $275 $250

MODEL 642 ENHANCED ACTION – .38 Spl. cal., DA only, 1 7/8 in. stainless steel barrel, 5 shot mag., aluminum alloy frame, front integral sight, fixed rear adj. sight, custom wood grip, matte silver finish, 15 oz. New 2017.

MSR $565 $490 $430 $365 $330 $295 $275 $250

MODEL 642 PRO SERIES – .38 S&W Spl. +P cal., DAO, J-frame, 1.875 in. stainless steel barrel, 5 shot, aluminum alloy frame/stainless steel cylinder, no internal lock, cut for moon clips, integral front and fixed rear sights, black synthetic grip, matte silver frame finish, 14.6 oz. New 2010.

MSR $531 $465 $395 $345 $300 $250 $200 $175

MODEL 642-2 POWER PORT – .38 Spl. cal., satin black finish, 2 1/8 in. ported barrel, Uncle Mike's grips, white dot front sight, no Performance Center trademark, internal lock. Mfg. 2008.

MODEL 646 – .40 S&W cal., 4 in. ribbed slabside barrel, 6 shot fluted titanium cylinder, drift adj. Patridge front sight, micrometer adj. rear sight, drilled and tapped for scope mount, smooth combat trigger, round butt, L-target frame, "Performance Center" on the left side and "40 S&W" on the right side of barrel, frosted glass bead stainless finish, Altamont wood combat grips, 2 sets of half moon clips and extraction tool, ser. no. prefix "RDA", 36 oz. Mfg. 2000.

Last MSR was $845.

MODEL 647-1 VARMINTER – .17 HMR cal., stainless steel K-frame, 12 in. Walther barrel, Weaver scope rail, includes bipod adapter, black Patridge front sight with adj. black blade rear sight, glass bead satin stainless finish, wood target square butt grips, internal trigger lock system, black Allen soft zipper case, distributed by Camfour and Hill Country.

Last MSR was $1,200.

MODEL 647-1 – .17 HMR cal., K-frame, 12 in. partially fluted barrel with raised black front sight, 6 shot, satin stainless steel, upper and lower Picatinny rails on back of barrel, red dot/green dot fixed sights, also includes optical sight and bipod, checkered wood grained brown synthetic grips, 54 oz. Mfg. 2011-2020.

$1,175 $975 $850 $750 $650 $550 $500 *$1,419*

MODEL 657 – .41 Mag. cal., 2 5/8 in. full shroud barrel, 6 shot, unfluted cylinder, glass bead stainless steel, wood grips with finger grooves, adj. rear sight, red ramp front sight, 39.6 oz. Mfg. 2010-2011.

$895 $700 $550 $450 $400 $350 $300 *$1,049*

MODEL 657 DEFENSIVE REVOLVER – .41 Mag. cal., 2 5/8 in. barrel, 6 shot non-fluted cylinder, ball detent lockup, full-length extractor, round butt, N-frame, adj. Millett red ramp front sight, micrometer adj. white outline rear sight, flash chromed teardrop hammer, chromed trigger with overtravel stop, Hogue combat grips, glass bead stainless steel finish, aluminum carry case, 39.6 oz. Distributed by Lew Horton, 1999.

Last MSR was $1,001.

MODEL 657 HUNTER – .41 Mag. cal., 6 in. Magna-Ported barrel, integral Weaver base, N-frame, round butt, 6 shot unfluted cylinder, ball detent lockup, adj. Millett red ramp front sight, adj. rear sight, 48 oz. Distributed by RSR, 1995-1999.

Retail pricing was not available for this model.

GRADING - PPGS™	100%	98%	95%	90%	80%	70%	60%	LAST MSR

MODEL 681-4 LEW HORTON SPECIAL – .357 Mag. cal., 3 in. Quadra-port barrel, 7 shot cylinder with chamfered charge holes, trigger overtravel stop, fixed sight, ser. no. prefix "LHB", 300 mfg. Distributed by Lew Horton, 1996.

Last MSR was $700.

MODEL 681-5 SPECIAL FOR CAMFOUR – .357 Mag. cal., 3 or 4 in. full lug barrel, 7 shot fluted cylinder, adj. black ramp front sight, Quad Porting, glass bead stainless steel finish, laminate checkered wood and Hogue Bantam Monogrip, 7 shot moon clips, chamfered cylinder charge holes, Performance Center case. Distributed by Camfour, 2001.

Last MSR was N/A.

MODEL 686 – .38 Super cal., 4 in. tapered lug barrel, interchangeable red ramp front sight, adj. black rear sight, Ahrends cocobolo finger groove grips, stainless steel, glass bead finish, 6 shot, unfluted cylinder, L-frame, internal key lock system, accepts full moon clips, includes PC aluminum carry case, 37 oz. Distributed by Banger's 2003.

Last MSR was N/A.

MODEL 686 (CURRENT MFG.) – .357 Mag. or .38 Special +P cal., SA/DA, PC tuned action, stainless steel frame, barrel, and cylinder, 4 in. vented rib barrel, unfluted cylinder, 6 shot, chromed custom teardrop hammer, chromed trigger with trigger stop, interchangeable orange front and adj. rear sight, black synthetic grips, Performance Center Speed Release thumbpiece, matte silver finish, 37.9 oz. New late 2017.

MSR $1,006	$850	$750	$650	$575	$475	$385	$325

MODEL 686 ACTION REVOLVER – .357 Mag. cal., 6 in. match grade barrel, barrel compensator.

Last MSR was N/A.

MODEL 686 MAG COMP – .357 Mag. cal., 3 in. barrel, integral compensator, adj. front red ramp sight, white outline rear sight, radiused full lug barrel, radiused hammer, radiused combat trigger w/overtravel stop, Uncle Mike's grips, Performance Center logo, contoured thumbpiece, full-length extractor rod, 350 mfg. Distributed by Lew Horton, 1992.

Last MSR was $1,000.

MODEL 686 CARRY COMP 4 IN. – .357 Mag. cal., 4 in. barrel, integral compensator, dovetailed front sight w/interchangeable post or red ramp, white outline rear sight, Uncle Mike's grips. Distributed by Lew Horton.

Last MSR was $1,000.

MODEL 686 CARRY COMP 6 IN. – .357 Mag. cal., 6 in. full underlug barrel, integral port, replaceable front sight, Hogue grips, semi-target hammer, smooth combat trigger. Mfg. 1994.

Last MSR was $1,099.

MODEL 686 "THE COMPETITOR" – .357 Mag. cal., 6 in. barrel, fluted cylinder w/chamfered charge holes, integral scope base, 6 ounce variable underweight, dovetailed front post, black blade rear sight, Hogue grips, semi-target hammer, smooth combat trigger, 52-58 oz. Distributed by Lew Horton.

Last MSR was $1,100.

MODEL 686 COMPETITOR – .357 Mag. cal., L-frame, 6 in. barrel with removable adj. barrel weights, tuned action, 6 shot, vented lower shroud contains up to five barrel weights, black Hogue synthetic grips with finger grooves, glass-beaded stainless steel, Picatinny rail on top of barrel, adj. Patridge front sight, 53 oz. New 2013.

MSR $1,466	$1,250	$1,095	$940	$850	$685	$575	$490

MODEL 686 DISTINGUISHED COMBAT MAGNUM – .357 Mag. or .38 Spl. +P cal., SA/DA, stainless steel frame and cylinder, 2 1/2 in. precision crowned barrel, unfluted cylinder, chrome teardrop hammer, 7 shot, red ramp front and adj. rear sights, custom checkered finger groove wood grips, chrome trigger with stop, glass bead finish, 34.6 oz. New 2014.

MSR $1,129	$950	$825	$700	$635	$515	$425	$350

MODEL 686 "THE HUNTER" – .357 Mag. cal., similar to the Model 657 Hunter, except has L-frame and wood grips. 200 mfg.

Last MSR was $1,153.

MODEL 686 PLUS – .357 Mag. cal., 6 in. tapered barrel, 7 shot fluted cylinder machined for full moon clips w/chamfered charge holes, L-frame drilled and tapped for scope mount, round butt, Altamont wood grips, flash chromed semi-target hammer and smooth combat trigger, gold bead Patridge front sight, micrometer adj. white outline rear sight, satin stainless steel finish, 44 oz. Distributed by Lew Horton, 1998.

Last MSR was $929.

GRADING - PPGS™	100%	98%	95%	90%	80%	70%	60%	LAST MSR

MODEL 686 PLUS (CURRENT MFG.) – .357 Mag. or .38 Special +P cal., SA/DA, PC tuned action, L-frame, stainless steel frame, cylinder and barrel, 5 in. vented ribbed barrel, 7 round unfluted cylinder cut for moon clips, chromed custom teardrop hammer, chromed trigger with trigger stop, interchangeable orange front and adj. rear sight, black synthetic grips, Performance Center Speed Release thumbpiece, matte stainless finish, 10.6 in. OAL, 38.4 oz. New late 2017.

MSR $1,006	$850	$750	$650	$575	$475	$385	$325

* ***Model 686 Plus Pro Series*** – .357 Mag./.38 S&W Spl.+P cal., SA/DA, stainless steel frame and cylinder, 5 in. stainless steel barrel, 7 shot, interchangeable front and adj. rear sight, black synthetic grips, cylinder cut for moon clips (included), matte silver finish, 38.2 oz. New 2018.

MSR $1,027	$875	$765	$650	$595	$475	$400	$325

MODEL 686-4 WITH ADJUSTABLE SIGHTS – .357 Mag. cal., 2 1/2 in. barrel, Magna Port, 7 shot cylinder, wood grips. Mfg. 1998.

Retail pricing was not available for this model.

MODEL 686 PPC REVOLVER – .357 Mag. cal., 6 in. barrel, custom underlug, integral barrel port.

Last MSR was N/A.

MODEL 686-6 LIGHT RAIL – 5 in. barrel with small rail under the full lug for accessories, 6 shot cylinder, green Hi-Viz front sight, white outline rear sight, synthetic rubber grip, internal lock. Mfg. 2007.

MODEL 686 SSR PRO SERIES – .357 Mag./.38 Spl. + P cal., SA/DA, tuned action, L-frame, 4 in. custom stainless steel barrel with recessed Precision crown, 6 shot, stainless steel frame and cylinder, teardrop hammer, adj. rear sight, interchangeable front sight, checkered wood grips, bossed mainspring, chamfered charge holes, matte silver frame finish, 38.6 oz. New 2007.

MSR $1,024	$865	$750	$650	$575	$500	$425	$350

MODEL 929 (JERRY MICULEK SIGNATURE) – 9mm Para. cal., SA/DA, PC tuned action, N-frame, 6 1/2 in. stainless steel barrel removable compensator, 8 shot, stainless steel frame, titanium cylinder cut for moon clips, chrome teardrop hammer, chrome trigger with stop, Patridge front and adj. rear sights, black rubber grips with finger grooves, Jerry Miculek signature, matte silver finish, 44.2 oz. New 2014.

MSR $1,229	$1,050	$920	$790	$715	$580	$475	$400

MODEL 940 SPECIAL – .356 TSW cal., ported barrel, dovetail front sight, barrel markings are ".356 TSW" on the right and "Smith & Wesson" on the left side. S/N prefix "APC". Limited Production of 300. Distributed by Lew Horton, 1994. Disc.

Last MSR was $575.

This model has also been referred to as the "Pocket Rocket."

MODEL 942 AIRWEIGHT 9MM CENTENNIAL – 9mm Para. cal., 2 in. ported barrel, one was made as a prototype using a Model 642-1 alloy frame, stainless steel cylinder, S/N CAN1706. Built as a T&E prototype, it was shipped to firearms journalist Wiley Clapp in 1999 for test and evaluation.

Last MSR was N/A.

MODEL 986 – 9mm Para. cal., SA/DA, PC tuned action, 2 1/2 in. stainless steel custom barrel with recessed precision crown, unfluted titanium cylinder, 7 shot, chromed custom teardrop hammer, chromed trigger with overtravel stop, red ramp front and adj. rear sights, custom wood grips, bossed mainspring, moon clips included, matte silver finish, 31.4 oz. New 2017.

MSR $1,129	$950	$825	$700	$635	$515	$425	$350

MODEL 986 PRO SERIES – 9mm Para. cal., SA/DA, 5 in. custom barrel with recessed precision crown, 7 shot, stainless steel L frame with gray titanium alloy fluted cylinder, teardrop hammer, Patridge front and adj. rear sights, black rubber finger groove grips, bossed mainspring, moon clips included, Glass Bead finish, 34.9 oz. New 2014.

MSR $1,189	$1,000	$875	$750	$680	$550	$455	$390

MODEL M&P R8 (MODEL 327 M&P R8) – .357 Mag. or .38 Spl. +P cal., N-frame, 8 shot, 5 in. two-piece barrel, Scandium alloy frame, stainless steel cylinder, interchangeable dot front sight, adj. V-notch rear sight, accessory rail, matte black finish, black synthetic grips with finger grooves, 36.3 oz. New mid-2007.

MSR $1,360	$1,160	$1,015	$875	$790	$640	$525	$450

Rifles: Performance Center Variations

M&P RIFLE – 5.56 NATO cal., GIO, 10 shot mag., 20 in. stainless steel barrel, synthetic stock with Hogue pistol grip, free floating forend, two-stage match trigger, billet aluminum receiver with Picatinny rail, no sights, hardcoat black or camo anodized finish, includes rifle case, 8 lbs. 2 oz. Mfg. 2008-2017.

	$1,150	$925	$825	$725	$675	$625	$575	*$1,549*

Add $40 for camo finish.

GRADING - PPGS™	100%	98%	95%	90%	80%	70%	60%	LAST MSR

M&P 10 CREEDMOOR – 6.5 Creedmoor cal., GIO, 20 in. barrel, rifle length gas system, 10 shot mag., alloy frame, two-stage match trigger, Magpul MOE stock, Magpul MOE Plus grip, ambi safety selector, 15 in. Troy Alpha free float handguard with 2 in. aluminum M-LOK accessory rail, 9 lbs. New 2017.

MSR $2,055	$1,550	$1,225	$1,100	$975	$900	$825	$750	

M&P 15 COMPETITION RIFLE – 5.56 NATO cal., GIO, 18 in. carbon steel barrel, rifle length gas system, 30 shot mag., two-stage trigger, 6-position adj. VLTOR IMOD stock, Hogue pistol grip, manual safety on lower, 15 in. Troy Alpha M-LOK free float handguard with 2 in. aluminum M-LOK accessory rail, Armornite black finish, 7.4 lbs. New 2017.

MSR $1,599	$1,200	$950	$850	$750	$700	$650	$600	

M&P 15-22 PC SPORT – .22 LR cal., blowback action, 18 in. carbon steel fluted threaded barrel, 10 shot mag., two-stage match trigger, Magpul MBUS sights, VLTOR adj. stock, Hogue pistol grip, M&P slim handguard with Magpul M-LOK, Picatinny rail, 5.2 lbs. New 2018.

MSR $724	$550	$425	$375	$350	$325	$300	$275	

M&P 15-22 PC TB – .22 LR cal., blowback operation, 18 in. fluted barrel, 10 shot detachable mag., fixed (compliant) or 6-position VLTOR adj. buttstock, polymer receiver with modular rail forend, adj. A2 post front sight and adj. dual aperture rear sight, black finish, 5.6 lbs. Mfg. 2011-2015.

	$600	$475	$425	$375	$350	$325	$300	*$789*

M&P 15PC LIMITED EDITION – 5.56 NATO cal., Wylde chambering, GIO, 20 in. barrel, 10 shot mag., skeletonized full-length buttstock, integral Picatinny style rail system, anodized streamlined free floating forend, black rubber pistol grip, swivel stud for sling or bipod attachment, PC marked soft carry case, master trigger lock and manual, marked "M&P 15PC" laser engraved on the right side, no forward assist on upper receiver, black matte finish. Mfg. 2006.

	$1,500	$1,200	$1,075	$950	$875	$825	$750	*$1,999*

PERFORMANCE CENTER T/C R22 – please refer to the listing under Thompson/Center Arms Co. Rifles: Semi-Auto.

PERFORMANCE CENTER T/C LRR – please refer to the listing under Thompson/Center Arms Co. Rifles: Bolt Action.

	100%	98%	95%	90%	80%	70%	60%	50%	40%	30%	20%	10%

RIFLES - ALL VARIATIONS

Rifles: Revolving

MODEL 320 REVOLVING RIFLE – .320 S&W cal., 6 shot cylinder, 16, 18, or 20 in. round barrel, hard rubber grips, detachable shoulder stock, blue or nickel (rare, add a premium) finish. 977 mfg. 1879-87.

* ***Model 320 Revolving Rifle 16 or 20 in. Barrel*** – 239 mfg. with 16 in., and 224 with 20 in. barrel.

N/A	$15,000	$12,000	$10,000	$8,700	$8,100	$7,675	$7,000	$6,375	$5,600	$4,800	$3,850

* ***Model 320 Revolving Rifle 18 in. barrel*** – 514 mfg.

N/A	$13,500	$11,000	$9,750	$9,350	$8,700	$8,100	$7,675	$7,000	$6,375	$5,600	$4,800

GRADING - PPGS™	100%	98%	95%	90%	80%	70%	60%	LAST MSR

Rifles: NFA

MODEL 1940 LIGHT RIFLE MARK I/II – 9mm Para. cal., 20 shot mag., fires from open bolt, 9 3/4 in. barrel, black tenonite stock. Mfg. for the British government during 1940.

	N/A	N/A	$6,750	$6,000	$5,250	$4,750	$3,950	

This model was done at the British Government's request in 1939 to Smith & Wesson for a 9mm paramilitary rifle. Smith & Wesson designed, built and sent a group of these production Mark I rifles to the British Government for testing in 1940. The Mark I failed the 5000 round test due to the rifle being made to shoot the 9mm American manufacture ammunition not the 'hotter" European manufacture. After this discovery, at the request of the British Government, the British wanted S&W to do further engineering on this rifle. Improvements were done and a group of the Mark II rifles were sent for additional testing. By this time, the British had lost interest in the rifle. In spite of its failure in testing, it was a very well made rifle with lots of steel and machining required in its manufacturing, unlike the Sten gun.

A total of 1227 known 9mm Light Rifles were built, of which 200 were of the Mark II variation. 1010 were sold to the British Government. More frames were made than guns built; therefore serial numbers range between 1-2200.

GRADING - PPGS™ 100% 98% 95% 90% 80% 70% 60% LAST MSR

At the end of WWII, all of the Light rifles in possession of the British government were supposedly cut in half and dumped in the English Channel, except for five that are in a British Military Museum.

A very interesting note: In 1974 S&W discovered some crated and unfired 1940 Light rifles in their facility. In 1975 they were then sold as a curio and relic to a distributor. These had a 9 3/4 inch barrel, blue finish and black tenonite stock.

Also noted: Any of the 1940 9mm Light Rifles should not be loaded with or fired with any modern manufactured 9mm ammunition.

Rifles: Bolt Action

In 1984 S&W discontinued importation of all Howa manufactured rifles. Mossberg continued importation utilizing leftover S&W parts in addition to fabricating their own.

MODEL A – .22-250 Rem., .243 Win., .270 Win., .308 Win., .30 - 06, 7mm Rem. Mag., or .300 Win. Mag. cal., 23 3/4 in. barrel, folding leaf sight, checkered Monte Carlo stock with rosewood forend tip and pistol grip cap. Mfg. by Husqvarna in Sweden 1969-1972.

$575 $500 $425 $350 $300 $250 $195

MODEL B – .243 Win., .270 Win., or .30-06 cal., similar to Model A, except has 20 3/4 in. barrel, Monte Carlo stock with Schnabel forend.

$575 $500 $425 $350 $300 $250 $195

MODEL C – similar to Model B, with sporting stock.

$575 $500 $425 $350 $300 $250 $195

MODEL D – similar to Model C, with full-length two-piece Mannlicher style stock.

$625 $550 $475 $395 $350 $300 $250

MODEL E – similar to Model D, with cheekpiece.

$625 $550 $475 $395 $350 $300 $250

MODEL 1500 MOUNTAINEER – .222 Rem., .22-250 Rem., .223 Rem., .243 Win, .25-06 Rem., .270 Win, .30-06, or .308 Win. cal., 22 in. barrel, 5 or 6 shot mag., no sights, walnut stock, approx. 7 lbs. 10 oz. Imported 1983-1984.

$400 $350 $300 $250 $245 $210 $185

Add $27 for sights.

* ***Model 1500 Mountaineer Magnum*** – 7mm Rem. Mag. or .300 Win. Mag. cal.

$425 $375 $325 $275 $250 $215 $195

MODEL 1500 DELUXE – same cals. as standard 1500, Monte Carlo stock, skip-line checkering, select walnut, no sights. Imported 1983-1984.

$450 $400 $350 $300 $265 $225 $200

Add 10% for 7mm Mag. and .300 Win. Mag.

MODEL 1500 DELUXE VARMINT – .222 Rem, .22-250 Rem., or .223 Rem. cal., heavy 24 in. barrel, skip-line checkering, no sights. Imported 1983-1984.

$475 $425 $375 $325 $275 $235 $200

MODEL 1700 LS "CLASSIC HUNTER" – .243 Win, .270 Win, or .30-06 cal., 22 in. barrel, removable 5 shot mag., solid recoil pad, no sights, Schnabel forend, finely checkered. Imported 1983-1984.

$495 $450 $400 $350 $315 $265 $245

I-BOLT RIFLE – .25-06 Rem., .270 Win., .30-06, 7mm Rem. Mag. (disc. 2008), or .300 Win. Mag. (disc. 2008), cal., short or long action, 4 shot mag., 23 or 25 (disc. 2008) in. barrel, black synthetic, Realtree camo synthetic, or Monte Carlo walnut (mfg. 2008) stock, blue carbon steel or stainless steel (disc. 2008) action and barrel, Picatinny rail integral with receiver, approx. 7 lbs. Mfg. mid-2007-2009.

$525 $475 $425 $375 $335 $285 $265 *$553*

Add $84 for camo.

Add approx. 10%-15% for walnut stock and stainless barrel (disc. 2008).

* ***I-Bolt Rifle w/Weathershield*** – .25-06 Rem., .270 Win., .30-06, 7mm Rem. Mag., or .300 Win. Mag. cal., short or long action, 23 in. barrel, similar to I-Bolt model, except has Weathershield coated black or camo synthetic stock. Mfg. 2009.

$525 $475 $425 $375 $335 $285 $265 *$588*

Add $70 for camo.

GRADING - PPGS™	100%	98%	95%	90%	80%	70%	60%	LAST MSR

Rifles: Semi-Auto

The following is a listing of abbreviations with related feature codes of both centerfire and rimfire semi-auto rifles: Stock: S/6 ADJ - 6 position adj., S/BLK - black synthetic, S/CAM - camo synthetic, S/SF - solid fixed, S/W - wood stock. Pistol Grip: PG - plastic grip, RG - rubber grip, WG - wood grip, NA - no grip. Rear Sight: R/ADJ - adjustable, R/FS - folding sight, R/FSADJ - folding adjustable, NA - no rear sight. Front Sight: F/BB - Black Blade, F/BP - Black Post, F/FO - fiber optic, F/FS - folding sight, F/FSADJ - folding adjustable, F/GB - Gold Bead, F/WBF - white bead front sight, NA - no front sight. Forend: CFF - custom free float, MR - modular rail, STD - standard, NA - no forend (one piece stock). Receiver Material: AL - alloy, CA - carbon, SS - Stainless steel, POLY - polymer. Action: BA - bolt action, FA - fixed action, SAT - semi-auto.

This database does not take into consideration the state compliant variations of the M&P10 and M&P15 rifles.

M&P10 OPTICS READY – .308 Win. cal., GIO, 18 in. barrel, enhanced flash hider, 5, 10 (disc. 2020), or 20 shot mag., fixed, Magpul MOE fixed (camo only), or 6-pos. CAR stock, pistol grip, ambidextrous controls, chromed gas key, bolt carrier, and firing pin, matte black or Realtree APG camo (disc. 2020) finish, 7 lbs. 11 oz. New 2013.

MSR $1,639	$1,395	$1,225	$1,050	$950	$775	$650	$600	

Add $110 for Realtree APG camo finish (disc. 2020).

M&P10 SPORT OPTICS READY – .308 Win. cal., 16 in. barrel with Armornite finish, A2 flash suppressor, 20 shot mag., optics ready, 6-position telescopic stock, synthetic grip, gas block with Picatinny rail, mid-length handguard, sling swivel, ambi controls, approx. 4.8 lbs. New 2018.

MSR $1,089	$825	$650	$575	$500	$475	$450	$400	

M&P15 CENTERFIRE SEMI-AUTO SERIES – .223 Rem./5.56 NATO or 5.45x39mm cal., GIO, AR-15 style design with 16 in. or longer chrome-lined barrel with muzzle brake, 1:9 or 1:7 (new 2017) rate of twist, aluminum upper and lower receiver, 10 or 30 shot mag. (most are Mil-Spec), one-piece fixed position, skeletonized, or 6-position CAR collapsible stock, hardcoat anodized black finish, features detachable carrying handle, A2 post front sight, adj. dual aperture rear sight, thinned handguard, M&P15T features extended Picatinny rail on receiver and barrel, in addition to RAS on both sides and bottom of barrel, supplied with hard carry case, approx. 6 1/2 lbs. New 2006.

The lowest serial number encountered to date is SW00200.

* ***M&P15 w/Removable Carry Handle*** – 5.56 NATO/.223 Rem. cal., GIO, 16 in. carbon steel barrel with Armornite finish, 30 shot PMAG, alloy receiver, adj. A2 post front sight, adj. rear sight, 6-position CAR stock, black polymer grip, removable carry handle, matte black finish, 6.98 lbs. Disc. 2020.

	$950	$750	$675	$600	$550	$525	$475	*$1,269*

Add $20 for 1:7 rate of twist barrel (mfg. 2017-2019).

* ***M&P15A*** – 5.56 NATO cal., GIO, AR-15 style, 16 in. barrel, 30 shot mag., similar to Model M&P15, except features a receiver Picatinny rail and adj. rear folding battle sight with ribbed handguard, 6 1/2 lbs. Mfg. 2006-2012.

	$975	$775	$675	$600	$575	$525	$475	*$1,289*

* ***M&P15T*** – 5.56 NATO cal., GIO, AR-15 style, fixed 10 (CA compliant) or detachable 30 shot PMAG, 16 in. barrel with Armornite finish, forged integral trigger guard, folding (disc. 2010) or fixed black post front sight (new 2011), fixed (new 2011) or folding (disc. 2010) adj. rear sight, modular rail (disc. 2010), 10 in. free float quad rail handguard (new 2011), 6-pos. telescopic stock, 6.85 lbs. Disc. 2017.

	$825	$700	$625	$550	$500	$475	$425	*$1,159*

* ***M&P15T w/M-LOK*** – 5.56 NATO/.223 Rem. cal., GIO, 16 in. lightweight contoured barrel with Armornite finish, flash suppressor, 30 shot PMAG, forged integral trigger guard, Magpul MBUS sights, 6-pos. telescopic stock, black synthetic grips, mid-length gas system, 13 in. M&P slim modular free float handguard with Magpul M-LOK capability, 2 in. M-LOK Picatinny-style rail panel included, with or w/o Crimson Trace LINQ System (disc. 2020), 6.71 lbs. New 2017.

MSR $1,189	$900	$700	$625	$550	$525	$475	$450	

Add $330 for Crimson Trace LINQ System (disc. 2020).

* ***M&P15FT*** – 5.56 NATO cal., AR-15 style, blowback operation, 16 in. barrel with Armornite finish, 10 shot mag., alloy receiver, forged integral trigger guard, Troy Folding Battle sights or folding Magpul MBUS front and rear sights, one-piece fixed pistol grip stock, 10 in. free float quad rail. Mfg. 2008-2011.

	$1,275	$1,025	$900	$800	$750	$700	$625	*$1,709*

* ***M&P15 Optic Ready*** – 5.56 NATO cal., GIO, 16 in. carbon steel barrel with flat-top Picatinny rail and gas block, 30 shot mag., optics ready alloy receiver, black alloy finish, 6-position adj. stock, no rear sight. Mfg. 2008-2018.

	$800	$625	$575	$500	$475	$425	$400	*$1,069*

GRADING - PPGS™	100%	98%	95%	90%	80%	70%	60%	LAST MSR

* ***Model M&P15ORC*** – 5.56 NATO cal., GIO, AR-15 style, 16 in. barrel, 10 shot mag. (compliant CT, MA, MD, NJ and NY), alloy receiver, optics ready, pistol grip stock, black synthetic grip, Picatinny rail, black alloy finish. Mfg. mid-2008-2017.

	$775	$625	$550	$500	$450	$425	$375	*$1,039*

* ***M&P15X*** – 5.56 NATO/.223 Rem. cal., GIO, AR-15 style, 16 in. barrel, 30 shot PMAG, alloy receiver, adj. A2 post front and Troy rear folding battle sights, 6-position adj. pistol grip stock, Troy carbine length handguard, black alloy finish, 6.35 lbs. Mfg. 2008-2017.

	$1,025	$825	$725	$650	$600	$550	$500	*$1,379*

* ***M&P15X w/M-LOK*** – 5.56 NATO/.223 Rem. cal., GIO, 16 in. barrel with Armornite finish, 30 shot PMAG, forged integral trigger guard, adj. A2 post front and folding Magpul MBUS rear sights, 6-pos. telescopic stock, M&P slim aluminum carbine length Magpul M-LOK handguard, 2 in. M-LOK aluminum Picatinny rail panel, Picatinny top rail, 6.4 lbs. Mfg. 2017-2020.

	$925	$725	$650	$575	$550	$500	$450	*$1,239*

* ***M&P15I*** – .223 Rem. cal., GIO, AR-15 style, 17 in. barrel, 10 shot mag. (compliant CT, MA, MD, NJ, and NY), black alloy finish, pistol grip stock, adj. rear sight, black post front sight, alloy receiver, 7 lbs. Mfg. mid-2008-2011.

	$950	$750	$675	$600	$550	$500	$475	*$1,259*

* ***M&P15R*** – 5.45x39mm cal., GIO, AR-15 style, 16 in. barrel, 30 shot mag., black alloy finish, pistol grip stock, adj. rear and black post front sight, alloy receiver, Picatinny rail, 6 1/2 lbs. Mfg. 2008-2011.

	$825	$650	$575	$500	$475	$450	$400	*$1,089*

M&P15MOE – 5.56 NATO cal., GIO, AR-15 style, 16 in. barrel, 30 shot mag., black alloy finish, 6-pos. adj. stock, alloy receiver, post front sight, folding rear sight. Mfg. 2010-2011.

	$925	$750	$675	$575	$550	$500	$450	*$1,249*

M&P15 MOE MID – 5.56 NATO cal., GIO, 16 in. barrel, 30 shot mag., alloy receiver, M4 A2 post front sight and Magpul MBUS rear sight, Magpul MOE stock, Magpul MVG (vertical grip), features Magpul hardware, black or FDE finish. Mfg. 2012-2017.

	$950	$750	$675	$600	$550	$500	$475	*$1,259*

* ***M&P15 MOE SL MID*** – 5.56 NATO/.223 Rem. cal., GIO, 16 in. barrel with Armornite finish, flash suppressor, 30 shot PMAG, alloy receiver, black post front sight and folding MBUS rear sight, 6-position Mil-Spec stock, Magpul MOE SL grip, mid-length gas system, features Magpul hardware, 2 in. M-LOK polymer Picatinny rail panel, mid-length handguard, black, FDE, or Stealth Gray (disc. 2019) finish, 6 1/2 lbs. Mfg. 2017-2020.

	$925	$725	$650	$575	$550	$500	$450	*$1,239*

* ***M&P15PS*** – 5.56 NATO cal., GIO, 16 in. barrel, fixed 10 (CA compliant) or 30 shot mag., black alloy finish, six position adj. stock with standard forend, alloy receiver, solid handguard, Picatinny rail above gas block, no sights, flat-top upper, chrome-lined bore, gas key, and bolt carrier, adj. gas plug with three settings. Mfg. 2010-2013.

	$1,025	$800	$725	$650	$600	$550	$500	*$1,359*

* ***M&P15PSX*** – 5.56 NATO cal., GIO, 16 in. barrel, 30 shot mag., black alloy finish, 6-pos. adj. stock with standard forend and tactical rail, alloy receiver. Mfg. 2010-2013.

	$1,125	$900	$800	$700	$650	$600	$550	*$1,499*

M&P15 300 WHISPER – .300 Whisper cal., GIO, 16 in. threaded barrel with or without sound suppressor, 10 shot (camo) or 30 shot PMAG (black), 6-pos. telescopic stock, low recoil and muzzle blast, gas block with integral Picatinny-style rail, black (new 2014) or Realtree APG camo on all surfaces except barrel, 6.11 lbs. Mfg. 2012-2020.

	$850	$675	$600	$525	$500	$450	$425	*$1,119*

M&P15-22 SPORT RIMFIRE SEMI-AUTO – .22 LR cal., blowback action, 16 1/2 in. barrel with or w/o threading, 10 or 25 shot mag., A2 post front sight and dual aperture rear sight, fixed or six position CAR adj. stock, quad rail handguard, matte black, Pink Platinum (mfg. 2014 -2015), Black and Tan (mfg. 2014-2015), Purple Platinum (mfg. 2014-2015), Harvest Moon Orange (mfg. 2014-2015), 100% Realtree APG HD (disc. 2015), Kryptek Highlander (new 2016), Muddy Girl (new 2016), or Robins Egg Blue Platinum (new 2018) camo finish, 5 1/2 lbs. New 2009.

MSR $461	$350	$275	$250	$225	$200	$185	$175	

Add 5% for threaded barrel (disc.).

Add $50 for 100% Realtree APG HD camo finish with threaded barrel (mfg. 2011-2015).

Add $50 for Pink Platinum, Black and Tan, Purple Platinum, or Harvest Moon Orange finish (mfg. 2014-2015).

Add $60 for Kryptek Highlander (new 2016), Muddy Girl (new 2016), or Robins Egg Blue Platinum (new

GRADING - PPGS™	100%	98%	95%	90%	80%	70%	60%	LAST MSR

2018) camo finish.

During 2015, the model nomenclature was changed from M&P15-22 to M&P15-22 Sport.

* ***M&P15-22 Sport MOE SL*** – .22 LR cal., blowback action, polymer frame, 16 1/2 in. carbon steel barrel with flash hider, 25 shot mag., folding Magpul MBUS front and rear sights, Magpul MOE SL stock, polymer grip, two-pos. safety, black or FDE finish, 5 1/2 lbs. New 2017.

MSR $521	$400	$300	$275	$250	$225	$200	$185	

* ***M&P15-22 Sport OR w/M&P Red/Green Dot Optic*** – .22 LR cal., blowback operation, 16 1/2 in. carbon steel barrel with A2 flash hider, 10 or 25 shot mag., fixed or 6-pos. adj. stock, black polymer grips, 2-pos. receiver mounted safety, 10 in. M&P Slim handguard with Magpul M-LOK rail panel included, includes factory mounted MP-100 red/green dot optic, black finish, 83.6 oz.

MSR $479	$350	$275	$250	$225	$200	$185	$175	

* ***M&P15-22 MOE Rimfire Semi-Auto*** – .22 LR cal., similar to Model M&P15-22, except has 16 in. threaded barrel, A1 style compensator, 25 shot detachable mag., folding front and rear sight and skeletonized Magpul MOE stock, flat black or FDE (new 2012) finish, approx. 5 1/2 lbs. Mfg. 2011-2016.

	$450	$350	$325	$275	$250	$225	$200	*$609*

* ***M&P15-22 PC TB***

Please see listing under Performance Center rifles.

M&P15 SPORT – 5.56 NATO cal., GIO, 16 in. Melonite treated barrel, A2 flash suppressor, fixed or detachable 10 or 30 shot mag., single stage trigger, hardcoat anodized black upper and lower receiver, polymer handguard, chrome-lined gas key and bolt carrier, adj. A2 post front sight, adj. dual aperture rear sight, 6-position telescoping buttstock. Mfg. 2011-2016.

	$550	$450	$400	$350	$325	$300	$275	*$739*

M&P15 SPORT II – 5.56 NATO cal., GIO, 16 in. threaded or non-threaded barrel w/1:9 twist, 10 or 30 shot mag., Magpul MBUS rear sight, fixed or 6-pos. adj. stock, forged integral trigger guard, forward assist and dust cover, chromed firing pin, Armornite barrel finish. New 2017.

MSR $772	$655	$575	$490	$445	$360	$300	$275	

* ***M&P15 Sport II M-LOK*** – 5.56 NATO cal., GIO, 16 in. threaded barrel with Armornite finish, 30 shot mag., forged integral trigger guard, adj. A2 front sight post, folding Magpul MBUS rear sight, 6-pos. adj. stock, black polymer grips, Magpul MOE M-LOK carbine length handguard, 2 in. M-LOK Picatinny-style rail panel, chromed firing pin, forward assist and dust cover, 6.78 lbs. New 2017.

MSR $793	$675	$600	$500	$450	$375	$300	$275	

* ***M&P15 Sport II OR*** – 5.56 NATO cal., GIO, 16 in. threaded barrel with Armornite finish, 30 shot PMAG, forged integral trigger guard, optics ready, 6-pos. stock, black polymer grips, gas block with integral Picatinny rail, forward assist and dust cover, chromed firing pin, QD sling swivel attachment point, 6 1/2 lbs. New 2017.

MSR $748	$635	$550	$475	$425	$350	$300	$275	

Add $43 for A2 flash hider and Crimson Trace CTS-103 red/green dot electronic sight.

* ***M&P15 Sport II OR M-LOK*** – 5.56 NATO cal., GIO, 16 in. threaded barrel with Armornite finish, 30 shot mag., forged integral trigger guard, adj. A2 front sight post, folding Magpul MBUS rear sight, 6-pos. adj. stock, black polymer grips, Magpul MOE M-LOK carbine length handguard, 2 in. M-LOK Picatinny-style rail panel, chromed firing pin, forward assist and dust cover, optics ready, black finish, 6.78 lbs. New 2019.

MSR $772	$655	$575	$490	$445	$360	$300	$275	

Add $42 for Crimson Trace CTS-103 red/green electronic sight.

M&P15 TS – 5.56 NATO/.223 Rem. cal., GIO, 14 1/2 in. chrome-lined barrel (16 in. including pinned and welded Smith Vortex flash suppressor), 30 shot PMAG, Magpul MBUS sights, Magpul MOE 6-pos. telescopic stock, Magpul MOE grip, full Troy TRX (disc.) or Troy Alpha Rail free floating handguard, 6 1/2 lbs. Mfg. 2011-2020.

	$1,175	$925	$825	$725	$675	$650	$575	*$1,569*

M&P15VTAC – 5.56 NATO cal., GIO, Viking Tactics Model, 16 in. barrel, 30 shot mag., black alloy finish, pistol grip stock, modular rail, alloy receiver. Mfg. mid-2008-2011.

	$1,500	$1,175	$1,050	$925	$875	$800	$725	*$1,989*

GRADING - PPGS™	100%	98%	95%	90%	80%	70%	60%	LAST MSR

M&P15 VTAC II – 5.56 NATO/.223 Rem. cal., GIO, 16 in. barrel, flash suppressor, 30 shot PMAG, Geissele Super-V trigger, VLTOR IMOD 6-pos. collapsible stock, mid-length gas system for lower recoil, 13 in. TRX Extreme (disc.) or VTAC/Troy 13 in. BattleRail Apha Rail free float handguard, includes Viking Tactics light mount, tactical sling, and LPSM low profile sling mount, Melonite/hardcoat anodized black finish, 6.28 lbs. Mfg. 2012-2019.

	$1,450	$1,150	$1,025	$925	$850	$800	$725	*$1,949*

SHOTGUNS

In 1984 S&W discontinued importation of all Howa manufactured shotguns. Mossberg continued importation utilizing leftover S&W parts in addition to fabricating their own.

MODEL 916 SLIDE ACTION SHOTGUN – 12, 16, or 20 ga., 20, 26, 28, or 30 in. barrels, various chokes, plain pistol grip stock, solid frame. Mfg. by S&W in Springfield, MA. 1972-disc.

	$175	$150	$140	$130	$120	$110	$100	

* ***Model 916 Slide Action Shotgun Vent. rib and pad***

	$200	$175	$155	$145	$135	$130	$120	

MODEL 916T SLIDE ACTION – similar to 916, except barrels can be interchanged. Disc.

	$195	$170	$155	$145	$135	$130	$125	

* ***Model 916T Slide Action Vent. rib and pad***

	$225	$200	$180	$170	$155	$145	$135	

MODEL 96 SLIDE ACTION – various gauges, disc.

	$125	$110	$100	$90	$75	$70	$65	

MODEL 1000 P SLIDE ACTION – 12 ga., various barrel lengths, chokes, VR. Disc.

	$350	$305	$270	$230	$210	$190	$170	

This model is the same as the Model 3000.

MODEL 1000 AUTOLOADER – 12 or 20 ga., 22-30 in. VR barrels, various chokes, gas operated, engraved alloy receiver, checkered pistol grip stock. Mfg. 1972-1984.

	$350	$325	$295	$260	$240	$220	$200	

Add $30 for multi-choke tubes.
Add approx. $125 for slug barrel.

* ***Model 1000 Autoloader Waterfowler*** – 3 in. chamber, parkerized finish, Magnum 28 or 30 in. barrel, multi-chokes, steel receiver, "M" suffix, camo sling and swivels. Disc.

	$500	$450	$375	$340	$310	$275	$255	

* ***Model 1000 Autoloader Super 12*** – handles all loads interchangeably, top-of-the-line model during its time. Disc.

	$500	$450	$400	$360	$330	$300	$280	

Add $50 for multi-choke.

* ***Model 1000 Autoloader Target*** – 12 or 20 ga., skeet, super skeet, and trap models available. Super skeet has 15 barrel muzzle vents to reduce recoil. Trap model has multi-choke tubes, Monte Carlo select walnut stock and forend. Both alloy and steel receivers available in Skeet model, Trap is steel only.

Skeet/Super Skeet	$400	$390	$335	$260	$235	$215	$190	
Trap (Model 1000T)	$595	$525	$450	$375	$325	$285	$235	

Note: Shotguns made for S&W by Howa Machinery, Ltd., Japan. This line was picked up by Mossberg after S&W discontinued them - these models may be more desirable.

MODEL 1012 SEMI-AUTO – 12 ga., 3 in. chamber, 24, 26, 28, or 30 in. barrel with vent. rib and 5 flush choke tubes, micro coated twin piston gas operated, checkered satin walnut, black synthetic, or synthetic stock with 100% Max-4 or APG camo treatment, includes four-piece shim kit, approx. 6 1/2 lbs., mfg. in Turkey. Imported 2007-2009.

	$525	$475	$425	$395	$350	$300	$275	*$644*

Add $35 for satin finished walnut stock and forearm.
Add $91 for 100% camo coverage.

* ***Model 1012 Super Semi-Auto*** – similar to Model 1012, except has 3 1/2 in. chamber, not available with walnut stock and forearm, approx. 7.3 lbs. Imported 2007-2009.

	$650	$575	$525	$475	$425	$395	$360	*$784*

Add $98 for full camo coverage.

GRADING - PPGS™	100%	98%	95%	90%	80%	70%	60%	LAST MSR

MODEL 1020 SEMI-AUTO – 20 ga., 3 in. chamber, otherwise similar to Model 1012, single piston gas operation, approx. 6 lbs.

	$525	$475	$425	$395	$350	$300	$275	*$644*

Add $35 for satin finished walnut stock and forearm.
Add $91 for 100% camo coverage.
Subtract $21 for Model 1020SS w/short stock and 24 in. barrel.

MODEL 3000 SLIDE ACTION – 12 or 20 ga., 3 in. chambers, 22-30 in. barrels, walnut stock and forend, 6 1/4-7 1/2 lbs.

	$350	$305	$270	$230	$210	$190	$170	

Add $30 for multi-choke tubes.
Subtract $40 for slug gun (rifle sights on 22 in. barrel).

This model was also available in a "Waterfowler" variation - values are approx. the same as listed.

MODEL 3000 POLICE – 12 ga. only, 18 or 20 in. barrel, blue or parkerized finish, many combinations of finishes, stock types, and other combat accessories were available for this model.

	$325	$255	$215	$185	$170	$155	$140	

Add $125 for folding stock.

ELITE GOLD GRADE I SxS – 20 ga., 3 in. chamber, scalloped boxlock action, 26 or 28 in. barrels with fixed chokes, ejectors, ST or DT, Grade III checkered walnut straight grip English or pistol grip stock, color case hardened frame with light scroll engraving, 6.5-6.7 lbs., mfg. in Turkey and imported 2007-2010.

	$1,250	$1,000	$825	$700	$575	$450	$375	*$2,380*

ELITE SILVER GRADE I O/U – 12 ga., scalloped boxlock action, 26, 28, or 30 in. VR barrels with 5 flush choke tubes, ST, ejectors, color case hardened frame with light scroll engraving, Grade III checkered walnut pistol grip stock, solid recoil pad, engine turned internal barrel parts, 7.6-7.8 lbs., mfg. in Turkey and imported 2007-2010.

	$1,250	$1,000	$825	$700	$575	$450	$375	*$2,380*

SMITHSON, J.P.

Current custom long arm manufacturer located in Provo, UT.

J.P. Smithson specializes in custom long arms, including bolt action and single shot rifles, as well as shotguns. J.P. Smithson also specializes in fiberglass and carbon stocked rifles, as well as wood stocks, custom metal work, and his own design of quick detachable scope mounts. Many options for long guns are available. Since each gun is built per customer specifications, please contact him directly for more information, including availability, delivery time, and pricing.

SNAKE CHARMER

Previously manufactured by Verney-Carron USA, Inc. located in Clay Center, KS a joint venture of Verney-Carron SA located in Saint-Etienne, France (please refer to the separate Verney-Carron listing) and Y.B.E., Inc. located in Clay Center, KS (distributor of Hastings barrels and choke tubes). Distributor sales only.

SHOTGUNS: SINGLE SHOT

SNAKE CHARMER II – .410 bore only, stainless steel, break open single shot, black molded plastic stock and forend, shell holder in stock, also available as Night Charmer (disc. 1988) and Sea Charmer (disc. 1988), 3 1/2 lbs. Disc. 2009.

	$180	$160	$145	$130	$115	$100	$90	*$216*

Add $10 for Night Charmer (disc. 1988).
Add $18 for Sea Charmer (disc. 1988).
Subtract $18 for black carbon steel barrel (New Generation Model).

SNOWY MOUNTAIN RIFLES

Current manufacturer located in Hamilton, MT. Previously located in Missoula, MT.

In addition to custom long range precision rifles, Snowy Mountain Rifles also offers a short barrel shotgun based on the Remington 870 for military and law enforcement, as well as gunsmithing services and a complete line of rifle accessories, including optics, suppressors, bipods, and slings.

RIFLES: BOLT ACTION

SMR ALASKAN – .30 Nosler, .338 Win. Mag., 300 Win. Mag., .35 Whelen, .300 PRC, .416 Rigby, 7mm Mag., or .375 H&H cal., Defiance Deviant Hunter w/controlled round feed action, right or left-hand configuration, 22, 24, or 26 in. Benchmark match grade barrel with Sendero contour, TriggerTech

GRADING - PPGS™	100%	98%	95%	90%	80%	70%	60%	LAST MSR

Special trigger, hinged BDL floorplate, carbon AG composite Alaskan stock, Graphite Black, Magpul FDE, Magpul OD Green, or Tactical Gray Cerakote finish, approx. 9 lbs. New 2019.

MSR $5,250	$4,475	$3,925	$3,350	$3,050	$2,475	$2,025	$1,575	

Add $300 for 22 or 24 in. Proof Research Carbon Sendero barrel.
Add $100-$190 for SMR stainless or titanium muzzle brake.

SMR ALPINE HUNTER – 6mm Creedmoor, 6.5 Creedmoor, 6.5x47 Lapua, .260 Rem., 6.5 PRC, .308 Rem. Mag., 7mm Rem. Mag., .28 Nosler, .30 Nosler, or .300 Win. Mag. cal., Defiance Deviant Hunter action, 22, 24, or 26 in. Benchmark match grade stainless steel hand-lapped threaded barrel w/thread cap, TriggerTech Special trigger, hinged floorplate, full carbon AG composite Alpine Hunter stock, Graphite Black, Magpul FDE, Magpul OD Green, or Tactical Gray Cerakote finish, 7 lbs. 4 oz. New 2019.

MSR $4,950	$4,200	$3,675	$3,150	$2,850	$2,310	$1,895	$1,475	

Add $300 for 22 or 24 in. Proof Research Carbon Sendero barrel.
Add $100-$240 for SMR stainless or titanium muzzle brake.
Add $100 for Hunter style detachable mag. or Snowy Mountain Rifles Tactical Box.

SMR AMBUSH – .243 Win., 6.5 Creedmoor, .260 Rem., 6XC, 7mm-08 Rem., 7mm Mag., .308 Win., .300 Win. Mag., or .338 Win. cal., SMR 3600 action, match grade stainless 5R #5 fluted barrel, BDL, Timney 510-U trigger, lightweight composite stock, Talley low ring and base set. Mfg. 2015-2018.

	$3,695	$3,250	$2,775	$2,525	$2,050	$1,675	$1,300	*$4,350*

SMR CARBON LRH – .243 Win., 6mm Creedmoor, 6.5 Creedmoor, 6.5x47, .260 Rem., .308 Win., 7mm Mag., .28 Nosler, .300 Win., .300 Norma, or .338 Norma cal., SMR Elite Hunter action, match grade carbon wrap barrel, SMR muzzle brake, detachable mag., Timney 510-U trigger, lightweight composite stock with adj. cheekpiece, integral 20 MOA rail. Mfg. 2015-2018.

	$5,000	$4,375	$3,750	$3,400	$2,750	$2,250	$1,750	*$5,900*

Add $200 for .300 Norma or .338 Norma cal.
Add $125 for Jewell trigger.

SMR ELITE PRECISION RIFLE – .260 Rem., .308 Win., .300 Win. Mag., .300 Norma, .338 Norma, or .338 Lapua cal., SMR Elite action, custom 5R match grade stainless M24 contour barrel, SMR muzzle brake, SMR DBM with 5 shot mag., Jewell trigger, Precision stock with adj. cheek and LOP, integral 20 MOA rail. Mfg. 2015-2018.

	$4,085	$3,575	$3,075	$2,775	$2,250	$1,850	$1,450	*$4,800*

Add $200 for .300 Norma or .338 Norma cal.
Add $400 for .338 Lapua cal.

SMR FULL CURL – 6mm Creedmoor, 6XC, 6.5 Creedmoor, 6.5x57 Lapua, .260 Rem., 6.5 SAUM, or .308 Win. cal., Defiance Rebel (full curl ultra light) action, right or left-hand configuration, 20 (disc.), 22, or 24 in. Proof Research Carbon Sendero Light barrel, TriggerTech Special trigger, hinged floorplate, full curl carbon ultra light stock, bottom metal BDL, Graphite Black, Magpul FDE, Magpul OD Green, or Tactical Gray Cerakote finish, 5 lbs. 8 oz. New 2019.

MSR $5,250	$4,475	$3,925	$3,350	$3,050	$2,475	$2,025	$1,575	

Add $100-$190 for SMR stainless or titanium muzzle brake.

SMR LONG RANGE HUNTER (OLDER MFG.) – .243 Win., 6.5 Creedmoor, 6.5x284, .260 Rem., .308 Win., .300 WSM, 7mm Mag., .300 Win., .300 Norma, or .338 Norma cal., SMR 3600 action, custom match grade stainless 5R #6 fluted barrel, SMR muzzle brake, HS Precision detachable box mag., Timney 510-U trigger, composite hunter stock with adj. cheekpiece. Mfg. 2014-2018.

	$4,200	$3,675	$3,150	$2,850	$2,325	$1,900	$1,500	*$4,950*

Add $200 for .300 Norma or .338 Norma cal.
Add $80 for Cerakoted barrel action.
Add $125 for Jewell trigger.

SMR LONG RANGE HUNTER (NEW MFG.) – 6.5 Creedmoor, 6.5 PRC, 7mm Rem. Mag., .28 Nosler, .30 Nosler, .300 WSM, .300 Norma, .338 Norma, or .300 Win. Mag. cal., Defiance Deviant Hunter action, right or left-hand configuration, 22, 24, or 26 in. Benchmark match grade stainless steel hand-lapped threaded barrel w/thread cap, TriggerTech Special trigger, Long Range Hunter adj. stock, BDL or hunter style box mag., Graphite Black, Magpul FDE, Magpul OD Green, or Tactical Gray Cerakote finish, 8 lbs. 8 oz. New 2019.

MSR $5,450	$4,650	$4,050	$3,500	$3,150	$2,550	$2,100	$1,600	

Add $300 for 22 or 24 in. Proof Research Carbon Sendero barrel.
Add $100-$240 for SMR stainless or titanium muzzle brake.
Add $100 for HS Hunter style detachable mag. or Snowy Mountain Rifles Tactical Box.

GRADING - PPGS™	100%	98%	95%	90%	80%	70%	60%	LAST MSR

SMR PALADIN – .260 Rem, .308 Win., or .300 Win. Mag. cal., SMR 3600 fluted bolt action, Benchmark match grade threaded and capped (.260 Rem. or .308 Win. cal.) barrel or with muzzle brake (.300 Win. Mag. cal. only), Accuracy International 5 shot mag., Timney trigger, Bell & Carlson stock with pistol grip and raised cheekpiece, Desert Tan finish. Disc. 2014.

	$2,095	$1,825	$1,575	$1,425	$1,150	$950	$735	*$2,450*

SMR TIMBERLINE – .243 Win., .260 Rem., 7mm-08 Rem., 6.5 Creedmoor, or .308 Win. cal., SMR 3600 fluted action, 22 in. custom match grade stainless steel fluted barrel, Manners carbon fiber filled stock and forearm, pistol grip, Timney trigger, Talley low ring and base set, gray camo stock finish, approx. 7 lbs. Mfg. 2014-2018.

	$3,575	$3,125	$2,675	$2,425	$1,975	$1,625	$1,250	*$4,200*

Add $125 for Jewell trigger.
Add $80 for Cerakoted barreled action.
Add $80 for SMR Picatinny rail.

SOCIETA SIDERURGICA GLISENTI

Previous manufacturer located in Brescia, Italy. Also see the Italian Military Arms listing.

PISTOLS: SEMI-AUTO

GLISENTI MODEL 1910 – 9mm Glisenti cal., 7 shot, 4 in. barrel, fixed sights, blue, checkered wood, rubber or plastic grips, Italian service pistol. Mfg. 1910-WWII.

	$1,800	$1,575	$1,350	$1,225	$1,000	$825	$625	

Warning: While some Glisentis may chamber and fire the 9mm Para. cartridge, it is extremely dangerous to do so.

SOCIETE FAYOUMI

Current manufacturer of shotguns using the trademarks Carina, Anakon, and MK-10, located in Beirut, Lebanon. No current U.S. importation - European distribution only.

SODIA, FRANZ

Previous manufacturer founded in 1871 in Ferlach, Austria with headquarters in Salzburg since 1961 and Vienna since 2008. The factory in Ferlach was closed in 1985.

Werner Sodia is the nephew of Franz Sodia, he is the last still working gunsmith in the Sodia family. No new models are currently being produced however some repair work is offered. For provenance and value of an old Franz Sodia gun, send good quality photos as well as the numbers and stamps that are on the gun to werner@sodia-exclusiv.com.

LONG GUNS: CUSTOM

Older Sodia arms are very high quality and are often excellently engraved and inlaid. Sodia is famous for its high quality long arms in many configurations. Previous models include: Model 557 Mountain Carbine O/U combination gun, Model 557 Super De Luxe O/U combination gun, Model 270 AD Drilling, Model 30 Drilling, Model 160 EJ Safari SxS double rifle, Model 260 EJ SxS double rifle, Model 158 AN Drilling, Model 360 EJ SxS double rifle, Model 560 EJ Safari SxS double rifle, Model 150 HH single barrel rifle, in addition to a bolt action model in many calibers.

To determine current values on older Franz Sodia rifles and shotguns, it is very important to consider the overall desirability of the gun's configuration (i.e. boxlock or sidelock action, caliber/gauge, special features, amount and quality of engraving (including gold inlays), type and quality of wood, checkering/carving, eye appeal, and original condition factor). All Franz Sodia guns are hand crafted, and need to be evaluated individually to determine value and shootability.

SOKOLOVSKY CORPORATION SPORT ARMS (SCSA)

Previous manufacturer until 1990 located in Sunnyvale, CA.

PISTOLS: SEMI-AUTO

SOKOLOVSKY .45 AUTOMASTER – .45 ACP cal. only, stainless steel, single action, 6 in. barrel, 6 shot mag., adj. Millet sights, unique action, no external operating levers, 55 oz. Mfg. 1984-90.

	$2,700	$2,200	$1,850	$1,620	$1,335	$1,115	$930	*$3,300*

Total production on this model is 50 pistols.

GRADING - PPGS™	100%	98%	95%	90%	80%	70%	60%	LAST MSR

SOG ARMORY

Previous rifle manufacturer located in Houston, TX until late 2013.

For individual model listings, please go to BlueBookOfGunValues.com/overflow.

SOLEIHAC ARMURIER

Previous manufacturer located in Saint Etienne, France.

This manufacturer produced copies of 1894 patent Darne R model guns until 1950. The guns produced were generally simple and less expensive than other manufacturers' sliding breech guns. Most unmarked sliding breech guns were probably manufactured by Soleihac Armurier. Quality and pricing will be similar to low grade (Halifax and RIO model) Darne guns in average condition.

SOL INVICTUS ARMS

Current manufacturer of AR-15 style pistols, rifles, and tactical pistols and shotguns, located in Melbourne, FL.

For individual model listings, please go to BlueBookOfGunValues.com/overflow.

SOMMER + OCKENFUSS GmbH

Previous manufacturer located in Baiersbronn, Germany until 2002. Previously imported by Lothar Walther Precision Tool, located in Cumming, GA. Previously imported by Intertex Carousels Corporation during 1998-2000, and located in Pineville, NC.

For individual model listings, please go to BlueBookOfGunValues.com/overflow.

SONS OF LIBERTY GUN WORKS

Current AR-15 style rifle and pistol manufacturer located in Laredo, TX. Previously located in San Antonio, TX until circa 2020.

Please refer to BlueBookOfGunValues.com to order the *Blue Book of AR-15s & Variations*, available as a book or online subscription.

SOROKA RIFLE COMPANY

Current rifle manufacturer located in New Zealand. Currently imported and distributed by Soroka Rifles USA, located in Sedona, AZ.

RIFLES: SINGLE SHOT

MODEL 07 ALPINE EXPRESS/AFRICAN EXPRESS MODEL – various standard magnum and dangerous game calibers, features the Gibbs Farquharson action, Alpine Express or African Express Model, engraved cased colored receiver, 24 or 26 in. barrel with quarter rib, barrel band, and integral Talley base, checkered deluxe Turkish walnut stock and forearm with ebony tip, solid rubber pad, top tang safety, finishes such as rust bluing, hot bluing, French gray, or satin black chrome available upon request.

MSR	100%	98%	95%	90%	80%	70%	60%
MSR $18,950	$17,000	$14,875	$12,750	$11,550	$9,350	$7,650	$5,950

SOUTHERN GUN COMPANY

Current custom rifle manufacturer located in the U.K.

RIFLES

Southern Gun Company manufactures single shot and manual repeating action rifles in several calibers and configurations built to customer specifications. Southern Gun Company also manufactures the LA-30 semi-auto rifle with features built to customer specifications. Please contact the company directly for more information including options, pricing, and availability.

SPARTAN GUN WORKS

Previous trademark of Remington Arms Company, Inc. for long arms imported from Russia (mostly Baikal) from 2004-2009.

For individual model listings, please go to BlueBookOfGunValues.com/overflow.

SPARTAN PRECISION RIFLES

Current rifle manufacturer established in early 2011, located in San Jose, CA. Previously located in Concord, CA.

Custom rifle maker Marc Soulie builds rifles per individual specifications, with a specialty in F-Class and sniper rifles. Complete rifle builds take approximately 10-12 months build time. Please contact him directly for more information, including pricing, configurations, options, availability and delivery time.

GRADING - PPGS™	100%	98%	95%	90%	80%	70%	60%	LAST MSR

SPECIAL WEAPONS LLC

Previous tactical rifle manufacturer 1999-2002, located in Mesa, AZ. Previously located in Tempe, AZ.

CARBINES: SEMI-AUTO

OMEGA 760 – 9mm Para. cal., reproduction of the S&W Model 76, 16 1/4 in. partially shrouded barrel, fixed wire stock, 30 shot mag., 7 1/2 lbs. Limited mfg. 2002.

	100%	98%	95%	90%	80%	70%	60%	LAST MSR
	$495	$450	$425	$395	$375	$350	$325	*$575*

SW-5 CARBINE – 9mm Para. cal., configuration styled after the HK-94 (parts interchangeable), stainless steel receiver, plastic lower housing, 16 1/4 in. stainless steel barrel, A2 style black synthetic stock with wide forearm, 10 shot mag. (accepts high capacity HK-94/MP-5 mags also), approx. 6 3/4 lbs. Mfg. 2000-2002.

	100%	98%	95%	90%	80%	70%	60%	LAST MSR
	$1,475	$1,225	$1,025	$875	$800	$750	$695	*$1,600*

SW-45 CARBINE – .45 ACP cal., otherwise similar to SW-5 Carbine. Mfg. 2000-2002.

	100%	98%	95%	90%	80%	70%	60%	LAST MSR
	$1,550	$1,275	$1,050	$895	$825	$775	$725	*$1,700*

RIFLES: SEMI-AUTO

SW-3 – .308 Win. cal., styled after the HK-91 (parts interchangeable), 17.71 in. stainless steel barrel, tooled receiver, sheet steel trigger housing, A2 style stock, approx. 10 lbs. Mfg. 2000-2002.

	100%	98%	95%	90%	80%	70%	60%	LAST MSR
	$1,425	$1,175	$995	$850	$800	$750	$695	*$1,550*

* ***SW-3 SP*** – similar to SW-3, except has PSG-1 style trigger assembly, 22 in. custom target barrel and Weaver rail welded to receiver top. Mfg. 2000-2002.

	100%	98%	95%	90%	80%	70%	60%	LAST MSR
	$2,250	$1,975	$1,700	$1,500	$1,250	$1,050	$895	*$2,500*

SPECIALIZED DYNAMICS

Current custom AR-15 style manufacturer located in Chandler, AZ since 2007.

Please refer to BlueBookOfGunValues.com to order the *Blue Book of AR-15s & Variations*, available as a book or online subscription.

SPECIALIZED TACTICAL SYSTEMS

Current OEM parts manufacturer and previous rifle manufacturer located in Ogden, UT. Previously located in Pleasant View, UT.

Please refer to BlueBookOfGunValues.com to order the *Blue Book of AR-15s & Variations*, available as a book or online subscription.

SPENCER CARBINES/RIFLES - CURRENT MFG.

Currently manufactured by Armi Sport di Chiappa Silvia & C., located in Brescia, Italy. Current reproductions are imported by Cimarron, Dixie Gun Works, and Taylor's & Co. Please refer to Chiappa Firearms LTD listing in the C section.

SPENCER REPEATING RIFLES CO.

Previous manufacturer located in Boston, MA between 1860-1868. Spencer manufactured approximately 144,000 rimfire rifles and carbines, of which approximately 107,000 were contracted to the United States Government during the Civil War.

The brainchild of young Christopher Miner Spencer, more than 13,500 Spencer M1860 Army rifles, 800 M1860 Navy rifles, and 48,000 M1860 Army carbines saw action during the Civil War.

In late 1864, the Chief of Ordnance directed modifications, including reducing the bore from .52 to .50 caliber, and shortening the barrel from 22 inches to 20 inches. The new carbine was designated the Spencer M1865 carbine. Nearly 19,000 were produced by the Spencer Repeating Rifle Company, and another 30,500 by the Burnside Rifle Company, although all were delivered too late to see action in the Civil War. Model 1865 carbines and refurbished M1860 carbines became the mainstay of America's troops on the Western Frontier until replaced by "Trap-Door" Springfield carbines after 1873.

The author wishes to express thanks to Roy Marcot, author of *Spencer Repeating Rifles*, for providing most of the information listed here.

100%	98%	95%	90%	80%	70%	60%	50%	40%	30%	20%	10%

RIFLES: LEVER ACTION

SMALL-FRAME MILITARY CARBINES AND SPORTING RIFLES – fewer than four dozen prototype small-frame .38 rimfire cal. sporting rifles and .44 rimfire cal. military carbines were made by Christopher Spencer in Hartford between 1860 and 1861. They are exceedingly rare, and only a few are in private hands.

100%	98%	95%	90%	80%	70%	60%	50%	40%	30%	20%	10%
N/A	N/A	N/A	$16,000	$14,000	$12,000	$10,000	$9,000	$8,000	$7,000	$5,000	$4,500

MODEL 1860 NAVY RIFLES – the rarest of production Spencer firearms, 803 Spencer Model 1860 Navy rifles with sword-type bayonets were produced for the U.S. Navy Bureau of Ordnance between 1862 and 1863.

100%	98%	95%	90%	80%	70%	60%	50%	40%	30%	20%	10%
N/A	N/A	$14,000	$12,000	$9,000	$8,000	$6,500	$5,000	$4,500	$4,000	$3,500	$3,000

Add $1,250 for correct Collins produced sword-type bayonet. Add $250 for the correct scabbard in at least very good condition.

Beware: a Collins-produced sword-type bayonet for the Sharps M1859 rifle can be made to fit the Spencer Navy rifle, but it is not a true Spencer Navy bayonet.

MODEL 1860 ARMY RIFLES – between 1863 and 1864, the Spencer factory in Boston produced 11,471 Spencer M1860 Army rifles for the Federal Ordnance Department, another 200 for the U.S. Navy, and approximately 2,000 for private purchase. All were issued with a Pattern M1855 style angular bayonet which fit only these rifles.

100%	98%	95%	90%	80%	70%	60%	50%	40%	30%	20%	10%
N/A	N/A	$10,000	$9,000	$7,000	$6,000	$5,000	$3,500	$3,000	$2,500	$2,000	$1,800

Add $600 for correct angular bayonet and scabbard.

MODEL 1860 CARBINES – beginning in October 1863, the Spencer factory began delivering the first of 45,733 Spencer M1860 carbines to the Ordnance Department for use by Federal cavalrymen. As many as 3,000 additional M1860 carbines went to private purchasers, and also saw action in the war. Because Spencer carbines were so important to the Federal war effort, nearly all saw hard use during the last 18 months of fighting. This resulted in very few weapons available today in excellent condition, and fewer yet with case colors remaining on the receiver.

100%	98%	95%	90%	80%	70%	60%	50%	40%	30%	20%	10%
N/A	N/A	$11,000	$10,000	$7,500	$6,000	$4,500	$3,750	$2,750	$2,000	$1,800	$1,500

Subtract 25% for Springfield Armory reconditioned Spencer Model 1860 carbines (modified after the war).

MODEL 1865 CARBINES – in 1865 and 1866, the Spencer factory delivered 18,959 Spencer M1865 carbines to the Federal Ordnance Department. Concurrently, the Burnside Rifle Company of Providence, Rhode Island manufactured and delivered 30,502 Spencer M1865 carbines to the Ordnance Department.

100%	98%	95%	90%	80%	70%	60%	50%	40%	30%	20%	10%
N/A	$7,000	$6,000	$5,000	$3,000	$2,750	$2,500	$2,000	$1,750	$1,500	$1,200	$1,000

MODEL 1865 ARMY RIFLES – as many as 3,000 Spencer M1865 Army rifles were made by the Spencer factory in 1865. While none were ordered by the U.S. Army Ordnance Department, 2,000 went to the Commonwealth of Massachusetts National Guard, and another 1,000 went to Canadian troops and to private purchasers.

100%	98%	95%	90%	80%	70%	60%	50%	40%	30%	20%	10%
N/A	$6,000	$5,000	$4,000	$3,000	$2,750	$2,500	$2,000	$1,750	$1,500	$1,200	$1,000

SPRINGFIELD ARMORY RIFLE MUSKET CONVERSION OF SPENCER CARBINES – in 1871, General Dyer, Chief of Ordnance, directed that 1,109 Spencer M1865 carbines be converted to two-band muskets. They were fitted with Springfield .50 caliber barrels which held the standard M1855 pattern bayonet. The conversion work was done at Springfield Armory.

100%	98%	95%	90%	80%	70%	60%	50%	40%	30%	20%	10%
N/A	$6,000	$5,000	$4,000	$3,000	$2,750	$2,500	$2,000	$1,750	$1,500	$1,200	$1,000

Note: There is no record that these rifles were ever issued to U.S. troops. This is the reason why so many examples are known in 80% or better condition.

MODEL 1867 ARMY RIFLES AND CARBINES – in 1867, the Spencer factory produced approx. 1,000 M1867 Army rifles and 12,000 carbines. All were intended for private domestic or foreign military sales.

100%	98%	95%	90%	80%	70%	60%	50%	40%	30%	20%	10%
N/A	$5,000	$4,500	$3,000	$2,500	$2,000	$1,750	$1,500	$1,400	$1,200	$1,000	$900

NEW MODEL ARMY RIFLES AND CARBINES – in their final year of production, 1868, the Spencer Repeating Rifle Company produced approx. 1,000 Army rifles and 5,000 carbines. These too, were intended for private domestic or foreign military sales.

100%	98%	95%	90%	80%	70%	60%	50%	40%	30%	20%	10%
N/A	$5,000	$4,500	$3,000	$2,500	$2,000	$1,750	$1,500	$1,400	$1,200	$1,000	$900

SPORTING RIFLES – between 1864-68, the Spencer factory produced approximately 2,000 sporting rifles for the civilian trade. The initial 200 or so were made from surplus military M1860 Army rifle receivers. Thereafter, approximately 1,800 sporting rifles were made expressly as such. The majority chambered the Spencer 56-46 bottleneck rimfire cartridge, but a small number were produced in .50 caliber, chambering 56-50 and the 56-52 cartridges. Spencer sporting rifles missing the rear tang sight are worth approximately 25% less than those listed, as factory tang sights are near-impossible to find. Most Spencer sporting rifles had 26-inch long round barrels, but more desirable versions with octagon barrels command a substantial premium, and 34 inch octagon barrels are a rarity.

Only a relatively few Factory engraved, Spencer sporting rifles are known, and will command a substantial premium. Over the past few years such rifles sold at auction from $15,000 to $45,000, depending on condition.

100%	98%	95%	90%	80%	70%	60%	50%	40%	30%	20%	10%
* ***Round Barrel Sporting Rifles***											
N/A	N/A	$9,000	$7,500	$4,000	$2,500	$2,250	$2,000	$1,750	$1,500	$1,300	$1,200
* ***Octagon Barrel Sporting Rifles***											
N/A	N/A	$10,000	$8,000	$5,000	$3,750	$3,000	$2,750	$2,250	$1,750	$1,500	$1,250

SPHINX SYSTEMS LTD.

Current trademark owned and operated by Kriss Arms. The Sphinx Systems Limited entity operated from 1876-2016, formerly located in Matten b. Interlaken, Switzerland. Previously imported by Kriss Arms USA, beginning 2011, located in Virginia Beach, VA. In late 2010, Kriss Arms acquired Sphinx Systems Ltd., including the Sphinx trademark. Previously distributed until 2009 by Sabre Defence Industries, LLC, located in Nashville, TN. Previously imported by Rocky Mountain Armoury, located in Silverthorne, CO. Previously manufactured by Sphinx Engineering S.A. located in Porrentruy, Switzerland, and by Sphinx U.S.A., located in Meriden, CT until 1996. Previously imported by Sile Distributors located in New York, NY. In 2016, Kriss USA took over production of the Sphinx pistols under the Sphinx trademark.

GRADING - PPGS™	100%	98%	95%	90%	80%	70%	60%	LAST MSR

PISTOLS: SEMI-AUTO

Please contact the importer directly for current U.S. availability and pricing on the following current models.

MODEL AT-380 – .380 ACP cal., DAO, 3.27 in. barrel, stainless steel frame, two-tone finish, 10 shot mag. with finger extension, checkered walnut grips. Disc. 1996.

$435	$375	$350	$325	$295	$275	$250	*$494*

Add $20 for black finish.
Add $71 for N/Pall finish.

MODEL 2000S STANDARD – 9mm Para. or .40 S&W (new 1993) cal., 4.53 in. barrel, DA/SA or DAO, stainless steel fabrication, 10 (C/B 1994), 15* (9mm Para.), or 11* (.40 S&W) shot mag., checkered walnut grips, fixed sights, 35 oz. Importation disc. 2002.

$1,650	$900	$700	$525	$450	$410	$375	

Add $117 for .40 S&W cal.

* ***Model 2000PS Standard Police Special*** – similar to Model 2000S, except has compact slide and 3.66 in. barrel. Disc.

$2,200	$1,000	$800	$550	$410	$380	$350	

Add $40 for .40 S&W cal.
Add $87 for N/Pall finish.

* ***Model 2000P Standard Compact*** – similar to Model 2000 Standard, except has 3.66 in. barrel and 13 shot mag., 31 oz. Disc.

$1,650	$900	$700	$450	$410	$380	$350	

Add $40 for .40 S&W cal.
Add $87 for N/Pall finish.

* ***Model 2000H Standard Sub-Compact*** – similar to Model 2000 Compact, except has 3.34 in. barrel and 10 shot mag., 26 oz. Disc. 1996.

$1,550	$950	$750	$500	$410	$380	$350	*$940*

Add $40 for .40 S&W cal.
Add $87 for N/Pall finish.

MODEL 2000 MASTER – 9mm Para., 9x21mm, or .40 S&W cal., SAO, two-tone finish only, designed for Master's stock class competition. Disc.

$2,500	$1,450	$1,100	$995	$895	$775	$650	*$2,035*

MODEL AT-2000 (NEW MODEL) – 9mm Para. or .40 S&W cal., 4.53 in. barrel, DA/SA, 10 shot mag., machined slide with electro deposited finish, decocking mechanism. Limited mfg. 2004-2005.

$2,000	$1,675	$1,450	$1,225	$1,000	$800	$675	*$1,995*

MODEL AT-2000CS COMPETITOR – 9mm Para., 9x21mm, or .40 S&W cal., DA/SA, competition model featuring many shooting improvements including 5.3 in. compensated barrel, 10 (C/B 1994), 11* (.40 S&W), or 15* shot mag., Bo-Mar adj. sights, two-tone finish. Imported 1993-1996.

$2,100	$1,275	$1,050	$950	$850	$750	$675	*$1,902*

Add $287 for Model AT-2000C (includes Sphinx scope mount).
Add $1,538 for AT-2000K conversion kit (new 1995).
Add $1,490 for Model AT-2000CKS (competition kit to convert AT-2000 to comp. pistol, disc. 1994).

GRADING - PPGS™	100%	98%	95%	90%	80%	70%	60%	LAST MSR

MODEL 2000 COMPETITION – similar to Model 2000 Master, except is SAO and includes more advanced competitive shooting features, Bo-Mar sights, top-of-the-line competition model. Imported 1993-96.

	$3,000	$1,925	$1,725	$1,500	$1,250	$1,050	$895	*$2,894*

Add $78 for Model AT-2000GM (includes Sphinx scope mount).

MODEL 3000 SERIES – 9mm Para., 9x21mm (disc.), .40 S&W, or .45 ACP cal., DA/SA, available in standard (4.53 in. barrel), tactical (3 3/4 in. barrel), or competition (4.53 in. barrel, adj. sights), configuration, choice of manual safety or decocker, titanium upper/lower frame with stainless slide, stainless steel slide with titanium lower frame or stainless steel frame/slide, front/rear gripstrap stippling or grooved, two-tone finish, approx. 40 oz. Imported 2001-circa 2012.

	$2,525	$2,275	$2,000	$1,800	$1,575	$1,375	$1,150	

Add $350 for titanium frame with stainless steel slide.
Add $800 for stainless steel slide with titanium upper/lower frame (disc.).
Add $75 for tactical model.
Add $350 for competition model.

SPHINX COMPETITION MODELS – currently available in either an Open (extended barrel with 3 port compensator and Aimpoint scope), Modified (2 port compensator and rear sight optics), or Standard. Disc. 2013.

This model was POR.

SPHINX .45 ACP – .45 ACP cal., DA/SA, steel construction, 3 3/4 in. barrel, double slide serrations, blue finish, 10 shot mag., fixed Trijicon night sights, black polymer grips, decocker mechanism, approx. 43 oz. New 2007.

MSR N/A	$2,850	$2,500	$2,150	$1,850	$1,500	$1,250	$1,000	

SDP SERIES – 9mm Para. cal., 3 1/8 (Sub-Compact), 3.7 (Compact), 4 1/2 (Standard) in. barrel, DA/SA, aluminum or hybrid alloy/polymer frame (Alpha series) and steel slide, full-length guide rails, 13, 15, or 17 shot mag., match grade trigger, six integrated safeties including loaded chamber indicator, notched Picatinny rail avail. on compact and standard models, forward and rear slide serrations, various sight combinations available per individual model, interchangeable aluminum/rubber grip system, 21-31 3/4 oz. New 2012.

* ***SDP Standard Alpha*** – 9mm Para. cal., DA/SA, 4 1/2 in. barrel, 17 shot mag., steel slide, alloy/polymer hybrid frame, matte black finish only, 31 3/4 oz., Mfg. 2014-2016.

	$950	$825	$725	$650	$525	$425	$350	*$1,295*

* ***SDP Compact Alpha*** – 9mm Para. cal., DA/SA, 3.7 in. barrel, 15 shot mag., steel slide, alloy/polymer hybrid frame, Black, Krypton, Sand, Duotone, stainless steel, or Wolf (mfg. 2016 only) finish, 27 1/2 oz., Mfg. 2014-2016.

	$800	$700	$600	$525	$450	$375	$300	*$949*

Add $96 for Wolf finish (new 2016).

* ***SDP Compact (SDP Compact Black)*** – 9mm Para. cal., DA/SA, ambi decocking lever, 3 3/4 in. threaded or non-threaded barrel barrel, 15 shot mag., reversible magazine catch, match grade trigger w/enlarged and undercut trigger guard, iron sights, interchangeable polymer grips w/ rubber overmolding, Picatinny rail, hard anodized aluminum frame, high cut beavertail, PVD coated steel slide, black, Sand, Krypton, Combat Grey, or Alpine finish, 29.06 oz. New 2016.

MSR $999	$850	$725	$650	$575	$500	$450	$375	

Add $50 for Sand, Krypton, Combat Grey, and Alpine finish.
Add $50 for threaded barrel.

* ***SDP Duty (SDP Compact Black Duty)*** – 9mm Para. cal., DA/SA, ambi decocking lever, 3 3/4 in. threaded barrel, 17 shot mag., match grade trigger, iron sights, interchangeable polymer grips w/rubber overmolding, Picatinny rail, hard anodized aluminum frame, high cut beavertail, steel slide, loaded chamber indicator, black, Sand, Krypton, Combat Grey, or Alpine (disc. 2016) finish, 30.18 oz. New 2016.

MSR $1,019	$875	$750	$675	$600	$525	$475	$400	

Add $50 for Sand, Krypton, Combat Grey, or Alpine finish.
Add $50 for threaded barrel.

* ***SDP Sub Compact Alpha*** – 3 1/8 in. barrel, 13 shot mag., matte black finish only, approx. 21 oz. Mfg. 2014-2016.

	$850	$750	$650	$575	$525	$475	$425	*$949*

GRADING - PPGS™	100%	98%	95%	90%	80%	70%	60%	LAST MSR

SPIDER FIREARMS

Current rifle manufacturer located in St. Cloud, FL.

RIFLES: SINGLE SHOT

These models can also be custom ordered in .510 DTC, .510BR-DTC, .50 Spider, .50 SFBR, .416 Barrett, .408 CheyTac, .338 Harris, .338 Lapua, and .338 Wby. Mag. cals.

SPORTSMAN FERRET 50 - .50 BMG cal., single shot bolt action, A2 style buttstock and pistol grip, Picatinny rail, choice of 18 to 36 in. barrel (LW-19 chrome moly is standard), matte black finish, perforated handguard with bipod, includes muzzle brake. Mfg. 2003-Disc.

	100%	98%	95%	90%	80%	70%	60%	LAST MSR
	$3,150	$2,750	$2,375	$2,150	$1,800	$1,600	$1,400	*$3,511*

Add $291 for LW-50 stainless steel barrel (SS Sportsman)

Add $583 for LW-50 Supermatch stainless super match barrel (SM Sportsman).

SUPERCOMP FERRET - .50 BMG cal., similar to Ferret 50, features solid steel construction, fixed scope rails, 18 to 36 in. Lothar Walther stainless or chrome moly Supermatch barrels, adj. 1 lb. competition style trigger, two-axis cheek rest, and detachable rear monopod. New 2004.

	100%	98%	95%	90%	80%	70%	60%	LAST MSR
MSR $6,694	$5,750	$5,000	$4,325	$3,900	$3,175	$2,600	$2,000	

Add $302 for LW-50 stainless steel barrel.

Add $583 for LW-50 stainless steel Supermatch barrel.

SPIKE'S TACTICAL LLC

Current AR-15 pistol and rifle manufacturer located in Apopka, FL.

Please refer to BlueBookOfGunValues.com to order the *Blue Book of AR-15s & Variations*, available as a book or online subscription.

SPIRIT GUN MANUFACTURING COMPANY LLC

Previous manufacturer located in West Palm Beach, FL until 2011.

Please refer to BlueBookOfGunValues.com to order the *Blue Book of AR-15s & Variations*, available as a book or online subscription.

SPITFIRE

Please refer to the JSL (Hereford) listing in the J section.

SPOHR, THOMAS (TS FINE GUNS)

Current custom gunmaker located in Grobmaischeid, Germany. No current U.S. importation.

Thomas Spohr is a top-quality gunmaker that manufactures many different configurations of guns including bolt action rifles, Drillings, Luger/Broomhandle carbines, etc. Please contact the company directly for more information, current pricing, and availability in the U.S.

SPORTCO/SPORTING ARMS CO.

Previous Australian manufacturer established 1947 in Adelaide, South Australia by Jack Warne (of Kimber fame) and business partner Kevin Koch. Sporting Arms Co. was taken over in 1965 by USA company Omark Industries, and the range of 22 rimfire and centerfire rifles were expanded until the company closed in 1983.

The company established itself by manufacturing sporting caliber barrels for the large number of military surplus SMLE rifles in the Australian community post WWII. In 1956, they purchased from the government the complete lot of some 65,000 310 Cadet caliber BSA Martini rifles, some of which were immediately shipped on to Golden State Arms in California.

Known to sporting shooters in Australia and overseas as "Sportco", this Adelaide based company produced sporting firearms for over 35 years for the Australian market and export to Great Britain, Rhodesia, Borneo, South Africa, Canada, New Zealand and the U.S. For more information on this company's history, please visit www.sportco.org.au.

Sportco's firearms were of good quality utilitarian manufacture, and to date, there has been little collector interest. Sportco manufactured the Winchester Model 310 and 320 actions before they were shipped to the U.S. for completion. Values for Sportco firearms must be based on their shooting value only in today's competitive marketplace involving new firearms.

RIFLES

Sportco .22 cal. rimfire rifles are currently priced in the $125-$500 range depending on the configuration and condition. Centerfire rifles are priced in the $350-$1,000 range depending on configuration and condition.

GRADING - PPGS™	100%	98%	95%	90%	80%	70%	60%	LAST MSR

SPORT-SYSTEME DITTRICH

Current manufacturer established in 2003, located in Kulmbach, Germany. No current U.S. importation. Previously imported in North America by Wolverine Supplies, located in Manitoba, Canada until 2014, and by Marstar Canada, located in Ontario, Canada.

Sport-Systeme Dittrich manufactures high quality semi-auto reproductions of famous military guns, including the MP38 (BD 38 €2,480), BD 38/L, Sturmgewehr 44 (BD 44) and the Gerät Neumünster (BD 3008, €1,950). Its latest model is a reproduction of the Fallschirmjägergewehr FG42 as the BD42/I (€7,560), BD42/II (€7,450), BD 43/I (€3,250), and BD 44 (€2,690). Other current models include MKB42 (€3,250), BD 1-5 (€10,500), BD 35/1 (€3,500), SG11 (€3,500), SG12 (€3,500), DC13- SG13 (€3,500), P18 (€1,800), and P18K (€1,800). Please contact the company directly for more information, including pricing and U.S. availability.

SPRINGER'S ERBEN, JOHANN

Current manufacturer, retailer, and auction house established in 1836, located in Vienna, Austria.

Joh. Springer's Erben is one of the leading retailers for hunting and sporting guns and rifles, shooting supplies, security equipment, and related accessories in Austria. Additionally, Springer's manufactures custom made long guns in a variety of configurations on a limited basis. This newest generation of family members includes Christian Johann Springer, whose great-great-great grandfather started the family business during 1836 in Vienna. He is the 6th generation to follow who owns and leads the company successfully.

Johann Springer's Erben also has several auctions annually, which include a wide variety of sporting firearms, especially older European trademarks and configurations.

Please contact the company directly for more information, including U.S. availability and an individualized price quotation based on the configuration.

SPRINGFIELD ARMORY

America's first federal armory located in Springfield, MA. Production began in 1795 and an Act of Congress made it an official federal arsenal in 1872. This government owned armory was closed in 1968 and the "Springfield Armory" trademark was sold to a private individual in the early 1970s, and evolved into the current Springfield Armory. Not associated with the private firm of the same name located in Geneseo, IL.

In recent years, collectors have realized that military specimens in 90%-100% original condition are very rare and desirable. Since the supply of these guns is limited, values listed for these condition factors may actually be a little under current market values, especially auction pricing. On Springfields and other U.S. military long arms, the importance of the wood being original, unsanded, and with crisp, clear cartouches cannot be overstated.

PISTOLS: SEMI-AUTO

M1911 MILITARY MFG. SPRINGFIELD ARMORY – approx. 30,000 mfg. 1914-1915, blue finish.

100%	98%	95%	90%	80%	70%	60%	LAST MSR
N/A	$5,950	$4,600	$3,500	$3,000	$2,500	$2,000	

Serialization is 72,751-83,855, 102,597-107,596, 113,497-120,566, and 125,567-133,186.

Most mint/100% specimens encountered in this model have been refinished - be careful.

RIFLES: BOLT ACTION, KRAG-JORGENSEN

Please refer to Krag-Jorgensen section for models and pricing.

RIFLES: BOLT ACTION, MODEL 1903 & VARIATIONS

On Springfields and other U.S. military long arms, the importance of the wood being original, unsanded, and with crisp, clear cartouches cannot be overstated.

Values listed for Model 1903s assume 100% original guns. Values listed for Model 1922s assume 100% original blued guns.

U.S. MODEL 1903 SPRINGFIELD – .30-06 cal., bolt action, mfg. by Springfield Armory and Rock Island Arsenal, 24 in. barrel. Mfg. 1903-1930.

* ***U.S. Model 1903 Springfield Pre-WWI Mfg.*** – values below represent original rifles.

100%	98%	95%	90%	80%	70%	60%	LAST MSR
$6,000	$4,500	$3,750	$3,250	$2,500	$2,250	$1,850	

Subtract 80% if reworked.

* ***U.S. Model 1903 Springfield Serialized 800,000 - 1,275,767*** – double heat treated receiver.

100%	98%	95%	90%	80%	70%	60%	LAST MSR
$4,500	$4,000	$3,300	$2,750	$2,000	$1,650	$1,250	

GRADING - PPGS™	100%	98%	95%	90%	80%	70%	60%	LAST MSR

* ***U.S. Model 1903 Springfield Serialized 1,275,768 +*** – nickel steel receiver.

	$4,950	$4,000	$3,300	$2,750	$2,500	$2,100	$1,650	

MODEL 1903 MARK I – .30-06 cal., similar to U.S. Model 1903 Springfield, except altered for the Pedersen device, a slot is milled into the left side of receiver to act as an ejection port for use of the semi-auto bolt insert.

	$4,500	$4,000	$3,500	$1,800	$1,200	$1,000	$850	

Values listed are w/o the Pedersen device.

* ***Model 1903 Mark I w/Pedersen*** – includes Pedersen device.

Current pricing for this model range from $20,000-$40,000, depending on original condition. Complete Pedersen devices in 98%+ original condition have sold for $35,000.

Be aware - inspect carefully for originality!

1903-A1 – .30-06 cal., similar to U.S. Model 1903 Springfield, except type C pistol grip stock. Mfg. 1930-1939.

	$4,500	$4,000	$3,500	$3,000	$1,800	$1,000	$850	

* ***1903 Remington Modified*** – Remington mfg. approx. 9,000 from October-December 1940.

	$6,500	$5,500	$4,000	$3,500	$3,000	$2,500	$1,500	

* ***1903 Remington*** – Remington mfg. approx. 345,000 1941-1942.

	$4,000	$3,500	$2,750	$2,500	$1,850	$1,500	$1,000	

1903 NATIONAL MATCH (PRE-1929)

	$6,000	$5,000	$4,500	$3,500	$2,500	$1,750	$1,250	

1903-A1 NATIONAL MATCH (1929 to 1939)

	$6,500	$6,000	$5,000	$4,000	$2,750	$1,950	$1,250	

1903-A3 – .30-06 cal., similar to 1903, with production modifications, aperture rear sight, no finger groove in forestock, lower quality finish, stamped floorplate and barrel band. Mfg. WWII by Remington and Smith Corona.

	$3,000	$2,500	$1,500	$850	$600	$450	$400	

Add 15% for Smith Corona mfg.

1903-A3 NATIONAL MATCH – 200 mfg., known as the "unmatched" match rifle.

	$3,700	$3,350	$3,000	$2,600	$2,200	$1,875	$1,625	

1903-A4 SNIPER (WWII) – .30-06 cal., with M73B1 or M84 scope in Redfield mount, no front sight.

	$6,500	$4,500	$4,000	$2,500	$1,800	$1,200	$1,000	

Subtract 30% if reworked with parkerized small parts.

1903 MARINE SNIPER – .30-06 cal., includes 8X Unertl scope.

	$22,500	$18,000	$15,000	$8,000	$5,000	$3,000	$2,000	

Original condition is key for values listed above. Be very careful and get an evaluation from a dealer/collector who knows the difference before buying/selling.

1903 NRA NATIONAL MATCH – .30-06 cal., similar to 1903, with hand selected and custom fit parts, produced for target shooting. "NRA" and flaming bomb proofed on trigger guard with 1915 date.

	$6,000	$5,500	$4,500	$3,000	$1,500	$995	$900	

1903 SPORTER – .30-06 cal., similar to National Match, with sporter stock and Lyman sight.

	$6,000	$4,800	$4,000	$3,000	$1,500	$1,000	$850	

1903 MATCH STYLE T – .30-06 cal., 26, 28, or 30 in. barrel, similar to Sporter, heavy barrel, globe sight, and target bases.

Excellent original condition specimens have been seen with asking prices in the $8,500-$10,000+ range.

1903 FREE RIFLE TYPE A – .30-06 cal., similar to Style T, with 28-30 in. barrel, and Swiss hook butt.

Excellent original condition specimens have been seen with asking prices in the $8,500-$10,000+ range.

1903 FREE RIFLE TYPE B – .30-06 cal., similar to Type A, with double-set triggers, cheekpiece stock, modified firing pin.

Excellent original condition specimens have been seen with asking prices in the $8,500-$15,000+ range.

SPRINGFIELD MODEL 1922 MATCH RIFLE – .30-06 cal., headless cocking piece, 24 in. tapered very heavy barrel, Lyman 48B and 48C receiver and undercut blade front sights.

Excellent original condition specimens have been seen with asking prices in the $10,000-$15,000 range.

GRADING - PPGS™	100%	98%	95%	90%	80%	70%	60%	LAST MSR

MODEL 1922-M1 – .22 LR cal., Target Rifle, 5 shot mag., 24 in. barrel, modified 1903, Lyman receiver sight, sporter stock, issued 1927.

Blue finish	$2,500	$1,800	$1,750	$1,500	$1,000	$600	$500	

MODEL 1922 NRA VARIATION – not tapped for scope, without forend grooves, blue finish. Issued 1922-26.

	$3,750	$3,400	$3,000	$2,000	$1,800	$1,500	$1,250	

M2 .22 TARGET RIFLE – similar to 1922 M1, except improved lock time, adj. head space bolt design.

	$2,500	$1,800	$1,500	$1,000	$700	$600	$550	

RIFLES: SEMI-AUTO

Please refer to the U.S. Military section for more information on previously manufactured military and commercial M1 carbines and Garands.

RIFLES/CARBINES: SINGLE SHOT

MODEL 1870 ROLLING-BLOCK RIFLE, U.S.N. – .50 cal. centerfire, 32 5/8 in. barrel, not serial numbered, 22,013 mfg.

	N/A	$2,500	$2,200	$1,950	$1,500	$1,100	$900	

MODEL 1871 ROLLING-BLOCK RIFLE, U.S.A. – .50 cal. centerfire, 36 in. barrel, not serial numbered, 10,001 mfg.

	N/A	$2,150	$1,750	$1,350	$1,000	$900	$750	

MODEL 1873 RIFLE "TRAPDOOR" – .45-70 Govt. cal., 32 5/8 in. barrel, 2 bands. Approx. 73,000 mfg. between 1873-77.

	$2,500	$2,200	$1,800	$1,500	$1,150	$775	$650	

Subtract 40% if stock cartouche faint or absent.

MODEL 1884 RIFLE "TRAPDOOR" – .45-70 Govt. cal., 32 5/8 in. barrel, 2 bands. Approx. 232,000 mfg. between 1885-1890.

	$2,250	$1,850	$1,450	$975	$725	$625	$525	

Subtract 40% if stock cartouche faint or absent.

MODEL 1884 CARBINE "TRAPDOOR" – .45-70 Govt. cal., similar to Model 1879 Carbine with 22 in. barrel, half stock, single barrel band, Buffington rear sight, barrel band grooved on top to allowing for sight leaf to rest, approx. ser. no. range 325,000 - 480,000. Approx. 20,000 mfg. 1886-1889.

	N/A	$3,500	$2,850	$2,300	$1,950	$1,500	$1,000	

MODEL 1873 CARBINE – 22 in. barrel, half stock, single barrel band/stacking swivel, 20,000 made, but semi-scarce.

	N/A	$6,000	$5,250	$4,250	$3,250	$2,750	$2,250	

Add up to 50% for Pre-Custer serial numbers below 43,700 (pre-1876 mfg.).
Subtract 50% for faint or no stock cartouche.

MODEL 1873 CADET RIFLE – .45-70 Govt. cal., 29 1/2 in. barrel, stacking swivel, no sling swivels.

	$2,500	$2,000	$1,475	$1,100	$925	$775	$650	

Subtract $100 for variation with sling-swivels.
Subtract 25-35% if restocked with buttplate and hole drilled for cleaning tools.

MODEL 1875 OFFICER'S RIFLE FIRST TYPE – .45-70 Govt. cal., 477 mfg. between 1875 and 1886, 26 in. barrel, single barrel band. Not serial numbered, some dated, three different types, with First Type being the most desirable (approx. 125 mfg. 1875-1877), Second Type had approx. 250 mfg. 1877-1881, and Third Type has approx. 100 mfg. during 1885 only, not issued by U.S. government, but sold to Army officers for sporting use.

	N/A	$39,000	$34,000	$27,000	$23,000	$17,500	$15,000	

Approx. 25 rifles were mfg. prior to the standardization of this model.

MODEL 1875 SPRINGFIELD LEE VERTICAL ACTION – 32 1/2 in. barrel, 143 rifles in .45-70 US Govt. cal. were manufactured at Springfield Armory in 1875, as per 1874 Congressional appropriation of $10,000. Rifles were issued to companies of the 1st and 20th Infantry Regiments for field trials. Rifles were withdrawn, declared surplus and purchased by Bannerman's who later sold them in his catalog for $36.

	N/A	$15,000	$12,000	$10,000	$8,000	$6,000	$4,000	

MODEL 1877 RIFLE – .45-70 Govt. cal., mfg. 3,943.

	N/A	$3,000	$2,650	$2,250	$1,875	$1,625	$1,325	

GRADING - PPGS™	100%	98%	95%	90%	80%	70%	60%	LAST MSR

MODEL 1877 CARBINE – .45-70 Govt. cal., 22 in. barrel, "C" rear sight to 1,200 yards. Mfg. 2,946.

	N/A	$4,750	$4,250	$3,850	$3,300	$2,850	$2,450	

MODEL 1877 CADET RIFLE – .45-70 Govt. cal., 29 1/2 in. barrel. 1,050 mfg.

	N/A	$2,000	$1,400	$1,100	$950	$900	$800	

MODEL 1879 RIFLE – .45-70 Govt. cal., approx. 140,000 mfg.

	$1,800	$1,400	$1,150	$950	$850	$700	$650	

MODEL 1879 CARBINE – .45-70 Govt. cal., no stacking swivel. Approx. 15,000 mfg.

	N/A	$3,500	$2,850	$2,300	$1,950	$1,500	$1,000	

MODEL 1879 CADET RIFLE – .45-70 Govt. cal., stacking swivel but no sling swivels. 5,000 mfg.

	$2,000	$1,600	$1,150	$950	$775	$650	$600	

MODEL 1880 – .45-70 Govt. cal., combination triangular, sliding type, bayonet-ramrod. 1,001 mfg.

	N/A	$2,800	$2,200	$1,950	$1,650	$1,325	$1,050	

SHOTGUNS: SINGLE SHOT

MODEL 1881 FORAGER – 20 ga., 1,376 mfg. 1881-1885. Be cautious when purchasing.

	N/A	$3,000	$2,500	$1,800	$1,500	$1,300	$1,150	

SPRINGFIELD ARMORY (MFG. BY SPRINGFIELD INC.)

Current trademark manufactured by Springfield Inc., located in Geneseo, IL. Springfield Inc. has also imported a variety of models. This company was named Springfield Armory, Geneseo, IL until 1992.

The government owned Springfield Armory closed in 1968, and the "Springfield Armory" trademark was purchased by a private individual in the early 1970s. Initially, the new company manufactured a semi-automatic M14, but when the BATF disapproved the model name, it became the M1A. The company was then sold to the Reese family, and it was moved to Geneseo, IL. Springfield Inc. manufactures commercial pistols and rifles, including reproductions of older military handguns and rifles. For more information and current pricing on both new and used Springfield Armory airguns, please refer to the *Blue Book of Airguns,* edited by Dennis A. Adler and Tom Gaylord (also available online).

COMBINATION GUNS

M6 SCOUT RIFLE – .22 LR, .22 WMR (disc.), or .22 Hornet cal. over smoothbore .410 bore w/3 in. chamber, O/U Survival Gun, 14 (legal transfer needed) or 18 1/4 in. barrels, parkerized or stainless steel (new 1995), approx. 4 lbs. Disc. 2004.

	100%	98%	95%	90%	80%	70%	60%	
.22 LR/.22 Win. Mag. cal.	$425	$375	$325	$275	$250	$225	$195	
.22 Hornet cal.	$775	$725	$650	$550	$475	$400	$325	

Last MSR was $215.

Add approx. 10% for stainless steel.
Add 10% for lockable Marine flotation plastic carrying case.

Early mfg. does not incorporate a trigger guard while late production had a trigger guard.

M6 SCOUT PISTOL/CARBINE – .22 LR or .22 Hornet cal. over .45 LC/.410 bore, 16 in. barrels, parkerized or stainless steel. Mfg. 2002-2004.

	100%	98%	95%	90%	80%	70%	60%	
.22 LR cal.	$425	$375	$325	$275	$250	$225	$195	
.22 Hornet cal.	$775	$725	$650	$550	$475	$400	$325	

Last MSR was $223.

Add 10% for stainless steel.
Add approx. $200 per interchangeable 10 in. pistol barrel assembly.
Add 15% for detachable stock.

This model was also available with an optional detachable stock ($49-$59 MSR, not legal with a rifled barrel less than 16 in. or smoothbore less than 18 in.).

M6 SCOUT PISTOL – .22 LR or .22 Hornet cal. over .45 LC/.410 bore, 10 in. barrels, parkerized or stainless steel. Mfg. 2002-2004.

	100%	98%	95%	90%	80%	70%	60%	
.22 LR cal.	$425	$375	$325	$275	$250	$225	$195	
.22 Hornet cal.	$775	$725	$650	$550	$475	$400	$325	

Last MSR was $199.

Add approx. 10% for stainless steel.
Add approx. $200 per interchangeable 16 in. carbine barrel.

GRADING - PPGS™	100%	98%	95%	90%	80%	70%	60%	LAST MSR

PISTOLS: SEMI-AUTO

HELLCAT 3 MICRO COMPACT – 9mm Para. cal., 3 in. hammer forged steel barrel, 11 shot (w/pinky extension) mag. and 13 shot extended mag., reversible mag. release and flush plate, flat trigger, U-dot Tritium/luminescent front and tactical rack rear sights, optional Viridian E Series laser sight, black polymer textured adaptive grips, billet machined slide, top slide serrations, dual captive recoil spring w/full length guide rod, loaded chamber indicator, standard accessory rail, black Melonite or Desert FDE (new 2020) Cerakote finish, 18.3 oz. (flush mag.) or 18.6 oz. (extended mag.). New late 2019.

MSR $569	$485	$425	$350	$325	$275	$225	$175	

Add 7.5% (MSR $610) for Desert FDE Cerakote finish (new 2020).

* ***Hellcat 3 Micro Compact OSP*** – 9mm Para. cal., 3 in. hammer forged steel barrel, 11 shot (w/pinky extension) and 13 shot extended mag., reversible mag. release and flush plate, flat trigger, U-dot Tritium/luminescent front and tactical rack rear sights, optics ready, optional Viridian E Series laser sight, black polymer textured adaptive grips, billet machined slide, top slide serrations, dual captive recoil spring w/full length guide rod, loaded chamber indicator, standard accessory rail, black Melonite or Desert FDE Cerakote (new 2020) finish, 17.9 oz. (flush mag.) or 18.3 oz. (extended mag.). New late 2019.

MSR $599	$500	$450	$375	$350	$275	$225	$175	

Add 7.5% (MSR $643) for Desert FDE Cerakote finish (new 2020).

» **Hellcat 3 Micro Compact OSP W/ Shield SMSC** – similar to the Hellcat 3 Micro Compact OSP except has a Shield SMSC, available in black Melonite finish. New 2021.

MSR $799	$680	$595	$510	$460	$375	$305	$240	

OMEGA PISTOL – .38 Super, 10mm Norma, or .45 ACP cal., SA, ported slide, 5 or 6 in. interchangeable ported or unported barrel with Polygon rifling, special lockup system eliminates normal barrel link and bushing, Pachmayr grips, dual extractors, adj. rear sight. Mfg. 1987-1990.

	$1,000	$875	$750	$675	$550	$450	$350	*$849*

Add 75% (Last MSR was $1,512) for interchangeable conversion units.
Add 40% (Last MSR was $1,185) for interchangeable 5 or 6 in. barrel (including factory installation).

Each conversion unit includes an entire slide assembly, one mag., 5 or 6 in barrel, recoil spring guide mechanism assembly, and factory fitting.

OMEGA MATCH – same cals. as Omega, except has low profile combat sights, 8 shot mag., and beveled magwell. Mfg. 1991-92 only.

	$1,100	$950	$825	$750	$600	$500	$400	*$1,103*

Pistols: Semi-Auto - P9 Series

MODEL P9 – 9mm Para., 9x21mm (new 1991), .40 S&W (new 1991), or .45 ACP cal., patterned after the Czech CZ-75, DA/SA, blue (standard beginning 1993), parkerized (standard until 1992), or duotone finish, various barrel lengths, checkered walnut grips. Mfg. in U.S. starting 1990.

* ***Model P9 Standard*** – 4.72 in. barrel, 15 shot (9mm Para.), 11 shot (.40 S&W), or 10 shot (.45 ACP) mag., parkerized finish standard until 1992 - blue finish beginning 1993, 32.16 oz. Disc. 1993.

	$475	$375	$335	$295	$275	$240	$215	*$518*

Add $61 for .45 ACP cal.
Add $182 for duotone finish (disc. 1992).
Subtract $40 for parkerized finish.

In 1992, Springfield added a redesigned stainless steel trigger, patented sear safety which disengages the trigger from the double action mechanism when the safety is on, lengthened the beavertail grip area offering less "pinch," and added a two-piece slide stop design.

* ***Model P9 Stainless*** – similar to P9 Standard, except is constructed from stainless steel, 35.3 oz. Mfg. 1991-93.

	$550	$425	$350	$285	$250	$215	$185	*$589*

Add $50 for .45 ACP cal.

* ***Model P9 Compact*** – 9mm Para. or .40 S&W cal., 3.66 in. barrel, 13 shot (9mm Para.) or 10 shot (.40 S&W) mag., shorter slide and frame, rounded trigger guard, 30 1/2 oz. Disc. 1992.

	$425	$350	$300	$275	$250	$225	$200	*$499*

Add $20 for .40 S&W cal.
Add $20-$30 for blue finish depending on cal.
Add $78 for duotone finish.

GRADING - PPGS™	100%	98%	95%	90%	80%	70%	60%	LAST MSR

* ***Model P9 Sub-Compact*** – 9mm Para. or .40 S&W cal., smaller frame than the P9 Compact, 3.66 in. barrel, 12 shot (9mm Para.) or 9 shot (.40 S&W) finger extension mag., squared-off trigger guard, 30.1 oz. Disc. 1992.

$425	$350	$300	$275	$250	$225	$200	*$499*

Add $20 for .40 S&W cal.

Add $20-$30 for blue finish depending on cal.

* ***Model P9 Factory Comp*** – 9mm Para., .40 S&W, or .45 ACP cal., 5 1/2 in. barrel (with compensator attached), extended sear safety and mag. release, adj. rear sight, slim competition checkered wood grips, choice of all stainless (disc. 1992) or stainless bi-tone (matte black slide), dual port compensator, 15 shot (9mm Para.), 11 shot (.40 S&W), or 10 shot (.45 ACP) mag., 33.9 oz. Mfg. 1992-93.

$650	$525	$450	$420	$390	$360	$330	*$699*

Add $36 for .45 ACP cal.

Add $75-$100 for all stainless finish.

* ***Model P9 Ultra IPSC (LSP)*** – competition model with 5.03 in. barrel (long slide ported), adj. rear sight, choice of parkerized (standard finish until 1992 when disc.), blue (disc. 1992), bi-tone (became standard 1993), or stainless steel (disc. 1992) finish, extended thumb safety, and rubberized competition (9mm Para. and .40 S&W cals. only) or checkered walnut (.45 ACP cal. only) grips, 15 shot (9mm Para.), 11 shot (.40 S&W), or 10 shot (.45 ACP) mag., 34.6 oz. Disc. 1993.

$700	$475	$415	$350	$300	$275	$250	*$694*

Add $30 for .45 ACP cal.

* ***Model P9 Ultra LSP Stainless*** – stainless steel variation of the P9 Ultra LSP. Mfg. 1991-92.

$725	$525	$425	$360	$315	$260	$225	*$769*

Add $30 for .40 S&W cal.

Add $90 for .45 ACP cal.

* ***Model P9 World Cup*** – see listing under 1911-A1 Custom Models heading.

Pistols: Semi-Auto - R-Series

PANTHER MODEL – 9mm Para., .40 S&W, or .45 ACP cal., DA/SA, 3.8 in. barrel, hammer drop or firing pin safety, 15 shot (9mm Para.), 11 shot (.40 S&W), or 9 shot (.45 ACP) mag., Commander hammer, frame mounted slide stop, narrow profile, non-glare blue finish only, walnut grips, squared-off trigger guard, 29 oz. Mfg. 1992 only.

$600	$500	$400	$350	$300	$275	$250	*$609*

FIRECAT MODEL – 9mm Para. or .40 S&W cal., SA, 3 1/2 in. barrel, 3-dot low profile sights, all steel mfg., firing pin block and frame mounted ambidextrous safety, 8 shot (9mm Para.) or 7 shot (.40 S&W) mag., checkered combat style trigger guard and front/rear gripstraps, non-glare blue finish, 35 3/4 oz. Mfg. 1992-1993.

$550	$450	$400	$350	$300	$275	$250	*$569*

BOBCAT MODEL – while advertised in 1992, this model was never mfg.

LINX MODEL – while advertised in 1992, this model was never mfg.

Pistols: Semi-Auto - Disc. 1911-A1 Models

MODEL 1911-A1 STANDARD MODEL – .38 Super, 9mm Para., 10mm (new 1990), or .45 ACP cal., patterned after the Colt M1911-A1, 5.04 (Standard) or 4.025 (Commander or Compact Model) in. barrel, SA, 7 shot (Compact), 8 shot (.45 ACP), 9 shot (10mm), or 10 shot (9mm Para. and .38 Super) mag., walnut grips, parkerized, blue, or duotone finish. Mfg. 1985-1990.

$450	$360	$330	$300	$280	$260	$240	*$454*

Add $35 for blue finish.

Add $80 for duotone finish.

This model was also available with a .45 ACP to 9mm Para. conversion kit for $170 in parkerized finish, or $175 in blue finish.

* ***Model 1911-A1 Standard Defender Model*** – .45 ACP cal. only, similar to Standard 1911-A1 Model, except has fixed combat sights, beveled magwell, extended thumb safety, bobbed hammer, flared ejection port, walnut grips, factory serrated front strap and two stainless steel magazines, parkerized or blue finish. Mfg. 1988-90.

$485	$435	$375	$340	$300	$280	$260	*$567*

Add $35 for blue finish.

GRADING - PPGS™	100%	98%	95%	90%	80%	70%	60%	LAST MSR

* ***Model 1911-A1 Standard Commander Model*** – .45 ACP cal. only, similar to Standard 1911-A1 Model, except has 3.63 in. barrel, shortened slide, Commander hammer, low profile 3-dot sights, walnut grips, parkerized, blue, or duotone finish. Mfg. in 1990 only.

	$450	$415	$350	$325	$285	$260	$245	*$514*

Add $30 for blue finish.
Add $80 for duotone finish.

* ***Model 1911-A1 Standard Combat Commander Model*** – .45 ACP cal. only, 4 1/4 in. barrel, bobbed hammer, walnut grips. Mfg. 1988-89.

	$435	$385	$325	$295	$275	$250	$230	

Add $20 for blue finish.

* ***Model 1911-A1 Standard Compact Model*** – .45 ACP cal. only, compact variation featuring shortened Commander barrel and slide, reduced M1911 straight gripstrap frame, checkered walnut grips, low profile 3-dot sights, extended slide stop, combat hammer, parkerized, blue, or duotone finish. Mfg. 1990 only.

	$450	$415	$350	$325	$285	$260	$245	*$514*

Add $30 for blue finish.
Add $80 for duotone finish.

* ***Model 1911-A1 Standard Custom Carry Gun*** – .38 Super (special order only), 9mm Para., 10mm (new 1990), or .45 ACP cal., similar to Defender Model, except has tuned trigger pull, heavy recoil spring, extended thumb safety, and other features. Mfg. 1988-disc.

	$860	$725	$660	$535	$460	$420	$385	*$969*

Add $130 for .38 Super Ramped, 10mm was POR.

* ***Model 1911-A1 Standard National Match Hardball Model*** – .38 Super (disc.), 9mm Para. (disc.), or .45 ACP cal., National Match barrel and bushing, specially fitted frame and slide, Bo-Mar adj. rear sight, Herrett walnut grips, plastic cased. Mfg. 1988-90.

	$780	$650	$565	$515	$460	$415	$385	*$897*

This model was made specifically for DCM competition shooting.

* ***Model 1911-A1 Standard Bullseye Wadcutter Model*** – .45 ACP cal. only, designed for wadcutter loads only, 5 or 6 (ported or unported) in. barrel, Bo-Mar rib mounted on slide, checkered gripstraps, match trigger, beavertail grip safety, polished feed ramp and throated barrel. Mfg. 1989-disc.

	$1,415	$1,200	$1,025	$925	$825	$750	$675	*$1,599*

Add $25 for 6 in. barrel.
Add $80 for 6 in. ported barrel.

* ***Model 1911-A1 Standard Trophy Master Competition Pistol*** – .38 Super, 9mm Para. (disc.), 10mm (new 1990), or .45 ACP cal., competition model which includes low profile combat sights, ambidextrous safety, long match trigger, bobbed hammer, Pachmayr wraparound grips. Mfg. 1988-90.

	$1,400	$1,100	$950	$875	$800	$730	$660	*$1,443*

Add $130 for .38 Super with supported chamber, 10mm was POR.

* ***Model 1911-A1 Standard Trophy Master Competition Expert Model*** – .38 Super, 9mm Para. (disc.), 10mm (new 1990), or .45 ACP cal., mfg. for IPSC competition shooting, dual chamber compensator system on match barrel, blue finish, ambidextrous thumb safety, beveled and polished magwell, lowered and flared ejection port, wraparound Pachmayr grips, shock buffer, includes 2 mags. and plastic carrying case. Mfg. 1988-90.

	$1,675	$1,450	$1,225	$1,025	$950	$890	$850	*$1,664*

Add $130 for .38 Super with supported chamber, 10mm was POR.

This model was an improved variation of the Master Grade Competition Pistol "A."

* ***Model 1911-A1 Standard Trophy Master Competition Distinguished Model*** – similar to Expert Model, except has brushed hard chrome finish, checkered gripstraps and trigger guard, top-of-the-line competition model. Mfg. 1988-1990.

	$2,000	$1,675	$1,450	$1,225	$1,025	$950	$875	*$2,275*

Add $130 for .38 Super with supported chamber, 10mm was POR.
Subtract $130 for "B" Model.

This model was an improved variation of the Master Grade Competition Pistol "B-1."

GRADING - PPGS™	100%	98%	95%	90%	80%	70%	60%	LAST MSR

Pistols: Semi-Auto - 1911-A1, Single Action (90s Series)

The initials "PDP" refer to Springfield's Personal Defense Pistol series.

Beginning in 2000, Springfield Armory started offering a Loaded Promotion package on their 1911-A1 pistol line. Many of these features and options are found on the FBI's Hostage Rescue Teams (HRT) pistol contract with Springfield Armory. Standard features of this Loaded Promotion package are hammer forged premium air-gauged barrel, front and rear cocking serrations, Novak patented low profile sights or Bo-Mar type adj. sights, extended thumb safety, tactical beavertail, flat mainspring housing, Cocobolo grips, High Hand grip, lightweight match trigger, full length guide rod, and machine beveled mag. well. This promotion includes all pistols except the Mil-Spec Model 1911 A1.

In 2001, Springfield's Custom Loaded 1911-A1 Series pistols came equipped standard with Springfield's integral locking system, carry bevel, hammer forged premium air-gauged barrel, front and rear cocking serrations, Novak patented low profile sights (some models come equipped with Tritium sights or Bo-Mar type adj. sights), extended thumb safety, tactical beavertail, flat mainspring housing, Cocobolo grips, high hand grip, lightweight adj. match trigger, full length guide rod, machine beveled magwell, and a "loaded" coupon ($600 consumer savings). These Custom Loaded features will vary by model. All models with less than a 5 in. and all alloy pistols supplied with ramped, fully supported barrels.

Beginning 2002, every Springfield pistol is equipped with a patented integral locking system (I.L.S., keyed in the rear gripstrap) at no extra charge.

Beginning 2007, most models were shipped with an 11 gear system, including one (GI models only) or two mags., belt holster, magazine pouch, and bore brush supplied in a lockable blue plastic case.

In 2015 all Loaded pistols include the 11 Gear System which consists of a paddle holster, double magazine pouch, and a new 1911 case.

PDP DEFENDER MODEL – .40 S&W (disc. 1992) or .45 ACP cal., standard pistol with slide and barrel shortened to Champion length (4 in.), tapered cone dual port compensator system, fully adj. sights, Videcki speed trigger, rubber grips, Commander style hammer, serrated front strap, parkerized (disc. 1992), duotone/bi-tone, or blue (disc. 1993) finish. Mfg. 1991-1998.

	100%	98%	95%	90%	80%	70%	60%	LAST MSR
	$850	$745	$635	$580	$465	$380	$295	*$992*

* ***PDP Defender Model Factory Comp*** – .38 Super (disc.) or .45 ACP cal. only, entry level IPSC gun, 5 5/8 in. barrel with compensator attached, adj. rear sight, Videki speed trigger, checkered walnut grips, beveled magwell, 10 shot (.38 Super) or 8 shot (.45 ACP) mag., blue finish only, 40 oz. Mfg. 1991-2000.

	100%	98%	95%	90%	80%	70%	60%	LAST MSR
	$900	$785	$675	$610	$495	$400	$315	*$1,049*

* ***PDP Defender Model High Capacity Factory Compensated*** – .38 Super (disc.) or .45 ACP cal. only, blue finish. Mfg. 1995-2000.

	100%	98%	95%	90%	80%	70%	60%	LAST MSR
	$955	$835	$715	$650	$525	$430	$335	*$1,109*

1911-A1 90s EDITION (CUSTOM LOADED) – .38 Super, 9mm Para., 10mm (disc. 1991), .40 S&W, or .45 ACP cal., patterned after the Colt M1911-A1, except has linkless operating system, 5.04 (Standard) or 4 (Champion or Compact Model) in. barrel, 7 shot (Compact), 8 shot (.40 S&W or .45 ACP Standard), 9 shot (9mm Para., 10mm, or .38 Super), or 10 shot (.38 Super) mag., checkered walnut grips, parkerized (.38 Super beginning 1994 or .45 ACP beginning 1993), blue or duotone (disc. 1992) finish. New 1991.

* ***1911-A1 90s Edition Mil-Spec "Defend Your Legacy"*** – .38 Super (disc. 2011) or .45 ACP cal., 5 in. stainless steel barrel, blue (disc.), 7 shot, parkerized, matte stainless, bi-tone (mfg. 2004 only), or OD Green (mfg. 2004 only) finish, 3-dot Hi-Viz fixed combat sights, standard loaded features include belt holster, double mag. pouch and extra set of grips (Mil-Spec Package), 39 oz. New 1991.

	100%	98%	95%	90%	80%	70%	60%	LAST MSR
MSR $640	$550	$480	$415	$375	$305	$250	$195	

Add $17 for blue finish (disc. 2001).

Add $21 for OD Green or bi-tone finish (mfg. 2004 only).

Subtract approx. $70 if without Mil-Spec package (became standard in 2012, includes belt holster, double mag. pouch and extra set of grips, introduced 2009).

Add $631 for .38 Super cal. in High Polish Nickel (Acusport exclusive 2004-2007).

Add $92 for matte stainless finish.

» **1911-A1 90s Edition Mil Spec Stainless Steel "Defend Your Legacy"** – .45 ACP cal., full size frame and slide, all stainless construction, 5 in. match grade stainless steel barrel, slanted serrations on rear of slide, standard spur hammer and grip safety, arched style mainspring housing with I.L.S., single-sided non-extended thumb safety, combat trigger, fixed combat 3-dot sights, lowered and flared ejection port, cross cannon emblazoned walnut grips, polished finish on flat surfaces, matte finish on rounded areas, includes Mil-Spec Package. New 2003.

	100%	98%	95%	90%	80%	70%	60%	LAST MSR
MSR $849	$725	$635	$550	$475	$400	$325	$250	

GRADING - PPGS™	100%	98%	95%	90%	80%	70%	60%	LAST MSR

* ***1911-A1 90s Edition Mil-Spec Operator*** – .45 ACP cal. only, similar to Mil-Spec 1911-A1, except has Picatinny light mounting system forged into lower front of frame, parkerized finish only. Disc. 2002.

	$615	$540	$460	$420	$340	$275	$215	*$756*

* ***1911-A1 90s Edition Loaded Operator*** – .45 ACP cal. only, similar to full size service model, except has Picatinny accessory rail forged into lower front of frame, checkered hardwood (disc. 2003), plastic grips, OD Green slide with black bi-tone Armory Kote finished frame, Novak low mount Tritium (disc.) or Trijicon night sights. New 2002.

MSR $1,308	$1,100	$950	$850	$750	$625	$500	$400	

* ***1911-A1 90s Edition Loaded Black Operator (Long Beach Contract Operator)*** – .45 ACP cal., 5 in. stainless steel match grade barrel, two 8 shot mags. with Slam pad, GI-style recoil system, forged steel slide with Black Armory Kote finish, forged steel frame with integral accessory rail and Black Armory Kote finish, extended ambidextrous thumb safety, ergonomic beavertail grip safety, Delta hammer, extended trigger, G10 grips, fixed combat 3-dot Tritium sights, includes 11 Gear System, 43 oz. New 2015.

MSR $1,409	$1,250	$1,075	$900	$795	$650	$525	$425	

* ***1911-A1 90s Edition Loaded Marine Corps Operator*** – .45 ACP cal., 5 in. stainless steel match grade barrel, two 7 shot mags., GI-style recoil system, full size steel frame with integral accessory rail and Olive Drab Armory Kote finish, forged steel slide with front and rear slanted serrations and Black Armory Kote finish, low profile combat 3-dot tritium sights, flat mainspring housing with I.L.S., Delta hammer, beavertail grip safety, long aluminum match grade trigger, extended ambidextrous thumb safety, lowered and flared ejection port, G10 grips, 43 oz. New 2015.

MSR $1,308	$1,100	$950	$850	$750	$625	$500	$400	

* ***1911-A1 90s Edition Loaded Lightweight Operator*** – .45 ACP cal. only, 5 in. stainless steel barrel, blue finish, 7 shot mag., fixed low profile combat rear sight, dovetail front sight, Cocobolo grips, 34 oz. Mfg. 2006-2020.

	$1,050	$925	$795	$725	$600	$495	$385	*$1,210*

* ***1911-A1 90s Edition Loaded Standard or Lightweight Model*** – .45 ACP cal. (current mfg.), Standard model has parkerized, blue (disc.), or OD Green with Armory Kote (mfg. 2002-2014) finish, Custom Loaded features became standard in 2001, Lightweight Model was mfg. 1995-2012 with either matte (disc. 2002), bi-tone (mfg. 2003-2012) or blue (mfg. 1993-disc.) finish, current mfg. is w/either Novak low mount or Trijicon night sights, 28.6 or 35.6 oz.

MSR $950	$845	$735	$625	$550	$475	$375	$295	

Add $52 for Lightweight Model (with Trijicon night sights), disc. 2012.
Subtract approx. 10%-25% if w/o Custom Loaded features (new 2001), depending on condition.

* ***1911-A1 90s Edition Loaded Stainless Standard Model*** – 9mm Para. (mfg. 1994-2012), .38 Super (disc.), .40 S&W (mfg. 2001-2002), or .45 ACP cal., 7 (.45 ACP cal.), 8 (.40 S&W), or 9 (9mm Para.) shot mag., Custom Loaded features became standard in 2001, wraparound rubber (disc.) or checkered hardwood grips, 11 Gear system holster became standard 2009, Novak Lo-Mount (disc.), Bo-Mar type (mfg. 1996-2001), or combat 3-dot sights, beveled magwell, 39.2 oz. New 1991.

MSR $1,004	$885	$795	$695	$585	$485	$395	$325	

Add $62 for 9mm Para. cal. (disc. 2012), or $32 for .40 S&W cal. (disc.).
Add $230 for Tactical Combat Model with combat features and black stainless steel (mfg. 2005-disc.).
Add $50 for Bo-Mar type sights (disc. 2001).
Add $202 for long slide variation in .45 Super cal. with V16 porting and Bo-Mar sights (disc.).

* ***1911-A1 90s Edition Stainless Super Tuned Standard*** – .45 ACP cal. only, super tuned by the Custom Shop, 7 shot mag., 5 in. barrel, Novak fixed Lo-Mount sights, 39.2 oz. Mfg. 1997-99.

	$875	$765	$655	$595	$480	$395	$305	*$995*

* ***1911-A1 90s Edition Target Model*** – 9mm Para. or .45 ACP cal., includes Custom Loaded features, stainless steel or black stainless steel (mfg. 2003-2012), with (.45 ACP cal. only) or w/o V12 ported barrel, adj. sights, 38 oz. Mfg. 2001-2014.

	$975	$850	$700	$630	$510	$415	$325	*$1,118*

Add $166 for black stainless steel with adj. Trijicon sights (.45 ACP cal. only). Disc. 2012.
Subtract approx. $15 for non-ported V12 barrel.

* ***1911-A1 90s Edition Trophy Match*** – .40 S&W (mfg. 2001-2005) or .45 ACP cal. only, top-of-the-line pistol featuring improved trigger pull, adj. rear sight, 5 in. match grade barrel and bushing, Custom Loaded features became standard in 2001, choice of Armory Kote (.40 S&W cal. only, new 2001), stainless steel, bi-tone (disc.), or blue (disc.) finish, 35.6 oz. Mfg. 1994-2014.

	$1,375	$1,195	$1,025	$920	$740	$605	$470	*$1,605*

Add $10 for bi-tone finish (disc.).
Add $8 for High Capacity Trophy Match (disc.).
Subtract $100 for blue finish (disc.).

GRADING - PPGS™	100%	98%	95%	90%	80%	70%	60%	LAST MSR

* ***1911-A1 90s Edition Standard High Capacity*** – 9mm Para. (disc.) or .45 ACP cal., 5 in. barrel, blue (disc. 2001) or matte parkerized (new 1996) finish with plastic grips, 3-dot fixed combat sights, 10 shot (except for law enforcement) mag. Mfg. 1995-2003.

	$635	$555	$475	$430	$350	$285	$220	*$756*

Add $50 for blue finish (disc.).

* ***1911-A1 90s Edition Stainless High Capacity*** – similar to Standard High Capacity, except is stainless steel. Mfg. 1996-2000.

	$675	$590	$505	$460	$370	$305	$235	*$819*

* ***1911-A1 90s Edition XM4 High Capacity Model*** – 9mm Para. or .45 ACP cal., features widened frame for high capacity mag., blue (mfg. 1993 only) or stainless finish only. Mfg. 1993-1994.

	$595	$520	$445	$405	$325	$270	$210	*$689*

1911-A1 TACTICAL RESPONSE PISTOL (TRP SERIES) – .45 ACP cal., forged National Match frame and slide, 5 in. stainless steel barrel, 7 shot mag., front strap checkering, low profile fixed combat 3-dot Tritium sights, extended beveled magwell, Black Armory Kote or stainless steel finish, checkered rosewood (disc.) or black/grey G10 grips, 36 oz. New 1999.

MSR $1,648	$1,395	$1,225	$1,025	$925	$775	$650	$550	

* ***1911-A1 TRP Operator*** – .45 ACP or 10mm (mfg. 2018-2020) cal., forged National Match frame with 1/2, 3/4 (6 in. barrel only), or full-length accesory rail, 5 or 6 (new 2018) in. stainless steel match grade barrel, 7 or 8 (10mm only) shot mag., adj. Trijicon night sights, Black/Grey G10 or OD green finish Octo-Grip texture (mfg. 2018-2020 on 10mm only) grips, Black Armory Kote or Tactical Gray (mfg. 2017-2020) finish, 4 1/2-5 1/2 lbs. New mid-2008.

MSR $1,730	$1,475	$1,275	$1,050	$950	$800	$675	$575	

Add $60 for 10mm cal. (mfg. 2018-2020).
Add $112 for 6 in. barrel.

1911-A1 TRP 10MM - RMR – 10mm cal., GI-style recoil system, forged National Match heavy frame, 5 or 6 in. match grade stainless steel barrel with Nitride finish, two 8 shot stainless steel mags. with Slam Pad, SA magwell, forged steel slide with rear cocking serrations, Trijicon Ruggedized Miniature Reflex (RMR) mount with integrated night sights, green/black (5 in. barrel) or black (6 in. barrel) G10 grips, Posi-Lock front strap and mainspring housing, Black-T finish on frame and slide, 6 in. model has OD Green finish on frame, 44-50 oz. Mfg. mid-2018-2020.

	$1,950	$1,700	$1,465	$1,325	$1,075	$885	$685	*$2,238*

Add $51 for 6 in. barrel.

1911-A1 LONG SLIDE CUSTOM LOADED STAINLESS – .45 ACP or .45 Super (mfg. 2001 only) cal., 6 in. ported (disc. 2004) or unported barrel, 7 shot mag., checkered wood grips, adj. sights, 41 oz. Mfg. 2001-2012.

	$1,095	$950	$825	$725	$575	$475	$365	*$1,237*

Add $72 for ported barrel (V16, disc. 2004).
Add $403 for Trophy Match Model (disc. 2004).

MODEL 1911-A1 GI – .45 ACP cal., 5 in. barrel, parkerized, OD Green Armory Kote finish or stainless steel, 7 (standard) or 13 (high capacity) shot mag., low profile military sights, diamond checkered walnut grips with U.S. initials, includes 5.11 Gear belt holster, 36 oz. Mfg. 2004-2011.

	$565	$485	$415	$375	$300	$245	$190	*$656*

Add $52 for stainless steel.
Add $61 for high capacity magazine (parkerized finish, new 2005).

1911-A1 RANGE OFFICER/(RO) TARGET – 9mm Para. (new 2014) or .45 ACP cal., 5 in. stainless match grade barrel, fully supported ramp (RO Target), beveled magwell, two 7 shot mags, lowered and flared ejection port, Delta hammer, speed trigger, fully adj. target rear sight, diamond checkered walnut or Cocobolo grips with Springfield Armory logo, beavertail grip safety, case and holster, blue frame/slide (disc.), parkerized finish, 40 oz. New 2011.

MSR $942	$800	$690	$575	$500	$425	$350	$295	

* ***1911-A1 Range Officer Champion*** – 9mm Para. or .45 ACP cal., lightweight aluminum frame, 4 in. fully supported ramped hammer forged barrel, extended lightweight trigger, fiber optic front and low profile combat rear sights, Cross Cannon™ double diamond checkered cocobolo grips, beavertail grip safety, single-sided thumb safety, flat mainspring housing, includes 11 Gear System, black finish, approx. 30 oz. New 2015.

MSR $924	$785	$685	$585	$500	$425	$350	$295	

GRADING - PPGS™	100%	98%	95%	90%	80%	70%	60%	LAST MSR

* ***1911-A1 Range Officer Compact (RO Compact)*** – 9mm Para. (new 2015) or .45 ACP cal., forged National Match frame and slide, 4 in. match grade steel barrel, 6 or 8 (9mm Para.) shot mag., checkered thinline cocobolo grips, low profile rear sight, red fiber optic front sight, beavertail grip safety, extended lightweight skeletonized trigger, flat mainspring housing, single-sided thumb safety, includes holster and dual mag. carrier, 28 1/2 oz. New mid-2014.

MSR $924	$785	$685	$585	$500	$425	$350	$295	

* ***1911-A1 Range Officer Operator*** – 9mm Para. or .45 ACP cal., GI-Style recoil system, forged carbon steel frame and slide with Parkerized finish, 5 in. stainless steel match grade barrel, two 7 shot blued steel mags., fully adj. target sights, Crossed Cannon double diamond cocobolo grips, includes 11 Gear System, 40 oz. New 2016.

MSR $1,042	$900	$800	$700	$600	$500	$400	$325	

* ***1911-A1 Range Officer/RO Target Stainless Steel*** – 9mm Para. or .45 ACP cal., GI-style recoil system, forged carbon stainless steel frame and slide, 5 in. stainless steel match grade barrel, two 9 shot stainless steel mags., fully adj. target sights, Crossed Cannon double diamond Cocobolo grips, includes 11 Gear System, 41 oz. New 2016.

MSR $1,057	$925	$825	$725	$625	$525	$425	$350	

1911 RO ELITE SERIES – 9mm Para. or .45 ACP cal., configurations include 1911 Range Officer Elite Compact, 1911 Range Officer Elite Champion, 1911 Range Officer Operator, and 1911 Range Officer Elite Target. New mid-2017.

* ***1911 Range Officer Elite Champion*** – 9mm Para. or .45 ACP cal., forged lightweight aluminum alloy full sized frame, 4 in. stainless steel match grade bull barrel, two 7 shot blued steel (.45 ACP) or two 9 shot stainless steel (9mm) mags., fully supported ramp, forged steel slide, SA tactical white dot rear sight with fiber optic front sight, Gen 2 trigger, ambidextrous safety, flat wire captive recoil system, custom thin-line G10 grips, Black-T surface treatment finish, 30-31.5 oz. Mfg. mid-2017-2020.

	$900	$800	$700	$600	$500	$400	$325	*$1,030*

Add $14 for 9mm Para. cal.

* ***1911 Range Officer Elite Compact*** – 9mm Para. or .45 ACP cal., lightweight forged alloy frame, 4 in. stainless steel match grade bull barrel with fully supported ramp, two 8 shot mags., forged steel slide, Gen 2 trigger, SA tactical white dot rear and fiber optic front sights, thin-line G10 grips, ambidextrous safety, flat wire recoil system with full-length guide rod, Black-T finish, 28.5-29.4 oz. Mfg. mid-2017-2020.

	$900	$800	$700	$600	$500	$400	$325	*$1,030*

Add $14 for 9mm Para. cal.

* ***1911 Range Officer Elite Operator*** – 9mm Para., 10mm (new 2019), or .45 ACP cal., GI recoil system, forged steel match grade frame and slide, 5 in. stainless steel match grade barrel, two 7 shot blued steel (.45 ACP) or two 9 shot stainless steel (9mm) mags., Gen 2 trigger, SA tactical white dot rear and fiber optic front sight, thin-line G10 grips, ambidextrous safety, accessory rail, front and rear slide serrations, Black-T finish, 41 oz. New mid-2017.

MSR $1,145	$1,000	$875	$775	$675	$575	$475	$400	

Add $14 for 9mm Para. cal.

* ***1911 Range Officer Elite Target*** – 9mm Para. or .45 ACP cal., GI recoil system, forged steel match grade frame and slide, 5 in. stainless steel match grade barrel, two 7 shot blued steel (.45 ACP) or 9 shot stainless steel (9mm) mags., Gen 2 trigger, fully adj. rear target sight and fiber optic front sight, custom thin-line G10 grips, ambidextrous safety, Black-T finish, 40-41 oz. Mfg. mid-2017-2020.

	$925	$825	$725	$625	$525	$425	$350	*$1,048*

Add $13 for 9mm Para. cal.

1911-A1 COMMANDER MODEL – .45 ACP cal. only, similar to Standard 1911-A1 Model, except has 3.63 in. barrel, shortened slide, Commander hammer, low profile 3-dot sights, walnut grips, parkerized, blue, or duotone finish. Mfg. 1991-92.

	$425	$370	$320	$290	$235	$190	$150	

* ***1911-A1 Commander Model Combat*** – .45 ACP cal. only, 4 1/4 in. barrel, bobbed hammer, walnut grips. Mfg. 1991 only.

	$425	$370	$320	$290	$235	$190	$150	

GRADING - PPGS™	100%	98%	95%	90%	80%	70%	60%	LAST MSR

1911-A1 CHAMPION MODEL – .380 ACP (Model MD-1, mfg. 1995 only) or .45 ACP cal., similar to Standard Model, except has 4 in. barrel and shortened slide, blue (disc. 2000) or parkerized (Mil-Spec Champion, new 1994) finish, Commander hammer, checkered walnut grips, 3-dot sights (Novak night sights became standard 2001), 7 shot mag., 33 1/2 oz. Mfg. 1992-2002.

100%	98%	95%	90%	80%	70%	60%	LAST MSR
$695	$610	$520	$470	$380	$315	$245	*$856*

Add $30 for Ultra Compact slide (mfg. 1997-98).
Add $79 for ported Champion V10 with Ultra Compact slide (disc.).
Subtract approx. 10%-25% if w/o Custom Loaded features (new 2001), depending on condition.
Subtract approx. $150 for .380 ACP cal. (Model MD-1, disc.).

* ***1911-A1 Champion Model (Custom Loaded)*** – .45 ACP cal. only, stainless steel or Lightweight bi-tone with OD Green with Black Armory Kote finish (new 2004), Trijicon night sights. Mfg. 1992-2012.

100%	98%	95%	90%	80%	70%	60%	LAST MSR
$900	$800	$675	$615	$500	$400	$315	*$1,031*

Add $42 for stainless steel.
Add $119 for Ultra Compact slide (mfg. 1997-98).
Add $52 for ported Champion V10 with Ultra Compact slide (disc. 2000).
Subtract approx. 10%-25% if w/o Custom Loaded features (new 2001), depending on condition.

* ***1911-A1 Champion Model Lightweight*** – .45 ACP cal., 4 in. barrel, aluminum frame, matte metal finish, night sights became standard during 2001, current mfg. has lower Picatinny rail. Mfg. 1999-disc.

100%	98%	95%	90%	80%	70%	60%	LAST MSR
$995	$850	$725	$625	$500	$425	$350	*$1,129*

Subtract approx. 10%-25% if w/o Custom Loaded features (new 2001), depending on condition.

* ***1911-A1 Champion Model Lightweight Operator*** – .45 ACP cal., 4 in. stainless steel match grade bull barrel, two 7 shot mags., forged aluminum alloy Operator frame with integral accessory rail, beavertail grip safety, flat mainspring housing, lightweight Delta hammer, extended ambidextrous thumb safety, extended trigger, low profile 3-dot tritium combat sights, lowered and flared ejection port, Crossed Cannon double diamond Cocobolo grips, Black Armory Kote finish, 34 oz. Mfg. 2006-2020.

100%	98%	95%	90%	80%	70%	60%	LAST MSR
$925	$825	$725	$625	$525	$425	$350	*$1,050*

* ***1911-A1 Champion Model GI*** – .45 ACP cal., parkerized or blued slide with black anodized frame (Lightweight Model, new 2005), low profile military sights, diamond checkered wood grips with U.S. initials, includes belt holster, 34 oz. Mfg. 2004-2012.

100%	98%	95%	90%	80%	70%	60%	LAST MSR
$560	$485	$410	$375	$300	$245	$190	*$656*

* ***1911-A1 Champion Model TRP*** – .45 ACP cal., 4 in. barrel, otherwise similar to TRP Tactical Response. Mfg. 1999-2001.

100%	98%	95%	90%	80%	70%	60%	LAST MSR
$1,045	$915	$785	$710	$575	$470	$365	*$1,249*

* ***1911-A1 Champion Model Comp PDP*** – .45 ACP cal. only, compensated version of the Champion Model, blue. Mfg. 1993-98.

100%	98%	95%	90%	80%	70%	60%	LAST MSR
$780	$680	$585	$530	$430	$350	$275	*$869*

* ***1911-A1 Champion Model Super Tuned*** – .45 ACP cal., super tuned by the Custom Shop, 7 shot mag., 4 in. barrel, blue or parkerized finish, Novak fixed Lo-Mount sights, 36.3 oz. Mfg. 1997-99.

100%	98%	95%	90%	80%	70%	60%	LAST MSR
$850	$745	$635	$580	$465	$380	$295	*$959*

Add $30 for blue finish.

* ***1911-A1 Champion Model XM4 High Capacity*** – 9mm Para. or .45 ACP cal., high capacity variation. Mfg. 1994 only.

100%	98%	95%	90%	80%	70%	60%	LAST MSR
$615	$540	$460	$420	$340	$275	$215	*$699*

1911-A1 COMPACT MODEL – .45 ACP cal. only, compact variation featuring shortened 4 in. barrel and slide, reduced M1911-A1 curved gripstrap frame, checkered walnut grips, low profile 3-dot sights, 6 or 7 shot mag., extended slide stop, standard or lightweight alloy (new 1994) frame, combat hammer, parkerized, blue, or duotone (disc. 1992) finish, standard or lightweight (new 1995) configuration, 27 or 32 oz. Mfg. 1991-96.

100%	98%	95%	90%	80%	70%	60%	LAST MSR
$415	$365	$310	$280	$230	$185	$145	*$476*

Add $66 for blue finish.
Add $67 for Compact Lightweight Model (matte finish only).

* ***1911-A1 Compact Model Stainless*** – stainless steel variation of the Compact Model. Mfg. 1991-96.

100%	98%	95%	90%	80%	70%	60%	LAST MSR
$495	$435	$370	$335	$270	$225	$175	*$582*

* ***1911-A1 Compact Model Lightweight*** – .45 ACP cal., forged alloy frame, matte metal finish, 6 shot mag., Novak night sights became standard 2001. Mfg. 1999-2003.

100%	98%	95%	90%	80%	70%	60%	LAST MSR
$585	$510	$440	$395	$320	$265	$205	*$733*

Subtract approx. 10%-25% if w/o Custom Loaded features (new 2001), depending on condition.

GRADING - PPGS™	100%	98%	95%	90%	80%	70%	60%	LAST MSR

» **1911-A1 Compact Model Lightweight Stainless** – similar to Compact Lightweight, except is stainless steel. Disc. 2001.

	$725	$635	$545	$495	$400	$325	$255	*$900*

Subtract approx. 10%-25% if w/o Custom Loaded features (new 2001), depending on condition.

* ***1911-A1 Compact Model Comp Lightweight*** – compensated version of the Compact Model, bi-tone or matte finish, regular or lightweight alloy (new 1994) frame. Mfg. 1993-98.

	$775	$680	$580	$525	$425	$350	$270	*$869*

* ***1911-A1 Compact Model High Capacity*** – blue or stainless steel, 3-dot fixed combat sights, black plastic grips, 10 shot (except for law enforcement) mag. Mfg. 1995-96 only.

	$550	$475	$400	$365	$295	$245	$190	*$609*

Add $39 for stainless steel.

* ***1911-A1 Compact Model High Capacity PDP Comp*** – .45 ACP cal. only, features compensated 3 1/2 in. barrel, 10 shot (except law enforcement) mag., blue finish only. Mfg. 1995-96 only.

	$830	$725	$620	$565	$455	$375	$290	*$964*

1911 A-1 ULTRA COMPACT (CUSTOM LOADED) – .380 ACP (lightweight only, mfg. 1995 only), 9mm Para. (new 1998, lightweight stainless only), or .45 ACP cal., 3 1/2 in. barrel, bi-tone (.45 ACP only, disc.), matte (.380 ACP, MD-1), or parkerized (Mil-Spec Ultra Compact) finish, 6, 7 (.380 ACP cal.) or 8 (9mm Para. cal.) shot mag., Custom Loaded features and night sights became standard in 2001, 24 or 30 oz. Mfg. 1995-2003.

	$680	$595	$510	$460	$375	$305	$240	*$837*

Add $12 for V10 porting.
Add $12 for Novak Tritium sights (not available on 9mm Para.cal.).
Add $110 for bi-tone finish (disc.).
Subtract $50 for MD-1 variation (.380 ACP only).
Subtract approx. 10%-25% if w/o Custom Loaded features (new 2001), depending on condition.

* ***1911 A-1 Ultra Compact Mil-Spec*** – .45 ACP cal., parkerized (disc.) or blued (new 2004) finish, similar to full size Mil-Spec Model, 6 shot mag., checkered grips, 3-dot fixed Hi-Viz combat sights. Mfg. 2001-2002, reintroduced 2004 only.

	$550	$480	$410	$375	$300	$245	$190	*$641*

Subtract approx. 10%-25% if w/o Custom Loaded features (new 2001), depending on condition.

* ***1911 A-1 Ultra Compact Stainless Custom Loaded*** – 9mm Para. (disc. 2004) or .45 ACP cal., stainless steel, Novak (disc.) or Fixed Combat Trijicon night sights became standard 2001. Mfg. 1998-2012.

	$925	$800	$675	$615	$490	$400	$315	*$1,073*

Add $17 for 9mm Para. cal. (lightweight, disc. 2004).
Subtract approx. 10%-25% if w/o Custom Loaded features (new 2001), depending on condition.

* ***1911 A-1 Ultra Compact Lightweight*** – .45 ACP cal., aluminum frame, matte metal finish, night sights became standard 2001. Mfg. 1999-2001.

	$695	$610	$520	$470	$380	$315	$245	*$867*

Subtract approx. 10%-25% if w/o Custom Loaded features (new 2001), depending on condition.

* ***1911 A-1 Ultra Compact V10 Lightweight Ported*** – .45 ACP cal., bi-tone finish. Mfg. 1999-2001.

	$750	$655	$560	$510	$410	$335	$260	*$737*

» **1911 A-1 Ultra Compact V10 Lightweight Stainless** – 9mm Para. or .45 ACP (exclusive) cal., similar to Ultra Compact Lightweight, except is stainless steel, Novak Lo-Mount sights. Mfg. 1999-2002.

	$725	$635	$545	$495	$400	$325	$255	*$870*

Add $31 for night sights (.45 ACP cal. only).
Subtract approx. 10%-25% if w/o Custom Loaded features (new 2001), depending on condition.

* ***1911 A-1 Ultra Compact High Capacity*** – 9mm Para. (disc.) or .45 ACP cal., parkerized (Mil-Spec) or blue (disc.) finish, and stainless steel (disc.) construction, 10 shot mag., 3-dot fixed combat (disc.) or Novak Lo-Mount (new 2002) sights, black plastic grips. Mfg. 1996-2002.

	$735	$645	$550	$500	$405	$330	$255	*$909*

Add $98 for stainless steel.
Add $145 for stainless steel with V10 ported barrel (disc.).
Subtract approx. 10%-25% if w/o Custom Loaded features (new 2001), depending on condition.

GRADING - PPGS™	100%	98%	95%	90%	80%	70%	60%	LAST MSR

* ***1911 A-1 Ultra Compact V10 Ported*** – .45 ACP cal. only, 3 1/2 in. specially compensated barrel/slide, blue (disc.), bi-tone, or parkerized (Mil-Spec Ultra Compact) finish, Novak Lo-Mount or 3-dot combat sights, 30 oz. Mfg. 1995-2002.

	$690	$605	$515	$470	$380	$310	$240	*$853*

Subtract approx. 10%-25% if w/o Custom Loaded features (new 2001), depending on condition.

* ***1911 A-1 Ultra Compact V10 Super Tuned Ported*** – .45 ACP cal. only, super tuned by the Custom Shop, 3 1/2 in. ported barrel, bi-tone finish or stainless steel (exclusive), Novak fixed Lo-Mount sights, 32.9 oz. Mfg. 1997-99.

	$925	$810	$695	$630	$510	$415	$325	*$1,049*

Add $70 for stainless steel (exclusive).

1911-A1 MICRO COMPACT – .45 ACP cal. only, 3 in. tapered barrel w/o bushing, matte finish, checkered grips, 6 shot mag., Novak Lo-Mount night sights. Mfg. 2002 only.

	$625	$545	$470	$425	$345	$280	$220	*$749*

* ***1911 A-1 Micro Compact Lightweight Custom Loaded*** – similar to Micro Compact 1911 A-1, except also available in .40 S&W (disc.) cal., bi-tone, OD Green (mfg. 2003 only), or black Armory Kote (mfg. 2003-2004) finish with forged steel slide (grey) and aluminum alloy frame (blue), checkered cocobolo grips, Trijicon night sights, 24 oz. Mfg. 2002-2012.

	$1,195	$995	$875	$750	$625	$525	$425	*$1,377*

Add $71 for Operator Model with XML X-treme mini light (disc. 2011).

* ***1911 A-1 Micro Compact Lightweight Stainless Custom Loaded*** – .45 ACP cal. only, similar to Micro Compact 1911 A-1 Custom Loaded, except is stainless or black stainless steel slide. Mfg. 2003 only.

	$825	$720	$620	$560	$455	$370	$290	*$993*

* ***1911 A-1 Micro Compact GI*** – .45 ACP cal., parkerized finish, checkered diamond walnut grips with U.S. initials, includes belt holster, 32 oz. Mfg. 2004-2011.

	$615	$535	$465	$400	$325	$270	$210	*$708*

1911-A1 EMP (ENHANCED MICRO PISTOL) – 9mm Para. or .40 S&W cal., 9 shot mag., 3 in. stainless steel bull barrel, polished stainless slide with blue frame, Tritium 3-dot sights, available in Standard or Lightweight configuration, reduced dimensions result in narrower profile, Cocobolo or G10 (disc. 2016) grips, bi-tone finish, 27 (Lightweight) or 33 oz. New 2007.

MSR $1,249	$1,095	$950	$825	$725	$625	$515	$400

Add $71 for G10 grips (mfg. 2008-2016).

* ***1911-A1 EMP LW Black*** – 9mm Para. cal., aluminum alloy frame, 3 in. stainless steel match grade bull barrel, 9 shot, forged steel slide with Black Armory Kote finish, low profile combat rear and fiber optic front sights, double diamond cocobolo grips, dual spring with full-length guide rod, 27 oz. New 2017.

MSR $1,104	$975	$850	$725	$625	$500	$425	$350

* ***1911-A1 EMP Champion*** – 9mm Para. or .40 S&W cal., lightweight, forged stainless steel slide with satin finish, forged aluminum alloy frame with black hardcoat anodized finish and double diamond Cocobolo grips, 4 in. stainless steel match grade bull barrel, three ten shot mags., fiber optic front and white dot rear sights, Bi-Tone finish, 31 oz. New 2016.

MSR $1,177	$1,025	$900	$775	$675	$575	$475	$400

Add $43 for forged carbon steel frame (new 2018).

1911-A1 EMP CHAMPION LW BITONE CONCEAL CARRY CONTOUR – 9mm Para. or .40 S&W (new mid-2017) cal., aluminum alloy frame with hardcoat anodized black finish (9mm only), carbon steel frame finished in Black-T (.40 S&W only), black slide with tactical gray frame (new 2019), desert FDE frame and slide (new 2019), or desert FDE frame with OD Green slide (new 2019), 4 in. stainless steel match grade bull barrel, 9 shot, low profile combat rear and fiber optic front sights, G10 grips, dual spring with full-length guide rod, forged stainless steel slide with satin finish and rear cocking serrations, 30.5 oz. New 2017.

MSR $1,220	$1,075	$950	$825	$725	$625	$515	$400

1911-A1 LOADED PARKERIZED WITH CRIMSON TRACE LASERGRIPS – .45 ACP cal., GI-Style recoil system, forged steel slide with Black Armory Kote finish, forged steel frame with integral accessory rail and Olive Drab Armory Kote finish, 5 in. stainless steel match grade barrel, two 7 shot blued steel mags., low profile combat 3-dot Tritium sights, G10 grips, Crimson Trace Lasergrips, includes 11 Gear System, 43 oz. Limited mfg. 2016 only.

	$975	$850	$725	$625	$500	$425	$350	*$1,104*

GRADING - PPGS™	100%	98%	95%	90%	80%	70%	60%	LAST MSR

GULF VICTORY SPECIAL EDITION – .45 ACP cal., special edition featuring presentation grade blue finish, gold etching on slide and other gold-plated small parts, includes specially padded and embroidered storage case with jacket patch, window decal, and cloisonné medallion honoring all U.S. Armed Forces. Mfg. 1991-92.

	$750	$655	$560	$510	$410	$335	$260	*$869*

1911-A1 RONIN OPERATOR – 9mm Para., 10mm (new late 2020), or .45 ACP cal., stainless steel frame, 4 1/4 or 5 in. forged stainless steel, match grade barrel, 8 or 9 shot, forged carbon steel blued slide, fiber optic front and tactical rack white dot rear sights, crossed cannon wood laminate grips, GI-style recoil system, satin aluminum/black (4.25 in.) or stainless/black (5 in.) finish, 31-41 oz. New 2020.

MSR $849	$700	$650	$550	$500	$400	$325	$250	

1911 VICKERS TACTICAL MASTER CLASS – .45 ACP cal., forged carbon steel, Black-T frame, 5 in. forged stainless steel, match grade barrel, 8 shot, forged carbon steel Black-T slide, Tritium/luminescent front and Vickers Elite Battle U-Notch Rear sights, "LAV" engraved into G10 grips and woven front strap checkering, GI-style recoil system, black finish, 41.5 oz. New 2021.

MSR $1,495	$1,275	$1,100	$950	$850	$700	$575	$450	

This model was developed with retired U.S. Army combat veteran Larry Vickers.

Pistols: Semi-Auto - 1911-A1 Custom Models

In addition to the models listed, Springfield also custom builds other configurations of Race Guns that are available through Springfield dealers.

1911-A1 CUSTOM COMPACT – .45 ACP cal. only, carry or lady's model with shortened slide and frame, compensated, fixed 3-dot sights, Commander style hammer, Herrett walnut grips, other custom features, blue only.

	$1,615	$1,325	$1,100	$950	$850	$750	$675	*$1,815*

1911-A1 CUSTOM CHAMPION – similar to Custom Compact, except is based on Champion model with full size frame and shortened slide.

	$1,615	$1,325	$1,100	$950	$850	$750	$675	*$1,815*

BASIC COMPETITION – .45 ACP (other cals. available upon request) cal., Bo-Mar adj. rear sight, blue finish, checkered walnut grips. Mfg. 1994-2017.

	$1,825	$1,475	$1,175	$975	$825	$725	$625	*$2,199*

BULLSEYE WADCUTTER – 9mm Para. or .45 ACP cal., specifically designed for wadcutter loads, 5 or 6 (disc.) in. barrel, Bo-Mar rib mounted on slide top.

MSR $2,595	$2,200	$1,925	$1,650	$1,495	$1,200	$950	$750	

COMPACT CARRY 1911-A1 – 9mm Para. or .45 ACP cal., custom fitted National Match bull barrel and bushing, many other Custom Shop features, Novak Lo-Mount rear and dovetail front Tritium 3-dot sights, checkered cocobolo grips, premium black T finish.

MSR $3,450	$2,950	$2,550	$2,200	$2,000	$1,600	$1,300	$1,050	

CUSTOM CARRY 1911-A1 – .45 ACP (other cals. available upon request) cal., similar to Defender Model, except has tuned trigger pull, 7 shot mag., heavy recoil spring, extended thumb safety, available in blue or phosphate (disc.) finish. New 1991.

MSR $2,395	$2,075	$1,800	$1,550	$1,400	$1,100	$950	$750	

CUSTOM HIGH CAPACITY LTD – .40 S&W cal. Mfg. 2004-2011.

	$2,200	$1,775	$1,425	$1,125	$975	$875	$775	*$2,650*

CUSTOM OPERATOR – .45 ACP cal. Mfg. 2001-2013.

	$2,495	$2,225	$1,775	$1,400	$1,100	$950	$850	*$2,810*

DISTINGUISHED BIANCHI/COMPETITION STEEL – .38 Super cal. Mfg. 2004-2018.

	$3,295	$2,850	$2,450	$2,050	$1,775	$1,500	$1,250	*$3,670*

DISTINGUISHED CLASSIC – 9mm Para. or .45 ACP. cal., National Match barrel and bushing, custom fit slide to National Match frame, many other Custom Shop features, deluxe low mount Springfield adj. target rear and dovetail with gold bead front sights, checkered brown grips, charcoal blue finish.

MSR $3,995	$3,395	$2,975	$2,550	$2,300	$1,850	$1,500	$1,185	

DISTINGUISHED LIMITED – .45 ACP cal. (other cals. available upon request), dual chamber compensator system on match barrel, brushed hard chrome finish, checkered gripstraps and trigger guard, top-of-the-line competition model. Disc. 2018.

	$2,995	$2,600	$2,150	$1,750	$1,350	$1,050	$875	*$3,340*

GRADING - PPGS™ 100% 98% 95% 90% 80% 70% 60% LAST MSR

ENTRY LEVEL WADCUTTER – .38 Super, .40 S&W, 10mm, or .45 ACP cal., 5 in. barrel, standard competition features. Disc.

$925 $800 $700 $600 $550 $475 $425 *$1,049*

Add $200 for .38 Super cal.

Add $391 for 10mm or .40 S&W cal.

This model featured supported chambers in all cals. except .45 ACP.

EXPERT LIMITED – .45 ACP (other cals. available upon request) cal., mfg. for IPSC competition shooting, dual chamber compensator system on match barrel, duotone finish. Disc. 2018.

$1,875 $1,525 $1,175 $975 $825 $725 $625 *$2,270*

This model is an improved variation of the Trophy Master Competition Model.

FULL HOUSE RACE GUN – .45 ACP cal., high capacity frame, chrome finish only. Mfg. 1998-2011.

$2,925 $2,475 $2,100 $1,800 $1,550 $1,350 $1,150 *$3,395*

Add $150 for STI/SV style frame (disc.).

LEATHAM LEGEND SERIES CUSTOM 1 – Disc. 2011.

$2,875 $2,475 $2,050 $1,775 $1,500 $1,250 $995 *$3,367*

These models were available exclusively through Davidson's until 2010.

LEATHAM TROPHY MATCH – .40 S&W cal., 5 in. barrel, high capacity model, Armory Kote finish. Mfg. 2005-2007.

This model was POR.

LOADED OPERATOR – .45 ACP cal., 5 in. barrel, OD Green or black Armory Kote finish and slide, Novak or Trijicon night sights. Limited mfg. 2005.

$1,025 $900 $800 $700 $600 $500 $400 *$1,218*

NATIONAL MATCH HARDBALL – 9mm Para. or .45 ACP cal., National Match barrel and bushing, specially fitted frame and slide, blue only, Bo-Mar (disc.) or low mount Springfield adj. rear and undercut front sights, Herrett walnut (disc.) or checkered cocobolo grips, plastic case.

MSR $2,595 $2,200 $1,925 $1,650 $1,495 $1,200 $950 $750

This model is made specifically for DCM competition shooting.

NRA PPC DISTINGUISHED – .45 ACP (other cals. available upon request) cal., designed to comply with NRA PPC competitive rules/regulations, factory test target, custom carrying case. Mfg. 1995-disc.

$1,875 $1,525 $1,175 $975 $825 $750 $675 *$2,195*

OPERATOR LIGHTWEIGHT – .45 ACP cal., 3 in. barrel, bi-tone finish, XML mini-light, includes Novak Trijicon night sights. Limited mfg. 2005.

$1,050 $925 $800 $700 $600 $500 $400 *$1,247*

OPERATOR TACTICAL RESPONSE – .45 ACP cal., 5 in. barrel, black Armory Kote finish, adj. Trijicon night sights. Limited mfg. 2005.

$1,395 $1,075 $900 $775 $675 $575 $475 *$1,639*

P9 WORLD CUP – 9x21mm or .40 S&W cal., state-of-the-art competition pistol, based on factory P9 Race gun, hard chrome finish only. Disc.

$2,550 $2,100 $1,775 $1,500 $1,250 $975 $795 *$2,935*

PROFESSIONAL MODEL – 9mm Para. or .45 ACP cal., FBI contract model, custom fitted National Match barrel and bushing, many other custom shop features, Novak Lo-Mount rear sight, checkered cocobolo grips, black T finish. New 1999.

MSR $3,363 $2,850 $2,500 $2,150 $1,950 $1,550 $1,250 $1,000

PROFESSIONAL LIGHT RAIL MODEL – 9mm Para. or .45 ACP cal., National Match light rail frame with lower Picatinny rail, custom fitted National Match barrel and bushing, many other Custom Shop features, Novak Lo-Mount rear and dovetail front 3-dot Tritium sights, checkered cocobolo grips, black T finish. New 1999.

MSR $3,465 $2,935 $2,550 $2,200 $1,985 $1,585 $1,285 $1,035

PPC DISTINGUISHED 1500 – 9mm Para. or .45 ACP. cal., National Match barrel and bushing, custom fit long slide to National Match frame, many other Custom Shop features, low mount Aristocrat Tri-set rear and undercut dovetail black target front sights, premium G10 grips, black T finish.

MSR $3,650 $3,150 $2,750 $2,350 $2,150 $1,750 $1,400 $1,100

PPC TROPHY MATCH – 9mm Para. cal. Mfg. 2004-2006.

$1,200 $1,000 $825 $700 $625 $525 $450 *$1,395*

GRADING - PPGS™	100%	98%	95%	90%	80%	70%	60%	LAST MSR

SILENT OPERATOR (MASTER CLASS SILENT OPERATOR) – .45 ACP cal., 5.28 in. threaded hammer forged barrel with Melonite finish and thread protector, Master Class stainless steel barrel bushing, two 7 shot mags., flared magwell, 2nd Gen 4.5 lb. speed trigger, suppressor height night sights, ext. thumb safety, beavertail grip safety, Picatinny rail dust cover, Master Class slide markings, black Nitride or FDE finish, 2 lbs. 6 oz. Mfg. 2017 only.

	$1,875	$1,650	$1,400	$1,275	$1,025	$850	$650	*$2,195*

SINGLE STACK CLASSIC (SSC) – 9mm Para. or .45 ACP cal., throated barrel, 7 shot mag. with checkered extended release, National Match heavy frame, barrel, and bushing, bobbed hammer, skeletonized trigger, low mount adj. rear and front fiber optic sight, checkered black plastic grips, beavertail safety, polished feed ramp, black Armory Kote finish. New 2016.

MSR $3,350	$2,850	$2,495	$2,150	$1,950	$1,550	$1,285	$1,000

TGO 1 – .45 ACP cal., 1911-A1 custom model, forged frame and slide, 5 in. National Match stainless steel barrel, Nowlin Match Grade throated barrel and bushing, 7 shot mag., lowered and flared ejection port, extended ejector, National Match lightweight adj. speed trigger, deluxe low mount BoMar fully adj. rear sight and Dawson fiber optic front sight with certificate, black Micarta double diamond grips and Leatham legend signature laser engraved thin lined cocobolo smooth wood grips, High-Hand beavertail grip safety, extended ambi thumb safety, hand checkered front strap 20 LPI, Carry Bevel treatment, Robar Industries Ltd. Bi-Tone finish, Roguard proprietary black finish on slide, NP-3 nickel/Teflon finish on frame, includes 4 mags. with Slam Pads, lifetime warranty, custom aluminum case, unique Legend series markings and serial number, Certificate of Authenticity, letter from Rob Leatham, autographed picture and autographed target shot from Rob Leatham, 8.5 in. OAL, 38 oz. New 2003.

MSR $4,127	$3,500	$3,050	$2,625	$2,375	$1,925	$1,575	$1,225

TGO 2 – .45 ACP cal., 1911-A1 custom model, forged frame and slide, 5 in. stainless steel throated match barrel and bushing, 7 shot mag., Springfield Armory wide mouth funneled magwell, Delta lightweight hammer, National Match lightweight adj. speed trigger, BoMar low mount adj. rear sight and Dawson fiber optic front sight with certificate, black Micarta double diamond grips and Leatham legend signature laser engraved thin lined cocobolo smooth wood grips, High-Hand beavertail grip safety, extended ambi thumb safety, machine checkered front strap 20 LPI, Carry Bevel treatment, double serrated slide, loaded chamber indicator, Robar Industries Ltd. Bi-Tone finish, Roguard proprietary black finish on slide, NP-3 nickel/Teflon finish on frame, includes 4 mags. with Slam Pads, lifetime warranty, custom aluminum case, unique Legend series markings and serial number, Certificate of Authenticity, letter from Rob Leatham, and autographed picture from Rob Leatham, 8.5 in. OAL, 38 oz. Mfg. 2003-disc.

Last MSR was $1,899.

TGO 3 – .45 ACP cal., 1911-A1 custom model, lightweight forged aluminum frame with Black Armory Kote finished stainless steel slide, 5 in. stainless steel throated match barrel and bushing, 7 shot mag., beveled magwell, lowered and flared ejection port, Delta lightweight hammer, National Match lightweight adj. speed trigger, Springfield Armory fully adj. rear sight with low mount BoMar cut Dawson fiber optic front sight, black Micarta double diamond grips and Leatham legend signature laser engraved thin lined cocobolo smooth wood grips, High-Hand beavertail grip safety, ambi thumb safety, Carry Bevel treatment, double serrated slide, loaded chamber indicator, includes 4 mags. with Slam Pads, lifetime warranty, custom aluminum case, unique Legend series markings and serial number, Certificate of Authenticity, letter from Rob Leatham, and autographed picture from Rob Leatham, 8.5 in. OAL, 30 oz. Mfg. 2003-disc.

Last MSR was $1,295.

TROPHY MASTER "COMPETITION" – .45 ACP (other cals. available upon request) cal., competition model which includes low profile combat sights, ambidextrous safety, long match trigger, bobbed hammer, Pachmayr wraparound grips. Disc. 1996.

	$1,420	$1,125	$950	$875	$800	$725	$650	*$1,598*

ULTIMATE CARRY 1911-A1 – 9mm Para. or .45 ACP cal., custom fitted National Match barrel and bushing, many other Custom Shop features, Novak Lo-Mount rear and dovetail front 3-dot Tritium sights, checkered G10 grips, black T finish.

MSR $3,395	$2,875	$2,500	$2,150	$1,950	$1,550	$1,250	$1,000

Pistols: Semi-Auto Legend Series

LEGEND SERIES LIMITED EDITION CHRIS KYLE TRP OPERATOR – .45 ACP cal., forged carbon steel frame, 5 in. stainless steel match grade bull barrel, 7 shot stainless steel mag. with slam pad, forged carbon steel slide with black Nitride treatment, adj. low profile 3-dot Tritium combat sights, black and gray G10 grips with American flag engraving, National Match full-length guide rod, includes mahogany presentation case, a Chris Kyle FROG Foundation commemorative coin, and a copy of American Sniper autographed by Taya Kyle, features unique serial number ranging from CK0001-CK1000, 45 oz. Limited 1,000 mfg. beginning 2016. Disc.

	$2,325	$2,100	$1,925	N/A	N/A	N/A	N/A	*$2,499*

GRADING - PPGS™	100%	98%	95%	90%	80%	70%	60%	LAST MSR

Pistols: Semi-Auto - XD Series

All XD pistols are manufactured by HS Produkt (formerly I.M. Metal) in Croatia. All XD pistols were originally shipped with two magazines. Beginning 2005, high capacity magazines are legal for civilian sales in those states that permit high cap. mags. During 2006, all XD pistols were shipped with the XD Gear System, consisting of belt holster, double magazine pouch, magazine loader, two magazines and cable lock.

In 2013, Springfield Armory USA released its XD-S Series in .45 ACP cal. with many compact features.

XD 5 IN. TACTICAL (X-TREME DUTY) – 9mm Para., .357 SIG (disc. 2014), .40 S&W, .45 ACP (new 2006), or .45 GAP (mfg. 2005-2007) cal., cold hammer forged 5 in. barrel, 9 (.45 GAP, disc.), 10, 12 (.40 S&W or .357 SIG), or 15 (9mm Para.) shot mag., lightweight polymer frame, matte black, bi-tone (.45 ACP only), Dark Earth (mfg. 2007-2012) or OD Green (disc.) finish, steel slide, single action striker fired with U.S.A. trigger system, firing pin and loaded chamber indicators, dual recoil spring system, polymer frame with lower Picatinny rail, ambidextrous mag. release, grip safety, front and rear slide serrations, external thumb safety version became separate model in 2008, approx. 29 (9mm Para. cal.) or 33 oz. Mfg. 2002-2015.

	100%	98%	95%	90%	80%	70%	60%	LAST MSR
	$475	$400	$350	$300	$265	$235	$200	*$539*

Add $31 for .45 ACP cal. (new 2006).
Add $31 for thumb safety (.45 ACP cal. only, black or bi-tone finish only).
Add $74 for bi-tone finish (.45 ACP cal. only).
Add $92 for Trijicon sights (disc.) or approx. $90 for Heinie (disc.) Tritium Slant Pro sights.
Subtract $7 for .45 GAP cal. black tactical (disc. 2007).

* ***XD Tactical Pro*** – limited mfg. 2003 only.

	100%	98%	95%	90%	80%	70%	60%	LAST MSR
	$875	$775	$675	$575	$475	$400	$350	*$1,099*

XD 4 IN. SERVICE MODEL DEFENDERS SERIES – 9mm Para. cal., single action striker fired with U.S.A. trigger system, cold hammer forged 4 in., 16 shot mag., black polymer frame, steel slide, fixed dovetail sights, grip safety, dual recoil spring system, integral accessory lower rail on frame, ambidextrous mag. release, front and rear slide serrations, matte black Melonite finish, 7.3 OAL, 28 oz. New 2019.

	100%	98%	95%	90%	80%	70%	60%	LAST MSR
MSR $399	$340	$290	$250	$210	$185	$150	$120	

XD 4 IN. SERVICE MODEL (X-TREME DUTY) – 9mm Para., .357 SIG (disc. 2015), .40 S&W, .45 ACP (mfg. 2006-2020), or .45 GAP (mfg. 2005-2007) cal., cold hammer forged 4 in. ported or unported barrel, 9 (.45 GAP), 10 (.45 ACP), 12 (.40 S&W or .357 SIG), or 15 (9mm Para.) shot mag., lightweight polymer frame, matte black (only finish available on .357 SIG cal.), bi-tone (mfg. 2003-2015), Dark Earth (mfg. 2007-2012) or OD Green (disc.) finish, steel slide, single action striker fired with U.S.A. trigger system, firing pin and loaded chamber indicators, dual recoil spring system, polymer frame with lower Picatinny rail, ambidextrous mag. release, grip safety, front and rear slide serrations, thumb safety version became separate model during 2008, approx. 28 (9mm Para.) or 30 oz. Mfg. 2002-2020.

	100%	98%	95%	90%	80%	70%	60%	LAST MSR
	$475	$395	$335	$275	$240	$220	$200	*$524*

Add $24 for .45 ACP cal.
Add $22 for thumb safety in .45 ACP cal. only. (disc. 2016).
Add $42 for bi-tone finish (mfg. 2003-2015).
Add $35 for V10 ported barrel (black or OD Green finish, not available in .45 ACP or .45 GAP cal.), disc.
Add $100 for stainless steel slide (.45 ACP cal. only), disc.
Add $96 for Trijicon or Heinie Tritium Slant Pro night sights (not available on .45 GAP cal.), disc.
Subtract $7 for .45 GAP cal. (disc. 2007).

XD 3 IN. SUB-COMPACT DEFENDERS SERIES – 9mm Para. cal., single action striker fired with U.S.A. trigger system, 3 in. cold hammer forged barrel, 13 shot mag., black polymer frame, steel slide, fixed dovetail 3-dot sights, grip safety, dual recoil spring system, integral accessory lower rail on frame, ambidextrous mag. release, black Melonite finish, 6 1/4 in. OAL, 26 oz. New 2019.

	100%	98%	95%	90%	80%	70%	60%	LAST MSR
MSR $399	$340	$290	$250	$210	$185	$150	$120	

XD 3 IN. SUB-COMPACT (X-TREME DUTY) – 9mm Para. or .40 S&W (mfg. 2004-2020) cal., cold hammer forged 3 in. barrel, 9 (.40 S&W), 10 (9mm Para.), 13 (9mm Para.) or 16 (9mm Para.) shot mag., lightweight polymer frame, black, bi-tone (mfg. 2004-2015), satin stainless (disc.), or OD Green (disc.) finish, steel slide, single action striker fired with U.S.A. trigger system, firing pin and loaded chamber indicators, dual recoil spring system, polymer frame with lower Picatinny rail, ambidextrous mag. release, grip safety, front and rear slide serrations, 26 oz. Mfg. 2003-2020.

	100%	98%	95%	90%	80%	70%	60%	LAST MSR
	$475	$395	$335	$275	$240	$220	$200	*$524*

Add $42 for bi-tone finish (mfg. 2004-2015).
Add $96 for Trijicon or Heinie Tritium Slant Pro night sights (disc.).
Add $100 for X-treme mini light (disc. 2011).

This model is not available with a thumb safety.

GRADING - PPGS™	100%	98%	95%	90%	80%	70%	60%	LAST MSR

XD COMPACT SERIES – 9mm Para. (mfg. 2007 only), .40 S&W (mfg. 2007 only), or .45 ACP cal., 4 or 5 (disc. 2014) in. barrel, shortened grip frame, Black, OD Green (disc. 2012), bi-tone (mfg. 2008-2014), or Dark Earth (disc. 2011) finish, stainless steel slide, OD Green (disc. 2012) or Dark Earth (disc. 2011), 10 or extended 13 shot mag., 29 or 32 oz. Mfg. 2007-2018.

	$475	$400	$350	$300	$265	$235	$200	*$541*

Add $46 for 5 in. barrel (disc. 2014).
Add $66 for bi-tone finish (disc. 2014) or stainless steel slide (4 in. barrel only, disc. 2012).
Add $94 for Trijicon night sights (disc. 2011).
Subtract $30 for 9mm or .40 S&W cal. (4 in. barrel only), w/o night sights (disc. 2007).

XD CUSTOM SERIES – the Springfield custom shop made three variations of the XD pistol, including the XD Carry, XD Production, and XD Custom Competition. Most calibers and sizes were available.

Last MSRs in 2015 on this series were as follows - XD Carry was $795, XD Production was $1,200, and XD Custom Competition was $1,460.

XD-E – 9mm Para. or .45 ACP (new 2018) cal., black polymer frame with exposed hammer and forged steel slide, 3.3, 3.8 (new 2019, 9mm only), or 4.5 (new 2019, 9mm only) in. hammer forged steel barrel with Melonite, 6 (.45 ACP), 8 (w/grip X-Tension), 7 (.45 ACP), or 9 (w/Mag X-Tension) shot mag., fiber optic front and low profile 3-dot rear sights with or w/o red Viridian "E" series laser, High-Hand beavertail grip with 3 texture zones for minimal slippage, dual spring with full-length guide rod, 23-26.2 oz. New 2017.

MSR $542	$475	$395	$335	$275	$240	$220	$200

Add $13-$18 for red Viridian "E" series laser.
Add 7.5% (MSR $580) for .45 ACP cal. (new 2018).

XD(M) SERIES – 9mm Para. (disc. 2020), .40 S&W, or .45 ACP (mfg. 2011-2017) cal., contoured frame is slightly modified from XD model, 3.8 (new 2010) or 4 1/2 in. match grade barrel, 10 (.45 ACP only, new 2012), 13, 16 or 19 shot mag., black polymer frame, forged steel or stainless steel slide, minimal reset trigger, includes 3 interchangeable backstraps, lower Picatinny rail, includes XD Gear holster and black plastic carrying case, black, bi-tone (disc. 2016), Desert FDE (mfg. 2019-2020), or OD Green (disc. 2014) Melonite oxide finish, 6 3/4-7 1/2 in. OAL, 28-31 oz. New mid-2008.

MSR $652	$560	$490	$425	$375	$300	$250	$200

Subtract $29 for 9mm Para. cal. (disc. 2020).
Add $62 for bi-tone finish (disc. 2016).
Add approx. $66 for OD Green w/stainless slide (not available in .45 ACP cal.), disc. 2014.
Add $118 for night sights (Tritium or Trijicon), disc.
Subtract approx. $50 if without XD Gear System (disc. 2015).

* ***XD(M) 10mm*** – 10mm cal., black polymer frame with changeable backstraps, 4 1/2 in. hammer forged steel barrel, 15 shot mag., forged steel slide, fiber optic front and low profile combat rear sights, one-piece full length guide rod, Melonite finish on slide and barrel, 7 3/4 in. OAL, 31.2 oz. New late 2018.

MSR $652	$560	$490	$425	$375	$300	$250	$200

XD(M) COMPACT SERIES – 9mm Para., .40 S&W, or .45 ACP (new 2012) cal., black polymer frame, 3.8 in. hammer forged match grade barrel, 9, 11, or 13 shot flush mag., low profile dovetail rear and fiber optic front sights, grip safety, lower Picatinny rail, includes the XD(M) Gear System (disc. 2015) or two mags., black Melonite or stainless steel (bi-tone, disc. 2017) slide finish, 28-29 oz. Mfg. 2011-2018.

	$550	$475	$425	$375	$335	$300	$265	*$630*

Add $29 for .45 ACP cal. (new 2012).
Add $63 for bi-tone finish (disc. 2017).

This model is also available with an extended 13 (.45 ACP), 16 (.40 S&W) or 19 (9mm Para.) shot mag. in states where legal.

XD(M) COMPETITION SERIES – 9mm Para. (disc. 2020), .40 S&W (disc. 2018), 10mm (new 2019), or .45 ACP cal., fully supported chamber, black polymer frame, 5 1/4 in. match grade hammer forged steel barrel with Melonite, 13 (.45 ACP), 15 (10mm), 16 (.40 S&W, disc. 2018), or 19 (9mm Para.) shot mag., forged steel slide, USA Trigger System, red fiber optic front and fully adj. target rear sight, grip safety, accessory rail, loaded chamber indicator, ambi mag. release, striker status indicator, includes the XD(M) Gear System (disc. 2015) or two magazines, Mega-Lock frame texture, Melonite slide finish, black or bi-tone (disc. 2016) finish, 8.2 in. OAL, 29-32 oz. New late 2011.

MSR $779	$660	$575	$500	$425	$375	$300	$230

Subtract $26 for 9mm Para. cal. (disc. 2020)
Add $62 for bi-tone finish (disc. 2016).
Subtract approx. $80 if without XD(M) Gear System (disc. 2015).

GRADING - PPGS™	100%	98%	95%	90%	80%	70%	60%	LAST MSR

XD(M) CUSTOM SERIES – the Springfield custom shop made three variations of the XD(M) pistol, including the XD(M) Carry, XD(M) Production, and XD(M) Custom Competition. Most calibers and sizes were available.

Current MSRs on this series are as follows - XD(M) Carry is $910, XD(M) Production is $1,365, and XD(M) Custom Competition is $1,525.

XD-M ELITE – 9mm Para. cal., polymer frame, 3.8 or 4 1/2 in. hammer forged steel barrel, Melonite finish, two 20 shot mags., extended flared magwell, META (Matched-Enhanced Trigger Assembly) trigger system, fiber optic front and Tactical Rack U-dot rear sights, one-piece recoil system w/full length guide rod, improved slide serrations, black finish, 29 oz. New 2020.

MSR $590	$500	$440	$375	$325	$275	$225	$175	

* ***XD-M Elite Compact*** – 9mm Para. cal., compact polymer frame, 3.8 in. hammer forged steel barrel, Melonite finish, two 14 shot mags., extended flared magwell, META (Matched-Enhanced Trigger Assembly) trigger system, fiber optic front and Tactical Rack U-dot rear sights, one-piece recoil system w/full length guide rod, improved slide serrations, black finish, 27 oz. New 2020.

MSR $590	$500	$440	$375	$325	$275	$225	$175	

* ***XD-M Elite Tactical OSP*** – 9mm Para. cal., polymer frame, 4 1/2 in. hammer forged steel barrel, Melonite finish, two 22 shot mags., extended flared magwell, META (Matched-Enhanced Trigger Assembly) trigger system, Co-Witness sights, one-piece recoil system w/full length guide rod, improved slide serrations, black or Desert FDE finish, 30 oz. New 2020.

MSR $709	$600	$500	$450	$400	$325	$275	$200	

XD-M ELITE PRECISION – 9mm Para. cal., black polymer frame, 5 1/4 in. hammer forged steel barrel, Melonite finish, three 22 shot mags., extended flared magwell, META (Matched-Enhanced Trigger Assembly) trigger system, one-piece recoil system w/full length guide rod, improved slide serrations, 30 oz. New 2020.

MSR $653	$550	$475	$425	$375	$300	$250	$200	

XD(M) OSP (OPTICAL SIGHT PISTOL) – 9mm Para. (disc. 2020) or 10mm (new mid-2019) cal., black or Desert FDE (mfg. 2019-2020) polymer frame, 4 1/2 or 5.3 (mfg. 2019-2020, shipped with additional 4 1/2 in. non-threaded barrel) in. threaded hammer forged and Melonite treated barrel with thread protector, two 15 (10mm, new 2019) or 19 shot stainless steel mags., factory milled forged steel slide with Melonite, Co-Witnessed suppressor height sights, three sight bases, with or without Vortex Venom red dot with fiber optic front and low profile combat rear sights, Mega-Lock grip texturing, three interchangeable backstraps, grip safety, one-piece full-length guide rod, accessory rail, ambi mag. release, loaded chamber indicator, striker status indicator, black or Desert FDE Cerakote (mfg. 2019-2020) slide finish, 29-31.1 oz. New 2017.

MSR $695	$600	$545	$485	$415	$365	$315	$275	

Add $15 for Desert FDE Cerakote finish (mfg. 2019-2020).
Add $248 for Vortex Venom red dot sight.

XD(M) THREADED BARREL – 9mm Para. (disc. 2018) or .45 ACP cal., FDE polymer frame, 4 1/2 in. threaded steel barrel with thread protector, includes three 13 or 19 (9mm) shot stainless steel mags., forged steel slide and barrel, USA Trigger System, dovetail front and rear suppressor height 3-dot sights, grip safety, one-piece full-length guide rod, accessory rail, loaded chamber indicator, status striker indicator, ambi mag. release, black Melonite finish, 8.4 in. OAL, 29-31 oz. New 2016.

MSR $673	$595	$495	$445	$385	$335	$300	$265	

XD-S – 9mm Para. or .45 ACP cal., hammerless striker ignition system, 3.3 or 4 (new 2014) in. steel barrel, 5, 7, or 9 (single stack with extension) shot mag., polymer frame with textured grip panels, fiber optic front and low profile dovetail rear sights, black or bi-tone Melonite metal finish, loaded chamber indicator, single position Picatinny rail system, short reset trigger, rear grip safety, two interchangeable backstraps, includes XD-S Gear System, 21 1/2 oz. Mfg. 2013-2015.

	$525	$450	$400	$350	$315	$280	$250	*$595*

Add $4 for .45 ACP cal.
Add $50 for bi-tone finish.

Springfield Armory has issued a voluntary safety recall on Springfield 3.3 XDS pistols in 9mm Para. cal. with serial numbers between XS900000 and XS938700, and in .45 ACP with serial numbers between XS500000 and XS686300 due to a remote possibility of unintentional discharge. For more information, please visit Springfieldrecall.com, or call 800.680.6866.

GRADING - PPGS™	100%	98%	95%	90%	80%	70%	60%	LAST MSR

* ***XD-S Essentials*** – 9mm Para., .40 S&W (new 2016), or .45 ACP cal., hammerless striker ignition system, 3.3 or 4 (new 2014) in. steel Melonite finish barrel, 5, 7, or 9 (single stack with extension) shot mag., fiber optic front and low profile dovetail rear sights, black, Melonite, or satin stainless slide, black, FDE (new 2016), or Tactical Gray (9mm Para. new 2017, .45 ACP new 2018) polymer frame with textured grip panels, loaded chamber indicator, single position Picatinny rail system, short reset trigger, rear grip safety, two interchangeable backstraps, includes two mags., 21 1/2 oz. Mfg. 2013-2018.

$450	$385	$325	$275	$240	$220	$200	*$499*

Add $50 for satin stainless slide.
Add $50 for .45 ACP cal. or $94 for .45 ACP cal. with satin stainless slide.
Add $109 for Crimson Trace Laserguard with 9mm or $153 for Crimson Trace with .45 ACP cal. (mfg. 2016 only).

Springfield Armory has issued a voluntary safety recall on Springfield 3.3 XDS pistols in 9mm Para. cal. with serial numbers between XS900000 and XS938700, and in .45 ACP with serial numbers between XS500000 and XS686300 due to a remote possibility of unintentional discharge. For more information, please visit Springfieldrecall.com, or call 800.680.6866.

XD-S MOD.2 – .40 S&W or .45 ACP cal., ultra slim contoured black, desert FDE (mfg. 2019-2020), or tactical gray polymer frame with enhanced grip texture, 3.3 in. hammer forged steel barrel with Melonite finish, 1-5 (flush) and 1-6 (Mid-Mag X-tension) shot mags., trigger safety, tactical rack U notch serrated white dot rear and fiber optic front sights with or w/o Viridian "E" series laser or tactical rack U notch serrated rear and Pro-Glo Tritium luminescent front sights, grip safety, loaded chamber indicator, posi-wedge slide serrations, ambidextrous mag. release, forged carbon with Melonite finish or satin stainless (mfg. 2019-2020) steel slide, 6 1/2 in. OAL, 23-24 oz. Mfg. 2018-2020.

$465	$385	$325	$275	$240	$220	$200	*$524*

Add $44 for .45 ACP cal.
Add $50 for Pro-Glo Tritium luminescent front sight.
Add $41 for satin stainless slide.
Add $31 for Viridian "E" series laser.

XD-S MOD.2 OSP – 9mm Para. cal., polymer frame with enhanced grip texture, 3.3 in. hammer forged steel barrel, 7 or 9 (extended) shot mag., forged steel slide, Melonite finish on slide and barrel, white dot front and serrated rear sights, with or w/out Crimson Trace CTS-1500 red dot, dual captive recoil spring w/full length guide rod, black finish, 21.5 oz. (w/flush mag.) or 22.5 oz. (w/extended mag.). New 2020.

MSR $425	$365	$325	$275	$250	$200	$165	$130

Add 30% (MSR $549) for Crimson Trace CTS-1500 red dot.

XD MOD.2 SUB-COMPACT – 9mm Para., .40 S&W (disc. 2018), or .45 ACP cal., ultra slim contoured black or FDE (mfg. 2016-2018) polymer frame, 3 or 3.3 (.45 ACP only) in. hammer forged barrel, two 9 (.45 or .40 S&W) or 13 (9mm) shot mags., USA Trigger System, low profile rear combat and fiber optic front sights, features GripZone grips with three zones of different textures, grip safety, loaded chamber indicator, striker status indicator, posi-wedge slide serrations, ambidextrous mag. release, high-hand beavertail, accessory rail, black Melonite or stainless steel (Bi-Tone disc. 2018) slide finish, 6 1/4-6 1/2 in. OAL, 26 oz. Mfg. 2015-2020.

$495	$425	$365	$315	$275	$240	$215	*$559*

Add $29 for .45 ACP cal.
Add $43 for stainless steel (Bi-Tone disc. 2018) finish.

XD MOD.2 SERVICE MODEL – 9mm Para., .40 S&W (disc. 2018), or .45 ACP cal., black or tactical gray (9mm Para. only) polymer frame with GripZone texture, 4 in. barrel, two 12, 13, or 16 shot stainless steel mags., forged steel w/Melonite finish or satin stainless steel (9mm Para. or .40 S&W only) slide, fiber optic front and low profile combat rear sights, grip safety, full-length guide rod, accessory rail, ambidextrous mag. release, loaded chamber indicator, 7 1/4 in. OAL, 28-30 oz. Mfg. 2017-2020.

$495	$425	$365	$315	$275	$240	$215	*$559*

Add $29 for .45 ACP cal.
Add $43 for stainless steel slide (9mm Para. or .40 S&W cal. only).

* ***XD MOD.2 Service Model Threaded*** – 9mm Para. cal., FDE polymer frame, 4.8 in. hammer forged threaded barrel, two 16 shot mags., USA Trigger System, dovetail front and rear suppressor height 3-dot sights, grip safety, dual spring with full-length guide rod, accessory rail, ambidextrous mag. release, loaded chamber indicator, GripZone texture, black Melonite slide finish, 29 oz. Mfg. 2017-2020.

$510	$425	$365	$315	$275	$240	$215	*$586*

GRADING - PPGS™	100%	98%	95%	90%	80%	70%	60%	LAST MSR

XD MOD.2 TACTICAL MODEL – 9mm Para. (mfg. 2017-2020) or .45 ACP cal., black polymer frame, 5 in. forged carbon steel barrel, two 13 or 16 (9mm) shot mags., USA Trigger System, full-length guide rod, fiber optic front and low profile combat rear sights, accessory rail, ambi mag. release, loaded chamber indicator, GripZone texture, grip safety, Melonite or stainless steel (9mm only, mfg. 2017-2020) slide finish, 29-31 oz. Mfg. 2016-2020.

	100%	98%	95%	90%	80%	70%	60%	LAST MSR
	$525	$425	$365	$315	$275	$240	$215	*$608*

Add $29 for .45 ACP cal.

Add $43 for stainless steel slide (9mm only, mfg. 2017-2020).

Pistols: Semi-Auto - 911 Series

MODEL 911 .380 ACP – .380 ACP cal., hardcoat anodized aluminum frame with Octo-Grip texture, 2.7 in. 416R stainless steel precision broached barrel, one 6 (flush) and 7 (extended) shot mag., stainless steel slide, Delta hammer, G10 enhanced pivoting trigger, Pro-Glo Tritium/luminescent front and white outlined Tritium rear night sights, Gray/Black or Green/Black Hogue G10 thin-line grips or Viridian Green laser, extended ambi thumb safety, loaded chamber indicator, rear slide serrations, Black Nitride or brushed stainless steel slide finish, 5 1/2 in. OAL, 12.6 oz. New 2018.

	100%	98%	95%	90%	80%	70%	60%
MSR $536	$450	$395	$340	$300	$250	$205	$160

Add $180 for Viridian Green laser grips.

* ***Model 911 .380 ACP Desert FDE*** – .380 ACP cal., 7075 T6 hardcoat anodized aluminum frame with Desert FDE Cerakote finish and Octo-Grip texture, 2.7 in. 416R stainless steel barrel with black Nitride finish, 1-6 shot (flush) and 1-7 shot extended stainless steel mag., black Nitride or Desert FDE Cerakote slide with ball cut and loaded chamber indicator, Pro-Glo Tritium/Luminescent front and white outlined rear Tritium night sights, Black G10 Sand Dune or rubber SA wrap-around Hogue grips, full-length guide rod w/flat wire spring, 12.6 oz. New 2019.

	100%	98%	95%	90%	80%	70%	60%
MSR $629	$535	$475	$400	$365	$300	$250	$200

* ***Model 911 .380 ACP Platinum/Graphite*** – .380 ACP cal., aluminum frame with Octo-Grip texture, 2.7 in. 416R stainless steel barrel, 1-6 shot (flush) and 1-7 shot extended mag., Pro-Glo Tritium/Luminescent front and white outlined rear Tritium night sights, engineered ivory grips, loaded chamber indicator, full-length guide rod, hardcoat anodized clear frame finish, Elite Concrete Cerakote slide finish, 12.6 oz. Mfg. 2019-2020.

	100%	98%	95%	90%	80%	70%	60%	LAST MSR
	$625	$550	$475	$425	$350	$285	$225	*$729*

* ***Model 911 .380 ACP Titanium*** – .380 ACP cal., 7075 T6 hardcoat anodized aluminum frame with Titanium Cerakote finish and Octo-Grip texture, 2.7 in. 416R stainless steel barrel with black Nitride finish, 1-6 shot (flush) and 1-7 shot extended stainless steel mag., Black Nitride or Titanium Cerakote slide with ball cut and loaded chamber indicator, Pro-Glo Tritium/Luminescent front and white outlined rear Tritium night sights, Blacked Out G10 or Black G10 Chevron grips, full-length guide rod with flat wire spring, 12.6 oz. New 2019.

	100%	98%	95%	90%	80%	70%	60%
MSR $649	$550	$480	$415	$375	$300	$250	$200

* ***Model 911 .380 ACP Vintage Blue*** – .380 ACP cal., 7075 T6 anodized hardcoat aluminum frame with Octo-Grip texture and Vintage Blue Cerakote finish, 2.7 in. 416R stainless steel barrel, 1-6 shot (flush) and 1-7 shot extended stainless steel mag., PVD Stainless steel slide with ball cut and loaded chamber indicator, Pro-Glo Tritium/Luminescent front and white outlined rear Tritium night sights, engineered ivory grips, full-length guide rod w/flat wire spring, 12.6 oz. New 2019.

	100%	98%	95%	90%	80%	70%	60%
MSR $729	$625	$550	$475	$425	$350	$285	$225

MODEL 911 (9MM PARA) – 9mm Para. cal., 7075 T6 anodized hardcoat aluminum frame with Octo-Grip texturing, 3 in. 416R stainless steel precision broached barrel with black Nitride finish, one 6 shot (flush) and one 7 shot extended stainless steel mag., Hogue short reset enhanced pivoting G10 trigger with shoe, Pro-Glo Tritium/Luminescent front and white outlined Tritium rear night sights with or w/o integrated green Viridian laser grips, G10 thin line, Viridian green laser, or Hogue rubber wrap around grips, ambi thumb safety, full-length guide rod w/flat wire spring, loaded chamber indicator, posi-wedge slide serrations, ambidextrous extended thumb safety, black Nitride, Desert FDE (new 2020), or brushed stainless steel slide finish, 15.3 oz. New 2019.

	100%	98%	95%	90%	80%	70%	60%
MSR $580	$500	$425	$375	$325	$275	$225	$175

Subtract $25 (MSR $555) for Hogue rubber grips.

Add $49 for Desert FDE finish w/Hogue grips (new 2020).

Add $20 for G10 thin line grips.

Add $210 for Viridian green laser grips.

MODEL 911 ALPHA – .380 ACP cal., 7075 T6 hardcoat anodized aluminum frame, 2.7 in. 416R stainless steel precision broached barrel with black Nitride finish, 6 shot stainless steel mag., stainless steel slide

GRADING - PPGS™	100%	98%	95%	90%	80%	70%	60%	LAST MSR

with ball cut and loaded chamber indicator, fiber optic front and white 2-dot rear sights, crossed cannon polymer grips, ambidextrous extended thumb safety, posi-wedge slide serrations, full-length guide rod with flat wire spring, black Nitride or brushed stainless slide finish, 5 1/2 in. OAL, 12.6 oz. New 2019.

MSR $429 $365 $325 $275 $250 $200 $165 $135

Pistols: Semi-Auto - Saint Series, AR-15 Style

SAINT PISTOL – 5.56 NATO or .300 AAC Blackout cal., GIO, pistol length gas port with low profile pinned gas block (5.56 NATO) or adj. gas block (.300 Blackout), 7 1/2 in. 416R stainless steel or 9 in. chrome moly (.300 Blackout only) barrel, Melonite treated, 30 shot Magpul PMAG, NiB coated GI trigger, Bravo Company trigger guard, no sights, SB Tactical SBX-K forearm brace, Magpul MOE (5.56 NATO) or Bravo Company Mod.3 (.300 Blackout) pistol grip, forged Type III hardcoat anodized 7075 T6 aluminum upper (forward assist available on .300 Blackout model) and lower receiver with Accu-Tite Tension System, carbine "H" heavy Tungsten buffer, GI-style charging handle, enhanced M16 BCG, M-LOK free floating handguard with SA locking tabs and forward handstop, includes soft pistol case, black or Desert FDE finish, also available with B5 Systems furniture (mfg. 2020 only), 5 lbs. 8 oz. Mfg. 2018-2020.

$760 $650 $575 $500 $425 $350 $275 ***$849***

Add $44 for 5.56 NATO cal.

* ***Saint Pistol 9.6 in.*** – 5.56 NATO cal., DI, carbine length gas system, 9.6 in. chrome moly Vanadium Melonite barrel, A2 flash hider, 30 shot Magpul Gen M3 mag., NiB coated GI trigger, BCM Gunfighter trigger guard, Trinity Force breech brace (1.0 standard pistol), single sided safety, forged aluminum upper and lower receiver, M4 feed ramps, Picatinny pinned gas block, M16 w/carpenter steel and HPT/MPI Melonite BCG, GI-style charging handle, carbine "H" heavy Tungsten buffer, Type III hardcoat anodized black finish, also available with B5 Systems furniture, 5 lbs. 8 oz. New 2020.

MSR $895 $760 $650 $575 $500 $425 $350 $275

SAINT EDGE PISTOL – 5.56 NATO cal., carbine length pinned adj. gas block, 5 1/2 (Saint Edge PDW, new 2020) or 3 in. Melonite treated CMV barrel, A2 flash hider or Maxim Defense muzzle brake (Saint Edge PDW, new 2020), 30 shot Magpul Gen 3 mag., SA match single stage trigger with short reset, spring loaded flip-up adj. front sight and dual aperture rear sight, Maxim Defense CQB or SCW (Saint Edge PDW, new 2020) brace, Bravo Company MOD 3 grip, ambi safety, forged aluminum upper receiver, billet aluminum lower receiver w/Accu-Tite Tension System, M-LOK SA aluminum free float handguard with locking tabs and hand stop, mid-size charging handle, Maxim system buffer assembly, enhanced M16 BCG, 24.6 OAL., 5 lbs. 11.5 oz. Also available as takedown system w/extended folding brace (Saint Edge Evac model, new 2020). New 2018.

MSR $1,559 $1,175 $925 $825 $725 $675 $625 $575

Add 15% (MSR $1,777) for Saint Edge PDW (new 2020).

Add 25% (MSR $1,949) for Saint Edge Evac (new 2020).

SAINT VICTOR PISTOL – 5.56 NATO or .300 AAC Blackout cal., GIO, pistol length gas port with adj. gas block, 7 1/2 in. 416R stainless steel (5.56 NATO) or 9 in. CMV (.300 Blackout) barrel with Melonite finish, A2 flash hider, 30 shot Magpul PMAG, enhanced NiB coated single stage flat trigger, Bravo Company trigger guard, no sights, SB Tactical SBX-K brace, Bravo Company Mod. 3 pistol grip, forged Type III hardcoat anodized aluminum upper and lower receiver with Accu-Tite Tension System, free float M-LOK handguard with SA locking tabs and forward handstop, includes soft pistol case, also available with B5 Systems furniture (new 2020), available in black, Desert FDE, OD Green, or Tactical Gray finish, 5 lbs. 8 oz. New 2019.

MSR $1,100 $940 $825 $700 $600 $500 $425 $330

Add 2.5% (MSR $1,125) for Desert FDE, OD Green, or Tactical Gray finish.

* ***Saint Victor Pistol .308 Win.*** – .308 Win. cal., DI, carbine length, low profile pinned gas block, 10.3 in. CMV barrel, SA two-piece forward blast diverter, 20 shot Magpul PMAG Gen M3 mag., NiB flat GI trigger, SB Tactical SBA3 brace, BCM GUNFIGHTER Mod 3 pistol grip, single side safety, forged aluminum upper and lower receiver, Accu-Tite Tension System, Picatinny rail, Melonite BCG, aluminum free float M-LOK handguard w/SA locking tabs, GI-style charging handle, QD endplate, hardcoat anodized black finish, 8.6 lbs. New 2020.

MSR $1,412 $1,200 $1,050 $900 $775 $650 $525 $425

PISTOLS: SINGLE SHOT, 1911-A2 SASS SERIES

1911-A2 SASS – various cals., single shot break open action featuring interchangeable barrels, Pachmayr grips, adj. front and rear sights, blue finish only, 61-66 oz. Mfg. 1990-1992.

* ***1911-A2 SASS 10 3/4 in. Barrel*** – .22 LR, 7mm BR, .243 Win., .357 Mag., or .44 Mag. cal.

$650 $560 $495 $450 $420 $390 $360 ***$749***

Add $399 per interchangeable conversion unit (includes barrel).

GRADING - PPGS™	100%	98%	95%	90%	80%	70%	60%	LAST MSR

* ***1911-A2 SASS 15 in. Barrel*** – .22 LR, .223 Rem., .243 Win. (new 1991), 7mm BR, 7mm-08 Rem., .308 Win., or .358 Win. cal.

	$650	$560	$495	$450	$420	$390	$360	*$749*

Add $399 per interchangeable conversion unit (includes barrel).

RIFLES: BOLT ACTION

CZ 98 HUNTER CLASSIC – .243 Win., .270 Win., .30-06, .308 Win., 6.5x55mm, 7x57 Mauser, 7x64mm, 7.29x57mm, .300 Win. Mag., or 7mm Rem. Mag. cal., features Mauser 98 Large Ring action, mfg. by CZ in the Czech Republic and Springfield Armory, controlled feeding, 24 in. hammer forged barrel, adj. trigger, choice of walnut or synthetic stock, 7.7 lbs. Limited mfg. 1995 only.

	$345	$315	$285	$260	$240	$220	$195	*$411*

Add $38 for walnut stock.

MAUSER M98 – 7x57mm Mauser cal., surplus rifles with standard military dimensions and features. Importation disc. 1989.

* ***Mauser M98 Hunting/Utility Grade***

	$70	$50	$45	$45	$40	$40	$35	*$75*

* ***Mauser M98 Collector Grade***

	$105	$90	$80	$70	$60	$50	$40	*$116*

* ***Mauser M98 Premium Grade***

	$170	$150	$130	$115	$100	$90	$80	*$194*

MODEL 2020 WAYPOINT – .308 Win., 6mm Creedmoor, 6.5 Creedmoor, or 6.5 PRC cal., 20 or 24 in. fluted stainless steel or carbon fiber barrel with Mil-Spec Green Cerakote (Evergreen Camo stock) or Desert Verde Cerakote (Ridgeline Camo stock) finish (Evergreen Camo stock) or 24 in. fluted, removable SA radial muzzle brake, 5 shot AICS pattern mag., enlarged ejection port, sliding extractor, adj. Triggertech trigger, Hybrid profile carbon fiber stock with five QD mounts, with or w/out adj. cheek comb, Pachmayr Decelerator recoil pad, hybrid dual plane feed ramp, Picatinny mount, M-LOK, Evergreen Camo or Ridgeline Camo hand-painted stock finish, 6 lbs. 10 oz.-8 lbs. 2 oz. New late 2020.

MSR $1,699	$1,450	$1,275	$1,095	$985	$800	$675	$550	

Add 7.5% (MSR $1,825) for adj. cheek comb.
Add 35% (MSR $2,275) for carbon fiber barrel.

RIFLES: SEMI-AUTO, TACTICAL DESIGN

Many models listed are CA legal, since they do not have a muzzle brake. MSRs are typically the same as those guns available with a muzzle brake. Pricing on CA legal firearms is not included within the scope of this listing - please contact a Springfield dealer directly for this information.

M1 CARBINE – .30 Carbine cal., features new receiver on older military M1 GI stocks. Disc.

	$495	$435	$370	$335	$270	$225	$175	

M1 GARAND AND VARIATIONS – .30-06, .270 Win. (disc. 1987), or .308 Win. cal., semi-auto, 24 in. barrel, gas operated, 8 shot mag., adj. sights, 9 1/2 lbs.

* ***M1 Garand Rifle*** – .30-06 or .308 Win. cal., mfg. with original U.S. government issue parts, with new walnut stock, 8 shot mag., 24 in. barrel, 9 1/2 lbs. Limited mfg. 2002-2007.

	$1,175	$1,030	$880	$800	$645	$530	$410	*$1,439*

Add $30 for .308 Win. cal.

* ***M1 Garand Standard Model*** – similar to M1 Garand Rifle, except optional camo GI fiberglass stock.

	$725	$635	$545	$495	$400	$325	$255	*$761*

Subtract $65 if with GI stock.

* ***M1 Garand National Match*** – walnut stock, match barrel and sights.

	$850	$745	$635	$580	$465	$380	$295	*$897*

Add $240 for Kevlar stock.

* ***M1 Garand Ultra Match*** – match barrel and sights, glass bedded stock, walnut stock standard.

	$950	$830	$710	$645	$520	$425	$330	*$1,033*

Add $240 for Kevlar stock.

* ***M1-D Sniper Rifle*** – .30-06 or .308 Win. cal., limited quantities, with original M84 scope, prong type flash suppressor, leather cheek pad and sling.

	$1,100	$960	$825	$750	$605	$495	$385	*$1,033*

GRADING - PPGS™	100%	98%	95%	90%	80%	70%	60%	LAST MSR

* ***M1 Garand Tanker Rifle*** – similar to T-26 authorized by Gen. MacArthur at the end of WWII, 18 1/4 in. barrel, .30-06 or .308 Win. cal., GI stock standard.

	$850	$745	$635	$580	$465	$380	$295	*$797*

Add $23 for walnut full stock.

* ***D-Day M1 Garand Rifle*** – .30-06 cal., 24 in. barrel, gas operated, military square post front sight, engraved stock, 8 shot mag., two 8 shot clips, leather sling, cleaning kit, includes wooden crate and limited edition lithograph print, 9 1/2 lbs. 1,944 mfg. 2004-2005.

	$1,375	$1,205	$1,030	$935	$755	$620	$480	*$1,490*

BM 59 – .308 Win. cal., mfg. in Italy and machined and assembled in the Springfield Armory factory, 19.32 in. barrel, 20 shot detachable box mag., 9 1/2 lbs.

* ***BM 59 Standard Italian Rifle*** – with grenade launcher, winter trigger, tri-compensator, and bipod.

	$1,750	$1,530	$1,310	$1,190	$960	$785	$610	*$1,950*

* ***BM 59 Alpine Rifle*** – with Beretta pistol grip type stock.

	$2,025	$1,770	$1,520	$1,375	$1,115	$910	$710	*$2,275*

This model was also available in a Paratrooper configuration with folding stock at no extra charge.

* ***BM 59 Nigerian Rifle*** – similar to BM 59, except has Beretta pistol grip type stock.

	$2,075	$1,815	$1,555	$1,410	$1,140	$935	$725	*$2,340*

* ***BM 59 E Model Rifle***

	$1,975	$1,730	$1,480	$1,345	$1,085	$890	$690	*$2,210*

M1A RIFLES – .243 Win. (disc.), .308 Win., or 7mm-08 Rem. (1991 mfg. only) cal., patterned after the original Springfield M14 - except semi-auto, walnut or fiberglass stock, 18 or 22 in. steel or stainless steel barrel, fiberglass handguard, "New Loaded" option (see separate listing) beginning 2001 includes NM air gauged barrel, trigger group, front and rear sights, and flash suppressor or Springfield proprietary muzzle brake, 9 lbs.

* ***M1A Standard/Basic Model*** – 7.62mm cal., 22 in. regular or National Match (disc.) barrel, two-stage military trigger, military square post front and adj. aperture rear sights, choice of Collector (original GI stock, disc. 2001), birch (disc. 2003), black fiberglass (M1A Basic Model, disc.), camo fiberglass (disc.), GI wood (disc. 1992), brown laminated fiberglass (disc.) or black laminated (M1A Standard Model mfg. 1996-2000) stock. Currently mfg. stock finishes for the M1A Standard model include Mossy Oak camo (mfg. 2003-16), Green (mfg. 2011-16), black, Highlander Camo (mfg. 2015-18), or FDE (new 2015) composite or walnut (new 1993) stock, approx. 9 lbs.

MSR $1,720	$1,525	$1,300	$1,075	$950	$825	$700	$595	

Add $19 for Highlander Camo stock (mfg. 2015-18).
Add 5% (MSR $1,823) for new walnut stock.
Add $59 for birch stock (disc. 2003).
Add $10 for green composite stock (mfg. 2011-16).
Add $45 for Mossy Oak camo finished stock (disc. 2016).
Add $44 for stainless steel barrel (disc.), $74 for bipod and stabilizer (disc.) or $159 for brown laminated stock (disc.), $59 for National Match barrel (disc.), $155 for National Match barrel and sights (disc.), $200 for folding stock (disc. 1994).
Subtract $58 for camo fiberglass stock (disc.).

Standard (entry level model) stock configuration for 1996 was black or camo fiberglass.

* ***M1A E-2*** – standard stock is birch. Disc.

	$975	$855	$730	$665	$535	$440	$340	*$842*

Add $30 for walnut stock.
Add $120 for Shaw stock with Harris bipod.

* ***M1A Bush Rifle*** – .308 Win. cal., 18 in. shrouded barrel, 8 lbs. 12 oz., collector GI, walnut, Mossy Oak camo finished (new 2003), black fiberglass folding (disc. 1994 per C/B), and black fiberglass (disc.) or laminated black (disc.) stock. Disc. 1999, reintroduced 2003 only.

	$1,300	$1,135	$975	$885	$715	$585	$455	*$1,529*

Add $29 for walnut stock (disc.), $15 for black fiberglass stock (disc.), $86 for black laminated stock (disc.), $235 for National Match variation (disc.), and $525 for Super Match variation (disc.)

GRADING - PPGS™	100%	98%	95%	90%	80%	70%	60%	LAST MSR

* ***M1A National Match*** – .308 Win. cal., 22 in. steel or stainless steel (new 1999) barrel, National Match sights, mainspring guide, flash suppressor, and gas cylinder, special glass bedded oil finished match stock, two-stage tuned trigger, walnut stock became standard in 1991, 9 lbs.

MSR $2,485	$2,150	$1,850	$1,600	$1,450	$1,150	$950	$750	

Add 2.5% (MSR $2,542) for stainless steel barrel.
Add $155 for heavy composition stock (disc.).
Add $250 for either fiberglass or fancy burl wood stock (disc.).

.243 Win. and 7mm-08 Rem. cals. were also available at extra charge until discontinued.

* ***M1A Super Match*** – .308 Win. cal., 22 in. Hart (disc.) or Douglas premium air gauged custom heavy carbon or stainless steel barrel, oversized walnut, McMillan Black fiberglass, or McMillan Marine Corps Green Camo fiberglass super match stock, modified operating rod guide, rear lugged receiver beginning 1991, approx. 11 1/2 lbs.

MSR $3,018	$2,625	$2,275	$1,950	$1,750	$1,425	$1,175	$950	

Add 7.5% (MSR $3,258) for stainless steel Douglas barrel.
Add $767 for McMillan Black or Marine Corps Green camo fiberglass stock with stainless steel barrel.
Add $250 for Krieger or Hart barrel (disc.).
Add $200 for fancy burl walnut stock (disc.).

.243 Win. and 7mm-08 Rem. cals. were also available at extra charge until discontinued.

M1A LOADED STANDARD – .308 Win. cal., 22 in. National Match steel or stainless steel (disc. 2018) barrel, features shooting upgrades such as National Match trigger assembly, front and rear sights, and National Match flash suppressor, 10 shot mag., Black or OD Green (disc. 2016) fiberglass, Collector GI walnut (disc. 2000), or new walnut stock, approx. 9 1/2 lbs. New 1999.

MSR $1,884	$1,675	$1,475	$1,250	$1,075	$875	$725	$575	

Add $100 for stainless steel barrel (disc. 2018).
Add 5% (MSR $2,001) for new walnut stock.
Add $213 for walnut stock with stainless steel barrel.
Add $15 for OD Green composite stock (disc. 2016).
Add $525 for extended cluster rail with black fiberglass stock and National Match stainless steel barrel (mfg. 2006-2011).
Add $100 for Collector GI walnut (disc. 2000).

M1A PRECISION ADJUSTABLE LOADED RIFLE – 6.5 Creedmoor (new 2018) or .308 Win./7.62 NATO cal., 22 in. National Match carbon or stainless steel (disc. 2016, reintroduced 2018-19, 6.5 Creedmoor only) barrel, 10 shot mag., NM blade front and aperture rear sights, precision adjustable composite stock, black or FDE (new 2016) finish, 11.25 lbs. New 2015.

MSR $2,045	$1,800	$1,525	$1,300	$1,150	$925	$750	$600	

Add $40 for stainless steel barrel (disc. 2016, reintroduced 2018-19, 6.5 Creedmoor only).

Add 2.5% (MSR $2,088) for 6.5 Creedmor cal.

M1A "GOLD SERIES" – .308 Win. cal., heavy walnut competition stock, gold medal grade heavy Douglas barrel. Mfg. 1987 only.

	$1,950	$1,700	$1,460	$1,320	$1,070	$875	$680	*$1,944*

Add $126 for Kevlar stock, add $390 for special Hart stainless steel barrel, add $516 for Hart stainless steel barrel with Kevlar stock.

M1A SCOUT SQUAD – .308 Win. cal., 18 in. carbon barrel, two-stage military trigger, military square post front sight and adj. aperture rear, choice of GI Collector (disc. 1998), green (disc. 2011), black laminated (disc. 1998), black, FDE (mfg. 2015-2020), Mossy Oak composite (disc. 2016), or walnut stock, muzzle stabilizer standard, supplied with Scout mount and handguard, approx. 9 lbs. New 1997.

MSR $1,886	$1,675	$1,400	$1,175	$1,050	$850	$675	$595	

Add 7.5% (MSR $2,026) for walnut stock.
Add $88 for Mossy Oak camo stock (disc. 2016).
Add $14 for Green composite stock (disc. 2011).

M1A SOCOM 16 – .308 Win. cal., 16 1/4 in. barrel with muzzle brake, upper handguard has been cut out for sight rail, 10 shot box mag., Tritium front sight with ghost ring aperture rear sight, forward scout-style Picatinny mount, two-stage military trigger, black, green (disc. 2016), FDE (mfg. 2015-2020), or multi-cam (mfg. 2015 only) composite stock with steel buttplate, black finish, 8.8 lbs. New 2004.

MSR $2,026	$1,800	$1,525	$1,275	$1,150	$925	$750	$650	

Add $15 for green composite stock (disc. 2016).
Subtract $148 for multi-cam composite stock (mfg. 2015 only).

GRADING - PPGS™	100%	98%	95%	90%	80%	70%	60%	LAST MSR

M1A SOCOM 16 II – .308 Win. cal., 16 1/4 in. carbon steel barrel with muzzle brake, black composite stock with steel buttplate, black or urban camo (disc. 2011) finish, 10 shot box mag., Tritium front sight with ghost ring aperture rear sight, two-stage military trigger, cluster rail or extended (new 2007) cluster rail, 10 lbs. Mfg. 2005-2014.

	$2,100	$1,875	$1,650	$1,450	$1,250	$1,000	$800	*$2,399*

Add $100 for extended cluster rail (Socom II, new 2007).

M1A SOCOM 16 CQB – 7.62 NATO/.308 Win. cal., 16 1/4 in. parkerized carbon steel barrel, 10 shot mag., XS Post front sight with Tritium insert and ghost ring rear sight, 5-position CQB composite stock with adj. cheekpiece and M-LOK Rail system, 9.2 lbs. New 2016.

MSR $2,188	$1,900	$1,625	$1,375	$1,225	$975	$875	$725	

Add 12.5% (MSR $2,470) for Vortex Venom sight and SA base.

M1A SOCOM 16 TANKER – 7.62 NATO/.308 Win. cal., patterned after the SOCOM 16 Tanker, 16 1/4 in. carbon steel barrel, 6 grooves, 10 shot Parkerized steel mag., XS post w/Tritium insert front sight, ghost ring aperture rear sight w/MOA adj., vintage walnut stock, 8 3/4 lbs. New 2020.

MSR $2,026	$1,800	$1,525	$1,275	$1,150	$925	$750	$650	

M1A/M21 TACTICAL – .308 Win./7.62mm cal., Garand action, 22 in. barrel, tactical variation of the Super Match mfg. with match grade parts giving superior accuracy, adj. walnut cheekpiece stock, choice of Douglas carbon steel or stainless Krieger barrel, 11.6 lbs. Mfg. 1990-late 2010s.

	$3,225	$2,875	$2,375	$2,100	$1,750	$1,450	$1,200	*$3,619*

Add $427 for Krieger stainless barrrel.

M25 "WHITE FEATHER" TACTICAL – .308 Win. cal., Garand action, includes black fiberglass M3A McMillan stock, 22 in. Kreiger heavy carbon steel barrel standard, Rader trigger, White Feather logo and Carlos Hathcock II signature, 10 shot box mag., includes Harris bipod, 12 3/4 lbs. Mfg. 2001-2009.

	$4,750	$4,155	$3,560	$3,230	$2,610	$2,135	$1,660	*$5,278*

SAINT – 5.56 NATO cal., GIO, mid-length gas system, 16 in. chrome moly barrel with Melonite coating, 30 shot Magpul PMAG, enhanced NiB SST, BCM trigger guard, A2 style front sight and gas block, optional pic-gas block variation (new 2020), dual aperture rear sight, 6-pos. stock, rubber buttpad, Bravo Company MOD 0 pistol grip, forged aluminum upper and lower receiver, M4 feed ramps, GI-style charging handle, M16 BCG, carbine "H" style heavy tungsten buffer assembly, BCM PKMR two-piece KeyMod or M-LOK aluminum SA free float (new 2017) handguard w/SA locking tabs and internal aluminum heat shield, QD and slotted sling attachment points, black, Tactical Gray (mfg. 2019-2020), OD Green (mfg. 2019-2020), or Desert FDE (mfg. 2018-2020) Type III hardcoat anodized finish, also available with B5 Systems furniture (new 2020), 6 lbs. 11 oz. New 2016.

MSR $995	$760	$650	$575	$500	$425	$350	$275	

SAINT EDGE – 5.56 NATO cal., adj. gas block, 16 in. CMV Melonite barrel, 30 shot mag., SST, dual aperture sights, adj. flip-up front sight, SOPMOD buttstock, Bravo Company Mod 3 pistol grip, forged aluminum upper and lower receiver, mid-size charging handle, M16 bolt carrier group, full-length M-LOK free floating handguard, includes case, black finish, 6 lbs. 3 oz. New 2017.

MSR $1,350	$1,025	$875	$800	$700	$575	$450	$375	

SAINT VICTOR – 5.56 NATO or .350 Legend (new 2021) cal., GIO, mid-length, low profile, compact frame, 16 in. stainless steel Melonite treated CMV barrel with muzzle brake, 30 shot Magpul PMAG Gen M3, NiB coated single stage flat trigger, Bravo Company trigger guard, spring loaded flip-up front and rear sights, black Bravo Company 6-pos.stock, 15 in. M-LOK aluminum SA free float handguard w/SA locking tabs and forward hand stop, Bravo Company Mod 3 pistol grip, Accu-Tite tension system, pistol length gas port, adj. gas block, forged aluminum upper and lower receiver, GI-style charging handle, heavy tungsten buffer system, Type III hardcoat anodized black finish, desert FDE (new 2021), OD green (new 2021), or Tactical Gray (new 2021) finish, also available with B5 Systems furniture (new 2020), 6 lbs. 9 oz. New 2019.

MSR $1,125	$850	$750	$650	$575	$475	$375	$300	

Add 5% (MSR $1,192) for Desert FDE, OD Green, or Tactical Gray finish.
Subtract 5% (MSR $1,073) for .350 Legend cal.

* ***Saint Victor AR-10 .308 Win.*** – similar to the Saint Victor, except in AR-10 configuration, .308 Win./7.62mm NATO cal., available in black finish, 7 lbs. 11 oz. New 2020.

MSR $1,452	$1,100	$950	$825	$750	$600	$500	$400	

SAR-3 – .308 Win. cal., licensed copy of the pre-ban import HK-91, predecessor to the SAR-8, mfg. in Greece.

	$995	$870	$745	$675	$545	$450	$350	

GRADING - PPGS™	100%	98%	95%	90%	80%	70%	60%	LAST MSR

SAR-8 - .308 Win. cal., patterned after the HK-91, roller lock delayed blowback action, fluted chamber, rotary adj. rear aperture sight, 18 in. barrel, recent mfg. incorporated a cast aluminum receiver with integrated Weaver rail, pistol grip, slim forearm, and green furniture (for law enforcement only), supplied with walnut (disc. 1994) or black fiberglass thumbhole sporter stock, 10 (C/B 1994) or 20 (disc. 1994) shot detachable mag., 8.7 lbs. Mfg. in U.S. starting 1990, disc. 1998.

$1,015 $890 $760 $690 $560 $455 $355 *$1,204*

SAR-8 parts are interchangeable with both SAR-3 and HK-91 parts.

* ***SAR-8 Tactical Counter Sniper Rifle*** - .308 Win. cal., tactical sniper variation of the SAR-8. Mfg. 1996-98.

$1,325 $1,160 $995 $900 $730 $595 $465 *$1,610*

SAR-48 MODEL - .308 Win. cal., GPO, authentic copy of the Belgian semi-auto FAL/LAR rifle, 21 in. barrel, 20 shot mag., walnut or synthetic stock, adj. sights, sling, and mag. loader. Mfg. 1985-89.

$1,675 $1,465 $1,255 $1,140 $920 $755 $585

Add approx. 20% for Israeli configuration with heavy barrel, bipod, flash hider, and flip-up buttplate.

The SAR-48 was disc. in 1989 and reintroduced as the Model SAR-4800 in 1990.

* ***SAR-48 Bush Rifle*** - similar to SAR-48 model, except has 18 in. barrel. Disc.

$1,750 $1,530 $1,310 $1,190 $960 $785 $610

* ***SAR-48 .22 Cal.*** - .22 LR cal., variation of the Sporter Model. Disc. 1989.

$725 $635 $545 $495 $400 $325 $255 *$760*

SAR-4800 SPORTER MODEL - .223 Rem. (new 1997) or .308 Win. cal., GPO, authentic copy of the Belgian semi-auto FAL/LAR rifle, 18 (.223 Rem. cal. only) or 21 in. barrel, 10 (C/B 1994) or 20 (disc.) shot mag., walnut (disc.) or black fiberglass thumbhole sporter stock, adj. sights, sling, and mag. loader. Mfg. 1990-1998.

$1,080 $945 $810 $735 $595 $485 $380

All SAR - 4800 parts are interchangeable with both SAR-48 and FN/FAL parts. This model is an updated variation of the pre-WWII FN Model 49.

* ***SAR-4800 Bush Rifle Sporter Model*** - similar to standard model, except has 18 in. barrel.

$1,085 $950 $815 $735 $595 $490 $380 *$1,216*

DR-200 SPORTER RIFLE - while advertised, this model never went into production. ($687 was planned MSR).

SPRINGFIELD ARMS CO.

Previous assumed business name of Stevens Arms during the Savage era. Many long arm variations were marked with this company listing even though Savage manufactured the guns. Most were average quality utilitarian firearms and most have a current value in the $75-$300 range depending on configuration and condition.

STACCATO (STI INTERNATIONAL)

Current manufacturer established in 1993 located in Georgetown, TX, previously known as STI International until 2020. Distributor and dealer sales.

Founded in 1993, STI International introduced the Staccato brand for their duty and defense oriented pistols in 2019. In 2020, they rebranded their entire line as Staccato. In addition to manufacturing the pistols listed, Staccato also makes parts and accessories for 1911 and 2011 style pistols - please contact the company directly for pricing and availability.

PISTOLS: SEMI-AUTO, SINGLE ACTION (STI PRODUCTION)

The beginning numerals on all STI pistols designate the barrel length, and most of the following models are listed in numerical sequence. STI offers a lifetime warranty on all their models.

2.5 NEMESIS - 7mm Penna/7x23mm cal., 2 1/2 in. barrel. Mfg. 2010-2011.

$840 $725 $625 $525 $450 $400 $350 *$870*

DUTY ONE (3.0 DUTY ONE, 4.0 DUTY ONE, 5.0 DUTY ONE) - 9mm Para., .40 S&W (disc. 2014), or .45 ACP cal., 3 (ramped bull), 4.4 (bull disc. 2013, bushing new 2014), or 5 in. ramped bull barrel, 6, 8, or 9 shot mag., forged steel frame with integral tactical rail, undercut trigger guard, front and rear slide serrations, fixed front and rear sights, G10 grip panels, Recoil Master (3 or 4 in. barrel) or full-length guide rod (5 in. barrel), high ride beavertail grip safety, matte blue or hard chrome (mfg. 2014 only) finish, 36.3 oz. Mfg. 2013-2016.

$1,275 $1,125 $1,025 $875 $750 $625 $525 *$1,499*

Add $79 for Tritium sights (4 in. barrel, disc.).
Add $363 for hard chrome finish (disc. 2014).

GRADING - PPGS™	100%	98%	95%	90%	80%	70%	60%	LAST MSR

* ***Duty One Lite (3.0 Duty One Lite, 4.0 Duty One Lite)*** - 9mm Para. or .45 ACP cal., 3 (bull) or 4 (bushing) in. barrel, 6, 8, 9, or 10 shot mag., aluminum frame, fixed front and rear sights, unique cocking serrations on slide and frame, tactical accessory rail, blued/anodized finish. Mfg. 2014-2016.

$1,350 $1,200 $1,075 $950 $815 $700 $575 ***$1,599***

ELEKTRA CTC (3.0 ELEKTRA) - 9mm Para., .40 S&W (disc. 2012), or .45 ACP cal., forged aluminum black anodized or silver frame with Crimson Trace Laser (new 2015, black anodized only, became standard 2017), 3.10 in. bull barrel, stainless steel slide with Cerakote finish, blue (disc. 2014), purple (disc. 2014), red (disc. 2014), or pink pearl (9mm only) grips, rear cocking serrations, beavertail grip safety, 6 or 8 shot mag., fixed Tritium 2 dot sights, Recoil Master. Mfg. 2010-2017.

$1,250 $1,095 $950 $850 $700 $600 $495 ***$1,799***

3.0 ESCORT - 9mm Para., .40 S&W (mfg. 2013-2014) or .45 ACP cal., 3.24 in. bull barrel, forged aluminum Officer length frame with silver Cerakote finish, STI Recoil Master, undercut trigger guard, bobbed grip safety, checkered cocobolo grips, round top slide with rear cocking serrations and blued finish, adj. 3-dot sights, 6 or 8 shot mag., stippled front strap, 22.8 oz. Mfg. 2009-2016.

$1,100 $995 $875 $735 $650 $550 $465 ***$1,299***

LAWMAN (3.0 LAWMAN, 4.0 LAWMAN) - .38 Super (3 in. barrel, mfg. 2014 only), 9mm Para. or .45 ACP cal., 3 or 4.15 in. STI ramped bull barrel, polished blue finish, carbon steel slide, 8 or 9 shot mag., forged steel frame with 30 LPI front strap checkering, undercut trigger guard, G10 (disc. 2015) or VZ Double Diamond black and gray G10 grips (new 2016), front and rear slide cocking serrations, long curved aluminum trigger, high ride beavertail safety, recoil master guide rod, ramped front sight, tactical adj. rear sight, optional Tritium sights, 6 or 8 shot mag., single sided thumb safety, blue (disc.), black/green (disc.), brown/tan (disc.), or black Cerakote (new 2015) finish, 24.8 oz. Mfg. 2012-2016.

$1,275 $1,125 $1,025 $875 $750 $625 $525 ***$1,499***

Add $79 for Tritium sights (disc. 2014).

3.0 OFF DUTY - 9mm Para. or .45 ACP cal., compact frame, blued or hard chrome matte finish, 3 in. barrel with blue slide, checkered cocobolo grips, stippled front strap, competition front sight, tactical rear sight, 31.3 oz. Mfg. 2009-2013.

$1,075 $950 $800 $725 $595 $485 $375 ***$1,265***

3.0 ROGUE - 9mm Para. cal., 3 in. bull barrel, forged aluminum compact frame, STI stippled front strap, undercut trigger guard, blued slide with Duracoated frame, integral sights, 21 oz. Mfg. 2009.

$925 $825 $725 $650 $575 $500 $425 ***$1,024***

3.0 SHADOW - 9mm Para., .40 S&W, or .45 ACP cal., 3 in. bull barrel, matte black KG coated finish, forged aluminum frame, undercut trigger guard, stippled front strap, ultra thin G10 grips with STI logo, rear cocking serrations, curved trigger, beavertail grip safety, fixed Tritium 2 dot sights, 6 or 8 shot mag., 23.4 oz. Mfg. 2010-2014.

$1,250 $1,095 $950 $850 $695 $565 $440 ***$1,472***

3.0 SPARTAN III - 9mm Para. or .45 ACP cal., 1911 Commander steel frame, parkerized finish, bald front strap, hand checkered double diamond mahogany grips, rear slide serrations, STI long curved trigger, 3.24 in. chrome non-ramped bull bushing barrel, STI high ride beavertail grip safety, competition front sights, fixed rear sights, 6 or 8 shot mag., 32.7 oz. Mfg. 2012-2014.

$650 $575 $495 $440 $360 $295 $225 ***$754***

TACTICAL SS (3.0 TACTICAL SS, 4.0 TACTICAL SS, 5.0 TACTICAL SS) - .38 Super (3 in. only, mfg. 2014), 9mm Para., .40 S&W (disc. 2014), or .45 ACP cal., SA, 3, 4, or 5 in. ramped bull or threaded (new 2014) barrel, long curved trigger, ramped front sight and fixed ledge rear sights or tall suppressor sights (threaded barrel models only, new 2016), 6, 8, or 9 shot mag., full-length guide rod (5 in. only), VZ Aliens black and gray (new 2016) G10 grip panels, high ride beavertail grip safety, ambi thumb safeties, forged steel frame with integral tactical rail, 30 LPI front strap checkering, undercut trigger guard, matte blue (disc. 2014), hard chrome (mfg. 2014 only), or black Cerakote finish, 34-41 oz. Mfg. 2013-2016.

$1,625 $1,425 $1,200 $1,075 $925 $795 $650 ***$1,899***

Add $100 for threaded barrel and Tritium sights.
Add $340 for hard chrome finish (mfg. 2014 only).

3.0 TACTICAL - .38 Super, 9mm Para., .40 S&W, or .45 ACP cal., matte blue or hard chrome finish, 3 in. bull or threaded barrel, modular steel frame with integral tactical rail, flat-top slide with rear cocking serrations, black glass filled nylon polymer grips, long curved trigger, high ride beavertail grip safety, fixed rear sight, ramped front sight, 10, 12, 14, or 17 shot mag., 34 oz. Mfg. 2014-2015.

$1,825 $1,595 $1,375 $1,240 $1,000 $825 $640 ***$2,144***

Add $102 for Tritium sights, or $167 for threaded barrel with Tritium sights.
Add $340 for hard chrome finish.

GRADING - PPGS™	100%	98%	95%	90%	80%	70%	60%	LAST MSR

* ***3.0 Tactical Lite*** – .38 Super, 9mm Para., .40 S&W, or .45 ACP cal., 3 in. bull or threaded barrel, 10, 12, 14, or 17 shot mag., with or w/o Tritium sights, blue finish. Mfg. 2014 only.

$1,825	$1,595	$1,375	$1,240	$1,000	$825	$640	*$2,144*

Add $62 for Tritium sights or $167 for threaded barrel and Tritium sights.

3.0 TOTAL ECLIPSE – 9mm Para., .40 S&W, or .45 ACP cal., 3 in. barrel, skeletonized trigger, aluminum frame, polymer grips, beavertail safety, fixed 2-dot Tritium sights, blue finish, 23.1 oz. Mfg. 2011-2013.

$1,575	$1,375	$1,175	$1,075	$865	$710	$550	*$1,870*

3.25 GP5 – 9mm Para. cal., 3 1/4 in. barrel, DAO, blue finish, chrome moly steel frame w/integral tactical rail, textured polymer grips, double slide serrations, ambi safety, internal extractor, adj. sights, 24.2 oz. Mfg. by Grand Power, Ltd. 2010-2011.

$595	$550	$500	$450	$400	$375	$350	*$663*

3.4 BLS9/BLS40 – 9mm Para. or .40 S&W cal., blue finish, Govt. length grips, Heinie low mount sights, single stack mag., 30 oz. Mfg. 1999-2005.

$765	$650	$565	$460	$400	$375	$350	*$889*

3.4 LS9/LS40 – 9mm Para. or .40 S&W (disc. 2008) cal., blue finish, Commander length grips, single stack mag., Heinie low mount rear sight, slide integral front sight, 28 oz. Mfg. 1999-2013.

$925	$825	$725	$650	$575	$500	$425	*$1,002*

3.4 ESCORT – 9mm Para. or .45 ACP cal., 1911 forged aluminum Commander style frame, 3.4 in. ramped bull barrel, slide with rear cocking serrations, Duracoat finish with blue slide, undercut trigger guard, stippled front strap, rosewood grips, STI high ride beavertail grip safety, fixed Novak style 3-dot sights, 22.8 oz. Mfg. 2007-2008.

$925	$825	$725	$650	$575	$500	$425	*$1,024*

3.9 FALCON – .38 Super, .40 S&W, or .45 ACP cal., STI standard frame, 3.9 in. barrel, size is comparable to Officers Model, adj. rear sight. Limited mfg. 1993-98.

$1,875	$1,375	$1,175	$925	$850	$775	$675	*$2,136*

3.9 GUARDIAN – 9mm Para. (new 2009), .40 S&W (mfg. 2014 only), or .45 ACP cal., 1911 Commander style aluminum blue frame, 3.9 in. ramped bull barrel, stainless steel slide w/polished sides, stippled front strap, undercut trigger guard, rosewood (disc.) or cocobolo wood grips, fixed 3-dot sights, 6 or 8 shot mag., stainless/blue or hard chrome (disc. 2014) finish, 32.4 oz. Mfg. 2007-2016.

$1,100	$995	$875	$735	$650	$550	$465	*$1,299*

Add $340 for hard chrome finish (disc. 2014).

3.9 STINGER – 9mm Para. or .38 Super cal., black frame, designed for IPSC and USPSA competition, 38 oz. Mfg. 2005-2008.

$2,500	$2,225	$1,975	$1,750	$1,575	$1,375	$1,150	*$2,773*

3.9 TACTICAL – 9mm Para., .40 S&W, or .45 ACP cal., matte blue finish, 3.9 in. bull barrel, modular steel frame with integral tactical rail, flat-top slide with rear cocking serrations, black glass filled nylon polymer grips, long curved trigger, high ride beavertail grip safety, fixed rear sight, ramped front sight, 34 oz. Mfg. 2012-2013.

$1,775	$1,500	$1,250	$1,000	$875	$800	$675	*$2,109*

3.9 V.I.P. – 9mm Para. (new 2009), .40 S&W (new 2009), or .45 ACP cal. only, aluminum frame, STI modular polymer frame, stainless steel slide, 3.9 in. bull barrel with STI Recoilmaster muzzle brake, 10, 13, or 16 shot double stack mag., STI fixed sights, blue or hard chrome finish or stainless steel, 25 oz. Mfg. 2001-2006, reintroduced 2009-2014.

$1,500	$1,325	$1,125	$1,025	$825	$675	$525	*$1,775*

Add $340 for hard chrome finish.

4.0 SPARTAN IV – 9mm Para. or .45 ACP cal., 1911 Commander steel frame, parkerized finish, bald front strap, hand checkered double diamond mahogany grips, rear slide serrations, STI long curved trigger, 4.26 in. chrome non-ramped bull bushing barrel, STI high ride beavertail grip safety, competition front sights, fixed rear sights, 8 or 9 shot mag., 34.3 oz. Mfg. 2012-2014.

$650	$575	$495	$440	$360	$295	$225	*$754*

4.0 TACTICAL – 9mm Para., .40 S&W, or .45 ACP cal., matte blue or hard chrome finish, 3 in. bull or threaded barrel, modular steel frame w/integral tactical rail, flat-top slide w/rear cocking serrations, black glass filled nylon polymer grips, long curved trigger, high ride beavertail grip safety, fixed rear sight, ramped front sight, 10, 12, 14, or 17 shot mag., 34 oz. Mfg. 2014-2015.

$1,825	$1,595	$1,375	$1,240	$1,000	$825	$640	*$2,144*

Add $102 for Tritium sights, or $167 for threaded barrel with Tritium sights.
Add $340 for hard chrome finish.

GRADING - PPGS™	100%	98%	95%	90%	80%	70%	60%	LAST MSR

* **4.0 Tactical Lite** – 9mm Para. or .45 ACP cal., 2011 platform, 4 in. bull or threaded barrel, 10, 12, or 17 shot mag., aluminum frame, full-length tactical rail, fixed rear and ramped front sight, ambidextrous safety, tactical magwell, black Cerakote finish, 32 oz. Mfg. 2014-2016.

$1,825 $1,595 $1,375 $1,240 $1,000 $825 $640 *$2,199*

Add $100 for threaded barrel.

4.15 TACTICAL – 9mm Para., .40 S&W, or .45 ACP cal., blue steel, fixed sights, short trigger, ambi safety, 34 1/2 oz. Mfg. 2004-2013.

$1,725 $1,500 $1,295 $1,175 $950 $775 $600 *$2,045*

4.15 RANGER II (3.9 RANGER) – 9mm Para. (new 2009), .40 S&W (new 2009), or .45 ACP cal. only, Officer's Model with 3.9 (Ranger, disc. 2004) or 4.15 (Ranger II, new 2005) in. bull barrel and 1/2 in. shortened grip frame, blue or hard chrome (new 2014) steel frame w/stainless steel slide, low mount STI/Heinie sights, 8 or 9 shot mag., 29 oz. Mfg. 2001-2014.

$1,000 $875 $750 $675 $550 $450 $350 *$1,181*

Add $340 for hard chrome finish.
Add $192 for Ranger III configuration (mfg. 2010-2013).

4.15 DUTY CT – 9mm Para., .40 S&W or .45 ACP cal., 5 in. bull barrel, matte blue finish, integral tactical rail, flat-top slide w/rear cocking serrations, ramped front sight, fixed rear sight, 36.6 oz. Mfg. 2006-2008.

$1,100 $950 $825 $700 $600 $525 $450 *$1,286*

MATCH MASTER (4.15 MATCH MASTER) – .38 Super or 9mm Para. (new 2014) cal., 2011 platform, 4.26 in. TruBor barrel with T2 compensator, 10 or 20 shot mag., sabertooth front and rear cocking serrations, stainless steel spur hammer, black glass filled nylon polymer grips with aluminum magwell, drilled and tapped, C-More red dot scope with blast shield and thumb rest, ambi safety, blue or hard chrome (mfg. 2014 only) finish with polished classic slide, 38.9 oz. Mfg. 2009-2017.

$2,550 $2,225 $1,825 $1,575 $1,300 $1,100 $950 *$2,999*

Add $395 for hard chrome finish (mfg. 2014 only).

STEEL MASTER (4.15 STEEL MASTER) – 9mm Para. cal., 2011 platform, 4.26 in. TruBor barrel, T1 compensator, 10 or 20 shot mag., blue or hard chrome (mfg. 2014 only) finish with polished classic slide, sabertooth cocking serrations, stainless steel spur hammer, ambi safety, C-More red dot scope w/blast shield and thumbrest, black glass filled nylon polymer grips w/aluminum magwell, 38.9 oz. Mfg. 2009-2017.

$2,395 $2,075 $1,750 $1,565 $1,225 $975 $810 *$2,799*

Add $395 for hard chrome finish (mfg. 2014 only).

4.25 GP6 – 9mm Para. cal., 4 1/4 in. barrel, DA/SA, blue finish, chrome moly steel frame with integral tactical rail, textured polymer grips, double slide serrations, ambi safety, internal extractor, adj. sights, 26.1 oz. Mfg. by Grand Power, Ltd. Mfg. 2009-2012.

$595 $550 $500 $450 $400 $375 $350 *$663*

Add $34 for GP6-C model with fiber optic front sight and adj. rear sight (mfg. 2010-2011).

4.25 EL COMMANDANTE – 9mm Para. cal., blue matte finish, Government steel frame, 4.25 in. non-ramped bushing barrel, beavertail grip safety, steel trigger, single sided thumb safety, one-piece original GI-style guide rod, GI steel sights, smooth wood grips, rear slide cocking serrations, 34 1/2 oz. Mfg. 2011 only.

$895 $725 $625 $525 $450 $400 $350 *$942*

4.3 HAWK – various cals., 4.3 in. barrel, STI standard frame (choice of steel or aluminum), 27 or 31 oz. Mfg. 1993-1999.

$1,725 $1,275 $1,075 $875 $800 $700 $600 *$1,975*

4.3 NIGHT HAWK – .45 ACP cal., 4.3 in. barrel, STI wide extended frame, blue finish, 33 oz. Limited mfg. 1997-99.

$1,875 $1,375 $1,175 $925 $850 $775 $675 *$2,136*

5.0 APEIRO – .38 Super (mfg. 2014 only), 9mm Para., .40 S&W, or .45 ACP cal., 2011 platform, 5 in. Schuemann Island style bull barrel, 10, 12, 14, or 17 shot mag., oversized magwell, long wide steel frame, stainless steel slide with sabertooth serrations and Cerakote black frame, blue finish, black glass filled nylon polymer grips, stainless flared and blended magwell, Dawson fiber optic front and adj. rear sights, ambi safety, 38 oz. Mfg. 2010-2017.

$2,550 $2,225 $1,825 $1,575 $1,300 $1,100 $950 *$2,999*

5.0 DUTY ONE – 9mm Para., .40 S&W (disc. 2014) or .45 ACP cal., 5.1 in. barrel with bushing, forged steel frame with integral tactical rail (new 2013), undercut trigger guard, front and rear slide serrations, checkered wood (disc. 2012) or G10 grip panels (new 2013), matte blue or hard chrome (mfg. 2014 only) finish, high ride beavertail grip safety, 8 or 9 shot mag., 37.2 oz. Mfg. 2005-2016.

$1,175 $1,025 $875 $800 $650 $525 $400 *$1,499*

Add $363 for hard chrome finish (disc. 2014). Add $79 for Tritium sights (disc.).

GRADING - PPGS™	100%	98%	95%	90%	80%	70%	60%	LAST MSR

* ***5.0 Duty One Lite*** – 9mm Para. or .45 ACP cal., 5 in. barrel with bushing, 8 or 10 shot mag., aluminum frame, fixed front and rear sights, 1911 slide serrations, full-length guide rod, tactical accessory rail, blued/anodized finish. Mfg. 2014-2016.

$1,350	$1,200	$1,075	$950	$815	$700	$575	*$1,599*

5.0 EAGLE – 9mm Para., .357 SIG, .38 Super (disc. 2011) .40 S&W, or .45 ACP cal., 5 in. barrel, STI standard full size wide body govt. model frame (choice of steel or aluminum), 10, 12, 14, or 17 shot double stack mag., fixed (new 2016) or adj. rear sight, fiber optic front sight, polished blue (disc. 2015), matte blue (new 2016), or hard chrome (mfg. 2014 only) finish, high ride beavertail grip safety, black glass filled nylon polymer grips, 31 or 35 oz. Disc. 2016.

$1,700	$1,500	$1,250	$1,100	$950	$825	$675	*$1,999*

Add $340 for hard chrome finish (disc. 2014).
Add $266 for .38 Super with .45 ACP conversion kit (disc. 2011).

5.0 EDGE – .38 Super (new 2014), 9mm Para., 10mm Norma (disc. 2008), .40 S&W, or .45 ACP cal., 5 in. bull barrel, designed for limited/standard IPSC competition, STI extended wide body frame, two 13 (.45 ACP), 18 (.40 S&W), or 21 (.38 Super/9mm) shot double stack mags., full-length dust cover and guide rod, fiber optic front sight, fully adj. rear sight, oversized magwell, stainless steel ambi safety, blue or hard chrome (disc. 2014) finish, 39 oz. Mfg. 1998-2017.

$1,860	$1,625	$1,395	$1,260	$1,025	$850	$700	*$2,199*

Add $340 for hard chrome finish (disc. 2014).

5.0 EXECUTIVE – 9mm Para., .40 S&W, or .45 ACP cal., 2011 platform, STI long/wide frame, 5 in. bull barrel, 10, 12, 14, or 17 shot double stack mag., extended mag. release, oversized magwell, ambi safety, stainless construction, grey nylon polymer grips and square trigger guard, hard chrome finish with black inlays, fiber optic front and STI adj. rear sights, Dawson Tool Less guide rod, approved for IPSC standard and USPSA limited edition, 38 oz. Mfg. 2001-2016.

$2,285	$1,995	$1,650	$1,425	$1,160	$1,000	$875	*$2,699*

* ***5.0 Executive Special Edition*** – 9mm Para., .40 S&W, or .45 ACP cal., ramped bull barrel, 24Kt. gold on all steel surfaces, checkered black grips, "Special Edition" engraved on slide, 39 oz. Mfg. 2005-2006.

$2,625	$2,325	$2,000	N/A	N/A	N/A	N/A	*$2,930*

* ***5.0 Executive IPSC 30th Commemorative*** – 9mm Para., .40 S&W, or .45 ACP cal., ramped bull barrel, two-tone hard chrome finish, special engraved slide with "IPSC 30th Anniversary" on side, 39 oz. Mfg. 2005-2006.

$2,500	$2,225	$1,975	N/A	N/A	N/A	N/A	*$2,775*

5.0 FB7 – 7mm or 9mm Para. cal., 5 in. barrel. Mfg. 2010-2011.

$1,750	$1,500	$1,250	$1,000	$875	$800	$675	*$1,940*

5.0 G.I. – .45 ACP cal., 5 in. non-ramped bushing barrel, matte blue finish, steel frame and trigger, beavertail grip safety, matte blue slide w/rear cocking serrations, smooth wood grips, GI steel sights, 8 shot mag., 35.3 oz. Mfg. 2010-2014.

$750	$650	$565	$510	$415	$340	$265	*$874*

5.0 GM – 9mm Para. or .38 Super cal., race gun, modular steel frame, 5 in. one-piece, rifle grade, stainless steel TruBor compensated barrel, mag. release, long curved trigger, C-More red dot reflex sight, stainless steel magwell, 2011 glass filled black polymer modular grips, high ride beavertail grip safety, ambi thumb safety, hard chrome finish with blue color inlay, lightened classic flat-top slide, drilled and tapped, sabertooth cocking serrations, recoil master guide rod, 17 or 20 shot mag., 44.6 oz. Mfg. 2014-2015.

$3,125	$2,735	$2,350	$2,125	$1,725	$1,400	$1,095	*$3,682*

5.0 HAWK – 9mm Para. cal., 5 in. barrel, 4 1/2 lb. trigger pull, fixed ledge rear w/fiber optic front sight, twin slide serrations, one-piece guide rod, matte blue metal finish. Mfg. 2018 only.

$1,295	$1,125	$925	$825	$725	$625	$525	*$1,499*

5.0 LAWMAN (LSA) – 9mm Para. (new 2013) or .45 ACP cal., 1911 Govt. style, 5 in. bushing barrel, hammer forged carbon steel frame, designed for duty, self-defense, IPSC, USPSA, and IDPA competition, fixed front sight with TAS rear sight, 8 or 9 shot mag., unique grip pattern (disc. 2015), VZ Double Diamond black and gray G10 grips (new 2016), 1911 slide serrations, blue (disc.), black/green (disc.), brown/tan (disc.) or black Cerakote (new 2015) finish, 36 oz. Mfg. 2005-2016.

$1,275	$1,125	$1,025	$875	$750	$625	$525	*$1,499*

GRADING - PPGS™	100%	98%	95%	90%	80%	70%	60%	LAST MSR

5.0 LEGEND – .38 Super, 9mm Para., .40 S&W, or .45 ACP cal., 5 in. bull barrel, STI modular steel long wide frame, Tri-top forged slide w/sabertooth cocking serrations and hard chrome w/black inlay and polished sides, blue frame, black glass filled nylon polymer grips w/hard chrome magwell, Dawson fiber optic front sights, adj. rear sight, 10, 12, 14, or 17 shot mag., 38 oz. Mfg. 2007-2015.

	$2,450	$2,150	$1,840	$1,665	$1,350	$1,100	$860	*$2,886*

5.0 MARAUDER – 9mm Para. cal., 2011 platform, 5 in. barrel w/bushing, 10 or 17 shot mag., fiber optic front and adj. TAS rear sights, short dust cover with tactical rail for light/laser mounting, tactical magwell with cutouts, 2011 molded black grips, black Cerakote finish. Mfg. 2014-2017.

	$2,050	$1,800	$1,500	$1,300	$1,075	$935	$795	*$2,399*

5.0 NITRO 10 – 10mm cal., 1911 style forged steel Government frame, 5 in. ramped bull barrel, 8 shot mag., one-piece steel guide rod, long curved trigger, undercut trigger guard, competition front sight, fixed "Ledge" style rear sight, "Nitro" cocobolo (disc. 2015) or VZ Operator II Marsoc G10 (new 2016) grips, polished blued slide, matte blued frame, high ride beavertail grip safety, single-sided thumb safety, classic slide w/front and rear cocking serrations, 38.9 oz. Mfg. 2014-2016.

	$1,350	$1,200	$1,075	$950	$815	$700	$575	*$1,599*

5.0 RANGEMASTER – .38 Super (mfg. 2014 only), 9mm Para. or .45 ACP cal., Master Series forged black frame, 5 in. ramped bull barrel, 8 or 9 shot mag., fully adj. rear sight, extended magwell, ambi stainless steel safety, 30 LPI checkering, STI Recoilmaster guide rod, 2011 style trigger guard, cocobolo wood grips, blue or hard chrome (disc. 2014) finish, 38 oz. Mfg. 2005-2016.

	$1,350	$1,200	$1,075	$950	$815	$700	$575	*$1,599*

Add $340 for hard chrome finish (disc. 2014).

5.0 RANGEMASTER II – similar to Rangemaster, except does not have extended frame dust cover. Mfg. 2006 only.

	$1,175	$965	$850	$725	$625	$525	$475	*$1,344*

5.0 SENTINEL – 9mm Para., .40 S&W, or .45 ACP cal., 1911 Govt. forged frame, 5 in. barrel, flat-top slide with rear cocking serrations, matte blue finish, front strap 30 LPI checkering, checkered steel D&T mainspring housing and flared magwell, STI competition front sights, adj. rear sight, thick rosewood grips, 38.3 oz. Mfg. 2007-2008.

	$1,395	$1,200	$1,025	$875	$750	$625	$550	*$1,598*

5.0 SENTINEL PREMIER – 9mm Para. or .45 ACP cal., 1911 Govt. style forged frame, 5 in. bull barrel with bushing, flush fit target crown, polished slide with rear cocking serrations, 8 (.45 ACP) or 10 shot mag., adj. Tritium sights, black (disc. 2015) or VZ ETC Zebra G10 (new 2016) grips, single-sided safety, front strap 30 LPI checkering, checkered steel D&T mainspring housing and flared magwell, hard chrome (disc.) or Tumbled Blue finish, 36.7 oz. Mfg. 2009-2017.

	$1,795	$1,575	$1,325	$1,150	$995	$850	$700	*$2,099*

5.0 SENTRY – 9mm Para., .40 S&W, or .45 ACP cal., 5 in. ramped barrel w/bushing, classic polished flat-top slide w/front and rear cocking serrations, checkered cocobolo grips, blue or hard chrome finish, competition front and adj. rear sights, 6 or 9 shot mag., 35.3 oz. Mfg. 2009-2014.

	$1,495	$1,300	$1,125	$1,000	$825	$675	$525	*$1,753*

Add $315 for hard chrome finish.

5.0 SPARROW – .22 LR cal. only, unlocked blowback action, STI standard extended frame, 5.1 in. ramped bull barrel, fixed sights, blue finish, 30 oz. Limited mfg. 1998-1999 only.

	$1,025	$900	$800	$700	$600	$500	$400	*$1,090*

5.0 SPARTAN V – 9mm Para. (new 2013), or .45 ACP cal., 1911 Govt. steel frame, parkerized finish, bald front strap, hand checkered double diamond wood grips, front and rear slide serrations, STI long curved trigger, 5 in. chrome ramped bushing barrel, STI high ride beavertail grip safety, fiber optic front sights, adj. rear sights, 9 shot mag., 35.3 oz. Mfg. 2007-2015.

	$650	$575	$495	$440	$360	$295	$225	*$754*

5.0 STI 20TH ANNIVERSARY – 9mm Para., .40 S&W, or .45 ACP cal., 5 in. bull barrel, steel frame, PVD and TIN (titanium nitride) finish, black glass filled nylon polymer filled grips, TIN coated magwell, beavertail grip safety, Dawson fiber optic front and STI adj. rear sight, 38 oz. Limited edition of 200 during 2010.

	$3,300	$2,950	$2,600	N/A	N/A	N/A	N/A	*$3,623*

5.0 100TH ANNIVERSARY SPECIAL EDITION – .45 ACP cal., consists of 2 pistols - one is traditional GI-style 1911, and the other gun is built on STI's patented high capacity modular frame, boxed with 2011 STI "challenge" coin, 500 sets mfg. 2011-2012.

	$3,875	$3,400	$2,900	$2,400	$2,100	$1,950	$1,700	*$4,154*

GRADING - PPGS™	100%	98%	95%	90%	80%	70%	60%	LAST MSR

5.0 TACTICAL – 9mm Para., .40 S&W, or .45 ACP cal., 5 in. bull or threaded barrel, short trigger, ambi safety, 10, 12, 14, or 17 shot mag., blue steel or hard chrome finish, fixed sights, 39 oz. Mfg. 2004-2015.

	$1,825	$1,595	$1,375	$1,240	$1,000	$825	$640	*$2,144*

Add $340 for hard chrome finish.
Add $102 for Tritium sights or $167 for Tritium sights and threaded barrel.

* ***5.0 Tactical Lite*** – similar to 5.0 Tactical, except stainless slide, alloy frame, fixed sights, 34 1/2 oz. Mfg. 2004-2005.

	$1,800	$1,525	$1,300	$1,050	$900	$825	$700	*$2,002*

TROJAN/TROJAN LITE (5.0) – 9mm Para., .40 S&W (disc. 2016), .38 Super (disc. 2016), or .45 ACP cal., 5 in. barrel with bushing, 8 (.45 ACP) or 10 shot single stack mag., cast steel or aluminum (Trojan Lite) frame, stainless steel available 2006-2011, fiber optic front and fully adj. rear sight, cocobolo wood grips, stippled front strap and mainspring housing, matte blue, blue/anodized (Trojan Lite), or hard chrome (disc. 2014) finish, 34-42 oz. Mfg. 1999-2017.

	$1,175	$1,025	$875	$800	$650	$525	$400	*$1,499*

Add $100 for aluminum frame (Trojan Lite).
Add $340 for hard chrome finish (disc. 2014).
Add $288 for .38 Super with .45 ACP conversion kit (disc. 2011).
Add $412 for stainless steel (disc. 2011).

5.0 TRUBOR (COMPETITOR) – 9mm Para. or .38 Super cal. only, standard frame, classic slide with front and rear serrations, square hammer, compensator, double stack mag., match sear, STI "Alchin" style blast deflector mount, TruBor compensator became standard 2005, C-More red dot reflex sight, wide ambi and grip safeties, 41.3 oz. Mfg. 1999-2011.

	$2,475	$2,050	$1,750	$1,450	$1,200	$995	$875	*$2,864*

5.0 TRUBOR GM – 9mm Para. or .38 Super cal., 5 in. TruBor bull barrel, hard chrome finish with blue color inlays, classic flat-top slide, sabertooth cocking serrations, blue glass filled nylon polymer grips w/ stainless steel magwell, drilled and tapped, C-More gray red dot reflex sight, 44.6 oz. Mfg. 2009-2011.

	$3,350	$3,000	$2,700	$2,250	$1,800	$1,400	$1,175	*$3,655*

5.0/5.5 TRUBOR – 9mm Para. or .38 Super cal., 2011 platform, modular steel frame, 5 or 5.5 (disc. 2013) in. TruBor barrel w/5-port competition proven compensator, 10 or 20 shot mag., full-length guide rod, stainless steel spur hammer, black glass filled nylon polymer grips w/aluminum magwell, lightened slide with front and rear cocking serrations, C-More railway red dot sight w/blast deflector mount, ambi thumb safety, polished blue or hard chrome (disc. 2014) finish, 41 oz. Mfg. 2012-2016.

	$2,475	$2,150	$1,775	$1,525	$1,250	$1,050	$925	*$2,899*

Add $347 for hard chrome finish (disc. 2014).

5.0 TRUSIGHT – 9mm Para., .40 S&W, or .45 ACP (disc. 2008) cal., 5 in. ramped bull barrel with expansion chamber, black glass filled nylon polymer grip with aluminum magwell, Dawson fiber optic front sight, adj. rear sight, blue finish with polished slide, 39 oz. Mfg. 2006-2009.

	$1,795	$1,525	$1,275	$1,050	$900	$825	$700	*$1,985*

5.0 USPSA SINGLE STACK – 9mm Para., .38 Super (new 2013), .40 S&W, or .45 ACP cal., 5 in. stainless steel barrel w/bushing, tri-top two-tone slide w/sabertooth cocking serrations, blue frame, 30 LPI front strap checkering, checkered steel D&T mainspring housing and magwell, competition front and adj. rear sight, 8 or 9 shot mag., 38.3 oz. Mfg. 2009-2015.

	$1,675	$1,475	$1,250	$1,140	$925	$750	$585	*$1,976*

5.0 USPSA DOUBLE STACK – 9mm Para., .40 S&W, or .45 ACP cal., 5 in. stainless steel barrel, tri-top two-tone slide w/sabertooth cocking serrations, blue frame, 30 LPI front strap checkering, checkered steel D&T mainspring housing and magwell, competition front and adj. rear sight, 38.3 oz. Mfg. 2009-2012.

	$2,425	$2,000	$1,750	$1,450	$1,200	$1,000	$900	*$2,818*

5.0 IPSC DOUBLE STACK – 9mm Para., .40 S&W, or .45 ACP cal., 5 in. bull barrel, blue frame, two-tone hard chrome slide w/sabertooth cocking serrations, Dawson fiber optic front and adj. rear sights, black glass filled nylon polymer grips w/stainless steel magwell, 38 oz. Mfg. 2009-2012.

	$2,425	$2,000	$1,750	$1,450	$1,200	$1,000	$900	*$2,818*

LEGACY MODEL – .45 ACP cal., 5 in. ramped STI bushing barrel, PVD finish, polished flat-top black slide, rear cocking serrations, front strap checkering, custom cocobolo grips, ambi thumb safety, ramped front sight, 36 oz. Mfg. 2006-2008.

	$1,750	$1,500	$1,250	$1,000	$900	$825	$700	*$1,929*

5.1 LIMITED – while advertised during 1998 with an MSR of $1,699, this model never went into production.

GRADING - PPGS™	100%	98%	95%	90%	80%	70%	60%	LAST MSR

5.5 EAGLE – various cals., features STI standard frame, 5 1/2 in. compensated barrel, 44 oz. Limited mfg. 1994-98.

	$2,100	$1,750	$1,475	$1,200	$995	$895	$775	*$2,399*

5.5 GRANDMASTER – .38 Super cal. standard, custom order gun with any variety of options available, double stack mag., 42 oz. Mfg. 2001-2008.

	$3,075	$2,650	$2,275	$1,900	$1,650	$1,425	$1,200	*$3,371*

5.5 STI GM – 9mm Para. or .38 Super cal., modular steel frame, 5.5 TruBor bull barrel w/two inch integral compensator, hard chrome finish with blue, red, or black inlay, C-More red dot sight, blue glass filled polymer grips w/stainless flared magwell, drilled and tapped mag. release, lightened slide w/ sabertooth cocking serrations, high ride beavertail grip safety, ambi thumb safety, 10 or 20 shot mag., 44.6 oz. Mfg. 2012-2016.

	$3,125	$2,735	$2,350	$2,125	$1,725	$1,400	$1,095	*$3,682*

6.0 EAGLE – .38 Super (disc.), 9mm Para., .40 S&W, or .45 ACP cal., features STI super ext. heavy steel frame, 6 in. barrel with bushing, blue or hard chrome (disc. 2014) finish, wide body with 10, 12, 14, or 17 shot double stack mag., fiber optic front and fully adj. target style rear sights, ambi safety, 42 oz. Mfg. 1998-2015.

	$1,900	$1,665	$1,425	$1,295	$1,050	$850	$665	*$2,199*

Add $340 for hard chrome finish (disc. 2014).
Add $267 for .38 Super with .45 ACP conversion kit (disc. 2008).

6.0 TROJAN – 9mm Para. or .45 ACP cal., similar to Trojan 5.0, except has 6 in. barrel and single stack mag., 36 oz. Mfg. 2000-2015.

	$1,325	$1,160	$995	$900	$725	$595	$465	*$1,555*

Add $143 for .38 Super with .45 ACP conversion kit (disc. 2008).

6.0 HUNTER – 10mm cal. only, 6 in. barrel, STI super ext. heavy frame with single stack mag., blue finish, 51 oz. Only 2 mfg. 1998, disc. 2000.

	$2,250	$1,875	$1,650	$1,425	$1,200	$995	$895	*$2,485*

Add $350 for Leupold 2X scope with terminator mount.

6.0 PERFECT 10 – 10mm Norma cal., 2011 platform, 6 in. bull barrel, blue or hard chrome (disc. 2014) finish with polished classic flat-top slide, front and rear cocking serrations, ramped front and Heinie fixed rear sights, 6 in. integral tactical rail, 10 or 14 shot mag., black glass filled nylon polymer grips with aluminum flared magwell, ambi safety, 37 1/2 oz. Mfg. 2009-2016.

	$2,285	$1,995	$1,650	$1,425	$1,160	$1,000	$875	*$2,699*

Add $340 for hard chrome finish (disc. 2014).

6.0 TARGETMASTER – 9mm Para. or .45 ACP cal., Master Series forged black frame, 6 in. ramped bull barrel, two-piece steel guide rod, 8 or 9 shot mag., undercut trigger guard, 30 LPI checkering, Aristocrat 3-pos. rear sight, ext. magwell, ambi stainless steel safety, cocobolo wood grips, matte blued finish, 40 oz. Mfg. 2005-2016.

	$1,525	$1,350	$1,175	$1,050	$900	$775	$625	*$1,799*

Add $315 for hard chrome finish in 9mm Para. cal. (disc. 2014), or $340 for hard chrome finish in .45 ACP cal. (disc. 2014).

6.0 .450 XCALIBER – .450 cal., single stack mag., V-10 barrel and slide porting, stainless grip and thumb safeties, adj. rear sight. Limited mfg. 2000-2002.

	$1,000	$850	$750	$650	$525	$450	$395	*$1,122*

6.0 .450+ XCALIBER – .450+ cal., otherwise similar to Xcaliber 6.0 .450, except has 6 in. frame with patented polymer grip and double stack mag. Limited mfg. 2000-2002.

	$1,775	$1,575	$1,350	$1,175	$995	$875	$775	*$1,998*

COMBAT MASTER – 9mm Para. cal., 5.4 in. match grade bull barrel, fiber optic front and adj. rear sights, full-length black 2011 DVC stipple grip, Combat Master slide cuts, extended slide release and mag. release, tool-less guide rod, black DLC w/polished serrations and Bronze Copper TiN finish, 36.8 oz., limited mfg. Mfg. 2019 only.

	$3,500	$3,050	$2,650	$2,400	$1,950	$1,600	$1,250	*$3,899*

This model was manufactured in conjuction with Taran Tactical Innovations.

COSTA 5.0 – 9mm Para. or .45 ACP cal., 5 in. bull barrel, 10, 12, or 17 shot mag., black Diamond Like Carbon (DLC) finish. Mfg. 2016 only.

	$2,200	$1,925	$1,600	$1,375	$1,125	$975	$850	*$2,599*

GRADING - PPGS™	100%	98%	95%	90%	80%	70%	60%	LAST MSR

COSTA CARRY COMP – 9mm Para. or .45 ACP cal., 4.15 in. carry comp barrel, 10, 12, or 17 shot mag., trigger system with ambi safety lever, fixed ledge rear and fiber optic front sights, 2011 TreeBark stippled tan grips, Recoil Master, slim tactical magwell, Picatinny under-rail, DLC black finish. Mfg. 2016-2017.

$3,250	$2,825	$2,400	$2,000	$1,725	$1,375	$1,200	*$3,699*

COSTA H.O.S.T. – 9mm Para. or .45 ACP cal., 4.15 in. threaded bull barrel and fluted slide, one each 18 and 21 (9mm Para.), 11, and 13 (.45 ACP) shot mag., trigger system with ambi safety lever, Vortex Viper red dot sight w/tall Tritium sights, 2011 Treebark stippled tan grips, Recoil Master, thread protector, slim tactical magwell, Picatinny under-rail, DLC black finish. Mfg. 2017-2018.

$3,100	$2,700	$2,300	$1,900	$1,675	$1,350	$1,150	*$3,499*

COSTA VIP – 9mm Para. or .45 ACP cal., 4.15 in. bull barrel, two 10 or 15 shot mags., trigger system with ambi safety lever, low profile Tritium front and fixed ledge rear sights, 2011 TreeBark stippled VIP length black grips, Recoil Master, Picatinny under-rail, DLC black finish. Mfg. 2016-2017.

$2,200	$1,925	$1,600	$1,375	$1,125	$975	$850	*$2,599*

DVC-C – 9mm Para. cal., 3.9 in. bull barrel, Dawson Precision Perfect Impact fiber optic front and Stealth Charger rear sights, Gen II 2011 grip, ambi thumb safety, Recoil Master, black DLC finish, 25.9 oz. Mfg. late 2018-2019.

$2,550	$2,225	$1,825	$1,575	$1,300	$1,100	$950	*$2,999*

This model replaces the DVC Carry.

DVC-L – 9mm Para. or .40 S&W cal., 5 in. bull barrel, 2.5 lb. trigger with ambi safeties, STI adj. rear with fiber optic front sight, Gen II 2011 grip, Dawson Precision tool-less guide rod, hard chrome with black DLC barrel, black DLC with TiN barrel, or black DLC with black barrel finish, 39.6 oz. Mfg. late 2018-2019.

$2,550	$2,225	$1,825	$1,575	$1,300	$1,100	$950	*$2,999*

This model replaced the DVC Limited.

DVC-O – 9mm Para. or .38 Super cal., 5.4 in. TX2 compensated barrel with TiN coating, 2.5 lb. trigger with ambi safeties, frame mounted C-More RTS2 sights, Gen II 2011 grip, Dawson Precision ICE magwell and tool-less guide rod, hard chrome with black DLC barrel, DLC with gold TiN barrel, or full black DLC finish, 40.4 oz. Mfg. late 2018-2019.

$3,400	$2,975	$2,475	$2,075	$1,725	$1,450	$1,250	*$3,999*

This model replaced the DVC Open.

DVC-P – 9mm Para. or .45 ACP cal., railed frame, 5 in. patented recoil compensation barrel, Tactical Slim magwell, 3 lb. trigger with ambi safety levers, HOST rear with fiber optic front sight, Gen II 2011 Double Stack grip, Dawson Precision Tool-Less guide rod, black DLC finish, 36 oz. Mfg. late 2018-2019.

$3,400	$2,975	$2,475	$2,075	$1,725	$1,450	$1,250	*$3,999*

This model replaced the DVC Omni.

DVC-S – 9mm Para. or .38 Super cal., 4.15 in. TX1 compensated barrel, ICE magwell, 2.5 lb. trigger with ambi safety levers, frame mounted C-More RTS2 sights, Gen II 2011 grip, Dawson tool-less guide rod, hard chrome with DLC barrel, black DLC with TiN barrel, or black DLC with DLC barren finish, 36.7 oz. Mfg. late 2018-2019.

$3,400	$2,975	$2,475	$2,075	$1,725	$1,450	$1,250	*$3,999*

This model replaced the DVC Steel.

DVC-3 – 9mm Para. cal., railed frame, 5.4 in. bull barrel with TiN coating, tactical magwell, 2.5 lb. trigger with ambi safety levers, fully adj. rear with fiber optic front sight, Gen II 2011 grip, Dawson Tool-Less guide rod, black DLC finish, 36.5 oz. Mfg. late 2018-2019.

$2,550	$2,225	$1,825	$1,575	$1,300	$1,100	$950	*$2,999*

This model replaced the DVC 3-Gun.

DVC 3-GUN – 9mm Para. cal., 5.4 in. TiAIN coated barrel with bushing, two 21 shot mags., STI tactical aluminum magwell, STI adj. rear and fiber optic front sights, black DVC 2011 grip, ambi safety lever, accessory rail for light/laser sight, black DLC finish. Mfg. 2016-2018.

$2,550	$2,225	$1,825	$1,575	$1,300	$1,100	$950	*$2,999*

DVC CARRY – 9mm Para. cal., 3.9 in. bull barrel with TiAIN coating, includes two 15 shot mags., trigger with ambi safety lever, low profile Tritium front sight, fixed ledge rear sight, 2011 DVC stippled VIP length black grips, Recoil Master, black DLC finish. Mfg. 2017-2018.

$2,550	$2,225	$1,825	$1,575	$1,300	$1,100	$950	*$2,999*

GRADING - PPGS™	100%	98%	95%	90%	80%	70%	60%	LAST MSR

DVC CLASSIC – 9mm Para., .40 S&W, or .45 ACP cal., forged Master Series frame, 5.4 in. bushing barrel, 8, 9, or 10 shot mag., extended base pads, Dawson Precision D&T mag. release, ICE magwell, fully adj. rear sight and fiber optic front, black VZ II Operator grips, tool-less guide rod, hard chrome finish. Mfg. 2016-2017.

$2,375 $2,075 $1,725 $1,475 $1,200 $1,025 $895 *$2,799*

DVC LIMITED – 9mm Para. or .40 S&W cal., 2011 platform, 5 in. bull barrel with TiAIN finish, two 18 (.40 S&W) or 21 shot mags., improved sear and hammer, new 2 lb. trigger, fiber optic front and adj. rear sights, Dawson Precision tool-less guide rod, slide porting on top and sides, textured grips, hard chrome finish. Mfg. 2015-2018.

$2,700 $2,325 $1,850 $1,600 $1,300 $1,100 $950 *$3,199*

DVC OMNI – 9mm Para. or .45 ACP cal., 4.15 in. barrel w/Island compensator, 3 lb. trigger pull, 2 dot Tritium fixed ledge style rear and Tritium front sight, black DVC stippled grips, full-length tactical rail, Tactical Slim magwell, DLC black slide finish. Mfg. 2018 only.

$3,400 $2,975 $2,475 $2,075 $1,725 $1,450 $1,250 *$3,999*

DVC OPEN – 9mm Para. cal., entirely new design based off the 2011, 5 or 5.4 in. precision fit bull barrel with TruBor style integrated compensator and TiAIN finish, 10 or 20 shot mag., Dawson Precision guide rod, reversible dual detent slide racker (a new slide racker was introduced during 2018), mounted C-More 6MOA red dot reflex sight, hand textured grips, oversized competition magwell, hard chrome finish on all steel parts, 48 oz. Mfg. 2015-2018.

$3,400 $2,975 $2,475 $2,075 $1,725 $1,450 $1,250 *$3,999*

DVC STEEL – 9mm Para. or .38 Super cal., 4.15 in. TX1 compensated barrel with TiAIN finish, 10, 21, or 27 shot mag., trigger w/ambi safety lever, mounted C-More dot sight, 2011 DVC stippled black grips, hard chrome finish, includes Dawson Precision tool-less guide rod, DVC Magwell, dual detent slide racker. Mfg. 2017-2018.

$3,400 $2,975 $2,475 $2,075 $1,725 $1,450 $1,250 *$3,999*

DVC TACTICAL – 9mm Para. or .45 ACP cal., 5 in. threaded bull barrel with TiAIN coating, two 10, 13, or 21 shot mags., trigger system with ambi safety lever, Tritium fixed ledge sights, 2011 DVC stippled black grips, Dawson Precision tool-less guide rod, tactical magwell, thread protector, Picatinny under-rail, DLC black finish. Mfg. 2017-2018.

$2,550 $2,225 $1,825 $1,575 $1,300 $1,100 $950 *$2,999*

GUARDIAN DS – 9mm Para. or .45 ACP (new 2017) cal., 2011 platform, lightweight aluminum narrow frame, 3.9 in. bull barrel, 10 or 15 shot double stack mag., stainless steel slide, TAS rear w/white dot front sights, black 2011 VIP grips, single side safety lever, black Cerakote frame finish. Mfg. 2016-2017.

$1,625 $1,425 $1,200 $1,075 $925 $795 $650 *$1,899*

HEXTAC 3.0 DS – 9mm Para. cal., 1911 or 2011 platform, aluminum frame, 3.7 in. bull barrel, two 10 or 15 shot mags., Hex profile hammer, trigger system w/single-sided safety lever, fiber optic front sight, fixed ledge rear sight, molded VIP length black grips (2011) or VZ Alien black/gray grips (1911), Recoil Master, Hex pattern serrations, black Cerakote finish. Mfg. 2017 only.

$1,860 $1,625 $1,395 $1,260 $1,025 $850 $700 *$2,199*

Add $400 for 2011 platform model.

HEXTAC DS – 9mm Para. or .45 ACP cal., 2011 platform, lightweight Tri-Topped slide, 4 or 5 in. bushing barrel, 10, 14, or 20 shot mag., extended base, flared magwell, rear ledge and fiber optic front sights, molded black double diamond grips, Picatinny under-rail, Recoil Master, black Cerakote finish. Mfg. 2016-2017.

$2,200 $1,925 $1,600 $1,375 $1,125 $975 $850 *$2,599*

HEXTAC SS – 9mm Para. or .45 ACP cal., 1911 platform, lightweight Tri-Topped slide, 4 in. bull or 5 in. bushing barrel, 8 or 9 shot mag., flared magwell, trigger system with ambi safety lever, fixed rear ledge and front fiber optic sights, VZ Alien grips, Picatinny under-rail, Recoil Master, Hex pattern serrations, black Cerakote finish. Mfg. 2016-2017.

$1,860 $1,625 $1,395 $1,260 $1,025 $850 $700 *$2,199*

H.O.S.T. DS (DOUBLE STACK) – 9mm Para., .45 ACP, or 10mm (5 in. only) cal., designed to "host" a sight, a light, and/or suppressor ready, 4.15 or 5 in. threaded barrel with bushing, one each 11 and 13 shot mag. (.45 ACP), 15 and 18 shot (.40 S&W), or 18 and 21 shot (9mm), trigger system with ambi safety lever, tall Tritium fixed suppessor sights, 2011 black Treebark stippled grips, Dawson Presicion tool-less guide rod (5 in. bbl.), Recoil Master (4 in. bbl.), tactical magwell, thread protector, Picatinny under-rail, DLC black finish. Mfg. 2017 only.

$2,750 $2,425 $2,000 $1,700 $1,450 $1,200 $1,050 *$3,199*

GRADING - PPGS™	100%	98%	95%	90%	80%	70%	60%	LAST MSR

H.O.S.T. SS (SINGLE STACK) – 9mm Para., .45 ACP, or 10mm cal., designed to "host" an optic, light, or a suppressor, 4.15 or 5 in. threaded barrel with bushing, two 8 or 10 shot mags. with extended basepads, trigger system with ambi safety lever, tall Tritium fixed suppressor sights, VZ Alien black/gray grips, Dawson Presicion tool-less guide rod (5 in. bbl.), Recoil Master (4 in. bbl.), slim magwell, thread protector, Picatinny under-rail, DLC black finish. Mfg. 2017 only.

	$2,275	$2,000	$1,650	$1,400	$1,150	$1,000	$875	$2,699

STACCATO-C – 9mm Para. cal., railed aluminum frame, 3.9 in. barrel, two 8 shot mags., Dawson Precision Perfect Impact fiber optic front and Stealth Charger rear sights, new 2011 Single Stack Carry grip, Recoil Master, black DLC finish, 25.6 oz. Mfg. late 2018-2019.

	$1,275	$1,125	$950	$875	$700	$575	$475	$1,499

STACCATO-P H.O.S.T. – 9mm Para. or .45 ACP cal.,1913 railed frame, 4 1/2 in. bull barrel, Tactical Slim magwell, fiber optic front sight and Gen II HOST plate rear, Gen II 2011 Double Stack grip, Recoil Master, black DLC finish, designed to work with the Leupold Delta Point Pro, Trijicon RMR, and other popular optics that use the same mounting platform. Mfg. 2018-2019.

	$2,125	$1,860	$1,600	$1,450	$1,175	$950	$750	$2,499

STACCATO-R – 9mm Para. or .45 ACP cal., single stack, Government length billet steel frame, 5 in. bushing barrel, three 8 (.45 ACP) or 10 (9mm Para.) mags., Dawson Precision fiber optic and STI adj. rear sights, 2011 black grips, ambi safety levers, Dawson 5.0 Adaptive Tool-less recoil system, accessory rail, black DLC finish. Mfg. 2020 only.

	$1,700	$1,500	$1,300	$1,150	$950	$750	$600	$1,999

TACTICAL DS – 9mm Para., .40 S&W (disc. 2016), or .45 ACP cal., 2011 platform, steel frame, 4 or 5 in. threaded or non-threaded bull barrel, 10, 12, 14, or 17 shot mag., tactical magwell, fixed ledge rear and ramped front sights or tall Tritium fixed suppressor sights (threaded model only), molded black grips, ambidextrous safety, Picatinny under-rail, Recoil Master, tactical magwell, black Cerakote finish. Mfg. 2015-2017.

	$1,860	$1,625	$1,395	$1,260	$1,025	$850	$700	$2,199

Add $100 for threaded barrel.

PISTOLS: SEMI-AUTO, SINGLE ACTION (STACCATO PRODUCTION)

Add $100 for DLC barrel coating.

STACCATO-C DPO (DUO) – 9mm Para. cal., lightweight alloy frame, 3.9 in. bull barrel w/flush fit 11 degree crown (new 2021), 3X single stack Officer mags. w/base pad, Dawson Precision Perfect Impact front fiber optic sight and DUO Carry Optic System, 2011 Single Stack Carry grip, Recoil Master Light system, black DLC finish. New 2020.

MSR $1,699	$1,450	$1,250	$1,100	$1,000	$800	$650	$500	

STACCATO C2/C2 DUO – 9mm Para. cal., lightweight alloy frame, 3.9 in. bull barrel, 16 or two 17 shot mags., Dawson Precision Perfect Impact front fiber optic sight and Dawson Charger or Carry DUO (Dawson Universal Optic System, C2 Duo model) rear sight, 2011 G2 black grips, ambi safety levers, Recoil Master Light system, accessory rail, black DLC finish. Mfg. 2020 only.

	$1,700	$1,500	$1,300	$1,150	$950	$750	$600	$1,999

Add $500 for C2 Duo model.

STACCATO C2 DPO CARRY/TACTICAL – 9mm Para. cal., lightweight alloy frame, 3.9 in. bull barrel w/flust fit 11 degree crown (new 2021), 3.9 Recoil Master Light recoil system, three 16 shot mags., fiber optic front sight, Dawson Universal Optic system and rear sight, 2011 Officer length G2 black grips, ambi safety levers, Picatinny accessory rail, black DLC finish. New 2020.

MSR $2,299	$1,950	$1,700	$1,465	$1,325	$1,075	$885	$750	

STACCATO-P/P DPO (DUO) – 9mm Para. or .45 ACP (disc. 2019) cal., Picatinny 1913 railed frame, 4.4 in. bull barrel w/flush fit 11 degree crown (new 2021), Dawson 4.4 Adaptive Tool-Less Recoil System, Tactical Slim magwell, Dawson Precision Perfect Impact fiber optic front and Stealth Charger or DUO Tactical (Dawson Universal Optic, P DUO, new 2020) rear sights, Gen II 2011 Double Stack grip, black DLC finish, 34 oz. New late 2018.

MSR $2,099	$1,785	$1,550	$1,325	$1,200	$950	$800	$700	

Add $200 for stainless steel threaded barrel (new 2021).
Add $300 for DLC coated threaded barrel (new 2021).
Add $300 for P DPO (Duo) model (new 2020).
Add $400 for chrome slide w/DLC bull barrel (new 2021) or $600 for chrome slide w/DLC threaded barrel (new 2021).

This model replaced the DVC Tactical.

GRADING - PPGS™	100%	98%	95%	90%	80%	70%	60%	LAST MSR

STACCATO XC – 9mm Para. cal., 5 in. compensated bull barrel, 15, 17, 18, or 20 shot mag., Tactical Advantage magwell, Dawson Precision fiber optic front and DUO Tactical rear sights, G2 grips, DLC black finish. New 2020.

MSR $4,299	$3,650	$3,200	$2,750	$2,480	$2,000	$1,650	$1,425	

STACCATO XL – 9mm Para. or .40 S&W cal., full-length slide and frame, 5.4 in. bull barrel w/flush fit 11 degree crown (new 2021), 15, 17, 18, or 20 shot mag., Tactical Advantage magwell, Dawson Precision long sight radius fiber optic front and STI adj. rear sights, G2 grips, DLC black finish. New 2020.

MSR $3,399	$2,900	$2,550	$2,150	$1,950	$1,600	$1,300	$1,000	

REVOLVERS

TEXICAN SAA – .45 LC cal., blue finish, color case hardened frame and hammer, 5 1/2 in. barrel, 6 shot, hard rubber grips with STI logo, floating firing pin, fixed sights, 36 oz. Mfg. 2007-2010.

	$1,195	$1,000	$875	$750	$600	$500	$400	*$1,344*

RIFLES/CARBINES: SEMI-AUTO

STi 10/22 FORCE – .22 LR cal., aluminum receiver, 21 in. Lothar Walther barrel, black synthetic Hogue stock, 7 lbs. Mfg. 2003-2006.

	$975	$850	$725	$625	$500	$400	$350	*$1,103*

STI SPORT 10-22 RIFLE/CARBINE – .22 LR cal., 16 in. lined aluminum barrel or 20 in. stainless steel bull barrel. Mfg. 2010-2011.

	$895	$825	$750	$675	$600	$525	$450	*$978*

STI SPORTING/TACTICAL CARBINE – .223 Rem. or 5.56 NATO cal., GIO, 16 in. stainless steel barrel, JP trigger group, STI Valkyrie handguard and gas block, Nordic tactical compensator, black Teflon coating, fixed A2 or collapsible buttstock, optional rails, approx. 7 lbs. Mfg. 2010-2014.

	$1,225	$825	$575	$475	$425	$375	$350	*$1,455*

STAG ARMS LLC

Current pistol, rifle, and accessories manufacturer established in 2003 and located in Cheyenne, WY beginning 2020. Previously located in New Britain, CT until 2019.

Please refer to BlueBookOfGunValues.com to order the *Blue Book of AR-15s & Variations*, available as a book or online subscription.

STAGGS-BILT

Previous manufacturer located in Phoenix, AZ circa 1970.

Staggs-Bilt manufactured a lever action combination gun, in addition to other firearms for Hunter Arms and several other gun companies. Approx. 2,000 combination lever action guns were manufactured with the Staggs-Bilt name, mostly in 20 ga./.30-30 Win. cal., with uncheckered straight grip walnut stock with recoil pad, DT, and iron sights.

Current values on this gun are in the $500-$750 range, depending on condition.

STALLARD ARMS

Current manufacturer of 9mm Para. pistols located in Mansfield, OH since 1991. Distributed by MKS Supply, Inc. located in Dayton, OH.

Please refer to the Hi-Point Firearms listing in the H section.

STANDARD ARMS & STANDARD ARMS MFG. CO.

Previous manufacturer that started production in Wilmington, DE, in Sept., 1909, and closed in 1912. The company was restarted in 1913 as Standard Arms Mfg. Co., and closed in April, 1914.

Nearly 5,000 rifles were manufactured at the actual factory. At the time the plant closed, approx. 2,200 rifles were in various stages of production, and a supply of parts remained. These were primarily purchased by Numrich Arms, made into complete rifles, and sold. Total production (Standard Arms, Standard Arms Mfg. Co. & those assembled by Numrich Arms) reached approx. 7,000 rifles. The highest known serial number is 9012. Within serialization, large blocks of numbers were abandoned, and this is thought to be due to changes and improvements made during production. In addition, as the factory closed with a large number of rifles in partial stages of production, it is often not possible to determine which rifles were actually made and completed at the factory, and which were completed outside the factory at a later date.

Many special order options were available, such as checkering, pistol grip, deluxe grades of woods, special sights, etc. Several grades of engraving were available, including Rocky Mountain, Adirondack, Sierra, and Selkirk. Lower priced "etched" models were also available and less frequently encountered than engraved models. A .50 caliber "Camp Carbine" was offered in smooth bore, slide action only. Approx. 25-30 were manufactured and utilized a special cartridge similar to the .50-70 shot cartridge. These are rarely encountered, although they are known to exist in collections.

GRADING - PPGS™	100%	98%	95%	90%	80%	70%	60%	LAST MSR

RIFLES: SEMI-AUTO

MODEL G AUTOLOADER – .25 Rem., .30 Rem., .32 Rem. (scarce), or .35 Rem. cal., bottom loading box mag., 22 in. barrel, open sight, straight stock. This was the first gas operated rifle in the U.S.A. Gas port can be closed and gun will function as a slide action. Approx. 7,000 mfg. 1910.

	100%	98%	95%	90%	80%	70%	60%	LAST MSR
	$2,000	$1,800	$1,500	$1,250	$1,000	$800	$650	

Add substantial premiums for higher grade examples.
Subtract 10% for slide action only (Model M).

STANDARD ARMS OF NEVADA, INC.

Previous pistol manufacturer from 1999-2000 located in Reno, NV.

PISTOLS: SEMI-AUTO

SA-9 – 9mm Para. cal., double action only, sub-compact design, 10 shot mag., 3.1 in. barrel, black polymer frame with matte black steel slide, 14 oz. Mfg. 1999-2000.

	100%	98%	95%	90%	80%	70%	60%	LAST MSR
	$220	$190	$175	$165	$150	$140	$130	*$249*

STANDARD 380 – while advertised, this model never went into production. MSR was $176.

STANDARD MANUFACTURING CO. LLC

Current manufacturer located in New Britain, CT. Previously located in Newington, CT. Dealer and consumer direct sales were through FFL dealer.

PISTOLS: SEMI-AUTO

1911 PISTOL – 1911 style pistol, 5 in. stainless steel match grade barrel w/match bushing, enhanced machined hammer, medium solid match grade trigger, high profile low-mount tactical sights, rosewood double diamond stock, upswept beavertail grip safety, extended mag. release, tactical thumb safety and slide stop, checkered front frame strap and flat mainspring housing, blued (with or w/o engraving), case color (with or w/engraving), nickel plated (new 2019), or stainless steel (disc. 2017) finish.

	100%	98%	95%	90%	80%	70%	60%	LAST MSR
MSR $1,329	$1,200	$1,025	$900	$775	$650	$550	$450	

Add 20% (MSR $1,599) for nickel plated finish (new 2019).
Add 20% (MSR $1,599) for engraved blued finish.
Add 22.5% (MSR $1,625) for case colored finish.
Add 42.5% (MSR $1,899) for engraving w/case colored finish.

REVOLVERS: DOUBLE ACTION

S333 THUNDERSTRUCK – .22 Win. Mag. cal., volley fire, DA, compact design, aluminum frame, 1 1/4 in. double barrels, 8 shot mag., 2 shots per pull, high strength steel construction, double cantilever trigger with integral blade style safety, red dot front and rear sights, black polymer grip, transfer bar blocks firing pins from hammers, titanium firing pin and cylinder inserts, black anodized finish, 18 oz. New mid-2019.

	100%	98%	95%	90%	80%	70%	60%	LAST MSR
MSR $429	$400	$350	$300	$260	$220	$180	$140	

REVOLVERS: SINGLE ACTION

SAA .38 – .38 Spl. cal., carbon steel frame, 4 3/4 in. barrel, 6 shot, fixed sights, custom walnut stock, two-piece walnut grip, cone shaped firing pin, nickel plated or bone and charcoal color case hardened finish, deep blued metal parts, available as "El Chingon" Model, 40 oz.

	100%	98%	95%	90%	80%	70%	60%	LAST MSR
MSR $1,899	$1,700	$1,500	$1,300	$1,150	$950	$750	$600	

SAA .45 – .45 LC cal., Colt 45 style, carbon steel frame, 4 3/4, 5 1/2, or 7 1/2 in. blued barrel, 6 shot, fixed blade front sight w/u-notch rear sight, custom walnut stock, choice of standard wood, fancy wood one-piece, two-piece walnut grip with or w/o checkering, or faux ivory grips, cone shaped firing pin, optional C-Coverage engraving, nickel plated or bone and charcoal color case hardened finish, deep blued metal parts, 40 oz.

	100%	98%	95%	90%	80%	70%	60%	LAST MSR
MSR $1,895	$1,700	$1,500	$1,300	$1,150	$950	$750	$600	

Add 5% for faux ivory grips (disc.).
Add 7.5% (MSR $2,045) for fancy wood one-piece grips.
Add 15% for two-piece checkered grips (disc.).
Add 5% (MSR $1,995) for nickel-plated finish.

* ***SAA .45 "C" Coverage Engraved Model*** – similar to the SAA .45, except has "C" coverage engraving, available in nickel plated or bone and charcoal case color hardened finish.

	100%	98%	95%	90%	80%	70%	60%	LAST MSR
MSR $3,250	$2,950	$2,575	$2,200	$2,000	$1,625	$1,325	$1,025	

Add 7.5% (MSR $3,495) for nickel-plated finish.

GRADING - PPGS™	100%	98%	95%	90%	80%	70%	60%	LAST MSR

RIFLES: SEMI-AUTO

STANDARD MODEL A SPORTING RIFLE (STD-15 SPORTING RIFLE MODEL A) – 5.56 NATO cal., GIO, rail height gas block, right or left-hand action, 16 or 18 (new 2020) in. Govt. profile barrel with A2 flash hider, 10 or 30 shot black aluminum mag., stainless steel single stage trigger, Roger's Super-Stoc, standard A2 pistol grip, M4 feed ramps, M-LOK compatible polymer drop-in handguard, A3 upper and aluminum lower receiver with anodized finish, 6-position carbine buffer tube, receiver endplate with ambi single point sling loops, matte black finish, 6 lbs. New late 2016.

MSR $999	$950	$825	$725	$650	$525	$425	$325	

Add $50 for left-hand action.
Add 20% (MSR $1,199) for 18 in. barrel (new 2020).

STANDARD MODEL B SPORTING RIFLE (STD-15 SPORTING RIFLE MODEL B) – 5.56 NATO or .300 AAC Blackout cal., GIO, right or left-hand action, extended low profile gas block, 16 in. Govt. profile barrel with Yankee Hill Machine Phantom flash hider, 10 or 30 shot Mission First Tactical polymer mag., stainless steel speed hammer and trigger, front and rear manual flip iron sights, MFT Minimalist adj. stock, MFT EPG16V2 grip, M4 feed ramps, extruded KeyMod 10 in. super light rail, A3 upper and aluminum lower receiver with anodized finish, standard charging handle, Nitride bolt carrier group, 6-position carbine buffer tube, receiver endplate with ambi single point sling loops, black, gold, FDE, tan, or Flat Foliage Green finish, 6.2 lbs. Mfg. late 2016-19.

	$1,125	$975	$850	$775	$625	$500	$400	*$1,199*

Add $50 for left-hand action.
Add $101 for gold finish.

STANDARD MODEL C SPORTING RIFLE (STD-15 SPORTING RIFLE MODEL C) – 5.56 NATO cal., GIO, right or left-hand action, carbine length gas system, 16 in. Govt. profile chrome moly barrel, A2 flash hider, 30 shot black aluminum mag., stainless steel Mil-Spec SST, A2 front sight and detachable carry handle A2 rear sight, 6-pos. M4 adj. or A2 fixed stock, standard A2 grip, ambi safety selector, M4 feed ramps, CAR single heat shield handguard, forged aluminum receiver, 7.5 lbs. Mfg. late 2016-19.

	$850	$750	$650	$575	$475	$375	$300	*$899*

Add $50 for left-hand action.

STANDARD MODEL D SPORTING RIFLE (STD-15 SPORTING RIFLE MODEL D) – .223 Wylde chamber, GIO, 18 in. fluted stainless steel heavy barrel, YHM Phantom muzzle brake, SST, MFT Minimalist (disc.) or 6-pos. Magpul STR stock, MFT EPG16v2 grip, ambi safety selector, mid-length gas system, low profile adj. gas block, 13 in. KeyMod super light rail, ambi charging handle with tactical latch, forged aluminum receivers, 7 1/2 lbs. Disc. 2019.

	$1,375	$1,200	$1,025	$925	$750	$625	$475	*$1,449*

Add $50 for left-hand action.

STANDARD MODEL E SPORTING RIFLE – 5.56 NATO cal., GIO, 16 in. Govt. profile barrel, A2 flash hider, red/green reflex sight, low profile gas block, carbine length gas system, M4 feed ramps, CAR single heat shield handguard, integral laser, 7 1/2 lbs. Mfg. 2018-19.

	$825	$725	$625	$550	$450	$375	$300	*$879*

THOMPSON MODEL 1922 – .22 LR cal., blowback action, 16.4 in. ribbed barrel, 10 shot (standard) or optional 50 shot aluminum drum magazine, receiver milled from aircraft grade aluminum, open sights, deluxe walnut stock and forearm, pistol grip, half scale replica patterned after the Thompson Model 1927, high gloss blue finish, 5 1/2 lbs. Mfg. 2014-18.

	$950	$835	$725	$650	$525	$425	$325	*$1,100*

Add $349 for additional drum and stick.

While advertised during 2012, this gun started mfg. during 2014.

SHOTGUNS: SEMI-AUTO

SKO-12 – 12 ga., 2 3/4 and 3 in. chamber, gas operating system with AR-style mag. and bolt release, 18 7/8 in. barrel threaded for door breacher w/Tru-Choke thread pattern for screw-in choke system, 5 (standard), optional 2 or 10 shot mag., adj. stock, polymer AR-style grip, ambidextrous safety, 22 in. Picatinny top rail, available as Works Packages (new 2018), 38 in. OAL, 7 lbs. 10 oz. New late 2017.

MSR $1,100	$980	$850	$725	$650	$550	$450	$350	

Add $400 for Works Package (new 2018).

Works Pacakge includes: Reflex sight, aluminum tactical grip w/red laser and flashlight, High 8 slot rise, two offset sight mounts, 2 point black tactical sling, swivel set, front mount rail w/screw, and Door Buster breaching chokes.

GRADING - PPGS™	100%	98%	95%	90%	80%	70%	60%	LAST MSR

SKO-BULL – 12 ga., gas operation system with AR-style mag. and bolt release, 18 7/8 in. barrel with screw in choke system threaded for stiletto and tactical chokes, 2, 5, 9, or 15 shot mag., adj. stock, 22 in. top rail mount, black finish, 30 3/4 in. OAL, 7 lbs. 10 oz. (without mag.). Mfg. mid-2018-19.

	$1,100	$995	$875	$735	$650	$550	$465	*$1,299*

SHOTGUNS: SLIDE ACTION

DP-12 – 12 ga., 3 in. chambers, bullpup configuration, inline feeding, two 18 7/8 in. threaded barrels with spreader choke tubes, 14 shot twin magazine capacity, bottom loading and ejection, single trigger, synthetic stock, rubber recoil pad with dual spring loaded recoil, composite foregrip, non-slip rubber pistol grip, ambidextrous safety, two Picatinny rails for accessories, ambidextrous pump slide release, slots to attach MOE rails, shell indicator window, front sling and sling swivel attachment, scannable QR code to access manual and FAQ, black, black and gold two-tone (disc. 2019), FDE, OD Green, gold (disc. 2019), or Desert Tan (disc. 2019) finish, 9 lbs. 12 oz. New late 2014.

MSR $1,499	$1,425	$1,250	$1,075	$975	$775	$650	$500

Add $605 for Gold finish (disc.).

Add $105 for black and gold two-tone finish (disc.).

One each with Blue Snakeskin, Red Snakeskin, or Wood Camo finish was also manufactured. Last MSR was $1,995.

* ***DP-12 With The Works #1*** – 12 ga., 2 3/4 in. chamber, spreader chokes with Tru-Choke thread pattern, 14 shot mag., synthetic stock, composite forend with slots for MOE rails, rubber recoil pad, non-slip rubber pistol grip, composite front vertical grip, aircraft grade aluminum receiver, ambi safety, works package #2 includes Reflex sight CXHD113, aluminum tactical grip with red laser and flashlight, flip-up iron AR-15 style backup sights, offset sight mounts, 1 in. high 8-slot riser, 4-piece MOE rail set, 2-point black tactical sling, 1 in. swivel set, front mounting rail w/ screw, Door Buster door breaching chokes, two Picatinny rails, choke tube wrench, and heavy duty lock, black, OD Green, tan (mfg. 2018-19), or FDE finish, 29.5 in. OAL, 9 lbs. 12 oz. New 2018.

MSR $1,825	$1,700	$1,500	$1,275	$1,150	$925	$775	$600

* ***DP-12 With The Works #2*** – 12 ga., 2 3/4 in. chamber, spreader chokes with Tru-Choke thread pattern, 14 shot mag., synthetic stock, composite forend with slots for MOE rails, rubber recoil pad, non-slip rubber pistol grip, composite front vertical grip, aircraft grade aluminum receiver, ambi safety, works package #2 includes Reflex sight CXHD113, flip-up iron AR-15 style backup sights, offset sight mounts, 1 in. high 8-slot riser, 4-piece MOE rail set, 2-point black tactical sling, 1 in. swivel set, tactical flashlight with strobe, remote switch for flashlight, offset flashlight mount, green laser, front mounting rail w/screw, Door Buster door breaching chokes, two Picatinny rails, choke tube wrench, and heavy duty lock, black, OD Green, tan (mfg. 2018-19), or FDE finish, 29.5 in. OAL, 9 lbs. 12 oz. New 2018.

MSR $1,825	$1,700	$1,500	$1,275	$1,150	$925	$775	$600

FIREARMS: OTHER

Per the manufacturer: these firearms are legally classified as "Firearm/Other", they are not considered a handgun or a rifle, nor are they NFA classified as an "Any Other Weapon" (AOW) or "Short Barreled Rifle" (SBR).

STANDARD MODEL 15 CTA – 5.56 NATO cal., GIO, 14.5 in. barrel with nickel boron barrel extension, A2 flash hider, pistol length gas system, low profile gas block, 10 shot Mission First Tactical poly mag., forged upper and lower receivers, stainless steel Mil-Spec trigger, KAK industries Shockwave 2.0 brace, 10 in. KeyMod Super Light Rail handguard, A2 grip, Mil-Spec charging handle, ambi single point sling loops, phosphate coated M16 BCG, black anodized finish, 5 lbs. 14 oz. Disc. 2019.

	$670	$530	$480	$420	$390	$370	$330	*$900*

SKO MINI – 12 ga., 2 3/4 and 3 in. chamber, gas operating system, 14 3/4 in. barrel threaded with Tru-Choke thread pattern for screw-in choke system, 2 (standard) and optional 5 and 10 shot detachable mag., receivers machined from 7075 aluminum, composite forend with slots for Magpul MOE accessories and bolt on rails, polymer AR-style grip, ambidextrous safety, AR-style magazine release and bolt release, forward vertical grip, black anodized finish, nitride internals, available as Works Package (Reflex Sight, aluminum tactical grip w/red laser and flashlight, High 8 slot rise, two offset sight mounts, 2 point black tactical sling, swivel set, front mount rail w/screw, and Door Buster breaching chokes, 38 in. OAL, 7 lbs. 10 oz. New late 2017.

MSR $750	$730	$625	$550	$475	$400	$325	$250

Add $400 for Works Package (new 2018).

GRADING - PPGS™ 100% 98% 95% 90% 80% 70% 60% LAST MSR

Works Pacakge includes: Reflex sight, aluminum tactical grip w/red laser and flashlight, High 8 slot rise, two offset sight mounts, 2 point black tactical sling, swivel set, front mount rail w/screw, and Door Buster breaching chokes.

SKO SHORTY – 12 ga., 2 3/4 and 3 in. chamber, gas operating system, 17 3/4 in. barrel threaded with Tru-Choke thread pattern for screw-in choke system, 2 (standard) and optional 5 and 10 shot detachable mag., receivers machined from 7075 aluminum, composite forend with slots for Magpul MOE accessories and bolt on rails, polymer AR-style grip, ambidextrous safety, AR-style magazine release and bolt release, forward vertical grip, black anodized finish, nitride internals, available as Works Package (Reflex Sight, aluminum tactical grip w/red laser and flashlight, High 8 slot rise, two offset sight mounts, 2 point black tactical sling, swivel set, front mount rail w/screw, and Door Buster breaching chokes, 28.75 in. OAL, 7 lbs. 2 oz. New 2020.

MSR $750 $730 $625 $550 $475 $400 $325 $250

Add $400 for Works Package.

Works Pacakge includes: Reflex sight, aluminum tactical grip w/red laser and flashlight, High 8 slot rise, two offset sight mounts, 2 point black tactical sling, swivel set, front mount rail w/screw, and Door Buster breaching chokes.

STANDARD PRODUCTS CO.

Previous WWII subcontractor of M1 carbines located in Port Clinton, OH.

Please refer to US Military Long Arms listing for more information.

STAR, BONIFACIO ECHEVERRIA S.A.

Previous manufacturer located in Eibar, Spain. Star, Bonifacio Echeverria S.A. closed its doors on July 28th, 1997, due to the intense financial pressure the Spanish arms industry experienced during the late 1990s. Previously imported by Interarms, located in Alexandria, VA.

PISTOLS: SEMI-AUTO

MODEL H – similar to Model HN, except 7.65mm, 7 shot.

$425 $375 $325 $290 $230 $190 $150

MODEL HN – .380 ACP cal., 6 shot, 2 3/4 in. barrel, blue, fixed sights, plastic grips. Mfg. 1934-41.

$450 $395 $340 $300 $250 $200 $165

MODEL I – .32 ACP cal., 9 shot, 4 3/4 in. barrel, blue, fixed sights, plastic grips. Mfg. 1934-36.

$400 $350 $300 $275 $225 $180 $150

MODEL IN – similar to Model I, except .380 ACP, 8 shot, 4 3/4 in. barrel, blue.

$395 $345 $295 $270 $215 $180 $140

MODEL 1920 – 9mm Bergmann Bayard or .38 Super cal., easily identified by unusual safety located on left rear slide. Issued to Spanish Guardia Civil.

$800 $700 $600 $500 $400 $300 $250

MODEL 1921 – 9mm Bergmann Bayard cal., this model was fitted with a grip safety that was later dropped when standardizing the Model A production. Issued to Spanish Guardia Civil.

$750 $600 $500 $475 $385 $315 $245

MODEL 1922 – designation for the early Model A. Issued to Spanish Guardia Civil.

$600 $500 $425 $375 $300 $250 $200

MODEL A – .38 Super cal., modified Government Colt, 5 in. barrel, no grip safety, blue, checkered wood grips. Mfg. 1934-disc.

$550 $425 $350 $300 $250 $225 $200

Add 50% for Spanish Air Force issue if in original box.

MODEL A CARBINE – usually 7.63mm cal., unusual variation, slotted with tangent rear sight and extended barrel.

$3,500 $3,000 $2,500 $2,250 $2,000 $1,750 $1,500

Add $500 for original stock (different from MB and MMS stock).

MODEL B – similar to Model A, but 9mm Para. cal. Mfg. 1934-1975.

$750 $650 $550 $450 $350 $275 $200

Add 125% for post-war German police if with two matching magazines.

GRADING - PPGS™	100%	98%	95%	90%	80%	70%	60%	LAST MSR

MODEL BS – 9mm Para. cal., similar to Model B. 83,129 mfg. 1968-1994.

	$650	$500	$400	$350	$300	$250	$200	

MODEL M – similar to Model A, except has large frame, available in 9mm Bergmann Bayard, 9mm Para., 8 shot, and .45 ACP, 7 shot, 5 in. barrel, blue, fixed sights, checkered wood or plastic grips.

	$750	$625	$525	$425	$350	$275	$200	

Add 100% for early variation with ser. no. under 4,835.

MODEL P – .45 ACP cal. only, similar to Model A, except has large frame, 7 shot mag. Mfg. 1934-1975.

	$800	$725	$625	$525	$450	$375	$275	

Add 100% for early variation with ser. no. under 5,112.

MODELS SUPER A (9mm Largo), M (9mm Largo), & P (.45 ACP) – similar to Models A, M, & P, except has loaded chamber indicator, mag. safety, and easier takedown feature. Mfg. 1946-89.

Super A	$750	$650	$550	$450	$350	$250	$200	
Super M	$1,250	$1,000	$800	$600	$550	$450	$350	
Super P	$1,500	$1,200	$900	$650	$550	$450	$350	*$340*

The Super A was a Spanish Service pistol. Recent imports in 80% condition were available in the $150 range.

MODEL SUPER B – 9mm Para. cal., similar to Model B, except has loaded chamber indicator, mag. safety and easier takedown feature, choice of blue or Starvel finish on Model B, late production models are poorly polished and have parkerized small parts. Importation disc. in 1990.

	$650	$525	$400	$350	$300	$275	$250	*$330*

Add $30 for Starvel finish.
Add 100% for Early guns.

SUPER TARGET MODEL – similar to Star Super, but target sights, extended trigger guard, modified trigger. Rare.

	$2,250	$1,750	$1,500	$1,100	$950	$850	$750	

MODEL MB – 9mm Para. cal., late production Model M cut for shoulder stock, mag. safety.

	$3,000	$2,500	$1,950	$1,725	$1,500	$1,200	$900	

Add $450 for shoulder stock.
Add 20% to rig if matching stock.

MODEL MMS – 7.63mm cal., late production Model M cut for shoulder stock, mag. safety.

	$2,500	$2,000	$1,725	$1,500	$1,200	$900	$600	

Add $450-$650 for shoulder stock.
Add 20% to rig for matching stock.

MODEL SI – .32 ACP cal., 8 shot, 4 in. barrel, blue, without grip safety, small version of Government .45 in appearance, plastic grips. Mfg. 1941-1965.

	$375	$300	$250	$225	$200	$175	$150	

MODEL S – similar to Model SI, except .380 ACP cal., 9 shot, mfg. 1941-1965. Importation of these Police contract models was disc. 1991.

	$300	$260	$225	$195	$160	$135	$100	*$237*

Add $30 for Starvel finish.
Add 100% for guns issued to the Spanish Air Force with original box and 2 matching mags.
Add $3,000 for gold damascene finish, if in 98%+ condition.

In 1989, Interarms imported factory reconditioned used Spanish Police Contract Model S pistols - these guns were available in either blue or Starvel finish and were supplied with a plastic box with accessories.

MODELS SUPER SI AND S – similar to Model S, with Super Star improvements. Mfg. 1946-1972.

	$400	$350	$300	$275	$225	$180	$150	

MODEL SUPER SM – similar to Model Super S, except adjustable sight and wood grips. Mfg. 1973-81.

	$500	$440	$375	$340	$275	$225	$175	

MODEL CO POCKET – .25 Auto cal., 2 3/4 in. barrel, blue, fixed sights, plastic grips. Mfg. 1929-56.

	$350	$300	$265	$240	$195	$160	$125	

MODEL CU STARLET – .25 Auto cal., 2 3/8 in. barrel, alloy frame, fixed sights, plastic grips, blue, or chrome slide, frame anodized in black, blue, green, grey, or gold. Mfg. 1957-72.

	$325	$280	$250	$225	$180	$145	$110	

Minor changes prompted a model redesignation as CK during 1973.

GRADING - PPGS™	100%	98%	95%	90%	80%	70%	60%	LAST MSR

MODEL D – .380 ACP cal., small steel frame version of the Model A with several minor variations, 40,416 mfg. 1922-47.

	$650	$575	$500	$450	$360	$300	$225	

MODEL DK (STARFIRE) – .380 ACP cal., 3 1/8 in. barrel, fixed sights, plastic stocks, finished in same color availability as Model CU. Mfg. 1957-1972, U.S. import ceased as of 1968 due to Federal GCA legislation.

	$500	$440	$375	$340	$275	$225	$175	

Add 30% for unusual alloy colors.

Minor changes prompted a redesignation as DKL (.380 ACP) 1972 and DKI (.32 ACP) 1972.

MODEL HK LANCER – similar to Model Starfire, except .22 LR cal. Mfg. 1955-68.

	$325	$285	$245	$185	$150	$125	$95	

MODEL F – .22 LR cal., 10 shot, 4 in. barrel, fixed sights, blue, plastic grips. Mfg. 1942-67.

	$350	$300	$260	$220	$180	$145	$115	

MODEL FS – similar to Model F, except 6 in. barrel, adj. sights. Mfg. 1942-67.

	$350	$300	$260	$220	$180	$145	$115	

MODEL F OLYMPIC RAPID FIRE – .22 Short cal., 9 shot, 7 in. barrel, adj. sight, aluminum slide, barrel weights and muzzle brake, blue, plastic grips. Mfg. 1942-67.

	$650	$550	$450	$400	$350	$300	$250	

MODEL FR – restyled Model F, with "squared" barrel, adj. sight and slide stop. Mfg. 1967-72.

	$325	$285	$245	$220	$180	$145	$115	

Add 15% for chrome finish.

MODELS FR SPORT AND MODEL FR TARGET – similar to Model FR, except FR Sport has 150mm barrel, and the Model FR Target has 180mm barrel, 65,534 mfg. 1967-83.

	$350	$305	$265	$240	$195	$160	$125	

Add 15% for chrome finish.

MODEL FM – similar to Model FR, except heavier frame, web ahead of trigger guard, 4 1/2 in. barrel. 8,799 mfg. 1972-83.

	$325	$285	$245	$220	$180	$145	$115	

MODEL BKS STARLIGHT – 9mm Para. cal., 8 shot, 4 1/4 in. barrel, plastic grips. Mfg. 1970-1981.

Blue	$450	$400	$350	$300	$250	$200	$150	

Add 10% for chrome finish.

MODEL BM – 9mm Para. cal., single action, 8 shot mag., 4 in. barrel, steel frame, Colt 1911 action, blue, chrome (disc. 1989), or Starvel (new 1990) finish, plastic grips, 35 oz. Importation disc. 1991.

	$400	$325	$275	$250	$200	$175	$150	*$415*

Add $30 for Starvel or chrome (disc. 1990) finish.
Add 150% for Navy issue with escutcheon grips.

MODEL BKM – identical to Model BM, except lightweight duraluminum frame, blue finish only, 26 oz. Importation disc. 1991.

	$450	$325	$275	$250	$200	$175	$150	*$415*

MODEL PD – .45 ACP cal., SA, 6 shot mag., 4 in. barrel, adj. rear sight, blue or Starvel (new 1990) finish only, walnut grips, alloy frame, 25 oz. Mfg. 1975-importation disc. 1991.

	$500	$425	$300	$250	$225	$200	$175	*$475*

Add $20 for Starvel finish (new 1990).
Add 20% for late variation with 30M rear sight.

MODEL 28 – 9mm Para. cal., DA/SA, 15 shot mag., 4 1/4 in. barrel, blue finish only, advanced design, 40 oz. Mfg. 1983 and 1984 only.

	$450	$400	$350	$300	$250	$200	$150	

Note: Model 28 is interesting since no screws were used in its manufacture. Hammer assembly (including spring, cocking lever, sear, disconnector and ejector) is housed under removable backstrap.

MODEL 30M – 9mm Para. cal. only, successor to the Model 28, DA/SA, 4.33 in. barrel, 15 shot mag., blue finish only, adj. rear sight, checkered wraparound plastic grips, steel frame, 40 oz. New 1985. Importation disc. 1991.

	$450	$400	$350	$300	$250	$200	$175	*$495*

GRADING - PPGS™	100%	98%	95%	90%	80%	70%	60%	LAST MSR

MODEL 30 PK DURAL FRAME – similar to Model 30M, except slightly shorter duraluminum frame, 3.86 in. barrel, 30 oz. Disc. 1989.

	$475	$400	$325	$275	$225	$175	$150	*$580*

MODEL 31P (STEEL FRAME)/31PK (DURAL FRAME) – 9mm Para. (disc. 1993) or .40 S&W (new 1990) cal., compact variation, DA/SA, features Acculine barrel (3.86 in.), 14 shot mag., ambidextrous safety with decocking lever, blue or Starvel finish, all steel construction, 39.4 oz. Imported 1990-94.

	$450	$375	$300	$250	$200	$175	$150	*$398*

Add $30 for Starvel finish (disc. 1993).

Prices are the same for Model 31PK Dural Frame (imported 1990-93).

MODEL M40 FIRESTAR – .40 S&W cal., SA, 6 shot mag., 3.39 in. Acculine barrel, checkered rubber grips, compact design utilizing all steel construction, 3-dot sighting system with adjustable rear sight, blue, Starvel, or nickel (new 1997) finish, 30.35 oz. Mfg. 1990-disc.

	$350	$300	$250	$220	$180	$145	$115	*$306*

Add $17 for nickel finish.
Add $20 for Starvel finish.

* ***Model M40 Firestar Plus*** – similar to M40 Firestar, except incorporates alloy frame, new grip design, ambidextrous easy-view safety, and fast button release 10 shot mag. Advertised initially during 1995.

This model was never released for commercial sale.

MODEL M43 FIRESTAR – 9mm Para. cal., 7 shot mag., otherwise similar to Model M40 Firestar. Disc.

	$400	$325	$250	$225	$200	$175	$150	*$296*

Add $17 for nickel finish.
Add $20 for Starvel finish.

* ***Model M43 Firestar Plus*** – similar to M43 Firestar, except incorporates alloy frame, and fast button release 10 shot double stack mag., new grip design, ambidextrous easy-view safety. Mfg. 1995-97.

	$450	$350	$250	$225	$200	$175	$150	*$351*

Add $12 for nickel finish.
Add $25 for Starvel finish.

MODEL M45 FIRESTAR – .45 ACP cal., SA, ultra compact design featuring 4 barrel lugs, steel frame and slide, 3.6 in. reverse taper Acculine barrel, 6 shot mag., black synthetic grips, blue or Starvel finish, 35 oz. Mfg. 1992-97.

	$450	$350	$275	$250	$225	$200	$175	*$351*

Add $12 for nickel finish.
Add $20 for Starvel finish.

* ***Model M45 Firestar Plus*** – similar to M45 Firestar, except incorporates alloy frame, new grip design, ambidextrous easy-view safety, and fast button release 10 shot mag. Advertised during 1995.

This model was never released for commercial sale.

MEGASTAR – 10mm or .45 ACP cal., DA/SA, larger variation of the Firestar featuring 4.6 in. barrel and 12 (.45 ACP) or 14 (10mm) shot mag., 47.6 oz. Imported 1992-1994.

	$450	$395	$340	$305	$250	$205	$160	*$653*

Add $35 for Starvel finish.

ULTRASTAR – 9mm Para. or .40 S&W (new 1996) cal., DA/SA, compact design, 3.57 in. barrel, 9 shot mag., blue steel metal, triple dot sights, steel internal mechanism, polymer exterior construction, 26 oz. Mfg. 1994-1997.

	$350	$300	$250	$225	$180	$145	$115	*$296*

STATE ARMS GUN CO.

Trademark found on .50 BMG cal. bolt action rifles manufactured by the East Ridge/State Arms Gun Co., Inc. located in Bancroft, WI. Please refer to the East Ridge/State Arms Gun Co., Inc. listing in the E section.

STEEL ACTION GmBH

Current bolt action rifle company, located in Koln, Germany. No current U.S. importation.

Steel Action manufactures high-quality hunting rifles using a solid rotating head-lock w/straight-pull bolt action technology. Models include: Steel Action HS (hunting short), Steel Action HM (medium cals.), and Steel Action HM (mag. cals.) in wood and synthetic stocks. Please contact the company directly for more information on their models including pricing, options, and delivery time.

GRADING - PPGS™	100%	98%	95%	90%	80%	70%	60%	LAST MSR

STEEL CITY ARMS, INC.

Previous manufacturer located in Pittsburgh, PA until 1990. In 1991, the name was changed to Desert Industries, Inc. and manufacture was moved to Las Vegas, NV. Very few guns exist with Steel City markings.

PISTOLS: SEMI-AUTO

DOUBLE DEUCE – .22 LR cal. or .25 ACP cal., DA/SA, matte finish stainless steel, 2 1/2 in. barrel, 6 (.25 ACP) or 7 (.22 LR) shot mag., unchecked rosewood grips, 18 oz. Mfg. 1984-1995.

	100%	98%	95%	90%	80%	70%	60%	LAST MSR
	$265	$230	$200	N/A	N/A	N/A	N/A	*$290*

Various select hardwood stocks were also available at an extra cost ($20-100).

STEEL CORE DESIGNS LTD

Current bolt action rifle manufacturer located in Kent, England. Currently imported by CS Tactical located in Elk Grove, CA beginning 2020. Previously imported by Steel Core Designs USA LLC and located in Folsom, CA. until 2019.

For individual model listings, please go to BlueBookOfGunValues.com/overflow.

STEERING GEAR (GRAND RAPIDS & SAGINAW LOCATIONS)

Previous WWII subcontractor of M1 carbines located in Saginaw and Grand Rapids, MI. Saginaw Steering Gear was a division of General Motors Corp.

Please refer to US Military Long Arms listing in the U section for more information.

STEINKAMP MASCHINENBAU GmbH & Co. KG

Previous long gun manufacturer located in Espelkamp, Germany.

LONG GUNS

STEINKAMP SW1 – various cals./gauges, configurations include: standard double rifle version in 8x57R cal., also available as a combination gun with either 20 ga. or .410 bore with 3 in. chamber and rifle calibers, including 5.6x50R Mag., 7x65R, 8x57R, or 9.3x74R, or an O/U shotgun, 24 in. barrels, bullpup with pistol grip styling, choice of plastic or wood, hinged buttplate opened by trigger guard mechanism allows access to chambers, falling block action, extractor or ejector, non-selective single trigger, manual cocking, Picatinny rail, designed by A. Görzen, OAL 26 3/4 in., 7 1/2 lbs. Mfg. 2007-disc.

Base price on this model was €3,495.

STERLING

Previous manufacturer located in Gasport and Lockport (1978-1986), NY until 1986.

PISTOLS

Rather than list individual models, the following generalizations will help in ascertaining values for this trademark. Models 300, 302 and 402 will average between $75 and $175 if in 70%+ condition. Models 283, 284, 285 (Husky), and 286 (Trapper) are semi-auto .22 cal. pistols with various barrel lengths - values will range between $100-$200. Models 400 (.380 ACP), PPL (.380 ACP short barrel, uncommon), and 450 (.45 ACP, prototype only - no mfg.) usually range between $150-$350. X-Caliber single shot pistols (8 or 10 in. barrels in .22 LR, .357 Magnum, or .44 Magnum) usually range between $200-$375 depending on caliber and if the gun comes with spare barrels, rimfire variants generally appraise for less on that value scale.

STERLING ARMAMENT, LTD.

Previous manufacturer established circa 1900, and located in Dagenham, Essex, England. Previously imported and distributed by Cassi Inc. located in Colorado Springs, CO until 1990.

CARBINES: SEMI-AUTO

AR-180 – please refer to the Armalite section for more information and pricing on this model.

STERLING MK 6 – 9mm Para. cal., blowback semi-auto with floating firing pin, shrouded 16.1 in. barrel, side mounted mag., folding stock, 7 1/2 lbs. Disc. 1989.

	100%	98%	95%	90%	80%	70%	60%	LAST MSR
	N/A	$1,750	$1,500	$1,400	$1,200	$1,000	$795	*$650*

PISTOLS: SEMI-AUTO

PARAPISTOL MK 7 C4 – 9mm Para. cal., 4 in. barrel, tactical design pistol, crinkle finish, same action as MK. 6 Carbine, fires from closed bolt, 10, 15, 20, 30, 34 or 68 shot mag., 5 lbs. Disc. 1989.

	100%	98%	95%	90%	80%	70%	60%	LAST MSR
	N/A	$1,500	$1,400	$1,200	$1,000	$800	$700	*$600*

Add $50 per 30 or 34 shot mag., $125 for 68 shot mag.

PARAPISTOL MK 7 C8 – 9mm Para. cal., similar to C4, except has 7.8 in. barrel, 5 1/4 lbs. Disc. 1989.

	100%	98%	95%	90%	80%	70%	60%	LAST MSR
	N/A	$1,500	$1,400	$1,250	$1,050	$900	$750	*$620*

Add $50 per 30 or 34 shot mag., $125 for 68 shot mag.

GRADING - PPGS™	100%	98%	95%	90%	80%	70%	60%	LAST MSR

STERLING ARSENAL

Current firearms manufacturer and custom shop located in Sterling, VA beginning 2010.

Please refer to BlueBookOfGunValues.com to order the *Blue Book of AR-15s & Variations*, available as a book or online subscription.

STEVENS, J., ARMS COMPANY

Current trademark of long arms produced by Savage Arms, Inc. Beginning in 1999, Savage Arms, Inc. began manufacturing/importing Stevens trademarked guns again, including rifles and shotguns. J. Stevens Arms Company was founded in 1864 at Chicopee Falls, MA as J. Stevens & Co. In 1886 the name was changed to J. Stevens Arms and Tool Co. In 1916, the plant became New England Westinghouse, and tooled up for Mosin-Nagant Rifles. In 1920, the plant was sold to the Savage Arms Corp. and manufactured guns were marked "J. Stevens Arms Co." This designation was dropped in the late 1940s, and only the name "Stevens" has been used up to 1990. On July 1, 2019, Vista announced that it sold Savage's (and its subsidiaries Stevens and Fox) firearms to Long Range Acquisition, LLC.

Depending on the remaining Stevens factory data, a factory letter authenticating the configuration of a particular specimen, along with dates produced may be obtained by contacting the company directly. The charge for this service is $25.00 per gun - please allow 8 weeks for an adequate response.

For more Stevens model information, please refer to the Serialization section in the back of this text.

COMBINATION GUNS

MODEL 22-410 - .22 LR cal. over .410 bore, selector on right side of frame, walnut or Tenite stock. Introduced mid-1939-disc.

$425 $375 $300 $250 $200 $165 $140

PISTOLS

NO. 10 TARGET SINGLE SHOT - .22 LR cal., 8 in. barrel, blue, adj. sights, rubber grips, squared-off like an automatic pistol, tip up action. Mfg. 1919-39.

$600 $525 $450 $400 $325 $275 $150

NO. 35 TARGET SINGLE SHOT - .22 LR or .25 Rimfire cal., 6, 8, 10, or 12 1/4 in. barrel, blue, walnut grips. Mfg. 1907-39.

$375 $325 $275 $225 $200 $185 $165

12 1/4 in. barrel variants carry a premium in higher grades.

NO. 35 "OFF-HAND" SHOTGUN - .410 smoothbore cal., 8 or 12 1/4 in. barrel. Mfg. 1923-35.

$350 $300 $250 $225 $200 $150 $125

This firearm is legally considered an "Any Other Weapon" (AOW) per the NFA and is subject to all relevant NFA regulations. Failure to comply with these regulations may result in fines/imprisonment.

NO. 35 "OFF-HAND" AUTOSHOT - similar to Off-Hand Shotgun. Mfg. 1929-34.

$300 $250 $225 $200 $150 $125 $100

This firearm is legally considered an "Any Other Weapon" (AOW) per the NFA and is subject to all relevant NFA regulations. Failure to comply with these regulations may result in fines/imprisonment.

RIFLES

Stevens made a wide variety of inexpensive, utilitarian rifles that, to date, have attracted mostly shooting interest, but little collector interest. A listing of these models may be found in the back of this text under "Serialization."

TIP-UP RIFLES - .22 S, .22 LR, .25 Stevens, .32, .38, or .44 Long RF or CF cal., variations No. 1 - No. 15 feature various weights, wood styles, sights, and other differences, later series has full loop at rear trigger guard. Mfg. circa 1870s-1895.

* ***Tip-Up Rifle Basic Model No. 1 without forearm***

$500 $475 $425 $375 $300 $250 $200

* ***Tip-Up Rifle Model 101*** - .44 shot cartridge, built on the No. 12 Marksman action, lever action opening, straight grip stock, 26 in. barrel. Mfg. 1914-20.

$250 $225 $195 $175 $150 $125 $100

NO. 12 MARKSMAN - .22 LR, .25 Long, or .32 RF cal., boys type single shot with traditional Stevens profile, operated with underlever that allows barrel to tip up for loading, 22 in. round tapered barrel,

GRADING - PPGS™	100%	98%	95%	90%	80%	70%	60%	LAST MSR

walnut stock and forend, silver blade front sight and "V" block rear sight, knurled thumbscrew for takedown. Mfg. 1912-1933.

	$425	$350	$275	$240	$215	$185	$160	

NO. 14 1/2 LITTLE SCOUT – .22 RF cal., 18 or 20 in. barrel, rolling breechblock action, iron sights. Mfg. 1909-36.

	$425	$350	$275	$240	$215	$185	$160	

STEVENS/SPRINGFIELD MODEL 15/120 – .22 S, L, or LR, bolt action single shot, one-piece integral barrel and receiver, manually operated cocking piece at rear of bolt, birch hardwood stock, open rear and bead front sight, thousands mfg. for companies such as Sears, Montgomery Wards, J.C. Penny, Cotter & Co., etc. Mfg. 1936-1971.

	$200	$185	$165	$135	$115	$95	$80	

POCKET RIFLES – detachable serially numbered nickel-plated stock, variations found within each frame size.

- ***Pocket Rifle Small Frame*** – .22 cal. (various issues).

	$450	$400	$350	$300	$275	$235	$200	

- ***Pocket Rifle Small Frame Without Stock***

	$300	$250	$200	$150	$125	$100	$80	

- ***Pocket Rifle Medium Frame*** – .22, .32, .38, .44 cals. (various issues).

	$500	$450	$400	$350	$300	$250	$200	

- ***Pocket Rifle Medium Frame Without Stock***

	$300	$250	$200	$150	$125	$100	$75	

- ***Pocket Rifle Large Frame*** – .22 to .44 cals.

	$600	$550	$500	$450	$400	$350	$300	

- ***Pocket Rifle Large Frame Without Stock***

	$425	$375	$325	$275	$225	$200	$175	

MODEL 44 IDEAL SINGLE SHOT – .22 LR through .44-40 WCF cals., rolling block, lever action, takedown, 24 or 26 in. barrels, straight grip stock and forearm. Mfg. 1894-1932.

	$700	$650	$575	$525	$450	$325	$300	

Subtract 20% for Rimfire cals.

MODEL 44 1/2 IDEAL SINGLE SHOT – similar to Model 44, except .22 LR through .44-40 WCF cals., falling block, lever action, takedown, 24 or 26 in. barrels, straight grip stock and forearm, action redesigned 1903. Mfg. 1903-16.

	$950	$850	$750	$625	$500	$425	$350	

Subtract 10% for rimfire cals.

MODELS 45-54 SINGLE SHOTS – .22 LR through .44-40 WCF cals., rolling and falling block receivers, lever action, takedown, deluxe versions of the Models 44 and 44 1/2, many special order features, including double-set triggers, types of finish, engraving, length and weight of barrels, stock configuration could be special ordered. Mfg. 1896-1916.

The higher grade Schuetzens and Stevens-Pope are very collectible. These models have to be appraised individually when determining value.

MODEL 200 BOLT ACTION – .22-250 Rem., .223 Rem., .243 Win., .25-06 Rem. (disc. 2011), .270 Win., .30-06, .308 Win., .300 Win. Mag., 7mm-08 Rem. (disc. 2011) or 7mm Rem. Mag. cal., short or long action, no sights, 3 or 4 shot internal mag., AccuTrigger not available on this model, 22 or 24 in. barrel, checkered synthetic stock and forend with pillar bedding, with or w/o camo (select cals. only, disc. 2011), Stevens laser etched on bolt, 6 1/2 lbs. Mfg. 2005-2013.

	$365	$325	$280	$240	$210	$190	$170	*$420*

Add $42 for camo (disc. 2011).

Add $50 for scope package that includes 3-9x40mm scope (mfg. 2010-2011).

MODEL 300 BOLT ACTION – .22 LR cal., 20 3/4 in. barrel, AccuTrigger not available, 10 shot detachable mag., grey checkered synthetic stock, adj. rear sight, swivel studs, approx. 5 lbs. Mfg. 2006-2013.

	$175	$155	$130	$110	$90	$80	$70	*$205*

Add $11 for 4x15mm scope (disc. 2012).

MODEL 305 BOLT ACTION – .22 WMR cal., similar to Model 300 bolt action, except has 5 shot detachable box mag. Mfg. 2006-2013.

	$190	$165	$135	$115	$95	$85	$75	*$230*

GRADING - PPGS™	100%	98%	95%	90%	80%	70%	60%	LAST MSR

MODEL 310 BOLT ACTION – .17 HMR cal., similar to Model 305 bolt action, except has 21 in. standard or heavy barrel w/o sights. Mfg. 2006-2013.

	$200	$175	$140	$120	$95	$85	$75	*$245*

Add $31 for heavy barrel (disc. 2008).

MODEL 315 BOLT ACTION YOUTH – .22 LR cal., single shot, uncheckered hardwood stock, shortened Youth dimensions, 19 in. barrel, 5 lbs. Mfg. 2006-2011.

	$175	$135	$100	$85	$75	$55	$45	*$218*

CADET BOLT ACTION – .22 LR cal., does not have AccuTrigger, single shot mini-Youth Model with 16 in. barrel, shortened hardwood stock, fixed sights w/rear aperture sight, 4 1/2 lbs. Mfg. 2006-2011.

	$165	$135	$100	$85	$75	$65	$60	*$211*

MODEL 322 BOLT ACTION (INCLUDING A, B, C, & S) – .22 Hornet cal., otherwise similar to Model 325. Mfg. 1947-50.

	$450	$395	$335	$275	$225	$185	$150

The Model 322S had an aperture sight.

MODEL 325 BOLT ACTION (INCLUDING A, B, C) – .30-30 Win. cal., 4 shot detachable mag. Introduced 1947. Disc. 1950.

	$375	$335	$275	$225	$185	$150	$135

NO. 414 ARMORY MODEL – .22 LR or .22 Short cal. only, lever action, 26 in. barrel, single shot, Lyman aperture sight. Mfg. 1912-32.

	$900	$750	$625	$550	$450	$375	$300

MODEL 416 – .22 LR cal., bolt action, 25 in. medium barrel, 5 shot mag. Disc.

	$250	$220	$190	$175	$140	$120	$90

This model was also mfg. as a U.S. military training rifle. Can be denoted by "U.S. Property" on rear of bolt housing. Healthy premiums exist for this variation. Originally, 10,000 were mfg. at a cost of $22.42 each.

NO. 417 WALNUT HILL MODEL – .22 LR, .22 Short, and .22 Hornet cal., lever action, 28 or 29 in. extra heavy barrel, target stock with full pistol grip, beavertail forend, made in 0-3 suffix variations (different sights). Mfg. 1932-47.

	$1,600	$1,400	$1,200	$1,000	$875	$725	$500

NO. 417 1/2 WALNUT HILL MODEL – similar to No. 417, except available in .25 RF cal. also. Mfg. 1932-40.

	$875	$675	$525	$475	$440	$395	$360

NO. 418 WALNUT HILL MODEL – .22 LR or .22 Short only, 26 in. barrel, pistol grip stock, semi beavertail forearm. Mfg. 1932-40.

	$950	$825	$700	$600	$500	$400	$360

NO. 425 HIGH POWER LEVER ACTION RIFLE – .25, .30, .32, or .35 Rem. cals., 22 in. round barrel with 2/3 length mag. tube, side ejection, blue only, plain walnut stock and forearm, originally designed by John Redfield. Approx. 26,000 mfg. 1910-17.

	$1,850	$1,700	$1,500	$1,250	$1,000	$850	$700

Variations of the No. 425 included the No. 430 (deluxe checkered stock and forearm), No. 435 (extra fancy checkered stock and forearm with engraved designs on receiver borders and lever), or No. 440 (best quality checkered walnut with fully engraved game scenes, and engraved forearm tip and lever). Values range respectively from $450-$950, $650-$1,400, and $1,000-$2,950.

NO. 430 HIGH POWER LEVER ACTION RIFLE – upgraded variation of the No. 425, deluxe checkered stock and forearm.

	$4,000	$3,500	$3,000	$2,500	$2,000	$1,700	$1,400

NO. 435 HIGH POWER LEVER ACTION RIFLE – upgraded variation of the No. 425, extra fancy checkered stock and forearm, with engraved designs on receiver border and lever.

	$8,000	$6,500	$5,500	$4,500	$3,500	$3,000	$2,500

NO. 440 HIGH POWER LEVER ACTION RIFLE – upgraded variation of the No. 425, best quality checkered walnut stock and forearm, with fully engraved game scenes and engraved forearm tip.

	$10,000	$8,500	$7,000	$6,000	$5,000	$4,500	$4,000

STEVENS FAVORITE NO.'S 17-29 – .22 LR, .25 RF or .32 RF cal., 24 in. barrel most common, other lengths available, Rocky Mountain front sight, straight grip stock, small tapered forearm. Mfg. 1894-1935.

	$450	$395	$300	$195	$165	$145	$125

Add 35% for octagon barrels.

GRADING - PPGS™	100%	98%	95%	90%	80%	70%	60%	LAST MSR

MODEL 1915 FAVORITE – .22 LR, .22 WRF (special order option), .25, or .32 cal., redesign of original Steven's Favorite, action slightly heavier and stronger, blue takedown frame, walnut stock and forearm, other internal changes, similar outward appearance, marked "SVG" after 1920, offered as the No. 27 with full octagon barrel, the No. 17 with round barrel, and the No. 20 with smoothbore barrel, 4 1/2 lbs. Mfg. 1915-1940.

$450 $395 $300 $195 $165 $145 $125

STEVENS FAVORITE MODEL 30 (RECENT MFG.) – .17 HMR (Model 30R17, mfg. 2004-2005), .22 LR (Model 30G), or .22 WMR (Model GM, mfg. 2002-2005) cal., choice of solid or takedown (new 2004) action, lever action falling block with inertia firing pin, 20 in. round or 21 (disc.) in. half octagon (Model 30G) or full octagon (Model GM) barrel, uncheckered wood stock and forearm, open sights, 4 1/4 lbs. New mfg. began in late 1998 by Savage Arms, Inc., limited availability 2007-2012.

$315 $245 $220 $195 $170 $155 $130 *$379*

Add $38 for .22 WMR cal. (mfg. 2002-2005).
Add $64 for .17 HMR cal. (mfg. 2004-2005).
Add $17 for takedown action (.22 LR or .17 HMR cal. only, TD Model).

NO. 65 LITTLE KRAG – .22 LR cal., bolt action takedown rifle, removable 20 in. round barrel, single shot, open or peep sights, straight grip walnut stock with rubber buttplate. Mfg. 1903-1910.

$450 $395 $300 $195 $165 $145 $125

NO. 70 "VISIBLE LOADING" SLIDE ACTION RIFLE – .22 S, L, or LR cal., exposed hammer, 22 in. barrel, open sights, straight grip stock, tube mag., grooved slide handle. Other variations with different barrel lengths and sights will command slight premiums.

$550 $475 $400 $350 $300 $250 $200

MODEL 71 "STEVENS FAVORITE" COMMEMORATIVE – .22 LR cal., replica of original, single shot lever action, 22 in. octagon barrel, color case hardened receiver with "Favorite" in gold-filled lettering, gold plated lever and hammer, brass front sight blade and rear sight elevator, portrait medallion commemorating Joshua Stevens inlaid into the right side of stock, oil finished plain straight walnut stock, Schnabel forearm, crescent shaped brass buttplate. Approx. 10,000 mfg. beginning 1971-disc.

$625 $550 $475 $425 $350 $275 $225 *$75*

NO. 80 GALLERY RIFLE – .22 S, L, LR, or .25 Stevens rimfire cal., slide acton repeater, 24 in. round barrel, bead front and adj. sporting rear sights, blue finish, smooth walnut straight grip stock with hard rubber buttplate and 12 groove round slide handle, 4 1/4 lbs. Mfg. 1906-1910.

$425 $350 $275 $240 $215 $185 $160

SIDE LEVER CRACKSHOT – .22 RF or .32 RF cal., boys type single shot rifle, breechblock is operated by a small lever on the side of the frame, side lever opening, 20 in. round barrel with fixed sights. Mfg. 1900-1913.

$295 $235 $195 $150 $100 $60 $50

NO. 20 FAVORITE – .22 RF or .32 RF smoothbore, 24 in. barrel, smoothbore variation of the No. 17 rifle.

$250 $225 $200 $165 $125 $95 $75

NO. 26 CRACKSHOT – .22 RF or .32 RF cal., boys type single shot rifle, under lever opening, 18 in. round barrel, hardwood straight grip stock and forend, open sights. Mfg. 1913-41.

$295 $235 $195 $150 $100 $60 $50

NO. 26 1/2 CRACKSHOT – .22 RF or .32 RF shotshell, smoothbore variation of the No. 26 rifle.

$225 $200 $175 $135 $110 $85 $65

MODEL 53/053 BOLT ACTION – .22 S, L, LR, .22 WMR, or .25 Stevens rimfire cal., single shot bolt action rifle, 24 in. round barrel, chrome bolt and trigger, gold bead front and open rear sights (Model 53) or hooded front with interchangeable inserts and rear apeture and folding middle sight (Model 053), walnut pistol grip stock, 5 lbs. Mfg. 1935-1947.

$200 $175 $150 $135 $110 $90 $70

Add 15% for .22 WMR, or 30% for .25 Stevens cal.

MODEL 72 CRACKSHOT – .22 LR cal., single shot falling block action, 22 in. octagon barrel with blue finish, open sights, color case hardened frame, straight stock, serial number noted with "B" prefix. Mfg. 1972-1989.

$300 $260 $225 $200 $175 $140 $100 *$165*

Some later manufactured Model 72 Crackshots have been noted to have black parkerized barrel and receiver finish, bronze-colored lever, and a squirrel on a branch engraved on both sides of the receiver. These were indicated by serial numbers with an "E" prefix.

GRADING - PPGS™	100%	98%	95%	90%	80%	70%	60%	LAST MSR

MODEL 74 – .22 LR cal., similar to Model 72 Crackshot, except has round barrel. Mfg. 1972-1974. Extremely scarce.

$360 $320 $275 $250 $200 $175 $125 *$165*

MODEL 987 – .22 LR cal. only, semi-auto, 15 shot tube mag., 20 in. barrel, hardwood Monte Carlo stock, adj. rear sight, 6 lbs. Disc. 1989.

$160 $140 $120 $100 $85 $70 $50 *$119*

MODEL 83/083 BOLT ACTION – .22 S, L, LR, .22 WMR, or .25 Stevens rimfire cal., single shot bolt action rifle, 24 in. round barrel, chrome bolt and trigger, gold bead front and open rear sights (Model 83) or hooded front with interchangeable inserts and #105 rear apeture and folding middle sight (Model 083), walnut finished hardwood pistol grip stock, walnut pistol grip stock, 5 lbs., Mfg. 1935-1942.

$175 $150 $125 $100 $85 $70 $60

Add 15% for .22 WMR, or 30% for .25 Stevens cal.

MODEL 84C – .22 S, L, LR cal., mag. fed bolt action rifle, 24 in. round barrel, detachable mag., chrome bolt and trigger, simple post front sight and open rear sights, finished walnut hardwood stock, left side thumb safety.

$175 $150 $125 $100 $85 $70 $60

MODEL 87 SEMI-AUTO – .22 LR cal., tube mag., round tapered barrel, over 1.8 million made in numerous variations, including the Model 6, 76, 87, 187, 188, 60, 90, 88, 388, 887 and many others under brand names for Sears, Montgomery Ward, Western Auto, CIL, Coast to Coast, etc., model numbers include letter suffix added as changes were made. Introduced in 1938, and continued through the early 1980s.

$150 $130 $110 $90 $70 $60 $50

MODEL 89 LEVER ACTION – .22 LR cal., single shot, 18 1/2 in. barrel, Martini type action, Western style lever, straight stock. Mfg. 1976-disc.

$150 $130 $115 $100 $85 $70 $50

SHOTGUNS

Stevens made a wide variety of inexpensive, utilitarian shotguns that, to date, have attracted mostly shooting interest, but little collector interest. A listing of these models may be found in the back of this text under "Serialization."

MODEL 67 SLIDE ACTION – 12, 20 ga., or .410 bore, 3 in. chamber, steel receiver, 5 shot, upper receiver safety, 6 1/4-7 1/2 lbs. Recent mfg. by Stevens. Disc. 1989.

$200 $180 $170 $155 $145 $135 $125 *$229*

Add $30 for choke tubes (with VR).
Add $10 for VR only.

* ***Model 67 Slide Action VTR-K Camo*** – 12 or 20 ga., 28 in. VR barrel with choke tubes, laminated camo stock. Mfg. 1986-88.

$250 $220 $190 $170 $155 $145 $135 *$295*

* ***Model 67 Slide Action Slug Model*** – 12 ga. only, 21 in. barrel, rifle sights. Disc. 1989.

$200 $165 $140 $110 $100 $90 $80 *$245*

* ***Model 67 Slide Action VRT-Y*** – 20 ga. only, 22 in. VR barrel with choke tubes, youth model with smaller stock dimensions. Mfg. 1987-88.

$205 $170 $140 $110 $100 $90 $80 *$259*

MODEL 69-RXL SLIDE ACTION – 12 ga. only, law enforcement version of the Model 67, 18 1/4 in. cylinder bore barrel with recoil pad, 6 1/2 lbs. Disc. 1989.

$250 $200 $175 $150 $130 $120 $90 *$245*

MODEL 77 SLIDE ACTION W/J, K, M, OR SC SUFFIX – 12 ("J" suffix), 16 ("K" suffix), or 20 ("M" suffix) ga. or .410 bore, "SC" designates Super Choke. Mfg. 1955-1971.

$175 $160 $140 $120 $100 $80 $60

MODEL 94 – 12, 16, 20, 28 ga., or .410 bore, single shot breakopen, hammer, 6 1/4 lbs. Mfg. 1929-disc.

$200 $175 $150 $135 $110 $90 $70 *$92*

MODEL 124 BOLT ACTION – 12 ga. only, straight pull action, 28 in. barrel, 3 shot, Tenite buttstock and forearm, circa 1950.

$300 $275 $240 $200 $180 $160 $140

NO. 200 SLIDE ACTION – 20 ga., 3 in. chamber, tube mag., 26, 28, 30, or 32 in. barrel, takedown, 5 shot, 6 1/2 lbs. Mfg. circa 1910.

$225 $190 $180 $150 $125 $95 $85

GRADING - PPGS™	100%	98%	95%	90%	80%	70%	60%	LAST MSR

MODEL 240 O/U – .410 bore, split hammers, double trigger.

GRADING - PPGS™	100%	98%	95%	90%	80%	70%	60%	LAST MSR
	$675	$600	$525	$475	$375	$325	$225	

MODEL 301 SINGLE SHOT – 12, 20 ga., or .410 bore, 3 in. chamber, single shot, break action, 26 in. carbon steel barrel, interchangeable choke tubes, rugged synthetic stock, soft recoil pad, two-position safety, matte black finish, 5.59 lbs. New 2017.

GRADING - PPGS™	100%	98%	95%	90%	80%	70%	60%	LAST MSR
MSR $189	$160	$145	$135	$125	$110	$100	$75	

* ***Model 301 Single Shot Compact*** – 20 ga. or .410 bore, 3 in. chamber, single shot, break action, 22 in. carbon steel barrel, interchangeable choke tubes, rugged synthetic stock, soft recoil pad, 12.75 in. LOP, two-position safety, matte black finish, 5.34 lbs. New 2017.

GRADING - PPGS™	100%	98%	95%	90%	80%	70%	60%	LAST MSR
MSR $189	$160	$145	$135	$125	$110	$100	$75	

MODEL 301 TURKEY SINGLE SHOT – 12 or 20 ga., or .410 bore, 3 in. chamber, break open action, 26 in. barrel, extra full win. choke, bead sight, synthetic stock with Mossy Oak Bottomland or Mossy Oak Obsession camo finish, recoil pad, 13.75 in. LOP, swivel studs on stock and forend, hammer blocking safety, one-piece rail, matte black metal finish, 5.07 lbs. New 2019.

GRADING - PPGS™	100%	98%	95%	90%	80%	70%	60%	LAST MSR
MSR $209	$180	$155	$135	$125	$115	$100	$75	

MODEL 301 TURKEY XP – 20 ga. or .410 bore, 3 in. chamber, single shot, break open action, 26 in. barrel, extra full Win. choke, front bead sight, 1x30 Red Dot, Mossy Oak Bottomland or Mossy Oak Obsession Camo, manual hammer blocking safety, recoil pad, one-piece rail,black receiver and barrel finish, 5.07 lbs. New 2020.

GRADING - PPGS™	100%	98%	95%	90%	80%	70%	60%	LAST MSR
MSR $249	$215	$190	$160	$145	$135	$125	$100	

MODEL 311 SxS – 12, 16, 20 ga., or .410 bore, 3 in. chambers, double triggers, extractors, VR. Disc. 1989.

GRADING - PPGS™	100%	98%	95%	90%	80%	70%	60%	LAST MSR
	$275	$235	$200	$175	$160	$145	$130	*$309*

Add 30% for .410 bore.
Add 20% for 16 or 20 ga.
Add 200% for early models in .410 bore w/walnut stocks and case colors.

* ***Model 311-R SxS*** – 12 or 20 ga., similar to Model 311, except has 18 1/4 in. cylinder bore barrels for law enforcement use, 3 in. chambers, 6 3/4 lbs. Disc. 1989.

GRADING - PPGS™	100%	98%	95%	90%	80%	70%	60%	LAST MSR
	$245	$205	$185	$150	$140	$125	$115	*$309*

MODEL 315 SxS – 12, 16, 20 ga., or .410 bore, DT, extractors, hammerless, case colored frame, walnut stock and forearm, model identification is on top lever, this model also was mfg. under various trade names, including Riverside and Springfield.

GRADING - PPGS™	100%	98%	95%	90%	80%	70%	60%	LAST MSR
	$425	$375	$325	$275	$225	$180	$150	

MODEL 320 SECURITY THUMBHOLE – 12 or 20 ga., slide action, 18 1/2 in. chrome alloy steel security barrel, 5 shot, bottom load, bead or ghost ring sight, synthetic thumbhole stock and forend, dual slide bars, rotary bolt, black finish, 7 lbs. New 2021.

GRADING - PPGS™	100%	98%	95%	90%	80%	70%	60%	LAST MSR
MSR $275	$230	$200	$175	$155	$125	$110	$100	

Add $30 for ghost ring sights.

MODEL 320 SLIDE ACTION FIELD – 12 or 20 ga., 3 in. chamber, 26 or 28 in. blued VR barrel with fixed modified choke, bead sight, bottom load, right eject, rotary bolt, black synthetic stock and forearm, approx. 7 1/2 lbs. New 2012.

GRADING - PPGS™	100%	98%	95%	90%	80%	70%	60%	LAST MSR
MSR $259	$220	$195	$165	$150	$125	$110	$100	

Add $40 for combo model with extra 18 1/2 in. cyl. bore barrel (disc. 2015).

* ***Model 320 Slide Action Field Youth*** – 20 ga., 3 in. chamber, 22 in. VR barrel with fixed modified choke, 12.75 in. LOP, 5 shot, dual slide bars, rotary bolt, bead sight, matte black metal finish, black synthetic stock and forearm, 6.8 lbs. New 2015.

GRADING - PPGS™	100%	98%	95%	90%	80%	70%	60%	LAST MSR
MSR $259	$220	$195	$165	$150	$125	$110	$100	

MODEL 320 SLIDE ACTION FIELD CAMO – 12 or 20 ga., 3 in. chamber, 26 (Muddy Girl only) or 28 (MO Shadow Grass Blades only) in. blued VR barrel, rotary bolt, 5 shot, green fiber optic sights, synthetic stock, bottom load, right eject, dual slide bars, drilled and tapped receiver, Muddy Girl or Mossy Oak Shadow Grass Blades camo finish, 7 1/2 lbs. New 2016.

GRADING - PPGS™	100%	98%	95%	90%	80%	70%	60%	LAST MSR
MSR $299	$255	$225	$190	$175	$140	$115	$100	

* ***Model 320 Slide Action Field Youth Camo*** – 12 or 20 ga., 3 in. chamber, 22 (Muddy Girl only) or 26 (MO Shadow Grass Blades only) in. blued VR barrel, mod chokes, rotary bolt, 5 shot, green fiber optic sight, drilled and tapped receiver, synthetic stock, bottom load, right eject, dual slide bars, 12 3/4 in. LOP, Mossy Oak Shadow Grass Blades or Muddy Girl camo finish, 6.8-7.2 lbs. New 2016.

GRADING - PPGS™	100%	98%	95%	90%	80%	70%	60%	LAST MSR
MSR $299	$255	$225	$190	$175	$140	$115	$100	

GRADING - PPGS™	100%	98%	95%	90%	80%	70%	60%	LAST MSR

MODEL 320 SLIDE ACTION FIELD GRADE TURKEY – 12 ga., 3 in. chamber, 22 in. VR barrel, EF choke, 5 shot rotary mag., fiber optic front sights, synthetic stock with Mossy Oak Obsession camo finish, 14.5 in. LOP, matte black metal finish, 7 lbs. New 2016.

MSR $309	$265	$230	$195	$180	$145	$120	$100	

MODEL 320 SLIDE ACTION SECURITY – 12 or 20 (new 2015) ga., 3 in. chamber, 18 1/2 in. cyl. bore barrel, side ejection, with or w/o pistol grip, bead, ghost ring, or rifle (mfg. 2012 only) sights, avail. with one-piece rail and heat shield, matte black metal finish, black synthetic stock and forearm, approx. 7 lbs. New 2012.

MSR $259	$220	$195	$165	$150	$120	$100	$85	

Add $30 for ghost ring or rifle (mfg. 2012 only) sights.
Add $40 for one-piece rail with heat shield.
Add $40 for Security Combo (includes 28 in. VR sporting barrel and 18 1/2 in. Security barrel with bead sight).

MODEL 320 SLIDE-ACTION WATERFOWL – 12 ga., bottom load, right-eject pump action, 28 in. VR barrel with interchangeable choke tubes, long green fiber optic front sight, rugged synthetic stock and forend, dual slide bars, rotary bolt, available in standard or compact length of pull, Mossy Oak Shadow Grass Blades camo finish, 7.45 lbs. New 2016.

MSR $280	$225	$195	$170	$150	$135	$125	$115	

MODEL 350 SLIDE ACTION FIELD – 12 ga., 28 in. barrel, 5 shot tube mag., bottom ejection, matte black synthetic stock, vent. rib, bead sights, 8.2 lbs. Mfg. mid-2010-2011.

	$250	$200	$175	$150	$135	$125	$115	*$294*

MODEL 350 SLIDE ACTION SECURITY – 12 ga., 3 in. chamber, 18 1/2 in. barrel, 5 shot tube mag., bottom ejection, matte black synthetic pistol grip stock, bead (disc. 2012), ghost ring, or rifle (disc. 2012) sights, 7.6 lbs. Mfg. mid-2010-2015.

	$225	$195	$170	$150	$135	$125	$115	*$276*

* ***Model 350 Slide Action Security/Field Combo*** – 12 ga., includes both 18 1/4 and 28 in. barrels. Mfg. mid-2010-2011.

	$275	$235	$200	$185	$170	$160	$150	*$339*

MODEL 411 SxS – 12, 20 (disc. 2004) ga. or .410 bore (disc. 2004), 28 in. monobloc barrels with choke tubes, boxlock action with laser engraved sideplates, SST, checkered walnut stock and splinter forearm, approx. 6 1/4 lbs., mfg. in Russia. Imported 2004-2005.

	$380	$330	$280	$235	$200	$180	$160	*$438*

MODEL 320 TURKEY THUMBHOLE – 12 or 20 ga., slide action, 22 in. chrome alloy steel barrel with matte black finish, extended extra full choke tubes, 5 shot, bottom load, adj. fiber optic turkey sights, OD Green synthetic thumbhole stock and forend, dual slide bars, rotary bolt, 7.6 lbs. New 2021.

MSR $323	$275	$240	$200	$185	$150	$125	$100	

MODEL 512 GOLD WING O/U – 12, 20, 28 ga., or .410 bore, boxlock action, 2 3/4 (28 ga.) or 3 in. chambers, 24 (Youth Model, 20 ga.), 26 or 28 in. VR barrels, choke tubes (except for .410 bore), ST, extractors, Turkish walnut pistol grip stock, Schnabel forearm, fleur-de-lis checkering, blue receiver with light relief engraving and gold pheasant inlays. Mfg. in Turkey. Mfg. 2007-2013.

	$575	$475	$425	$375	$340	$300	$265	*$690*

MODEL 520 SLIDE ACTION – this model was designed by John M. Browning, slight humpback in receiver.

	$475	$425	$350	$325	$275	$225	$150	

MODEL 520-30 TRENCH/RIOT MILITARY SHOTGUNS – see the "Trench/Riot Shotgun" category in the T section for more information and prices.

MODEL 530A SxS – 12, 16, 20 ga. or .410 bore, 2 3/4 in. chambers, boxlock action similar to Model 311, DT, extractors, 28 in. barrels, F/Mod. chokes, handcut checkered walnut stock, splinter forearm, case colored hardened finish, light engraving with dog, no ser. no.

	$275	$235	$200	$175	$160	$145	$130	

Add 30% for .410 bore.
Add 20% for 16 or 20 ga.

MODEL 555 O/U – 12, 16 (new 2019), 20, 28 ga., or .410 bore, 3 in. chambers, 26 or 28 (12 ga. only) in. chrome-lined barrels, lightweight aluminum receiver, manual extractors, SST, tang mounted safety, Turkish walnut stock, 5.5-6.2 lbs. New 2015.

MSR $709	$600	$525	$450	$410	$325	$275	$225	

GRADING - PPGS™	100%	98%	95%	90%	80%	70%	60%	LAST MSR

* ***Model 555 Compact O/U*** – 20, 28, or .410 ga., 3 in. chamber, 24 in. chrome-lined barrels, 5 chokes, 2 shot, SST, Turkish walnut stock, tang mounted safety, scaled to gauge, lightweight aluminum receiver, 5 lbs. New 2017.

MSR $709	$600	$525	$450	$410	$325	$275	$225	

* ***Model 555 Enhanced O/U*** – 12, 16 (new 2019), 20, 28 ga., or .410 bore, 3 in. chamber, 26 or 28 (12 ga. only) in. chrome-lined barrels, 5 interchangeable choke tubes, 2 shot, automatic shell extractor, SST, Imperial walnut stock and forend, tang mounted safety, lightweight aluminum and laser-engraved Filigree ornament receiver, includes a steel insert to reinforce the breech, 5.6-6.45 lbs. New 2016.

MSR $859	$725	$635	$550	$500	$400	$325	$280	

MODEL 555 TRAP – 12 or 20 ga., 3 in. chamber, shotgun, single barrel trap gun, single shot, right or left-hand action, 26 (compact model) or 30 (full size) in. chrome-lined, carbon steel VR barrel, 3 chokes, lightweight aluminum alloy silver receiver w/semi-gloss finish, manual extractor, bead sight, oil-finish, Turkish walnut stock and forend, tang mounted manual safety, 7.3-7.5 lbs. New 2020.

MSR $709	$600	$525	$450	$410	$325	$275	$225	

MODEL 612 GOLD WING SxS – 12, 20, 28 ga., or .410 bore, boxlock action, 2 3/4 (28 ga.) or 3 in. chambers, 26 or 28 in. VR barrels, choke tubes (except for .410 bore), ST, extractors, Turkish walnut pistol grip stock, fleur-de-lis checkering, lightweight alloy receiver with light relief engraving and gold pheasant inlays. Mfg. 2010-2011.

	$625	$525	$450	$375	$340	$300	$265	*$799*

MODEL 612 SxS TRAIL GUN – 12 or 20 ga., 20 in. barrels, 3 in. chambers, checkered walnut stock and forearm, blue receiver. Mfg. 2010-2011.

	$625	$525	$450	$375	$340	$300	$265	*$799*

MODEL 620 SLIDE ACTION – an improved version of the Model 520 with streamlined receiver.

	$275	$240	$215	$180	$160	$135	$100	

MODEL 620 TRENCH/RIOT MILITARY SHOTGUNS – see the "Trench/Riot Shotgun" category in the T section for more information and prices.

MODEL 675 SLIDE ACTION – 12 ga. only, 24 in. VR multi-choked barrel with iron sights (including removable rear ramp), hardwood stock with recoil pad, 6 1/2 lbs. Mfg. 1987-88.

	$250	$220	$190	$170	$155	$145	$135	*$295*

MODEL 9478 – 10, 12, 20 ga., or .410 bore, single shot break open, inertia firing pin, external hammer. Mfg. 1978-85.

	$200	$175	$150	$135	$110	$90	$70	

FOX/STEVENS MODEL B SxS – please refer to this listing in the Fox, A.H. section.

FOX/STEVENS MODEL B-SE SxS – please refer to this listing in the Fox, A.H. section.

SHOTGUNS: SEMI-AUTO

S1200 – 12 ga., 3 in. chamber, inertia system, 26 or 28 in. VR blued steel barrel with five interchangeable chokes (accepts Beretta MobilChoke system), 5 shot mag., bead sight, all-weather black matte synthetic or walnut (12 ga. only) stock, bottom load, right eject, 6.4-7 lbs. Mfg. 2016-2017.

	$485	$425	$365	$330	$265	$225	$175	*$573*

Add $112 for walnut stock.

* ***S1200 Camo*** – 12 ga., 3 in. chamber, inertia system, 28 in. VR barrel with five interchangeable chokes (accepts Beretta MobilChoke system), 5 shot mag., bead sight, synthetic stock, bottom load, right eject, 100% Mossy Oak Bottomlands or Mossy Oak Shadow Grass Blades camo finish, 6.6 lbs. Mfg. 2016-2017.

	$535	$475	$400	$365	$295	$240	$185	*$629*

STEYR AUSTRIAN MILITARY

Previously manufactured for the Austrian military in Steyr, Austria.

RIFLES: BOLT ACTION

MODEL 95 RIFLE – 8x56R Mannlicher cal., straight pull bolt action, 30 in. barrel, adj. sights, military full stock.

	$295	$265	$225	$195	$170	$135	$100	

These rifles were converted (rechambered) from 8x50R caliber, which was the original round during WWI until 1930. The chamber is marked with a large "S" for S-Patrone (round). Conversion began in 1930.

GRADING - PPGS™	100%	98%	95%	90%	80%	70%	60%	LAST MSR

MODEL 95 CARBINE – similar to Model 95 Rifle, except has 19 1/2 in. barrel.

	$395	$360	$315	$275	$225	$175	$125	

STEYR DAIMLER PUCH A.G.

Previous manufacturer located in Steyr, Austria 1911 to circa 1960.

PISTOLS

POCKET AUTO (MODEL 1909) – 6.35mm or 7.63mm cal., tip-down barrel, mag. fed., N. Pieper patent. Mfg. 1909-1914 and 1921-1939.

	$450	$350	$275	$225	$175	$150	$125	

Add 10% for 7.63mm cal.

ROTH STEYR MODEL 1907 (ROTH/KRNKA M.7) – 8mm Steyr cal., 10 shot, 5 1/8 in. barrel, fixed magazine top loaded by stripper clip. Total production in Steyr and Budapest is approx. 100,000.

	$1,800	$1,500	$1,200	$900	$800	$700	$600	

Add 25% for "Budapest" markings.

STEYR-HAHN MODEL AUTOMATIC – 9mm Steyr cal., 8 shot, 5.1 in. barrel, fixed magazine top loaded by stripper clip, blue, checkered wood grips, may be encountered with mixed numbers on parts, Chile adopted in 1911 (Model 1911), Romania adopted in 1912 (Model 1912), and Austro-Hungary in 1914 with the beginning of WWI (most common). Mfg. 1911-1919, with total production reaching nearly 300,000. In 1938, the Germans confiscated and converted a quantity of these to 9mm Para., "08" was stamped on the left side of these guns.

	$1,200	$1,000	$800	$600	$450	$400	$350	

Add 100% if marked "08" or with Romanian Crest.
Add 50% for Chilean Crest.

MODEL SP (SICHERHEITSPISTOLE) – .32 ACP cal., semi-auto, DAO, trigger cocking mechanism, very rare. Mfg. in 1959 only, total production was 912.

	$875	$750	$650	$550	$500	$450	$400	

Sicherheitspistole means "security pistol".

STEYR ARMS (STEYR MANNLICHER)

2008-Current

Pre-2008

Currently manufactured by Steyr-Mannlicher AG & Co. KG in Austria. Founded in Steyr, Austria by Joseph Werndl circa 1864. Currently imported beginning mid-2005 by Steyr Arms, Inc., located in Bessemer, AL. Previously located in Trussville, AL until 2013. Previously located in Cumming, GA. Previously imported 2004-mid-2005 by Steyr USA, located in West Point, MS. Previously imported 2002-2003 by Dynamit Nobel, located in Closter, NJ. Previously imported and distributed until 2002 by Gun South, Inc. (GSI) located in Trussville, AL.

In 2007, the firm of Steyr-Mannlicher was sold to new owners and the factory was relocated to Kleinraming, approx. 12 miles from the original site in Steyr, Austria. The new firm, Steyr Arms, was purchased by Dr. Ernst Reichmayr and his friend and partner, Gerhard Unterganschnigg.

Note: also see Mannlicher Schoenauer Sporting Rifles in the M section for pre-WWII models.

For more information and current pricing on both new and used Steyr airguns, please refer to the *Blue Book of Airguns* - also available as an online subscription.

COMBINATION GUNS

MANNLICHER DUETT – .222 Rem., .243 Win., .308 Win., 7x65R, .30-06, .30R Blaser, 8x57 IRS, 9.3x74R over 12 ga. cal., 3 in. chamber, 23.6 in. barrel, satin finished aluminum receiver with etched panels, two single staged triggers, open sights with integral scope mount rail, fancy checkered European walnut stock and forearm, manual cocking system, fine (Duett Earl) or deep (Duett Duke) hand engraving on sideplates, sling swivels, Mannox finish, 6.6 lbs. Limited importation 2016-2017.

	$3,650	$3,300	$2,950	$2,600	$2,300	$2,000	$1,650	*$3,995*

Add $2,000 for fine hand engraving (Duett Earl).
Add $3,700 for deep hand engraving (Duett Duke).

PISTOLS: SEMI-AUTO

A2 MF SERIES – 9mm Para. cal., compact, medium, or large frame sizes, 3.8, 4, or 4.5 in. cold hammer forged barrel, 10 or 17 shot mag. (optional 15 shot mag.), trapezoid sights, textured ergonomic grip, four safety variations (trigger, drop, indirect firing pin, or manual safety), loaded chamber indicator, full

GRADING - PPGS™	100%	98%	95%	90%	80%	70%	60%	LAST MSR

Picatinny rail, ambidextrous mag. release, key lock and takedown lever, manual lock, flared magwell, forward slide serrations, 7- 7.9 in. OAL, 1.6-1.7 lbs. Importation began 2019.

* ***C9-A2*** – 9mm Para. cal., compact frame size, 3.8 in. cold hammer forged barrel, 10 or 17 shot mag. (optional 15 shot mag.), trapezoid sights, textured ergonomic grip, 4 safety variations (trigger, drop, indirect firing pin, or manual safety), loaded chamber indicator, full Picatinny rail, ambidextrous mag. release, key lock and takedown lever, manual lock, flared magwell, forward slide serrations, 7 in. OAL, approx. 1.68 lbs. Importation began 2019.

MSR $685	$600	$550	$450	$425	$350	$275	$225	

* ***L9-A2*** – 9mm Para. cal., large frame size, 4.5 in. cold hammer forged barrel, 10 or 17 shot mag. (optional 15 shot mag.), trapezoid sights, textured ergonomic grip, 4 safety variations (trigger, drop, indirect firing pin, or manual safety), loaded chamber indicator, full Picatinny rail, ambidextrous mag. release, key lock and takedown lever, manual lock, flared magwell, forward slide serrations, 7.9 in. OAL, 1.7 lbs. Importation began 2019.

MSR $685	$600	$550	$450	$425	$350	$275	$225	

* ***M9-A2*** – 9mm Para. cal., medium size frame, 4 in. cold hammer forged barrel, 10 or 17 shot mag. (optional 15 shot mag.), trapezoid sights, textured ergonomic grip, four different safety variations (trigger, drop, indirect firing pin, or manual lock safety), loaded chamber indicator, full Picatinny rail, ambidextrous mag. release, key lock and takedown lever, manual lock, flared magwell, forward slide serrations, 7.4 in. OAL, 1.6-1.7 lbs. Importation began 2019.

MSR $685	$600	$550	$450	$425	$350	$275	$225	

C-A1 SERIES – 9mm Para. (C9 A-1), or .40 S&W (C40 A-1, importation disc. 2011, reintroduced 2017) cal., 3.6 or 3.8 in. barrel, similar to M-A1 Series, 12 or 17 shot mag., compact frame. Importation disc. 2018.

	$500	$450	$395	$350	$300	$275	$250	*$575*

Add $175 for TFX optical sights (9mm Para. cal. only, new 2017).

L-A1 SERIES – 9mm Para., .40 S&W, or .357 SIG (disc. 2016) cal., right or left-hand action, full size polymer frame, 4 1/2 or 5 (threaded, new 2017) in. cold hammer forged barrel, full-length slide, adj. sights, 12 (.40 S&W or .357 SIG) or 17 (9mm Para. only) shot mag., ergonomic high grip, newly designed loaded chamber indicator, reversible magazine release, lower Picatinny rail, matte black finish. Imported 2014-2018.

	$500	$450	$395	$350	$300	$275	$250	*$575*

Add $40 for threaded barrel (9mm Para. cal. only, new 2017).
Add $175 for TFX optical sights (9mm Para. cal. only, new 2017).

M-A1 SERIES – .357 SIG (M357 A-1, disc. 2013), 9mm Para. (M9 A-1), or .40 S&W (M40 A-1) cal., DAO, SFO, updated Model M with Picatinny rail on lower front of frame, redesigned grip frame, 1/2 (not available in .357 SIG cal, disc.), 4, or 4 1/2 (threaded, new 2018) in. barrel, 10, 12 (.40 S&W or .357 SIG) or 15 (9mm Para.) shot mag., black polymer or OD Green (new 2018) frame with matte black finished slide, trigger safety, white outlined triangular sights, redesigned grip frame, trigger safety and lockable safety system, updated Model M with Picatinny rail on lower front of frame, matte black finished slide, approx. 27 oz. Imported 2004-2009, reintroduced late 2010 to late 2018.

	$500	$450	$395	$350	$300	$275	$250	*$575*

Add $25 for OD Green frame (new 2017).
Add $40 for threaded barrel (9mm Para. cal. only, new 2017).
Add $175 for TFX optical sights (9mm Para. cal. only).
Add $23 for triangle sights with Trilux (disc.).
Add $40 for night sights (disc. 2013).

S-A1 SERIES – 9mm Para. (S9 A-1), or .40 S&W (S40 A-1) cal., similar to M-A1 Series, 10 shot mag., smaller compact frame. Importation disc. late 2018.

	$500	$450	$395	$350	$300	$275	$250	*$575*

Add $175 for TFX optical sights (9mm Para. cal. only, new 2017).

MODEL GB – 9mm Para. cal., DA/SA, delayed blowback action, 5 1/4 in. barrel with Polygon rifling, 18 shot mag., steel construction, non-glare checkered plastic grips, matte finish, 2 lbs. 6 oz. Importation disc. 1988.

Commercial	$675	$600	$525	$450	$400	$350	$300	
Military	$900	$800	$700	$600	$525	$450	$400	*$514*

In 1987, Steyr mfg. a military variation of the Model GB featuring a phosphate finish - only 937 were imported into the U.S.

GRADING - PPGS™	100%	98%	95%	90%	80%	70%	60%	LAST MSR

MODEL M SERIES – 9mm Para., .357 SIG, or .40 S&W cal., DAO, SFO, features first integrated limited access key lock safety in a semi-auto pistol, 3 different safety conditions, black synthetic frame, 10 shot mag., matte black finish, loaded chamber indicator, triangle/trapezoid sights, 28 oz. Limited importation 1999-2002.

$500	$450	$400	$350	$300	$275	$250	*$610*

Add $65 for night sights.

MODEL RFP – .22 LR cal., recoil operated, 4 in. barrel, 10 shot mag., fixed sights, black polymer frame w/ finger groove grips and serrated backstrap, trigger safety w/decocking function, dual slide serrations, lower Picatinny rail, approx. 21 oz. Imported 2017 only.

$365	$325	$285	$260	$240	$220	$195	*$435*

MODEL S – 9mm Para., .357 SIG, or .40 S&W cal., DAO, SFO, 3 1/2 in. barrel, 10 shot mag., shorter grip frame, loaded chamber indicator, triangle/trapezoid sights, matte black finish, 22 1/2 oz. Limited importation 2000-2002.

$475	$435	$385	$350	$325	$300	$280	*$610*

MODEL SPP – 9mm Para. cal., SA, delayed blow back system, rotating 5.9 in. barrel, 15 or 30 shot mag., adj. sights, utilizes synthetic materials and advanced ergonomics, grooved receiver for scope mounting, matte black finish, 44 oz. Limited importation 1992-1993.

$995	$895	$725	$550	$495	$450	$400	*$895*

RIFLES: BOLT ACTION, CURRENT/RECENT PRODUCTION

The Steyr-Mannlicher models were in production 1968-1996.

Current production guns are now called Steyr-Mannlicher models. For models manufactured 1903-1971, please refer to the Mannlicher Schoenauer Sporting Rifles section in this text. All known calibers are listed for each model. Caliber offerings varied often throughout the 28 year run of the Steyr-Mannlicher, stock designs evolved, and sights and magazine styles changed. The only truly rare caliber is the 6mm Rem., which was always special order. Next in North American rarity is the .25-06. Certain additional European calibers are rare in the USA because they were not imported due to lack of popularity - 5.6x57mm, 6.5x57mm, 6x62mm Freres, 6.5x65mm, and 9.3x62mm.

All four action lengths, SL, L, M, S, were offered in numerous deluxe variations with engraving and stock carving on special order blued metal and highly polished engraved actions. Stock carving is heavy and elegant. The "twisted appearance" of the hammer rifles barrels on all firearms of this group lends a unique and unmistakable look to these rifles.

A major irritant for hardcore Steyr-Mannlicher collectors is the continued misidentification of Luxus models by online sellers. First, a standard USA version Luxus has the word "Luxus" engraved on the left side of the receiver. A Luxus also has a steel box magazine instead of a rotary plastic one and a rotary shotgun style safety, although some apparently early Luxus models exist with the sliding side safety.

Pricing shows the result of continued cost increases at Steyr, which finally caused the end of the production run and redesign to the SBS-96 model to save costs, regain competition, and take advantage of improved safety features.

ZEPHYR 22 – .22 LR cal., single or double-set triggers, open sights, features full-length Mannlicher stock, checkered walnut stock with metallic cap or half stock and no checkering (Standard model), sling swivels, sights, trigger guard and forend cap are original Mannlicher Schoenauer parts. Mfg. 1953-late 1970, with total production of 3,913 rifles.

$2,600	$2,275	$1,950	$1,750	$1,400	$1,100	$900

ZEPHYR II – .17 HMR, .22 LR, or .22 WMR cal., 19.7 in. threaded or standard barrel w/o sights, 5 shot detachable mag., gold trigger, select oil-finished checkered European walnut half or full stock w/ Schnabel forearm, 5.8 lbs. Importation began 2018.

MSR $1,130	$950	$850	$700	$650	$550	$425	$350

Add $369 for full stock.

MODEL ML-79 – various U.S. and metric cals., European predecessor of the Luxus, factory literature shows both L and M actions with various calibers, detachable magazine, marked on the receiver as ML-79, set trigger, adj. sights, full or half-stock design of the Luxus, sliding side safety of standard Steyr-Mannlicher Sporter, marked on receiver as "ML-79". Mfg. 1977-1979, extremely rare in the USA.

Extreme rarity factor precludes accurate pricing on this model.

GRADING - PPGS™	100%	98%	95%	90%	80%	70%	60%	LAST MSR

PROFESSIONAL RIFLE – 6.5x55mm, .270 Win., 7x57mm, 7x64mm, .30-06, 7.5x55mm Swiss, 8x57mm, or 9.3x62mm cal., double set trigger, sights optional, brown (disc. 1970) or green (new 1970) synthetic half stock. Mfg. 1968-1993.

$1,000 $800 $700 $600 $550 $500 $400 *$995*

The 6.5x55mm cal. Professionals were totally unknown in the U.S.A. until a small lot was imported by GunSouth in the mid-1990s.

JAGDMATCH – .222 Rem., .243 Win., or .308 Win. cal., match rifle for European sports competition, 23.6 in. barrel, 5 shot rotary mag., single or double set trigger, laminated half stock only, special Steyr SSG match type receiver, 8 1/2 lbs. Disc.

$1,600 $1,200 $1,000 $800 $725 $625 $550 *$2,450*

MODEL S – 6.5x68mm, .257 Wby., .264 Win. Mag., 7mm Rem. Mag., .300 H&H, .300 Win. Mag., 8x68mm, .338 Win. Mag., 9.3x64mm, or .375 H&H cal., 25.6 in. barrel with half stock, 4 shot rotary mag., double set or single trigger, half stock, optional with reserve magazine in butt-stock, 8.4 lbs. Mfg. 1968-1996.

$1,600 $1,200 $1,000 $800 $725 $625 $550 *$2,745*

* ***Model S/T (Tropical Model)*** – 9.3x64mm, .375 H&H, .458 Win. Mag. cal., 25.6 in. barrel with half stock, 4 shot rotary mag., double set or single trigger, reserve magazine in buttstock, 9.02 lbs. Mfg. 1968-1996.

$1,750 $1,300 $1,000 $800 $700 $600 $550 *$2,850*

* ***Model S Luxus*** – same calibers as Model S, in-line, non-rotary, 3 shot steel mag.,single set trigger, open sights, stock design, magazine, and safety are different from other Steyr-Mannlichers, full or half stock with better checkering, rotary thumb safety, 8 lbs. Mfg. 1980-1996.

$1,950 $1,700 $1,500 $1,400 $1,200 $1,000 $800 *$3,250*

MANNLICHER CL LUXUS – .243 Win., .270 Win., .30-06, 6.5x55mm, 7x64R, 7mm-08 Rem., 7mm Rem. Mag. (new 2014), .308 Win., 9.3x62mm, .270 WSM, .300 WSM, 8x68mm, or .375 H&H cal., 23 1/2 or 25.6 in. barrel, open sights, Luxus wood stock, Picatinny rail. Importation disc. 2017.

$2,900 $2,575 $2,175 $1,800 $1,500 $1,275 $1,075 *$3,299*

MANNLICHER (STEYR) ULTRA LIGHT – .222 Rem., .223 Rem., .243 Win., .308 Win., or 7mm-08 Rem. cal., bolt has 4 locking lugs and a 70 degree bolt throw, 3-position roller tang safety, 19 in. fluted barrel, Weaver rail, 4 shot detachable mag., checkered European walnut stock with rosewood pistol grip and forend caps, approx. 6 lbs. Imported 2004-2013.

$2,400 $2,100 $1,825 $1,475 $1,200 $1,050 $925 *$2,799*

STEYR SCOUT SERIES (MANNLICHER) – .223 Rem. (new 2000), .243 Win., .308 Win., 7mm-08 Rem. (new 2000), or .376 Steyr (mfg. 1999-2000, reintroduced 2005-disc.) cal., designed by Jeff Cooper, 19 1/4 in. fluted barrel, features grey, black synthetic Zytel with wood panel inserts or camo (.308 Win. cal. only beginning 2005) stock, Picatinny optic rail, integral bipod, Package includes Steyr or Leupold (disc. 2005) M8 2.5x28 IER scope with factory Steyr mounts, and luggage case. Mfg. 1998-2017.

$1,850 $1,575 $1,375 $1,125 $900 $750 $650 *$2,099*

Add $100 for camo (disc. 2013).

Add $600 for Steyr Scout Package with Steyr or Leupold (disc. 2004) scope, mounts and luggage case (disc. 2013).

* ***Steyr Scout (Older Mfg.)*** – .243 Win. cal., similar to Jeff Cooper Package, except does not include scope, mounts, or case. Mfg. 1998-2014.

$1,450 $1,275 $1,100 $975 $800 $650 $550 *$1,969*

Add $100 for .376 Steyr cal. (black stock only, disc. 2000).

Add $100 for Jeff Cooper grey stock.

* ***Steyr Scout (New Mfg.)*** – .223 Rem., .243 Win., .308 Win., 6.5 Creedmoor (new 2019), or 7mm-08 Rem. cal., 19 or 22 (new 2017) in. fluted or unfluted threaded barrel, 4 grooves, detachable double stack 5 or 10 shot mag., single stage adj. trigger, flip-up iron sights and integral top rail, choice of black, grey (disc. 2016), mud, or green finish stock with Elastomer buttpad with spacers, 3-position safety, five removable push-and-turn-style sling swivel positions, three sling swivels included, integrated bipod, extra mag. storage compartment in the stock., stainless or Mannox finish, includes extra mag., owner's manual, 39.4 in. OAL, 6.6 lbs. New 2015.

MSR $1,749 $1,500 $1,300 $1,100 $1,000 $800 $650 $550

* ***Steyr Scout Tactical*** – .223 Rem. (new 2000) or .308 Win. cal., similar to Steyr Scout, emergency ghost ring sights, except has black synthetic stock with removable spacers, oversized bolt handle. Mfg. 1999-2002.

$1,600 $1,400 $1,250 $1,050 $900 $750 $625 *$2,069*

GRADING - PPGS™	100%	98%	95%	90%	80%	70%	60%	LAST MSR

» **Steyr Scout Tactical Stainless** – .223 Rem. or .308 Win. cal., similar to Steyr Scout Tactical, except has stainless steel barrel. Mfg. 2000-2002.

	$1,650	$1,425	$1,150	$1,025	$830	$710	$590	*$2,159*

* ***Steyr Scout Jeff Cooper*** – .223 Rem., .308 Win. or .376 Steyr (disc. 2000, reintroduced 2005) cal., grey synthetic Zytel stock with Jeff Cooper logo and integral bipod, certificate of authenticity with test target, Package (disc. 2004) included Leupold M8 2.5x28 IER scope with factory Steyr mounts, and luggage case. Mfg. 1999-2009.

	$2,375	$2,050	$1,750	$1,425	$1,175	$1,050	$900	*$2,699*

Add approx. 15% for Steyr Scout Package with Leupold scope, mounts and luggage case (disc. 2004).

» **Steyr Scout Jeff Cooper Limited Edition** – .308 Win. cal., 20 in. fluted barrel, 10 shot polymer double stack detachable box mag., single stage trigger, flip-up iron sights, Scout stock with integrated bipod and UIT rail, 3-position safety, integral top rail, "JC" crest of arms, special ser. no., two removable sling swivels, includes Leupold 2.5X28mm Scout Scope, Galco Ching Sling, Boyt hard and soft case, Steyr scope mounts, extra magazine, and copy of Cooper's book *Art of the Rifle*, gray Mannox finish, approx. 8 lbs., limited mfg. of 300. Mfg. 2010-2017.

	$2,625	$2,250	$1,875	$1,550	$1,275	$1,050	$925	*$2,995*

STEYR SCOUT RFR – .17 HMR, .22 LR, or .22 WMR cal., 20 in. threaded barrel, 10 shot detachable mag., black polymer stock, Picatinny rail, 7.3 lbs. Mfg. 2017-2018.

	$525	$450	$415	$375	$335	$300	$275	*$600*

MODEL SM 12 – various cals., available in various stock configurations, 20, 23.6, or 25 in. stainless steel barrel w/o sights, including Mannlicher or checkered European walnut stock with Bavarian cheekpiece and forend, hand cocking system, sling swivels, Mannox or stainless steel finish, approx. 7 1/2 lbs. New 2016.

* ***Model SM 12 Full Stock*** – .243 Win., .308 Win., 7mm-08 Rem., 7x64R, .270 Win., 6.5x55SE, .30-06 Spr., 8x57JS, or 9.3x62 cal., 23.6 in. barrel stainless steel barrel w/o sights, checkered European walnut stock with Bavarian cheekpiece and forend, hand cocking system, sling swivels, Mannox or stainless steel finish, approx. 7 1/2 lbs. New 2016.

MSR $2,999	$2,550	$2,250	$1,900	$1,750	$1,400	$1,150	$900

* ***Model SM 12 Half Stock*** – .243 Win., .300 Win. Mag., .300 Wby., .308 Win. Mag., .7mm-08 Rem., 7x64R, .270 Win., .270 WSM, .300 WSM, 6.5x55SE, .30-06 Spr., 8x57JS, 9.3x62, 7mm Rem. Mag., or 8x68S cal., 23.6 in. barrel stainless steel barrel w/o sights, Combi Trigger, checkered European walnut stock with Bavarian cheekpiece and forend, optional aluminum bedding inside synthetic stock (SM 12 SX Model), hand cocking system, sling swivels, Mannox or stainless steel finish, approx. 7 1/2 lbs. New 2016.

MSR $2,799	$2,400	$2,100	$1,800	$1,600	$1,300	$1,050	$850

Add $200 for .300 Win. Mag., .300 Wby., 7x64R, .270 WSM, .300 WSM, 8x68S, 7mm Rem. Mag., or 8x68S cal.

* ***Model SM 12 Light*** – .243 Win., .308 Win. Mag., ,270 Win., .7mm-08 Rem. (disc. 2020), 7x64R, 6.5x55SE (disc. 2020), .30-06, 8x57JS (disc. 2020), or 9.3x62 (disc. 2020) cal., 20 in. stainless steel barrel w/o sights, Mannlicher or checkered European walnut stock with Bavarian cheekpiece and forend, hand cocking system, sling swivels, Mannox or stainless steel finish, approx. 7 1/2 lbs. New 2016.

MSR $2,999	$2,550	$2,250	$1,900	$1,750	$1,400	$1,150	$900

* ***Model SM 12 Mountain*** – .243 Win., .308 Win. Mag., .270 Win., .7mm-08 Rem., 7x64R, 6.5x55SE, .30-06 Spr., 8x57JS, or 9.3x62, cal., 20 in. stainless steel barrel w/o sights, Mannlicher or checkered European walnut stock with Bavarian cheekpiece and forend, hand cocking system, sling swivels, Mannox or stainless steel finish, approx. 7 1/2 lbs. New 2016.

MSR $2,799	$2,400	$2,100	$1,800	$1,600	$1,300	$1,050	$850

MODEL SM 12 SX HALF STOCK – .243 Win., .300 Win. Mag., .300 Wby., .308 Win. Mag., .7mm-08 Rem., 7x64R, .270 Win., .270 WSM, .300 WSM, 6.5x55SE, .30-06 Spr., 8x57JS, 9.3x62, 7mm Rem. Mag., or 8x68S cal., 23.6 in. barrel stainless steel barrel w/o sights, fine tuned trigger w/forward set trigger, synthetic stock w/polymer inlays and aluminum bedding block, hand cocking system, sling swivels, Mannox or stainless steel finish, 7.5 lbs. New 2016.

MSR $2,299	$1,950	$1,700	$1,450	$1,350	$1,100	$900	$700

Add $200 for 7mm Rem. Mag. , 8x68S, .300 Win. Mag., .300 WBY, .270 WSM, or .300 WSM cal.

GRADING - PPGS™	100%	98%	95%	90%	80%	70%	60%	LAST MSR

MANNLICHER/SBS PROHUNTER MODEL – .222 Rem. (new 2004), .223 Rem. (new 2004), .243 Win., .25-06 Rem., .260 Rem. (mfg. 2000-2004), .270 Win., .280 Rem. (mfg. 2000-2013), .30-06, .308 Win., 7mm-08 Rem., 7mm Rem. Mag. (new 2014), 6.5x55mm, 6.5x57mm (disc. 1999), 7x64mm (disc. 1999, reintroduced 2014), 9.3x62mm (disc. 1999), or .338 Federal (new 2014) cal., features safe bolt system (SBS), detachable mag., black synthetic or camo (mfg. 2000-2013) adjustable with included spacers (new 2014) stock, matte blue finish, 24 or 26 in. hammer forged barrel without sights, drilled and tapped, 7 lbs. 7 oz. Mfg. 1996-2017.

$1,000 $895 $775 $650 $525 $465 $400 ***$1,150***

Add $75 for camo stock (mfg. 2000-2013).
Add $152 for heavy barrel (.308 Win. cal. only, disc. 2005).

SBS stands for Safe Bolt System, which indicates the use of a relatively complicated bolt action designed with hunter safety in mind.

* ***SBS Pro Hunter*** – .270 Win., .30-06, .308 Win., .300 Win. Mag., or 7mm-08 Rem. cal., 20, 23.6, or 25.6 in. steel or stainless steel barrel w/o sights, two-stage mag., black synthetic stock with adj. buttpad, Safe Bolt System (SBS). Mfg. 2016-2017.

$725 $635 $550 $500 $400 $350 $325 ***$850***

Add $100 for stainless steel barrel.

* ***SBS ProHunter Model Magnum*** – .270 WSM (new 2004), .300 WSM (new 2004), .300 Win. Mag., 7mm WSM (new 2004), 7mm Rem. Mag., 6.5x68mm (disc. 1999), or 8x68S (disc. 1999) cal., similar to SBS ProHunter Model, except has 23.6 in. or 25.6 (disc.) in. barrel. Imported 1997-2013.

$1,000 $895 $775 $650 $525 $465 $400 ***$1,150***

Add $75 for camo stock (new 2000).
Add $152 for heavy barrel (.300 Win. Mag. only, disc.).
Add $150 for metric cals (disc.).

* ***SBS ProHunter Model SS*** – similar to SBS ProHunter, except has stainless steel barrel with matte finish. Mfg. 2000-2017.

$1,100 $975 $850 $725 $625 $525 $425 ***$1,250***

Add $129 for camo stock (.270 Win. or .30-06 cal.).

» ***SBS ProHunter Model SS Magnum*** – similar to SBS ProHunter Magnum, except has stainless steel barrel with matte finish. Mfg. 2000-2017.

$1,100 $975 $850 $725 $625 $525 $425 ***$1,250***

Add $75 for camo stock (.300 Win. Mag. or 7mm Rem. Mag. cal. only).
Add $165 for black finish (7mm Rem. Mag. cal. only, mfg. 2005).

* ***SBS ProHunter Model .376 Steyr*** – .376 Steyr cal. only, 20 in. barrel with iron sights, black synthetic or camo (new 2000) stock, matte blue finish. Mfg. 1999-2004.

$695 $600 $500 $450 $395 $350 $300 ***$799***

Add $60 for camo.

* ***SBS ProHunter Model Compact (Youth/Ladies) Rifle*** – .243 Win., .260 Rem. (new 2000) 7mm-08 Rem., or .308 Win. cal., shortened stock with 2 butt spacers for adj. length, 20 in. barrel with iron sights, matte blue finish. Mfg. 1999-2002.

$710 $640 $570 $500 $450 $395 $350 ***$819***

* ***SBS ProHunter Model Compact (Youth/Ladies) SS*** – similar to ProHunter Compact, except has stainless steel barrel with matte finish. Mfg. 2000-2002.

$780 $675 $600 $495 $430 $365 $315 ***$909***

* ***SBS ProHunter Model Mountain Rifle*** – .243 Win., .25-06 Rem., .260 Rem. (new 2000), .270 Win., .270 WSM (mfg. 2004), .30-06, .300 WSM (mfg. 2004), .308 Win., .376 Steyr (new 2005), 7mm-08 Rem., 7mm WSM (mfg. 2004), or 6.5x55mm (new 2000) cal., 20 in. barrel, no sights, matte blue finish, black or camo (mfg. 2000-2002) synthetic stock, detachable mag. Mfg. 1999-2008.

$895 $775 $650 $525 $465 $400 $350 ***$991***

* ***SBS ProHunter Model Mountain Rifle SS*** – similar to ProHunter Mountain Rifle, except has stainless steel barrel with matte finish. Mfg. 2000-2008.

$1,050 $850 $700 $600 $495 $430 $375 ***$1,195***

Add $129 for camo stock (.243 Win., .270 Win. or .30-06 cal. only).

* ***SBS ProHunter Model Tactical*** – .308 Win. cal., features 20 in. barrel and 10 shot mag. Limited mfg. 2005.

$850 $700 $575 $500 $450 $400 $350 ***$983***

GRADING - PPGS™	100%	98%	95%	90%	80%	70%	60%	LAST MSR

PRO HUNTER II – .223 Rem., .243 Rem., .308 Win., or 7mm-08 Rem. cal., SBS action, 20 in. cold hammer forged and threaded standard or stainless steel (7mm-08 Rem. cal. only), 4 shot two-stage detachable mag., Boyds Prairie Hunter laminated wood stock with choice of Mossy Oak Elements Terra Gila pattern or Pepper wood grain, 3-pos. safety, MANNOX finish, 7.7 lbs. New 2020.

MSR $1,199	$1,025	$900	$775	$700	$575	$475	$375	

MANNLICHER PRO VARMINT – .223 Rem. cal., 23.6 in. heavy fluted barrel, black synthetic or camo vented stock, includes tactical rail. Imported 2009-2013.

	$1,600	$1,450	$1,275	$1,075	$900	$775	$650	$1,799

Add $200 for camo.

PRO ALASKAN – .30-06, .338 RCM, or .375 Ruger cal., 23.6 in. barrel, stainless steel action, set trigger, 4 shot detachable mag., open sights, soft touch camo stock. Mfg. 2009-2017.

	$1,625	$1,425	$1,225	$1,100	$895	$725	$575	$1,899

PRO AFRICAN – .30-06 (disc. 2013), 9.3x62mm (disc. 2013), .338 RCM, or .375 Ruger cal., black soft touch synthetic stock, 4 shot detachable box mag., two-piece Weaver style scope bases, tactical bolt, black finish. Mfg. 2009-2017.

	$1,625	$1,425	$1,225	$1,100	$895	$725	$575	$1,899

PRO THB – .308 Win. or 6.5 Creedmoor (new 2018) cal., SBS action, 16, 20, 24 1/2 (6.5 Creedmoor only, new 2018) or 26 (.308 Win. only) in. threaded cold hammer forged barrel, 4 shot mag., two-stage mag., black, green, or Boyd Multicam ventilated stock, optional Manners (6.5 Creedmoor only) or McMillan stock (new 2019), 3-position safety, 20 in. MOA Picatinny rail, tactical bolt, adj. LOP, black Mannox finish, 36.7-45.2 in. OAL, 8.2-9.3 lbs. Importation began late 2016.

MSR $1,399	$1,200	$1,050	$900	$800	$650	$550	$425	

Add $580 for McMillan stock.
Add $600 for Manners stock.
Add $100 for Boyd Multicam stock.

* ***PRO Long Pic Rail*** – .308 Win. cal., SBS action, 16, 20, or 26 in. threaded cold hammer forged barrel, 4 shot mag., two-stage mag., 3-position safety, full-length rail, tactical bolt, adj. LOP, black Mannox finish, 36.7-45.2 in. OAL, 8.2-9.3 lbs. Imported 2017-2019.

	$1,900	$1,650	$1,400	$1,300	$1,050	$850	$650	$2,115

SBS FORESTER MODEL – similar to SBS Pro Hunter Model, except has wood stock and standard blue finish. Mfg. 1997-2002, reintroduced 2005.

	$925	$800	$700	$600	$525	$425	$350	$1,051

* ***SBS Forester Model Mountain Rifle*** – .243 Win. (disc. 2002), .25-06 Rem., .260 Rem. (new 2000), .270 Win. (disc. 2002, reintroduced 2005), .30-06 (disc. 2002), .308 Win. (disc. 2002), 7mm-08 Rem., 6.5x55mm (mfg. 2000-2002) cal., 20 in. barrel, no sights, matte blue finish, checkered walnut stock, detachable mag. Mfg. 1999-2002, reimported 2004-2005.

	$925	$800	$700	$600	$525	$425	$350	$1,051

* ***SBS Forester Model Magnum*** – .300 Win. Mag., 7mm Rem. Mag., 6.5x68mm (disc. 1999), or 8x68S (disc. 1999) cal., similar to SBS Forester Model, except has 25.6 in. barrel. Mfg. 1997-2002.

	$720	$635	$565	$510	$450	$395	$350	$829

CLASSIC MANNLICHER (SBS) HALF STOCK (AMERICAN) – .222 Rem., .223 Rem., .243 Win., .25-06 Rem. (disc. 2013), .260 Rem. (disc. 2002), .270 Win., .280 Rem. (disc. 2002), .30-06, .308 Win., 7mm-08 Rem., 6.5x55mm, 6.5x57mm (disc. 2013), 6.5x58mm (disc. 2013), 7x64mm, 8x57JRS (disc. 2013), or 8x68mm (new 2014) cal., features deluxe checkered walnut stock with full pistol grip and forend cap, deep blue finish, 23.6 in. barrel with exterior hammer forged swirls, with or w/o sights. Mfg. 2000-2017.

	$2,175	$1,900	$1,500	$1,200	$1,050	$925	$825	$2,495

Add $1,000 for case colors (disc 2013).

* ***SBS Classic Mannlicher Half Stock Magnum*** – .270 WSM (new 2004), .300 WSM (new 2004), .300 Win. Mag., 7mm WSM (mfg. 2004-2013) or 7mm Rem. Mag. cal., 25.6 in. barrel. Mfg. 2000-2017.

	$2,400	$2,100	$1,825	$1,475	$1,200	$1,050	$925	$2,799

Add $1,000 for case colors (disc. 2013).

* ***SBS Classic Mannlicher Half Stock Mountain*** – similar cals. as SBS Classic Mannlicher Full Stock, features 20 in. barrel with open sights. Mfg. 2006-2008.

	$2,050	$1,625	$1,250	$1,025	$875	$750	$650	$2,269

GRADING - PPGS™	100%	98%	95%	90%	80%	70%	60%	LAST MSR

SBS CLASSIC MANNLICHER FULL STOCK – various cals., similar to SBS Classic Mannlicher Half Stock, except has deluxe full-length stock and 20 in. barrel with sights. Mfg. 2000-2017.

	$2,325	$1,975	$1,550	$1,250	$1,075	$950	$850	*$2,695*

Add $1,200 for case colors (disc. 2013).

* ***SBS Classic Mannlicher Goiserer*** – .270 Win., .30-06, or .308 Win. cal., similar to Classic Mannlicher Half Stock, except has iron sights and 20 in. barrel, 4 shot mag. Mfg. 2003-2005.

	$1,725	$1,325	$1,100	$950	$775	$675	$575	*$2,014*

CLASSIC MANNLICHER ANTIQUE – various cals., 20 or 23 in. barrel with open sights, choice of half-stock or Mannlicher full stock, case colored receiver, barrel, and bolt. Imported 2006-2013.

	$4,400	$3,850	$3,400	$2,900	$2,450	$2,000	$1,650	*$4,899*

Add $300 for Mannlicher full stock.

MANNLICHER CLASSIC LIGHT – .270 Win., .30-06, or 7x64R cal., half-stock, 20 in. fluted barrel, set trigger, open sights. Disc. 2017.

	$2,400	$2,100	$1,825	$1,475	$1,200	$1,050	$925	*$2,799*

SBS TACTICAL – .308 Win. cal. only, 20 in. barrel w/o sights, features oversized bolt handle and high capacity 10 shot mag. with adapter, matte blue finish. Mfg. 1999-2002.

	$840	$735	$625	$550	$500	$450	$395	*$969*

* ***SBS Tactical Heavy Barrel*** – .300 Win. Mag. (new 2000) or .308 Win. cal., features 20 (carbine, new 2000, .308 Win. only) or 26 in. heavy barrel w/o sights and oversized bolt handle, matte blue finish or stainless steel (carbine only, new 2000). Mfg. 1999-2002.

	$865	$745	$635	$550	$500	$450	$395	*$1,019*

Add $30 for .300 Win. Mag. cal.
Add $40 for stainless steel.

* ***SBS Tactical McMillan*** – similar to SBS Tactical Heavy Barrel, except has custom McMillan A-3 stock with adj. cheekpiece and oversized bolt handle, matte blue finish. Mfg. 1999-2002.

	$1,465	$1,245	$1,035	$850	$725	$600	$550	*$1,699*

Add $30 for .300 Win. Mag. cal.

* ***SBS Tactical CISM*** – .308 Win. cal., 20 in. heavy barrel w/o sights, laminated wood stock with black lacquer finish, adj. cheekpiece and buttplate, 10 shot detachable mag., vent. forend. Mfg. 2000-2002.

	$3,050	$2,650	$2,300	$1,950	$1,600	$1,300	$1,150	*$3,499*

Subtract approx. 35% for Swiss contract CISM Match in 7.5x55mm cal. with match diopter sights and 23 1/2 in. barrel. (Only 100 were imported.)

MANNLICHER BIG BORE – .450 Marlin cal., 22 in. barrel, open sights, black synthetic stock, 3 shot mag. Disc. 2017.

	$1,600	$1,450	$1,275	$1,075	$900	$775	$650	*$1,799*

MODEL CL II – various cals., SBS action, available in Half Stock, Full Stock, Light, Mountain, Semi Weight, or Stainless variations, 20 (Light or Mountain Model) or 23.6 (Half Stock, Full Stock, or Stainless), 3 or 4 shot detachable synthetic mag., two-stage, forward-set, or double-set trigger, European walnut, Bavarian cheekpiece w/double flame and fish scale pattern, trigger safety, includes soft-side carry case, branded hat, and range notebook, 7.4-8.3 lbs. Importation began 2016.

* ***CL II Carbon*** – .308 Win., 6.5 Creedmoor, or .338 Lapua Mag. cal., 22, 25, 25.6 (new 2021), or 26 (disc.) in. heavy threaded barrel, detachable double column box mag., Combi trigger, FlexSight, FBT carbon fiber stock, 3-pos. safety wheel, includes soft-side carry case, branded hat, and range notebook, 6.7-7.7 lbs. New late 2018.

MSR $4,299	$3,850	$3,400	$3,000	$2,600	$2,200	$1,800	$1,400	

Add $300 for 6.5 Creedmoor.
Add $400 for .338 Lapua Mag.

* ***CL II Full Stock*** – .222 Rem., .223 Rem., .243 Win., .308 Win., 7mm-08 Rem., 7x64, .270 Win., .30-06 Spr., .25-06 Rem., 6.5x55SE, 8x57JS, or 9.3x62 cal., SBS action, 23.6 in. barrel, 4 shot detachable synthetic mag., two-stage, forward-set, or double-set trigger, full European walnut stock, Bavarian cheekpiece w/double flame and fish scale pattern, 3-position or trigger safety, 7.7 lbs. Importation began 2016.

MSR $2,799	$2,400	$2,100	$1,800	$1,600	$1,300	$1,050	$850	

GRADING - PPGS™	100%	98%	95%	90%	80%	70%	60%	LAST MSR

* ***CL II Half Stock*** – .243 Win., .223 Rem., .300 Win. Mag., .308 Win., 7mm-08 Rem., 7x64, .270 Win., .270 WSM, .300 WSM, .300 WBY, .375 H&H Mag., .458 Win. Mag., .30-06 Spr., .25-06 Rem., 6.5x55SE, 7mm Rem. Mag., 8x68 S,8x57JS, or 9.3x62 cal., SBS action, 23.6 in. barrel, 3 or 4 shot detachable synthetic mag., two-stage, forward-set, or double-set trigger, European walnut half stock, Bavarian cheekpiece w/double flame and fish scale pattern, 3-position or trigger safety, 7.3-7.9 lbs. Importation began 2016.

MSR $2,549	$2,150	$1,900	$1,600	$1,500	$1,200	$1,000	$750	

Add $200 for .300 Win. Mag., 7mm Rem. Mag., 8x68S, .270 WSM, .300 WSM, or .300 WBY cal.
Add $450 for .375 H&H or .458 Win. Mag.

* ***CL II Light*** – .243 Win., .308 Win., 7x64, .270 Win., or .30-06 Spr. cal., SBS action, 20 in. barrel, 4 shot detachable synthetic mag., two-stage, forward-set, or double-set trigger, European walnut, Bavarian cheekpiece w/double flame and fish scale pattern, trigger safety, 7.45 lbs. Importation began 2016.

MSR $2,599	$2,200	$1,950	$1,650	$1,500	$1,200	$1,000	$800	

* ***CL II Mountain*** – .223 Rem., .223 Rem., .243 Win., .308 Win., 7mm-08 Rem., 7x64, .270 Win., .30-06 Spr., .25-06 Rem., 6.5x55SE, 8x57JS, or 9.3x62 cal., SBS action, 20 in. barrel, 4 shot detachable synthetic mag., two-stage, forward-set, or double-set trigger, European walnut, Bavarian cheekpiece w/double flame and fish scale pattern, trigger safety, 7.45 lbs. Importation began 2016.

MSR $2,549	$2,150	$1,900	$1,600	$1,500	$1,200	$1,000	$750	

MODEL CL II SX HALF STOCK – .243 Win., .300 Win. Mag., .308 Win., 7mm-08 Rem., 7x64, .270 Win., .270 WSM, .300 WSM, .300 WBY, .375 H&H Mag., .458 Win. Mag., .30-06 Spr., .25-06 Rem., 6.5x55SE, 7mm Rem. Mag., 8x57JS, or 9.3x62 cal., SBS action, 23.6 in. barrel, 4 shot detachable synthetic mag., two-stage, forward-set, or double-set trigger, synthetic stock w/polymer inlays and aluminum bedding, 3-position or trigger safety, 7.3-7.9 lbs. Importation began 2016.

MSR $1,782	$1,575	$1,350	$1,175	$1,025	$900	$750	$625	

Add $277 for .300 Win. Mag., 7mm Rem. Mag., 8x68S, .270 WSM, .300 WSM, or .300 WBY cal.
Add $1,050 for .375 H&H or .458 Win. Mag.

STEYR ELITE (SBS TACTICAL) – .223 Rem. (disc. 2008) or .308 Win. cal., 20 (carbine, disc.), 22.4 (new 2006) or 26 (disc. 2005) in. barrel, two 5 shot detachable mags. (with spare buttstock storage), adj. black synthetic stock, full-length Picatinny spec. mounting rail, oversize bolt handle, oversize bolt handle, matte blue finish or stainless steel. Imported 2000-2017.

	$1,950	$1,725	$1,500	$1,275	$1,050	$875	$775	*$2,299*

* ***Steyr Elite 08*** – .308 Win. cal., 23.6 in. blue or stainless steel barrel, 10 shot high capacity box mag., Dural aluminum folding stock, extra long Picatinny rail. Imported 2009-2013.

	$5,325	$4,650	$4,325	$3,750	$3,250	$2,600	$1,995	*$5,999*

150TH YEAR FERDINAND RITTER VON MANNLICHER COMMEMORATIVE – 6.5x54mm Mannlicher Schoenauer cal. only, euro-style trigger guard, SST, open sights, checkered high grade full stock carbine or half stock rifle, polished blue metal, gold filled engraving, originally specified production was announced to be six units, then 150 units, and finally 250 units. Mfg. 1999 only.

	$3,500	$3,150	$2,700	$2,250	$1,850	$1,500	$1,250	*$3,500*

MANNLICHER SBS EUROPEAN MODEL – .243 Win., .25-06 Rem., .270 Win., .30-06 (disc. 1998), .308 Win., 7mm-08 Rem., 6.5x55mm, 6.5x57mm, 7x64mm, 7.5x55mm, or 9.3x62mm cal., features safe bolt system (SBS), 23.6 in. barrel with sights, checkered walnut stock and forearm. Mfg. 1997-99.

	$2,300	$1,850	$1,600	$1,325	$1,100	$925	$850	*$2,795*

* ***Mannlicher SBS European Model Magnum*** – .300 Win. Mag., 7mm Rem. Mag., 6.5x68mm, or 8x68S cal., 25.6 in. barrel with sights, checkered walnut stock and forearm. Mfg. 1997-99.

	$2,375	$1,900	$1,625	$1,350	$1,100	$925	$850	*$2,895*

* ***Mannlicher SBS European Model "Goiserer"*** – similar to Mannlicher SBS European Model, except has 20 in. barrel. Mfg. 1997-99.

	$2,500	$2,000	$1,650	$1,350	$1,100	$925	$850	*$2,995*

* ***Mannlicher SBS European Model Full Stock*** – similar to Mannlicher SBS European Model, except has full-length Mannlicher stock. Mfg. 1997-99.

	$2,500	$2,000	$1,650	$1,350	$1,100	$925	$850	*$2,995*

MODEL SSG – .243 Win. (disc., PII Sniper only) or .308 Win cal., for competition or law-enforcement use. Marksman has regular sights, detachable rotary mag., Teflon coated bolt with heavy duty locking lugs, synthetic stock has removable spacers, parkerized finish. Match version has heavier target barrel and "match" bolt carrier, can be used as single shot. Extremely accurate.

GRADING - PPGS™	100%	98%	95%	90%	80%	70%	60%	LAST MSR

* ***Model SSG Carbon*** – .243 Win., .308 Win., .300 Win. Mag., or .338 Lapua Mag. cal., 20 or 22 1/4 in. cold hammer forged heavy barrel, polymer double-stack 6, 8, or 10 shot mag., top Picatinny rail, adj. carbon fiber thumbhole stock with grooved pistol grip and Elastomer recoil pad, includes bipod, Mannox finish, 11 lbs. 2 oz. Mfg. 2016-2017.

$3,300 $2,975 $2,625 $2,300 $2,000 $1,700 $1,375 ***$3,695***

* ***Model SSG 69 Sport (PI Rifle)*** – .243 Win. or .308 Win. cal., 26 in. barrel with iron sights, 3 shot mag., black or green ABS Cycolac synthetic stock. Disc.

$1,775 $1,500 $1,225 $1,000 $850 $725 $650 ***$1,989***

Add 15% for walnut stock (disc. 1992, retail was $448).

* ***Model SSG PII/PIIK Sniper Rifle*** – .22-250 Rem. (new 2004), .243 Win. (disc.) or .308 Win. cal., 20 (Model PIIK) or 26 in. heavy barrel, no sights, green or black synthetic Cycolac or McMillan black fiberglass stock, modified bolt handle, choice of single or set triggers. Disc. 2017.

$1,695 $1,500 $1,300 $1,050 $875 $750 $625 ***$1,899***

Add 15% for walnut stock (disc. 1992, retail was $448).

* ***Model SSG PIII Rifle*** – .308 Win. cal., 26 in. heavy barrel with diopter match sight bases, H-S Precision Pro-Series stock in black only. Importation 1991-93.

$2,300 $1,875 $1,425 $1,050 $825 $700 $600 ***$3,162***

* ***Model SSG PIV (Urban Rifle)*** – .308 Win. cal., carbine variation with 16 1/2 in. heavy barrel and flash hider (disc.), ABS Cycolac synthetic stock in green or black. Imported 1991-2002, 2004-2017.

$1,695 $1,500 $1,300 $1,050 $875 $750 $625 ***$1,899***

* ***Model SSG Jagd Match*** – .222 Rem., .243 Win., or .308 Win. cal., checkered wood laminate stock, 23.6 in. barrel, Mannlicher sights, DT, supplied with test target. Mfg. 1991-1992.

$1,550 $1,050 $950 $800 $675 $600 $540 ***$1,550***

* ***Model SSG Match Rifle*** – .308 Win. only, 26 in. heavy barrel, brown ABS Cycolac stock, Walther Diopter sights, 8.6 lbs. Mfg. disc. 1992.

$2,000 $1,500 $1,225 $925 $800 $700 $600 ***$2,306***

Add $437 for walnut stock.

* ***Model SPG-T*** – .308 Win. cal., Target model. Mfg. 1993-98.

$3,225 $2,850 $2,550 $2,200 $1,850 $1,500 $1,200 ***$3,695***

* ***Model SPG-CISM*** – .308 Win. cal., 20 in. heavy barrel, laminated wood stock with adj. cheekpiece and black lacquer finish. Mfg. 1993-99.

$2,995 $2,600 $2,300 $1,950 $1,700 $1,450 $1,200 ***$3,295***

* ***Model SSG Match UIT*** – .308 Win. cal. only, 10 shot steel mag., special single set trigger, free floating barrel, Diopter sights, raked bolt handle, 10.8 lbs. Disc. 1998.

$3,000 $2,500 $2,000 $1,800 $1,500 $1,200 $1,000 ***$3,995***

UIT stands for Union Internationale de Tir.

* ***Model SSG M1 (Performance Edition)*** – .308 Win. Mag. or .338 Lapua Mag. cal., interchangeable barrel, 10 shot mag., adj. two-stage trigger, folding aluminum stock, adj. buttstock, KeyMod or M-LOK forend, exchangeable grip straps, ambi thumb safety, trigger, bold handleand firing pin lock, 30 MOA top Picatinny rail, tan finish, optional drag bag, side loading option, 13.93 - 15.03 oz. Importation began 2019.

MSR $9,999 $8,500 $7,450 $6,400 $5,800 $4,700 $3,800 $3,000

Add $501 for .338 Lapua Mag. cal.

MODEL SSG 04/MODEL SSG 04-A1 – .308 Win. or .300 Win. Mag. cal., 20 (disc. 2005, reintroduced 2017) or 23.6 in. heavy hammer forged barrel with muzzle brake, 8 or 10 shot mag., two-stage trigger, black synthetic stock, 20 MOA Picatinny rail, matte metal finish, optional full-length rail (A1 Model, new 2009), 10.1 lbs. Imported 2004-2020.

$2,050 $1,800 $1,540 $1,395 $1,130 $925 $775 ***$2,415***

Add $284 for .300 Win. Mag. cal.

Add $514 for A1 Model (new 2009) or $784 for A1 Model with .300 Win. Mag. cal.

MODEL SSG 08 – .243 Win., .308 Win., .300 Win. Mag. (new 2014), or .338 Lapua Mag. (new 2014) cal., 20, 23.6, or 25.6 in. barrel, 6, 8, or 10 shot detachable mag., two-stage trigger, aluminum folding stock w/ adj. cheekpiece, buttplate, and telescopic butt spike, trigger safety, various adj. Picatinny rails, trail spade, black, Bush Camo (disc. 2019), Camo (standard, disc. 2019), or stainless (disc. 2019) finish, 12-13 1/2 lbs.

MSR $4,999 $4,250 $3,700 $3,200 $2,900 $2,350 $1,900 $1,500

Add $500 for .338 Lapua Mag. cal.

Add $525 for .308 Win. w/camo finish cal. (disc. 2019).

Add $510 for camo finish or stainless steel action/barrel (disc. 2019).

GRADING - PPGS™	100%	98%	95%	90%	80%	70%	60%	LAST MSR

* ***Model SSG-08 A1*** – .308 Win. cal. or .338 Lapua Mag. cal., SBS action, 20, 23.6, or 25.6 in. match grade barrel w/Mannox finish and muzzle brake, aluminum folding stock, adj. cheekpiece and recoil pad, monopod, pistol grip w/interchangeable backstraps, heavy duty fluted bolt, full-length modular Picatinny rail, heavy duty bipod, dust cover, 15.2-16.3 lbs.

MSR $6,999	$5,950	$5,200	$4,450	$4,050	$3,300	$2,700	$2,100	

Add $800 for .338 Lapua Mag. cal.

HS .50 – .460 Steyr (disc. 2013) or .50 BMG cal., single shot, 33 in. barrel with muzzle brake, includes Picatinny rail and bipod, approx. 28 lbs. Importation began 2004.

MSR $5,999	$5,100	$4,475	$3,825	$3,475	$2,800	$2,300	$1,775	

* ***HS .50 M1/HS .50 M1 Mountain*** – .50 BMG cal., repeater action, takedown design, 24 (HS-M1 Mountain) or 33 in. barrel with muzzle brake, 5 shot mag., two-stage trigger, pistol grip, Picatinny rail and bipod, black or Bush Camo finish, 30.4 lbs.

MSR $8,099	$6,900	$6,000	$5,150	$4,700	$3,800	$3,100	$2,400	

MONOBLOC – .308 Win. or .30-06 cal., short action, hand cocking system, 22 in. cold-hammer forged steel threaded barrel, 4 shot, SST, synthetic stock w/aluminum bedding, available in many colors, pistol grip, leather inlays, 8.2 lbs. Importation began 2020.

MSR $5,250	$4,450	$3,900	$3,350	$3,050	$2,450	$2,000	$1,550	

Rifles: Bolt Action, Model 72 Series (Mannlicher Schonauer M 72)

There is no model designation on the Model 72 Series. Only the caliber is stamped on the left-hand side of the barrel in front of the rear sight. There are two different action lengths - L/M (light and middle) and S/T (heavy and tropics). Production started on May 4, 1972 with ser. no. 1500 in .30-06 cal., and was exported to America, the last rifle in the series was ser. no. 10026, and was in .243 Win. cal. Total production was 8,526.

MODEL M72 (MODEL M) – 5.6x57mm, .243 Win., .270 Win., 7x57mm, 7x64mm, .30-06, or .308 Win. cal., available in rifle and full stock carbine versions, single and double set triggers, 5 shot rotary mag., this is a hybrid design resembling the original Mannlicher-Schoenauer with features from the new (1968) Steyr-Mannlicher Sporter to reduce costs. Mfg. 1973-circa 1980.

	$875	$795	$725	$650	$575	$500	$460	*$525*

* ***Model 72 (Model S & S/T Mag.)*** – 6.5x68mm, 8x68mm, 9.3x64mm, 7mm Rem. Mag., .300 Win. Mag., .375 H&H, or .458 Win. Mag. cal., 4 shot rotary mag., half stock, 25.6 in. barrel, DT or optional ST, S/T Model has heavy tropical barrel, which was also optional in 23.6 inches, and only offered in 9.3x64mm, .375 H&H, or .458 Win. Mag. Mfg. 1973-1975.

	$1,750	$1,600	$1,450	$1,300	$1,150	$1,000	$900	

Note: some rare catalogs show these S and S/T Magnum action versions, though none appear to have been imported into the U.S.A. by U.S. importers.

MODEL SL – .222 Rem., .222 Rem. Mag., .223 Rem, .22-250 Rem, or 5.6x50mm cal., 23.6 in. barrel, double set or single trigger, 5 shot rotary mag., 6.27 lbs. Mfg. 1968-1996.

	$1,400	$1,100	$900	$700	$600	$495	$450	*$2,540*

* ***Model SL Carbine Model*** – .222 Rem., .222 Rem. Mag., .223 Rem., .22-250 Rem., or 5.6x50mm cal., 20 in. barrel with full stock, early models possess slimmer stock design, 38 1/2 inches overall, 6.16 lbs. (some list 5.95 lbs.) Disc.

	$1,600	$1,200	$1,000	$900	$700	$650	$500	*$2,450*

* ***Model SL Varmint Rifle*** – .222 Rem., .222 Rem. Mag., .223 Rem., .22-250 Rem., or 5.6x50mm cal., 25.6 in. barrel, two heavy barrel varmint versions with either traditional heavy stock and heavy barrel or square forearm vented stock, double set or single trigger, no sights, 7.92 lbs. Disc.

	$1,625	$1,325	$900	$800	$650	$550	$500	*$2,450*

MODEL L – 5.6x50mm, 5.6x57mm, .22-250, .243 WCF, 6mm Rem., or .308 Win. cal., 23.6 in. barrel, double set and single trigger, 5 shot rotary mag., 6.38 lbs. Mfg. 1968-1996.

	$1,500	$1,300	$900	$750	$675	$600	$540	*$2,250*

This model is most often seen in .243 Win. and .308 Win. - special order calibers included 6mm Rem. and .22-250 Rem.

* ***Model L Carbine Model*** – 5.6x50mm, 5.6x57mm, .22-250, .243 WCF, 6mm Rem., or .308 Win. cal., 20 in. barrel with full stock, early models possess a slimmer stock design, 38 1/2 inches overall, approx. 6.2 lbs.

	$1,600	$1,300	$995	$825	$700	$600	$540	*$2,450*

GRADING - PPGS™	100%	98%	95%	90%	80%	70%	60%	LAST MSR

* ***Model L Varmint Rifle*** – 5.6x50mm, 5.6x57mm, .22-250, .243 WCF, 6mm Rem., or .308 Win. cal., 25.6 in. barrel, two heavy barrel varmint versions with either traditional stock and heavy barrel square forearm vented stock, double set or single trigger, no sights, 7.92 lbs.

	$1,600	$1,325	$875	$800	$650	$550	$500	*$2,450*

* ***Model L Luxus*** – same calibers as L, stock design, magazine, and safety are different from other Steyr-Mannlichers, full or half stock with better checkering, rotary thumb safety, single set trigger, and in-line, non-rotary 3 shot steel magazine, open sights, available in full stock and half-stock versions. Mfg. 1980-1996.

	$1,700	$1,450	$1,100	$950	$800	$700	$650	*$3,150*

* ***Model L Luxus Carbine (Full Stock)*** – similar to L Luxus rifle, except has full stock and 20 in. barrel. Disc. 1996.

	$1,800	$1,500	$1,200	$1,000	$800	$700	$650	*$3,150*

MODEL M – 6x62mm Freres, .25-06 Rem., 6.5x55mm, 6.5x57mm, 6.5x65mm, .270 Win., 7x57mm, 7x64mm, .30-06, 7.5x55mm Swiss, 8x57mm, or 9.3x62mm cal., available in carbine (20 in. barrel), and rifle (23.6 in. barrel), double set and single trigger, 5 shot rotary mag. Mfg. 1968-1996.

	$1,500	$1,300	$900	$700	$650	$600	$540	*$2,250*

Add $400 for left-hand action.

Special order and unlisted calibers varied and included .25-06, 6.5x55mm, and 7.5x55mm.

* ***Model M Carbine Model*** – 6.5x55mm, 6.5x57mm, .270 Win., .30-06, 8x57mm, or 9.3x62mm cal., full stock, 20 in. barrel, 7.26 lbs. Disc.

	$1,600	$1,400	$900	$825	$700	$600	$540	*$2,450*

* ***Model M Luxus*** – same calibers as Model M, stock design, magazine, and safety are different from other Steyr-Mannlichers, full or half stock with better checkering, rotary thumb safety, single set trigger, and in-line, non-rotary, 3 shot steel mag., open sights, 7.7 lbs. Mfg. 1980-1996.

	$1,750	$1,500	$1,200	$900	$800	$700	$650	*$2,950*

* ***Model M Luxus Carbine (Full Stock)*** – similar to Model M Luxus, except with full stock and 20 in. barrel. Disc. 1996.

	$1,900	$1,650	$1,300	$950	$825	$700	$650	*$3,150*

* ***Model M "1000 Year City of Steyr Commemorative" Luxus Carbine*** – .30-06 cal., deluxe full stock, gold inlaid on receiver and trigger guard, single set trigger, in-line, non-rotary, 3 shot steel mag., open sights, approx. 7.7 lbs. Mfg. 1980-1983.

	$3,650	$2,850	$2,400	N/A	N/A	N/A	N/A	*$4,200*

RIFLES: SEMI-AUTO

AUG S.A. A3 M1 – 5.56 NATO/.223 Rem. cal., short stroke GPO, rotating bolt, bullpup configuration, 16, 20 (disc. 2020), or 24 (disc. 2020) in. quick detach barrel, 10, 30 or 42 shot AUG mag., NATO variants use AR-15 mags., design incorporates use of advanced plastics, green, black, white, or mud colored composite stock with rubber buttpad, folding vertical foregrip, crossbolt safety, integral 1.5 or 3 power Swarovski scope or short, medium, or extended length Picatinny top rail, 7.9 lbs. Importation resumed mid-2006.

MSR $2,050	$1,850	$1,600	$1,400	$1,250	$1,000	$850	$650	

Add approx. 10% for 24 in. heavy barrel with Picatinny rail and bipod (disc.).
Add $520 for 1.5X or $620 for 3X optic.

AUG S.A. COMMERCIAL – similar to AUG S.A., grey (3,000 mfg. circa 1997), green, or black finish.

SP receiver (Stanag metal)	$2,950	$2,750	$2,450	$2,150	$1,750	$1,575	$1,400	
Grey finish	$3,150	$2,875	$2,600	$2,250	$1,825	$1,625	$1,450	
Green finish (last finish)	$3,400	$2,975	$2,700	$2,300	$1,875	$1,675	$1,500	
Black finish	$4,125	$3,750	$3,300	$2,950	$2,750	$2,500	$2,250	

Last MSR was $1,362 (1989) for Green finish.

STEYR USR (UNIVERSAL SPORTING RIFLE) – .223 Rem. cal., unthreaded barrel, USR thumbhole stock, AUG barrels are not interchangeable with this model. Approx. 3,000 imported circa 1996 before the sporting arms ban began.

	$1,650	$1,450	$1,250	$1,050	$900	$775	$650	

MODEL MAADI AKM – 7.62x39mm cal., copy of Soviet AKM design rifle, 30 shot mag., open sights.

	$2,250	$2,000	$1,800	$1,600	$1,450	$1,250	$1,125	

GRADING - PPGS™	100%	98%	95%	90%	80%	70%	60%	LAST MSR

SHOTGUNS

MODEL 300 SxS – boxlock, cocking indicators, DT, pistol grip stock with cheekpiece, 28 in. barrels, selector switch to change from extractors to ejectors, sling swivels, light scroll engraving. Mfg. circa mid 1920s - late 1930s, scarce.

	100%	98%	95%	90%	80%	70%	60%	LAST MSR
	N/A	N/A	$1,500	$1,300	$1,100	$925	$700	

STINGER MANUFACTURING CORP.

Previous company located in Sault Sainte Marie, MI circa 2002-2004.

PISTOLS: PEN DESIGN

STINGER – .22 LR cal. (most common), pen pistol design, originally marketed by R. J. Braverman Corp. located in Meredith, NH, manufactured by Remcon North Corp. from Meredith, NH, in 2002 a new company called Stinger Manufactured Corp. revived this pen pistol design and went back into production until early 2004.

	100%	98%	95%	90%	80%	70%	60%	LAST MSR
	$550	$475	$425	$375	$350	$325	$300	

STOCK, FRANZ

Previous manufacturer located in Berlin, Germany.

PISTOLS: SEMI-AUTO

.22 LR PISTOL – .22 LR cal. Mfg. in Germany 1920-40.

	100%	98%	95%	90%	80%	70%	60%	LAST MSR
	$650	$450	$300	$250	$200	$175	$150	

Add 200% for long barrel.

.25 ACP PISTOL – .25 ACP or .32 ACP cal. Mfg. in Germany 1920-40.

	100%	98%	95%	90%	80%	70%	60%	LAST MSR
	$350	$300	$250	$200	$175	$150	$100	

STOCKWORKS

Please refer to Robert Hisserich Co. listing in the R section.

STOEGER INDUSTRIES, INC.

Current importer/trademark established in 1924, currently located in Accokeek, MD, previously located in Wayne, NJ until 2000. Stoeger Industries, Inc. was purchased by Beretta Holding of Italy in 2000 and is now a division of Benelli USA.

Stoeger has imported a wide variety of firearms during the past nine decades. Most of these guns were good quality and came from known makers in Europe (some were private labeled). Stoeger carried an extensive firearms inventory of both house brand and famous European trademarks - many of which were finely made with beautiful engraving, stock work, and other popular special order features. As a general rule, values for Stoeger rifles and shotguns may be ascertained by comparing them with a known trademark of equal quality and cal./ga. Certain configurations will be more desirable than others (i.e. a Stoeger .22 caliber Mannlicher with double-set triggers and detachable mag. will be worth considerably more than a single shot target rifle).

Perhaps the best reference works available on these older Stoeger firearms (not to mention the other trademarks of that time) are the older Stoeger catalogs themselves - quite collectible in their own right. You are advised to purchase these older catalogs (some reprints are also available) if more information is needed on not only older Stoeger models, but also the other firearms being sold at that time.

For more information and current pricing on both new and used Stoeger airguns, please refer to the *Blue Book of Airguns* - also available as an online subscription.

PISTOLS: SEMI-AUTO

Stoeger Lugers can be found in the Luger section.

COUGAR – 9mm Para., .40 S&W, or .45 ACP (new 2010) cal., DA/SA, copy of Beretta, 3.6 in. barrel, 8 (.45 ACP), 11 (.40 S&W), or 15 (9mm Para.) shot mag., ambidextrous safety, 3-dot sights, Bruniton black (disc.) Nitride hardened matte black, silver, or two-tone finish, checkered plastic grips, blowback action with rotating bolt, removable front sight, approx. 32 oz. Mfg. in Turkey. Imported 2007-2016.

	100%	98%	95%	90%	80%	70%	60%	LAST MSR
	$385	$340	$275	$240	$215	$195	$180	*$469*

Add $30 for silver or two-tone finish.
Add $40 for .45 ACP cal. in black finish with Picatinny rail.

* ***Cougar Compact*** – 9mm Para. cal., DA/SA, compact frame, 3.6 in. barrel, 13 shot mag., checkered plastic grips, Nitride-hardened matte black finish, 28.8 oz. Mfg. 2011-2016.

	100%	98%	95%	90%	80%	70%	60%	LAST MSR
	$385	$340	$275	$240	$215	$195	$180	*$469*

GRADING - PPGS™	100%	98%	95%	90%	80%	70%	60%	LAST MSR

PRO SERIES 95 – .22 LR cal., target pistol with choice of either 5 1/2 or 7 1/4 in. VR, fluted, or bull barrel, adj. rear sight, adj. trigger, push-button takedown, Pachmayr rubber grips, gold accents, 10 shot mag., 45-47 oz. Mfg. 1995-96.

5 1/2 in. bull barrel	$440	$375	$335	$300	$275	$250	$225	
5 1/2 in. VR barrel	$515	$425	$365	$325	$285	$255	$225	
7 1/4 in. fluted barrel	$455	$385	$340	$300	$275	$250	$225	

Last MSR's were $495 for 5 1/2 in. bull barrel, $595 for 5 1/2 in. VR barrel, and $525 for 7 1/4 in. fluted barrel.

STR-9 – 9mm Para. cal., striker fired, polymer frame, 4.17 in. barrel, 10 (new 2020) or 15 shot double stack mag., reversible mag. release, drift adj. 3-dot sights, integrated rail, interchangeable backstraps, black finish, 24-26 oz. New 2019.

MSR $329	$280	$245	$210	$190	$155	$125	$110	

Add $70 for 1 mag., 1 backstrap, and night sights (new 2021).
Add $60 for 3 mags. and 3 backstraps (disc. 2020).
Add $120 for 3 mags., 3 backstraps, and night sights (disc. 2020).

* ***STR-9 Compact*** – 9mm Para. cal., striker fired, compact polymer frame, 3.8 in. barrel, 10 or 13 (new 2021) shot standard or extended (new 2021) mag., 3-dot, or Tritium night sights, tactile loaded chamber indicator, interchangeable backstraps, black finish. New 2020.

MSR $329	$280	$245	$210	$190	$155	$125	$110	

Add $70 for 1 extended mag., 1 backstrap, and night sights (new 2021).
Add $60 for 3 mags. and 3 backstraps (disc. 2020).
Add $120 for 3 mags., 3 backstraps, and Tritium night sights (disc. 2020).

* ***STR-9 Combat*** – 9mm Para. cal., striker fired, 4.67 in. threaded barrel, three 10 or 20 shot mags., flared magwell, quick read 3-dot sight, trigger safety, drilled and tapped receiver, 4 mounting plates and cover, includes 3 interchangeable backstraps, black synthetic or Nitride-Hardened matte black finish, 28.8 oz. New 2021.

MSR $549	$470	$410	$350	$325	$260	$215	$185	

* ***STR-9 Optic Ready Pistol*** – 9mm Para. cal., striker fired, polymer frame, 4.17 in. barrel, includes one (new 2021) or three (mfg. 2020 only) 10 or 15 shot mags., 3 backstraps, black finish, 26 oz. New 2020.

MSR $379	$325	$285	$245	$220	$180	$150	$125	

SHOTGUNS: O/U

CLASSIC MODEL – 12 ga., 3 1/2 in. chambers, engraved boxlock action, 26, 28, or 30 in. vent. barrels with VR and 3 choke tubes, gold SST, AE, checkered walnut stock and forearm, approx. 7 1/2 lbs. Disc.

While advertised for $919 by Stoeger Industries during 2000, this model was never imported by Stoeger Industries. However, it has had limited importation to date from domestic distributors.

CONDOR FIELD – 12, 20, 28 ga., or .410 bore, 2 3/4 or 3 in. chambers, 24 (mfg. 2015-2017), 26, or 28 in. VR barrels, screw in choke tubes or fixed chokes (.410 bore only), blued receiver, A-Grade satin walnut stock, high polish finish, 6-7.4 lbs.

MSR $449	$380	$335	$285	$260	$210	$175	$145	

Add $200 for 12 ga./28 in. and 20 ga./26 in. combo (new 2017).

* ***Condor Field Stainless*** – 12 ga., 3 in. chambers, 28 in. stainless steel barrels, screw-in chokes, A-Grade satin walnut stock, stainless steel receiver.

MSR $559	$475	$415	$350	$325	$260	$215	$195	

* ***Condor Field Synthetic*** – 12 ga., 2 3/4 or 3 in. chamber, 28 in. barrel, IC/M chokes, 2 shot mag., SST, brass bead sight, black synthetic stock, 7.3 lbs. New 2021.

MSR $349	$300	$265	$225	$200	$165	$135	$115	

CONDOR I SINGLE TRIGGER – 12, 16 (mfg. 2006-2013), 20, 28 (new 2012) ga., or .410 bore (new 2005), 3 in. chambers, boxlock action, deluxe checkered walnut, extractors, 24 (28 ga. only, new 2012), 26 or 28 in. VR separated barrels with choke tubes on 12 and 20 ga. (standard beginning 1992), 7.7 lbs. Importation disc.

	$375	$335	$275	$240	$215	$195	$180	*$449*

Add $170 for Condor combo, including set of 12 ga. and 20 ga. barrels (mfg. 2004-2012).

CONDOR I SPECIAL – similar to Condor I, except features matte stainless steel receiver, oil finished hardwood stock and forearm. Imported 2002-2006.

	$365	$325	$275	$235	$215	$195	$180	*$415*

Add $135 for Condor combo, including set of 12 ga. and 20 ga. barrels (new 2004).

GRADING - PPGS™	100%	98%	95%	90%	80%	70%	60%	LAST MSR

CONDOR COMPETITION – 12 or 20 ga., 3 in. chambers, 30 in. ported barrels with choke tubes, SST, AE, checkered AA grade select gloss walnut stock (with or w/o adj. comb, LH or RH) and forearm, 7.3-7.8 lbs. New 2005.

MSR $669	$575	$500	$430	$390	$315	$260	$220	

Add $230 for Condor combo with 12 and 20 ga. barrels (mfg. 2007-2012, available in right or left hand).

CONDOR LONGFOWLER – 12 or 20 (new mid-2013) ga., 3 in. chambers, 30 in. vented barrels with VR and two extended choke tubes, single trigger, extractors, checkered A-Grade satin walnut stock and semi-beavertail forearm, top tang safety, 7 1/2 lbs. New 2013.

MSR $449	$380	$335	$285	$260	$210	$175	$145	

CONDOR OUTBACK – 12 or 20 (disc.) ga., 3 in. chambers, 20 in. barrels with screw-in chokes, ST, extractors, choice of checkered A-Grade satin walnut or black painted walnut stock and forearm, rifle sights, separated barrels, blue or polished nickel finish, 6 1/2-7 lbs. New 2007.

MSR $449	$380	$335	$285	$260	$210	$175	$145	

Add $50 for black finished walnut stock and polished nickel metal finish.

CONDOR SKEET – 12 ga., 3 in. chambers, break action, 22 in. barrels, screw-in chokes, fiber optic front sight, A-Grade satin walnut stock, rubber buttpad, tang mounted thumb safety, 7.1 lbs. New 2019.

MSR $449	$380	$335	$285	$260	$210	$175	$145	

CONDOR SUPREME (DELUXE) – 12 or 20 ga., 3 in. chambers, 24 (20 ga. only, disc. 2010), 26, 28, or 30 (disc. 2001) in. VR barrels with choke tubes, high polish blue, gold SST, AE, checkered AA grade high gloss American walnut stock and forearm, 6.8-7.4 lbs. Importation began 2000.

MSR $619	$525	$460	$395	$355	$290	$240	$200	

Add $190 for Condor combo, including set of 12 ga. and 20 ga. barrels (mfg. 2004-2012).

CONDOR YOUTH – 20 ga. or .410 bore, 2 1/2-3 in. chambers, 22 in. barrels, 13 in. LOP, blued receiver, available with screw-in or fixed chokes, A-Grade satin walnut stock, high polish finish, 5 1/2 lbs.

MSR $449	$380	$335	$285	$260	$210	$175	$145	

DOUBLE DEFENSE – 12 or 20 ga., 3 in. chambers, 20 in. barrels with fixed IC chokes, black finished walnut stock, approx. 7 lbs.

MSR $449	$380	$335	$285	$260	$210	$175	$145	

SHOTGUNS: SxS

COACH GUN MODEL – 12, 20 ga., or .410 (new 1991) bore, 2 3/4 or 3 in. chambers, 20 in. barrels with choke tubes (disc.) or fixed IC/M chokes, single or double triggers, choice of blue, polished nickel, or matte nickel (new 1996) finish, choice of dark (nickel finish only) or light hardwood stock, ST or DT, 6 1/2-7 lbs.

MSR $449	$380	$335	$285	$260	$210	$175	$145	

Add $100 for black finished walnut and polished matte nickel finish.
Add $110 for polished nickel.
Add $64 for carved stagecoach scene on stock (mfg. 1996-99).

* ***Coach Gun Model Deluxe*** – similar to Coach Gun Model, includes deluxe checkered walnut stock and forearm, fixed (IC/M) or choke tubes (new 1998), gold triggers. Mfg. 1997-99.

	$385	$325	$290	$260	$230	$195	$170	*$499*

COACH GUN SILVERADO – similar to Coach Gun, except features a matte nickel metal finish and oil finished hardwood pistol grip or straight English (not available in .410 bore) stock and forearm. Imported 2002-2004.

	$320	$270	$215	$180	$150	$130	$110	*$375*

COACH GUN SUPREME – 12, 20 ga. or .410 bore (disc. 2005), 20 or 24 (disc. 2005) in. barrels with choke tubes (except for .410 bore), hammerless, blue, polished nickel, or blue/stainless steel finish, checkered AA grade walnut stock with recoil pad and beavertail forearm, ST or DT, extractors, approx. 6 1/2 lbs. Importation began 2004.

MSR $549	$470	$410	$350	$325	$260	$215	$185	

DOUBLE DEFENSE – 12 or 20 ga., 3 in. chambers, hammerless, matte blue finish, 20 in. ported barrels, fixed IC chokes, single trigger, non-reflective matte black hardwood or black synthetic (new 2014) stock, fiber optic front sight, top and bottom Picatinny rails, 6 1/2 lbs. New mid-2009.

MSR $489	$415	$365	$315	$285	$230	$185	$160	

UPLANDER FIELD – 12, 16 (mfg. 1996-disc.), 20, 28 ga., or .410 bore, 2 3/4 or 3 in. chambers, 24 (English style stock only, disc.), 26, or 28 in. barrels with extractors, DT, underlug lockup, checkered A Grade satin finished walnut pistol grip or straight English (20 ga. or .410 bore only) stock, 7-7 1/2 lbs.

MSR $449	$380	$335	$285	$260	$210	$175	$145	

Subtract approx. 10% if w/o choke tubes.

GRADING - PPGS™	100%	98%	95%	90%	80%	70%	60%	LAST MSR

* ***Uplander Youth*** – 20 ga. or .410 bore, 2 1/2 or 3 in. chambers, 22 in. barrels, A-Grade satin walnut stock, 6 1/2 lbs.

MSR $449	$380	$335	$285	$260	$210	$175	$145	

UPLANDER LONGFOWLER – 12 or 20 ga., 2 3/4 or 3 in. chambers, 30 in. barrels with two extended choke tubes, single trigger, extractors, checkered A-Grade satin walnut stock and semi-beavertail forearm, top tang safety, 7 1/2 lbs. New 2013.

MSR $449	$365	$325	$275	$235	$200	$165	$135	

UPLANDER SPECIAL – 12, 20, or 28 ga., 3 in. chambers (not available in 28 ga.), 24 or 26 in. barrels, fixed chokes on 28 ga., features straight grip Brazilian hardwood checkered English stock and forearm, DT, approx. 7.3 lbs. Mfg. 2002-2005.

	$340	$300	$260	$230	$200	$165	$125	*$375*

UPLANDER SUPREME – 12 or 20 ga., 3 in. chambers, 24 (20 ga. only, disc. 2010), 26, or 28 in. barrels with choke tubes, extractors, gold ST, high gloss AA grade checkered walnut stock and forearm, approx. 7 1/2 lbs. Importation began 2000.

MSR $549	$470	$410	$350	$325	$260	$215	$185	

Add $140 for combo package (includes 12 and 20 ga. or 20 and 28 ga. barrels, mfg. 2005-2012).

SHOTGUNS: SEMI-AUTO

MODEL 2000 – 12 ga. only, 3 in. chamber, Benelli licensed inertia recoil operating system, 18 1/2 (new 2012), 24 (new 2010), 26, 28, or 30 in. VR barrel with 5 choke tubes, checkered walnut or black synthetic (new 2002) stock and forearm, matte metal, 100% Advantage Timber HD (mfg. 2002-2010), Realtree APG HD (new 2007), or Advantage Max-4 camo (new 2004) finish, approx. 7.1 lbs. Mfg. by Vursan Manufacturing located in Istanbul, Turkey. Imported 2001-2013.

	$435	$365	$315	$265	$230	$195	$175	*$509*

Add $60 for 100% camo coverage.
Add $90 for Turkey configuration with Timber HD steady grip and 24 in. barrel.
Add $59 (11 oz.) or $89 (13 oz.) for recoil reducer.
Add $121 for Model 2000 Deluxe with upgraded wood and floral etched receiver trim (disc. 2003).
Add $146 for synthetic combo package which includes a smoothbore slug barrel with screw-in IC choke and rifle sights, $226 if with camo, or $81 if with walnut (disc. 2002).

* ***Model 2000 Slug*** – 12 ga. only, 3 in. chamber, available with walnut or synthetic with 100% Advantage Timber HD finish, 24 in. smoothbore barrel with adj. rifle sights, 6.7 lbs. Imported 2003-2004.

	$365	$320	$285	$250	$225	$195	$175	*$430*

Add $15 for walnut stock and forearm.
Add $75 for 100% camo coverage.

MODEL 3000 – 12 ga., 3 in. chamber, Benelli inertia system, 24 (mfg. 2014-2020), 26, or 28 in. barrel with chokes, drilled and tapped, 4 shot mag., red bar sights, with (new 2019) or w/o Bronze Cerakote receiver, A Grade satin finished walnut (new 2015) or synthetic stock with black, Mossy Oak Bottomland, Realtree APG (disc. 2018), Realtree Max-4 (disc.), or Realtree Max-5 camo finish, approx. 7 1/2 lbs. New 2013.

MSR $559	$475	$415	$350	$325	$260	$215	$195	

Add $60 for camo finish or A Grade walnut stock (new 2015).
Add $90 for Bronze Cerakote finished receiver (new 2019).
Add $110 for SteadyGrip stock with 24 in. barrel and Realtree APG camo finish (disc. 2018).

* ***Model 3000 Compact*** – 12 ga., 3 in. chamber, 26 in. barrel with chokes, 4 shot mag., fiber optic front sight, black synthetic stock, 7 lbs. New 2015.

MSR $559	$475	$415	$350	$325	$260	$215	$195	

MODEL 3000 DEFENSE – 12 ga., 3 in. chamber, inertia driven, 18 1/2 in. VR barrel, fiber optic front sight, black synthetic stock, with or without pistol grip, 6.9 lbs. New 2017.

MSR $559	$475	$415	$350	$325	$260	$215	$195	

Add $60 for pistol grip stock.

* ***Model 3000 Defense Freedom Series*** – 12 ga., 3 in. chamber, inertia driven, 18 1/2 in. VR barrel, 7 shot extended mag., fiber optic front sight, black synthetic stock, with or without pistol grip, 6.9 lbs. New 2018.

MSR $619	$525	$460	$395	$355	$290	$240	$200	

Add $50 for pistol grip stock.

GRADING - PPGS™	100%	98%	95%	90%	80%	70%	60%	LAST MSR

MODEL 3000 M3K 3-GUN – 12 ga., 3 in. chamber, inertia driven, 24 in. barrel, 4 shot mag., extended tactical style bolt handle, enlarged and beveled loading port, oversized bolt release and safety, black synthetic stock, 7.3 lbs. New 2015.

MSR $669	$575	$500	$430	$390	$315	$260	$220	

* ***Model M3K 3-GUN Freedom Series*** – 12 ga., 3 in. chamber, inertia driven, 24 in. barrel, 10 shot extended mag., extended tactical style bolt handle, enlarged and beveled loading port, oversized bolt release and safety, black synthetic stock, 7.3 lbs. New 2018.

MSR $699	$600	$525	$450	$410	$325	$275	$225	

MODEL 3000 R RIFLED SLUG – 12 ga., 3 in. chamber, inertia driven, 24 in. barrel, black synthetic stock, 7.3 lbs. New 2015.

MSR $619	$525	$445	$385	$350	$300	$250	$200	

MODEL 3000 SPORTING – 12 ga., 3 in. chamber, inertia driven, 30 in. VR barrel, fiber optic front sight, black synthetic stock, 7 1/2 lbs. New 2017.

MSR $669	$575	$500	$430	$390	$315	$260	$220	

MODEL 3020 – 20 ga., 3 in. chamber, Benelli inertia system, 24 (new 2020), 26, or 28 in. VR barrel with chokes, drilled and tapped, 4 shot mag., red fiber optic front sight, synthetic stock with Black, Realtree APG (disc. 2018), Mossy Oak Bottomland (new 2019), Mossy Oak Obsession (new 2020), Realtree Max-5 stock with Cerakote Burnt Bronze receiver (new 2020), or Realtree Max-5 camo finish, or satin walnut stock with Burnt Bronze Cerakote receiver (new 2019), approx. 5 1/2 lbs. New 2014.

MSR $559	$475	$415	$350	$325	$260	$215	$195	

Add $60 for camo finish.
Add $90 for satin walnut stock and Burnt Bronze Cerakote receiver (new 2019).
Add $90 for Realtree Max-5 camo stock and Burnt Bronze Cerakote receiver (new 2020).
Add $90 for Mossy Oak Obsession camo stock (new 2020).

* ***Model 3020 Compact*** – 20 ga., 3 in. chamber, inertia driven, 26 in. barrel, black synthetic stock, 5 1/2 lbs. New 2015.

MSR $559	$475	$415	$350	$325	$260	$215	$195	

* ***Model 3020 Defense*** – 20 ga., 2 3/4 or 3 in. chamber, 18 1/2 in. VR barrel, ghost ring fiber optic front sight, black synthetic stock and forearm, 6.9 lbs. New 2018.

MSR $619	$525	$460	$395	$355	$290	$240	$200	

* ***Model 3020 Upland Special*** – 20 ga., 2 3/4 or 3 in. chamber, inertia driven system, 26 in. barrel, gloss walnut stock, 5.6 lbs. New 2020.

MSR $649	$550	$480	$415	$375	$310	$260	$215	

MODEL 3500 – 12 ga. only, 2 3/4, 3, or 3 1/2 in. chamber, Benelli inertia recoil operating system, 24 (disc. 2020), 26, or 28 in. VR barrel with 5 choke tubes, fiber optic front sight, black synthetic or satin walnut (new 2018) stock and forearm, 100% Realtree APG (disc. 2018), 100% Realtree Max-4 (disc.), 100% Realtree Max-5, 100% Mossy Oak Bottomland (new 2019) camo coverage, or Realtree Max-5 camo with Bronze Cerakote receiver finish (new 2019), straight or SteadyGrip (Realtree APG only) stock. New 2011.

MSR $669	$560	$490	$420	$380	$310	$250	$200	

Add $100 for 100% camo coverage or satin walnut (new 2018) stock and forearm.
Add $130 for Realtree Max-5 camo coverage with Bronze Cerakote receiver (new 2019).
Add $130 for SteadyGrip (disc. 2018).

MODEL 3500 PREDATOR/TURKEY SPECIAL – 12 ga., 2 3/4, 3, or 3 1/2 in. chamber, inertia driven system, 24 in. barrel with screw-in chokes, Mossy Oak Overwatch camo stock, 7.5 lbs. New 2020.

MSR $929	$795	$695	$595	$540	$435	$375	$300	

M3500 SNOW GOOSE – 12 ga., 2 3/4, 3, or 3 1/2 in. chamber, 28 in. VR barrel, five extended choke tubes w/choke wrench, 10 shot mag., red-bar front sight, receiver is drilled and tapped, oversized bolt handle and release button, beveled loading port, rugged paracord sling included, Distressed White Cerakote finish, 8.2 lbs. New 2021.

MSR $899	$750	$650	$600	$500	$425	$350	$275	

MODEL 3500 WATERFOWL SPECIAL – 12 ga., 3 in. chamber, inertia driven, 28 in. VR barrel, extended choke tubes, 4 shot mag., red bar front sights, Realtree Max-5 camo stock, drilled and tapped, FDE Cerakote metal finish, 7.8 lbs. New 2019.

MSR $849	$725	$635	$550	$500	$400	$325	$280	

GRADING - PPGS™	100%	98%	95%	90%	80%	70%	60%	LAST MSR

ULTRA-LIGHT MODEL – 12 ga. only, 3 in. chamber, gas operated, 26 or 28 in. VR barrel with 3 choke tubes, checkered walnut stock and forearm, approx. 6 1/2 lbs. Disc.

	$295	$260	$230	$210	$195	$180	$165	

While advertised by Stoeger Industries during 2000, this model was never imported by Stoeger Industries. However, it has had limited importation to date from domestic distributors.

SHOTGUNS: SINGLE BARREL, TRAP

THE GRAND – 12 ga., 2 3/4 or 3 in. chamber, 30 in. barrel with stepped ventilated trap rib and choke tubes, barrel extractor lifts the shell from the chamber, A Grade satin walnut stock with fully adj. comb, red fiber optic front sight, automatic safety, matte black finish, 9.1 lbs. New 2014.

MSR $629	$535	$475	$400	$365	$300	$275	$250	

SHOTGUNS: SLIDE ACTION

P350 – 12 ga. only, 3 or 3 1/2 in. chamber, 18 1/2 (Home Security, cyl. fixed choke, disc.), 24, 26, or 28 in. barrel, includes 5 screw-in chokes, choice of black synthetic, Timber HD (disc. 2008), Realtree APG HD, Realtree Max-4 HD, or Realtree Max-5 camo coverage, approx. 6.9 lbs. Mfg. 2005-2016.

	$285	$240	$200	$170	$150	$125	$110	*$349*

Add $100 for 100% camo coverage.
Add $130 for SteadyGrip stock with 24 in. barrel and Realtree APG finish.
Add $30 for pistol grip (18 1/2 in. barrel only), disc.
Add $63 for 13 oz. recoil reducer (disc. 2010).

P350 DEFENSE – 12 ga., 2 3/4-3 1/2 in. chamber, 18 1/2 in. barrel, fixed cylinder, blade front sight attached at the muzzle, field or pistol grip synthetic stock, matte black finish, 7 lbs. Mfg. 2014-2016.

	$285	$240	$200	$170	$150	$125	$110	*$349*

Add $30 for pistol grip stock.

MODEL P3000 – 12 ga. only, 2 3/4 and 3 in. chamber, 26 (new 2017) or 28 in. VR barrel w/screw-in chokes, black synthetic or satin walnut (new 2018) stock and forearm, 5 shot mag., black finish. New 2016.

MSR $289	$250	$220	$190	$170	$140	$125	$100	

Add $50 for satin walnut (new 2018) stock and forearm.

* ***Model P3000 Camo*** – 12 ga., 3 in. chamber, 26 or 28 in. VR barrel w/screw-in chokes, synthetic stock, Realtree Max-5 camo finish, 6.9 lbs. New 2017.

MSR $339	$290	$255	$220	$195	$160	$130	$125	

MODEL P3000 DEFENSE – 12 ga., 3 in. chamber, 18 1/2 in. VR barrel with screw-in or fixed choke, 5 shot mag., red bar front sight, black synthetic stock, with or without pistol grip, 6.4 lbs. New 2017.

MSR $289	$250	$220	$190	$170	$140	$125	$100	

Add $50 for pistol grip stock and fixed choke.

* ***Model P3000 Defense Freedom Series*** – 12 ga., 2 3/4 or 3 in. chamber, 18 1/2 in. VR barrel with screw-in or fixed choke, 7 shot mag., red bar front sight, black synthetic stock, 6.4 lbs. New 2018.

MSR $339	$290	$255	$220	$195	$160	$130	$125	

* ***Model P3000 Defense Freedom Series Supreme*** – 12 ga., 2 3/4 or 3 in. chamber, inertia driven, 18 1/2 in. barrel, cylinder fixed, extended choke tubes, ghost ring sights, P3000 Supreme black synthetic side-folding collapsible pistol grip stock, 7.3 lbs. New 2020.

MSR $469	$400	$350	$300	$275	$225	$185	$155	

MODEL P3500 – 12 ga., 2 3/4, 3, or 3 1/2 in. chamber, 26 or 28 in. barrel with screw-in chokes, 5 shot mag., red bar front sight, synthetic stock, black or Realtree Max-5 camo finish, 7 lbs. New 2017.

MSR $339	$290	$255	$220	$195	$160	$130	$125	

Add $50 for Realtree Max-5 camo finish.

STONER RIFLE

Please refer to the Knight's Armament Company listing in the K section.

STRANK, ANDREAS

Current long gun manufacturer established in 1995, located in Baesweiler, Germany. No current U.S. importation.

Andreas Strank manufactures high quality shotguns and bolt action rifles per individual special order. Please contact the company directly for more information and current pricing.

GRADING - PPGS™	100%	98%	95%	90%	80%	70%	60%	LAST MSR

STRASSER

Current trademark of straight pull bolt action rifles (the Modular RS-14 Series) manufactured by HMS PRÄZISIONSTECHNIK GmbH, located in Eugendorf, Austria. Please refer to the HMS PRÄZISIONSTECHNIK GmbH listing in the H section. Currently imported by International Firearm Corp. located in Midwest City, OK.

STRATEGIC ARMORY CORPS, LLC

Current manufacturer located in Phoenix, AZ.

Strategic Armory Corps, LLC was formed in August of 2011 and is the parent company of AWC Systems Technology LLC, which manufactures sound supressors, AWC Ammo, Armalite, Inc., Surgeon Rifles, and McMillan Firearms Manufacturing LLC. Please refer to these listings for current firearms manufacture.

STRAYER TRIPP INTERNATIONAL

Please refer to the STI International listing in this section.

STRAYER-VOIGT, INC.

Current manufacturer of Infinity pistols located in Gordon, TX.

Please refer to the Infinity Firearms listing in the I section for more information.

STREET SWEEPER

Previously manufactured by Sales of Georgia, Inc. located in Atlanta, GA.

SHOTGUNS

STREET SWEEPER – 12 ga. only, 12 shot rotary mag., tactical configuration with 18 in. barrel, double action, folding stock, 9 3/4 lbs. Restricted sales following the ATF classification as a "destructive device." Mfg. 1989-approx. 1995.

	100%	98%	95%	90%	80%	70%	60%	LAST MSR
	$1,495	$1,350	$1,100	$995	$895	$795	$695	

Unless this model was registered with the ATF before May 1st, 2001, it is subject to seizure with a possible fine/imprisonment.

STRIKE INDUSTRIES

Current AR-15 style pistol, rifle, and parts manufacturer located in Santa Ana, CA. Dealer and distributor sales.

Please refer to BlueBookOfGunValues.com to order the *Blue Book of AR-15s & Variations*, available as a book or online subscription.

STURM, RUGER & CO., INC.

RUGER

Current manufacturer with production facilities located in Newport, NH, Prescott, AZ, and Mayodan, NC. Previously manufactured in Southport, CT 1949-1991 (corporate and administrative offices remain at this location). A second factory was opened in Newport, NH in 1963, and still produces single action revolvers, rifles and shotguns. During September 2013, Ruger purchased a 220,000 square foot facility in Mayodan, NC. New production began in late fall of 2013.

In January of 1949, partners William B. Ruger and Alexander Sturm began manufacturing .22 pistols in a leased 4,400 square foot wooden structure on Station St. in Southport, CT. By 1956 they acquired an additional 2,300 square feet that is today affectionately known as the Red Barn. By January of 1959 they completely moved into a newly finished building on Lacey Place, not too far from Station St. The company continued to expand its product line and in 1967 began producing long guns in a factory building located in Newport, NH. By 1988 Ruger set up another facility in Prescott, AZ to make the P-series center-fire pistols. In July 1991 they completely suspended production at Southport. The corporate offices remain there to this day. Then, in 2013 Ruger opened a third large factory in Mayodan, NC. Over time production of the extensive variety of products was divided up and dispersed among these facilities.

Red Barn on Station St. 1949-1959 pistols & revolvers

Lacey Place 1959-1991 pistols, revolvers & rifles

Pinetree Casting Newport, NH 1963 - current investment castings

Newport, NH 1967 - current shotguns, rifles, and since 1992 revolvers

Prescott, AZ 1988 - current all centerfire pistols and since 1992 rimfire pistols

Mayodan, NC 2013 - current modern rifles. In 2015 an additional line was also made up for producing SR22 pistols.

Late 2018 - Ruger establishes a custom shop which modifies standard production models with extra features/options and accuracy enhancements.

From 2004-2007 the Ruger Studio of Art & Decoration offered factory engraving on any current Ruger model. The engraving could range from presentation inscriptions to bas-relief and extensive gold in-laid masterpieces. Prices could

GRADING - PPGS™	100%	98%	95%	90%	80%	70%	60%	LAST MSR

range from a few hundred dollars to $40,000 or more.

Ruger emerged as America's largest small arms maker, and offers a complete line of firearms for sportsmen, law enforcement and military. Over a 70 year span, from five separate factories Ruger has shipped over 42 million firearms.

Alex Sturm passed away in November 1951. Bill Ruger carried on until July 6, 2002 when he too passed away at his home in Prescott, AZ. Ruger, America's greatest 20th century arms inventor, is buried on his estate Corbin Park at Croydon, NH.

On November 23, 2020, Ruger finalized a deal to purchase Marlin as a result of the breakup of the Remington Arms Company. It was announced that Marlin branded firearms would be produced at existing Ruger facilities and will become available during the second half of 2021.

RUGER COLLECTIBILITY OVERVIEW

Since the mid-1970s collecting Ruger firearms has become a very popular hobby, as a result, many of the early pistols, revolvers and rifles are actively sought after. Some models and sub-models were produced in such small quantities that they were not cataloged. The engraving project in the mid-50s yielded 275 ornamented handguns, mostly single-action revolvers. Certain of these are regarded as a holy grail of Ruger collecting.

The most popular among collectors are the early single-action revolvers, the early Standard Pistols 1949-1959 and then the early rifles. The single-action revolvers fall into three distinct categories identified by the time frames they were produced; 1953-1963, 1963-1973 and 1973-date (New Model). As in most collectables the earliest time frame encompasses the rarest and most collectable specimens; certain of these guns command the highest prices.

All Ruger firearms produced in 1976 were marked MADE IN THE 200th YEAR OF AMERICAN LIBERTY, collectors refer to them as "Liberty Models". Guns that fall into this category will sell for a slight premium if in NIB condition.

Some guns of all models can have special markings, "S" denoting sold as seconds, "D" duplicate, "U" used, "US" on guns shipped to the military. A star designates a single cylinder. Foreign proof marks and ATF marked guns appear occasionally. A negotiable premium will be added to specimens featuring any of the markings. The premium can sometimes equal the value of the basic gun.

The 100% condition factor in this section assumes the gun is new or in mint like original condition, in the original packaging with all paperwork. This can sometimes require additional evaluation and/or appraisal due to wide varying values that packaging and paperwork can add to certain individual pieces.

The publisher would like to thank Bill Hamm, Richard Machniak, John C. Dougan and Chad Hiddleson for their contributions in this and previous editions.

RUGER CUSTOM SHOP

The Ruger Custom Shop was established at the end of October 2018 and specializes in high performance variations/versions in some of Ruger's more popular models. Ruger Custom Shop products have been designed by Ruger's in-house team of engineers, input from firearms industry professionals, competitive shooters, noted hunters, and outdoor writers. Ruger Custom Shop variations cannot be individually ordered directly with customer special order features/options. These variations need to be purchased directly through Ruger's established dealer network. These models can be found within their respective categories in this section.

PISTOLS: SEMI-AUTO, RIMFIRE

Many distributors and customizers have produced special/limited editions of this popular series of .22 cal. pistols; these editions are not listed in the *Blue Book of Gun Values*. After 1999, all non-22/45 model pistols were fitted with Ruger logo medallions with a red background. Note that Ruger's 22/45 series did not have red eagle logo medallions in either grip panel until the P512MKIIRP was introduced in 2010.

Ruger recalled all Mark IV pistols produced prior to June 1, 2017. This includes Mark IV™ Target, Hunter, Competition, 22/45™, 22/45™ Lite and 22/45™ Tactical models. These models bear serial numbers beginning with "401" (2017 models) or "WBR" (2016 models).

Add $449 for the Silent-SR suppressor, available on select models (new 2016, NFA regulations apply).

"RED EAGLE" STANDARD & TARGET MODEL – Ruger's first offerings, popular designation with red grip medallions, changed to black medallions in memory of Alexander Sturm in 1952, ser. no. range 0001-35000. Approx. 27,000 mfg. 1949-1952.

Standard Model	$1,000	$650	$475	$350	$265	$235	$175	
Standard Model w/"salt cod" box	$4,500	$4,125	$3,000	$2,100	$1,500	$1,000	$800	
Target w/6 7/8 in. barrel	$950	$750	$600	$450	$375	$350	$300	

Produced until early 1952. Serialized approx. 0001 - 25,300 and 30001 to 35000 with Mark I Auto occupying blocks from 15,000-16,999 and 25,000-25,300.

GRADING - PPGS™	100%	98%	95%	90%	80%	70%	60%	LAST MSR

"BLACK OR SILVER EAGLE" STANDARD MODEL (POST RED EAGLE) – .22 LR cal., 9 shot, 4 3/4 in. or 6 in. barrel, blue, fixed sights, checkered walnut or hard rubber grips, some minor parts variants, most common configuration, ser. no. above 33,000. Mfg. 1952-1982.

	100%	98%	95%	90%	80%	70%	60%	LAST MSR
Standard	$550	$400	$350	$275	$225	$175	$100	
"HECHO EN MEXICO" marked (250 mfg. total, 200 w/4.75" bbl. and 50 w/6" bbl.)	$2,500	$2,100	$1,750	$1,300	$850	$775	$700	
Stainless 1 of 5000 Signature Series w/box (grips have silver eagle with red background)	$575	$425	$350	N/A	N/A	N/A	N/A	

* ***"Black or Silver Eagle" Standard Model (Post Red Eagle) Stainless Steel 1 of 5,000 w/California Freedom Inscription*** – engraved "CAL. FREEDOM '82" on chamber, donated by Ruger to the California Citizens Against the Gun Initiative in 1982, and raffled to NRA members and CA gun owners, known ser. no. range is 17-03379 to 17-04792. 26 mfg., including one prototype.

100%	98%	95%	90%	80%	70%	60%	LAST MSR
$1,250	$950	$800	N/A	N/A	N/A	N/A	

"BLACK OR SILVER EAGLE" MARK I TARGET – similar to Standard, except has 5 1/2 in. heavy, 5 1/4 in. tapered (scarce, mfg. 1952 - 1955 only) barrel, or 6 7/8 in. heavy tapered barrel, adj. target sights, some minor part variants, ser. no. starts at approx. 25300. Mfg. 1952-1982.

	100%	98%	95%	90%	80%	70%	60%	LAST MSR
5 1/4 in. tapered bbl.	$950	$800	$650	$475	$325	$250	$200	
5 1/2 in. bull bbl.	$550	$400	$325	$275	$200	$175	$150	
6 7/8 in. tapered bbl.	$650	$450	$375	$300	$225	$175	$150	
6 7/8 in. U.S. marked	N/A	$1,200	$950	$700	$500	$350	$300	

Add $150 for Ruger marked muzzle brake.

MARK II STANDARD – .22 LR cal., 4 3/4 or 6 in. barrel, checkered black Delrin synthetic grips, blue finish, 10 shot mag., approx. 2 1/4 lbs., ser. nos. start at 18-00001. Mfg. 1982-2004.

100%	98%	95%	90%	80%	70%	60%	LAST MSR
$350	$275	$150	$125	$110	$100	$95	*$299*

* ***Mark II Standard Stainless Steel*** – variation of the Mark II Standard. Disc. 2004.

100%	98%	95%	90%	80%	70%	60%	LAST MSR
$375	$300	$225	$175	$125	$100	$85	*$390*

Stainless serial numbers start at 211-00001 and thereafter are intermixed with the blue model.

MARK II STANDARD 50TH ANNIVERSARY – .22 LR cal., blue receiver without scallops at rear (similar to pre-Mark II models), stainless steel bolt with Ruger eagle logo, 50th Anniversary Ruger crest on top of frame in front of ejection port, black grips with Ruger medallion in red background, lockable red case. Approx. 55,000 mfg. 1999 only.

100%	98%	95%	90%	80%	70%	60%	LAST MSR
$350	$300	$225	$175	$125	$110	$100	*$287*

After 1999, all Ruger .22 pistols (except the 22/45 models) were fitted with Ruger logo medallions having a red background.

MARK II TARGET – .22 LR cal., blued steel, 4 (mfg. 1996-99) bull, 5 1/4 (disc. 1994), 5 1/2 bull, 6 7/8 tapered, or 10 in. bull barrel, 2 5/8 - 3 1/4 lbs. depending on barrel. Disc. 2004.

100%	98%	95%	90%	80%	70%	60%	LAST MSR
$550	$400	$350	$300	$225	$150	$110	*$365*

Add $25 for 4 in. bull barrel.
Add $100 for 5 1/4 in. tapered or 10 in. bull barrel.

* ***Mark II Target Stainless Steel*** – stainless variation of the Mark II Target, includes choice of 5 1/4 (disc. 1994), 5 1/2 bull, 6 7/8 tapered or 10 in. bull barrel. Disc. 2004.

100%	98%	95%	90%	80%	70%	60%	LAST MSR
$550	$450	$375	$250	$175	$115	$95	*$460*

Add $100 for 5 1/4 in. tapered or 10 in. bull barrel.

MARK II MODEL 22/45 – .22 LR cal., Zytel frame is patterned after the Model 1911 .45 ACP Govt., 4, 4 3/4, 5 1/4 (Target, disc. 1994), or 5 1/2 in. bull barrel, 10 shot mag. (push-button release), fixed (4 3/4 in. barrel only) or adj. sights, 28-35 oz. Mfg. 1993-2004.

* ***Mark II Model 22/45 Blue Finish*** – 4 in. regular barrel with adj. sights (Model P4, new 1997) or 5 1/2 in. bull barrel with adj. sights (Model P512). Mfg. 1994-2004.

100%	98%	95%	90%	80%	70%	60%	LAST MSR
$250	$200	$165	$135	$125	$115	$100	*$290*

* ***Mark II Model 22/45 Stainless*** – 4 3/4 in. regular barrel with fixed sights (Model KP4, new 1997), 5 1/4 in. tapered barrel (Model KP514 disc. 1994) or 5 1/2 in. bull barrel with adj. sights (Model KP512). Disc. 2004.

100%	98%	95%	90%	80%	70%	60%	LAST MSR
$275	$235	$200	$175	$135	$125	$115	*$315*

Add $65 for adj. sights (5 1/2 in. bull barrel only).
Add $165 for 5 1/4 in. barrel.

GRADING - PPGS™	100%	98%	95%	90%	80%	70%	60%	LAST MSR

GOVERNMENT TARGET MODEL (MK678G) - commercial variation of the government training model without "U.S." markings, 6 7/8 in. bull barrel, adj. rear sight, blue finish, black plastic grips, 46 oz., at least first 30,000 were individually test targeted. Mfg. 1987-2004.

	$475	$350	$275	$200	$165	$150	$125	*$445*

* ***Government Target Model (MK678G) Military "U.S." Marked*** – blue finish, adj. sights, 6 7/8 in. bull barrel, U.S. marking on chamber, issued to U.S. military personnel for training purposes, must be factory verified, ser. no. range 210-00001 - 210-19300, approx. 35 believed to be in civilian hands. Disc. 1999.

	$1,400	$1,100	$850	$550	$400	$350	$325	

* ***Government Target Model (KMK678G) Stainless Steel*** - .22 LR cal., stainless steel, black polymer grips, 6 7/8 in. bull barrel, adj. rear sight, fixed front sight, 46 oz. Mfg. 1991-2004.

	$500	$375	$325	$225	$175	$150	$125	*$535*

As least some of these are also thought to have been test targeted.

* ***Government Target Model (KMK678GC) Competition Slabside*** - .22 LR cal., stainless steel, black polymer grips, 6 7/8 in. slabside barrel, adj. sights, drilled and tapped, includes two magazines. Mfg. 1992-2004.

	$500	$375	$325	$225	$175	$150	$125	*$555*

* ***Blued Stainless (KMK512B or KMK512N) United States Navy Contract*** - .22 LR cal., black phosphate finish over stainless steel, black polymer grips, with blackened Ruger medallion, 5 1/2 in. bull barrel with narrow aperture rear sight blade and thin front sight blade, contract overrun of 84 pistols sold to U.S. domestic market, ser. no. range 212-89651 - 213-52645.

	$950	$800	$600	$500	$400	$350	$300	

"FRIENDS OF NRA" MK6 - .22 LR cal., high polish blue finish, NRA logo, faux ivory grips, "NATIONAL RIFLE ASSOCIATION" in gold on left side of barrel, ser. no. range 221-78058 to 221-89364, 650 mfg. for NRA auction events in the U.S. during 1997.

	$525	$450	$400	N/A	N/A	N/A	N/A	

"FRIENDS OF NRA" KMK6 - .22 LR cal., stainless steel with black enamel type ornamentation highlights, two-line "Limited Edition" appearing on one side of the barrel, two-line "NATIONAL RIFLE ASSOCIATION" on other side of barrel with NRA logo on rear of bolt, ser. no. range 223-76165 to 224-33634, 750 mfg. for NRA auction events in the U.S. during 2001.

	$525	$450	$400	N/A	N/A	N/A	N/A	

KMK4 "ONE OF ONE THOUSAND" - .22 LR cal., stainless steel, produced as a commemoration of the last 1,000 Mark II pistols mfg. before the introduction of the Mark III series, ser. no. range 226-17150 to 226-18143.

	$550	$300	$250	N/A	N/A	N/A	N/A	*$390*

MARK III STANDARD - .22 LR cal., 4 3/4 or 6 in. tapered barrel with fixed sights, the Mark III action is an evolution of the Mark II design, featuring a relocated mag. release button on the left side of the grip, behind the trigger guard, recontoured ejection port and tapered bolt ears, blue finish, loaded chamber indicator, internal lock, 10 shot mag., magazine disconnector safety, checkered composition grip panels, 35-37 oz. Mfg. 2005-2016.

	$365	$300	$275	$250	$225	$200	$180	*$429*

MARK III TARGET - .22 LR cal., 5 1/2 in. bull or 6 7/8 (disc. 2009) in. tapered barrel, fixed front and adj. rear sights, operating mechanism is the same as the Mark III Standard, blue finish, checkered black plastic or laminate target finger groove grips (new 2013), approx. 42 oz. Mfg. 2005-2016.

	$425	$370	$320	$290	$235	$190	$150	*$499*

Add $60 for laminate target finger groove grips (new 2013).

A few hundred of the MKIII678G Mark III Government models were produced in 2005 in the serial range 227-04601 to 227-06937. Add $150 if NIB.

* ***Mark III Target (KMKIII) Stainless*** - .22 LR cal., similar to Mark III Target, except has stainless steel construction, 5 1/2 in. bull barrel, 42 oz. Mfg. 2005-2016.

	$480	$370	$285	$225	$185	$165	$140	*$629*

* ***Mark III Target Government Competition*** - .22 LR cal., 6 7/8 in. slab sided bull barrel, stainless steel construction, brown laminated cocobolo (disc. 2012) or laminate target (new 2013) grip panels with thumb rest, fixed front and adj. rear sight, satin stainless finish, 45 oz. Mfg. 2005-2016.

	$575	$465	$385	$330	$275	$230	$195	*$729*

GRADING - PPGS™	100%	98%	95%	90%	80%	70%	60%	LAST MSR

MARK III HUNTER – .22 LR cal., stainless steel construction, 4 1/2 (mfg. 2006-2013) or 6 7/8 in. target crowned fluted barrel, checkered cocobolo (disc. 2012), checkered laminate, target laminate finger groove (new 2013), or Crimson Trace (mfg. 2008-2010) grips, V-notch rear sight blade, Hi-Viz/Fiber optic front sights with interchangeable LitePipes, adj. rear sight, drilled and tapped, 41 oz. Mfg. 2005-2016.

$575 $465 $385 $330 $275 $230 $195 *$729*

Add $70 for target laminate finger groove grips (new 2013).

Add $173 for Crimson Trace Lasergrips (4 1/2 in. barrel only, disc. 2010).

MARK III 22/45 – .22 LR cal., Zytel frame is patterned after the Model 1911 .45 ACP Govt., push-button mag. release, 4 in. slab-sided bull (2,000 mfg., disc. 2005), 4 in. bull, 4 1/2 slab-sided bull (disc. 2010), or 5 1/2 in. bull barrel, fixed dot or adj. sights, blue finish, tapered bolt ears, approx. 31 oz. Mfg. 2005-2016.

$340 $285 $250 $225 $175 $150 $115 *$399*

Add $40 for 5 1/2 in. bull barrel.

Add $160 for 5 1/2 in. slab-sided bull barrel (disc. 2011).

Add $46 for brown or black (new 2013) replaceable laminate grip panels.

Add $50 for 5 1/2 in. bull barrel with blue titanium Cerakote grip frame and removable rubber grips (Ruger model 10162). Note that this model was given to dealers as a promotion during Ruger's 2016 Winter Retailer Program (Catalog number P512MKIIIRP-BT). Serial number example 275-61617.

* ***Mark III 22/45 Threaded Barrel*** – .22 LR cal., SA, 4 1/2 in. threaded bull barrel, 10 shot mag., Zytel polymer grip frame, fixed front and adj. rear sights or Picatinny rail, blue finish, 32 oz. Mfg. 2011-2016.

$425 $370 $320 $290 $235 $190 $150 *$499*

Add $449 for Silent-SR suppressor (new 2016, NFA regulations apply).

* ***Mark III 22/45 Stainless*** – .22 LR cal., similar to Mark III 22/45, except is stainless steel, 5 1/2 in. bull or 5 1/2 in. slab side bull (mfg. 2011 only) barrel only with adj. rear sight, 35 oz. Mfg. 2005-2011.

$350 $265 $200 $170 $150 $130 $125 *$448*

Note that the 5 1/2 in. slab side bull barrel model was rollmarked on the receiver with "COMPETITION TARGET MODEL".

* ***Mark III 22/45 Hunter*** – .22 LR cal., stainless with 4 1/2 (new 2006) or 6 7/8 in. fluted barrel, green case, scope base adapter, six interchangeable Litepipes and internal lock. Mfg. 2005-2010.

$435 $350 $260 $210 $165 $140 $120 *$548*

* ***Mark III 22/45 Hunter, Interchangeable Cocobolo Grips*** – .22 LR cal., similar to Model 22/45 Hunter, except has interchangeable Model 1911-style cocobolo grip panels, 5 1/2 or 6 7/8 in. stainless steel fluted barrel, fiber optic front adj. rear sight, 32-34 oz. Mfg. 2011 only.

$450 $350 $275 $215 $175 $160 $140 *$593*

22/45 LITE – .22 LR cal., 10 shot mag., 4.4 in. stainless steel threaded barrel sleeve, upper receiver with fluted barrel shroud, gold anodized finish with slant machine cuts on receiver (disc. 2012), black anodized finish with fluted barrel (mfg. 2012-2013), Cobalt anodize finish with ventilated barrel shroud (new 2014), blue anodized with "shark grill" ventilated barrel shroud (new 2015), or OD Green finish with ventilated barrel shroud (new 2016), fixed front and adj. rear sights, Zytel polymer or black molded rubber grips, push-button mag. release on left side of frame, marked "RUGER 22/45 LITE" in front of ejection port, loaded chamber indicator, includes two magazines, internal lock key and soft case, 23 oz. Mfg. 2012-2016.

$475 $365 $330 $300 $275 $250 $225 *$549*

Add $150 for raspberry anodized variant (less than 72 made, model 3904) or gray anodized model (less than 104 made, model 3905). Disc. 2013.

Add $75 for bronze anodized variant made as a bonus for Ruger's 4R Program sales (mfg. 2014-2016).

MARK IV STANDARD – .22 LR cal., one-piece aluminum grip frame, 4 3/4 or 6 in. tapered barrel, push-button takedown, 10 shot mag., fixed front and rear sight, checkered synthetic grips, ambi manual safety, blued finish, 28.2-30.1 oz. New 2018.

MSR $449 $375 $300 $275 $250 $225 $200 $180

* ***Mark IV Standard 70th Anniversary Special Edition*** – .22 LR cal., aluminum frame, 4 3/4 in. tapered cold hammer forged barrel, 10 shot mag., fixed front and rear sights, checkered synthetic grips, features a commemorative 70th Anniversary laser engraving and limited edition "70TH" serial number prefix, shipped in custom wood case, includes 70th Anniversary pin and decal, blued finish, 28.2 oz. 5,000 produced 2019.

$450 $395 $340 $300 $275 $250 $225 *$529*

GRADING - PPGS™	100%	98%	95%	90%	80%	70%	60%	LAST MSR

MARK IV COMPETITION – .22 LR cal., 6.88 in. slab-sided bull barrel, push-button takedown, 10 shot mag., stainless steel construction, fixed front and adj. rear sights, checkered laminate grips with thumbrest, ambi manual safety, drilled and tapped receiver, satin stainless finish, 45.8 oz. New 2017.

MSR $749	$635	$560	$485	$440	$365	$295	$250	

MARK IV HUNTER – .22 LR cal., one-piece grip frame, 6 3/4 in. fluted bull barrel, push-button takedown, 10 shot mag., stainless steel, fiber optic front sight, adj. rear sight, checkered laminate or target laminate grips, ambi manual safety, satin stainless finish, 44 oz. New late 2016.

MSR $769	$650	$575	$495	$450	$375	$300	$250	

Add $30 for target laminate grips.

MARK IV TACTICAL – .22 LR cal., aluminum anodized frame, 4.4 in. threaded bull barrel, push-button takedown, 10 shot mag., fixed front and adj. rear sights, black checkered synthetic grips, factory installed top and bottom Picatinny rails, blued finish, 34.6 oz. New 2018.

MSR $569	$485	$425	$365	$325	$295	$260	$230	

MARK IV TARGET – .22 LR cal., one-piece aluminum grip frame, 5 1/2 or 10 (new 2020) in. heavy bull barrel, push-button takedown, 10 shot mag., fixed iron front sight, adj. rear sight, checkered synthetic or target laminate (5 1/2 in. only) grips, blued finish, 35.6-46.3 oz. New late 2016.

MSR $529	$450	$395	$340	$300	$275	$250	$225	

Add $40 for target laminate grips.
Add $116 for 10 in. barrel (new 2020).

* ***Mark IV Target Stainless*** – .22 LR cal., 5 1/2 or 10 (new 2020) in. heavy bull or threaded (new 2018, 5 1/2 in. only) barrel, 10 shot mag., stainless steel construction, fixed front and adj. rear sights, checkered synthetic grips, satin stainless finish, 42.8-53.5 oz. New 2017.

MSR $689	$585	$500	$425	$350	$300	$265	$235	

Add $10 for threaded barrel (new 2018).
Add $30 for 10 in. barrel (new 2020).

MARK IV 22/45 – .22 LR cal., polymer frame, 5 1/2 in. heavy bull barrel, 10 shot mag., fixed front and adj. rear sights, checkered synthetic grips, push-button takedown, blued finish, 34.4 oz. New 2018.

MSR $409	$350	$300	$275	$250	$225	$200	$180	

MARK IV 22/45 LITE – .22 LR cal., polymer grip frame with serrated front strap and checkered back strap, 4.4 in. threaded (black or gold, new 2019) or stainless non-threaded barrel, push-button takedown, two 10 shot mags., contoured ejection port, fixed front and adj. rear sights, checkered 1911 style grip panels or target laminate (new 2019) grips, ambi manual safety, Picatinny rail, vented aluminum receiver with Bronze (mfg. 2017 only), Black, Gold, or Diamond Gray (new 2019) anodized finish, 25-27 oz. New 2017.

MSR $559	$475	$415	$350	$315	$295	$260	$230	

Add $40 for stainless barrel and target laminate grips (new 2019).
Add 75% for Black Hills Ammunition special edition with green anodized barrel/receiver assembly, "BLACK HILLS" on right rear portion of the receiver, brown hardwood grip panels with BLACK HILLS AMMUNITION logo on the right panel, Ruger eagle logo on the left panel and special BH18-0001 through BH18-0200 serial number sequence. 200 produced 2018 (Ruger model 43919).

MARK IV 22/45 TACTICAL – .22 LR cal., 4.4 in. threaded barrel, push-button takedown, 10 shot mag., push-button mag. release, alloy steel receiver, contoured ejection port, fixed front and adj. rear sights, checkered 1911-style grips with polymer grip frame, ambi manual safety, ergonomic bolt stop, top and bottom Picatinny rails, black oxide finish, 33.3 oz. New 2017.

MSR $529	$450	$395	$340	$300	$275	$250	$225	

22 CHARGER – .22 LR cal., features 10/22 action with 10 in. barrel and 10 shot rotary mag. with mag. release in front of trigger guard, black/grey laminated pistol grip stock and forend, scope rail and bipod included, matte black metal finish, 3 1/2 lbs. Mfg. 2008-2012.

	$325	$265	$230	$195	$175	$150	$125	*$389*

22 CHARGER (CURRENT MFG.) – .22 LR cal., 8 or 10 in. cold hammer forged threaded barrel, shot detachable flush-mounted BX-10 rotary (disc. 2016) or 15 shot BX-15 mag. (black polymer stock only), alloy steel construction with matte black finish, brown laminate (disc. 2016) or black polymer stock, A2-style grip, features improved ergonomics, Picatinny rail, with or w/o rail brace mount and integrated QD cup (new late 2019), includes adj. bipod and soft case, alloy steel construction with matte black finish, 3.13-3.25 lbs. New 2015.

MSR $309	$265	$230	$200	$180	$145	$120	$95	

Add $40 for rail brace mount (new late 2019).
Add $449 for Silent-SR suppressor (new 2016, NFA regulations apply).

GRADING - PPGS™	100%	98%	95%	90%	80%	70%	60%	LAST MSR

* ***22 Charger Takedown*** – .22 LR cal., 10 in. cold hammer forged threaded barrel, threaded cap, detachable flush-mounted BX-1 10 shot rotary (disc. 2016) or 15 shot BX-15 mag. (black polymer stock only), alloy steel construction, Green Mountain laminate (disc. 2016) or black polymer stock, A2 style grip, features 10/22 takedown quick disconnect feature that allows the pistol to be taken down quickly and easily, Picatinny rail, with or w/o rail brace mount and integrated QD cup (new late 2019), includes adj. bipod and hard plastic case, matte black finish, 3.22-3.43 lbs. New 2015.

MSR $419 $350 $300 $275 $250 $225 $200 $180

Add $180 for rail brace w/integrated QD cup and threaded cap (new late 2019).

Add $449 for Silent-SR suppressor (new 2016, NFA regulations apply).

SR-22 – .22 LR cal., SA/DA operation with external hammer, 3 1/2 or 4 1/2 (new 2016) in. stainless steel or threaded (new 2013, 3 1/2 in. only) barrel, 10 shot mag., aluminum/black or aluminum/silver (new 2013) anodized slide with front and rear serrations, black, Raspberry (Ruger model 3608, mfg. 2013-2016), Toxic camo (mfg. 2018-2019), or Harvest Moon camo (mfg. 2018-2019) polymer frame and two interchangeable black rubberized grips, adj. 3-dot sights with fully adj. rear, Picatinny rail in front of trigger guard, ambidextrous manual thumb safety/decocking lever and magazine release, includes two 10 shot mags in soft case, 17 1/2-18.7 oz. New 2012.

MSR $439 $370 $300 $275 $250 $225 $200 $180

Add $20 for 4 1/2 in. barrel (new 2016).

Add $30 for aluminum/silver anodized finish (new 2013).

Add $40 for threaded barrel (new 2013).

Add $40 for Toxic camo (mfg. 2018-2019) or Harvest Moon camo (mfg. 2018-2019) polymer frame finish.

Add $50 for blue titanium grip frame (Ruger model 3621) given as a Ruger 2016 Winter Retailer promotion with the purchase of any six SR22 pistols. Known serial number range 366-33243 to 367-87793.

Add $50 for Tungsten Cerakote grip frame and green Hi-Viz front sight (Ruger model 3627) given as a promotion through Ruger's "Retailer Exclusive's Program" during the Winter of 2016. Unknown quantity produced. Known serial number range 366-95794 to 367-24566.

Add $449 for Silent-SR suppressor (new 2016, NFA regulations apply).

PISTOLS: SEMI-AUTO, CENTERFIRE

AMERICAN PISTOL – 9mm Para. or .45 ACP cal., 4.2 or 4 1/2 (.45 ACP) in. barrel, 10 or 17 (9mm Para.) shot mag., includes two nickel-Teflon plated steel magazines, stainless steel slide with black Nitride finish, Novak LoMount Carry 3-dot sights, small, medium, or large modular wrap-around grips, Picatinny rail, ambidextrous manual safety, integrated trigger safety, ambidextrous slide stop and magazine release, 31-32 1/2 oz. New mid-2016.

MSR $579 $500 $435 $375 $335 $275 $225 $195

* ***American Pistol Pro*** – 9mm Para. or .45 ACP cal., 10 or 17 (9mm Para. only) shot mag., stainless steel slide with black Nitride finish, 4.2 or 4 1/2 (.45 ACP) in. barrel, one-piece high performance glass-filled nylon grip frame, Novak LoMount Carry 3-dot sights, integrated trigger safety, modular wrap-around grip system, ambi slide stop and mag. release, Picatinny rail, 30 oz. New 2017.

MSR $579 $500 $435 $375 $335 $275 $225 $195

AMERICAN PISTOL COMPACT – 9mm Para. or .45 ACP (new 2017) cal., one-piece, high performance glass-filled nylon frame, 3.55 or 3.75 (.45 ACP, new 2017) in. barrel, 7 (new 2020), 10, or 17 (9mm Para. only) shot mag., includes two nickel-Teflon plated steel magazines, stainless steel slide with black Nitride or Gray Cerakote (new 2020) finish, pre-tensioned striker system, short takeup trigger, Novak LoMount Carry 3-dot sights, modular wrap-around grips, ambidextrous manual safety, integrated trigger safety, ambidextrous slide stop and mag. release, Picatinny rail, black or gray (new 2020) Cerakote finish, 29.2 oz. New late 2016.

MSR $579 $500 $435 $375 $335 $275 $225 $195

* ***American Pistol Compact Pro*** – 9mm Para. or .45 ACP cal., one-piece, high performance glass-filled nylon frame, 3.55 or 3.75 in. barrel, 10 or 17 (9mm Para. only) shot mag., includes two nickel-Teflon plated steel magazines, stainless steel slide with black Nitride finish, pre-tensioned striker system, short takeup trigger, Novak LoMount Carry 3-dot sights, modular wrap-around grips, integrated trigger safety, ambidextrous slide stop and mag. release, Picatinny rail, 28.6 oz. New 2017.

MSR $579 $500 $435 $375 $335 $275 $225 $195

GRADING - PPGS™	100%	98%	95%	90%	80%	70%	60%	LAST MSR

AMERICAN PISTOL COMPETITION – 9mm Para. cal., striker fired, 5 in. stainless steel competition barrel, two nickel-Teflon plated steel 17 shot mags., ported stainless steel slide with top of slide serrations, fiber optic front and adj. target rear sights, one-piece glass-filled Nylon grip frame, ergonomic wrap-around grip module, integrated trigger safety, Mil-Std 1913 Picatinny rail, black Nitride finish, 34.1 oz. New 2020.

MSR $579	$500	$435	$375	$335	$275	$225	$195	

AR-556 PISTOL – 5.56 NATO, .350 Legend (new 2020), or .300 AAC Blackout cal., carbine or pistol (.300 Blackout and .350 Legend) length gas system, 9 1/2 (.350 Legend only, new 2020) or 10 1/2 in. cold hammer forged chrome moly threaded barrel with flash suppressor, 5 (.350 Legend) or 30 shot Magpul PMAG, adj. SB Tactical SBA3 Pistol Stabilizing Brace, 7075-T6 forged aluminum flat-top upper receiver with forward assist, dust cover, and brass deflector, 9 in. free float handguard with M-LOK attachment, integral QD sling sockets, Type III hardcoat anodized black or American Flag Cerakote (new 2020) finish, 6.2 lbs. New 2019.

MSR $899	$675	$525	$475	$425	$400	$375	$325	

Add $50 for .350 Legend (new 2020) or .300 AAC Blackout cal.
Add $50 for American Flag Cerakote finish (new 2020).

EC9s – 9mm Para. cal., striker fired, evolutionary replacement for the LC9/LC380 series, Black, Purple (new mid-2019), FDE (new mid-2019), Turquoise (new mid-2019), or Gray (new mid-2019) glass-filled nylon grip frame, 3.12 in. blued alloy steel barrel, 7 shot mag., integral sights, black oxide or aluminum Cerakote (new mid-2019) slide finish, 17.2 oz. New 2018.

MSR $299	$250	$220	$190	$170	$140	$115	$95	

Add $20 for FDE or Gray frame with black oxide slide finish (new mid-2019).
Add $30 for Purple or Turquoise frame with aluminum Cerakote slide finish (new mid-2019).
Add $30 for Hogue Beavertail HandALL grip sleeve with Cobblestone texturing, finger grooves, and gentle palm swells (new late 2020).

* ***EC9s with IWB Holster*** – 9mm Para. cal., striker fired, black glass-filled nylon grip frame, 3.12 in. alloy steel barrel, 7 shot mag., finger grip extension floorplate, integral sights, includes polymer IWB holster, black oxide barrel and slide finish, 17.2 oz. Mfg. 2019-2020.

	$275	$240	$200	$185	$150	$125	$100	*$319*

LCP (LIGHTWEIGHT COMPACT PISTOL) – .380 ACP cal., DAO, black, Toxic camo (mfg. 2018-2019), or Harvest Moon camo (mfg. 2018-2019) glass filled nylon frame with molded checkering, 2 3/4 in. barrel, 6 or 7 (mfg. 2013-2019) shot mag., blued steel slide, bobbed hammer, fixed sights, Lasermax Centerfire laser (mfg. 2012-2014), Crimson Trace Laserguard (mfg. 2011-2016), or Viridian E-Series red laser (new 2016), black Ruger logos inset in grip panels, includes external locking device, pocket holster, 9.65-10 oz. New 2008.

MSR $259	$220	$195	$165	$150	$120	$100	$85	

Add $90 for Viridian E-Series red laser (new 2016).
Add $170 for Crimson Trace Laserguard (mfg. 2011-2016).
Add $70 for Lasermax Centerfire laser (mfg. 2012-2014).
Add $40 for Toxic camo (mfg. 2018-2019) or Harvest Moon camo (mfg. 2018-2019) glass filled nylon frame.

* ***LCP Stainless*** – .380 ACP cal., DAO, 2 3/4 in. barrel, 7 shot mag., stainless steel slide, fixed front and rear sights, black glass-filled nylon grip frame, brushed stainless (disc. 2016) or matte stainless finish, 9.65 oz. Mfg. 2014-2016, reintroduced 2019 with skeletonized aluminum trigger and "chevron" slide serrations.

MSR $299	$250	$220	$185	$160	$125	$115	$90	

* ***LCP 10th Anniversary Limited Edition*** – .380 ACP cal., one-piece glass-filled nylon checkered grip frame, 2 3/4 in. alloy steel barrel with blued finish, 6 shot mag., stainless steel slide with forward cocking serrations, aluminum skeletonized trigger, integral sights, "Tenth Anniversary" laser engraving to commemorate the anniversary of the LCP pistol introduction and "chevron" slide serrations, 9.6 oz. Mfg. 2019 only.

	$250	$220	$185	$160	$125	$115	$90	*$299*

* ***LCP With American Flag*** – .380 ACP cal., glass-filled Nylon textured grip frame, 2 3/4 in. barrel with black oxide finish, 6 shot mag., steel slide with American Flag Cerakote finish, integral sights, includes finger grip extension floorplate, 9.6 oz. New 2020.

MSR $289	$250	$220	$190	$170	$140	$115	$95	

GRADING - PPGS™	100%	98%	95%	90%	80%	70%	60%	LAST MSR

* ***LCP with IWB Holster*** – .380 Auto cal., black high-performance glass filled nylon frame, 2 3/4 in. alloy steel barrel, 6 shot, finger grip extension floorplate, recessed hammer, fixed front and rear sights are integral to the slide, includes IWB holster, blued slide and barrel finish, 9.6 oz. Mfg. 2019-2020.

	$235	$200	$175	$160	$125	$115	$90	*$279*

LCP CUSTOM – .380 ACP cal., 2 3/4 in. barrel, blued alloy steel slide, 6 shot mag., photo luminescent front and drift adj. rear sights, polished stainless steel guide rod, wide red anodized skeletonized aluminum trigger, finger grip extension mag. floorplate, black glass-filled nylon grips, 9.75 oz. Mfg. 2015-2016.

	$225	$195	$170	$155	$125	$100	$80	*$269*

LCP II – .380 ACP cal., black, Toxic camo (mfg. 2018-2019), or Harvest Moon camo (mfg. 2018-2019) high-performance glass-filled nylon grip frame, 2 3/4 in. alloy steel barrel, 6 or 7 (new 2019)shot mag., hammer recessed within slide, single action trigger, fixed front and rear sights, textured grip, with or w/o Viridian E-Series red laser, includes pocket holster, finger grip extension floorplate, blued finish, 10.6 oz. New late 2016.

MSR $349	$295	$275	$235	$200	$165	$125	$100	

Add $50 for 7 shot mag. (new 2019).
Add $50 for Toxic camo (mfg. 2018-2019) or Harvest Moon camo (mfg. 2018-2019) glass-filled nylon grip frame.
Add $90 for Viridian E-Series red laser (new mid-2017).

LCP II LITE RACK – .22 LR cal., Secure Action, black high-performance glass-filled Nylon grip frame, 2 3/4 in. stainless steel barrel, 10 shot mag. and mag. loader, alloy steel slide with black oxide finish, recessed hammer, fixed front and rear sights, black textured grips with or w/o Hogue HandALL Grip Sleeve (new 2021), manual safety, features the Lite Rack system, satin stainless finish, 11.2 oz. New 2020.

MSR $349	$295	$275	$235	$200	$165	$125	$100	

Add $20 for Hogue HandALL Grip Sleeve (new 2021).
Add $100 for Viridian E-Series green laser (new 2021).

LC9 – 9mm Para. cal., DAO, 3.12 in. barrel, alloy steel slide, blue finish, black glass filled nylon grip frame, 7 or 9 (new 2013) shot mag., 3-dot fixed front and adj. rear sights, slightly larger (less than 1 in. in both height and width) than the LCP, finger grip extension, loaded chamber indicator, includes soft case, optional Lasermax Centerfire laser (new 2012) or Crimson Trace Lasergrips, 17.1 oz. Mfg. 2011-2014.

	$375	$335	$275	$240	$215	$195	$180	*$449*

Add $80 for Lasermax Centerfire laser (mfg. 2012-2014).
Add $180 for Crimson Trace "Laserguard" laser (mfg. 2013-2014).

* ***LC9s*** – 9mm Para. cal., SFO, 3.12 in. barrel, alloy steel slide, black glass-filled nylon checkered grip frame, 7 shot mag., adj. 3-dot or HiViz Lightwave fiber optic (mfg. 2017 only) sights, finger grip extension floorplate, integrated trigger safety, manual safety, and magazine disconnect, compatible with all existing LC9 accessories, including lasers, holsters and extended 9 shot mag., black oxide finish, 17.2 oz. Mfg. mid-2014-2017, reintroduced 2021.

MSR $529	$450	$395	$340	$300	$250	$200	$175	

Add $20 for HiViz Lightwave fiber optic sights (mfg. 2017).

* ***LC9s Pro*** – 9mm Para. cal., SFO, 3.12 in. barrel, alloy steel slide, blue finish, black glass-filled nylon grip frame with aggressive texturing, 7 shot mag., adj. 3-dot sights, finger grip extension mag. floorplate, visual loaded chamber view port, internal striker blocker, internal trigger safety, compatible with all existing LC9 accessories, including lasers, holsters and extended 9 shot mag., includes soft case, and one 7 shot mag., 17.2 oz. Mfg. 2015-2017.

	$390	$335	$275	$240	$215	$185	$165	*$479*

* ***LC9s Stainless*** – 9mm Para. cal., striker fired action, 3.12 in. barrel, 7 shot mag., stainless steel slide, adj. 3-dot sights, finger grip extension, black glass filled nylon grip frame, finger grip extension, includes soft case, loaded chamber indicator, brushed stainless slide and blued alloy steel barrel finish, 17.2 oz. Mfg. 2017 only.

	$400	$350	$300	$250	$225	$200	$175	*$499*

Add $20 for HiViz Lightwave fiber optic sights.

LC380 – .380 ACP cal., DAO, 3.12 in. barrel, alloy steel slide and barrel, blued finish, 7 shot mag., black glass-filled checkered nylon grip frame, adj. 3-dot sights, Crimson Trace Laserguard Laser (mfg. 2014-2016) or LaserMax Centerfire (mfg. 2014 only), internal lock, manual safety, magazine disconnect, loaded chamber indicator, finger grip extension mag. floorplate, includes one 7 shot mag. and soft case, 17.2 oz. New 2013.

MSR $539	$460	$400	$345	$315	$255	$215	$175	

Add $190 for Crimson Trace Laserguard Laser (mfg. 2014-2016).
Add $80 for Lasermax Centerfire laser (mfg. 2014 only).

GRADING - PPGS™	100%	98%	95%	90%	80%	70%	60%	LAST MSR

P85 – 9mm Para. cal., DA/SA, 4 1/2 in. barrel, aluminum frame with steel slide, 3-dot fixed sights, 15 shot mag., oversized trigger, polymer grips, matte black finish, 2 lbs. Mfg. 1987-1990.

$350 $295 $265 $235 $215 $200 $185 *$410*

Subtract $30 if without case and extra mag.

Any P85 models without the "MKIIR" stamp on either the left or right side of the safety must be returned to the factory for a free safety modification.

* ***KP85*** – stainless variation of the P85. Mfg. 1990 only.

$375 $315 $280 $230 $200 $165 $140 *$452*

Subtract $30 if without case and extra mag.

Variants included a decocking or double action only version at no extra charge. Any KP85 models without the "MKIIR" stamp on either the left or right side of the safety must be returned to the factory for a free safety modification.

P85 MARK II – 9mm Para. cal., DA/SA, 4 1/2 in. barrel, aluminum frame with steel slide, 3-dot fixed sights, 15 shot mag., ambidextrous safety beginning in 1991, oversized trigger, polymer grips, matte black finish, 2 lbs. Mfg. 1990-1992.

$350 $295 $265 $235 $215 $200 $185 *$410*

Subtract $30 if without case and extra mag.

* ***KP85 Mark II*** – stainless variation of the P85. Mfg. 1990-1992.

$375 $315 $280 $230 $200 $165 $140 *$452*

Subtract $30 if without case and extra mag.

P89 – 9mm Para. cal., DA/SA, improved variation of the P85 Mark II, 10 (C/B 1994) or 15 (new late 2005) shot mag., ambidextrous safety or decocker (Model P89D), blue finish, 32 oz. Mfg. 1992-2007.

$380 $330 $280 $250 $215 $200 $185 *$475*

Variants were available in a decocking (P89DC) or double action only (P-89DAO, disc. 2004) version at no extra charge.

KP89 STAINLESS – stainless variation of the P89, also available in double action only (disc. 2004). Mfg. 1992-2009.

$425 $360 $305 $250 $215 $200 $185 *$525*

Add $45 for convertible 7.65mm Luger cal. barrel (Model KP89X, approx. 5,750 mfg. during 1994 only).

P90 – .45 ACP cal., DA/SA, similar to KP90 Stainless, except has blue finish, 8 shot mag., 33 1/2 oz. Disc. 2010.

$475 $395 $335 $265 $215 $200 $185 *$591*

Add $50 for Tritium night sights (disc. 2006).

P90 models were produced in a variety of models for law enforcement or government contracts and will be found with any combination of safety model, decocker or double action only with fingergroove tactical rubber grip and/or Tritium night sights.

KP90 STAINLESS – .45 ACP cal., DA/SA 4 1/2 in. barrel, oversized trigger, aluminum frame with stainless steel slide, 8 shot single column mag., KP90 or decocking (KP90D), polymer grips, 3-dot fixed sights, ambidextrous safety began approx. ser. no. 660-12800. Mfg. 1991-2010.

$495 $415 $360 $295 $250 $225 $200 *$636*

Add $50 for Tritium night sights (disc. 2006).

KP90 models were produced in a variety of models for law enforcement or government contracts and will be found with any combination of safety model, decocker or double action only with fingergroove tactical rubber grip and/or Tritium night sights.

KP91 STAINLESS – .40 S&W cal., similar to Model KP90 Stainless, except is not available with external safety and has 11 shot double column mag. Mfg. 1991-1994.

$385 $335 $295 $240 $210 $180 $155 *$489*

This model was available in a decocking variation (KP91D) or double action only (KP91DAO). Approx. 39,600 of all models were mfg. before being discontinued in favor of the tapered slide KP944 model.

P93 CHICAGO POLICE SPECIAL CONTRACT – produced in the late 1990s for a Chicago Police Department contract, this blued stainless P93 was ordered with a special P89M rollmark on the slide so that those who were concerned about having a "compact" pistol would not be alerted to the fact that it was indeed a P93. Extremely rare in civilian hands.

Extreme rarity precludes accurate pricing on this model, and should be examined for authenticity. NIB specimens have been noted at $550.

GRADING - PPGS™	100%	98%	95%	90%	80%	70%	60%	LAST MSR

KP93 STAINLESS – 9mm Para. cal., compact variation with 3 9/10 in. tilting barrel - link actuated, matte blue or REM (mfg. 1996 only) finish, 3-dot sights, 10 (C/B 1994) or 15* shot mag., available with DA/SA ambidextrous decocker action or DAO, 31 oz. Mfg. 1994-2004.

$450	$370	$315	$260	$220	$200	$185	*$575*

Add $50 for tritium night sights.

KP93 models were produced in a variety of models for law enforcement or government contracts and will be found with any combination of decocker model or double action only with fingergroove tactical rubber grip and/or Tritium night sights.

P93D BLUE – similar to KP93 Stainless, except has blue finish, compact model, ambidextrous decocker, 31 oz. Mfg. 1998-2004.

$395	$330	$285	$240	$215	$200	$185	*$495*

Add $50 for Tritium night sights.

P93 models were produced in a variety of models for law enforcement or government contracts and will be found with any combination of decocker model or double action only with fingergroove tactical rubber grip and/or Tritium night sights.

* ***P94/KP94 w/Integral Tac-Star Laser Sight*** – 9mm Para. cal., 10 (C/B 1994) or 15* shot mag., integral Tac-Star laser sight, tritium night sights, ambidextrous safety, ambidextrous decocker, or double action only. Mfg. 1994 only.

$650	$575	$495	$440	$360	$295	$225	

Add $50 for Tritium night sights.

These factory laser sighted pistol models were also produced in any combination with fingergroove tactical rubber grip and/or Tritium night sights. Some were also produced with Ruger's "REM" finish. Reportedly 1,836 made total of all models.

KP94 STAINLESS – 9mm Para. or .40 S&W cal., available with ambidextrous safety, matte stainless or REM (mfg. 1996 only) finish, DA/SA ambidextrous decocker action or DAO, 10 (C/B 1994), or 15* (9mm Para.) shot mag., 33 oz. Mfg. 1994-2004.

$450	$370	$315	$260	$220	$200	$185	*$575*

Add $50 for Tritium night sights.

KP94 models have been produced in a variety of models for law enforcement or government contracts and will be found with any combination of safety model, decocker or double action only with fingergroove tactical rubber grip and/or Tritium night sights.

P94 BLUE – similar to KP94 Stainless, except has blue finish. Mfg. 1998-2004.

$395	$330	$285	$240	$215	$200	$185	*$495*

Add $50 for Tritium night sights.

P94 models have been produced in a variety of models for law enforcement or government contracts and will be found with any combination of safety model, decocker or double action only with fingergroove tactical rubber grip and/or Tritium night sights.

P95PR (P95) – 9mm Para. cal., available in DA/SA ambidextrous decocker (D/DPR suffix), ambidextrous safety, or DAO configuration (DAO suffix, mfg. 1996-2004), polymer frame, 3.9 in. barrel, fixed sights, blue finish, 10 or 15 (new late 2005) shot mag., lower Picatinny rail became standard in 2006, (non-Picatinny rail models discontinued 2005), 27 oz. Mfg. 1996-2013.

$320	$275	$235	$195	$165	$150	$135	*$399*

Add $50 for Tritium night sights (disc. 2006).

During 2006, this model's nomenclature changed from P95 to P95PR to reflect the Picatinny style rail.

P95 models have been produced in a variety of models for law enforcement or government contracts and will be found with any combination of safety model, decocker or double action only with fingergroove tactical rubber grip and/or Tritium night sights. The P95DAO double action only model was disc. 2004.

KP95PR STAINLESS (KP95) – stainless variation of Model P95 and P95PR. Mfg. 1997-2013.

$355	$310	$250	$200	$175	$140	$120	*$439*

Add $50 for Tritium night sights.

During 2006, this model's nomenclature changed from KP95 to KP95PR to reflect the Picatinny style rail. Non-Picatinny rail models were disc. 2005. KP95 models have been produced in a variety of models for law enforcement or government contracts, and will be found in any combination of safety model, decocker, or double action only with fingergroove tactical rubber grips and/or Tritium night sights. The KP95DAO double action only model was disc. 2004.

GRADING - PPGS™	100%	98%	95%	90%	80%	70%	60%	LAST MSR

P97D – .45 ACP cal., DA/SA, ambidextrous decocker, 8 shot mag., blue finish, 30 1/2 oz. Mfg. 2002-2004.

	$370	$315	$275	$235	$215	$200	$185	*$460*

Add $50 for Tritium night sights.

KP97 STAINLESS – .45 ACP cal., similar to KP95 Stainless, except has 8 shot mag., 27 oz. Mfg. 1999-2004.

	$395	$315	$265	$235	$215	$200	$185	*$495*

Add $50 for Tritium night sights.

P345PR (P345) – .45 ACP cal., ambidextrous safety or decocker (P345DPR, disc. 2006), DA/SA, black polymer frame with blue steel slide, 4.2 in. barrel, fixed sights, polyurethane grips, slimmer profile frame, 8 shot single column mag., with or w/o (disc. 2006) Picatinny rail, loaded chamber indicator, 29 oz. Mfg. 2005-2012.

	$485	$425	$335	$275	$225	$210	$195	*$599*

KP345PR (KP345) – .45 ACP cal., decocker (KP345DPR, disc. 2006), similar to P345, except has stainless steel slide, Picatinny rail became standard 2007 (KP345PR), 29 oz. Mfg. 2005-2012.

	$515	$440	$345	$280	$230	$210	$195	*$639*

P944 – .40 S&W cal., similar to P94, ambidextrous safety, blue finish, 34 oz. Mfg. 1999-2010.

	$445	$360	$300	$245	$215	$200	$185	*$557*

Add $50 for tritium night sights (disc. 2006).

This model has been produced in many versions for law enforcement or government contracts and will be found with any combination of safety type, decocker, or double action only, fingergroove tactical rubber grip, and/or Tritium night sights.

KP944 STAINLESS – similar to P944, except is stainless steel, also available as decocker (KP944D). Mfg. 1999-2010.

	$500	$400	$345	$275	$230	$195	$170	*$647*

Add $50 for tritium night sights (disc. 2006).

This model has been produced in many versions for law enforcement or government contracts and will be found with any combination of safety type, decocker, or double action only, fingergroove tactical rubber grip, and/or Tritium night sights. The KP944DAO double action only model was disc. 2004.

PC CHARGER – 9mm Para. cal., dead blow action, 6 1/2 in. cold hammer forged threaded barrel with blued finish, 10 or 17 shot mag., flared mawell, interchangeable magwells for use with Ruger or Glock mags., aluminum alloy receiver, no sights, ergonomic pistol grip with extended trigger reach, aluminum billet receiver with integrated rear Picatinny rail, glass-filled polymer chassis system, CNC-milled handguard with M-LOK compatible slots, reversible charging handle, Type III hardcoat anodized finish, 5.2 lbs. New 2020.

MSR $799	$680	$595	$510	$460	$375	$300	$250	

RUGER-57 – 5.7x28mm cal., Secure Action fire control, textured ergonomic frame, 4.94 in. alloy steel barrel w/black Nitride finish, two 20 shot steel mags., fiber optic front and adj. rear sights, 1911-style ambi manual safety, all steel slide is drilled and tapped, Picatinny rail, black oxide finish, 24.5 oz. New 2020.

MSR $799	$700	$595	$510	$460	$375	$300	$250	

SECURITY-9 – 9mm Para. cal., 4 in. barrel, 1:10 twist, 10 or 15 shot mag., alloy steel slide, internal hammer, drift adj. 3-dot sights, with or w/o Viridian E red laser sight (new 2019), black high performance glass-filled nylon textured grip frame or Hogue grip sleeve (new 2019), bladed trigger safety/external manual safety, front cocking serrations, aluminum chassis with full-length guide rails, blued finish, 23.8-24.5 oz. New 2018.

MSR $379	$325	$285	$245	$220	$180	$150	$125	

Add $20 for Hogue grip sleeve (new 2019).

Add $60 for Viridian E-Series red laser (new 2019).

* ***Security-9 Compact*** – 9mm Para. cal., compact frame, 3.42 in. alloy steel barrel, 1:10 twist, 10 shot mag., drift adj. 3-dot sights, with or w/o Viridian E red laser sight (new mid-2019), high-performance glass-filled nylon textured grip frame or Hogue grip sleeve (new late 2019), integrated trigger safety, front cocking serrations, blued finish, 21.9 oz. New 2019.

MSR $379	$325	$285	$245	$220	$180	$150	$125	

Add $20 for Hogue grip sleeve (new late 2019).

Add $60 for Viridian E red laser sight (new mid-2019).

GRADING - PPGS™	100%	98%	95%	90%	80%	70%	60%	LAST MSR

SECURITY-9 PRO – 9mm Para. cal., striker fired, glass-filled Nylon textured grip frame, 4 in. barrel, 15 shot mag., alloy steel slide and barrel, steel Tritium sights, integrated trigger safety, front cocking serrations, blued finish, 23.8 oz. New late 2019.

MSR $549	$470	$410	$350	$320	$260	$215	$175	

* ***Security-9 Compact Pro*** – 9mm Para. cal., striker fired, glass-filled Nylon textured grip frame, 3.42 in. alloy steel barrel, 10 shot mag., steel Tritium sights, integrated trigger safety, full-length guide rails, front cocking serrations, blued finish, 21.9 oz. New late 2019.

MSR $549	$470	$410	$350	$320	$260	$215	$175	

SR9 – 9mm Para. cal., SFO, semi-double action trigger pull, 4 1/8 in. barrel, 10 or 17 shot mag., reversible backstrap, low profile 3-dot sights, glass filled nylon frame, choice of black stainless (disc.), brushed stainless steel, alloy steel/Nitridox Pro Black (SR9B Model, disc.), alloy steel/Black Nitride, or OD Green (mfg. 2009-2010), Picatinny rail, ambidextrous safety, 26 1/2 oz. Mfg. late 2007-2018.

	$475	$415	$350	$315	$275	$240	$210	*$569*

Note that all SR9 models serial numbered 330-29999 and earlier are subject to a factory recall at no charge. If your pistol has not yet had the new parts installed, please contact Sturm, Ruger & Company at 1-800-784-3701 or email SR9Recall@ruger.com and they will provide you with shipping instructions.

* ***SR9C*** – 9mm Para. cal., similar to the Model SR9, except has compact frame and 3 1/2 in. barrel, stainless steel/brushed stainless, alloy/Nitridox Pro Black (disc.), or alloy steel/black Nitride slide finish, 10 or 17 shot mag., adj. 3-dot sights, 23.4 oz. Mfg. mid-2010-2018.

	$475	$415	$350	$315	$275	$240	$210	*$569*

9E – 9mm Para. cal., 4.14 in. barrel, 10 or 17 shot mag., fixed 3-dot sights, black glass-filled nylon grip frame, reversible back strap, integral accessory mounting rail, 27.2 oz. Mfg. 2015-2017.

	$365	$315	$280	$260	$240	$220	$195	*$459*

SR40 – .40 S&W cal., hammerless SFO, 10 or 15 shot mag., 4.14 in. barrel, alloy or stainless steel slide with brushed stainless or Nitridox Pro Black finish, adj. 3-dot sights, black glass filled nylon grips, reversible backstrap, integral mounting rail, ambidextrous thumb safety, loaded chamber indicator, includes two mags., 27 1/4 oz. Mfg. 2011-2018.

	$475	$415	$350	$315	$275	$240	$210	*$569*

* ***SR40C*** – .40 S&W cal., similar to SR40, except has compact frame, 3 1/2 in. barrel, brushed stainless or Nitridox Pro Black finish, 9 or 15 shot mag., adj. 3-dot sights, 23.4 oz. Mfg. mid-2011-2018.

	$475	$415	$350	$315	$275	$240	$210	*$569*

SR45 – .45 ACP cal., 4 1/2 in. barrel, 10 shot mag., black glass -filled nylon grip frame, adj. 3-dot sights, choice of brushed stainless slide or alloy steel with black Nitride finish, includes two magazines, 30.15 oz. Mfg. 2013-2018.

	$475	$415	$350	$315	$275	$240	$210	*$569*

SR1911 – .45 ACP cal., patterned after the Colt M1911 Series 70, SA, 5 in. barrel, supplied with one 7 and one 8 shot stainless steel mag., extended mag. release, matte stainless steel frame and slide, oversized ejection port, bobbed hammer, skeletonized trigger, Novak 3-dot adj. sights, diamond checkered cocobolo grips with silver Ruger medallion inserts, oversized beavertail grip safety, extended thumb safety, standard recoil guide system, rear slide serrations, 39 oz. New mid-2011.

MSR $939	$800	$700	$600	$550	$440	$360	$300	

* ***SR1911 Commander*** – .45 ACP cal., Commander style, similar to SR-1911, except has 4 1/4 in. barrel, 7 shot mag., 36.4 oz. New 2013.

MSR $939	$800	$700	$600	$550	$440	$360	$300	

* ***SR1911 Competition*** – 9mm Para. or .45 ACP (new 2019) cal., Competition style, black Nitride stainless steel grip frame, 5 in. barrel, 8 (.45 ACP) or 10 (9mm Para.) shot mag., stainless steel slide with two-tone finish (black Nitride and stainless), match trigger, undercut trigger guard, fiber optic front sight and adj. serrated rear target sight, Hogue Piranha (9mm Para.) or textured (.45 ACP) G10 grip panels, ambidextrous safety, extended mag. release, forged slide stop and integral plunger tube, includes fitted hard case, two 10 shot competition mags., Ruger Custom Shop Certificate of Authenticity, challenge coin, cleaning cloth, gun peg, and decal, 41 oz. Mfg. by Ruger Custom Shop beginning 2018.

MSR $2,299	$2,050	$1,800	$1,550	$1,400	$1,150	$950	$700	

Add $200 for 9mm Para. cal.

GRADING - PPGS™	100%	98%	95%	90%	80%	70%	60%	LAST MSR

* ***SR1911 Lightweight Commander-Style*** – 9mm Para. (new 2016) or .45 ACP cal., aluminum grip frame with black or gray anodized finish, 4 1/4 in. stainless steel barrel, 7 or 9 (9mm Para. only) shot mag., stainless steel slide with low-glare finish, oversized ejection port and extended mag. release, skeletonized hammer, aluminum skeletonized trigger, drift adj. Novak 3-dot sights, hardwood or black rubberized (9mm, new 2016) grip panels, checkered backstrap, oversized beavertail grip safety, extended thumb safety, standard recoil guide system, rear slide serrations, includes two stainless steel mags. and soft case, 29.3 oz. New 2015.

MSR $979	$825	$720	$620	$560	$455	$375	$325	

* ***SR1911 Officer-Style*** – 9mm Para. or .45 ACP (new mid-2018) cal., black anodized aluminum or stainless steel (.45 ACP, new mid-2018) frame, 3.6 in. Officer-style barrel, 8 shot mag., stainless steel slide, oversized ejection port, skeletonized hammer, skeletonized trigger, drift adj. Novak 3-dot sights, deluxe checkered G10 grip panels, oversized beavertail grip safety, extended thumb safety, 27.2-31 oz. New 2018.

MSR $979	$825	$720	$620	$560	$455	$375	$325	

* ***SR1911 Officer-Style Custom Shop Model*** – .45 Auto cal., Custom Shop Officer-style 1911, black Nitride-coated stainless steel frame with 25 LPI checkered front strap and mainspring housing, 3.6 in. bull barrel with polished feed ramp, fitted barrel lug, and target crown, 7 shot mag., extended mag. release, hand-fitted stainless steel slide with black Nitride/brushed stainless finish, match trigger, undercut trigger guard, Tritium front sight and fully adj. rear combat sight, deluxe G10 grip panels, beavertail grip safety, ambi safety, inspection port, includes fitted lockable hard case, Ruger Custom Shop Certificate of Authenticity, challenge coin, cleaning cloth, gun peg, and decal, 33 oz. Mfg. late 2019-2020.

	$1,625	$1,425	$1,225	$1,100	$900	$750	$625	*$1,899*

* ***SR1911 Target*** – 9mm Para. (new 2018), 10mm (new mid-2017), or .45 ACP cal., stainless steel slide and frame with low-glare finish, 5 in. stainless steel barrel, 8 shot mag., extended mag. release, oversized ejection port, skeletonized hammer, aluminum skeletonized trigger, Bomar adj. sights, deluxe checkered G10 or black rubberized (new mid-2017) grips, checkered backstrap, oversized beavertail grip safety, extended thumb safety, standard recoil guide system (.45 ACP) or bushingless Nitride finish bull barrel (10mm), satin finished stainless steel, 39 or 40.4 (10mm) or 41.9 (.45 ACP) oz. New mid-2017.

MSR $1,019	$865	$755	$650	$590	$475	$400	$325	

REVOLVERS: SINGLE ACTION, OLD MODELS

These vintage revolvers without a hammer block safety were manufactured between 1953 and 1973, and are chambered in .22 RF and several popular centerfire calibers. There are models and sub-models with variants in the Single-Six, Bearcat, Blackhawk & Super Blackhawk families. The single-shot Hawkeye is considered as part of the Old Model classification. The Old Model or Three Screw Single-Six, Blackhawk and Super Blackhawk models are visually identified apart from the New Model by the presence of three screws on the side of the cylinder frame - the New Model features two pins at the same location.

Ruger offers a free conversion kit that will upgrade the lock work, similar to the New Model, thereby offering the best of both technologies. Ruger will fit these parts-sets at their Service Dept. at no charge and return the original parts to the customer.

If the original parts are not with the revolver, subtract $100 for Single-Six internal parts, $150 for Blackhawk internal parts and $200 for Super Blackhawk internal parts.

SINGLE SIX – .22 LR cal., 4 5/8 (mfg. 1959-1962), 5 1/2 (mfg. 1953-1973), or 9 1/2 (mfg. 1959-1962) in. barrel, fixed sights, checkered rubber or walnut (new 1960) grips, blue finish. Mfg. 1953-1973.

Add $650 for Factory stag XR3 grips on models that apply.

Add $2,500 for Factory ivory XR3 grips on models that apply.

A negotiated premium can be added for examples with S (seconds) or D (duplicate) marking.

Due to large price fluctuations of original two-piece boxed examples, an individual expert appraisal is recommended.

After 1962, only the 5 1/2 gun was available as an LR only model (RSS5W). Walnut grips became standard equipment in 1960 and from 1960 to 1962 hard rubber grips were available only as an option on this model. Genuine stag and ivory grips were also available as an accessory for the XR3 grip frame and due to their rarity, authentication by an expert is necessary. Varnished walnut grips appear at ser. no. 160000. XR3 grip frame changed to XR3-RED in 1962, and was standard with oiled walnut grip panels and fitted with anodized aluminum ejector rod housing (1963).

GRADING - PPGS™	100%	98%	95%	90%	80%	70%	60%	LAST MSR

* ***Single Six Flat Loading Gate*** – 5 1/2 in. barrel only, approx. 62,000 mfg. from 1953-1957. Four variations with ser. no. range 1-62000.

	$1,050	$750	$600	$450	$350	$275	$225	

Add 75% for those serial numbered under 2000 with a non-serrated front sight.

* ***Single Six Round Loading gate*** – with round loading gate, serial numbered up to approximately 194000.

4 5/8 in. bbl. (1959-1962 mfg.)	$1,250	$875	$675	$425	$350	$250	$225	
5 1/2 in. bbl. (1953-1973 mfg.)	$650	$475	$375	$250	$195	$165	$150	
9 1/2 in. bbl. (1959-1962 mfg.)	$1,200	$850	$650	$400	$325	$225	$200	

Add $75 for extra .22 WMR cylinder w (4 5/8 in. bbl., mfg. 1961-1962, ser. no. range 173000 to 189000) or (9 1/2 in. bbl., mfg. 1961-1962, ser. no. range 164000 to 193700).

1953-1962 mfg. ser. no. range for the 5 1/2 in. barrel is 62000-194000. 4 5/8 in. barrel ser. no. range is 128500-187400. 9 1/2 in. barrel ser. no. range is 139030-193700.

1963-1973 mfg. ser. no. range for the 5 1/2 in. barrel is 194000-196942, 244020-244320, 342700-approx. 500430, 800000-833352, 20-00000-20-99999, and 21-00000 - 21-56105.

Factory letter mandatory as RSS4X, RSS5X, or RSS9X.

* ***Single Six Factory Engraved Models*** – factory cased with varnished walnut grip panels, several groups of engraving patterns, each commanding a separate valuation, considered the most desirable of entire SA line. Except for 22 guns engraved in Spain, all others engraved by Charles H. Jerred, limited to only 260 examples. Mfg. 1954-1958.

Subtract $1,000 if w/o presentation case.

Add a premium for consecutively numbered pairs that are verified as being shipped together.

» **Spanish Engraved** – ser. nos. 7 and 8, 5,100-5,119.

	$25,000	$21,000	$18,000	N/A	N/A	N/A	N/A	

» **All Blue Engraved** – ser. no. range 24, 4177, 135XX-243XX, 26 mfg.

	$18,000	$15,000	$12,000	N/A	N/A	N/A	N/A	

» **Standard Pattern** – ser. no. ranges 308XX, 355XX, 449XX, 50XXX, and 74XXX, and eight individual guns numbered 75070 to 100955, 210 mfg.

	$11,000	$9,000	$8,000	N/A	N/A	N/A	N/A	

SINGLE SIX .22 MAGNUM – 6 1/2 in. barrel only, serial numbered between 300000-340100, left side of frame rollmarked in two lines with "RUGER SINGLE-SIX WIN. .22RF MAG.CAL." The last few thousand of this variety were fitted with XR3-RED grip frame. Walnut grips became standard equipment in 1960 at about serial number 320000 and from 1960 to 1962 hard rubber grips were available only as an option on this model. Approx. 40,100 mfg. 1959-1962.

	$700	$575	$475	$375	$275	$175	$150	

Add $75 if revolver was originally shipped as a convertible with extra .22 LR cylinder (factory letter mandated for RSSMX designation).

A very few Mag. only Single-Sixes (not magnum marked) were produced after 340200. These are very rare and authentication through factory letter (as RSSMW) is necessary - add $200.

SINGLE SIX CONVERTIBLE – similar to Single Six, except .22 LR and .22 WMR interchangeable cylinders, redesigned grip frame (XR3-Red), wood grips, 4 5/8, 5 1/2, 6 1/2, or 9 1/2 in. barrel with 4 5/8 in. being the rarest. Mfg. 1962-1972.

* ***Single Six Convertible 5 1/2, 6 1/2 in. barrel***

	$575	$475	$350	$225	$175	$150	$125	

Ser. no. range for 5 1/2 in. barrel begins about 194000.

Ser. no. range for 6 1/2 in. barrel begins about 340200.

* ***Single Six Convertible 4 5/8 or 9 1/2 in. barrel***

	$1,200	$700	$600	$500	$350	$250	$175	

Ser. no. range for 4 5/8 in. barrel begins about 428000.

Ser. no. range for 9 1/2 in. barrel begins about 360000.

LIGHTWEIGHT SINGLE SIX – similar to Single Six, except aluminum alloy frame, XR3 grip frame, 4 5/8 in. barrel, 200,000-212,000 serial range, alloy or steel cylinder, black hard rubber grips, steel ejector rod housing. Three variations, 12,530 mfg. 1956-1959.

GRADING - PPGS™	100%	98%	95%	90%	80%	70%	60%	LAST MSR

* ***Lightweight Single Six Tri-color*** – silver colored aluminum cylinder frame, aluminum cylinder with green/brown colored "martin hard coat" finish, ser. no. range 200000-205250.

	$2,100	$1,300	$1,000	$850	$600	$450	$350

* ***Lightweight Single Six Tri-color w/S Marking*** – "S" (seconds) marked (verified), ser. nos. are random, 266 mfg.

	$2,150	$1,600	$1,250	$1,000	$850	$600	$475

Add $250 if the "S" marking on bottom of cylinder frame is ahead of the trigger guard.

The S marking will be found as a serial number suffix or on the bottom of the cylinder frame ahead of the trigger guard. Due to the rarity of this variety, factory authentication as an LWSC is mandatory.

* ***Lightweight Single Six Blue Alloy*** – all blue with black anodized aluminum cylinder frame and alloy cylinder, ser. no. range 205238-207300.

	$2,600	$1,600	$1,200	$1,000	$700	$500	$400

* ***Lightweight Single Six Blue Steel*** – steel cylinder, with black anodized aluminum cylinder frame, ser. no. range 206200-212530.

	$1,100	$900	$700	$600	$500	$400	$300

SUPER SINGLE SIX CONVERTIBLE – similar to Single Six Convertible, except adj. sights. 5 1/2 or 6 1/2 barrel lengths std. 183,170 mfg. 1964-1972.

4 5/8 in. bbl.	$2,500	$2,300	$1,850	$1,500	$1,200	$1,000	$750
5 1/2 in. bbl.	$575	$450	$325	$250	$200	$175	$150
6 1/2 in. bbl.	$575	$450	$325	$250	$200	$175	$150
Nickel plated w/ 6 1/2 in. bbl.	$2,450	$2,200	$1,800	$1,400	$1,000	$850	$500

A negotiated premium can be added for examples with S (seconds) or D (duplicate) marking.

For the 4 5/8 in. and nickel plated examples noted above, factory authentication is necessary for the prices noted above to be applicable.

OLD MODEL BEARCAT – .22 LR cal., 6 shot, 4 in. barrel, black anodized alloy frame, black (73,200-76,400 and 914XX ser. no. range) or brass anodized trigger guard, epoxy resin rosewood grips w/o medallion on early models, models mfg. after 1963 had oiled walnut with insert eagle medallion and anodized aluminum housing, gold tone trigger guard, steel ejector rod housing until 1964, early guns were marked with a letter of the alphabet before the ser. no., 17 oz. Mfg. 1958-1970.

Early Mfg. w/epoxy resin rosewood grips	$725	$575	$475	$425	$325	$275	$225
w/alphabetical prefix	$875	$650	$525	$450	$350	$300	$250
Later Mfg. w/walnut grips	$650	$425	$350	$300	$250	$180	$175
Black trigger guard variation (73,200-76,400 and 914XX ser. no. range)	$2,500	$1,800	$1,200	$975	$775	$635	$495

A negotiated premium can be added for examples with S (seconds) or D (duplicate) marking.

Numerous variations exist within this model incorporating production changes.

Total production was 143,195 guns.

OLD MODEL SUPER BEARCAT – similar to Bearcat, except steel frame, made with brass anodized aluminum trigger guard (early model), or blue steel guard, 25 oz. Mfg. 1971-74.

	$650	$475	$375	$275	$225	$200	$175

A negotiated premium can be added for examples with S (seconds) marking.

Total production was 64,420 guns.

BLACKHAWK "FLATTOP" – .357 Mag. cal., 6 shot, 4 5/8 (27,200 mfg.), 6 1/2 (14,200 mfg.), or 10 (1,300 mfg.) in. barrel, flat-top cylinder frame, adj. sight, blue, black rubber or varnished walnut grip panels (became standard at approx. ser. no. 30000). Approx. 42,690 mfg. between 1955-1962 in ser. no. range 1-42689.

4 5/8 in. bbl.	$1,400	$950	$800	$750	$550	$400	$325
6 1/2 in. bbl.	$1,150	$900	$750	$550	$400	$300	$225
10 in. bbl.	$3,850	$2,150	$1,750	$1,250	$900	$750	$650

Add $650 for Factory stag grips.

Add $2,500 for Factory ivory grips.

A negotiated premium can be added for examples with S (seconds) or D (duplicate) marking.

GRADING - PPGS™	100%	98%	95%	90%	80%	70%	60%	LAST MSR

BLACKHAWK – .30 Carbine, .357 Mag., .41 Mag., or .45 LC cal., this model is the 1962 variation with protected rear sight, ramp front sight, and 4 5/8 (.357 Mag., .41 Mag. or .45 Colt), 6 1/2 (.357 Mag. or .41 Mag.), or 7 1/2 (.30 Carbine or .45 LC) in. barrel.

.30 Carbine cal.	$900	$700	$550	$400	$350	$275	$225
.357 Mag. cal.	$575	$425	$400	$350	$300	$250	$200
.357 Mag. cal. w/brass frame (570 mfg.)	$1,750	$1,425	$1,000	$750	$500	$400	$300
.41 Mag. cal.	$900	$650	$600	$550	$475	$400	$300
.41 Mag. cal. w/brass frame 4 5/8 in. bbl. (62 mfg.)	$6,800	$5,150	$3,750	$2,750	$2,100	$1,700	$1,300
.41 Mag. cal. w/brass frame 6 1/2 in. bbl. (160 mfg.)	$3,250	$2,600	$1,800	$1,200	$950	$650	$500
.45 Colt cal.	$1,150	$950	$750	$525	$400	$350	$300
.45 Colt cal. w/brass frame (620 mfg.)	$2,250	$1,800	$1,500	$1,000	$750	$500	$425

A negotiated premium can be added for examples with S (seconds) or D (duplicate) marking.

Note that the values listed above for revolvers with brass grip frames must be for guns that have been factory authenticated.

Total production was 32,985 for .30 carbine (mfg. 1967-1973), 245,059 for .357 Mag. (mfg. 1962-1973), 39,371 for .41 Mag. (mfg. 1965-1973), and 23,030 for .45 LC (mfg. 1970-1973).

BLACKHAWK CONVERTIBLE – similar to Blackhawk, with extra cylinder, .357 Mag. and 9mm Para., or .45 LC and .45 ACP cals.

.357 Mag./9mm Para. cal.	$950	$675	$550	$350	$275	$225	$175
.45 LC/.45 ACP cal.	$1,250	$950	$750	$650	$550	$500	$400

Add $700 for 4 5/8 in. bbl. .357/9mm Para. with non-prefix serial number (103000 to 141000). Factory authentication necessary.

Add $325 for 6 1/2 in. bbl. with non-prefix ser. no. (103000-141000).

Add $200 for .45 Colt/.45 ACP with 4 5/8 in. barrel.

This model did not feature a brass grip frame.

BLACKHAWK FLATTOP .44 MAGNUM – similar to .357 Mag. cal. Blackhawk Flat-top, except heavier frame and cylinder, .44 Mag., 6 1/2 (25,660 mfg.), 7 1/2 (2,700 mfg.), or 10 in. (1,500 mfg.) barrel. 29,860 guns mfg. between 1956-1963 in ser. no. range 1-29860.

6 1/2 in. bbl.	$1,650	$1,100	$950	$750	$475	$325	$250
7 1/2 in. bbl.	$2,800	$1,750	$1,250	$950	$750	$600	$400
10 in. bbl.	$4,500	$2,500	$1,900	$1,250	$1,000	$800	$650

Add $650 for Factory stag grips.

Add $2,250 for Factory ivory grips.

A negotiated premium can be added for examples with S (seconds) marking.

Distinguishable from Super Blackhawk by fluted cylinder, rounded trigger guard, and lack of protective topstrap ribs to sides of rear sight.

SUPER BLACKHAWK – .44 Mag. cal., 6 1/2 (rare) or 7 1/2 in. barrel, larger "Dragoon" grip frame with square back trigger guard, unfluted cylinder, adj. sights, walnut grips. Mfg. 1959-1972.

7 1/2 in. barrel	$825	$700	$625	$425	$350	$225	$200

*** *Super Blackhawk Early & Other Rare Variations***

Mahogany cased	$1,500	$1,250	$1,000	$850	$750	$650	$550
Long frame cased	$2,850	$2,500	$1,850	$1,500	$1,100	$850	$700
White box cased	$2,750	$2,250	$1,850	$1,500	$1,100	$850	$700
6 1/2 in. bbl. (ser. range 24300-27200)	$1,850	$1,650	$1,450	$1,200	$1,000	$750	$550
Brass frame, Prefix S/N	$1,850	$1,700	$1,250	$1,000	$750	$500	$425

A negotiated premium can be added for examples with S (seconds) or D (duplicate) marking.

Add $3,500 to the Brass frame Super Blackhawk price, if without 80- prefix serial number (serial number range 282xx to 36xxx). Must be factory verified.

Production totals are as follows: mahogany cased (approx. 3,850), long frame cased (approx. 950), white box cased (approx. 7,350, few surviving cases), non-cased (94,360), 6 1/2 in. bbl. (approx. 600), and brass frame (approx. 1,660).

GRADING - PPGS™	100%	98%	95%	90%	80%	70%	60%	LAST MSR

HAWKEYE SINGLE SHOT – .256 Mag. cal., XR3-RED grip frame, round cylinder replaced by rectangular rotating breech block, 8 1/2 in. barrel, blue, oiled walnut grips, adj. sight, barrel tapped for one inch scope base, very rare, 45 oz. 3,043 mfg. Mfg. 1963-64 only.

	$2,950	$2,300	$1,850	$1,500	$1,200	$1,000	$900	

A negotiated premium can be added for examples shipped as factory "second" (only 10 mfg.).

REVOLVERS: SINGLE ACTION, NEW MODELS

The following single actions are known as "New Models." They have 2 pins through the frame and cock without the clicks associated with Ruger's Old Model mechanism. The changeover occurred as a result of incorporating safety features. The "New Models" have a transfer bar similar to those found on modern double action revolvers and do not accidentally discharge if dropped. Manufacture started 1973. During certain years of manufacture, Ruger's changes in production on certain models (calibers, barrel markings, barrel lengths, etc.) have created rare variations that are now considered premium niches. These areas of low manufacture will add premiums to the values listed on standard models. Beginning 1996, Ruger started supplying all New Model revolvers with a case and lock.

From 2007-2012 all blued steel and stainless New Model flat-top single actions and blued steel Super Single Six and Blackhawk models were manufactured with unobtrusive internal lock and checkered black plastic grips (the blue flat-top models were assembled with laminate grips). Beginning mid-2012, Ruger discontinued the use of the unobtrusive internal lock and in 2014 reintroduced wood laminate grips.

SUPER SINGLE SIX "STAR" MODEL – .22 LR cal., so named because of star stamped on bottom of frame, blue or stainless, single cylinder (not convertible). Mfg. 1974-1975 only with 63-ser. no. prefix.

Blue 5 1/2 or 6 1/2 in. bbl.								
	$575	$500	$400	$350	$300	$250	$225	
Blue 9 1/2 in. bbl. (rare)								
	$875	$750	$650	$550	$425	$350	$300	
Blue 4 5/8 in. bbl.(very rare)								
	$1,200	$1,000	$850	$750	$625	$500	$400	
Stainless 5 1/2 or 6 1/2 in. bbl.								
	$600	$500	$415	$375	$305	$250	$195	
Stainless 9 1/2 in. bbl.	$850	$750	$575	$500	$425	$350	$275	
Stainless 4 5/8 in. bbl.(rare)								
	$850	$750	$575	$500	$425	$350	$275	

* ***Super Single Six "Arrow" Model*** – .22 S, L, or LR cal., similar to Star Model, except produced with an arrow stamp (also resembles the shape of a house) on bottom of frame. Blue models only. Models SSR4, SSR5, SSR6, and SSR9. Mfg. 1986 only in serial no. range 261-10000 to 261-32000.

	$575	$500	$450	$375	$310	$260	$200	

Add $100 for 4 5/8 in. or 9 1/2 in. barrel.

NEW MODEL SINGLE SIX .17 HMR (SUPER SINGLE SIX .17 HMR) – .17 HMR cal., 6 shot, 6 1/2 in. barrel with special crown, blue finish, adj. rear sight, smooth rosewood (disc. 2007) or black checkered hard rubber grips, 35 oz. New 2003.

MSR $629	$535	$475	$400	$365	$300	$250	$200	

Add $100 for "Friends of NRA" model NR6-17NRA produced in 2004.

Beginning in 2007, this model was supplied with unobtrusive internal lock and black checkered grips as standard. Beginning in mid-2012, Ruger discontinued the use of the unobtrusive internal lock.

SINGLE SIX .17 HMR, STAINLESS STEEL – .17 HMR cal., 6 shot, 5 1/2 in or 6 1/2 in. barrel with special crown, stainless steel, adj. rear sight, smooth rosewood, red laminate or cocobolo grips (mfg. 2009 to 2011 only).

	$650	$550	$450	$400	$350	$300	$225	

Not more than 200 to 300 of each model produced.

NEW MODEL SINGLE SIX CONVERTIBLE (SUPER SINGLE SIX CONVERTIBLE) – .22 LR cal., includes interchangeable .22 WMR cylinder, 4 5/8, 5 1/2, 6 1/2, or 9 1/2 in. barrel, blue finish, 6 shot, similar to old Super Single Six, except has transfer bar safety, adj. rear sight, walnut (disc.), rosewood (disc.), wood laminate or black checkered hard rubber grips (new 2007), 33 oz. (with 5 1/2 in. barrel). New 1973.

MSR $629	$535	$475	$400	$365	$300	$250	$200	

Beginning in 2007, this model in blue finish was supplied with unobtrusive internal lock and black checkered grips as standard. Beginning mid-2012, Ruger discontinued the use of the unobtrusive internal lock, and reintroduced wood laminate grips in 2014.

GRADING - PPGS™	100%	98%	95%	90%	80%	70%	60%	LAST MSR

* ***Single Six Convertible Stainless Steel*** – .22 LR cal., includes .22 WMR cylinder, stainless steel construction, 4 5/8 (disc. 1976 - rare), 5 1/2, 6 1/2, or 9 1/2 (disc. 1975-rare) in. barrel, 6 shot, walnut grips, ramp front and adj. rear sights, satin stainless finish, 40 oz. Introduced 1974.

MSR $699	$600	$525	$450	$410	$325	$275	$225	
4 5/8 or 9 1/2 in. bbl.	$675	$575	$490	$440	$375	$300	$230	

Add 50% for stainless 4 5/8 in. barrel with "LIBERTY" roll marking, approx. 300 produced.

Add 10% for "Friends of NRA" model KNR6-NRA issue of 750 produced in 2000.

* ***Super Single Six High Gloss Stainless*** – 5 1/2 (disc. 1996) or 6 1/2 in. barrel, features high gloss stainless steel finish. Mfg. 1994-97.

	$450	$350	$275	$150	$120	$110	$95	*$425*

A model with simulated ivory grips (GKNR6-I) was also offered in 1996 for one year only. Last MSR was $425. Add 10% to pricing shown above.

* ***New Model Single Six Convertible w/Vaquero Sights*** – .22 S, L, or LR cal., 4 5/8 (uncatalogued, rare - ajpprox. 1,000 produced), 5 1/2 or 6 1/2 (disc. 2017) in. barrel, 6 shot, fixed Vaquero style sights, black checkered grips, includes interchangeable .22 WMR cylinder, blued finish, approx. 34 oz. New 1994.

MSR $699	$600	$525	$450	$410	$325	$275	$225	
4 5/8 in. bbl.	$625	$600	$500	$400	$375	$275	$225	

* ***Single Six Convertible 50th Anniversary*** – similar to Single Six Convertible with Vaquero style sights, 4 5/8 in. barrel only, cocobolo wood grips, special high polish, and "50th Anniversary 1953-2003" Ruger logo, includes red plastic case. Over 22,000 mfg. 2003 only.

	$450	$350	$300	$200	$150	$140	$125	*$425*

* ***Super Single Six Convertible Stainless Steel w/Vaquero Sights*** – .22 S, L, or LR cal., stainless steel, 4 5/8 (extremely rare!!), 5 1/2, or 6 1/2 in. barrel, fixed Vaquero style sights, black checkered grips. Mfg. 1994-1997, with a few additional revolvers produced through 2011.

	$475	$415	$350	$325	$260	$215	$165	*$415*

Note that extreme rarity of the 4 5/8 in. variation precludes accurate pricing (21 produced, only 5 known). 4,300+ mfg. with 5 1/2 in. barrel and 5,300+ mfg. with 6 1/2 in. barrel.

SUPER SINGLE SIX STAINLESS STEEL HUNTER – .17 HMR (disc. 2006) cal., similar to Super Single Six Stainless Steel, 7 1/2 in. barrel, black laminate grips, integral scope mounts with one inch rings, 45 oz. Mfg. 2004-09.

	$650	$575	$495	$400	$325	$265	$225	*$617*

Note that although this model was last listed in Ruger's 2006 price listings, factory "cleanup" groups continued to be shipped to 2009.

NEW MODEL SINGLE-SIX HUNTER (SUPER SINGLE SIX STAINLESS STEEL HUNTER CONVERTIBLE) – .17 HMR/.17 Mach 2 (rare, mfg. 2005 only), or .22 LR/.22 WMR cal., 7 1/2 in. barrel, 6 shot, stainless steel, bead front, adj. rear sight, black laminate grips, integral scope mounts with one inch rings, satin stainless finish, 45 oz. New 2004.

MSR $879	$750	$650	$550	$500	$400	$350	$285	

Add 60% for .17 HMR/.17 Mach 2 cal. (very rare, only a few hundred produced).

COLORADO CENTENNIAL SUPER SINGLE SIX – similar to Super Single Six Convertible, except produced to commemorate the 100th anniversary of Colorado statehood, 15,000 mfg. 1975 only, includes walnut case with medallion insert, stainless steel grip frame, rosewood grips, both cylinders roll marked with the Colorado Centennial motif, 6 1/2 in. barrel, issue price was $250.

	$650	$450	$300	N/A	N/A	N/A	N/A	*$250*

Although a single example has yet to be uncovered, rumors persist of a few of this model having the "MADE IN THE 200th YEAR OF AMERICAN LIBERTY" rollmark on the barrel in addition to the standard Colorado Centennial/US Bicentennial rollmark and the Sturm, Ruger & Co., Inc. rollmark.

SUPER SINGLE SIX SSM – similar to original Super Single-Six except .32 H&R Mag. cal., 4 5/8, 5 1/2, 6 1/2 or 9 1/2 in. barrel, blue frame, 6 shot, adj. sights, wood grips, 32-35 oz. Mfg. 1984-1994.

	$675	$550	$500	$450	$400	$350	$300	

Add $50 for 4 5/8 or 9 1/2 in. barrel.

Add 10% if frame is marked "SSM" (5-1/2 in. and 6-1/2 in. most common although only three in 4 5/8 in. with this marking were produced).

NEW MODEL SINGLE SIX .32 H&R MAG. W/VAQUERO STYLE SIGHTS – .32 H&R Mag. cal., 4 5/8 in. barrel, case colored frame or high gloss stainless steel (new 2001), 6 shot, choice of steel XR3-RED grip frame or shortened XR3-RED grip frame with faux ivory, bird's head with black Micarta grips (new

GRADING - PPGS™	100%	98%	95%	90%	80%	70%	60%	LAST MSR

2002) or rosewood grips, 32-35 oz. Mfg. 2001-2004, with intermittent "cleanup" quantities produced between 2004-2010.

	$550	$475	$425	$375	$200	$175	$150	*$576*

Add $75 for stainless steel or bird's head grip frame.
Add $40 for faux ivory or black Micarta grips.

SINGLE NINE – .22 WMR cal., 6 1/2 in. barrel, 9 shot, stainless steel finish, Williams adj. fiber optic sights, laminate Gunfighter grips, 39 oz. New 2013.

MSR $699	$600	$525	$450	$410	$325	$275	$225

SINGLE TEN – .22 LR cal., 5 1/2 in. barrel, 10 shot, stainless steel with satin stainless finish, laminate Gunfighter grips, Williams adj. fiber optic sights, 38 oz. New 2012.

MSR $699	$600	$525	$450	$410	$325	$275	$225

SUPER SINGLE SIX BISLEY MODEL .22 LR OR .32 H&R MAG. – .22 LR (mfg. 1986-2017) cal., 6 1/2 in. barrel with fixed (disc. 1987) or adj. sights, available with fluted cylinder (disc. 1987) or unfluted roll marked cylinder (disc. 2006), although small "cleanup" quantities continued to be produced through 2011 and again in 2017, satin blue finish only. .32 H&R Mag. cal. has same features as the .22 LR, fixed (disc. 1989) or adj. sights (disc. 1994), available with fluted cylinder (disc. 1989), or unfluted roll marked cylinders (disc. 1994), Goncalo Alves smooth grips changed to walnut, then rosewood, then red laminate grips during last production.

	$650	$500	$425	$300	$250	$200	$175	*$475*

Add 10% for adj. sights/fluted cylinder combination or fixed sights/roll marked cylinder combination (rare).
Add 50% for .32 H&R Mag. cal. (disc. 1994).

* ***Super Single Six Bisley Stainless Steel*** – .22 LR cal., 6 1/2 in. barrel, 6 shot, stainless steel construction, ramp front and adj. rear sights, laminate grips, satin stainless finish, 40 oz. Only a few hundred mfg. beginning in 2017.

	$675	$525	$425	$300	$250	$200	$175

SUPER SINGLE SIX BISLEY MODEL SHOOTIST – .22 LR cal., special limited edition, stainless steel, 4 5/8 in. barrel, adj. sights, marked "In Memory of Our Friend, Tom Ruger, The Shootists", inscribed with the name of the recipient on backstrap, only 52 or 53 mfg. 1994 in ser. no. range 262-97333 to 263-01864.

	$2,500	$1,800	$1,200	$1,000	$850	$650	$500

NEW BEARCAT – .22 LR cal., frame slightly longer than old Bearcat, engraved non-fluted cylinder, 4 (disc.) or 4.2 (new 2010) in. cold hammer forged barrel, 6 shot, transfer bar hammer block safety, blue finish, smooth rosewood (disc. 2010) or laminate (new 2010) grips, blade front and integral notch rear sights, includes hard plastic case, 24 oz. New 1996.

MSR $639	$575	$475	$400	$365	$300	$250	$210

Add $110 for LR cylinder without firing pin groove (only five known in serial range 93-01966 to 93-11000).

* ***New Bearcat Stainless Steel*** – .22 LR cal., similar to New Bearcat, except is stainless steel. New 2002.

MSR $689	$600	$510	$440	$400	$325	$275	$230

Add $110 for LR cylinder without firing pin groove (approx. 300 produced in error in 2001).

* ***New Bearcat Convertible*** – similar to New Bearcat, except has convertible interchangeable .22 WMR cyl., early production, recalled by the factory. Mfg. 1993-1994 only.

	$2,500	$1,700	$1,250	$1,050	$900	$750	$550

The .22 WMR cylinder was recalled to the factory in 1994. It is estimated that up to 60% of the 1,000 New Bearcat Convertibles produced had their .22 WMR cylinders returned to the factory due to the recall.

NEW BEARCAT 50th ANNIVERSARY – .22 LR cal. only, gold plated trigger guard, cylinder with two gold bands and "RUGER BEARCAT" in gold, gold filled "50TH ANNIVERSARY BEARCAT - 2008" rollmark on barrel, smooth cocobolo grip panels without medallions (reminiscent of original 1958 to 1963 production plastic impregnated rosewood Bearcat panels), "SBC" prefix serial number and special white cardboard packaging with Ruger logo carrying case. Mfg. 2008 only. Only 2,539 produced.

	$850	$675	$625	N/A	N/A	N/A	N/A	*$758*

NEW MODEL BLACKHAWK – .30 Carbine (disc. 1996, reintroduced 1998), .357 Mag., .41 Mag. (disc. 1996, reintroduced 1999), or .45 LC cal., similar to Old Model Blackhawk, 4 5/8 (.357 Mag., .41 Mag., and .45 LC), 5 1/2 (.45 LC only), 6 1/2 (.357 Mag. and .41 Mag. only), or 7 1/2 in. (.30 Carbine and .45 LC only) cold hammer forged barrel, transfer bar safety, adj. sight, alloy grip frame, 6 shot, current mfg. has black

GRADING - PPGS™	100%	98%	95%	90%	80%	70%	60%	LAST MSR

checkered grips, ramp front and adj. rear sights, includes hard plastic case, 40-44 oz. New 1973.

MSR $669	$575	$500	$430	$390	$315	$260	$220	

New Model .357 Mag. Blackhawks are serial numbered 32-00001 on up. New Model .45 LC Blackhawks are serial numbered 46-00001 on up. New Model .30 Carbine Blackhawks are serial numbered 51-00001 on up and the earliest .41 Blackhawks were serial numbered 41-00001 on up only to be included within the 46- prefix beginning in 1980. Note that in 2015, all regular production Blackhawks were merged into the 38- prefix at serial number 38-30081.

Beginning in 2007, this model in blue was supplied with unobtrusive internal lock and black checkered grips as standard. Beginning mid-2012, Ruger discontinued the use of the unobtrusive internal lock and in 2014 reintroduced laminate grip panels.

* ***New Model Blackhawk Bisley*** – .357 Mag (disc. 2006, with factory "cleanup" guns manufactured into 2012), .41 Mag. (disc. 2006 with factory "cleanup" guns mfg. into 2012), or .45 LC cal., 7 1/2 in. barrel, 6 shot mag., incorporated Bisley raked hammer, ramp front and adj. rear sights, longer steel grip frame, goncalo alves (disc.), walnut (disc.), rosewood (disc.), Bisley-style hardwood, or brown laminated (disc.) grips, available with fluted cylinder (disc. 1987) or unfluted rollmarked cylinder, 48-50 oz. Mfg. 1986-2017.

	$775	$650	$575	$525	$450	$350	$300	*$899*

Add 20% for .41 Mag. Cal (with fluted or non-fluted cylinder) or for .45 LC cal. with fluted cylinder.

Note that the fluted models are generally more scarce than the rollmarked cylinder models, especially in .45 LC.

* ***New Model Blackhawk Stainless Steel*** – .327 Fed. Mag. (mfg. 2011-2012), .357 Mag. or .45 LC (mfg. 1993-2009) cal., 4 5/8 (.357 Mag. or .45 LC, disc. 2011), 5 1/2 (.327 Fed. Mag. or .45 LC both disc.), 6 1/2 (.357 Mag. only) or 7 1/2 (.45 LC only, disc. 2009) in. barrel, 6 shot, ramp front, adj. rear sights, hardwood or laminate (disc.) grips, satin stainless finish, 46-48 oz.

MSR $799	$680	$600	$500	$465	$375	$315	$265	

Add 20% for .327 Fed. Mag. cal.

Add approx. 20% for .357 Mag./9mm Para. convertible revolvers with 32-prefix serial number (300 were made in this model).

The 5 1/2 in. .45 LC is very scarce in stainless.

* ***New Model Blackhawk High Gloss Stainless Steel*** – .357 Mag. or .45 LC cal., 4 5/8, 6 1/2 (.357 Mag. only), or 7 1/2 (.45 LC only) in. barrel, features high gloss stainless steel finish. Mfg. 1994-1996 in 37-30xxx to 37-46xxx (.357 Mag.) and 47-59xxx to 47-69xxx (.45 LC) serial number range.

	$725	$635	$550	$495	$400	$325	$250	*$443*

All models are considered rare.

* ***New Model Blackhawk Arizona Ranger Commemorative*** – .45 Colt cal., 4 5/8 in. barrel, stainless steel grip frame. 304 produced in 46-44228 to 46-44550 serial range for the Arizona Rangers in 1979.

	$875	$750	$625	N/A	N/A	N/A	N/A	

NEW MODEL BLACKHAWK 50th ANNIVERSARY MATCHED SET – Includes one .44 Mag. and one .357 Mag. revolver, flat-top frame, 4 5/8 (.357 Mag.) and 6 1/2 (.44 Mag.) in. barrel, gold rollmark "50 Years of Blackhawk 1955-2005", or "50 Years of .44 Magnum 1956-2006", black checkered grips with medallions, matched serial numbers, collector's wood case. Mfg. 2007-2008.

	$1,050	$875	$825	N/A	N/A	N/A	N/A	*$1,350*

These models were also available individually - MSR was approx. $600 each.

NEW MODEL BLACKHAWK 50th ANNIVERSARY – .357 Mag. cal., 4 5/8 in. barrel, flat-top frame, smaller, pre-1962 XR-3 grip frame with checkered hard rubber grips with black Ruger medallions, cylinder indexing aligns loading gate cutout with cylinder borings, unobtrusive internal lock, "50 YEARS OF BLACKHAWK 1955-2005" gold rollmark, supplied with red case. Mfg. 2005-2006.

	$650	$400	$350	$300	$275	$250	$225	*$605*

* ***50 Years of .44 Magnum Blackhawk*** – similar to 50th Anniversary Blackhawk, except has "50 YEARS OF .44 MAGNUM 1956-2006" rollmarked on barrel, hard rubber style grips with black medallions. Mfg. 2006 only.

	$700	$550	$500	$425	$400	$350	$300	*$605*

Note that production of the .44 Mag. model initially began in Ruger's Newport, New Hampshire facility and these were rollmarked with an 89- prefix serial number up to ser. no. 89-05067 (89-00001 through 89-00500 were not produced in 2006 with the block of 500 guns being produced at a later date as Super Blackhawk models instead of flattop framed Blackhawks). Approximately 1,200 of the last 89- prefixed cylinder frames

GRADING - PPGS™	100%	98%	95%	90%	80%	70%	60%	LAST MSR

were transferred to Ruger's Prescott, Arizona facility for completion. All new 50th Anniversary .44 Blackhawk production at Prescott then received an 870- prefix serial number. All Prescott production of this model has the "WARNING" statement located on the bottom of the barrel.

* ***50th Anniversary .357 Blackhawk 1 of 500 Special Edition*** - .357 Mag. cal., gold plated hammer, trigger, and grip medallions, selective gold highlights on cylinder and grip frame, known serial number range 520-09632 to 520-16731.

	$850	$750	$640	$575	$470	$385	$300	

NEW MODEL BLACKHAWK CONVERTIBLE - similar to New Model Blackhawk, except interchangeable cylinders, .357 Mag./9mm Para. with 4 5/8 or 6 1/2 in. barrel or .45 LC/.45 ACP (disc. 1985, reintroduced 1999 w/o 7 1/2 in. barrel) cal. 6 shot, alloy steel construction, blued finish, ramp front and adj. rear sights, black checkered hard rubber grips, 39-45 oz.

MSR $749	$635	$550	$475	$425	$350	$300	$250	

Beginning in 2007, this model was supplied with unobtrusive lock and black checkered grips as standard. Beginning mid-2012, Ruger discontinued the use of the unobtrusive internal lock and in 2014 reintroduced laminate grips.

* ***New Model Blackhawk Buckeye Special*** - 10mm Auto/.38-40 Win. or .32/.32-20 WCF cal., 6 1/2 in. barrel. Mfg. 1988-1990.

	$1,000	$850	$750	$500	$400	$300	$225	

Add 10% for Buckeye Special in .32/.32-20 cal. (mfg. for Buckeye Sports in 1988).

BLACKHAWK-SRM .357 REM. MAXIMUM - similar to New Model Blackhawk, except is chambered for .357 Rem. Maximum, 7 1/2 or 10 1/2 in. barrels available, target sights, 53 oz., 11,500 mfg. 1982-84; production suspended due to unresolvable engineering problems.

	$950	$850	$650	$500	$400	$350	$300	

Add $100 for 10 1/2 in. barrel.

BLACKHAWK FLAT-TOP .44 SPL. - .44 Spl. cal., flat-top frame, smaller, pre-1962 XR-3 grip frame with checkered hard rubber grips and black Ruger medallions, 4 5/8 in. or 5 1/2 in. barrel, cylinder indexing aligns loading gate cut out with cylinder borings, unobtrusive internal lock (disc. 2012) or without internal lock (new 2012). Mfg. 2009-2014.

	$475	$400	$325	$250	$200	$165	$140	*$609*

Note that revolvers without the internal lock are identified with a 521- prefix serial number and have laminate grips.

BLACKHAWK "FLAT-TOP" RUGER COLLECTORS ASSOCIATION 35TH ANNIVERSARY COMMEMORATIVE - .357 Mag. cal., flat-top frame, 10 in. barrel, high polish finish, smaller, pre-1962 XR-3 grip frame with checkered hard rubber grips and black Ruger medallions, cylinder indexing aligns loading gate cut out with cylinder borings, unobtrusive internal lock, special RCA-00001 - RCA-00054 serial number range. 54 guns produced during 2010 only.

	$1,450	$1,100	$900	$650	$500	$425	$350	

BLACKHAWK RUGER COLLECTORS ASSOCIATION .44 FLATTOP 40TH ANNIVERSARY COMMEMORATIVE - .44 Spl. cal., flat-top frame, 10 1/2 in. bull barrel, high polish finish, longer steel ejector housing, smaller, undercut front sight, pre-1962 XR-3 grip frame with checkered hard rubber grips and black Ruger medallions, cylinder indexing aligns loading gate cut out with cylinder borings, special RCA-40001-RCA-40120 serial number range.120 guns produced during 2016 only.

	$1,050	$900	$800	$700	$550	$450	$400	

BLACKHAWK "SHOOTISTS" BISLEY FLAT-TOP - .44 Spl. cal., high polish finish, 7 1/2 inch barrel, special "MEN WHO STAND IN THE GAP" inscription on barrel, steel Bisley grip frame with brown laminate grips and black Ruger medallions, cylinder indexing aligns loading gate cut out with cylinder borings, special SH25-001 to SH25-100 serial number range. 100 guns produced during 2010 only.

	$1,500	$1,100	$900	$775	$630	$515	$400	

BLACKHAWK "SHOOTISTS" BISLEY FLAT-TOP "MISTAKE GUN" - .44 Spl. cal., regular blue finish, 7 1/2 inch barrel, steel Bisley grip frame with brown laminate grips and black Ruger medallions, cylinder indexing aligns loading gate cutout with cylinder borings, known serial number range 520-21224 - 520-21582. 101 guns produced in 2010 by mistake with regular serial numbers. An additional 30 revolvers produced in 2012, serial number range 520-30581 to 520-30610.

	$1,250	$1,000	$850	$700	$600	$500	$450	

GRADING - PPGS™ 100% 98% 95% 90% 80% 70% 60% LAST MSR

NEW MODEL SUPER BLACKHAWK – .44 Mag. cal., 4 5/8 (new 1994), 5 1/2 (new 1987), 7 1/2, 10 1/2 tapered (mfg. 1979-1983), or 10 1/2 (bull/target, new 1984) in. barrel, 6 shot, blue finish, Dragoon style grip frame with square back trigger guard or XR3-RED shape steel grip frame with round trigger guard (4 5/8 or 5 1/2 in. models only), unfluted cylinder except for 5 1/2 in. barrel, walnut, rosewood (disc.), or brown laminate (mfg. 2009-disc.) grips, square back trigger guard (avail. on 7 1/2 or 10 1/2 in. barrel models only), ramp front (target front on 10 1/2 in. bull) and adj. rear sights, similar to old model in appearance, but has new action, steel ejector housing was introduced in 2000, 45-55 oz. New 1973.

MSR $829 $700 $615 $525 $485 $385 $325 $275

The new model Super Blackhawk started with serial number 81-00001.

* ***New Model Super Blackhawk 50th Anniversary*** – .44 Mag. cal., 6 shot, 7 1/2 in. barrel, blue gloss finish, gold anniversary trim and rollmarked "50TH ANNIVERSARY SUPER BLACKHAWK - 2009" in gold on barrel, commemorates 50th anniversary of the Super Blackhawk, gold band at front and rear of cylinder, smooth cocobolo grips with black eagle medallions, included special white cardboard packaging with Ruger logo carrying case. 1,660 mfg. 2009 only.

$1,000 $750 $650 $550 $475 $400 $350 *$880*

* ***New Model Super Blackhawk Stainless Steel*** – .44 Mag. cal., 4.62, 5 1/2, 7 1/2, or 10 1/2 in. barrel, 6 shot, stainless steel, square back trigger guard (7 1/2 or 10 1/2 in. bbl. only), ramp front and adj. rear sights (target front on 10 1/2 in. bbl.), hardwood grips, satin stainless finish.

MSR $829 $700 $615 $525 $485 $385 $325 $275

Add $30 for 10 1/2 in. bull/target barrel.

* ***New Model Super Blackhawk High Gloss Stainless Steel*** – high gloss stainless steel finish, not available in 10 1/2 in. bull barrel. Mfg. 1994-1996 in 86-57xxx to 87-04xxx serial number range.

$725 $635 $550 $495 $400 $325 $250 *$450*

NEW MODEL SUPER BLACKHAWK BISLEY – .44 Mag., blue finish only, 7 1/2 in. barrel, 6 shot, incorporates Bisley raked hammer, adj. sights, longer grip frame, goncalo alves, walnut, rosewood (disc) or brown laminate grips, available with fluted cylinder (disc. 1986) or unfluted rollmarked cylinder. Mfg. 1986-2013, reintroduced 2018 only.

$725 $635 $550 $500 $400 $335 $250 *$899*

NEW MODEL SUPER BLACKHAWK STAINLESS HUNTER – .44 Mag. cal., 6 shot, 7 1/2 in. ribbed barrel only, gray (early) or black laminated wood grips, ramp front and adj. rear sights, includes scope rings and integral scope mounts (new 2002), satin stainless finish, 52 oz. Mfg. 1992-95, reintroduced 2002.

MSR $959 $825 $775 $610 $550 $450 $370 $320

NEW MODEL SUPER BLACKHAWK BISLEY STAINLESS HUNTER – .44 Mag. cal., 7 1/2 in. barrel with scope mounts built into solid rib, stainless steel construction, unfluted cylinder, round trigger guard, 6 shot, ramp front and adj. rear sights, black laminate grips, satin stainless finish, 52 oz. New 2009.

MSR $959 $825 $775 $610 $550 $450 $370 $320

VAQUERO – .357 Mag. (new 1997), .44-40 WCF (new 1994), .44 Mag. (new 1994), or .45 LC cal., 6 shot, 4 5/8, 5 1/2, or 7 1/2 (not available in .357 Mag.) in. barrel, color case finished frame, blue steel grip frame, barrel, and cylinder, steel ejector housing became standard in 2000, transfer bar hammer safety, smooth rosewood or simulated ivory (new 1996) grips, patterned after the Colt SAA, fixed sights, 39-41 oz. Mfg. 1993-2004.

$650 $550 $450 $375 $250 $200 $175 *$555*

Add $40 for simulated ivory grips (new 1996).

Add approx. $150 for simulated ivory grips and engraved cylinder (mfg. 1998-99).

Note that the last of the Vaquero model to be produced were "cleanup" runs and that these "cleanup" runs are identified as having the "WARNING" rollmark on the bottom of the barrel. Ser. range beginning at 58-96020. The most recent of these "cleanup" guns also have brown laminate grips.

* ***Vaquero High Gloss Stainless Steel*** – similar to Vaquero models, except high gloss stainless steel finish, smooth rosewood grips. Mfg. 1993-2004.

$650 $525 $400 $325 $200 $170 $160 *$555*

Add $40 for simulated ivory grips (new 1996).

Add 10% for .40 S&W caliber (very limited quantities produced from 2000 to 2010)

Add approx. $150 for simulated ivory grips and engraved cylinder (mfg. 1998-99).

Note that the last of the Vaquero models to be produced were "cleanup" runs and that these "cleanup" runs are identified as having the "WARNING" rollmark on the bottom of the barrel. Ser. range beginning at 58-96020. The most recent of these "cleanup" guns also have brown laminate grips.

GRADING - PPGS™	100%	98%	95%	90%	80%	70%	60%	LAST MSR

* ***Vaquero "Friends of NRA" Special Production*** – .44-40 WCF cal., blue/case colored cylinder frame, 6 1/2 in. barrel, serial number range 55-99260 to 56-13146. 550 produced for the various Friends of NRA events held around the country in 1999.

	$625	$500	$425	$395	$315	$260	$200	

* ***Vaquero San Diego Sheriff's Association Commemorative*** – .40 S&W cal., high gloss stainless steel, 4 5/8 inch barrel, "SAN DIEGO SHERIFF" laser etched in large black letters on right side of barrel, right grip panel has the 150th inscription on the backstrap, cased in an oak presentation case with glass top and French fitted with green material, nickel plated San Diego Sheriff's deputy badge including Sheriff signature and date 2000.

	$825	$725	$625	$550	$450	$375	$285	

Subtract $90 for models that were left unsold by the Sherriff's Association, and then sold w/o engraving or presentation case - approx. 200, ser. nos. up to 58-93524.

* ***Vaquero "Dealer Special"*** – .45 Colt cal., blue/case colored or high polish stainless finish, 5 1/2 inch barrel, simulated ivory grip panels with Ruger Eagle logo scrimshawed on the panel and "RUGER" above, special red plastic lockable case. Approximately 1,000 of each produced in 2002 and 2003 in serial range 57-89268 to 58-73129 as a special program by Ruger for those dealers who purchased a "12-pack" of Ruger firearms from a distributor. BNV-455DS and KBNV-455DS.

	$600	$500	$400	$325	$200	$175	$160	

* ***Vaquero Class of 2003 West Point Commemorative*** – .45 Colt cal., high polish blue, 5 1/2 in. barrel, gold band at front of barrel, gold plated hammer and trigger, simulated ivory grips with gold grip screw and ferrules, grip medallions are gold plated West Point crest, 70% etch scroll engraving on cylinder frame, barrel, grip frame, ejector housing, and between the cylinder flutes, two gold bands at rear of cylinder with "COUNTRY DUTY HONOR" repeating itself between the gold lines and a gold star between each of the words, "WEST POINT CLASS OF 2003" appears in gold into lines on the right side of the barrel above the ejector housing and "UNITED STATES MILITARY ACADEMY" also into lines on left side of the barrel, "PROTECTORS OF THE FREE" is in gold on the backstrap, as is the West Point crest at the top of the grip frame, traditional "WARNING" statement was moved to the bottom of the barrel near the ejector housing, cased in natural finished oak display case with etched glassed window in the lid. 452 produced in serial range USMA03001 to USMA03453.

	$2,450	$2,150	$1,850	$1,675	$1,350	$1,100	$850	

* ***Vaquero Bird's Head*** – .357 Mag. (4 5/8 in. barrel) or .45 Colt (3 3/4 in. barrel) cal., color case finished frame or high polish stainless steel with bird's head frame, choice of black Micarta or simulated ivory (new 2003) grips. Disc. 2004, although small groups of "cleanup" guns were shipped from the factory as late as 2010 (identified by the "Warning" rollmark on the bottom of the barrel).

	$650	$550	$425	$325	$225	$195	$165	*$595*

BISLEY VAQUERO – .357 Mag. (new 1999, 5 1/2 in. barrel only), .44 Mag. or .45 LC cal., 4 5/8 (new 1999) or 5 1/2 in. barrel, incorporates Bisley raked hammer and longer grip frame, case colored finished frame with blue steel grip frame, barrel, and cylinder, steel ejector housing became standard in 2000, fixed sights, approx. 40 oz. Mfg. 1998-2004, although small groups of "cleanup" guns were shipped from the factory as late as 2010 (identified by the "Warning" rollmark on the bottom of the barrel).

	$650	$550	$450	$325	$225	$180	$160	*$575*

Add $40 for simulated ivory grips.

* ***Bisley Vaquero Stainless*** – similar to Bisley Vaquero, except is high gloss stainless steel. Disc. 2004.

	$650	$550	$450	$325	$225	$180	$160	*$575*

Add $40 for simulated ivory grips.

NEW VAQUERO – .357 Mag. or .45 LC cal., 4 5/8, 5 1/2, or 7 1/2 (.45 LC cal. only, disc. 2009) in. barrel, 6 shot, redesigned using a slimmer pre-1962 XR-3 style grip frame, color case hardened finished (disc. 2009) or blued cylinder frame (new 2009) frame with blued gripstraps, cylinder indexing aligns loading gate cutout with cylinder borings, recontoured hammer, new hammer spring, unobtrusive internal lock (disc. 2012), beveled cylinder, checkered hard rubber (disc.) or hardwood grips, crescent-shaped ejector rod head, 37-41 oz. New 2005.

MSR $829	$700	$615	$525	$485	$385	$325	$275	

Note that Ruger discontinued the use of the unobtrusive internal lock in mid-2012 (510 and 511- serial number prefix). Revolvers without the lock are identified with a 512- prefix serial number and will generally be found with laminate grips.

GRADING - PPGS™	100%	98%	95%	90%	80%	70%	60%	LAST MSR

* ***New Vaquero High Gloss Stainless*** – .357 Mag. or .45 LC cal., similar to New Vaquero, except is stainless steel, 41-44 oz. New 2005.

MSR $829	$700	$615	$525	$485	$385	$325	$275	

* ***New Vaquero Stainless Steel Engraved*** – .45 LC cal., stainless steel, 5 1/2 in. barrel, 6 shot, black checkered grips, factory machine engraved with hand engraved highlights, approx. 75% engraving coverage. Mfg. 2005-2006 only.

	$900	$750	$650	N/A	N/A	N/A	N/A	

Last MSR was $1,000 or $1,950 for consecutively numbered pair.

* ***New Model Vaquero Stainless Steel Engraved Matched Pair*** – .45 LC cal., matched pair, stainless steel, 5 1/2 in. barrel, 6 shot, simulated ivory panel grips with black eagle medallions, factory machine engraved with hand engraved highlights, approximately 75% engraving coverage, cased as a consecutively serial numbered pair. No more than 178 pairs mfg. during 2006-2007 only.

	$3,450	$3,150	$2,850	N/A	N/A	N/A	N/A	*$3,893*

* ***New Vaquero Bisley High Gloss Stainless*** – .357 Mag. or .45 LC cal., 5 1/2 in. barrel only, 6 shot, high gloss stainless steel, simulated ivory grips, fixed sights, Bisley-style hammer, 41-45 oz. New 2009.

MSR $899	$765	$670	$575	$520	$420	$350	$300	

NEW VAQUERO "FRIENDS OF NRA" MATCHED PAIR – .45 LC cal., case colored hardened finished frame, 5 1/2 in. barrel, 6 shot, Hogue ivory grips with black Eagle medallions, rollmarked "NRA '2009 GUN OF THE YEAR' MATCHED SET in gold on right side of barrel, special double red plastic case with certificate of authenticity, each matched set of revolvers also has a matching serial number (i.e. NRAL-0001 and NRAR-0001" for "left" and "right"). Reportedly serial numbered from NRAL-0001 and NRAR-0001 to NRAL-1125 and NRAR-1125. Only 1,125 sets produced for Friends of NRA events during 2009.

	$1,400	$1,225	$1,050	$950	$775	$625	$495	

NEW VAQUERO COWBOY PAIR – Matched pairs of consecutively numbered Vaqueros were available for order from Ruger for a period of time. Refer to individual New Vaquero pricing to determine the price of a matched pair.

NEW VAQUERO SASS PAIR – .357 Mag. or .45 LC cal., 4 5/8 (.357 Mag. only), or 5 1/2 (.45 LC only) in. barrel, 6 shot, fixed sights, black checkered grips with SASS logo grip medallions, high gloss stainless steel, lower and wider Montado-style hammer, only available in set of two with consecutive SASS prefix serial numbers, early production included grooved front strap, includes commemorative red case, 43-45 oz. New 2010.

MSR $1,699	$1,450	$1,275	$1,095	$985	$800	$695	$625	

WRANGLER – .22 LR cal., SA, aluminum alloy frame, 4.62 in. cold hammer forged barrel, 6 shot, blade front and integral notch rear sights, checkered synthetic grips, Black, Silver, or Burnt Bronze Cerakote finish, 30 oz. New 2019.

MSR $249	$215	$190	$160	$145	$120	$95	$80	

REVOLVERS: DOUBLE ACTION

During certain years of manufacture, Ruger's changes in production on certain models (cals., barrel markings, barrel lengths, etc.) have created rare variations that are now considered premium niches. These areas of low manufacture will add premiums to the values listed on standard models.

SPEED SIX (MODELS 207, 208 & 209) – .38 Spl., .357 Mag., or 9mm Para. cal., 2 3/4, or 4 in. barrel, fixed sights, checkered walnut grips, round butt, blue finish, some guns have factory speed hammer (no hammer spur). Mfg. 1973-1988. Model 207 and 208 disc. 1988.

	$550	$375	$300	$225	$175	$150	$140	*$292*

Add $300 for 9mm Para. (Model 209 disc. 1984).
Add 10% for "low-back" grip frame with 150-prefix.

* ***Speed Six Models 737 & 738*** – stainless steel versions of Models 207 and 208, .357 Mag and .38 Spl. cals., 2 3/4, 3 (Postal Inspector contract) or 4 in. barrel. Disc. 1988.

	$575	$400	$325	$225	$175	$150	$140	*$320*

Add 100% for "U.S." and "N.I.S." marked with 2 3/4 in. barrel.

* ***Speed Six Model 739*** – stainless steel, 9mm Para. Disc. 1984.

	$875	$600	$550	$450	$300	$225	$200	

GRADING - PPGS™	100%	98%	95%	90%	80%	70%	60%	LAST MSR

SECURITY SIX (MODEL 117) – .357 Mag. cal., 6 shot, 2 3/4, 3 (late production only), 4, 4 (heavy), or 6 in. barrel, adj. sights, checkered walnut grips, square butt. Mfg. 1970-1985.

	$550	$375	$300	$225	$175	$150	$140	*$309*

Add $15 for target grips.
Add 50% for .38 Special cal with 6 in. barrel and 150- prefix serial number
Add 50% for .357 Mag. Cal. With 2 3/4 in barrel, adj. sights and round butt (Model RDA-32RB - extremely rare).

Note that beginning late in the 150- serial number prefix, the grip frame was changed to have a more outward "highback" shape. Revolvers with the earlier "lowback" grip frame are generally considered more collectible (add 10%). 500 of this model were mfg. for the California Highway Patrol during 1983 (.38 Spl. cal.) in stainless steel only. They are distinguishable by a C.H.P. marking. Other Security Six Model 117 special editions have been made for various police organizations - premiums might exist in certain regions for these variations.

* ***Security Six Model 717*** – stainless steel version of Model 117. Disc. 1985.

	$550	$375	$300	$225	$175	$150	$140	*$338*

Add 20% for "low back" grip frame with 150- prefix.
Add 30% for this model in .38 Special with 4, 4 (heavy) or 6 in. barrel.
Add 50% for .357 Mag. Cal with 2 3/4 in. barrel, adj. sights and round butt (model GA-32RB - extremely rare).

POLICE SERVICE SIX – .357 Mag, .38 Spl., or 9mm Para. cal., blue finish only, square butt, fixed sights, checkered walnut grips. All revolvers having fixed sights and square butt grip frame with "lowback" shape to the backstrap were also marked "SECURITY-SIX". Such revolvers are found only with a 150-prefix serial number. Only when the new highback grip frame came out were the fixed sight and square butt revolvers marked "SERVICE-SIX".

* ***Police Service Six Model 107*** – .357 Mag. cal., 2 3/4 or 4 in. barrel, fixed sights. Disc. 1988.

	$550	$375	$300	$225	$175	$150	$140	*$287*

Add 10% for "low back" grip frame with 150- prefix.

* ***Police Service Six Model 108*** – .38 Spl. cal., 2 3/4 or 4 in. barrel, fixed sights. Disc. 1988.

	$500	$350	$275	$200	$175	$150	$140	*$287*

Add 40% for this model with low-back grip frame, 6 in. barrel, and 150- prefix serial number, and 10% for all other low-back models.
Add 125% for "U.S." marked with or without lanyard loop.
Add 100% for .380 rimmed cartridge, with or without lanyard loop.

* ***Police Service Six Model 109*** – 9mm Para. cal., 2 3/4 or 4 in. barrel, fixed sights. Disc. 1984.

	$850	$550	$500	$400	$275	$195	$175	

POLICE SERVICE SIX STAINLESS STEEL – stainless construction, 2 3/4 or 4 in. barrel, fixed sights, checkered walnut grips.

* ***Police Service Six Stainless Steel Model 707*** – .357 Mag. cal., 2 3/4 or 4 in. barrel, square butt. Disc. 1988.

	$600	$450	$350	$275	$225	$175	$140	*$310*

* ***Police Service Six Stainless Steel Model 708*** – .38 Spl. cal., 2 3/4 or 4 in. barrel, square butt. Disc. 1988.

	$550	$375	$300	$250	$200	$150	$140	*$310*

GP-100 – .357 Mag. or .38 Spl. (disc.) cal., 4 (disc. 2009), 4.2, or 6 (.357 Mag. only) in. standard (disc.) or heavy full shrouded barrel, 6 shot, triple-locking cylinder, strengthened design intended for constant use with all .357 Mag. ammunition, easy takedown, rubber cushioned grip panels with polished Goncalo Alves wood inserts (disc.) or black rubber Hogue Monogrip, fixed (mfg. 1989-2006) or adj. sights with white outlined rear and interchangeable front, transfer bar safety, 35-46 oz. depending on barrel configuration. New 1986.

MSR $769	$655	$575	$490	$445	$360	$295	$250	

* ***GP-100 Stainless Steel*** – .327 Fed. Mag. (mfg. 2009-2013), .38 Spl. (disc.), .44 Special (mfg. 2017-2019), or .357 Mag. cal., 3 (new 1990, .357 Mag. only), 4 (disc. 2009), 4.2, or 6 in. barrel, 6 or 7 (.327 Fed. Mag. only, disc. 2013) shot, ramp front and fixed (3 in. only) or adj. sights, Hogue grips, satin stainless finish, 36-45 oz. New 1987.

MSR $799	$680	$600	$500	$450	$375	$300	$265	

Add $30 for adj. sights.
Add $30 for .44 Special cal. (mfg. 2017-2019).

GRADING - PPGS™	100%	98%	95%	90%	80%	70%	60%	LAST MSR

* ***GP-100 High Gloss Stainless Steel*** – .357 Mag. or .38 Special (rare) cal., high gloss stainless steel finish, adj. sights, 3 or 4 in. heavy barrel. Mfg. 1996 only in serial number range 173-30xxx to 173-65xxx.

	$485	$375	$295	$250	$195	$165	$140	*$457*

Fixed sights were cataloged but not known to have been produced in this model.

* ***GP-100 .22 LR*** – .22 LR cal., 5 1/2 in. barrel, 10 shot, stainless steel construction, fiber optic front and adj. rear sights, cushioned rubber grip with hardwood insert, 42 oz. New 2016.

MSR $829	$700	$615	$525	$475	$385	$315	$275

GP-100 7-ROUND – .357 Mag. or .327 Fed. Mag. (disc. 2019) cal., 2 1/2, 4.2, or 6 in. barrel, 7 shot mag., stainless steel construction, fiber optic front and adj. rear sight, cushioned rubber grip with hardwood insert or Hogue Monogrip (disc. 2019), satin stainless finish, 36-43.5 oz. New 2018.

MSR $899	$765	$670	$575	$520	$420	$350	$300

GP-100 MATCH CHAMPION – .357 Mag. or 10mm Auto (new mid-2018) cal., 4.2 in. slab-sided half-lug stainless steel barrel, 6 shot, Novak fixed or adj. (new 2015) rear sights and fiber optic front sights, contoured cylinder, Hogue stippled hardwood grip, satin stainless finish, 38 oz. New 2014.

MSR $969	$825	$720	$620	$560	$455	$375	$325

SUPER GP100 – 9mm Para. (new late 2019) or .357 Mag. cal., Super Redhawk action, 5.5 or 6 (new late 2019) in. cold hammer forged stainless steel barrel, 1:16 twist, 8 shot, fiber optic front and adj. rear sight, Hogue hand-finished hardwood grips, stainless steel barrel, cylinder, and frame with PVD coating, ships with three full moon clips, fitted hard case, a Ruger Custom Shop Certificate of Authenticity, challenge coin, cleaning cloth, gun peg, and decal, PVD or satin stainless (new late 2019) finish, 45.6-47 oz. Mfg. by the Ruger Custom Shop beginning 2019.

MSR $1,549	$1,320	$1,155	$990	$900	$725	$600	$515

SP101 – .357 Mag. cal., alloy steel frame, 2.25 in. barrel, 5 shot, black ramp front and integral rear sights, cushioned rubber grip with engraved hardwood inserts, blued finish, 26 oz. New 2019.

MSR $719	$615	$540	$460	$425	$345	$275	$225

SP101 MATCH CHAMPION – .357 Mag. cal., small frame variation of the GP-100 Stainless, 4.2 in. full lug barrel with 11° target crown, 5 shot, fluted, triple locking cylinder, stainless steel, fiber optic ramp front and adj. rear sights, Altamont hardwood grip with stippled and checkered sides, 30 oz. New mid-2017.

MSR $859	$725	$635	$550	$515	$415	$345	$280

SP101 STAINLESS STEEL – 9mm Para. (new 2018), .22 LR (6 shot - mfg. 1990-2004), .32 H&R (6 shot - mfg. 1991-2012), .327 Federal (6 shot - mfg. 2007-2011, 2016), .38 Spl. +P (5 shot), 9mm Para. (5 shot - mfg. 1991-2000), or .357 Mag. (5 shot - new 1991) cal., 2 1/4, 3 1/16, 4 (mfg. 1990-2007), or 4.2 (new 2012) in. barrel, small frame variation of the GP-100 Stainless, fiber optic (new 2012) or black ramp front sight, fixed or adj. rear (new 1996) sights, cushioned rubber grips with black plastic or engraved hardwood insert (new 2012), satin stainless finish, 25-34 oz. New 1989.

MSR $719	$615	$540	$460	$425	$345	$275	$225

Add $30-$50 for .327 Fed. Mag. with ramp front sights (new 2018) or fiber optic front sights and engraved hardwood inserts.

Add $170 for Crimson Trace Lasergrips (mfg. 2008-2011).

Add $100 for .357 Mag. models with "125 GR. BULLET" rollmarked on barrel lug (disc. 1991).

Add $300 for 9mm Para. caliber (disc. 2000, reintroduced 2018).

Add $150 for .22 LR caliber without fiber optic sights (disc. 2004).

The .327 Federal caliber configuration will also shoot .32 H&R Mag., ,32 S&W, and .32 S&W Long cartridges.

The first few thousand SP-101s in .38 Special had green grip inserts. Also, approximately 3,000 total of the earliest KSP-321 and KSP-331 .357 Mag. models were rollmarked with "125 GR. BULLET" on the barrel under the caliber designation (serial range 570-59359 to 570-67976).

Ruger introduced a .357 Mag./2 1/4 in. (new 1993) or .38 Spl./2 1/4 (mfg. 1994-2005) in. configuration featuring a spurless hammer, double action only.

SP-101 barrel lengths are as follows: .22 cal. is available in 2 1/4 or 4 in. standard or heavy barrel, .32 H&R is available in 3 1/16 or 4 (mfg. 1994-2008) in. heavy barrel, .38 Spl. is available in 2 1/4 or 3 1/16 in. length only, 9mm Para. is available in 2 1/4 (mfg. 1989-2000) or 3 1/16 in. (mfg. 1989-2000) length only, and .357 Mag. is available in 2 1/4 or 3 1/16 in. length only.

* ***SP101 Stainless Steel .22 LR*** – .22 LR cal., 4.2 in. barrel, 8 shot, satin stainless steel, black rubber grips with checkered wood panel inserts, adj. rear sight, fiber optic front sight, 30 oz. New late 2011.

MSR $769	$655	$575	$490	$445	$360	$295	$250

GRADING - PPGS™	100%	98%	95%	90%	80%	70%	60%	LAST MSR

* ***SP101 Stainless Steel High Gloss*** – .38 Spl. (disc. 1996), 9mm Para. (disc. 1996), or .357 Mag. cal., similar to SP-101 Stainless Steel, except has high gloss stainless steel finish. Mfg. 1996-1997.

	$650	$475	$350	$275	$225	$195	$150	*$443*

Add $300 for 9mm Para. cal.

Estimated 100 produced in .38 Spl, 1,500 produced in .357 Mag. and an unknown quantity in 9mm (very rare). Serial range 571-81675 to 572-44777.

REDHAWK – .41 Mag. (mfg. 1984-1991) or .44 Mag. cal., 6 shot fluted cylinder, 5 1/2 and 7 1/2 (disc. 2005) in. barrel, blue finish, square butt, smooth hardwood grips, 49-54 oz. Disc. 2009.

	$650	$460	$375	$285	$225	$180	$165	*$789*

Add $40 for scope rings (disc. 2005).

.41 Mag. cals. will bring collector premium.

* ***Redhawk Stainless Steel/Redhawk and Redhawk Hunter*** – .357 Mag. (mfg. 1984-1985), .41 Mag. (mfg. 1984-1991), .44 Rem. Mag., or .45 LC (mfg. 1998-2005, 4 in. barrel only, mfg. 2007-2017 in 4.2 in.) cal., stainless steel construction, 4.2 (new 2007), 5 1/2, or 7 1/2 in. barrel, choice of hardwood, laminate (new 2009), or Hogue Monogrip (4.2 in. barrel only) grips, 6 shot, ramp front and adj. rear sights, integral scope mounts and scope rings (Redhawk Hunter 7 1/2 in. model only), satin stainless finish, 49-54 oz. New 1979.

MSR $1,079	$915	$800	$685	$620	$500	$400	$325	

Add $80 for integral scope mounts and scope rings (Redhawk Hunter model).
Models in .357 Mag., .41 Mag. or .45 LC will bring collector premiums.

.357 Mag. produced only with 5 1/2 or 7 1/2 in. barrel without integral scope mount/rings.

Beginning in 2018, Ruger began transitioning an engineering change within their Redhawk models by eliminating the solid barrel and replacing it with a cold hammer forged sleeve and barrel shroud. The change began occurring in certain Redhawk models by the beginning of the 504- prefix serial number and will eventually be found in all Redhawk models. The new type barrel is identified as a "stepped" looking barrel crown. Old style solid barrels have a flat barrel crown.

* ***Redhawk .357 Magnum - 8 Shot*** – .357 Mag. cal., 2 3/4 ("J" style grip frame), 4.2, or 5 1/2 in. barrel, 8 shot, cylinder relieved for full moon clips (three included), stainless steel construction, ramp front and adj. rear sights, smooth hardwood grips, satin stainless finish, 44-52 oz. New 2018.

MSR $1,079	$865	$745	$615	$550	$445	$365	$285	

* ***Redhawk (Dual Caliber)*** – .45 Auto/.45 Colt cal., 4.2 in. half-lug barrel, all stainless steel construction, 6 shot, triple-locking cylinder, single spring mechanism, round butt frame, fully adj. black blade rear and red ramp front sights, checkered hardwood grips, satin stainless finish, includes three full moon clips, 44 oz. Mfg. mid-2015-2018.

	$865	$745	$615	$550	$445	$365	$285	*$1,079*

* ***Redhawk with Cold Hammer Forged Sleeve and Shroud Barrel*** – .357 Mag., .44 Rem. Mag. (new 2019), or .45 Auto (new 2019) cal., 2.75 (new 2019, .357 Mag.), 4.2, 5 1/2, or 7 1/2 (new 2019, .44 Rem. Mag.) in. cold hammer forged sleeve and shroud barrel, 6 shot fluted (new 2019) or 8 shot unfluted (.357 Mag. only) cylinder, stainless steel construction, ramp front and adj. rear sights, hardwood, engraved hardwood (new 2019), or Hogue (new 2019) grips, standard Redhawk grip frame or round butt grip frame (2.75 in., .357 Mag. or .45 Auto only), includes three full moon clips, satin stainless finish, 44-54 oz. New 2018.

MSR $1,079	$915	$800	$685	$620	$500	$410	$360	

SUPER REDHAWK STAINLESS – .44 Mag., .454 Casull, or .480 Ruger (mfg. 2001-2007, reintroduced 2013) cal., 6 shot, 7 1/2 or 9 1/2 in. barrel, fluted (.44 Mag. cal. only) or non-fluted cylinder, choice of regular or high gloss (mfg. 1996 only), Target Gray (.454 Casull and .480 Ruger only, disc. 2009), or satin stainless steel finish, ramp front and adj. rear sights, cushioned grip panels (GP-100 style, disc.) or Hogue Tamer Monogrips (new 2008), stainless steel scope rings, includes hard plastic case, 53-58 oz. New late 1987.

MSR $1,159	$985	$860	$740	$675	$550	$450	$385	

Add $30 for .454 Casull or .480 Ruger cal.
Add $75 for early .44 Mag. with "SUPER REDHAWK" rollmarked on both sides of cylinder frame extension, serial range 550-00500 to at least 550-00659.

* ***Super Redhawk Stainless Alaskan*** – .44 Mag. (new 2008), .454 Casull, or .480 Ruger (disc. 2007, reintroduced 2013) cal., stainless steel, 5 shot (some .480 Ruger only) or 6 shot, 2 1/2 in. barrel, ramp front and adj. rear sights, Hogue Tamer Monogrip, unfluted cylinder, satin stainless finish, 44-45 oz. New 2005.

MSR $1,189	$1,000	$875	$750	$680	$550	$475	$390	

Add 50% for .480 Ruger with 5-shot cylinder (less than 30 believed to have been shipped commercially).

GRADING - PPGS™	100%	98%	95%	90%	80%	70%	60%	LAST MSR

* ***Super Redhawk 10mm Auto*** – 10mm Auto cal., 6 1/2 in. stainless steel barrel, 6 shot, ramp front and adj. rear sights, cushioned rubber grips with hardwood inserts, includes three full moon clips, satin stainless finish, 54 oz. Mfg. 2018-2020.

	$985	$860	$740	$675	$550	$450	$385	*$1,159*

LCR – 9mm Para. (new 2015), .22 LR (new 2012), .22 WMR (new 2013), .38 Spl. +P, .327 Federal Mag. (new mid-2015), or .357 Mag. cal., 5 (.38 Spl. or .357 Mag.), 6 (.22 WMR or .327 Federal), or 8 (.22 LR only, new 2012) shot, DAO, hammerless, 1 7/8 in. barrel, monolithic aluminum frame, stainless steel cylinder, polymer fire control housing, matte black or blackened stainless (.357 Mag. or 9mm only) finish, Hogue Tamer Monogrip or Crimson Trace Lasergrips (disc. 2015), integral rear sight with pinned ramp front sight, 13 1/2-17 oz. New 2010.

MSR $579	$495	$435	$375	$335	$275	$225	$195

Add $90 for .357 Mag., .327 Federal Mag. (new mid-2015), or 9mm Para. (new 2015) cal.
Add $280 for Crimson Trace Lasergrips (disc. 2015).
Add $50 for LCR-XS model with standard dot Tritium front sight (.38 Spl. +P cal. only) and U-notch integral rear sight (mfg. 2011-2013).

LCRX – .38 Spl. +P, .357 Mag. (new 2019), .22 WMR (new 2018), or .22 LR (new 2017, 3 in. model only) cal., 1 7/8 or 3 (new 2015) in. barrel, 5 shot, external hammer, monolithic aluminum frame, stainless steel cylinder, polymer fire control housing, matte black finish, compact with finger grooves (1 7/8 in. only) or full size (3 in. only, new 2015) Hogue Tamer Monogrip, integral rear sight or adj. black blade rear (new 2015, 3 in. model) with pinned ramp front sight, 13 1/2-15.7 oz. New 2014.

MSR $579	$495	$435	$375	$335	$275	$225	$195

* ***LCRX Stainless Steel*** – 9mm Para. (new 2018), .327 Fed. Mag. (new 2018), or .357 Mag. cal., 1.87 or 3 (new 2019) in. barrel, 5 or 6 shot, stainless steel monolithic frame construction, external hammer, replaceable pinned ramp front and integral U-notch rear sights or adj. black blade rear sight (new 2019), Hogue Tamer Monogrip with finger grooves, matte black frame finish, 17.4 oz. New mid-2017.

MSR $679	$580	$510	$435	$395	$320	$265	$225

RIFLES: BOLT ACTION, RIMFIRE

MODEL 77/17 (CURRENT MFG.) – .17 WSM cal., 20 in. cold hammer forged standard or threaded (with thread protector, new 2020) barrel, 6 shot detachable rotary mag., no sights, integral scope mounts, American walnut stock, sling swivel studs, 3-pos. safety, blued finish, 5.7 lbs. New mid-2018.

MSR $999	$850	$750	$650	$575	$475	$385	$325

MODEL 77/17 – .17 Mach 2 (disc. 2006) or .17 HMR cal., 22 in. barrel, blue finish, 9 shot rotary mag., no sights, checkered American walnut or black laminate (mfg. 2003-2012, .17 HMR cal. only) stock, 6 1/2 lbs. Mfg. 2002-2016.

	$825	$725	$625	$550	$450	$375	$300	*$979*

MODEL 77/22 (R/RS) – .22 LR cal., 10 shot rotary mag., 20 in. barrel, all steel construction, 3-position safety, checkered walnut stock, blue finish, non-adj. trigger, available with either optional iron sights (RS suffix, disc. 2004) or plain barrel (no sights) with scope rings (included), 2.7 millisecond lock time on trigger, 6 lbs. 2 oz. Mfg. 1984-2016.

	$750	$625	$550	$450	$375	$300	$250	*$979*

Add $25 for iron sights (disc. 2004).
Add 125% if w/o 77/22 roll mark or with green laminated stock.

* ***Model 77/17 Stainless*** – .17 HMR (disc. 2016), .17 WSM (new 2015), or .17 Hornet (new 2013) cal., similar to Model 77/17, 18 1/2 (new 2019), 20 (mfg. 2019-2020), 22 (disc. 2005), or 24 (mfg. 2006-2020) in. cold hammer forged threaded (new late 2019) or standard stainless steel barrel, 6 (.17 Hornet, .17 WSM), 9 (.17 HMR), or 10 (disc.) shot detachable rotary mag., no sights, integral scope mounts, black laminate (became standard 2006-2016), Green Mountain laminate (new 2013), or American walnut (mfg. 2015-disc.) stock, includes sling swivel studs, target grey (disc.) or matte stainless finish, 7-7 1/2 lbs. New 2002.

MSR $1,069	$800	$695	$600	$525	$425	$350	$295

* ***Model 77/22-RP/RSP All-Weather Stainless*** – .22 LR cal., similar to Model 77/22, except has brushed stainless steel finish, metal with matte black DuPont Zytel or Next G1 Vista camo (mfg. 2011 only) synthetic stock, no sights, 6 lbs. Mfg. 1989-2014.

	$695	$550	$450	$350	$295	$250	$225	*$899*

Add $25 for iron sights (disc. 2004). Add $26 for camo (disc. 2011).

GRADING - PPGS™	100%	98%	95%	90%	80%	70%	60%	LAST MSR

* ***Model 77/22 Stainless (VBZ Varmint Stainless Laminated)*** – .22 LR cal., similar to Model 77/22, except stainless steel (target grey finish became standard 2005-disc.), 24 in. heavy stainless barrel, laminated brown hardwood (disc. 2013), American Walnut (new 2014) stock, no sights, 7 1/2 lbs. Mfg. 1995-2016.

	$785	$675	$595	$495	$400	$315	$265	*$1,069*

MODEL 77/22-RM/RSM MAG. – .22 WMR cal., similar to Model 77/22-R/RS, except has 20 in. barrel, 9 shot rotary mag., blue finish, checkered walnut stock, iron (RSM suffix, disc. 2004) or no sights, 6 1/2 lbs. Mfg. 1990-2016.

	$750	$625	$550	$450	$375	$300	$250	*$979*

Add $25 for iron sights (disc. 2004, RSM suffix).

* ***Model 77/22-RMP/RSMP Mag. All-Weather Stainless*** – .22 WMR cal., 20 in. barrel, similar to Model 77/22-RM/RSM Mag., except has brushed stainless steel metal with matte black DuPont Zytel synthetic stock, 6 lbs. Mfg. 1990-2014.

	$695	$550	$450	$350	$295	$250	$225	*$899*

Add $25 for iron sights (disc. 2005).

* ***Model 77/22-VMBZ Mag. Varmint Stainless Laminated*** – .22 WMR cal., similar to Model 77/22 RM/RSM MAG., except stainless steel (target grey finish became standard 2005), 24 in. heavy stainless barrel, laminated brown hardwood (disc. 2013) or American Walnut (new 2014) stock, 7 1/2 lbs. Mfg. 1993-2016.

	$785	$675	$610	$495	$400	$315	$265	*$1,069*

MODEL 77/22 (CURRENT MFG.) – .22 Hornet cal., 18 1/2 in. threaded CHF steel or stainless steel barrel with thread protector, 6 shot detachable rotary mag., no sights, American walnut or Green Mountain laminate stock, sling swivels, 3-pos. safety, blued or matte stainless finish, 6.5-7 lbs. New mid-2020.

MSR $999	$850	$750	$650	$575	$475	$385	$325

Add $70 for stainless steel barrel and Green Mountain laminate stock.

AMERICAN RIMFIRE RIFLE – .17 HMR (new 2014), .22 LR or .22 WMR cal., 18 (threaded, new 2015) or 22 in. satin blued, hammer forged barrel, detachable, flush mounted 9 or 10 shot rotary mag., Marksman adj. trigger, Williams fiber optic front sight and 10/22 style adj. "V" notch folding leaf rear sight, black composite stock and forearm, drilled and tapped, 60 degree bolt, integral bedding block system, sling swivels, includes two interchangeable stock modules (new 2014) that provide comb height options for scope or iron sight use, 5 1/2-6 lbs. New mid-2013.

MSR $359	$310	$270	$235	$210	$170	$140	$120

Add $30 for threaded barrel (new 2015).
Add $449 for Silent-SR suppressor (new 2016, threaded model only, NFA regulations apply).

* ***American Rimfire Compact Rifle*** – .17 HMR (new 2014), .22 LR or .22 WMR cal., 18 in. threaded (new 2015) or non-threaded barrel, 12 1/2 in. LOP, Williams fiber optic front and adj. rear sights, black synthetic stock, satin blued finish, 5.38 lbs. New mid-2013.

MSR $359	$310	$270	$235	$210	$170	$140	$120

Add $30 for threaded barrel (new 2015).
Add $449 for Silent-SR suppressor (new 2016, threaded model only, NFA regulations apply).

* ***American Rimfire Wood Stock*** – .22 LR cal., 22 in. hammer forged barrel with satin blued finish, Power Bedding integral bedding block system, detachable 10 shot rotary mag., Marksman adj. trigger, tang safety, drilled and tapped, Williams fiber optic front and folding leaf rear sights, wood stock with checkering on grip and forend, rubber buttpad, front and rear sling swivels, 6.1 lbs. New mid-2015.

MSR $509	$425	$375	$325	$295	$235	$195	$165

* ***American Rimfire Rifle Stainless*** – .17 HMR, .22 LR, or .22 WMR cal., 18 in. stainless steel threaded barrel, detachable, flush mounted 9 or 10 (.22 LR cal. only) shot rotary mag., Marksman adj. trigger, no sights, factory installed one-piece aluminum scope rail, black synthetic stock with modern forend contouring and grip serrations, 60 degree bolt, integral bedding block system, sling swivels, includes interchangeable standard LOP high comb stock module that provides comb height for scope, satin stainless finish, 5.3 lbs. New mid-2017.

MSR $429	$365	$320	$275	$250	$215	$185	$150

Add $449 for Silent-SR suppressor (NFA regulations apply).

AMERICAN RIMFIRE GO WILD CAMO – .22 LR, .22 WMR, or .17 HMR cal., 18 in. threaded barrel with factory installed muzzle brake, 9 or 10 shot rotary mag., Ruger Marksman adj. trigger, no sights, synthetic stock with GO Wild Camo I-M Brush camo finish, includes two interchangeable stock modules, sling swivel studs, 5.9 lbs. New 2020.

MSR $469	$400	$350	$300	$270	$220	$185	$150

GRADING - PPGS™	100%	98%	95%	90%	80%	70%	60%	LAST MSR

AMERICAN RIMFIRE LONG-RANGE TARGET – .22 LR cal., 22 in. cold hammer forged threaded bull barrel, knurled thread protector, 10 shot detachable rotary mag., extended mag. release, Ruger Marksman Adjustable trigger, no sights (scope base installed), speckled black/brown laminate stock with two-way adj. comb, adj. LOP with soft rubber buttpad, QD attachment points, sling swivel studs, tang safety, Power Bedding integral bedding block system, one-piece aluminum scope rail, matte blued finish, 8 lbs. New late 2019.

MSR $599	$510	$450	$385	$350	$275	$225	$200	

AMERICAN RIMFIRE TARGET RIFLE – .17 HMR, .22 LR, or .22 WMR cal., 18 in. cold hammer forged, threaded bull barrel with knurled thread protector, detachable, flush mounted 9 or 10 (.22 LR cal. only) shot rotary mag., Marksman adj. trigger, no sights, black laminate stock with Alexander Henry forend, integral bedding block system, sling swivels, and rubber buttpad, 60 degree bolt, one-piece aluminum Picatinny scope rail, satin blue finish, 6.7 lbs. New mid-2017.

MSR $499	$425	$375	$325	$300	$250	$215	$185	

Add $449 for Silent-SR suppressor (NFA regulations apply).

* ***American Rimfire Target Stainless*** – .17 HMR, .22 LR, or .22 WMR cal., 18 in. cold hammer forged stainless steel threaded bull barrel with knurled thread protector, 9 or 10 shot detachable rotary mag., extended mag. release, adj. trigger, no sights, black laminate stock features an Alexander Henry forend, rubber buttpad, sling swivel studs, factory installed one-piece aluminum scope rail, satin stainless finish, 6.7 lbs. New 2019.

MSR $529	$450	$395	$340	$300	$250	$200	$175	

* ***American Rimfire Target With Thumbhole Stock*** – .22 LR cal., 18 in. cold hammer forged threaded bull barrel with factory installed knurled thread protector, 10 shot rotary mag., alloy steel or stainless steel (new 2019), adj. trigger, no sights, black laminate stock with thumbhole and LOP spacers, factory installed one-piece aluminum scope rail, sling swivel studs, satin blued or stainless (new 2019) finish, 6.7 lbs. New 2018.

MSR $559	$475	$415	$350	$325	$260	$215	$185	

Add $20 for stainless steel (new 2019).

PRECISION RIMFIRE RIFLE – .17 HMR, .22 WMR, or .22 LR cal., 18 in. threaded target barrel, 6 grooves, one 9 shot mag., two 10 shot BX-1 mags., or one 15 shot BX-15 mag., Marksman adj. trigger, Quick-Fit Precision Rimfire adj. stock, AR-15 style pistol grip, 15 in. free float M-LOK handguard w/optional Magpul slots, Picatinny rail, molded one-piece chassis, hardcoat anodized black or American Flag Cerakote (new 2020) finish, 6.8 lbs. New 2018.

MSR $529	$450	$395	$340	$300	$250	$200	$175	

Add $50 for American Flag Cerakote finish (new 2020).

RIFLES: BOLT ACTION, CENTERFIRE

During certain years of manufacture, Ruger's changes in production on certain models (cals., barrel markings, barrel lengths, etc.) have created rare variations that are now considered premium niches. These areas of low manufacture will add premiums to the values listed on standard models.

Earlier mfg. had flat-bolt handle or hollow round bolt, and will bring $150+ premium, depending on configuration.

Early (pre-1972) mfg. with flat-bolt handle are desirable in the rarer cals. and will command a 100% premium if in 98%+ original condition.

MODEL 77/22-RH/RSH HORNET – .22 Hornet cal., features lengthened receiver, detachable 6 shot rotary mag. (not interchangeable with other 77/22 mags.), 20 in. blue barrel, checkered American walnut stock, includes scope rings, 6 1/2 lbs. Mfg. 1994-2019.

	$750	$650	$575	$475	$385	$300	$265	*$999*

Add $20 for iron sights (RSH suffix, disc. 2002).

* ***Model 77/22 Matte Stainless/Green Mountain Laminate (VHZ Hornet Varmint Stainless Laminated)*** – .17 Hornet (new 2013) or .22 Hornet cal., similar to Model 77/22 Hornet, stainless steel action, 24 in. heavy stainless barrel (target grey finish became standard 2005), no sights, laminated brown hardwood (disc. 2011), or Green Mountain (new 2012) stock, 7 1/2 lbs. New 1995.

MSR $1,069	$800	$775	$650	$575	$465	$385	$335	

MODEL 77/357 – .357 Mag. cal., 18 1/2 in. standard or threaded CHF barrel with thread protector, 5 shot detachable rotary mag., gold bead front and adj. rear sights, black synthetic stock, sling swivel studs, 3-pos. safety, brushed stainless finish, 5.5 lbs. Mfg. 2012-2016, reintroduced late 2017.

MSR $999	$850	$750	$650	$575	$475	$385	$325	

Add 10% for blued steel, .357 Mag. cal. (rare).

GRADING - PPGS™	100%	98%	95%	90%	80%	70%	60%	LAST MSR

MODEL 77/44 – .44 Rem. Mag. cal., 18 1/2 in. standard barrel or threaded CHF barrel with thread protector (new 2021), 4 shot detachable rotary mag., bead front and adj. rear sights, American walnut with checkered grip and forearm (mfg. 1997-2004, reintroduced 2017) or black synthetic stock, sling swivel studs, 3-pos. safety, blued finish, 5.2 lbs, Mfg. 1997-2004, reintroduced 2009-2016, again in late 2017.

MSR $939	$800	$700	$600	$545	$440	$360	$310	

Add $60 for walnut stock.

* ***Model 77/44 Stainless*** – .44 Rem. Mag. cal., 18 1/2 in. standard barrel or threaded CHF barrel with thread protector (new 2021), stainless steel construction, 4 shot detachable rotary mag., bead front and adj. rear sights, black synthetic or Next G1 Vista camo (mfg. 2011-2018) stock, sling swivel studs, 3-pos. safety, brushed stainless finish, 5.2 lbs. Mfg. 1999-2004, reintroduced 2009.

MSR $999	$850	$750	$650	$575	$475	$385	$325	

MODEL 77R – .22-250 Rem., .220 Swift, 6mm Rem., .243 Win., .250 Savage, .257 Roberts, .25-06 Rem., .270 Win., 7x57mm, 7mm-08 Rem., 6.5mm Rem. Mag. (scarce), 7mm Rem. Mag., .280 Rem., .284 Win. (scarce), .308 Win., .30-06, .300 Win. Mag., .338 Win Mag., .350 Rem. Mag. (scarce), or .358 Win. (scarce) cal., long or short action, blue finish, 5 shot mag., 3 shot in Mag. cals., 22 or 24 in. barrel, available with integral bases or round top, stock is checkered walnut with red rubber buttplate, approx. 7 lbs. Mfg. 1968-1992.

Common calibers	$600	$475	$425	$325	$300	$250	$200	
.250 Savage cal.	$650	$450	$385	$350	$285	$230	$180	
6.5 Rem. Mag., .284 Win., .350 Rem., .358 Win.	$950	$900	$825	$750	$600	$450	$300	

Last MSR was $558.

Add 50% for flatbolt in .350 Rem.

The rarity of the M77R with flatbolt in .338 Win. Mag. precludes pricing - authentication by an expert is necessary.

* ***Model 77 RL*** – .22-250 Rem., .243 Win., .250 Sav., .257 Roberts, .270 Win., .30-06, or .308 Win. cal., ultra light variation weighing 6 lbs., black forearm tip. Disc. 1992.

	$550	$450	$375	$325	$270	$250	$225	*$592*

Add 75% for .250 Sav. cal.

* ***Model 77 RS*** – .243 Win., .250 Sav., 6mm Rem., 6.5mm Rem. Mag. (very scarce), 7x57mm, .25-06 Rem., .270 Win., .280 Rem., .284 Win. (very scarce), .30-06, .308 Win., 7mm Rem. Mag., .300 Win. Mag., .338 Win. Mag, .35 Whelen, .350 Rem. Mag. (scarce), or .358 Win. (scarce) cal., similar to Model 77R, except has open sights. Disc. 1992.

Common calibers	$600	$475	$425	$325	$300	$250	$225	
.250 Savage cal.	$700	$550	$430	$390	$315	$260	$200	
6.5mm Rem. Mag., .284 Win., .350 Rem., or .358 Win.	$1,000	$875	$750	$680	$550	$450	$350	

Last MSR was $616.

Add 200% for short action flatbolt in .22-250 or .250 Savage cal.

Add 200% for long action flatbolt in 7mm Rem. or .30-06 cal.

The rarity of the M77RS with flatbolt in .270 Win. or 7x57 cal. precludes pricing - authentication by an expert is necessary.

* ***Model 77PL*** – .25-06 Rem., .270 Win., .30-06, .300 Win., .338 Win. Mag., 7mm Rem. Mag., or 7x57mm cal., differs from R Model in that it has a round top, drilled to take Redfield scope mounts, w/o sights. Disc.

	$550	$450	$375	$300	$245	$200	$200	

* ***Model 77ST*** – .25-06 Rem., .257 Roberts, 7x57mm, .300 Win. Mag., .338 Win. Mag., 7mm Rem. Mag., .30-06, or .270 Win. cal., differs from RS Model in that it has round top drilled to take Redfield scope mounts with iron sights on barrel. Disc.

	$625	$550	$475	$395	$325	$265	$245	

The rarity of the M77ST with flatbolt in .257 Roberts, .270 Win., 7x57, 7mm Rem. Mag., and .30-06 cal. precludes pricing - authentication by an expert is necessary.

The 77ST in calibers .25-06, .300 Win. Mag., or .338 Win. Mag. with flatbolt may not have been produced. Authentication by an expert is necessary.

* ***Model 77V Varmint*** – .22-250 Rem., .220 Swift, .243 Win., 6mm Rem., .25-06 Rem., .280 Rem., .308 Win., or .30-06 cal., 24 in. heavy barrel (26 in. on .220 Swift), drilled and tapped for target bases, approx. 9 lbs. Mfg. 1968-1992.

	$625	$550	$475	$395	$325	$265	$245	*$574*

Add 200% for M77V long action flatbolt in .25-06 or .270 Win. cal.

GRADING - PPGS™	100%	98%	95%	90%	80%	70%	60%	LAST MSR

* ***Model 77 RS African*** – similar to Model 77R, except in .458 Win. Mag. cal. Disc. 1991.

	$650	$550	$475	$395	$335	$315	$300	$680

This model was supplied standard with a steel trigger guard and steel floorplate.

Estimated 12-15 produced total in .416 Taylor circa 1973 to 1976 in this M77RS model as well as the M77RSC listed below. Extreme rarity precludes accurate pricing. Examples must be authenticated through factory letter.

* ***Model 77 RSC*** – similar to Model 77 RS African, except has Circassian walnut stock (C suffix). Mfg. 1976-78.

	$850	$650	$500	$450	$400	$365	$335	

Estimated 12-15 produced total in .416 Taylor circa 1973 to 1976 in this M77RSC model as well as the M77RS listed below. Extreme rarity precludes accurate pricing. Examples must be authenticated through factory letter.

* ***Model 77 RLS*** – .243 Win. (disc. 1989), .270 Win., .30-06, or .308 Win. cal. (disc. 1989), ultra light, 18 1/2 in. barrel, open sights, 6 lbs. Mfg. 1987-93.

	$500	$400	$325	$300	$275	$250	$225	$592

* ***Model 77 RSI*** – .22-250 Rem. (disc. 1991), .243 Win. .250-3000 Sav. (disc. 1986), .270 Win., .30-06, .308 Win. (disc. 1991), 7x57mm (rare), or 7mm-08 Rem. cal., International Mannlicher (full-length stock) with 18 1/2 in. barrel and open sights (includes scope rings), approx. 7 lbs. Disc. 1993.

	$650	$450	$375	$300	$265	$230	$210	$623

Add 50% for 7mm-08, .250-3000 Sav., or 7x57mm cal.

MODEL 77R MARK II SERIES – various cals. as listed in the submodels below, evolutionary design of the Ruger Model 77R featuring slenderized proportioning, 3-position swing-back safety, new trigger, trigger guard and floorplate latch, stainless steel bolt with Mauser extractor design, various barrel lengths, receiver with integral scope bases, hand checkered American walnut stock, includes scope rings, various weights. New 1989.

The Hawkeye Model was introduced during 2007, and please refer to separate model listings.

* ***Model 77R Mark II*** – .204 Ruger (new 2004), .220 Swift (new 1995), .22-250 Rem. (new 1993), .223 Rem. (new 1992), .243 Win., .25-06 Rem. (new 1993), .257 Roberts (new 1993), .260 Rem. (new 1999), .270 Win. (new 1993), .270 WSM (new 2004), .280 Rem. (new 1993), 6mm Rem., 6.5x55mm Swedish (new 1993), 7x57mm (new 1993), .30-06 (new 1993), .308 Win., 7mm WSM (new 2004), 7mm Rem. Mag. (new 1993), 7mm RSUM (new 2002), .300 Win. Mag. (new 1993), .300 WSM (new 2004), .300 RSUM (new 2002), .338 Win. Mag. (new 1993). or .350 Rem. Mag. (new 2004) cal., checkered walnut stock is standard, 22 or 24 in. barrel, standard model of the Mark II Series, approx. 7 lbs. Disc. 2006.

	$500	$450	$400	$345	$295	$250	$200	$695

* ***Model 77LR Mark II*** – .25-06 Rem., .270 Win., .30-06, .300 Win. Mag., or 7mm Rem. Mag. cal., left-hand variation of the Model 77R. Mfg. 1991-2007.

	$525	$475	$425	$365	$315	$275	$225	$749

* ***Model 77RL Mark II*** – .223 Rem., .243 Win., .257 Roberts (new 1993), .270 Win. (new 1993), .30-06 (mfg. 1993-2004, reintroduced 2006), or .308 Win. cal., 20 in. barrel, black forend tip, ultra light variation weighing approx. 6 lbs. Mfg. 1990-2008.

	$650	$575	$495	$425	$375	$295	$250	$837

* ***Model 77RLFP Mark II Stainless*** – .204 Ruger, .223 Rem. (new 2005), .243 Win., .270 Win., or .30-06 cal., 20 in. barrel, black synthetic stock, ultralight variation of the Model 77, w/o sights, 6 1/2 lbs. Mfg. 1999-2008.

	$550	$425	$350	$275	$245	$225	$200	$779

* ***Model 77RS Mark II*** – 6mm Rem., .243 Win., .25-06 Rem. (new 1993), .270 Win. (new 1993), .30-06 (new 1993), .308 Win., 7x64 Brenneke (mfg. 1998 to 2001), 7mm Rem. Mag. (new 1993), .300 Win. Mag. (new 1993), .338 Win Mag. (new 1993), or .458 Win. Mag. (mfg. 1994-98) cal., 22 or 24 in. barrel, similar to Model 77R, except has open sights. Mfg. 1990-2004.

	$550	$425	$350	$275	$245	$225	$200	$780

Add $200 for 7x64 Brenneke cal. (less than 300 sold domestically in United States as an overrun to a foreign contract).

GRADING - PPGS™	100%	98%	95%	90%	80%	70%	60%	LAST MSR

* ***Model 77CR Mark II Compact*** – .223 Rem., .243 Win., .260 Rem., .308 Win., or 7mm-08 Rem. cal., features 16 1/2 in. barrel, checkered walnut stock, includes scope rings, no sights, approx. 5 3/4 lbs. Mfg. 2002-2008.

$550	**$425**	**$350**	**$275**	**$245**	**$225**	**$200**	***$779***

» **Model 77CRBBZ Mark II Compact Stainless** – stainless variation of the Model 77CR Compact, black laminate stock. Mfg. 2002-2008.

$575	**$500**	**$450**	**$395**	**$325**	**$265**	**$235**	***$837***

* ***Model 77FRBBZ Mark II Frontier*** – .243 Win., .308 Win., .300 WSM (disc. 2006), or 7mm-08 Rem. cal., compact design features 16 1/2 in. barrel, and shortened grey laminate stock, barrel cantilever base allows scope to be mounted over barrel in front of action, blue finish, includes scope rings and Weaver style scope base adapter. Mfg. 2005-2008.

$595	**$525**	**$465**	**$415**	**$350**	**$285**	**$250**	***$831***

» **Model 77FRTG Mark II Frontier Stainless** – .338 Federal (new 2007), .358 Win. (new 2008), .325 WSM (disc. 2007), or other cals. similar to Frontier model disc. 2007, stainless variation of the Model 77 FRBBZ Frontier, target grey finish stainless steel barrel/action. Mfg. 2006-2008.

$725	**$625**	**$525**	**$400**	**$335**	**$290**	**$245**	***$936***

Add 100% for .325 WSM cal.

* ***Model 77RSI Mark II*** – .243 Win., .270 Win., .30-06, or .308 Win. cal., International Mannlicher (full-length stock) with 18 1/2 in. barrel and open sights (includes scope rings), approx. 7 lbs. Mfg. 1993-2008.

$725	**$625**	**$525**	**$400**	**$335**	**$290**	**$245**	***$911***

* ***Model 77RLS Mark II*** – .243 Win. or .308 Win. cal., ultra light, 18 1/2 in. barrel, open sights. Mfg. 1990 only.

$500	**$450**	**$400**	**$345**	**$295**	**$250**	**$200**	***$564***

* ***Model K77RFP Mark II All-Weather Stainless*** – .204 Ruger (new 2005), .22-250 (new 1996), .223 Rem., .243 Win., .25-06 Rem. (new 1999), .260 Rem. (new 1999), .270 Win., .270 WSM (new 2004), .280 Rem. (new 1993), 7.62x39mm (disc. 2000), .30-06, .308 Win., .325 WSM (New 2006), .350 Rem. Mag. (new 2006), 7mm-08 Rem. (new 2005), 7mm Rem. Mag., 7mm WSM (new 2004), 7mm RSUM (new 2002), .300 Win. Mag., .300 WSM (new 2004), .300 RSUM (new 2002), or .338 Win. Mag. (new 1992) cal., 22 or 24 in. barrel, similar to Model 77R Mark II except has stainless steel metal with matte black DuPont Zytel synthetic stock, no sights. Mfg. 1990-2006.

$950	**$900**	**$825**	**$750**	**$600**	**$450**	**$350**	***$695***

Add 50% for .325 WSM cal.

* ***Model K77RSFP Mark II All-Weather Stainless*** – .223 Rem. (new 2002), .243 Win., .270 Win., .30-06, 7mm Rem. Mag., .300 Win. Mag., or .338 Win. Mag. cal., otherwise similar to Model K77RFP All-Weather Stainless, except has open sights. Disc. 2004.

$795	**$650**	**$550**	**$475**	**$395**	**$350**	**$295**	***$780***

* ***Model K77RBZ Mark II Satin Stainless*** – .22-250 Rem. (new 1999), .223 Rem., .243 Win., .270 Win., .280 Rem. (disc. 2006), .30-06, .308 Win., 7mm Rem. Mag., .300 Win. Mag., .338 Win. Mag., or .350 Rem. Mag. (disc. 2005) cal., features brown wood laminate stock with sling swivels, 22 or 24 in. barrel without sights, approx. 7 5/16 lbs. Mfg. 1997-2008.

$575	**$500**	**$450**	**$395**	**$325**	**$265**	**$245**	***$837***

* ***Model K77RSBZ Mark II*** – .243 Win., .270 Win., .30-06, .300 Win. Mag., .338 Win. Mag., or 7mm Rem. Mag. cal., 22 or 24 in. barrel, laminated stock, open sights, includes scope rings, approx. 7 3/8 lbs. Disc. 2004.

$525	**$475**	**$425**	**$365**	**$315**	**$275**	**$225**	***$825***

* ***Model K77RVT (VBZ) Mark II*** – .22 PPC (disc. 1996), .204 Ruger (new 2004), .220 Swift (disc. 2006), .22-250 Rem., .223 Rem., .243 Win., .25-06 Rem., .308 Win., 6.5 Creedmoor (new 2009), or 6mm PPC (disc. 1996) cal., 26 or 28 (new 2009, 6.5 Creedmoor cal. only) in. heavy barrel, features stainless steel construction, target grey finish was standard 2005-2009, brown (new 2009) laminated stock, approx. 9 3/4 lbs. Mfg. 1993-2012.

$750	**$615**	**$500**	**$425**	**$375**	**$325**	**$275**	***$963***

This model's nomenclature changed from VBZ to VT during 1994.

* ***Model KM77VTBBZ Mark II Target*** – .204 Ruger, .22-250 Rem., .223 Rem., .243 Win. (disc. 2012), .25-06 Rem. (disc. 2012), 6.5 Creedmoor, or .308 Win. cal., 26 or 28 (6.5 Creedmoor only) in. stainless steel barrel, black laminate stock, 4 or 5 shot mag., no sights, 9 1/2-9 3/4 lbs. Disc.

$795	**$650**	**$550**	**$475**	**$395**	**$350**	**$295**	***$1,029***

GRADING - PPGS™	100%	98%	95%	90%	80%	70%	60%	LAST MSR

* ***Model 77LRBBZ Mark II Stainless*** – .25-06 Rem. (new 2004), .270 Win., .30-06, 7mm Rem. Mag., or .300 Win. Mag. cal., left-hand action, 22 in. barrel, uncheckered grey laminated stock, includes scope rings. Mfg. 1999-2008.

	$575	$500	$450	$395	$325	$265	$245	*$837*

MODEL 77 COMPACT MAGNUM – .300 RCM, .308 Win. (new 2011) or .338 RCM cal., 20 in. barrel, matte finish, American walnut stock, U-type notch rear sight with elevated brass bead front sight, 3 or 4 shot mag., left-hand became available in 2010, 7 1/4 lbs. Mfg. mid-2008-2012.

	$765	$625	$500	$425	$375	$325	$275	*$929*

* ***Model 77 Compact Magnum Stainless*** – .300 RCM or .338 RCM cal., 20 in. barrel, matte stainless finish, black synthetic stock, U-type notch rear sight with elevated brass bead front sight, 3 shot mag., 6 3/4 lbs. New mid-2008-2011.

	$750	$615	$500	$425	$375	$325	$275	*$914*

MODEL 77 RSM – .375 H&H, .416 Rigby, or .458 Lott (new 2002) cal., 23 or 24 (.375 H&H cal.) in. barrel, 3 or 4 (.375 H&H cal.) shot mag., premium grade Circassian walnut with hand cut checkering and ebony forend tip, integral barrel and sighting quarter rib with two folding sights, approx. 9 1/2 lbs. Mfg. 1990-2010.

	$1,950	$1,425	$1,100	$975	$850	$725	$675	*$2,404*

MODEL 77 RS EXPRESS – .270 Win., .25-06 (rare), .30-06, 7mm Rem. Mag., .300 Win. Mag., .300 H&H (extremely rare!), or .338 Win. Mag. (new 1994) cal., 22 or 24 in. barrel, 3 or 4 shot mag., similar construction to Model 77RSM with premium grade wood and other materials, 7 1/2 lbs. Mfg. 1991-2002.

	$1,250	$875	$815	$750	$700	$675	$595	*$1,625*

Add 60% for .25-06 cal. (reportedly 12 produced).
Add 100% for .300 H&H cal. (reportedly only 1 produced).

MODEL 77-GS GUNSITE SCOUT – .308 Win. or 5.56 NATO (mfg. 2015-2018) cal., right or left (mfg. 2012-2018) hand action, 16.1 in. cold hammer forged barrel with flash suppressor, 10 shot detachable box mag., alloy steel receiver, non-rotating Mauser type controlled round feed extractor, protected front sight and adj. ghost ring rear sight, checkered grey laminate or composite (new 2015) stock, soft rubber buttpad with 3 1/2 in. spacers, sling swivels, forward mounted Picatinny rail, Gunsite name rollmarked on the receiver and engraved on the grip cap, matte black finish, approx. 7 lbs. New 2011.

MSR $1,139	$1,000	$850	$725	$675	$550	$450	$375	

Note that the earliest few hundred Gunsite Scouts produced had a 711- serial number prefix from the M77 Hawkeye series. The Gunsite Scout was soon after given its exclusive serial number prefix of 680-.

* ***Model 77-GS Gunsite Scout Stainless*** – .308 Win. or 5.56 NATO (mfg. 2015-2018) cal., 16.1, 16 1/2 (disc. 2012) or 18 in. barrel with flash suppressor, 10 shot detachable box mag., alloy steel receiver, matte stainless finish, forward mounted Picatinny rail, checkered grey/black laminate or composite (new 2015) stock, soft rubber buttpad with 3 1/2 in. spacers, sling swivels, protected front sight and adj. ghost ring rear sight, Gunsite engraved logo grip cap, non-rotating Mauser type controlled round feed extractor, right or left-hand (new 2012) action, approx. 7 lbs. New 2011.

MSR $1,199	$1,050	$900	$775	$700	$575	$475	$400	

GUNSITE SCOUT .450 BUSHMASTER – .450 Bushmaster cal., 16 in. free floated barrel, Hybrid muzzle brake, 4 shot detachable box mag., alloy steel receiver, controlled round feed extractor, fixed blade-type ejector, ghost ring adj. rear and blade front sights, American walnut or black synthetic (mfg. mid-2018-2019) stock, soft rubber buttpad with spacers, sling swivel studs, 3-pos. safety, forward mounted Picatinny rail, Gunsite name is rollmarked on the receiver and engraved on the grip cap, matte black finish, 6.2-6.6 lbs. New 2017.

MSR $1,199	$1,050	$900	$775	$700	$575	$475	$400	

GUNSITE SCOUT .350 LEGEND – .350 Legend cal., 16 1/2 in. free floating cold hammer forged threaded barrel with muzzle brake, 5 shot detachable box mag., alloy steel, non-rotating Mauser-type controlled round feed extractor, fixed blade-type ejector, non-glare protected front sight and adj. rear sight, integral scope mounts, black synthetic stock, soft rubber buttpad with spacers, sling swivel studs, 3-pos. safety, forward mounted Picatinny rail, matte black finish, 6.3 lbs. New late 2019.

MSR $1,139	$975	$850	$725	$675	$550	$450	$375	

MODEL HM77R HAWKEYE SERIES – various cals., newest variation of the M77, featuring one-piece stainless bolt, new LC6 trigger, rotating Mauser type controlled round extractor, slimmer profile, checkered American walnut stock with solid red recoil pad, matte bluing on barrel and action (disc. on most models 2010) or satin blue finish, redesigned steel floorplate and latch, left-hand available in certain cals. beginning 2008, includes scope rings, various weights. New 2007.

GRADING - PPGS™	100%	98%	95%	90%	80%	70%	60%	LAST MSR

* ***Hawkeye (Model HM77R)*** – .204 Ruger, .22-250 Rem. (disc. 2013), .223 Rem., .243 Win., .25-06 Rem. (disc. 2013), .257 Roberts (disc. 2013), .270 Win., .280 Rem. (may not have been produced), .30-06, .308 Win., 7mm Rem. Mag., 7mm-08 Rem., .300 Win. Mag., .300 RCM (disc. 2012), .338 Win. Mag. (disc. 2013), .338 RCM (mfg. 2011-2012), .338 Federal (mfg. 2008-2010), 6.5 Creedmoor (mfg. 2010-2013), or .358 Win. (mfg. 2008-2009) cal., newest variation of the M77, featuring one-piece stainless bolt, 3, 4, or 5 shot mag., 22 or 24 in. barrel, rotating Mauser type controlled round extractor, slimmer profile, checkered American walnut stock with solid red recoil pad, extensive cut checkered grip and wrap-around checkered forend, matte bluing on barrel and action (disc. 2010) or satin blue (new 2011), new LC6 trigger, redesigned steel floorplate and latch, no sights, includes scope rings, 7-8 1/4 lbs. Mfg. 2007-2019.

	$825	$725	$625	$565	$455	$375	$325	*$979*

This model was available in left-hand action in most popular cals. at no extra charge (disc. 2014).

* ***Hawkeye All-Weather Stainless (Model HM77RFP)*** – same cals. as Model HM77R Hawkeye, except not available in .257 Roberts, 22 or 24 in. barrel, matte finish stainless steel, black checkered synthetic stock, no sights, similar Hawkeye features as the HM77R. Mfg. 2007-2014.

	$675	$525	$400	$315	$265	$225	$195	*$899*

* ***Hawkeye Laminated Stainless (Model HM77R)*** – .25-06 Rem., .270 Win., .30-06, 7mm Rem. Mag., or .300 Win. Mag. cal., left-hand action, 22 in. barrel, matte finish stainless steel, black laminated stock, includes scope rings. Mfg. mid-2008-2010.

	$675	$575	$450	$400	$350	$300	$250	*$862*

* ***Model HM77RBH*** – .30-06 cal., 22 in. blue or stainless steel barrel, brown Hogue overmolded stock. Limited mfg. 2008.

	$575	$450	$365	$315	$275	$230	$210	*$821*

* ***Model HM77RGH*** – .270 Win. cal., 22 in. blue or stainless steel barrel, green Hogue overmolded stock. Limited mfg. 2008.

	$575	$450	$365	$315	$275	$230	$210	*$821*

* ***Hawkeye Alaskan (Model HM77R)*** – .375 Ruger or .416 Ruger (new 2010) cal., 20 in. stainless steel (disc. 2010) or alloy steel (new 2011) barrel with choice of Diamondblack corrosion resistant coating or stainless Hawkeye matte finish, express sights with adj. V-notch rear sight, black Hogue overmolded stock with recoil pad, 8 lbs. Mfg. 2007-2012.

	$950	$900	$825	$750	$600	$450	$300	*$1,099*

* ***Hawkeye Alaskan (Current Mfg.)*** – .375 Ruger, .338 Win. Mag., or .300 Win. Mag. cal., 20 in. cold hammer forged stainless steel barrel, radial port muzzle brake, barrel band mounted swivel stud, 3 shot mag., hinged solid steel floorplate, Mauser-type controlled round feed extractor, fixed blade-type ejector, LC6 trigger, white bead front and V-notch adj. rear sights, black Hogue overmolded stock, 3-pos. safety, integral scope mounts on receiver, one-piece stainless steel bolt, Hawkeye Matte stainless finish, 8.1 lbs. New 2019.

MSR $1,279	$1,100	$955	$810	$725	$600	$500	$425

* ***Hawkeye African (Model HM77RS)*** – .223 Rem. (mfg. 2011-2013), 9.3x62mm (mfg. 2011-2012), .375 Ruger, .300 Win. Mag., or .338 Win. Mag. cal., satin blue finish, right or left (.375 Ruger cal only) hand action, 23 in. alloy steel barrel, checkered American walnut stock and forearm with ebony forend cap (not available in .223 Rem. cal.), 3 or 5 shot mag., bead front sight, adj. rear sight, 7 3/4 lbs. Mfg. 2007-2012.

	$1,025	$875	$750	$650	$575	$525	$475	*$1,199*

* ***Hawkeye African with Muzzle Brake (Model HM77RSB)*** – .300 Win. Mag. (disc. 2019), .338 Win. Mag. (disc. 2019), .375 Ruger, or .416 Ruger cal., 3 shot mag., 23 in. barrel with removable radial port muzzle brake and barrel band, satin blue finish, American walnut stock with ebony forend cap, LC6 trigger, right or left (.375 Ruger, or new for 2017 in .416 Ruger) hand action, Express style bead front and adj. rear sights, non-rotating Mauser-type round feed extractor, fixed blade-type ejector, hinged steel floorplate with engraved Ruger logo, three position safety, integral scope mounts, 8 lbs. New 2013.

MSR $1,279	$1,100	$955	$810	$725	$600	$500	$425

* ***Hawkeye Compact (Model HM77-CR)*** – .223 Rem. (mfg. 2009-2016), .243 Win. (mfg. 2009-2017), .260 Rem. (mfg. 2009-disc.), 7mm-08 Rem., 7.62x39mm (disc. 2012), .308 Win., or 6.8 SPC (disc. 2011) cal., 16 1/2 in. barrel w/o sights, LC6 trigger, 12 1/2 in. LOP, American walnut stock, matte blueing on barrel and action (disc. 2010) or satin blue (new 2011) finish, approx. 6 lbs. Mfg. 2009-2017, reintroduced 2020.

MSR $979	$830	$725	$625	$565	$455	$375	$325

GRADING - PPGS™	100%	98%	95%	90%	80%	70%	60%	LAST MSR

* ***Hawkeye Compact Laminate Stainless (Model HKM77-CRBBZ)*** – .223 Rem.(disc. 2016), .243 Win., .260 Rem. (disc. 2011), 7mm-08 Rem., .308 Win., 6.8 SPC (mfg. 2009-disc.), or .300 RCM (mfg. 2009-disc.) cal., 16 1/2 in. barrel, stainless steel matte finish, black laminate stock, no sights, 6-6 1/2 lbs. New 2009.

MSR $1,069	$910	$795	$685	$620	$500	$410	$350	

* ***Hawkeye Ultra Light (Model HM77RL)*** – .223 Rem., .243 Win., .257 Roberts, .270 Win., .30-06, or .308 Win. cal., 20 in. barrel w/o sights, matte blue metal finish, checkered walnut stock with black forend cap, approx. 6 1/2 lbs. Mfg. 2009-2010.

	$695	$585	$460	$410	$350	$300	$250	*$888*

» **Hawkeye All-Weather Ultra Light (Model HM77RLFP)** – .204 Ruger, .223 Rem., .243 Win., .270 Win., or .30-06 cal., similar to Ultra Light, except has stainless steel action with matte finish and black synthetic stock, approx. 6 1/2 lbs. Mfg. 2009 only.

	$575	$450	$375	$325	$275	$250	$220	*$803*

* ***Hawkeye International (Model HM77R)*** – .243 Win., .270 Win., .30-06, or .308 Win. cal., 18 1/2 in. barrel with adj. rear express sight and blade front sight, matte blued metal finish, checkered Mannlicher walnut stock with sling swivels, 6 1/4 - 7 lbs. Mfg. 2009-2010.

	$750	$650	$550	$425	$350	$315	$275	*$967*

* ***Hawkeye Magnum Hunter (Model HKM77-MH)*** – .300 Win. Mag. cal., 3 shot mag., 24 in. stainless steel barrel with removable radial-port muzzle brake, stainless steel receiver, no sights, LC6 trigger, All-Weather Green Hogue overmolded stock, matte stainless finish, 8 lbs. Mfg. 2013-2015.

	$900	$790	$650	$525	$450	$350	$300	*$1,139*

* ***Hawkeye Sporter (Model HKM77-RBBZ)*** – .22-250 Rem. (disc. 2011), .223 Rem. (disc. 2011), .243 Win., .270 Win., .280 Rem. (new 2012), .30-06, .308 Win., .300 Win. Mag., .338 Win. Mag., or 7mm Rem. Mag. cal., features matte finished stainless steel action with 22 or 24 in. barrel w/o sights, brown (disc.) or black (new 2010) laminate stock, 7 1/2 - 8 1/2 lbs. Mfg. 2009-2013.

	$760	$550	$400	$315	$265	$225	$195	*$959*

* ***Hawkeye Tactical (Model HM77-VLEHFS)*** – .223 Rem., .243 Win. (disc. 2010), or .308 Win. cal., 4 or 5 shot mag., matte finished blued action and 20 in. bull barrel with flash suppressor, no sights, adj. two-stage target trigger, black Hogue overmolded stock with Harris bipod, 8 3/4 lbs. Mfg. 2009-2013.

	$1,050	$900	$765	$650	$575	$525	$475	*$1,199*

* ***Hawkeye Varmint Target*** – .204 Ruger, .22-250 Rem., .223 Rem., .308 Win., or 6.5 Creedmoor cal., 26 in. heavy contour cold hammer forged stainless steel barrel with target crown, 4 or 5 shot mag., no sights, two-stage adj. trigger, target forend, black laminate stock, Hawkeye matte stainless finish, 9 1/4-9 3/4 lbs. Mfg. 2014-2019.

	$965	$845	$725	$655	$530	$435	$340	*$1,139*

HAWKEYE GUIDE GUN – .300 RCM (disc. 2017), .300 Win. Mag. (disc. 2019), .338 RCM (disc. 2017), .338 Win. Mag., .375 Ruger, .30-06, or .416 Ruger (new 2014) cal., 3 or 4 shot mag., 20 in. stainless steel barrel with removable radial-port muzzle brake, Mauser-type controlled round feed extractor, fixed blade-type ejector, Hawkeye matte finish, Green Mountain laminate stock, soft rubber recoil pad with buttpad spacers, Express style bead front and adj. rear sights, right or left (.375 Ruger cal. only) hand action, LC6 trigger, three position safety, hinged steel floorplate with engraved Ruger logo, integral scope mounts, 8.1 lbs. New 2013.

MSR $1,279	$1,100	$955	$810	$725	$600	$500	$425	

HAWKEYE HUNTER – 6.5 Creedmoor, 6.5 PRC, .308 Win., .30-06, .300 Win. Mag., 7mm Rem. Mag., or .204 Ruger cal., 20, 22, or 24 in. cold hammer forged stainless steel threaded barrel, 5R rifling, 3 or 4 shot mag., non-rotating Mauser-type round feed extractor, LC6 trigger, checkered American walnut stock and forend, pistol grip, 3-pos. safety, one-piece stainless steel bolt, mounting sling swivels, 20 MOA Picatinny rail, right or left-hand action, satin stainless finish, 7.2-8.1 lbs. New late 2019.

MSR $1,099	$950	$825	$700	$650	$515	$425	$365	

HAWKEYE FTW HUNTER – .30-06 (disc. 2018), .300 Win. Mag. (disc. 2019), .308 Win. (disc. 2018), .375 Ruger (disc. 2017, reintroduced 2019), 6.5 Creedmoor, 7mm Rem. Mag. (disc. 2017), or .260 Rem. (disc. 2017) cal., right or left-hand (.375 Ruger, 6.5 Creedmoor, or .300 Win. Mag. only) action, 22 or 24 in. cold hammer forged barrel, Ruger Muzzle Brake System, thread protector, 3 or 4 shot mag., stainless steel construction, Mauser-type controlled round feed extractor, fixed blade-type ejector, no sights, Natural Gear Camo laminate stock with soft rubber buttpad and buttpad spacers, three position safety, one-piece stainless steel bolt, hinged solid steel floorplate, integral scope mounts, features engraved FTW logo and patented latch, includes scope rings, Hawkeye matte stainless finish, 7.6-8.2 lbs. New mid-2016.

MSR $1,279	$1,100	$955	$810	$725	$600	$500	$425	

GRADING - PPGS™	100%	98%	95%	90%	80%	70%	60%	LAST MSR

HAWKEYE LONG-RANGE HUNTER - 6.5 Creedmoor or 6.5 PRC cal., 22 in. cold hammer forged stainless steel barrel with 5R rifling, radial-port muzzle brake, 3 or 5 shot, LC6 trigger, no sights, speckled black/brown laminate stock with adj. LOP, soft rubber buttpad, 3-pos. safety, 20 MOA Picatinny rail, Hawkeye matte stainless finish, 7.2 lbs. New 2020.

MSR $1,279	$1,100	$955	$810	$725	$600	$500	$425	

HAWKEYE LONG-RANGE TARGET - .300 Win. Mag., 6.5 Creedmoor (new 2019), 6.5 PRC (new 2019), .204 Ruger (new late 2019), or .308 Win. (new late 2019) cal., 24 in. heavy contour target barrel featuring Ruger Precision Rifle Hybrid muzzle brake, 3, 5, or 10 shot AI-Style mag., alloy steel receiver, no sights, speckled black/brown painted laminate stock, two-way adj. comb, Picatinny rail, matte black finish, 10.7 lbs. New 2018.

MSR $1,279	$1,100	$955	$810	$725	$600	$500	$425	

HAWKEYE PREDATOR (MODEL HKM77R-Z) - .204 Ruger, .22-250 Rem., .223 Rem., .308 Win. (mfg. 2013-2018), or 6.5 Creedmoor (new 2013) cal., 22 or 24 in. heavy barrel, 4 or 5 shot mag., stainless steel action with adj. two-stage target trigger, no sights, Green Mountain laminate stock, Hawkeye matte stainless finish, approx. 8 lbs. New 2009.

MSR $1,139	$975	$850	$725	$675	$550	$450	$375	

* ***Hawkeye FTW Predator*** - .308 Win. (disc. 2018) or 6.5 Creedmoor cal., 22 (disc.) or 24 in. medium contour barrel, stainless steel construction, 4 shot mag., no sights, two-stage adj. trigger, three position safety, Green Mountain laminate stock with adj. LOP, Hawkeye matte stainless finish, 8-8.12 lbs. New 2015.

MSR $1,159	$985	$850	$725	$675	$550	$450	$385	

MODEL 77 50TH ANNIVERSARY M77 HAWKEYE (RUGER MODEL 47190) - .243 Win. cal., 22 in. cold hammer forged barrel, 6 grooves, 4 shot mag., alloy steel construction, non-rotating Mauser-type controlled round feed extractor, features a fixed blade-type ejector, high grade American walnut ergonomic stock, wrap around checkering on grip and forend, 3-position safety, hinged floorplate, custom 50th Anniversary "M77 50 Years" bolt handle and floorplate engravings, integral scope mounts, satin blued finish, includes red drawstring bag for accessories, 42 in. OAL, 7 lbs. Mfg. 2018 only.

	$1,550	$1,350	$1,165	$1,050	$850	$700	$550	*$1,799*

Note that an "Employee Edition" of the M77 50th Anniversary rifle was also produced (Ruger model 47193) with "EMPLOYEE EDITION" selectively gold layered on the stainless round bolt handle, high polish blue finish on the barreled action, and selective gold and silver layer engraved floorplate identical to the Ruger collector edition 50th Anniversary Rifle. This model was also serial numbered within the regular M77 Hawkeye sequence (i.e. 712-477xx range). Unknown quantity produced.

MODEL 77 50TH ANNIVERSARY M77 HAWKEYE (COLLECTOR EDITION - RUGER MODEL 47191) - The earliest version of the Model 77 50th Anniversary M77 Hawkeye was produced through collaboration of the Ruger factory and Ruger collector Terry Wolosek. It has additional features of a blued steel "flatbolt" style bolt handle, selective gold/silver layer engraving on the sides of the receiver in lieu of the selective gold of the regular production model, and selective silver layered engraving on the floorplate instead of selective gold on the regular production model and high polish blue. 77 produced in serial no. range 7750-00001 through 7750-00077 (Ruger model 47191).

	$3,000	$2,625	$2,250	$2,040	$1,650	$1,350	$1,100	

AMERICAN RIFLE - .223 Rem. (mfg. 2014-2018), .22-250 Rem. (mfg. 2013-2018), .243 Win., .270 Win., .30-06, .308 Win., or 7mm-08 Rem. (new 2013) cal., 22 in. hammer forged barrel, flush fitting 4 or 5 (.223 Rem. cal. only, mfg. 2014-2018) shot rotary mag., right or left (mfg. 2015-2018, .308 still offered) hand action, black composite stock, matte black finish, soft rubber recoil pad, w/o sights, Power Bedding allows free floating barrel, 3-5 lb. Marksman adj. trigger, tang safety, drilled and tapped, approx. 6 1/4 lbs. New 2012.

MSR $489	$415	$365	$315	$285	$250	$225	$200	

* ***American Rifle Compact*** - .22-250 (mfg. 2014-2017), .223 Rem. (mfg. 2014-2017), .243 Win., .308 Win., or 7mm-08 Rem. cal., similar to American Rifle, except features 18 in. barrel, 4 or 5 (.223 Rem. only, disc. 2017), shot rotary mag., 12 1/2 in. LOP, 6 lbs. New 2013.

MSR $489	$415	$365	$315	$285	$250	$225	$200	

* ***American Rifle Magnum*** - .300 Win. Mag. or 7mm Rem. Mag. (disc. 2017) cal., 24 in. stainless steel threaded barrel with thread protector, 3 shot detachable box mag., stainless steel construction, no sights, black nylon synthetic stock, one-piece aluminum scope rail, matte stainless finish, 7 1/2 lbs. Mfg. 2016-2019.

	$595	$525	$450	$400	$325	$275	$225	*$699*

GRADING - PPGS™	100%	98%	95%	90%	80%	70%	60%	LAST MSR

* ***American Rifle Ranch (Standard or Compact Length Stock)*** – 5.56 NATO, .300 AAC Blackout, .450 Bushmaster (new 2017), 7.62x39mm (new late 2017), .350 Legend (new late 2019), or 6.5 Grendel (new 2020) cal., 16.12 in. cold hammer forged barrel with matte black finish, 3 (new 2017) or 5 shot flush fit rotary mag. or 10 shot AR-style mag. (new 2018), no sights, one-piece aluminum scope rail, soft rubber buttpad, Power Bedding integral bedding block system, tang safety, Marksman adj. trigger, FDE composite stock, includes magazine and sling swivel studs, 36 in. OAL (standard, disc. 2015) or 34.75 in. OAL (Compact), approx. 6 lbs. New 2015.

MSR $549 $470 $410 $350 $325 $265 $230 $200

* ***American Rifle with Redfield Revolution Riflescope*** – .22-250 Rem., .223 Rem., .243 Win., .270 Win., .30-06, .308 Win., or 7mm-08 Rem. cal., 22 in. barrel, 4 or 5 (.223 Rem. only) shot mag., black composite stock, matte black finish, Redfield Revolution riflescope, 7-7 1/4 lbs. Mfg. 2014-2015.

$610 $525 $450 $410 $325 $275 $215 ***$699***

* ***American Rifle with Vortex Crossfire II Riflescope*** – .243 Win., .270 Win., .30-06, .223 Rem. (mfg. 2018-2019), or .308 Win. cal., 22 in. barrel, 4 or 5 (mfg. 2018-2019) shot, alloy steel, black synthetic stock, includes Vortex Crossfire II Riflescope, matte black finish, 7 lbs. New 2016.

MSR $639 $540 $475 $400 $365 $300 $250 $210

AMERICAN RIFLE HUNTER – 6.5 Creedmoor or .308 Win. cal., 20 in. heavy contour barrel, Hybrid muzzle brake, 5 shot Magpul PMAG, Ruger Marksman adj. trigger, Gray Magpul Hunter American stock with fully adj. LOP, spacers included, tang safety, one-piece Picatinny scope base, matte black finish, 9.2 lbs. New 2020.

MSR $799 $680 $600 $500 $450 $375 $300 $265

AMERICAN RIFLE PREDATOR – .204 Ruger, .223 Rem., .22-250 Rem., .243 Win., 6.5 Creedmoor, 6mm Creedmoor (new 2017), .308 Win., 6.5 Grendel (new 2018), or 7mm-08 Rem. (new 2019) cal., alloy steel construction, 18 (.308 Win. cal. only) or 22 in. cold hammer forged heavy tapered threaded barrel, right or left-hand (new late 2017) action, integral bedding block system free floats barrel, ergonomic, lightweight, moss green composite stock with forend contouring and grip serrations, soft rubber recoil pad, pistol grip, 3 shot AI-style mag. (new 2018), 4 or 5 (disc. 2017) shot rotary mag., or 10 shot AR-style mag. (new 2018), Ruger Marksman adj. trigger, factory installed one-piece of aluminum scope rail, one-piece three-lug 70° bolt, swivel studs, matte black finish, 6 1/4-6.62 lbs. New mid-2014.

MSR $529 $450 $395 $340 $300 $265 $230 $200

Add $40 for left-hand action (new late 2017).

Add $20 for 3 shot AI-style or 10 shot AR-style mag. (new 2018).

* ***American Rifle Predator Camo*** – .243 Win., 7mm-08 Rem., 6.5 Creedmoor, .308 Win., .30-06, .450 Bushmaster, .300 Win. Mag., .350 Legend (new 2020), or 6.5 PRC (new 2020) cal., 16.1 (new 2020, compact), 22, or 24 in. cold hammer forged alloy steel threaded barrel with Bronze Cerakote finish, muzzle brake, 3 or 5 shot AI-style, rotary, or single stack mag., Marksman adj. trigger, no sights, GO WILD camo I-M brush synthetic stock, soft rubber buttpad, sling swivel studs, tang safety, Power Bedding system, one-piece Picatinny scope base, 6.6-7.1 lbs. New 2018.

MSR $629 $535 $475 $400 $365 $300 $250 $210

* ***American Rifle Predator with Vortex Crossfire II Riflescope*** – .223 Rem., .204 Ruger, 6.5 Creedmoor, or .308 Win. (disc. 2019) cal., 18 (disc. 2019) or 22 in. alloy steel threaded barrel with matte black finish, 3, 4, or 10 shot AI-style, rotary, or AR-style mag., Moss Green synthetic stock, includes Vortex Crossfire II Riflescope, 7.2-7.6 lbs. New 2018.

MSR $699 $600 $525 $450 $410 $325 $275 $225

AMERICAN RIFLE ALL-WEATHER – .22-250 Rem., .223 Rem., .243 Win., .270 Win., .30-06, .308 Win., or 7mm-08 Rem. cal., 22 in. stainless steel cold hammer forged barrel, 4 shot rotary mag., right or left (new 2016) hand action, drilled and tapped receiver, no sights, Power Bedding integral bedding blocks, adj. trigger, ergonomic lightweight black composite stock with soft rubber recoil pad, tang safety, matte stainless finish, approx. 6 1/4 lbs. Mfg. 2014-2017.

$535 $475 $400 $365 $295 $245 $210 ***$629***

* ***American Rifle All-Weather Compact*** – .22-250 Rem., .223 Rem., .243 Win., .308 Win., or 7mm-08 Rem. cal., similar to American Rifle All-Weather, except features 18 in. barrel, 4 or 5 shot rotary mag., right or left (new 2017) hand action, 12 1/2 in. LOP, 6 lbs. Mfg. 2014-2017.

$535 $475 $400 $365 $295 $245 $210 ***$629***

Left-hand action available only in .243 Win., 7mm-08 Rem., or .308 Win. cal.

GRADING - PPGS™	100%	98%	95%	90%	80%	70%	60%	LAST MSR

PRECISION RIFLE – .243 Win. (disc. 2016), .308 Win., 6mm Creedmoor (new 2017), 6.5 Creedmoor, 5.56 NATO (mfg. 2017 only), .300 Win. Mag. (new late 2018), .338 Lapua Mag. (new late 2018), .300 PRC (new 2019), or 6.5 PRC (new 2019) cal., in-line recoil path, 20 (.308 Win.), 24 (6mm or 6.5 Creedmoor), or 26 (.300 Win. Mag., .338 Lapua Mag., 6.5 PRC, 6mm Creedmoor, .243 Win. - disc. 2016) in. free floating cold hammer forged barrel, with or without Hybrid muzzle brake (new mid-2016) or muzzle brake with tunable compensator (new late 2018), features a Multi-Magazine Interface and two 10 shot Magpul PMAGs, Ruger Marksman adj. trigger, MSR stock is foldable and adj. for comb and LOP, soft rubber buttpad, AR-style grip, oversized bolt handle, Samson Evolution KeyMod handguard (disc.), short action handguard (mfg. mid-2016-2017), or 15 or 18 (.300 Win. Mag. or .338 Lapua Mag.) in. free float M-LOK handguard (new 2018), multiple QD sling attachment points, bottom Picatinny rail, left-folding stock hinge is attached to AR-style buffer tube and accepts AR-style stocks, with or without billet aluminum bolt shroud (new mid-2016), 9.8-15.2 lbs. New mid-2015.

MSR $1,599	$1,275	$1,075	$950	$850	$725	$600	$525	

Add $200 for Hybrid muzzle brake, short action handguard, and billet aluminum bolt shroud (mfg. 2016 only).
Add $500 for .300 Win. Mag. (new late 2018), .338 Lapua Mag. (new late 2018), or .300 PRC (new 2019).

* ***Precision Magpul MOE K2+*** – 6mm Creedmoor cal., 26 in. CHF stainless steel barrel with 5R rifling, APA muzzle brake, 10 shot Magpul PMAG, TriggerTech trigger, Ruger Precision MSR stock with QD attachment points feature bottom M-LOK slots, soft rubber buttpad, adj. LOP and comb height, Sorbothane cheek pad, Magpul MOE K2+ grip, ambi safety, aluminum free float handguard with M-LOK slots, 20 MOA Picatinny rail, Type III hardcoat anodized with Gray Cerakote finish, 12.8 lbs. New 2021.

MSR $2,399	$2,050	$1,795	$1,540	$1,395	$1,130	$925	$800	

RIFLES: LEVER ACTION

MODEL 96 CARBINE – .17 HMR (new 2002), .22 LR (disc. 2003), .22 WMR, or .44 Mag. (disc. 2007) cal., 18 1/2 in. barrel with single barrel band, uncheckered hardwood stock with curved buttplate, 10 (.17 HMR or .22 LR), 9 (.22 WMR), or 4 (.44 Mag.) shot detachable rotary mag., crossbolt safety on trigger guard, adj. rear sight, .44 Mag. has case hardened finish lever, rimfire receivers are drilled and tapped while the .44 Mag. has a receiver with integral bases, scope rings (became standard 1997), approx. 5 1/4 - 6 lbs. Mfg. 1996-2008.

	$800	$525	$450	$350	$275	$200	$175	*$451*

Add $200 for .44 Mag. cal. with scope rings (disc. 2007).

RIFLES: SEMI-AUTO, RIMFIRE

During certain years of manufacture, Ruger's changes in production on certain models (calibers, barrel markings, barrel lengths, etc.) have created rare variations that are now considered premium niches. These areas of low manufacture will add premiums to the values listed on standard models. The Model 10/22 has been manufactured in a variety of limited production models including a multi-colored or green laminate wood stock variation (1986), a brown laminate stock (1988), a Kittery Trading Post Commemorative (1988), a smoke or tree bark laminate stock (1989), a Chief AJ Model, Wal-Mart (stainless with black laminated hardwood stock - 1990), etc. These limited editions will command premiums over the standard models listed, depending on the desirability of the special edition.

Note: Ruger firearms produced during 1976 were rollmarked "MADE IN THE 200th YEAR OF AMERICAN LIBERTY". Add $50-$75 when in 100% in the original box condition.

10/17 CARBINE – .17 HMR cal., steel receiver, birch stock only, 18 1/2 in. barrel.

While advertised with an MSR of $510, this model never went into production.

10/22 COLLECTOR'S SERIES FIRST EDITION – .22 LR cal., 18 1/2 in. barrel, one BX-25 mag. and one BX-1 mag. (Model 21104) or three BX-1 mags. (Model 21105), black composite stock, 50th Anniversary bolt marking, "RCS1-" serial number prefix, commemorative 50th Anniversary box with an exclusive Collector's Series box decal and "The Ruger 10/22 Rifle * 22 LR - Fifty Years * 1964-2014" special receiver marking, also included was a Collector's Series pin, 10/22 50th Anniversary bumper sticker, replica of the original 1964 10/22 ad and a limited edition Ruger Collector's Series street sign. Over 31,000 mfg. 2014-2015.

	$265	$220	$180	$150	$130	$120	$100	*$349*

10/22 COLLECTOR'S SERIES SECOND EDITION (MODEL 21125) – .22 LR cal., 18 1/2 in. barrel, 10 shot detachable rotary mag., protected, non-glare blade front and ghost ring adj. rear aperture sights, "RCS2-" serial number prefix, Modular Stock System with low comb and standard LOP on dark gray composite stock, satin black finish, exclusive Collector's Series bolt marking, includes $25 ShopRuger.com gift certificate and one-of-a-kind Ruger Collector's Series memorabilia, including Limited Edition street sign, 5 lbs. Over 30,000 produced 2015-2017.

	$265	$220	$180	$150	$130	$120	$100	*$349*

GRADING - PPGS™	100%	98%	95%	90%	80%	70%	60%	LAST MSR

10/22 CARBINE COLLECTOR'S SERIES THIRD EDITION (MODEL 31115) – .22 LR cal.,18 1/2 in. cold hammer forged barrel w/two-screw V-block system, 6 grooves, 10 shot rotary mag., alloy steel, polymer trigger, protective blade front sight, ghost ring adj. rear sight, "RCS3-" serial number prefix, OD Green synthetic modular stock w/low comb, crossbolt manual safety, one-piece aluminum scope rail, satin black finish, includes $25 ShopRuger.com gift certificate and one-of-a-kind Ruger Collector's Series memorabilia, including Limited Edition "Man's Best Friend" street sign and dog tag, 37 in. OAL, 5 lbs. Over 10,000 mfg. 2018-2020.

$340 $300 $255 $230 $185 $155 $130 *$399*

10/22 COLLECTOR'S SERIES FOURTH EDITION, "VOTE 2020" (MODEL 31154) – .22 LR cal., 18 1/2 in. cold hammer forged alloy steel barrel with satin black finish, thread protector, 6 grooves, 10 shot detachable rotary mag., polymer trigger, protected blade front sight, ghost ring adj. rear sight, American Flag synthetic stock, crossbolt manual safety, one-piece aluminum scope rail, "Collector Series" bolt marking, includes "Vote 2020" metal street sign and pin, $25 ShopRuger.com gift certificate, and one-of-a-kind Ruger Collector's Series memorabilia, 37 in. OAL, 4.8 lbs. Limited mfg. beginning mid-2020.

MSR $369 $325 $275 $235 $225 $175 $150 $120

10/22 CARBINE WITH VIRIDIAN EON 3-9x40 SCOPE – .22 LR cal., 18 1/2 in. cold hammer forged alloy steel barrel, 10 shot detachable rotary mag., gold bead front and adj. rear sight, black synthetic or hardwood (new 2010) stock, push-button crossbolt manual safety, includes factory mounted Viridian EON 3-9x40 scope, combination scope base adapter for both Weaver-style and .22 tip-off scope mounts, and Ruger hard case, satin black finish, 5.4-6.1 lbs. New late 2019.

MSR $399 $340 $300 $255 $230 $185 $155 $130

10/22 CARBINE "ECONOMY" MODEL – .22 LR cal., 18 1/2 in. CHF barrel, 10 shot detachable rotary mag., factory installed combination scope base adapter for both Weaver-style and .22 tip-off scope mounts, Charcoal or Gray synthetic stock, push-button crossbolt manual safety, satin black finish, 4.5 lbs. New mid-2019.

MSR $309 $265 $230 $195 $180 $145 $120 $100

10/22 COMPACT – .22 LR cal., 16 1/2 in. barrel, 10 shot mag., fiber optic front sight and adj. rear sight (although a few with standard 10/22 sights were also produced), hardwood stock with rubber buttpad, 12 3/4 in. LOP, satin black finish, 4 1/2 lbs. Mfg. 2005-2017.

$300 $265 $225 $200 $150 $125 $100 *$359*

10/22 COMPACT (CURRENT MFG.) – .22 LR cal., 16.12 in. cold hammer forged barrel, 10 shot rotary mag., extended mag. release, fiber optic front and adj. fiber optic rear sight, black synthetic modular stock with low comb, 12.5 in. LOP, push-button crossbolt manual safety, satin black finish, 4.6 lbs. New late 2018.

MSR $309 $265 $230 $195 $180 $145 $120 $100

10/22 COMPETITION – .22 LR cal., aluminum frame, 16 1/8 in. cold hammer forged fluted bull alloy steel barrel with satin black finish or stainless steel barrel with satin stainless/black Cerakote accents (new 2019), detachable 10 shot rotary mag., BX-Trigger, no sights, speckled black/gray (with "CS2-" prefix serial number), Green Mountain (new late 2019 with "CS4-" prefix serial number), or natural brown (new 2019 with "CS7-" prefix serial number) laminated stock, fully adj. cheek rest, crossbolt manual safety, aluminum receiver, optics-ready 30 MOA Picatinny rail, hardcoat anodized black metal finish, includes hard case, 13 1/2 in. OAL, 6 lbs. Mfg. by the Custom Shop beginning 2018.

MSR $899 $775 $675 $575 $525 $425 $350 $300

10/22 STANDARD CARBINE – .22 LR cal., 10 shot rotary mag., 18 1/2 in. barrel with barrel band, birch or uncheckered walnut (disc. 1989) with contoured buttplate, satin black finish, adj. folding rear and gold bead front sights, 5 lbs. New 1964.

MSR $309 $265 $230 $195 $180 $145 $120 $100

Add $90 for Taylor Targets Rimfire Animal Spinner Target and Ruger-branded Flambeau hard case (mfg. 2019 only).

* ***10/22 Standard Carbine Synthetic*** – .22 LR cal., 10 shot rotary mag., 18 1/2 in. barrel with barrel band, black synthetic stock with contoured buttplate (boatpaddle style manufactured 1997 to 2001, full buttstock and forearm style new 2001), satin black finish, folding adj. rear and gold bead front, or LaserMax laser (mfg. 2013 only) sights integrated into forend, 5 lbs. New 1999.

MSR $309 $265 $230 $195 $180 $145 $120 $100

Add $90 for factory installed Weaver 3-9x40 scope and hard case (mfg. 2018-2020).
Add $120 for Lasermax laser sights (mfg. 2013 only).

* ***10/22 Standard Carbine Stainless*** – .22 LR cal., 18 1/2 in. stainless steel barrel and action, 10 shot, gold bead front, adj. folding rear sights, choice of birch (disc. 2008) or black synthetic (new 1997) stock, clear satin finish, 5 lbs. New 1992.

MSR $339 $290 $255 $220 $195 $160 $130 $110

GRADING - PPGS™	100%	98%	95%	90%	80%	70%	60%	LAST MSR

* ***10/22 Standard Carbine 40th Anniversary*** – similar to 10/22 Standard Carbine, except includes 40th Ruger anniversary medallion in buttstock. Mfg. 2004 only.

$275 $225 $200 $150 $120 $110 $100 *$279*

* ***10/22 Carbine GO WILD Camo Rock-Star (Model 31113)*** – .22 LR cal., 18 1/2 in. alloy steel barrel with threaded muzzle and thread cap, 10 shot mag., GO WILD Camo Rock-Star camouflage stock, gold bead front and adj. rear sights, ships with soft sided case, satin black finish, 5 lbs. New 2019.

MSR $399 $340 $300 $255 $230 $185 $155 $130

10/22 STANDARD SPORTER – .22 LR cal., 10 shot rotary mag., 18 1/2 in. barrel, deluxe hand checkered American walnut stock, flat grooved buttplate (disc. 1987) or rubber buttpad and sling swivels, satin black finish, adj. rear and gold bead front sights, 5 3/4 lbs. New 1971.

MSR $419 $450 $325 $275 $245 $200 $160 $140

10/22 RIFLE – similar to 10/22 Standard Carbine, except has 20 in. barrel with hardwood stock. Mfg. 2004-2006.

$220 $190 $150 $135 $115 $100 $90 *$275*

10/22 TAKEDOWN TD – .22 LR cal., stainless steel, 18 1/2 in. barrel, 10 shot rotary mag., takedown action with recessed locking lever, black synthetic stock, clear matte finish, polymer trigger housing, adj. rear sight, gold bead front sight, includes black synthetic backpack style bag, 4 2/3 lbs. New mid-2012.

MSR $439 $370 $320 $275 $250 $200 $165 $145

* ***10/22 Takedown with Mica Bronze Synthetic Stock*** – .22 LR cal., takedown action, 16.4 in. cold hammer forged threaded barrel, 10 shot detachable rotary mag., extended mag. release, gold bead front and adj. rear sight, Mica Bronze synthetic stock, push-button crossbolt manual safety, includes carry case, satin black finish, 4.4 lbs. Mfg. 2017-2018. This model was promoted by Ruger through their 2017 Summer Retailer Program.

$360 $300 $265 $240 $195 $160 $125 *$439*

* ***10/22 Takedown TDT (Ruger Model 11112)*** – .22 LR cal., similar to 10/22 Takedown TD, except has 16.62 in. threaded barrel with Mini-14 style flash suppressor, satin black finish, 4 2/3 lbs. New 2013.

MSR $459 $390 $340 $295 $265 $215 $175 $150

* ***10/22 Takedown Threaded (Ruger Model 21133)*** – .22 LR cal., 16.1 in. threaded, fluted target barrel, 10 shot mag., no sights, black synthetic stock featuring the Ruger Modular Stock System, satin black finish, 5.3 lbs. New 2016.

MSR $629 $535 $475 $400 $365 $300 $250 $200

Add $629 for Silent-SR suppressor (new 2016, NFA regulations apply).

10/22 TAKEDOWN BACKPACKER (MODEL 31152) – .22 LR cal., 16.4 in. precision rifled, cold hammer forged, stainless threaded barrel, 10 shot rotary mag., includes four BX-1 mags., polymer trigger housing, fiber optic front and adj. fiber optic rear sight, Stealth Gray Magpul X-22 Backpacker stock, MOE SL non-slip rubber buttpad, w/ergonomic handguard, integrated storage compartment in grip, push-button, crossbolt manual safety, 4.2 lbs. New 2020.

MSR $529 $450 $400 $350 $300 $250 $200 $175

10/22 TAKEDOWN LITE (RUGER MODEL 21152) – .22 LR cal., 16.1 in. cold hammer forged barrel in aluminum alloy barrel sleeve with threaded muzzle, detachable 10 shot mag., extended mag. release, no sights, black synthetic stock featuring the Ruger Modular Stock System, polymer trigger, crossbolt manual safety, includes carry case, satin black finish, 4 1/2 lbs. New mid-2016.

MSR $659 $560 $490 $420 $380 $310 $260 $215

10/22 TACTICAL (FS TACTICAL, RUGER MODEL 1261) – .22 LR cal., 10 shot rotary mag., 16 1/8 in. barrel with SR-556/Mini 14 style flash suppressor and barrel band, no sights, black synthetic stock with contoured buttplate, Picatinny rail on top of receiver, satin black finish, 4.3 lbs. New late 2010.

MSR $359 $310 $270 $235 $210 $170 $140 $120

10/22 TACTICAL w/HEAVY BARREL – .22 LR cal., 10 shot rotary mag., 16 1/8 in. heavy hammer forged barrel w/o sights and spiraled exterior, black Hogue overmolded stock, target trigger, adj. bipod, 6.8 lbs. Mfg. late 2010-2016.

$500 $395 $335 $275 $240 $215 $175 *$629*

10/22 TARGET LITE – .22 LR cal., 16.13 in. cold hammer forged threaded barrel tensioned in black anodized aluminum alloy barrel sleeve, 10 shot mag., BX trigger, no sights, black or red/black (mfg. 2018-2019) laminate thumbhole stock with adj. LOP, satin blued finish, 5 lbs. New 2017.

MSR $649 $550 $480 $415 $375 $310 $260 $215

GRADING - PPGS™	100%	98%	95%	90%	80%	70%	60%	LAST MSR

10/22-T TARGET MODEL – .22 LR cal., 20 in. cold hammer forged heavy barrel with recessed target crown and spiral design, 10 shot mag., target trigger, no sights, brown laminated American hardwood stock, rubber buttpad, and sling swivels, satin black finish, 7 1/2 lbs. Mfg. 1996-2017.

	$465	$385	$315	$260	$230	$200	$165	*$579*

* ***10/22 Target Model Stainless (K10/22-T)*** – .22 LR cal., 20 in. cold hammer forged heavy barrel with recessed target crown and spiral design, 10 shot mag., stainless steel, target trigger, no sights, brown (disc. 2010) or black laminated American hardwood stock (mfg. 2011-2017) with flat rubber buttpad and sling swivels, clear satin finish, 7 1/2 lbs. Mfg. 1998-2008, reintroduced 2010-2017.

	$525	$460	$395	$355	$290	$235	$185	*$629*

* ***K10/22-TNZ Target Model Stainless (Ruger Model 1147)*** – features 20 in. barrel w/o sights, stainless steel action and barrel, laminated thumbhole stock with slanted forend, 7 lbs. Mfg. 2001-2002.

	$525	$450	$375	$325	$260	$225	$185	*$649*

* ***K10/22-T Target Tactical*** – similar to 10/22-T Target Model, except available in black matte finish, black Hogue overmolded stock, receiver with Picatinny style rail, 16.1 in. barrel with no sights, includes precision adj. bipod, 6.9 lbs. Mfg. 2010 only.

	$500	$425	$345	$295	$250	$215	$175	*$555*

10/22 FINGERGROOVE SPORTER – similar to 10/22 Standard, except Monte Carlo stock and beavertail forearm. Mfg. 1966-1971.

w/o checkered stock	$850	$650	$550	$450	$375	$350	$325	
w/checkered stock	$1,200	$950	$800	$650	$550	$450	$400	

This variation will be found with a non-prefix serial number ranging from 43xxx to 200xxx, as well as with a 110 prefix serial number.

10/22 INTERNATIONAL (OLD PRODUCTION) – similar to 10/22 Standard, except walnut full stock Mannlicher style. Mfg. 1966-69.

	$800	$650	$550	$450	$375	$350	$325	

Add 50% for checkered stock.

This variation will be found with a non-prefix serial number ranging from 15xxx to 200xxx, as well as a few with a 110 prefix serial number.

10/22RBI INTERNATIONAL (NEW PRODUCTION) – features Mannlicher style international birch full stock. Mfg. 1994-2003.

	$250	$210	$170	$140	$120	$110	$100	*$279*

* ***K10/22RBI International (New Production) Stainless*** – stainless variation of the 10/22RBI International. Disc. 2003.

	$350	$280	$245	$215	$180	$155	$130	*$299*

10/22 MAGNUM – .22 WMR cal., steel receiver, longer and heavier bolt, 10 shot rotary mag., 18 1/2 in. barrel, uncheckered birch stock, blue metal, folding rear sight, 6 1/2 lbs. Mfg. 1999-2006.

	$950	$775	$650	$550	$425	$325	$225	*$536*

10/22 50TH ANNIVERSARY DESIGN CONTEST RIFLE – .22 LR cal., 18 1/2 in. stainless steel barrel with flash suppressor, push-button, crossbolt manual safety, non-glare post front sight, ghost ring adj. rear sight, detachable 10 shot mag., black composite synthetic stock with stippled forend, interchangeable stock modules provide comb height options for scope or iron sight use, pistol grip, Scout style Picatinny top rail, 13 1/2 in. LOP, sling swivels, clear satin finish, includes special 50th anniversary bolt and receiver markings and commemorative box, celebrating 50 years of the 10/22, 5 lbs. Limited mfg. during 2014.

	$325	$285	$250	$225	$180	$150	$115	*$379*

This model was created as the result of a nationwide design contest. Ruger narrowed the entries down to 10 finalists, and asked the public to vote for their favorite design.

RUGER/REMINGTON CANADIAN CENTENNIAL MATCHED NO. 3 SET – includes a Remington Model 742 in .308 Win. cal. and a Ruger 10/22 Sporter (hand-checkered or uncheckered) with special commemorative appointments, with green lined double presentation case or each gun individually boxed with outer brown cardboard shipping carton. 1,908 sets mfg. 1967 only.

	$950	$650	$550	N/A	N/A	N/A	N/A	

Note that the set with hand-checkered 10/22 exists in quantities roughly twice that of the set with an uncheckered 10/22.

GRADING - PPGS™	100%	98%	95%	90%	80%	70%	60%	LAST MSR

* ***Ruger/Remington Canadian Centennial Matched No. 2 Set*** – 70 sets mfg. 1967 only, hand-checkered 10/22 with "B" grade wood, presentation case, serial numbered C31 through C100.

	$1,150	$775	$550	N/A	N/A	N/A	N/A	

* ***Ruger/Remington Canadian Centennial Matched No. 1 Special Deluxe Set*** – 30 sets mfg. 1967 only, hand-checkered 10/22 with "C" grade wood, presentation case, serial numbered C1 through C30.

	$1,400	$895	$675	N/A	N/A	N/A	N/A	

10/22 CANADIAN CENTENNIAL – 2,000 to 2,400 mfg. in 1967.

	$550	$400	$350	N/A	N/A	N/A	N/A	*$100*

Note that the single 10/22 Canadian Centennial will be found with serial numbers ranging from C2009 through C4424. Within this group are as few as 200 with a stock that does not have hand-checkering.

SR-22 RIFLE – .22 LR cal., 16.1 in. barrel with Mini-14 flash suppressor or target crown, 10 shot rotary mag., Hogue monogrip pistol grip, six position telescoping or fixed buttstock, integrated Picatinny rail on top of receiver, mid-length vented circular handguard with Picatinny rail, Ruger Rapid Deploy sights, 6 1/2 lbs. Mfg. 2013-2017.

	$600	$490	$425	$375	$325	$275	$250	*$709*

Add $449 for Silent-SR suppressor (new 2016, NFA regulations apply).

RIFLES: SEMI-AUTO, CENTERFIRE

MODEL 44 STANDARD CARBINE – .44 Mag. cal., 4 shot mag., 18 1/2 in. barrel, blowback action, folding sight, curved butt. Mfg. 1959-1985.

	$950	$850	$650	$450	$400	$325	$300	*$332*

* ***Model 44 Standard Carbine Deerstalker*** – .44 Mag. cal., approx. 3,750 mfg. with "Deerstalker" marked on rifle until Ithaca lawsuit disc. manufacture (1962).

	$1,450	$1,100	$950	$850	$650	$500	$450	

* ***Model 44 Standard Carbine 25th Year Anniversary*** – .44 Mag. cal., 18 1/2 in. barrel, folding sight, has medallion in stock. Limited production, mfg. 1985 only.

	$950	$750	$550	N/A	N/A	N/A	N/A	*$495*

MODEL 44RS – .44 Mag. cal., blowback action, 18 1/2 in. barrel, 4 shot mag., aperture receiver sight, curved buttstock and swivels.

	$1,200	$1,000	$850	$650	$500	$450	$350	

Add 60% for 44RS with barrel rollmarked "MADE IN THE 200th YEAR OF AMERICAN LIBERTY".

MODEL 44 FINGERGROOVE SPORTER – .44 Mag. cal., Monte Carlo stocked version of 44 Standard. Mfg. until 1971.

	$1,350	$950	$800	$700	$550	$425	$350	
w/factory checkered stock	$1,850	$1,400	$1,200	$1,020	$825	$675	$525	

Note that a few factory hand-checkered .44 Fingergroove Sporter's do exist and can be lettered by the factory as either "44SPC" or "44SP HAND CHECKERED".

MODEL 44 INTERNATIONAL – .44 Mag. cal., similar to Model 44 Standard Carbine, except full-length Mannlicher style stock. Mfg. until 1971.

	$1,350	$950	$800	$700	$550	$425	$350	

Add 50% for factory checkered stock.

Note that a few factory hand-checkered .44 Internationals do exist and can be lettered by the factory as either "44XC" or "44XC HAND CHECKERED".

MODEL 99/44 DEERFIELD CARBINE – .44 Mag. cal., 4 shot rotary mag., 18 1/2 in. barrel with folding aperture rear sight, rotating bolt with dual front locking lugs, blue finish only, uncheckered hardwood stock, includes integral scope mounts and rings, 6 1/4 lbs. Mfg. 2000-2006.

	$850	$750	$600	$500	$400	$300	$260	*$702*

MINI-14 – .223 Rem. or .222 Rem. (disc.) cal., 5 (standard mag. starting in 1989), 10 (disc.), or 20* shot detachable mag., 18 1/2 in. barrel, gas operated, blue finish, aperture rear sight, military style stock, approx. 6 3/4 lbs. Mfg. 1975-2004.

	$650	$445	$385	$350	$325	$300	$285	*$655*

Add 20% for .222 Rem. cal.
Add $300 for folding stock (disc. 1989).
Add 25% for Southport Model with gold bead front sight.
Add 100% for Mini-14 GB (primarily used for law enforcement) with a flash hider and bayonet lug (blue or stainless) if in 95%+ original condition.

GRADING - PPGS™	100%	98%	95%	90%	80%	70%	60%	LAST MSR

* ***Mini-14 Stainless*** – mini stainless steel version, choice of wood or black synthetic (new 1999) stock. Disc. 2004.

	$650	$450	$395	$365	$335	$315	$295	*$715*

Add 20% for .222 Rem. cal.
Add $300 for folding stock (disc. 1990).

MINI-14 RANCH RIFLE – .223 Rem. cal., 5 (standard mag. starting in 1989), 10 (disc.), or 20 shot detachable mag., blued finish, 18 1/2 in. barrel, choice of black synthetic or hardwood stock, receiver cut for factory rings, similar to Mini-14, supplied with scope rings, folding (disc.) or adj. ghost ring aperture rear sight, blade or protected front sight, and flat style recoil pad (became standard 2005), drilled and tapped receiver (new 2013), 7 lbs. New 1982.

MSR $999	$900	$750	$650	$585	$515	$450	$395	

Add $50 for 20 shot mag. (new 2008).
Add $260 for Mini 14 NRA-ILA Limited Edition with 16 1/8 in. barrel and black Hogue overmolded stock (ltd. mfg. 2008-2009).

Due to 1994 Federal legislation and public sentiment at the time, the Mini-14 and the Mini-14 Ranch Rifle was only produced for the public with a 5 shot detachable mag., 1994-2004.

* ***Mini-14 Stainless Ranch Rifle*** – 5.56 NATO (current mfg.), .223 Rem. (older mfg.), or 6.8 SPC (mfg. 2007-2011) cal., 16 1/2 (special order only, disc. 2017) or 18 1/2 in. stainless steel barrel, 5 or 20 (not available in 6.8mm SPC) shot mag., stainless steel construction, folding (disc.) or adj. ghost ring aperture rear sight, choice of wood (disc, reintroduced mid-2016) or black synthetic (new 1999) stock, drilled and tapped receiver (new 2013), matte stainless finish, 6 3/4 lbs. New 1986.

MSR $1,069	$950	$795	$685	$620	$500	$410	$350	

Add $70 for 20 shot mag. (not available in 6.8mm SPC cal.).
Add $70 for 16 1/2 in. barrel (special order only, disc. 2017).
Add $300 for folding stock (disc. 1990).

MINI-14 TARGET RIFLE w/THUMBHOLE STOCK – .223 Rem. cal., 22 in. stainless steel heavy barrel with adj. harmonic tuner, no sights, ergonomic black or grey (disc.) laminated thumbhole stock, stainless scope rings, 5 shot mag., 3-position rubber recoil pad with adj. LOP, drilled and tapped receiver (new 2013), 9 1/2 lbs. Mfg. 2007-2016.

	$1,070	$925	$800	$725	$585	$475	$375	*$1,259*

Add $16 for 20 shot mag. (mfg. 2009-disc.).

MINI-14 TARGET RIFLE w/BLACK SYNTHETIC STOCK – .223 Rem. cal., 22 in. stainless steel heavy barrel with adj. harmonic tuner, 5 shot mag., no sights, black Hogue overmolded stock, stainless scope rings, drilled and tapped receiver (new 2013), matte stainless finish, 8 1/2 lbs. Mfg. 2007-2016.

	$1,070	$925	$800	$725	$585	$475	$375	*$1,259*

Add $16 for 20 shot mag. (mfg. 2009-disc.).

MINI-14 TACTICAL RIFLE FIXED STOCK – 5.56 NATO or .300 AAC Blackout (new 2015) cal., blued steel or stainless steel action and barrel, compact 16 1/8 in. blue barrel with flash suppressor, 5 (disc. 2019) or 20 shot mag., fixed black synthetic or speckled black/brown hardwood (new 2020) stock with vents on upper forend, blade front and adj. rear sights, drilled and tapped receiver (new 2013), matte stainless finish, 6 3/4 lbs. New 2009.

MSR $1,089	$950	$800	$685	$620	$500	$410	$360	

Add $80 for stainless steel action and barrel.
Subtract $20 for speckled black/brown hardwood stock (new 2020).

MINI-14 TACTICAL RIFLE w/COLLAPSIBLE STOCK – 5.56 NATO cal., compact 16 1/8 in. CHF barrel with flash suppressor, 5 (disc.) or 20 shot mag., black Strikeforce ATI 6-position collapsible and folding stock, includes quad Picatinny accessory rails on forend, blade front and adj. rear sights, blued finish, 7 1/4 lbs. New 2009.

MSR $1,089	$950	$800	$685	$620	$500	$410	$360	

MINI-THIRTY – 7.62x39mm Russian cal., 16 1/8 (with flash suppressor) or 18 1/2 in. barrel, 5 or 20 shot detachable mag., black synthetic or hardwood stock, folding leaf rear sight and blade front (disc. 2004) or adj. ghost ring aperture rear sight and protected front sight (new 2004), includes scope rings, 7 lbs. 3 oz. Mfg. 1987-2004.

	$650	$450	$400	$375	$335	$300	$260	*$695*

* ***Mini-Thirty Stainless*** – 7.62x39mm cal., 18 1/2 in. barrel, stainless steel variation of the Mini-Thirty, black synthetic or hardwood (reintroduced mid-2016) stock, folding leaf rear sight and blade front sight (disc. 2004) or adj. ghost ring aperture rear sight and protected front sight (new 2005), 5 or 20 shot mag., integral sling swivels, 6 3/4 lbs. New 1990.

MSR $1,069	$950	$795	$685	$620	$500	$410	$350	

Add $70 for 20 shot mag.

GRADING - PPGS™	100%	98%	95%	90%	80%	70%	60%	LAST MSR

* ***Mini-Thirty Tactical*** – 7.62x39mm cal., 16 1/8 in. barrel with flash suppressor, 20 shot mag., adj. ghost ring aperture rear sight and non-glare post front sight, black synthetic stock, integral sling swivels, Ruger scope bases, blued or matte stainless (new 2017) finish, 6.7 lbs. New late 2010.

MSR $1,089	$950	$800	$685	$620	$500	$410	$360	

Add $80 for stainless steel (new 2017).

AR-556 – 5.56 NATO or .300 AAC Blackout (new late 2019) cal., GIO, 16.1 in. cold hammer forged alloy barrel and Ruger flash suppressor with matte black oxide finish, M4 feed ramp cuts, 10 (new 2019) or 30 shot Magpul PMAG, single stage trigger, enlarged trigger guard, Ruger Rapid Deploy folding rear sight, milled F-height gas block with post front sight, or no sights, black synthetic 6-pos. collapsible, Magpul MOE synthetic collapsible (new 2018), or fixed (new 2016) stock, ergonomic pistol grip, forged aluminum upper and lower receivers, forward assist, dust cover, brass deflector, 11 in. aluminum free float handguard w/Magpul M-LOK /attachment slots (new 2019), 6.5-7.1 lbs. New 2015.

MSR $799	$680	$600	$500	$450	$375	$325	$300	

Add $20 for 11 in. free floating aluminum handguard with M-LOK attachment slots and no sights (new 2019).
Add $50 for Magpul MOE synthetic collapsible stock (new 2018).
Add $50 for fixed 10 shot mag. (new 2019).

* ***AR-556 with B5 Bravo Stock*** – 5.56 NATO cal., 16.1 in. cold hammer forged alloy threaded barrel and Ruger flash suppressor with matte black oxide finish, 30 shot Magpul PMAG, Ruger Elite 452 AR-Trigger, no sights, B5 Bravo collapsible buttstock, B5 Systems Type P23 grip, mid-length gas system, lightweight 13.5 in. free float handguard with M-LOK attachment slots, forged aluminum lower and flat-top upper receiver with Picatinny rail, Type III hardcoat anodized finish, 6.7 lbs. New late 2019.

MSR $899	$765	$670	$575	$520	$420	$375	$325	

* ***AR-556 with Monsterman Grip (Model 8513)*** – 5.56 NATO cal., 16.1 in. barrel with factory installed thread protector, 10 shot mag., fixed A2 stock, MonsterMan grip, 7 1/2 lbs. Mfg. 2018-2019.

	$625	$500	$450	$400	$375	$350	$325	*$849*

AR-556 MPR (MULTI-PURPOSE RIFLE) – 5.56 NATO, .450 Bushmaster (new late 2018), or .350 Legend (new mid-2019) cal., 16.38 (.350 Legend only, new mid-2019), 18, or 18.63 in. cold hammer forged threaded barrel, muzzle brake, 5 (.450 Bushmaster or .350 Legend) or 30 shot Magpul PMAG, Ruger Elite 452 AR-Trigger, no sights, black synthetic Magpul MOE SL collapsible buttstock, Magpul MOE grip, rifle or carbine length gas system, forged aluminum flat-top upper with forward assist, dust cover, and brass deflector, lower receiver with Mil-Spec buffer tube, free floating 15 in. handguard with Magpul M-LOK accessory attachment slots, Type III hardcoat anodized black or American Flag Cerakote (new 2020) finish, 6.8-7.4 lbs. New late 2017.

MSR $899	$765	$670	$575	$520	$420	$375	$325	

Add $50 for American Flag Cerakote finish (new 2020).
Add $200 for .450 Bushmaster (new late 2018) or .350 Legend (new mid-2019) cal.

AR-556 OPTICS CARBINE – 5.56 NATO cal., GIO, 16.1 in. cold hammer forged alloy barrel with matte black oxide finish, M4 feed ramps, 10 or 30 shot Magpul PMAG, single stage trigger, enlarged trigger guard, no sights, black synthetic 6-pos. collapsible stock, ergonomic pistol grip, forged aluminum lower and flat-top upper receiver with forward assist, dust cover, and brass deflector, gas block with integral Picatinny rail, glass-filled Nylon handguard, Type III hardcoat anodized black finish, 6.7 lbs. Mfg. 2019-2020.

	$600	$475	$425	$375	$350	$325	$300	*$789*

RUGER CARBINE (FORERUNNER TO THE NAMED "PISTOL CALIBER" CARBINE) – 9mm Para. (PC9) or .40 S&W (PC4) cal., 16 1/4 in. barrel, 10 (PC4) or 15 (PC9) shot detachable mag., with or w/o sights, with fully adj. rear sight or rear receiver sight, black synthetic stock, crossbolt safety, matte metal finish, 6 lbs. Mfg. 1998-2006.

	$675	$595	$500	$450	$375	$300	$250	*$623*

Add $24 for adj. rear receiver sight.

The earliest produced guns were rollmarked "RUGER POLICE CARBINE" on the receiver. Later marked "RUGER CARBINE". Beginning 2005, this model came standard with an adjustable ghost ring aperture rear sight and protected blade front sight.

PC CARBINE ("PISTOL CALIBER" CARBINE) – 9mm Para. or .40 S&W (new mid-2019) cal., dead blow action, 16 in. cold hammer forged standard or fluted and threaded barrel, 10, 15 (new 2019), or 17 shot mag., interchangeable magazine wells, aluminum alloy frame, non-glare protected blade front sight, adj. ghost ring rear aperture sight, black synthetic stock, soft rubber buttpad with spacers, sling swivel stud, textured grip, integrated Picatinny rail, reversible magazine release and reversible charging handle, Type III hardcoat anodized black finish, 6.8 lbs. New 2018.

MSR $649	$550	$485	$415	$375	$310	$260	$215	

GRADING - PPGS™	100%	98%	95%	90%	80%	70%	60%	LAST MSR

* ***PC Carbine With AR Chassis*** – 9mm Para. cal., dead-blow action, 16.12 in. fluted or threaded and fluted cold hammer forged chrome moly steel barrel, 6 grooves, 10 or 17 shot mag., flared magwell, no sights, adj. black synthetic stock w/6-pos. Magpul MOE buttstock, glass-filled polymer chassis system, ergonomic pistol grip with extended trigger reach, aluminum free float handguard with Magpul M-LOK accessory attachment slots, aluminum billet receiver with integrated Picatinny style rail, reversible mag. release and charging handle, Type III hardcoat anodized black finish, includes one SR-Series pistol mag. and hex wrench, 7.3 lbs. New late 2019.

MSR $799	$680	$600	$500	$450	$375	$300	$265	

* ***PC Carbine With Free Float Handguard*** – 9mm Para. cal., Dead blow action, 16.12 in. threaded and fluted cold hammer forged barrel, 10 or 17 shot mag., protected blade front and adj. ghost ring rear sight, black synthetic stock, rubber buttpad with spacers, aluminum free float handguard with Magpul M-LOK accessory attachment slots, 7075-T6 aluminum billet receiver with integrated Picatinny style rail, Type III hardcoat anodized black or American Flag Camo (new 2020) finish, 7 lbs. New 2019.

MSR $729	$625	$550	$475	$425	$350	$280	$225	

Add $50 for American Flag Camo finish (new 2020).

SR-556/SR-556 CARBINE – 5.56 NATO or 6.8 SPC (mfg. mid-2010-2011) cal., GPO, 10, 25 (6.8 SPC only, disc. 2011), or 30 shot mag., 16.1 in. barrel with flash suppressor or target crown, matte black finish, four position chrome plated gas regulator, quad rail handguard, with or without Troy folding sights, fixed (556SC) or 6-position telescoping M4 style buttstock, Hogue monogrip pistol grip with finger grooves, upper receiver has integrated Picatinny rail, chrome plated bolt, bolt carrier, and extractor, includes rail covers, soft sided carry case and three magazines, 7.4 (Carbine) or 7.9 lbs. Mfg. mid-2009-2015.

	$1,525	$1,225	$1,100	$950	$900	$825	$750	*$2,049*

* ***SR-556E*** – 5.56 NATO cal., GPO (two-stage with regulator), 10 (SR-556ESC) or 30 shot mag., 16.1 in. cold hammer forged barrel with flash suppressor, Ruger Rapid Deploy folding sights (new 2013), A2 style pistol grip, 6-position telescoping M4 style buttstock, vented aluminum handguard with full-length Picatinny rail, upper receiver has integrated Picatinny rail, 7.35 lbs. Mfg. mid-2011-2014.

	$1,025	$825	$725	$650	$600	$550	$500	*$1,375*

SR-556 TAKEDOWN – 5.56 NATO cal., GPO, 16.1 in. takedown threaded barrel with flash suppressor, three 30 shot Magpul PMAGs, Elite 452 AR trigger, folding iron sights, black synthetic collapsible stock, Magpul MOE grip, Mil-Spec buffer tube, KeyMod handguard (new 2016, for reduced overall weight), includes ballistic nylon case, three rail covers, and a lock, manganese phosphate/hardcoat anodized finish, 7.1 lbs. Mfg. mid-2015-2018.

	$1,650	$1,300	$1,175	$1,025	$975	$900	$800	*$2,199*

SR-556VT – 5.56 NATO cal., GPO, 5 shot mag., 20 in. hammer forged stainless steel barrel, round, lightweight adaptable vented handguard with Picatinny rail on top, fixed A2-style buttstock, Magpul MOE grip, two-stage trigger, charging handle with tactical latch, 8 1/2 lbs. Mfg. 2013-2014.

	$1,500	$1,175	$1,050	$925	$875	$800	$725	*$1,995*

Ruger has issued a recall on this model because the disconnector in the two-stage trigger system was not properly heat-treated by a vendor and can wear prematurely. This can result in an unsafe condition in which the rifle delays firing or doubles. No incidents have been reported, but this is an important safety issue. Please contact Ruger customer service at 603.865.2442 or at recall@Ruger.com to determine if your gun is part of the recall.

SR-762 CARBINE – 7.62 NATO cal., two-stage piston driven, AR-15 style, 16.1 in. heavy contour chrome-lined cold hammer forged barrel, includes three 20 shot Magpul PMAGs, folding backup iron sights, 6-pos. adj. M4-style stock, Hogue monogrip, lightweight adj. adapatable handguard, full-length top Picatinny rail and two side rails, one-piece bolt carrier, four position gas regulator, sight adjustment tool, includes soft side carry case, matte black finish, 8.6 lbs. Mfg. late 2013-2018.

	$1,750	$1,400	$1,250	$1,100	$1,025	$950	$875	*$2,349*

XGI – while advertised, this model was never shipped commercially because it could not maintain Ruger accuracy standards.

MSR was originally targeted at $425.

RIFLES: SINGLE SHOT

During certain years of manufacture, Ruger's changes in production on certain models (cals., barrel markings, barrel lengths, etc.) have created rare variations that are now considered premium niches. These areas of low manufacture will add premiums to the values listed on standard models.

Non-prefix rifles are known in .222, .22-250, .243, 6mm, .25-06, .270, .280, 7mm Rem. Mag., 7x57,

GRADING - PPGS™	100%	98%	95%	90%	80%	70%	60%	*LAST MSR*

.300 Win. Mag., .30-06, .308, .375 H&H., 45-70 and .458 cal.

Calibers 6.5mm Rem., .264 Win. Mag., 7x65R, .300 H&H and .338 were also rumored or cataloged during the 1966-1968 time period but are not known to have been produced.

One rifle chambered in .225 Win. is known to be in the factory collection.

For the calibers listed above that are known to have been produced with non-prefix serial numbers, the Number 1 during this time period could be ordered with nearly any combination of barrel length and weight (22" light weight or 26" medium weight barrel). The .375 H&H and .458 were available with a 24" heavy weight barrel and most in .45-70 were produced with a 22" medium weight barrel.

For all but the .375 H&H, .45-70 and .458, the 1966-1968 period rifles could also be ordered with any combination of no sights/open sights/target blocks or either Alex Henry or Semi-Beavertail forearm.

Pre-1969, non-prefix rifles will command a 30%-50% premium (ser. no. 1-8XXX).

NO. 1-A LIGHT SPORTER – similar to No. 1-B Standard, .204 Ruger (mfg. 2005-2006), .22 Hornet (disc., 355 mfg.), .222 Rem. (mfg. 2013), .223 Rem. (rare), .243 Win. (disc. 2012), .270 Win. (disc. 2012), 7mm-08 (rare), 7x57mm (disc. 2009), .30-06 (disc. 2012), .280 Rem. (mfg. 2014), .300 RCM (mfg. 2009-2012), .303 British (mfg. 2011-2012), .308 Win. (mfg. 2011-2012), 7.62x39mm (approx. 300 mfg. 2015), or 6.5 Creedmoor (mfg. 2011-2012) cal., 22 in. barrel, folding sight on quarter rib, ramp front sight, no rings, American walnut stock, Alexander Henry forearm, front swivel in barrel band, 7 1/4 lbs. Mfg. 1966-2014. Although uncatalogued beginning in 2015, very limited runs of this model in various calibers have continued to be produced by Ruger.

$1,250 $900 $800 $650 $500 $400 $325 ***$1,399***

The "A" suffix designates an Alexander Henry classic forearm with light barrel and open sights.

NO. 1-AB – various cals., .204 Ruger (mfg. 2006-2008) cal., 22 in. barrel, checkered walnut stock and forearm. Mfg. 1967-1968, 1982-1983, 2006, 2008. Although uncataloged beginning in 2009, very limited runs of this model in various calibers have continued to be produced by Ruger including a rare chambering in .338 Federal in 2016 and 2017.

$1,000 $750 $625 $500 $400 $350 $300 ***$1,147***

Add 20% for .338 Federal cal.

The "AB" suffix designates semi-beavertail forearm with light barrel.

NO. 1-B STANDARD – falling block action with curved Farquharson lever, popular cals. include .204 Ruger (new 2004), .218 Bee (disc. 2006), .22 Hornet (mfg. 1988-2006), .22-250 Rem. (disc. 2006), .220 Swift (disc. 2006), .223 Rem. (disc. 2009), .257 Roberts (disc. 2003), .243 Win. (disc. 2006), 6.5 Creedmoor (new 2010), 6mm Rem (disc. 2003), .25-06 Rem., .270 Win. (disc. 2009), .280 Rem. (disc. 2003), .30-06, .308 Win. (mfg. 2002-2008), 6.5mm Rem. Mag. (disc.), 7x57 (disc.), 7mm Rem. Mag. (disc. 2009), .270 Wby. Mag. (mfg. 1990-2006), .300 Wby. Mag. (mfg. 1990-2006), .300 Win. Mag., or .338 Win. Mag. (disc. 2006) cal., 22 or 26 in. barrel, quarter rib with integral scope bases, supplied with rings and no sights, checkered stock and semi-beavertail forearm, approx. 8 1/4 lbs. Mfg. 1966-2010.

$1,000 $700 $550 $425 $350 $300 $275 ***$1,182***

Add 50% for 6.5mm Rem. Mag. or 30% for 7x57 cal.

Although uncataloged beginning in 2011, very limited runs of this model in various calibers have continued to be produced by Ruger. The "B" suffix designates semi-beavertail forearm with medium barrel and was available in all cals. under .375 H&H.

NO. 1-H TROPICAL RIFLE – similar to Medium Sporter, except .45-70 Govt. (rare, mfg. 1976), .375 H&H (disc. 2013), .404 Jeffery (rare, mfg. 1993-95), .416 Rem. (mfg. 1993-2003), .416 Rigby (mfg. 1991-2009), .416 Ruger (mfg. 2009-2011), .450/400 NE (mfg. 2007-2012 and 2014), .458 Lott (mfg. 2003-2012), .458 Win. Mag. (disc. 2008), or .405 Win. (mfg. 2004-2008) cal., 24 in. heavy barrel, blued finish, walnut stock, open sights, 7 3/4-9 1/4 lbs. Disc. 2014.

Common calibers	**$1,050**	**$835**	**$650**	**$475**	**$375**	**$325**	**$295**
.404 Jeffrey cal.	**$1,850**	**$1,620**	**$1,390**	**$1,260**	**$1,020**	**$835**	**$650**
.45-70 Govt. cal.	**$3,700**	**$3,240**	**$2,775**	**$2,515**	**$2,035**	**$1,665**	**$1,295**

Last MSR was $1,399.

Add 40% for 1-H model in .450/.400 NE with heavier than standard "D" weight barrel (about 30 made 2015).

NO. 1-RSI INTERNATIONAL – .243 Win. (disc. 2006), .257 Rob. (mfg. 2014), .270 Win. (disc. 2012), 7x57mm (disc. 2013), .300 RCM (mfg. 2011 only), or .30-06 (disc. 2012), or .308 (rare, only 6 made) cal., features 20 in. lightweight barrel with full-length walnut Mannlicher stock, includes swivels and open sights, 7 lbs. Disc. 2014.

$1,100 $835 $650 $500 $400 $350 $295 ***$1,399***

GRADING - PPGS™	100%	98%	95%	90%	80%	70%	60%	LAST MSR

NO. 1-S MEDIUM SPORTER – .218 Bee (disc. 2003), 7mm Rem. Mag. (disc. 2003), 9.3x62 (mfg. 2014), 9.3x74R (mfg. 2007-2011), .45-70 Govt. (disc. 2013), .300 Win. Mag. (disc. 2003, reintroduced 2011-2012), .300 H&H (mfg. 2010-2012), .338 RCM (mfg. 2009-2011), .338 Win. Mag. (disc. 2003), .375 Ruger (mfg. 2009-2011), .38-55 Win. (mfg. 1989), .460 S&W Mag. (mfg. 2009-2012), .475 Linebaugh/.480 Ruger (mfg. 2009-2012), 9.3x62 (new 2014) cal., similar to Light Sporter, 22 or 26 (.300 H&H cal. only) in. medium barrel, open sights, 7 1/4-8 lbs. Disc. 2014.

$1,150 $835 $650 $475 $375 $325 $295 *$1,399*

* ***No. 1-S Medium Sporter 50th Anniversary*** – .45-70 Govt. cal. only, engraved action with selective gold layering, including the Ruger logo and 50 years, William B. Ruger signature on receiver bottom, checkered Circassian walnut stock and forearm. 1,500 mfg. 1999 only.

$2,100 $1,500 $1,300 $1,100 $995 $850 $700 *$1,950*

NO. 1-V VARMINTER – similar to No. 1-B Standard, except .22 PPC (mfg. 1993-96), .22-250 Rem. (disc.), .220 Swift (disc., reintroduced 2014 only), .223 Rem. (disc. 2012), .243 Win. (disc.), .25-06 Rem. (disc. 2012), 6mm Rem. (disc. 2005), 6mm PPC (mfg. 1993-96), 6.5 Creedmoor (mfg. 2011-2012), 6.5-284 Norma (new 2013), 7mm Rem. (disc.), .280 Rem. (disc.), or .300 Win. Mag. (disc.) cal., 24 or 26 (disc., was .220 Swift only) in. heavy barrel, without rib, no sights, checkered walnut stock and forearm, target scope blocks, approx. 8 3/4 lbs. Mfg. 1970-2014.

$1,100 $835 $650 $475 $375 $325 $295 *$1,399*

Add 20% for .22 PPC cal. or 6mm PPC cal.

NO. 1 K1-BBZ STAINLESS – various cals. and configurations, satin stainless steel action and barrel, grey laminate hardwood stock with black recoil pad, drilled and tapped rear quarter rib w/o sights. Mfg. 2001-2009.

* ***No. 1 K1-B-BBZ Stainless Standard*** – .243 Win. (disc. 2009), .25-06 Rem. (disc. 2009), .270 Win. (disc. 2009), .30-06, .308 Win. (mfg. 2002-2006), .300 Win. Mag. (disc. 2009), 7mm STW (disc. 2004), or 7mm Rem. Mag. (disc. 2009) cal., 26 in. barrel, 8 lbs. Mfg. 2001-2009.

$975 $725 $575 $475 $400 $350 $300 *$1,222*

* ***No. 1 K1-H-BBZ Stainless Tropical*** – .375 H&H, .416 Rigby (mfg. 2002-2006), .405 Win. (mfg. 2004, reintroduced 2006-2008), .416 Ruger (new 2009, rare), .458 Win. (mfg. 2005-2006), or .458 Lott (mfg. 2002-2004, reintroduced 2007) cal., 24 in. barrel, 9 lbs. Mfg. 2001-2009.

$925 $675 $550 $425 $350 $300 $250 *$1,186*

Note that a very small "cleanup" run of K1-H barreled receivers in .458 Lott were manufactured with walnut forearm and buttstock in 2016.

* ***No. 1 K1-S-BBZ Stainless Sporter*** – .45-70 Govt. or .375 Ruger (mfg. 2008-2009) cal., 22 in. barrel with iron sights, black laminated stock, 7 1/4 lbs. Disc.

$975 $725 $575 $475 $400 $350 $300 *$1,222*

* ***No. 1 K1-V-BBZ Stainless Varminter*** – .204 Ruger (new 2004), or .22-250 Rem. cal. only, 24 in. bull barrel, black laminate stock, 9 lbs. Mfg. 2001-2009.

$925 $675 $550 $425 $350 $300 $250 *$1,186*

NO. 1 .450 BUSHMASTER – .450 Bushmaster cal., single shot, 20 in. cold hammer forged stainless steel barrel, muzzle brake, no sights, black laminate stock, sporting style buttpad, sling swivel studs, sliding tang safety, 7 1/2 lbs. New 2018.

MSR $1,899 $1,575 $1,275 $950 $825 $700 $575 $495

NO. 1 .450 MARLIN – .450 Marlin cal., single shot 20 in. cold hammer forged barrel, blade sights, American walnut stock, sporting style buttpad, sling swivel studs, sliding tang safety, satin blued finish, 7.1 lbs. Mfg. 2018-2019.

$1,575 $1,275 $950 $825 $700 $575 $495 *$1,899*

NO. 1 50TH ANNIVERSARY LIMITED EDITION – .308 Win. cal., falling block, 22 in. cold hammer forged barrel, ejector, blade sights, American walnut stock with sporting style recoil pad, grip cap, sliding tang safety, sling swivel studs, features custom engraving on right and left-hand sides of the breech block, Ruger scope mounting system, satin blued finish, 7 lbs. Limited mfg. 2017-2018.

$2,000 $1,700 $1,475 $1,325 $1,075 $900 $700 *$2,299*

Add 30% for "High Grade" model with circassian walnut buttstock and forearm (model 21315), special serial number sequence in selective gold "50YR-01" through "50YR-50" and additional engraving at top of receiver and "1 of 50" through "50 of 50" on bottom of receiver with scroll engraving at each side. 50 produced 2018 only.

Add 25% for 50th Anniversary "Employee Edition", 6.5 Creedmoor (Ruger model 21316) with additional scroll engraving on top of receiver and selective gold "Employee Edition" at bottom front of receiver with scroll engraving to each side. Reportedly 178 produced 2018 only.

GRADING - PPGS™	100%	98%	95%	90%	80%	70%	60%	LAST MSR

NO. 3 CARBINE – same basic action as No. 1, except simpler lever design, uncheckered stock with barrel band on forearm, available in .22 Hornet, .30-40 Krag, .45-70 Govt. (only cal. available 1986), .223 Rem., .44 Mag., or .375 Win. cal., 22 in. barrel, folding sight. Mfg. 1972-87.

	$900	$800	$650	$550	$450	$350	$300	*$284*

Add 20% for .44 Mag. (900 to 1,000 produced) or .375 Win. cal.

RUGER/LYMAN 1878 CENTENNIAL RIFLE – .45-70 Govt. cal., 101 sets mfg. in Grade I and 1,000 in Grade II. Grade I has hand engraving, custom stock, 28 in. D weight barrel, tubular 4X Lyman Century scope, ser. nos. L-001-1878 to L-101-1978. Grade II had photo engraved frame, ser. nos. L-78-0001 to L-78-1000. Mfg. 1978 only.

Grade I	$2,500	$2,000	$1,200	$900	$800	$700	$600	
Grade II	$1,750	$1,425	$1,050	$850	$725	$600	$525	

One William Lyman commemorative cased rifle was also mfg., preceeding Grades I & II. This model was auctioned off at the 1978 NRA Show.

SHOTGUNS: O/U

RED LABEL (PREVIOUS MFG.) – 12, 20, or 28 (new 1994) ga., 3 in. chambers (except 28 ga.), various barrel lengths and choke (including skeet) combinations, boxlock, SST, 26 or 28 in. VR barrels, auto ejectors, choice of checkered pistol grip or English straight grip (new 1992, Red Label English Field) stock, stainless steel frame became standard on 12 ga. and 20 ga. 1985, choke tubes became optional in 1988, standard 1990, 6-7 3/4 lbs. Mfg. 1977-2011.

* ***Red Label Standard Grade*** – Disc. 2011.

	$1,650	$1,175	$900	$775	$650	$550	$475	*$2,015*

Add 20% for 28 ga.
Add $622 for .410 bore Briley conversion tube set for 28 ga. only (disc. 2005).
Subtract 15%-20% without choke tubes.

During late 1994, some 12 and 20 ga. Red Label boxes were marked "EZ", indicating the new easy-opening feature (this is not mechanically spring-assisted, but rather works on tight machining tolerances). All Red Label shotguns have the "EZ" opening feature beginning 1995.

Earlier all-steel 12 ga. models (approx. 500 mfg.) with short field tubes could command 10%-15% premiums over values listed from collectors interested in acquiring this variation. 20 ga. models w/o choke tubes are blue only.

* ***Red Label 20 Gauge Engraved "21 Club" Presentation Shotgun*** – Approximately 20 produced for leading gun writers at the time the Red Label was introduced. This series features photo-etch engraving on left and right sides of the receiver by James Triggs as well as hand-engraved presentation inscriptions by Bob Kain, metal grip cap, serial numbers known to range between 400-00009 and 400-00158.

Extreme rarity precludes accurate pricing on this model. Individual specimens should be professionally appraised.

* ***Red Label 20 Gauge Pre-Production With Stainless Receiver*** – 51 pre-production stainless receiver shotguns with 26 in. blue barrels were produced in 1979 and sold to employees and friends of the company, engraved "1 of 51" on the bottom of the trigger guard. Stainless steel break lever, serial numbered 400-13490 to 400-13552. Quantities produced: 12 F/M; 15 IC/M; 24 SK/SK.

Extreme rarity precludes accurate pricing on this model. Individual specimens should be professionally appraised.

* ***Red Label All Weather Stainless*** – 12 ga. only, stainless steel (disc.) or target grey stainless steel (new 2003) receiver and barrels, checkered black synthetic stock and forearm, 26, 28, or 30 in. VR barrels with choke tubes, 7 1/2 lbs. Mfg. 1999-2006.

	$1,275	$975	$800	$700	$600	$500	$450	*$1,702*

* ***Red Label Sporting Clays*** – 12 or 20 (mfg. 1994-2007) ga., features 30 in. separated barrels, choice of walnut or synthetic (12 ga. only) stock, Briley choke tubes with forcing cones back bored to .744 in., 3/8 in. VR with middle bead, sporting clays recoil pad, approx. 7 1/2 lbs. Mfg. 1992-2011.

	$1,550	$1,175	$900	$775	$650	$550	$475	*$2,015*

* ***Red Label English Field*** – 12, 20, or 28 (new 1995) ga., similar to Red Label, except has English style straight grip stock. Mfg. 1992-2000.

	$965	$775	$685	$600	$550	$500	$450	*$1,276*

GRADING - PPGS™	100%	98%	95%	90%	80%	70%	60%	LAST MSR

* ***Red Label Engraved (2001-2011 Mfg.)*** – 12, 20, or 28 ga., 26, 28, or 30 (disc. 2004) in. barrels, 4 different gold inlay options depending on ga., with receiver scroll engraving, pheasant standard on 12 ga., grouse on 20 ga., and woodcock on 28 ga., available in Standard Model, All-Weather Stainless (disc. 2004), and Sporting Clays (disc. 2004, reintroduced 2009) configurations. Mfg. 2001-2011.

$1,750	**$1,375**	**$1,000**	**$825**	**$700**	**$600**	**$500**	***$2,245***

Add 20% for 28 ga. with non-standard roughed grouse motif (reportedly 20 produced).

* ***Red Label Hand Engraved (1997-2000 Mfg.)*** – available in 12 (203 made), 20 (50 made), or 28 (80 made) ga., available in 2/3 "C" coverage, 1/3 "B" coverage or dit-dot border "A" pattern coverage (standard). Only the earliest hand engraved guns had circassian walnut buttstock and forearm. Later guns were produced with circassian walnut buttstock and black walnut forearm or black walnut for both pieces. The contracted engravers of this series were John J. Adams, Sr., John J. Adams, Jr., Carmine Lombardy, Alvin White, Andrew Bourbon, and Jon Ashford. Mfg. 1997-2000.

$2,200	**$1,900**	**$1,650**	**$1,300**	**$1,000**	**$850**	**$725**	***$2,552***

Add $190 for 1/3 engraving coverage.
Add $532 for 2/3 engraving coverage.

28 ga production quantities: KRL-2826A (30); KRL-2827A (27); KRL-2826B (20); KRL-2827B (1); KRL-2826C (1); KRL-2827C (1).

20 ga. production quantities: KRL-2029B (38); KRL-2030B (9); KRL-2029C (2); KRL-2030C (1).

12 ga. production quantities: KRL-1226A (31); KRL-1227A (18); KRL-1226B (75); KRL-1227B (64); KRL-1236B (1); KRL-1226C (9) and KRL-1227C (6)

In all, only 333 Red Label special hand engraved models were produced.

* ***Red Label 50th Anniversary Engraved*** – 12, 20, or 28 ga., 26 or 28 in. barrels, receiver scroll engraving, 3 different gold inlay options (depending on ga.) on right side of receiver and Ruger 50th Anniversary logo on left side of receiver. Mfg. 1999 only. Probably not more than 1,500 of each model produced.

$1,450	**$1,125**	**$850**	**N/A**	**N/A**	**N/A**	**N/A**	

WILDLIFE FOREVER SPECIAL EDITION – 12 ga. only, limited edition to celebrate the 50th anniversary of Wildlife Forever, features Baron & Son engraving with gold pheasant and mallard inlays on receiver sides, 300 mfg. 1993 only.

$1,595	**$900**	**$775**	**N/A**	**N/A**	**N/A**	**N/A**	***$1,595***

Add $125 for hard case.

RED LABEL "WOODSIDE" – 12 ga. only, 3 in. chambers, 26, 28, or 30 (Sporting Clays Model only with special chokes, new 1996) in. barrels, straight or pistol grip stock, features premium checkered walnut, satin nickel finish, unique stock design permitting wood to fill-in where frame boxlock action would normally be, 7 1/2-8 lbs. Mfg. 1995-2002.

$1,950	**$1,750**	**$1,300**	**$1,000**	**$850**	**$650**	**$550**	***$1,889***

* ***Red Label "Woodside" Engraved*** – available in 2/3 "C" coverage, 1/3 "B" coverage or dit-dot border "A" pattern coverage (standard) with pistol grip and 26 or 28 in. barrels. Only the earliest hand engraved guns had circassian walnut buttstock and forearm. Later guns were produced with circassian walnut buttstock and black walnut forearm or black walnut for both pieces. The contracted engravers of this series were John J. Adams, Sr., John J. Adams, Jr., Carmine Lombardy, Alvin White, Andrew Bourbon, and Jon Ashford. Only 81 mfg. 1997-2000.

$2,500	**$2,050**	**$1,725**	**$1,350**	**$1,050**	**$875**	**$750**	***$2,805***

Add $190 for 1/3 engraving coverage.
Add $532 for 2/3 engraving coverage.

Production quantities: KWS-1226A (45); KWS-1227A (17); KWS-1226B (6); KWS-1227B (5); KWS-1226C (1) and KWS-1227C (7).

RED LABEL (RECENT MFG.) – 12 ga., 3 in. chambers, 26, 28, or 30 in. hammer forged separated barrels with Briley choke tubes, VR, SST, brass bead front sights, ejectors, polished stainless steel receiver, satin blued finish, checkered American Walnut stock and forearm with solid rubber pad, two-position tang safety/barrel selector, includes custom molded case, approx. 7 3/4 lbs. Approx. 9,000 mfg. 2014 only.

$1,250	**$1,175**	**$900**	**$775**	**$650**	**$550**	**$475**	***$1,399***

Note that approximately 250 of this model in 20 ga. were also reportedly produced with barrel lengths of 26, 28, and 30 in. These were sold to Ruger employees and other friends of the factory. Extreme rarity precludes accurate pricing for this model.

GRADING - PPGS™	100%	98%	95%	90%	80%	70%	60%	LAST MSR

SHOTGUNS: SxS

GOLD LABEL SxS – 12 ga. only, 3 in. chambers, 28 in. barrels with solid rib and choke tubes, rounded stainless boxlock action, SST, blue barrel finish, ejectors, choice of deluxe 22 LPI checkered English straight grip or pistol grip stock and splinter forearm, approx. 6 1/2 lbs. Mfg. late 2002-2008.

	$3,850	$2,850	$2,200	$1,725	$1,250	$1,050	$925	*$3,226*

Add 25% pistol grip stock.

SHOTGUNS: SINGLE BARREL

TRAP MODEL – 12 ga., 34 in. stainless barrel with straight grooves and 2 choke tubes, fully adj. high post rib, engraved stainless receiver with gold Ruger name, adj. deluxe checkered walnut stock, beavertail forearm, adj. trigger, 9 lbs. Serial numbered 440-00001 through 440-00633 (only 551 shipped). Mfg. 2001 only.

	$3,850	$3,200	$2,500	$2,000	$1,500	$1,300	$1,200	*$2,850*

SUHLER JAGDGEWEHR MANUFAKTUR GmbH

Previous manufacturer and firearms restorer located in Suhl, Germany.

Suhler Jagdgewehr manufactured a variety of SxS shotguns, in addition to restoring both antique and historical guns.

SUNDANCE INDUSTRIES, INC.

Previous manufacturer located in Valencia, CA.

For individual model listings, please go to BlueBookOfGunValues.com/overflow.

SUN DEVIL MANUFACTURING LLC

Previous rifle and billet aluminum parts and accessories manufacturer located in Mesa, AZ until circa-2019.

Please refer to BlueBookOfGunValues.com to order the *Blue Book of AR-15s & Variations*, available as a book or online subscription.

SUPER SIX LIMITED

Previous manufacturer located in Brookfield, WI until 1992.

REVOLVERS

GOLDEN BISON SERIES – .45-70 Govt. cal., 6 shot revolver, 8 or 10 1/2 in. octagon barrel, large size (OAL 15-17 1/2 in.), manganese bronze frame, crossbolt manual safety, smooth hardwood grips, approx. 6 lbs. 177 total mfg. (including special/limited editions). Disc. approx. 1992.

	$1,675	$1,475	$1,275	$1,000	$875	$775	$675	*$1,895*

Low serialization specimens (ser. nos. 1-15) have asking prices of $2,250-$2,950.

* ***Golden Bison Series Centennial Limited Edition*** – .45-70 Govt. cal., 8 or 10 1/2 in. octagon barrel, 6 shot, smooth hardwood grips, crossbolt manual safety, features special engraving and case, 20 total mfg.

	$2,950	$2,275	$1,675	N/A	N/A	N/A	N/A	*$3,995*

SUPER SIX LLC

Previous manufacturer located in Milwaukee, WI from 1999-2004.

During late 1998, Super Six LLC purchased the previous trademark of Super Six Limited. This trademark had very limited manufacture.

SUPER SIX CLASSIC, LLC

Previous trademark manufactured by Defense Supply & Manufacturing, located in Fort Atkinson, WI. Previously distributed exclusively by Zanders Sporting Goods.

REVOLVERS

BISON BULL – .45-70 Govt. cal., 10 in. octagon custom Badger barrel, manganese bronze frame, chrome moly steel cylinder, 6 shot, manual crossbolt safety, adj. Millett rear sight, ramp blade front sight, integral scope mount, deluxe custom hardwood grips, 6 lbs. Disc.

	$1,375	$1,200	$995	$875	$750	$675	$600	*$1,495*

SUPERIOR AMMUNITION

Previous custom rifle and current ammunition manufacturer located in Sturgis, SD. Consumer direct sales only.

RIFLES: BOLT ACTION

SUPERIOR CLASSIC LIGHTWEIGHT – various cals. up to .375 H&H, Rem. Mod. 700, Win. Mod. 70 Classic, or Dakota Mod. 76 action, blind box mag. or hinged floorplate, approx. 5 3/4 lbs.

	$1,850	$1,650	$1,350	$1,100	$900	$750	$625	*$2,000*

GRADING - PPGS™	100%	98%	95%	90%	80%	70%	60%	LAST MSR

SUPERIOR VARMINT MODEL – various smaller cals., Rem. Mod. 700, Dakota Varmint, or Searcy action, stainless match grade barrel, heavy or light variations.

$1,900	$1,725	$1,400	$1,125	$900	$750	$625	*$2,100*

SUPERIOR PROFESSIONAL MODEL – various large cals. up to .470 Capstick, only available in Win. Mod. 70 Classic or Dakota Mod. 76 action, blind box mag. (optional) or hinged floorplate.

$2,350	$2,050	$1,850	$1,600	$1,350	$1,150	$900	*$2,500*

SUPERIOR ARMS

Current AR-15 style pistol and rifle manufacturer established in 2004, and located in Wapello, IA.

Please refer to BlueBookOfGunValues.com to order the *Blue Book of AR-15s & Variations*, available as a book or online subscription.

SURGEON RIFLES, INC.

Current custom rifle manufacturer established circa 2000 and located in Phoenix, AZ. Previously located in Prague, OK. In 2011, Strategic Armory Corps acquired Surgeon Rifles.

For individual model listings, please go to BlueBookOfGunValues.com/overflow.

SURVIVAL ARMS, INC.

Previous manufacturer established in 1990 located in Orange, CT. Previously located in Cocoa, FL, until 1995.

In 1990, Survival Arms, Inc. took over the manufacture of AR-7 Explorer rifles from Charter Arms located in Stratford, CT.

RIFLES: SEMI-AUTO

AR-7 EXPLORER RIFLE – .22 LR cal., takedown or normal wood stock, takedown barreled action stores in Cycolac synthetic stock, 8 shot mag., adj. sights, 16 in. barrel, black matte finish on AR-7, silvertone on AR-7S, camouflage finish on AR-7C, 2 1/2 lbs. Disc.

$150	$125	$100	$85	$75	$65	$55	*$150*

Add 20% for takedown action.

AR-20 SPORTER – similar to AR-22, except has shrouded barrel, tubular stock with pistol grip, 10 or 20 shot mag. Mfg. 1996-98.

$195	$165	$140	$120	$105	$95	$80	*$200*

AR-22/AR-25 – .22 LR cal., 16 in. barrel, black rifle features pistol grip with choice of wood or metal folding* stock, includes 20 (1995 only) or 25 (disc. 1994) shot mag. Disc. 1995.

$175	$150	$125	$100	$80	$70	$60	*$200*

Subtract $50 for wood stock model.

SVENDSEN, ERL, F.A. MFG. CO.

Previous manufacturer located in Itasca, IL.

DERRINGERS

LITTLE ACE – .22 S cal., patterned after the Ethan Allen "HIDE-A-WAY", bronze frame, blue steel barrel with case hardened hammer and spur trigger.

$85	$75	$70	$65	$60	$55	$50

4-ACES – .22 S cal., 4 barrel derringer with rotating firing pin and spur trigger, bronze frame with blue rifled steel barrels and case hardened parts.

$175	$150	$135	$120	$105	$90	$75

SWING

Previously manufactured by Schutzen Bohme GmbH located in Rintein, Germany.

RIFLES: BOLT ACTION

SWING BOLT ACTION – .308 Win. cal., target bolt action rifle with thumbhole stock and vented forearm, target sights, 30 in. barrel, 12.1 lbs. Mfg. 1994.

$850	$750	$650	$575	$500	$450	$395

SWISS MILITARY

Previously manufactured Swiss military rifles.

REVOLVERS

MODEL 1878 MILITARY ISSUE, WAFFENFABRIK BERN – 10.4mm cal., rust blued with strawed small parts, black hard rubber grips. Sequentially serialed from 1-6000 (approximately). The majority

GRADING - PPGS™	100%	98%	95%	90%	80%	70%	60%	LAST MSR

arsenal refurbished in Switzerland.

	N/A	$3,500	$3,150	$2,650	$2,350	$1,975	$1,750	

Subtract 30% if arsenal refurbished.

MODEL 1882 WAFFENFABRIK NEUHAUSEN (SIG) – several hundred revolvers assembled by SIG in late 1920s from parts made by Bern, marked Waffenfabrik Neuhausen, black HR or fluted wood grips, independently serialed 1-300 (approximately).

	N/A	$1,500	$1,300	$1,100	$900	$775	$650	

MODEL 1882 COMMERCIAL ("P" PREFIX) AND MILITARY ISSUE, WAFFENFABRIK BERN – 7.5mm cal., made from 1882-1929. Rust blued with strawed small parts. Sequentially serialed from 1-32,250. Antique production serial number cutoff is #8108. Several variations.

Add $2,000-$3,000 for elongated and fixed lanyard loop for the Swiss Bicycle troops. Only a small number were assembled - beware of fakes!

Add $1,500-$3,500 for black leather covered shoulder stock whose projecting lug would attach to base of the M1882 frame (depending on condition).

In 1882, Colonel Schmidt manufactured the black leather covered shoulder stock, which was never adopted by the military and production was limited. Correct for first and early second variation revolvers.

* ***First Variation*** – octagonal barrel that does not flare at frame juncture, thin top strap, no recoil shield reinforcement and black hard rubber grips. Serialed from 1-1500 (approximately).

	N/A	$1,500	$1,300	$1,100	$900	$775	$650	

Add 25% for commercial pistols with police markings.

Add 100% for special order versions with long barrel.

* ***Second Variation*** – octagonal barrel that flares at frame juncture, thick top strap, reinforced recoil shield around firing pin hole and black hard rubber grips. Serialed from 1500-20,000 (approximately).

	N/A	$750	$650	$550	$450	$350	$250	

Add 35% if serial number under 8108, regardless if military or commercial.

Add 25% for commercial pistols with police markings.

* ***Third Variation*** – similar to Second Variation except has fluted, wood grips. Serialed from 20,001-32,250 (approximately).

	N/A	$650	$575	$500	$425	$325	$250	

MODEL 1929 COMMERCIAL ("P" PREFIX) AND MILITARY ISSUE – 7.5mm cal., made from 1929 to 1946, assembled with red (scarcest), brown and black grips. Serialed from 50,000-68,500 (approximately). Red grips on the first 7,000 revolvers. Relatively few Commercial M1929s, those earmarked for the Zoll (border patrol) were issued with an unusual Luger-like holster.

	N/A	$550	$475	$400	$325	$250	$175	

Add $200-$600 for Zoll holster, depending on condition.

Add 20% for early Model 1929s with red grips.

RIFLES: BOLT ACTION

These models were designed by Schmidt and Rubin (Rubin designed the cartridge, and Schmidt designed the actions). Schmidt was in charge of designing the 1889 and 1896 actions, later forming the basis of the 1911 and 1931 rifles. Manufactured by Eidgenossische Waffenfabrik Bern, which was a Swiss federal armory.

MODEL 1889 – usually encountered between 85%-95% condition.

	$995	$870	$745	$675	$545	$450	$350	

MODEL 1908 MILITARY TEST RIFLES – Experimental series of about 900 guns, carbines and rifles, numbered sequentially from 1-900 approximately. The first 200 were carbines, the balance rifles. All with fluted receivers with three flutes of unequal length - the longest on the center of the receiver, the shortest off to the side. Also, the bolt locking lug sleeve has three holes, a feature that was deleted in the M1911.

Carbine	N/A	$2,000	$1,750	$1,500	$1,250	$1,000	$750	
Rifle	N/A	$1,650	$1,300	$1,100	$925	$800	$650	

MODEL 1911 – available in either carbine or rifle configuration.

Carbine	$1,695	$1,485	$1,270	$1,155	$930	$765	$595	
Rifle	$750	$655	$565	$510	$415	$340	$265	

GRADING - PPGS™	100%	98%	95%	90%	80%	70%	60%	LAST MSR

MODEL 1926 VATICAN AND BORDER PATROL CARBINE – 210 carbines (10 made 1924, 200 made 1926), based on the M1911 but with a heavy barrel and no bayonet lug, serialed independently with a "V" prefix.

N/A	$1,750	$1,500	$1,300	$1,100	$900	$700	

MODEL 1931 & VARIATIONS – The Bern factory assembled about 2,240 sniper rifles based on the K31 between 1944 and 1946 beginning with SN 450,001. The earliest rifles had a 1.8 power scope, the latest a 2.8 power scope. As standard rifles were also assembled at the same time, sniper rifles have been recorded with serial numbers into the 453,xxx range.

$1,250	$950	$700	$550	$450	$375	$300	

Add 25% if fitted w/diopter target sights.

* ***K31/42 Sniper (Designation ZFK 31/42)*** – 7.5x55 cal., 1.8 power flip-up scope and 1-10 marked rear sight, first 50 rifles had a scope, slightly different from standard production, that was marked with a matching sn.

N/A	$4,000	$3,500	$3,000	$2,500	$2,150	$1,750	

Add 20% if one of the first 50 rifles.

* ***K31/43 Sniper (Designation ZFK 31/43)*** – 7.5x55 cal., 2.8 power flip-up scope and 1-7 marked rear sight.

N/A	$4,500	$3,750	$3,000	$2,500	$2,150	$1,750	

* ***K31 Experimental Snipers*** – 7.5x55 cal., same designations as above but with detachable scopes, based on K31/42 (1.8x scope) or K31/43 (2.8x scope), an estimated 50 rifles, closely serialed around #4523xx. Very rare.

N/A	$8,500	$7,500	$6,500	$5,500	$4,500	$3,500	

* ***K31/55 (Designation ZFK 31/55, Sometimes ZFK 55 Or M1955)*** – 7.5x55 cal., with matching 3.5 power detachable scope, originally issued in matching numbered can. Rifle has a large, integral muzzle brake/flash suppressor and comes with a bipod. Independent serial range 1000-5150.

N/A	$6,500	$5,500	$5,000	$4,500	$4,000	$3,500	

Subtract 25% if mismatched scope, subtract another $200 if missing can.

VETTERLI – .41 Swiss or 10.4mm Swiss cal., not mfg. by Schmidt-Rubin.

$750	$675	$600	$525	$450	$375	$295	

SWORD INTERNATIONAL INC.

Current manufacturer of AR-15 style carbines, rifles, and accessories, located in Sparks, NV.

Please refer to BlueBookOfGunValues.com to order the *Blue Book of AR-15s & Variations*, available as a book or online subscription.

SYMES & WRIGHT LTD.

Previous manufacturer located in London, England.

Symes & Wright Ltd. manufactured approx. 25 best quality shotguns and double rifles annually. Values must be determined after evaluating each firearm individually.

SYREN

Current trademark of shotguns manufactured by Caesar Guerini and Fabarm, located in Cambridge, MD. Dealer sales. Currently imported by Syren USA, located in Cambridge, MD.

For individual model listings, please go to BlueBookOfGunValues.com/overflow.

SZECSEI & FUCHS FINE GUNS GmbH

Please refer to listing under Fuchs Fine Guns GmbH in the F section.

TJF

Previous firearms manufacturer located in Suhl, Germany until 2014. Previously imported by Heirloom Armes located in Howard Lake, MN.

SHOTGUNS: SXS

TJF offered a scalloped Anson & Deeley boxlock action with double triggers, ejectors, and game scene engraving. There were two frame sizes - one was the normal for 12, 16, and 20 ga., and the petite frame was available in 28 ga. or .410 bore.

TNW FIREARMS, INC.

Current firearms manufacturer located in Vernonia, OR. Consumer direct sales.

For individual model listings, please go to BlueBookOfGunValues.com/overflow.

TPS ARMS LLC

Current rifle and shotgun manufacturer located in Rush City, MN with manufacturing located in Mesquite, TX.

GRADING - PPGS™	100%	98%	95%	90%	80%	70%	60%	LAST MSR

RIFLES: O/U

M6-100 TAKEDOWN – .22 LR/.410 ga., 3 in. chambers, 18 1/4 in. barrels, interchangeable choke tubes, 2 shot mag., all steel construction, flip-up rear peep and stationary front sight, aluminum stock and grip, AR style takedown pin for quick breakdown, includes full choke tube/wrench and shell storage in stock, blued finish, approx. 5 lbs.

MSR $589	$500	$440	$375	$340	$275	$225	$175

M6-120 TAKEDOWN – .22 WMR/.410 ga., 3 in. chambers, 18 1/4 in. barrels, interchangeable choke tubes, 2 shot mag., all steel construction, flip-up rear peep and stationary front sight, aluminum stock and grip, AR style takedown pin for quick breakdown, includes full choke tube/wrench and shell storage in stock, blued finish, approx. 5 lbs.

MSR $589	$500	$440	$375	$340	$275	$225	$175

M6-130 TAKEDOWN/M6-140 TAKEDOWN – .22 WMR/.410 ga (M6-130). or .22 Hornet/.410 ga. (M6-140), 3 in. chamber, 18 1/4 in. barrel, interchangeable choke tubes, 2 shot mag., all steel construction, flip-up rear peep and stationary front sight, aluminum stock and grip, AR style takedown pin for quick breakdown, includes full choke tube/ wrench and shell storage in stock, blued finish, approx. 5 lbs.

MSR $589	$500	$440	$375	$340	$275	$225	$175

M6-150 TAKEDOWN – .357 Mag./.410 ga., 3 in. chamber, 18 1/4 in. barrel, interchangeable choke tubes, 2 shot mag., all steel construction, adj. "Y" style front post and flip-up rear sight, aluminum stock and grip, AR style takedown pin for quick breakdown, includes full choke tube/wrench and shell storage in stock, blued finish, approx. 5 lbs. New circa 2020.

MSR $625	$550	$475	$400	$350	$300	$250	$175

SHOTGUNS: O/U

M6-160 TAKEDOWN – .410 ga., 3 in. chamber, O/U, 18 1/4 in. barrel, 2 shot mag., all steel construction, aluminum stock and grip, fiber optic front and STD rear grooved sights, AR style takedown pin for quick breakdown, full choke tube, wrench, and additional shell storage in stock, blued finish. New circa 2020.

MSR $575	$500	$425	$375	$325	$275	$225	$175

TR IMPORTS

Current importer located in Fort Worth, TX. Previously located in Keller, TX.

TR Imports - imports the Silver Eagle line of shotguns that are manufactured in Central Turkey and the Titan Series manufactured by Rossler located in Austria. They also specialize in importing lesser known European manufacturers/trademarks. For Titan Series models, please see the Rossler listing in the R section. For all lesser known models and manufacturers, please contact the importer directly for pricing and U.S. availability.

For more information and individual model listings, please go to BlueBookOfGunValues.com/overflow.

TS FINE GUNS

Current custom rifle and shotgun manufacturer located in Großmaischeid, Germany. No current U.S. importation.

Please refer to Spohr, Thomas located in the S section.

TACONIC FIREARMS, LTD.

Previous rifle manufacturer located in Cambridge, NY until 2003.

GRADING - PPGS™	100%	98%	95%	90%	80%	70%	60%	LAST MSR

RIFLES: BOLT ACTION, CUSTOM

TACONIC 98 ULTIMATE MOUNTAIN HUNTER – various cals., features double square bridge, titanium alloy M-98 action, XXX Grade English or Circassian walnut, stainless or chrome moly barrel, matte finished metal, available with a variety of options, base prices are listed below. Disc. 2003.

$5,750	$5,100	$4,500	$4,000	$3,500	$3,000	$2,500	*$5,995*

TACTICAL 73

Current AR-15 style firearm and parts manufacturer, located in Val della Torre, Italy. No current U.S. importation.

Please contact the manufacturer directly for information on their model lineup, including pricing, options, and availability.

TACTICAL ARMS MANUFACTURER, INC.

Previous manufacturer located in Huntersville, NC until circa 2016.

RIFLES: SEMI-AUTO

Tactical Arms Manufacturer, Inc. manufactured AR-15 M4 or M16 style rifles in various calibers and configurations. Base prices started at $1,195.

TACTICAL ARMS OF TEXAS

Previous AR-15 rifle manufacturer and customizer located in Stafford, TX 2011-2018.

Please refer to BlueBookOfGunValues.com to order the *Blue Book of AR-15s & Variations*, available as a book or online subscription.

TACTICAL ARMZ

Previous rifle and suppressor manufacturer located in Springfield, MO until early 2018.

Please refer to BlueBookOfGunValues.com to order the *Blue Book of AR-15s & Variations*, available as a book or online subscription.

TACTICAL EDGE ARMS

Current AR-15 style pistol and rifle manufacturer located in Clarksville, TN.

Please refer to BlueBookOfGunValues.com to order the *Blue Book of AR-15s & Variations*, available as a book or online subscription.

TACTICAL RIFLES

Current rifle manufacturer located in Zephyrhills, FL. Previously located in Dade City, FL until 2010.

Please refer to BlueBookOfGunValues.com to order the *Blue Book of AR-15s & Variations*, available as a book or online subscription.

TACTICAL SOLUTIONS, INC.

Current rifle and components manufacturer located in Boise, ID.

Please refer to BlueBookOfGunValues.com to order the *Blue Book of AR-15s & Variations*, available as a book or online subscription.

TACTICAL SUPPLY

Previous rifle and parts manufacturer, located in Yakima, WA.

Please refer to BlueBookOfGunValues.com to order the *Blue Book of AR-15s & Variations*, available as a book or online subscription.

TACTICAL WEAPONS

Current law enforcement/military division of FNH USA, located in McLean, VA.

Tactical Weapons currently manufactures machine guns only for law enforcement/military.

TACTICAL WEAPONS SOLUTIONS

Previous manufacturer located in Apopka, FL until 2015.

Please refer to BlueBookOfGunValues.com to order the *Blue Book of AR-15s & Variations*, available as a book or online subscription.

TALO DISTRIBUTORS, INC.

Current wholesale buying cooperative established in 1965, located in Framingham, MA.

Over the years, Talo Distributors, Inc. has released a wide variety of both special and limited editions for many major firearms companies. More research is underway to compile a listing of all special/limited editions made to date. Please contact the company directly for more information on both its current and older special/limited editions. For Talo's current Special/Limited Editions, please visit www.taloinc.com for more information.

TALON ARMAMENT

Current AR-15 style rifle manufacturer located in Kennesaw, GA.

Please refer to BlueBookOfGunValues.com to order the *Blue Book of AR-15s & Variations*, available as a book or online subscription.

GRADING - PPGS™	100%	98%	95%	90%	80%	70%	60%	LAST MSR

TALON INDUSTRIES, INC.

Previous pistol manufacturer located in Ennis, MT until 2001.

PISTOLS: SEMI-AUTO

T100 – .380 ACP cal., double action only, 3.3 in. barrel, black polymer frame with choice of black (T100B) or satin (T100S) slide finish, or alloy frame and slide, 10 shot mag., failsafe loaded chamber indicator positioned on top of slide in back of breech bolt, 3-dot sights, 20 1/2 oz. Mfg. 2000-2001.

$115 $95 $85 $75 $65 $55 $50 ***$135***

T200 – 9mm Para. cal., otherwise similar to Model T100. Mfg. 2000-2001.

$145 $125 $100 $90 $75 $65 $55 ***$170***

TALON ORDNANCE

Previous AR-15 style rifle manufacturer located in Richland, MS.

Please refer to BlueBookOfGunValues.com to order the *Blue Book of AR-15s & Variations*, available as a book or online subscription.

TANFOGLIO, FRATELLI, Srl

Current pistol, rifle, and parts manufacturer located in Gardone, Italy. Currently imported by European American Armory located in Sharps, FL, and on a limited basis by the Italian Firearms Group (IFG) beginning 2011, located in Amarillo, TX. Previously imported by K.B.I., located in Harrisburg, PA, and also by Excam, F.I.E., and others.

Tanfoglio manufactures a wide variety of high quality semi-auto pistols, including the Witness Series and the Appeal semi-auto rifle which is currently imported by European American Armory Corp. The company also released a series of Signature models during 2012 - these guns are imported exclusively by the Italian Firearms Group (IFG), and are listed in this section. Tanfoglio also manufactures a proprietary line of pistols, including competition models and the Raptor single shot, which has been mostly distributed in Europe.

PISTOLS: SEMI-AUTO

1911 CUSTOM – .45 ACP cal., SA, 5 in. barrel, blue or two-tone finish, ambidextrous extended safety, cocked and locked safety on frame, adj. rear sight, removable front sight, wood grips, 38 oz. Limited importation 2013-2014.

$665 $580 $500 $450 $365 $300 $235 ***$787***

BULLS EYE – 9mm Para., .38 Super, .40 S&W, 10mm, or .45 ACP cal., SA, 6 in. barrel, chrome finish, auto firing pin block, checkered front and back strap, extended mag. release, adj. rear sight, removable front sight, full-length dust cover, 10 (.45 ACP), 13 (10mm or .40 S&W), or 17 (9mm Para. or .38 Super) shot mag., drilled and tapped, 44 oz. Limited importation 2013-2014.

$1,125 $985 $850 $765 $625 $500 $395 ***$1,329***

DEFIANT FORCE PLUS – 9mm Para. or .40 S&W cal., SA/DA, competition, full size polymer frame, 4.4 in. barrel, hammer fired, square trigger guard, fixed front and interchangeable fixed rear sights, standard manual safety mounted on frame, stainless steel slide, full-length rail, dust cover, 32 oz. Importation began 2018.

Please contact the importer directly for pricing and availability on this model.

DEFIANT LIMITED PRO – .40 S&W, .38 Spl., 10mm, or .45 ACP cal., SA/DA, competition, small or large frame, 4.8 in. barrel w/polygonal rifling, custom mag. release, square trigger guard, interchangeable front and adj. rear Supersight, walnut checkered grips, extended manual safety, slide checkering, full length rail, dust cover, hard chrome finish, 42 oz. Limited mfg. Importation began 2018.

Please contact the importer directly for pricing and availability on this model.

DEFIANT STOCK 1 – .40 S&W, .38 Spl., 10mm, or .45 ACP cal., SA/DA, small or large steel frame similar to the STOCK III model, 4 1/2 in. barrel, fixed or interchangeable sights, standard frame mounted safety, slide checkering, full-length rail, dust cover, black finish, 42 oz. Importation began 2017.

Please contact the importer directly for pricing and availability on this model.

GOLD CUSTOM ERIC – 9mm Para., .38 Super, .40 S&W, 10mm, or .45 ACP cal., SA, 5.7 in. barrel, chrome finish, auto firing pin block, ambidextrous safety, beveled magwell, checkered front and back strap, extended mag. release, full-length dust cover, 11 (.45 ACP), 14 (10mm), 15 (.40 S&W), or 18 (9mm Para. or .38 Super) shot mag., three port compensator, drilled and tapped, 44 oz. Limited importation 2013-2014.

$2,100 $1,840 $1,575 $1,425 $1,150 $950 $735 ***$2,489***

GRADING - PPGS™	100%	98%	95%	90%	80%	70%	60%	LAST MSR

LIMITED CUSTOM ERIC – 9mm Para., .38 Super, .40 S&W, 10mm, or .45 ACP cal., SA, 4.92 in. barrel, chrome finish, auto firing pin block, ambidextrous safety, beveled magwell, checkered front and back strap, extended mag. release, full-length dust cover, adj. rear sight, removable front sight, 11 (.45 ACP), 13 (.40 S&W), 14 (10mm), 18 (9mm Para. or .38 Super) shot mag., three port compensator, drilled and tapped, 42 oz. Limited importation 2013-2014.

$1,235 $1,080 $925 $840 $680 $550 $430 ***$1,453***

STOCK II – 9mm Para., .38 Super, .40 S&W, 10mm, or .45 ACP cal., DA/SA, 4.92 in. barrel, auto firing pin block, accessory rail, checkered front and back strap, extended mag. release, extended safety, full-length dust cover, adj. rear sight, removable front sight, 10 (.45 ACP), 13 (.40 S&W or 10mm), or 17 (9mm Para. or .38 Super) shot mag., blue finish, 42 oz. Limited importation 2013-2014.

$975 $850 $725 $665 $535 $440 $340 ***$1,152***

STOCK III – 9mm Para., .38 Super, .40 S&W, 10mm, or .45 ACP cal., DA/SA, 4.92 in. barrel, auto firing pin block, accessory rail, checkered front and back strap, extended mag. release, extended safety, full-length dust cover, adj. rear sight, removable front sight, 10 (.45 ACP), 13 (.40 S&W or 10mm), or 17 (9mm Para. or .38 Super) shot mag., blue finish, 42 oz. Limited importation 2013-2014.

$875 $765 $650 $595 $480 $395 $300 ***$1,037***

WITNESS 1911 – .45 ACP cal., steel frame, 5 in. standard barrel, 8 shot mag., long hole hammer, skeletonized trigger, adj. super sight, wood checkered grips, extended beavertail safety, interchangeable parts, integral accessory rail, flat mainspring housing, framed steel inserts, two-tone finish. Imported 2014-2019.

$750 $650 $550 $500 $425 $350 $275 ***$895***

WITNESS 1911 COMMANDER SINGLE STACK (OLDER MFG.) – 9mm Para. or .45 ACP cal., 4 1/8 in. barrel, lightweight polymer frame, 7 shot single stack mag., smooth polymer grips, matte black finish, fixed sights, checkered "Double D" grips, integral accessory rail, flat mainspring housing, extended beavertail safety, 29 oz. Imported 2017-2018.

$525 $465 $415 $375 $335 $300 $275 ***$627***

WITNESS 1911 FULL SIZE SINGLE STACK (OLDER MFG.) – .45 ACP cal., 5 in. barrel, lightweight polymer or steel frame, 7 shot single stack mag., smooth polymer grips or checkered "Double D" grips, matte black finish, integral accessory rail, skeletonized hammer and trigger, extended beavertail safety, 32 or 38 oz. Imported 2013-disc.

$500 $450 $400 $365 $335 $300 $275 ***$580***

Add $255 for steel frame (includes skeletonized trigger, fully adj. rear sight, checkered "Double D" grips.)

WITNESS 1911 OFFICER'S MODEL SINGLE STACK (OLDER MFG.) – 9mm Para. or .45 ACP cal., 3 1/2 in. barrel, lightweight polymer frame, 7 shot single stack mag., smooth polymer grips, matte black finish, fixed sights, checkered "Double D" grips, integral accessory rail, flat mainspring housing, extended beavertail safety, 26 oz. Imported 2017-2018.

$525 $465 $415 $375 $335 $300 $275 ***$627***

WITNESS 1911 P – .45 ACP cal., polymer frame, 5 in. barrel, 8 shot single stack mag., long hole hammer, interchangeable parts, integral accessory rail, flat mainspring housing, framed steel inserts, matte black finish, 32 oz. Disc. 2019.

$500 $450 $375 $350 $275 $225 $175 ***$598***

WITNESS 1911 P COMMANDER – .45 ACP or 9mm Para. cal., lightweight polymer frame, 4 1/4 in., 8 or 9 shot single stack mag., long hole hammer, windage adj. sight, smooth polymer grips, extended beavertail grip safety, flat mainspring housing, steel action inserts, integral accessory rail, interchangeable parts, matte black finish, 28.8 oz. Imported 2017-2019.

$525 $465 $415 $375 $335 $300 $275 ***$627***

WITNESS 1911 P OFFICER – .45 ACP or 9mm Para. cal., lightweight polymer frame, 4 1/4 in. standard barrel, 7 shot single stack mag., long hole hammer, fixed or windage adj. sight, smooth polymer grips, extended beavertail grip safety, flat mainspring housing, steel action inserts, integral accessory rail, interchangeable parts, matte black finish, 28.8 oz. Imported 2017-2019.

$525 $465 $415 $375 $335 $300 $275 ***$627***

WITNESS CARRY COMP GUN – .38 Super (disc. 1997), 9mm Para. (disc. 1997), .40 S&W cal. (disc. 1997), 10mm (disc. 1994, reintroduced 1999), or .45 ACP cal., DA/SA, full size frame with compact slide and 1 in. compensator, 10 (C/B 1994), 12* (.40 S&W), or 16* (9mm Para.) shot mag., Wonder (new 1997), blue, Duo-Tone (disc. 1994) finish. Imported 1992-2004.

$425 $370 $320 $290 $235 $190 $150 ***$479***

Add $10 for Wonder finish.

GRADING - PPGS™	100%	98%	95%	90%	80%	70%	60%	LAST MSR

WITNESS COMBO PACKAGE – includes one built up frame and 9mm Para./.40 S&W complete conversion kits, blue, chrome, or Duo-Tone (disc. 1994) finish, full size variation with 4 1/2 in. barrel. Imported 1992-97.

	$515	$450	$385	$350	$285	$230	$180	*$588*

Add $29 for chrome or Duo-Tone finish.

* ***Witness Combo Package (L) Compact*** – similar to Witness Combo Package, except has 3 5/8 in. barrels, blue only. Imported 1994-97.

	$515	$450	$385	$350	$285	$230	$180	*$588*

WITNESS DOMINA XTREME – 9mm Para. or .38 Super cal., SA, 5 1/4 in. coned ported barrel w/polygonal rifling, compensator, 18 shot reversible mag., extended magwell, ported slide, adj. trigger, includes Benthley TSX6 optics, scope mount w/blast shield, Xtreme aluminum grips, ambi safety, blue/black finish with two-tone ceramic coating, 3 lbs. New 2020.

MSR $5,449	$4,635	$4,050	$3,475	$3,150	$2,550	$2,085	$1,815	

WITNESS EA 9 SERIES – 9mm Para. or 10mm cal., action patterned after the CZ-75, selective DA, 4 1/2 in. unported or ported (polymer, New Frame only, new 2002) barrel, 10 (C/B 1994, disc.), 14, 16, 17 (new 2020), or 18 (new late 2004) shot mag., steel or polymer frame/steel slide (new 1997), combat sights, black neoprene grips, integral accessory rail, Wonder (new 1997), stainless steel (disc. 1996), blue (disc.), blue/chrome (disc. 1993), or brushed chrome (disc. 1996) finish, 2.1 lbs. Imported late 1990-disc.

	$585	$510	$440	$400	$325	$275	$230	*$693*

Add $108 for steel frame.

* ***Model EA 9 Stainless*** – similar to EA 9, except is stainless steel. Imported 1992-96.

	$420	$365	$315	$285	$230	$190	$145	*$480*

* ***Model EA 9 (L)*** – similar to EA 9, except has 3 5/8 in. unported or ported (polymer frame only, mfg. 2002-2006) barrel and 10 (C/ B 1994), 12 (new late 2004), or 13* shot mag., 27 oz. Importation disc.

	$585	$510	$440	$400	$325	$275	$230	*$693*

Add $108 for steel frame.
Add $10-$20 for ported barrel (polymer frame only, disc. 2006).

WITNESS EA 10 SUPER SERIES – 10mm cal., action patterned after the CZ-75, DA/SA, 4 1/2 in. barrel, polymer or steel frame, 10, 12*, or 15 (new late 2004) shot mag., choice of stainless steel (disc.), blue, chrome (disc.), or Wonder (new 1999) finish, combat sights, black neoprene grips, 33 oz. Imported 1994 only, reintroduced 1999-disc.

	$550	$450	$385	$335	$285	$230	$185	*$665*

Add $30 for chrome finish (disc.).
Add $65 for stainless steel (disc.).
Subtract $76 for polymer frame.

* ***Model EA 10 Stainless*** – similar to EA 10, except is stainless steel.

	$495	$435	$370	$335	$270	$225	$175	*$566*

* ***Model EA 10 Carry Comp*** – similar to EA 10, except has 4 1/2 in. compensated barrel, blue or Wonder (new 2005) finish. Mfg. 1999-2005.

	$415	$365	$310	$280	$230	$185	$145	*$489*

Subtract $20 for blue finish.

* ***Model EA 10 Compact*** – similar to EA 10, except has 3 5/8 in. barrel, 8 or 12 (new late 2004) shot mag., 27 oz. Importation disc.

	$550	$450	$385	$335	$285	$230	$185	*$665*

Subtract $76 for polymer frame.

WITNESS EA 38 SUPER SERIES – .38 Super cal., action patterned after the CZ-75, DA/SA, 4 1/2 in. barrel, steel or polymer frame/steel slide (mfg. 1997-2004), 10 (C/B 1994), 18 (new late 2004) or 19* shot mag., choice of Wonder (heat treated grey satin finish, new 1997), stainless steel (disc. 1996), blue (disc.), blue/chrome (disc. 1994), or brushed chrome (disc. 1996) finish, combat sights, black neoprene grips, 33 oz. Imported 1994-disc.

	$550	$450	$385	$335	$285	$230	$185	*$665*

Subtract $31 for polymer frame (disc. 2004).

* ***Model EA 38 Stainless*** – similar to EA 38, except is stainless steel. Imported 1994-96.

	$525	$460	$395	$355	$290	$235	$185	*$595*

* ***Model EA 38 Compact*** – similar to EA 38 Super Series, except has 3 5/8 in. unported or ported barrel, choice of matte blue or Wonder finish, 30 oz. Imported 1999-2004.

	$370	$325	$275	$250	$205	$165	$130	*$449*

Subtract $20 for polymer frame.
Add $20 for Wonder finish or ported barrel (polymer frame only).

GRADING - PPGS™	100%	98%	95%	90%	80%	70%	60%	LAST MSR

WITNESS EA 40 SERIES – .40 S&W cal., action patterned after the CZ-75, DA/SA, 4 1/2 in. barrel, steel or polymer frame/steel slide (new 1997), 10 (C/B 1994), 12*, or 15 (new late 2004) shot mag., choice of Wonder (new 1997), stainless steel (disc. 1996), blue, blue/chrome (disc.), or brushed chrome (disc. 1996) finish, combat sights, black neoprene grips, 33 oz. Imported late 1990-disc.

	$550	$450	$385	$335	$285	$230	$185	*$665*

Subtract $76 for polymer frame.

* ***Model EA 40 Stainless*** – similar to EA 40, except is stainless steel. Imported 1992-96.

	$455	$400	$340	$310	$250	$205	$160	*$509*

* ***Model EA 40 (L) Compact*** – similar to EA 40, except has 3 5/8 in. unported or ported barrel, 9 or 12 (new late 2004) shot mag. Importation disc.

	$550	$450	$385	$335	$285	$230	$185	*$665*

Subtract $36 for polymer frame.
Add $10-$20 for ported barrel (polymer frame only, disc. 2005).

WITNESS EA 41 SERIES – .41 Action Express cal., action patterned after the CZ-75, DA/SA, 4 1/2 in. barrel, steel frame, 11 shot mag., blue, blue/chrome, or brushed chrome finish, combat sights, black neoprene grips, 33 oz. Importation disc. 1993.

	$450	$395	$335	$305	$245	$200	$155	*$595*

Add $40 for blue/chrome or brushed chrome finish.

* ***Model EA 41 Compact*** – similar to EA 41, except has 3 1/2 in. barrel and 8 shot mag.

	$495	$435	$370	$335	$270	$225	$175	*$625*

Add $40 for blue/chrome or brushed chrome finish.

WITNESS EA 45 SERIES – .45 ACP cal., action patterned after the CZ-75, DA/SA, 4 1/2 in. standard or compensated (mfg. 1998-2005) barrel, steel frame, polymer full size frame (new 2004), or polymer frame/steel slide (new 1997), 10 (C/ B 1994) or 11* shot mag., choice of Wonder (new 1997), stainless steel (disc. 1996), blue, blue/chrome (disc. 1993), or brushed chrome (disc. 1996) finish, combat sights, walnut grips, 35 oz. Importation began late 1990.

MSR $665	$550	$450	$385	$335	$285	$230	$185	

Add $109 for .45 ACP/.22 LR combo.
Add $40 for ported barrel (steel only, with Wonder finish, disc. 2004).
Subtract $76 for polymer frame.

* ***Model EA 45 Stainless*** – similar to EA 45, except is stainless steel. Imported 1992-96.

	$510	$445	$380	$345	$280	$230	$180	*$595*

* ***Model EA 45 (L) Compact*** – similar to EA 45, except has 3 5/8 in. unported or ported barrel and 8 shot mag., 26 oz. Importation disc.

	$550	$450	$385	$335	$285	$230	$185	*$665*

Add $30 for ported barrel (polymer frame only, disc. 2004).
Add $50 for single port barrel compensator or carry configuration with compensator (disc.).
Subtract $36 for polymer frame.

WITNESS ELITE MATCH – 9mm Para., 10mm, .38 Super, .40 S&W, or .45 ACP cal., SA w/over-travel and take up adj., 4 3/4 in. barrel, 10 (.45 ACP), 14 (.40 S&W or 10mm), 15 (.40 S&W or 10mm, disc.), or 17 (9mm Para. or .38 Super) shot mag., heart shaped hammer, checkered black polymer grips, extended safety, extended mag. release, two-tone finish, approx. 44 oz. Importation began mid-2013.

MSR $1,053	$895	$785	$675	$600	$495	$425	$350	

WITNESS ELITE STOCK I – 9mm Para., 10mm, .40 S&W, or .45 ACP cal., SA/DA, full size frame, 4 1/2 in. cone barrel w/lock-up, polygonal rifling, heart-shaped hammer, fully adj. sight, checkered walnut grip, extended safety, extended beavertail, 39 oz. Imported 2018-2020.

	$950	$800	$700	$650	$500	$425	$325	*$1,102*

WITNESS ELITE STOCK II – 9mm Para., 10mm, .38 Super, .40 S&W, or .45 ACP cal., SA/DA w/over-travel stop, checkered frame and back strap, 4 1/2 tapered cone slide/barrel lock up, polygonal rifling, 10 (.45 ACP), 14 (.40 S&W or 10mm), 15 (disc.), or 17 (9mm Para. and .38 Super) shot mag., extended mag. release, hard chrome frame, heart-shaped hammer, fully adj. super sights, with or w/o red-dot optics (Witness Elite Stock II Optic model, 9mm Para. only, new 2021), diamond checkered walnut grips, extended ambi safety, extended beavertail, full dust cover, 33 oz. Importation began 2005.

MSR $1,301	$1,100	$965	$825	$750	$600	$500	$425	

Add $128 for red-dot optics (Witness Elite Stock II Optic model, new 2021).

GRADING - PPGS™	100%	98%	95%	90%	80%	70%	60%	LAST MSR

WITNESS ELITE STOCK III – 9mm Para., 10mm, .38 Super, .40 S&W (disc. 2020), or .45 ACP cal., SA/DA w/over-travel stop, semi-auto pistol, checkered frame and back strap, 4 3/4 in. tapered cone slide/barrel lock up, polygonal rifling, 10 (.45 ACP), 14 (.40 S&W or 10mm), 15 (.40 S&W or 10mm, disc.), 17 (.38 Super or 9mm Para.), or 18 (9mm Para., disc.) shot mag., hard chrome frame, heart shaped hammer, fully adj. super sights, diamond checkered walnut grips, extended ambi safety, extended beavertail, integral accessory rail, full dust cover, full shroud, blue/black finish, 33 oz. Importation began 2005.

MSR $1,197	$1,700	$1,490	$1,275	$1,155	$935	$775	$660	

WITNESS FCP – .380 ACP, .38 Super, .38 Spl., 9mm Para., .40 S&W, or .45 ACP cal., polymer frame, DAO, blue finish, 6 shot non-detachable mag., 4 in. barrel, fast cycle tube chamber, utitlizes simple reusable tubes that encase each round, no detachable mag., 26 oz. Importation disc. 2007.

	$185	$160	$140	$125	$100	$85	$65	*$219*

WITNESS GOLD TEAM – .38 Super, 9mm Para., 9x21mm, 10mm (disc. 1994), .40 S&W, or .45 ACP cal., triple chamber compensator, SA trigger, super sight, drilled and tapped for scope mount, top-of-the-line competition model featuring hand-fitted major components and 25 LPI checkering, hard chrome finish. Imported 1992-98.

	$1,875	$1,640	$1,405	$1,275	$1,030	$845	$655	*$2,150*

This model was also available as a frame only - retail was $389.

* ***Witness Gold Team Elite*** – 9mm Para., .38 Super, .40 S&W (disc. 2020), or .45 ACP cal., 5 1/4 in. barrel, triple chamber compensator, 10, 14, 15 (disc.), 17, or 18 (disc.) shot mag., competition hard chrome frame, tapered cone slide/barrel lock up, checkered frame and backstrap, competition hammer and safety, super sight, aluminum grips, 41 oz. Importation began 2005.

MSR $2,438	$2,070	$1,815	$1,555	$1,410	$1,140	$930	$725	

* ***Witness Gold Team Xtreme*** – 9mm Para. or .38 Super cal., SA, 5 1/4 in. barrel with polygonal rifling, 17 shot extended mag., specially tuned by the Tanfoglio custom shop, white checkered aluminum grips, features many Xtreme components such as hammer, trigger, guide rod, and firing pin, ported barrel and slide, two-tone ceramic coating with matte silver frame, slide, and matte black frame, includes some shooting accessories, approx. 48 oz. Mfg. by Tangfolio. Importation began 2015.

MSR $5,480	$4,675	$3,800	$3,150	$2,500	$2,000	$1,750	$1,500	

WITNESS HUNTER – 10mm or .45 ACP (disc.) cal., SA w/over-travel stop, auto firing bin block, competition hard chrome checkered (disc.) or competition steel frame, 6 in. barrel, polygonal rifling, 10 (.45 ACP, disc.), 14 (10mm), or 15 (10mm, disc.) shot mag, extended mag. release, low profile heavy duty adj. dovetail front sight, adj. super sight, extended manual safety, tapered cone slide/barrel lock up, drilled and tapped, blue/black or camo (disc.) finish, 41 oz. Importation began 2005.

MSR $1,361	$1,155	$1,000	$865	$780	$635	$525	$450	

WITNESS LIMITED CLASS – .38 Super, 9mm Para., .40 S&W, or .45 ACP cal., match frame, competition grips, high capacity mag., single action trigger, long slide with match barrel and super sight, extended safety, blue finish only. Imported 1994-98.

	$855	$750	$640	$580	$470	$385	$300	*$967*

* ***Witness Limited Custom*** – 9mm Para., 10mm, .40 S&W, .45 ACP, or .38 Super cal., SA, 4 3/4 in. coned barrel w/slide lock-up, polygonal rifling, 10, 14, 17, 18 (disc.), or 19 (disc.) shot extended mag. release, beveled mag., heart-shaped hammer, fully adj. super sight, ported and lightened slide, full dust cover, drilled and tapped for scope mount, ambi controls, 1.9 lbs. Importation began 2017.

MSR $1,498	$1,275	$1,115	$950	$865	$700	$600	$500	

* ***Witness Limited Custom Xtreme*** – 9mm Para. or .40 S&W cal., SA, 4 3/4 in. barrel with polygonal rifling, 14 (.40 S&W, disc.) 15 (.40 S&W, new 2020), 17 (9mm Para., disc.), or 18 (9mm Para., new 2020) shot extended mag., white checkered grips, features many Xtreme components such as aluminum blue or white grips, hammer, trigger, guide rod, firing pin, and fiber optic front sight, black ceramic coated, includes some shooting accessories, blue/black (new 2020) or white/black (disc.) finish, approx. 45 oz. Importation began 2015.

MSR $2,576	$2,190	$1,915	$1,645	$1,490	$1,205	$1,000	$765	

Add $76 for white/black finish (disc.).

* ***Witness Limited Elite*** – 9mm Para., 10mm, .38 Super, .40 S&W, or .45 ACP cal., SA w/over-travel stop and take-up adj., competition hard chrome frame, 4 3/4 in. coned barrel w/lock-up, polygonal rifling, 10 (.45 ACP), 15 (.40 S&W or 10mm), or 18 (9mm Para. or .38 Super) shot mag., extended magwell, skeletonized (heart shaped) hammer, square trigger guard, fully adj. super sight, low profile checkered walnut grips, extended ambi safety, extended beaver tail, checkered frame and backstrap, full-length dust shroud, 45 oz. Importation began 2005.

MSR $1,498	$1,275	$1,115	$950	$865	$700	$600	$500	

GRADING - PPGS™ 100% 98% 95% 90% 80% 70% 60% *LAST MSR*

* ***Witness Limited Pro*** – similar to Witness Limited, except that small parts, including trigger, mag. release, hammer, rear sight, and frame controls are finished in black. Imported 2012-disc.

$975 $850 $725 $650 $550 $450 $395 ***$1,119***

* ***Witness Limited Xtreme*** – 9mm Para. or .40 S&W cal., SA, 4 3/4 in. coned barrel w/polygonal rifling, extended magwell, Xtreme components such as aluminum grips, hammer, trigger, guide rod, firing pin, and fiber optic front sight and fully adj. supersight, drilled and tapped for scope mount, large slide serrations, includes cleaning set, two recoil springs, steel front sight and three extra mags. w/Xtreme aluminum base bad, special ceramic coating, 2.8 lbs. Imported 2020 only.

$2,150 $1,900 $1,600 $1,500 $1,200 $1,000 $750 ***$2,552***

WITNESS MATCH – 9mm Para., 10mm, .38 Super, .40 S&W, or .45 ACP cal., 4 3/4 in. polygonal rifled barrel, competition frame, SA, trigger over-travel, adj. rear sights, extended mag. release, rubber grips, two-tone finish, 33 oz. Imported 2006-2017.

$950 $825 $675 $575 $475 $395 $350 ***$1,106***

WITNESS MATCH XTREME – 9mm Para., .40 S&W (disc. 2020), 10mm, or .45 ACP cal., SA/DA, 6 in. barrel with polygonal rifling, 10 (.45 ACP.), 14 (.40 S&W, disc.), 15 (10mm only), 17 (9mm Para., disc. 2020), or 18 (9mm Para. only, new 2020) shot extended mag., black aluminum checkered grips, features many Xtreme components such as hammer, trigger, guide rod, firing pin, and fiber optic front sight, blue/black (new 2020) or two-tone ceramic coated finish, includes some shooting accessories, approx. 47 oz. Importation began 2015.

MSR $2,379 $2,000 $1,750 $1,500 $1,400 $1,100 $900 $700

WITNESS MULTI-CLASS PISTOL PACKAGE – .38 Super, 9mm Para., 9x21mm, .40 S&W, or .45 ACP cal., consists of one Witness Limited Class Pistol and complete Unlimited Class top half (slide and barrel), dual chamber steel compensator, blue finish only. Imported 1994 only.

$1,450 $1,270 $1,085 $985 $795 $650 $505 ***$1,638***

WITNESS P CARRY – 9mm Para. (disc. 2020), 10mm, .40 S&W (disc. 2020), or .45 ACP (disc. 2020) cal., DA/SA, Commander style, full size polymer frame, compact slide with Wonder finish, 3.6 in. coned barrel, 10 (.45 ACP), 14 (10mm or .40 S&W), 15 (10mm or .40 S&W, disc.), or 17 (9mm Para.) shot mag., windage adj. sight, integral M-1913 rail, slide lockup, two-tone finish, 1.7 lbs. New 2006.

MSR $710 $600 $525 $450 $410 $325 $275 $225

WITNESS P COMPACT – 9mm Para., 10mm, .40 S&W, or .45 ACP cal., SA/DA, polymer or steel frame, 3.6 in. barrel, 8 (.45 ACP), 12 (10mm or .40 S&W), 13 (9mm Para.), or 14 (9mm Para., disc.) shot mag., low profile adjustable sights, integral M-1913 rail, matte black, pink or purple, 28 oz. New 2014.

MSR $585 $500 $440 $375 $340 $275 $225 $195

Add $108 for steel frame.

WITNESS P FULL SIZE – 9mm Para., 10mm, .40 S&W, or .45 ACP cal., SA/DA, large full size polymer or steel frame, 4 1/2 in. barrel, 10 (.45 ACP), 14 (10mm or .40 S&W), or 17 (9mm Para.) shot mag., low profile windage adj. sight, integral M-1913 rail, matte black, 30.4 oz. Importation began 2014.

MSR $585 $500 $440 $375 $340 $275 $225 $195

Add $108 for steel frame.

WITNESS P MATCH – 9mm Para., .38 Super, .40 S&W, 10mm, or .45 ACP cal., SA w/overtravel stop, large black polymer frame with steel slide, 4 3/4 in. barrel, 10 (.45 ACP), 14 (10mm and .40 S&W), or 17 (9mm and .38 Super) shot mag., heart shaped (disc.) or standard hammer, fully adj. super sight, extended safety, extended magwell housing, lower Picatinny rail, extended mag. release, requires base pad, 30.4 oz. Imported 2018-disc.

$700 $600 $500 $475 $375 $300 $250 ***$815***

* ***Witness P Match Pro*** – 9mm Para., .38 Super (disc.), .40 S&W (disc. 2020), 10mm, or .45 ACP cal., DA/SA, black polymer competition (large) frame, 4 3/4 in. barrel, 10 (.45 ACP), 14 (10mm and .40 S&W, new 2018), 17 (9mm Para., new 2018), 18 (10mm, 2017 only), or 19 (.38 Super, 2017 only) shot mag., heart shaped (disc.) or standard hammer, fully adj. super sight, extended safety, extended magwell housing, integrated accessory rail, extended mag. release, features red "T" on polymer grips, blue/black finish, 1.9 lbs. New 2017.

MSR $812 $700 $610 $520 $475 $380 $315 $270

WITNESS PAVONA COMPACT POLYMER SERIES – .380 ACP, 9mm Para., or .40 S&W (disc. 2015) cal., DA/SA, compact sparkling polished polymer frame, 3.6 in. barrel, 9 (.40 S&W cal. only) or 13 shot mag., white dot front and rear sight, external hammer system, ambidextrous mag. release, serrated slide stop and thumb safety, blue/black/gold, blue/black/silver, blue/imperial/silver, blue/sapphire/silver, chrome/

GRADING - PPGS™	100%	98%	95%	90%	80%	70%	60%	LAST MSR

charcoal/silver, or blue/fandango/silver finish, 25 oz. Mfg. by Tanfoglio. Imported 2014-late 2018.

	$425	$375	$325	$275	$225	$200	$150	*$495*

Add $25 for chrome/charcoal/silver finish.
Add $56 for D'Wedge Purse Insert with holster (disc. 2016).
Add $223-$273 for D'Wedge Purse Insert with Pavona Concealed Carry purse, depending on cork or leather construction.

WITNESS SILVER TEAM – .38 Super, 9mm Para., 9x21mm, 10mm (disc. 1994), .40 S&W, or .45 ACP cal., dual chamber compensator, SA trigger, super sight, drilled and tapped for scope mount, competition features include hammer, extended safety, paddle mag. release, black rubber grips, double-dip blue finish, high capacity mag. Imported 1992-98.

	$855	$750	$640	$580	$470	$385	$300	*$967*

WITNESS SPORT – .38 Super, 9mm Para., .40 S&W, 10mm (disc. 1994), or .45 ACP cal., 4 1/2 in. barrel, full size frame, standard slide length, Duo-Tone finish, extended safety and high capacity mag., target sights. Imported 1994-95.

	$535	$470	$400	$365	$295	$240	$185	*$616*

Add $86 for .38 Super, 10mm, or .45 ACP cal.

WITNESS SPORT LONG SLIDE – .38 Super, 9mm Para., .40 S&W, 10mm (disc. 1994), or .45 ACP cal., long slide variation of the EA Series, except has 4 3/4 in. ported or unported barrel and slide, Duo-Tone finish, extended safety and high capacity mag., competition sights, 34 1/2 oz. Importation disc. 1995.

	$595	$520	$445	$405	$325	$270	$210	*$681*

Add $79 for .38 Super, 10mm, or .45 ACP cal.

WITNESS STOCK II XTREME – 9mm Para. or .40 S&W cal., SA/DA, 4 1/2 in. barrel with polygonal rifling, 14 (.40 S&W, disc.), 15 (40 S&W, new 2021), 17 (9mm Para., disc.), or 18 (9mm Para., new 2021) shot extended mag., white checkered grips, features many Xtreme components such as aluminum grips, hammer, trigger, guide rod, firing pin, and fiber optic front sight, two-tone ceramic finish with bronze colored (disc.) slide and matte blue/black frame, includes some shooting accessories, approx. 44 oz. Importation began 2015.

MSR $2,369	$2,000	$1,750	$1,500	$1,350	$1,100	$900	$700	

WITNESS STOCK III XTREME – 9mm Para. or .40 S&W cal., SA/DA, 4 1/2 in. barrel with polygonal rifling, 14 (.40 S&W, disc.), 15 (40 S&W), 17 (9mm Para., disc.), or 18 (9mm Para.) shot extended mag., black checkered aluminum grips, features many Xtreme components such as hammer, trigger, guide rod, firing pin, and fiber optic front sight, two-tone ceramic finish with bronze colored frame and matte black slide, includes some shooting accessories, approx. 45 oz. Importation began 2015.

MSR $2,320	$1,975	$1,730	$1,480	$1,350	$1,085	$900	$775	

WITNESS TRI-CALIBER PACKAGE – includes one built up frame and caliber conversions (9mm Para., .40 S&W, and .41 AE), which include slide, barrel, recoil guide, and spring, matte blue or chrome finish, compact or full size variations, includes carry case. Imported 1992-1993 only.

	$975	$855	$730	$665	$535	$440	$340	*$1,195*

Add $40 for chrome finish.

RIFLES

WITNESS APPEAL SEMI-AUTO – .22 LR or .22 WMR cal., bullpup design, 16 (disc.) or 18 in. barrel with muzzle brake, elevated Picatinny rail, adj. front and rear sights, ambidextrous controls, black polymer thumbhole stock with pistol grip has adj. LOP, 10 shot mag., front and rear sling mounts, black or blue/black finish, 4.8 lbs. Importation began 2012.

MSR $462	$390	$340	$295	$265	$215	$175	$155	

Add $36 for extra mags.

TANNER, ANDRÉ

Previous manufacturer located in Switzerland. Previously imported and distributed by Mandall Shooting Supplies, Inc. located in Scottsdale, AZ, and by Osborne's located in Cheboygan, MI.

Tanner rifles are noted for their superior accuracy and limited production - less than 150 were mfg. annually.

RIFLES: BOLT ACTION

300 METER MATCH RIFLE – 7.5 Swiss (special order) or 7.62mm cal. only, single shot, top-of-the-line 300 meter match rifle incorporating all match shooting features including deluxe palm rest, aperture sights. Importation disc.

	$4,650	$3,995	$3,400	$2,775	$2,250	$1,900	$1,600	*$4,900*

Add $100 for adj. cheekpiece.
Subtract $190 for repeating model with similar features.

GRADING - PPGS™	100%	98%	95%	90%	80%	70%	60%	LAST MSR

* ***300 Meter Match Rifle UIT Standard*** – similar to Model 300, except is without palm rest and adj. Swiss buttplate, 10 shot mag., aperture sights. Importation disc.

	$4,450	$3,850	$3,350	$2,750	$2,225	$1,925	$1,600	*$4,700*

Add $100 for adj. cheekpiece.

SUPERMATCH MODEL 50 M – .22 LR cal. only, 50 meter free rifle, deluxe palm rest, adj. buttplate, thumbhole stock. Importation disc.

	$3,600	$3,200	$2,850	$2,450	$2,050	$1,800	$1,600	*$3,900*

Add $100 for adj. cheekpiece.

TARHUNT CUSTOM RIFLES, INC.

Current custom rifled shotgun & manufacturer established in 1989, located in Bloomsburg, PA. Dealer and consumer direct sales.

In addition to rifles and shotguns, TarHunt also builds custom XP-100 bolt action pistols on a customer supplied action. Contact the company directly for a price quotation.

RIFLES: BOLT ACTION

TarHunt builds custom bolt action rifles on a customer supplied M-7 or M-700 action. Base price begins at $1,495. TarHunt also builds precision Hunting, Wildcat, and Competition Bench Rest rifles. Most any caliber, based on BAT (precision) actions. Base price is POR.

SHOTGUNS: BOLT ACTION

All RSG models of bolt action slug gun are stainless steel as of 2015. In 2009, the RSG-20 and RSG-12 (Rifled Slug Gun) was selected for an industry award.

Add $130 for left-hand action on all current models, add $110 for McMillan Utility molded camo-finished stocks, $300 for high gloss metal, $495 for nickel, dipped camouflage stock finish is POR.

PROFESSIONAL MODEL RSG-12 – 12 ga., 2 3/4 or 3 (new 2003) in. chamber, bolt action slug gun featuring 21 1/2 or 23 (new 2003) in. E.R. Shaw barrel and 2 lug bolt, 1 shot mag. (new 1998), matte black finish, McMillan fiberglass stock with Pachmayr Decelerator rifle pad, receiver drilled and tapped for standard Leupold windage bases (included, new 1997), muzzle brake became standard 1994, various finish options, 7 3/4 lbs. Mfg. 1991-2017.

	$2,450	$2,150	$1,850	$1,675	$1,350	$1,100	$850	*$2,895*

* ***Professional Model RSG-12 Combo Slug Gun*** – includes standard Professional RSG-12, clip model, Slug Gun stock and second 3 in. wide forearm, heavy weight bench rest to install on sported barrel action for ease of testing slug ammo. Mfg. 1994-2004.

	$2,400	$1,575	$1,250	$1,000	$850	$750	$600	*$2,175*

* ***RSG-12/RSG-20 10th Anniversary/Millennium 2000 Edition*** – a combination of 12 and 20 ga., hand selected actions and barrels, muzzle brake, controlled feed, stanadard Jewell trigger, NP-3 nickel/Teflon gray metal finish, black McMillan stock with Pachmayr Decelerator pad, 25 Millennium guns were mfg. in 2000 only - serial no. range 1 of 25 through 25 of 25. Disc. 2000.

	$3,000	$1,525	$1,275	$1,050	$900	$800	$625	*$2,395*

* ***Profession Model RSG-12 Stainless Steel*** – 12 or 20 (RSG-20) ga., 3 in. chamber, TarHunt control feed 2 lug bolt action, drilled and tapped for standard Leupold windage bases, free floating 23 in. threaded in, heavy wall, E.R. Shaw stainless steel barrel with muzzle brake, 1:28 in. twist, 1 shot blind mag., 2 1/2 lb. pull Jewell trigger, black McMillan fiberglass stock with Pachmayr Decelerator rifle pad, 13 1/2 in. LOP, matte black finish, approx. 43 in. OAL, 7 1/4-8 3/4 lbs. New 2017.

MSR $3,495	$3,150	$2,750	$2,365	$2,145	$1,735	$1,420	$1,100	

MATCHLESS MODEL RSG-12 – upgraded variation featuring 400 grit polished gloss metal finish, muzzle brake, 1-28tr, McMillan (high gloss) standard black or optional "Fiber" grain stock finish (wood looking finish, disc. 2000). Mfg. 1993-1997.

	$2,795	$2,295	$1,975	$1,785	$1,450	$1,175	$925	*$3,100*

PEERLESS MODEL RSG-12/RSG-20 – upgraded variation featuring NP-3 (nickel/Teflon) metal finish. optional Jewell trigger, muzzle brake, McMillan standard black or utility camo, or "Fiber" grain stock (wood grain finish, disc. 2000). Mfg. 1995-2015.

	$3,250	$2,675	$2,295	$2,075	$1,675	$1,375	$1,075	*$2,995*

ELITE MODEL RSG-16 – 16 ga., 2 3/4 in. chamber, 23 in. E.R. Shaw rifled barrel, and 2 lug bolt, 1 shot mag., matte black or blue finish, black McMillan fiberglass stock with Pachmayr Decelerator pad, drilled and tapped for Rem. 700 long action style bases. Mfg. 2003-2004, 2010-2017.

	$2,950	$2,150	$1,850	$1,675	$1,350	$1,100	$850	*$2,895*

GRADING - PPGS™	100%	98%	95%	90%	80%	70%	60%	LAST MSR

RSG 20 MOUNTAINEER MODEL – 20 ga., 2 3/4 or 3 in. chambers, TarHunt 2 lug bolt, control feed, glass bedded action with cocking indicator, drilled and tapped, free floating 21 or 23 (including muzzle brake) in. E.R. Shaw matte black heavy wall rifled (1:23 in. twist) barrel, 1 shot blind mag., 2 1/2 lbs. Optional Jewell custom trigger, black textured epoxy painted McMillan fiberglass stock with Pachmayr Decelerator pad, matte blue finish, 13 1/2 in. LOP, 43 in. OAL, 6 1/2-8 3/4 lbs. Mfg. 1997-2013.

	$2,850	$2,150	$1,850	$1,675	$1,350	$1,110	$850	*$3,195*

* ***RGS-20 Mountaineer Stainless Steel*** – RSG-20 ga., 2 3/4 or 3 in. chambers, TarHunt 2 lug bolt, control feed, glass bedded action with cocking indicator, drilled and tapped, free floating 21 or 23 (including muzzle brake) in. E.R. Shaw matte stainless steel heavy wall rifled (1:23 in. twist) barrel, 1 shot blind mag., 2 1/2 lbs. Jewell custom trigger, black textured epoxy painted McMillan fiberglass stock with Pachmayr Decelerator pad, 13 1/2 in. LOP, 43 in. OAL, 6 1/2-8 3/4 lbs. New 2014.

MSR $3,495	$3,195	$2,600	$2,250	$2,000	$1,650	$1,350	$1,000

RSG-TACTICAL (SNIPER) MODEL – 12 ga., similar to RSG-12, except has M-86 McMillan fiberglass black tactical stock with Pachmayr Decelerator pad and heavy barrel front stud mount for bipod, 2 round clip, 3 rounds total, matte blue finish. Mfg. 1992-1998.

	$2,195	$995	$875	$750	$700	$650	$450	*$1,695*

Add $150 for bipod.

BLOCK CARD MODEL – 12 ga., 2 3/4 in. chamber, special length and forcing cone chamber, various barrel lengths (up to 36 in.), cartridge type chokes, special 3 in. wide McMillan fiberglass stock, Pachmayr Decelerator pad, fluted barrels optional, weighted stocks optional, single shot actions, matte blue finish. Total of 15 mfg. Disc.

Last MSR was $1,775.

ENVY MODEL RSG-12/RSG-20 – 12 or 20 (3 in. chamber available) ga., Jewell trigger, choice of fancy grade or high figure walnut stock, control feed action, rings and bases, muzzle brake, glass beaded stainless steel metal finish. New 2016.

MSR $6,295	$5,375	$4,700	$4,025	$3,650	$2,950	$2,425	$2,050

Custom 20 ga. Shrifle chamber, and fluted barrel or fluted bolt is POR.
Upgrading of the walnut stocks is POR.

Due to custom walnut stock, delivery time takes a minimum of 10 to 18 months.

SHOTGUNS: SLIDE ACTION

DSG (DESIGNATED SLUG GUN) – DSG 12 or 16 (disc.) ga., based on Rem. 870, non-removable custom fit Shaw 23 in. rifled slug barrel with muzzle brake, includes Leupold two-piece windage bases which accept any standard rings, available Wingmaster 2 3/4 in., Wingmaster 3 in. configurations. Disc.

	$795	$725	$650	$550	$475	$400	$350	*$840*

Add $356 for Wingmaster Mag.
Add $69 for left-hand (disc.).

DSG-12 REM. 870 EXPRESS/WINGMASTER – 12 ga., 2 3/4, 3, or 3 1/2 in. chamber, Rem. 870 receiver, drilled and tapped, non-removable E.R. Shaw 23 in. threaded in, rifled barrel with muzzle brake, 1:28 in. twist, TarHunt two-piece windage bases which accept any standard turn-in rings, wood or matte black synthetic stock and forearm, recoil pad, also available Express Mag. (3 in. chamber), Wingmaster Mag. (3 in. chamber), or Express Super Mag. (3 1/2 in. chamber) configurations, matte black metal finish.

MSR $1,200	$1,025	$900	$775	$700	$575	$475	$400

Add $50 for left-hand.
Add $35 for Super Cell recoil pad.
Add $85 for ShurShot thumbhole black w/synthetic stock.
Add $349 for Wingmaster 3 in. Magnum.
3 1/2 in. Super Mag is POR.

TarHunt DSG-12 conversion to customer suplied right-hand Rem. Model 870 is $550, left-hand $570.

DTG-12 REM. 870 EXPRESS/WINGMASTER "BOSS-S" TURKEY – 12 ga., 2 3/4 or 3 in. chamber, Rem. 870 receiver, drilled and tapped, non-removable E.R. Shaw 23 in. threaded in, straight rifled barrel, threaded for Rem. Chokes, optional trigger prep., TarHunt two-piece windage bases which accept any standard turn-in rings, wood or matte black or camo synthetic stock and forearm, recoil pad, also available Express Mag. (3 in. chamber), or Wingmaster Mag. (3 in. chamber, disc.) configurations, matte black metal finish.

MSR $1,099	$985	$865	$745	$675	$545	$445	$345

Left-hand model is POR.
Add $35 for Super Cell recoil pad.
Add $85 for ShurShot thumbhole black w/synthetic stock.

GRADING - PPGS™	100%	98%	95%	90%	80%	70%	60%	LAST MSR

DTG-12 REM. 870 SUPER MAG. EXPRESS/ "BOSS-C" TURKEY – 12 ga., 3 1/2 in. chamber, Rem. 870 receiver, drilled and tapped, non-removable E.R. Shaw 23 in. threaded in, straight rifled barrel, threaded for Rem. Chokes, TarHunt two-piece windage bases which accept any standard turn-in rings, synthetic stock and forearm, recoil pad, 100% Mossy Oak camo finish.

MSR $1,395	$1,190	$1,050	$900	$815	$675	$550	$450	

Add $35 for Super Cell recoil pad.
Add $85 for ShurShot thumbhole black w/synthetic stock.

TASK FIREARMS

Previous importer located in Miami, FL.

FIREARMS

Task Firearms previously imported SAR semi-auto and slide action shotguns, in addition to pistols. Task Firearms also imported the Fatih model semi-auto pistol manufactured by Trabzon Gun Industry Corp. located in Ankara, Turkey, and a line of Diamond Doubles shotguns manufactured by Vega in Turkey.

TATE GUNMAKERS LLC

Previous shotgun manufacturer 1995-2010, located in Ione, CA.

SHOTGUNS: CUSTOM

Dale Tate, formerly of J. Purdey & Sons, made custom order shotguns per individual customer specifications in 12, 16, 20, or 28 ga. until mid-2010. All models were POR. Tate Gunmakers also specialized in gun repair and restoration. An individual expert appraisal is recommended before buying or selling a Tate shotgun.

TAURUS INTERNATIONAL MFG., INC.

Currently manufactured by Taurus Forjas S.A., located in Porto Alegre, Brazil and in Bainbridge, GA, beginning late 2019. Previously located in Miami, FL (certain models) until 2019. Currently, handguns made in Brazil are imported by Taurus International Mfg., Inc. located in Miami, FL since 1982. Beginning 2007, Taurus Tactical, a separate entity, was created for law enforcement/military sales and service. Distributor sales only.

From late 2012-2015, Taurus Holdings held an exclusive global distribution agreement with Diamondback Firearms, LLC. Taurus assumed all sales and marketing efforts of the Diamondback branded products from its Miami office during that time.

All Taurus products are known for their innovative design, quality construction, and proven value, and are backed by a lifetime repair policy.

Taurus order number nomenclature is as follows: the first digit followed by a dash refers to type (1 = pistol, 2 = revolvers, 3 = longuns, 4 = Magazines/Accessories, 5 = grips, and 10 = scope mount bases), the next 2 or 3 digits refer to model number, the next digit refers to type of hammer (0 = exposed, 1 = concealed), the next digit refers to barrel length (w/o fractions), the last digit refers to finish (1 = blue, 9 = stainless), and the suffix at the end refers to special features (T = total titanium, H = case hardened, M = matte finish, PLY = polymer, UL = Ultra-Lite, C = ported (compensation), G = gold accent, PRL = mother-of-pearl grips, R = rosewood grips, NS = night sights, MG = magnesium, and FO = fiber optic). Hence, 2-454089M refers to a Model 454 Raging Bull revolver in .454 Casull cal. with an exposed hammer and a 8 3/8 in. barrel in matte stainless finish.

PISTOLS: SEMI-AUTO

From 1990-92, certain models became available with a Laser Aim LA1 sighting system that included mounts, rings (in matching finish), a 110 volt AC recharging unit, a 9 volt DC field charger, and a high impact custom case.

Taurus incorporated their keyed Taurus security system on most models during 2000, except the PT-22 and PT-25, and this is now available with all models. When the security system is engaged (via a keyed button on the bottom of rear grip strap), the pistol cannot be fired, cocked, or disassembled, and the gun's manual safety cannot be disengaged. This security key also works for the revolvers.

Recent variations that are CA approved are not broken out separately, as pricing is usually the same as the standard model.

Add approx. $30 for the Deluxe Shooter's Pack option (includes extra mag. and custom case) on the 92, 99, 100, and 101 Series (disc. 2000).

GRADING - PPGS™ 100% 98% 95% 90% 80% 70% 60% *LAST MSR*

22 POLY (22 PLY) – .22 LR cal., DAO, blowback action, black, white (new 2020), lavender (new 2020), or cyan (new 2020) sub-compact polymer frame, 2.33 in. tip up barrel, 8 shot mag., fixed sights, black or raspberry (new 2020) polymer grips, manual safety, Taurus Security System, magazine disconnect, blue steel or matte stainless steel slide with fish scale serrations, 10.8 oz. New mid 2014.

MSR $255 $230 $200 $170 $155 $140 $125 $110

Add 5% (MSR $270) for matte stainless steel.

Add 17.5% (MSR $299) for lavender or white polymer frame (new 2020).

25 PLY – .25 ACP cal., otherwise similar to 22 Ply. Mfg. late 2014-2015.

$230 $210 $185 $170 $155 $140 $125 ***$276***

CURVE – .380 ACP cal., blowback action, subcompact polymer frame with metallic sub-frame, 2 1/2 in. barrel, 6 shot mag., hammerless, contoured trigger, with or w/o LED light and laser built into the frame or Viridian laser/light (new 2017), short grip frame assembly, magazine disconnect, unique curved design with belt clip allows pistol to follow body contours, loaded chamber indicator, Taurus Security System, black oxide finish, 10.2 oz. Mfg. 2015-2018.

$335 $295 $275 $250 $225 $200 $185 ***$369***

Add $50 for LED light and laser or Viridian laser/light (new 2017).

G2C – 9mm Para. or .40 S&W cal., SA, striker fired, compact polymer frame available in black, OD Green, Cyan, Gray, Light Purple or Deep Purple (Special Edition frame colors became available during 2018), 3 1/4 in. barrel, 10 or 12 shot mag., reversible mag. release, carbon steel or stainless steel slide, fixed white dot front and adj. white dot rear sights or night sights (mfg. mid-2019-2020), integrated Picatinny rail, precision cut slide serrations, matte black or matte stainless finish, 21.15 oz. New late 2018.

MSR $273 $270 $235 $210 $190 $175 $165 $150

Add $14 for night sights (mfg. mid-2019-2020).

Add 5% (MSR $288) for stainless steel.

G2 MILLENNIUM – 9mm Para. or .40 S&W cal., DA/SA, 3.2 in. barrel, 10 (.40 S&W) or 12 (9mm Para.) shot mag., blue polymer or matte stainless slide, 3-dot low profile sights, loaded chamber indicator, manual and trigger safety, ambidextrous thumb rest, matte black finish, stippled grips with finger indexing memory pads, Picatinny under rail, 22 oz. Mfg. 2013-2018.

$275 $235 $210 $190 $175 $165 $150 ***$319***

Add $20 for stainless steel.

G2S – 9mm Para. or .40 S&W cal., striker fired, polymer frame available in black, OD Green, Tan, Cyan, Brown, or Deep Purple (Special Edition frame colors became available during 2018), 3 1/4 in. barrel, 6 or 7 shot, single action trigger, fully adj. white dot rear and fixed white dot front sight or night sights (new mid-2019), polymer grip, slide serrations, integrated Picatinny rail, matte black carbon steel or matte stainless steel, 20.25 oz. New mid-2018.

MSR $253 $250 $220 $190 $170 $140 $115 $90

Add 5% (MSR $268) for stainless steel.

Add 12.5% (MSR $286) for .40 S&W cal.

Add $30 for night sights (new mid-2019).

Add $137 for Viridian laser (new 2020).

G3 – 9mm Para. cal., SA w/restrike capability, Black, OD Green, or Tan full size polymer frame, 4 in. barrel, 10, 15, or 17 shot mag., carbon and stainless steel construction, fixed front and drift adj. rear white dot sights, stipple patch grips w/ergonomic palm swell and side frame memory pads, striker block, manual, trigger, or loaded chamber indicator safety options, integrated Mil-Std 1913 Picatinny rail, matte black or matte stainless finish, 25 oz. New 2020.

MSR $298 $280 $245 $210 $190 $150 $125 $100

Add 5% (MSR $314) for stainless finish.

Add $16 for night sights.

G3C – 9mm Para. cal., SA w/Restrike, compact polymer frame, 3.2 in. stainless steel barrel, 10 or 12 shot mag., fixed front and drift adj. rear sight, striker block, manual, and trigger safety, accessory rail, loaded chamber indicator, Tenifer matte black finish, 22 oz. New 2020.

MSR $309 $265 $230 $200 $180 $150 $125 $100

PT-22 – .22 LR cal., DAO, tip-up design, 2 3/4 in. barrel, 8 shot mag., fixed sights, polymer (new 2011) or steel frame, stainless (new 2011) or steel slide, blue, nickel (new 1995), blue/nickel (mfg. 1997-2000), Duo-tone (new 2000), or deluxe blue/gold (new 1997) finish, wood (new 1999), mother-of-pearl (mfg. 2000-2011, deluxe blue/gold finish only), black pearl (mfg. 2006-2011), rosewood, checkered wood, or black synthetic (new 2012) grips, reverse fish-scale serrations on slide, Taurus Security System, 12.3 oz. Mfg. 1992-2015.

$230 $210 $185 $170 $155 $140 $125 *$276*

Add $23 for blue/gold or nickel/gold finish with rosewood or $38 for blue/gold or nickel/gold finish with black pearl (mfg. 2006-2011) or mother-of-pearl grips (disc. 2011).

Add $22 for pink pearl grips with blue or nickel finish (disc. 2011) or $38 for pink pearl grips with blue/nickel and gold finish (Model PP-22), disc. 2011.

Add $17 for polymer frame with stainless steel slide (new 2011).

Subtract $7 for black synthetic grips (new 2012).

PT-24/7 – 9mm Para., .40 S&W, or .45 ACP (new 2005) cal., DAO, SFO, large black polymer frame with blued steel or satin stainless steel slide, 4 in. barrel with 3-dot sights, grips have Ribber grip overlays, 10, 12 (.45 ACP cal.), 15 (.40 S&W cal.), or 17 (9mm Para. cal.) shot mag., built-in Picatinny rail system on bottom of frame, includes 3 safeties, 27 1/2 oz. Mfg. late 2004-2005.

$450 $395 $345 $295 $260 $225 $195 *$578*

Add $16 for stainless steel.

PT-24/7 PRO FULL SIZE – 9mm Para., .40 S&W, or .45 ACP cal., SA first shot, and follows continually in SA model, SFO, large black polymer frame with blued steel, Duo Tone (new 2009), titanium (9mm Para. cal. only), or satin stainless steel slide, 4 in. barrel with Heinie front and Slant Pro rear sight, Ribber grips (.45 ACP cal.) or Ribber overmold grips (grip inlays), 10, 12 (.45 ACP cal.), 15 (.40 S&W cal.), or 17 (9mm Para. cal.) shot mag., built-in Picatinny rail system on bottom of frame, includes 3 safeties, 27.2 oz. Mfg. 2006-2010.

$415 $350 $310 $280 $240 $210 $185 *$498*

Add $16 for stainless steel or $188 for titanium.

This model uses a SA trigger mechanism. However, if a cartridge does not fire, a DA feature allows the shooter a second firing pin strike via the DA trigger pull. If the cartridge still does not fire, then extraction by slide operation will insert a fresh round while reverting to the SA model automatically.

* ***PT-24/7 Pro Long Slide*** – similar to Full Size 24/7-Pro, except has 5.2 in. barrel, also available in .38 Super cal. (new 2010), similar mag. capacities, Tenifer finish (2010 only), 29.1 oz. Mfg. 2006-2010.

$445 $385 $340 $295 $260 $225 $195 *$530*

Add $15 for stainless steel. Add $31 for Tenifer finish (new 2010). Add $197 for Tenifer finish with night sights (.40 S&W cal. only, new 2010).

* ***PT-24/7 Pro Compact*** – similar to Full Size 24/7-Pro, except has 3 1/3 in. barrel, similar mag. capacities. Mfg. 2006-2010.

$415 $350 $310 $280 $240 $210 $185 *$498*

Add $16 for stainless steel or $188 for titanium.

PT-24/7 G2 – 9mm Para., .40 S&W, or .45 ACP cal., advanced DA/SA trigger system, SFO, 4.2 in. barrel, large black polymer frame, horizontally grooved grips with metallic inserts and 3 interchangeable backstraps, ambidextrous thumb rests, matte black or stainless steel slide, Strike Two trigger with safety, ambidextrous manual decocker latch and safety, fixed front and low profile adj. rear sight, vertical loaded chamber indicator, built-in Picatinny rail system on bottom of frame, 10, 12 (.45 ACP cal. only), 15 (.40 S&W cal. only) or 17 (9mm Para. only) shot mag., 28 oz. Mfg. 2011-2016.

$315 $265 $235 $210 $185 $160 $140 *$362*

Add $15 for stainless steel.

* ***PT-24/7 G2 Compact*** – 9mm Para., .40 S&W, or .45 ACP cal., similar to PT-24/7 G2, except has 3 1/2 in. barrel, 27 oz. Mfg. 2011-2016.

$315 $265 $235 $210 $185 $160 $140 *$362*

Add $15 for stainless steel.

PT-24/7 OSS – 9mm Para., .40 S&W, or .45 ACP cal., similar operating system as PT-24/7 Pro Full Size, including SA/DA trigger system, choice of tan or black frame, 5 1/4 in. match grade barrel, Novak sights, lower frame Picatinny rail, 10, 12, 15, or 17 shot mag., ambidextrous decocking safety, black Tenifer steel or stainless (new 2009) slide with front and rear serrations, approx. 32 oz. Mfg. 2007-2010.

$475 $415 $370 $325 $285 $240 $210 *$623*

Add $63 for Novak Lo-Mount night sights.

Add $18 for matte finished stainless steel slide (new 2009).

PT-25 – .25 ACP cal., similar to PT-22, except has 9 shot mag., 12.3 oz. Mfg. 1992-2015.

$230 $210 $185 $170 $155 $140 $125 *$276*

Add $17 for polymer frame with stainless steel slide (new 2011).

Add $22 for blue/gold or nickel/gold finish with rosewood or $38 for blue/gold or nickel/gold finish

GRADING - PPGS™	100%	98%	95%	90%	80%	70%	60%	LAST MSR

with mother-of-pearl grips (disc. 2011).
Add $22 for pink pearl grips with blue or nickel finish (disc. 2011) or $38 for pink pearl grips with blue/nickel and gold finish (Model PP-25), disc. 2011.

PT-38S – .38 Super cal., 4 1/4 in. barrel, DA/SA utilizes Model PT-945 alloy frame, choice of blue, stainless steel, or stainless/gold finishes, 3-dot fixed sights, 10 shot mag., checkered rubber (standard) or smooth faux mother-of-pearl grips, 30 oz. Mfg. 2005-2010.

	$525	$480	$425	$375	$325	$280	$230	*$695*

Add $16 for stainless steel slide.
Add $48 for stainless steel slide, gold accents, and faux mother-of-pearl grips.

PT-58 – .380 ACP cal., similar to PT-99AF, except in .380 ACP cal., 4 in. barrel, 10 (C/B 1994) or 12* shot mag. Mfg. 1988-96.

	$360	$300	$260	$220	$200	$180	$165	*$429*

Add $32 for satin nickel finish (disc. 1994).

Beginning 1993, the PT-58 utilized the Taurus Tri-Position safety system which features hammer-drop or "cocked-and-locked" options.

* ***PT-58SS (Stainless Steel)*** – similar to PT-58, except is stainless steel. Mfg. 1992- 96.

	$415	$350	$310	$280	$240	$210	$185	*$470*

PT-58 HC PLUS – .380 ACP cal., medium frame, similar to PT-58, except has 19 shot mag., ambidextrous safety, fixed sights, 18.7 oz. Mfg. 2006-2010.

	$495	$450	$395	$350	$295	$260	$220	*$664*

Add $16 for stainless steel slide.

PT-91AF – .41 Action Express cal., action similar to PT-92AF, except is in .41 AE cal., 10 shot mag., 34 oz. Imported 1990 only.

	$425	$360	$315	$280	$240	$210	$185	*$446*

Add $36 for satin nickel finish.
Add $25 for shooter's pack (includes custom case and extra mag.).

92 (PT-92) (AF) – 9mm Para. cal., DA/SA, design similar to Beretta Model 92 SB-F, exposed hammer, ambidextrous safety, 5 in. barrel, current mfg. has frame accessory rail in front of trigger guard, 10 (C/B 1994), 15*, or 17 (new late 2004) shot mag., smooth Brazilian walnut (disc.), checkered black rubber (new 1999), white pearl (mfg. 2020 only), Hogue (mfg. 2020 only), or G10 black/blue (mfg. 2020 only) grips, black oxide (current mfg.), blue (disc.), satin nickel (disc. 1994), or Blue Sapphire polished PVD (mfg. 2020 only) finish, fixed or night (mfg. 2000-2004) sights, loaded chamber indicator, Taurus Security System, 34 oz.

MSR $544	$460	$390	$325	$280	$240	$210	$185	

Add $45 for white pearl grips (mfg. 2020 only).
Add $139 for Hogue grips and Blue Sapphire polished PVD slide finish (mfg. 2020 only).
Add $164 for G10 blue/black grips and Blue Sapphire polished PVD slide finish (mfg. 2020 only).
Add $40 for satin nickel finish (disc. 1994).
Add $78 for night sights (disc. 2004).
Add $415 for Laser Aim Sight (disc. 1991).
Add $266 for blue or stainless conversion kit to convert 9mm Para. to .22 LR (mfg. 1999-2004).

* ***92 SS (Stainless Steel) (PT-92SS)*** – 9mm Para. cal., large frame, 5 in. barrel, 17 shot mag., integrated front sight, drift adj. rear sight, Mil-Std 1913 Picatinny rail, black rubber or white pearl (mfg. 2020 only) grips, combat matte (new 2006, high cap. mag. only) or regular stainless steel, 34 oz. New 1992.

MSR $557	$460	$395	$330	$280	$240	$210	$185	

Add $45 for white pearl grips (mfg. 2020 only).
Add $78 for night sights (disc. 2004).

* ***PT-92 Deluxe*** – choice of blue/gold (disc. 2004) or stainless steel with gold finish, rosewood, or mother-of-pearl (new 2000) grips. Mfg. 1999-2011.

	$515	$460	$400	$350	$295	$260	$220	*$655*

Add $25 for faux mother-of-pearl grips.
Add $40 for stainless gold finish with rosewood grips (new 2011).
Subtract approx. $15 for blue/gold finish (disc. 2004).

* ***PT-92AFC*** – compact variation of the Model PT-92AF, 4 in. barrel, 10 (C/B 1994) or 13* shot mag., fixed sights. Disc. 1996.

	$395	$345	$300	$260	$220	$195	$175	*$449*

Add $38 for satin nickel finish (disc. 1993).

GRADING - PPGS™	100%	98%	95%	90%	80%	70%	60%	LAST MSR

* ***PT-92AFC (Stainless Steel)*** – similar to PT-92AFC, except stainless steel. Mfg. 1993-96.

	$425	$360	$315	$280	$240	$210	$185	*$493*

PT 92 BRAZILIAN WALNUT – 9mm Para. cal., DA/SA, matte black hard anodized frame, 5 in. barrel, two 17 shot mags., alloy steel, hammer firing system, integrated front sight and drift adj. rear sight, Brazilian walnut wood grips, manual safety and ambi decocker, firing pin block, matte black and polished stainless slide, 34 oz. Mfg. mid-2019-2020.

MSR pricing was not available for this model.

PT-99 (AF) – 9mm Para. cal., similar to Model PT-92AF, except has adj. rear sight, 10 or 17 shot mag., 34 oz. Disc. 2011.

	$495	$450	$395	$350	$295	$260	$220	*$617*

Add $45 for satin nickel finish (disc. 1994).
Add $266 for blue or stainless conversion kit to convert 9mm Para. to .22 LR (mfg. 1999-2004) or .40 S&W (mfg. 2000-2004).

This action is similar to the Beretta Model 92SB-F.

* ***PT-99SS (Stainless Steel)*** – similar to PT-99, except is fabricated from stainless steel. Mfg. 1992-2011.

	$495	$450	$395	$350	$295	$260	$220	*$633*

PT-100 – .40 S&W cal., DA/SA, large frame, 5 in. barrel, 10 (C/B 1994), 11* (reintroduced late 2004) shot mag., safeties include ambidextrous manual, hammer drop, inertia firing pin, and chamber loaded indicator, choice of blue, satin nickel (disc. 1994), or stainless steel finish, accessory rail, smooth Brazilian hardwood (disc.) or rubber grips, 34 oz. Mfg. 1992-97, reintroduced 2000-2012.

	$495	$450	$395	$350	$295	$260	$220	*$641*

Add $40 for satin nickel finish (disc. 1994).
Add $78 for night sights (mfg. 2000-2004).
Add $266 for blue or stainless conversion kit to convert .40 S&W to .22 LR cal. (disc. 2004).

* ***PT-100SS (Stainless Steel)*** – .40 S&W cal., similar to PT-100, except is fabricated from stainless steel, and 16 shot mag. Mfg. 1992-96, reintroduced 2000-2013.

	$515	$460	$400	$350	$295	$260	$220	*$668*

Add $78 for night sights (disc. 2005).

* ***PT-100 Deluxe*** – choice of blue/gold (disc. 2004) finish or stainless steel with gold, rosewood, or mother-of-pearl grips. Mfg. 2000-2011.

	$525	$480	$425	$375	$325	$280	$230	*$670*

Add $25 for faux mother-of-pearl grips.
Subtract approx. $15 for blue/gold finish (disc. 2004).

PT-101 – .40 S&W cal., similar to PT-100, except has adj. rear sight., 10 or 11 shot mag., 34 oz. Mfg. 1992-96, reintroduced 2000-2011.

	$495	$450	$395	$350	$295	$260	$220	*$617*

Add $266 for blue or stainless conversion kit to convert .40 S&W to .22 LR cal. (disc. 2004).
Add $45 for satin nickel finish (disc. 1994).

* ***PT-101SS (Stainless Steel)*** – similar to PT-101, except is stainless steel. Mfg. 1992-96, reintroduced 2000-2011.

	$495	$450	$395	$350	$295	$260	$220	*$633*

PT-111 MILLENNIUM – 9mm Para. cal., DAO, SFO, 3 1/4 in. barrel with fixed 3-dot sights, black polymer frame with steel slide, 10 shot mag. with push-button release, 18.7 oz. Mfg. 1998-2004.

	$375	$310	$265	$220	$200	$180	$165	*$422*

Add $78 for night sights (new 2000).
Add $47 for pearl or burl walnut grips (limited mfg. 2003).

* ***PT-111 Millennium Stainless*** – similar to Model PT-111, except has stainless steel slide. Mfg. 1998-2004.

	$385	$335	$295	$260	$220	$195	$175	*$438*

Add $78 for night sights (new 2000).
Add $46 for pearl or burl walnut grips (limited mfg. 2003).

* ***PT-111 Millennium Titanium*** – similar to Model PT-111, except has titanium slide and night or 3-dot (new 2004) sights. Mfg. 2000-2004.

	$435	$385	$340	$295	$260	$225	$195	*$508*

Add $78 for night sights.

GRADING - PPGS™	100%	98%	95%	90%	80%	70%	60%	LAST MSR

PT-111 MILLENNIUM PRO – 9mm Para. cal., SA/DA trigger, SFO, 10 or 12 (new late 2004) shot mag., blue steel frame, current mfg. has Heinie Straight 8 sights, improved ergonomics, Posi-Traction slide serrations, recessed magazine release, manual safety lever, trigger block mechanism, firing pin block, and lightweight frame, 18.7 oz. Mfg. 2003-2012.

$375	$310	$265	$220	$200	$180	$165	*$467*

Add $78 for night sights (disc. 2004).

* ***PT-111 Millennium Pro Stainless*** – similar to Model PT-111 Millennium Pro, except has stainless steel slide. Mfg. 2003-2012.

$395	$330	$285	$260	$210	$170	$135	*$483*

Add $78 for night sights (mfg. 2004).

* ***PT-111 Ti Millennium Pro Titanium*** – similar to Model PT-111 Millennium Pro, except has titanium slide and 3-dot sights, 16 oz. Mfg. 2005-2011.

$525	$480	$425	$375	$325	$280	$230	*$655*

PT-132 MILLENNIUM – .32 ACP cal., double action only, 3 1/4 in. barrel, black polymer frame, manual safety, 10 shot mag., fixed 3-dot (disc. 2002) or adj. (new 2003) sights, blue steel slide, 18.7 oz. Mfg. 2001-2004.

$355	$300	$260	$220	$200	$180	$165	*$422*

* ***Model PT-132 Millennium Stainless*** – similar to Model PT-132, except has stainless steel slide. Mfg. 2001-2004.

$360	$300	$260	$220	$200	$180	$165	*$438*

PT-132 MILLENNIUM PRO – .32 ACP cal., similar to Model PT-132 Millennium, SA/DA trigger, current mfg. has Heinie Straight 8 sights, improved ergonomics, Posi-Traction slide serrations, recessed magazine release, manual safety lever, trigger block mechanism, firing pin block, adj. rear sight, and lightweight frame, 19.9 oz. Mfg. 2003, reintroduced 2005-2011.

$375	$310	$265	$220	$200	$180	$165	*$467*

* ***PT-132 Millennium Pro Stainless*** – similar to Model PT-132 Millennium Pro, except has stainless steel slide. Mfg. 2003, reintroduced 2005-2011.

$395	$345	$300	$260	$220	$195	$175	*$483*

PT-138 MILLENNIUM – .380 ACP cal., double action only, 3 1/4 in. barrel, black polymer frame, manual safety, 10 shot mag., fixed 3-dot sights, blue steel slide, 18.7 oz. Mfg. 1999-2004.

$355	$300	$260	$220	$200	$180	$165	*$422*

Add $78 for night sights (mfg. 2000-2003).

* ***Model PT-138 Millennium Stainless*** – similar to Model PT-138, except has stainless steel slide. Mfg. 1999-disc.

$360	$300	$260	$220	$200	$180	$165	

Add $78 for night sights (mfg. 2000-2003).

PT-138 MILLENNIUM PRO – .380 ACP cal., similar to Model PT-138 Millennium, SFO, 10 or 12 shot (new 2005) mag., SA/DA trigger, current mfg. has Heinie Straight 8 sights, improved ergonomics, Posi-Traction slide serrations, recessed magazine release, manual safety lever, trigger block mechanism, firing pin block, and lightweight frame, 18.7 oz. Mfg. 2003, reintroduced 2005-2011.

$375	$310	$265	$220	$200	$180	$165	*$467*

Add $78 for night sights (disc. 2003).

* ***PT-138 Millennium Pro Stainless*** – similar to Model PT-138 Millennium Pro, except has stainless steel slide. Mfg. 2003, reintroduced 2005-2011.

$395	$345	$300	$260	$220	$195	$175	*$483*

PT-140 MILLENNIUM – .40 S&W cal., DAO, SFO, 3 1/4 in. barrel, black polymer frame, manual safety, 10 shot mag., fixed 3-dot sights, blue steel slide, 18.7 oz. Mfg. 1999-2004.

$375	$310	$265	$220	$200	$180	$165	*$461*

Add $78 for night sights (new 2000).
Add $47 for pearl or burl walnut grips (mfg. 2003).

* ***PT-140 Millennium Stainless*** – similar to Model PT-140, except has stainless steel slide. Mfg. 1999-2004.

$380	$335	$295	$260	$220	$195	$175	*$476*

Add $78 for night sights (new 2000).
Add $46 for pearl or burl walnut grips (mfg. 2003).

GRADING - PPGS™	100%	98%	95%	90%	80%	70%	60%	LAST MSR

PT-140 MILLENNIUM PRO – .40 S&W cal., similar to Model PT-140 Millennium, except has SA/DA trigger, current mfg. has Heinie Straight 8 sights, improved ergonomics, Posi-Traction slide serrations, recessed magazine release, manual safety lever, trigger block mechanism, firing pin block, and lightweight frame, 23 1/2 oz. Mfg. 2003-2012.

	$395	$345	$300	$260	$220	$195	$175	*$483*

Add $78 for night sights (disc. 2004).

* ***PT-140 Millennium Pro Stainless*** – similar to Model PT-140 Millennium Pro, except has stainless steel slide. Mfg. 2003-2012.

	$415	$350	$310	$280	$240	$210	$185	*$498*

Add $78 for night sights (disc. 2004).

PT-145 MILLENNIUM – .45 ACP cal., otherwise similar to Model PT-140 Millennium, 23 oz. Mfg. 2000-2003.

	$400	$350	$310	$280	$240	$210	$185	*$484*

Add $79 for night sights (new 2000).

* ***PT-145 Millennium Stainless*** – similar to Model PT-140, except has stainless steel slide. Mfg. 1999-2003.

	$400	$350	$310	$280	$240	$210	$185	*$500*

Add $78 for night sights (new 2000).

PT-145 MILLENNIUM PRO – .45 ACP cal., similar to Model PT-145 Millennium, except has SA/DA trigger, current mfg. has Heinie Straight 8 sights, improved ergonomics, Posi-Traction slide serrations, recessed magazine release, manual safety lever, trigger block mechanism, firing pin block, and lightweight frame, 22.2 oz. Mfg. 2003-2012.

	$395	$345	$300	$260	$220	$195	$175	*$483*

Add $78 for night sights (disc. 2004).

* ***PT-145 Millennium Pro Stainless*** – similar to Model PT-145 Millennium Pro, except has stainless steel slide. Mfg. 2003-2013.

	$415	$350	$310	$280	$240	$210	$185	*$498*

Add $78 for night sights (mfg. 2000-2004).

PT-400 – .400 Cor-Bon cal., similar to Model PT-940, except has 4 1/4 in. ported barrel and 8 shot mag., 29 1/2 oz. Mfg. 1999 only.

	$415	$350	$310	$280	$240	$210	$185	*$523*

* ***PT-400 Stainless*** – similar to Model PT-400, except has stainless steel slide. Mfg. 1999 only.

	$415	$350	$310	$280	$240	$210	$185	*$539*

PT-609/609TI-PRO – 9mm Para. cal., DA/SA, 3 1/4 in. barrel with titanium slide, fixed sights, black polymer grips, lower rail on frame, 13 shot mag., 19.7 oz. Mfg. 2007-2010.

	$535	$490	$430	$375	$325	$280	$230	*$670*

PT-638 PRO COMPACT – .380 ACP cal., SA target style trigger with trigger safety, 3.2 in. barrel, low mount sights with adj. rear, 15 shot mag., ambidextrous manual safety, loaded chamber indicator, blue or matte stainless slide, black polymer frame with Memory Pad, 28 oz. Mfg. 2011 only.

	$395	$345	$300	$260	$220	$195	$175	*$483*

Add $15 for matte stainless steel slide.

PT-709 SLIM – 9mm Para. cal., SA (disc.) or DA/SA trigger (current mfg.), 3 in. barrel, 7 shot mag., black polymer compact frame with grip texturing, 3-dot sights, loaded chamber indicator, advanced "Strike Two" trigger system, Taurus Security System, blue finish, 19 oz. Mfg. late 2008-2012, reintroduced 2014-2017.

	$275	$235	$210	$190	$175	$165	$155	*$319*

Add $14 for Bulldog Case (mfg. 2010-2011).

* ***PT-709 Slim Stainless*** – 9mm Para. cal., similar to PT-709 Slim, except has matte finished stainless steel slide, 19 oz. Mfg. late 2008-2017.

	$285	$240	$215	$195	$175	$165	$155	*$339*

Add $15 for Bulldog Case (mfg. 2010-2011).

* ***PT-709 Slim Titanium*** – similar to Model 709 Slim, except has titanium slide, 17 oz. Disc. 2010.

	$515	$460	$400	$350	$295	$260	$220	*$623*

Add $15 for Bulldog Case (new 2010).

PT-709 G2 SLIM – 9mm Para. cal., sub-compact frame, 7 or 9 (extended) shot mag., 3.2 in. barrel with low profile adj. rear sights, loaded chamber indicator, black polymer frame and blue or matte stainless slide, 19.4 oz. Limited mfg. 2011 only.

	$395	$345	$300	$260	$220	$195	$175	*$483*

GRADING - PPGS™	100%	98%	95%	90%	80%	70%	60%	LAST MSR

* ***PT-709 G2 Slim Stainless*** – similar to PT-709 G2 Slim, except has matte finished stainless steel slide. Limited mfg. 2011 only.

	$415	$350	$310	$280	$240	$210	$185	*$498*

PT-732 TCP (TAURUS COMPACT PISTOL) – .32 ACP cal., 3.3 in. barrel, DAO, 6 shot mag., blue or matte stainless steel slide, low profile fixed sights, loaded chamber indicator, checkered black or pink polymer frame, 10.2 oz. Mfg. 2011-2012.

	$295	$250	$215	$185	$170	$155	$145	*$352*

PT-738 TCP (TAURUS COMPACT PISTOL) – .380 ACP cal., 3.3 in. barrel, DAO, choice of pink or black polymer frame, matte black, matte stainless, black stainless (new 2011), or titanium (disc. 2011) slide, 6 shot mag., fixed front sight, checkered polymer grips, loaded chamber indicator, integrated sights, 10.2 oz. Mfg. mid-2009-2016.

	$260	$220	$200	$175	$155	$135	$125	*$295*

Subtract $45 for matte black carbon slide.
Add $110 for titanium slide (disc. 2011).

PT-738 TCP W/WINGS (TAURUS COMPACT PISTOL) – .380 ACP cal., 3.3 in. barrel, 6 shot mag., grooved black polymer frame, blue or stainless steel slide, hammerless, DAO trigger, low profile fixed sights, unique retractable wings that fold out from rear of slide allowing racking the slide easier, loaded chamber indicator, matte black or matte stainless finish, 10.2 oz. Mfg. 2015-2016.

	$235	$200	$185	$165	$150	$135	$125	*$266*

Add $45 for stainless steel slide.

PT-738FS – .380 ACP cal., DAO, 3.3 in. barrel, blue slide, polymer frame, loaded chamber indicator, low profile fixed sights, hammerless, 10.2 oz. Mfg. 2013-2015.

	$225	$195	$170	$155	$140	$125	$120	*$250*

PT-740 SLIM – .40 S&W cal., DA/SA trigger, 3 in. barrel, 6 shot mag., black polymer compact frame with grip texturing, 3-dot sights, loaded chamber indicator, advanced "Strike Two" trigger system, Taurus Security System, blue finish, 19 oz. Mfg. 2011-2017.

	$275	$235	$210	$190	$175	$165	$155	*$319*

* ***PT-740 Slim Stainless*** – .40 S&W cal., similar to PT-740 Slim, except has matte stainless steel slide. Disc. 2017.

	$285	$240	$215	$195	$175	$165	$155	*$339*

PT-740 G2 SLIM – While advertised during 2010 this model never went into production.

PT-745 COMPACT MILLENNIUM PRO – .45 ACP cal., DA/SA, SFO, compact variation of Millennium Pro with 3 1/4 in. barrel, Heinie Straight 8 sights, 6 shot mag. with finger extension, matte blue steel slide, loaded chamber indicator, black polymer grip frame, Desert Tan grips were added 2006 (disc.), 20.8 oz. Mfg. 2005-2012.

	$395	$345	$300	$260	$220	$195	$175	*$483*

* ***PT-745 Compact Millennium Pro Stainless*** – similar to PT-745 Compact Millennium Pro, except has stainless steel slide. Mfg. 2005-2012.

	$415	$350	$310	$280	$240	$210	$185	*$498*

PT-809 – 9mm Para. cal., similar design to the PT-24/7 OSS, 4 in. barrel, DA/SA with Strike Two capability, SFO, Novak sights, 17 shot mag., external hammer, loaded chamber indicator, blue or stainless (disc. 2012), front and rear slide serrations, lower Picatinny rail, ambidextrous 3-position safety and decocker, ambidextrous mag. release, extended grip, small, medium, and large interchangeable backstraps, double stack magazines, unique takedown levers, Taurus Security System, 30.2 oz. Mfg. 2007-2016.

	$275	$240	$210	$185	$170	$150	$130	*$347*

Add $15 for stainless steel slide (disc. 2012).
Add $188 for .22 LR conversion kit (10 shot mag., mfg. 2011 only).

* ***PT-809 Compact*** – 9mm Para. cal., 3 1/2 in. barrel, 17 shot mag., 3-dot fixed sights, polymer grips with metallic inserts, loaded chamber indicator, ambidextrous mag. release, Strike Two trigger, external hammer, shortened grip frame, Taurus Security system, matte black finish, 24.7 oz. Mfg. 2011-2016.

	$275	$240	$210	$185	$170	$150	$130	*$347*

Add $15 for stainless steel slide (disc. 2012).

PT-840 – .40 S&W cal., similar design to the PT-24/7 OSS, 4 in. barrel, DA/SA with Strike Two capability, Novak sights, 15 shot mag., matte blue or matte stainless slide (disc. 2012), front and rear slide serrations, lower frame Picatinny rail, ambidextrous 3-position safety and decocker, ambidextrous mag. release, extended grip, small, medium, and large interchangeable backstraps, external hammer, double stack magazines, Taurus Security System, approx. 30 oz. Mfg. 2008-2016.

	$275	$240	$210	$185	$170	$150	$130	*$347*

Add $15 for stainless steel slide (disc. 2012).
Add $188 for .22 LR conversion kit (10 shot mag., mfg. 2011 only).

GRADING - PPGS™	100%	98%	95%	90%	80%	70%	60%	LAST MSR

* ***PT-840 Compact*** – .40 S&W cal., 3 1/2 in. barrel, 15 shot mag., 3-dot sights, polymer grips with metallic inserts, loaded chamber indicator, ambidextrous mag. release, Strike Two capability, shortened grip frame, external hammer, matte black finish, 24.7 oz. Mfg. 2011-2016.

$275	$240	$210	$185	$170	$150	$130	*$347*

Add $16 for stainless steel slide (disc. 2012).

PT-845 – .45 ACP cal., similar design to the PT-24/7 OSS, 4 in. barrel, DA/SA with Strike Two capability, SFO, Novak sights, 12 shot mag., blue or stainless (disc.), front and rear slide serrations, lower frame Picatinny rail, ambidextrous 3-position safety and decocker, ambidextrous mag. release, extended grip, small, medium, and large interchangeable backstraps, external hammer, double stack magazines, takedown lever, approx. 30 oz. Mfg. 2008-2016.

$275	$240	$210	$185	$170	$150	$130	*$347*

Add $15 for stainless steel slide (disc. 2012).
Add $188 for .22 LR conversion kit (10 shot mag., mfg. 2011 only).

PT-908 – 9mm Para. cal., compact version of the PT-92 with 3.8 in. barrel, DA/SA, 8 shot mag., fixed sights, blue or nickel finish. Mfg. 1993-1997.

$360	$300	$260	$220	$200	$180	$165	*$435*

* ***PT-908D SS (Stainless Steel)*** – similar to Model PT-908, except is stainless steel. Mfg. 1993-97.

$385	$335	$295	$260	$220	$195	$175	*$473*

PT-909 – 9mm Para. cal., DA/SA, 4 in. barrel, lower frame Picatinny rail, 10 or 17 shot mag., blue finish, fixed rear sight, alloy medium frame with steel slide, checkered rubber grips, 28.2 oz. Mfg. 2006-2010.

$500	$450	$395	$350	$295	$260	$220	*$648*

Add $16 for stainless steel slide.

PT-911 COMPACT – 9mm Para. cal., DA/SA, 4 in. barrel, 10 or 15 (new late 2004) shot mag., checkered rubber grips, fixed sights, 28.2 oz. Mfg. 1997-2010.

$500	$450	$395	$350	$295	$260	$220	*$648*

Add $79 for night sights (disc. 2004).

* ***PT-911 Compact SS (Stainless Steel)*** – stainless variation of the PT-911 Compact. Disc. 2010.

$530	$480	$425	$375	$325	$280	$230	*$664*

Add $78 for night sights (disc. 2004).

* ***PT-911 Compact Deluxe*** – choice of blue/gold finish or stainless steel with gold, rosewood, or mother-of-pearl grips. Mfg. 2000-2010.

$550	$495	$450	$395	$350	$295	$245	*$702*

Add $15 for stainless steel with gold or faux mother-of-pearl grips.

PT-917 COMPACT PLUS – 9mm Para. cal., DA/SA, 4 in. barrel with fixed sights, rubber grips, 19 shot mag., medium frame, blue finish or stainless steel, 31.8 oz. Mfg. 2007-2010.

$500	$450	$395	$350	$295	$260	$220	*$609*

Add $18 for stainless steel.

PT-922 – .22 LR cal., sport model with 10 shot mag., 6 in. tapered barrel, adj. sights, medium frame, blue finish, angled synthetic grip frame with Taurus medallions on bottom, 25 oz. Limited mfg. 2004.

$285	$250	$215	$185	$170	$155	$145	*$370*

PT-938 COMPACT – .380 ACP cal., DA/SA, 3 3/4 in. barrel, ambidextrous safety, 10 or 15 (new late 2004) shot mag., blue finish with alloy frame and steel slide, rubber grips, fixed sights, 34 oz. Mfg. 1997-2005.

$410	$350	$310	$280	$240	$210	$185	*$516*

* ***PT-938 Compact SS (Stainless Steel)*** – stainless slide variation of the PT-938 Compact with matte stainless finish.

$420	$360	$315	$280	$240	$210	$185	*$531*

PT-940 – .40 S&W cal., compact version of the PT-100 with 3 5/8 in. barrel, DA/SA, 10 shot mag., fixed sights, 28.2 oz. Mfg. 1996-2010.

$500	$450	$395	$350	$295	$260	$220	*$648*

Add $79 for night sights (disc. 2004).

* ***PT-940 SS (Stainless Steel)*** – similar to PT-940, except is stainless steel. Mfg. 1996-2010.

$530	$480	$425	$375	$325	$280	$230	*$664*

Add $80 for night sights (disc. 2009).

* ***PT-940 Deluxe*** – choice of blue/gold or stainless steel with gold finish, rosewood, or mother-of-pearl grips. Mfg. 2000-2010.

$545	$490	$430	$375	$325	$280	$230	*$702*

Add $15 for stainless steel with gold with rosewood grips or for mother-of-pearl grips.

GRADING - PPGS™	100%	98%	95%	90%	80%	70%	60%	LAST MSR

PT-945 – .45 ACP cal., DA/SA, 4 1/4 in. ported (mfg. 1997-2003) or unported barrel, 8 shot single stack mag., ambidextrous 3-position safety and decocker, chamber loaded indicator, 3-dot sights, 29 1/2 oz. Mfg. 1995-2010.

	$560	$495	$450	$395	$350	$295	$245	*$695*

Add $78 for night sights (disc. 2004).
Add $39 for ported barrel (disc. 2003).

* ***PT-945 SS (Stainless Steel)*** – stainless steel variation of the PT-945. Mfg. 1995-2010.

	$575	$510	$455	$395	$350	$295	$245	*$711*

Add $78 for night sights (disc. 2004).
Add $39 for ported barrel (disc. 2003).

* ***PT-945 Deluxe*** – choice of blue/gold (disc. 2004) or stainless steel finish, mother-of-pearl (new 2000), or rosewood grips. Mfg. 1999-2010.

	$615	$550	$485	$430	$380	$325	$275	*$764*

Add $16 for mother-of-pearl grips.
Subtract approx. $15 for blue/gold finish.

PT-957 – .357 SIG cal., DA/SA, compact model with 3 5/8 in. ported (available only with night sights or in 957 Deluxe beginning 2002) or non-ported (new 2002) barrel and slide, 10 shot mag., ambidextrous 3-position safety and decocker, blue finish, checkered rubber grips, fixed sights, 28 oz. Mfg. 1999-2003.

	$425	$360	$315	$280	$240	$210	$185	*$523*

Add $90 for night sights.
Add $40 for ported barrel (disc. 2002).

* ***PT-957 SS (Stainless Steel)*** – stainless steel variation of the PT-957. Mfg. 1999-2003.

	$430	$385	$340	$295	$260	$225	$195	*$539*

Add $40 for ported (disc. 2001) barrel, or $130 for ported barrel and night sights (disc. 2003).

* ***PT-957 Deluxe*** – choice of blue/gold or stainless steel with gold finish, rosewood, or mother-of-pearl grips. Mfg. 2000-2002.

	$475	$415	$370	$325	$285	$240	$210	*$610*

Add $15 for stainless steel.
Add $15 for mother-of-pearl grips.

TAURUS 1911 (PT-1911) – .38 Super (mfg. 2006-2011), 9mm Para. (new 2006), .40 S&W (mfg. 2006-2010), or .45 ACP cal., SA, 5 in. barrel, choice of Heinie front and rear sights or Picatinny rail, 8 (.40 S&W or .45 ACP) or 9 (.38 Super or 9mm Para.) shot mag., blue, Duo-tone (new 2008), or Cerakote finish (Tungsten Gray, Desert Sand, Bronze (new 2021), or Mil-Spec OD Green, new 2019), Special Editions became available during 2019 w/various colored frame/slide and grip configurations, choice of steel or aluminum (new 2008) frame with steel slide, black checkered diamond pattern, bull's head wood (disc. 2015), Altamont (new 2020), or Custom VZ (Cerakote only) grips, bobbed hammer, front and rear serrations on slide, accurized hand tuned action, 42 oz. New mid-2005.

MSR $615	$525	$465	$390	$325	$285	$240	$210	

Add $6 for 9mm Para. cal. with matte black finish (new 2006).
Add $16 for Altamont wood grips/black finish or $31 for Altamont wood grips and Cerakote Bronze finish (both new 2020).
Add $38 for U.S. Flag Cerakote finish (new 2020).
Add $52 for Picatinny rail (.45 ACP cal. only).
Add $80 for Tungsten Gray, Desert Sand, or Mil-Spec OD Green Cerakote finish (new 2019).
Add $93 for Duo-Tone finish (.45 ACP cal. only), not available with Picatinny rail.
Add $147 for bull's head grips (.45 ACP cal. only, disc. 2015).
Add approx. $75 for aluminum frame (disc. 2011).

* ***PT-1911 Compact*** – .45 ACP cal., only, similar to PT-1911, except has 4 1/4 in. barrel, 6 shot mag. Mfg. 2006 only.

	$490	$430	$365	$335	$270	$220	$170	*$599*

Add $20 for stainless steel slide.

* ***Taurus 1911 Stainless (PT-1911 Stainless)*** – 9mm Para. (disc. 2018), or .45 ACP cal., SAO, 5 in. barrel, 8 or 9 shot mag., stainless steel frame and slide, Novak drift adj. sights, bull's head (disc. 2015) or checkered black grips, matte stainless finish, lower frame Picatinny rail, 42 oz.

MSR $707	$635	$540	$440	$375	$320	$270	$240	

Add $17 for lower frame Picatinny rail.
Add $68 for bull's head grips (disc. 2015).
Subtract $30 for 9mm Para. cal. (disc. 2018).

GRADING - PPGS™	100%	98%	95%	90%	80%	70%	60%	LAST MSR

TAURUS 1911 COMMANDER – .45 ACP or 9mm Para. (new 2020) cal., SAO, 4.2 in. barrel, 8 shot mag., carbon steel slide, Novak drift adj. front and rear sight, checkered black, Magpul MOE (new 2019, in black, FDE, Gray, or OD Green), Custom VZ (new 2019), or checkered wood (new 2020) grips, extended beavertail, matte black finish, Cerakote (Tungsten Gray, Desert Sand, or Mil-Spec Green, new 2019), Cerekote aluminum (new 2020), Midnight Bronze (new 2020), or Prizm PVD (new 2021) slide finish, 38 oz. New 2018.

MSR $616 $520 $460 $390 $325 $285 $240 $210

Subtract $23 for checkered black grips.
Add $34 for Aluminum or Midnight Bronze Cerakote finish (new 2020).
Add $107 for Cerakote finish (new 2019).
Add $113 for custom VZ grips (new 2019).

* ***Taurus 1911 Commander Flag Limited Edition*** – .45 ACP cal., SA, 4.2 in. barrel, 8 shot mag., carbon steel slide, Novak drift adj. front and rear sight, custom U.S. flag engraved altamount rosewood w/bonded ivory inlay or stars and stripes VZ G10 grips, extended beavertail, matte black finish, 38 oz. Limited mfg. 2019-2020.

$575 $500 $4325 $390 $315 $275 $225 *$672*

TAURUS 1911 OFFICER – .45 ACP or 9mm Para. (new 2020) cal., SAO, alloy steel frame, 3 1/2 in. barrel, 6 shot mag., carbon steel slide, Novak drift adj. front and rear sights, checkered black, Altamont wood (new 2020), black (new 2020), or custom VZ (new 2020) grips, matte black or Cerakote (new 2020, Tungsten, MS Green, Desert Sand, Desert Aluminum, or Desert Bronze) finish, 35 oz. New 2018.

MSR $639 $525 $465 $390 $325 $285 $240 $210

Add $26 for Altamont wood grips with Cerakote finish in Desert Aluminum or Desert Bronze (new 2020).
Add $75 for VZ grips with Cerakote finish in Tungsten, MS Green, or Desert Sand (new 2020).
Subtract $77 for Altamond wood grips with matte black finish (new 2020).

PT-1911FS – .45 ACP cal., 5 in. barrel, blued steel slide and frame, skeletonized trigger, double slide serrations, fixed sights, double diamond black synthetic grips, 7 shot mag., 38 oz. Mfg. 2013-2015.

$485 $435 $375 $320 $280 $240 $210 *$574*

PT-1911B SERIES – .38 Super (1911B-38, disc.), 9mm Para. (1911B-9), or .45 ACP (1911BHC-12) cal., 5 in. barrel, SA, blue, stainless, 9, 11, or 12 shot mag., with or w/o Novak night sights (disc. 2010), Heinie sights became standard 2011, 38-40 oz. Mfg. mid-2009-2011.

$535 $490 $430 $375 $325 $280 $230 *$677*

Add $103 for stainless steel. Add $17 for 11 shot mag. Add $79 for .45 ACP with 12 shot mag. Add $63 for Novak night sights. Add $93 for Hi-Polish with bull's head walnut grips. Add $16 for pearl grips.

PT-2011 DT INTEGRAL – .380 ACP or 9mm Para. cal., DA/SA with trigger safety, SFO, 3.2 in. barrel, 11 (.380 ACP), 13 or 15 (.380 ACP) shot mag., aluminum frame with black polymer grips, loaded chamber indicator, matte black metal finish, removable backstraps, adj. rear sight, 21 or 24 oz. Mfg. 2012 only.

$475 $415 $370 $325 $285 $240 $210 *$572*

* ***PT-2011 DT Integral Stainless*** – similar to PT-2011 DT Integral, except has stainless steel slide. Mfg. 2012 only.

$485 $425 $375 $325 $285 $240 $210 *$588*

PT-2011 DT HYBRID – 9mm Para. or .40 S&W cal., DA/SA with trigger safety, SFO, 3.2 in. barrel, 11 (.40 S&W) or 13 (9mm Para.) shot mag., black polymer lower frame with steel upper frame and slide, loaded chamber indicator, matte black metal finish, removable backstraps, adj. rear sight, 24 oz. Mfg. 2012-2013.

$490 $425 $375 $325 $285 $240 $210 *$589*

* ***PT-2011 DT Hybrid Stainless*** – similar to PT-2011 DT Hybrid, except has stainless upper frame and slide. Mfg. 2012-2013.

$500 $450 $395 $350 $295 $260 $220 *$605*

PT-2045 – .45 ACP cal., SFO, 4.2 in. barrel, blue or stainless, 12 shot mag., checkered polymer grips, with or w/o Novak night sights, approx. 32 oz. Limited mfg. 2009 only.

$450 $395 $345 $295 $260 $225 $195 *$561*

Add $16 for stainless steel. Add $62 for night sights.

SPECTRUM – .380 ACP cal., striker fire, DAO, 2.8 in. barrel, 6 or 7 shot with extended mag., stainless steel slide with matte black or matte stainless finish, integrated low profile sights, with (new mid-2018) or without Viridian laser, soft-touch panels integrated into the grip and slide in standard or various two-tone frame combinations, 10 oz. Mfg. 2017-2019, reintroduced 2021.

MSR $224 $200 $175 $150 $135 $110 $90 $70

Add $10 for two-tone frame combinations.
Add $62 for red Viridian laser (new 2018).

GRADING - PPGS™	100%	98%	95%	90%	80%	70%	60%	LAST MSR

TH9 – 9mm Para. cal., SAO, hammer fired, full size black, brown, cyan, Gray, OD Green, or Tan polymer frame, 4 1/4 in. barrel, carbon steel slide, includes two 17 shot mags., Novak drift adj. sights, interchangeable backstraps, firing pin block safety, matte black finish, 28.2 oz. New 2019.

MSR $347	$320	$280	$240	$220	$175	$145	$110	

Add 7.5% (MSR $377) for Brown, Cyan, Gray, OD Green, or Tan frame color.

TH9C COMPACT – 9mm Para. cal., SAO, hammer fired, compact black, brown, cyan, gray, OD Green, or tan polymer frame, 3.54 in. barrel, 13 shot mag., Novak drift adj. sights, firing pin block safety, matte black finish, 25 oz. New 2019.

MSR $347	$320	$280	$240	$220	$175	$145	$110	

Add 7.5% (MSR $377) for Brown, Cyan, Gray, OD Green, or Tan frame color.
Add $93 for Viridian laser (new 2020).

TH40 – .40 S&W cal., SAO, hammer fired, Black, Brown, Gray, OD Green, or Tan full size polymer frame, 4 1/4 in. barrel, carbon steel slide, includes two 15 shot mags., Novak drift adj. sights, polymer grips, firing pin block safety, interchangeable backstraps, matte black finish, 28.2 oz. New 2019.

MSR $347	$320	$280	$240	$220	$175	$145	$110	

Add 7.5% (MSR $377) for Brown, Gray, OD Green, or Tan frame color.

TH40C COMPACT – .40 S&W cal., SAO, hammer fired, Black, Brown, Gray, OD Green, or Tan compact polymer frame, 3.54 in. barrel, carbon steel slide, 11 or 15 shot mag., Novak drift adj. sights, polymer grips, firing pin block safety, matte black finish, 25 oz. New 2019.

MSR $347	$320	$280	$240	$220	$175	$145	$110	

Add 7.5% (MSR $377) for Brown, Gray, OD Green, or Tan frame color.

TX22 – .22 LR cal., SAO, striker fired, black, FDE, or OD Green polymer frame, 4.1 in. threaded barrel, 10 shot mag., Taurus Pittman Trigger System (PTS), fixed white dot front sight and adj. white dot rear sight, ergonomic grip, Mil-Std 1913 accessory rail, hard anodized matte black finish, 17.3 oz. New 2019.

MSR $317	$280	$245	$210	$185	$155	$125	$100	

* ***TX22 Competition*** – similar to the TX22, except has a red dot optics-ready slide and 5 in. threaded Bull barrel assembly, 10 or 16 mag., hard anodized matte black finish, 23.2 oz. New 2021.

MSR $485	$435	$380	$325	$295	$240	$195	$150	

REVOLVERS: RECENT PRODUCTION

From 1990-1992, certain models became available with a Laser Aim LA1 sighting system that included mounts, rings (in matching finish), a 110 volt AC recharging unit, a 9 volt DC field charger, and a high impact custom case.

The following Taurus revolvers have been listed in numerical order. All currently manufactured revolvers listed are rated for +P ammunition.

Tracker model nomenclature refers to a heavy contoured barrel with full shroud, porting, and with or w/o VR.

All currently manufactured Taurus revolvers are equipped with the patented Taurus Security System, introduced in 1998, which utilizes an integral key lock on the back of the hammer, locking the action.

Add approx. $45 for scope base mount on currently produced models that offer this option.
Add $31 for carrying case on Raging Bull & Raging Hornet Models listed (disc. 2006).

GAUCHO SA – .357 Mag. (new 2006), .44-40 WCF (mfg. 2006), or .45 LC cal., SA Western style revolver, large frame, 4 3/4 (new 2006), 5 1/2, 7 1/2 (new 2006), or 12 (mfg. 2006) in. barrel, fixed sights, four click action, choice of all blue, blue/color case hardened, matte stainless, or polished stainless steel, 36.7 oz (5 1/2 in. barrel). Mfg. 2005-2007.

	$425	$360	$315	$280	$240	$210	$185	*$520*

Add $16 for stainless steel or blue/color case hardened finish.
Add $26 for 12 in. barrel (mfg. 2006).

RAGING HUNTER – .357 Mag./.38 Special +P (new 2019), .44 Mag., .454 Casull (new 2019), or .460 S&W Mag. (new 2021) cal., DA/SA, large frame, 5 1/8 (new 2019), 6 3/4 (new 2019), or 8 3/8 in. ported barrel, 5, 6, or 7 shot mag., spurred hammer, fixed front and adj. rear sights, soft rubber grips with cushioned insert, optics ready Picatinny rail, matte black or two-tone finish, 55 oz. New 2018.

MSR $929	$825	$675	$550	$495	$450	$400	$350	

Add $10 for two-tone finish.
Add 5% (MSR $968) for .460 S&W Mag. cal. (new 2021).
Add $30 for Taurus BK case.

GRADING - PPGS™	100%	98%	95%	90%	80%	70%	60%	LAST MSR

MODEL 17C – .17 HMR or .17 Mach 2 (mfg. 2004-2006) cal., small frame, 8 shot, 2, 4, or 5 in. barrel, blue only, adj. sights, full underlug on 4 and 5 in. barrels, soft rubber grips, 24-27 1/2 oz. Mfg. 2003-2007.

$295 $250 $215 $185 $170 $155 $145 *$391*

* ***Model 17C Ultra-Lite*** – ultra light hammer forged frame, 2 in. barrel, available in matte blue (disc. 2004, reintroduced 2006) or bright stainless steel, 18 1/2 oz. Mfg. 2003-2006.

$340 $285 $235 $200 $180 $160 $150 *$453*

Subtract $47 for matte blue finish.

* ***Model 17CSS (Stainless Steel)*** – similar to Model 17C, except is polished (disc.) or matte stainless steel, 5 in. barrel disc. 2006. Mfg. 2003-2007.

$330 $275 $230 $200 $180 $160 $150 *$439*

MODEL 17-IB (INSTANT BACKUP) – .17 HMR or .17 Mach 2 cal., small steel frame, 1 3/4 in. barrel, concealed hammer, blue finish, 8 (.17 HMR) or 9 (.17 Mach 2) shot, checkered rubber grips, adj. rear sight, transfer bar safety, 22.2 oz. Mfg. 2005-2007.

$295 $250 $215 $185 $170 $155 $145 *$391*

* ***Model 17 Instant Backup Stainless*** – .17 HMR or .17 Mach 2 cal., similar to Model 17 Instant Backup, except is matte stainless steel. Mfg. 2005-2007.

$330 $275 $230 $200 $180 $160 $150 *$439*

MODEL 17 TRACKER – .17 HMR cal., compact frame, 7 shot, adj. sights, 4 (mfg. 2012 only), 6 1/2 or 8 3/8 (mfg. 2004 only) in. Tracker VR barrel, matte black (current mfg.), blue (mfg. 2004-2005, 2007-2018), duo-tone (mfg. 2004 only, 6 1/2 in. barrel only) finish or matte stainless steel, Ribber grip, 41 or 45 oz. New 2003.

MSR $541 $460 $400 $350 $315 $255 $205 $160

Add 10% (MSR $595) for matte stainless steel.

Subtract approx. 10% for blue finish (disc. 2007).

MODEL 17-12 SILHOUETTE – .17 HMR cal., compact frame, features 12 in. barrel, adj. sights, includes scope mount. Mfg. 2003-2004.

$320 $275 $230 $200 $180 $160 $150 *$430*

MODEL 21T TRACKER – .218 Bee cal., compact frame, 6 1/2 in. Tracker barrel with VR, 7 shot, matte stainless steel, adj. sights. Mfg. 2003-2004.

$325 $275 $230 $200 $180 $160 $150 *$438*

MODEL 22H SS RAGING HORNET – .22 Hornet cal., large frame, 8 shot, stainless steel construction, 10 in. VR barrel with full shroud, fully adj. sights, scope mount bases included, contoured rubber grips, 50 oz. Mfg. 1999-2004.

$795 $685 $600 $525 $450 $395 $330 *$898*

MODEL 30C SS RAGING THIRTY HUNTER – .30 Carbine cal., large frame, 8 shot, 10 in. heavy VR barrel with full shroud and adj. sights, matte stainless steel, includes scope mounts and full moon clips, 50 oz. Mfg. 2003-2004.

$795 $685 $600 $525 $450 $395 $330 *$898*

MODEL 30S SILHOUETTE/HUNTER – .30 Carbine cal., large frame, 8 shot, 12 in. VR barrel with partial shroud, matte stainless steel, adj. hammer tension, trigger overtravel stop, includes scope mounts, 50 oz. Mfg. 2003-2004.

$625 $560 $490 $430 $380 $325 $275 *$743*

MODEL 44 – .44 Mag. cal., 6 shot, large frame, integral porting compensator, exposed or concealed (3 in. barrel only, mfg. 1997-98) hammer, bright blue finish, adj. sights, rubber grips, 3 (mfg. 1997-98), 4, 6 1/2 (VR), or 8 3/8 (VR) in. ported or non-ported (disc. 2002) barrel, 45-57 oz. Mfg. 1994-2004.

$400 $350 $310 $280 $240 $210 $185 *$500*

Add $23 for 6 1/2 or 8 3/8 in. ported barrel.

Subtract approx. 10% for non-ported barrel.

* ***Model 44SS (Stainless Steel)*** – .44 Mag. cal., DA/SA, large frame, 4, 6 1/2, or 8 3/8 in. ported barrel, 6 shot, adj. sights, Taurus Security System, soft rubber black grips, matte finished stainless steel, 45-57 oz. New 1994.

MSR $661 $525 $440 $385 $330 $285 $240 $200

Add 2.5% (MSR $676) for 8 3/8 in. ported barrel.

Add $46 for 3 in. ported barrel with fixed sights and round butt grips (mfg. 1996-1997).

* ***Model 44 Silhouette*** – similar to Model 44, except has 12 in. VR non-ported barrel, adj. hammer tension and trigger overtravel stop, includes scope base mounts. Mfg. 2003-2004.

$485 $425 $375 $325 $285 $240 $210 *$602*

GRADING - PPGS™	100%	98%	95%	90%	80%	70%	60%	LAST MSR

MODEL 44 TRACKER (44C) - .44 Mag. cal., DA/SA, compact frame, 2 (new 2020, stainless only) or 4 in. ported barrel, 5 shot, adj. rear sight, Ribber grips, blue (disc.), black oxide, or matte stainless steel, 34 oz. New 2005.

MSR $578	$475	$415	$350	$325	$270	$215	$165	

Add 2.5% (MSR $595) for matte stainless steel.

MODEL 45-410 "THE JUDGE" (44-TEN TRACKER) - .45 LC/.410 shotshell cal., 2 1/2 or 3 (new 2008) in. chamber, DA, compact frame, 2 1/2 (disc.), 3 (new 2007), or 6 1/2 in. barrel, 5 shot, fiber optic front sight, Ribber grips, blue (disc.) or matte black oxide (current) finish, 29 or 32 oz. New 2006.

MSR $512	$435	$385	$350	$325	$295	$260	$220	

Add $128 for orange night sights and Hogue grips (new 2020).
Add $39 for 2 1/2 in. cylinder with ported barrel and accessory rail (mfg. 2010-2012).
Add $156 for Crimson Trace Lasergrips (mfg. 2010-2012).

During late 2007, this model's nomenclature changed to the Model 45-410 Judge.

* ***Model 45-410 The Judge Stainless (44-Ten Tracker Stainless)*** - similar to Model 45-410, except is matte stainless steel, 29, 32, or 36.8 (3 in. chamber) oz. New 2006.

MSR $559	$460	$415	$350	$325	$295	$260	$220	

Add $129 for orange night sights and Hogue grips (new 2020).
Add $31 for 2 1/2 in. cylinder with ported barrel and accessory rail (mfg. 2010-2012).
Add $157 for Crimson Trace Lasergrips (mfg. 2010-2012).

* ***Model 45-410 The Judge Ultra-Lite*** - similar to Model 45-410 Judge, 2 1/2 in. barrel, except has alloy frame, choice of blued steel or stainless steel cylinder, not available in 3 in. cylinder, 22.4 oz. Mfg. 2008-2011.

	$575	$510	$455	$395	$350	$295	$245	*$648*

Add $32 for stainless steel barrel and cylinder. Add $313 for Crimson Trace Lasergrips (new 2010).

MODEL 45-410 "THE JUDGE" PUBLIC DEFENDER - .45/.410 shotshell, 2 1/2 in. chamber, DA/SA, 2 1/2 in. barrel, 5 shot, fiber optic front and fixed rear sights, matte black or matte stainless finish, steel or titanium (disc. 2011) cylinder, reduced profile hammer, Ribber grips, 28.2 oz. New mid-2009.

MSR $512	$435	$385	$350	$325	$295	$260	$220	

Add $49 for stainless steel cylinder or $78 for titanium cylinder (disc. 2011).
Add $47 for pink Ribber grips (mfg. 2010-2011) or $82 for pink Ribber grips and Bulldog Case (mfg. 2010-2011).

* ***Model 45-410 "The Judge" Public Defender Ultra-Lite*** - similar to Model 45-410 The Judge Public Defender, except has ultra-lite aluminum frame and choice of blue steel or stainless, 2 1/2 in. cylinder, 20.7 oz. Mfg. 2011 only.

	$575	$510	$455	$395	$350	$295	$245	*$648*

Add $32 for stainless steel barrel and cylinder.

* ***Model 45-410 "The Judge" Public Defender Polymer*** - .45 LC/.410 shotshell, DA/SA, 2 1/2 in. barrel, 5 shot mag., black or FDE (new 2020) lightweight polymer frame, blue (disc. 2011), black oxide, or matte stainless cylinder, spurred hammer, fiber optic front and adj. rear sights, Ribber grips, 27 oz. New 2011.

MSR $456	$415	$365	$335	$315	$280	$260	$220	

Add $16 for matte stainless steel.
Add $29 for FDE lightweight polymer frame (new 2020).
Subtract approx. 10% for blue cylinder (disc. 2011).

* ***Model 45-410FS Polymer*** - .45 LC/.410 shotshell, 2 1/2 in. chamber, 2 in. barrel, polymer frame with blued steel cylinder, 5 shot, fiber optic front sight, transfer bar, Ribber grip, matte black finish, 27 oz. Mfg. 2013-2016.

	$425	$360	$315	$280	$250	$225	$195	*$483*

JUDGE MAGNUM - .45 LC/.410 shotshell, 3 in. chamber, 3 or 6 1/2 (new 2018) in. barrel, 5 shot, fiber optic front sight, Ribber grip, scroll engraving on cylinder/back of frame and checkered black Altamont wood grips w/finger grooves (new 2019), black oxide (new 2019) or matte black finish, 37 oz. New 2016.

MSR $512	$435	$385	$350	$325	$295	$260	$220	

Add $171 for scroll engraving/checkered black Altamont wood grips (new 2019).

* ***Judge Magnum Stainless*** - .45 LC/.410 shotshell, 3 in. chamber, DA/SA, 3 or 6 1/2 in. barrel, 5 shot, matte stainless steel, spurred hammer, fiber optic front and fixed rear sights, Ribber grip, transfer bar safety, 37-48 oz.

MSR $559	$460	$415	$350	$325	$295	$260	$220	

GRADING - PPGS™	100%	98%	95%	90%	80%	70%	60%	LAST MSR

MODEL 45 RAGING BULL – .45 LC cal., 6 shot, 6 1/2 or 8 3/8 in. VR ported barrel, adj. sights, soft rubber grips, 53 or 63 oz. Mfg. 1999-2001.

$475 $415 $370 $325 $285 $240 $210 *$575*

* ***Model 45 .45 LC Raging Bull Stainless*** – similar to Model 45 Raging Bull, except is stainless steel. Disc. 2001.

$530 $480 $425 $375 $325 $280 $230 *$630*

MODEL 65 – .357 Mag./.38 Spl. +P cal., medium frame, DA, 6 shot, 2 1/2 (mfg. 1993-97), 3 (disc. 1992) or 4 in. full underlug barrel, fixed sights, checkered walnut (disc.), Hogue (new 2020, in black rubber, Pau Ferro, or Lamo Camo), or soft rubber (new 1999) grips, blue finish (disc.) or matte black finish, 38 oz. Disc. 1997, reintroduced 1999.

MSR $487 $410 $360 $310 $280 $225 $185 $150

Add $34 for Pau Ferro or Lamo Camo Hogue grips (both new 2020).
Add $58 for soft rubber grips.

* ***Model 65SS (Stainless Steel)*** – .357 Mag./.38 Spl. +P cal., similar to Model 65, except is matte finished stainless steel, soft rubber or Hogue (new 2020, Pau Ferro or Lamo Camo) grips. Mfg. 1993-97, reintroduced 1999.

MSR $503 $425 $375 $325 $290 $235 $190 $150

Add $34 for Hogue Pau Ferro or Lamo Camo grips (new 2020).
Add $94 for soft rubber grips.

MODEL 66 – .357 Mag./.38 Spl. +P cal., medium frame, DA, 6 (disc. 2001) or 7 (new 1999) shot, 2 1/2 (mfg. 1993-97), 3 (disc. 1992), 4 (disc., reintroduced 2018) or 6 in. barrel, checkered walnut (disc. 1999), rubber (mfg. 2000-2019), Hogue rubber (new 2020), Hogue wooden Pau Ferro (mfg. 2020 only), or Hogue wooden Lamo Camo (mfg. 2020 only) grips, black oxide or matte black oxide finish, ramped front and adj. rear sights, 38-40 oz. Disc. 1997, reintroduced 1999.

MSR $502 $450 $395 $340 $305 $250 $205 $160

Subtract 5% (Last MSR was $518) for Hogue wood Pau Ferro or Hogue Lamo Camo grips (new 2020).
Add $15 for satin nickel finish (disc.).
Add $10 for 4 or 6 in. compensated (66CP) barrel (mfg. 1993-94).

* ***Model 66SS (Stainless Steel)*** – .357 Mag./.38 Spl. +P cal., similar to Model 66, but in stainless steel. Mfg. 1987-97, reintroduced 1999.

MSR $518 $470 $410 $355 $320 $260 $210 $165

Subtract 5% (Last MSR was $537) for Hogue Pau Ferro or Hogue Lamo Camo grips (mfg. 2020 only).
Add $10 for 4 or 6 in. compensated (66CP) barrel (mfg. 1993-94).

* ***Model 66 Silhouette/Hunter*** – .357 Mag./.38 Spl. cal., 7 shot, 12 in. barrel with adj. sights, rubber grips, adj. hammer tension and trigger overtravel stop became standard 2003, includes scope mount. Mfg. 2001-2004.

$375 $310 $265 $220 $200 $180 $165 *$430*

* ***Model 66 Silhouette/Hunter SS (Stainless Steel)*** – similar to Model 66 Silhouette/Hunter, except is matte finished stainless steel. Mfg. 2001-2004.

$415 $350 $310 $280 $240 $210 $185 *$477*

MODEL 73 – .32 Long cal. only, DA, 6 shot, 3 in. heavy barrel only, checkered walnut grips, 20 oz. Disc. 1992.

$215 $185 $165 $145 $130 $120 $115 *$223*

Add $20 for satin nickel finish.

MODEL 76 – .32 H&R Mag. cal., DA, 6 shot, 6 in. heavy barrel with solid rib, fully adj. rear sight, transfer bar safety, checkered hardwood grips, blue only, 34 oz. Mfg. 1991-94.

$260 $225 $190 $165 $150 $135 $125 *$308*

MODEL 80 – .38 Spl. cal. only, DA, 6 shot, 3 or 4 in. barrel, checkered walnut grips, fixed sights, 30 oz. Disc. 1996.

$225 $195 $170 $155 $140 $125 $120 *$252*

Add $15 for satin nickel finish (disc. 1992).

* ***Model 80SS (Stainless Steel)*** – similar to Model 80, except stainless steel. Mfg. 1993-97.

$275 $230 $200 $175 $160 $145 $135 *$313*

MODEL 82 (SECURITY) – .38 Spl. +P cal., medium frame, DA, 6 shot, 3 (disc. 1998) or 4 in. heavy barrel, checkered walnut (disc.) or rubber (new 1999) grips, full underlug, fixed sights, satin nickel (disc.) or blue finish, 36.5 oz.

MSR $431 $370 $325 $280 $250 $205 $165 $130

Add $15 for satin nickel finish (disc.).

GRADING - PPGS™	100%	98%	95%	90%	80%	70%	60%	LAST MSR

* ***Model 82SS (Stainless Steel) Security*** – similar to Model 82, except is polished stainless steel. Mfg. 1993-2013.

$400 $350 $310 $280 $240 $210 $185 ***$514***

MODEL 83 – .38 Spl. cal. only, DA, 6 shot, 4 in. heavy barrel, checkered walnut grips, adj. sights, 34 1/2 oz. Disc. 1998.

$250 $215 $185 $165 $150 $135 $125 ***$278***

Add $13 for satin nickel finish.

* ***Model 83SS (Stainless Steel)*** – similar to Model 83, except stainless steel. Mfg. 1993-98.

$285 $250 $215 $185 $170 $155 $145 ***$324***

MODEL 85 – .38 Spl. +P cal. only, small frame, DA, 5 shot, 2 or 3 (disc. 2001, reintroduced 2006) in. heavy ported (new 1997) or unported barrel, hammer forged frame, bobbed (mfg. 2011 only) or exposed hammer, checkered walnut (disc. 2000) or soft rubber boot grips, fixed sights, 21-24 1/2 oz. Disc. 2012.

$345 $285 $235 $200 $180 $160 $150 ***$445***

Add $53 for pink pearl grips (disc. 2011).
Add $16 for bobbed hammer (mfg. 2011 only) or ported barrel (disc. 2003).
Add $20 for satin nickel finish (3 in. barrel only, disc. 1992).
Subtract $15 for Hy-Lite magnesium grey finish (disc.).

* ***Model 85SS (Stainless Steel)*** – stainless version of Model 85. Disc. 2012.

$385 $335 $295 $260 $220 $195 $175 ***$492***

Add $53 for pink pearl grips (disc. 2011).
Add $47 for gold accents and rosewood grips (disc. 2011).
Add $16 for ported barrel (mfg. 1997-2003).

* ***Model 85CH (Blue or Stainless)*** – similar to Model 85, DAO, except has 2 in. barrel, Brazilian hardwood combat (disc. 2000) or soft rubber grips and spurless concealed hammer that fits flush with the frame, 21 oz. Mfg. 1992-2004.

$285 $250 $215 $185 $170 $155 $145 ***$375***

Add $16 for ported barrel (disc. 2003).
Add $47 for polished stainless steel.

* ***Model 85 Titanium Ultra-Lightweight*** – features titanium barrel and cylinder and choice of matte aluminum or stainless steel (disc. 2001) small frame, fixed sight, rubber grips, choice of hammer or concealed hammer (Police Model 85), 17 oz. Mfg. 1999-2010.

$535 $490 $430 $375 $325 $280 $230 ***$648***

Add $94 for Crimson Trace Lasergrips (disc. 2008).

* ***Model 85PLYB2/Protector Ply*** – .38 Spl. +P cal., small frame, 1 1/4 or 1 3/4 in. barrel with VR in high vis. fiber optic front sight, 5 shot, features lightweight polymer frame and checkered wood colored polymer grips, blued or stainless cylinder assembly, ambidextrous thumb rest, 16.5 oz. Mfg. 2011-2012.

$355 $300 $260 $220 $200 $180 $165 ***$461***

* ***Model 85T*** – similar to Model 85, except 100% titanium construction, 2 in. ported barrel only, choice of bright spectrum blue, matte spectrum blue, matte spectrum gold, stealth grey (mfg. 2000 only), or shadow grey (new 2000) finish, 15.4 oz. Mfg. 1999-2006.

$530 $480 $425 $375 $325 $280 $230 ***$625***

Add $39 for blue and gold titanium finish and mother-of-pearl grips (disc. 2004, reintroduced 2006).

* ***Model 85 Special Edition/Deluxe*** – features blue finish with gold trim or stainless/gold trim, ported 2 in. barrel, rosewood or mother-of-pearl grips, includes integral key lock. Mfg. 1998-2011.

$380 $335 $295 $260 $220 $195 $175 ***$492***

Add $47 for stainless/gold trim with rosewood grips.
Add $16 for blue/gold trim with faux mother-of-pearl grips.
Add $57 for stainless/gold trim with faux mother-of-pearl grips.

* ***Model 85 Ultra-Lite*** – ultra-lightweight version of Model 85 using an alloy frame, choice of blue or gray finish, 17 oz. Disc. 2012.

$335 $275 $230 $200 $180 $160 $150 ***$430***

Add $53 for pink pearl grips (disc. 2011).
Add $177 for LG185 (new 2012) or $312 (disc. 2011) for Crimson Trace Lasergrips (new 2009).

» ***Model 85SSUL Ultra-Lite Stainless*** – matte stainless variation of the Model 85 Ultra-Lite, 17 oz. Disc. 2012.

$360 $300 $260 $220 $200 $180 $165 ***$461***

Add $125 for LG-185 (new 2012) or $312 (disc. 2011) for Crimson Trace grips.
Add $53 for pink pearl grips (mfg. 2010-2011).

GRADING - PPGS™	100%	98%	95%	90%	80%	70%	60%	LAST MSR

» **Model 85 Ultra-Lite Deluxe** – ported barrel, choice of blue/gold or stainless/gold, mother-of-pearl (new 2000) or rosewood grips, 17 oz. Mfg. 1999-2011.

$400 $350 $310 $280 $240 $210 $185 *$530*

Add $9 for matte stainless/gold and rosewood grips.

Add $31 for matte stainless/gold finish with faux mother-of-pearl grips.

MODEL 85FS SERIES – .38 Spl. +P cal., DA, 2 in. barrel, 6 shot, spurred hammer, fixed sights, textured rubber grips with finger grooves, transfer bar safety, matte black finish, 21 oz. New 2013.

$300 $260 $230 $200 $180 $160 $140

* ***Model 85FS Stainless*** – .38 Spl. +P cal., DA, 2 in. barrel, 5 shot, stainless steel, spurred hammer, fixed sights, textured rubber grips with finger grooves, transfer bar safety, matte stainless finish, 21 oz. Mfg. 2013-2018.

$310 $275 $250 $215 $190 $170 $150 *$389*

* ***Model 85FS Polymer*** – .38 Spl. +P cal., DA, black polymer frame and steel cylinder, 2 1/2 in. barrel, 5 shot, spurred hammer, fiber optic front and fixed rear sights, textured rubber grips with finger grooves, transfer bar safety, matte black finish, 18 oz. Mfg. 2013-2018.

$300 $260 $230 $200 $180 $160 $140 *$379*

» **Model 85FS Polymer Stainless** – .38 Spl. +P cal., similar to Model 85FS Polymer, except features polymer frame and stainless steel cylinder, 16 1/2 oz. Mfg. 2013-2018.

$310 $275 $250 $215 $190 $170 $150 *$389*

* ***Model 85FS Ultra-Lite*** – .38 Spl. +P cal., DA, black anodized ultra-lite aluminum frame, 2 in. barrel, 5 shot, spurred hammer, fixed sights, textured rubber grips with finger grooves, matte black finish, 17 oz. Mfg. 2013-2018.

$310 $275 $250 $215 $190 $170 $150 *$389*

» **Model 85FS Stainless Ultra-Lite** – .38 Spl. +P cal., similar to Model 85FS Ultra-Lite, except features aluminum frame and stainless steel cylinder, 17 oz. Mfg. 2013-2018.

$325 $280 $250 $215 $195 $175 $155 *$409*

MODEL 85 VIEW – .38 Spl. +P cal., DAO trigger, 1 in. barrel, ultra-lite aluminum alloy frame, titanium cylinder and barrel, 5 shot, fixed front sight, clear-view Lexan sideplate, contoured grip, pink or matte stainless finish, Taurus Security System, 9 oz. Mfg. 2014-2015.

$385 $350 $315 $280 $250 $220 $190 *$453*

MODEL 85 W/CONVERTIBLE HAMMER – .38 Spl. +P cal., DA, 2 in. barrel, 6 shot, fixed sights, choice of stainless steel or aluminum alloy (Ultra-Lite) frame, convertible hammer allows it to be easily removed for concealment purposes, textured black synthetic grips, blue or matte stainless finish, 17-21 oz. Mfg. 2015 only.

$295 $260 $235 $210 $190 $170 $150 *$371*

Add $15 for stainless steel finish.

Add $15 for Ultra-Lite frame or $31 for Ultra-Lite frame and stainless steel finish.

MODEL 86 CUSTOM TARGET – .38 Spl. cal. only, DA target model, 6 shot, 6 in. barrel, specially contoured smooth walnut grips, adj. rear sight, blue only, 34 oz. Disc. 1994.

$270 $230 $200 $175 $160 $145 $135 *$352*

This model was available in either single or double action with adj. counterweight and interchangeable front sight inserts.

MODEL 94 – .22 LR cal., small frame, DA, 9 shot, 2 (new 1997), 3 (mfg. 1991-98), 4 or 5 (new 1996) in. barrel, full underlug on 4 or 5 in. barrel, blue finish, adj. rear sight, target features, 25 oz. Mfg. 1989-2013.

$340 $285 $235 $200 $180 $160 $150 *$438*

* ***Model 94 Ultra-Lite*** – .22 LR cal., ultra light hammer forged frame, 2 in. barrel, available in matte blue or bright stainless steel, 18 oz. Mfg. 1999-2013.

$370 $310 $265 $220 $200 $180 $165 *$481*

Add $32 for matte stainless steel construction.

* ***Model 94SS (Stainless Steel)*** – .22 LR cal., stainless version of Model 94. Mfg. 1990-2013.

$375 $310 $265 $220 $200 $180 $165 *$486*

MODEL 96 TARGET SCOUT – .22 LR cal. only, DA, 6 shot, 6 in. barrel, checkered walnut grips, same features as Model 86, 34 oz. Disc. 1998.

$275 $230 $200 $175 $160 $145 $135 *$376*

GRADING - PPGS™ 100% 98% 95% 90% 80% 70% 60% *LAST MSR*

MODEL 218 RAGING BEE – .218 Bee cal., large frame, 8 shot, 10 in. heavy VR barrel with full shroud and adj. sights, matte stainless steel, includes scope mounts, 50 oz. Mfg. 2003-2004.

$795 $685 $600 $525 $450 $395 $330 *$898*

MODEL 218 SILHOUETTE/HUNTER – .218 Bee cal., DA, large frame, 7 shot, 12 in. VR barrel with partial shroud, matte stainless steel, rubber boot grips, adj. hammer tension and trigger overtravel stop, includes scope mounts, 49.8 oz. Mfg. 2003-2004.

$400 $350 $310 $280 $240 $210 $185 *$461*

MODEL 327 – .327 Federal cal., small frame, 2 in. barrel, blue or matte stainless, with or w/o concealed hammer, 6 shot, fixed sights, rubber grips. Mfg. mid-2009-2010.

$360 $300 $260 $220 $200 $180 $165 *$467*

Add $47 for stainless steel. Add $10 for blue frame with concealed hammer. Add $63 for stainless steel frame with concealed hammer.

MODEL 380 (IB) – .380 ACP cal., DAO, 5 shot, 1 3/4 in. barrel, adj. rear sight, fixed front sight, textured rubber grips, marked "Taurus Ultra-Lite" on left side of frame, bobbed hammer, matte black finish, uses Taurus Stellar Clip, 15 1/2 oz. New 2012.

MSR $488 $370 $325 $270 $225 $200 $180 $165

* ***Model 380 (IB) Stainless*** – .380 ACP cal., similar to Model 308, except is matte stainless steel. New 2012.

MSR $524 $415 $335 $285 $230 $200 $180 $165

MODEL 405 – .40 S&W cal., DA, medium frame, 5 shot mag., fixed sights, blue finish, Ribber grips, 29 oz. Mfg. 2011-2012.

$365 $310 $265 $220 $200 $180 $165 *$477*

* ***Model 405SS (Stainless Steel)*** – .40 S&W cal., similar to Model 405, except has stainless steel finish. Mfg. 2011-2012.

$400 $350 $310 $280 $240 $210 $185 *$523*

MODEL 415SS – .41 Mag. cal., compact frame, 5 shot, similar to Model 415T, except has matte stainless steel construction, Ribber grips, 30 oz. Mfg. 1999-disc.

$435 $385 $340 $295 $260 $225 $195 *$508*

MODEL 415T – .41 Mag. cal., compact frame, 5 shot, all titanium construction, 2 1/2 in. ported barrel with fixed sights, choice of bright spectrum blue (disc. 2001), matte spectrum blue (disc. 2001), matte gold (mfg. 1999 only), stealth grey (mfg. 2000 only), or shadow grey (new 2000) finish, Ribber grips. Mfg. 1999-2003.

$500 $450 $395 $350 $295 $260 $220 *$602*

MODEL 415SS TRACKER – .41 Mag. cal., medium frame, 5 shot, 2 1/2 in. barrel, stainless steel, fixed sights, Ribber grips, 30 oz. Mfg. 2006-2011.

$500 $450 $395 $350 $295 $260 $220 *$623*

MODEL 416 SS RAGING BULL – .41 Mag. cal., large frame, 6 shot, 6 1/2 or 8 3/8 in. ported heavy barrel with VR, adj. sights, matte stainless steel, rubber grips with cushion inserts, 53 or 63 oz. Mfg. 2003-2011.

$650 $575 $500 $450 $395 $335 $285 *$780*

MODEL 425 SS TRACKER – .41 Mag. cal., medium frame, 5 shot, similar to Model 415T, 4 in. ported barrel with full shroud, adj. sights with red inserts, Ribber grips, stainless steel with matte finish, 34.8 oz. Mfg. 2000-2012.

$515 $460 $400 $350 $295 $260 $220 *$655*

MODEL 425T TRACKER – similar to Model 425 Tracker, except is all titanium construction, choice of stealth grey (mfg. 2000 only) or matte shadow grey finish, 4 or 6 in. barrel, adj. sights, 24.3 oz. Mfg. 2000-2006.

$625 $560 $490 $430 $380 $325 $275 *$766*

MODEL 431 – .44 Spl. cal., 5 shot, 2 (new 1995), 3, or 4 in. barrel, blue only, fixed sights. Mfg. 1993-97.

$265 $230 $200 $175 $160 $145 $135 *$286*

* ***Model 431SS (Stainless Steel)*** – similar to Model 431, except stainless steel. Mfg. 1993-97.

$315 $260 $220 $185 $170 $155 $145 *$368*

MODEL 441 – similar to Model 431, except has 3, 4, or 6 in. barrel, adj. sights. Mfg. 1993-97.

$275 $230 $200 $175 $160 $145 $135 *$313*

* ***Model 441SS (Stainless Steel)*** – similar to Model 441, except is stainless steel. Mfg. 1993-97.

$375 $310 $265 $220 $200 $180 $165 *$468*

GRADING - PPGS™	100%	98%	95%	90%	80%	70%	60%	LAST MSR

MODEL 444 RAGING BULL – .44 Mag. cal., large frame, 6 shot, 6 1/2 or 8 3/8 in. VR ported barrel with full shroud and adj. sights, soft rubber grips with cushion inserts, matte black finish, 53 or 63 oz. Mfg. 1999-2016.

	$625	$560	$490	$430	$380	$325	$275	*$753*

* ***Model 444 Raging Bull Stainless*** – .44 Mag. cal., large frame, 6 1/2 or 8 3/8 in. VR ported barrel with full shroud, 6 shot, adj. sights, soft rubber grips with cushion inserts, matte stainless steel. Mfg. 1999-2019.

	$735	$625	$540	$475	$400	$335	$285	*$900*

* ***Model 444 Multi Raging Bull Ultra-Lite*** – .44 Mag. cal., 6 shot, 2 1/2 or 4 in. barrel, blue alloy (disc.) or matte stainless steel Raging Bull style frame with titanium cylinder, rubber grips with finger grooves and insert cushion, fiber optic front sight, 28.3 oz. New 2005.

MSR $945	$795	$675	$585	$535	$425	$350	$285	

Subtract approx. $100 for blue alloy frame (disc.).
Add $15 for 4 in. barrel with adj. rear sight (disc. 2011).

MODEL 445 – .44 Spl. cal., compact frame, 5 shot, 2 in. ported (new 1999) or standard barrel, fixed sights, blue or stainless, Ribber or rubber grips, 28 oz. Mfg. 1997-2003.

	$295	$250	$215	$185	$170	$155	$145	*$359*

Add $16 for ported barrel (new 1999).

* ***Model 445 Concealed Hammer*** – similar to Model 445, except w/o hammer, ported or unported barrel. Mfg. 1999-2003.

	$295	$250	$215	$185	$170	$155	$145	*$359*

Add $16 for ported barrel.

* ***Model 445 Concealed Hammer Stainless*** – similar to Model 445 Concealed Hammer, except is stainless steel. Mfg. 1999-2003.

	$310	$260	$220	$185	$170	$155	$145	*$406*

Add $16 for ported barrel.

* ***Model 445 SS (Stainless Steel)*** – stainless variation of the Model 445. Mfg. 1997-2003.

	$310	$260	$220	$185	$170	$155	$145	*$406*

Add $16 for ported barrel.

* ***Model 445 Ultra-Lite*** – .44 Spl. cal., features ported (disc. 2002) or unported (new 2012) 2 in. barrel, blue or matte stainless steel, 22 oz., Ribber grips on new mfg. Mfg. 1999-2002, reintroduced 2012 only.

	$395	$345	$300	$260	$220	$195	$175	*$508*

Add $31 for matte stainless steel.

* ***Model 445 Ultra-lite Concealed Carry*** – features stainless steel or titanium frame, ported 2 in. barrel, walnut combat grips. Mfg. 2002 only.

	$370	$310	$265	$220	$200	$180	$165	*$500*

Add $100 for titanium construction.

MODEL 445T – .44 Spl. cal., 5 shot, all titanium construction, 2 in. ported barrel with fixed sights, choice of bright spectrum blue, matte spectrum blue, matte gold (mfg. 1999 only), stealth grey (new 2000), or shadow grey (new 2000) finish, Ribber grips. Mfg. 1999-2002.

	$500	$450	$395	$350	$295	$260	$220	*$600*

MODEL 450 – .45 LC cal., 5 shot, compact frame, similar to Model 450T, except is matte stainless steel, also available in Ultra-Lite variation, Ribber grips, 20 (Ultra Lite) or 28 oz. Mfg. 1999-2005.

	$425	$360	$315	$280	$240	$210	$185	*$492*

Add $31 for Ultra-Lite Model.

MODEL 450T – .45 LC cal., 5 shot, all titanium construction, 2 in. ported barrel with fixed sights, choice of bright spectrum blue, matte spectrum blue, matte gold (mfg. 1999 only), stealth grey (new 2000), or shadow grey (new 2000) finish, Ribber grips. Mfg. 1999-2002.

	$500	$450	$395	$350	$295	$260	$220	*$600*

MODEL 454 RAGING BULL – .454 Casull cal., large frame, DA, 2 1/4 (mfg. 2005-2006), 5 (case colored, disc. 2000), 6 1/2 or 8 3/8 in. full lug ported barrel with integral VR, 5 shot, front and rear cylinder locks, bright blue or case colored (new 1999) finish, soft black rubber grips with recoil absorbing insert, micrometer adj. rear sight, transfer bar safety, integral key lock, 53-63 oz. Mfg. 1998-2012.

	$850	$750	$650	$550	$475	$420	$350	*$1,016*

Add $96 for case colored frame (disc. 2000).
Subtract $53 for 2 1/4 in. ported barrel (disc.).

GRADING - PPGS™	100%	98%	95%	90%	80%	70%	60%	LAST MSR

* ***Model 454 Casull Raging Bull Stainless*** – .454 Casull cal., similar to Model 454 Casull Raging Bull, except is stainless steel, 2 1/2 (new 2007), 5, 6 1/2, or 8 3/8 in. VR barrel, fiber optic front (2 1/2 in. barrel only) and adj. rear sights, Taurus Security System, satin (6 1/2 in. barrel only, disc. 2000) or matte (new 1999) stainless finish. New 1998.

MSR $1,187	$985	$825	$700	$585	$490	$430	$360	

Add 2.5% (MSR $1,204) for 5, 6 1/2, or 8 3/8 in. barrel.
Add 2.5% (MSR $1,204) for stainless finish.

* ***Model 454 Casull Raging Bull Silhouette*** – similar to Model 454 Casull Raging Bull Stainless, except has 12 in. non-ported barrel with adj. sights, adj. hammer tension and trigger overtravel stop. Mfg. 2003-2004.

	$725	$635	$545	$475	$425	$365	$315	*$859*

MODEL 455 TRACKER – .45 ACP cal., compact frame, 5 shot, 2, 4 or 6 in. ported barrel, adj. rear sight, matte stainless steel, includes 5 Stellar full moon clips, Ribber grips. Mfg. 2002-2004.

	$450	$395	$345	$295	$260	$225	$195	*$523*

* ***Model 455 Tracker Titanium*** – similar to Model 455 Tracker, except has titanium construction with shadow gray finish. Mfg. 2004 only.

	$525	$480	$425	$375	$325	$280	$230	*$625*

MODEL 460 TRACKER – .45 LC cal., compact frame, 5 shot, 4 or 6 1/2 in. VR ported barrel, adj. sights, matte stainless steel. Mfg. 2003-2004.

	$445	$385	$340	$295	$260	$225	$195	*$516*

* ***Model 460T Tracker*** – similar to Model 460 Tracker, except has titanium construction, 4 VR or non-VR 6 1/2 in. barrel. Mfg. 2003-2004.

	$565	$510	$455	$395	$350	$295	$245	*$688*

MODEL 465 RAGING BULL – .460 S&W Mag. cal., large frame, 2 1/2, 4, 6 1/2, or 10 in. ported barrel, matte stainless steel construction, fixed or adj. sights, soft rubber grips. Mfg. 2006.

	$750	$650	$575	$495	$440	$375	$325	*$880*

MODEL 480 RUGER RAGING BULL – .480 Ruger cal., large frame, 5 shot, 5 (limited mfg.), 6 1/2, or 8 3/8 in. VR barrel, matte stainless finish only, otherwise similar to Model 454 Casull, 51-63 oz. Mfg. 2001-2005.

	$525	$480	$425	$375	$325	$280	$230	*$641*

MODEL 500 – .500 S&W Mag. cal., 5 shot, 2 1/2 (fixed sights only, new 2006), 4 (new 2006), 6 1/2 (new 2006), or 10 in. ported barrel, adj. rear sight, soft rubber cushioned grips, stainless steel only, 68-72 oz. Mfg. mid-2005-2007.

	$775	$675	$595	$525	$450	$395	$330	*$934*

Subtract $17 for 2 1/2 in. barrel.

MODEL 513 RAGING JUDGE MAGNUM – interchangeably shoots .454 Casull, .45 LC, or .410 ga., DA, large frame, 6 shot, 3 (non-ported) or 6 1/2 (VR) in. barrel with Hi-Viz fiber optic front sight, 3 in. non-fluted cylinder, rubber grips with cushion inserts and red "Raging Bull" backstrap, blue finish, 60.6 or 72.7 oz. Mfg. 2011-2013.

	$850	$750	$650	$550	$475	$420	$350	*$1,012*

* ***Model 513 Raging Judge Magnum SS*** – .45 LC, .454 Casull, or .410 ga., DA/SA, large frame, 3 or 6 1/2 in. barrel, 6 shot, stainless steel, spurred hammer, fiber optic front and fixed rear sights, rubber grips with cushioned inserts, transfer bar safety, matte stainless finish, 61-73 oz.

MSR $1,168	$975	$825	$700	$575	$485	$430	$360	

MODEL 513 RAGING JUDGE MAGNUM ULTRA-LITE – .45 LC cal./.410 bore with 3 in. cylinder, SA/DA, 7 shot, 3 or 6 1/2 in. barrel with high vis. fiber optic front sights, features Ultra-Lite frame, blue finish, rubber grips with cushion inserts, 41.4 or 47.2 oz. Mfg. 2011-2012.

	$825	$735	$630	$540	$465	$410	$340	*$983*

* ***Model 513 Raging Judge Magnum Ultra-Lite SS*** – similar to Model 513 Raging Judge Magnum Ultra-Lite, except is matte stainless steel. Mfg. 2011-2012.

	$885	$775	$675	$565	$485	$430	$360	*$1,030*

MODEL 528 RAGING JUDGE – 28 ga., large frame, 5 shot, DA, 6 1/2 in. VR rifled barrel with high vis. fiber optic front sight, unfluted cylinder, blue or matte stainless finish, black rubber grips with cushion inserts and red "Raging Bull" backstrap, 67 oz. While advertised during 2011, this model never went into production.

MODEL 590 TRACKER – 5mm Rem. Rimfire Mag. cal., medium frame, DA, 6 1/2 in. barrel, blue finish, 9 shot, adj. sights, Ribber grips, 43.7 oz. Mfg. late 2008-2011.

	$360	$300	$260	$220	$200	$180	$165	*$467*

GRADING - PPGS™	100%	98%	95%	90%	80%	70%	60%	LAST MSR

* ***Model 590 Tracker SS*** – similar to Model 590 Tracker, except is matte stainless steel. Mfg. late 2008-2011.

	$400	$350	$310	$280	$240	$210	$185	*$514*

MODEL 605 – .357 Mag. cal., small frame, 5 shot, 2 in. unported (new 2002), 2 1/4 (disc. 2005), or 3 (mfg. 1996-98, reintroduced 2006-disc.) in. barrel, blue (disc.) or matte black finish, 4 port compensated barrel (2 1/4 in. only) with fixed sights, exposed or concealed (Model 605CH, mfg. 1997-2005, 2 1/4 in. barrel) hammer, full barrel shroud, oversized finger grooved rubber grips, 24 1/2 oz. New 1995.

MSR $353	$315	$275	$235	$200	$180	$160	$140	

Add $16 for ported barrel (disc. 2003).
Add $303 for Crimson Trace Lasergrips (disc. 2011).

* ***Model 605 SS (Stainless Steel)*** – .357 Mag. cal., stainless variation of the Model 605.

MSR $369	$320	$280	$245	$210	$190	$170	$150	

Add $16 for ported barrel (disc. 2003).
Add $303 for Crimson Trace Lasergrips (mfg. 2008-2011).

* ***Model 605T Titanium*** – similar to Model 605, except is titanium with shadow grey finish. Mfg. 2005-2006.

	$535	$490	$430	$375	$325	$280	$230	*$625*

* ***Model 605 Protector (605PLYB2/Protector Ply)*** – .357 Mag. cal., lightweight black polymer frame, blued or stainless cylinder assembly, 1 (disc.) or 2 in. barrel with VR, 5 shot, spurred hammer, fiber optic front and fixed rear sights, Ribber grips, ambidextrous thumb rest, matte black or matte stainless finish, 19 3/4 oz. New 2011.

MSR $361	$315	$275	$235	$200	$180	$160	$140	

Add 5% (MSR $377) for black/stainless steel cylinder (new 2012).

MODEL 606 – .357 Mag. cal., 6 shot, 2 or 2 1/4 in. uncompensated or compensated barrel, exposed or concealed hammer, fixed sights. Mfg. 1997-98.

	$285	$250	$215	$185	$170	$155	$145	*$296*

Add $19 for ported barrel (2 in. only).

* ***Model 606 SS (Stainless Steel)*** – stainless variation of the Model 606. Disc. 1998.

	$315	$260	$220	$185	$170	$155	$145	*$344*

Add $20 for ported barrel (2 in. only).

MODEL 607 – .357 Mag. cal., 7 shot, 4 or 6 1/2 (VR) in. compensated barrel, adj. rear sight, Santoprene synthetic grips, 44 oz. Mfg. 1995-97.

	$335	$285	$235	$200	$180	$160	$150	*$447*

Add $18 for 6 1/2 in. VR barrel.

* ***Model 607SS (Stainless Steel)*** – stainless variation of the Model 607. Mfg. 1995-97.

	$375	$310	$265	$220	$200	$180	$165	*$508*

Add $20 for 6 1/2 in. VR barrel.

MODEL 608 – .357 Mag. cal., large frame, 8 shot, 3 (mfg. 1997-98), 4, 6 1/2 (VR), or 8 3/8 (VR, new 1997) in. barrel with integral compensator, rubber finger grooves, exposed or concealed (mfg. 1997-2010, 3 in. barrel) hammer, adj. sights, 44-56 oz. Mfg. 1996-2004.

	$355	$300	$260	$220	$200	$180	$165	*$469*

Add $15 for 6.5 or 8 3/8 in. VR ported barrel.

* ***Model 608SS (Stainless Steel)*** – .357 Mag. cal., DA/SA, large frame, 3 (mfg. 1997-98), 4, 6 1/2, or 8 3/8 (disc. 2012) in. VR ported barrel, 8 shot, stainless steel, exposed or concealed hammer, adj. sights, soft rubber grips, matte stainless finish, 51 or 56 oz. New 1996.

MSR $775	$630	$540	$450	$385	$335	$280	$230	

MODEL 617 – .357 Mag. cal., medium frame, DA, 7 shot, 2 in. regular or ported (disc.) barrel, fixed sights, exposed or concealed (Model 617CH, disc. 2005) hammer, rubber (disc. 2006) or Ribber (new 2007) grips, 28.3 oz. Mfg. 1998-2012.

	$415	$350	$310	$280	$240	$210	$185	*$508*

Add $15 for ported barrel (disc. 2003).

* ***Model 617SS (Stainless Steel)*** – .357 Mag. cal., similar to Model 617, except is polished (disc. 2007) or matte stainless steel, 28.3 oz. New 1998.

MSR $618	$500	$430	$360	$310	$260	$225	$195	

Add $15 for ported barrel (disc. 2003).

GRADING - PPGS™	100%	98%	95%	90%	80%	70%	60%	LAST MSR

* ***Model 617 ULT*** – similar to Model 617, except is 5 shot, aluminum alloy receiver and titanium cylinder, matte stainless finish, 2 in. regular or ported barrel, soft rubber grips. Mfg. 2001-2002.

	$455	$395	$345	$295	$260	$225	$195	*$530*

Add $15 for ported barrel.

* ***Model 617T*** – .357 Mag. cal., compact frame, 7 shot, all titanium construction, 2 in. ported barrel with fixed sights, choice of bright spectrum blue, matte spectrum blue (disc. 2001), matte gold (mfg. 1999 only), stealth grey (mfg. 2000 only), or shadow grey (new 2000) finish, Ribber grips, 19.9 oz. Mfg. 1999-2006.

	$550	$495	$450	$395	$350	$295	$245	*$680*

MODEL 627 SS TRACKER – .357 Mag. cal., medium frame, 7 shot, 4 or 6 1/2 (new 2001, VR) in. ported barrel, adj. sights, heavy full underlug, matte stainless steel finish, Ribber grips, 28.8 or 40 oz. New 2000.

MSR $535	$480	$420	$365	$325	$295	$260	$220	

* ***Model 627T Tracker*** – .357 Mag. cal., 7 shot, all titanium construction, 4 or 6 1/2 (new 2001, non-VR) in. ported barrel, adj. sights, choice of stealth grey (disc. 2001) or shadow grey finish, Ribber grips, 24.3 or 28 oz. Mfg. 2000-2006.

	$610	$550	$485	$430	$380	$325	$275	*$766*

MODEL 650 CIA – .38 Spl. +P (new 2013) or .357 Mag. cal., DAO, small frame, 2 in. barrel, 5 shot, hammerless, fixed sights, soft rubber boot grips, matte black finish, 24.2 oz. Mfg. 2001-2017.

	$415	$360	$310	$265	$220	$195	$175	*$539*

* ***Model 650 CIA SS (Stainless Steel)*** – similar to Model 650 CIA, except is matte stainless steel. Mfg. 2001-2012.

	$415	$360	$315	$280	$240	$210	$185	*$555*

MODEL 651 PROTECTOR (CIA) – .357 Mag. cal., small frame, 5 shot, 2 in. barrel, DA, shrouded zero profile hammer, soft rubber boot grips, 25 oz. Mfg. 2003-2012.

	$365	$310	$265	$220	$200	$180	$165	*$477*

* ***Model 651T Protector*** – similar to Model 651 CIA Protector, except is shadow grey titanium construction, 17.3 oz. Mfg. 2004-2006.

	$510	$460	$400	$350	$295	$260	$220	*$625*

* ***Model 651 Protector SS (CIA)*** – similar to Model 651 Protector, except has matte stainless steel. Mfg. 2003-2012.

	$400	$350	$310	$280	$240	$210	$185	*$523*

MODEL 669 – similar to Model 66 except has fully shrouded 4 or 6 in. barrel, blue finish, 37 oz. Disc. 1998.

	$285	$250	$215	$185	$170	$155	$145	*$344*

Add $10 for VR barrel (mfg. 1989-1992).
Add $400 for Laser Aim Sight (offered 1990-1992).
Add $19 for compensated (669CP) barrel (new 1993).

* ***Model 669SS (Stainless Steel)*** – similar to Model 669, but in stainless steel. Disc. 1998.

	$340	$285	$235	$200	$180	$160	$150	*$421*

Add $21 for compensated (669CP) barrel (new 1993).

MODEL 689 – similar to Model 669, except has VR. Disc. 1998.

	$300	$260	$220	$185	$170	$155	$145	*$358*

Add $390 for Laser Aim Sight (mfg. 1990-91 only).

* ***Model 689SS (Stainless Steel)*** – similar to Model 669, but in stainless steel. Disc. 1999.

	$350	$300	$260	$220	$185	$155	$135	*$435*

MODEL 692 TRACKER – .38 Special +P/.357 Mag. or 9mm Para. cal., DA/SA, 3 or 6 1/2 in. barrel, 7 shot, spurred hammer, fixed front sight, Ribber grips, carbon steel or stainless steel cylinder, black oxide (mfg. 2019 only), matte black, or matte stainless finish, 35.27 oz. New 2018.

MSR $653	$530	$465	$415	$375	$300	$250	$210	

* ***Model 692 Tracker SS (Stainless Steel)*** – similar to Model 692 Tracker, but in stainless steel. New 2018.

MSR $706	$580	$510	$435	$395	$320	$260	$215	

MODEL 731 SS ULTRA-LITE – .32 H&R Mag. cal., small frame, 2 in. ported barrel, 6 shot, aluminum frame with matte stainless steel cylinder, fixed sights, rubber boot grips, 17 oz. Mfg. 1998-2011.

	$390	$335	$295	$260	$220	$195	$175	*$514*

GRADING - PPGS™	100%	98%	95%	90%	80%	70%	60%	LAST MSR

* ***Model 731T*** – .32 H&R Mag. cal., small frame, 6 shot, all titanium construction, 2 in. ported barrel with fixed sights, bright blue (disc. 1999), matte blue, shadow grey (new 2003) or matte gold (disc. 1999) finish, rubber grips. Mfg. 1999, reintroduced 2003-2004.

	$455	$395	$345	$295	$260	$225	$195	*$531*

Subtract $64 for matte blue finish.

MODEL 741 – .32 H&R Mag. cal., 6 shot, 3 or 4 in. barrel, blue only, adj. sights. Mfg. 1993-94.

	$235	$200	$175	$155	$140	$125	$120	*$254*

* ***Model 741SS (Stainless Steel)*** – similar to Model 741, except is stainless steel. Mfg. 1993-94.

	$295	$250	$215	$185	$170	$155	$145	*$342*

MODEL 761 – .32 H&R Mag. cal., 6 shot, 6 in. barrel, blue only, adj. sights. Mfg. 1993-94.

	$265	$230	$200	$175	$160	$145	$135	*$326*

MODEL 817 ULTRA-LITE – .38 Spl. +P cal., medium frame, 7 shot, 2 in. ported (disc. 2002) or unported solid rib barrel, soft rubber (disc. 2006) or Ribber (new 2007) grips, bright blue finish, 21 oz. Mfg. 1999-2012.

	$400	$350	$310	$280	$240	$210	$185	*$508*

Add $20 for ported barrel (disc. 2002).

* ***Model 817 Ultra-Lite Stainless*** – similar to Model 817 Ultra-Lite, except is matte stainless steel. Mfg. 1999-2012.

	$425	$360	$315	$280	$240	$210	$185	*$555*

Add $20 for ported barrel (disc. 2003).

MODEL 827 – .38 Spl. +P cal., 7 shot, 4 in. heavy solid rib barrel, fixed sights, rubber grips, 36 1/2 oz. Mfg. 1999 only.

	$285	$250	$215	$185	$170	$155	$145	*$317*

* ***Model 827 Stainless*** – similar to Model 827, except is stainless steel. Mfg. 1999 only.

	$315	$260	$220	$185	$170	$155	$145	*$364*

MODEL 850 CIA – .38 Spl. +P cal., small frame, 5 shot, hammerless, DAO, 2 in. barrel with fixed sights, rubber boot grips, blue finish, approx. 23 oz. Mfg. 2001-2010.

	$350	$300	$260	$220	$200	$180	$165	*$452*

* ***Model 850 CIA SS (Stainless Steel)*** – similar to Model 850 CIA, except is matte stainless steel. Mfg. 2001-2010.

	$380	$335	$295	$260	$220	$195	$175	*$498*

* ***Model 850 CIA Ultra Lite*** – .38 Spl. +P cal., DAO, black anodized lightweight aluminum frame, 2 in. barrel, 5 shot, hammerless, fixed sights, matte black finish, 16 oz. Mfg. 2005, reintroduced 2008-2017.

	$365	$315	$260	$210	$185	$165	$150	*$459*

Add $47 for aluminum frame and matte stainless cylinder (disc. 2012).

* ***Model 850T CIA*** – .38 Spl. cal., similar to Model 850 CIA, except has shadow grey finish and all titanium construction, spectrum blue/titanium gold finish and mother-of-pearl grips optional 2005. Mfg. 2001-2009.

	$560	$495	$450	$395	$350	$295	$245	*$701*

Add $47 for blue and gold finish with mother-of-pearl grips (disc. 2006).

MODEL 851 PROTECTOR (CIA) – .38 Spl. +P cal., small frame, 5 shot, 2 in. full underlug barrel, DAO, shrouded hammer, rubber boot grips, 25 oz. Mfg. 2003-2010.

	$350	$300	$260	$220	$200	$180	$165	*$452*

* ***Model 851 Protector SS (Stainless Steel)*** – similar to Model 851 Protector, except is matte stainless steel. Mfg. 2003-2010.

	$380	$335	$295	$260	$220	$195	$175	*$498*

* ***Model 851 Protector Ultra-Lite*** – similar to Model 851 Protector, except is Ultra-Lite model with blue finish and adj. sight. Mfg. 2003-2012.

	$385	$335	$295	$260	$220	$195	$175	*$492*

* ***Model 851 Protector Ultra-Lite Aluminum/Titanium*** – similar to Model 851 Protector Ultra-Lite, except is aluminum/stainless steel or aluminum/titanium. Mfg. 2003-2012.

	$430	$385	$340	$295	$260	$225	$195	*$530*

Add $118 for aluminum/titanium construction (disc. 2010).

GRADING - PPGS™	100%	98%	95%	90%	80%	70%	60%	LAST MSR

* ***Model 851 Protector Titanium*** – similar to Model 851 Protector, except is shadow grey titanium. Mfg. 2003-2004, reintroduced 2006.

	$525	$480	$425	$375	$325	$280	$230	*$625*

Add $39 for spectrum blue/titanium gold finish and mother-of-pearl grips (disc. 2004).

MODEL 856 – .38 Spl. +P cal., DA, compact frame, 6 shot, 2 in. barrel, fixed sights, rubber boot grips, blue finish, 22.2 oz. Mfg. late 2008-2012.

	$350	$300	$260	$220	$200	$180	$165	*$461*

* ***Model 856SS*** – .38 Spl.+P cal., similar to Model 856, except is matte stainless steel. Mfg. late 2008-2012.

	$395	$335	$295	$260	$220	$195	$175	*$508*

Add $8 for adj. sight (disc. 2010).

MODEL 856 (CURRENT MFG.) – .38 Spl.+P cal., DA/SA, 2 in. barrel, 6 shot, carbon steel or stainless steel, spurred hammer, serrated ramp front and fixed rear sight, black soft rubber grips, matte blue or matte stainless finish, 22 oz. New 2018.

MSR $364	$315	$275	$235	$205	$175	$140	$110

Add 5% (MSR $379) for matte stainless.
Add 37.5% (MSR $500) for Viridian red laser grip.

* ***Model 856CH (Concealed Hammer)*** – .38 Spl.+P cal., DAO, lightweight aluminum, carbon steel, or stainless steel small frame, 2 in. barrel, 6 shot, matte carbon steel cylinder, concealed hammer, serrated ramp front and fixed rear sight, black soft rubber grips, transfer bar safety, matte black oxide, matte black, or matte stainless cylinder finish, anodized Azure (mfg. 2019 only), Bronze (mfg. 2019 only) finish, 16 oz. New mid-2019.

MSR $342	$300	$265	$225	$190	$165	$135	$105

Add 5% (MSR $358) for matte stainless.

* ***Model 856 Ultra-Lite*** – .38 Spl.+P cal., DA/SA, Ultra-Lite frame, 2 in. barrel, spurred or concealed hammer, serrated ramp front sight, fixed rear sight, black soft rubber or VZ grips in Operator II Black (mfg. 2019 only) or Cyclone Black/Grey finish, matte black, matte stainless, or exclusive frame colors in Azure, Bronze, Burnt Orange, Cobalt Blue (new mid-2019), or Rouge, 15.7 oz. New 2019.

MSR $342	$300	$265	$225	$190	$165	$135	$105

Add 5% (MSR $358) for matte stainless steel.
Add 7.5% (MSR $370) for exclusive frame colors.
Add 27.5% (MSR $441) for VZ grips with Black/Gray Cyclone finish.
Add $92 for VZ Black Operator II grips (mfg. 2019 only).

MODEL 856 DEFENDER – .38 Spl.+P cal., DA/SA, small stainless steel or ultralight aluminum alloy frame, 3 in. barrel, 6 shot, night sight with bright orange outline or fixed rear sight, Hogue black rubber, VZ custom, or Altamont wood grips, matte black, matte stainless, or Tungsten Cerakote (with Altamont wood grips only) finish, 16 (ultralight) or 35 oz. New 2020.

MSR $390	$350	$305	$265	$240	$195	$160	$125

Add 5% (MSR $406) for matte stainless finish.
Add 7.5% (MSR $423) for Altamont wood grips and Tungsten Cerakote finish.
Add $30 for night sights.
Add 17.5% (MSR $455) for VZ custom grips.

MODEL 905 – 9mm Para. cal., small frame, 5 shot, 2 in. barrel, rubber boot grips, exposed or concealed (CH Model, DAO, disc. 2005) hammer, fixed sights, includes 5 Stellar full moon clips, blue finish, 21 oz. New 2003.

MSR $370	$335	$295	$250	$230	$185	$150	$115

* ***Model 905SS (Stainless Steel)*** – 9mm Para. cal., similar to Model 905, except is stainless steel. New 2003.

MSR $385	$350	$305	$265	$240	$195	$160	$125

* ***Model 905 Ultra-Lite*** – ultra light frame, blue finish. Mfg. 2003-2004.

	$310	$260	$220	$185	$170	$155	$145	*$414*

» ***Model 905 Ultra-Lite Stainless*** – matte stainless variation of the Model 905 Ultra-Lite. Mfg. 2003-2004.

	$380	$335	$295	$260	$220	$195	$175	*$461*

MODEL 941 – .22 WMR cal., small frame, 8 shot, 2 (new 1997), 3 (disc. 1998), 4, or 5 (disc. 2012) in. barrel, blue only, adj. sights, full underlug on 4 and 5 in. barrels, soft rubber or wood (disc. 2000, 5 in. barrel only) grips, 24-27 1/2 oz. Mfg. 1993-2013.

	$355	$300	$260	$220	$200	$180	$165	*$465*

GRADING - PPGS™	100%	98%	95%	90%	80%	70%	60%	LAST MSR

* ***Model 941 Ultra-Lite*** – ultra light hammer forged frame, available in matte blue or bright stainless steel, 2 in. barrel standard beginning 2007, 18 1/2 oz. Mfg. 1999-2013.

	$380	$335	$295	$260	$220	$195	$175	*$499*

Add $32 for matte stainless steel construction (2 in. barrel only).

* ***Model 941SS (Stainless Steel)*** – similar to Model 941, except is polished (disc.) or matte stainless steel. Mfg. 1993-2013.

	$400	$350	$310	$280	$240	$210	$185	*$513*

MODEL 942 – .22 LR or .22 WMR cal., DA/SA, standard or ultralight small frame, 2 or 3 in. steel alloy or stainless steel barrel, 8 shot, spurred hammer, serrated ramp front and drift adj. rear sight, black soft rubber grips, transfer bar safety, matte black or matte stainless finish, 17.8-23.6 oz. New 2020.

MSR $370	$320	$265	$225	$190	$170	$155	$145	

Add 5% (MSR $385) for stainless steel.

MODEL 970 TRACKER – .22 LR cal., DA, medium frame, 7 shot, 6 1/2 in. heavy VR barrel, adj. rear sight, Ribber grips, matte stainless steel or blue finish (new 2007), 45.6 oz. Mfg. 2001-2010.

	$375	$310	$265	$220	$200	$180	$165	*$445*

Add $47 for matte stainless steel.

MODEL 971 TRACKER SS (STAINLESS STEEL) – .22 WMR cal., otherwise similar to Model 970 Tracker, 45.2 oz. Mfg. 2001-2004, and 2006-2010.

	$415	$320	$275	$250	$200	$165	$130	*$498*

MODEL 980 SILHOUETTE/HUNTER SS (STAINLESS STEEL) – .22 LR cal., DA, compact frame, 7 shot, 12 in. heavy barrel, adj. rear sight, Ribber grips, adj. trigger tension and trigger stop, includes scope mount, 56.8 oz. Mfg. 2001-2004.

	$375	$310	$265	$220	$200	$180	$165	*$414*

MODEL 981 SILHOUETTE/HUNTER SS (STAINLESS STEEL) – .22 WMR cal., otherwise similar to Model 980 Silhouette SS, 56.2 oz. Mfg. 2001-2004.

	$400	$350	$310	$280	$240	$210	$185	*$430*

MODEL 990 TRACKER – .22 LR cal., medium frame, 9 shot, 4 or 6 1/2 in. VR barrel with low mount adj. sights, blue finish, rubber boot (disc.) or Ribber grips, 44 oz. Mfg. late 2008-2012.

	$385	$335	$295	$260	$220	$195	$175	*$492*

* ***Model 990 Tracker SS*** – .22 LR cal., similar to Model 990 Tracker, except is matte stainless steel. Mfg. late 2008-2013.

	$430	$385	$340	$295	$260	$225	$195	*$555*

MODEL 991 TRACKER – .22 WMR cal., medium frame, 9 shot, 4 or 6 1/2 in. VR barrel with low mount adj. sights, blue finish, rubber boot (disc.) or Ribber grips, 38 or 44 oz. Mfg. late 2008-2012.

	$395	$345	$300	$260	$220	$195	$175	*$492*

* ***Model 991 Tracker SS*** – similar to Model 991 Tracker, except is matte stainless steel. Mfg. late 2008-2013.

	$430	$385	$340	$295	$260	$225	$195	*$555*

MODEL 992 TRACKER – includes interchangeable 9 shot .22 LR and .22 WMR cylinders, DA, 4 or 6 1/2 in. VR barrel with low profile adj. rear sights, blue (disc.) or black oxide finish, Ribber grips, 55 oz. New 2011.

MSR $639	$550	$480	$415	$375	$300	$250	$210	

This model has a quick change feature - pressing a button located on the right side of the frame will unlock the cylinder yoke and allow it to be removed w/o tools.

* ***Model 992 Tracker SS*** – similar to Model 992 Tracker, except is matte stainless steel. New 2011.

MSR $706	$620	$540	$475	$400	$350	$295	$245	

RIFLES: LEVER ACTION

MODEL 62 LA RIFLE/CARBINE – .22 LR cal., blue finish, 16 1/2 (mfg. 2006 only) or 23 in. barrel, uncheckered walnut hardwood stock, adj. rear sight, 11 or 12 shot tube mag., 4 1/2 lbs. Mfg. 2006-07.

	$400	$350	$300	$270	$220	$180	$140	*$329*

* ***Model 62 Rifle/Carbine Stainless*** – similar to Model 62 Rifle/Carbine, except is polished stainless steel, 4 1/2 lbs. Mfg. 2006-07.

	$425	$370	$320	$290	$235	$190	$150	*$349*

GRADING - PPGS™	100%	98%	95%	90%	80%	70%	60%	LAST MSR

RIFLES: REVOLVING

CIRCUIT JUDGE – .410 bore/.45 LC cal., DA, 18 1/2 in. barrel, shotgun/rifle crossover, revolver action based on the original "Judge" with fluted cylinder, 5 shot, bright blue finish, fiber optic sights, Brazilian hardwood Monte Carlo stock with vent. recoil pad, available as smoothbore shotgun or back bored rifle barrel, 4 lbs. Mfg. mid-2010-11.

	100%	98%	95%	90%	80%	70%	60%	LAST MSR
	$700	$600	$525	$475	$385	$315	$250	*$618*

RIFLES: SEMI-AUTO

MODEL 63 – .22 LR cal., patterned after the Winchester Model 63, 10 shot tube mag., blue finish, takedown design, 23 in. round barrel, adj. rear sight, 4 1/2 lbs. Imported 2003-07.

	100%	98%	95%	90%	80%	70%	60%	LAST MSR
	$325	$285	$245	$220	$180	$145	$115	*$329*

Add $33 for tang sight (mfg. 2005-06).
Add $30 for scope mount (mfg. 2007 only).

* ***Model 63 Stainless*** – similar to Model 63, except is stainless steel. Mfg. 2003-07.

	100%	98%	95%	90%	80%	70%	60%	LAST MSR
	$350	$305	$265	$240	$195	$160	$125	*$349*

Add $33 for tang sight (mfg. 2005-06).

MODEL 73 – .22 WMR cal., similar to Model 63, except mag. has less capacity. Imported late 2003-04.

	100%	98%	95%	90%	80%	70%	60%	LAST MSR
	$325	$285	$245	$220	$180	$145	$115	*$311*

* ***Model 73 Stainless*** – similar to Model 73, except is stainless steel. Imported 2003-04.

	100%	98%	95%	90%	80%	70%	60%	LAST MSR
	$350	$305	$265	$240	$195	$160	$125	*$342*

MODEL 173 – .17 HMR cal., similar to Model 73. Imported late 2003-04.

	100%	98%	95%	90%	80%	70%	60%	LAST MSR
	$325	$285	$245	$220	$180	$145	$115	*$342*

* ***Model 173 Stainless*** – similar to Model 173, except is stainless steel. Imported 2003-04.

	100%	98%	95%	90%	80%	70%	60%	LAST MSR
	$350	$305	$265	$240	$195	$160	$125	*$358*

CARBINE CT G2 SERIES – 9mm Para. (Model CT9G2L), .40 S&W (Model CT40G2M), or .45 ACP (Model GT45G2M) cal., tactical design featuring hybrid aluminum/polymer frame with steel reinforcement, 10 (.45 ACP cal), 15 (.40 S&W cal.), or 34 (9mm Para. cal) shot mag., 16 in. barrel, fixed black polymer pistol grip skeletonized stock, ribbed polymer forearm with lower Picatinny rail, flat-top aluminum upper receiver with built-in full-length Picatinny rail, fixed front and adj. rear sights, 9 1/4 lbs.

While advertised in 2011, this model was never mass manufactured.

CTG2 – 9mm Para. or .40 S&W cal., blowback action, 16 in. barrel, 10 shot mag., aluminum upper with integral full-length Picatinny rail, fully adj. rear and square post front sights, convertible charging handle, polymer handguard, ambidextrous bolt catch and mag. release, Black or Tan stock, 6.6 lbs. Mfg. 2014 only.

	100%	98%	95%	90%	80%	70%	60%	LAST MSR
	$775	$675	$595	$525	$450	$395	$330	*$879*

T4SA – 5.56 NATO or .223 Rem. cal., GIO, 16 in. Melonite chrome moly M4 profile barrel, Magpul 30 shot PMAG, AR/M4 Gen M2 window, oversized Magpul trigger guard, 6-pos. Magpul CTR buttstock with QDs and sling mounts, friction lock, Magpul MOE black grip with storage, carbine length low profile gas system, forged aluminum lower and A3 flat-top upper receiver with T-Markings, aluminum KeyMod, 1913 top rail with four integrated quick disconnect points, aluminum M-LOK, or 1913 top rail handguard, Mil-Spec buffer tube, matte black, Cerakote Elite Sand, or Jungle finish, 6 1/2 lbs. Mfg. 2017-18.

	100%	98%	95%	90%	80%	70%	60%	LAST MSR
	$1,025	$925	$800	$685	$595	$515	$440	*$1,199*

RIFLES: SLIDE ACTION

Add $30 for Weaver style scope base mount.
Add $14 for Taurus Rimfire Recharger (2 pack without ammo, new 2002).

MODEL 62 RIFLE/CARBINE – .22 LR or .22 WMR (disc. 2000) cal., patterned after the Win. Model 62, 16 1/2 (carbine) or 23 (rifle) in. barrel, open adj. sights, 11 or 12 shot tube mag., includes switchable manual firing pin block safety on top of receiver and integral Taurus Security System lock on hammer, uncheckered hardwood stock and grooved forearm, blue or case colored receiver, approx. 4 1/2 lbs. Imported 1999-2007.

	100%	98%	95%	90%	80%	70%	60%	LAST MSR
	$400	$350	$300	$270	$220	$180	$140	*$299*

Add $34 for rear tang sight (new 2002).

* ***Model 62 Rifle/Carbine Stainless*** – similar to Model 62 Rifle/Carbine, except is stainless steel. Mfg. 2000-07.

	100%	98%	95%	90%	80%	70%	60%	LAST MSR
	$425	$370	$320	$290	$235	$190	$150	*$319*

Add $78 for rear tang sight (mfg. 2002-2004).

GRADING - PPGS™	100%	98%	95%	90%	80%	70%	60%	LAST MSR

* ***Model 62 Rifle/Carbine "Upstart" Youth/Adult Combo*** – similar to Model 62 Rifle/Carbine, except is available with both youth (shortened LOP), and adult stocks. Imported 2002-04.

	$350	$305	$265	$240	$195	$160	$125	*$311*

Add $16 for stainless steel.

MODEL 72 RIFLE/CARBINE – .22 WMR cal., 10 or 11 shot tube mag., blue or case colored receiver, similar to Model 62 Rifle/Carbine, 4 1/2 lbs. Imported 2001-07.

	$325	$285	$245	$220	$180	$145	$115	*$329*

Add $34 for rear tang sight (new 2002).
Add $20 for case colored receiver.

Beginning 2001, this model's nomenclature changed from Model 62 to Model 72 (.22 WMR cal. only).

* ***Model 72 Rifle/Carbine Stainless*** – similar to Model 72 Rifle/Carbine, except is stainless steel, 80 oz. Imported 2001-07.

	$350	$305	$265	$240	$195	$160	$125	*$349*

Add $34 for rear tang sight (new 2002).

MODEL 172 RIFLE/CARBINE – .17 HMR cal., 16 1/2 (carbine, disc. 2005) or 23 (rifle) in. barrel, adj. sights, 4 1/2 oz. Imported 2003-06.

	$325	$285	$245	$220	$180	$145	$115	*$327*

* ***Model 172 Rifle/Carbine Stainless*** – similar to Model 172 Rifle/Carbine, except is stainless steel. Imported 2003-06.

	$350	$305	$265	$240	$195	$160	$125	*$342*

THUNDERBOLT RIFLE/CARBINE – .357 Mag./.38 Spl. or .45 LC cal., 20 (carbine) or 26 in. (rifle) round barrel with full mag., patterned after the Colt Lightning rifle, 11 (carbine) or 13 (rifle) shot tube mag., choice of case colored or blue finish, short stroke action, uncheckered hardwood stock and forearm, hammer drop release button hidden in the hammer, solid metal curved crescent buttplate, long horn adj. rear sight, 8 lbs. Mfg. 2006-09.

	$450	$395	$340	$305	$250	$205	$160	*$705*

Add $43 for case colors.

* ***Thunderbolt Rifle/Carbine Stainless*** – similar to Thunderbolt Rifle/Carbine, except is polished stainless steel. Mfg. 2006-09.

	$500	$440	$375	$340	$275	$225	$175	*$813*

TAVOR

Current trademark established during 2013. Imported by IWI US, Inc., located in Middletown, PA. IWI US, Inc. is a member of the SK Group.

CARBINES/RIFLES: SEMI-AUTO

Conversion kits are produced in 9mm Para., 5.45x39mm or .300 AAC Blackout cal. Please contact the importer directly for pricing and availability.

TAVOR SAR – 5.56 NATO, .300 AAC Blackout (new 2016), or 9mm Para cal., bullpup design, long stroke GPO, 16 1/2, 17 (9mm Para. cal.), or 18 in. chrome-lined barrel, 10 or 30 shot STANAG pattern (AR-15) mag., reinforced polymer frame and stock, integral folding adj. backup sights with Tritium front post, fully ambi controls, flat-top with full Picatinny rail or Meprolight reflex sight mounted directly to the receiver (TSIDF16, disc. 2016), short forward rail on forend, LRBHO, matte black, Flat Dark Earth or OD Green (new 2014) finish, approx. 8-8 1/2 lbs. Importation began early 2013.

MSR $1,999	$1,700	$1,495	$1,275	$1,150	$935	$775	$660

Add $50 for .300 AAC Blackout cal.
Add $50 for 2 3/8 in. permanently attached or 3 7/8 in. removable muzzle brake.
Add $600 for TAR-21/IDF16 (TSIDF16) configuration with Mepro-21 reflex sight.

Available in left-hand model with all controls situated for left-hand operation including the cocking handle, safety lever, QD swivel receptacles, relocation of the forward 45° Picatinny rail to the left side and left side ejection.

TAVOR X95 – 5.56 NATO, 9mm Para., or .300 AAC Blackout cal., bullpup design, long stroke GPO, 16 1/2 or 18 1/2 (new 2018) in. chrome-lined, CHF barrel, 6 grooves, 30 STANAG pattern (AR-15) mag. or 32 (9mm Para. cal. only) shot mag., integral folding adj. backup sights with Tritium front post, reinforced polymer frame and stock, modular Tavor style pistol grip, ambi controls, flat-top with full Picatinny rail, ambi mag. release above trigger guard, forearm with Picatinny rails at the 3, 6, and 9 o'clock positions with removable rail covers, charging handle located close to center mass, low profile

GRADING - PPGS™	100%	98%	95%	90%	80%	70%	60%	LAST MSR

bolt release button, LRBHO, matte black, FDE or ODG finish, 26 1/8 in. OAL, approx. 8 lbs. Imported beginning early 2016.

MSR $1,999	$1,700	$1,495	$1,275	$1,150	$935	$775	$660	

Add $50 for .300 AAC Blackout cal.

This model is also available in left-hand configuration at no extra charge.

TAVOR 7 – 7.62x51 NATO cal., bullpup configuration, GPO, 4-pos gas regulator, 16 1/2 in. chrome-lined, CHF threaded barrel w/muzzle brake, 4 grooves, 20 shot mag. (LR/SR25 magazine type), M-LOK handguard, QD sling sockets on stock, ambi controls, full-length Picatinny rail, matte black, FDE, or OD Green finish, 26.7 in. OAL, 9 lbs. Importation began 2018.

MSR $2,099	$1,785	$1,550	$1,325	$1,200	$950	$800	$700	

SHOTGUNS: SEMI-AUTO

TS12 – 12 ga., 3 in. chamber, reinforced polymer bullpup design, 2-pos. gas regulator, short stroke gas piston, 18 1/2 in. barrel w/Benelli/Beretta choke tubes, three mag. tubes that hold five cartridges each, polymer stock, pistol grip, crossbolt safety, full-length Picatinny rail, M-LOK compatible rails, matte black, FDE (new 2020), OD Green (new 2020) finishes available, 28 in. OAL., 8 lbs. Importation began 2018.

MSR $1,399	$1,190	$1,050	$900	$815	$675	$550	$450	

TAYLOR, F.C. FUR CO.

Previous company which marketed animal trap guns circa 1921-1941.

PISTOLS: SINGLE SHOT

.22 CAL. TAYLOR FUR GETTER – .22 LR cal., designed to shoot animal at close range once trigger mechanism has been activated (usually with bait attached to a lever). Mfg. by O.F. Mossberg for Taylor, ser. range 1-3,100. Introduced circa 1921.

N/A	$2,300	$1,850	$1,650	$1,300	$1,000	$750	

Add 15% for very early serial number with stake made from two pieces and capable of swiveling, usually found in the 1-300 serial number range.

Subtract $150 if w/o stake.

.38 CAL. TAYLOR FUR GETTER – .38 cal., believed to have been mfg. by Lovelace, markings cast in top of frame (brass) with iron barrel - all bearing the 1914 patent date.

N/A	$1,500	$1,300	$1,050	$825	$650	$500	

Add 10%-15% premium for alloy frame with top plate attached with two screws and uncracked frame.

This model was mfg. on the April 1914 patent of C.D. Lovelace, who worked mainly in the San Angelo, TX area and manufactured two variations of this gun in .38 cal. The first variation was marked "Texas Gun Co." around the cocking rod. The second variation has "The Texas Gun Co, San Angelo, TX" cast into the top of the action. The Lovelace patent was issued in 1914 and an arrangment was made with F.C. Taylor Fur Co. to market these guns under the name of SureShot, with the F.C. Taylor logo and 1914 patent date cast into the top of two variations of the gun, a rounded top brass frame and a flattop brass frame. An alloy or pot metal frame version had two screws attaching the top frame cover. Most of this variation will be found badly damaged, with cracked frames (rarely seen). From 1914-1921, three variations of the Taylor .38 cal. were marketed in this seven-year period, which indicates the rarity of the .38 cal. It took from 1921 to 1939 for F.C. Taylor to sell just over 3,100 .22 cal. guns. A fourth variation .38 cal. will be found with the Taylor logo ground off the round top frame variation, with the 1914 patent date. These guns were sold to and marketed by Biggs Fur Co. of Kansas City.

TAYLOR'S & CO., INC.

TAYLOR'S & CO. INC.

Current importer and distributor established during 1988, located in Winchester, VA.

Taylor's & Co. is an importer and distributor of Uberti, Pietta, Pedersoli, and Chiappa products. Taylor's is also a distributor for Bond Arms Inc. - please refer to the Bond Arms Inc. section. For more information and up-to-date pricing regarding current Taylor's & Co., Inc. black powder models, please refer to the *Blue Book of Modern Black Powder Arms* (also available online). This book features information, complete pricing, and reference guides.

DERRINGERS: REPRODUCTIONS

DEADWOOD DOUBLE DERRINGER – .22 LR or .22 WMR cal., coal black, antique black, bright nickel, or gold plated finish, 3 in. barrels. Mfg. 2009-2010.

	$130	$110	$100	$90	$80	$70	$60	*$149*

GRADING - PPGS™	100%	98%	95%	90%	80%	70%	60%	LAST MSR

PISTOLS: SxS

DOUBLE BARREL HOWDAH PISTOL – .45 LC/.410 (3 in. shells), 10 1/4 in. rifled barrels, manual shell extractors, flip-up rear sight with brass bead front sight, checkered walnut or rubberized (Alaskan) stock, tang safety, case hardened blued (Original), browned (Vintage), or matte chrome (Alaskan) finish. New 2017.

MSR $1,584	$1,350	$1,180	$1,010	$920	$750	$610	$530	

Add $473 for Vintage model.
Subtract $34 for Alaskan model.

PISTOLS: SEMI-AUTO

1911-A1 MODEL – .45 ACP cal., 5 in. barrel, straight checkered mainspring housing, arched straight "grain" (disc. 2014, reintroduced 2018), or arched checkered mainspring housing, 8 shot single stack mag., smooth (disc.) or checkered walnut, cocobolo diamond (disc.), olive diamond (disc.), olive with ashlar diamond (disc.), or walnut diamond checkered (disc. 2013) grips, blue finish, with or w/o lanyard ring, includes black carrying case and two mags. Mfg. by Armscor. New 2011.

MSR $532	$450	$395	$340	$300	$250	$200	$175	

Add $20 for lanyard ring (disc. 2017).
Add $19 for olive diamond, olive with Ashlar diamond, or for cocobolo diamond checkered grips (mfg. 2013-2017).
Add $31 for walnut diamond checkered grips (mfg. 2013-2014).
A Combat model with adj. sights was also available - retail was POR.

* ***1911-A1 Nickel*** – .45 ACP cal., 5 in. barrel, 8 shot mag., fixed front sight, dovetail rear sight, checkered walnut grip, includes black carrying case and two mags., nickel finish, 2.47 lbs. Mfg. 2018 only.

1911-A1 FS TACTICAL – 9mm Para. (mfg. 2015-2018), .45 ACP, or 10mm (mfg. 2015-2016) cal., 5 in. barrel, 8 shot mag., combat hammer, skeletonized trigger, ambidextrous safety, extended beavertail, Picatinny underrail, green fiber optic front sight, black or Gun Metal Grey (disc. 2020) parkerized finish, checkered walnut grips, 3 1/4 lbs. Mfg. by Armscor. Importation began 2013.

MSR $669	$575	$500	$430	$390	$315	$260	$220	

Add $220 for Gun Metal Grey finish (disc. 2020).
Add $187 for 9mm Para. cal. (mfg. 2015-2018).

* ***1911 Compact Carry Tactical*** – 9mm Para. (mfg. 2015-2018) or .45 ACP cal., 3 5/8 in. barrel, 7 shot mag., combat hammer, skeletonized trigger, GI thumb safety, hi-sweep beavertail grip, Novak style rear and dovetail mounted front sights, rear slide serrations, parkerized, Gun Metal Grey (disc. 2020), Dark Earth (disc. 2018), OD Green (disc. 2018), or Coyote Tan Cerakote (disc. 2018) finish, checkered walnut grips, 2.43 lbs. Mfg. by Armscor. Importation began 2013.

MSR $661	$560	$490	$420	$380	$310	$260	$215	

Add $178 for Gun Metal Grey (disc. 2020), Dark Earth (disc. 2018), OD Green (disc. 2018), or Coyote Tan (disc. 2018) Cerakote finish.

1911 .22 – .22 LR cal., 5 in. barrel, SA, black frame with black or olive green slide, checkered wood grips, 10 shot mag., mfg. by Chiappa. Mfg. 2011-2013.

	$250	$225	$195	$175	$140	$115	$90	*$300*

Add $79 for black slide (disc. 2012).
Add $65 for target model (disc. 2012).

CUSTOM 1911 HAND ENGRAVED – .45 ACP cal., 5 in. barrel, 8 shot mag., hand engraved floral and scroll by Jim Downing, diamond patterned checkered walnut grips, polished blue or matte nickel finish. Mfg. 2014-2016.

	$865	$750	$650	$595	$475	$395	$300	*$1,019*

Add $700 for matte nickel finish.

CUSTOM 1911 TACTICAL – 9mm Para. (mfg. 2015-2018), 10mm (mfg. 2015-2017), or .45 ACP cal., 3 5/8 (compact, new 2015) or 5 in. barrel, 8 shot mag., combat hammer, skeletonized trigger, ambidexrous safety, extended beavertail, front and back slide serrations, Picatinny rail, green fiber optic front sight, special multi-color or black grips, Gun Metal Gray, Dark Earth (disc. 2018), OD Green (disc. 2018), or Coyote Tan (disc. 2018) Cerakote finish. Mfg. by Armscor. Mfg. 2014-disc.

	$710	$625	$535	$485	$395	$325	$250	*$836*

Add $188 for 9mm Para. cal. (disc. 2018).

BLACK ROCK 1911 – 9mm Para. (mfg. 2015-2018), .45 ACP or 10mm (mfg. 2015-2017) cal., 3 5/8 (compact, new 2015) or 5 in. barrel, 8 shot mag., combat hammer, skeletonized trigger, extended beavertail, ambidextrous safety, front and rear slide serrations, Black Rock finish, checkered walnut grips. Mfg. by Armscor, 2014-disc.

	$675	$595	$500	$460	$375	$300	$235	*$791*

Add $8 for 5 in. barrel.
Add $187 for 9mm Para. cal. (mfg. 2015-2018).

GRADING - PPGS™	100%	98%	95%	90%	80%	70%	60%	LAST MSR

M4 TACTICAL SERIES – .22 LR cal., GIO, 6 in. solid steel barrel, 10 or 28 shot mag., fire control group, dust cover, adj. sights, pseudo flash hider, bayonet lug, forward assist, and bolt release, quad rail capable forearm, includes two mags. Imported 2011-2012.

	$350	$315	$275	$235	$200	$180	$165	*$419*

REVOLVERS: REPRODUCTIONS, CONVERSIONS

1858 REMINGTON CONVERSION – .32-20 WCF (mfg. 2009), .38 Spl., .38-40 WCF (mfg. 2009), .44-40 WCF, or .45 LC cal., 5 1/2, 7 3/8, or 8 in. barrel, steel frame and backstrap, brass trigger guard, smooth walnut grips, blue finish, case colored hammer. New 2009.

MSR $600	$510	$450	$385	$350	$275	$225	$200	

Add $8 for .44-40 WCF.

1871-1872 OPEN TOP CONVERSION EARLY MODEL – .38 Spl., .38 LC (disc. 2011), .44 Colt (disc. 2011), .44 Spl. (disc. 2011), .45 Schofield (disc. 2011), or .45 LC cal., 4 3/4, 5 1/2, or 7 1/2 in. round barrel, Early Model frame, 1851 Navy size grips, with or w/o brass backstrap and trigger guard, walnut or black polymer (Cavalier, new 2020) grips, case hardened frame, blue or nickel finish. New 2007.

MSR $549	$470	$410	$350	$325	$260	$215	$185	

Add $118 for nickel finish.
Add $209 for Cavalier model (new 2020).

1871-1872 OPEN TOP CONVERSION LATE MODEL – .38 Spl., .38 LC (disc. 2011), .44 Colt (disc. 2011), .44 Spl. (disc. 2011), .45 Schofield (disc. 2011), or .45 LC cal., 7 1/2 in. round barrel, Late Model frame, 1860 Army grips, steel backstrap and trigger guard, case hardened frame, blue or nickel finish. New 2006.

MSR $577	$495	$435	$375	$335	$275	$225	$195	

Add $117 for nickel finish.

1871 C. MASON (1860 ARMY) – .38 Spl., .38 LC (disc. 2011), .44 Colt (disc. 2011), .44 Spl. (disc. 2011), .45 LC, or .45 Schofield (disc. 2011) cal., 4 3/4, 5 1/2, or 8 in. round barrel, 1860 Army frame (forged), 6 shot, steel backstrap and trigger guard, blade front sights, blue or nickel finish with case hardened frame, 2.23 lbs. New 2007.

MSR $615	$525	$460	$395	$355	$290	$240	$200	

Add $117 for nickel finish.

1871 C. MASON (1851 NAVY) – .38 Spl., .38 LC (disc. 2011), .44 Colt (disc. 2011), .44 Spl. (disc. 2011), or .45 Schofield (disc. 2011) cal., 4 3/4, 5 1/2, or 7 1/2 in. octagonal barrel, 1851 Navy frame (forged), 6 shot, brass backstrap and trigger guard, brass post front sight, blue or nickel finish with case hardened frame, 2.32 lbs. New 2007.

MSR $583	$500	$440	$375	$340	$275	$225	$195	

Add $118 for nickel finish.

REVOLVERS: REPRODUCTIONS, SAA

Add $146-$147 for Taylor tuned action (hand-tuned and polished, lightened hammer and trigger pull with custom springs) on all Cattleman models, unless otherwise noted.
Add $600 for half-coverage hand engraving, or $1,000 for full coverage hand engraving on all Cattleman models (limited availability).

1875 ARMY OUTLAW – .357 Mag., .44-40 WCF, .45 LC, or .45 ACP cal., 5 1/2 or 7 1/2 in. barrel, case hardened frame with blue, nickel, or white finish, smooth two-piece walnut or ivory (Rambler model only, new 2020) grips, steel backstrap. New 2011.

MSR $606	$515	$450	$385	$350	$285	$230	$200	

Add $107 for .45 LC/.45 ACP cylinder.
Add $118 for nickel finish.
Add $208 for Rambler model (blue finish, ivory grips).
Add $385 for white finish with photo engraving (new 2014).

1890 ARMY POLICE – .357 Mag., .44-40 WCF, .45 LC, or .45 ACP cal., 5 1/2 in. barrel, blue finish, lanyard ring, two-piece smooth walnut grips. Mfg. 2011-2016.

	$475	$415	$355	$325	$260	$215	$165	*$560*

Add $6 for .44-40 WCF or $8 for .45 ACP cal.
Add $97 for .45 LC/.45 ACP cal. cylinder.

CATTLEMAN VARIATIONS – available in .32-20 WCF, .357 Mag., .38-40 WCF, .44 Spl., .44-40 WCF, .45 ACP (new 2003), or .45 LC cal., 3 1/2, 4 3/4, 5 1/2, and 7 1/2 in. barrel lengths, brass (New Model frame) or steel (Old Model frame) backstrap and trigger guard. Mfg. by Uberti. New 2002.

* ***Cattleman Antique Finish*** – .357 Mag. or .45 LC cal., 3 1/2, 4 3/4 or 5 1/2 in. barrel, New Model forged frame, 6 shot, blade front sights, walnut grips, antique finish, 2.3 lbs.

MSR $707	$600	$530	$450	$410	$335	$275	$235	

GRADING - PPGS™	100%	98%	95%	90%	80%	70%	60%	LAST MSR

* ***Cattleman Brass Backstrap and Trigger Guard*** – .357 Mag. (disc. 2008, reintroduced 2011), or .45 LC cal. Disc. 2011.

	$390	$330	$285	$250	$215	$175	$150	*$456*

* ***Cattleman Carbine*** – .357 Mag., .44-40 WCF, or .45 LC cal., 18 in. barrel with shoulder stock. Mfg. 2009-2013.

	$675	$595	$500	$450	$375	$300	$225	*$800*

Add $6 for .44-40 WCF cal.

* ***Cattleman Charcoal Finish*** – .357 Mag. or .45 LC cal., 4 3/4 or 5 1/2 in. barrel, New Model forged frame, 6 shot, blade front sights, walnut grips, charcoal blue finish, 2.3 lbs.

MSR $665	$575	$500	$430	$390	$315	$260	$220	

* ***Cattleman Millenium*** – .45 LC cal., 4 3/4 in. barrel, brass backstrap and trigger guard. Mfg. 2000-2008.

	$300	$265	$225	$200	$175	$155	$125	*$365*

* ***Cattleman Nickel Finish*** – .357 Mag. or .45 LC cal., 4 3/4, 5 1/2, or 7 1/2 in. barrel, New Model forged frame, 6 shot, blade front sights, walnut, polymer black buffalo, polymer pearl, or polymer ivory grips, nickel plated finish with charcoal blue screws, approx. 2 1/2 lbs.

MSR $690	$585	$510	$440	$400	$325	$275	$230	

Add $209 for polymer black buffalo, pearl, or ivory grips.

* ***Cattleman Steel Backstrap and Trigger Guard*** – .32-20 WCF, .38-40 WCF, .44 Spl., .44-40 WCF, .45 ACP or .45 LC cal., 4 3/4, 5 1/2, or 7 1/2 in. barrel, choice of New or Old Model (disc.) frame.

MSR $572	$485	$425	$365	$330	$265	$225	$190	

Add $9 for .44-40 WCF or .44 Spl. cal.
Add $17 for .38-40 WCF or .32-20 WCF cal.
Add $108 for .45 LC/.45 ACP cal.

* ***Cattleman "TR" Presidential*** – .45 LC cal. only, 5 1/2 in. barrel, features unique photo engraving on frame, cylinder, and barrel (Taylor's exclusive), white heat treated finish with charcoal blue screws, simulated ivory, wood, or black hard rubber grips. Mfg. 2005-2006.

	$565	$450	$375	$315	$275	$240	$215	*$685*

Add $30 for black grips, or $100 for simulated ivory grips.

CATTLEMAN .44 MAG. – .44 Mag. cal., 6 in. barrel, non-fluted cylinder, forged frame, 6 shot, blade front sights, Army grips, blue finish, 2.6 lbs.

MSR $627	$530	$460	$400	$360	$290	$240	$210	

CATTLE BRAND REVOLVER – .357 Mag. or .45 LC cal., case hardened or nickel frame, 4 3/4 or 5 1/2 in. barrel, 6 shot, brass backstrap and trigger guard (with Stag grips, standard) or nickel, white PVC or Stag grips, features laser engraved patterns of cattle brands. New 2017.

MSR $537	$460	$400	$350	$315	$250	$200	$175	

Add $242 for nickel finish with white PVC grips.
Add $327 for nickel finish with Stag grips.

CATTLEMAN BISLEY – .357 Mag. (disc. 2008, reintroduced 2011), .38-40 WCF (disc. 2008) or .45 LC cal., patterned after the Colt Bisley Model, 4 3/4, 5 1/2, or 7 1/2 in. barrel, forged and case colored New Model frame, steel trigger guard and backstrap, wood grips, blue finish, 2 1/2-2 3/4 lbs. Mfg. 1997-2008, reintroduced 2010.

MSR $617	$525	$460	$395	$350	$290	$240	$200	

CATTLEMAN DEVIL ANSE – .45 LC or .357 Mag. cal., 4 3/4 in. barrel, 6 shot, case hardened hammer, fixed front and rear frame notch sights, matte black wood grips, blued finish, 2.43 lbs. New 2019.

MSR $599	$510	$450	$385	$350	$275	$225	$200	

CATTLEMAN DRIFTER – .357 Mag. or .45 LC cal., forged frame, 4 3/4, 5 1/2, or 7 1/2 in. full octagonal barrel, steel backstrap and trigger guard, case hardened frame finish. New 2019.

MSR $594	$510	$450	$385	$350	$275	$225	$200	

GUNFIGHTER CATTLEMAN – .357 Mag. or .45 LC cal., forged steel frame, 4 3/4 (new 2015) or 5 1/2 in. barrel, steel backstrap and trigger guard, smooth or checkered (new 2014) walnut large Army-size grips, color case hardened finish, 2.4 lbs. Importation began 2011.

MSR $587	$500	$440	$375	$340	$275	$225	$195	

Add $36 for checkered grips.
Add $117 for nickel finish.

* ***Gunfighter Cattleman Short-Stroke Competition Series*** – .357 Mag. or .45 LC cal., case hardened frame, 5 1/2 in. barrel, 6 shots, large Army size checkered walnut grips, 2.3 lbs. New 2017.

MSR $667	$575	$500	$430	$390	$315	$260	$220	

Add $116 for Taylor polished.

GRADING - PPGS™	100%	98%	95%	90%	80%	70%	60%	LAST MSR

CATTLEMAN ISLAND GIRL QUICK DRAW - .38 Spl., 4 3/4 in. barrel, nickel finish with one-piece white checkered polymer grips, fire blued screws, beveled cylinder, Ruger style coil spring. Mfg. 2006-2008.

	$595	$525	$465	$400	$345	$275	$240	*$710*

CATTLEMAN OLD RANDALL - .357 Mag. or .45 LC cal., steel frame, 4 3/4 or 5 1/2 in. barrel, 6 shot, case hardened hammer, matte brass backstrap and trigger guard, walnut Navy size grips, blued finish, 2.5 lbs. New 2020.

MSR $511	$435	$380	$325	$295	$240	$195	$175	

CATTLEMAN FLORAL ENGRAVED/PHOTO ENGRAVED (CATTLEMAN VARIATIONS ENGRAVED) - .357 Mag. or .45 LC cal., 4 3/4, 5 1/2, or 7 1/2 in. barrel, forged frame, 6 shot, blade front sights, Taylor's & Co. original featuring unique photo engraving (laser engraved and hand chased) on frame, cylinder, and barrel, choice of blue (mfg. 2006-2013), color case hardened (disc. 2013), white heat-treated steel, coin finish hardening (new 2014), or white laser floral engraved (new 2017) on the steel frame and bluing on remaining parts, smooth walnut grips, 2.27-2.76 lbs. New 2003.

MSR $751	$635	$550	$475	$425	$350	$285	$250	

Add $195 for 29 for coin finish hardening (new 2014).
Add $230 for white heat-treated steel finish.

1873 CATTLEMAN-OLD MODEL(CATTLEMAN QUICK DRAW) - .357 Mag. or .45 LC cal., 4 (disc.), 4 3/4, 5 1/2, or 7 1/2 in. barrel, forged frame, blue finish with case hardened New (disc. 2008) or Old Model frame, approx. 2 1/2 lbs. New 2006.

MSR $579	$495	$435	$375	$335	$275	$225	$195	

Add $49 for military stamp on grip (Calvary model, new 2017).

1873 BIRDSHEAD/CATTLEMAN SHERIFF BIRDSHEAD - .357 Mag. or .45 LC cal., 3 1/2 or 4 3/4 in. barrel, patterned after the Colt 1877 Thunderer, 6 shot, forged and case hardened frame, steel backstrap, blade front sights, smooth or checkered (new 2014) walnut bird's head grips, blue finish, 2.16 lbs. Mfg. by Uberti. New 1997.

MSR $581	$495	$435	$375	$335	$275	$225	$195	

Add $36 for checkered grips (new 2014).
Add $188 polymer ivory grips (mfg. 2011 only).
Add $79 for nickel finish (.357 Mag. cal. only, with 4 3/4 in. barrel, disc. 2008).

* ***1873 Birdshead/Flattop Birdshead*** - .357 Mag or .45 LC cal., 3 1/2 (Flattop) or 4 3/4 (Birdshead), 6 shot, with (blue finish) or w/o (nickel plated), fixed front blade and rear frame notch sights, walnut or polymer ivory (nickel plated), blue or nickel plated (Flattop) finish, 2.35-2.43 lbs. New 2021.

MSR $507	$435	$380	$325	$295	$240	$195	$175	

Add $9 for 1873 Flattop Birdshead (3.5 in. barrel, walnut grips).
Add $122 for 1873 SA Nickel Flattop Birdshead Ivory (3.5 in. barrel, ivory grips).

CATTLEMAN STAINLESS (OUTFITTER) - .357 Mag. (disc. 2008, reintroduced 2017) or .45 LC cal., all stainless construction, 4 3/4, 5 1/2, or 7 1/2 in. barrel, forged frame, two-piece walnut grips, approx. 2 1/2 lbs. New 2003.

MSR $739	$630	$550	$475	$430	$345	$285	$245	

Add $12 for .357 Mag. (reintroduced 2017).

CATTLEMAN TAYLOR GAMBLER - .357 Mag. or .45 LC cal., 4 3/4 (new 2015) or 5 1/2 in. barrel, fancy checkered walnut grips, forged frame, blue color case hardened finish, includes deluxe custom tuning. Importation began 2012.

MSR $619	$525	$460	$395	$350	$290	$240	$200	

CATTLEMAN TAYLOR MARSHAL - .45 LC or .357 Mag. cal., forged steel color case hardened frame, 5 1/2 in. round barrel, steel backstrap and trigger guard, checkered antique polymer ivory grip, includes deluxe custom tuning. Importation began 2012.

MSR $715	$610	$535	$460	$415	$335	$275	$240	

CHIAPPA SINGLE ACTION - .22 LR cal., 4 3/4 in. barrel, 6 shot, blue finish, black plastic checkered or wood grips. Mfg. 2013 only.

	$150	$125	$115	$100	$85	$70	$55	*$179*

Add $16 for wood grips.

NEW MODEL BLACKHAWK - .357 Mag. cal., 4 5/8 in. barrel, flat-top frame with adj. rear sight and pre-1962 XR3 grip frame, choice of blue or stainless, hard rubber grips with Handlebar Doc white medallions. Mfg. 2006-2008.

	$575	$500	$450	$395	$340	$275	$240	*$675*

GRADING - PPGS™	100%	98%	95%	90%	80%	70%	60%	LAST MSR

NEW VAUQUERO "HANDLEBAR DOC SIGNATURE SERIES" – .357 Mag. or .45 LC cal., color case hardened blue or stainless steel frame, 4 5/8, 5 1/2, or 7 1/2 in. barrel, checkered black grips with white "HD" medallions, "Handlebar Doc Series" etched on barrel, Taylor's exclusive. Mfg. 2005-2009.

$595 $525 $450 $395 $340 $275 $240

QUICK DRAW REVOLVING CARBINE – .357 Mag., .44-40 WCF, or .45 LC cal., 18 in. barrel, straight grip smooth walnut stock with brass buttplate, blue finish with case hardened forged frame, 4.4 lbs.

MSR $820 $700 $615 $525 $475 $385 $315 $275

Add $4 for .44-40 WCF cal.

OUTLAW LEGACY REVOLVER – .357 Mag. or .45 LC cal., 4 3/4 in. barrel, 6 shot, ivory grips, blued laser engraved fnish, 2.3 lbs. Mfg. by Pietta. Importation began 2017.

MSR $580 $495 $435 $375 $335 $275 $225 $195

* ***Outlaw Legacy Nickel Engraved*** – .357 Mag. or .45 LC cal., 4 3/4, 5 1/2 (new 2019), or 7 1/2 (new 2019) in. barrel, 6 shot, ivory grips, nickel laser engraved fnish, 2.3 lbs. Mfg. by Pietta. Importation began 2017.

MSR $649 $550 $480 $415 $375 $310 $260 $215

RUNNIN' IRON – .357 Mag. or .45 LC cal., 3 1/2, 4 3/4, or 5 1/2 in. barrel, checkered black polymer (disc. 2011) or checkered walnut grips, designed by Deke Rivers for cowboy action shooting, low and wide hammer spur, crescent style ejector rod, blue finish. New 2010.

MSR $654 $550 $490 $420 $380 $310 $260 $215

Add $26 for 4 3/4 or 5 1/2 in. barrel.
Add $44 for checkered polymer grips (disc. 2011)
Add $44 for short-stroke competition model (new 2017).
Add $116 for Deluxe Edition (custom tuning with lightened trigger and hammer pull, disc.).

* ***Runnin' Iron Black Rock Finish Series*** – .45 LC cal., 3 1/2 or 4 3/4 in. barrel, checkered walnut grips, low and wide hammer spur, crescent style ejector rod, Black Rock (scratch resistant black satin) finish. New 2014.

MSR $723 $615 $540 $460 $420 $340 $275 $240

Add $25 for 4 3/4 in. barrel.
Add $43 for short-stroke competition model (new 2017).
Add $146 for Deluxe Edition (custom tuning with lightened trigger and hammer pull, disc.).

* ***Runnin' Iron Stainless*** – .357 Mag. or .45 LC cal., 3 1/2, 4 3/4, or 5 1/2 in. barrel, stainless steel, checkered black polymer (disc. 2011) or walnut grips, designed by Deke Rivers for cowboy action shooting, low and wide hammer spur, crescent style ejector rod. New 2010.

MSR $836 $710 $625 $535 $485 $390 $325 $280

Add $15 for .357 Mag. cal.
Add $44 for checkered polymer grips (disc. 2011).
Add $44 for short stroke model (.45 LC, 3 1/2 in. barrel).
Add $146 for Deluxe Edition (custom tuning with lightened trigger and hammer pull, disc.).

RUNNIN' REVOLVING CARBINE – .44-40 WCF or .45 LC cal., similar to Runnin' Iron, 18 in. revolving carbine barrel, straight grip walnut stock with brass buttplate, deluxe tuned action. Imported 2012-2016.

$785 $675 $575 $525 $425 $350 $275 *$940*

Add $7 for .44-40 WCF cal.

SMOKE WAGON – .38 Spl (disc. 2011)., .357 Mag., .44-40 WCF, or .45 LC cal., 3 1/2, 4 3/4 or 5 1/2 in. barrel, blue finish with case color hardened frame, checkered wood grips, low profile hammer, wider style sights. New 2008.

MSR $623 $530 $460 $400 $360 $290 $240 $210

Add $8 for .44-40 WCF cal.

* ***Smoke Wagon Short-Stroke Competition Series*** – .357 Mag. or .45 LC cal., case hardened frame, 4 3//4 or 5 1/2 in. barrel, 6 shot, steel backstrap and trigger guard, Navy size checkered walnut grips, 2.3 lbs. New 2017.

MSR $666 $575 $500 $430 $390 $315 $260 $220

Add $117 for Taylor tuned action with lightened trigger and hammer pull.

STALLION 1873 POCKET – .22 LR (new 2008) or .38 Spl. cal., 3 1/2, 4 3/4, or 5 1/2 in. round tapered blue barrel, scaled down SAA with small case hardened frame, 6 shot, one-piece walnut standard or bird's head smooth grips, steel or brass backstrap and trigger guard. Mfg. 1999-2004, reintroduced 2006.

MSR $524 $450 $400 $340 $300 $250 $200 $175

Add $21 for .38 Spl. (steel frame).
Add $27 for bird's head grips.
Add $36 for .22 LR/.22 WMR convertible cylinder.

GRADING - PPGS™	100%	98%	95%	90%	80%	70%	60%	LAST MSR

THE RANCH HAND – .22 LR, .357 Mag. or .45 LC cal., 4 (.45 LC cal. only, disc. 2013), 4 3/4, 5 1/2, or 7 1/2 in. barrel, forged frame, brass backstrap and trigger guard, smooth or checkered (mfg. 2014-2016) grips, blue finish with case hardened frame, approx. 2 1/2 lbs. Importation began 2012.

MSR $537	$460	$400	$350	$315	$250	$200	$180	

Add $14 for .357 Mag. or .45 LC cal.
Add $33 for checkered grips (mfg. 2014-2016).

UBERTI SINGLE ACTION/CATTLEMAN 12 SHOT – .22 LR cal., 4 3/4 or 5 1/2 in. barrel, 6 or 12 shot, brass (disc. 2018) or steel backstrap and trigger guard, case colored frame, smooth walnut grips. New 2013.

MSR $558	$475	$415	$350	$325	$260	$215	$185	

Add $25 for 12 shot.
Subtract approx. $30 for brass backstrap and trigger guard (mfg. 2013-2018).

REVOLVERS: REPRODUCTIONS, SCHOFIELD

1875 NO. 3 NEW MODEL RUSSIAN – .38 Spl. (disc. 2011), .44 Russian, .44-40 WCF (disc. 2011), or .45 LC cal., 6 shot, top-break action, 3 1/2 (disc. 2008), 5 (disc. 2008), or 6 1/2 (with lanyard ring and trigger guard spur, special order only until 2008 with case colored trigger guard), or 7 (disc. 2008) in. barrel with solid rib, automatic ejection, blue finish with smooth walnut grips. New 2007.

MSR $1,182	$1,000	$875	$750	$680	$550	$455	$390	

Add $17 for .44 Russian cal.
Subtract approx 12% for 3 1/2, 5, or 7 in. barrel.

NEW MODEL NO. 3 FRONTIER – .45 LC or .44 Spl. (new 2020) cal., forged steel frame, 5 or 6 1/2 in. barrel, blade rear sight, smooth or checkered (optional add-on) walnut grips, charcoal blue finish, approx. 2 1/2 lbs. New mid-2009.

MSR $1,182	$1,000	$875	$750	$680	$550	$455	$390	

Add $9 for .44 Spl. cal. (new 2020).

NO. 3 SECOND MODEL SCHOFIELD – .38 Spl., .44-40 WCF, .44 Russian (disc. 2013), or .45 LC cal., 3 1/2, 5, or 7 in. barrel with solid rib, case colored trigger guard, opening lever and hammer, smooth walnut grips, blued finish. New 2009.

MSR $1,170	$995	$870	$745	$675	$545	$450	$390	

Add $8 for .44-40 WCF cal.
Add $107 for charcoal blue finish with case hardened frame.
Add $210 for nickel finish.
Add $412 for nickel finish and pearl grip (.45 LC, 7 in. bbl. only).

RIFLES: REPRODUCTIONS, LEVER ACTION

1860 HENRY RIFLE – .44-40 WCF or .45 LC cal., 24 1/4 in. barrel, brass or steel frame, 13 shot mag., available in brass, case hardened, in-the-white, or laser engraved finish, with or w/o sling swivels.

MSR $1,463	$1,250	$1,095	$940	$850	$690	$565	$450	

Add $76 for steel frame (without sling swivels).
Add $88 for sling swivels.
Add $165 for in-the-white finish (without sling swivels).
Add $275 for charcoal blue barrel finish (with sling swivels).
Add $348 for laser engraving with hand chasing (without sling swivels).
Add $120 for transition model with hinged loading port (mfg. 2006-2008).

1860 HENRY TRAPPER RIFLE – .45 LC cal., 18 1/2 in. octagonal tapered blue barrel, brass frame and buttplate, no sling swivels, 8.8 lbs. Mfg. 2014-2016.

	$1,200	$1,050	$900	$815	$660	$550	$425	*$1,417*

1865 SPENCER CARBINE/RIFLE (160 SERIES) – .44 Russian (limited mfg., disc. 2006), .44-40 WCF (new 2005), .45 Schofield (disc. 2011), .45 LC (new 2012) or .56-50 cal., reproduction of the Civil War Spencer carbine, case colored receiver, lock, and hammer, 20 or 30 (rifle, new 2005) in. barrel, 7-9 shot mag., walnut stock and forearm, includes slings, mfg. by Armi-Sport. Imported 2002-2012, reintroduced 2016.

MSR $1,925	$1,640	$1,440	$1,235	$1,120	$900	$740	$575	

Add $118 for rifle.
Add $130 for Spencer carbine sling.

1866 SPORTING RIFLE – .32-20 WCF (disc. 2011), .38 Spl., .44-40 WCF, or .45 LC cal., 20 or 24 1/4 in. octagonal barrel, 13 shot, adj. rear with front blade sights, blue finish with forged brass frame, straight walnut stock, 8.8 lbs. Mfg. by Uberti. New 2002.

MSR $1,241	$1,050	$920	$795	$715	$580	$475	$375	

GRADING - PPGS™	100%	98%	95%	90%	80%	70%	60%	LAST MSR

1866 TRANSITION – .44-40 WCF or .45 LC cal., 24 1/4 in. barrel, side-hinged loading port, round magazine tube, brass frame, blue barrel finish, with or without custom wooden forend. Limited mfg. 2008-2011.

	$1,160	$1,000	$850	$725	$600	$500	$400	*$1,359*

Add $106 for custom wooden forend.

1866 TRAPPER RIFLE – .38 Spl. or .45 LC cal., 18 in. octagon barrel, 10 shot, blue finish with brass frame, adj. rear with front blade sights, straight walnut stock, 7.39 lbs. Mfg. by Uberti. Disc. 2016.

	$1,000	$875	$750	$680	$550	$450	$350	*$1,183*

1866 YELLOWBOY CARBINE – .32-20 (disc. 2007), .32 H&R Mag. (mfg. 2005-2007), .38 Spl., .44-40 WCF, or .45 LC cal., 19 in. round barrel, 10 shot, rear ladder sight with front blade on front barrel band, blue barrel with forged brass frame, walnut straight stock, with saddle ring, approx. 7 1/2 lbs. New 2003.

MSR $1,272	$1,085	$950	$815	$750	$595	$495	$380	

Add $5 for .44-40 WCF cal.

1873 CARBINE – .32-20 WCF (disc. 2010), .38-40 WCF (mfg. 2002 only), .357 Mag., .44 Spl. (disc. 2011), .44 Mag. (new 2011), .44-40 WCF (new 2008), or .45 LC cal., 16 1/8 or 19 in. round barrel, 9 or 10 (19 in. bbl. only) shot, front blade with rear ladder sights, carbine walnut stock, rubber stock pad (.44 Mag. cal. only), blue or case hardened finish, without saddle ring, 7.2- 7.48 lbs. New 2002.

MSR $1,281	$1,085	$950	$815	$740	$595	$490	$380	

Add $4 for .44-40 WCF cal.
Add $61 for case hardened frame (.357 Mag. cal. only).
Add $71 for .44 Mag. cal. with rubber stock pad.

* ***1873 Compact Carbine*** – .357 Mag. cal., 16 1/8 in. round barrel, blued frame, rear ladder and blade front sights, shortened (12.8 in. LOP) walnut stock with rubber pad, 7.2 lbs. New 2015.

MSR $1,281	$1,085	$950	$815	$740	$595	$490	$380	

1873 COMANCHERO – .357 Mag. or .45 LC cal., 18 or 20 in. octagonal barrel, 10 shot, case hardened frame, gold bead front sight, uncheckered (disc. 2018) or checkered (new 2013) straight grip stock or uncheckered (disc. 2018) or checkered pistol grip stock, custom tuning by Cody Conagher, buckskin lever covering and laced buckskin buttstock cover, blue finish, 7.39 lbs. New 2010.

MSR $1,916	$1,625	$1,420	$1,225	$1,100	$895	$725	$575	

Add $38 for pistol grip checkered stock.
Subtract approx. $75-$100 for uncheckered straight or uncheckered pistol grip stock (disc. 2018).
Add $71 for half round/half octagon barrel on pistol grip stock (mfg. 2010-2016, reintroduced 2019).
Add $560 for Comanchero action (includes action work, leather accessories, and gold bead sight), mfg. 2014-2018.
Add $33 for half round/half octagon barrel on straight stock (disc. 2016).

1873 LADIES & YOUTH CARBINE – .357 Mag./.38 Spl. cal., 16 1/8 in. round tapered barrel, 10 shot mag., forged steel frame, walnut stock with dark leather buttpad, gold bead front sight, blued receiver and furnishings. Mfg. by Uberti. Imported 2012-2016.

	$1,175	$1,025	$875	$750	$625	$525	$410	*$1,378*

* ***1873 Ladies & Youth Carbine Version II*** – .357 Mag./.38 Spl. cal., similar to 1873 Ladies & Youth Carbine, except features shortened stock for a shorter length of pull (12.8 in. LOP). New 2015.

MSR $1,465	$1,250	$1,095	$950	$850	$690	$565	$450	

1873 MAVERICK – .357 Mag. or .45 LC cal., 18 or 20 in. octagon barrel, choice of straight or pistol grip checkered stock, custom tuned by Cody Conager. Imported 2009 only.

	$1,475	$1,275	$1,050	$895	$750	$625	$525	*$1,600*

Add $105 for checkered pistol grip stock.

1873 RIFLE – .357 Mag., .44-40 (disc.), or .45 LC cal., 16 1/8 (disc.), 18, or 20 in. octagon barrel, 10 shot, adj. rear sight, case hardened frame, checkered straight stock, 7.59 lbs. New 2011. Mfg. by Uberti.

MSR $1,383	$1,175	$1,025	$875	$795	$650	$525	$425	

Add $312 for Taylor tuned action.

1873 RUNNIN' COMMANCHERO CARBINE – .44-40 WCF or .45 LC cal., short stroke action, 16 1/8 in. round barrel, 9 shot, blue frame, filled rear dovetail sight, walnut straight stock, buckskin lever wrap, elk leather buttstock cover, includes ladder-style factory sight, custom tuning, 7.2 lbs. New 2012.

MSR $1,932	$1,645	$1,440	$1,235	$1,120	$900	$740	$575	

Add $4 for .44-40 WCF cal.

GRADING - PPGS™	100%	98%	95%	90%	80%	70%	60%	LAST MSR

1873 SPECIAL SPORTING RIFLE – .45 LC, .44-40 WCF, or .357 Mag. cal., 18 or 24 1/4 (disc. 2018) in. 1/2 octagonal barrel, 13 shot, buckhorn rear and blade front sights, straight or checkered pistol grip walnut stock, blue finish with case hardened frame, 8.2 lbs.

MSR $1,350	$1,150	$1,000	$865	$780	$635	$525	$400	

Add $4 for .44-40 WCF cal.
Add $105 for checkered pistol grip stock.

1873 SPECIAL SPORTING RIFLE DELUXE – .357 Mag., .44-40 WCF, or .45 LC cal., 20, 24 1/4 (.45 LC only), or 30 (.45 LC only) in. octagonal barrel, 13 shot, buckhorn rear and blade front sights, checkered pistol grip walnut stock, blue finish with case hardened frame or white heat-treated steel barrel and frame (new 2012), 8.7 lbs. Current Mfg. by Uberti.

MSR $1,421	$1,210	$1,060	$910	$825	$665	$550	$425	

Add $9 for .44-40 WCF cal.
Add $57 for 30 in. barrel.
Add $113 for white heat-treated steel barrel and frame (new 2012).

1873 SPORTING RIFLE – .32-20 WCF (disc. 2004, reintroduced 2007-disc.), .357 Mag., .38-40 WCF (disc. 2004, reintroduced 2007), .44-40 WCF, .44 Spl. (disc.), or .45 LC cal., 20 or 24 1/4 in. octagonal barrel, 13 shot, buckhorn rear and blade front sights, straight walnut stock, blue finish with case hardened frame, or antique (new 2011) barrel and frame finish, 8.2 lbs. New 2002.

MSR $1,314	$1,120	$980	$840	$760	$615	$500	$390	

Add $5 for .44-40 WCF cal.
Add $17 for .38-40 WCF cal.
Add $113 for white finish.
Add $208 for Antique finish (new 2011).

1873 TAYLOR'S TRAPPER – .44-40 WCF (new 2008), .357 Mag., or .45 LC cal., forged steel frame, 18 in. tapered full octagonal barrel, 10 shot, buckhorn rear and blade front sights, straight or checkered pistol grip (disc. 2018) walnut stock, blue finish with case hardened frame, 7.39 lbs. New 2006.

MSR $1,314	$1,120	$980	$840	$760	$615	$500	$390	

Add $98 for checkered pistol grip walnut stock (disc. 2018).

1876 CENTENNIAL CARBINE/RIFLE (SPORTING) – .40-60 (disc. 2011), .45-60, .45-75 (disc. 2011), or .50-95 cal., 22 (disc. 2015) or 28 in. round (carbine, disc. 2015) or octagon (rifle) barrel, 11 shot, buckhorn rear and blade front sights, blue finish with case colored frame, 10 lbs. New 2006.

MSR $1,647	$1,400	$1,225	$1,050	$950	$775	$650	$525	

Add $21 for .50-95 cal.
Add $83 for round barrel (disc. 2015).

1883 BURGESS CARBINE – .44-40 WCF or .45 LC cal., 20 or 25 1/2 in. round barrel, 10 or 13 (.45 LC, 25 1/2 in.) shot, front blade with rear ladder sights, uncheckered straight grip walnut stock, blue finish, no saddle ring, 7.6 lbs. Mfg. 2009-2016.

	$1,225	$1,075	$925	$835	$675	$550	$450	*$1,440*

Add $21 for 25 1/2 in. barrel.

1883 BURGESS RIFLE – .44-40 WCF (disc. 2016) or .45 LC cal., case hardened frame, 20 or 25 1/2 (disc. 2016) in. round (disc. 2016) or octagon barrel, 10 or 13 (.45 LC, 25 1/2 in. bbl., disc. 2016), adj. rear sights, uncheckered straight grip walnut stock, 7.6 lbs. New 2009.

MSR $1,505	$1,280	$1,110	$950	$850	$700	$575	$450	

1886 CARBINE – .444 Marlin or .45-70 Govt. cal., 22 in. round barrel with saddle ring, case colored frame with blue barrel and mag. tube. Mfg. 2008-2013.

This model was listed as P.O.R.

1886 RIDGE RUNNER RIFLE – .45-70 Govt. cal., 18 1/2 in. octagonal barrel, muzzle brake, 4 shot, integrated Skinner peep and Picatinny rail rear sight, front fiber optic sight, sling swivels, "D" shaped lever, soft touch black stock with rubber buttpad, matte black or hard chrome finish, 7.8 lbs. New 2015.

MSR $1,728	$1,465	$1,275	$1,100	$995	$800	$675	$525	

Add $102 for hard chrome finish.

1886 RIFLE – .444 Marlin (disc. 2013) or .45-70 Govt. cal., 26 in. octagonal barrel, 8 shot, adj. rear with front blade sights, case colored frame, straight walnut stock, 9 lbs. Mfg. by Chiappa. New 2008.

MSR $1,709	$1,450	$1,275	$1,090	$985	$800	$650	$510	

1886 SPORTING RIFLE – .45-70 Govt. cal., 26 in. octagonal barrel with blue finish, 5 shot, case hardened receiver, front dovetail blade and rear buckhorn sights, checkered stock and forend. Mfg. by Pedersoli. Importation began 2017.

MSR $1,909	$1,625	$1,420	$1,225	$1,100	$895	$730	$575	

GRADING - PPGS™	100%	98%	95%	90%	80%	70%	60%	LAST MSR

1886 TAKEDOWN CLASSIC – .45-70 Govt. cal., 26 in. octagonal barrel, 8 shot, adj. rear with front blade sights, case hardened frame, takedown receiver, checkered straight walnut stock, 9 lbs. Mfg. by Chiappa. New 2015.

MSR $1,623	$1,380	$1,210	$1,035	$940	$750	$625	$485	

1886/71 BOARBUSTER RIFLE – .444 Marlin cal., 19 in. barrel, 5 shot, adj. rear sight, European Picatinny style base with integral rear sight, half cock safety on the hammer and a safety on the slide catch at rear of frame, walnut checkered pistol grip stock and forend, metal parts are blued, tang is drilled and tapped, 7.26 lbs. Mfg. by Pedersoli. Mfg. 2013-2016.

	$1,740	$1,525	$1,300	$1,185	$955	$785	$625	*$1,940*

1886/71 PEDERSOLI CLASSIC RIFLE – .45-70 Govt. cal., 24 in. PMG (Pedersoli Match Grade) barrel, 5 shot mag., solid steel locking lugs, drilled and tapped for Creedmoor sight, tunnel front sight, blue barrel and magazine plug, checkered walnut pistol grip stock and forend, ultra light microcell memory buttplate, 7 1/2 lbs.

MSR $1,740	$1,480	$1,295	$1,110	$1,000	$815	$665	$525	

1886/71 WILDBUSTER RIFLE – .45-70 Govt. cal., 24 in. barrel, 5 shot, ramp rear sight, walnut forend and pistol grip stock with a checkered buttplate, blue finish, 8.15 lbs. Mfg. by Pedersoli. New 2013.

MSR $1,697	$1,445	$1,265	$1,085	$985	$795	$650	$500	

1892 ALASKAN TAKEDOWN CARBINE/RIFLE – .357 Mag. (new 2014), .45 LC (mfg. 2017-2018), or .44 Mag. cal., 16 or 20 in. standard or threaded (new 2019, 16 in. only) barrel, 7 or 10 shot, large loop lever, matte chrome or matte black (new 2017) finish, overmolded black rubber coated wood stock, recoil pad, Skinner Express rear sight, drilled and tapped, takedown action, "Alaskan" engraved on receiver. New 2013.

MSR $1,412	$1,200	$1,050	$900	$815	$660	$550	$450	

Add $88 for matte chrome finish.
Add $50 for survival bag.
Add $118 for matte chrome standard loop lever.

1892 CARBINE – .32-20 WCF (disc. 2006), .32 H&R Mag. (disc. 2006), .38-40 WCF (disc. 2006), .38 Spl. (disc. 2006), .44 S&W (disc. 2006), .357 Mag., .44-40 WCF, or .45 LC cal., 20 in. round barrel, 10 shot, rear ladder and blade front sights, straight walnut stock with standard loop, blue finish with case hardened frame, 6.2 lbs. Current Mfg. by Chiappa.

MSR $1,310	$1,120	$980	$840	$760	$615	$500	$390	

Add $19 for .357 Mag. or .45 LC cal.

1892 RIFLE – .32-20 (disc. 2005), .32 H&R Mag. (disc. 2005), .357 Mag., .38-40 (disc. 2010), .38 Spl. (disc. 2010), .44 S&W (disc. 2005), .44-40 WCF, .45 LC, or .44 Mag. (20 in. only, new 2014) cal., 16 (new 2017), 20, or 24 in. octagonal barrel, 11 shot, buckhorn rear and blade front sights, straight walnut stock with oil finish, blue barrel finish with case hardened frame or chrome (mfg. 2017-2018), 7.3 lbs. Current Mfg. by Chiappa.

MSR $1,310	$1,120	$980	$840	$760	$615	$500	$390	

Add $15 for .44-40 cal.
Add $19 for 20 or 24 in. barrel.
Add $204 for chrome finish (16 in. bbl., .357 Mag. cal. only, mfg. 2017-2018).

1892 RIO BRAVO CARBINE – .357 Mag. (new 2014), .44-40 WCF or .45 LC cal., 20 in. round barrel, 10 shot, 6 grooves, rear ladder and blade front sights, straight walnut stock with oil finish, large loop lever, blue finish with case hardened frame, 6.2 lbs. Mfg. by Chiappa. New 2007.

MSR $1,350	$1,150	$1,000	$865	$780	$635	$525	$425	

1892 TAKEDOWN RIFLE – .32-20 (disc. 2005), .32 H&R Mag. (disc. 2005), .38 Spl. (disc. 2005), .38-40, .357 Mag., .44-40 (disc.), .44 S&W (disc. 2005), or .45 LC cal., 20 or 24 in. octagonal barrel, 10 shot, buckhorn rear and blade front sights, blue barrel finish with case hardened receiver, walnut stock with oil finish, rifle is able to be broke down into two pieces for easy transport, 6.2 lbs. Mfg. by Chiappa 2003-2008, reintroduced 2014.

MSR $1,370	$1,165	$1,025	$875	$795	$650	$525	$425	

1892 TAYLOR HUNTSMAN – .357 Mag., .45 LC, or .44 Mag. cal., 16 in. round barrel, deluxe Skinner rear sight and fluorescent high visibility front sight, matte blue finish, 5 1/2 lbs. Mfg. 2017-2018.

	$1,080	$945	$800	$730	$575	$475	$375	*$1,273*

1892 TRAPPER RIFLE – .357 Mag. or .45 LC cal., 16 in. octagonal barrel, 7 shot, buckhorn rear and blade front sights, blue finish with case hardened frame or chrome (disc. 2018) finish, straight walnut stock, 6 lbs. Current Mfg. by Chiappa.

MSR $1,310	$1,120	$980	$840	$760	$615	$500	$390	

Add $204 for chrome finish (disc. 2018).

GRADING - PPGS™	100%	98%	95%	90%	80%	70%	60%	LAST MSR

UBERTI SCOUT RIFLE – .22 LR or .22 Mag. (new 2015) cal., 19 in. blue barrel, chrome plated alloy receiver, 15 shot, Dovetail rear and front blade sights, straight grip walnut finished hardwood, black soft touch (mfg. 2015), or pink soft touch (mfg. 2015) stock, 5.8 lbs. New 2013.

MSR $581	$495	$435	$370	$335	$270	$225	$175	

Add $92 for .22 Mag. cal. (new 2015).
Add $43 for black or pink soft touch stock (mfg. 2015 only).

RIFLES: REPRODUCTIONS, SINGLE SHOT

1863 SHARPS CARBINE – .50-70 cal., 22 in. round barrel, fixed front sight. Mfg. 2014-2016.

	$1,135	$995	$850	$770	$625	$510	$400	*$1,332*

1874 CAVALRY CARBINE – .45-70 Govt. or .50-70 (mfg. 2005-2006) cal., 22 in. round blue barrel with color case hardened frame, single trigger, fixed front sight, walnut stock, 9.7 lbs. Current Mfg. by Chiappa.

MSR $1,300	$1,100	$965	$825	$750	$600	$500	$400	

Add approx. 10% for .50-70 cal.

1874 SHARPS BUSINESS – .45-70 Govt. cal., 28 in. octagon barrel, double set trigger, Buckhorn rear sight, blue finish with color case hardened receiver, classic walnut stock and Schnabel forend, 8.59 lbs. Mfg. by Chiappa. New 2014.

MSR $1,418	$1,200	$1,050	$900	$815	$660	$550	$450	

1874 SHARPS CAVALRY CARBINE – .45-70 Govt. cal., 22 in. round barrel retained by steel bands, fixed front sight, drilled and tapped, 8.37 lbs. Mfg. by Pedersoli. New 2014.

MSR $1,563	$1,325	$1,160	$995	$900	$725	$595	$465	

1874 SHARPS INFANTRY/BERDAN MODEL – .45-70 Govt. cal., 30 in. barrel, musket configuration with 3 barrel bands and patchbox. Disc. 2006.

	$925	$775	$625	$500	$425	$375	$350	*$1,045*

Add $45 for Berdan model with DT.

1874 SHARPS LIGHT – .17 Hornet, .22 Hornet, or .22 LR (new 2015) cal., 24 in. round barrel, double set trigger, straight grip uncheckered walnut stock and forearm, drilled and tapped, color case hardened frame, matte blue finish, 7.7 lbs. Mfg. by Pedersoli, 2014-2018.

	$1,350	$1,180	$1,015	$925	$750	$625	$500	*$1,582*

Add $23 for .22 Hornet or POR for .17 Hornet cal.

1874 SHARPS QUIGLEY DOWN UNDER – .45-70 Govt., .45-120, or .38-55 (mfg. 2014-2015) cal., 32 (.45-70 cal. only) or 34 in. octagon barrel, exact reproduction of rifle used in the "*Quigley Down Under*" movie, includes Hartford style pewter forend tip, double set trigger, fixed front and rear ladder sights, case hardened frame, checkered walnut stock with patchbox. Current Mfg. by Chiappa.

MSR $1,670	$1,425	$1,250	$1,075	$975	$785	$650	$550	

Add $129 for 34 in. barrel.
Add $134 for .45-120 cal. with 34 in. barrel.
Add $149 for .38-55 cal. with 34 in. barrel (disc. 2015).

1874 SHARPS QUIGLEY DOWN UNDER SPORT – .45-70 Govt. cal., 34 in. barrel, European walnut stock with patchbox, German silver forearm cap, case colored frame, blade front and rear ladder sights, 13.21 lbs. Mfg. by Pedersoli. New 2008.

MSR $2,146	$1,825	$1,595	$1,375	$1,240	$1,000	$825	$650	

1874 SHARPS SPORTING RIFLE – .45-70 Govt. cal., 32 in. octagon barrel, case hardened or white (disc. 2013) frame and blue barrel finish, Schnabel forearm or pewter Hartford-style forend tip, double set trigger, oil-finished walnut stock, receiver, breechblock, and trigger plate all machined from a solid piece of steel, one-piece pre-drilled tang, dovetail front sight.

MSR $1,418	$1,200	$1,050	$900	$815	$660	$550	$450	

Add $83 for Hartford-style pewter forend tip.
Add $269 for white frame finish (disc. 2013).

1885 HIGH WALL – .38-55 WCF (new 2005), .45 LC (mfg. 2009-disc.), or .45-70 Govt. cal., 30 or 32 in. octagon barrel, forged steel, Buckhorn rear and blade front sights, straight walnut stock and forearm, single or double set triggers, blue barrel finish and case hardened frame, includes brass rod cleaning kit in the buttstock, 9 1/2 lbs. Mfg. by Uberti. New 1999.

MSR $981	$835	$730	$625	$570	$460	$375	$290	

Add $105 for .45-70 Govt. cal.
Add $128 for .38-55 WCF cal.
Add $147 for 32 in. barrel (.45-70 cal. only).
Add $170 for double set trigger.

GRADING - PPGS™	100%	98%	95%	90%	80%	70%	60%	LAST MSR

* ***1885 High Wall Checkered Pistol Grip*** – .38-55 WCF or .45-70 Govt. cal., similar to 1885 High Wall, except has checkered pistol grip stock.

MSR $1,239	$1,050	$925	$795	$715	$580	$475	$375	

Add $25 for .38-55 WCF cal.
Add $25 for 32 in. barrel (.45-70 cal. only).
Add $170 for double set trigger.

1885 LOW WALL – .17 HMR (mfg. 2005-2007), .17 Mach II (mfg. 2005-2007), .22 LR, .32-20 (disc. 2016), .38-40 WCF (disc. 2016), or .45 LC (new 2008) cal., 30 in. octagon barrel, forged steel, Buckhorn rear and blade front sights, single or double set trigger, color case hardened frame and blue barrel finish, checkered pistol grip walnut stock, 9 lbs. Current Mfg. by Uberti.

MSR $1,149	$975	$855	$730	$665	$535	$440	$340	

Add $170 for double set trigger.
Add $34 for .32-20 (disc. 2016) or .38-40 WCF (disc. 2016) cal.

HALF-PINT SHARPS – .22 Win. Mag., .22 LR, .45 LC, .44-40 Win., .38-55, .22 Hornet, .30-30 Win., .17 HMR, or .218 Bee cal., 24 or 26 in. barrel, 20% smaller version of the original Sharps rifle, double trigger, rear Creedmoor and blade front sights, blue barrel finish and case hardened frame, walnut stock, 5 1/2 lbs. Current Mfg. by Armi Chiappa.

MSR $1,389	$1,175	$1,025	$875	$795	$650	$525	$425	

HALF-PINT SPORTING RIFLE – .22 LR cal., 24 in. barrel, chrome plated alloy frame, double set trigger, walnut stock. Limited availability 2013 only.

This model was only listed as P.O.R.

HIGH WALL CLASSIC – .38-55 or .45-70 Govt. cal., 30 or 32 in. carbon steel barrel in matte blue finish, single set trigger, Winchester-type rear and blade front sights, drilled and tapped, original style lever, pistol grip stock with checkered grip panels and cheekpiece, large buttplate, case hardened frame. Mfg. by Pedersoli. New 2014.

MSR $2,135	$1,815	$1,590	$1,360	$1,235	$1,000	$815	$635	

* ***High Wall Sporting*** – .38-55 or .45-70 Govt. cal., 30 or 32 in. carbon steel barrel in matte blue finish, single set trigger, Winchester-type rear and blade front sights, pistol grip stock with checkered grip panels and cheekpiece, large buttplate, drilled and tapped, Schuetzen style lever. Mfg. by Pedersoli. New 2014.

MSR $2,135	$1,815	$1,590	$1,360	$1,235	$1,000	$815	$635	

LITTLE BADGER – .22 LR or .22 Mag. (new 2015) cal., 16 1/2 in. barrel, adj. rear sight, folding stock, includes nylon carry bag and special cartridge holder, 3 1/2 lbs. Mfg. 2014-2018.

	$185	$160	$140	$125	$100	$85	$75	*$217*

LITTLE SHARPS HUNTER – .17 Hornet cal., 24 in. half round/half octagon barrel with matte blue finish, double trigger, drilled and tapped, no sights, walnut stock and forend, rubber buttpad, color case hardened finish, 5 1/2 lbs. Mfg. by Chiappa 2014-2016.

	$935	$810	$695	$630	$510	$425	$325	*$1,110*

LITTLE SHARPS TARGET – .17 Hornet cal., 26 in. matte blue heavy octagon barrel, double trigger, spirit level front globe sight with interchangeable blades and a middle range diopter tang sight, drilled and tapped, checkered walnut stock, white satin frame with blued screws, 5 1/2 lbs. Mfg. by Chiappa 2014-2016.

	$1,090	$955	$820	$740	$600	$500	$400	*$1,281*

ROLLING BLOCK BABY CARBINE – .22 LR (new 2012), .22 WMR (new 2012), .357 Mag., .44-40 WCF (disc. 2011), or .45 LC (disc. 2011) cal., 22 in. round blued barrel, adj. rear with Dovetail front blade sights, case hardened receiver, brass buttplate and trigger guard, uncheckered straight grip walnut stock, 5.04 lbs. Mfg. by Uberti. New mid-2009.

MSR $736	$625	$545	$470	$425	$345	$275	$225	

Add $15 for .357 Mag. cal.

ROLLING BLOCK CREEDMORE NO. 2 – .45-70 Govt. cal., 30 in. round blue barrel, coin finished frame, double set triggers, Long Range Creedmore and front globe sights, checkered walnut pistol grip stock and forend, 9 1/4 lbs. Mfg. by Pedersoli. New mid-2009.

MSR $1,909	$1,625	$1,425	$1,225	$1,100	$895	$725	$575	

ROLLING BLOCK JOHN BODINE – .45-70 Govt. or .45-90 cal., 30 or 34 in. blue octagon barrel, case hardened frame, double set triggers, includes Long Range Creedmore and front globe sights, walnut checkered pistol grip stock, forend has inlet German silver cap, 11.9 lbs. Mfg. by Pedersoli. New mid-2009.

MSR $2,024	$1,725	$1,510	$1,295	$1,175	$950	$775	$600	

Add $44 for .45-90 cal.

GRADING - PPGS™	100%	98%	95%	90%	80%	70%	60%	LAST MSR

ROLLING BLOCK MISSISSIPPI – .45 LC or .357 Mag. cal., alloy frame is engraved with old silver finish, 26 in. broach rifled carbon steel barrel, brass trigger guard, blue finish. Mfg. by Pedersoli. Importation began 2017.

MSR $984 $835 $730 $625 $570 $460 $375 $290

SPRINGFIELD TRAPDOOR CARBINE – .45-70 Govt. cal., 22 in. round barrel with barrel band, Buckhorn rear and blade front sights, uncheckered straight grip walnut stock, blue finish with case colored trapdoor, 7.27 lbs. Mfg. by Pedersoli. New 2008.

MSR $1,551 $1,325 $1,160 $995 $900 $730 $595 $465

RIFLES: REPRODUCTIONS, SLIDE ACTION

LIGHTNING SLIDE ACTION CARBINE/RIFLE – .357 Mag. (disc. 2011), .44-40 WCF (disc. 2011), or .45 LC cal., 20 in. round, 24 1/4 (rifle only), or 26 in. octagon barrel, case colored frame, straight grip walnut stock with checkered forearm. Mfg. 2007-2014.

$935 $820 $700 $635 $515 $425 $325 *$1,098*

Add $37 for 26 in. round barrel.
Add $65 for 20 in. octagon barrel or $92 for 24 1/4 in. octagon barrel.

PREMIUM LIGHTNING – .357 Mag. or .45 LC cal., case hardened frame, 20, 24 (new 2017), or 26 (new 2017) in. octagon barrel, 10 or 12 shot mag., checkered semi-fancy walnut stock, 6.39 lbs. New 2014.

MSR $1,836 $1,565 $1,375 $1,175 $1,065 $860 $700 $550

Add $21 for 24 in. barrel (new 2017).

STANDARD LIGHTNING – .357 Mag. or .45 LC cal., 20 or 26 (new 2017) in. round barrel, blue receiver and furniture, walnut stock, 6.39 lbs. New 2014.

MSR $1,563 $1,320 $1,150 $995 $900 $725 $600 $475

Add $32 for 26 in. barrel (new 2017).

RIFLES: SEMI-AUTO

M4 22 – .22 LR cal., blowback action, 16 in. solid steel barrel, 10 or 28 shot mag., fire control group, dust cover, adj. sights, pseudo flash hider, bayonet lug, forward assist, and bolt release, quad rail capable forearm, includes two mags, 5 1/2 lbs. Mfg. 2011-2012.

$350 $295 $260 $230 $200 $180 $165 *$419*

RIFLES/SHOTGUNS: O/U COMBINATIONS

DOUBLE BADGER – .410/.22 Mag. or .410/.22 LR cal., 19 in. barrels, adj. fiber optic sights, drilled and tapped, front trigger fires the bottom barrel and the rear trigger fires the top barrel, blue finish. Mfg. 2015-2016.

$325 $285 $245 $220 $180 $145 $115 *$376*

X CALIBER SURVIVAL RIFLE – 12 ga./.22 LR cal., 18 1/2 in. round barrel, this rifle can fire up to 12 different calibers due to the 8 steel adapters supplied (also allows user to shoot 8 additional pistol cals. and two shotgun cals.), 2 shot, Picatinny rails, fiber optic front and adj. rear sights, polypropylene foam stock with storage space, black finish, 5.9 lbs. Mfg. 2015-2018.

$750 $650 $565 $510 $415 $350 $275 *$887*

SHOTGUNS: LEVER ACTION

1887 "BOOTLEG" – 12 ga., 18 1/2 in. barrel, 5 shot mag., matte black or case hardened (deluxe model) receiver and barrel, walnut stock, 7.9 lbs. New 2015.

MSR $1,275 $1,075 $925 $800 $725 $585 $485 $400

Add $81 for Deluxe model with case hardened frame.
Add $50 for Survival bag.

1887 COWBOY HUNTER – 12 ga., 22 in. blue barrel, includes coversion kit to transform from 1887 standard model to a Fast Load System shotgun and back again, brass bead front sight, case hardened frame, walnut stock, 9 lbs. Mfg. by Chiappa 2014-2016.

$1,175 $1,030 $880 $800 $650 $550 $425 *$1,381*

1887 LEVER ACTION SHOTGUN (STANDARD MODEL) – 12 ga., 2 3/4 in. chamber, matte chrome (disc. 2016) or color case hardened frame, 22 or 28 in. barrel, includes three Old-style Beretta chokes and wrench, uncheckered pistol grip American walnut stock, with (22 in. barrel only) or without Fast Load (disc. 2013), 6.6 lbs. Mfg. by Chiappa. New mid-2009.

MSR $1,480 $1,250 $1,100 $950 $850 $700 $575 $450

Add $39 for 22 in. barrel with matte chrome or $81 for 28 in. barrel with matte chrome finish (disc. 2016).

GRADING - PPGS™	100%	98%	95%	90%	80%	70%	60%	LAST MSR

1887 T-MODEL – 12 ga., 18 1/2 in. barrel, 5 shot mag., drilled and tapped, black rubber overmolded stock with softtouch coating, matte black finish. New 2015.

MSR $1,312	$1,115	$975	$835	$760	$615	$500	$400	

Add $50 for Survival bag.
Add $189 for wood stock attachment.

1887 ZOMBIE BLASTER – 12 ga., 18 1/2 in. round barrel, 5 shot mag., Soft Touch stock, matte black finish, 7.9 lbs. Mfg. 2015-2016.

	$1,050	$925	$795	$715	$575	$475	$375	*$1,201*

SHOTGUNS: REPRODUCTIONS

1878 COACH GUN – 12 ga., 20 in. barrel, blue frame, steel buttplate, uncheckered (disc.) or checkered (new 2011) walnut pistol grip stock, double triggers, 6.7 lbs. Mfg. by CZ, mid-2009-2015.

	$800	$750	$695	$595	$450	$375	$300	*$905*

DOUBLE BARREL HAMMER COACH GUN – 12 ga., 3 in. chambers, color case hardened frame, 20 in. barrels, rebounding mule-ear external hammers, double triggers, no sights, checkered walnut pistol grip stock and forearm, 6.7 lbs. Current Mfg. by CZ USA.

MSR $963	$825	$725	$625	$560	$450	$375	$300	

SxS MODEL – 12 ga., 28 9/16 in. barrels with chokes, approx. 7 lbs. Mfg. by Pedersoli.

	$695	$595	$475	$350	$275	$200	$150	*$1,122*

TAYLOR'S DOUBLE BARREL – 28 ga., 3 in. chamber, 28 in. barrel, interchangeable chokes, manual extractor, double trigger action, floral engraving on receiver, white engraved frame and blued barrel. New 2019.

MSR $1,795	$1,525	$1,335	$1,150	$1,035	$850	$685	$550	

TRIPLE CROWN – 12 ga., three 28 in. barrels, includes five Remington chokes, fixed front sight, firing sequence is bottom right, bottom left, then top barrel, white finished receiver, checkered pistol grip stock, 8.7 lbs. Mfg. by Chiappa. New 2014.

MSR $1,929	$1,640	$1,435	$1,225	$1,115	$900	$740	$600	

TRIPLE THREAT – 12 ga., three 18 1/2 in. barrels, includes Rem Chokes, 3 shot, blue receiver, fixed front sight, two-piece walnut stock, 8 lbs. Mfg. by Chiappa. New 2014.

MSR $1,955	$1,665	$1,450	$1,250	$1,125	$915	$750	$600	

WYATT EARP COACH GUN – 12 ga., SxS, 20 in. chrome bored barrels, checkered pistol grip walnut stock, color case hardened frame with or w/o (new 2013) Wyatt Earp stamp, fast shell loading, blue finish, approx. 7 lbs. Mfg. by Pedersoli. New 2011.

MSR $1,535	$1,300	$1,140	$975	$885	$715	$585	$450	

TECHNO ARMS (PTY) LIMITED

Previous manufacturer located in Johannesburg, S. Africa circa 1994-1996. Previously imported by Vulcans Forge, Inc. located in Foxboro, MA.

SHOTGUNS: SLIDE ACTION

MAG-7 SLIDE ACTION SHOTGUN – 12 ga. (60mm chamber length), 5 shot detachable mag. (in pistol grip), 14, 16, 18, or 20 in. barrel, straight grip or pistol grip stock, matte finish, 8 lbs. Imported 1995-96.

	$795	$675	$625	$550	$500	$450	$400	*$875*

TEDNA

Previous brand name of shotguns manufactured in Turkey and imported by Zenith Firearms located in Afton, VA until 2017.

SHOTGUNS

All shotguns came with a rugged plastic carry case, factory cleaning kit, combination trigger lock, and a 5-year warranty.

AVANTGARDE O/U – 12 or 20 ga., 3 in. chamber, O/U, 26, 28, or 30 in. barrels, 5-piece mobile choke set, 2 shot, steel receiver, 14 1/2 in. LOP, single trigger, auto ejector, red fiber optic front with brass mid-bead sight, Turkish walnut stock, silver or case hardened sideplates, rubber recoil pad, includes plastic carry case, 6.7-7.9 lbs., mfg. in Turkey by Tedna. Imported until 2017.

	$500	$435	$370	$335	$275	$225	$175	*$578*

GRADING - PPGS™	100%	98%	95%	90%	80%	70%	60%	LAST MSR

EXCELLENCE O/U – 12 or 20 ga., 2 3/4-3 in. chamber, O/U, 26, 28, or 30 in. steel barrels, 5-piece mobile choke set, 2 shot, auto ejector, single trigger, red fiber optic front sight with brass mid-bead, Turkish walnut stock with silver or case hardened sideplates, rubber recoil pad, 14.5 in. LOP, monobloc steel receiver, 6 3/4-7.95 lbs., mfg. in Turkey by Tedna. Imported until 2017.

$515	$450	$385	$350	$285	$235	$185	*$609*

EXCELLENCE COACH SxS – 12 or 20 ga., 2 3/4-3 in. chamber, SxS, 18 1/2 in. steel, chrome-lined barrel, IC/M chokes, 2 shot, monobloc steel receiver, single trigger, brass bead sight, Turkish walnut stock, case hardened sideplates, metal buttplate or rubber recoil pad, 6 1/2-6 3/4 lbs., mfg. in Turkey by Tedna. Imported until 2017.

$565	$495	$425	$385	$315	$250	$200	*$652*

EXCELLENCE SPORTING SxS – 12 or 20 ga., 2 3/4-3 in. chamber, SxS, 26 in. steel, chrome-lined barrel, 5-piece mobile choke set, 2 shot, monobloc steel receiver, single trigger, white bead sights, Turkish walnut stock, case hardened sideplates, rubber recoil pad, 14 1/2 in. LOP, 6.85-7.25 lbs., mfg. in Turkey by Tedna. Imported until 2017.

$565	$495	$425	$385	$315	$250	$200	*$652*

G125 – 12 ga., 2 3/4-3 in. chamber, semi-auto, gas operated, 28 in. steel, chrome-lined barrel, 5-piece mobile choke set, 4 shot mag., matte black alloy receiver, red fiber optic front sight with brass mid-bead, Turkish walnut stock, rubber recoil pad, 14 1/4 in. LOP, 7.55 lbs., mfg. in Turkey by Tedna. Imported until 2017.

$335	$295	$250	$230	$185	$150	$115	*$399*

G125P – 12 ga., 2 3/4-3 in. chamber, semi-auto, gas operated, 28 in. steel, chrome-lined barrel, 5-piece mobile choke set, 4 shot, matte black alloy receiver, red fiber optic front sight, synthetic stock, rubber recoil pad, 14 1/4 in. LOP, 7.6 lbs., mfg. in Turkey by Tedna. Imported until 2017.

$335	$295	$250	$230	$185	$150	$115	*$394*

K125 – 12 ga., 2 3/4-3 in. chamber, semi-auto, kinetic operation, 28 in. steel, chrome-lined barrel, 5-piece mobile choke set, 4 shot mag., matte black alloy receiver, red fiber optic front sight with brass mid-bead, Turkish walnut stock, rubber recoil pad, 14 1/4 in. LOP, 7 lbs., mfg. in Turkey by Tedna. Imported until 2017.

$335	$295	$250	$230	$185	$150	$115	*$399*

P12/P20 – 12 or 20 ga., 2 3/4-3 in. chamber, slide action, 26 (20 ga.) or 28 (12 ga.) in. steel, chrome-lined barrel, 5-piece mobile choke set, 4 shot, matte black alloy receiver, red fiber optic front sight, Turkish walnut stock, rubber recoil pad, 14 1/4 in. LOP, 6.2-7 lbs., mfg. in Turkey by Tedna. Imported until 2017.

$235	$200	$175	$150	$125	$100	$75	*$278*

P12T PUMP TACTICAL – 12 ga., 2 3/4-3 in. chamber, slide action, 18 1/2 in. steel, chrome-lined barrel, external knurled breaching choke, 4 shot, matte black alloy receiver, protected red fiber optic front and ghost ring rear sights, black synthetic stock, rubber recoil pad, 14 1/4 in. LOP, 6 1/2 lbs., mfg. in Turkey by Tedna. Imported until 2017.

$215	$195	$165	$145	$125	$95	$65	*$262*

PRIME S/SE O/U – 12 or 20 ga., 2 3/4-3 in. chamber, O/U, 26, 28, or 30 in. steel, chome-lined barrel, 5-piece mobile choke set, 2 shot mag., monobloc steel receiver, extractor (S) or auto ejector (SE), single trigger, white bead sights (S) or red fiber optic front with brass mid-bead (SE), Turkish walnut stock with black sideplates (S) or silver or case hardened sideplates (SE), rubber recoil pad, 6.9-7.7 lbs. Mfg. in Turkey by Tedna. Imported until 2017.

$425	$375	$325	$295	$235	$195	$150	*$494*

Add $60 for silver or case hardened sideplates.

TELO, RENATO

Current manufacturer located in Brescia, Italy. Currently imported by Kevin's Fine Outdoor Gear & Apparel, located in Thomasville, GA.

Renato Telo manufactures best quality O/U long guns with and without sideplates, with prices starting at $15,995. Please contact the importer directly for more information, including models, availability, delivery time and U.S. pricing.

TEMPLAR CUSTOM ARMS

Current custom pistol, AR-15 style rifle/shotgun, and bolt action rifle manufacturer located in Windham, OH since 2010.

Templar Custom Arms specializes in combative pistols, bolt action rifles, and AR-15 style rifles/shotguns built to customer specifications. Please contact the company directly for more information including pricing, options, and availability.

GRADING - PPGS™	100%	98%	95%	90%	80%	70%	60%	LAST MSR

TEMPLAR CUSTOM, LLC (TEMPLAR CONSULTING)

Previous AR-15 rifle and component manufacturer located in Apex, NC 2008-2017.

Please refer to BlueBookOfGunValues.com to order the *Blue Book of AR-15s & Variations*, available as a book or online subscription.

TEMPLAR TACTICAL ARMS LLC

Previous AR-15 manufacturer located in Bozeman, MT 2008-2014.

Please refer to BlueBookOfGunValues.com to order the *Blue Book of AR-15s & Variations*, available as a book or online subscription.

TEMPLAR TACTICAL FIREARMS

Previous bolt action rifle and current suppressor manufacturer located in Spring, TX.

For individual model listings, please go to BlueBookOfGunValues.com/overflow.

TERRIER ONE

Previous trademark distributed by Serrifile located in Lancaster, CA.

REVOLVERS

TERRIER ONE – .32 S&W cal., double action, 2 1/4 in. barrel, 5 shot, nickel-plated, 17 oz. Mfg. 1984-87.

$90	$80	$70	$60	$45	$30	$25	*$55*

TESRO SPORTWAFFEN GMBH & CO. KG

Current manufacturer located in Bächingen, Germany. Previously located in Niederstotzingen, Germany. No current U.S. importation.

Tesro also manufactures high quality air pistols and air rifles. Please contact the company directly for more information regarding U.S. availability and pricing.

PISTOLS: SEMI-AUTO

TS 22-3 – .22 LR cal., 4.45 in. barrel, target model with ergonomic wood grips, 5 shot mag., black finish, adj. rear sight, 2 1/4 lbs.

Please contact the company directly for U.S. availablity and pricing.

TS 32-3 – .32 Wadcutter cal., 4.45 in. barrel, target model with ergonomic wood grips, 5 shot mag., black finish, adj. rear sight, 2 1/4 lbs.

Please contact the company directly for U.S. availablity and pricing.

TEXAS ARMS

Previous manufacturer located in Waco, TX, until circa 1999.

DERRINGERS: O/U

DEFENDER – .357 Mag., .38 Spl., 9mm Para., .44 Mag., .45 ACP, .45 LC cal., or .45 LC cal./.410 bore shotshell, features stainless steel 3 in. interchangeable octagon barrels, shell ejector for rimmed cartridges, rebounding hammer and retracting firing pins, spur trigger, crossbolt safety, bead blasted grey finish, 16-21 oz. Mfg. 1993-circa 1999.

$275	$235	$200	$175	$160	$145	$130	*$310*

Add $100 per interchangeable set of barrels.

TEXAS BLACK RIFLE COMPANY

Previous semi-auto pistol and rifle manufacturer located in Shiner, TX until circa 2018.

Please refer to BlueBookOfGunValues.com to order the *Blue Book of AR-15s & Variations*, available as a book or online subscription.

TEXAS CUSTOM GUNS

Previous AR-15 style custom rifle manufacturer located in Alvin, TX 2009-2017.

Please refer to BlueBookOfGunValues.com to order the *Blue Book of AR-15s & Variations*, available as a book or online subscription.

TEXAS GUNFIGHTERS

Previous importer located in Irving, TX circa 1988-1990.

REVOLVERS: SINGLE ACTION

SHOOTIST EDITION – .45 LC cal., patterned after the Colt SAA, 4 3/4 in. barrel, nickel-plated black powder frame, one-piece walnut grips, mfg. by A. Uberti of Italy. Mfg. 1988-disc.

* ***Shootist Edition Standard Model*** – 1,000 total mfg., cased.

$625	$525	$440	N/A	N/A	N/A	N/A	*$649*

* ***Shootist Edition 1 of 100*** – 100 total mfg., fully engraved, genuine mother-of-pearl one-piece grips, cased.

$1,275	$1,050	$775	N/A	N/A	N/A	N/A	*$1,395*

This model was also supplied with an extra set of walnut grips.

GRADING - PPGS™	100%	98%	95%	90%	80%	70%	60%	LAST MSR

TEXAS LONGHORN ARMS, INC.

Previous manufacturer located in Richmond, TX circa 1988-1997.

REVOLVERS

SINGLE-ACTION – various cals., patterned after Colt's SAA, except the loading gate and ejector rod have been moved to left side of frame enabling left-hand loading, mfg. from 4140 steel, 1-piece grip, adj. trigger, case-hardened and blue finish, entirely handmade, supplied with lifetime warranty. Models included the Texas Border Special (last MSR was $1,595), South Texas Army (last MSR was $1,595), West Texas Flat-Top Target (last MSR was $1,595), Grover's Northpaw (last MSR was $685), and Grover's Improved Number Five (last MSR was $1,195). Special editions and sets were also advertised (ranging from $1,500 MSR - $7,650 MSR), but very few were actually built. Mint examples are currently in the $1,350-$1,500 range, except for Grover's Northpaw, which is in the $650 range. While production plans called for 1,000 of each model to be manufactured, very few pistols were actually made.

THOMAS

Previous trademark manufactured by Alexander James Ordnance, Inc. located in Covina, CA.

Please refer to listing under A.J. Ordnance in this text.

THOMPSON & CAMPBELL

Previous rifle manufacturer located in Cromarty, the Black Isle, Scotland.

RIFLES: BOLT ACTION

Thompson & Campbell manufactured high quality bolt action rifles that featured the patented Inver action. The Inver action utilized a rear extension plate and reinforcement rod that was inletted into the stock for additional strength. Individual models included the Inver, Cromie, the Islay, and Jura (Mannlicher configuration). Thompson & Campbell manufactured approx. 20-24 rifles annually.

THOMPSON

Thompson
Auto-Ordnance Corporation

Current trademark of pistols and carbines manufactured by Auto Ordnance located in Worcester, MA and Greeley, PA. Corporate offices are currently located in Greeley, PA (previously located in Blauvelt, NY). Auto Ordnance became a division of Kahr Arms in 1999. Dealer and distributor sales.

Auto-Ordnance Corp. manufactures an exact reproduction of the original 1927 Thompson sub-machine gun. They are currently available from Kahr Arms in semi-auto only since production ceased on fully automatic variations (Model 1928 and M1) in 1986 (mfg. 1975-1986 including 609 M1s). All current models utilize the Thompson trademark, are manufactured in the U.S., and come with a lifetime warranty.

PISTOLS: SEMI-AUTO

1911 BOOTLEGGER PISTOL – .45 ACP cal., slide and receiver engraved with "Bootlegger Prohibition Edition" and "Proof Tennessee Moonshine", 5 in. barrel w/marking "White Lightning", 7 shot mag., steel construction, blade front and drift adj. for windage rear sight, scroll engraved American walnut wood grips, distressed Midnight Blue Cerakote finish w/clear coating overlay, 36.8 oz. Mfg. 2020 only.

	100%	98%	95%	90%	80%	70%	60%	LAST MSR
	$1,100	**$950**	**$800**	**$750**	**$600**	**$500**	**$375**	***$1,215***

1911 THOMPSON CUSTOM (1911TC) – .45 ACP cal., stainless steel or aluminum (Lightweight model, mfg. 2005-2007) construction, Series 80 design, 5 in. barrel, SA, Thompson bullet logo on left side of double serrated slide, 7 shot mag., grip safety, checkered laminate grips with medallion, skeletonized trigger, combat hammer, low profile sights, 31 1/2 (Lightweight) or 39 oz. Mfg. 2004-2017.

	100%	98%	95%	90%	80%	70%	60%	LAST MSR
	$825	**$700**	**$575**	**$475**	**$375**	**$325**	**$295**	***$977***

THOMPSON 1927 A-1 DELUXE – .45 ACP cal., SA, blowback design, 10 1/2 in. finned barrel, 10 (standard), 50, or 100 shot drum mag. and 10 or 30 shot stick mag., blade front sight, adj. rear sight, grooved walnut forearm with sling swivel and smooth walnut pistol grip, marked "MODEL OF 1927A-1" and "THOMPSON SEMI-AUTOMATIC CARBINE" / "CALIBER .45 AUTOMATIC CARTRIDGE" on the left side and "AUTO-ORDNANCE CORPORATION" / "WORCESTER MASSACHUSETTS USA" on the right side, approx. 6 lbs. New 2008.

	100%	98%	95%	90%	80%	70%	60%	LAST MSR
MSR $1,462	**$1,240**	**$1,085**	**$930**	**$850**	**$685**	**$575**	**$475**	

Add $104 for 50 shot drum mag.
Add $295 for 100 shot drum mag.

CARBINES: SEMI-AUTO

The Auto-Ordnance Thompson replicas listed below are currently supplied with a 10, 15 (disc.), 20, or 30 shot stick or 10 (resembling the older 50 shot L-type drum) - new 1994, 50, or 100 (mfg. 1990-93,

GRADING - PPGS™	100%	98%	95%	90%	80%	70%	60%	LAST MSR

reintroduced 2006) shot drum mag. Tommy Guns are not currently legal in CA, CT, or NY.

Add $73 for rifle hard case with Thompson logo.
Add $160 for padded rifle soft case with Thompson logo.
Add $173 for 1927 A-1 pistol violin case.
Add $209 for 1927 A-1 rifle violin case.
Add $214 for Thompson FBI hard case.

1927 A3 - .22 CAL. - .22 LR cal., 16 or 18 in. finned barrel with compensator, alloy frame and receiver, fixed or detachable walnut stock, pistol grip, and forearm pistol grip, 7 lbs. Disc. 1994.

	$995	$875	$750	$650	$550	$500	$450	*$510*

1927 A5 PISTOL/CARBINE - .45 ACP cal., 13 in. finned barrel, alloy construction, 10 (C/B 1994) shot mag., 26 in. OAL, 7 lbs. Disc. 1994.

	$1,050	$925	$825	$750	$650	$600	$500	*$765*

BOOTLEGGER THOMPSON - .45 ACP cal., 16 in. finned barrel, 20 shot stick and 50 shot drum mags., fixed blade front and open rear drift adj. sights, walnut fixed stock w/vertical foregrip, engraved historical images from 1920s w/"Bootlegger Prohibition Edition", "White Lightning", and "Proof Tennessee Moonshine" on slide, distressed Midnight Blue Cerakote w/clear coating finish, 12.5 lbs. Mfg. 2020 only.

	$1,950	$1,700	$1,450	$1,350	$1,100	$900	$700	*$2,309*

THOMPSON M1 CARBINE (.45 ACP CAL.) - .45 ACP cal., combat model, 16 1/2 in. smooth barrel w/o compensator, 10 (new 2017) or 30 shot original surplus mag. (current mfg. will not accept drum mags.), walnut pistol grip stock and grooved horizontal forearm, side-cocking lever, matte black finish, 11 1/2 lbs. New 1986.

MSR $1,518	$1,295	$1,135	$970	$880	$700	$600	$500	

* ***Thompson M1- Lightweight Carbine*** - 9mm Para. (new 2018) or .45 ACP cal., 16 1/2 in. smooth barrel w/o compensator, 30 shot original surplus mag., lightweight alloy receiver, walnut pistol grip stock and grooved horizontal forearm, side-cocking lever, matte black finish, 9 1/2 lbs. Mfg. 2001-2002, reintroduced 2005.

MSR $1,373	$1,175	$1,025	$875	$800	$650	$550	$450	

During 2006, this model incorporated a large machined radius on the bottom of the receiver to improve magazine insertion.

* ***Thompson M1 "Tanker WWII Thompson"*** - .45 ACP cal., 16 1/2 in. smooth barrel, 20 and 30 shot stick mag., steel receiver, blade front, fixed battle rear sights, walnut buttstock with "U.S" logo, pistol grip, and grooved horizontal forearm, side-cocking lever, army OD Green Cerakoted finish, white star of the Sherman tank engraved forward of the magwell, Kerr sling and WWII 3 mag. pouch carrier, 38 in. OAL, 11 1/2 lbs. New 2019.

MSR $1,824	$1,550	$1,355	$1,165	$1,055	$875	$750	$625	

THOMPSON M1 SBR "TOMMY GUN" - .45 ACP cal., closed bolt, 10 1/2 in. barrel, 30 shot stick mag., blade front and fixed battle rear sights, fixed walnut buttstock, pistol grip, grooved horizontal foregrip and sling swivels, blue metal finish, 32 in. OAL, 10.5-12 lbs. New 2004.

MSR $2,234	$1,900	$1,660	$1,425	$1,290	$1,045	$855	$675	

This carbine model may only be shipped from the factory to an NFA Class II manufacturer or NFA Class III dealer.

THOMPSON 1927 A-1 COMMANDO - .45 ACP cal., 16 1/2 in. finned barrel with compensator, 20 or 30 (disc.) shot mag., black finished stock and forearm, parkerized metal, black nylon sling, 13 lbs. New 1997.

MSR $1,541	$1,310	$1,150	$985	$890	$725	$625	$590	

During 2006, this model incorporated a spherical cocking knob.

THOMPSON 1927 A-1 DELUXE CARBINE 16 1/2 IN. - 10mm (mfg. 1991-93) or .45 ACP cal., 16 1/2 in. finned barrel with compensator, includes one 10 or 20 shot stick (new 2017), one 10 (new 2018) or 50 shot drum, 30 shot stick original surplus mag. (disc. 2020), current mfg. accepts drum mags., solid steel construction, matte black finish, adj. rear sight, walnut stock, pistol grip, and finger grooved forearm grip, 13 lbs.

MSR $1,569	$1,335	$1,165	$1,000	$905	$750	$625	$525	

Add $148 for 10 shot drum mag. (new 2018).
Add $260 for 50 shot drum mag.
Add $47 for 10 shot drum mag. and horizontal foregrip.
Add $543 for detachable buttstock and vertical foregrip w/20 shot stick mag.

GRADING - PPGS™	100%	98%	95%	90%	80%	70%	60%	LAST MSR

Add $320 for 10 shot drum mag. and violin case package (mfg. 2018-2020).
Add $663 for 100 shot drum mag.
Add $451 for 50 round drum, 20, or 30 (disc. 2020) shot stick mag. and violin case package (new 2015).
Add $790 for detachable buttstock and vertical foregrip with 50 round drum and 20 or 30 (disc. 2020) shot stick mag., or $1,158 with detachable buttstock and vertical foregrip with 100 round drum and 20 (new 2017), or 30 (disc. 2020) shot stick mag. (2016).
Add $462 for detachable buttstock and horizontal foregrip (mfg. 2007-disc).

During 2006, design changes included a more authentic spherical cocking knob, improved frame to receiver fit, and a large machined radius at the bottom of the receiver to help with magazine insertion.

* ***Thompson 1927 A-1 Deluxe Carbine 14 1/2 In.*** - .45 ACP cal., 14 1/2 in. barrel with permanently affixed Cutts Compensator (approved by the BATFE), 20 shot stick mag., blade front and open rear adj. sights, polished American walnut fixed or detachable buttstock and vertical foregrip, 12 1/2 lbs. New 2016.

MSR $1,699	$1,450	$1,275	$1,095	$985	$800	$650	$560	

Add $494 for detachable buttstock and vertical foregrip.

* ***Thompson 1927 A-1 Deluxe Carbine SBR*** - .45 ACP cal., closed bolt, 10 1/2 in. finned barrel with 1 1/2 in. compensator, 20 shot stick mag., blade front and adj. rear sights, walnut fixed or detachable buttstock with vertical foregrip, blue metal finish, 25.5- 35 in. OAL, 12 lbs. New 2004.

MSR $2,331	$1,980	$1,735	$1,485	$1,345	$1,090	$890	$725	

Add $569 for detachable buttstock.

This carbine model may only be shipped from the factory to an NFA Class II manufacturer or NFA Class III dealer.

* ***Thompson 1927 A-1 Deluxe Carbine Special Limited Ed.*** - .45 ACP cal., 10 or 20 shot drum mag., marked "TIG 13 Hours Benghazi" Tiegan model or engraved w/"TIG" and "Beyond the Battlefield" logo and TIG. Limited mfg. of 1,000 units. Mfg. 2018-2019.

	$1,350	$1,175	$1,050	$925	$825	$725	$625	*$1,544*

* ***Thompson 1927 A-1 Deluxe Case Hardened*** - .45 ACP cal., 16 1/2 in pinned barrel (18 in. with compensator), one 20 round stick mag., blade front and open rear adj. sights, walnut fixed stock and vertical foregrip, standard or Bisley grips, case hardened w/clear protective coat, optional Tiger Stripe (disc. 2020), 41 in. OAL, 13 lbs. New 2018.

MSR $1,872	$1,590	$1,390	$1,195	$1,080	$875	$715	$600	

Add $742 for Tiger Stripes (disc. 2020).

* ***Thompson 1927 A-1 Deluxe .22 LR Cal.*** - .22 LR cal., very limited mfg., 30 shot mag. standard. Disc.

	$1,100	$995	$925	$800	$700	$650	$575	

* ***Thompson 1927 A-1 Deluxe Hard Chrome*** - .45 ACP cal., 16 1/2 in. finned barrel (18 in. w/ compensator), 50 round drum and 20 round stick mag., blade front and open rear adj. sights, walnut fixed stock and vertical foregrip, hard chrome finish, includes hard case with Thompson logo and the word "Chicago Typewriter", 41 in. OAL, 13 lbs. New 2016.

MSR $3,431	$2,900	$2,550	$2,175	$1,875	$1,650	$1,350	$1,075	

Add $742 for Tiger Stripes.

* ***Thompson 1927 A-1 Deluxe Semi-Auto "Bonnie & Clyde Special Edition"*** - .45 ACP cal., 16 1/2 in. finned barrel with 1 1/2 in. compensator, one 20 shot stock and one 50 shot drum mag., solid steel construction, blade front and adj. rear sight, fixed walnut stock and vertical foregrip, finger grooved pistol grip is engraved with badge of the Texas Rangers, each gun is engraved with reminders of Bonnie & Clyde's escapades including photos, wanted posters, and news headlines, custom rust Cerakote finish, 41 in. OAL, 13 lbs. Limited mfg. 2018-2020.

	$2,195	$1,920	$1,650	$1,495	$1,250	$995	$775	*$2,583*

* ***Thompson 1927 A-1 Presentation Walnut Carbine*** - .45 ACP cal., similar to 1927 A-1 Deluxe, except has presentation grade walnut buttstock, pistol grip, and foregrip, supplied with plastic case. Limited mfg. 2003.

	$850	$675	$525	$425	$350	$325	$295	*$1,121*

* ***Thompson 1927 A-1 Titanium Gold*** - .45 ACP cal., 16 1/2 in. finned barrel (18 in. w/compensator), 50 round drum and 20 round stick mag., blade front and open rear adj. sights, walnut fixed stock and vertical foregrip, gold-plated finish, includes hard case with Thompson logo and the word "Chicago Typewriter", 41 in. OAL, 13 lbs. New 2016.

MSR $3,431	$2,900	$2,550	$2,175	$1,875	$1,650	$1,350	$1,075	

Add $742 for Tiger Stripes.

GRADING - PPGS™ 100% 98% 95% 90% 80% 70% 60% LAST MSR

THOMPSON 1927 A-1C LIGHTWEIGHT DELUXE – 9mm Para. (new 2018) or .45 ACP cal., similar to 1927 A-1 Deluxe, except receiver made of a lightweight alloy, currently shipped with 20 (new 2018) or 30 shot stick mag. (where legal, disc.), current mfg. accepts drum mags., 9 1/2 lbs. New 1984.

MSR $1,462 $1,240 $1,085 $930 $850 $685 $575 $475

Add $474 for 100 shot drum mag.

DELUXE 1927 A-1 CARBINE/1911A-1 GI PISTOL MATCHED SET – .45 ACP cal., 16 1/2 in. finned (18 in. w/compensator (carbine), 5 in. barrel (pistol), 20 round stick mag., 7 round mag. (pistol), pinned front blade and open rear adj. sight, iron front and rear dovetail cut low profile sight (pistol), fixed stock and vertical foregrip, matte black steel frame, 13 lbs. Mfg. 2016-disc.

$1,700 $1,525 $1,350 $1,175 $1,000 $900 $800 ***$1,971***

"TRUMP THOMPSON" 1927 A-1 EDITION – .45 ACP cal., 16 1/2 in. finned barrel, 20 shot stick mag., 50 shot drum mag., steel construction, American walnut fixed stock and vertical foregrip, right side of stock engraved w/Presidential Seal, American flag, and White House, "First Freedom" quote on grip, receiver engraved "Donald J. Trump" and "45th", Armor Black and Clear Cerakote finish, 12 1/2 lbs. Limited mfg. beginning 2019.

MSR $2,794 $2,375 $2,075 $1,780 $1,615 $1,305 $1,070 $830

THOMPSON/CENTER ARMS CO., INC.

Current manufacturer established during 1967, located in Springfield, MA. Previously located in Rochester, NH. Distributor and dealer sales.

On Dec. 18, 2006 Smith & Wesson holding corp. announced that it purchased Thompson Center Arms Co., Inc. During late 2010, Smith & Wesson moved their production to its Springfield, MA facility.

Thompson/Center also has created a custom shop to enable customers to create custom pistols, rifles, shotguns, and muzzleloaders. Please contact the factory for availability and an individualized quotation.

Please refer to the *Blue Book of Modern Black Powder Arms* (also available online) for more information and prices on Thompson/Center's lineup of modern black powder models.

PISTOLS: SINGLE SHOT

Caution: older and newer TC components do not interchange safely. Although parts will fit, they may not function properly. Special ordering of barrels, frames, and calibers started in 1988. Values listed are for complete guns - including frame and barrel.

CONTENDER – .22 LR, .22 Rem., 5mm Rem., .218 Bee, .22 Hornet, .22 Jet, .221 Fireball, .222 Rem., .25-35 WCF, .256 Mag., .30 Carbine, .30-30 Win., .38 Spl., .357 Mag., .17 Ackley Bee, .17 Bumblebee, .17 Hornet, .17K Hornet, .17 Rem., .300 Whisper (new 1994), .30 Herrett, .357 Herrett, .357-44 B&D, 7x30 Waters, .32 H&R Mag., .32-20 WCF, 6mm TCU, 6.5mm TCU, or 9mm Para. cal., barrels are interchangeable, 8 3/4 (disc.), 10, or 14 in. barrel, hinged break open action, trigger guard action lever, blue, .44, .357 Mag., and .45 Colt available with detachable choke for hot shot cartridges, VR, 10 in. barrel available, 10 in. bull barrel, adj. sights, checkered walnut grip and forearm. Mfg. 1967-2000.

The Contender action was made in 3 variations, and a wide variety of changes were made to grips, stocks, sights, etc. during 1967-2000. These production variances do not necessarily add premiums to values listed.

* ***Contender Bull Barrel*** – available in 13 cals. between .17 Rem. and .45 Win. Mag., 10 in. round barrel only.

$415 $325 $240 $200 $180 $170 $155 ***$510***

Add $22 for .45 Colt/.410 bore with internal chokes.
Add $11 for .22 LR match grade chamber (new 1996).
Add approx. $230-$267 per additional barrel.

* ***Contender Armour Alloy II Bull Barrel*** – 7 cals. between .22 LR and .30-30 Win., similar to regular Bull Barrel, except has Armour Alloy II satin finish which is harder than stainless steel. Mfg. 1986-89.

$350 $325 $295 $240 $180 $170 $155 ***$415***

Add $5 for .45 Colt/.410 bore internal choke.

* ***Contender Vent. Rib*** – .357 Mag. (disc.), .44 Mag. (disc.) or .45 Colt/.410 bore cal., 10 in. VR barrel only, adj. front and flip-up rear sight, internal choke became standard in 1985.

$425 $325 $240 $200 $195 $160 $150 ***$533***

* ***Contender Armour Alloy Vent. Rib*** – .45/.410 bore cal., internal choke, has Armour Alloy II satin finish which is harder than stainless steel. Mfg. 1986-disc.

$375 $315 $245 $190 $175 $155 $130 ***$435***

GRADING - PPGS™	100%	98%	95%	90%	80%	70%	60%	LAST MSR

* ***Contender Stainless Steel*** – various cals., 10 in. bull barrel. Mfg. 1993-2000.

	$450	$325	$250	$200	$175	$160	$150	$578

Add approx. $240 per additional barrel.
Add $5 for .45/.410 bore with adj. sights.
Add $20 for .45/.410 bore with VR.

* ***Contender Octagon Barrel*** – .22 LR, .22 WMR (disc.), .22 Hornet (disc.), .22K Hornet (disc.), .222 Rem. (disc.), or .357 Mag. (disc.) cal., 10 in. barrel. Disc. 1998.

	$375	$275	$215	$180	$170	$160	$150	$474

* ***Contender Match Grade Barrel*** – .22 LR cal. only, choice of 10 or 14 in. match barrel. Mfg. 1992-98.

	$375	$275	$215	$180	$170	$160	$150	$460

Add $10 for 14 in. barrel.

CONTENDER SHOOTERS PACKAGE – .22 LR Match, .223 Rem., .30-30 Win., or 7-30 Waters cal., includes blue frame and 14 in. barrel w/o sights, 2.5-7X scope, composite grips and forend, Weaver style base and rings, pistol case. Mfg. 1998-2000.

	$650	$575	$550	$450	$400	$360	$330	$754

CONTENDER SUPER (14 & 16 IN.) – 13 cals. available from .17 Rem.-.45 Win. Mag. (disc.), 14 or 16 in. bull barrel only, special grips, beavertail forearm, adj. sight, 3 1/2 lbs. Disc. 1997.

	$360	$265	$200	$180	$170	$160	$150	$474

Add $5 for 16 in. barrel.
Add $31 for .17 Rem. cal. (new 1992).
Add $10 for .45-70 Govt. cal. in 16 in. barrel only with muzzle brake (new 1992).
Add approx. $224 per additional barrel.
Add $31 for VR barrel (.45 LC/.410 bore only).
Thompson Center also made special order guns in cals. other than those listed above. If factory work, these pistols will be worth a premium.

* ***Contender Super Stainless*** – various cals., choice of 14 or 16 in. barrel. Mfg. 1993-97.

	$385	$275	$215	$165	$130	$120	$100	$505

Add $5 for 16 in. barrel.
Add $25 for .45-70 Govt. bull barrel with muzzle tamer.
Add $30-$35 for .45 LC/.410 bore with internal choke.
Add approx. $240 per additional barrel.

* ***Contender Super Armour Alloy II*** – 5 cals. between .22 LR and 7mm Rem. Mag., similar to regular Super Contender, except has Armour Alloy II satin finish which is harder than stainless steel. Mfg. 1986-89.

	$355	$295	$240	$185	$160	$135	$115	$425

G2 CONTENDER 50TH ANNIVERSARY – .22 LR cal., 10 in. octagon barrel, steel sights, adj. rear and ramped blade front, checkered walnut grip forearm, engraved and gold plated anniversary logo on both side of receiver and barrel, includes walnut presentation case, blue finish, 15 1/2 in. OAL, 3 1/2 lbs. 500 mfg. circa 2017.

	$1,200	$1,050	$900	$825	$665	$545	$425	$1,400

G2 CONTENDER – various rimfire and centerfire cals., current cals are .22 LR and .357 Mag., 12 or 14 (disc.) in. barrel, adj. sights, blued finish, walnut finger groove grip and forearm, replacement for the Contender model, will accept older Contender barrels w/o frame alteration, automatic hammer block safety with built-in interlock, hammer recocking w/o breaking open the gun, opening has been made easier, approx. 3 1/2 lbs. New 2002.

MSR $729	$650	$550	$450	$395	$350	$300	$250	

Add approx. $10 for 14 in. barrel (disc.).
Add approx. 5% for .17 HMR or 17 Mach 2 cal.
Add $333-$458 per additional barrel, depending on length and caliber.

* ***G2 Contender Stainless*** – various cals., similar to G2 Contender, except is stainless steel with black rubber grips, 14 in. barrel only. Mfg. 2006-2011.

	$695	$550	$475	$425	$350	$300	$265	$809

CONTENDER HUNTER PACKAGE – .223 Rem., .7-30 Waters, .30-30 Win., .35 Rem., .357 Rem. Max. (disc. 1994), .375 Win. Mag. (new 1992), .44 Mag., or .45-70 Govt. cal., special 12 (disc.) or 14 (new 1992) in. barrel with muzzle brake, 2.5 power scope with lighted reticle, walnut grip has nonslip rubber insert to cushion recoil, includes studs, swivels, sling, and deluxe carrying case, approx. 4 lbs. Mfg. 1990-97.

	$695	$575	$495	$430	$365	$315	$275	$798

GRADING - PPGS™	100%	98%	95%	90%	80%	70%	60%	LAST MSR

CONTENDER 25TH ANNIVERSARY – .22 LR cal. only, 10 in. octagon barrel, laser etched anniversary logo on receiver sides and barrel, checkered stock and forearm, limited mfg. in 1992 only.

	$610	$535	$465	$410	$360	$315	$275	*$700*

* ***Contender 25th Anniversary Cased Set*** – cased set with 5 barrels including .22 LR, .22 WMR, .22 Jet, .22 Hornet, and .38 Spl. cal., 50 sets mfg. 1992 only.

	$1,850	$1,550	$1,225	$1,050	$900	$775	$650	*$1,975*

SUPER CONTENDER (14 & 16 IN.) – various cals. between .22 LR-.45-70 Govt., wood grips with rear stippling, configurations include 14 or 16 in. bull (with or w/o VR) barrel, adj. sights, blue finish only. Mfg. 1999-2000.

	$410	$345	$285	$255	$220	$195	$170	*$520*

Add $35 for 14 in. VR barrel.
Add $5 for 16 in. tapered barrel.

* ***Super Contender Stainless*** – similar to Super Contender, except only available in 14 in. barrel. Mfg. 1999-2000.

	$430	$320	$215	$165	$135	$120	$100	*$578*

Add $35 for VR barrel.
Add $22 for .45/.410 ga. barrel.

ENCORE – various cals. between .22 LR and .480 Ruger (new 2002), walnut grip with finger grooves and forend, blue finish, 10 (disc. 1999), 12 (new 1999), or 15 in. barrel with adj. sights, VR barrel on .45 LC/.410 bore, hammer block safety with bolt interlock, 4-4 1/2 lbs. Mfg. 1998-2012.

	$575	$485	$415	$335	$285	$250	$225	*$679*

Add $228 for extra 10 in. (disc.), approx. $313 for extra 12 in. barrel, or $318 for extra 15 in. barrel, depending on caliber.
Add $40 for .45 LC/.410 bore barrel, depending on barrel length.
Values are for base caliber - most calibers will add approx. 5% to base price.

Encore pistol barrels ARE NOT interchangeable with Contender pistol barrels.

* ***Encore Stainless*** – .22-250 Rem., .223 Rem., .243 Win., .30-06, .308 Win., 7mm-08 Rem., .44 Mag., .45 LC/.410 bore, or .480 Ruger (mfg. 2003) cal., black synthetic finger groove grips and forearm, 12 (disc.) or 15 in. barrel. Mfg. 1999-2012.

	$625	$525	$475	$425	$350	$300	$265	*$729*

Add $23 for .480 Ruger cal. (mfg. 2003).
Add $40 for .45LC/.410 bore.

* ***Encore Hunter Package*** – .22-250 Rem., .270 Win., or .308 Win. cal., features 15 in. barrel w/o sights and 2.5-7X scope, Weaver base and rings, composite grip and forend, includes case. Mfg. 1998-2005, reintroduced 2010-2012.

	$875	$750	$650	$550	$450	$375	$325	*$969*

ENCORE PRO HUNTER – .223 Rem., or .308 Win. cal., 15 in. stainless steel drilled and tapped, fluted barrel, swing hammer, adj. sights, ambidextrous rubber grip with finger grooves and forearm, frame is etched with "Pro Hunter", 4 1/2 lbs. New 2015.

MSR $779	$700	$615	$525	$475	$385	$325	$265	

Add $347-$420 for extra new barrel depending on caliber and length.

PRO-HUNTER – various cals., 15 in. fluted stainless steel barrel, adj. sights, hardwood (disc. 2007) or rubber grips. Mfg. 2006-2012.

	$650	$550	$475	$425	$350	$300	$250	*$779*

Add $30 for hardwood grips (disc. 2007).
Add $413-$450 per extra barrel, depending on caliber.

RIFLES: BOLT ACTION

A recall has been issued for all Venture rifles manufactured prior to October 28, 2011. To determine if your rifle is affected, please visit Smith & Wesson's website: smith-wesson.com or call 1-800-713-0356.

COMPASS RIFLE – .204 Ruger, .22-250 Rem., .223 Rem., .243 Win., .270 Win., .300 Win. Mag., .308 Win., .30-06, 6.5 Creedmoor (new 2017), 7mm-08 Rem., or 7mm Rem. Mag. cal., 22 or 24 (Mag. cals. only) in. threaded barrel w/o sights, 4 or 5 shot rotary mag., adj. trigger, black composite stock with aluminum pillar bedding and textured grip panels, 3-position safety on rear of bolt, 3 lug bolt design with 60 degree lift, blue metal finish, 7 1/4-7 1/2 lbs. Mfg. 2016-2019.

	$350	$325	$295	$275	$250	$225	$200	*$399*

Thompson Center has issued a recall on Compass rifles manufactured prior to Sept.16, 2016. Please contact the manufacturer directly at (855)-512-5935 for more information on how to get one of these early rifles serviced.

GRADING - PPGS™	100%	98%	95%	90%	80%	70%	60%	LAST MSR

COMPASS II – .243 Win., .270 Win., .300 Win. Mag., .308 Win., .223 Rem./5.56 NATO, .30-06, 6.5 Creedmoor, or 7mm Rem. Mag. cal., 21.6 (with 5R rifling) or 24 in. barrel with threaded muzzle, 4 or 5 shot detachable rotary mag., Generation II trigger, no sights, blued/black composite stock, 13.25 in. LOP, 3-pos. safety, with Weaver style bases or Crimson Trace scope combo, 7-8.5 lbs. New 2020.

MSR $417	$375	$325	$275	$250	$200	$175	$125	

Add $178 for Crimson Trace scope combo.

* ***Compass II Compact*** – .243 Win., .308 Win., .223 Rem./5.56 NATO, or 6.5 Creedmoor cal., 16 1/2 in. barrel with 5R rifling and threaded muzzle, 4 or 5 shot detachable rotary mag., Generation II trigger, no sights, blued/black composite stock, extended buttpad/spacer, with or w/o Crimson Trace scope combo, 3-pos. safety, 6.5-7.5 lbs. New 2020.

MSR $417	$375	$325	$275	$250	$200	$175	$125	

Add $178 for Crimson Trace scope combo.

COMPASS UTILITY – .243 Win., .270 Win., .308 Win., .223 Rem./5.56 NATO, .30-06, or 6.5 Creedmoor cal., 21.6 in. barrel with 5R rifling, 5 shot detachable mag., Generation I trigger, no sights, black composite stock, 13.25 in. LOP, with Weaver style bases installed, with or w/o scope combo, blued finish, 7-8 lbs. New 2020.

MSR $370	$325	$300	$250	$225	$175	$150	$125	

Add $89 for scope combo.

DIMENSION – various cals., short or long action, 22 or 24 in. 5R rifled barrel, 3 shot detachable box mag., adj. trigger, textured grip black synthetic stock with competition cheekpiece and removable stock spacers, drilled and tapped, 3 lug fluted bolt, right or left-hand action, matte blue finish, 7 lbs. Mfg. 2012-2018.

	$595	$525	$450	$375	$300	$250	$225	*$689*

ICON – .22-250 Rem., .243 Win., .270 Win., .280 Rem., .30-06, .300 Win. Mag., .338 Win. Mag., .308 Win., .30 TC (disc. 2011), 6.5 Creedmoor (new 2010), or 7mm Rem. Mag. cal., medium or long action, black synthetic (medium action), Realtree camo (medium action), checkered American walnut (long action only), Classic Sporter style walnut (Icon Classic, new 2008), or choice of Ultra Wood pistol grip stock and forearm, 24 in. barrel, hinged floorplate on long action, cocking indicator, adj. trigger, detachable 3 shot mag. on medium action, interlocked bedding system, butterknife jeweled bolt handle, 60 degree bolt lift, Weaver style base, guaranteed to shoot 1 in. or less at 100 yards, approx. 7 1/2 lbs. Mfg. 2007-2012.

	$795	$650	$550	$475	$400	$350	$295	*$889*

Subtract $80 for synthetic stock with Weathershield dull nickel finish (medium action only).
Add $10 for camo stock.
Subtract $10 for Ultrawood stock (.22-250 Rem., .243 Win., .30 TC, or .308 Win. cal.).

ICON PRECISION HUNTER – .204 Ruger, .223 Rem., .22-250 Rem., .243 Win., 6.5 Creedmoor (mfg. 2010-2011), or .308 Win. cal., 22 in. heavy fluted barrel with 5R button rifling, fat bolt design with tactical style handle, classic varminter style brown synthetic stock with cheekpiece and beavertail forend, detachable 3 shot mag. with single shot adapter, Picatinny rail, adj. trigger, two position safety, sling swivel studs, 8 lbs. Mfg. 2009-2012.

	$900	$775	$675	$575	$475	$425	$350	*$1,019*

ICON WARLORD – .308 Win. or .338 Lapua cal., 5 or 10 shot mag., hand lapped stainless steel fluted barrel, carbon fiber tactical style stock with adj. cheekpiece, available in OD Green, Flat Black, or Desert Sand, Weather Shield finish on all metal, adj. trigger, Picatinny rail, tactical bolt handle, 12 3/4-13 3/4 lbs. Mfg. 2010-2011.

	$3,000	$2,600	$2,200	$1,800	$1,500	$1,250	$1,125	*$3,499*

PERFORMANCE CENTER T/C LRR – .243 Win., .308 Win., or 6.5 Creedmoor cal., 20, 24, or 26 in. threaded, free floating, fluted barrel, 5R rifling, muzzle brake, 10 shot detachable box mag., PC adj. trigger, stock/chassis system with adj. cheekpiece and buttplate, Magpul M-LOK forend slots, Calwell bipod, 2-position safety lever, 20 in. MOA Picatinny-style rail, visible and tactile cocking indicator, includes soft gun case, matte black or FDE finish, 43 1/2-47 1/2 in. OAL, 11-12 lbs. New 2019.

MSR $1,231	$1,110	$975	$835	$750	$625	$525	$425	

Add $292 for Vortex Diamondback riflescope 4-12x40mm Dead-Head BDC Reticle.

VENTURE WEATHER SHIELD – .204 Ruger (disc. 2017), .223 Rem., .22-250 Rem., .243 Win. (disc. 2017), .25-06 (disc. 2017), .270 Win., .280 Rem. (disc. 2017), .30-06, 6.5 Creedmoor (new 2017), 7mm-08 Rem., 7mm Rem. Mag., .270 WSM (disc. 2017), .300 WSM (disc. 2017), .308 Win., .30 TC (disc.), .300 Win. Mag., or .338 Win. Mag. (disc. 2017) cal., 22 or 24 in. match grade tapered barrel with 5R button rifling, fat bolt design, classic sporter black synthetic stock with Hogue overmolded panels on grip and forearm (disc. 2017) or Weathershield composite stock, detachable 3 shot mag., Weaver style base, adj. trigger, two position safety, blue finish, 7 lbs. Mfg. 2009-2019.

	$495	$435	$375	$335	$275	$225	$175	*$578*

Subtract approx. $40 for classic sporter black synthetic stock with Hogue overmolded panels on grip and forearm (disc. 2017).

GRADING - PPGS™	100%	98%	95%	90%	80%	70%	60%	LAST MSR

* ***Venture Compact*** – .22-250 Rem., .223 Rem. (new 2015), .243 Win., 7mm-08 Rem., or .308 Win. cal., similar configuration to the Venture, 20 in. barrel, detachable 3 shot mag., adj. trigger, black synthetic stock with Hogue overmolded panels on grip and forearm, 2-position safety, 1 in. adj. spacer, and short (12 1/2 to 13 1/2 in.) LOP, drilled and tapped, 39 3/4 in. OAL, 6 3/4 lbs. Mfg. 2012-2019.

	$450	$395	$340	$300	$250	$200	$160	*$537*

VENTURE PREDATOR – .204 Ruger, .243 Win. (new 2018), .223 Rem., .22-250 Rem., 7mm-08 (new 2018), or .308 Win. cal., 22 in. fluted barrel, 3 shot detachable box mag., adj. trigger, composite stock with 100% Realtree Max-1 or AP Snow (new 2012) camo coverage, Hogue panels, Weather Shield bolt handle, 6 3/4 lbs. Mfg. 2010-2019.

	$540	$475	$400	$365	$295	$245	$190	*$638*

VENTURE II – .243 Win., .270 Win., .300 Win. Mag., .308 Win. Mag., .223 Rem./5.56 NATO, .30-06, .350 Legend, 6.5 Creedmoor, or 7mm Rem. Mag. cal., 22 or 24 in. barrel with 5R rifling, 3 shot detachable mag., Generation II trigger, no sights, black composite stock with Hogue panels, 13.5 in. LOP, Weather Shield Exterior, 7.3-7.5 lbs. New 2020.

MSR $540	$475	$425	$375	$325	$275	$225	$175	

RIFLES: SEMI-AUTO

PERFORMANCE CENTER T/C R22 RIFLE – .22 LR cal., 20 in. stainless or carbon steel heavy contour fluted, threaded barrel with button-rifling, 10 shot rotary detachable mag., Hogue overmolded textured polymer or Altamont laminated wood thumbhole stock, push-button safety, 6061 aluminum receiver, built-in Picatinny rail, stainless steel bolt, sling swivel studs, matte black or matte silver finish, 38 1/2 in. OAL, approx. 7 lbs. New 2019.

MSR $497	$425	$375	$325	$295	$225	$195	$160	

Add $121 for Altamont laminated wood thumbhole stock.

* ***Performance Center T/C R22 Carbon Fiber*** – .22 LR cal., 17 in. stainless steel/carbon fiber barrel with muzzle brake, 10 shot rotary mag., Hogue overmolded textured thumbhole stock or blue, brown, or red hardwood laminated thumbhole stock, right-hand cheekpiece, push-button safety, 6061 aluminum receiver, built-in Picatinny rail, stainless steel bolt, sling swivel studs, 5.2 lbs. New 2020.

MSR $523	$475	$415	$350	$325	$265	$235	$200	

Add $119 for brown, blue, or red laminated hardwood thumbhole stock.

R-55 CLASSIC – .17 Mach 2 (mfg. 2006-2007) or .22 LR cal., blowback action, all steel construction, 5 (new 2003) or 8 (disc. 2002) shot mag., 22 in. match grade barrel with muzzle crown, adj. rear sight, blue finish, uncheckered Monte Carlo walnut stock, 5 1/2 lbs. Mfg. 2000-2009.

	$475	$400	$335	$285	$240	$195	$160	*$586*

R-55 CLASSIC BENCHMARK TARGET – same action as Classic, 18 in. heavy target barrel, brown laminated hardwood Monte Carlo target stock, matte blue finish, 10 shot mag., no sights, receiver is drilled and tapped, 6.8 lbs. Mfg. 2003-2009.

	$475	$400	$335	$285	$240	$195	$160	*$586*

R-55 SPORTER – .17 Mach 2 (disc.) or .22 LR cal., blue steel, 20 in. barrel, brown laminate or black composite stock, fiber optic sights, 6.25-7.25 lbs. Mfg. 2005-2011.

	$460	$400	$335	$285	$240	$215	$180	*$545*

Add $92 for brown laminate stock.

* ***R-55 Sporter Stainless*** – .22 LR cal., similar to Sporter, except with All-Weather stainless steel and black composite stock, 7 1/4 lbs. Disc. 2011.

	$625	$550	$495	$450	$400	$325	$250	*$705*

SILVER LYNX – .22 LR cal., 20 in. match grade barrel with adj. fiber optic open sights, 5 shot mag., stainless steel action and barrel, black composite stock with Monte Carlo cheekpiece, 5 1/2 lbs. Mfg. 2004-2005.

	$340	$295	$240	$200	$165	$145	$120	*$423*

T/C R22 RIFLE – .22 LR cal., 17 in. button rifled threaded barrel, 10 shot rotary detachable mag., green fiber optic front and adj. rear peep sight, OD Green, Realtree Edge, Mossy Oak Break-Up Country, TrueTimber Strata camo (new mid-2019), FDE with Black Grit (new 2020) composite stock or Hardwood stock (new 2020), push-button safety, aluminum receiver with stainless steel bolt and Picatinny style top rail, blue finish, 35 in. OAL, 4.4 lbs. New 2019.

MSR $399	$340	$300	$250	$225	$175	$150	$125	

Add $20 for Realtree Edge, Mossy Oak Break-Up Country, TrueTimber Strata (new mid-2019) camo or FDE with Black Grit finish (new 2020).

Add $73 for Hardwood stock (new 2020).

GRADING - PPGS™	100%	98%	95%	90%	80%	70%	60%	LAST MSR

RIFLES: SINGLE SHOT

ENCORE RIFLE – available in many rimfire and centerfire cals. between .17 Mach 2 (mfg. 2005-2009) and .45-70 Govt., interchangeable standard 24 or heavy 26 in. barrel, automatic hammer block safety, trigger guard opening lever, choice of black synthetic (new 1999), Realtree camo (new 2005), Realtree Hardwoods HD camo, or American walnut uncheckered forearm and Monte Carlo stock with pistol grip, adj. rear sight, approx. 7 lbs. Mfg. 1997-2012.

$575 $475 $375 $325 $275 $250 $225 *$689*

Add $50 for walnut.
Add $50 for camo.
Add $35 for .17 Mach 2 cal. (disc.).
Add $352 per extra blue finish barrel.
Add $173 for thumbhole stock (disc.).

Encore rifle barrels ARE NOT interchangeable with Contender Carbine barrels.

* ***Encore Rifle Stainless*** – similar to Encore Rifle, except has black synthetic stock and forearm or Realtree/Realtree Hardwoods HD (new 2005) camo treatment, and is stainless steel. Mfg. 1999-2012.

$650 $525 $425 $350 $300 $265 $235 *$769*

Add $399 per extra barrel.
Add $70 for camo.
Add $265 for thumbhole stock (camo only, disc.).

* ***Encore Rifle Katahdin Carbine*** – .444 Marlin (disc. 2003), .450 Marlin, or .45-70 Govt. cal., 18 in. barrel with muzzle tamer, blue steel, black composite stock and forearm, fiber optic sights, drilled and tapped, 6 lbs., 10 oz. Mfg. 2002-2005.

$525 $400 $275 $235 $195 $180 $170 *$617*

Add $292 for extra barrel.

* ***Encore Rifle Hunter Package*** – .300 Win. Mag., or .308 Win. cal., includes 3-9x40mm scope, Weaver style base and rings, and hard case. Mfg. 2002-2005.

$770 $640 $585 $475 $400 $360 $330 *$905*

PRO HUNTER RIFLE – various cals., 28 in. fluted barrel only w/o sights, drilled and tapped, stainless steel, features recoil reducing Flex Tech stock and choice of black, Hardwoods camo, with or w/o thumbhole, 7 3/4 lbs. Mfg. 2006-2012.

$725 $575 $475 $400 $350 $315 $275 *$839*

Add $70 for camo.
Add $99 for .416 Rigby cal. (disc. 2011).
Add $333 per extra barrel.

ENCORE PRO HUNTER CENTERFIRE RIFLE – .243 Win., .30-06, or .308 Win. cal., 28 in. fluted stainless steel barrel, swing hammer, SIMS recoil pad, FlexTech stock and forend, 42 1/2 in. OAL, 7 1/2 lbs.

MSR $839 $715 $625 $535 $485 $390 $320 $250

ENCORE PRO HUNTER PREDATOR – .204 Ruger, .223 Rem., .22-250 Rem., or .308 Win. cal., single shot rifle, 28 in. fluted barrel, synthetic Flextech stock with 100% Realtree Max-1 camo coverage, recoil pad, scope base, 42 1/2 in. OAL, 7 3/4 lbs. Mfg. 2010-disc.

$750 $650 $565 $510 $415 $340 $265 *$882*

ENCORE PRO HUNTER KATAHDIN CARBINE – .45-70 Govt., .460 S&W, or .500 S&W cal., similar configuration to Encore Pro Hunter Predator, 20 in. fluted stainless steel barrel, adj. peep sights, features recoil reducing Flex Tech stock with or w/o thumbhole, Simms recoil pad, drilled and tapped, 34 1/2 in. OAL, 7 lbs. New 2010.

MSR $852 $725 $635 $545 $490 $400 $325 $255

CONTENDER CARBINE – available in 15 cals. between .17 Rem. and .44 Rem. Mag., also .410 bore (3 in.), Contender action with pistol grip full stock and forearm, 21 in. interchangeable barrel, drilled for scope mounts, iron sights standard. Mfg. 1986-2000.

$440 $350 $275 $225 $190 $175 $160 *$540*

Add $31 for .17 Rem. cal. (disc. 1997).
Add $21 for .410 bore barrel. (disc. 1997).
Add approx. $244 per extra barrel.
Add $11 for match grade .22 LR barrel.
Subtract $36 for Youth Model (16 1/4 in. barrel w/o VR - disc. 1998).
Add $175 for Survival Carbine System (disc. - includes Rynite stock, 16 1/4 in. .223 Rem. barrel, extra .45 Colt/.410 bore barrel, and soft camo cordura case).

GRADING - PPGS™	100%	98%	95%	90%	80%	70%	60%	LAST MSR

* ***Contender Carbine Rynite*** – similar to Contender Carbine, except has Rynite stock and forend. Mfg. 1990-93.

	$360	$285	$225	$195	$180	$165	$155	*$425*

Add $30 for .17 Rem. cal.
Add $10 for match grade barrel.
Add $25 for 21 in. VR smoothbore .410 bore barrel.

* ***Contender Carbine Stainless*** – various cals., 21 in. barrel, choice of walnut (disc. 1993) or Rynite synthetic stock. Mfg. 1993-2000.

	$440	$350	$275	$225	$190	$175	$160	*$546*

Add $35 for walnut stock (disc.).
Add $11 for .22 LR match barrel (new 1995).
Add $26 for .410 bore smoothbore barrel with screw-in full choke (disc.).

This model was also available in a Youth Model with walnut stock at no extra charge (disc. 1993).

HUNTER RIFLE MODEL – single shot, top lever break open action w/interchangeable barrels, .22 Hornet, .223 Rem., .22-250 Rem., .243 Win., .270 Win., 7x57mm, .30-06, .308 Win., .375 H&H (new 1992), or .416 Rem. Mag. (new 1992) cal., 23 in. barrel, 6 lbs. 14 oz., checkered walnut stock, choice of medium or light sporter weight barrel. New 1983 and improved in 1987. Available in left-hand at no extra charge. Disc. 1992.

	$625	$495	$415	$350	$285	$250	$220	*$595*

Add $20 for .375 H&H or .416 Rem. Mag. cal.
Add approx. $275 per extra rifle barrel.

* ***Hunter Rifle Model Deluxe*** – similar to Hunter Model, except features double triggers and upgraded walnut stock and forearm. Mfg. 1992 only.

	$550	$450	$375	$325	$285	$250	$225	*$675*

Add $20 for .375 H&H or .416 Rem. Mag. cal.

* ***Hunter Rifle Model Shotgun*** – same action as Hunter Rifle, except is supplied with 12 ga. barrel (field choke with 3 1/2 in. chamber or slug barrel with 3 in. chamber and iron sights) or 10 ga. barrel (3 1/2 in. chamber). Disc. 1992.

	$500	$415	$350	$295	$265	$240	$220	*$595*

Add $275 per additional shotgun barrel.

TCR '83 ARISTOCRAT – similar to Hunter Model, except stock has cheekpiece and forearm is checkered, stainless steel, double set triggers. Disc. 1986.

	$750	$575	$450	$395	$350	$315	$275	*$475*

Add $175 for each additional barrel(s) (including 12 ga. slug).

HOTSHOT – .22 LR cal., 19 in. barrel, synthetic stock with black, Realtree AP camo, or AP Pink camo, short LOP, designed for Youth, automatic safety, drilled and tapped, 3 lbs. Mfg. 2010-2012.

	$175	$150	$130	$110	$95	$80	$70	*$219*

Add $30 for camo finish.

G2 CONTENDER – various rimfire and centerfire cals., .30-30 Win. is only current cal., single shot rifle, compact, 23 in. blue or stainless steel (disc.) barrel, newer mfg. features manual firing pin selector allows shooting both rimfire and centerfire cartridges with safety position in the center, no sights, uncheckered walnut (blue finish only) or black composite (disc.) stock, drilled and tapped, blue or stainless steel (disc.) finish, 36 3/4 in. OAL, 5 1/2 lbs. New 2009.

MSR $729	$625	$545	$475	$425	$345	$275	$225	

Add $20 for .17 HMR cal. (disc.).

SHOTGUNS: SINGLE SHOT

ENCORE SHOTGUN – 12 (new 2004) or 20 ga., 3 in. chamber, action based on Encore pistol with trigger guard for barrel opening, 26 in. VR barrel with three choke tubes (Field model only, N/A in Slug or Turkey model), recoil pad. Mfg. 1998-2009.

	$725	$600	$500	$400	$325	$250	$200	*$876*

Add approx. $408 per additional shotgun VR barrel with choke tubes.
Subtract $23 for 20 ga.

* ***Encore Shotgun Slug Gun*** – 12 or 20 ga. only, 3 in. chamber, 24 or 26 (20 ga. only) in. rifled barrel with fiber optic sights, walnut stock and forearm. Mfg. 2000-2005, reintroduced 2008-2009.

	$750	$625	$515	$400	$325	$250	$200	*$895*

Subtract approx. $25 for 20 ga.
Add $20 for fluted barrel.

GRADING - PPGS™	100%	98%	95%	90%	80%	70%	60%	LAST MSR

* ***Encore Shotgun Turkey Gun*** – 12 (disc. 2005) or 20 ga., 3 in. chamber, 24 in. smoothbore barrel with screw-in turkey choke tube, 100% Realtree Hardwoods (new 2003) or Advantage Timber (mfg. 2002 only) camo coverage, and fiber optic sights. Mfg. 2002-2011.

	100%	98%	95%	90%	80%	70%	60%	LAST MSR
	$825	$725	$625	$525	$450	$400	$325	*$978*

Add $71 for muzzleloading barrel (disc. 2003).
Subtract $21 if w/o camo coverage.

* ***Encore Shotgun Katahdin Turkey Gun*** – 12 ga., 3 in. chamber, 20 in. barrel with turkey choke tube, composite stock with Realtree Hardwoods HD camo pattern, fiber optic sights. Limited mfg. 2005.

	100%	98%	95%	90%	80%	70%	60%	LAST MSR
	$590	$510	$410	$325	$275	$225	$200	*$748*

ENCORE PRO HUNTER RIFLED SLUG GUN – 12 or 20 ga., 3 in. chamber, 28 in. fluted rifled barrel, drilled and tapped, engraved stainless steel frame, swing hammer, no sights, FlexTech stock with SIMS recoil pad, 42 1/2 in. OAL, 7 1/2 lbs.

	100%	98%	95%	90%	80%	70%	60%	LAST MSR
MSR $892	$750	$650	$550	$500	$425	$350	$275	

Add $20 for 12 ga.

ENCORE PRO HUNTER TURKEY GUN – 12 or 20 ga., 24 or 26 in. rifled bore barrel, adj. fiber optic sights, Flextech synthetic stock with 100% Realtree AP camo coverage, extra full turkey choke tube, 6 1/4-6 3/4 lbs. Mfg. 2010-2020.

	100%	98%	95%	90%	80%	70%	60%	LAST MSR
	$750	$650	$565	$510	$415	$340	$265	*$892*

THOR

Current trademark established during 2001 and manufactured by Thor Global Defense Group, located in Van Buren, AR. Distributed by Knesek Guns, located in Van Buren, AR.

For individual model listings, please go to BlueBookOfGunValues.com/overflow.

THUNDER-FIVE

Previous trademark manufactured by MIL Inc., located in Piney Flats, TN. Previous company name was Holston Enterprises, Inc. Previously manufactured by Mil, Inc. located in Piney Flats, TN. Previously distributed by C.L. Reedy & Associates, Inc. located in Jonesborough, TN.

REVOLVERS

While previously advertised as the Spectre Five (not mfg.), this firearm was re-named the Thunder-Five.

THUNDER-FIVE – .45 LC cal./.410 bore (T-45) with 3 in. chamber or .45-70 Govt. (T-70 mfg. 1994-98) cal., single or double action, unique 5 shot revolver design permits shooting .45 LC or .410 bore shotshells interchangeably, 2 in. rifled barrel, phosphate finish, external ambidextrous hammer block safety, internal transfer bar safety, combat sights, hammer, trigger, and trigger guard, Pachmayr grips, padded plastic carrying case, 48 oz., serialization started at 1,101. Mfg. 1992-circa 2007.

	100%	98%	95%	90%	80%	70%	60%	LAST MSR
	$495	$450	$400	$375	$350	$325	$300	*$545*

Sub-caliber sleeve inserts were available until 1998 for 9mm Para., .357 Mag./.38 Spl., and .38 Super cals.

THUREON DEFENSE

Current manufacturer located in Germantown, WI.

For individual model listings, please go to BlueBookOfGunValues.com/overflow.

TIKKA

Current trademark imported by Beretta U.S.A. Corp., located in Accokeek, MD. Previously imported until 2000 by Stoeger Industries, located in Wayne, NJ. Tikka rifles are currently manufactured by Sako, Ltd. located in Riihimäki, Finland. Previously manufactured by Oy Tikkakoski Ab, of Tikkakoski, Finland (pre-1989).

TIKKA

During 2000, Tikka was purchased by Beretta Holding of Italy. All currently produced Tikkas are imported by Beretta U.S.A. Corp., located in Accokeek, MD.

Also see listings under Ithaca combination guns and bolt action rifles for older models.

COMBINATION GUNS: O/U

Previously manufactured in Jyvaskyla, Finland. In 1989, under a joint venture agreement, the 412 O/U shooting system was manufactured in Italy. Older models may be found in the Valmet trademark section of this text.

GRADING - PPGS™	100%	98%	95%	90%	80%	70%	60%	LAST MSR

During 1993, the new models of the 512S series replaced the older 412S series. Separate listings have not been provided, since they are almost identical in most respects.

Add $745-$765 for extra shotgun barrels (includes screw-in chokes), $810 for extra shotgun/rifle combo, and $1,040 for double rifle barrels.

MODEL 512S/412S SHOOTING SYSTEM - interchangeable barrel assemblies permit a double rifle, shotgun/rifle, and O/U shotgun configuration, user installed interchangeable barrels, monobloc locking, rifle barrel positioning by adjustment, SST, extractors or ejectors, checkered walnut stock and forend, cocking indicators, blue finish.

* ***Model 512S Field Grade*** - 12 ga. only, 3 in. chambers, auto ejectors, screw-in choke tubes (includes 5), 26 or 28 in. barrels, matte nickel finish. New 1986-importation disc. 1997, reintroduced 2000 only.

$1,050	$750	$595	$550	$475	$440	$400	*$1,134*

Subtract 10% if w/o choke tubes.

Add $45 for Sporting Clays Model (new 2000).

The Premium Grade became standard issue beginning 1995. This model was reintroduced in 2000 only, and new features included back boring and ported barrels (Sporting Clays Model only).

* ***Model 412ST Trap*** - 12 ga., Monte Carlo stock, 30 in. barrels, screw-in chokes standard. Disc.

$1,125	$925	$725	$650	$580	$540	$475	*$1,325*

This variation was made by Valmet in Finland.

* ***Model 412ST Premium Grade Trap*** - 12 ga., 30 in. barrels, screw-in chokes, better quality walnut Monte Carlo stock and checkering. Disc.

$1,425	$1,000	$875	$750	$625	$580	$515	*$1,665*

This variation was made by Valmet in Finland.

* ***Model 512S Sporting Clays*** - 12 ga. only, sporting clays configuration with 28 or 30 (new 1994) in. VR barrels and choke tubes. Imported 1992-97.

$1,160	$950	$735	$650	$580	$540	$475	*$1,360*

* ***Model 512S Combination Gun*** - combination rifle/shotgun, 12 ga, 3 in. chambers, 24 in. barrels, under rifle barrel in .222 Rem., .30-06, or .308 Win. cal., extractors. Importation disc. 1997.

$1,425	$1,000	$875	$750	$625	$580	$515	*$1,770*

* ***Model 512S Double Rifle*** - .30-06 (new 1994), .308 Win. (new 1994), 9.3x74R cal., 24 in. barrels, extractors. Importation disc. 1997.

$1,525	$1,200	$1,000	$875	$750	$650	$550	*$1,890*

RIFLES: BOLT ACTION

In 2016, Tikka made significant upgrades to the T3 line of models and created the T3x Series. New features/upgrades included an improved grip, new modular stock with wide forend, new recoil pad, stock noise reduction, metallic bolt shroud, improved rail attachment, and redesigned ejection port. All rifles are manufactured by Sako in Finland. About 3,000 rifles sold under the Tikka name have been recalled following operational failures, but a small number of guns sold in the American market remain in the hands of consumers who may not have heard about this recall affecting some rifles manufactured circa 2003-2004. Consumers are urged to contact the Tikka Recall Center at 800-503-8869 with their rifle's serial number to find out if their firearm is part of the recall.

NEW GENERATION RIFLE (MODELS 595/695) - .22-250 Rem., .223 Rem., .243 Win., .270 Win., .30-06, .308 Win., 7mm Rem. Mag, .300 Win. Mag., or .338 Win Mag. cal., 22 1/2 (non-Mag.) or 24 1/2 (Mag. cals.) in. barrel, detachable 3 (standard) or 5 (optional) shot mag., forged and milled right or left-hand action in two lengths, checkered walnut stock, 7-7 1/2 lbs. Sako mfg. 1989-94.

$725	$600	$550	$500	$450	$400	$360	*$835*

Add $25 for Mag. cals.

Cals. .22-250 Rem., .308 Win., and .300 Win. Mag. were introduced in late 1989.

This model's nomenclature also included the Models 595 (short actions with cals. up to .308 Win. cal.) and 695 (long action, including Mag. cals.).

PREMIUM GRADE MODEL - .22-250 Rem., .223 Rem., .243 Win., .270 Win., .30-06, .308 Win., 7mm Rem. Mag, .300 Win. Mag., or .338 Win Mag. cal., high polished blue barrel, select walnut stock with rollover cheekpiece and rosewood pistol grip cap and forend tip. Imported 1989-1994.

$860	$715	$600	$550	$500	$450	$400	*$1,030*

Add $40 for Mag. cals.

GRADING - PPGS™	100%	98%	95%	90%	80%	70%	60%	LAST MSR

VARMINT MODEL – .22-250 Rem., .223 Rem., .243 Win., or .308 Win. cal., 24 1/2 in. heavy barrel, no sights. Mfg. 1991-94.

	$895	$750	$625	$550	$500	$450	$400	*$1,090*

T1X MTR – .22 LR or .17 HMR cal., right or left (new 2020) hand configuration, 16 (new 2021) or 20 in. cold hammer forged barrel, 10 shot rotary mag., stainless steel bolt, SST, black synthetic changeable pistol grip and stock, 6-6.5 lbs. New 2018.

MSR $579	$495	$435	$375	$335	$275	$225	$195	

Add $20 for left-hand configuration (new 2020).

T3 FOREST – various cals., 22 7/16 or 24 3/8 in. free floating cold hammer forged blued barrel, Monte Carlo oiled walnut stock, black rubber recoil pad, single stage trigger, blued finish. Mfg. 2015 only.

	$850	$750	$650	$550	$450	$385	$350	*$950*

WHITETAIL HUNTER/SYNTHETIC (BATTUE) – .22-250 Rem. (new 1995), .223 Rem. (new 1995), .243 Win. (new 1995), .25-06 Rem.(new 1995), .270 Win., .30-06, .308 Win. (not available in synthetic), 6.5x55mm Swedish (new 2002), 7mm Rem. Mag., 7mm-08 Rem. (new 1999), .300 Win. Mag., or .338 Win. Mag. cal., 20 1/2 (disc. 1994), 22 1/2 (new 1995), or 24 1/2 (new 1995, Mag. cals. only), in. barrel, 3 or 5 (optional) shot detachable mag., choice of wood or black synthetic (new 1996) stock, no sights (Hunter Model), or open sights on raised rib (disc., Battue Model), approx. 7 1/4 lbs. Mfg. 1991-2002.

	$525	$450	$390	$350	$325	$300	$275	*$615*

Add $30 for Mag. cals.

Add $60 for carved elk or deer game scene stock (mfg. 1996-97).

* ***Whitetail Hunter/Synthetic Left Hand*** – similar cals. as Whitetail Hunter, left-hand action. Importation disc. 2003.

	$590	$530	$460	$395	$360	$325	$295	*$680*

Add $30 for Mag. cals.

* ***Whitetail Hunter/Synthetic/Battue Stainless*** – similar cals. as Whitetail Hunter, except not available in 6.5x55mm Swedish cal., black synthetic stock only and satin finished stainless steel, 7 1/4 lbs. Mfg. 1997-2002.

	$590	$530	$460	$395	$360	$325	$295	*$680*

Add $30 for Mag. cals.

* ***Whitetail Hunter/Synthetic Stainless Laminate*** – .25-06 Rem., .270 Win., .30-06, .300 Win. Mag., or 7mm Rem. Mag. cal., similar to Whitetail Hunter Stainless, except has grey laminate wood stock and forend with checkering, satin finished stainless steel, 3 shot detachable mag., 7 1/4 lbs. Imported 2002-2003.

	$650	$565	$500	$430	$375	$315	$270	*$745*

Add $30 for Mag. cals.

* ***Whitetail Hunter/Synthetic Deluxe*** – similar cals. as Whitetail Hunter, gloss finished deluxe checkered walnut stock and forearm with rollover cheekpiece. Imported 1999-2003.

	$650	$565	$500	$460	$400	$360	$330	*$745*

Add $30 for Mag. cals.

T3 HUNTER – .22-250 Rem. (disc. 2009), .223 Rem. (disc. 2009), .243 Win., .25-06 Rem. (disc. 2009), .270 Win., .270 WSM (disc. 2012), .30-06, .308 Win., 6.5x55mm (disc. 2009), 7mm-08 Rem. (mfg. 2006-2009), 7mm Rem. Mag. (disc. 2009, reintroduced 2013), .300 WSM (disc. 2012), .300 Win. Mag., .338 Federal (disc. 2008), .338 Win. Mag. (disc. 2009), or 6.5x55 SE (new 2015) cal., cold hammer forged 22 7/16-24 3/8 in. barrel, similar action as the Whitetail Hunter, choice of checkered walnut or black synthetic stock (disc. 2003), black rubber recoil pad, 3-4 shot detachable mag., 2 position rear safety, right or left (new 2015) hand action, designed by Giugiaro of Italy, approx. 6 3/4 lbs. Importation began mid-2003-2015.

	$690	$580	$485	$415	$365	$315	$285	*$825*

Add $75 for left-hand action (new 2015).

Subtract 10% for synthetic stock.

* ***T3 Deluxe*** – similar cals. as T3 Hunter, oil finished deluxe Tripartiti checkered walnut stock with rosewood forend tip and pistol grip cap. Mfg. 2006-2007.

	$895	$725	$600	$550	$500	$450	$400	*$1,075*

* ***T3 Lite*** – various cals., similar to T3 Hunter, except has TrueBody glass fiber reinforced polymer black stock, adj. buttplate, approx. 6 1/4 lbs. Imported 2004-2015.

	$550	$475	$415	$365	$310	$275	$250	*$675*

Add $50 for WSM cals.

GRADING - PPGS™	100%	98%	95%	90%	80%	70%	60%	LAST MSR

* ***T3 Lite Stainless*** – various cals., similar to T3, except has stainless action and barrel, available with black synthetic stock only. Importation began mid-2003.

  $680 $565 $485 $415 $365 $315 $285 *$800*

Add $50 for WSM cals.
Add $75 for left-hand action (available in most right-hand cals.).

* ***T3 Lite Compact*** – .204 Ruger, .223 Rem., .22-250 Rem., .243 Win., 7mm-08 Rem., or .308 Win. cal., short or medium action, 20 in. barrel, 3-4 shot detachable mag., TrueBody glass fiber reinforced polymer black stock, black rubber recoil pad, 12 1/2 inch LOP, two position rear safety. Mfg. mid-2014-2015.

  $550 $475 $415 $365 $310 $275 $250 *$675*

* ***T3 Camo Stainless*** – similar to T3 Lite Stainless, except has Realtree HD Hardwoods camo stock finish. Mfg. 2006-2007.

  $650 $575 $495 $425 $350 $300 $260 *$795*

* ***T3 Laminated Stainless*** – .243 Win., .25-06 Rem. (disc.), .260 Rem. (new 2016), .270 Win., .270 WSM, .30-06, .300 WSM, .300 Win. Mag., .308 Win., 7mm Rem. Mag., or .338 Win. Mag.(disc.) cal., similar to T3 Stainless, available with grey matte laminated hardwood stock, approx. 6 3/4 lbs. Imported 2004-2015.

  $875 $750 $650 $550 $450 $400 $350 *$1,000*

Add $50 for WSM cals.

* ***T3 Scout CTR*** – .223 Rem. or .308 Win. cal., 20 in. heavy barrel w/o sights, black synthetic stock with built in Monte Carlo cheekpiece, 5 or 6 shot mag., Picatinny rail on receiver. Mfg. 2010-2012.

  $825 $725 $625 $525 $425 $365 $330 *$950*

* ***T3 CTR*** – .260 Rem. or .308 Win. cal., medium action, 20 in. semi-heavy contoured barrel, 10 shot steel detachable box mag., mag. release on aluminum trigger guard, no sights, checkered synthetic pistol grip stock with adj. cheekpiece, black rubber recoil pad, sling swivels, Teflon bolt, top Picatinny rail, 7 1/2 lbs. Mfg. mid-2014-2015.

  $950 $825 $725 $650 $525 $450 $350 *$1,100*

* ***T3 CTR Stainless*** – .260 Rem. or .308 Win. cal., stainless steel, medium action, 20 in. semi-heavy contoured stainless steel barrel, 10 shot steel detachable box mag., aluminum trigger guard, checkered synthetic pistol grip stock with adj. cheekpiece, Teflon bolt, top Picatinny rail, sling swivels. Mfg. 2015 only.

  $1,050 $950 $825 $750 $650 $525 $425 *$1,225*

* ***T3 Big Boar Synthetic*** – .30-06, .308 Win. or .300 WSM cal., black synthetic stock, 19 in. barrel, features Giugiaro design, 6.1 lbs. Imported 2005-2007.

  $585 $515 $460 $400 $350 $300 $275 *$695*

* ***T3 Varmint*** – .22-250 Rem., .223 Rem., or .308 Win. (disc. 2009) cal., choice of steel or stainless steel action/barrel, 23 3/8 in. heavy barrel, black synthetic stock, 3-6 shot detachable mag., 8 lbs. Imported 2004-2011, reintroduced 2015.

  $795 $700 $600 $500 $400 $350 $300 *$900*

* ***T3 Super Varmint*** – .22-250 Rem., .223 Rem., or .308 Win. cal., 23 3/8 in. heavy stainless barrel, 3 or 4 shot mag., laminated synthetic stock with adj. comb, Picatinny rail, extra swivel stud, adj. trigger. Imported 2005-2007.

  $1,250 $1,000 $800 $695 $585 $485 $415 *$1,425*

* ***T3 Tactical*** – .223 Rem. or .308 Win. cal., T3 action, 20 or 24 (disc. 2007) in. free floating match grade barrel with protected threaded muzzle, 5 shot mag., fiberglass-reinforced copolymer polypropylene stock with adj. comb, wide forearm, Picatinny rail, 7 1/4 lbs. Imported 2004-2015.

  $1,550 $1,225 $1,050 $875 $750 $650 $550 *$1,775*

T3x CAMO STAINLESS – .222 Rem., .223 Rem., .22-250, .30-06, .243 Win., 7mm-08 Rem., .308 Win., .270 Win., .270 WSM, or .300 WSM cal., 20, 22, or 24 in. cold hammer forged stainless steel barrel, 3 or 4 shot mag., SST, synthetic stock with Realtree Hardwoods HD pattern camo finish. Mfg. 2016 only.

Retail pricing was not available for this model.

T3x COMPACT TACTICAL RIFLE (CTR) – .260 Rem., .308 Win., or 6.5 Creedmoor cal., 20 or 24 (new 2017) in. semi-heavy threaded barrel, 10 shot steel mag., widened angular ejection port, aluminum trigger guard and mag. release lever, black modular synthetic stock, cheekpiece, upgraded recoil pad, vertical angled interchangeable non-slip pistol grips, Picatinny rail, Teflon bolt, 7.4 lbs. New 2016.

MSR $1,099 $935 $825 $700 $635 $515 $425 $365

GRADING - PPGS™	100%	98%	95%	90%	80%	70%	60%	LAST MSR

* ***T3x Compact Tactical Rifle Stainless (CTR)*** – .260 Rem., .308 Win., or 6.5 Creedmoor cal., 20 or 24 (new 2017) in. semi-heavy threaded stainless steel barrel, 10 shot steel mag., widened angular ejection port, aluminum trigger guard and mag. release lever, black modular synthetic stock, cheekpiece, upgraded recoil pad, vertical angled interchangeable non-slip pistol grips, Picatinny rail, Teflon bolt, 7.4 lbs. New 2016.

MSR $1,199	$1,025	$900	$775	$700	$575	$475	$400

T3x FOREST – .22-250 Rem. (2016 only), .243 Win. (2016 only), .260 Rem. (2016 only), 7mm-08 Rem. (2016 only), .308 Win., .25-06 Rem. (2016 only), 6.5x55 SE (2016 only), .270 Win., .30-06, 7mm Rem. Mag., or .300 Win. Mag. cal., 22.4 or 24.3 in. cold hammer forged Sako barrel, 3 or 4 shot detachable mag., widened angular ejection port, walnut stock, rollover cheekpiece, black rubber buttpad, sling swivel studs, metallic bolt shroud, steel recoil lug, 6.6-7 lbs. New 2016.

MSR $1,099	$935	$825	$700	$635	$515	$425	$365

T3x HUNTER – .243 Win., .308 Win., .270 Win., .30-06, .260 Rem. (mfg. 2016 only), .300 Win. Mag., .300 WSM (2016 only), 6.5x55 SE, 7mm Rem. Mag., 7mm-08 Rem. (new 2018), or 6.5 Creedmoor (new 2018) cal., right or left-hand action, 22.4 or 24.3 in. cold hammer forged Sako blued steel fluted or non-fluted barrel, 3 shot detachable mag., SST, widened angular ejection port, checkered walnut stock, black rubber recoil pad, sling swivel studs, two-stage safety, metallic bolt shroud, steel recoil lug, 6.6-7 lbs. New 2016.

MSR $949	$810	$710	$610	$550	$445	$365	$315

Add $50 for .300 WSM cal. (mfg. 2016 only).

* ***T3x Hunter Stainless*** – .243 Win., .308 Win., .270 Win., .30-06, .260 Rem., 6.5x55 SE, 7mm Rem. Mag., or 6.5 Creedmoor (new 2018) cal., right or left-hand action, 22.4 or 24 1/3 (new 2018) in. cold hammer forged Sako stainless steel fluted or non-fluted (disc. 2020) barrel, 3 shot detachable mag., SST, checkered walnut stock, black rubber recoil pad, sling swivel studs, two-stage safety, 6.6-7 lbs. New 2016.

MSR $1,149	$975	$850	$725	$675	$550	$450	$375

T3x LAMINATED STAINLESS – .243 Win., .308 Win., .270 Win., .30-06, .260 Rem., .270 WSM, .300 WSM, 7mm Rem. Mag., or 6.5 Creedmoor (new 2018) cal., 22.4 or 24.3 in. cold hammer forged Sako stainless steel barrel, 3 shot detachable mag., widened angular ejection port, SST, no sights, hand laminated grey wood stock, black rubber buttpad, sling swivels, two-position safety, metallic bolt shroud, steel recoil lug, 6.6-7 lbs. New 2016.

MSR $1,129	$960	$840	$720	$650	$525	$430	$335

T3x LITE – .223 Rem., .22-250 Rem., .243 Win., .308 Win., .25-06 Rem., .270 Win., .30-06, .300 Win. Mag., .270 WSM, .300 WSM, 7mm-08 Rem., 7mm Rem. Mag., or 6.5 Creedmoor (new mid-2017) cal., 22 2/5 or 24 1/3 in. cold hammer forged Sako blued barrel, 3 shot detachable mag., widened angular ejection port, SST, black synthetic modular stock with all new features, black recoil pad, low angled grip, metallic bolt shroud, steel recoil lug, improved rail attachment, 5.9-7 lbs. New 2016.

MSR $749	$650	$575	$500	$450	$375	$300	$250

* ***T3x Lite Compact*** – .204 Ruger, .223 Rem., .22-250 Rem., .243 Win., 7mm-08 Rem., .308 Win., or 6.5 Creedmoor (mfg. 2018-2019, reintroduced 2021) cal., 20 in. cold hammer forged Sako barrel, 3 or 4 shot detachable mag., SST, black synthetic modular stock with all new features, includes 1 in. spacer and larger recoil pad, sling swivel studs, 12 1/2 in. LOP, 5.9 lbs. New 2016.

MSR $749	$650	$575	$500	$450	$375	$300	$250

* ***T3x Lite Roughtech*** – .308 Win., .270 Win., 6.5 PRC, .300 Win. Mag., .270 WSM, .300 WSM, 7mm Rem. Mag., or 6.5 Creedmoor cal., 22.4 or 24.3 in. barrel, muzzle brake, wide angular ejection port, modular synthetic stock w/interchangeable pistol grips, recoil pad, metallic bolt shroud, steel recoil lug, black or tan Cerakote finish. New 2021.

MSR $1,099	$935	$825	$700	$635	$515	$425	$365

* ***T3x Lite Stainless*** – .223 Rem., .22-250 Rem., .243 Win., .308 Win., .25-06 Rem., .270 Win., .30-06, .300 Win. Mag., .270 WSM, .300 WSM, 7mm-08 Rem., 7mm Rem. Mag., or 6.5 Creedmoor (new 2018) cal., right or left-hand action, 22.4 or 24.3 in. cold hammer forged Sako stainless steel barrel, 3 or 4 shot detachable mag., stainless steel metal parts, widened angular ejection port, SST, black synthetic modular stock with all new features, black recoil pad, low angled grip, metallic bolt shroud, steel recoil lug, improved rail attachment, 5.9-6.3 lbs. New 2016.

MSR $849	$725	$635	$550	$500	$400	$325	$280

Add $50 for left-hand action.

GRADING - PPGS™ 100% 98% 95% 90% 80% 70% 60% LAST MSR

* ***T3x Lite Veil*** – .308 Win., .270 Win., 6.5 PRC, .300 Win. Mag., .270 WSM, .300 WSM, 7mm Rem. Mag., or 6.5 Creedmoor cal., 22.4 or 24.3 in. barrel, muzzle brake, wide angular ejection port, modular synthetic stock w/interchangeable pistol grips, recoil pad, metallic bolt shroud, steel recoil lug, Alpine or Wideland Cerakote finish. New 2021.

MSR $1,299 $1,100 $965 $825 $750 $605 $495 $385

T3x SPORTER – .222 Rem., .223 Rem., .260 Rem., .308 Win., or 6.5x55 cal., right or left-hand action, 20 in. threaded barrel, 5 or 6 shot mag., SST, colored laminate stock, cheekpiece with integrated memory feature can also be adjusted both vertically and horizontally, recoil pad is vertically adjustable and may be extended with optional spacers. Mfg. 2016 only.

Retail pricing was not available for this model.

T3x TAC A1 – .223 Rem. (mfg. 2016 only), .300 Win. (mfg. 2016 only), .260 Rem. (new 2017), 6.5 Creedmoor (new 2017), or .308 Win. cal., right or left (new 2018) hand action, 16 (new 2018), 20, or 24 (new 2017) in. semi-heavy blued barrel, 5 or 6 shot mag., extractor claw, spring loaded ejector plunger, black modular synthetic stock, wide forend, cheekpiece with adjusting wheel, heavy duty sling swivel studs, vertical grip, Picatinny rail, Teflon bolt. New 2016.

MSR $1,949 $1,650 $1,450 $1,250 $1,100 $900 $750 $625

Add $50 for left-hand action (new 2018, 6.5 Creedmoor or .308 Win. cal. only).

T3x UPR (ULTIMATE PRECISION RIFLE) – .308 Win. or 6.5 Creedmoor cal., 24.3 in. barrel, muzzle threaded, 10 shot mag., adj. SST, adj. stock, two-stage safety, QD slings, satin matte finish, 8.5 lbs. New 2021.

MSR $1,499 $1,275 $1,115 $950 $865 $700 $600 $500

T3x VARMINT – .22-250 Rem., .223 Rem., or 6.5 Creedmoor (new 2018) cal., 23.7 or 24.3 (new 2018) in. cold hammer forged Sako free floating barrel, 5 or 6 shot detachable mag., widened angular ejection port, SST, no sights, black modular synthetic stock with extra wide forend and foam insert for noise reduction, swivel studs, ergonomic cheekpiece, upgraded recoil pad, interchangeable non-slip vertical pistol grips, two-position safety, metallic bolt shroud, steel recoil lug, improved rail attachment, 7.9 lbs. New 2016.

MSR $1,000 $850 $750 $650 $575 $475 $385 $325

* ***T3x Varmint Stainless*** – .204 Ruger, .222 Rem., .223 Rem., .22-250, .243 Win., .308 Win., .270 WSM, .300 WSM, .25-06 Rem., 6.5x55, 7mm Rem., .270 Win., .30-06, or .338 Win. cal., similar to T3x Varmint, except is stainless steel. Mfg. 2016 only.

Retail pricing was not available for this model.

CONTINENTAL VARMINT MODEL – .17 Rem. (mfg. 2000-2002), .22-250 Rem., .223 Rem., or .308 Win. cal., heavy 26 in. barrel w/o sights, adj. trigger, quick release 3 shot detachable mag., integral scope mount rails, checkered walnut stock with beavertail forend, recoil pad spacer system, 8 1/8 lbs. Mfg. 1996-2003.

$615 $520 $460 $400 $350 $325 $300 *$720*

CONTINENTAL LONG RANGE HUNTER – .25-06 Rem. (disc. 2002), .270 Win. (disc. 2002), 7mm Rem. Mag., or .300 Win. Mag. cal., heavy 26 in. barrel w/o sights, checkered walnut stock and forend, 8 3/8 lbs. Mfg. 1996-2003.

$640 $540 $475 $415 $365 $325 $300 *$750*

Subtract 5% for non-Mag. cals. (disc. 2002).

TARGET (SPORTER) MODEL – .22-250 Rem., .223 Rem., .308 Win., 7mm-08 Rem. (new 2002), or 6.5x55mm Swedish (new 2003) cal., 23 3/8 in. barrel w/o sights, competition style stock with adj. buttplate and cheekpiece, detachable 5 shot mag., stippled pistol grip and forend, 9 lbs. Mfg. 1998-2003.

$845 $765 $660 $580 $515 $450 $395 *$950*

This model was designated the Tikka Sporter until 2003.

TIMBERWOLF

Previous trademark manufactured by I.M.I. (Israel Military Industries) located in Israel. Previously imported and distributed by Action Arms located in Philadelphia, PA until 1994.

RIFLES: SLIDE ACTION

TIMBERWOLF – .357 Mag. or .44 Mag. (disc.) cal., slide action, straight grip shotgun style stock with adj. drop, blue or satin chrome finish, takedown, 18 1/2 in. barrel, 10 shot tube mag., sear locking and firing pin safeties, integral scope base, approx. 5 1/2 lbs. Imported 1989-93.

.357 Mag. cal. $850 $775 $700 $625 $525 $425 $350

.44 Mag. cal. (blue only) $1,100 $1,000 $875 $725 $625 $525 $425 *$299*

Add $80 for satin chrome finish.

This model was designed by Evan Whildin, and imported/distributed by Action Arms Ltd. Springfield Armory imported 1,000 .44 Mag. Timberwolf models during 1990-91.

GRADING - PPGS™	100%	98%	95%	90%	80%	70%	60%	LAST MSR

TIME PRECISION ARMS

Current custom riflemaker located in Bethel, CT. Previously located in New Milford, CT, and Brookfield, CT. Consumer direct sales.

RIFLES: BOLT ACTION

All Time Precision Arms models are available in 4 different configurations - Hunting, Benchrest, Sporting, and Target rifles. Current MSR's are as follows: Hunting Model (base MSR range $2,202-$2,322), Benchrest Model (base MSR $2,202), Target Model (base MSR range $2,202-$2,220), Sporting Model (base MSR $1,980). Please contact the company directly for more information, current availability, and delivery time.

TIPPMANN ARMORY

Current rifle manufacturer established in 2014, located in Fort Wayne, IN.

FIREARMS: OTHER

Tippmann Armory also manufactures reduced scale Gatling Gun style firearms.

GATLING GUN – 9mm Para. cal., manually operated Gatling style gun, eight 10 in. barrels, 33 shot Glock mag., brass and steel construction, fixed sights, comes on its own pintle/carriage, w/steel wheels with rubber tires, black and brass finishes, 65 lbs.

MSR $5,000	$4,275	$3,775	$3,250	$2,950	$2,375	$1,950	$1,700	

RIFLES: SINGLE SHOT

ROLLING BLOCK MODEL – .357 Mag., .44 Mag., or .45-70 Govt. cal., rolling block action, black or case hardened investment cast 1018 steel frame, 27 in. round barrel, coil spring driven hammer, fixed front sight, adj. Buckhorn rear sight, walnut forearm and stock w/steel buttplate, 8.2-9.2 lbs.

MSR $899	$775	$675	$575	$475	$425	$375	$325	

Add $100 for .45-70 Govt. cal.
Add $250 for case hardened frame.
Add $350 for for .44-70 Govt. cal. w/case hardened frame.

TIPPMANN ARMS CO., LLC

Current AR-15 style rifle and pistol manufacturer located in Fort Wayne, IN.

Please refer to BlueBookOfGunValues.com to order the *Blue Book of AR-15s & Variations*, available as a book or online subscription.

TISAS TRABZON GUN INDUSTRY CORP.

Current manufacturer of semi-auto pistols established in 1993, located in Ankara, Turkey. Currently imported (Regent models only) by LKCI LLC, located in Newark, OH, Brownells, located in Grinnell, IA, Omega Arms, located in Heath, OH, and SDS Imports (Zigana models only), located in Knoxville, TN. Select models were previously imported by Zenith Firearms until 2017, located in Afton, VA. Previously imported by Umarex USA Inc. late 2011-2016 (Regent model only), by American Tactical Imports, located in Rochester, NY 2008-2011, and imported briefly by Interstate Arms located in Billerica, MA.

PISTOLS: SEMI-AUTO

Tisas Trabzon manufactures a full line of high quality semi-auto pistols that are based on three main series - Zigana (Zig), Kanuni, Fatih, and Regent.

All models include a rugged plastic carry case, factory cleaning kit, keyed cable lock, three magazines, and a 5-year warranty. Umarex USA still handles warranty repairs on Regent 1911 .45 firearms.

FATIH 13 – .380 ACP cal., SA/DA, 3.9 in. barrel, 13 shot, fixed front and dovetailed rear sights, ambidextrous thumb safety, black or white finish, 1 1/2 lbs. Mfg. in Turkey by Tisas. Disc.

	$345	$300	$250	$215	$185	$150	$125	*$406*

Add $16 for white finish.

FATIH 380 – .380 ACP cal., SA/DA, 3.98 in. semi-fixed barrel, two 13 shot mags., white chrome finish, includes cleaning brush and owner's manual, 21 oz. Imported by SDS Imports beginning 2019.

MSR $390	$335	$300	$250	$225	$175	$150	$135	

R100 1911-A1 – .45 ACP cal., patterned after the Govt. M1911-A1, black steel frame, SA, 7 shot mag., 5 in. barrel, bar stock slide, low cut ejection port, wide spur hammer, brown checkered synthetic grips, serrated ramp front sight, fixed notch rear sight, blue finish, accepts most aftermarket M1911 style parts, approx. 40 oz. Imported by Umarex 2011-2016.

	$375	$325	$295	$275	$250	$225	$200	*$440*

GRADING - PPGS™	100%	98%	95%	90%	80%	70%	60%	LAST MSR

R200S – .45 ACP cal., 5 in. barrel, 7 shot mag., satin nickel finished frame and slide with double serrations, skeletonized trigger and bobbed hammer, combat style sights, double diamond checkered synthetic grips, 40 oz. Imported by Umarex 2012-2016.

	$475	$425	$375	$350	$325	$300	$275	*$550*

R350CR – .45 ACP cal., 4 in. barrel, 7 shot mag., lower Picatinny rail, bobbed hammer and skeletonized trigger, checkered front grip strap, double diamond checkered Hogue synthetic grips, 35 oz. Imported by Umarex 2012-2016.

	$425	$375	$350	$325	$300	$275	$250	*$499*

REGENT BR9 – 9mm Para. cal., patterned after the Browning Hi-Power, locked breech, blued steel frame, 4.6 in. barrel, 13 shot mag., round hammer, drift adj. rear and post front sights, black synthetic or optional checkered walnut grips, black Cerakote finish, 29.5 oz. Imported by LKCI beginning 2018.

MSR $559	$475	$415	$350	$325	$260	$215	$185

* ***Regent BR9 SS*** – 9mm Para. cal., 5 in. barrel, similar to the BR9, except is stainless steel w/black trigger and hammer. Imported by LKCI beginning 2018.

MSR $599	$510	$450	$385	$350	$285	$230	$185

REGENT B45 – .45 ACP cal., 5 in. barrel, 8 shot mag., SA trigger, checkered wood grips, black Cerakote finish, 35.5 oz. Imported by Omega Arms beginning 2018.

MSR $435	$375	$325	$275	$250	$200	$175	$150

REGENT CC45 – .45 ACP cal., SA, 4 in. barrel, 8 shot mag., three hole trigger, checkered grips, black Cerakote or stainless steel finish, 34 oz. Imported by LKCI beginning 2018.

MSR $447	$380	$335	$285	$260	$210	$175	$145

Add $140 for stainless steel finish.

REGENT M9 – 9mm Para. cal., 5 in. barrel, front and rear slide serrations, black chrome finish. Mfg. by Tisas, imported by LKCI beginning 2018.

Please contact the importer directly for pricing and availability.

REGENT P9 – 9mm Para. cal., SA/DA, 4 in. barrel, polymer frame, lower Picatinny rail, black finish, 25 oz. Imported by LKCI beginning 2018.

Please contact the importer directly for U.S. availability and pricing on this model.

REGENT P45 SERIES – .45 ACP cal., SA, 5 in. barrel, 8 shot mag., 3-hole trigger, checkered grips, black Cerakote (P45 model) or stainless steel (P45R or P45 SS model) finish, 35.5 oz. Mfg. by Tisas, imported by LCKI and Omega Arms beginning circa 2018.

MSR $445	$380	$335	$285	$260	$210	$175	$145

Add $142 for stainless steel finish (P45 SS model).
Add $100 for stainless steel finish and rail (P45R model).

REGENT SP1/REGENT SP2 – 9mm Para. cal., SA/DA, 5.1 in. barrel, textured grips, lower Picatinny rail, black Cerakote (SP1 model) or white chrome (SP2 model) finish, 31.5 oz. Imported by LKCI beginning 2019.

MSR $435	$370	$325	$275	$250	$205	$165	$150

Add $10 for white chrome finish (SP2 model).

REGENT T1/REGENT T2 – 9mm Para. cal., SA/DA, 5.1 in. barrel, textured grips, no rail, black Cerakote (TP1 model) or white chrome (TP2 model) finish, 31.5 oz. Imported by LKCI beginning 2019.

Please contact the importer for U.S. availability and pricing on this model.

ZIG M 45 – .45 ACP cal., SA, 4 in. barrel, 8 shot mag., dovetailed sights, ambidextrous thumb safety, black finish or stainless steel, 7.64 in. OAL, 2.13 lbs. Mfg. in Turkey by Tisas. Disc.

	$465	$400	$350	$315	$250	$215	$185	*$549*

Add $50 for stainless steel.

* ***ZIG M 45 Custom Carry Package*** – .45 ACP cal., SA, action smoothed and tuned, 4 in. barrel, target crowned, 8 shot mag., beveled magwell, custom ejection port, trigger stop installation, dovetailed sights, ambidextrous thumb safety, polished feed ramp and barrel throat, includes 3 Metalform mags., choice of custom Duracoat frame and slide color, 2.13 lbs. Custom work done by Zenith Firearms. Disc.

	$650	$575	$495	$435	$375	$315	$250	*$749*

ZIG PC 1911 – .45 ACP cal., SA, 5 in. barrel, 8 shot mag., dovetailed sights, ambidextrous thumb safety, black finish, 8.62 in. OAL, 2.25 lbs. Mfg. in Turkey by Tisas. Disc.

	$465	$400	$350	$315	$250	$215	$185	*$549*

GRADING - PPGS™	100%	98%	95%	90%	80%	70%	60%	LAST MSR

* ***ZIG PC 1911 Custom Tactical/Target Package*** – .45 ACP cal., SA, action smoothed and tuned, 5 in. barrel, target crowned, 8 shot mag., beveled magwell, 3 Metalform mags., extended mag. release, custom ejection port, trigger stop installation, adj. rear and fiber optic front sights, ambidextrous thumb safety, polished feed ramp and barrel throat, full-length guide rod, shock buffer, extended magwell and mainspring housing, custom Duracoat finish, 2.25 lbs. Custom work done by Zenith Firearms. Disc.

	$775	$685	$585	$525	$425	$350	$275	*$899*

ZIG PCS 1911 – .45 ACP cal., SA, 4 in. stainless steel barrel, 8 shot mag., ambidextrous thumb safety, matte finish, 7.64 in. OAL, 2.13 lbs. Mfg. in Turkey by Tisas. Disc.

	$500	$450	$395	$345	$295	$250	$195	*$599*

ZIG PCS 9 – 9mm Para. cal., SA, 4 in. stainless steel barrel, 10 shot mag., dovetailed sights, ambidextrous thumb safety, matte finish, 7.64 in. OAL, 2.13 lbs. Mfg. in Turkey by Tisas. Disc.

	$500	$450	$395	$345	$295	$250	$195	*$599*

ZIGANA FC – 9mm Para. cal., SA/DA, 4.6 in. ported barrel, 15 shot, dovetailed sights, ambidextrous thumb safety, white finish, 1.83 lbs. Mfg. in Turkey by Tisas. Disc.

	$375	$325	$275	$235	$200	$175	$150	*$447*

ZIGANA KC – 9mm Para. cal., SA/DA, 4.1 in. ported barrel, 15 shot, dovetailed sights, ambidextrous thumb safety, white finish, 1.79 lbs. Mfg. in Turkey by Tisas. Disc.

	$365	$315	$265	$225	$195	$165	$145	*$437*

ZIGANA F/ZIGANA K – 9mm Para. cal., SA/DA, 4.1 (Zigana K) or 4.6 (Zigana F) in. barrel, Browning type locking system, two 15 shot mag., exposed hammer, auto firing pin blocking device, two-position manual safety, lower Picatinny rail, black finish, 29 oz. Imported by SDS Imports beginning circa 2018.

MSR $299	$255	$225	$190	$175	$140	$115	$100	

ZIGANA PX-9 – 9mm Para. cal., 4 in. hammer forged barrel, two 15 shot mags., Tritium post front and adj. rear sights, front and rear cocking serrations, includes hard case, holster, and loader, black finish. Imported by SDS Imports beginning 2020.

MSR $380	$325	$285	$245	$220	$180	$150	$125	

TITAN

Current trademark of bolt action rifles manufactured by Rossler (Robler) Waffen GmbH.

Please refer to the Rossler (Robler) Waffen GmbH listing in the R section.

TOBIN ARMS

Previous SxS shotgun manufacturer located in Norwich, CT circa 1909-1910 and in Woodstock, Ontario, 1910-1923. During 1923, a sporting goods distributor, G.B. Crandall, purchased Tobin Arms and continued to manufacture Tobin style guns until 1951, and are marked accordingly.

SHOTGUNS: SxS

Tobin Arms manufactured good quality, sidelock SxS hammerless shotguns in 12 or 16 ga. in a variety of makes and configurations. These shotguns were referred to as Tobin Simplex guns. Some of the models included the No. 250, No. 200, No. 55L, Model 40, and Model 25. Models varied in quality of wood, finish, and engraving. Values for average condition guns without engraving and ejectors typically range from $295-$850. Variations with strong original case colors, ejectors, SST, and light engraving have values ranging from $1,450-$2,950, depending on overall condition.

TOKAREV

Please refer to the Russian Service Pistols and Rifles listing in the R section.

TOLLEY, J & W

Current trademark owned by F.J. Wiseman & Co., Ltd., located in Staffordshire, England.

J & W Tolley was renowned for big bore wildfowl guns, as well as express and big game rifles. Current double rifles are built to order. Please contact the company directly for a price quotation, available options, and delivery time.

RIFLES: SxS

J & W TOLLEY BOXLOCK – various cals. and options, custom made to order.

J & W TOLLEY SIDELOCK – various cals. between .375 H&H-.600 NE, true H&H style action, custom made to order, approx. 12-18 months delivery time.

GRADING - PPGS™	100%	98%	95%	90%	80%	70%	60%	LAST MSR

TOMAHAWK

Current trademark of shotguns manufactured by M&U, located in Konya, Turkey. No current U.S. importation.

M&U manufactures a complete line of hunting and tactical style shotguns under the Tomahawk trademark, including semi-auto, slide action, O/U, SxS, lever action, and single barrel configurations. A wide variety of configurations are available, including receiver finishes and stock options. Currently, these guns have had little or no importation into the U.S. Please contact the company directly for more information, including pricing and domestic availability.

TOMPKINS

Previous pistol trademark manufactured under license by Varsity Manufacturing Co., located in Springfield, MA circa 1947-1953. Also manufactured by Walter Woodman in limited quantities after 1953.

PISTOLS: SINGLE SHOT

TOMPKINS PRECISION PISTOL – .22 LR cal., single shot pistol utilizing flexible sear mechanism and trap door style breech block, checkered walnut grips with full-length forend, adj. sights, approx. 200 mfg. through 1953, late mfg. will be marked WE Woodman (approx. 2 dozen) on receiver top, instead of AH Tompkins.

	100%	98%	95%	90%	80%	70%	60%	LAST MSR
	$1,100	$900	$750	$600	$500	$400	$350	

TORNADO

Currently manufactured by AseTekno located in Helsinki, Finland. No current U.S. importation.

RIFLES: BOLT ACTION

TORNADO MODEL – .338 Lapua Mag. cal., unique straight line design with free floating barrel, 5 shot mag., pistol grip assembly is part of frame, limited importation into the U.S.

Please contact the company directly regarding domestic availability and pricing.

TOROS ARMS

Current shotgun manufacturer established in 1998, located in Konya, Turkey. No current U.S. importation.

Toros Arms currently manufactures a complete line of the following shotguns: O/U, SxS, single barrel, semi-auto, lever-action, slide action, tactical, magazine fed, and accessories. Please contact the company directly for more information, including pricing and domestic availability.

TORUN ARMS

Current shotgun manufacturer located in Konya, Turkey. Previously imported on a private label basis by Savage Arms, Inc., located in Westfield, CT.

Torun Arms manufactures a complete line of good quality O/U, SxS, semi-auto, slide action, and single shot shotguns. The company also manufactures air rifles. Previously, select models were being manufactured on a private label basis for Savage Arms, Inc. Please contact the company directly for more information, including pricing and domestic availability.

TOZ

Current manufacturer established in 1712, located in Tula, Russia. Previously imported by Larry's Guns, located in Gray, ME until 2019, and by Tula Firearms, located in San Diego, CA. TOZ is an abbreviation for Tulsky Oruzheiny Zavod. Dealer sales.

PISTOLS: SINGLE SHOT

TOZ-35 FREE PISTOL – .22 LR cal., falling block action, single shot pistol, 12 in. barrel, adj. trigger, fully adjustable rear sight, fixed front post sight, anatomically fit target grips (with or w/o Rink laminate grip and forestock), employs virtually every shooting refinement possible in a single shot target pistol, breech lever located on the bottom of pistol grip, cocking lever on the left side of the pistol above the trigger, black matte finish, comes with wooden case, tool kit, and spare parts. Limited mfg.

	100%	98%	95%	90%	80%	70%	60%	LAST MSR
No MSR	$650	$575	$500	$450	$350	$275	$200	

Factory examples of these pistols lack formed grips, and as such will need to be fit to the shooter before use. Pre-formed replacement grips are also available from various manufacturers.

GRADING - PPGS™	100%	98%	95%	90%	80%	70%	60%	LAST MSR

FIREARMS

TOZ manufactures a wide variety of quality O/U, SxS, single shot, and semi-auto shotguns, in addition to pistols, rifles and combination guns. TOZ also provides a complete line of custom services, including elaborate inlays (gold, silver, and platinum) and wood carving. Please contact the importer directly for more information on the TOZ pistol. For more information on TOZ long guns, please refer to the Tula Arms Plant section.

TRABZON

Please refer to the Tisas Trabzon Gun Industry Corp. listing in this section.

TRACKER ARMS

Current trademark of various shotgun configurations and manufactured by Tracker Arms Ind. & Trade Co. Ltd. located in Istanbul, Turkey. No current U.S. importation.

TRACKINGPOINT

Current bolt action rifle manufacturer established late 2011, located in Pflugerville, TX. Previously located in Austin, TX.

Please refer to BlueBookOfGunValues.com to order the *Blue Book of AR-15s & Variations*, available as a book or online subscription.

TRADEWINDS

Previous importer located in Tacoma, WA.

RIFLES

HUSKY MODEL 5000 – .22-250 Rem., .243 Win., .270 Win., .308 Win., or .30-06 cal., bolt action, 23 3/4 in. barrel, adj. sight, removable mag., hand-checkered walnut stock. Disc.

$325	$310	$290	$250	$225	$200	$175

NORAHAMMER 900 SERIES – .270 Win., .308 Win., or .30-06 cal., similar to Husky Model, 20 1/2 in. barrel, 6 lbs. 8 oz.

$325	$310	$290	$250	$225	$200	$175

MODEL 311-A – .22 LR cal., bolt action, 5 shot, 22 1/2 in. barrel, folding leaf rear sight, walnut checkered stock. Disc.

$180	$170	$150	$130	$120	$100	$85

MODEL 260-A – .22 LR cal., semi-auto, 5 shot, 22 1/2 in. barrel, 3 leaf folding sight, checkered walnut stock. Disc.

$200	$190	$175	$150	$130	$120	$100

SHOTGUNS: SEMI-AUTO

MODEL H-170 – 12 ga., 2 3/4 in. chamber, 26 in. mod. or 28 in. full choked barrel, recoil action, alloy receiver, 5 shot tube mag., VR, checkered walnut stock. Disc.

$275	$265	$250	$225	$200	$180	$150

TRADITIONS PERFORMANCE FIREARMS

Current firearms, black powder replicas and muzzleloading importer located in Old Saybrook, CT. Distributor and dealer sales.

For individual model listings, please go to BlueBookOfGunValues.com/overflow.

TRANSFORMATIONAL DEFENSE INDUSTRIES, INC.

Previous name of a manufacturer of civilian and law enforcement firearms 2008-late 2010, located in Virginia Beach, VA.

Transformational Defense Industries, Inc. was part of the Gamma Applied Visions Group SA. On Sept. 1, 2010, the company name was changed to Kriss USA. Please refer to the Kriss Systems SA listing for current information.

TRAILBLAZER FIREARMS

Current manufacturer of pistols established in 2014, located in Asheville, NC.

PISTOLS: SINGLE SHOT

LIFECARD – .22 LR or .22 WMR (new 2019) cal., SA, sleek no snag folding design, approx. the size of a credit card when folded, full size metal handle, built-in ambi safety features (does not fire when closed), corrosion resistant isonite steel, optional custom-fit black or brown leather sleeve (limited

GRADING - PPGS™	100%	98%	95%	90%	80%	70%	60%	LAST MSR

availability), hardcoat black anodized, OD Green (new late 2019), Cobalt (new late 2019), Desert Sand (new late 2019), Magpul FDE (new late 2019), Graphite Black (new late 2019), or Tequila Sunrise (new 2020) finish, approx. 7 oz. New 2018.

MSR $299	$250	$225	$190	$175	$140	$115	$100

Add $39 for leather sleeve.
Add $50 for .22 WMR cal. (new 2019).

Limited Edition models were made available in 2019. They include: American Flag Special Edition (.22 LR cal.), "We The People" Special Edition (.22 LR or .22 WMR cal.), and Talo Member Exclusives in Burnt Bronze or Robin Egg Blue (.22 WMR or .22 LR cal.). Please contact the manufacturer directly for pricing and availability on these models.

* ***LifeCard Polymer*** – .22 LR cal., sleek no snag folding design, built in ambidextrous safety features (does not fire when closed), corrosion resistant isonite steel, approx. the size of a credit card when folded, full size polymer handle makes overall weight lighter than standard model, optional custom-fit black or brown leather sleeve (limited availability), hardcoat anodized black finish. New late 2019.

MSR $299	$275	$225	$200	$175	$150	$125	$100

Add $39 for leather sleeve.

TREJO PISTOLS

Current trademark of M-1911 style semi-auto pistols manufactured by Industrias Trejo S.A de C.V. beginning in 1948 located in Zacatlan (Puebla), Mexico. Currently imported exclusively by Armamentos, Inc. located in West Palm Beach, FL.

Please contact the importer directly for availability and pricing.

TRENCH/RIOT SHOTGUNS

The following is a chronological listing beginning with WWI of the various U.S. commercial Riot and military Trench and Riot shotguns mfg. to date.

The publisher wishes to express thanks to the late Pat Redmond and Rick Crosier for the information in this section.

Some 100% values have been intentionally omitted in this section as they are seldom seen or sold.

Values listed below are for original, unmodified shotguns with proper parts makers, and unsanded wood with crisp stock cartouches.

All Trench/Riot shotguns listed are in 12 ga. only.

SHOTGUNS: MILITARY TRENCH, WWI

WINCHESTER MODEL 1897 MILITARY TRENCH GUN – high-polish commercial blue finish, solid frame with 6 row ventilated handguard for bayonet attachment, walnut high comb stock with hard rubber buttplate (no cartouches in stock). Guns used by the U.S. Army for trench warfare in WWI, most have "U.S." and ordnance "flaming bomb" hand stamped on the right side of the receiver above ejection port. Military markings were added in the 1920s to about 10% of the trench guns kept in the Army's inventory after the war. Serial range 650,000-695,000.

Trench Gun	N/A	N/A	$8,500	$7,000	$5,250	$3,750	$2,500
Trench Gun w/military markings	N/A	$9,500	$8,000	$6,000	$4,250	$3,250	$2,250

REMINGTON MODEL 10 MILITARY TRENCH GUN – high polish commercial blue finish with wood handguard on top of barrel, separate bayonet adaptor attaches to front of barrel for bayonet attachment. "U.S." and ordnance bomb marked on left side receiver, stock is unmarked. Extremely rare and hard to find complete and in original condition. Trench gun barrel length is 22 in. as compared to 20 in. Riot gun. Prices quoted only for complete guns with wood handguard and bayonet adaptor. Serial range 160,000-165,000.

Trench Gun	N/A	$15,000	$12,750	$4,800	$3,500	$2,000	$1,800
Riot Gun	N/A	$5,000	$3,000	$1,200	$650	$500	$400

SHOTGUNS: MILITARY RIOT/TRENCH, WWII

ITHACA MODEL 37 MILITARY SHOTGUNS – rarest of all Trench shotguns, high polish commercial blue finish, "RLB" and ordnance bomb on left side of receiver, ordnance bomb on barrel, stocks not proofed, blue vent. handguard for bayonet attachment, only 1,420 Trench guns were ordered in 1941. Ithaca supplied mostly long barrel martially marked shotguns. Serial range 49,000-62,000.

Trench Gun	N/A	$20,000	$15,000	$12,500	$7,500	$4,000	$3,250
Riot Gun	N/A	$6,000	$5,000	$3,500	$2,000	$1,000	$750
Long Barrel	N/A	$2,500	$1,850	$1,500	$1,000	$750	$600

GRADING - PPGS™	100%	98%	95%	90%	80%	70%	60%	LAST MSR

REMINGTON MODEL 31 MILITARY SHOTGUNS - commercial blue finish (high polish and flat blue finishes noted). Can be marked "U.S. Property" on receiver and/or barrel. Some examples noted with only ordnance mark on stock. Serial range 39,500-60,500.

Riot Gun	N/A	$2,800	$1,800	$1,000	$750	$650	$500	
Long Barrel	N/A	$1,200	$1,000	$650	$500	$400	$300	
Trainer w/ comp.	N/A	$1,300	$1,100	$750	$600	$500	$400	

REMINGTON MODEL 11 MILITARY SHOTGUNS - this is the most commonly found military shotgun. Examples of 5 shot and 3 shot Sportsman Model. Examples with plain or engraved receivers and plain or fancy checkered wood. Military marked with "U.S." and ordnance bomb on receiver and barrel. Later models are marked "Military Finish". These shotguns all have highly polished commercial blue finish and ordnance marked stocks. Serial range 450,000-500,000 and 700,000-711,000.

Riot Guns	N/A	$1,800	$1,350	$875	$650	$500	$350	
Long Barrel	N/A	$850	$500	$350	$300	$250	$200	
Aerial Trainer w/machine gun mount	N/A	$8,500	$7,250	$5,250	$4,000	$3,000	$2,250	

* ***Remington Model 11 Military Shotgun Riot*** - this configuration was sold by the government as surplus as late as the 1970s and can occasionally be found NIB with packing materials and instruction manual. Mint in factory box - $2,800.

SAVAGE MODEL 720 MILITARY SHOTGUNS - appears identical to Remington Model 11. This was mfg. by Stevens/Savage in very limited quantities, 20in. barrel w/cylinder bore, plain and engraved receivers noted with high quality commercial blue finish. Stocks are unmarked and must have ramp sights to be original. Watch for altered guns made into Riots. Serial range 69,000-90,000.

Riot Gun	N/A	$2,800	$2,500	$1,850	$1,250	$925	$750	
Long Barrel	N/A	$1,000	$800	$750	$500	$350	$300	

STEVENS MODEL 620 MILITARY SHOTGUNS - this was the current model being sold by Stevens and has a commercial blue finish, but not of the same quality as the other companies. Trench guns are equipped with handguards that have a definite purple/reddish color to the front and dark blue vent. shroud. Model 620s are much rarer than 520s and have "U.S." and ordnance bomb on receiver, ordnance bomb on barrel and unmarked stock. Serial range 1,000-30,000.

Trench Gun	N/A	$5,500	$4,500	$3,150	$2,000	$1,500	$925	
Riot Gun	N/A	$1,800	$750	$450	$400	$350	$250	
Long Barrels	N/A	$700	$600	$400	$250	$200	$175	

STEVENS 520-30 MILITARY SHOTGUNS - this model was resurrected due to available machinery and is the most commonly found Trench gun. Riot guns in mint condition are hard to find. Same finish as Model 620, "U.S." and ordnance bomb on receiver, ordnance bomb on barrel and no proofing on stocks, except for reworks. Trench gun has same style handguard as Model 620. Serial range 30,000-70,000.

Trench Gun	N/A	$4,500	$3,250	$2,150	$1,500	$800	$600	
Riot Gun	N/A	$2,000	$1,000	$750	$350	$300	$250	
Long Barrels	N/A	$700	$500	$400	$225	$175	$150	

STEVENS SINGLE & DOUBLE BARREL MILITARY SHOTGUNS - these guns were procured by the government from distributors and gun dealers. "U.S." and oversized flaming bomb hand stamped on left side receiver.

Single Barrel	N/A	$750	$600	$400	$350	$300	$250	
Double Barrel	N/A	$1,750	$1,450	$1,200	$950	$725	$500	

WINCHESTER MODEL 97 MILITARY SHOTGUNS - takedown model, high polish commercial blue finish, finger groove walnut stock with hard rubber buttplate. All early riot and trench guns have "WB" and crossed cannons cartouches on the left side of stock, left side of receiver is machined marked "U.S." with or w/o ordnance "flaming bomb". All "WB" trenchguns have a 6 row ventilated handguard. All 97s will have ordnance "flaming bomb" on top of barrel. Around serial range 950,000, receivers were all marked on left side with a machined "U.S." and ordnance "flaming bomb" proofs, ventilated handguard was changed to a 4 row, "GHD" and ordnance crossed cannons cartouches on left side of stock. During this transition, a very few examples with 6 row handguards were mfg. Serial range 920,000-960,000.

Riot Gun w/ WB	N/A	$2,500	$2,000	$1,700	$800	$600	$500	
Trench Gun w/ WB	N/A	$10,000	$8,500	$6,500	$4,500	$2,850	$1,800	
Trench Gun w/ GHD	N/A	$10,000	$8,500	$6,500	$4,500	$2,850	$1,800	
Long Barrel	N/A	$2,000	$1,500	$1,200	$800	$650	$500	

GRADING - PPGS™	100%	98%	95%	90%	80%	70%	60%	LAST MSR

WINCHESTER MODEL 12 MILITARY SHOTGUNS – takedown model with improved hammerless receiver. These were made to supplement Model 97 production. Riot guns and Trench guns share same serial range. Finished in high polished commercial blue, except for some Trench guns (only) which were the only WWII shotguns to have factory parkerized finishes. All Model 12s have "U.S." and ordnance bomb on right side of receiver, ordnance bomb on barrel and cross cannons ordnance mark and inspector initials on left side of stock. Trench guns have 4 row vent. handguards.

* ***Winchester Model 12 Military Shotgun Blue finish*** – serial range 926,000-1,030,000.

Trench Gun w/ WB	N/A	$10,000	$8,500	$6,500	$4,500	$2,850	$1,800	
Riot Gun	N/A	$2,000	$1,850	$1,500	$750	$650	$500	
Long Barrel	N/A	$1,500	$1,200	$1,000	$750	$600	$450	

* ***Winchester Model 12 Military Shotgun Parkerized finish*** – serial range 1,030,000-1,040,000.

Trench Gun w/ WB	N/A	$10,000	$8,500	$6,500	$4,500	$2,850	$1,800	

WINCHESTER MODEL 37 MILITARY SHOTGUNS – high polish, commercial blue, single barrel, procured from Winchester. "U.S." and ordnance bomb proofmarks were applied to left side of receiver. Winchester records show shipment of 5,410 guns to the military - very few examples of this model have ever been found.

Single Barrel	N/A	$3,500	$2,500	$1,500	$1,200	$1,000	$750	

SHOTGUNS: MILITARY RIOT/TRENCH, VIETNAM

ITHACA MODEL 37 – parkerized finish with "U.S." marks on right side of receiver. Receiver and barrel are also marked "P". Serial range, applied on gun upside-down, is from S1,000-S23,500. Used in the Vietnam era. A very few original Trench guns with parkerized handguards have been noted.

Riot Gun	N/A	$3,500	$2,500	$1,800	$800	$600	$500	
Trench Gun	N/A	$8,500	$7,150	$5,750	$4,000	$2,500	$2,000	

SAVAGE-STEVENS 77E – parkerized finish with sling swivels and red rubber buttpad. "U.S." marked on right side of receiver and military "P" proofmark on receiver and barrel. Hard to find in excellent condition.

Riot Gun	N/A	$1,800	$1,400	$1,200	$800	$400	$300	

WINCHESTER MODEL 1200 – parkerized barrel, mag. tube, and bayonet adapter with U.S. marking on barrel. Aluminum receiver with black or matte type finish, "U.S." is marked under serial number. Very rare as few examples have been released by the government due to its continued use by military forces.

Trench Gun	N/A	$5,000	$4,250	$3,400	$2,500	$1,450	$850	

SHOTGUNS: RIOT/TRENCH GUN, COMMERCIAL SALES

WINCHESTER MODEL 12 RIOT – thousands mfg. late 1930s-1960s.

	N/A	$550	$450	$395	$350	$295	$240	

WINCHESTER MODEL 97 – commercial high polish blue, changed from solid frame to takedown in 1935. Trench guns made through 1945 and Riot gun mfg. continued until 1960s.

* ***Winchester Model 97 Solid Frame*** – Serial range 700,000+.

Trench Gun	N/A	$4,500	$3,500	$2,800	$1,500	$1,200	$1,000	
Riot Gun	N/A	$2,000	$1,600	$1,100	$850	$600	$500	

* ***Winchester Model 97 Takedown*** – Serial range 800,000+.

Trench Gun	N/A	$3,500	$2,750	$2,000	$1,450	$1,100	$900	
Riot Gun	N/A	$1,500	$800	$600	$500	$400	$300	

REMINGTON MODEL 10 – commercial high polish blue, sold in the 1920s to various government and banking agencies.

Riot Gun	N/A	$800	$600	$300	$275	$250	$200	

REMINGTON MODEL 11 – made in 1930s for law enforcement use.

Riot Gun	N/A	$700	$575	$450	$350	$300	$275	

MODEL 31R RIOT GUN – similar to 31A, with 20 in. barrel.

	N/A	$600	$475	$350	$275	$175	$150	

ITHACA MODEL 37 – parkerized models made in 1960s for police agencies and commercial sales.

Trench Gun	N/A	$1,950	$1,750	$1,500	$1,250	$1,000	$750	
Riot Gun	N/A	$575	$475	$375	$275	$225	$175	

GRADING - PPGS™	100%	98%	95%	90%	80%	70%	60%	LAST MSR

U.S. MILITARY SHOTGUN ACCESSORIES

WWI BAYONETS – military acceptance proofs, leather scabbards, and two variations of attachments to belt, two-toned blue handle and parkerized blade.

* ***WWI Bayonet Winchester 1917 date***

Prices range from $150-$400, depending on original condition.

* ***WWI Bayonet Remington 1917-1918 dates***

Prices range from $125-$300, depending on original condition.

LEATHER SLING – WWI dates, w/brass hardware.

Prices range from $75-$300, depending on original condition. Mint condition will bring $400.

SHOTGUN SHELL POUCHES

* ***Shotgun Shell Pouch 32 round with sling***

Prices range approx. $500, depending on original condition. Mint condition prices are approx. $1,200.

* ***Shotgun Shell Pouch 12 round dated 1921-1922***

Prices range approx. $400, depending on original condition. Mint condition will bring $1,200.

WWII BAYONETS – same as from WWI, but have plastic scabbard w/large ordnance bomb, or original WWI leather scabbard.

Prices range approx. $125-$650, depending on original condition.

LEATHER SLING – WWII dates, w/steel hardware.

Prices range from $50-$300, depending on original condition. Mint condition will bring $400.

SHOTGUN SHELL POUCHES – 12 round pouches with contract dates from 1960s-1990s.

Prices range from $50-$125.

SHOTGUN SHELL POUCHES – 12 round pouches dated 1942-45, various manufacturers, watch for recent 1943 JQMD fake pouches - they have extreme two-tone colors.

Prices range approx. $350, depending on original condition.

VIETNAM BAYONETS – new contracts to supplement large quantities of shotguns being sent to Vietnam, black plastic handles, green plastic scabbards, marked "M-1917".

Gen. Cut - mfg. by General Cutlery prices range from $150-$250.
CA-mfg. by Canadian Arsenal prices range from $150-$300.

TRIPLE ACTION LLC

Previous gun design firm located in Logan, UT.

PISTOLS: SINGLE SHOT

Triple Action LLC planned to manufacture a .50 BMG single shot pistol with 13.2 in. barrel, with muzzle brake and nitrogen recoil controller. Only a few prototypes were manufactured. Construction materials included titanium and aircraft grade aluminum, and the weight was 10 or 12 lbs.

TRISTAR ARMS INC.

Current importer established in 1994, located in N. Kansas City, MO. Distributor and dealer sales.

In 2015, the company name changed from TriStar Sporting Arms, Ltd. to TriStar Arms Inc.

PISTOLS: SEMI-AUTO

The following semi-auto pistol variations are manufactured by Canik55 in Turkey.

C-100 – 9mm Para., and .40 S&W (disc. 2017) cal., DA/SA, 3.7 in. barrel, steel slide, 10 (9mm, disc.), 11 (.40 S&W, disc.), or 15 (9mm Para.) shot mag., rear snag-free dovetail sights and fixed blade front sight, black polycoat, chrome (mfg. 2017), Tungsten finish (new 2018), black polymer checkered grips, includes two magazines and hard plastic case, approx. 25 oz. Imported 2013-2020.

100%	98%	95%	90%	80%	70%	60%	LAST MSR
$385	$340	$300	$275	$250	$225	$200	*$460*

Add $20 for chrome (disc. 2017) or Tungsten (new 2018) finish.

T-100 – 9mm Para. cal., DA/SA, 15 shot mag., 3.7 in. barrel, black polymer grips, rear snag-free dovetail and fixed blade front sights, Black Cerakote, Titanium Cerakote (mfg. 2014-2015), or chrome (disc. 2014) finish, includes black plastic case, approx. 26 oz. Imported 2013-2020.

100%	98%	95%	90%	80%	70%	60%	LAST MSR
$385	$340	$300	$275	$250	$225	$200	*$460*

Add $20 for chrome (disc. 2014) or Titanium Cerakote (mfg. 2014-2015) finish.

GRADING - PPGS™	100%	98%	95%	90%	80%	70%	60%	LAST MSR

L-120 – 9mm Para. cal., DA/SA, 4.7 in. barrel, 17 shot mag., steel slide, alloy frame, black polymer grips, rear snag-free dovetail and fixed blade front sights, Black Cerakote or chrome finish, includes black plastic case and extra mag., 28 oz. Mfg. 2013-2015.

	$385	$340	$300	$275	$250	$225	$200	*$459*

Add $20 for chrome finish.

P-100 – 9mm Para. or .40 S&W (disc. 2017) cal., 3.7 in. barrel, 11 (disc. 2017) or 15 shot mag., black Cerakote finish, includes two mags., gun lock, cleaning kit, and hard carrying case, approx. 36 oz. Imported 2015-2020.

	$415	$350	$325	$295	$250	$225	$200	*$490*

P-120 – 9mm Para. or .40 S&W (mfg. 2015-2017) cal., DA/SA, 4.7 in. barrel, 14 (.40 S&W, disc. 2017) or 17 shot mag., steel slide, alloy frame, black polymer grips, rear snag-free dovetail and fixed blade front sights, Black Cerakote or chrome finish, includes two mags., gun lock, cleaning kit, and black plastic carrying case, 41.6 oz. Imported 2013-2020.

	$415	$350	$325	$295	$250	$225	$200	*$490*

Add $20 for chrome finish.

S-120 – 9mm Para. cal., DA/SA, 17 shot mag., 4.7 in. barrel, steel frame, steel slide, black polymer grips, rear snag-free dovetail and fixed blade front sights, Black Cerakote or chrome finish, includes extra mag. and black plastic case, approx. 36 oz. Imported 2013-2020.

	$400	$345	$315	$285	$250	$225	$200	*$470*

Add $25 for chrome finish.

T-120 – 9mm Para. cal., DA/SA, full size, 17 shot mag., steel alloy frame, steel slide, 4.7 in. barrel, rail under barrel for laser or flashlight mount, scalloped ridges on slide for better grip, black polymer grips, rear snag-free dovetail and fixed blade front sights, Black Cerakote, Desert Sand Cerakote (new 2014), Titanium Cerakote (mfg. 2014-2017), Tungsten (new 2018), or chrome (disc. 2014) finish, 30 oz. Imported 2013-2020.

	$400	$345	$315	$285	$250	$225	$200	*$470*

Add $25 for Desert Sand Cerakote (new 2014), Titanium Cerakote (mfg.2014-2017), Tungsten (new 2018), or chrome (disc. 2014) finish.

TP-9C – 9mm Para. cal., DA/SA, SFO, 10 shot mag., 3 1/2 in. barrel, polymer frame, 1.39 lbs. Mfg. 2013 only.

	$400	$345	$315	$285	$250	$225	$200	*$469*

TXI – .22 LR cal., SFA, 4 in. barrel, 10 shot mag., adj. rear dovetail and fixed front sight, textured grips w/finger grooves, firing pin block, plastic carrying case, trigger safety and decocker, lower Picatinny rail, black polymer frame w/lightweight aluminum slide, black anodized metal finish, 18 oz. Limited importation 2018 only.

	$295	$265	$245	$225	$200	$185	$170	*$349*

Z-919 – 9mm Para. cal., 4.1 or 4.5 in. barrel, 17 shot mag., fixed combat sights, black polymer Tenifer frame with rib panels and lower Picatinny rail, matte black slide, approx. 1.7 lbs. Mfg. 2019 only.

	$400	$345	$315	$285	$250	$225	$200	*$470*

Add $20 for Perfomance variation.
Subtract $10 for Compact variation.

REPRODUCTIONS: REVOLVERS, SAA

REGULATOR – .357 Mag. (disc. 2005) or .45 LC cal., 4 3/4 or 5 1/2 in. barrel, choice of brass or steel backstrap/trigger guard, two-piece smooth walnut grips. Mfg. by Uberti. Disc.

	$385	$335	$295	$260	$225	$200	$180	*$455*

Add $34 for Regulator DLX with steel backstrap/trigger guard (.45 LC only).

STALLION – .17 HMR/.17 Mach 2 cal., 5 1/2, 7 1/2 (mfg. 2005 only), or 9 (mfg. 2005 only) in. barrel. Mfg. by Uberti. Imported 2005-2006.

	$435	$395	$350	$300	$265	$235	$200	*$459*

Add $94 for Stallion DLX with steel backstrap/trigger guard (mfg. 2005 only).

REPRODUCTIONS: RIFLES

HENRY LEVER ACTION – .44-40 WCF (disc. 2005) or .45 LC cal., brass frame only, 18 1/2 (Trapper, disc. 2005) or 24 1/4 (rifle) in. barrel, 9.4 lbs. Mfg. by Uberti. Disc.

	$1,125	$875	$750	$625	$525	$425	$325	*$1,359*

MODEL 1866 LEVER ACTION – .38 Spl. (disc. 2005), .44-40 WCF (disc. 2005) or .45 LC cal., 19 (Yellowboy), 20 (disc. 2005), or 24 1/4 in. barrel, 7.2 (Yellowboy) or 8.4 (rifle) lbs. Mfg. by Uberti. Disc.

	$840	$700	$600	$500	$450	$400	$350	*$999*

Add $110 for Sport configuration (20 or 24 1/4 in. barrel).

GRADING - PPGS™	100%	98%	95%	90%	80%	70%	60%	LAST MSR

MODEL 1873 SPORT LEVER ACTION – .44-40 WCF (disc. 2005) or .45 LC cal., 24 1/4 or 30 (disc. 2005) in. barrel, 8.4 lbs. Mfg. by Uberti. Disc.

$1,075	$800	$675	$575	$500	$425	$325	*$1,259*

Add $45 for 30 in. barrel (disc. 2005).

MODEL 1885 SINGLE SHOT HIGH WALL – .45-70 Govt. cal., 28 in. barrel. Mfg. by Uberti, importation disc. 2005.

$725	$595	$535	$475	$400	$325	$250	*$852*

MODEL 1874 SHARPS – .45-70 Govt. cal., 28, 32, or 34 (disc. 2006) in. barrel, double set triggers, adj. rear sight, case hardened frame, approx. 10 lbs. Mfg. by Pedersoli. Importation disc. 2004, resumed 2006-2009.

$950	$850	$750	$650	$550	$450	$350	*$1,099*

Add $60 for Bridgeport Model with higher sideplate (disc. 2006).

RIFLES: BOLT ACTION

PEE-WEE .22 – .22 LR cal., single shot, manual cocking bolt, 16 1/2 in. barrel, steel construction, blue finish, adj. rear leaf sight, 12 in. LOP, uncheckered walnut Monte Carlo stock, 2 3/4 lbs. Limited mfg. 1998 only.

$170	$140	$130	$120	$110	$100	$90	*$189*

STRAIGHT PULL ACTION (SPA) – .22 LR cal., straight pull action, 20 in. barrel w/o sights, 10 shot detachable mag., black synthetic stock and forend, black anodized metal finish, 6.3 lbs. Limited importation 2018 only.

$425	$365	$325	$285	$240	$220	$195	*$519*

RIFLES: SEMI-AUTO

MK 22 – .22 LR cal., blowback action, 16 1/2 in. barrel w/flash hider, includes two 22 shot detachable mag., flip-up w/upper and rear sight, folding buttstock, pistol grip, tactical configuration w/upper, lower, and side Picatinny rails, choice of black or Desert Sand Cerakote finish, 6.5 lbs. Mfg. by ISSC located in Austria. Limited importation 2018 only.

$450	$395	$365	$325	$295	$265	$235	*$549*

Add $30 for Desert Sand Cerakote finish.

SHOTGUNS: LEVER ACTION

MODEL 1887 – 12 ga. only, patterned after the Winchester Model 1887, "WRA Co." logo on left side of receiver, 30 in. barrel, 5 shot tube mag., blue finish, 2-piece walnut forearm and rounded pistol grip stock, 8 lbs. Limited importation 1997-98.

$535	$475	$435	$400	$360	$330	$295	*$599*

SHOTGUNS: O/U

MODEL 300 – 12 ga. only, 3 in. chambers, underlug action, double triggers, extractors, etched engraving, standard checkered Turkish walnut stock and forearm, 26 or 28. in. VR barrels with fixed chokes. Imported 1994-98 from Turkey.

$425	$375	$330	$300	$275	$250	$225	*$429*

MODEL 333 FIELD GRADE – 12 or 20 ga., 3 in. chambers, engraved boxlock frame with satin finish, SST, ejectors, fancy grade Turkish walnut with hand-cut checkering, 26 (12 ga. only), 28, or 30 in. VR barrels, supplied with 5 choke tubes, approx. 7 1/2 lbs. Imported from Turkey 1994-98.

$735	$625	$550	$500	$450	$400	$360	*$800*

* ***Model 333 Field Grade Sporting Clays*** – similar to Model 333 Field Grade, except has sporting recoil pad, elongated forcing cones, 28 or 30 in. ported barrels with extended stainless steel choke tubes, 7 3/4 lbs. Imported from Turkey 1994-97.

$825	$725	$625	$550	$500	$450	$400	*$900*

* ***Model 333SCL Ladies Sporting Clays*** – similar to Model 333 Sporting Clays, except is fitted with special ladies stock, 28 in. barrels only with four choke tubes. Imported from Turkey. Disc. 1997.

$825	$725	$625	$550	$500	$450	$400	*$900*

MODEL 330 – 12 or 20 ga., 3 in. chambers, etched satin finished frame, SST, extractors, fixed chokes, checkered standard Turkish walnut stock and forearm, approx. 7 1/2 lbs. Imported from Turkey 1994-99.

$475	$415	$375	$325	$295	$280	$265	*$549*

* ***Model 330D*** – similar to Model 330, except has ejectors and three choke tubes. Imported from Turkey 1994-99.

$615	$500	$450	$400	$365	$335	$300	*$689*

GRADING - PPGS™	100%	98%	95%	90%	80%	70%	60%	LAST MSR

SILVER HUNTER – 12 or 20 ga., 3 in. chambers, underlug action, SST, extractors, silver receiver with etched engraving, standard checkered Turkish walnut stock and forearm, 26 or 28. in. VR barrels with choke tubes, 7 lbs. Imported from Spain 2002-2004.

	$615	$500	$450	$400	$365	$335	$300	*$737*

SILVER II – 12, 16, or 20 ga., similar to Silver Hunter, except has ejectors, approx. 7.4 lbs. Imported from Spain 2002-2006.

	$750	$625	$525	$465	$415	$365	$315	*$915*

SILVER CLASSIC – 12 or 20 (new 2002) ga., similar to Silver II, except has case colored receiver and long forcing cones. Imported from Spain 2002-2004.

	$750	$625	$525	$465	$415	$365	$315	*$899*

SILVER SPORTING – 12 ga., similar to Silver II, except has 3 in. chambers and 28 or 30 in. ported barrels with broadway VR, 7 lbs., 6 oz. Imported from Spain 2002-2004.

	$750	$625	$525	$465	$415	$365	$315	*$899*

WS/OU MAGNUM – 12 ga., 3 1/2 in. chambers, ejectors, SST, 28 in. VR barrels with choke tubes, 100% Skyline Excel camo (new 2003) coverage (except frame) or matte black metal and checkered black finished walnut stock and forearm. 7 lbs. 2 oz. Imported 2002-2004.

	$650	$550	$475	$425	$395	$375	$350	*$779*

Add $84 for Skyline Excel camo coverage.

HUNTER – 12 or 20 ga., 3 in. chambers, 26 or 28 in. VR barrels with choke tubes, blued boxlock action, SST, extractors, checkered walnut stock and forearm, 6-7 1/4 lbs. Imported 2006-2007.

	$425	$375	$330	$300	$275	$250	$225	*$499*

* ***Field Hunter*** – similar to Hunter, 12 or 20 (disc. 2010) ga., has auto ejectors and vent. recoil pad, 6-7 1/4 lbs. Imported 2007-2013.

	$625	$525	$450	$400	$350	$295	$250	*$729*

* ***Hunter Lite*** – similar to Hunter, except has lightweight construction with silver alloy frame, 5 1/2 or 6 lbs. Imported 2006-2007.

	$440	$380	$340	$310	$285	$260	$235	*$529*

* ***Hunter Gold Combo*** – 12/20 or 20/28 ga. two barrel sets, extractors, ST, 28 in. barrels with Beretta style choke tubes, distinguishable by gold pheasants on receiver and styling grooves next to checkering, 7.4 lbs. Imported 2009 only.

	$875	$750	$675	$600	$525	$475	$425	*$999*

HUNTER EX – 12, 16 (new 2011), 20, 28 (disc. 2017) ga., or .410 bore, 3 in. chambers, 26 or 28 in. VR barrels, extractors, blued steel, choke tubes, fiber optic front sight, SST, checkered walnut, black synthetic (mfg. 2010 only) or camo (mfg. 2011 only) pistol grip stock and forearm, 5.7-7.4 lbs. Imported 2008-2019.

	$565	$500	$450	$415	$375	$350	$325	*$640*

Add $30 for 28 ga. (disc. 2017) or .410 bore (28 in. barrels).

Subtract $55 for black synthetic stock and forearm (mfg. 2010 only) or camo stock/forearm and fiber optic night sight (mfg. 2011 only).

HUNTER EX LT – 12, 20, or 28 (disc. 2015, reintroduced 2018) ga., 2 3/4 or 3 in. chambers, 26 or 28 in. VR barrels w/5 Mobil chokes, checkered Turkish walnut stock and forearm, extractors, gold SST, engraved lightweight alloy receiver, fiber optic sight, 5.4-6.8 lbs. Imported 2013-2019.

	$580	$500	$450	$415	$375	$350	$325	*$670*

HUNTER MAG. CAMO 3-1/2 IN. – 12 ga., 3 1/2 in. chambers, 26, 28, or 30 (new 2016) in. barrels with 5 choke tubes, fiber optic front sight, synthetic stock and forearm, 100% Mossy Oak Duck Blind or Mossy Oak Blades camo coverage, 7.3-7.6 lbs. Mfg. 2009-2019.

	$635	$525	$465	$425	$395	$375	$350	*$730*

Add $15 for bronze/Mossy Oak Blades camo (new 2019).

* ***Hunter Mag. Black 3-1/2 In.*** – 12 ga., 28 in. barrel, similar to Hunter Mag. Camo, except has 100% matte black finish on wood and metal, 7.6 lbs. Mfg. 2012-2019.

	$565	$500	$450	$415	$375	$350	$325	*$640*

HUNTER MAG II – 12 ga. 3 1/2 in. chamber, 26, 28, or 30 in. barrels, five Beretta mobil choke tubes, fiber optic front sight, synthetic stock and forearm, Mossy Oak Break Up, Mossy Oak Duck Blind, Bronze/Mossy Oak Blades, or Midnight Bronze/Mossy Oak Bottomlands, 7.3 lbs. New 2020.

MSR $790	$670	$585	$500	$455	$370	$300	$265	

Add $20 for Bronze/Mossy Oak Blades or Midnight Bronze/Mossy Oak Bottomlands finish.

GRADING - PPGS™	100%	98%	95%	90%	80%	70%	60%	LAST MSR

SETTER MODEL – 12 ga., 3 in. chambers, boxlock action, 28 in. VR barrels with 3 Beretta style chokes, extractors, DT, silver finished steele receiver with laser etching, checkered walnut stock and forearm, brass bead front sight, 7.4 lbs. Limited importation 2011 only.

	$385	$340	$295	$260	$230	$210	$195	*$444*

SETTER S/T MODEL (CURRENT MFG.) – 12, 20, 28 (new 2016) ga., or .410 bore (new 2016), 2 3/4 or 3 in. chambers, 26 (20 ga. only) or 28 in. VR barrels w/5 Mobil choke tubes, fiber optic front sight, high gloss walnut stock, SST, extractors, 6.3-7.2 lbs. New 2013.

MSR $610	$520	$455	$390	$355	$285	$235	$200	

Add $30 for 28 ga. or .410 bore (new 2016).

SPORTING MODEL – 12 ga., 3 in. chambers, 28 (disc. 2010) or 30 in. chrome-lined ported VR barrels w/ extended Mobil choke tubes, checkered walnut pistol grip stock, semi-beavertail forend, coin finished steel frame, self-adj. locking bolts, ejectors, gold SST, approx. 7 1/2 lbs. Imported 2008-2019.

	$715	$600	$525	$450	$395	$350	$295	*$825*

TRINITY – 12, 16, or 20 ga., 2 3/4 or 3 in. chamber, 24 kt. gold inlaid steel frame, 28 in. VR barrel, five Beretta Mobil chokes, fiber optic front sights, Turkish walnut stock, 6.3-6.9 lbs. New 2020.

MSR $730	$625	$545	$475	$425	$345	$275	$225	

TRINITY LT – 12, 20, 28 ga., or .410 bore, 2 3/4 (28 ga. only) or 3 in. chamber, lightweight aluminum frame, 26 (20 ga. only) or 28 in. VR barrel, five Beretta Mobil chokes, fiber optic front sights, Turkish walnut stock, 5.3-6.3 lbs. New 2020.

MSR $730	$625	$545	$475	$425	$345	$275	$225	

Add $20 for 28 ga. or .410 bore.

TT-15 DTA – 12 ga., 2 3/4 in. chambers, 30 in. barrels, 5 Beretta extended color coded MobilChoke tubes, fiber optic sights, wood stock, adj. comb, palm swell, adj. buttpad, 8.7 lbs. Limited importation 2017 only.

	$1,300	$1,140	$975	$885	$715	$585	$455	*$1,450*

TT-15 DOUBLE TRAP – 12 ga., 2 3/4 in. chambers, Trap configuration, 32 in. barrels, skeet chokes, 8.9 lbs. New 2016.

MSR $1,585	$1,350	$1,180	$1,010	$920	$750	$610	$530	

TT-15 COMBO – 12 ga., 2 3/4 in. chambers, Trap configuration, includes 32 in. O/U barrels and unsingle 34 in. barrel, CT-5 chokes. Imported 2016-2017 only.

	$1,550	$1,375	$1,175	$975	$850	$750	$650	*$1,725*

TT-15 COMBO TRAP/CTA DELUXE DOUBLE COMBO – 12 ga., 2 3/4 in. chambers, Trap configuration, includes 32 in. O/U barrels and unsingle barrel w/fully adj. skeletonized top rib, with (TT-15 CTA Deluxe Model) or w/o detachable trigger assembly, adj. aluminum buttpad, cheekpiece, and comb, includes 5 Mobil extended color coated choke tubes Importation began 2016.

MSR $2,015	$1,700	$1,500	$1,300	$1,150	$950	$750	$725	

Add $395 or deluxe variation w/detachable trigger assembly and better grade walnut stock and forearm (TT-15 CTA Deluxe Combo model).

TT-15 FIELD – 12, 20, 28 ga., or .410 bore, 2 3/4 or 3 in. chamber, steel frame, 28 in. chrome-lined VR barrel, 5 color-coded extended Beretta/Benelli mobile chokes (SK, IC, M, IM, F), steel monobloc construction, automatic ejectors, SST, fiber optic front sight, Turkish walnut stock and forearm, coin-finished steel frame w/laser etching, 5.7-7 lbs. New 2019.

MSR $900	$765	$670	$575	$520	$420	$350	$300	

Add $30 for 28 ga. or .410 bore.

TT-15 SPORTING – 12 ga., 3 in. chambers, 30 in. vented barrels w/VR and 5 ported extended choke tubes, ejectors, SST, fiber optic front and brass mid-bead rear sight, checkered walnut stock and forearm w/solid buttpad, coin finished receiver, 7.9 lbs. Importation began 2018.

MSR $990	$845	$740	$635	$575	$465	$380	$325	

SHOTGUNS: SxS

MODEL 311 – 12 or 20 ga., 3 in. chambers, Greener boxlock action, 26 or 28 in. barrels, standard checkered Turkish walnut stock and forearm, DTs, supplied with five choke tubes, white chrome frame finish, extractors. Imported 1994-97 from Turkey.

	$535	$475	$435	$400	$360	$330	$295	*$599*

* ***Model 311R*** – 12 or 20 ga., 20 in. cylinder bore barrels designed for cowboy re-enactment shooting or home defense, other features similar to Model 311. Imported from Turkey. Disc. 1997.

	$375	$325	$300	$275	$250	$225	$200	*$429*

GRADING - PPGS™	100%	98%	95%	90%	80%	70%	60%	LAST MSR

MODEL 411 – 12, 16 (mfg. 1999-2004), 20 (disc. 2004), 28 (disc. 2004) ga., or .410 bore (disc. 2004), 3 in. chambers (except 28 ga.), 26 or 28 (12 ga. only) in. barrels with (12 and 20 ga.) or w/o (28 ga. or .410 bore) choke tubes, boxlock action, DT, extractors, steel shot compatible, case colored frame, checkered walnut stock and forearm, recoil pad, 6.5-7.25 lbs. Mfg. by Luciano Rota (R.F.M.). Imported 1998-2005.

$710 $650 $575 $525 $450 $400 $350 *$849*

* ***Model 411D*** – similar to Model 411, except not available in 16 ga., features engraved case colored frame, single trigger, ejectors, and English style stock, 6 1/2-7 1/4 lbs. Imported 1999-2005.

$915 $800 $700 $600 $500 $400 $325 *$1,110*

* ***Model 411F*** – 12, 20 (disc. 2004), 28 (disc. 2004) ga., or .410 bore (disc. 2004), 3 in. chambers (except 28 ga.), silver engraved sideplates, gold SST, English straight stock with cut checkering, ejectors, choke tubes (except for 28 ga. and .410 bore), 6 1/2-7 1/4 lbs. Imported 2000-2005.

$1,425 $1,200 $995 $850 $725 $650 $575 *$1,608*

* ***Model 411R Coach Gun*** – 12 or 20 ga., 3 in. chambers, hammerless, 20 in. fixed choke (C/C) barrels, case colored frame, DT, extractors, 6-6 1/2 lbs. Imported 1999-2003.

$650 $575 $525 $475 $425 $375 $325 *$745*

This model was designed for both cowboy competition shooting and quail hunting.

GENTRY – 12, 16, 20, 28 ga., or .410 bore, 3 in. chambers, engraved coin finished boxlock action with sideplates, SST, extractors, 20 (Gentry Coach Model, 12 or 20 ga. only), 26 or 28 in. barrels with matted rib and three choke tubes (fixed chokes on 16, 20 ga. and .410 bore), checkered pistol grip stock and semi-beavertail forearm, approx. 6 1/2 lbs. Imported 2003-2006.

$775 $600 $500 $440 $380 $325 $275 *$929*

Add $16 for 28 ga. or .410 bore.
Subtract $14 for Gentry Coach Model (hammerless, disc. 2003).

BRISTOL – 12, 20, 28 ga., or .410 bore, 2 3/4 (28 ga.) or 3 in. chamber, steel frame, chrome-lined chamber and barrel, five Beretta choke tubes, auto ejectors, SST, brass bead sight, English stock w/ case colored receiver, select Turkish walnut, select top tang safety, laser engraving, oil finish, 5.08-6.74 lbs. Importation began 2021.

MSR $1,100 $935 $825 $700 $635 $515 $425 $365

Add $30 for 28 ga. or .410 bore.

* ***Bristol Silver*** – 12, 20, 28 ga., or .410 bore, 2 3/4 (28 ga.) or 3 in. chamber, steel frame, chrome-lined chamber and barrel, five Beretta choke tubes, auto ejectors, SST, brass bead sight, English stock w/nickel finish receiver w/24K gold inlay, select Turkish walnut, select top tang safety, laser engraving, oil finish, 5.08-6.74 lbs. Importation began 2021.

MSR $1,040 $885 $775 $665 $600 $485 $415 $350

Add $30 for 28 ga. or .410 bore.

BRITTANY – 12, 16 (new 2006), 20, 28 (new 2006) ga., or .410 bore (disc. 2006), 3 in. chambers, boxlock action, case colored frame, SST, ejectors, 26 in. barrels with matted rib and three choke tubes, checkered straight grip stock and semi-beavertail forearm, 6.2-7.4 lbs. Imported 2003-2007.

$950 $775 $650 $525 $450 $400 $350 *$1,150*

Add $30 for 28 ga. or .410 bore.

* ***Brittany Classic*** – 12, 16, 20, 28 ga., or .410 bore, similar to Brittany, except has 27 in. barrels, upgraded features, including fancy checkered pistol grip walnut stock and forearm with oil finish, engraved frame, 6.3-6.7 lbs. Imported 2007-2008.

$1,185 $1,025 $875 $745 $630 $525 $425 *$1,419*

Add $40 for 28 ga. or .410 bore.

BRITTANY SPORTING – 12 or 20 ga., 3 in. chambers, boxlock action with sideplates, engraved case colored frame, SST, ejectors, 28 in. barrels with matted rib and three choke tubes, checkered pistol grip stock and semi-beavertail forearm, approx. 6 3/4 lbs. Imported 2003-2005.

$875 $725 $625 $525 $475 $425 $375 *$1,049*

DERBY CLASSIC – 12 or 20 ga., 3 in. chambers, true sidelock case colored action, DT, ejectors, checkered straight grip stock and splinter forearm, 7 3/4 lbs. Mfg. by Zabala Hermanos in Spain 2002-2005.

$1,300 $1,075 $900 $775 $675 $600 $525 *$1,550*

YORK – 12 or 20 ga., boxlock action, 26 or 28 in. barrels with choke tubes, approx. 7 lbs. Imported during 2006.

$525 $450 $400 $350 $300 $260 $230 *$609*

GRADING - PPGS™	100%	98%	95%	90%	80%	70%	60%	LAST MSR

PHOENIX – 12, 20, or 28 ga., 3 in. chambers, boxlock action, 28 in. barrels with Beretta style choke tubes, SST, top tang safety, checkered pistol grip walnut stock, engraved blue frame with engraved gold pheasant, 6.8 lbs. Mfg. 2009-2010.

	$925	$800	$675	$575	$475	$400	$325	*$1,049*

* ***Phoenix Combo*** – includes 12/20 or 20/28 ga., 28 in. barrels. Mfg. 2009-2010.

	$1,225	$1,075	$900	$775	$675	$575	$475	*$1,359*

SHOTGUNS: SEMI-AUTO

Shim kits and fiber optic sights became standard on all hunting models beginning 2011.

COMPACT – 12 ga., 3 in. chamber, gas operated, 20 in. barrel, extended/ported cylinder choke tube, two 5 shot mags., adj. sights, forward grip, full size carry handle, black finish, 30 in. OAL, 8 lbs. Mfg. mid-2018-2019.

	$675	$600	$525	$465	$395	$350	$295	*$790*

COMPACT BULLPUP TACTICAL – 12 ga., 3 in. chamber, AK style controls, 20 in. barrel, 5 shot detachable mag., fixed pistol grip, removable carry handle, full Picatinny rail, mattle black finish, 8.6 lbs. New 2019.

MSR $760	$650	$570	$490	$440	$360	$295	$250

PHANTOM SERIES – 12 ga. only, 3 or 3 1/2 (Phantom Field/Synthetic Mag. only) in. chamber, various VR (except Phantom HP) barrel lengths with choke tubes, available in Field (blue metal finish, gold accents, and checkered walnut stock and forearm), Synthetic (black non-glare matte metal and flat black synthetic stock and forearm), or HP (home security with open sights, matte finished metal, and synthetic stock and forearm), 6 lbs. 13 oz.-7 lbs. 6 oz. Italian mfg., limited importation 2001-2002.

	$385	$350	$315	$285	$265	$245	$225	*$425*

Subtract $44 for Phantom Synthetic.
Add $74 for 3 1/2 in. Mag. (Field).
Add $44 for Mag. Synthetic.

KRX TACTICAL – 12 ga., 2 3/4 or 3 in. chamber, detachable 5 shot mag., 20 in. barrel, front sight, fixed pistol grip stock, removable carry handle, full-length upper and partial lower Picatinny rails, black or FDE or forearm (new 2018) finish 7.4 lbs. New 2016.

MSR $540	$460	$400	$350	$315	$250	$200	$175

Add $30 for FDE finish (new 2018).

RAPTOR – 12 or 20 ga., 3 in. chamber, 26 or 28 in. barrel with three Beretta choke tubes, fiber optic sight, matte black synthetic stock, 6.4-6.8 lbs. New 2013.

MSR $455	$375	$350	$300	$275	$225	$175	$135

* ***Raptor Camo*** – 12 or 20 (new 2016) ga., 3 in. chamber, 28 in. barrel with one extended Beretta turkey choke, fiber optic sight, 100% Next Micro Print finish, 7.1 lbs. New 2015.

MSR $540	$460	$400	$350	$315	$250	$200	$175

* ***Raptor Youth*** – 20 ga., 3 in. chamber, 24 in. barrel with 3 Beretta choke tubes, fiber optic sight, black synthetic, Muddy Girl (new 2014), Vista Camo (new 2014), or Next Micro Print (mfg. 2015 only) stock and forearm, 6.1 lbs. New 2013.

MSR $455	$375	$350	$300	$275	$225	$175	$135

Add $45 for Muddy Girl (new 2014) or $85 for Vista Camo (new 2014) finish.
Add $75 for Next Micro Print (mfg. 2015 only).

RAPTOR A-TAC – 12 ga., 3 in. chamber, gas operated, 20 in. barrel with extended choke, fixed pistol grip black synthetic stock, Picatinny rail, swivel studs, tactical style operating handle, bridge front sight with fiber optic bead, 7 lbs. New 2013.

MSR $470	$400	$350	$300	$275	$225	$185	$155

* ***Raptor A-TAC Turkey*** – 12 ga., 3 in. chamber, 24 in. barrel with one extended Beretta turkey chokes, raised bridge front fiber optic sight, mounted Picatinny rail with ghost ring sight, fixed pistol grip, Digital Camo (mfg. 2014 only), 1/2 Kryptek Typhon (mfg. 2014 only), or 1/2 Mossy Oak Break-Up coverage, 7.2 lbs. Mfg. 2014-2015.

	$425	$375	$325	$295	$250	$225	$200	*$489*

Add $30 for Digital Camo finish (mfg. 2014 only).

TEC12 – 12 ga., 3 in. chamber, capable of operating in pump or semi-auto mode by the turn of a dial, inertia rotary bolt action, 20 or 28 (mfg. 2013 only) in. barrel with choke tubes, external ported cyl. choke, black synthetic stock with rubber fixed pistol grip plus one set of military sling swivels and swivel studs, matte black finish, Picatinny rail, ghost ring sight and raised front bridge sight with fiber optic bead, 7.2 lbs. Imported 2013-2017.

	$585	$525	$450	$395	$365	$335	$295	*$690*

GRADING - PPGS™	100%	98%	95%	90%	80%	70%	60%	LAST MSR

TSA SERIES (DIANA SERIES) – 12, 20, or 28 (disc. 2003) ga., 3 or 3 1/2 in. chamber, various VR barrel lengths with choke tubes, available in Marine (19 in. barrel), Field (blue metal finish, gold accents, and checkered walnut stock and forearm), Synthetic (black non-glare matte metal and flat black synthetic stock and forearm), Slug (24 in. rifled barrel with iron sights), or camo model (100% camo coverage), 6 3/4-7 1/2 lbs. Imported 2003-2007.

	$340	$310	$285	$255	$225	$200	$185	*$399*

Add $30 for Field Grade.
Add $30 for 20 ga. (disc.) or Youth Model with synthetic stock, or $60 for Youth with walnut stock.
Add $200 for Synthetic Model with 3 1/2 in. chamber.
Add $200 for camo model with 3 1/2 in. chamber.
Add $100 for camo model with 3 in. chamber.
Add $25 for Slug Model (24 in. rifled barrel, disc. 2004).
Add $34 for Marine Model with 19 in. barrel and choke tubes (mfg. 2004).

This model was designed by CD Europe of Italy and manufactured in Turkey.

* ***TSA Black 3-1/2 In.*** – 12 ga., 3 1/2 in. chamber, twin GPO, 26 (disc. 2015) or 28 in. chrome-lined barrel, 5 shot, fiber optic front sight, black stock and forearm, flat black metal finish, 7.4 lbs. Imported 2012-2017.

	$565	$500	$450	$415	$375	$350	$325	*$640*

* ***TSA Camo 3-1/2 In.*** – 12 ga., 3 (disc.) or 3 1/2 in. chamber, twin GPO, 24 (disc.), 26, 28, or 30 in. chrome-lined barrel, fiber optic front sight, vent. rib with matted sight plane, 5 shot, 100% Realtree Advantage Timber (24 in. barrel only, disc.), 100% Mossy Oak Obsession (disc., 24 in. barrel only), Duck Blind (disc.), or Realtree Max-4 camo coverage, 7.2-7.6 lbs. Importation 2008-2017.

	$650	$575	$500	$450	$395	$350	$295	*$730*

Subtract 10% for 3 in. chambers.

VIPER G2 SERIES – 12, 20, or 28 (wood stock or silver only) ga., 2 3/4 or 3 in. chamber, gas operated, 24, 26 or 28 in. barrel, choke tubes, 5 shot mag., G2 action became standard 2010, configurations include wood, synthetic, camo, and silver, fiber optic front sight, mag. cut off, vent. rib with matted sight plane, choice of wood, black synthetic, camo, or carbon fiber (disc. 2009) stock, approx. 5.7-6.9 lbs. Importation began 2007.

* ***Viper G2 Bronze*** – 12, 16 (new 2021), 20, 28 (new 2016) ga., or .410 bore (new 2018), 3 in. chamber, 26 or 28 in. VR barrel with 3 Beretta MobileChoke tubes, 5 shot mag., fiber optic front sight, high grade Turkish walnut stock with cut checkering and high gloss finish, rubber recoil pad, shim kit, Cerakote receiver finish, 5.2-6.8 lbs. New 2015.

MSR $845	$720	$630	$540	$490	$395	$325	$275	

Add $55 for 16 ga. (new 2021), 28 ga. (new 2016) or .410 bore (new 2018).

* ***Viper G2 Camo*** – 12, 20 ga., or .410 bore (new 2019), 3 in. chamber, 26, 28, or 30 in. VR barrel with 3 Beretta MobileChoke tubes, fiber optic sights, features 100% Realtree Advantage Timber, Realtree Max-4 (disc. 2020), or Realtree Max-5 (new 2020) camo finish, 6.2-6.9 lbs. New 2012.

MSR $685	$600	$500	$425	$400	$325	$265	$225	

Add $45 for left-hand action 28 in. barrel in Realtree Max-4 camo (disc. 2020) or Realtree Max-5 (new 2020).
Add $35 for .410 bore (new 2019).

* ***Viper G2 Silver*** – 12, 20, or 28 ga., 2 3/4 or 3 in. chamber, silver alloy receiver, 26 or 28 in. barrel, Beretta style choke tubes, extended skeet choke (28 ga.), 5 shot mag., fiber optic sights, TriStar checkered walnut stock and forearm, 5-6.8 lbs. New 2010.

MSR $725	$615	$540	$460	$420	$340	$275	$225	

Add $45 for 28 ga. with extended skeet choke.

* ***Viper G2 Synthetic*** – 12, 20 ga., or .410 bore (new 2019), 2 3/4 (disc.) or 3 in. chamber, 26 or 28 in. barrel, choke tubes, 5 shot mag., fiber optic sights, mag. cut off, vent. rib with matted sight plane, carbon fiber (disc. 2009) or black synthetic stock and forearm, 6.1-6.9 lbs. Importation began 2007.

MSR $595	$500	$450	$375	$350	$275	$225	$195	

Add $55 for .410 bore (new 2019).
Add $45 for left-hand action.
Add $120 for carbon fiber stock (disc. 2009).

Soft touch finish became standard on synthetic models beginning 2011.

GRADING - PPGS™	100%	98%	95%	90%	80%	70%	60%	LAST MSR

* ***Viper G2 Wood*** – 12, 16 (new 2021), 20, 28 (disc. 2013, reintroduced 2016) ga., or .410 bore (new 2018), 2 3/4 or 3 in. chamber, G2 action became standard 2010, 26 or 28 in. barrel w/choke tubes, 5 shot mag., fiber optic sights, checkered walnut stock and forearm, mag. cut off, vent. rib with matted sight plane, 5.2-6.9 lbs. Importation began 2007.

MSR $660 $560 $490 $420 $380 $310 $260 $215

Add $60 for 16 ga., 28 ga., or .410 bore (new 2018).

VIPER G2 YOUTH/COMPACT – 12, 20 ga., or .410 bore, 24 in. barrel, 5 shot mag., fiber optic sights, black synthetic stock (two-stock combo) and forearm with soft touch finish, adult stock included, also available in Compact model configuration w/single stock w/o extension, 5.7-6.5 lbs.

MSR $610 $520 $455 $390 $355 $285 $235 $200

Add $40 for .410 bore.

Add $45 for two-stock combo (includes both youth and adult stocks, 20 ga. only).

* ***Viper G2 Youth Camo*** – 12 (disc.) or 20 ga., 3 in. chamber, 24, 26 (disc) or 28 (disc.) in. barrel, G2 action became standard during 2010, similar to Viper Series, except has 100% Mossy Oak Duck Blind (disc.), or 100% Realtree Advantage Timber camo coverage, soft touch stock/forearm finish became standard 2011, 6 lbs. New 2008.

MSR $685 $600 $500 $425 $400 $325 $265 $225

Add $16 for Viper G2 TW (Turkey/Waterfowl) Model with 12 or 20 ga., 24 or 28 in. barrel (disc.).

* ***Viper G2 Youth Wood*** – 20 ga. or .410 bore, 24 in. barrel with choke tubes, checkered wood stock and forearm, 5.7 lbs.

MSR $680 $580 $510 $435 $395 $320 $265 $225

Add $60 for .410 bore.

VIPER G2 SPORTING – 12 or 28 (mfg. 2013-2015) ga., 3 in. chamber, 30 in. ported barrel, four Beretta extended MobilChoke tubes, ventilated raised target rib, 5 shot mag., fiber optic front and brass mid-bead sights, Tristar checkered walnut stock with adj. comb, 6-7.4 lbs. New 2010.

MSR $885 $750 $650 $550 $500 $420 $350 $295

Subtract approx. $30 for 28 ga. (disc. 2015).

VIPER G2 SR/SRB SPORT – 12 ga., 3 in. chamber, 30 in. ported barrel with 4 extended Beretta chokes, wide target rib, red (SB model) or blue (SRB model, new 2020) anodized receiver, fiber optic sight, manual E-Z Load magazine cut-off, Soft Touch on stock and forearm, 7.2 lbs. New 2014.

MSR $685 $600 $500 $425 $400 $325 $265 $225

* ***Viper G2 SR/SRB Youth*** – 20 ga., 3 in. chamber, 26 in. barrel, red (SR Youth model) or blue (SRB Youth model, new 2020) anodized receiver, Soft Touch on stock and forearm, black finish, 6.2 lbs. New 2015.

MSR $610 $520 $455 $390 $355 $285 $235 $200

VIPER G2 TACTICAL – 12 ga., 20 in. barrel, matte black finish, fiber optic sights, 5 shot mag., cylinder choke, swivel studs, 6 1/2 lbs. Mfg. 2010-2012.

$395 $350 $300 $265 $235 $200 $175 ***$444***

VIPER G2 TURKEY – 12, 20 ga., or .410 bore, 3 in. chamber, 24 in. barrel with extended Turkey choke, fixed black soft rubber pistol grip stock, fiber optic front sight, Picatinny rail, 100% Realtree Advantage Timber (disc.) or Midnight Bronze/Bottomlands (new 2020) camo finish, 6.8 lbs. Importation began 2011.

MSR $720 $615 $540 $460 $425 $345 $275 $225

Add $50 for .410 bore.

Add $16 for Viper G2 TW (Turkey/Waterfowl) Model with 12 or 20 ga., 24 or 28 in. barrel (disc. 2014).

VIPER MAX – 12 ga., 3 1/2 in. chamber, two-piston system, 28 in. barrel, Beretta Optima Plus choke tubes, fiber optic front sight, synthetic stock, overmolded rubber grips, 7.4 lbs. New 2017.

MSR $700 $600 $525 $450 $410 $325 $275 $225

* ***Viper Max Camo*** – 12 ga., 3 1/2 in. chamber, two-piston system, 26, 28, or 30 in. VR barrel, 4 Beretta Optima Plus choke tubes, 5 shot mag., fiber optic front sights, recoil pad, swivel studs, overmolded rubber grips on stock and forearm, 100% Realtree Max-5HD finish, 7.3 lbs. New 2017.

MSR $795 $675 $590 $510 $460 $370 $310 $245

Add $15 bronze/Mossy Oak Blades (new 2019) camo finish.

SHOTGUNS: SINGLE BARREL

TT-09 TRAP – 12 ga., 2 3/4 in. chamber, 34 in. ported VR barrel with extended choke tubes, ejector, select Monte Carlo walnut stock (drilled for recoil reducer), fiber optic front and brass mid-rib bead sight, acid etched alloy receiver, rubber buttpad, 8 1/2 lbs. Mfg. 2009-2012.

$750 $675 $600 $525 $475 $425 $375 ***$899***

GRADING - PPGS™	100%	98%	95%	90%	80%	70%	60%	LAST MSR

TT-15 MONO TRAP – 12 ga., 3 1/2 in. chamber, 34 in. VR barrel with 3 ported Beretta Mobil extended choke tubes, checkered walnut stock and forearm with cheekpiece, adj. comb, 7.8-8 lbs. Importation began 2018.

MSR $1,250	$1,065	$930	$800	$725	$585	$480	$415	

TT-15 TOP SINGLE/UNSINGLE – 12 ga., 3 1/4 in. chamber, choice of 34 in. top single or unsingle barrel w/fully adj. skeletonized rib and 3 Mobil extended color coated choke tubes, adj. aluminum buttpad and cheekpeice, approx. 8 1/2 lb. New 2018.

MSR $1,435	$1,220	$1,065	$915	$830	$685	$565	$475	

Add $75 for unsingle variation.

SHOTGUNS: SLIDE ACTION

DIANA SERIES – 12 or 20 ga., 3 or 3 1/2 in. chamber, choice of Field, camo Mag., or black synthetic configuration, dual slide rails, 20, 24, or 28 (VR) in. barrel with choke tubes, 5 shot mag., crossbolt safety behind trigger, 6-7 lbs. Imported 2004 only.

	$160	$140	$120	$100	$90	$80	$70	*$188*

Add $51 for Field or synthetic Mag.
Add $31 for synthetic stock/forearm.
Add $147 for Mag. camo in 12 ga., or $94 for Mag. w/o camo.

COBRA SERIES – 12 ga. only, 3 in. chamber, various barrel lengths, includes 1-3 choke tubes. Importation began 2007.

* ***Cobra Field Black*** – 12 or 20 (new 2015) ga., 3 in. chamber, 26 or 28 in. barrel with 3 Beretta choke tubes, fiber optic front sight, extended forearm, swivel studs, matte black finish, 5.6-6.9 lbs. Disc.

	$285	$250	$225	$200	$185	$175	$165	*$350*

* ***Cobra Field Camo*** – 12 or 20 ga., 3 in. chamber, 26 or 28 in. barrel, 3 Beretta MobileChoke tubes, fiber optic front sight, extended forearm, swivel studs, Next Micro Print camo finish, 5.6-6.9 lbs. Imported 2012-2017.

	$360	$315	$275	$250	$225	$200	$185	*$425*

* ***Cobra Field Turkey*** – 12 ga., 3 in. chamber, 24 in. barrel with 3 Beretta MobileChoke tubes, fiber optic sight, fixed pistol grip synthetic stock, 100% Next Micro Print camo finish, 6.7 lbs. Disc.

	$425	$375	$325	$295	$250	$225	$200	*$490*

* ***Cobra Field Youth*** – 20 ga., 3 in. chamber, 24 in. barrel with 3 Beretta MobileChoke tubes, fiber optic sight, black receiver, Black, Muddy Girl, or Next Micro Print camo finish on stock and forearm, 5.4 lbs. Imported 2015-2017.

	$285	$250	$225	$200	$185	$175	$165	*$350*

Add $45 for Muddy Girl or $75 for Next Micro Print camo finish.

* ***Cobra Force*** – 12 ga., 3 in. chamber, 18 1/2 (new 2014) or 20 (disc. 2013) in. barrel, one (new 2014) or 2 (disc. 2013) choke tubes, Picatinny rail under forearm and on top of receiver, fiber optic bridge front sight, rear sight, swivel studs, fixed pistol grip stock with soft rubber grip, matte black finish, 6 1/2 lbs. Disc. 2017.

	$335	$295	$260	$240	$220	$200	$185	*$400*

* ***Cobra Mag.*** – 12 ga., 3 (disc.) or 3 1/2 in. chamber, 28 in. barrel with choke tubes, synthetic stock, black, or Realtree Max-5 camo finish, 6.9 lbs. Importation began 2016.

MSR $380	$325	$285	$245	$220	$180	$150	$125	

Add $80 for Realtree Max-5 camo finish.

* ***Cobra Marine*** – 12 ga., 3 in. chamber, 18 1/2 in. barrel with Beretta cyl. MobilChoke, spring-loaded forearm, swivel studs, Picatinny rail under forearm, blade front sight, synthetic Marine stock and forearm, brushed nickel finish, 6.2 lbs. Imported 2014-2017.

	$325	$285	$250	$225	$180	$150	$125	*$370*

* ***Cobra Tactical*** – 12 ga., 3 in. chamber, 18 1/2 (new 2014) or 20 (disc. 2013) in. barrel, spring-loaded forearm, faux extended mag tube, Beretta cyl. choke tube, blade front sight, Picatinny rail under forearm, Black synthetic stock, swivel studs, 6.3 lbs. Disc.

	$275	$235	$215	$190	$175	$150	$125	*$320*

COBRA SERIES II – 12 ga. only, 3 in. chamber, various barrel lengths, includes 1-3 choke tubes. Importation began 2017.

* ***Cobra II Field Black*** – 12 or 20 ga., 3 in. chamber, 28 in. VR barrel with 3 Beretta choke tubes, fiber optic front sight, extended forearm, swivel studs, matte black finish, 6.8 lbs. Disc. 2019.

	$235	$215	$190	$175	$165	$150	$135	*$275*

GRADING - PPGS™	100%	98%	95%	90%	80%	70%	60%	LAST MSR

* ***Cobra II Field Camo*** – 12 or 20 ga., 3 in. chamber, 24, 26, or 28 in. VR barrel, 3 Beretta MobileChoke tubes, fiber optic front sight, extended forearm, swivel studs, 100% RealTree Advantage Timber (24 in. barrel only) or RealTree Max-5 camo finish, 5.6-6.9 lbs. Mfg. 2018-2019.

	$285	$250	$225	$200	$190	$180	$170	*$335*

Add $30 for turkey variation w/24 in. barrel.

* ***Cobra II Field Youth*** – 20 ga., 3 in. chamber, 24 in. VR barrel with 3 Beretta Mobile choke tubes, fiber optic front sight, choice of black or 100% RealTree Max 5 camo finish on stock and forearm, 5.4 lbs. Mfg. 2018-2019.

	$235	$215	$190	$175	$165	$150	$135	*$275*

Add $60 for 100% RealTree Max 5 camo finish.

* ***Cobra II Force*** – 12 ga., 3 in. chamber, 18 1/2 in. ported barrel w/raised front sight, receiver Picatinny rail, spring loaded forearm, open rear sight, swivel studs, fixed pistol grip stock with soft rubber grip, matte black finish, 6 1/2 lbs. Mfg. 2018-2019.

	$265	$240	$220	$200	$180	$170	$160	*$320*

* ***Cobra II Marine*** – 12 ga., 3 in. chamber, 18 1/2 in. barrel, spring-loaded forearm, swivel studs, bead front sight, black synthetic stock and grooved forearm, brushed nickel or black (new 2019) metal finish, 6.2 lbs. Mfg. 2018-2019.

	$240	$220	$200	$185	$170	$160	$150	*$290*

Add $70 for black finish (new 2019).

* ***Cobra II Tactical*** – 12 ga., 3 in. chamber, 18 1/2 in. barrel, spring-loaded forearm, swivel studs, bead front sight, black synthetic stock and grooved forearm, matte black metal finish, 6.2 lbs. Mfg. 2018-2019.

	$230	$210	$190	$175	$160	$150	$140	*$259*

COBRA III SERIES – 12 or 20 ga., 3 or 3 1/2 in. chamber, 24, 26, or 28 in. barrel. New 2020.

* ***Cobra III Field*** – 12, 20, 28 ga. or .410 bore, 3 in. chamber, 26 (20 ga. only) or 28 in. VR barrel, CT-3 chokes, walnut or black (12 or 20 ga. only) synthetic stock, 5.2-7 lbs. New 2020.

MSR $345	$295	$255	$220	$200	$160	$130	$115	

Add $30 for walnut stock.
Add $70 for 28 ga. or .410 bore w/walnut stock.

* ***Cobra III Field Camo*** – 12 or 20 ga., 3 in. chamber, 24, 26, or 28 in. barrel, synthetic stock in Realtree Max-5 or Realtree Advantage Timber finish, 6.9 lbs. New 2020.

MSR $410	$350	$300	$265	$240	$195	$160	$135	

Add $40 for Realtree Advantage Timber.

* ***Cobra III Field Youth*** – 20 ga., 3 in. chamber, 24 in. barrel, CT-3 chokes, walnut or synthetic stock in black or Realtree Max-5 finish, 5.4-6.5 lbs. New 2020.

MSR $345	$295	$255	$220	$200	$160	$130	$115	

Add $70 for walnut stock.
Add $65 for Realtree Max-5 finish.

* ***Cobra III Force*** – 12 ga., 3 in. chamber, 18 1/2 in. barrel, muzzle brake, 1 Beretta/Benelli mobil choke, 5 shot mag. (plug included), ghost ring sight mounted on top of receiver, fixed pistol grip stock w/soft rubber grip, swivel studs, black finish, 6.5 lbs. Importation began 2020.

MSR $365	$310	$270	$235	$210	$170	$140	$120	

* ***Cobra III Marine/Tactical*** – 12 ga., 3 in. chamber, 18 1/2 in. chrome-lined barrel, 1 Beretta/Benelli mobil style choke tube, 5 shot mag., blade front sight, black synthetic stock, Picatinny rail on spring loaded forearm, swivel studs, black or Marine finish, 6.2 lbs. Importation began 2020.

MSR $320	$275	$240	$200	$185	$150	$125	$100	

Add $15 for Marine model.

TROJAN FIREARMS

Current AR-15 style pistol, rifle, and accessories manufacturer located in Phoenix, AZ.

Please refer to BlueBookOfGunValues.com to order the *Blue Book of AR-15s & Variations*, available as a book or online subscription.

TROMIX CORPORATION

Previous firearms manufacturer established in 1999, located in Inola, OK. Previously located in Broken Arrow, OK.

RIFLES: SEMI-AUTO

Tromix manufactured AR-15 style rifles until 2008. Tromix lower receivers bear no caliber designation. Serialization was TR-0001-0405.

The models listed were also available with many custom options.

GRADING - PPGS™	100%	98%	95%	90%	80%	70%	60%	LAST MSR

TR-15 SLEDGEHAMMER – .44 Rem. Mag. (disc. 2001), .440 Cor-Bon Mag., .458 SOCOM, .475 Tremor, or .50 AE cal., GIO, 16 3/4 in. barrel, other lengths and weights available by custom order. Mfg. 1999-2006.

	$1,125	$700	$525	$450	$400	$350	$325	*$1,350*

TR-15 TACKHAMMER – various cals., GIO, 24 in. bull barrel, other lengths and weights were available by custom order. Mfg. 1999-2006.

	$1,125	$700	$525	$450	$400	$350	$325	*$1,350*

SHOTGUNS

Tromix manufactures Class II short barrel shotguns based on the Saiga model. Please contact the company directly for more information.

TROY DEFENSE

Current AR-15 style rifle and pistol manufacturer located in West Springfield, MA.

Please refer to BlueBookOfGunValues.com to order the *Blue Book of AR-15s & Variations*, available as a book or online subscription.

TRUVELO ARMOURY

Current manufacturer located in Midrand, South Africa. Truvelo Armoury is a division of Truvelo Manufacturers (Pty) Ltd. No current U.S. importation.

Truvelo Armoury entered into the field of barrel and rifle manufacturing in 1994. The success of the manufacturing of highly accurate barrels led to the development of a combination of their own barrel range and sophisticated sniper rifle technology. The result of this combination is Truvelo's range of highly accurate, long range rifles with calibers up to 20x110 Hispano. The Truvelo range of rifles is called the Counter Measure Sniper Rifle (CMS). Truvelo Armory also previously manufactured the Neostead shotgun, the BXP 9mm Tactical pistol, and various custom hunting and sporting rifles. Please contact the factory directly for more information, delivery time, and availability.

TULA ARMS PLANT

Current manufacturer established during 1712, located in Tula, Russia. Previously imported by SSME Deutsche Waffen, Inc., located in Plant City, FL until 2010. Previously distributed by Tulsky Souvenir, LLC, located in San Diego, CA.

For individual model listings, please go to BlueBookOfGunValues.com/overflow.

TURKISH FIREARMS CORPORATION

Please refer to the Huglu listing in the H section.

TURKUAZ

Current shotgun manufacturer located in Turkey. Currently distributed and exported by Dorkas Foreign Trade, located in Konya, Turkey.

Turkuaz manufactures a line of good quality semi-auto shotguns in a variety of configurations, including hunting and tactical. Many finishes and stock options are also available. Please contact the exporter directly for more information, including pricing and domestic availability.

TURNBULL RESTORATION CO., INC.

Current firearms restoration and manufacturing company established in 1990, located in Bloomfield, NY, specializes in the faithful and accurate restorations of period firearms from initial polishing to final finishing. These finishes include period correct bone charcoal color case hardening, charcoal bluing, rust bluing, and Nitre bluing.

Turnbull Restoration Co., Inc. (formerly know as Doug Turnbull Restoration and Turnbull Manufacturing), specializes in the restoration of Colt 1911s, early Colt semi-auto pistols, Colt SAAs, USFA SAAs, shotguns from makers A.H. Fox, L.C. Smith, Parker Brothers and lever action rifles from Winchester, Browning, Marlin, and others. In addition to full, historically-accurate restorations Turnbull Restoration also offers services including upgrades and antique finishes that replicate natural aging and patina.

Model	Qty. Made	Year Issue	Retail Price
PISTOLS: SEMI-AUTO LISTINGS			
TURNBULL CENTENNIAL 1911	20	2011-2014	MSR was $3,895
TURNBULL 1911 WWI (BASE MODEL)	N/A	New 2013	MSR is $2,625
TURNBULL 1911 WWI HERITAGE MODEL	N/A	New 2013	MSR is $3,225
TURNBULL 1911 A COVERAGE ENGRAVED MODEL	N/A	New 2013	MSR is $3,750

Model	Qty. Made	Year Issue	Retail Price
TURNBULL 1911 B COVERAGE ENGRAVED MODEL	N/A	New 2013	MSR is $4,350
TURNBULL 1911 C COVERAGE ENGRAVED MODEL	N/A	New 2013	MSR is $5,000
TURNBULL 1911 COMMANDER	N/A	2013-disc.	MSR was $3,050
TURNBULL 1911 COMMANDER HERITAGE	N/A	2016-disc.	MSR was $3,250
TURNBULL 1911 COMMERCIAL MODEL	N/A	New 2018	Base is $4,995
TURNBULL 1911 CUSTOM COMMANDER	50	2013-2014	MSR was $2,950
TURNBULL 1911 GOVERNMENT HERITAGE MODEL	N/A	New 2016	MSR is $3,225
TURNBULL 1911 GOVERNMENT MODEL	N/A	New 2016	MSR is $3,025
REVOLVERS: SAA LISTINGS			
GEORGE PATTON SERIES COLT SAA	10	2003-2004	MSR was $5,500
CATTLE BRAND COLT SAA	N/A	2003-2004	MSR was $7,995
THEODORE ROOSEVELT COLT SAA	25	2003	MSR was $7,500
COWBOY CLASSIC SAA	999	2004-2008	MSR was $1,250
OPEN RANGE SAA	N/A	2009-2013	MSR was $1,450
OPEN RANGE SAA SHERIFF'S MODEL	N/A	2009-2013	MSR was $2,200
CUSTOM OPEN RANGE SAA	N/A	2011-2013	MSR was $4,250
CAVALRY SAA	5	2011-2013	MSR was $1,575
BUNTLINE SAA	N/A	Mfg. 2011	MSR was $1,650
CUSTOM COWBOY CLASSIC SAA	N/A	2013-2014	MSR was $2,200
RIFLES: LISTINGS			
THEODORE ROOSEVELT WINCHESTER MODEL 1876	25	2006-disc.	MSR was $28,000
THEODORE ROOSEVELT WINCHESTER MODEL 1886 TENNIS MATCH GUN	3 to date	2013-2017	MSR was $12,000
TURNBULL MODEL 1886	N/A	New 2006	Base is $3,500
TURNBULL MODEL 1886 .475 TURNBULL CAL.	N/A	New 2006	MSR is $4,700
1886 THUMPER	N/A	2014-disc.	MSR was $29,995
USRAC/WINCHESTER MODEL 1892 TAKE-DOWN	N/A	Mfg. 2011	MSR was $2,200
RUGER NO. 1 1-H TROPICAL	N/A	Mfg. 2011	MSR was $2,200.
TAR-10 SEMI-AUTO	35	2012-2013	MSR was $4,995
TAR-10 SEMI-AUTO HUNTING HERITAGE TRUST 2013 SHOT SHOW AUCTION GUN	1	2013	$134,000
TAR-15 SEMI-AUTO	N/A	2013-disc.	MSR was $2,750
TAR-40 SEMI-AUTO	100	2013-disc.	MSR was $4,995
TURNBULL, DOUG SIGNATURE MODEL 71 475	N/A	New 2018	Base is $20,000
HENRY-TURNBULL RIFLE	1,750	2019	$1,495

TURNER RICHARDS GUNMAKERS

Previous gunmaker located in Bromsgrove, U.K.

Robert Turner grew up in Birmingham and was trained by Westley Richards craftsmen while still a teenager. While only a handful of long guns have been manufactured under his own name, his craftsmanship can be found in guns bearing some of Britain's best names, including Boss & Co., Churchill, Atkin, Grant & Lang, Dickson & MacNaughton, William Evans, Holland & Holland, P.V. Nelson, William Powell, and Westley Richards.

While Turner no longer makes guns for the gun trade, he is currently one of the fifteen elected Guardians of the Birmingham Proof House.

It is highly recommended that an expert individual appraisal be done on any Turner long gun in order to determine current value before buying or selling.

Information appears courtesy of Vic Venters and Shooting Sportsman *magazine.*

2 VETS ARMS CO.

Please see listing at the beginning of the "A" section.

NOTES

U.S.R.A.

Previous organization (United States Revolver Association) that established certain rules for target pistol shooting. Target pistols were manufactured by Harrington & Richardson - please refer to the Handgun section under Harrington & Richardson.

U.S. ARMAMENT CORP.

Current manufacturer located in Ephrata, PA since 2007.

U.S. Armament Corp. manufactures full size replicas of the 1877 Bulldog Gatling Gun and other iconic pieces. Please contact the company directly for more information, including options, pricing, and availability.

U.S. ARMS COMPANY

Previous manufacturer located in Riverhead, NY.

GRADING - PPGS™	100%	98%	95%	90%	80%	70%	60%	LAST MSR

REVOLVERS: SINGLE ACTION

ABILENE .357 MAG. – 6 shot, 4 5/8, 5 1/2, or 6 1/2 in. barrel, adj. sights, transfer bar ignition, smooth walnut grips, blue finish only. Mfg. 1976-83.

$325	$275	$240	$200	$185	$170	$155	

* ***Abilene .357 Mag. Stainless Steel*** – similar to Abilene, only in stainless steel.

$350	$285	$240	$200	$185	$170	$155	

ABILENE .44 MAG. – 7 1/2 and 8 1/2 in. barrel, unfluted cylinder blue finish only, otherwise similar to .357 Mag.

$325	$265	$240	$220	$200	$165	$150	

* ***Abilene .44 Mag. Stainless Steel*** – similar to Abilene .44 Mag., only stainless steel.

$375	$330	$290	$235	$210	$180	$155	

U.S. GENERAL TECHNOLOGIES, INC.

Previous manufacturer located in S. San Francisco, CA circa 1994-96.

RIFLES: SEMI-AUTO

P-50 SEMI-AUTO – .50 BMG cal., includes 10 shot detachable mag., folding bipod, muzzle brake, matte black finish. Mfg. 1995-96.

$5,600	$4,950	$4,475	$3,975	$3,500	$3,050	$2,600	*$5,995*

U.S. HISTORICAL SOCIETY

Previous organization which marketed historically significant firearms reproductions until April, 1994. Located in Richmond, VA. Most firearms were manufactured by the Williamsburg Firearms Manufactory and the Virginia Firearms Manufactory.

For individual model listings, please go to BlueBookOfGunValues.com/overflow.

U.S. MACHINE GUN ARMORY LLC

Please refer to MGA (Machine Gun Armory) located in the M section.

U.S. MILITARY HANDGUNS

Please refer to listings in the Colt (includes subcontracted variations of the M1911 and M1911A1) and Smith & Wesson sections.

U.S. MILITARY & COMMERCIAL LONG ARMS MFG'S

Also see listings under Colt, Enfield, Krag-Jorgensen, Springfield Armory, and Winchester. U.S. Military Trench and Riot guns may be found under the "Trench/Riot Shotguns" category in the T section.

CARBINES: SEMI-AUTO

Values are for original unmodified carbines, with proper parts makers, unsanded wood, and crisp stock cartouches.

U.S. M1 CARBINE (MILITARY & COMMERCIAL) – .30 Carbine cal., 18 in. barrel, 15 or 30 shot box mag., wood stocked, two or four position aperture rear, blade front sight with protective ears, with or without bayonet lug. This weapon was designed by Winchester for the U.S. government, over 6 million were produced by 12 different companies. Plainfield mfg. after WWII was for civilian sales. It is a gas operated lightweight carbine which was also used by other countries' armed forces. Makers and values as follows. Some variations have the type III barrel band.

GRADING - PPGS™	100%	98%	95%	90%	80%	70%	60%	LAST MSR

* ***Carbines: Semi-Auto, Reworks & Commercial Mfg.*** – includes carbines that have been factory reworked at U.S. arsenals.

Underwood	$850	$675	$495	$400	$350	$300	$275
S.G. Saginaw	$825	$650	$475	$400	$350	$300	$275
Quality Hardware	$850	$675	$495	$415	$370	$325	$295
Nat'l Postal Meter	$950	$775	$525	$425	$375	$325	$295
IBM	$950	$775	$525	$425	$370	$325	$295
Standard Products	$800	$650	$495	$415	$370	$325	$295
Inland	$850	$675	$495	$415	$370	$325	$295
SG Grand Rapids	$950	$775	$525	$425	$375	$325	$295
Winchester	$1,150	$850	$750	$550	$425	$350	$325
Irwin Pedersen	$1,700	$1,400	$995	$850	$775	$675	$580
Rockola	$995	$925	$700	$525	$425	$350	$325
Plainfield	$395	$360	$330	$295	$260	$230	$195
Commercial Mfg. (43 mfgs.)	$350	$300	$265	$235	$200	$185	$170

An Inland presentation carbine with white stock was also mfg. in limited quantities for military service organizations (i.e. V.F.W., American Legion, etc.). Values for original guns are currently in the $1,750-$2,000 range.

Recent imports can usually be denoted by visible import markings and/or alterations to original finish.

* ***Carbines: Semi-Auto, Original Type I*** – includes original carbines with flip rear sight and no bayonet lug.

Underwood	$2,125	$1,675	$1,250	$1,000	$875	$750	$675
S.G. Saginaw	$2,250	$1,800	$1,300	$1,050	$950	$800	$750
Quality Hardware	$2,125	$1,675	$1,250	$1,000	$875	$750	$675
Nat'l Postal Meter	$2,375	$1,950	$1,325	$1,050	$950	$800	$750
IBM	$2,375	$1,950	$1,325	$1,050	$950	$800	$750
Standard Products	$2,000	$1,625	$1,250	$1,050	$925	$800	$750
Inland	$2,125	$1,675	$1,250	$1,000	$875	$750	$675
SG Grand Rapids	$2,375	$1,950	$1,325	$1,050	$950	$800	$750
Winchester	$2,875	$2,200	$1,875	$1,375	$1,075	$875	$800
Irwin Pedersen	$4,250	$3,500	$2,500	$2,125	$1,925	$1,675	$1,425
Rockola	$2,500	$2,275	$1,750	$1,300	$1,050	$875	$800

Subtract 30% for original finish guns that have been changed back to the original configuration by switching parts.

* ***Carbines: Semi-Auto, Original Type II*** – includes original carbines with adj. rear sight and no bayonet lug.

S.G. Saginaw	$1,825	$1,450	$1,050	$875	$775	$650	$600
Quality Hardware	$1,875	$1,650	$1,075	$875	$775	$650	$600
IBM	$2,100	$1,700	$1,150	$925	$825	$715	$650
Standard Products	$1,750	$1,425	$1,050	$875	$775	$650	$600
Inland	$1,875	$1,475	$1,075	$875	$775	$650	$600
SG Grand Rapids	$2,100	$1,700	$1,150	$925	$825	$715	$650
Winchester	$2,525	$1,875	$1,650	$1,200	$925	$775	$700
Irwin Pedersen	$3,750	$3,050	$2,175	$1,875	$1,700	$1,475	$1,275
Rockola	$2,175	$2,025	$1,550	$1,150	$925	$775	$700

Subtract 30% for original finish guns that have been changed back to the original configuration by switching parts.

* ***Carbines: Semi-Auto, Original Type III*** – includes original carbines with adj. rear sight and bayonet lug.

Inland	$1,700	$1,350	$1,000	$800	$700	$600	$550
Winchester	$2,300	$1,700	$1,500	$1,100	$850	$700	$650

Subtract 30% for original finish guns that have been changed back to the original configuration by switching parts.

Subtract 50% for modified guns with adj. sight and bayonet lug.

M1 A1 PARATROOPER CARBINE – .30 Carbine cal., mfg. by Inland - WWII production, folding stock, crossed cannon proofed on bottom, OAL 26 1/2 in. with stock folded. 140,000 mfg. 1942-1945.

Beware of after-market fakes.

* ***M1 A1 Paratrooper Carbine Type I*** – values assume original guns with flip rear sight and no bayonet lug.

$5,500	$5,000	$3,250	$2,500	$2,150	$1,750	$1,450

GRADING - PPGS™	100%	98%	95%	90%	80%	70%	60%	LAST MSR

* ***M1 A1 Paratrooper Carbine Type II*** – values assume original guns with adj. rear sight and no bayonet lug.

	$5,500	$5,000	$2,700	$2,100	$1,750	$1,450	$1,150	

* ***M1 A1 Paratrooper Carbine Type III*** – values assume original guns with adj. rear sight and bayonet lug.

	$3,200	$2,800	$2,150	$1,750	$1,500	$1,250	$1,000	

RIFLES: BOLT ACTION

For U.S. Military Enfields, please refer to the Enfield section.

RIFLES: SEMI-AUTO

On original (non-reworked) variations listed, it is absolutely critical that rifles have not been rebuilt and must have original cartouche stock.

Values are for original unmodified rifles, with proper parts makers, unsanded wood, and crisp stock cartouches. Without original wood and non-original parts, values drop to rework prices. Beware of fake stock cartouches.

M1 GARAND – .30-06 cal., semi-auto, 8 shot en bloc clip fed, gas operated, adj. aperture sight, wooden stock. Made 1937-57 by Springfield, Winchester, H&R, and International Harvester.

* ***M1 Garand Reworks*** – includes rifles reworked at U.S. Arsenals.

	$1,250	$1,050	$900	$800	$700	$600	$500	

* ***M1 Garand Early Type I*** – identified by gas trap barrel up to ser. no. 50,000, all were mfg. by Springfield.

	N/A	$45,000	$40,000	$35,000	$20,000	$15,000	$10,000	

* ***M1 Garand Type II*** – identified by gas port barrel and ser. no. over 50,000.

	$1,450	$1,200	$1,035	$925	$800	$695	$575	

* ***M1 Garand Pre-WWII Winchester Mfg.***

	$3,750	$3,150	$2,700	$2,400	$2,100	$1,800	$1,500	

* ***M1 Garand Pre-WWII Springfield Mfg.***

	$3,750	$3,150	$2,700	$2,400	$2,100	$1,800	$1,500	

* ***M1 Garand WWII Mfg.*** – serialization starts at approx. 400,000.

	$5,000	$4,200	$3,600	$3,200	$2,800	$2,400	$2,000	

* ***M1-C or M1-D Garand Sniper*** – with scope and mounts (beware of fakes and rewelds with boxes and papers). M1-D values assume paperwork for values listed.

M1-D	N/A	$4,500	$3,400	$2,800	$2,200	$1,725	$1,350	
M1-C	N/A	N/A	$8,500	$7,500	$6,250	$5,000	$4,000	

Top values require original DCM shipping box, paperwork, and all listed accessories.

* ***M-1 Garand Post-WWII H & R, IHC, SA Mfg.*** – .30-06 cal., semi-auto, 8 shot internal mag., some may be arsenal refinished, mfg. for the U.S. military during the 1950s.

	$1,750	$1,550	$1,350	$1,150	$950	$750	$650	

Add 15% if IHC mfg.

Subtract 60% if w/o correct parts.

M1 GARAND NATIONAL MATCH – target version of the Garand, using National Match barrel and sights, glass bedding, etc. Must have serialized N.M. paperwork for prices listed below.

	$2,800	$2,500	$1,800	$1,400	$1,000	$800	$650	

U.S. ORDNANCE

Current manufacturer and distributor located in McCarran, NV. Commercial sales through Desert Ordnance, located in Sparks, NV.

U.S. Ordnance is licensed by Saco Defense to be the exclusive manufacturer and distributor for the M60 Series machine gun and spare parts.

RIFLES: SEMI-AUTO

U.S. Ordnance has manufactured semi-auto reproductions (BATFE approved) of belt fed machine guns. Recent models include the M-60/M-60E3 (MSR is POR), M60E4/Mk43 (MSR $12,500-$13,000, new 2004) and more. Previous models included the .303 Vickers (last MSR was $4,500 w/o tripod), Browning M-1919 (last MSR was $1,995), and the M-1919A4 (last MSR was $2,095). These belt fed variations are machined to military specifications, and have a 5 year warranty. Please contact the distributor directly for more information, including pricing and availability.

GRADING - PPGS™	100%	98%	95%	90%	80%	70%	60%	LAST MSR

U.S. TRINITY CUSTOM

Current manufacturer of custom bolt action rifles and other custom firearms, located in Northlake, TX.

U.S. Trinity Custom builds precision rifle and custom 1911s hand fit by a master gunsmith built to customer specifications. Gunsmithing services, custom coating, laser engraving, and NFA items are also available. Please contact the company directly for more information, including pricing, options, and availability.

USAS 12

Previous trademark manufactured by International Ordnance Corporation located in Nashville, TN circa 1992-95. Previously manufactured (1990-91) by Ramo Mfg., Inc. located in Nashville, TN. Previously distributed by Kiesler's Wholesale located in Jeffersonville, IN until 1994. Originally designed and previously distributed in the U.S. by Gilbert Equipment Co., Inc. located in Mobile, AL. Previously manufactured under license by Daewoo Precision Industries, Ltd. located in South Korea.

SHOTGUNS: SEMI-AUTO

USAS 12 – 12 ga. only, gas operated action available in either semi or fully auto versions, 18 1/4 in. cylinder bore barrel, closed bolt, synthetic stock, pistol grip, and forearm, carrying handle, 10 round box or 20 round drum mag., 2 3/4 in. chamber only, parkerized finish, 12 lbs. Mfg. 1987-1995.

	100%	98%	95%	90%	80%	70%	60%	LAST MSR
	$1,500	$1,250	$1,050	$925	$850	$750	$650	*$995*

Add $300-$500 for extra 20 shot drum magazine (banned by the BATFE).

Values above are for a semi-auto model. This model is currently classified as a destructive device and necessary federal NFA Class III transfer paperwork must accompany a sale.

USA TACTICAL FIREARMS

Current AR-15 style pistol and rifle manufacturer located in Catawba, NC. Previously located in Statesville, NC.

Please refer to BlueBookOfGunValues.com to order the *Blue Book of AR-15s & Variations*, available as a book or online subscription.

USFA/ZIP FACTORY, LLC

Previous handgun manufacturer located in Hartford, CT 2012-2017.

PISTOLS: SEMI-AUTO

ZIP .22 – .22 LR cal., modular construction allows many types of configurations, 5 1/4 in. barrel, accepts Ruger 10/22 mags., fixed sights, black finish, 15 1/2 oz. Mfg. 2013-2017.

	100%	98%	95%	90%	80%	70%	60%	LAST MSR
	$180	$160	$150	$140	$130	$120	$115	*$200*

Add $20 for Ruger BX-1 magazine.

UBERTI, A. Srl

Current firearms, black powder, replica firearms, and accessories manufacturer established in 1959, located in Serezzo, Italy. Currently imported and distributed by Uberti USA (previous company name was Stoeger Industries 2003-2017) located in Accokeek, MD, Taylor's & Co, located in Winchester, VA, Cimarron F.A. Co, located in Fredricksburg, TX, E.M.F., located in Santa Ana, CA, Navy Arms, located in Martinsburg, WV, Cabela's (certain models only), located in Sidney, NE, and Dixie Gun Works, located in Union City, TN. Previously imported by Tristar Sporting Arms, located in N. Kansas City, MO, and until Dec. 31st, 2002 by Uberti USA, Inc., located in Lakeville, CT.

In late 1999, Beretta purchased Aldo Uberti & Co. S.r.l.

The current importers listed above import Uberti guns with their own importer stamp. However, all guns will also have the Uberti name listed as the manufacturer. Please refer to the individual importers for additional information on Uberti firearms.

For more information and up-to-date pricing regarding current Aldo Uberti black powder models, please refer to the *Blue Book of Modern Black Powder Arms* (also available online).

PISTOLS: REPRODUCTIONS, SINGLE SHOT

1871 ROLLING BLOCK TARGET PISTOL – available in .22 LR, .22 WMR, .22 Hornet (disc. 2004), .357 Mag. (disc. 2002), or .45 LC (Navy Model with open sights only, mfg. 1992-95) cal., 9 1/2 in. half-round, half-octagon barrel, case colored frame and backstrap, brass trigger guard. Imported 2002-2006.

	100%	98%	95%	90%	80%	70%	60%	LAST MSR
	$385	$300	$250	$210	$175	$155	$135	*$480*

GRADING - PPGS™	100%	98%	95%	90%	80%	70%	60%	LAST MSR

REVOLVERS: DOUBLE ACTION

INSPECTOR MODEL – .32 S&W or .38 Spl. cal., 3, 4, or 6 in. barrels, double action, blue or chrome finish. Imported 1985-89.

	$390	$295	$245	$210	$170	$145	$125	*$406*

Add $35 for target sights.
Add $25 for chrome plating.

REVOLVERS: REPRODUCTIONS, SA/SAA & VARIATIONS

Factory engraving and other embellishments or finishes (including antique charcoal blue, in-the-white steel, nickel, etc.) may be special ordered by contacting the importer(s) directly.

Add $85 for antique patina finish (disc.), $45 for antique charcoal blue finish (disc.) on all Cattleman variations, $130 for silver plating (disc.), $40 for in-the-white finish (disc.), $85 for nickel plating (not available on Schofield, disc.), $85 for select grade walnut one-piece fitted grips (disc.), $49 for walnut grip, $250 or $575 (solid silver) for Army/Navy Tiffany grips (disc.), $45 for checkered grips (disc.), $50 for stag horn grips (disc.), $69 for gunfighter grip, $189 for faux ivory, $189 for black bison horn grips, $189 for faux pearl, $350 for mother-of-pearl grips (disc.), or $650-$1,450 for Cattleman engraving, depending on amount, and if with gold inlays (disc.).

COLT 1851 NAVY CONVERSION – .38 Spl. cal. only, 4 3/4 (disc. 2020), 5 1/2, or 7 1/2 in. barrel, patterned after original 1851 Navy, brass backstrap and trigger guard, 2.6 lbs. Importation began 2007.

MSR $589	$500	$440	$375	$340	$275	$225	$195	

REMINGTON 1858 NEW ARMY CONVERSION – .45 LC cal., 8 in. barrel, brass backstrap and trigger guard, case hardened frame, one-piece walnut grips, 2.6 lbs. Importation began 2007.

MSR $599	$510	$450	$385	$350	$275	$225	$200	

COLT 1860 ARMY CONVERSION – .38 Spl. (disc.) or .45 LC cal., 4 3/4 (.38 Spl. cal. only, disc. 2017), 5 1/2, 7 1/2 (disc.), or 8 in. barrel, patterned after original 1860 Army, blued steel backstrap and trigger guard, 2.6 lbs. Importation began 2007.

MSR $619	$525	$460	$395	$350	$290	$240	$200	

COLT 1871 RICHARDS/MASON CONVERSION – .38 Spl., .38 LC, .44 Colt (8 in. barrel only), or .45 Schofield cal., choice of brass (New Model) or steel BS/TG (Old Model), 5 1/2, 7 1/2, or 8 in. round or octagon barrel, one-piece walnut grips, approx. 2.6 lbs. Imported 2002 only.

	$385	$350	$315	$275	$250	$225	$200	*$450*

COLT 1871-1872 OPEN TOP EARLY/LATE MODEL – .38 Spl., .38 LC (disc. 2002), .44 Russian (disc. 2002), .44 Colt (disc. 2002), .44 LC (disc. 2002), .44 Spl. (disc. 2002), .45 Schofield (disc. 2002), or .45 LC cal., open top frame, 4 3/4 (Early Model only, disc.), 5 1/2 (Early Model only), or 7 1/2 in. octagon barrel, Army (Late Model) or Navy (Early Model) size grips. Imported 2002, reintroduced 2007.

MSR $579	$495	$435	$375	$335	$275	$225	$195	

Subtract $30 for Early Model Navy with brass backstrap and trigger guard.

BUCKHORN SAA – .44 Mag., .44 Spl. (disc.), or .44-40 WCF (disc.) cal., 4 3/4, 5 1/2 (new 2002), 6 (disc.), or 7 1/2 in. barrel, brass or steel backstrap. Importation disc. 2002.

* ***Buckhorn New Model Frame SAA*** – steel or brass backstrap and trigger guard. Disc.

	$415	$360	$315	$280	$230	$190	$140	*$410*

Add $69 for convertible cylinder.
Add $40 for Target Model (disc.).
Subtract $51 for New Model frame (brass BS & TG).

* ***Buckhorn Buntline SAA*** – .44-40 WCF (disc.) or .44 Mag. cal., 18 in. barrel, includes non-detachable shoulder stock with brass hardware and lanyard ring. Importation disc. 1989, resumed 2001-2002.

	$415	$360	$315	$280	$230	$190	$140	*$455*

Add $40 for target sights.
Add $40 for extra .44-40 WCF cylinder combo (disc.).
Add $122 for detachable shoulder stock (disc.).
Subtract $45 for New Model frame (BB & TG).

1873 CATTLEMAN FLAT-TOP SAA ("FIRST ISSUE") – .357 Mag. (mfg. 2001-2002), .38-40 WCF (disc. 2002), .44-40 WCF, or .45 LC cal., 4 3/4, 5 1/2, or 7 1/2 in. barrel, choice of regular (disc. 2002) or flat-top receiver. Imported 1997-2004.

	$435	$375	$325	$280	$230	$190	$140	*$430*

GRADING - PPGS™	100%	98%	95%	90%	80%	70%	60%	LAST MSR

1873 CATTLEMAN SAA & VARIATIONS – available in .22 LR (disc. 1990), .22 WMR (disc. 1990), .32-20 WCF (mfg. 2001-2003), .357 Mag., .38 Spl. (disc. 2003), .38-40 WCF (mfg. 1989-2003), .44 Spl. (disc. 2003), .44-40 WCF, or .45 LC cal., 3 3/4 (.45 LC only, disc.), 4 (.45 LC only, disc.), 4 3/4, 5 1/2, or 7 1/2 in. barrel, brass or steel backstrap and trigger guard, Old Model (with cylinder pin retainer) or New Model (with plunger) frame, 2.3 lbs. (with 5 1/2 in. barrel). New 2002.

* ***1873 Cattleman SAA with Steel Grip Strap and Trigger Guard*** – choice of New or Old Model frame, case colored or nickel finished, charcoal blue barrel/cylinder also available on Old Model. Disc.

	$450	$395	$340	$300	$250	$200	$160	*$529*

Add $110 for charcoal blue finish or $150 for charcoal blue finish and martially marked grips (.45 LC cal. only).
Add $219 for faux ivory, black buffalo horn, or faux pearl grips (new 2006).
Add $60 for charcoal blue barrel, cylinder, and grip frame/trigger guard (.45 LC cal. only).
Add $75 for convertible cylinder (.45 LC/.45 ACP, .22 LR/.22 WMR in 5 1/2 in. barrel only, disc. 2002).

* ***1873 Cattleman SAA with Brass Grip Strap and Trigger Guard*** – .357 Mag., .38-40 WCF (mfg. 2001-2002), .44 Mag. (mfg. 2001-2002), .44 Spl. (mfg. 2001-2002), .44-40 WCF, or .45 LC cal., 3 3/4 (.45 LC only, disc.), 4 (.45 LC only, disc.), 4 3/4, 5 1/2, or 7 1/2 in. barrel. Disc.

	$425	$375	$325	$295	$235	$195	$150	*$519*

Add $51 for convertible cylinder (.45 LC/.45 ACP, disc. 2002).

* ***1873 Cattleman SAA Polished Nickel New Model*** – .45 LC cal., full nickel-plated New Model steel frame, 4 3/4, 5 1/2, or 7 1/2 in. barrel, polished nickel finish.

MSR $689	$585	$510	$440	$400	$325	$265	$210

* ***1873 Cattleman SAA Stainless Steel*** – .45 LC cal., similar to 1873 Cattleman SAA with New Model frame, 4 3/4 (disc. 2018), 5 1/2, or 7 1/2 in. barrel, stainless steel.

MSR $739	$625	$550	$475	$425	$350	$280	$225

» **1873 Cattleman Stainless Engraved** – .45 LC cal., 4 3/4 or 5 1/2 in. barrel, engraved frame, faux pearl grips. Mfg. 2011-2017.

	$1,050	$925	$825	$750	$650	$550	$450	*$1,199*

* ***1873 Cattleman SAA Matched Set*** – .45 LC or .357 Mag. (new 2011) cal., 4 3/4 (disc. 2010) or 5 1/2 in. barrel, New Model frame, choice of blue/case colored, nickel/faux ivory grips (disc. 2010), or matte blue (disc. 2010) with walnut grips. Mfg. mid-2008-2016.

	$985	$875	$775	$700	$625	$550	$495	*$1,099*

Add $580 for nickel finish with faux ivory grips (disc. 2010, reintroduced 2013).
Add $40 for matte blue finish with walnut grips (disc. 2010).

* ***1873 Cattleman SAA Engraved*** – .45 LC cal., 4 3/4 or 5 1/2 in. barrel, engraved action, New Model frame, choice of white finish/AAA walnut grips, blue coin finish/bison horn grips, or silver plated finish/faux pearl grips. Mfg. mid-2008-2010.

	$950	$850	$750	$650	$550	$450	$375	*$1,069*

Add $40 for blue coin finish with buffalo horn grips.
Add $110 for silver plated finish and faux pearl grips.

* ***1873 Cattleman SAA Target Model*** – similar to standard Cattleman Model, only fully adj. rear blade sight, brass backstrap. Importation disc. 1990.

	$540	$450	$375	$310	$250	$215	$190	*$335*

Add $25 for steel backstrap and trigger guard.
Add $60 for stainless steel construction (disc.).

1873 CATTLEMAN .22 REVOLVER – .22 LR cal., color case hardened frame, 5 1/2 or 7 1/2 in. barrel, 12 shot fluted cylinder, fixed sights, one-piece oil finished walnut grips, blue finish, 2.3 lbs. New 2021.

MSR $589	$500	$440	$375	$340	$275	$225	$195

1873 CATTLEMAN U.S. SAA CAVALRY – .45 LC cal., 7 1/2 in. barrel, Old Model frame, charcoal blue finish, steel backstrap and trigger guard, one-piece walnut grips, 2.3 lbs. Disc. 2009.

	$540	$450	$375	$310	$250	$215	$190	*$629*

1873 CATTLEMAN ARTILLERY SAA – .45 LC cal., 5 1/2 in. barrel, Old Model frame, charcoal blue finish, steel backstrap and trigger guard, one-piece walnut grips, 2.3 lbs. Disc. 2009.

	$540	$450	$375	$310	$250	$215	$190	*$629*

1873 CATTLEMAN BIRD'S HEAD SAA – .357 Mag. (new 2001), .44 Spl. (disc. 2002), .44-40 WCF (disc. 2004), or .45 LC cal., 3 (Sheriff's Model, .44-40 WCF or .45 LC cal. only, disc.), 3 1/2 (OM frame only) 4, 4 3/4, or 5 1/2 in. barrel, choice of Old or New Model frame, patterned after the Colt 1877 Thunderer, case colored frame, checkered (disc.) or smooth walnut bird's head grips, 2.3 lbs. New 1997.

MSR $579	$495	$435	$375	$335	$275	$225	$195

Add $10 for Old Model frame.

GRADING - PPGS™	100%	98%	95%	90%	80%	70%	60%	LAST MSR

1873 CATTLEMAN BISLEY SAA – .357 Mag., .38-40 WCF (disc. 2002), .44 Spl. (disc. 2002), .44-40 WCF (disc. 2004), or .45 LC cal., New Model frame, patterned after the Colt Bisley Model, 4 3/4 (disc. 2020), 5 1/2, or 7 1/2 (disc. 2020) in. barrel, case colored frame, wood grips. New 1997.

MSR $619	$525	$460	$395	$355	$290	$240	$200	

* ***1873 Cattleman Bisley Flat-top SAA*** – similar to Cattleman Bisley, except has flat-top frame with fixed or target (.44-40 WCF - disc. or .45 LC cal., 7 1/2 in. barrel only) sights. Importation disc. 2004.

	$425	$375	$325	$295	$235	$195	$150	*$435*

Add $25 for target sights (disc.).

1873 CATTLEMAN BUNTLINE SAA – .22 LR/.22 WMR combo (disc. 2000), .357 Mag. (disc. 2018), .44-40 WCF (disc. 2010), .44 Mag. (mfg. 2001-2002), or .45 LC cal., 12 (mfg. 2001-2002, .45 LC only) or 18 in. barrel, New Model frame with steel or brass (disc. 2002) backstrap cut for shoulder stock, field sights with round frame (disc. 2020) or target sights on flat-top frame. Importation disc. 1989, reintroduced 1993.

MSR $709	$600	$525	$450	$410	$325	$275	$225	

Subtract approx. 10% for field sights with round frame (disc. 2020).
Subtract $56 for brass backstrap and trigger guard (disc. 2002).

* ***1873 Cattleman Buntline Carbine SAA*** – similar to Cattleman Buntline, 18 in. barrel, detachable or non-detachable shoulder stock with brass hardware and lanyard ring. Importation disc. 1989, reintroduced 1993-95.

	$425	$375	$325	$295	$235	$195	$150	*$475*

Add $34 for target sights.
Add $34 for .22 LR/.22 WMR combo. (disc. 1989).
Add $175 for detachable shoulder stock.

1873 CATTLEMAN CALLAHAN SAA – .44 Mag. cal., New Model frame, 4 3/4 (disc. 2019), 6, or 7 1/2 (Target only, disc. 2016) in. barrel, 100% blue finish, smooth walnut grips. New 2010.

MSR $639	$545	$475	$410	$375	$300	$250	$210	

Add $50 for Target Model in 6 or 7 1/2 (disc. 2016) in. barrel, includes ramped front sight and adj. rear sight (disc. 2020).

1873 CATTLEMAN CHARCOAL BLUE OLD MODEL – .45 LC cal., Old Model frame, 4 3/4, 5 1/2, or 7 1/2 in. barrel, steel backstrap and trigger guard, charcoal blue finish.

MSR $669	$575	$500	$430	$390	$315	$260	$220	

Add $50 for Artillery or Cavalry markings.

1873 CATTLEMAN CHISHOLM SAA – .45 LC cal., New Model frame, 4 3/4, 5 1/2 (disc. 2020), or 7 1/2 (disc. 2010) in. barrel, matte metal finish with case colored hammer and checkered walnut grips, 2.3 lbs. Importation began 2006.

MSR $599	$510	$450	$385	$350	$275	$225	$200	

1873 CATTLEMAN CODY NEW MODEL SAA – .45 LC cal., full nickel plated steel frame, 4 3/4, 5 1/2, or 7 1/2 (disc. 2019) in. barrel, 6 shot fluted cylinder, ivory style grips, 2.3 lbs. New mid-2013.

MSR $899	$765	$675	$575	$525	$425	$350	$300	

* ***1873 Cattleman Cody Limited Edition Set*** – .45 LC cal., New Model frame, full nickel plated finish, 5 1/2 in. barrel only, 6 shot fluted cylinder, ivory style grips, matching serial numbers. Mfg. mid-2013-2020.

	$1,515	$1,325	$1,135	$1,025	$835	$685	$575	*$1,778*

1873 CATTLEMAN COWBOY MOUNTED SHOOTER (CMS) TRAINER – .22 LR. cal., 3 1/2 in. barrel, 12 shot cylinder, blue/case colored. New 2016.

MSR $650	$550	$480	$415	$375	$310	$260	$215	

1873 CATTLEMAN DESPERADO SAA – .45 LC cal., New Model frame, choice of 4 3/4 (disc. 2020), 5 1/2, or 7 1/2 (disc. 2010) in. barrel, nickel finish and black buffalo horn grips. Importation began 2006.

MSR $889	$750	$650	$565	$510	$415	$340	$265	

1873 CATTLEMAN EL PATROL – .45 LC or .357 Mag. cal., 3 1/2 or 4 in. barrel, blue finish with color case hardened or stainless steel frame, 3 1/2 or 4 in. barrel, lower profile hammer, checkered walnut grips, front blade sight. Mfg. 2013-2014.

	$540	$475	$400	$365	$295	$245	$190	*$639*

Add $140 for stainless steel.

1873 CATTLEMAN EL PATRON SAA – .357 Mag. or .45 LC cal., New Model frame, 4 3/4 (stainless steel disc. 2016) or 5 1/2 in. barrel, blue or stainless, checkered walnut grips. New 2009.

MSR $649	$550	$480	$415	$375	$310	$260	$215	

Add $150 for stainless steel (.45 LC cal. only).

GRADING - PPGS™	100%	98%	95%	90%	80%	70%	60%	LAST MSR

* ***1873 Cattleman El Patron Cowboy Mounted Shooter (CMS) SAA*** – .357 Mag. or .45 LC cal., New Model frame, 3 1/2 or 4 in. barrel, blue or stainless (disc. 2016), checkered walnut grips. Mfg. 2011-2020.

	$575	$500	$430	$390	$315	$260	$220	*$669*

Add $140 for stainless steel (3 1/2 in. barrel only, disc. 2016).

* ***1873 Cattleman El Patron Competition*** – .357 Mag. or .45 LC cal., blue, case hardened (disc.) frame, or stainless steel, 4 3/4 or 5 1/2 in. barrel, 6 shot fluted cylinder, one-piece checkered walnut grips, 2.3 lb. New mid-2013.

MSR $669	$575	$500	$430	$390	$315	$260	$220	

Add $180 for stainless steel.

1873 CATTLEMAN EL PATRON GRIZZLY PAW NEW MODEL – .45 LC or .357 Mag. cal., color case hardened frame, 4 3/4 or 5 1/2 in. barrel, checkered 1860 Army grips, blued finish. Importation began 2018.

MSR $659	$560	$490	$420	$380	$310	$260	$215	

1873 CATTLEMAN FRISCO SAA – .45 LC cal., case hardened New Model frame, charcoal blue finish, 4 3/4 (disc. 2020), 5 1/2, or 7 1/2 (disc. 2020) in. barrel, 6 shot fluted cylinder, steel backstrap and trigger guard, pearl style grips, 2.3 lbs. New mid-2013.

MSR $869	$740	$650	$550	$500	$400	$340	$285	

1873 CATTLEMAN GUNFIGHTER SAA – .45 LC cal., 4 3/4, 5 1/2, or 7 1/2 in. barrel, steel backstrap and trigger guard, matte metal finish, black checkered synthetic grips, New Model frame, 2.3 lbs. Mfg. 2005-2009.

	$400	$350	$300	$260	$230	$210	$180	*$479*

1873 CATTLEMAN HOMBRE SAA – .357 Mag. or .45 LC cal., New Model frame, 4 3/4 in. barrel, brass grip strap and trigger guard, matte blue metal finish with case colored hammer, smooth walnut grips, 2.3 lbs. Importation began 2007.

MSR $509	$430	$375	$325	$295	$235	$195	$165	

1873 CATTLEMAN MILLENIUM SAA – .357 Mag. or .45 LC cal., 4 3/4 in. barrel, matte finished metal, brass backstrap and trigger guard, New Model frame only. Imported 2000-2006.

	$260	$215	$190	$165	$150	$130	$120	*$300*

1873 CATTLEMAN NEW MODEL SPECIAL EDITION – .45 LC cal., 4 3/4 or 5 1/2 in. barrel, pearl grips, full scroll engraving, stainless steel finish. New 2018.

MSR $1,199	$1,020	$895	$765	$695	$560	$460	$395	

1873 CATTLEMAN OLD WEST SAA – .357 Mag. (disc. 2020) or .45 LC cal., Old Model case hardened frame, Old West Antique finish, 4 3/4 (disc. 2020), 5 1/2, or 7 1/2 (disc. 2018) in. barrel, 6 shot fluted cylinder, steel backstrap and trigger guard, one-piece walnut grips, 2.3 lbs. New mid-2013.

MSR $709	$600	$525	$450	$410	$330	$275	$225	

1873 CATTLEMAN SHORT STROKE COWBOY MOUNTED SHOOTER (CMS) PRO NEW MODEL – .45 LC cal., 3 1/2 in. round barrel, 6 shot fluted cylinder, walnut stock, one-piece checkered walnut grip, custom grade mainspring, wide hammer with aggressive checkering, EasyView sights, blued case hardened or stainless steel (new 2020) frame, 2 lbs. New 2017.

MSR $739	$625	$550	$475	$425	$350	$280	$225	

Add $170 for stainless steel (new 2020).

* ***1873 Cattleman Short Stroke CMS Kenda Lenseigne Pro New Model*** – .45 LC cal., 3 1/2 in. round barrel, 6 shot fluted cylinder, blued case hardened or stainless steel (new 2020) frame, walnut stock, modified bird's head walnut grips bearing Kenda Lenseigne brand, custom grade mainspring, wide hammer with aggressive checkering, EasyView sights, 2 lbs. New 2017.

MSR $739	$625	$550	$475	$425	$350	$280	$225	

Add $170 for stainless steel (new 2020).

1873 CATTLEMAN SHORT STROKE SASS PRO NEW MODEL – .357 Mag. or .45 LC cal., case hardened frame, 4 3/4 or 5 1/2 in. barrel, 6 shot fluted cylinder, one-piece checkered walnut grip, custom grade mainspring, EasyView sights, steel backstrap and trigger guard, blue finish.

MSR $729	$625	$550	$475	$425	$350	$275	$225	

* ***1873 Cattleman Short Stroke SASS Pro Nickel*** – .357 Mag. or .45 LC cal., nickel-plated steel frame, 4 3/4 or 5 1/2 in. barrel, 6 shot fluted cylinder, ivory-style grip, custom grade mainspring, EasyView sights, polished nickel finish, 2.3 lbs. Mfg. 2017-2020.

	$775	$680	$580	$525	$425	$350	$300	*$909*

GRADING - PPGS™	100%	98%	95%	90%	80%	70%	60%	LAST MSR

1873 CATTLEMAN SHERIFF'S MODEL SAA – .44-40 WCF or .45 LC cal., choice of steel or brass grip strap and trigger guard, 3 or 4 in. barrel. Importation disc. 2002.

	$345	$265	$210	$175	$160	$150	$135	*$410*

Subtract approx. 10% with brass grip strap and trigger guard.

1873 CATTLEMAN SAA REVOLVER CARBINE – .357 Mag. (disc. 2002), .44-40 WCF (disc. 2002), or .45 LC cal., New Model frame, 18 (new 2004) or 19 (disc. 2003) in. barrel, fixed stock with brass rifle buttplate, finger rest extension on trigger guard, choice of quick detachable mounts (disc. 2020) or target sights, 4.4 lbs. New 1997.

MSR $909	$775	$680	$580	$525	$425	$350	$300

Subtract approx. 10% for quick detachable mounts (disc. 2020).

1873 CATTLEMAN II SAA MATCHED SET – .357 Mag. or .45 LC. cal, 5 1/2 in. barrel, steel backstrap and trigger guard. New 2016.

MSR $1,158	$1,050	$950	$850	$725	$650	$550	$495

1873 CATTLEMAN II NEW MODEL BRASS – .357 Mag., .44-40 WCF., or .45 LC. cal., 4 3/4, 5 1/2, or 7 1/2 in. barrel, brass backstrap and trigger guard. New 2016.

MSR $549	$470	$410	$350	$325	$265	$215	$185

Add $10 for .44-40 WCF cal.

1873 CATTLEMAN II NEW MODEL STEEL – .357 Mag., .44-40 WCF., or .45 LC cal., 4 3/4, 5 1/2, or 7 1/2 in. barrel, steel backstrap and trigger guard. New 2016.

MSR $579	$495	$435	$375	$335	$275	$225	$195

1873 STALLION COLT SAA – .22 LR/.22 WMR cal. combo only, 4 3/4, 5 1/2, or 6 1/2 in. barrel, case hardened frame, 1-piece walnut grip, 2.4 lbs. Importation disc. 1989.

	$325	$265	$225	$195	$175	$155	$135	*$325*

Add $27 for steel backstrap and trigger guard.
Add $26 for Target Model.

* ***1873 Stainless Colt Stallion SAA*** – similar to standard Stallion, except is stainless steel. Importation disc. 1989.

	$400	$315	$250	$210	$185	$165	$155	*$425*

1873 STALLION STEEL GRIP STRAP/TG SAA – .22 LR (mfg. 2000-2016) or .38 Spl. cal., 3 1/2 (disc. 2002), 4 3/4 (disc. 2015), or 5 1/2 in. barrel, smaller, scaled-down SAA case colored New Model frame, approx. 32 oz. Mfg. 1999-2020.

	$470	$410	$350	$325	$260	$215	$185	*$549*

Add $60 for target sights (disc. 2016).
Add $39 for Target Model (38 Spl. cal. only, not available with 3 1/2 in. barrel, disc. 2002).
Add $90 for .22 LR/.22 WMR combo (disc. 2002, reintroduced 2014).

* ***1873 Stallion Brass Grip Strap/TG SAA*** – .22 LR cal., 4 3/4 (new 2011) or 5 1/2 in. barrel, 6 or 10 (new 2010) shot mag.

MSR $489	$415	$365	$315	$285	$230	$185	$160

Add $40 for 10 shot variation (new 2010).
Add $80 for Target Model (disc. 2016) or $110 for Target Model with 10 shot (disc. 2016).
Add $39 for dual cylinder (.22 LR/.22 WMR, disc. 2002).
Add $90 for Target Model with dual cylinder (disc.).

* ***1873 Stallion Bird's Head SAA OWD*** – .38 Spl. cal., New Model frame, 3 1/2 in. barrel, checkered walnut grips, Old West Defense (OWD) features. New 2011.

MSR $589	$500	$440	$375	$340	$275	$225	$195

* ***1873 Stallion Conversion SAA*** – .22 LR/.22 WMR cal. includes .22 LR and .22 WMR cylinders, 4 3/4 (previously available w/o extra .22 WMR cylinder, disc. 2017), 5 1/2, or 6 1/2 (disc. 2020) in. barrel, choice of blue/case colored frame or brass grip strap and trigger guard with case colored frame, one-piece smooth walnut grips, 24 oz. New mid-2009.

MSR $559	$475	$415	$350	$325	$265	$215	$185

Add $20 for steel grip strap (disc. 2019).
Add $80 Target Model (disc. 2020).
Subtract approx. $70 if without .22 WMR cylinder (disc. 2010).

1873 CATTLEMAN .22 LR SAA – .22 LR cal., case hardened frame, charcoal blue finish, 4 3/4, 5 1/2, or 7 1/2 in. barrel, 6 or 12 shot fluted cylinder, steel or brass (6 shot only) backstrap and trigger guard, one-piece walnut grips, 2.3 lbs. New mid-2013.

MSR $549	$470	$410	$350	$325	$260	$215	$185

GRADING - PPGS™	100%	98%	95%	90%	80%	70%	60%	LAST MSR

1873 HORSEMAN SAA - .357 Mag., .45 LC, .22 LR (new 2015), or .44 Mag. (new 2015) cal., case hardened frame, charcoal blue finish, 4 3/4, 5 1/2, or 7 1/2 in. barrel, steel back strap and trigger guard, wide trigger, one-piece smooth walnut grips, transfer bar safety. Mfg. mid-2013-2016.

	$460	$400	$340	$300	$250	$200	$160	*$549*

Add $10 for .45 LC and .357 Mag.
Add $30 for .44 Mag.

1875 REMINGTON ARMY/FRONTIER SA - .357 Mag. (disc. 2002), .44-40 WCF (disc. 2002), .45 ACP (mfg. 1992-2002, extra cylinder only), or .45 LC cal., 5 1/2 (Frontier configuration, disc. 1995, resumed 2001) or 7 1/2 (Outlaw configuration) in. barrel, brass (disc.) or steel (new 1993) trigger guard, blue/case colored frame or nickel (new 2006) finish, two-piece walnut grips, approx. 2.6 lbs. Imported 2002, reimported beginning 2005.

MSR $609	$520	$455	$390	$355	$285	$235	$200	

Add $42 for convertible cylinder (.45 LC/.45 ACP, disc.).
Add $120 for nickel finish and walnut grips in Outlaw configuration only (new 2006).

* ***1875 Remington SA Carbine*** – .357 Mag. .44-40 WCF, or .45 LC cal., 18 in. barrel, includes non-detachable shoulder stock with brass hardware and lanyard ring. Importation disc. 1989.

	$425	$285	$230	$200	$185	$180	$175	*$440*

Add $110 for nickel plating.

1890 REMINGTON POLICE SA - .357 Mag., .44-40 WCF (disc. 2002), .45 ACP (mfg. 1993-2002, dual cylinder only), or .45 LC cal., 5 1/2, or 7 1/2 (disc. 1995) in. barrel, blue finish with lanyard ring, brass (disc. 2002) or steel (new 1993) trigger guard, two-piece walnut grips, 2.6 lbs. Imported 2002, reimported beginning 2005.

MSR $619	$525	$460	$395	$355	$290	$240	$200	

Add $42 for dual cylinder (disc.).

PHANTOM MODEL SAA - .357 or .44 Mag. cal. only, 10 1/2 in. barrel for silhouette use. Imported 1985-89.

	$475	$395	$325	$290	$260	$230	$215	*$509*

1874 SCHOFIELD RUSSIAN SA - .44 Russian cal., 6 shot, break open, 6 (disc.), 6 1/2 (new 2002) or 7 (new 2002) in. barrel. Imported 2000-2002.

	$675	$585	$475	$425	$365	$300	$275	*$800*

1875 SCHOFIELD SA - .44-40 WCF or .45 LC cal., 3, 5, or 7 in. barrel. Imported 2000-2002.

	$635	$550	$465	$400	$350	$300	$275	*$750*

RUSSIAN NEW MODEL NO. 3 SA - .44 Russian or .45 LC (new 2006) cal., break open, blued steel frame and backtrap, 6 1/2 in. barrel, trigger guard finger extension, 6 shot with automatic extraction, Cyrillic barrel stamping, case colored opening mechanism and trigger guard, 2.7 lbs. Importation began 2005.

MSR $1,189	$1,015	$890	$760	$690	$560	$450	$395	

Add $10 for .44 Russian cal.
Add $410 for nickel finish with faux ivory grips (.45 LC cal. only, disc. 2020).

1875 NO. 3 SECOND MODEL TOP BREAK SA - .38 Spl. (new 2006), .44-40 WCF or .45 LC cal., patterned after the Schofield break open action, 3 1/2, 5, or 7 in. barrel, 6 shot, blue finish, walnut grips, case colored opening lever and trigger guard, available in First or Second Model (disc.), approx. 2 1/2 lbs. Importation began 2005.

MSR $1,179	$1,010	$885	$760	$690	$560	$450	$390	

* ***1875 No. 3 Second Model Top Break Nickel*** – .38 Spl. or .45 LC cal., break open, 3 1/2 (disc. 2017), 5, or 7 in. barrel, 6 shot, walnut (mfg. 2005-disc.) or pearl (new 2006) grips, full nickel plated steel. New 2005.

MSR $1,589	$1,350	$1,180	$1,015	$925	$750	$610	$525	

Add $2,000-$2,140 for nickel finish engraved model with pearl/wood grips (.45 LC cal. only, mfg. 2010-2011).

* ***1875 No. 3 Second Model Top Break Premium*** – .45 LC cal. only, 6 shot, faux pearl or walnut grips, blue or nickel finish, extensive scroll engraving with blue screws (nickel) or gold-lined border (blue), available from World Class dealers only. Imported 2007-2011.

	$2,550	$2,100	$1,800	$1,500	$1,200	$900	$700	*$2,999*

Add $140 for blue finish with faux pearl grips.

REVOLVERS: REPRODUCTIONS, OUTLAWS & LAWMEN SERIES

Each piece in Uberti's limited edition Outlaws and Lawmen collection draws its inspiration from the actual gun carried by the historical figure after which it is named.

GRADING - PPGS™	100%	98%	95%	90%	80%	70%	60%	LAST MSR

1851 NAVY CONVERSION OUTLAWS & LAWMEN "WILD BILL" – .38 Spl. cal., 7 1/2 in. barrel, ivory style grips, case hardened finish. Importation began 2019.

MSR $809	$685	$600	$515	$465	$375	$310	$265	

1873 SINGLE ACTION CATTLEMAN NEW MODEL OUTLAWS & LAWMEN "BONNEY" – .45 LC or .357 Mag. (new 2020) cal., New Model blued steel frame, 5 1/2 in. barrel, bison style grips, case hardened finish. Importation began 2019.

MSR $799	$680	$600	$500	$460	$375	$300	$265	

1873 SINGLE ACTION CATTLEMAN OUTLAWS & LAWMEN "DALTON" – .45 LC or .357 Mag. (new 2021) cal., 5.5 in. barrel, 6 shot fluted cylinder, pearl-style grip, fully decorated with engraving replicating the design found on Bob Dalton's Colt, hand-chased engraving work by Atelier Giovanelli, blue steel finish, 2.3 lbs. New 2020.

MSR $1,089	$915	$800	$685	$620	$500	$410	$360	

Add $20 for .45 LC cal.

1873 SINGLE ACTION CATTLEMAN NEW MODEL OUTLAWS & LAWMEN "DOC" – .45 LC or .357 Mag. (new 2020) cal., 4 3/4 in. barrel, 6 shot fluted cylinder, nickel-plated steel frame, pearl-style grips, 2.2 lbs. New 2018.

MSR $869	$740	$650	$550	$500	$400	$340	$285	

1873 SINGLE ACTION CATTLEMAN NEW MODEL OUTLAWS & LAWMEN "JESSE" – .45 LC or .357 Mag. (new 2020) cal., 5 1/2 in. barrel, 6 shot fluted cylinder, fully blued steel frame, backstrap, and trigger guard, bison horn style grips, 2.3 lbs. New 2018.

MSR $759	$650	$570	$490	$440	$360	$295	$250	

1873 CATTLEMAN OUTLAWS & LAWMEN "TEDDY" – .45 LC cal., 5 1/2 in. barrel, 6 shot fluted cylinder, full nickel-plated steel, simulated ivory grips, full laser engraving closely replicating the looks of Roosevelt's Colt, nickel finish, 2.3 lbs. New 2021.

MSR $1,249	$1,065	$930	$800	$725	$585	$480	$415	

1875 NO. 3 2ND MODEL TOP-BREAK OUTLAWS & LAWMEN "HARDIN" – .45 LC cal., 7 in. barrel, 6 shot fluted cylinder, case hardened frame, two-piece buffalo-horn grips, blued finish. New 2021.

MSR $1,479	$1,260	$1,100	$950	$850	$700	$560	$490	

1875 SINGLE ACTION ARMY OUTLAWS & LAWMEN "FRANK" – .45 LC or .357 Mag. (new 2021) cal., nickel-plated steel frame, 7 1/2 in. barrel, 6 shot fluted cylinder, ivory-style grip, nickel finish, 2.8 lbs. Importation began 2018.

MSR $949	$810	$710	$610	$550	$445	$365	$315	

Add $20 for .45 LC cal.

RIFLES: REPRODUCTIONS, LEVER ACTION

Add $140 for antique patina finish, $80 for charcoal blue finish, $75 for in-the-white finish, $235 for silver plating, $210 for nickel plating, $90 for checkered wood, $210 for select wood, or $475 for deluxe wood.

Add $850-$3,500 for hand-engraving options, depending on the amount of engraving and gold inlays.

All special order options, including wood upgrades and engraving were discontinued in 2011.

SILVERBOY RIFLE – .22 LR or .22 WMR (new 2013) cal., 19 in. round barrel, 15 shot mag., chrome plated alloy receiver, straight grip uncheckered walnut stock, controlled round feed, 5.8 lbs. Mfg. 2012-2016.

	$515	$465	$435	$400	$375	$325	$275	*$559*

Add $10 for .22 WMR cal.

1860 HENRY RIFLE/CARBINE – .44-40 WCF or .45 LC (rifle only) cal., iron (disc. 2010), brass, or steel frame, 10 or 13 shot mag., 24 1/4 in. barrel on rifle, 22 1/2 in. barrel on carbine (disc. 2002), metal finishes include case colored frame/blue barrel, charcoal blue (disc.), white (disc.), or chrome (disc.) finish, approx. 9 lbs.

MSR $1,499	$1,275	$1,115	$950	$865	$700	$600	$500	

Add $80 for steel frame.

Add $20 for iron frame (disc.).

The carbine was disc. in 1989, re-introduced 1992-2002.

* ***1860 Henry Carbine Trapper*** – .45 LC cal., 16 1/2 (disc. 2002) or 18 1/2 in. octagonal barrel, 8 shot mag., brass frame and buttplate, case hardened lever. New 1990.

MSR $1,519	$1,295	$1,135	$975	$880	$710	$600	$500	

* ***1860 Henry Rifle/Carbine 1 of 1,000*** – disc.

	$1,450	$1,150	$975	$850	$700	$575	$425	

GRADING - PPGS™ 100% 98% 95% 90% 80% 70% 60% LAST MSR

1866 YELLOWBOY CARBINE – .22 LR (disc. 1989), .22 WMR (disc. 1989), .38 Spl., .44-40 WCF (disc. 2018), or .45 LC cal., brass receiver, 10 shot mag., 19 in. round barrel, 7.4 lbs. Importation disc. 1995, resumed 2002.

MSR $1,239 $1,055 $925 $795 $715 $580 $475 $415

* ***1866 Yellowboy Carbine Trapper*** – .22 LR, .38 Spl., or .44-40 WCF cal., 16 in. barrel. Importation disc. 1989.

$650 $475 $395 $340 $285 $260 $235 *$686*

* ***1866 Yellowboy Carbine Indian*** – .22 LR, .22 WMR, .32-20 WCF (new 2002), .38 Spl., .44-40 WCF, or .45 LC (new 1996) cal., 19 in. barrel. Imported 2002 only.

$670 $535 $430 $360 $310 $275 $240 *$760*

Subtract $50 without brass tacks (disc.).

* ***1866 Yellowboy Carbine Red Cloud Commemorative*** – same cals., special engraving and brass tacks in forearm and stock. Importation disc. 1989.

$720 $600 $475 $400 $350 $330 $300 *$850*

1866 YELLOWBOY SPORTING RIFLE – .22 LR (mfg. 2001-2002), .22 WMR (mfg. 2001-2002), .32-20 WCF (mfg. 2002-2011), .38 Spl. (disc. 2020), .38-40 WCF (mfg. 2002-2011), .44-40 WCF, or .45 LC (new 1996) cal., brass receiver, 10 or 13 shot mag., 24 1/4 in. octagon barrel, 8.2 lbs.

MSR $1,269 $1,080 $950 $810 $725 $595 $485 $425

* ***1866 Sporting Rifle Deluxe Uberti Model*** – .44-40 WCF cal., features high polished receiver with fire blue small parts, ladder rear sight. Imported 1995 only.

$895 $675 $525 N/A N/A N/A N/A *$895*

This model was sold exclusively by Cherry's, located in Greensboro, NC.

* ***1866 Sporting Rifle "L.D. Nimschke" Special Edition*** – .44-40 WCF cal., receiver, buttplate, and forend cap feature recreations of Nimschke scroll engraving by Giovanelli of Italy, silver plated, deluxe walnut. Only 300 mfg. 1995-disc.

$1,650 $1,150 $800 N/A N/A N/A N/A *$1,495*

This model was sold exclusively by Cherry's, located in Greensboro, NC.

Optional 2nd Edition of Nimschke pattern book by R.L. Wilson ($100).

* ***1866 Sporting Rifle Yellowboy Indian Rifle*** – .22 LR (disc. 1989), .22 WMR (disc. 1989), .38 Spl., or .44-40 WCF cal., 24 1/4 in. barrel. Importation disc. 1989, reintroduced 1993-95.

$700 $560 $475 $385 $300 $260 $235 *$800*

1866 YELLOWBOY SHORT RIFLE BRASS – .22 LR (mfg. 2001-2002), .22 WMR (mfg. 2001-2002), .32-20 WCF (mfg. 2002-2011), .38 Spl., .38-40 WCF (mfg. 2002-2011), .44-40 WCF (disc. 2018), or .45 LC (new 1996) cal., brass receiver, 10 or 13 shot mag., 20 in. octagon barrel, 8.2 lbs.

MSR $1,269 $1,080 $950 $810 $725 $595 $485 $425

1866 FLATSIDE – .45 LC. cal., 20 in. barrel, 150th Anniversary Edition of the 1866 Yellowboy Rifle with engraving. Limited mfg. 2016 only.

$1,500 $1,250 $1,075 $975 $825 $725 $625 *$1,779*

1866 MUSKET – .44-40 WCF or .45 LC cal., features 27 in. barrel with barrel bands. Imported 1999-2002.

$810 $600 $500 $425 $360 $320 $280 *$910*

1873 125th ANNIVERSARY – .44-40 WCF cal., special anniversary offering featuring engraved gold plated metal with fire blue receiver and small parts, long rifle configuration with deluxe pistol grip and forearm. 125 mfg. 1998 only, marketed exclusively by Cherry's.

$3,250 $2,500 $1,750 N/A N/A N/A N/A *$3,500*

1873 CARBINE – .22 LR (disc. 1991), .22 WMR (disc. 1991), .32-20 WCF (mfg. 2001-2005), .357 Mag. (disc. 2020), .38 Spl. (disc. 1991) .38-40 (mfg. 2002-2011), .44 Mag. (disc. 2020), .44-40 WCF (disc. 2018), or .45 LC (new 1992) cal., 10 shot mag., steel receiver, 19 in. round barrel with forearm barrel bands, 7.4 lbs.

MSR $1,309 $1,115 $975 $835 $760 $615 $500 $425

Add $110 for .44 Mag. cal. (disc. 2020).

Add $35 for case colored frame (disc.).

* ***1873 Carbine Trapper*** – .357 Mag., .44-40 WCF, or .45 LC cal. only, 16 1/8 in. barrel. Importation disc. 1990.

$750 $600 $500 $425 $360 $320 $280 *$750*

GRADING - PPGS™	100%	98%	95%	90%	80%	70%	60%	LAST MSR

1873 COMPETITION RIFLE – .357 Mag. or .45 Colt. cal., short stroke lever and action job, 20 in. octagon blue barrel, 10 shot mag., A-grade walnut stock and forearm with rubber recoil pad, color case hardened finished receiver, designed for cowboy action shooting. Importation began mid-2014.

MSR $1,499 $1,275 $1,115 $950 $865 $700 $600 $500

1873 LIMITED EDITION SHORT RIFLE DELUXE – .45 LC cal., case hardened steel frame and lever, 20 in. blue octagonal barrel, 10 shot mag., A-Grade satin finished walnut stock, 8.2 lbs. Importation began 2018.

MSR $1,929 $1,650 $1,445 $1,250 $1,125 $910 $750 $640

1873 MUSKET – .44-40 WCF or .45 LC cal., features 30 in. round barrel with barrel bands. Imported 1999-2002.

$875 $700 $575 $450 $375 $325 $300 *$999*

1873 SPORTING RIFLE – .32-20 WCF (mfg. 2001-2002), .357 Mag. (new 1995), .38-40 WCF (mfg. 2002-2011), .44-40 WCF (new 1995), or .45 LC cal., case hardened receiver, 10 or 13 shot mag., 18 (half-round/half-octagon), 20 in. octagon (new 1990, Short Rifle), 24 1/4 in. octagon, or 30 (mfg. 1990-2002) in. octagon barrel, can be drilled and tapped for Uberti rear tang aperture sight (new 1993), 8.2 lbs.

MSR $1,339 $1,150 $1,000 $865 $780 $635 $525 $445

Add $10 for .44-40 WCF cal.
Add $40 for half-round/half-octagon barrel.
Add $17 for 30 in. barrel (.44-40 WCF or .45 LC cal. only, disc. 2002).
Add $77 for Deluxe Model with 30 in. barrel (disc. 2002).

* ***1873 Special Sporting Rifle Steel*** – .357 Mag., .44-40 WCF, or .45 LC cal., 24 1/4 in. half round/half octagon barrel, hand checkered pistol grip stock and forearm, case hardened frame, buttplate, and lever.

MSR $1,449 $1,235 $1,080 $925 $840 $680 $555 $450

Add $10 for .357 Mag. or .44-40 WCF cal.

* ***1873 Special Sporting Short Rifle Steel*** – .357 Mag., .44-40 WCF (disc. 2017), or .45 LC (disc. 2020) cal., 20 in. half round/half octagon barrel, hand checkered pistol grip stock and forearm, case hardened frame, buttplate, and lever.

MSR $1,449 $1,235 $1,080 $925 $840 $680 $555 $450

1873 TRAPPER RIFLE – .357 Mag. or .45 LC cal., 16 1/8 in. barrel, otherwise similar to 1873 Sporting Rifle. Mfg. 2010-2020.

$1,130 $990 $850 $775 $625 $510 $445 *$1,329*

1876 CENTENNIAL RIFLE – .40-60 WCF (disc. 2010), .45-60 WCF (disc. 2020), .45-75 WCF (disc. 2020), or .50-95 WCF cal., 28 in. octagon barrel, blue finish and case hardened frame, full mag., iron sights, walnut stock and forearm, 10 lbs. Importation began 2008.

MSR $1,709 $1,450 $1,275 $1,095 $985 $800 $650 $570

1883 BURGESS LEVER ACTION RIFLE/CARBINE – .45 LC cal., case colored frame with blued barrel and mag. tube, 20 (carbine) or 25 1/2 (rifle) in. barrel. Mfg. 2010-2016.

$1,275 $1,115 $950 $865 $700 $575 $450 *$1,499*

1886 WINCHESTER HUNTER LITE – .45-70 cal., 22 in. round barrel, 8 shot mag., case hardened frame, A-Grade walnut stock, blue barrel finish, 7.1 lbs. New 2017.

MSR $2,189 $1,865 $1,625 $1,400 $1,275 $1,025 $850 $700

1886 WINCHESTER SPORTING – .45-70 Govt. cal., 26 in. blue octagonal barrel, 8 shot mag., case hardened frame, straight A Grade checkered walnut stock, 9.1 lbs. New 2017.

MSR $2,259 $1,925 $1,685 $1,450 $1,310 $1,060 $875 $750

RIFLES: REPRODUCTIONS, SINGLE SHOT

1871 ROLLING BLOCK TARGET CARBINE/RIFLE – available in .22 LR, .22 WMR, .22 Hornet (disc. 2004), or .357 Mag. (disc.) cal., 22 in. round (carbine) or 26 in. octagon barrel, color case hardened receiver and hammer, brass trigger guard, open sights, approx. 5 lbs. Disc. 2007.

$440 $350 $295 $240 $200 $175 $155 *$535*

Add $65 for rifle model.

1871 ROLLING BLOCK HUNTER CARBINE – .30-30 Win., .38-55 WCF, or .45-70 Govt. cal., 22 in. barrel, otherwise similar to Rolling Block Target. Mfg. 2010-2016.

$675 $595 $500 $460 $375 $300 $235 *$799*

GRADING - PPGS™	100%	98%	95%	90%	80%	70%	60%	LAST MSR

1871 ROLLING BLOCK HUNTER CARBINE RIMFIRE – .17 HMR, .22 LR, or .22 WMR cal., 22 in. barrel, otherwise similar to Rolling Block Hunter Carbine. Mfg. 2011-2016.

	$600	$525	$450	$410	$325	$275	$210	*$709*

1874 SHARPS CARBINE RIFLE – .45-70 Govt. cal., patterned after the original 1874 Sharps action, 22 in. (carbine, new 2007), 32 (disc.), or 34 in. octagon barrel, available in standard (disc. 2011), Adobe Walls (disc.), or Long Range (disc. 2011) configuration. Imported 2006-2018.

	$1,585	$1,400	$1,200	$1,025	$895	$750	$600	*$1,829*

Add $110 for Cavalry carbine with 22 in. barrel and barrel band (disc. 2009).
Add $820 for Long Range (34 in. half-round, half-octagon barrel, disc. 2009).
Add $550 for Adobe Walls configuration (disc.).

* ***1874 Sharps Buffalo Hunter*** – .45-70 Govt. cal., 32 in. barrel, straight A-Grade checkered walnut stock, case hardened levers and buttplate.

MSR $3,079	$2,600	$2,275	$1,950	$1,775	$1,425	$1,175	$1,000

* ***1874 Sharps Deluxe Rifle*** – .45-70 Govt. cal., 34 in. barrel, gold inlaid bison head on receiver, straight AA Grade checkered walnut stock, case hardened levers and buttplate.

MSR $3,849	$3,275	$2,865	$2,450	$2,225	$1,800	$1,475	$1,285

* ***1874 Sharps Down Under*** – .45-70 Govt. cal., 34 in. barrel, straight A-Grade checkered walnut stock, case hardened levers and buttplate.

MSR $3,179	$2,700	$2,365	$2,025	$1,835	$1,485	$1,215	$1,050

* ***1874 Sharps Extra Deluxe Rifle*** – .45-70 Govt. cal., 32 in. barrel, AAA grade walnut stock, elaborate scroll engraving with gold buffalo inlays. Imported 2007-2018.

	$4,375	$3,825	$3,300	$2,900	$2,475	$2,075	$1,600	*$5,169*

* ***1874 Sharps Special Rifle*** – .45-70 Govt. cal., 32 in. barrel, checkered pistol grip walnut stock and flat buttplate, case hardened levers and buttplate.

MSR $2,429	$2,065	$1,800	$1,550	$1,400	$1,135	$925	$800

SPRINGFIELD TRAPDOOR CARBINE/RIFLE – .45-70 Govt. cal., choice of 22 (carbine) or 32 1/2 (rifle) in. round barrel, case colored receiver, uncheckered walnut stock and forearm. Importation began 2006.

MSR $2,109	$1,785	$1,550	$1,325	$1,200	$950	$800	$700

Add $280 for rifle configuration.

1885 WINCHESTER HIGH WALL CARBINE – .22 Hornet (mfg. 2004-2011), .30-30 Win. (disc. 2004), .38-55 WCF (disc. 2002), .40-65 WCF (disc. 2002), .44 Mag. (mfg. 2004-2011), .44-40 WCF (disc. 2002), .45 LC (disc. 2004), .45-70 Govt., .45-90 WCF (disc. 2002, reintroduced 2005-2017), or .45-120 (disc. 2002, reintroduced 2005-2017) cal., 28 in. octagon barrel, straight grip walnut stock and forearm, case colored receiver, 7.7 or 9.9 lbs. Mfg. 1999-2020.

	$910	$795	$685	$620	$500	$410	$350	*$1,069*

* ***1885 Winchester High Wall Sporting Rifle*** – .45-70 Govt. or .45-90 WCF (disc. 2017) cal., 30 or 32 (disc. 2020) in. octagon barrel, straight grip walnut stock with crescent blued buttplate, case hardened frame and lever.

MSR $1,149	$975	$850	$725	$675	$550	$450	$375

Add $50 for 32 in. barrel (disc. 2020).

* ***1885 Winchester High Wall Special Sporting Rifle*** – .45-70 Govt., .45-90 (disc. 2017) or .45-120 (disc. 2017) cal., 30 (disc. 2018) or 32 in. octagon barrel, aperture sights, checkered pistol grip walnut stock, blued buttplate, case hardened frame and lever.

MSR $1,350	$1,150	$1,000	$865	$780	$635	$525	$450

1885 WINCHESTER HIGH WALL BIG GAME RIFLE – .45-70 Govt. cal., 22 in. round barrel, A-Grade checkered pistol grip walnut stock, rubber buttpad, blue finish, 37.5 in. OAL, 6.7 lbs. Mfg. 2016-2020.

	$1,050	$920	$790	$715	$580	$475	$400	*$1,229*

1885 HIGH WALL COURTENEY STALKING RIFLE – .303 British or .45-70 (new 2021) cal., 24 in. round blue steel barrel, case hardened receiver, A-Grade walnut checkered pistol grip stock and forend, rubber buttpad, 7.1 lbs. New 2020.

MSR $1,689	$1,440	$1,260	$1,080	$980	$790	$650	$560

RIFLES: REPRODUCTIONS, SLIDE ACTION

COLT LIGHTNING CARBINE/RIFLE – .357 Mag. (disc. 2015) or .45 LC cal., patterned after the Colt Lightning carbine/rifle, 20 (carbine (disc. 2011) or short rifle) or 24 1/4 (rifle) in. barrel, blue (disc. 2010) or case colored frame finish, uncheckered walnut stock and forearm, 6.2-6 1/2 lbs. Imported 2006-2016.

	$1,125	$985	$850	$775	$625	$500	$400	*$1,319*

Subtract approx. $100 for blue metal finish on rifle (disc. 2010).
Subtract approx. $50 for carbine variation (disc. 2011).

GRADING - PPGS™	100%	98%	95%	90%	80%	70%	60%	LAST MSR

SHOTGUNS: SxS

DOUBLE BARREL – 12 ga. only, 2 3/4, 3, or 3 1/2 in. chambers, 20, 21 1/2, 24, or 26 in. barrels, exposed hammers, checkered walnut pistol grip stock and forearm. Imported 1999-2001.

	$875	$700	$575	$450	$375	$325	$300	*$999*

UGARTECHEA, ARMAS

Previous manufacturer located in Eibar, Spain. Previously imported by Aspen Outfitting Co., located in Aspen, CO, and by Lion Country Supply, located in Port Matilda, PA. Armas Ugartechea closed its doors circa 2017.

For individual model listings, please go to BlueBookOfGunValues.com/overflow.

UGARTECHEA, IGNACIO

Previous manufacturer located in Eibar, Spain. Previously imported exclusively by Aspen Outfitting Company, located in Aspen, CO.

For individual model listings, please go to BlueBookOfGunValues.com/overflow.

ULTIMATE

Please refer to the Blaser listing in the B section.

ULTIMATE ARMS LLC (UA/ARMS)

Current manufacturer located in Gallatin, TN. Previously located in Franklin and Madison, TN.

For individual model listings, please go to BlueBookOfGunValues.com/overflow.

ULTIMATE FIREARMS

Current bolt action rifle manufacturer located in Okemos, MI.

RIFLES: BOLT ACTION

GAME BREAKER – .450 Bushmaster cal., Remington Model 700 action, 20, 22, or 24 in. stainless steel Lothar Walther barrel, enhanced trigger, synthetic stock (various finishes), optional Cerakote finishes on barrel, bolt, and action, optional fluting available, scope, bases, and rings sold separately.

MSR $2,500	$2,100	$1,850	$1,600	$1,450	$1,150	$950	$750	

Add $1,000 for Cerakote finish.

ULTRA LIGHT ARMS, INC.

Previous manufacturer located in Granville, WV. Ultra Light Arms, Inc. was purchased by C.F. Holding Corp. in 1999.

PISTOLS: BOLT ACTION

MODEL 20 HUNTERS PISTOL – various cals., 14 in. Douglas heavy barrel, 5 shot mag., Kevlar graphite reinforced stock in choice of 4 colors, Timney trigger, left or right-hand bolt, approx. 4 lbs. Mfg. 1987-89.

	$1,295	$1,150	$975	$850	$700	$640	$575	*$1,600*

MODEL 20 REB – popular cals. from .22-250 Rem. through .308 Win. (other cals. on request), 14 in. Douglas #3 barrel, 5 shot mag., composite Kevlar graphite reinforced stock, green, brown, black, or camo DuPont Imron paint, Timney adj. trigger, includes hard case, 4 lbs. Mfg. 1994-95, reintroduced 1998 only.

	$1,475	$1,200	$1,000	$875	$750	$625	$500	*$1,600*

RIFLES: BOLT ACTION

ULTRA LIGHT RIFLE – caliber to customer specs., various actions, 2-position 3-function safety in top of stock, Timney trigger, Douglas 22 or 24 in. barrel, no sights, graphite reinforced stock with recoil pad, matte finish standard, other finishes at extra cost. Many special order features and services were available on these models, 4 3/4-5 3/4 lbs. Mfg. 1985-1999.

MODEL 20 – many cals. available between .17 Rem. and .358 Win., short action, Kevlar stock. Disc.

	$2,225	$1,675	$1,225	$950	$800	$700	$640	*$2,500*

Add $100 for left-hand action.

* ***Model 20 RF*** – .22 LR cal., convertible from repeater to single shot, 22 in. Douglas premium barrel, DuPont composite stock with Imron paint (some color options available), no sights, drilled and tapped, 5 1/4 lbs. Mfg. 1983-1999.

	$750	$650	$550	$475	$400	$350	$300	*$800*

Add $50 for repeater action.

The first 100 pre-production rifles in this model were marked "1-of-100" consecutively, with owner's initials.

GRADING - PPGS™	100%	98%	95%	90%	80%	70%	60%	LAST MSR

MODEL 24 – .25-06 Rem., .270 Win., .280 Rem. (mfg. 1992 only), .30-06, or 7mm Exp. Rem. cal., long action, Kevlar stock, 5 1/4 lbs. Disc. 1999.

	$2,325	$1,775	$1,300	$995	$825	$700	$640	*$2,600*

Add $100 for left-hand action.

MODEL 28 MAGNUM – .264 Win. Mag., .300 Win. Mag., .338 Win. Mag., 7mm Rem. Mag., or .416 Rigby (mfg. 1992 only) cal., Kevlar stock, 5 3/4 lbs. Disc. 1999.

	$2,625	$1,975	$1,550	$1,225	$950	$700	$600	*$2,900*

Add $100 for left-hand action.

MODEL 40 MAGNUM – .300 Wby. Mag. or .416 Rigby cal., otherwise similar to Model 28 Series. Mfg. 1993-99.

	$2,625	$1,975	$1,550	$1,225	$950	$700	$600	*$2,900*

Add $100 for left-hand action.

ULTRAMATIC

Previous trademark with manufacture located in Enzesfeld, Austria. Ultramatic Productions, GmbH, changed its name to Wolf Sporting Pistols in 1997.

PISTOLS: SEMI-AUTO

ULTRAMATIC PISTOL – 9mm Para. cal., DA/SA, various barrel lengths, competition model with muzzle brake. Disc. approx. 1996.

	$1,150	$975	$850	$700	$640	$575	$500	

Add 20% for early mfg.

UMAREX SPORTWAFFEN GmbH & Co. KG.

Current firearms, airguns, air soft, and signal pistol manufacturer established in 1972 as Uma Mayer Ussfeller GmbH, with headquarters located in Arnsberg, Germany. Firearms are currently imported by Walther Arms located in Fort Smith, AR.

Initially, the company was founded to produce look alike over the counter guns, after a more restrictive gun law was introduced in Germany. Umarex first manufactured tear gas and signal pistols, and then started producing air rifles. After acquiring Reck Sportwaffen Fabrick Karl Arndt in 1979, the company was reorganized under the Umarex name. Umarex purchased Walther during 1993, and also manufactures ammunition, optics, and accessories. During 2006, Umarex purchased Hämmerli, and production equipment was moved from Lenzburg, Switzerland to Ulm, Germany. During mid-2006, Umarex purchased RUAG Ammotec USA Inc., and moved the company to Fort Smith, AR, and the company's name was changed to Umarex USA. During 2008, Colt Industries licensed Umarex to manufacture the Colt AR-15 in .22 LR cal. From 2009-2018, H&K licensed Umarex to manufacture replicas in .22 LR cal. During 2011, Colt Industries licensed Umarex to manufacture a Govt. 1911-A1 Model in .22 LR cal. These guns were previously imported exclusively by Umarex USA located in Fort Smith, AR until 2013. Since then all firearm products produced by Umarex GmbH & Co. KG. and imported into the U.S. are sold and marketed by Walther Arms, Inc., a subsidiary of Carl Walther, Germany, located on the same premises as Umarex USA in Fort Smith.

Please refer to the Colt, H&K, Hämmerli, Regent (trademark only), UZI, and Walther listings for information and values on currently imported firearms. For more information on currently manufactured (beginning circa 1984) Umarex airguns, including many major U.S. trademark mfg. under license, please refer to the *Blue Book of Airguns* - also available as an online subscription.

UNDERWOOD-ELLIOT-FISHER CORP.

Previous WWII subcontractor of M1 carbines located in Chicago, IL.

Please refer to U.S. Military & Commercial Long Arms section.

UNERTL ORDNANCE COMPANY, INC.

Previous manufacturer located in Las Vegas, NV circa 2004-2006.

Unertl Ordnance Company manufactured a .45 ACP cal. semi-auto pistol in various configurations, including MEU (SOC) $2,795 last MSR, UCCP $2,195 last MSR, and the DLX $2,195 last MSR. The company also manufactured the UPR bolt action sniper rifle in .308 Win. cal. Last MSR was $5,900.

UNIQUE

Previous manufacturer 1923-2006 located in Patin, France. Previously located in Hendaye, France until 2001. Previously imported by Nygord Precision Products located in Prescott, AZ.

For individual model listings, please go to BlueBookOfGunValues.com/overflow.

GRADING - PPGS™	100%	98%	95%	90%	80%	70%	60%	LAST MSR

UNIQUE-ALPINE

Current manufacturer of bolt action rifles established in 2002, located in Bavaria, Germany, with manufacturing sites in Germany and Switzerland. No current U.S. importation.

RIFLES: BOLT ACTION

Unique Alpine manufactures both high quality sport and hunting bolt action rifles. Current sport models include: TPG-3 A4, UPG-1 Festschaft, UPG-1 AR-15 Klappschaft, JPR-1 Nordland, JPR-1 Nordland Scout, and JPR-1 Highland. Current hunting models include: JPR-1 Nordland, JPR-1 Nordland Scout, JPR-1 Highland, JPR-1 Kodiak, and JPR-1 Europa. Previous sport models included: TPG-1 and TPG-2.

UNIQUE-ARS

Current custom AR-15 style rifle and related accessories manufacturer established circa 2014, located in McCall, ID.

Please refer to BlueBookOfGunValues.com to order the *Blue Book of AR-15s & Variations*, available as a book or online subscription.

UNITED SPORTING ARMS, INC.

Previous manufacturer located in Tombstone and Tucson, AZ and Post Falls, ID.

For individual model listings, please go to BlueBookOfGunValues.com/overflow.

UNITED STATES FIREARMS CORP.

Current manufacturer of Wildey trademarked semi-auto gas operated pistols. Please refer to listings under Wildey (New Mfg.) in the W section.

UNITED STATES FIRE ARMS MFG. CO., INC./USFA

Previous manufacturer located in Hartford, CT 1995-2012. Previously located at Colt's original old armory in Hartford, CT. Previous company name was United States Patent Firearms Manufacturing Company until 1997 and was distributed exclusively beginning 2008 by AcuSport.

PISTOLS: SEMI-AUTO

1910 COMMERCIAL MODEL – .45 ACP cal., 5 in. barrel, high polish Armory Blue, hand checkered fancy walnut grips, 7 shot mag., fire blue appointments, 1905 patent dates, grip safety, checkered thumb safety, round 1905 fire blue hammer with hand cut checkering, original Colt 1910 rollmarks on both sides of slide. Limited mfg. 2006-2009.

$1,650	$1,425	$1,275	$1,075	$925	$800	$700	*$1,895*

1911 MILITARY MODEL – .45 ACP cal., 5 in. barrel, military polish Armory Blue, hand checkered standard walnut grips, 7 shot mag., fire blue appointments, 1905 patent dates, grip safety, small contoured checkered thumb safety, spur hammer with hand cut checkering, original Colt 1911 military rollmarks on both sides of slide, including choice on right side of U.S. Navy or U.S. Army. Limited mfg. 2006-2009.

$1,650	$1,425	$1,275	$1,075	$925	$800	$700	*$1,895*

1911 SUPER 38 – .38 Super cal., features original 1911 Super 38 metal finishes and blue appointments, 1905 patent dates, grip safety, small thumb safety and spur hammer. Limited mfg. 2007-2009.

$1,650	$1,425	$1,275	$1,075	$925	$800	$700	*$1,895*

REVOLVERS

SHOOTING MASTER – .357 Mag. cal., 7 1/2 in. barrel, 6 shot, full blue finish, adj. rear sight, U.S. hard rubber grips, large heavy frame, knurled takedown pin, large loop trigger guard. Limited mfg. 2011-2012 only.

$1,350	$1,200	$995	$825	$700	$600	$450	*$1,495*

SPARROWHAWK – .327 Federal cal., 7 1/2 in. barrel, 8 shot, full blue finish, adj. rear sight, U.S. hard rubber grips, scaled down frame, knurled takedown pin, large loop trigger guard. Limited mfg. 2011-2012.

$1,350	$1,200	$995	$825	$700	$600	$450	*$1,495*

GRADING - PPGS™	100%	98%	95%	90%	80%	70%	60%	LAST MSR

REVOLVERS: SAA

USFA also had a custom shop offering the following levels of engraving: Armory Grade A ($830 MSR), Armory Grade B ($1,135 MSR), Armory Grade C ($1,395 MSR), Armory Grade D ($1,650 MSR), Master Grade A ($1,260 MSR), Master Grade B ($2,615 MSR), Master Grade C ($3,725 MSR) or Master Grade D ($5,045 MSR).

Add $725 for elephant ivory grips, $495 for stag, $275 Tru-Ivory two-piece Natural White, Slightly Aged, or Antique Ultra Aged, $75 for ivory, $330 for standard American one-piece walnut, $250 for two-piece American walnut, $400 for smooth fancy European one-piece walnut, $330 for fancy grade European two-piece walnut, or $175 for diamond checkered grips.

COLT 1851 RICHARDS NAVY CONVERSION – .38 Spl. cal. only, 7 1/2 in. barrel with ejector, Old Armory Bone Case finish frame, gate, hammer, and conversion ring, Dome Blue barrel, cylinder, and ejector housing, smooth walnut grips. Disc.

$1,175	$950	$825	$700	$600	$500	$400	*$1,300*

THE SINGLE ACTION – .32-20 WCF, .44-40 WCF, .44 Spl., .38-40 WCF, .38 Spl., or .45 LC cal., 4 3/4, 5 1/2, or 7 1/2 in. barrel, Bone Case and Dome Blue finish, or nickel, white sided hammer, U.S. hard rubber grips. Mfg. 2009-2012.

$1,050	$925	$850	$725	$550	$475	$350	*$1,150*

Add $275 for nickel finish.

SINGLE ACTION ARMY PREMIUM GRADE – .22 LR (mfg. 1996-2001), .22 WMR (mfg. 1996-2001), .32-20 (new 1998), .357 Mag. (disc. 1998), .38 Spl. (new 2004), .38-40 WCF, .41 Colt (mfg. 1999-2003), .44 Spl. (new 2004), .44-40 WCF, .45 ACP (disc. 2006), or .45 LC cal., 3 (no ejector), 4 (no ejector), 4 3/4, 5 1/2, 7 1/2, or 10 (new 1997) in. barrel, original screw cylinder release, white sided hammer standard beginning 2005, choice of Dome Blue, Dome Blue/Old Armory Bone Case, or nickel finish, checkered U.S. hard rubber grips. Disc.

$895	$775	$650	$525	$450	$375	$325	*$975*

Add $205 for nickel finish.

The barrel marking for this revolver is "U.S.F.A. MFG. Co. HARTFORD CT. U.S.A."

* ***SAA Flat-top Target*** – similar to SAA, except has flat-top receiver with target sights, full Dome Blue finish is standard. Mfg. 1997-2002, reintroduced 2004-2012.

$1,500	$1,325	$1,165	$975	$800	$700	$600	*$1,695*

Add $195 for full Armory Blue or nickel finish.
Add $195 for case colored frame and hammer.
Add $55 for Dome Blue/Old Armory Bone Case finish (disc.).
Add $179 for Armory Blue/Old Armory Bone Case finish (disc.).

* ***SAA U.S. Pre-War*** – similar cals. as the SAA Premium, except also available in .41 Colt, most historically correct and accurate pre-war SAA reproduction available. Mfg. 2000-2012.

$1,350	$1,200	$995	$825	$700	$600	$450	*$1,495*

* ***SAA New Buntline Special*** – .45 LC cal. only, 16 in. barrel, includes correct skeleton shoulder stock, ser. numbered 28,8xx and up. Mfg. 2000-2002.

$1,850	$1,675	$1,500	$1,250	$1,000	$900	$800	*$2,199*

Add $396 for nickel finish.

CUSTER BATTLEFIELD GUN – .45 LC cal., 7 1/2 in. barrel, has Orville W. Ainsworth inspector cartouche on one-piece walnut grips, antique patina finish, script barrel legend with slanted cross at each end, ser. range 200-14,343. Mfg. 2006-2012.

$1,550	$1,350	$1,200	$975	$775	$700	$600	*$1,725*

PATRIOT SERIES – .30 Carbine or .45 ACP cal., 5 1/2 (.45 ACP) or 7 1/2 (.30 Carbine) in. barrel with lanyard loop, Old Armory Bone case colored frame, Dome Blue (.30 Carbine) or Armory Blue (.45 ACP) finish, "AUTOMATIC 45" rollmark. Mfg. 2005-2008.

$1,125	$925	$800	$650	$525	$450	$400	*$1,280*

Add $210 for .45 ACP cal.

GOVERNMENT INSPECTOR SERIES – .45 LC cal., exact recreations of guns inspected by government inspectors, including Henry Nettleton, Orville Ainsworth, David Clark, and Rinaldo Carr, exact cartouche stampings and hand-stamped markings, 5 1/2 or 7 1/2 in. barrel, historically correct, one-piece walnut grips, Old Armory Bone case color hardened frame, Armory Blue, antique, or nickel finish. Mfg. 2005-2012.

$1,500	$1,325	$1,165	$975	$800	$700	$600	*$1,695*

Add $40 for antique finish.
Add $134 for nickel finish (disc. 2007).

GRADING - PPGS™	100%	98%	95%	90%	80%	70%	60%	LAST MSR

BISLEY MODEL SAA – same cals. as SAA, 4 3/4, 5 1/2, 7 1/2, or 10 (disc.) in. barrel, patterned after the Colt Bisley Model, smooth walnut grips, standard or target configuration, choice of Bone Case/Dome Blue, Bone Case/Armory Blue, or nickel finish. Disc. 1998, reintroduced 2000-2002, again 2004-2012.

	$1,550	$1,350	$1,200	$975	$775	$700	$600	*$1,725*

Add $225 for Armory Blue/Old Armory Bone Case finish.
Add $225 for nickel finish.
Add $200 for Bisley Target variation.

BIRDSHEAD MODEL SAA – same cals. as SAA, patterned after the Colt Model 1877 Thunderer, 3 1/2, 4, or 4 3/4 in. barrel with ejector, case colored frame. Mfg. 1997-2002.

	$975	$825	$725	$625	$525	$425	$325	*$1,150*

Add $149 for nickel finish.

CHINA CAMP – various cals., designed for competition shooting, silver steel competition finish with two-piece hard rubber grips. Mfg. 2000-2003.

	$975	$850	$725	$625	$525	$425	$325	*$1,200*

SHERIFF'S MODEL – similar cals. as the SAA, 2 1/2, 3, 3 1/2, or 4 in. barrel w/o ejector rod housing, U.S. hard rubber grips, choice of bone case/blue or nickel finish. Mfg. 2004-2012.

	$1,050	$925	$850	$725	$550	$475	$350	*$1,150*

Add $370 for nickel finish. Add $200 for bird's head grip (new 2010).

RODEO – .32-20 WCF (mfg. 2005-2006), .38 Spl., .38-40 WCF (mfg. 2005-2006), .44-40 WCF (disc. 2006), .44 Spl. (mfg. 2005-2006), or .45 LC cal., 4 3/4, 5 1/2, or 7 1/2 (new 2004) in. barrel, matte blue finish, fixed firing pin, square notch rear sight, hard rubber or Tru-Ivory grips, white sided hammer became standard 2005, entry level cowboy action shooting model. Mfg. 2002-2012.

	$675	$595	$475	$425	$375	$325	$295	*$760*

Add $131 for Rodeo Heritage Model with Tru-Ivory grips (disc. 2005).
Add $358 for Rodeo Race Groove (limited mfg. 2006).

* ***Rodeo II*** – .38 Spl. or .45 LC cal., 4 3/4 or 5 1/2 in. barrel, similar to Rodeo, except has satin nickel finish with U.S. burlwood grips. Mfg. 2008-2012.

	$750	$650	$550	$475	$365	$335	$295	*$825*

COWBOY – .38 Spl. or .45 LC cal., 4 3/4, 5 1/2, or 7 1/2 in. barrel, full Dome Blue metal finish, U.S. brown hard rubber grips, cross pin frame, square notch rear and square front blade sights. Mfg. 2007-2008.

	$775	$675	$575	$500	$425	$375	$325	*$790*

* ***Cowboy Convertible*** – .357 Magnum/.38 Spl cal., cross pin frame, 4 3/4, 5 1/2, or 7 1/2 in. barrel, square notch rear and square front blade sights, U.S. brown hard rubber grips, full Dome Blue metal finish. Mfg. 2007-2008.

	$1,100	$975	$825	$750	$600	$500	$375	

Add 50% for 9mm Para. cal. conversion cylinder.

GUNSLINGER – .32-20 WCF, .38-40 WCF, .38 Spl., .44-40 WCF, .44 Spl., or .45 LC cal., 4 3/4, 5 1/2, or 7 1/2 in. barrel, cross-pin frame, cowboy action aged bluing, hard rubber grips, antique finish, square notch rear and front blade sights. Mfg. 2005-2012.

	$1,250	$1,025	$995	$850	$625	$475	$375	*$1,375*

Add $70 for black powder frame (disc. 2006).
Add 50% if w/convertible .38 Spl. and 9mm Para. cylinders.

DOUBLE EAGLE – .44-40 WCF, .44 Spl., or .45 LC cal., 3, 3 1/2, or 4 in. barrel with ejector, blue finish with bone color case hardening or nickel finish, US hard rubber grips, large loop trigger guard, bird's head hammer. Mfg. 2010-2012.

	$1,225	$1,000	$975	$850	$625	$475	$375	*$1,350*

Add $250 for nickel finish.

OLD ARMORY ORIGINAL – .32-20 WCF, .38 WCF, .38 Spl., .44-40 WCF, .45 LC, or .455 Eley cal., historically correct 1st Generation Colt frame or blackpowder frame, 4 3/4, 5 1/2, or 7 1/2 in. barrel, U.S. hard rubber grips, color case hammer, bone case and Armory blue finish, available in standard original, correct 1890 British proofed (.455 Eley cal. only), or ejectorless model (7 1/2 in. barrel, blackpowder frame, .45 LC cal. only). Mfg. 2011-2012.

	$1,895	$1,750	$1,625	$1,500	$1,250	$995	$750	*$2,095*

OMNI-POTENT SIX SHOOTER – various cals., 4 3/4, 5 1/2, or 7 1/2 in. barrel, choice of case colored, Old Armory Bone Case or Armory Blue finish, checkered Bisley style walnut grips with round butt and lanyard loop. Mfg. 2000-2002, reintroduced 2004-2009.

	$1,450	$1,275	$1,050	$900	$750	$650	$525	*$1,625*

Add approx. $200 for nickel finish. Add $270 for Omni-Target Model with raised adj. sights.

GRADING - PPGS™	100%	98%	95%	90%	80%	70%	60%	LAST MSR

OMNI-POTENT SNUBNOSE – various cals., 2, 3, or 4 in. barrel, full Armory Blue or nickel finish, checkered Bisley style walnut grips with round butt and lanyard loop. Mfg. 2000-2002, reintroduced 2004-2009.

	$1,300	$1,100	$900	$750	$625	$500	$450	*$1,475*

Add $200 for nickel finish.

PLINKER – .22 LR or .22 WMR cal., 4 3/4, 5 1/2, or 7 1/2 in. barrel, Old Armory Bone Case/Dome Blue finish, U.S. hard rubber grips, square notch rear and square front blade sights, includes extra .22 WMR cylinder. Mfg. 2004-2012.

	$1,050	$925	$850	$725	$550	$475	$350	*$1,150*

Add $545 for Target Model with adj. sights and Dome Blue finish.
Add $245 for nickel.

USFA 12/22 – .22 LR cal., Dome Blue or nickel finish, 4 3/4, 5 1/2, or 7 1/2 in. barrel, U.S. hard rubber grips. Mfg. 2009-2012.

	$950	$825	$725	$650	$525	$450	$400	*$1,095*

Add $330 for nickel finish.

HUNTER – .17 HMR cal., 7 1/2 in. barrel, matte blue finish, adj. rear sight, replaceable front blade sight, drilled and tapped, U.S. hard rubber grips, 3 1/2 lbs. Limited mfg. 2004-2005.

	$750	$650	$550	$475	$400	$325	$275	*$839*

JOHN WAYNE CENTENNIAL LTD. ED. – .45 LC cal., 5 1/2 in. barrel, nickel or Color Case and Armory Blue finish, cross pin frame, ser. nos. begin at JW-1, 25 sets and 50 singles mfg. 2007-2010.

	$4,500	$4,000	$3,500	$3,000	$2,500	$2,000	$1,750	*$4,999*

JOHN WAYNE RED RIVER D CLASSIC – .45 LC cal., 4 3/4 or 5 1/2 in. black powder style cross pin frame, faux ivory grips, V-notch rear sight, "Duke's Movie Gun Blue" finish, could be ordered as a pair with holster and belt. Disc.

	$1,725	$1,550	$1,325	$1,150	$995	$875	$675	*$1,899*

SHOT PISTOL – .45 LC/.410 bore, 2 1/2 in. chambers, 2 in. standard barrel with front bead sight, or with M4 muzzle brake (M4-410), 6 shot, blue finish, larger open trigger guard, black checkered grips with USFA markings. Approx. 20 mfg. late 2011.

	$2,000	$1,750	$1,500	$1,350	$1,100	$900	$700	

RIFLES: REPRODUCTIONS, LEVER ACTION

STANDARD LIGHTNING MAGAZINE RIFLE – .38-40 WCF, .44-40 WCF, or .45 LC cal., patterned after the Colt Lightning rifle, 26 in. round, half-round or octagon barrel, 15 shot mag., straight grip uncheckered walnut stock and small checkered forearm. Disc. 2009.

	$1,325	$1,150	$950	$825	$700	$600	$500	*$1,480*

Add $270 for octagon barrel.
Add $245 for half-round/half-octagon barrel.
Nickel finish was POR.

* ***Standard Lightning Deluxe Rifle*** – similar to Standard, except has deluxe checkered semi-pistol grip stock and forearm, choice of 26 in. octagon, round or half-round, half-octagon barrel with half mag. Disc. 2009.

	$2,225	$1,950	$1,750	$1,500	$1,250	$1,000	$875	*$2,559*

Add $100 for half-round, half-octagon barrel.

STANDARD LIGHTNING MAGAZINE CARBINE – similar to Lightning Rifle, except has 16 (Trapper) or 20 in. round barrel and 8 (Trapper, new 2006) or 12 shot mag. Disc. 2009.

	$1,325	$1,150	$950	$825	$700	$600	$500	*$1,480*

Add $515 for Lightweight Baby Carbine with 20 in. special tapered barrel and lightweight forearm with special checkering.
Add $675 for Trapper Model with 16 in. special taper barrel and checkering.
Add $270 for checkered stock and forearm.

STANDARD LIGHTNING COWBOY RIFLE/CARBINE – .38-40 WCF, .44-40 WCF, or .45 LC cal., 20 in. (carbine) or 26 (rifle) in. round barrel with ladder (carbine) or buckhorn rear sight, matte blue metal and matte wood finish. Disc. 2006.

	$1,175	$1,025	$900	$800	$700	$600	$500	*$1,345*

UNIVERSAL FIREARMS

Previous manufacturer located in Hialeah, FL 1958-1987. Previous company name was Bullseye Gunworks, located in Miami, FL. The company moved to Hialeah, FL in 1958 and began as Universal Firearms.

GRADING - PPGS™	100%	98%	95%	90%	80%	70%	60%	LAST MSR

Universal Firearms M1 carbines were manufactured and assembled at the company's facility in Hialeah starting in the late 1950s. The carbines of the 1960s were mfg. with available surplus GI parts on a receiver subcontracted to Repp Steel Co. of Buffalo, NY. The carbines of the 1970s were mfg. with commercially manufactured parts due to a shortage of GI surplus. In 1983, the company was purchased by Iver Johnson Arms of Jacksonville, AR, but remained a separate division as Universal Firearms in Hialeah until closed and liquidated by Iver Johnson Arms in 1987.

PISTOLS: SEMI-AUTO

MODEL 3000 ENFORCER PISTOL - .30 Carbine cal., walnut stock, 11 1/4 in. barrel, 17 3/4 in. overall, 15 and 30 shot. Mfg. 1964-83. Also see listing under Iver Johnson.

Blue finish	$450	$375	$325	$275	$235	$200	$185	
Nickel-plated	$500	$425	$350	$295	$250	$235	$220	
Gold-plated	$500	$425	$350	$275	$250	$225	$200	
Stainless	$600	$550	$450	$350	$275	$225	$195	

Add $50 for Teflon-S finish.

RIFLES: SEMI-AUTO, CARBINES

1000 MILITARY - .30 Carbine cal., "G.I." copy, 18 in. barrel, satin blue finish, birch stock. Disc.

	$375	$325	$275	$235	$200	$180	$170	

MODEL 1003 - 16, 18, or 20 in. barrel, .30 M1 copy, blue finish, adj. sight, birch stock, 5 1/2 lbs. Also see listing under Iver Johnson.

	$375	$325	$275	$235	$200	$180	$170	*$203*

* ***Model 1010*** - nickel finish, disc.

	$425	$375	$325	$275	$235	$200	$180	

* ***Model 1015*** - gold electroplated, disc.

	$425	$375	$325	$275	$235	$200	$180	

Add $45 for 4X scope.

1005 DELUXE - .30 Carbine cal., custom Monte Carlo walnut stock, high polish blue, oil finish on wood.

	$425	$365	$325	$275	$235	$200	$180	

1006 STAINLESS - .30 Carbine cal., stainless steel construction, birch stock, 18 in. barrel, 6 lbs.

	$475	$425	$375	$325	$275	$235	$200	*$234*

1020 TEFLON - .30 Carbine cal., DuPont Teflon-S finish on metal parts, black or grey color, Monte Carlo stock.

	$425	$375	$325	$275	$235	$200	$180	

1025 FERRET A - .256 Win. Mag. cal., M1 Action, 18 in. barrel, satin blue finish, birch stock, 5 1/2 lbs.

	$400	$350	$300	$265	$235	$200	$175	*$219*

2200 LEATHERNECK - .22 LR cal., blowback action, 18 in. barrel, birch stock, satin blue finish, 5 1/2 lbs.

	$350	$300	$250	$215	$185	$170	$160	

5000 PARATROOPER - .30 Carbine cal., metal folding extension or walnut stock, 16 or 18 in. barrel.

	$550	$475	$400	$350	$295	$250	$225	*$234*

5006 PARATROOPER STAINLESS - similar to 5000, only stainless with 18 in. barrel only.

	$650	$575	$500	$425	$350	$285	$250	*$281*

1981 COMMEMORATIVE CARBINE - .30 Carbine cal., "G.I Military" model, cased with accessories. Mfg. for 40th Anniversary 1941-1981.

	$700	$625	$550	$475	$400	$325	$275	

RIFLES: SLIDE ACTION

MODEL 440 VULCAN - .44 Mag. cal., slide action, 18 1/4 in. barrel with adj. rear and front ramp sight, 5 shot detachable mag.

	$400	$350	$300	$250	$215	$185	$165	

SHOTGUNS

All Universal shotguns were disc. after 1982.

MODEL 7312 O/U - 12 ga., 30 in. full and mod., VR barrel, boxlock, vent. barrel spacer, SST, auto ejectors, barrels ported to reduce recoil, engraved, color case hardened receiver, trap or skeet style, checkered select stock.

	$1,650	$1,540	$1,485	$1,430	$1,320	$1,210	$1,045	

GRADING - PPGS™	100%	98%	95%	90%	80%	70%	60%	LAST MSR

MODEL 7412 O/U – similar to 7312, without ejectors, blue and silver receiver.

	$1,430	$1,210	$1,155	$1,100	$9,900	$880	$825	

MODEL 7712 O/U – 12 ga., 26 or 28 in. barrel, VR, non-selective single trigger, extractors, light engraving, checkered pistol grip stock.

	$440	$415	$385	$360	$330	$275	$220	

MODEL 7812 O/U – similar to 7712, with auto ejectors and more engraving.

	$605	$580	$550	$525	$470	$415	$385	

MODEL 7912 O/U – similar to 7812, with selective single trigger and gold damascene engraving.

	$1,210	$1,155	$1,100	$1,045	$965	$880	$825	

MODEL 7112 SxS – 12 ga., 26 or 28 in. barrels, various chokes, boxlock, extractors, engraved case hardened frame, checkered pistol grip stock.

	$330	$305	$275	$250	$195	$165	$140	

DOUBLE WING SxS – 10, 12, 20 ga., or .410 bore, 26, 28, or 30 in. barrels, various chokes, DT, boxlock, extractors, checkered pistol grip stock.

12/20 ga. or .410 bore	$330	$305	$275	$250	$195	$165	$140	
10 gauge	$385	$360	$330	$305	$250	$220	$165	

MODEL 7212 SINGLE BARREL TRAP – 12 ga., 30 in. full, Simmons type VR, engraved case colored frame, ported barrel to reduce recoil, boxlock, auto ejector, select checkered trap style stock.

	$1,100	$990	$935	$880	$770	$715	$605	

UTAS

Current shotgun manufacturer located in Antalya, Turkey. The UTS-15 is currently imported by UTAS-USA, located in Des Plaines, IL.

SHOTGUNS: SEMI-AUTO

XTR-12 – 12 ga., 3 in. chamber, gas operated with rotating bolt, 18.7 (disc. 2016) or 20 (new 2017) in. barrel with muzzle, two 5 or 10 (new 2018) shot mags., sights are optional, 5-position telescopic stock, integrated quad Picatinny rail, 8-position sling attachment housing, standard Cerakote black or optional Burnt Bronze, FDE, OD Green, or Tungsten finish, approx. 8 lbs. Mfg. 2015-disc.

	$800	$650	$575	$525	$475	$450	$400	*$1,099*

Add $69 for 10 shot mag. (new 2018).
Add $100 for Burnt Bronze, FDE, OD Green, or Tungsten finish.
Add $138 for front and rear sights.

UTS-15A – 12 ga., 2 1/2, 2 3/4, or 3 in. chamber, bullpup configuration, 19.6 in. barrel, 14 shot mag. (dual 7 shot mags.) w/auto-alternating or selectable feed, snap open loading ports and cartridge counter mag. followers, spring assisted pin ejector, adj. rear sight w/flip-up large aperture peep or big game V elevation, fiber flip-up stock and reinforced buttplate, full-length integrated top Picatinny rail, matte black, Burnt Bronze, FDE, OD Green, or Tungsten Cerakote finish, 10 lbs.

While advertised in 2019 this model has yet to be produced. MSR was set at $1,475.

SHOTGUNS: SLIDE ACTION

UTS-15/UTS-9 – 12 ga., 3 in. chamber, bullpup configuration, 18 1/2 in. barrel threaded for Beretta-style choke tubes, 9 (UTS-9) or 15 (UTS-15) shot, two 7 shot alternately feeding or selectable mag. tubes with selector switch, no sights, pistol grip, polymer receiver, top Picatinny rail, choice of black (UTS-15), Hunting Camo (UTS-15 Hunting), Muddy Girl camo (UTS-15 Muddy Girl), OD Green (UTS-15 OD Green), Sand (UTS-15 Desert, disc. 2015), or blue camo (UTS-15 Marine, with corrosion resistant satin nickel plating on metal parts, disc. 2015), FDE, Tungsten, or Burnt Bronze finish, 6.9 lbs. Mfg. by UTAS in Turkey beginning late 2012.

MSR $1,099	$995	$875	$750	$625	$575	$525	$475	

Add $100 for OD Green, Sand (disc. 2015), Burnt Bronze, FDE, or Tungsten finish.
Add $200 or Hunting Camo (disc. 2017, reintroduced 2018) or Muddy Girl Camo finish.
Add $229 for flashlight with red laser or $329 for flashlight with green laser (new 2018).
Add $400 for blue Camo finish with satin nickel plating on metal parts (disc.).

UZI

Current trademark manufactured by Israel Weapon Industries (IWI, previously called Israel Military Industries) and Carl Walther Sportwaffen GmbH (.22 cal. pistols/rifles only). Centerfire semi-auto pistols are currently imported beginning 2015 by IWI US, Inc., located in Harrisburg, PA. .22 cal. Uzi pistols and rifles were imported by Umarex USA, located in Fort Smith, AR. Uzi

GRADING - PPGS™	100%	98%	95%	90%	80%	70%	60%	LAST MSR

America, a partnership between IMI and Mossberg, imported a 9mm Para. and .40 S&W cal. carbine built on the mini-Uzi receiver for the law enforcement market. During 1996-1998, the Uzi Eagle pistols were imported by UZI America, Inc., subsidiary of O.F. Mossberg & Sons, Inc.

Serial number prefixes used on Uzi Firearms are as follows: "SA" on all 9mm Para. semi-auto carbines Models A and B; "45 SA" on all .45 ACP Model B carbines; "41 SA" on all .41 AE Model B carbines; "MC" on all 9mm Para. (only cal. made) semi-auto mini-carbines; "UP" on 9mm Para. semi-auto Uzi pistols, except Eagle Series pistols; and "45 UP" on all .45 semi-auto Uzi pistols (disc. 1989). There are also prototypes or experimental Uzis with either "AA" or "AAL" prefixes - these are rare and will command premiums over values listed below.

PISTOLS: SEMI-AUTO

UZI PISTOL – 9mm Para. or .45 ACP cal., 4 1/2 in. barrel, SA, parkerized finish, 10 (.45 ACP) or 20 (9mm Para.) shot mag., supplied with molded carrying case, sight adj. key and mag. loading tool, 3.8 lbs. Importation disc. 1993.

$2,000	$1,825	$1,700	$1,350	$1,100	$900	$775	*$695*

Add $100 for original blue plastic case and accessories.
Add $300 when packaged with a caliber conversion kit.
Add $400 for importation by Springfield Armory.
Add approx. 10% for two-line slide marking "45 ACP Model 45".

UZI .22 CAL. PISTOL – .22 LR cal., patterned after the Uzi centerfire pistol, blowback semi-auto action, 5 in. barrel with muzzle brake slots on top, black metal receiver, lower Picatinny rail, adj. sights, grip safety, 20 shot mag., 3.9 lbs. Imported by Umarex USA 2012-2015.

$675	$625	$550	$425	$375	$300	$280	*$499*

UZI EAGLE SERIES – 9mm Para. or .40 S&W cal., DA/SA, based off the CZ-75 design, various configurations, matte finish with black synthetic grips, 10 shot mag. Mfg. by IMI. Imported 1997-1998 by Uzi America. Also imported as the Jericho 941 by K.B.I. and later by IWI, and as the Baby Eagle imported by Magnum Research.

* ***Uzi Eagle Series Full-Size*** – 9mm Para. or .40 S&W cal., 4.4 in. barrel, steel construction, decocking feature, Tritium night sights, polygonal rifling. Imported 1997-98.

$650	$600	$550	$500	$450	$425	$375	*$535*

Subtract 5%-10% for .40 S&W cal.

* ***Uzi Eagle Series Short Slide*** – 9mm Para. or .40 S&W cal., similar to Full Size Eagle, except has 3.7 in. barrel. Imported 1997-98.

$650	$600	$550	$500	$450	$425	$375	*$535*

Subtract 5%-10% for .40 S&W cal.

* ***Uzi Eagle Series Compact*** – 9mm Para. or .40 S&W cal., available in double action with decocking or double action only, 3 1/2 in. barrel. Imported 1997-98.

$650	$600	$550	$500	$450	$425	$375	*$535*

Subtract 5%-10% for .40 S&W cal.

* ***Uzi Eagle Series Polymer Compact*** – 9mm Para. or .40 S&W cal., similar to Compact Eagle, except has compact polymer frame. Imported 1997-98.

$650	$600	$550	$500	$450	$425	$375	*$535*

Subtract 5%-10% for .40 S&W cal.

UZI PRO PISTOL – 9mm Para. cal., SA, blowback operation, closed bolt, 4 1/2 in. Mil-Spec cold hammer forged CrMoV barrel, matte black finish, includes 20 and 25 shot mag., adj. sights, polymer pistol grip lower, firing pin block, thumb operated manual safety, recent mfg. includes top and extended lower Picatinny rails, approx. 3 2/3 lbs. Importation began 2015.

MSR $1,109	$950	$850	$800	$725	$650	$575	$500

Add $200 for side folding stabilizing brace.

RIFLES/CARBINES: SEMI-AUTO

CARBINE MODEL A – 9mm Para. cal., 16.1 in. barrel, parkerized finish, 25 shot mag. Last three digits of the serial number are stamped on the end of the barrel. Mfg. by IMI 1980-1983 and ser. range is SA01,001-SA037,000. Imported by Action Arms.

$2,400	$2,200	$2,050	$1,625	$1,325	$1,100	$925

Add $100 for original cardboard box numbered to the gun with accessories.

Approx. 100 Model As were mfg. with a nickel finish. These are rare and command considerable premiums over values listed above.

GRADING - PPGS™	100%	98%	95%	90%	80%	70%	60%	LAST MSR

CARBINE MODEL B – 9mm Para., .41 Action Express (new 1987), or .45 ACP (new 1987) cal., 16.1 in. barrel, baked enamel black finish over phosphated (parkerized) base finish, 16 (.45 ACP), 20 (.41 AE) or 25 (9mm Para.) shot mag., metal folding stock, includes molded case and carrying sling, 8.4 lbs. Last three digits of the serial number are stamped on the end of the barrel. Mfg. by IMI 1983 - until Federal legislation disc. importation 1989 and ser. range is SA037,001-SA073,544. Imported by Action Arms.

$2,275	$2,100	$1,950	$1,550	$1,250	$1,050	$875	*$698*

Subtract approx. $150 for .41 AE or .45 ACP cal.
Add $150 for .22 LR cal. conversion kit (new 1987).
Add $215 for .45 ACP to 9mm Para./.41 AE conversion kit.
Add $150 for 9mm Para. to .41 AE (or vice-versa) conversion kit.
Add $215 for 9mm Para. to .45 ACP conversion kit.
Add $100 for original plastic case with accessories.
Add $200 for early Model B in the cardboard box used for the Model A.

MINI CARBINE – 9mm Para. cal., similar to Carbine Model B except has 19 3/4 in. barrel, 20 shot mag., side-folding metal stock, scaled down version of the regular carbine, 7.2 lbs. Last three digits of the serial number are stamped on the end of the barrel. New 1987. Federal legislation disc. importation 1989.

$3,700	$3,275	$2,900	$2,450	$1,975	$1,650	$1,475	*$698*

Add $150 for original plastic case and accessories.

UZI RIFLE – .22 LR cal., patterned after the Uzi Carbine Model B, 17.9 in. barrel with faux suppressor, blowback semi-auto action, features metal receiver, folding stock, traditional Uzi handguard, hidden Picatinny rail, adj. front and rear sights, grip safety, 10 or 20 shot mag., black finish, 7.7 lbs. Last three digits of the serial number are stamped on the end of the barrel. Imported by Umarex 2012-2015.

$675	$625	$550	$425	$375	$300	$275	*$599*

UZKON ARMS DEFENSE

Current manufacturer located in Konya, Turkey. Currently imported by Uzkon USA, located in Las Vegas, NV beginning 2015. Previously imported on a limited basis by Century International Arms, located in Delray Beach, FL.

Uzkon Arms Defense manufactures a complete line of good quality semi-auto AR-15 style tactical rifles, hunting and tactical semi-auto shotguns, in addition to slide action, SxS, and O/U shotguns. Uzkon also makes airguns and blank pistols, as well as less lethal products for security forces. Please contact the importer directly for more information, including domestic availability and pricing.

VM HY-TECH LLC

Previous rifle manufacturer located in Phoenix, AZ.

Please refer to BlueBookOfGunValues.com to order the *Blue Book of AR-15s & Variations*, available as a book or online subscription.

VO VAPEN AB

Current rifle manufacturer established in 1977, located in Fjälkinge, Sweden. No current U.S. importation.

VO Vapen AB is a small family company founded by Master Gunsmith Viggo Olsson that manufactures hand made high quality hunting rifles utilizing a patented takedown system allowing interchangeable barrels. Since all guns are built per custom order, please contact the company directly for more information, U.S. availability, and current pricing.

VAIL, ROY

Previous custom shotgun and rifle maker located in Warwick, NY circa 1950s - early 1970s.

Roy Vail was a top quality custom gunmaker who manufactured approx. 150 custom shotguns and 200 custom rifles. Francotte actions were typically used on his SxSs, and he would add the wood, engraving inlays, and checkering. Secondary values are difficult to establish, and each gun must be evaluated individually for its overall desirability factor, which includes configuration, condition, embellishments, and quality of wood and checkering.

VALKYRIE ARMS LTD.

Current manufacturer located in Olympia, WA. Dealer sales.

Valkyrie Arms Ltd. manufactures custom suppressors made to order. Previously, Valkyrie Arms manufactured the DeLisle 2000, Browning M1919-SA and the DeLisle Sporter Carbine.

GRADING - PPGS™	100%	98%	95%	90%	80%	70%	60%	*LAST MSR*

PISTOLS: SEMI-AUTO

M3A1 GREASE GUN – improved design using several USGI parts, 8 in. barrel, black finish.

MSR $1,450	$1,230	$1,075	$925	$835	$675	$550	$450	

STEN MKII – modified AR-15 parts, one-piece S-7 tool steel hardened firing pin, similar to original, semi-gloss baked on "GunKoat 2300" finish.

MSR $1,250	$1,065	$930	$800	$725	$585	$480	$415	

RIFLES: SEMI-AUTO

M3A1 GREASE GUN – new and improved design using several USGI parts, 16 1/2 in. barrel, collapsible stock optional.

MSR $1,550	$1,320	$1,155	$990	$900	$725	$600	$515	

STEN MKII CARBINE – modified AR-15 parts, one-piece S-7 tool steel hardened firing pin, similar to original, semi-gloss baked on "GunKoat 2300" finish, carbine conversion kit also available.

MSR $1,450	$1,230	$1,075	$925	$835	$675	$550	$450	

Add $250 for carbine conversion kit.

DELISLE COMMANDO CARBINE – reproduction of WWII original, uncheckered wood stock and forearm, parkerized finish, sling swivels, optional dummy suppressor.

MSR $2,495	$2,125	$1,850	$1,600	$1,450	$1,175	$950	$825	

Subtact $500 for Dummy Suppressor Model.

VALMET

Previous trademark manufactured in Finland. Previously imported 2004-2005 by Tristar, located in N. Kansas City, MO.

For information on the Finnish L-35 pistol refer to Lahti Pistol in the "L" section.

VALMET, INC.

Previous manufacturer located in Jyvaskyla, Finland. Previously imported by Stoeger Industries, Inc. located in South Hackensack, NJ.

The Valmet line was discontinued in 1989 and replaced by Tikka in 1990. Please refer to Tikka in the T section.

PISTOLS: SEMI-AUTO

For information on the Finnish L-35 pistol refer to Lahti Pistol in the "L" section.

RIFLES: SEMI-AUTO

Magazines for the following models are a major consideration when purchasing a Valmet semi-auto rifle and prices can run anywhere from $200-$500. Model 76 .308 mags. will function in a Model 78, but not vice versa.

HUNTER MODEL – .223 Rem., .243 Win., .30-06 (scarce), or .308 Win. cal., gas operated semi-auto, Kalashnikov action, 20 1/2 in. barrel, checkered walnut stock and forearm, matte finished metal, 5, 9, or 20 shot mag., 8 lbs. New 1986, Federal legislation disc. importation 1989.

	$2,000	$1,750	$1,500	$1,350	$1,100	$900	$700	*$795*

GRADING - PPGS™	100%	98%	95%	90%	80%	70%	60%	LAST MSR

M62/S – 7.62x39mm cal., semi-auto version of Finnish M-62, 15 or 30 shot mag., 16 5/8 in. barrel, gas operated, rotating bolt, adj. rear sight, tube steel or wood stock. Mfg. 1962-disc.

$5,500 $4,825 $4,125 $3,750 $3,000 $2,475 $1,925

Tube steel stock variants carry a premium over the wood stock variants.

M71/S – similar to M62/S, except .223 Rem. cal., stamped metal receiver, tube steel, reinforced resin, or wood stock. Disc.

$2,800 $2,450 $2,100 $1,900 $1,550 $1,250 $975

MODEL 76 – .223 Rem., 7.62x39mm, or .308 Win. cal., long stroke GPO, 16 3/4 in. or 20 1/2 (.308 only) in. barrel, 15 or 30 (7.62x39mm only) shot mag., stamped or milled receiver, fixed or folding tube steel, plastic, or wood stock, parkerized finish., Federal legislation disc. importation 1989.

$3,750 $3,300 $2,850 $2,650 $2,200 $1,750 $1,375 *$740*

Add approx. 10% for folding tube steel stock.

Add 20% for wood stock in .308 Win. cal.

MODEL 78 – .223 Rem., 7.62x39mm, or .308 Win. cal., similar to Model 76, except has 24 1/2 in. barrel, stamped or milled receiver, reinforced trunnion on stamped receiver variant, wood stock and forearm, and barrel bipod, 11 lbs. New 1987. Federal legislation disc. importation 1989.

$3,600 $3,100 $2,750 $2,575 $2,000 $1,700 $1,300 *$1,060*

Add 10% for 7.62x39mm cal.

MODEL 82 BULLPUP – .223 Rem. cal., long stroke GPO, bullpup design, 17 in. barrel, 15 or 30 shot mag., steel receiver encased in plastic stock housing, fixed dioptical iron offset sights, urethane stock, 7.75 lbs. Mfg. 1978-1986 with limited importation.

$4,200 $3,675 $3,150 $2,850 $2,300 $1,875 $1,475

SHOTGUNS/RIFLES: O/U

Engraving was available on a limited basis as price on request from the manufacturer. Options included field or target configuration with extensive bank note engraving on the receiver in a choice of four patterns, select Triple-X hand checkered wood, and satin finish.

Extra barrel assemblies were available for the following 412 models. Last MSRs ranged from $505-$605 each for a shotgun (including screw-in chokes), $579 each for shotgun/rifle combo, and $660 each for double rifle ($100 more for ejectors).

LION MODEL – 12 ga., 26, 28, or 30 in. barrels, various chokes, boxlock, SST, checkered stock. Mfg. 1947-68.

$800 $700 $600 $550 $450 $375 $300

MODEL 412 O/U SHOOTING SYSTEM – interchangeable barrel assemblies permit a double rifle, shotgun/rifle, and O/U shotgun configuration, user-installed interchangeable barrels, monobloc locking, rifle barrel positioning by adjustment, SST, extractors or ejectors, checkered walnut stock and forend, cocking indicators, blue finish. Importation on all models was disc. 1989.

Add $100 for synthetic stock on all 412 models.

* ***Model 412S O/U Shooting System Field Grade*** – 12 ga. was standard, auto ejectors, screw-in choke tubes, matte nickel finish. Imported 1986-89.

$950 $850 $725 $650 $525 $425 $350 *$999*

Add 15% for 20 ga.

* ***Model 412S O/U Shooting System Field and Target*** – 12 ga. only, 2 3/4 and 3 in. chambers, ejectors. Disc. 1988.

$850 $750 $650 $580 $475 $380 $300 *$874*

* ***Model 412ST O/U Shooting System Trap and Skeet*** – 12 ga., Monte Carlo stock on Trap model, 28 in. barrels on Skeet model, screw-in chokes standard. Disc.

$1,150 $1,000 $875 $780 $640 $525 $400 *$1,215*

* ***Model 412ST O/U Shooting System Premium Grade Target*** – similar to Model 412ST Trap and Skeet, except has better walnut and checkering. Imported 1987-89.

$1,475 $1,300 $1,100 $1,000 $800 $675 $525 *$1,550*

* ***Model 412S O/U Shooting System Combination Gun*** – combination, 12 ga, 3 in. chamber over choice of .222 Rem., .223 Rem., .243 Win., .30-06, or .308 Win. cal., extractors. Disc.

$1,125 $975 $850 $775 $625 $500 $400 *$1,615*

* ***Model 412S O/U Shooting System Double Rifle*** – .243 Win. (disc. 1987), .30-06, .308 Win. (disc. 1987), .375 H&H Mag. (disc. 1987), or 9.3x74R cal., extractors, 24 in. barrels. Disc.

$1,175 $1,025 $875 $800 $650 $525 $420 *$1,275*

Add $100 for 9.3x74R cal. or .375 H&H Mag. cal.

This model in .30-06 cal. has extractors only while in 9.3x74R cal. ejectors are standard.

GRADING - PPGS™	100%	98%	95%	90%	80%	70%	60%	LAST MSR

* ***Model 412K O/U Shooting System Double Rifle*** – .30-06 or .308 Win. cal. only, 24 in. separated barrels, extractors. Importation disc. 1986.

$880 $775 $675 $600 $480 $400 $320 *$899*

VALOR ARMS

Curent rifle manufacturer established in 1997, located in Akron, OH.

Please refer to BlueBookOfGunValues.com to order the *Blue Book of AR-15s & Variations*, available as a book or online subscription.

VALTRO

Current trademark established during 1988 manufactured by Italian Arms, located in Collebeato, Brescia, Italy. Currently imported by Valtro USA, located in Hayward, CA. Previously located in San Rafael, CA.

Valtro manufactures both excellent quality slide action and semi-auto shotguns, in addition to a very high quality semi-auto pistol, and a variety of signal pistols. Currently Valtro USA is importing only semi-auto pistols. Please contact them directly for more information and availability.

PISTOLS: SEMI-AUTO

1998 A1 .45 ACP – .45 ACP cal., forged National Match frame and slide, 5 in. barrel, SA, deluxe wood grips, 8 shot mag., dovetail front sightambidextrous safety, blue finish, flat checkered mainspring housing, front and rear slide serrations, beveled magwell, speed trigger, 40 oz., lifetime guarantee. Very limited importation.

$5,500 $5,200 $4,950 $4,650 $4,250 $3,850 $3,500

SHOTGUNS: SLIDE ACTION

TACTICAL 98 SHOTGUN – 12 ga. only, 18 1/2 or 20 in. barrel featuring MMC ghost ring sights and integral muzzle brake, 5 shot mag., internal chokes, receiver sidesaddle holds 6 exposed rounds, pistol grip or standard stock, matte black finish, lightweight. Imported 1998-disc.

$790 $630 $525 $475 $425 $400 $360

PM5 – 12 ga., 3in. chamber, 20 in. chrome-lined barrel, 7 shot mag., removable prismatic box mag. feed, ultra lightweight, alloy receiver, black synthetic stock with matte black finish, available with or w/o ghost ring sights, optional folding stock. Limited importation disc.

$995 $900 $800 $725 $650 $575 $500

VAN DYKE RIFLE DESIGNS

Previous rifle manufacturer located in Plainville, KS until 2017.

For individual model listings, please go to BlueBookOfGunValues.com/overflow.

VARBERGER

Previous rifle manufacturer located in Varberg, Sweden. Previously imported by Hill Country Wholesale, Inc. located in Austin, TX, and distributed by Paul & Associates, located in Wellsville, KS until late 1995.

For individual model listings, please go to BlueBookOfGunValues.com/overflow.

VARNER SPORTING ARMS, INC.

Previous manufacturer located in Marietta, GA circa 1988-1989.

RIFLES: SINGLE SHOT

VARNER FAVORITE HUNTER – .22 LR cal., patterned after J. Stevens Favorite Model, 1/2 round - 1/2 octagon 21 1/2 in. takedown barrel, blue frame, walnut stock and forearm, aperture rear sight, 5 lbs. Mfg. 1988-89.

$325 $270 $220 $185 $150 $130 $110 *$369*

* ***Varner Favorite Hunter Deluxe*** – similar to Favorite Hunter, except has case colored frame and lever, and deluxe walnut stock and forearm. Mfg. 1988-89.

$450 $375 $285 $225 $175 $150 $135 *$500*

* ***Varner Favorite Hunter Presentation Grade*** – includes target hammer and trigger, AAA quality checkered stock and forearm, includes takedown case. Mfg. 1988-1989.

$480 $400 $310 $250 $195 $170 $155 *$569*

PRESENTATION ENGRAVED – previously available in a No. 1 Grade for $649, a No. 2 for $779, or a No. 3 for $1,099.

VASKENT

Current rifle manufacturer located in Brada, Czech Republic. No current U.S. importation.

RIFLES: BOLT ACTION

Vaskent manufactures a competition bolt action rifle for ISSF Shooting, featuring an aluminum frame/adj. stock with finger grooved wooden pistol grip and adj. cheekpiece. They also make Benchrest, Biathlon, and hunting rifles. Please contact the company directly for U.S. availability and pricing.

VATAN HUNTING FIREARMS COMPANY

Previous manufacturer located in Konya, Turkey from 1965-circa 2012.

Vatan manufactured good quality O/U, SxS, semi-auto, slide action, and single barrel rifles under their trademark name Egemen. Additionally, Vatan manufactured a line of blank pistols and airguns. These guns were not imported into the U.S. in any sizeable quantity.

VECTOR ARMS, INC.

Previous tactical rifle, pistol, and parts manufacturer located in N. Salt Lake, UT until 2017.

For individual model listings, please go to BlueBookOfGunValues.com/overflow.

VEGA

Current rifle and shotgun manufacturer located in Istanbul, Turkey. Shotguns were previously imported by Task Firearms, located in Miami, FL, and by Adco Sales, located in Woburn, MA.

Vega manufactures private label Diamond shotguns, which were imported into the U.S until circa 2012. Additionally, Vega offers a complete line of SxS shotguns (current models include the H12, H14, H16, H410, and the Coach Gun), O/U shotguns (current models include: De Luxe, S10, S20, S30, S40, S50, S28, S410), as well as semi-auto shotguns (current models include: D-2170, D-2171, Camo, FD-2170, D-1371, D-1171, S-Camo, F-1010, and the FF-1010), and slide action shotguns (current models include: PW-1001, PS-1001, and the FP-1001).

Vega also manufactures bolt action and single barrel rifles. Current models include: BA-1002, SB-1003, SB-1004, and the SB-410. These models have had little or no recent importation into the U.S. Please contact the factory directly for more information, including pricing and availability.

VEKTOR

Current trademark established during 1953 as part of LEW (Lyttelton Engineering Work, a subsidiary part of commercial network from Armscor). In 1995, Vektor became a separate division of Denel Land Systems of South Africa.

For individual model listings, please go to BlueBookOfGunValues.com/overflow.

VEPR

Current trademark manufactured by Molot JSC (Vyatskie Polyany Machine Building Factory) located in Russia. Previously imported beginning 2014 by I.O., Inc., located in Palm Bay, FL, Krebs Custom, located in Wauconda, IL, Mach 1 Arsenal, located in Maryville, TN, and beginning in 2013 by Molot USA, located in Walnut Creek, CA. Previously imported by ZDF Import/Export, Inc., located in Salt Lake City, UT. Previously imported during 2004 by European American Armory, located in Sharps, FL.

For individual model listings, please go to BlueBookOfGunValues.com/overflow.

VERITAS TACTICAL

Current AR-15 style pistol, rifle, and parts manufacturer, located in Orlando, FL.

Please refer to BlueBookOfGunValues.com to order the *Blue Book of AR-15s & Variations*, available as a book or online subscription.

VERNEY-CARRON

Current manufacturer of shotguns and rifles established during 1820, located in St. Etienne, France. Currently imported by Kebco LLC, located in Hanover, PA. Previously imported until 2008 by Verney-Carron USA, Inc., located in Clay Center, KS. Previously distributed until 2002 by the Graystone Group, located in Chicago, IL. Previously imported by Yellow Brick Enterprises, located in Clay Center, KS during 1998 only.

VERNEY-CARRON HISTORY

The company was established during 1820 by Claude Verney-Carron, whose ancestors were "Faiseur de fusils" - gunmakers since at least 1650. Verney-Carron is proud to reflect on six generations of family ownership, and is the largest French manufacturer of hunting shotguns and rifles. Please contact the manufacturer directly for more information, including current model availability and domestic pricing regarding these fine firearms.

In 2000, Verney-Carron SA and Y.B.E., Inc., located in Clay Center, KS (distributor of Hastings barrels & choke tubes) established a joint venture, Verney-Carron USA, Inc., located in Clay Center, KS. This joint venture purchased Sporting Arms Manufacturing, Inc., the manufacturer of the Snake Charmer II shotgun. During 2001, Sporting Arms Manufacturing was dissolved, and the Snake Charmer II is now manufactured by Verney-Carron USA, Inc. Please refer to the separate Snake Charmer listing.

In 2002, Verney-Carron SA and Club Interchasse SAS established another joint venture, Ligne Verney-Carron SAS, located in Bourges, France to develop and sell hunting clothes and accessories.

In 2004, Verney-Carron SA purchased 100% of Ets. Demas SAS (please refer to the separate Demas listing), maker of fine handcrafted shotguns and double rifles (SxS or O/U).

During December 2008, Verney-Carron legally absorbed its subsidiary and moved its facility to the Verney-Carron factory. The custom workshop is now known as L'Atelier Verney-Carron.

RIFLES: CUSTOM

Verney-Carron functions almost like a custom shop, where any combination of features, finishes, calibers, and wood options can be selected per individual customer order. Current SxS models include: Azur XA SxS double rifle, Azur XB SxS double rifle, Azur XC SxS double rifle, Azur Eloge SxS double rifle, Azur Eloge FC SxS double rifle, Azur Damascus SxS double rifle (special order only), Azur Full Damascus (special order only), Azur Legend SxS sidelock double rifle(special order only), Azur PH SxS Safari double rifle with round body, Azur PH SxS Safari double rifle with ejectors, Azur Imperial SxS Safari double rifle, Azur Luxe SxS Safari double rifle, Azur Eloge SxS Safari double rifle. Previous SxS models include: AVC RL, AVC R models.Current O/U models include: SX Passion O/U double rifle, SX Prodige O/U double rifle, SX Eloge FC O/U double rifle, SX (Eloge) Elegance, SX Supreme O/U double rifle. Current single shot models include: Azur Legend Single Shot rifle, BT single shot falling block rifle. Current bolt action models include: Mauser 98 type bolt action rifle. Please contact Kebco LLC for more information, including a quotation and delivery time.

RIFLES: STANDARD MFG.

The following models are standard Verney-Carron production guns. Current/recent models include: Impact LA Series (semi-auto), Impact NT (semi-auto), Sagittaire O/U Series, and SpeedLine (manual repeating). Please contact Kebco LLC for U.S. availability and pricing.

SHOTGUNS: CUSTOM

Verney-Carron functions almost like a custom shop, where any combination of features, finishes, calibers, and wood options can be selected per individual customer order. Current SxS models include: Azur Legend sidelock double shotgun, Azur AD210 shotgun, Azur AD230, Azur AD Absolu, Azur AD Eloge, and the Azur AD Eloge FC. Current O/U models include: SL 1030 SL 1040, SL 1050, SL Eloge, SL Elegance, and the SL 1060 (special order only).

Please contact Kebco for more information, including a quotation and delivery time.

SHOTGUNS: STANDARD MFG.

The following models are standard Vernay-Carron production guns. Current/recent models include the: Matrix (semi-auto), P12 (slide action), Sagittaire series (O/U), SOLO (single barrel), V Series (gas operated semi-auto), Veloce (manual repeating) and Vercar (SxS). Please contact Kebco LLC for U.S. availability and pricing.

VERONA

Previous trademark of shotguns manufactured by F.A.I.R., Fausti, and Pietta, located in Brescia, Italy. Previously imported 2009-2011 by Legacy Sports International, located in Reno, NV. Previously imported until late 2005 by B.C. Outdoors, located in Boulder City, NV.

For individual model listings, please go to BlueBookOfGunValues.com/overflow.

VICKERS LIMITED

Previous manufacturer located in Crayford/Kent, England.

RIFLES: SINGLE SHOT, TARGET

JUBILEE SINGLE SHOT TARGET RIFLE – Martini type action, .22 LR cal., 28 in. heavy barrel, target sights, one-piece pistol grip, target stock, pre-WWII.

100%	98%	95%	90%	80%	70%	60%
$440	$330	$305	$275	$250	$220	$165

EMPIRE MODEL – similar to Jubilee, with 27 or 30 in. barrel, straight grip stock.

100%	98%	95%	90%	80%	70%	60%
$415	$310	$285	$260	$220	$195	$150

VICTOR ARMS CORPORATION

Previous manufacturer located in Houston, TX.

Victor Arms Corporation manufactured limited quantities of a .22 LR upper unit for the AR-15. The V22 and its .22 LR cal. magazine replaced the standard .223 upper assembly/magazine. Additionally, a complete protoype gun was also manufactured.

GRADING - PPGS™	100%	98%	95%	90%	80%	70%	60%	LAST MSR

VICTORY ARMS CO. LIMITED

Previously manufactured in prototype format only by Modern Manufacturing Company located in Phoenix, AZ.

PISTOLS: SEMI-AUTO

MODEL MC5 – while a few prototypes were mfg. for trade shows (circa 1991-92), this model was never commercially manufactured. Last advertised retail was $465.

VICTRIX ARMAMENTS

Current rifle manufacturer located in Cazzano Sant'Andrea, Brescia, Italy. No current U.S. importation.

RIFLES: BOLT ACTION

Victrix Armaments manufactures high quality bolt action rifles in various calibers and configurations. Current trademarks include Pugio, Gladio, Scorpio, Corvo, Tormento, Venus, Target, Target Blackbelt, Absolute, Challenge, Crown, Throne, Performance, Minerva Tactical (Stubby, Gladius, and Scorpio variants), Victoria Sport (Carbon Performance, F-Class TR, F-Class Open, and Sport Series variants), and Lunae Hunting (Lunae Model).

VIERLINGS

The German word *Vierling* denotes a four-barrel long arm configuration, mostly manufactured in Germany and Austria.

This configuration of long arm has four barrels, usually a mixture of centerfire/rimfire caliber barrel(s) and shotgun barrel(s). Some Vierlings may also have all-shotgun barrels (rare) or all-rifle barrels (rare). Vierlings typically have two triggers, both single-set for use with the rifle barrels. Barrel selectors are usually on the top tang. In order to reduce weight, quite a few have actions made from high grade aluminum (Dural) with steel reinforcements in critical areas. This unusual configuration is mostly of German mfg., although there are a few Austrian specimens also (the gunmakers of Ferlach still custom-make this model). All Vierlings are mfg. one at a time, with fabrication being very complicated, lengthy, and expensive. Perhaps the most rare Vierling configuration is a gun with four shotgun barrels. Every Vierling must be appraised individually: most older-manufactured specimens, however, are priced in the $6,000-$15,000 range, depending on the desirability of the configuration, and overall condition. Recently and currently manufactured special-order Vierlings are expensive, with pricing typically starting at $35,000 +, depending on features, engraving, and other options.

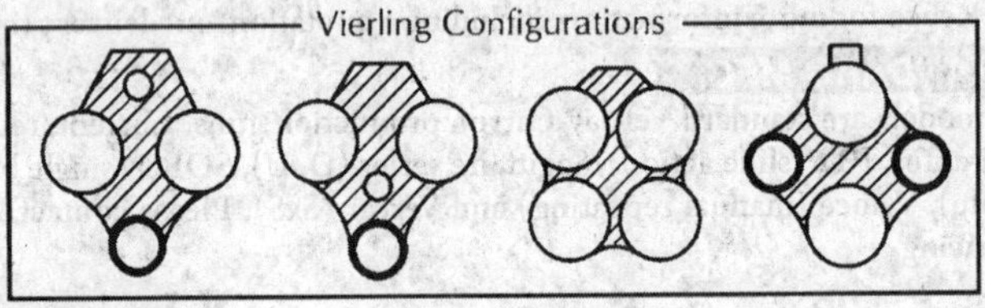
Vierling Configurations

VIGILANCE RIFLES INC.

Current rifle manufacturer located in Chino Valley, AZ beginning 2012. Previously located in Banning, and Redlands, CA.

RIFLES: BOLT ACTION

MODEL 12 WINDRUNNER – .223 Rem. (disc. 2017), 6.5 Creedmoor, or .308 Win. cal., 4 (disc.) or 10 shot detachable mag., all steel construction, Savage Accutrigger, collapsible stock with adjustable cheekpiece and monopod, heavy recoil pad, Picatinny rail, includes drag bag and pivoting bipod, matte black finish, 18 lbs. New late 2013.

MSR $4,699 $4,000 $3,500 $3,000 $2,710 $2,200 $1,800 $1,575

Add $99 for extra 10 shot mag.
Add $199 for soft case.

MODEL 18 WINDRUNNER – .50 BMG or 12.7x108mm (M18 Russian) cal., chrome moly upper receiver, one-piece chrome moly bolt, Windrunner bolt handle, oversized chrome moly AR design extractor, aluminum lower, Remington trigger, pocket locked 2 places, 29 in. rifle cut chrome moly bull barrel with muzzle brake, 1:15 in. twist, single or 10 shot detachable mag., all steel construction, Savage AccuTrigger, adj. AR stock, Picatinny 0 MOA rail, pivoting bipod with folding legs, matte black finish, 29.5 lbs. New 2018.

MSR $4,699 $4,000 $3,500 $3,000 $2,710 $2,200 $1,800 $1,575

Add $149 for Accushot foldable adj. monopod M14 / M18.
Add $299 for hard cover case.
Add $329 for XLR Tactical rear stock M14 / M18.
Add $349 for XLR Extreme .50 BMG rear stock.

GRADING - PPGS™	100%	98%	95%	90%	80%	70%	60%	LAST MSR

Add $349 for Timney two-stage trigger.
Add $499 for adj. bipod legs up & down.
Add $499 for heavy duty Vigilance folding stock adapter.
Add $600 for 10 shot repeater.
Add $999 for heat shroud w/matched Picatinny rail.
Add $1,299 for extra barrel w/brake or an extra bolt (make your rifle a mulit-caliber).

RIFLES: SEMI-AUTO

M14 – .50 BMG cal., precision machined chrome moly upper receiver, carrier and bolt, chrome chamber and piston cylinder, 29 in. chrome moly barrel, M16 safety, 10 shot push-button release extruded aluminum magazine with bolt catch system, M16 trigger, SRS rear stock system, front tube stock threads onto the receiver, integrated with 360° pivoting bipod, extendable cheekpiece, butt, and LOP, pistol grip, Mil-Spec actuating handle, drilled and tapped to accept standard Picatinny rails, black oxide finish, 48 lbs. New mid-2014.

MSR $14,999	$12,750	$11,150	$9,560	$8,675	$7,010	$5,740	$5,000

Add $175 for match front Picatinny rail.
Add $299 for extra 10 shot magazine.
Add $399 for drag bag.
Add $400 for fifth wheel universal mounting rails.
Add $499 for premium muzzle brake.
Add $699 for hard case.
Add $1,999 for Humvee mount stand for fifth wheel or boat.
Add $2,200 for Night Force scope and rings.
Add $4,000 for any order outside the U.S.
Add $3,999 for recoiling M14 mount.
Add $9,500 for removable retractable helicopter stand and rails.

M20 – 9mm Para. cal., quick change carbine barrel with muzzle brake, 10, 18, 25, 32, or 50 shot mag., built to take PROMAG, fixed ejector doubles as mag. stop, controlled feed extractor, integrated fixed sights, MOE featureless, fold, and extendable stock, shark fin grip, fire pin lock (if the lid is open the firing pin is blocked), w/XLR or Vigilance folder, Picatinny rails. New 2020.

MSR $1,349	$1,150	$1,000	$865	$780	$635	$525	$450

Add $299 for hard case or travel upgrade.
Add $350 for Vigilance folder.
Add $399 for full set upgrade.

VR1 – .338 Lapua, .375 CheyTac, .408 CheyTac, or .505 Gibbs (disc. 2012) cal., GPO, stainless steel upper receiver, bull barrel, titanium muzzle brake, premium wood stock in a variety of colors or synthetic tactical stock, two-stage trigger, detachable 5 or 10 shot mag., many options available, weights vary according to configuration.

MSR $14,999	$12,750	$11,150	$9,560	$8,675	$7,010	$5,740	$5,000

Add $299 for extra 5 shot or $499 for extra 10 shot magazine.
Add $199 for soft case or $399 for hard case.

VIGILANT ARMS

Previous AR-15 style manufacturer located in Jacksonville, FL until late 2018.

Vigilant Arms manufactured high quality AR-15 pistols and rifles built to customer specifications.

VIKING ARMAMENT, INC.

Current AR-15 style and bolt action rifle manufacturer located in Grand Junction, CO.

For individual model listings, please go to BlueBookOfGunValues.com/overflow.

VI-MA SNC.

Previous rifle and shotgun manufacturer located in Brescia, Italy until circa 2017.

RIFLES: SINGLE SHOT

Vi-Ma manufactured a high quality single shot boxlock rifle with a unique sliding breech that was available in various cals. between .222 Rem. and .375 H&H. Six variations were available and included the Pegaso, Pegaso SL, Pegaso XL, Pegaso XLO, Pegaso OXL, and Pegaso Black Gold. Vi-Ma also manufactured SxS hammer shotguns.

VINTAGE ORDNANCE COMPANY, LLC

Current single shot pistol manufacturer located in Elizabethtown, KY. Dealer sales.

For individual model listings, please go to BlueBookOfGunValues.com/overflow.

VIPER

Current trademark imported by Tristar Sporting Arms, LTD, located in North Kansas City, MO.

Please refer to the Tristar (Sporting) Arms listing in the T section.

VIRGIN VALLEY CUSTOM GUNS

Previous manufacturer of custom bolt action rifles located in Hurricane, UT until 2005.

RIFLES: BOLT ACTION

Virgin Valley offered custom barrels, stocks, wildcat chamberings, many other options and riflesmithing services.

SAFARI RIFLE – various big game cals., choice of Dakota Mod. 76, Mauser, or Win. Mod. 70 action, individually custom ordered.

This model was POR.

VIRGINIAN

Please refer to the Interarms listing in the I section.

VIS

Currently manufactured by the F.B. Radom arsenal in Radom, Poland. Please refer to the Radom listing in the R section.

VLTOR WEAPON SYSTEMS

Current manufacturer of AR-15 style rifles, receivers, parts, and related accessories located in Tucson, AZ.

Please refer to BlueBookOfGunValues.com to order the *Blue Book of AR-15s & Variations*, available as a book or online subscription.

VOERE (AUSTRIA)

Current manufacturer established in 1948, and currently located in Kufstein, Austria. Previously distributed in the U.S. by CC INTNL beginning 2014, located in Houston, TX. No current U.S. importation.

For individual model listings, please go to BlueBookOfGunValues.com/overflow.

VOERE (GERMAN)

Previous manufacturer located in Vohrenvach, Germany. Voere was absorbed by Mauser-Werke circa 1986, and most of the company machinery was moved to Oberndorf during that time. Voere of Germany should not be confused with the current Austrian firm of the same name.

Voere of Germany manufactured a wide variety of rifles in many configurations, including both bolt action and semi-auto (closed and open bolt) .22 cal. rifles. Bolt action centerfire rifles were also produced in many styles and calibers, including some private label contracts with such firms as Shikar, Frankonia, Akah, and others. While not considered as highly collectible today, most German Voere rifles were noted for their quality craftsmanship and above-average accuracy. Secondary values today depend on the desirability of the rifle configuration (stock design, finish, caliber, etc.) and original condition, but most .22 cal. rifles sell in the $150 - $350 range, while centerfire rifles are typically priced in the $425 - $725 range, if complete with magazines.

VOLCANIC

Previous trademark manufactured 1855-1860 by the Volcanic Repeating Arms Company, and New Haven Firearms Company, located in New Haven, CT.

The author and publisher would like to express his thanks to Mr. Casey Nanz for providing the following information.

HISTORY OF VOLCANIC REPEATING ARMS COMPANY

In 1855 Smith & Wesson changed their name to the Volcanic Repeating Arms Company and began adding additional investors. One of the new investors was a successful shirt maker with an interest in firearms named Oliver F. Winchester. Over the next year, Winchester increased his ownership in the company until he eventually purchased the company from Smith & Wesson and became the president and largest shareholder. The company was still using .41 caliber ammunition and had expanded to offer different models of firearms. By this time, all of the guns being produced were designed with a new style, corrosion resistant brass frame in hopes of securing Navy contracts. Blued steel barrels were now standard with the same rotating barrel assembly for loading the weapon. Early guns were engraved in the floral type scroll pattern sometimes called a grapevine pattern and will command an extra premium. The barrel address had been changed to: "THE VOLCANIC REPEATING ARMS CO. NEW HAVEN CONN. PATENTED FEB.14 1854." Serial numbers began with 1 and ran throughout the estimated production of 3500 guns.

By mid 1857, Winchester had reorganized the Volcanic Repeating Arms Company into the New Haven Arms Company. The company would remain in business until 1860 when Winchester introduced the Henry Rifle based on the Volcanic's lever action design. The main way to distinguish a "Volcanic" from a "New Haven" is the change in the barrel address with the omission of "Volcanic" and the addition of "New Haven" in the address. The New Haven

	Above Average	Average	Below Average

Arms company began producing guns in .31 and .41 caliber like Smith & Wesson had done years before. The guns are serial numbered beginning with one and ascending throughout the end of production of an estimated 3,500 guns.

CARBINES

NAVY CARBINE – .41 cal., lever action carbine with 16 in. barrel, perch belly walnut stock with piano type varnish, brass crescent buttplate, produced with excess barrels from the Navy No. 3 pistol production, approx. 500 mfg.

	$20,000 - $25,000	$15,000 - $20,000	$12,500 - $15,000

NEW HAVEN PISTOL CARBINE – .41 cal., lever action, 16 in. barrel with attachable shoulder stock and crescent brass buttplate, this is the rarest variation of the New Haven guns and production numbers are unknown but estimated to be less than 100.

	$25,000 - $40,000	$20,000 - $30,000	$15,000 - $20,000

Prices are for original matching shoulder stock, if missing subtract 40%-50%.

This model is almost impossible to obtain in excellent condition with few known specimens. It is highly recommended to seek a competent appraisal before selling/purchasing.

NEW HAVEN CARBINES – .41 cal., lever action, 16, 21, or 25 in. barrel, engraved or plain brass frame with piano finish, walnut perch belly stock, standard barrel markings and serial numbered on the frame and internal parts, resembles a miniature Henry rifle at a glance. Approx. 1,000 mfg.

Add a premium for 21 or 25 in. barrel.

* ***16 in. Model***	$20,000 - $30,000+	$15,000 - $20,000	$12,500 - $15,000

* ***21 in. Model*** – .41 cal., lever action carbine, 21 in. octagon steel barrel with blued finish, brass receiver and buttplate, color case hardened finish on hammer, trigger, lever and a piano finish on perch belly walnut stock.

	$20,000 - $30,000+	$15,000 - $20,000	$12,500 - $15,000
* ***25 in. Model***	$30,000 - $40,000+	$20,000 - $30,000	$15,000 - $20,000

PISTOLS

These models are rarely seen and desirable in almost any condition. Higher condition guns are seldom seen and pricing escalates quickly for better condition.

NAVY PISTOL NO. 1 – .41 cal., lever action, 6 in. barrel, approx. 1,200 mfg.

	$15,000 - $20,000+	$8,000 - $15,000	$6,000 - $8,000

NAVY PISTOL NO. 2 – .41 cal., lever action, 8 in. barrel, approx. 1,500 mfg.

	$15,000 - $22,500+	$7,000 - $15,000	$5,000 - $7,000

NAVY PISTOL NO. 3 – .41 cal., lever action, 16 in. barrel, attachable shoulder stock, approx. 300 mfg.

	$25,000 - $40,000+	$20,000 - $30,000	$15,000 - $20,000

Subtract 20% for mismatched shoulder stock or 35% if w/o shoulder stock.

This model is the rarest variation, and an individual appraisal is highly recommended before buying or selling.

NEW HAVEN NO. 1 3 1/2 IN. – .31 cal., lever action, 3 1/2 in. barrel, brass frame, some of which were engraved and gold or silver washed, varnished walnut grips (some examples of ivory have been encountered), most common model produced and encountered. Approx. 1,000 mfg.

	$10,000 - $15,000	$6,000 - $10,000	$4,000 - $6,000

Add 20% for factory engraving.

Any special features will command an extra premium if original.

NEW HAVEN NO. 1 6 IN. – .31 cal., lever action, 6 in. barrel, brass frame, some of which were engraved and gold or silver washed, varnished walnut grips (some examples of ivory have been encountered), rare example. Approx. 250 mfg.

	$12,000 - $16,000	$8,000 - $12,000	$6,000 - $8,000

Add 20% for factory engraving.

Any special features will command an extra premium if original.

This model is rarely found in higher condition factors.

NEW HAVEN NO. 2 – .41 cal., lever action, 6 (rare) or 8 in. barrel, brass frame, some of which were engraved and gold or silver washed, varnished walnut grips (some examples of ivory have been encountered). Approx. 1,250 mfg.

	$15,000 - $22,500	$10,000 - $15,000	$7,500 - $10,000

Add 20% for factory engraving.

Any special features will command an extra premium if original.

This model is rarely found in higher condition factors.

GRADING - PPGS™	100%	98%	95%	90%	80%	70%	60%	LAST MSR

VOLKMANN PRECISION, LLC

Current pistol manufacturer established in 2007, located in Littleton, CO. Previously located in Lakewood, CO until 2011. Consumer direct sales through FFL.

For individual model listings, please go to BlueBookOfGunValues.com/overflow.

VOLQUARTSEN CUSTOM (LTD.)

Current pistol/rifle customizer and manufacturer established in 1974, located in Carroll, IA. Dealer sales.

PISTOLS: SEMI-AUTO

Volquartsen also previously customized a wide variety of pistols based on the Ruger Mark II & III action (built from customer's existing MKIII or MK IV pistol). The prices on these previously customized guns do not include the base pistol price. These custom pistol conversions include: V-6 $1,150, V-2000 $1,150, V-Magic II $899, Olympic $760, Stingray $772, Lightweight $760-$867, Classic $571, or the Compact $496. Please contact the company directly for more information including options and availability for any current custom offerings.

Pricing listed in this section reflects base model pricing only.

BLACK MAMBA – .22 LR cal., retrofitted MK IV 22/45 frame, 4 1/2 or 6 in. stainless steel barrel in aluminum shroud, threaded muzzle, target sights, Tandemkross hiveGrip (disc.) or Hogue Overmolded grip, integral Picatinny rail, single-port compensator, Volquartsen competition bolt, accurizing kit installed, black, FDE, or OD Green Cerakote finish, 1 lb. 13 oz. New 2019.

MSR $1,442	$1,225	$1,075	$925	$840	$675	$550	$480	

CHEETAH – .17 HMR, .17 Mach 2 (disc. 2005), .22 LR, or .22 WMR cal., titanium 7 in. (.22 LR cal. only) or 10 in. barrel, 9 or 10 shot mag., synthetic finger groove stock with ambi grip, CNC aluminum frame, Weaver style scope mount, available with black, blue, red, green, or silver stock, 46 oz. Mfg. 2003-2006.

	$825	$725	$625	$550	$450	$375	$300	*$972*

MAMBA-TF (HABU) – .22 LR cal., push-button takedown, Ruger MK IV standard aluminum frame retrofitted w/Volquartzen accurizing kit, 4 1/2 or 6 in. stainless steel barrel, laser hardened stainless steel breech, Volthane checkered grip, competition upper and lower receiver, integral top and bottom Picatinny rail, black finish. New 2020.

MSR $1,554	$1,320	$1,150	$1,000	$900	$725	$600	$515	

MAMBA-TFX – .22 LR cal., push-button takedown, Ruger MK IV standard aluminum frame retrofitted w/Volquartzen accurizing kit, 4 1/2 or 6 in. stainless steel barrel, laser hardened stainless steel breech, LLV-4X upper, no sights, optics ready with multiple mounting locations, Volthane checkered grip, black finish. New 2021.

MSR $1,554	$1,320	$1,150	$1,000	$900	$725	$600	$515	

MAMBA-X – .22 LR cal., available on Ruger MK IV target frame or Ruger MK IV 22/45 frame, 4.5 in. stainless steel barrel, laser-hardened breech, single-port compensator, LLV-4X upper, no sights, optics ready, DLC coated bolt and accurizing kit, Type III hardcoat anodized black finish. New 2021.

MSR $1,342	$1,140	$1,000	$850	$775	$625	$515	$445	

MINI MAMBA – .22 LR cal., blowback operated, retrofitted MK IV 22/45 frame, 3 in. stainless steel barrel in aluminum shroud, threaded muzzle, target fiber optic sights, Hogue Overmolded grip, integral Picatinny rail, Volquartsen competition bolt, accurizing kit installed, black Cerakote finish, 1 lb. 13 oz. New 2021.

MSR $1,369	$1,175	$1,025	$875	$800	$650	$550	$460	

PREDATOR – .17 HMR or .22 WMR cal., choice of brown laminate wood grips (disc. 2006) or black McMillan grips, 12 in. stainless steel bull barrel, wedge locking block system, includes scope mount. Mfg. 2005-2009.

	$1,150	$1,000	$875	$775	$625	$525	$400	*$1,353*

Add $220 for barrel only.
Subtract approx. $300 if w/o black McMillan grips (became standard 2007).

SCORPION – .22 LR cal., blowback operated, 4 1/2 or 6 in. stainless steel barrel with muzzle threads and thread protector or compensator, 10 shot mag., built on lightweight aluminum VC Target 1911 style or MKIII style frame in silver, blue (disc. 2016), red (disc. 2016), black, OD Green or other finishes, optional tritium, HIVIZ, or target sights, various factory installed optics options available, Volthane Target grips, laminated wood target grips, or Hogue monogrips, left side thumb safety, competition bolt, flat-top or Picatinny top rail upper, bottom Picatinny accessory rail optional, 28 oz. New 2012.

MSR $1,343	$1,140	$1,000	$850	$775	$625	$515	$445	

For custom/semi-custom Scorpion models, apply the following adjustments:
Add $21 for 1911 style frame.
Add $50 for Picatinny lower accessory rail.
Add $100 for adj. target sights
Add $138 for Target rear and HIVIZ front sights.

GRADING - PPGS™	100%	98%	95%	90%	80%	70%	60%	LAST MSR

Add $168 for Tritium rear and HIVIZ front sights.
Add $74 for black aluminum grips.
Add $158 for laminated
Add $215 for walnut grips.
Add $95 for compensator.
Add $94 for Tiger Stripe finish.
Add $125 for black Nitride finish.
Add $200 for Urban Camo finish.
Add $219 for hard chrome finish.

Beginning in mid-2013, this model can also be ordered in a 1911 style grip frame.

* ***Scorpion .22 WMR Competition Pistol*** – .22 WMR cal., 6 in. barrel with or w/out compensator, includes two 9 shot mags., with or w/o ramped post or Hi-Viz Front and adj. target or Tritium rear sights, black, Hyena brown, or Predator green VZ grips, black Nitride or hard chrome finish. New 2017.

MSR $1,842	$1,565	$1,370	$1,175	$1,065	$860	$705	$550	

* ***Scorpion American Flag*** – .22 LR cal., lightweight 1911 style Target frame, 4 1/2 or 6 in. multi-port stainless steel barrel, compensator, target sights, black Hogue grips, black DLC competition bolt, black accessory rail, American Flag finish, approx. 2 lbs.

MSR $1,765	$1,500	$1,320	$1,125	$1,020	$825	$675	$525	

* ***Scorpion Battleworn*** – .22 LR cal., lightweight 1911 style Target frame, 4 1/2 or 6 in. multi-port stainless steel barrel, compensator, Hi-Viz front and target rear sights, black Hogue grips, black accessory rail, Battleworn finish, approx. 2 lbs.

MSR $1,715	$1,450	$1,275	$1,100	$980	$800	$650	$510	

* ***Scorpion Limited Model*** – .22 LR cal., lightweight VC Target or 1911 style black alloy frame, 6 in. stainless steel barrel, Hi-Viz front and target rear sights, competition bolt, Hogue or Volthane (MK III only) grips, hardcoat anodized black finish, 1 lb. 12 oz.

MSR $1,370	$1,175	$1,025	$875	$800	$650	$550	$460	

* ***Scorpion Open Model*** – .22 LR cal., 1911 or target style black alloy frame, 4 1/2 in. stainless steel barrel, compensator, with or without Hi-Viz front and target rear sights, competition bolt, Hogue or Volthane grips, Type III hardcoat anodized black or OD Green (new 2019) finish, 1 lb. 12 oz.

MSR $1,343	$1,140	$1,000	$850	$775	$625	$515	$445	

* ***Scorpion MKIII LLV 4.5 In. Target*** – .22 LR cal., lightweight VC Target silver NP3 alloy frame, 4 1/2 in. stainless steel barrel, Hi-Viz front and target rear sights, competition bolt, Volthane grips, metallic silver CrN finish, 2 lbs. 1 oz. Disc. 2020.

	$1,125	$975	$850	$775	$625	$500	$400	*$1,259*

* ***Scorpion MKIII LLV 6 In. Target*** – .22 LR cal., lightweight VC Target black alloy frame, 6 in. multi port stainless steel barrel, Hi-Viz front and target rear sights, competition bolt, Volthane grips, hardcoat anodized black finish, 2 lbs. 6 oz.

MSR $1,375	$1,175	$1,025	$875	$800	$650	$550	$460	

* ***Scorpion FTV Model*** – .22 LR cal., 1911 style black alloy frame, 4 1/2 or 6 in. multi port stainless steel barrel, compensator, Vortex Venom 3 MOA dot sight on flat-top upper, competition bolt, Hogue grips, anodized black finish, 2 lb.-2 lb. 3 oz. Disc. 2020.

	$1,225	$1,075	$925	$825	$650	$550	$425	*$1,447*

V-10X – .22 LR cal., aluminum frame, 6 in. stainless steel barrel, ergonomic finger groove laminated wood (disc.), black, or silver grips, target trigger, TL rear adj. target sight, optional Picatinny rail, drilled and tapped, black hard anodized finish. Mfg. mid-2009-2016.

	$1,025	$900	$775	$700	$575	$450	$375	*$1,199*

Add $150 for compensator.

RIFLES: BOLT ACTION

SUMMIT RIFLE – .17 Mach 2 (new 2019) or .22 LR cal., rimfire, biathalon style straight-pull action, 10 shot mag., uses Ruger or Volquartsen rotary mags., lightweight carbon fiber threaded barrel, Hogue Overmold or Magpul stock, other stocks optional, crossbolt safety on trigger guard, integral 20 MOA Picatinny rail, black finish, 5 lb. 5 oz. New 2018.

MSR $1,267	$1,075	$940	$800	$730	$590	$485	$375	

Add $248 for laminate ambi stock (new 2021).
Add $263 for a laminated sporter (disc. 2020) or $233 for a laminated lightweight or silhouette thumbhole stock.
Add $650 for McMillan sporter or thumbhole (disc. 2020) or $473 for a VX-5000 (disc. 2020) stock.
Add $683 for an Inferno (disc. 2020) or $975 for a signature series Bastogne walnut (disc. 2020) stock.

While .17 WSM was advertised as new in 2020, Volquartsen later made a decision not to manufacture Summit models with that caliber.

GRADING - PPGS™ 100% 98% 95% 90% 80% 70% 60% LAST MSR

RIFLES: SEMI-AUTO

Volquartsen stock configurations include: Laminated Lightweight Thumbhole, Laminated Thumbhole Silhouette, Laminated Sporter, Signature Series Bastogne Walnut, VX-5000, McMillan Fiberglass Thumbhole, McMillan Fiberglass Sporter, or Hogue Overmolded Stock. Laminated stocks are available in brown, blue, gray, green, orange, pink, yellow, red, turquoise, or brown/grey. Base prices listed typically represent standard Hogue synthetic stock.

Beginning 2014, rifles have been organized by actions and barrel combinations - Ultralite, Superlite, Lightweight, Stainless, Deluxe, IF-5, or SF-1. Previously, the nomenclature for these guns were the Standard Models listed in different calibers.

Please contact the manufacturer for pricing and availability of various options.

BATTLEWORN – .22 LR cal., stainless steel bull barrel, forward blow compensator, I-Fluting, stainless steel receiver, Black, Gray, OD Green, or FDE Magpul stock, integral Picatinny rail, Battleworn finish. New mid-2018.

MSR $1,899 $1,620 $1,420 $1,210 $1,100 $900 $725 $560

CLASSIC 17 WSM – .17 WSM cal., 20 in. threaded stainless steel bull barrel, stainless steel receiver and integral Picatinny rail, 8 shot mag., brown, grey, or brown/grey laminated or laminated wood thumbhole stock, 9 lbs. 7 oz. New 2014.

MSR $1,720 $1,460 $1,275 $1,100 $1,000 $800 $660 $510

Add $105 for thumbhole stock (disc.)
Add $356 for McMillan sporter stock (disc.)

CLASSIC STAINLESS – .17 HMR, .17 Mach 2 (mfg. 2006-2012), .22 LR, or .22 WMR cal., stainless bull barrel, stainless receiver with integral Picatinny rail, TG2000 trigger guard, Hogue stock, laminated sporter or lightweight laminated thumbhole silhouette (disc. 2016) stock, various finishes available.

MSR $1,504 $1,275 $1,120 $950 $865 $700 $575 $450

Add $216 for .17 HMR or .22 WMR cal.
Add $524 for .17 WSM cal.
Add $143 for laminated sporter stock.
Add $221 for laminated thumbhole silhouette stock (disc. 2016).

DELUXE STAINLESS – .17 HMR, .17 Mach 2 (mfg. 2006-2012), .17 WSM (new 2017), .22 LR, or .22 WMR cal., stainless bull barrel with straight flutes and 32-hole comp, stainless steel receiver with integral Picatinny rail, TG2000 trigger guard, Hogue, laminated sporter, laminated thumbhole silhouette (disc. 2016), or McMillan sporter (disc. 2017) stock, various finishes available.

MSR $1,632 $1,400 $1,225 $1,050 $950 $775 $625 $500

Add $216 for .17 HMR or .22 WMR cal.
Add $590 for .17 WSM (new 2017).
Add $123 for laminated sporter stock.
Add $387 for McMillan sporter stock (disc.)
Add $221 for laminated thumbhole silhouette stock (disc. 2016).

IF-5 STAINLESS – .17 HMR, .17 Mach 2 (mfg. 2006-2012), .17 WSM (disc. 2020), .22 LR, or .22 WMR cal., 20 1/2 in. stainless bull barrel with unique I-fluting and forward blow comp, stainless receiver with integral Picatinny rail, TG2000 trigger guard, Hogue, laminated sporter, or laminated lightweight thumbhole silhouette stock, various finishes available, 38 1/2 in. OAL, 7 lbs. 6 oz.

MSR $1,664 $1,425 $1,250 $1,075 $975 $780 $650 $500

Add $216 for .17 HMR or .22 WMR cal.
Add $629 for .17 WSM cal. (disc. 2020)
Add $143 for laminated sporter stock.
Add $248 for laminated lightweight thumbhole silhouette stock.
Add $251 for McMillan Fiberglass Stock (disc.)

SF-1 STAINLESS – .17 HMR, .17 Mach 2 (mfg. 2006-2012), .22 LR, or .22 WMR cal., stainless steel bull barrel with unique snake fluting and forward blow comp, stainless receiver with integral Picatinny rail, TG2000 trigger guard, Hogue, laminated sporter, lightweight laminated thumbhole silhouette, or McMillan thumbhole stock (disc.), various finishes available.

MSR $1,664 $1,425 $1,250 $1,075 $975 $780 $650 $500

Add $216 for .17 HMR or .22 WMR cal.
Add $143 for laminated sporter stock.
Add $530 for McMillan thumbhole stock. (disc.)
Add $248 for laminated lightweight thumbhole silhouette stock.

GRADING - PPGS™	100%	98%	95%	90%	80%	70%	60%	LAST MSR

SIGNATURE SERIES – .17 HMR, .22 LR, or .22 WMR cal., top-of-the-line model, 20 1/2 in. stainless steel snake fluted and compensated barrel, features hand cut engraving on the receiver, trigger guard and Nova scope rings, integral Picatinny rail, includes Zeiss Conquest 4.5x14 scope, checkered Bastogne walnut stock with cheekpiece, many finish options are available. Disc. 2018.

	$2,075	$1,825	$1,550	$1,425	$1,150	$925	$725	*$2,439*

Add $216 for .17 HMR or .22 WMR cal.
Add $735 for Signature Series factory engraved.

TF SERIES – .17 HMR (TF-17) or .22 WMR (TF-22) cal., matte black stainless steel 18 1/2 in. bull barrel, machined counterweight system attached to CNC machined bolt, aluminum receiver, ambi birch stock with 14 in. LOP, 9 shot mag., Picatinny rail, approx. 8 1/2 lbs. Mfg. 2011-2017.

	$1,075	$950	$800	$725	$600	$475	$375	*$1,265*

EVOLUTION MODEL – .204 Ruger or .223 Rem. cal., gas operated, 20 or 24 (.204 Ruger only) in. standard barrel, stainless steel receiver, trigger guard, and bolt, integral machined Picatinny rail on receiver top, brown or gray laminate sporter stock or brown/gray laminated thumbhole silhouette stock, with or w/o extended Monte Carlo cheekpiece, 10 shot AR-15 style mag., 11 1/2 lbs. Mfg. 2005-2016.

	$2,125	$1,875	$1,600	$1,450	$1,175	$950	$750	*$2,483*

Add $115 for brown/gray laminated thumbhole silhouette stock.
Add $226 for camo (now avail. only as part of camo package w/scope), disc. 2011.
Add $1,271 for Evolution Camo package with scope (disc. 2014).

FUSION TAKE DOWN MODEL – .17 HMR, .17 Mach 2 (disc. 2012), .22 LR (disc.), or .22 WMR cal., 18 3/8 in. interchangeable barrels with muzzle brake, Picatinny rails on top of receiver and bottom of barrel shroud, 9 shot rotary mag., black finished alloy receiver, 37 1/2 in. OAL, 6 1/2-7 lbs. Limited mfg. 2004, reintroduced 2006-disc.

	$1,725	$1,500	$1,300	$1,175	$950	$775	$600	*$2,039*

Add $229 for extra (different caliber) barrel only.
Subtract $250 for .17 Mach 2 (disc. 2012) or .22 LR (disc.) cal.

INFERNO – .17 HMR (disc. 2010, reintroduced 2017) .17 Mach 2 (disc. 2013), .22 LR, or .22 WMR (disc. 2010, reintroduced 2017) cal., Superlite aluminum receiver with Weaver style scope mount and carbon fiber THM tension barrel threaded into the receiver, barreled action fits into specially designed CNC machined aluminum stock with adj. LOP and adj. cheekpiece, black, blue, red, purple, silver (new 2012), or OD Green (new 2012) stock, TG2000 trigger group, EDM extractor, Inferno muzzle compensator. Mfg. 2010-2013, reintroduced 2017-2020.

	$1,900	$1,675	$1,425	$1,300	$1,050	$850	$675	*$2,232*

Add $216 for .17 HMR or .22 WMR cal.
Add $46 for .17 Mach 2 cal. (disc. 2013).

LIGHTWEIGHT – .17 HMR, .17 Mach 2 (disc. 2012), .17 WSM (mfg. 2018-2020), .22 LR, or .22 WMR cal., 16 1/2 in. lightweight THM tension carbon fiber barrel, forward blow comp, integral Picatinny rail, stainless receiver, Hogue stock, various finishes available.

MSR $1,579	$1,340	$1,175	$1,000	$900	$740	$600	$475

Add $30 for open sights (.22 LR cal.).
Add $216 for .17 HMR or .22 WMR cal.
Add $567 for .17 WSM cal. (mfg. 2018-2020).
Add $248 for laminated lightweight thumbhole stock.
Add $385 for VX5000 Lightweight (disc. 2012).

OPEN SIGHT – .22 LR cal., CNC machined stainless steel receiver with DLC coated machined bolt, 16 1/2 in. lightweight THM tension carbon fiber tension barrel, TG2000 trigger guard with 2.25 lb. trigger pull, XS ghost ring rear and Hi-Viz fiber optic front sights, FDE, OD Green, or black Magpul X-22 Hunter stock, 35 in. OAL, 6 lbs. 5 oz. New 2018.

MSR $1,589	$1,350	$1,175	$1,025	$925	$750	$600	$475

SUPERLITE – .17 HMR, .17 Mach 2 (disc. 2012), .22 LR, or .22 WMR cal., alloy receiver, lightweight barrel with carbon fiber sleeve, 32-hole comp, matte black finish, integral Picatinny rail, available with standard Hogue stock, various other stock options and colors are additional.

MSR $1,459	$1,240	$1,080	$925	$850	$675	$560	$425

Add $216 for .17 HMR or .22 WMR cal.
Add $248 for lightweight thumbhole stock.

* ***VM-22 Rifle*** – .22 LR cal., Superlite barreled action, 18 3/4 in. barrel with aluminum forward Blow compensator, black or FDE Mapgul X-22 Hunter stock, adj. LOP, integral Picatinny rail, Type III hardcoat anodized black receiver finish, 36 1/2 in. OAL, 5 lbs. 4 oz. New 2016.

MSR $1,474	$1,250	$1,100	$940	$850	$700	$560	$440

GRADING - PPGS™	100%	98%	95%	90%	80%	70%	60%	LAST MSR

ULTRALITE – .22 LR, .22 WMR, or .17 HMR cal., Ultralite Lightweight THM tension carbon fiber barrel, hardcoat anodized alloy receiver, TG2000 trigger, Hogue Overmold or lightweight thumbhole laminated stock, integral Picatinny rail, 4 lbs. 9 oz. New 2013.

MSR $1,432	$1,220	$1,075	$920	$825	$675	$550	$425	

Add $248 for red or blue laminated lightweight thumbhole stock.
Add $379 for ModShot Stock.
Add $530 for McMillan Sporter stock.

VG-1 – .17 HMR, .17 Mach 2 (disc.), .22 LR, or .22 WMR cal., 20 in. stainless steel fluted and compensated barrel, matte black epoxy coated action, military green McMillan fiberglass sporter stock, NOVA rings. Disc. 2018.

	$1,450	$1,275	$1,100	$975	$800	$650	$500	*$1,710*

Add $216 for .17 HMR for .22 WMR cal.
Add $56 for .17 Mach cal. (disc.).

VOLTRAN

Current trademark manufactured by Ücyilidiz Arms Ind. Co. Ltd., located in Istanbul, Turkey.

Voltran is one of several trademarks manufactured by Ücyilidiz Arms Ind. Co. Ltd. - others include Akdal and Blow. Please refer to these sections for more information.

VOLUNTEER ENTERPRISES

Previous manufacturer located in Knoxville, TN.

Volunteer Enterprises became Commando Arms after 1978.

CARBINES

COMMANDO MARK III CARBINE – .45 ACP cal., semi-auto, blowback action, 16 1/2 in. barrel, aperture sight, stock styled after the Auto-Ordnance "Tommy Gun." Mfg. 1969-1976.

	$750	$675	$625	$565	$525	$475	$425	

Add 10% for vertical grip.

COMMANDO MARK 9 – similar to Mark III in 9mm Para. cal.

	$675	$625	$565	$525	$475	$425	$375	

Add 10% for vertical grip.

VOUZELAUD

Previous manufacturer located in France. Previously imported by Waverly Arms Co. located in Suffolk, VA.

SHOTGUNS: SxS

MODEL 315 E – 12, 16 or 20 ga., boxlock, 28 in. barrels, auto ejectors, straight grip French walnut stock, double triggers, case colored receiver, light engraving. Importation disc. 1987.

Values generally range between $1,350-$2,000 for this model.

MODEL 315 EL – similar to Model 315 E, except has satin finish receiver engraved with bouquets of fine English scrollwork, trigger guard and forearm also engraved. Importation disc. 1987.

Values generally range between $1,475-$2,250 for this model.
Add $600 for 28 ga. or .410 bore (Model 315 EL-S, special order only).

MODEL 315 EG – 12, 16 or 20 ga., sidelock, 28 in. barrels, selective ejectors, double triggers, extensive scroll engraving on coin finish receiver, English style stock of extra fancy French walnut. Importation disc. 1987.

Values generally range between $1,750-$2,750 for this model.

MODEL 315 EGL-S – same general features as the Model 315 EGL, except monobloc barrel construction, extensive game scene engraving, and grand deluxe walnut stock and forearm with extra fine hand-checkering. Importation disc. 1987.

Last MSR was $5,895.

Values generally range between $1,950-$2,950 for this model.

VUDOO GUN WORKS

Current custom bolt action rifle manufacturer located in Saint George, UT.

For individual model listings, please go to BlueBookOfGunValues.com/overflow.

VULCAN ARMAMENT, INC.

Previous rifle manufacturer located in Inver Grove Heights, MN, 1991-circa 2013. Previously located in South St. Paul, MN.

Please refer to BlueBookOfGunValues.com to order the *Blue Book of AR-15s & Variations*, available as a book or online subscription.

WMD GUNS

Current manufacturer of pistols, AR-15 style rifle/carbines, and proprietary coating (NiB-X) located in Stuart, FL.

Please refer to BlueBookOfGunValues.com to order the *Blue Book of AR-15s & Variations*, available as a book or online subscription.

JAGDWAFFEN OUTSCHAR (W. SCHASCHL-OUTSCHAR) GmbH

Current long arm manufacturer established during 1864 and located in Ferlach, Austria.

W. Schaschl-Outschar has been making high quality long arms in Ferlach since 1864. Many rifle and shotgun configurations are possible - please contact the manufacturer directly for more information, U.S. availability, and pricing.

W.W. GREENER LIMITED

Current manufacturer established in 1829 in Newcastle Upon Tyne, and currently located in Hagley, England, with sales and administration offices located in Wiltshire, England. While there is no current U.S. agent, Kirk Merrington, located in Kerryville, TX has a good knowledge of W.W. Greener guns and can repair most types. Until 1994, Gibbs Rifle Co. located in Martinsburg, WV was the U.S. agent.

For individual model listings, please go to BlueBookOfGunValues.com/overflow.

WAFFENFABRIK HEIN

Previous bolt action rifle manufacturer located in Tekoa, WA until 2009.

RIFLES

Hein was known for its N-Series rifle action. Recent bolt action rifles include Palouse Custom Trophy ($2,900 last MSR) and the Palouse Custom Classic ($4,700 last MSR). A single shot rifle, the Model C-97 was POR.

WAFFEN GLATZ

Previous manufacturer located in Erlendorf, Austria.

Johann Glatz manufactured high quality rifles, including a stalking rifle, a bolt action, and a drilling. All guns were custom ordered, and must be appraised individually for value.

WAFFEN HIENDLMAYER

Current manufacturer located in Eggenfelden, Germany. No current U.S. importation.

Klaus Hiendlmayer specializes in custom guns and engraving, and manufactures a version of the SIG 550 sniper rifle. Prices range from €1,999-€2,750. Please contact the company directly for more information, including domestic availability.

WAFFEN JUNG GMBH

Current custom rifle manufacturer located in Lohmar, Germany. No current U.S. importation.

Waffen Jung GmbH manufactures a high quality Stutzen style Rominten edition bolt action rifle, in addition to a takedown model, Mauser sporter, Mauser Magnum sporter, and a Jagen Weltweit (synthetic stock) bolt action rifles. All guns are custom order. Please contact the company directly for more information, including U.S. availability.

WAFFEN KESSLER

Current rifle manufacturer located in Deggendorf, Germany. No current U.S. importation.

Waffen Kessler builds high quality bolt action rifles in a variety of configurations, including a Mannlicher. Many options are available. Please contact the company directly for more information, including pricing and U.S. availability.

WAFFEN SCHUMACHER GmbH

Current manufacturer of bolt action and semi-auto rifles located in Krefeld, Germany.

Waffen Schumacher GmbH also sells some original military make/models in addition to selling guns from other European manufacturers. Also see listing under Schmeisser Germany GmbH.

WAFFENSTUBE GUGGI

Current long gun manufacturer and custom order stock carver established during 1978, located in Graz, Austria. No current U.S. importation.

Waffenstube Guggi manufactures custom order sidelock combination guns, single barrel and SxS rifles, bolt action rifles, and shotguns. They also perform outstanding stock carving and checkering services. Please contact the company directly for more information and an individual price quotation.

GRADING - PPGS™	100%	98%	95%	90%	80%	70%	60%	LAST MSR

WAFFEN VERATSCHNIG

Previous manufacturer located in Ferlach, Austria.

Waffen Veratschnig manufactured a variety of high grade, made to individual special order rifles, shotguns, Combination Guns, Drillings, and Vierlings. A wide variety of engraving scenes, wood carvings, and other special features were available at an extra cost. Very few models were actually imported into the U.S.

WALTHER

Current manufacturer established in 1886, and currently located in Ulm, Germany 1953 to date. Sport and defense models, in addition to target pistols and rifles, are currently imported by Walther Arms, Inc. located in Fort Smith, AR. Previously imported, distributed, and manufactured (Models PPK and PPK/S only) by Smith & Wesson circa 2002-2012, located in Springfield, MA. Earl's Repair Service has imported limited quantities of Walther target pistols and rifles in the past as well. Previously imported and distributed 1998-2001 by Walther USA LLC, located in Springfield, MA, and by Interarms, located in Alexandria, VA circa 1962-1999. Previously manufactured in Zella-Mehlis, Germany 1886 to 1945. Walther was sold to Umarex Sportwaffen GmbH circa 1994, and company headquarters are located in Arnsberg, Germany. Smith & Wesson was the primary distributor for most Walther firearms and accessories in the United States from 2002-2012. During 2012, Carl Walther GmbH Sportwaffen and Umarex announced the formation of Walther Arms, Inc. located in Fort Smith, AR to import, sell, and market all Walther products in the U.S. beginning Jan. 1, 2013.

The calibers listed in the Walther Pistol sections are listed in American caliber designations. The German metric conversion is as follows: .22 LR - 5.6mm, .25 ACP - 6.35mm, .32 ACP - 7.65mm, and .380 ACP - 9mm kurz. The metric caliber designations in most cases will be indicated on the left slide legend for German mfg. pistols listed in the Walther section.

For more information and current pricing on both new and used Walther airguns, please refer to the *Blue Book of Airguns* - also available as an online subscription.

PISTOLS: SEMI-AUTO, PRE-WAR & WWII MFG.

MODEL 1 - .25 ACP cal., 2.1 in. barrel, fixed sights, blue, checkered hard rubber grips, pre-WWI, 13.1 oz. Mfg. 1908-1909.

$1,200 $1,000 $800 $600 $450 $350 $250

MODEL 2 - .25 ACP cal., 2.1 in. barrel, blue finish, hard rubber grips, pop-up rear sight on early models, fixed on late models, 9 3/4 oz. Mfg. 1902-1909.

$650 $525 $400 $275 $225 $175 $125

This model can usually be distinguished by its knurled barrel ring.

* ***Model 2 Early*** - differentiated by its pop-up rear sight.

$3,000 $2,500 $2,000 $1,500 $1,250 $1,000 $750

Beware of fakes!

MODEL 3 - .32 ACP cal., 2.6 in. barrel, blue, fixed sights, hard rubber grips, ejection port on left side, 16 1/2 oz. Mfg. 1910-1913.

$4,500 $3,500 $2,500 $2,000 $1,500 $1,000 $750

MODEL 4 - .32 ACP cal., 8 shot, 3 1/2 in. barrel, blue, hard rubber grips, ejection port on left side, 19.4 oz. Mfg. 1910-1928.

$550 $425 $325 $250 $200 $150 $100

Add 10% for WWI "Eagle" proofs.

MODEL 5 - better quality version of Model 2, fixed rear sight, 9.71 oz. Mfg. 1913-1915.

$600 $500 $400 $275 $145 $135 $125

MODEL 6 - 9mm Para. cal., 4 7/8 in. barrel, blue, hard rubber grips, ejection port on right side, 34 oz. Approx. 1,000 mfg. 1915-1917.

$12,000 $10,000 $8,000 $6,000 $4,000 $3,000 $2,000

Add 50% if Imperial proofed.

MODEL 7 - .25 ACP cal., 3 in. barrel, blue, fixed sights, hard rubber grips, ejection port on right side, 12 oz. Mfg. 1917-1918.

$850 $700 $550 $465 $385 $285 $200

GRADING - PPGS™	100%	98%	95%	90%	80%	70%	60%	LAST MSR

MODEL 8 – .25 ACP cal., 2 7/8 in. barrel, blue or nickel finish, fixed sights, black checkered plastic grips with round medallions, three variations (including 1st and 2nd runs), 12.7 oz. Approx. 145,000 mfg. 1920-1943.

	$750	$600	$475	$325	$240	$150	$125

Add 25% for nickel.
Add 25% for engraved slide.

MODEL 9 VEST POCKET – .25 ACP cal., engineering revision of Model 1, 2 in. barrel, blue finish standard, upward ejection, 6 shot bottom release mag., fixed sights, black checkered plastic grips with round medallions, safety lever on left frame side behind trigger, 9 oz. Mfg. 1921-45.

	$750	$650	$575	$495	$395	$285	$160

Add 100% for engraved slide.
Add 20% for nickel.
Add 10% for "Eagle N" proofing.

MODEL PP DOUBLE ACTION – .22 LR, .32 ACP, or .380 ACP cal., PP designates "Polizei Pistole," 3 7/8 in. barrel, blue, fixed sights, plastic grips. Mfg. 1929-1945. "Crown N" proof until 1939, "Eagle N" Nazi commercial proof until 1945. Approx. serialization 750,000 (1929) - 1,000,000 (combined with PPK, late 1930s), then PP was assigned its own ser. no. range beginning at 100,000P, and by 1945, serialization had reached approx. 396,000P.

.22 LR cal.	$1,750	$1,350	$1,000	$850	$700	$550	$450
.32 ACP cal.	$1,000	$800	$600	$475	$375	$275	$225
.380 ACP cal.	$2,000	$1,750	$1,500	$1,200	$1,050	$875	$650

Add 15% for alloy frame.
Values assume original guns without import markings. Recently imported WWII/surplus police used guns are stamped on the frame or receiver, indicating the current importer and address - subtract 20%-30% from values listed for these recent imports.

Original nickel finished Model PPs are very rare; this precludes accurate price evaluation.

* ***Model PP .32 ACP Bottom Release Magazine*** – safety rotates 90 degrees.

	$1,750	$1,250	$1,000	$750	$650	$550	$450

* ***Model PP .380 ACP Bottom Release Magazine*** – safety rotates 90 degrees.

	$2,750	$2,325	$1,950	$1,650	$1,250	$900	$700

* ***Model PP Pre-War Persian Contract*** – 9mm kurz cal., BMR proof.

	$5,500	$4,500	$3,500	$2,500	$2,250	$2,000	$1,750

Subtract 75% for recent imports which have been relisted.

* ***Model PP Pre-War Verchromt .32 or .380 ACP cal.***

	$3,500	$3,000	$2,500	$1,850	$1,400	$1,200	$800

Add 50% for .380 ACP cal.

* ***Model PP Pre-War Stoeger*** – .32 ACP cal. only.

	$2,500	$2,125	$1,650	$1,400	$1,050	$800	$625

MODEL PP WARTIME PRODUCTION – mfg. 1940-1945, "Eagle N" Proof (Nazi commercial nitro proof after April 1940) or "Crown N" proof (German commercial proof mark used until April, 1940) found on pre-WWII military production. Variations are listed either by proof marks or frame/slide markings.

* ***Model PP "Waffenamt" Proofed*** – .32 ACP or .380 ACP cal., "Eagle N" military acceptance marking.

.32 ACP cal.							
Milled finish	$1,350	$1,000	$750	$550	$450	$350	$250
.380 ACP cal.	$3,500	$3,000	$2,500	$2,000	$1,000	$700	$600

Add 25%-50% if Waffenamt proofed, depending on condition (late war PPs are sometimes encountered with Walther marked beechwood grips).

All .380 ACP cal. Waffenamt Proofed PP's have hi-gloss finish. In most cases, the .380 ACP cal. has the bottom mag. release.

* ***Model PP "Eagle N" Proofed*** – .22 LR or .32 ACP cal., with lanyard loop.

.32 ACP cal.	$900	$775	$650	$550	$425	$350	$250
.22 LR cal.	$1,500	$1,250	$1,000	$800	$650	$500	$450

Add 50% to .32 ACP cal., Waffenamt proofed PPs that have hi-gloss finish.
Subtract 25% for post-WWII French added lanyard to the left side of the grip.

* ***Model PP "Eagle C & F" Marked (Nazi Police)*** – .32 ACP cal., "Eagle F" or "Eagle C" proofed on left side of frame.

	$2,000	$1,750	$1,250	$1,000	$800	$600	$400

Add 25% if Eagle C marked. All hi-gloss are early productions.

GRADING - PPGS™	100%	98%	95%	90%	80%	70%	60%	LAST MSR

* ***Model PP RFV Marked*** - .32 ACP cal., "Crown N". Mfg. for "Reichsfinanzverwaltung" Reich Finance Administration.

$2,500 $2,000 $1,500 $1,000 $800 $500 $450

* ***Model PP RJ Marked*** – .32 ACP cal., "Crown N". Mfg. for "Reichsjustizministerium" Reich Justice Ministry.

$2,500 $2,200 $1,450 $1,100 $850 $500 $450

* ***Model PP SA Marked*** – .22 LR or .32 ACP cal., "Crown N". Mfg. for SA (Sturm Abteilung - group leaders) of the Nazi party.

$3,250 $2,650 $2,100 $1,675 $1,250 $925 $600

Add 25% for .22 LR.

Rare SA markings may bring as much as 50% more over values listed.

There were 28 SA groups.

* ***Model PP NSKK Marked*** – .32 ACP cal., "Crown N" or "Eagle N" proofed. Mfg. for "National-sozialistischer Kraftfahrkorps" Nazi Party Transport Corps, rare.

$5,500 $4,500 $3,500 $2,500 $1,750 $1,250 $1,000

* ***Model PP RRZ Proofed*** – .32 ACP cal., mfg. for "Reichsrundfunkzentrale" Reich Radio Broadcasting - only 3 known.

Extreme rarity precludes accurate pricing.

* ***Model PP PDM Marked*** – .32 ACP cal., "Crown N" for "Polizeidirektion München" Munich Police Department, all have bottom mag. release.

$2,750 $2,325 $1,775 $1,450 $1,075 $750 $550

* ***Model PP AC Marked*** – .32 ACP cal., replaced Walther Banner during 1945, "Eagle N".

$800 $675 $525 $400 $300 $250 $200

Some are mismatched (assembled at factory by GIs after the factory was captured). Subtract 20% if mismatched.

* ***Model PP Czech. Contract*** – stamped with "Rampant Lion" design.

$1,500 $1,100 $875 $700 $600 $500 $400

* ***Model PP Panagraph Slide***

$2,000 $1,675 $1,425 $1,150 $875 $675 $475

* ***Model PP Danish Rplt.***

$1,500 $1,250 $1,000 $800 $700 $550 $400

MODEL PP LIGHTWEIGHT – aluminum alloy frame version.

$1,500 $1,150 $875 $725 $550 $400 $275

Add 20% to Standard Model prices.

Add 20%-40% for original nickel finish (very rare).

Add 25% for early hi-gloss finish.

MODEL PPK PRE-WAR PRODUCTION – .22 LR, .25 ACP, .32 ACP, or .380 ACP cal., PPK designates "Polizei Pistole Kriminal" 3 1/4 in. barrel, blue, gold, nickel, or chrome silver, fixed sights, plastic grips. Mfg. circa 1930-1940.

.22 LR cal.	$2,500	$1,750	$1,200	$900	$650	$525	$400
.25 ACP cal.	$15,000	$10,000	$7,500	$5,500	$4,500	$3,500	$2,500
.32 ACP cal.	$1,750	$1,250	$950	$700	$575	$450	$325
.380 ACP cal.	$4,500	$2,500	$1,750	$1,500	$900	$700	$500

Add 60% for bottom release mag (.32 ACP cal.).

MODEL PPK WARTIME PRODUCTION – mfg. 1940-1945, "Eagle N" proofed after April 1940, "Crown N" proofs appear on pre-1940 production with frame/slide markings. Variations are listed either by proof-marks, frame/slide markings, configuration, or type of finish.

* ***Model PPK Commercial "Eagle N" Proofed*** – .22 LR, .32 ACP, or .380 ACP cal., Nazi Eagle over N (standard Nazi commercial acceptance proof).

.22 LR cal.	$2,500	$1,850	$1,350	$900	$750	$525	$460
.32 ACP cal.	$1,500	$1,225	$950	$725	$450	$350	$300
.380 ACP cal.	$3,750	$2,900	$2,200	$1,500	$1,000	$750	$550

This variation is normally encountered with semi-polished, exterior metal showing milling marks to various degrees.

* ***Model PPK Waffenamt Proofed With High Polish Finish***

$2,800 $2,150 $1,500 $1,200 $700 $500 $400

* ***Model PPK "Eagle C" Marked*** – .32 ACP cal., "Crown N", "Eagle N", and "Eagle C", mfg. for Nazi Police.

$2,250 $1,750 $1,250 $900 $600 $500 $400

Add 25% for high polish finish.

GRADING - PPGS™	100%	98%	95%	90%	80%	70%	60%	LAST MSR

* ***Model PPK "Eagle F" Marked*** – .32 ACP cal., "Crown N" "Eagle F", Nazi Police, all have the lightweight aluminum frame.

$3,000 $2,500 $2,000 $1,500 $1,000 $650 $500

* ***Model PPK RZM Marked*** – .32 ACP cal., "Crown N" proof-marking for "Reichszeugmeisterei" Reich Party Purchasing Office.

$3,250 $2,750 $2,250 $1,750 $1,250 $1,000 $750

* ***Model PPK Party Leader*** – .32 ACP cal., named because grips (brown or black plastic) have the German eagle holding a Swastika, "Crown N" or "Eagle N" proofed, honor weapon awarded 3rd Reich political leaders, rare. Beware of fake grips (especially black color), as reproductions have been made recently. Unfortunately, the grips on a Party Leader (mfg. 1936-41) are the only distinguishing feature on this very desirable configuration.

$8,500 $6,800 $5,250 $3,650 $3,000 $2,500 $2,000

* ***Model PPK RFV Marked*** – .32 ACP cal., "Crown N", mfg. for "Reichsfinanzverwaltung" Reich Finance Administration.

$3,500 $3,000 $2,350 $1,625 $1,100 $800 $600

* ***Model PPK PDM Marked*** – .32 ACP cal., "Crown N", mfg. for "Polizeidirektion München" Police Dept. Munich, all have the bottom mag. release.

$3,500 $3,000 $2,350 $1,625 $1,100 $800 $600

* ***Model PPK DRP Marked*** – .32 ACP cal., "Crown N", mfg. for "Deutsche Reichspost" German Postal Service.

$3,250 $2,850 $2,275 $1,700 $1,050 $800 $600

* ***Model PPK Panagraph Slide***

$2,250 $1,825 $1,500 $1,250 $1,025 $800 $600

* ***Model PPK Verchromt*** – .32 ACP or .380 ACP cal., differentiated by dull silver satin type finish.

$4,500 $3,850 $3,100 $2,550 $2,000 $1,500 $1,000

Add 50% for .380 ACP cal.

* ***Model PPK "K" Suffix*** – "K" beneath ser. no., with numbered slide.

$2,500 $2,000 $1,500 $1,200 $1,000 $750 $600

Add 20% for matching mag.

* ***Model PPK "W" Suffix*** – .32 ACP cal., "Crown N" proofed, "W" suffix ser. no.

$1,500 $1,250 $1,000 $850 $650 $475 $375

* ***Model PPK Early 90 Degree Safety***

$2,000 $1,500 $1,100 $925 $800 $700 $600

* ***Model PPK Early Bottom Release Mag.***

$3,750 $3,100 $2,500 $2,000 $1,500 $1,250 $1,000

* ***Model PPK 7-Digit Ser. No.***

$2,250 $1,750 $1,250 $1,000 $850 $700 $550

* ***Model PPK Dural Frame*** – .22 LR, .32 ACP, or .380 ACP cal., chrome finish (very rare), "Eagle N".

.32 ACP cal.	$2,500	$1,750	$1,250	$950	$800	$700	$600
.380 ACP cal.	$6,000	$4,800	$3,800	$2,800	$2,400	$2,000	$1,600
.22 LR cal.	$3,500	$3,000	$2,400	$1,900	$1,400	$1,200	$1,000

Add 100% for early production with high-gloss finish (brown cast and green cast).

* ***Model PPK Czech Contract*** – stamped "Rampant Lion" design.

$2,000 $1,575 $1,250 $1,000 $750 $625 $550

* ***Model PPK Danish Rplt.***

$1,750 $1,400 $1,025 $850 $625 $550 $425

MODEL PPK LIGHTWEIGHT – aluminum alloy frame version.

Add 20% to .32 cal. commercial price listing.

MODEL 1925 – .22 S or LR cal. (known as Standard Model in Germany).

$2,500 $2,000 $1,500 $1,200 $1,000 $725 $600

1932 OLYMPIA MODEL – .22 S or LR cal., 10 shot, 6 or 9 in. barrel, target sights, one-piece grip, introduced in 1928 and used in 1932 Olympics. Marketed by Stoeger and Chas. Heyer-Nairobi. Very similar to Model 1925, except with checkered trigger, front strap, bullet counterweight, and fuller grip.

$3,000 $2,500 $1,500 $1,000 $800 $700 $600

GRADING - PPGS™	100%	98%	95%	90%	80%	70%	60%	LAST MSR

1936 OLYMPIA MODEL – .22 LR cal., 7.4 in. barrel, adj. target sights, blue, wood grips, 4 barrel weights available. Mfg. 1936-1940.

	$2,000	$1,625	$1,275	$1,050	$900	$800	$700	

Add 20% for weight set.

1936 OLYMPIA "JÄGERSCHAFTS" HUNTING MODEL – similar to Sport, with 4 in. barrel. Mfg. 1936-1940. Also seen with "Eagle N" proofs.

	$2,750	$2,250	$1,650	$1,250	$1,000	$800	$700	

OLYMPIA RAPID FIRE MODEL – .22 Short cal. only, 7.4 in. barrel, blue, adj. sight, wood grip, has alloy slide. Mfg. 1936-1940.

	$2,500	$2,100	$1,600	$1,200	$995	$600	$525	

1936 OLYMPIA FÜNFKAMPF MODEL – .22 Short or LR cal., 9 1/4 in. barrel, blue, adj. sight, wood grips, barrel weights, circa 1936.

	$3,250	$2,750	$2,250	$1,750	$1,500	$1,200	$900	

PISTOLS: SEMI-AUTO, POST-WAR

Smith & Wesson has placed a recall on all Walther PPK and PPK/S pistols manufactured by Smith & Wesson from March 21, 2002-Feb. 3, 2009. Ser. no. ranges subject to this recall are as follows: 0010BAB-9999BAB, 0000BAC-9999BAC, 0000BAD-9999BAD, 0000BAE-999BAE, 0000BAF-9999BAF, 0000BAH-9999BAH, 00000BAJ-9999BAJ, 0000BAK-9999BAK, 0000BAL-5313BAL, 0000BAM-1320BAM, 0000LTD-0499LTD, 0001PPK-1500PPK, 0026REP-0219REP, and 0001WLE-0459WLE. Smith & Wesson has advised all owners to discontinue usage and return the pistol to S&W for free repair. Please contact S&W directly for more information.

CCP (CONCEALED CARRY PISTOL) – 9mm Para. cal., Softcoil gas-delayed blowback system, SA, black polymer compact frame, 3.54 in. barrel with or w/o stainless steel slide, interchangeable front sight, adj. rear sight, manual thumb safety, 8 shot mag., reversible mag. release, non-slip textured high grip, passive firing pin block, lower accessory rail, loaded chamber indicator, includes two mags., optional Viridian red laser (new 2018), black Cerakote finish, 22.3 oz. Mfg. mid-2014-2018.

	$445	$395	$350	$310	$280	$250	$225	*$469*

Add $20 for stainless steel slide.
Add $30 for Viridian red laser mounted to front of trigger guard (new 2018).

In March 2017, Walther issued a recall for this model due to its possibility of drop-firing, regardless of the manual safety being on or off. If you own a CCP, please do not load or fire your Walther CCP pistol. Please contact Walther immediately to arrange to have your pistol upgraded free of charge at 1-866-503-3389.

CCP M2 – 9mm Para. or .380 ACP (new 2020) cal., Softcoil Technology (gas delayed blowback system), 3.54 in. barrel, easy cocking slide, two 8 shot, ambi mag. release, 3-dot polymer sights, ergonomic Walther grip, manual thumb safety and firing pin block safety, Picatinny rail, front and rear slide serrations, with or without Viridian laser (disc. 2020), black, stainless steel, Angel Blue (new 2020), Tungsten Gray (new 2021), or Blue Titanium (new 2021) Cerakote finish, 22.33 oz. New mid-2018.

MSR $499	$460	$400	$350	$310	$280	$250	$225	

CREED – 9mm Para. cal., polymer frame, 4 in. barrel, includes two 10 or 16 shot mags., ambidextrous mag. release, bobbed hammer, pre-cocked double action trigger system, low profile steel 3-dot sights, non-slip grip texturing, front and rear cocking serrations, Picatinny accessory mounting rail, matte black Tenifer coating, 27 oz. Mfg. late 2016-2018.

	$350	$320	$280	$250	$225	$200	$185	*$399*

MODEL PP & VARIATIONS – .22 LR, .32 ACP, or .380 ACP cal., double action, specifications similar to pre-war PP, 3 7/8 in. barrel. Imported 1963-2000. German manufacture.

* ***Model PP .380 ACP cal.*** – 7 shot mag.

	$750	$600	$450	$350	$300	$275	$250	*$999*

* ***Model PP .32 ACP cal.*** – 8 shot mag.

	$650	$500	$395	$295	$275	$250	$225	*$999*

* ***Model PP .22 LR cal.*** – 10 shot mag., disc. 1984.

	$800	$650	$425	$375	$325	$300	$275	*$783*

* ***Model PP Blue Engraved*** – .22 LR (disc.) or .380 ACP cal. Disc. 1984.

	$1,425	$1,125	$950	$835	$685	$585	$485	*$1,650*

Add 5% for .22 LR cal.

GRADING - PPGS™	100%	98%	95%	90%	80%	70%	60%	LAST MSR

* ***Model PP Chrome Engraved*** – .22 LR or .380 ACP cal. Disc. 1984.

	$1,450	$1,125	$900	$785	$655	$550	$465	*$1,600*

Add $50 for .22 LR cal.

* ***Model PP Silver Engraved*** – .22 LR (disc.) or .380 ACP cal. Disc. 1984.

	$1,750	$1,200	$1,000	$885	$715	$610	$515	*$1,948*

* ***Model PP Gold Engraved*** – .22 LR (disc.) or .380 ACP cal. Disc. 1984.

	$1,950	$1,500	$1,150	$1,025	$830	$710	$590	*$2,053*

* ***Model PP Manurhin*** – .22 LR, .32 ACP, or .380 ACP cal. Disc. 1984.

	$525	$440	$350	$225	$180	$165	$150

Add 10% for .380 ACP cal.

* ***Model PP 50th Anniversary Commemorative*** – .22 LR., .32 ACP, or .380 ACP cal., gold-plated parts, hand-carved grips, presentation case. 500 imported to U.S. 1979. 800 mfg.

	$1,625	$1,175	$650	N/A	N/A	N/A	N/A	*$1,700*

* ***Model PP "100 Jahre" 1886-1986*** – 7.65mm cal., 100th anniversary PP edition, primarily made for the German marketplace, inscription marked on right side of slide.

Plastic Grips	$1,050	$750	$625	N/A	N/A	N/A	N/A
Extended Wood Grips	$1,150	$850	$675	N/A	N/A	N/A	N/A

* ***Model PP Last Edition*** – supplied with fitted hard case, certificate, and video of Walther history, 400 mfg. in .32 ACP cal., 100 mfg. in .380 ACP cal., 500 total mfg. in Germany 1999 only.

	$1,350	$1,050	$900	N/A	N/A	N/A	N/A

Add $100 for .380 ACP cal.

This model was the last of the PP, PPK, PPK/S models to be manufactured when Germany stopped production in 1999.

PP SPORT – double action, thumbrest grips, round hammer with spur, adj. rear sight, 6.1 or 8.1 in. barrel, 25.6 or 27.2 oz. Mfg. 1953-70.

Manurhin Mfg.	$900	$750	$625	$550	$495	$425	$350
Mark II (1955-1957)	$1,000	$775	$650	$600	$545	$500	$450
Walther Mfg.	$1,250	$1,000	$750	$625	$575	$525	$450

Subtract 10% if not marked.

Add $75 for barrel weight, $100 for factory case, 20% for factory nickel, 5% for single action.

* ***PP Sport "C" Model C*** – mfg. for competition shooting, single action, 7 5/8 in. barrel, spur hammer.

	$1,250	$1,000	$750	$675	$575	$525	$450

MODEL PP SUPER – .380 ACP cal., 3.6 in. barrel, 7 shot, fixed sights, plastic grips, blue, 1,000 mfg. in .380 ACP cal., 26.8 oz. Mfg. 1973-79.

	$975	$750	$550	$395	$285	$250	$235

* ***Model PP Super Ultra/Police*** – 9x18mm Ultra (aka 9x18mm Police) cal., recently imported West German police trade-ins, approx. 4,000 mfg.

	$700	$550	$400	$300	$275	$250	$225

* ***Model PP Super Super-Cutaway***

	$795	$650	$550	N/A	N/A	N/A	N/A

MODEL PPK – similar to pre-war PPK, .22 LR, .32 ACP, or .380 ACP cal., 3.31 in. barrel. Mfg. post-war-1999, U.S. import stopped by GCA 68 on W. German and French production.

.32 ACP Cal.	$775	$550	$425	$350	$325	$295	$275
.22 LR Cal.	$1,200	$950	$600	$525	$450	$375	$325
.380 ACP Cal.	$1,200	$950	$600	$475	$425	$350	$300
Blue Engraved	$1,675	$1,300	$950	$835	$685	$585	$485
Silver Engraved	$1,950	$1,400	$1,000	$885	$715	$610	$515
Gold Engraved	$2,275	$1,675	$1,250	$1,100	$895	$785	$630

100% column assumes NIB condition - subtract 15% if not boxed.

MODEL PPK LAST EDITION – similar to PP Last Edition, but was never imported into the U.S. because of the GCA of 1968.

MODEL PPK LIGHTWEIGHT – similar to Standard, with dural frame, .22 LR or .32 ACP cal.

	$995	$725	$500	$375	$325	$295	$275

Add 20% for .22 LR cal.

GRADING - PPGS™	100%	98%	95%	90%	80%	70%	60%	LAST MSR

MODEL PPK: 1980-CIRCA 1999 U.S. MFG. – .380 ACP cal. only, 3.35 in. barrel, similar specifications as previous W. German and French manufacture, blue or bright nickel (new 1997) finish, 7 shot finger extension mag., black plastic grips, 21 oz. Mfg. 1980-circa 1999 in the U.S. by Emco, located in Gadsden, AL.

	$750	$600	$450	$365	$320	$295	$265	*$543*

Manufacture in the U.S. was under an exclusive licensing agreement with Walther of Germany.

MODEL PPK: 2001-2012 U.S. MFG. – .380 ACP cal., stainless steel construction. Mfg. 2001-2012 by Smith & Wesson in Springfield, MA.

	$450	$350	$325	$295	$265	$235	$210	

MODEL PPK STAINLESS: 1996-CIRCA 1999 U.S. MFG. – .32 ACP (new 1998) or .380 ACP cal., stainless steel construction. Mfg. 1996-circa 1999 in the U.S. by Emco, located in Gadsden, AL.

	$750	$600	$450	$365	$320	$295	$265	*$543*

MODEL PPK STAINLESS: 2001-2012 U.S. MFG. – .32 ACP (new 2008) or .380 ACP cal., stainless steel construction. Mfg. 2001-2012 in the U.S. by Smith & Wesson, located in Springfield, MA.

	$475	$375	$325	$285	$250	$225	$200	

MODEL PPK: 2019-CURRENT U.S. MFG. – .380 ACP cal., DA/SA, 3.3 in. barrel, 6 shot, stainless steel construction, beavertail extension, fixed front and rear sights, rear slide serrations, classic black checkered panel grips, black or stainless finish, 22.1 oz. Reintroduced late 2019 in the U.S. by Walther Arms, Inc. located in Fort Smith, AR.

MSR $849	$725	$635	$550	$500	$400	$325	$280	

MODEL PPK (RECENT MFG.) – .32 ACP (stainless only 2008-2013) or .380 ACP cal., 3.35 in. barrel, choice of blue or stainless steel, 6 (.380 ACP cal.) or 7 shot mag., 20.8 oz. Mfg. by Walther in Ulm, Germany. Disc.

	$565	$475	$395	$335	$295	$265	$225	*$699*

Add $230 for Crimson Trace Lasergrips (disc. 2009).
Add $270 for machine engraving and case (mfg. 2011-2012).

* ***Model PPK 75th Anniversary*** – .380 ACP cal. only, blue finish scroll engraving on frame and slide, "75th Anniversary" script on frame, gold Walther banner and PPK on left side, smooth wood grips, includes wooden presentation case, 1,500 mfg. 2006.

	$875	$750	$675	N/A	N/A	N/A	N/A	*$996*

MODEL PPK/E – .380 ACP cal., 3.4 in. barrel, high polish blue, 7 (.380 ACP) or 8 (.32 ACP) shot mag., 23 oz.

	$525	$465	$435	$395	$360	$330	$295	

While advertised in America during 2000 with a MSR of $294, this model was distributed in Europe only until circa 2008, and was produced with the cooperation of F.E.G., located in Hungary.

Century Arms International began importing used guns circa 2009.

MODEL PPK/S & VARIATIONS – .22 LR, .32 ACP, or .380 ACP cal., similar to PPK, except has larger PP frame to meet import requirements of 1968, 3 1/4 in. barrel, production in W. Germany, Manurhin of France (disc. 1986), and in the U.S. (mfg. under license from Walther by Interarms), 10 (.22 LR) or 8 (.32 ACP and .380 ACP) shot, double action, fixed sights.

* ***American Model PPK/S*** – .380 ACP cal. only, blue or two-tone (.380 ACP cal. only) finish, 8 shot, one finger extension and one flat bottom mag., approx. 26 oz. Made by S&W under licensing agreement. Disc. 2001, reintroduced 2007-2012.

	$450	$350	$325	$295	$260	$235	$210	*$630*

Add $170 for machine engraving and case (mfg. 2010-2012).

* ***Model PPK/S Stainless U.S. Mfg.*** – .32 ACP (new 1998) or .380 ACP cal. Mfg. by Emco located in Gadsden, AL circa 1983-circa 1999, and S&W circa 2001-2012.

1983-Circa 1999 mfg.	$750	$600	$450	$395	$350	$300	$275	
2001-2012 mfg.	$450	$375	$325	$280	$250	$225	$200	*$629*

Add $230 for Crimson Trace Lasergrips (.380 ACP cal. only, new 2008).

* ***Model PPK/S (Current Mfg.)*** – .380 ACP cal., DA/SA, 3.3 in. barrel, two 7 shot mags., fixed front and rear sights, classic grip, hammer drop decocking safety, rear slide serrations, beavertail extension, black or walnut (new 2021) grips, black or stainless finish, 23.6 oz. New 2019.

MSR $849	$725	$635	$550	$500	$400	$325	$280	

Add $50 for walnut grips (new 2021).

GRADING - PPGS™	100%	98%	95%	90%	80%	70%	60%	LAST MSR

* ***Model PPK/S First Edition*** – .380 ACP cal., 3.3 in. barrel, two 7 shot mags., cocobolo wood grips (additional extended grip), hammer drop decocking safety, rear slide serrations, beavertail extension, marked "First Edition" on right side under ejection port, Ser. No. range 101-1350, stainless steel finish, 23.6 oz., U.S. limited mfg. 1,250. New 2019.

MSR $799	$700	$600	$500	$450	$375	$300	$250	

This model is a Talo Exclusive and available through a Talo distributor.

* ***Model PPK/S German*** – .22 LR (disc. 1984), .32 ACP (disc. 1999), or .380 ACP (disc. 1999, reintroduced 2013) cal., 3.35 in. barrel, 7 shot mag., choice of blue finish or stainless steel. Disc. 2017.

.380 ACP cal.	$565	$475	$395	$335	$295	$265	$225	
.22 LR cal. (pre-2013)	$850	$725	$595	$450	$375	$325	$300	
.32 ACP cal.	$600	$525	$450	$400	$325	$295	$275	

Last MSR on the .380 ACP cal. was $699.

* ***Model PPK/S .22 LR*** – .22 LR cal., 3.3 in. barrel, 10 shot mag. with finger extension, fixed sights, checkered black synthetic grips, black or nickel (new 2016) finish or stainless steel construction (disc. 2015), 20-24 oz. Manufactured in Ulm, Germany. New 2013.

MSR $349	$300	$285	$265	$245	$225	$210	$195	

Add $50 for stainless steel (disc. 2015).

* ***American Model PPK/S Blue Engraved*** – blue engraved. Disc. 1985.

	$875	$850	$800	$695	$585	$485	$415	*$990*

* ***American Model PPK/S Gold-Engraved Commemorative*** – 500 total mfg. Disc. 1987.

	$1,000	$875	$700	N/A	N/A	N/A	N/A	*$1,200*

* ***American Model PPK/S Gold-Engraved*** – disc. 1985.

	$975	$850	$700	$585	$500	$415	$365	*$1,070*

* ***West German Model PPK/S Blue Engraved*** – inventory depleted 1990.

	$1,475	$1,050	$850	$740	$620	$515	$440	*$1,550*

* ***West German Model PPK/S Chrome Engraved*** – importation disc. 1991.

	$1,525	$1,075	$950	$835	$685	$585	$485	*$1,700*

* ***West German Model PPK/S Silver Engraved*** – disc. 1988.

	$1,675	$1,150	$975	$860	$700	$600	$500	*$1,700*

* ***West German Model PPK/S Gold Engraved*** – disc. 1985.

	$1,950	$1,250	$1,000	$885	$715	$610	$515	*$1,800*

MANURHIN PPK/S – see listings under Manurhin in the M Section.

PDP (PERFORMANCE DUTY PISTOL) – 9mm Para. cal., modular design, full size polymer frame, steel slide, 4 or 4 1/2 in. barrel, two 10 or 18 shot mags., PDT (Performance Duty Trigger), red-dot ready, textured grips, auto safety, SuperTerrain serrations, black finish, 21.5 oz. New 2021.

MSR $649	$550	$470	$425	$375	$325	$295	$275	

* ***PDP Compact*** – 9mm Para. cal., modular design, compact polymer frame, steel slide, 4 in. barrel, two 10 or 15 shot mags., PDT (Performance Duty Trigger), red-dot ready, textured grips, auto safety, SuperTerrain serrations, medium backstrap, black finish, 21.4 oz. New 2021.

MSR $649	$550	$470	$425	$375	$325	$295	$275	

PK380 – .380 ACP cal., DA/SA, steel frame, 3.6 in. barrel, 8 shot mag., steel frame, 3-dot steel sights, lightweight ergonomic polymer grip, ambidextrous manual safety, Picatinny bottom rail, patterned after the P22, black, nickel, or Angel Blue (new 2016) finish, approx. 21 oz. New 2009.

MSR $449	$385	$335	$285	$260	$225	$200	$185	

Add $50 for nickel finish.
Add $50 for laser sight (black finish only).
Add $50 for Angel Blue finish (new 2016).
Add 10% for First Edition model (limited mfg. 2009 only).

PPS – 9mm Para. (disc. 2016) or .40 S&W cal., SFO, 3.2 in. barrel, 5 (.40 S&W cal. only), 6, 7, or 8 (9mm Para. cal. only) shot single stack mag., black polymer frame, matte black metal finish, fixed sights, thinner profile than the PPK (1.04 in.), ambidextrous safety, interchangeable back straps, pre-cocked striker ignition, magazine extension, 6.1 lbs. trigger pull, 21 oz. Limited importation 2008-2018.

	$525	$450	$400	$350	$315	$295	$275	*$629*

Subtract approx. $200 for 9mm Para. cal. (disc. 2016).
Add $153 for night sight kit (mfg. 2010-2012).

A first edition was also available in this model in anthracite finish. First edition marking appears on left side of slide. This edition sold out during late 2008.

GRADING - PPGS™	100%	98%	95%	90%	80%	70%	60%	LAST MSR

PPS M2 – 9mm Para. cal., 3.18 in. barrel, Tenifer coating on slide and barrel, 6, 7, or 8 shot mag., smoothlight trigger, 3-dot metal sights or XS F8 Tritium night sights (mfg. 2019-2020), ergonomic Walther grip, front and rear slide serrations, cocking indicator, extended slide stop, matte black finish, 21.1 oz. New 2016.

MSR $499	$460	$400	$350	$310	$280	$250	$225	

Add $30 for LE Edition (features phosphoric night sights and three magazines).
Add $150 for Crimson Trace laser.
Add $100 for XS F8 Tritium night sights (mfg. 2019-20).

* ***PPS M2 RMSC*** – 9mm Para. cal., 3.18 in. barrel, 6, 7, or 8 shot mag., smoothlight trigger, features the RMSc optic reflex mini sight, ergonomic Walther grip, front and rear slide serrations, Tenifer coating on slide and barrel, cocking indicator, extended slide stop, matte black finish, 21.7 oz. Mfg. mid-2018-2020.

	$595	$500	$450	$385	$335	$300	$275	*$699*

PPQ – 9mm Para. or .40 S&W cal., SFO, synthetic frame with steel slide, 4 (.40 S&W cal. only), or 4.1 (threaded barrel available on first edition only) in. barrel, 12 (.40 S&W cal. only), 15, or 17 shot mag., black finish, textured synthetic grips, night sights (first edition only) or adj. front and rear sights, Quick Defense Trigger, 24 1/2 oz. Mfg. 2011-2012.

	$525	$450	$415	$365	$325	$295	$275	*$600*

Add $300 for first edition model.

PPQ M2 CLASSIC – 9mm Para. cal., SFO, 4 in. barrel, 15 shot, ambi mag. release, short reset Quick Defense Trigger, 3-dot polymer sights, ergonomic grip, lower Picatinny rail, front and rear slide serrations, interchangeable backstrap, black Tenifer coating, 24.5 oz. Reintroduced 2017-2019.

	$550	$470	$425	$375	$325	$295	$275	*$649*

PPQ M2 .45 – .45 ACP cal., 4, 4.25 (new 2019), or 4.9 (SD barrel, mfg. 2018-2020) in. polygonal rifled barrel, 10, 12, or 15 (new 2019) shot mag., front and rear slide serrations, low profile 3-dot sights or XS F8 night sights (new 2019), fully ambidextrous controls, short reset quick defense trigger, serrated square trigger guard, tactical grip, three safeties including trigger, lower Picatinny rail, black finish, 28 oz. New mid-2015.

MSR $699	$595	$500	$450	$385	$335	$300	$275	

Add $30 for 4 7/8 in. SD barrel (mfg. 2018-2020).
Add $100 for XS F8 night sights (4.25 in. barrel only, new 2019).

PPQ M2 – 9mm Para. or .40 S&W (disc. 2018) cal., SFO, 4 (9mm Para. only), 4.1 (.40 S&W cal., disc. 2018), or 5 (disc. 2018) in. barrel, 10, 15, or 17 (disc. 2018) shot mag., low profile combat sights or XS F8 night sights (new 2019), appearance and most features similar to Model PPQ, ambidextrous mag. release button, black, Coyote Tan (limited mfg., new 2019), FDE, OD Green, or Tungsten Cerakote finish, 24 oz. Mfg. 2013-2019.

	$550	$470	$425	$375	$325	$295	$275	*$649*

Add $50 for XS F8 night sights (new 2019).

* ***PPQ M2 .22 LR Cal.*** – .22 LR cal., SFO, 4 or 5 in. barrel, 10 or 12 shot mag., lower Picatinny rail, 3 safeties, quick defense trigger, polymer front sight with dot or fiber optic front sight (5 in. barrel only), metal adj. rear sight, ambi slide stop, interchangeable backstraps, front and rear slide serrations, 20.8-23.6 oz. New 2014.

MSR $399	$340	$300	$265	$245	$225	$210	$195	

Add $100 for 5 in. barrel with fiber optic front sight.

* ***PPQ M2 SD Tactical .22 LR Cal.*** – .22 LR cal., 4.6 in. threaded barrel, 10 or 12 shot mag. with adapter, ambi slide stop and mag. release button, Mil-Std 1913 Picatinny rail, front and rear slide serrations, 21 oz. New 2014.

MSR $449	$385	$335	$285	$260	$225	$200	$185	

PPQ M2 5 INCH – 9mm Para. cal., 5 in. barrel, 10 or 15 shot, Tenifer coating on slide, barrel, and inside action parts, quick defense trigger, low profile 3-dot polymer sights, interchangeable backstraps, ambi slide stop, Mil-Std 1913 Picatinny accessory rail, front and rear slide serrations, black finish, 26 oz. Mfg. 2018-2020.

	$625	$575	$465	$395	$345	$310	$285	*$749*

PPQ M2 Q4 TAC – 9mm Para. cal., 4.6 in. threaded barrel, 15 or 17 shot extended mag., quick defense trigger, LPA fiber optic front sights and adj. competition rear iron sights, includes RMR mounting plates, optics ready slide, ergonomic grip, three safeties, front and rear slide serrations, ambi slide stop, three interchangeable backstraps, Mil-Std 1913 Picatinny accessory rail, Tenifer coating on slide and barrel, 26 oz. Mfg. late 2017-2019.

	$625	$575	$465	$395	$345	$310	$285	*$749*

GRADING - PPGS™	100%	98%	95%	90%	80%	70%	60%	LAST MSR

PPQ M2 Q5 MATCH – 9mm Para. cal., 5 in. barrel, includes three 10 or 15 shot mags., ambidextrous mag. release and slide stop, quick defense trigger, fiber optic front and adj. rear target sights, optic mounting platform, ergonomic Walther grip, three safeties, lower Picatinny rail, front and rear slide serrations, Tenifer coating on slide, barrel, and inside action parts, matte finish, 26 oz. Mfg. 2016-2019.

	$750	$675	$600	$500	$450	$400	$350	*$849*

* ***PPQ M2 Q5 Match SF/PPQ M2 Q5 Match SF Pro*** – 9mm Para. cal., all steel construction w/extended frame rails, 5 in. barrel, includes three 15 or 17 (Pro Model) shot mags., ambidextrous mag. release and slide stop, quick defense trigger, fiber optic front and adj. rear competition sights, optic mounting platform, three safeties, ergonomic Walther grip, extended Mil-Std 1913 lower Picatinny rail, front and rear slide serrations, Tenifer coating on slide, barrel, and inside action parts, matte finish, 41.6 or 42.3 oz. New 2019.

MSR $1,499	$1,350	$1,185	$1,015	$925	$745	$600	$475

Add $151 for 17 shot mag. (Pro Model).

PPQ NAVY – 9mm Para. cal., SFO, 4.6 in. threaded barrel, 15 or 17 shot extended mag., quick defense trigger, lower Picatinny rail, dual slide serrations, three interchangeable backstrap inserts, black finish, 25 oz. Disc. 2020.

	$595	$500	$450	$385	$335	$300	$275	*$699*

PPQ M2 SC (SUB-COMPACT) – 9mm Para. cal., DA, black polymer frame, 3 1/2 in. barrel, 10 or 15 shot mag., 3-dot polymer or XS F8 night sights (new 2019), ergonomic black grip, 3 safeties, lower Picatinny rail, front and rear slide serrations, ambi slide stop, Tenifer coating on slide and barrel, interchangeable backstrap, matte finish, 21.2 oz. Mfg. mid-2018-2020.

	$550	$470	$425	$375	$325	$295	$275	*$649*

Add $50 for XS F8 night sights (new 2019).

PPX M1 – 9mm Para. or .40 S&W cal., hammer fired, DAO, 4 or 4.6 (PPX SD) in. barrel, low profile 3-dot sights, lower Picatinny rail, checkered trigger guard, ergonomic textured synthetic grips, ambidextrous slide stop, bobbed hammer, polymer frame with steel or stainless steel slide, 14 or 16 shot mag., 27.2 oz. Manufactured in Ulm, Germany 2013-2014.

	$395	$350	$315	$285	$260	$240	$220	*$449*

Add $50 for stainless steel slide.

MODEL TP – .22 LR or .25 ACP cal., DA/SA, updated version of Model 9, 6 shot, 2.6 in. barrel, concealed hammer, 12 oz. Mfg. 1961-1971.

.22 LR cal.	$950	$750	$550	$350	$300	$260	$225
.25 ACP cal.	$750	$600	$500	$300	$275	$250	$200

MODEL TPH – .22 LR or .25 ACP cal., DA/SA, 2.8 in. barrel, 6 shot, alloy frame, blue, fixed sights, plastic grips, 11 1/2 oz. Mfg. 1968-98 in W. Germany, U.S. import stopped by GCA of 1968.

.22 LR cal.	$1,750	$1,500	$1,000	$850	N/A	N/A	N/A
.25 ACP cal.	$1,850	$1,600	$1,100	$900	N/A	N/A	N/A

Add 100% for factory engraving.

Subtract 10% on the 100% values if not boxed with all accessories.

TPH cutaways were also mfg. in small quantities for instructional use. Current pricing for a mint specimen is approx. $1,500.

100% price assumes NIB condition.

AMERICAN MODEL TPH – .22 LR or .25 ACP (new 1992) cal., DA/SA, blue finish or stainless steel, black plastic grips, 6 shot mag., 2 1/4 in. barrel, 14 oz. Mfg. 1987-2000.

	$900	$800	$750	$650	N/A	N/A	N/A	*$460*

Add 10% for .25 ACP cal.

* ***American Model TPH Stainless*** – stainless steel fabrication. Disc. 2000.

	$650	$600	$500	$450	N/A	N/A	N/A	*$460*

Add 10% for .25 ACP.

Deduct $90 for missing magazine (always came with two).

MODEL P.38 & VARIATIONS – Please refer to listings under the P.38 entries in the P section. Only the currently imported Walther P.38 appears in this section.

* ***Model P.38 (Recent Importation)*** – .22 LR, 7.65mm Luger, or 9mm Para. cal., DA/SA, alloy or steel frame. Previously imported by Earl's Repair Service. Disc.

	$850	$750	$635	$575	$465	$380	$325	*$995*

Add $1,000 for steel frame.

MODELS P1 & P4 – Please refer to listings under the P.38 entries in the P section.

GRADING - PPGS™	100%	98%	95%	90%	80%	70%	60%	LAST MSR

MODEL P5 – 7.65mm Luger, 9mm Para., or 9x21mm cal., DA, alloy frame, ejection port on left side, frame mounted decocking lever, 3 1/2 in. barrel, adj. rear sight, blue finish only, 8 shot mag., auto safeties, 28 oz. Mfg. 1977-disc. Previously imported by Earl's Repair Service.

	$1,950	$1,500	$1,150	$1,025	$830	$710	$590	

P-5 cutaways were also mfg. in small quantities for instructional use. Current pricing for a mint specimen is approx. $2,000.

* ***Model P5 Compact*** – compact variation of P-5 with 3.1 in. barrel, 26 1/2 oz. Limited importation 1987-disc.

	$2,500	$2,000	$1,500	$1,000	$750	$600	$500	

* ***Model P5 Long*** – special edition, 5.3 in. barrel, wood grips, 29.6 oz. 50 mfg. 1988 only.

	$4,500	$3,500	$2,500	N/A	N/A	N/A	N/A	

* ***Model P5 100th Year Commemorative*** – marked "1886-1986 100 Jahre" with Walther banner, elaborate grip carving, presentation walnut case. Imported 1986-91.

	$2,650	$1,750	$1,100	N/A	N/A	N/A	N/A	*$2,890*

MODEL P5 - L102A1 – P5 compact variation, DA/SA, green phosphate, plastic grips. Mfg. for the British Special Air Service (SAS), 20-30 imported.

	$3,500	$2,000	$1,500	$1,250	$1,000	$750	$500	

P22 – .22 LR cal., DA/SA, 3/4 scale of the P99, 3.42 in. barrel, hammer fired, black polymer frame with grooved and stippled grip, matte black finish, military green frame or nickel slide, or brushed chrome slide and anthracite frame finish (disc. 2010), internal trigger lock with loaded chamber indicator and mag. disconnect, 10 shot mag., firing pin drop safety, safety key lock on right side of frame, interchangeable backstrap, adj. rear (disc.) or 3-dot sights, 15.2 oz. Mfg. 2001-2017, reintroduced in Angel Blue finish only 2019-2020.

	$295	$280	$265	$245	$225	$210	$195	*$339*

Add $20 for nickel finish.
Add $20 for laser sight (black finish only).
Add $20 for Angel Blue finish (mfg. 2016-2017, reintroduced 2019).
Add $71 for brushed chrome slide and anthracite frame finish (mfg. 2007-2010).
Add $257 for red dot sight (mfg. 2006-2007).

Walther offered a limited P22 first edition which included two barrels, stabilizer assembly/frame extension for 5 in. barrel, and a blue plastic case. These were marked "Limited Edition P22" and 1,000 were mfg. Current value for a mint gun with all accessories is in the $400-$450 range.

A special edition two barrel set of this model was available exclusively through Davidson's during 2006 - MSR was $370.

* ***P22 Tactical*** – .22 LR cal., similar to P22, except has 3.42 in. threaded barrel and FDE finish. Mfg. 2014-2017.

	$350	$320	$280	$250	$225	$200	$185	*$399*

* ***P22 Target*** – .22 LR cal., similar to P22, except has 5 in. barrel, and frame extension that slides over barrel, available in black frame with nickel slide or black slide and OD Green (disc. 2016) or black frame, 18 1/2 oz. w/o mag. Mfg. 2001-2019.

	$350	$300	$295	$265	$235	$200	$175	*$419*

Add $40 for nickel finish.

* ***P22 Military*** – .22 LR cal., similar to P22, except has light brown graphite frame, 17.6 oz. Mfg. 2013-2017.

	$275	$240	$215	$190	$175	$160	$150	*$329*

P22QD – .22 LR cal., SA/DA, 3.42 in. threaded barrel, 10 shot mag., extended mag. release, 3-dot polymer sights, ergonomic grip, front and rear slide serrations, lower Picatinny rail, decocking safety, updated safety markings from "S" and "F" to a traditional red dot, and fully captured recoil spring, black, Angel Blue, nickel, camo (new 2020), Tungsten Gray (new 2020), Hot Pink (new 2020), or Military (OD Green) finish, 17 oz. New mid-2017.

MSR $329	$280	$245	$210	$190	$175	$160	$150	

Add $20 for P22QD Military model with OD Green finish.
Add $20 for nickel, camo (new 2020), Hot Pink (new 2020), Tungsten (new 2020), or Angel Blue finish.
Add $70 for laser sight (black finish only).

* ***P22QD Tactical*** – .22 LR cal., SA/DA, 3.42 in. threaded barrel with adapter, 10 shot mag., extended mag. release, 3-dot polymer sights, ergonomic grip, front and rear slide serrations, lower Picatinny rail, decocking safety, updated safety markings from "S" and "F" to a traditional red dot, and fully captured recoil spring, FDE finish on slide and frame, 17 oz. New mid-2017.

MSR $399	$350	$320	$280	$250	$225	$200	$185	

GRADING - PPGS™	100%	98%	95%	90%	80%	70%	60%	LAST MSR

SP22-M1 – .22 LR cal., 4 in. barrel, 10 shot, SA, polymer frame, stainless steel slide, target trigger, wide variety of options, including accessory rails, grips, and optics, 27 oz. Mfg. 2008-2010.

	$325	$265	$225	$200	$180	$160	$140	*$399*

Add $173 for red dot sight, $132 for laser sight, $317 for adj. match grips, $22 for Picatinny rail, and $59 for TruGlo fiber optic sights.

* ***SP22-M2*** – .22 LR cal., similar to SP22-M1, except has 6 in. barrel, vertical cutouts under barrel in front of frame assembly. Mfg. 2008-2010.

	$350	$300	$250	$225	$195	$175	$150	*$421*

* ***SP22-M3 Target*** – .22 LR cal., similar to SP22-M2, except has upper and lower accessory rails. Mfg. 2008-2010.

	$425	$350	$300	$260	$240	$220	$200	*$485*

* ***SP22-M4 Match Sport*** – .22 LR cal., 6 in. match grade barrel, ergonomic black stippled wood target grips, 10 shot mag., SA, match trigger, 32 1/2 oz. Mfg. 2008-2010.

	$675	$600	$525	$450	$400	$350	$295	*$784*

P88 & VARIATIONS – 9mm Para. or 9x21mm cal., DA/SA, alloy frame, 4 in. barrel, 15 shot button release mag., fully ambidextrous, decocking lever, matte finish, adj. rear sight, internal safeties, plastic grips, 31 1/2 oz. Mfg. 1987-93.

	$1,400	$800	$650	$550	$500	$475	$450	*$1,129*

P88 cutaways were also mfg. in small quantities for instructional use. Current pricing for a mint specimen is approx. $2,000.

* ***P88 Compact*** – 9mm Para. or 9x21mm cal., 3.93 in. barrel, 14* (disc.) or 10 (C/B 1994) shot mag., 29 oz. Imported 1993-2003.

	$1,950	$1,500	$1,150	$1,025	$830	$710	$590	*$900*

Add 25% for 14 shot mag.

* ***P88 Champion*** – 9mm Para. cal. only, 6 in. barrel, SA only, 14* shot mag., 30.9 oz. Very limited mfg. 1992-disc.

	$3,200	$1,850	$1,500	$1,250	$995	$775	$625	

* ***P88 Competition*** – 9mm Para. cal., similar to P88 Champion, except has 4 in. barrel, SA only, 14* shot mag., 28.2 oz. Very limited mfg. 1992-disc.

	$2,600	$1,500	$1,250	$995	$775	$625	$550	

* ***P88 Sport*** – .22 LR cal. only, 6 in. barrel, SA only, 10 shot mag. Very limited mfg. 1995-disc.

	$2,450	$1,900	$1,550	$1,250	$995	$775	$625	

P99 AS & VARIATIONS – 9mm Para., 9x21mm (ltd. importation 1996), or .40 S&W (new 1999) cal., SFO, 4 (9mm Para.) or 4.1 (.40 S&W) in. barrel, polymer frame, 10, 12 (.40 S&W cal. only), 15, or 16 (disc. 2006, 9mm Para. cal. only) shot mag., standard, anti-stress (DA AS Model, new 2004), or quick action (QA, allowing consistent SA trigger performance) trigger, decocking, and internal striker safeties, cocking and loaded chamber indicators, ambi mag. release, ergonomic black, desert tan (disc. 2008), or green (Military model, new 1999) synthetic grip with interchangeable backstrap, adj. rear sight, matte black, titanium coated (mfg. 2003-2006), or QPQ with silver slide (mfg. 1999-2003) finish, 25 oz. Ltd. importation 1995-disc.

	$650	$485	$435	$375	$315	$275	$250	*$629*

Add $140 for Tritium sight set with green 3-dot system (.40 S&W only), or $109 for white 3-dot metal sights (disc. 2011).
Add $260 for night sight kit (mfg. 2010-2011).
Add $31 for titanium finish (mfg. 2003-2006).
Add $125 for 9x21mm cal. (ltd. importation 1996).
Engraved P99s (9mm Para. cal. only) were available in the following configurations- Grade I Arabesque ($3,700 last MSR), Grade II Goldline ($4,200 last MSR), Grade III Arabesque w/gold ($4,660 last MSR).

* ***P99 AS (Current Mfg.)*** – 9mm Para. cal., DA/SA, 4 in. barrel, 10 or 15 shot mag., polymer white dot sights, ambi mag. release, interchangeable backstraps, black finish, 24 oz.

MSR $699	$600	$525	$450	$410	$325	$275	$225	

* ***P99 Compact*** – 9mm Para. or .40 S&W cal., SFO, 3 1/2 in. barrel, 8 (.40 S&W cal.) or 10 shot mag. with finger extension, available in QA, AS, or DAO (disc. 2006), Weaver rail, compact frame, blue finish only, 20 oz. Mfg. 2004-2018.

	$550	$485	$435	$375	$315	$275	$250	*$629*

* ***P99 QSA*** – 9mm Para. or .40 S&W cal., first introduced before the QA, slide marked with QSA inscription, large decocking plate. Very few mfg.

	$900	$750	$525	N/A	N/A	N/A	N/A	

GRADING - PPGS™	100%	98%	95%	90%	80%	70%	60%	LAST MSR

* ***P99 2000 Commemorative*** – 9mm Para. or .40 S&W cal., features high polish blue slide with laser inscription "Commemorative for the Year 2000". Limited mfg. 1,000 (only 500 for the U.S.) of each cal. in 2000 only, cased with Walther videotape.

	$850	$650	$495	N/A	N/A	N/A	N/A	*$840*

* ***P99 La Chasse DU Engraved*** – 9mm Para. or .40 S&W cal., similar to Model P-99 Military, except has laser engraved slide, wooden backstrap and green lanyard, luminescent sights, special case. Mfg. 1998-2000.

	$950	$800	$725	N/A	N/A	N/A	N/A	*$1,078*

* ***P99 La Chasse Engraved*** – features choice of elaborate oak leaf, Arabesque, or English style hand scroll engraving on polished slide. Mfg. 1998-2000.

	$1,995	$1,600	$1,400	N/A	N/A	N/A	N/A	*$2,126*

* ***P99 Canada Edition*** – 9mm Para. cal. only, 105mm barrel, black finish only, scarce in the U.S., includes two 16 shot mags.

	$1,000	$750	$600	N/A	N/A	N/A	N/A	

* ***P99 Malta Arms Act Special Edition*** – special edition commemorating the Malta Arms Act of 2005, 99 mfg. 2005 only.

	$950	$725	$550	N/A	N/A	N/A	N/A	

P990 – similar to P99, SFO, except is double action only, features Walther's constant pull trigger system, black, QPQ slide finish, or Military Model (green), 25 oz. Mfg. 1998-2003.

	$550	$475	$425	$385	$350	$325	$295	*$644*

Q4 STEEL FRAME – 9mm Para. cal., steel frame, 4 in. barrel, 15 shot mag., phosphoric sights, wrap-around grip panel, extended beavertail, full length Picatinny rail, recessed slide release, front and rear slide serrations, 39.7 oz. New 2020.

MSR $1,449	$1,230	$1,075	$925	$835	$675	$550	$450	

* ***Q4 Steel Frame OR*** – 9mm Para. cal., steel frame, 4 in. barrel, 15 shot mag., LPA sights, optic ready, wrap-around grip panel, extended beavertail, full length Picatinny rail, recessed slide release, front and rear slide serrations, 40 oz. New 2020.

MSR $1,549	$1,320	$1,155	$990	$900	$725	$600	$515	

Q4 TAC M1/Q4 TAC M2 – 9mm Para. cal., right or left-hand action, 4 or 6 in. barrel, 15 shot mag., paddle-style (M1) or reversible button-style (M2) mag. release, quick-defense trigger, ability to swap from iron sights to optics, ambi slide stop, 25 oz. New 2020.

MSR $799	$680	$600	$500	$450	$375	$300	$265	

Q5 MATCH STEEL FRAME – 9mm Para. cal., machined solid steel billet frame, 5 in. barrel, ported and optic ready slide, 15 shot mag., reversible button-style mag. release, LPA red fiber optic front and LPA black adj. rear sight, wrap-around grip panel, interchangeable backstraps, extended beavertail, front and rear serrations, ambi slide stop, full length Picatinny rail, recessed slide release, 27.9 oz. New 2020.

MSR $1,699	$1,450	$1,275	$1,095	$985	$800	$650	$560	

* ***Q5 Match SF Arabesque*** – 9mm Para. cal., steel frame, 5 in. barrel, 15 shot mag., Dynamik performance trigger, black serrated target front and adj. match rear sights, checkered Circassian walnut grips, Tenifer Nitride finish, 24K gold inlay, coin finish, full coverage engraving by Dario Cortini, 41.6 oz. New 2020.

MSR $30,000	$27,000	$23,625	$20,250	$18,360	$14,850	$12,150	$9,450	

* ***Q5 Match SF Black Diamond*** – 9mm Para. cal., steel frame, 5 in. barrel, 15 shot, pure steel mag. base plate, Dynamik performance trigger, black serrated target front and adj. match rear sights fully integrated, checkered aerospace grade aluminum alloy w/one-piece wrap around grips, Tenifer Nitride treated and polished, diamond like carbon coated, satin anodizing, 41.6 oz. New 2020.

MSR $2,999	$2,700	$2,375	$2,025	$1,825	$1,475	$1,200	$950	

* ***Q5 Match SF Black Tie*** – 9mm Para. cal., steel frame, 5 in. barrel, 15 shot, pure steel mag. base plate, Dynamik performance trigger, black serrated target front and adj. match rear sights, fully integrated, checkered aerospace grade aluminum alloy one-piece wrap around grip, Tenifer Nitride treated and polished, Stinox coated, satin anodizing, 41.6 oz. New 2020.

MSR $2,699	$2,425	$2,125	$1,825	$1,650	$1,350	$2,000	$850	

* ***Q5 Match SF Patriot*** – 9mm Para. cal., steel frame, patriotic engraving done at Bottega Giovanelli, 5 in. barrel, 15 shot, pure steel mag. base plate, Dynamik performance trigger, black serrated target front and adj. match rear sights fully integrated, checkered aerospace grade aluminum alloy w/one-piece wrap around grips, Tenifer Nitride treated and polished, satin anodizing, 41.6 oz. New 2020.

MSR $3,999	$3,600	$3,150	$2,700	$2,450	$1,975	$1,625	$1,250	

GRADING - PPGS™	100%	98%	95%	90%	80%	70%	60%	LAST MSR

Q5 MATCH STEEL FRAME PRO – 9mm Para. cal., machined solid steel billet frame, 5 in. barrel, ported and optic ready slide, 17 shot mag., reversible button-style mag. release, Carl Walther Performance magwell, two aluminum base plates, LPA red fiber optic front and LPA black adj. rear sight, wrap-around grip panel, interchangeable backstraps, extended beavertail, front and rear serrations, ambi slide stop, full length Picatinny rail, recessed slide release, 42.3 oz. New 2020.

MSR $1,849	$1,575	$1,380	$1,180	$1,075	$875	$725	$600	

PISTOLS: SEMI-AUTO, TARGET

Walther target pistols are imported by Champions Choice located in La Vergne, TN. Previously imported by Interarms until 1993, Nygord Precision Products until 1996, and by Earl's Repair Service, located in Tewksbury, MA.

Add 10% to the values listed for left-hand stocks (available on most models).

MODEL GSP TARGET STANDARD – .22 LR cal., SA, 4 1/2 in. barrel, 5 shot mag. standard, 8 or 10 shot mag. optional, adj. sights, nickel, two-tone, or blue finish, walnut target grips, two-stage trigger became optional in 1995, optional carrying case, 42.3 oz. Mfg. 1969-2001.

	$1,350	$1,200	$995	$650	$550	$475	$425	*$1,450*

This model was also available as a complete international package, including a GSP with .22 Short and .32 S&W Wadcutter conversion units, including triggers. MSR was approx. $3,100.

* ***Model GSP Target Junior*** – similar to GSP Target, except has slimmer 4 1/4 in. barrel design, smaller walnut grips, 40.1 oz. Importation disc. 1992.

	$1,350	$1,200	$995	$650	$550	$495	$425	*$1,810*

* ***Model GSP-C Target*** – similar to Model GSP Target, except in .32 S&W Wadcutter, and 4 1/4 in. barrel, 49.4 oz. Mfg. 1971-2001.

	$1,350	$1,200	$995	$650	$550	$475	$425	*$1,595*

Add $1,095 for OSP-2000 .22 Short conversion unit.
Add $995 for GSP .22 LR cal. conversion unit.

* ***Model GSP Target Expert*** – .22 LR or .32 cal., similar to GSP Standard, except for recoil compensation system located in barrel weight, sight radius has been changed, and sights are located further to the rear of the gun, modified frame (cut on an angle) behind the trigger area, stippled blonde/blue ergonomic laminated wood grips, 42.3 oz. Mfg. 2001-disc.

	$1,850	$1,525	$1,325	$1,125	$900	$750	$650	*$2,060*

Add $190 for .32 cal.

* ***Model GSPC Target Expert*** – similar to Model GSP Expert, except available in .32 S&W Wadcutter cal., 45.1 oz. Mfg. 2001-2005.

	$2,275	$1,695	$1,100	$850	$675	$575	$495	*$1,695*

* ***Model GSP Target Atlanta*** – .22 LR cal., "Special Edition for the 1996 Olympic Games, Atlanta" inscribed on right side of bolt housing, black laminate grips, titanium plated bolt, otherwise same as GSP Target Standard. Disc.

	$1,800	$1,450	$1,000	N/A	N/A	N/A	N/A	

* ***Model GSP Target 25th Year Commemorative Special Limited Edition*** – .22 LR cal., aluminum carrying case, options included two-tone finish, laminated Canadian black birch grip, titanium plated bolt, special 70 g. barrel weight with "25 Jahre GSP" engraved, adj. front sight, two-stage trigger, 3 lbs. 1,000 mfg. 1994.

	$2,500	$2,150	$1,850	N/A	N/A	N/A	N/A	

This model was only available from Earl's Repair Service.

* ***Model GSP-C Target 25th Year Commemorative Special Limited Edition*** – similar to GSP 25th Year Commemorative, except in .32 S&W Wadcutter, engraved 65 g. barrel weight, 1,000 mfg. as complete pistols or conversion units. Mfg. 1996 only.

	$1,995	$1,600	$1,250	N/A	N/A	N/A	N/A	

* ***Model GSP Target Special Anniversary Pistol/Rifle Combination*** – only 50 sets mfg. for 2000, includes scope, pistol, and rifle conversion kit, includes carry case. Disc.

	$5,000	$3,750	$2,750	N/A	N/A	N/A	N/A	*$5,500*

This combo was only available from Earl's Repair Service.

GRADING - PPGS™	100%	98%	95%	90%	80%	70%	60%	LAST MSR

* ***Model GSP Target Rifle Conversion Kit*** – .22 LR cal., unique conversion allows inserting a GSP action in a rifle stock, includes 16 3/4 in. (18 1/4 with GSP compensator) stainless barrel, black, brown, camo, or Walther blue, laminate stock, right or left-hand, 5, 8, or 10 shot mag. Mfg. 1996-disc.

$995 $850 $725 $610 $515 $425 $375 ***$995***

Add $155 with Super Match stock.
Add $300 for Super Match Kit.
Add $75 for left-hand stock.

This rifle conversion kit is only available from Earl's Repair Service, Inc.

MODEL KSP 200 – .22 LR cal., SA, adj. laminated ergonomic grips, target trigger and sights, two-tone slide finish, mfg. in cooperation with Baikal. Mfg. 2000-2004.

$500 $450 $415 $385 $350 $325 $295 ***$575***

MODEL OSP – similar to GSP, in .22 Short cal. Mfg. 1961-1994 for international competition (meets ISU and NRA regs.), 3.35 (new 1994, current model is OSP 2000) or 4 1/4 in. barrel, 44.4 oz. Importation disc. 2017.

$1,400 $1,200 $1,000 $800 $700 $600 $500 ***$1,795***

MODEL SSP EXPERT – .22 LR cal., SA, 6 in. barrel, lightweight construction, black synthetic ergonomic grips in three different sizes, pneumatic buffer, cocking indicator, extended rear sight, 5 shot mag., 34 oz. Importation 2006-disc.

$2,150 $1,900 $1,675 $1,450 $1,225 $950 $825 ***$2,420***

WALTHER/HAMMERLI MODEL SP 20 RRS – .22 LR or .32 S&W Wadcutter cal., SA, state-of-the-art target pistol featuring composite frame with redesigned ergonomic grips, RRS designates recoil reducing system, fully hand adj. rear sight, various slide colors available. Imported by Larry's Guns circa 2006-2017.

$1,749 $1,425 $1,250 $1,075 $950 $825 $725

Add $246 for .32 S&W Wadcutter cal.
Add $795 for .22 LR conversion, or $850 for .32 Wadcutter conversion.

FREE PISTOL – .22 LR cal., single shot, electronic trigger, 11.8 in. heavy barrel, advanced target design with fully adj. grips and sights, 49.4 oz. Mfg. 1977-91.

$1,450 $1,200 $1,000 $850 $675 $575 $500 ***$2,140***

HÄMMERLI-WALTHER – please refer to Hämmerli AG in the H section.

REVOLVERS

MODEL R99 – .357 Mag. cal., 6 shot, double action, 3 in. barrel, adj. rear sight, blue or stainless steel, unique Duo-grip allows for different hand sizes (2 grips included), 28 1/2 oz. Mfg. by Smith & Wesson 1999 only for the European market with no U.S. importation.

This model was basically a variation of the S&W Models 19 (blue) or 66 (stainless).

RIFLES: DISC.

MODEL B – .30-06 cal., bolt action, post-war mfg., 22 in. barrel. Disc.

$775 $625 $500 $400 $300 $250 $200

Add 20% for double-set triggers.

MODEL 1 AUTOLOADING – .22 LR cal., Carbine model, autoloading, 20 1/2 in. barrel, 5 or 9 (optional) shot detachable mag., could be used as bolt action or semi-auto, checkered pistol grip, walnut sporter stock, 5 1/2 lbs. Disc.

$895 $800 $700 $600 $500 $400 $300

MODEL 2 AUTOLOADING – .22 LR cal., similar to Model 1, except has 24 1/2 in. barrel, finger grooved forearm, tangent sight, adj. trigger, checkered sporter stock, pre-war, 7 lbs. Disc.

$995 $875 $775 $625 $500 $400 $300

MODEL V CHAMPION – micrometer adj. sight and checkered pistol grip stock. Disc.

$775 $625 $500 $400 $300 $250 $200

MODEL DSM 34 – .22 LR cal., single shot, military stock, tangent sight. Pre-war and wartime mfg. Disc.

$1,000 $650 $550 $500 $450 $375 $300

Add 50% for stamp in stock.
Add 20% for AS stamp in stock.

MODEL KKM INTERNATIONAL MATCH – .22 LR cal., single shot bolt action, 28 in. heavy barrel, adj. aperture sight, adj. hook butt, thumbhole stock, accessory rail, post-war mfg. Disc.

$880 $770 $715 $660 $550 $495 $440

MODEL KKM-S – similar to KKM, with adj. cheekpiece. Disc.

$935 $825 $770 $715 $605 $550 $495

GRADING - PPGS™	100%	98%	95%	90%	80%	70%	60%	LAST MSR

MODEL KKJ SPORTER – .22 LR cal., bolt action, 5 shot, 22 1/2 in. barrel, open sight, checkered sporter stock, post-war. Disc.

	$1,250	$995	$650	$550	$450	$385	$330	

Add 20% for double-set triggers.

MODEL KKJ-MA – .22 WMR cal. Disc.

	$1,250	$1,100	$775	$650	$550	$450	$385	

MODEL KKJ-HO – .22 Hornet cal., repeater or single shot (Model KKJ-E). Disc.

	$1,450	$1,225	$825	$700	$575	$450	$385	

Add 20% for double-set triggers.

MODEL KKW – .22 LR cal., single shot, military stock, tangent sight, pre-war and wartime mfg.

	$750	$600	$420	$300	$260	$220	$195	

Add 50% for SA stamp on stock.

MODEL SSV VARMINT – .22 LR cal., single shot bolt action, 25 1/2 in. barrel, no sights, Monte Carlo pistol grip stock, post-war mfg. Disc.

.22 LR cal.	$700	$600	$525	$495	$415	$360	$330	
.22 Hornet cal.	$825	$725	$600	$550	$475	$415	$385	

MODEL UIT BV UNIVERSAL – .22 LR cal., single shot bolt action, 25.6 in. heavy barrel, adj. aperture sight, target stock with palm rest, adj. butt, meets ISU regs., 11 lbs. Disc. 1990.

	$1,325	$1,050	$850	$700	$635	$580	$530	*$1,700*

This model was previously known as the Model UIT Special.

MODEL UIT MATCH – .22 LR cal., similar to Model UIT, except with improved stock design which includes fully stippled lower forearm and pistol grip, 25.6 in. barrel, 8.6 lbs. Importation disc. 1993.

	$1,125	$925	$800	$660	$610	$555	$510	*$1,400*

* ***Model UIT-E Match*** – electronic trigger, 25.6 in. barrel, 10.4 lbs. Disc. 1986.

	$1,350	$940	$860	$770	$670	$630	$560	*$1,250*

GX-1 – .22 LR cal., similar to Model UIT Match, 25 in. barrel with fully adj. free rifle stock, all accessories included, 16 1/2 lbs. Importation disc. 1991.

	$1,895	$1,375	$1,125	$985	$860	$775	$680	*$2,350*

MODEL PRONE 400 – similar to UIT Match, with Prone style competition stock and no sights. Disc.

	$750	$635	$580	$525	$415	$360	$305	

MODEL KK/MS SILHOUETTE – .22 LR cal. only, designed for silhouette shooting, no sights, thumbhole stock with adj. butt, fully stippled forend and stock grip, front barrel weight, 23.6 in. barrel, 16.3 lbs. Imported 1984-91.

	$975	$795	$625	$560	$495	$435	$395	*$1,175*

RUNNING BOAR MODEL 500 – similar to KK/MS Silhouette, no sights, thumbhole stock with adj. wood buttplate and cheekpiece, 23.6 in. barrel, 8.4 lbs. Disc. 1990.

	$1,195	$900	$675	$575	$500	$435	$395	*$1,300*

MODEL WA-2000 – .300 Win. Mag. (55 mfg., standard) or .308 Win. (92 mfg., optional) cal., ultra-deluxe semi-auto, 25.6 in. barrel, 5 or 6 shot mag., optional extras include aluminum case, spare mags., integral bipod, adj. tools and leather sling, regular or night vision scope, special order only, 16 3/4 lbs. Disc. 1988.

	$36,000	$32,000	$29,000	$27,000	$25,000	$22,500	$20,000	

A 7.5 Swiss cal. conversion kit was also optional on this model.

RIFLES: CURRENT/RECENT MFG.

HAMMERLI TAC R1 22 C – .22 LR cal., 16.1 in. barrel, removable flash hider, 10, 20, or 30 shot mag., flip-up sights, minimal adj. stock w/QD sling point, ergonomic grip, aluminum upper and lower receiver, 13 in. free float M-LOK handguard, Picatinny rail, black finish, 5.6 lbs. Mfg. in Germany by Umarex beginning mid-2019.

MSR $449	$385	$335	$285	$260	$210	$175	$150	

MODEL G22 SEMI-AUTO – .22 LR cal., bullpup design, 20 in. barrel, 10 shot mag., fire control and mag. integrated in rear of stock, black synthetic, carbon fiber, or camo (disc. 2006) thumbhole stock, adj. sliding sights, right or left-hand controls and ejection, blue or military green finish, Weaver style rails on rear sight/carry handle, lower forearm, and on front right mount, approx. 6 lbs. Mfg. 2004-2011.

	$435	$380	$330	$290	$250	$225	$195	*$509*

Add $39 for scope or $67 for laser or $102 for red-dot sights (disc. 2009).
Add $56 for carbon fiber stock (disc. 2007) or $50 for camo stock (disc. 2006).

GRADING - PPGS™	100%	98%	95%	90%	80%	70%	60%	LAST MSR

MODEL HK G36 – .22 LR cal., semi-auto, copy patterned after the H&K G36, blowback operation, black polymer frame, 18.1 in. barrel with muzzle brake, 20 shot, elevated Picatinny rail with front and adj. rear sights, ambidextrous safety, skeletonized folding stock, 6 3/4 lbs. Mfg. by Walther in Germany. Imported 2015-2018.

$525 $450 $400 $360 $330 $300 $275 *$599*

MODEL KK200 – .22 LR cal., available in standard rifle laminated stock, power match, and sport configurations, top-of-the-line competition model, 19.7 in. barrel, 11.57 lbs. Disc.

$1,995 $1,675 $1,375 $1,050 $850 $725 $600

Add approx. $1,000 for machined KK200 Power Match Model with nickel plated stippled stock and forend, 25 1/2 in. barrel, 13 lbs. (limited mfg. 1995).

Add approx. $500 for KK200 S (sport configuration).

Add $265 for electronic trigger on Power Match or Sport Models.

MODEL KK300 – similar to Model KK200, except has target or adj. aluminum competition stock. Imported 2006-disc.

$2,625 $2,350 $1,900 $1,600 $1,300 $995 $750

Add $1,200 for adj. aluminum competition stock.

MODEL KK CLUB SPORT RIFLE – .22 LR cal. Mfg. 2000-disc.

$525 $450 $400 $350 $275 $260 $230

MODEL GSP RIFLE – .22 LR cal., utilizes GSP sport pistol action, 16 3/4 in. stainless fluted barrel, through engraved compensator, laminated "silhouette style" thumbhole stock, 5 shot standard, 8 or 10 shot optional, optics or scope optional, 8.55 lbs. Imported 1996-2007.

$2,400 $2,100 $1,800 $1,500 $1,250 $1,125 $1,000 *$2,590*

This model was only available from Earl's Repair Service.

SHOTGUNS: SxS

MODEL WSF – 12 or 16 ga., checkered walnut stock, double triggers, boxlock, sling swivels, 28.4 in. barrel. Introduced 1932-disc.

$725 $575 $425 $325 $275 $240 $200

MODEL WSFD – 12 or 16 ga., cheekpiece, checkered walnut stock, double triggers, boxlock, sling swivels, 6.3 (16 ga.) or 6.6 (12 ga.) lbs. Introduced 1932-disc.

$925 $725 $575 $450 $400 $350 $300

SHOTGUNS: SEMI-AUTO

WALTHER SEMI-AUTO – 12 ga. only, 2 3/4 in. chamber, 25 1/2 in. barrel, crossbolt safety, checkered walnut stock and forearm. Mfg. in Zella-Mehlis 1921-1931.

$975 $895 $795 $675 $550 $450 $375

WALTHER, FRENCH-MADE BY MANURHIN

Previously manufactured in Mulhouse, France. Previously imported 1984-86 by Matra-Manurhin International, Inc. located in Alexandria, VA.

PISTOLS: SEMI-AUTO

Manufacture of these Walther PP type pistols commenced in Mulhouse, France in 1951. They were marked "MANURHIN" on the slide until 1954. Since then they were designated Walther MKII. They were imported into the USA by Interarms up to 1983.

In 1984, following a disagreement regarding the use of the Walther trademark, a few pistols were manufactured using the standard Walther slide legend, w/o the "under license of" above the legend. Additionally, the Manurhin name, logo, and the words "Made in France" were stamped on the heel of the gun in very small letters. Following this French production, pistols were made in Germany and marked Walther, or made in France and marked Manurhin. Manurhin briefly set up an office in New York to do its own importation, and later moved to Florida.

In 1984, Manurhin was imported directly with no Interarms logo or Walther trademark appearing on Models PP and PPK/S. Importation was discontinued 1986, when all production resumed in Ulm, Germany.

MODEL PP – .22 LR, .32 ACP, or .380 ACP cal., DA/SA, 3 7/8 in. barrel, 10 shot mag. (.22 LR), 8 shot mag. (.32 ACP), 7 shot mag. (.380 ACP), blue only, all steel construction, positive hammer block safety, 24 oz.

$450 $350 $300 $230 $205 $185 $170 *$419*

Add 20% for .22 LR or .380 ACP cal.

Add $46 for Durgarde finish.

GRADING - PPGS™	100%	98%	95%	90%	80%	70%	60%	LAST MSR

* ***Model PP Collector*** – blue finish, special engraving. Imported 1986 only.

	$465	$415	$350	$285	$250	$215	$185	*$529*

* ***Model PP Presentation*** – blue finish, special ornamentation. Imported 1986 only.

	$720	$650	$500	$430	$375	$315	$270	*$819*

* ***Model PP Interarms Import*** – various engraving options available in either blue, nickel, or gold finish. Prices ranged from $222-$450. Disc.

	$395	$325	$285	$235	$200	$170	$145	

PP SPORT – .22 LR cal. only, DA/SA, 6.1 or 8.1 in. barrel, blue finish only, precision adj. sights, contoured plastic grips with thumbrest, 25 oz. New Manurhin design beginning 1985-disc.

	$750	$650	$550	$450	$350	$300	$250	*$635*

* ***PP Sport-C*** – similar to PP Sport, except is single action. Disc.

	$700	$600	$500	$400	$350	$300	$250	*$635*

MODEL PPK – .22 LR, .32 ACP, or .380 ACP cal., DA/SA, 3 1/4 in. barrel, 7 (.380 ACP), 8 (.32 ACP), or 10 (.22 LR) shot mag., blue only, all steel construction, positive hammer block safety, 23 oz. Disc.

	$550	$475	$425	$375	$350	$325	$300	

Add 20% for .22 LR or .380 ACP cal.

MODEL PPK/S – .22 LR, .32 ACP, or .380 ACP cal., DA/SA, 3 1/4 in. barrel, 7 (.380 ACP), 8 (.32 ACP), or 10 (.22 LR) shot mag., blue only, all steel construction, positive hammer block safety, 23 oz. Disc.

	$400	$350	$300	$230	$205	$185	$170	*$419*

Add 20% for .22 LR cal.

* ***Model PPK/S Durgarde*** – similar to Model PPK/S, only with bonded brushed chrome finish. Disc.

	$450	$400	$350	$300	$275	$250	$240	*$465*

Add 20% for .22 LR cal.

* ***Model PPK/S Collector*** – blue finish, special engraving. Imported 1986 only.

	$465	$415	$350	$300	$275	$250	$225	*$529*

* ***Model PPK/S Presentation*** – blue finish, special ornamentation. Imported 1986 only.

	$720	$650	$500	$430	$375	$315	$270	*$819*

* ***Model PPK/S Interarms Import*** – various engraving options available in either blue, nickel, or gold finish. Prices ranged from $222-$540. Disc.

	$395	$340	$300	$230	$205	$185	$170	

WALTTER

Current trademark of shotguns and air rifles manufactured by Target Silah Sanayi, located in Konya, Turkey. No current U.S. importation.

Target manufactures a complete line of good quality semi-auto, slide action, O/U, single barrel, and SxS shotguns with a variety of receiver finishes and stock options. Currently, this trademark has had little or no U.S. importation. Please contact the company directly for more information, including pricing and domestic availability.

WAMO MFG.

Previous manufacturer located in San Gabriel, CA.

In addition to making air guns, Wamo also manufactured the .22 LR Powermaster pistol, the Hamilton pirate pistol, and the Tommygun. Pistol values are currently in the $150-$350 range, while the Tommygun ranges from $195-$350 (must be original and complete).

WAR SPORT

Previous AR-15 style pistol and rifle manufacturer located in Robbins, NC until 2017. War Sport also manufactured a line of parts and accessories including upper build kits, barrels, muzzle devices, and related small parts.

Please refer to BlueBookOfGunValues.com to order the *Blue Book of AR-15s & Variations*, available as a book or online subscription.

WARNER ARMS CORPORATION

Previous manufacturer located in Norwich, CT.

PISTOLS: SEMI-AUTO

INFALLIBLE POCKET AUTO PISTOL – .32 ACP cal., 7 shot, 3 in. barrel, fixed sights, rubber grips. Mfg. 1917-19.

	$450	$350	$250	$150	$125	$100	$90	

GRADING - PPGS™	100%	98%	95%	90%	80%	70%	60%	LAST MSR

WARRIOR ARMS LLC

Current AR-15 style pistol and rifle manufacturer established during 2011, located in Valparaiso, IN.

Please refer to BlueBookOfGunValues.com to order the *Blue Book of AR-15s & Variations*, available as a book or online subscription.

WARWICK TACTICAL

Current manufacturer of single and double stack competition pistols, located in Landisville, PA.

For individual model listings, please go to BlueBookOfGunValues.com/overflow.

WASATCH PRECISION ARMS

Previous custom bolt action rifle manufacturer located in Ogden, UT until 2011.

RIFLES: BOLT ACTION

Wasatch Precision Arms manufactured custom bolt action rifles based on the Rem. 700 action with synthetic and carbon fiber stocks until 2011. All prices reflect the last manufactured suggested price for 2011. Models included: Wasatch Summit ($3,995), Wasatch Summit Carbon ($3,995), Open Country ($2,295), Open Country Carbon ($2,495), Ridge Top Carbon ($1,895), and the Flat Lander ($1,695).

WATSON BROS.

Current long gun manufacturer established in 1885, located in London, England.

Watson Bros. manufactures distinct round body actions with self-opening locks in both SxS and O/U shotgun configurations. Back action sidelock double rifles are also available. All guns are built to custom order. Please contact the factory directly for more information including current pricing.

WEATHERBY

Current trademark manufactured and imported by Weatherby located in Sheridan, WY, beginning April 2019. Previously located in Paso Robles, CA 2006-early 2019, Atascadero, CA 1995-2006, and in South Gate, CA, 1945-1995. Weatherby has had many rifles and shotguns private labeled from various manufacturers in Europe and Japan. Weatherby began manufacturing select rifles in the U.S. during early 1995. Dealer and distributor sales.

Weatherby is an importer and manufacturer of long arms. Earlier production was from Germany and Italy, and German mfg. is usually what is collectible. Select rifle models are currently produced in the U.S., while O/U shotguns are made in Italy and semi-autos shotguns are mfg. in Turkey.

Weatherby is well-known for their high-velocity proprietary rifle calibers.

Early Weatherby rifles used a Mathieu Arms action in the 1950s - primarily since it was available in left-hand action. Right-handed actions were normally mfg. from the FN Mauser type.

DRILLINGS

WEATHERBY DRILLING – mfg. by J.P. Sauer during the late 1960s-early 1970s for Weatherby importation (marked "Weatherby" on right barrel), identical to Sauer Model 3000, except was not available in all metric cals. Disc.

	100%	98%	95%	90%	80%	70%	60%	LAST MSR
	$2,850	$2,450	$2,100	$1,800	$1,500	$1,250	$1,000	

PISTOLS: BOLT ACTION

SILHOUETTE PISTOL – .22-250 Rem. or .308 Win. cal., mfg. in Japan during late 1970s, 14 1/2 in. barrel, Lyman or Williams sights, fitted case. Only 50 were mfg. in .22-250 Rem. and 150 in .308 Win. cal. Disc. 1981.

	100%	98%	95%	90%	80%	70%	60%	LAST MSR
	$3,750	$3,300	$2,750	$2,450	$2,100	$1,850	$1,650	

MARK V CFP (CENTERFIRE PISTOLS) – .22-250 Rem., .223 Rem. (new 2000), .243 Win., 7mm-08 Rem., or .308 Win. cal., features 15 in. fluted stainless steel barrel with recessed crown, ambidextrous designed multi-layer brown laminate stock with finger grooves and swivel studs, blue Mark V lightweight action, no sights, 3 shot internal mag., 5 1/4 lbs. Mfg. 1997-2000.

	100%	98%	95%	90%	80%	70%	60%	LAST MSR
	$935	$815	$735	$650	$600	$550	$500	*$1,099*

* ***Mark V CFP Accumark*** – same cals. as Mark V CFP, features specially designed synthetic stock with Kevlar and other fibers, matte black finish with grey spider web pattern, 5 lbs. Limited mfg. 2000 only.

	100%	98%	95%	90%	80%	70%	60%	LAST MSR
	$935	$815	$735	$650	$600	$550	$500	*$1,099*

GRADING - PPGS™	100%	98%	95%	90%	80%	70%	60%	LAST MSR

MARK V CFP (COMPACT FIRING PLATFORM) – .22-250 Rem., .223 Rem., .243 Win., or 7mm-08 Rem. cal., 16 in. unfluted matte blue barrel w/o sights, matte blue action, right-hand Mark V one-piece bolt with 54 degree lift, tan Fibermark composite stock with black spider webbing and ambidextrous grip, 5 shot internal mag., Talley rings and bases became standard 2007, 5 1/4 lbs. Mfg. 2006-2010.

	$1,425	$1,150	$875	$750	$625	$525	$475	*$1,689*

RIFLES: RIMFIRE

ACCUMARK CLASSIC & DELUXE BOLT ACTION – while these models were advertised in 1990 ($635 retail), they never went into production.

MARK XXII CLIP MAG OR TUBE FEED SEMI-AUTO – .22 LR cal., mag. feed, skip-line checkered walnut stock with or without rosewood forend and pistol grip cap, clip models have 5 or 10 shot detachable mag., 24 in. barrel, open V rear fold down sight, grooved alloy receiver, all XXIIs had a right side lever that allowed changing from semi-auto to single shot, tube feed model weighs approx. 6 lbs., 10 oz., clip model weighs 5 lbs., 13 oz. Approx. 100,000 mfg. 1964-1988.

Italian/Japanese mfg.	$875	$785	$675	$550	$425	$325	$275	*$454*

Subtract 5% if trigger guard and floorplate is discolored (should be dark black like the receiver NOT turning gray).

Subtract 5% without original sling swivels.

Subtract 5-10% for stocks with knots (usually JC or JT serial number prefix guns).

Add 20% for guns with boxes if box in good condition and with original papers.

These guns were made 1964-1988. There were 81,618 clip fed models made and 28,017 tube fed models made. The first tube feed models were made by Nikko in 1973, and the last tube feed models were made by Howa in 1988. During that period of time, there were more tube feed models than clip fed models manufactured.

During this time, the type and quality of the wood and finish, rosewood spacers, safety, side lever, rear sight, bolt, trigger, floorplate design, magazines, and magazine release were just some of the many changes that occurred during this manufacturing period. Because of these variations and what a given buyer may find desirable, prices could fluctuate approx. 10%-50%, depending on what features have become more desirable today. A slight premium may be asked for U.S. mfg. Weatherby Mark XXII.

A Weatherby Mark XXII 4x50 scope was also marketed with these .22 cal rifles. The scope was made in Japan. It is a 4x28mm and not 4x50mm. The 4x was the magnification power. The 50 was a measure of the relative brightness or light gathering capabilities and not the diameter of the objective lens. If new in original box with papers the value is approx. $275. If used in good condition with original box, the value is approx. $200. If used without box, the value is approx. $75 to $150 (depending upon condition).

This model was originally mfg. in Italy by Beretta 1964-1971 (no letter prefix to the serial numbers). From 1967 to 1971 Beretta added a rosewood forend tip and pistol grip cap to the stock. Next was KTG-Japan 1967-1971 "J" serial number prefix. KTG and Beretta XXIIs were the only ones to have the desirable trigger pull adjustment screw in front of the trigger guard. Target shooters are finding these guns to be excellent "shooters" (especially when using the single shot mode). As a result, there has been an increased interest and price over the past year for the Beretta and KTG made XXIIs. Next was Nikko-Japan 1972-1980 with "N" serial number prefix for the clip model and "T" prefix for the tube feed model. Nikko was the first one to make the tube feed models and the first to have laser checkering, which is desired by some collectors as well as wood spacers between the stock and rosewood and the improved rear sight that folds down. Next was Mossberg USA 1981-1982 with serial number prefix "AC" for clip and "AT" for the tube feed model. About 1,300 were made by Mossberg and prices for 98% condition or better are selling for over $1,000. Next and last was Howa Japan 1984-1988 with serial number prefix "JC" for clip and "JT" for tube. The Weatherby Mark XXII .22 cal. semi-auto or single shot rifle was marketed for a stylish appearance and most buyers took good care of these guns and as a result, it is common to find these guns in 95% condition or better. In recent years, there has been a wide difference between the "advertised prices" and the "actual selling prices". More sellers are realizing how to price the gun to sell based on which features are more desirable.

MARK XXII BOLT ACTION – .17 HMR or .22 LR cal., features Anschutz action/barrel, 23 in. target grade barrel w/o sights, blue finish, deluxe checkered gloss finished Monte Carlo full pistol grip stock and forearm with rosewood caps, target type bolt handle with special cam cocking, 4 or 5 shot mag., adj. single stage trigger, supplied w/test target, approx. 6 1/2 lbs. Mfg. 2007-2011.

	$1,400	$1,300	$1,100	$895	$695	$495	$325	*$999*

Add $200 for .17 HMR cal.

Add $100-$200 for new in box (as came from factory).

Add $100-$200 if over 50% figuring. Standard was 25% figuring on one side of buttstock.

GRADING - PPGS™	100%	98%	95%	90%	80%	70%	60%	LAST MSR

RIFLES: BOLT ACTION, CUSTOM SHOP

CHRIS KYLE LIMITED EDITION – .300 Win. Mag. cal., button rifled free floated fluted stainless steel barrel with recessed target crown, fully adj. trigger, hand laminated raised comb Monte Carlo composite stock with Kryptek Highlander camo pattern, FDE Cerakote metal finish, Chris Kyle Frog logo laser etched on floorplate, Pachmayr Decelerator pad, swivel studs and a special edition CD are also included. Mfg. 2014 only.

$3,400	$3,150	$2,800	$2,500	$2,250	$2,000	$1,750	*$3,400*

Special limited edition commemorative rifles numbered 1 through 26 in honor of Navy Seal Chief Chris Kyle, the most lethal sniper in American military history, who died in Feb. 2013. Weatherby donated a portion of the proceeds to Chris Kyle's family.

CROWN CUSTOM MODEL – .257 Wby. Mag., .270 Wby. Mag., .300 Wby. Mag., .340 Wby. Mag., or 7mm Wby. Mag. cal., custom order only, engraved barrel, receiver, and scope mount, top-of-the-line model. Disc. 2010.

$8,250	$7,225	$6,200	$5,625	$4,550	$3,725	$2,900	*$9,699*

CUSTOM GRADE – various cals. from .240 Wby. Mag. to .340 Wby. Mag., 24 or 26 in. barrel, super fancy walnut stock featuring No. 7 style inlays, floorplate is engraved "Weatherby Custom", 6-8 months delivery time. Disc. 2001.

$4,250	$3,720	$3,190	$2,890	$2,340	$1,915	$1,490	*$5,099*

OUTFITTER CUSTOM – various cals. between .243 Win.-.338-06 A-Square (disc.), ultra lightweight bolt action, 5 shot mag., 24 or 26 in. stainless steel fluted barrel with titanium nitride hardcoating (disc.) or black Teflon coating, raised comb, Monte Carlo composite Kevlar stock in Desert Camo, 5 3/4 lbs. Mfg. 2001-Disc.

$2,650	$2,050	$1,725	$1,500	$1,250	$1,050	$850	*$3,000*

OUTFITTER KREIGER CUSTOM – same cals. as Outfitter Custom, ultra lightweight action, 24 or 26 in. Kreiger ultra lightweight contoured barrel with cut rifling, trued receiver and bolt face, lapped locking lugs, titanium nitride coating, desert camo stock. Mfg. 2001-2002.

$2,995	$2,620	$2,245	$2,035	$1,645	$1,350	$1,050	*$3,499*

Add $50 for Mag. cals.

TRCM (THREAT RESPONSE CUSTOM MAGNUM) – .300 Win. Mag., .300 Wby. Mag., .30-378 Wby. Mag., or .338-.378 Wby. Mag. cal., Mark V action with ergonomic, fully adjustable composite stock, black finished metal, various barrel lengths, optional Picatinny style ring and base system. Mfg. 2002-2009.

$2,325	$2,035	$1,745	$1,580	$1,280	$1,045	$815	*$2,899*

Add $270 for .30-378 Wby. Mag. or .338-378 Wby. Mag. cals.
Add $499 for desert camo stock and titanium nitride coating.

RIFLES: BOLT ACTION, MARK V SERIES

Pre-Mark V production started in 1945 and ended in 1961. Initially, rifles were customized from customer supplied guns, and this ended circa 1949. Between 1949-1963, Weatherby manufactured rifles in Southgate from FN Mauser actions in various cals., including the .257, .270, 7mm, .300, and .375 Wby. Mag. cals. From 1955-1959, Southgate also manufactured guns using the Mathieu left-hand action. Additionally, Schultz & Larson from Denmark was subcontracted to make rifles in .378 Wby. Mag. circa 1955-1962. Between 1956-1962, Southgate manufactured a .460 Wby. Mag. cal. using the Brevex Magnum action. Sako of Finland was also subcontracted circa 1957-1961 to produce rifles using a FN Mauser action. Initial Mark V production began in Southgate circa 1958-1959. During 1959-1973, J.P. Sauer of W. Germany was subcontracted to make the Mark V in a variety of calibers up to .460 Wby. Mag. These earlier pre-Mark V rifles will have a 20%-30% premium, depending on original condition and caliber.

In 1992, 24 in. barrels were disc. on most calibers of .300 or greater (including Models Mark V Deluxe, Fibermark, Lazermark, and Euromark). The Mark V action has also been manufactured in Japan.

All recently manufactured Weatherby Magnums in .30-378, .338-378, .378, .416, and .460 cal. are equipped with an Accubrake.

In 2016, Weatherby made significant refinements to the Mark V rifle for the first time since its introduction in 1958. These changes include ergonomically enhanced stock with a slimmer forearm and more distinct lines and contours, a right-hand palm swell was added, and the overall weight was reduced. These new features also include the LXX™ trigger (precision ground/polished and wider trigger face), hand-lapped barrels, and a SUB-MOA accuracy guarantee.

MARK V ACCUMARK (MAG. CALS.) – .240 Wby. Mag., .257 Wby. Mag., .270 Wby. Mag., .300 Win. Mag., .300 Wby. Mag., .30-378 Wby. Mag. (new 1997), .338-378 Wby. Mag. (new 1998), 7mm STW (mfg. 1998-2004), 6.5-300 Wby. Mag. (new 2016), 7mm Rem. Mag., 7mm Wby. Mag., .338 Lapua Mag. (new 2012) or .340 Wby. Mag. cal., LXX™ trigger (new 2016), Bell & Carlson hand laminated fiberglass

GRADING - PPGS™	100%	98%	95%	90%	80%	70%	60%	LAST MSR

(disc.) or raised comb Monte Carlo composite stock with matte gel coat finish and spiderweb accents, right side palm swell (new 2016), Pachmayr Decelerator pad, 2 or 3 shot mag., 24, 26, or 28 (.30-378 or .338-378 Wby. Mag. cals. only) in. stainless steel fluted barrel, aluminum bedding plate, fully adj. trigger, approx. 8 3/4 lbs. Mfg. 1996-2018.

	$1,950	$1,700	$1,465	$1,325	$1,075	$885	$750	*$2,300*

Add $300 for .338 Lapua Mag. (new 2012), .30-378 Wby. Mag., or .338-378 Wby. Mag. cals. with Accubrake barrel.

Add $100 for left-hand action (.257 Wby., 6.5-300 Wby. Mag., .300 Wby. Mag., or .30-378 Wby. Mag. cals. only, other cals. available 1999-2004, reintroduced 2006).

* ***Mark V Accumark (Reg. Cals.)*** – .22-250 Rem. (disc.), .223 Rem. (mfg. 2000-2004), .243 Win. (disc. 2011), .25-06 Rem. (disc. 2010), .270 Win., .280 Rem. (disc.), 7mm-08 Rem. (disc.), .30-06 (disc. 2009, reintroduced 2013), 6.5 Creedmoor (new 2017), or .308 Win. cal., 5 shot mag., hand laminated fiberglass stock (disc.) or raised comb Monte Carlo composite stock with matte gel coat finish and spiderweb accents, right side palm swell (new 2016), LXX™ trigger (new 2016), Pachmayr Decelerator pad, 24 in. fluted stainless barrel w/o sights, 7 1/4 lbs. Mfg. 1998-2004, reintroduced 2007-2018.

	$1,950	$1,700	$1,465	$1,325	$1,075	$885	$750	*$2,300*

MARK V ACCUMARK (CURRENT MFG.) – .240 Wby. Mag., .257 Wby. Mag., .270 Wby. Mag., .300 Win. Mag., .300 Wby. Mag., .30-378 Wby. Mag., .338-378 Wby. Mag., .340 Wby. Mag., 6.5 Creedmoor, 6.5 Wby. RPM, 6.5-300 Wby. Mag., 7mm Rem. Mag. (disc. 2020), 7mm Wby. Mag., or .338 Lapua Mag. cal., 24 or 26 in. #3 contour two-tone fluted barrel, 3 or 4 shot mag., TriggerTech Mark V trigger, hand-laid, raised Monte Carlo fiberglass stock w/matte gel coat and spiderweb accents, safety and extended bolt knob, Graphite Black Cerakote and stainless finish, some cals. available in left-hand action, 7.3 (standard action) or 8.3 (mag. action) lbs. New late 2019.

MSR $1,999	$1,700	$1,490	$1,275	$1,150	$935	$775	$650	

Add $100 for left-hand action in .257 Wby. Mag., .300 Wby. Mag., or 6.5-300 Wby. Mag.

Add $200 for .338 Lapua Mag., .30-378 Wby. Mag., or .338-378 Wby. Mag cals.

* ***Mark V Accumark Limited*** – .257 Wby. Mag., .300 Wby. Mag., 6.5 Creedmoor, 6.5 Wby. RPM, or 6.5-300 Wby. Mag. cal., 6 or 9-lug Mark V receiver in FDE Cerakote finish, 24 or 26 in. #3 contour spiral fluted barrel, Accubrake ST, 3 or 4 shot mag., TriggerTech Mark V trigger, hand-laid, raised Monte Carlo fiberglass stock w/ matte gel coat and aluminum bedding blocks, safety and extended bolt knob in Graphite Black, spiral fluted bolt, Graphite Black/FDE Cerakote finish. New 2021.

MSR $2,400	$2,050	$1,800	$1,550	$1,400	$1,100	$900	$700	

MARK V ACCUMARK ELITE – .240 Wby. Mag., .257 Wby. Mag., .270 Wby. Mag., .300 Win. Mag., .300 Wby. Mag., .30-378 Wby. Mag., .338-378 Wby. Mag., .340 Wby. Mag., 6.5 Creedmoor, 6.5 Wby. RPM, 6.5-300 Wby. Mag., 7mm Rem. Mag. (disc. 2020), 7mm Wby. Mag., or .338 Lapua Mag. cal., 24 or 26 in. #3 contour fluted barrel, 3 or 4 shot mag., TriggerTech Mark V trigger, Monte Carlo fiberglass or carbon fiber stock w/ brown sponge pattern accents, adj. comb, safety and extended bolt knob, spiral fluted bolt, Coyote Tan and Graphite Black Elite Cerakote finish, some cals. available in left-hand action, 7.6 lbs. New late 2019.

MSR $2,799	$2,385	$2,085	$1,785	$1,625	$1,325	$1,125	$925	

Add $100 for left-hand action in .257 Wby. Mag., .300 Wby. Mag., or 6.5-300 Wby. Mag.

Add $200 for .338 Lapua Mag., .30-378 Wby. Mag., or .338-378 Wby. Mag cals.

MARK V ACCUMARK PRO – .240 Wby. Mag., .257 Wby. Mag., .270 Wby. Mag., .300 Win. Mag., .300 Wby. Mag., .30-378 Wby. Mag., .338-378 Wby. Mag., .340 Wby. Mag., 6.5 Creedmoor, 6.5 Wby. RPM, 6.5-300 Wby. Mag., 7mm Rem. Mag. (disc. 2020), 7mm Wby. Mag., or .338 Lapua Mag. cal., 24 or 26 in. #3 contour fluted barrel, 3 or 4 shot mag., TriggerTech Mark V trigger, visible carbon fiber stock w/gray sponge pattern accents, adj. comb, safety and extended bolt knob, Graphite Black and Tungsten Cerakote finish, some cals. available in left-hand action, 7.1 (standard action) or 7.9 (mag. action) lbs. New late 2019.

MSR $2,499	$2,125	$1,850	$1,600	$1,450	$1,175	$950	$825	

Add $100 for left-hand action in .257 Wby. Mag., .300 Wby. Mag., or 6.5-300 Wby. Mag.

Add $200 for .338 Lapua Mag., .30-378 Wby. Mag., or .338-378 Wby. Mag cals.

MARK V ACCUMARK RC (MAG. CALS.) – .240 Wby. Mag., .257 Wby. Mag., .270 Wby. Mag., .300 Win. Mag., .300 Wby. Mag., .340 Wby. Mag. (disc. 2016), .338 Lapua Mag., .30-378 Wby. Mag., .338-378 Wby. Mag., 7mm Wby. Mag., 6.5-300 Wby. Mag. (new 2016), or 7mm Rem. Mag. (disc. 2016) cal., 2, 3, or 5 (.240 Wby. Mag. only) shot mag., 24, 26, or 28 in. free floating stainless steel fluted barrel, LXX™ trigger (new 2016), hand laminated raised comb Monte Carlo composite stock with matte gel coat finish and spiderweb accents, right side palm swell (new 2016), Pachmayr Decelerator pad, fully adj. trigger, special RC engraved floorplate, range certified with guaranteed sub-MOA accuracy, 7 1/4-8 1/4 lbs. Mfg. 2013-disc.

	$2,385	$2,085	$1,785	$1,625	$1,325	$1,125	$925	*$2,800*

Add $300 for .30-378 Wby. Mag., .338-378 Wby. Mag., or .338 Lapua Mag. cals. with Accubrake.

GRADING - PPGS™	100%	98%	95%	90%	80%	70%	60%	LAST MSR

MARK V ACCUMARK RC (REG. CALS.) – .270 Win. (disc. 2016), .30-06 (disc. 2016), .308 Win. (disc. 2016), or 6.5 Creedmoor (new 2017) cal., 5 shot mag., 24 in. free floating stainless steel fluted barrel, hand laminated raised comb Monte Carlo composite stock with matte gel coat finish and spiderweb accents, Pachmayr Decelerator pad, fully adj. trigger, Special RC engraved floorplate, 7 1/4 lbs. Mfg. 2013-disc.

	$2,385	$2,085	$1,785	$1,625	$1,325	$1,125	$925	*$2,800*

MARK V ALTITUDE/ALTITUDE RC – .240 Wby. Mag., .257 Wby. Mag., 6.5 Creedmoor, 6.5-300 Wby. Mag., .270 Win., .270 Wby. Mag., 7mm Wby. Mag. (mfg. 2018 only), .308 Win., .30-06, or .300 Wby. Mag. cal., 22, 24, 26, or 28 in. stainless steel fluted barrel with recessed target crown, 3, 4, or 5 shot mag., Kryptek Altitude camo carbon fiber hand laminated raised comb Monte Carlo composite stock with full-length aluminum bedding block, right side palm swell, Pachmayr Decelerator recoil pad, Tungsten Cerakote finish, 5.75-6.75 lbs. Mfg. 2018-2019.

	$2,295	$2,025	$1,725	$1,575	$1,275	$1,050	$875	*$2,700*

Add $200 for 6.5-300 Wby. Mag. or .300 Wby. Mag. cal.
Add $500 for Altitude RC model.

RC model is range certified with guaranteed sub-MOA accuracy and includes a printout from Oehler Ballistic Imaging System, signed and certified by Adam Weatherby.

MARK V ARROYO/ARROYO RC – 15 cals. available between .240 Wby. Mag.-.340 Wby. Mag., 24, 26, or 28 in. stainless fluted barrel w/o sights, Accubrake available on some cals., 2-5 shot non-detachable mag., LXX™ trigger (new 2016), hand-laminated raised comb Monte Carlo composite stock with full-length aluminum bedding block, right side palm swell (new 2016), and KUIU® Cias camo, two-tone Cerakote finish with Desert Sand and FDE added flutes, RC models include certified sub-MOA accuracy, RC engraved floorplate, and signed and certified by Ed or Adam Weatherby, 7 1/4-8 1/4 lbs. Mfg. by the Custom Shop 2015-2018.

	$2,385	$2,085	$1,785	$1,625	$1,325	$1,125	$925	*$2,800*

Add $200 for Accubrake.
Add $200 for .338 LM, .30-378 Wby. Mag., or .338-378 Wby Mag. cal.
Add $500 for Mark V Arroyo RC model.

MARK V BACKCOUNTRY – .240 Wby. Mag., .257 Wby. Mag., .270 Wby. Mag., 6mm Creedmoor, 6.5 Wby. RPM, 6.5-300 Wby. Mag., 6.5 Creedmoor, 7mm Wby. Mag., .270 Win., .280 Ackley, or .300 Wby. Mag. cal., 24 or 26 in. fluted barrel, 3 or 5 shot mag., TriggerTech trigger, carbon fiber stock, 3D HEX recoil reducer, Accubrake ST, 6-lug receiver, Cerakote finish, left-hand action available, approx. 5 1/2-6 lbs. New 2019.

MSR $2,499	$2,125	$1,850	$1,600	$1,450	$1,175	$950	$825	

Add $100 for left-hand action.

* ***Mark V Backcountry Ti*** – .240 Wby. Mag., .257 Wby. Mag., .270 Wby. Mag. (new 2020), 6mm Creedmoor, 6.5 Wby. RPM, 6.5-.300 Wby. Mag., 6.5 Creedmoor, 7mm Wby. Mag., .270 Win., .280 Ackley, or .300 Wby. Mag. cal., 24 or 26 in. fluted barrel, muzzle brake, 3 or 5 shot mag., TriggerTech trigger, carbon fiber stock, 3D HEX recoil reducer, Accubrake ST, Titanium receiver, KUIU Verde 2.0 or Gray Sponge Cerakote finish, left-hand action available, approx. 6.1 lbs. New 2019.

MSR $3,349	$2,850	$2,500	$2,150	$1,950	$1,575	$1,285	$1,100	

Add $100 for left-hand action.

MARK V CAMILLA DELUXE – .240 Wby. Mag., .243 Win. (new 2020), .270 Win. (disc. 2019), .280 Ackley Imp. (new 2020), 6.5 Creedmoor, .308 Win. (disc. 2019), .30-06 (disc. 2019), 6.5 Wby. RPM (new 2020), or 6mm Creedmoor (new 2020) cal., 6-lug Mark V action, 24 in. hand-lapped barrel, fluted bolt body, LXX trigger, AA fancy grade claro walnut Monte Carlo stock with right side palm swell, fineline diamond point Fleur-de-lis checkering, exotic hardwood forend and grip cap with maplewood spacers, Pachmayr Decelerator recoil pad, stock designed to properly fit a woman's body, blued metalwork in high lustre finish, 6 1/2 lbs. New 2018.

MSR $2,399	$2,050	$1,800	$1,550	$1,400	$1,150	$900	$700	

MARK V CAMILLA SUBALPINE – .240 Wby. Mag., .270 Win., 6.5 Creedmoor, .308 Win., or .30-06 cal., 22 or 24 in. chrome moly barrel with field crown and FDE Cerakote finish, hand-laminated raised comb Monte Carlo composite stock, shorter, slimmer forearm and grip with right-side palm swell, Pachmayr Decelerator recoil pad, 13 in. LOP, LXX trigger, aluminum bedding block, fluted bolt body, integral recoil lug, cocking indicator, Gore Optifade Subalpine camo finish, 5 3/4 lbs. Mfg. mid-2018-2019.

	$2,295	$2,025	$1,725	$1,575	$1,275	$1,050	$875	*$2,700*

This model was specifically designed to fit a woman's body.

GRADING - PPGS™	100%	98%	95%	90%	80%	70%	60%	LAST MSR

MARK V CAMILLA ULTRA LIGHTWEIGHT – .240 Wby. Mag., .243 Win. (new 2020), .270 Win. Mag. (mfg. 2019 only), .280 Ackley (new 2020).30-06 (mfg. 2019 only), .308 Win. Mag. (mfg. 2019 only), 6.5 Creedmoor, 6.5 Wby. RPM (new 2020), or 6mm Creedmoor (new 2020) cal., standard 6-Lug action, 22 or 24 in. fluted stainless steel barrel, 3, 4, or 5 shot mag., LXX trigger, raised comb Monte Carlo composite stock in Forest Green with black gel coat webbing, slender forearm, Pachmayr Decelerator recoil pad, 13 in. LOP, full length aluminum bedding block, integral recoil lug, cocking indicator, 5.75 lbs. New 2019.

MSR $1,999	$1,700	$1,490	$1,275	$1,150	$935	$775	$650

MARK V CARBONMARK – .257 Wby. Mag, .300 Wby. Mag., 6.5 Creedmoor, 6.5 WBY RPM, or 6.5-300 WBY Mag. cal., right or left-hand action, 26 in. Proof Research carbon fiber barrel, stainless steel core in #4 contour, threaded muzzle with flush thread cap, 3 shot mag., Triggertech trigger, black hand-laid raised Monte Carlo fiberglass stock with gray and tan sponge pattern, FDE and Graphite Black Cerakote finish, 7 3/4 lbs. New mid-2018.

MSR $2,499	$2,125	$1,850	$1,600	$1,450	$1,175	$950	$825

Add $100 for left-hand action.

MARK V CARBONMARK ELITE – .257 Wby. Mag., .300 Wby. Mag., 6.5 Creedmoor, 6.5 Wby. RPM, or 6.5-300 Wby. Mag. cal., 26 or 28 in. #4 contour 416R stainless steel threaded barrel roll-wrapped with a carbon fiber sleeve, Accubrake, 3 shot mag., TriggerTech trigger, carbon fiber stock with brown sponge pattern and adj. comb, 13.625 in. LOP, dual swivel stud attachments, extended bolt knob, right or left-hand action, Coyote Tan and Graphite Black Cerakote finish, 8.4 lbs. New late 2019.

MSR $3,299	$2,800	$2,450	$2,100	$1,900	$1,540	$1,275	$1,000

Add $100 for left-hand action.

MARK V CARBONMARK PRO – .257 Wby. Mag., .300 Wby. Mag., 6.5 Creedmoor, 6.5 Wby. Mag., 6.5 Wby. RPM, or 6.5-.300 Wby. Mag. cal., 24 or 26 in. #4 contour 416R stainless steel threaded barrel roll-wrapped with a carbon fiber sleeve, Accubrake, 4 shot mag., TriggerTech trigger, charcoal finish carbon fiber stock, dual swivel stud attachments, right or left-hand action, Tungsten and Graphite Black Cerakote finish, 6.7 lbs. New late 2019.

MSR $2,999	$2,550	$2,250	$1,900	$1,750	$1,400	$1,150	$900

Add $100 for left-hand action.

MARK V COWPOKE EDITION – .257 Wby. Mag., .30-378 Wby. Mag., .300 Wby. Mag., 6.5 Wby. RPM, or 6.5-300 Wby. Mag. cal., brown receiver, 24 in. #3 fluted contour two-toned barrel, Accubrake ST, TriggerTech trigger, hand-laid fiberglass, raised comb Monte Carlo stock, built on 6 and 9-lug, gold bolt knob, brown base w/gold and white sponge pattern Cerakote finish. New 2020.

MSR $2,500	$2,125	$1,850	$1,600	$1,450	$1,175	$950	$825

MARK V DGR (DANGEROUS GAME RIFLE) CUSTOM – .300 Win. Mag. (mfg. 2002-2004, reintroduced 2013-2015), .300 Wby. Mag. (new 2002), .338 Win. Mag. (mfg. 2002-2004, reintroduced 2013-2015), .340 Wby. Mag. (new 2002), .375 H&H, .375 Wby. Mag., .378 Wby. Mag., .416 Rem. Mag. (disc. 2015), .416 Wby. Mag., .458 Win. Mag. (disc. 2015), .458 Lott (mfg. 2005-2015), or .460 Wby. Mag. cal., 24 or 26 in. button rifled chrome moly barrel with express sights (rear is adj.), recessed target crown, barrel band with swivel stud (new 2016), LXX™ (new 2016-2018) or TriggerTech (new 2019) trigger, black fiberglass stock (disc.) with CNC machined aluminum bedding block and Pachmayr Decelerator pad (disc.) or Monte Carlo tan stock with black spiderweb accents, black oxide metal finish, 8 3/4 or 9 1/2 (.460 Wby. Mag.) lbs. New 2001.

MSR $3,200	$2,725	$2,385	$2,050	$1,855	$1,500	$1,225	$1,050

Add $300 for .460 Wby. Mag. with Accubrake.
Add $200 for .375 H&H, .375 Wby. Mag., .378 Wby. Mag., or .416 Wby. Mag.
Add $399 for snow or desert camo stock with titanium nitride coating (disc.).

MARK V DELUXE – .22-250 Rem. (mfg. 1999-2004), .240 Wby. Mag. (disc. 1996, reintroduced 1999-2004, 2007-2011), .243 Win. (mfg. 1999-2004, reintroduced 2007-2011), .25-06 Rem. (mfg. 1999-2004), .257 Wby. Mag., .270 Win. (mfg. 1999-2004, reintroduced 2007-2011), .270 Wby. Mag., .280 Rem. (mfg. 1999-2004), 7mm Wby. Mag., 7mm-08 Rem. (mfg. 1999-2004, reintroduced 2007), .30-06 (disc. 1996, reintroduced 1999-2004, again beginning 2007), .308 Win. (mfg. 1999-2004, reintroduced 2007), .300 Wby. Mag., .340 Wby. Mag., .375 H&H (mfg. 1993 only), .378 Wby. Mag., .416 Wby. Mag., or .460 Wby. Mag. cal., bolt action, 3-5 shot mag., 24 (short action cals.) or 26 (Wby. Mag. cals) in. barrel, current mfg. has 9 locking lugs (Mag. cals.) or 6 locking lugs (standard cals. and .240 Wby. Mag.), LXX™ trigger (new 2016), deluxe skip line checkered (disc.) or fineline checkered pistol grip walnut stock with rosewood tipped forearm and pistol grip (disc. 2015), new for 2016 is an ergonomically designed "AA" fancy grade Claro walnut Monte Carlo stock with right side palm swell, fineline diamond point checkering, and rosewood forend and grip cap with maplewood spacers, current production includes Pachmayr Decelerator pad, no sights, 8 lbs. Left-hand actions (.270 Wby. Mag. and .300 Wby. Mag.) were available at no extra charge through 1997. Mfg. began 1957.

Add 15%-25% for German manufacture (J.P. Sauer) in calibers under .35 if condition is 95% or better.

GRADING - PPGS™	100%	98%	95%	90%	80%	70%	60%	LAST MSR

* ***Mark V Deluxe Short Action Cals.*** – .22-250 Rem. (disc.), .243 Win. (disc. 2011), .25-06 Rem. (disc.), .270 Win., .240 Wby. (disc. 2010, reintroduced 2013), .280 Rem. (disc.), .30-06, .308 Win., or 7mm-08 Rem. (disc. 2010) short action cals. Mfg. 1999-2004, reintroduced 2007-2019.

	$2,295	$2,025	$1,725	$1,575	$1,275	$1,050	$875	*$2,700*

* ***Mark V Deluxe Wby. Mag. Cals.*** – .240 Wby. Mag. (new 2020), .257 Wby. Mag., 6.5-300 Wby. Mag., .270 Wby. Mag., .300 Wby. Mag., 7mm Wby. Mag., .340 Wby. Mag., 6.5 Wby. RPM (new 2020), or .375 H&H (disc. 1993) cal., 8 1/2 lbs.

MSR $2,349	$1,995	$1,750	$1,500	$1,350	$1,095	$900	$775	

Add approx. $200 for .375 H&H cal. (disc. 1993).

* ***Mark V Deluxe .30-378 or .378 Wby. Mag. Cals.*** – .30-378 Wby. Mag. (mfg. 2006), .378 Wby. Mag. cal., 26 (disc.) or 28 (with muzzle brake) in. barrel, 8 1/2 lbs.

MSR $2,699	$2,295	$2,025	$1,725	$1,575	$1,275	$1,050	$875	

* ***Mark V Deluxe .416 Wby. Mag. Cal.*** – first new caliber (introduced 1989) since the .240 Wby. Mag. was released 1965, 26 (disc.) or 28 in. barrel, includes muzzle brake, 9 lbs.

MSR $2,699	$2,295	$2,025	$1,725	$1,575	$1,275	$1,050	$875	

* ***Mark V Deluxe .460 Wby. Mag. Cal.*** – .460 Wby. Mag. cal., 24 (disc.), 26 (disc.), or 28 (new 2004) in. barrel, includes custom stock, integral muzzle brake, gloss AA French walnut stock with right-hand palm swell, Pachmayr Decelerator recoil pad, 10 lbs.

MSR $2,699	$2,295	$2,025	$1,725	$1,575	$1,275	$1,050	$875	

This model is available in left-hand at no extra charge. All .460 Wby. Mag. cal. rifles are manufactured in the Custom Shop and the floorplate is engraved with "WEATHERBY CUSTOM" in a banner.

MARK V FIRST LITE/FIRST LITE RC – .257 Wby. Mag., 6.5 Creedmoor, 6.5-.300 Wby. Mag., .270 Wby. Mag., or .300 Wby. Mag. cal., Magnum 9-Lug or Standard 6-Lug action, 24 or 26 in. #3 contour fluted barrel, recessed target crown, 3 or 4 shot mag., LXX trigger, raised comb Monte Carlo composite stock, slim forearm, slight right-hand palm swell, Pachmayr Decelerator recoil pad, First Lite Fusion camo finish, fluted bolt body, integral recoil lug, cocking indicator, aluminum bedding block, FDE Cerakote metal finish, 7 1/4-8 1/4 lbs. Mfg. 2019 only.

	$2,200	$1,925	$1,650	$1,495	$1,210	$1,000	$850	*$2,600*

Add $500 for First Lite RC model.

RC model is range certified with guaranteed sub-MOA accuracy and includes a printout from Oehler Ballistic Imaging System, signed and certified by Adam Weatherby.

MARK V KCR/KCR RC (KRIEGER CUSTOM RIFLE) – .257 Wby. Mag., 6.5-300 Wby. Mag., .300 Wby. Mag., or .30-378 Wby. Mag. cal., 28 in. Krieger Custom match grade hand-lapped free floated fluted barrel with recessed target crown, hand-laminated raised comb Monte Carlo composite stock with full-length aluminum bedding block, matte gel coat finish and right side palm swell, Pachmayr Decelerator recoil pad, Accubrake, KCR engraved floorplate, oversized bolt knob, FDE and Graphite Black Cerakote finish, 8 1/2 lbs. Mfg. 2018-2019.

	$3,050	$2,680	$2,300	$2,080	$1,685	$1,400	$1,200	*$3,600*

Add $500 for KCR RC model.

RC model is range certified with guaranteed sub-MOA accuracy and includes a printout from Oehler Ballistic Imaging System, signed and certified by Adam Weatherby.

MARK V LAZERMARK – .257 Wby. Mag., .270 Wby. Mag., 7mm Wby. Mag. (disc. 2016), .300 Wby. Mag., 6.5-300 Wby. Mag. (new 2019), or .340 Wby. Mag. (disc. 2016) cal., 3 shot mag., 24 (disc.) or 26 in. barrel, LXX trigger (new 2016), raised comb Monte Carlo stock with laser carved oak leaf pattern and right side palm swell (new 2016), maplewood spacers and rosewood forend and grip cap, Pachmayr Decelerator pad, high lustre finish, 8 1/2 lbs. Mfg. 1985-2019.

	$2,385	$2,085	$1,785	$1,625	$1,325	$1,125	$925	*$2,800*

* ***Mark V Lazermark .378 Wby. Mag. or .416 Wby. Mag. Cals.*** – first new caliber (introduced 1989) since the .240 Mag. was released 1965, includes muzzle brake. Disc. 2002.

	$1,850	$1,620	$1,390	$1,260	$1,020	$835	$650	*$2,266*

* ***Mark V Lazermark .460 Wby. Mag. Cal.*** – 24 (disc. 2000), 26 (disc. 2000), or 28 in. barrel, includes custom stock, internal muzzle brake, no extra charge for left-hand. Disc. 2002.

	$2,150	$1,880	$1,615	$1,460	$1,185	$970	$755	*$2,661*

* ***Mark V Lazermark Varmintmaster*** – .22-250 Rem. or .224 Varmintmaster cal., 24 or 26 in. barrel. Disc. 1991.

	$1,085	$950	$815	$740	$595	$490	$380	*$675*

Add $25 for 26 in. barrel.

Not available in left-hand action.

GRADING - PPGS™ 100% 98% 95% 90% 80% 70% 60% LAST MSR

MARK V OUTFITTER/OUTFITTER RC – .240 Wby. Mag., .257 Wby. Mag., 6.5 Creedmoor, 6.5-300 Wby. Mag. (new 2016), .270 Win., .270 Wby. Mag., 7mm Wby. Mag., .308 Win., .30-06, or .300 Wby. Mag. cal., 22, 24, 26, or 28 (new 2016) in. stainless fluted barrel w/o sights, Accubrake available on some cals., 2-5 shot non-detachable mag., fully adj. trigger (disc. 2015) or LXX™ trigger (new 2015), hand-laminated raised comb Monte Carlo carbon fiber stock with aluminum bedding plate, right-hand palm swell (new 2016), and matte gel coat finish in High Desert camo (with spiderweb accents), Armor Black (disc.) or FDE (new 2018) Cerakote finish on metalwork, RC models are range certified with guaranteed sub-MOA accuracy, include an engraved floorplate, and are signed and certified by Ed or Adam Weatherby, 5 1/2-6 3/4 lbs. Mfg. by the Custom Shop 2015-2016.

$2,385 $2,085 $1,785 $1,625 $1,325 $1,125 $925 *$2,800*

Add $200 for 6.5-300 Wby. Mag. (new 2016) or .300 Wby. Mag. cal.
Add $500 for Mark V Outfitter RC model.

MARK V ROYAL ULTRAMARK CUSTOM – .257 Wby. Mag., .270 Wby. Mag., .300 Wby. Mag., .340 Wby. Mag., or 7mm Wby. Mag. cal., 26 in. barrel, LXX™ trigger (new 2016), features high grade fancy American Claro checkered walnut stock with rosewood pistol grip cap and forend, damascened bolt and follower, engraved receiver and floorplate, select 24Kt. gold and nickel plating, custom order only, 8 lbs. Mfg. by the Custom Shop 2002-2016.

$5,100 $4,400 $3,750 $3,200 $2,550 $2,100 $1,675 *$5,800*

MARK V SAFARI GRADE CUSTOM – .257 Wby. Mag. (new 2000), .270 Wby. Mag. (new 2000), .300 Wby. Mag., .340 Wby. Mag., .375 H&H (new 2000), .375 Wby. Mag. (disc. 2006, reintroduced 2014), .378 Wby. Mag., .416 Wby Mag., .416 Rem. Mag. (mfg. 2007-2015), .458 Lott (mfg. 2007-2015), .458 Win. Mag. (disc. 2015), .460 Wby. Mag., or 7mm Wby. Mag. (mfg. 2000-2012, 2015) cal., 2 shot mag., 24, 26, or 28 in. barrel, LXX™ trigger (new 2016), fancy French walnut Monte Carlo stock with satin oil finish, ebony forend and pistol grip cap with fleur-de-lis checkering, damascened bolt and follower with engraved floorplate "Safari Custom", adj. express ramp rear and hooded front sights, 8 3/4 lbs. 6-8 month delivery. Mfg. by the Custom Shop until 2019.

$5,875 $5,125 $4,400 $3,995 $3,225 $2,650 $2,300 *$6,900*

Add $300 for .378 Wby. Mag. and .416 Wby. Mag. with Accubrake.
Add $400 for .460 Wby. Mag. with Accubrake.

Left-hand action became available during 2013 at no extra charge.

MARK V SLS (STAINLESS LAMINATE SPORTER) – .257 Wby. Mag., .270 Wby. Mag., .300 Wby. Mag., .300 Win. Mag., .338 Win. Mag., .340 Wby. Mag., 7mm Wby. Mag., or 7mm Rem. Mag. cal., 24 or 26 (Wby. Mag. cals. only) in. barrel, features grey laminate stock with recoil pad, stainless steel with matte blue finish, approx. 8 1/2 lbs. Mfg. 1997-2002.

$1,125 $985 $845 $765 $620 $505 $395 *$1,393*

MARK V SPM (SUPER PREDATORMASTER) – .22-250 Rem., .223 Rem., .243 Win., .308 Win., or 7mm-08 Rem. cal., features 24 in. Criterion button rifled barrel with flutes, black spider webbing on tan Accumark type stock with slim forend and CNC aluminum bedding block, Pachmayr Decelerator pad, 6 1/2 lbs. Mfg. 2001-2004.

$1,375 $1,205 $1,030 $935 $755 $620 $480 *$1,670*

MARK V SPORTER (LONG ACTION) – .240 Wby. Mag. (mfg. 1996 only), .257 Wby. Mag., .270 Wby. Mag., 7mm Wby. Mag., 7mm Rem. Mag. (disc. 2016), .270 Win. (mfg. 1996 only), .30-06 (disc. 1996), .300 Wby. Mag., .300 Win. Mag., .338 Win. Mag. (disc. 2004), .340 Wby. Mag. (disc. 2016), or .375 H&H (disc. 2002) cal., 3 shot mag., 24 or 26 in. barrel, LXX trigger (new 2016), checkered walnut stock without forearm or pistol grip caps (disc.) or raised comb Monte Carlo walnut stock with satin (disc.) or semi-gloss (new 2016) finish and fineline diamond checkering and rosewood forend and grip cap, low luster (disc.) or bead blasted matte blue metalwork, vent. recoil pad (disc.) or Pachmayr Decelerator pad, no sights, approx. 8 lbs. Mfg. 1993-2019.

$1,450 $1,175 $775 $850 $725 $625 $525 *$1,800*

* ***Mark V Sporter Standard Action*** – .22-250 Rem., .243 Win., .240 Wby. Mag., .25-06 Rem., .270 Win., .280 Rem., .30-06, .308 Win., or 7mm-08 Rem. cal., features raised comb, checkered walnut stock, 54 degree bolt lift, no sights, 24 in. barrel, approx. 6 3/4 lbs. Mfg. 1997-2004.

$1,000 $875 $750 $680 $550 $450 $350 *$1,249*

MARK V SUBALPINE/SUBALPINE RC – .257 Wby. Mag., 6.5 Creedmoor, 6.5-300 Wby. Mag., .270 Wby. Mag., or .300 Wby. Mag. cal., Magnum 9-Lug or Standard 6-Lug action, 22, 26, or 28 in. hand-lapped fluted stainless steel barrel (in #1 or #2 Mod. contour), recessed target crown, LXX trigger, hand-laid raised comb Monte Carlo composite stock with Gore Optifade Subalpine camo finish, slight right-hand palm swell, slim forearm, aluminum bedding block, Pachmayr Decelerator recoil pad, fluted bolt body,

GRADING - PPGS™	100%	98%	95%	90%	80%	70%	60%	LAST MSR

with (28 in. barrel only) or w/o Accubrake, integral recoil lug, cocking indicator, FDE Cerakote metal finish, 5 3/4-6 3/4 lbs. Mfg. 2019 only.

	$2,295	$2,025	$1,725	$1,575	$1,275	$1,050	$875	$2,700

Add $200 for 6.5-300 Wby. Mag.
Add $500 for Subalpine RC model.

RC model is range certified with guaranteed sub-MOA accuracy and includes a printout from Oehler Ballistic Imaging System, signed and certified by Adam Weatherby.

MARK V SVM (SUPER VARMINTMASTER) – .220 Swift (single shot only, disc., reintroduced 2005 only), .22-250 Rem., .223 Rem., .243 Win., .308 Win. (disc. 2004), or 7mm-08 Rem. (disc. 2004) cal., features 26 in. Criterion button rifled fluted barrel with crown, 4 or 5 shot mag., available as repeater or single shot, black spider webbing on tan Accumark type stock with beavertail forend and CNC aluminum bedding block, Pachmayr Decelerator pad, approx. 8 1/2 lbs. Mfg. 2000-2009.

	$1,600	$1,400	$1,200	$1,090	$880	$720	$560	$1,959

MARK V SVR (SPECIAL VARMINT RIFLE) – .22-250 Rem. or .223 Rem. cal., features 22 in. free floating Kreiger barrel, 4 or 5 shot mag., black Monte Carlo composite stock with grey spider webbing, aluminum bedding block, Pachmayr Decelerator pad, 7 1/4 lbs. Mfg. 2003-2005.

	$925	$810	$695	$630	$510	$415	$325	$1,176

MARK V SVR (SPECIAL VARMINT RIFLE) – .22-250 Rem. or .223 (new 2008) cal., similar to Super Varmintmaster, except has 22 in. barrel. Mfg. 2007-2009.

	$1,025	$895	$770	$695	$565	$460	$360	$1,259

MARK V TACMARK – .30-378 Wby. Mag., .338 Lapua Mag., .338-378 Wby. Mag., 6.5-300 Wby. Mag. (new 2018), .300 Win. Mag. (mfg. 2018 only), or .300 Wby. Mag. (new 2018) cal., 28 in. hand-lapped free floated fluted barrel with Accubrake, 5 shot detachable box mag., LXX™ trigger, fully adj. stock with aluminum bedding plate, black finish, 11 1/4 lbs. Mfg. by the Custom Shop 2016-2019.

	$3,485	$3,050	$2,615	$2,375	$1,915	$1,575	$1,350	$4,100

MARK V TACMARK ELITE – .30-378 Wby. Mag., .338 Lapua Mag., .338-.378 Wby. Mag., 6.5-300 Wby. Mag. (new 2018), .300 Win. Mag. (mfg. 2018 only), or .300 Wby. Mag. (new 2018) cal., hand-honed action, 28 in. hand-lapped Krieger custom match grade free floated #3 contour barrel, muzzle brake with gas dispersion ports, 5 shot detachable box mag., LXX™ trigger, fully adj. stock with aluminum bedding plate, DD Ross tactical bolt knob, range certified with guaranteed sub-MOA accuracy, High Desert camo finish with black spiderweb accents, 11 3/4 lbs. Mfg. by the Custom Shop 2016-2019.

	$5,350	$4,500	$3,995	$3,550	$3,000	$2,500	$1,875	$6,200

MARK V TERRAMARK/TERRAMARK RC – .240 Wby. Mag., .257 Wby. Mag., .270 Win. (disc. 2016), .270 Wby. Mag., .30-06 (disc. 2016), .300 Win. Mag., .300 Wby. Mag., .308 Win. (disc. 2016), .340 Wby. Mag. (disc. 2016), .30-378 Wby. Mag., .338 Lapua Mag., .338-378 Wby. Mag., 7mm Rem. Mag. (disc. 2016), 6.5 Creedmoor (new 2017), 6.5-300 Wby. (new 2017), or 7mm Wby. Mag. cal., 24 (new 2017), 26, or 28 (new 2017) in. button rifled free floated fluted stainless barrel with muzzle brake, recessed target crown, 3, 4, or 5 shot mag., LXX™ trigger (new 2016), hand laminated raised comb Monte Carlo composite stock with right-hand palm swell (new 2016) and matte gel coat finish in Desert Camo, Pachmayr Decelerator pad, FDE Cerakote finish on metalwork, RC models include special RC engraved floorplate and range certified to shoot sub-moa, 8 3/4 lbs. Mfg. by the Custom Shop 2014-2018.

	$2,385	$2,085	$1,785	$1,625	$1,325	$1,125	$925	$2,800

Add $200 for .338 Lapua Mag., .30-378 Wby. Mag., or .338-378 Wby. Mag. cal.
Add $500 for Mark V Terramark RC model.

MARK V TRR CUSTOM MAGNUM – .300 Win. Mag., .300 Wby. Mag., .30-378 Wby. Mag., .338 Lapua Mag. (new 2012), or .338-378 Wby. Mag. cals., 26 (disc. 2013) or 28 in. barrel with Accubrake, fully adj. black tactical stock, adj. trigger, w/o sights, approx. 9 lbs. Mfg. 2011-2015.

	$2,385	$2,085	$1,785	$1,625	$1,325	$1,125	$925	$2,800

Add $200 for .30-378 Wby. Mag., .338 Lapua Mag. (new 2012) or .338-378 Wby. Mag. with 28 in. barrel and Accubrake.

MARK V TRR RC (RANGE CERTIFIED) – .300 Win. Mag., .300 Wby. Mag., .30-378 Wby. Mag., .338 Lapua Mag. (new 2012), or .338-378 Wby. Mag. cal., 26 in. Kreiger barrel with Accubrake, adj. trigger, 2 shot mag., laminated stock with T-6 aluminum bedding system with three position buttstock, includes Leupold 4.5-14x50 LRT M1 scope (disc. 2012), Talley ring rail, bipod, and hard case, 9 1/4 lbs. Mfg. 2010-2015.

	$3,575	$3,050	$2,575	$2,250	$1,900	$1,650	$1,375	$4,200

Add approx. $1,700 for TRR Package including Leupold scope, ring rail, bipod, and hard case (disc. 2012).

GRADING - PPGS™	100%	98%	95%	90%	80%	70%	60%	LAST MSR

MARK V TRR (THREAT RESPONSE RIFLE) – .223 Rem., .308 Win., .300 Win. Mag. (disc. 2002), .300 Wby. Mag. (disc. 2002), .30-378 Wby. Mag. (disc. 2002), or .338-.378 Wby. Mag. (disc. 2002) cal., 22 in. barrel, 5 shot mag., Mark V action with black finished metal and black hybrid composite stock, various barrel lengths, optional Picatinny style ring and base system, 8 1/2-10 1/2 lbs. Mfg. 2002-2005.

	$1,400	$1,225	$1,050	$950	$770	$630	$490	*$1,737*

Add $52 for .300 Win. Mag. or .300 Wby. Mag. cals. (disc. 2002).
Add $208 for .30-378 Wby. Mag. or .338-378 Wby. Mag. cals. (disc. 2002).

MARK V ULTRA LIGHTWEIGHT – .243 Win. (disc. 2011), .240 Wby. Mag., .257 Wby. Mag. (new 1999), 6.5 Creedmoor (new 2017), .25-06 Rem. (disc. 2011), .270 Win., .270 Wby. Mag. (new 1999), .280 Rem. (disc. 2010), .300 Wby. Mag. (new 1999), .300 Win. Mag. (new 1999), 7mm-08 Rem. (disc. 2015), 7mm Rem. Mag. (new 1999), 7mm Wby. Mag. (new 1999), .30-06, .308 Win., 6.5-.300 Wby. Mag. (new 2016), or .338-06 A-Square (mfg. 2001-2003) cal., 22, 24, 26, or 28 (new 2016) in. blackened stainless steel fluted barrel with recessed target crown, 3 or 5 shot mag., LXX™ trigger (new 2016), lightweight synthetic stock (disc.) or hand-laminated raised comb Monte Carlo composite stock with aluminum bedding block, matte gel coat finish, spiderweb accents, and right side palm swell (new 2016), Pachmayr Decelerator pad, 5 3/4 or 6 3/4 lbs. Mfg. 1998-2019.

	$1,950	$1,700	$1,465	$1,325	$1,075	$885	$750	*$2,300*

Add $100 for .300 Wby. Mag. cal. with Accubrake or $100 for 6.5-300 Wby. Mag. cal. (new 2016, 28 in. barrel only).
Add $100 for left-hand action (.257 Wby. Mag., .270 Wby. Mag. (disc.), .300 Win. Mag. (disc.), 7mm Rem. Mag. (disc.), or 7mm Wby. Mag. (disc.).
Add $200 for left-hand action (.300 Wby. Mag. or 6.5-300 Wby. Mag. cal.).

MARK V ULTRA LIGHTWEIGHT RC – .240 Wby. Mag., .257 Wby. Mag., .270 Win., .270 Wby. Mag., .30-06, .300 Win. Mag., .300 Wby. Mag., .308 Win., 7mm Rem. Mag., or 7mm Wby. Mag. cal., 22, 24, or 26 in. free floated stainless steel fluted barrel with recessed target crown, 3 or 5 shot mag., fully adj. trigger, hand laminated raised comb Monte Carlo composite stock, matte gel coat finish and spiderweb accents, Special RC engraved floorplate, Pachmayr Decelerator pad, swivel studs included, 5 3/4-6 3/4 lbs. Mfg. 2014-2015.

	$2,000	$1,775	$1,525	$1,375	$1,115	$925	$750	*$2,400*

Add $200 for .300 Wby. Mag. cal.

MARK V ULTRAMARK (OLDER MFG.) – .240 Wby. Mag., .257 Wby. Mag., .270 Wby. Mag., .30-06, 7mm Wby. Mag., .300 Wby. Mag., .378 Wby. Mag. (mfg. 1989 only), or .416 Wby. Mag. (mfg. 1989 only) cal., fancy American walnut, individually hand-bedded, high luster finish, customized action, 24 or 26 in. barrel, basket weave checkering (including pistol grip). Imported 1989-90 only.

	$1,125	$985	$845	$765	$620	$505	$395	*$1,315*

Add $25 for 26 in. barrel.
Add $220 for .378 Wby. Mag. cal. (26 in. barrel only).
Add $325 for .416 Wby. Mag. cal. (26 in. barrel only).

MARK V ULTRAMARK (RECENT MFG.) – .257 Wby. Mag. or .300 Wby. Mag. cal., 3 shot mag., 26 in. barrel, fancy checkered American walnut stock with rosewood forend and pistol grip caps with maplewood/ebony spacers, Pachmayr Decelerator pad, fully adj. trigger, individually hand-bedded, high gloss finish, customized blue action, 8 1/2 lbs. Mfg. 2007-2015.

	$2,675	$2,200	$1,850	$1,575	$1,325	$1,100	$900	*$3,200*

MARK V WEATHERMARK – .240 Wby. Mag., .243 Win., .257 Wby. Mag., .270 Wby. Mag., .30-378 Wby. Mag., .300 Wby. Mag., .338-378 Wby. Mag., .340 Wby. Mag., 6.5 Creedmoor, 6.5-300 Wby. RPM, .270 Win. (disc. 2019), 6mm Creedmoor, 7mm Rem. Mag. (disc. 2019), 7mm Wby. Mag., .308 Win. (disc. 2019), .30-06 (disc. 2019), .300 Win. Mag. (disc. 2019), or .375 H&H Mag. (disc. 2019) cal., 24 or 26 in. hand-lapped chrome moly barrel with field crown, with or w/o Accubrake, 3 or 5 shot mag., LXX™ trigger, hand laminated raised comb Monte Carlo composite stock with full-length aluminum bedding block, right side palm swell, Pachmayr Decelerator pad, black matte gel coat finish with spiderweb accents, Tactical Grey Cerakote finish, 6 1/4-8 1/4 lbs. New 2016.

MSR $1,499	$1,275	$1,115	$950	$865	$700	$575	$500	

Add $100 for .30-378 Wby. Mag. or .338-378 Wby. Mag. cal. with Accubrake.

* ***Mark V Weathermark Bronze*** – .240 Wby. Mag., .243 Win., .257 Wby. Mag., .270 Wby. Mag., .30-378 Wby. Mag., .300 Wby. Mag., .338-378 Wby. Mag., .340 Wby. Mag., 6.5 Creedmoor, 6.5 Wby. RPM, 6.5-300 Wby. Mag., 6mm Creedmoor, or 7mm Wby. Mag. cal., 22, 24, or 26 in. #1, #2, or #3 contour threaded barrel with protector, spiral fluted bolt body, Accubrake ST (.30-378 and .338-378 Wby. Mag. cals. only), 4 shot mag., Triggertech trigger, black hand-laid raised comb Monte Carlo fiberglass stock with matte gel coat finish and Burnt Bronze spider web accents, aluminum bedding blocks, Graphite Black or Burnt Bronze Cerakote finish, 6.1-7.75 lbs. New 2020.

MSR $1,499	$1,275	$1,115	$950	$865	$700	$575	$500	

Add $100 for .30-378 Wby. Mag. or .338-378 Wby. Mag. cal.

GRADING - PPGS™	100%	98%	95%	90%	80%	70%	60%	LAST MSR

* ***Mark V Weathermark LT*** – .240 Wby. Mag., .257 Wby. Mag., .270 Wby. Mag., .300 Wby. Mag., 6.5 Creedmoor, 6.5 WBY RPM, 6.5-300 Wby. Mag., 6mm Creedmoor, or 7mm Wby. Mag. cal., right or left-hand action, #2 contour fluted barrel with FDE Cerakote finish, 4 shot mag., Triggertech trigger, green hand-laid raised comb Monte Carlo fiberglass stock with FDE speckle pattern, aluminum bedding blocks, Graphite Black Cerakote finish on bolt, knob, and safety, 5.9 lbs. New 2020.

MSR $1,899 $1,625 $1,425 $1,225 $1,100 $900 $750 $625

Add $100 for left-hand action.

* ***Mark V Weathermark Limited*** – .257 Wby. Mag., .300 Wby. Mag., 6.5 Creedmoor, 6.5 Wby. RPM, or 6.5-300 Wby. Mag. cal., 24 or 26 in. spiral fluted barrel, Accubrake, 3 or 5 shot mag., flat-face TriggerTech trigger, black base hand laid, raised comb Monte Carlo composite stock w/grey and brown accents, spiral fluted bolt knob, Burnt Bronze and Graphite Black Cerakote finish, 6 1/4 lbs. Ltd. mfg. beginning 2021.

MSR $2,299 $1,950 $1,700 $1,465 $1,325 $1,075 $885 $750

Add $100 for .30-378 Wby. Mag. or .338-378 Wby. Mag. cal. with Accubrake.

MARK V WYOMING GOLD EDITION COMMEMORATIVE RIFLE – .300 Wby. Mag. cal., 26 in. #2 contour barrel with gold and silver accent rings, LXX trigger, Exhibition Grade fancy French walnut stock with oil rubbed finish, custom fine line checkering, exotic wood forend, Pachmayr Decelerator recoil pad, cocking indicator, integral recoil lug, fluted bolt body, Damascened bolt, hand checkered bolt knob, gold engraved scroll work on receiver, gold lace Wyoming bucking horse and rider on floorplate, includes fully wrapped leather logo case, serial number starting with WY000001. Limited mfg. mid-2018-2019.

$9,000 $7,875 $6,750 $6,125 $4,950 $4,050 $3,150 *$10,000*

MARK V WYOMING SILVER EDITION COMMEMORATIVE RIFLE – .300 Wby. Mag., 26 in. #2 contour barrel, AAA Grade fancy French walnut stock with oil rubbed finish, custom fine line checkering, exotic wood forend, Pachmayr Decelerator recoil pad, Damascened aluminum alloy follower, silver engraved scroll work on receiver, floorplate features silver Wyoming bucking horse and rider. Limited mfg. mid-2018-2019.

$5,850 $5,125 $4,395 $3,985 $3,225 $2,650 $2,100 *$6,500*

CLASSICMARK I – available in 9 Wby. Mag. cals. in addition to .270 Win., 7mm Rem. Mag., .30-06, or .375 H&H cal., oil finished American Claro walnut stock with no cheekpiece and ebony forend cap, 1 in. solid recoil pad, panel point checkering. Mfg. 1992-1993.

$1,075 $940 $805 $730 $590 $485 $375 *$1,295*

Add $15 for 26 in. barrel.
Add $130 for .375 H&H cal.

* ***Classicmark I .300 or .340 Wby. Mag. Cals.*** – 26 in. barrel only, right or left-hand action, 8 1/2 lbs.

$1,095 $960 $820 $745 $600 $495 $385 *$1,323*

* ***Classicmark I .378 Wby. Mag. Cal.*** – 26 in. barrel only, right or left-hand action, 8 1/2 lbs.

$1,125 $985 $845 $765 $620 $505 $395 *$1,356*

* ***Classicmark I .416 Wby. Mag. Cal.*** – 26 in. barrel only, right or left-hand action, integral muzzle brake.

$1,150 $1,005 $865 $780 $635 $520 $405 *$1,411*

* ***Classicmark I .460 Wby. Mag. Cal.*** – 26 in. barrel only, includes custom stock, integral muzzle brake, 10 lbs. No extra charge for left-hand.

$1,250 $1,095 $940 $850 $690 $565 $440 *$1,573*

CLASSICMARK II – available in 9 Wby. Mag. cals. in addition to .270 Win., 7mm Rem. Mag., or .30-06, similar to Classicmark I, except has deluxe American walnut with 22 LPI multiple point checkering, steel grip cap, satin finished wood and metal, guaranteed 1 1/2 in. or less 3 shot grouping at 100 yards, right-hand action only. Mfg. 1992 only.

$1,525 $1,335 $1,145 $1,035 $840 $685 $535 *$1,775*

Add $28 for 26 in. barrel.

* ***Classicmark II .300 or .340 Wby. Mag. Cals.*** – 26 in. barrel only.

$1,550 $1,355 $1,165 $1,055 $855 $700 $545 *$1,803*

* ***Classicmark II .378 Wby. Mag. Cal.*** – 26 in. barrel only.

$1,700 $1,490 $1,275 $1,155 $935 $765 $595 *$1,976*

* ***Classicmark II .416 Wby. Mag. Cal.*** – 26 in. barrel only, integral muzzle brake.

$1,875 $1,640 $1,405 $1,275 $1,030 $845 $655 *$2,128*

* ***Classicmark II .460 Wby. Mag. Cal.*** – 26 in. barrel only, includes custom stock, integral muzzle brake, 10 lbs.

$1,925 $1,685 $1,445 $1,310 $1,060 $865 $675 *$2,207*

GRADING - PPGS™	100%	98%	95%	90%	80%	70%	60%	LAST MSR

* ***Classicmark II Safari Classic*** – .375 H&H cal., 24 in. barrel only, right-hand action, limited edition featuring custom action, quarter rib express and front ramp sights, barrel band swivel and engraved floorplate, stock similar to Classicmark II. Mfg. 1992 only.

$2,300 $2,015 $1,725 $1,565 $1,265 $1,035 $805 *$2,693*

EUROMARK – .257 Wby. Mag., .270 Wby. Mag., .300 Win. Mag., .300 Wby. Mag., .340 Wby. Mag., .375 H&H Mag., .375 Wby. Mag. (disc. 2013), .416 Wby. Mag. (disc. 2013), 7mm Rem. Mag., or 7mm Wby. Mag., 2 (.416 Wby. Mag. only, disc. 2013) or 3 shot mag., 24, 26, or 28 (.416 Wby. Mag. only, disc. 2013) in. barrel, oil finished, hand checkered, deluxe American Claro (disc.) or Monte Carlo select walnut stock with ebony pistol grip cap and forend tip, diamond point checkering, low luster bluing, and solid black (disc.) or Pachmayr Decelerator recoil pad, 8-9 lbs. Mfg. 1986-92, reintroduced 1995-2002, again 2010-2015.

$2,000 $1,775 $1,525 $1,375 $1,115 $925 $750 *$2,400*

Add $100 for .375 Wby. Mag. (disc. 2013) or $400 for .416 Wby. Mag. (disc. 2013) cal.
Add approx 10% for .378 Wby. Mag. (disc. 2011).

* ***Euromark .460 Wby. Mag. Cal.*** – 24 or 26 in. barrel, includes custom stock, internal muzzle brake, no extra charge for left-hand. Disc. 1992.

$1,450 $1,270 $1,090 $985 $800 $655 $510 *$1,708*

EUROSPORT – various cals., features hand-rubbed satin oil finished American Claro walnut stock with low luster blue metal work. Mfg. 1995-2002.

$915 $800 $685 $620 $505 $410 $320 *$1,143*

FIBERMARK – available in .240 Wby. Mag., .257 Wby. Mag., .270 Wby. Mag., .30-06, 7mm Wby. Mag., .300 Wby. Mag., or .340 Wby. Mag. cal., black non-glare fiberglass with wrinkle finish stock, metal has non-glare matte finish, 24 or 26 in. barrel, available in right (disc. 1991) or left-hand action, 7 1/4 lbs. Mfg. 1983-92.

$1,195 $1,045 $895 $815 $655 $540 $420 *$1,376*

Add $118 for .300 or .340 Mag. cal.

This model was available in left-hand action (22 in. barrel) in .270 Win. or .30-06 cal. only.

FIBERMARK (RECENT MFG.) – available in many cals. between .22-250 Rem.-.375 H&H, Mag. cals. only beginning 2005, 2 (.30-378 Wby. Mag. only), 3, or 5 shot internal mag., pillar bedded black composite Monte Carlo stock of Aramid cross-directional fibers, Pachmayr Decelerator pad, matte blue metal, 24, 26 (Mag. cals. only), or 28 (.30-378 Wby. Mag. cal. only) in. steel barrel, 6 3/4-8 1/2 lbs. Mfg. 2001-2015.

$1,275 $1,115 $950 $865 $700 $600 $500 *$1,500*

Add $300 for .30-378 Wby. Mag. or .338-378 Wby. Mag. cal.

* ***Fibermark Mark V Stainless*** – similar to Mark V Fibermark, except has stainless steel action and barrel with matte finish. Mfg. 2001-2004.

$1,075 $940 $805 $730 $590 $485 $375 *$1,334*

Add $98 for Mag. cals.
Add $301 for .30-378 Wby. Mag. cal.

SBGM (SUPER BIG GAME MASTER) – various cals. between .240 Wby. Mag. - .338-06 A-Square (disc.), 24 or 26 (Mag. cals. only) in. Criterion hand-lapped fluted Krieger barrel, barreled action is bedded to a specially-designed, hand-laminated, raised comb, Monte Carlo composite stock (a combination of Aramid, graphite and unidirectional fibers, and fiberglass) with black spiderweb patterning, Pachmayr Decelerator pad, 6 3/4 lbs. Mfg. 2002-disc.

$1,375 $1,205 $1,030 $935 $755 $620 $480 *$1,670*

Add $66 for Mag. cals.

SYNTHETIC (MAG. CALS.) – .240 Wby. Mag (disc. 2010), .257 Wby. Mag., .270 Wby. Mag., .300 Wby. Mag., .30-378 Wby. Mag. (new 1998), .300 Win. Mag., .338 Win. Mag. (disc. 2004), .338-378 Wby. Mag. (new 2001), .340 Wby. Mag., 7mm Wby. Mag., 7mm Rem. Mag., 7mm STW (mfg. 2001-2004), or .375 H&H cal., 24, 26, or 28 in. barrel, 2 or 3 shot mag., features lightweight black synthetic stock, bead blasted matte metal finish, approx. 8 lbs. Mfg. 1997-2012.

$1,075 $925 $775 $700 $600 $500 $425 *$1,300*

Add $300 for .30-378 Wby. Mag. or .338-378 Wby. Mag. cal. (28 in. barrel only).

* ***Synthetic (Standard Cals.)*** – .22-250 Rem. (disc. 2009), .243 Win., .25-06 Rem., .270 Win., .280 Rem., .30-06, .308 Win., or 7mm-08 Rem. cal., 4 or 5 shot mag., features raised comb, matte black injection mold synthetic stock, no sights, 20 (carbine, .243 Win., .308 Win., or 7mm-08 Rem., disc. 2002) or 24 in. barrel, approx. 6 1/2 lbs. Mfg. 1997-2011.

$1,050 $925 $775 $700 $600 $500 $425 *$1,235*

GRADING - PPGS™	100%	98%	95%	90%	80%	70%	60%	LAST MSR

* ***Synthetic Fluted*** – .257 Wby. Mag., .270 Wby. Mag., .300 Wby. Mag., .300 Win. Mag., 7mm Wby. Mag., or 7mm Rem. Mag. cal., features 24 or 26 in. fluted barrel, black synthetic stock with Monte Carlo cheekpiece, approx. 7 1/2 lbs. Mfg. 1997-98.

	$785	$685	$590	$535	$430	$355	$275	*$949*

* ***Synthetic Weathermark Alaskan Model*** – same cals. as Weathermark, similar to Weathermark, except has non-glare electroless nickel-plated metal parts, right or left-hand (mfg. 1992 only) action. Mfg. 1992-94.

	$750	$655	$565	$510	$415	$340	$265	*$875*

Add $37 for Wby. Mag. cals.
Add $164 for .375 H&H cal.
Add $375 for left-hand action (disc.).

SYNTHETIC STAINLESS MODEL (MAG. CALS.) – same cals. as Synthetic, except not available in .338-378 Wby. Mag. or 7mm STW, features bead blasted matte stainless construction, synthetic Monte Carlo stock. Mfg. 1995-2004.

	$1,075	$940	$805	$730	$590	$485	$375	*$1,282*

Add $200 for .30-378 Wby. Mag. (28 in. barrel only).

* ***Synthetic Stainless (Standard Cals.)*** – .22-250 Rem., .243 Win., .240 Wby. Mag., .25-06 Rem., .270 Win., .280 Rem., .30-06, .308 Win., or 7mm-08 Rem. cal., features raised comb, matte black injection molded synthetic stock, no sights, 20 (carbine, .243 Win., .308 Win., or 7mm-08 Rem. cal.) or 24 in. stainless barrel and action, approx. 6 1/2 lbs. Mfg. 1997-2004.

	$975	$855	$730	$665	$535	$440	$340	*$1,166*

* ***Synthetic Fluted Stainless*** – .257 Wby. Mag., .270 Wby. Mag., .300 Wby. Mag., .300 Win. Mag., 7mm Wby. Mag., or 7mm Rem. Mag., features 24 or 26 in. fluted stainless barrel and action, black synthetic stock with Monte Carlo cheekpiece, approx. 7 1/2 lbs. Mfg. 1997-98.

	$1,025	$895	$770	$695	$565	$460	$360	*$1,149*

VARMINTMASTER – .22-250 Rem. or .224 Wby. Mag., (also called .224 Varmintmaster in Weatherby catalogs - disc. 1994) cal., 24 (disc. 1991) or 26 in. barrel, 6 1/2 lbs. Disc. 1995.

	$1,075	$940	$805	$730	$590	$485	$375	*$1,297*

Add 100% for .224 Wby. Mag. cal. (scarce).
Not available in left-hand action.

WEATHERMARK – available in various Wby. Mag. cals. from .240 (disc. 1996) to .340 and .257 Roberts (disc. 1994), .270 Win., 7mm Rem. Mag., .300 Win. Mag., .30-06, .338 Win. Mag., or .375 H&H (disc.) cal., design is similar to Classicmark II, except is fitted with black checkered composite stock, satin finish black metal, 22 (disc. 1995, .270 Win. or .30-06 only), 24, or 26 in. barrel, right-hand only, 7 1/2 lbs. Mfg. 1992-94.

	$685	$600	$515	$465	$375	$310	$240	*$799*

WHITETAIL – .257 Sav. cal., limited edition features deluxe high grade American Claro walnut, hand checkered bolt knob and engraved floorplate, 22 in. #1 contoured barrel, 6 lbs. Mfg. 1993 only.

	$1,150	$1,005	$865	$780	$635	$520	$405	*$1,366*

1976 BICENTENNIAL MARK V – .257 Wby. Mag., .270 Wby. Mag., 7mm Wby. Mag., or .300 Wby Mag. cal., 1,000 mfg. in 1976 only.

	$1,495	$1,310	$1,120	$1,015	$820	$675	$525	*$2,000*

1984 MARK V OLYMPIC COMMEMORATIVE – .257 Wby. Mag., .270 Wby. Mag., 7mm Wby. Mag., or .300 Wby. Mag. cal., special gold accenting, extra-fancy walnut stock with burnished brass oval depicting the Olympic "Star In Motion" emblem inlay. Mfg. 1984, only 1,000 mfg. at $2,000 retail.

	$2,000	$1,676	$1,450	N/A	N/A	N/A	N/A	

MARK V 35TH ANNIVERSARY COMMEMORATIVE – .257 Wby. Mag., .270 Wby. Mag., 7mm Wby. Mag., or .300 Wby. Mag. cal., limited mfg. 1980, 1,000 produced total.

	$2,000	$1,676	$1,450	N/A	N/A	N/A	N/A	

MARK V 40TH ANNIVERSARY COMMEMORATIVE – .257 Wby. Mag. (35 mfg.), .270 Wby. Mag. (35 mfg.), 7mm Wby. Mag. (35 mfg.), or .300 Wby. Mag. (95 mfg.) cal. Limited mfg. 1985, 200 produced total.

	$2,000	$1,676	$1,450	N/A	N/A	N/A	N/A	

MARK V 50TH ANNIVERSARY COMMEMORATIVE – .300 Wby. Mag. cal., 26 in. barrel, checkered high grade Claro Monte Carlo walnut stock with cheekpiece and brass Weatherby anniversary logo plaque, gold trigger, rosewood pistol grip cap, engraved floorplate, 9 lbs. Limited mfg. 1995.

	$2,250	$1,850	$1,500	N/A	N/A	N/A	N/A	

GRADING - PPGS™	100%	98%	95%	90%	80%	70%	60%	LAST MSR

MARK V 70TH ANNIVERSARY COMMEMORATIVE – .257 Wby. Mag. cal., 24 in. barrel, checkered high grade Claro Monte Carlo walnut stock with cheekpiece, rosewood pistol grip and forend caps, engraved floorplate, Pachmayr waffle-style recoil pad, high gloss finish on all metal work, bottom metal features 70th Anniversary logo in gold, includes custom leather case and commemorative knife and sheath by Dan Weatherby, 7 3/4 lbs. 70 mfg. during 2015.

$5,450 $4,900 $3,995 N/A N/A N/A N/A *$5,900*

RIFLES: BOLT ACTION, VANGUARD SERIES 1

The Vanguard Series 1 rifles were discontinued in 2011. All guns were shipped with a factory three shot target, guaranteeing 1.5 in. accuracy at 100 yards.

VANGUARD – .243 Win., .25-06 Rem., .270 Win., .30-06, .308 Win., 7mm Rem. Mag., .264 Win. Mag., or .300 Win. Mag. cal., mfg. circa late 1960s-early 1970s.

$435 $380 $325 $295 $240 $195 $150

Add 10% for .264 Win. Mag. cal.

VANGUARD ALASKAN – .223 Rem., .243 Win., .270 Win., 7mm-08 Rem., 7mm Rem. Mag., .30-06, or .308 Win. cal., no sights, electroless nickel metal plating. Mfg. 1993-1994.

$625 $545 $470 $425 $345 $280 $220 *$699*

VANGUARD AXIOM BIG GAME – .25-06 Rem., .270 Win., .30-06, .257 Wby. Mag., 7mm Rem. Mag., .300 Win. Mag., or .300 Wby Mag., 24 in. blue barrel, patented Knoxx adj. stock with pistol grip, black finish. Limited mfg. 2009.

$875 $775 $675 $575 $475 $375 $325 *$969*

VANGUARD AXIOM VARMINT – .22-250 Rem., .223 Rem., or .308 Win. cal., similar to Axiom Big Game, except has 22 in. barrel, 8 3/4 lbs. Limited mfg. 2009.

$775 $680 $580 $525 $425 $350 $270 *$879*

VANGUARD BACK COUNTRY CUSTOM – .257 Wby. Mag., .270 Win., .30-06, .300 Win. Mag., or .300 Wby. Mag., features stainless steel action and 24 in. fluted barrel, Ultralight composite stock with spider webbing and Pachmayr Decelerator pad, 6 3/4 lbs. Mfg. 2008-2009.

$900 $790 $675 $610 $495 $405 $315 *$1,119*

VANGUARD CARBINE – .22-250 Rem., .223 Rem., .243 Win., 7mm-08 Rem., .308 Win. cal., 20 in. contoured barrel, matte black metal finish, adj. trigger, composite stock, 6 3/4 lbs. Mfg. 2009-2011.

$450 $395 $340 $300 $250 $200 $160 *$523*

VANGUARD CLASSIC I – .223 Rem., .243 Win., .270 Win., 7mm-08 Rem., 7mm Rem. Mag., .30-06, or .308 Win. cal., checkered walnut stock with satin finish, black buttpad, 24 in. barrel, 3 (7mm Rem. Mag.) or 5 shot mag., No. 1 barrel contour, approx. 7 lbs. 5 oz. Mfg. 1989-1993.

$480 $420 $360 $325 $265 $215 $170 *$549*

This model was the replacement for the Vanguard VGS and VGL.

VANGUARD CLASSIC II – .22-250 Rem., .243 Win., .270 Wby. Mag., .270 Win., 7mm Rem. Mag., .30-06, .300 Win. Mag., .300 Wby. Mag., or .338 Win. Mag. cal., 24 in. No. 2 barrel contour, 3 or 5 shot mag., custom checkered deluxe walnut stock with pistol grip cap and black forend cap, solid black recoil pad, matte finished metal, approx. 7 3/4 lbs. Mfg. 1989-92.

$675 $590 $505 $460 $370 $305 $235 *$750*

This model was also available in a No. 3 barrel contour in .22-250 Rem. cal. only.

VANGUARD COMPACT – .22-250 Rem., .223 Rem. (new 2008), .243 Win., .308 Win. or 7mm-08 Rem. (new 2006) cal., 20 in. barrel, shortened 12 1/2 LOP, 5 shot mag., matte black hardwood stock, 6 3/4 lbs. Mfg. 2005-2009.

$575 $505 $430 $390 $315 $260 $200 *$649*

VANGUARD DELUXE – .257 Wby. Mag., .270 Win., .30-06, .300 Win. Mag. (new 2007), .300 Wby. Mag., or 7mm Rem. Mag. (new 2007) cal., 24 in. barrel w/o sights, features high gloss walnut Monte Carlo stock with rosewood forend tip and pistol grip cap, high gloss bluing, 3 or 5 shot mag., 7 3/4 lbs. Mfg. 2006-2009.

$835 $730 $625 $570 $460 $375 $290 *$989*

Add $133 for matte stainless steel action/barrel (Deluxe SS, disc. 2006).

VANGUARD FIBERGUARD – .223 Rem., .243 Win., .270 Win., 7mm Rem. Mag., .30-06, or .308 Win. cal., 20 in. barrel, green fiberglass stock, 3 to 6 shot mags., no sights, blue metal parts, approx. 6 1/2 lbs. Disc. 1988.

$500 $440 $375 $340 $275 $225 $175 *$560*

Not available in left-hand action.

GRADING - PPGS™	100%	98%	95%	90%	80%	70%	60%	LAST MSR

VANGUARD PREDATOR – .22-250 Rem., .223 Rem., or .308 Win. cal., 22 in. contoured barrel, injection molded composite stock with 100% Natural Gear camo coverage (including barrel and action), adj. trigger, low density recoil pad, 8 lbs. Mfg. 2009-2011.

$735	$640	$550	$495	$400	$325	$255	*$866*

VANGUARD SAGE COUNTRY CUSTOM – available in various cals. between .22-250 Rem. - .338 Win. Mag., injection molded stock with desert camo, 24 in. barrel, low density recoil pad. Mfg. 2008-2009.

$575	$505	$430	$390	$315	$260	$200	*$659*

Add $30 for .270 WSM or .300 WSM cals.

VANGUARD SPORTER – .22-250 Rem., .223 Rem., .243 Win., .25-06 Rem. (new 2007), .257 Wby. Mag., .270 Win., .270 WSM (new 2005), .30-06, .308 Win., .300 WSM, .300 Win. Mag., .300 Wby. Mag., .338 Win. Mag., 7mm-08 Rem. (new 2008), or 7mm Rem. Mag. cal., 24 in. barrel, 3 or 5 shot fixed or detachable box mag., checkered walnut stock with rosewood forend tip, satin finish and checkering, matte blue metal, 7 3/4 lbs. Mfg. 2005-2011.

$595	$520	$445	$400	$325	$270	$210	*$754*

Add $55 for detachable box magazine (Sporter DBM, new 2010).
Add $200 for matte stainless steel action/barrel (Sporter SS, disc. 2009).
Add $30 for WSM cals.

VANGUARD SUB-MOA – .22-250 Rem., .223 Rem., .243 Win., .25-06 Rem. (new 2007), .257 Wby. Mag., .270 Win., .270 WSM (new 2005), .30-06, .308 Win., .300 WSM, .300 Win. Mag., .300 Wby. Mag., .338 Win. Mag., 7mm-08 Rem. (new 2008), or 7mm Rem. Mag. cal., matte finished steel or stainless steel action and 24 in. barrel, choice of light tan or charcoal Monte Carlo Fiberguard stock with Pachmayr Decelerator pad, no sights, guaranteed to shoot a three shot .99 in. group at 100 yards, 3 or 5 shot mag., 7 3/4 lbs. Mfg. 2005-2011.

$865	$750	$650	$580	$475	$385	$300	*$1,019*

Add $31 for WSM cals.
Add $150 for stainless steel action/barrel (disc. 2009).

* ***Vanguard Sub-MOA TR*** – .223 Rem. or .308 Win. cal., 22 in. contoured barrel with recessed target crown, 5 shot mag., laminated Monte Carlo composite stock with beavertail forearm and Pachmayr Decelerator pad, three swivel studs, adj. trigger, guaranteed to shoot 3-shot group of .99 in. or less with factory or premium ammo, 8 3/4 lbs. Mfg. 2010-2011.

$875	$750	$640	$580	$470	$385	$300	*$1,016*

* ***Vanguard Sub-MOA TRR Package*** – .300 Win. Mag., .300 Wby. Mag., .30-378 Wby. Mag., or .338-378 Wby. Mag. cal., 28 in. barrel with Accubrake, adj. trigger, laminated stock with T-6 aluminum bedding system with three position buttstock, includes Leupold 4.5-14x50 LRT M1 scope, Talley ring rail, bipod, and hard case. Mfg. 2010 only.

$3,350	$2,975	$2,550	$2,200	$1,875	$1,550	$1,300	*$3,999*

VANGUARD SUB-MOA VARMINT – .204 Ruger (mfg. 2007-2010), .22-250 Rem., .223 Rem., or .308 Win. cal., features hand laminated composite stock with oversized vented forend and CNC machined aluminum bedding plate, Pachmayr Decelerator pad, three sling swivels, 22 in. barrel, 5 shot mag., 8 1/4 lbs. Mfg. 2006-2011.

$925	$800	$700	$600	$500	$425	$375	*$1,101*

Add $59 for .204 Ruger cal. (disc. 2010).

VANGUARD SYNTHETIC (RECENT MFG.) – .22-250 Rem., .223 Rem., .243 Win., .25-06 Rem. (new 2007), .257 Wby. Mag., .270 Win., .270 WSM (new 2005), .30-06, .308 Win., .300 WSM, .300 Win. Mag., .300 Wby. Mag., .338 Win. Mag., 7mm-08 Rem. (new 2008), or 7mm Rem. Mag. cal., choice of matte black metal or satin stainless steel action/barrel, black synthetic stock, includes many Mark V features, including one-piece fluted bolt with 3 gas ports, 2 locking lugs, and 90-degree bolt lift, 3 or 5 shot mag., 24 in. barrel, adj. trigger, each gun supplied with 3 shot factory target, approx. 7 1/2 lbs. Domestic mfg. 1997-2011.

$450	$395	$340	$305	$250	$205	$160	*$523*

Add $20 for WSM cals.
Add $76 for detachable box magazine (Synthetic DBM, new 2010).
Add $106 for Vanguard Combo with Simmons 3.5-10x40mm scope and Leupold rings/bases (new 2011).
Add $206 for Vanguard package (includes Bushnell Banner 3-9x40mm scope mounted and bore sighted, Uncle Mike's nylon sling, and Plano molded case, new 2005).
Add $210 for stainless steel action/barrel (disc. 2009).
Add $263 for Vanguard stainless package (disc. 2006).

GRADING - PPGS™	100%	98%	95%	90%	80%	70%	60%	LAST MSR

* ***Vanguard Synthetic HB-ST*** – .223 Rem. or .308 Win. cal., 22 in. matte blue barrel, 5 shot mag., adj. trigger, features black synthetic injection molded stock with textured Silent-Tek SureGrip finish, recessed target crown, low density recoil pad, 8 lbs. Mfg. 2010-2011.

$560	$485	$450	$375	$325	$270	$230	*$642*

VANGUARD THUMBHOLE LAMINATE – .204 Ruger (disc. 2009), .22-250 Rem. (disc. 2009), .223 Rem., .25-06 Rem. (new 2010), .257 Wby. Mag. (new 2010), .270 Win. (new 2010), 7mm Rem. Mag. (new 2010), .30-06 (new 2010), .300 Win. Mag. (new 2010), or .300 Wby. Mag. (new 2010) cal., 24 in. hammer forged barrel, nutmeg laminate stock with thumbhole and barrel vents, Pachmayr Decelerator pad, adj. trigger. Mfg. 2009-2010.

$725	$635	$545	$495	$400	$325	$255	*$799*

Add $60 for .204 Ruger cal. (disc. 2009).

VANGUARD VARMINT SPECIAL – .204 Ruger (new 2007), .22-250 Rem., .223 Rem., or .308 Win. cal., features checkered hand laminated tan Monte Carlo composite stock with aluminum bedding plate, 22 in. barrel w/o sights, 5 shot mag., 8 1/4 lbs. Mfg. 2006-2008, reintroduced 2010-2011.

$600	$525	$450	$400	$340	$295	$250	*$713*

Add $61 for .204 Ruger (new 2007).

VANGUARD YOUTH – .22-250 Rem., .223 Rem., .243 Win., 7mm-08 Rem., or .308 Win. cal., 5 shot mag., 20 in. contoured barrel, lighter Vanguard action, adj. trigger, black synthetic stock with removable elongated spacer to adj. length of pull, low density recoil pad, approx. 6 1/2 lbs. Mfg. 2010-2011.

$450	$395	$340	$300	$250	$200	$160	*$523*

VANGUARD VGD – .22-250 Rem., .243 Win., .25-06 Rem., .270 Win., 7mm Rem. Mag., .30-06, or .300 Win. Mag. cal., bolt action, checkered deluxe walnut stock with rosewood tip forearm and pistol grip, 24 in. barrel, no sights, 5 shot mag. (except 3 shot for .300 Win. Mag.), high luster bluing, about 8 lbs. Disc. 1988.

$525	$460	$395	$355	$290	$235	$185	*$600*

Not available in left-hand action.

VANGUARD VGL – .223 Rem., .243 Win., .270 Win., 7mm Rem. Mag., .30-06, or .308 Win. cal., lightweight bolt action, checkered walnut stock, 5 shot mag. (6 on .223 Rem.), 20 in. barrel, no sights, 6 1/2 lbs. Disc. 1988.

$415	$365	$310	$280	$230	$185	$145	*$467*

Not available in left-hand action.

VANGUARD VGS – same cals. as Vanguard VGX, bolt action, checkered satin finished walnut stock, 24 in. barrel, no sights, approx. 8 lbs. Disc. 1988.

$415	$365	$310	$280	$230	$185	$145	*$467*

Not available in left-hand action.

VANGUARD VGX DELUXE – .22-250 Rem., .243 Win., .270 Win., .270 Wby. Mag., .300 Win. Mag., .300 Wby. Mag., .30-06, .338 Win. Mag., or 7mm Rem. Mag. cal., 24 in. barrel, Monte Carlo stock with skipline checkering, high gloss wood and metal, rosewood grip cap and forend tip. Mfg. 1989-1993.

$625	$545	$470	$425	$345	$280	$220	*$699*

VANGUARD WEATHERGUARD – same cals. as Classic I, replacement for Fiberguard, wrinkle black finished synthetic stock, entry level Weatherby, similar specs. as Classic I, approx. 8 lbs. Mfg. 1989-1993.

$440	$385	$330	$300	$240	$200	$155	*$499*

RIFLES: BOLT ACTION, VANGUARD SERIES 2

Weatherby discontinued its Vanguard Series 1 in 2011, and released the Vanguard Series 2 in 2012. Differences on the Series 2 include a creep-free, match quality, two-stage trigger, 3-position safety, and Griptonite synthetic stock with special inserts and palm swell (select models). All Series 2 Vanguards come with a Sub-MOA accuracy guarantee.

VANGUARD SERIES 2 ACCUGUARD – .240 Wby., 6.5-300 Wby. Mag. (new 2018), .257 Wby. Mag., .270 Win. (disc. 2018), .30-06, .300 Win. Mag., or .300 Wby. Mag. cal., 24 or 26 in. #3 contour fluted stainless steel barrel, recessed target crown, hand-laminated, raised comb Monte Carlo composite stock with full-length aluminum bedding plate, matte gel coat finish and spiderweb accents, bead blasted matte finish, 8 3/4 lbs. Mfg. 2016-disc.

$935	$825	$700	$635	$515	$425	$350	*$1,099*

VANGUARD SERIES 2 ADAPTIVE COMPOSITE (VAC) – .223 Rem., 6.5 Creedmoor, or .308 Win. cal., 20 in. #3 contour threaded barrel, 5 shot, fully adj. composite target stock with quick adjustments and rubberized grip panels, matte bead blasted blued finish, 8.75 lbs. Mfg. 2017 only.

$1,080	$950	$810	$725	$595	$485	$400	*$1,269*

GRADING - PPGS™	100%	98%	95%	90%	80%	70%	60%	LAST MSR

VANGUARD SERIES 2 BACKCOUNTRY – .240 Wby. Mag., .257 Wby. Mag., 6.5 Creedmoor (new 2019), .270 Win., .300 Wby. Mag., .30-06, .308 Win. (mfg. 2015-2018), or .300 Win. Mag. cal., pillar bedded action, fluted 24 in. barrel w/o sights, blue metal finish, Cerakote treated Tactical Grey finished Monte Carlo composite stock with spiderweb accents, Pachmayr Decelerator pad, approx. 6 3/4 lbs. Mfg. 2013-disc.

	$1,025	$900	$775	$700	$575	$475	$400	*$1,199*

VANGUARD SERIES 2 BADLANDS – .256 Rem., .257 Wby. Mag., 6.5-300 Wby. Mag., 6.5 Creedmoor, 6.5 PRC (new 2020), .270 Win., .25-06 (new 2019), 7mm-08 Rem., 7mm Rem. Mag., .300 Win. Mag., .300 Wby. Mag., .30-06, or .308 Win. cal., 24 or 26 in. #2 contour cold hammer forged barrel, hinged floorplate, adj. two-stage trigger, Monte Carlo polymer stock with textured forearm and grip areas in Badlands Approach camo pattern finish, Vanguard recoil pad, 3-pos. safety, integral recoil lug, fully enclosed bolt sleeve, one-piece machined fluted bolt body, Burnt Bronze Cerakote metal finish, 7 1/4-7 1/2 lbs. New 2019.

MSR $799	$680	$600	$500	$450	$375	$300	$250	

VANGUARD SERIES 2 CAMILLA – .243 Win., 6.5 Creedmoor, 7mm-08 Rem., .22-250 Rem. (new 2020), or .308 Win. cal., 20 in. barrel, 4 or 5 shot mag., raised comb Monte Carlo A-grade Turkish stock designed to properly fit a woman's body with satin finish, rosewood forend and grip cap, Fleur-de-lis checkering pattern, pistol grip with trigger finger groove, right side palm swell, 13 in. LOP, matte bead blasted blued finish, 6 1/2 lbs. New 2017.

MSR $749	$635	$550	$475	$425	$350	$285	$250	

VANGUARD SERIES 2 CAMILLA WILDERNESS – .243 Win., .308 Win., 6.5 Creedmoor, or 7mm-08 Rem. cal., 20 in. #1 contour cold hammer forged threaded barrel with matte blued finish, hinged floorplate, adj. two-stage trigger, green hand-laid fiberglass stock with high comb and black webbing, recoil pad, 13 in. LOP, slender forend, slim pistol grip, 3-pos. safety, fluted bolt body, fully enclosed bolt sleeve. New 2020.

MSR $849	$725	$635	$550	$495	$425	$325	$275	

VANGUARD SERIES 2 CARBINE – .22-250 Rem., .223 Rem., .243 Win., 7mm-08 Rem., or .308 Win. cal., 20 in. contoured barrel, 5 shot mag., matte blue finish, lightweight composite Monte Carlo Griptonite stock features pistol grip and forend inserts, right side palm swell, 7 lbs. Mfg. 2012-2016.

	$550	$480	$415	$375	$300	$250	$200	*$649*

VANGUARD SERIES 2 DELUXE – .257 Wby. Mag., .270 Win., .30-06, .300 Win. Mag. (disc. 2018), or .300 Wby. Mag. cal., 24 in. barrel, raised comb, features Monte Carlo Claro walnut stock in high gloss finish, rosewood forend and grip cap with maplewood spacers, fineline checkering, high gloss bluing, 3 or 5 shot mag., 7 lbs. Mfg. 2012-disc.

	$975	$850	$725	$675	$550	$450	$375	*$1,149*

VANGUARD SERIES 2 DGR (DANGEROUS GAME RIFLE) – .375 H&H cal., 24 in. barrel, 3 shot mag., NECG adj. rear sight and Williams Gun Sight Company hooded front sight, hand-laminated raised comb Monte Carlo composite stock with full-length aluminum bedding plate, matte gel coat finish and spiderweb accents, matte bead blasted blued finish, 7 3/4 lbs. Mfg. 2016-disc.

	$975	$850	$725	$675	$550	$450	$375	*$1,149*

VANGUARD SERIES 2 FIRST LITE – .240 Wby. Mag., .25-06 Rem. Mag., .257 Wby. Mag., 6.5 Creeedmoor, 6.5 PRC (new 2020), 6.5-300 Wby. Mag., .270 Win., .300 Win. Mag., .300 Wby. Mag., .30-06, or .308 Win. cal., 26 or 28 in. #2 contour fluted cold hammer forged barrel, hinged floorplate, 3, 4, or 5 shot mag., adj. two-stage trigger, Monte Carlo stock with textured forearm and grip areas, right side palm swell, First Lite Fusion camo finish, Vanguard recoil pad, 3-pos. safety, Accubrake is standard, integral recoil lug, fully enclosed bolt sleeve, one-piece machined fluted bolt body, FDE Cerakote metal finish, 7 1/4 lbs. New 2019.

MSR $999	$850	$750	$650	$585	$475	$400	$325	

VANGUARD SERIES 2 H-BAR RC – .223 Rem., .22-250 Rem. (disc. 2016), 6.5 Creedmoor (new 2017), or .308 Win. cal., 22 in. cold hammer forged barrel, 5 shot, hand-laminated Monte Carlo composite stock with beavertail forearm and vents to dissipate heat, CNC machined aluminum bedding plate, range certified with Sub-MOA accuracy, range certified engraved floorplate, signed and certified by Ed Weatherby, 8 3/4 lbs. Mfg. 2016-2018.

	$1,175	$1,025	$875	$800	$650	$550	$450	*$1,369*

VANGUARD SERIES 2 LAMINATE H-BAR – .22-250 Rem., .223 Rem., or .308 Win. cal., 22 in. heavy barrel, 5 shot, fully adj. oil finished, laminate target stock with quick adjustments and wide forend, Limbsaver® recoil pad, matte blued finish, 9 1/4 lbs. Limited mfg. 2016 only.

	$1,230	$1,075	$925	$835	$675	$550	$450	*$1,449*

GRADING - PPGS™	100%	98%	95%	90%	80%	70%	60%	LAST MSR

VANGUARD SERIES 2 LAMINATE SPORTER – .22-250 Rem., .223 Rem., .243 Win., .25-06 Rem., .237 Wby. Mag., .270 Win., .30-06 Sprg., .300 Wby. Mag., .300 Win. Mag., .308 Win., 6.5 Creedmoor, 6.5-300 Wby. Mag., 7mm Rem. Mag., or 7mm-08 Rem. Mag. cal., 24 or 26 (Mag. cals. only) in. #2 contour cold-hammer forged, matte bead blasted blued barrel, adj. match two-stage trigger, raised comb, Monte Carlo "A" grade Turkish walnut stock w/stain urethane finish, rosewood forend cap and fine line diamond point checkering, 3-pos. safety, fluted bolt body and fully enclosed bolt sleeve, one-piece machined bolt body, Vanguard recoil pad, hinged floorplate, internal recoil lug. New 2020.

MSR $799	$680	$600	$500	$450	$375	$300	$250	

VANGUARD SERIES 2 LAZERGUARD – .223 Rem. (disc. 2016), .243 Win. (disc. 2018), .257 Wby. Mag., .270 Win. Mag. (new 2019), .300 Win. Mag. (new 2019), .30-06, .308 Win. (disc. 2019), or .300 Wby. Mag. cal., 24 or 26 in. contoured barrel, 5 shot, raised comb Monte Carlo AA Grade Claro walnut stock with high gloss finish and laser carved oak leaf pattern, rosewood forend and grip cap with maplewood spacers, blued metalwork in high luster finish, 7 3/4 lbs. Mfg. 2016-disc.

	$935	$825	$700	$635	$515	$425	$350	*$1,099*

VANGUARD SERIES 2 LEUPOLD PACKAGE – .243 Win., .257 Wby. Mag., .270 Win., 7mm Rem. Mag., .308 Win., .30-06, .300 Win. Mag., or .300 Wby. Mag. cal., 24 in. barrel, 3 or 5 shot, package includes Vanguard synthetic rifle, Leupold 3-9x40 VX-2 riflescope with matte finish and duplex reticle, scope is mounted and boresighted by Weatherby gunsmith, Talley designed Weatherby Vanguard lightweight mounts, 8 1/2 lbs. Mfg. 2016-2018.

	$895	$785	$675	$610	$495	$425	$350	*$1,049*

VANGUARD SERIES 2 MEATEATER – 6.5 Creedmoor, 6.5-300 Wby. Mag., .300 Win. Mag., .308 Win., .300 Wby. Mag., or 7mm Rem. Mag., 24 or 26 (magnum) in. #2 spiral fluted cold hammer forged barrel, adj. match two-stage trigger, Monte Carlo stock w/black base and gray/brown accents, textured forearm, right-side palm swell, 3-pos. safety, integral recoil lug, Vanguard recoil pad, one-piece bolt body w/fully enclosed bolt sleeve, laser engraved Meateater hinged floorplate, Tungsten Cerakote finish. New 2020.

MSR $999	$850	$750	$650	$585	$475	$400	$325	

VANGUARD SERIES 2 MODULAR CHASSIS – .223 Rem., 6.5 Creedmoor (new 2017), or .308 Win. cal., 20 in. heavy barrel, 10 shot detachable box mag., fully adj. LUTH-AR MBA-1 buttstock, Hogue overmolded grip with finger grooves, hole spacing for Magpul rails, CNC-machined hard anodized aluminum chassis, matte blued finish, 8 3/4 lbs. Mfg. 2016-2018.

	$1,300	$1,135	$970	$880	$700	$600	$500	*$1,519*

VANGUARD SERIES 2 RC – .22-250 Rem. (disc. 2016), .223 Rem. (disc. 2016), .243 Win., .25-06 Rem., .240 Wby. Mag. (mfg. 2013-2016), .257 Wby. Mag., .270 Win., 6.5 Creedmoor (new 2016), .30-06, .300 Wby. Mag., .300 Win. Mag., .308 Win., .338 Win. Mag. (disc. 2014), 7mm-08 Rem. (disc. 2016), or 7mm Rem. Mag. cal., 24 in. forged barrel with matte blue finish, pillar-bedded composite stock with Monte Carlo raised cheekpiece and non-slip black spiderwebbing, 3 or 5 shot mag., Special RC engraved floorplate, approx. 7 3/4 lbs. Mfg. 2012-2018.

	$1,100	$965	$825	$750	$600	$500	$425	*$1,299*

VANGUARD SERIES 2 RC VARMINT – .223 Rem., .22-250 Rem., or .308 Win. cal., 22 in. free floated barrel with recessed target crown and matte blue finish, hand laminated Monte Carlo composite stock with beavertail forend, Pachmayr Decelerator pad, aluminum bedding plate, 5 shot mag., Special RC engraved floorplate, 8 3/4 lbs. Mfg. 2012-2015.

	$1,025	$900	$775	$700	$575	$475	$400	*$1,199*

VANGUARD SERIES 2 REALTREE XTRA – .243 Win., .257 Wby. Mag., .270 Win., .308 Win., or .30-06 cal., 24 in. barrel, 3 or 5 shot, Monte Carlo stock features hard textured forearm and grip areas, right side palm swell, and Realtree Xtra camo pattern finish, matte bead blasted blued metal finish, 7 3/4 lbs. Limited mfg. 2016 only.

	$650	$575	$500	$400	$335	$295	$240	*$749*

VANGUARD SERIES 2 SAFARI – .375 H&H, .300 Wby. Mag., or .30-06 cal., 24 in. hammer forged barrel, NECG adj. rear sight and Williams Gun Sight Company hooded front sight (.375 H&H only), .30-06 version does not have sights, European walnut stock with hand rubbed oil finish, Monte Carlo cheekpiece, diamond point Fleur-de-lis checkering, exotic hardwood grip cap and forend tip, Pachmayr Decelerator recoil pad, matte bead blasted blued finish, 7.5-7.75 lbs. Mfg. 2018-circa 2020.

	$935	$825	$700	$635	$515	$425	$350	*$1,099*

Add $200 for .375 H&H cal.

VANGUARD SERIES 2 SELECT – .243 Win., 6.5 Creedmoor (new 2019), .270 Win., 7mm Rem. Mag., .308 Win., .30-06, or .300 Win. Mag. cal., 24 or 26 in. barrel, 3 or 5 shot, black Monte Carlo stock with hard, textured forearm and grip areas, right side palm swell, matte bead blasted blued finish, 7 3/4 lbs. New 2016.

MSR $549	$475	$415	$350	$325	$260	$225	$175	

GRADING - PPGS™	100%	98%	95%	90%	80%	70%	60%	LAST MSR

VANGUARD SERIES 2 SPORTER – .22-250 Rem., .223 Rem., .240 Wby. Mag. (mfg. 2014-2016), .243 Win., .25-06 Rem., .257 Wby. Mag., .270 Win., .270 WSM (disc. 2012), .30-06, .300 Wby. Mag., .300 Win. Mag., .300 WSM (disc. 2012), .308 Win., .338 Win. Mag. (disc. 2015), 7mm-08 Rem., or 7mm Rem. Mag. cal., 24 in. barrel, 3 or 5 shot mag., raised comb, Monte Carlo Turkish walnut stock with satin urethane finish, rosewood forend and fineline diamond point checkering, matte blue finish, approx. 7 3/4 lbs. New 2012.

MSR $799	$680	$600	$500	$450	$375	$300	$265	

An optional detachable box magazine (Vanguard Series 2 Sporter DBM) is available in .25-06 Rem., .270 Win., or .30-06 cal. only at no additional charge.

VANGUARD SERIES 2 SYNTHETIC – .22-250 Rem., .223 Rem., .240 Wby. Mag., .243 Win., .25-06 Rem., .257 Wby. Mag., 6.5 Creedmoor (new 2017), 6.5 PRC (new 2020), 6.5-300 Wby. Mag. (new 2018), .270 Win., .270 WSM (disc. 2012), .30-06, .308 Win., .300 WSM (disc. 2012), .300 Win. Mag., .300 Wby. Mag., .338 Win. Mag. (disc. 2015), .375 H&H Mag. (new 2016, features adj. iron sights with hooded front sight), 7mm Rem. Mag., or 7mm-08 Rem. cal., 3 or 5 shot mag., 24 or 26 in. barrel, lightweight composite Monte Carlo Griptonite stock with pistol grip and forend inserts, matte blue or green (new 2020) finish, 7 1/2 lbs. New 2012.

MSR $599	$510	$450	$385	$350	$275	$225	$195	

Add $20 for for green finish (new 2020).

Add $100 for Series 2 Synthetic Combo (includes Simmons 3.5-10x40mm Truplex Reticle scope, and Leupold Rifleman rings and bases), mfg. 2012 only.

Add $200 for Series 2 Synthetic Package (includes Simmons 3.5-10x40mm Truplex Reticle scope, Leupold Rifleman rings and bases, adj. nylon sling, and injection-molded scoped rifle case), mfg. 2012 only.

Add $350 for Series 2 Synthetic Package (includes 3-9x42mm Redfield Revenge riflescope with matte finish and 4-plex reticle, mounted and boresighted, Talley-designed Weatherby Vanguard mounts, adj. nylon sling, injection-molded scoped rifle case), mfg. 2013-2015.

An optional detachable box magazine (Vanguard Series 2 Synthetic DBM) is available in .240 Wby. Mag., .25-06 Rem., .270 Win., or .30-06 cal. only at no additional charge.

* ***Vanguard Series 2 Synthetic Stainless*** – .223 Rem. (disc. 2018), .243 Win., .257 Wby. Mag., .270 Win., .30-06, .308 Win., .300 Win. Mag., .300 Wby. Mag., or 7mm Rem. Mag. cal., 24 or 26 in. barrel, similar to Vanguard Series 2 Synthetic, except features stainless steel. Mfg. 2012-disc.

	$680	$600	$500	$450	$375	$300	$250	*$799*

VANGUARD SERIES 2 SYNTHETIC COMPACT (YOUTH) – .22-250 Rem. (disc. 2016), .223 Rem. (disc. 2016), .243 Win., 6.5 Creedmoor (new 2017), 7mm-08 Rem., or .308 Win. cal., 5 shot mag., 20 in. contoured barrel, injection molded composite stock with removable elongated spacer to adj. length of pull, 3-pos. safety, matte blued or black base w/blue and grey accents (Compact Blue model, new 2020) finish, 6 1/2 lbs. New 2012.

MSR $549	$475	$415	$350	$325	$260	$225	$175	

Add $80 for for Compact Blue model (new 2020).

VANGUARD SERIES 2 TRR RC – .223 Rem. or .308 Win. cal., 22 in. barrel with recessed target crown, hand laminated Monte Carlo composite stock with aluminum bedding plate, beavertail forend, Pachmayr Decelerator recoil pad, includes factory-shot target certified and signed by Ed Weatherby and special RC engraved floorplate, 8 3/4 lbs. Mfg. 2012-2015.

	$1,025	$900	$775	$700	$575	$475	$400	*$1,199*

VANGUARD SERIES 2 VARMINT SPECIAL – .22-250 Rem., .223 Rem., or .308 Win. cal., 22 in. contoured barrel with recessed target crown, 5 shot mag., matte blue finish, lightweight composite Monte Carlo Griptonite stock with pistol grip and forend inserts, 8 3/4 lbs. Mfg. 2012-2014.

	$725	$650	$575	$475	$425	$375	$325	*$849*

VANGUARD SERIES 2 WEATHERGUARD CARBINE – .223 Rem. (mfg. 2016 only), .22-250 Rem. (mfg. 2016 only), .243 Win., 7mm-08 Rem., or .308 Win. cal., 20 in. lightweight barrel, 5 shot, Monte Carlo Griptonite® stock features pistol grip and forend inserts, right side palm swell, Tactical Grey Cerakote finish, 7 lbs. Mfg. 2016-2017.

	$635	$550	$475	$425	$350	$285	$250	*$749*

VANGUARD SERIES 2 WEATHERGUARD/WEATHERGUARD DBM – .223 Rem., .257 Wby. Mag., .22-250 Rem., 7mm Rem. Mag., .243 Win., .300 Win. Mag., .240 Wby. Mag., .300 Wby. Mag., .25-06 Rem., 6.5 Creedmoor, .270 Win., 7mm-08 Rem., .308 Win., or .30-06 cal., 24 or 26 in. barrel, 3 or 5 shot mag., optional detachable box mag. avail. in some cals., Monte Carlo Griptonite stock features pistol grip and forend inserts and right side palm swell, 3-pos. safety, Tactical Grey Cerakote finish, 7 3/4 lbs. New 2016.

MSR $649	$550	$480	$415	$375	$300	$250	$200	

GRADING - PPGS™ 100% 98% 95% 90% 80% 70% 60% LAST MSR

VANGUARD SERIES 2 WEATHERGUARD BRONZE – .22-250 Rem., .223 Rem., .240 Wby. Mag., .243 Win., .25-06, .257 Wby. Mag., .270 Win., .30-06, .300 Wby. Mag., .300 Win. Mag., .308 Win., 6.5 Creedmoor, 6.5-300 Wby. Mag., 7mm Rem. Mag., or 7mm-08 Rem. cal., 24 or 26 in. #2 contour cold hammer forged barrel with Burnt Bronze Cerakote finish, hinged floorplate, adj. two-stage trigger, black base stock with bronze webbing, right side palm swell, 3-pos. safety, fluted bolt body, fully enclosed bolt sleeve, 7.5 lbs. New 2020.

MSR $699 $595 $525 $450 $400 $325 $275 $225

VANGUARD SERIES 2 WEATHERGUARD H-BAR – .223 Rem., .22-250 Rem. (mfg. 2016 only), 6.5 Creedmoor (new 2017), or .308 Win. cal., 22 in. #3 contoured heavy threaded barrel, 5 shot, Monte Carlo Griptonite® stock features pistol grip and forend inserts, right side palm swell, Tactical Grey Cerakote finish, 8 1/4 lbs. Mfg. 2016-2018.

$675 $600 $500 $450 $375 $300 $250 *$789*

VANGUARD SERIES 2 (WEATHERGUARD) MULTICAM – .240 Wby. Mag., .243 Win., .25-06, .257 Wby. Mag., .270 Win., .30-06, .300 Wby. Mag., .300 Win. Mag., .308 Win., 6.5 Creedmoor, 6.5-300 Wby. Mag., 7mm Rem. Mag., or 7mm-08 Rem. cal., 24 or 26 in. cold hammer forged #2 contour threaded barrel, hinged floorplate, adj. two-stage trigger, MultiCam Camo polymer stock, right side palm swell, recoil pad, 3-pos. safety, fluted bolt body, FDE Cerakote finish on all metalwork, 7.5 lbs. New 2020.

MSR $849 $725 $635 $550 $495 $425 $325 $275

VANGUARD SERIES 2 WILDERNESS/WILDERNESS DBM – .240 Wby. Mag., .257 Wby. Mag., .25-06 Rem., 6.5 Creedmoor, 6.5-300 Wby. Mag., .270 Win., .300 Win. Mag., .308 Win., .300 Wby. Mag., or .30-06 cal., 24or 26 in. fluted barrel, 3 or 5 shot, optional detachable box mag. available in some cals., hand-laminated raised comb Monte Carlo carbon fiber composite stock with aluminum bedding plate, matte gel coat finish, and spiderweb accents, matte bead blasted blued finish, 6 3/4 lbs. Mfg. 2016-disc.

$765 $675 $575 $525 $425 $350 $300 *$899*

RIFLES: BOLT ACTION, WBY-X SERIES

WBY-X SERIES – various cals., built on Vanguard Series 2 platform, 20 (#1 contour), 22 (#3 contour) or 24 (cold hammer forged) in. barrel with matte bead blasted blued finish, with or w/o recessed target crown, 3 or 5 shot mag., two-stage adj. trigger, 3-position safety, lightweight composite Monte Carlo stock with Proveil, Next, Boneyard, or Kryptek patterns, no sights, drilled and tapped, swivel studs included, 6 1/2-8 1/2 lbs. Mfg. 2014-2016.

* ***WBY-X Black Reaper TR*** – .223 Rem. or .308 Win. cal., 22 in. #3 contour barrel with recessed target crown, hand laminated Monte Carlo composite stock dipped in Proveil Reaper Black pattern, 8 1/4 lbs. Mfg. 2014-2015.

$650 $575 $500 $400 $335 $295 $240 *$749*

* ***WBY-X Blaze*** – .223 Rem., .243 Win., .270 Win., .308 Win., or .30-06 cal., 24 in. barrel, 5 shot mag., features stock dipped in Boneyard Camo Blaze pattern, 7 1/4 lbs. Mfg. 2014-2015.

$650 $575 $500 $400 $335 $295 $240 *$749*

* ***WBY-X GH2 (Girls Hunt 2)*** – .22-250 Rem., .223 Rem., .243 Win., .308 Win. or 7mm-08 cal., 20 in. barrel, 5 shot mag., Monte Carlo composite black stock with pink spider web accents, adj. LOP with stock spacer, matte blued metal finish, 6 1/2 lbs. Mfg. mid-2013-2016.

$650 $575 $500 $400 $335 $295 $240 *$749*

* ***WBY-X Hog Reaper*** – .223 Rem., .243 Win., .308 Win., or 7mm-08 Rem. cal., 20 in. barrel, 5 shot mag., features stock dipped in Proveil Hog Reaper pattern, 7 lbs. Mfg. 2014-2015.

$650 $575 $500 $400 $335 $295 $240 *$749*

* ***WBY-X Kryptek*** – .223 Rem., .243 Win., .270 Win., .308 Win., or .30-06 cal., 24 in. barrel, 5 shot mag., composite Monte Carlo stock features hard textured forearm and grip areas, right side palm swell, fully dipped in Kryptek Highlander Reduced camo pattern, matte blued finish, 7 1/4-7 1/2 lbs. Mfg. 2015-2016.

$650 $575 $500 $400 $335 $295 $240 *$749*

* ***WBY-X Kryptek H-BAR*** – .223 Rem. or .308 Win. cal., 22 in. cold hammer forged barrel, 5 shot, composite Monte Carlo stock fully dipped in Kryptek Highlander Reduced camo pattern, 8 1/4 lbs. Mfg. 2015-2016.

$650 $575 $500 $400 $335 $295 $240 *$749*

» **WBY-X Kryptek TR** – .223 Rem. or .308 Win. cal., similar to Kryptek, except features 22 in. barrel with recessed target crown, 8 1/4 lbs. Mfg. 2015 only.

$650 $575 $500 $400 $335 $295 $240 *$749*

GRADING - PPGS™	100%	98%	95%	90%	80%	70%	60%	LAST MSR

* ***WBY-X Saratoga*** – .223 Rem., .243 Win., .270 Win., .308 Win, or .30-06 cal., 24 in. barrel, injection molded composite Monte Carlo stock dipped in One Nation Vintage American Flag camo pattern, bead blasted metal finish, approx. 7 1/4 lbs. Mfg. 2015 only.

$650 $575 $500 $400 $335 $295 $240 ***$749***

* ***WBY-X Typhon*** – .223 Rem., .243 Win., .270 Win., .308 Win., or .30-06 cal., 24 in. barrel, features stock dipped in Kryptek Typhon pattern, 7 1/4-7 1/2 lbs. Mfg. 2014-2015.

$650 $575 $500 $400 $335 $295 $240 ***$749***

» **WBY-X Typhon TR** – .223 Rem. or .308 Win. cal., similar to Typhon, except features 22 in. # 3 contour barrel with recessed target crown, 8 1/4 lbs. Mfg. 2014-2015.

$650 $575 $500 $400 $335 $295 $240 ***$749***

* ***WBY-X Volt*** – .22-250 Rem., .223 Rem., .243 Win., 7mm-08 Rem., or .308 Win. cal., 20 in. barrel w/o sights, 5 shot mag., lightweight composite Monte Carlo stock with bright green spiderweb accents, adj. LOP w/stock spacer included, bead blasted matte blue metal finish, 6 3/4 lbs. Mfg. 2015-2016.

$650 $575 $500 $400 $335 $295 $240 ***$749***

* ***WBY-X Whitetail Bonz*** – .240 Wby., .243 Win., .257 Wby., .270 Win., .300 Win. Mag., .300 Wby. Mag., .30-06, or .308 Win. cal., 24 in. barrel, 3 or 5 shot mag., features stock dipped in Next Camo Whitetail Bonz pattern, 7 1/4-7 1/2 lbs. Mfg. mid-2013-2015.

$650 $575 $500 $400 $335 $295 $240 ***$749***

» **WBY-X Whitetail Bonz Compact (Youth)** – .22-250 Rem., .223 Rem., .243 Win., .308 Win., or 7mm-08 Rem. cal., similar to WBY-X Whitetail Bonz, except features 20 in. barrel, 5 shot mag., adj. LOP with stock spacer, 6 1/2 lbs. Mfg. mid-2013-2015.

$650 $575 $500 $400 $335 $295 $240 ***$749***

SHOTGUNS: O/U

Recent Weatherby O/U shotguns were previously manufactured by Fausti of Italy until 2011. Previous manufacture was by SKB of Japan, and by Nikko Firearms of Japan from May 1972 to 1981.

Japanese manufacture utilized the IMC choke system (integral multi-choke), which allows interchangeability with Briley choke tubes.

REGENCY FIELD GRADE – 20 (new 1968) or 12 ga., checkered stock, VR, engraved sideplates, SST, early importation beginning in 1967 was from Italy, later mfg. was switched to Japan.

$1,395 $1,250 $1,095 $940 $850 $690 $565

Add 10%-15% for early Italian mfg. (note proof marks).

REGENCY TRAP GRADE – 12 ga., checkered trap stock, engraved, VR, SST. Imported from Italy.

$1,200 $1,050 $850 $725 $650 4550 $450

OLYMPIAN STANDARD – 12 and 20 ga., lightly engraved sideplates. Disc. 1980.

$850 $745 $640 $580 $470 $385 $300

OLYMPIAN SKEET – 26 or 28 in. barrel.

$885 $775 $665 $600 $485 $400 $310

OLYMPIAN TRAP – 30 or 32 in. barrel, VR.

$850 $745 $640 $580 $470 $385 $300

ATHENA GRADE III CLASSIC FIELD – 12, 20, or 28 (new 2001) ga., 2 3/4 (28 ga. only) or 3 in. chambers, 26 or 28 in. barrels, features oil finished American Claro walnut stock with rounded pistol grip and slender forearm, gold SST (push-button on trigger), silver grey nitride sideplates with rose and scroll engraved gold pheasant and quail hunting scenes, gold "W" on opening lever, 6 1/2-8 lbs. Mfg. 1999-2007.

$2,125 $1,860 $1,595 $1,445 $1,170 $955 $745 ***$2,510***

ATHENA D'ITALIA III – 12 or 20 ga., 3 in. chambers, vented 26 or 28 in. VR barrels with choke tubes, ejectors, four-lock boxlock action with chrome plated sideplates with gold game bird scenes, SST (tang operated), checkered oil finished walnut stock and forearm, pierced top lever, trigger guard features Weatherby flying "W", 6 1/2-8 lbs. Mfg. by Fausti 2008-2011.

$2,200 $1,925 $1,650 $1,495 $1,210 $990 $770 ***$2,599***

ATHENA GRADE IV FIELD – 12, 20, 28 (mfg. 1989-1993) ga., or .410 bore (mfg. 1989-1993) bore, 3 in. chambers, 26 or 28 in. VR barrels with or without choke tubes, boxlock with Greener Crossbolt, SST, ejectors, high luster finish on hand checkered Claro walnut stock (full pistol grip with rosewood cap) and forearm, recoil pad, engraved sideplates with satin nickel finish, vent. barrels and rib, multi-chokes became standard (except .410 bore) 1986 and 1992 (28 ga.), 6 1/2-8 lbs. Mfg. 1982-2002.

$2,085 $1,825 $1,565 $1,420 $1,145 $940 $730 ***$2,549***

Subtract 10% if without choke tubes.

This model was redesignated the Grade IV in 1989.

GRADING - PPGS™	100%	98%	95%	90%	80%	70%	60%	LAST MSR

* ***Athena Grade IV Field Skeet & Trap Models*** – 12 (Trap only) or 20 ga., special stock dimensions, target sights. Disc. 1992.

$1,675 $1,465 $1,255 $1,140 $920 $755 $585 *$1,965*

Skeet models were available in fixed choke only.

* ***Athena Grade IV Field Single Trap Model*** – 12 ga., 32 or 34 in. barrels with multi-choke feature. Disc. 1992.

$1,675 $1,465 $1,255 $1,140 $920 $755 $585 *$1,975*

* ***Athena Grade IV Field Trap Combo*** – 12 ga., includes a set of O/U barrels and oversingle barrel with multi-choke feature. Disc. 1992.

$2,300 $2,015 $1,725 $1,565 $1,265 $1,035 $800 *$2,616*

* ***Athena Grade IV Field Master Skeet Set*** – 12 ga., includes 6 fitted full-length Briley tubes with integral extractors (20, 28 ga., and .410 bore), cased. Imported 1988-91.

$3,100 $2,715 $2,325 $2,110 $1,705 $1,395 $1,085

ATHENA D'ITALIA IV – similar to Athena D'Italia III, except also available in 28 ga. Mfg. 2008-2010 by Fausti.

$2,500 $2,190 $1,875 $1,700 $1,375 $1,125 $875 *$2,799*

Add $300 for 28 ga.

ATHENA GRADE V CLASSIC FIELD – 12 or 20 ga., 3 in. chambers, similar to Grade IV, except has more elaborate engraving w/o gold inlays, gold SST, and better walnut, 6 1/2 - 8 lbs. Mfg. by SKB 1989-2007.

$2,375 $2,080 $1,780 $1,615 $1,305 $1,070 $830 *$2,773*

In 1993, Weatherby changed the styling of this gun to incorporate European shooting features including an oil finished, round knob stock and slim forearm, tight rose-and-scroll engraving, and matted VR.

ATHENA D'ITALIA V – 12 or 20 ga., vented 26 or 28 in. VR barrels with choke tubes, ejectors, four-lock boxlock action with chrome plated sideplates featuring intricate rose and scroll engraving, raised and engraved hingepin, extra select checkered oil finished walnut stock and forearm, 7 1/2 - 8 lbs. Mfg. by Fausti 2008-2011.

$3,350 $2,930 $2,515 $2,280 $1,845 $1,510 $1,175 *$3,999*

ORION UPLAND CLASSIC FIELD – 12 or 20 ga., 3 in. chambers, features high luster checkered Claro walnut stock and forearm, blue frame, gold SST, gold Weatherby flying "W" on trigger guard, rounded checkered pistol grip stock and slender forearm, ejectors, 26 or 28 in. VR barrels with choke tubes, 6 1/2-8 lbs. Mfg. 1999-2007.

$1,225 $1,070 $920 $835 $675 $550 $430 *$1,500*

ORION I FIELD (OLDER MFG.) – 12 or 20 ga., 3 in. chambers, 26, 28, or 30 (12 ga. only) in. VR barrels with multi-chokes, SST, ejectors, checkered walnut full pistol grip stock and forearm, recoil pad, blue receiver with engraved upland and waterfowl scenes, 6 1/2-8 lbs. Mfg. 1989-2002.

$1,240 $1,085 $930 $845 $680 $560 $435 *$1,539*

* ***Orion I Field Ducks Unlimited*** – 12 ga. (sponsor gun in 1986) or 20 ga. (sponsor gun in 1987), deluxe walnut with gold duck scenes, blue frame, multi-chokes, includes presentation case.

$1,395 $1,220 $1,045 $950 $765 $630 $490

ORION I FIELD (CURRENT MFG.) – 12 ga., 3 in. chambers, 26 or 28 in. VR barrels with 3 choke tubes, steel receiver/barrels, ejectors, ST, brass bead front sight, checkered walnut stock and forearm with recoil pad, blue finish, 7 lbs. New 2015.

MSR $949 $800 $700 $600 $550 $450 $375 $300

ORION D'ITALIA I – 12 or 20 ga., 3 in. chambers, vented 26 or 28 in. VR barrels, ejectors, high lustre checkered walnut stock and forearm, blue boxlock action with game and floral engraving, engraved forearm iron and hinge pin, trigger guard has Weatherby flying "W" engraved in gold, 6.5-8 lbs. Mfg. by Fausti 2008-2011.

$1,425 $1,245 $1,070 $970 $785 $640 $500 *$1,699*

ORION II FIELD – 12, 20, 28 ga., or .410 bore, 3 in. chambers (except 28 ga.), boxlock with Greener Crossbolt, SST, ejectors, walnut with high-gloss finish, blue (early mfg.) or silver nitride receiver with light engraving. Multi-chokes became standard 1986. Field Grade disc. 1993.

$1,075 $940 $805 $730 $590 $485 $375 *$1,207*

Subtract 10% without choke tubes on older models.

Subtract $14 for Skeet grade (12 and 20 ga., fixed chokes only).

This model was redesignated Grade II in 1989. In 1993, the Standard Field Models in this variation were discontinued (Classic Grade took its place) - only Field and Sporting Clays variations were available.

GRADING - PPGS™	100%	98%	95%	90%	80%	70%	60%	LAST MSR

* ***Orion II Field Classic*** – 12, 20, or 28 ga., multi-choked barrels with matted VR, features rounded pistol grip stock and oil finished Claro walnut stock and forearm, gold SST, ejectors, waterfowl and upland game scenes on silver grey nitride finish, 6 1/2-8 lbs. Mfg. 1993-2007.

	$1,500	$1,315	$1,125	$1,020	$825	$675	$525	*$1,873*

ORION II FIELD/CLASSIC SPORTING – 12 ga. only, Sporting Clays configuration, early mfg. was blue finish, recent mfg. had silver nitride finish, choice of Field Sporting (with rosewood pistol grip cap and grooved upper forearm) or Classic Field Sporting (rounded pistol grip and smaller forearm), acid etched engraving, rounded recoil pad, matte finish VR, lengthened forcing cones. Mfg. 1991-2002.

	$1,400	$1,225	$1,050	$950	$770	$630	$490	*$1,753*

ORION D'ITALIA II – 12, 20, or 28 ga., vented 26, 28, or 30 (12 ga. only) in. VR barrel, ejectors, fancy grade checkered walnut stock and forearm, hard chrome receiver with game and floral engraving, engraved forearm iron and hinge pin, trigger guard has Weatherby flying "W" engraved in gold, 6 1/2-8 lbs. Mfg. 2008-2010 by Fausti.

	$1,600	$1,400	$1,200	$1,090	$880	$720	$560	*$1,899*

Add $80 for 28 ga.

SUPER SPORTING CLAYS (SSC) – 12 ga. only, 3 in. chambers, 28, 30, or 32 in. vented barrels with 12mm target VR and gas ports, choke tubes, fully adj. trigger, satin oil finished sporter style pistol grip stock with Schnabel forearm, Pachmayr Decelerator pad, approx. 8 lbs. Mfg. 1999-2007.

	$1,875	$1,640	$1,405	$1,275	$1,030	$845	$655	*$2,378*

ORION D'ITALIA SC (SPORTING CLAYS) – 12 ga., 28, 30, or 32 in. ported barrels, ejectors, four-lock boxlock action, satin oil finished checkered walnut stock with adj. comb, pistol grip, and Schnabel forend, chrome plated receiver with engraved Weatherby logo, trigger guard has gold engraved flying "W", 8 lbs. Mfg. by Fausti 2008-2009.

	$2,250	$1,970	$1,690	$1,530	$1,240	$1,015	$790	*$2,599*

ORION III FIELD – 12 or 20 ga. only, similar to Grade II, except has silver grey receiver with custom engraving including mallard and pheasant game scenes, multi-chokes standard. Mfg. 1989-2002.

	$1,545	$1,350	$1,160	$1,050	$850	$695	$540	*$1,917*

* ***Orion III Field Classic*** – 12 or 20 ga., multi-choked 26 or 28 in. VR barrels, features rounded pistol grip stock and oil finished Claro walnut stock and forearm, extensive engraving on silver grey nitride finish with gold game scene inlays, matted VR, 7 1/4-8 lbs. Mfg. 1993-2007.

	$1,800	$1,575	$1,350	$1,225	$990	$810	$630	*$2,258*

* ***Orion III Field English*** – 12 or 20 ga., 3 in. chambers, features straight grip stock and silver grey nitride receiver with engraving and gold inlays, approx. 6 1/2 lbs. Mfg. 1997-2002.

	$1,595	$1,395	$1,195	$1,085	$875	$720	$560	*$1,998*

ORION D'ITALIA III – similar to Orion D'Italia II, except has better walnut and gold inlays. Mfg. 2008-2010 by Fausti.

	$1,850	$1,620	$1,390	$1,260	$1,020	$835	$650	*$2,199*

ORION SPORTING – 12 ga., 3 in. chambers, 30 in. ported barrels, knurled, extended chokes, tapered ventilated top rib, fiber optic front sight, ambidextrous top tang safety, low profile receiver, automatic ejectors, high gloss finished A-grade walnut stock with diamond point checkering and adj. comb, 7 1/2 lbs. New 2018.

MSR $1,099	$950	$825	$715	$650	$525	$450	$350	

SHOTGUNS: SxS

Recent SxS manufacture was by Fausti of Italy until 2011. SxS manufacture utilizes the IMC choke system (integral multi-choke), which allows interchangeability with Briley choke tubes. Importation was disc. during 2003, and reintroduced during 2005.

ORION – 12, 20, 28 ga. or .410 bore, 3 in. chambers standard except for 28 ga., ejectors, case colored boxlock action, gold SST, 18 LPI checkered half-round pistol grip Turkish walnut stock and semi-beavertail forearm, 26 or 28 in. barrels, solid pad, 6 3/4-7 lbs., approx. 400 mfg. (including Athena) in Spain by Abolla 2002-2003.

	$960	$840	$720	$655	$530	$430	$335	*$1,149*

ORION D'ITALIA SBS – 12 or 20 ga., 3 in. chambers, SST, 26 (20 ga. only) or 28 (12 ga. only) in. back bored barrels with choke tubes, coin finished boxlock action, gloss finished checkered pistol grip stock and beavertail forearm, Weatherby flying "W" in gold on trigger guard, 6 3/4-7 1/4 lbs. Mfg. by Fausti 2008-2011.

	$1,875	$1,650	$1,425	$1,250	$1,025	$875	$725	*$2,199*

GRADING - PPGS™	100%	98%	95%	90%	80%	70%	60%	LAST MSR

ATHENA – 12 or 20 ga., 3 in. chambers, ejectors, case colored engraved boxlock action with sideplates, gold SST, 22 LPI checkered straight grip select Turkish walnut stock and splinter forearm, 26 or 28 in. barrels with IMC choke system (interchangeable with Briley), solid pad, 6 3/4-7 lbs., approx. 400 (including Orion) mfg. in Spain by Abolla 2002-2003.

$1,285	$1,125	$965	$875	$705	$580	$450	*$1,599*

ATHENA D'ITALIA – 12, 20, or 28 ga., 2 3/4 (28 ga. only) or 3 in. chambers, engraved coin finished Anson & Deeley boxlock action with sideplates, double locking system, monobloc barrels with ejectors and stainless steel choke tubes, DT, oil finished English straight grip select walnut stock and slim forearm with new Scottish checkering, gold "W" on trigger guard, supplied with hardshell takedown case, 6 3/4-7 1/4 lbs. Mfg. by Fausti of Italy 2005-2011.

$2,725	$2,385	$2,045	$1,855	$1,500	$1,225	$955	*$3,129*

Add $140 for 28 ga.

* ***Athena D'Italia PG*** – 12, 20, or 28 ga., similar boxlock action, except has more engraving, gold SST, deluxe checkered walnut rounded pistol grip stock and semi-beavertail forearm, 6 3/4-7 1/4 lbs. Mfg. by Fausti of Italy. Mfg. 2006-2010.

$3,250	$2,845	$2,450	$2,210	$1,790	$1,465	$1,150	*$3,799*

Add $130 for 28 ga.

* ***Athena D'Italia Deluxe*** – 12, 20, or 28 ga., coin finished boxlock action with sideplates featuring Bulino style game scene engraving and gold inlays by A. Posilini (hand signed), relief engraved shoulders, AAA straight grip 24 LPI checkered Turkish walnut stock with wood buttplate and splinter forearm, gold SST, ejectors, 6 3/4-7 1/4 lbs. Mfg. by Fausti of Italy. Mfg. 2006-2008.

$6,900	$6,040	$5,175	$4,690	$3,795	$3,105	$2,415	*$7,625*

Add $164 for 28 ga.

SHOTGUNS: SEMI-AUTO

Beginning 2008, all semi-autos are manufactured in Turkey. Previous manufacture was by ITI of Italy until 2007, and utilized the IMC choke system (integral multi-choke), which allows interchangeability with Briley choke tubes.

Add $359 for interchangeable SAS rifled 22 in. slug barrel (mfg. 2004-2007).

18i DELUXE – 12 or 20 ga., 3 in. chamber, Inertia-driven, 26 or 28 in. barrel, five choke tubes, full length ventilated top rib, 4 shot mag., LPA fiber sights, matte finish walnut stock with texturing in the palm and foregrip, red ring on safety release button, custom LaserTech engraving on receiver. New 2020.

MSR $1,899	$1,625	$1,425	$1,225	$1,100	$895	$750	$600

18i SYNTHETIC – 12 ga., 3 1/2 in. chamber, Inertia-driven system, full length ventilated top rib, 4 shot mag., LPA fiber sights, synthetic stock and forearm wiith soft touch area on cheek rest, aggressive texture on the palm and foregrip, red ring safety, matte finish. New 2020.

MSR $1,099	$935	$825	$700	$635	$515	$425	$350

18i WATERFOWLER CAMO – 12 ga., 3 1/2 in. chamber, Inertia-driven system, full length ventilated top rib, includes 5 choke tubes, 4 shot mag., LPA fiber sights, elastomer stock, red ring safety release button, 100% Realtree Max-5, Realtree Timber, Mossy Oak Bottomlands, or Mossy Oak Shadow Grass Blades camo finish. New 2020.

MSR $1,199	$1,025	$895	$775	$695	$575	$475	$400

CENTURION FIELD GRADE – 12 ga., gas operation, VR, full pistol grip checkered walnut stock. Mfg. 1972-1981.

$300	$265	$225	$205	$165	$135	$105

CENTURION TRAP GRADE – 12 ga., checkered stock, VR.

$335	$295	$250	$230	$185	$150	$115

CENTURION DE LUXE – 12 ga., VR, checkered stock, lightly engraved.

$375	$330	$280	$255	$205	$170	$130

Add 20% for deluxe wood.

* ***Centurion De Luxe DU*** – mfg. 1980 for DU chapters.

$550	$480	$415	$375	$305	$250	$195

ELEMENT DELUXE – 12, 20, or 28 (disc. 2017) ga., inertia operated action, 26 or 28 in. VR barrel with 3 choke tubes, 4 shot mag., drop out trigger system, AA Grade American walnut stock, fineline diamond point checkering with wrap-around pattern on forearm, aluminum alloy receiver with gold-etched Weatherby logo on sideplate, chrome-plated bolt, gloss finished metalwork. Mfg. 2015-2018.

$950	$825	$700	$625	$475	$395	$325	*$1,099*

Add $50 for 28 ga. (disc. 2017).

GRADING - PPGS™	100%	98%	95%	90%	80%	70%	60%	LAST MSR

ELEMENT SYNTHETIC – 12 or 20 ga., 3 in. chamber, 26 or 28 in. VR barrel with 4 choke tubes, 4 shot mag., Griptonite stock features pistol grip and forend inserts in gray/black design, matte bead blasted finish, 6 1/4-6 3/4 lbs. New 2016.

MSR $549	$465	$400	$350	$315	$250	$210	$185	

ELEMENT UPLAND – 12 or 20 ga., 3 in. chamber, inertia operated action, 26 or 28 in. chrome-lined VR barrel, integral multi-choke system (IC/M/F), drop-out trigger system, fiber optic front sights, walnut stock with matte oil finish, aircraft grade aluminum receiver, dual purpose bolt release, high luster finish, 6 1/4-6 3/4 lbs. New 2019.

MSR $699	$595	$520	$450	$400	$325	$275	$225	

ELEMENT WATERFOWLER MAX-5 – 12 or 20 ga., 3 in. chamber, 26 or 28 in. VR barrel with 4 choke tubes, 4 shot, Griptonite stock with rubberized pistol grip and forend inserts, 100% Realtree Max-5 camo pattern, 6 1/4-6 3/4 lbs. New 2016.

MSR $699	$595	$520	$450	$400	$325	$275	$225	

MODEL 82 – 12 ga. only, 2 3/4 or 3 in. chamber, gas operation, alloy receiver, VR, deluxe walnut stock, multi-chokes became standard in 1985, Trap Grade was disc. 1984. Mfg. 1983-89.

	$395	$345	$295	$270	$215	$180	$140	*$500*

Subtract $30 without multi-chokes.
Subtract $35 for Trap Grade (disc. 1984).

* ***Model 82 Buckmaster*** – 22 in. barrel choked skeet, rifle sights, 7 1/2 lbs. Disc. 1989.

	$395	$345	$295	$270	$215	$180	$140	*$500*

MODEL SAS FIELD – 12 ga., 3 in. chamber, self-compensating gas operated mechanism, 26, 28 (disc. 2001, reintroduced 2005), or 30 (12 ga. only. disc. 2001) in. VR barrel with Briley choke tubes, "Weatherby" outlined in gold on right side of receiver, high grade satin oil finished checkered American Claro walnut stock and forearm, includes stock shim system, 6 3/4-7 3/4 lbs. Mfg. in Italy 1999-2007.

	$775	$680	$580	$525	$425	$350	$270	*$926*

* ***Model SAS Field Sporting Clays*** – similar to SAS Field, except has choice of 26 (disc. 2004), 28, or 30 (new 2005) in. ported VR barrel with extended choke tubes, includes molded plastic case, 7-7 3/4 lbs. Mfg. 2002-2005.

	$850	$745	$640	$580	$470	$385	$300	*$999*

* ***Model SAS Field Synthetic*** – similar to Model SAS Field, except has black synthetic stock and forearm. Mfg. late 2000-2007.

	$745	$650	$560	$505	$410	$335	$260	*$879*

* ***Model SAS Field Camo*** – 12 ga. only, 24 (Mossy Oak Breakup only, new 2001) 26, or 28 (Shadow Grass only) in. VR barrel with 5 extended Briley choke tubes, HiViz front sight, 100% camo coverage in either Mossy Oak Breakup (disc. 2006), Shadow Grass (disc. 2006), Skyline Fall Flight (new 2007), or Skyline Apparition Excel (new 2007), 7 1/4-7 3/4 lbs. Mfg. late 2000-2007.

	$810	$710	$610	$550	$445	$365	$285	*$977*

* ***Model SAS Field Slug Gun*** – 12 ga. only, 3 in. chamber, 22 in. rifled barrel w/o sights, includes cantilever base, checkered Monte Carlo walnut stock and forearm with sling swivels, 7 3/4 lbs. Mfg. 2003-2007.

	$825	$720	$620	$560	$455	$370	$290	*$987*

SA-08 DELUXE – 12, 20, or 28 (mfg. 2013-2017) ga., 3 in. (12 or 20 ga.) chamber, 26 or 28 in. VR barrel with choke tubes, matte black receiver with "Weatherby" in gold on right side, oil finished checkered walnut stock and forearm with high gloss finish, dual valve system, 5 1/2-6 3/4 lbs. Mfg. 2010-circa 2019.

	$550	$480	$415	$375	$300	$250	$210	*$649*

Add $50 for 28 ga. (disc. 2017).

SA-08 ENTRE RIOS – 28 ga. only, scaled down frame, 26 or 28 in. VR barrel with 3 choke tubes, checkered walnut stock and forearm, 5 1/4 lbs. Mfg. 2011 only.

	$625	$550	$475	$425	$375	$325	$275	*$749*

SA-08 KRYPTEK COMPACT (PREVIOUS MFG.) – 20 ga., 24 in. barrel with choke tubes, vented top rib, dual valve system, lightweight injection-molded synthetic stock, Kryptek Highlander camo pattern on stock and forend, shorter LOP, swivel studs included, 5 3/4 lbs. Mfg. 2014 only.

	$695	$595	$525	$450	$375	$315	$275	*$799*

GRADING - PPGS™	100%	98%	95%	90%	80%	70%	60%	LAST MSR

SA-08 UPLAND – 12 or 20 ga., 3 in. chamber, gas action with dual valves for light or heavy loads, 26 or 28 in. VR barrel with choke tubes, matte black receiver with "Weatherby" in gold on right side, oil finished checkered walnut stock and forearm with satin finish, 5 1/2-6 3/4 lbs., mfg. in Turkey. Mfg. 2008-2016.

	$675	$585	$500	$450	$375	$300	$265	*$799*

This model was also available as a SA-08 Youth in 20 ga. with 12 1/2 LOP at no extra charge (disc. 2011).

SA-08 SYNTHETIC/SA-08 SYNTHETIC COMPACT – 12 (disc. 2019) or 20 ga., 3 in. chamber, dual valve gas operated system, 24 (compact), 26, or 28 in. VR barrel, 3 screw-in choke tubes, brass bead front sight, black synthetic stock, swivel studs, 12 1/2 in. LOP (compact model), push-button safety, matte black finish. New 2009.

MSR $499	$425	$375	$325	$290	$235	$195	$165	

SA-08 WATERFOWLER – 12 ga. only, 3 in. chamber, 26 or 28 in. VR barrel with choke tubes, similar to Synthetic model, except has 100% Realtree Max-5 (new 2015) or Mothwing Marsh Mimicry (disc. 2014) camo coverage, special dipping process adheres camo to all exterior stock and metalwork, 6 1/2 lbs. Mfg. 2010-2017.

	$675	$585	$500	$450	$375	$300	$265	*$799*

Subtract approx. $50 for Mothwing Marsh Mimicry camo (disc. 2014).

* ***SA-08 Waterfowler Max-5 Compact*** – 20 ga., 3 in. chamber, 26 or 28 in. VR barrel, 3 choke tubes, 5 shot mag., swivel studs, 12 1/2 in. LOP, 100% Realtree Max-5 camo finish, 5 3/4 lbs. Mfg. 2016-2017.

	$675	$585	$500	$450	$375	$300	$265	*$799*

SA-459 BLACK REAPER TR – 12 or 20 ga., 3 in. chamber, gas operated, 18 1/2 in. barrel, 5 shot, oversized bolt handle, Proveil Reaper Black pattern on stock and forend, features trimmer forend for easy handling, includes swivel studs, 6-6 1/2 lbs. Disc. 2015.

	$650	$575	$500	$400	$335	$295	$240	*$749*

SA-459 TR – 12 or 20 ga., 3 in. chamber, 18 1/2 in. ported barrel, 5 or 8 (new 2015) shot mag., tactical configuration with black synthetic pistol grip stock and forearm, includes ghost ring rear sight on Picatinny receiver rail, M16 front sight, oversized bolt handle, approx. 7 lbs. Mfg. 2011-2016

	$595	$525	$450	$400	$325	$275	$225	*$699*

Add $150 for 8 shot mag. (new 2015).

SA-459 TURKEY (PREVIOUS MFG.) – 12 or 20 ga., 3 in. chamber, 21-1/4 in. barrel with removable extended choke tube, gas operated action, fiber optic front and ghost ring rear sights, features Mothwing Spring Mimicry camo finish, oversized hourglass bolt handle, 6-6 1/2 lbs. Mfg. 2012-2014.

	$625	$550	$495	$425	$350	$295	$250	*$699*

SA-459 TURKEY (CURRENT MFG.) – 12 or 20 ga., 3 in. chamber, gas operated action, 22 in. VR barrel with removable extended choke tube, fiber optic front sight, oversized hourglass bolt handle, 100% Realtree Xtra Green camo finish, includes Picatinny rail, rubberized pistol grip, 6 1/4 or 6 3/4 lbs. New 2015.

MSR $649	$550	$480	$415	$375	$300	$250	$210	

WBY-X SA-08 KRYPTEK COMPACT (RECENT MFG.) – 20 ga., 3 in. chamber, 24 in. barrel w/choke tubes, vented top rib, dual valve system, lightweight injection-molded synthetic stock, 100% camo coverage on stock and forend, shorter LOP, swivel studs included, 6 3/4 lbs. Mfg. 2015-2016.

	$675	$585	$500	$450	$375	$300	$265	*$799*

WBY-X SA-08 GH2 (GIRLS HUNT 2) – 20 ga., 24 in. barrel with choke tubes, vented top rib, unique dual valve system, shorter LOP, lightweight injection-molded synthetic stock featuring a pink spiderweb pattern, 5 3/4 lbs. Mfg. 2014-2016.

	$650	$575	$500	$425	$350	$295	$250	*$749*

WBY-X SA-08 VOLT COMPACT – 20 ga., 3 in. chamber, 24 in. VR barrel with 3 choke tubes, 5 shot mag., black synthetic stock and forearm, 12 1/2 in. LOP, 5 3/4 lbs. Mfg. 2015-2016.

	$650	$575	$500	$425	$350	$295	$250	*$749*

SHOTGUNS: SLIDE ACTION

PATRICIAN FIELD GRADE – 12 ga., checkered stock, VR. Mfg. 1972-81.

	$275	$240	$205	$185	$150	$125	$95	

PATRICIAN TRAP GRADE – 12 ga., checkered stock, VR.

	$295	$260	$220	$200	$160	$135	$105	

PATRICIAN DE LUXE – 12 ga., checkered stock, lightly engraved, fancy wood, VR.

	$325	$285	$245	$220	$180	$145	$115	

GRADING - PPGS™	100%	98%	95%	90%	80%	70%	60%	LAST MSR

MODEL 92 – 12 ga. only, 2 3/4 and 3 in. chambers, ultra-short slide action w/twin rails, 26-30 in. VR barrels, engraved black alloy receiver, checkered pistol grip walnut stock and forearm. Mfg. 1982-89.

$325 $285 $245 $220 $180 $145 $115 *$400*

Subtract 10% for Trap grade (disc. 1984).
Subtract 10% if fixed choke (multi-chokes became standard 1985) barrel.

* ***Model 92 Buckmaster*** – 22 in. skeet bore barrel, rifle sights, 7 1/2 lbs. Disc. 1987.

$345 $300 $260 $235 $190 $155 $120 *$400*

WBY-X PA-08 BLACK REAPER TR – 12 or 20 ga., 3 in. chamber, 18 1/2 in. barrel with fixed cyl. bore, 4 shot, matte black metalwork, blade white dot front sight, swivel studs included, lightweight synthetic stock dipped in Proveil Reaper Black pattern, 6-6 1/2 lbs. Mfg. 2014-2016.

$395 $340 $295 $260 $230 $200 $175 *$469*

PA-08 KNOXX STRUTTER X – 12 ga., 24 in. VR barrel with choke tubes, features adj. Knoxx recoil reduction system stock with pistol grip, fiber optic sights, drop out trigger system, choice of matte black metal finish and black synthetic stock and forearm or 100% Apparition Excel camo coverage, 7 lbs., mfg. in Turkey. Mfg. 2008 only.

$425 $370 $320 $290 $235 $190 $150 *$499*

Add $80 for 100% camo coverage.

PA-08 KNOXX HD – 12 ga., 3 in. chamber, 18 in. barrel with fixed IC choke, features black synthetic Knoxx SpecOps adj. stock with pistol grip, extended mag. (5 shot capacity), 7 lbs. Mfg. in Turkey 2008 only.

$425 $370 $320 $290 $235 $190 $150 *$499*

PA-08 UPLAND – 12 or 20 ga., 3 in. chamber, 26 or 28 in. VR ribbed barrel with choke tubes, dual slide bar action, brass bead front sight, matte black metal, checkered low lustre walnut stock and forearm, 6 1/2 lbs. Mfg. 2008-2017.

$365 $335 $285 $250 $225 $200 $185 *$449*

This model is also available as a PA-08 Upland Compact in 20 ga. with 12 1/2 LOP and 22 in. barrel at no extra charge (new 2012).

PA-08 UPLAND SLUG GUN COMBO – 12 ga., 3 in. chamber, 24 in. rifled barrel with cantilever scope mount in matte black, 28 in. field barrel with IMC chokes, brass bead front sight, and has gloss black finish, walnut stock with gloss finish, 7 1/4 lbs. Mfg. 2012-2017.

$550 $475 $395 $340 $300 $265 $240 *$629*

PA-08 SYNTHETIC – 12 or 20 (new 2013) ga., 3 in. chamber, 26 or 28 in. chrome-lined VR ribbed barrel with choke tubes, dual slide bar action, brass bead front sight, matte black metal, lightweight black injection-molded synthetic stock and forearm, 6 1/2 lbs. Mfg. 2010-2017.

$350 $310 $270 $240 $210 $180 $160 *$399*

* ***PA-08 Synthetic Compact*** – 20 ga., 3 in. chamber, dual slide bar action, 22 in. chrome-lined VR ribbed barrel with choke tubes, 4 shot, brass bead front sight, lightweight black injection-molded synthetic stock and forearm, matte black metal finish, 5 3/4 lbs. Mfg. 2015-2017.

$350 $310 $270 $240 $210 $180 $160 *$399*

PA-08 SYNTHETIC SLUG GUN COMBO – 12 ga., 3 in. chamber, 24 in. rifled barrel with cantilever scope mount in matte black, 28 in. field barrel with IMC chokes, brass bead front sight, and has gloss black finish, black synthetic stock and forearm, 7 1/4 lbs. Mfg. 2012-2017.

$450 $395 $350 $295 $265 $235 $210 *$549*

PA-08 SYNTHETIC WATERFOWLER – 12 ga., 3 in. chamber, 26 or 28 in. barrel, lightweight and durable injection-molded synthetic stock with Mothwing Marsh Mimicry camo pattern, special dipping process adheres camo directly to all stock components, brass bead front sight, 7 1/4 lbs. Mfg. 2012-2014.

$350 $310 $270 $240 $210 $180 $160 *$399*

PA-08 TR – 12 or 20 (new 2013) ga., 3 in. chamber, 18 1/2 in. barrel with fixed cylinder choke and bladed white dot front sight, matte black finish, black synthetic stock and forearm, crossbolt trigger guard safety, 5 shot mag., dual action slide bars, 6 3/4 lbs. Mfg. 2011-2016.

$350 $310 $270 $240 $210 $180 $160 *$399*

Add $20 for TR accessory rail that attaches to screw-on magazine end cap.

PA-08 TURKEY – 12 ga., 3 in. chamber, 22 in. VR barrel with removable full choke tube, white dot blade front sight, dual action bar system, 5 shot mag., choice of Mothwing Spring Mimicry (disc. 2014) or Realtree Xtra Green (new 2015) camo finish, matte metal finish, 7 lbs. Mfg. 2012-2017.

$350 $315 $265 $235 $215 $195 $185 *$429*

GRADING - PPGS™	100%	98%	95%	90%	80%	70%	60%	LAST MSR

PA-08 TYPHON TR – 12 or 20 ga., 3 in. chamber, 18 1/2 in. barrel with fixed cyl. choke, 4 shot, matte black metalwork, blade white dot front sight, lightweight synthetic stock dipped in Kryptek Typhon pattern, swivel studs, 5 3/4-6 1/2 lbs. Mfg. 2014-2015.

$350 $310 $270 $240 $210 $180 $160 *$399*

PA-08 WATERFOWLER MAX-5 – 12 ga., 3 in. chamber, 26 or 28 in. VR barrel with 3 choke tubes, 4 shot mag., synthetic stock and forearm with Realtree Max-5 camo coverage, swivel studs, 7 1/4 lbs. Mfg. 2015-2017.

$350 $315 $265 $235 $215 $195 $185 *$429*

PA-459 BLACK REAPER TR – 12 or 20 ga., 3 in. chamber, 18 1/2 in. chrome-lined barrel with extended ported cyl. choke tube, 5 or 8 (new 2015, 12 ga. only) shot, 13 1/2 in. LOP, adj. rear LPA-style ghost ring sight, ergonomic buttstock with textured grip, stock dipped in Proveil Reaper black pattern, 5 3/4-6 1/2 lbs. Mfg. 2014-2015.

$465 $400 $350 $295 $265 $235 $210 *$569*

Add $80 for 8 shot mag. (new 2015, 12 ga. only).

PA-459 HOME DEFENSE – 12 ga. only, 3 in. chamber, 19 in. barrel, black synthetic stock and forearm. Mfg. 2010 only.

$350 $305 $265 $240 $195 $160 $125 *$469*

PA-459 TR – 12 or 20 (mfg. 2013-2015) ga. only, 3 in. chamber, 18 1/2 in. ported removable cylinder choke tube, M16 style fiber optic front sight, black synthetic grooved pistol grip stock and forearm, alloy receiver with integral Picatinny rail and adj. ghost ring sight, 13 1/2 in. LOP, 5 (disc. 2015) or 7 (new 2015, 12 ga. only) shot mag., matte black metalwork, 6 1/2 lbs. Mfg. 2011-2016.

$475 $400 $340 $295 $265 $235 $210 *$599*

Subtract approx. $100 for 20 ga. with 5 shot mag. (mfg. 2013-2015).

* ***PA-459 Digital TR*** – 12 ga. only, otherwise similar to PA-459 TR, except has green/tan digital camo pattern on stock (not pistol grip) and forearm, choice of 6 or 7 (new 2015) shot mag. Mfg. 2011-2015.

$465 $400 $350 $295 $265 $235 $210 *$569*

Add $80 for 7 shot mag. (new 2015).

PA-459 TURKEY – 12 ga., 3 in. chamber, 21-1/4 in. barrel with removable extended ported choke tube, 13-1/2 in. LOP, 5 shot mag., fiber optic front and ghost ring rear sight, ergonomic pistol grip buttstock with rubber texturized grip, Picatinny accessory rail, 100% Mothwing Spring Mimicry (disc. 2015) or Realtree Xtra Green (new 2015) camo finish, 7 1/4 lbs. Mfg. 2012-2016.

$475 $400 $340 $295 $265 $235 $210 *$599*

PA-459 TYPHON TR – 12 or 20 ga., 3 in. chamber, 18 1/2 in. chrome-lined barrel with extended ported cyl. choke tube, 5 shot, shorter LOP, adj. rear LPA-style ghost ring sight, ergonomic buttstock with textured grip, stock dipped in Kryptek Typhon pattern, swivel studs included, 5 3/4-6 1/2 lbs. Mfg. 2014-2015.

$450 $395 $350 $295 $265 $235 $210 *$549*

WEAVER ARMS CORPORATION

Previous manufacturer located in Escondido, CA circa 1984-1990.

CARBINES

NIGHTHAWK CARBINE – 9mm Para. cal., semi-auto design carbine, fires from closed bolt, 16.1 in. barrel, retractable shoulder stock, 25, 32, 40, or 50 shot mag. (interchangeable with Uzi), ambidextrous safety, parkerized finish, 6 1/2 lbs. Mfg. 1987-90.

$675 $600 $525 $450 $375 $325 $300 *$575*

PISTOLS: SEMI-AUTO

NIGHTHAWK PISTOL – 9mm Para. cal., closed bolt semi-auto, 10 or 12 in. barrel, alloy upper receiver, ambidextrous safety, black finish, 5 lbs. Mfg. 1987-90.

$800 $700 $625 $550 $475 $425 $350 *$475*

WEBLEY & SCOTT AG (LIMITED)

Current trademark of firearms manufactured in Turkey and airguns manufactured in England with headquarters located in Luzern, Switzerland beginning 2010. Currently imported (bolt actions only) beginning 2016 by Legancy International, located in Reno, NV. Previously imported beginning mid-2013 by Centurion International, located in Reno, NV. Previously imported mid-2011-mid-2013 by Webley & Scott USA, located in Reno, NV. Previously located in West Midlands, England, with history dating back to 1790, and Birmingham, England.

GRADING - PPGS™	100%	98%	95%	90%	80%	70%	60%	LAST MSR

SxS shotguns were previously imported and distributed late 2007-2008 by Legacy Sports International, located in Reno, NV.

Webley & Scott is one of the oldest names in the UK gun industry, being able to trace its origins back to 1790 when William Davis started making bullet moulds in his small factory in Birmingham, England. In this early period Birmingham flourished as the greatest manufacturing centre of firearms in the world. Yet the only official proof house was in London, then in 1813 the world famous Birmingham Proof House was established by an Act of Parliament.

For more information and current pricing on both new and used Webley & Scott airguns, please refer to the *Blue Book of Airguns* - also available as an online subscription.

For detailed Webley & Scott history, please go to BlueBookOfGunValues.com/overflow.

PISTOLS: SEMI-AUTO

MODEL 1903 – .38 ACP cal., experimental model.

Extreme rarity precludes accurate pricing on this model.

MODEL 1904 – .455 Webley Auto cal., limited production, approx. 35 mfg.

Extreme rarity precludes accurate pricing on this model.

MODEL 1905 – 7.65mm/.32 ACP cal., ser. no. range 1-22,309, approx. 13,000+ mfg. from 1906-1909.

$1,500	$1,300	$1,100	$750	$600	$400	$300

MODEL 1906 – .45 cal., military trials pistol, never reached serial production.

Extreme rarity precludes accurate pricing on this model.

MODEL 1907 – 6.35mm/.25 ACP cal., hammer model, ser. no. range 7,060-163,109, approx. 50,000 mfg. from 1906-1939.

$1,000	$900	$800	$700	$600	$500	$400

MODEL 1908 – 7.65mm/.32 ACP cal., ser. no. range 22,310-163,709, approx. 90,000 mfg. from 1909-1940.

$1,500	$1,400	$1,300	$1,000	$750	$500	$400

MODEL 1909 – 9mm Browning Long cal., ser. no. range 16,000-137,416, approx. 1,700 mfg. from 1909-1922.

$2,700	$2,400	$2,100	$1,800	$1,400	$1,000	$800

MODEL 1910 – .380 ACP cal., ser. no. range 55,047-156,175, approx. 1,700 mfg. from 1910-1932.

$2,000	$1,900	$1,800	$1,700	$1,600	$1,500	$1,400

MODEL 1910 HIGH VELOCITY – .38 ACP (.38 Auto) cal., ser. no. range 40,000-66,664, less than 1,000 mfg. from 1909-1911.

$3,500	$3,000	$2,500	$2,000	$1,750	$1,500	$1,400

METROPOLITAN POLICE MODEL (M.P. MODEL) – 7.65mm (.32 ACP) cal., fixed standing leaf rear sight, ser. no. range 57,000-163,382, approx. 15,000 mfg. from 1911-1940.

$1,500	$1,400	$1,300	$1,000	$750	$500	$400

MODEL 1911

Please refer to the 1911 Target Model listing in the "PISTOLS: SINGLE SHOT" category.

MODEL 1912 – 6.35mm/.25 ACP cal. hammerless version of the Model 1907, ser. no. range 41,000-161,859, approx. 15,000 mfg. from 1909-1938.

$1,000	$900	$800	$700	$600	$500	$400

NAVY MODEL .455 MKI (SELF LOADING) – .455 Webley Auto cal., Royal Navy contract version of the Model 1913, marked MKI, ser. no. range 1-8,000. Mfg. 1913-1919.

Navy	$3,500	$3,000	$2,500	$2,000	$1,500	$1,000	$600
Commercial	$5,500	$5,000	$4,000	$3,500	$2,500	$2,000	$1,500

Commercially produced (in limited quantity) from 1911-1933. Serial no. range for the commercial pistols (including 500 for Australian contract) is scattered between 63130-158919. Commercial production probably never reached 1,000 with number 158919 being finished in Dec. 1933.

ROYAL HORSE ARTILLERY MODEL .455 MKI – .455 Webley Auto cal., rotary rear sights from 50-200 yards and a manual safety attached to the hammer, most are slotted at the base of the left grip for attachment of a shoulder stock, ser. no. range 2,501-8,050, less than 500 mfg. 1913-1919.

$10,000	$8,500	$7,500	$6,500	$5,500	$4,500	$3,500

Add 100% for original shoulder stock.

Add $1,250 for high quality reproduction stock.

GRADING - PPGS™	100%	98%	95%	90%	80%	70%	60%	LAST MSR

MODEL 1921 – 7.65mm/.32 ACP cal., improved Model 1908, Webley's final attempt at modernizing the .32 ACP, with a manual safety on the slide. Serial no. range 106,824-160,499, approx. 1,000 mfg. from 1914-1937 (pre-1921 pistols were later upgraded by addition of the slide safety).

	$3,000	$2,750	$2,500	$2,250	$1,750	$1,500	$1,250	

MODEL 1922 – 9mm Browning Long cal., also known as the New Military & Police Model, the (South) African Model, and the Romanian Model, ser. no. range 130,000-160,000, less than 1,900 mfg. from 1920-1932.

	$3,750	$3,500	$2,750	$2,500	$2,250	$1,750	$1,500	

"HUMANE KILLER" MODEL – 7.65mm/.32 ACP cal., single shot variation based on the .32 ACP cal. models, designed specifically for the humane put-down of livestock, used by vets, the Royal Society for the Prevention of Cruelty to Animals, and the Ministry of Agriculture and Fisheries, ser. no. range 100,000-200,000, less than 1,000 mfg. 1920-1940.

	$1,000	$900	$800	$700	$550	$450	$350	

PISTOLS: SINGLE SHOT

SINGLE SHOT TARGET MODELS – usually found in .22 LR cal., tip-up 10 3/8 in. barrel, target model, checkered walnut grips, early model grip terminates with steel weight to provide balance, also provides a means to attach a shoulder stock on some models, original model is improved with thumbrest grip as part of the wood grip, by the 1950s, thumbrest was enlarged and made of plastic with a compartment for steel weight at the bottom.

	$1,500	$1,400	$1,300	$1,200	$1,100	$1,000	$900	

Add 100% for special order .32 S&W or .38 S&W cals.
Add $1,000-$1,250 for shoulder stock.

M1911 TARGET MODEL – .22 LR cal., developed as companion piece for the Metropolitan Police .32 cal. service semi-auto, interchangeable 4 1/2 or 9 1/4 in. barrel, shoulder stock, could be ordered with both barrels, ser. no. range 58536-156398. Approx. 1,400 mfg. 1911-1932.

	$2,000	$1,800	$1,600	$1,200	$1,000	$800	$600	

Add $1,000-$1,250 for shoulder stock.
Add 100%-150% for cased sets with both barrel lengths.

WEBLEY PERCUSSION MODELS

The first patents for the Webley revolver were issued to brothers James and Phillip Webley in February and March of 1853. Prior to 1853 and up to 1867, Webley revolvers went through a period of development, including the percussion system, the pinfire, rimfire, and finally, the more common centerfire system. Webley made the early Webley pistols, while other makers in England and on the continent made pistols to the Webley design.

The early percussion revolvers were of the open frame design similar to the Colt 1851 or 1860. Of particular note are the three single action Longspur models. The Longspur was easily identified by its overly long hammer spur, and made in a pocket, holster or belt model, with barrel lengths from 3 1/2 to 7 inches, and in calibers from 48 ga. to 120 ga.

FIRST MODEL LONGSPUR – barrel hinged to frame, sides of frame obscure hammer except for spur, and no attached rammer, ser. no. range 131-388. Mfg. 1853-1855.

Extreme rarity preclues accurate pricing on this model.

SECOND MODEL LONGSPUR – barrel still hinged to frame, hammer more visible, also featured rammer attached to frame, ser. no. range 199-969. Mfg. 1855-1857.

Extreme rarity precludes accurate pricing on this model.

THIRD MODEL LONGSPUR – barrel not hinged to frame but attached via barrel over cylinder pin and is secured with thumb screw to frame with screw through cylinder pin, compound rammer is attached to barrel side, ser. no. range 985-1602. Mfg. 1857-1867.

Extreme rarity precludes accurate pricing on this model.

WEDGE FRAME MODELS – between 1857 and 1859, Webley developed the "wedge frame" as a transition between the "open frame" of the Longspur and the final "solid frame" percussion pistol which would develop into the solid frame cartridge pistols that became a hallmark of the Webley brand. This model met with great success with numerous guns being produced during a short time, most were made with attached ram under barrel or side barrel, five or six shot cylinder, numerous calibers and barrel lengths. Few examples have survived. Mfg. 1857-1859.

Extreme rarity precludes accurate pricing on this model.

GRADING - PPGS™	100%	98%	95%	90%	80%	70%	60%	LAST MSR

SOLID FRAME MODELS – the development of the solid frame percussion revolver offered a rigidity in frame design that would last into the modern revolver, few of the percussion revolvers with the solid frame were produced by Webley because of the development of more modern cartridge systems. Final development of the Webley solid frame revolver culminates with the arrival in 1867 of Webely's RIC No. 1, the model officially adopted by the Royal Irish Constabulary in Jan. 1868, presented to George A. Custer in 1869, and the model produced by Webley until the 1930s in one form or another.

Extreme rarity factor of solid frame percussion, pinfire, and rimfire models precludes accurate pricing.

REVOLVERS

R.I.C. MODELS – .320, .380, .442, .450, .455, or .476 cal., adopted by the Royal Irish Constabulary in Jan., 1868, recognized worldwide and produced in one variation or another from 1867-1939.

* ***R.I.C. Model No. 1*** – .380, .442, .450, .455, or .476 cals., 6 shot, fluted cylinder, most common with 4 1/2 in. barrel, but also found with 2 1/2 and 6 in. lengths, first of the series was offered in .442 cal. with 4 1/2 in. barrel, later No. 1 New Model was offered in .455 cal., ser. nos. exceeded 60,300 by Oct., 1884, serial nos. to approx. 102052 in 1914.

  $2,200 $1,900 $1,600 $1,200 $1,000 $800 $600

* ***R.I.C. Model No. 2*** – .320, .380, .442, or .450 cal., 2 to 4 in. barrels, ser. nos. reached 100139 by 1914.

  $2,000 $1,800 $1,500 $1,200 $1,000 $800 $600

* ***R.I.C. Model No. 3*** – typically found in .442 cal., 2 to 4 in. barrels, ser. nos. range from single digits to 15,000, 16,000, 30,000, and 70,000, 4 in. barrel variation was chosen as the official police weapon of the Queensland Govt., Australia.

  $2,000 $1,800 $1,500 $1,200 $1,000 $800 $600

* ***R.I.C. Model 83*** – .320, .380, .450, or .455 cal., 2 1/4, 2 1/2, 3, or 3 1/2 in. barrel, ser. no. 102,634. Mfg. until 1939.

  $2,200 $1,900 $1,600 $1,200 $1,000 $800 $600

* ***M. P. (Metropolitan Police) Model*** – .450 cal., introduced after the R.I.C. New Model No. 1, 6 shot, adopted by the London Metropolitan Police in 1883 and remained in service until 1911.

  $2,000 $1,800 $1,500 $1,200 $1,000 $800 $600

WEBLEY NO. 1 1/2 MODEL – .442 or .450 cal., 4 1/4 in. octagon barrel, limited examples of ser. nos. 28,000 and 60,000 have been observed.

$1,000 $900 $800 $700 $600 $500 $400

WEBLEY NO. 2 BRITISH BULL DOG PATTERN – .320, .380, .442, .450 centerfire, or .44 Short rimfire cal., short (2 1/2 in.) barrel, designed and manufactured by Webley as pocket models for civilians, with model names such as British Bulldog, The Pug, The Ulster Bulldog, or The Tower Bulldog, serial numbers vary by model.

$900 $800 $700 $600 $500 $400 $300

WEBLEY NO. 5 EXPRESS MODEL – .360, .380, .450, .455, .45 Colt, or .476 cal., include the large caliber military version and the small caliber civilian version, early military versions were based on the R.I.C. No. 1 frame with 6 in. barrel and came in .450 or .455 cal., New Model Express had new bird's head grip frame, .455 cal., and 5 1/2 in. barrel, military versions also included a single action in .476 cal., with 5 1/2 in. barrel issued to the Cape Mounted Rifles in 1881, civilian version offered in .360 or .380 cal., with a 2 1/2 - 4 1/2 in. barrel being the most common, ser. nos. range from the low 1,000 to excess of 10,000,000.

Large Cals. (Military)	$2,000	$1,900	$1,800	$1,700	$1,200	$900	$600
Small Cals. (Civilian)	$1,000	$900	$800	$700	$600	$500	$400

Cased, engraved, or unusual examples will command a premium.

REVOLVERS: HINGED FRAME, CENTERFIRE

Mark I-V .455 in. " service revolvers are all very similar, with bird's head grip frames and [usually] 4 in. barrels, differing primarily on the mechanism for cylinder removal, types of springs and steel used, and trigger guard and hammer configurations. The last model, the Mk. VI, differed from the earlier marks by having a square grip frame and a 6 in. barrel, though Mks. IV and V can often be found with the longer barrel.

Numerous surplus service Webleys (and Enfields), primarily the square-butt Mk. VI, were converted by U.S. gunsmiths to use .45 ACP ammunition; this will drastically decrease their value to collectors, up to 50% for high condition specimens.

Many commercial examples of service revolvers were privately owned by officers, and individual weapons may be engraved with their owner's name. Revolvers with such an attribution may command a premium of 20%, or more if adequate documentation can be provided to support provenance.

GRADING - PPGS™	100%	98%	95%	90%	80%	70%	60%	LAST MSR

While the production life for the service Mark III was relatively short, the commercial variants were very popular for private purchase, and exhibit some unique features sought after by collectors. Variations, which include a flared butt and/or a half-cock, may bring an additional 30% over service revolvers if in 90%, or better condition.

Shoulder stocks and Pritchard bayonets for Mark VI revolvers were never officially sanctioned accessories and, now, are often faked. Theoretically, shoulder stocks from the Webley 1.5 in. (No.1 Mk. I) signal pistol may have been fitted to the Mk. VI by armorers during World War I, but this procedure was somewhat complicated by requiring the milling of a longitudinal slot at the base of the left grip frame. There is no foolproof way of telling whether a signal pistol stock was fitted to a pistol a hundred years ago, or last week. However, recent "reproductions" of shoulder stocks do not require the slot milled into the revolver's grip frame. Also, during the Great War, the gun-making firm of W.W. Greener produced approximately 200 Pritchard bayonets for private purchase, to fit the Mk. VI revolver. These bayonets had either gunmetal or casehardened steel (very rare) hilts and engraved markings, whereas the markings on today's Pritchards are stamped.

WOODS PATTERN - .450 cal., 6 shot, double action, 5 in. barrel, mfg. circa 1870.

Extreme rarity precludes accurate pricing on this model.

PRYSE PATTERN-WEBLEY NO. 4 - .32, .38, .44, .450, .455, .476, or .577 cal., double action revolver, 3 to 5 3/4 in. barrel for Webley mfg., 3 to 7 1/2 barrel for other mfgs. Most barrel ribs were marked with either mfg. or retailer name w/address (most common.), blue or nickel finish. The pattern was designed by Charles Pryse Jr., utilizing his patented innovations and the patented barrel lock with tongs/paddles from the Belgian inventor Philippe Counet. Mfg. by Pryse, Webley, Francotte (Belgium), and other British or Belgian makers, mfg. from 1877 onward. Webley production covered a ser. no range from 364 to 81,035.

$2,500 $2,000 $1,500 $1,000 $800 $700 $600

Cased, engraved, or inscribed examples will also command a premium.

Engraved or (owner) inscribed examples will command a premium.

Period oak display and leather travel cases will command a minimum of $500 premium, depending on condition and accessories.

Add 15% for Wilkinson special orders with Wilkinson retailer barrel markings.

WEBLEY IMPROVED GOVT. - .455 cal., 5 3/4 in. barrel, 6 shot, bird's head grips, blue or nickel finish, identified as the "Kaufmann" pattern. Mfg. circa early 1880s.

* ***Webley Improved Govt. First Pattern*** - Kaufmann serial numbers 33-121.

$5,500 $5,200 $4,800 $4,500 $3,700 $3,200 $2,500

* ***Webley Improved Govt. Second Pattern*** - Kaufmann serial numbers 165-1,228.

$5,000 $4,600 $4,200 $3,700 $3,200 $3,000 $2,500

* ***Webley Improved Govt. Third Pattern*** - Kaufmann serial numbers 1,245-1,316.

$4,700 $4,400 $4,000 $3,700 $3,200 $3,000 $2,500

WEBLEY IMPROVED GOVT. MODEL 1886 - .455 or .476 cal., 6 shot "church steeple" cylinder, 6 in. barrel, bird's head grips, ser. no. range 1,467-1,876. Mfg. circa mid-1880s.

$2,500 $2,000 $1,500 $1,000 $800 $700 $600

WEBLEY GOVT. MODEL 1889 - .455 or .476 cal., 6 shot "church steeple" cylinder, 6 in. barrel, flared or bird's head grips, ser. no. range 1,982-3,933. Mfg. late 1880s.

$2,500 $2,000 $1,500 $1,000 $800 $700 $600

WEBLEY GOVT. MODEL 1891 - .450 or .476 cal., 6 shot "church steeple" cylinder, 7 1/2 in. barrel, flared grips, ser. no. range 4,100-4,200. Approx. 200 mfg. early 1890s.

$3,500 $3,000 $2,500 $2,000 $1,500 $1,400 $1,300

WEBLEY GOVT. MODEL 1892 - .450, .455, or .476 cal., 6 shot "church steeple" cylinder, 7 1/2 in. barrel, flared grips, blue or nickel finish, ser. no. range 4197-6499. Mfg. circa early 1890s.

$3,000 $2,500 $2,000 $1,500 $1,400 $1,300 $1,200

WEBLEY GOVT. MODEL 1893 - .450 or .455 cal., 6 shot "church steeple" cylinder, 7 1/2 in. barrel, flared grips, ser. no. range 5,000-6,000. Mfg. early 1890s.

$3,300 $2,800 $2,300 $1,800 $1,700 $1,600 $1,500

WEBLEY GOVT. MODEL 1894 - .450 or .455 cal., 6 shot fluted cylinder, 6 or 7 1/2 (Target Model) in. barrel, bird's head or flared grips, ser. no. range 6,000-10,000. Mfg. early-mid 1890s.

$2,500 $2,000 $1,500 $1,000 $800 $700 $600

Target models command 10-20% premium.

GRADING - PPGS™	100%	98%	95%	90%	80%	70%	60%	LAST MSR

WEBLEY GOVT. ARMY (TARGET) MODEL 1896 – .450, .455, or .476 cal., 6 (Army) or 7 1/2 (Target) in. barrel, bird's head (Army) or flared (Target) grips, ser. no. range 10,000-23,000. Mfg. late 1890s.

	100%	98%	95%	90%	80%	70%	60%	LAST MSR
	$2,500	$2,000	$1,500	$1,000	$800	$700	$600	

Target models command a 10-20% premium.

Cased, engraved, or inscribed examples will command additional premium.

WEBLEY W.S. NEW MODEL – .455 cal., 4, 6, or 7 1/2 (Target) in. barrel, ser. no. range 88,056-454,229. Mfg. early 1900s to 1935.

	100%	98%	95%	90%	80%	70%	60%	LAST MSR
	$2,200	$1,900	$1,500	$1,000	$800	$650	$600	
Target Model w/accessories	$2,650	$2,275	$1,800	$1,450	$1,200	$950	$775	

WEBLEY-FOSBERY AUTOMATIC MODELS – .455 cal., 6 shot, hinged frame, 4, 6, or 7 1/2 in. barrel, blue or nickel finish, walnut or hard rubber grips, ser. nos. less than 5,000. Mfg. 1901-1924.

* ***Webley-Fosbery Automatic Model First 1901*** – ser. nos. under 300, production prior to Dec. 1901.

	100%	98%	95%	90%	80%	70%	60%	LAST MSR
	$20,000	$17,500	$15,000	$12,500	$10,000	$8,500	$7,000	

Add 20% for earliest guns with hook safety and serial number under 50.

* ***Webley-Fosbery Automatic Model 1902*** – .38 ACP cal., 8 shot, ser. no. range is just over 1,000 to just below 1,400, extremely rare, less than 800 mfg. 1902-1903.

This model is extremely rare, and values may exceed 100% of values for the Model 1901.

* ***Webley-Fosbery Automatic Model First 1903*** – .455 cal., 6 shot, large and small frame, ser. nos. between 100 and 4930.

	100%	98%	95%	90%	80%	70%	60%	LAST MSR
	$15,000	$12,500	$10,000	$9,000	$8,000	$7,000	$6,000	

Add 20% for target revolvers.

WEBLEY WILKINSON MODELS – .450/.455, or .455/.476 cal., during production of the Webley No. 4 Model, Webley produced the Wilkinson Models, well-made and finished, which Henry Wilkinson sold through his retail business, barrels were typically 5 3/4 or 6 in., with Target models in 7 1/2 in. Mfg. 1884-1914.

* ***Webley Wilkinson Model First 1884 Small Hinge Pattern*** – Wilkinson serial numbers 7,896-8,301.

	100%	98%	95%	90%	80%	70%	60%	LAST MSR
	$3,500	$3,000	$2,500	$2,000	$1,800	$1,600	$1,500	

* ***Webley Wilkinson Model Second 1888 Large Hinge Pattern*** – Wilkinson serial numbers 8,357-8,741.

	100%	98%	95%	90%	80%	70%	60%	LAST MSR
	$3,500	$3,000	$2,500	$2,000	$1,800	$1,600	$1,500	

* ***Webley Wilkinson Model 1892*** – Wilkinson serial numbers 8,788-9,385.

	100%	98%	95%	90%	80%	70%	60%	LAST MSR
	$3,500	$3,000	$2,500	$2,000	$1,800	$1,600	$1,500	

* ***Webley Wilkinson Model 1900*** – Wilkinson serial numbers W467-W967.

	100%	98%	95%	90%	80%	70%	60%	LAST MSR
	$3,500	$3,000	$2,500	$2,000	$1,800	$1,600	$1,500	

* ***Webley Wilkinson Model 1905*** – Wilkinson serial numbers W1102-W2977.

	100%	98%	95%	90%	80%	70%	60%	LAST MSR
	$3,000	$2,500	$2,000	$1,500	$1,300	$1,100	$1,000	

* ***Webley Wilkinson Model 1910*** – transitional model, Wilkinson serial numbers around 3,000. Mfg. 1910 as a transition between 1905 and 1911 models.

	100%	98%	95%	90%	80%	70%	60%	LAST MSR
	$4,500	$4,000	$3,500	$3,000	$2,500	$2,000	$1,500	

* ***Webley Wilkinson Model 1911*** – Wilkinson serial numbers 3,104-4,400.

	100%	98%	95%	90%	80%	70%	60%	LAST MSR
	$3,000	$2,500	$2,000	$1,500	$1,300	$1,100	$1,000	

WEBLEY MARK II POCKET MODEL – .380 cal., 3 or 4 in. barrel, 6 shot, blue or nickel finish, folding trigger, ser. no. range 1-808. Mfg. circa early 1890s.

	100%	98%	95%	90%	80%	70%	60%	LAST MSR
	$1,000	$900	$800	$700	$600	$500	$400	

WEBLEY MARK III POCKET MODEL .320 CAL. – .320 cal., 3 in. barrel, 6 shot, blue or nickel finish, ser. no. range 10,000-22,000. Mfg. early 1900s.

	100%	98%	95%	90%	80%	70%	60%	LAST MSR
	$1,000	$900	$800	$700	$600	$500	$400	

WEBLEY MARK III POCKET MODEL .380 CAL. – .380 cal., 3, 4, 6 (Target), or 10 (Target) in. barrel, 6 shot, blue or nickel finish, ser. no. range 1,656-55,627. Mfg. mid-1890s.

	100%	98%	95%	90%	80%	70%	60%	LAST MSR
	$1,000	$900	$800	$700	$600	$500	$400	

Add a 30% premium on Target models.

.380 WEBLEY REVOLVER (MK III AND MK IV) – .320 or .380 Webley cal., some purchased privately by officers as well as by police forces and security, early Marks by P. Webley & Son, the Mark or designation usually stamped on left side of revolver frame, wood or composition grips. Mfg. by Webley & Scott.

	100%	98%	95%	90%	80%	70%	60%	LAST MSR
	$750	$650	$550	$475	$400	$325	$275	
Earlier Marked	$1,200	$1,050	$900	$815	$660	$550	$425	
Engraved/cased	$1,950	$1,700	$1,500	$1,350	$1,050	$950	$750	

There exists a rare Mk IV variant with a sideplate which is almost identical to the No.2 Mk.1 Enfield revolver

with values similar to the earlier marked revolvers.

WEBLEY W.P. – .32 S&W or .320 cal., 2 or 3 in. barrel, 6 shot, hammerless or hammer type, blue or nickel finish, ser. no. range 1000-8527. Mfg. circa early 1900s to mid-1930s.

$1,000 $900 $800 $700 $600 $500 $400

WEBLEY MARK IV – .22 LR (scarce), .32 (scarce), .38 S&W, or .380 cal., 3, 4, 5, or 6 (Target) in. barrel, 6 shot, wartime production exceeded 125,000, commercial production approx. 50,000. Mfg. early 1920s to late 1970s.

$800 $750 $700 $600 $400 $350 $300

Add 75%-100% for .22 LR or .32 cal.

Deduct 20% for Century Arms imports fitted with a hammer block safety. These can be identified with a prominent screw head protruding from the frame below the hammer.

MARK IV (NEW SERVICE) – .38 S&W cal., 5 in. barrel, 6 shot, the model that Enfield used to produce their No. 2 Mk.I .380 revolver, with only minor differences, and differing from the common Mk.IV by having a sideplate. Only a few examples known, but to be on the lookout for.

$5,000 $4,500 $4,200 $4,000 $3,700 $3,200 $3,000

REVOLVERS: SERVICE MODELS

Mark I-V .455 cal. service revolvers are all very similar, with bird's head grip frames and [usually] 4 in. barrels, differing primarily on the mechanism for cylinder removal, types of springs and steel used, and trigger guard and hammer configurations. The Mark VI, differed from the earlier marks by having a square grip frame and a 6 in. barrel, though Marks IV and V can often be found with the longer barrel. Shoulder stocks and Pritchard bayonets for Mark VI revolvers were never officially sanctioned accessories and, now, are often faked. Theoretically, shoulder stocks from the Webley 1.5" (No.1 Mk.I) signal pistol may have been fitted to the Mk. VI by armorers during World War I, but this procedure was somewhat complicated, requiring milling of the left grip frame. W.W. Greener produced approximately 200 Pritchard bayonets, for private purchase, to fit the Mk. VI revolver. These bayonets had either gunmetal or casehardened steel (very rare) hilts and engraved markings, markings on today's Pritchards are stamped.

Many surplus service Webleys (and Enfields), primarily the square-butt Mark VI were modified to use .45 ACP cal. ammo - this will decrease their value by 50% or more.

Cased, engraved, or inscribed examples with their owner's name have also been seen (usually in the commercial examples of service revolvers), and will bring a 20% premium or more with documented provenance.

Mark III variations which include flared butt and half-cock models may bring a 20%-30% premium, if in 90% or better condition.

.455 WEBLEY REVOLVERS – .455 Webley cal., purchased privately by officers as well on War Office contracts. Mk I model approved in 1887, Mk II in 1894, Mk III in 1897, Mk IV in 1899, Mk V in 1913, and the Mk VI in 1915, the Mark number is stamped on the revolver frame, Vulcanite hardened rubber grips. Enfield also made the Mk VI Webley during 1921-1926. Mfg. by P. Webley & Son until 1897 when Webley acquired W.C. Scott and the name changed to Webley & Scott.

$1,900 $1,600 $1,350 $1,200 $1,050 $950 $800

Add 30%-50% for Mk I, Mk II, Mk III, and Mk IV revolvers.

Add 30% for scarce Enfield production (1921-1926).

Add 10% for 4 in. barrel Mk V.

Add 20% for 6 in. barrel Mk V.

Add 20% for commercial MK V and Mk VI revolvers with a "C" in a box stamped on the left side of frame.

Subtract 50% for cut cylinder for .45 ACP with rim clips.

MARK I SERVICE – .455 cal. and commercial .450 Revolver or .476 Enfield MK III cal., DA, bird's head grip frame with a hump (prawl) behind the hammer, cylinder retention/removal was via a crossbolt through the barrel lug, 4 in. barrel, fixed sights, blue finish, top break 6 shot, over 40,000 service and commercial examples produced. Mfg. 1890-1894.

$2,000 $1,800 $1,250 $1,000 $750 $600 $500

Add 10% for a Mk.I* variant (Naval, MK.II specification) and 20% for a Mk.I variant (Naval, Mk.V specification).**

MARK II SERVICE – .455 cal. and commercial .450 Revolver or .476 Enfield MK III cal., DA, rounded bird's head grip frame, cylinder retention/removal was via a crossbolt through the barrel lug, 4 in. barrel, fixed sights, blue finish, top break 6 shot, service and commercial ser. no. range 41,675-63,584. Mfg. 1894-1897.

$2,000 $1,800 $1,600 $1,200 $1,000 $800 $600

Add 20% for a Mk.II variant (Naval, Mk.V specification).**

GRADING - PPGS™	100%	98%	95%	90%	80%	70%	60%	LAST MSR

MARK III SERVICE – .455 cal., and commercial .450 Revolver or .476 Enfield MK III cal., DA, rounded birdshead grip frame, cylinder retention/removal via a cam lever at the hinge on the left side of the frame, 4 in. barrel, fixed sights, blue finish, top break 6 shot, commercial models may have a flared butt or a half-cock notch, ser. no. range commercial (approx. 12-10,000) and service (approx. 76,000-80,000) revolvers. Mfg. 1897-1899.

	100%	98%	95%	90%	80%	70%	60%	LAST MSR
	$2,000	$1,800	$1,600	$1,200	$1,000	$800	$600	

Commercial variations with flared butt and half-cock may bring an additional 30% premium over service revolvers, if in 90% or better condition.

MARK IV SERVICE - .455 cal., and commercial .450 Revolver or .476 Enfield MK III cal., DA, rounded bird's head grip frame, cylinder retention/removal via a cam lever at the hinge on the left side of the frame, 4 in. barrel, fixed sights, blue finish, top break 6 shot, "Boer War" model, ser. no. range 79,462-129,185. Mfg. 1899-1913.

	100%	98%	95%	90%	80%	70%	60%	LAST MSR
	$1,800	$1,500	$1,200	$1,000	$800	$600	$500	

Add 20% for the rare Mk.IV variant of 1924 (Naval, Mk.VI specification).**

This revolver's introduction corresponded with the beginning of the 2nd Boer War, thus referred to as the "Boer War Model".

MARK V SERVICE - .455 cal., and commercial .450 Revolver or .476 Enfield MK III cal., DA, rounded birdshead grip frame, cylinder retention/removal via a cam lever at the hinge on the left side of the frame, 4 or 6 in. barrel, fixed sights, blue finish, top break 6 shot, ser. no. range 129,900-215,000. Mfg. 1913-1915.

	100%	98%	95%	90%	80%	70%	60%	LAST MSR
	$1,800	$1,500	$1,200	$1,000	$800	$600	$500	

Add 10% for 6 in. barrel service revolvers.

Add 20% for commercial revolvers.

Commercial revolvers were designated with a "C" in a small square box, on the left side of the frame below the hammer.

MARK VI SERVICE - .455 cal., DA, square butt frame, cylinder retention/removal via a cam lever at the hinge on the left side of the frame, 6 in. barrel, fixed sights, blue finish, top break 6 shot, ser. no. range 135,000-430,000. Mfg. 1915-1919.

	100%	98%	95%	90%	80%	70%	60%	LAST MSR
	$1,600	$1,400	$1,100	$900	$700	$600	$500	

Add 20% for rare wartime commercial models.

Add approx. $1,000 for either an original fitted buttstock or a Pitchard bayonet with a gunmetal (brass) hilt; double this price for a steel hilted Pritchard.

Deduct 50% if cut for .45 ACP cal.

Commercial revolvers were designated with a "C" in a small square box, on the left side of the frame below the hammer.

MARK VI SERVICE (LATER MFG.) - .455 cal., DA, square butt frame, cylinder retention/removal via a cam lever at the hinge on the left side of the frame, 4 (commercial, Irish, Canadian, and South African purchases) or 6 in. barrel, fixed sights, blue finish, top break 6 shot, ser. no. range 430,000-455,000. Mfg. by Webley circa 1919-late 1930s.

	100%	98%	95%	90%	80%	70%	60%	LAST MSR
	$1,800	$1,500	$1,200	$1,00	$800	$650	$500	

Add 10% for short 4 in. barreled variants and for commercial models.

The Royal Small Arms Factory at Enfield Lock also produced approximately 27,600 of its version of the Webley Mk. VI (the No.1 Mk. VI) for the military from 1921-1926, with a serial number range: 1-9,999, A1-A9,999, and B1-B7,600.

MARK VI/.22 - .22 RF cal., round barrel, with similar weight and dimensions to Mark VI Service, two variants, one with a shortened cylinder, and the other with a stepped cylinder, a few commercial examples are found with serial numbers above 450,000.

	100%	98%	95%	90%	80%	70%	60%	LAST MSR
	$2,400	$2,200	$1,900	$1,600	$1,100	$900	$700	

Produced by Webley and initially offered to the British army as an inexpensive alternative to the .455 cal. revolver for pistol practice between WWI and WWII. Never adopted, a few commercial examples are found with serial numbers above 450,000. A rare revolver in this country.

RIFLES: BOLT ACTION

EMPIRE RIFLE - .243 Win., .270 Win., .308 Win., .30-06, 7mm-08, or .300 Win. Mag. cal., 22 or 24 (disc.) in. cold hammer forged barrel w/o sights, 3 or 4 shot detachable mag., two-stage trigger, checkered walnut stock and forend with rosewood capped pistol grip and forend tip, jeweled bolt, satin finished wood or synthetic stock w/blued metal finish, approx. 8 lbs. New 2015.

	100%	98%	95%	90%	80%	70%	60%	LAST MSR
MSR $799	$675	$575	$500	$450	$400	$365	$335	

Add $87 for package (includes Nikko Sterling Panamax 3-9x40 scope and one-piece base and rings. Offered 2016-2017).

GRADING - PPGS™	100%	98%	95%	90%	80%	70%	60%	LAST MSR

XOCET RIMFIRE RIFLE – .17 HMR, .22 LR, or .22 WMR cal., 19 in. threaded carbon-steel standard or carbon/Kevlar composite bull barrel, 10 shot detachable mag., skeletonized trigger, black polymer stock, sling swivel studs, top Picatinny rail, black finish, 7 1/2 lbs. New 2016.

MSR $439	$365	$325	$275	$250	$225	$195	$165	

Add $60 for bull barrel.

SHOTGUNS: OVER & UNDER

Webley & Scott imported a line of private label shotguns manufactured for them in Turkey by Komando Av Sa. Tic. Ltd. Sti. until 2017.

MODEL 900 EXTREME O/U – 12 or 20 ga., 3 in. chambers, 28 or 30 in. VR barrels, 5 interchangeable chokes, auto ejectors, single trigger, fiber optic sights, oil finished select walnut stock and forend, manual safety, with or w/out presentation case, 6.5-7.25 lbs. Importation disc. 2017.

Retail pricing was not available for this model.

* ***Model 900 Extreme Junior O/U*** – 20 ga., 3 in. chambers, 28 in. VR barrels, 5 interchangeable chokes, auto ejectors, single trigger, fiber optic sights, oil finished select walnut stock, manual safety, with or w/o presentation case, 6.3 lbs. Importation disc. 2017.

Retail pricing was not available for this model.

MODEL 900 EXTREME TRAP O/U – 12 ga., 3 in. chambers, 30 in. VR barrel, 5 interchangeable chokes, single trigger, fiber optic sight, oil finished select walnut stock with fixed or adj. comb, manual safety, with or w/out presentation case, 8.2 lbs. Imported 2015-2017.

Retail pricing was not available for this model.

MODEL 900 SPORTING O/U – 12, 20, 28 ga. or .410 bore, 2 3/4 or 3 in. chambers, 26, 28, or 30 (12 ga. only) in. chrome-lined VR barrels, 5 interchangeable chokes, auto ejectors, fiber optic sight, oil finished select Turkish walnut stock and forearm, manual safety, light engraving, jeweled monobloc walls, with or w/out leather hard case, matte black receiver, 5.3-7.25 lbs. Importation disc. 2017.

	$1,050	$925	$795	$715	$575	$475	$375	*$1,250*

* ***Model 900 Sporting Deluxe O/U*** – 12 ga., 3 in. chambers, 28 in. VR barrels, 5 interchangeable chokes, auto ejectors, single trigger, fiber optic sight, oil finished select walnut stock and forearm, manual safety, silver alloy receiver with engraved waterfowl scene, jeweled monobloc walls, with or w/out leather hard case, 7.15 lbs. Importation disc. 2017.

	$1,100	$965	$825	$750	$600	$500	$400	*$1,300*

* ***Model 900 Sporting Junior O/U*** – 20 ga., 3 in. chambers, 26 or 28 in. chrome-lined VR barrels, 5 interchangeable chokes, auto ejectors, single trigger, fiber optic sight, oil finished select Turkish walnut stock and forearm, manual safety, matte black receiver with light engraving, jeweled monobloc walls, with or without presentation case, 6.3 lbs. Importation disc. 2017.

	$1,100	$965	$825	$750	$600	$500	$400	*$1,300*

MODEL 2000 PREMIUM O/U – 12 ga., 3 in. chambers, 28 or 30 in. chrome-lined barrels, five interchangeable Teague style chokes, boxlock, heavy hammer springs, CNC machined receiver with bone charcoal color case hardening, jeweled monobloc walls, manual safety, V-spring action, auto ejectors, brass bead front sight pin, oil finished select Turkish pistol grip walnut stock, includes presentation case, 7.1 lbs. Importation disc. 2017.

	$2,125	$1,850	$1,595	$1,450	$1,175	$950	$750	*$2,500*

MODEL 3000 SIDELOCK O/U – 12 or 20 ga., 3 in. chambers, 28 in. chrome-lined barrels, sidelock, heavy hammer springs, CNC machined receiver with bone charcoal color case hardening, jeweled monobloc walls, manual safety, V-spring action, ejectors, brass bead front sight pin, oil finished select Turkish pistol grip walnut stock, includes five Teague style chokes and presentation case. Importation disc. 2017.

	$5,100	$4,475	$3,825	$3,475	$2,800	$2,295	$1,785	*$6,000*

SHOTGUNS: SxS

MODEL 700 – 12 or 20 ga., boxlock, case hardened receiver, minimum engraving, single trigger. Mfg. 1949-80.

	$3,000	$2,600	$2,200	$1,850	$1,550	$1,200	$995	

Subtract $50 for double trigger.

MODEL 701 – similar to Model 700 but fanciest walnut, most engraving. Mfg. 1949-80.

	$3,500	$3,150	$2,600	$2,300	$1,995	$1,675	$1,350	

This model is hard to differentiate from the Model 702.

MODEL 702 – similar to Model 700 but middle grade. Mfg. 1949-80.

	$3,250	$2,800	$2,400	$2,200	$1,700	$1,425	$1,175	

Subtract $75 for double trigger.

GRADING - PPGS™	100%	98%	95%	90%	80%	70%	60%	LAST MSR
MODEL 712 – 12 ga., specifically designed for the American market.	$2,500	$2,250	$1,875	$1,600	$1,350	$1,100	$895	
MODEL 720 – 20 ga.	$4,500	$3,995	$3,500	$3,100	$2,600	$2,150	$1,625	
MODEL 728 – same action as the Model 700, except is 28 ga. and designed specifically for the American market, only 40 were mfg. 1966-68.	$5,000	$4,500	$4,000	$3,500	$2,800	$2,350	$1,800	
MODEL 700 SERIES (RECENT MFG.) – 12, 20, or 28 ga., boxlock, Mfg. in Turkey. Imported by Legacy Sports 2007-2008.	$2,950	$2,580	$2,215	$2,000	$1,625	$1,350	$1,150	*$3,477*

Add $167 for 28 ga.

MODEL 2000 SxS – 12 or 20 ga., 3 in. chambers, 26 or 28 in. tapered and raised barrels, includes 5 interchangeable chokes or fixed/mod. chokes, auto ejectors, single trigger, bead sight, checkered oil finished select grade Turkish walnut pistol grip stock with splinter forend, English scroll engraving, includes choke wrench and presentation carrying case, color case hardened receiver, 6.5-6.72 lbs. Mfg. in Turkey. Importation disc. 2017.	$2,125	$1,850	$1,595	$1,450	$1,175	$950	$750	*$2,500*
MODEL 3000 SxS – 12 or 20 ga., 3 in. chambers, 28 in. tapered raised barrels, 5 interchangeable chokes, auto ejectors, bead sight, single trigger, hand checkered oil finished select grade Turkish walnut pistol grip stock with splinter forend, color case hardened receiver with English scroll engraving, includes choke wrench and presentation carrying case, 6.5-6.72 lbs. Mfg. in Turkey. Importation disc. 2017.	$5,100	$4,475	$3,825	$3,475	$2,800	$2,295	$1,785	*$6,000*

SHOTGUNS: SEMI-AUTO

During 2007-2008, Webley & Scott had a line of private label, gas operated semi-auto shotguns manufactured in Turkey. Models included: the 812 (12 ga.), 820 (20 ga.) and 828 (28 ga.). These guns were not imported into the U.S.

MODEL 800 SERIES SEMI-AUTO – 12 ga., 3 in. chamber, inertia driven, 28 in. nickel chrome-lined barrel, raised vent rib, includes 5 interchangeable chokes using Beretta Mobil choke thread pattern, 4 shot mag., single trigger, bead front sight, black synthetic or synthetic walnut stock, rubber recoil pad, textured foregrip and palm swell, includes optional sling swivels, matte black finish, 6.4 lbs. Importation disc. 2017.	$635	$550	$475	$425	$350	$285	$225	*$750*

SHOTGUNS: SLIDE ACTION

Webley & Scott imported a line of private label shotguns manufactured for them in Turkey by Komando Av Sa. Tic. Ltd. Sti. until 2017.

MODEL 600 DELUXE TACTICAL SLIDE ACTION – 12 ga., 3 in. chamber, 20 in. chrome-lined barrel with flash suppressor, matte blue receiver, 5 shot, black polymer tactical stock with pistol grip and extra ammo storage, AR style fiber optic front and ghost ring rear sights, heat shield, top Picatinny rail, spring loaded extended forend, swivel studs, rubber recoil pad, 6.6 lbs. Importation disc. 2017.	$375	$325	$265	$235	$200	$175	$150	*$450*
MODEL 612B HOME DEFENSE SLIDE ACTION – 12 ga., 3 in. chamber, 20 in. chrome-lined barrel, matte blue receiver, 5 shot, black polymer stock and forearm, crossbolt safety, spring loaded extended forend, swivel studs, black rubber recoil pad, 6.3 lbs. Importation disc. 2017.	$295	$260	$220	$200	$175	$150	$135	*$350*
MODEL 612P20T TACTICAL SLIDE ACTION – 12 ga., 3 in. chamber, 20 in. chrome-lined barrel with flash suppressor, matte blue receiver, 5 shot, black polymer tactical stock with pistol grip, AR style fiber optic front and ghost ring rear sights, heat shield, top Picatinny rail, spring loaded extended forend, swivel studs, rubber recoil pad, 6.6 lbs. Importation disc. 2017.	$340	$300	$250	$225	$185	$150	$135	*$400*

WEIHRAUCH & WEIHRAUCH SPORT GmbH & CO. KG SPORTWAFFENFABRIK

Current manufacturer of rifles, airguns, and blank pistols located in Mellrichstadt, Germany.

Weihrauch manufactures air rifles, air pistols, and small bore repeating rifles under the name Weihrauch Sport GmbH & Co. KG. Please contact the company directly for more information, including model availability and pricing.

GRADING - PPGS™	100%	98%	95%	90%	80%	70%	60%	*LAST MSR*

For more information and current pricing on both new and used Weihrauch airguns, please refer to the *Blue Book of Airguns* - also available as an online subscription.

RIFLES: BOLT ACTION

MODEL HW 60 TARGET – .22 LR cal., target rifle featuring adj. sights, 26 3/4 in. barrel, single shot, match walnut stock and other match features, aperture sights, 10.8 lbs. Importation disc. 1995.

$625	$550	$450	$395	$350	$295	$275	*$705*

Add $220 for left-hand action.

MODEL HW 60J – .22 LR or .222 Rem. cal., sporter model with checkered walnut stock. Importation disc. 1992.

$525	$475	$425	$395	$345	$300	$250	*$585*

Add $300 for .222 Rem. cal.

MODEL HW 60J (CURRENT MFG.) – .17 Mach 2, .17 HMR, .22 LR, .22 Win. Mag., .22 Hornet, or .222 Rem. cal., 23 in. heavy barrel, adj. double pull trigger or direct trigger with lateral slide safety, bead front and folding rear sight, walnut stock with cheekpiece, fine checkered forearm and pistol grip, rubber buttplate and two sling swivels, receiver tube with dovetail rail and screw holes for scope mounting. New 2016.

Please contact the company directly for pricing and availability for this model.

MODEL HW 66 – .22 Hornet or .222 Rem. cal., match grade. Imported 1989-1990.

$575	$495	$395	$325	$285	$250	$215	*$688*

Add $80 for double set triggers. Add $50 for stainless steel barrel in .22 Hornet cal.

MODEL HW 66 JAGD-MATCH – .17 Mach 2, .17 HMR, .22 LR, .22 Hornet, or .222 Rem. cal., 22 in. cylindrical match barrel, double pull trigger or direct trigger with lateral slide safety, no sights, oiled walnut match stock with stippling and rubber buttplate. New 2016.

Please contact the company directly for pricing and availability for this model.

MODEL HW 66 PRODUCTION – .17 HMR, .22 LR, .22 Win. Mag., .22 Hornet, or .222 Rem. cal., 22 in. extra heavy barrel, adj. double pull trigger with lateral slide safety, open sights, classic American sporter style walnut stock, with or without thumbhole (also includes checkering on the pistol grip and forearm), ambidextrous, rubber buttplate, receiver tube with dovetail rail. New 2016.

Please contact the company directly for pricing and availability for this model.

MODEL HW 660 MATCH – .22 LR cal., match rifle variation featuring adj. comb, vent. forend, with or w/o aperture sights, 10.8 lbs. Imported 1991-2005.

$850	$725	$600	$500	$400	$350	$300	*$999*

Add $150 for laminate stock (new 1998). Subtract $150 if w/o Anschütz aperture sights.

WEIHRAUCH, HERMANN REVOLVER GmbH

Please refer to Hermann Weihrauch Revolver GmbH listing in the H section.

WELLS

Previous custom rifle manufacturer located in Prescott, AZ.

RIFLES: BOLT ACTION

Wells manufactured a custom rifle based on a Mauser double square bridge action, using the finest materials available. Action prices started at $5,500, and stocks were priced from $5,500 on up. Many custom features and options were available, including engraving by Rachel Wells. Delivery time was approx. 24 months. Additionally, Wells also had a complete barrel manufacturing facility, specializing in cut rifle barrels in almost every caliber.

WERNER BARTOLOT

Current custom gun manufacturer established in 1986, located in Hermagor, Austria. Consumer direct sales only.

Werner Bartolot manufactures very high quality SxS and O/U double rifles, drillings, and single shot rifles. Please contact the company for more information, including availability and an individual price quotation.

WESSON, FRANK

Previous manufacturer located in Worcester, MA 1854-1865, and Springfield, MA circa 1865-1875.

100%	98%	95%	90%	80%	70%	60%	50%	40%	30%	20%	10%

PISTOLS: SINGLE SHOT

SMALL FRAME FIRST MODEL – .22 cal., tip up action, 3 1/2 in. 1/2 octagon barrel, brass frame, spur trigger, rosewood grips, round frame, irregular sideplate. 2,500 mfg. 1859-1862.

100%	98%	95%	90%	80%	70%	60%	50%	40%	30%	20%	10%
$600	$550	$495	$440	$385	$330	$275	$220	$195	$165	$140	$110

SMALL FRAME SECOND MODEL – similar to First Model, with flat sided frame and circular sideplate. 12,000 mfg. 1862-1880.

100%	98%	95%	90%	80%	70%	60%	50%	40%	30%	20%	10%
$550	$495	$440	$385	$330	$305	$250	$195	$165	$110	$105	$85

MEDIUM FRAME FIRST MODEL – .30 S-L or .32 S rimfire cal., 4 in. 1/2 octagon barrel, iron frame, same as Small Frame in other respects, narrow hinge and short trigger. 1,000 mfg. 1859-1862.

100%	98%	95%	90%	80%	70%	60%	50%	40%	30%	20%	10%
$525	$470	$415	$360	$305	$275	$220	$195	$165	$110	$105	$85

MEDIUM FRAME SECOND MODEL – similar to First Model Medium Frame, with wider hinge and longer trigger. 1,000 mfg. 1862-1870.

100%	98%	95%	90%	80%	70%	60%	50%	40%	30%	20%	10%
$495	$440	$385	$330	$275	$250	$220	$195	$165	$110	$105	$85

RIFLES: SINGLE SHOT

NO. 1 LONG RANGE – .44-100 or .45-100 standard cal., side hammer, falling block lever actuated, 34 in. octagon barrel, aperture rear sight on upper tang, select checkered pistol grip stock. Less than 50 mfg. circa 1870-1880.

100%	98%	95%	90%	80%	70%	60%	50%	40%	30%	20%	10%
$4,950	$4,675	$4,400	$3,850	$3,575	$3,080	$2,860	$2,475	$2,200	$2,035	$1,760	$1,540

NO. 2 HUNTING RIFLE – similar to No. 1, with finger loop lever. Less than 100 mfg.

100%	98%	95%	90%	80%	70%	60%	50%	40%	30%	20%	10%
$4,400	$4,180	$3,850	$3,520	$3,025	$2,750	$2,420	$2,255	$2,035	$1,925	$1,760	$1,540

NO. 1 SPORTING RIFLE – .38-100, .40-100, or .45-100 standard cal., similar to No. 2, with center hammer, less than 25 mfg.

100%	98%	95%	90%	80%	70%	60%	50%	40%	30%	20%	10%
N/A	$4,400	$4,180	$3,850	$3,520	$3,025	$2,750	$2,420	$2,255	$2,035	$1,925	$1,760

MODEL 1870 SMALL FRAME FIRST TYPE – .22 rimfire cal., 6 in. half octagon barrel rotates on its axis to load, brass frame, spur trigger, rosewood grips, detachable stock. Approx. 3,000 mfg. 1870-1890.

100%	98%	95%	90%	80%	70%	60%	50%	40%	30%	20%	10%
$550	$495	$470	$440	$415	$385	$360	$305	$275	$220	$195	$165

Subtract 25% if without stock.

MODEL 1870 SMALL FRAME SECOND TYPE – full octagon barrel.

100%	98%	95%	90%	80%	70%	60%	50%	40%	30%	20%	10%
$525	$470	$440	$415	$385	$360	$330	$275	$250	$195	$165	$140

MODEL 1870 SMALL FRAME THIRD TYPE – iron frame, push-button half cock.

100%	98%	95%	90%	80%	70%	60%	50%	40%	30%	20%	10%
$495	$440	$415	$385	$360	$330	$305	$250	$220	$165	$140	$110

MODEL 1870 MEDIUM FRAME FIRST TYPE – similar to Small Frame First Type, except in size and availability of .32 cal. Approx. 5,000 mfg. 1870-1893.

100%	98%	95%	90%	80%	70%	60%	50%	40%	30%	20%	10%
$525	$495	$470	$440	$415	$385	$360	$305	$275	$250	$195	$165

Subtract 25% if without stock.

MODEL 1870 MEDIUM FRAME SECOND TYPE – external push-button half cock and iron frame.

100%	98%	95%	90%	80%	70%	60%	50%	40%	30%	20%	10%
$440	$415	$385	$330	$305	$275	$220	$195	$165	$140	$110	$90

Subtract 25% if without stock.

MODEL 1870 MEDIUM FRAME THIRD TYPE – has three screws in iron frame.

100%	98%	95%	90%	80%	70%	60%	50%	40%	30%	20%	10%
$440	$415	$385	$330	$305	$275	$220	$195	$165	$140	$110	$90

Subtract 25% if without stock.

MODEL 1870 LARGE FRAME FIRST TYPE – .32, .38, .42, or .44 rimfire cal., 15-24 in. barrel, similar to smaller frame models, auto extractor. Approx. 500 mfg. 1870-1880.

100%	98%	95%	90%	80%	70%	60%	50%	40%	30%	20%	10%
$825	$770	$715	$660	$605	$550	$525	$495	$440	$385	$305	$275

Subtract 25% if without stock.

MODEL 1870 LARGE FRAME SECOND TYPE – similar to First Type, with standard sliding extractor.

100%	98%	95%	90%	80%	70%	60%	50%	40%	30%	20%	10%
$825	$770	$715	$660	$605	$550	$525	$495	$440	$385	$305	$275

Subtract 25% if without stock.

RIFLES: SINGLE SHOT, TIP UP

SMALL FRAME TIP UP – .22 rimfire cal., 6 in. half octagon barrel, brass frame, spur trigger, rosewood grips. Approx. 500 mfg. 1865-1875.

100%	98%	95%	90%	80%	70%	60%	50%	40%	30%	20%	10%
$605	$550	$525	$495	$470	$440	$415	$360	$330	$275	$220	$165

Subtract 25% if without stock.

100%	98%	95%	90%	80%	70%	60%	50%	40%	30%	20%	10%

MEDIUM FRAME TIP UP – .22, .30, or .32 rimfire cal., 10 or 12 in. barrel, same as small frame, with exceptions noted and larger frame. Approx. 1,000 mfg. 1862-1870.

$600	$550	$525	$495	$470	$440	$415	$360	$330	$275	$220	$165

Subtract 25% if without stock.

WESSON & HARRINGTON

Previous trademark of special/limited editions manufactured by H&R 1871, LLC 1995-2001. During 2000, Marlin Firearms Co. purchased the assets of H&R 1871, Inc., and the name was changed to H&R 1871, LLC. Factory Wesson & Harrington products were manufactured in Gardner, MA.

RIFLES: SINGLE SHOT

Please refer to the H & R 1871 section for earlier Wesson & Harrington Buffalo Classic & Target Models.

GRADING - PPGS™	100%	98%	95%	90%	80%	70%	60%	LAST MSR

SHOTGUNS: SINGLE SHOT

WESSON & HARRINGTON NWTF LONG TOM CLASSIC – 12 ga., top lever break open action, 32 in. FC barrel, case hardened frame, checkered straight grip walnut stock and forearm, 7 1/2 lbs. Mfg. 1995-2001.

	$300	$240	$195	$150	$125	$110	$95	*$350*

DAN WESSON FIREARMS

Please refer to Dan Wesson listing in the D section.

WESSON FIREARMS CO. INC.

Previous manufacturer located in Palmer, MA 1992-1995. Previously located in Monson, MA until 1992. In late 1990, ownership of Dan Wesson Arms changed (within the family), and the new company was renamed Wesson Firearms Co. Inc.

For models manufactured by Wesson Firearms Co. Inc., please refer to listings under Dan Wesson located in the D section.

WEST COAST WEAPONWORKS, LLC

Current AR-15 style rifle manufacturer established in 2016, located in San Diego, CA.

Please refer to BlueBookOfGunValues.com to order the *Blue Book of AR-15s & Variations*, available as a book or online subscription.

WESTERN ARMS COMPANY

Previous manufacturer located in Ithaca, NY.

Western Arms Corporation factory letters for 1990-1939 production may be obtained through the Cody Firearms Records Office at the Buffalo Bill Center of the West.

SHOTGUNS: SxS

WESTERN LONG RANGE – 12, 16, 20 ga., or .410 bore, 26-32 in. barrels, mod. and full choke, boxlock, extractors, double or single trigger, plain pistol grip stock, Western Arms Co. was a division of Ithaca Gun. Mfg. 1929-1946.

Double Trigger	$275	$225	$200	$175	$150	$125	$100
Single Trigger	$325	$275	$250	$225	$200	$150	$125

WESTERN FIELD

Previous trademark used on Montgomery Ward rifles and shotguns.

The Western Field trademark has appeared literally on hundreds of various models (shotguns and rifles) sold through the Montgomery Ward retail network. Most of these models were manufactured through subcontracts with both domestic and international firearms manufacturers. Typically, they were "spec." guns made to sell at a specific price to undersell the competition. Most of these models were derivatives of existing factory models with less expensive wood and perhaps missing the features found on those models from which they were derived. To date, there has been very little interest in collecting Western Field guns, regardless of rarity. Rather than list Western Field models, a general guideline is that values generally are under those of their "1st generation relatives." As a result, prices are ascertained by the shooting value of the gun, rather than its collector value. See Store Brand Crossover List located in the back of this text.

WESTERN PRECISION RIFLES

Previous custom rifle builder and gunsmith located in Arizona from 2008-2018.

In 2018, Western Precision Rifles stopped production of custom rifles and moved their remaining information to the www.vtoptics.com.

RIFLES: BOLT ACTION

Previous standard rifle packages were available in the following calibers: .300 Norma Mag., .300 Ultra Mag., .300 Win. Mag., 7mm Rem. Mag., 28 Nosler, 6.5x284 Norma, 6.5 SAUM, 6.5mm Creedmoor, 6.5x47 Lapua, .243 Win., or 6mm Creedmoor cal. Because each rifle was built to customer specifications, many other options and upgrades were available.

Optional upgrades for rifle packages included:
Add $200 for Jewell trigger upgrade.
Add $400 for complete load development.
Add $2,100 for Nightforce NXS 5.5x22x50 scope with precision rings.

PACKAGE 1 – various cals., 26 in. Proof Research carbon fiber barrel with side discharge brake, Timney trigger, Manners EH3 carbon fiber stock, pillar and glass bedded, Defiance deviant hunter receiver with fluted bolt and integral rail. Disc. 2018.

Last base MSR was $5,500.

PACKAGE 2 – various cals., 26 in. fluted match grade stainless steel barrel with brake, Timney trigger, Manners EH3 carbon fiber stock, pillar and glass bedded, Defiance deviant hunter receiver with fluted bolt and integral rail. Disc. 2018.

Last base MSR was $5,200.

PACKAGE 3 – various cals., 26 in. Proof Research carbon fiber barrel with side discharge brake, Timney trigger, Manners EH3 carbon fiber stock, pillar and glass bedded, Stiller Predator/Tac 300 receiver. Disc. 2018.

Last base MSR was $5,200.

PACKAGE 4 – various cals., 26 in. fluted stainless match grade barrel with brake, Timney trigger, Manners EH3 carbon fiber stock, pillar and glass bedded, Stiller Predator/Tac 300 receiver. Disc. 2018.

Last base MSR was $4,900.

PACKAGE 5 – various cals., 26 in. Proof Research carbon fiber barrel with side discharge brake, Timney trigger, Manners EH3 carbon fiber stock, pillar and glass bedded, Trued Rem. 700 receiver with fluted bolt and tactical bolt knob. Disc. 2018.

Last base MSR was $4,600.

PACKAGE 6 – various cals., 26 in. stainless fluted match barrel with brake, Timney trigger, Manners EH3 carbon fiber stock, pillar and glass bedded, Trued Rem. 700 receiver with fluted bolt and tactical bolt knob. Disc. 2018.

Last base MSR was $4,200.

TACTICAL MATCH RIFLE – .308 Win., 6.5 Creedmoor, 6mm Creedmoor, .243 Win., or 6.5x47 LM cal., 22 in. heavy varmint contour threaded barrel with muzzle brake, Timney trigger, Manners stock, Defiance S/A receiver with fluted bolt, tactical knob, and integral rail. Disc. 2018.

Last base MSR was $4,800.

WESTLEY RICHARDS & CO. LTD.

Current manufacturer located in Birmingham, England 1812 to date. In 1995, Westley Richards opened its own agency in the U.S. currently located in Gulf Breeze, FL. Previously located in Bozeman, MT until June 2016, and Springfield, MO. Originally William Westley Richards was located in Birmingham, England.

Note: Westley Richards guns are essentially custom ordered - only 40-45 guns are made annually. They make many guns that are impossible to list and evaluate, except on an individual basis. Professional appraisal is necessary upon purchase or sale.

To obtain a quotation for a new Westley Richards shotgun or rifle, an inquiry should be submitted to the manufacturer or importer.

IDENTIFYING WESTLEY RICHARDS & CO. LONG GUNS

There seems to be a lot of confusion regarding W. Richards, W. R. Richards, William Richards, and other generic derivatives of the famous English gunmaker, Westley Richards. Part of the problem is that there are seventeen registered firms in England, including several in London, who have made guns by the name of Richards. A genuine Westley Richards gun never has the first name abbreviated, and the London address is usually found on the rib panel. Further compounding the problem, a previous Belgian gunmaker, identifiable by W. Richards on the locks or rib, had many shotguns exported into the United States, which

are commonly confused with the real London maker. These Belgian guns are commonly hammer guns with damascus twist barrels most frequently encountered in either 10, 12, or 16 ga. The easiest way to determine this maker is to recognize the Liege proof marks on the barrel flats and chamber length given in millimeters. Most of these Belgian guns sell in the $375-$750 range, depending on condition and configuration.

WESTLEY RICHARDS & CO. HISTORY

Since its founding in Birmingham in 1812, Westley Richards and Co. pushed the boundaries of firearms technology, including notable improvements in percussion, breech loading, and military gunmaking, as well as with ammunition. With their revolutionary patent of 1875, Westley's William Anson and John Deeley created the genesis for the modern sporting shotgun - a gun with concealed hammers as well as locks that cocked with the fall of the barrels. Other innovations included the doll's head top extension and bolting system, mechanical single trigger and ejector systems, forend fasteners, detachable locks (known in America as droplocks), and the Ovundo shotgun of 1914. Production ground to a halt during WWI, but unlike some other Birmingham firms, Westley emerged from post-World War I healthier than many of its competitors, mostly due to a burgeoning American marketplace and the patronage of wealthy Indian princes. The 1930s on the other hand, ushered in tougher times, and WWII essentially wrecked a firm dependent on a rapidly shrinking empire. Capt. E.D. Barclay purchased the bankrupt business from liquidators in 1946, and the company muddled through another decade before being sold to Capt. Walter Clode in 1957. Clode kept the firm running and concentrated on modernizing the company's high-tech engineering and toolmaking operations until his son Simon joined the company in 1987. Simon integrated the technology and the skills of the bench trained craftsmen - a process that is still in use today. Founder William Wesley Richards had a simple motto: "To make as good a gun as can be made." During mid-2014, Westley Richards & Co announced the acquisition of Teague Precision Chokes.

Information appears courtesy of Vic Venters & David Grant.

RIFLES

MSR values for currently manufactured rifles are listed in English pounds. On older rifles, a knowledgeable appraisal/evaluation should be procurred before buying.

Deluxe scroll and game scene engraving is POR.

FIXED LOCK (BOXLOCK) DOUBLE RIFLE – .470 NE or .500 NE cal., standard features include type 'C' doll's head, disc set strikers, two triggers, automatic ejectors, chopper lump barrels, quarter rib, express sights, ramp foresight, standard walnut stock, and traditional scroll engraving.

* ***Fixed Lock Double Rifle Current Mfg.*** – .470 NE, .500 NE, and .577 NE cal.

Current MSR for the base model is £59,500.

Add £7,500 for traditional scroll engraving.

The values listed represent the standard model without additional options (of which there is a wide array).

* ***Fixed Lock Double Rifle Older & Recent Mfg.***

100%	98%	95%	90%	80%	70%	60%
N/A	$29,500	$25,000	$22,000	$20,000	$18,000	$16,000

HAND DETACHABLE LOCK (DROPLOCK) DOUBLE RIFLE – nearly all calibers available; standard features include type 'C' doll's head, disc set strikers, hand detachable locks, two triggers, automatic ejectors, manual or automatic safety, chopper lump barrels, quarter rib, express sight.

* ***Hand Detachable Lock Double Rifle Current Mfg.***

Current MSR for the base model is £79,500.

Add £5,000 for .577 NE or .600 NE cal.

The values listed represent the standard model without additional options (of which there is a wide array).

* ***Hand Detachable Lock Double Rifle Older & Recent Mfg.***

100%	98%	95%	90%	80%	70%	60%
N/A	$40,000	$34,000	$29,000	$25,000	$21,500	$16,750

Add 20% for Mag. cals. .460 NE or higher.

SIDELOCK DOUBLE RIFLE – nearly all calibers available, standard features include type 'C' doll's head, disc set strikers, two triggers, automatic ejectors, scroll engraving standard, manual or automatic safety, chopper lump barrels, quarter rib, express sight.

Current MSR for the base model is £104,500.

Add £4,000 for .577 NE or .600 NE cal.

The values listed represent the standard model without additional options (of which there is a wide array).

GRADING - PPGS™	100%	98%	95%	90%	80%	70%	60%	LAST MSR

BOLT ACTION MAGAZINE RIFLE – nearly all calibers available; choice of standard, Magnum, or short action, adjustable trigger, Model 70 style 3-position safety, express sight, ramp foresight.

* ***Bolt Action Magazine Rifle Current Mfg.***

Current MSR for the base model is £35,500.
Add £3,500 for exhibition wood.
Add £6,500 for traditional scroll engraving.

The values listed represent the standard model without additional options (of which there is a wide array).

* ***Bolt Action Magazine Rifle Older & Recent Mfg.***

	100%	98%	95%	90%	80%	70%	60%	LAST MSR
	N/A	$11,000	$9,000	$7,750	$6,750	$5,750	$4,750	

SHOTGUNS: PRE-WWII MFG.

Add 50% for 20 ga.
Add 100% for 28 ga.
Add $1,500 for cased extra set of locks.

OVUNDO O/U – detachable lock boxlock, optional sideplates. Disc.

	100%	98%	95%	90%	80%	70%	60%	LAST MSR
	$18,000	$15,000	$12,500	$9,750	$8,500	$7,250	$6,000	

MODELE DE GRANDE LUXE - SxS – scalloped receiver, detachable locks, profuse scroll & game scene engraving. Disc.

	100%	98%	95%	90%	80%	70%	60%	LAST MSR
	$15,000	$13,000	$11,000	$9,750	$8,500	$7,250	$6,000	

MODEL DE LUXE - SxS – scalloped receiver, detachable locks, fine scroll & game scene engraving. Disc.

	100%	98%	95%	90%	80%	70%	60%	LAST MSR
	$11,000	$9,500	$8,500	$7,500	$6,000	$5,500	$5,000	

HAMMERLESS EJECTOR PLAIN QUALITY - SxS – scalloped receiver, Anson & Deeley fixed locks. Disc.

	100%	98%	95%	90%	80%	70%	60%	LAST MSR
	$6,000	$5,000	$4,000	$3,500	$3,000	$2,500	$2,000	

"B" QUALITY EJECTOR - SxS – boxlock with plain (unscalloped) receiver, light scroll engraving. Disc.

	100%	98%	95%	90%	80%	70%	60%	LAST MSR
	$5,000	$4,000	$3,500	$3,000	$2,500	$2,250	$2,000	

SHOTGUNS: O/U, RECENT MFG.

BEST QUALITY O/U – 16 or 20 ga. only. 2 1/2 or 2 3/4 in. chambers, standard features include Westley Richards top lever, automatic ejectors, automatic safety, two triggers or Westley Richards patent single trigger, hand detachable locks, hinged coverplate, sideplates with inspection port, chopper lump barrels.

Please contact the importer directly for a price quotation on this model.

SHOTGUNS: SxS, RECENT & CURRENT MFG.

MSR values for currently manufactured rifles are listed in English pounds. For used values, an appraisal/evaluation should be procured before buying.

CONNAUGHT MODEL – 12, 20, or 28 ga., Anson & Deeley scalloped boxlock action, scroll engraving, 26 or 28 in. barrels, ejectors, about 6 1/2 lbs. Disc.

	100%	98%	95%	90%	80%	70%	60%	LAST MSR
	$9,250	$8,000	$6,600	$5,600	$4,800	$4,000	$3,400	*$10,900*

HAND DETACHABLE LOCK (DROPLOCK) – available in 8, 10, 12, 16, 20, 28 ga., or .410 bore, 2 3/4 in. or 3 in. chambers, standard features include model 'C' doll's head, Westley Richards top lever, automatic ejectors, automatic safety, two triggers, hand detachable locks, hinged coverplate, chopper lump barrels.

* ***Hand Detachable Lock (Droplock) Current Mfg.***

Current MSR for the base model is £64,500.
Add £15,000 for 8 or 10 ga., or £25,000 for 4 ga.
Add £4,950 for SST.
Add £4,250 for spare detachable locks.
Add £3,850 for side plates.
Deluxe scroll or game scene engraving is POR.

The values listed represent the standard model without engraving and additional options (of which there is a wide array).

* ***Hand Detachable Lock (Droplock) Older & Recent Mfg.***

	100%	98%	95%	90%	80%	70%	60%	LAST MSR
	N/A	$21,000	$17,500	$14,250	$11,000	$9,500	$7,750	

Add 50% for 20 ga.
Add 100% for .410 bore or for 28 ga.

Only six .410 best quality boxlocks have been mfg. to date.

100%	98%	95%	90%	80%	70%	60%	50%	40%	30%	20%	10%

BEST QUALITY SIDELOCK – 12, 16, 20, 28 ga., or .410 bore, 2 3/4 in. or 3 in. chambers, standard features include Best London sidelock action, assisted opening system, automatic ejectors, automatic safety, two triggers, chopper lump barrels, scroll engraving standard.

* ***Best Quality Sidelock Current Mfg.***

Current MSR for the base model is £79,500.
Add £4,500 for SNT.
Add £3,500 for exhibition wood.
Add £1,150 for Prince of Wales, Round, or Woodward Grip.
Deluxe scroll or game scene engraving is POR.

The values listed represent the standard model without engraving and additional options (of which there is a wide array).

* ***Best Quality Sidelock Older & Recent Mfg.***

N/A	$27,500	$24,000	$21,500	$17,500	$13,750	$9,950

Add 50% for 20 ga.
Add 100% for 28 ga. or .410 bore.
Add $1,000 for SST.

Most specimens in this model were custom ordered, so each gun should be evaluated individually.

WHITNEY ARMS COMPANY

Previous manufacturer located in New Haven, CT, 1798-1886.

Whitney Arms Company began firearms production in 1798. Eli Whitney Sr. & Eli Whitney Jr. were prominent figures and prolific producers in the arms manufacturing world for a great many years, and their production plant in New Haven is credited as being the first major manufacturer of commercial firearms in America. The Whitneys produced a tremendous variety of firearms under family ownership for approximately 90 years before selling the company to Winchester in 1888. Numerous long arms, starting with the Whitney 1798 U.S. Contract Musket, and moving forward through various other flintlock, percussion, rimfire, and centerfire rifles, handguns, and shotguns, contributed to the vast broadness of the Whitney line. Whitney collaborated with Burgess, Kennedy, Morse, Tiesing, Howard, Cochran, Scharf, and many others. Many of the early Whitney rifles, such as the historic 1798 Flintlock muskets, are rare and highly collectible, commanding substantial premiums when found in original configuration, and not converted to percussion. The Whitney lever action repeaters are also quite popular among collectors. A fair number remain in circulation.

The author wishes to express his thanks to Mr. Steve Engleson for providing the following information on Whitney Arms Company.

100%	98%	95%	90%	80%	70%	60%	50%	40%	30%	20%	10%

RIFLES: LEVER ACTION

WHITNEY-KENNEDY LEVER ACTION MAGAZINE RIFLES – a repeating rifle with loading port on right side, top ejection, approx. 15,000 mfg. between 1879-1886, barrels are typically marked "Whitney Arms Co." or "Whitneyville Armory" with some variations having the Kennedy name included, often referred to as the Kennedy rifle, two basic frame styles, large and small caliber, frame sizes were the same, but internal parts and configuration had several differences, both frame styles also available in carbines and muskets, two other basic variations were the standard loop lever, a serpentine or "S" shaped finger lever, ser. nos. were sequential from 1-5,000, and from there a letter prefix was added, these appeared from "A" through "S", with numbers 1-999 following.

* ***Whitney-Kennedy Lever Action Magazine Rifles Large Caliber*** – .40-60 WCF, .45-60 WCF, .45-75 WCF, or .50-95 Express cal., 26 or 28 in. round or octagon barrels, walnut stocks, crescent steel buttplate, full magazine capacity of 9 rounds in standard rifle.

100%	98%	95%	90%	80%	70%	60%	50%	40%	30%	20%	10%
N/A	N/A	$4,800	$4,200	$3,500	$3,000	$2,700	$2,500	$2,300	$2,000	$1,900	$1,500

Add 400% for .50-95 Express cal. (extremely rare).
Add 10% for .45-75 cal. (rare).
Add 50% for carbine or musket.
Add 100% for half-round, half-octagon barrel.
Add 20% for non-prefix (early) serial numbers.
Add 10% for serpentine lever.

100%	98%	95%	90%	80%	70%	60%	50%	40%	30%	20%	10%

* ***Whitney-Kennedy Lever Action Magazine Rifles Small Caliber*** – .44-40 WCF, .38-40 WCF, or .32-20 WCF cal., 24 in. round or octagon barrel, walnut stock and crescent buttplate, full magazine capacity of 13 rounds in standard rifle.

100%	98%	95%	90%	80%	70%	60%	50%	40%	30%	20%	10%
N/A	N/A	$4,000	$3,500	$3,000	$2,700	$2,400	$2,000	$1,800	$1,600	$1,350	$1,200

Add 50% for carbine or musket (extremely rare).
Add 100% for half-round, half-octagon barrel.
Add 20% for half-magazine.
Add 20% for 26 or 28 in. barrel.
Add 20% for .38-40 WCF and .32-20 WCF cals.

1878 BURGESS REPEATING RIFLE – .45-70 Govt. cal., standard sporting rifle, 28 in. octagon or round barrel, loading port on right side, serpentine shaped lever, walnut stock, blue receiver and full magazine capacity of 9 rounds, typically w/o Whitney markings, barrels marked "G.W. Morse Patented Oct. 28th 1856", and tangs are marked "A. Burgess Patented Jan. 7th 1873", several variations, including the first, second, and third models, as well as military carbines and muskets.

100%	98%	95%	90%	80%	70%	60%	50%	40%	30%	20%	10%
N/A	N/A	$7,500	$6,500	$5,200	$4,000	$3,500	$3,000	$2,750	$2,500	$2,250	$2,100

Add 300% for the first model top loader (few made and most converted by the factory to sideloader).
Add 100% for military carbine or musket (certain variations will command a higher premium).
Add 30% for first or second model.

Values shown are for the most typically encountered variation, the third model sporting rifle.

This model was also known as the Whitney-Burgess-Morse lever action repeating rifle, mfg. through a license agreement with Andrew Burgess, total production of approx. 2,000 were made between 1878-82.

WHITNEY FIREARMS COMPANY

Previous manufacturer from 1956-1959 located in Hartford, CT.

GRADING - PPGS™	100%	98%	95%	90%	80%	70%	60%	LAST MSR

PISTOLS: SEMI-AUTO

WOLVERINE OR LIGHTNING – .22 LR cal., unique futuristic sci-fi appearance, 10 shot, 4 5/8 in. barrel, plastic grips, aluminum alloy frame and barrel shroud, blue model is more common (approx. 13,000 mfg.), nickel is rare (approx. 900 mfg.). Mfg. 1955-1962.

GRADING - PPGS™	100%	98%	95%	90%	80%	70%	60%	LAST MSR
Blue finish	$850	$700	$600	$500	$400	$350	$300	
Nickel finish	$2,500	$2,000	$1,500	$1,000	$800	$700	$600	

WHITWORTH

This trademark can be found in the Interarms listing in the I section.

WICHITA ARMS, INC.

Previous manufacturer located in Wichita, KS.

PISTOLS

WICHITA INTERNATIONAL PISTOL (WIP) – available in 8 cals. between .22 LR and .357 Mag., single shot, break open action, stainless steel, adj. sights, 10 or 14 in. barrel, adj. sights or scope mounts, smooth walnut stocks and forearm. Disc. 1994.

100%	98%	95%	90%	80%	70%	60%	LAST MSR
$680	$465	$350	$285	$250	$215	$185	*$775*

Add $100 for 14 in. barrel.

WICHITA CLASSIC PISTOL – assorted cals. to .308 Win., 11 1/4 in. barrel, action has left-hand bolt for shooting with right hand, deluxe walnut, custom made, 3 lbs. 15 oz. Disc. 1997.

100%	98%	95%	90%	80%	70%	60%	LAST MSR
$3,280	$2,550	$2,150	$1,865	$1,715	$1,295	$1,075	*$3,495*

* ***Wichita Classic Pistol Engraved*** – similar to Wichita Classic, except is extensively engraved.

100%	98%	95%	90%	80%	70%	60%	LAST MSR
$5,250	$3,750	$2,750	N/A	N/A	N/A	N/A	*$5,250*

WICHITA SILHOUETTE PISTOL (WSP) – .308 Win. or 7mm/IHMSA cal., adj. trigger and sights, 14 15/16 in. barrel, center grip walnut stock, rear grip, 4 1/2 lbs. Left-hand action for shooting with right hand. Disc. 1994.

100%	98%	95%	90%	80%	70%	60%	LAST MSR
$1,520	$1,050	$850	$740	$620	$515	$440	*$1,800*

WICHITA MAGAZINE PISTOL – .308 Win. or 7mm/IHMSA cal., fiberthane (disc. 1987) or walnut (new 1988) stock, choice of MK-40, Silhouette, or Classic configuration, 13 in. barrel, adj. trigger, multi-range sights, 4 1/2 lbs. Disc. 1994.

100%	98%	95%	90%	80%	70%	60%	LAST MSR
$1,250	$875	$700	$585	$500	$415	$365	*$1,550*

GRADING - PPGS™	100%	98%	95%	90%	80%	70%	60%	LAST MSR

* ***Wichita Magazine Pistol Classic*** – features 11 1/4 in. octagon barrel, AAA walnut stock, 3 lbs. 15 oz. Disc. 1994.

	$2,975	$2,450	$2,000	$1,740	$1,495	$1,215	$1,000	*$3,400*

WICHITA BENCH PISTOL – .222 Rem., 6 PPC, or .22 Cheetah cal., uses WBR 1200 action, rear grip, 18 in. stainless steel Douglas barrel. Mfg. 1994-98.

	$1,875	$1,500	$1,250	$1,100	$895	$785	$630	*$1,875*

RIFLES: BOLT ACTION

WICHITA CLASSIC RIFLE (WCR) – .17-222, .17-222 Mag., .222 Rem., .222 Rem. Mag., .223 Rem., 6x47mm, and other cals. up to and including .308 Win. cal., single shot, select walnut, 21 in. octagon barrel, Canjar trigger, no sights, 7 lbs. Disc.

	$3,275	$2,500	$2,150	$1,865	$1,715	$1,295	$1,075	*$3,495*

Add $175 for left-hand action.

* ***Wichita Classic Rifle Varmint (WVR)*** – similar to WCR, except available only in Varmint cals. (up to and including .308 Win.) and round barrel. Disc. 1997.

	$2,500	$1,795	$1,375	$1,215	$985	$855	$685	*$2,695*

Add $175 for left-hand action.

* ***Wichita Classic Rifle Silhouette (WSR)*** – available in most cals., grey fiberthane stock, 24 in. match grade barrel, 2 oz. Canjar trigger, no sights, 9 lbs. Disc. 1995.

	$2,475	$1,775	$1,375	$1,215	$985	$855	$685	*$2,650*

Add $175 for left-hand action.

* ***Wichita Classic Rifle Magnum*** – Mag. cals., stainless steel only. Disc. 1984.

	$1,725	$1,300	$1,175	$1,040	$845	$735	$600

WICKLIFFE RIFLES

Previously manufactured by Triple S Development located in Wickliffe, OH.

For individual model listings, please go to BlueBookOfGunValues.com/overflow.

WIDFORSS

Please refer to Mauritz Widforss AB listing in the M section.

WIENER WAFFENFABRIK

Previous manufacturer located in Vienna, Austria.

PISTOLS: SEMI-AUTO

LITTLE TOM – 6.35mm (.25 ACP) or 7.65mm (.32 ACP) cal., 2 1/2 (.25 ACP) or 3 1/2 (.32 ACP) in. barrel, DA, designed by Alois Tomiska, small quantities mfg. in Czechoslovakia circa 1908-1918, later production in Austria circa 1919-1925.

.25 ACP cal.	$500	$450	$400	$350	$300	$250	$200
.32 ACP cal.	$600	$550	$500	$450	$400	$350	$300

Values assume Austrian production. Czech production will bring a premium. The .32 ACP cal. model is more scarce.

WIFRA

Please refer to the Saleri, W.R. di Saleri William & C. snc listing in the S section.

WILD WEST GUNS

Current custom gunsmith and manufacturer established in 1992, located in Anchorage, AK and in Las Vegas, NV beginning 2013. Dealer and consumer direct sales.

Wild West Guns offers firearms engraving by Guild Engraver Jim White. Please contact the company directly for a price quotation.

PISTOLS: SEMI-AUTO

Wild West Guns builds custom 1911 style handguns per customer order. Please contact the company directly for pricing and available options. Wild West Guns previously manufactured a customized M1911 style semi-auto model called the ShadowLite package - 1997 retail was $2,495.

REVOLVERS

WOLVERINE – .45 ACP-.454 Casull cal., DA, 5 in. barrel, 6 shot cylinder, adj. rear sight, finger grooved rubber grips, cut for moon clips, custom made to customer specifications, many options available, bead blast finish.

MSR $3,500	$2,975	$2,600	$2,230	$2,025	$1,630	$1,340	$1,165

WWG customizes the Wolverine starting with a factory Ruger Super Redhawk revolver.

GRADING - PPGS™	100%	98%	95%	90%	80%	70%	60%	LAST MSR

RIFLES: BOLT ACTION

SUMMIT LITE – various short action cals., Rem. or Win. action, lightweight configuration, 18-26 in. fluted match grade barrel, Alaska Magnum muzzle brake, Timney trigger, custom ultra light Kevlar reinforced stock, with or w/o thumbhole, Pachmayr Decelerator pad, matte blue, IonBond, parkerized, or stainless steel finish, 4 1/4 lbs. New 1998.

MSR $5,000	$4,350	$3,800	$3,265	$2,965	$2,395	$1,965	$1,550	

Add $175 for stainless steel. Add $110 for thumbhole stock.
Left-hand action is POR.

PRO GUIDE – .375 H&H, .416 Rem., .458 Win., or .458 Lott cal., Win. controlled feed action, slab side barrel with muzzle brake and quarter rib, parkerized finish, camo or black synthetic stock with Pachmayr Decelerator pad. Disc. 2014.

	$3,650	$3,250	$2,850	$2,500	$2,200	$1,800	$1,600	*$3,995*

Add $175 for stainless steel.
Left-hand action is POR.

RIFLES: LEVER ACTION

All current models listed in this section are subject to FET (Federal Excise Tax) - approx. 15%.

ALASKAN WWG COPILOT RIFLE – .30-30 Win. (disc. 1999, reintroduced 2011), .35 Rem. (new 2011), .357 Mag. (disc. 1999, reintroduced 2011-disc.), .44 Mag. (disc. 1999, reintroduced 2011-disc.), .444 Marlin (disc. 1999), .45 LC (mfg. 2011-disc.), .45-70 Govt., .457 WWG Mag. (new 2000), or .50 Alaskan (new 2000-disc.) cal., 16 1/2 (current) or 24 (disc.) in. ported barrel, 6 shot tube mag., red fiber optic front sight with skeletonized hood, ghost ring rear sight with threaded aperture, laminated wood pistol grip buttstock with WWG logo, Pachmayr decelerator pad, features customized Marlin lever action with takedown conversion, WWG big loop lever, includes Cordura case or optional hard case, matte blue, IonBond, parkerized, stainless steel, or hard chrome finish, 37 in. OAL, 6 1/2 lbs. New 1996.

MSR $3,500	$3,150	$2,750	$2,365	$2,145	$1,735	$1,425	$1,100	

Add $250 for .50 Alaskan cal. conversion package.
Subtract approx. 20% for older disc. cals.

* ***Alaskan CoPilot Rifle Limited*** – .457 WWG Mag. or .45-70 Govt. cal., takedown action, features most of Wild West Guns custom shop options, includes hard case. Only 150 to be mfg. beginning 2001 with custom ser. nos.

	$3,175	$2,850	$2,300	$1,800	$1,500	$1,300	$1,100	*$2,995*

ALASKAN WWG COPILOT .44 MAG. – .357 Mag. (mfg. 2018-2020) or .44 Mag. cal., smoothed and tuned takedown action, 8 shot mag., open sights, checkered walnut stock and forearm, large loop lever, Picatinny rail on top of barrel, 35 in. OAL, 6 lbs. New 2016.

MSR $3,500	$3,150	$2,750	$2,365	$2,145	$1,735	$1,425	$1,100	

ALASKAN GUIDE – .457 WWG Mag.-.45/70 Govt. cal., (also available as.50 Alaskan cal. conversion package), 18 1/2 in. ported barrel, 6 shot tube mag., ghost ring rear sight, fiber optic front sight, straight style laminated wood stock with WWG logo, big loop lever, Pachmayr Decelerator pad, matte blue, IonBond, parkerized, or stainless steel finish. New 1997.

MSR $4,500	$3,825	$3,345	$2,870	$2,600	$2,105	$1,720	$1,345	

Add $250 for .50 Alaskan cal. conversion package.
Add $150 for stainless steel.

CUSTOM 49 ER COPILOT – various centerfire cals., customized Marlin Model 1895 action w/special WWG serialization, stainless steel, black synthetic stock and forearm, includes fitted red velvet lined display case, engraved by Jim White, available in Tier I, Tier II, or Tier III. New 2016.

Current MSR's are as follows: Tier I - MSR $5,979, Tier II - MSR $7,979, and Tier III - MSR $12,000.

MASTER GUIDE – .457 WWG Mag., .45-70 Govt., or .50 Alaskan cal., takedown action, 18 1/2 in. barrel, 6 shot tube mag., ghost right rear and fiber optic front sight, laminated wood straight buttstock with WWG logo, Pachmayr decelerator pad, WWG big loop lever, matte blue, IonBond, parkerized, stainless steel, or hard chrome finish. Disc.

	$2,025	$1,775	$1,525	$1,375	$1,115	$910	$710	*$2,399*

Add $250 for .50 Alaskan cal. conversion package.
Add $125 for stainless steel.

MODEL 04 – .454 Casull or .500 S&W cal., stainless steel CNC machined frame, takedown or solid rifle, 16 1/2, 18 1/2, or 20 in. barrel, walnut, laminate or synthetic stock, ghost ring sights, Pachmayr decelerator pad. Limited mfg. 2005.

	$1,350	$1,150	$975	$860	$700	$600	$500	*$1,499*

Add $300 for synthetic stock.
Add $400 for takedown.

GRADING - PPGS™	100%	98%	95%	90%	80%	70%	60%	LAST MSR

RIFLE – various cals., big loop lever, bear proof ejector, ghost ring rear sight, fiber optic front sight with cut hood, straight grip walnut stock, hand fitted max recoil pad, stainless steel. Mfg. 2013-disc.

	100%	98%	95%	90%	80%	70%	60%	LAST MSR
	$1,700	$1,500	$1,300	$1,075	$950	$800	$675	*$1,899*

WWG 1895 45/70 RIFLE – .45-70 Govt. cal., WWG big loop lever, 18 1/2 in. ported stainless steel barrel, 6 shot tube mag., trigger Happy Kit, ghost ring rear and XS blade front sights w/full-length rail, checkered black synthetic stock and forearm with Pachmayr decelerator pad, matte finish, 37 in. OAL, 6 1/2 lbs. Disc. 2018.

	100%	98%	95%	90%	80%	70%	60%	LAST MSR
	$1,225	$1,075	$925	$835	$675	$550	$435	*$1,349*

RIFLES: SEMI-AUTO

Wild West Guns builds a custom AR-15 rifle per customer order. Please contact the company directly for pricing and available options.

WILDEY (NEW MFG.)

Current trademark of semi-auto gas operated pistols manufactured by USA Firearms Corp. located in Winsted, CT.

PISTOLS: SEMI-AUTO

During 2016, USA Firearms Corp. announced that it would start manufacturing the Wildey pistol again to the same specifications as the original. In January 2019, USA Firearms Corp. announced they are accepting pre-orders for the Wildey Survivor pistol with many options. Current model below reflects base MSRP only. Please contact the company directly for more information and availability.

WILDEY SURVIVOR – .475 Wildey Mag., .45 Win. Mag., or .44 Auto Mag. cal., 8, 10, or 12 in. barrel, black, red, or orange high and low front sight, smooth or textured Pau Ferro or Special grips, matte, high buff, or brushed stainless finish. New late 2018.

	100%	98%	95%	90%	80%	70%	60%
MSR $2,750	$2,500	$2,150	$1,850	$1,700	$1,350	$1,100	$850

Add $150 for matte stainless or $250 for high buff stainless finish.
Add $90 for Pau Ferro or $120 for Special grips.

WILDEY, INC.

Previous manufacturer located in Warren, CT 2000-circa 2011. Previously located in New Milford, CT until 1999.

Originally, the company was named Wildey Firearms Co., Inc. located in Cheshire, CT. At that time, serialization of pistols was 45-0000. When Wildey, Inc. bought the company out of bankruptcy from the old shareholders, there had been approximately 800 pistols mfg. To distinguish the old company from the present company, the serial range was changed to 09-0000 (only 633 pistols with the 09 prefix were produced). These guns had the Cheshire, CT address. Pistols produced by Wildey, Inc., New Milford, CT are serial numbered with 4 digits (no numerical prefix).

CARBINES: SEMI-AUTO

WILDEY CARBINE – .44 Auto Mag., .45 Wildey Mag., .45 Win. Mag., or .475 Wildey Mag. cal., features 18 in. barrel with forearm and detachable skeleton walnut stock, polished or matte stainless steel. Mfg. 2003-2011.

	100%	98%	95%	90%	80%	70%	60%	LAST MSR
	$2,700	$2,225	$1,750	$1,500	$1,235	$1,030	$855	*$3,110*

Add $237 for matte stainless steel finish.

PISTOLS: SEMI-AUTO

Add $585-$1,950 per interchangeable barrel assembly, depending on barrel length and finish.

WILDEY AUTO PISTOL – .45 Win. Mag., .45 Wildey Mag., or .475 Wildey Mag., gas operated, 5, 6, 7, 8, 10, or 14 in. VR barrel, SA, selective single shot or semi-auto, 3 lug rotary bolt, fixed barrel (interchangeable), polished stainless steel construction, 7 shot, double action, adj. sights, smooth or checkered wood grips, designed to fire proprietary new cartridges specifically for this gun including the .45 Win. Mag. cal., 64 oz. with 5 in. barrel.

Add $560-$1,148 per interchangeable barrel.

* ***Wildey Survivor Model*** – .357 Mag., .44 Auto Mag. (new 2003), .45 Win. Mag., 45 Wildey Mag., or .475 Wildey Mag. cal., 5, 6, 7, 8, 10, 12, 14 (new 2000), or 18 (new 2003) in. VR barrel, polished stainless steel finish. Mfg. 1990-2011.

	100%	98%	95%	90%	80%	70%	60%	LAST MSR
	$1,575	$1,225	$950	$810	$670	$565	$475	*$1,571*

Add $26-$125 for 5-12 in. barrel, depending on length, and $1,206 for 18 in. Silhouette model.
Add $26 for .45 Wildey Mag. or .475 Wildey Mag. cal.

The .475 Wildey cal. is derived from a factory cartridge.

GRADING - PPGS™	100%	98%	95%	90%	80%	70%	60%	LAST MSR

* ***Wildey Survivor Guardsman*** – similar to Survivor Model, except has squared-off trigger guard, same options apply to this model as for the Survivor model. Mfg. 1990-2011.

	$1,575	$1,225	$950	$810	$670	$565	$475	*$1,571*

* ***Wildey Hunter Model*** – .45 Win. Mag., .45 Wildey Mag., or .475 Wildey Mag. cal., 5, 6, 7, 8, 10, 12, 14 (new 2000) or 18 (new 2003) in. VR barrel, matte finish on all metal parts, adj. sights. Mfg. 1990-2011.

	$1,750	$1,550	$1,400	$1,235	$1,000	$870	$700	*$1,829*

Add $15 - $582 for 8 in. - 14 in. barrel, depending on length, or $1,210 for 18 in. silhouette model.
Add $25 for .45 Wildey Mag. or .475 Wildey Mag. cal.

.475 Wildey Mag. was available in 8, 10, or 12 in. barrel only.

* ***Wildey Hunter Guardsman*** – similar to Hunter Model, except has squared-off trigger guard, same options apply to this model as for the Hunter model. Mfg. 1990-2011.

	$1,750	$1,550	$1,400	$1,235	$1,000	$870	$700	*$1,829*

Add $100 for 12 in. barrel.
Add $625 for 14 in. barrel.
Add $1,175 for 18 in. silhouette barrel.

* ***Wildey Presentation Model*** – same specifications as Hunter Guardsman model, except is engraved with hand-checkered or smooth stocks.

	$2,500	$2,000	$1,600	$1,410	$1,160	$980	$800	*$2,000*

WILDEY AUTO PISTOL OLDER MFG. – .475 Wildey Mag. cal. was available in 8 or 10 in. barrel only.

* ***Older Wildey Serial Nos. 1-200.***

	N/A	$4,000	$3,500	$3,000	$2,500	$2,000	$1,500	*$2,180*

Add $20 for 8 or 10 in. barrel.

* ***Older Wildey Serial Nos. 201-400.***

	N/A	$3,800	$3,300	$2,750	$2,250	$1,750	$1,250	*$1,980*

Add $20 for 8 or 10 in. barrel.

* ***Older Wildey Serial Nos. 401-600.***

	N/A	$3,500	$3,100	$2,500	$2,000	$1,500	$1,000	*$1,780*

Add $20 for 8 or 10 in. barrel.

* ***Older Wildey Serial Nos. 601-800.***

	N/A	$3,250	$2,750	$2,250	$1,750	$1,250	$750	*$1,580*

Add $20 for 8 or 10 in. barrel.

* ***Older Wildey Serial Nos. 801-1,000.***

	N/A	$3,000	$2,500	$2,000	$1,500	$1,000	$650	*$1,275*

Add $25 for 8 or 10 in. barrel.

* ***Older Wildey Serial Nos. 1,001-2,489.***

	N/A	$3,000	$2,500	$2,000	$1,500	$1,000	$650	*$1,175*

Add $20 for 8 or 10 in. barrel.

JOHN WILKES GUN AND RIFLE MANUFACTURERS (WILKES, JOHN GUNMAKERS LTD.)

Current manufacturer established circa 1830, located in Arundel, West Sussex, U.K.

For individual model listings, please go to BlueBookOfGunValues.com/overflow.

WILKINSON ARMS

Previous trademark established circa 1996 and manufactured by Ray Wilkinson circa 1996-1998 (limited production), and by Northwest Arms located in Parma, ID circa 2000-2005.

CARBINES

LINDA CARBINE – 9mm Para. cal., 16 3/16 in. barrel, aluminum receiver, pre-ban configuration (limited supplies), fixed tubular stock with wood pad, vent. barrel shroud, aperture rear sight, small wooden forearm, 18 or 31 shot mag., beginning 2002, this model came standard with many accessories, 7 lbs. Mfg. circa 1996-2005.

	$1,295	$1,075	$850	$725	$600	$500	$425	*$1,800*

Only 2,200 Linda Carbines were marked "Luger Carbine" on the receiver. The last 1,500 distributed by Northwest Arms include a longer stock, and matched bolt and barrel (Rockwell 57).

GRADING - PPGS™	100%	98%	95%	90%	80%	70%	60%	LAST MSR

* ***Linda Carbine L2 Limited Edition*** – mfg. from the last 600 of the original 2,200 pre-ban Linda Carbines, includes many upgrades and accessories. Mfg. 2002-2005.

Last MSR was $4,800.

There isn't enough activity in the secondary marketplace to accurately predict values on this limited ed. Linda carbine.

TERRY CARBINE – 9mm Para. cal., blowback semi-auto action, 31 shot mag., 16 3/16 in. barrel, closed breech, adj. sights, 7 lbs. Disc.

	100%	98%	95%	90%	80%	70%	60%	LAST MSR
With black P.V.C. stock	$475	$395	$325	$295	$260	$230	$200	
With maple stock	$625	$525	$400	$350	$340	$325	$300	

PISTOLS: SEMI-AUTO

DIANE MODEL – .25 ACP cal., 6 shot, 2 1/8 in. barrel, fixed sight, matte blue, plastic grips. Disc.

	100%	98%	95%	90%	80%	70%	60%	LAST MSR
	$150	$125	$95	$80	$65	$55	$50	

LINDA MODEL – 9mm Para. cal., blowback action firing from closed bolt, 8.3 in. barrel, 31 shot mag., PVC pistol grip, maple forearm, Williams adj. rear sight. Disc.

	100%	98%	95%	90%	80%	70%	60%	LAST MSR
	$675	$625	$550	$475	$425	$350	$295	

SHERRY MODEL – .22 LR cal., 2 1/2 in. barrel, aluminum frame, fully machined steel slide, trigger group, and bolt insert, available in various colors, 9 1/4 oz. Mfg. 2000-2005.

	100%	98%	95%	90%	80%	70%	60%	LAST MSR
	$245	$200	$160	$140	$125	$110	$100	*$280*

Add $25 for gold anodized frame.
Add $20 for collector's edition.
Add $100 for Robar coating.

WILKINSON TACTICAL

Current AR-15 style pistol, rifle, and shotgun manufacturer located in Laramie, WY.

Please refer to BlueBookOfGunValues.com to order the *Blue Book of AR-15s & Variations*, available as a book or online subscription.

WILLIAM & SON

Current firearms manufacturer and luxury retailer established in 1999, located in London, England. Previous company name was William R. Asprey. William R. Asprey is the 7th generation of the renowned Asprey family who established their first business in 1781. William & Son continues the family tradition of building best quality English guns.

A competent appraisal is highly suggested for used Asprey and William & Son rifles and shotguns, as all guns have been built to custom order, and older guns need to be appraised individually based on condition, gauge, engraving, and possible accessories.

Prices do not include English VAT.

RIFLES: BOLT ACTION

BEST QUALITY MAGAZINE RIFLE – standard cals. include .243 Win., .270 Win., .308 Win., or .375 H&H, Mauser or Mannlicher action, 3/4 rib with standard and two-folding leaf rear sight, best quality pistol grip walnut stock with traditional cheekpiece, custom order only, Magnum or short action and scopes are priced upon individual quotation only.

Last MSR in 2018 started at £23,500, depending on caliber.

RIFLES: SxS, SIDELOCK

BEST QUALITY DOUBLE RIFLE – various cals. up to .577, sidelock ejector with engraved reinforced action, DT, pinless lockplates, best quality walnut, folding leaf rear sight on 3/4 rib, includes scroll engraving, leather case with accessories. Limited mfg. until 2018.

Last MSR started at £115,000, depending on caliber.
Add £10,000 for .375 H&H cal., add £15,000 for .465/.500 cals. or, £20,000 for .577 NE.
Add £5,100 for detachable scope mounts.
Deluxe or game scene engraving was POR.

SHOTGUNS: O/U, SIDELOCK

BEST QUALITY GAME GUN – 12, 16, or 20 ga., best quality sidelock ejector model, DTs, scroll engraving standard, best quality checkered walnut, custom order only. Disc. Reintroduced circa 2020.

MSR starts at £89,000.
Interchangeable chokes, deluxe or game scene engraving are all POR.

BEST QUALITY SPORTER GUN – 12 or 20 ga., trigger plate action, best quality sidelock ejector model, SST, best quality checkered walnut, large scroll engraving standard, custom order only. Disc.

MSR started at £46,500.
Add £1,000 for 20 ga.
Interchangeable chokes, deluxe or game scene engraving were all POR.

GRADING - PPGS™	100%	98%	95%	90%	80%	70%	60%	LAST MSR

SHOTGUNS: SxS, SIDELOCK

BEST QUALITY GAME GUN – available in 12 ga.-.410 bore, best quality sidelock ejector model, scroll engraving standard, DTs, best quality checkered walnut, custom order only.

MSR starts at £81,500.
Add £2,000 for 28 ga. or .410 bore.
Add £18,500+ for extra barrels.
Interchangeable chokes, deluxe or game scene engraving are all POR.

WILLIAM DOUGLAS & SONS

Previous manufacturer located in Staffordshire, England. Limited U.S. importation by Cape Outfitters located in Cape Girardeau, MO until circa 2004.

RIFLES: SxS

EXPRESS RIFLE – .375 H&H cal., H&H type back action sidelock with bolster fences, DTs, ejectors, 24 in. regulated barrels, folding leaf rear sight, oil finished European walnut stock with 20 LPI checkering, light engraving, case hardened action.

$19,750	$15,250	$11,000	$8,750	$7,400	$6,200	$5,300	

BOXLOCK EXPRESS RIFLE – .470 NE or .500 NE (new 1998) cal., Anson & Deeley action with DT (front trigger is articulated), case colored action with deep blue small parts, 24 in. regulated barrels, checkered European walnut stock and forearm with oil finish, light border engraving.

$12,975	$9,950	$9,000	$8,250	$7,500	$6,750	$6,000	

Add $1,000 for .500 NE cal.

* ***Boxlock Express Rifle Deluxe*** – includes better walnut and fully engraved receiver.

$15,650	$12,750	$10,750	$9,500	$8,750	$7,500	$6,750	

SHOTGUNS: SxS

WILLIAM DOUGLAS BOXLOCK – 16, 20, or 28 ga., 2 3/4 in. chambers, case colored receiver, chopper lump barrels, DT, 26 or 28 in. barrels.

$4,650	$4,200	$3,750	$3,250	$2,750	$2,250	$1,750	

Add $800 for ST.

WILLIAM EVANS LIMITED

Current manufacturer of long arms established during 1883, located in London, England.

William Evans Limited, Gun & Rifle Makers, have been manufacturing high quality shotguns and rifles for over 130 years. Most William Evans shotguns and double rifles must be appraised individually since they were all custom ordered initially. All new guns must be ordered from the factory directly. All prices are FOB England, less VAT. Please contact William Evans directly for more information, including any special orders.

RIFLES

MSR values for currently manufactured rifles are listed in English pounds, and used prices are not listed, since these models are only infrequently encountered in today's marketplace.

BEST QUALITY SIDELOCK DOUBLE RIFLE – various cals., traditional bold scroll-engraved sidelock action, many options available, custom order only.

* ***Best Quality Sidelock Double Rifle Current Mfg.***

Current MSR on this model is £POA (£85,000+).
Add £5,000 for .500 NE-.577 NE cals.
Cals. .600 NE and above are POR.

BOLT ACTION MAGAZINE RIFLE – various cals., Mauser standard or Magnum action, many options available, custom order only.

* ***Bolt Action Magazine Rifle Current Mfg.***

Current MSR on this model is £POA (£18,500+).
Add £6,000 for Mauser Magnum action.

SHOTGUNS: O/U & SxS

Delivery time on custom guns ranges from 24-30 months.

BEST QUALITY O/U SIDELOCK – 12, 16, 20, 28 ga., or .410 bore, best quality sidelock gun with DT, bold scroll engraving standard, custom order only.

Current MSR on this model is from £75,000.
Add £8,000 for 28 ga. or .410 bore.

BEST QUALITY SxS SIDELOCK – 12, 16, 20, 28 ga., or .410 bore, best quality sidelock gun with DT, bold scroll engraving standard, custom order only.

Current MSR on this model is from £60,000
Add £2,000 for 28 ga. or .410 bore.

CONNAUGHT – 12, 16, 20, 28 ga., or .410 bore, 2 3/4 or 3 in. chambers, 25 to 32 in. barrels, fixed or Briley/Teague multi-chokes, DT, square or rounded body action, choice of straight or pistol grip walnut stock with splinter forend, Anson style pushrod, hand engraved with traditional rose and scroll, produced in collaboration with Grulla Armas, 6-7 1/2 lbs. New 2011.

Current MSR on this model is from £9,000

Delivery time on this model is approx. 9 months.

CONNAUGHT PREMIUM – 12, 16, 20, 28 ga., or .410 bore, 2 3/4 or 3 in. chambers, 25 to 30 in. barrels, fixed or Briley multi-chokes, DT, square or rounded body action, choice of straight or pistol grip walnut stock with splinter forend, Anson style pushrod, hand engraved with traditional rose and scroll, produced in collaboration with Grulla Armas, 6 -7 1/2 lbs. New 2011.

Current MSR on this model is from £14,150

Delivery time on this model is approx. 9 months.

PALL MALL SxS – 12, 16, 20, 28 ga., or .410 bore, 2 3/4 or 3 in. chambers, 25 to 32 in. barrels, fixed or Briley/Teague multi-chokes, DT, choice of straight or pistol grip walnut stock with splinter forend, assisted opener, Anson style pushrod, hand engraved with traditional rose and scroll, produced in collaboration with Grulla Armas, 6 -7 1/2 lbs. New 2011.

Current MSR on this model is £17,500.

Delivery time on this model is approx. 9 months.

ST. JAMES – 12, 16, or 20 ga., 3 in. chambers, based on Perazzi X12, MX16 and MX20 style actions, 28, 30, or 32 in. barrels, fixed chokes, single, selective trigger, English-style trigger guard, oil-finished Turkish walnut stock, classic rounded forend, Prince of Wales grip, includes gold oval plate for personalized initials, traditional scroll engraving, optional leather case, approx. 7 1/2 lbs.

Current MSR on this model is £18,000

Delivery time on this model is approx. 12 months.

WILLIAM LARKIN MOORE

Current importer and dealer established in 1973, located in Scottsdale, AZ. Previously located in Agoura, CA, and Westlake Village, CA.

William Larkin Moore imports a variety of high grade quality shotguns and double rifles. Currently, the company imports Arrieta, S.L., Pedro Arrizabalaga, Armas Garbi, Chapuis Armes, LeBeau Courally, B. Rizzini, F.lli. Rizzini, and is the exclusive U.S. importer for F.lli Piotti. Please refer to the individual listings for information on current models and pricing.

WILLIAM POWELL (WILLIAM POWELL & SONS)

Current manufacturer established in 1802, located in Oxfordshire, England. Previously located in Birmingham, England until 2008. The company was controlled by the descendants of William Powell I until 2008. Previous company names were William Powell & Sons Gunmakers Ltd., and William Powell & Sons (until 2018). No current U.S. importation. Previously imported 1999-2002 by John Higgins, located in Richmond Hill, GA, and by Bells Legendary Countrywear located in New York, NY, until 1999. The Heritage Series was introduced into the U.S. in 1984.

For individual model listings, please go to BlueBookOfGunValues.com/overflow.

WILSKA & LANDEN (W&L) FIREARMS

Current bolt action rifle and parts manufacturer established circa 2018, located in Kukkila, Finland. No current U.S. importation.

W&L Firearms manufactures a line of complete rifles and bolt actions called the C Series Rifle. Please contact the company directly for more information, including pricing and U.S. availability.

WILSON COMBAT

Current firearms manufacturer, customizer, and supplier of custom firearms parts and accessories established in 1978, located in Berryville, AR.

PISTOLS: SEMI-AUTO

Prices reflect .45 ACP cal. base model w/o upgrades. A wide variety of options are available - contact the company directly for pricing.
Add $325 for the WCR-22 pistol suppressor (new 2016).

GRADING - PPGS™	100%	98%	95%	90%	80%	70%	60%	LAST MSR

40th ANNIVERSARY BOX SET – This set features the 40th Anniversary EDC X9 1911 in 9mm Para. cal., 4 in. barrel, polished stainless slide, 5 shot mag., gold bead front sight, gold inlaid markings on the slide, "EDC X9" is inlaid by Baron on right side of slide, Wilson Combat logo inlaid on the top, and "40 Years of Innovation" is inlaid on the left, 29 oz. The 40th Anniversary Supergrade 1911 in .45 ACP cal., with 5 in. barrel, 8 shot mag., mammoth ivory grips by Dan Chinnock, silver bead front sight, high polished Baron blue finish with silver inlays, "Supergrade" is inlaid on the right side of the slide, Wilson Combat logo inlaid behind right rear cocking serrations, "40 Years of Tradition" inlaid on left side, 42 oz., Out the Front Knife by Hogue (representing commitment to be on the cutting edge of weapon technology), the knife has polished flats, X-TAC grip pattern, and "Forty Years of Cutting Edge" laser engraved on the blade, set also includes 40th Anniversary Wilson Combat coins and custom fit shadow box. Limited mfg. 2017 only.

Retail pricing wasn't available for this set.

40th ANNIVERSARY CQB ELITE – 9mm Para., .45 ACP, or .38 Super cal., full size carbon steel frame, 5 in. stainless match grade cone barrel, flush cut reverse crown, fluted chamber and barrel with black flutes, Bullet Proof mag. release and round butt magwell, 5 in. carbon steel slide, Battlesight with green fiber optic front sight, Desert ironwood burl grips with sterling silver medallions, ambi Bullet Proof thumb safety, high grip Bullet Proof beavertail grip safety, high cut checkered front strap, front and rear cocking serrations, "40th Anniversary" over "1977-2017" on left side of slide, specialized serial numbers WC40-001 through WC40-400, 38.3 oz. Limited mfg. of 400 models beginning 2017.

MSR $3,900	$3,500	$3,075	$2,625	$2,380	$1,925	$1,575	$1,225	

Add $110 for 9mm Para. or .38 Super cal.

BERETTA/WILSON COMBAT 92G BRIGADIER TACTICAL – 9mm Para. cal., M9A1 frame, 4.7 in. stainless barrel with recessed crown and black finish, three 15 shot M9A1 Beretta mags., oversized steel mag. release, beveled magwell, skeletonized Elite II hammer, steel trigger, 92A1 round trigger guard profile, Trijicon tritium dovetail front sight, rear u-notch battlesight, G10 Dirty Olive grips with Wilson Combat logo medallion, dehorned 92G Brigadier slide, fluted steel guide rod, steel decocking levers, G configuration ambidextrous decocker only, aluminum lanyard loop, checkered front strap and back strap, Wilson Combat logo on slide, rail for mounting light or laser, special serial number range with WC prefix, 36 oz. New 2018.

MSR $1,195	$1,025	$895	$775	$700	$575	$475	$375	

BERETTA/WILSON COMBAT 92G CENTURION TACTICAL – 9mm Para. cal., M9A1 frame, 4.3 in. stainless barrel with recessed crown and black Bruniton finish, 17 or 20 shot Beretta mags., oversized steel mag. release, Wilson Combat mag. guide, beveled magwell, all steel components, skeletonized Elite II hammer, 92A1 round trigger guard profile, Ameriglo "Hackathorn" design Tritium with orange ring, dovetail front sight, Wilson Combat rear u-notch battlesight, G10 gray/black ultra thin grips with Wilson combat logo medallion, shortened 92G Vertec slide, G configuration ambidextrous decocker only, checkered front strap and back strap, Wilson Combat logo on slide, rail for mounting light or laser, special serial number range with WC prefix, 33.2 oz. New 2018.

MSR $1,250	$1,050	$950	$800	$700	$600	$475	$375	

BERETTA/WILSON COMBAT 92G COMPACT CARRY – 9mm Para. cal., checkered compact frame, 4.3 in. blackened stainless barrel with recessed target crown, 13 shot, beveled magwell, 16 lb. hammer spring, rounded trigger guard, white dot integral front sight and Wilson Combat rear battlesight, Wilson Combat G10 grips, steel ambidextrous decocker-only levers, steel guide rod and extended steel magazine catch, marked with Wilson Combat logo and special serialization, Beretta black Bruniton finish. Limited mfg. 2016-disc.

	$935	$825	$700	$635	$515	$425	$325	*$1,095*

BERETTA/WILSON COMBAT 92G VERTEC/BRIGADIER TACTICAL – 9mm Para. cal., modified M9A1 style/Vertec checkered frame with accessory rail, 4.7 in. "Elite" style match grade stainless barrel with recessed target crown, 15 shot mag., oversized steel mag. release, beveled magwell, skeletonized Elite II hammer, rounded trigger guard, Trijicon dovetail Tritium front and Wilson Combat rear sights, G10 Vertec black cherry grips with Wilson Combat logo medallion, enhanced Brigadier slide with Wilson Combat logo, Wilson Combat fluted steel guide rod, checkered front strap and Vertec backstrap, matte black Armor-Tuff finish, 32 oz. New 2018.

MSR $1,495	$1,275	$1,125	$950	$875	$700	$575	$500	

BERETTA/WILSON COMBAT 92G VERTEC/CENTURION TACTICAL – 9mm Para. cal., M9A1 frame with 92A1 round trigger guard profile and improved checkering, 4.3 in. stainless barrel with recessed crown, two 17 shot and one 20 shot Beretta mags., oversized steel mag. release, shortened 92G Vertec slide, skeletonized Elite II hammer, steel trigger, AmeriGlo "Hackathorn" design Tritium with orange ring, dovetail front sight, Wilson Combat rear u-notch battlesight, G10 Vertec black grips with Wilson Combat logo medallion, steel G Model decocking levers, black Bruniton finish, 33.2 oz. New 2019.

MSR $1,495	$1,275	$1,125	$950	$875	$700	$575	$500	

GRADING - PPGS™	100%	98%	95%	90%	80%	70%	60%	LAST MSR

ACP (AMERICAN COMBAT PISTOL) – 9mm Para. or .45 ACP cal., carbon steel frame, 4 (Compact), 4 1/4 (Commander), or 5 (full size) in. stainless match grade barrel and bushing, 7 (compact model only), 8 (.45 ACP), or 10 (9mm Para.) shot mag., contoured magwell, Battlesight w/red fiber optic front sight, choice of black or black/gray G10 Eagle Claw grips w/black medallions, Tactical Bullet Proof thumb safety, High Grip Bullet Proof beavertail grip safety, Eagle Claw front strap/mainspring housing treatment, Eagle Claw rear cocking serrations, Armor Tuff finish, 36.9-41.6 oz. New late 2019.

MSR $2,495	$2,250	$1,950	$1,700	$1,500	$1,250	$1,000	$800	

Add $100 for 9mm Para. cal.

AR9 – 9mm Para. cal., 8 or 11.3 in. barrel, threaded muzzle with QComp flash hider, Wilson Combat two-stage TTU (Tactical Trigger Unit), standard AR furniture, BCM pistol grip, billet aluminum flat-top upper and lower receiver, Wilson Combat T.R.I.M. rail, Shockwave Blade pistol firearm support, Armor-Tuff finish, 5-6 lbs. New 2016.

MSR $1,995	$1,750	$1,575	$1,450	$1,325	$1,100	$875	$675	

ARP TACTICAL – 5.56 NATO, .300 AAC Blackout, .300 HAM'R or 6.8 SPC II cal., carbine length gas system with low 3 Rem. profile gas block, 11.3 in. ARP Tactical match grade barrel, threaded muzzle with Accu-Tac flash hider, Wilson Combat tactical trigger guard, single stage TTU (Tactical Trigger Unit), BCM pistol grip, forged flat-top upper and lower receiver, 10.4 in. Wilson Combat T.R.I.M. rail, Shockwave Blade pistol forearm support, Armor-Tuff finish, 6 lbs. New 2016.

MSR $2,250	$1,975	$1,775	$1,625	$1,475	$1,250	$975	$775	

Add $50 for 6.8 SPC II cal.

BILL WILSON CARRY PISTOL – .45 ACP cal., compact carbon steel round butt frame, 4 in. stainless match grade cone barrel, 7 shot mag., carbon steel slide, blue finish, 30 LPI high cut checkered front strap, rear slide serrations, tactical thumb safety, contoured magwell, G10 starburst grips, high ride beavertail grip safety, BattleSight rear with fiber optic front sight, approx. 39 oz. Disc. 2016.

	$2,775	$2,350	$2,025	$1,775	$1,475	$1,275	$1,075	*$3,205*

BILL WILSON CARRY II PISTOL – 9mm Para. or .45 ACP cal., compact aluminum frame, 4 in. stainless steel match grade fluted barrel (flush cut, reverse crown), 4 in. carbon steel slide, 7 shot, integral light rail, contoured magwell, black cherry G10 ultra thin grips, X-TAC treatment on front strap/mainspring housing, and rear cocking serrations, Bullet Proof beavertail grip safety and hammer, Tactical Bullet Proof thumb safety, Battlesight rear with gold bead front sight, 29.63 oz. Mfg. 2017-mid-2020.

	$3,475	$3,100	$2,650	$2,225	$1,875	$1,575	$1,275	*$3,850*

CONTEMPORARY CLASSIC CENTENNIAL – .45 ACP cal., 100th anniversary of the 1911, full size carbon steel frame and slide, 5 in. carbon match grade barrel and bushing, 8 shot mag., Turnbull charcoal blue finish, French walnut double diamond grips, beavertail grip safety, contoured magwell, lanyard loop mainspring housing, 30 LPI high cut checkered front grip strap, "1911-2011" engraving, Battlesight rear and gold bead front sights, tactical thumb safety, top and rear slide serrations, special serial numbers (JMB001-JMB100) includes walnut presentation box, 45 oz. Limited edition of 100 mfg. during 2011.

	$3,550	$3,150	$2,725	$2,350	$1,950	$1,650	$1,350	*$3,995*

CLASSIC – 9mm Para., 10mm, .38 Super, .40 S&W, or .45 ACP cal., full size carbon steel frame, 5 in. stainless match grade barrel and bushing, carbon steel slide, two-tone finish, 30 LPI high cut checkered front strap, rear slide serrations, tactical thumb safety, contoured magwell, cocobolo double diamond grips, high ride beavertail grip safety, Lo-Mount adj. rear sight with improved ramp front sight.

MSR $3,030	$2,575	$2,250	$1,925	$1,750	$1,450	$1,175	$1,000	

CLASSIC SUPERGRADE – 9mm Para., 10mm, .38 Super, .40 S&W, or .45 ACP cal., full size stainless steel frame, 5 in. stainless match grade barrel and bushing, carbon steel slide, blue finish, 30 LPI high cut checkered front strap, top and rear slide serrations, Lo-Mount adj. rear sight, improved ramp front sight, ambi safety, Speed-Chute magwell, cocobolo double diamond grips, beavertail grip safety, full-length guide rod, each gun hand built. Ltd. mfg. disc. mid-2020.

	$4,675	$4,225	$3,750	$3,150	$2,650	$2,200	$1,700	*$5,195*

Add $105 for 9mm Para., 10mm, .38 Super, or .40 S&W cal.

CARRY COMP – 9mm Para. (disc. 2011), .38 Super, or .45 ACP cal., lightweight aluminum (disc. 2012) or compact carbon steel frame, 4 or 4 1/2 (disc.) in. compensated match grade barrel, 7 shot mag., contoured magwell, 4 in. carbon steel slide, skeletonized ultra light hammer, combat tactical sight system (disc.) or Battlesight rear and fiber optic front sights, Dymondwood (disc.) or G10 Starburst grips, High Ride Bullet Proof beavertail grip safety, 30 LPI front strap checkering, black, green (disc.), tan (disc.), or grey (disc.) Amor-Tuff finish, 38.4 oz.

MSR $3,200	$2,775	$2,350	$2,025	$1,775	$1,475	$1,225	$1,075	

Add $165 for Carry Comp Lightweight (disc. 2012).

GRADING - PPGS™	100%	98%	95%	90%	80%	70%	60%	LAST MSR

* ***Carry Comp Professional*** – 9mm Para. (disc. 2011), .38 Super, or .45 ACP cal., similar to Carry Comp, except has compact frame that is 1/2 in. shorter. Disc. 2012.

	$3,425	$3,025	$2,600	$2,175	$1,850	$1,550	$1,250	*$3,765*

Add $165 for Carry Comp Professional Lightweight.

CARRY COMP PROFESSIONAL (CURRENT MFG.) – 9mm Para., .45 ACP, or .38 Super cal., Professional size carbon steel frame, 4 in. stainless match grade compensated barrel with carbon steel slide, Battlesight with fiber optic front sight, black G10 starburst grips with pewter medalions, High-Ride beavertail grip safety, Tactical Bullet Proof thumb safety, 30 LPI front strap checkering, rear cocking serration, Armor-Tuff finish, 40.5 oz. New 2017.

MSR $3,200	$2,775	$2,350	$2,025	$1,775	$1,475	$1,225	$1,075	

Add $110 for 9mm Para. or .38 Super cal.

CQB – 9mm Para., .38 Super, .40 S&W (new 2012), 10mm (new 2012), or .45 ACP cal., full size aluminum round butt frame, 5 in. stainless match grade barrel and bushing, flush cut and crowned, carbon steel slide, blue finish, 30 LPI high cut checkered front strap, top and rear slide serrations, tactical thumb safety, contoured magwell, G10 starburst grips, beavertail grip safety and hammer, Battlesight rear and fiber optic front sights, countersunk slide stop.

MSR $2,865	$2,575	$2,150	$1,825	$1,550	$1,225	$1,050	$925	

Add $110 for 9mm Para., .38 Super, or .40 S&W cal.
Add $225 for 10mm cal.

* ***CQB Compact*** – 9mm Para., .38 Super or .45 ACP cal., compact carbon steel frame, 4 in. stainless match grade cone barrel, carbon steel slide, blue finish, 30 LPI high cut checkered front strap, top and rear slide serrations, tactical thumb safety, contoured magwell, G10 starburst grips, high ride beavertail grip safety, Battlesight rear and fiber optic front sights.

MSR $2,890	$2,575	$2,150	$1,850	$1,575	$1,250	$1,075	$950	

Add $205 for CQB Compact Lightweight (disc.).

* ***CQB Lightweight*** – 9mm Para., 10mm, .38 Super, .40 S&W, or .45 ACP cal., full size aluminum frame, 5 in. stainless match grade barrel and bushing, 5 in. carbon steel slide, blue finish, 30 LPI high cut checkered front strap, top and rear slide serrations, tactical thumb safety, contoured magwell, G10 starburst grips, beavertail grip safety, Battlesight rear and fiber optic front sights, weighs 14% less than steel model. Disc. 2014.

	$2,650	$2,225	$1,950	$1,700	$1,400	$1,175	$1,125	*$3,030*

CQB ELITE – 9mm Para., 10mm, .38 Super, .40 S&W, or .45 ACP cal., full size carbon steel frame, 5 in. stainless match grade barrel and bushing, 5 in. carbon steel slide, blue finish, 30 LPI high cut checkered front strap, top and rear slide serrations, tactical thumb safety, Speed-Chute magwell with lanyard loop, G10 diagonal flat bottom grips, beavertail grip safety, Battlesight rear and fiber optic front sights, 41 oz.

MSR $3,425	$3,100	$2,700	$2,400	$2,000	$1,700	$1,400	$1,150	

Add $110 for 9mm Para., .38 Super, or .40 S&W cal.
Add $225 for 10mm cal.

* ***CQB Elite 40th Anniversary*** – .45 ACP, 9mm Para., or .38 Super cal., full size carbon steel frame, 5 in. stainless match grade cone barrel, flush cut reverse crown, fluted chamber and barrel with back flutes, 5 in. carbon steel slide, Desert Ironwood burl grips with sterling silver medallions, Bullet Proof beavertail grip safety and ambidextrous thumb safety, 30 LPI high cut checkered front strap and slide top serrations, front and rear cocking serrations, Wilson Combat logo behind right rear cocking serration, "Wilson Combat" on right side of slide, "40th Anniversary" over "1977-2017" on left side of slide, specialized serial numbers WC40-001 through WC40-400, 38.3 oz. New 2017.

MSR $3,900	$3,525	$3,100	$2,650	$2,225	$1,875	$1,575	$1,275	

Add $110 for 9mm Para. or .38 Super cal.

* ***CQB Elite Commander/Professional*** – 9mm Para., .38 Super, or .45 ACP cal., Professional size carbon steel frame, 4 (Professional) or 4 1/4 (Commander) in. stainless match grade barrel and bushing, flush-cut reverse crown, 8 shot mag., Bullet Proof magwell and mag. release, 4 (Professional) or 4 1/4 (Commander) in. carbon steel slide, Battlesight with fiber optic front sight, G10 diagonal flat bottom black grips with pewter medallions, High-Ride Bullet Proof beavertail grip safety, Tactical Bullet Proof thumb safety, high cut checkered front strap, 30 LPI top and 40 LPI rear slide serrations, 38.3-38.6 oz. New 2020.

MSR $3,425	$3,100	$2,700	$2,400	$2,000	$1,700	$1,400	$1,150	

Add $110 for 9mm Para. or .38 Super cal.

GRADING - PPGS™ 100% 98% 95% 90% 80% 70% 60% LAST MSR

* ***CQB Elite Compact*** – 9mm Para., .38 Super, or .45 ACP cal., Compact size carbon steel frame, 4 in. stainless match grade cone barrel, flush-cut reverse crown, 8 shot mag., Bullet Proof mag. release and round butt magwell, 4 in. carbon steel slide, Battlesight with fiber optic front sight, G10 starburst flat bottom black grips with pewter medallions, High-Ride Bullet Proof beavertail grip safety, Tactical Bullet Proof thumb safety, high cut checkered front strap, 30 LPI top and 40 LPI rear slide serrations, 36.8 oz. New 2020.

MSR $3,425 $3,100 $2,700 $2,400 $2,000 $1,700 $1,400 $1,150

Add $110 for 9mm Para. or .38 Super cal.

CQB LIGHT-RAIL – 9mm Para., 10mm, .38 Super, .40 S&W, or .45 ACP cal., full size aluminum frame, 5 in. stainless match grade barrel and bushing, carbon steel slide, blue finish, integral light rail, 30 LPI high cut checkered front strap, top and rear slide serrations, tactical thumb safety, contoured magwell, G10 starburst grips, beavertail grip safety, Battlesight rear and fiber optic front sights. Disc. 2012.

$2,625 $2,225 $1,950 $1,700 $1,400 $1,175 $1,025 ***$3,005***

* ***CQB Light-rail Lightweight*** – 9mm Para., 10mm (disc. 2014), .38 Super, .40 S&W (disc.), or .45 ACP cal., full size aluminum frame, 5 in. stainless match grade barrel and bushing, 5 in. carbon steel slide, integral light rail, 30 LPI high cut checkered front strap, top and rear slide serrations, contoured magwell, Bullet Proof thumb safety, contoured magwell, G10 starburst grips, high ride Bullet Proof beavertail grip safety, Battlesight rear and fiber optic front sights, 60% lighter than comparable steel frame, blue finish, 36.6 oz.

MSR $3,145 $2,725 $2,275 $1,975 $1,700 $1,400 $1,175 $1,125

Add $110 for 9mm Para., .38 Super, or .40 S&W (disc.) cal.

* ***CQB Light-Rail Lightweight Compact*** – 9mm Para., .38 Super (disc. 2011, reintroduced 2017), or .45 ACP cal., compact aluminum round butt frame, 4 in. stainless match grade cone barrel, 4 in. carbon steel slide, blue finish, integral light rail, 30 LPI high cut checkered front strap, top and rear slide serrations, tactical thumb safety, contoured magwell, G10 starburst grips, high ride Bullet Proof beavertail grip safety, Battlesight rear and fiber optic front sights, weighs 14% less than steel model, 27.3 oz.

MSR $3,280 $2,825 $2,375 $2,050 $1,800 $1,500 $1,200 $1,125

* ***CQB Tactical LE Light-Rail*** – 9mm Para., 10mm, .38 Super, .40 S&W, or .45 ACP cal., full size stainless steel frame, 5 in. stainless match grade bull barrel, 5 in. carbon steel slide, 8 shot, blue finish, integral light rail, 30 LPI high cut checkered front strap, top and rear slide serrations, tactical thumb safety, Speed-Chute magwell with lanyard loop, G10 diagonal flat bottom grips, Bullet Proof beavertail grip safety, Battlesight rear and fiber optic front sights.

MSR $3,115 $2,700 $2,300 $2,000 $1,750 $1,450 $1,200 $1,050

Add $115 for 9mm Para., .38 Super, or .40 S&W cal.

Add $230 for 10mm cal.

CQB COMMANDER – 9mm Para. or .45 ACP cal., professional size carbon steel round butt frame, 4 1/4 in. stainless match grade barrel and bushing, fluted chamber, 4 1/4 in. carbon steel slide, 8 shot, contoured magwell, Bullet Proof mag. release, Battlesight rear and fiber optic front sight, G10 starburst pattern beveled bottom black grips with pewter medallions, Concealment Bullet Proof beavertail grip safety and hammer, Tactical Bullet Proof thumb safety, 30 LPI high cut checkered front strap, top and rear slide serrations, 35.14 oz. New 2016.

MSR $3,600 $3,300 $2,925 $2,550 $2,150 $1,825 $1,525 $1,225

* ***CQB Commander Compact*** – 9mm Para. or .45 ACP cal., compact carbon steel round butt frame, 4 1/4 in. stainless match grade barrel and bushing, flush cut reverse crown, fluted chamber, 4 1/4 in. carbon steel slide, 30 LPI high cut checkered front strap, Bullet Proof mag. release, beavertail grip safety and hammer, Tactical Bullet Proof thumb safety, G10 starburst pattern black grips with pewter medallions, Battlesight rear and fiber optic front sights, top and rear slide serrations. New 2017.

MSR $3,600 $3,300 $2,925 $2,550 $2,150 $1,825 $1,525 $1,225

Add $110 for 9mm Para. cal.

EDC9 COMPACT – 9mm Para. cal., compact carbon steel frame with enhanced frame rails, 4 in. stainless cone barrel, fluted chamber/barrel, Bullet Proof round butt magwell and mag. release, 4 in. stainless steel tri-top slide with external extractor, black G10 aggressive Starburst grips with pewter medallions, adj. Battlesight with fiber optic front sight, concealment Bullet Proof beavertail grip safety and hammer, tactical thumb safety, top and rear slide serrations. New 2017.

MSR $3,695 $3,375 $2,975 $2,575 $2,150 $1,825 $1,525 $1,225

GRADING - PPGS™	100%	98%	95%	90%	80%	70%	60%	LAST MSR

EDC9 PROFESSIONAL – 9mm Para. cal., professional size carbon steel frame with reliability enhanced frame rails, 4 in. stainless fluted barrel with reliability enhancing lock-up, 4 in. carbon steel tri-top slide with external extractor, Bullet Proof round butt magwell, beavertail grip safety, hammer, and thumb safety, G10 aggressive starburst black grips with pewter medallions, X-TAC treatment on front strap/mainspring housing and front/rear cocking serrations, Wilson Combat tactical adj. Battlesight rear and fiber optic front sights. New 2017.

MSR $3,695	$3,375	$2,975	$2,575	$2,150	$1,825	$1,525	$1,225

EDC X9 – 9mm Para. cal., 1911-style pistol, high-capacity compact size aluminum X-frame with enhanced frame rails, 4 in. stainless steel fluted cone barrel, two 15 shot mags., Bullet Proof mag. release, 4 in. stainless steel tri-top slide with external extractor, concealment Bullet Proof hammer, elevation adj. tactical Battlesight with fiber optic front sight, black G10 starburst grips with pewter medallions, ambidextrous thumb safety, X-TAC treatment on front strap/mainspring housing and front cocking serrations, top and rear slide serrations, black, gray, green, Federal Brown, FDE or Burnt Bronze finishes, 35 oz. New 2017.

MSR $2,895	$2,475	$2,150	$1,775	$1,525	$1,250	$1,050	$925

EDC X9L – 9mm Para. cal., compact size aluminum X-frame with enhanced frame rails, 5 in. stainless steel match grade barrel, flush cut reverse crown, fluted chamber, 5 in. stainless steel tri-top slide with external extractor, two 15 or 18 shot mags., Bullet Proof mag. release, Concealment Bullet Proof hammer, tactical adj. Battlesight with fiber optic front sight, black G10 Starburst grips with pewter medallions, Bullet Proof thumb safety, X-TAC front strap/backstrap treatment, top and rear slide serrations, 32.4 oz. New 2019.

MSR $2,995	$2,695	$2,350	$2,025	$1,850	$1,475	$1,225	$950

EDC X9S – 9mm Para. cal., X9S sub-compact aluminum X-frame, 3 1/4 in. stainless steel fluted cone barrel, fluted chamber, one 10 and one 15 shot extended mag., 3 1/4 in. SS Tri-Top slide with external extractor, T6-7075 aluminum frame, with or w/o accessory rail, 25.5 oz. New 2020.

MSR $2,695	$2,295	$2,025	$1,725	$1,575	$1,260	$1,050	$895

ELITE PROFESSIONAL – 9mm Para., .38 Super or .45 ACP cal., professional size carbon steel frame, 4 in. stainless match grade heavy flanged cone barrel, carbon steel slide, blue finish, 30 LPI high cut checkered front strap, rear slide serrations, ambidextrous thumb safety, Speed-Chute magwell, G10 diagonal flat bottom grips, full-length guide rod with reverse plug, high ride beavertail grip safety, Battlesight rear and fiber optic front sights, 39.6 oz.

MSR $3,650	$3,350	$2,950	$2,550	$2,150	$1,825	$1,525	$1,225

Add $165 for Elite Professional Lightweight (disc.).

EXPERIOR COMMANDER – 9mm Para. or .45 ACP cal., Professional size carbon steel slide and frame with WAVE cut rails, 4 1/4 in. stainless match grade barrel, fluted chamber w/lowered front locking lug, flash cut reverse crown, 8 (.45 ACP) or 10 (9mm Para.) shot mag., Bullet Proof mag. release and round butt magwell, Battlesight w/red fiber optic front sight, G10 black TRAK pattern grips w/pewter medallions, Tactical Bullet Proof thumb safety, concealment Bullet Proof beavertail grip safety and hammer, 1911-style slide serrations, TRAK texture front strap/mainspring housing, countersunk slide stop, Ryan Wilson high grip frame modification, 37.9 oz. New late 2019.

MSR $3,750	$3,450	$3,150	$2,700	$2,300	$1,875	$1,550	$1,250

Add $100 for 9mm Para. cal.

* ***Experior Commander Compact*** – 9mm Para. or .45 ACP cal., single stack, compact carbon steel slide and frame w/WAVE cut rails, 4 1/4 in. carbon steel barrel, fluted chamber, 7 (.45 ACP) or 9 (9mm Para.) shot mag., Bullet Proof mag. release and round butt magwell., Battlesight w/red fiber optic front sight, G10 black TRAK pattern grips w/pewter medallions, Tactical Bullet Proof thumb safety, concealment beavertail grip safety and hammer, 1911-style serrations, countersunk slide stop, TRAK texture on front strap/mainspring housing, Ryan Wilson high grip frame modification, black with other finishes available, 36.7 oz. New late 2019.

MSR $3,750	$3,450	$3,150	$2,700	$2,300	$1,875	$1,550	$1,250

Add $100 for 9mm Para. cal.

EXPERIOR COMMANDER DOUBLE STACK – 9mm Para. cal., double stack, high capacity compact size aluminum frame, 4 1/4 in. stainless match grade barrel, fluted chamber, flush cut reverse crown, two 18 shot mag., Bullet Proof mag. release and aluminum magwell, concealment Bullet Proof hammer, Battlesight w/red fiber optic front sight, black G10 aggressive starburst grips w/pewter medallions, Bullet Proof thumb safety, 1911 style slide serrations, TRAK texture on front and backstrap, countersunk slide stop, black finish, optional finishes available, optional 15 shot mag., 30.2 oz. New late 2019.

MSR $3,045	$2,600	$2,250	$1,950	$1,750	$1,400	$1,150	$900

GRADING - PPGS™	100%	98%	95%	90%	80%	70%	60%	LAST MSR

EXPERIOR COMPACT – 9mm Para. or .45 ACP cal., compact carbon steel slide and frame with WAVE cut rails, 4 in. stainless match grade cone, fluted barrel, 7 (.45 ACP) or 9 (9mm Para.) shot mag., Bullet Proof mag. release and round butt magwell, Battlesight w/red fiber optic front sight, G10 black TRAK pattern grips w/pewter medallions, Tactical Bullet Proof thumb safety, beavertail grip safety and hammer, 1911-style serrations, countersunk slide stop, TRAK texture on front strap/mainspring housing, Ryan Wilson high grip frame modification, black finish, optional finishes available, 36.9 oz. New late 2019.

MSR $3,750	$3,450	$3,150	$2,700	$2,300	$1,875	$1,550	$1,250	

Add $100 for 9mm Para. cal.

EXPERIOR COMPACT DOUBLE STACK – 9mm Para. cal., 1911 stainless steel slide, high-capacity compact aluminum frame, 4 in. stainless match grade fluted barrel and chamber, two 18 shot mag., Bullet Proof mag. release and aluminum magwell, concealment Bullet Proof hammer, Battlesight w/red fiber optic front sight, black G10 aggressive Starburst grips w/pewter medallions, Bullet Proof thumb safety, 1911-style slide serrations, countersunk slide stop, TRAK texture on front strap/mainspring housing, Ryan Wilson high grip frame modification, black finish, optional finishes available, optional 15 shot mag., 38.8 oz. New late 2019.

MSR $2,995	$2,695	$2,350	$2,025	$1,850	$1,475	$1,225	$950	

Add $100 for 9mm Para. cal.

EXPERIOR DOUBLE STACK – 9mm Para. cal., double stack, high capacity compact size aluminum frame, 5 in. stainless match grade barrel w/lowered front locking lug, flash cut reverse crown, two 18 shot mag., Bullet Proof mag. release and aluminum magwell, Concealment Bullet Proof hammer, Battlesight w/red fiber optic front sight, black G10 aggressive starburst grips w/pewter medallions, Bullet Proof thumb safety, 1911 style slide serrations, TRAK texture on front and backstrap, countersunk slide stop, black finish, optional finishes available, optional 15 shot mag., 41 oz. New late 2019.

MSR $3,095	$2,700	$2,250	$1,950	$1,700	$1,400	$1,175	$1,000	

EXPERIOR FULL SIZE/LONGSLIDE – 9mm Para. or .45 ACP cal., carbon steel slide and full size frame with (Longslide only) or w/o WAVE cut rails, 5 (Full Size) or 6 (Longslide) in. stainless match grade barrel, fluted chamber, lowered front locking lug, flash cut reverse crown, 8 (.45 ACP) or 10 (9mm Para.) shot mag., Bullet Proof mag. release and round butt magwell, Battlesight w/red fiber optic front sight, G10 black TRAK pattern grips w/pewter medallions, Tactical Bullet Proof thumb safety, beavertail grip safety and hammer, 1911-style slide serrations, TRAK texture on front strap/mainspring housing, countersunk slide stop, Ryan Wilson high grip frame modification, black finish, optional colors available, approx. 40 oz. New late 2019.

MSR $3,750	$3,450	$3,150	$2,700	$2,300	$1,875	$1,550	$1,250	

Add $100 for 9mm Para. cal.

EXPERIOR PROFESSIONAL – 9mm Para. or .45 ACP cal., Professional size 4 in. carbon steel slide and frame with WAVE cut rails, 4 in. stainless match grade cone, fluted barrel and chamber w/lowered front locking lug, flash cut reverse crown, 8 (.45 ACP) or 10 (9mm Para.) shot mag., Bullet Proof mag. release and round butt magwell, Battlesight w/red fiber optic front sight, G10 black TRAK pattern grips w/pewter medallions, Tactical Bullet Proof thumb safety, concealment Bullet Proof beavertail grip safety and hammer, 1911-style slide serrations, TRAK texture front strap/mainspring housing, countersunk slide stop, Ryan Wilson high grip frame modification, 38.2 oz. New late 2019.

MSR $3,750	$3,450	$3,150	$2,700	$2,300	$1,875	$1,550	$1,250	

Add $100 for 9mm Para. cal.

EXPERIOR SUB COMPACT – 9mm Para. cal., Sentinel size carbon steel frame w/WAVE cut rails, 3 1/2 in. stainless match grade cone, fluted barrel and chamber, lowered front locking lug, flush cut reverse crown, 8 shot mag., Bullet Proof mag. release and round butt magwell, Battlesight w/red fiber optic front sight, black G10 TRAK pattern grips w/pewter medallions, Tactical Bullet Proof thumb safety, concealment bullet proof beavertail grip safety and hammer, 1911-style slide serrations, countersunk slide stop, TRAK texture on front strap/mainspring housing, full-length guide rod w/reverse plug, Ryan Wilson high grip frame modification, black finish, optional finishes available, 36.4 oz. New late 2019.

MSR $3,850	$3,475	$3,100	$2,650	$2,225	$1,875	$1,575	$1,275	

HACKATHORN SPECIAL – 9mm Para., .38 Super, or .45 ACP cal., full size carbon steel frame, 5 in. stainless match grade barrel, 5 in. carbon steel slide, fluted chamber, 8 shot mag., checkered front strap, black G10 starburst flat bottom grips, Bullet Proof tactical thumb safety, magwell and mag. release, beavertail grip safety and hammer, Battlesight rear and fiber optic front sights, top and rear slide serrations, approx. 40 oz.

MSR $3,750	$3,450	$3,150	$2,700	$2,300	$1,875	$1,550	$1,250	

GRADING - PPGS™	100%	98%	95%	90%	80%	70%	60%	LAST MSR

HACKATHORN SPECIAL COMMANDER – 9mm Para. or .45 ACP cal., professional size carbon steel frame, 4 1/4 in. stainless match grade fluted barrel and bushing, flush cut reverse crown, 8 shot mag., Bullet Proof round butt magwell, 4 1/2 in. carbon steel slide, black G10 Starburst flat bottom grips, Battlesight with fiber optic front sight, top and rear slide serrations, rear cocking serrations, countersunk slide stop, high cut checkered front strap, Concealment Bullet Proof beavertail grip safety and hammer, tactical thumb safety, 38.2 oz. New 2018.

MSR $3,750	$3,450	$3,150	$2,700	$2,300	$1,875	$1,550	$1,250	

HUNTER – 10mm or .460 Rowland cal., 5 1/2 in. single port compensated barrel with fully supported chamber, full size carbon steel frame and slide, 30 LPI high cut checkered front strap, tactical thumb safety, contoured magwell, high ride beavertail grip safety, Crimson Trace Lasergrips, countersunk slide stop, full-length guide rod with reverse plug, approx. 40 oz.

MSR $4,100	$3,650	$3,150	$2,750	$2,350	$1,875	$1,550	$1,350	

LIMITED TEN SERIES 1 – .45 ACP cal., full size carbon steel frame, 5 in. stainless match grade barrel, 8 shot mag., lo-mount adj. Battlesight with white gold bead front sight, mammoth ivory grips, Bullet Proof beavertail grip and ambi thumb safety, blued finish, custom hand engraved by Wayne D'Angelo, includes custom case and letter of authenticity, 41.9 oz.

LIMITED TEN SERIES 2 – .45 ACP cal., full size stainless steel frame, 5 in. match grade barrel, 8 shot mag., carbon steel slide, Battlesight with white gold bead front sight, mammoth tusk bark ivory grips, Bullet Proof beavertail grip and thumb safety, blued finish, custom hand engraved by Layne Zuelke, unique Limited Ten ser. no., includes custom case and letter of authenticity.

LIMITED TEN SERIES 3 – .45 ACP cal., professional size carbon steel frame, 4.75 in. stainless match grade barrel, 8 shot mag., carbon steel slide, commander hammer, Battlesight with white gold bead front sight, desert iron wood grips with sterling silver medallions, Bullet Proof beavertail grip and retro checkered thumb safety, custom hand engraved by Wayne D'Angelo, unique limited ten serial number, custom case, and letter of authenticity, blued finish, 39.1 oz. New 2020.

Please contact the manufacturer directly for price and availability.

LIMITED TEN SERIES 4 – .45 ACP cal., professional size stainless steel slide and frame, 4.75 in. stainless match grade barrel, 8 shot mag., commander hammer, Battlesight with white gold bead front sight, desert iron wood grips with sterling silver medallions, Bullet Proof beavertail grip and retro checkered thumb safety, custom engraving by Layne Zuelke, unique limited ten serial number, custom case, and letter of authenticity, 39.1 oz. New 2021.

Please contact the manufacturer directly for price and availability.

PAUL HOWE PACKAGE FOR GLOCK – 9mm Para. cal., Glock Gen 4 stippled starburst pattern frame, full fit Wilson Combat barrel, 15 (Glock 19) or 17 (Glock 26) shot mag., Paul Howe cut on trigger guard, Wilson Combat square notch Battlesight with AmeriGlo Tritium with green outline front sight, stippled thumb pads with Wilson Combat logo, black Armor-Tuff slide CSAT logo on slide, Paul Howe wide slide top serrations. New 2019.

MSR $1,500	$1,275	$1,125	$950	$875	$700	$575	$450	

PINNACLE – .45 ACP cal., based on the Classic Supergrade model, full size frame, 5 in. stainless match grade barrel, 8 shot, full-length spiral fluted guide rod, 5 in. carbon steel slide, blued steel trigger, beavertail grip safety, deluxe burl wood smooth grips with gold plated grip medallions, lo-mount adj. rear sight with Battleblade, gold bead front sight, checkered front strap, hand fitted and finished, classic scroll pattern hand engraving, deluxe blue finish with polished sides of frame and slide, deluxe walnut presentation case, letter of authenticity, detailed inside & out with options selected by Bill Wilson, highest grade of craftsmanship, 45 oz. Mfg. disc. mid-2020.

	$7,250	$6,500	$5,750	$4,995	$4,250	$3,500	$2,700	*$7,995*

PROFESSIONAL – 9mm Para., .38 Super, .40 S&W (disc. 2011), or .45 ACP cal., professional size carbon steel frame, 4 in. stainless match grade cone barrel, carbon steel slide, blue finish, 30 LPI high cut checkered front strap, top and rear slide serrations, tactical thumb safety, contoured magwell, G10 starburst grips, high ride beavertail grip safety, Battlesight rear and fiber optic front sights.

MSR $2,920	$2,475	$2,175	$1,850	$1,685	$1,350	$1,125	$975	

* ***Professional Lightweight*** – 9mm Para., .38 Super or .45 ACP cal., similar to Professional, except has lightweight aluminum frame.

MSR $3,090	$2,700	$2,250	$1,950	$1,700	$1,400	$1,175	$1,000	

* ***Professional Light-Rail Lightweight (CQB)*** – 9mm Para., .38 Super or .45 ACP cal., professional size aluminum frame, integral light rail.

MSR $3,205	$2,775	$2,350	$2,025	$1,775	$1,475	$1,225	$1,075	

GRADING - PPGS™	100%	98%	95%	90%	80%	70%	60%	LAST MSR

PROTECTOR – 9mm Para., 10mm, .38 Super, .40 S&W, or .45 ACP cal., full size carbon steel frame, 5 in. stainless match grade barrel and bushing, carbon steel slide, contoured magwell, Battlesight rear and fiber optic front sights, G10 starburst grips, tactical thumb safety, high cut checkered front strap, front and rear slide serrations, two-tone finish. Disc. 2016.

	$2,475	$2,175	$1,850	$1,685	$1,350	$1,125	$975	*$2,920*

Add $110 for 9mm Para. cal.

* ***Protector Compact*** – 9mm Para. or .45 ACP cal., integral light-rail lightweight frame, 4 in. stainless match grade cone barrel, 4 in. carbon steel slide, fluted barrel and chamber, 7 shot mag., Bullet Proof round butt magwell and mag. release, Battlesight rear and fiber optic front sight, G10 starburst grips with black medallions, High-Ride Bullet Proof beavertail grip safety, Tactical Bullet Proof thumb safety, 30 LPI high cut checkered front strap, slide top and rear and front cocking serrations, 28.2 oz. New 2016.

MSR $3,875	$3,500	$3,100	$2,650	$2,225	$1,875	$1,575	$1,275

Add $110 for 9mm Para. cal.

PROTECTOR (CURRENT MFG.) – 9mm Para. or .45 ACP cal., integral light rail steel or lightweight frame, 5 in. stainless match grade fluted barrel, 5 in. carbon steel slide, 8 (.45) or 10 (9mm) shot mag., Battlesight with fiber optic front sight, G10 starburst grips with black medallions, Bullet Proof round-butt magwell, high ride beavertail grip safety, and tactical thumb safety, high cut checkered front strap, top, rear, and cocking serrations, 41.6 oz. New 2018.

MSR $3,875	$3,500	$3,100	$2,650	$2,225	$1,875	$1,575	$1,275

Add $110 for 9mm Para. cal.

PROTECTOR PROFESSIONAL – 9mm Para. or .45 ACP cal., integral light-rail steel or lightweight frame, 4 in. fluted barrel, 4 in. carbon steel slide, 8 or 10 shot mag., Bullet Proof round butt magwell and mag. release, Battlesight rear and fiber optic front sight, G10 starburst grips with black medallions, High-Ride Bullet Proof beavertail grip safety and Tactical Bullet Proof thumb safety, 30 LPI high cut checkered front strap, front cocking serrations and carry cuts, 37.5 oz. New 2016.

MSR $3,875	$3,500	$3,100	$2,650	$2,225	$1,875	$1,575	$1,275

Add $110 for 9mm Para. cal.

PROTECTOR SERIES AR PISTOL – 5.56 NATO, .300 AAC Blackout, or .300 HAM'R cal., GIO, 11.3 in. match grade stainless barrel with Q-Comp flash hider/muzzle brake, D&H 20 shot mag., M2 two-stage TTU trigger, oversized tactical trigger guard, Tailhook Mod 2 adj. brace, BCM Starburst pistol grip, Mil-Spec forged upper and lower receiver, low profile gas block, mid-length gas system, M-LOK compatible handguard with 4 in. accessory rail, black Armor-Tuff finish, left-handed models available, 5 lbs. 10 oz. New 2019.

MSR $2,000	$1,700	$1,490	$1,275	$1,150	$950	$775	$650

STEALTH (S.D.S.) – 9mm Para., .38 Super, .40 S&W (disc. 2011) or .45 ACP cal., compact carbon steel frame, 4 in. stainless match grade heavy flanged cone barrel, carbon steel slide, blue finish, 30 LPI high cut checkered front strap, rear slide serrations, ambidextrous thumb safety, contoured magwell, G10 starburst grips, high ride beavertail grip safety, Battlesight rear and fiber optic front sights, full-length guide rod with reverse plug.

MSR $3,535	$3,225	$2,875	$2,500	$2,100	$1,775	$1,475	$1,175

Add $280 for Stealth Lightweight (disc.).

SENTINEL – 9mm Para. cal., Sentinel steel frame that is 1/2 in. shorter than compact, 3 1/2 in. stainless match grade cone barrel, 8 shot mag., carbon steel slide, blue finish, 30 LPI high cut checkered front strap, rear slide serrations, Bullet Proof tactical thumb safety, contoured magwell, G10 slimline grips, high ride Bullet Proof beavertail grip safety, Battlesight rear and fiber optic front sights, full-length guide rod with reverse plug, approx. 32 oz.

MSR $3,310	$2,850	$2,375	$2,050	$1,800	$1,500	$1,225	$1,125

Add $115 for Sentinel Lightweight (disc.).

* ***Ms. Sentinel*** – 9mm Para. cal., Sentinel aluminum frame that is 1/2 in. shorter than compact, 3 1/2 in. stainless match grade cone fluted barrel, 8 shot mag., carbon steel slide, 30 LPI high cut checkered front strap, rear slide serrations, tactical thumb safety, contoured magwell, cocobolo starburst grips, concealment Bullet Proof beavertail grip safety and hammer, Bullet Proof shortened/rounded mag. release, Battlesight rear and fiber optic front sights, full-length guide rod with reverse plug, blue finish, approx. 31 oz.

MSR $3,875	$3,500	$3,100	$2,650	$2,225	$1,875	$1,575	$1,275

GRADING - PPGS™	100%	98%	95%	90%	80%	70%	60%	LAST MSR

* ***Sentinel Compact*** – 9mm Para. or .38 Super (new 2016) cal., compact size carbon steel round butt frame, 3.6 in. stainless match grade barrel, 8 shot mag., Bullet Proof mag. release (new 2016), 3.6 in. carbon steel slide, Battlesight with fiber optic front sight, G10 slimline (mfg. 2012 only) or Wilson Combat Black Cherry slant grips with pewter medallions (new 2016), Concealment Bullet Proof beavertail grip safety and hammer (new 2016), tactical thumb safety, 30 LPI high cut checkered front strap, top and rear slide serrations, blue finish, 36.8 oz. Mfg. 2012 only, reintroduced 2016.

MSR $3,750	$3,450	$3,150	$2,700	$2,300	$1,875	$1,550	$1,250	

Last MSR in 2012 was $3,255.

Add $170 for Sentinel Compact Lightweight (mfg. 2012 only).

* ***Sentinel Professional*** – 9mm Para. or .38 Super (new 2016) cal., professional size carbon steel round butt frame, 3.6 in. stainless match grade barrel (fluted, new 2016), updated 3.6 in. carbon steel slide design, 8 shot mag., Bullet Proof mag. release (new 2016), Battlesight with fiber optic front sight, G10 slimline (mfg. 2012 only) or Wilson Combat Black Cherry slant grips with pewter medallions (new 2016), Concealment Bullet Proof (new 2016) beavertail grip safety and hammer, Tactical Bullet Proof (new 2016) thumb safety, 30 LPI high cut checkered front strap, blue finish, 38 oz. Mfg. 2012, reintroduced 2016.

MSR $3,750	$3,450	$3,150	$2,700	$2,300	$1,875	$1,550	$1,250	

Last MSR in 2012 was $3,310.

Add $115 for Sentinel Professional Lightweight (mfg. 2012 only).

SENTINEL XL – 9mm Para., .38 Super, or .45 ACP cal., sub-compact aluminum round butt frame, 4 in. stainless match grade fluted barrel, 4 in. carbon steel slide with top serrations, 8 shot mag., Battlesight with fiber optic front sight, Wilson Combat Black Cherry ultra thin grips with pewter medallions, Torx Head grip screws, Concealment Bullet Proof beavertail grip safety and hammer, Tactical Bullet Proof thumb safety, 30 LPI high cut checkered front strap, approx. 30 oz. New mid-2016.

MSR $3,800	$3,475	$3,100	$2,650	$2,225	$1,875	$1,575	$1,275	

Add $110 for 9mm Para. or .38 Super cal.

SUPER SENTINEL – .38 Super cal., 8 shot mag., 3.6 in. match grade barrel, carbon steel slide, Sentinel aluminum frame, 30 LPI high cut checkered front strap, High Ride Bullet Proof beavertail grip safety, Bullet Proof thumb safety, contoured magwell, G10 slimline grips, fiber optic front sight, full-length guide rod with reverse plug, 25.2 oz. New 2012.

MSR $3,875	$3,500	$3,100	$2,650	$2,225	$1,875	$1,575	$1,275	

SPEC-OPS 9 – 9mm Para. cal., 4 1/4 in. stainless steel match grade barrel, mid-size polymer frame with fully machined stainless steel rail insert, 16 shot mag., blue finish, 20 LPI checkered front strap, concealment Bullet Proof beavertail grip safety and Spec-Ops ultralight hammer, tactical thumb safety, Starburst grip pattern with textured grip radiuses, countersunk slide stop, contoured magwell, 30 LPI slide top serrations, Spec-Ops Lo-Profile rear sight, inline dovetail improved ramp fiber optic front sight, 37 oz. Disc. 2017.

	$2,000	$1,750	$1,525	$1,300	$1,100	$900	$775	*$2,285*

SUPERGRADE COMMANDER SPECIAL – 9mm Para., .45 ACP, or .38 Super cal., Professional size carbon steel round butt frame, 4 1/4 in. stainless match grade barrel with flush-cut reverse crown, fluted chamber, 8 shot mag., Bullet Proof mag. release, contoured magwell, blued 4 1/4 in. carbon steel flat-top slide with polished sides, Commander hammer, Battlesight with white gold bead front sight, deluxe burl wood smooth grips with sterling silver medallions, bobbed High-Ride Bullet Proof beavertail grip safety, Bullet Proof Retro checkered thumb safety, forward angled rear cocking serrations, full length guide rod, high cut checkered front strap, hand polished blued finish or stainless steel and blue two-tone finish, 37.2 oz. New 2019.

MSR $5,350	$4,550	$3,980	$3,425	$3,100	$2,500	$2,050	$1,625	

Add $105 for 9mm Para. or .38 Super cal.

TACTICAL CARRY – 9mm Para., .45 ACP, or .38 Super cal., full size carbon steel frame, 5 in. stainless match grade barrel, flush cut reverse crown, fluted chamber, 8 shot mag., Bullet Proof mag. release and round-butt magwell, 5 in. carbon steel slide, Battlesight rear and fiber optic front sights, G10 starburst grips, Bullet Proof beavertail grip safety and hammer, slide top and rear serrations, 39.6 oz. New 2015.

MSR $3,750	$3,450	$3,150	$2,700	$2,300	$1,875	$1,550	$1,250	

* ***Tactical Carry Commander*** – 9mm Para., .38 Super, or .45 ACP cal., Professional size carbon steel frame, 4.25 in. stainless match grade barrel and bushing, flush cut reverse crown, fluted chamber, 4.25 in. carbon steel slide, 8 shot mag., Bullet Proof round butt one-piece magwell, Battlesight with fiber optic front sight, black G10 starburst grips with pewter medallions, Concealment Bullet Proof beavertail grip safety and hammer, Tactical Bullet Proof thumb safety, 30 LPI high cut checkered front strap, rear cocking serrations, 37.8 oz. New mid-2019.

MSR $3,750	$3,450	$3,150	$2,700	$2,300	$1,875	$1,550	$1,250	

Add $110 for 9mm Para. or .38 Super cal.

GRADING - PPGS™	100%	98%	95%	90%	80%	70%	60%	LAST MSR

* ***Tactical Carry Compact*** – 9mm Para., .38 Super, or .45 ACP cal., compact size carbon frame, 4 in. stainless match grade cone barrel, 4 in. carbon steel slide, fluted chamber and barrel, 7 shot, Bullet Proof round butt magwell and mag. release, Battlesight rear and fiber optic front sight, G10 starburst grips, Torx Head grip screws, Concealment Bullet Proof beavertail grip safety and hammer, Tactical Bullet Proof thumb safety, 30 LPI high cut checkered front strap, top and rear slide serrations, 37.2 oz. New 2016.

MSR $3,750	$3,450	$3,150	$2,700	$2,300	$1,875	$1,550	$1,250	

* ***Tactical Carry Professional*** – 9mm Para., .38 Super, or .45 ACP cal., full size carbon steel frame, 4 in. stainless match grade fluted barrel, 4 in. carbon steel slide, high cut checkered front strap, Bullet Proof round butt magwell, Tactical Bullet Proof thumb safety, beavertail grip safety and hammer, G10 starburst grips, Battlesight rear and fiber optic front sights, top and rear slide serrations. New 2017.

MSR $3,750	$3,450	$3,150	$2,700	$2,300	$1,875	$1,550	$1,250	

TACTICAL ELITE – 9mm Para., 10mm (disc.), .38 Super, .40 S&W (disc.), or .45 ACP cal., full size carbon steel frame, 5 in. stainless match grade heavy flanged cone barrel, carbon steel slide, blue finish, 30 LPI high cut checkered front strap, front and rear slide serrations, ambidextrous thumb safety, Speed-Chute magwell, G10 starburst grips, high ride beavertail grip safety, Battlesight rear and fiber optic front sights, 43.6 oz.

MSR $3,650	$3,350	$2,950	$2,550	$2,150	$1,825	$1,525	$1,225	

Add $165 for Tactical Elite Lightweight (disc.).

TACTICAL SUPERGRADE – 9mm Para., 10mm (disc. 2011, reintroduced 2015), .38 Super, .40 S&W (disc. 2011, 2015), or .45 ACP cal., full size stainless steel frame, 5 in. stainless match grade barrel and bushing, carbon steel slide, blue finish, 30 LPI high cut checkered front strap, top and rear slide serrations, ambidextrous safety, Speed-Chute magwell, G10 starburst grips, beavertail grip safety, Battlesight rear and white outline Tritium front sights.

MSR $5,045	$4,550	$4,125	$3,700	$3,100	$2,600	$2,100	$1,650	

Add $110 for .38 Super, 9mm Para., 10mm, or .40 S&W cal.

* ***Tactical Supergrade Compact*** – 9mm Para., .38 Super, or .45 ACP cal., compact carbon steel frame, 4 in. stainless match grade cone barrel, carbon steel slide, blue finish, 30 LPI high cut checkered front strap, top and rear slide serrations, ambidextrous thumb safety, Speed-Chute magwell, G10 starburst grips, beavertail grip safety, Battlesight rear and white outline Tritium front sights, full-length guide rod and reverse plug.

MSR $5,045	$4,550	$4,125	$3,700	$3,100	$2,600	$2,100	$1,650	

Add $105 for 9mm Para. or .38 Super cal.

* ***Tactical Supergrade Professional*** – 9mm Para., .38 Super, or .45 ACP cal., carbon steel frame, 4 in. stainless match grade cone barrel, carbon steel slide, 8 shot mag., blue finish, 30 LPI high cut checkered front strap, top and rear slide serrations, ambidextrous thumb safety, Speed-Chute magwell, G10 starburst grips, beavertail grip safety, Battlesight rear and white outline Tritium front sights, full-length guide rod and reverse plug, 44.8 oz. New 2010.

MSR $5,045	$4,550	$4,125	$3,700	$3,100	$2,600	$2,100	$1,650	

Add $110 for .38 Super or 9mm Para. cal.

TEXAS BBQ SPECIAL – 9mm Para. or .45 ACP cal., full size stainless steel frame, 5 in. stainless match grade fluted barrel, reverse crown, 5 in. stainless steel slide (no front cocking serrations or carry cuts), 8 shot mag., Bullet Proof round butt magwell and mag. release, Battlesight rear and gold bead front sights, Wilson Combat Black Cherry slant grips with sterling medallions, Torx Head grip screws, Concealment Bullet Proof beavertail grip safety and hammer, Tactical Bullet Proof thumb safety, high cut checkered front strap, three levels of coverage of hand engraving by Wayne D'Angelo, 37.8 oz. Mfg. 2016-mid-2020.

	$4,450	$4,000	$3,500	$3,100	$2,600	$2,200	$1,775	*$4,960*

Add $110 for 9mm Para. cal.
Add $535 for Level Two base price.
Add $1,085 for Level Three base price.

ULTRALIGHT CARRY – 9mm Para., .38 Super, or .45 ACP cal., full size aluminum round butt frame, 5 in. stainless match grade barrel and bushing, flush cut and crowned, fluted chamber, contoured magwell, 5 in. carbon steel slide, Battlesight rear and fiber optic front sight, G10 starburst grips, tactical thumb safety, beavertail grip safety, 30 LPI high cut checkered front strap, top and rear slide serrations, countersunk slide stop, blue finish, 31.4 oz.

MSR $3,650	$3,350	$2,950	$2,550	$2,150	$1,825	$1,525	$1,225	

GRADING - PPGS™	100%	98%	95%	90%	80%	70%	60%	LAST MSR

* ***Ultralight Carry Compact*** – 9mm Para., .38 Super, or .45 ACP cal., compact aluminum round butt frame, 4 in. stainless match grade fluted barrel, 4 in. carbon steel slide, contoured magwell, G10 Starburst grips, Battlesight rear and fiber optic front sight, high cut checkered front strap, Concealment Bullet Proof beavertail grip safety and hammer, Tactical Bullet Proof thumb safety, top and rear slide serrations, 28.6 oz.

MSR $3,650	$3,350	$2,950	$2,550	$2,150	$1,825	$1,525	$1,225	

* ***Ultralight Carry Sentinel*** – 9mm Para. cal., Sentinel aluminum round butt frame, 3 1/2 in. stainless match grade cone fluted barrel, 8 shot mag., carbon steel slide, blue finish, 30 LPI high cut checkered front strap, top and rear slide serrations, tactical thumb safety, contoured magwell, G10 starburst grips, beavertail grip safety and hammer, Battlesight rear and fiber optic front sights, shortened rounded mag. release, countersunk slide stop, approx. 31 oz.

MSR $3,875	$3,500	$3,100	$2,650	$2,225	$1,875	$1,575	$1,275	

ULTRA LIGHT CARRY COMMANDER – 9mm Para. cal., Professional size round butt aluminum frame, 4 1/4 in. stainless match grade fluted barrel with flush cut reverse crown, 8 shot mag., Bullet Proof mag. release, 4 1/4 in. carbon steel slide, Battlesight with fiber optic front sight, G10 Starburst grips with pewter medallions, high cut checkered front strap, aluminum mainspring housing, concealment Bullet Proof beavertail grip safety and hammer, tactical Bullet Proof thumb safety, Torx head grip screws, top and rear slide serrations, 28.8 oz. New 2018.

MSR $3,825	$3,485	$3,150	$2,700	$2,300	$1,875	$1,550	$1,250	

* ***Ultralight Carry Commander Compact*** – 9mm Para. or .45 ACP cal., compact round butt lightweight aluminum alloy frame, 4 1/4 in. stainless steel match grade barrel and bushing, flush cut reverse crown, fluted chamber, 4 1/4 in. carbon steel slide, 7 shot, top and rear slide serrations, 30 LPI high cut checkered front strap, G10 starburst grips with pewter medallions, Bullet Proof mag. release, beavertail grip safety, and hammer, Tactical Bullet Proof thumb safety, Battlesight rear and fiber optic front sights, 28.7 oz. New 2017.

MSR $3,825	$3,485	$3,150	$2,700	$2,300	$1,875	$1,550	$1,250	

Add $110 for 9mm Para. cal.

ULTRA LIGHT CARRY PROFESSIONAL – 9mm Para. or .45 ACP cal., Professional size round butt aluminum frame, 4 in. stainless match grade cone barrel, flush cut reverse crown, fluted chamber/barrel, Bullet Proof mag. release, 4 in. carbon steel slide, G10 Starburst grips, Concealment Bullet Proof beavertail grip safety and hammer, tactical thumb safety, high cut checkered front strap, aluminum mainspring housing, top and rear slide serrations, 29.2 oz. New 2018.

MSR $3,650	$3,350	$2,950	$2,550	$2,150	$1,825	$1,525	$1,225	

Add $115 for 9mm Para. cal.

VICKERS ELITE – .45 ACP or 9mm Para. cal., full size carbon steel frame, 5 in. stainless match grade fluted barrel, 5 in. carbon steel slide with top serrations, 8 shot mag., Bullet Proof round-butt magwell, Battlesight with gold bead front sight, G10 Vickers Elite logo grips, bobbed high-ride Bullet Proof beavertail grip safety, Tactical Bullet Proof thumb safety, 30 LPI high cut checkered front strap, wide front and rear cocking serrations, 38 oz. New 2016.

MSR $3,850	$3,475	$3,100	$2,650	$2,225	$1,875	$1,575	$1,275	

Add $110 for 9mm Para. cal.

* ***Vickers Elite Commander*** – .45 ACP or 9mm Para. cal., Professional size carbon steel frame, 4 1/4 in. stainless match grade barrel, fluted chamber, flush cut reverse crown, 8 shot, one-piece Bullet Proof magwell, 4 1/4 in. carbon steel slide, Battlesight with gold bead front sight, G10 Vickers Elite logo grips, bobbed High-Ride Bullet Proof beavertail grip safety, Tactical Bullet Proof thumb safety, high cut checkered front strap, top and rear slide serrations, wide rear cocking serrations, 39.6 oz. New 2018.

MSR $3,850	$3,475	$3,100	$2,650	$2,225	$1,875	$1,575	$1,275	

Add $110 for 9mm Para. cal.

VICKERS ELITE PACKAGE FOR GLOCK – 9mm Para. cal., Glock Gen 5 stippled frame with Vickers Tactical logo, 4 in. barrel, 15 (Glock 19) or 17 (Glock 17) shot mag., Tango Down/Vickers Tactical mag. release, Tango Down/Vickers Tactical grip plug, Battlesight with green fiber optic front sight, wide slide top serrations, front cocking serrations, stippled thumb pads with Wilson Combat logo, black Armro-Tuff slide finish, 30.3 oz. New 2018.

MSR $1,350	$1,150	$1,000	$850	$800	$650	$500	$400	

X-TAC – 9mm Para., .45 ACP, or .38 Super cal., full size carbon steel frame, 8 shot mag., 5 in. stainless match grade barrel and bushing, carbon steel slide, parkerized finish, X-Tac front strap/mainspring housing, X-Tac rear cocking serrations, tactical thumb safety, contoured magwell, G10 starburst grips, beavertail grip safety, Battlesight rear and fiber optic front sights, 46.2 oz.

MSR $2,760	$2,495	$2,100	$1,800	$1,550	$1,225	$1,050	$925	

GRADING - PPGS™	100%	98%	95%	90%	80%	70%	60%	LAST MSR

* ***X-TAC Commander*** – 9mm Para., .45 ACP, or .38 Super cal., Professional size carbon steel frame, 4 1/4 in. stainless match grade barrel and bushing, flush-cut reverse crown, 8 shot mag., contoured magwell, 4 1/4 in. carbon steel slide, high profile U-Notch rear sight, black G10 X-TAC pattern grips with pewter medallions, High-Ride Bullet Proof beavertail grip safety, Tactical Bullet Proof thumb safety, bi-directional X-TAC front strap/mainspring housing slide treatment, X-Tac rear cocking serrations, black parkerized finish, 38 oz. New 2020.

MSR $2,760	$2,495	$2,100	$1,800	$1,550	$1,225	$1,050	$925	

Add $110 for 9mm Para. or .38 Super cal.

* ***X-TAC Compact*** – .45 ACP, 9mm Para., or .38 Super cal., compact carbon steel round butt frame, 4 in. stainless match grade barrel, 7 (.45), 8 (9mm), or 9 (.38 Super) shot mag., 4 in. carbon steel slide, contoured magwell, G10 X-TAC pattern grips with pewter medallions, X-TAC front strap, high ride Bullet Proof beavertail grip safety, thumb safety, Battlesight with fiber optic front sight, X-TAC rear cocking serration treatment on slide, black parkerized finish, 37.4 oz.

MSR $2,785	$2, 575	$2,150	$1,825	$1,550	$1,225	$1,050	$925	

X-TAC ELITE – 9mm Para., .38 Super, or .45 ACP cal., full size carbon steel frame, 5 in. stainless match grade barrel and bushing, reverse crown fluted chamber, 5 in. carbon steel slide, 8 shot, Bullet Proof magwell and mag. release, Battlesight rear and fiber optic front sights, black G10 aggressive starburst grips with pewter medallions, Torx Head grip screws, Concealment Bullet Proof beavertail grip safety and hammer, Tactical Bullet Proof thumb safety, unique X-Tac front strap/mainspring housing and rear cocking serration treatment, top and rear slide serrations, 40.32 oz. New 2016.

MSR $3,650	$3,350	$2,950	$2,550	$2,150	$1,825	$1,525	$1,225	

Add $110 for 9mm Para. and .38 Super cal.

* ***X-TAC Elite Commander*** – 9mm Para., .38 Super, or .45 ACP cal., Professional size carbon steel frame, 4 1/4 in. stainless match grade barrel and bushing, flush-cut reverse crown, fluted chamber, 8 shot mag., Bullet Proof magwell and mag. release, 4 1/4 in. carbon steel slide, Battlesight with fiber optic front sight, black G10 aggressive starburst grips with pewter medallions, Concealment Bullet Proof beavertail grip safety and hammer, Tactical Bullet Proof thumb safety, X-TAC front strap/mainspring housing and rear cocking serration treatment, top and rear slide serrations, 38.4 oz. New 2020.

MSR $3,650	$3,350	$2,950	$2,550	$2,150	$1,825	$1,525	$1,225	

Add $110 for 9mm Para. or .38 Super cal.

* ***X-TAC Elite Compact*** – 9mm Para., .38 Super, or .45 ACP cal., compact size carbon steel frame, 4 in. stainless match grade cone fluted barrel, flush cut reverse crown fluted chamber, 4 in. carbon steel slide, 7 shot mag., Bullet Proof magwell and mag. release, Battlesight rear and fiber optic front sights, black G10 aggressive starburst grips with pewter medallions, Torx Head grip screws, Concealment Bullet Proof thumb safety, unique X-TAC front strap/mainspring housing and rear cocking serration treatment, top and rear slide serrations, 36.8 oz. New 2016.

MSR $3,650	$3,350	$2,950	$2,550	$2,150	$1,825	$1,525	$1,225	

Add $110 for 9mm Para. or .38 Super cal.

* ***X-TAC Elite Carry Comp*** – 9mm Para. or .45 ACP cal., compact carbon steel frame, 4 in. match grade stainless barrel, fluted chamber, 4 in. steel slide, 7 shot mag., Bullet Proof round butt magwell, Battlesight rear and fiber optic front sights, black G10 grips with pewter medallions, Bullet Proof thumb and beavertail grip safety, slide top and rear serrations, X-TAC treatment, 39.36 oz. New 2016.

MSR $3,850	$3,475	$3,100	$2,650	$2,225	$1,875	$1,575	$1,275	

Add $110 for 9mm Para. cal.

X-TAC PROFESSIONAL – 9mm Para., .38 Super, or .45 ACP cal., professional size carbon steel frame, 4 in. stainless match grade barrel, 4 in. carbon steel slide, X-TAC treatment on front strap/mainspring housing and rear cocking serrations, high ride Bullet Proof beavertail grip safety, Tactical Bullet Proof thumb safety, G10 X-TAC pattern black grips with pewter medallions, BattleSight rear and fiber optic front sights, black parkerized finish. New 2017.

MSR $2,785	$2, 575	$2,150	$1,825	$1,550	$1,225	$1,050	$925	

Add $110 for 9mm Para. and .38 Super cal.

* ***X-TAC Elite Professional*** – 9mm Para., .38 Super, or .45 ACP cal., professional size carbon steel frame, 4 in. stainless match grade fluted barrel, 4 in. carbon steel slide, 8 shot, X-TAC treatment on front strap/mainspring housing and rear cocking serrations, G10 aggressive starburst black grips with pewter medallions, Battlesight rear and fiber optic front sights, Bullet Proof magwell, beavertail grip safety, and hammer, Tactical Bullet Proof thumb safety. New 2017.

MSR $3,650	$3,350	$2,950	$2,550	$2,150	$1,825	$1,525	$1,225	

Add $110 for 9mm Para. and .38 Super cal.

GRADING - PPGS™	100%	98%	95%	90%	80%	70%	60%	LAST MSR

* ***X-TAC Elite Carry Comp Professional*** – 9mm Para. or .45 ACP cal., professional size carbon steel frame, 4 in. stainless match grade compensated barrel, fluted chamber, Bullet Proof magwell and mag. release, 4 in. carbon steel slide, G10 slant pattern black grips with pewter medallions, Battlesight with fiber optic front sight, X-TAC treatment on front strap/mainspring housing and rear cocking serrations, top and rear slide serrations, Concealment Bullet Proof beavertail grip safety and hammer, Tactical Bullet Proof thumb safety, 39.6 oz. New 2017.

MSR $3,850	$3,475	$3,100	$2,650	$2,225	$1,875	$1,575	$1,275	

Add $110 for 9mm Para. cal.

X-TAC SENTINEL/X-TAC ELITE SENTINEL – 9mm Para. or .38 Super. cal., 1/2 in. shorter than compact, carbon steel frame and 3.5 in. X-TAC serration treated slide, 3.5 in. barrel with (Sentinel) or w/o (Elite) fluted chamber and stainless match grade cone barrel w/flush cut reverse crown, 8 shot contoured (Sentinel) or Bullet Proof (Elite) mag. and mag. release, Battlesight w/fiber optic front sight, black G10 X-TAC (Sentinel) or aggressive starburst (Elite) grips w/Pewter medallions, High-Ride or Concealment Bullet Proof beavertail grip and tactical thumb safety, black parkerized finish, 40 oz. New 2021.

MSR $2,860	$2,430	$2,125	$1,825	$1,650	$1,330	$1,095	$950	

Add $890 for X-TAC Elite Sentinel model.

X-TAC SUPERGRADE – 9mm Para., .38 Super, or .45 ACP cal., 1911 style, full size carbon steel round butt frame, 5 in. stainless match grade barrel and bushing, flush cut reverse crown, 5 in. carbon steel X-Top slide, 8 shot mag., contoured magwell, Bullet Proof mag. release, Battlesight with fiber optic front sight, black G10 X-TAC pattern grips with black medallions, High-Ride Bullet Proof beavertail grip safety, Tactical Bullet Proof thumb safety, enhanced bi-directional X-TAC front strap/mainspring housing treatment, unique X-TAC rear cocking serration treatment on slide, 40.6 oz. Limited mfg. beginning mid-2019.

MSR $4,795	$4,325	$3,785	$3,250	$2,950	$2,380	$1,950	$1,575	

Add $110 for 9mm Para. or .38 Super cal.

* ***X-TAC Supergrade Commander*** – 9mm Para., .38 Super, or .45 ACP cal., 1911 style, Commander size carbon steel round butt frame, 4 1/4 in. stainless match grade barrel and bushing, flush cut reverse crown, 4 1/4 in. carbon steel X-Top slide, 8 shot mag., contoured magwell, Bullet Proof mag. release, Battlesight with fiber optic front sight, black G10 X-TAC pattern grips with black medallions, High-Ride Bullet Proof beavertail grip safety, Tactical Bullet Proof thumb safety, enhanced bi-directional X-TAC front strap/mainspring housing treatment, unique X-TAC rear cocking serration treatment on slide, 38.4 oz. Limited mfg. beginning mid-2019.

MSR $4,795	$4,325	$3,785	$3,250	$2,950	$2,380	$1,950	$1,575	

Add $110 for 9mm Para. or .38 Super cal.

* ***X-TAC Supergrade Compact*** – 9mm Para., .38 Super, or .45 ACP cal., 1911 style, Compact size carbon steel round butt frame, 4 in. stainless match grade cone barrel, flush cut reverse crown, 4 in. carbon steel X-Top slide, 7 shot mag., contoured magwell, Bullet Proof mag. release, Battlesight with fiber optic front sight, black G10 X-TAC pattern grips with black medallions, High-Ride Bullet Proof beavertail grip safety, Tactical Bullet Proof thumb safety, enhanced bi-directional X-TAC front strap/mainspring housing treatment, unique X-TAC rear cocking serration treatment on slide, 37 oz. Limited mfg. beginning mid-2019.

MSR $4,795	$4,325	$3,785	$3,250	$2,950	$2,380	$1,950	$1,575	

Add $110 for 9mm Para. or .38 Super cal.

* ***X-TAC Supergrade Professional*** – 9mm Para., .38 Super, or .45 ACP cal., 1911 style, Professional size carbon steel round butt frame, 4 in. stainless match grade cone barrel, flush cut reverse crown, 4 in. carbon steel X-Top slide, 8 shot mag., contoured magwell, Bullet Proof mag. release, Battlesight with fiber optic front sight, black G10 X-TAC pattern grips with black medallions, High-Ride Bullet Proof beavertail grip safety, Tactical Bullet Proof thumb safety, enhanced bi-directional X-TAC front strap/mainspring housing treatment, unique X-TAC rear cocking serration treatment on slide, 38 oz. Limited mfg. beginning mid-2019.

MSR $4,795	$4,325	$3,785	$3,250	$2,950	$2,380	$1,950	$1,575	

Add $110 for 9mm Para. or .38 Super cal.

WILSON COMBAT/SIG SAUER WCP320 – 9mm Para. cal., carry cut, 4.7 in. barrel w/black DLC finish, two 17 shot mags., SIG mag. release and slide stop, SIG P320 X full size steel trigger, Wilson Combat Battlesight w/red fiber optic front sight, X-TAC pattern on slide top, front, and rear cocking serrations, lower rail, ser. no. w/WC prefix, black or tan finish, Wilson Combat logo on slide, 29.2 oz. New 2020.

MSR $1,195	$1,025	$895	$775	$700	$575	$475	$375	

RIFLES: SEMI-AUTO

All rifles come standard with nylon tactical case.

A variety of accessories are available for additional cost - please contact the company directly for more information on available options.

Add $325 for WCR-22 rimfire rifle suppressor (new 2016).

GRADING - PPGS™	100%	98%	95%	90%	80%	70%	60%	LAST MSR

.308 SUPER SNIPER – .308 Win. cal., GIO, 20 in. button rifled stainless steel fluted or non-fluted (disc.) barrel, billet AR machined aluminum upper and lower receivers, 12 or 14 in. free floating T.R.I.M. rail, customer's choice of tactical trigger unit and Armor-Tuff finish colors, 9.2 lbs. New 2015.

MSR $3,120	$2,650	$2,325	$1,990	$1,800	$1,460	$1,195	$1,050	

Subtract approx. $50 for non-fluted barrel.

AR9 CARBINE – 9mm Para. cal., closed bolt blowback, 16 in. fluted or non-fluted barrel, QComp flash hider, T.R.I.M. rail, two-stage tactical trigger, BCM Starburst Gunfighter grip, Wilson/Rogers Super-Stoc, billet aluminum flat-top upper and lower receiver, standard AR furniture/sight compatibility, hard anodized black finish, 6 lbs. New 2017.

MSR $1,995	$1,750	$1,575	$1,450	$1,325	$1,100	$875	$675	

Add $100 for fluted barrel.

BILL WILSON RANCH RIFLE – .300 HAM'R cal., 18 in. Bill Wilson Ranch Rifle round threaded match grade barrel with Circle WC Ranch logo, threaded muzzle with thread protector, 5, 10, 20, or 30 shot mag., Wilson Combat Tactical Trigger Unit M2, Trijicon Accupoint 3-9x40 green dot rifle scope mounted and zeroed, Smoke composite carbon fiber closed shoulder buttstock, black BCM Starburst Gunfighter grip, lightweight billet upper (flat-top) and billet lower receiver, 12 in. M-LOK rail with three green Wilson Combat rail covers, black Ergo Ladder top rail cover, Wilson Combat lightweight scope rings, Armor-Tuff finish applied over green/black hardcoat anodized upper/lower receivers, 6 lbs. 2 oz. New 2019.

MSR $3,350	$2,850	$2,500	$2,150	$1,950	$1,575	$1,285	$1,115	

M4 TACTICAL CARBINE – .223 Rem. cal., GIO, 16 1/4 in. fluted match grade barrel with muzzle brake, 20 shot mag., aluminum flat-top upper and lower receiver, quad rail free float aluminum handguard, single stage trigger, Ergo pistol grip, 6-position collapsible stock, black, green, tan or gray anodized finish, 6.9 lbs. Disc. 2011.

	$1,775	$1,575	$1,450	$1,325	$1,100	$875	$675	*$2,000*

PAUL HOWE TACTICAL CARBINE – 5.56 NATO cal., 14.7 in. stainless steel fluted barrel with permanently attached Accu-Tac flash hider (meets the 16 in. barrel requirement), two-stage TTU, Daniel Defense fixed front sight tower, CSAT rear aperture flip-up sight, BCM Starburst Gunfighter grip, 10.4 in. T.R.I.M. rail, Armor-Tuff camo finish, 6 1/4 lbs. New 2018.

MSR $2,700	$2,295	$2,025	$1,725	$1,575	$1,275	$1,050	$900	

Add $1,475 for the Paul Howe Carbine Kit (V3 ultralight scope mount, Blue Force Gear Vickers Combat applications sling, and Leupold VX-6HD scope).

PAUL HOWE TACTICAL CARBINE 6.5 CREEDMOOR – 6.5 Creedmoor cal., intermediate length gas system w/low profile gas block, standard or lightweight configuration, 16 in. fluted Paul Howe match grade barrel, threaded muzzle w/Accu-Tac flash hider, Daniel Defense fixed front sight post w/flip-up rear BUS w/CSAT aperture sight, Wilson/Rogers Super-Stoc in FDE finish, Starburst Gunfighter grip w/FDE finish, billet aluminum flat-top upper and lower receiver, 12 in. M-LOK rail, NiB BCG, Camo Armor-Tuff finish, available as a kit that includes: Ultralight scope mount, Leupold VX-6HD, Streamlight TLR-1 HL, and Vickers sling w/push-button sling swivels, 8.4 lbs. New 2020.

MSR $3,345	$2,950	$2,650	$2,425	$2,200	$1,850	$1,450	$1,150	

Add $100 for lightweight configuration.
Additional kit option has an MSR of $1,475.

PROTECTOR SERIES AR CARBINE – 5.56 NATO, .300 AAC Blackout, or .300 HAM'R cal., GIO, 16 1/4 in. match grade stainless barrel with Q-Comp flash hider/muzzle brake, 30 shot mag., M2 two-stage TTU trigger, oversized tactical trigger guard, Rogers Super-Stoc buttstock, BCM Starburst pistol grip, forged upper and lower receivers, low profile gas block, mid-length gas system, M-LOK compatible handguard with 4 in. accessory rail and QD sling mount, black or Coyote Tan Armor-Tuff finish, 6 lbs. New 2019.

MSR $2,000	$1,775	$1,575	$1,450	$1,325	$1,100	$875	$675	

Add $225 for left-handed model.

SPR (SPECIAL PURPOSE RIFLE) – 5.56 NATO cal., GIO, 18 in. stainless steel match grade barrel with Accu-Tac flash hider, low profile gas block, forged flat-top upper and lower receiver, quad rail free float aluminum handguard (disc.) or T.R.I.M. rail, 20 shot mag., single stage trigger, Ergo (disc.) or Bravo pistol grip, A2 fixed (disc.) or Wilson/Rogers Super-Stoc buttstock, black, green, tan or gray anodized finish, 6.9 lbs. Disc. 2020.

	$2,150	$1,925	$1,775	$1,625	$1,350	$1,075	$850	*$2,450*

SS-15 SUPER SNIPER RIFLE – .223 Rem./5.56 NATO (.223 Wylde chamber, new 2012) cal., GIO, 18 in. fluted heavy match grade stainless steel barrel with muzzle brake, aluminum flat-top upper and lower receiver, aluminum free float handguard, black, green, tan, federal brown, green base camo, or gray anodized finish, 20 shot mag., single stage trigger, Ergo pistol grip, fixed A2 stock, 8.7 lbs. Disc.

	$1,975	$1,750	$1,600	$1,475	$1,225	$975	$750	*$2,225*

Add $400 for green base camo.

GRADING - PPGS™	100%	98%	95%	90%	80%	70%	60%	LAST MSR

RANGER – 5.56 NATO, 6.8 SPC, .300 AAC Blackout, .243 Win., 6.5 Creedmoor (disc. 2020), .300 HAM'R (new 2018), .308 Win., or .358 Win. cal., GIO, 16 in. Ranger match grade fluted or non-fluted barrel, threaded muzzle with QComp, Rogers/Wilson Super-Stoc, black BCM Starburst Gunfighter grip, M2 Tactical Trigger Unit, SLR Rifleworks adj. gas block, 10 in. M-LOK rail with three Falcon/Ergo rail covers, lightweight billet lower and flat-top upper receiver, hard anodized black or green finish, 8 lbs. New 2017.

MSR $2,300	$1,950	$1,700	$1,465	$1,325	$1,075	$885	$765	

Add $100 for .300 AAC Blackout cal.
Add $150 for 6.8 SPC cal.
Add $845 for AR-10 platform.

RECON TACTICAL .458 SOCOM – .458 SOCOM cal., GIO, 16 or 18 in. match grade stainless steel fluted barrel, threaded muzzle with QComp muzzle brake, single stage TTU, Rogers/Wilson Super-Stoc, mid-length gas system with adj. gas block, billet lower and flat-top upper receivers, M-LOK rail, NP3 coated BCG, Armor-Tuff finish over hardcoat anodized black or green finish, 7 lbs. New 2018.

MSR $2,400	$2,040	$1,780	$1,530	$1,380	$1,125	$925	$800	

Add $200 for green finish.

RECON TACTICAL 5.56 NATO/.224 VALKYRIE – 5.56 NATO or .224 Valkyrie (new 2018) cal., 16 in. medium weight stainless steel match grade barrel, threaded muzzle with QComp flash hider, BCM Starburst Gunfighter grip, tactical trigger guard, Rogers/Wilson Super-Stoc, single stage TTU, T.R.I.M. rail, mid-length gas system with low profile gas block, billet lower and flat-top upper receiver, NP3 coated BCG, black, FDE (disc.), Gray (disc.) or Green finish, 7 lbs.

MSR $2,350	$2,000	$1,750	$1,500	$1,360	$1,100	$900	$780	

Add $50 for .224 Valkyrie cal.

RECON TACTICAL 6.5mm CREEDMOOR – 6.5 Creedmoor cal., 16, 18, or 20 in. match grade stainless steel fluted (disc. 2020) or non-fluted barrel, threaded muzzle with QComp flash hider, single stage TTU, Rogers/Wilson Super-Stoc, rifle length gas system with low profile gas block, billet lower and flat-top upper receiver, 14 in. T.R.I.M. rail, NP3 coated BCG, Armor-Tuff finish over hardcoat anodized finish, 7.85 lbs. New 2018.

MSR $3,095	$2,635	$2,300	$1,975	$1,795	$1,450	$1,185	$1,025	

Add $50 for fluted barrel.

RECON TACTICAL 6.8 SPC II/6.5 GRENDEL – 6.8 SPC II or 6.5 Grendel (new 2018) cal., GIO, 16, 18, or 20 in. match grade stainless steel barrel, threaded muzzle with Accu-Tac (6.8 SPC II) or QComp (6.5 Grendel) flash hider, tactical trigger guard, single stage TTU, Rogers/Wilson Super-Stoc, Bravo Company pistol grip, billet upper and lower receivers, mid-length gas system with low profile gas block, T.R.I.M. (6.8 SPC) or M-LOK (6.5 Grendel) rail, Armor-Tuff finish over black, green, or camo hardcoat anodized finish, 7 lbs.

MSR $2,400	$2,040	$1,780	$1,530	$1,380	$1,125	$925	$800	

Add $25 for 20 in. barrel.
Add $50 for fluted barrel.
Add $125 for camo finish.

RECON TACTICAL .300 AAC BLACKOUT/.204 RUGER – .300 AAC Blackout or .204 Ruger (new 2018) cal., GIO, 16 or 18 in. stainless steel match grade barrel, QComp muzzle brake, Rogers/Wilson Super-Stoc, Bravo Company pistol grip, carbine or mid (18 in. barrel) length gas system with low profile gas block, forged upper and lower receivers, T.R.I.M. or M-LOK rail, single stage TTU, tactical trigger guard, NP3 coated BCG, Armor-Tuff finish over hard anodized finish, 7 lbs.

MSR $2,350	$2,000	$1,750	$1,500	$1,360	$1,100	$900	$780	

RECON TACTICAL .308 WIN./.338 FEDERAL/7mm-08 REM./6mm CREEDMOOR – .308 Win., .338 Federal (16 in. barrel only), 6mm Creedmoor (mfg. 2018-2020, 16 in. only), or 7mm-08 Rem. (mfg. 2018-2020, 16 in. only) cal., GIO, 16, 18, or 20 in. match grade stainless steel barrel, threaded muzzle with Accu-Tac or QComp flash hider, billet lower and flat-top upper receiver, mid-length gas system with low profile gas block, T.R.I.M. or M-LOK (7mm-08 Rem. or 6mm Creedmoor only) rail, single stage Tactical Trigger Unit, Rogers/Wilson Super-Stoc, NP3 coated BCG, Armor-Tuff finish applied over hardcoat anodized black finish, 7.85-8 lbs.

MSR $2,995	$2,650	$2,375	$2,175	$1,975	$1,650	$1,300	$1,000	

Add $150 for .308 Win. cal.

RECON TACTICAL 7.62x40 WT – 7.62x40 WT cal., GIO, 20 in. match grade stainless steel barrel, threaded muzzle with Accu-Tac flash hider, tactical trigger guard, single stage TTU, Rogers/Wilson Super-Stoc, black Ergo grip, mid-length gas system with low profile gas block, forged lower and flat-top upper receivers, T.R.I.M. rail, Armor-Tuff finish over hardcoat anodized black finish, 7 lbs.

MSR $2,350	$2,000	$1,750	$1,500	$1,360	$1,100	$900	$780	

GRADING - PPGS™	100%	98%	95%	90%	80%	70%	60%	LAST MSR

SUPER SNIPER – .260 Rem. (disc. 2020), 6mm Creedmoor (disc. 2020), 6.5 Creedmoor, 6.5 Grendel, .224 Valkyrie, or .223 Wylde chamber (compatible with .223/5.56) cal., rifle length gas system, 20, 22 (6.5 Creedmoor only), or 24 (6.5 Creedmoor only) in. stainless match grade barrel, single stage TTU, Rogers Super-Stoc buttstock, Wilson Combat/BCM Starburst Gunfighter grip, low profile gas block, 13.8 or 14 (6.5 Creedmoor) in. T.R.I.M. rail, billet lower and flat-top upper receiver, NP3 coated BCG, Armor-Tuff finish over hard anodized finish, 8 lbs. 11 oz.-10 lbs. 2 oz. New 2018.

MSR $2,225	$1,975	$1,750	$1,600	$1,475	$1,225	$975	$750	

Add $50 for .223 Wylde cal. w/fluted barrel.
Add $200 for .224 Valkyrie or 6.5 Grendel cal.
Add $895 for 6.5 Creedmoor cal.

TACTICAL HUNTER – .22 Nosler (mfg. 2018-2020), .204 Ruger, .308 Win., 7mm-08 Rem., 6.8 SPC (mfg. 2018-2020), 6.5 Grendel (mfg. 2018-2020), .300 HAM'R (mfg. 2018-2020), .338 Federal, 6.5 Creedmoor, 6mm Creedmoor (disc. 2020), .260 Rem., or .458 SOCOM (mfg. 2018-2020) cal., GIO, 18 or 20 in. threaded match grade fluted or non-fluted barrel, threaded muzzle with thread protector, 14.6 in. Wilson Combat M-LOK rail, billet lower and flat-top upper receiver, rifle-length gas system with SLR Rifleworks adj. gas block, Rogers/Wilson Super-Stoc, Tactical Trigger Unit, BCM charging handle, standard buffer, black Starburst Gunfighter grip, black or green hardcoat anodized finish. New 2017.

MSR $3,095	$2,630	$2,300	$1,975	$1,790	$1,450	$1,180	$1,030	

Add $50 for 7mm-08 Rem. cal.
Add $100 for .308 Win. or .338 Federal cal.
Add $125 for .260 Rem. cal.

* ***Tactical Hunter .458 HAM'R*** – .458 HAM'R cal., 18 in. fluted match grade barrel, threaded muzzle with thread protector, 7 or 9 shot mag., Rogers/Wilson Super-Stoc, Wilson Combat/BCM Starburst Gunfighter grip, mid-length gas system with SLR Rifleworks adj. gas block, billet lower and flat-top upper receiver, 13.8 in. M-LOK rail with three Falcon/Ergo rail covers, custom length buffer, NP3 coated BCG, Armor-Tuff finish applied over hard anodized finish, green/black finish is standard, additional color/camo options available, 7 lbs. 11 oz. New 2018.

MSR $2,750	$2,340	$2,050	$1,750	$1,590	$1,280	$1,050	$915	

TACTICAL LIGHTWEIGHT – 5.56 NATO, 6.8 SPC II, or 7.62x40 WT cal., GIO, 16.2, 18 (7.62x40 WT cal. only), or 20 (7.62x40 WT cal. only) in. match grade barrel, low profile gas block, Picatinny rail, Ergo pistol grip, tactical trigger guard, two-stage trigger, black Armor-Tuff finish, 20 shot mag., adj. black synthetic Rogers/Wilson Super-Stoc buttstock. Mfg. 2012-2016.

	$1,975	$1,775	$1,625	$1,475	$1,250	$975	$775	*$2,250*

UT-15 URBAN TACTICAL CARBINE – .223 Rem. cal., GIO, 16 1/4 in. fluted match grade barrel with muzzle brake, aluminum flat-top upper and lower receiver, quad rail free float aluminum handguard, black, green, tan or gray anodized finish, 20 shot mag., single stage trigger, Ergo pistol grip, 6-position collapsible stock, 6.9 lbs. Disc. 2011.

	$1,775	$1,600	$1,475	$1,325	$1,125	$875	$700	*$2,025*

ULTIMATE HUNTER – .204 Ruger (new 2018), .243 Win., .308 Win., .338 Federal, .358 Win., 6.8 SPC (new 2018), 6.5 Creedmoor, or .458 SOCOM (new 2018) cal., GIO, 18, 20, or 22 in. fluted button rifled, stainless steel match grade barrel, crowned muzzle, Smoke Composite carbon fiber closed shoulder buttstock with Limbsaver pad, black Mission First Tactical pistol grip, lightweight billet lower and flat-top upper receiver, Wilson/SLR click-adjustable gas block, Tactical Trigger Unit, BCM charging handle, 14.6 in. Wilson Combat M-LOK rail, green or black finish, 7 lbs. 5 oz. New 2017.

	$2,950	$2,650	$2,425	$2,200	$1,850	$1,450	$1,150	*$3,345*

* ***Ultimate Hunter .458 HAM'R*** – .458 HAM'R cal., 18 in. fluted match grade barrel, crowned muzzle, 7 or 9 shot mag., Tactical Trigger Unit, Smoke Composite carbon fiber closed shoulder buttstock with Limbsaver pad, MFT black pistol grip, mid-length gas system with SLR Rifleworks adj. gas block, billet lower and lightweight flat-top upper receiver, 13.8 in. M-LOK rail with three Falcon/Ergo rail covers, NP3 coated BCG, custom length buffer, Armor-Tuff Finish applied over hard anodized green/black (standard) finish, other colors/camo is optional, 7 lbs. 4 oz. New 2018.

MSR $3,055	$2,600	$2,275	$1,950	$1,775	$1,430	$1,175	$1,025	

ULTRALIGHT HUNTER – .204 Ruger (new 2018), 6.8 SPC (new 2018), .458 SOCOM (mfg. 2018-2020), .300 HAM'R (mfg. 2018-2020), .308 Win. (disc. 2020), .338 Federal (disc.), or .358 Win. cal., GIO, 16.2 in. Ultralight Hunter match grade barrel, crowned muzzle, Tactical Trigger Unit, Smoke Composite carbon fiber closed shoulder buttstock with Limbsaver pad, black Mission First Tactical pistol grip, intermediate-length gas system with SLR Rifleworks adj. gas block, BCM charging handle, standard buffer, lightweight billet lower and flat-top upper receiver, 12.6 in. M-LOK rail, black or green hardcoat anodized finish, 7 lbs. New 2017.

MSR $3,310	$2,815	$2,465	$2,110	$1,915	$1,550	$1,265	$1,100	

GRADING - PPGS™	100%	98%	95%	90%	80%	70%	60%	LAST MSR

ULTRALIGHT RANGER – 5.56 NATO, 6.8 SPC, .300 AAC Blackout, .243 Win., 6.5 Creedmoor, .300 HAM'R (new 2018), .308 Win., or .358 Win. cal., GIO, 16 in. Ranger match grade fluted or non-fluted barrel, threaded muzzle with QComp, Smoke Composite carbon fiber closed shoulder buttstock, M2 Tactical Trigger Unit, black Mission First Tactical pistol grip, 10 in. M-LOK rail with three Falcon/Ergo rail covers, lightweight billet upper and lower receiver, SLR Rifleworks adj. gas block, hard anodized black or green finish, 7 lbs. 6 oz. New 2017.

MSR $2,415	$2,050	$1,795	$1,540	$1,395	$1,130	$925	$800	

Add $100 for .300 AAC Blackout cal.
Add $150 for 6.8 SPC cal.
Add $845 for AR-10 platform model.

URBAN SUPER SNIPER – 6.8 SPC cal. (disc. 2020) or .223 Wylde chambered, GIO, 18 in. stainless steel Urban Super Sniper match grade barrel, M4 feed ramps, mid-length gas system with low profile gas block, Rogers Super-Stoc buttstock, single stage Tactical Trigger Unit, 10.4 in. T.R.I.M. rail, BCM Starburst Gunfighter grip, billet lower and flat-top upper receiver, Armor-Tuff finish, 7 lbs. 5 oz.

MSR $2,200	$1,875	$1,640	$1,400	$1,275	$1,025	$850	$735	

Add $50 for fluted barrel.

SHOTGUNS

Please refer to Scattergun Technologies in the S section for complete listing of shotguns and accessories.

WINCHESTER

Current trademark established in 1866 in New Haven, CT.

Currently manufactured by Miroku of Japan since circa 1992, Herstal, Belgium (O/U shotguns since 2004), and in Columbia, SC (Model 70 only beginning 2008). Previously manufactured in New Haven, CT, 1866-2006, and by U.S. Repeating Arms from 1981-2006 through a licensing agreement from Olin Corp. to manufacture shotguns and rifles domestically using the Winchester Trademark. Corporate offices are located in Morgan, UT. Olin Corp. previously manufactured shotguns and rifles bearing the Winchester Hallmark at the Olin Kodensha Plant (closed 1989) located in Tochigi, Japan, Cobourg, Ontario, Canada, and also in European countries. In 1992, U.S. Repeating Arms was acquired by GIAT located in France. In late 1997, the Walloon region of Belgium acquired controlling interest of both Browning and U.S. Repeating Arms.

For more information and current pricing on both new and used Winchester airguns and current black powder models, please refer to the *Blue Book of Airguns* and the *Blue Book of Modern Black Powder Arms* (also available online).

In addition to the models listed within this section, Winchester also offered various models/variations that were available only at the annual SHOT SHOW beginning 2004. For complete model descriptions of all SHOT Show Specials, please go to BlueBookOfGunValues.com/overflow.

WINCHESTER TIMELINE 1855-TO DATE

1855 - Horace Smith and Daniel Wesson form Volcanic Repeating Arms Co. in Norwich, CT.

1856 - Volcanic Repeating Arms Co. moves to New Haven, CT. Oliver Winchester purchases majority of company stock.

1857 - Volcanic Repeating Arms Co. becomes insolvent, Smith & Wesson sell remaining stock to Oliver Winchester. Winchester reorganizes as New Haven Arms Co.

1866 - New Haven Arms Co. is renamed Winchester Repeating Arms Co.

1919 - Company releases Winchester branded consumer products that are sold at Winchester stores and independent retailers.

1923 - The first Winchester 3 in. Magnum is released.

1931 - Winchester Repeating Arms Co. is sold to Olin Industries. Olin merges Winchester with its Western Cartridge Co., forming the Winchester-Western Division of Olin Industries.

1936 - Winchester releases the legendary Model 70 centerfire bolt action rifle.

1941 - Winchester engineers develop an M1 Carbine working model and the .30 M1 Carbine cartridge in thirteen days for government testing.

1964 - Winchester releases its first Commemorative, the Wyoming Diamond Jubilee Model 1894.

1969 - Winchester introduces the Winchoke on some of its shotguns.

1980 - Olin sells New Haven manufacturing plant to employees. Manufacturing of firearms continues under license with the name of U.S. Repeating Arms Co. (USRAC).

1992 - U.S. Repeating Arms bought by GIAT (Groupement des Industries de l' Amree de Terre), a French owned arms conglomerate.

1997 - Belgian Walloon Region government acquires U.S. Repeating Arms Co., Browning Arms Co., and Fabrique Nationale.

2006 - U.S. Repeating Arms Co. plant in New Haven, CT closes.

2007 - Winchester Repeating Arms Co. formed by FN/Browning.

2008 - Winchester Model 70s begin production in FN's Columbia, SC plant.

2009 - Winchester Model 1892s made by Miroku.

2010 - Winchester Model 1894s re-introduced.

2013 - Winchester Model 1873 re-introduced mfg. by Miroku Corp. in Japan.

2016 - Winchester's 150th Anniversary - Commemorative Sesquicentennial Models 1866, 1873, 94, 70, and 101 released.

2017 - Winchester releases its XPR centerfire rifle designed for shooters with a smaller stature.

WINCHESTER OVERVIEW

Note: Winchester Rifles are a field in themselves. Models Henry, 1866, 1873, 1876, 1885, 1886, 1892, 1894, and 1895 all were produced with a multitude of special order options. Special orders included front and rear special sights, half or 2/3 magazines, takedown, various barrel lengths (barrel lengths from 14 to 36 inches could be special ordered for many models), configurations, and weights, special metal finishes, deluxe wood (either checkered or carved) in a variety of finishes, an impressive range of engraving options, different butt plates, etc. All of these special orders act independently and interdependently to determine the correct value of a particular Winchester. Some of the finest rifles ever made are special order Winchesters engraved by the Ulrichs, G. Young, L.D. Nimschke, and others. For these reasons, a Model 1886 Winchester can range in price from $1,000 to over $500,000 - quite a price range for one model alone! When contemplating a purchase on the higher dollar range, qualified and professional opinions should be secured, preferably from at least 2 sources. Unfortunately many fakes and upgraded (non-original) guns have surfaced in the last 10 years with the sudden increase in prices. Winchesters shown in this section are priced assuming a standard model with no special orders. Any special orders will further add to the prices shown. Caliber rarities must also be considered. Many of the early Winchesters are broken down by year of manufacture. Refer to the "Model Serialization" section in this book.

A factory letter specifying original configuration and manufacturing dates by serial number will help solidify values for older/out-of-production Winchester rifles and shotguns. Letters may be obtained through the Cody Firearms Records Office at the Buffalo Bill Center of the West. To use this service, verify the model/ser. no. falls within the ranges listed on the Records Office website and mail your informational request to Cody Firearms Records Office, 720 Sheridan Ave., Cody, WY 82414.

Research results will include (if available): gun type, caliber, barrel length, any special orders or finishes, return(s) to the factory, and any additional information pertinent to serial number contained in the ledger.

With the recent price appreciation of most upper condition Winchester rifles, excellent original condition has become so expensive that the many special order features Winchester offered do not cost that much more. However, on lesser condition guns that are much less expensive, these same special order features will cost more percentage-wise since the condition factor does not cost a premium.

Model 1866 Lever Action Rifle - ser. no. range 125,000-170,101.
Approx. 33 specimens have been researched outside of this ser. no. range.
Model 1873 Lever Action Rifle - ser. no. range 1-720,496.
Approx. 160 specimens have been researched outside of this ser. no. range.
Model 1876 Lever Action Rifle - ser. no. range 1-63,871.
Model 1883 Bolt Action Rifle (Hotchkiss Repeater) - ser. no. range 1-84,555.
May be referred to as Model 1879, 1880, or 1883.
Model 1885 Single Shot Rifle or Shotgun - ser. no. range 1-109,999.
Not available in ser. nos. 74,459-74,556. Also known as High and Low Wall.
Model 1886 Lever Action Rifle - ser. no. range 1-156,599.
Not available in ser. nos. 135,125-135,144 and 146,000-150,799.
Model 1887 & 1901 Lever Action Shotguns - ser. no. range 1-72,999.
Model 1890 Slide Action Rifle - ser. no. range 1-329,999.

GRADING - PPGS™	100%	98%	95%	90%	80%	70%	60%	LAST MSR

Not available in ser. nos. 10,809-10,884, 20,000-29,999, 32,629-32,698, 37,599-37,627, 234,061-234,140, and 234,142-234,160.

Model 1892 Lever Action Rifle - ser. no. range 1-379,999.

Not available in ser. nos. 374,851-376,100.

Model 1893 Slide Action Shotgun - ser. no. range 1-34,050.

Model 1894 Lever Action Rifle - ser. no. range 1-353,999.

Model 1895 Lever Action Rifle - ser. no. range 1-59,999.

Model "Lee" Bolt Action Rifle - ser. no. range 1-19,999.

Model 1897 Slide Action Shotgun - ser. no. range 34,051-377,999.

Model 1903 Semi-Auto .22 Cal. Rifle - ser. no. range 1-39,999.

Model 1905 Semi-Auto Rifle - ser. no. range 1-29,078.

Model 1906 Slide Action Rifle - ser. no. range 1-79,999.

Model 1907 Semi-Auto Rifle - ser. no. range 1-9,999.

Winchester factory data on models produced between approx. 1907-1961 is almost non-existent (except Custom Shop mfg.) since there was a fire at the Winchester factory in 1961.

A NOTE ON WINCHESTER FINISHES: It is very important to understand that there is a big value difference between a Model 1873 with 90% bright blue as opposed to a gun that has patina finish (turning brown). A bright blue specimen might bring several times more, because it is closer to the way it originally left the factory - with bright bluing. "Brown" guns are simply not as desirable as guns that show little or no use and retain bright blue finish.

COMBINATION GUNS

SHOTGUN/RIFLE COMBINATION – combination 12 ga. and .222 Rem., .223 Rem., .243 Win., .270 Win., .30-06, .308 Win., .300 Win. Mag., 5.6x57Rmm, 6.5x55mm, 7x65Rmm, 7x57mm Mauser, or 9.3x74R cal. rifle, O/U, 25 in. barrels, top barrel is WinChoked, Grand European engraving and finish, 8 1/2 lbs. Mfg. 1983-1985.

100%	98%	95%	90%	80%	70%	60%	LAST MSR
$2,795	$2,475	$2,100	$1,875	$1,650	$1,550	$1,425	*$2,550*

Add 50% for .300 Win. Mag. or 6.5x55mm cal.

This model was advertised in .222 Rem., .223 Rem., 6.5x55mm, or .300 Win. Mag. cal., but very few 6.5x55mm or .300 Win. Mag. cals. have been encountered to date.

PISTOLS: SINGLE SHOT

SINGLE SHOT PISTOL – .22 LR cal., bolt action, walnut, brass, or pot metal grips, 9 in. barrel with open sights, no two are exactly alike, and quality can run from very good to crude, ser. nos. under 20.

Prices on this model typically range from $3,750 - $4,950, depending on original condition.

100%	98%	95%	90%	80%	70%	60%	50%	40%	30%	20%	10%

RIFLES: BOLT ACTION

On Models 52, 54, 56, 57, 58, 59, 60, 60A, 67, 677, 68, 69, 69A, 697, and 70 values in 50% or less original condition have been omitted since values in those conditions will approximate the 60% price. This reflects the fact that while these lower condition specimens are not as desirable to collectors, they are still sought after as shooters.

MODEL 1883 (HOTCHKISS REPEATER) – .45-70 Govt. cal., designed by Benjamin D. Hotchkiss, unique tube mag. located in buttstock attached to receiver, up-turn/pull-back bolt action, 26 in. round or octagon barrel standard on rifle. Over 84,000 mfg. between 1879-1889. Carbine extremely rare in Third Model (20 in. barrel).

Subtract 25% for carbine configuration (24 in. round barrel with one band), or musket (32 in. round barrel with cleaning rod and two barrel bands).

Add 25% for Deluxe Model with fancy pistol grip checkered wood.

* ***Model 1883 First Style*** – approx. 6,419 mfg. with magazine cut off and safety control incorporated into one unit.

100%	98%	95%	90%	80%	70%	60%	50%	40%	30%	20%	10%
N/A	N/A	$2,750	$2,375	$1,975	$1,650	$1,475	$1,325	$1,150	$1,000	$925	$875

* ***Model 1883 Second Style*** – approx. 16,102 mfg., magazine cut off on right receiver top, safety on left side.

100%	98%	95%	90%	80%	70%	60%	50%	40%	30%	20%	10%
N/A	N/A	$2,750	$2,375	$1,975	$1,650	$1,475	$1,325	$1,150	$1,000	$925	$875

100%	98%	95%	90%	80%	70%	60%	50%	40%	30%	20%	10%

* ***Model 1883 Third Style*** - most commonly encountered Hotchkiss, 2-piece stock, approx. 62,034 mfg. 1883-1899.

100%	98%	95%	90%	80%	70%	60%	50%	40%	30%	20%	10%
N/A	N/A	$2,375	$1,975	$1,650	$1,475	$1,325	$1,150	$1,000	$925	$825	$725

The Model 1883 Hotchkiss was the first bolt action designed for the U.S. military .45-70 Govt. cartridge. On the First and Second models, inspect wood directly below bolt and left frame side for cracks, breaks, or older repairs as it is frequently encountered on these early models with thin wrists.

LEE STRAIGHT PULL RIFLE - 6mm Lee (.236 U.S.N. cal.), 5 shot non-detachable box mag., 24 (Sporting Rifle) or 28 (Musket) in. barrel, folding leaf sight, blue metal, military style full stock, mfg. 1897-1902, Navy Issue Model is the Musket with "236 U.S.N." on barrels. Approx. 20,000 mfg. (including 15,000 Muskets for the U.S. Navy military contract) between 1895-1902 with parts clean up occurring in 1916.

* ***Lee Straight Pull Rifle U.S.N. Military Musket***

100%	98%	95%	90%	80%	70%	60%	50%	40%	30%	20%	10%
N/A	$3,025	$2,575	$2,200	$1,975	$1,650	$1,375	$1,200	$1,100	$950	$825	$675

* ***Lee Straight Pull Rifle Sporting*** - similar to Musket, with 24 in. barrel, sporter style stock. Approx. 1,700 mfg. 1897-1902.

100%	98%	95%	90%	80%	70%	60%	50%	40%	30%	20%	10%
N/A	$3,300	$2,925	$2,525	$2,200	$1,925	$1,650	$1,375	$1,150	$1,075	$950	$875

This design was originally patented by James Paris Lee and assigned to the Lee Arms Company. Winchester obtained manufacturing rights to produce this model for the U.S Navy military contract 1895-1902.

MODEL 43 - .218 Bee, .22 Hornet, .25-20 WCF, or .32-20 WCF cal., dubbed "Poor Man's Model 70," 24 in. round tapered barrel, box type mag. Approx. 62,617 mfg. between 1949-1957.

100%	98%	95%	90%	80%	70%	60%	50%	40%	30%	20%	10%
$1,050	$880	$750	$600	$525	$475	$375	$325	$275	$220	$190	$165

Add 100% for Deluxe Model with fancy checkered wood.
Add 150% for .32-20 WCF and .25-20 WCF cal.
Add 20% for .218 Bee cal.
Subtract 25% if non-factory drilled and tapped (early models).

GRADING - PPGS™	100%	98%	95%	90%	80%	70%	60%	LAST MSR

MODEL 52 TARGET - .22 S (rare) or LR cal., 5 shot mag., 28 in. standard or heavy barrel (1st cataloged 1933), target sights and target style stock, speedlock trigger feature was introduced in 1929. Approx. 125,233 Model 52s in all variations were mfg. between 1919-79.

GRADING - PPGS™	100%	98%	95%	90%	80%	70%	60%	LAST MSR
	$900	$825	$725	$600	$550	$500	$450	
Altered w/aftermarket speedlock	$850	$750	$650	$575	$525	$475	$375	

Barrel drilling and tapping for scope blocks was not standard until ser. no. 5200.

A few Model 52 Target models with stainless steel barrels have been encountered. Values range from $1,500-$2,100, depending on condition.

* ***Model 52A Target*** - similar to Model 52, except all "A" suffix Model 52s have a speedlock trigger. Values are similar to Model 52 Target with speedlock trigger. In terms of rarity, it seems the "E" suffix is probably the scarcest (also the most poorly mfg.), followed by the "A" suffix variation.

MODEL 52A HEAVY BARREL - similar to Standard Target, with heavy barrel.

GRADING - PPGS™	100%	98%	95%	90%	80%	70%	60%	LAST MSR
	$1,150	$1,000	$850	$750	$600	$500	$450	

MODEL 52-B TARGET - extensively redesigned action, improved stock design, offered with a variety of sights. Approx. mfg. 1940-47.

GRADING - PPGS™	100%	98%	95%	90%	80%	70%	60%	LAST MSR
	$1,350	$1,200	$1,100	$1,000	$825	$725	$600	

MODEL 52-B HEAVY BARREL - similar to 52-B, with heavy barrel, with adj. sling swivel as to position of front swivel, and single shot adapter became available.

GRADING - PPGS™	100%	98%	95%	90%	80%	70%	60%	LAST MSR
	$1,450	$1,325	$1,200	$1,100	$1,000	$875	$775	

MODEL 52-B BULL GUN - extra heavy weight barrel.

GRADING - PPGS™	100%	98%	95%	90%	80%	70%	60%	LAST MSR
	$2,150	$1,925	$1,650	$1,250	$1,075	$925	$750	

MODEL 52 SPORTER (SPORTING RIFLE) - 24 in. round lightweight barrel with front sight cover, sporting type select walnut stock with cheekpiece, hard rubber pistol grip cap, black plastic tipped forearm, checkered steel buttplate, 5 shot mag. is standard, about 7 1/4 lbs. Mfg. 1934-1958. There is some controversy as to whether any of the Model 52 Sporters were drilled and tapped per factory worksmanship. Be cautious of "factory" drilled and tapped receivers on all model 52s, as there are many "gunsmith" Sporters that have been made with turned down, shortened target barrels.

GRADING - PPGS™	100%	98%	95%	90%	80%	70%	60%	LAST MSR

* ***Model 52 Sporter*** – advertised approx. 1936.

	$4,950	**$4,125**	**$3,000**	**$2,475**	**$1,825**	**$1,550**	**$1,200**	

* ***Model 52A Sporter*** – introduced approx. 1937, receiver and locking lug were strengthened.

	$6,600	**$6,000**	**$5,500**	**$4,400**	**$3,300**	**$2,200**	**$1,650**	

* ***Model 52B Sporter*** – introduced approx. 1940.

	$4,950	**$3,950**	**$3,000**	**$2,475**	**$1,825**	**$1,550**	**$1,200**	

* ***Model 52B (1993 Re-issue) Sporter*** – .22 LR cal., patterned after the original Model 52B and includes steel buttplate, 24 in. barrel w/o sights, Micro Motion trigger with adjustment screw on bottom plate, high-polish blue, 5 shot mag., checkered 52B style stock with ebony forend tip, 7 lbs. Mfg. by Miroku in Japan 1993-2002.

	$1,200	**$1,100**	**$1,000**	**$875**	**$650**	**$550**	**$500**	***$662***

* ***Model 52C Sporter*** – introduced 1947 with adj. Micro Motion trigger, approx. 500-1,000 mfg., 2 screws in trigger guard.

	$6,000	**$4,775**	**$4,350**	**$3,250**	**$2,475**	**$1,825**	**$1,550**	

A few Model 52 Sporters & Targets were mfg. with stainless steel barrels (17,XXX-27,XXX serial range) - these guns will command a premium over values shown. Stainless steel barrels were also offered by Winchester as after market parts.

MODEL 52-C STANDARD TARGET – "Micro Motion" trigger and "Marksman" stock, single shot adaptor, 5 or 10 shot mag. was avail., standard barrel, otherwise similar to 52-B. Mfg. 1947-61.

	$1,425	**$1,325**	**$1,200**	**$1,100**	**$875**	**$650**	**$550**	

MODEL 52-C HEAVY TARGET – similar to Standard Target, with heavy barrel.

	$1,475	**$1,375**	**$1,200**	**$1,100**	**$875**	**$775**	**$725**	

MODEL 52-C BULL TARGET – extra heavy (bull) barrel model of Heavy Target 52-C. Mfg. approx. 1947-1961.

	$2,375	**$1,925**	**$1,600**	**$1,450**	**$1,325**	**$1,150**	**$1,000**	

MODEL 52-D TARGET – improved version of 52-C with free floating standard or heavy barrel and adj. bedding device, all 52-Ds were single shot. Fewer than 750 rifles were shipped.

	$1,300	**$1,150**	**$1,000**	**$900**	**$800**	**$700**	**$600**	

MODEL 52-D INTERNATIONAL MATCH – similar to 52-D, with free rifle stock, accessory rail. Mfg. 1969-1975.

	$1,650	**$1,400**	**$1,125**	**$925**	**$775**	**$650**	**$525**	

Previous Model 52s had ser. no. suffixes - either A, B, C, or D" After approx. 1975, rifles started appearing with an "E" serial prefix. Both Model 52 International and Prone could have factory stocks that were not Winchester mfg.

MODEL 52-D PRONE – similar to International Match, with prone style stock. Mfg. 1960-75.

	$1,525	**$1,350**	**$1,150**	**$900**	**$750**	**$600**	**$550**	

MODEL 52-E TARGET – similar to Model 52-D Target, approx. 652 mfg. 1975-1980.

	$1,925	**$1,650**	**$1,350**	**$1,075**	**$895**	**$765**	**$650**	

MODEL 52-E INTERNATIONAL PRONE – similar to 52-D, with lighter colored wood stock, removable roll over cheekpiece. Approx. 37 mfg. 1975-1980.

	$1,525	**$1,350**	**$1,150**	**$900**	**$750**	**$600**	**$550**	

MODEL 52-E INTERNATIONAL MATCH – heavy match barrel, lower accessory rail, uncheckered light colored walnut thumbhole stock with adj. buttplate and beavertail forend, no sights, scattered in ser. no. range E-123,000 - E125,000. Approx. 44 mfg. 1975-1980.

	$2,150	**$1,750**	**$1,450**	**$1,325**	**$1,200**	**$1,050**	**$900**	

MODEL 54 HIGH POWER SPORTER – .22 Hornet, .220 Swift (rare, mfg. 1935-1936), .250-3000 Sav., .257 Roberts (rare, mfg. 1935-1936), .270 Win., 7x57mm, 7.65x57mm Mauser (rare, mfg. 1929-1936), .30-30 Win., .30-06, 9x57mm Mauser (rare, mfg. 1929-1939) cal., 24 in. barrel, open sights, checkered pistol grip stock, blue finish, mfg. 1925-1936.

	$1,650	**$1,375**	**$1,100**	**$950**	**$800**	**$650**	**$550**	

Rare cals. will add premiums to the values listed. This model was also mfg. with a stainless steel barrel during the late 1920s-early '30s with premiums also being asked.

MODEL 54 CARBINE – introduced 1927, similar to Rifle, with 20 in. barrel, plain stock.

	$1,825	**$1,425**	**$1,175**	**$1,025**	**$875**	**$725**	**$550**	

GRADING - PPGS™	100%	98%	95%	90%	80%	70%	60%	LAST MSR

MODEL 54 IMPROVED SPORTER – .22 Hornet, .220 Swift, .250-3000 Savage, .257 Roberts, .270 Win., 7x57mm, or .30-06 cal., 5 shot mag., 24 or 26 in. barrel, one-piece firing pin, checkered pistol grip stock. Mfg. 1930-1936.

$1,650 $1,400 $1,150 $1,025 $875 $775 $650

Rare calibers will add premiums to the values listed.

MODEL 54 CARBINE IMPROVED – similar to Rifle, with 20 in. barrel.

$2,125 $1,775 $1,450 $1,150 $975 $825 $725

MODEL 54 SUPER GRADE – introduced 1934, similar to Sporter, with better wood and black forend tip and pistol grip cap.

$3,625 $3,100 $2,575 $1,975 $1,675 $1,500 $1,325

Add 15%-50% for .220 Swift and .257 Roberts cals., depending on original condition.
Add approx. 75%-100% for 7x57mm cal., depending on condition.

MODEL 54 SPORTING SNIPER'S RIFLE – .30-06 cal., similar to Sporter, with 26 in. heavy barrel, Lyman #48 W receiver sight. Mfg. 1929-1935.

$2,875 $2,175 $1,750 $1,475 $1,275 $1,100 $1,000

MODEL 54 NATIONAL MATCH – introduced 1935, similar to Standard, with Lyman sights and Marksman stock.

$2,150 $1,925 $1,650 $1,275 $1,075 $925 $750

MODEL 56 SPORTER – .22 S or LR cal., 5 or 10 shot box mag., 22 in. round barrel, open sights, plain pistol grip stock. Approx. 8,297 mfg. between 1926-29.

$1,825 $1,475 $1,200 $1,100 $925 $800 $650

Approx. 1,000 mfg. in .22 Short cal.

MODEL 57 TARGET – .22 S (disc. 1930) or LR cal., 22 in. barrel with barrel band, open sights, stock cutaway for aperture sight on left side, drilled and tapped receiver, heavy target uncheckered pistol grip walnut stock, 5 (standard) or 10 shot mag., left side push-button mag. release, checkered steel buttplate approx. 5 lbs. Approx. 18,600 were mfg. between 1927-1936.

$1000 $850 $725 $575 $475 $420 $360

MODEL 57 SPORTING SNIPER'S MATCH – .30-06 cal., 26 in. extra heavy barrel (1 1/4 at breech and 7/8 at the muzzle), Lyman #48 W receiver sight, Marksman stock, approx. 12 lbs., rare. Introduced late 1935.

N/A $4,750 $4,250 $3,850 $3,450 $2,950 $2,500

MODEL 69 & 69A – .22 S, L, or LR cal., 5 or 10 shot repeater, 25 in. barrel, aperture or open rear sight, not serial numbered. Approx. 355,000 mfg. between 1935-63.

$425 $365 $300 $235 $150 $100 $85

Add 40% for Target Model.
Add 20% for grooved receiver (Model 69A only).
Add 5% for chrome plated bolt handle and trigger guard.

The Model 69 was cocked by the closing motion of the bolt and had a non-swept back bolt handle, whereas the 69A was cocked by the opening motion of the bolt and had a swept back bolt handle. Number 97B rear aperture sight and 80A hooded front target sights and standard open sights were offered on both the Model 69 and 69A.

MODEL 72/72A – .22 LR and Gallery Model (.22 short only), tube mag., bolt action, 25 in. round, tapered barrel, aperture or open rear sight, not serial numbered. Over 161,000 mfg. between 1938-59.

$500 $425 $325 $275 $125 $110 $95

Add 30% for Target Model.
Add 100% for Gallery Model (mfg. 1939-1942) - rare.
Add 20% for grooved receiver (Model 72A only).
Add 5% for chrome plated bolt handle and trigger guard.

The Model 72 and 72A both cocked on opening. The Model 72A has a swept back bolt handle and some minor internal mechanical improvements. Same open sight options as Models 69/69A.

MODEL 75 TARGET – .22 LR cal., 5 or 10 shot mag., 28 in. barrel, target sights, slight variation used by Government in WWII. Approx. 88,715 Model 75 Target and Model 75 Sporter rifles were mfg. between 1938-1958.

$850 $725 $600 $525 $450 $375 $325

Add 25% for Olympic sights.
Add 20% for original Winchester leather sling.

GRADING - PPGS™	100%	98%	95%	90%	80%	70%	60%	LAST MSR

MODEL 75 SPORTER – similar to Model 75, except 24 in. tapered barrel, detachable mag., non-target sights and select checkered walnut.

	$1,500	$1,300	$1,000	$725	$650	$600	$500	

Add 20%-25% for "grooved" receiver allowing "tip-off" scope mounts.

MODEL 131 – .22 S, L, and LR cal., 7 shot mag.

	$225	$200	$175	$150	$125	$95	$75	

MODEL 141 – .22 S, L, and LR cal., butt loading tube mag.

	$225	$200	$175	$150	$125	$95	$75	

MODEL 320 RIFLE – .22 LR cal., similar to Single Shot Model 310, with 5 shot mag. Mfg. 1972-74.

	$325	$325	$300	$265	$235	$185	$150	

MODEL 325 RIFLE – .22 WMR cal., otherwise similar to Model 320, limited mfg. 1972-74.

	$375	$350	$325	$300	$250	$200	$100	

MODEL 670 RIFLE – another economy version of the Model 70, .225 Win., .243 Win., .270 Win, .308 Win., or .30-06 cal., 22 in. barrel, open sights, no hinged floorplate, pistol grip stock. Mfg. 1967-73.

	$325	$275	$235	$195	$175	$165	$140	

MODEL 670 CARBINE – similar to 670, with 19 in. barrel, not available in .308 Win. Mfg. 1967-70.

	$325	$275	$235	$195	$175	$165	$140	

MODEL 670 MAGNUM – similar to 670, with reinforced stock, .264 Mag., 7mm Mag., or .300 Win. Mag. cal. Mfg. 1967-70.

	$365	$295	$265	$225	$205	$195	$165	

MODEL 697 – .22 WRF cal., same general specifications as the Model 69, except no iron sights or sight cuts in barrel and no ramp or sight cover. Telescope bases attached to barrel were standard.

	$2,750	$2,425	$2,200	$1,650	$1,425	$1,200	$1,100	

MODEL 770 – .22-250 Rem., .222 Rem., .243 Win., .270 Win., .30-06, or .308 Win. cal., 22 in. barrel, open sights, no floorplate or forend tip. Mfg. 1969-71.

	$425	$375	$325	$300	$275	$250	$225	

MODEL 770 MAGNUM – similar to Model 770, .264 Mag., 7mm Mag., or .300 Win. Mag. cal., recoil pad. Mfg. 1969-71.

	$500	$450	$400	$325	$300	$275	$250	

MODEL 777 – .30-06 cal., bolt action, 4 shot mag., mfg. by Nikko in Japan during 1979-80 for sale to Winchester subsidiaries in Australia, Germany, Italy, and Scandinavia, only 3 were shipped to the U.S., checkered Monte Carlo stock with Wundhammer swell grip, lightweight barrel, engraved action, "Winchester" is cast on the left side of the receiver near the top, approx. 1,000 mfg. with 250 in .30-06 cal. - 750 mfg. in different cal. and sold elsewhere, 8 1/2 lbs.

	$1,850	$1,675	$1,500	$1,350	$1,200	$1,100	$1,000	

WILDCAT – .22 LR cal., 21 in. regular or heavy (Target/Varmint model) barrel with (Sporter) or w/o (Target/Varmint) sights, detachable 5 or 10 shot mag., checkered hardwood stock and forend (Target or Sporter configuration), sling swivels, fold down rear sight, includes one 5 and three 10 shot mags., two-stage trigger, two-position safety on trigger guard, 4 1/2 or 5 1/2 (Target/Varmint) lbs. Imported from Russia 2007-2009.

	$215	$185	$150	$130	$110	$90	$80	*$259*

Add $50 for Wildcat Target/Varmint variation with heavy barrel and beavertail forend (no sights).

This model with 21 in. Sporter barrel was featured as a SHOT Show Special during 2006.

RIFLES: BOLT ACTION - PRE-1964 MODEL 70

The Pre-'64 Model 70 Bolt Action Rifle (advertised by Winchester throughout much of its production history as "The Rifleman's Rifle") was produced from 1936 through 1963. Collectors recognize three major manufacturing periods: "Pre-War" (1936-1941); "Transition" (1946-1948); and "Latter" (1949-1963). There were only eighteen (18) original chamberings, these are: .22 Hornet, .220 Swift, .243 Win.(standard cal.), .250 Savage (.250-3000), .257 Roberts, .264 Win. Mag.(standard cal.), .270 Win.(standard cal.), 7x57mm Mauser, .300 Savage (standard cal.), .300 H&H, .300 Win. Mag., .30-06 (standard cal., .30 Govt. '06 Springfield - approx. 80% of total mfg. by cal.), .308 Win. (standard in Featherweight Style only), .338 Win. Mag.(standard cal.), .35 Rem.(standard cal.), .358 Win. (in Featherweight Style only), .375 H&H, and .458 Win. Mag. (in Super Grade AFRICAN Style only). It is important to note that every caliber was not available during each manufacturing period. Any other caliber encountered (including 7.65mm Argentine and 9x57mm Mauser) may be regarded as either special ordered or non-original. Magazine capacities are as follows: "Standard Calibers" (including .22 Hornet) five (5) rounds; "H&H Magnums" (.300 & .375) four (4) rounds; and "Winchester Short Magnums" (.264, .300, .338, .458) three (3) rounds. The rifle was produced in

GRADING - PPGS™	100%	98%	95%	90%	80%	70%	60%	LAST MSR

a myriad of styles and variations - most of which are covered individually. Unfortunately, a veritable "cottage industry" has developed involving the alteration, "upgrading," and/or outright faking of these guns. Be careful when contemplating a purchase of any rare Model 70 (and get a receipt describing the purchase accurately).

MODEL 70 PRE-WWII PRODUCTION STANDARD GRADE – 12 standard cals., 5 shot mag., 4 shot mag. on Magnums, 24, 25, or 26 in. barrel, open sights, checkered walnut pistol grip stock, approx. ser. range is 1-41,750. Mfg. 1937-1941.

Standard Cals. (see listings above)	$2,275	$1,975	$1,725	$1,150	$875	$725	$525
.22 Hornet	$3,675	$3,300	$2,800	$2,125	$1,675	$1,325	$1,050
.220 Swift	$2,850	$2,550	$2,125	$1,275	$1,075	$875	$725
.257 Roberts	$4,000	$3,500	$2,925	$1,825	$1,450	$1,050	$775
.270 Win.	$2,650	$2,475	$2,125	$1,375	$1,075	$875	$725
.300 H&H	$3,850	$3,400	$2,775	$2,025	$1,575	$1,225	$900
.375 H&H	$5,125	$4,300	$3,800	$2,700	$2,175	$1,750	$1,325
7x57mm Mauser	$6,600	$5,950	$4,950	$4,200	$3,400	$2,875	$2,300
.250-3000 Savage	$6,175	$5,600	$5,125	$4,300	$3,525	$2,875	$2,300

Add approx. 100% for Super Grades in common cals.

Values listed assume original, unaltered specimens - modifications/alterations to either the metal or wood surfaces can reduce prices by large amounts. All pre-war Model 70s have only 2 holes drilled in the front of the receiver (none in the back). An extra set of "holes" can decrease value as much as 50%. Some pre-WWII Model 70s have a "D" suffix indicating a doubled up serial number - this variation will command a premium because of its rarity. The Model 70 is one gun for which caliber ranks before condition in terms of desirability. Specimens encountered in under 60% condition will not decrease in price substantially since almost any shooter is worth $500-$600.

There are more fakes than legitimate specimens in cals. 7x57mm and .250-3000 Savage!

Rare cals. such as the .300 Savage, .35 Rem., 7.65mm, and 9x57mm Mauser are seldom encountered, and their scarcity precludes accurate price evaluation. Cals. 7.65mm and 9x57mm Mauser were special order only and were made up from leftover Model 54 barrels. Also, the original factory box, papers, and hanging tag will add 25%-30% to the values listed. Believe it or not, there are getting to be a lot of fake Model 70 boxes that have been intentionally aged. Carefully screen NIB (watch the hanging tag also) specimens in this model for possible expert refinishing.

MODEL 70 CARBINE (MFG. 1936-1946) – available in most cals. during its period, 20 in. barrel, short rifle variation of the Pre-'64 Model 70 (Winchester never officially used the "Carbine" terminology). If original, front sight base will be an integral part of the barrel. All carbines were disc. shortly after WWII. Beware of fakes.

Add 50%-100% for carbine variations mfg. 1936-1946 with 20 in. barrel to pre-war .22 Hornet caliber values (watch for fakes with cut off barrels, rechambered "K" models, and examine the front sight carefully), .250-3000 Savage, .257 Roberts, .270 Win., 7mm, or .30-06 (most common) cal.

MODEL 70 TRANSITION (MFG. 1946-1948) – several of the post-war Model 70s mfg. between 1946-48 exhibit the pre-war receiver characteristics and have a transition safety. This variation is more rare than normal models, ser. no. range is 60,000-100,000.

Add 10% to Model 70 Pre-WWII standard grade values.

On this Transitional Model, the receiver bridge may or may not be factory drilled.

MODEL 70 STANDARD GRADE (1946-1963 PRODUCTION) – 18 standard cals. including .22 Hornet, .220 Swift, .243 Win., .250 Savage (.250-3000), .257 Roberts, .264 Win. Mag., .270 Win., 7x57mm Mauser, .300 Savage, .300 H&H, .300 Win. Mag., .30-06, .308 Win., .338 Win. Mag., .35 Rem., .358 Win., and .375 H&H, 5 shot mag., 4 shot mag. on Magnums, 24, 25, or 26 in. barrel, open sights, checkered walnut pistol grip stock, ser. range is 52,549-581,471. Mfg. 1946-1963.

Standard cals. (those cals. not listed below)	$1,450	$1,200	$1,100	$900	$650	$550	$500
.22 Hornet	$3,750	$3,350	$2,700	$2,350	$1,625	$1,225	$1,050
.220 Swift	$2,450	$1,975	$1,800	$1,125	$825	$625	$550
.243 Win.	$2,100	$1,875	$1,475	$1,050	$900	$775	$700
.257 Roberts	$3,250	$2,500	$2,075	$1,650	$1,150	$800	$625
.264 Mag. (Westerner)	$2,200	$1,900	$1,750	$1,125	$850	$650	$550
.270 Win.	$1,850	$1,625	$1,375	$1,100	$825	$625	$525
.300 H&H	$2,650	$2,300	$1,775	$1,175	$975	$750	$625
.300 Win. Mag.	$3,850	$3,400	$2,900	$2,375	$1,800	$1,325	$1,050
.338 Win. Mag.	$3,350	$2,700	$2,400	$1,650	$1,250	$1,000	$825
.375 H&H	$4,000	$3,500	$3,150	$2,375	$2,150	$1,850	$1,500

Add 10% for .300 H&H or .375 H&H if rear receiver is not drilled and tapped.

Add 30% for stainless steel barrel in .300 H&H or .270 Win. cal.

Values listed assume original, unaltered specimens - modifications/alterations to either the metal or wood surfaces

GRADING - PPGS™	100%	98%	95%	90%	80%	70%	60%	LAST MSR

can reduce prices by large amounts. Most post-war Model 70s are drilled on top of the receiver (2 holes in front and 2 holes in back) to accept scope mounts (except early .300 and .375 H&H cals.). Pre-1964 mfg. Model 70s are desirable since Winchester implemented manufacturing techniques that lowered the quality beginning in 1964.

Rare cals. such as the .250-3000, .300 Savage, .308 Win. (extremely rare, so watch for fakes), .35 Rem., and 7x57mm Mauser are seldomly seen or sold. Premiums depend on the rarity of the caliber and original condition.

Believe it or not, there are getting to be a lot of fake Model 70 boxes that have been intentionally aged. Carefully screen NIB (watch the hanging tag also) specimens in this model.

MODEL 70 SUPER GRADE – similar to Standard Model, except has deluxe wood, black pistol grip cap and forend tip, all Super Grades have a raised cheekpiece with deluxe wraparound checkering, and Super Grade marked floorplate. Disc. 1960.

.375 H&H	$7,000	$6,150	$5,250	$4,600	$4,000	$3,500	$3,000	

A general rule for Super Grades is that if you add 100% to the standard grade in similar cals., values should be rather close. For .375 H&H cal., values are listed.

Later Model 70 Super Grades have jeweled action components and rust blued barrels.

MODEL 70 SUPER GRADE AFRICAN – .458 Win. Mag. cal. only, front swivel base relocated and attached to bottom of barrel, nearly all possess one or two visible stock crossbolts (usually covered with Bakelite). Most have all action components (bolt body, extractor, extractor ring and magazine follower) jeweled (i.e., engine turned), rust blued barrel. 1,226 mfg. 1956-63.

	$8,000	$7,500	$7,000	$6,500	$5,500	$4,500	$4,000	

While other Super Grades were disc. approx. 1960, the "AFRICAN" continued in that style until the end of all production. Normal attrition and collectors owning more than one contribute to extreme rarity. Retains considerable "shooter" value in lesser external conditions. Watch for cracked and/or repaired stocks.

MODEL 70 FEATHERWEIGHT – lightened version of Standard, .243 Win., .264 Win. Mag. (Westerner, mfg. 1962-1963), .270 Win., .308 Win., .30-06, or .358 Win. cal., 22 (standard) or 26 (Westerner only) in. barrel, aluminum trigger guard and floorplate, plastic (introduced circa 1958) or aluminum buttplate, ser. range is 206,626-581,471. Mfg. 1952-1963.

.243 Win.	$1,700	$1,475	$1,200	$950	$775	$650	$575	
.264 Mag. (Westerner)	$2,600	$2,200	$1,875	$1,550	$1,250	$1,000	$850	
.270 Win.	$1,625	$1,450	$1,275	$1,050	$900	$775	$650	
.30-06	$1,700	$1,475	$1,200	$950	$775	$650	$575	
.308 Win.	$1,700	$1,475	$1,200	$950	$775	$650	$575	
.358 Win. Alum. butt only	$4,350	$3,750	$2,950	$2,450	$1,950	$1,600	$1,250	

Add 10-20% for .30-06, .308 Win., .243 Win., or .270 Win. cal. models with aluminum buttplate, depending on condition.

The .358 Win. cal. is rare because Winchester had problems with this cal. Many of them were exchanged for other calibers, and the result is that original guns are rare in this cal. The .264 Mag. Westerner was only mfg. with a Win. recoil pad.

MODEL 70 SUPER GRADE FEATHERWEIGHT – .243 Win., .270 Win., .30-06, or .308 Win. cal. only, because of inconsistencies of Super Grade action component jeweling (i.e., engine turning), a simple stock and hinged floorplate change can create an "instant" Super Grade Featherweight (check stock carefully for wood filling near area of Standard Super Grade rear sight "boss" in barrel channel), all Super Grade Featherweights have a raised cheekpiece with wraparound "fish tail" checkering, all have rust blued barrels, less than 1,000 mfg.

	$7,700	$7,150	$6,600	$5,500	$4,400	$3,300	$2,750	

This is perhaps the rarest variation of the Pre-'64 Model 70 - beware of fakes.

MODEL 70 NATIONAL MATCH – similar to Standard, with target stock and scope bases, .30-06 only. Disc. 1960.

	$3,850	$3,475	$2,850	$2,425	$2,200	$1,875	$1,650	

MODEL 70 TARGET – similar to Model 70 Standard, in .243 Win. or .30-06 cal. (mfg. 1955-1963), earlier pre-'51 Target guns were available in virtually any cal. (i.e., .22 Hornet, .220 Swift, etc.), 24 in. medium weight barrel and target stock. Disc. 1963.

Add 50%-75% over standard values if condition is over 90%. 60% condition will be priced the same.

MODEL 70 BULL GUN – similar to Standard Model 70, with 28 in. heavy barrel, .300 H&H or .30-06 cal. only, .30-06 cal is much rarer.

.300 H&H cal.	$4,500	$4,000	$3,750	$3,500	$3,000	$2,500	$2,250	
.30-06	$4,950	$4,250	$3,875	$3,600	$3,100	$2,800	$2,400	

GRADING - PPGS™	100%	98%	95%	90%	80%	70%	60%	LAST MSR

MODEL 70 VARMINT – similar to Standard Model 70, in .220 Swift or .243 Win. cal., 26 in. heavy barrel, scope bases, varmint style stock. Mfg. 1956-63.

	$2,300	$1,925	$1,625	$1,325	$1,050	$800	$700	

Add 40% for .220 Swift cal. Add 10% for steel buttplate.

Less than 900 were mfg. in .220 Swift cal. Stainless steel barrels are also encountered in this model with 3 different types of finishes.

MODEL 70 ALASKAN – similar to Standard Model 70, in .300 Win. Mag. (mfg. 1963 only with 25 in. barrel - known as Alaskan), .338 Win. Mag., or .375 H&H cal., 24 (Westerner Alaskan) or 25 in. barrel, recoil pad. Mfg. 1960-63.

.375 H&H	$3,750	$3,200	$2,650	$2,100	$1,500	$1,300	$1,200	
.300/.338 Win. Mag.	$3,850	$3,400	$2,900	$2,375	$1,800	$1,325	$1,050	

RIFLES: BOLT ACTION - MODEL 70, 1964-2006 MFG.

Beginning 1994, Winchester began using the Classic nomenclature to indicate those models featuring a pre-1964 style action with controlled round feeding.

U.S. Repeating Arms closed its New Haven, CT manufacturing facility on March 31, 2006, and an auction was held on Sept. 27-28, 2006, selling the production equipment and related assets.

WSM cals. will bring an approx. 10% premium, and WSSM cals. will bring an approx. 15% premiums on most of the following models, if in 95%+ condition.

MODEL 70 STANDARD – .22-250 Rem., .222 Rem., .225 Win. (mfg. 1964-1972), .243 Win., .25-06 Rem., .270 Win., .308 Win., or .30-06 cal., 5 shot, 22 or 24 in. heavy barrel, open sights, Monte Carlo stock with sling swivels. Mfg. 1964-1980.

Other cals.	$725	$575	$475	$375	$325	$275	$225	
.225 Win. cal.	$1,450	$1,100	$900	$775	$650	$550	$450	

MODEL 70 WESTERNER – .22-250 Rem. (new 1983), .223 Rem. (new 1983), .243 Win., .270 Win., .30-06, .300 Win. Mag., or 7mm Rem. Mag. cal., 22 or 24 (Mag. cals. only) in. barrel, checkered satin finished straight comb stock with recoil pad, folding rear sight in middle of barrel, polished blue barrel with satin finished receiver, no forend tip or sling swivels. Mfg. 1982-1985.

	$825	$650	$550	$475	$400	$350	$300	

MODEL 70 MAGNUM – .264 Win. Mag., 7mm Rem. Mag., .300 H&H Mag., .300 Win. Mag., .338 Win. Mag., .375 H&H, or .458 Win. Mag. cal., 24 in. barrel. Disc.

	$825	$650	$550	$475	$415	$350	$300	

Add 25%-35% for .375 H&H or .458 Win. Mag. (African Model) cal.

MODEL 70 SUPER GRADE – various cals., deluxe wood with ebony forend cap, Super Grade appears on the floorplate. Disc.

	$1,050	$875	$750	$600	$525	$500	$475	

MODEL 70 DELUXE – .243 Win., .270 Win., .30-06, or .300 Win. Mag. cal., 22 in. barrel, open sight, hand-checkered, black forend tip. Mfg. 1964-71.

	$850	$675	$575	$475	$400	$300	$250	

The Model 70 Deluxe was redesignated the Standard Model 70 in 1972.

MODEL 70 TARGET RIFLE 1964-1971 – .308 Win. or .30-06 cal., 24 in. heavy barrel, no sights, target bases, heavy target style stock with hand stop. Disc. 1971.

	$925	$800	$725	$600	$500	$450	$350	

MODEL 70 1968 PALMA MATCH – .308 Win. cal., 26 in. heavy barrel with counterbored muzzle, blued finish, glass bedded action and breech end of barrel, Marksman stock, black rubber buttpad with white spacer, contoured aluminum hand stop, short accessory rail, furnished with Redfield International Match front and rear sights, marked on right side of barrel "PALMA TROPHY MATCH". Limited production by the Winchester Custom Shop. Mfg. 1968 only.

Retail values were not available for this model.

* ***Model 70 1971 Palma Match*** – .308 Win. cal., similar to Model 70 1968 Palma Match, except has externally adj. trigger, Champion Target front sight and Redfield International Match rear sight, and is marked on right side of barrel "PALMA MATCH/NRA CENTENNIAL 1871-1971" (two lines), matte finish. Limited production by the Winchester Custom Shop. Mfg. 1971 only.

* ***Model 70 1976 Palma Match*** – .308 Win. cal., similar to Model 70 1968 Palma Match rifle, except is marked on right side of barrel "PALMA MATCH 1876-1976". 140 rifles mfg. by the Winchester Custom Shop 1976 only.

GRADING - PPGS™	100%	98%	95%	90%	80%	70%	60%	LAST MSR

MODEL 70 INTERNATIONAL ARMY MATCH 1970-1979 – .308 Win. cal. (while only catalogued in .308 Win., several are known in .30-06 cal. also), 24 in. heavy barrel with matte finish, counterbored muzzle, glass bedded action and breech end of barrel, externally adj. trigger, special stock conforming to ISU requirements with pronounced cheepiece and deep forend which extends to bottom of trigger guard, blind mag., black rubber buttpad with white spacer, clamp lever and front swivel assembly, long accessory channel, no sights. Limited production by the Winchester Custom Shop on a special order only basis 1970-1979.

$1,200	$1,050	$925	$800	$650	$575	$500	

MODEL 70 MANNLICHER 1969-1971 – .243 Win., .270 Win., .30-06, or .308 Win. cal., 19 in. barrel, open sight, full-length Monte Carlo stock with steel forend cap. Disc. 1971.

$1,150	$1,000	$875	$775	$625	$550	$475	

MODEL 70A – economy version of 1972 type Model 70, same cals., no hinged floorplate or forend tip. Mfg. 1972-78.

$550	$450	$375	$300	$275	$225	$175	

MODEL 70A MAGNUM – similar to Model 70A, except in Mag. cals. but not .375 H&H or .458. Mfg. 1972-78.

$600	$500	$425	$325	$275	$225	$185	

MODEL 70 FEATHERWEIGHT – .22-250 Rem., .223 Rem., .243 Win., .25-06 Rem. (disc. 1993), .257 Roberts (disc.), .270 Win., .280 Rem., 6.5x55mm Swedish (new 1991), 7x57mm Mauser (disc.), .30-06, .308 Win., 7mm-08 Rem. (new 1992), 7mm Rem. Mag. (mfg. 1991-92 only), or .300 Win. Mag. (mfg. 1991-92 only) cal., bolt action, both short and medium action, 5 shot mag., 22 in. barrel (24 in. with .300 Win. Mag.), checkered walnut stock, with or w/o sights, approx. 6 1/2 lbs. Mfg. 1981-94.

$825	$725	$550	$450	$350	$300	$275	*$562*

In 1981, during U.S.R.A. takeover transition, guns were distinguishable by the U.S.R.A. trademark on the recoil pad. Some collectors will pay a premium for Win. marked pads. Cals. .257 Robts. and 7x57mm Mauser were disc. 1985.

This model had an "XTR" suffix until 1989.

MODEL 70 CLASSIC FEATHERWEIGHT – .22-250 Rem. (new 1994), .223 Rem. (mfg. 1994 only), .243 Win. (new 1994), .270 Win., .280 Rem. (disc. 2000), .30-06, .308 Win. (new 1994), 6mm Rem. (limited mfg. circa 1995), 6.5x55mm Swedish (new 1997), or 7mm-08 Rem. (new 1994) cal., 22 in. barrel, 5 shot mag., blue action, features claw-controlled round feeding action bedded into standard grade walnut stock, jewelled bolt, knurled bolt handle, includes rings and bases, approx. 7 lbs. Mfg. 1992-2006.

$825	$725	$550	$450	$350	$300	$275	*$762*

* ***Model 70 Classic Featherweight WSM*** – .270 WSM (new 2002), .300 WSM, .325 WSM (new 2005) or 7mm WSM (new 2002) cal., controlled round feeding, 24 in. round barrel, 3 shot internal mag., approx. 7 1/4 lbs. Mfg. 2001-2006.

$900	$800	$600	$500	$400	$325	$280	*$792*

Add $39 for left-hand action (new late 2003, not available in .325 WSM cal.).

* ***Model 70 Classic Featherweight Super Short WSSM*** – similar to Model 70 Classic Featherweight, except available in .223 WSSM, .243 WSSM, and .25 WSSM (new 2004) cals., 22 in. barrel, 3 shot mag., 6 lbs. Mfg. 2003-2006.

$900	$800	$600	$500	$400	$325	$280	*$814*

* ***Model 70 Classic Featherweight BOSS*** – similar to Model 70 Classic Featherweight, except has 22 in. barrel with BOSS. Mfg. 1996 only.

$875	$775	$575	$475	$360	$300	$275	*$735*

* ***Model 70 Classic Featherweight Stainless (Recent Mfg.)*** – .223 WSSM, .243 WSSM, .25 WSSM, .270 WSM, .300 WSM, .325 WSM, or 7mm WSM cal., 22 or 24 in. stainless barrel and action, no sights, three position safety, controlled round feed, Pachmayr Decelerator pad on WSM models, 3 shot mag., cut checkering with Schnabel forend, 6-7 1/4 lbs. Mfg. 2005-2006.

$925	$850	$625	$400	$375	$325	$275	*$806*

* ***Model 70 Classic Featherweight Stainless*** – .22-250 Rem., .243 Win., .270 Win., .30-06, .308 Win., .300 Win. Mag. (disc. 1998), or 7mm Rem. Mag. cal., 22 or 24 (Mag. cals. only) in. stainless barrel, checkered walnut stock, 3 or 5 shot mag., approx. 7-7 1/2 lbs. Mfg. 1997-99.

$825	$725	$550	$450	$375	$300	$275	*$746*

* ***Model 70 Classic Featherweight All-Terrain*** – .270 Win., .30-06, .300 Win. Mag., or 7mm Rem. Mag. cal., 22 or 24 in. matte finish stainless steel barrel/receiver, black fiberglass/graphite stock with checkering, with (1996-1997 only) or without BOSS, 3 or 5 shot mag., 7 1/4 lbs. Mfg. 1996-98.

$825	$725	$550	$450	$375	$300	$275	*$672*

Add 20% for BOSS (disc. 1997).

GRADING - PPGS™	100%	98%	95%	90%	80%	70%	60%	LAST MSR

* ***Model 70 Classic Featherweight Win-Tuff Rifle*** - .22-250 Rem., .223 Rem., .243 Win., .270 Win., .30-06, or .308 Win. cal., features brown laminated checkered stock with Schnabel forend, includes base and rings, pistol grip cap, 7 lbs. Mfg. 1988-90. Reintroduced 1992-93.

$625 $550 $500 $425 $350 $300 $275 *$572*

* ***Model 70 Classic Featherweight Special*** - .243 Win. cal., features custom fitted stock, hand-honed action, barrel, and bolt/follower, custom shop proof stamp, select American walnut with rounded pistol grips, no sights. Only 50 mfg.

$950 $775 $725 $550 $475 $425 $375

This model is distinguishable by the Super Grade floorplate marking.

MODEL 70 XTR EUROPEAN FEATHERWEIGHT - 6.5x55 Swedish Mauser cal., 22 in. barrel, 5 shot mag., rifle sights, 6 3/4 lbs. Made 1986 only.

$600 $525 $450 $400 $325 $300 $275 *$460*

MODEL 70 LIGHTWEIGHT RIFLE - .22-250 Rem. (disc. 1992), .223 Rem., .243 Win., .270 Win., .280 Rem. (mfg. 1988-92), .30-06, or .308 Win. cal., 22 in. barrel, checkered walnut stock, no sights, 6 1/2 lbs. Mfg. 1987-1995.

$650 $550 $500 $375 $325 $275 $250 *$513*

* ***Model 70 Lightweight Rifle Win-Tuff*** - .22-250 Rem. (mfg. 1988-89), .223 Rem. (new 1989), .243 Win. (new 1988), .270 Win. .30-06 or .308 Win. (new 1989) cal., similar to Model 70 Lightweight Rifle, except has laminated brown hardwood stock with checkering. Mfg. 1987-92.

$600 $525 $450 $375 $300 $250 $200 *$471*

* ***Model 70 Lightweight Rifle Win-Cam*** - .270 Win. or .30-06 cal., greenish laminated hardwood stock with checkering, 22 in. barrel. Mfg. 1987-disc.

$600 $525 $450 $375 $300 $250 $200 *$471*

This model was previously designated Featherweight before 1989.

MODEL 70 CARBINE/LIGHTWEIGHT CARBINE - .22-250 Rem., .222 Rem. (scarce), .223 Rem., .243 Win., .250 Savage (new 1986), .308 Win., .270 Win., or .30-06 cal., bolt action, 5 shot mag., both short and medium action, 20 in. barrel, checkered walnut stock, no sights, approx. 6 lbs. Mfg. 1984-87.

$650 $550 $500 $400 $325 $275 $250 *$395*

Add $15 for open sights.

MODEL 70 SPORTER - .22-250 Rem. (mfg. 1989-1993), .223 Rem. (mfg. 1989-93), .243 Win. (mfg. 1989-93), .25-06 Rem. (mfg. 1985-87 and reintroduced 1990), .264 Win. Mag., .270 Win., .270 Wby. Mag. (new 1988), .30-06, .300 Win. Mag., .300 Wby. Mag. (new 1989), .300 H&H (mfg. 1989- 1992), .308 Win. (mfg. 1986-89), .338 Win. Mag., or 7mm Rem. Mag. cal., 24 in. barrel, 3 or 5 shot mag., custom Sporter styling, Monte Carlo cheekpiece, detachable sling swivels, 7 3/4 lbs. Disc. 1994.

$800 $650 $525 $425 $325 $300 $275 *$556*

Add approx. 5% for iron sights (.270 Win., .30-06, .300 Win. Mag., or 7mm Rem. Mag. only).

This model had an "XTR" suffix until 1989.

* ***Model 70 Sporter Win-Tuff*** - .270 Win., .30-06, 7mm Rem. Mag., .300 Win. Mag., .300 Wby. Mag., or .338 Win. Mag. cal., similar to Model 70 Sporter, except has checkered brown laminate stock with sling swivels, solid recoil pad, 24 in. barrel, approx. 7 3/4 lbs. Mfg. 1992 only.

$650 $550 $500 $425 $325 $275 $250 *$572*

MODEL 70 CLASSIC SPORTER III (LT) - .25-06 Rem., .264 Win. Mag. (disc. 2000), .270 Win., .270 Wby. Mag. (disc. 1998), .270 WSM (new 2004), .30-06, .300 Win. Mag., .300 WSM (new 2004), .300 Wby. Mag. (disc. 2000), .325 WSM (new 2005), .338 Win. Mag., 7mm STW (mfg. 1997-2002), 7mm WSM (new 2004), or 7mm Rem. Mag. (disc. 2005) cal., similar to Model 70 Sporter, except features controlled round feeding, 3 (Mag. cals. only) or 5 shot internal mag., 24 or 26 in. barrel, checkered walnut stock, blue finish, stock was redesigned by David Miller in 1999 (denoted by "LT" Model suffix), approx. 7 3/4-8 lbs. Mfg. 1994-2006.

$850 $750 $550 $450 $350 $300 $275 *$742*

Add 10% for Mag. cals.
Add 10% for left-hand action (new 1997).
Add 10% for iron sights - disc. 1998 (available in .270 Win., .30-06, .300 Win. Mag., .338 Win. Mag., or 7mm Rem. Mag.).

This model's nomenclature was changed from Model 70 Classic Sporter LT to Model 70 Classic Sporter III during 2005. Sporter III improvements include a trimmer forend and stock, Pachmayr Decelerator pad, and a more open pistol grip.

GRADING - PPGS™	100%	98%	95%	90%	80%	70%	60%	LAST MSR

* ***Model 70 Classic Sporter Stainless*** – .270 Win., .30-06, .300 Win. Mag., .338 Win. Mag., or 7mm Rem. Mag. cal., 24 or 26 in. barrel with (1997 only) or without BOSS, checkered walnut stock, controlled round feeding, 3 or 5 shot mag., right or left-hand action, approx. 7 3/4 lbs. Mfg. 1997-98.

	$925	$800	$600	$525	$425	$325	$300	*$716*

Add 10% for BOSS.
Add 5% for left-hand action.

* ***Model 70 Classic Sporter BOSS*** – .25-06 Rem. (disc. 1996), .270 Win., .30-06, .264 Win. Mag. (disc. 1996), 7mm STW (new 1997), 7mm Rem. Mag., .270 Wby. Mag. (mfg. 1996 only), .300 Win. Mag., .300 Wby Mag. (mfg. 1996 only), or .338 Win. Mag. cal., 24 or 26 in. barrel with BOSS, 3 or 5 shot mag., checkered walnut stock, approx. 7 3/4 lbs. Mfg. 1995-98.

	$925	$800	$575	$475	$375	$300	$275	*$728*

Add approx. 10% for left-hand action (new 1997).

* ***Model 70 Classic Sporter Laredo*** – .300 Win Mag., 7mm STW (mfg. 1997-98), or 7mm Rem. Mag. cal., features claw extraction and controlled round feeding, 26 in. round or fluted (new 1998) barrel with (.300 Win. Mag. and 7mm Rem. Mag. disc. 1997) or without BOSS. Mfg. 1996-99.

	$1,050	$875	$675	$550	$450	$350	$325	*$794*

Add approx. 20% for BOSS (disc. 1998).
Add approx. $130 for fluted barrel.

* ***Model 70 Classic Sporter Safari Express*** – .375 H&H, .416 Rem. Mag., or .458 Win. Mag. cal., features Express style rear sight with standing blade, redesigned stock with negative drop and Pachmayr Decelerator recoil pad, trigger guard and floorplate are one assembly, 3 shot mag., controlled round feed, 24 in. barrel with barrel band swivel attachment, checkered walnut stock and forearm, 8 1/2 lbs. Mfg. 1999-2006.

	$1,700	$1,425	$1,025	$825	$650	$550	$500	*$1,149*

* ***Model 70 Classic Sporter Super Express Mag.*** – .375 H&H, .416 Rem. Mag. (new 1994), or .458 Win. Mag. cal., 3 shot mag., claw extractor controlled round feeding (new 1993), open sights, 22 or 24 in. (.375 H&H or .416 Rem. Mag.) barrel, 8 1/2 lbs. Disc. 1998.

	$1,525	$1,325	$1,000	$800	$650	$550	$500	*$865*

This model had an "XTR" suffix until 1989.

MODEL 70 CLASSIC LAMINATED WSM – .270 WSM, .300 WSM, .325 WSM (new 2005) or 7mm WSM cals., claw extractor controlled round feed, brown laminate stock, 24 in. barrel w/o sights, one inch deluxe recoil pad, blued receiver and barrel, 3 shot mag., 7 3/4 lbs. Mfg. 2003-2005.

	$850	$675	$550	$475	$375	$325	$300	*$810*

MODEL 70 DBM (DETACHABLE BOX MAGAZINE) – .22-250 Rem. (mfg. 1993 only), .223 Rem. (mfg. 1993 only), .243 Win. (new 1993), .270 Win., .30-06, .308 Win. (mfg. 1993 only), 7mm Rem. Mag., or .300 Win. Mag. cal., checkered walnut stock and forend, features 3 shot detachable box mag., 24 or 26 in. barrel with or without sights, includes bases and rings or iron sights (new 1993, optional) in .30-06, .300 Win. Mag., or 7mm Rem. Mag., 7 3/4 lbs. Mfg. 1992-94.

	$850	$675	$550	$475	$375	$325	$300	*$598*

Add $35 for iron sights.

MODEL 70 CLASSIC DBM – .22-250 Rem., .243 Win., .270 Win., .284 Win., .30-06, .308 Win., .300 Win. Mag., or 7mm Rem. Mag. cal., similar to Model 70 DBM, except has controlled round feeding, 24 or 26 in. barrel. Mfg. 1994 only.

Most cals.	$925	$775	$650	$500	N/A	N/A	N/A	
.284 Win. (268 mfg.)	$1,650	$1,475	$1,325	$1,225	$1,000	N/A	N/A	*$619*

Add $50 for iron sights (.270 Win., .30-06, .300 Win. Mag., or 7mm Rem. Mag.).

* ***Model 70 Classic DBM-S*** – .270 Win., .30-06, .300 Win. Mag., or 7mm Rem. Mag. cal., similar to Model 70 DBM, except has black synthetic stock, this model became a Classic series in 1994 (featuring controlled round feeding). Mfg. 1993-94.

	$850	$675	$550	$475	$375	$325	$300	*$619*

MODEL 70 STAINLESS – .270 Win., .30-06, 7mm Rem. Mag., .300 Win. Mag., or .338 Win. Mag. cal., matte finished stainless steel receiver, barrel, and bolt, black synthetic composite stock, 22 (.270 Win. or .30-06 only, disc. 1992) or 24 in. barrel, approx. 6 3/4 lbs. Mfg. 1992-94.

	$800	$625	$550	$475	$375	$325	$275	*$616*

MODEL 70 CLASSIC STAINLESS – .22-250 Rem. (disc. 1999), .223 Rem. (disc. 1994), .243 Win. (disc. 1998), .270 Win., .270 WSM (mfg. 2002), .30-06, .308 Win. (disc. 1998), .270 Wby. Mag. (mfg. 1997 only), .300 Win. Mag., .300 Wby. Mag. (disc. 2000), .300 RUM (disc. 2002), .300 WSM (mfg. 2001-

GRADING - PPGS™	100%	98%	95%	90%	80%	70%	60%	LAST MSR

2003), .338 Win. Mag., .375 H&H, 7mm STW (mfg. 2001-2002), 7mm WSM (mfg. 2002), or 7mm Rem. Mag. (disc. 2003, reintroduced 2004) cal., features controlled round feeding, 22 (disc. 2001), 24, or 26 in. barrel, black synthetic composite stock, 3, 5, or 6 shot mag., without sights except for .375 H&H cal., 6 3/4-7 1/2 lbs. Mfg. 1994-2005.

$925 $800 $600 $475 $350 $300 $250 *$817*

Add $30 for Mag. cals., or $125 for .375 H&H cal.

* ***Model 70 Classic Stainless BOSS*** – .22-250 Rem. (disc. 1996), .243 Win. (disc. 1996), .270 Win., .30-06, .308 Win. (disc. 1996), .270 Wby. Mag. (mfg. 1997 only), .300 Win. Mag., .300 Wby. Mag. (mfg. 1996-97), .338 Win. Mag., or 7mm Rem. Mag. cal., 22, 24, or 26 in. barrel with BOSS, black synthetic stock, 6 3/4-7 1/2 lbs. Mfg. 1995-98.

$975 $825 $625 $500 $375 $325 $275 *$788*

MODEL 70 CLASSIC LAMINATED STAINLESS – .270 Win., .30-06, .300 Win. Mag., .338 Win. Mag., or 7mm Rem. Mag. cal., 24 or 26 (Mag. cals. only) in. barrel without sights, checkered grey/black laminate stock with sporter style dimensions, stainless action and barrel, 3 or 5 shot mag., approx. 8 lbs. Mfg. 1998-99.

$975 $825 $625 $500 $375 $325 $275 *$753*

* ***Model 70 Classic Laminated Stainless Camo*** – .270 Win., .30-06, .300 Win. Mag., or 7mm Rem. Mag. cal., similar to Model 70 Classic Stainless, except has Mossy Oak Treestand finish composite stock, approx. 7 1/4 lbs. Mfg. 1998 only.

$875 $775 $600 $500 $375 $325 $275 *$745*

MODEL 70 COYOTE STAINLESS LAMINATED – various standard, WSSM, or WSM cals., push feed (non-WSM/WSSM cals.) or controlled round feed (WSM/WSSM cals. only) action, 24 in. medium heavy stainless steel sporter barrel, uncheckered brown or grey (new 2006) laminate stock with reverse taper on forend, 3 (WSM cals. only), 5, or 6 (.223 Rem. or .204 Ruger only) shot mag., 8 3/4 lbs. Mfg. 2000-2006.

$825 $725 $525 $425 $350 $300 $275 *$689*

Add 10% for WSM cals.
Add 15% for WSSM cals.

MODEL 70 COYOTE LAMINATED BLUE – .223 Rem., .270 WSM, .300 WSM, .325 WSM, 7mm WSM, .223 WSSM, .243 WSSM, or .25 WSSM cal., similar to Model 70 Coyote Laminated Stainless, except has blued barrel/receiver finish. Mfg. 2005 only.

$875 $775 $600 $475 $375 $325 $275 *$689*

Add 10% for WSM cals.
Add 15% for WSSM cals.

MODEL 70 COYOTE OUTBACK STAINLESS LAMINATED – various standard, Mag., or WSM cals., grey laminate stock with three oval holes in buttstock and four in forend, matte finished stainless receiver and 24 in. fluted barrel w/o sights, 3-6 shot mag., controlled round push feeding, approx. 7 3/4 lbs. Limited mfg. 2006.

$1,450 $1,200 $975 $775 $625 $475 $375 *$1,016*

Add 10% for WSM and standard Mag. cals.

MODEL 70 COYOTE LITE – similar cals. as Model 70 Coyote Laminated Blue, except also available in .22-250 Rem., .243 Win., and .308 Win. (new 2006) cal., features 24 in. blued steel (WSSM cals. only) or stainless steel fluted barrel/action, controlled round feed action, floorplate, carbon fiber/fiberglass composite Bell & Carlson stock with vented forend, Pachmayr Decelerator pad, 7 1/2 lbs. Mfg. 2005-2006.

$1,000 $850 $625 $500 $425 $350 $300 *$889*

Add 10% for WSM cals.

MODEL 70 CLASSIC SM (SYNTHETIC MATTE) – .22-250 Rem. (mfg. 1993 only), .223 Rem. (mfg. 1993 only), .243 Win. (mfg. 1993 only), .270 Win., .30-06, .308 Win. (mfg. 1993 only), 7mm Rem. Mag., .300 Win. Mag., .338 Win. Mag., or .375 H&H (new 1993) cal., features black composite stock with checkering and sling swivels, 22 (.22-250 Rem., .223 Rem., .243 Win., or .308 Win. - mfg. 1993 only), 24, or 26 in. barrel with matte metal finish, 3 or 5 shot, approx. 7 1/2 lbs. Mfg. 1992-96.

$825 $725 $575 $475 $375 $325 $300 *$620*

Add 10% for Mag. cals.

Until 1993, this model was called the Model 70 SSM. In 1994, this model became the Model 70 Classic SM featuring controlled round feeding.

MODEL 70 CLASSIC SM BOSS – .270 Win., .30-06, 7mm Rem. Mag., .300 Win. Mag., or .338 Win. Mag. cal., 24 or 26 in. barrel with BOSS, 3 or 5 shot, approx. 7 1/4 lbs. Mfg. 1995-96 only.

$925 $750 $600 $475 $375 $325 $300 *$735*

GRADING - PPGS™	100%	98%	95%	90%	80%	70%	60%	LAST MSR

MODEL 70 CLASSIC COMPACT – .243 Win., .308 Win. (disc. 2003), or 7mm-08 Rem. cal., features 12 1/2 in. LOP, 20 in. barrel and shallow profile, pre-'64 type action, 4 shot mag., checkered walnut stock and forearm, blue action and barrel, 6-6 1/2 lbs. Mfg. 1998-2006.

	$825	$750	$575	$425	$325	$300	$275	$762

MODEL 70 VARMINT – same general specifications as standard Sporter, .22-250 Rem., .223 Rem., .225 Win., .243 Win., or .308 Win. cal., 26 in. cold hammer forged heavy barrel, counter-sunk muzzle, no sights, 5 shot mag., target scope bases, 7 3/4 lbs. Mfg. 1964-1993.

	$775	$600	$525	$450	$375	$325	$275	$720

Add 50% for .225 Win. cal.

This model had an "XTR" suffix 1978-89.

* ***Model 70 Varmint Heavy (HBV)*** – .220 Swift (mfg. 1994-98), .22-250 Rem., .222 Rem. (mfg. 1997-98), .223 Rem., .243 Win., or .308 Win. cal., push-feed action, 26 in. heavy stainless fluted (new 1997) or plain barrel (countersunk muzzle) without sights, black synthetic beavertail H-S Precision stock with aluminum bedding block, 10 3/4 lbs. Mfg. 1993-1999.

	$900	$725	$575	$500	$450	$375	$325	$795

Add approx. $125 for fluted barrel.

MODEL 70 SHB (SYNTHETIC HEAVY BARREL) – .308 Win. cal., features checkered black composite stock, 26 in. barrel with matte metal finish, jeweled bolt, 9 lbs. Mfg. 1992 only.

	$750	$600	$525	$450	$375	$325	$275	$563

MODEL 70 WINLIGHT – .25-06 Rem., .270 Win., .280 Rem. (new 1987), .30-06, 7mm Rem. Mag., .300 Win. Mag., .300 Wby. Mag., or .338 Win. Mag. cal., McMillan fiberglass stock, thermoplastic receiver bedding, blue metal parts, 22 or 24 (Mag. cals. only) in. barrel, 3 or 4 shot mag., no sights, approx. 6 1/2 lbs. Mfg. 1986-90.

	$900	$775	$725	$600	$550	$500	$450	$637

MODEL 70 RANGER RIFLE – .22-250 Rem. (new 1999), .223 Rem. (new 1992), .243 Win. (new 1991), .270 Win., .30-06, or 7mm Rem. Mag. cal., push-feed action, 22 or 24 in. barrel, 3 (7mm Rem. Mag.), 5, or 6 shot mag., plain hardwood stock without checkering, open sights, approx. 7 lbs. Disc. 1999.

	$575	$475	$375	$325	$275	$225	$200	$503

* ***Model 70 Ranger Rifle Compact (Ladies/Youth)*** – .22-250 Rem. (mfg. 1999 only), .223 Rem. (disc. 1989, reintroduced 1997, disc. 1998), .243 Win., .308 Win. (new 1991), or 7mm-08 Rem. (mfg. 1997-98, reintroduced 2000) cal., push-feed action, 20 (disc. 1992) or 22 (new 1993) in. barrel, 5 or 6 shot mag., shorter hardwood stock dimensions, open sights, 6 1/2 lbs. Disc. 2000.

	$600	$525	$375	$325	$275	$250	$225	$528

MODEL 70 STEALTH – .22-250 Rem., .223 Rem., .308 Win. cal., push-feed action, 26 in. heavy barrel w/o sights, non-glare matte metal finish, Accu-Block black synthetic stock with full-length aluminum bedding block, 5 or 6 shot mag., 10 3/4 lbs. Mfg. 1999-2003.

	$1,025	$850	$775	$650	$600	$550	$500	$800

MODEL 70 STEALTH II – .22-250 Rem., .223 WSSM, .243 WSSM, .25 WSSM, or .308 Win. cal., push-feed action, 26 in. heavy barrel w/o sights, matte blue finish, redesigned black synthetic stock with aluminum pillar bedding, 3 or 5 shot mag., 10 lbs. Mfg. 2004-2006.

	$900	$750	$600	$475	$400	$375	$325	$886

Add 10% for WSSM cals.

MODEL 70 BLACK SHADOW – .270 Win., .30-06, .300 Win. Mag., or 7mm Rem. Mag cal., push-feed action, 3 (Mag. cals.) or 5 shot internal mag., 24 or 26 (Mag. cals.) in. barrel w/o sights, matte receiver and barrel finish, black composite stock with conventional floorplate mag., 7 1/4 lbs. Mfg. 1998-2003.

	$575	$425	$325	$300	$275	$250	$225	$523

Add approx. 10% for Mag. cals.

MODEL 70 CLASSIC/CAMO ULTIMATE SHADOW – .223 WSSM (new 2004), .243 WSSM (new 2004), .25 WSSM (new 2004), .270 WSM, .300 WSM, .325 WSM (new 2005) or 7mm WSM cal., features controlled round feed, black or Dura-Touch armor coated Mossy Oak New Break-Up camo finished molded synthetic stock with rubber grip inserts and new recoil pad, matte black metal, 3 shot mag., 24 in. blued steel or stainless steel barrel, 6 3/4 lbs. Mfg. 2003-2005.

	$850	$700	$575	$500	$425	$375	$325	$817

Add 10% for WSM cals. or 15% for WSSM cals.

Add 10% for stainless steel action.

Add approx. $100 Mossy Oak New Break-Up camo finish.

GRADING - PPGS™	100%	98%	95%	90%	80%	70%	60%	LAST MSR

MODEL 70 SUPER SHADOW – various cals., similar to Classic Ultimate Shadow, except has oval dot textured gripping surfaces on pistol grip and forearm, blue finish, controlled round push feed action, available in either short or super short action, blind mag., 22 (.223 WSSM, .243 WSSM, or .25 WSSM cal.) or 24 in. barrel w/o sights, 6 (WSSM cals.) or 6 3/4 lbs. Mfg. 2003-2006.

$575	$450	$325	$275	$225	$200	$175	*$525*

Add 10% for WSM and Mag. cals. or 15% for WSSM cals.

MODEL 70 SHADOW ELITE STAINLESS – various standard, WSM, and Mag. cals., short or long action, lightweight black synthetic stock with rubberized overmolded gripping surfaces on pistol grip and forearm, and Dura-Touch Armor coating, WinSorb recoil pad, 24 or 26 in. stainless fluted barrel, no sights, except .375 H&H cal., controlled round feed action, 3 or 5 shot mag., 6 3/4-7 3/4 lbs. Limited mfg. 2006 only.

$800	$625	$475	$375	$300	$250	$225	*$739*

Add 10% for WSM and standard Mag. cals.
Add approx. $125 for .375 H&H cal.

* ***Model 70 Shadow Elite Stainless Camo*** – similar to Model 70 Shadow Elite Stainless, except available in Mossy Oak Break-Up camo. Limited mfg. 2006 only.

$875	$650	$550	$450	$375	$325	$275	*$808*

Add 10% for standard Mag. and WSM cals.
Add $200 for .375 H&H cal.

MODEL 70 PRO SHADOW – various standard, WSM, and Mag. cals., short or long action, 22 or 24 in. blue barrel, black synthetic stock with Dura-Touch Armor coating and oval-dot gripping surfaces, controlled round push feed, 3 or 5 shot mag., 6 1/2-7 lbs. Limited mfg. 2006 only.

$775	$600	$525	$450	$375	$325	$275	*$594*

Add 10% for standard Mag. and WSM cals.

* ***Model 70 Pro Shadow Stainless*** – similar to Model 70 Pro Shadow, except has stainless barrel/action. Limited mfg. 2006 only.

$825	$650	$575	$500	$450	$375	$325	*$638*

Add 10% for standard Mag. and WSM cals.
Add $125 for .375 H&H cal.

MODEL 70 CLASSIC SUPER GRADE III – .25-06 Win. (new 2001), .270 Win. (mfg. 1991-2003), .270 WSM (new 2004), .30-06 (new 1991), 7mm STW (230 mfg. 1999 only), 7mm WSM (new 2004), 7mm Rem. Mag. (disc. 1998, reintroduced 2000-2003), .264 Win. Mag. (limited mfg. 2000 only), .300 WSM (new 2004), .300 Win. Mag. (disc. 2003, reintroduced 2005), .325 WSM (new 2005), or .338 Win. Mag. cal., 24 or 26 in. barrel, 3 (Mag. cals.) or 5 shot mag., jewelled bolt, stainless steel extractor for true claw controlled round feeding and ejecting, three-position safety, checkered satin finish walnut stock with wood cheekpiece, black forend tip, bases and rings included, approx. 7 3/4-8 lbs. Mfg. 1990-2006.

$1,650	$1,275	$1,100	$975	$800	$650	$550	*$1,036*

Add 10% for WSM and Mag. cals.

This model was designated the Model 70 Super Grade until 1995. During 1999, this model was redesigned to include a new Express style rear sight with standing blade, negative stock drop, Pachmayr Decelerator pad, one-piece floorplate and full barrel band swivel attachment. This model was on its third generation of design improvements (now called the Super Grade III) with trimmer sporter style stock, steel stock crossbolt, and inlaid swivel studs.

* ***Model 70 Classic Super Grade III RMEF*** – .300 WSM or .325 WSM (new 2005) cal., similar to Model 70 Classic Super Grade, except is Rocky Mountain Elk Foundation special edition, includes Super Grade Stock with ebony forend and Pachmayr Decelerator pad, special RMEF emblem on grip cap, 26 in. barrel, 8 lbs. Limited mfg. 2003-2006.

$1,875	$1,475	$1,225	$1,100	$975	$825	$600	*$1,183*

This model was redesignated the Super Grade III RMEF in 2005.

* ***Model 70 Classic Super Grade III BOSS*** – similar to Model 70 Classic Super Grade, except has BOSS. Mfg. 1995-97.

$1,125	$900	$775	$600	$500	$375	$325	*$956*

MODEL 70 SUPER GRADE CENTENNIAL – .30-06 cal., deluxe checkered walnut stock, black forend cap, controlled round feed with engraved "1906-2006 - 100 Years of .30-06 Springfield" on bolt face, 24 in. blue steel barrel, 3 shot mag., polished engraved floorplate with special gold and nickel accents, 8 lbs. 306 mfg. 2005-2006.

$1,700	$1,450	$1,325	N/A	N/A	N/A	N/A	*$1,259*

GRADING - PPGS™	100%	98%	95%	90%	80%	70%	60%	LAST MSR

MODEL 70 50TH ANNIVERSARY MODEL – .300 Win. Mag. cal., 24 in. barrel, deluxe walnut stock, engraving and special motifs on metal surfaces, serial numbered 50 ANV 1 - 50 ANV 500, 7 3/4 lbs. 500 mfg. 1987 only.

$1,925 $1,650 $1,375 N/A N/A N/A N/A *$939*

MODEL 70 TARGET (1972-1979 MFG.) – .308 Win. or .30-06 cal., 26 in. heavy barrel with counterbored muzzle, Marksman stock, black rubber buttpad with white spacer, contoured aluminum hand stop, long accessory channel, no sights, scope blocks. Mfg. 1972-1979.

Retail pricing was not available for this model.

MODEL 70 ULTRA MATCH – .308 Win. or .30-06 cal., 26 in. heavy barrel with counterbored muzzle, glass bedded action and breech end of barrel, externally adj. trigger, Marksman stock, black rubber buttpad with white spacer, contoured aluminum hand stop, long accessory channel, no sights, matte finish. Limited production by the Winchester Custom Shop on a special order only basis 1972-1979.

Retail values were not available for this model.

RIFLES: BOLT ACTION - POST 1964 MODEL 70 CUSTOM GRADES

MODEL 70 CUSTOM GRADE – various cals., old style Model 70 action, semi-fancy American walnut checkered stock, engine turned bolt and follower, hand honed internal parts. Mfg. 1988-89 only.

$2,200 $1,775 $1,375 $1,100 $925 $775 $650 *$1,172*

MODEL 70 XTR FEATHERWEIGHT ULTRA GRADE "1 OF 1,000" – .270 Win. cal., extensively engraved, finely checkered deluxe French walnut stock, with mahogany presentation case.

$3,975 $3,125 $2,375 N/A N/A N/A N/A *$5,000*

MODEL 70 CLASSIC CUSTOM GRADE – .264 Win. Mag. (new 1994), .270 Win., .30-06, 7mm Rem. Mag., .300 Win. Mag., .300 Wby. Mag. (new 1994) or .338 Win. Mag. cal., 24 or 26 in. barrel, similar to Model 70 Super Grade, but had to be special ordered through the Custom Gun Shop, and with many custom features including semi-fancy walnut with satin finish and hand-honed internal parts. Mfg. 1990-1994.

$2,650 $2,200 $1,650 $1,325 $1,150 $875 $775 *$1,757*

A Model 70 Collector Grade was also a variant of this model which was mfg. in the Custom Gun Shop - this model was priced on request only.

* ***Model 70 Classic Custom Grade Featherweight*** – .22-250 Rem. (new 1994), .223 Rem. (new 1994), .243 Win. (new 1994), .270 Win., .280 Rem., .30-06, .308 Win. (new 1994), 7mm-08 Rem. (new 1994) cal., 22 in. barrel, Featherweight features, controlled round feeding, higher grade wood. Mfg. 1992-1994.

$2,200 $1,975 $1,550 $1,225 $1,100 $875 $775 *$1,757*

* ***Model 70 Classic Custom Grade Sharpshooter I/II*** – .22-250 Rem. (new 1993), .223 Rem. (mfg. 1993-94), .30-06, .308 Win., or .300 Win. Mag. cal., specially designed McMillan A2 (disc. 1995) or H-S Precision heavy target stock, Schneider (disc. 1995) or H-S Precision (new 1996) 24 (.308 Win. cal. only) or 26 in. stainless steel barrel, choice of blue or grey finish starting 1996. Mfg. 1992-1998.

$2,150 $1,650 $1,150 $1,000 $925 $825 $750 *$1,994*

Subtract $100 if without stainless barrel (pre-1995).

This model was designated the Sharpshooter II in 1996 (features H-S Precision stock and stainless steel barrel).

This model was also available in left-hand action beginning 1998 (.30-06 and .300 Win. Mag. cals. only).

* ***Model 70 Classic Custom Grade Sporting Sharpshooter I/II*** – .270 Win. (disc. 1994), 7mm STW, or .300 Win. Mag. cal., 1/2-minute of angle sporting version of the Custom Sharpshooter, custom shop only, Sharpshooter II became standard in 1996. Mfg. 1993-98.

$2,075 $1,575 $1,100 $975 $900 $825 $750 *$1,875*

This model was also available in left-hand action in 1998.

* ***Model 70 Classic Custom Grade Sporting Sharpshooter*** – .220 Swift cal., 26 in. Schneider barrel, controlled round feeding, available with either McMillan A2 or Sporting synthetic (disc. 1994) stock. Mfg. 1994-95 only.

$2,150 $1,675 $1,325 $1,075 $925 $825 $725 *$1,814*

* ***Model 70 Classic Custom Grade Express*** – .300 Petersen (mfg. 1995 only), .375 H&H, .375 JRS (mfg. 1992-96), 7mm STW (mfg. 1993-94), .416 Rem. Mag., .458 Win. Mag., or .470 Capstick (disc. 1995) cal., 24 in. (22 in. on .458 Win. Mag.) barrel, claw controlled round feeding, deluxe walnut with satin finish and checkering, 3-leaf express (disc. 1995) or pre-64 style adj. rear sight (new 1996), high luster metal finish, bolt and follower are engine turned, available by special order through the custom gun shop only. Mfg. 1990-1998.

$3,025 $2,425 $1,975 $1,650 $1,325 $1,150 $1,000 *$2,512*

Subtract $200 for 7mm STW cal.

In 1994, the model nomenclature was changed from Model 70 Custom Grade Express, and in 1996 it was changed from Model 70 Classic Express.

GRADING - PPGS™	100%	98%	95%	90%	80%	70%	60%	LAST MSR

MODEL 70 CUSTOM ULTIMATE CLASSIC – .25-06 Rem., 6.5x55mm Swedish (new 2001), .270 Win., .280 Rem. (mfg. 1996, reintroduced 1999), .30-06, 7mm STW (disc. 2006), .264 Win. Mag. (disc. 2006), .270 Wby. Mag. (disc. 1996), .35 Whelen (new 1998), 7mm Rem. Mag., 7mm RUM, .300 Win. Mag., .300 Wby. Mag., .300 H&H (mfg. 1996-99), .300 RUM (new 2000), .338 Win. Mag., .338-06 (mfg. 1999-2001), .338 RUM (new 2001), .340 Wby. Mag. (mfg. 1998), .375 H&H (1995 only), .416 Rem. Mag. (1995 only), or .458 Win. Mag. (1995 only) cal., controlled round feeding, engine turned bolt, checkered fancy walnut stock, choice of 22 (.458 Win. Mag. only), 24 or 26 in. tapered round full-fluted, 1/2 round, 1/2 octagonal, or full octagonal tapered stainless barrel, one inch black decelerator recoil pad, choice of blue or stainless barreled action, 3 or 5 shot mag., includes bases/rings except on some Mag. cals., approx. 7 3/4 lbs., except for large disc. cals., included hard case. Mfg. 1995-2006.

$3,300 $3,025 $2,750 $2,425 $1,975 $1,650 $1,100 *$3,060*

Add $100 for stainless steel barrel, $110 for fluted round barrel, or $235 for full or half octagon barrel.
Add approx. 15% for .375 H&H and larger Mag. cals (disc. 1995).

This model was previously designated the Model 70 Ultimate Classic until 2000, and was changed to the Model 70 Custom Ultimate Classic.

Left-hand action (new 1997) was available in all recent cals.

MODEL 70 CLASSIC CUSTOM SHORT ACTION – .243 Win. (disc. 2000, reintroduced 2002 only), .257 Roberts, .260 Rem. (disc. 2006), .270 WSM (new 2002), .284 Win. (new 2006), .308 Win., .358 Win., .300 WSM (new 2001), .325 WSM (new 2005), 7mm-08 Rem., 7mm WSM (new 2002), or .450 Marlin (mfg. 2001-2004) cal., 22 (disc. 2002) or 24 (new 2003) in. match grade tapered stainless or chrome moly barrel with cut rifling, controlled round feed, no sights, deluxe high gloss checkered walnut stock and forend, one inch black decelerator recoil pad, satin matte blue finished action and barrel, 3-5 shot mag., approx. 7 1/2 lbs. Mfg. 2000-2006.

$2,925 $2,250 $1,825 $1,475 $1,250 $1,050 $875 *$2,866*

Left-hand action was available on this model.

MODEL 70 CLASSIC CUSTOM FEATHERWEIGHT – .223 WSSM (mfg. 2004), .243 WSSM (mfg. 2004), .25 WSSM (mfg. 2004), .243 Win. (new 2006), .25-06 Rem. (new 2006), .270 Win., .280 Rem. (new 2004), .284 Win. (new 2006), .30-06, .308 Win. (new 2006), 6.5x55mm Swedish (new 2006), or 7mm-08 Rem. (mfg. 2003) cal., 5 shot mag., Featherweight stock with Schnabel forend, match grade 22 in. barrel w/o sights, matte blue or stainless action/barrel, 7 1/4 lbs. Mfg. 2003-2006.

$2,925 $2,250 $1,825 $1,475 $1,250 $1,050 $875 *$2,866*

MODEL 70 CLASSIC CUSTOM CARBON – .25-06 Rem., .270 WSM, .300 WSM, .338 Win. Mag., or 7mm WSM cal., satin stainless action, 24 or 26 in. carbon fiber barrel with Shilen stainless barrel liner, controlled round feed, reinforced black composite stock, 6 1/2 - 7 lbs. Mfg. 2003-2004.

$3,350 $2,575 $2,000 $1,550 $1,275 $1,075 $900 *$3,233*

MODEL 70 CLASSIC CUSTOM EXTREME WEATHER – .25-06 Rem. (disc. 2001), .270 Win. (disc. 2000), .270 WSM (new 2004), .30-06, .300 Win. Mag., .300 RUM (new 2001), .300 WSM (new 2004), .308 Win. (new 2004), .325 WSM (new 2005), .338 Win. Mag., 7mm WSM (new 2004), 7mm Rem. Mag., or .375 H&H (new 2001) cal., controlled round feed, matte finished stainless action and match grade 22 lightweight (.375 H&H only), 24, or 26 in. fluted stainless barrel w/o sights, black McMillan fiberglass stock with cheekpiece and 1 in. Pachmayr Decelerator pad, 3 or 5 shot mag., available in either right or left-hand action, approx. 7 1/2 lbs. Mfg. 2000-2005.

$2,575 $2,100 $1,725 $1,525 $1,275 $1,050 $825 *$2,576*

MODEL 70 CUSTOM EXTREME LIGHTWEIGHT WEATHER II – various standard, WSM, and Mag. cals., 22, 24, or 26 in. fluted Krieger barrel w/o sights, black lightweight McMillan Hunter's Edge fiberglass stock with Pachmayr Decelerator recoil pad, 3 or 5 shot mag., matte finished stainless steel action/barrel, 6 1/4 - 7 lbs. Limited mfg. 2006 only.

$2,850 $2,225 $1,825 $1,550 $1,300 $1,075 $850 *$2,800*

This model was also available with left-hand action, except in WSM cals.

MODEL 70 CUSTOM STAINLESS LAMINATE – .270 WSM, .300 WSM, .325 WSM, or 7mm WSM cal., choice of brown or black/grey featherweight stock with Pachmayr Decelerator recoil pad, controlled round feed, 24 in. stainless sporter barrel w/o sights, engine turned bolt, 8 lbs. Limited mfg. 2006 only.

$2,375 $2,025 $1,600 $1,325 $1,150 $1,000 $800 *$2,332*

MODEL 70 CLASSIC CUSTOM MANNLICHER – .260 Rem., .308 Win., or 7mm-08 Rem. cal., 19 in. barrel w/o sights (sights optional), 4 shot internal mag., full-length checkered walnut stock, smooth tapered barrel and blue action, approx. 6 3/4 lbs. Mfg. 1999-2000.

$2,725 $2,175 $1,700 $1,400 $1,100 $925 $825 *$2,595*

This model was designated the Model 70 Custom Mannlicher until 2000.

GRADING - PPGS™	100%	98%	95%	90%	80%	70%	60%	LAST MSR

MODEL 70 CUSTOM MAPLE – .270 Win., .284 Win., .30-06, or .308 Win. cal., 24 in. sporter barrel w/o sights, gloss finished checkered hand-made fiddleback curly maple stock with black forend cap, custom shop pistol grip cap, right or left-hand blue or stainless steel action, 7 3/4 lbs. Limited mfg. 2006 only.

$4,500	$3,825	$3,325	$2,675	$2,150	$1,725	$1,450	*$4,355*

MODEL 70 CUSTOM CONTINENTAL HUNTER – .270 Win., .284 Win., .30-06, or .308 Win. cal., 22 in. Krieger stainless or blue sporter barrel w/o sights, gloss finished Claro walnut stock with round pistol grip and Schnabel forend, Niedner style steel buttplate, controlled round feed, right or left-hand action, 4 or 5 shot mag., 6 3/4 lbs. Limited mfg. 2006 only.

$5,400	$4,775	$4,225	$3,475	$2,875	$2,325	$1,775	*$5,226*

MODEL 70 CLASSIC CUSTOM SAFARI EXPRESS – .340 Wby. Mag. (disc. 1999), .358 STA (disc. 2000), .375 H&H, .375 RUM (new 2001), .404 Jeffery (mfg. 2004), .416 Rem. Mag., .416 Rigby (mfg. 2001), .458 Win. Mag., .458 Lott, or .470 Capstick (new 2002) cal., honed internal parts, engine turned bolt and follower, adj. Dietrich Apel Express rear and front sights, deluxe checkered walnut stock and forend, 22 (.458 Win. Mag. & .458 Lott) or 24 in. barrel with sling stud, 3 shot mag., approx. 9 1/4 lbs. Mfg. 1999-2006.

$3,350	$2,625	$1,950	$1,525	$1,125	$975	$850	*$3,252*

Add $490 for .416 Rigby cal. (mfg. 2001 only).

Beginning in 2000, this model was available in left-hand action in all cals. except .470 Capstick.

This model was designated the Model 70 Custom Safari Express until 2000.

MODEL 70 WSM CUSTOM NORTH AMERICAN BIG GAME SERIES – .270 WSM, .300 WSM, or 7mm WSM cal., controlled round feed, checkered XXX American walnut stock with Schnabel forend, Pachmayr Decelerator recoil pad, engraved receiver, trigger guard, and floorplate, high lustre bluing. Only 125 of each edition (Whitetail Deer - .270 WSM, Elk - .300 WSM, and Antelope - 7mm WSM) mfg. 2004-2005 with matching serial numbers.

$3,175	$2,600	$1,950	$1,500	$1,125	$975	$850	*$3,030*

This model was sold in sets only (all 3 calibers.)

MODEL 70 CLASSIC CUSTOM AFRICAN EXPRESS – .340 Wby. Mag. (disc. 1999), .358 STA (disc. 2000), .375 H&H, .416 Rem. Mag., .416 Rigby (mfg. 2001 only), .458 Win. Mag., .458 Lott, or .470 Capstick (mfg. 2001 only) cal., drop down floorplate, increasing mag. capacity to 4, checkered fancy English walnut stock with black Pachmayr Decelerator pad and ebony pistol grip and forend caps, adj. Dietrich Apel Express rear and front sights, 22 (.458 Win. Mag. only) or 24 in. barrel with sling stud, approx. 9 1/2 lbs. Mfg. 1999-2006.

$5,025	$4,075	$3,475	$2,775	$2,175	$1,675	$1,450	*$4,867*

Add $437 for .416 Rigby cal. (disc. 2001).

Beginning in 2000, this model was available in left-hand action in all cals. except .458.

This model was designated the Model 70 Custom African Express until 2000.

MODEL 70 CLASSIC CUSTOM TAKE-DOWN – .300 RUM, .300 Win. Mag. (new 2002), .375 H&H, .416 Rem. Mag., or 7mm Rem. Mag. cal., all stainless construction with blue Teflon finish, takedown receiver/barrel assembly, brown synthetic stock and forearm, .75 MOA guaranteed for takedown action assembly/reassembly, 24 (.375 H&H or .416 Rem. Mag. cal. only) or 26 (fluted only) in. barrel, 3 shot internal mag., 8 1/2-9 lbs. Limited mfg. 2001-2006.

$3,825	$3,250	$2,800	$2,375	$1,975	$1,700	$1,375	

While advertised beginning in 1998 with a MSR of $2,495, this model was finally produced during 2001.
This model was only available from the Bass Pro Shops.

MODEL 70 ULTRA GRADE – .270 Win. cal., gold line engraved, includes wood display case, 500 mfg.

$3,300	$2,750	$2,200	$1,975	$1,650	$1,325	$1,100	*$5,000*

MODEL 70 CUSTOM 100TH ANNIVERSARY .30-06 – 30-06 cal., 22 in. blue sporter barrel with "100th Anniversary Custom 1 of 100" engraved in gold, 5 shot mag., semi-fancy checkered American walnut stock with recoil pad, single steel crossbolt, controlled round feed action, gold and nickel engraved floorplate with WWI Allied soldiers and sport hunter with whitetail deer, 7 1/4 lbs. 100 mfg. 2006 only.

$2,750	$2,150	$1,825	N/A	N/A	N/A	N/A	*$2,660*

MODEL 70 CUSTOM SPECIAL "70 YEARS OF THE MODEL 70" – .270 Win., .30-06, or .300 Win. Mag. cal., 24 or 26 (.300 Win. Mag. only) in. blue barrel with "One of Seventy" engraved in gold, semi-fancy checkered walnut stock with inletted sling swivel bases, controlled round feed action, each caliber has special engraved floorplate, 7 1/2-7 3/4 lbs. 70 of each caliber mfg. 2006 only.

$2,650	$2,100	$1,725	N/A	N/A	N/A	N/A	*$2,547*

GRADING - PPGS™	100%	98%	95%	90%	80%	70%	60%	LAST MSR

MODEL 70 COLLECTOR GRADE – various cals., this variation was a special order through the Winchester Custom Shop and values will vary per individual gun.

MODEL 70 CUSTOM BUILT – various cals., this variation was a special order through the Winchester Custom Shop and values will vary per individual gun.

MODEL 70 EXHIBITION GRADE – various cals., fancy checkered American walnut stock with hardwood forend tip. Mfg. 1988-89 only.

	100%	98%	95%	90%	80%	70%	60%	LAST MSR
	$2,250	$1,775	$1,175	N/A	N/A	N/A	N/A	*$2,192*

RIFLES: BOLT ACTION - MODEL 70, 2007-CURRENT MFG.

In late 2007, Olin announced that its famous Winchester Model 70 would be reintroduced with a new MOA trigger system, and manufactured by FN Manufacturing located in Columbia, SC. Winchester continues to introduce more variations of the new Model 70.

MODEL 70 ALASKAN – .30-06, .300 Win. Mag., .338 Win. Mag., or .375 H&H cal., 25 in. barrel with folding adj. rear sight and hooded gold bead front sight, satin finished Monte Carlo walnut stock and forearm with cut checkering, MOA trigger system, Pachmayr Decelerator recoil pad, Pre-64 style controlled round feed with claw extractor, 8-1/2 lbs. New 2012.

	100%	98%	95%	90%	80%	70%	60%	LAST MSR
MSR $1,440	$1,225	$1,075	$920	$830	$675	$550	$480	

Add $40 for .375 H&H Mag. cal.

This model in .375 H&H cal. was featured as a 2012 SHOT Show Special.

MODEL 70 COYOTE LIGHT – .22-250 Rem., .243 Win., .308 Win., .270 WSM, .300 WSM, or .325 WSM cal., 22 (disc. 2010) or 24 in. heavy stainless fluted free floating barrel, 3 or 5 shot mag., charcoal gray textured lightweight carbon fiber/fiberglass Bell & Carlson composite stock with diagonally vented forend, matte blue receiver, Pachmayr Decelerator recoil pad, 7 1/2 lbs. Mfg. 2009-disc.

	100%	98%	95%	90%	80%	70%	60%	LAST MSR
	$1,175	$925	$800	$650	$550	$475	$450	*$1,270*

Add $40 for WSM cals.

MODEL 70 COYOTE LIGHT, BLUED – .223 Rem., .270 WSM, .300 WSM, 7mm WSM, .223 WSSM, .243 WSSM, .25 WSSM, .204 Ruger, or .325 WSM cal., 24 in. medium heavy 24 in. fluted stainless steel barrel, 3 or 6 shot mag., hinged floorplate, matte blued receiver, carbon fiber/fiberglass composite Bell and Carlson stock with flow-through vents on the forend, Pachmayr Decelerator pad, skeletonized aluminum bedding block, 7 lbs. 8 oz. Disc.

	100%	98%	95%	90%	80%	70%	60%	LAST MSR
	$775	$675	$575	$525	$450	$350	$275	*$839*

Add $29 for WSM cals. or $50 for WSSM cals.

MODEL 70 COYOTE LIGHT SR – .22-250 Rem., .243 Win., 6.5 Creedmoor (new 2019), .308 Win., .270 WSM, .300 WSM, or .325 WSM cal., 24 in. free floating fluted stainless steel barrel, recessed target crown, threaded muzzle, blade-type ejector, Pre-64 style controlled round feed with claw extractor, MOA Trigger System, Bell and Carlson synthetic stock with charcoal gray textured finish and multiple forend vents, Pachmayr Decelerator recoil pad, dual front sling swivel studs, 3-pos. safety, one-piece aluminum bedding block, forged steel receiver, matte finished metal surfaces, 7 lbs. 8 oz. Disc. 2020.

	100%	98%	95%	90%	80%	70%	60%	LAST MSR
	$1,175	$925	$800	$650	$550	$475	$450	*$1,270*

Add $40 for WSM cals.

MODEL 70 COYOTE LIGHT STAINLESS – .223 Rem., .243 Win., .308 Win., .300 WSM, .270 WSM, 7mm WSM, .223 WSSM, .243 WSSM, .25 WSSM, .204 Ruger, .325 WSM, or .22-250 Rem. cal., 24 in. medium heavy fluted stainless steel barrel, carbon fiber/fiberglass composite Bell and Carlson stock with flow-through vents on the forend, Pachmayr Decelerator pad, skeletonized aluminum bedding block, 7 lbs. 8 oz. Disc.

	100%	98%	95%	90%	80%	70%	60%	LAST MSR
	$825	$725	$600	$550	$450	$375	$325	*$881*

Add $29 for WSM cals. or $49 for WSSM cals.

MODEL 70 EXTREME TRUE TIMBER VSX MB – .243 Win., 6.5 Creedmoor, 7mm-08 Rem., .308 Win., 6.5 PRC, 6.8 Western, .270 WSM, .300 WSM, .25-05 Rem., .270 Win., .30-06 Springfield, .265 Win. Mag., 7mm Rem. Mag., or .300 Win. Mag. cal., Pre-64 action, 22, 24, or 26 in. free floating barrel in Tungsten Cerakote finish, muzzle brake, 3 or 5 shot mag., hinged floorplate, controlled ejection, M.O.A. trigger system, TrueTimber VSX Bell and Carlson synthetic stock, sculpted cheekpiece, 3-pos. safety, controlled round feed, Pachmayr Decelerator recoil pad, knurled bolt handle, sling swivel studs, 6 lbs. 12 oz. New 2021.

	100%	98%	95%	90%	80%	70%	60%	LAST MSR
MSR $1,650	$1,400	$1,225	$1,050	$950	$775	$630	$550	

Add $40 for 6.5 Creedmoor, 6.5 PRC, 6.8 Western, WSM, and Mag. cals.

GRADING - PPGS™	100%	98%	95%	90%	80%	70%	60%	LAST MSR

MODEL 70 EXTREME WEATHER MB – .243 Win., 6.5 Creedmoor, 7mm-08 Rem., .308 Win., 6.5 PRC, .270 WSM, .300 WSM, .25-06 Rem., .270 Win., .30-06, .264 Win. Mag., 7mm Rem. Mag., .300 Win. Mag., or 6.8 Western cal., 22, 24, or 26 in. free floating fluted stainless steel sporter barrel, threaded with muzzle brake, recessed target crown, 3 shot mag., forged steel receiver, Pre-64 style controlled round feed with claw extractor, blade-type ejector, MOA trigger system, Bell and Carlson black synthetic stock with sculpted cheekpiece and gray web finish, Pachmayr Decelerator recoil pad, 3-pos. safety, 7 lbs. New 2021.

MSR $1,600	$1,375	$1,195	$1,020	$925	$750	$625	$530	

Add $40 for 6.8 Western, 6.5 PRC, Mag., or WSM cals.

MODEL 70 EXTREME WEATHER SS – .243 Win., 6.5 Creedmoor (new 2019), 7mm-08 Rem., .308 Win., .270 WSM, .300 WSM, .325 WSM, .25-06, .270 Win., .30-06, .264 Win. Mag. (new 2014), 7mm Rem. Mag., .300 Win. Mag., or .338 Win. Mag. cal., 3 or 5 shot mag., stainless steel action, 22, 24, or 26 in. free floating, stainless steel fluted barrel, charcoal gray textured Bell & Carlson synthetic stock with alloy skeletal bedding block and cheekpiece, MOA trigger system, one-piece trigger guard and mag. frame, no sights, 6 3/4-7 1/4 lbs. New 2008.

MSR $1,340	$1,200	$900	$750	$600	$525	$475	$425	

Add $40 for standard Mag. or WSM cals.

During the first year of manufacture (2008), this model featured an engraved custom one-piece floorplate marked "2008 Model 70 Limited Edition".

MODEL 70 FEATHERWEIGHT (DELUXE) – .22-250 Rem., .243 Win., 6.5 Creedmoor (new 2019), .264 Win. Mag., .270 Win., .300 Win. Mag., .308 Win., .30-06, .25-06 Rem., 7mm-08 Rem., .270 WSM, .300 WSM, .325 WSM, 6.8 Western (new 2021), or 6.5 PRC (new 2021) cal., pre-64 style controlled round feeding, new MOA trigger system adj. from 3-5 lbs., blade type ejector, 3 or 5 shot mag., 22 or 24 in. hammer forged blue barrel w/o sights, one-piece trigger guard and hinged mag. floorplate, high polish bluing, satin finished Grade II fleur-de-lis checkered walnut stock with Schnabel forend, jeweled bolt, knurled bolt handle, 3-position safety, Pachmayr Decelerator recoil pad, 6 3/4-7 1/4 lbs. New 2008.

MSR $1,050	$1,000	$840	$675	$600	$500	$425	$350	

Add $40 for 6.8 Western (new 2021), 6.5 PRC (new 2021), standard Mag., or WSM cals.

During the first year of manufacture (2008), this model featured an engraved custom one-piece floorplate marked "2008 Model 70 Limited Edition".

* ***Model 70 Featherweight Compact*** – .22-250 Rem. (disc. 2020), .243 Win. (disc. 2020), 6.5 Creedmoor (new 2019), .308 Win., 7mm-08 Rem., 6.8 Western (new 2021), or 6.5 PRC (new 2021) cal., similar to Model 70 Featherweight except has 20 in. barrel and 13 in. LOP, 6 1/2 lbs. New 2011.

MSR $1,050	$1,000	$840	$675	$600	$500	$425	$350	

Add $40 for 6.8 Western (new 2021) or 6.5 PRC (new 2021) cal.

MODEL 70 JACK O'CONNOR TRIBUTE – .270 Win. cal., pre-64 action with controlled feed and ejection, 22 in. barrel, blue finish, jeweled bolt body and engraved handle, drilled and tapped, 5 shot mag., finely checkered French AA walnut stock and forearm with Shadowline cheekpiece, alloy floorplate with ram's head engraving, Pachmayr Decelerator pad, Jack O'Connor gold signature on trigger guard, engraved steel grip cap, three position safety, Hex guard screws, 7 lbs. 8 oz. Limited mfg. mid-2013-2014.

	$1,875	$1,650	$1,400	$1,275	$1,025	$850	$650	*$2,000*

This model was featured as a 2012 SHOT Show Special with the following variations, free-floating barrel, ebony forearm tip, Jack O'Connor signature in nickel on trigger guard, included voucher to purchase an embroidered custom case from the Jack O'Connor Center.

* ***Model 70 Jack O'Connor Custom Tribute*** – .270 Win. cal., similar to Model 70 Jack O'Connor Tribute, except features French AAA walnut stock and forearm, 7 lbs. 8 oz. Limited mfg. mid-2013-2014.

	$2,525	$2,200	$1,900	$1,725	$1,400	$1,150	$875	*$2,600*

This model was featured as a 2012 SHOT Show Special with the following variations: M.O.A. Trigger System, ebony forearm tip, Jack O'Connor signature in nickel on trigger guard, included voucher for free custom embroidered case that was redeemable through the Jack O'Connor Center.

MODEL 70 LONG RANGE MB – .22-250 Rem., .243 Win., 6.5 Creedmoor, .308 Win., 6.5 PRC, .270 WSM, .300 WSM, or 6.8 Western cal., 24 in. free floating fluted blued steel barrel, threaded with muzzle brake, recessed target crown, 5 shot mag., hinged floorplate, forged steel receiver, Pre-64 style controlled round feed with claw extractor, blade type ejector, MOA trigger system, Bell and Carlson tan synthetic stock with flow-through forend vents and black web finish, Pachmayr Decelerator recoil pad, molded checkering, 3-pos. safety, drilled and tapped, matte blued finish, 7 lbs. 8 oz. New 2021.

MSR $1,050	$1,000	$840	$675	$600	$500	$425	$350	

Add $40 for 6.8 Western, 6.5 PRC, and WSM cals.

GRADING - PPGS™	100%	98%	95%	90%	80%	70%	60%	LAST MSR

MODEL 70 SAFARI EXPRESS – .375 H&H, .416 Rem. Mag., or .458 Win. Mag. cal., 24 in. blue barrel with hooded blade front sight, express rear barrel sight, 3 shot mag., pre-'64 type claw extractor, dual recoil lugs, reinforced crossbolts, checkered satin finished walnut stock with cheekpiece, one-piece steel trigger guard, flush mount hinged magazine floorplate, barrel band front swivel base, Pachmayr Decelerator recoil pad, 9 lbs. New 2010.

MSR $1,610	$1,375	$1,195	$1,020	$925	$750	$625	$530	

MODEL 70 SPORTER (DELUXE) – .25-06 Rem., .270 Win., .30-06, .264 Win. Mag., 7mm Rem. Mag., .300 Win. Mag., .338 Win. Mag., .300 WSM, .270 WSM, or .325 WSM cal., 3 or 5 shot mag., 24 or 26 in. barrel w/o sights, satin finished Grade I walnut stock with cheekpiece and cut checkering, Pachmayr Decelerator recoil pad, 3-position safety, MOA trigger, Pre-64 style round feed with claw extractor, sling swivel studs, high polish blued receiver/barrel, 7 1/4-7 3/4 lbs. Mfg. 2008-2019.

MSR $1,010	$975	$825	$700	$575	$500	$425	$350	

Add $40 for standard Mag./WSM cals.

During the first year of manufacture (2008), this model featured an engraved custom one-piece floorplate marked "2008 Model 70 Limited Edition".

MODEL 70 SUPER GRADE – .243 Win. (new 2020), 6.5 Creedmoor (new 2019), 7mm-08 Rem. (new 2020), .308 Win. (new 2020), .270 WSM (new 2009), .300 WSM (new 2009), .270 Win. (new 2009), .30-06, .264 Win. Mag. (new 2020), .280 Rem. (new 2020), 7mm Rem. Mag. (new 2012), .300 Win. Mag., .338 Win. Mag. (new 2010), or 6.8 Western (new 2021) cal., 22 (new 2020), 24, or 26 in. free floating barrel, recessed target crown, 3 or 5 shot mag., pre-64 style round feed with claw extractor, blade type ejector, MOA trigger system, no sights, Grade IV/V full fancy walnut stock with shadowline cheekpiece, inletted swivel studs, Pachmayr Decelerator recoil pad, 3-pos. safety, one-piece steel floorplate marked "Super Grade", engraved steel crossbolt, forged steel receiver with integral recoil lug, highly polished metal surfaces, 8-8 1/2 lbs. New 2008.

MSR $1,490	$1,275	$1,115	$955	$865	$700	$575	$495	

Add $40 for standard Mag. and WSM cals.

During the first year of manufacture (2008), this model featured an engraved custom one-piece floorplate marked "2008 Model 70 Limited Edition".

MODEL 70 75TH ANNIVERSARY SUPER GRADE – .30-06 cal., 24 in. barrel w/o sights, features Grade IV/V fancy walnut stock with cut checkering and shadowline cheekpiece, floorplate features "75th Anniversary Model 70" with scroll engraving, right side of upper receiver has engraved banner "The Rifleman's Rifle", engraved steel grip cap, 8-1/4 lbs. Mfg. 2012 only.

	$1,950	$1,750	$1,550	$1,325	$1,100	$975	$825	*$2,000*

MODEL 70 SUPER GRADE 150TH COMMEMORATIVE – .270 Win. cal., 24 in. round barrel with gold band at muzzle, "The American Legend 1866-2016" marked in gold on barrel, High Grade V/VI American black walnut stock with cut fleur-de-lis checkering and deluxe shadowline cheekpiece, Pachmayr Decelerator pad, black forend tip and recessed steel sling swivel studs, jeweled bolt, deep relief scroll engraving with gold embellishments on the highly polished blued receiver, barrel, trigger guard, floorplate, and grip cap including the Winchester 150th Anniversary logo and the WRA scroll trademark, steel trigger guard and one-piece bottom metal, three-position safety, 8 1/4 lbs. Limited mfg. 2016 only.

	$2,025	$1,875	$1,700	$1,550	$1,375	$1,200	$1,100	*$2,070*

MODEL 70 ULTIMATE SHADOW – various cals., 3 or 5 shot mag., 22, 24, or 26 in. blue barrel, black pistol grip composite stock with oval dot gripping surfaces, controlled round feed action, hinged mag. floorplate, external claw extractor, Winsorb recoil pad, no sights, MOA trigger system, approx. 6 1/2-7 lbs. Mfg. 2009-2015.

	$750	$675	$600	$500	$450	$400	$375	*$800*

Add $40 for Mag. cals.

* ***Model 70 Ultimate Shadow SS*** – various cals., similar to Model 70 Ultimate Shadow, except has matte stainless steel action and barrel, 6-3/4-7/14 lbs. Mfg. 2012-2015.

	$925	$800	$700	$600	$525	$425	$375	*$990*

Add $40 for Mag. cals.

MODEL 70 ULTIMATE SHADOW HUNTER – various standard and Mag. cals., Pre-64 style controlled round feed with claw extractor, 3 or 5 shot mag., 22, 24, or 26 in.Sporter free floating barrel, lightweight synthetic Mossy Oak Break-Up Infinity (disc. 2014), or Mossy Oak Break-Up Country (new 2015) camo finish, gray overmolded rubberized gripping surfaces, satin blued metal finish, three position safety, recessed target crown, MOA trigger system, blade type ejector, Winsorb technology recoil pad, no sights, approx. 6 3/4-7 1/4 lbs. Mfg. 2013-2015.

	$825	$750	$650	$575	$500	$450	$400	*$870*

Add $50 for Mag. cals.

GRADING - PPGS™	100%	98%	95%	90%	80%	70%	60%	LAST MSR

* ***Model 70 Ultimate Shadow Hunter SS*** – various cals., similar to Model 70 Ultimate Shadow Hunter, except has matte stainless steel action and barrel, 6-3/4-7/14 lbs. Mfg. 2013-2015.

	$1,025	$900	$800	$675	$575	$500	$425	*$1,100*

Add $40 for Mag. cals.

RIFLES: BOLT ACTION, MISC., 2015-CURRENT MFG.

In 2015, after 50 years, Winchester released its new XPR bolt action rifle.

XPR – .223 Rem. (new 2021), .243 Win. (new 2016), 6.5 Creedmoor (new 2018), .270 Win., .350 Legend (new 2019), .30-06, .300 Win. Mag., 7mm-08 Rem. (new 2016), .308 Win. (new 2016), .338 Win. Mag., .270 WSM (new 2016), .300 WSM (new 2016), .325 WSM (mfg. 2016-2020), 7mm Rem. Mag. (new 2016), 6.5 PRC (new 2021), or 6.8 Western (new 2021) cal., free floating 22 (new 2016), 24, or 26 in. barrel w/o sights and recessed target crown, 3 shot detachable box mag., steel receiver, controlled round feed and claw extractor with blade-type ejector, MOA trigger system with stainless steel components, black polymer stock with textured panels and Inflex Technology recoil pad, 3-position safety on back of bolt, bolt unlock button, nickel Teflon coated bolt body, matte black finish, 6 3/4-7 1/4 lbs. New 2015.

MSR $550	$525	$450	$400	$375	$350	$325	$300

XPR COMPACT – .223 Rem. (new 2021), .243 Win., 6.5 Creedmoor (new 2018), 7mm-08 Rem., .308 Win., .350 Legend (new 2019), .270 WSM, .300 WSM, .325 WSM (disc. 2020), or 6.5 PRC (new 2021) cal., 20 or 22 in. barrel, 3 shot detachable box mag., MOA trigger system, black polymer stock, 13 in. LOP, Inflex Technology recoil pad, two-position thumb safety, Perma-Cote matte gray metal surfaces, nickel Teflon bolt body, 6 1/2-6 3/4 lbs. New 2017.

MSR $550	$525	$450	$400	$375	$350	$325	$300

XPR HUNTER CAMO – .223 Rem. (new 2021), .243 Win., 6.5 Creedmoor (new 2018), .270 Win., .30-06, .300 Win. Mag., 7mm-08 Rem., .308 Win., .350 Legend (new 2019), .338 Win. Mag., .270 WSM, .300 WSM, .325 WSM (disc. 2020), 7mm Rem. Mag., or 6.5 PRC (new 2021) cal., free floating 22, 24, or 26 in. barrel w/o sights and recessed target crown, 3 shot detachable box mag., steel receiver, controlled round feed and claw extractor with blade-type ejector, MOA trigger system with stainless steel components, 2-position thumb safety with cocking indicator, bolt unlock button and nickel Teflon coated bolt body, Mossy Oak Break-Up Country or Mountain Country Range (mfg. 2017 only) polymer stock with textured panels and Inflex Technology recoil pad, 6 3/4-7 1/4 lbs. New 2016.

MSR $630	$590	$500	$425	$400	$350	$325	$300

XPR HUNTER COMPACT MOSSY OAK BREAK-UP COUNTRY – .223 Rem. (new 2021), .243 Win., 6.5 Creedmoor (new 2018), 7mm-08 Rem., .308 Win., .350 Legend (new 2019), .270 WSM, .300 WSM, .325 WSM (disc. 2020), or 6.5 PRC (new 2021) cal., 20 or 22 in. barrel, 3 shot detachable box mag., MOA trigger system, Mossy Oak Break-Up Country camo stock, 13 in. LOP, Inflex Technology recoil pad, 2-position thumb safety, Perma-Cote matte gray metal surfaces, nickel Teflon bolt body, 6 1/2-7 lbs. New 2017.

MSR $630	$590	$500	$425	$400	$350	$325	$300

XPR HUNTER HIGHLANDER – .243 Win., 6.5 Creedmoor, 7mm-08 Rem., .308 Win., .350 Legend, .270 WSM, .300 WSM, .325 WSM, .270 Win., .30-06, 7mm Rem. Mag., .300 Win. Mag., or .338 Win. Mag. cal., 22, 24, or 26 in. button rifled free floated steel barrel, recessed target crown, 3 shot detachable box mag., MOA trigger system, advanced polymer stock in Kryptek Highlander Camo finish with textured panels, Inflex recoil pad, two-position thumb safety and cocking indicator, receiver is machined from solid steel bar stock, bolt unlock button, nickel Teflon bolt body, steel recoil lug, Perma-Cote FDE finish on barrel, receiver, and bolt handle, 6 3/4-7 1/4 lbs. Mfg. 2019-2020.

	$575	$500	$425	$400	$350	$325	$300	*$600*

XPR HUNTER TRUE TIMBER STRATA – .223 Rem. (new 2021), .243 Win., 6.5 Creedmoor, 7mm-08 Rem., .308 Win., .350 Legend, .270 WSM, .300 WSM, .325 WSM (disc. 2020), .270 Win., .30-06, 7mm Rem. Mag., .300 Win. Mag., .338 Win. Mag., 6.5 PRC (new 2021), or 6.8 Western (new 2021) cal., 22, 24, or 26 in. button rifled free floated steel barrel, recessed target crown, 3 shot detachable box mag., MOA trigger system, advanced polymer stock in TrueTimber Strata finish with textured panels, Inflex recoil pad, two-position thumb safety and cocking indicator, receiver is machined from solid steel bar stock, bolt unlock button, nickel Teflon bolt body, steel recoil lug, Perma-Cote FDE finish on barrel, receiver, and bolt handle, 6 3/4-7 1/4 lbs. New 2019.

MSR $630	$590	$500	$425	$400	$350	$325	$300

XPR RENEGADE LONG RANGE SR – .243 Win., 6.5 Creedmoor, 7mm-08 Rem., .308 Win., .270 WSM, .300 WSM, 6.5 PRC (new 2021), or 6.8 Western (new 2021) cal., 22 or 24 in. button rifled free floated steel barrel, threaded muzzle, recessed target crown, 3 shot detachable box mag., MOA Trigger System, advanced Grayboe Renegade long range stock, Inflex Technology recoil pad, two 1/4 in. LOP spacers, two position thumb safety, enlarged bolt knob, nickel Teflon on bolt body, Perma-Cote matte black finish on barrel, receiver, and bolt handle, 8.5-8.75 lbs. New 2020.

MSR $1,100	$1,015	$875	$750	$675	$525	$450	$365

GRADING - PPGS™	100%	98%	95%	90%	80%	70%	60%	LAST MSR

XPR SPORTER – .223 Rem. (new 2021), .243 Win., 6.5 Creedmoor, 7mm-08 Rem., .308 Win., .350 Legend (new 2019), .270 WSM, .300 WSM, .325 WSM (disc. 2020), .270 Win., .30-06, 7mm Rem. Mag., .300 Win. Mag., .338 Win. Mag., 6.5 PRC (new 2021), or 6.8 Western (new 2021) cal., 22, 24, or 26 in. button rifled, free floated steel barrel, recessed target crown, 3 shot detachable box mag., MOA trigger system, Grade I walnut stock with checkering on the pistol grip and forend, Inflex Technology recoil pad, two-position thumb safety, bolt unlock button, steel recoil lug, solid steel receiver, cocking indicator, nickel Teflon bolt body, Perma-Cote matte black finish on metal surfaces, 6 3/4-7 1/4 lbs. New 2018.

MSR $630	$590	$500	$425	$400	$350	$325	$300	

XPR STEALTH SR (SUPPRESSOR READY) – .223 Rem., .243 Win., 6.5 Creedmoor, 7mm-08 Rem., .308 Win., .350 Legend, 6.5 PRC, .270 WSM, .300 WSM, or 6.8 Western cal., 16 1/2 in. button rifled free floating steel barrel, threaded muzzle with knurled thread protector, recessed target crown, 3, 4, or 5 shot detachable box mag., nickel Teflon coating on bolt body, MOA trigger system, green composite sporter stock, Inflex Technology recoil pad, two-pos. thumb safety, Talley Picatinny pattern scope mounting rail, Perma Cote matte black finish, 6.5 lbs. New 2021.

MSR $670	$615	$515	$425	$400	$350	$325	$300	

GRADING EXPLANATION FOR WINCHESTER LEVER ACTIONS

A combination of grading systems is being used exclusively for Winchester Models 1873 and 1876 in this section to assist the reader in ascertaining the value of a particular specimen more accurately. They work as follows - the top pricing line contains three value ranges (Above Average, Average, or Below Average) which have been created to encompass most of the specimens commonly encountered within these models.

Since there is a drastic value difference between 95%-50% bright blue and 30% dull patina/fading finish on older Winchesters, a traditional grading/value line has been included to give you examples of values from 100% down to 10% providing you a better perspective of the top end of the marketplace.

The three value groupings include "Below Average," "Average," and "Above Average" condition factors. These value ranges indicate the following conditions:

BELOW AVERAGE VALUE RANGE - a specimen with no finish remaining, perhaps some parts have been replaced, deteriorated metal may be lightly pitted with faint barrel/frame markings, rounded edges of wood and metal, wood showing much wear with possible repairs or cracks, must be in working order.

AVERAGE VALUE RANGE - a specimen with all original parts, exhibits gun metal patina finish, metal mostly smooth (perhaps lightly pitted), principal lettering and markings legible throughout, wood showing honest wear with little finish remaining (may have small cracks and other imperfections), good working order.

ABOVE AVERAGE VALUE RANGE - a specimen featuring unpolished brass (on Henrys and Model 1866s) or plum brown patina with traces of bluing in protected areas (on all steel frame models), sharp corners, crisp barrel markings, traces of original finish remaining, metal should exhibit nice patina or older flaking finish, wood should have some original stock varnish remaining and minor handling marks and dings, good bore, perfect working order with no replacement parts.

VALUES FOR 10%-100% CONDITION FACTORS - this includes the entire range of condition factors from 10% - 100% in many cases. N/As indicate that the condition factor is so infrequently encountered, it does not have a value. Normally, below average value ranges will approximately correspond to the 0%-10% pricing line values, average value range represents 10%-20%, and above average can range from 20%-40%, depending on the model. Typically, over 50% refers to a rifle which exhibits over 30% bright bluing/case colors or unpolished brass on the frame.

See PPGS for percentage grading examples.

RIFLES: LEVER ACTIONS - 1860-1964

Values by percentages are not listed on the Models Henry and 1866, as original condition over 30% is seldom encountered.

Volcanic pistols and carbines may be found under the Volcanic listing.

For the following lever action rifles, multiple special order features that add value are not cumulative (i.e., do not add 30% for an octagon barrel to the premium for a Deluxe rifle). Also, as a general rule, premiums for calibers, options, and special order features become less important on the following lever action models in under 90% original condition (i.e., do not add a 50% premium for .44-40 WCF on a Model 1892 rifle if original condition is under 90%).

Subtract 40%-60% on the following models if metal is pitted or poorly refinished (i.e., rounded edges on metal because of over buffing, and/or wood has been excessively sanded). Note: even well-done refinishing of metal or wood refinishing will reduce values for most collectors.

GRADING - PPGS™	Above Average	Average	Below Average

HENRY RIFLE – .44 Henry Flat (rimfire) cal., 15 shot, 24 in. barrel with integral slotted tube mag. and loading lever, blue barrel, brass or iron frame. Approx. 13,000 total production, mfg. 1860-1866.

Because almost all Henrys have little or no original finish remaining, values are in ranges rather than listed by separate condition factors.

* ***Henry Rifle Iron Frame Model*** – frame made of iron, round type buttplate, without lever latch, adj. sporting type rear leaf sight, serial numbers are in three digits only. Total production is believed to be less than 300.

	$75,000 - $120,000	$50,000 - $75,000	$25,000 - $35,000

* ***Henry Rifle First Model*** – approx. 5,000 mfg., generally serialized below 5,000, with or without lever latch, perch belly stock and slotted receiver for rear sight.

	$50,000 - $75,000	$25,000 - $40,000	$15,000 - $25,000

* ***Henry Rifle Martial Marked*** – contracted by U.S. military for Civil War use, denoted by "C.G.C." inspector markings on upper barrel breech and stock, approx. 1,900 with serialization scattered. All First Model Martials were in the 3000 S/N range.

	$45,000 - $75,000	$25,000 - $45,000	$13,000 - $25,000

This rifle was the most revolutionary shoulder weapon introduced in the Civil War.

* ***Henry Rifle Late Model*** – similar to first model, except buttplate heel has pointed profile, lever latch became standard and receiver is not slotted for rear sight, serial numbers over approx. 5,000, most commonly encountered Henry with approx. 8,000 mfg.

	$25,000 - $50,000	$18,000 - $25,000	$12,000 - $18,000

MODEL 1866 – .44 rimfire or centerfire, 24 in. barrel, blue barrel with brass frame, differs from Henry in that it has a wood forearm, frame cartridge loading port, and separate tube mag. Total production reached 170,101 for all models, mfg. 1866-98.

Because almost all Model 1866s have little or no original finish remaining, values are in ranges rather than listed by separate condition factors.

* ***Model 1866 First Model Rifle*** – "Improved Henry" action, .44 cal. rimfire, without forend cap, serialization is concealed on lower tang inside buttstock, serial range is from mid-12,000 to mid-15,000 (in Henry serial range sequence) Very Rare.

	$50,000 - $75,000	$35,000 - $50,000	$18,000 - $35,000

Buyer beware - watch for fakes!

* ***Model 1866 Carbine First Model*** – same action as Rifle, only with 20 in. barrel, 2 barrel bands and saddle ring.

	$25,000 - $40,000	$10,000 - $25,000	$4,000 - $10,000

* ***Model 1866 Rifle Second Model*** – "New Model" with redesigned frame, with Henry barrel markings, serial number inside on the earlier guns after ser. no. 19,000, outside lower tang beneath lever (approx. after ser. no. 20,000).

	$25,000 - $35,000	$15,500 - $75,000	$7,500 - $15,000

* ***Model 1866 Carbine Second Model*** – frame and other changes similar to Second Model Rifle.

	$18,000 - $25,000	$9,000 - $17,000	$3,000 - $9,000

* ***Model 1866 Rifle Third Model*** – block style serial numbers usually located behind trigger, improved frame. Serial numbered approx. 25,000-149,000.

	$17,000 - $23,000	$9,000 - $16,000	$3,000 - $8,000

* ***Model 1866 Carbine Third Model*** – same changes as Model 1866 Third Model Rifle, 20 in. barrel with 2 bands.

	$12,000 - $20,000	$8,000 - $12,000	$4,000 - $7,000

* ***Model 1866 Musket Third Model*** – 27 in. round barrel, 24 in. magazine, 3 barrel bands.

	$12,000 - $18,000	$7,000 - $12,000	$3,000 - $7,000

* ***Model 1866 Rifle/Carbine/Musket Fourth Model*** – .44 cal., twin rimfire and centerfire, script style serial number on lower tang near lever latch, improved frame, serial range approx. 149,000-170,101.

	$12,000 - $18,000	$7,000 - $15,000	$3,000 - $6,000

All 4th Model Rifles had steel buttplates and forend caps.

100%	98%	95%	90%	80%	70%	60%	50%	40%	30%	20%	10%

MODEL 1873 – .32-20 WCF, .38-40 WCF, or .44-40 WCF cal., iron frame with sideplates, frame loading port, 20 or 24 in. round or octagon barrel, rifles have forearm caps and carbines have forearm bands, tube mag., blue finish with case hardened parts, oil finished stock, serial numbered on lower tang, 720,610 mfg. between 1873-1919.

Since early Model 1873s were only made in .44 cal., no caliber markings are present. With the introduction of additional calibers, barrels (just in front of the receiver) and the brass elevator were stamped with the caliber. Model 1873s are serial numbered sequentially on the lower tang. On guns serial numbered 80,000 to 170,000, an "A" followed the number. From 170,000 to 190,000, either "A" or "B" may be found, while after 200,000, usually "B" was used. The letter does not seem to have any definite meaning. The earliest guns had no marking on the upper tang, but were marked "Model 1873" on the lower tang next to the ser. no. up to number 350, after which "Model 1873" is marked on the upper tang, where it remained through the model run.

* ***Model 1873 First Model Rifle*** – serial numbers approx. 1-30,000, sliding thumbprint dust cover on 2 guides which are an integral part of upper frame, absence of any cal. marking.

100%	98%	95%	90%	80%	70%	60%	50%	40%	30%	20%	10%
N/A	N/A	$16,500	$13,200	$9,900	$8,250	$6,000	$4,000	$3,750	$3,500	$2,750	$2,000

A below average Model 1873 First Model Rifle is currently valued in the $900-$1,650 range.
An average Model 1873 First Model Rifle is currently valued in the $1,650-$2,500 range.
An above average Model 1873 First Model Rifle is currently valued in the $2,500-$3,500 range.

Percentage values listed above are for original guns with corresponding percentages of bright blue finish remaining (refer to PPGS for accurate grading).

* ***Model 1873 Carbine First Model*** – 20 in. round barrel with carbine style forearm band. Distinctive curved buttplate, with saddle ring.

100%	98%	95%	90%	80%	70%	60%	50%	40%	30%	20%	10%
N/A	N/A	$27,500	$24,200	$19,800	$16,500	$13,200	$9,900	$6,000	$5,000	$4,000	$3,000

A below average Model 1873 Carbine First Model is currently valued in the $1,100-$2,100 range.
An average Model 1873 Carbine First Model is currently valued in the $2,500-$3,500 range.
An above average Model 1873 Carbine First Model is currently valued in the $3,500-$5,000 range.

Percentage values listed above are for original guns with corresponding percentages of bright blue finish remaining (refer to PPGS for accurate grading).

* ***Model 1873 Musket First Model*** – 30 in. round barrel, 27 in. mag. with 3 barrel bands, approx. 500 mfg.

100%	98%	95%	90%	80%	70%	60%	50%	40%	30%	20%	10%
N/A	N/A	$15,000	$12,000	$11,000	$10,000	$9,000	$8,000	$7,000	$6,000	$5,000	$3,500

A below average Model 1873 Musket First Model is currently valued in the $1,100-$2,150 range.
An average Model 1873 Musket First Model is currently valued in the $2,150-$2,800 range.
An above average Model 1873 Musket First Model is currently valued in the $2,800-$4,800 range.

Percentage values listed above are for original guns with corresponding percentages of bright blue finish remaining (refer to PPGS for accurate grading).

* ***Model 1873 Rifle Second Model*** – improved dust cover which slides on center rail on rear section of frame top which is held in place by two screws, serial range 31,000-90,000.

100%	98%	95%	90%	80%	70%	60%	50%	40%	30%	20%	10%
N/A	N/A	$12,000	$11,000	$9,000	$8,700	$6,600	$4,500	$3,000	$2,000	$1,500	$1,000

A below average Model 1873 Rifle Second Model is currently valued in the $675-$1,325 range.
An average Model 1873 Rifle Second Model is currently valued in the $1,325-$1,825 range.
An above average Model 1873 Rifle Second Model is currently valued in the $1,825-$2,750 range.

Percentage values listed above are for original guns with corresponding percentages of bright blue finish remaining (refer to PPGS for accurate grading).

* ***Model 1873 Carbine Second Model*** – changes similar to 1873 Second Model Rifle, with 20 in. round barrel and 2 barrel bands.

100%	98%	95%	90%	80%	70%	60%	50%	40%	30%	20%	10%
N/A	N/A	$22,000	$19,800	$17,600	$13,200	$9,900	$7,700	$5,500	$4,400	$3,300	$2,200

A below average Model 1873 Carbine Second Model is currently valued in the $875-$1,550 range.
An average Model 1873 Carbine Second Model is currently valued in the $2,000-$2,500 range.
An above average Model 1873 Carbine Second Model is currently valued in the $2,500-$3,500 range.

Percentage values listed above are for original guns with corresponding percentages of bright blue finish remaining (refer to PPGS for accurate grading).

* ***Model 1873 Musket Second Model*** – changes similar to 1873 Second Model Rifle, with 30 in. barrel and 3 barrel bands.

100%	98%	95%	90%	80%	70%	60%	50%	40%	30%	20%	10%
N/A	N/A	$6,875	$6,150	$5,500	$4,625	$3,850	$3,300	$2,750	$1,975	$1,550	$1,325

A below average Model 1873 Musket Second Model is currently valued in the $1,000-$1,400 range.
An average Model 1873 Musket Second Model is currently valued in the $1,400-$1,800 range.
An above average Model 1873 Musket Second Model is currently valued in the $1,800-$2,500 range.

Percentage values listed above are for original guns with corresponding percentages of bright blue finish remaining (refer to PPGS for accurate grading).

100%	98%	95%	90%	80%	70%	60%	50%	40%	30%	20%	10%

* ***Model 1873 Rifle Third Model*** – dust cover rail integral with frame, serial 90,000-end of production.

100%	98%	95%	90%	80%	70%	60%	50%	40%	30%	20%	10%
N/A	N/A	$8,250	$6,925	$6,000	$4,950	$4,125	$3,575	$3,300	$1,875	$1,650	$875

Add 20% for .44-40 WCF cal.
Add 30% for octagon barrel for .44-40 WCF cal. only.
A below average Model 1873 Rifle Third Model is currently valued in the $750-$1,000 range.
An average Model 1873 Rifle Third Model is currently valued in the $1,000-$1,650 range.
An above average Model 1873 Rifle Third Model is currently valued in the $1,650-$2,300 range.

Percentage values listed above are for original guns with corresponding percentages of bright blue finish remaining (refer to PPGS for accurate grading).

* ***Model 1873 Carbine Third Model*** – changes similar to 1873 Rifle Third Model, with 20 in. barrel and 2 barrel bands.

100%	98%	95%	90%	80%	70%	60%	50%	40%	30%	20%	10%
N/A	N/A	$19,800	$16,500	$14,300	$12,100	$8,800	$6,600	$5,500	$3,300	$2,200	$1,650

A below average Model 1873 Carbine Third Model is currently valued in the $1,200-$1,800 range.
An average Model 1873 Carbine Third Model is currently valued in the $1,800-$2,200 range.
An above average Model 1873 Carbine Third Model is currently valued in the $2,500-$3,500 range.

Percentage values listed above are for original guns with corresponding percentages of bright blue finish remaining (refer to PPGS for accurate grading).

* ***Model 1873 Musket Third Model*** – 30 in. round barrel and 3 barrel bands.

100%	98%	95%	90%	80%	70%	60%	50%	40%	30%	20%	10%
N/A	N/A	$5,625	$4,950	$4,400	$3,750	$3,200	$2,650	$2,025	$1,650	$1,325	$1,100

A below average Model 1873 Musket Third Model is currently valued in the $800-$1,200 range.
An average Model 1873 Musket Third Model is currently valued in the $1,200-$1,500 range.
An above average Model 1873 Musket Third Model is currently valued in the $1,500-$2,000 range.

Percentage values listed above are for original guns with corresponding percentages of bright blue finish remaining (refer to PPGS for accurate grading).

* ***Model 1873 .22 Rimfire Rifle*** – .22 S, L, or Extra L (very rare) cal., 24 in. barrel, no loading gate, the first .22 caliber repeater, 19,552 produced, mfg. 1884-1904. Made in rifle configuration only.

100%	98%	95%	90%	80%	70%	60%	50%	40%	30%	20%	10%
N/A	N/A	$13,200	$11,000	$9,775	$7,475	$5,750	$4,600	$4,000	$2,300	$1,725	$1,375

Add 50% for takedown model.
A below average Model 1873 .22 Rimfire Rifle is currently valued in the $725-$1,375 range.
An average Model 1873 .22 Rimfire Rifle is currently valued in the $1,375-$1,875 range.
An above average Model 1873 .22 Rimfire Rifle is currently valued in the $1,875-$2,500 range.

The takedown mechanism is unique in that a pin is driven out of the receiver, and is very prone to wear.

Percentage values listed above are for original guns with corresponding percentages of bright blue finish remaining (refer to PPGS for accurate grading).

* ***Model 1873 Deluxe Rifle*** – distinguishable by color case hardened frame and deluxe checkered stock and forearm, this model was special order only with many features and options available at an extra cost.

100%	98%	95%	90%	80%	70%	60%	50%	40%	30%	20%	10%
N/A	N/A	N/A	$37,500	$31,250	$27,500	$25,000	$22,500	$18,750	$15,625	$12,500	$9,375

A below average Model 1873 Deluxe Rifle is currently valued in the $2,750-$4,500 range.
An average Model 1873 Deluxe Rifle is currently valued in the $4,500-$7,500 range.
An above average Model 1873 Deluxe Rifle is currently valued in the $7,500-$12,000 range.

Values are for standard deluxe gun, w/o any special orders.

Percentage values listed above are for original guns with corresponding percentages of bright blue finish remaining (refer to PPGS for accurate grading).

* ***Model 1873 Trapper's Carbine*** – all features similar to .22 rimfire model, except available with 14, 15, or 16 in. barrel.

100%	98%	95%	90%	80%	70%	60%	50%	40%	30%	20%	10%
N/A	N/A	$30,000	$25,000	$20,000	$15,000	$14,000	$13,000	$12,000	$10,000	$8,000	$6,000

A below average Model 1873 Trapper's Carbine is currently valued in the $2,250-$3,500 range.
An average Model 1873 Trapper's Carbine is currently valued in the $3,500-$4,500 range.
An above average Model 1873 Trapper's Carbine is currently valued in the $4,500-$6,000 range.

Other barrel lengths were also available on this model, but are much rarer.

Percentage values listed above are for original guns with corresponding percentages of bright blue finish remaining (refer to PPGS for accurate grading).

100%	98%	95%	90%	80%	70%	60%	50%	40%	30%	20%	10%

* ***Model 1873 "One of One Thousand"*** – special care taken during assembly and testing to guarantee better accuracy, markings on top of breech designate model, deluxe walnut, extremely rare, barrel marked "One of One Thousand" in most cases, 136 mfg. Original cost was $100.

Values can range from $75,000 - $500,000, depending on condition.

A factory letter is a must for any "One of One Thousand" Winchester. Watch for fake letters. Note: Rarity of the "One of One Thousand" and the "One of One Hundred" models has made unethical upgrading of this model fairly common. Use extreme caution in purchasing.

* ***Model 1873 "One of One Hundred"*** – similar to "One of One Thousand" only rarer, 8 known. Sold new for $20 over the list price of a similarly equipped Model 1873.

Values can range from $75,000 - $500,000, depending on condition.

A factory letter is a must for any "One of One Hundred" Winchester. Watch for fake letters.

MODEL 1876 – .40-60 WCF, .45-60 WCF, .45-75 WCF (first caliber offered), or .50-95 Express cal., 22, 26, or 28 in. round or octagon barrel, similar but larger frame than Model 1873, tube mag., rifles have forearm caps while carbines and muskets have forearm bands and caps, crescent butt, blue finish, straight grip stock, 63,871 mfg. between 1876-1897.

The Model 1876 was also called the Centennial Model since its introduction coincided with the U.S. Centennial Exposition held in Philadelphia, PA in 1876. Popularity for this model decreased ten years later when the more powerful and advanced Model 1886 was introduced.

1876 Deluxe Models with 90%+ original case colors are extremely rare.

* ***Model 1876 Rifle First Model*** – serial numbered approx. 1-3,000, distinguishable by no dust cover on frame top.

N/A	N/A	$25,000	$22,150	$19,525	$16,800	$14,000	$11,675	$9,250	$6,800	$4,350	$3,850

A below average Model 1876 Rifle First Model is currently valued in the $1,875-$2,525 range.
An average Model 1876 First Model is currently valued in the $2,525-$3,600 range.
An above average Model 1876 First Model is currently valued in the $3,600-$4,400 range.

Percentage values listed above are for original guns with corresponding percentages of bright blue finish remaining (refer to PPGS for accurate grading).

* ***Model 1876 Carbine First Model*** – 22 in. round barrel, one barrel band, saddle ring, full-length forearm giving a musket appearance.

N/A	N/A	$23,650	$20,900	$18,425	$15,950	$11,000	$8,800	$6,600	$5,500	$4,400	$3,850

A below average Model 1876 Carbine First Model is currently valued in the $2,000-$2,500 range.
An average Model 1876 Carbine First Model is currently valued in the $2,500-$3,250 range.
An above average Model 1876 Carbine First Model is currently valued in the $3,250-$4,500 range.

Percentage values listed above are for original guns with corresponding percentages of bright blue finish remaining (refer to PPGS for accurate grading).

* ***Model 1876 Musket First Model*** – 32 in. round barrel with 1 band, scarce model because no foreign military contracts.

N/A	N/A	$30,000	$25,250	$21,350	$19,250	$15,000	$10,000	$8,000	$7,000	$6,000	$5,000

A below average Model 1876 Musket First Model is currently valued in the $2,500-$3,750 range.
An average Model 1876 Musket First Model is currently valued in the $3,750-$5,500 range.
An above average Model 1876 Musket First Model is currently valued in the $5,500-$6,200 range.

Percentage values listed above are for original guns with corresponding percentages of bright blue finish remaining (refer to PPGS for accurate grading).

* ***Model 1876 Rifle Second Model*** – dust cover rail held on by screw, early "Thumbprint" approx. S/N range 3000-7000, later with serrated rear edges approx. S/N range 7000-30000.

N/A	N/A	$16,500	$14,300	$12,100	$11,000	$9,900	$7,700	$5,500	$4,400	$3,300	$2,200

Add 35% for .50-95 WCF cal.
A below average Model 1876 Rifle Second Model is currently valued in the $1,500-$1,800 range.
An average Model 1876 Rifle Second Model is currently valued in the $1,750-$2,500 range.
An above average Model 1876 Rifle Second Model is currently valued in the $2,750-$3,750 range.

Percentage values listed above are for original guns with corresponding percentages of bright blue finish remaining (refer to PPGS for accurate grading).

* ***Model 1876 Carbine Second Model*** – changes similar to Model 1876 Rifle Early Second Model, with 22 in. round barrel and full-length forearm giving a musket appearance.

100%	98%	95%	90%	80%	70%	60%	50%	40%	30%	20%	10%
N/A	N/A	$22,000	$19,800	$17,600	$15,400	$13,200	$11,000	$7,700	$4,400	$3,300	$2,200

A below average Model 1876 Carbine Second Model is currently valued in the $1,200-$1,500 range.
An average Model 1876 Carbine Second Model is currently valued in the $1,500-$2,500 range.
An above average Model 1876 Carbine Second Model is currently valued in the $2,500-3,500 range.

Percentage values listed above are for original guns with corresponding percentages of bright blue finish remaining (refer to PPGS for accurate grading).

* ***Model 1876 Musket Second Model*** – changes similar to Model 1876 Rifle Early Second Model, with 32 in. round barrel and carbine forend tip.

100%	98%	95%	90%	80%	70%	60%	50%	40%	30%	20%	10%
N/A	N/A	$21,450	$19,250	$15,400	$14,000	$12,375	$11,550	$9,350	$6,325	$3,575	$2,200

A below average Model 1876 Musket Second Model is currently valued in the $1,200-$2,500 range.
An average Model 1876 Musket Second Model is currently valued in the $2,500-$3,750 range.
An above average Model 1876 Musket Second Model is currently valued in the $3,750-$5,000 range.

Percentage values listed above are for original guns with corresponding percentages of bright blue finish remaining (refer to PPGS for accurate grading).

* ***Model 1876 Rifle Third Model*** – dust cover rail integral with frame, serial range 30,000-end of production.

100%	98%	95%	90%	80%	70%	60%	50%	40%	30%	20%	10%
N/A	N/A	$15,000	$12,750	$10,750	$9,000	$7,500	$6,000	$4,750	$3,750	$3,000	$2,000

Add 25% for .50-95 WCF cal.
A below average Model 1876 Rifle Third Model is currently valued in the $1,000-$1,600 range.
An average Model 1876 Rifle Third Model is currently valued in the $1,600-$2,500 range.
An above average Model 1876 Rifle Third Model is currently valued in the $2,750-$3,750 range.

Percentage values listed above are for original guns with corresponding percentages of bright blue finish remaining (refer to PPGS for accurate grading).

* ***Model 1876 Carbine Third Model*** – frame similar to Model 1876 Rifle Third Model, with 22 in. round barrel and full-length forearm giving a musket appearance.

100%	98%	95%	90%	80%	70%	60%	50%	40%	30%	20%	10%
N/A	N/A	$22,500	$18,000	$13,000	$10,500	$8,500	$6,750	$5,000	$3,500	$3,000	$2,000

A below average Model 1876 Carbine Third Model is currently valued in the $1,200-$1,500 range.
An average Model 1876 Carbine Third Model is currently valued in the $1,500-$2,500 range.
An above average Model 1876 Carbine Third Model is currently valued in the $2,500-$3,500 range.

Percentage values listed above are for original guns with corresponding percentages of bright blue finish remaining (refer to PPGS for accurate grading).

* ***Model 1876 Musket Third Model*** – frame similar to Model 1876 Rifle Third Model, with 32 in. round barrel.

100%	98%	95%	90%	80%	70%	60%	50%	40%	30%	20%	10%
N/A	N/A	$18,700	$16,500	$14,300	$12,100	$10,450	$8,250	$6,600	$5,500	$4,400	$3,300

A below average Model 1876 Musket Third Model is currently valued in the $2,000-$2,500 range.
An average Model 1876 Musket Third Model is currently valued in the $2,500-$3,500 range.
An above average Model 1876 Musket Third Model is currently valued in the $3,500-$4,500 range.

Percentage values listed above are for original guns with corresponding percentages of bright blue finish remaining (refer to PPGS for accurate grading).

* ***Model 1876 Deluxe Rifle*** – distinguishable by color case hardened frame and deluxe checkered stock and forearm, this model was special order only with many features and options available at extra cost.

100%	98%	95%	90%	80%	70%	60%	50%	40%	30%	20%	10%
N/A	N/A	N/A	$60,000	$48,000	$42,000	$36,000	$30,000	$24,000	$21,600	$18,000	$14,400

Values are for standard deluxe gun.
A below average Model 1876 Deluxe Rifle is currently valued in the $5,000-$7,500 range.
An average Model 1876 Deluxe Rifle is currently valued in the $7,500-$10,000 range.
An above average Model 1876 Deluxe Rifle is currently valued in the $10,000-$13,000 range.

Percentage values listed above are for original guns with corresponding percentages of bright blue finish remaining (refer to PPGS for accurate grading).

* ***Model 1876 "One of One Thousand"*** – special care taken in manufacture to guarantee better accuracy, markings on top of breech designate model, deluxe walnut, extremely rare, 54 mfg. Original cost was $100.

Values can range from $75,000 - $500,000, depending on condition.

100%	98%	95%	90%	80%	70%	60%	50%	40%	30%	20%	10%

A factory letter is a must for any "One of One Thousand" Winchester. Watch for fake letters. Values are not listed because too few original specimens are bought or sold to accurately establish pricing.

Note: Rarity of the "One of One Thousand" and the "One of One Hundred" models has made unethical upgrading of this model fairly common. Use extreme caution in purchasing.

* ***Model 1876 "One of One Hundred"*** – similar to "One of One Thousand" only rarer, 8 mfg. Sold new for $20 over the list price of a similarly equipped Model 1876.

Values can range from $75,000 - $500,000, depending on condition.

A factory letter is a must for any "One of One Hundred" Winchester. Believe it or not, watch for fake letters. Values are not listed because too few original specimens are bought or sold to accurately establish pricing.

* ***Model 1876 Northwest Mounted Police Carbine*** – .45-75 WCF cal. only, 22 in. barrel, "NWMP" or "MP" marking may appear on stock (with wear, this cartouche may not be visible - the majority were not marked) approx. 1,600 mfg., factory records can only verify 150.

N/A	N/A	$22,000	$19,800	$13,200	$11,000	$9,900	$8,250	$6,600	$5,500	$4,950	$4,400

A below average Model 1876 Northwest Mounted Police Carbine is currently valued in the $2,750-$4,500 range.
An average Model 1876 Northwest Mounted Police Carbine is currently valued in the $4,500-$5,750 range.
An above average Model 1876 Northwest Mounted Police Carbine is currently valued in the $5,750-$7,200 range.

Above average specimens in this model should have traces of blue. Be very wary of the stock cartouche since these buttstocks were sold as surplus back in the 1920s. A letter of authenticity is a good idea on this model.

Percentage values listed above are for original guns with corresponding percentages of bright blue finish remaining (refer to PPGS for accurate grading).

MODEL 1886 – .33 WCF, .38-56 WCF, .38-70 WCF (830 mfg.), .40-65 WCF, .40-70 WCF (629 mfg.), .40-82 WCF, .45-70 Govt., .45-90, .50-110 Express, or .50-100-450 (234 mfg.) cal. available, Browning's first high power lever action design distinguishable by vertical locking bars, .45-70 Govt. most popular cal., 26 in. round or octagon barrel, tube mag., steel forend cap, straight grip stock. Case colored receiver was standard finish until 1901, then blue became the standard finish. Approx. 159,990 mfg. between 1886-1935.

On the following Model 1886 variations add the percentages non-cumulative for special order features and/or configuration.
Add 20% for octagon barrel.
Add 30% for octagon barrel with takedown (not on Lightweight).
Add 25% for .45-70 Govt. or .45-90 cal.
Add 100% for .50-110 or 150% for .50-100-450 cal.
Add 100%-150% for case colored receivers on standard guns only (pre-1902 mfg.), depending on original condition.
Add 200% for WWI British government purchase for RFC/RNAS with British military proofmarks and ownership marks. Purchased at the London Arms Co. to use against Zeppelins and other lighter than air craft using incendiary bullets. Very rare - 17 known sold to the public during the 1920s.

* ***Model 1886 Standard Rifle*** – various cals., color case hardening was standard on the frame, buttplate, and forend cap until 1901 (approx. 122,000 ser. no. range), when the standard finish became blue.

N/A	N/A	$18,000	$15,600	$13,200	$10,800	$8,400	$7,200	$6,000	$4,800	$3,600	$2,400

* ***Model 1886 Carbine*** – same general specifications as Rifle, except 22 in. round barrel and saddle ring, solid frame only.

N/A	N/A	$30,000	$24,000	$19,200	$16,800	$14,400	$13,200	$12,000	$9,600	$8,400	$4,200

Add 50% for full stock carbine (very rare).

.33 WCF cal. is the rarest caliber in this model.

* ***Model 1886 Musket*** – almost all are chambered in .45-70 Govt. cal., 30 in. round barrel, full-length military style forearm, military sights, only 350 mfg., very rare.

N/A	N/A	$22,000	$18,700	$15,950	$13,200	$11,000	$8,800	$7,700	$6,600	$5,500	$4,400

Most specimens encountered in this variation are in very good condition. A pitted musket is almost never encountered.

* ***Model 1886 Deluxe Rifle*** – distinguishable by deluxe checkered pistol grip walnut stock and forearm, color case hardened frame, this model was special order only with many features and options available at an extra cost.

N/A	N/A	N/A	$42,000	$36,000	$24,000	$18,000	$14,400	$10,800	$9,600	$8,400	$7,200

Values are for standard deluxe gun, w/o any special orders.

100%	98%	95%	90%	80%	70%	60%	50%	40%	30%	20%	10%

* ***Model 1886 Lightweight Rifle*** – .45-70 Govt. or .33 WCF cal. only, 22 (.45-70 Govt. cal.) or 24 (.33 WCF cal.) in. round nickel steel tapered barrel, half mag., rubber shotgun buttplate.

» **Model 1886 Lightweight .33 cal.**

N/A	N/A	$3,300	$2,800	$2,500	$2,200	$2,000	$1,850	$1,750	$1,600	$1,400	$1,200

» **Model 1886 Lightweight .45-70 Govt. cal.**

N/A	N/A	$7,150	$6,325	$5,500	$4,625	$4,000	$3,450	$3,000	$2,200	$1,875	$1,650

Since lightweight rifles were fairly late production, all specimens are blue and in very good condition usually.

* ***Model 1886 Deluxe Lightweight Rifle*** – distinguishable by fancy checkered wood stock.

N/A	N/A	$18,750	$15,625	$12,500	$10,000	$7,500	$6,250	$5,250	$3,750	$3,125	$2,500

Since lightweight rifles were fairly late production, all specimens are blue and in very good condition usually.

MODEL 1892 RIFLE – .25-20 WCF, .32-20 WCF, .38-40 WCF, or .44-40 WCF cal., 24 in. round or octagon barrel, blue, tube mag., forend cap, crescent butt. Approx. 1,000,000 mfg. between 1892-1941.

N/A	N/A	$3,750	$3,125	$2,500	$2,200	$1,875	$1,575	$1,250	$1,125	$1,000	$875

Add 50% for .44-40 WCF cal.
Add 25% for .38-40 WCF cal.
Add 25% for Takedown Model.

A short rifle configuration was available in this model with special order barrels under 16 inches, 12 in. being the rarest. These guns are very rare (most went to South America) and prices typically range $2,750-$8,000, depending on original condition.

* ***Model 1892 Rifle Antique*** – .25-20 WCF, .32-20 WCF, .38-40 WCF, or .44-40 WCF cal., 24 in. round or octagon barrel, blue, tube mag., forend cap, crescent butt, ser. no. range under 168,000. Mfg. 1892-1898.

N/A	N/A	$4,800	$4,200	$3,600	$3,300	$3,000	$2,700	$2,400	$1,800	$1,500	$1,250

Add 100% for .44-40 WCF cal.
Add 25% for .38-40 WCF cal.
Add 25% for Takedown Model.

* ***Model 1892 Deluxe Rifle*** – distinguishable by fancy pistol grip checkered wood. Mfg. 1892-1941.

N/A	$20,000	$16,800	$15,600	$14,400	$12,000	$10,800	$9,600	$7,800	$6,000	$3,600	$2,400

MODEL 1892 CARBINE – 20 in. round barrel, 2 barrel bands, and saddle ring, except one barrel band and one rifle style mag. tube retainer on cals. .25-20 WCF and .32-20 WCF.

N/A	N/A	$4,800	$4,200	$3,600	$3,000	$2,700	$2,100	$1,500	$1,325	$1,075	$850

Add 50% for .44-40 WCF cal. or 25% for .38-40 WCF cal.

MODEL 1892 TRAPPER'S CARBINE – all features similar to standard SRC, except has a 12, 14, 15, 16, or 18 in. barrel, so called Trapper's Model because it was handy for trappers who had to carry a powerful but lightweight repeating rifle.

N/A	N/A	$14,400	$12,000	$10,800	$8,400	$7,200	$6,000	$5,400	$4,800	$3,600	$2,400

Most 1892 Trapper's Carbines are in the 15 in., .44-40 WCF cal. configuration. Most of the 1892 Trapper's Carbine were shipped to South America or Australia. This variation is almost never encountered over 30% condition - most are brown guns. Check federal laws regarding 12, 14 and 15 inch barrels.

MODEL 1892 MUSKET – most are chambered in .44-40 WCF cal., 30 in. round, full-length military style forearm with military style rear sight.

N/A	N/A	$18,700	$16,500	$14,300	$13,200	$12,100	$11,000	$8,800	$6,600	$4,400	$3,300

Add $1,500 - $2,000 for correct bayonet.

MODEL 1894 RIFLE – .25-35 WCF, .30-30 Win. (.30 WCF), .32-40 WCF, .32 Spl., or .38-55 WCF cal., most common (and popular) is .30-30 Win. cal., tube mag., 24 or 26 in. round or octagon barrel was standard, blue, straight grip stock, Model 1894 barrel marking changed just before ser. no. 500,000 circa 1908, tang marking changed after ser. no. 500,000, "18" was removed around ser. no. 1,000,000 circa 1927. Over 5,000,000, mfg. 1894-2006.

Add 25% for WWI French contract variant with metric rear sight and sling swivels on left side of buttstock and barrel band. Saddle ring was removed on many French contract 1894s. Mfg. 1899-1929.

Newer Model 94 mfg. may be found in the RIFLES: MODEL 94 LEVER ACTION - POST 1964 PRODUCTION section. The Model 1894 rifle configuration (forearm stock with forearm cap) was discontinued circa 1925 at approx. ser. no. 950,000-995,000. The Model 1894 rifle was replaced by the Model 55 (mfg. 1924-1932), and the Model 64 (mfg. 1933-1957 and 1972-1973).

100%	98%	95%	90%	80%	70%	60%	50%	40%	30%	20%	10%

* ***Model 1894 Rifle 1894-1898 Mfg.*** – antique mfg., pre-148,000 ser. no.

N/A	$6,900	$5,750	$5,175	$4,600	$4,000	$3,450	$2,875	$2,300	$1,725	$1,425	$1,150

Add 20% for takedown variation.
Add approx. 25% for cals. other than .30-30 Win. or .32 Spl.

The Model 1894 Winchester has the distinction of being the world's most popular rifle.

* ***Model 1894 Rifle 1899-1929 Mfg.*** – Model 94s built 1899-1929. After 1929, only the Model 1894 carbine was produced up until 1940.

N/A	$4,400	$3,850	$3,300	$2,750	$2,200	$1,650	$1,375	$1,225	$1,100	$1,000	$825

Add 25% for takedown variation.
Add approx. 50% for cals. other than .30-30 Win. or .32 Spl.

The Model 1894 Winchester has the distinction of being the world's most popular sporting rifle.

* ***Model 1894 Deluxe Rifle*** – distinguishable by fancy pistol grip checkered wood. Mfg. 1894-1929.

N/A	$17,000	$13,200	$12,000	$10,800	$10,200	$9,600	$8,400	$7,200	$6,000	$4,800	$3,600

MODEL 1894 TRAPPER'S CARBINE – all features similar to the standard SRC, except with a 14, 15, or 16 in. barrel.

N/A	N/A	$8,525	$7,200	$5,775	$4,775	$3,900	$3,300	$2,750	$2,475	$2,200	$1,650

The large majority of this variation are encountered in .30-30 Win. cal. with 15 in. barrel. Any other caliber or barrel length will create a premium. Most of these carbines are brown and rusty. Rarely, if ever, encountered with very much finish remaining.

Note: Check federal laws on legality of 14 and 15 in. barrels.

MODEL 1894 SADDLE RING CARBINE – 20 in. round barrel.

N/A	N/A	$3,300	$3,025	$2,725	$2,420	$1,825	$1,525	$1,200	$1,100	$975	$850

Add 30% for any cal. other than .30-30 Win. or .32 Spl.
Carbines with special order features such as pistol grip, deluxe wood, checkering, etc. can bring even greater premiums than the rifle.

* ***Model 1894 Saddle Ring Carbine Antique*** – 20 in. round barrel, antique mfg., pre-148,000 ser. no.

N/A	N/A	$6,250	$5,250	$4,400	$3,225	$2075,	$1,875	$1,575	$1,200	$1,000	$900

Add 30% for any cal. other than .30-30 Win.

Carbines with special order features such as pistol grip, deluxe wood, checkering, etc. can bring even greater premiums than the rifle.

* ***Model 1894 Saddle Ring Carbine Eastern*** – features long forearm, early stock design, early style carbine post or hooded ramp (later mfg.) front sight, and without saddle ring, mfg. late 1920s-early 1930s.

N/A	N/A	$2,725	$2,400	$2,125	$1,825	$1,575	$1,350	$1,125	$925	$800	$600

MODEL 1894 1940-1964 PRODUCTION CARBINE – 1940-1964 mfg. without saddle ring, barrel is marked Model 94.

$1,100	$900	$750	$650	$500	$425	$375	$325	$275	$250	$225	$200

Add 100% for .25-35 WCF cal.

Some WWII carbines with special U.S. markings will bring a premium over prices listed.

MODEL 1895 RIFLE FLATSIDE – .30 US (most common), .38-72, or .40-72 cal., early model, distinguishable in that frame does not have fluting or ridge contouring, serial range approx. 1-5000. Mfg. 1895-1896.

N/A	N/A	$9,675	$8,475	$7,250	$6,050	$4,850	$3,625	$3,025	$2,425	$1,825	$1,200

Add 20% for octagon barrel on cals. .38-72 or .40-72.

MODEL 1895 RIFLE – .30-03, .30-06, .30-40 Krag, .303 Brit., .35 Win., .38-72, .40-72, .405 Win., or 7.62mm Russian cal., 24-28 in. barrel, blue action, box mag., straight grip stock, 425,881 mfg. from 1896-1931.

N/A	N/A	$5,875	$5,175	$4,500	$3,900	$3,400	$2,825	$2,325	$1,775	$1,200	$900

Add 100% for octagon barrel.
Add 50% for .405 Win. cal.
Add 20% for takedown model.

The Model 1895 was a Browning design incorporating the first box type mag. in a lever action repeating rifle. .30 US is the most commonly encountered cal. in this model. A large Russian military contract was secured in 1915 with chambering for the 7.62mm Russian cartridge (over 293,000 mfg. or over 66% of total production).

100%	98%	95%	90%	80%	70%	60%	50%	40%	30%	20%	10%

* ***Model 1895 Deluxe Rifle*** – distinguishable by fancy pistol grip checkered wood. Mfg. 1894-1929.

N/A	N/A	$16,800	$14,400	$13,200	$10,800	$8,400	$6,600	$4,200	$3,600	$3,000	$1,800

MODEL 1895 CARBINE – .30 US (.30-40 Krag Army - most common cal.), .30-03, .30-06, or .303 Brit. cal., 22 in. round barrel, military style top handguard wood and military sights, with or without saddle ring.

N/A	N/A	$6,275	$5,725	$4,950	$3,750	$3,625	$2,975	$2,300	$1,975	$1,650	$1,325

Add 20% for caliber other than .30 U.S.
Add 50% for U.S. government marked.

MODEL 1895 FLATSIDE MUSKET – early models have serial range under 5,000, no flutes on frame, .30-40 Krag only.

Rarity on this model means only a few specimens in several museums.

MODEL 1895 MUSKET – .30-03, .30-06, or .30-40 Krag cal., 28 in. round barrel with handguard over barrel, military sights.

N/A	N/A	$6,600	$5,775	$5,225	$4,625	$3,975	$3,475	$2,925	$2,200	$1,650	$1,375

Add 10%-15% if U.S. Govt. marked.

MODEL 1895 NRA MUSKET – .30-03, .30-06, or .30-40 Krag cal., similar to Standard Musket grade with 24 or 30 in. barrel, 1901 Krag style rear sight. NRA approved for official NRA competition.

N/A	N/A	$5,800	$5,200	$4,525	$3,825	$3,275	$2,625	$2,200	$1,700	$1,375	$1,100

Add 30% if U.S. government marked.

MODEL 1895 RUSSIAN MUSKET – 7.62mm Russian cal. (7.62x54R), over 293,000 mfg. for Imperial Russian Govt., mfg. 1915-16, various Russian Ordnance stamps should be present.

N/A	N/A	$4,850	$4,750	$4,175	$3,600	$3,100	$2,525	$2,000	$1,675	$1,375	$1,150

MODEL 53 RIFLE – .25-20 WCF, .32-20 WCF, or .44-40 WCF cal., 22 in. round barrel, 1/2 tube mag. holding 6 cartridges, solid frame or takedown, blue finish, pistol grip or straight grip stock, serial numbered both separately and within the Model 92 range. Mfg. 24,916 between 1924-32.

N/A	N/A	$2,100	$1,875	$1,625	$1,350	$1,175	$900	$725	$600	$500	$375

Add 100% for .44-40 WCF cal.
Add 25% for Takedown Model.

* ***Model 53 Deluxe Rifle*** – distinguishable by fancy pistol grip checkered wood.

N/A	N/A	$5,275	$4,825	$4,400	$3,975	$3,425	$3,050	$2,575	$2,175	$1,775	$1,325

MODEL 55 RIFLE – .25-35 WCF (rare), .30-30 Win. (takedown only), or .32 Win. Spl. cal., lever action design, solid frame (less common) and takedown (more common), 24 in. lightweight rapid taper round barrel, shotgun style buttstock with serrated steel buttplate, tube mag., holds 3 cartridges. Approx. 20,500 mfg. between 1924-1932. Serial numbered independently to approx. 2,865, then serialized with Model 1894 production on underside of receiver. Simply could not compete with the Model 1894. Note that a small number of rifles were made during a parts clean-up from 1933-1942.

* ***Model 55 Rifle Standard Cals.*** – .30-30 Win. or .32 Win. Spl. cal.

N/A	$2,000	$1,750	$1,500	$1,250	$1,000	$900	$800	$700	$600	$500	$400

Add 20% for solid frame model.

* ***Model 55 Rifle .25-35 WCF Cal.***

N/A	$5,000	$4,500	$4,000	$3,500	$3,000	$2,750	$2,500	$2,250	$2,000	$1,750	$1,500

MODEL 64 RIFLE – .219 Zipper (very rare), .25-35 WCF (rare), .30-30 Win., or .32 Win. Spl. cal., 20 (may be referred to as carbine) or 24 in. round barrel, with standard 26 in. on the .219 Zipper, blue metal, pistol grip stock, revamped Model 55 action with increased mag. capacity, 66,783 mfg. between 1933-1957 and 1972-73 (over 8,250 mfg. in .30-30 Win. cal. only - these last two years with minor changes).

N/A	$1,350	$1,200	$1,000	$900	$850	$750	$650	$550	$500	$450	$400

Add 150% for 20 in. barrel (sometimes referred to as Carbine).
Add 400% for .25-35 WCF cal. (rare).
Add 500% for .219 Zipper cal. (very rare).

Many of this variation now have extra holes drilled on the top of the receiver to accept scope mounts - subtract 50% for this alteration. The Model 64 is usually found in excellent condition.

Model 64 1972-73 mfg. may be found in the post-'64 section.

* ***Model 64 Deluxe Rifle*** – distinguishable by fancy checkered wood stock with pistol grip.

N/A	N/A	$2,500	$2,150	$1,875	$1,700	$1,525	$1,325	$1,150	$950	$800	$725

100%	98%	95%	90%	80%	70%	60%	50%	40%	30%	20%	10%

MODEL 65 RIFLE – .218 Bee (introduced 1939), .25-20 WCF, or .32-20 WCF cal., 22 in. round barrel (except .218 Bee - 24 in.), 1/2 tube mag. holding 7 cartridges, blue with pistol grip stock. Mfg. 5,704 between 1933-1947.

N/A	$5,500	$4,950	$4,400	$3,850	$3,300	$2,750	$2,475	$2,200	$1,925	$1,650	$1,375

While the .25-20 WCF cal. is the rarest, the .218 Bee has the most demand.

The Model 65 was a design evolved from the Model 53. The Model 65 was not tapped on receiver side for scope mounts. As a rule, most specimens are in either pretty nice or refinished condition.

* ***Model 65 Deluxe Rifle*** – distinguishable by fancy pistol grip checkered wood.

N/A	$9,625	$8,525	$7,525	$6,600	$5,500	$4,700	$4,125	$3,525	$2,750	$2,200	$1,650

MODEL 71 RIFLE – .348 Win. cal., 2/3 tube mag. holding 4 cartridges, improved Model 1886 frame, blue metal with pistol grip stock, 20 or 24 in. barrel, short or long tang. Mfg. 47,254 between 1935-1957.

N/A	$2,100	$2,000	$1,900	$1,800	$1,700	$1,600	$1,500	$1,450	$1,350	$1,250	$1,000

Add 30%-40% for early variation long tang, depending on condition.
Add 150% for short rifle with 20 in. barrel.
Add $250 for bolt peep sight.

* ***Model 71 Deluxe Rifle*** – distinguishable by fancy pistol grip cap, sling swivel studs, checkered wood.

N/A	$3,500	$2,750	$2,500	$2,250	$2,000	$1,750	$1,500	$1,400	$1,300	$1,200	$1,000

Add 20% for long tang.

GRADING - PPGS™	100%	98%	95%	90%	80%	70%	60%	LAST MSR

MODEL 88 RIFLE – pre-'64 version with diamond cut checkering, no barrel band, 22 in. barrel. Mfg. 1955-63. Total production for all varieties of the Model 88 Lever Action was approx. 284,000 units. Mfg. 1955-1963.

.308 Win. (1955-1963)	$1,000	$875	$700	$500	$425	$365	$300	
.243 Win. (1956-1963)	$1,375	$1,175	$925	$765	$650	$550	$375	
.358 Win. (1956-1962)	$3,995	$3,500	$2,850	$2,000	$1,550	$1,250	$950	
.284 Win. (Intro-1963)	$3,200	$3,000	$2,500	$2,000	$1,500	$1,000	$725	

RIFLES: LEVER ACTION - POST 1964 PRODUCTION

MODEL 64 1972-1974 MODEL – .30-30 Win. cal., 5 shot, 2/3 tube mag., 24 in. barrel, open sight, plain pistol grip stock. Mfg. 1972-1974.

	$500	$450	$400	$350	$300	$275	$225	

MODEL 71 STANDARD – .348 Win. cal., 24 in. round tapered barrel with buckhorn rear and hooded ramp front sight, top tang safety, 4 shot half mag., uncheckered walnut stock with steel buttplate and forearm, approx. 8 lbs. Mfg. by Miroku 2012 only.

	$1,625	$1,400	$1,175	$1,050	$900	$775	$625	*$1,470*

MODEL 71 DELUXE – .348 Win. cal., similar to Model 71 Standard, except has deluxe checkered walnut stock and forearm. Mfg. 2012 only.

	$1,475	$1,275	$1,075	$950	$825	$700	$575	*$1,660*

MODEL 88 RIFLE (1955-1963 MFG.) – Please see listing under Rifles: Lever Action - 1860-1964.

MODEL 88 RIFLE (1964-1973 MFG.) – .243 Win., .284 Win., or .308 Win. cal., 1964 model with impressed basket weave checkering, no barrel band, 22 in. barrel. Mfg. 1964-1973.

.308 Win. cal.	$800	$700	$500	$425	$365	$300	$250	
.243 Win. cal.	$1,350	$900	$600	$575	$495	$450	$350	
.284 Win. cal.	$2,000	$1,700	$1,500	$1,200	$1,000	$750	$600	

MODEL 88 CARBINE – introduced 1968, no checkering, one-piece stock, barrel band, 19 in. barrel. Mfg. 1968-1973.

.308 Win. cal. (1968-1973)	$1,625	$1,350	$975	$775	$575	$475	$425	
.243 Win. cal.	$2,100	$1,650	$1,400	$1,125	$975	$825	$650	
.284 Win. cal.	$3,250	$2,750	$2,325	$2,050	$1,600	$1,300	$1,000	

MODEL 150 – .22 LR, 20 1/2 in. barrel, tube mag., hammerless, uncheckered hardwood stock and forearm, sling swivels, approx. 47,400 mfg. 1967-74.

	$150	$125	$100	$80	$65	$55	$45	

MODEL 250 – .22 LR, 20 1/2 in. barrel, tube mag., hammerless, checkered pistol grip stock. Mfg. 1963-73.

	$300	$260	$200	$160	$125	$100	$80	

GRADING - PPGS™	100%	98%	95%	90%	80%	70%	60%	LAST MSR

* ***Model 250 Deluxe*** – similar to Model 250, with select wood and sling swivels. Mfg. 1965-71.

	$395	$335	$265	$195	$160	$120	$80	

MODEL 255 – .22 WMR, otherwise similar to Model 250. Mfg. 1964-70.

	$395	$325	$265	$225	$185	$160	$135	

* ***Model 255 Deluxe*** – .22 WMR cal., with select wood and swivels. Mfg. 1965-73.

	$875	$750	$625	$475	$300	$225	$150	

MODEL 1866 150TH COMMEMORATIVE – .44-40 WCF cal., 24 in. octagon barrel with gold ring on muzzle, barrel marked "Winchester Repeating Arms 1866-2016", blade front and ladder-type carbine rear sight, Grade 5/6 satin oil finished uncheckered straight grip walnut stock and forearm, extensively engraved brass receiver with Winchester horse and rider on right side and WRA scroll trademark on left, engraved brass crescent buttplate and forearm cap, 7 1/2 lbs. Limited mfg. 2016 only.

	$3,000	$2,650	$2,300	$2,100	$1,900	$1,700	$1,500	*$3,330*

MODEL 1866 SHORT RIFLE – .38 Spl., .45 LC (new 2018), or .44-40 WCF cal., 20 in. octagon barrel, 10 (.44-40 WCF or .45 LC) or 11 shot full-length mag., bright polished brass frame, folding ladder rear sight with Marbles bold bead front sight, Grade I uncheckered American black walnut straight grip stock with satin oil finish, crescent brass buttplate and forearm with brass tip, open top ejector port, blued steel action screws and loading gate, 7 1/4 lbs. Mfg. 2017-2019.

	$1,150	$995	$850	$725	$625	$525	$425	*$1,300*

MODEL 1873 150TH COMMEMORATIVE – .44-40 WCF cal., 24 in. octagon barrel marked "The American Legend 1866-2016", gold band on muzzle, 13 shot mag., Marbles gold bead front sight, buckhorn rear, and upper tang mounted aperture sights, silver Nitride finished receiver with Winchester 150th Anniversary logo and the WRA scroll trademark, Grade 5/6 checkered walnut straight grip stock and forearm, crescent buttplate and forearm cap are engraved, 7 1/2 lbs. Limited mfg. 2016 only.

	$3,000	$2,650	$2,300	$2,100	$1,900	$1,700	$1,500	*$3,330*

MODEL 1873 CARBINE – .357 Mag./.38 Spl., .44-40 Win., or .45 LC cal., 20 in. barrel with blued barrel band, 10 or 11 shot mag., ladder style rear and blade front sights, walnut straight grip stock with satin oil finish, classic carbine style forearm, blued steel carbine strap buttplate and saddle ring, steel loading gate, drilled and tapped receiver top tang, 7 1/4 lbs. New 2018.

MSR $1,350	$1,150	$1,000	$865	$780	$635	$525	$450	

MODEL 1873 SHORT RIFLE – .357 Mag./.38 Spl., .44-40 Win. (new 2014) or .45 Colt (new 2014) cal., 10 or 11 shot full mag., 20 in. round barrel with semi-buckhorn rear sight and Marbles gold bead front sight, straight grip satin oil finished walnut stock and forearm, crescent buttplate, blue or color case hardened (new 2014) finish, firing pin/striker block safety, rear tang is drilled and tapped, brass carrier block, 7 1/4 lbs. New 2013.

MSR $1,350	$1,150	$1,000	$865	$780	$635	$525	$450	

Add $280 for color case hardened finish (new 2014).

MODEL 1873 SPORTER RIFLE – .357 Mag./.38 Spl., .44-40 WCF, or .45 LC (new 2016) cal., 20 (mfg. 2016-2017) or 24 in. octagon barrel with full mag., 13 or 14 shot mag., Marble Arms front sight and semi-buckhorn rear sight, satin finished uncheckered stock and forearm, upper rear tang is drilled and tapped, case colored receiver, lever, crescent buttplate, and forearm cap, 7 1/2 lbs. New 2015.

MSR $1,790	$1,600	$1,400	$1,190	$1,035	$850	$725	$600	

MODEL 1873 SPORTER PISTOL GRIP – .357 Mag./.38 Spl., .45 LC, or .44-40 WCF cal., 24 in. octagon barrel with full mag., 13 or 14 shot mag., Marble Arms front sight and semi-buckhorn rear sight, pistol grip satin finished uncheckered stock and forearm, upper rear tang is drilled and tapped, blue (mfg. 2016-2019) or case colored receiver, lever, crescent buttplate, and forearm cap, 8 lbs. New 2016.

MSR $1,790	$1,600	$1,400	$1,190	$1,035	$850	$725	$600	

Subtract approx. $270 for blue finish (mfg. 2016-2019).

MODEL 1886 GRADE I – .45-70 Govt. cal., 26 in. octagon barrel. Mfg. 1997-1998.

	$1,175	$1,050	$975	$825	$725	$650	$550	*$996*

This model was originally manufactured in Japan w/o a top tang safety. However, once these guns were imported, the BATF decided not to approve the configuration unless the guns were shipped back to Japan for a top tang safety update.

* ***Model 1886 High Grade*** – .45-70 Govt. cal., features gold-line receiver engraving with multiple gold animals, polished blue, deluxe checkered walnut stock and forearm with metal cap, 1,000 mfg. 1997 only.

	$1,925	$1,550	$1,175	N/A	N/A	N/A	N/A	*$1,588*

GRADING - PPGS™	100%	98%	95%	90%	80%	70%	60%	LAST MSR

MODEL 1886 TAKEDOWN – .45-70 Govt. cal., features original takedown action design, uncheckered semi-pistol grip walnut stock with crescent buttplate, 26 in. octagon barrel with buckhorn rear sight, forend has ebony cap, 9 1/4 lbs. Mfg. 1999 only.

	$1,425	$1,275	$1,050	$850	$775	$650	$550	*$1,140*

MODEL 1886 EXTRA LIGHT GRADE I – .45-70 Govt. cal., 22 in. round tapered barrel, shotgun buttplate, half magazine, high polish receiver and barrel bluing, open sights, uncheckered walnut stock and forearm, 7 1/4 lbs. 3,500 mfg. 2000-2001, and 2010-2012.

	$1,375	$1,075	$875	$800	$725	$625	$550	*$1,270*

* ***Model 1886 Extra Light High Grade*** – similar to Model 1886 Extra Light Grade I, except features engraved elk and whitetail deer and game scenes on blue receiver, extra fancy checkered walnut stock and forearm, 7 1/4 lbs. 1,000 mfg. 2000-2001.

	$1,650	$1,200	$1,000	N/A	N/A	N/A	N/A	*$1,440*

MODEL 1886 DELUXE RIFLE – .45-70 Govt. or .45-90 WCF (new 2021) cal., 24 in. octagon barrel with bead front and buckhorn rear sight, 8 shot mag., color case hardened receiver, lever, crescent buttplate, grip cap, lower tang, and forearm cap, blued barrel and mag. tube, Grade 3/4 satin finished checkered pistol grip stock and forearm, 8 3/8 lbs. New 2016.

MSR $1,790	$1,750	$1,550	$1,300	$1,075	$925	$800	$650	

MODEL 1892 GRADE I – .357 Mag. (new 1998), .44-40 WCF (new 1998), or .45 LC cal., similar to original Model 1892 Winchester, 24 in. round barrel, top tang mounted manual hammer stop, blue finish with etched receiver engraving, gold trigger, satin finished walnut straight grip stock and forend with metal cap, 6 1/4 lbs. Mfg. 1997-99.

	$875	$700	$525	$450	$375	$325	$275	*$744*

MODEL 1886 SHORT RIFLE – .45-70 Govt. or .45-90 WCF (new 2019) cal., 24 in. round barrel with full-length mag. tube, adj. buckhorn rear sight and gold bead Marble's front sight, 8 shot mag., blued metal finish, uncheckered satin finished walnut stock and forearm, crescent steel buttplate, approx. 8 3/8 lbs. New 2011.

MSR $1,370	$1,315	$1,025	$900	$775	$650	$550	$475	

* ***Model 1892 Grade I Short Rifle*** – .44 Mag. cal., 20 in. round barrel with full mag., uncheckered staight grip walnut stock with crescent buttplate, buckhorn rear sight, high polish blue finish only, 6 lbs. Mfg. 1999-2000.

	$900	$750	$575	$475	$400	$350	$300	*$752*

* ***Model 1892 Grade I Short Rifle (2009-2012 Mfg.)*** – .44 Rem. Mag. or .357 Mag. cal., 20 in. round gloss blue barrel, steel receiver, tube mag., oil finished Grade I straight grip walnut stock with crescent buttplate, short forearm with steel cap, Marble's gold bead front sight, buckhorn style rear sight, tang safety, 6 lbs., 8 oz. Mfg. 2009-2012.

	$1,100	$925	$800	$675	$550	$450	$325	*$1,069*

* ***Model 1892 Trapper*** – .44-40 WCF, .44 Rem. Mag., .357 Mag., or .45 LC cal., 16 in. round gloss blue barrel, high polish blue steel receiver, tube mag., oil finished Grade I straight grip walnut stock with plastic shotgun style buttplate, Marble's gold bead front sight, buckhorn style rear sight, tang safety, 5 lbs. 14 oz. Mfg. mid-2011-2012.

	$1,100	$925	$800	$675	$550	$450	$325	*$1,069*

* ***Model 1892 Trapper Takedown*** – .44-40 WCF, .44 Rem. Mag., .357 Mag., or .45 LC cal., 16 in. octagon gloss blue barrel, takedown action, high polish blue steel receiver, tube mag., oil finished Grade I pistol grip checkered walnut stock with polished crescent buttplate, rifle forearm, Marble's gold bead front sight, buckhorn style rear sight, tang safety, 6 lbs. 4 oz. Mfg. mid-2011-2012.

	$1,650	$1,400	$1,150	$1,000	$850	$725	$575	*$1,549*

This model was originally featured as a 2010 SHOT Show Special.

* ***Model 1892 Case Hardened Sporter*** – .44-40 WCF, .44 Rem. Mag., .357 Mag., or .45 LC cal., 24 in. octagon gloss blue barrel, case colored steel receiver, tube mag., oil finished Grade I straight grip uncheckered walnut stock with case colored crescent buttplate, rifle forearm, with case colored forearm cap, Marble's gold bead front sight, buckhorn style rear sight, tang safety, 7 lbs., 4 oz. Mfg. mid-2011-2012.

	$1,375	$1,075	$875	$800	$725	$625	$500	*$1,269*

* ***Model 1892 High Grade*** – .45 LC cal., features gold accents and receiver game scene, 1,000 mfg. 1997 only.

	$1,525	$1,250	$900	N/A	N/A	N/A	N/A	*$1,285*

GRADING - PPGS™	100%	98%	95%	90%	80%	70%	60%	LAST MSR

MODEL 1892 CARBINE – .357 Mag., .44 Rem. Mag., .44-40 Win., or .45 LC cal., top tang safety, 20 in. round button rifled barrel with barrel band and full-length mag., rebounding hammer, blade front and semi-buckhorn rear sight, uncheckered straight grip walnut stock and forearm w/satin finish, steel contoured carbine strap buttplate, loop lever, 10 shot mag., saddle ring, approx. 6 lbs. Mfg. by Miroku in Japan. Mfg. 2011-2013, reintroduced 2018.

MSR $1,110	$1,050	$940	$825	$725	$625	$550	$475	

Last MSR in 2013 was $1,160.

* ***Model 1892 Large Loop Carbine*** – .357 Mag., .44 Rem. Mag., .44-40 Win., or .45 LC cal., 20 in. round barrel with blued steel barrel band, 10 shot mag., carbine ladder rear sight (disc. 2012), semi-buckhorn rear sights with Marble Arms front sight (mfg. 2014-2017), or ladder rear sight and Marble Arms gold bead front sight (new 2019), walnut straight grip stock with satin finish, blued steel carbine strap buttplate, large loop lever, steel loading gate, top tang is drilled and tapped, 6 lbs. Mfg. 2011-2012, reintroduced 2014-2017, 2019-present.

MSR $1,310	$1,200	$1,050	$875	$750	$600	$500	$425	

MODEL 1892 SHORT RIFLE – .357 Mag., .44 Rem. Mag., .44-40 Win. (new 2019), or .45 LC cal., 20 in. round barrel with full-length mag. tube, 10 shot mag., semi-buckhorn rear sight with Marble Arms gold bead front, steel loading gate, walnut straight grip stock with satin finish, classic rifle-style forearm with blued steel cap and crescent buttplate, 6 lbs. New 2014.

MSR $1,110	$1,050	$940	$825	$725	$625	$550	$475	

MODEL 1892 JOHN WAYNE HIGH GRADE – .44-40 WCF cal., 18 1/2 in. barrel, 9 shot, silver nickel nitride receiver with engraved John Wayne portrait, initials, and flowing banner with "Courage, Strength, Grit" on right side, two portraits and banner with "John Wayne American 1907-2007" on left side, blue loading gate and action screws, ladder style adj. rear sight, saddle ring, blue hammer and trigger, large loop lever, uncheckered walnut stock, limited mfg. of 4,000, first 1,000 offered as match set with Custom Grade. Disc. 2009.

	$2,250	$1,775	$1,550	N/A	N/A	N/A	N/A	*$1,999*

MODEL 1892 JOHN WAYNE CUSTOM GRADE – .44-40 WCF cal., 18 1/2 in. barrel with gold signature, 9 shot, blue receiver with engraved John Wayne portrait, initials, and flowing banner with "Courage, Strength, Grit" on right side, two portraits and banner with "John Wayne American 1907-2007" on left side, blue loading gate and action screws, ladder style adj. rear sight, saddle ring, blue hammer and trigger, large loop lever, checkered Grade 5/6 satin walnut stock and forearm, limited mfg. of 1,000. Disc. 2009.

	$3,925	$3,300	$2,700	N/A	N/A	N/A	N/A	*$3,499*

MODEL 1895 GRADE I – .270 Win. (disc. 1999), .30-06 (mfg. 1998-1999, reintroduced 2010), .30-40 Krag (new 2010), or .405 Win. (mfg. 2000-2004, reintroduced 2010) cal., similar to original Model 1895 Winchester, checkered straight grip stock and Schnabel forearm, 24 in. round barrel, with buckhorn rear sight, 4 shot mag., top tang safety, blue finish, 8 lbs. Mfg. 1997-2004, and limited production 2010.

	$1,150	$975	$825	$700	$575	$525	$475	*$1,179*

MODEL 1895 LIMITED EDITION – .30-06 cal., similar to original Model 1895 Winchester, blue receiver, 24 in. round barrel, 4 shot mag. (box mag.), uncheckered woodstock and forearm, rear buckhorn sight, two-piece cocking lever, 8 lbs. 4,000 mfg. 1995-97.

	$1,050	$750	$575	N/A	N/A	N/A	N/A	*$853*

* ***Model 1895 Limited Edition High Grade*** – .30-06 (mfg. 1995-99) or .405 Win. (mfg. 2000-2002) cal., same general specifications as the Model 1895 Limited Edition, features older No. 3 engraving pattern with double scenes, gold borders with multiple gold inlays, deluxe checkered walnut stock and forearm. 4,000 mfg. 1995-2002.

	$1,925	$1,400	$1,150	N/A	N/A	N/A	N/A	*$1,532*

Add 20% for .405 Win. cal.

MODEL 1895 THEODORE ROOSEVELT 150TH ANNIVERSARY CUSTOM GRADE – .405 Win. cal., high polish blue receiver engraved with North American big game scenes, extensive gold plating, gold "Theodore Roosevelt" signature on receiver, top of barrel is matted, deluxe high grade walnut stock, includes commemorative brochure. 500 mfg. in sets with High Grade matching serial numbers 2008.

	$3,000	$2,500	$1,950	$1,525	$1,200	$995	$795	*$3,299*

This model was featured as a 2008 SHOT Show Special.

MODEL 1895 THEODORE ROOSEVELT 150TH ANNIVERSARY HIGH GRADE – .405 Win. cal., nitride finished receiver engraved with North American big game scenes, gold accents, gold "Theodore Roosevelt" signature on receiver, top of barrel is matted, deluxe high grade walnut stock, includes commemorative brochure. 1,000 mfg. 2008.

	$1,650	$1,375	$1,100	$900	$775	$650	$525	*$1,599*

This model was featured as a 2008 SHOT Show Special.

GRADING - PPGS™	100%	98%	95%	90%	80%	70%	60%	LAST MSR

MODEL 1895 THEODORE ROOSEVELT SAFARI HIGH GRADE – .405 Win. cal., 4 shot mag., 24 in. blue barrel, checkered Grade II/III walnut stock and forearm, silver nitride receiver with deep engraving, gold African big game inlays and embellishments, matte blue finish, TR "Safari Centennial 1909-2009" medallion on stock, gold signature on trigger guard, buckhorn rear sight, Marbles front sight, drilled and tapped, special matching ser. nos., includes full color box sleeve, special edition hang tag, owner's manual, and hardcover copy of Roosevelt's book, *African Game Trails,* and deluxe double gun case, 8 lbs. Ltd. mfg. of 1,500, the first 1,000 sold as a set with the Custom Grade, remaining 500 sold individually. Mfg. 2009 only.

$1,725 $1,450 $1,175 N/A N/A N/A N/A ***$1,749***

MODEL 1895 THEODORE ROOSEVELT SAFARI CUSTOM GRADE TWO GUN SET – .405 Win. cal., 4 shot mag., 24 in. blue barrel, checkered Grade III/IV walnut stock and forearm, blue receiver with deep engraving, gold African big game inlays and embellishments, matte blue finish, TR "Safari Centennial 1909-2009" medallion on stock, jeweled hammer, special matching ser. nos., patterned after Roosevelt's 1895 rifle featured in Cody Firearms Museum, includes full color box sleeve, special edition hang tag, owner's manual, and hardcover copy of Roosevelt's book, *African Game Trails,* and deluxe double gun case, 8 lbs. Ltd. mfg. of 1,000 two gun sets, sold only with Model 1895 Safari High Grade. Mfg. 2009 only.

$3,650 $3,150 $2,550 N/A N/A N/A N/A ***$3,649***

RIFLES: LEVER ACTION - MODEL 94, 1964-2006 MFG.

Due to engineering changes in 1992, all Model 94s and variations (not including the 9422 models) had a crossbolt safety in the upper rear of the receiver which prevents the hammer from contacting the firing pin.

100th Anniversary Model 1894s (mfg. 1994) are marked "1894-1994" on the receiver. During 2003, Winchester discontinued the crossbolt receiver safety, and introduced the new top tang safety.

U.S. Repeating Arms closed its New Haven, CT manufacturing facility on March 31, 2006, and an auction was held on Sept. 27-28, 2006, selling the production equipment and related assets.

AE suffix on the following models indicates angle eject.

Winchester made a major change in Model 94 production when it went to an investment cast receiver during 1964. The Model 94s listed below w/crossbolt safety (1992-2006 mfg.) are not as desirable as those models w/o the crossbolt safety manufactured pre-1992, unless a rare variation, configuration and/or caliber is involved.

MODEL 94 STANDARD MODEL – .30-30 Win., .32 Win. Spl. (disc. 1973, reintroduced 1992), 7-30 Waters (new 1989), .44 Mag. (mfg. circa late 1960s-1970s), .44 Spl. (mfg. 1984), .444 Marlin (mfg. 1984), or .45 LC (mfg. 1984) cal., 6 or 7 (24 in. barrel only) shot tube mag., 20 or 24 (mfg. 1987-88 only) in. round barrel, open sights, straight walnut stock, two barrel bands on forearm, Angle Eject became standard 1984, 6 1/2 lbs. Mfg. 1964-1997.

$550 $450 $380 $325 $225 $200 $160 ***$363***

Add 25% for 7-30 Waters cal.

MODEL 94 TRADITIONAL (DELUXE WALNUT) – .30-30 Win., .44 Mag. (new 1999), or .480 Ruger Big Bore (mfg. 2002-2003) cal., similar to Standard Rifle, except has plain (new 1998, not available in .44 Mag. cal.) or checkered walnut stock and forearm, 6 (.30-30 Win. cal.) 10 (.480 Ruger cal.), or 11 (.44 Mag. cal.) shot mag., 6 1/4 lbs. Mfg. 1988-2004.

$725 $600 $500 $375 $300 $250 $225 ***$436***

Add $34 for Traditional-CW Model (w/checkered stock and forearm).

Add $57 for .44 Mag. cal. (Traditional-CW Model with checkered stock, mfg. 1999-2004).

Add for .480 Ruger Big Bore cal. (mfg. 2002-2003) - $43 (Traditional) or $105 (Traditional-CW).

Add $55 for 1.5 - 4.5X scope with low mounts (disc.).

MODEL 94 LEGACY ROUND – .30-30 Win., .357 Mag. (new 1997), .44 Mag. (new 1997), or .45 LC (new 1997) cal., 7 (.30-30 Win. cal. only) or 12 shot mag., pistol grip checkered walnut stock and forearm, 20 (disc. 1999) or 24 (new 1997) in. round barrel, 6 3/4 lbs. Mfg. 1995-2006.

$720 $525 $475 $360 $275 $250 $225 ***$497***

Subtract $15 for 20 in. barrel.

* ***Model 94 Legacy Round 26 In.*** – .30-30 Win. or .38-55 Win. cal., 7 shot mag., adj. Marble's rear tang sight, similar to Model 94 Legacy Round, except features blue or color case hardened receiver and 26 in. round barrel, 7 lbs. Mfg. 2004-2006.

$975 $750 $550 $425 $375 $300 $250 ***$783***

Add 15% for case colored receiver.

Add a slight premium for .38-55 WCF cal.

GRADING - PPGS™	100%	98%	95%	90%	80%	70%	60%	LAST MSR

MODEL 94 LEGACY OCTAGON – .30-30 Win. or .38-55 Win. cal., 7 shot mag., adj. Marble's rear tang sight, crescent buttplate, blue or color case hardened receiver and 26 in. octagon barrel, 7 1/4 lbs. Mfg. 2004-2006.

$1,000 $800 $575 $475 $375 $350 $325 *$882*

Add 20% for case colored receiver.

Add a slight premium for .38-55 WCF cal.

MODEL 94 RANGER – .30-30 Win. cal. only, 20 in. barrel, uncheckered hardwood stock and forearm, 6 shot mag., 6 1/4 lbs. Mfg. 1985-2006.

$525 $425 $360 $275 $250 $225 $200 *$386*

Add approx. 15% for 4x32 scope with see-through mounts (disc. 1999).

* ***Model 94 Ranger Compact*** – .30-30 Win. or .357 Mag. cal., 16 in. barrel, uncheckered hardwood stock with 12 1/2 LOP with recoil pad, post-style front sight, 5 (.30-30 Win. cal.) or 9 shot mag., 5 7/8 lbs. Mfg. 1998-2004.

$675 $550 $375 $300 $225 $200 $160 *$402*

MODEL 94 TRAILS END – .357 Mag., .44-40 WCF (mfg. 1998-99), .44 Mag., or .45 LC cal., similar to standard rifle, except has 11 shot tube mag., 20 in. barrel, choice of standard or large loop lever (disc. 1998), crossbolt safety, 6 1/2 lbs. Mfg. 1997-2006.

$925 $750 $575 $375 $275 $225 $200 *$480*

Add approx. $20 for large loop lever (disc. 1998).

* ***Model 94 Trails End Takedown*** – similar to Model 94 Trails End, except has takedown action. Limited mfg. 2006.

$900 $725 $525 $425 $350 $325 $300 *$559*

* ***Model 94 Trails End Octagon*** – similar to Model 94 Trails End, except has octagon barrel, choice of blue or case colored receiver finish, 6 3/4 lbs. Mfg. 2004-2006.

$1,000 $850 $675 $475 $325 $275 $225 *$757*

Add 15% for case colored receiver.

MODEL 94 TRAILS END HUNTER ROUND – .25-35 Win., .30-30 Win., or .38-55 Win. cal., 20 in. round barrel, 6 shot mag., uncheckered walnut stock and forearm, shotgun buttplate, 6 1/2 lbs. Mfg. 2005-2006.

$825 $650 $525 $375 $275 $200 $175 *$480*

Add a premium for .25-35 WCF or .38-55 WCF cal.

* ***Model 94 Trails End Hunter Round Takedown*** – similar to Model 94 Trails End Hunter Round, except has takedown action. Limited mfg. 2006.

$925 $725 $550 $375 $300 $250 $225 *$559*

* ***Model 94 Trails End Hunter Octagon*** – similar to Model 94 Trails End Hunter, except has blued (new 2006) or case colored receiver and octagon barrel, crescent buttplate. Mfg. 2005-2006.

$975 $825 $625 $475 $350 $300 $275 *$757*

Add 15% for case colored receiver.

Add a premium for .25-35 WCF or .38-55 WCF cal.

MODEL 94 SHORT HUNTER TAKEDOWN – .30-30 Win., .44 Mag., or .450 Marlin cal., takedown action, 18 in. barrel, 6 or 10 (.44 Mag. only) shot mag., uncheckered walnut stock, XS ghost ring sight, 6 lbs. Limited mfg. 2006.

$925 $725 $550 $400 $300 $250 $225 *$587*

MODEL 94 PACK RIFLE – .30-30 Win. or .44 Mag. cal., 18 in. barrel, 4 or 5 shot 3/4 mag., over-dimension walnut stock and forearm cap w/o checkering, removable hood sight, 6 1/4 lbs. Mfg. 2000-2001.

$550 $450 $360 $275 $225 $200 $160 *$496*

MODEL 94 TIMBER CARBINE – .444 Marlin (disc. 2001) or .450 Marlin (new 2004) cal., 18 in. ported barrel with 4 (.450 Marlin cal. only) or 5 (disc. 2001) shot 2/3 mag., top tang safety, checkered semi-pistol grip stock and forearm, blue finish only, adj. XS ghost ring rear sight (new 2004), hooded front sight (disc. 2001) or ramp style front sight, 6 lbs. Mfg. 1999-2001, reintroduced 2004-2006.

$1,100 $975 $825 $675 $550 $400 $275 *$623*

* ***Model 94 Timber Carbine Scout*** – .30-30 Win. or .44 Mag. cal., similar to Model 94 Timber Carbine, 18 in. non-ported barrel with rail base, 4 (.30-30 Win.) or 8 (.44 Mag.) shot mag., XS ghost ring sights, uncheckered walnut stock and forearm, 6 lbs. Mfg. 2005-2006.

$875 $675 $500 $380 $325 $275 $225 *$623*

* ***Model 94 Timber Carbine Scout Takedown*** – similar to Model 94 Timber Scout, except has takedown action and Pachmayr recoil pad. Limited mfg. 2006 only.

$975 $825 $650 $475 $325 $275 $225 *$699*

GRADING - PPGS™	100%	98%	95%	90%	80%	70%	60%	LAST MSR

MODEL 94 WIN-TUFF RIFLE – .30-30 Win. cal., similar to Model 94 Rifle, except has laminated hardwood stock and forearm with checkering, drilled and tapped for scope mounts. Mfg. 1987-disc.

$425	$325	$275	$225	$200	$175	$150	*$404*

MODEL 94 BLACK SHADOW – .30-30 Win. or .44 Mag./.44 Spl. cal., 20 or 24 (.30- 30 Win. cal. only) in. barrel, 4 or 5 shot mag., non-glare finish, black composite synthetic stock with recoil pad and fuller forearm, approx. 6 1/4 lbs. Mfg. 1998-2000.

$625	$500	$375	$250	$200	$175	$150	*$381*

* ***Model 94 Black Shadow Big Bore*** – .444 Marlin cal., 20 in. barrel only, otherwise similar to Model 94 Black Shadow, 6 1/2 lbs. Mfg. 1998-2000.

$600	$475	$375	$275	$225	$175	$150	*$394*

MODEL 94 TRAPPER – .30-30 Win., .357 Mag. (mfg. beginning 1992), .44 Mag./.44 Spl. (new 1985), or .45 LC (new 1985) cal., 16 in. barrel, side ejection, walnut stock, 5 (.30-30 Win. cal.) or 9 shot tube mag., blue finish, dovetailed front sight, 6 lbs. Mfg. 1980-2006.

$825	$650	$525	$360	$275	$200	$175	*$470*

* ***Model 94 Trapper Compact*** – .357 Mag. cal., similar to Model 94 Trapper, except has 12 1/2 in. LOP stock. Limited mfg. 2006 only.

$925	$725	$550	$400	$300	$250	$225	*$486*

MODEL 94 BIG BORE – .307 Win. (disc. 1998), .356 Win. (disc. 1998), or .375 Win. (disc. 1987), or .444 Marlin (new 1998) cal., angled ejection port provides scope mounting, checkered walnut Monte Carlo stock with recoil pad, 20 in. barrel, 6 shot mag., sling swivels, 6 1/2 lbs. Mfg. 1983-disc.

$1,025	$800	$500	$400	$325	$275	$250	*$465*

Add 25% for .356 Win. or .375 Win. cal.

Also mfg. in a top eject (pre-USRA). This model had an "XTR" suffix until 1989.

MODEL 94 HERITAGE CUSTOM 1 OF 100 – .38-55 WCF cal., special edition for the NSSF Heritage Fund, features Winchester's historic No. 2 pattern hand engraved with 24Kt. gold inlays and individually signed by the engraver, deluxe spade checkered straight grip stock and forearm with metal cap, 1/2 round, 1/2 octagon 26 in. barrel, 6 3/4 lbs. Mfg. by the custom shop 2002-2003.

$5,750	$4,125	$2,475	N/A	N/A	N/A	N/A	*$5,200*

MODEL 94 HERITAGE HIGH GRADE 1 OF 1000 – .38-55 WCF cal., special edition for the NSSF Heritage Fund, features Winchester's historic No. 3 engraving pattern with 24Kt. gold inlays, deluxe checkered straight grip stock and forearm with metal cap, 1/2 round, 1/2 octagon 26 in. barrel, signed by engraver with factory letter, ser. no. prefix HER, 6 3/4 lbs. Mfg. 2002 only. While 1,000 rifles were scheduled to be manufactured, only 255 were mfg.

$2,650	$2,075	$1,875	N/A	N/A	N/A	N/A	*$1,883*

MODEL 94 CUSTOM LIMITED EDITION – .44-40 WCF (mfg. 2000 only) or .38-55 WCF (new 2001) cal., case colored receiver and 24 in. octagon match (.44-40 WCF cal. only) or 1/2 round, 1/2 octagon (.38-55 WCF cal. only) barrel with satin bluing, full (.44-40 WCF only) or 3/4 mag. tube, spade checkered straight grip walnut stock and forearm with metal cap, 7 1/4 (.38-55 WCF cal.) or 7 3/4 lbs. Only 75 mfg. in .44-40 WCF cal. 2000-2002.

$2,875	$2,225	$1,975	N/A	N/A	N/A	N/A	*$2,393*

MODEL 94 NEW GENERATION CUSTOM – .30-30 Win. cal., fancy pistol grip stock and long forearm with spade checkering, high lustre bluing with custom scroll engraving and hand engraved gold moose on right side of frame and gold doe/buck on left, new tang safety, 20 in. barrel. Limited mfg. 2003-2004.

$3,300	$2,675	$2,175	N/A	N/A	N/A	N/A	*$2,995*

MODEL 94 LIMITED EDITION CENTENNIAL – .30-30 Win. cal., crossbolt safety, manufactured to commemorate the 100th anniversary of the Model 94 in 1994.

* ***Model 94 Limited Edition Centennial Grade I*** – features No. 9 style Winchester engraving pattern (rolled) on both sides of receiver, 26 in. half-round half-octagonal barrel, pistol grip stock and forearm with cut checkering, half mag., open sights, crescent buttplate, 12,000 mfg. 1994 only.

$1,300	$1,025	$825	N/A	N/A	N/A	N/A	*$811*

* ***Model 94 Limited Edition Centennial High Grade*** – features No. 6 style Winchester engraving pattern (rolled) on both sides of receiver with gold outlines and 2 gold animals (mountain sheep and deer), Lyman No. 2 tang mounted rear sight, F-style checkering and carving, deluxe walnut, 26 in. half-round half-octagonal barrel, half-mag., crescent buttplate, 3,000 mfg. 1994 only.

$2,600	$2,100	$1,525	N/A	N/A	N/A	N/A	*$1,272*

GRADING - PPGS™	100%	98%	95%	90%	80%	70%	60%	LAST MSR

* ***Model 94 Limited Edition Centennial Custom High Grade*** – .30 WCF cal., features No. 5 style Winchester engraving pattern (hand-executed) on both sides of greyed receiver, etched by Baron Technology, gold outline panel scenes featuring caribou and pronghorns, Lyman No. 2 upper tang sight, F-style checkering and carving, 26 in. half-round half-octagonal barrel, half-mag., crescent buttplate, 94 mfg. in 1994 only.

$6,600 $5,325 $4,350 N/A N/A N/A N/A *$4,684*

MODEL 94 XTR – .30-30 Win. or 7-30 Waters (new 1985) cal., 20 or 24 (7-30 Waters only) in. barrel, checkered select walnut, hooded front sight (except 7-30 Waters which has dovetailed front blade), 6 1/2 lbs. Disc. 1988.

$825 $725 $550 $425 $300 $225 $200 *$285*

Add $100 for 7-30 Waters cal. rifle.

The XTR nomenclature was disc. 1988.

* ***Model 94 XTR Deluxe*** – .30-30 Win. cal. only, deluxe American walnut stock and lengthened forearm with fancy checkering, 20 in. barrel with deluxe script, rubber buttpad. Mfg. 1987-88 only.

$875 $750 $575 $425 $300 $225 $200 *$426*

MODEL 94 .44 MAG. S.R.C. – .44 Mag. cal., top eject, 20 in. barrel, SRC. Mfg. 1967-1972.

$800 $625 $400 $300 $225 $200 $175

MODEL 94 CLASSIC SERIES – .30-30 Win. cal., 20 or 26 in. octagon barrel. Approx. 47,000 mfg. 1967-1970.

$700 $525 $325 $250 $200 $175 $150

MODEL 94 ANTIQUE CARBINE – similar to Standard, with case hardened scroll engraved receiver, gold-plated saddle ring. Mfg. 1964-1983.

$675 $550 $450 $325 $250 $225 $200

MODEL 94 CARBINE – .30-30 Win. cal., uncheckered walnut stock and hooded front sight, w/o saddle ring. Manufactured circa 1976.

$675 $550 $450 $325 $250 $225 $200

MODEL 94 WRANGLER – .32 Win. Special, top ejection, saddle ring, 16 in. barrel, oversized loop lever, western scene roll engraved on receiver, "Wrangler" logo on barrel, 5 shot mag. Only 7,947 mfg. 1983-1984.

$700 $525 $350 $250 $200 $175 $150

MODEL 94 WRANGLER IA – .30-30 Win. cal., top ejection, 18 in. barrel, small loop lever, western scene roll engraved on receiver, "Wrangler IA" logo on barrel. Limited mfg. 1983 only.

$775 $650 $500 $375 $275 $200 $175

MODEL 94 WRANGLER II – .32 Win. Spl. (disc. 1984) or .38-55 WCF cal., angle ejection, 16 in. barrel, saddle ring, oversized loop-shaped lever, western scene roll-engraved receiver, 5 shot mag., uncheckered stock and forearm, "Wrangler II" logo on barrel, 6 1/8 lbs. Made 1983-85 only.

$675 $525 $325 $250 $200 $175 $150 *$275*

MODEL 94 WRANGLER LARGE LOOP – .30-30 Win., .44 Mag., or .45 LC (new 1999) cal., 16 in. barrel, has large loop lever, uncheckered walnut stock and forearm, blue finish, open sights, 6 lbs. Mfg. 1992-99.

$525 $425 $325 $250 $200 $175 $150 *$400*

MODEL 94 DU – .30-30 Win. cal., approx. 2,800 rifles were mfg. in the U.S. during 1986. Serial numbered DU-860001-DU-8628000.

$1,175 $925 $750 $600 $475 $375 $275

MODEL 94 DU GOLD – .30-30 Win. cal., gold plated receiver, 300 mfg. 1986. Serial numbered DU-863000-DU-863299.

$1,500 $1,325 $1,050 $800 $675 $550 $450

MODEL 9417 TRADITIONAL – .17 HMR cal., 11 shot mag., 20 1/2 in. barrel, checkered straight grip stock and forearm, full mag., 6 lbs. Limited mfg. 2003-2004.

$1,150 $1,050 $900 $675 $550 $450 $325 *$515*

MODEL 9417 LEGACY – .17 HMR cal., 11 shot mag., 22 1/2 in. barrel, checkered pistol grip stock and longer forearm, 6 lbs. Limited mfg. 2003-2004.

$1,275 $1,125 $925 $650 $550 $450 $325 *$551*

MODEL 9422 XTR TRADITIONAL (STANDARD WALNUT) – .22 LR or .22 WMR cal., takedown, 20 1/2 in. round barrel, 15 shot (LR) or 11 shot (Mag. cal.) mag., grooved forged steel receiver, uncheckered (early mfg.) or checkered straight grip, uncheckered or checkered high gloss (disc.) or satin weather

GRADING - PPGS™	100%	98%	95%	90%	80%	70%	60%	LAST MSR

resistant finish (new 1988) walnut stock and forearm, regular or large loop (mfg. 1998-99) lever, sights, 6 lbs. Mfg. 1972-2004.

	$900	$725	$525	$425	$350	$325	$300	*$479*

Add 25% for early pre-XTR mfg. with uncheckered straight grip stock.
Add 25% for large loop lever (disc. 1999).
Add approx. 15% for .22 WMR cal.

This model had an "XTR" suffix until 1989. Earlier mfg., including pre-XTR and early XTR rifles, had no checkering.

MODEL 9422 XTR CLASSIC – same general specifications as Model 9422 XTR Standard, except has 22 1/2 in. barrel and non-checkered, satin finished, pistol grip walnut stock and extended forearm, stock also has fluted comb with crescent steel buttplate, curved finger lever, 6 1/2 lbs. Mfg. 1985-1987.

	$1,100	$975	$850	$775	$650	$525	$375	*$301*

MODEL 9422 LEGACY – .22 LR or .22 WMR (new 1999) cal., 22 1/2 in. barrel with deluxe checkered semi-pistol grip stock, 11 (.22 WMR) or 15 shot non full-length mag., 6 lbs. Mfg. 1998-2004.

	$1,100	$975	$850	$775	$650	$525	$375	*$512*

Add 15% for .22 WMR cal.

MODEL 9422 CUSTOM TRIBUTE – .22 LR cal., 20 1/2 in. barrel, engraved silver plated receiver with gold inlaid Model 9422 Tribute banner on left side of receiver and gold horse and rider on right, engine turned bolt and extractor, gold plated trigger, select walnut with fleur-de-lis checkering on straight grip stock and forearm, 6 lbs. 222 mfg. by the Custom Shop 2005 with a "CTS" serial number prefix.

	$3,750	$2,825	$2,025	N/A	N/A	N/A	N/A	*$2,313*

MODEL 9422 SPECIAL EDITION TRADITIONAL TRIBUTE – .22 LR or .22 WMR cal., 20 1/2 in. round barrel, features a Winchester horse and rider engraved on right side of receiver, and Model 9422 Tribute banner on left, checkered straight grip walnut stock and forearm, 6 lbs. 4300 in .22 LR cal. and 3200 in .22 WMR cal. Special Edition Traditional and Legacy Tribute rifles were mfg. in 2005 with a "FTS" serial number prefix.

	$1,050	$875	$700	$475	$325	$275	$225	*$516*

Add 10% for .22 WMR cal.

MODEL 9422 SPECIAL EDITION LEGACY TRIBUTE – .22 LR or .22 WMR cal., similar to Model 9422 Special Edition Traditional, except has 22 1/2 in. barrel and pistol grip stock with crescent recoil pad. 4300 in .22 LR cal. and 3200 in .22 WMR cal. Special Edition Traditional and Legacy Tribute rifles were mfg. in 2005 with a "FTS" serial number prefix.

	$1,350	$1,225	$975	$650	$550	$450	$325	*$551*

Add 10% for .22 WMR cal.

MODEL 9422 HIGH GRADE TRADITIONAL TRIBUTE – .22 LR or .22 WMR cal., 20 1/2 in. round barrel, features silver banner with Model 9422 Tribute on left receiver side and horse and rider on right side, etched engraving on blued receiver, checkered straight grip walnut stock and forearm, 6 lbs. 1072 in .22 LR cal. and 850 in .22 WMR cal. High Grade Traditional and Legacy Tribute rifles were mfg. in 2005 with a "FTS" serial number prefix.

	$2,025	$1,775	$1,375	$925	$750	$600	$500	*$1,050*

Add 10% for .22 WMR cal.

MODEL 9422 HIGH GRADE LEGACY TRIBUTE – .22 LR or .22 WMR cal., similar to High Grade Traditional Tribute, except has 22 1/2 in. barrel and crescent recoil pad, pistol grip stock, 6 lbs. 1072 in .22 LR cal. and 850 in .22 WMR cal. High Grade Traditional and Legacy Tribute rifles were mfg. in 2005 with a "FTS" serial number prefix.

	$2,200	$1,925	$1,475	$1,050	$850	$725	$600	*$1,085*

Add 5% for .22 WMR cal.

MODEL 9422 TRAPPER – .22 S, L, LR, or .22 WMR (new 1998), 16 1/2 in. barrel, checkered walnut stock and forearm, 11 (.22 LR), 8 (.22 WMR), 15 (.22 S), or 12 (.22 L) shot tube mag., 5 3/4 lbs. Mfg. 1996-2001.

	$1,275	$1,025	$900	$650	$550	$450	$325	*$437*

Add $150 for .22 WMR cal.

500 Trapper special edition models were made for W.A.C.A. with engraving and silver and gold wash. Current estimated value is $1,300 for NIB condition. C.D.N.N. Sports Inc. in Abilene, TX ordered 1,002 Trapper models (501 in .22 WMR and 501 in .22 S, L, LR cal.) with case colored receivers and special serial numbers. Current estimated value is $1,200 for NIB condition.

Some barrel markings on this model may not have the "S" for .22 Short cal.

GRADING - PPGS™	100%	98%	95%	90%	80%	70%	60%	LAST MSR

MODEL 9422 WIN-CAM – .22 WMR cal. only, similar to 9422 XTR Standard, except has checkered greenish laminated hardwood stock and forearm. Mfg. 1987-1997.

	$975	$825	$650	$475	$325	$275	$225	$424

MODEL 9422 WINTUFF – .22 LR or .22 WMR cal., 20 1/2 in. barrel, checkered laminated brown hardwood stock and forearm, 6 1/4 lbs. Mfg. 1988-1999.

	$825	$650	$525	$350	$275	$200	$175	$423

Add 10% for .22 WMR cal.

MODEL 9422 HIGH-GRADE – .22 LR cal., features engraved receiver with raccoon and coonhound, deluxe checkered walnut stock and forearm. Mfg. 1995-96 only.

	$1,050	$875	$675	$475	$325	$275	$225	$489

MODEL 9422 HIGH GRADE SERIES II – .22 LR cal., 20 1/2 in. barrel, high grade walnut stock and forearm with cut checkering, engraved receiver includes dog and squirrels, 6 lbs. Mfg. 1998-99.

	$1,075	$900	$700	$475	$325	$275	$225	$504

MODEL 9422 25TH ANNIVERSARY GRADE I – .22 LR cal., deluxe checkered walnut stock and forearm, engraved receiver with Winchester Horse and Rider, 2,500 mfg. 1997 only, inventory remained through 1999.

	$1,225	$975	$875	$650	$550	$450	$325	$606

MODEL 9422 25TH ANNIVERSARY HIGH GRADE – .22 LR cal., extra deluxe checkered walnut stock and forearm, high gloss blue and engraved receiver with Winchester Horse and Rider, featuring silver borders and lever accents, 250 mfg. 1997 only.

	$2,000	$1,550	$1,050	N/A	N/A	N/A	N/A	$1,348

RIFLES: LEVER ACTION - MODELS 94 AND 1894, 2010-CURRENT

The following models in this category are manufactured in Miroku, Japan beginning 2010.

MODEL 1894 OLIVER WINCHESTER 200TH ANNIVERSARY CUSTOM GRADE – .30-30 Win. cal., 24 in. half-round, half-octagon barrel, top tang safety, buckhorn rear sight, Marble's front sight, checkered Grade IV/V walnut stock with high gloss finish, 8 shot mag., blue receiver with deep scroll engraving, left side has Winchester Repeating Arms crest, right side has "Two Hundred Years, Oliver F. Winchester" and "1810-2010" in gold, Oliver F. Winchester signature in gold on top of bolt, approx. 8 lbs. 500 mfg. in sets with High Grade during 2010 only.

	$2,250	$1,850	$1,475	N/A	N/A	N/A	N/A	$1,959

MODEL 1894 OLIVER WINCHESTER 200TH ANNIVERSARY HIGH GRADE – .30-30 Win. cal., 24 in. half-round, half-octagon barrel, top tang safety, buckhorn rear sight, Marble's front sight, checkered Grade II/III walnut stock with high gloss finish, 8 shot mag., silver nitride receiver with delicate scroll engraving, left side has Winchester Repeating Arms crest, and right has "Two Hundred Years, Oliver F. Winchester" and "1810-2010" in gold, Oliver F. Winchester signature in gold on top of bolt, approx. 8 lbs. 500 mfg. in sets with Custom Grade during 2010 only, remaining quantities were sold individually.

	$1,595	$1,175	$975	N/A	N/A	N/A	N/A	$1,469

MODEL 94 CARBINE – .30-30 Win. or .38-55 Win. cal., 7 shot tube mag., 20 in. button rifled barrel with barrel band, semi-buckhorn rear sight and Marbles blade front sight, uncheckered satin finished plain walnut stock and forearm, blue metal finish, top tang safety, drilled and tapped, 6 1/2 lbs. New 2013.

MSR $1,240	$1,075	$940	$825	$715	$600	$500	$415	

MODEL 94 SHORT RIFLE – .30-30 Win., .38-55 Win. (new 2012), or .450 Marlin (new 2015) cal., 20 in. round barrel (ported on .450 Marlin cal.), 7 shot mag., steel construction, rebounding hammer, adj. semi-buckhorn rear sight and Marbles front sight, uncheckered walnut stock and forearm, black synthetic shotgun style buttplate or Pachmayr Decelerator recoil pad on .450 Marlin cal., top tang safety, articulated cartridge stock, blue finish, satin finished stock, 6 3/4 lbs. New 2011.

MSR $1,270	$1,100	$965	$825	$725	$600	$500	$425	

MODEL 94 SPORTER – .30-30 Win. or .38-55 Win. cal., 24 in. half-round, half-octagon barrel, 8 shot full-length mag., all steel construction, includes knurled hammer spur, rebounding hammer, Marble's front sight and semi-buckhorn rear sight, checkered satin finished walnut stock and forearm with crescent buttplate, top tang safety, articulated cartridge stop, blue finish, satin finished stock, approx. 7 1/2 lbs. New 2011.

MSR $1,440	$1,300	$1,090	$950	$825	$675	$550	$480	

MODEL 94 TRAILS END TAKEDOWN – .30-30 Win., .38-55 Win. (new 2014) or .450 Marlin cal., top tang safety, 20 in. ported round barrel with Marble's front sight and semi buckhorn rear sight, satin finished plain walnut stock and forearm, .450 Marlin cal. has Pachmayr Decelerator recoil pad, 6 shot mag., approx. 6-3/4 lbs. New 2012.

MSR $1,510	$1,285	$1,125	$965	$875	$700	$580	$500	

GRADING - PPGS™	100%	98%	95%	90%	80%	70%	60%	LAST MSR

MODEL 94 125TH ANNIVERSARY CUSTOM – .30-30 Win. cal., 24 in. triple-checked, button rifled full octagon barrel, 8 shot mag., hammer is drilled and tapped for a knurled hammer spur extension, gold bead front sight and adj. semi-buckhorn rear sight, straight grip Grade V/VI walnut stock with oil finish, blued steel forearm band, steel crescent buttplate, full bordered cut checkering with spade insets on both the grip and forearm, deep relief hand engraving by Giovanelli of Italy of a classic running deer scene on the right side of the receiver and horse and rider with Winchester banner on the left side of the receiver, with gold embellished accents on both sides of the receiver, highly polished deeply blued metalwork, special barrel markings commemorate this collectable rifle, steel loading gate, articulated cartridge stop, coin finished, 7 1/2 lbs. Limited mfg. 2019 only.

	100%	98%	95%	90%	80%	70%	60%	LAST MSR
	$3,100	$2,725	$2,325	$2,110	$1,700	$1,400	$1,125	*$3,450*

MODEL 94 125TH ANNIVERSARY HIGH GRADE – .30-30 Win. cal., 24 in. triple-checked button rifled full octagon barrel, 8 shot mag., hammer is drilled and tapped for a knurled hammer spur extension, gold bead front sight and adj. semi-buckhorn rear sight, straight grip Grade III/IV walnut stock with oil finish, blued steel forearm band, full bordered cut checkering with spade insets on both the grip and forearm, steel crescent buttplate, hand-chased engraving designed by Giovanelli of Italy of the horse and rider and the Winchester banner on the left side of the receiver and a trophy whitetail buck and the Winchester banner on the right, highly polished deeply blued metalwork, special barrel markings commemorate this rifle, steel loading gate, articulated cartridge stop, 7 1/2 lbs. Limited mfg. 2019 only.

	100%	98%	95%	90%	80%	70%	60%	LAST MSR
	$2,150	$1,880	$1,625	$1,460	$1,185	$975	$800	*$2,400*

MODEL 94 150TH COMMEMORATIVE – .30-30 Win. cal., 24 in. octagon barrel marked "The American Legend 1866-2016", gold band on muzzle, 8 shot mag., gold bead front and buckhorn rear sight, Grade 5/6 checkered walnut straight grip stock and forearm, crescent buttplate and forearm cap are engraved, silver Nitride finished receiver with Winchester 150th Anniversary logo and the WRA scroll trademark, 7 1/2 lbs. Limited mfg. 2016 only.

	100%	98%	95%	90%	80%	70%	60%	LAST MSR
	$2,400	$2,100	$1,900	$1,700	$1,500	$1,350	$1,200	*$2,670*

RIFLES: O/U

DOUBLE XPRESS RIFLE – .30-06, .257 Roberts, .270 Win., 7x57mmM, 7x57Rmm, 7x65Rmm, or 9.3x74Rmm cal., 23 1/2 in. O/U barrels, iron sights with claw scope mounts, ejectors, fully engraved satin finish receiver with game scene engraving, walnut specially hand checkered, sling swivels, 8 1/2 lbs. Mfg. 1984-1985 only.

	100%	98%	95%	90%	80%	70%	60%	LAST MSR
	$4,950	$4,500	$3,000	$2,500	$2,250	$2,000	$1,750	*$2,995*

In 1984, Aero Marine located in Birmingham, AL special ordered 200 deluxe double rifles in 7x57mm Mauser cal. They featured better engraving and game scenes with bottom of receiver marked Jaeger. Of the 200, 100 were rifles with 90 being standard grade and 10 being deluxe. The other 100 were supplied with an extra set of O/U shotgun barrels. Sales were slow on these special guns and eventually they were liquidated to another wholesaler. Recently, prices are in the $3,500-$3,950 range for the rifle alone and $5,000-$5,500 for the Combo, depending on condition.

100%	98%	95%	90%	80%	70%	60%	50%	40%	30%	20%	10%

RIFLES: SEMI-AUTO

MODEL 1903 – .22 Win. Auto rimfire cal., 10 shot tube mag., 20 in. round barrel, open sights, straight grip stock cut out for partial magazine filling. Approx. 126,000 mfg. between 1903-1932.

100%	98%	95%	90%	80%	70%	60%	50%	40%	30%	20%	10%
N/A	$1,595	$1,375	$1,050	$900	$775	$650	$550	$475	$400	$325	$250

Add 150% for deluxe checkered model.

First U.S. semi-auto rifle designed for a special .22 cal. rimfire cartridge. Regular .22 cal. rimfire will not function or chamber properly in this model. Early models up to around ser. no. 1,800 were mfg. w/o a safety. Safety became standard around ser. no. 5,400. Watch for fake boxes.

MODEL 1905 – .32 Win. or .35 Win. cal., 5 or 10 shot box mag., 22 in. round barrel, open sights, straight or plain pistol grip stock. Approx. 29,113 mfg. between 1905-20.

100%	98%	95%	90%	80%	70%	60%	50%	40%	30%	20%	10%
N/A	$800	$725	$625	$575	$525	$450	$400	$360	$325	$300	$275

MODEL 1907 – .351 Win. cal., 5 or 10 shot box mag., 20 in. round barrel, open sights, plain pistol grip stock, an improved version of the Model 1905. Approx. 58,490 mfg. between 1907-57.

100%	98%	95%	90%	80%	70%	60%	50%	40%	30%	20%	10%
N/A	$750	$650	$575	$500	$425	$350	$325	$295	$250	$215	$195

MODEL 1910 – .401 Win. cal., 4 shot box mag., 20 in. barrel, open sight, plain pistol grip stock. Mfg. 20,786 between 1910-36.

100%	98%	95%	90%	80%	70%	60%	50%	40%	30%	20%	10%
N/A	$950	$825	$700	$600	$550	$500	$450	$400	$360	$325	$300

Add 50% for Fancy Sporting Rifle (special checkered walnut).

100%	98%	95%	90%	80%	70%	60%	50%	40%	30%	20%	10%

MODEL 55 – please refer to listing in Rifles: Single Shot.

MODEL 63 – .22 LR cal., styling similar to Model 1903, takedown, 10 shot tube mag., 20 (disc. 1936) or 23 in. barrel, open sights, plain pistol grip stock. Approx. 174,692 mfg. between 1933-1958.

$1,250	$1,075	$900	$750	$675	$600	$475	$375	$325	$275	$230	$200

Add 100%-150% for 20 in. barrel (carbine) depending on condition.

The Model 63 was introduced to take advantage of the new .22 LR cartridge, which the older Model 1903 couldn't chamber.

Watch for fake boxes and hanging tags on this model, especially with rifles in over 95%+ original condition.

* ***Model 63 w/Grooved Receiver*** – with grooved receiver.

$1,975	$1,775	$1,600	$1,375	$1,000	$800	$675	$600	$500	$375	$300	$250

GRADING - PPGS™	100%	98%	95%	90%	80%	70%	60%	LAST MSR

MODEL 63 GRADE I - RECENT PRODUCTION – .22 LR cal., similar to original Model 63, 10 shot mag., 23 in. barrel, checkered walnut stock and forearm, blue finish with engraved receiver, 6 1/4 lbs. Mfg. 1997-98.

	$675	$600	$550	$500	$430	$375	$315	*$678*

* ***Model 63 High Grade - Recent Mfg.*** – .22 LR cal., similar to original Model 63, 10 shot mag., deluxe checkered walnut stock and forearm, blue finish with engraved gold animals and accents on receiver, 6 1/4 lbs. 1,000 mfg. 1997 only.

	$1,050	$875	$750	N/A	N/A	N/A	N/A	*$1,083*

MODEL 74 – .22 S or LR (introduced in 1940) cal., tubular mag. in stock, pop-out bolt assembly. Approx. 406,574 mfg. between 1939-1955. Distinguishable by squared-off rear receiver.

	$395	$325	$250	$200	$165	$140	$90	

Add 25% for .22 Short cal. (mfg. 1939-1952).
Add 25% for pre-WWII mfg.

MODEL 77 – .22 LR cal., detachable box mag. or tubular mag. under barrel. Over 217,000 mfg. between 1955-62.

	$350	$300	$250	$200	$150	$130	$100	

Add $50 for tube mag.

MODEL 100 RIFLE PRE-1964 MFG.

	$800	$675	$600	$550	$475	$375	$325	

Add $100 for .243 Win. cal.
Add $350 for .284 Win. cal.

MODEL 100 RIFLE – .243 Win., .284 Win., or .308 Win. cal., 4 shot detachable mag., 22 in. round barrel with open sights, gas operated, basket weave checkering impressed on stock, pistol grip cap. Over 262,000 mfg. 1964-1973 with some production occurring in Japan.

	$675	$600	$500	$425	$275	$225	$200	

The pre-1964 .284 Win. cal. with cut checkering was made for less than one year (WFF, ser. range 72,XXX with no letter suffix or prefix).

MODEL 100 CARBINE – similar to rifle, with 19 in. barrel, plain pistol grip stock, barrel band. Mfg. 1967-1973.

	$875	$750	$600	$525	$450	$350	$325	

Add $100 for .243 Win. cal.
Add $400 for .284 Win. cal.

MODEL 190 RIFLE – .22 S, L, or LR cal., 15 shot LR tube mag., alloy receiver, uncheckered walnut finished hardwood stock, 20 1/2 (Carbine Model) or 24 (Rifle Model) in. barrel, approx. 2,150,000 (including the Model 290 listed also) during 1967-1980.

	$175	$150	$125	$100	$85	$75	$65	

MODEL 290 DELUXE RIFLE – similar to 190, with select Monte Carlo stock. Mfg. 1965-1973.

	$375	$325	$265	$225	$175	$140	$125	

MODEL 490 RIFLE – .22 LR cal., 5 shot mag., 22 in. barrel, folding sight, checkered one-piece stock. Mfg. 1975-1980.

	$325	$265	$225	$185	$155	$145	$130	

GRADING - PPGS™	100%	98%	95%	90%	80%	70%	60%	LAST MSR

SUPER X RIFLE GRADE I (SXR) – .30-06, .270 WSM, .300 WSM, or .300 Win. Mag. cal., gas operated action with multi-lug rotating bolt locking system, blued alloy receiver, 22 (.30-06 cal.) or 24 in. blue barrel w/o sights, hinged floorplate with 3 or 4 shot detachable box mag., enlarged trigger guard with crossbolt safety, walnut stock and raked forearm featuring unique circle pattern checkering on stock and forearm for grip, removable trigger assembly, approx. 7 1/4 lbs. Mfg. 2006-2009.

	100%	98%	95%	90%	80%	70%	60%	LAST MSR
	$925	$825	$675	$550	$500	$425	$350	*$949*

Add $30 for Mag. cals.

SUPER X RIFLE GRADE II (SXR) – similar to Super X Grade I, except also available in .325 WSM cal., deluxe wood ergonomic stock with adj. LOP and recoil reduction system, with or w/o TruGlo fiber optic sight system, 7 1/2 lbs. Mfg. 2007 only.

	100%	98%	95%	90%	80%	70%	60%	LAST MSR
	$750	$675	$575	$500	$425	$375	$325	*$864*

Add $28 for Mag. cals.

Add $68 for adj. LPA Sights with TruGlo fiber optic elements (.300 Win. Mag. or .325 WSM cal. only).

MODEL SX-AB – .308 Win. cal., 20 in. heavy barrel w/o sights, fully adj. stock with textured pistol grip and forearm, includes three interchangeable cheekpieces, 10 shot detachable mag., Picatinny bottom rail on forearm, 100% Mossy Oak Brush camo coverage, 10 lbs. Approx. 2,000 mfg. during 2009 only.

	100%	98%	95%	90%	80%	70%	60%	LAST MSR
	$1,250	$1,075	$950	$825	$700	$600	$550	*$1,379*

WILDCAT – .22 LR cal., striker fired, 18 in. precision button rifled chrome moly steel barrel, recessed target crown, 10 shot rotary mag., fully ambidextrous mag. release, spring-assisted magazine ejection, fully adj. ghost ring rear and ramped post front sight, ambidextrous molded polymer stock with skeletonized buttstock, front and rear sling eyelets molded into the stock, reversible manual safety button, bolt release button, upper assembly has an integral Picatinny top rail and rear access port, Picatinny rail section on underside of forearm, 4 lbs. New 2019.

	100%	98%	95%	90%	80%	70%	60%	LAST MSR
MSR $270	$230	$200	$175	$155	$125	$110	$90	

WILDCAT SR – .22 LR cal., striker fired, 16 1/2 in. precision button rifled chrome moly steel barrel, recessed target crown, threaded muzzle with knurled thread protector, 10 shot rotary mag., fully ambidextrous mag. release, spring-assisted mag. ejection, fully adj. ghost ring rear and ramped post front sight, ambi molded polymer stock with skeletonized buttstock, front and rear sling eyelets molded into the stock, reversible manual safety button, integral Picatinny sight rail, Picatinny rail section on underside of forearm, 4 lbs. New 2021.

	100%	98%	95%	90%	80%	70%	60%	LAST MSR
MSR $300	$255	$225	$190	$175	$140	$115	$100	

100%	98%	95%	90%	80%	70%	60%	50%	40%	30%	20%	10%

RIFLES: SINGLE SHOT

MODEL 1885 – available in most popular rimfire and centerfire cals. between .22 S, L, or LR and .50, falling block trigger guard activated action, John Browning's first high power single shot rifle design, many variations were made and we will list the standard types. Over 139,725 mfg. between 1885-1920.

This design was originally mfg. as the Model 1878 by the Browning Brothers in Ogden, UT, in the early 1880s. Fewer than 600 were mfg. - see the Browning section for values.

* ***Model 1885 Sporting Rifle Low Wall*** – 24 or 26 in. round or octagon barrel was standard, open sights, solid frame, standard trigger.

100%	98%	95%	90%	80%	70%	60%	50%	40%	30%	20%	10%
N/A	N/A	$1,650	$1,450	$1,275	$1,150	$975	$825	$700	$550	$400	$300

Add 30% for centerfire cal.

Add 25%-50% for case colored frame, depending on original condition.

* ***Model 1885 Sporting Rifle High Wall*** – 30 in. barrel, standard trigger, open sights, solid frame. Available in various size and weight barrels numbered (in front of forearm) from lightest to heaviest: 1, 2, 3, 3 1/2 (introduced 1910), 4, and 5. Case hardened frames standard until 1901 when bluing became standard, three different frames depending on caliber. Heavier barrels in rare calibers will bring a premium.

100%	98%	95%	90%	80%	70%	60%	50%	40%	30%	20%	10%
N/A	N/A	$5,500	$3,850	$3,000	$2,600	$2,050	$1,725	$1,500	$1,325	$1,100	$875

Add 30% for 20 ga. shotgun.

Add 30% for Takedown Model.

Add 25% for No. 5 barrel.

Add 10% for set trigger.

Add 25%-50% for case colored frame, depending on original condition.

Add 25%-50% for .405, .45, and .50 caliber.

100%	98%	95%	90%	80%	70%	60%	50%	40%	30%	20%	10%

* ***Model 1885 Schuetzen Rifle*** – high wall, 30 in. octagon barrel, double-set triggers, spur lever, aperture sight, Schuetzen style stock, adj. palm rest and buttplate.

N/A N/A $9,750 $7,000 $5,250 $4,350 $3,650 $3,200 $2,850 $2,500 $2,250 $1,875

Add 30% for Takedown frame.

Add 25%-50% for case colored frame, depending on original condition.

Prices are for factory original guns only. Since this model had many shooting alterations performed by various aftermarket suppliers of its time, perhaps only 10% of remaining specimens are unaltered (or 100% factory).

* ***Model 1885 Deluxe Sporting Rifle*** – various cals., available in Low Wall, High Wall, or Schuetzen configuration, distinguishable by case colored receiver and fancy pistol grip checkered wood.

N/A N/A $10,500 $8,250 $6,825 $5,625 $4,950 $4,475 $4,000 $3,450 $2,775 $2,175

Add 50%-100% for Deluxe Schuetzen Model with fancy pistol grip checkered wood and case colored receiver, depending on original condition.

* ***Model 1885 High Wall Musket*** – usually found in .22 LR cal.

N/A N/A $1,500 $1,350 $1,150 $975 $850 $750 $650 $550 $475 $400

Add 100% for .45-70 Govt. or .45-90 cal.

* ***Model 1885 Low Wall Musket (Winder Musket)*** – low wall, 3rd model, .22 Short or LR (most common) cal., 28 in. barrel, standard trigger and lever, military style stock and sights, grooved forearm, one barrel band.

N/A N/A $1,550 $1,325 $1,125 $950 $800 $700 $600 $500 $400 $300

MODEL 1885 (RECENT MFG.) – please refer to the RIFLES: SINGLE SHOT, POST 1964 MFG. section for these listings.

MODEL 1900 SINGLE SHOT – .22 S and L cal., bolt action, 18 in. round barrel, blue metal, open sights, one-piece straight grip gumwood stock without fitted buttplate, takedown, not serial numbered. Approx. 105,000 mfg. between 1899-1902.

N/A N/A $1,100 $900 $675 $425 $300 $200 $165 $145 $125 $110

Add 100% for later models marked M1900 on barrel, and Win. stamped butt.

This model is usually encountered with flaked frames.

MODEL 1902 SINGLE SHOT – similar to 1900, bolt action, with minor improvements. Distinguishable by specially shaped extended trigger guard. Not serial numbered. Approx. 640,299 mfg. between 1902-1931.

N/A $650 $525 $400 $275 $200 $150 $100 $90 $80 $70 $60

Chambering included .22 cal. Extra Long cal. in 1914 (interchangeable with S&L).

THUMB TRIGGER MODEL 99 – similar to 1902, with button behind cocking piece used to fire with thumb instead of trigger, not serial numbered. Approx. 75,433 were mfg. between 1904-1923.

N/A $2,000 $1,800 $1,575 $1,350 $1,000 $900 $725 $625 $550 $350 $325

MODEL 1904 SINGLE SHOT – improved version of 1902, 21 in. round barrel, chambering included .22 Extra Long in 1914, not serial numbered. Approx. 302,859 mfg. between 1904-31.

N/A $525 $450 $375 $300 $200 $175 $160 $150 $125 $100 $90

* ***Model 1904-A Single Shot*** – introduced 1927 with new sear bar and chambered for .22 LR.

N/A $525 $450 $375 $300 $200 $175 $160 $150 $125 $100 $90

MODEL 47 – .22 S, L, or LR cal., single shot bolt action, 25 in. round barrel, unique bolt design, uncheckered walnut stock, 5 1/4 lbs., approx. 43,000 (not serial numbered) mfg. during 1948-54.

$525 $450 $325 $250 $200 $175 $150 $135 $125 $120 $115 $110

MODEL 52 – please refer to listings in the Rifles: Bolt Action section.

MODEL 55 – .22 cal. only, top loading single shot, bottom ejection, 22 in. round barrel, open sporting sights, not serial numbered. Over 45,000 mfg. between 1958-61.

$225 $190 $175 $140 $125 $110 $100 $90 $80 $75 $70 $65

GRADING - PPGS™	100%	98%	95%	90%	80%	70%	60%	LAST MSR

MODEL 58 SINGLE SHOT – similar to Models 1902 and 1904, .22 LR cal., 18 in. round barrel, open sights, takedown. Approx. 38,992 mfg. between 1928-31.

	$1,100	$950	$800	$700	$550	$450	$350	

GRADING - PPGS™	100%	98%	95%	90%	80%	70%	60%	LAST MSR

MODEL 59 SINGLE SHOT – improved Model 58 with 23 in. round barrel and pistol grip stock with buttplate. Approx. 9,200 mfg. between 1930-1931.

	$1,325	$1,095	$950	$825	$600	$500	$350	

MODEL 60 – .22 S, L, or LR cal., improved Model 59, 23 in. round barrel increased to 27 in. 1933. Approx. 160,754 mfg. between 1930-34.

	$465	$395	$335	$275	$195	$160	$125	

Add 20% for 23 in. barrel.

MODEL 60A SPORTER – .22 S, L, or LR cal., sporter variation of Model 60, pistol grip walnut stock. Disc.

	$600	$495	$435	$375	$325	$250	$225	

MODEL 60A TARGET – similar to Model 60 with Lyman 55W aperture rear sight, heavier target stock, and 27 in. round tapered barrel. Approx. 6,118 mfg. between 1932-39.

	$725	$625	$550	$475	$425	$350	$295	

MODEL 67/67A – .22 S, L, LR or .22 WRF (introduced 1935) cal., 20 in. (Boys Rifle), 24 (miniature target boring), and 27 in. (sporting or smoothbore) round barrels, same basic action as the Model 60, not serial numbered. Approx. 383,000 mfg. between 1934-1963.

	$300	$250	$225	$175	$125	$100	$75	
.22 WRF cal.	$685	$600	$500	$465	$375	$310	$240	

Add 30% for Boys rifle.

Add 100%-150% for smoothbore, depending on condition.

MODEL 677 – same basic specifications as Model 67, except no iron sights or sight cuts in barrel, not serial numbered, supplied with Win. 5-A scope, .22 WRF is scarce. Approx. 2,240 mfg. between 1937-39.

	$2,525	$2,215	$1,850	$1,625	$1,295	$1,050	$805	

MODEL 68 – .22 LR or .22 WRF cal., bolt action single shot, similar to Model 67, walnut stock, supplied with aperture sight (no rear sight), not serial numbered. Approx. 100,000 mfg. between 1934-46.

.22 LR cal.	$400	$350	$275	$225	$200	$150	$125	
.22 WRF cal.	$1,325	$1,125	$950	$825	$650	$525	$400	

MODEL 121 SINGLE SHOT RIFLE – .22 LR cal., bolt action, 20 3/4 in. barrel, open sights, plain pistol grip stock. Mfg. 1967-73.

	$125	$110	$95	$90	$70	$55	$45	

MODEL 121Y SINGLE SHOT RIFLE – similar to 121, with shorter stock.

	$125	$110	$95	$90	$70	$55	$45	

MODEL 121 DELUXE – similar to 121, with ramp front sight and sling swivels.

	$140	$120	$105	$95	$80	$60	$50	

MODEL 310 SINGLE SHOT – .22 LR cal., bolt action, 22 in. barrel, open sights, checkered pistol grip stock, swivels. 13,544 mfg. 1972-1975.

	$265	$220	$190	$165	$140	$110	$95	

WINGO "ICE PALACE" RIFLE – 5mm shot cartridge, 22 in. round barrel with vent. rib, modified lever action Martini type single shot, walnut Monte Carlo stock and forearm, marked "WINGO" on both sides of receiver, mfg. in England for Winchester "Ice Palace" shooting center, electrical cord extends from the magazine connecting to a target throwing device which threw black clay mini-pigeons, approx. 20 mfg.

	$3,000	$2,650	$2,275	$2,075	$1,675	$1,375	$1,075	

Add approx. 33% if with electric cables, operating trap mechanism, and at least 50 rounds of 5mm ammo and mini-pigeons.

RIFLES: SINGLE SHOT, POST 1964 MFG.

MODEL 1885 LOW WALL GRADE I .22 LR CAL. – .22 LR cal., 24 1/2 in. half-round, half-octagon barrel with buckhorn rear sights, uncheckered straight grip walnut stock and forearm, crescent buttplate, blue finish only, 8 lbs. 2,400 mfg. late 1999-2001.

	$735	$625	$525	$450	$400	$350	$300	*$828*

* ***Model 1885 Low Wall High Grade*** – similar to Model 1885 Low Wall Grade I, except features frame engraving, 24Kt. squirrel/cottontail scenes, fancy walnut stock and forearm with cut checkering. 1,100 mfg. late 1999-2001.

	$1,050	$875	$750	$650	$550	$450	$350	*$1,180*

MODEL 1885 LOW WALL – .17 HMR (disc. 2006), .17 Mach 2 (new 2005), .22 Hornet, .223 Rem., .22-250 Rem., or .243 Win. cal., 24 in. octagon barrel, checkered straight grip or pistol grip walnut stock and Schnabel forearm, open sights, sling swivels, drilled and tapped, 8 lbs. Mfg. 2003-2006.

	$875	$700	$575	$500	$450	$400	$350	*$1,069*

GRADING - PPGS™	100%	98%	95%	90%	80%	70%	60%	LAST MSR

MODEL 1885 HIGH WALL – .22-250 Rem. (new 2006), .223 Rem. (new 2006), .270 WSM, .300 WSM, .325 WSM (new 2006), or 7mm WSM cal., 28 in. full octagon barrel without sights, checkered walnut stock, Schnabel forearm, adj. trigger, Pachmayr Decelerator pad, blued receiver, 8 1/2 lbs. Mfg. 2005-2006.

	$1,100	$800	$675	$575	$500	$425	$375	
.325 WSM & 7mm WSM	$1,600	$1,200	$1,000	$700	$500	$425	$375	*$1,085*

MODEL 1885 BPCR – .45-70 Govt. cal., 30 in. half round, half octagon barrel, case colored receiver, lever, buttplate, and pistol grip cap, drilled and tapped, oil finished Grade III/IV walnut Creedmor style stock with Schnabel forearm, no sights, 10 lbs., 8 oz.

	$1,450	$1,275	$1,075	$925	$800	$700	$600	*$1,779*

This model was featured as a 2009 SHOT Show Special.

MODEL 1885 HIGH WALL CENTENNIAL HUNTER – .30-06 cal., features gold embellished .30-06 seal on right side of engraved receiver, special barrel inscription, 28 in. octagon barrel, 8 1/2 lbs. Limited mfg. 2006.

	$1,525	$1,275	$975	N/A	N/A	N/A	N/A	*$1,617*

MODEL 1885 HUNTER RIMFIRE – .17 HMR, .17 WSM, .22 LR, or .22 WMR cal., low wall lever action, 24 in. octagon barrel with button rifling, semi-buckhorn rear sight and Marbles gold bead front sight, checkered walnut stock and Schnabel forearm with sling swivels, Pachmayr rubber recoil pad, blued frame and barrel, approx. 7 1/2 lbs. Mfg. by Miroku. New 2014.

MSR $1,520	$1,325	$1,135	$970	$880	$700	$600	$500	

100%	98%	95%	90%	80%	70%	60%	50%	40%	30%	20%	10%

RIFLES: SLIDE ACTION, DISC.

MODEL 1890 – .22 S, L, LR, or WRF, cals. are non-interchangeable (don't shoot a .22 S in a gun chambered for .22 L) and the barrel is marked for single cal. only, visible hammer, solid-frame (first 15,000) or takedown, 24 in. octagonal barrel, case hardened receiver was standard until 1901, optional metal finishes included full or partial coverage nickel, silver, and gold - all were special order, model nomenclature changed to Model 90 circa 1919 at approx. ser. no. range 640,000. Approx. 849,000 mfg. between 1890-1932.

* ***Model 1890 First Model Solid Frame*** – color case hardened receiver, mfg. 1890-1892.

N/A	$12,600	$10,800	$8,100	$7,650	$5,850	$4,500	$4,250	$3,600	$3,150	$2,475	$2,000

Add 20% for .22 L or WRF cal.

* ***Model 1890 Second Model Takedown*** – color case hardened or blue receiver, takedown feature was added in 1892 after over 15,000 solid frames had been made, approx. ser. no. range 15,500-326,000. Mfg. 1892-1907.

» **Model 1890 Second Model Takedown w/Case Colored Receiver**

N/A	$5,400	$4,500	$4,050	$3,600	$3,325	$3,150	$2,875	$2,250	$1,800	$1,350	$1,125

» **Model 1890 Second Model Takedown w/Blue Finish**

N/A	$2,700	$2,250	$2,150	$1,800	$1,275	$1,000	$800	$675	$525	$450	$400

* ***Model 1890 Third Model Takedown w/Blue Finish*** – most commonly encountered Model 1890, post-1901 manufacture.

N/A	$2,650	$1,800	$1,125	$750	$575	$500	$400	$350	$300	$275	$225

Add 50% for .22 LR cal. (mfg circa 1919-1932, starting at ser. no. approx. 610,000).

.22 LR cal. accounted for approx. 10% of the total production on this model.

Deluxe model will bring premiums over values listed. There were also a limited amount of guns mfg. with stainless steel barrels which will add to values of post-1901 mfg.

The Model 1890 was Winchester's first slide action repeating rifle. It replaced the Model 1873 .22 cal. It was an excellent and inexpensive .22 rifle that rapidly became the universal firearm used in shooting galleries. Even though production reached approx. 849,000 units, most guns were heavily used and specimens existing today in 98%+ condition are rare. Check carefully for rebarreling (notice proof marks on barrel).

MODEL 1906 – .22 S, L, or LR, 20 in. round barrel, tube mag., visible hammer, open sights, straight stock with shotgun buttplate. Approx. 848,000 mfg. between 1906-1932.

N/A	$3,225	$2,975	$1,975	$1,075	$550	$450	$350	$275	$250	$200	$175

Add 20% for non-grooved forearm.

Add 20% for .22 S cal. only.

This model is seldom encountered in over 90% original condition - original mint specimens can top $2,000.

Model nomenclature was changed to the Model 06 circa 1918.

100%	98%	95%	90%	80%	70%	60%	50%	40%	30%	20%	10%

* ***Model 1906 Expert*** – similar to Model 1906, except has a pistol grip stock and different shaped slide handle, finish choices included blue, nickel trimmed receiver, guard, and bolt, or full nickel trimmed, .22 S cal. only until approx. 70,000, mfg. 1917-1925.

N/A	$4,400	$3,500	$3,300	$1,650	$1,000	$825	$650	$525	$375	$300	$250

Add 25% for walnut stock.

MODEL 61 HAMMERLESS – .22 S, L, LR, WRF or Mag. cal., 24 in. round or octagon barrel (disc. 1947), with rifling or smoothbore (either small bore or Routledge), tube mag., open sights, plain grip stock. Approx. 350,000 mfg. between 1932-1963.

$1,125	$1,050	$875	$800	$650	$500	$400	$300	$250	$225	$175	$150

Add up to 100% for single cal. barrel marking (S or LR, Short is very rare).
Add $300 for pre-war mfg. w/small forearm.
Add 20% for grooved receiver.
Add 10% for pre-WWII rust blue metal finish.
Mint original pre-war Model 61s in the proper picture box are selling in the $3,800-$4,500 range. Post-war boxed Model 61s (Kraft box) are selling in the $2,800-$3,200 range. Smoothbore small diameter shot variations are selling in the $3,000-$4,000 range, while the Routledge shot variation with .410 diameter bore are selling in the $8,500-$10,000 range.

Pre-war manufacture has small forearm. "WRF" marked round barrel is rare - front of receiver must be marked "W.R.F."

Watch for fake boxes and hanging tags on this model, especially with rifles in over 95%+ original condition.

* ***Model 61 WRF*** – .22 WRF cal. only, front of the receiver, bottom side, must be stamped "WRF", octagon barrel mfg. 1932-1946, and round barrel mfg. 1947-1950.

$3,150	$2,825	$2,575	$2,100	$1,750	$1,250	$1,000	$750	$575	$475	$400	$250

Add 20% for round barrel.
Mint original pre-war WRF Model 61s in the proper picture box are selling in the $3,750-$4,000 range. Post-war boxed WRF Model 61s (Kraft box) are selling in the $3,800-$4,500 range.

* ***Model 61 Octagon .22 LR*** – .22 LR cal., octagon barrel variation of the Model 61. Disc. approx. 1947.

$4,000	$3,500	$3,000	$2,600	$2,100	$1,750	$1,425	$1,100	$900	$750	$575	$500

* ***Model 61 Octagon .22 WRF*** – .22 WRF cal., octagon barrel variation of the Model 61. Disc. approx. 1947.

$3,500	$3,250	$2,850	$2,475	$1,975	$1,675	$1,375	$1,125	$900	$675	$450	$350

* ***Model 61 Magnum*** – similar to Standard 61, but chambered for .22 WMR, three variations include two barrel marking differences and the third has an additional letter "A" stamped on the bottom of the trigger guard assembly, indicating a factory update. Mfg. 1959-1961.

$2,275	$2,075	$1,800	$1,425	$1,175	$950	$775	$675	$550	$450	$400	$325

Add $600-$1,000 for rare "WMRF" barrel marking.
Mint original rifles in the proper Kraft box are currently selling for approx. in the $3,500-$4,000 range.

* ***Model 61 Octagon .22 Short*** – .22 Short cal., octagon barrel variation of the Model 61. Disc. approx. 1947.

$4,250	$3,950	$3,625	$3,225	$2,750	$2,200	$1,850	$1,525	$1,250	$1,000	$750	$500

* ***Model 61 Smoothbore*** – .22 cal. shot cartridge only, 24 in. round smoothbore barrel, three variations include the Routledge bore with 3/8 in. (.375 in.) muzzle bore diameter and matted frame top (approx. 75 mfg. in the 45,000-47,000 ser. range), second variation is referred to as the Winchester Counter Bore (approx. .265 in.), third variation is the Straight Smoothbore with bore diameter the same as the .22 cartridge.

$4,150	$3,750	$3,300	$2,825	$2,200	$1,850	$1,525	$1,250	$1,000	$750	$500	$400

Add 100% for Routledge bore.
Mint original boxed guns with the Winchester Counter Bore and Straight Smoothbore are currently selling for $4,500-$6,000. Mint original boxed Routledge Bore guns are $8,000-$10,000.

MODEL 62/62A VISIBLE HAMMER – modern version of 1890, will shoot calibers interchangeably, 23 in. round tapered or octagon barrel. Over 409,000 mfg. between 1932-1958.

$1,300	$1,000	$650	$475	$375	$300	$250	$200	$185	$170	$155	$130

Add 50% for Gallery model (Gallery style loading port).
Add 50% for pre-WWII mfg.

Pre-war Model is 62, distinguishable by small forearm. The Model 62-A was introduced 1940 at approx. serial number 99,200 with minor changes. Model 62A single cal. barrel markings do not add premiums. .22 Short only models without the Winchester roll die receiver marking are more scarce than the so-called "Gallery Rifle" - mint specimens without the roll die marking are approx. $2,000. Also watch for fake roll die markings. Gallery variations of these models will also command sizable premium. Watch for fake boxes and hanging tags on this model, especially with rifles in over 95%+ original condition.

GRADING - PPGS™	100%	98%	95%	90%	80%	70%	60%	LAST MSR

MODEL 270 – .22 LR cal., tube mag., 20 1/2 in. barrel, checkered walnut pistol grip stock. Mfg. 1963-73.

	$210	$180	$160	$150	$120	$100	$85	

* ***Model 270 Plastic Forearm Variation***

	$180	$160	$140	$120	$100	$85	$75	

* ***Model 270 Deluxe*** – similar to 270, with select wood, Monte Carlo stock. Mfg. 1965-73.

	$300	$250	$180	$130	$100	$85	$70	

MODEL 275 – similar to 270, in .22 WMR cal.

	$240	$210	$180	$165	$120	$100	$85	

* ***Model 275 Deluxe*** – similar to 270 Deluxe, in .22 WMR cal.

	$420	$350	$300	$240	$180	$150	$110	

100%	98%	95%	90%	80%	70%	60%	50%	40%	30%	20%	10%

SHOTGUNS: 1879-1963

BREECH LOADING SxS – 10 or 12 ga., imported from England for sales through the Winchester New York City office only, exposed hammers, available in 5 grades ranging from Class D - Class A and Match gun (lowest to highest). Higher grades were mfg. by W.C. Scott & Sons, C.G. Bonehill, W.C. McEntree, Richard Redmond, and H. & E. Hammond Gun Mfg.'s. Approx. 10,000 were imported between 1879-84.

Prices vary greatly due to condition and grade. Prices can range from $350 (poor condition Class D) to over $5,500 (95%+ condition specimen in Class A or Match gun).

This SxS model was the first shotgun bearing the Winchester name sold in the U.S. Identifiable by "Winchester Repeating Arms Co., New Haven, Connecticut, USA" marking on barrel rib top.

MODEL 1887 LEVER ACTION – 10 or 12 ga., 4 shot tube mag., 30 or 32 in. full choke fluid steel barrels, plain pistol grip stock, first Browning patent shotgun mfg. by Winchester, first lever action repeating shotgun mfg. domestically. Mfg. 1887-1901. Approx. 64,855 mfg.

N/A	$4,575	$3,850	$3,375	$2,925	$2,425	$2,000	$1,450	$1,200	$1,000	$850	$750

Standard frame finish on this model was color case hardening. Premiums exist for original bright case colored specimens. 10 ga. began production with serial number 22148. Also mfg. in Riot configuration (20 in. cylinder bore barrel). Gauges were chambered for 2 5/8 in. (12 ga.) and 2 7/8 in. (10 ga.). A very small amount was also made up in .70-150 cal. - add a significant premium.

* ***Model 1887 Lever Action Deluxe*** – damascus barrel, checkered stock, and other special order features.

N/A	$9,475	$7,600	$6,325	$5,175	$3,575	$2,800	$2,275	$1,900	$1,525	$1,275	$1,000

MODEL 1893 SLIDE ACTION – 12 ga., 30 (standard) and 32 in. barrel, black powder only. First Winchester shotgun with sliding forearm action, first Browning slide action patent, disc. 1897 after run of some 34,050. Note: chambered for 2 5/8 shells only, damascus barrels were available at extra cost, as were fancy stocks.

N/A	$1,275	$1,075	$925	$800	$675	$600	$550	$500	$450	$375	$325

This gun had limited sales because mechanical weaknesses developed when shooting smokeless powder. Winchester offered a brand new shotgun of the customer's choice when they returned their Model 1893.

MODEL 1897 SLIDE ACTION – 12 or 16 ga. (introduced 1900), improved Model 1893 action, 26-32 in. barrels, visible hammer, various chokes, takedown or solid frame, plain pistol grip stock. Over 1,024,700 mfg. between 1897-1957.

N/A	$950	$750	$600	$550	$450	$325	$275	$250	$225	$200	$175

Add 50% for 16 ga.

Early 16 ga. Model 1897s were chambered for 2 9/16 in. shotshells, and are not as valuable because of the 2 3/4 in. shell length currently manufactured. This model was marked "Model 1897" on the slide action rails until circa 1912 (approx. ser. no. 500,000). After approx. ser. no. 500,000, the marking was moved to the barrel and changed to Model 97. The Model 1897 was the first Winchester shotgun chambered for 2 3/4 in. smokeless ammunition. This model was also manufactured with a damascus barrel for a short period of time, and is rare.

MODEL 1897 RIOT GUNS – see the "Trench/Riot Shotgun" category in the T section for more information and prices.

MODEL 1897 TRENCH GUNS – see the "Trench/Riot Shotgun" category in the T section for more information and prices.

This model changed its stock configuration after WWI.

100%	98%	95%	90%	80%	70%	60%	50%	40%	30%	20%	10%

MODEL 1897 TRAP – higher grade version of Standard, checkered stock, could have black diamond inlay in stock until 1919 (Black Diamond Trap), breechblock marked "Trap" until approx. 1926. Mfg. 1897-1931.

N/A	$3,000	$2,575	$2,200	$1,925	$1,600	$1,200	$900	$750	$550	$500	$450

* ***Model 1897 Trap Black Diamond Trap*** – distinguishable by diamond ebony inlays in stock pistol grip.

N/A	$2,500	$2,200	$1,975	$1,750	$1,450	$1,100	$825	$675	$500	$450	$400

MODEL 1897 PIGEON – higher grade version of Standard 97, should have engraved pigeon behind hammer on frame, breechblock marked "Pigeon", most exhibit black diamond stock inlays until 1919. Mfg. 1897-1939.

N/A	$12,750	$9,950	$8,550	$6,600	$4,950	$3,850	$3,300	$2,200	$1,650	$1,100	$900

MODEL 1901 – 10 ga. only, strengthened Model 1887 action to accept smokeless powder, lever action, standard barrel 32 in., blue barrel and frame, 5 shot mag., barrel address on upper tang. 13,500 mfg. between 1901-1920, starting with serial number 64,856.

N/A	$4,225	$3,850	$3,625	$3,000	$2,425	$2,175	$1,825	$1,500	$1,000	$850	$600

Add 50% for Deluxe Grade (checkered wood).

This shotgun was chambered for 2 7/8 in. smokeless powder ammunition.

MODEL 1911 SL AUTOLOADER – 12 ga., recoil operated, 26 or 28 in. barrel, various chokes, pistol grip laminated birch stock. Mfg. 1911-1921, with some production occurring between 1921-1928, 103,246 produced, action had design problems, nicknamed "The Widowmaker" or "Head Buster."

$1,000	$875	$750	$600	$550	$450	$350	$275	$225	$175	$150	$125

Values assume original wood without splitting, repair, or replacement. The Model 1911 was Winchester's first semi-auto shotgun. It did not prove to be satisfactory partly because the design had to avoid infringing the patents for Browning's famous A-5 model. Interestingly enough, this was a design which Winchester originally had helped Browning patent.

GRADING - PPGS™	100%	98%	95%	90%	80%	70%	60%	LAST MSR

MODEL 12 SLIDE ACTION – 12 (introduced 1914), 16 (introduced 1914), 20 (initial ga., mfg. 1912, 2 1/2 in. chamber mfg. until 1927), or 28 (introduced 1937) ga., 25 (20 ga. only, mfg. 1912-14), 26, 28, 30, or 32 in. standard, nickel, or stainless steel (scarce) barrel with or without rib (matted, solid, or VR), 2 9/16 (early 16 or 20 ga., until 1927, at ser. no. 464,565), 2 3/4 (became standard 1927) or 3 in. chamber, 6 shot, blue metal, various chokes, hammerless, plain pistol grip or straight walnut stock and forearm, marked Model 1912 from 1912-1919, approx. ser. no. 172,000. 14 in. LOP was original standard, then changed to 14 1/2 in. circa 1930. Mfg. 1912-1976. Most 28 ga. guns offered for sale today are fabrications and are not authentic. Very few original 28 ga. guns were built in this model and original specimens are rare and very collectible, even in lower percentage condition.

12 ga.(plain FC barrel)	$650	$525	$425	$350	$275	$225	$175
16 ga.(plain FC barrel)	$850	$700	$575	$475	$375	$295	$250
20 ga.(plain FC barrel)	$1,100	$900	$725	$625	$525	$475	$450
28 ga.(plain FC barrel)	N/A	$5,750	$4,625	$4,200	$3,575	$2,950	$2,550

Subtract 50% if with non-factory Cutts compensator (has choke marked on barrel).
Add 50% for factory installed Cutts compensator (no choke marking on barrel).
Add 20% for 32 in. barrel.
Add 50% for original box with papers.
The following add-ons DO NOT apply to 28 ga. values.
Add 20%-40% for Win. solid rib, depending on original condition.
Add 50%-60% for Win. milled VR.
Add 25%-50% for "Deluxe Field Grade" with fancy checkered wood, depending on condition.
Add 10% for pre-WWII mfg.
Add 60% for each extra barrel(s).
Add 40%-50% for Win. special VR (offset barrel proofmark).

"Y" prefix appears on Model 12s built 1964-1980 - see listing under Post-64 Models. Publisher's Note: The "Y" was actually added in front of the already applied serial numbers to be shipped after the 1968 Gun Control Act took effect (1970). The "left over" pre "64" receivers were used up on custom orders until that law became effective, and then the "Y" was added.

Nickel steel barrel Model 12s (mfg. 1912-1931) have become very popular in recent years, and some collectors are actually specializing on nickel steel Model 12s only. Winchester proofed steel barrels were introduced in 1931.

Stainless steel barrel Model 12s were introduced during 1926 as a special order only, and discontinued in 1931 (65X,XXX

GRADING - PPGS™	100%	98%	95%	90%	80%	70%	60%	LAST MSR

serial range). Values typically range between $1,450 - $3,500, and are very rare in over 95% original condition, as the bluing easily wore off the stainless steel barrel since it was a "Japaned" finish, not regular bluing. Original gauge can be determined by removing the buttstock and observing the gauge marking on the stock screw boss.

"Donut" post Winchester VRs are more desirable than the rectangular post.

13-15 in. LOPs could be special ordered on Model 12s until 1964.

Special order features on field guns have captured much collector interest in recent years. Combinations of these features can add a considerable percentage to the base values listed. Rare special orders on rare variations are very desirable and prices can double and more if the combination is right. As is the case with most other collectible shotguns at this time, Model 12s with open choked barrels in shorter lengths are A LOT more desirable (and expensive) than a specimen with a 30 in. full choke barrel (most common). Values listed are for standard configuration (28 or 30 in. full choke barrel with no rib). For most Model 12s, values for condition factors less than 60% will approximate the 60% price, because of shooter demand. Premiums must be added for the rarer open choked barrels in shorter length on all gauges.

Recently, some non-original, re-stamped 28 ga. barrels have been added to 16 or 20 ga. frames "creating" a more desirable (and expensive) gun to unsuspecting buyers. Roll die markings are getting better and better so be very cautious when considering a non-Cutts 28 ga. (as in get a receipt specifying originality). 28 ga. ser. no. range is approx. 720,138 to 1,857,XXX. 28 ga. Model 12s were available with both 2 3/4 (common) or 2 7/8 (infrequent) in. chamber. The 28 ga. has a magazine tube which is crimped, swaged, and necked at the rear and is visible with barrel assembly off and slide pulled back, enabling mag tube to protrude slightly at the rear of receiver extension. Believe it or not, there are getting to be a lot of fake Model 12 boxes that have been intentionally aged. Carefully screen NIB (watch the hanging tag also) specimens in this model.

* ***Model 12 Special Information***

Editor's Note: The Model 12 Winchester was produced continuously from 1912-1980. Over 2,027,500 were produced both in standard and deluxe (Pigeon) grades. Pigeon grades were first listed in 1914 and disc. during the war (1941). Reintroduced in 1948, they were disc. permanently in 1964, after which the Super Pigeon Grade became available only on a custom-order basis from Winchester's Custom Gun Shop. These guns are worth 50%-300% premiums depending on gauge, barrel lengths, stock options, engraving patterns, etc.

With an attrition rate of approximately 33%, Model 12s with rare features produced 50 years ago will only be much rarer today (and expensive). 28 ga. guns were built between 1937 and 1960. Gauge rarity in increasing order is 12 ga. (approx. 360,000 mfg. 1925-1943), 16 ga. (approx. 190,000 mfg. 1925-1943), 20 ga. (approx. 71,000 mfg. 1925-1943), .410 bore (Model 42), and 28 ga. (approx. 2,600 mfg. 1937-1943). Serialization breakdown by year of manufacture is provided under the "Serialization" section of this book. When collecting Model 12s, ser. nos. on the underside of receiver (forward end), should match ser. no. on bottom rear of Mag. tube.

MODEL 12 FEATHERWEIGHT – similar to Standard, except with alloy guard and different takedown system. Mfg. 1959-62. "F" suffix after ser. no.

	100%	98%	95%	90%	80%	70%	60%	LAST MSR
	$825	$725	$600	$475	$375	$300	$250	

MODEL 12 RIOT GUNS – see the "Trench/Riot Shotgun" category in the T section for more information and prices.

MODEL 12 MILITARY TRENCH GUNS – see the "Trench/Riot Shotgun" category in the T section for more information and prices.

MODEL 12 HEAVY DUCK GUN – 12 ga., 3 in. chamber, 30 or 32 in. barrel, solid rubber recoil pad, 1/2 in. shorter pull than regular Model 12 (13 5/8 in LOP.). Mfg. 1935-1963.

	100%	98%	95%	90%	80%	70%	60%	LAST MSR
	$1,350	$1,175	$1,050	$925	$800	$600	$500	

Add 50% for solid rib.

Add 50% for 32 in. barrel.

* ***Model 12 Heavy Duck Gun Vent. Rib*** – factory Winchester or 2 different rib styles mfg. by Simmons, notice barrel proof marking - rare.

	100%	98%	95%	90%	80%	70%	60%	LAST MSR
	$3,600	$3,200	$2,800	$2,500	$2,000	$1,650	$1,450	

Add 25%-50% for "Deluxe Field Grade" with fancy checkered wood, depending on condition.

MODEL 12 SKEET GUN – 12, 16, 20, or 28 ga., 26 in. barrel, skeet choke, checkered pistol grip stock, 14 in. LOP standard on pre-war guns. Mfg. 1933-1976.

	100%	98%	95%	90%	80%	70%	60%	LAST MSR
12 ga.	$2,150	$1,625	$1,150	$1,000	$900	$750	$650	
16 ga.	$3,350	$2,875	$2,400	$2,000	$1,750	$1,500	$1,250	
20 ga.	$5,875	$4,500	$3,375	$2,875	$2,250	$1,800	$1,500	
28 ga.	$9,750	$8,300	$7,200	$6,100	$5,000	$4,850	$3,500	

Add 10% for solid rib.

GRADING - PPGS™	100%	98%	95%	90%	80%	70%	60%	LAST MSR

Add 20% for Win. Special VR.
Add 50% for Win. milled VR.
Subtract 50% for non-Factory-Cutts compensator.
Add approx. 10% for brown plastic Hydrocoil stock, 12 ga. only.
Add approx. 10% for white plastic Hydrocoil stock (approx. 50 mfg, 12 ga. only).

MODEL 12 TRAP GUN – various gauges, full choke barrel, deluxe straight or pistol grip stock, solid recoil pad, 14 3/8 in. LOP standard on pre-war guns. Mfg. 1940-1964.

$1,900 $1,450 $1,250 $1,075 $850 $725 $625

Add 20% for milled VR.
Add approx. 20% for brown plastic Hydrocoil stock.
Add approx. 50% for white plastic Hydrocoil stock (approx. 50 mfg).

While plain barreled variation is rare, it is not as desirable.

Another variation of the Model 12 Trap Gun was called the "Ladies or Junior Model", with a factory LOP of 13 in., supplied with an original Jostom specially designed two-ply sponge rubber pad - it was standard in 12 ga. and also available for special order in 16 or 20 ga. It was only manufactured for three years and is marked "Model 12 Trap" on the receiver extension.

MODEL 12 SUPER GRADE – 12, 16, or 20 ga., 26, 28, or 30 in. matted rib barrel, deluxe walnut with checkered pistol grip (metal grip cap) stock and forearm. Mfg. 1955-1959.

$2,250 $2,000 $1,800 $1,575 $1,350 $1,000 $850

Add 60% for 20 ga.
Add 50% for 16 ga.

MODEL 12 "BLACK DIAMOND" TRAP GRADE – various configurations, straight or pistol grip stock, features a small ebony diamond inlaid on each side of the pistol grip, 30 or 32 in. barrel with solid rib.

$3,675 $3,400 $2,885 $2,625 $1,900 $1,725 $1,475

Add 50% for milled VR.

MODEL 12 TOURNAMENT GRADE – 12 ga. only, straight grip stock, small checkered forearm, usually stamped "Tourn" in wood on buttstock under buttplate. Mfg. 1914-1930.

$3,250 $2,750 $2,500 $2,250 $1,800 $1,500 $1,300

MODEL 12 PIGEON GRADE – finer and more deluxe version of Model 12, many variations. Mfg. 1914-41 and 1948-64, engine turned breechblock and shell follower, usually with engraved pigeon on bottom rear of mag. tube.

	$4,000	$3,750	$3,100	$2,600	$2,100	$1,650	$1,400
28 ga.	N/A	$7,250	$6,500	$5,500	$4,750	$4,000	$3,600

Add 25% for VR.
Add 100% for 20 ga.

Beware of potential fakes (i.e., inspect the engraved pigeon carefully if engraved on gun and also note the quality and finish of the extra grade wood).

MODEL 20 – .410 bore, single shot, hammer, boxlock, 26 in. full choke (a few guns have been observed with cylinder choking), 6 lbs. 23,616 mfg. between 1919-1924.

$1,200 $950 $800 $650 $500 $350 $300

Add 50% to the value, if original.

While most Model 20s have 2 1/2 in. chambers, late parts cleanup guns could be chambered for 3 in. also. Very few of the Winchester Model 20's came with "deluxe" features.

* ***Model 20 Winchester Junior Trap Shooting Outfit*** – complete Shooting Outfit includes: Winchester Model 20, .410 bore sport gun, a Model 20 stock hang tag, six boxes of Winchester .410 shot shells, 100 midget-sized Winchester clay targets, a hand throwing trap, and three-section cleaning rod. The Outfit also includes an instructional manual, two informative brochures, a score sheet pad, Winchester gun grease, rust remover and gun oil. All of the Winchester Junior Trap Shooting Outfit components are packed in a sturdy carrying case (with lock and key) for transporting.

$8,500 $8,000 $7,500 $7,000 $6,500 $6,000 $5,500

Prices for this model assume all accessories are included - if not, subtract substantially. Just the shotshell boxes and accessories from this outfit are worth $2,500+ in nice condition.

MODEL 21 – 12, 16, 20, 28 ga., or .410 bore, boxlock action, after years in the design stage, production began in 1929 with guns being shipped to the warehouse in 1930 and first offered in Winchester's 1931 price list. Regular production continued for thirty years, through 1959. Approx. 32,500 mfg.

GRADING - PPGS™	100%	98%	95%	90%	80%	70%	60%	LAST MSR

1931-1988. Approx. 1,100 were mfg. by the Custom Shop (including Custom, Pigeon, and Grand American Grades) during 1960-1982. Factory records for these models (early mfg. is sketchy) are available by contacting the Cody Firearms Museum located in Cody, WY. The following retail prices are for a standard field gun with average wood, beavertail forearm, ejectors, and single selective trigger with no alterations.

12 ga.	$7,750	$6,750	$5,750	$5,000	$4,500	$4,000	$3,750
16 ga.	$9,750	$8,750	$7,750	$6,750	$6,000	$5,500	$5,000
20 ga.	$11,000	$9,250	$8,000	$7,000	$6,500	$6,000	$5,500

Add 15%-25% for VR depending on condition.

Add 15%-30% per extra barrel assembly, depending on original condition.

Add 25% for 3 in. chambers (Duck Gun, 12 ga. only).

Add 20% for "Deluxe" marked guns, depending on original condition.

Subtract approx. 20% for double triggers w/extractors.

Subtract 10% for double triggers with ejectors (normally encountered with splinter forearm).

The early guns were plain, standard 12 gauge models with double triggers and extractors. Later in 1931, 16 and 20 gauge chamberings became available, as did selective single trigger and automatic ejectors.

The Model 21 Trap Grade gun was introduced in 1932 followed in 1933 by Tournament Grade, Custom Built Grade and the Model 21 Skeet gun. By about this time options included fancier wood, beavertail or semi-beavertail forends, checkered butts (standard on skeet guns) or skeleton steel buttplates, recoil pads and almost any variation the customers might desire. Metal finishes on a Model 21 are unusual in that they have salt blue frames and rust blue barrels - this explains the difference in coloration between these metal surfaces.

The Tournament Grade was dropped in 1936 and the Trap Grade in 1940. A Standard Grade Trap Gun was added in 1941. The early Custom Built Grade was dropped in 1942 and the Deluxe Grade was added. This grade included as standard many of the previously available extra cost options.

Relatively few guns were produced in chamberings smaller than 20 gauge. 28 gauge first appeared in the 1936 catalog, although a few were probably produced before that. Winchester records are unclear as to the total but it is generally believed that fewer than 100 original factory guns were made. In addition, a number of original 20 gauge guns have been modified at the factory or elsewhere with factory 28 gauge barrels. These latter guns are just as valuable if the conversion was done at the Winchester Custom Gun Shop. Authenticity of the original guns should be established by factory letter.

.410 bore guns were first listed in 1955 but, again, some had been produced earlier, one having been built for John Olin in 1950. Throughout Winchester history all the rules seem to have had exceptions and nowhere is this more apparent than with respect to the Model 21 which, after all, has been pretty much a custom gun from the very beginning. Factory records and tallies among dealers indicate the existence of 40 to 50 original factory guns. As in the case of the 28 gauge, extra barrels were available and at least some of those have been added to original 20 gauge guns.

The 3 inch Magnum 12 gauge Duck gun (stamped "Duck" on floor plate) was offered in Winchester catalogs from 1940 through 1952. Selective single triggers and automatic ejectors were standard as were the solid red Winchester recoil pads and 30 in. or 32 in. barrels. Some cases of non-factory upgrading of 2 3/4 or 3 inch Magnum guns have been reported. If authenticity is important to the buyer, a factory letter should be requested available from the Cody Firearms Museum at $85 per gun. With respect to such letters, in cases where records may be missing or incomplete, the resultant letters may be less conclusive than desired. In some instances, consultation with, or a written appraisal from an authoritative collector arms dealer might be helpful. As can be seen, values are partly based on a certain interdependence between options. Higher grade guns, of course, will bring somewhat higher prices, although much of their increased value results from the many "options" being included as standard features.

Buyers or sellers with limited experience should always seek expert advice or appraisals in dealing with a Model 21. This is especially true with regard to higher grade guns and those with extra ornamentation.

Six standard patterns of engraving and several stock checkering and carving styles evolved during the production years. Values added by these and other embellishments such as precious metal inlays are beyond the scope of this work.

There is disagreement as to the effects of refinishing or restoration on a Model 21. Many shooters and at least some collectors prefer a professionally refinished gun to a badly worn one. Higher grade guns restored by a master craftsman may approach factory original guns in value.

* ***Model 21 Skeet Gun*** – available in Tournament Grade 1933-1935, Trap Grade 1933-1940, Custom Built Grade 1936-1941 and 1953-1959, Skeet Grade 1936-1959, Deluxe Grade 1942-1950, Custom Deluxe Grade 1951-1952.

Add 10% to standard Model 21 values. Larger premiums exist for special order grades.

GRADING - PPGS™	100%	98%	95%	90%	80%	70%	60%	LAST MSR

* ***Model 21 Tournament Skeet Grade*** – 12 ga., marked "TOURNAMENT SKEET" on the floorplate in front of the trigger guard. Mfg. 1933-1936.

Add 20%-25% to standard Model 21 values.

* ***Model 21 Trap Gun*** – introduced 1940, Trap Grade disc. same year.

Add 10%-25% to standard Model 21 values (be wary of non-factory modifications, especially to the stock).

* ***Model 21 3 Inch Duck Gun*** – 12 ga. only, 30 or 32 in. barrels, introduced in 1940, must be so stamped (observe the 3 in. and Duck markings very carefully).

	100%	98%	95%	90%	80%	70%	60%
	$8,100	$7,200	$6,300	$5,900	$5,400	$4,950	$4,500

Add 10% for 32 in. barrels.

* ***Model 21 .410 Bore*** – retail prices for original guns may be expected to range between $37,500 and $50,000 for mechanically sound guns depending on quality of finish. Non-original guns with add-on factory barrels would probably be reduced by one-third.

* ***Model 21 28 Ga.*** – factory original guns will probably bring from $25,000 to $30,000 and, as with the .410 bore guns, 20 gauge guns modified to 28 gauge with factory barrels would be worth approx. the same if done at the factory.

MODEL 21: RECENT PRODUCTION – refer to listing under SHOTGUNS: RECENT PRODUCTION SxS.

MODEL 24 SxS – 12, 16, or 20 ga., boxlock, hammerless, double triggers. Introduced 1940, disc. 1957 after approx. 116,280 mfg.

	100%	98%	95%	90%	80%	70%	60%
12 ga.	$825	$725	$625	$475	$350	$275	$225
16 ga.	$950	$775	$675	$525	$400	$325	$275
20 ga.	$1,000	$900	$800	$675	$550	$425	$350

MODEL 25 SLIDE ACTION – 12 ga. only, non-takedown version of the Model 12, 26 or 28 in. barrel. 87,937 mfg. between 1949-1954.

	100%	98%	95%	90%	80%	70%	60%
	$550	$475	$400	$350	$300	$250	$200

MODEL 36 SINGLE SHOT – 9mm Rimfire cal., long shot, short shot, and ball, 18 in. round barrel, single shot bolt action, guns were not serial numbered, one-piece plain stock and forearm, special shaped trigger guard, 2 3/4 lbs. Approx. 20,000 mfg. between 1920-27.

	100%	98%	95%	90%	80%	70%	60%
	N/A	$1,700	$1,500	$1,300	$1,050	$895	$750

MODEL 37 SINGLE SHOT – 12, 16, 20, 28 ga., or .410 bore, top-lever break-open action, all barrels are full choke. Note on pricing that there is a big difference between a 100% gun without a box and NIB condition. Not serial-numbered. Over 1,015,000 mfg. between 1936-63.

	100%	98%	95%	90%	80%	70%	60%
12 gauge	$450	$325	$250	$200	$125	$100	$90
16 gauge	$450	$325	$250	$200	$125	$100	$90
20 gauge	$495	$395	$325	$250	$150	$110	$90
28 gauge	$2,500	$1,825	$1,325	$995	$725	$575	$450
.410 bore	$650	$500	$450	$375	$325	$200	$150

If models are truly NIB, add $125-$175 to 100% condition values only, depending on gauge.
Add 20% for "Red Letter" models.
Add 15% for 32 in. barrel (12, 16, or 20 ga. only).

Most 28 ga. Model 37s have the "Red Letter."

* ***Model 37 Single Shot Youth/Boys/Red Dot*** – 20 ga. only, 26 in. barrel marked Mod. Choke on barrel, solid red factory pad, identifiable by red dot inset into metal that is visible when hammer is cocked.

	100%	98%	95%	90%	80%	70%	60%
	N/A	$500	$400	$325	$250	$195	$150

MODEL 40 SEMI-AUTO – 12 ga. only, long recoil action, 28 or 30 in. barrel, walnut stock, skeet model also, poorly designed, many recalled by Winchester. Approx. 12,000 mfg. 1940-41.

	100%	98%	95%	90%	80%	70%	60%
	$900	$750	$600	$475	$400	$300	$225

MODEL 41 BOLT ACTION – .410 bore, 2 1/2 in. chamber until 1933 when it changed to 3 in., bolt action, single shot, 24 in. round barrel bored F, one-piece plain walnut stock and forearm, not serialized, approx. 22,145 were mfg. 1920-34.

	100%	98%	95%	90%	80%	70%	60%
	$800	$700	$575	$500	$425	$350	$300

Add 15% for 3 in. chamber.

This model is rarely encountered with over 80% original condition.

GRADING - PPGS™	100%	98%	95%	90%	80%	70%	60%	LAST MSR

MODEL 42 SLIDE ACTION – first pump specifically designed for the .410 bore, hammerless, 2 1/2 (introduced 1935) or 3 in. chamber, 26 or 28 in. barrel, plain walnut pistol grip stock with circular grooved forearm (modified 1947), invented by William Roemer, approx. 6 1/2 - 7 lbs. Approx. 164,800 mfg. in 4 grades between 1933-1963.

Add 30% to any Model 42 chambered for 2 1/2 in. shells.
Add 25% for factory installed Cutts compensator (no choke marking on barrel).
Add 25% for pre-war guns.
Subtract 50% for non-factory installed Cutts compensator (choke marked on barrel).

Special order features on field guns have captured much collector interest in recent years. Combinations of these features can add a considerable percentage to the base values listed. Special orders on rare variations are very desirable, and prices can double, or more than double, if the combination is right.

A note on Model 42 Vent. Ribs:

Early Model 42 vent. ribs were designed "Winchester Special Ventilated Rib" circa 1954 in the 125,000 ser. no. range. This rib had a wavy line matting on top of the rib, no stamping on the side, is known as the "Doughnut" post rib, and were in production until the end of 1957 with approx. ser. no. 149,000. The second variation Model 42 rib appears on guns in the approx. ser. no. range 141,000-149,000. This rib was made with both solid and hollow round posts. All parts for the vent. rib were made at the Winchester plant. A third variation was introduced at the end of 1957, when Winchester decided to send its Model 42 barrels to the Simmons Gun Specialty Co. in Kansas City for installation of the vent. ribs. In-the-white barrels were proofed in New Haven and marked on the left side so that the rib would not cover up the proofmark before shipment to Simmons. The ser. no. was not stamped on the receiver extension until the gun was completely assembled. This last variation, or oval post, appears on Model 42s starting at approx. ser. no. 150,000. This third variation is marked either "SIMMONS PATENTED" or "SIMMONS GUN SPECIALTY CO., KANSAS CITY, MO". The longer Simmons marking was stamped on the rib until the end of production.

* ***Model 42 Slide Action Standard Grade*** – 26 or 28 in. plain, solid rib or vent. rib (after market) barrel, plain walnut straight or pistol grip stock, walnut grooved forearm. Mfg. 1933-1963.

Plain barrel	$2,000	$1,750	$1,475	$1,275	$1,100	$995	$875
Solid rib	$3,300	$2,850	$2,500	$2,150	$1,900	$1,750	$1,575

A factory vent. rib on this model is very rare and desirable, as only a very few have been encountered.

* ***Model 42 Slide Action Skeet Grade*** – 26 or 28 in. plain, solid rib or vent. rib barrel, select checkered walnut straight grip or pistol grip stock and checkered forearm extension, 4 different chokes (full, modified, skeet, or cylinder) during pre-war (approx. ser. no. 1-52,000), post-war (approx. ser. no. 52,000-164,000) had same chokes available through 1953, when cylinder choke was dropped, and improved cylinder was added.

Plain barrel	$4,150	$3,750	$3,400	$3,100	$2,750	$2,475	$1,995
Solid rib	$5,500	$5,000	$4,450	$3,950	$3,500	$3,100	$2,700
Vent. rib	$6,500	$5,950	$5,350	$4,650	$4,000	$3,600	$3,100

* ***Model 42 Slide Action Trap Grade/Trap Grade Skeet*** – first variation had small checkered forearm with one diamond in center, field choke (full, modified, or cylinder), second variation has large checkered forearm with 2 diamonds in center, both variations had 26 or 28 in. plain or solid rib barrel, select checkered walnut straight grip (one closed diamond on underside of grip) or pistol grip (one closed diamond on each side of grip) stock, usually choked skeet, stamped "TRAP" at bottom of receiver under the ser. no. Only 231 mfg.

	$15,125	$12,500	$10,725	$9,000	$7,700	$6,325	$5,225

Add 10% for small slide handle.

* ***Model 42 Slide Action Deluxe Grade*** – same configurations as Trap Grade, 20 LPI checkering, most are fitted with special vent. rib after 1954 in 3 styles: round post-donut base, round post, and rectangle post, pre-1954 mfg. had plain or solid rib barrel, 1946-1950 mfg. may have "DELUXE" stamp under ser. no. on receiver. Mfg. 1946-63.

» **Model 42 Slide Action Deluxe Grade Solid Rib**

	$15,125	$12,650	$10,725	$9,000	$7,975	$6,600	$5,500

» **Model 42 Slide Action Deluxe Grade Vent. Rib (factory)**

	$16,500	$14,850	$12,100	$10,950	$9,625	$7,975	$6,875

* ***Model 42 Slide Action Pigeon Grade*** – same configurations as Deluxe Grade, except has pigeon engraved on underside of mag. tube, most were factory engraved, very few mfg.

Must be appraised individually. Before purchasing any factory engraved Model 42, it is advised that a reputable dealer/collector be consulted.

GRADING - PPGS™	100%	98%	95%	90%	80%	70%	60%	LAST MSR

MODEL 50 SEMI-AUTO – 12 or 20 ga., 3 shot, recoil-operated (non-recoiling barrel), 26-30 in. barrels, VR optional, steel frame or Feather Weight Model (aluminum receiver, FTW) introduced 1958. Over 196,000 mfg. between 1954-61, starting with serial number 1,000.

Standard Model	$650	$525	$450	$400	$350	$300	$250	
Trap or Skeet Model	$1,300	$1,050	$950	$800	$700	$600	$500	

Add $100 for VR (Simmons installed).
Add $50 for Feather Weight Model (denoted by "A" suffix in ser. no.).
Add $150 for 20 ga.

* ***Model 50 Semi-Auto Pigeon Grade*** – can be denoted by PIGEON stamped above the serial number on the barrel assembly, deluxe wood.

	$2,300	$2,100	$1,850	$1,625	$1,400	$1,200	$995	

MODEL 59 SEMI-AUTO – 12 ga. only, 3 shot, short recoil operation, Win-lite (steel and fiberglass) ribless barrels, 26-30 in. barrel lengths, alloy receiver inscribed with hunting scenes, Versalite (first interchangeable choke tubes) option introduced 1961, 6 1/2 lbs. 82,085 mfg. between 1960-1965.

	$750	$625	$500	$400	$300	$250	$200	

Add 30% for barrel with all three choke tubes.

Inspect carefully for either cracked receiver (by bolt handle cutout and over serial numbers) or separating fiberglass on end of barrel. Winchester also mfg. 20 and 14 gauges experimentally in this model, which are extremely rare and expensive.

* ***Model 59 Semi-Auto Pigeon Grade*** – mfg. 1962-1965.

	$3,000	$2,500	$2,000	$1,600	$1,200	$1,000	$800	

SHOTGUNS: POST-1964

Winchester introduced WinChokes in 1969.

Shotguns: Post-1964, Lever Action

MODEL 9410 TRADITIONAL – .410 bore, 2 1/2 in. chamber, lever action based on the Model 94 rifle, 24 in. round barrel with cylinder bore or Standard Invector chokes (new 2003), 9 shot tube mag., iron sights with TruGlo front and modified V adj. rear, checkered straight grip walnut stock and forearm, top tang safety became standard in 2003, approx. 6 3/4 lbs. Mfg. 2001-2006.

	$995	$825	$675	$495	$400	$325	$250	*$626*

Subtract approx. $50 if w/o Invector chokes.

* ***Model 9410 Traditional Semi-Fancy*** – similar to Model 9410 Traditional, except has checkered semi-fancy walnut stock and Standard Invector choke system. Mfg. 2004 only.

	$1,350	$1,075	$875	$750	$575	$425	$325	*$789*

* ***Model 9410 Traditional Packer*** – cylinder bored or Standard Invector chokes (new 2003, includes 3 chokes), 20 in. barrel, 5 shot, 2/3 mag., open sights, checkered semi-pistol grip walnut stock and forearm with sling swivel studs, also available in Packer Compact Model (12 1/2 in. LOP, new 2003), 6 1/4 - 6 1/2 lbs. Mfg. 2002-2006.

	$995	$825	$675	$495	$400	$325	$250	*$647*

Subtract approx. $50 if w/o standard Invector chokes (includes 3).

* ***Model 9410 Traditional Ranger*** – similar to Model 9410 Traditional, except has uncheckered hardwood stock and forearm, 24 in. barrel with fixed cylinder bore barrel, 6 3/4 lbs. Mfg. 2003-2006.

	$825	$650	$525	$400	$325	$250	$200	*$532*

* ***Model 9410 Traditional TS Custom Case Colored*** – similar to Model 9410 Traditional, case colored receiver, lever, crescent buttplate, lower tang, and barrel bands, deluxe straight grip checkered walnut stock and extended forearm, matte bluing, 24 in. round barrel, gold trigger, top safety, 7 lbs. Mfg. 2005 only.

	$2,250	$1,800	$1,425	$1,150	$950	$800	$600	*$1,418*

Shotguns: Post-1964, Semi-Auto

Winchester introduced WinChokes in 1969.

MODEL 140 RANGER SEMI-AUTO – 12, 16, or 20 ga., entry level model. Disc.

	$275	$250	$220	$200	$175	$155	$140	

GRADING - PPGS™	100%	98%	95%	90%	80%	70%	60%	LAST MSR

MODEL 1400 SEMI-AUTO – 12, 16, or 20 ga., 26, 28, or 30 in. barrel, 2 3/4 in. chamber, alloy receiver, various chokes, gas operated, 2 shot mag., checkered pistol grip stock. Mfg. 1964-1981.

	100%	98%	95%	90%	80%	70%	60%	LAST MSR
	$275	$250	$220	$200	$175	$155	$140	
Vent. rib	$315	$265	$240	$220	$195	$165	$150	

Add 33% for Winchester recoil reduction system (mfg. 1964-1970).

Note: In 1968 the model 1400 series was modified. The action release was improved and the checkering redesigned. From 1968-72, they were designated MKII, which was then dropped. The values for the later guns mfg. from 1968-73 may run approx. 10% higher - values shown are for guns mfg. from 1965-1968. A left-hand version was also available, and was disc. in 1973.

NEW MODEL 1400 WALNUT – 12 or 20 ga., 2 3/4 in. chamber, 22 (disc.), 26 (mfg. 1991-93), or 28 in. VR barrel, checkered walnut stock and forearm, WinChokes standard, 3 shot mag., rotary bolt system, 7-7 1/2 lbs. Mfg. 1989-94.

$350	$290	$260	$240	$220	$190	$165	*$419*

Add $15 for limited mfg. 1993 Quail Unlimited Model (2,500 mfg. 1993).

MODEL 1400 CUSTOM HIGH GRADE – 12 ga. only, 28 in. VR WinChoke barrel, special order only through the Custom Gun Shop, features deluxe hand checkered walnut and special engraving. Mfg. 1991-92.

$1,295	$995	$750	N/A	N/A	N/A	N/A	*$1,695*

MODEL 1400 SKEET GRADE – similar to 1400, 12 or 20 ga., with 26 in. VR barrel, skeet bore, select skeet style stock. Mfg. 1965-73.

$425	$350	$300	$275	$220	$195	$165

MODEL 1400 TRAP GRADE – similar to 1400, with 30 in. full choke VR barrel, select trap style stock. Mfg. 1965-73.

$360	$330	$305	$275	$220	$195	$165

MODEL 1400 DEER GUN – similar to 1400, with 22 in. barrel, rifle sights, 12 ga. only. Mfg. 1965-74.

$265	$240	$220	$200	$175	$165	$140

MODEL 1400 SLUG HUNTER – 12 ga. only, 22 in. smoothbore cyl. or rifled Sabot choke-tubed barrel, drilled and tapped for scope, includes bases or iron sights, 7 1/4 lbs. Mfg. 1990-92.

$355	$310	$270	$250	$225	$195	$165	*$420*

MODEL 1400 RANGER – 12 or 20 ga., gas operation, alloy receiver, 22 cyl. deer, 26 (mfg. 1991-93), or 28 in. WinChoke barrel, checkered walnut finished hardwood stock and forearm, VR became standard 1985, 7 1/4 lbs. Disc. 1994.

$285	$235	$200	$180	$160	$140	$120	*$377*

Add $53 for deer combo. (includes extra 22 in. cyl. bore barrel).
Subtract $40 without VR.

MODEL 1500 XTR – 12 or 20 ga., 2 3/4 inch only, 28 inch barrel, plain or VR, WinChoke tubes, gas operation. Mfg. 1978-82.

$300	$260	$240	$220	$200	$180	$160

SUPER X MODEL 1 – 12 ga., 26, 28, or 30 in. VR barrel, various chokes, steel receiver, self compensating gas operation, checkered pistol grip stock and forearm. Mfg. 1974-1981.

$500	$450	$400	$350	$300	$250	$225

SUPER X MODEL 1 SKEET – 12 ga., similar to Standard, with 26 in. skeet bore barrel, select skeet style stock. Mfg. 1974-1981.

$695	$595	$500	$475	$450	$425	$400

Add 20% if NIB condition.

SUPER X MODEL 1 TRAP – 12 ga., similar to Standard, with 30 in. barrel, imp. mod. or full choke, select trap style stock.

$595	$550	$475	$425	$415	$395	$350

Add 20% if NIB condition.

SUPER X MODEL 1 CUSTOM TRAP OR SKEET – 12 ga. only, limited production from the Custom Shop, deluxe checkered walnut stock and forearm, extensive scroll engraving on receiver, built to custom order. Limited mfg. 1987-92.

$1,295	$925	$725	N/A	N/A	N/A	N/A

* ***Super X Model 1 Custom Trap or Skeet Engraved*** – 12 ga., features number 5 engraving pattern with 7 gold inlays. Disc.

$2,395	$1,900	$1,350	N/A	N/A	N/A	N/A	*$1,295*

Add $700 for factory gold inlays (8 flying ducks).

GRADING - PPGS™	100%	98%	95%	90%	80%	70%	60%	LAST MSR

SUPER X2 3 IN. MAGNUM FIELD – 12 ga. only, 3 in. chamber, self-adjusting gas operation, 26 or 28 in. VR back-bored barrel with Invector chokes, 5 shot mag., choice of checkered walnut or black synthetic stock and forearm with recoil pad, high gloss blue or matte metal finish, approx. 7 1/4-8 lbs. Mfg. 1999-2004.

$750	$650	$575	$525	$465	$400	$325	*$874*

* ***Super X2 3 in. Magnum Field Light*** – 12 ga., 26 or 28 in. VR back-bored barrel with Invector Plus chokes, alloy receiver, checkered pistol grip walnut stock and forearm, 6 1/2 - 6 3/4 lbs. Mfg. 2005-2006.

$835	$710	$600	$560	$500	$450	$375	*$945*

* ***Super X2 3 in. Magnum Field Sporting Clays*** – 12 ga., 28 or 30 in. VR back-bored barrel with Invector chokes, adj. stock using spacers, includes 2 gas pistons, checkered walnut or Signature Red Dura-Touch finished (new 2003) hardwood stock and forearm, approx. 8 lbs. Mfg. 2001-2007.

$875	$730	$610	$560	$500	$450	$375	*$999*

Add $16 for Signature Red Dura-Touch finish on stock and forearm.

* ***Super X2 3 in. Magnum Field Sporting Clays Signature II*** – 12 ga., 28, 30, or 32 (mfg. 2005 only) in. barrel, red anodized alloy receiver and forearm cap, two gas pistons provided, black metallic paint on stock and forearm, adj. stock spacers provided, approx. 8 lbs. Mfg. 2005-2006.

$885	$735	$625	$575	$500	$450	$375	*$1,015*

* ***Super X2 3 in. Magnum Field Composite*** – 12 ga., 26 or 28 in. VR barrels with three Invector chokes, black composite stock and forearm with Dura-Touch armor coating, matte metal finish, includes sling swivel studs, approx. 7 3/4 lbs. Mfg. 2004-2005.

$775	$665	$585	$525	$465	$400	$325	*$908*

* ***Super X2 3 in. Magnum Field Rifled Deer*** – 12 ga., 22 in. rifled barrel with cantilever scope base and TruGlo sights (rear sight folds down), black synthetic stock and forearm, 7 1/4 lbs. Mfg. 2002-2005.

$800	$675	$585	$530	$455	$395	$325	*$957*

* ***Super X2 2 3/4 in. Magnum Field Practical MK I*** – 12 ga., similar to Super X2 Practical MKII, except is 2 3/4 in. chamber, has regular TruGlo iron sights, and does not have Dura-Touch, cylinder bore Invector choke standard, 8 lbs. Mfg. 2003-2007.

$960	$800	$675	$575	$500	$465	$435	*$1,116*

* ***Super X2 3 in. Magnum Field Practical MK II*** – 12 ga., home defense configuration featuring black composite stock and forearm, black metal finish, 22 in. barrel with Invector choke system and removable LPA ghost ring sights, 8 shot extended mag., includes sling swivels, Dura-Touch armor coated composite finish became standard during 2003, 8 lbs. Mfg. 2002-2006.

$1,075	$885	$715	$635	$550	$495	$440	*$1,287*

Subtract 10% if w/o Dura-Touch finished stock and forearm.

SUPER X2 3 1/2 IN. MAG. COMPOSITE – 12 ga. only, 3 1/2 in. chamber, similar to Super X2, black synthetic stock and forearm with vent. recoil pad, Dura-Touch armor coated stock/forearm treatment became standard during 2003 for all models, 24 (disc. 2000), 26, or 28 in. VR back-bored barrel with Invector chokes, 7 1/2-8 lbs. Mfg. 1999-2005.

$885	$725	$625	$565	$500	$450	$375	*$1,027*

* ***Super X2 3 1/2 In. Mag. Composite Universal Hunter*** – 12 ga., similar to Super X2 3 1/2 In. Mag., except has full coverage Mossy Oak Break-Up camo composite stock and forearm, 26 in. VR barrel with 3 Invector Plus chokes, including optional extended extra full (standard beginning 2006), TruGlo sights, 7 3/4 lbs. Mfg. 2002-2007.

$1,050	$875	$700	$600	$515	$455	$375	*$1,252*

Subtract approx. 5% for standard Invector Plus chokes.

* ***Super X2 3 1/2 In. Mag. Composite Greenhead*** – 12 ga., similar to Super X2 3 1/2 In. Mag., except has green Dura-Touch stock and forearm for enhanced durability and non-slip hold during cold/wet conditions, 28 in. VR barrel, matte metal finish, 8 lbs. Mfg. 2002-2005.

$900	$740	$620	$565	$500	$450	$375	*$1,036*

* ***Super X2 3 1/2 In. Mag. Composite Turkey*** – 12 ga., similar to Super X2 3 1/2 In. Mag., except has 24 in. VR barrel with TruGlo sights and extra full turkey choke tube, matte finish only, 7 1/2 lbs. Mfg. 1999-2002.

$880	$730	$615	$555	$495	$450	$375	*$1,018*

During 2001-2002, this model incorporated a "Team NWTF" logo on the stock.

GRADING - PPGS™	100%	98%	95%	90%	80%	70%	60%	LAST MSR

* ***Super X2 3 1/2 In. Mag. Composite Camo Turkey (NWTF)*** – 12 ga., similar configuration as regular Turkey, except has 100% Mossy Oak Break-Up or Mossy Oak Obsession camo treatment and TruGlo sights, 7 1/2 lbs. Mfg. 2000-2007.

$1,035 $850 $700 $550 $495 $425 $375 *$1,236*

Beginning in 2001, this model incorporates a "Team NWTF" logo on the stock.

* ***Super X2 3 1/2 In. Mag. Composite Camo Waterfowl*** – 12 ga., similar to Super X2 3 1/2 In. Mag., except has 100% Mossy Oak Shadow Grass treatment, 28 in. VR back-bored barrel with Invector chokes, 8 lbs. Mfg. 1999-2005.

$1,000 $840 $685 $565 $495 $425 $375 *$1,185*

SX3 (SUPER X3) 3 IN. MAGNUM WALNUT FIELD – 12 or 20 (new 2009) ga., 3 in. chamber, self-adjusting Active Valve gas operation, 26 or 28 in. VR barrel with Invector Plus chokes, variable checkered walnut stock with second generation Pachmayr Decelerator pad, adj. LOP, alloy receiver and 4 shot mag. tube, grey Perma-Cote Ultra Tough or Dura-Touch Armor coating (current) surface finish, 6 3/8-7 lbs. Mfg. 2006-2011.

$1,025 $875 $750 $650 $575 $500 $450 *$1,220*

* ***SX3 (Super X3) Compact Field*** – 12 or 20 ga., similar to Super X3 3 in. Magnum Walnut Field, except has shortened 13 in. LOP. Mfg. 2011 only.

$1,025 $875 $750 $650 $575 $500 $450 *$1,220*

* ***SX3 (Super X3) 3 in. Magnum Classic Field*** – 12 or 20 ga., similar to 3 in. Walnut Field, except has traditional diamond pattern checkering and non-adj. Decelerator recoil pad. Mfg. 2008-2009.

$975 $850 $750 $650 $575 $500 $450 *$1,159*

* ***SX3 (Super X3) 3 in. Flanigun Exhibition/Sporting*** – 12 or 20 ga., 28 or 30 (new 2010) in. VR barrel with Invector Plus chokes, black composite stock and forearm with Dura-Touch armor coating and red annodized frame and forearm cap, designed for Winchester exhibition shooter Patrick Flanigan, 7 1/4 lbs. Mfg. 2008-2010.

$1,195 $995 $850 $725 $625 $550 $475 *$1,479*

This model was featured as a 2009 SHOT Show Special in 12 ga. only, 30 in. VR barrel, TruGlo fiber optic front sight, three signature Invector Plus choke tubes, and Inflex Technology recoll pad.

* ***SX3 (Super X3) 3 in. Magnum Field Composite*** – 12 or 20 (new 2011) ga., similar to 3 in. Mag. Walnut Field, black composite stock and forearm, alloy receiver, 26 or 28 in. barrel with Invector Plus chokes, approx. 6 3/4 lbs. Mfg. 2006-2011.

$975 $850 $725 $625 $525 $475 $425 *$1,140*

Add $10 for 12 ga.

* ***SX3 (Super X3) 3 in. Magnum Field Cantilever Deer*** – 12 or 20 (new 2011) ga., 22 in. rifled barrel with Weaver style cantilever scope base and TruGlo sights, alloy receiver, black synthetic stock and forearm, approx. 7 1/2 lbs. Mfg. 2006-2011.

$1,025 $895 $775 $650 $575 $500 $450 *$1,200*

Add $20 for 12 ga.

SX3 FIELD – 12 (disc. 2016) or 20 ga., 3 in. chamber, 26 or 28 in. VR back bored barrel with three Invector Plus chokes, matte black aluminum alloy receiver with red accents, active valve system, satin oil finished walnut stock and forearm with cut checkering, Pachmayr Decelerator recoil pad, ambidextrous crossbolt safety, drop out trigger, 6 1/2-6 3/8 lbs. Mfg. 2012-2016, but inventory remained until 2019.

$900 $800 $695 $600 $525 $425 $375 *$1,070*

This model was originally featured as a SHOT Show Special in 2011.

* ***SX3 Field Compact*** – 12 (disc. 2016) or 20 ga., 3 in. chamber, compact, 24 (new 2014), 26 or 28 in. VR back bored barrel with three Invector Plus choke tubes, 4 shot mag., matte black aluminum alloy receiver, drop out trigger, brass front sight bead, 13 in. LOP, satin oil finished walnut stock and forearm with cut checkering, Pachmayr Decelerator recoil pad, ambidextrous crossbolt safety, active valve system, 6 1/4-6 3/8 lbs. Mfg. 2012-2016, but inventory remained until 2019.

$900 $800 $695 $600 $525 $425 $375 *$1,070*

This model was originally featured as a 2010 SHOT Show Special.

SX3 BLACK SHADOW – 12 (disc. 2016) or 20 ga., 3 in. chamber, 24 (new 2017), 26, or 28 in. VR back bored barrel with three Invector Plus choke tubes, Quadra-Vent ports, drop out trigger, brass bead front sight, matte black synthetic stock with textured gripping surface and matching forearm, Inflex Technology recoil pad, drop shims and LOP spacers, ambidextrous crossbolt safety, active valve system, matte black receiver with red accents, 6 1/2-6 3/4 lbs. Mfg. 2012-2018.

$900 $800 $695 $600 $525 $425 $375 *$1,070*

Subtract 5% for 12 ga. (disc. 2016).

This model was originally featured as a 2011 SHOT Show Special.

GRADING - PPGS™	100%	98%	95%	90%	80%	70%	60%	LAST MSR

SX3 CANTILEVER BUCK – 12 (disc. 2017) or 20 ga., 3 in. chamber, 22 in. rifled barrel, 4 shot mag., drop out trigger, TruGlo fiber optic front sight and rear Weaver style cantilever, matte black synthetic stock with textured gripping surfaces, Inflex technology recoil pad, ambidextrous crossbolt safety, active valve system, matte black receiver, 7 1/2 lbs. Mfg. 2012-2016, but inventory remained until 2019.

$1,025	$875	$750	$650	$575	$500	$425	*$1,200*

Subtract $50 12 ga. (disc. 2017).

SX3 COMPOSITE SPORTING – 12 ga. 2 3/4 in. chamber, 4 shot mag., 28, 30, or 32 in. ported Perma-Cote gray barrel with vent. rib, extended signature Invector Plus choke tubes, TruGlo fiber optic sight and white mid-bead, active valve system, ambidextrous crossbolt safety, matte nickel plated receiver, signature Red Briley bolt handle, release button and magazine cap weight system, black synthetic stock with or without carbon fiber finish, Inflex technology recoil pad, includes shims and LOP spacers, 7 1/4-7 1/2 lbs. Mfg. 2016-2019.

$1,450	$1,175	$1,000	$875	$750	$625	$550	*$1,680*

Add $60 for carbon fiber finish.

SX3 WATERFOWL HUNTER – 12 (disc. 2016) or 20 ga., 3 in. chamber, 26 or 28 in. VR back bored barrel with three Invector Plus choke tubes, 4 shot mag., drop out trigger, TruGlo fiber optic front sight, synthetic stock w/textured gripping surfaces, cast/drop shims and LOP spacers, Inflex Technology recoil pad, ambidextrous crossbolt safety, active valve system, Quadra-Vent ports, 100% Mossy Oak Duck Blind (disc. 2016) or Mossy Oak Shadow Grass Blades (new 2017) camo finish, approx. 6-5/8-7 lbs. Mfg. 2012-2018.

$1,025	$875	$750	$650	$575	$500	$425	*$1,200*

SX3 ULTIMATE SPORTING ADJUSTABLE – 12 ga., 2 3/4 in. chamber, 28, 30, or 32 in. Perma-Cote gray ported barrel with VR, extended signature Invector Plus choke tubes, drop out trigger group, TruGlo fiber optic sight and white mid-bead, satin oil finished Grade II/III walnut stock with adj. comb and cut checkering, Pachmayr Decelerator recoil pad, ambidextrous crossbolt safety, active valve system, signature Red Briley bolt handle, release button and magazine cap weight system, includes red ABS hard sided case, matte nickel plated receiver, 7 1/2-7 5/8 lbs. Mfg. 2016-2018.

$1,575	$1,275	$1,050	$925	$800	$700	$600	*$1,870*

SX3 UNIVERSAL HUNTER – 12 or 20 ga., 3 or 3 1/2 in. chamber, 26 or 28 in. VR back bored barrel with three invector plus shoke tubes, drop out trigger, TruGlo fiber optic front sight, Inflex technology recoil pad, ambidextrous safety, active valve system, 100% Mossy Oak Break-Up Infinity (disc. 2014) or Mossy Oak Break-Up Country (new 2015) camo coverage. Mfg. 2012-2016.

$1,050	$900	$775	$675	$575	$500	$425	*$1,240*

SX3 (SUPER X3) SPORTING – 12 ga. only, 2 3/4 in. chamber, 28, 30, or 32 in. ported VR barrel with 5 extended choke tubes and TruGlo front sight, checkered adj. comb walnut stock and forearm, Active Valve gas system, gun metal grey receiver finish, Pachmayr Decelerator recoil pad, approx. 7 1/2 lbs., includes red ABS hard case with Winchester logo. Mfg. 2011-2015.

$1,450	$1,175	$1,000	$875	$750	$625	$550	*$1,700*

This model was originally featured as a 2010 SHOT Show Special.

SX3 (SUPER X3) 3 1/2 IN. MAGNUM COMPOSITE – 12 ga. only, 3 1/2 in. chamber, features black composite stock and forearm, alloy receiver, grey Perma-Cote Ultra Tough (disc.) or Dura-Touch Armor coating (current) surface finish, 26 or 28 in. VR barrel with Invector Plus chokes, 4 shot mag., approx. 7 1/4 lbs. Mfg. 2006-2011.

$1,050	$925	$800	$675	$575	$525	$475	*$1,280*

* ***SX3 (Super X3) 3 1/2 In. Magnum Composite Waterfowl*** – 12 or 20 (new 2011, 3 in. chamber) ga., similar to Super X3 3 1/2 In. Mag., except has 100% Mossy Oak New Shadow Grass (disc.) or Mossy Oak New Duck Blind (new 2007) treatment, 26 or 28 in. VR barrel with 3 choke tubes, approx. 6 1/2 (20 ga.) or 7 lbs. Mfg. 2006-2011.

$1,225	$975	$825	$725	$625	$525	$450	*$1,480*

Subtract $140 for 20 ga. (new 2011).

* ***SX3 (Super X3) 3 1/2 In. Magnum Composite All Purpose Field*** – 12 or 20 (new 2011, 3 in. chamber), similar to Super X3 3 1/2 In. Mag., except has 100% Mossy Oak New Break-Up (disc. 2009) or Mossy Oak Infinity (new 2010) camo treatment, 26 or 28 in. VR barrel with 3 choke tubes, approx. 6 1/2 (20 ga.) or 7 lbs. Mfg. 2006-2011.

$1,225	$975	$825	$725	$625	$525	$450	*$1,480*

GRADING - PPGS™	100%	98%	95%	90%	80%	70%	60%	LAST MSR

* ***SX3 (Super X3) 3 1/2 in. Mag. NWTF Cantilever Extreme Turkey*** – 12 ga., 24 in. cantilever barrel with extra-full extended turkey choke tube, composite stock with full Mossy Oak New Break-Up camo treatment and Dura-Touch Armor coating, Active Valve system, Pachmayr Decelerator recoil pad, steel sling swivels, includes TruGlo deluxe red dot scope and Weaver style mount, includes hardshell case, approx. 7 1/2 lbs. Mfg. 2008-2010.

  $1,225 $1,000 $850 $725 $600 $525 $450 ***$1,539***

* ***SX3 (Super X3) 3 1/2 In. Mag. Gray Shadow*** – 12 ga., 3 1/2 in. chamber, gray Perma-Cote UT surface finish, 26 or 28 in. barrel, gray composite stock with Dura-Touch Armor coating, Active Valve System, three Invector-Plus chokes, sling swivel studs, red "W" embedded in stock, 7-7 1/4 lbs. Mfg. 2009.

  $1,050 $900 $800 $700 $625 $550 $475 ***$1,299***

This model was originally featured as a 2008 SHOT Show Special.

SX3 BLACK SHADOW 3 1/2 IN. MAG. – 12 ga., 3 1/2 in. chamber, otherwise similar to the SX3 3 in. Black Shadow, 7 1/4 lbs. Mfg. 2012-2016.

$925 $800 $700 $600 $500 $400 $350 ***$1,070***

SX3 WATERFOWL HUNTER 3 1/2 IN. MAG. – 12 ga., 3 1/2 in. chamber, otherwise similar to SX3 3 in. Waterfowl Hunter, approx. 7 1/8 lbs. Mfg. 2012-2016.

$1,050 $925 $825 $700 $600 $500 $400 ***$1,200***

SX3 UNIVERSAL HUNTER 3 1/2 IN. MAG. – 12 ga., 3 1/2 in. chamber, otherwise similar to SX3 Universal Hunter 3 in., 7-7 1/8 lbs. Mfg. 2012-2016.

$1,025 $875 $750 $650 $575 $500 $425 ***$1,240***

SX3 (SUPER X3) NWTF CANTILEVER (EXTREME) TURKEY – 12 (3 1/2 in.) or 20 (3 in.) ga., 24 in. cantilever barrel with extra-full extended turkey choke tube and TruGlo front sight, composite stock with full Mossy Oak New Break-Up Infinity (disc. 2014) or Mossy Oak Break-Up Country (new 2015) camo treatment and Dura-Touch Armor coating, Active Valve system, Inflex Technology recoil pad, steel sling swivels, approx. 7 1/2 lbs. Mfg. 2011-2018.

$1,025 $875 $750 $650 $575 $500 $425 ***$1,200***

SX3 LONG BEARD – 12 or 20 (new 2018) ga., 3 (new 2018) or 3 1/2 in. chamber, 24 in. barrel with Briley X-full Long Beard Invector Plus extended choke tube, Quadra-Vent ports, 4 shot mag., drop out trigger group, TruGlo fiber optic front sight, fully adj, folding rear sight, Weaver style cantilever scope mount rail design, synthetic pistol grip stock with textured gripping surfaces, 3 interchangeable recoil pads and comb inserts, ambi crossbolt safety, 100% Realtree Xtra green leaf (disc. 2014) or Mossy Oak Break-Up Country (new 2015) camo finish, 7 1/2-7 3/8 lbs. Mfg. 2014-2018.

$1,075 $950 $825 $700 $600 $500 $425 ***$1,270***

SX4 (SUPER X4) – 12 or 20 (new 2019) ga., 3 or 3 1/2 in. chamber, 24 (new 2019, 20 ga. only), 26, or 28 in. VR back bored barrel with three Invector Plus choke tubes, Quadra-Vent ports, 4 shot mag., drop-out trigger group, TruGlo long bead fiber optic front sight, matte black synthetic stock with rounded pistol grip and textured gripping surfaces, Inflex Technology recoil pad, LOP spacers, ambidextrous crossbolt safety, active valve system, 6 7/8-7 1/8 lbs. New 2017.

MSR $830 $700 $625 $550 $475 $420 $365 $335

Add $130 for 3 1/2 in. chamber.

Add $130 for 20 ga. (new 2019).

SX4 CANTILEVER BUCK – 12 or 20 (new 2020) ga., 3 in. chamber, 22 in. rifled barrel, drop out trigger group, TruGlo fiber optic front and adj. rear sight, synthetic stock with rounded pistol grip and textured gripping surfaces, Weaver-style cantilever rail design, LOP spacers, Inflex Technology recoil pad, ambidextrous crossbolt safety, active valve system, matte black finish, 7 1/2 lbs. New 2018.

MSR $990 $845 $740 $635 $575 $475 $400 $350

Add $130 for 20 ga. (new 2020).

SX4 COMPACT – 12 or 20 ga., 3 in. chamber, gas operated with active valve system, 24, 26, or 28 in. VR barrel, three Invector Plus choke tubes, 3 shot mag., hard chrome-plated chamber and bore, aluminum alloy receiver, drop-out trigger group, TruGlo Long Bead fiber optic front sight, black composite stock with rounded pistol grip and textured gripping surfaces, Pachmayr Decelerator recoil pad, 13 in. LOP with spacers, ambidextrous crossbolt safety, Quadra-Vent ports, back-bored technology, larger bolt handle and bolt release button, matte black finish, 6.4-7 lbs. New 2019.

MSR $830 $700 $625 $550 $475 $420 $365 $335

Add $130 for 20 ga.

GRADING - PPGS™	100%	98%	95%	90%	80%	70%	60%	LAST MSR

SX4 FIELD – 12 or 20 (new 2019) ga., 3 in. chamber, 26 or 28 in. VR back bored barrel with three Invector Plus choke tubes, 4 shot mag., drop out trigger group, TruGlo long bead fiber optic front sight, satin oil finished checkered walnut stock and forearm, Inflex Technology recoil pad, ambidextrous crossbolt safety, matte black receiver with horizontal red accent line in back of ejector port, active valve system, large bolt handle and bolt release button, approx. 6 3/4 lbs. New 2017.

MSR $960	$815	$715	$625	$550	$475	$400	$350

Add $140 for 20 ga. (new 2019).

SX4 FIELD COMPACT – 12 or 20 (new 2019) ga., 3 in. chamber, 24, 26, or 28 in. VR barrel with 3 Invector Plus choke tubes, 4 shot mag., TruGlo fiber optic front sights, drop out trigger group, satin oil finished checkered walnut stock, Inflex Technology recoil pad, ambidextrous crossbolt safety, 13 in. LOP, matte black receiver, approx. 6 1/2 lbs. New 2017.

MSR $960	$815	$715	$625	$550	$475	$400	$350

Add $140 for 20 ga. (new 2019).

SX4 NWTF CANTILEVER TURKEY – 12 or 20 (new 2020) ga., 3 1/2 in. chamber, 24 in. back bored barrel, Invector Plus Extra-Full Turkey choke tube, Quadra-Vent ports, drop out trigger group, TruGlo fiber optic front and adj. rear sights, synthetic stock with rounded pistol grip and textured gripping surfaces, Weaver style cantilever rail design, Inflex Technology recoil pad, LOP spacers, ambidextrous crossbolt safety, 100% Mossy Oak Obsession camo finish, 7 1/2 lbs. New 2018.

MSR $1,100	$935	$825	$700	$635	$525	$425	$375

SX4 UNIVERSAL HUNTER – 12 or 20 (new 2019) ga., 3 1/2 in. chamber, 24, 26, or 28 in. back bored VR barrel, three Invector Plus Choke tubes, Quadra-Vent ports, drop out trigger group, TruGlo long bead fiber optic front sight, synthetic stock with rounded pistol grip and textured gripping surfaces, LOP spacers, Inflex Technology recoil pad, ambidextrous crossbolt safety, active valve system, larger bolt handle and bolt release button, 100% Mossy Oak Break-Up Country camo finish, approx. 7 lbs. New 2018.

MSR $1,100	$935	$825	$700	$635	$525	$425	$375

SX4 UPLAND FIELD – 12 or 20 (new 2020) ga., 3 in. chamber, gas operated with active valve system, 26 or 28 in. VR barrel, three Invector Plus choke tubes, 3 shot mag., matte nickel-plated receiver with engraved upland game scene, drop-out trigger group, TruGlo Long Bead fiber optic front sight, Grade II/III walnut stock with straight line cut checkering, improved ergonomics, rounded pistol grip, and satin oil finish, Inflex Technology recoil pad, ambidextrous crossbolt safety, back-bored technology, hard chrome-plated chamber and bore, larger bolt handle and bolt release button, 7 lbs. New 2019.

MSR $1,150	$975	$850	$725	$675	$550	$450	$375

Add $130 for 20 ga. (new 2020).

SX4 WATERFOWL HUNTER – 12 or 20 (new 2019) ga., 3 or 3 1/2 in. chamber, 26 or 28 in. VR back bored barrel with three Invector Plus choke tubes, Quadra-Vent ports, 4 shot mag., drop-out trigger group, TruGlo long bead fiber optic front sight, rounded pistol grip stock with textured gripping surfaces, Inflex Technology recoil pad, LOP spacers, ambidextrous crossbolt safety, large bolt handle and bolt release button, active valve gas system, 100% Mossy Oak Shadow Grass Blades (disc. 2020) or Mossy Oak Shadow Grass Habitat (new 2021) camo finish, approx. 7 lbs. New 2017.

MSR $960	$815	$715	$625	$550	$475	$400	$350

Add $140 for 3 1/2 in. chamber.
Add $140 for 20 ga. (new 2019).

SX4 WATERFOWL HUNTER COMPACT – 12 or 20 ga., 3 in. chamber, gas operated with active valve system, 24, 26, or 28 in. VR barrel, three Invector Plus choke tubes, 3 shot mag., hard chrome-plated chamber and bore, drop-out trigger group, TruGlo long bead fiber optic front sight, synthetic stock with rounded pistol grip and textured gripping surfaces, 13 in. LOP, two 1/4 in. LOP spacers, Pachmayr Decelerator recoil pad, ambidextrous crossbolt safety, Quadra-Vent ports, back-bored technology, larger bolt handle and bolt release button, 100% Mossy Oak Shadow Grass Blades camo finish, 6 1/2-6 3/4 lbs. New 2019.

MSR $960	$815	$715	$625	$550	$475	$400	$350

Add $140 for 20 ga.

SX4 WATERFOWL HYBRID HUNTER – 12 or 20 ga., 3 or 3 1/2 in. chamber, gas operated with active valve system, 26 or 28 in. VR back bored barrel, Invector Plus choke tube system, Quadra-Vent ports, TruGlo Long Bead fiber optic front sight, Mossy Oak Shadow Grass Blades Habitat camo finshed synthetic stock with rounded pistol grip and textured gripping surfaces, LOP spacers, Infex Technology recoil pad, ambi crossbolt safety, Cerakote FDE finish on barrel and receiver, approx. 7 lbs. New 2021.

MSR $930	$790	$690	$595	$535	$435	$355	$310

Add $150 for 20 ga.
Add $150 for 3 1/2 in. chamber.

GRADING - PPGS™	100%	98%	95%	90%	80%	70%	60%	LAST MSR

Shotguns: Single Barrel, 1968-1980 mfg.

MODEL 370 – 12, 16, 20, 28 ga., or .410 bore, 28-32 in. full choke plain barrel, replaced the Model 37, top lever break open, exposed hammer, plain pistol grip stock. Approx. 221,578 were mfg. between 1968-73.

12 ga.	$150	$125	$100	$90	$85	$80	$75	
16 ga.	$175	$150	$110	$90	$85	$80	$75	
20 ga.	$195	$165	$130	$110	$90	$85	$75	
28 ga.	$275	$225	$175	$140	$120	$100	$85	
.410 bore	$275	$225	$175	$140	$120	$100	$85	

The Model 370 was mfg. in Winchester's Canadian plant in Cobourg, Ontario.

MODEL 370 YOUTH – similar to 370, with 26 in. barrel, 12 1/2 in. stock, with recoil pad.

	$175	$145	$110	$95	$85	$80	$75	

MODEL 37A – single barrel shotgun, 26-36 in. full choke barrel, concave hammer spur, gold plated trigger, updated checkering pattern on pistol grip and bottom of forearm, roll engraved receiver, optional 36 in. goose barrel, 5 1/2-6 lbs. Approx. 391,168 mfg. between 1973-1980 in the Winchester plant in Cobourg, Ontario.

12 ga.	$150	$125	$100	$90	$85	$80	$75	
16 ga.	$150	$125	$100	$90	$85	$80	$75	
20 ga.	$150	$125	$100	$90	$85	$80	$75	
28 ga.	$225	$195	$150	$130	$110	$90	$80	
.410 bore	$275	$225	$175	$140	$120	$100	$85	

Add 15% for 36 in. goose barrel (12 ga. only)

MODEL 37A YOUTH – similar to 37A, except 20 ga. or .410 bore with 12 1/2 in. LOP stock.

	$175	$145	$110	$95	$85	$80	$75	

MODEL 840 – various gauges, mfg. in Canada until 1980.

	$140	$110	$95	$85	$75	$65	$55	

MODEL 1370 SLAGBLASTER – 12 ga., 26 in. heavy barrel, shoots special Winchester/Western CE8Z industrial ammunition with extended 3 oz. zinc slug (rare), industrial sales only - used to clean slag from steel kilns, 9 lbs. Mfg. in Canada, disc.

	$750	$700	$650	$575	$525	$450	$400	

SHOTGUNS: SLIDE ACTION, 1964-CURRENT

Winchester introduced WinChokes in 1969.

U.S. Repeating Arms closed its New Haven, CT manufacturing facility on March 31, 2006. There may be some speculation on recently manufactured Model 1300 shotguns. All Model 1300 last MSRs listed are from the Winchester 2006 price sheet.

MODEL 12 SUPER PIGEON GRADE – 12 ga., slide action, 26, 28, or 30 in. barrel, VR, any choke, hand honed action, engine turned breechblock and loading flap, "B" checkering and No. 5 engraving, custom order grade walnut stock. Limited production between 1964-72.

	$3,750	$3,275	$2,650	$2,275	$1,995	$1,650	$1,400	

Subtract 20% for Super Pigeon Grades mfg. 1984-85 (480 total).

MODEL 12 "Y" SERIES FIELD GRADE – 12 ga., 26, 28, or 30 in. VR barrel, various chokes, jeweled bolt, "Y" Series Model 12's had a forged receiver, while pre-64 Model 12's had a milled receiver, hand checkered select walnut stock, "Y" ser. no. prefix. Mfg. 1972-1975.

	$750	$650	$600	$550	$500	$450	$400	

In 1984, Y series Model 12s were once again available through a private contract with U.S.R.A. Co. which included engraving on Grades 1A-1C and 2-5. These guns were available in either Field, Trap, or Skeet configurations. Since there was no manufacturer's suggested retail, Model 12 values shown are established by analyzing the sales of the two private contractors - no more of these variations are available.

MODEL 12 "Y" SERIES PIGEON GRADES – 12 ga. only, available in Field, Trap, or Skeet configuration. 480 were mfg. 1985 only in the U.S. Repeating Arms Custom Shop. All receivers were sent in the white to Giovanelli in Italy for various levels of engraving, then sent back to the Custom Shop for bluing and assembly. Each had a U.S. Repeating Arms letter of authentication.

	$1,425	$1,250	$1,025	$875	$785	$695	$600	*$1,375*

* ***Model 12 "Y" Series Pigeon Grades 1A, 1B, & 1C*** – 12 ga., three different receiver patterns featuring ducks and dogs, standard machine cut checkering. Mfg. 1985 only.

	$1,500	$1,300	$1,050	$900	$800	$700	$600	*$1,195*

The breakdown of grades and configurations is as follows:

GRADING - PPGS™	100%	98%	95%	90%	80%	70%	60%	LAST MSR

Grade 1A - Trap (40 mfg.), Skeet (15 mfg.), Field (15 mfg.)
Grade 1B - Trap (25 mfg.), Skeet (15 mfg.), Field (13 mfg.)
Grade 1C - Trap (30 mfg.), Skeet (10 mfg.), Field (12 mfg.)

* ***Model 12 "Y" Series Pigeon Grade 2*** – 12 ga., engraving features two ducks on right side of receiver and a dog on left side, machine cut checkering. Mfg. 1985 only.

	$1,875	$1,650	$1,500	$1,300	$1,150	$900	$800	*$1,495*

The breakdown of grade and configurations is as follows:
Grade 2 - Trap (10 mfg.), Skeet (5 mfg.), Field (5 mfg.)

* ***Model 12 "Y" Series Pigeon Grade 3*** – 12 ga., features dog on right side of receiver and three ducks on left side. Mfg. 1985 only.

	$1,875	$1,650	$1,500	$1,300	$1,150	$900	$800	*$1,495*

The breakdown of grade and configurations is as follows:
Grade 3 - Trap (20 mfg.), Skeet (10 mfg.), Field (5 mfg.)

* ***Model 12 "Y" Series Pigeon Grade 4*** – 12 ga., multiple ducks and dogs on both sides of the receiver, machine cut checkering, also available with gold inlays. Mfg. 1985 only.

	$2,200	$1,875	$1,600	$1,400	$1,200	$1,050	$950	*$1,695*

Add $1,300 for gold inlays (only 25 mfg., Last MSR was $2,695).
The breakdown of grade and configurations is as follows:
Grade 4 - Trap (16 mfg.), Skeet (13 mfg.), Field (6 mfg.)
Grade 4 Gold - Trap (14 mfg.), Skeet (7 mfg.), Field (4 mfg.)

* ***Model 12 "Y" Series Pigeon Grade 5*** – 12 ga., features full fancy "B" carved and checkered stock/forearm, elaborate game scene engraving with or without gold inlays. Mfg. 1985 only.

	$2,750	$2,300	$1,900	$1,600	$1,350	$1,200	$995	*$1,995*

Add $1,500 for gold inlays (55 mfg. Last MSR was $2,995).
The breakdown of grade and configurations is as follows:
Grade 5 - Trap (42 mfg.), Skeet (20 mfg.), Field (13 mfg.)
Grade 5 Gold - Trap (33 mfg.), Skeet (15 mfg.), Field (7 mfg.)

* ***Model 12 "Y" Series Pigeon Grade 5 Three Barrel Set*** – 12 ga., features Grade 5 engraving with gold inlays, three barrel assemblies, and a presentation case. Only 45 mfg. 1985 only.

	$6,500	$5,750	$4,800	$4,300	$4,000	$3,500	$2,800	*$4,995*

MODEL 12 SKEET GRADE – similar to Field Grade, with 26 in. VR skeet bore barrel, skeet style stock, with recoil pad. Mfg. 1972-75.

	$1,195	$995	$895	$750	$650	$550	$500	

MODEL 12 TRAP GRADE – similar to Field grade, with 30 in. VR full choke barrel, trap style stock, straight or Monte Carlo, recoil pad. Mfg. 1972-80.

	$1,095	$950	$850	$750	$650	$500	$450	

MODEL 12 DU – 800 mfg. during 1975 for auction at Ducks Unlimited chapter banquets. Please refer to the Ducks Unlimited listing in the D section, available online at BlueBookofGunValues.com/overflow.

MODEL 12 LIMITED EDITION

* ***Model 12 Limited Edition Grade I 20 Ga.*** – 20 ga. only, 2 3/4 in. chamber only, reproduction of the famous Winchester Model 12 with slight design improvements, 26 in. VR barrel bored modified, 5 shot mag., high post floating rib, walnut stock and forearm with semi-gloss finish, takedown, 7 lbs. 4,000 mfg. by Miroku 1993-95.

	$995	$825	$650	N/A	N/A	N/A	N/A	*$879*

* ***Model 12 Limited Edition Grade IV 20 Ga.*** – similar specifications to Grade I, except has select walnut checkered 22 lines per inch with high gloss finish, extensive game scene engraving including multiple gold inlays. 1,000 mfg. by Miroku 1993-95.

	$1,500	$1,250	$995	N/A	N/A	N/A	N/A	*$1,431*

MODEL 42 HIGH GRADE LIMITED EDITION – .410 bore, 26 in. full choke VR barrel, Grade V-VI wood with special scroll and gold border engraving, 850 mfg. by Miroku 1993 only.

	$1,850	$1,425	$1,100	N/A	N/A	N/A	N/A	*$1,617*

MODEL 120 RANGER – 12, 16, or 20 ga., entry level model, VR and WinChokes. Disc.

	$200	$180	$165	$140	$110	$100	$90	

GRADING - PPGS™	100%	98%	95%	90%	80%	70%	60%	LAST MSR

MODEL 1200 FIELD GRADE – 12, 16, or 20 ga., 26, 28, or 30 in. barrel, alloy receiver, various chokes, checkered pistol grip stock, pad. Mfg. 1964-1981.

	100%	98%	95%	90%	80%	70%	60%	LAST MSR
	$200	$180	$165	$140	$110	$100	$90	
Vent. rib	$220	$205	$195	$165	$140	$110	$100	
WinChoke	$240	$215	$200	$190	$180	$160	$140	

Add 33% for Winchester recoil reduction system (mfg. 1966-1970).

MODEL 1200 MAGNUM – similar to 1200, chambered for 12 or 20 ga., 3 in. magnum shells. Mfg. 1964-80.

	100%	98%	95%	90%	80%	70%	60%	LAST MSR
	$210	$190	$175	$165	$140	$110	$100	
Vent. rib	$240	$215	$200	$185	$150	$140	$110	

MODEL 1200 SKEET GUN – similar to 1200, 12 or 20 ga., 26 in. VR barrel, skeet bore, 2 shot mag. and select style stock. Mfg. 1965-74.

	100%	98%	95%	90%	80%	70%	60%	LAST MSR
	$325	$275	$235	$200	$165	$140	$120	

MODEL 1200 TRAP GUN – similar to 1200, with 12 ga., VR, 30 in. full choke barrel, select trap style stock. Mfg. 1965-74.

	100%	98%	95%	90%	80%	70%	60%	LAST MSR
	$295	$275	$250	$195	$165	$140	$120	
WinChoke	$330	$305	$275	$250	$220	$165	$140	

MODEL 1200 DEER GUN – similar to 1200, with 22 in. barrel, rifle sights, 12 ga. only. Mfg. 1965-74.

	100%	98%	95%	90%	80%	70%	60%	LAST MSR
	$250	$200	$165	$110	$100	$85	$75	

MODEL 1200 POLICE STAINLESS – 12 ga. only, 18 in. barrel, 7 shot mag. Disc.

	100%	98%	95%	90%	80%	70%	60%	LAST MSR
	$250	$195	$165	$125	$105	$90	$75	

MODEL 1200 DEFENDER – 12 ga. only, 18 in. cylinder bore barrel, 7 shot mag., 6 lbs. Disc.

	100%	98%	95%	90%	80%	70%	60%	LAST MSR
	$250	$200	$180	$155	$140	$125	$110	

MODEL 1300 FEATHERWEIGHT – 12 or 20 ga., 3 in. chamber, takedown, 26 (new 1991) or 28 in. barrel, 5 shot, plain or VR (became standard 1990), WinChoke tubes, checkered walnut stock and grooved forearm, alloy frame, recoil pad, 6 3/4-7 1/8 lbs. Mfg. 1978-93.

	100%	98%	95%	90%	80%	70%	60%	LAST MSR
	$300	$260	$230	$195	$175	$160	$145	*$374*

Subtract $30 without VR.

This model had an "XTR" suffix until 1989. Older Model 1300 Featherweights had roll-engraving but no premiums are being asked at this time.

MODEL 1300 WALNUT FIELD – 12 or 20 (disc. 1994) ga., 3 in. chamber, 26 or 28 in. VR barrel with WinChokes (includes 3), checkered satin (disc. 2003) or gloss finished (new 2004) walnut stock and forearm, approx. 7 1/4 - 7 1/2 lbs. Mfg. 1994-2006.

	100%	98%	95%	90%	80%	70%	60%	LAST MSR
	$350	$250	$200	$160	$140	$120	$110	*$444*

Beginning 2003, Winchester started engraving "Speed Pump" on receiver on all Model 1300 variations.

* ***Model 1300 Walnut Black Shadow Field*** – 12 or 20 (new 1996) ga., 3 in. chamber, 26 or 28 in. (12 ga. only) VR WinChoke barrel, black composite stock and forearm, 6 3/4-7 1/4 lbs. Mfg. 1995-2006.

	100%	98%	95%	90%	80%	70%	60%	LAST MSR
	$275	$210	$170	$135	$120	$110	$95	*$357*

* ***Model 1300 Walnut Field Sporting*** – 12 ga., 3 in. chamber, 24 (compact) or 28 in. VR barrel with 5 WinChokes, satin finished checkered walnut full-length or compact (13 in. LOP) stock and forearm with radiused recoil pad, TruGlo front sight, matte metal finish, 6 3/4 or 7 1/2 lbs. Mfg. 2002-2006.

	100%	98%	95%	90%	80%	70%	60%	LAST MSR
	$350	$255	$205	$165	$135	$120	$110	*$444*

* ***Model 1300 Walnut Field Advantage Camo*** – 12 ga. only, 28 in. barrel with choke tubes, full coverage. Advantage Camo. Mfg. 1997 only.

	100%	98%	95%	90%	80%	70%	60%	LAST MSR
	$340	$265	$235	$195	$165	$145	$125	*$432*

* ***Model 1300 Walnut Field New Shadow Grass*** – 12 ga. only, 26 or 28 in. VR barrel with 3 WinChokes, 100% Mossy Oak New Shadow Grass camo coverage, approx. 7 lbs. Mfg. 2004-2006.

	100%	98%	95%	90%	80%	70%	60%	LAST MSR
	$365	$275	$215	$180	$150	$130	$115	*$472*

MODEL 1300 UPLAND SPECIAL FIELD – 12 or 20 (new 2000) ga., 3 in. chamber, features gloss finished (new 2004) or satin finished (disc. 2003) checkered straight grip walnut stock and forearm, solid recoil pad, 24 in. VR barrel with choke tube, blue only, 6 3/4 lbs. Mfg. 1999-2006.

	100%	98%	95%	90%	80%	70%	60%	LAST MSR
	$350	$255	$205	$165	$135	$120	$110	*$444*

MODEL 1300 CUSTOM HIGH GRADE – while advertised, this model never went into production. Advertised retail was $1,395.

GRADING - PPGS™	100%	98%	95%	90%	80%	70%	60%	LAST MSR

MODEL 1300 WATERFOWL – 12 ga. only, 3 in. chamber, 28 or 30 (disc.) in. VR barrel, matte finished metal, choice of low luster walnut finish or brown Win-Tuff wood stock, recoil pad, camo sling, and swivels, WinChokes standard, 7 lbs. Mfg. 1984-1991.

	$295	$260	$235	$200	$180	$165	$150	*$367*

MODEL 1300 TURKEY GUN – 12 ga. only, 3 in. chamber, 22 in. VR barrel, WinChoked, walnut stock and forearm with low luster finish, metal surfaces have matte finish, supplied with camouflaged fabric sling, 6 3/8 lbs. Mfg. 1985-88.

	$290	$265	$235	$200	$180	$165	$150	*$348*

* ***Model 1300 Turkey Gun Win-Cam*** – similar to Model 1300 Turkey Gun, except has greenish laminated hardwood stock and forearm. Mfg. 1987-93.

	$350	$295	$250	$200	$180	$165	$150	*$435*

* ***Model 1300 Turkey Gun Win-Cam Combo Pack*** – 12 ga., supplied with 22 and 30 in. VR non-glare finished barrels, greenish laminated hardwood stock and forearm, camo sling, matte finished metal. Mfg. 1987-88 only.

	$375	$330	$290	$260	$230	$200	$185	*$425*

* ***Model 1300 Turkey Gun Ladies-Youth Win-Cam Turkey Gun*** – 20 ga. only, 3 in. chamber, 22 in. VR barrel, green camo laminate shortened stock and forearm, includes sling and National Wild Turkey Federation engraving, 6 lbs. Mfg. 1992 only.

	$340	$295	$250	$200	$180	$165	$150	*$411*

* ***Model 1300 Turkey Gun Win-Cam NWTF Series I-IV*** – 12 or 20 ga., Series I was released 1989 (12 ga. only) and included special receiver engraving featuring National Wild Turkey Federation motifs, Series II was released 1990 with a choice of either 12 (disc.) or 20 ga. Ladies/Youth model, Series III was released 1991-92, Series IV was released 1993. Disc. 1994.

	$365	$300	$250	$200	$180	$165	$150	*$458*

MODEL 1300 TURKEY - SYNTHETIC STOCK – 12 or 20 (mfg. 1996-99, Black Shadow only) ga., 3 in. chamber, 22 in. VR barrel with choke tube, choice of 2 color Realtree camo patterns on synthetic stock and forearm, full camo coverage available in Realtree or Advantage (new 1996), or non-glare black (Black Shadow) finish on all surfaces, approx. 6 3/4 lbs. Mfg. 1994-2000.

* ***Model 1300 Turkey Synthetic Stock Black Shadow Finish*** – disc. 2000.

	$260	$195	$160	$135	$120	$110	$95	*$328*

* ***Model 1300 Turkey Synthetic Stock Mossy Oak Break-Up*** – 12 ga. only, 3 in. chamber, 22 in. VR barrel with TruGlo sights, high density X-full turkey choke tube, 100% Mossy Oak coverage on wood and metal, 6 3/4 lbs. Mfg. 2000 only.

	$375	$295	$260	$225	$200	$185	$170	*$459*

This model was also available with iron sights and rifled sabot choke tube for deer hunting - add approx. $30.

* ***Model 1300 Turkey Synthetic Stock RealTree/Advantage Camo Finish*** – RealTree covered synthetic stock and forearm or full coverage camo. Disc. 1998.

	$290	$240	$180	$150	$130	$115	$100	*$370*

Add $62 for full coverage camo.
Add $40 for full coverage without sling (disc. 1997).
Add $40 for smoothbore barrel (Advantage full camo only).

MODEL 1300 UNIVERSAL HUNTER/TURKEY – 12 ga. only, 3 in. chamber, 26 in. VR barrel with 3 WinChokes, full coverage standard or New Mossy Oak Break-Up (new 2003) camo, with or w/o TruGlo 3-dot sights, composite stock and forearm, 7 lbs. Mfg. 2002-2006.

	$400	$350	$300	$255	$200	$165	$140	*$517*

Subtract 5% if w/o TruGlo sights (Hunter Model).

MODEL 1300 NWTF TURKEY MODELS – 12 ga. only, 3 in. chamber, 18 (Short Turkey, new 2002) or 22 in. barrel, choice of Black Shadow (black synthetic stock and forearm with non-glare metal finish and extra full choke tube, mfg. 2001 only), Turkey Superflauge with full coverage TreBark Superflauge (mfg. 2001) or Mossy Oak Break-Up camo with TruGlo sights, Buck & Tom Superflauge with full coverage TreBark Superflauge (mfg. 2001) or Mossy Oak Break-Up (new 2002) camo with 2 choke tubes including rifled sabot, or Short Turkey (18 in. barrel with rifled sights and full coverage Mossy Oak Break-Up camo) configurations, "Team NWTF" logo printed on stock, 6 3/4 lbs. Mfg. 2001-2006.

	$425	$360	$260	$225	$175	$150	$125	*$514*

Subtract approx. $160 for Black Shadow configuration.
Add $42 for Buck & Tom Superflauge configuration.

GRADING - PPGS™	100%	98%	95%	90%	80%	70%	60%	LAST MSR

MODEL 1300 LADIES-YOUTH – 20 ga. only, 3 in. chamber, 22 in. VR barrel, shortened stock dimensions, walnut stock with recoil pad and rearward positioned, grooved forearm, 6 1/4 lbs. Mfg. 1992 only.

$315 $260 $220 $180 $165 $150 $135 *$355*

MODEL 1300 SLUG HUNTER – 12 ga. only, 3 in. chamber, 22 in. rifled or smoothbore barrel with iron sights, checkered stock and forearm, satin walnut finish or brown laminate stock (Win-Tuff). Supplied with camo fabric sling and rings and bases. Mfg. 1988-disc.

$360 $300 $250 $200 $180 $165 $150 *$445*

Add $10 for smoothbore barrel with Sabot rifled tubes (disc. 1992).
Add $4 for "Whitetails Unlimited" Model (new 1991).

MODEL 1300 WALNUT DEER – 12 ga. only, 3 in. chamber, 22 in. rifled barrel, non-glare metal surfaces, rifle sights, checkered walnut stock with recoil pad and forearm, 7 1/4 lbs. Mfg. 1994-1999.

$350 $285 $255 $225 $200 $185 $170 *$429*

* ***Model 1300 Walnut Deer Black Shadow*** – 12 or 20 (mfg. 1996-97, reintroduced 2000) ga., 3 in. chamber, 22 in. smoothbore (12 ga. only, disc. 2003) or rifled (new 1996) barrel with IC WinChoke, matte black stock, forearm, and metal parts, rifle sights, drilled and tapped receiver, approx. 6 3/4 lbs. Mfg. 1994-2006.

$300 $225 $175 $150 $125 $115 $95 *$382*

Add $44 for Cantilever scope mount, available in 12 ga. only (new 2000).
Add $77 for deer combo package that includes 22 in. cyl. bore (disc. 1998) or rifled (new 2000) barrel and 28 in. VR WinChoke barrels.
Subtract approx. $25 for smoothbore barrel (disc. 2003).

* ***Model 1300 Walnut Deer Ranger*** – 12 or 20 (Ranger regular or compact) ga., 3 in. chamber, 22 in. rifled barrel with rifle or TruGlo sights, smaller dimensions on 20 ga. Deer Ranger Compact (13 in. LOP, disc. 2005), brown composite stock and forearm, non-glare finish, 6 3/4 lbs. Mfg. 2000-2006.

$305 $230 $170 $145 $125 $110 $100 *$396*

* ***Model 1300 Walnut Deer Full Advantage Camo*** – 12 ga. only, 3 in. chamber, choice of 22 in. rifled or smoothbore barrel, entire gun is in Full Advantage camo pattern, drilled and tapped receiver, iron sights, 7 lbs. Mfg. 1995-98.

$350 $295 $260 $225 $200 $185 $170 *$432*

Subtract $22 for smoothbore barrel.

MODEL 1300 RANGER – 12 or 20 ga., 3 in. chamber, 22 cyl. or rifled (deer only, disc.), 24 1/8 cyl. (disc. deer barrel), 26 (mfg. 1991-98), 28, or 30 (disc. 1992) in. plain or VR barrel, walnut finished hardwood stock, alloy receiver, approx. 7 1/4 lbs. Mfg. 1983-2004.

$285 $215 $170 $135 $120 $110 $95 *$367*

Subtract $40 without VR or WinChokes.

This model was also available in a deer combination package which included either a 22 in. rifled or smoothbore deer barrel and a 28 in. VR WinChoke barrel in either 12 or 20 ga. (disc.). - add approx. 25% to values listed.

* ***Model 1300 Ranger Gloss*** – 12 or 20 ga., 3 in. chamber, 26 or 28 in. VR barrel, gloss finished checkered hardwood stock and forearm, 7 1/4-7 1/2 lbs. Limited mfg. 2006.

$300 $225 $180 $140 $125 $110 $95 *$391*

» **Model 1300 Ranger Gloss Compact** – similar to Model 1300 Ranger Gloss, except has 22 or 24 in. barrel and 13 in. LOP. Limited mfg. 2006.

$285 $215 $170 $135 $120 $110 $95 *$366*

* ***Model 1300 Ranger Ladies/Youth Model*** – 20 ga. only, 3 in. chamber, 22 in. VR barrel, shorter stock dimensions - 13 in. LOP and rearward positioned forearm. Disc. 1998.

$285 $235 $200 $170 $150 $125 $110 *$309*

Subtract $40 if without WinChoke and VR.

* ***Model 1300 Ranger Compact*** – 12 or 20 ga., 3 in. chamber, features shorter dimensions (13 LOP), 22 (20 ga. only) or 24 (12 ga. only) in. VR barrel with WinChoke and TruGlo sights, uncheckered hardwood stock and grooved forearm, blue only, approx. 6 3/4 lbs. Mfg. 1999-2005.

$300 $225 $175 $140 $120 $110 $95 *$391*

MODEL 1300 CAMP DEFENDER – 12 ga. only, 3 in. chamber, 8 shot mag., 22 in. barrel with rifle sights and WinChoke, choice of black synthetic (disc. 2000) or hardwood (new 2001) stock and forearm, matte metal finish, 6 7/8 lbs. Mfg. 1999-2004.

$300 $230 $180 $150 $125 $110 $100 *$392*

GRADING - PPGS™ 100% 98% 95% 90% 80% 70% 60% LAST MSR

MODEL 1300 DEFENDER – 12 or 20 (disc. 1996, reintroduced 2001) ga., 3 in. chamber, available in Police (disc. 1989), Practical (new 2005), Marine, and Defender variations, 18 or 24 (mfg. 1994-98) in. cyl. bore barrel, 5 (disc. 1998), 7 (disc. 1998), or 8 shot mag., matte metal finish, choice of hardwood (disc. 2001), composite (matte finish), or pistol grip (matte finish, 12 ga. only) stock, TruGlo sights became standard 1999, 5 3/4-7 lbs. Disc. 2006.

$270 $210 $160 $130 $110 $95 $85 *$341*

Add $13 for short pistol grip and full length stocks.

Add approx. $100 for Combo Package (includes extra 28 in. VR barrel - disc. 1998).

* ***Model 1300 Defender NRA*** – 12 or 20 ga., 18 in. barrel with removable TruGlo fiber optic front sight, composite stock, 8 shot mag., features NRA medallion on pistol grip, also available in 12 ga. combo with pistol grip stock, 6 1/4-6 1/2 lbs. Limited mfg. 2006.

$285 $215 $175 $140 $120 $110 $95 *$364*

Add $13 for combo with pistol grip and full length stock.

* ***Model 1300 Defender Practical*** – 12 ga. only, 3 in. chamber, 8 shot mag., 22 in. barrel with TruGlo adj. open sights, designed for practical shooting events, black synthetic stock and forearm. Mfg. 2005 only.

$300 $230 $170 $145 $125 $110 $100 *$392*

» **Model 1300 Defender Practical NRA** – 12 ga. only, 3 in. chamber, 8 shot mag., 22 in. barrel with TruGlo sights, black synthetic stock and forearm, Winchoke system, adj. open sights, NRA logo grip cap, 6 1/2 lbs. Limited mfg. 2006 only.

$315 $240 $180 $150 $130 $110 $100 *$414*

* ***Model 1300 Defender Stainless Coastal Marine*** – 12 ga. only, 18 in. cyl. bore stainless steel barrel and mag. tube, a Sandstrom 9A phosphate coating was released late 1989 to give long lasting corrosion protection to all receiver and internal working parts, Dura-Touch armor coating stock treatment added 2004, 6 shot mag., synthetic pistol grip (disc. 2001) or full black stock configuration, approx. 6 3/8 lbs. Mfg. 2002-2005.

$465 $380 $275 $225 $195 $165 $140 *$575*

» **Model 1300 Defender Stainless Coastal Marine NRA** – 12 ga. only, 18 in. nickel plated stainless steel barrel, anodized aluminum alloy receiver and plated parts for corrosion resistance, Dura-Touch Armor coating on composite stock, 7 shot mag., sling swivel studs, removable TruGlo fiber optic front sight, 6 1/2 lbs. Limited mfg. 2006 only.

$480 $390 $280 $230 $200 $165 $140 *$598*

* ***Model 1300 Lady Defender*** – 20 ga. only, 3 in. chamber, choice of synthetic regular or pistol grip stock, 4 (disc. 1996) or 7 shot mag., 18 in. cyl. bore barrel (new 1996), 5 3/8 lbs. Disc. 1998.

$235 $190 $150 $120 $105 $90 $80 *$290*

SPEED PUMP FIELD – 12 ga., 3 in. chamber, side ejection, four lug rotary bolt, 26 or 28 in. VR barrel with Invector Plus chokes, choice of gloss finished checkered walnut or black synthetic stock and forearm, approx. 7 1/4 lbs. Mfg. by Miroku during 2008.

$295 $250 $215 $200 $185 $170 $155 *$349*

Add $50 for checkered walnut stock and forearm.

SPEED PUMP DEFENDER – 12 ga., 3 in. chamber, side ejection, 5 shot mag., 18 in. plain barrel with fixed cylinder choke, black composite stock with non-glare finish and ribbed forearm. Mfg. by Miroku during 2008.

$240 $210 $190 $170 $150 $135 $120 *$299*

SXP (SUPER X PUMP) FIELD – 12 or 20 (new 2015) ga., 3 in. chamber, 4 shot mag., 26 or 28 in. barrel, full, mod., or IC Invector plus choke tubes, checkered satin finished stock and forearm with premium recoil pad, brass bead front sight, drop out trigger, crossbolt safety, 6 3/4-7 1/8 lbs. New 2013.

MSR $410 $360 $315 $285 $250 $220 $195 $175

Add $30 for 20 ga. (new 2015).

* ***SXP Field Compact*** – 12 or 20 (new 2015) ga., 3 in. chamber, 24, 26 or 28 in. barrel, full, mod., or IC Invector plus choke tubes, 4 or 5 shot mag., drop out trigger, brass bead front sight, checkered satin finished stock and forearm with Inflex Technology recoil pad, crossbolt safety, 6 3/4 lbs. New 2014.

MSR $410 $360 $315 $285 $250 $220 $195 $175

Add $30 for 20 ga. (new 2015).

GRADING - PPGS™	100%	98%	95%	90%	80%	70%	60%	LAST MSR

SXP BLACK SHADOW DEER – 12 or 20 (new 2017) ga., 3 in. chamber, 4 or 5 shot mag., 22 in. fully rifled barrel, black synthetic stock with textured gripping surfaces, Inflex Technology recoil pad, TruGlo fiber optic front and adj. rear sights, receiver mounted Picatinny rail, rotary bolt, drop out trigger, crossbolt safety, 6 7/8 lbs. New 2013.

MSR $530	$460	$400	$350	$300	$265	$235	$195	

Add $30 for 20 ga. (new 2017).

This model was originally featured as a 2012 SHOT Show Special.

SXP BLACK SHADOW FIELD – 12 or 20 (new 2015) ga., 3 or 3 1/2 (new 2012) in. chamber, 24 (new 2017), 26, or 28 in. VR barrel with 3 Invector Plus choke tubes, rotary bolt with dual steel action slide bars, black pistol grip composite stock, non-glare matte metal finish with red accents, crossbolt trigger guard safety, styling similar to Super X3 semi-auto, Inflex recoil pad, approx. 6 3/4-7 lbs. New 2009.

MSR $390	$335	$275	$240	$215	$185	$170	$150	

Add $20 for 3 1/2 in. chamber (new 2012).
Add $20 for 20 ga. (new 2015).

SXP DEFENDER – 12 or 20 ga. (new 2015), 3 in. chamber, 8 in. fixed cylinder bore barrel, 5 shot mag., drop-out trigger group, brass bead front sight, black composite pistol grip stock with textured gripping surfaces, deep groove forearm, Inflex Technology recoil pad, crossbolt safety, drilled and tapped alloy receiver, non-glare metal finish, 6 1/4 lbs. New 2009.

MSR $360	$310	$270	$235	$210	$175	$150	$125	

Add $30 for 20 ga. (new 2015).

SXP EXTREME DEER – 12 ga., 3 in. chamber, 22 in. rifled barrel with fiber optic front and adj. rear sights, alloy receiver, black synthetic pistol grip stock with two interchangeable comb pieces, Inflex recoil pad, non-glare matte metal finish with red receiver accents, 7 lbs. New 2016.

MSR $570	$485	$425	$365	$330	$275	$240	$200	

SXP EXTREME DEER HUNTER – 12 ga., 3 in. chamber, 22 in. fully rifled barrel, 3-shot adaptor with Speed-Plug System, alloy receiver, drop out trigger group, TruGlo fiber optic front and adj. rear sight, synthetic pistol grip stock with textured gripping surfaces, two interchangeable comb pieces and LOP spacers, Inflex Technology recoil pad, crossbolt safety, rotary bolt, 100% Mossy Oak Break-Up Country camo finish, 7 lbs. New 2016.

MSR $640	$540	$475	$400	$365	$300	$275	$250	

SXP HYBRID HUNTER – 12 or 20 ga., 3 or 3 1/2 in. chamber, 26 or 28 in. back bored barrel, Invector Plus choke tubes, 3 shot adaptor with Speed-Plug System, rotary bolt, drilled and tapped alloy receiver, TruGlo Long Bead fiber optic front sight, Mossy Oak Shadow Grass Habitat camo synthetic stock with textured gripping surfaces, Inflex Technology recoil pad, reversible crossbolt safety, FDE Perma-Cote finish on barrel and receiver, 6 1/2-7 lbs. New 2021.

MSR $430	$365	$320	$275	$250	$200	$165	$145	

Add $20 for 3 1/2 in. chamber or 20 ga.

SXP LONG BEARD – 12 or 20 (new 2018) ga., 3 or 3 1/2 in. chamber, slide action shotgun, 24 in. back bored barrel with Invector Plus Extra-Full Long Beard turkey choke tube, 4 or 5 shot mag., alloy receiver, TruGlo fiber optic adj. sights, synthetic pistol grip stock with textured gripping surfaces, two interchangeable comb pieces and LOP spacers, Inflex Technology recoil pad, crossbolt safety, rotary bolt, black chrome protection, 100% Mossy Oak Break-Up Country or Mossy Oak Obsession (new 2018) camo finish, 7 1/4 lbs. New 2016.

MSR $550	$470	$410	$365	$335	$300	$265	$235	

Add $40 for 3 1/2 in. chamber.
Add $40 for 20 ga. (new 2018).

SXP MARINE DEFENDER – 12 or 20 (new 2016) ga., 3 in. chamber, 18 in. barrel with Invector Plus cylinder choke tube, black synthetic stock with textured gripping surfaces, Inflex Technology recoil pad, non-glare matte black alloy drilled and tapped receiver with hard chrome barrel and mag. tube, tactical ribbed forearm, includes both brass bead and TruGlo fiber optic front sights, drop out trigger, crossbolt safety, 4-lug rotary bolt, 6 1/4 lbs. New 2013.

MSR $410	$360	$315	$285	$250	$220	$195	$175	

Add $30 for 20 ga. (new 2016).

SXP SHADOW DEFENDER – 12 or 20 ga., 3 in. chamber, 18 in. barrel, Invector Plus cylinder choke tube, 5 shot mag., alloy receiver, brass bead front sight, synthetic pistol grip stock with two interchangeable comb pieces, tactical ribbed forearm, Inflex Technology recoil pad, textured gripping surfaces, crossbolt safety, matte black finish, 6-6 1/4 lbs. Mfg. 2017-2020.

	$375	$335	$300	$275	$250	$225	$200	*$450*

Add $20 for 20 ga.

GRADING - PPGS™	100%	98%	95%	90%	80%	70%	60%	LAST MSR

SXP SHADOW MARINE DEFENDER – 12 or 20 ga., 3 in. chamber, 18 in. barrel, Invector Plus cylinder choke tube, 5 shot mag., alloy receiver, brass bead front sight, synthetic pistol grip stock with textured gripping surfaces, two interchangeable comb pieces and LOP spacers, tactical ribbed forearm, Inflex Technology recoil pad, crossbolt safety, matte hard chrome plating on barrel, mag. tube and slide arms, 6 1/4 lbs. Mfg. 2017-2020.

	$425	$350	$315	$285	$250	$225	$200	*$500*

Add $20 for 20 ga.

SXP TRAP – 12 ga., 3 in. chamber, 30 or 32 in. back bored barrel with VR (5/16 in.), three Invector Plus choke tubes, 4 shot mag., drop out trigger group, TruGlo fiber optic front sight and ivory mid-bead, satin finished checkered Monte Carlo stock and forearm, Inflex Technology recoil pad, crossbolt safety, 3-shot adaptor with Speed-Plug System, matte black finish, approx. 7 1/2 lbs. New 2015.

MSR $490	$435	$365	$315	$265	$235	$210	$185	

* ***SXP Trap Compact*** – 12 or 20 (new 2019) ga., similar to SXP Trap, except has 28 or 30 in. barrel and 13 in. LOP. New 2015.

MSR $490	$435	$365	$315	$265	$235	$210	$185	

Add $30 for 20 ga. (new 2019).

SXP TURKEY – 12 (3 1/2 in.) or 20 (3 in. chamber) ga., 24 in. barrel with TruGlo fiber optic adj. sights on the barrel, Invector Plus extra-full turkey choke tube, alloy receiver, matte black synthetic stock with textured gripping surfaces, Inflex Technology recoil pad, crossbolt safety, matte black metal finish, 6 1/4-6 5/8 lbs. New 2017.

MSR $450	$390	$350	$300	$275	$250	$225	$195	

SXP TURKEY HUNTER – 12 or 20 (new 2015) ga., 3 or 3-1/2 in. chamber, 4 or 5 (20 ga.) shot mag., 22 (disc. 2014) or 24 in. VR barrel with TruGlo sights, 100% Mossy Oak Break-Up Infinity (disc. 2014), Mossy Oak Break-Up Country (new 2015), or Mossy Oak Obsession (new 2018) camo coverage, Inflex Technology recoil pad, 6 1/4-6 5/8 lbs. New 2012.

MSR $530	$460	$400	$365	$335	$300	$265	$235	

SXP ULTIMATE DEFENDER – 12 ga., 3 in. chamber, 18 in. barrel with extended ported door-breacher choke tube, 4 shot mag., drop out trigger group, ghost ring rear sight and protected front blade front sight, black synthetic stock with textured gripping surfaces and Inflex Technology recoil pad, includes receiver Picatinny rail and 2 additional rails in front of forearm, 7 1/2 lbs. Mfg. 2015-2016.

	$425	$375	$335	$300	$275	$250	$225	*$500*

SXP ULTIMATE MARINE DEFENDER – 12 ga., 3 in. chamber, 18 in. barrel with extended porter breacher choke tube, 4 shot mag., drop out trigger group, ghost ring rear sight with protected front sight blade, includes receiver Picatinny rail and 2 additional rails in front of forearm, matte hard chrome plating on barrel and mag., 7 1/2 lbs. Mfg. 2015-2016.

	$465	$415	$375	$335	$300	$275	$250	*$540*

SXP UNIVERSAL HUNTER – 12 or 20 ga., 3 or 3 1/2 in. chamber, 24, 26, or 28 in. back bored barrel, three Invector Plus choke tubes, drilled and tapped alloy receiver, drop out trigger group, TruGlo long bead fiber optic front sight, synthetic stock with textured gripping surfaces, Inflex Technology recoil pad, crossbolt safety, 3-shot adaptor with Speed-Plug System, rotary bolt, 100% Mossy Oak Break-Up Country camo finish, black chrome protection on bolt and metal components, 6 1/2-7 lbs. New 2016.

MSR $480	$410	$360	$315	$280	$225	$185	$160	

Add $30 for 3 1/2 in. chamber or 20 ga.

SXP WATERFOWL HUNTER – 12 or 20 (new 2016) ga., 3 or 3 1/2 (new 2012) in. chamber, 26 or 28 in. back bored barrel with three Invector Plus choke tubes, 3-shot adaptor with Speed-Plug System, drop out trigger group, TruGlo long bead fiber optic front sight, synthetic stock with textured gripping surfaces, Inflex Technology recoil pad, crossbolt safety, rotary bolt, 100% Mossy Oak Duck Blind (disc. 2012), Mossy Oak Shadow Grass Blades (mfg. 2013-2020), or Mossy Oak Shadow Grass Habitat (new 2021) camo coverage, black chrome protection, approx. 6 3/4-7 lbs. New 2011.

MSR $470	$400	$350	$300	$275	$225	$185	$155	

Add $30 for 20 ga. (new 2016) or 3 1/2 in. chamber (new 2012).

SXP YOUTH FIELD – 12 or 20 ga., 3 in. chamber, 18, 20, 22, or 24 in. VR barrel, three Invector Plus choke tubes, 3 shot mag., drop-out trigger group, brass bead front sight, satin finished stock and forearm with traditional checkering, 12 in. LOP, Inflex Technology recoil pad, crossbolt safety, back-bored technology, 3-shot adaptor with speed-plug system, matte finish, 5 7/8-6 7/8 lbs. New 2019.

MSR $410	$360	$315	$285	$250	$220	$195	$175	

Add $30 for 20 ga.

GRADING - PPGS™	100%	98%	95%	90%	80%	70%	60%	LAST MSR

SHOTGUNS: O/U - RECENT PRODUCTION

Model 101 dates of manufacture and serialization data can be found in the SERIALIZATION section in the back of this text.

In November of 1987 Olin/Winchester disc. the Model 101. Classic Doubles (listed separately in this text) imported this model under their own trademark until approx. 1990. With the discontinuance of the Model 101 and its many variations, both dealers and collectors have created a lot more demand for this model recently. As a result, prices have escalated and the scramble is on to try and pick off those rare and desirable variations. Since there have been a lot of limited editions and production changes in the 101 O/U series, it could very well be that this model might become very collectible in upcoming years (as happened to the Model 12).

Note: Model 101 and Model 96 Xpert guns were made by Olin Kodensha located in Tochigi, Japan.

Add 10% for the following discontinued Model 101s listed in this section if in NIB condition only.

MODEL 91 – 12 ga. only, mfg. by Laurona in Spain for international sales including Europe, SST, ejectors optional, VR, distinguishable by black chrome finish on metal parts. Disc.

Prices are difficult to evaluate because of limited importation domestically. In some regions they are bought as medium priced field guns ($550-$650), while in others they are sold as a rare Winchester O&U ($900-$1,100).

MODEL 96 XPERT FIELD GRADE – 12 or 20 ga., similar action to Model 101, 3 in. chambers, auto ejectors, SST, various barrel lengths and chokes, action similar to 101, no engraving, checkered pistol grip stock and forearm. Mfg. 1976-82.

$875	$775	$650	$550	$475	$425	$375	

Add 10% for 20 ga.

This model has become known as the "Poor Man's 101".

MODEL 96 XPERT SKEET GRADE – 2 3/4 in. chambers, similar to Field Grade, with 27 in. skeet barrels, skeet style stock. Mfg. 1976-82.

$925	$850	$725	$600	$500	$450	$410	

Add 10% for 20 ga.

MODEL 96 XPERT TRAP GRADE – 12 ga. only, 2 3/4 in. chambers, similar to Field, 30 in. imp. mod./full or full/full choke, trap style stock. Mfg. 1976-82.

$875	$775	$650	$550	$475	$425	$375	

MODEL 99 – 12 ga., DT, no engraving. Disc.

$700	$575	$525	$470	$430	$395	$360	

MODEL 101 FIELD VARIATION – 12, 20 ga., or .410 bore, 26, 28, or 30 in. barrels, various chokes, boxlock, auto ejectors, SST, engraved receiver, checkered American walnut pistol grip stock. Mfg. 1963-87.

Values assume WinChokes (standard since 1983) - subtract $60 if without.

* ***Model 101 Field Variation Older Production*** – checkered walnut stock and forearm, ejectors, SST, blue metal with light engraving on receiver, various barrel lengths, w/o choke tubes.

$995	$850	$725	$625	$585	$550	$500	

Add 50% for 28 ga. or .410 bore.

Add 20% for 20 ga.

* ***Model 101 Field Variation 25th Anniversary Model*** – 12 ga., 32 in. F/M barrels, 2 3/4 in. chambers, engraved "1 of 101" with silver inlays, cased. Mfg. 1988.

$5,000	$4,500	$4,000	$3,500	$3,000	$2,000	$1,500	*$3,500*

* ***Model 101 Field Variation Special*** – 12 ga., 3 in. chambers, VR, 27 in. barrels with WinChokes, blue receiver with scroll engraving, ejectors, 7 lbs. Disc. 1987.

$1,350	$1,225	$995	$875	$775	$695	$600	*$1,185*

* ***Model 101 Field Variation Lightweight*** – 12 or 20 ga., similar to regular Field Grade, except has coin finished receiver, vent. barrels, and solid rubber recoil pad, w/o WinChokes, 6 1/2 - 7 lbs. Disc. 1987.

$1,200	$1,100	$1,000	$900	$800	$600	$500	*$1,425*

Add 20% for 20 ga.

* ***Model 101 Field Variation Waterfowl Model*** – 12 ga. only, 3 in. chambers, 30 or 32 (disc.) in. WinChoked barrels, VR, matte blue receiver with moderate engraving, low gloss walnut stock with vent. recoil pad, 7 3/4 lbs. Disc. 1987.

$1,895	$1,700	$1,500	$1,250	$1,050	$800	$700	*$1,570*

GRADING - PPGS™	100%	98%	95%	90%	80%	70%	60%	LAST MSR

* ***Model 101 Field Variation Grade 2 Barrel Hunting Set*** – 12 or 20 ga. barrels, both with WinChokes, 26 in. barrels - 20 ga., 28 in. barrels - 12 ga., scroll engraved, blue receiver with game scene engraving and borders, cased. Mfg. 1984-87.

	$3,300	$2,800	$2,600	$2,400	$2,200	$2,000	$1,800	*$2,345*

* ***Model 101 Field Variation Quail Special*** – 12, 20 (disc. 1984), 28 (new 1987) ga., or .410 bore (new 1987), 25 1/2 in. WinChoke barrels, straight grip stock, vent. barrels and rib, coin finished receiver with game scene engraving, 6 3/4 lbs. 500 of each ga. were mfg. Imported 1984-86.

12 ga.	$2,900	$2,495	$2,250	$1,995	$1,750	$1,550	$1,450
20 ga.	$3,500	$3,100	$2,650	$2,200	$1,850	$1,750	$1,650
28 ga.	$5,250	$4,500	$3,950	$3,600	$3,200	$2,700	$2,500
.410 bore	$4,500	$3,850	$3,250	$2,800	$2,350	$1,900	$1,800

Last MSR was $1,950.

All 28 ga. models are baby frames.

* ***Model 101 Field Variation National Wild Turkey Federation Commemorative*** – features golden turkeys on receiver sides, 27 in. VR barrels with choke tubes, only 300 mfg.

	$3,000	$2,400	$1,900	$1,700	$1,500	$1,300	$1,000

Original issue price was $1,950.

* ***Model 101 Field Variation American Flyer Live Bird*** – 12 ga. only, 28 or 29 1/2 (new 1988) in. separated barrels with special competition VR, blue frame with gold wire borders and pigeon inlay, 8-8 1/2 lbs. Imported 1987 only.

	$2,595	$2,275	$1,950	$1,775	$1,600	$1,425	$1,300	*$2,910*

Add $925 for Combo Model (with extra set of 28 & 29 1/2 in. barrels with WinChokes - 45 mfg.).
Add $265 for 29 1/2 in. barrel with WT4 choke tubes.

Approx. 200 of this model were mfg.

MODEL 101 MAGNUM – similar to 101 Field, 12 or 20 ga., 3 in. Mag. chambering, recoil pad, 30 in. barrels, full and mod., or full and full choke. Mfg. 1966-81.

	$1,300	$1,100	$1,000	$800	$700	$600	$500

Add 20% for 20 ga.

MODEL 101 SKEET VARIATION – similar to 101 Field, with 26 1/2 (12 or 20 ga.) or 28 (28 ga. or .410 bore) in. skeet bored barrels, skeet style stock. Mfg. 1966-84.

	$1,200	$1,000	$825	$770	$700	$650	$595

Add 50% for 28 ga. or .410 bore.
Add 30% for 20 ga.

MODEL 101 THREE GAUGE SKEET SET – similar to Skeet 101, with 20, 28 ga., and .410 bore barrels, cased. Mfg. 1974-84.

	$3,800	$3,475	$3,150	$2,850	$2,600	$2,250	$1,900

MODEL 101 TRAP VARIATION – 12 ga. only, 30 or 32 in. barrels with normal or wide VR, imp. mod. and full or full and full chokes, trap style stock. Mfg. 1966-84.

	$1,320	$1,100	$935	$825	$715	$660	$605

MODEL 101 SINGLE BARREL TRAP – similar to O/U Trap, with 32 or 34 in. F or IM choke barrel, Monte Carlo trap style stock. Mfg. 1967-71.

	$880	$660	$550	$495	$385	$360	$330

Add 100% for an extra O/U barrel (Trap Set).

MODEL 101 PIGEON GRADE (XTR) – 12, 20, 28 ga., or .410 bore (disc. 1986), vent. barrels, deluxe engraved silver receiver version of 101, select checkered wood. Mfg. 1974-1987.

* ***Model 101 Pigeon Grade Lightweight Field Model*** – lightweight variation, WinChokes standard, 28 ga. baby frame has 27 in. barrels, 6 1/2-7 lbs. Disc. 1987.

12 ga.	$2,195	$2,000	$1,800	$1,450	$1,350	$1,250	$1,150
20 ga.	$2,700	$2,350	$2,000	$1,800	$1,700	$1,600	$1,500
28 ga. standard	$3,750	$3,300	$2,900	$2,500	$2,200	$2,100	$1,700
28 ga. baby frame	$5,000	$4,650	$4,250	$3,800	$3,350	$2,750	$2,500
.410 bore	$3,500	$3,250	$2,925	$2,500	$2,200	$2,100	$1,700

Last MSR was $1,950.

Subtract 5% if without WinChokes (available in all gauges).

* ***Model 101 Pigeon Grade Lightweight recent mfg.*** – 20 ga. only, 27 in. barrels only with WinChokes, previously manufactured guns that have been photo-chemically engraved and gold plated, 101 (total mfg.) shotguns were sold by Guns Unlimited Inc. located in Omaha, NE 1995-96.

	$2,495	$2,200	$2,000	$1,800	$1,600	$1,500	$1,300	*$1,795*

GRADING - PPGS™	100%	98%	95%	90%	80%	70%	60%	LAST MSR

* ***Model 101 Pigeon Grade Lightweight two barrel set*** – includes either 12/20 ga. with WinChokes (28 in. barrels on 12 ga. and 27 in. on 20 ga.) or 28 ga./.410 bore (27 in. barrels, 28 ga. has WinChokes; .410 bore has fixed M/F chokes), 250 sets mfg. serial numbered HS1-HS250. Disc. 1986.

	$3,595	$3,350	$2,950	$2,750	$2,300	$2,150	$1,900	*$2,500*

Add 30% for 28 ga./.410 bore combo.

* ***Model 101 Pigeon Grade 3 barrel set*** – coin finished Pigeon Grade frame, approx. 250 mfg.

	$4,750	$4,350	$3,900	$3,400	$2,750	$2,450	$2,250	

* ***Model 101 Pigeon Grade Featherweight*** – 12 or 20 ga., English straight stock, 25 1/2 in. barrels bored IC/IM, 6 1/2-6 3/4 lbs. Disc. 1987.

	$1,950	$1,750	$1,450	$1,275	$950	$850	$750	*$1,580*

Add 20% for 20 ga.
Add 20% for WinChokes.

* ***Model 101 Pigeon Grade Skeet*** – 12, 20, 28 ga., or .410 bore.

	$1,850	$1,650	$1,450	$1,225	$1,100	$875	$775	

Add 25% for 20 ga.
Add 50% for 28 ga. or .410 bore.

* ***Model 101 Pigeon Grade Trap (Disc.)*** – 12 ga. only, vent. barrels and rib, coin finish receiver with fine scroll engraving, engraved pigeon on floorplate, WinChoke standard, 8 1/4 lbs. Disc. 1985.

	$1,550	$1,350	$1,100	$925	$825	$725	$650	*$1,475*

Subtract 15% if w/o WinChokes.

* ***Model 101 Pigeon Grade Super*** – 12 ga. only, blue receiver with elaborate engraving including multiple gold inlays, extra select walnut with fleur-de-lis checkering on stock and forearm, WinChoke standard, 7 1/2 lbs. Imported 1985-87 only.

	$5,000	$4,800	$4,500	$3,800	$3,000	$2,750	$2,200	*$4,590*

MODEL 101 PIGEON GRADE TRAP (CURRENT) – 12 ga., 2 3/4 in. chambers, 30 or 32 in. 10mm VR ported barrels with Invector Plus choking, adj. trigger, TruGlo interchangeable fiber optic front sights, high gloss checkered Grade II/III or Grade III/IV (disc.) walnut stock, with or w/o adj. comb, white line spacer Pachmayr Decelerator pad, low profile nickel plated receiver with classic Pigeon engraving, includes ABS hard case, approx. 7 1/2 lbs. Mfg. in Belgium. New 2008.

MSR $2,600	$2,200	$1,925	$1,650	$1,500	$1,210	$1,000	$850	

Add $160 for adj. comb.

MODEL 101 PIGEON SPORTING – 12 ga., 30 or 32 in. ported barrels, 2 3/4 in. chambers, 10mm rib, gloss finished checkered Grade II/III walnut stock with adj. comb, five choke tubes, adj. trigger, silver Nitride receiver with light scroll engraving, TruGlo front sight, includes hard case, 7 - 7 1/4 lbs. Mfg. 2009-2010.

	$2,275	$1,850	$1,625	$1,375	$1,100	$900	$825	*$2,619*

MODEL 101 DIAMOND GRADE – Trap or Skeet O/U, 12 (Trap only), 20, 28 ga., or .410 bore, vent. barrels and rib, WinChoke standard on Trap - add $75 on Skeet model (disc. 1986), select hand checkered walnut, engraved satin-finish receiver. Trap model has extra high VR. Skeet model has raised rib and muzzle vents.

* ***Model 101 Diamond Grade Standard Trap*** – 12 ga. only, 30 or 32 in. vent. barrels, 8 3/4 - 9 lbs. Disc. 1987.

	$1,700	$1,500	$1,275	$1,100	$900	$780	$640	*$1,860*

* ***Model 101 Diamond Grade Unsingle Trap*** – 12 ga. only, lower single barrel, 32 or 34 in. barrel, extended rib. Disc. 1986.

	$1,900	$1,675	$1,425	$1,200	$1,000	$800	$600	*$1,760*

Add $60 for WinChoke.

* ***Model 101 Diamond Grade Oversingle Trap*** – 12 ga. only, WinChokes, 34 in. upper barrel only, 8 1/2 lbs. Imported 1986-87 only.

	$2,100	$1,795	$1,600	$1,425	$1,200	$995	$895	*$2,145*

* ***Model 101 Diamond Grade Oversingle Combo*** – includes one set of O/U barrels and an oversingle barrel, cased. Imported 1987 only.

	$2,950	$2,725	$2,500	$2,250	$2,000	$1,800	$1,600	*$3,550*

Add $275 for ATA Trap set.

* ***Model 101 Diamond Grade Trap Combo*** – 12 ga. only, includes a set of 30 or 32 in. vent. O/U barrels and a 32 or 34 in. high ribbed unsingle (lower) barrel, standard or Monte Carlo stock, approx. 9 lbs. Disc. 1987.

	$2,950	$2,600	$2,325	$1,975	$1,800	$1,600	$1,400	*$2,940*

GRADING - PPGS™	100%	98%	95%	90%	80%	70%	60%	LAST MSR

* ***Model 101 Diamond Grade Standard Skeet*** – 12, 20, 28 ga., or .410 bore, 27 1/2 in. vent. barrels and competition rib, 6 1/2 - 7 1/4 lbs. Disc. 1987.

	$1,725	$1,525	$1,300	$1,125	$950	$850	$700	*$1,950*

Add 30% for 28 ga. or .410 bore.
Add 20% for 20 ga.

Certain design features may increase/decrease the values of this model.

* ***Model 101 Diamond Grade Four Gauge Skeet Set*** – includes 12, 20, 28 ga., and .410 bore 27 1/2 in. separated barrel assemblies, cased. Imported 1985-87 only.

	$4,500	$4,000	$3,500	$3,000	$2,800	$2,500	$2,000	*$5,025*

* ***Model 101 Diamond Grade Sporting Clay*** – 12 ga. only, marked Diamond Sporter, 28 in. barrels with WinChokes, designed for Sporting Clay competition. Disc. 1987.

	$2,250	$1,875	$1,550	$1,225	$1,025	$875	$725	*$1,965*

MODEL 101 150TH COMMEMORATIVE – 12 ga., 3 in. chambers, 28 in. high gloss blued barrels, Invector Plus choke tubes, white front bead sight, deep relief scroll engraving with gold embellishments on the silver Nitride finished receiver, trigger guard, top lever, forearm bracket, latch lever, and safety barrel selector, includes the Winchester 150th Anniversary logo and the WRA scroll trademark, gloss finished high Grade IV/V walnut stock with cut checkering, white line spacer Pachmayr Decelerator recoil pad, 7 lbs. Limited mfg. 2016 only.

	$2,750	$2,500	$2,250	$2,000	$1,850	$1,700	$1,550	*$3,070*

MODEL 101 SPORTING - CURRENT MFG. (SELECT) – 12 ga., 2 3/4 in. chambers, 28, 30, or 32 in. lightweight ported barrels, Invector Plus chokes with 5 signature extended choke tubes, 10mm broadway rib, ejectors, adj. trigger shoe, white mid-bead and TruGlo interchangeable fiber optic front sight, high gloss Grade II/III walnut stock and forearm with 20 LPI checkering, Pachmayr Decelerator pad, traditional 101 styling with low profile blue engraved receiver, steel grip cap, includes ABS case, 7 1/4-7 3/8 lbs. Mfg. by FN in Belgium. New 2007.

MSR $2,450	$2,085	$1,825	$1,565	$1,425	$1,150	$940	$815

This model was featured as a SHOT Show Special for 2006 and 2008.

Select was dropped from this model's nomenclature beginning 2008.

MODEL 101 FIELD - CURRENT MFG. (SELECT) – 12 ga., 3 in. chambers, 26 or 28 in. lightweight barrels, Invector Plus flush chokes with three choke tubes, 10mm broadway rib, ejectors, adj. SST, brass bead front sight, high gloss Grade II/III walnut stock and forearm with 20 LPI checkering, vented white line spacer Pachmayr Decelerator pad, low profile blue receiver with deep relief engraving, steel grip cap, 6 3/4-7 lbs. Mfg. by FN in Belgium. New 2007.

MSR $1,960	$1,720	$1,450	$1,250	$1,125	$910	$775	$675

Select was dropped from this model's nomenclature beginning 2008.

MODEL 101 DELUXE FIELD (SELECT) – 12 ga. only, 3 in. chambers, 26, 28, or 30 in. barrels, ejectors, oil finished Grade II checkered walnut stock and forearm, Pachmayr Decelerator pad, adj. SST, Invector-Plus chokes and three Signature flush choke tubes, silver nitride receiver with engraving, includes hard case, 7-7 1/2 lbs. Mfg. by FN in Belgium. Mfg. 2007-2010.

	$1,395	$1,150	$950	$850	$750	$650	$575	*$1,679*

Select was dropped from this model's nomenclature beginning 2009.

MODEL 101 LIGHT – 12 ga., 3 in. chambers, 26 or 28 in. barrels, Grade II/III checkered gloss finished walnut stock and forearm, engraved aluminum alloy receiver with quail and pheasants, springer spaniel on bottom, Pachmayr Decelerator pad, three Invector Plus choke tubes, 6-6 1/4 lbs. Mfg. 2009-2010.

	$1,725	$1,475	$1,250	$1,050	$925	$800	$675	*$2,039*

This model was originally featured as a 2008 SHOT Show Special.

501 GRAND EUROPEAN – Trap or Skeet, 12 or 20 (Skeet only) ga., 27, 30, or 32 in. vent. barrels and rib, extra select hand checkered walnut with oil finish, Schnabel forearm, extensive scroll engraving on satin-finished receiver. Mfg. 1981-1986.

	$2,300	$2,100	$2,000	$1,800	$1,600	$1,400	$1,200	*$1,720*

Add 20% for 20 ga. Skeet.

* ***501 Grand European Featherweight*** – 20 ga. only, straight grip stock, 25 1/2 in. VR barrels, 5 3/4 lbs. Disc. 1986.

	$3,150	$2,750	$2,500	$2,175	$1,900	$1,700	$1,500	*$1,720*

GRADING - PPGS™	100%	98%	95%	90%	80%	70%	60%	LAST MSR

PRESENTATION GRADE – 12 ga. only, available in both Trap and Skeet models, blue action extensively engraved with gold inlays, special crotch walnut, 27 (Skeet) or 30 in. vent. barrels, hand checkered, silver wire borders on perimeter of receiver. Imported 1984-87 only.

$3,950 $3,395 $3,075 $2,400 $2,000 $1,800 $1,600 *$3,840*

Subtract 10% for Trap Model.

MODEL 1001 FIELD GRADE – 12 ga. only, 3 in. chambers, boxlock action, 28 in. VR (8mm) barrel with WinPlus chokes, blue metal featuring 40% engraving coverage, Grade I stock and forearm, high luster finish, mfg. in Italy by Marocchi 1993, disc. 1998.

$975 $795 $725 $650 $595 $550 $495 *$1,099*

* ***Model 1001 Field Grade Sporting Clays*** – 12 ga. only, 2 3/4 in. chambers, 28 or 30 in. VR (10mm) vent. barrels with WinPlus chokes, full engraving (includes scroll and flying W with clay bird), silver nitride receiver with remaining parts blue, Grade II-III stock and forearm, satin finish, mfg. in Italy by Marocchi 1993, disc. 1998.

$1,075 $925 $795 $725 $650 $595 $550 *$1,253*

* ***Model 1001 Field Grade Sporting Clays Lite*** – 12 ga. only, 3 in. chambers, blue finish, 28 in. VR barrels with WinPlus chokes, checkered walnut stock and forearm, gold SST, 7 lbs. Mfg. 1995-98.

$1,000 $795 $725 $650 $595 $550 $495 *$1,153*

MODEL G5500 SPORTER – 12 ga. only, marked Sporter, 28 or 30 in. barrels with fixed chokes (bored IC/M, IM/F, or XF/F) or WinChokes.

$1,795 $1,475 $1,275 $1,075 $900 $780 $640

Add 20% for WinChokes.

MODEL G6500 SPORTER – 12 ga. only, marked Sporter, barrels and chokes same as G5500.

$2,295 $1,925 $1,625 $1,400 $1,225 $1,050 $900

Add 20% for WinChokes.

SELECT FIELD (SUPREME) – 12 ga. only, 3 in. chambers, low profile boxlock action with dual tapered locking lugs positioned between the barrels, SST, ejectors, game scene engraved receiver, 26 (new 2001) or 28 in. 6mm VR back-bored barrels with Invector Plus choking (high polish barrels became standard in 2005), redesigned barrels in 2003, checkered walnut stock and forearm, blue action and barrels, barrel selector on safety switch, approx. 7 lbs. Mfg. 2000-2005.

$1,265 $1,025 $900 $800 $700 $600 $500 *$1,498*

During 2004, this model's nomenclature was changed from Supreme Select Field to Select Field.

SELECT WHITE FIELD TRADITIONAL/EXTREME – 12 ga. only, 3 in. chambers, 26 or 28 in. barrels, engraved low profile silver nitride receiver, walnut stock with oval (Extreme) or standard (Traditional) checkering, Invector-Plus choke system, 7-7 1/4 lbs., mfg. by Miroku. Limited mfg. 2006.

$1,295 $1,050 $900 $800 $700 $600 $500 *$1,533*

SELECT ELEGANCE (SUPREME) – 12 ga. only, 3 in. chambers, grey game scene engraved low profile receiver with dual locking pin design, choice of regular checkered (Traditional Elegance) or oval checkered (Extreme Elegance, new 2004) Grade III walnut stock and Schnabel forearm, 26 or 28 in. non-ported barrels with Invector Plus choke system (high polish barrels became standard in 2005), includes red hardshell case, approx. 7 lbs., mfg. by FN Belgium. Mfg. 2003-2006.

$1,950 $1,625 $1,275 $995 $875 $775 $675 *$2,320*

SELECT MIDNIGHT – 12 ga. only, 3 in. chambers, 26 or 28 in. barrels, high gloss blued receiver with gold bird accents on both sides and bottom, satin finished Grade II/II walnut stock with oval checkering pattern, deluxe recoil pad, approx. 7 lbs., limited mfg. by Miroku 2006 only.

$1,995 $1,650 $1,300 $1,025 $900 $800 $700 *$2,380*

SUPREME SELECT SPORTING – 12 ga. only, 2 3/4 in. chambers, satin finished bi-tone receiver w/o engraving, 28 or 30 in. 10mm VR back-bored barrels with porting, redesigned barrels in 2003, SST with adj. trigger shoe system, sharply checkered walnut stock and Schnabel style forearm, approx. 7 1/2 lbs. Mfg. 2000-2003.

$1,200 $995 $900 $800 $700 $600 $500 *$1,406*

SELECT ENERGY SPORTING – 12 ga. only, 2 3/4 in. chambers, 28, 30, or 32 in. ported and vented side rib high polish barrels with Invector Plus chokes (high polish barrels became standard in 2005), marked "Select Energy Sporting" on contrasting chrome finished receiver, 10mm VR, select American walnut stock with oval checkering and palm swell, with or w/o adj. cheekpiece, adj. trigger shoe, TruGlo front sight, approx. 7 1/2 lbs., mfg. by Miroku 2004-2006.

$1,635 $1,425 $1,125 $965 $855 $750 $650 *$1,950*

Add $165 for adj. comb stock.

GRADING - PPGS™	100%	98%	95%	90%	80%	70%	60%	LAST MSR

SELECT ENERGY TRAP – 12 ga. only, 2 3/4 in. chambers, 30 or 32 in. VR barrels with Invector Plus chokes (high polish barrels became standard in 2005), similar features as the Select Energy Sporting, features oval checkering on stock and forearm, palm swell, TruGlo front sight, Monte Carlo or adj. comb stock with solid recoil pad, approx. 7 1/2 lbs., made by FN in Belgium. Mfg. 2004-2007.

	$1,635	$1,425	$1,125	$965	$855	$750	$650	*$1,948*

Add $164 for adj. comb stock.

SELECT PLATINUM FIELD – 12 ga. only, 3 in. chambers, 26 or 28 in. barrels, ejectors, oil finished Grade II/III checkered walnut stock and Schnabel forearm, Invector-Plus chokes and three Signature extended choke tubes, adj. SST, silver nitride receiver with deep relief engraving, includes hard case, 7-7 1/2 lbs. Mfg. by FN in Belgium. Mfg. 2007-2008.

	$1,975	$1,650	$1,300	$1,025	$900	$800	$700	*$2,359*

This model was featured as a SHOT Show Special during 2006.

SELECT PLATINUM SPORTING – 12 ga. only, 2 3/4 in. chambers, 28, 30, or 32 in. ported barrels, ejectors, oil finished Grade II/III checkered walnut stock and forearm, Invector-Plus chokes and five Signature extended choke tubes, silver nitride receiver with light game scene engraving, adj. SST system, 10mm broadway rib, mid-bead and TruGlo competition front sight, includes hard case, approx. 7 -7 1/2 lbs. Mfg. by FN in Belgium. Mfg. 2007-2008.

	$2,200	$1,925	$1,650	$1,400	$1,200	$1,000	$875	*$2,625*

SHOTGUNS: RECENT PRODUCTION SxS

Values for recently manufactured side-by-sides assume NIB condition - subtract 10%-15% if without box, warranty card, and original shipping container (with packing materials).

MODEL 21: RECENT MFG. – between 1960-1987, Model 21 production was limited to high grades, built to special order only, and 1987 was the last year Winchester carried Model 21 pricing in its catalog. On custom shop guns mfg. 1960-1969, there is no Winchester name on the barrels, but the Winchester proof mark is on the water table, along with a designation "Model 21" or "New Haven, CT" plus the ser. no. On Model 21s produced from 1969-1988, the water tables are stamped as already noted, and the designation "Model 21 - Winchester" is stamped on the top of the left barrel adjacent to the rib, next to the receiver. Connecticut Shotgun Manufacturing Company is currently manufacturing Model 21 shotguns (marked "Model 21" only), including Grades 21-1, 21-5, 21-6, Grand American, and the Royal Exhibition. These guns are not marked "Winchester", and will not letter from the Cody Firearms Museum. Please refer to the Connecticut Shotgun Manufacturing Company listing for more information regarding these newer custom Model 21s. Also refer to previously mfg. Winchester Model 21 listings under SHOTGUNS: 1879-1963.

Add 25% for 16 or 20 ga.
Add $1,500 for vent. rib.

* ***Model 21 Custom Built*** – standard model with no engraving.

	$8,000	$7,000	$5,000	N/A	N/A	N/A	N/A	*$8,100*

* ***Model 21 Custom Grade*** – includes No. 6 engraved receiver and VR.

	$12,500	$10,500	$9,000	N/A	N/A	N/A	N/A	*$11,080*

* ***Model 21 Pigeon Grade*** – single set of barrels, No. 6 engraved, w/o gold inlays, 37 mfg. total in 12, 16, and 20 ga.

	$21,000	$19,000	$16,000	N/A	N/A	N/A	N/A	

* ***Model 21 Grand American Grade*** – includes 2 sets of barrels with forearms, No. 6 engraved with gold inlays, cased. Must letter from CFM.

	$28,500	$23,000	$19,500	N/A	N/A	N/A	N/A	*$22,745*

* ***Model 21 Grand American Small Gauge*** – 28 ga. or .410 bore. Must letter from CFM.

	$39,000	$31,000	$24,500	N/A	N/A	N/A	N/A	*$34,460*

Add 25% for 28 ga./.410 bore combo.

* ***Model 21 Grand American ("1 of 8" set)*** – includes 20, 28 ga., and .410 bore VR barrels. Only 4 of 8 sets actually mfg. Must letter from CFM.

	N/A	$65,000	$45,000	N/A	N/A	N/A	N/A	*$55,000*

* ***Model 21 Grand Royal (2 barrel set)*** – the highest grade of Model 21s ever produced, originally made in a .410 bore 2 barrel set for John Olin, only 4 others were ever manufactured, and all were 2 barrel sets.

Extreme rarity precludes accurate pricing on this model.

GRADING - PPGS™	100%	98%	95%	90%	80%	70%	60%	LAST MSR

MODEL 22 – 12 ga. only, subcontracted by Winchester and manufactured in Spain by Laurona circa 1975 for international sales including Europe, field configuration only with 28 in. barrels, DT, oil finished checkered walnut stock and semi-beavertail forearm, matted rib, black-chrome finish on metal parts, hand engraved receiver, limited mfg.

	$1,200	$995	$825	$700	$600	$525	$475	

MODEL 23 XTR – 12 or 20 ga., 3 in. chambers, 25 1/2, 26, 28, or 30 in. blue barrels, various chokes, single trigger, VR, auto ejectors, scroll engraved, silver grey satin finish, checkered select walnut stock and forearm, first commercial gun to employ interchangeable chokes. Mfg. 1978-disc.

* ***Model 23 Grade 1***

	$1,900	$1,750	$1,600	$1,350	$1,100	$950	$800	

Add 20% for 20 ga.
Subtract 10% for fixed chokes.

* ***Model 23 XTR Pigeon Grade*** – standard weight model, 6 1/2-7 lbs., coin finished receiver with scroll engraving. WinChoke option became standard in 1986. Disc. 1986.

	$2,300	$2,100	$1,850	$1,600	$1,300	$1,100	$900	*$1,460*

Add 20% for 20 ga.
Subtract 10% if w/o WinChokes.

* ***Model 23 XTR Pigeon Grade Lightweight*** – 25 1/2 in. barrels only bored IM/IC (12 ga.) or IC/M (20 ga.) or with WinChokes, 6 1/4-6 3/4 lbs., coin finished receiver with bird scene engraving, English stock. Disc. 1986.

	$2,495	$2,150	$1,925	$1,750	$1,250	$1,000	$800	*$1,420*

Add 15% for 20 ga.
Subtract 10% if w/o WinChokes.

MODEL 23 PIGEON GRADE DUCKS UNLIMITED – 12 or 20 ga., 500 mfg. in 1981 (12 ga.), and 500 mfg. in 1983 (20 ga.), 1981 12 ga. serialization is 81-DU-XXX, 1983 20 ga. serialization is 83-DU-XXX, cased.

	$2,500	$2,300	$2,200	$2,000	$1,800	$1,500	$1,200	

Add 20 % for 20 ga. (1983 mfg.).

MODEL 23 GOLDEN QUAIL SERIES – 12 ga. (1986), 20 ga. (1984), 28 ga. (1985), or .410 bore (1987), 25 1/2 in. solid rib barrels bored IC/M, monoblocs are marked "IC/M" but the barrels are marked "Q1/Q2", coin finished receiver with one gold inlay on floorplate, beavertail forearm, straight grip English stock with recoil pad. Only 500 mfg. each year per gauge. Disc. 1987.

12 ga.	$2,995	$2,775	$2,500	$2,150	$1,850	$1,475	$1,325	
20 ga.	$3,400	$3,100	$2,700	$2,300	$1,975	$1,750	$1,475	
28 ga. (20 ga. frame)	$4,750	$4,350	$3,950	$3,650	$3,300	$2,900	$2,450	
.410 bore (small frame)	$4,750	$4,350	$3,950	$3,650	$3,300	$2,900	$2,450	

Last MSR was $1,950.

MODEL 23 LIGHT DUCK – 20 ga., blue receiver and 28 in. barrels F/F, select walnut, 8 1/2 lbs. Limited edition, 500 mfg., introduced 1985.

	$2,895	$2,400	$2,075	$1,775	$1,350	$1,100	$975	*$1,660*

MODEL 23 HEAVY DUCK – 12 ga., 30 in. barrels, F/F, blue receiver, select walnut, 8 1/2 lbs. Limited edition, 500 mfg. 1984 only.

	$2,995	$2,895	$2,695	$2,495	$2,195	$1,895	$1,595	

MODEL 23 CUSTOM 2 BARREL SET – interchangeable 20 and 28 ga. 26 in. barrels, blue engraved receiver with gold inlays, "B" checkering on stock and forearm, leather cased with accessories, only 500 sets mfg. 1986. Disc. 1987.

	$5,975	$5,325	$4,975	$4,075	$3,525	$3,375	$3,075	*$4,625*

MODEL 23 GRANDE CANADIAN – 12 or 20 ga., 25 1/2 in. barrels with fixed chokes, coin finished receiver with oak leaf engraving and one gold leaf inlay on receiver bottom, English AAA select walnut stock with beavertail forearm, 51 mfg. in 12 ga., 450 mfg. in 20 ga., approx. 50 two-gun sets were also offered with cases (approx. ser. nos. 1-51).

Single Gun	$2,850	$2,400	$1,950	$1,700	$1,500	$1,250	$1,125	
Cased set	$6,750	$6,050	$5,150	$4,450	$4,000	$3,450	$3,000	

Add 20% for 20 ga.

MODEL 23 CUSTOM – 12 ga. only, 27 in. WinChoke barrels, high luster bluing, no engraving, SST, ejectors, solid red rubber recoil pad, 7 lbs. Imported 1987 only.

	$2,800	$2,600	$2,400	$2,200	$1,900	$1,600	$1,200	*$1,975*

GRADING - PPGS™	100%	98%	95%	90%	80%	70%	60%	LAST MSR

MODEL 23 CLASSIC SERIES – 12, 20, 28 ga., or .410 bore, 26 in. VR barrels, single trigger, deluxe hand-checkered walnut stock and beavertail forearm, solid recoil pad, brass nameplate, gold inlay on bottom of receiver, ebony inlay in forearm, 5 3/4 - 7 lbs. Imported 1986-1987 only.

12 ga.	$2,650	$2,375	$2,100	$1,825	$1,400	$1,250	$1,150	
20 ga.	$2,950	$2,550	$2,225	$1,900	$1,675	$1,395	$1,295	
28 ga. (small frame)	$5,400	$5,000	$4,000	$3,500	$3,000	$2,500	$2,250	
.410 bore (small frame)	$4,495	$4,100	$3,600	$3,350	$3,100	$2,750	$2,400	

Last MSR was $1,975.

100% values assume NIB for this model.

The 28 ga. on this model features a smaller frame, and was the only 28 ga. small frame produced in the Model 23 Series.

FACTORY WINCHESTER COMMEMORATIVES: U.S. PRODUCTION

During the course of a year, we receive many phone calls, emails, and letters on Winchester non-factory special editions and limited editions which do not appear in this section. It should be noted that a factory commemorative issue is a gun that has been manufactured, marketed, factory cataloged, and sold through the auspices of the specific trademark. There have literally been hundreds of non-factory special and limited editions which, although mostly made by Winchester (some were subcontracted), were not marketed or retailed by Winchester. These guns are NOT considered Winchester factory commemoratives in this publication, and for the most part, do not have the desirability factor that the factory commemoratives have. Non-factory cataloged special/limited editions are not listed in this text, because there are literally hundreds of them and collector interest is not as great as for the factory commemoratives. Remember, the least your special/limited edition can be worth is a little more than the standard edition value. Do not concentrate on the rarity or you will be disappointed.

Typically, special and limited editions are made for distributors and typically manufactured by sub-contract for an organization, state, special event, personality, etc. and are typically sold and marketed through a distributor to dealers, or a company/individual to those people who want to purchase them. These special editions may or may not have a retail price and many times, the demand may be regional with values decreasing rapidly in other areas of the country. Also, most special/limited editions do not have alphabetical prefixes/suffixes within their serial ranges. Desirability is the key to determining values on these editions.

As a reminder on commemoratives, especially for the beginning collector, here are a few facts applicable to all manufacturers of commemoratives. Commemoratives were guns specifically designed as a reproduction of an historically famous gun model, or as a tie-in with historically famous persons or events. They are generally of very excellent quality and often embellished with select woods and finishes such as silver, nickel, or gold plating. Obviously, they are manufactured to be instant collectibles and to be pleasing to the eye. As with firearms in general, not all commemorative models have achieved collector status, although most enjoy an active market. Consecutive-numbered pairs as well as collections based on the same serial number will bring a premium. Remember that handguns usually are in some type of wood presentation case, and that rifles may be cased or in packaging with graphics styled to the particular theme of the collectible.

The original factory packaging and papers should always accompany the firearm as they are necessary to realize full value. All commemorative firearms should be absolutely new, unfired, and as issued since any obvious use or wear removes it from collector status and lowers its value significantly. Many owners have allowed their commemoratives to sit in their boxes and plastic bags (could be serious if there is moisture where storage occurs) for years without inspecting them for corrosion or oxidation damage. Periodic inspection should be implemented to ensure no damage occurs - this is important, since even light "freckling" created from touching the metal surfaces can reduce values significantly. A fired gun with obvious wear or without its original packaging can lose as much as 50% of its normal value - many used commemoratives get sold as "fancy shooters" with little, if any, premiums being asked.

The values listed reflect actual prices paid recently through dealer offerings, at gun shows, and both online and brick and mortar auctions. In some regions it may be possible to purchase a Winchester 94 commemorative made in substantial quantity for a slight premium over a standard production Winchester 94. Because of this, prices could fluctuate over 25% depending on the geographic location of purchase or sale.

A final note on factory commemoratives: One of the characteristics of commemoratives/special editions is that over the years of ownership, most of the original amount manufactured stays in the same NIB condition. Thus, if supply always is constant and in one condition, demand has to increase before price appreciation can occur. Many commemorative dealers have told me that recent changes in overseas currency rates have made domestic guns less expensive to own - for Europeans especially. For this reason, more commemoratives are being

GRADING - PPGS™	100%	Issue Price	Qty. Made

sold overseas resulting in less supply for the domestic market. After almost 50 years of factory commemoratives and non-factory commemorative/special editions, the performance of these older guns can now be accurately analyzed and the appreciation (or depreciation) can be compared against other purchases of equal vintage. A definitive series of articles has been written on Commemoratives and how they have performed as investments against other traditional economic items - please visit BlueBookOfGunValues.com and look under Articles at the bottom of the page - click S.P. Fjestad's Lethal Blogging - Archived Articles - then click on Commemorative Firearms - Beauty or the Beast Parts 1-4. You be the judge.

U.S. Repeating Arms announced in 1990 that they would once again resume the production of factory commemorative firearms.

There are no factory records available on Winchester Commemoratives from the Buffalo Bill Historical Center, and as a result, no factory letters are available.

1964 WYOMING DIAMOND JUBILEE 94 CARBINE – published ser. no. range WJ1- WJ1500.

	$1,395	$100	1,501

1966 CENTENNIAL '66 RIFLE – no ser. no. prefix or suffix.

	$695	$125	N/A

1966 CENTENNIAL '66 CARBINE – total mfg. of both the rifle and carbine was 102,309, no ser. no. prefix or suffix.

	$695	$125	102,309

Add $50-$75 over individual prices for consecutively serial numbered rifle and carbine set.

1966 NEBRASKA CENTENNIAL 94 RIFLE – ser. no. range NC1- NC2500.

	$1,295	$100	2,500

1967 CANADIAN '67 CENTENNIAL RIFLE – no ser. no. prefix or suffix.

	$650	$125	N/A

1967 CANADIAN '67 CENTENNIAL CARBINE – total mfg. of both the rifle and carbine was 90,301, no ser. no. prefix or suffix.

	$650	$125	90,301

Add $50-$75 over individual prices for consecutively serial numbered rifle and carbine set.

1967 ALASKAN PURCHASE CENTENNIAL CARBINE – ser. no. range AP1- AP1500, w/rack.

	$1,595	$125	1,501

1968 ILLINOIS SESQUICENTENNIAL 94 CARBINE – ser. no. range IS1- IS37468.

	$695	$110	37,468

1968 BUFFALO BILL RIFLE "1 OF 300" PRES. – ser. no. range WCF1- WCF300.

	$3,995	$1,000	300

1968 BUFFALO BILL RIFLE – ser. no. range WC1- WC112923.

	$695	$130	N/A

1968 BUFFALO BILL CARBINE – total mfg. of both the rifle and carbine was 112,923, ser. no. range WC1- WC112923.

	$695	$130	112,923

Add $50-$75 over individual prices for consecutively serial numbered rifle and carbine set.

1969 GOLDEN SPIKE CARBINE – ser. no. range GS1- GS69996.

	$750	$120	69,996

1969 THEO. ROOSEVELT RIFLE – ser. no. range TR1- TR52386.

	$695	$135	N/A

1969 THEO. ROOSEVELT CARBINE – total mfg. of both the rifle and carbine was 52,386, ser. no. range TR1- TR52386.

	$695	$135	52,386

1970 COWBOY COMMEMORATIVE CARBINE – ser. no. range CB1- CB27549.

	$750	$125	27,549

1970 COWBOY CARBINE "1 OF 300" – ser. no. range NCHF1- NCHF300.

	$3,995	$1,000	300

1970 LONE STAR RIFLE – ser. no. range LS1- LS38385.

	$695	$140	N/A

GRADING - PPGS™	100%	Issue Price	Qty. Made

1970 LONE STAR CARBINE – total mfg. of both the rifle and carbine was 38,385, ser. no. range LS1-LS38385.

	$695	$140	38,385

1971 NRA CENTENNIAL MUSKET – ser. no. range NRA1- NRA47380, not all shipped.

	$695	$150	23,400

1971 NRA CENTENNIAL RIFLE – ser. no. range NRA1- NRA47380, not all shipped.

	$695	$150	21,000

1974 TEXAS RANGER CARBINE – ser. no. range RA151- RA5000.

	$795	$135	4,850

1974 TEXAS RANGER PRESENTATION – ser. no. range RA1- RA150.

	$3,995	$1,000	150

1976 U.S. BICENTENNIAL CARBINE – includes factory wall rack, ser. no. range USA1- USA19999.

	$750	$325	19,999

1977 WELLS FARGO – ser. no. range WFC1- WFC19999.

	$850	$350	19,999

1977 "LIMITED EDITION I" – ser. no. range 77L1- 77L1500.

	$1,595	$1,500	1,500

1977 LEGENDARY LAWMEN – ser. no. range LL1- LL19999.

	$895	$375	19,999

1978 ANTLERED GAME CARBINE – ser. no. range AG1- AG19999.

	$895	$375	19,999

1979 LEGENDARY FRONTIERSMAN RIFLE – ser. no. range LF1- LF19999.

	$995	$425	19,999

1979 "LIMITED EDITION II" – ser. no. range 78L1- 78L1500.

	$1,595	$1,750	1,500

1979 MATCHED SET ONE OF ONE THOUSAND – ser. no. range MC1- MC1000 and MR1- MR1000.

	$3,995	$3,000	1,000

1980 "OLIVER WINCHESTER" – ser. no. range OFW1- OFW1999.

	$995	$375	19,999

1981 U.S. BORDER PATROL - MEMBERS MODEL – ser. no. range USBP1- USBP800.

	$995	$695	800

1981 JOHN WAYNE – ser. no. range JW1- JW49000.

	$1,495	$600	49,000

Optional accessories were also available for this model: the gun rack with leather insert is currently selling for approx. $395 and the leather scabbard is trading for $395.

1981 "DUKE" – ser. no. range DUKE1- DUKE1000.

	$3,500	$2,250	1,000

1981 JOHN WAYNE "1 OF 300" SET – ser. no. range JWM1- JWM300 and JWDM1-JWDM300.

	$6,500	$10,000	300

1982 ANNIE OAKLEY – ser. no. range AOK1- AOK6000.

	$1,500	$699	6,000

1982 OKLAHOMA DIAMOND JUBILEE – ser. no. range ODJ-1 - ODJ-1001.

	$1,750	$2,250	1,001

1982 AMERICAN BALD EAGLE - SILVER – ser. no. range ABE1984- ABE4784.

	$895	$895	2,800

1982 AMERICAN BALD EAGLE - GOLD – ser. no. range ABE1782- ABE1983.

	$5,000	$2,950	200

1983 CHIEF CRAZY HORSE – ser. no. range CCH1- CCH19999.

	$995	$600	19,999

GRADING - PPGS™	100%	Issue Price	Qty. Made

1984 WINCHESTER-COLT COMMEMORATIVE SET – 1 each of the Model 1894 Carbine and Colt Peacemaker, serial numbered 1 WC-4440 WC., .44-40 WCF cal., elaborate gold etching, cased.

	$3,500	$3,995	2,300

Approx. 2,300 sets were actually put together in this combination. Some sets were split up with individual prices being discounted. Colt SAAs have been selling individually in the $1,350-$1,495 range.

1985 BOY SCOUTS 75TH ANNIVERSARY – Model 9422 action, .22 cal., rifle configuration, 6 1/4 lbs.

* ***1985 Boy Scouts 75th Anniversary*** – 15,000 mfg., serial numbered BSA 1 - BSA 15,000, roll engraved, antique pewter receiver, hooded front sight.

	$1,275	$495	15,000

* ***1985 Eagle Scouts 75th Anniversary*** – 1,000 mfg., serial numbered EAGLE 1 - EAGLE 1,000, receiver has triple level gold etching, select American walnut stock and forearm, gold-plated lever, hammer, and forearm cap.

	$5,500	$1,710	1,000

1985 MODEL 94 TEXAS SESQUICENTENNIAL – .38-55 WCF cal., available in carbine or rifle.

* ***1985 Model 94 Texas Sesquicentennial Rifle*** – 24 in. round barrel, elaborate gold etching, includes Bowie knife, oak cased, 586 mfg, ser. no. range TSR1- TSR586.

	$2,995	$2,995	586

* ***1985 Model 94 Texas Sesquicentennial Carbine*** – 18 1/2 in. round barrel, gold finished receiver and barrel bands, roll engraved receiver, 2,600 mfg., serial numbered TEX1 -TEX2600.

	$995	$695	2,600

* ***1985 Model 94 Texas Sesquicentennial Rifle/Carbine Set*** – includes one each of the Model 94 rifle and carbine, Bowie knife, 150 mfg., ser. no. range Carbine: TEXM1- TEXM150 and Rifle: TSRM1-TSRM150.

	$6,500	$7,995	150

1986 120TH ANNIVERSARY MODEL 94 CARBINE – .44-40 WCF cal. only, 20 in. barrel, large loop type finger lever, crescent buttplate, deluxe checkered walnut stock and forearm, extensive gold etching on barrel and framesides, 1,000 mfg. ser. no. WRA001-WRA1000.

	$1,250	$995	1,000

1986 STATUE OF LIBERTY MODEL 94 – Model 94 rifle in .30-30 Win. cal. with octagon barrel, extensive C. Giovanelli scroll engraving with multiple 22Kt. gold inlays, deluxe walnut with fine checkering, also includes 29 in. hand-carved wooden statue of the Statue of Liberty, serial numbers can range from SL001-SL100, while 100 were scheduled to be produced, only 62 were mfg. on a special order basis only, and the customer could pick out the serial number. This model is a USRAC factory commemorative.

	$12,500	$6,500	62

Must have matching carved statue.

1987 U.S. CONSTITUTION 200th ANNIVERSARY – .44-40 WCF cal., 20 in. octagon barrel, deluxe checkered walnut, crescent buttplate, full coverage master engraving, No more than 50 guns were to be mfg., the serial number is the name of the state and is done in gold on the top of the tang, cased in a leather luggage style case.

	$22,500	$12,000	19

This model was distributed exclusively by Cherry's, located in Greensboro, NC.

1990 WYOMING CENTENNIAL – .30-30 Win. cal., 20 in. round barrel, deluxe checkered walnut, engraved by Bottega C. Giovanelli, coin finished receiver. Originally advertised as an issue of 999 guns, the Winchester strike caused the edition to be reduced in size to only 500 pieces. Serial numbered WYC001-WYC500.

	$1,795	$895	500

This model was distributed exclusively by Cherry's, located in Greensboro, NC.

1991 125th ANNIVERSARY – .44-40 WCF cal., 24 in. octagon barrel, deluxe checkered walnut, crescent style buttplate, engraving by Bottega C. Giovnaelli utilizing some of Winchester's most historic engraving patterns, includes walnut display case. Serial numbered from WRAC001-WRAC125. Serial numbers were made to order.

	$7,500	$4,995	61

This model was distributed exclusively by Cherry's, located in Greensboro, NC.

GRADING - PPGS™	100%	Issue Price	Qty. Made

1992 KENTUCKY BICENTENNIAL - .30-30 Win. cal., lever action, 20 in. round barrel, receiver, lever and hammer case hardened and lacquered by Doug Turnbull, semi-fancy checkered American walnut stock, optional display case. Serial numbered KY001-KY500.

	$1,795	$995	500

This model was distributed exclusively by Cherry's, located in Greensboro, NC.

1992 ARAPAHO - .30-30 Win. cal., 20 in. round barrel, checkered walnut stock, lever, receiver and barrel bands gold plated, etched receiver scenes by Baron technology, optional display case. Originally advertised as uncheckered, Winchester made the mistake of checkering all the wood when it was on the production line. The advertisement showed the gun as uncheckered but all guns were delivered as checkered. Serial number ARAP001-ARAP500.

	$1,795	$895	500

This model was distributed exclusively by Cherry's, located in Greensboro, NC.

1993 NEZ PERCE MODEL 94 CARBINE - .30-30 Win. cal., 20 in. round barrel, receiver, lever, and barrel bands nickel plated, etched receiver scenes done by Baron Technology, includes suede leather soft case with trim and a branded head and shoulders image of Chief Joseph. Serial numbered NEZ001-NEZ600.

	$1,795	$950	600

This model was distributed exclusively by Cherry's, located in Greensboro, NC.

1995 FLORIDA SESQUICENTENNIAL 94 CARBINE - .30-30 Win. cal., 20 in. round barrel, brushed gold plate on the receiver, lever and barrel bands, scenes are roll dyed with hand touch up by Bottega C. Giovanelli. All 500 receivers were mfg., but not all of these receivers were used to make the Florida guns. Other special issue receivers were used that bear this serial number as the reception to this commemorative was poor, optional presentation case. Serial numbered FL001-FL500.

	$1,795	$1,195	350

This model was distributed exclusively by Cherry's, located in Greensboro, NC.

1996 WILD BILL HICKOK RIFLE - .45 LC cal., 20 in. round barrel, "John Wayne" style lever loop, receiver, lever, and bands are brushed nickel, left side of the receiver features a full coverage engraving pattern, right side of the receiver has his famous engraved 1851 Navy Colts, surrounded by scrollwork, a banner with his birth and date of death along with his famous "Dead Man's Hand" (Aces & Eights), deluxe uncheckered walnut. Serial numbered WBH001-WBH350.

	$1,795	$1,195	350

This model was distributed exclusively by Cherry's, located in Greensboro, NC.

WINCHESTER COMMEMORATIVES: NON-DOMESTIC - 1970 TO DATE

Between 1970-1982, Winchester Model 94 Commemoratives were made by Cooey, located in Cobourg, Ontario, Canada.

1970 NORTHWEST TERRITORIES (CANADIAN) - ser. no. range NWT501- NWT3106.			
	$1,395	$150	2,500
1970 NORTHWEST TERRITORIES DELUXE (CANADIAN) - ser. no. range NWT1- NWT500.			
	$1,750	$250	500
1973 YELLOW BOY (SOLD IN EUROPE ONLY) - ser. no. range YB1- YB4903.			
	$1,795	$150	4,903
1973 M.P.X. (MADE ESPECIALLY FOR A MOVIE) - ser. no. range MPX1- MPX32.			
	$9,000	$78	32
1973 R.C.M.P. (CANADIAN) - ser. no. range RCMP1- RCMP10442, not all shipped.			
	$995	$190	9,500
1973 R.C.M.P. MEMBERS ISSUE (CANADIAN) - ser. no. range MP1- MP5100, not all shipped.			
	$995	$190	4,850
1973 R.C.M.P. PRESENTATION - (CANADIAN) - ser. no. range RCMP1P- RCMP10P.			
	$11,500	N/A	10
1974 APACHE (CANADIAN) - ser. no. range AC1- AC10200, not all shipped.			
	$995	$150	8,600
1975 KLONDIKE GOLD RUSH (CANADIAN) - ser. no. range KGR1- KGR10200.			
	$995	$230	10,200

GRADING - PPGS™	100%	Issue Price	Qty. Made

1975 K.G.R. (DAWSON CITY ISSUE) - (CANADIAN) – ser. no. range D1KGR- D25KGR.

	$8,500	N/A	25

1975 COMANCHE (CANADIAN) – ser. no. range CC1- CC11511.

	$995	$230	11,511

1976 SIOUX (CANADIAN) – ser. no. range SU1- SU12000, not all shipped.

	$995	$280	10,000

1976 LITTLE BIG HORN (CANADIAN) – ser. no. range LBH1- LBH11000.

	$995	$230	11,000

1977 CHEYENNE .44-40 WCF CAL. (CANADIAN) – .44-40 WCF Cal., ser. no. range CH1- CH13000, not all shipped.

	$995	$300	11,225

1977 CHEYENNE .22 LR CAL. (CANADIAN) – .22 LR Cal., ser. no. range CHF1- CHF8221, not all shipped.

	$1,500	$320	5,000

1978 CHEROKEE .30-30 WIN. CAL. (CANADIAN) – .30-30 Win. Cal., ser. no. range CK1- CK9000.

	$995	$385	9,000

1978 CHEROKEE .22 LR CAL. (CANADIAN) – .22 LR cal., ser. no. range CHF1- CHF4286, not all shipped.

	$1,500	$385	3,950

1978 ONE OF ONE THOUSAND (SOLD IN EUROPE ONLY) – no ser. no. prefix or suffix.

	$9,995	$5,000	250

This model was not advertised in the U.S.

1980 ALBERTA DIAMOND JUBILEE (CANADIAN) – ser. no. range ADJ301- ADJ3000.

	$995	$650	2,700

1980 A.D.J. DELUXE PRESENTATION (CANADIAN) – ser. no. range ADJ1- ADJ300.

	$1,795	$1,900	300

1980 BAT MASTERSON CARBINE – ser. no. range BM1-BM8000.

	$995	$650	8,000

1980 SASKATCHEWAN DIAMOND JUBILEE (CANADIAN) – ser. no. range SDJ301- SDJ3000.

	$995	$695	2,700

1980 S.D.J. DELUXE PRESENTATION (CANADIAN) – ser. no. range SDJ1- SDJ300.

	$1,795	$1,995	300

1981 U.S. BORDER PATROL – ser. no. range BP1- BP1000.

	$995	$1,195	1,000

1981 CALGARY STAMPEDE (CANADIAN) – ser. no. range CS1- CS1000.

	$1,795	$2,200	1,000

1981 CANADIAN PACIFIC CENTENNIAL (CANADIAN) – ser. no. range CPC301- CPC3000.

	$895	$800	2,700

1981 CANADIAN PACIFIC CENTENNIAL PRESENTATION (CANADIAN) – ser. no. range CPC1- CPC300.

	$1,795	$2,200	300

1981 CANADIAN PACIFIC (EMPL.) - (CANADIAN) – ser. no. range CP1- CP2000.

	$895	$800	2,000

1981 JOHN WAYNE (CANADIAN) – ser. no. range CJW1- CJW1000.

	$1,595	$995	1,000

1982 GREAT WESTERN ARTIST I – no ser. no. prefix or suffix.

	$1,995	$2,200	999

1982 GREAT WESTERN ARTIST II – no ser. no. prefix or suffix.

	$1,995	$2,200	999

1986 SECOND SERIES EUROPEAN 1 OF 1,000 – mfg. for European sales only 1986, ser. no. range N/A.

	$9,995	$6,000	150

1992 ONTARIO CONSERVATION – this model was marketed in Canada only, ser. no. range 001CO-400CO.

	$1,750	$1,195	400

GRADING - PPGS™	100%	98%	95%	90%	80%	70%	60%	LAST MSR

SHOT SHOW SPECIALS

Since 2006 Winchester has introduced SHOT (Shooting, Hunting, Outdoor Trade) Show Specials annually for its dealers who attend the SHOT Show. These are typically variations of existing models, but with different features, finishes, calibers/gauges, etc. These guns can only be ordered during the SHOT Show, and the quantity depends on the amount of dealer orders received during the show. Unfortunately, the quantity of each SHOT Show Special variation is not available. If a SHOT Show Special is well received by the dealers, it may go into production as a standard model. If this happens, these variations can be found in the regular categories. These SHOT Show Specials are not Limited or Special Editions. Models listed in this section have only the MSRs at the time of their releases, and secondary values must be based off the variation from which they are derived. SHOT Show Specials manufactured during 2008-present will appear alphabetically according to category. For complete model descriptions and information, please go to BlueBookOfGunValues.com/overflow. Unfortunately, Winchester does not have records on the quantities produced on these SHOT Show Special models.

WINDHAM WEAPONRY

Current manufacturer of AR-15 style pistols, rifles, receivers, parts, barrels, and related accessories established in 2011, located in Windham, ME. Windham Weaponry is located in the former Bushmaster Manufacturing plant in Windham, ME.

Please refer to BlueBookOfGunValues.com to order the *Blue Book of AR-15s & Variations*, available as a book or online subscription.

WINSLOW ARMS COMPANY

Previous manufacturer located in Camden, SC.

RIFLES: BOLT ACTION

WINSLOW SPORTING RIFLE – offered with various actions, FN Supreme, Mark X Mauser, Rem. 700 and 788, Sako, and Win. 70, offered in all popular calibers from .17 Rem. to .458 Mag., standard calibers have 24 in. barrels and 3 shot magazines, magnum calibers have 26 in. barrels and 2 shot magazines, two style stocks, "Bushmaster Conventional", slender pistol grip and beavertail forearm, "Plainsmaster", full curl, hooked pistol grip and flat wide forearm, both are Monte Carlo with cheekpieces, recoil pads and swivels, walnut, maple, and myrtle are used with rosewood forend tip and pistol grip cap, rifle comes in 8 basic grades, custom embellishments can increase values greatly, discretion must be used, values are for basic models.

Grade	100%	98%	95%	90%	80%	70%	60%	LAST MSR
* ***Commander Grade***	$1,750	$1,500	$1,275	$1,025	$850	$725	$600	
* ***Regal Grade***	$1,875	$1,625	$1,300	$1,050	$875	$750	$625	
* ***Regent Grade***	$1,995	$1,675	$1,350	$1,100	$925	$800	$675	
* ***Regimental Grade***	$2,750	$2,350	$2,050	$1,750	$1,500	$1,250	$1,000	
* ***Crown Grade***	$3,000	$2,500	$2,175	$1,850	$1,575	$1,325	$1,100	
* ***Royal Grade***	$3,450	$2,950	$2,500	$2,150	$1,750	$1,500	$1,250	
* ***Imperial Grade***	$3,850	$3,500	$3,050	$2,700	$2,375	$2,000	$1,750	
* ***Emperor Grade***	$6,200	$5,650	$5,000	$4,400	$3,700	$3,000	$2,350	

WISCHO JAGD-UND SPORTWAFFEN GmbH & CO. KG

Previous division of Frankonia Handels GmbH & Co.KG, a European firearms and airgun importer previously located in Rottendorf, Germany and Erlangen, Germany.

Wischo had a complete line of shotguns, rifles, pistols, and revolvers.

GRADING - PPGS™	100%	98%	95%	90%	80%	70%	60%	LAST MSR

WISEMAN, BILL AND CO.

Current custom rifle and action manufacturer established in 1980, located in College Station, TX.

Bill Wiseman also manufactures top quality actions and test barrels used throughout the firearms industry. Additionally, Wiseman/McMillan manufactures rifle barrels and custom stocks. He also performs many gunsmithing services to customer supplied rifles. Please contact the company directly for more information on these products.

PISTOLS

SILHOUETTE PISTOL – various cals., Sako action, 14 in. Wiseman/McMillan fluted stainless barrel, 5 or 7 shot magazine, laminate or fiberglass (new 1999) pistol grip stock, no sights, 4 1/2-5 1/2 lbs. Limited mfg. 1989-2002.

$1,295	$1,000	$900	$800	$750	$700	$650	*$1,295*

Subtract $200 for fiberglass stock.

RIFLES: BOLT ACTION

Add 11% excise tax to prices shown for new manufacture. Some models listed have very limited production.

HUNTER MODEL – available in various cals., Sako action, similar to TSR2, stainless steel barrel by Wiseman/McMillan, laminate stock, Teflon finished metal parts, Pachmayr Decelerator pad, sling swivels.

$4,395	$3,650	$3,150	$2,500	$2,200	$1,850	$1,500	*$4,395*

HUNTER DELUXE – similar to Hunter Model except had TSR1 action and custom checkering.

$6,995	$6,000	$5,250	$4,500	$3,750	$3,000	$2,500	*$6,995*

Add $500 for detachable mag.

MAVERICK – similar to Hunter but with black fiberglass stock. Disc. 2003.

$1,995	$1,575	$1,200	$1,050	$900	$775	$675	*$1,995*

RAMPAGE – .300 WSM cal., 24 in. barrel, with or w/o muzzle brake, no sights, Certa metal coating, pillar bedded Hogue composite stock, hinged floorplate, guaranteed 1/2 MOA accuracy. Mfg. 2011-disc.

$1,999	$1,775	$1,550	$1,350	$1,150	$875	$675	*$1,999*

VARMENTER – similar to Hunter but with thumbhole stock. Disc. 2003.

$2,395	$1,925	$1,500	$1,250	$1,025	$875	$775	*$2,395*

TEXAS SAFARI RIFLE (TSR) SERIES – various cals., stainless steel fluted or non-fluted barrel, with or w/o integral muzzle brake, no floorplate (hidden mag.), standard floorplate, or 4 shot detachable mag., standard, 2, or 3-pos. tang safety, synthetic stock. New 1996-disc.

Add $375 for extra mag. concealed in stock.
Add $195 for 2 or 3-pos. tang safety.
Add $225 for fluted barrel or muzzle brake.
Add $175 for extra straight in-line feed mag.
TSRs were available in short (last MSR $2,000) or long (last MSR $2,250) action.

* ***TSR I*** – various cals., 4 shot inline feed detachable mag.

$2,995	$2,750	$2,200	$1,950	$1,750	$1,500	$1,200	*$2,995*

* ***TSR II*** – various cals., features standard floorplate.

$2,595	$2,300	$2,000	$1,700	$1,500	$1,250	$950	*$2,595*

* ***TSR III*** – various cals., features hidden magazine (no floorplate).

$2,295	$1,850	$1,575	$1,225	$1,025	$875	$750	*$2,295*

TSR TACTICAL (OLDER MFG.) – .300 Win. Mag., .308 Win., or .338 Lapua Mag. cal., 5 shot detachable mag., or standard floorplate, synthetic stock with adj. cheekpiece, stainless steel fluted barrel with integral muzzle brake, guaranteed 1/2 MOA accuracy. Mfg. 1996-2003.

$2,795	$2,200	$1,700	$1,500	$1,235	$1,030	$855	*$2,795*

Add $195 for fluted barrel.
Add $195 for muzzle brake.
Add $150 for 3 position safety.

TSR TACTICAL (NEW MFG.) – various cals., various barrel lengths with or w/o muzzle brake, receiver features integral Picatinny rail, Certa metal coating, adj. black composite Hogue stock (2 options available), detachable mag., guaranteed 1/4 MOA accuracy. Mfg. 2011-disc.

Base MSR was $3,850.
Tactical TSRs were available in short (last MSR $850) or long (last MSR $1,925) action.

GRADING - PPGS™	100%	98%	95%	90%	80%	70%	60%	LAST MSR

WOLF SPORTING PISTOLS

Previous trademark of pistols manufactured in Vienna, Austria. Previously imported and distributed by J R Distributing, located in Moorpark, CA until 1999.

Wolf pistols were noted for their features, quality construction, and resembled the Colt M1911, but had an entirely different action and internal design.

WOLFPACK ARMORY

Current AR-15 style pistol, rifle, and parts manufacturer located in Fairmont, WV.

Please refer to BlueBookOfGunValues.com to order the *Blue Book of AR-15s & Variations*, available as a book or online subscription.

WOODWARD, JAMES AND SONS

Acquired by James Purdey & Sons in January 1949 (previously manufactured in London, England). In 1996, James Purdey & Sons once again started manufacturing a best quality Woodward shotgun.

SHOTGUNS: DOUBLE AND SINGLE BARREL

Woodward made one of the world's finest shotguns. They were formally acquired by J. Purdey and Sons on January 1, 1949. Most of the long guns they made were custom built and grading and pricing should be done individually. It is strongly recommended to obtain competent professional appraisals when contemplating a Woodward purchase or sale.

All new prices do not include VAT.

BEST QUALITY SxS SHOTGUN – custom-built in all gauges, barrel lengths and chokes, sidelock, auto ejectors, stocked to specifications, pre-WWII and new mfg. circa 1996-2003.

	100%	98%	95%	90%	80%	70%	60%
12 ga.	$29,950	$26,205	$22,465	$20,365	$16,475	$13,480	$10,485
20 ga.	$44,925	$39,310	$33,695	$30,550	$24,710	$20,215	$15,725
28 ga.	$60,000	$52,500	$45,000	$40,800	$33,000	$27,000	$21,000
.410 bore	$74,875	$65,515	$56,150	$50,915	$41,180	$33,695	$26,200

Last MSR was £40,100 (20 ga. only).

Add $1,000 for SST

BEST QUALITY O/U SHOTGUN – custom-built in all gauges, barrel lengths, and chokes, VR, sidelock, auto ejectors, stocked to customer specifications, pre-WWII and new mfg. by special order only beginning 1996.

* ***Best Quality O/U Shotgun - 1996-Current Mfg.*** – 12, 16, 20, 28 ga., or .410 bore.

This model is POR. The last posted MSR was £55,000.

* ***Best Quality O/U Shotgun - Pre-WWII Mfg.***

	100%	98%	95%	90%	80%	70%	60%
12 ga.	N/A	$42,750	$37,405	$33,775	$26,935	$22,230	$17,100
20 ga.	N/A	$61,250	$53,595	$48,390	$38,590	$31,850	$24,500
28 ga.	N/A	$140,000	$122,500	$110,600	$88,200	$72,800	$56,000

.410 bore - 2 mfg., too rare to accurately predict.

Add $1,000 for ST.

BEST QUALITY SINGLE BARREL TRAP GUN – 12 ga. only, limited mfg. pre-WWII only.

100%	98%	95%	90%	80%	70%	60%
$12,750	$11,155	$9,565	$8,670	$7,015	$5,740	$4,465

WUTTI, MANFRED

Current manufacturer of custom made long arms established in 1990, located in Geistthal, Austria.

Manfred Wutti manufactures high quality long guns in a variety of configurations, including underlever back action shotguns with hammers. Since every gun is a custom order, please contact the manufacturer directly for availability and a pricing quotation.

WYOMING ARMORY

Current owner of Pentheny de Pentheny rifle trademark beginning 2009, located in Cody, WY.

Currently, Wyoming Armory is not producing rifles under the Pentheny de Pentheny name, but specializes in gunsmithing, firearms restoration, and builds custom precision bolt action rifles based on customer's specifications. Please contact the company directly for more information including prices, options, and availability.

GRADING - PPGS™	100%	98%	95%	90%	80%	70%	60%	LAST MSR

WYOMING ARMS LLC

Current manufacturer of AR-15 style carbines/rifles and pistols located in Cody, WY.

Please refer to BlueBookOfGunValues.com to order the *Blue Book of AR-15s & Variations*, available as a book or online subscription.

WYOMING ARMS MFG. CORP.

Previous manufacturer located in Thermopolis, WY. Very small quantities of Parker pistols were mfg.

PARKER PISTOLS: STAINLESS STEEL

STANDARD PISTOL – 9mm Para., 10mm, .40 S&W, or .45 ACP cal., 3 3/8, 5, or 7 in. barrel, 7 (.45 ACP), 8 (10mm & .40 S&W), or 9 (9mm Para.) shot mag., Millett adj. sights, grooved synthetic grips, 29-39 oz. Disc. 1992.

$450	$300	$250	$195	$165	$140	$120	*$399*

Add $50 for 7 in. barrel.

Add 50%-75% for 9mm Para. cal., only approx. 12 produced.

.357 MAG. – .357 Mag. cal., single action semi-auto, 7 in. barrel, adj. sights, 8 shot mag., lifetime warranty, 44 oz. Disc. 1992.

$425	$350	$300	$240	$210	$180	$155	*$479*

XN ARMS INDUSTRY AND TRADE CO.

Previous tactical semi-auto shotgun manufacturer located in Istanbul, Turkey. Previously imported by EAA Corp, located in Rockledge, FL.

GRADING - PPGS™	100%	98%	95%	90%	80%	70%	60%	LAST MSR

SHOTGUNS: SEMI-AUTO

EKSEN MKE 1919 – 12 ga. only, 2 3/4 or 3 in. chamber, gas operated, AR-15 style, 19.7 in. barrel, 3 chokes, two 5 shot detachable mags., ribbed handguard with A2 front post sight, detachable carrying handle, integral Picatinny rail, black finish or 100% "BONZ" camo coverage, 6 1/2 lbs. Disc.

	100%	98%	95%	90%	80%	70%	60%	LAST MSR
	$625	$550	$495	$475	$450	$425	$395	*$699*

XTREME MACHINING

Previous rifle manufacturer located in Drifting, PA until 2017. Previously located in Grassflat, PA. Previously distributed until 2012 by American Tactical Imports, located in Rochester, NY.

Please refer to BlueBookOfGunValues.com to order the *Blue Book of AR-15s & Variations*, available as a book or online subscription.

YANKEE HILL MACHINE CO., INC. (YHM)

Current manufacturer of AR-15 style rifles, receivers, parts, suppressors, and related accessories, established in 1951, located in Florence, MA. Consumer direct and dealer sales.

Please refer to BlueBookOfGunValues.com to order the *Blue Book of AR-15s & Variations*, available as a book or online subscription.

YAZICILAR AV

Current manufacturer of rifles, shotguns, and airguns located in Trabzon, Turkey. Previously imported by International Firearms Corp. (IFC), located in Midwest City, OK.

SHOTGUNS: SEMI-AUTO

YAZ MAXIMUS – 12 ga., 3 in. chamber, GIO, 24-28 in. barrel, raised rib, full set of choke tubes, 10 shot mag., synthetic stock, grey anodized aluminum receiver, black or Mossy Oak Obsession/Shadow Grass Blades camo finish. Imported 2016-disc.

	100%	98%	95%	90%	80%	70%	60%	LAST MSR
	$425	$375	$325	$275	$225	$200	$150	*$492*

YILDIZ SILAH SANAYI

Current shotgun manufacturer located in Burdur, Turkey. Currently imported exclusively by Academy Sports (multiple locations).

For individual model listings, please go to BlueBookOfGunValues.com/overflow.

Z-B RIFLE

Previous trademark of rifles manufactured by Brno & Uhersky Brod, located in Czechoslovakia.

RIFLES: BOLT ACTION

Z-B MAUSER VARMINT RIFLE – .22 Hornet cal., short Mauser bolt action, 23 in. barrel, double set triggers, 3 leaf sight, checkered pistol grip stock (also known as Brno Hornet).

	100%	98%	95%	90%	80%	70%	60%	LAST MSR
	$825	$745	$690	$605	$550	$470	$415	

ZDF IMPORT EXPORT INC.

Previous importer located in Salt Lake City, UT, 1995-circa 2011.

Please refer to Robinson Armament Co. and Vepr listings.

Z-HAT CUSTOM

Previous custom rifle manufacturer and current custom gunsmithing shop located in Casper, WY.

RIFLES: CUSTOM

Z-Hat Custom manufactured four basic bolt action rifles, with a variety of options and special features, based on a customer supplied action. Previous models included the Hunter, Pro Stalker, Varmint Hunter, and the Mountaineer. Base price for all models was $1,000.

Z-M WEAPONS

Previous rifle manufacturer and pistol components maker located in Richmond, VT. Previously located in Bernardston, MA.

Please refer to BlueBookOfGunValues.com to order the *Blue Book of AR-15s & Variations*, available as a book or online subscription.

ZRO DELTA

Current pistol and rifle manufacturer located in Connelly Springs, NC.

Please refer to BlueBookOfGunValues.com to order the *Blue Book of AR-15s & Variations*, available as a book or online subscription.

ZVI

Previous manufacturer located in Prague, Czech Republic.

ZVI manufactured the Kevin line of small frame .380 ACP cal. semi-auto pistols. ZVI also manufactured the Falcon, a .50 BMG bolt action repeater (2 shot mag.).

ZVS IMPEX

Previous semi-auto pistol manufacturer located in Slovakia 1937-circa 2020.

ZVS Impex manufactured a semi-auto U.S. Model P20/P21 chambered for either 9mm Para. or .40 S&W cal.

ZABALA HERMANOS, S.A.

Previous manufacturer circa 1932-2010, located in Eibar, Spain. Zabala Hermanos was acquired by Norica during 2010, and is currently offering a line of shotguns under the Laurona Zabala trademark. Z. Hermanos built private label shotguns for Tristar, located in N. Kansas City, MO. The company also built private labeled shotguns for KBI, Inc. (Charles Daly SxSs only) until early 2010. Previously imported and distributed by American Arms located in Kansas City, MO, until 2000, and by Galef Shotguns.

SHOTGUNS

Zabala Hermanos manufactured good quality boxlock SxS shotguns (Models 213 €370 - €430 last MSR, Kestrel €370 last MSR, Berri €380 - €510 last MSR, Vencedor Magnum (sideplates) €550 - €590 last MSR, Sporting Magnum €535 last MSR, and the Anthea Magnum €560 - €600 last MSR, O/U shotguns (XL 90 Series €445 - €690 last MSR, Suprema Magnum €510 last MSR, and Century Classic Magnum €530 last MSR) and sidelock SxS shotguns (Vencedor Model €720 - €758 last MSR). The company produced over 600,000 long guns, and was family owned.

ZAKLADY MECHANICZNE TARNÓW S.A.

Current heavy industry conglomerate that also manufactures tactical bolt action rifles located in Tarnów, Poland.

Zaklady manufactures the Alex Tactical Sport bolt action rifle in .308 Win. cal. This bullpup design has an extended upper Picatinny rail and forward detachable bipod. Please contact the manufacturer directly for pricing, options, and availability.

ZANARDINI

Previous manufacturer circa 1946-2014, located in Brescia, Italy. Previously imported by Kevin's Fine Outdoor Gear & Apparel, located in Thomasville, GA. Previously imported by S.O.G. Arms, located in Hacienda Heights, CA. Several U.S. firms stocked a few Zanardini models in the past, but not the complete line.

For individual model listings, please go to BlueBookOfGunValues.com/overflow.

ZANOTTI

Previous manufacturer located in Bologna, Italy. Previous company names were Zanotti 1625 and Fabio Zanotti. Previously imported and distributed by New England Arms Corp. located in Kittery Point, ME until 1999. Zanotti became part of the Renato Gamba Group in 1985.

For individual model listings, please go to BlueBookOfGunValues.com/overflow.

ZANOTTI, R. (ARMERIA RENATO ZANOTTI)

Current manufacturer established during 1625, located in Bologna, Italy. No current U.S. importation. Previously imported circa 2008-2010 by Zanotti USA, located in Houston, TX.

Please contact the manufacturer directly for current pricing and U.S. availability.

ZANOTTI FAMILY & COMPANY HISTORY

Cassiano Zanotti began in 1625 producing some of Italy's finest handmade firearms. Giacinto Zanotti opened a shop in Bologna around 1861 and soon become the most famous in the family. Maria and Stefano Zanotti continued the manufacture of guns in 1871. Production was briefly halted during World War I and in 1932 Stefano's nephew, Tomaso, re-opened the shop and Fabio Zanotti soon followed. After Fabio left Bologna, Renato, the last of the Zanotti branch in Bologna continued production. Renato died in 1975, and at his death, his legacy would be destined for oblivion if not for the efforts of the youngest of his shop boys of the time, Giorgio Simoni. Giorgio decided to give it a try, took over the shop, and now with his son Andrea, is continuing production as a Master Armorer using the very same techniques used by the Zanotti family.

RIFLES: SxS

Express SxS rifles are also available, built based on Zanotti's shotgun design, up to .300 H&H caliber.

SHOTGUNS: SxS

Renato Zanotti shotguns are completely handmade one at a time by master craftsmen and have many innovative trademark features available only in Zanotti firearms. Today Zanotti Armoria continues in that tradition by producing world class handcrafted SxS shotguns.

These fine handmade guns require from 12 to 18 months from time of order to delivery because each one is custom built to the buyer's specifications. The price is the same no matter the gauge of the shotgun. A 50% down payment is required before fabrication can begin.

ZANOTTI, STEFANO

Please refer to Gamba, Renato listing in the G section.

ZASTAVA ARMS

Current manufacturer established in 1853, located in Serbia. Currently imported and distributed exclusively beginning 2018 by Zastava Arms USA located in Des Plaines, IL. Previously imported and distributed by Century International Arms, located in Delray Beach, FL. Some models were imported by EAA, located in Rockledge, FL; please refer to EAA in the E section. Remington previously imported certain models until 2009, as well as KBI until 2005. Previously distributed by Advanced Weapons Technologies, located in Athens, Greece, and by Nationwide Sports Distributors located in Southampton, PA. Previously imported by T.D. Arms, followed by Brno U.S.A., circa 1990.

Zastava Arms makes a wide variety of quality pistols, rifles, and sporting shotguns. Zastava Arms was subcontracted by Remington Arms Co. to make certain bolt action rifle models.

HANDGUNS: SEMI-AUTO

MODEL CZ99 – 9mm Para. or .40 S&W cal., DA/SA, 15 shot, 4 1/4 in. barrel, short recoil, choice of various finishes, SIG locking system, hammer drop safety, ambi controls, 3-dot Tritium sighting system, alloy frame, firing pin block, loaded chamber indicator, squared-off trigger guard, checkered dark grey polymer grips, 32 oz.

	100%	98%	95%	90%	80%	70%	60%	Last MSR
	$550	$400	$375	$330	$300	$285	$265	*$495*

While a Z9 was advertised, it was never commercially imported. All guns were CZ99 or CZ40.

Zastava CZ99 configurations (with finishes) included matte blue with synthetic grips (500 imported), commercial blue with synthetic grips (750 imported), military "painted finish" with synthetic grips (1,000 imported), matte blue finish with checkered wood grips (115 imported), high polish blue with checkered grips (115 imported), and military "painted finish" with wood grips (2 prototypes only).

MODEL CZ999 – 9mm Para. cal., DA/SA, alloy frame, 4 1/4 in. barrel, 15 shot double stack mag., hammer drop safety, squared-off trigger guard, white 3-dot sighting system, checkered dark grey polymer grips, ambi slide release/decocker and mag. release, loaded chamber indicator, blue or chrome slide, blued frame finish, 32 oz. Importation beginning 2019.

	100%	98%	95%	90%	80%	70%	60%
MSR $599	$510	$450	$385	$350	$280	$235	$300

Add $40 for chrome/matte chrome slide and blued frame.

MODEL CZ999 SCORPION – 9mm Para. cal., similar to CZ99, except has indicator for the last three rounds in the magazine.

Please refer to the Skorpion listing in the S section for current information on this model. This pistol was imported by K.B.I. as the ZDA model.

MODEL CZ40 – .40 S&W cal., 55 prototypes were imported for testing, but most had a feeding problem due to improper magazine design, mag. design changes were planned, but were cancelled due to the Serbian/Croatian war.

Suggested retail was $495.

MODEL CZ70 – 9mm Para. cal., SA, Tokarev style, no slide safety, blue finish, limited importation.

	100%	98%	95%	90%	80%	70%	60%
	$1,000	$850	$775	$675	$575	$510	$460

GRADING - PPGS™	100%	98%	95%	90%	80%	70%	60%	LAST MSR

MODEL EZ9/EZ40 – 9mm Para. or .40 S&W cal., DA/SA, 3.86 (compact) or 4.25 in. barrel, 15 shot, paint/phosphate aluminium alloy frame, with or w/o lower Picatinny rail, hammer drop safety, squared-off trigger guard, white 3-dot sighting system, checkered dark grey polymer grips, ambi slide release/decocker, and mag. release, loaded chamber indicator, blue finished steel slide, approx. 7 3/4 in. OAL, 33 oz. Importation began 2019.

MSR $610	$515	$450	$385	$350	$280	$235	$300	

Add $50 for chrome/matte chrome slide, blued frame.

MODEL M57A – 7.62x25mm Tokarev cal., SA, 4 1/2 in. barrel, 9 shot, steel frame and slide, hammer drop safety, rounded trigger guard, fixed sights, grooved dark grey polymer grips, external safety, blue or chrome finish, approx. 7.87 in. OAL, 30 oz. Importation began 2019.

MSR $399	$350	$300	$275	$250	$200	$150	$125	

Add $100 for chrome finish.

MODEL M70AA – 9mm Para. cal., SA, 4 1/2 in. barrel, 9 shot, steel frame and slide, hammer drop safety, rounded trigger guard, fixed sights, grooved dark grey polymer grips, external safety, blue or chrome finish, approx. 7.87 in. OAL, 32 oz. Importation began 2019.

MSR $399	$340	$300	$250	$230	$185	$155	$120	

Add $100 for chrome finish.

MODEL M88 – 9mm Para. or .40 S&W cal., SA, 6 or 8 shot mag., 3.6 in. barrel, blue finish, compact frame, limited importation, 28 oz.

	$600	$525	$465	$415	$360	$330	$295	

The Zastava M88 loosely resembles a modernized Tokarev pistol.

MODEL ZPAP85 – 5.56x45mm cal., 10 in. CHF barrel, dimpled stamped steel receiver, hard nickel moly steel bolt carrier, chrome bolt, hinged top cover, 30 shot mag., Krinkov style rear and post front sights, synthetic grip and light or dark wood handguard, bolt hold-open notch on the safety selector, black finish, 19.3 in. OAL, 6.6 lbs. Importation began 2019.

MSR $819	$725	$625	$550	$500	$400	$325	$250	

Add $281 for booser, dark wood, top/rear rail, and SB3 brace.
Add $375 for night brake, quad rail, top/rear rail, SB3 brace, and angled foregrip.

MODEL ZPAP92 – 7.62x39mm cal., 10 in. CHF barrel, dimpled stamped steel receiver, hard nickel moly steel bolt carrier, chrome bolt, hinged top cover, 30 shot mag., Krinkov style rear and post front sights, synthetic grip and wood handguard, bolt hold-open notch on the safety selector, black finish, 19.3 in. OAL, 6.6 lbs. Importation began 2019.

MSR $843	$715	$625	$535	$485	$400	$320	$280	

Add $50 for stained foregrips and walnut grip.
Add $110 for dark wood and top/rear rail.
Add $260 for dark wood, top/rear rail, SB3 brace.
Add $310 for dark wood, top/rear rail, and SB Tactical FS1913 folding brace.
Add $379 for night brake, quad rail, top/rear rail, SB3 brace, and angled foregrip.

RIFLES: BOLT ACTION

Since 1881, Zastava Arms has remained loyal to the Mauser bolt action system while incorporating all the innovations which followed. Zastava Arms produces sporting rifles based on the Mauser system, in many calibers. Barrels for sporting rifles are made of high quality chrome-vanadium steel, by cold forging. Options for Zastava Arms rifles provide a choice of three types of triggering mechanism, three types of stock, various optical sights, and engraving styles.

MODEL CZ22 – .22 LR, .22 WMR, or .22 Hornet cal., 35 of each cal. imported circa 1990. Suggested retail was $275.

	$250	$225	$195	$175	$150	$135	$120	

Add 15% for .22 WMR or .22 Hornet cal.

MODEL CZ99 PRECISION – .22 LR or .22 WMR cal., rotating bolt.

Please refer to the Remington Model Five listing in the Remington section under the category Rifles: Rimfire, Bolt Action.

MODEL LK M85 – .22 Hornet (disc. 2020), .222 Rem. (disc. 2018), .222 Rem. Mag. (disc. 2018), .22-250 Rem. (disc. 2018, reintroduced 2021), .223 Rem. (disc. 2018, reintroduced 2021), or 7.62x39mm cal. (disc. 2018, reintroduced 2021), Mauser bolt action, drilled and tapped, forged chrome-vanadium steel barrel, detachable mag., single or double set trigger, adj. rear and hooded rear post sights, pig back or Monte Carlo style checkered, polished, and oiled walnut stock with rubber recoil pad and sling swivels, lever-type safety, blue finish. Importation began 2018.

MSR $750	$635	$550	$475	$425	$350	$285	$250	

Previously imported by Interarms, American Arms, Remington, and K.B.I. Please refer to the Remington Model 799 listing in the Remington section.

GRADING - PPGS™	100%	98%	95%	90%	80%	70%	60%	LAST MSR

MODEL LK M70 – .22-250 Rem., 6mm Rem. (disc. 2018), 6.5x57mm (disc. 2018), 7x57mm (disc. 2018), 8x57mm (disc. 2018), .270 Win., 7x57, 7x64mm (disc. 2018), .30-06, .25-06 Rem., 6.5x55mm (disc. 2018), 9.3x62mm (disc. 2018), .243 Win., .308 Win., .264 Win. Mag. (disc. 2018), 7mm Rem. Mag. (disc. 2018), .300 Win. Mag., .375 H&H (disc. 2020), or .458 Win. Mag. cal., Mauser bolt action, drilled and tapped, forged chrome-vanadium steel barrel, single or double set trigger, adj. rear and hooded rear post sights, pig back or Monte Carlo style checkered, polished and oiled walnut stock with rubber recoil pad and sling swivels, lever-type safety, blue finish. Importation began 2019.

MSR $799	$680	$600	$500	$450	$375	$300	$265	

Previously imported by Interarms, American Arms, Remington, and K.B.I. Please refer to the Remington Model 799 listing in the Remington section.

MODEL MP 22 – .22 LR cal., Mauser bolt action, drilled and tapped, forged steel barrel, detachable mag., single or double set trigger, adj. rear and hooded rear post sights, checkered, polished and oiled walnut stock with rubber recoil pad and sling swivels, lever-type safety, blue finish. Importation began 2018.

MSR $459	$390	$340	$295	$265	$215	$175	$150	

RIFLES: SEMI-AUTO

The PAP 762 semi-auto rifle carbine is currently imported by EAA Corp. Please refer to the EAA listing in the E section for current information and pricing.

MODEL M70 AKM – 7.62x39mm cal., 16 1/4 in. chrome-lined barrel, removable ported muzzle brake, 30 shot mag., side-mounted optics rail, Magpul Zhukov folding stock, Tango Down pistol grip, full length aluminum handguard w/cut-out on left side, 45-degree mini rail, black finish. Importation began 2021.

Please contact the importers or the factory directly for pricing and availability on this model.

MODEL ZPAPM70 – 7.62x39mm cal., gas operated action, 16.3 in. CHF or chrome-lined (new 2020) barrel, 10 or 30 shot mag., stamped steel receiver, double stack bolt, adj. front and rear iron sights, fixed dark walnut wood or collapsible black poly furniture, FDE or Olive Drab poly stock and forearm with poly pistol grip, bolt hold open notch on safety selector, black finish, 37 in. OAL, 7.9 lbs. Importation began 2018.

MSR $769	$650	$575	$495	$450	$365	$295	$235	

Add $110 for dark walnut oiled wood furniture, Black, OD Green, or FDE stock.
Add $130 for chrome-lined barrel (new 2020).

SNIPER RIFLE MODEL M91 – 7.62x54R cal., GPO, 24 in. CHF chrome-lined threaded barrel w/tack welded muzzle nut, adj. gas block, two 10 shot mags., 1.5mm steel bulged trunnion receiver, POSP 4x24 scope, ergonomic Dragunov style polymer stock and forearm w/Picatinny rails, AK style safety, black finish. New 2020.

MSR $3,500	$2,975	$2,600	$2,230	$2,025	$1,630	$1,340	$1,165	

ZBROJOVKA BRNO

Current manufacturer located in Brno, Czech Republic. This company remains part of CZ Uhersky Brod. It is important not to confuse this new Zbrojovka Brno (formerly Brno Rifles), with the original Zbrojovka Brno which closed its doors in 2006.

COMBINATION GUNS

COMBO RIFLE/SHOTGUN – .243 Win., .30-06, or .308 Win. cal. over 12 ga., 23 1/2 in. barrels, black receiver, checkered pistol grip walnut stock, extractors, sling mount on barrel, shotgun barrel fired by rear trigger, front trigger has set function for precision rifle shooting, 7 1/2 lbs. Imported 2009-2013.

	$1,875	$1,625	$1,400	$1,250	$900	$800	$700	*$2,181*

RIFLES: SINGLE SHOT

EFFECT – .30-06 or .308 Win. cal., 23.6 in. barrel, single set trigger, light engraved blue receiver, iron sights, sling swivels, checkered walnut stock, 6 lbs. Imported 2009-2013.

	$1,295	$1,135	$970	$880	$710	$585	$455	*$1,585*

Add $114 for FS Model with Mannlicher full stock.

RIFLES: O/U

STOPPER – .375 H&H (new 2010), .416 Rigby (new 2010), or .458 Win. Mag. cal., black or hand engraved silver receiver with gold trigger, 23.7 in. separated barrels, checkered walnut stock with Schnabel forend, 9 lbs. Imported 2009-2013.

	$4,500	$4,000	$3,650	$3,350	$3,000	$2,750	$2,500	*$4,999*

Add $3,000 for hand engraved silver receiver and gold trigger.

GRADING - PPGS™	100%	98%	95%	90%	80%	70%	60%	LAST MSR

SHOTGUNS: O/U

MODEL 801.1 – 12 ga., 3 1/2 in. chambers, 30 in. barrels, engraved silver receiver, barrel selector, fixed chokes, checkered pistol grip walnut stock and forearm, SST, 7 lbs. Limited importation 2009-2010.

	100%	98%	95%	90%	80%	70%	60%	LAST MSR
	$2,650	$2,320	$1,985	$1,800	$1,455	$1,190	$925	*$2,999*

MODEL 801.2 – 12 ga., 3 in. chambers, 30 in. barrels, engraved silver receiver, barrel selector, three screw in chokes, checkered pistol grip walnut stock and forearm, SST, 7 lbs. Limited importation 2009-2010.

	100%	98%	95%	90%	80%	70%	60%	LAST MSR
	$2,650	$2,320	$1,985	$1,800	$1,455	$1,190	$925	*$2,999*

ZELENY SPORT s.r.o.

Current manufacturer located in the Czech Republic. No current U.S. importation.

Please contact the manufacturer directly for current pricing and U.S. availability.

PISTOLS: SEMI-AUTO

HS SERIES – 9x19, .40 S&W, or .45 ACP cal., 12, 13, or 16 shot mag., standard or sub-compact variation, black, two-tone, or tan finish. Imported 2015-disc.

Retail pricing was not available for this model.

RIFLES: SEMI-AUTO

Zeleny Sport manufactures a AK-47 design Model 96 Beryl semi-auto in .223 Rem. cal., the company also makes a Works 11 Series with fixed wood, fixed synthetic, or folding stock.

ZENITH FIREARMS

Current pistol and rifle manufacturer located in Afton, VA.

For individual model listings, please go to BlueBookOfGunValues.com/overflow.

ZEPHYR

Previous Stoeger trademark of guns manufactured in Spain, and imported by Stoeger circa 1930s-1972.

RIFLES

Stoeger has imported a wide variety of bolt action rifles during the past 60 years. Rather than list the many models individually, each Zephyr rifle should be compared to a gun of equal caliber, quality, and features to ascertain an approximate value range.

SHOTGUNS: SxS

WOODLANDER II – 12 or 20 ga., various chokes, boxlock, double triggers, extractors, engraved, checkered pistol grip stock.

	100%	98%	95%	90%	80%	70%	60%
	$495	$440	$385	$360	$305	$275	$250

UPLANDER (4E) – 12, 16, 20, 28 ga., or .410 bore, sidelock action, double triggers, ejectors, engraved.

	100%	98%	95%	90%	80%	70%	60%
	$775	$695	$640	$585	$570	$480	$440

STERLINGWORTH II – similar to Woodlander, with sidelock action.

	100%	98%	95%	90%	80%	70%	60%
	$825	$725	$660	$605	$580	$525	$495

VICTOR SPECIAL – 12 ga., 25, 28, or 30 in. barrels, various chokes, double triggers, extractors, checkered pistol grip stock.

	100%	98%	95%	90%	80%	70%	60%
	$440	$385	$330	$305	$250	$220	$195

UPLAND KING – 12 or 16 ga., sidelock, single trigger, VR, ejectors, fully engraved.

	100%	98%	95%	90%	80%	70%	60%
	$1,000	$900	$800	$725	$650	$600	$550

THUNDERBIRD – 10 ga. Mag., 32 in. barrels, double triggers, French walnut, engraved.

	100%	98%	95%	90%	80%	70%	60%
	$925	$825	$675	$575	$525	$490	$475

Add $175 for ejectors.

SHOTGUNS: SINGLE SHOT

HONKER – 10 ga. Mag., 36 in. VR barrel, lightly engraved.

	100%	98%	95%	90%	80%	70%	60%
	$500	$460	$420	$350	$310	$290	$270

VANDALIA TRAP – 12 ga. Trap Model, 32 in. barrel, engraved.

	100%	98%	95%	90%	80%	70%	60%
	$700	$620	$575	$525	$475	$425	$390

ZEV TECHNOLOGIES

Current manufacturer of modular handguns, AR-15 firearms, parts, and accessories, located in Centralia, WA. Previously located in Oxnard, CA.

Please refer to BlueBookOfGunValues.com to order the *Blue Book of AR-15s & Variations*, available as a book or online subscription.

ZIEGENHAHN & SOHN OHG

Current custom gun manufacturer established in 1928, located in Zella-Mehlis, Germany. No current U.S. importation. Previously imported by Heirloom Armes until 2014, located in Howard Lake, MN. Previously imported by New England Custom Gun Service, Ltd., located in Plainfield, NH.

LONG ARMS

Ziegenhahn & Sohn manufactures high quality, classic Anson & Deeley boxlock "Big Five" double rifles with Holland & Holland pattern sidelocks and ejectors, and sidelocks in calibers up to .500 NE, with larger calibers also available upon request. Ziegenhahn & Sohn also manufactures high quality boxlock and sidelock shotguns. Large caliber bolt action rifles are available by special order, and the company also makes a Heeren falling block single shot rifle. A variety of custom order options including traditional bone charcoal color case hardening is also available. Each gun is individually built per customer specifications. Please contact the company directly for current pricing, availability, and delivery time.

Ziegenhahn currently is building the Krieghoff Essencia SxS with back action - please refer to the Krieghoff section for more information.

ZIMMERSTUTZEN

Refers to a single shot target rifle in rimfire caliber usually used indoors on a 50 foot range. Most Zimmerstutzens were either manufactured in Germany or Austria pre-WWII.

The Zimmerstutzen was the ancestor of the ten meter target rifle, and its German history dates back to at least 1840. The rough English translation of the word is "Parlor Rifle." The most common Zimmerstutzen caliber is 4mm, but there have been over 25 calibers noted that range from 4mm to 5.55mm. Both fixed (standard rimfire cartridge) and separate (percussion cap and separate lead ball) ammunition have been used during the course of its manufacture. The most identifiable feature of a Zimmerstutzen is that typically, only the last eight inches of the rifle barrel are used when firing and the loading mechanism at the end of the barrel is very unique and discernable. When shooting a Zimmerstutzen, the hammer strikes a protruding transfer bar situated inside the barrel and contacts the rimfire ammunition for detonation.

Pricing on Zimmerstutzen pistols varies on the elaborateness, embellishments, and condition of every pistol, as no two are exactly the same. Average condition guns with not a lot of special features typically sell in the $650-$995 range. Fancy pistols with engraving and carving typically sell in the $850-$1,600 range, depending on condition.

Pricing on Zimmerstutzen rifles depends on the same factors as the pistols. Average condition Zimmerstutzens with not a lot of special features typically sell in the $650-$1,300 range. Elaborate guns with extra fancy stocks and embellishments are usually priced in the $1,450-$2,250 range, depending on the condition factor.

ZIP FACTORY, LLC

Please refer to listing under USFA/Zip Factory, LLC located in the U section.

ZOLI, ANGELO

Previous manufacturer located in Brescia, Italy. Previously imported and distributed exclusively by Angelo Zoli USA located in Addison, IL. Mfg. 1985-87.

For individual model listings, please go to BlueBookOfGunValues.com/overflow.

ZOLI, ANTONIO

Historic gun making family dating back to the late 1860s. Current manufacturing established at the end of WWII in 1945 when the factory was re-started, located in Brescia, Italy. Currently imported by and distributed beginning 2013 by Zoli International LLC, located in San Antonio, TX, previously located in Bulverde, TX. Previously imported and distributed 2006-2013 by Antonio Zoli America, located in Canandaigua, NY. Previously located in Weston, FL. O/U rifles were previously imported by Cape Outfitters, located in Cape Girardeau, MO. Previously imported and distributed (1990-91 only) by European American Armory Corp. located in Hialeah, FL. Prior to 1990, A. Zoli was imported and distributed exclusively by Antonio Zoli U.S.A., Inc. located in Fort Wayne, IN.

These guns all bear the Zoli Bow and Arrow logo.

During early 2013, Zoli announced a joint venture with Norbert Hausmann, former president of Blaser USA, called Zoli International LLC. This new company now provides all business activities for Zoli, including importation, distribution, sales, and service.

GRADING - PPGS™	100%	98%	95%	90%	80%	70%	60%	LAST MSR

Antonio Zoli firearms are totally unrelated to guns produced by Angelo Zoli (guns marked "A. Zoli" make it hard to determine the correct manufacturer). Parts are not interchangeable and warranties from Antonio Zoli firearms DO NOT apply to Angelo Zoli guns.

COMBINATION GUNS

Zoli currently makes a Corona O/U combination gun with set trigger. This model is imported into the U.S. on a limited basis - please contact the importer directly.

COMBINATO – 12 or 20 ga. over .243 Win. or .222 Rem. cal., double triggers, folding rear sight, game scene engraved frame, double triggers, skipline checkereing, sling swivels, silver finish. Importation disc. 1993.

$1,750	$1,500	$1,300	$1,100	$950	$775	$600	*$1,995*

* ***Combinato Set*** – includes one set of either 20 or 12 ga. barrels and an additional rifle/shotgun barrel set, same cals. as Combinato, boxlock action, cased. Importation disc. 1993.

$2,400	$2,150	$1,850	$1,600	$1,400	$1,200	$995	*$2,700*

SAFARI DELUXE – similar to Combinato, except has sideplates with elaborate game scene engraving. Importation disc. 1993.

$4,850	$4,400	$3,950	$2,100	$2,675	$2,400	$2,225	*$5,200*

Add approx. 50% for Safari Deluxe 2 (includes 2 sets of shotgun barrels).

EXPRESS ELE3 SET – includes one set of .30-06 cal. O/U barrels, one set of 20 ga./.243 Win. cal. barrels, one set of 20 ga./20 ga. barrels, special order, elaborate game scene engraving, includes German claw mount 4X scope and case. Disc.

$7,950	$7,250	$6,500	$5,750	$5,000	$4,500	$3,950

DRILLINGS

Zoli manufactures a MG92 (boxlock) and MG92 EL (boxlock with sideplates and skipline checkering) Drilling in 12 ga. and various U.S. and metric cals. These models do not currently have U.S. importation.

RIFLES: BOLT ACTION

Antonio Zoli was contract manufacturer of the Karl Gustav 1900 design for Husqvarna. Over 55,000 produced.

The AZ 1900 Series has many variations, and the models listed in this section were for U.S. export only. Please contact the factory directly for more information and availability on its other bolt action models.

AZ 1900C – .243 Win., .270 Win., 6.5x55mm, .30-06, .308 Win., 7mm Rem. Mag., or .300 Win. Mag. cal., 21 or 24 (Mag. cals.) in. barrel, checkered walnut stock with weatherproof stock finish, sling swivels, iron sights, 7.4 lbs. Importation disc. 1993.

$1,100	$850	$740	$660	$585	$500	$450	*$1,295*

Add approx. 10% for AZ 1900 Deluxe (better walnut).
Add 60% for AZ 1900 Super Deluxe (select walnut and moderate engraving).
Add approx. 10% for Model AZ 1900 DL (photo engraved receiver and floorplate).

MODEL AZ 1900M – .243 Win., 6.5x55mm, .270 Win., .30-06, or .308 Win. cal., 21 in. barrel, fiberglass, Kevlar, and graphite composite stock with baked on walnut wood grain finish with checkering, drilled and tapped receiver. Imported 1991 only.

$725	$625	$550	$495	$450	$415	$375	*$840*

Add approx. 10% for Model AZ 1900M DL (photo engraved receiver and floorplate).

AZ 1900 SERIES – .243 Win., .270 Win. .30-06, .308 Win., .270 Wby. Mag., 7x64R, 7mm Rem. Mag., .300 Win. Mag., or .338 Win. Mag. cal., Gustav action, checkered walnut pistol grip Monte Carlo stock with cheekpiece, blue barrel, available in Pro, Pro Lux, or Pro CL configuration. Importation began 2009.

This model was POR.
Add $195 for AZ 1900 Pro CL Model.
Add $455 for AZ 1900 Pro Lux Model.

RIFLES: O/U

EXPRESS – 7x65R, 7x57mm, .30-06, .308 Win., or 9.3x74Rmm cal., 25.6 in. barrels, hand checkered walnut stock with cheekpiece, set trigger for bottom barrel, extractors. Importation disc. 1993.

$3,875	$3,250	$2,900	$2,600	$2,200	$1,950	$1,650	*$4,400*

Add $600 for E Model (with ejectors).

GRADING - PPGS™	100%	98%	95%	90%	80%	70%	60%	LAST MSR

EXPRESS EM – 7x65R, .30-06, .308 Win., or 9.3x74Rmm cal., mechanical single trigger, ejectors. Importation disc. 1990, reintroduced 1992 only.

	$4,850	$3,975	$3,300	$2,900	$2,600	$2,200	$1,900	*$5,300*

Add $2,395 for De Luxe Model (disc.).
Add $7,200 for E3 De Luxe Model (disc.).

The Express E3 De Luxe Model includes 2 extra sets of barrels - 1 set is shotgun (20 ga. - 2 3/4 or 3 in. chambers).

Z EXPRESS – 9.3x74Rmm, .30-06, or 8x57mm cal., 22 in. barrel with open sights, standard features include Boss locking system, ejectors, monolithic forged frame, hand detachable mechanical trigger, express rib with folding sights, oil finished Turkish walnut stock, scope mount and rings, includes aluminum case. Importation began 2008.

MSR $7,250	$6,475	$5,600	$4,800	$4,150	$3,600	$3,100	$2,500

Add $3,540 for interchangeable 20 or 28 ga. shotgun barrels.

Z EXPRESS SAFARI (AFRICAN) – .450/400 NE 3 in. Nitro cal., otherwise similar to Z Express Model.

MSR $11,880	$10,600	$9,100	$7,650	$6,250	$5,175	$4,100	$3,400

Z EXPRESS AMBASSADOR ELB – similar to Z Express Model, except has better quality wood and more engraving. Importation began 2008.

MSR $12,420	$11,000	$9,500	$7,950	$6,600	$5,500	$4,400	$3,650

Add $3,540 for interchangeable 20 or 28 ga. barrels.

Z SAFARI AMBASSADOR AFRICAN – similar to Z Express African Model, except has extra select walnut and more elaborate engraving. Importation began 2008.

MSR $19,480	$17,900	$15,250	$13,000	$11,000	$9,000	$7,750	$6,500

Add $3,540 for interchangeable 20 or 28 ga. barrels.

Z CUSTOM GRADE – Zoli's top-of-the-line double rifle, custom order only.

Base price on this model is POR.

RIFLES: SxS

SAVANA E – 7x65Rmm, .30-06, .308 Win., or 9.3x74Rmm cal., boxlock action, ejectors. Importation disc. 1990.

	$5,850	$4,850	$3,975	$3,300	$2,800	$2,350	$2,000	*$6,600*

Add $400 for Savana EM Model (single trigger).

* ***Savana E Deluxe*** – similar to Savana E, except has elaborate game scene engraving. Importation disc. 1990.

	$7,750	$7,100	$6,500	$6,000	$5,500	$5,000	$4,600	*$8,295*

SHOTGUNS: O/U, RECENT PRODUCTION

Designed by Marini (ex-Perazzi employee). All newer manufactured Z guns from Antonio Zoli feature a Boss locking system with fitted recoil shoulders, detachable posi-lock trigger system, and ultra high quality barrels.

Please contact the importer directly for pricing on available options for currently manufactured shotguns.

GOLDEN SNIPE – 12 or 20 ga., various barrel lengths, VR, single trigger, ejectors, engraved.

	$560	$520	$475	$430	$395	$360	$330

DELFINO – 12 or 20 ga., 3 in. chambers, 26 or 28 in. barrels, ejectors, VR, single non-selective trigger, blue frame with delicate engraving, walnut pistol grip stock and forearm. Disc.

	$500	$425	$375	$325	$295	$280	$265

RITMO HUNTING – 12 ga. only, 3 in. chambers, 26 or 28 in. vent. rib barrels, SST, ejectors, select checkered walnut, blue frame and barrels with moderate engraving, recoil pad, 7 1/4 lbs. Disc.

	$575	$510	$465	$410	$370	$350	$335

RITMO PIGEON GRADE IV – 12 ga. only, live pigeon gun, 28 in. VR barrels, SST, ejectors, superbly engraved silver finished receiver, extra fine checkering on deluxe walnut, cased, 7 1/2 lbs. Disc.

	$1,250	$1,100	$950	$800	$675	$600	$550

M85 RITMO TRAP OR SKEET – 12 ga. only, 28 in. (Skeet only), 30, or 32 in. barrels, ejectors, SST, special stock dimensions, engraved blue receiver, select checkered walnut stock and forearm, cased, 7 3/4 lbs. Disc.

	$595	$500	$465	$440	$415	$395	$370

This model was also available in a single barrel trap model at no extra charge.

* ***M85 Ritmo Trap Combination*** – 12 ga. only, supplied with O/U and single barrel sets, various barrel lengths, cased. Disc.

	$995	$895	$800	$700	$620	$575	$500

GRADING - PPGS™	100%	98%	95%	90%	80%	70%	60%	LAST MSR

SILVER FALCON – 12 or 20 ga., 3 in. chambers, boxlock action, SST, ejectors, 26 or 28 in. barrels with multi-chokes, coin finished receiver with engraving, checkered Turkish walnut stock and forearm with weatherproof finish. Importation disc. 1991.

	$1,050	$600	$500	$400	$350	$300	$250	*$1,695*

WOODSMAN – 12 ga. only, 3 in. chambers, 23 in. VR barrels are designed to shoot rifle slugs at 55 yards and to accept 5 interchangeable choke tubes, SST, ejectors, quarter rib on barrels with pop-up rifle sights, checkered Circassian walnut stock and forearm with swivels (waterproof finish).

	$1,200	$1,000	$875	$750	$650	$550	$400	*$1,895*

* ***Woodsman Combo*** – includes 2 sets of barrels (3 in. chambers) with Zoli interchangeable choke system.

	$1,800	$1,550	$1,400	$1,200	$1,050	$925	$800	*$2,320*

MODEL Z-90 TARGET MODEL – 12 ga. only, boxlock action, adj. SST, black competition receiver, deluxe checkered Turkish walnut stock with recoil pad and forearm, vent. barrels and rib, SST, ejectors.

* ***Model Z-90 Target Model Trap Gun*** – 29 1/2 or 32 in. barrels with screw-in chokes and raised VR, Monte Carlo stock, blue finish. Importation disc. 1993.

	$1,700	$1,450	$1,050	$825	$775	$625	$500	*$2,495*

* ***Model Z-90 Target Model Mono Trap Gun*** – 32 or 34 in. barrel with screw-in chokes and raised VR, Monte Carlo stock. Importation disc. 1993.

	$1,650	$1,450	$1,125	$850	$775	$625	$500	*$2,495*

* ***Model Z-90 Target Model Combo Trap Set*** – includes O/U trap barrels as well as mono trap barrel on same receiver, available as 30/32 in. sets or 32/34 in. sets. Imported 1991-92.

	$1,800	$1,750	$1,650	$925	$825	$750	$500	*$2,700*

* ***Model Z-90 Target Model Skeet Gun*** – 28 in. barrels only with screw-in chokes. Importation disc. 1993.

	$1,800	$1,300	$1,200	$995	$850	$700	$600	*$2,495*

* ***Model Z-90 Target Model Sporting Clays Gun*** – 28 in. barrels with screw-in chokes, coin finished receiver with engraved sideplates, separated barrels, Schnabel forend, solid recoil pad. Importation disc. 1990.

	$1,700	$1,450	$1,200	$995	$850	$700	$600	*$2,495*

KRONOS SPORT/COMPETITION – 12, 20, or 28 ga., competition model with detachable trigger group and best quality Zoli barrels, titanium flush or extended choke tubes, deluxe checkered walnut stock and forearm, cased. Importation began 2009.

MSR $5,400	$4,600	$4,025	$3,450	$3,125	$2,525	$2,075	$1,800	

Add $1,995 for 20/28 ga. combination set.

KRONOS SKEET – 12 ga. only, similar to Kronos Sport, but is designed for Skeet shooting. Importation began 2009.

MSR $5,400	$4,600	$4,025	$3,450	$3,125	$2,525	$2,075	$1,800	

KRONOS DOUBLE TRAP – 12 ga., 29 1/2 or 32 in. barrels, otherwise similar to Kronos Sport. Imported 2009-2013.

	$4,275	$3,650	$3,100	$2,600	$2,200	$2,000	$1,675	*$4,750*

KRONOS TOP SINGLE TRAP – 12 ga., 34 in. barrel only. Importation began 2009.

MSR $5,400	$4,600	$4,025	$3,450	$3,125	$2,525	$2,075	$1,800	

Add $1,495 for Trap Combo with extra O/U barrels.

KRONOS SILVER – 12 ga., 28, 30, 32, or 34 in. flat rib barrels.

MSR $6,600	$5,625	$4,925	$4,225	$3,825	$3,095	$2,530	$2,300	

EXPEDITION – 12, 20, 28 ga, or .410 bore, 26-32 in. barrel, coin finished boxlock action, SST, ejectors, detachable trigger group, Boss locking system, deluxe checkered Prince of Wales grip walnut stock and forearm with checkered wood buttplate. Importation began 2009.

MSR $5,600	$4,750	$4,150	$3,550	$3,250	$2,600	$2,150	$1,850	

Add $3,200 for barrel (12 ga.) and $3,300 for 20, 28, or .410 bore (small ga. action).
Add $2,350 for 20/28 ga. combo (disc.).

EXPEDITION EL – 12, 20, 28 ga., or .410 bore, 26, 28, 29 1/2, 30, or 32 in. barrels, coin finished boxlock action, SST, ejectors, detachable trigger group, Boss locking system, deluxe checkered walnut stock and forearm with checkered wood buttplate, scroll engraved receiver with gold bird inlays. New 2011.

MSR $6,700	$5,700	$5,000	$4,250	$3,900	$3,150	$2,550	$2,300	

Add $500 for CCH model (disc. 2013) or $2,100 for 20/28 ga. combo (disc. 2013).

GRADING - PPGS™	100%	98%	95%	90%	80%	70%	60%	*LAST MSR*

Z EXTRA HR – 12 ga., 30 or 32 in. barrels. Importation began 2014.

MSR $8,800	$7,850	$6,750	$5,700	$4,800	$3,900	$3,200	$2,600	

* ***Z Extra HR Bilanx*** – 12 ga., 30 or 32 in. barrels. Importation began 2014.

MSR $9,100	$8,100	$7,000	$5,850	$4,950	$4,000	$3,350	$2,850	

Z SPORT – 12 or 20 (new 2008) ga., various barrel lengths to 32 in., 3 choke tubes, choice of blue or French grey receiver finish, border engraved with gold logo, fancy oil finished checkered Turkish walnut stock, detachable posi-lock trigger system, includes hard case with tools. Importation began 2007.

MSR $6,420	$5,725	$4,950	$3,850	$3,150	$2,700	$2,200	$1,750	

Add $375 for adj. stock.
Add $2,380 for 20/28 ga. combination set.

* ***Z Sport Bilanx*** – 12, 20, or 28 ga., 28, 29 1/2, or 32 in. barrels, similar to Z Sport, except has Zoli BHB balancing system (barrel weight and stock grip), fine nickel or deep blue finish. Imported 2011-disc.

	$6,125	$5,100	$3,950	$3,350	$2,825	$2,200	$1,800	*$6,720*

Add $2,380 for Combo in 20 and 28 ga.

* ***Z Sport Extra*** – similar to Z Sport, except has 80% engraving coverage in bold English scroll and checkered extra fancy Turkish walnut. Importation began 2007.

MSR $7,950	$7,275	$6,400	$5,400	$4,650	$3,800	$3,000	$2,550	

Add $375 for adj. stock.
Add $2,450 for 20/28 ga. combination set.

* ***Z Sport Extra Bilanx*** – 12, 20, or 28 ga., 28, 29 1/2, or 32 in. barrels, similar to Z Sport, except has Zoli BHB balancing system (barrel weight and stock grip). New 2011.

MSR $8,250	$7,000	$6,125	$5,250	$4,750	$3,850	$3,150	$2,750	

Add $2,450 for Combo in 20 and 28 ga.

Z SPORT HR – 12 ga., 30 or 32 in. high rib barrels, beavertail forearm, adj. comb. Importation began 2014.

MSR $8,300	$7,050	$6,175	$5,300	$4,800	$3,850	$3,150	$2,750	

* ***Z Sport HR Bilanx*** – similar to Z Sport HR. Importation began 2014.

MSR $7,500	$6,375	$5,580	$4,780	$4,350	$3,500	$2,875	$2,500	

Z SPORT FR – 12, 20, 28 ga., or .410 bore, 28, 30, 32, or 34 in. flat rib barrels, silver or black action.

MSR $7,500	$6,375	$5,580	$4,780	$4,350	$3,500	$2,875	$2,500	

Z SPORT MR – 12 ga., 30 or 32 mid rib barrels w/adj. comb, silver or black action.

MSR $8,000	$6,800	$5,950	$5,100	$4,600	$3,750	$3,050	$2,400	

Z TRAP HR COMBO – 12 ga., 30, 32, or 34 in. barrels w/adj. comb, additional O/U barrel included.

MSR $10,950	$9,300	$8,150	$7,000	$6,350	$5,100	$4,200	$3,250	

Z AMBASSADOR ROUND BODY SPORTING – 12 or 20 ga., 28, 30, or 32 in. barrels with 6 choke tubes, Boss coin finished action, hand engraved with deep floral scroll and 24Kt. gold shield logo, exhibition grade oil finished Turkish walnut stock with hand checkering, includes leather hard case. Limited importation 2007.

	$7,500	$6,500	$5,500	$4,750	$4,000	$3,300	$2,750	*$8,690*

Z AMBASSADOR EL SPORTING – similar to Round Body Sporting, except has 100% deep scroll engraving and three Bulino style game scenes, hand carved oil finished exhibition grade Turkish walnut stock with hand-cut checkering, includes leather hard case, tools, parts kits, and snap caps. Importation began 2007.

MSR $13,800	$12,000	$10,250	$8,950	$7,750	$6,500	$5,500	$4,400	

Add $5,100 for 20/28 ga. combination set (new 2008).
Add $1,050 for gold accent (Model Z Ambassador EL Sporting Gold).

Z AMBASSADOR BILANX EL – 12, 20, or 28 ga., 28, 29 1/2, or 32 in. barrels, similar to Z Ambassador EL, except has Zoli BHB balancing system (barrel weight and stock grip). Imported 2011-2013.

	$9,950	$9,250	$8,250	$7,250	$6,250	$5,250	$4,250	*$10,500*

Add $2,200 for Combo in 20 and 28 ga.

Z AMBASSADOR EL HUNTING – choice of standard boxlock or Boss action, similar to Z Expedition EL, except has better wood and engraving with gold inlays. Importation began 2009.

MSR $15,200	$12,925	$11,310	$9,695	$8,790	$7,110	$5,815	$5,065	

Add $1,450 for gold accent (Model Z Ambassador EL Gold).
Add $3,350-$3,550 for extra flat rib barrels.
Add $5,650 for extra set of 20 and 28 ga. barrels (disc.2015).

GRADING - PPGS™	100%	98%	95%	90%	80%	70%	60%	LAST MSR

Z AMBASSADOR SL HUNTING – top-of-the-line model with round action and extensive scroll engraving on coin finished frame, supplied with aluminum motor case. Imported 2009-2010, reintroduced circa 2018.

MSR $20,400	$17,350	$15,200	$13,000	$11,800	$9,550	$7,800	$6,050	*$13,000*

Add $2,500 for Z-Ambassador SLG model.
Add $2,600 for 20/28 ga. combo (disc.).

Z AMBASSADOR SUPER LUXUS (BILANX) – 12, 20, or 28 ga., 28, 29 1/2, or 32 in. barrels, Zoli BHB balancing system (barrel weight and stock grip), hand rounded receiver, hand carved fences, deep scroll hand engraving (with or w/o game scenes), oil finished exhibition grade Turkish walnut stock, detachable trigger mechanism, SST or DT, 6.2-7 lbs. New 2011.

MSR $17,900	$14,950	$12,000	$9,750	$8,000	$6,250	$5,500	$5,000	

Add $4,400 for Combo in 20 and 28 ga.
Add $2,350 for Z Ambassador Super Luxus RB (round body).

R.B. PERNICE – 20, 28 ga., or .410 bore, monolithic Boss type action, 26, 28, 30, or 32 in. silver soldered barrels, 5 exchangeable choke tubes, SST, adj. trigger blade for LOP, bolt Boss type locking system, case color hardened, polished and engraved/silver-carbon nitride or black hot blued finish.

Current MSR is $7,200
Add $7,750 for R.B. Pernice Ambassador EL model.
Add $1,400 for color case hardening w/gold plated trigger and gold inlay.
Add $3,500 for additional barrel.

SHOTGUNS: SxS, RECENT PRODUCTION

UPLANDER – 12 or 20 ga., 3 in. chambers, 25 in. barrels with fixed chokes (IC/M), ST, ejectors, color case hardened receiver, English style checkered Circassian walnut stock and forearm with oil or polyurethane finish. Importation disc. 1990.

	$750	$625	$560	$520	$485	$450	$425	*$1,295*

SILVER FOX – 12 or 20 ga., 3 in. chambers, 26 or 28 (12 ga. only) in. barrels with fixed chokes, ST, ejectors, hand engraved silver finished receiver with "AZ" in gold, straight grip checkered Circassian walnut stock and forearm. Importation disc. 1990.

	$1,400	$1,300	$1,200	$995	$875	$750	$625	*$2,995*

ARIETE M3 – 12 ga. only, 26 or 28 in. barrels, matted rib, single non-selective trigger, ejectors, blue receiver with fine scroll engraving, cased. Disc.

	$550	$475	$400	$360	$330	$310	$285	

EMPIRE – 12 or 20 ga. Mag., 27 or 28 in. barrels, moderate engraving, coin finished receiver. Disc.

	$1,100	$1,075	$975	$875	$795	$725	$650	

Add $100 for 3 in. Mag. chambers.

This model was distributed by Euroarms of America, Inc.

VOLCANO RECORD – 12 ga. only, 28 in. barrels, H&H type sidelocks, ejectors, SST, treble Purdey locks, silver finished receiver with elaborate engraving, best quality fine checkered walnut, special order only. Disc.

	$4,100	$4,000	$3,800	$3,400	$2,950	$2,650	$2,300	

* ***Volcano Record ELM*** – 12 ga. only, built to individual customer specifications, best quality H&H style sidelock. Disc.

	$10,750	$9,800	$8,800	$7,100	$6,850	$6,200	$4,400	

This model was distributed by Euroarms of America, Inc.

CUSTOM SERIES – SxS, individual custom order only, every refinement is used in the construction of these extremely rare and expensive shotguns. The Volcano Extra Lusso shotgun is probably the most elaborate Antonio Zoli shotgun. Disc. 2005.

Last MSR was $58,850.

SHOTGUNS: SINGLE SHOT

Z TRAP UNSINGLE HR – 12 ga., boxlock action, 34 in. barrel with raised rib and external choke tubes. New 2014.

MSR $6,800	$6,100	$5,200	$4,350	$3,600	$3,000	$2,500	$2,175	

Add $300 Z Trap Unsingle HR Bilanx.
Add $2,500 for combo with extra set of barrels.

ZOMBIE DEFENSE

Previous custom manufacturer located in Henrico, VA 2009-2016.

Please refer to BlueBookOfGunValues.com to order the *Blue Book of AR-15s & Variations*, available as a book or online subscription.

Listed below are the names, websites, and/or email addresses of various firearms/shooting organizations, associations, and advocacy groups throughout the U.S. You are encouraged to join those organizations which pertain to your region and area of interest. For full contact information including address, phone numbers, and membership pricing and information, please visit our website at BlueBookOfGunValues.com and scroll down to the bottom of the page, under Content Information, click on Gun Values. As thorough as we try to be, it's impossible to keep up on the constant changes made within these organizations. If your club does not appear on the following pages or doesn't have the correct contact information, please contact us for inclusion in the next edition/online update.

For more than 50 years, the NRA's affiliated Gun Collecting clubs (identified in the following listings with an *) have been a vital part of NRA's educational outreach programs. With over 100 of these clubs, there is one for almost every collecting interest and area. Collector affiliates are leaders in firearms safety programs for gun shows, and they sponsor some of the most popular and successful shows in the country. They participate in the NRA's Annual Meetings and Exhibits with spectacular displays of rare and historically important arms. Affiliates also sponsor the annual National Gun Show and the annual National Gun Collecting Seminar. An annual awards ceremony for collector affiliates is held every year at the NRA's Annual Meetings.

*** Alabama Gun Collectors Association (ALGCA)**
Email: agcanow@gmail.com

Alaska Gun Collectors Association
Website: www.agca.net
Email: akguncollectors@gmail.com

American Custom Gunmakers Guild (ACGG)
Website: www.acgg.org
Email: admin@acgg.org

*** American Single Shot Rifle Association**
Website: www.assra.com

*** American Society of Arms Collectors**
Website: www.americansocietyofarmscollectors.org

*** The American Thompson Association**
Website: www.nfatoys.com/tsmg/tata

Arizona Citizen's Defense League
Website: www.azcdl.org
Email: President@azcdl.org

Arizona State Rifle and Pistol Association
Website: www.asrpa.com
Email: asrpapresident@gmail.com

*** Arkansas Gun & Cartridge Collectors Club**
Website: www.arkgccc.com

Arkansas Rifle and Pistol Association
Email: President@arpa-online.org

*** Ark - La - Tex Gun Collectors**
Website: www.arklatexguncollectorsla.com
Email: web@arklatexguncollectorsassn.com

*** Arms Collectors of Southwest Washington (ACSWW)**
Website: www.acsww.org
Email: armscsww@gmail.com

*** Association of Ohio Longrifle Collectors**
Website: www.aolrc.com
Email: ogdenjim@sbcglobal.net

*** Browning Collectors Association**
Website: www.browningcollectors.com
Email: markhannahjr@aol.com

BamaCarry
Website: www.bamacarry.us
Email: efulmer@bamacarry.us

Buckeye Firearms Association (Ohio)
Website: www.buckeyefirearms.org
Email: drieck@buckeyefirearms.org

Cody Firearms Museum
Website: www.centerofthewest.org

California Rifle & Pistol Association, Inc.
Website: www.crpa.org
Email: contact@crpa.org

*** Central Wisconsin Gun Collectors Association**
Website: www.centralwisconsingun.org
Email: cwgca@yahoo.com

Colorado Gun Collectors Association (CGCA)
Website: www.cgca.com
Email: cgcashow@cgca.com

Colorado State Shooting Association
Website: www.cssa.org
Email: president@cssa.org

*** Colt Collectors Association**
Website: www.coltcollectors.com
Email: secretary@coltcollectors.com, coltsecretary@gmail.com

Contemporary Longrifle Association
Website: www.longrifle.ws
Email: cla@longrifle.com

Connecticut Citizens Defense League
Website: www.ccdl.us
Email: president@ccdl.us

Connecticut State Rifle and Revolver Association
Website: www.thecsrra.org
Email: president@thescrra.org

*** Dakota Territory Gun Collectors Association**
Website: www.dtgca.org

Deleware State Sportsmen's Association
Website: www.brpc-de.com
Email: jeff.hague@bville-rifle-pistol.org

DIVA – Women Outdoors Worldwide
Website: www.divawow.org

*** Eastern Shore Arms Collectors**
Website: easternshorearmscollectors.org

*** Egyptian Collectors Association**
Email: bobleck202@gmail.com

Firearm Owners Against Crime (Pennsylvania)
Website: www.foacpac.org
Email: kimstolger@foacpac.org

Florida Carry
Website: www.floridacarry.org
Email: contact@floridacarry.org

Florida Sport Shooting Association
Email: president@fissa.org

*** Forks of the Delaware Historical Arms Society, Inc.**
Website: www.allentownshow.net

A.H. Fox Collectors Association
Website: www.foxcollectors.com

*** Garand Collectors Association**
Website: www.thegca.org
Email: info@thegca.org

Georgia Carry
Website: www.georgiacarry.org
Email: jhenry@georgiacarry.org

Georgia Sport Shooting Association
Email: rosenqvist@windstream.net

German Gun Collectors Association
Email: sales@germanguns.com
Questions about German Guns
Website: www.germanguns.com
Email: inquiries@germanguns.com.

*** Glock Collectors Association**
Website: glockcollectorsassociation.org
Email: contact@glockcollectorsassociation.org

Great Western Arms Collector
Website: www.greatwesternarmsco.com
Email: sackpeterson@gmail.com

Gun Owners Action League of Massachusetts
Website: www.goal.org
Email: jimwallace@goal.org

Gun Owners Action League of Washington
Website: www.wagoal.org
Email: jwaldron@wagoal.org

Gun Owners of America
Website: www.gunowners.org
Email: goamail@gunowners.org

Gun Owners of California
Website: www.gunownersca.com
Email: contact@crpa.org

Gun Owners of Maine
Website: www.gunownersofmaine.org
Email: info@gunownersofmaine.org

Gun Owners of South Carolina
Website: www.gosc.org
Email: lmgs@sc.rr.com

Gun Owners of Vermont
Website: www.gunownersofvermont.org
Email: info@gunownersofvermont.org

*** Hawaii Historic Arms Association**
Website: hawaiihistoricarms.com

Hawaii Firearms Coalition
Website: www.hifico.org
Email: info@hifico.org

Hawaii Rifle Association
Email: hghawaii@gmail.com

*** Houston Gun Collectors Association**
Website: www.hgca.org

Idaho State Rifle and Pistol Association
Website: www.idahosrpa.org
Email: president@idahosrpa.org

Illinois State Rifle Association
Website: www.isra.org
Email: donm@isra.org

Indiana State Rifle Association
Website: www.isrpa.org
Email: vp@isrpa.org

*** International Ammunition Association**
Website: www.cartridgecollectors.org

Iowa Firearms Coalition
Website: www.iowafc.org
Email: info@iowafc.org

Iowa State Rifle and Pistol Association
Website: www.iasrpa.org
Email: president@iasrpa.org

Jews for the Preservation of Firearms Ownership
Website: www.jpfo.org
Email: jpfo@jpfo.org

Kansas State Rifle Association
Email: bwilliams@ksraweb.org

Kentucky Concealed Carry Coalition
Website: www.kc3.com

*** Kentucky Rifle Association**
Website: kentuckyrifleassociation.org

League of Kentucky Sportsmen
Email: enighbert@gmail.com

*** Lancaster Muzzle Loading Rifle Association**
Email: LMLRA@comcast.net

Lefever Arms Collectors Association
Website: www.lefevercollectors.com
Email: laca@hughes.net

The Liberal Gun Club
Website: www.theliberalgunclub.com
Email: kimstolger@foacpac.org

Louisiana Shooting Association
Website: www.louisianashooting.com

Maine Rifle and Pistol Association
Website: www.mainerpa.org
Email: jfmerrill@tds.net

*** Mannlicher Collectors Association**
Website: www.mannlicher.org
Email: armand.martell@gmail.com

*** Marlin Firearms Collectors Association, Ltd.**
Website: www.marlin-collectors.com

*** Maryland Arms Collectors Association (MACA)**
Website: www.Baltimoreshow.com
Email: MACA@baltimoreshow.com

Maryland Shall Issue
Website: www.marylandshallissue.org
Email: info@marylandshallissue.org

Maryland State Rifle & Pistol Association
Website: www.msrpa.org
Email: jandrews@msrpa.org

*** Maumee Valley Gun Collectors Association**
Website: www.mvgca.com
Email: jtsnyder@bex.net

Merwin Hulbert Collectors Association
Website: www.merwinhulbert.com
Email: MerwinMan@triad.rr.com

*** Michigan Antique Arms Collectors**
Website: www.michiganantiquearms.com
Email: MAAC@michiganantiquearms.com

Michigan Coalition for Responsible Gun Owners
Website: www.mcrgo.org
Email: brady@mcrgo.org

Michigan Rifle & Pistol Association
Website: www.michrpa.org
Email: Lcebula@hotmail.com

*** Midwest Gun Traders Inc.**
Website: www.midwestguntrader.com
Email: admin@midwestguntrader.com

*** Miniature Arms Collectors/Makers Society, Ltd.**
Website: miniaturearms.org
Email: wdriskill@hotmail.com

*** Minnesota Gun Owners Caucus**
Website: www.gunowners.mn/
Email: contact@gunowners.mn

Minnesota Rifle & Revolver Association
Website: www.mrra.org
Email: mrrapresident@gmail.com

Minnesota Weapons Collectors
Website: www.mwca.org
Email: info@mwca.org

*** Missouri Valley Arms Collectors Association, Inc. (MVACA)**
Website: www.mvaca.org
Email: membership@mvaca.org

Mississippi State Firearm Owners Association
Website: www.msfoa.tripod.com
Email: douglasmbowser@yahoo.com

Missouri Firearms Coalition
Website: www.missourifirearmscoalition.org
Email: Alexandra.salsman@gmail.com

Mohave Arms Collectors Association
Website: www.mohavesportsmanclub.com
Email: suggest2msc@gmail.com

Montana Rifle & Pistol Association
Website: www.mtrpa.org
Email: kragjorgensen@bresnan.net

Montana Rifle & Pistol Association
Website: www.mtssa.org
Email: gary@mtssa.org

*** Nat'l Automatic Pistol Collectors Association (NAPCA)**
Website: www.napca.net
Email: info@napca.net

National Rifle Association (NRA)
Website: www.nra.org
Email: membership@nrahq.org

National Shooting Sports Foundation (NSSF)
Website: www.nssf.org

Nebraska Firearms Owners Association
Website: www.nebraskafirearms.org
Email: Info@NebraskaFirearms.org

Nebraska Marksmanship Association
Website: www.nemarksmanship.com
Email: michaelnollett@outlook.com

Nevada Firearms Coalition
Website: www.nvfac.org
Email: Don@nvfac.org

New Eastcoast Arms Collectors Associates, (NEACA, Inc.)
Website: www.neaca.com
Email: sales@neaca.com

New Jersey Second Amendment Society
Website: www.nj2as.org
Email: aroubian@nj2as.org

*** New Mexico Gun Collectors Association**
Website: www.nmgca.net
Email: contact@nmgca.net

New Mexico Shooting Sports Association
Website: www.nmssa.org
Email: president@nmssa.org

New York State Rifle and Pistol Association
Website: www.nysrpa.org
Email: tking@nysrpa.org

North Carolina Firearms Coalition
Website: www.ncfirearmscoalition.org
Email: director@ncfirearmscoalition.org

North Carolina Rifle & Pistol Association
Website: www.ncrpa.org
Email: frededgecomb@gmail.com

North Dakota Shooting Sports Association
Website: www.ndssa.org
Email: mgodbout@hotmail.com

*** Northwest Montana Arms Collectors Association (NWMACA)**
Website: https://2therange.com

*** Ohio Gun Collectors Association**
Website: www.ogca.com
Email: ogca@ogca.com

Ohio Rifle & Pistol Association
Website: www.orpa.net
Email: president@orpa.net

Oklahoma Rifle Association
Website: www.oklarifle.com
Email: jerry@oklarifle.com

Oklahoma Second Amendment Association
Website: www.ok2a.org
Email: ok2aassociation@gmail.com

Operation Blazing Sword/Pink Pistols
Website: www.blazingsword.org,www.pinkpistols.org
Email: erin@blazingsword.org

*** Oregon Arms Collectors, Inc. (OAC)**
Website: www.oregonarmscollectors.com
Email: m1903@yahoo.com

Oregon Firearms Federation
Website: www.oregonfirearms.org
Email: off@oregonfirearms.org

Oregon State Shooting Association
Website: www.ossa.org
Email: president@ossa.org

Parker Gun Collectors Association
Website: www.parkerguns.org
Email: PGCAmembership@gmail.com

PA Rifle & Pistol Association
Website: www.pennarifleandpistol.org
Email: EGestl1969@gmail.com

*** Paso Del Norte Gun Collectors**
Website: https://pasodelnorteguncollectors.com

*** Penn Antique Gun Collectors Association (PAGCA)**
Website: www.pagca.com
Email: brucepowell1506@verizon.net

*** Penn Gun Collectors Association, Inc.**
Website: www.paguncollectors.org
Email: president.pgca@verizon.net

*** Potomac Arms Collectors Association, Inc. (PACA)**
Website: www.paca-club.org
Email: JLeahigh@comcast.net

*** Remington Society of America**
Website: www.remingtonsociety.org
Email: remingtonsa.sec@gmail.com

Rhode Island 2nd Amendment Coalition
Website: www.ri2nd.org
Email: info@ri2nd.org

Rhode Island Firearms Owners League
Website: www.rifol.org
Email: info@rifol.org

*** Ruger Collectors Association, Inc.**
Website: www.rugercollectorsassociation.com
Email: contactus@rugercollectorsassociation.com

SAAMI (Sporting Arms & Ammunition Manufacturers' Institute)
Website: www.saami.org

SASS (Single Action Shooting Society)
Website: www.sassnet.com
Email: SASS@sassnet.com

*** Santa Barbara Historical Arms Association**
Website: www.sbhaa.org
Email: sbhaa1957@gmail.com

*** Santa Barbara Historical Arms Association**
Website: www.sbhaa.org
Email: sbhaa1957@gmail.com

Second Amendment Foundation
Website: www.saf.org
Email: info@saf.org

*** Smith & Wesson Collectors Association**
Website: www.theswca.org
Email: swca357@hotmail.com

L.C. Smith Collectors Association (LSCA)
Website: www.lcsmith.org
Email: frankfinch@msn.com

*** South Carolina Arms Collectors Association**
Website: www.scaca.net
Email: showdirector@scgunshows.com

South Dakota Shooting Sports Association
Website: www.sdshootingsports.org
Email: tom@sdshootingsports.org

*** Stark Gun Collectors**
Website: https://www.starkguncollectors.org/
Email: starkcollectors@gmail.com

*** Tennessee Military Collectors Assn.**
Website: www.tmcaonline.org
Email: tmca@comcast.net

Tennessee Firearms Association
Website: www.tennesseefirearms.com
Email: inquiry@tennesseefirearms.com

Tennessee Shooting Sports Association
Website: www.tennesseeshootingsportsassociation.org
Email: ray.harvey@earthlink.net

Texas Gun Collectors Association (TGCA)
Website: https://www.tgca.org/
Email: MurryCathlina@gmail.com

Texas State Rifle Association
Website: www.tsra.com
Email: president@tsra.com

Thompson/Center Association
Website: http://thompsoncenterassociation.org/
Email: tcaogs@metrocast.net

*** Tri-State Gun Collectors, Inc.**
Website: www.tristategunshow.org

*** Tulsa Arms Collectors Association**
Website: http://www.tulsaarmsshow.com/

*** Utah Gun Collectors Association**
Website: www.ugca.org
Email: john2008@oldguns.net

Utah Shooting Sports Council
Website: www.utahshootingsportscouncil.org
Email: clark.aposhian@gmail.com

Utah State Rifle & Pistol Association
Website: www.usrpa.org
Email: LarryScanlan@msn.com

Vermont Federation of Sportsmen's Clubs
Website: www.vtfsc.com
Email: vtfsc.president@gmail.com

Virgina Citizens Defense League
Website: www.vcdl.org
Email: president@vcdl.org

*** Virginia Gun Collectors Association, Inc.**
Website: www.vgca.net
Email: rpebecker@verizon.net

Virginia Shooting Sports Association
Website: www.foacpac.org
Email: vssamain@verizon.net

Washington Arms Collectors
Website: www.washingtonarmscollectors.org
Email: office@washingtonarmscollectors.org

Washington State Rifle & Pistol Association
Website: www.wsrpa.org
Email: president@wsrpa.org

*** Weapons Collectors Society of Montana**
Website: www.wsofmt.net

West Virginia Citizens Defense League
Website: www.wvcdl.org
Email: imasters@wvcdl.org

West Virginia State Rifle & Pistol Association
Website: www.wvasrpa.org
Email: gunsandammo@yahoo.com

Willamette Valley Arms Collectors Association, Inc.
Website: www.wvaca.org
Email: wvaca.show@outlook.com

*** Winchester Arms Collectors Association (WACA)**
Website: www.winchestercollector.org
Email: GHill@winchestercollector.org

Wisconsin Force (Firearm Owners)
Website: www.wisconsinforce.org
Email: president@wisconsinforce.org

Wyoming State Shooting Association
Website: www.wyossa.com
Email: wssapres@wyoming.com

*** Wyoming Weapons Collectors**
Website: http://wyomingweaponscollectors.com
Email: pistolmama15@yahoo.com

*** Ye Conn Gun Guild**
Website: http://ycgg.org/
Email: peterkuck@comcast.net

CONSERVATION ORGANIZATIONS

The following are not firearms associations, but are conservation organizations that may or may not have links to hunting/shooting sports. These organizations are dedicated to preserving wildlife and natural habitat. You are encouraged to contact these organizations to learn more.

Ducks Unlimited, Inc.
One Waterfowl Way
Memphis, TN 38120
Phone: 901-758-3825 or 1-800-45DUCKS
Fax: 901-758-3850
Website: www.ducks.org
Membership fee of $35

Global Sporting & Conservation Alliance
340 West Putnam Avenue
Greenwich, CT 06830
Phone: 203-340-9633
Fax: 203-618-0419
Email: globalsportingca@aol.com

Hunting Heritage Trust
428 Spalding Lake Circle
Aiken, SC 29803
Phone: 803-641-1030
Fax: 803-641-1070
Website: www.huntingheritagetrust.org

The Mule Deer Foundation
1939 S 4130 W, Ste. H
Salt Lake City, UT 84104-4875
Phone: 888-375-DEER
Fax: 801-973-1177
Website: www.muledeer.org
Email: askmdf@muledeer.org
$35 Annual Membership Fee, includes 6 issues of MDF magazine

The National Wild Turkey Federation
P.O. Box 530
Edgefield, SC 29824
Phone: 803-637-3106
Website: nwtf.org
Email: info@nwtf.net
Membership fee of $35

North American Moose Foundation
Shannon James, Executive Director
P.O. Box 30
610 W. Custer, Ste. B
Mackay, ID 83251
Phone: 208-588-2939
Fax: 208-588-2980
Email: moose@atcnet.net
Membership fee of $35

North American Pronghorn Foundation
P.O. Box 1383
Rawlins, WY 82301
Phone: 307-324-5238
Website: www.pronghornfoundation.homestead.com
Membership fee of $20

Pheasants Forever
1783 Buerkle Circle
Saint Paul, MN 55110
Phone: 651-773-2000
Fax: 651-773-5500
Website: www.pheasantsforever.org
Email: contact@pheasantsforever.org
$35 Annual Membership Fee includes five issues of Pheasants Forever magazine

Quail Forever
1783 Buerkle Circle
Saint Paul, MN 55110
Phone: 866-457-8245
Fax: 651-773-5500
Website: www.quailforever.org
Email: contact@quailforever.org
$35 Annual Membership, includes 4 issues of Quail Forever magazine

The Ruffed Grouse Society
Ronald P. Burkert
451 McCormick Rd.
Coraopolis, PA 15108
Phone: 888-564-6747
Website: www.ruffedgrousesociety.org
Email: rgs@ruffedgrousesociety.org
$35 Annual Membership Fee
$60 Conservation Membership Fee
$150 Sustaining Membership Fee
$250+ Various Sponsor Membership Fee
All memberships include a subscription to Ruffed Grouse Society magazine.

Safari Club International & SCI Foundation
4800 W. Gates Pass Rd.
Tucson, AZ 85745-9490
Phone: 520-620-1220
Website: www.safariclub.org
$65 Annual Membership Fee USA/CAN/MEX (includes subscription to monthly Safari magazine and bi-monthly Safari Times newsletter)

Whitetails Unlimited
P.O. Box 720
2100 Michigan Street
Sturgeon Bay, WI 54235
Phone: 800-274-5471 or 920-743-6777
Fax: 920-743-4658
Website: www.whitetailsunlimited.com
Email: nh@whitetailsunlimited.com

Wild Sheep Foundation
Gray Thornton, President
412 Pionghoin Trail
Bozeman, MT 59718
Phone: 406-404-8750
Website: www.wildsheepfoundation.org
Email: info@wildsheepfoundation.org
1 year membership $45; 3 years $120

REFERENCE SOURCES

Adler, Dennis, *Colt Black Powder Reproductions & Replicas.* Minneapolis, MN: Blue Book Publications, Inc. 1998.

Adler, Dennis, *Black Powder Revolvers - Reproductions & Replicas.* Minneapolis, MN: Blue Book Publications, Inc., 2008.

Adler, Dennis, *Black Powder Long Arms & Pistols - Reproductions & Replicas.* Minneapolis, MN: Blue Book Publications, Inc., 2009.

Adler, Dennis, *Colt Single Actions - From Patersons to Peacemakers.* Edison, NJ: Chartwell Books, 2007.

Adler, Dennis, *Metallic Cartridge Conversions.* Iola, WI: Krause Publications, 2002.

Adler, Dennis, *Winchester Shotguns*, Edison, NJ: Chartwell Books, 2006.

Allen, John & Adler, Dennis, The 4th Edition *Blue Book of Modern Black Powder Arms.* Minneapolis, MN: Blue Book Publications, Inc., 2004.

Allen, John, The 5th Edition *Blue Book of Modern Black Powder Arms* (2007), 6th Edition (2009), 7th Edition (2011), 8th Edition (2013), 9th Edition (2016). Minneapolis, MN: Blue Book Publications, Inc.

Antaris, Leonardo, Dr., *Astra Automatic Pistols.* Sterling, CO: FIRAC Publishing Co., 1988.

Antaris, Leonardo, Dr., *Star Firearms*, Davenport, IA: Firac Publishing, 2002.

Bady, Donald B., *Colt Automatic Pistols.* Los Angeles, CA: Borden Publishing Co., 1973.

Baker, D.J., *British Handloading Cartridge Tools,* Ceredigion, U.K., The Cambrian Press, 2014.

Baer, Larry L., *The Parker Book* North Hollywood, CA: Beinfeld Publishing Co., 1974.

Ball, Robert, *Mauser Military Rifles of the World*, Iola, WI: Krause Publications, 1996.

Ball, Robert, *Remington Firearms: The Golden Age of Collecting*, WI: Krause Publications, 1995.

Barnes, Frank C., *Cartridges of the World.* Northbrook, IL: DBI Books, Inc., 2009.

Barnes, Frank C., *Cartridges of the World.* Northbrook, IL: DBI Books, Inc., 2012.

Beeman, Robert, Dr. & Allen, John, The 7th Edition *Blue Book of Airguns* (2008), 8th Edition (2009), 9th Edition (2011), 10th Edition (2012), 11th Edition (2014), 12th Edition (2016). Minneapolis, MN: Blue Book Publications, Inc.

Belford, James N. and Dunlap, Jack, *Mauser Self Loading Pistol.* Alhambia, CA: Borden Publishing Co., 1969.

Bender, Roy G. III, *Mauser.* Houston, TX: Collector's Press, 1971.

Bleile, Roger, *American Engravers – The 21st Century*, Blue Book Publications, Inc., 2010

Bleile, Roger, *American Engravers III – Masterpieces in Metal by America's Engraving Artisans*, Blue Book Publications, Inc., 2015

Boothroyd, Geoffry & Susan M., *Boothroyd's Directory of British Gunmakers.* Amity, OR: Sand Lake Press, 1994.

Braceras, Saul, *Express Rifle - A Different Weapon.* Madrid, Spain: Valmayor Ediciones, S.L., 2007.

Breathed and Schroeder, *System Mauser.* Chicago, IL: Handgun Press, 1967.

Brophy, William S., *L.C. Smith Shotguns.* North Hollywood, CA: Beinfeld Publishing Co., 1977.

Brophy, William S., *Marlin Firearms.* Harrisburg, PA: Stackpole Books, 1989.

Brown, Gurney, *Colt's Python – King of the Seven Serpents.* Minneapolis, MN: Blue Book Publications, Inc. 2018.

Brown, Gurney, *Seven Serpents – The History of Colt's Snake Guns* - 1st (2015) and 2nd (2016) printing. Minneapolis, MN: Blue Book Publications, Inc., 2015

Butzer, David F., *The American Shotgun.* Middlefield, CT: Lyman Publications, 1973.

Bussard, Michael, *The Ammo Encyclopedia* (2008), 2nd Edition (2010), 3rd Edition (2011), 4th Edition (2012), 5th Edition (2014), 6th Edition (2017). Minneapolis, MN: Blue Book Publications, Inc.

Buxton, Warren H., *The P-38 Pistol.* Volumes I, II & III. Los Alamos, NM: U.C. Ross Books.

Byron, David, *Gunmarks, Tradenames, Codemarks, and Proofs from 1870 to the Present.* New York, NY: Crown Publishers, 1979.

Carder, Charles, *Side by Sides of the World.* Delphos, OH: AVIL ONZE Publishing.

Carder, Charles, *Side by Sides of the World Y2K.* Delphos, OH: AVIL ONZE Publishing, 2000.

Carpenter, Mel, *An Introduction to MBA Gyrojets And Other Ordnance*, Orange Park, FL, MRC3 Publishing, 2010.

Condry, Ken, & Jones, Larry, *The Colt Commemoratives, 1961-1986.* Dallas, TX: Taylor Publishing Co., 1989.

Costanza, Sam, *World of Lugers. Volume I.* Mayfield Heights, OH: World of Lugers, 1977.

Eastman, Matt, *Browning, Sporting Arms of Distinction.* Fitzgerald, GA: Published by Author, 1994.

Ezell, Edward Clinton, *Handguns of the World.* Harrisburg, PA: Stackpole Books, 1981.

Ezell, Edward Clinton, *Small Arms of the World.* (12th Ed). Harrisburg, PA: Stackpole Books, 1983.

Dance, Tom, *High Standard; A Collector's Guide to the Hamden & Hartford Target Pistols.* Lincoln, RI: Andrew Mobray Publishers, 1991.

Flayderman, Norm, *Flayderman's Guide to Antique American Firearms.* Iola, WI: Gun Digest Books, 2009.

Fjestad, S.P., 2nd Edition *Blue Book of Antique American Firearms & Values.* Minneapolis, MN: Blue Book Publications, Inc. 2018.

Gardner, Col. Robert, *Small Arms Makers.* New York, NY: Bonanza Books, 1963.

Grant, James. J., *Boys' Single Shot Rifles.* Prescott, AZ: Wolfe Publishing Company, 1991.

Groenewold, John, *Quackenbush Guns.* Mundelein, IL, published by author, 2000.

Gunther, Mullins, Price, and Cote', *The Parker Story. Vol. I.* Knoxville, TN: Parker Story Joint Venture Group, 1998.

Gunther, Mullins, Price, and Cote', *The Parker Story. Vol. II.* Knoxville, TN: Parker Story Joint Venture Group, 2000.

Hogg, Ian V., *Pistols of the World*, 4th Ed.

Houchins, John, *L.C. Smith - The Legend Lives*, Winston-Salem, NC: Published by Author, 2006.

Hill and Anthony, *Confederate Long Arms and Pistols.* Charlotte, NC: Confederate Arms, 1978.

Jinks, Roy G., *History of Smith & Wesson.* North Hollywood, CA: Beinfeld Publishing Co., 1977.

Karr and Karr, Jr., *Remington Handguns.* Stackpole Co., Second Edition, 1951.

Kenyon, Charles Jr., *Lugers at Random.* Chicago, IL: Handgun Press, 1969.

Kersten, Manfred, *Walther: A German Legend*, Long Beach, CA: Safari Press, Inc., 2001.

Kimmel, J., *Savage & Stevens Arms.* Portland, OR: Corey/Stevens Pub., Inc., 1990.

Kopec, Graham, and Moore, *A Study of the Colt Single Action Army Revolver.* Redding, CA: Kopec, Graham, and Moore Publishers, 2006. www.johnakopec.com

Krasne, Jerry A., *Encyclopedia and Reference Catalog for Auto Loading Guns.* San Diego, CA: Triple K Manufacturing, 1989.

Lamboy, Stephen & Elena Micheli-Lamboy, *Mario Terzi – Master Engraver*, Minneapolis, MN: Blue Book Publications, Inc., 2011.

Law, Richard D., *Backbone of the Wehrmacht: The German K98k Rifle.* Coburg, Ontario, Canada: Collector Grade Publications, 2006.

Lee, Jerry (Ed.), *Standard Catalog of Firearms,* Iola, WI, Gun Digest Books, 2012.

Leithe, Frederick, *Japanese Handguns.* California: Borden Publishing Co., 1968.

Madis, George, *The Model 12.* Lancaster, TX: Privately published by Author, 1981.

Madis, George, *The Winchester Book.* Lancaster, TX: Privately published by Author, 1975.

Marcot, Roy, *Remington, America's Oldest Gunmaker.* Peoria, IL: Primedia Special Interest Publications, 1998.

Marcot, Roy & Gyde, John, *Remington .22 Rimfire Rifles.* Creswell, OR: Remington Armory Press, 2007.

Marcot, Roy. *Remington Rolling Block Rifles, Carbines & Shotguns.* Tucson, AZ: Northwood Heritage Press, 2009.

Maxwell, Samuel L., Sr., *Lever Action Magazine Rifles.* Published by Author, 1978.

Muderlak, Ed, *Parker Guns, The Old Reliable.* Long Beach, CA: Safari Press, 1997.

Murray, Douglas, *The Ninety-Nine.* Published by Author, 1985.

Nonte, Jr., George C., *Firearms Encyclopedia.* Outdoor Life: New York, NY, 1973.

Ogle, John, *The Book of Colt Paper.* Blue Book Publications, Inc.: Minneapolis, MN, 2011

Olson, Ludwig, *Mauser Bolt Action Rifles.* Montezuma, IA: F. Brownell & Son Publishers, Inc., 1976.

Price, Charlie & Parker Story Joint Venture Group, *Parker Gun Identification & Serialization,* Minneapolis, MN: Blue Book Publications, Inc. 2002.

Rankin, James L., *Walther. Vols. I, II, III.* Coral Gables, FL: Published by Author, 1976.

Ricciardelli, Stephen, *Firearms Owner's Manual Compilation* (web only), http://stevespages.com/page7b.htm

Rule, Roger C., *The Rifleman's Rifle.* Northridge, CA: Alliance Books, Inc., 1982.

Sellers, Frank, *American Gunsmiths,* 2nd Edition. Minneapolis, MN: Blue Book Publications, Inc., 2008.

Sellers, Frank, *Sharp's Firearms.* North Hollywood, CA: Beinfeld Publishing Co., 1978.

Serven, editor, *The Collecting of Guns.* Bonanza Books, 1964.

Sharpe, Phillip B., *The Rifle in America.* Funk and Wagnalls, 1947.

Shideler, Dan, *Standard Catalog of Remington Firearms,* Iola, WI, Gun Digest Books, 2008.

Shooter's Bible. S. Hackensack, NJ: Published annually by Skyhorse Publishing.

Skennerton, Ian, *British Small Arms of World War II,* Labrador, Australia: self-published, 1988.

Skennerton, Ian, *The Lee Enfield Story,* Labrador, Australia: self-published, 1992.

Skennerton, Ian & Stamps, *.380 Enfield Revolver,* Labrador, Australia: self-published, 1992.

Skennerton, Ian, *Small Arms Identification Series. Vols. 1-17.* Labrador, Australia: self-published, 1993-2003.

Steindler, *Steindler's New Firearms Dictionary.* Phoenix, AZ: Stackpole Books, 1985.

Still, Jan C., *Axis Pistols.* Marceline, MO: Walsworth Publishing Co., 1986.

Still, Jan C., *Imperial Lugers.* Marceline, MO: Walsworth Publishing Co., 1991.

Still, Jan C., *Third Reich Lugers.* Marceline, MO: Walsworth Publishing Co., 1988.

Stubbendieck, James, *L.C. Smith Production Records: The Numbers Behind the Legend.* Minneapolis, MN: Blue Book Publications, Inc., 2013

Supica, Jim and Nahas, Richard, *Standard Catalog of Smith & Wesson.* Iola, WI: Krause Publications, 1996.

Supica, Jim, *Standard Catalog of Smith & Wesson. Vol. II.* Iola, WI: Krause Publications, 2001.

Supica, Jim and Nahas, Richard, *Standard Catalog of Smith & Wesson*, 3rd Ed. Iola, WI: Gun Digest Books, 2006.

Tanner, Hans, *Guns of the World.* Bonanza Books, 1972, 1977.

Tinker, Edward & Johnson, Graham, *Simson Lugers, Simson & Co, Suhl - The Weimar Years.* Galesburg, IL: Brad Simpson Publishing, 2007.

Trolard, Tom, *Winchester Commemoratives,* Plano, TX: Commemorative Investments Press, 1985.

Vanderlinden, Anthony, *Belgian Browning Pistols 1889-1949,* Greensboro, NC: Wet Dog Publications, 2001.

Vanderlinden, Anthony, & H.M. Shirley, *Browning Auto-5 Shotgun - The Belgian FN Production,* Greensboro, NC: Wet Dog Publications, 2003.

Vanderlinden, Anthony, *FN Browning Pistols - Side-Arms That Shaped World History,* Greensboro, NC: Wet Dog Publications, 2010.

Vanderlinden, Anthony, *ARS Mechanica - The Ultimate FN Book,* Greensboro, NC: Wet Dog Publications, 2011.

Webster, Donald B. Jr., *Suicide Specials.* Harrisburg, PA: Stackpole, Co., 1958.

West, Bill, *Browning Arms & History.* Santa Fe Springs, CA: Stockton Trade Press, Inc., 1972.

West, Bill, *Marlin and Ballard Firearms & History.* Norwalk, CA: Stockton Trade Press, Inc., 1977.

West, Bill, *Remington Arms & History.* Whittier, CA: Stockton Trade Press, Inc., 1970.

West, Bill, *Savage and Stevens Arms & History.* Whittier, CA: Stockton Trade Press, Inc., 1971.

Whitaker, Dean H., *Model 70 Winchester 1937-1964.* Dallas, TX: Taylor Publishing Co., 1978.

Wilkerson, Don, *Post-War Colt Single Action Army.* Published by Author, 1978.

Wilkerson, Don, *Post-War Colt Single Action Revolver, 1976-1986.* Dallas, TX: Taylor Publishing, 1986.

Wilkerson, Don, *Colt Scouts, Peacemakers, and New Frontiers in .22 Caliber,* Marceline, MO: Walsworth Publishing Co., 1993.

Wilkerson, Don, *Colt Single Action Army Revolver, Pre-War/Post-War Model,* Minneapolis, MN, Broughton Printing Inc., 1991.

Wilson, R.L., *The Colt Engraving Book. Vols. I & II.* New York, NY: Bannerman's Limited Edition, 2001.

Wilson, R.L., 2nd Ed. *The Book of Colt Firearms.* Minneapolis, MN: Blue Book Publications, Inc., 1993.

Wilson, R.L., 3rd Ed. *The Book of Colt Firearms.* Minneapolis, MN: Blue Book Publications, Inc., 2008.

Wilson, R.L., *The Blue Book Pocket Guide for Colt Dates of Manufacture.* Minneapolis, MN: Blue Book Publications, Inc., 2008.

Wilson, R.L., *Colt, An American Legend.* New York, NY: Abbeville Press.

Wilson, R.L., *Colt Commemorative Firearms.* Geneseo, IL: Robert E.P. Cherry Publishing Co., 1973.

Wilson, R.L., *The Colt Heritage.* New York, NY: Simon and Schuster.

Wilson, R.L., *Silk & Steel,* New York: Random House. 2003

Wilson, R.L., *Winchester: An American Legend,* New York: Random House. 1991.

Wilson, R.L., *The World of Beretta: An International Legend,* New York: Random House. 2000.

Wilson, R.L., *Ruger & His Guns.* New York: Simon and Schuster. 1996.

Wirnsberger, Gerhard, *The Standard Directory of Proofmarks.* Jolex, Inc.

Wood, J.B., *Beretta Automatic Pistols, The Collector's & Shooter's Comprehensive Guide.* Harrisburg, PA: Stackpole Books, 1985.

Zhuk, A.B., *The Illustrated Encyclopedia of Handguns.* London: Greenhill Books. 1995.

STORE BRAND CROSS-OVER LIST

The following listing is provided as a cross-reference of Store Brands to original manufacturer and model number. Although not exhaustive, this list covers most major stores and chains that have had their name put on guns by other manufacturers. The values for the firearms listed on these pages are approximately 15% – 40% less than the original manufacturers' model(s).

Our thanks goes out to Numrich Gun Parts Corp., West Hurley, NY. They can be reached at (845) 679-4867.

House Brand	Model No.	Orig. Mfgr.	Orig. Model
Aldens	670	Springfield	67
Aldens	670	Savage	67
Belknap	964A	Stevens	87N
Belknap	B63	Springfield	947
Belknap	B63	Savage	947B
Belknap	B63E	Savage	940E
Belknap	B64	Savage	67
Belknap	B65C	Springfield	745
Belknap	865C	Savage	745
Belknap	B68	Savage	94C
Belknap	B68D	Savage	94D
Belknap	B963	Springfield	120
Belknap	B963	Savage	120
Belknap	B964	Savage	87J
Belknap	B967	Savage	87N
Coast to Coast	180	Savage	58
Coast to Coast	1800	Savage	18D
Coast to Coast	182	Savage	18S
Coast to Coast	184	Savage	951
Coast to Coast	267	Savage	77
Coast to Coast	285	Savage	7J
Coast to Coast	286	Savage	46
Coast to Coast	288	Savage	87J
Coast to Coast	320	Savage	120
Coast to Coast	367	Savage	30
Coast to Coast	40	Marlin	99C
Coast to Coast	42	Marlin	70
Coast to Coast	650	Marlin	55
Coast to Coast	779	Mossberg	479
Coast to Coast	843	Savage	340
Coast to Coast	843	Springfield	840
Coast to Coast	843V2DS	Savage	340(.222)
Coast to Coast	843V3DS	Savage	340(.30/30)
Coast to Coast	946	Stevens	940
Coast to Coast	946	Springfield	947
Coast to Coast	946E	Stevens	940E
Coast to Coast	946Y	Stevens	940Y
Cotter & Co	10-40	Glenfield	10
Cotter & Co	10-40	Marlin	101
Cotter & Co	121	Stevens	120-15
Cotter & Co	167	Springfield	67
Cotter & Co	167T	Savage	30
Cotter & Co	168	Savage	30
Cotter & Co	168	Springfield	67VR
Cotter & Co	287	Springfield	87J
Cotter & Co	33	Marlin	336C
Cotter & Co	410	Savage	110E
Cotter & Co	424	Savage	24F
Cotter & Co	434	Savage	34
Cotter & Co	474	Savage	170
Cotter & Co	474	Springfield	174
Cotter & Co	487T	Springfield	187
Cotter & Co	489	Savage	89
Cotter & Co	60-50	Glenfield	60
Cotter & Co	60-50	Marlin	99C
Cotter & Co	645	Savage	745
Cotter & Co	645C	Savage	745C
Cotter & Co	75-46	Marlin	99M1
Cotter & Co	75-45	Glenfield	75
Cotter & Co	842	Springfield	840
Cotter & Co	911	Springfield	511
Cotter & Co	918	Springfield	18
Cotter & Co	948	Stevens	940
Cotter & Co	948E	Savage	948E
Cotter & Co	949	Springfield	944
Cotter & Co	949C	Savage	940
Cotter & Co	949Y	Savage	944Y
C.I.L.	125	Anschutz	184
C.I.L.	212	Savage	7J
C.I.L.	221	Savage	7J
C.I.L.	227	Savage	871
C.I.L.	233	Savage	85N
C.I.L.	266	Savage	187
C.I.L.	470	Anschutz	520/61
C.I.L.	607	Savage	67
C.I.L.	607 TD	Savage	30 FLD GR.
C.I.L.	621	Savage	30
C.I.L.	621 TD	Savage	30D
C.I.L.	710	Savage	311
C.I.L.	725	Savage	FOX BDE
C.I.L.	830	Savage	340
C.I.L.	871	Savage	170
C.I.L.	950C.D	Savage	110C.D
C.I.L.	MKVII	H & R	865
Eastern Arms	101.1	Stevens	94B
Eastern Arms	IOI.23	Savage	416
Foremost See J.C.Penney			
Gamble Skogmo, Hiawatha			
Gamble Skogmo	130	Savage	30
Gamble Skogmo	1300-567 VR	Savage	67-VR
Gamble Skogmo	180N	Savage	87N
Gamble Skogmo	189J	Savage	87J
Gamble Skogmo	189N	Stevens	87N
Gamble Skogmo	521	Savage	120
Gamble Skogmo	567	Savage	67
Gamble Skogmo	S87	Savage	187
Gamble Skogmo	594	Savage	944
Gamble Skogmo	594Y	Savage	944Y
Gamble Skogmo	GU12-5517A	J.C.Higgins	60 & 66
Glenfield	10	Marlin	101
Glenfield	20	Marlin	80
Glenfield	25	Marlin	80 W/swivels
Glenfield	30A	Marlin	336
Glenfield	35	Marlin	336 .35 cal
Glenfield	50	Marlin	55
Glenfield	60	Marlin	5
Glenfield	60	Marlin	99C
Glenfield	65	Marlin	99M1
Glenfield	70	Marlin	989M2
Glenfield	75	Marlin	989MI
Globco	Mohawk	Russian	Tokarev

House Brand	Model No.	Orig. Mfgr.	Orig. Model
Hawthorn See Wards			
Hercules	50	Stevens	5100
Hiawatha See Gambles			
J.C. Higgins See Sears			
J.C. Penney common name, F - Foremost			
J.C.Penney	2025	Marlin	80C
J.C.Penney	2035	Marlin	80
J.C.Penney	2035	Glenfield	20
J.C.Penney	2066	Marlin	49DL
J.C.Penney	2935	Marlin	336
J.C.Penney	3040	Marlin	336
J.C.Penney	3040	Glenfield	30A
J.C.Penney	4011	High Standard	FLIGHT KING
J.C.Penney	6400	Savage	340
J.C.Penney	6610	Savage	120
J.C.Penney	6630	Glenfield	50
J.C.Penney	6630	Marlin	66
J.C.Penney	6647	Savage	944
J.C.Penney	6647	Springfield	944
J.C.Penney	6660	Glenfield	60
J.C.Penney	6660	Marlin	99C
J.C.Penney	6670	Springfield	67H
J.C.Penney	6670	Savage	67
J.C.Penney	6870	Savage	30
J.C.Penney	6870H	Savage	30H
Katz	F-1282	Marlin	989M2
Katz	F-1282	Glenfield	70
Katz	F-1287	Marlin	55
Katz	F-1287	Glenfield	50
Kresge	151	Boito	CBC
K-Mart	151	Boito	CBC
Marlin/new	780	Marlin/old	80
Marlin/new	781	Marlin/old	81
Marlin/new	782	Marlin/old	980
New Haven	220K	Mossberg	320K-A
New Haven	240K	Mossberg	340K
New Haven	246K	Mossberg	346K-A
New Haven	250K	Mossberg	152K
New Haven	250K8	Mossberg	350K-A
New Haven	273	Mossberg	173
New Haven	273A	Mossberg	173A
New Haven	283.D	Mossberg	183D
New Haven	284	Mossberg	173
New Haven	285	Mossberg	185D-C
New Haven	290	Mossberg	190D-A
New Haven	453	Mossberg	353
New Haven	600AT	Mossberg	500A
New Haven	600C	Mossberg	500C
New Haven	600E	Mossberg	500E
New Haven	679	Mossberg	472
New Haven	740	Mossberg	640
Otasco	30	Marlin	336
Otasco	30	Glenfield	30A
Otasco	65	Glenfield	60
Otasco	65	Marlin	99C
Palmetto	11	Stevens	85,89
Premier	Trail Blazer	Stevens	29A

House Brand	Model No.	Orig. Mfgr.	Orig. Model
Revelation, see Western Auto			
Sears. Ranger. J.C. Higgins			
J.C.Higgins	30	High Standard	30
J.C.Higgins	101.1	Savage	94
J.C.Higgins	101.24	Savage	15-120
J.C.Higgins	20	High Standard	200
J.C.Higgins	42 DL	Marlin	80
J.C.Higgins	52	Sako	L46
J.C.Higgins	S4	Browning	FN-300
J.C.Higgins	583.13 to.23	High Standard	10
J.C.Higgins	583.2078-79	High Standard	20ga pump
J.C.Higgins	583.514-730	High Standard	20ga pump
J.C.Higgins	6670H	Stevens	67H
J.C.Higgins	80	High Standard	101
Ranger	101.2	Savage	238
Ranger	101.8	Stevens	83
Ranger	104.7	H&R	120
Ranger	105.20	H&R	120
Ranger	120	Winchester	1200
Ranger	30	Stevens	520A
Ranger	34A	Marlin	80.C,780
Ranger	34A	Marlin	50-50E
Ranger	35A	Stevens	66A
Ranger	36	Marlin	80 Adj. Trigger
Ranger	400	Stevens	311
Sears	101.1	Savage	94
Sears	101.100	Savage	96/96Y
Sears	101.10040	Savage	94
Sears	101.10041	Savage	94
Sears	101.10080	Stevens	940
Sears	101.1120	Savage	51 and 951
Sears	101.12	Stevens	39
Sears	101.13	Stevens	86-7
Sears	101.138	Savage	38A and 58A
Sears	101.138	Springfield	18.410
Sears	101.1380	Springfield	18,18C
Sears	101.1380	Stevens	58,C
Sears	101.1381	Springfield	18,951 E,F
Sears	101.1381	Stevens	58,51, E,F
Sears	101.16	Savage	6,87
Sears	101.1610	Savage	540 DL
Sears	101.1610	Savage	FOX BDL
Sears	101.1610	Fox BST	EC,BD,BE,B-F
Sears	101.1620-1670	Stevens	530,A;311,A,C
Sears	101.1700	Savage	94
Sears	101.1701	Fox BSE	C,D,Ser F,H
Sears	101.1701-C	Savage	BSE
Sears	101.1710	Savage	FOX BDE
Sears	101.1710	Savage	540 BDE
Sears	101.1750	Savage	94
Sears	101.1760	Savage	94
Sears	101.19	Stevens	827-7
Sears	101.20	Stevens	15
Sears	101.22	Stevens	87M(MUSKET)
Sears	101.25	Stevens	39A,59A,BandC
Sears	101.2830	Savage	63-73
Sears	101.2830	Savage	73
Sears	101.3	Stevens	237
Sears	101.3538830	Stevens	89
Sears	101.4	Stevens	38
Sears	101.40	Springfield	947,D,Y
Sears	101.40	Stevens	940,D,Y,DY
Sears	101.451	Marlin	336
Sears	101.5	Stevens	37
Sears	101.51004	Savage	94
Sears	101.510070	Savage	94

House Brand	Model No.	Orig. Mfgr.	Orig. Model
Sears	101.51009	Springfield	944,Yseries A
Sears	101.51013	Springfield	944,Yseries A
Sears	101.51024	Savage	94
Sears	101.510270	Savage	94
Sears	101.51044	Savage	94
Sears	101.510660	Stevens	9478
Sears	101.510660	Springfield	944,Y series A
Sears	101.510670	Stevens	9478
Sears	101.510680	Stevens	9478
Sears	101.512220	Stevens	5100,530,311
Sears	101.512230	Stevens	5100,530,311
Sears	101.51451	Springfield	67
Sears	101.51452	Springfield	67
Sears	101.51454	Springfield	67
Sears	101.51472	Springfield	67 Series B
Sears	101.52701	Stevens	71,74 S/S
Sears	101.52772	Savage	34,65,34M.65M
Sears	101.52773	Savage	34,65,34M,65M
Sears	101.5350	Springfield	18.58
Sears	101.5350-D	Stevens	18D
Sears	101.53521	Savage	340
Sears	101.53527	Savage	340
Sears	101.5380	Savage	18/18AC.58
Sears	101.5380	Springfield	18,12,16,20ga.
Sears	101.5380D	Stevens	18ADC
Sears	101.538840	Savage	34,65,34M,65M
Sears	101.540	FOX	B-BST,BDL
Sears	101.5410	Springfield	18,58
Sears	101.5410D	Savage	18D
Sears	101.5410D	Springfield	18DS
Sears	101.54880	Stevens	80 Series A
Sears	101.54880	Springfield	187 Series A
Seem	101.64881	Marlin	980 DL,987
Sears	101.600	Stevens	39A,59A,B,C
Sears	101.7	Stevens	311
Sears	101.750	SpringField	18.410
Sears	101.750	Savage	38A and 58A
Sears	101.7C	Stevens	311-C
Sears	101.8	Stevens	83
Sears	102	Stevens	240
Sears	102.25	Stevens	520A
Sears	102.35	Savage	M521
Sears	102.35	Savage	M29-D2
Sears	103.13	Marlin	81
Sears	103.16	Marlin	80
Sears	103.18	Marlin	100
Sears	103.181	Marlin	101
Sears	103.1977	Marlin	101
Sears	103.19770	Marlin	101
Sears	103.19771	Marlin	101
Sears	103.19780	Marlin	101
Sears	103.19790	Marlin	80
Sears	103.19791	Marlin	80
Sears	103.19800	Marlin	80
Sears	103.19801	Marlin	80
Sears	103.1981	Marlin	81
Sears	103.19810	Marlin	81
Sears	103.19811	Marlin	81
Sears	103.1982	Marlin	81DL
Sears	103.19820	Marlin	81
Sears	103.19821	Marlin	81
Sears	103.19840	Marlin	56
Sears	103.19880	Marlin	57 LR-MAG.
Sears	103.19881	Marlin	57 LR-MAG.
Sears	103.19890	Marlin	57 LR-MAG.
Sears	103.2	Marlin	80
Sears	103.228	Marlin	80
Sears	103.229	Marlin	81
Sears	103.273	Marlin	782

House Brand	Model No.	Orig. Mfgr.	Orig. Model
Sears	103.273	Marlin	980
Sears	103.274	Marlin	122
Sears	103.275	Marlin	122
Sears	103.2751	Marlin	122
Sears	103.2840	Marlin	80
Sears	103.2850	Marlin	81
Sears	103.2870	Marlin	56
Sears	103.350	Marlin	M90
Sears	103.360	Marlin	90
Sears	103.4	Marlin	A1
Sears	103.450	Marlin	336
Sears	103.451	Marlin	336
Sears	103.720	Marlin	59
Sears	103.740	Marlin	59
Sears	103.8	Marlin	100
Sears	10.19790	Marlin	80
Sears	11.2	Stevens	238
Sears	153.512350	Laurona	S/S
Sears	153.512351	Laurona	S/S
Sears	153.512360	Laurona	S/S
Sears	153.512361	Laurona	S/S
Sears	153.512740	Laurona	71 O/U
Sears	18	Mossberg	183K
Sears	18AC	Savage	18C
Sears	2C	Winchester	131
Sears	20	High Standard	200
Sears	200	Winchester	1200
Sears	200	Mossberg	G4
Sears	201	Mossberg	80
Sears	202	Mossberg	80
Sears	203	Mossberg	85
Sears	204	Mossberg	83
Sears	205	Mossberg	73
Sears	206	Mossberg	70
Sears	207	Mossberg	75
Sears	209	Stevens	84-7
Sears	21	High Standard	K2011
Sears	210	Mossberg	85B
Sears	211	Mossberg	83B
Sears	211	Stevens	86-7
Sears	212	Mossberg	73B
Sears	213	Mossberg	75B
Sears	215	Mossberg	85C
Sears	216	Mossberg	83C
Sears	217	Mossberg	75C
Sears	217	Stevens	87M (MUSKET)
Sears	218	Mossberg	73C
Sears	218	Stevens	22/410
Sears	231	Stevens	83
Sears	232	Stevens	87-7
Sears	233	Stevens	87-7
Sears	234	Savage	234
Sears	238	Stevens	827-7
Sears	25	High Standard	A1041 .22 auto
Sears	273.2400	Winchester	190
Sears	273.27S10(2C)	Winchester	131
Sears	273.27520(2M)	Winchester	131
Sears	273.510770	Winchester	37A
Sears	273.510780	Winchester	37A
Sears	273.510790	Winchester	37A
Sears	273.53421	Winchester	100
Sears	277	Stevens	1S
Sears	278.28180	Cooey	64
Sears	281.512650	Antonio Zoli	O/U
Sears	281.512651	Antonio Zoli	O/U
Sears	281.512660	Antonio Zoli	O/U
Sears	281.512661	Antonio Zoli	O/U
Sears	281.512750	Antonio Zoli	O/U
Sears	282.510821	Boito	ERA Single Bbl

House Brand	Model No.	Orig. Mfgr.	Orig. Model	House Brand	Model No.	Orig. Mfgr.	Orig. Model
Sears	282.510831	Boito	ERASingle Bbl	Sears	97	Savage	94
Sears	282.510841	Boito	ERA Single Bbi	Sears	97AC	Savage	94AC
Sears	282.5227740	CBC	122	Sears	98	Stevens	37
Sears	282.527740	FIE	122	Sears	98	Springfield	944
Sears	2C	Winchester	131	Sears	M30	Stevens	M520
Sears	2T	Winchester	121,131,141	Sears	mzm	Savage	34
Sears	2/57	Stevens	66	Sears 100	273.532141	Winchester	NM 94
Sears	2/58	Stevens	66	Sears 200	2732.5320	Winchester	1200
Sears	30	High Standard	22 PUMP	Sears 200	273.2011	Winchester	1200
Sears	300	Winchester	1400	Sears 200	273.21010	Winchester	1200
Sears	31	J.C. Higgins	31	Sears 200	273.2160	Winchester	1200
Sears	33	J.C. Higgins	33	Sears 200	273.2250	Winchester	1200
Sears	34	J.C. Higgins	34	Sears 200	273.2251	Winchester	1200
Sears	340.530430	Ithaca	49SS	Sears 200	273.2280	Winchester	1200
Sears	35A	Stevens	66A	Sears 200	273.4310	Winchester	1200
Sears	36	Marlin	80	Sears 200	273.4320	Winchester	1200
Sears	375	Mossberg	45B	Sears 200	273.4340	Winchester	1200
Sears	377	Mossberg	42C	Sears 200	273,4350	Winchester	1200
Sears	381	Mossberg	46B	Sears 200	273.4410	Winchester	1200
Sears	382	Mossberg	46B	Sears 200	273.4420	Winchester	1200
Sears	384	Mossberg	45A	Sears 200	273.4450	Winchester	1200
Sears	385	Mossberg	45B	Seem 200	273.514010	Winchester	1200
Sears	387	Mossberg	42C	Sears 200	273.614010	Winchester	1200
Sears	388	Mossberg	42C	Sears 200	273.514011	Winchester	1200
Sears	389	Mossberg	42A OR 26C	Sears 200	273.514020	Winchester	1200
Sears	390	Mossberg	26C	Seem 200	273.514040	Winchester	1200
Sears	3T	Winchester	190	Sears 200	273.514050	Winchester	1200
Sears	41	Marlin	101	Sears 200	273.514051	Winchester	1200
Sears	41 DLA	Marlin	122	Sears 200	273.514210	Winchester	1200
Sears	42	Marlin	80	Sears 200	273.514220	Winchester	1200
Sears	42DL	Marlin	80	Sears 200	273,514250	Winchester	1200
Sears	42DLM	Marlin	980	Sears 200	273.514251	Winchester	1200
Sears	43	Marlin	81	Sears 200	273.514810	Winchester	1200
Sears	43DL	Marlin	81	Sears 200	273.614820	Winchester	1200
Sears	44DL	Marlin	57	Sears 200	273.514830	Winchester	1200
Sears	44DLM	Marlin	57M	Sears 200	273.514840	Winchester	1200
Sears	45	Marlin	336C	Sears 200	273.515010	Winchester	1200
Sears	46	Marlin	56	Sears 200	273.515020	Winchester	1200
Sears	46DL	Marlin	56	Sears 200	273.515050	Winchester	1200
Sears	4980	Stevens	94-2 W/PAD	Sears 200	273.515051	Winchester	1200
Sears	49.11830/30	Savage	99 A	Sears 200	273.515080	Winchester	1200
Sears	53	Winchester	70	Sears 200	273.515090	Winchester	1200
Sears	54	Winchester	94	Sears 200	273.515220	Winchester	1200
Sears	583.1	High Standard	N/A	Sears 200	273.515221	Winchester	1200
Sears	583,126	Sako	L46	Sears 200	273.515250	Winchester	1200
Sears	583.13	High Standard	N/A	Sears 200	273.515251	Winchester	1200
Sears	583.14	H & R	120	Sears 200	273.515280	Winchester	1200
Sears	583.15	H&R	121	Sears 200	273.515290	Winchester	1200
Sears	583.16	High Standard	10	Sears 200	273.515410	Winchester	1200
Sears	583.17	High Standard	N/A	Sears 200	273.515420	Winchester	1200
Sears	583.18	H & R	120	Sears 200	273.515470	Winchester	1200
Sears	583.2	H & R	M120	Sears 200	273.515710	Winchester	1200
Sears	583.20	High Standard	Flight King	Sears 200	273.515720	Winchester	1200
Sears	583.2085-87	High Standard	20ga pump	Sears 200	273.515920	Winchester	1200
Sears	583.21	H&R	M120	Sears 200	273.5310	Winchester	1200
Sears	583.25	H&R	M121	Sears 200	273.5350	Winchester	1200
Sears	583.3	H&R	M121	Sears 2T	273.27530	Winchester	141
Sears	583.4	High Standard	10	Sears 300	273.1310	Winchester	1400
Sears	583.7	High Standard	10	Sears 300	273.1320	Winchester	1400
Sears	583.91	H & R	121	Sears 300	273.1350	Winchester	1400
Sears	6C (Canada)	Winchester	Cooy 64,64B	Sears 300	273.21550	Winchester	1400
Sears	6C(American)	Winchester	490	Sears 300	273.2500	Winchester	1400
Sears	66	High Standard	66	Sears 300	273.2540	Winchester	1400
Sears	73	Savage	73	Sears 300	273.32060	Winchester	1400
Sears	870.528140	Voere	Clip .22	Sears 300	273.32070	Winchester	1400
Sears	92	Stevens	39	Sears 300	273.521050	Winchester	1400
Sears	93	Stevens	38	Sears 300	273.521051	Winchester	1400
Sears	94	Stevens	237	Sears 300	273.521080	Winchester	1400
Sears	95	Stevens	238	Sears 300	273.521090	Winchester	1400

House Brand	Model No.	Orig. Mfgr.	Orig. Model
Sears 300	273.521160	Winchester	1400
Sears 300	273.521161	Winchester	1400
Sears 300	273.521250	Winchester	1400
Sears 300	273.521251	Winchester	1400
Sears 300	273.521260	Winchester	1400
Sears 300	273.521280	Winchester	1400
Sears 300	273.521290	Winchester	1400
Sears 300	273.521580	Winchester	1400
Sears 300	273.521680	Winchester	1400
Sears 300	273.521710	Winchester	1400
Sears 300	273.521770	Winchester	1400
Sears 300	273.521780	Winchester	1400
Sears 300	273.523251	Winchester	1400
Sears 300	273.52151	Winchester	1400
Sears 3T-A	273.2390	Winchester	190-290
Sears 3T-A	273.2400	Winchester	190-290
Sears 3T-A	273.528110	Winchester	190-290
Sears 3T-A	273.528111	Winchester	190-290
Sears 4T	273.2360	Winchester	270
Sears 53A	273.532780	Winchester	70A
Sears 54	273.2120	Winchester	NM 94
Sears 54	273.532140	Winchester	NM 94
Sears 54	273.53419	Winchester	NM 94
Sears 54	273.810	Winchester	NM 94
Sears 54	273.811	Winchester	NM 94
Sears 6C	273.28130	Winchester	490
Sears 6C	273.528131	Winchester	490
Sears 6C	273.528132	Winchester	490
Sears MI	273.27010	Winchester	121
Sears M5,M-5T	273.2340	Winchester	150-250
Sears M5,M-5T	273.2341	Winchester	150-250
Sears M5,M-5T	273.2350	Winchester	150-250
Sears M5,M-5T	273.2351	Winchester	150-250
Sears T.W. 73	273.532730	Winchester	670 Mag.
Sears T.W. 73	23.31020	Winchester	New Mod 70
Sears T.W. 73	273.1390	Winchester	MN 30-06
Sears T.W. 73	273.1400	Winchester	MN 70 (.270)
Sears T.W. 73	273.1830	Winchester	New Mod 70
Sears T.W. 73	273.1840	Winchester	New Mod 70
Sears T.W. 73	273.1850	Winchester	New Mod 70
Sears T.W. 73	273.1860	Winchester	New Mod 70
Sears T.W. 73	273.1870	Winchester	New Mod 70
Sears T.W. 73	273.31010	Winchester	New Mod 70
Sears T.W. 73	273.31060	Winchester	New Mod 70
Sears T.W. 73	273.32020	Winchester	New Mod 70
Sears T.W. 73	273.32030	Winchester	New Mod 70
Sears T.W. 73	273.32040	Winchester	New Mod 70
Sears T.W. 73	273.532061	Winchester	New Mod 70
Sears T.W. 73	273.532071	Winchester	New Mod 70
Sears T.W. 73	273.532081	Winchester	New Mod 70
Sears T.W. 73	273.53403	Winchester	New Mod 70
Sears T.W. 73	273.53406	Winchester	New Mod 70
Sears T.W. 73	273.53409	Winchester	New Mod 70
Sears T.W. 73	273.32010	Winchester	Now Mod 70
Ted Williams	340.530430	Ithaca	49SS
Shapleigh's	KING NITRO	Savage	15
Simmons	411	Savage	540DL
Simmons	411	Savage	Fox BDE 20ga
Simmons	411 E	Savage	540 BDE
Simmons	411 E	Savage	Fox BDE 20ga
Talo	12DL	Stevens	120
Talo	176 VR	Springfield	67 VR
Talo	176DL	Springfield	67
Western Auto, Revelation			
Revelation	300	Savage	30 D,E,F

House Brand	Model No.	Orig. Mfgr.	Orig. Model
Revelation	394 Series P	Stevens	94P
Revelation	76	High Standard	Double Nine
Revelation	R310	Mossberg	500AB
Western Auto	100	Mossberg	321
Western Auto	101Y	Savage	73Y
Western Auto	101.1701	Savage	540BS
Western Auto	101.171	Savage	540BD
Western Auto	101.2830	Savage	73
Western Auto	101.52772	Savage	65M
Western Auto	101.535D	Savage	18
Western Auto	101.53500	Savage	18D
Western Auto	101.53521	Savage	340
Western Auto	101.5380	Savage	18AC
Western Auto	101.5380D	Savage	18DAC
Western Auto	101.5410	Savage	18DS,S
Western Auto	103	Savage	89
Western Auto	103.13	Marlin	81
Western Auto	103.16	Marlin	80
Western Auto	103.18	Marlin	80
Western Auto	103.181	Marlin	101
Western Auto	103.19780	Marlin	101
Western Auto	103.19790	Marlin	80
Western Auto	103.19800	Marlin	80
Western Auto	103.1981	Marlin	81
Western Auto	103.1982	Marlin	81DL
Western Auto	103.19820	Marlin	81
Western Auto	103.19840	Marlin	56
Western Auto	103.19880	Marlin	57
Western Auto	103.19890	Marlin	57M
Western Auto	103.1997	Marlin	101
Western Auto	103.2	Marlin	80
Western Auto	103.228	Marlin	80
Western Auto	103.229	Marlin	81
Western Auto	103.273	Marlin	980
Western Auto	103.274	Marlin	122
Western Auto	103.2751	Marlin	122
Western Auto	103.2840	Marlin	80
Western Auto	103.2850	Marlin	81
Western Auto	103.2870	Marlin	56
Western Auto	103.360	Marlin	90
Western Auto	103.450	Marlin	336
Western Auto	103.451	Marlin	336
Western Auto	103.720	Marlin	59
Western Auto	103.740	Marlin	59
Western Auto	105-2060	Marlin	780
Western Auto	105-2060	Marlin	80
Western Auto	107	Mossberg	640K
Western Auto	107A	Mossberg	640
Western Auto	110-2140	Marlin	81
Western Auto	110-2140	Marlin	781
Western Auto	115	Savage	46
Western Auto	115-2277	Marlin	57
Western Auto	116-2276	Marlin	57M
Western Auto	117	Mossberg	402
Western Auto	120-2220	Marlin	99
Western Auto	125	Mossberg	353
Western Auto	135	Savage	187
Western Auto	135	Springfield	187A
Western Auto	150m	Marlin	49
Western Auto	150-2225	Marlin	49
Western Auto	160	Springfield	187A
Western Auto	160	Savage	80
Western Auto	200-2280	Marlin	39A
Western Auto	200-2282	Marlin	39A
Western Auto	200-2550	Marlin	336
Western Auto	200-2554	Marlin	336(.44MAG)
Western Auto	205	Mossberg	472PCA
Western Auto	210A	Mossberg	810AH

House Brand	Model No.	Orig. Mfgr.	Orig. Model
Western Auto	220A	Mossberg	800A
Western Auto	220AD	Mossberg	800AD
Western Auto	220B	Mossberg	800B
Western Auto	220BD	Mossberg	800BD
Western Auto	220C	Mossberg	800C
Western Auto	220CD	Mossberg	800CD
Western Auto	225	Savage	340
Western Auto	2280	Marlin	39A
Western Auto	2282	Marlin	39A Mountie
Western Auto	230	Savage	340
Western Auto	250	Savage	110E
Western Auto	250A	Savage	110D
Western Auto	250D	Savage	110
Western Auto	260	Savage	170
Western Auto	260	Springfield	174
Western Auto	300	Springfield	67
Western Auto	300	Stevens	30
Western Auto	300A	Savage	30AC
Western Auto	300F	Stevens	77C
Western Auto	300H	Savage	30,HAC
Western Auto	300-300AC	Springfield	67
Western Auto	310	Mossberg	500
Western Auto	310A	Mossberg	500A
Western Auto	310AB	Mossberg	500AB
Western Auto	310B	Mossberg	500B
Western Auto	310C	Mossberg	500C
Western Auto	310E	Mossberg	500E
Western Auto	312	Mossberg	395
Western Auto	312AK	Mossberg	395K
Western Auto	312SB	Mossberg	395T
Western Auto	316	Mossberg	390
Western Auto	316BB	Mossberg	390T
Western Auto	316BK	Mossberg	390K
Western Auto	325B	Mossberg	385T
Western Auto	325BK	Mossberg	385K
Western Auto	330	Mossberg	183 & 183K
Western Auto	330B	Mossberg	183T
Western Auto	335-3725	Marlin	59
Western Auto	336	Springfield	951
Western Auto	350	Stevens	94
Western Auto	350A	Savage	94D
Western Auto	350M	Stevens	94
Western Auto	355	Stevens	947
Western Auto	355Y	Savage	94Y
Western Auto	355YE	Springfield	947YE
Western Auto	356Y	Springfield	944Y
Western Auto	360	Savage	540
Western Auto	360	Savage	FOX mod B
Western Auto	360C	Savage	540C
Western Auto	400	Stevens	745
Western Auto	400C	Savage	745C
Western Auto	420	High Standard	Supmatic C-011
Western Auto	425	High Standard	Supmatic C-120
Western Auto	460	Springfield	511
Western Auto	SD52A	Stevens	311
West Point	45	Marlin	60

Wards, Western Field, and Hawthorne

House Brand	Model No.	Orig. Mfgr.	Orig. Model
Hawthorne	110	Unknown	S shot SG
Hawthorne	580 EJN	Colt	Colteer/bolt
Hawthorne	814 EJN	Colt	Colteer/SS
Hawthorne	820B	Mossberg	340
Hawthorne	880	Colt	Colteer/semi
Hawthorne	880 EJN	Colt	Colteer/bolt
Wards	24M 419A	Mossberg	9
Wards	472	Noble	50
Wards	850	Mossberg	353
Wards Triumph	52	Stevens	315

House Brand	Model No.	Orig. Mfgr.	Orig. Model
Western Field	04M-489A	Mossberg	50
Western Field	04M-218A	Mossberg	73C
Western Field	04M-2117A	Mossberg	9
Western Field	04M-217A	Mossberg	75C
Western Field	04M-214A	Mossberg	85C
Western Field	04M-216A	Mossberg	83C
Western Field	I	Mossberg	RF-1
Western Field	10-SD247A	Stevens	94B (Tenite)
Western Field	14	Savage	39A
Western Field	14	Savage	59A
Western Field	14M-215A	Mossberg	85
Western Field	14M-497B	Mossberg	M42
Western Field	14M-488A	Mossberg	50
Western Field	15	Mossberg	80
Western Field	150	Mossberg	183K
Western Field	151X	Kessler	N/A
Western Field	155	Mossberg	173
Western Field	15A	Mossberg	83
Western Field	16	Mossberg	85
Western Field	160	Mossberg	385K
Western Field	16A	Mossberg	85
Western Field	17	Mossberg	73
Western Field	170	Mossberg	395K
Western Field	172	Mossberg	395K
Western Field	173	Mosaberg	395
Western Field	175	Mossberg	385K
Western Field	17A	Mossberg	73
Western Field	I8	Mossberg	75
Western Field	20	Mossberg	9R
Western Field	215A	Mossberg	85
Western Field	24M,488A	Mossberg	51
Western Field	30	Stevens	520
Western Field	31A	Mossberg	44
Western Field	31A	Mossberg	40
Western Field	32	Mossberg	21
Western Field	32	Mossberg	20
Western Field	33	Marlin	336
Western Field	35A	Mossberg	30
Western Field	36	Stevens	521
Western Field	36	Mossberg	10
Western Field	36B	Mossberg	25A
Western Field	36B	Mossberg	10
Western Field	36C	Mossberg	25A
Western Field	360	Mossberg	26C
Western Field	37	Mossberg	30
Western Field	39	Mossberg	25
Western Field	390A	Mossberg	26C
Western Field	40,D	Mossberg	44
Western Field	40	Marlin	101
Western Field	40N	Noble	40NA
Western Field	40M-215A	Mossberg	185
Western Field	41	Mossberg	45
Western Field	45	Marlin	989M2
Western Field	45	Mossberg	42
Western Field	45B	Mossberg	26C
Western Field	45C	Mossberg	25A
Western Field	46	Mossberg	42
Western Field	466	Mossberg	RA1
Western Field	469	Mossberg	RA1-Kit
Western Field	46A	Mossberg	42
Western Field	46C	Moseborg	42A
Western Field	46D	Mossberg	42C
Western Field	47	Mossberg	45A
Western Field	472	Noble	50
Western Field	47A,L	Mossberg	45A
Western Field	48	Mossberg	45A
Western Field	488A	Mossberg	51
Western Field	48A	Mossberg	45B
Western Field	48A	Mossberg	46MLB

House Brand	Model No.	Orig. Mfgr.	Orig. Model
Western Field	5-4	Mossberg	8-M4
Western Field	50	Glenfield	60
Western Field	502-26FR	Mossberg	500
Western Field	505	Mossberg	500
Western Field	509	Mossberg	500
Western Field	524	Mossberg	500
Western Field	534	Mossberg	500
Western Field	536	Mossberg	500
Western Field	539	Mossberg	500
Western Field	550A	Mossberg	500A
Western Field	550AS	Mossberg	500AB
Western Field	550B	Mossberg	500B
Western Field	550C	Mossberg	500B
Western Field	550E	Mossberg	500E
Western Field	550E	Mossberg	500E
Western Field	60	Savage	620A
Western Field	600ERI 12 GA	Remington	SPT 58
Western Field	60SB	Savage	620A
Western Field	679	Mossberg	472
Western Field	710	Savage	110
Western Field	72	Noble	50
Western Field	72C	Mossberg	472
Western Field	730	Mossberg	8l0AH
Western Field	732	Mossberg	810AH
Western Field	734	Mossberg	810A
Western Field	740	Marlin	336
Western Field	765	Mossberg	810A
Western Field	766	Mossberg	810B
Western Field	767	Mossberg	800A
Western Field	768	Mossberg	800A
Western Field	771	Mossberg	472BA
Western Field	772	Mossberg	472PCA
Western Field	775	Mossberg	800AD
Western Field	776	Mossberg	800BD
Western Field	778	Mossberg	472BAS
Western Field	780	Mossberg	800A
Western Field	782	Mossberg	800B
Western Field	79	Mossberg	472 PRA
Western Field	50	Savage	29
Western Field	807A ECH	Colt	Colteer S.S.
Western Field	808	Savage	87
Western Field	808C	Savage	87J
Western Field	815	Mossberg	321
Western Field	820B	Mossberg	340
Western Field	822	Mossberg	640K
Western Field	828	Mossberg	353
Western Field	830	Mossberg	340K
Western Field	832	Mossberg	341
Western Field	836	Savage	187N
Western Field	840	Mossberg	640
Western Field	842	Mossberg	346K
Western Field	846	Mossberg	351C
Western Field	850 855	Mossberg	353
Western Field	852	Mossberg	341
Western Field	865	Mossberg	402
Western Field	880	Colt	Colteer Semi.
Western Field	894	Mossberg	430-432
Western Field	895	Mossberg	402
Western Field	9-2 3/4	Mossberg	9-2 1/2
Western Field	93M	Mossberg	26C
Western Field	93M-213A	Mossberg	75B
Western Field	93M-2116A	Mossberg	9
Western Field	93M-212A	Mossberg	738
Western Field	93M-211A	Mossberg	83B
Western Field	93M-210A	Mossberg	85B
Western Field	93M-497A	Mossberg	42C
Western Field	93M-491A	Mossberg	465
Western Field	93M-495A	Mossberg	45B
Western Field	EMN 171	Marlin	50
Western Field	EMN 176	Marlin	55
Western Field	M-SD57	Stevens	M87
Western Field	M025	Savage	520A
Western Field	M040 0/U	Marlin	90
Western Field	M040N	Stevens	820
Western Field	M051	Stevens	515
Western Field	M059	Stevens	M87
Western Field	M060	Stevens	620
Western Field	M080	Savage	29 & 75
Western Field	M087	Stevens	M87
Western Field	M10	Stevens	94 Short tang
Western Field	M150	Mossberg	183T
Western Field	M155	Mossberg	183D
Western Field	M160	Mossberg	385T
Western Field	M170	Mossberg	395S
Western Field	M172	Mossberg	395K
Western Field	M175	Mossberg	385K
Western Field	M23 NH402A	Stevens	820
Western Field	M35	Savage	520 POLY
Western Field	M36	Savage	521
Western Field	M60	Savage	620 DELUX
Western Field	M61	Savage	621 DELUX
Western Field	M72	Mossberg	472 PRA
Western Field	M734	Mossberg	810BH
Western Field	M771	Moseberg	472SBA
Western Field	M772	Mossberg	472PCA
Western Field	M7 75	Mossberg	800AD
Western Field	M776	Mossberg	800BD
Western Field	M778	Mossberg	472BAS
Western Field	M780	Mossberg	800A
Western Field	M782	Mossberg	800B
Western Field	M808.C	Stevens	87,C,J
Western Field	M808N	Stevens	87N
Western Field	M80A	Savage	M29-D1
Western Field	M815	Mossberg	320
Western Field	M822	Mossberg	640K
Western Field	M85	Stevens	85
Western Field	M-SD57	Stevens	87
Western Field	SS 94B	Stevens	94C
Western Field	SB033	Savage	520 W/POLY
Western Field	SB066	Savage	621 DELX POLY
Western Field	SB067	Savage	621 DELX COMP
Western Field	S5112C	Savage	540C
Western Field	SB115	Savage	115
Western Field	SB300,C	Stevens	311,C
Western Field	SB30A	Savage	520
Western Field	SB311C	Savage	311C
Western Field	SB312	Savage	540D
Western Field	SB312	Savage-Fox	BDL
Western Field	SB33	Savage	520 POLY
Western Field	SB60A	Savage	620 DELUX
Western Field	SB61A	Savage	621 DELUX
Western Field	SB620A	Stevens	620A
Western Field	SB66	Savage	621 DELX POLY
Western Field	SB712	Savage	840
Western Field	SB80A	Savage	29-DI
Western Field	SB85TA	Stevens	85
Western Field	SB87,TA	Stevens	M87
Western Field	XNH 175	Marlin	55
Western Field	XNH 565	Noble	60-66
Widgeon	SA 650	Marlin	55 12 GA

SERIALIZATION INDEX

AGUIRRE Y ARANZABAL (AYA)
SERIALIZATION 1945 to 1994 2436
BOSS & CO., LTD. SERIALIZATION 2436
BROWNING SERIALIZATION PRE-1975 2436
A-5 (AUTOMATIC 5) SHOTGUN -12 ga. 2436
A-5 (AUTOMATIC 5) SHOTGUN -16 ga. 2437
A-5 SHOTGUN - 20 ga. 2437
SUPERPOSED MODEL - O & U - 12 ga. 2438
SUPERPOSED MODEL - O & U - 20 ga. 2438
SUPERPOSED MODEL - O & U - 28 ga. & .410 bore 2438
LIEGE O & U - Approximately 10,000 produced 2438
DOUBLE AUTOMATIC SHOTGUN 2438
HI-POWER (9mm) PISTOL 2439
BROWNING .380 ACP CAL. 2439
.25 ACP CAL. BABY BROWNING 2439
.22 CAL. (Nomad-Challenger-Medalist) 2439
BOLT ACTION RIFLES (Safari, Medallion, & Olympian Models). 2439
B.A.R. 2439
.22 AUTO RIFLE (Grades I, II, and III) 2439
T-BOLT RIFLE (T1 and T2) 2440
BROWNING SERIALIZATION
1975 TO CURRENT 2440
BROWNING MODEL CONFIGURATION CODES .. 2440
Shotguns O/U 2440
Superposed Grade I 2440
Superposed Pigeon Grade 2440
Superposed Pointer Grade 2440
Superposed Diana Grade 2440
Superposed Midas Grade 2440
Citori Grade I 2440
Citori Grade III 2440
Citori Grade VI 2441
Citori Golden Clays 2441
Citori Gran Lightning 2441
Shotguns Semi-Auto 2441
Auto 5 2441
A-500 2441
Gold 2441
Shotguns Slide Action 2441
BPS 2441
Model 42 Limited Edition 410 Bore 2441
Shotguns Side by Side 2441
B-SS 2441
Rifles 2441
Pistols 1975-1998 2441
Pistols 1999-Current 2441
E.J. CHURCHILL GUNMAKERS SER. 2442
COLT'S FIREARMS SERIALIZATION 2442
MODEL 1849 POCKET REVOLVER 2442
MODEL 1849 POCKET REVOLVER - LONDON BARREL ADDRESS 2442
MODEL 1851 NAVY 2442
MODEL 1851 NAVY - LONDON BARREL ADDRESS 2442
MODEL 1860 ARMY 2442
MODEL 1861 NAVY 2442
MODEL 1862 POLICE 2443
MODEL 1873 - SINGLE ACTION ARMY 2443
(SAA) - PRE-WAR 2443
1ST GENERATION COLT SINGLE ACTION ARMY - CALIBER
BREAKDOWN 2443
COLT SINGLE ACTION ARMY – POST-WAR PRODUCTION 2444
NEW FRONTIER SINGLE ACTION ARMY 2444
MODEL 1911 AND 1911A1 – Commercial
production Capital "C" prefix - .45 cal. 2444
MODEL 1911 AND 1911A1 MILITARY PRODUCTION 2445
COLT SINGLE-ACTION MODEL NUMBERS 2445
STANDARD MODEL P REVOLVER CODES 2446
NEW FRONTIER MODEL 2446
SHERIFF'S MODELS 2447
REVOLVERS WITH FULL BLUE FRAMES 2447
FULL BLUE NEW FRONTIERS 2447
MISCELLANEOUS MODEL NUMBERS 2447
BLACK POWDER MODEL P REVOLVERS 2447
MODEL 1877 LIGHTNING & THUNDERER DA 2447
MODEL 1878 SxS HAMMER SHOTGUN 2448
MODEL 1883 SxS HAMMERLESS SHOTGUN 2448
LIGHTNING SLIDE ACTION - SMALL FRAME 2448
LIGHTNING SLIDE ACTION - MEDIUM FRAME 2448
LIGHTNING SLIDE ACTION - LARGE FRAME 2448
AR-15 - SPORTER MODELS 2448
COLT BLACKPOWDER 2ND GENERATION
SERIALIZATION 2448
MODEL1851 NAVY 2448
MODEL 1851 NAVY, R. E. LEE 2448
1851 NAVY, U. S. GRANT 2448
MODEL 1851 GRANT-LEE PAIR 2448
3rd MODEL DRAGOON 2448
MODEL 1851 NAVY 2448
MODEL 1860 ARMY 2448
1861 NAVY 2449
1862 POCKET NAVY 2449
1862 POCKET POLICE 2449
1847 WALKER 2449
1st MODEL DRAGOON 2449
2nd MODEL DRAGOON 2449
3rd MODEL DRAGOON 2449
BABY DRAGOON 2449
1860 ARMY 2449
HERITAGE WALKER 2449
JOHN DICKSON & SON SERIALIZATION 2449
A.H. FOX SERIALIZATION 2449
GRADE A-F 12 GAUGE 2449
GRADE A-F 16 GAUGE 2449
GRADE A-F 20 GAUGE 2450
STERLINGWORTH 12 GAUGE 2450
STERLINGWORTH 16 GA. 2450
STERLINGWORTH 20 GAUGE 2450
SINGLE BARREL TRAP - GRADE J, K, L, M 2451
GERMAN EARLY DATE CODES 2451
GERMAN MODERN DATE CODES 2451
STEPHEN GRANT SERIALIZATION 2451
GREAT WESTERN ARMS CO. PRODUCTION
PERCENTAGES AND NUMBERS 2451
W. W. GREENER SERIALIZATION 2452

HARRINGTON & RICHARDSON SERIALIZATION 1940 - 1982 ..... **2452**
HIGH STANDARD SERIALIZATION **2452**
HOLLAND & HOLLAND SERIALIZATION **2453**
ITALIAN YEAR OF MFG. DATE CODES **2455**
ITHACA GUN CO. SERIALIZATION **2456**
CHARLES LANCASTER SERIALIZATION **2456**
JOSEPH LANG SERIALIZATION **2457**
MARLIN FIREARMS COMPANY SERIALIZATION **2457**
MAUSER BROOMHANDLES SERIALIZATION 1896 - late 1930 ..... **2457**
PARKER BROTHERS SHOTGUNS SERIALIZATION 1866 - 1942 ..... **2458**
PIOTTI SERIALIZATION **2459**
JAMES PURDEY & SONS, LTD. SERIALIZATION **2459**
REMINGTON DATE CODE DATA & SxS SHOTGUN SERIALIZATION **2460**
E. REMINGTON & SONS WHITMORE MODELS 2461
E. REMINGTON & SONS MODELS 1882, 1883, 1885 AND 1887 2461
REMINGTON ARMS COMPANY MODEL 1889 TOTAL Mfg. 134200 2461
REMINGTON ARMS COMPANY MODEL 1900 TOTAL Mfg. 98508 2462
REMINGTON ARMS COMPANY MODEL 1894 TOTAL Mfg. 41194 2462
REMINGTON ARMS COMPANY MODEL 1894 REM. SPCL. 2462
SAVAGE/STEVENS PRODUCTION DATA **2462**
SAVAGE ARMS CO. 2462
J. STEVENS ARMS CO. 2462
SAVAGE MODEL NINETY-NINE SERIALIZATION 2463
L.C. SMITH SERIALIZATION **2463**
L.C. Smith (Manufactured by Hunter Arms Co. 1890-1918) 2463
Hammer Shotguns 2463
Hammerless Shotguns 2464
1918-1950 (These serial numbers include all types of L.C. Smith, Fulton and Hunter Shotguns) 2464
SMITH & WESSON PERFORMANCE CENTER PRODUCT CODE INFO. **2465**
S & W PERFORMANCE CENTER PRODUCT CODES 2465
S & W ABBREVIATIONS 2467
SPANISH YEAR OF MFG. DATE CODES **2468**
STURM, RUGER & CO., INC. **2468**
THOMPSON/CENTER ARMS CO., INC. **2469**
WINCHESTER RIFLES SERIALIZATION **2469**
MODEL 1866 2469
MODEL 1873 2469
MODEL 1873, cont. 2470
MODEL 1876 2470
MODEL 1885 SINGLE SHOT 2470
MODEL 1886 2470
MODEL 1890 2471
MODEL 1890 2471
MODEL 1892 2471
MODEL 1894 2471
Model 1894 facts 2472
MODEL 9422 2472
MODEL 1895 2473
MODEL 1903 2473
MODEL 1905 2473
MODEL 1906 2473
MODEL 1907 2474
MODEL 1910 2474
MODEL 1911 S.L. 2474
MODEL 52 2474
MODEL 53 2475
MODEL 54 2475
MODEL 55 2475
MODEL 61 2475
MODEL 62 2476
MODEL 63 2476
MODEL 70 2476
MODEL 70 CLASSIC 2477
MODEL 71 2477
MODEL 74 2477
MODEL 88 2477
MODEL 100 2477
WINCHESTER RIFLE AND SHOTGUN SERIAL **2477**
NUMBER PREFIXES **2477**
POST-1968 ..... **2477**
WINCHESTER SHOTGUNS **2478**
MODEL 1887 2478
Model 1893 2478
Model 1897 2478
MODEL 1897 TRENCH/RIOT SHOTGUN 2478
MODEL 1901 2479
MODEL 1911 2479
MODEL 12 2479
MODEL 12, cont. 2479
MODEL 12 TRENCH/RIOT SHOTGUN 2479
Blue Finish 2479
Parkerized Finish 2479
NEW STYLE M/12 2480
MODELS 120/1200/1300 2480
MODEL 24 2480
MODEL 36 2480
MODEL 37 2480
MODEL 40 2480
MODEL 42 2480
MODEL 50 2480
WINCHESTER MODEL 101 ..... **2480**
SERIALIZATION **2480**
12 gauge 2480
MODEL 101, 20 gauge. 2482
MODEL 101, 28 ga. & .410 bore 2482
MODEL 101, 28 ga. & .410 bore 2482

SERIALIZATION

This section has once again been expanded to help you identify the year of manufacture on many popular manufacturers and trademarks. To use these tables, compare your serial number(s) to the correct manufacturer and model, and ascertain which bracket it falls into based on the year of manufacture and corresponding serial number. In several cases, caliber rarity can also be determined. Date codes are now also provided on some manufacturers and countries to allow you to determine the year of manufacture by the date code on the barrel or frame/receiver.

The publisher wishes to thank Galazan's and Dixie Gun Works for providing a portion of this serialization information.

AGUIRRE Y ARANZABAL (AYA) SERIALIZATION 1945 to 1994

From 1945 to 1994 AYA had manufactured over 600,000 shotguns of all models and grades with all serial numbers assigned in chronological order. For 1927-1944 year of manufacture date codes, see "Spanish Year Of MFG. Date Codes" in this section..

YEARS	SER. # START	SER. # END
1945-1948	0001	19999
1949-1954	20000	71999
1955-1959	72000	115286
1960-1965	115287	222508
1966-1971	222509	378548
1972-1977	378549	481401
1978-1983	481402	576551
1984-1987	576553	599999
1988-1993	600000	602422
1994	602423	602642

AYA 1995-2006

Beginning 1995 the Spanish proof house implemented a new serial number system. The new system consists of four sets of digits separated by a hyphen. The first set is the manufacturers code, the second designates the type of firearm, the third set is the firearms chronological number, the fourth set shows the year of mfg.

YEAR	SER. # START	SER. # END
1995	16-03-001-95	16-03-800-95
1996	16-03-001-96	16-03-755-96
1997	16-03-001-97	16-03-642-97
1998	16-03-001-98	16-03-677-98
1999	16-03-001-99	16-03-719-99
2000	16-03-001-00	16-03-758-00
2001	16-03-001-01	16-03-645-01
2002	16-03-001-02	16-03-645-02
2003	16-03-001-03	16-03-781-03
2004	16-03-001-04	16-03-703-04
2005	16-03-001-05	16-03-652-05
2006	16-03-001-06	16-03-750-06

BOSS & CO., LTD. SERIALIZATION

YEAR STARTING	SER. # END
1830	680
1850	1400
1857	1600
1900	4700
1920	6618
1930	7730
1945	8711
1951	8912
1953	8920

BOSS & CO., LTD. SERIALIZATION, cont.

YEAR STARTING	SER. # END
1963	9219
1970	9559

BROWNING SERIALIZATION PRE-1975 SERIALIZATION

Since 1968-1969 was a transition period in Browning serialization, firearms may be serialized with either 1968 or 1969 style markings. Browning firearms historical letters by model and serial number are available for $39.95 through Browning Customer Service at 800-333-3288.

A-5 (AUTOMATIC 5) SHOTGUN -12 ga.

YEAR	SER. # START	SER. # END
1903	1	4121
1904	4122	15300
1905	15301	19920
1906	19921	22320
1907	22321	26970
1908	26971	30446
1909	30447	33431
1910	33432	35630
1911	35631	35925
1912	35926	38988
1913	38989	44250
1914	44251	47298
1915-1918	No Production	
1919	47719	47950
1920	47299	47718
1921	48951	53500
1922	53501	58150
1923	58151	62600
1924	62601	69300
1925	69301	79150
1926	79151	88000
1927	88001	106250
1928	106251	127650
1929	127651	154500
1930	154501	177100
1931	177101	182300
1932	182301	182788
1933	182789	183152
1934	183153	185560
1935	185561	191604
1936	191605	194535
1937	194536	199200
1938	199201	208400
1939	208401	218808
1940	218809	224596
1941-1943	No Production	
1944	Production limited to servicemen	
1945	Production limited to servicemen	
1946	228729	240950

A-5 (AUTOMATIC 5) SHOTGUN -12 ga., cont.

YEAR	SER. # START	SER. # END
1947	240951	256500
1948	256501	274100
1949	274101	288550
1950	288551	316750
1951	316751	352050
1952	352051	387499
1953	387500	437400
1954	437401	447750
1955	447751	454700
1956	454701	459900
1957	459901	463700

In 1953 Browning added an alpha prefix to the serial number to differentiate between Lightweight and Standardweight guns.

YEAR	STD.12	LT.WT. 12
1953	H1-H6600	L1-L4450
1954	H6601-H39700	L4451-L45250
1955	H39701-H83450	L45251-L83600
1956	H83451-H100000	L83601-L99877
1956	M1-M35250	G1-G35450
1957	M35251-M86300	G35451-G85950
1958	M86301-M99999	G85951-G99663

1958-1976 Ser. No. sequence changed to include a one or two digit numeral followed by an alpha character.

YEAR	STD. WT.	LT. WT.	MAGNUM
1958	8M	8G	8V
1959	9M	9G	9V
1960	0M	0G	0V
1961	1M	1G	1V
1962	2M	2G	2V
1963	3M	3G	3V
1965	5M	5G	5V
1966	6M	6G	6V
1964	4M	4G	4V
1967	7M	7G	7V
1968	8M	8G	8V
1969	69M	69G	69V
1970	Disc.	70G	70V
1971	Disc.	71G	71V
1972	Disc.	72G	72V
1973	Disc.	73G	73V
1974	Disc.	74G	74V
1975	Disc.	75G	75V
1976	Disc.	76G	76V

A-5 (AUTOMATIC 5) SHOTGUN -16 ga.

YEAR	SER. # START	SER. # END
1909	1	3200
1910-1912	3201	15000
1913	15001	19000
1914-1918	No Production	
1919	19671	20500
1920	20501	22237
1921	22238	24050
1922	24051	26000
1923	26001	28400
1924	28401	35650
1925	35651	40010
1926	40011	51600
1927	51599	57900
1928	57901	65100
1929	65101	82750
1930	82751	90500
1931	90501	94000

A-5 (AUTOMATIC 5) SHOTGUN -16 ga., cont.

YEAR	SER. # START	SER. # END
1932	94001	96072
1933	96073	96143
1934	96144	99500
1 Year	Ser. # Start	Ser. # End
935	99501	103500
1936	103501	105850
1937	105851	111000
1938	111001	118200
1939	118201	126123
1940	126123	126175
1941-1943	No Production	
1944	Production limited to servicemen	
1945	Production limited to servicemen	
1946	128117	128646
1947	128647	130616
1947	X1001	X13666
1948	X13667	X23501
1949	X23502	X34600
1950	X34601	X43700
1951	X43701	X59400
1952	X59401	X77700
1953	X77701	X99999

In 1953 Browning changed the Ser. No. alphabetic character to differentiate between Lightweight (Sweet 16) & Standard weight guns.

YEAR	STD.16	SWEET 16
1953	R1-R3100	S1-S3700
1954	R3100-R20800	S3701-S24850
1955	R20801-R48750	S24851-S49350
1956	R48751-R74700	S49350-S72300
1957	R74701-R99999	S72301-S99908

1957-58 Prefix "T" for Standardweight and Prefix "A" for Sweet 16 numbers mixed, but range from 1-10900.
1958-1976 Ser. No. sequence changed to include a one or two digit numeral followed by an alpha character.

YEAR	STD.16	SWEET 16
1958	8R	8S
1959	9R	9S
1960	0R	0S
1961	1R	1S
1962	2R	2S
1963	3R	3S
1964	Disc.	4S
1965	Disc.	5S
1966	Disc.	6S
1967	Disc.	7S
1968	Disc.	8S
1969	Disc.	69S
1970	Disc.	70S
1971	Disc.	71S
1972	Disc.	72S
1973	Disc.	73S
1974	Disc.	74S
1975	Disc.	75S
1976	Disc.	Disc.

A-5 SHOTGUN - 20 ga.

YEAR	LT.WT. 20	MAGNUM 20
1958	8Z	Introduced in
1959	9Z	1967
1960	0Z	
1961	1Z	
1962	2Z	

A-5 SHOTGUN - 20 ga., cont.

YEAR	LT.WT. 20	MAGNUM 20
1963	3Z	
1964	4Z	
1965	5Z	
1966	6Z	
1967	7Z	7X
1968	68Z	68X
1969	69Z	69X
1970	70Z	70X
1971	71Z	71X
1972	72Z	72X
1973	73Z	73X
1974	74Z	74X
1975	75Z	75X
1976	76Z	76X

SUPERPOSED MODEL - O & U - 12 ga.

YEAR	SER. # START	SER. # END
1931	1	2000
1932	2001	4000
1933	4001	6000
1934	6001	8000
1935	8001	10000
1936	10001	12000
1937	12001	14000
1938	14001	16000
1939	16001	17000
1939-1947 NO PRODUCTION		
1948	17001	17200
1949	17201	20000
1950	20001	21000
1951	21001	27000
1952	27001	33000
1953	33001	37000
1954	37001	43000
1955	43001	48000
1956	48001	54000
1957	54001	59000
1958	59001	68500
1959	68501	76500
1960	76501	86500
1961	86501	96500
1962	96501	99999
1962	1	6500

Serial number change to letter and number suffix.

YEAR	SER. # PREFIX CODE
1962	S2 suffix after Ser. No.
1963	S3 suffix after Ser. No.
1964	S4 suffix after Ser. No.
1965	S5 suffix after Ser. No.
1966	S6 suffix after Ser. No.
1967	S7 suffix after Ser. No.
1968	S8 suffix after Ser. No.
1969	S69 suffix after Ser. No.
1970	S70 suffix after Ser. No.
1971	S71 suffix after Ser. No.
1972	S72 suffix after Ser. No.
1973	S73 suffix after Ser. No.
1974	S74 suffix after Ser. No.
1975	S75 suffix after Ser. No.
1976	S76 suffix after Ser. No.
1976 to 1984	"P" or Presentation Models only

SUPERPOSED MODEL - O & U - 20 ga.

YEAR	SER. # START	SER. # END
1949	201	1700
1950	1701	2800
1951	2801	3200
1952	3201	5300
1953	5301	6700

SUPERPOSED MODEL - O & U - 20 ga., cont.

YEAR	SER. # START	SER. # END
1954	6701	8400
1955	8401	9400
1956	9401	10500
1957	10501	11500
1958	11501	14180
1959	14181	17060
1960	17061	20640
1961	20641	23820
1962	23821	27300

Serial number change to letter and number suffix.

YEAR	SER. # PREFIX CODE
1963	V3 suffix after Ser. No.
1964	V4 suffix after Ser. No.
1965	V5 suffix after Ser. No.
1966	V6 suffix after Ser. No.
1967	V7 suffix after Ser. No.
1968	V8 suffix after Ser. No.
1969	V69 suffix after Ser. No.
1970	V70 suffix after Ser. No.
1971	V71 suffix after Ser. No.
1972	V72 suffix after Ser. No.
1973	V73 suffix after Ser. No.
1974	V74 suffix after Ser. No.
1975	V75 suffix after Ser. No.
1976	V76 suffix after Ser. No.

SUPERPOSED MODEL - O & U - 28 ga. & .410 bore

YEAR	28 GA.	.410 BORE
1960-1962	NOT AVAILABLE	
1963	F3	J3
1964	F4	J4
1965	F5	J5
1966	F6	J6
1967	F7	J7
1968	F8	J8
1969	F69	J69
1970	F70	J70
1971	F71	J71
1972	F72	J72
1973	F73	J73
1974	F74	J74
1975	F75	J75
1976	F76	J76

LIEGE O & U - Approximately 10,000 produced

YEAR	SER. # PREFIX CODE
1973	73J prefix before Ser. No.
1974	74J prefix before Ser. No.
1975	75J prefix before Ser. No.

DOUBLE AUTOMATIC SHOTGUN

YEAR	SER. # START	SER. # END
1952 -	N/A	
1959	N/A	
1960 -	N/A	
1971	N/A	

1st or both digits indicate last 2 digits in year of manufacture (i.e. - OA1947 - 1960 mfg., 70A245671 - 1970 mfg.)

HI-POWER (9mm) PISTOL

YEAR	SER. # START	SER. # END
1945-1954 no data for the annual breakdown		
	1	72250
1955	72251	75000
1956	75001	77250
1957	77251	80000
1958	80001	85267
1959	85268	89687
1960	89688	93027
1961	93028	109145
1962	109146	113548
1963	113549	115822
1964	115823	T136538
1965	T136569	T146372
1966	T146373	T173285
1967	T173286	T213999
1968	T214000	T258000
1969	T258001	T261000

During 1969 the Hi-Power pistol Serial Number code was changed to a two digit year and "C" prefix. Serial Numbers for "T" prefix Hi-Power pistols exceeded T300000 and were shipped into 1970.

YEAR	SER. # PREFIX CODE
1969	69C prefix before Ser. No.
1970	70C prefix before Ser. No.
1971	71C prefix before Ser. No.
1972	72C prefix before Ser. No.
1973	73C prefix before Ser. No.
1974	74C prefix before Ser. No.
1975	75C prefix before Ser. No.
1976	76C prefix before Ser. No.
1977 to date	New style serialization

BROWNING .380 ACP CAL.

YEAR	SER. # START	SER. # END
1955	N/A	
1964	N/A	
1965	500000	598804
1966	598805	603890
1967	603891	619474
1968	619475	N/A
1969	N/A	
1970 Discontinued due to GCA of 1968. New model has longer barrel, adj. rear sight, modified grip.		

YEAR	SER. # PREFIX CODE
1971	71N prefix before Ser. No.
1972	72N prefix before Ser. No.
1973	73N prefix before Ser. No.
1974	74N prefix before Ser. No.
1975	75N prefix before Ser. No.

.25 ACP CAL. BABY BROWNING

YEAR	SER. # START	SER. # END
1955-1958 Records not available		
1959	181000	206349
1960	206350	230999
1961	231000	250999
1962	251000	278999
1963	279000	286099
1964	286100	308499
1965	308500	329999
1966	333000	367443
1967	367444	412999
1968	413000	479000
1969 Discontinued because of GCA of 1968		

.22 CAL. (Nomad-Challenger-Medalist)

YEAR	NOMAD	CHALLENGER	MEDALIST
1959	P9	U9	T9
1960	P0	U0	T0
1961	P1	U1	T1
1962	P2	U2	T2
1963	P3	U3	T3
1964	P4	U4	T4
1965	P5	U5	T5
1966	P6	U6	T6
1967	P7	U7	T7
1968	P8	U8	T8
1969	P69	U69	T69
1970	P70	U70	T70
1971	P71	U71	T71
1972	P72	U72	T72
1973	P73	U73	T73
1974	Disc.	U74	T74
1975	Disc.	Disc.	Disc.

BOLT ACTION RIFLES
(Safari, Medallion, & Olympian Models)

YEAR	SER. # CODE
1959	N/A
1962	No prefix (numeral-letter) before Ser. No. (i.e., only digits)
1963	3-single letter prefix or suffix by Ser. No.
1964	4-single letter prefix or suffix by Ser. No.
1965	5-single letter prefix or suffix by Ser. No.
1966	6-single letter prefix or suffix by Ser. No.
1967	7-single letter prefix or suffix by Ser. No.
1968	8-single letter prefix or suffix by Ser. No.
1969	Single letter (Y, Z, or L) followed by last 2 digits of year of mfg. Prefix only.
1970	"Y70" prefix
1971	"L71" prefix
1972	"Z72" prefix
1973	"Y73" prefix
1974	"Z74" prefix
1975	"L75" prefix

B.A.R.

YEAR	SER. # SUFFIX CODE
1967	"M7" suffix after Ser. No.
1968	"M8" suffix after Ser. No.
1969	"M69" suffix after Ser. No.
1970	"M70" suffix after Ser. No.
1971	"M71" suffix after Ser. No.
1972	"M72" suffix after Ser. No.
1973	"M73" suffix after Ser. No.
1974	"M74" suffix after Ser. No.
1975	"M75" suffix after Ser. No.
1976	"M76" suffix after Ser. No.
1976 to date	New sequence with "RT" appearing in middle of Ser. No.

.22 AUTO RIFLE (Grades I, II, and III)

YEAR	SER. # CODE
1956-Mid. 1961 "T" prefix = LR, "A" prefix = short	
Mid. 1961 "A" changed to "E" prefix 5 digits or less.	
1961	"1T" or "1A" or "1E" prefix before Ser. No.
1962	"2T" or "2E" prefix before Ser. No.
1963	"3T" or "3E" prefix before Ser. No.
1964	"4T" or "4E" prefix before Ser. No.
1965	"5T" or "5E" prefix before Ser. No.
1966	"6T" or "6E" prefix before Ser. No.
1967	"7T" or "7E" prefix before Ser. No.

.22 AUTO RIFLE (Grades I, II, and III), cont.

YEAR	SER. # CODE
1968	"8T" or "8E" prefix before Ser. No.
1969	"69T" or "69E" prefix before Ser. No.
1970	"70T" or "70E" prefix before Ser. No.
1971	"71T" or "71E" prefix before Ser. No.
1972	"72T" or "72E" prefix before Ser. No.
1973	Japan production

T-BOLT RIFLE (T1 and T2)

YEAR	SER. # CODE
1965	"X5" suffix after Ser. No.
1966	"X6" suffix after Ser. No.
1967	"X7" suffix after Ser. No.
1968	"X8" suffix after Ser. No.
1969	"X69" suffix after Ser. No.
1970	"X70" suffix after Ser. No.
1971	"X71" suffix after Ser. No.
1972	"X72" suffix after Ser. No.
1973	"X73" suffix after Ser. No.
1974	"X74" suffix after Ser. No.
1975	"X75" suffix after Ser. No.

BROWNING SERIALIZATION 1975 TO CURRENT

In 1975 Browning began using the two (2) letter code system (located in the middle of the serial number) for determining the year of manufacture. For example "PN" would be "89" indicating 1989. Browning firearms historical letters by model and serial number are available for $39.95 through Browning Customer Service at 800-333-3288.

LETTER	NUMBER
Z	1
Y	2
X	3
W	4
V	5
T	6
R	7
P	8
N	9
M	10

BROWNING MODEL CONFIGURATION CODES

Beginning in 1976 Browning started identifying a model and its configuration using a three number (or possibly a combination of letters and numbers) code in the serial number.

SHOTGUNS O/U

Superposed Grade I

CONFIGURATION	CODE
12 Ga. Hunting	214
12 Ga. Superlight	204
20 Ga. Hunting	264
20 Ga. Superlight	224

Superposed Pigeon Grade

CONFIGURATION	CODE
12 Ga. Hunting	314
12 Ga. Superlight	304
20 Ga. Hunting	364
20 Ga. Superlight	324

Superposed Pointer Grade

CONFIGURATION	CODE
12 Ga. Hunting	414
12 Ga. Superlight	404
20 Ga. Hunting	464
20 Ga. Superlight	424

Superposed Diana Grade

CONFIGURATION	CODE
12 Ga. Hunting	514
12 Ga. Superlight	504
20 Ga. Hunting	564
20 Ga. Superlight	524

Superposed Midas Grade

CONFIGURATION	CODE
12 Ga. Hunting	614
12 Ga. Superlight	604
20 Ga. Hunting	664
20 Ga. Superlight	624

Citori Grade I

CONFIGURATION	CODE
12 Ga. 3-1/2	103
12 Ga. Trap Monte Carlo Stock	143
12 Ga. Trap Conventional Stock	N43
12 Ga. Skeet	1B3
12 Ga. Hunting	153
12 Ga. Lightning	753
12 Ga. Superlight	A13
12 Ga. Upland	B13
325 20 Ga. Sporting	C33
20 Ga. Skeet	1C3
20 Ga. Hunting	163
20 Ga. Lightning	763
20 Ga. Micro Lightning	H33
20 Ga. Superlight	A33
20 Ga. Upland	B33
28 Ga. Skeet	1E3
28 Ga. Hunting	173
28 Ga. Lightning	773
28 Ga. Superlight	A73
.410 Bore Skeet	1F3
.410 Bore Hunting	183
.410 Bore Lightning	783
.410 Bore Superlight	A83
Three Barrel Set	1K3
Four Barrel Set	1A3

Citori Grade III

CONFIGURATION	CODE
12 Ga. Trap Monte Carlo Stock	343
12 Ga. Trap Conventional Stock	R43
12 Ga. Skeet	3B3
12 Ga. Hunting	353
12 Ga. Lightning	853
12 Ga. Superlight	M13
20 Ga. Skeet	3C3
20 Ga. Hunting	363
20 Ga. Lightning	863
20 Ga. Superlight	M33
28 Ga. Skeet	3E3
28 Ga. Lightning	873

Citori Grade III, cont.

CONFIGURATION	CODE
28 Ga. Superlight	M73
.410 Bore Skeet	3F3
410 Lightning	883
410 Superlight	M83
Three Barrel Set	3K3
Four Barrel Set	3A3

Citori Grade VI

CONFIGURATION	CODE
12 Ga. Trap Monte Carlo Stock	643
12 Ga. Trap Conventional Stock	S43
12 Ga. Skeet	6B3
12 Ga. Hunting	653
12 Ga. Lightning	953
12 Ga. Superlight	F13
20 Ga. Skeet	6C3
20 Ga. Hunting	663
20 Ga. Lightning	963
20 Ga. Superlight	F33
28 Ga. Skeet	6E3
28 Ga. Lightning	973
.410 Bore Skeet	6F3
.410 Bore Lightning	983
.410 Bore Superlight	F83
Citori Grade VI, cont.	
Configuration	Code
Three Barrel Set	6K3
Four Barrel Set	6A3

Citori Golden Clays

CONFIGURATION	CODE
12 Ga. Trap Monte Carlo Stock	143
12 Ga. Trap Conventional Stock	N43
12 Ga. Skeet	1B3
20 Ga. 325 Sporting	C33
20 Ga. Skeet	6C3
28 Ga. Skeet	6E3
.410 Bore Skeet	6F3
GTI Sporting	P13
325 Sporting	C13
Special Sporting	T13
Lightning Sporting	W53
PLUS Trap	J43
PLUS Combo	1P3
Three Barrel Set	6K3
Four Barrel Set	6A3

Citori Gran Lightning

CONFIGURATION	CODE
12 Ga.	253
20 Ga.	263
28 Ga.	273
.410 Bore	283

Shotguns Semi-Auto

Auto 5

CONFIGURATION	CODE
Magnum 12 Ga.	151
Magnum Stalker 12 Ga.	T51
Light 12 Ga.	211
Light 12 Stalker 12 Ga.	T11

Auto 5, cont.

CONFIGURATION	CODE
Sweet 16 Ga.	221
Magnum 20 Ga.	161
Light 20 Ga.	231

A-500

CONFIGURATION	CODE
12 Ga. Recoil	751
12 Ga. Gas	351
12 Ga. Gas Sporting Clays	S51

Gold

CONFIGURATION	CODE
10 Ga.	R91
12 Ga.	F51
20 Ga.	F61

Shotguns Slide Action

BPS

CONFIGURATION	CODE
10 Ga.	192
10 Ga. Stalker	T92
12 Ga. 3-1/2	102
12 Ga. 3-1/2" Stalker	T02
12 Ga. Pigeon	P52
12 Ga. Game	152
12 Ga. (includes all hunting & Upland Models)	152
12 Ga. Stalker	T52
20 Ga. (includes all hunting & Upland Models)	162
28 Ga.	172

Model 42 Limited Edition 410 Bore

CONFIGURATION	CODE
Grade I	882
High Grade	982

Shotguns Side by Side

B-SS

CONFIGURATION	CODE
Sidelock 12 Ga.	918
Sidelock 20 Ga.	938

Rifles

MODEL	CODE
BAR Grade IV	437
BAR 22 Grade I	146
BAR 22 Grade II	246
A-Bolt 22 Grade I	136
A-Bolt 22 Gold Med.	G36
Trombone 22	337
B-92	167

Pistols 1975-1998

MODEL	CODE
Hi-Power 9mm	245
Hi-Power .40 S&W	2W5
Hi-Power Military	215

Pistols 1999-Current

MODEL	CODE
Hi-Power 9mm	510

E.J. CHURCHILL GUNMAKERS SER.

YEAR	GUN #
1891	156
1892	339
1893	384
1894	480
1895	569
1896	655
1897	761
1898	923
1899	1047
1900	1156
1911	1851
1920	2250
1924	2834
1930	4315
1940	6401
1948	6601
1957	6901
1960	7400
1967	8300

COLT'S FIREARMS SERIALIZATION

For additional Colt serialization on most Colt models through 1998, please refer to Blue Book Pocket Guide for Colt Dates of Manufacture by R.L. Wilson. This publication is available in book-form only. Visit www.bluebookofgunvalues.com to order.

MODEL 1849 POCKET REVOLVER

YEAR	SER. # START	SER. # END
1849	1	11999
1850	12000	15999
1851	16000	24999
1852	25000	54999
1853	55000	84999
1854	85000	99999
1855	100000	109999
1856	110000	129999
1857	130000	139999
1858	140000	149999
1859	150000	159999
1860	160000	183999
1861	184000	196999
1862	197000	222999
1863	223000	249999
1864	250000	269999
1865	270000	279999
1866	280000	289999
1867	290000	299999
1868	300000	309999
1869	310000	319999
1870	320000	324999
1871	325000	329999
1872	330000	330999
1873	331000	340000

MODEL 1849 POCKET REVOLVER - LONDON BARREL ADDRESS

YEAR	SER. # START	SER. # END
1853	1	999
1854	1000	4999
1855	5000	8999
1856	9000	11000

MODEL 1851 NAVY

YEAR	SER. # START	SER. # END
1850	1	2499
1851	2500	9999
1852	10000	19999
1853	20000	34999
1854	35000	39999
1855	40000	44999
1856	45000	64999
1857	65000	84999
1858	85000	89999
1859	90000	92999
1860	93000	97999
1861	98000	117999
1862	118000	131999
1863	132000	174999
1864	175000	179999
1865	180000	184999
1866	185000	199999
1867	200000	203999
1868	204000	206999
1869	207000	209999
1870	210000	211999
1871	212000	213999
1872	214000	214999
1873	215000	215348

MODEL 1851 NAVY - LONDON BARREL ADDRESS

YEAR	SER. # START	SER. # END
1853	1	3999
1854	4000	14999
1855	15000	40999
1856	41000	42000

MODEL 1860 ARMY

YEAR	SER. # START	SER. # END
1860	1	1999
1861	2000	24999
1862	25000	84999
1863	85000	149999
1864	150000	152999
1865	153000	155999
1866	156000	161999
1867	162000	169999
1868	170000	176999
1869	177000	184999
1870	185000	189999
1871	190000	197999
1872	198000	198999
1873	199000	200500

MODEL 1861 NAVY

YEAR	SER. # START	SER. # END
1861	1	4599
1862	4600	9999
1863	10000	16999
1864	17000	24999
1865	25000	27999
1866	28000	29999
1867	30000	30999
1868	31000	32999
1869	33000	33999
1870	34000	34999
1871	35000	35999
1872	36000	36999
1873	37000	38843

MODEL 1862 POLICE

YEAR	SER. # START	SER. # END
1861	1	8499
1862	8500	14999
1863	15000	25999
1864	26000	28999
1865	29000	31999
1866	32000	34999
1867	35000	36999
1868	37000	39999
1869	40000	41999
1870	42000	43999
1871	44000	44999
1872	45000	45999
1873	46000	47000

MODEL 1873 - SINGLE ACTION ARMY

(SAA) - PRE-WAR

YEAR	CALIBER	SER. # START
1873	.45 Colt Caliber, Standard	1
1874	.450 Boxer	200
1875	.44 Rimfire series (own serials, 1-1863 made through 1880)	15000
1876	.476 Eley introduced	22000
1877		33000
1878	.44-40 introduced in quantity	41000
1879		49000
1880		53000
1881		62000
1882	Sheriff's model introduced	73000
1883	.22 rimfire introduced	85000
1884	.32-20 and .38-40 introduced	102000
1885	.41 Colt introduced	114000
1886	.38 Colt introduced	117000
1887	.32 Colt and .32 S&W introduced	119000
1888	Flattop Target	125000
	S.A.A. began; no.	126530
1889	.32 rimfire; ,32-44 S&W, .38 S&W; and .44 Russian introduced	128000
1890	.44 Smoothbore; .380 and .450 Eley; and .44 S&W introduced	130000
1891	.38-44 introduced	136000
1892		144000
1893		149000
1894	Beginning of Bisley models	154000
1895		159000
1896	Transverse cylinder latch introduced, screw lock at front of frame dropped	163000
1897		168000
1898		175000
1899		182000
1900		192000
1901		203000
1902		220000
1903		238000
1904	Revolvers built to handle smokeless powder, Intro. VP Proof on trigger guard	250000
1905		261000
1906		273000
1907		288000
1908		304000
1909		308000

MODEL 1873 - SINGLE ACTION ARMY

(SAA) - PRE-WAR cont.

YEAR	CALIBER	SER. # START
1910		312000
1911		316000
1912	Discontinue Bisley model	321000
1913	S&W Special introduced	325000
1914		328000
1915	Long flute cylinders; range no. 330001 to 331480	329500
1916		332000
1917		335000
1918		337000
1919		337200
1920		338000
1921		341000
1922		343000
1923		344500
1924	.45 ACP introduced, requiring special cylinders	346400
1925		347300
1926		348200
1927		349800
1928		351300
1929		352400
1930	.38 Special introduced	353800
1931		354100
1932		354500
1933		354800
1934		355000
1935	.357 Magnum introduced	355200
1936		355300
1937		355400
1938		356100
1939		356600
1940	A few S.A.A. during and just after the war	357000 thru 357859

1ST GENERATION COLT SINGLE ACTION ARMY - CALIBER BREAKDOWN

CALIBER	S.A.A	FLATTOP TARGET	BISLEY	BISLEY TARGET
.22 Rimfire	107	93	0	0
.32 Rimfire	1	0	0	0
.32 Colt	192	24	160	44
.32 S&W	32	30	18	17
.32-44	2	9	14	17
.32-20	29,812	30	13,291	131
.38 Colt (through 1914)	1,011	122	412	96
.38 Colt (post-1922)	1,365	0	0	0
.38 S&W	9	39	10	5
.38 Colt Special	82	7	0	0
.38 S&W Special	25	0	2	0
.38-44	2	11	6	47
.357 Magnum	525	0	0	0
.380 Eley	1	3	0	0
.38-40	38,240	19	12,163	98
41 LC	16,402	91	3,159	24
.44 Smoothbore	15	0	1	0
.44 Rimfire	1,863	0	0	0
.44 German	59	0	0	0

1ST GENERATION COLT SINGLE ACTION ARMY - CALIBER BREAKDOWN, cont.

CALIBER	S.A.A	FLATTOP TARGET	BISLEY	BISLEY TARGET
.44 Russian	154	51	90	62
.44 S&W	24	51	29	64
.44 S&W Special	506	1	0	0
.44-40	64,489	21	6,803	78
.45	150,683	100	8,005	97
.45 Smoothbore	4	0	2	0
.45 ACP	44	0	0	0
.450 Boxer	729	89	0	0
.450 Eley	2,697	84	5	0
.455 Eley	1,150	37	180	196
.476 Eley	161	2	0	0
TOTAL QUANTITIES	310,386	914	44,350	976

COLT SINGLE ACTION ARMY – POST-WAR PRODUCTION

YEAR	SER. # START	SER. # END
"SA" suffix from 1956 to 1978, "SA" prefix 1978 to 1984		
1956	0001SA	8799SA
1957	8800SA	18499SA
1958	18500SA	23399SA
1959	23400SA	28499SA
1960	28500SA	33599SA
1961	33600SA	35649SA
1962	35650SA	37299SA
1963	37300SA	38499SA
1964	38500SA	39999SA
1965	40000SA	41499SA
1966	41500SA	43799SA
1967	43800SA	46299SA
1968	46300SA	48999SA
1969	49000SA	52599SA
1970	52600SA	59399SA
1971	59400SA	61699SA
1972	61700SA	64399SA
1973	64400SA	69399SA
1974	69400SA	73319SA
1975	NONE PRODUCED	
1976 (start of 3rd generation of production)		
	80000SA	82000SA
1977	82001SA	95999SA
1978	96000SA	99999SA
Mid-1978Start of "SA" prefix on front of ser. no.		
1978	SA01000	SA14808
1979	SA14809	SA30254
1980	SA30255	SA46919
1981	SA46920	SA58627
1982	SA58628	SA65255
1983	SA65256	SA66495
1984	SA66496	C.S. PROD.

NEW FRONTIER SINGLE ACTION ARMY

YEAR	SER. # START	SER. # END
1961	3000NF	3005NF
1962	3006NF	3849NF
1963	3850NF	4699NF
1964	4700NF	4974NF
1965	4975NF	5399NF
1966	5400NF	5674NF
1967	5675NF	5699NF
1968	5700NF	5899NF
1969	5900NF	5924NF

NEW FRONTIER SINGLE ACTION ARMY, cont.

YEAR	SER. # START	SER. # END
1970	5925NF	6874NF
1971	6875NF	7049NF
1972	7050NF	7074NF
1973	7075NF	7174NF
1974	7175NF	7264NF
1975	7265NF	7288NF
1978	7501NF	N/A
REINTRODUCED IN SEPTEMBER		
1978	01001NF	04424NF
1979	04425NF	06274NF
1980	06275NF	11374NF
1981	11375NF	16584NF
1982	16584NF	DISC. 1982

MODEL 1911 AND 1911A1 – Commercial production Capital "C" prefix - .45 cal.

YEAR	SER. # START	SER. # END
1912	C1	C1899
1913	C1900	C5399
1914	C5400	C16599
1915	C16600	C27599
1916	C27600	C74999
1917	C75000	C98999
1918	C99000	C105999
1919	C106000	C120999
1920	C121000	C126999
1921	C127000	C128999
1922	C129000	C133999
1923	C134000	C134999
1924	C135000	C139999
1925	C140000	C144999
1926	C145000	C150999
1927	C151000	C151999
1928	C152000	C154999
1929	C155000	C155999
1930	C156000	C158999
1931	C159000	C160999
1932	C161000	C164799
1933	C164800	C174599
1934	C174600	C177999
1935	C178000	C179799
1936	C179800	C183199
1937	C183200	C188699
1938	C188700	C189599
1939	C189600	C198899
1940	C198900	C199299
1941	C199300	C208799
1942	C208800	C215018
1943-1945: Commercial production interrupted by WWII		
1946	C221001	C222000
1947	C222001	C231999
1948	C232000	C238500
1949	C238501	C240000
1950	C240000	247701C
"C" SUFFIX STARTED WITH SER. NO. 240228		
1951	247701C	253179C
1952	253180C	259549C
1953	259550C	266349C
1954	266350C	270549C
1955	270550C	272549C
1956	272550C	276699C
1957	276700C	281999C
1958	282000C	283799C
1959	283800C	285799C
1960	285800C	287999C
1961	288000C	289849C

MODEL 1911 AND 1911A1 – Commercial production Capital "C" prefix - .45 cal., cont.

YEAR	SER. # START	SER. # END
1962	289850C	291299C
1963	291300C	293799C
1964	293800C	295999C
1965	296000C	300299C
1966	300300C	308499C
1967	308500C	315599C
1968	315600C	324499C
1969	324500C	332649C
1970	332650C	336169C
Mid-1970 New	70G01001	70G05550
1971	70G05551	70G18000
1972	70G18001	70G34400
1973	70G34401	70G43000
1974	70G43001	70G73000
1975	70G73001	70G88900
1976	70G88901	70G99999
Mid-1976 New	01001G70	13900G70
1977	13901G70	45199G70
1978	45200G70	N/A

MODEL 1911 AND 1911A1 MILITARY PRODUCTION

YEAR	SER. # START	SER. # END	MFG.
1912	1	500	COLT
	501	1000	COLT USN
	1001	1500	COLT
	1501	2000	COLT USN
	2001	2500	COLT
	2501	3500	COLT USN
	3501	3800	COLT USMC
	3801	4500	COLT
	4501	5500	COLT USN
	5501	6500	COLT
	6501	7500	COLT USN
	7501	8500	COLT
	8501	9500	COLT USN
	9501	10500	COLT
	10501	11500	COLT USN
	11501	12500	COLT
	12501	13500	COLT USN
	13501	17250	COLT USN
1913	17251	36400	COLT
	36401	37650	COLT USMC
	37651	38000	COLT
	38001	44000	COLT USN
	44001	60400	COLT
1914	60401	72570	COLT
	72571	83855	
SPRINGFIELD-(THESE NUMBERS RESERVED FOR SPRINGFIELD)			
	83856	83900	COLT
	83901	84400	COLT USMC
	84401	96000	COLT
	96001	97537	COLT USN
	97538	102596	COLT
	102597	107596	
SPRINGFIELD (RESERVED NO. RANGE)			
1915	107597	109500	COLT
	109501	110000	COLT USN
	110001	113496	COLT
	113497	120566	SPRING-FIELD
		(RESERVED FOR SPRINGFIELD)	
1915	120567	125566	COLT
	125567	133186	
SPRINGFIELD-(RESERVED FOR SPRINGFIELD)			
1916	133187	137400	COLT
1917	137401	151186	COLT

MODEL 1911 AND 1911A1 MILITARY PRODUCTION, cont.

YEAR	SER. # START	SER. # END	MFG.
1917	151187	151986	COLT USMC
	151987	185800	COLT
	185801	186200	COLT USMC
	186201	209586	COLT
	209587	210386	COLT USMC
	210387	215386	COLT
FRAMES (RESERVED FOR RECEIVERS)			
	215387	216186	COLT USMC
	216187	216586	COLT
	216587	216986	COLT USMC
1918	216987	217386	COLT USMC
1918	217387	223952	COLT
	223953	223990	COLT USN
	223991	232000	COLT
	232001	233600	COLT USN
	233601	580600	COLT
	1	13152	REM. UMC
1919	13153	21676	REM. UMC
	580601	629500	COLT
	629501	717386	COLT
1924	700001	710000	COLT
1937	710001	712349	COLT USN
1938	712350	713645	COLT
1939	713646	717281	COLT USN
1940	717282	721977	COLT
1941	721978	756733	COLT
1942	756734	793657	COLT
	793658	797639	COLT USN
	797640	800000	COLT
	S800001	S800500	SINGER
	800501	801000	H&R
	801001	856100	COLT
1943	856101	958100	COLT
	**856101	856404	Replacement No
	**856405	916404	ITHACA
	**916405	1041404	REM. RAND
	1041405	1096404	US&S
	1088726	1208673	COLT
	1208674	1279673	ITHACA
	1279674	1279698	RE NO AA
	1279699	1441430	REM. RAND
	1441431	1471430	ITHACA
	1471431	1609528	REM. RAND
1944	1609529	1743846	COLT
	1743847	1816641	REM. RAND
	1816642	1890503	ITHACA
	1890504	2075103	REM. RAND
1945	2075104	2134403	ITHACA
	2134404	2244803	REM. RAND
	2244804	2380013	COLT
	2380014	2619013	REM. RAND
	2619014	2693613	ITHACA

** Denotes double issue ranges.

COLT SINGLE-ACTION MODEL NUMBERS

The author wishes to express thanks to the late Mr. Don Wilkerson for allowing the edited information published below from his 1986 Post-War Single-Action Revolver, 1976-1986 publication.

A working knowledge of model numbers for the various Colt single-action revolvers is a must for even a novice collector. Since the mid - 1970s Colt has placed the model number on the end label of the shipping cartons of virtually all their firearms. Many collectors and publications regularly use the model number to describe or differentiate between revolvers. Using the model number is an accurate and efficient method to delineate

COLT SAA MODEL NOS., cont,

a particular variation. Example: .45 caliber revolver with a 4 3/4 in. barrel, blue and casehardened finish and eagle stocks can be described as a simple "P-1840." Each Colt model is specified by an alphabetical letter and 4 numerical digits. The basic model number as it pertains to single-action revolvers can be broken down as follows:

MODEL P - basic type of frame. The letter "P" is used to delineate the single-action type of frame.

FIRST NUMERAL - "1" is the first model built on a particular type of frame. Numerals 2, 3, 4, etc. indicate later versions. These versions are not always numbered in numerical order and the same number has been used for different models at different times. A "1" denotes the basic standard single-action frame. A "2" denotes the new black powder frame available through the Colt Custom Gun Shop. A "3" has been used at various times to denote a non-standard frame or cylinder. The "4" is used to specify the New Frontier style of frame. Numbers such as "7" and "8" are frequently used to specify commemorative or special editions.

SECOND NUMERAL - specifies caliber. A "4" denotes .32-20, a "6" denotes .357 Magnum, a "7" denotes .44 Special, an "8" denotes .45 caliber, and a "9" specifies .44-40 caliber.*

THIRD NUMERAL - denotes barrel length. "3" is used to denote both a 3 inch and a 4 inch barrel. "4" is 4 3/4 inch or 5 inch, "5" is 5 1/2 inch, "7" is 7 1/2 inch, and "1" is 12 inch.*

FOURTH NUMERAL - is used to denote several different variations of the standard model. Some of the most common examples are: "1," "2," or "6" for nickel finish, "1" for full blue finish in the case of P-1871, and "2," "3," and "4" as used for the Sheriff's Model series to denote blue and casehardened finish, nickel finish, and Royal Blue and casehardened finish, respectively. The fourth numeral can also denote the type of stocks as in P-1673. The fourth numeral in the basic model designation must be used in conjunction with the preceding three numerals to determine its exact meaning. The fourth numeral is kind of a "catch-all" number. Many times this number serves only to differentiate a later model from a similar model assembled years earlier.

*The .32-20 caliber and the 5 inch barrel length are listed in the 1984 Colt Buyer's Guide, but as of this date neither have been produced.

STANDARD MODEL P REVOLVER CODES

The primary model numbers used by Colt for Model P revolvers produced since 1976 are as follows:

P-1640 - .357 Magnum, 4 3/4 in. barrel, blue finish, eagle stocks.
P-1641 - .357 Magnum, 4 3/4 in. barrel, nickel finish, wood stocks.
P-1650 - .357 Magnum, 5 1/2 in. barrel, blue finish, eagle stocks.
P-1656 - .357 Magnum, 5 1/2 in. barrel, nickel finish, wood stocks.
P-1670 - .357 Magnum, 7 1/2 in. barrel, blue finish, eagle stocks.
P-1673 - .357 Magnum, 7 1/2 in. barrel, blue finish, wood stocks.

STANDARD MODEL P REVOLVER CODES, cont,

P-1676 - .357 Magnum, 7 1/2 in. barrel, nickel finish, wood stocks.
P-1740 - .44 Special, 4 3/4 in. barrel, blue finish, eagle stocks.
P-1746 - .44 Special, 4 3/4 in. barrel, nickel finish, wood stocks.
P-1750 - .44 Special, 5 1/2 in. barrel, blue finish, eagle stocks.
P-1756 - .44 Special, 5 1/2 in. barrel, nickel finish, wood stocks.
P-1770 - .44 Special, 7 1/2 in. barrel, blue finish, eagle stocks.
P-1776 - .44 Special, 7 1/2 in. barrel, nickel finish, wood stocks.
P-1716 - .44 Special, 12 in. barrel, nickel finish, wood stocks.
P-1840 - .45 Colt, 4 3/4 in. barrel, blue finish, eagle stocks.
P-1841 - .45 Colt, 4 3/4 in. barrel, nickel finish, wood stocks.
P-1850 - .45 Colt, 5 1/2 in. barrel, blue finish, eagle stocks.
P-1856 - .45 Colt, 5 1/2 in. barrel, nickel finish, wood stocks.
P-1870 - .45 Colt, 7 1/2 in. barrel, blue finish, eagle stocks.
P-1876 - .45 Colt, 7 1/2 in. barrel, nickel finish, wood stocks.
P-1813 - .45 Colt, 12 in. barrel, blue finish, eagle stocks.
P-1816 - .45 Colt, 12 in. barrel, nickel finish, wood stocks.
P-1940 - .44-40 caliber, 4 3/4 in. barrel, blue finish, eagle stocks.
P-1941* - .44-40 caliber, 4 3/4 in. barrel, nickel finish, wood stocks.
P-1950 - .44-40 caliber, 5 1/2 in. barrel, blue finish, eagle stocks.
P-1970 - .44-40 caliber, 7 1/2 in. barrel, blue finish, eagle stocks.
P-1976* - .44-40 caliber, 7 1/2 in. barrel, nickel finish, wood stocks.
P-1911 - .44-40 caliber, 12 in. barrel, nickel finish, wood stocks.

**These model numbers were used primarily for engraved or special ordered revolvers as the two models indicated were never produced as a regular model. "Blue finish" in the above chart denotes the standard blue finish, i.e., blue with case hardened frame.*

NEW FRONTIER MODEL

P-4671 - .357 Magnum, 7 1/2 in. barrel, nickel finish, wood stocks.
P-4750 - .44 Special, 5 1/2 in. barrel, Royal Blue finish, wood stocks.
P-4770 - .44 Special , 7 1/2 in. barrel, Royal Blue finish, wood stocks.
P-4840 - .45 Colt, 4 3/4 in. barrel, Royal Blue finish, wood stocks.
P-4850 - .45 Colt, 5 1/2 in. barrel, Royal Blue finish, wood stocks.
P-4870 - .45 Colt, 7 1/2 in. barrel, Royal Blue finish, wood stocks.
P-4940 - .44-40 caliber, 4 3/4 in. barrel, Royal Blue finish, wood stocks.
P-4970 - .44-40 caliber, 7 1/2 in. barrel, Royal Blue finish, wood stocks.

Note: The term "Royal Blue" in the New Frontier chart denotes a revolver with a casehardened frame and a Royal (high polish) Blue finish on the other major components.

SHERIFF'S MODELS

P-1932 - .44-40 caliber, 3 in. barrel, blue finish, eagle stocks.
P-1933* - .44-40/.44 Special, 3 in. barrel, nickel finish, wood stocks.
P-1934* - .44-40/.44 Special, 3 in. barrel, Royal Blue finish, wood stocks.
*Circa 1984 all Sheriff's Models are listed as single calibers: .44-40 or .45 caliber.

REVOLVERS WITH FULL BLUE FRAMES

Some of the "full blue" models have had more than one model number assigned to the same variation. As a result, a particular model may have been identified by different model numbers at different times. Following the model numbers and descriptions in this chart will be an approximate time frame during which that particular model was in use. No date following the description indicates that only one model number for that particular variation is known to the author (Don Wilkerson).

P-1640 - FB - .357 Magnum, 4 3/4 in. barrel, fluted cylinder, eagle stocks.
P-1650 - FB - .357 Magnum, 5 1/2 in. barrel, fluted cylinder, eagle stocks.
P-1740 - FB - .44 Special, 4 3/4 in. barrel, fluted cylinder, eagle stocks.
P-1750 - FB - .44 Special, 5 1/2 in. barrel, fluted cylinder, eagle stocks.
P-1770 - FB - .44 Special, 7 1/2 in. barrel, fluted cylinder, eagle stocks.
P-1770 - UB - .44 Special, 7 1/2 in. barrel, unfluted cylinder, eagle stocks.
P-3840 - .45 Colt, 4 3/4 in. barrel, both fluted and unfluted cylinders, eagle stocks (early to mid -1982).
P-1840 - FB - .45 Colt, 4 3/4 in. barrel, fluted cylinder, eagle stocks (mid to late 1982 to date).
P-1840 - UB - .45 Colt, 4 3/4 in. barrel, unfluted cylinder, eagle stocks (mid to late 1982 to date).
P-1850 - FB - .45 Colt, 5 1/2 in. barrel, fluted cylinder, eagle stocks.
P-1850 - UB - .45 Colt, 5 1/2 in. barrel, unfluted cylinder, eagle stocks.
P-1871 - .45 Colt, 7 1/2 in. barrel, fluted cylinder, wood stocks (1977 to 1979).
P-1870 - FB - .45 Colt, 7 1/2 in. barrel, fluted cylinder, wood stocks (1982 to date).
P-1870 - UB - .45 Colt, 7 1/2 in. barrel, unfluted cylinder, wood stocks (1982 to date).
P-1871 - FB - .45 Colt, 12 in. barrel, fluted cylinder, eagle stocks.

FULL BLUE NEW FRONTIERS

P-4770 - FB - .44 Special, 7 1/2 in. barrel, fluted cylinder, wood stocks.
P-4870 - FB - .45 Colt, 7 1/2 in. barrel, fluted cylinder, wood stocks.
P-4870 - UB - .45 Colt, 7 1/2 in. barrel, unfluted cylinder, wood stocks.

MISCELLANEOUS MODEL NUMBERS

1750 - AA - .44 Special, 5 1/2 in. barrel, blue finish with nickel cylinder, eagle stocks.
1750 - AB - .44 Special, 5 1/2 in. barrel, blue finish with nickel cylinder with blue flutes, eagle stocks.
1840 - UC - .45 Colt, 4 3/4 in. barrel, blue finish, unfluted cylinder, eagle stocks.

MISCELLANEOUS MODEL NUMBERS, cont.

1850 - UC - .45 Colt, 5 1/2 in. barrel, blue finish, unfluted cylinder, eagle stocks.
1870 - UC - .45 Colt, 7 1/2 in. barrel, blue finish, unfluted cylinder, eagle stocks.
Note: The term "blue finish" in this chart is the standard blue finish with a casehardened frame.

BLACK POWDER MODEL P REVOLVERS

P-2830 - .45 Colt, 3 in. barrel, blue finish.
P-2833 - .45 Colt, 3 in. barrel, nickel finish.
P-2834* - .45 Colt, 3 in. barrel, Royal Blue finish.
P-2836 - .45 Colt, 4 in. barrel, Royal Blue finish.
P-2837 - .45 Colt, 4 in. barrel, nickel finish.
P-2840 - .45 Colt, 4 3/4 in. barrel, blue finish.
P-2841 - .45 Colt, 4 3/4 in. barrel, nickel finish.
P-2847* - .45 Colt, 5 in. barrel, nickel finish.
P-2870 - .45 Colt, 7 1/2 in. barrel, blue finish.
P-2871 - .45 Colt, 7 1/2 in. barrel, nickel finish.
P-2940 - .44-40 caliber, 4 3/4 in. barrel, blue finish.
P-2941 - .44-40 caliber, 4 3/4 in. barrel, nickel finish.
P-2970 - .44-40 caliber, 7 1/2 in. barrel, blue finish.
P-2971 - .44-40 caliber, 7 1/2 in. barrel, nickel finish.
P-2437* - .32-20 caliber, 4 in. barrel, nickel finish.
P-2474* - .32-20 caliber, 7 1/2 in. barrel, Royal Blue finish.

**As of this writing these calibers have not been produced. The terms "blue finish" and "Royal" in this chart refer to Colt's standard single-action finish, i.e., casehardened frame with all components finished in either standard blue or Royal Blue.*

MODEL 1877 LIGHTNING & THUNDERER DA

YEAR	SER. # START	SER. # END
1877	1	2900
1878	3000	13499
1879	13500	18999
1880	19000	27999
1881	28000	33999
1882	34000	39999
1883	40000	47999
1884	48000	51499
1885	51500	52999
1886	53000	57499
1887	57500	62699
1888	62700	72499
1889	72500	73499
1890	73500	80499
1891	80500	85399
1892	85400	88999
1893	89000	94999
1894	95000	96999
1895	97000	101699
1896	101700	105199
1897	105200	107499
1898	107500	111499
1899	111500	115499
1900	115500	122699
1901	122700	130299
1902	130300	139999
1903	140000	148499
1904	148500	156199
1905	156200	158999
1906	159000	161999
1907	162000	163999
1908	164000	164999
1909	165000	166849

MODEL 1878 SxS HAMMER SHOTGUN

YEAR	SER. # START	SER. # END
1878	1	99
1879	100	2249
1880	2250	7849
1881	7850	11799
1882	11800	14999
1883	15000	17399
1884	17400	18549

MODEL 1883 SxS HAMMERLESS SHOTGUN

YEAR	SER. # START	SER. # END
1885	18550	20349
1886	20350	21199
1888	22000	22499
1889	22500	22683
1883	1	249
1884	250	849
1885	850	1399
1886	1400	2199
1887	2200	3055
1888	3056	4057
1889	4058	4449
1890	4450	5349
1891	5350	6249
1892	6250	6749
1893	6750	7249
1894	7250	7549
1895	7550	8366

LIGHTNING SLIDE ACTION - SMALL FRAME

YEAR	SER. # START	SER. # END
1887	1	999
1888	1000	7999
1889	8000	11749
1890	11750	14299
1891	14300	14699
1892	14700	15399
1893	15400	16599
1894	16600	19799
1895	19800	22999
1896	23000	25999
1897	26000	29599
1898	29600	35299
1899	35300	42799
1900	42800	52299
1901	52300	63299
1902	63300	73699
1903	73700	81999
1904	82000	89912

LIGHTNING SLIDE ACTION - MEDIUM FRAME

YEAR	SER. # START	SER. # END
1884	1	3074
1885	3075	12649
1886	12650	20499
1887	20500	24999
1888	25000	32999
1889	33000	40999
1890	41000	49999
1891	50000	63199
1892	63200	65999
1893	66000	70999
1894	71000	75999
1895	76000	78999
1896	79000	80499
1897	80500	82499
1898	82500	83999
1899	84000	85799
1900	85800	87799
1901	87800	89299
1902	89300	89777

LIGHTNING SLIDE ACTION - LARGE FRAME

YEAR	SER. # START	SER. # END
1887	1	999
1888	1000	2399
1889	2400	3799
1890	3800	5199
1891	5200	5699
1892	5700	5999
1893	6000	6299
1894	6300	6496

AR-15 - SPORTER MODELS

YEAR	SER. # START	SER. # END
1963	SP00001	SP00023
SP00024-SP00100 Specials		
1964	SP00101	SP02500
1965	SP02501	SP05599
1966	SP05600	SP08249
1967	SP08250	SP10749
1968	SP10750	SP13999
1969	SP14000	SP14653
1970	SP15001	SP15473
1971	SP16001	SP19400
1972	SP19401	SP24200
1973	SP24201	SP32600
1974	SP32601	SP43800
1975	SP43801	SP55300
1976	SP55301	N/A

COLT BLACKPOWDER 2ND GENERATION SERIALIZATION

MODEL NO.	SER. # RANGE	TOTAL	START	END
MODEL1851 NAVY				
C-1121	4201 25100	20900	1971	1978
C-1122				
As above but at higher range of numbers Unk'n - 1978				
MODEL 1851 NAVY, R. E. LEE				
C-9001	251 REL 5000 REL	4750	-	1971
1851 NAVY, U. S. GRANT				
C-9002	251 USG5000 USG	4750	-	1971
MODEL 1851 GRANT-LEE PAIR				
C-9003	01 GLP 250 GLP	250	-	1971
3rd MODEL DRAGOON				
C-1770	20801 20826	25	1974	1978
Prototype	20901 24501	3601		
C-1770MN	S/N As Above	20	1984	1984
MODEL 1851 NAVY				
F-1100	24900 29150	4250	5/80	10/81
F-1101	S/N As Above	300	10/81	11/81
W/Blank Cylinders				
F-1110	29151 S 29640 S	489	6/82	10/82
Stainless Steel				
MODEL 1860 ARMY				
F-1200	201000212835	7593	11/78	11/82
Rebated Cylinder				

MODEL 1860 ARMY, cont.

MODEL NO.	SER. # RANGE	TOTAL	START	END
F-1200 EBO				
	S/N As Above	500	1979	1979
Butterfield				
F-1200 LNK				
	S/N As Above	Unk'n	Unk'n	Unk'n
Electroless Nickel				
F-1200 MN				
	S/N As Above	12	1984	1984
Nickel/Ivory				
F-1202				
	S/N As Above	500	1979	1979
Limited Edition				
F-1203	207330211250	2670	7/80	10/81
Fluted Cylinder				
F-1210	211263 S 212540 S	1278	1/82	4/82
Stainless Steel				

1861 NAVY

F-1300	40000 43165	3166	9/80	10/81

1862 POCKET NAVY

F-1400	48000 58850	5765	12/79	11/81
	and skip odd no.			
F-1400MN				
	S/N As Above	25	1984	1984
Nickel/Ivory				
F-1401				
	S/N As Above	500	1979	1980
Limited Edition				

1862 POCKET POLICE

F-1500	49000 57300	4801	1/80	9/81
	and skip even no.			
F-1500 MN				
	S/N As Above	25	1984	1984
Nickel/Ivory				
F-1501				
	S/N As Above	500	1979	1980
Limited Edition				

1847 WALKER

F-1600	1200 4120	2573	6/80	4/82
	32256 32500	245	5/81	9/81

1st MODEL DRAGOON

F-1700	25100 34500	3878	1/80	2/82

2nd MODEL DRAGOON

F-172	S/N As Above and Mix at Random for			
	1st, 2nd & 3rd	2676	1/80	2/82

3rd MODEL DRAGOON

F-140	S/N As Above and Mix at Random for			
	1st, 2nd & 3rd	2856	1/80	2/82
	31401 31450	50	10/81	11/81
F-1740EGA	Unk'n Unk'n	200	1982	1982
(Garabaldi Model<- "GCA" prefix)				

BABY DRAGOON

F-1760	16000 17851	1852	2/81	4/81
F-1761	S/N As Above	500	1979	1980
Limited Edition				

1860 ARMY

MODEL NO.	SER. # RANGE	TOTAL	START	END
F-9005	US 001/001 US to			
	US 3025/3025 US	3025	9/77	1/80
Cavalry Commemorative (Two Gun Set)				

HERITAGE WALKER

F-9006	01 1853	1853	6/80	6/81

JOHN DICKSON & SON SERIALIZATION

YEAR STARTING	SER. # END
1812-1854	1-1500
1860	2000
1864	2500
1870	3000
1878	3500
1885	3933
1886	4000
1889	4889
1892	4500
1898	5000
1903	5500

A.H. FOX SERIALIZATION

For a factory letter on an A.H. Fox, contact the Cody Firearms Records Office at the Buffalo Bill Center of the West at 720 Sheridan Ave., Cody, WY 82414, go to www.centerofthewest.org, call 307-578-4031, or email cfmrecords@centerofthewest.org. This is a fee service.

GRADE A-F 12 GAUGE

YEAR STARTING	SER. # END
1907	7500
1908	7600
1909	9900
1910	15000
1911	18700
1912	20000
1913	20700
1914	21500
1915	22000
1916	23200
1917	24300
1918	24700
1919	25000
1920	25900
1921	27000
1922	27900
1923	29000
1924	30000
1925	30900
1926	31600
1927	32000
1928	32900
1929	33850
1930	33900
1931	33999
1932	34100
1933	34200
1934	34300
1935	34400
1936	34500

GRADE A-F 16 GAUGE

YEAR STARTING	SER. # END
1937	34750
1938	34900
1939	35150
1940	35280
1912	300075
1913	300200
1914	300400

GRADE A-F 16 GAUGE, cont.

YEAR STARTING	SER. # END
1915	300600
1916	300700
1917	300750
1918	300800
1919	300900
1920	301100
1921	301300
1922	301500
1923	301800
1924	302000
1925	302300
1926	302500
1927	302650
1928	302800
1929	303000
1930	303050
1931	303100
1932	303200
1933	303300
1934	303350
1935	303400
1936	303500
1937	303650
1938	303800
1939	303850
1940	303870
Highest no.	303875

GRADE A-F 20 GAUGE

YEAR STARTING	SER. # END
1912	200100
1913	200250
1914	200500
1915	200700
1916	200800
1917	200900
1918	201000
1919	201300
1920	201500
1921	201600
1922	201800
1923	202000
1924	202200
1925	202400
1926	202500
1927	202800
1928	202950
1929	203100
1930	203150
1931	203200
1932	203300
1933	203350
1934	203500
1935	203700
1936	203750
1937	203800
1938	203830
1939	203900
1940	203970
Highest no.	203974

STERLINGWORTH 12 GAUGE

YEAR STARTING	SER. # END
1910	53800
1911	59000
1912	63500

STERLINGWORTH 12 GAUGE, cont.

YEAR STARTING	SER. # END
1913	66500
1914	74200
1915	75600
1916	77500
1917	79000
1918	82000
1919	84500
1920	89500
1921	92300
1922	94500
1923	97500
1924	99000
1925	100600
1926	105500
1927	113500
1928	119000
1929	122600
1930	128500
1931	130000
1932	132000
1933	134000
1934	136000
1935	138000
1936	139000
1937	145000
1938	150000
1939	155000
1940	161500
Highest no.	161556

STERLINGWORTH 16 GA.

YEAR STARTING	SER. # END
1913	351000
1914	351600
1915	352300
1916	353000
1917	353700
1918	354200
1919	355000
1920	356500
1921	357000
1922	357800
1923	358500
1924	359500
1925	359900
1926	360300
1927	362000
1928	364500
1929	366400
1930	367500
1931	368000
1932	368600
1933	369200
1934	369900
1935	372000
1936	373500
1937	374200
1938	374800
Highest no.	378481

STERLINGWORTH 20 GAUGE

YEAR STARTING	SER. # END
1912	250100
1913	252000
1914	253000
1915	254500
1916	254600

STERLINGWORTH 20 GAUGE, cont.

YEAR STARTING	SER. # END
1917	254700
1918	255000
1919	255300
1920	255800
1921	256100
1922	256400
1923	256800
1924	257200
1925	257700
1926	258200
1927	259300
1928	260500
1929	262000
1930	263600
1931	263800
1932	264000
1933	264300
1934	264600
1935	266500
1936	268500
1937	270500
1938	270800
1939	271200
1940	271225
Highest no.	271304

SINGLE BARREL TRAP - GRADE J, K, L, M

YEAR STARTING	SER. # END
1919	400090
1920	400250
1921	400275
1922	400300
1923	400325
1924	400350
1925	400375
1926	400385
1927	400395
1928	400400
1929	400410
1930	400415
1931	400425
1932	400500
1933	400525
1934	400540
1935	400568

GERMAN EARLY DATE CODES

Determining the date of manufacture for early German arms is not as simple as looking up a serial number. If the manufacturer is still in existence, contacting the manufacturer with model and serial number information may result in determining a date of manufacture. There are, however, some numeric stampings on German arms that, when present, indicate a month and year of manufacture. They will appear as three or four digit date codes that may appear with or without punctuation.

Examples

Code	Date
535	May 1935
5.35	May 1935
5/35	May 1935
1163	November 1963
11.63	November 1963
11/63	November 1963

GERMAN MODERN DATE CODES

Determining the year of manufacture for modern German arms is much simpler. The two letter code is found as part of or near the proof marks and can be interpreted using the following chart.

A	B	C	D	E	F	G	H	I	K
0	1	2	3	4	5	6	7	8	9

Examples

Code	Date
KK	99 or 1999
IF	85 or 1985

STEPHEN GRANT SERIALIZATION

YEAR STARTING	SER. # END
1867	2480
1870	3000
1875	3900
1880	4750
1885	5450
1890	6100
1895	6700
1896	6857
1900	7300

GREAT WESTERN ARMS CO. PRODUCTION PERCENTAGES AND NUMBERS

The Great Western Arms Co. manufactured a total of approximately 22,238 single action revolvers circa 1954-1964. The following information was compiled using the Great Western Survivor List (a list of GW revolver serial numbers that has been inspected and recorded) and filling the S/N gaps with intelligent guesses. The revised list was then broken down by approximate percentage of production showing caliber, barrel length, and finish. Model information is shown in approximate numbers produced. This information was compiled by Mr. Carlyle H. Pack.

CALIBER	PERCENTAGE
.22	46.94%
.45 LC	16.13%
.38 SPEC	13.83%
.357 ATOMIC	9.79%
.44 SPEC	4.93%
.44 MAG	3.85%
.357 MAG	3.14%
.22 HORNET	.88%
.44-40	.26%
.22 MAG	.12%
.45 ACP	.09%

BARREL LENGTH	PERCENTAGE
5 1/2 "	71.44%
7 1/2 "	16.52%
4 3/4 "	10.90%
4 "	.78%
12 "	.35%

FINISHES	PERCENTAGES
BLUE/CCH	47.91%
BLUE	42.48%
PARKERIZED	4.39%
NICKEL	4.29%
CHROME	.824%
GOLD	.05%
SILVER	.02%

GREAT WESTERN ARMS CO. PRODUCTION PERCENTAGES AND NUMBERS, cont.

MODEL TYPE	NUMBER
FRONTIER	20,462
KITS	799
FAST DRAW	641
DEPUTIES	124
SHERIFF	98
BUNTLINE	76
TARGET	39

W. W. GREENER SERIALIZATION

YEAR STARTING	SER. # END
1878	19304
1880	22860
1895	38917
1902	50911
1915	58536
1920	62621
1930	68635
1967	79259

HARRINGTON & RICHARDSON SERIALIZATION 1940 - 1982

The following serial numbered prefixes are related to the corresponding year of manufacture:

YEAR STARTING	S.N. PREFIX
1940	A
1941	B
1942	C
1943	D
1944	E
1945	F
1946	G
1947	H
1948	I
1949	J
1950	K
1951	L
1952	M
1953	N
1954	P
1955	R
1956	S
1957	T
1958	U
1959	V
1960	W
1961	X
1962	Y
1963	Z
1964	AA
1965	AB
1966	AC
1967	AD
1968	AE
1969	AF
1970	AG
1971	AH
1972	AJ
1973	AL
1974	AM
1975	AN
1976	AP
1977	AR

HARRINGTON & RICHARDSON SERIALIZATION 1940 - 1982, cont.

YEAR STARTING	S.N. PREFIX
1978	AS
1979	AT
1980	AU
1981	AX
1982	AY

H&R SINGLE BARREL SHOTGUNS

The following is a years of production listing for all Main Line single barrel shotguns produced by Harrington & Richardson with a cross reference to Deluxe and Youth variations.

MODEL	DATES	YEARS MFG.
1900	1901-1916	15 Years
1905 (Small Frame)	1906-1915	10 Years
1908	1909-1930	32 Years
1915 (Small Frame)	1916-1930	15 Years
No. 5	1931-1942	12 Years
No. 8	1931-1942	12 Years
48 (First use of the TOPPER name)	1943-1956	14 Years
188 (Deluxe variant of Model 48)	1943-1956	14 Years
148	1957-1961	5 Years
488 (Deluxe variant of Model 148)	1957-1961	5 Years
480 (Youth variant of Model 148)	1957-1961	5 Years
158	1962-1973	12 Years
198 (Deluxe variant of Model 158)	1962-1973	12 Years
490 (Youth variant of Model 158)	1962-1981	20 Years
058	1974-1981	8 Years
098 (Deluxe variant of Model 058)	1974-1981	8 Years
088 (Economy model)	1979-1986	5 Years
088 JR (Youth variant of Model 088)	1979-1986	5 Years
099 Deluxe	1982-1986	5 Years

HIGH STANDARD SERIALIZATION

The author wishes to express thanks to Mr. John J. Stimson, Jr. for the following information.

The serial numbers listed represent the highest serial number shipped for the year. Regular serial numbers began with 5,000 which was shipped October 15, 1932. Although it appears the guns were generally assembled in numerical sequence, the shipments were not and some guns may have remained in inventory for weeks, months, or even years between assembly and shipment.

YEAR	SER. # END
1932	5,102
1933	6,567
1934	8,313
1935	11,651
1936	18,751
1937	30,026

YEAR	SER. # END
1938	39,430
1939	50,619
1940	70,715
1941	91,986
1942	104,520
1943	115,423
1944	135,659
1945	145,817
1946	174,194
1947	233,402
1948	301,349
1949	326,123
1950	335,693
1951	356,899
1952	357,295
1953	442,984
1954	475,186
1955	508,613
1956	652,405
1957	776,129
1958	913,111
1959	1,044,802
1960	1,147,641
1961	1,224,652
1962	1,285,049
1963	1,353,764
1964	1,418,870
1965	1,507,541
1966	1,610,707
1967	1,853,513
1968	2,030,404
1969	2,172,356
1970	2,232,503
1971	2,828,293
1972	2,356,207
1973	2,424,175
1974	2,469,497

1975 is the last year of the regular serial number series (except for Sr. No. 2,500,811 shipped August 28, 1976) and marks the beginning of the letter prefix serialization.

YEAR	SR. NO.	SR. NO.	SR. NO.
1975	2,500,810	G 04,566	ML 06,747
1976		G 13,757	ML 23,065
1977	G 18,298	G 162,590	ML 29,707
1978	G 20,223		ML 41,270
1979			ML 63,483

HIGH STANDARD SERIALIZATION, cont.

YEAR	SR. NO.	SR. NO.	SR. NO.
1980	MLG 20,408		ML 81,629
1981	SH 18,446		ML 90,000
1982	SH 25,964		
1983	SH 31,558		
1984	SH 34,034		

HOLLAND & HOLLAND SERIALIZATION

PARADOX SERIES

YEAR STARTING	SERIAL NUMBER
1885	11500
1886	N/A
1887	N/A
1888	11691
1889	11788
1890	11865
1891	11948
1895	15036
1892	15075
1895	15347
1900	15558
1903	15655
1905	15750
1906	15825
1907	15860
1911	15900
1914	15950
1919	19560
1922	15970
1930	15980
1956	15979

RECORDED DATES

YEAR STARTING	SERIAL NUMBER
March 1856 (First Recorded Date)	565
October 1868	580
February 1857	584
August 1859	700
A gap in records	728-1059
1864	1060
1865	1101
1868	1352
1869	1439
1870	1578
1871	1769
1872	2002
1873	2401
1874	2759
1875	3174
1876	3649
1877	4179
1878	4774
1879	5274
1880	5819
1881	6382
1882	7009
1883	7473
1884	7904
1885	8406
1886	8809
1887	8999
Unused	9000-10000
Missing	10000-10849
Rook Rifles	10850-10999
Normal Series	11000-11499
Paradox Guns	11500-11999
Normal Series	12000-12999
Rook Rifles	13000-13999
Normal Series	14000-14999
Paradox Guns	15000-15999
Normal Series	16000-16999
Normal Series	17000-17399
Rifles and Rook Rifles	17400-17999
Believed Unused	18000-18999
Rifles	19000-19999
Misc. Guns and Rifles	20000-21999
See separate lists	22000+

ROOK RIFLES

YEAR STARTING	SERIAL NUMBER
1887	10850-10999
Assumed 1888 records missing	11000-11499
1889	13106
1890	13465
1891	13566
1892	13674
1893	13885-13999
1894 Rook/other rifles	17401
1899	17999

MAGAZINE RIFLES

YEAR STARTING	SERIAL NUMBER
1910	28000
1911	28100
1913	28199
1913	28300
1919	28399
1920-29	1-581
1930-33	582-880
1920-32	881-1181
1935-49	1182-1782
1949-60	1783-2179
1951-58	2180-2577
1952-62	2578-2977
1958-65	2978-3377
1964-74	3378-3783
1975-80	3784-4000
1981-87	4001-4250
1988-92	4251-4330

PLAIN GUNS

YEAR STARTING	SERIAL NUMBER
1907	26200
1908	26300
1909	26400
1909	26500
1910	26600
1911	26700
1912	26800
1913	26900
1913	26999
1913	28600
1914	28700
1914	28800
1915	28900
1915	28999
1915	29500
1915	29600
1916	29700
1919	29800
1919	29900
1919	30000
1920	30100
1922	30200
1924	30300
1925	30334
1925	31100
1926	31200
1928	31300
1929	31399
1929	32200
1931	32300
1933	32400
1935	32499
1935	34000
1936	34100

PLAIN GUNS, cont.

YEAR STARTING	SERIAL NUMBER
1937	34200
1939	34300
1949	34400
1953	34500
1956	34600
1961	34700
1975	34800

ROYAL GUNS

YEAR STARTING	SERIAL NUMBER
1899	22000
1900	22500
1902	23000
1903	23500
1906	25000
1907	25500
1910	25599
1910	27000
1911	27250
1912	27500
1913	27750
1914	27999
1914	29000
1915	29100
1919	29200
1920	29300
1920	29400
1921	29499
1921	30500
1922	30600
1922	30700
1924	30800
1925	30900
1926	30999
1926	31500
1927	31600
1927	31700
1928	31800
1929	31900
1929	32900
1934	32999
1934	33000
1935	33100
1936	33200
1937	33300
1937	33400
1939	33500
1946	33600
1948	33700
1950	33800
1952	33900
1954	33999
1954	36251
1956	36300
1958	36400
1959	36500
1962	36600
1964	36700
1965	36800
1970	36900
1970	40006
1972	40100
1974	40200
1979	40300
1980	40400
1981	40500
1982	40530
1983	40560

ROYAL GUNS, cont.

YEAR STARTING	SERIAL NUMBER
1984	40590
1985	40650
1986	40770
1987	40820
1988	40880
1989	40920
1990	41000
1991	41075
1992	41150
1993	41210

ROYAL OVER & UNDER GUNS

YEAR STARTING	SERIAL NUMBER
1950	36000
1952	36010
1954	36020
1958	36029
1993	51001

SPORTING OVER & UNDER GUNS

YEAR STARTING	SERIAL NUMBER
1993	50500

CAVALIER GUNS

YEAR STARTING	SERIAL NUMBER
1986	50001
1989	50150
1992	50250

ROYAL DOUBLE RIFLES - .450 & .465 cals.

YEAR STARTING	SERIAL NUMBER
1910	28200
1914	28299
1914	28500
1919	28535
1921	30335
1921	30415
1925	31042
1925	31049
1927	32000
1941	32099

ROYAL DOUBLE RIFLES - .375 cals.

YEAR STARTING	SERIAL NUMBER
1911	28400
1920	28499
1920	30416
1925	30499
1925	31050
1927	31099
1927	32100
1933	32199

ROYAL DOUBLE RIFLES - .240 & Small Bores Cals.

YEAR STARTING	SERIAL NUMBER
1920	28566
1923	28599
1923	31000
1926	31041
1926	31400
1931	31450
1955	31499

ROYAL DOUBLE RIFLES ALL CALS.

YEAR STARTING	SERIAL NUMBER
1933	35000
1939	35100
1950	35200
1953	35250
1956	35300
1963	35350
1968	35450
1975	35495
1977	35498
1980	35500
1981	35505
1984	35524
1985	35527
1988	35540
1989	35542
1990	35552
1991	35590

ITALIAN YEAR OF MFG. DATE CODES

Additional information regarding Italian Proof marks, and dates of manufacture can be found in THE WORLD OF BERETTA *An International Legend by R. L. Wilson.*

All Dates Prior to 1945 Have Year in Digits.

CODE	YEAR
I	1945
II	1946
III	1947
IV	1948
V	1949
VI	1950
VII	1951
VIII	1952
IX	1953
X	1954
XI	1955
XII	1956
XIII	1957
XIV	1958
XV	1959
XVI	1960
XVII	1961
XVIII	1962
XIX	1963
XX	1964
XXI	1965
XXII	1966
XXIII	1967
XXIV	1968
XXV	1969
XXVI	1970
XX7	1971
XX8	1972
XX9	1973
XXX	1974
AA	1975
AB	1976

ITALIAN YEAR OF MFG. DATE CODES, cont.

CODE	YEAR
AC	1977
AD	1978
AE	1979
AF	1980
AH	1981
AI	1982
AL	1983
AM	1984
AN	1985
AP	1986
AS	1987
AT	1988
AU	1989
AZ	1990
BA	1991
BB	1992
BC	1993
BD	1994
BF	1995
BH	1996
BI	1997
BL	1998
BM	1999
BN	2000
BP	2001
BS	2002
BT	2003
BU	2004
BZ	2005
CA	2006
CB	2007
CC	2008
CD	2009
CF	2010
CH	2011
CI	2012
CL	2013
CM	2014
CN	2015

ITHACA GUN CO. SERIALIZATION

For a factory letter on an Ithaca, Lefever Arms Company, or Western Arms Corporation shotgun, contact the Cody Firearms Records Office at the Buffalo Bill Center of the West at 720 Sheridan Ave., Cody, WY 82414, go to www.centerofthewest.org, call 307-578-4031, or email cfmrecords@centerofthewest.org. This is a fee service.

BAKER MODEL ITHACA DOUBLES

YEAR STARTING	SERIAL NUMBER
1880-1885	2447
1886	4104
1887	7003
1888	8787
1889 (Jan.-Aug.)	10534

CRASS MODEL ITHACA DOUBLES

YEAR STARTING	SERIAL NUMBER
1892	17235-21999
1893	25421
1894	25759
1895	27762
1896	28713
1897	30222
1898	33026
1899	38399
1900	46627
1901	61609
1902	76599
1903	94108

FLUES MODEL ITHACA DOUBLE & SINGLE

YEAR STARTING	SERIAL NUMBER
1908	175000-182031
1909	192499
1910	205399
1911	216499
1912	230099
1913	242599
1914	256699
1915	268199
1916	276899
1917	289299
1918	299799
1919	315399
1920	343335
1921	356513
1922	361849
1923	372099
1924	390499
1925	398352
1926	398365

N.I.D. MODEL ITHACA DOUBLE

YEAR STARTING	SERIAL NUMBER
1925	425000-425299
1926	439199
1927	451099
1928	454530
1929	457299
1930	458399
1931	459139
1932	459162
1933	459195
1935	459637
1936	459649
1935	460799
1936	462399
1937	464699
1938	464827
1939	464850
1940	464899
1938	465199
1939	465999
1940	466999
1941	467146
1946	467199
1941	468099
1946	468699
1947	468794
1948	468799
1947	469949
1948	469979
1948	470099

CHARLES LANCASTER SERIALIZATION

YEAR STARTING	SERIAL NUMBER
1826	100
1830	600
1840	1200
1850	2100
1860	3200
1861	3400
1862	3540
1863	3693
1864	3805
1865	3914
1866	3999
1867	4087
1868	4183

CHARLES LANCASTER SERIALIZATION, cont.

YEAR STARTING	SERIAL NUMBER
1869	4271
1870	4328
1871	4401
1872	4477
1873	4562
1874	4644
1875	4714
1876	4769
1877	4833
1878	4892
1879	4924
1880	4949
1881	4982
1882	5079
1883	5186
1884	5359
1885	5497
1886	5627
1887	5764
1888	5926
1889	6136
1890	6406
1891	6671
1892	6988
1893	7189
1894	7360
1895	7548
1896	7709
1897	7940
1898	8132
1899	8353
1900	8529
1901	8700

JOSEPH LANG SERIALIZATION

YEAR STARTING	SERIAL NUMBER
1858	2085
1860	2332
1865	2970
1870	3916
1875	5180
1880	6000
1885	7031
1890	7546
1895	8150
1900	9100

MARLIN FIREARMS COMPANY SERIALIZATION

Approximate serialization for Marlin rifles from 1883 to 1906 including Models 1881, 1888, 1889, 1891, 1892, 1894, and 1897. Marlin did not assign a specific block of serial number to these models. Using this list will place the year of manufacture plus or minus one year.

For a factory letter on Marlin, contact the Cody Firearms Records Office at the Buffalo Bill Center of the West at 720 Sheridan Ave., Cody, WY 82414, go to www.centerofthewest.org, call 307-578-4031, or email cfmrecords@centerofthewest.org. This is a fee service.

Older Rifles Mfg.

YEAR	FROM #	TO #
1883	4001	6700
1884	6701	8850
1885	8851	11300
1886	11301	15000
1887	15001	17800
1888	17801	21500
1889	21501	30000
1890	30001	45000
1891	45001	63250
1892	63251	80250
1893	80251	95750
1894	95751	115000
1895	115001	133000
1896	133001	144400
1897	144401	161200
1898	161201	175500
1899	175501	196000
1900	196001	213000
1901	213001	233300
1902	233301	262500
1903	262501	287300
1904	287301	310500
1905	310501	329000
1906	329001	355300

1948-1968 Mfg.

YEAR	SERIAL NO. PREFIX
1948	E
1949	F
1950	G
1951	H
1952	J
1953	K
1954	L
1955	M
1956	N
1957	P
1957-1958	R
1958-1959	S
1960	T
1960-Aug. 1961	U
1961-Aug. 1962	V
1963	W
1964	Y & Z
1965	AA
1966	AB
1967	AC
1968	AD

MAUSER BROOMHANDLES SERIALIZATION 1896 - late 1930

SER. #	DATE	NATURE OF CHANGES
before	1896	- The cone hammer used in place of spur hammer.
#25	1896	- "SYSTEM MAUSER" marked on top of the chamber.
before	1897	- The locking system changed from one to two lugs.
#200		- The barrel contour at the chamber is tapered instead of stepped.
#390	1897	- "WAFFENFABRIK MAUSER OBERNDORF A/N" marked on top of the chamber.

MAUSER BROOMHANDLES
SERIALIZATION 1896 - late 1930, cont.

SER. #	DATE	NATURE OF CHANGES
#975	1897	- The center section of the rear panel on the left side of the frame is not milled out (this feature appears earlier on a few 20-shot pistols). This area is sometimes used for special markings on contract pieces such as the Turkish and Persian.
#12,200 to #14,999	1898	- The large ring hammer replaces the cone hammer.
#21,000	1899	- There is no panel milling on either side of the frame.
		- A single lug bayonet type mount adopted for retaining the firing pin instead of the dovetail plate.
		- The trigger is mounted directly to the frame by two integral lugs rather than attached to a removable block.
		- The position of the serial number moved from the rear of the frame above the stock slot to the left side of the chamber.
#22,000	1900	- Two integral lugs used to mount the rear sight instead of a pin.
#29,000	1902	- Very shallow panels milled into the frame on both sides.*
#31,200	1903	- "WAFFENFABRIK MAUSER OBERNDORF A NECKAR" added to the right rear frame panel.*
#34,000	1904	- The depth of the frame panel milling increased.*
#35,000	1904	- The barrel extension side rails lengthened about a half inch.*
		- An additional lug for mounting added to the firing pin.*
		- The hammer changed to the small ring pattern.*
		- The safety mechanism altered to require that the lever be pushed up to engage it instead of down.*
		- The center of the safety lever knob is no longer milled out.*
#38,000	1905	- The short extractor with two ribs replaces the long thin extractor.*
#100,000	1910	- The rifling changed from four groove to six groove.
#130,000	1911	
#270,000	1915	- "NS" (Neues Sicherung or New Safety) appears on the back of the hammer. The hammer must be moved back beyond the cocked position to engage the safety.
#440,000	1921	- The lanyard ring stud is rotated 90 degrees.
#501,000	1923	- The Mauser "banner" appears on the left rear frame panel.
#800,000	1930	- The Mauser banner is enlarged.
		- A step is added to the barrel contour just ahead of the chamber.
		- The safety is changed to allow the hammer to be dropped from a cocked position, without danger, by pulling the trigger (called Universal Safety).
		- The front of the grip frame widened to equal the rear part where the stock slot is.
#850,000	1932	- "D.R.P.u.A.P." (Deutsches Reich Patenten und Anderes Patenten) added below the inscription on the right rear frame panel.
#860,000	1932	- The lettering in the frame inscription is slanted forward.
#900,000	1934	- The serial number is moved to the rear of the barrel extension behind the sight.
		- The two grooves in each side of the barrel extension side rails are eliminated.

MAUSER BROOMHANDLES
SERIALIZATION 1896 - late 1930, cont.

These nine changes appear out of sequence on three small batches of guns (29,000 to 29,900, 40,000 to 41,000, and 42,600 to 43,900). Most of these pistols are of the "bolo" style, that is they have 3.9 inch barrels, small grips, six or 10-shot magazines and fixed or adjustable rear sights. A few of these pistols show non-standard barrel contours, barrel extension milling and hammer safety devices. Apparently the factory withheld these numbers from the regular production series and reissued them at later dates.

PARKER BROTHERS SHOTGUNS SERIALIZATION 1866 - 1942

Additional information regarding Parker shotguns is available in PARKER GUN IDENTIFICATION & SERIALIZATION *compiled and edited by Charles E. Price & S.P. Fjestad available on www.bluebookofgunvalues.com.*

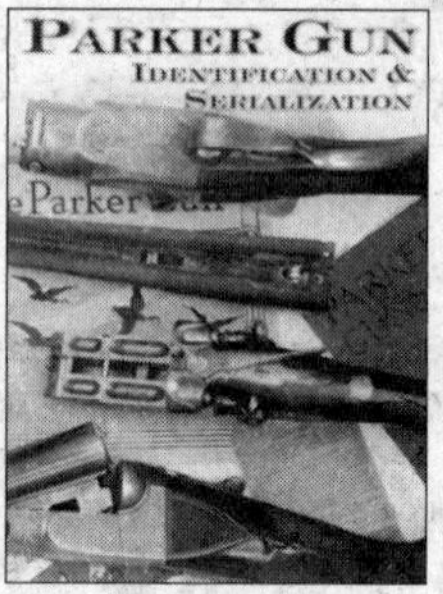

YEAR STARTING	SERIAL NUMBER
1866-1868	0-6,800
1868-1877	9,700
1877-1879	15,700
1880	17,600
1881	22,700
1882	27,300
1883	34,900
1884	36,000
1885	46,450
1886	48,125
1887	56,650
1889	59,500

PARKER BROTHERS
SHOTGUNS SERIALIZATION 1866 - 1942, cont.

YEAR STARTING	SERIAL NUMBER
1890	61,350
1891	66,800
1892	71,600
1893	77,000
1894	80,300
1895	82,400
1896	85,200
1897	86,450
1898	89,350
1899	92,450
1900	97,300
1901	105,750
1902	113,100
1903	121,900
1904	129,200
1905	132,000
1906	138,300
1907	144,250
1908	148,250
1910	153,000
1911	157,050
1912	157,800
first year of Trojan grade	
1913	165,000
1914	168,200
1915	171,500
1916	173,450
1917	175,650
first single barrel trap gun	
1918	180,250
1919	184,900
1920	190,100
1921	195,000
1922	200,500
first Parker single trigger	
1923	205,150
1924	207,150
first beaver tail forend	
1925	214,400
1926	218,050
first ventilated rib, first .410	
1927	222,650
1928	228,200
PH grade dropped	
1929	230,700
1930	234,200
1931	235,950
1932	236,100
1933	236,300
1934	236,650
first skeet guns, takeover of factory by Remington	
1935	237,000
1936	239,900
last regular catalog	
1937	240,300
1938-1942	242,385

PIOTTI SERIALIZATION

YEAR STARTING	SERIAL NUMBER
1962	1
1962	515
1963	1285
1964	1913
1965	2594
1966	2988
1967	3351
1968	3954

PIOTTI SERIALIZATION, cont.

YEAR STARTING	SERIAL NUMBER
1969	4787
1970	5018
1971	5499
1972	5815
1973	6180
1974	6437
1975	6650
1976	6839
1977	7025
1978	7236
1979	7388
1980	7524
1981	7663
1982	7797
1983	7918
1984	8038
1985	8179
1986	8318
1987	8465
1988	8605
1989	8753
1990	8878
1991	8978
1992	9063

JAMES PURDEY & SONS, LTD. SERIALIZATION

YEAR STARTING	SERIAL NUMBER
1814-1825	974
1826	1149
1827	1324
1828	1549
1829	1874
1830	1999
1831	2247
1832	2421
1833	2497
1834	2697
1835	2773
1836	2848
1837	3098
1838	3223
1839	3298
1840	3473
1841	3623
1842	3698
1843	3848
1844	3998
1845	4048
1846	4098
1847	4223
1848	4348
1849	4473
1850	4599
1851	4720
1852	4844
1853	4944
1854	5093
1855	5167
1856	5267
1857	5443
1858	5542
1859	5747
1860	5997
1861	6271
1862	6422
1863	6671
1864	6871

JAMES PURDEY & SONS, LTD. SERIALIZATION, cont.

YEAR STARTING	SERIAL NUMBER
1865	7121
1866	7420
1867	7646
1868	7896
1869	8246
1870	8322
1871	8646
1872	8821
1873	9096
1874	9288
1875	9505
1876	9648
1877	10153
1878	10440
1879	10800
1880	10900
1881	11082
1882	11342
1883	11669
1884	12036
1885	12171
1886	12530
1887	12875
1888	13150
1889	13468
1890	13662
1891	14000
1892	14520
1893	14851
1894	15134
1895	15362
1896	15726
1897	16095
1898	16420
1899	16736
1900	17078
1901	17227
1902	17547
1903	17849
1904	18148
1905	18400
1906	18686
1907	18987
1908	19272
1909	19546
1910	19813
1911	20147
1912	20400
1913	20770
1914	21086
1915	21332
1916	21465
1917	21541
1919	21574
1920	21892
1921	22111
1922	22312
1923	22491
1924	22896
1925	22937
1926	23283
1927	23284
1928	23551
1929	23854
1930	24139
1931	24387
1932	24567
1933	24647
1934	24743

JAMES PURDEY & SONS, LTD. SERIALIZATION, cont.

YEAR STARTING	SERIAL NUMBER
1935	24920
1936	25130
1937	25325
1938	25526
1939	25711
1940	25783
1941	25793
1942	25813
1943	25844
1945	25851
1946	25901
1947	25990
1948	26051
1949	26128
1950	26206
1951	26275
1952	26349
1953	26423
1955	26531
1975	28003
1979	28546
1981	28569

REMINGTON DATE CODE DATA & SxS SHOTGUN SERIALIZATION

Firearms Identification (Code located on barrel, left side of frame) Month of Manufacture (Code letter corresponds to numeral underneath).
The following barrel code information is reliable when used to identify the month and year of manufacture of Remington rifles since Remington seldom replaced barrels. When used to date Remington shotguns, where the barrel is easily changed, make sure the barrel is original to the shotgun.
For example "KP" would be 5 (May) 1923, and "RYY" would be 11 (November) 1952.

B	L	A	C	K	P	O	W	D	E	R	X
1	2	3	4	5	6	7	8	9	10	11	12

YEAR OF MANUFACTURE AND LETTER CODE	
1921	M
1922	N
1923	P
1924	R
1925	S
1926	T
1927	U
1928	W
1929	X
1930	Y
1931	Z
1932	A
1933	B
1934	C
1935	D
1936	E
1937	F
1938	G
1939	H
1940	J
1941	K
1942	L
1943	MM
1944	NN

REMINGTON DATE CODE
DATA & SxS SHOTGUN SERIALIZATION, cont.

YEAR OF MANUFACTURE AND LETTER CODE	
1945	PP
1946	RR
1947	SS
1948	TT
1949	UU
1950	WW
1951	XX
1952	YY
1953	ZZ
1954	A
1955	B
1956	C
1957	D
1958	E
1959	F
1960	G
1961	H
1962	J
1963	K
1964	L
1965	M
1966	N
1967	P
1968	R
1969	S
1970	T
1971	U
1972	W
1973	X
1974	Y
1975	Z
1976	I
1977	O
1978	Q
1979	V
1980	A
1981	B
1982	C
1983	D
1984	E
1985	F
1986	G
1987	H
1988	J
1989	K
1990	L
1991	M
1992	N
1993	O
1994	P
1995	Q
1996	R
1997	S
1998	T*
1999	U*
2000	V*
2001	W
2002	X
2003	Y
2004	Z
2005	A
2006	B
2007	C
2008	D
2009	E
2010	F
2011	G

REMINGTON DATE CODE
DATA & SxS SHOTGUN SERIALIZATION, cont.

YEAR OF MANUFACTURE AND LETTER CODE	
2012	H
2013	J
2014	K
2015	L
2016	M

Additional markings if present will indicate the following.

2	Part order replacement bbl.
3	Service section repair.
4	Returned as received.
5	Employee sale.

** Remington suspended barrel date code stamping circa August 1999 - October 2001, but did continue to mark shipping box end flaps with the date code.*

The author wishes to express thanks to Mr. Charles Semmer for the following Remington SxS shotgun serialization information.

E. REMINGTON & SONS
WHITMORE MODELS

MODEL	YEARS	SER. BLOCK	EST. TOTAL
1873	1873-1878	1-5000	5000
1875	1875-1877	1-3350	3350
1876	1876-1882	3350-5900	2250
1878	1878-1882	1-2400	2400
1879	1879-1888	W/ 1878	N/A

E. REMINGTON & SONS
MODELS 1882, 1883, 1885 AND 1887

MODEL	YEARS	SER. BLOCK	EST. TOTAL
1882	1882-1888	1000-17000	16000
1883	1882-1884	W/ 1882	N/A
1885	1885-1886	16700-20200	3500
1887	1886-1888	20200-23700	3500

REMINGTON ARMS COMPANY
MODEL 1889 TOTAL Mfg. 134200

YEAR STARTING	SERIAL NUMBER
1888	W/ 1887
1889	30000-32199
1890	32200-36949
1891	36950-43012
1892	43013-49844
1893	49845-58879
1894	58880-66016
1895	66017-73571
1896	73572-76980
1897	76981-80389
1898	80390-89123
1899	89124-97714
1900	EST. 97715-105000
1900	EST. 200000-205934
1901	205935-221450
1902	221451-234803
1903	234804-240530
1904	240531-247581
1905	247582-251192
1906	251193-254394
1907	254395-257745
1908	257746-259246
1909	N/A
1910	259247-259262

REMINGTON ARMS COMPANY
MODEL 1900 TOTAL Mfg. 98508

YEAR STARTING	SERIAL NUMBER
1900	300000-305000
1901	305001-317502
1902	317503-337038
1903	337039-343893
1904	343894-350207
1905	350208-354620
1906	354621-363060
1907	363061-372117
1908	372118-377925
1909	377926-382072
1910	382073-398507
1911	398508

REMINGTON ARMS COMPANY
MODEL 1894 TOTAL Mfg. 41194

YEAR STARTING	SERIAL NUMBER
1894	100,000-100,660
1895	100,661-103,106
1896	103,107-104,144
1897	104,145-106,916
1898	106,917-110,895
1899	110,896-116,139
1900	116,140-120,932
1901	120,933-123,913
1902	123,914-127,017
1903	127,018-129,349
1904	129,350-131,263
1905	131,264-133,042
1906	133,043-134,627
1907	134,628-136,292
1908	136,293-137,319
1909	137,320-137,988
1910	137,989-141,194

REMINGTON ARMS COMPANY
MODEL 1894 REM. SPCL.

TOTAL Mfg. Approx. 12, W/ 4 recorded

YEAR STARTING	SERIAL NUMBER
1902-1910	400000-400012

SAVAGE/STEVENS PRODUCTION DATA

The information below represents a listing of most Savage/Stevens rifles and shotguns mfg. in the past (some data has been approximated). Rather than list these models separately, they have been provided in this section for quick reference. Values on many of the models listed below typically range between $75-$500, depending on rarity and condition.

For a factory letter on an older Savage, contact the Cody Firearms Records Office at the Buffalo Bill Center of the West at 720 Sheridan Ave., Cody, WY 82414, go to www.centerofthewest.org, call 307-578-4031, or email cfmrecords@centerofthewest.org. This is a fee service.

SAVAGE ARMS CO.

MODEL	DATES	APPROX.GUNS
1903	1912-20	13,000
1904	1912-32	62,000
1905	1912-15	6,500
1909	1912-15	3,500
1911	1912-15	22,500
1912	1913-15	12,000

SAVAGE ARMS CO., cont.

MODEL	DATES	APPROX.GUNS
23A	1924-45	88,000
1914	1914-26	49,500
19	1933-45	16,000
1920	1920-32	12,000
1922	1922-25	16,000
23B	1924-45	16,500
23C	1924-42	14,500
23D	1932-45	15,000
3	1931-45	121,000
4	1933-45	38,000
5	1936-45	22,000
6	1938-45	45,500
7	1939-45	6,000
40	1928-42	16,000
45	1928-42	6,000
1925	1925-32	36,000
29	1933-45	23,500
CS22	1926-45	87,500
219	1938-45	12,500
220	1937-45	50,000
420	1937-42	13,500
430	1937-42	11.000
1921	1921-32	13,000
1928	1928-32	6,500
721	1930-32	12,000
FOX	1933-45	31,000
FOX B	1940-45	20,000

J. STEVENS ARMS CO.

MODEL	DATES	APPROX.GUNS
No. 12	1912-35	166,500
No. 14-1/2	1912-41	592,500
Fav.	1912-42	462,000
No. 26	1912-45	501,500
No. 44+414	1912-35	23,000
No. 70	1912-31	295,500
No. 71	1930-34	10,000
No. 75	1928-34	19,000
No. 15+425	1912-17	11,500
No. 35	1912-19	12,500
No. 35	1923-42	43,000
No. 41-43	1912-18	18,500
No. 10	1919-34	9,500
No. 85-89	1912-42	38,500
No. 93	1912-19	12,500
No. 97	1912-19	16,000
No. 101	1914-20	5,000
No. 105	1912-45	221,500
No. 107	1912-45	443,500
No. 106-08	1916-35	56,500
No. 115	1912-31	23,000
No. 124	1949-55	N/A
No. 125	1912-23	5,000
No. 180-85	1912-23	16,000
No. 958	1925-33	5,000
No. 116-17	1926-35	5,000
No. 946-48	1928-34	7,000
No. 215	1913-32	61,000
No. 235	1912-32	61,500
No. 315	1914-36	192,000
No. 385	1912-31	67,500
No. 345	1916-31	3,500
No. 311	1926-45	145,500
No. 330	1926-35	33,500
No. 335	1926-35	2,000
No. 520	1912-32	191,000
No. 521	1930-32	5,000
No. 60&61	1930-34	6,500
No. 620-21	1926-45	66,500
Mod. 30	1933-34	26,000
Mod. 31	1933-34	2,000
No. 15	1936-45	224,000
No. 11	1923-33	141,500
No. 95	1926-35	55,000

J. STEVENS ARMS CO., cont.

MODEL	DATES	APPROX.GUNS
No. 52	1933-37	88,000
No. 55	1935-36	3,500
No. 54	1933-42	23,500
No. 56	1933-45	97,500
No. 57	1939-42	500
No. 58	1933-45	29,500
No. 37	1936-42	29,000
No. 38	1936-45	33,500
No. 39	1938-45	64,000
No. 59	1938-45	21,000
No. 76	1938-45	6,000
No. 65-66	1929-45	174,000
No. 82	1936-37	35,500
No. 83	1936-42	159,000
No. 84	1936-45	99,500
No. 85	1939-43	14,000
No. 86	1936-43	82,500
No. 87	1938-45	200,000
No. 872	1940-42	3,500
No. 89	1926-37	12,000
No. 94	1926-45	934,000
No. 96	1926-33	3,500
No. 416	1937-42	2,000
No. 417	1932-42	1,000
No. 418	1932-42	1,500
No. 419	1932-36	1,000
No. 237	1936-43	16,000
No. 254	1936-42	1,000
No. 238	1936-45	40,000
No. 258	1936-45	11,000
No. 102-04	1936-42	500
No. 116	1936-42	1,000
No. 944	1936-42	1,500
No. 600	1936-42	5,500
No. 900	1936-42	2,000
No. 515	1936-42	500
No. 5151	1936-42	95,000
No. 530	1936-42	8,000
No. 500	1936-42	500
No. 22-410	1939-45	105,000
M.240	1940-45	20,500

SAVAGE MODEL NINETY-NINE SERIALIZATION

SERIAL NUMBERS AT YEAR END:	
10,000	1899
13,400	1900
19,500	1901
25,000	1902
35,000	1903
45,000	1904
53,000	1905
67,500	1906
73,500	1907
81,000	1908
95,000	1909
110,000	1910
119,000	1911
131,000	1912
146,500	1913
162,000	1914
175,500	1915
187,500	1916
193,000	1917
N/A	1918
212,500	1919
229,000	1920
237,500	1921
244,500	1922
256,000	1923
270,000	1924

SAVAGE MODEL NINETY-NINE SERIALIZATION, cont.

SERIAL NUMBERS AT YEAR END:	
280,000	1925
292,500	1926
305,000	1927
317,000	1928
324,500	1929
334,500	1930
338,500	1931
341,000	1932
344,500	1933
345,800	1934
350,800	1935
359,800	1936
N/A	1937
381,351	1938
388,640	1939
398,400	1940
416,000	1941
438,000	1946
464,000	1947
494,000	1948
528,000	1949
566,000	1950

L.C. SMITH SERIALIZATION

Existing L.C. Smith shotgun records include: Hunter Arms Company factory records circa 1890-1919, Hunter Arms Company shipping records circa 1918-1946, L.C. Smith Gun Company , 1946-1950 (FWS prefix), Marlin Firearms Company 1969-1971 (FWM prefix).

For a factory letter on an L.C. Smith, contact the Cody Firearms Records Office at the Buffalo Bill Center of the West at 720 Sheridan Ave., Cody, WY 82414, go to www.centerofthewest.org, call 307-578-4031, or email cfmrecords@centerofthewest.org. This is a fee service.

L.C. Smith (Manufactured by Hunter Arms Co. 1890-1918).

Hammer Shotguns

GAUGE	YEAR	SERIAL NO.
20	1907	5000-5131
20	1908	5379
20	1909	5677
20	1910	6238
20	1911	6593
20	1912	7076
20	1913	7521
20	1914	7828
20	1915	7935
20	1916	8149
20	1917	8250
10, 12, & 16	1894	50000-50867
10, 12, & 16	1895	51735
10, 12, & 16	1896	52602
10, 12, & 16	1897	55301
10, 12, & 16	1898	58000
10, 12, & 16	1900	79000-84943
10, 12, & 16	1901	89999
10, 12, & 16	1902	125000-129700
10, 12, & 16	1903	133039
10, 12, & 16	1904	137445
10, 12, & 16	1905	144409
10, 12, & 16	1906	150221
10, 12, & 16	1907	156901

Hammer Shotguns, cont.

GAUGE	YEAR	SERIAL NO.
10, 12, & 16	1908	159519
10, 12, & 16	1909	163160
10, 12, & 16	1910	166705
10, 12, & 16	1911	168761
10, 12, & 16	1912	171415
10, 12, & 16	1913	173371
10, 12, & 16	1914	175483
10, 12, & 16	1915	176091
10, 12, & 16	1916	176576
10, 12, & 16	1917	178522
10, 12, & 16	1918	179841

Hammerless Shotguns

GAUGE	YEAR	SERIAL NO.
20	1907	1000-1204
20	1908	1329
20	1909	1788
20	1910	2587
20	1911	3615
20	1912	4630
20	1913	4999
20	1913	10000-10786
20	1914	11451
20	1915	11873
20	1916	12361
20	1917	12666
20	1918	12753
10 & 12	1890	30000-32527
10 & 12	1891	34381
10 & 12	1892	36615
10 & 12	1893	37324
10 & 12	1894	38892
10 & 12	1895	40334
8, 10, 12, & 16	1896	40335-42219
8, 10, 12, & 16	1897	44104
8, 10, 12, & 16	1898	45999
16	1895	60000-60144
16	1896	60289
16	1897	60434
16	1898	60579
16	1899	60724
16	1900	60869
16	1901	61014
16	1902	61159
16	1903	61402
16	1904	61685
16	1905	62156
16	1906	62653
16	1907	63698
16	1908	64226
16	1909	65021
16	1910	65861
16	1911	66821
16	1912	67683
16	1913	68704
16	1914	69681
16	1915	69999
16	1915	400000-401758
10 & 12	1899	105210
10 & 12	1900	105917
10 & 12	1901	111681
10 & 12	1902	119035
10 & 12	1903	120767
10 & 12	1904	124419
10 & 12	1905	124999
10 & 12	1904	300000-300301
10 & 12	1905	305787
10 & 12	1906	311528

L.C. SMITH, cont.

Hammerless Shotguns, cont.

GAUGE	YEAR	SERIAL NO.
10 & 12	1907	318079
10 & 12	1908	322129
10 & 12	1909	329476
10 & 12	1910	333081
10 & 12	1911	336572
10 & 12	1912	341717
10 & 12	1913	345493
10 & 12	1914	350857
10 & 12	1915	352431
10 & 12	1916	355068
10 & 12	1917	359624
10 & 12	1918	361071
10, 12, & 16	1891	500-559
10, 12, & 16	1898	3173
10, 12, & 16	1901	6959
10, 12, & 16	1902	9000
10, 12, & 16	1902	200000-200025
10, 12, & 16	1903	201758
10, 12, & 16	1904	203272
10, 12, & 16	1905	205098
10, 12, & 16	1906	207093
10, 12, & 16	1907	209368
10, 12, & 16	1908	210579
10, 12, & 16	1909	211885
10, 12, & 16	1910	213084
10, 12, & 16	1911	214246
10, 12, & 16	1912	215615
10, 12, & 16	1913	216939
10, 12, & 16	1914	218260
10, 12, & 16	1915	218829
10, 12, & 16	1916	219603
10, 12, & 16	1917	219750

1918-1950 (These serial numbers include all types of L.C. Smith, Fulton and Hunter Shotguns).

YEAR	SERIAL NO.
1918	101-3850
1919	18252
1920	35228
1921	44566
1922	51985
1923	64187
1924	75897
1925	86695
1926	93841
1927	103900
1928	114817
1929	125347
1930	132827
1931	134242
1932	137779
1933	138371
1934	140146
1935	144296
1936	151123
1937	162670
1938	171179
1939	181701
1940	190280
1941	197124
1942	201794
1943	202959
1944	204084
1945	205423
1946	1-8595
1947	25661

1918-1950 (These serial numbers include all types of L.C. Smith, Fulton and Hunter Shotguns)., cont.

YEAR	SERIAL NO.
1948	41825
1949	55608
1950	56800

SMITH & WESSON PERFORMANCE CENTER PRODUCT CODE INFO.

The following Smith & Wesson Performance Center product code information appears courtesy of Mr. Jim Supica and Mr. Richard Nahas. I would like to thank them for making these product codes available. For additional information on Smith & Wesson firearms, the Standard Catalog of Smith & Wesson by Jim Supica and Richard Nahas is highly recomended. This book is available through www.bluebookofgunvalues.com.

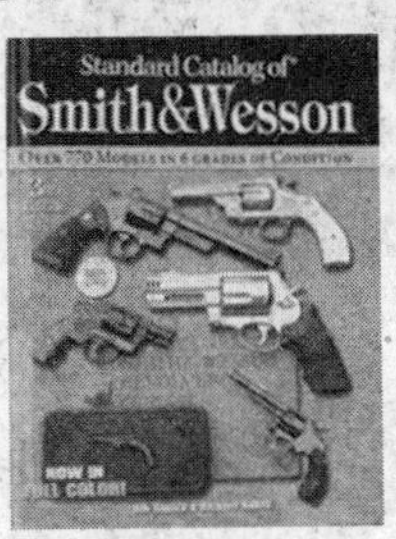

S & W PERFORMANCE CENTER PRODUCT CODES

170 = Designed/made from scratch
178 = Used existing Product / and improved

CODE	CONFIGURATION
170002	M-5906
170008	M-626 HUNTER
170009	M-686 C. C. 6"
170010	M-686 C. C. 3"
170011	SHORTY 40
170012	M-629 3" MAG.COMP.
170014	M-640 3" C. C.
170015	M-686 6" COMPETITOR
170016	M-686 4" C. C.
170020	Tactical Forty
170021	M-686 6" HUNTER
170023	M-442 ULTRALITE
170024	M-66 3" F-COMP.
170025	M-19 3" K-COMP.
170026	M-629 3" UNFLUTED
170027	M-356 COMPACT
170028	S/S SHORTY 40
I70029	M-60 3"FL ET-COMP.
170030	SHORTY 9mm
170032	M-356 LIMITED
170033	M-40 LIMITED
170034	M-686 6" HUNTER (BRAZIL)
170035	M-I9 3" K-COMP (BRAZIL)
170036	M-52 PERF. CTR.
170037	M-356 BRILEY CHASSIS
170038	M-845 WISCHO LIMITED
170039	M-356 PARKER HALE
170040	M-9mm WISCHO LIMITED
170042	M-640 2" Carry Comp.
170043	M-64O 2" Carry Comp.
170044	M-9mm WISCHO LTD. (2TONE)
170046	M-629 6" HUNTER (UNFLUTED)

S & W PERFORMANCE CENTER PRODUCT CODES, cont.

CODE	CONFIGURATION
170047	M-356 2" Carry Comp.
170048	M-629-4 3" Quad Port
170049	M-629 5" Carry Comp
170050	M-629 6.5" Carry Comp.
170052	356 TSW 4 1/4" Stocking Dealer
170053	9mm 4 1/4" Stocking Dealer
170054	40 S&W 4 1/4" Stocking Dealer
170055	M-460 Airweight
170056	M-629 Light Hunter: Duplicate PC
170056	M-625 V Comp 4" : Duplicate PC
170057	M-9mm Horton Limited
170058	M-629 3" DBL Magna Ported
170059	M-13 3" FS DBL Port (Eagle)
170060	Shorty 40 Mark II
170061	Shorty 40 MK III
170062	M-657 .41 Mag Light Hunter
170063	M-13 3" FS Dbl Port (Uncle Mikes)
170064	M-845 HORTON LIMITED
170065	M-629 7.5" HUNTER PLUS
170066	M-617 WISCHO Target
170067	M-9mm Compact
170068	M-640-.357 J-COMP
170069	not active
170070	M-625 5"
170071	not active
170072	M-625 HUNTER (PORTLESS)
170073	M-640-357 2 1/8 FL GB (RSR)
170074	M-686 7SH 3" FL CARRY COMP.
170075	SHORTY 45
170076	SHORTY 40 MARK III-S
170077	M-686 7SH 2.5" FL MAGPORT
170078	M-640.357 2 I/8 FL QUAD GB
170079	M-686 7SH 6" Hunter
170080	M-681 3" Quad Port
170081	M-625 45LC Fluted Hunter
170082	M-686 6" Supertarget
170083	PPC 9mm Limited
170084	M-629 7.5" Hunter
170085	M-625 6" GB Hunter
170086	M-686 7Shot 6" GB Hunter
170087	M-629 7.5" Master Hunter/Scope only
170088	Shorty 45 MKII
170089	M-627 5" 8SH Lew Horton GB
170090	M-66 3" Contour Frame/ bbl
170091	40 S&W Tactical-RSR
170092	M-627 5" 8 Shot Ported
170093	9mm 4" DA/SA FS
170094	M-629 7.5" Master Hunter
170095	M-627 6" 8 Shot Hunter
170096	M-1006 9SH 3 1/2" GB DA SS
170097	M-845 .45 ACP 5" FS MOD '845 OF 1998"
170098	45 RECON 45 ACP
170099	Shorty 4006 RECON 40 S&W
170100	M-629 6" Compensated Hunter
170101	M-745 5" AS SS
170102	M-627 6.5" 8 Shot
170103	M-686 6" 7 Shot Profile Bbl
170104	M-945 5" Stainless
170105	CQB Stainless 45 ACP
170106	CQB Alloy 45 ACP
170107	M-3953 Classic 4" 9mm DA only
170108	M-41 classic 7" 10SH 10 Mfg.
170109	M-610 6 1/2"
170110	Shorty 40 Mark III FS Two Tone (not used)
170111	M-686 6" 6 Shot Profile Bbl
170112	M-4516-7 Sh 3 1/2" GB DA SS
170113	M-586 .357 Mag. GB 4 1/8" FLT

S & W PERFORMANCE CENTER PRODUCT CODES, cont.

CODE	CONFIGURATION
170114	M- 657 4" PBP TH TT "Classic Series" Approx. 25 Mfg.
170115	M-657-6 SH 3" RR SS
170116	M-627 5" 8 Shot unfluted
170117	M-5906 5" 9mm LTD CS Slide (Wischo)
170118	M-4563 CQB Two Tone
170119	M-5906 5" 9mm/356Mag SuperPC
170120	M-629 44 6" 6 shot Competitor
170121	M-686 6" 6 shot Fluted Competitor
170122	M-617 New Profile Barrel
170123	M-627 5" Profile Barrel 6 Shot Fluted
170124	M-629 44 6.5" 6 shot fluted full lug comp & cap
170125	M-657 41 6.5" 6 shot fluted full lug comp & cap
170126	M-629 Compensated Hunter- New Frame/Hammer
170127	M-4566 4" 8SH 45 CQB AS Two-Tone
170128	.45 4515 RECON -RSR w/Knife
170129	M-4587 4.25"
170130	M-629 Classic 7 1/2" Barrel w/ Case
170131	M-29 Classic 7 1/2" Barrel w/Case
170132	M-625 6" .45 Long Colt Light Hunter Fluted GB
170133	M-627 2 5/8" 8 shot Defensive Revolver
170134	M-657 2 5/8" Defensive Revolver
170135	M-629 2 5/8" Defensive Revolver
170136	M-625 Light Hunter 6"
170137	M-629 V Comp 4" -RSR
170138	M-629 7 1/2" Light Hunter RSR
170139	M-4006
170140	9mm M-6906 RECON 3 1/2"
170141	45 RECON Black
170142	M-627-3 V-Comp Jerry Miculek Spcl. 5"
170143	M- 9mm Full Lug
170144	M-332 Never Made
170145	M-632 Never Made
170146	Schofield Model of 2000
170147	M-945 5" Blue 1998
170147	M-945 Two Tone 1999
170148	M-629 5" V-Comp RSR Special
170149	6" 629 Hunter Unfluted
170150	M-627 5 1/2" UnFluted RD
170151	M-27 Classic Series
170152	M-945 4" Black
170153	M-945 4" Stainless-RSR
170154	M-14 4"
170155	M-5906 5" 9mm 10 RDv Mag PPC
170156	M-945 3-3/4" RSR Special
170157	M-629 Extreme Hunter 12"
170158	M-629 12" w/sling
170159	M-629 8.5" Revolver w/sling
170160	M-657 12" Revolver w/sling
170161	M-657 12" Revolver w/sling
170162	M-657 8.5" Revolver w/sling
170163	M-19 K COMP Y2000
170164	M-4006 Shorty Forty -Y2000- Camfour
170165	M-646 4" 40 S&W
170166	M-27-7 8 Shot 4"
170167	M-27-7 8 Shot 6 1/2"
170168	M-952 9mm
170169	M-945 3 3/4" Black -Camfour
170170	M-586 L-Comp 3"
170171	M-629 7 1/2" Stealth Hunter
170172	M-681 4" Quad Port for Camfour
170173	M-945 5" RSR Special
170174	M-945 5" Two Tone RSR Special

S & W PERFORMANCE CENTER PRODUCT CODES, cont.

CODE	CONFIGURATION
170175	M-629 2 5/8" unfluted cyl
170176	M-625 5 1/4" 45 ACP for Camfour
170177	M-945 3 1/4" 45 ACP for Camfour
170178	M-681 3" Quad Port for Camfour
170179	M-25-10 6" for Sports South
170180	M-945 3 3/4" .40 S&W for Sports South
170181	M-629 7 1/2" Compensated Hunter for TALO
170182	M-627 4" w/ Comp RSR Special
170183	M-627 4" w/ Comp RSR Special
170184	M-945 3 1/4" 45ACP for RSR
170185FC	M-24-5 6 1/2" Case Color Frame 44 Spl Heritage
170186FC	FC M-25-11 6 1/2" Case Color Frame 45 Colt Heritage
170187FC	M-25 44-40 6" 6 Sh AS WG Color Case Frame Heritage
170188FC	M-25 38-40 6" 6 Sh AS WG Blue
170189FC	M-24 44 Spl 6.5" AS WG All Blue Finish Heritage
170190FC	M-25 44-40 6" 6Sh AS WG Blue
170191FC	M-25 38-40 6" 6Sh AS WG Blue
170192FC	M-625 FL 5" 45 ACP 6 Sh AS IFS S
170193FC	M-629 7 1/2" Unfluted Green/ Black
170194FC	M-629 7-1/2" Black Unfluted
170195FC	M- 4006 4" SA/DA FS IDPA
170196FC	M-25 Colt 6" Taper Bbl 6 Sh Fluted Blue
170197FC	M-25-12 5 1/2" Fixed Sight Model of 1917 45ACP
170198FC	FC KT-22 6" 6 Sh Fluted Adj Blue Model 17-8 Heritage
170199FC	M-15-9 5" Blue
170200FC	M-681 357 3" FS WG 7 Sh Birdsong
170201FC	M-5906 6" Pistol
170202FC	M-952
170203	Mfg Purposes Only
170204	Mfg Purposes Only
170205FC	M-627 38 Super 8 shot
170206FC	M-586 357 GB 4-1/8"
170207FC	M-3 5" nickel
170208FC	M-3 5" blue
170209FC	M-3 Nickel Schofield 7" 45
170210FC	M-627-5 357 w/Internal Lock
170211FC	M-25-12 Case Colored, 45 ACP
170212FC	M-17-8 6" Heritage Series
170213FC	M-29 Heritage Series Blue
170214FC	M-29 Heritage Series Nickel
170215FC	M-29 Nickel ?
170216FC	M-15-9 Heritage Series 6" Blue (McGivern Model)
170217FC	M-15-9 Heritage Series 6" Nickel (McGivern Model)
170218FC	M-25 45ACP 5-1/2" 1917 w/Military Finish
170219FC	M-629 7 1/2" unflutted Big Rock
170220FC	M-952 5" 9mm Firing Pin Block Safety 2003
170221FC	M-5906 Singapore
170222FC	M-945 Big Rock
170223FC	M-5906 6"
170224FC	M-5906 4" DA SA Mexico
170225FC	M-686-7 .38 Super for Bangers 2003
170226FC	M-625-10 2" .45 ACP Sc Clear/Stainless 2003
170227FC	M-945 5" Big Rock
170228FC	M-629-6 7 1/2" two-tone
170229FC	M-647-1 "Varminter" .17 HMR 12" 2003
170230FC	M-629-6 7 1/2" Unfluted-Birdsong Gn & BI-IL
170231FC	M-500 Magnum Hunter 10 1/2" X Frame 2003
170232FC	M-329-1 Black recalled June 2004 2003
170233FC	M-329-1 Clear recalled June 2004 2003

S & W PERFORMANCE CENTER PRODUCT CODES, cont.

CODE	CONFIGURATION
170234FC	M-629 8 3/8" for Davidson's
170235FC	M-657 8 3/8" for Davidson's
170236FC	M-952-1 6" w/ grip safety
170237FC	M-627-5 5" .357 Mag. V-8
170238FC	M-625 4" Wedge .45 ACP GB Unfluted comp/cap wood
170239FC	M-647 6 1/2" hi-vis Not Mfg.
170240FC	M-627-5 5" .357 Mag. 8 shot blk. Acusport
170241FC	M-629 7 1/2" .44 Mag. scope mount wg.
170242FC	M-647 8 3/8" SS GB black Acusport Not Mfg.
170243FC	M-1911PC 5" SA Stainless
170244FC	M-952-2 5" 9mm Stainless
170245FC	M-327 2" .357 Mag. 8 shot Ti Cyl. Shroud Black
170246FC	M-500 Compensated Hunter 6 1/2" Unfluted
170247FC	M-952-2 6" 9mm Stainless
170248FC	M-856 .357 Mag. 7 shot
170249FC	M-627-5 5" 8 shot black Acusport
170250FC	M-381 2" 7 shot Lew Horton
170251FC	M-327Sc 2" .357 Mag. 8 shot Ti Cyl. Shroud Clear
170252FC	M-625-10 Sc Stainless black Lew Horton 2004
170253FC	M-29 6 1/2" "American Pride" 2005
170254FC	M-327Sc 5" 8 shot Target Sights Ti 2005
170255FC	M-500 Hunter 7 1/2" black finish 2005
170800FC	M-686 6" 7 shot Competitor Unfluted
178001FC	M-686 6" 6 shot Hunter Unfluted
178002FC	M-627 2 5/8" 6 shot .357 Mag.
178003FC	M-657 2 5/8" 6 shot .41 Mag.
178004FC	M-586 3" 7 shot
178005FC	M-29-5 8 3/8 RB TT TH RR WO B Wood Grips
178006FC	M-10 4 1/4" Case Color Frame Square Butt Heritage Series
178007FC	M-19 2 1/2" Nickel
178008FC	M-15-8 4" Nickel
178009FC	M-15-8 4" Heritage Series

S & W ABBREVIATIONS

A2D	Adj. 2-Dot Sight
AA	Aluminum Alloy Frame
AB	Adj. Black Sight
AMSF	Ambidextious Safety
AS	Adj. Rear Sight
ATS	Adj. Target Sight
AV	Adj. V-Notch Sight
AWO	Adj. White Outline Sight
B	Blue
BB	Bead Blast Finish
BBL	Barrel
B/G	Black/Gray Finish
BK	Black Finish
BK/M	Black/Melonite Finish
BP	Black Polymer Grip
BPF	Black Polymer Frame
BULL	Bull Barrel
CB	Curved Backstrap Grip
CC	Clear Cote™ Finish
CS	Carbon Steel
CWG	Checkered Wood Grip
CWP	Checkered Wood Panel
DA	Double Action
DAO	Double Action Only
DBP	Dovetail Black Post
DFS	Dovetail Front Sight
DT	Drilled & Taped
ER	Equipment Rail
F2D	Fixed 2-Dot Sight
FN	Fixed Notch Sight

S & W PERFORMANCE CENTER PRODUCT CODES, cont.

CODE	CONFIGURATION
FNS	Fixed Tritium Night Sight (Fr. & Rr.)
FS	Fixed Sight
FV	Fixed V-Notch Sight
G	NATO Green
GB	Glass Bead Finish
GD	Green Dot
GY	Grey Finish
#SH	Magazine Capacity/Rds
HB	Heavy Barrel
HIVIS®	Light Gathering Sight
HR	Hogue Rubber Grip
HT	Hardwood Target Grip
HV	HIVIS® Front Sight
HWA	Hogue Wrap Around Rubber Grip
I	Integral or Interchangeable Sight
IB	Interchangeable Backstraps
IC	Integral Compensator
IFS	Interchangeable Front Sight
IL	Internal Lock
ISBR	Interchangeable Serrated Black Ramp Sight
LS	LadySmith®
M	Melonite Finish
MCA	Micrometer Click Adj.
MNSF	Manual Safety (Single Side)
MS	Matte Stainless
NG	Nato Green Polymer Grips
NLMC	Novak Lo-Mount Carry 2-Dot Sight
OD	Orange Dot
P	Partridge Sight
PBP	Pinned Black Partridge Sight
PBSR	Pinned Black Serrated Ramp Sight
PF	Polymer Frame
PP	PowerPort™ Ported Barrel
RB	Round Butt
RR	Red Ramp Sight
S	Stainless Finish
SA	Single Action
SB	Black Straight Backstrap Grip
SC	Scandium Alloy Frame
SG	Synthetic Grip
SNS	Satin Stainless Finish
SR	Serrated Ramp Sight

S & W ABBREVIATIONS, cont.

S Code	Configuration
S	Stainless Steel
STD	Standard Barrel
STG	Soft Touch Grip
T	Tritium
T2D	Tritium 2-Dot Rear Night Sight
TD	Tritium Dot Front Night Sight
TDA	Traditional Double Action
TR	Thumbrest
TS	Target Stock
UC	Unfluted Cylinder
UMB	Uncle Mike's Boot Grip
UMC	Uncle Mike's Combat Grip
UMR	Uncle Mike's Rubber Grip
VR	Vented Rib
WAS	Wilson Adj. Rear Sight
WC	Wood Combat Grip
WD	White Dot Sight
WG	Dymondwood® Grip
WO	White Outline Rear Sight
WT	Wooden Target Grip

SPANISH YEAR OF MFG. DATE CODES

The following Spanish year of manufacture information appears courtesy of Leonardo M. Antaris, M.D., author of *Astra Automatic Pistols*, and *Star Firearms*. For additional information regarding Spanish pistols, particularly Astras and Stars, see www.firac.us.

CODE	YEAR
A	1927
B	1928
C	1929
CH	1930
D	1931
E	1932
F	1933
G	1934
H	1935
I	1936
J	1937
K	1938
L	1939
LL	1940
M	1941
N	1942
Ñ	1943
O	1944
P	1945
Q	1946
R	1947
S	1948
T	1949
U	1950
V	1951
X	1952
Y	1953
Z	1954
A1	1955
B1	1956
C1	1957
D1	1958
EI	1959
F1	1960
G1	1961
H1	1962
I1	1963
J1	1964
K1	1965
L1	1966
M1	1967
N1	1968
Ñ1	1969
O1	1970
P1	1971
Q1	1972
R1	1973
S1	1974

SPANISH YEAR OF MFG. DATE CODES, cont.

CODE	YEAR
T1	1975
U1	1976
V1	1977
X1	1978
Y1	1979
Z1	1980
A2	1981
B2	1982
C2	1983
D2	1984
E2	1985
F2	1986
G2	1987
H2	1988
I2	1989
J2	1990
K2	1991
L2	1992
M2	1993
N2	1994
N2	1995
O2	1996
P2	1997
Q2	1998
R2	1999
S2	2000

Beginning in January 1995 the Spanish proof house implemented a new serial number system. Requirements included: 1) all guns would be numbered in a new sequential series starting with the number 1 at the beginning of the year, 2) the serial number was to be followed by the last two digits of the production year, 3) each manufacturer was assigned a code to be stamped on every gun, and 4) weapons were to be marked as to type. The new system consists of four sets of digits separated by a hyphen. The first set is the manufacturer's code, the second set designates the type of weapon, and the third set is the firearms chronological number irrespective of model, the fourth set shows the year of mfg.
The new weapons coding system includes, Carbines 01, Shotguns 03, Pistols 04, Revolvers 05, Rifles 06, Muzzleloaders 13, Short carbines 14, Submachine guns 15; etc.

STURM, RUGER & CO., INC.

Additional information regarding Sturm, Ruger & Co., Inc. firearms (including serialization) can be found in Ruger & His Guns; A History of the Man, the Company and Their Firearms *by R.L. Wilson.*

THOMPSON/CENTER ARMS CO., INC.

The following Thompson/Center Contender serial numbers appear courtesy of Tim Pancurak, T/C's Customer Service Rep. I would like to thank Thompson/Center Arms Co., Inc. and Mr. Pancurak for making these production figures available.

Approximate Contender Production Dates
Blue Steel Frame Serial Number Ranges

YEAR	JAN.-JUNE	JULY-DEC.
1967 -		1001-2250
1968 -	2251-3060	3061-4330
1969 -	4331-7500	7501-11075
1970 -	11076-14500	14501-15360
1971 -	15631-16850	16851-17885
1972 -	17886-19800	19801-22400
1973 -	22401-24750	24751-26090
1974 -	27091-30100	30101-34500
1975 -	34501-38401	38402-47890
1976 -	47891-60670	60671-67875
1977 -	67876-74825	74826-80398
1978 -	80399-91872	91873-108344
1979 -	108345-133856	133857-153636
1980 -	153637-169090	169091-173516
1981 -	173517-181663	181664-196703
1982 -	196704-208412	208413-220806
1983 -	220807-227176	227177-234850
1984 -	234851-246791	246792-256525
1985 -	256526-265000	265001-273800
1986 -	273801-287000	287001-297200
1987 -	297201-310599	310600-317009
1988 -	317010-327999	328000-335200
1989 -	335201-351700	351701-357200
1990 -	357201-366900	366901-370677
1991 -	370678-382852	382853-386697
1992 -	386698-399679	399680-407884
1993 -	407885-411796	411797-418410
1994-2000 -	418411	Disc.

Alloy II Frame Serial Number Ranges

YEAR	JAN.-JUNE	JULY-DEC.
1985 -		A2001-A2220
1986 -	A2221-A5485	A5486-A6760
1987 -	A6761-A8228	A8229-A8719
1988 -	A8720-A8763	A8764-A9035
1989 -	A9036-A10897	Disc.
1993 -	S11000-S11666	S11667-S14723
1994 -	S14724-S18041	S18042-S23103
1995-2000 -	S23104	Disc.

WINCHESTER RIFLES SERIALIZATION

The following Winchester serial numbers appear courtesy of U.S. Repeating Arms, New Haven, CT. I would like to thank U.S. Repeating Arms and Mr. Pardee for making these production figures available.
Shipping room records at the factory indicate the following serial numbers were assigned to guns at the end of the calendar year. Polishing Room SNA (Serial Number Application date) column information comes from the Polishing Room Ledgers held by the Center of the West.
For a factory letter on an older Winchester, contact the Cody Firearms Records Office at the Buffalo Bill Center of the West at 720 Sheridan Ave., Cody, WY 82414, go to www.centerofthewest.org, call 307-578-4031, or email cfmrecords@centerofthewest.org. This is a fee service.

MODEL 1866

YEAR	APPROX. LAST NO.
1866 -	12476 to 14813
1867 -	15578
1868 -	19768
1869 -	29516
1870 -	52527
1871 -	88184
1872 -	109784
1873- -	118401
1874 -	125038
1875 -	125965
1876 -	131907
1877 -	148207
1878 -	150493
1879 -	152201
1880 -	154379
1881 -	156107
1882 -	159513
1883 -	162376
1884 -	163649
1885 -	163664
1886 -	165071
1887 -	165912
1888 -	167155
1889 -	167401
1890 -	167702
1891 -	169003
1892 -	NONE
1893 -	169007
1894 -	169011
1895 -	NONE
1896 -	NONE
1897 -	169015
1898 -	170100
1899 -	DISCONTINUED

MODEL 1873

SNA records available from SN 272801 to the end

YEAR	APPROX. LAST NO.
1873 -	1 to 126
1874 -	2726
1875 -	11325
1876 -	23151
1877 -	23628
1878 -	27501
1879 -	41525
1880 -	63537
1881 -	81620
1882 -	109507
1883 -	145503
1884 -	175126
1885 -	196221
1886 -	222937
1887 -	225922
1888 -	284529
1889 -	323220
1890 -	363220
1891 -	405026
1892 -	441625
1893 -	466641
1894 -	481826
1895 -	499308

MODEL 1873, cont.

YEAR	APPROX. LAST NO.
1896 -	507545
1897 -	513421
1898 -	525922
1899 -	541328
1900 -	554128
1901 -	557236
1902 -	564557
1903 -	573957
1904 -	588953
1905 -	602557
1906 -	613780
1907 -	NONE
1908 -	NONE
1909 -	630385
1910 -	656101
1911 -	669324
1912 -	678527
1913 -	684419
1914 -	686510
1915 -	688431
1916 -	694020
1917 -	698617
1918 -	700734
1919 -	702042
No last # available	
20, 21, 22, 23,	720609

MODEL 1876

YEAR	APPROX. LAST NO.
1876 -	1 to 1429
1877 -	3579
1878 -	7967
1879 -	8971
1880 -	14700
1881 -	21759
1882 -	32407
1883 -	42410
1884 -	54666
1885 -	58714
1886 -	60397
1887 -	62420
1888 -	63539
1889 -	NONE
1890 -	NONE
1891 -	NONE
1892 -	63561
1893 -	63670
1894 -	63678
1895 -	NONE
1896 -	63702
1897 -	63869
1898 -	63871

MODEL 1885 SINGLE SHOT

YEAR	APPROX. LAST NO.	POLISHING ROOM SNA
1885 -	1 to 375	no entry
1886 -	6841	8193
1887 -	18328	20006
1888 -	30571	30132
1889 -	45019	37662
1890 -	N/A	45109
1891 -	53700	54099
1892 -	60371	60305
1893 -	69534	66163
1894 -	N/A	71024
1895 -	73771	74649

MODEL 1885 SINGLE SHOT, cont.

YEAR	APPROX. LAST NO.	POLISHING ROOM SNA
1896 -	78253	77255
1897 -	78815	80877
1898 -	84700	82492
1899 -	85086	85257
1900 -	88501	88302
1901 -	90424	91733
1902 -	92031	94738
1903 -	92359	96553
1904 -	92785	98953
1905 -	93611	102084
1906 -	94208	104603
1907 -	95743	107063
1908 -	96819	108004
1909 -	98097	109327
1910 -	98506	110870
1911 -	99012	112555
1912 -	N/A	113267
1913 -	100352	114726

No further serial numbers were recorded until the end of 1923. Last No. known was: 139700

MODEL 1886

YEAR	APPROX. LAST NO.	POLISHING ROOM SNA
1886 -	1 to 3211	3528
1887 -	14728	12497
1888 -	28577	28609
1889 -	38401	38652
1890 -	49723	51068
1891 -	63601	63738
1892 -	73816	74898
1893 -	83261	85144
1894 -	94543	97034
1895 -	103708	107346
1896 -	109670	111243
1897 -	113997	115106
1898 -	119192	118646
1899 -	120571	120795
1900 -	122834	No further entries
1901 -	125630	
1902 -	128942	
1903 -	132213	
1904 -	135524	
1905 -	138838	
1906 -	142249	
1907 -	145119	
1908 -	147322	
1909 -	148237	
1910 -	150129	
1911 -	151622	
1912 -	152943	
1913 -	152947	
1914 -	153859	
1915 -	154452	
1916 -	154979	
1917 -	155387	
1918 -	156219	
1919 -	156930	
1920 -	158716	
1921 -	159108	
1922 -	159337	

No further serial numbers were recorded until the discontinuance of the Model 1886 which was in 1935 at serial no. 159994.

MODEL 1890

Records on the Model 1890 are somewhat incomplete. Factory records indicate the following serial numbers were assigned to guns at the end of calendar year beginning with 1908. Actual records on the firearms which were manufactured between 1890 and 1907 are available from the Cody Firearms Records Office located at the Buffalo Bill Center of the West.

MODEL 1890

YEAR	APPROX. LAST NO.	POLISHING ROOM SNA
1890	N/A	245
1891 -	N/A	10884
1892 -	N/A	16454
1893 -	N/A	25954
1894 -	N/A	32554
1895 -	N/A	40218
1896 -	N/A	46525
1897 -	N/A	55855
1898 -	N/A	64748
1899 -	N/A	80268
1900 -	N/A	100554
1901 -	N/A	127181
1902 -	N/A	154985
1903 -	N/A	186724
1904 -	N/A	228104
1905 -	N/A	276637
1906 -	N/A	302204
1907 -	N/A	349947
1908 -	NONE	398006
1909 -	393427	431483
1910 -	423567	450000
1911 -	451264	484700
1912 -	478595	509100
1913 -	506936	527500
1914 -	531019	562400
1915 -	551290	594300
1916 -	570497	608741
1917 -	589204	612979
1918 -	603438	617978
1919 -	630801	649452
1920 -	NONE	678928
1921 -	634783	679313
1922 -	643304	683470
1923 -	654837	693040
1924 -	664613	701941
1925 -	675774	711462
1926 -	687049	736246
1927 -	698987	767898
1928 -	711354	795605
1929 -	722125	824623
1930 -	729015	837448
1931 -	733178	844278
1932 -	734454	846022
1933 -	N/A	846524
1934 -	N/A	848044
1935 -	N/A	848584
1936 -	N/A	848936
1937 -	N/A	No further entries

The Model 1890 was discontinued in 1932, however, a clean up of the production run lasted another 8+ years and included another 14 to 15000 guns. Our figures indicate approximately 849,000 guns were made.

MODEL 1892

YEAR	APPROX. LAST NO.	POLISHING ROOM SNA
1892 -	1 to 23701	7121
1893 -	35987	22804
1894 -	73508	38744
1895 -	106721	53616
1896 -	144935	67853
1897 -	159312	85930
1898 -	165431	103328
1899 -	171820	129983
1900 -	183411	155567
1901 -	191787	183683
1902 -	208871	209770
1903 -	253935	233451
1904 -	278546	280321
1905 -	315425	324168
1906 -	376496	366950
1907 -	437919	413705
1908 -	476540	471652
1909 -	522162	512627
1910 -	586996	581623
1911 -	643483	645931
1912 -	694752	694420
1913 -	742675	747502
1914 -	771444	776016
1915 -	804622	799690
1916 -	830031	811052
1917 -	853819	841881
1918 -	870942	854878
1919 -	903649	881258
1920 -	906754	917240
1921 -	910476	No further entries
1922 -	917300	
1923 -	926329	
1924 -	938641	
1925 -	954997	
1926 -	973896	
1927 -	990883	
1928 -	996517	
1929 -	999238	
1930 -	999730	
1931 -	1000727	
1932 -	1001324	

MODEL 1894

Records at the factory, and in some years, estimates, indicate the following serial numbers were assigned to guns at the end of the calendar year.

YEAR	APPROX. LAST NO.	POLISHING ROOM SNA
1894 -	1 to 14579	1674
1895 -	44359	14222
1896 -	76464	18571
1897 -	111453	33108
1898 -	147684	53941
1899 -	183371	80148
1900 -	204427	103932
1901 -	233975	137058
1902 -	273854	168420
1903 -	291506	204565
1904 -	311363	249782
1905 -	337557	291706
1906 -	378878	331895
1907 -	430985	381524
1908 -	474241	429757
1909 -	505831	449102
1910 -	553062	479073
1911 -	599263	534429

MODEL 1894, cont.

YEAR	APPROX. LAST NO.	POLISHING ROOM SNA
1912 -	646114	591281
1913 -	703701	645304
1914 -	756066	722280
1915 -	784052	825186
1916 -	807741	840846
1917 -	821972	873425
1918 -	838175	882032
1919 -	870762	895365
1920 -	880627	926851
1921 -	908318	935778
1922 -	919583	951501
1923 -	938539	964709
1924 -	953198	974121
1925 -	978523	987148
1926 -	997603	997938
1927 -	1027571	1012753
1928 -	1054465	1038665
1929 -	1077097	1060899
1930 -	1081755	1071420
1931 -	1084156	1079689
1932 -	1087836	1088141
1933 -	1089270	1092328
1934 -	1091190	1095364
1935 -	1099605	1099625
1936 -	1100065	1119104
1937 -	1100679	1158835
1938 -	1100915	1198405
1939 -	1101051	1216165
1940 -	1142423	1259563
1941 -	1191307	1313301
1942 -	1221289	1343183
1943 -	N/A	no entry
1944 -	N/A	1343196
1945 -	N/A	1352066
1946 -	N/A	No further entries
1947 -	N/A	
1948 -	1500000	
1949 -	1626100	
1950 -	1724295	
1951 -	1819800	
1952 -	1910000	
1953 -	2000000	
1954 -	2071100	
1955 -	2145296	
1956 -	2225000	
1957 -	2290296	
1958 -	2365887	
1959 -	2410555	
1960 -	2469821	
1961 -	2500000	
1962 -	2551921	
1963 -	2586000	
*1964	2700000 - 2797428	
1965 -	2894428	
1966 -	2991927	
1967 -	3088458	
1968 -	3185691	
1969 -	3284570	
1970 -	3381299	
1971 -	3557385	
1972 -	3806499	
1973 -	3929364	
1974 -	4111426	
1975 -	4277926	
1976 -	4463553	
1977 -	4565925	
1978 -	4662210	
1979 -	4826596	

MODEL 1894, cont.

YEAR	APPROX. LAST NO.	POLISHING ROOM SNA
1980 -	4892951	
1981 -	5024957	
1982 -	5103248	
1983-	N/A	
1984-	5309432	
1985-	5362944	
1986-	5409249	
1987-	5463790	
1988-	5517897	
1989-	5574822	
1990-	5615397	
1991-	6008296	

Model 1894 facts.

** The post-64 Model 94 began with serial number 2,700,000.*

**Serial number 1,000,000 was presented to President Calvin Coolidge in 1927.*

**Serial number 1,500,000 was presented to President Harry S. Truman in 1948.*

**Serial number 2,500,000 and 3,000,000 were presented to the Winchester Gun Museum, now located in Cody, Wyoming.*

**Serial number 3,500,000 was not constructed until 1979 and was sold at auction in Las Vegas, Nevada.*

**Serial number 4,000,000 - whereabouts unknown at this time.*

**Serial number 4,500,000 - shipped to Italy by Olin in 1978. Whereabouts unknown.*

**Serial number 5,000,000 - in New Haven, not constructed as of March 1983.*

MODEL 9422

YEAR	APPROX. LAST NO.
1972 -	F48558
1973 -	F121182
1974 -	F169044
1975 -	F229666
1976 -	F293472
1977-	F323197
1978-	F367976
1979-	F398044
1980-	F431532
1981-	F489918
1982-	F527632
1983-	F531722
1984-	F539305
1985-	F550843
1986-	F557835
1987-	F571623
1988-	F590039
1989-	F605281
1990-	F617848
1991-	F633224
1992-	F646000
1993-	F658316
1994-	F671391

MODEL 1895

YEAR	APPROX. LAST NO.	POLISHING ROOM SNA
1895 -	1 to 287	56
1896 -	5715	2783
1897 -	7814	5734
1898 -	19871	19567
1899 -	26434	24311
1900 -	29817	29808
1901 -	31584	34615
1902 -	35601	39459
1903 -	42514	43963
1904 -	47805	48444
1905 -	54783	52099
1906 -	55011	56688
1907 -	57351	62041
1908 -	60002	64326
1909 -	60951	68094
1910 -	63771	72565
1911 -	65017	76030
1912 -	67331	80423
1913 -	70823	84889
1914 -	72082	99264
1915 -	174233	211410
1916 -	377411	400166
1917 -	389106	403773
1918 -	392731	403791
1919 -	397250	405391
1920 -	400463	409662
1921 -	404075	412928
1922 -	407200	416355
1923 -	410289	419730
1924 -	413276	420874
1925 -	417402	421337
1926 -	419533	423100
1927 -	421584	423370
1928 -	422676	423779
1929 -	423680	424651
1930 -	424181	424662
1931 -	425132	425523
1932 -	425825	425825
1933 -	N/A	425881

MODEL 1903

Model 1903 SNA records available to SN 126221.

YEAR	APPROX. LAST NO.
1903 -	N/A
1904 -	6944
1905 -	14865
1906 -	23097
1907 -	31852
1908 -	39105
1909 -	46496
1910 -	54298
1911 -	61679
1912 -	69586
1913 -	76732
1914 -	81776
1915 -	84563
1916 -	87148
1917 -	89501
1918 -	92617
1919 -	96565
1920 -	N/A
1921 -	97650
1922 -	99011
1923 -	100452
1924 -	101688
1925 -	103075
1926 -	104230
1927 -	105537

MODEL 1903, cont.

YEAR	APPROX. LAST NO.
1928 -	107157
1929 -	109414
1930 -	111276
1931 -	112533
1932 -	112992

This model was discontinued in 1932, however, a clean up of parts was used for further production of approximately 2000 guns. Total production was approx. 126000 rifles through 1936.

MODEL 1905

Model 1905 SNA records available to SN 29913.

YEAR	APPROX. LAST NO.
1905 -	1 to 5659
1906 -	15288
1907 -	19194
1908 -	20385
1909 -	21280
1910 -	22423
1911 -	23503
1912 -	24602
1913 -	25559
1914 -	26110
1915 -	26561
1916 -	26910
1917 -	27297
1918 -	27585
1919 -	28287
1920 -	29113

MODEL 1906

YEAR	APPROX. LAST NO.	POLISHING ROOM SNA
1906 -	1 to 52278	55911
1907 -	89147	96820
1908 -	114138	134258
1909 -	165068	187450
1910 -	221189	250850
1911 -	273355	304600
1912 -	327955	355400
1913 -	381922	422600
1914 -	422734	458300
1915 -	453880	497200
1916 -	483805	500700
1917 -	517743	523127
1918 -	535540	538247
1919 -	593917	604917
1920 -	N/A	652563
1921 -	598691	652584
1922 -	608011	652780
1923 -	622601	663549
1924 -	636163	670684
1925 -	649952	683119
1926 -	665484	685999
1927 -	679892	No further entries
1928 -	695915	
1929 -	711202	
1930 -	720116	
1931 -	725978	
1932 -	727353	

A clean up of production took place for the next few years (approx. 1932-1937) with a record of production reaching approximately 848000.

MODEL 1907

Model 1907 SNA records available to SN 50000.

YEAR	APPROX. LAST NO.
1907 -	1 to 8657
1908 -	14486
1909 -	19707
1910 -	23230
1911 -	25523
1912 -	27724
1913 -	29607
1914 -	30872
1915 -	32272
1916 -	36215
1917 -	38235
1918 -	39172
1919 -	40448
1920 -	N/A
1921 -	40784
1922 -	41289
1923 -	41658
1924 -	42029
1925 -	42360
1926 -	42688
1927 -	43226
1928 -	43685
1929 -	44046
1930 -	44357
1931 -	44572
1932 -	44683
1933 -	44806
1934 -	44990
1935 -	45203
1936 -	45482
1937 -	45920
1938 -	46419
1939 -	46758
1940 -	47296
1941 -	47957
1942 -	48275
1943 -	N/A
1944 -	N/A
1945 -	48281
1946 -	48395
1947 -	48996
1948 -	49684
**1949 -	50662
**1950 -	51640
**1951 -	52618
**1952 -	53596
**1953 -	54574
**1954 -	55552
**1955 -	56530
**1956 -	57508
**1957 -	58486

** Actual records on serial numbers stops in 1948. The serial numbers ending each year from 1948 to 1957 were derived at by taking the last serial number recorded (58486) and the last number from 1948, (49684) and dividing the years of production (9), which relates to 978 guns each year for the nine year period.

MODEL 1910

YEAR	APPROX. LAST NO.
1910 -	1 to 4766
1911 -	7695
1912 -	9712
1913 -	11487
1914 -	12311

MODEL 1910, cont.

YEAR	APPROX. LAST NO.
1915 -	13233
1916 -	13788
1917 -	14255
1918 -	14625
1919 -	15665
1920 -	N/A
1921 -	15845
1922 -	16347
1923 -	16637
1924 -	17030
1925 -	17281
1926 -	17696
1927 -	18182
1928 -	18469
1929 -	18893
1930 -	19065
1931 -	19172
1932 -	19232
1933 -	19281
1934 -	19338
1935 -	19388
1936 -	19445

A cleanup of production continued into 1937 when the total of the guns was completed at approximately 20786

MODEL 1911 S.L.

YEAR	APPROX. LAST NO.
1911 -	1 to 3819
1912 -	27659
1913 -	36677
1914 -	40105
1915 -	43284
1916 -	45391
1917 -	49893
1918 -	52895
1919 -	57337
1920 -	60719
1921 -	64109
1922 -	69132
1923 -	73186
1924 -	76199
1925 -	78611

The Model 1911 was discontinued in 1925. However, guns were produced for three years after that date to clean up production and excess parts. When this practice ceased there were approximately 82774 guns produced.

MODEL 52

Model 52 SNA records available to SN 74125.

YEAR	APPROX. LAST NO.
1920 -	None indicated
1921 -	397
1922 -	745
1923 -	1394
1924 -	2361
1925 -	3513
1926 -	6383
1927 -	9436
1928 -	12082
1929 -	14594
1930 -	17253
1931 -	21954
1932 -	24951
1933 -	26725
1934 -	29030
1935 -	32448

MODEL 52, cont.

YEAR	APPROX. LAST NO.
1936 -	36632
1937 -	40419
1938 -	43632
1939 -	45460
1940 -	47519
1941 -	50317
1942 -	52129
1943 -	52553
1944 -	52560
1945 -	52718
1946 -	56080
1947 -	60158
1948 -	64265
1949 -	68149
1950 -	70766
1951 -	73385
1952 -	76000
1953 -	79500
1954 -	80693
1955 -	81831
1956 -	96869
1957 -	97869
1958 -	98599
1959 -	98899
1960 -	102200
1961 -	106986
1962 -	108718
1963 -	113583
1964 -	118447
1965 -	120992
1966 -	123537
1967 -	123727
1968 -	123917
1969 -	E 124107
1970 -	E 124297
1971 -	E 124489
1972 -	E 124574
1973 -	E 124659
1974 -	E 124744
1975 -	E 124828
1976 -	E 125019
1977 -	E 125211
1978 -	E 125315

This Model was discontinued in 1978. A small clean up of production was completed in 1979 with a total of 125419.

MODEL 53

The Model 53 was serial numbered in both its own series (1 to slightly over 15,000) as well as within the Model 1892 series. Early guns predominate the Model 53 serial number series with Model 1892 series serial numbers appearing more frequently mid to late production.

This Model was discontinued in 1932, however, a clean up of production continued for 9 more years. Some later Model 53s are numbered in with the Model 92s without differentiation.

YEAR	APPROX. LAST NO.	POLISHING ROOM SNA
1924 -	1 to 1488	2458
1925 -	4350	6086
1926 -	6882	10302
1927 -	9180	10874
1928 -	11139	No further entries
1929 -	12873	
1930 -	13794	

MODEL 53, cont.

YEAR	APPROX. LAST NO.	POLISHING ROOM SNA
1931 -	14416	
1932 -	14623	
1933 -	14727	
1934 -	14817	
1935 -	14976	
1936 -	15047	
1937 -	15078	
1938 -	15092	
1939 -	15099	
1940 -	15109	
1941 -	15118	

Total Production Approximately 24,916.

Records at the factory indicate the following serial numbers were assigned to guns at the end of the calendar year.

MODEL 54

YEAR	APPROX. LAST NO.
1925 -	1 to 3140
1926 -	8051
1927 -	14176
1928 -	19587
1929 -	29104
1930 -	32499
1931 -	36731
1932 -	38543
1933 -	40722
1934 -	43466
1935 -	47125
1936 -	50145

MODEL 55

Some later Model 55s are numbered in with the Model 94s without differentiation.

YEAR	APPROX. LAST NO.	POLISHING ROOM SNA
1924 -	1 to 836	1304
1925 -	2783	3296
1926 -	4957	6748
1927 -	8021	11563
1928 -	10467	12002
1929 -	12258	No further entries
1930 -	17393	
1931 -	18198	
1932 -	19204	
1933 -	Clean up 20580	

MODEL 61

YEAR	APPROX. LAST NO.
1932 -	1 to 3532
1933 -	6008
1934 -	8554
1935 -	12379
1936 -	20615
1937 -	30334
1938 -	36326
1939 -	42610
1940 -	49270
1941 -	57493
1942 -	59871
1943 -	59872
1944 -	59879
1945 -	60512
1946 -	71629
1947 -	92297
1948 -	115281
1949 -	125461

MODEL 61, cont.

YEAR	APPROX. LAST NO.
1950 -	135461
1951 -	145821
1952 -	156000
1953 -	171000
1954 -	186000
1955 -	200962
1956 -	216923
1957 -	229457
1958 -	242992
1959 -	262793
1960 -	282594
1961 -	302395
1962 -	322196
1963 -	342001

This Model was discontinued in 1963. For some unknown reason there are no actual records available from 1949 through 1963. The serial number figures for these years are arrived at by taking the total production figure of 342001, subtracting the last known # of 115281, and dividing the difference equally by the amount of remaining years available (15).

MODEL 62

YEAR	APPROX. LAST NO.
1932 -	1 to 7643
1933 -	10695
1934 -	14090
1935 -	23924
1936 -	42759
1937 -	66059
1938 -	80205
1939 -	96534
1940 -	116393
1941 -	137379
1942 -	155152
1943 -	155422
1944 -	155425
1945 -	156073
1946 -	183756
1947 -	219085
1948 -	252298
1949 -	262473
1950 -	272648
1951 -	282823
1952 -	293000
1953 -	310500
1954 -	328000
1955 -	342776
1956 -	357551
1957 -	383513
1958 -	409475

MODEL 63

YEAR	APPROX. LAST NO.
1933 -	1 to 2667
1934 -	5361
1935 -	9830
1936 -	16781
1937 -	25435
1938 -	30934
1939 -	36055
1940 -	41456
1941 -	47708
1942 -	51258
1943 -	51631
1944 -	51656
1945 -	53853

MODEL 63, cont.

YEAR	APPROX. LAST NO.
1946 -	61607
1947 -	71714
1948 -	80519
1949 -	88889
1950 -	97259
1951 -	105629
1952 -	114000
1953 -	120500
1954 -	127000
1955 -	138000
1956 -	150000
1957 -	162345
1958 -	175223

MODEL 70

YEAR	APPROX. LAST NO.
1935 -	1 to 19
1936 -	2238
1937 -	11573
1938 -	17844
1939 -	23991
1940 -	31675
1941 -	41753
1942 -	49206
1943 -	49983
1944 -	49997
1945 -	50921
1946 -	58382
1947 -	75675
1948 -	101680
1949 -	131580
1950 -	173150
1951 -	206625
1952 -	238820
1953 -	282735
1954 -	323530
1955 -	361025
1956 -	393595
1957 -	425283
1958 -	440792
1959 -	465040
1960 -	504257
1961 -	545446
1962 -	565592
1963 -	581471
1964	Model 70s began with the serial number 700,000.
1964 -	740599
1965 -	809177
1966 -	833795
1967 -	869000
1968 -	925908
1969 -	G941900
1970 -	G957995
1971 -	G1018991
1972 -	G1099257
1973 -	G1128731
1974 -	G1175000
1975 -	G1218700
1976 -	G1266000
1977 -	G1350000
1978 -	G1410000
1979 -	G1447000
1980 -	G1490709
1981 -	G1537134
1982-	G1632872

MODEL 70, cont.

YEAR	APPROX. LAST NO.
1983-	G1656883
1984-	G1782457
1985-	G1783276
1986-	G1808838
1987-	G1845122
1988-	G1893903
1989-	G1950701
1990-	G1987984
1991-	G2037985

The controlled round feed Model 70 was reintroduced in 1990 as the Model 70 Classic at serial number G15000.

MODEL 70 CLASSIC

YEAR	APPROX. LAST NO.
1990-	G16859
1991-	G23072
1992-	G26709

MODEL 71

YEAR	APPROX. LAST NO.
1935 -	1 to 4
1936 -	7821
1937 -	12988
1938 -	14690
1939 -	16155
1940 -	18267
1941 -	20810
1942 -	21959
1943 -	22048
1944 -	22051
1945 -	22224
1946 -	23534
1947 -	25728
1948 -	27900
1949 -	29675
1950 -	31450
1951 -	33225
1952 -	35000
1953 -	37500
1954 -	40770
1955 -	43306
1956 -	45843
1957 -	47254

MODEL 74

YEAR	APPROX. LAST NO.
1939 -	1 to 30890
1940 -	67085
1941 -	114355
1942 -	128293
1943 -	NONE
1944 -	128295
1945 -	128878
1946 -	145168
1947 -	173524
1948 -	223788
1949 -	249900
1950 -	276012
1951 -	302124
1952 -	328236
1953 -	354348
1954 -	380460
1955 -	406574

MODEL 88

YEAR	APPROX. LAST NO.
1955 -	1 to 18378
1956 -	36756
1957 -	55134
1958 -	73512
1959 -	91890
1960 -	110268
1961 -	128651
1962 -	139838
1963 -	148858
1964 -	160307
1965 -	162699
1966 -	192595
1967 -	212416
1968 -	230199
1969 -	H239899
1970 -	H258229
1971 -	H266784
1972 -	H279014
1973 -	H283718

MODEL 100

YEAR	APPROX. LAST NO.
1961 -	1 to 32189
1962 -	60760
1963 -	78863
1964 -	92016
1965 -	135388
1966 -	145239
1967 -	209498
1968 -	210053
1969 -	A210999
1970 -	A229995
1971 -	A242999
1972 -	A258001
1973 -	A262833

WINCHESTER RIFLE AND SHOTGUN SERIAL NUMBER PREFIXES POST-1968

The following serial number prefixes are found on Winchester rifles and shotguns as a result of the Gun Control Act of 1968.

MODEL NO. (S)	S.N. PREFIX
Super X Model 1	M
Super X Model 1 (Ducks Unlimited)	IDU
12	Y
12 (Ducks Unlimited)	DU
21	W
22	WS
MODEL NO. (S)	S.N. PREFIX
23	PWK
52	E
60 (Cooey)	C
40-70A-770-670	G
88	H
91	KS or WS
94	No Prefix used
94 Big Bore	BB
96	K
100	A
101	K
101 Pigeon Grade	PK
Bolt Action Rimfires 121-131 & 141	Z

WINCHESTER RIFLE AND SHOTGUN SERIAL NUMBER PREFIXES POST-1968, cont.

MODEL NO. (S)	S.N. PREFIX
Rimfire 150-190-250-255-270	
275 & 290	B
Rimfire 300-310 & 320	D
370 & 37A	C
490	J
1200	L
1300	LX
1400	N
1500	NX
1500 (European)	NE
9422	F

WINCHESTER SHOTGUNS

Records at the factory indicate the following serial numbers were assigned to guns at the end of the calendar year.

MODEL 1887

Model 1887 SNA records available from SN 129 to end.

YEAR	APPROX. LAST NO.
1887 -	1 to 7431
1888 -	22408
1889 -	25673
1890 -	29105
1891 -	38541
1892 -	49763
1893 -	54367
1894 -	56849
1895 -	58289
1896 -	60175
1897 -	63952
1898 -	64855

According to these records no guns were produced during the last few years of this model and it was therefore discontinued in 1901.

Model 1893

YEAR	APPROX. LAST NO.	POLISHING ROOM SNA
1893 -	N/A	7958
1894 -	N/A	16985
1895 -	N/A	24109
1896 -	N/A	32908

Model 1897

YEAR	APPROX. LAST NO.	POLISHING ROOM SNA
1897 -	1 to 32335	46190
1898 -	64668	63867
1899 -	96999	90099
1900 -	129332	121740
1901 -	161665	155949
1902 -	193998	192780
1903 -	226331	232089
1904 -	258664	269816
1905 -	296037	310112
1906 -	334059	352757
1907 -	377999	398919
1908 -	413618	438586
1909 -	446888	474392
1910 -	481062	514224
1911 -	512632	544663
1912 -	544313	574649
1913 -	575213	609337
1914 -	592732	621155

Model 1897, cont.

YEAR	APPROX. LAST NO.	POLISHING ROOM SNA
1915 -	607673	634255
1916 -	624537	645018
1917 -	646124	673277
1918 -	668383	705627
1919 -	691943	713785
1920 -	696183	744268
1921 -	700428	748404
1922 -	715902	760622
1923 -	732060	780537
1924 -	744942	793623
1925 -	757629	806826
1926 -	770527	816294
1927 -	783574	829515
1928 -	796806	845320
1929 -	807321	857216
1930 -	812729	865591
1931 -	830721	875213
1932 -	833926	885034
1933 -	835637	885040
1934 -	837364	885843
1935 -	839728	886094
1936 -	848684	895261
1937 -	856729	901405
1938 -	860725	905660
1939 -	866938	909925
1940 -	875945	918793
1941 -	891190	930412
1942 -	910072	950579
1943 -	912265	965000
1944 -	912327	968160
1945 -	916472	968160
1946 -	926409	975755
1947 -	936682	981005
1948 -	944085	985270
1949 -	953042	989410
1950 -	961999	995605
1951 -	970956	1001930
1952 -	979913	1007515
1953 -	988860	1013730
1954 -	997827	1017760
1955 -	1006784	1021610
1956 -	1015741	1024700
1957 -	1024700	1024701

Records on this Model are incomplete. The above serial numbers are estimated from 1897 through 1903 and again from 1949 through 1957. The actual records are in existence from 1904 through 1949.

MODEL 1897 TRENCH/RIOT SHOTGUN

This information is provided by Mr. Pat Redmond, after many years of research and collecting. Reference a Winchester Repeating Arms Co. Memorandum dated September 1945. Trench, Riot, and Long Barrel Contract Dates 1/31/42 - 3/23/43, Contract Shipments 24829 shotguns.

YEAR	SER. NOS.	TYPE	CONFIGURATION
1937 -	902117-903762	Mil.	Long Barrel
1939 -	911788-911813	Mil.	Trench Gun
1940 -	914087	Com.	Trench Gun
1940 -	924312	Com.	Trench Gun
1941 -	920235-956126	Mil.	Trench Gun
1942 -	930537-956216	Mil.	Trench Gun
1943 -	956628	Mil.	Trench Gun
1944 -	965482	Com.	Trench Gun
1944 -	966144	Com.	Trench Gun
1944 -	967371	Com.	Riot Gun
1949 -	993750	Com.	Riot Gun

MODEL 1901

Model 1907 SNA records available from where Model 1887 ends to SN 78356.

YEAR	APPROX. LAST NO.
1904 -	64,856 to 64,860
1905 -	66453
1906 -	67486
1907 -	68424
1908 -	69197
1909 -	70009
1910 -	70753
1911 -	71441
1912 -	72167
1913 -	72764
1914 -	73202
1915 -	73509
1916 -	73770
1917 -	74027
1918 -	74311
1919 -	74872
1920 -	77000

MODEL 1911

YEAR	APPROX. LAST NO.
1911 -	1-3819
1912 -	27659
1913 -	36677
1914 -	40105
1915 -	43284
1916 -	45391
1917 -	49843
1918 -	52895
1919 -	57337
1920 -	60719
1921 -	64109
1922 -	69132
1923 -	73186
1924 -	76199
1925 -	78611
1926-1928 - parts clean-up ending at.	82744

MODEL 12

YEAR	APPROX. LAST NO.	POLISHING ROOM SNA
1912 -	5308	9266
1913 -	32418	49344
1914 -	79765	110370
1915 -	109515	143142
1916 -	136412	157861
1917 -	159391	191510
1918 -	183461	196269
1919 -	219457	230343
1920 -	247458	281302
1921 -	267253	303678
1922 -	304314	333678
1923 -	346319	379021
1924 -	385196	417326
1925 -	423056	462132
1926 -	464564	498101
1927 -	510693	541109
1928 -	557850	594589
1929 -	600834	637335
1930 -	626996	673015
1931 -	651255	684476
1932 -	660110	698596
1933 -	664544	698662

MODEL 12, cont.

YEAR	APPROX. LAST NO.	POLISHING ROOM SNA
1934 -	673994	704074
1935 -	686978	723448
1936 -	720316	749429
1937 -	754250	788635
1938 -	779455	813810
1939 -	814121	849225
1940 -	856499	888006
1941 -	907431	903580
1942 -	958303	1002163
1943 -	975640	1034440
1944 -	975727	1042155
1945 -	990004	1060683
1946 -	1029152	1092085
1947 -	1102371	1145110
1948 -	1176055	1218845
1949 -	1214041	1281025
1950 -	1252028	1354540
1951 -	1290015	1418315
1952 -	1328002	1477650
1953 -	1399996	1568660
1954 -	1471990	1635300
1955 -	1541929	1684790
1956 -	1611868	1727280
1957 -	1651435	1784325
1958 -	1690999	1837879
1959 -	1795500	1887319
1960 -	1800000	1917780
1961 -	1930999	1932638
1962 -	1956990	1942598
1963 -	1962001	1968260
1964 -	N/A	1970885
1965-	N/A	No further entry
1966 -	1970875	

A clean up of production took place from 1964 through 1966 with the ending serial # 1970875.

MODEL 12 TRENCH/RIOT SHOTGUN

This information is provided by Mr. Pat Redmond after many years of research and collecting. Reference a Winchester Repeating Arms Co. Memorandum dated September 1945. Trench/Riot and long barrel Contract Dates 4/1/42 - 3/21/44, Contract Shipments 61014 shotguns.

Blue Finish

YEAR	SER. NOS.	TYPE	CONFIGURATION
1941 -	926558--956504	Mil.	Riot & Long Barrel
1942 -	961934-1001014	Mil.	Trench/Riot/ Long
1943 -	996899-1028856	Mil.	Trench & Riot

Parkerized Finish

YEAR	SER. NOS.	TYPE	CONFIGURATION
1943 -	1030000-1035214	Mil.	Trench Gun
1944 -	1035458	Mil.	Trench Gun
1945 -	1035525	Mil.	Trench Gun
1946 -	1071586	Com.	Riot Gun
1949 -	1740610	Com.	Riot Gun

NEW STYLE M/12

YEAR	APPROX. LAST NO.
1972 -	Y200 011-Y2006396
1973 -	Y2015662
1974 -	Y2022061
1975 -	Y2024478
1976 -	Y2025482
1977 -	Y2025874
1978 -	Y2026156
1979 -	Y2026399

MODELS 120/1200/1300

YEAR	APPROX. LAST NO.
1972 -	L739617
1973-	L828677
1974-	L898065
1975-	L967242
1976-	L1063788
1977-	L1163671
1978-	L1202123
1979-	L1235083
1980-	L1269765
1981-	L1320354
1982-	L1434776
1983-	L1567997
1984-	L1755346
1985-	L1894542
1986-	L1983657
1987-	L2075117
1988-	L2178816
1989-	L2306558
1990-	L2386211
1991-	L2498813
1992-	L2599825

MODEL 24

YEAR	APPROX. LAST NO.
1939 -	1 to 8118
1940 -	21382
1941 -	27045
1942 -	33670
1943 -	NONE RECORDED
1944 -	33683
1945 -	34965
1946 -	45250
1947 -	58940
1948 -	64417

There were no records kept on this model from 1949 until its discontinuance in 1958. The total production was approximately 116280.

MODEL 36

Approximately 20,000 Model 36 single shot 9mm shotguns were manufactured 1920-1927. These shotguns were not serial numbered.

MODEL 37

Approximately 1,000,000 Model 37 single shot shotguns were manufactured 1936-1963. These shotguns were not serial numbered.

MODEL 40

YEAR	APPROX. LAST NO.
1939 -	1 to 2671
1940 -	10592
1941 -	13265
1942 -	18929

MODEL 42

YEAR	APPROX. LAST NO.
1933 -	1 to 9398
1934 -	13963
1935 -	17728
1936 -	24849
1937 -	30900
1938 -	34659
1939 -	38967
1940 -	43348
1941 -	48203
1942 -	50818
1943 -	50822
1944 -	50828
1945 -	51168
1946 -	54256
1947 -	64853
1948 -	75142
1949 -	81107
1950 -	87071
1951 -	93038
1952 -	99000
1953 -	108201
1954 -	117200
1955 -	121883
1956 -	126566
1957 -	131249
1958 -	135932
1959 -	140615
1960 -	145298
1961 -	149981
1962 -	154664
1963 -	164800

MODEL 50

YEAR	APPROX. LAST NO.
1954 -	1 to 24550
1955 -	49100
1956 -	73650
1957 -	98200
1958 -	122750
1959 -	147300
1960 -	171850
1961 -	196400

WINCHESTER MODEL 101 SERIALIZATION

12 gauge

SER. NO.	MFG.MO.	YEAR
50,50,000	10	1959
50,500	3	1960
51,000	5	1960
51,500	6	1960
52,000	9	1961
52,500	3	1962
53,000	4	1962
53,500	5	1962
54,000	8	1962
54,500	9	1962
55,000	10	1962
55,500	12	1962
56,000	1	1963
56,500	2	1963
57,000	3	1963
57,500	3	1963
58,000	4	1963
58,500	5	1963
59,000	6	1963
59,500	6	1963

12 gauge, cont.

SER. NO.	MFG.MO.	YEAR
60,000	7	1963
60,500	8	1963
61,000	8	1963
61,500	11	1963
62,000	11	1963
62,500	11	1963
63,000	12	1963
63,500	1	1964
64,000	1	1964
64,500	2	1964
65,000	3	1964
65,500	3	1964
66,500	3	1964
67,000	5	1964
67,500	5	1964
68,000	5	1964
68,500	5	1964
69,000	6	1964
69,500	6	1964
70,000	7	1964
70,500	7	1964
71,000	8	1964
71,500	9	1964
72,000	9	1964
72,500	10	1964
73,000	10	1964
73,500	11	1964
74,000	11	1964
74,500	12	1964
75,000	12	1964
75,500	1	1965
76,000	2	1965
76,500	2	1965
77,000	3	1965
77,500	4	1965
78,000	4	1965
78,500	4	1965
79,000	4	1965
79,500	4	1965
80,000	5	1965
80,500	6	1965
81,000	6	1965
81,500	6	1965
82,000	6	1965
82,500	8	1965
83,000	8	1965
83,500	8	1965
84,000	9	1965
84,500	9	1965
85,000	10	1965
85,500	10	1965
86,000	10	1965
86,500	10	1965
87,000	10	1965
87,500	10	1965
88,000	11	1965
88,500	11	1965
89,000	11	1965
90,000	12	1965
90,500	12	1965
91,000	12	1965
91,500	1	1966
92,000	1	1966
92,500	2	1966
93,000	2	1966
93,500	2	1966
94,000	3	1966
94,500	3	1966

12 gauge, cont.

SER. NO.	MFG.MO.	YEAR
95,000	5	1966
95,500	5	1966
96,000	6	1966
96,500	7	1966
97,000	7	1966
97,500	7	1966
98,000	8	1966
98,500	8	1966
99,000	9	1966
99,500	9	1966
100,000	10	1966
100,500	10	1966
101,000	10	1966
101,500	11	1966
102,000	11	1966
102,500	12	1966
103,000	1	1967
103,500	1	1967
104,000	2	1967
104,500	3	1967
105,000	4	1967
105,500	5	1967
106,000	5	1967
106,500	5	1967
107,000	9	1967
107,500	10	1967
108,000	10	1967
108,500	11	1967
109,000	11	1967
109,500	11	1967
110,000	12	1967
110,500	1	1968
111,000	2	1968
111,500	3	1968
112,000	3	1968
112,500	3	1968
113,000	3	1968
113,500	4	1968
114,000	5	1968
114,500	5	1968
115,000	6	1968
115,500	6	1968
116,000	7	1968
116,500	7	1968
117,000	9	1968
117,500	10	1968
118,000	1	1969
118,500	1	1969
119,000	2	1969
119,500	3	1969
120,000	4	1969
120,500	4	1969
121,000	4	1969
121,500	4	1969
122,000	5	1969
122,500	6	1969
123,000	6	1969
123,500	6	1969
124,000	7	1969
124,500	7	1969
125,000	7	1969
125,500	8	1969
126,000	8	1969
126,500	9	1969
127,000	9	1969
127,500	10	1969
128,000	11	1969
128,500	11	1969

12 gauge, cont.

SER. NO.	MFG.MO.	YEAR
129,000	11	1969
129,500	2	1970
130,000	2	1970
130,500	3	1970
131,000	3	1970
131,500	4	1970
132,000	4	1970
132,500	4	1970
133,000	4	1970
133,500	5	1970
134,000	5	1970
134,500	5	1970
135,000	6	1970
135,500	6	1970
136,000	6	1970
136,500	8	1970
137,000	8	1970
137,500	8	1970
138,000	8	1970
139,000	12	1970
139,500	12	1970
140,000	12	1970
140,500	1	1971
141,000	2	1971
141,500	2	1971
142,000	2	1971
142,500	3	1971
143,000	3	1971
143,500	4	1971
144,000	4	1971
144,500	4	1971
145,000	4	1971
145,500	5	1971

MODEL 101, 20 gauge.

SER. NO.	MFG.MO.	YEAR
200,000	3	1966
200,500	3	1966
201,000	3	1966
201,500	3	1966
202,000	4	1966
202,500	4	1966
203,000	4	1966
203,500	5	1966
204,000	6	1966
204,500	6	1966
205,000	7	1966
205,500	8	1966
206,000	8	1966
206,500	8	1966
207,000	9	1966
207,500	9	1966
208,000	9	1966
208,500	12	1966
209,000	2	1967
209,500	7	1967
210,000	10	1967
210,500	12	1967

MODEL 101, 28 ga. & .410 bore

SER. NO.	MFG.MO.	YEAR
211,000	1	1968
211,500	1	1968
212,000	10	1968
212,500	10	1968
213,000	10	1968
213,500	11	1968
214,000	12	1968
214,500	12	1968
215,000	1	1969
215,500	2	1969
216,000	5	1969
216,500	6	1969
217,000	9	1969
217,500	10	1969
218,500	12	1969
219,000	12	1969
219,500	12	1969
220,000	12	1969

MODEL 101, 28 ga. & .410 bore

SER. NO.	MFG.MO.	YEAR
220,500	1	1970
221,000	1	1970
221,500	2	1970
222,000	3	1970
222,500	7	1970
223,000	9	1970
223,500	9	1970
224,000	9	1970
224,500	9	1970
225,000	10	1970
225,500	10	1970
226,000	11	1970
226,500	11	1970
227,000	11	1970
227,500	12	1970
228,000	12	1970
228,500	4	1971
229,000	4	1971
229,500	4	1971

PROOF MARKS

The proof marks shown below will assist in determining nationality of manufacturers when no other markings are evident. Since the U.S. has no proofing houses (as in England, France, Germany and other European countries), most U.S. manufacturers voluntarily proof their firearms with a specifed style of proofmark (i.e. the interlocked ©WPª synonymous with the Winchester trademark can be fired using modern smokeless powder) shells. Pre-1850 European firearms oftentimes do not exhibit any commercial proof marks and, with the exception of an occasional barrel address, they represent the single hardest category of firearms one can research properly. Captured weapons from major wars occasionally show two different nationalities of proof marks. This is acceptable since the gun was proofed in a national proof house after original manufacture and again when the gun was exported to a different country as a military acquisition. Please refer to the References section in this text for proof mark source information.

AUSTRIAN PROOF MARKS

PROOF MARK	CIRCA	PROOF HOUSE	TYPE OF PROOF AND GUN
	since 1891	Vienna	provisional proof for multi barrel guns
	since 1891	Ferlach	provisional proof for multi barrel guns
	1892-1918	Prague	provisional proof for rifles
	1892-1918	Ferlach	black powder proof for rifles
	1892-1918	Prague	black powder proof for rifles
	1892-1918	Weipert	black powder proof for rifles
	1892-1918	Vienna	black powder proof for rifles
	1918-1938	Ferlach	black powder proof for rifles
	1918-1938	Vienna	black powder proof for rifles
	1938-1940	Ferlach	black powder proof for rifles
	1938-1940	Vienna	black powder proof for rifles
	since 1945	Vienna	black powder proof for multi barrel guns
	since 1945	Ferlach	black powder proof for multi barrel guns
 BH	since 1891	Bundesheer	preliminary proof for multi barrel guns

PROOF MARK	CIRCA	PROOF HOUSE	TYPE OF PROOF AND GUN
	1891-1928	Budapest	smokeless powder proof for parabellum pistols
	Since 1981	Ferlach	smokeless powder proof for parabellum pistols
	1891-1931	Ferlach	smokeless powder proof for parabellum pistols
	since 1891	Vienna	smokeless powder proof for parabellum pistols
	1891-1931	Weipert	smokeless powder proof for parabellum pistols

BELGIAN PROOF MARKS

PROOF MARK	CIRCA	PROOF HOUSE	TYPE OF PROOF AND GUN
	since 1852	Liege	provisional black powder proof for breech loading guns and rifled barrels
	-	Liege	double proof marking for unfurnished barrels
	-	Liege	triple proof provisional marking for unfurnished barrels
	since 1893	Liege	definitive black powder proof for breech loading guns, small bore guns and handguns
	since 1853	Liege	View stamp and inspectors mark for firearms "Perron"
	since 1924	Liege	Nitro proof for rifled barrel and parabellum pistols
	since 1852	Liege	rifled arms defense for smokeless proof parabellum pistols
	-	Liege	Superior nitro proof
	1811-1892	Liege	black powder proof for rifles
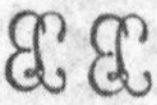	1897-1923	Liege	black powder proof for rifles

PROOF MARK	CIRCA	PROOF HOUSE	TYPE OF PROOF AND GUN
	1891-1968	Liege	type EC. smokeless powder proof for rifles
	1898-1968	Liege	type Pt. smokeless powder proof for rifles
	1898-1968	Liege	smokeless powder proof for rifles
	since 1968	Liege	smokeless powder proof for rifles

BRITISH PROOF MARKS

PROOF MARK	CIRCA	PROOF HOUSE	TYPE OF PROOF AND GUN
	since 1856	London	provisional proof for barrels
	since 1856	Birmingham	provisional proof for barrels
	since 1637	London	definitive black powder proof for shotguns,muzzle loader barrels
	since 1904	London	definitive nitro proof for all guns - parabellum pistols
	since 1954	Birmingham	definitive nitro proof for barrel and action
	since 1904	Birmingham	black powder proof only for parabellum pistols
	1868-1925	London	definitive special super power proof for parabellum pistols
	1868-1925	Birmingham	voluntary special black powder proof
	1868-1925	London	reproof marking for black powder rifles
	1868-1925	Birmingham	reproof marking for black powder rifles
	1868-1925	Birmingham	definitive black powder proof for shotguns
	since 1904	Birmingham	definitive nitro proof for all guns
	since 1670	London	view mark
	since 1904	Birmingham	view mark

FRENCH PROOF MARKS

PARIS HOUSE	ST ETIENNE HOUSE	CIRCA	TYPE OF PROOF AND GUN
		since 1897	provisional proof unfinished short barreled guns
EP	ST ETIENNE	1897	standard proof for finished guns
EP EP	ST ETIENNE	1897	double proof finished and joined barrels
EP N.A.	N.A ST ETIENNE	1897	single barrel proof for non-assembled guns
	F	1897	finished black powder guns
	F	since 1962	black powder proof for rifles
R		1962-1972	final black powder proof for rifles
	S	1926-1962	final black powder proof for rifles
	R	since 1962	final black powder proof for rifles
	PT PT	since 1900	smokeless powder proof for rifles
☆ PJ		1896-1926	smokeless powder proof for rifles
☆ PS		1896-1926	smokeless powder proof for rifles
☆ PM		1896-1926	smokeless powder proof for rifles
☆ PT		1900-1972	smokeless powder proof for rifles
☆☆ P.T		1926-1972	smokeless powder proof for rifles
☆ PT R		1962-1972	final smokeless powder proof for rifles
R		since 1962	final smokeless powder proof for rifles
R		since 1982	final smokeless powder proof for rifles

PARIS HOUSE	ST ETIENNE HOUSE	CIRCA	TYPE OF PROOF AND GUN
		1897	special proof for finished guns
		1897	ordinary smokeless powder proof
		1897	superior smokeless powder proo

GERMAN PROOF MARKS

Research continues for the inclusion of Pre-1950 German Proofmarks.

PROOF MARK	CIRCA	PROOF HOUSE	TYPE OF PROOF AND GUN
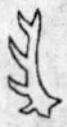	since 1952	Ulm	
	since 1968	Hannover	
	since 1968	Kiel (W. German)	
	since 1968	Munich	
	since 1968	Cologne (W. German)	
	since 1968	Berlin (W. German)	
	since 1952	Ulm	voluntary proof for hand/long guns
	since 1952	Ulm	repair proof for major gun parts
	since 1952	Ulm	provisional black powder for shotgun & multi barreled rifles
	since 1952	Ulm	definitive nitro proof for all guns
	since 1952	Ulm	definitive black powder for smokeless ammo guns
	since 1952	Ulm	Flobert for special purpose guns signal, flare, gas, & stun guns
	since 1945	E. German, Suhl	smokeless powder proof
	since 1950	E. German, Suhl	1st black powder proof for rifled barrels
	since 1950	E. German, Suhl	nitro powder proof

PROOF MARK	CIRCA	PROOF HOUSE	TYPE OF PROOF AND GUN
	since 1950	E. German, Suhl	repair proof
	since 1950	E. German, Suhl	1st black powder proof for smooth bored barrels
	since 1950	E. German, Suhl	inspection mark
	since 1950	E. German, Suhl	choke-bore barrel mark

ITALIAN PROOF MARKS

PROOF MARK	CIRCA	PROOF HOUSE	TYPE OF PROOF AND GUN
	since 1951	Brescia	provisional proof for all guns
	since 1951	Gardone	provisional proof for all guns
	since 1951	Gardone & Brescia	definitive proof for guns with smokeless powder
	since 1951	Gardone & Brescia	finish proof for firearms ready for sale
	since 1951	Gardone & Brescia	1st black powder proof

SPANISH PROOF MARKS

PROOF MARK	CIRCA	PROOF HOUSE	TYPE OF PROOF AND GUN
	since 1910	Eibar	provisional black powder proof for shotguns
	since 1910	Eibar	temporary black powder proof for shotguns
	since 1910	Eibar	final black powder proof for breech loading shotguns
	since 1910	Eibar	final smokeless powder proof for breech loading shotguns
	since 1910	Eibar	reinforced smokeless powder proof for breech loading shotguns
	since 1910	Eibar	provisional proof for shotguns
	since 1910	Eibar	final black powder proof for breech loading shotgun

PROOF MARK	CIRCA	PROOF HOUSE	TYPE OF PROOF AND GUN
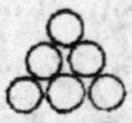	since 1923	Eibar	final and single black powder proof for double barreled muzzle loading shotun
	since 1923	Eibar	final and single black powder proof for single barrel smooth bored breechloading guns
	since 1923	Eibar	final black powder proof for double barreled breechloading rifles
	since 1923	Eibar	final black powder proof for single proof breechloading rifles
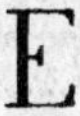	since 1923	Eibar	reinforced voluntary proof for single and double barrel shotguns
	since 1923	Eibar	final proof of military-style rifle
	since 1923	Eibar	single and final proof of non-self loading pistols
	since 1923	Eibar	single and final proof for self loading pistols and revolvers
	since 1929	Eibar	admission proof for guns with old marks
	since 1929	Eibar	proof used in Barcelona for guns with old marks
	since 1929	Eibar	final proof for revolver
	since 1929	Eibar	proof for semiautomatic pistols
	since 1929	Eibar	special manufacturer's mark for guns made for foreign sales
	since 1929	Eibar	smokeless proof for shotgun barrels
	since 1929	Eibar	reinforced smokeless proof for shotgun barrels

INDEX

Title Page 1
Publisher's Note/Copyright 2
Table Of Contents 3
Online Subscriptions/Credits 4
General Information 5
Acknowledgements 6-7
Fallen Comrades 7
About the Cover 8
Introduction by Zachary R. Fjestad 9-10
Foreword by Lisa Beuning 11-12
A Year in Review – What Happened?
by Zachary R. Fjestad 13-17
Collecting in the Time of COVID
by Mark Rendina 18-23
Blue Book of Gun Values Collectible Firearms
Average Index 24-25
How To Use This Book 26-29
Anatomy Of A Handgun 30
Anatomy Of A Rifle 31
Anatomy Of A Shotgun 32
Gun Questions/Appraisals Policy 33
Glossary 34-56
Abbreviations 57-61
Grading Criteria 62
NRA Condition Standards 63
The PPGS - Firearms Grading Made Easy 64
Photo Percentage Grading System™ 65-142
Identifying/Buying Older Editions 143-144
Modern Firearms/Antiques
Text & Pricing 145-2,418

A

2 VETS ARMS CO., LLC 145
2A ARMAMENT LLC 145
5TC (5 TOES CUSTOM) 145
A.A. 145
A.A.A. 145
A.A. ARMS INC 145
A & B HIGH PERFORMANCE FIREARMS 145
A.R. SALES 145
A06 ARMS 146
ADC (ARMI DALLERA CUSTOM) 146
AFC 146
A. J. ORDNANCE 146
AK-47 DESIGN CARBINES, RIFLES, & PISTOLS 146
AMAC 148
AMP TECHNICAL SERVICE GmbH 148
A.M.S.D. (ADVANCED MILITARY SYSTEM DESIGN) 149
AMT (ARCADIA MACHINE & TOOL) 149
APF 152
AR 57 LLC 152
AR-7 INDUSTRIES, LLC 152
AR-15 STYLE CARBINES, RIFLES, PISTOLS, & SHOTGUNS 153
ASAI AG (ADVANCED SMALL ARMS INDUSTRIES) . 154
ASI ARMS (ARAL ARMS) 154
A-SQUARE (CURRENT MFG.) 154
A-SQUARE (PREVIOUS MFG.) 154
ATCSA 154
ATA ARMS 154
AWA USA INC. 154
AWC SYSTEMS TECHNOLOGY, LLC 155
AYA (AGUIRRE Y ARANZABAL) 155
ABADIE 160
ABBEY, GEORGE T. 160
ABBEY, F.J. & COMPANY 160
ABBIATICO & SALVINELLI (FAMARS) 160
ACCU-MATCH INTERNATIONAL INC. 160
ACCU-TEK 160
ACCURACY INTERNATIONAL LTD. 162
ACCURACY X, INC. 163
ACCURATE ARMS RIFLES LLC 163
ACCURATE-MAG PRODUCTS 163
ACCURATE TOOL & MFG. CO. 164
ACHA 164
ACME 164
ACME ARMS 164
ACME HAMMERLESS 164
ACTION (M.S.) 164
ACTION ARMS LTD 164
ACTION LEGENDS MFG., INC. 165
ADAMS 165
ADAMS ARMS 165
ADAMS, JOSEPH 166
ADAMY, GEBR. JAGDWAFFEN 166
ADCO ARMS CO., INC. (ADCO SALES INC.) 166
ADCOR DEFENSE 166
ADEQ FIREARMS COMPANY 166
ADIRONDACK ARMS COMPANY 167
ADLER 167
ADLER HUNTING ARMS COMPANY 167
ADVANCED ARMAMENT CORP. 167
ADVANTAGE ARMS USA, INC. 167
AERO PRECISION USA 167
AERON CZ s.r.o. 167
AETNA 168
AETNA ARMS COMPANY 168
AGNER 168
AIM SURPLUS, LLC 168
AIRBORNE ARMS 168
AIR MATCH 168
AJAX ARMY 168
AKDAL 168
AKDAS ARMS 168
AKKAR 169
AKLYS DEFENSE LLC 169
AKRILL, E. 169
AKSA ARMS 169

AKUS ... 169
ALAMO RANGER ... 169
ALAN & WILLIAM ARMS, INC. ... 169
ALASKA ... 169
ALASKA MAGNUM AR'S ... 170
ALASKAN COMMEMORATIVES ... 170
ALBERTA TACTICAL RIFLE SUPPLY ... 170
ALCHEMY ARMS COMPANY ... 170
ALCHEMY CUSTOM WEAPONRY ... 170
ALDAZABAL ... 171
ALERT ... 171
ALESSANDRI, LOU, AND SON ... 171
ALEXANDER ARMS LLC ... 171
ALEXIA ... 172
ALEX PRO FIREARMS ... 172
ALFA ... 172
ALFA PROJ ... 172
ALKARTASUNA FABRICA DE ARMAS, S.A. ... 172
ALLEN & THURBER ... 173
ALLEN FIREARMS ... 173
ALMAR ... 173
ALPHA ARMS (ALPHARMS) ... 173
ALPHA ARMS INC. ... 173
ALPHA FOXTROT ... 173
ALPINE INDUSTRIES ... 173
ALTOBELLI ARMS COMPANY ... 173
ALTOR CORP. ... 174
AMBUSH FIREARMS ... 174
AMERICA REMEMBERS ... 174
AMERICAN ARMS ... 174
AMERICAN ARMS CO. ... 174
AMERICAN ARMS, INC. ... 174
AMERICAN BARLOCK WONDER ... 180
AMERICAN BUILT ARMS CO. ... 180
AMERICAN CLASSIC ... 181
AMERICAN CUSTOM GUNMAKERS GUILD, INC. (ACGG) ... 182
AMERICAN DEFENSE MFG. LLC ... 182
AMERICAN DERRINGER CORPORATION ... 182
AMERICAN FIREARMS MANUFACTURING CO., INC. 186
AMERICAN FRONTIER FIREARMS MFG., INC. ... 186
AMERICAN GUN CO. ... 187
AMERICAN GUN COMPANY, LLC ... 187
AMERICAN HISTORICAL FOUNDATION, THE ... 187
AMERICAN HUNTING RIFLES (AHR) ... 187
AMERICAN INDUSTRIES ... 188
AMERICAN INTERNATIONAL CORP. ... 188
AMERICAN LEGACY FIREARMS ... 188
AMERICAN LEGENDS ... 188
AMERICAN PRECISION ARMS ... 188
AMERICAN RIFLE COMPANY ... 189
AMERICAN SPIRIT ARMS ... 189
AMERICAN SPIRIT ARMS CORP. ... 189
AMERICAN TACTICAL (AMERICAN TACTICAL IMPORTS - ATI) ... 189
AMERICAN WESTERN ARMS, INC. ... 197
AM-TAC PRECISION ... 197
AMTEC 2000, INC. ... 197
ANATOLIA MANUFACTURING COMPANY LLC ... 197
ANATOLIAN DEFENSE INDUSTRY ... 197
ANCIENS ETABLISSEMENTS PIEPER ... 197
ANDERSON MANUFACTURING ... 197
ANDERSON WHEELER ... 197
ANDREAS STRANK BUCHSENMACHERMEISTER ... 198
ANGEL ARMS INC ... 198
ANGSTADT ARMS ... 198
ANSCHÜTZ ... 198
ANTREG ... 214
ANZIO IRONWORKS CORP. ... 214
APACHE ... 214
ARCHER MANUFACTURING ... 214
ARCHON FIREARMS ... 214
ARCUS CO. ... 214
ARDESA ... 215
ARES DEFENSE SYSTEMS INC. ... 215
AREX ... 215
ARISAKA ... 216
ARIZONA ARMORY ... 216
ARLINGTON ORDNANCE ... 216
ARMALITE ... 216
ARMALITE, INC. ... 217
ARMAMENT TECHNOLOGY ... 224
ARMAMENT TECHNOLOGY CORP. ... 224
ARMAS AZOR, S.A. ... 224
ARMATIX ... 225
ARMED GUNS ... 225
ARMERIA DE MADRID, LA ... 225
ARMES DE CHASSE LLC ... 225
ARMES MATHELON ... 225
ARMES PIERRE ARTISAN ETS. (P. CHAPUIS) ... 225
ARMI MAGAP ... 225
ARMI PERUGINI-VISINI ... 226
ARMI SALVINELLI ... 226
ARMI SAN MARCO ... 226
ARMI SAN PAOLO ... 226
ARMI SPORT di CHIAPPA SILVIA & C. Snc ... 226
ARMINEX LTD. ... 226
ARMINIUS ... 226
ARMITAGE INTERNATIONAL, LTD. ... 227
ARMORY USA LLC ... 227
ARMS CORPORATION OF THE PHILIPPINES ... 227
ARMS LLC ... 227
ARMS MORAVIA, LTD. ... 227
ARMS RESEARCH ASSOCIATES ... 227
THE ARMS ROOM (ARMS ROOM LLC) ... 228
ARMS TECH LTD. ... 228
ARMSAN ... 228
ARMSCO ... 228
ARMSCOR ... 228
ARMSCORP USA, INC. ... 231

ARM SPORT LLC 233
ARMSPORT, INC. 233
ARMY & NAVY 233
ARMY SERRA 233
ARNOLD ARMS CO., INC. 234
ARRIETA, S.L. 234
ARRIZABALAGA, PEDRO 235
ARSENAL DEMOCRACY 236
ARSENAL FIREARMS 236
ARSENAL INC. 236
ARSENAL JSCOMPANY (ARSENAL BULGARIA) 236
ARSENAL USA LLC 237
ART MANIFATTURA ARMI/ART ARMI 237
ASELKON 237
ASHBURY PRECISION ORDNANCE MANUFACTURING 237
ASILSAN 239
ASP 240
ASPREY 240
ASTRA 240
ASTRA ARMS S.A. 244
ATKIN, GRANT & LANG 244
ATKIN, HENRY 244
ATLAS FORCES 244
ATLAS GUNWORKS 244
AUSTRIAN SPORTING ARMS 246
AUSTRALIAN AUTOMATIC ARMS PTY. LTD. 246
AUSTRALIAN INTERNATIONAL ARMS 247
AUTAUGA RIFLES, INC. 248
AUTO MAG 248
AUTO MAG LTD. CORP. 250
AUTO-ORDNANCE CORP. 250
AUTO-POINTER 253
AVIDITY ARMS 253
AXELSON TACTICAL 253
AXIAL PRECISION 253
AXTELL RIFLE CO. 254
AZRA 16 254
AZTEK ARMS 254

B

BCI DEFENSE LLC 255
BCM EUROPEARMS 255
BJT (BELLMORE JOHNSON TOOL CO.) 255
BNTI ARMS 255
BSA GUNS LIMITED 255
BWE FIREARMS 258
B-WEST 259
BADROCK PRECISION RIFLES 259
BAER, LES 259
BAFORD ARMS, INC. 259
BAIKAL 259
BAILONS GUNMAKERS LIMITED 263
BAKER, W.H. & CO. 263
THE BAKER GUN & FORGING CO. 264
BALISTIK (SAVUNMA) DEFENSE INDUSTRY AND TRADE INC. 265
BALLARD ARMS, INC. 265
BALLESTER MOLINA/RIGAUD (HAFDASA) 266
BALTIMORE ARMS COMPANY 266
BANSNER'S ULTIMATE RIFLES, L.L.C. 266
BARAK HUNTING ARMS (BARAK SILAH) 268
BARNES PRECISION MACHINE, INC. 268
BARRETT FIREARMS MANUFACTURING, INC. 268
BAR-STO 272
BARTOLOT, WERNER 272
BASERRI 272
BATTAGLIA, MAURO 272
BATTLE ARMS DEVELOPMENT, INC. (B.A.D., INC.) . 272
BATTLE RIFLE COMPANY 272
BAUER FIREARMS CORPORATION 272
BAYARD 273
BAZOOKA BROTHERS MFG. 274
BEAR CREEK ARSENAL 274
BECAS 274
BEEMAN OUTDOOR SPORTS 274
BEHOLLA PISTOL 275
BENELLI 275
BENSON FIREARMS LTD. 288
BENTON & BROWN FIREARMS, INC. 289
BERETTA, DR. FRANCO 289
BERETTA 290
PISTOLS: SEMI-AUTO, PRE-WWII MFG. 291
PISTOLS: SEMI-AUTO, POST WWII MFG. 292
Pistols: Semi-Auto, Model 92 & Variations - 5.9 in. barrel 299
Pistols: Semi-Auto, Model 92, M9, & Variations - 4.9 or 5.1 in. barrel 299
Pistols: Semi-Auto, Model 92 & Variations - 4.3 and 4.7 in. barrels 302
Pistols: Semi-Auto, Model 96 & Variations, Recent Mfg. 304
REVOLVERS: SINGLE ACTION 306
RIFLES: BOLT ACTION, RECENT MFG. 307
RIFLES: LEVER ACTION 308
RIFLES: SEMI-AUTO, RECENT MFG. 308
RIFLES: O/U, CUSTOM 309
RIFLES: SxS, CUSTOM 309
RIFLES: SLIDE ACTION 310
SHOTGUNS: O/U, DISC. 310
SHOTGUNS: O/U, FIELD - CURRENT / RECENT MFG. 312
SHOTGUNS: O/U, SKEET - RECENT MFG. 317
SHOTGUNS: O/U, SPORTING CLAYS - CURRENT / RECENT MFG. . 318
SHOTGUNS: O/U, TRAP - RECENT MFG. 322
SHOTGUNS: O/U, CUSTOM GRADE - CURRENT / RECENT MFG. 324
SHOTGUNS: SxS, CURRENT / RECENT MFG. 327
SHOTGUNS: SxS, CUSTOM GRADE 329
SHOTGUNS: SINGLE BARREL, DISC. 330
SHOTGUNS: SLIDE ACTION, MFG. 1960-1996 331
SHOTGUNS: SEMI-AUTO 331
COMMEMORATIVES 340
BERGARA 341
BERGMANN 346
WAYNE BERGQUIST CUSTOM PISTOLS 347
BERNARDELLI, GIULIO 347

BERNARDELLI, VINCENZO 347
BERSA 347
BERTUZZI, F.LLI 350
BESCHI, MARIO 350
BEST ARMS (BEST HUGLU) 351
THE BEST OF THE WEST 351
BETTINSOLI, TARCISIO, Srl 351
BIG BEAR ARMS & SPORTING GOODS INC. 352
BIG HORN ARMORY INC. 352
BIG HORN ARMS CORP. 354
BIGHORN RIFLE CO. 354
BILL HANUS BIRDGUNS LLC 354
BINGHAM, LTD. 354
BISHOP AMMUNITION & FIREARMS 354
BITTNER 354
BLACK ACES TACTICAL 354
BLACK COLLAR ARMS 354
BLACK CREEK PRECISION 355
BLACK DAWN ARMORY (BLACK DAWN INDUSTRIES) .. 355
BLACK FORGE LLC 355
BLACKHEART FIREARMS (BLACKHEART INTERNATIONAL LLC) 355
BLACKOPS TECHNOLOGIES 355
BLACK RAIN ORDNANCE, INC. 355
BLACK RIFLE COMPANY LLC 355
BLACK WEAPONS ARMORY 355
BLAND, THOMAS & SONS GUNMAKERS LTD. 355
BLASER 355
BLEIKER, HEINRICH 364
BLUEGRASS ARMORY 364
BOBCAT WEAPONS INC. 364
BOBERG ARMS CORPORATION 364
BOHICA 364
BOITO 365
BOLLIGER, JOHN 365
BOND ARMS, INC. 365
BORA HUNTING ARMS COMPANY 368
BORCHARDT 368
BORDEN RIFLES 368
BOROVNIK, LUDWIG KG 368
BOSIS, LUCIANO 368
BOSS & CO., LTD. 369
BOSWELL, CHARLES 369
BOWEN, BRUCE & COMPANY 371
BOXALL & EDMISTON LTD. 371
BOY'S RIFLES 372
BRAVO COMPANY MFG., INC. (BCM) 372
BRAZIER, JOSEPH, LTD. 372
BREDA FUCILI (BREDA MECCANICA BRESCIANA) .. 372
BREEDING, RYAN 376
BRE-MAC Srl 376
BREN 10 (PREVIOUS MFG.) 376
BREN 10 (RECENT MFG.) 377
BRETTON-GAUCHER 377
BRIGADE FIREARMS 378
BRIGNOLI, SILVIO 378
BRILEY 378
BRITARMS 378
BRITISH ORDNANCE COMPANY 378
BRIXIA SHOTGUNS Srl 379
BRNO ARMS (ZBROJOVKA BRNO) 379
BRNO RIFLES 384
BROADSWORD GROUP 384
BROCKMAN'S RIFLES 384
BROLIN ARMS, INC. 385
BRONCO 387
BRONCO (PISTOLS) 387
BRONCO (LONG ARMS) 387
A.A. BROWN & SONS 387
DAVID MCKAY BROWN (GUNMAKERS) LTD. 388
ED BROWN CUSTOM, INC. 388
ED BROWN PRODUCTS, INC. 388
BROWN PRECISION, INC. 388
BROWNELLS, INC. 390
BROWNING 390
BROWNING HISTORY 390
BROWNING FACTS 391
BROWNING VALUES INFORMATION 391
BROWNING SERIALIZATION 391
BROWNING CUSTOM SHOP 392
PISTOLS: SEMI-AUTO, CENTERFIRE, F.N. PRODUCTION UNLESS OTHERWISE NOTED 392
PISTOLS: SEMI-AUTO, .22 CAL. RIMFIRE 399
RIFLES: BOLT ACTION 406
RIFLES: BOLT ACTION, CENTERFIRE A-BOLT I SERIES 408
RIFLES: BOLT ACTION, CENTERFIRE A-BOLT II SERIES 410
RIFLES: BOLT ACTION, CENTERFIRE X-BOLT SERIES 413
RIFLES: BOLT ACTION, RIMFIRE A-BOLT SERIES 419
RIFLES: LEVER ACTION 419
RIFLES: O/U 423
RIFLES: SEMI-AUTO, .22 LR 424
RIFLES: SEMI-AUTO, BAR SERIES 426
RIFLES: SEMI-AUTO, FAL & CAL SERIES 429
RIFLES: SINGLE SHOT 429
RIFLES: SLIDE ACTION 431
SHOTGUNS: BOLT ACTION, A-BOLT SERIES 431
SHOTGUNS: O/U, CYNERGY SERIES 432
SHOTGUNS: O/U, CITORI HUNTING SERIES 435
SHOTGUNS: O/U, CITORI SKEET 441
SHOTGUNS: O/U, CITORI SPORTING CLAYS 443
SHOTGUNS: O/U, CITORI TARGET 447
SHOTGUNS: O/U, CITORI TRAP 447
SHOTGUNS: O/U, SUPERPOSED GENERAL INFO & CHOKE CODES 450
SHOTGUNS: O/U, JOHN M. BROWNING COLLECTION 450
SUPERPOSED: 1931-1940 MFG. (PRE-WWII) 450
SUPERPOSED: 1948-1960 MFG. (POST-WWII) 451
SUPERPOSED: 1960-1976 MFG. 453
SHOTGUNS: O/U, SUPERPOSED HIGH GRADES: 1985-PRESENT ... 459
Superposed: Custom Shop Current Pricing & Models 459
SHOTGUNS: SxS 460
SHOTGUNS: SEMI-AUTO, AUTO-5 1903-1998, 2012-CURRENT MFG. 461
SHOTGUNS: SEMI-AUTO, DOUBLE AUTO MODELS 467
SHOTGUNS: SEMI-AUTO, MISC. - CURRENT / RECENT MFG. 467

SHOTGUNS: SINGLE BARREL, BT-99 & BT-100 475
SHOTGUNS: SINGLE BARREL, RECOILLESS TRAP 478
SHOTGUNS: SLIDE ACTION 478
SPECIAL EDITIONS, COMMEMORATIVES, & LIMITED MFG. 481
SHOT SHOW SPECIALS 482
BROZ ARMS CZ 482
BRUCHET 482
BRUGGER & THOMET 482
BRYCO ARMS 482
BUDISCHOWSKY 483
BUEHLER CUSTOM SPORTING ARMS 483
BUFFALO ARMS 483
BULA DEFENSE SYSTEMS 484
BULLARD REPEATING ARMS COMPANY 484
BULLSEYE GUN WORKS 485
BUL ARMORY / BUL LTD. (TRANSMARK) 485
BUMAR 490
THE BURGESS GUN CO. 490
BUSHMASTER FIREARMS 490
BUTLER ARMS USA 498
BUTLER ASSOC., INC. 498
BÜYÜK HUGLU 498

C

C3 DEFENSE, INC. 499
C&H PRECISION WEAPONS 499
CEO GUNS 499
CETME 499
CFS GUNS 499
CK ARMS 499
CMMG INC. 499
C-MORE COMPETITION 499
C.O. ARMS 500
CVA 500
CZ (CESKÁ ZBROJOVKA) 500
CZ (STRAKONICE) 528
CZ CUSTOM 529
CABANAS 530
CABELA'S INC. 530
CABOT GUN COMPANY LLC 530
CADEX DEFENCE 535
CAEM, RENATO 537
CAESAR GUERINI, Srl 537
CALICO LIGHT WEAPON SYSTEMS 544
CAMDON DEFENSE 545
CAMEX-BLASER USA, INC. 545
CANIK (55) 545
CAPRINUS 546
CARACAL 546
CARBON 15 546
CARL GUSTAF 546
CAROLINA ARMS GROUP 547
CASARTELLI, CARLO 547
CASPIAN ARMS, LTD. 547
CASULL ARMS CORPORATION 547
CATMA ARMS 547
CAVALRY 548
CAVALRY ARMS CORPORATION 548
CENTURION ARMS 548
CENTURION ORDNANCE, INC. 548
CENTURY ARMS 548
CENTURY ARMS (CENTURY INTERNATIONAL ARMS, INC.) 548
CENTURY MFG., INC. 557
CHAMPLIN FIREARMS, INC. 558
CHAPARRAL ARMS 558
CHAPUIS ARMES 558
CHAPUIS, P. ETS 559
CHARLES DALY: PRUSSIAN MFG. 559
CHARLES DALY: JAPANESE MFG. 560
CHARLES DALY: 1976-2010 562
CHARLES DALY: 2011-PRESENT 574
CHARLIN ARMS 580
CHARTER ARMS (1964-1996 MFG.) 580
CHARTER ARMS (CURRENT MFG.) 582
CHATTAHOOCHEE GUN WORKS, LLC 587
CHEROKEE FIREARMS 587
CHEYTAC USA, LLC 587
CHIAPPA FIREARMS USA LTD. 588
CHIAPPA FIREARMS Srl (ARMI SPORT di CHIAPPA SILVIA & C. Snc) 598
CHINA SOUTH INDUSTRIES 599
CHIPMUNK RIFLES 599
CHRISTENSEN ARMS 600
CHRISTIAN ARMORY WORKS 607
CHRISTOPH FUNK GEWEHRFABRIK SUL 608
CHURCHILL 608
E.J. CHURCHILL GUNMAKERS 608
CIMARRON F.A. CO. 608
CITADEL 625
CIVILIAN FORCE ARMS 627
CLARIDGE HI-TEC INC. 627
CLARK CUSTOM GUNS, INC. 627
CLASSIC DOUBLES 628
CLERKE ARMS, LTD. 630
CLERKE PRODUCTS 630
CLIFTON ARMS 630
COACH GUNS 630
COBALT KINETICS 632
COBB MANUFACTURING, INC. 632
COBRA 632
COBRA FIREARMS (COBRA ENTERPRISES OF UTAH, INC.) 632
COBRAY INDUSTRIES 633
COGSWELL & HARRISON (GUNMAKERS), LTD. 633
COLE ARMS INC. 635
COLT'S MANUFACTURING COMPANY, LLC 635
REVOLVERS: PERCUSSION 636
Revolvers: Percussion, Paterson Variations 636
Revolvers: Percussion, Walker Model 637
Revolvers: Percussion, Dragoon Series 638

Revolvers: Percussion, Models 1849, 1851, 1855, 1860, 1861, 1862, & 1865 639
REVOLVERS: PERCUSSION CONVERSIONS 642
Colt Thuer Conversions 642
Richards Conversions: All Variations 642
Richards-Mason Conversions: All Variations 643
Conversions with Round Cartridge Barrel 644
REVOLVERS: "OPEN TOP" MODELS 644
REVOLVERS: PERCUSSION, 2ND & 3RD GENERATION BLACK POWDER SERIES 645
DERRINGERS 645
REVOLVERS: POCKET MODELS 646
REVOLVERS: NEW LINE SERIES & VARIATIONS 646
REVOLVERS: SAA, 1873-1940 MFG. (SER. NOS. 1-357,000) 646
SAA 1st Generation Civilian/Commercial (Mfg. 1873-1940) 647
SAA 1st Generation Commercial, Non-Standard Mfg. 650
SAA U.S. Military, Mfg. 1873-1903 653
REVOLVERS: SAA, 2ND GENERATION: 1956-1975 MFG. 656
REVOLVERS: SAA, 3RD GENERATION: 1976-CURRENT MFG. 658
COLT CUSTOM SHOP ENGRAVING, SAA & SEMI-AUTO, 1976-PRESENT 662
Large Frame Size: Current SAAs and M1911s 663
Medium Frame Size 663
Small Frame Size 664
POPULAR SAA CUSTOM SHOP SPECIAL ORDER OPTIONS 664
REVOLVERS: SAA, SCOUT MODEL 664
PISTOLS: SEMI-AUTO, DISC. 665
PISTOLS: SEMI-AUTO, GOVT. MODEL 1911 COMMERCIAL VARIATIONS 667
PISTOLS: SEMI-AUTO, GOVT. MODEL 1911 MILITARY VARIATIONS 667
PISTOLS: SEMI-AUTO, GOVT. MODEL 1911A1 COMMERCIAL VARIATIONS 670
PISTOLS: SEMI-AUTO, GOVT. MODEL 1911A1 MILITARY VARIATIONS 672
PISTOLS: SEMI-AUTO, ACE MODELS, 1931-1947 MFG. 674
PISTOLS: SEMI-AUTO, NATIONAL MATCH MODELS - PRE-WWII 674
PISTOLS: SEMI-AUTO, NATIONAL MATCH MODELS - WWII & POST-WWII 674
PISTOLS: SEMI-AUTO, CUSTOM SHOP ENGRAVING PRICING, PRE-1991 676
PISTOLS: SEMI-AUTO, CURRENT CUSTOM SHOP ENGRAVING PRICING 676
PISTOLS: POPULAR 1911 CUSTOM SHOP SPECIAL ORDER OPTIONS 676
PISTOLS: SEMI-AUTO, SINGLE ACTION, RECENT/CURRENT MFG. 676
PISTOLS: SEMI-AUTO, DOUBLE ACTION - RECENT MFG. 688
PISTOLS: SEMI-AUTO, .22 CAL. - WOODSMAN SERIES & VARIATIONS 689
REVOLVERS: DOUBLE ACTION 692
REVOLVERS: DOUBLE ACTION, SWING OUT CYLINDER 694
RIFLES/CARBINES: PRE-1904 709
RIFLES: BOLT ACTION, CENTERFIRE 711
RIFLES: BOLT/SEMI-AUTO ACTION, RIMFIRE 712
RIFLES: SINGLE SHOT, CENTERFIRE 712
DRILLINGS 713
RIFLES: SEMI-AUTO, CENTERFIRE, AR-15 & VARIATIONS 713
AR-15, Pre-Ban, 1963-1989 Mfg. w/Green Label Box 713
AR-15, Pre-Ban,1989-Sept. 11,1994 Mfg. w/Blue Label Box 715
AR-15, Post-Ban, Mfg. Sept. 12, 1994-2019 716
RIFLES: SEMI-AUTO, RIMFIRE, AR-15 & VARIATIONS 723
RIFLES: SEMI-AUTO, MISC. CENTERFIRE 723
SHOTGUNS: O/U 724
SHOTGUNS: PERCUSSION 724
SHOTGUNS: SxS, DISC. 724
SHOTGUNS: SEMI-AUTO 724
SHOTGUNS: SLIDE ACTION 725
FACTORY COMMEMORATIVES & SPECIAL/LIMITED EDITIONS 725
COMANCHE 736
COMBINATION GUNS 736
COMMANDO ARMS 737
COMMANDO ARMS (NEW MFG.) 737
COMPETITIVE EDGE GUNWORKS LLC 737
COMPETITOR CORPORATION 737
CONCO ARMS 738
CONNECTICUT SHOTGUN MANUFACTURING CO. 738
CONNECTICUT VALLEY ARMS 742
CONNECTICUT VALLEY CLASSICS, INC. 744
CONQUEST 745
CONSTITUTION ARMS 745
CONTENTO/VENTURA 745
CONTINENTAL ARMS CORPORATION 745
CONTROLLED CHAOS ARMS 746
COOEY, H.W., MACHINE & ARMS CO. LTD. 746
COONAN ARMS 747
COONAN, INC. 748
COOPER FIREARMS OF MONTANA, INC. 749
COP 758
CORCIL 758
CORE RIFLE SYSTEMS 759
CORONADO ARMS 759
CORTONA 759
COSMI, AMERICO & FIGLIO 760
COSMOS 760
COSTER, GEORGE & SON 760
COUNTY, S.A.L. 760
CRESCENT FIRE ARMS CO. & CRESCENT-DAVIS ARMS CORP. 761
CRICKETT RIFLE 762
CROSS CANYON ARMS 764
CROSSFIRE LLC 764
CROWN CITY ARMS 764
CRUSADER WEAPONRY 764
CUMBERLAND MOUNTAIN ARMS, INC. 764
CUSTOM GUN GUILD 764
CYLINDER & SLIDE, INC. 765
CZECHPOINT, INC. 765
CZECH SMALL ARMS (CSA) 765

D

D&L SPORTS, INC. 767
D.A.R. GmbH (DYNAMICS ARMS RESEARCH) 767
DDI ARMS (DESTRUCTIVE DEVICES INDUSTRIES, LLC) 767
DGS, INC. 767
DNO FIREARMS 767
DP-12 767
DPMS FIREARMS (LLC) 767
DRD TACTICAL 774
DS ARMS INC. (DSA INC.) 774

DSP ARMORY 783
DWM 783
D.Z. ARMS 783
DAEWOO 783
DAISY 784
DAIWA 785
DAKIN GUN CO. 785
DAKOTA ARMS, INC. 785
DAKOTA SINGLE ACTION REVOLVERS 789
DALVAR OF USA 791
DALY, CHARLES 791
DAMKO / DK PRECISION OUTDOOR LLC 791
DAN ARMS OF AMERICA 791
DAN WESSON 792
DANE ARMORY LLC 803
DANIEL DEFENSE 803
DARDICK 807
D'ARCY ECHOLS & CO. 808
DARK STORM INDUSTRIES LLC (DSI) 808
DARNE S.A. 808
DASAN 810
DAUDSONS ARMOURY 810
DAVID MILLER CO. 810
DAVIDSON FIREARMS 810
DAVIDSON'S 811
DAVIS INDUSTRIES 811
DAVIS N.R. 811
DEAD FOOT ARMS LLC 811
DEFOURNEY 811
DEHAAN SHOTGUNS LTD. 811
DEL-TON INCORPORATED 811
DEMAS, ETS (L'ATELIER VERNEY-CARRON) 812
DEMRO 812
DEMYAN 812
DEPAR 812
DERYA INTERNATIONAL ARMS COMPANY (DERYA HUNTING ARMS) 812
DESENZANI 812
DESERT EAGLE 813
DESERT INDUSTRIES, INC. 813
DESERT ORDNANCE 813
DESERT TECH (DESERT TACTICAL ARMS) 813
DESERT TOYS 813
DETONICS DEFENSE TECHNOLOGIES, LLC 813
DETONICS FIREARMS INDUSTRIES 813
DETONICS USA 814
DEVIL DOG ARMS LLC 814
DEVIL DOG ARMS INC. 814
DEZ TACTICAL ARMS, INC. 814
DIAMOND 814
DIAMOND SHOTGUNS 814
DIAMONDBACK FIREARMS 814
DIAMONDHEAD 814
DIARM S.A. 815
DICKINSON, LLC 815
DICKSON & MACNAUGHTON 815
JOHN DICKSON & SON, LTD 815
DISSIDENT ARMS 815
DIXIE GUN WORKS 815
DLASK ARMS CORP. 815
DOLPHIN GUN COMPANY 816
DOMINGO, ACHA 816
DOMINION ARMS 816
DOMINO, IGI 816
DOUBLE D ARMORY, LTD 816
DOUBLESTAR CORP. 816
DOUBLETAP DEFENSE, LLC 816
DORKAS FOREIGN TRADE 816
DORUK SILAH CO. 816
DOWNSIZER CORPORATION 817
DRAGON 817
DRAKE ASSOCIATES 817
DREYSE 819
DRILLINGS 819
DRULOV 822
DUBIEL ARMS COMPANY 822
DUCKS UNLIMITED, INC. 822
DUMOULIN, ERNEST S.P.R.L. 822
DUMOULIN, FRANCOIS 823
DUMOULIN, HENRI & FILS 823
DUMOULIN HERSTAL S.A. 823

E

84 GUN CO. 825
E. ARTHUR BROWN COMPANY INC. 825
EAA CORP. 825
E.D.M. ARMS 825
E.M.F. CO., INC. 826
E.R. SHAW INC. 832
EAGLE ARMS, INC. 833
EAST RIDGE/STATE ARMS GUN COMPANY, INC. 835
ED BROWN CUSTOM, INC. 835
ED BROWN PRODUCTS, INC. 835
EDGE ARMS 841
EDWARD ARMS COMPANY 841
EFFEBI SRL 841
EGE SPORTING ARMS 841
EGEMEN 841
EGO ARMAS, S.A. 841
EGYPTIAN MILITARY 841
EMPEROR ARMS 841
EMPIRE RIFLE COMPANY LLC 841
EMTAN KARMIEL LTD 841
ENFIELD AMERICA, INC. 841
ENFIELDS 842
ENGLISH SHOTGUNS 849
ENTRÉPRISE ARMS INC. 850
ERA 850
ERHARDT, DENNIS 850
ERMA SUHL, GmbH 850

ERMA-WERKE 850
ERN, MAX 852
ESCALADE 852
ESCORT 852
ETERNAL 857
EUROARMS ITALIA Srl 857
EUROARMS OF AMERICA 857
EUROPEAN AMERICAN ARMORY CORP. 858
EVANS MACHINING SERVICE (EVANS ARMS) 862
EVANS, WILLIAM, GUN & RIFLE MAKERS 862
EVOLUTION USA 862
EXCAM 864
EXCEL ARMS 864
EXEL ARMS OF AMERICA, INC. 866

F

57 CENTER LLC 867
F-1 FIREARMS 867
F4 DEFENSE 867
F. DARNE FILS AINÉ 867
F&D DEFENSE 869
F.A.I.R. Srl 869
F.A.V.S. di FRANCESCO GUGLIELMINOTTI 869
FAS 869
FEG 869
FIAS 871
F.I.E. 871
FK BRNO 871
FM (FOXTROT MIKE) PRODUCTS 872
FMJ 872
FMK FIREARMS 872
FMR 872
FN AMERICA LLC (FNH USA) 872
FTL 880
FABARM, S.p.A. 880
FABBRI s.n.c. 880
FABRIQUE NATIONALE 881
FABRYKA BRONI LUCZNIK - RADOM SP.ZO.O 886
FALCO, Srl 886
FALCON FIREARMS 886
FALKOR DEFENSE 886
FAMARS di ABBIATICO & SALVINELLI Srl (CURRENT MFG.) 886
FAMARS di ABBIATICO & SALVINELLI Srl (MFG. 1967-2012) 886
FANZOJ, JOHANN 887
FARQUHARSON 887
FAUSTI STEFANO Srl 887
FAXON FIREARMS 887
FEATHER INDUSTRIES, INC. 887
FEATHER USA/AWI LLC 888
FEDERAL 888
FEDERAL ENGINEERING CORPORATION 888
FEDERAL ORDNANCE, INC. 889
FEINMECHANISCHE ENTWICKLUNGEN GmbH 889
FEINWERKBAU 889
FELIXTEAM 890
FELK TRAILERS PTY LTD. 890
FEMARU 891
FERLACH GUNS 891
FERLACHER WAFFEN PRÄZISIONSTECHNIK PRODUCTIONS GmbH & CO. KG. 892
FERLIB 892
FERRELL, ROGER 892
FIALA ARMS AND EQUIPMENT CO. 892
FIERCE FIREARMS, LLC 892
FIGHTLITE INDUSTRIES (ARES DEFENSE SYSTEMS INC.) 894
FINNCLASSIC 894
FINNISH LION 894
FIOCCHI OF AMERICA, INC. 895
FIREARMS INTERNATIONAL CORP. (F.I.C.) 895
FIREARMS INTERNATIONAL, INC. 895
FIREBIRD PRECISION 895
FIREPOWER XTREME 895
FIRESTORM 895
FLAVIO FARÈ 896
FLINT RIVER ARMORY LLC 896
FLODMAN GUNS 896
FORBES RIFLE, LLC 896
FORT DISCOVERY, INC. 897
FORT SOE SIA 897
FORT WORTH FIREARMS 897
FOSTECH MFG. 897
FOX, A.H. 897
FOX CARBINE 901
FRANCHI, LUIGI 901
FRANCOLIN INTERNATIONAL ARMS CO. 911
FRANCOTTE, AUGUSTE & CIE. S.A. 911
FRANKLIN ARMORY 913
FRASER, DANIEL (FRASER, DANL. & CO.) 913
FRASER FIREARMS CORP. 914
FREEDOM ARMS 914
FREEDOM ORDNANCE 916
FRENCH MILITARY 916
FRIGON GUNS, INC. 918
FROMMER PISTOLS 918
FUCHS FINE GUNS GmbH 918
FULTON ARMORY 918
FURR ARMS 918
FUSION FIREARMS 918

G

G2 PRECISION, LLC 919
GA PRECISION 919
G.A.C. RIFLES Srl 919
G.A.R. ARMS 919
GWACS ARMORY 919
GALAZAN 919
GALEF SHOTGUNS 919

GALENA INDUSTRIES INC. 919
GALIL 920
GAMBA, RENATO 921
GARBI, ARMAS 922
GARRAY RIFLES LTD 922
GASTINNE RENETTE 922
GATEWAY PRECISION ARMS 922
GATLING GUNS (OLDER MFG.) 922
GATLING GUNS (RECENT MFG.) 922
GAUCHER 922
GAZELLE ARMS 923
GAZELLE SHOTGUNS 923
GAVAGE 923
GEAR HEAD WORKS 923
GEISSELE AUTOMATICS 923
GELAN TRANSFORMER 923
GENTRY CUSTOM LLC 923
GERMAN P.38 MILITARY & COMMERCIAL PISTOLS 923
GERMAN SPORT GUNS GmbH 924
GEVARM 924
GIANI, VITTORIO 924
GIB 924
GIBBS, GEORGE 924
GIBBS GUNS, INC. 924
GIBBS RIFLE COMPANY, INC. 924
GIL, ANTONIO & CO 927
GILA RIVER GUN WORKS 927
GILBOA 927
GILL ARMS 927
GIRSAN MACHINE & LIGHT WEAPON INDUSTRY COMPANY 928
GLANZIG PRÄZISIONS-UND SPORTWAFFEN JAGDZUBEHÖR 930
GLENFIELD 930
GLISENTI 930
GLOCK 930
GOLAN 941
GOLDEN EAGLE 941
GOLDEN STATE ARMS 941
GONCZ ARMAMENT, INC. 942
GRAHAM BROTHER RIFLEWORKS 942
GRAND POWER s.r.o. 942
GRANGER, G. 942
GRANITE MOUNTAIN ARMS, INC. 942
GRANT, STEPHEN 942
GREAT WESTERN 942
GREAT WESTERN ARMS COMPANY 943
GREEN, ROGER 945
GREENER, W.W., LIMITED 945
GREIFELT AND COMPANY 945
GRENDEL, INC. 945
GREYBULL PRECISION 946
GREY GHOST PRECISION 946
GRIFFIN & HOWE 946
GRIFFIN ARMAMENT 949
GRIFFON 949
GRISEL, H.L. 949
GRULLA ARMAS 949
GRUND, KARL 950
GRÜNIG & ELMIGER AG 950
GUERINI, CAESAR 950
GUN 1 950
GUNCRAFTER INDUSTRIES 950
GUN ROOM CO., LLC 952
GUNSMOKE 953
GUNWERKS, LLC 953
GUN WORKS, LTD. 955
GUSTAF, CARL 955
GYROJET 955
GYC ARMAS (GIL, ANTONIO & CO.) 955

H

HHF 957
H.J.S. INDUSTRIES, INC. 957
HM DEFENSE & TECHNOLOGY 957
HMS PRÄZISIONSTECHNIK GmbH 957
H & R 1871, LLC. (HARRINGTON & RICHARDSON) 957
H-S PRECISION, INC. 962
HWP INDUSTRIES 964
HAENEL, C.G. (OLD MFG.) 965
HAENEL, C.G., GmbH (NEW MFG.) 965
HAGELBERG ARMS DESIGN 965
HAHN TACTICAL 965
HAILEY ORDNANCE CO. 965
HAKIM 965
HALO ARMS, LLC 965
HAMBRUSCH JAGDWAFFEN GmbH 965
HÄMMERLI AG 965
HÄMMERLI-WALTHER 969
HARDENED ARMS 969
HARDY 970
HARRINGTON & RICHARDSON, INC. 970
HARRIS GUNWORKS 995
HARRISON & HUSSEY LTD. 997
HARTFORD 997
HARTFORD ARMORY 998
HARTFORD ARMS AND EQUIPMENT COMPANY 998
HARTMANN & WEISS GmbH 999
HASKELL MANUFACTURING 999
HATCHER GUN COMPANY 999
HATFIELD GUN CO., INC. 1000
HATFIELD GUN COMPANY LLC 1000
HATFIELD'S 1001
HATSAN ARMS COMPANY 1001
KARL HAUPTMANN JAGDWAFFEN 1001
HAUSMANN & CO. GmbH 1001
HAWES FIREARMS 1001
HAWK GROUP CO LTD 1001
HEAD DOWN FIREARMS (HEAD DOWN PRODUCTS, LLC) 1001

HECKLER & KOCH 1002
HEDEF ARMS COMPANY 1012
HEGMANS, THEO 1012
N.L. HEINEKE, INC. 1012
HEINIE SPECIALTY PRODUCTS 1013
HEIRLOOM PRECISION 1013
HEIZER DEFENSE 1013
HELLIS, CHARLES 1013
HELWAN 1014
HENDRY, RAMSAY & WILCOX 1014
HENRY, ALEXANDER 1014
HENRY REPEATING ARMS COMPANY 1014
HENRY RIFLE 1024
HERA ARMS 1024
HERITAGE MANUFACTURING, INC. 1025
HERMANN WEIHRAUCH REVOLVER GmbH 1025
HERO GEAR (HERO GUNS) INC. 1026
HEROLD RIFLE 1026
HERTERS 1026
HESSE ARMS 1026
HEUBERG JAGDWAFFEN 1026
HEYM AG 1026
HIENDLMAYER, KLAUS 1030
HI-POINT FIREARMS 1030
HIGGINS, J.C. 1034
HIGH STANDARD 1034
DERRINGERS 1034
PISTOLS: SEMI-AUTO, LETTER SERIES 1035
PISTOLS: SEMI-AUTO, LETTER SERIES W/HAMMER 1037
PISTOLS: SEMI-AUTO, LEVER LETTER SERIES 1038
PISTOLS: SEMI-AUTO, LEVER NAME SERIES 1039
PISTOLS: SEMI-AUTO, 100 SERIES 1040
PISTOLS: SEMI-AUTO, 101 SERIES 1041
PISTOLS: SEMI-AUTO, DURA-MATIC SERIES 1042
PISTOLS: SEMI-AUTO, 102 SERIES 1043
PISTOLS: SEMI-AUTO, 103 SERIES 1044
PISTOLS: SEMI-AUTO, 104 SERIES 1046
PISTOLS: SEMI-AUTO, 105 SERIES 1047
PISTOLS: SEMI-AUTO, 106 SERIES, MILITARY MODELS 1047
PISTOLS: SEMI-AUTO, 107 SERIES 1048
PISTOLS: SEMI-AUTO, CONVERSION KITS 1050
PISTOLS: SEMI-AUTO, SH SERIES 1050
REVOLVERS: POLICE STYLE 1051
REVOLVERS: WESTERN STYLE 1054
RIFLES/CARBINES 1055
SHOTGUNS: BOLT ACTION 1056
SHOTGUNS: SEMI-AUTO 1056
SHOTGUNS: SLIDE ACTION 1057
SHOTGUNS: IMPORTED 1058
SHOTGUNS: DEFENSE & LAW ENFORCEMENT 1058
HIGH STANDARD MANUFACTURING CO. 1058
HIGH TECH CUSTOMS
(HIGH TECH CUSTOM RIFLES) 1061
HILL & MAC GUNWORKS (HMG STURMGEWEHR) . 1061
HILL COUNTRY RIFLES
(HILL COUNTRY RIFLE COMPANY) 1061
HISPANO ARGENTINO FABRICADE
AUTOMOVILES SA (HAFDASA) 1061
HODGE DEFENSE SYSTEMS INC. 1061
GEORGE HOENIG, INC. 1061
HOFER-JAGDWAFFEN, PETER 1062
HOGAN MANUFACTURING LLC 1062
P.L. HOLEHAN, INC. 1062
HOLLAND & HOLLAND LTD. 1062
HOLLENBECK GUN COMPANY 1066
HOLLOWAY & NAUGHTON GUNMAKERS 1067
HOLLOWAY ARMS CO. 1067
HOLMES FIREARMS 1067
HONOR DEFENSE LLC 1067
HOPKINS & ALLEN ARMS COMPANY, 1902-1914 . 1068
HORIZON FIREARMS 1071
HORSLEY, THOMAS 1071
HORTON, LEW, DIST. CO. 1071
HOULDING PRECISION FIREARMS 1071
HOUSTON ARMORY 1071
HOWA 1071
HUDSON MFG. 1080
HUG-SAN 1080
HUGLU 1080
HULDRA ARMS 1081
HUNTER ARMS COMPANY 1081
HUNT GROUP INTERNATIONAL
ARMS & SECURITY 1081
HUSAN ARMS 1081
HUSQVARNA 1081
HY-HUNTER INC.
FIREARMS MANUFACTURING CO. 1082
HYPER 1082

I

I.A.B. Srl 1083
IAC 1083
IAI 1083
IAI INC. - AMERICAN LEGENDS 1083
I A I 1083
IAR, Inc. 1083
I.F.G. 1084
I G A 1084
IMI 1084
I.O., INC. (INTER ORDNANCE) 1084
ISSC HANDELSGESELLSCHAFT 1084
IWI 1085
IBERIA FIREARMS 1085
IDAHO ARMORY 1085
IMPALA PLUS 1085
IMPALA PRECSION 1085
IMPERIAL GUN CO. LTD 1085
INDIAN ARMS 1085
INDUSTRIA ARMI GALESI 1085
INDUSTRY ARMAMENT 1086
INFALLIBLE 1086
INFINITY FIREARMS 1086
INGLIS HI-POWERS 1086
INGRAM 1087

INLAND MANUFACTURING (NEW MFG.) 1087
INLAND (PREVIOUS MFG.) 1089
INNOGUN 1089
INTACTO ARMS 1089
INTEGRITY ARMS & SURVIVAL 1089
INTERARMS 1089
INTERARMS ARSENAL 1091
INTERCONTINENTAL ARMS INC 1091
INTERDYNAMIC OF AMERICA, INC. 1091
INTERNATIONAL BUSINESS MACHINE CORP. (IBM) 1092
INTERNATIONAL FIREARMS CORP. (IFC) 1092
INTERNATIONAL HARVESTER CORP. 1092
INTERSTATE ARMS CORP 1092
INTRAC ARMS INTERNATIONAL INC 1093
INTRATEC 1093
INTRATEC U.S.A., INC 1094
INVESTARM, Srl 1094
INVESTMENT ARMS INC. 1094
INVINCIBLE ARMS LLC 1094
IRON ARMI Srl 1094
IRON BRIGADE ARMORY 1095
IRON RIDGE ARMS CO. 1095
IRWIN PEDERSON ARMS CO. 1095
IRWINDALE ARMS, INC. (IAI) 1095
ISRAEL ARMS INTERNATIONAL, INC. 1095
ISRAEL ARMS LTD. 1095
ISRAEL MILITARY INDUSTRIES (IMI) 1096
ISRAEL WEAPON INDUSTRIES LTD. (IWI) 1096
ISTANBUL SILAH 1096
ITALIAN MILITARY ARMS 1096
ITHACA CLASSIC DOUBLES 1097
ITHACA GUN COMPANY (NEW MFG.) 1098
ITHACA GUN COMPANY LLC (OLDER MFG.) 1100
IVER JOHNSON ARMS, INC. (NEW MFG.) 1110
IVER JOHNSON ARMS & CYCLE WORKS 1115
IZHMASH 1129
IZMIRLIOGLU 1130

J

J.B. CUSTOM INC. 1131
J.C. HIGGINS 1131
J.C SHOTWELL & SONS 1131
J.L.D. ENTERPRISES, INC. 1131
J.O. ARMS 1131
J. ROBERTS & SON (GUNMAKERS) LTD. 1131
JMC FABRICATION & MACHINE, INC 1131
JO. LO. AR. 1131
JP ENTERPRISES, INC 1132
J R CARBINES 1140
J R DISTRIBUTING 1140
JSL (HEREFORD) 1140
JTS GROUP 1140
JACKSON HOLE FIREARMS 1140
JACKSON RIFLES 1141
JAEGER, FRANZ 1141
JAGD-UND SPORTWAFFEN SUHL GmbH 1141
JAMES RIVER ARMORY 1141
JANZ GmbH 1141
JAPANESE MILITARY 1142
JARD, INC 1144
JARRETT RIFLES, INC. 1144
JEAN-MARC STEVAUX, S.P.R.L. 1147
JEFFERY, W.J. & CO. LTD 1147
JEFFERY SHARPS 1148
JENNINGS FIREARMS 1148
JERICHO (CURRENT MFG.) 1148
JERICHO (PREVIOUS MFG.) 1149
JESSE JAMES FIREARMS UNLIMITED 1149
JIEFFECO 1149
JIMENEZ ARMS INC. 1149
JOHANNSEN RIFLES 1149
JOHNSON AUTOMATICS, INC. 1150
J. JONGMANS ARMS COMPANY PTY. LTD. 1150
J. JONGMANS ARMS COMPANY 1150
JUCH-GRUND JAGDWAFFEN INH. KARL GRUND 1150
JUGGERNAUT TACTICAL 1150
JUNG, WAFFEN, GMBH 1150
JURRAS, LEE E. 1150
JUST, JOSEF 1151
J. SIP & SONS (JUSTIN SIP CUSTOM GUNS) 1151
JUST RIGHT CARBINES 1151

K

K.B.I., INC. 1153
KDF, INC 1153
KE ARMS 1153
K.F.C 1153
K&M ARMS 1154
KSN INDUSTRIES LTD. 1154
K-VAR CORP. 1154
KAHR ARMS 1155
KALASHNIKOV USA 1161
KASSNAR IMPORTS, INC. 1163
KEBERST INTERNATIONAL 1163
KEKKI 1163
KELBLY'S INC. 1163
KEL-TEC CNC INDUSTRIES, INC. 1163
KEMEN 1167
KENDALL INTERNATIONAL 1167
KENTUCKY RIFLES 1167
KEPPELER - TECHNISCHE ENTWICKLUNGEN GmbH 1168
KEPPLINGER, ING. HANNES 1168
KESSLER ARMS CORPORATION 1168
KESSLER, WAFFEN 1168
KEVIN'S 1168
KEYSTONE SPORTING ARMS 1168
KHAN ARMS 1169
KIFARU ARMS 1170

KILIMANJARO RIFLES 1170
KIMAR Srl 1170
J. KIMBALL ARMS CO. 1170
KIMBER 1171
KIMBER OF OREGON, INC. 1197
KIMEL INDUSTRIES, INC. 1202
KING'S ARSENAL 1203
KING'S GUN WORKS, INC. 1203
KINGSTON ARMORY 1203
KINTREK, INC. 1203
KIRICI SILAH 1203
KLEINGUENTHER FIREARMS CO. 1203
KNIGHT'S ARMAMENT COMPANY 1204
KOC ARMS 1206
KODIAK CO. 1206
KODIAK DEFENCE, INC. 1206
KOFS FIREARMS 1206
KOLAR ARMS 1206
KOLIBRI 1206
KONGSBERG 1207
KORA BRNO 1207
KORRIPHILA 1207
KORSTOG 1208
KORTH 1208
KOSCHAT, JAKOB 1211
KRAG-JORGENSEN (30/40 KRAG) 1211
KRAL AV 1212
KRASSNIK, VALENTIN 1212
KRICO 1213
H. KRIEGHOFF GUN CO. (SHOTGUNS OF ULM) 1213
KRISS ARMS GROUP (KRISS SYSTEMS SA) 1221
KUFSTEINER WAFFENSTUBE 1222
KUPEC, PAVEL 1222

L

L2D COMBAT 1223
L.A.R. MANUFACTURING, INC. 1223
L E S INCORPORATED 1225
LKCI LLC 1225
LMT 1225
LRB ARMS 1225
L.W. SEECAMP CO. 1225
LWRC INTERNATIONAL, INC. 1225
LA ARMERIA DE MADRID 1225
LABANU INCORPORATED 1226
LAHTI PISTOL 1226
LAKE FIELD ARMS LTD. 1226
LAKELANDER 1227
LAKESIDE MACHINE LLC 1227
LAMBOY, S.R. & CO. INC. 1227
LAMES 1227
LANBER 1228
LANCER SYSTEMS 1228
LANG, JOSEPH 1228
LANGDON TACTICAL 1228
LANTAC USA, LLC 1229
LAPORTE HOLDING 1230
LARM (ARMERIA DE MADRID, LA) 1230
LARUE TACTICAL 1230
LASERAIM ARMS, INC. 1231
LASALLE 1231
LATEK LTD. 1231
LAUER CUSTOM WEAPONRY 1231
LAUGO ARMS 1231
LAURONA ZABALA 1232
LAW ENFORCEMENT ORDNANCE CORPORATION 1232
LAYKE TACTICAL 1232
HARRY LAWSON LLC 1232
LAZZERONI ARMS COMPANY 1232
LEAD STAR ARMS 1235
LEADER ARMS TECHNOLOGY 1235
LEBEAU-COURALLY 1235
LECHNER & JUNGL GES.m.b.H. 1236
LEE ARMS COMPANY 1236
LEFEVER ARMS COMPANY 1237
LEFEVER, D.M. 1239
LE FORGERON 1240
LE FRANCAIS PISTOLS 1240
LEGACY SPORTS INTERNATIONAL 1241
LEGEND 1241
LEGENDARY ARMS WORKS 1241
LEGION FIREARMS LLC 1242
LEGION USA INC. 1242
LEITNER-WISE DEFENSE, INC. 1242
LEITNER-WISE RIFLE CO. INC. 1242
LES BAER CUSTOM, INC. 1242
LEW HORTON DIST. CO. 1249
LEWIS MACHINE & TOOL COMPANY (LMT) 1249
LIBERATOR 1249
LIBERTY 1249
LIBERTY ARMS INTERNATIONAL LLC 1249
LIBERTY ARMS WORKS, INC. 1249
LIEGEOISE D'ARMES 1250
LIGNOSE (BERGMAN) 1250
LILIPUT 1250
LIND, AL 1250
LINDNER GUN COMPANY 1250
LINEBAUGH CUSTOM SIXGUNS 1250
LINGARD, MICHAEL 1250
LINIE HABSBURG JAGDWAFFEN 1250
LIONHEART INDUSTRIES USA 1251
LIPPARD, KARL 1251
LITHGOW ARMS 1252
LITTLE SHARPS RIFLE MFG 1252
LJUNGMAN 1253
LJUTIC LLC 1253
LLAMA - Fabrinor S.A.L. (PREVIOUS MFG.) 1254
LLAMA (NEW MFG.) 1257
LOHMAN GUNSMITHING 1257
LOKI WEAPON SYSTEMS, INC. 1257

LON PAUL CUSTOM GUNS 1257
LONE STAR ARMAMENT, INC. 1258
LONE STAR ARMORY 1258
LONE STAR RIFLE CO., INC. 1258
LONE STAR TACTICAL SUPPLY 1259
LONE WOLF DISTRIBUTORS 1259
LONGTHORNE GUNMAKERS LTD 1259
LORCIN ENGINEERING CO., INC. 1260
LORENZO, CRESS 1261
LOSOK CUSTOM ARMS 1261
LUCCHINI, SANDRO 1261
LUGERS WITH VARIATIONS 1261
REFERENCE GUIDE BY TOGGLE MARKING 1262
DWM TOGGLE IDENTIFICATION 1262
DWM COMMERCIAL LUGERS 1262
ERFURT TOGGLE IDENTIFICATION 1263
SIMSON & CO. TOGGLE IDENTIFICATION 1264
SWISS TOGGLE IDENTIFICATION 1264
MAUSER TOGGLE IDENTIFICATION 1264
KRIEGHOFF TOGGLE IDENTIFICATION 1264
VICKERS TOGGLE IDENTIFICATION 1265
LUGERS: MATCHING MAGAZINE(S) & MILITARY HOLSTER ADD ONS 1265
PISTOLS: SEMI-AUTO, LUGERS & VARIATIONS 1265
Lugers: Pre-1900 & 1900 DWM Mfg. 1265
Lugers: 1902-DWM Mfg. 1265
Lugers: 1903-1904 DWM Mfg. 1266
Lugers: 1906-DWM Mfg. 1266
Lugers: 1908 DWM & Erfurt Mfg. 1267
Lugers: 1910-1918 Dated DWM & Erfurt Mfg. 1268
Lugers: 1920-1930 DWM 1268
Lugers: Krieghoff Mfg. 1270
Lugers: Mauser Mfg. 1270
Lugers: Reworks 1272
Lugers: Simson Mfg. 1272
Lugers: Swiss Bern 1272
Lugers: KDF, Interarms, Stoeger, & Recent Import 1272
Lugers: Special Interest 1273
LUGERS: ACCESSORIES 1274
Conversion Units - .22 cal. 1275
Detachable Stocks 1275
"Snail" Drum Magazines 1275
SHOTGUNS: O/U 1275
SHOTGUNS: SEMI-AUTO 1275
LU-MAR Srl 1275
LUNA 1275
LUSA USA 1276
LUVO PRAGUE LTD 1276
LUXUS ARMS LLC 1276
LYMAN 1276
LYNX 1276

M

MAB 1277
MAC (METROARMS CORP.) 1277
MAC (MILITARY ARMAMENT CORP.) 1277
MAG CUSTOM RIFLES 1277
MAS 1277
MBA ASSOCIATES 1277
MGA (MACHINE GUN ARMORY) 1278
MG ARMS INCORPORATED 1278
MGI 1279
M-K SPECIALTIES INC. 1279
MK ARMS INC. 1280
MKA ARMS 1280
MKE 1280
MKS SUPPLY, INC. 1281
MMC ARMORY 1282
MNR CUSTOM LLC 1282
M.O.A. CORPORATION 1282
MOA RIFLES, LLC 1283
M.R. NEW SYSTEM ARMS 1284
MTs ARMS 1284
JAMES MacNAUGHTON & SONS 1284
MAADI-GRIFFIN CO. 1285
MAGNUM RESEARCH, INC. 1285
MAGTECH AMMUNITION CO., INC. (MAGTECH) 1294
MAJESTIC ARMS, LTD. 1294
MAKAROV 1294
MAKURA HUNTING RIFLES 1295
MALIN, F.E. 1295
MAMBA 1295
MANCHESTER ARMS INC. 1295
MANDALL SHOOTING SUPPLIES, INC. 1295
MANIFATURRA ARMI ART 1295
MÄNNEL SPORT SHOOTING GmbH 1296
MANNLICHER PISTOLS 1296
MANNLICHER SCHOENAUER SPORTING RIFLES 1296
MANU-ARM 1299
MANUFRANCE 1299
MANURHIN 1300
MARATHON PRODUCTS, INC. 1301
MARBLE ARMS & MFG. CO. 1302
MARCEL THYS & SONS 1303
MARCOLMAR FIREARMS 1303
MARGOLIN 1303
MARLIN FIREARMS COMPANY 1304
MAROCCHI 1332
MARTIN, ALEX 1332
MARTINI 1332
MARTINI GUNMAKERS 1332
MASTERPIECE ARMS (MPA) 1333
MASTERPIECE ARMS, INC. 1333
MASQUELIER S.A. 1333
MATCHGUNS Srl 1333
MATCH GRADE ARMS & AMMUNITION 1333
MATEBA 1333
MATEBA ITALIA Srl 1334
MATHELON ARMES 1334
MATRA MANURHIN DEFENSE 1334
MATRIX ARMS 1334
MAUNZ MATCH RIFLES, LLC 1334
MAUNZ MFG., INC. 1334
MAURITZ WIDFORSS AB 1334
MAUSER JAGDWAFFEN GmbH 1334

MAVERICK ARMS, INC. 1362
MAWHINNEY, CHUCK.......... 1364
MAXIM DEFENSE.......... 1364
MAXIM FIREARMS 1364
MAXIMUS ARMS, LLC 1364
MAYFAIR ENGINEERING.......... 1364
MAYZUS GUNSMITH COMPANY s.r.o. 1364
McCANN INDUSTRIES.......... 1364
MCDUFFEE ARMS 1364
McMILLAN BROS. RIFLE CO. 1364
McMILLAN FIREARMS MANUFACTURING, LLC...... 1365
McMILLAN, G. & CO., INC.......... 1368
MCREES PRECISION 1370
MEACHAM TOOL & HARDWARE, INC. 1370
MEDWELL & PERRETT LIMITED.......... 1370
MELIOR - ROBAR & CO. 1370
MENZ, AUGUST 1370
MERCURY (PISTOLS).......... 1370
MERCURY (SHOTGUNS) 1370
MERKEL 1370
MERRILL.......... 1381
MERTMAK 1381
MERWIN HULBERT & CO. 1381
MERWIN HULBERT & CO. (RECENT MFG.) 1383
MESA PRECISION ARMS 1384
METROARMS CORPORATION (MAC).......... 1384
MICHIGAN ARMS 1385
MICOR DEFENSE, INC. 1385
MICROTECH SMALL ARMS
RESEARCH, INC. (MSAR) 1385
MIDLAND ARMS.......... 1385
MIDLAND RIFLES.......... 1386
MIDWEST INDUSTRIES, INC. 1386
MIIDA 1386
MILLER ARMS 1386
MILLER, DAVID CO. 1387
MILLER PRECISION ARMS 1387
MIL-SPEC INDUSTRIES CORP. 1387
MILTAC INDUSTRIES, LLC 1387
MILTEX, INC. 1387
MIROKU, B.C. 1387
MITCHELL ARMS, INC. 1387
MITCHELL'S MAUSERS 1387
MODULO MASTERPIECE 1389
MOHAWK ARMORY 1389
MOLL, M.F. 1389
MOLOT ARMS.......... 1390
MONTANA ARMORY, INC. 1390
MONTANA RIFLE COMPANY 1390
MONTGOMERY WARD 1392
MORIARTI ARMAMENTS 1392
MORINI COMPETITION ARM SA.......... 1393
MORTIMER, THOMAS.......... 1393
MOSIN-NAGANT 1393
MOSSBERG, O.F. & SONS, INC. 1393
DERRINGERS.......... 1393
PISTOLS: SEMI-AUTO.......... 1394
RIFLES: DISC., 1919-1987 MFG........... 1394
Mossberg "Targo" Smoothbore Models.......... 1400
RIFLES: BOLT ACTION.......... 1402
RIFLES: LEVER ACTION.......... 1406
RIFLES: SEMI-AUTO.......... 1407
SHOTGUNS: BOLT ACTION - DISC.......... 1409
SHOTGUNS: O/U.......... 1410
SHOTGUNS: SxS, RECENT PRODUCTION.......... 1411
SHOTGUNS: SEMI-AUTO.......... 1412
SHOTGUNS: SLIDE ACTION.......... 1418
SHOTGUNS: SLIDE ACTION, MODEL 835, 935, & 3000 SERIES.... 1434
SHOTGUNS: SLIDE ACTION MAGPUL SERIES.......... 1438
MOUNTAIN RIFLERY, LLC 1438
MOUNTAIN RIFLES INC. 1438
MUSGRAVE (PREVIOUS MFG.) 1439
MUSGRAVE (NEW MFG.) 1439
MUSKETEER RIFLES.......... 1439

N

NS FIREARMS CORP.......... 1441
NAMBU PISTOLS.......... 1441
NAROH ARMS 1442
NATIONAL POSTAL METER.......... 1442
NATIONAL WILD TURKEY FEDERATION (NWTF).. 1442
NAVY ARMS COMPANY.......... 1442
P.V. NELSON GUNMAKERS LTD. 1450
NEMESIS ARMS.......... 1450
NEMO ARMS (NEW EVOLUTION
MILITARY ORDNANCE).......... 1450
NESIKA.......... 1450
NEW ADVANTAGE ARMS, INC. 1451
NEW DETONICS MANUFACTURING
CORPORATION.......... 1452
NEW ENGLAND ARMS CORP. 1453
NEW ENGLAND CUSTOM GUN SERVICE, LTD.
(NECG LTD.).......... 1453
NEW ENGLAND FIREARMS 1453
NEW FRONTIER ARMORY.......... 1457
NEW ULTRA LIGHT ARMS LLC 1457
NEWTON ARMES.......... 1458
NEWTON ARMS CO. 1458
NEWTOWN FIREARMS 1459
NEXT GENERATION ARMS.......... 1459
NIGHTHAWK CUSTOM 1459
NIKKO FIREARMS CO., LTD.......... 1467
NOBLE MFG. CO. 1469
NOR-CAL PRECISION.......... 1469
NOREEN FIREARMS LLC.......... 1469
NORICA LAURONA.......... 1470
NORINCO 1470
NORINCO USA 1473
NORSMAN SPORTING ARMS & OUTFITTERS 1473
NORTH AMERICAN ARMS, INC. 1474
NORTH AMERICAN SAFARI EXPRESS 1477
NORTHERN COMPETITION.......... 1477

NORTHWEST ARMS 1477
NOSLER, INC. 1477
NOVESKE RIFLEWORKS LLC 1480
NOWLIN MFG., INC. 1480
NUOVA JAGER 1480

O

O'BRIEN RIFLE CO. 1481
O.D.I. (OMEGA DEFENSIVE INDUSTRIES) 1481
OBERLAND ARMS 1481
OBREGON 1481
OBSIDIAN ARMS 1481
OHIO ORDNANCE WORKS, INC. 1481
OLD-WEST GUN CO. 1482
OLLENDORFF, PHILIPP 1482
OLYMPIC ARMS, INC. 1483
OMEGA 1491
OMEGA ARMS 1491
OMEGA FIREARMS 1491
OMEGA PISTOL 1491
OMEGA RIFLES 1491
OMEGA RIFLES/SHOTGUNS 1492
OMEGA WEAPONS SYSTEMS INC. 1493
OMNI 1493
OMNI (CURRENT MFG.) 1493
ONLY LONG RANGE 1493
OPTIMA 1493
OPUS SPORTING ARMS, INC. 1493
OREGON ARMS 1494
ORISKANY ARMS INC. 1494
ORSI & ORSI 1495
ORSIS 1495
ORTGIES PISTOLS 1495
ORVIS 1495
OSPREY ARMAMENT 1497
OTTOMANGUNS 1497
OVERMATCH PRECISION ARMS 1498
OWEN, KEN 1498
ÖZKANLAR 1498

P

P.38 MILITARY & COMMERCIAL PISTOLS 1499
P.A.F. 1503
P.A.W.S., INC. 1504
PGW DEFENCE TECHNOLOGIES, INC. 1504
PHSADC (PAKISTAN HUNTING & SPORTING ARMS DEVELOPMENT COMPANY) ... 1504
PHX PHOENIX AG 1504
PKP, INC. 1504
POF USA 1504
PPK s.r.o. 1504
PSD MANUFACTURING (PALMETTO STATE DEFENSE, LLC) 1504
P.S.M.G. GUN COMPANY 1504
PTK INTERNATIONAL, INC. 1505
PTR 1505
PTR INDUSTRIES, INC. (PTR 91, INC) 1507
P.V. NELSON, (GUNMAKERS) 1510
PACIFIC INTERNATIONAL 1510
M. PADRÓNE 1510
PALMETTO ARMS CO. 1510
PALMETTO STATE ARMORY 1510
PARAMOUNT 1510
PALM PISTOL 1511
PAOLO PELI 1511
PARA USA, LLC 1511
PARDINI, ARMI Srl 1520
PARDUS 1522
PARKER BROS. MAKERS 1522
PARKER BROTHERS 1522
PARKER GUNMAKERS 1527
PARKER PISTOLS 1527
PARKER REPRODUCTIONS 1527
PARKER-HALE LIMITED 1529
PASTUSEK INDUSTRIES 1529
PATRIOT ORDNANCE FACTORY (POF) 1529
PATRIOT PRECISION 1529
PATRIOT WEAPONRY 1530
PAUZA SPECIALTIES 1530
PAVONA 1531
PEACE RIVER CLASSICS 1531
PEDERSEN CUSTOM GUNS 1531
PEDERSEN DEVICE 1531
PEDERSOLI, DAVIDE & C. Snc. 1531
PEERLESS RIFLE COMPANY 1531
PENTHENY de PENTHENY 1532
PERAZZI 1532
PEREGRINE INDUSTRIES, INC. 1544
PERODEAU, J.J. GUNMAKER 1545
PERUGINI-VISINI 1545
PETERS STAHL GmbH 1545
PFEIFER-WAFFEN 1545
PHASE 5 TACTICAL 1545
PHELPS MFG. CO. 1545
PHILLIPS & ROGERS, INC. 1546
PHOENIX ARMS 1546
PHOENIX ARMS CO. 1547
PHOENIX WEAPONRY 1547
PICKERT (PICKERT ARMINIUS) 1547
PIETTA, F.LLI 1547
PIONEER ARMS CORP. 1551
PIOTTI 1552
PIRANHA 1552
PISTOL DYNAMICS 1552
PLAINFIELD CARBINES 1552
PLAINS RIFLE 1552
POINTER 1552
POLI, ARMI F.LLI 1555
POLI NICOLETTA & C. snc. 1556
POLY TECHNOLOGIES, INC. 1556

POWELL & BROWN KNIFE PISTOL 1556
POWELL, WILLIAM & SON (GUNMAKERS) LTD. 1556
POWERS METAL WORKS, LLC 1556
PRAIRIE GUN WORKS 1557
PRANDELLI-GASPERINI 1557
PRECHTL JAGD & SPORTWAFFEN 1557
PRECISION FIREARMS 1557
PRECISION REFLEX, INC. 1557
PRECISION SMALL ARMS, INC. (PSA) 1557
PREDATOR CUSTOM SHOP 1559
PREDATOR TACTICAL LLC 1559
PREMIER 1559
PRENSES ARMS 1560
PRIMARY WEAPONS SYSTEMS (PWS) 1560
PRINZ 1560
PRINZ-WAFFEN 1560
PROARMS ARMORY s.r.o. 1560
PROCISION ARMS 1560
PROFESSIONAL ORDNANCE, INC. 1561
PROOF RESEARCH 1561
PUMA 1562
PURDEY, JAMES & SONS, LTD. 1563
PUSKARSTVO SPENDAL d.o.o. 1565

Q

Q.S. ARMI 1567
QFI (QUALITY FIREARMS INC.) 1567
QIQIHAR HAWK INDUSTRIES CO., LTD 1567
QUACKENBUSH, H.M. 1567
QUAIL UNLIMITED, INC. 1567
QUALITY ARMS 1568
QUALITY PARTS CO./BUSHMASTER 1568

R

R GUNS 1569
RAAC 1569
RAF 1569
RBA 1569
R.F.M. 1569
R.G. INDUSTRIES 1569
RGS LLC 1570
R.I.P. TACTICAL 1570
RND MANUFACTURING 1570
RPA DEFENCE LTD. (RPA SYSTEMS LTD. / RANGEMASTER PRECISION ARMS / RPA INTERNATIONAL LTD.) 1571
RPB INDUSTRIES 1571
RPM 1571
RWC (RUSSIAN WEAPON COMPANY) 1571
RWS 1572
RADIAN WEAPONS 1572
RADICAL FIREARMS, LLC 1572
RADOM 1572
RAINIER ARMS 1574
RAM-LINE, INC. 1574
RAMIREZ, TODD 1574
RAMO DEFENSE SYSTEMS 1575
RANDALL FIREARMS COMPANY 1575
RANGEMASTER PRECISION ARMS 1577
RANGER ARMS INC. 1577
RAPTOR ARMS CO., INC. 1577
RASHEED (RASHID) 1578
RAVELL 1578
RAVEN ARMS 1578
REBEL ARMS CORP. 1578
REC-ARMS 1578
RECORD-MATCH 1578
RED ARROW WEAPONS 1579
RED DESERT RIFLES 1579
RED ROCK ARMS 1579
RED ROCK PRECISION 1579
RED X ARMS 1580
REDOLFI F.LLI S.N.C. 1580
GARY REEDER CUSTOM GUNS 1580
REGENT 1580
REIMER JOHANNSEN GmbH (JOHANNSEN RIFLES) 1580
REISING ARMS COMPANY 1581
RELLIM ARMS 1581
REMINGTON ARMS COMPANY, INC. 1581
REMINGTON TRADEMARKS - 1816-PRESENT 1582
HANDGUNS: 1857-1945 PRODUCTION 1582
PISTOLS: BOLT ACTION 1588
PISTOLS: SEMI-AUTO, POST-WWII PRODUCTION 1588
PISTOLS: SINGLE SHOT, XP-100 & VARIATIONS 1591
RIFLES: DISC 1592
RIFLES: CANE VARIATIONS 1597
RIFLES: ROLLING BLOCK, MODERN MFG. 1598
RIFLES: SEMI-AUTO, CENTERFIRE 1598
RIFLES: SLIDE ACTION, CENTERFIRE 1602
RIFLES: RIMFIRE, BOLT ACTION 1606
RIFLES: RIMFIRE, "NYLON SERIES" 1610
RIFLES: RIMFIRE, SEMI-AUTO 1611
RIFLES: RIMFIRE, SLIDE ACTION 1614
RIFLES: BOLT ACTION, CENTERFIRE 1615
RIFLES: BOLT ACTION, MODEL 700 & VARIATIONS 1621
RIFLES: BOLT ACTION, MODEL 40X & VARIATIONS 1634
SHOTGUNS: O/U 1637
SHOTGUNS: SxS 1639
SHOTGUNS: SEMI-AUTO, MISC. MODELS 1643
Shotguns: Semi-Auto, Model 11 & Variations 1643
Shotguns: Semi-Auto, Model 48 & Variations 1644
Shotguns: Semi-Auto, Model 58 & Variations 1644
Shotguns: Semi-Auto, Model 1100 & Variations 1645
Shotguns: Semi-Auto, Model 11-87 & Variations 1649
Shotguns: Semi-Auto, SP-10 Models 1652
Shotguns: Semi-Auto, V3 & Versa Models 1653
SHOTGUNS: SINGLE SHOT 1654
SHOTGUNS: SLIDE ACTION, MODELS 10, 17, & 29 & VARIATIONS 1654
SHOTGUNS: SLIDE ACTION, MODEL 31 & VARIATIONS 1655
SHOTGUNS: SLIDE ACTION, MODEL 870 & VARIATIONS 1656
RENATO GAMBA 1665
RENETTE, GASTINNE 1665
REPUBLIC ARMS, INC. 1665
REPUBLIC ARMS OF SOUTH AFRICA 1666

REPUBLIC FORGE 1666
RETAY ARMS CORP. 1667
REVOLUTIONARY ROLLER LOCKS 1667
REX 1667
REXIO 1667
RHINO RIFLES (RHINO ARMS) 1667
RHODE ISLAND ARMS COMPANY 1667
RIB MOUNTAIN ARMS, INC. 1668
RICHLAND ARMS COMPANY 1668
RIEDL RIFLE COMPANY 1669
RIFLE CRAFT, LTD. 1669
RIFLES, INC. 1669
RIGANIAN, RAY (RIFLEMAKER) 1670
RIGBY, JOHN & CO. (GUNMAKERS), INC. 1670
RISE ARMAMENT 1671
RITTER & STARK 1671
RIVERMAN GUN WORKS 1671
RIZZINI & TANFOGLIO Srl 1672
RIZZINI, BATTISTA 1672
RIZZINI, EMILIO 1680
RIZZINI, F.LLI 1681
RIZZINI, I. (ISIDORA) 1682
ROAM 1682
THE ROBAR COMPANIES, INC. 1682
ROBERT HISSERICH COMPANY 1682
ROBERTS DEFENSE 1683
ROBERTS, J & SON (GUNMAKERS) LTD. 1683
ROBERTSON 1683
ROBINSON ARMAMENT CO. 1683
ROBINSON CUSTOM GUNS LLC 1684
ROCHE, CHRISTIAN 1684
ROCK ISLAND ARMORY 1684
ROCK ISLAND ARMORY (CURRENT MFG.) 1684
ROCK-OLA MANUFACTURING CO. 1691
ROCK RIVER ARMS, INC. 1691
ROCKY MOUNTAIN ARMS CORP. 1705
ROCKY MOUNTAIN ARMS, INC. 1705
ROCKY MOUNTAIN ELK FOUNDATION 1707
ROEDALE PRECISION 1707
ROGAK 1707
ROGER'S GUN WORKS, INC. 1707
ROGUE RIVER RIFLEWORKS 1707
RÖHM 1707
ROHRBAUGH FIREARMS CORP. 1708
ROPER 1708
ROSS RIFLE COMPANY 1708
ROSSI 1712
ROESSLER (ROBLER) WAFFEN GmbH 1719
ROTA, LUCIANO 1720
ROTH PERFORMANCE 1720
ROTTWEIL 1720
ROYAL AMERICAN SHOTGUNS 1720
ROYAL ARMS INTERNATIONAL 1720
RUBY 1721
RUGER 1721
RUKO SPORTING GOODS, INC. 1721
RUSSIAN AMERICAN ARMORY COMPANY 1721
RUSSIAN SERVICE PISTOLS AND RIFLES 1721
RUTTEN HERSTAL 1722

S

S.A.C.M. 1723
S.A.M. 1723
S.I.A.C.E. 1723
S.P.S. 1723
S.W.A.T. FIREARMS 1723
S.W.D., INC. 1723
SAE 1724
SBR (SOUTHERN BALLISTIC RESEARCH) 1724
SCCY INDUSTRIES 1724
SD TACTICAL ARMS 1725
SI DEFENSE, INC. 1725
SKB SHOTGUNS 1725
SKS 1738
SMI ARMS 1739
SRM ARMS 1739
SSK FIREARMS (SSK INDUSTRIES) 1740
STI INTERNATIONAL 1740
ST. GEORGE ARMS 1740
STL 1740
STP (MFG. BY PROMMERSBERGER) 1741
SWS 2000 1741
SABATTI s.p.a 1741
SABRE 1744
SABRE DEFENCE INDUSTRIES LLC 1744
SACO DEFENSE INC. 1744
SAFARI ARMS 1744
SAFARI CLUB INTERNATIONAL 1745
SAFETY HARBOR FIREARMS, INC. 1746
SAIGA 1746
SAKO, LTD. 1747
SALERI, W.R. di SALERI WILLIAM & C. snc 1755
SALIENT ARMS INTERNATIONAL 1755
SAMCO GLOBAL ARMS, INC. 1756
SAN JUAN ENTERPRISE 1756
SAN SWISS ARMS AG 1756
SAN TAN TACTICAL 1756
SAR ARMS 1756
SARASQUETA, FELIX 1756
SARASQUETA, J.J. 1756
SARASQUETA, VICTOR 1756
SARCO, INC. 1756
SARDIUS 1756
SARRIUGARTE, FRANCISO S.A. 1757
SARSILMAZ (SAR ARMS) 1757
SATTERLEE ARMS, LLC 1757
SAUER, J.P., & SOHN 1757
SAVAGE ARMS, INC. 1767
SAVIN, J.C. 1812
SAXONIA 1812

SCATTERGUN TECHNOLOGIES INC. (S.G.T.) 1812
SCHALL & CO. (SCHALL) 1814
SCHEIRING GmbH 1814
SCHELLER SPEZIALWAFFEN 1814
SCHERZ, MICHAEL 1814
SCHILLER BUCHSENMACHER 1814
SCHILLING, FA. ALFRED 1814
SCHMEISSER GmbH 1814
SCHMIDT-RUBIN RIFLES 1815
SCHMITT FRERES 1815
SCHROEDER BAUMAN 1815
SCHUERMAN ARMS, LTD. 1815
SCHUETZEN PISTOL WORKS 1815
SCHUETZEN RIFLES 1815
SCHULTZ & LARSEN 1816
SCHWABEN ARMS GMBH 1816
SCORPION 1816
SCORPION TACTICAL 1817
SCOTT, W.C., LTD. 1817
SEARCY, B. & CO. 1817
SEARS, ROEBUCK AND CO. 1818
SECURITY INDUSTRIES 1818
SEDCO INDUSTRIES, INC 1818
SEDGLEY, R.F., INC. 1818
SEECAMP, L.W. CO., INC. 1818
SEEKINS PRECISION 1819
SEITZ 1819
SEMMERLING 1819
SENNI ARMS CO. 1819
SENTINEL ARMS 1819
SERBU FIREARMS, INC. 1820
SERENGETI RIFLES, INC. 1820
SERO LTD. 1820
SHADOW SYSTEMS LLC 1820
C. SHARPS ARMS, INC. 1821
SHARPS, CHRISTIAN 1824
SHARPS MILSPEC 1827
SHARPS RIFLE COMPANY 1827
SHAW PRECISION GUNS 1827
SHERIDAN PRODUCTS INCORPORATED 1827
SHILEN RIFLES, INCORPORATED 1827
SHILOH SHARPS RIFLE MANUFACTURING COMPANY 1828
SHOOTERS ARMS MANUFACTURING INCORPORATED 1828
SIBERGUN 1828
SIDEWINDER 1828
SIG ARMS AG 1828
SIG-HÄMMERLI 1830
SIGNAL 9 DEFENSE 1830
SIG SAUER 1831
SILE DISTRIBUTORS 1864
SILMA SPORTING GUNS 1864
SILVA ARMS 1864
SILVER EAGLE 1865
SILVER SEITZ 1865
SILVER SHADOW ADVANCED SECURITY SYSTEMS LTD. 1865
SIMILLION, GENE 1865
SIMSEK 1865
SIMSON 1866
SINO DEFENSE MANUFACTURING (SDM) 1866
SIONICS WEAPON SYSTEMS 1866
SIPAHILER 1866
SIRKIS INDUSTRIES, LTD. 1866
SISK RIFLES LLC 1866
SJOGREN 1867
SKELI, LLC 1867
SKORPION 1867
SMITH-CORONA 1867
SMITH, L.C. 1867
SMITH & WESSON 1873
PISTOLS: LEVER ACTION, ANTIQUE 1874
TIP-UPS 1874
TOP-BREAKS 1876
SINGLE SHOTS 1882
EARLY HAND EJECTORS (NAMED MODELS) 1882
REVOLVERS: NUMBERED MODEL/RECENT MFG. (MODERN HAND EJECTORS) 1896
PISTOLS: SEMI-AUTO, CENTERFIRE 1917
PISTOLS: SEMI-AUTO, M&P/M&P M2.0 SERIES 1930
PISTOLS: SEMI-AUTO, RIMFIRE 1934
PRE-2009 ENGRAVING OPTIONS FOR HANDGUNS 1936
CURRENT ENGRAVING OPTIONS FOR HANDGUNS 1936
S&W SPECIAL/LIMITED EDITIONS 1937
S&W FACTORY COMMEMORATIVES 1937
S&W PERFORMANCE CENTER FIREARMS 1938
Pricing of Performance Center Firearms 1938
Heritage Series From Lew Horton & Performance Center Handguns 1939
Pistols: Semi-Auto, Performance Center Variations 1939
Revolvers: Performance Center Variations 1946
Rifles: Performance Center Variations 1957
RIFLES - ALL VARIATIONS 1958
Rifles: Revolving 1958
Rifles: NFA 1958
Rifles: Bolt Action 1959
Rifles: Semi-Auto 1960
SHOTGUNS 1963
SMITHSON, J.P. 1964
SNAKE CHARMER 1964
SNOWY MOUNTAIN RIFLES 1964
SOCIETA SIDERURGICA GLISENTI 1966
SOCIETE FAYOUMI 1966
SODIA, FRANZ 1966
SOKOLOVSKY CORPORATION SPORT ARMS (SCSA) 1966
SOG ARMORY 1967
SOLEIHAC ARMURIER 1967
SOL INVICTUS ARMS 1967
SOMMER + OCKENFUSS GmbH 1967
SONS OF LIBERTY GUN WORKS 1967
SOROKA RIFLE COMPANY 1967
SOUTHERN GUN COMPANY 1967

SPARTAN GUN WORKS 1967
SPARTAN PRECISION RIFLES 1967
SPECIAL WEAPONS LLC 1968
SPECIALIZED DYNAMICS 1968
SPECIALIZED TACTICAL SYSTEMS 1968
SPENCER CARBINES/RIFLES - CURRENT MFG. 1968
SPENCER REPEATING RIFLES CO. 1968
SPHINX SYSTEMS LTD. 1970
SPIDER FIREARMS 1972
SPIKE'S TACTICAL LLC 1972
SPIRIT GUN MANUFACTURING COMPANY LLC 1972
SPITFIRE 1972
SPOHR, THOMAS (TS FINE GUNS) 1972
SPORTCO/SPORTING ARMS CO. 1972
SPORT-SYSTEME DITTRICH 1973
SPRINGER'S ERBEN, JOHANN 1973
SPRINGFIELD ARMORY 1973
SPRINGFIELD ARMORY (MFG. BY SPRINGFIELD INC.) 1976
SPRINGFIELD ARMS CO. 2000
STACCATO (STI INTERNATIONAL) 2000
STAG ARMS LLC 2011
STAGGS-BILT 2011
STALLARD ARMS 2011
STANDARD ARMS & STANDARD ARMS MFG. CO. 2011
STANDARD ARMS OF NEVADA, INC. 2012
STANDARD MANUFACTURING CO. LLC 2012
STANDARD PRODUCTS CO. 2015
STAR, BONIFACIO ECHEVERRIA S.A. 2015
STATE ARMS GUN CO. 2018
STEEL ACTION GmBH 2018
STEEL CITY ARMS, INC. 2019
STEEL CORE DESIGNS LTD 2019
STEERING GEAR (GRAND RAPIDS & SAGINAW LOCATIONS) 2019
STEINKAMP MASCHINENBAU GmbH & Co. KG. 2019
STERLING 2019
STERLING ARMAMENT, LTD. 2019
STERLING ARSENAL 2020
STEVENS, J., ARMS COMPANY 2020
STEYR AUSTRIAN MILITARY 2027
STEYR DAIMLER PUCH A.G. 2028
STEYR ARMS (STEYR MANNLICHER) 2028
STINGER MANUFACTURING CORP. 2040
STOCK, FRANZ 2040
STOCKWORKS 2040
STOEGER INDUSTRIES, INC. 2040
STONER RIFLE 2045
STRANK, ANDREAS 2045
STRASSER 2046
STRATEGIC ARMORY CORPS, LLC 2046
STRAYER TRIPP INTERNATIONAL 2046
STRAYER-VOIGT, INC. 2046
STREET SWEEPER 2046
STRIKE INDUSTRIES 2046
STURM, RUGER & CO., INC. 2046
RUGER COLLECTIBILITY OVERVIEW 2047
RUGER CUSTOM SHOP 2047
PISTOLS: SEMI-AUTO, RIMFIRE 2047
PISTOLS: SEMI-AUTO, CENTERFIRE 2052
REVOLVERS: SINGLE ACTION, OLD MODELS 2059
REVOLVERS: SINGLE ACTION, NEW MODELS 2063
REVOLVERS: DOUBLE ACTION 2070
RIFLES: BOLT ACTION, RIMFIRE 2074
RIFLES: BOLT ACTION, CENTERFIRE 2076
RIFLES: LEVER ACTION 2085
RIFLES: SEMI-AUTO, RIMFIRE 2085
RIFLES: SEMI-AUTO, CENTERFIRE 2089
RIFLES: SINGLE SHOT 2092
SHOTGUNS: O/U 2095
SHOTGUNS: SxS 2097
SHOTGUNS: SINGLE BARREL 2097
SUHLER JAGDGEWEHR MANUFAKTUR GmbH 2097
SUNDANCE INDUSTRIES, INC. 2097
SUN DEVIL MANUFACTURING LLC 2097
SUPER SIX LIMITED 2097
SUPER SIX LLC 2097
SUPER SIX CLASSIC, LLC 2097
SUPERIOR AMMUNITION 2097
SUPERIOR ARMS 2098
SURGEON RIFLES, INC. 2098
SURVIVAL ARMS, INC. 2098
SVENDSEN, ERL, F.A. MFG. CO. 2098
SWING 2098
SWISS MILITARY 2098
SWORD INTERNATIONAL INC. 2100
SYMES & WRIGHT LTD. 2100
SYREN 2100
SZECSEI & FUCHS FINE GUNS GmbH 2100

T

TJF 2101
TNW FIREARMS, INC. 2101
TPS ARMS LLC 2101
TR IMPORTS 2101
TS FINE GUNS 2101
TACONIC FIREARMS, LTD. 2101
TACTICAL 73 2102
TACTICAL ARMS MANUFACTURER, INC. 2102
TACTICAL ARMS OF TEXAS 2102
TACTICAL ARMZ 2102
TACTICAL EDGE ARMS 2102
TACTICAL RIFLES 2102
TACTICAL SOLUTIONS, INC. 2102
TACTICAL SUPPLY 2102
TACTICAL WEAPONS 2102
TACTICAL WEAPONS SOLUTIONS 2102
TALO DISTRIBUTORS, INC. 2102
TALON ARMAMENT 2102
TALON INDUSTRIES, INC. 2103
TALON ORDNANCE 2103
TANFOGLIO, FRATELLI, Srl 2103

TANNER, ANDRÉ 2109
TARHUNT CUSTOM RIFLES, INC. 2110
TASK FIREARMS 2112
TATE GUNMAKERS LLC 2112
TAURUS INTERNATIONAL MFG., INC. 2112
TAVOR 2138
TAYLOR, F.C. FUR CO. 2139
TAYLOR'S & CO., INC. 2139
TECHNO ARMS (PTY) LIMITED 2152
TEDNA 2152
TELO, RENATO 2153
TEMPLAR CUSTOM ARMS 2153
TEMPLAR CUSTOM, LLC
(TEMPLAR CONSULTING) 2154
TEMPLAR TACTICAL ARMS LLC 2154
TEMPLAR TACTICAL FIREARMS 2154
TERRIER ONE 2154
TESRO SPORTWAFFEN GMBH & CO. KG 2154
TEXAS ARMS 2154
TEXAS BLACK RIFLE COMPANY 2154
TEXAS CUSTOM GUNS 2154
TEXAS GUNFIGHTERS 2154
TEXAS LONGHORN ARMS, INC. 2155
THOMAS 2155
THOMPSON & CAMPBELL 2155
THOMPSON 2155
THOMPSON/CENTER ARMS CO., INC. 2158
THOR 2165
THUNDER-FIVE 2165
THUREON DEFENSE 2165
TIKKA 2165
TIMBERWOLF 2170
TIME PRECISION ARMS 2171
TIPPMANN ARMORY 2171
TIPPMANN ARMS CO., LLC 2171
TISAS TRABZON GUN INDUSTRY CORP. 2171
TITAN 2173
TOBIN ARMS 2173
TOKAREV 2173
TOLLEY, J & W 2173
TOMAHAWK 2174
TOMPKINS 2174
TORNADO 2174
TOROS ARMS 2174
TORUN ARMS 2174
TOZ 2174
TRABZON 2175
TRACKER ARMS 2175
TRACKINGPOINT 2175
TRADEWINDS 2175
TRADITIONS PERFORMANCE FIREARMS 2175
TRANSFORMATIONAL
DEFENSE INDUSTRIES, INC. 2175
TRAILBLAZER FIREARMS 2175
TREJO PISTOLS 2176
TRENCH/RIOT SHOTGUNS 2176
TRIPLE ACTION LLC 2179
TRISTAR ARMS INC. 2179
TROJAN FIREARMS 2189
TROMIX CORPORATION 2189
TROY DEFENSE 2190
TRUVELO ARMOURY 2190
TULA ARMS PLANT 2190
TURKISH FIREARMS CORPORATION 2190
TURKUAZ 2190
TURNBULL RESTORATION CO., INC. 2190
TURNER RICHARDS GUNMAKERS 2191
2 VETS ARMS CO. 2191

U

U.S.R.A. 2193
U.S. ARMAMENT CORP. 2193
U.S. ARMS COMPANY 2193
U.S. GENERAL TECHNOLOGIES, INC. 2193
U.S. HISTORICAL SOCIETY 2193
U.S. MACHINE GUN ARMORY LLC 2193
U.S. MILITARY HANDGUNS 2193
U.S. MILITARY & COMMERCIAL
LONG ARMS MFG'S 2193
U.S. ORDNANCE 2195
U.S. TRINITY CUSTOM 2196
USAS 12 2196
USA TACTICAL FIREARMS 2196
USFA/ZIP FACTORY, LLC 2196
UBERTI, A. Srl 2196
UGARTECHEA, ARMAS 2207
UGARTECHEA, IGNACIO 2207
ULTIMATE 2207
ULTIMATE ARMS LLC (UA/ARMS) 2207
ULTIMATE FIREARMS 2207
ULTRA LIGHT ARMS, INC. 2207
ULTRAMATIC 2208
UMAREX SPORTWAFFEN GmbH & Co. KG. 2208
UNDERWOOD-ELLIOT-FISHER CORP. 2208
UNERTL ORDNANCE COMPANY, INC. 2208
UNIQUE 2208
UNIQUE-ALPINE 2209
UNIQUE-ARS 2209
UNITED SPORTING ARMS, INC. 2209
UNITED STATES FIREARMS CORP. 2209
UNITED STATES FIRE ARMS
MFG. CO., INC./USFA 2209
UNIVERSAL FIREARMS 2212
UTAS 2214
UZI 2214
UZKON ARMS DEFENSE 2216

V

VM HY-TECH LLC 2217
VO VAPEN AB 2217

VAIL, ROY 2217
VALKYRIE ARMS LTD. 2217
VALMET 2217
VALMET, INC. 2217
VALOR ARMS 2219
VALTRO 2219
VAN DYKE RIFLE DESIGNS 2219
VARBERGER 2219
VARNER SPORTING ARMS, INC. 2219
VASKENT 2219
VATAN HUNTING FIREARMS COMPANY 2220
VECTOR ARMS, INC. 2220
VEGA 2220
VEKTOR 2220
VEPR 2220
VERITAS TACTICAL 2220
VERNEY-CARRON 2220
VERONA 2221
VICKERS LIMITED 2221
VICTOR ARMS CORPORATION 2221
VICTORY ARMS CO. LIMITED 2222
VICTRIX ARMAMENTS 2222
VIERLINGS 2222
VIGILANCE RIFLES INC. 2222
VIGILANT ARMS 2223
VIKING ARMAMENT, INC. 2223
VI-MA SNC 2223
VINTAGE ORDNANCE COMPANY, LLC 2223
VIPER 2223
VIRGIN VALLEY CUSTOM GUNS 2224
VIRGINIAN 2224
VIS 2224
VLTOR WEAPON SYSTEMS 2224
VOERE (AUSTRIA) 2224
VOERE (GERMAN) 2224
VOLCANIC 2224
VOLKMANN PRECISION, LLC 2226
VOLQUARTSEN CUSTOM (LTD.) 2226
VOLTRAN 2230
VOLUNTEER ENTERPRISES 2230
VOUZELAUD 2230
VUDOO GUN WORKS 2230
VULCAN ARMAMENT, INC. 2230

W

WMD GUNS 2231
JAGDWAFFEN OUTSCHAR (W. SCHASCHL-OUTSCHAR) GmbH 2231
W.W. GREENER LIMITED 2231
WAFFENFABRIK HEIN 2231
WAFFEN GLATZ 2231
WAFFEN HIENDLMAYER 2231
WAFFEN JUNG GMBH 2231
WAFFEN KESSLER 2231
WAFFEN SCHUMACHER GmbH 2231
WAFFENSTUBE GUGGI 2231
WAFFEN VERATSCHNIG 2232
WALTHER 2232
PISTOLS: SEMI-AUTO, PRE-WAR & WWII MFG. 2232
PISTOLS: SEMI-AUTO, POST-WAR 2236
PISTOLS: SEMI-AUTO, TARGET 2245
REVOLVERS 2246
RIFLES: DISC. 2246
RIFLES: CURRENT/RECENT MFG. 2247
SHOTGUNS: SxS 2248
SHOTGUNS: SEMI-AUTO 2248
WALTHER, FRENCH-MADE BY MANURHIN 2248
WALTTER 2249
WAMO MFG. 2249
WAR SPORT 2249
WARNER ARMS CORPORATION 2249
WARRIOR ARMS LLC 2250
WARWICK TACTICAL 2250
WASATCH PRECISION ARMS 2250
WATSON BROS. 2250
WEATHERBY 2250
DRILLINGS 2250
PISTOLS: BOLT ACTION 2250
RIFLES: RIMFIRE 2251
RIFLES: BOLT ACTION, CUSTOM SHOP 2252
RIFLES: BOLT ACTION, MARK V SERIES 2252
RIFLES: BOLT ACTION, VANGUARD SERIES 1 2263
RIFLES: BOLT ACTION, VANGUARD SERIES 2 2265
RIFLES: BOLT ACTION, WBY-X SERIES 2269
SHOTGUNS: O/U 2270
SHOTGUNS: SxS 2272
SHOTGUNS: SEMI-AUTO 2273
SHOTGUNS: SLIDE ACTION 2275
WEAVER ARMS CORPORATION 2277
WEBLEY & SCOTT AG (LIMITED) 2277
WEIHRAUCH & WEIHRAUCH SPORT GmbH & CO. KG SPORTWAFFENFABRIK 2286
WEIHRAUCH, HERMANN REVOLVER GmbH 2287
WELLS 2287
WERNER BARTOLOT 2287
WESSON, FRANK 2287
WESSON & HARRINGTON 2289
DAN WESSON FIREARMS 2289
WESSON FIREARMS CO. INC. 2289
WEST COAST WEAPONWORKS, LLC 2289
WESTERN ARMS COMPANY 2289
WESTERN FIELD 2289
WESTERN PRECISION RIFLES 2290
WESTLEY RICHARDS & CO. LTD. 2290
WHITNEY ARMS COMPANY 2293
WHITNEY FIREARMS COMPANY 2294
WHITWORTH 2294
WICHITA ARMS, INC. 2294
WICKLIFFE RIFLES 2295
WIDFORSS 2295
WIENER WAFFENFABRIK 2295
WIFRA 2295
WILD WEST GUNS 2295

WILDEY (NEW MFG.) 2297
WILDEY, INC. 2297
JOHN WILKES GUN AND RIFLE MANUFACTURERS (WILKES, JOHN GUNMAKERS LTD.) 2298
WILKINSON ARMS 2298
WILKINSON TACTICAL 2299
WILLIAM & SON 2299
WILLIAM DOUGLAS & SONS 2300
WILLIAM EVANS LIMITED 2300
WILLIAM LARKIN MOORE 2301
WILLIAM POWELL (WILLIAM POWELL & SONS) .. 2301
WILSKA & LANDEN (W&L) FIREARMS 2301
WILSON COMBAT 2301
WINCHESTER 2318
WINCHESTER TIMELINE 1855-TO DATE 2318
WINCHESTER OVERVIEW 2319
COMBINATION GUNS 2320
PISTOLS: SINGLE SHOT 2320
RIFLES: BOLT ACTION 2320
RIFLES: BOLT ACTION - PRE-1964 MODEL 70 2324
RIFLES: BOLT ACTION - MODEL 70, 1964-2006 MFG. 2327
RIFLES: BOLT ACTION - POST 1964 MODEL 70 CUSTOM GRADES 2334
RIFLES: BOLT ACTION - MODEL 70, 2007-CURRENT MFG. 2337
RIFLES: BOLT ACTION, MISC., 2015-CURRENT MFG. 2340
GRADING EXPLANATION FOR WINCHESTER LEVER ACTIONS 2341
RIFLES: LEVER ACTIONS - 1860-1964 2341
RIFLES: LEVER ACTION - POST 1964 PRODUCTION 2351
RIFLES: LEVER ACTION - MODEL 94, 1964-2006 MFG. 2355
RIFLES: LEVER ACTION - MODELS 94 AND 1894, 2010-CURRENT 2360
RIFLES: O/U 2361
RIFLES: SEMI-AUTO 2361
RIFLES: SINGLE SHOT 2363
RIFLES: SINGLE SHOT, POST 1964 MFG. 2365
RIFLES: SLIDE ACTION, DISC. 2366
SHOTGUNS: 1879-1963 2368
SHOTGUNS: POST-1964 2375
Shotguns: Post-1964, Lever Action 2375
Shotguns: Post-1964, Semi-Auto 2375
Shotguns: Single Barrel, 1968-1980 mfg. 2382
SHOTGUNS: SLIDE ACTION, 1964-CURRENT 2382
SHOTGUNS: O/U - RECENT PRODUCTION 2390
SHOTGUNS: RECENT PRODUCTION SxS 2395
FACTORY WINCHESTER COMMEMORATIVES: U.S. PRODUCTION 2397
WINCHESTER COMMEMORATIVES: NON-DOMESTIC - 1970 TO DATE 2401
SHOT SHOW SPECIALS 2403
WINDHAM WEAPONRY 2403
WINSLOW ARMS COMPANY 2403
WISCHO JAGD-UND SPORTWAFFEN GmbH & CO. KG 2403
WISEMAN, BILL AND CO. 2404
WOLF SPORTING PISTOLS 2405
WOLFPACK ARMORY 2405
WOODWARD, JAMES AND SONS 2405
WUTTI, MANFRED 2405
WYOMING ARMORY 2405
WYOMING ARMS LLC 2406
WYOMING ARMS MFG. CORP. 2406

X

XN ARMS INDUSTRY AND TRADE CO. 2407
XTREME MACHINING 2407

Y

YANKEE HILL MACHINE CO., INC. (YHM) 2407
YAZICILAR AV 2407
YILDIZ SILAH SANAYI 2407

Z

Z-B RIFLE 2407
ZDF IMPORT EXPORT INC. 2407
Z-HAT CUSTOM 2407
Z-M WEAPONS 2407
ZRO DELTA 2408
ZVI 2408
ZVS IMPEX 2408
ZABALA HERMANOS, S.A. 2408
ZAKLADY MECHANICZNE TARNÓW S.A. 2408
ZANARDINI 2408
ZANOTTI 2408
ZANOTTI, R. (ARMERIA RENATO ZANOTTI) 2408
ZANOTTI, STEFANO 2409
ZASTAVA ARMS 2409
ZBROJOVKA BRNO 2411
ZELENY SPORT s.r.o. 2412
ZENITH FIREARMS 2412
ZEPHYR 2412
ZEV TECHNOLOGIES 2412
ZIEGENHAHN & SOHN OHG 2413
ZIMMERSTUTZEN 2413
ZIP FACTORY, LLC 2413
ZOLI, ANGELO 2413
ZOLI, ANTONIO 2413
ZOMBIE DEFENSE 2418

NRA Membership Information *766*
NRA National Firearms Museum (NFM) *824*
Buffalo Bill Center of the West Information/Membership *1,152*
NRA National Sporting Arms Museum *1,440*
Firearms/Shooting/Advocacy Organizations .. 2419
Conservation Organizations 2422
Reference Sources 2423
Store Brand Cross-Over List 2427
Serialization Index 2434
Serialization 2436
Proof Marks 2483
Index 2490
P.S. 2512

P.S.

NEW

COVID GUN

MSRP: $995

Another revolutionary award-winning design developed by Blue Book University, the COVID Gun can remove the virus from anyone with as few as five simple treatments.

Selector switch allows user to pick from COVID-19 or any of the other variants found.
Self-disinfecting, no need to clean or sanitize in between uses.
Picatinny rail allows for mounting of additional accessories such as:

- **Mask shooter**
- **Sanitizer sprayer**
- **Programmable voiceover recorder with suggested sayings such as:**
  - **"Social Distance"**
  - **"Put Your Mask On"**
  - **"Flatten the Curve"**